Chinwe Ada Crokwu

Resources + Aquisitions

AFRICAN HISTORY
AND
LITERATURES

HARVARD UNIVERSITY LIBRARY

WIDENER LIBRARY SHELFLIST, 34

AFRICAN HISTORY
AND
LITERATURES

CLASSIFICATION SCHEDULE
CLASSIFIED LISTING BY CALL NUMBER
CHRONOLOGICAL LISTING
AUTHOR AND TITLE LISTING

Published by the Harvard University Library
Distributed by the Harvard University Press
Cambridge, Massachusetts
1971

Preface

As part of its effort to computerize certain of its operations, the Harvard University Library is converting to machine-readable form the shelflist and classification schedules of Widener Library, which houses Harvard's central research collection. After each class or group of related classes is converted, it is published in the *Widener Library Shelflist* series.

This volume is the thirty-fourth in the series. It includes the *Afr* class, originally published as Volume 2, and 1200 document titles in the *Afr Doc* class, presented here for the first time. As a result of retrospective buying as well as acquisition of current materials, the *Afr* class has grown by one third in the five years which have elapsed since the earlier publication. The present volume lists more than 20,000 titles.

This catalogue is arranged in four parts. The classification schedule is the first of these. It serves as an outline of the second part, which presents the entries in shelflist order; that is, in order by call number, as the books are arranged on the shelves. Together these two parts form a classified catalogue and browsing guide to each class. Part three lists the same items (excluding periodicals and other serials) in chronological order by date of publication. In addition to its obvious reference use, this list yields information on the quantity and rate of publication in the field. It can be helpful in determining patterns of collection development and in identifying existing strengths and weaknesses. Access to the collection by author and by title is provided by the alphabetical list which constitutes the fourth part of the catalogue. Computer-generated entries are included for titles of works listed elsewhere by author. (In these added entries the author's name follows the title and is enclosed in parentheses.) This section equips the reader with a subject-oriented subset of the card catalogue — a finding list which offers substantial advantages of conciseness and portability over the catalogue as a whole.

A note of caution is in order. A shelflist has traditionally served as an inventory record of the books in the library and as an indispensable tool for assigning call numbers to books as they are added to the collection. Designed and maintained to fulfill these two functions, the Widener shelflist was never intended to serve the purposes now envisaged for it. The bibliographical standards are not equal to those that prevail in the public card catalogues; shelflist entries are less complete than the public catalogue entries and may contain errors and inconsistencies which have not been eliminated during the conversion process. Cross references and name added entries are not included. Entries for serials rarely reflect changes in title, and serial holding statements give only the year or volume number of the first and last volumes in the library with no indication of gaps. If there is a plus sign after the beginning volume number or date, it can be inferred that the title is being currently received. For a complete record of the holdings of serial titles, the conventional serial records in the Widener Library should be consulted.

The list has other deficiencies. No classification system is perfect, and books are not always classified where the reader would expect to find them. Some books formerly in Widener and subsequently transferred to the Houghton Library or the New England Deposit Library are still to be found in the list; but others had been dropped from the original shelflist and could not be re-inserted.

Special notations indicate the locations of books which are in the shelflist but not in the Widener building. Books transferred to the Houghton Library (for rare books and special collections) are indicated by the letters *Htn*. Books that have been moved to special storage areas are designated by one of the following notations; *NEDL*, *X Cg*, or a *V* as the first letter of a call number prefix. These books should be requested, by their current numbers, through the Widener Circulation Desk. The letters *RRC* designate books in the Russian Research Center Library. The letter A following a call number in the alphabetical or chronological section indicates that the Library holds more than one copy of the book on this number. The classified list, however, includes all copies.

The shelflists of libraries not having classified catalogues have long been used by librarians and readers as implements for systematically surveying holdings in a particular subject. When perusing a shelflist one sees all the titles that have been classified in a given area, and not merely those which happen to be on the shelves and whose spine lettering is legible. In addition, one can take in at a glance the essential bibliographical description of a book — author, title, place and date of publication. However, the potential bibliographical usefulness of the shelflist has been difficult to exploit because it exists in only one copy, which is generally kept in a relatively inaccessible location. In Widener this problem is intensified because the handwritten sheaf shelflist is peculiarly awkward to read and difficult to interpret. Computer technology has made it possible to enlarge the concept of the shelflist and to expand its usefulness and accessibility while improving the techniques of maintaining it.

This shelflist catalogue will be of greatest utility to those using the libraries at Harvard, but in spite of its limitations, it can serve as a general bibliography of the subject and is therefore being made available to other interested libraries and individuals. The computer-based shelflist files are being maintained on a continuing basis so that updated editions of volumes in the series can be published as the need arises.

CHARLES W. HUSBANDS
Systems Librarian

Contents

Statistical Summaries of Classes in this Volume

August 1970

Analysis of Shelflist Entries by Language

Entries in the *Afr* Class   17,696

English	9,396	Polish	38
French	4,808	Ukrainian	1
German	945	Serbo-Croatian	3
Russian	216	Bulgarian	1
Greek	3	Turkish	7
Latin	28	Finnish	3
Italian	711	Estonian	1
Spanish	452	Lithuanian	1
Portuguese	496	Arabic	1
Afrikaans & Dutch	416	Celtic Languages	1
Swedish	39	African Languages	14
Danish	16	Uncoded	77
Norwegian	5		

Entries in the *Afr Doc* Class   1,195

English	946	Portuguese	51
French	174	Afrikaans	7
Italian	5	Uncoded	10
Spanish	2		

Count of Titles

		Widener	Elsewhere	Total
Afr	Monographs	16,194	231	16,425
	Serials	909	16	925
	Pamphlets in Tract Volumes	1,558	29	1,587
	Pamphlet Boxes	118	5	123
	Total *Afr*	18,779	281	19,060
Afr Doc	Monographs	272	0	272
	Serials	911	0	911
	Pamphlets in Tract Volumes	34	0	34
	Pamphlet Boxes	3	0	3
	Total *Afr Doc*	1,220	0	1,220
Total Titles		19,999	281	20,280

Count of Volumes

		Widener	Elsewhere	Total
Afr	Monograph	17,308	285	17,593
	Serial	3,091	80	3,171
	Tract	217	6	223
	Total *Afr*	20,616	371	20,987
Afr Doc	Monograph	349	0	349
	Serial	656	0	656
	Tract	9	0	9
	Total *Afr Doc*	1,014	0	1,014
Total Volumes		21,630	371	22,001

WIDENER LIBRARY SHELFLIST, 34

AFRICAN HISTORY
AND
LITERATURES

CLASSIFICATION SCHEDULES

NOTE ON THE CLASSIFICATION

The Afr class provides for works on all the countries of the African continent and some of the neighboring islands. It contains primarily works on history, civilization and government, general geography and travel, general social and economic conditions (but not some specific aspects, such as crime or agriculture, which are in the Soc and Econ classes), religious affairs, and the various races of these countries. For North Africa (the Barbary States and Egypt), works on the ancient period (before the Arab conquest) are in the AH and Eg classes. Many government documents are in the Afr Doc class.

The organization of the Afr class requires some comment. The scheme was originally constructed before 1914, and it naturally reflects the situation existing at that time. The countries of northern Africa are in a geographical arrangement, going from west to east. But those of central and southern Africa are grouped according to the spheres of influence of the various European countries in the early 20th century -- Great Britain, France, Germany, etc. Some adjustments have been made recently to provide more adequately for the countries which became independent after World War II -- but within the framework of the original scheme. It has not always been possible to reclassify all the books in accordance with these changes.

About 1960 an addition was made at the end of the scheme to provide for the literature of Africa in both the European and indigenous languages. The scheme does not provide, however, for Afrikaans literature, which goes in the Neth class, or for the literatures in the Semitic and Hamitic languages found in northern Africa (e.g. Arabic, Amharic, Berber), which go in the OL class. Generally speaking, only currently acquired books are put in this new part of the Afr class. Thus, there are many older books, which would rightfully belong in the Afr class, that are still in the various classes for European literatures or in the linguistics class.

Bartol Brinkler
Chief Subject Cataloguer
June 15, 1965

OUTLINE

African history

1-870	Africa in general
	Barbary States
1001-1280	General
1301-1769	Morocco (including Spanish Morocco)
1801-2397	Algeria
2401-2699	Tunisia
2700-2798	Sahara
2800-2999	Libya
3001-4199	Egypt (including United Arab Republic)
3669-3849	Egyptian Sudan, Sudan Republic
4201-4699	Ethiopia
	Italian Africa
4700	General
4701-4749	Eritrea
4750-4799	Italian Somaliland, Somalia
4800-4899	French Somaliland
4900-4999	British Somaliland
	French Africa
5000-5049	General
	French West Africa
5050-5059	General
5060-5099	Mauritania
5100-5199	Senegal
5200-5249	Sudan, Mali Republic
5250-5269	Niger
5270-5289	Upper Volta
5300-5324	French Guinea
5325-5349	Ivory Coast
5350-5399	Dahomey
	French Equatorial Africa
5400-5409	General
5410-5429	Gabon
5430-5449	Congo Republic (Brazzaville)
5450-5469	Central African Republic, Ubangi-Shari
5470-5489	Chad
5501-5798	Madagascar
5800-5809	Mascarenes
5810-5849	Mauritius
5850-5879	Réunion
5881-5889	Rodriguez
5891-5899	Seychelles
	Spanish Africa
5900-5924	General
5925-5948	Rio de Oro (incl. Spanish Sahara)
5949	Ifni
5950-5998	Spanish Guinea (incl. Muni, Corisco, Fernando Po, etc.)
	Canary Islands. See Span
	British Africa
6000-6049	General
	British West Africa
6050-6099	General
6100-6124	Gambia
6125-6149	Sierra Leone
6150-6198	Ghana, Gold Coast
6200-6298	Nigeria

African history (cont.)

British Africa (cont.)
    British East Africa
6300-6398	General
6400-6470	Kenya
6475-6549	Uganda
6550-6599	Zanzibar

German Africa
6600-6649	General
6650-6699	Togo
9700-6749	Camerun
6750-6899	Tanganyika, Tanzania
6900-6990	Southwest Africa

Portuguese Africa
7000-7049	General
7050-7074	Portuguese Guinea
7075-7099	Cabinda
7100-7199	Angola
	Azores, Madeira, and Cape Verde Islands. See Port
7200-7349	Mozambique
7350-7499	Liberia
7500-7926	Congo (Leopoldville), Belgian Congo
7930-7949	Ruanda-Urundi

South Africa
8001-8695	General
8700-8849	Cape Colony
8850-8931	Basutoland, Lesotho
8950-9073	Natal
9075-9170	Transvaal
9190-9199	Swaziland
9200-9295	Orange River Colony
9325-9424	Bechuanaland, Botswana
9425-9525	Southern Rhodesia (incl. Federation of Rhodesia and Nyasaland)

British Central Africa
9535-9619	General
9625-9748	Northern Rhodesia, Zambia
9750-9860	Nyasaland, Malawi

African literatures
10000-10099	General
10100-11999	In English
12000-13699	In French
13700-13999	In Italian
14000-14499	In Spanish
14500-14899	In Portuguese
	In other European languages. See Neth, Ger L, etc.

In Hamitic and Semitic languages. See OL

In the indigenous languages (Bantu, etc.)
20000-21999	General and in special areas
22000-22999	Special language groups
23000-49999	Individual languages, A-Z

Africa in general
  [Include also Subsaharan Africa in general]
1-24   Periodicals (A-Z)

           Special organizations, etc.
             [See also Afr 5001]
25.1-.99   General works on all the organizations

           Organization of African Unity
             Publications of the whole body
24.100   Periodicals
25.101   Bibliographies
25.102   Pamphlet volumes
25.103   Charter
25.104   Others
               Works about the whole body
25.105   Periodicals
25.106   Bibliographies
25.107   Pamphlet volumes
25.108   General works
25.109   Special topics
               Special organs, etc.
                 [Divide each like .100-.109]
25.110-.119   Assembly of Heads of State
25.120-.129   Council of Ministers
25.130-.139   Secretariat
25.150-.159   Arbitration Commission
25.160-.169   Economic and Social Commission
25.170-.179   Education and Cultural Commission
25.180-.189   Defence Commission
25.190-.199   Health, Sanitation and Nutrition Commission
25.200-.209   Scientific, Technical and Research Commission
25.210-.219   Commission of Jurists
25.220-.229   Transport and Communications Commission
25.250-   Special committees, etc.
                 [Develop as needed]
[26]   Portfolios [Discontinued]
28   Bibliographies
29   Pamphlet volumes
30   Dictionaries

           Collected source materials
31   General
32   Statutes
33   Treaties
35   Others
36   Historiography
38   Archives

           Government and administration
40   General works
45   Special topics
50   General politics; political parties
55   Collected political biographies

           Military affairs
60   General works
63   Special topics
104-110   General history (By date)
115   General special

           History by periods
125   Ancient to Arab Invasion (To 7th century)
               [See also AH]
150   Medieval (7th to 16th centuries)
175   16th century to ca. 1850
               [Include modern in general]
200   Nineteenth century (1850-1900)

             Twentieth century
210   General works and 1900-1960
212   1960-

           Shares of foreign powers and their exploitations
500   General works
505   England
510   France
520   Spain

Africa in general (cont.)
  Shares of foreign powers and their... (cont.)

             Others
               [See also various local divisions, e.g.
               Portuguese Africa, South Africa, Congo]
530.1-.19   Germany
                 [See also Afr 6600-6649]
530.20-.30   Italy
                 [See also Afr 4700]
530.31-.39   Portugal, etc.
530.50-   U.S.
                 [See also Afr 7350-7499]

           Religion
545   General works

             Christian missions
550   General works
555   Sectional
                 [See also Missions in various countries]
575   Islam in Africa
580   Jews in Africa
590   Slavery in Africa

           Geography, description, etc.
603-610   General works (By date)
618   Special customs
620   Guidebooks
623   Views
625   Maps
626   Economic history and conditions
628   The negro race in general, especially
             "The world over" (By date, e.g. .258 for 1958)

           Races
630   General works (i.e. the negro race in Africa)
632   Sociological aspects
635   Other special aspects
640   Pygmies
650   Local in general
             [Include urbanization, etc.]

           Local divisions
655-660   The North (i.e. Egypt plus the Barbary States)
               (By date)
674-680   The West coast (By date)
695-700   The East coast (By date)
710   Tropical Africa
               [For Subsaharan Africa in general, see
               Afr 1-650.]

             Journeys across the interior
715   General works
718   East to West
724   Cape to Cairo
725   Region of the great lakes
730   Circumnavigation of Africa

           Lakes
750   General works
755   Chad
760   Western group
765   Victoria
770   Tanganyika
775   Nyassa
790   Others

           Rivers
800   General works
810   Niger
820   Zambesi
825   Others
               [See also the Nile with Egypt, the Congo
               with Congo, etc.]

           Islands
850   General works
852   West coast in general
854   East coast in general

Africa in general (cont.)

Local divisions (cont.)

Islands (cont.)

855	St. Helena
860	Ascension
861	Tristan da Cunha
870	Others
	[See also special islands and island groups below in local history]

Barbary States in general

1001-1024	Periodicals (A-Z)
[1025]	Folios [Discontinued]
1026	Bibliographies
1028	Pamphlet volumes

Collected source materials

1030	General
1032	Statutes
1033	Treaties
1035	Others
1036	Historiography

Government and administration

1038	General works
1040	Special topics
1042	General politics; political parties
1044	Collected political biographies

Military affairs

1046	General works
1047	Special topics
1065-1070	General history (By date)
1075	General special

History by periods

Ancient to Moorish conquest. See AH

Moorish conquest to 16th century

1080	General works
1081	Arab conquest
1082	Arab conquest to 800
1083	Aglabite dynasty (800-909)
1084	Fatimite dynasty (903-975)
	[See also Afr 3135-3138]
1085	Ziride dynasty (972-1148)
1086	Hammadide dynasty (1007-1152)
1087	Almoravide dynasty (1056-1147)
1088	Almohade dynasty (1130-1275)
1089	Other special

History since 16th century

1095	General works
	Barbary Piracy (1500-1830)
1100	General works
1103	Special topics
1105	19th and 20th centuries together
1110	20th century
1200	General relations with foreign powers

Geography, description, etc.

1254-1260	General works (By date)
1268	Special customs
1270	Guidebooks
1271	Views
1272	Maps

Economic history and conditions

1273.1-.199	Historical works
1273.500-.999	Contemporary works (By date)

Finance

1274.1-.199	Historical works
1274.500-.999	Contemporary works (By date)
1280	Races
1285	Religion

Morocco

1301-1324	Periodicals (A-Z)
[1325]	Folios [Discontinued]
1326	Bibliographies
1328	Pamphlet volumes

Collected source materials

1330	General works
1332	Statutes
1333	Treaties
1335	Others
1336	Historiography

Government and administration

1338	General works
1340	Special topics
1342	General politics; political parties
1344	Collected political biographies

Military affairs

1346	General works
1347	Special topics
1365-1370	General history (By date)
1375	General special

History by periods

Ancient to Arab conquest. See AH

Mohammedan conquest (690-788)

1380	General works
1385	Special topics

Medieval history (788-1550)

1390	General works
	Merinide dynasty (1195-1551)
1393	General works
1395	Special topics
1398	Portuguese wars

Piratical period (1529-1795)

1400	General works
1401	Rise of Sherif dynasty
1403	Battle of El Kasar (1578)
1405	Conquest of Timbuctoo (1580)
1406	Sherif dynasty (1580-1672)
1407	Stories of piracy and captivity
1408	Ismail (1672-1727)
1409	Other special (1529-1795)

Nineteenth century

1410	General works
	Sulaiman (1795-1822)
1415	General works
1418	Special topics
	Abd'er Rahman II (1822-1859)
1420	General works
1422	Relations and war with France (1844)
1425	Other special topics
	Sidi Mohammed (1859-1873)
1430	General works
1432	War with Spain (1859-1860)
1435	Other special topics
	El Hasan III (1873-1894)
1440	General works
1442	Troubles with Spain (1894)
1445	Other special topics
	Abd el Aziz (1894-1907)
1450	General works
1453	Tourmaline Expedition (1897-1898)
1470	Diplomatic negotiations concerning Morocco
1485	Other special topics (incl. Casablanca)

20th century

1487	General works
1490	Mulai Hafid (1907-1912)
1493	Mulai Yusoef (1912-1927) (incl. Abd-el Krim)
1494	Mulai Mohammad (Nov. 1929-1961)
1495	Hassan II (1961-)

Morocco (cont.)

General relations with foreign powers
The Morocco question

1550	General works
1555	Special topics

Other Mohammedan

1560	General works
1563	Special topics

United States

1565	General works
1567	Special topics

Great Britain

1568	General works
1569	Special topics

France

1570	General works
1571	Special topics

Spain

1573	General works
1574	Special topics

Portugal

1575	General works
1576	Special topics

Italy

1578	General works
1579	Special topics

Belgium

1581	General works
1582	Special topics

Germany

1583	General works
1584	Special topics

1585	Austria

1590	Other Christian

Geography, description, etc.

1605-1610	General works (By date)
1618	Special customs
1620	Guidebooks
1621	Views
1622	Maps

Economic history and conditions

1623.1-.199	Historical works
1623.500-.999	Contemporary works (By date)

Finance

1624.1-.199	Historical works
1624.500-.999	Contemporary works (By date)

Races

1625	General works
1630	Arabs
1635	Berbers
1640	Others
1645	Religion

Provinces of French Morocco

1650	General works

Fez

1655	General works
1658	Riff
	[Include Riff Revolt]
1660	Other districts
1665	Sus
1675	Marrakesh

Morocco (cont.)
Provinces of French Morocco (cont.)

Atlas and Transatlas

1680	General works
1685	Tafilelt
1688	Figig

Cities, towns, etc. of French Morocco

1700	General works
1703	A
1705	B
1706	C
1708	Dar-el-Baida
1709	D (Others)
1711	E
1713	Fez
1714	F (Others)
1716	G
1717	H
1718	I
1719	J
1720	K
1721	Laraiche
1722	L (Others)
1723	Marrakesh
1724	Mazagan
1725	Mequinez
1726	Mogador
1727	M (Others)
1729	N
1730	O
1731	P
1732	Q
1733	R
1734	Saffi
1735	Sale
1736	S (others)
1738	Tangier
1739	Tetuan
1740	T (Others)
1742	U
1744	V
1745	Wazzan
1746	W (Others)
1747	X
1748	Y
1749	Z

Spanish possessions in Morocco and environs

1750	General works
1752	Alhucemas
1753	Ceuta
1755	Melilla
1757	Peñon de Velez (Gomera, Peñon de la)
1759	Zaffarine Islands
1765	Heraldry

Genealogy

1766	General
1767	Special

Biographies

1768	Collected
1769.1-.26	Individual (A-Z)

Algeria

1801-1824	Periodicals (A-Z)
[1825]	Folios [Discontinued]
1826	Bibliographies
1828	Pamphlet volumes

Collected source materials

1830	General
1832	Statutes
1833	Treaties
1835	Others
1836	Historiography

Algeria (cont.)

	Government and administration
1838	General works
1840	Special topics
1842	General politics
	[Include political parties]
1844	Collected political biographies
1846	Military history
1848	Naval history
1865-1870	General history (By date)
1878	General special

	History by periods -
	Ancient to Arab conquest. See AH

	7th to 16th centuries
1880	General works
1881	Saracens (To 908)
1885	Zeianide dynasty (1239-1554)

	16th century to 1830
1900	General works
	Relations and wars with Spain (1515-1830)
1903	General works
1905	Special topics
	Foreign relations and Piracy (1515-1830)
1910	General works
	France
1915	General works
1918	Beaufort
1920	Duquesne
1922	Others
	England
1925	General works
1928	Blake
1930	Exmouth
1935	Holland
1940	Portugal
1942	United States
1945	Other foreign powers
1947	Stories of piracy and captivity

	French conquest (1830-1860)
1955	General works
1957	Expedition against Algiers (1830)
1960	Earlier military operations in the interior
1965	Abd-el-Kadar (1847)
1967	Capture of Abd-el-Kadar (1847)
1973	Two sieges of Constantine (1836, 1837)
1975	Conquest of Khabyla
1980	Conquest of desert tribes (1859?)
1990	Other special topics

	History from the Conquest to Independence (1860-1962)
2000	General works
2005	Wars with Arabs in the south
2010	Rising of 1871
2012	Rising of Bou Anama (1871?)
2015	Affair of Marquerite (1900?)
2020	Other risings
2025	Speical topics (1860-1914)
2026	1914-1945
2030	1945-1962

	History since Independence (1962-)
2035	General works
2037	Special topics

	Geography, description, etc.
2205-2210	General works (by date)
2218	Special customs
2220	Guidebooks
2221	Views
2222	Maps

	Economic history and conditions
2223.1-.199	General works
2223.500-.999	Contemporary works (By date)

Algeria (cont.)

	Finance
2224.1-.199	General works
2224.500-.999	Contemporary works (By date)

	Races
2225	General works

	African and Asiatic elements
2228	Arabs
2230	Berbers and Kabyles
	[Include works on the Kabyle country]
2232	The Mzab
2235	Moors in towns
2238	Negroes
2248	Others

	European elements and colonization
2250	General works
2260	French
2265	Spanish
2268	Italian
2270	Maltese
2272	German
2274	Others

2275	Religion

	Provinces, etc.
2279	General works

	Description by regions
2280	The Tell and Littoral
2283	The Plateau (incl. Aures Mts.)
2285	The Desert

	Administrative divisions
2287	Northern Territory
2288	Southern Territory
2290	Oran
2292	Algiers
2295	Constantine

	Cities, towns, etc.
2300	General works
2305	Adrar
2306	Ain Sefra
2308	Algiers
2310	A (Others)
2312	Biskra
2313	Blidah
2314	Bone
2315	Boufarik
2316	Bougie
2317	B (Others)
2318	Constantine
2320	C (Others)
2322	D
2324	E
2326	F
2328	Geryville
2330	Ghardaia
2331	Gourara
2332	Guelma
2335	G (Others)
2336	H
2338	Igla
2339	In Salah
2340	I (others)
2341	J
2342	Kantara, Al
2343	K (Others)
2344	Laghouat
2345	L (Others)
2346	Maghnia
2347	Medea
2348	Miliana
2349	Mostaganem
2350	Mustapha

Algeria (cont.)
Cities, towns, etc. (cont.)

2352	M (Others)
2354	Nemours
2355	N (Others)
2357	Oran
2358	Orleansville
2359	Ouargia
2360	O (Others)
2362	Philippeville
2363	P (Others)
2365	Q
2367	R
2368	S
2370	Tebessa
2371	Tidikelt
2372	Tizd-Ouzon
2373	Tlemcen
2374	Touat
2376	T (Others)
2377	U
2378	V
2380	W
2382	X
2384	Y
2386	Z
2390	Heraldry

Genealogy
2392	General
2393	Special

Biographies
2396	Collected
2397	Individual

Tunisia
2401-2424	Periodicals (A-Z)
[2425]	Folios [Discontinued]
2426	Bibliographies
2428	Pamphlet volumes
2430	Collected source materials
2436	Historiography
2438	Government and administration
2442	General politics, political parties
2444	Collected political biographies
2446	Military affairs
2448	Naval affairs
2455-2460	General history (By date)
2465	General special

History by periods
Ancient to Arab conquest. See AH

To 16th century
2470	General works

Hafside dynasty (1236-1574)
2475	General works
2480	English siege of Mahdiya (1390)
2482	Other special topics

16th century to 1819
2485	General works
2487	Spanish conquests (1535-1573)
2489	Turkish conquest (1573)
2492	Military revolution (ca. 1580)

1580-1705
2494	General works
2496	Blake's bombardment of Porte Farina (1655)

1702-1819 (Decadence of piracy)
2498	General works
2500	Relations with France

1819-1881
2505	General works
2508	Relations with France
2510	Relations with Italy
2512	Relations with England
2514	Relations with other powers
2518	Enfida affair

Tunisia (cont.)
History by periods (cont.)

1881-1956
2525	General works
2527	French invasion (1881)
2528	Treaty of Kasr-es-Said (May, 1881-April, 1882)

1882-1945
2530	General works
2532	Speical topics
2533	1945-1956

1956- (Independence)
2535	General works
2536	Biographies
2539	Special topics

Geography, description, etc.
2605-2610	General works (By date)
2618	Special customs
2620	Guidebooks
2621	Views
2622	Maps

Economic history and conditions
2623.1-.199	General works
2623.500-.999	Contemporary works (By date)

Finance
2624.1-.199	General works
2624.500-.999	Contemporary works (By date)

Races
2625	General works
2628	Natives
2630	French
2632	Italians
2634	Maltese
2636	Other European
2640	Religion
2650	Provinces, regions, etc.

Cities, towns, etc.
2660	A
2661	Beja
2662	Bizerta
2663	B (Others)
2664	Cabes
2665	C (Others)
2666	D
2667	E
2668	F
2669	Gafsa
2670	G (Others)
2671	Hammamet
2672	H (Others)
2673	I
2674	J
2675	Kairwan
2676	K (Others)
2677	L
2678	Monastir
2679	M (Others)
2680	N
2681	O
2682	P
2683	Q
2684	R
2685	Sfax
2686	Susa
2687	S (Others)
2688	Tunis
2689	T (Others)
2690	U
2691	V
2692	W
2693	X
2694	Y
2695	Z
2696	Heraldry

	Tunisia (cont.)
2697	Genealogy
	Biographies
2698	Collected
2699.1-.99	Individual (A-Z, 99 scheme, by person)
	Sahara
2700	Periodicals (A-Z)
[2702]	Folios [Discontinued]
2704	Bibliographies
2705	Pamphlet volumes
2706	Collected source materials
2708	Government and administration
2710	General politics
2714-2720	General history (By date)
2725	General special
	History by periods
2730	Flooding of the Sahara Railway
2731	20th century
	Geography, description, etc.
2745-2750	General works (By date)
2753	Special customs
2755	Guidebooks
2756	Views
2757	Maps
2758	Economic history and conditions
	Races
2760	General works
2762	Tuareg
2764	Tibbu
2765	Others
	Regions, etc.
2767	El Hamada (Stony Plateau)
3769	El Erg (Sandy Plateau)
	Cities, towns, etc.
2780	Air
2782	Assuad
2790	Tasili
2793	Tibesti
2798	Others
	Libya
2800	Periodicals (A-Z)
[2802]	Folios [Discontinued]
2804	Bibliographies
2805	Pamphlet volumes
2806	Collected source materials
2807	Historiography
2808	Government and administration
2810	General politics; political parties
2811	Collected political biographies
2812	Military affairs
2813	Naval affairs
2815-2820	General history (By date)
2825	General special
	History by periods
	Early to 1509. Class with Tunisia
2830	1509-1528
2833	1528-1531
2835	First Turkish period (1551-1715)
2840	Period of the Deys (1815-1833)
	Second Turkish period (1833-1911)
2845	General works
	Relations with foreign powers
2848	General works
2850	Italy
2860	France
2862	Other powers
	Italian period (1912-1951)
2870	General works
2875	Turco-Italian War

	Libya (cont.)
	History by periods (cont.)
	Italian period (1912-1951) (cont.)
2880	Other special topics
	Period of Independence (1951-)
2885	General works
	Geography, description, etc.
2925-2930	General works (By date)
2933	Special customs
2935	Guidebooks
2936	Views
2937	Maps
2938	Economic history and conditions
2939	Finance
2940	Races
2943	Religion
	Provinces, etc.
2945	Cyrenaica (Barca)
2948	Fessan
2949	Gebel
2950	Sirte
	Cities, towns, etc.
2960	A
2962	B
2964	C
2966	D
2967	E
2968	F
2970	G
2972	H
2973	I
2974	J
2975	Kupfra
2976	K (Others)
2977	L
2978	Murzuk
2979	M (Others)
2980	N
2981	O
2982	P
2983	Q
2984	Rhadames (Ghadames)
2985	Rhat
2986	R (Others)
2988	S
2990	Tripoli
2991	T (Others)
2992	U-V
2993	W
2994	X-Z
2995	Heraldry
	Genealogy
2996	General
2997	Special
	Biographies
2998	Collected
2999.1-.99	Individual (A-Z, scheme, by person)
	Egypt
3001-3024	Periodicals (A-Z)
[3025]	Folios [Discontinued]
3026	Bibliographies
3028	Pamphlet volumes
	Collected source materials
3030	General works
3032	Statutes
3033	Treaties
3035	Others
3037	Historiography
	Government and administration
3038	General works
3040	Special topics

Egypt (cont.)
3042	General politics; political parties
3044	Collected political biographies
3046	Military affairs
3050	Naval affairs
3065-3070	General history (By date)
3074-3080	General special (By date)

    History by periods
      Ancient to Arab conquest. See Eg

      Arab conquest to 1250 (or to 1517)
3120	General works
3125	Arab Conquest (638)

        First period (638-972)
3128	General works
3132	Special topics

        Fatimite dynasty (972-1171)
3135	General works
3138	Special topics

        Ayubite dynasty (1171-1250)
3140	General works
3143	Special topics
	[See also Crus]

      Mameluke dynasties (1250-1517)
3150	General works

        First Mameluke dynasty (Tartar, 1250-1382)
3155	General works
3158	Special topics

        Second Mameluke dynasty (Circassian, 1382-1517)
3160	General works
3163	Special topics

      Period of Tukish rule (1517-1798)
3170	General works

        1517-1650
3175	General works
	Turkish conquest. See Ott
3178	Special topics

        1650-1798
3180	General works
3183	Special topics

      French expedition (1798-1801). See Fr

      Period after French expedition (1801-1806)
3190	General works (By date)
3193	Special topics

      Nineteenth century
3198-3200	General works (By date)
3204	Special topics

        Mehemet Ali (1806-1849)
3205	General works
3207	Early years
	[Include English expedition of 1801-1807, etc.]
3209	Destruction of Mamelukes (1811-)
3215	Other special
3217	Ibrahim (Regent 1841-1848)

        Abbas I (Regent 1848; Pasha, 1849-1854)
3220	General works
3223	Special topics

        Said (1854-1863)
3225	General works
3228	Special topics

        Ismail (1863-1879)
3230	General works

          Foreign influence and control
3240	General works
3243	England to 1882
3245	France to 1904
3248	Dual control (1876-1883)
3250	Deposition (June 26, 1879)
3252	Other special topics

        Tewfik (1879-1892)
3255	General works

Egypt (cont.)
  History by periods (cont.)
    Nineteenth century (cont.)
      Tewfik (1879-1892) (cont.)
        Revolt of Arabi (1882)
3258	General works
3260	Bombardment of Alexandria (11 July 1882)
3262	Battle of Tel-el-kebir (13 Sept. 1882)
3265	Other special events
3267	Trial of Arabi and settlement
3269	Other special topics
3275	England in Egypt (1882-1904)

      Abbas II (1892-1914)
3280	General works
3285	Special topics

    20th century
3290	General works
3295	Special topics

      1914-1952
3300	General works
3305	Special topics

      1952-1958
3310	General works
3315	Special topics
	[Include the Suez War of 1956, Aqaba dispute]

  Egypt, 1958- ; United Arab Republic
3320	Periodicals
3321	Bibliographies
3322	Collected source materials
3325	General works
	[Do not use yet. See Afr 3340]
3326	Government and administration
3328	Political parties, etc.

    Political biographies
3329.1-.99	Collected (A-Z, 99 scheme)
3329.101-.899	Individual (A-Z, 800 scheme)
3330	Military affairs
3335	Foreign relations
3339	Other special topics

    1958-
3340	General works
3342	Special topics

Egypt (cont.)

Geography, races, local history, etc.
See Afr 3970-4199

Egyptian Sudan; Sudan Republic
3669	Bibliographies
3670	Pamphlet volumes
3671	Periodicals
3672	Collected source materials
3673	Historiography
3674	Government and administration
3675	General history
3678	General special

History by periods
3680	Before 1820
3685	Egyptian conquest (1820-1823)
3690	Governorship of Baker (1869-1873)
3695	First Governorship of Gordon (1874-1880)
	Revolt of Mahdi (1881-1885)
3700	General works
3705	Siege of Khartum (1884-1885)
3708	Expedition of Wolseley (1884-1885)
3710	Other special topics
	History from Evacuation (1885-1899)
3715	General works
3718	Special topics
3725	Emin Pasha in Equatoria (1878-1889)
3730	Stories of captivities
3735	Reconquest of the Sudan (1898-1899)
3740	Fashoda question (1898-1899)
3745	The Sudan since the conquest (1900-1956)
	History since independence (1956-)
3750	General works
3752	Special topics

Geography, description, etc.
3805-3810	General works (By date)
3811	Special customs
3812	Guidebooks, gazetteers, etc.
3813	Economic history and conditions
3814	Finance

Races
3816	General works
3817	Special
3818	Religion; missions

Provinces
3820	Northern
3821	Kordofan
3822	Darfur
3823	Bahr el Ghazal
3824	Equatoria
3825	Upper Nile
3826	Blue Nile, Gezira
3827	Kassala
3829	Others

Cities, towns, etc.
3830	General works
3831	Atbara
3832	Dongola
3833	Kassala
3834	Khartoum
3835	Omdurman
3836	Port Sudan
3837	Suakin
3838	Wad Medani
3839	Wadi Halfa
3843	Others
3845	Heraldry

Genealogy
3846	General
3847	Special

Biographies
3848	Collected
3849	Individual (A-Z, 299 scheme, by person)

Egypt (cont.)

Goegraphy, description, etc. of Egypt
3974-3980	General works (By date)
3982	History of travel
[3986]	Economic history and conditions [Discontinued]
3988	Special customs
3990	Guidebooks
3991	Gazetteers
3992	Maps

Economic history and conditions
3993.1-.199	General works
3993.500-.999	Contemporary works (By date)

Finance
3994.1-.199	General works
3994.500-.999	Contemporary works (By date)
3998	Registers, directories, etc.

Races
4000	General works
[4005]	Shilluks [Discontinued. See Afr 3817]
4008	Copts
4010	Arabs
4012	Ishmaelites
4015	Bejas
4020	Other indigenous races [See also Afr 3816-3817]
4025	European elements
4040	Religion

Districts, etc.
4045	Isthmus of Suez
4050	Libyan Desert
4055	Arabian Desert
4060	Nubia

Egyptian Sudan
[4070]	Geography, description, etc. [Discontinued. See Afr 3805-3812]
	Local
[4072]	Gezira [Discontinued. See Afr 3826]
[4080]	Kordofan [Discontinued. See Afr 3821]
[4085]	Darfur [Discontinued. See Afr 3822]
[4090]	Bahr-el-Gazel [Discontinued. See Afr 3823]
[4091]	Economic conditions, etc. [Discontinued. See Afr 3813-3814]
[4092]	Missions [Discontinued. See Afr 3818]
[4093]	Races [Discontinued. See Afr 3816-3817]
4095	Equatorial Egypt [Include here general works about the exploration of the upper Nile. See also with Sudan in Afr 3805-3810 and 3820-3829]

Cities, towns, etc. of Egypt
[See also Afr 3830-3843]
4098	Egyptian cities in general
4105	Alexandria
4108	A (Others)
4110	Berber
4113	B (Others)
4115	Cairo
4118	C (Others)
4120	Damietta
4125	D (Others)
4128	E
4130	F
4133	G
4135	H
4138	Ismailia
4140	I (Others)
4143	J
4150	K
4153	L
4155	M
4158	N
4163	O
4165	Port Said

	Egypt (cont.)
	Cities, towns, etc. of Egypt (cont.)
4168	P (Others)
4170	Q
4173	R
4178	Suez
4180	S Others)
4183	T
4185	U
4187	V
4190	W
4191	X
4192	Y
4193	Z
4195	Heraldry
	Genealogy
4196	General
4197	Special
	Biographies
4198	Collected
4199	Individual (A-Z, 800 scheme, by person)
	Ethiopia
4201-4224	Periodicals (A-Z)
[4225]	Folios [Discontinued]
4226	Bibliographies
4228	Pamphlet volumes
	Collected source materials
4230	General
4232	Statutes
4233	Treaties
4234	Other
4235	Historiography
4236	Church history in general
	Government and administration
4238	General works
4240	Special topics
4242	General politics; political parties
4244	Collected political biographies
4255-4260	General history (By date)
4265	General special
	History by periods
	Ancient Ethiopia to 4th century
4280	General works
4285	Special topics
	Christianization (4th to 6th centuries)
4290	General works
4295	Special topics
	6th to 16th centuries
4300	General works
4301	7th century
4302	8th century
4303	9th century
4304	10th century
4305	11th century
4306	12th century
4307	13th century
4308	14th century
4309	15th century
	16th century
4310	General works
4313	Lebna Dengel (1508-1540)
4315	Mohammedan conflicts and conquest
4317	Mohammed Gragne
4320	Relations with the Portuguese in general
	Galawdewos (1540-1559)
4330	General works
4335	Expedition of Da Gama
4338	Other special
4339	Minas
4340	Later Portuguese expeditions

	Ethiopia (cont.)
	History by periods (cont.)
	17th century
4345	General works
4349	Susemyos (1606-1632)
	Facilidas and end of Catholic missions (1633-1665)
4350	General works
4355	Special topics
4357	Christianity in the 18th century
	18th century to rise of Theodore (to 1855)
4360	General works
4365	Special topics
4368	Missions in the 19th century
	Theodore (1855-1868)
4370	General works
4375	English expedition (1867-1868)
4378	Other special topics
	John (1871-1889)
4380	General works
4382	War with Egypt (1875-1876)
4384	Wars with Italy in general
4385	Italian war with John (1886)
4386	Battles of Saati and Dogali (1887)
4387	War with the Dervishes (1888-1889)
4388	Other special topics
	20th century
4389	General works
	Menelek II (1889-1913)
4390	General works
4392	War with Italy (1895-1896)
4393	Siege of Nakalleh (8 Dec.-2 Jan. 1895-1896)
4394	Battle of Adua (March 1896)
4396	Policy of the Powers
4410	Lij Yasu (1913-1916)
4420	Zauditu (1916-1928)
	Haile Selassie I (1928-)
4430	General works
4431	War with Italy (1934-1935)
4432	Italian rule (1936-1941)
4433	1941-
4434	Other special topics
	General relations with foreign powers
4500	General works
	Egypt
4505	General works
4506	Special topics
	England
4508	General works
4509	Special topics
	Italy
4512	General works
4513	Special topics
	France
4515	General works
4516	Special topics
	Russia
4518	General works
4519	Special topics
	Other powers
4522	General works
4523	Special topics
	Geography, description, etc.
4555-4560	General works (By date)
4568	Special customs
4570	Guidebooks
4571	Views

Ethiopia (cont.)

Geography, description, etc. (cont.)

4572	Maps
4573	Economic history and conditions
4574	Finance

Races

4575	General works
4580	Abyssinians Proper
4582	Afars (Danakil)
4585	Falasha (i.e. Jews)
4590	Gallas
4591	Gurages
4592	Konsos
4593	Mensa
4598	Others

Religion. See Afr 4236, 4290, 4357, etc.

Provinces

4600	General works
4603	Tigre
4605	Amhara
4608	Godjam
4610	Shoa
4612	Harrar
4615	Nile
4618	Kaffa
4620	Equatorial
	Eritrea. See Afr 4701-4749

Cities, towns, etc.

4635	General works
4640	Addis Ababa
4641	Adua
4642	Aksum
4643	Amba-Mariam
4644	Ankober
4645	Antala
4646	A (Others)
4648	Besso
4649	B (Others)
4651	C
4653	Debra-Tabor
4654	D (Others)
4655	E
4656	F
4658	Gondar
4659	G (Others)
4660	H
4662	I
4664	J
4665	K
4667	L
4669	Magdala
4670	Mahdera-Mariam
4671	Makalle
4673	M (Others)
4674	N
4676	O
4678	P
4680	Q
4682	R
4684	Sokoto
4685	S (Others)
4688	T
4689	U
4690	V
4691	W
4692	X
4693	Y
4694	Z
4695	Heraldry

Genealogy

4696	General
4697	Special

Ethiopia (cont.)

Biographies

4698	Collected
4699.1-.99	Individual (A-Z, 99 scheme, by person)

4700	**Italian Africa in general (By date, e.g. .40 for 1940)**
	[See also Eritrea, Somaliland, Libya, etc.]

Eritrea

4701	Periodicals
4702	Bibliographies
4703	Pamphlet volumes
4705	Collected source materials
4707	Historiography
4710	Government and administration
4712	General politics; political parties
4715-4720	General history (By date)
4725	General special

History by periods

4728	Before 1869
4730	1869-1890
4731	Wars with Dervishes (1890-)
4732	1890-1952
4734	1952-

Geography, description, etc.

4742	General works
4743	Special customs
4744	Guidebooks, maps, etc.
4745	Economic history and conditions

Provinces, cities, towns, etc.

4746	Assab
4747	Others
4748	Heraldry; Genealogy

Biographies

4749.1-.99	Collected (A-Z, 99 scheme, by author)
4749.101-.399	Individual (A-Z, 299 scheme, by person)

Italian Somaliland; Somalia

4750	Periodicals
4753	Bibliographies
4755	Pamphlet volumes
4757	Collected source materials
4758	Historiography
4760	Government and administration
4762	General politics; political parties
4764	General history
4766	General special

History by periods

4768	Before 1889
4770	1889-1960
4772	1960-
4785	Geography, description, etc.
4787	Economic history and conditions
4788	Races
4789	Religion; missions
4790	Local
4795	Heraldry

Genealogy

4796	General
4797	Special

Biographies

4798	Collected
4799.1-.99	Individual (A-Z, 99 scheme, by person)

French Somaliland

4800	Periodicals
4801	Bibliographies
4803	Pamphlet volumes
4805	Collected source materials
4807	Historiography
4810	Government and administration

	French Somaliland (cont.)
4812	General politics; political parties
4815-4820	General history (By date)
4825	General special
	History by periods
4830	History to 1881
	1881-1946
4833	General works
4835	Building of railway
4839	Other special topics
	1946-
4840	General works
	Geography, description, etc.
4865-4870	General works (By date)
4875	Special customs
4876	Guidebooks
4877	Maps
4878	Economic history and conditions
4879	Finance
4880	Races
4882	Religion; missions
4883	Provinces
	Cities, towns, etc.
4886	Obock
4888	Sagallo
4890	Tadjura
4892	Djibuti
4894	Others
4895	Heraldry
	Genealogy
4896	General
4897	Special
	Biographies
4898	Collected
4899.1-.99	Individual (A-Z, 99 scheme, by person)
	British Somaliland
4900	Periodicals
4901	Bibliographies
4903	Pamphlet volumes
4905	Collected source materials
4907	Historiography
4908	Government and administration
4910	General politics; political parties
4915-4920	General history (By date)
4925	General special
	History by periods
4930	History to 1884
4933	British protectorate (1884-1894)
	1894-1960
4935	General works
4937	The Mad Mulla
4939	Other special topics
	1960-
4940	General works
	Geography, description, etc.
4965-4970	General works (By date)
4975	Special customs
4976	Guidebooks
4977	Maps
4978	Economic history and conditions
4979	Finance
4980	Races
4982	Religion; missions
4983	Provinces
	Cities, towns, etc.
4986	Berbera
4988	Zeila

	British Somaliland (cont.)
	Cities, towns, etc. (cont.)
4990	Bulhar
4992	Karam
4993	Zeilaof
4994	Others
4995	Heraldry
	Genealogy
4996	General
4997	Special
	Biographies
4998	Collected
4999.1-.99	Individual (A-Z, 9. scheme, by person)
	French Africa in general
5000	Periodicals
	Special organizations, etc.
5001.1-.99	General works on all the organizations together
	Union Africaine et Malgache; Organization Commune Africaine et Malgache (1965-)
5001.100	Periodicals issued by
5001.102	Monographs issued by
	Works about
5001.105	Bibliographies
5001.107	General works
5001.109	Special topics
	Specialized agencies of UAM [Divide each like .100-.109]
5001.110-.119	Organization africaine et malgache de coopération économique
5001.120-.129	Pacte de défense commune
5001.130-.139	Union africaine et malgache des postes et télé-communications
5001.140-.149	Comité des ministres des transports
5001.150-.159	Air Africaine
5003	Bibliographies
5005	Pamphlet volumes
5008	Collected source materials
5010	Government and administration
5012	General politics; political parties
5014-5020	General history (By date)
5023	General special
	History by periods
5025	Ancient
5030	Medieval
5032	Modern in general
5035	19th century
5040	20th century
5045	Geography, description, etc.
5046	Economic and financial conditions
5048	Races
5049	Religion
	French West Africa in general
5050	Periodicals
5051	Bibliographies
5052	Collected source materials
5053	Government and administration
5054	General history
5055.1-.99	General special
	History by periods
5055.100-.199	Before 1895
5055.200-.399	1895-1946
5055.400-.599	1946-1958
5055.600-	1958-
5056	Geography, description, etc. (By date, e.g. .131 for 1931)
5057	Economic and financial conditions
5058.1-	Races
5058.501-	Religion
5059	Collected biographies

Mauritania

5060	Periodicals
5063	Bibliographies
5065	Pamphlet volumes
5066	Collected source materials
5068	Historiography
5070	Government and administration
5072	General politics; political parties
5074	General history
5076	General special

	History by periods
5078	Before 1800
5079	1800-1900
5080	1900-1946
5081	1946-1958
5082	1958-
5090	Geography, description, etc.
5091	Economic and financial conditions
5093	Races
5094	Religion; missions
5095	Special customs

	Local
5096	Adrar
5098	Others

	Biographies
5099.1-.99	Collected (A-Z, 99 scheme, by author)
5099.101-.399	Individual (A-Z, 299 scheme, by person)

Senegal

5100	Periodicals
5103	Bibliographies
5105	Pamphlet volumes
5106	Collected source materials
5108	Historiography
5110	Government and administration
5112	General politics; political parties
5114-5120	General history (By date)
5125	General special

	History by periods
5128	Before 1800
5130	1800-1900
8135	1900-1946
5140	1946-1958
5145	1958-1960
5150	1960-
5180	Geography, description, etc.

	Economic conditions
5183.1-.199	General works
5183.500-.999	Contemporary works (By date)

	Finance
5184.1-.199	General works
5184.500-.999	Contemporary works (By date)
5185	Races
5187	Religion; missions
5188	Special customs
5190	Local

	Biographies
5199.1-.99	Collected (A-Z, 99 scheme, by author)
5199.101-.399	Individual (A-Z, 299 scheme, by person)

Sudan; Mali

[Include the former Upper Senegal and Niger
Colony, French Sudan, and Mali Federation]

5200	Periodicals
5203	Bibliographies
5205	Pamphlet volumes
5206	Collected source materials
5208	Historiography
5210	Government and administration
5212	General politics; political parties
5217-5220	General history (By date)
5223	General special

Sudan; Mali (cont.)

	History by periods
5225	To 1870
5227	French conquest
5228	1900-1960 (French rule)
5230	1960- (Republic)
5235	Geography, description, etc. (By date, e.g. .250 for 1950)
5240	Economic conditions
5241	Finance
5243	Races (299 scheme, by race)
	[Include Bambara, Fulah, Sangara, Solima, Tuat]
5245	Religion; missions
5246	Special customs

	Local
5247	Timbuctu
5248	Others

	Biographies
5249.1-.99	Collected (A-Z, 99 scheme, by author)
5249.101-.399	Individual (A-Z, 299 scheme, by person)

Niger

5250	Periodicals
5251	Bibliographies
5252	Collected source materials
5253	Historiography
5254	Government and administration
	[Include general politics; political parties]
5255	General history
5256	General special

	History by periods
5257.1-.99	Before 1900
5257.100-.299	1900-1946
5257.300-.499	1946-1958
5257.500-	1958-
5260	Geography, description, etc.
5262	Economic conditions
5263	Finance
5265	Races
5266	Religion; missions
5267	Special customs
5268	Local

	Biographies
5269.1-.99	Collected (A-Z, 99 scheme, by author)
5269.101-.399	Individual (A-Z, 299 scheme, by person)

Upper Volta

5270	Periodicals
5271	Bibliographies
5272	Collected source materials
5273	Historiography
5274	Government and administration
	[Include general politics; political parties]
5275	General history
5276	General special

	History by periods
5277.1-.99	Before 1900
5277.100-.299	1900-1946
5277.300-.499	1946-1958
5277.500-	1958-
5280	Geography, description, etc.
5282	Economic conditions
5283	Finance
5285	Races (299 scheme, by race)
	[Include Mossi]
5286	Religion; missions
5287	Special customs
5288	Local

	Biographies
5289.1-.99	Collected (A-Z, 99 scheme, by author)
5289.101-.399	Individual (A-Z, 299 scheme, by person)

French Guinea

5300	Periodicals
5303	Bibliographies
5305	Pamphlet volumes
5306	Collected source materials
5308	Historiography
5310	Government and administration
5312	General politics; political parties
5314	General history
5315	General special

History by periods
5316.1-.99	Before 1860
5316.100-.299	1860-1900
5316.300-.499	1900-1946
5316.500-.699	1946-1958
5316.700-	1958-
5318	Geography, description, etc.
5319	Economic and financial conditions
5320	Races
	[Include Baga, Mande, Mandingo, Tene]
5321	Religion; missions
5322	Special customs
5323	Local

Biographies
5324.1-.99	Collected (A-Z, 99 scheme, by author)
5324.101-.399	Individual (A-Z, 299 scheme, by person)

Ivory Coast

5325	Periodicals
5326	Bibliographies
5329	Pamphlet volumes
5331	Collected source materials
5332	Historiography
5333	Government and administration
5335	General politics; political parties
5337	General history
5338	General special

History by periods
5340.1-.99	Before 1840
5340.100-.299	1840-1893
5340.300-.499	1893-1946
5340.500-.699	1946-1958
5340.700-	1958-
5342	Geography, description etc.
5343	Economic and financial conditions
5344	Races
5345	Religion; missions
5346	Local

Biographies
5349.1-.99	Collected (A-Z, 99 scheme, by author)
5349.101-.399	Individual (A-Z, 299 scheme, by person)

Togo. See Afr 6650-6699

Dahomey; Slave Coast

5350	Periodicals (A-Z)
5353	Bibliographies
5355	Pamphlet volumes
5358	Collected source materials
5359	Historiography
5360	Government and administration
5362	General politics; political parties
5365	General history
5366	General special

History by periods
5368	Early to 1818
5370	1818-1894
5372	1894-1946
5374	1946-1960
5376	1960-
5385	Geography, description, etc.
5387	Economic conditions
5388	Finance
5390	Races
5392	Religion; missions

Dahomey; Slave Coast (cont.)

5394	Special customs
5396	Local

Biographies
5399.1-.99	Collected (A-Z, 99 scheme, by author)
5399.101-.399	Individual (A-Z, 299 scheme, by person)

French Equatorial Africa in general

5400	Periodicals
5401	Bibliographies
5402	Collected source materials
5403	Government and administration
5404	General history

History by periods
5405.1-.99	Before 1840
5405.100-.199	1840-1910
5405.200-.399	1910-1946
5405.400-.499	1946-1958
5405.500-	1958-
5406	Geography, description, etc. (By date, e.g. .231 for 1931)
	[Include du Chaillu]
5407	Economic and financial conditions
5408	Special customs, etc.
5409	Collected biographies

Gabon

5410	Periodicals
5411	Bibliographies
5412	Collected source materials
5413	Historiography
5414	Government and administration
	[Include general politics; political parties]
5415	General history
5416	General special

History by periods
5417.1-.99	Before 1840
5417.100-.299	1840-1910
5417.300-.499	1910-1946
5417.500-.699	1946-1958
5417.700-	1958-
5420	Geography, description, etc.
5422	Economic conditions
5423	Finance
5425	Races
	[Include Pahuin, Fan]
5426	Religion; missions
	[Include Schweitzer and Lambaréné]
5427	Special customs
5428	Local

Biographies
5429.1-.99	Collected (A-Z, 99 scheme, by author)
5429.101-.399	Individual (A-Z, 299 scheme, by person

Congo Republic (Brazzaville); Middle or Lower Congo

5430	Periodicals
5431	Bibliographies
5432	Collected source materials
5433	Historiography
5434	Government and administration
	[Include general politics; political parties]
5435	General history
5436	General special

History by periods
5437.1-.99	Before 1840
5437.100-.299	1840-1910
5437.300-.499	1910-1946
5437.500-.699	1946-1958
5437.700-	1958-
5440	Geography, description, etc.
5442	Economic conditions
5443	Finance
5445	Races
5446	Religion; missions
5447	Special customs

Congo Republic... (cont.)

5448	Local

	Biographies
5449.1-.99	Collected (A-Z, 99 scheme, by author)
5449.101-.399	Individual (A-Z, 299 scheme, by person)

Central African Republic; Ubangi-Shari

5450	Periodicals
5451	Bibliographies
5452	Collected source materials
5453	Historiography
5454	Government and administration
	[Include general politics; political parties]
5455	General history
5456	General special

	History by periods
5457.1-.99	Before 1840
5457.100-.299	1840-1910
5457.300-.499	1910-1946
5457.500-.699	1946-1958
5457.700-	1958-
5460	Geography, description, etc.
5462	Economic conditions
5463	Finance
5465	Races
5466	Religion; missions
5467	Special customs
5468	Local

	Biographies
5469.1-.99	Collected (A-Z, 99 scheme, by author)
5469.101-.399	Individual (A-Z, 299 scheme, by person)

Chad

5470	Periodicals
5471	Bibliographies
5472	Collected source materials
5473	Historiography
5474	Government and administration
	[Include general politics; political parties]
5475	General history
5476	General special

	History by periods
5477.1-.99	Before 1840
5477.100-.299	1840-1920
5477.300-.499	1920-1946
5477.500-.699	1946-1958
5477.700-	1958-
5480	Geography, description, etc.
5482	Economic conditions
5483	Finance
5485	Races
5486	Religion; missions
5487	Special customs
5488	Local

	Biographies
5489.1-.99	Collected (A-Z, 99 scheme, by author)
5489.101-.399	Individual (A-Z, 299 scheme, by person)

Cameroun. See Afr 6700-6749

Madagascar

5501-5526	Periodicals (A-Z)
5530	Bibliographies
5533	Pamphlet volumes

	Collected source materials
5536	Treaties, etc.
5538	Others
5539	Historiography
5540	Government and administration
5542	General politics; political parties
5544-5550	General history (By date)
5555	General special

Madagascar (cont.)

	History by periods
5565	Early to 1600

	1600-1700
5570	General works
5573	Early colonization
	[French in 1642 and English in 1644]
5575	Pirates
5580	1700-1808

	19th century
5585	General works
	Radama I (1808-1828)
5590	General works
5593	Introduction of Christianity
5600	Ranavalona I (1828-1861)
5605	Radama II (1861-1868)
5615	Ranavalona II (1868-1883)
	Ranavalona III (1883-1897)
5620	General works
5625	War with France, 1882-1884
5630	Anglo-French Agreement, 1890
5635	French expedition, 1895
5640	French colony (1896-1958)

	Malagasy Republic (1958-)
5645	General works
5647	Special topics

	Geography, description, etc.
5744-5750	General works (By date)
5753	Special customs
5755	Guidebooks
5757	Maps
5758	Economic and financial conditions
5760	Races

	Religion
5765	General works; Christian missions
5767	Islam in Madagascar
5770	Provinces

	Cities, towns, etc.
5780	General
5781	Tamatave
5783	Tananarive
5785	Diego Suarez
5787	Others

	Biographies
5789.1-.99	Collected (A-Z, 99 scheme, by author)
5789.101-.399	Individual (A-Z, 299 scheme, by person)

Islands near Madagascar

5790	General
5792	Sainte Marie
5794	Nosi Be

	Comoro Islands
5796	General
5798	Special islands
5799	Others

Mascarenes in general

5800	Periodicals
5801	Bibliographies
5802	Pamphlet volumes
5803	Collected source materials
5804	Government and administration
5805	General history

	History by periods
5806.1-.99	Before 1800
5806.100-.299	1800-1900
5806.300-	1900-
5807	Geography, description, etc.
5808	Races
5809	Collected biographies

Mauritius; Isle de France
5810	Periodicals
5813	Bibliographies
5815	Pamphlet volumes
5817	Collected source materials
5820	Government and administration
5822	General politics; political parties
5824-5830	General history (By date)

History by periods
5832	To 1800
5833	1800-1900
5835	1900-
5840	Religion; missions
5842	Geography, description, etc.
5843	Economic and financial conditions
5844	Races
5845	Special customs
5846	Local Mauritius
5847	Dependencies of Mauritius collectively

Biographies
5849.1-.99	Collected (A-Z, 99 scheme, by author)
5849.101-.399	Individual (A-Z, 299 scheme, by person)

Réunion
5850	Periodicals
5853	Bibliographies
5855	Pamphlet volumes
5857	Collected source materials
5860	Government and administration
5862	General politics; political parties
5864-5870	General history (By date)

History by periods
5871	Before 1700
5872	1700-
5874	Geography, description, etc.
5875	Races
5876	Local

Biographies
5879.1-.99	Collected (A-Z, 99 scheme, by author)
5879.101-.399	Individual (A-Z, 299 scheme, by person)

Rodriguez
5880	Periodicals
5881	Bibliographies
5882	Pamphlet volumes
5883	Collected source materials
5884	Government and administration
5885	General history

History by periods
5886.1-.99	Before 1810
5886.100-	1810-
5887	Geography, description, etc.
5888	Local

Biographies
5889.1-.99	Collected (A-Z, 99 scheme, by author)
5889.101-.399	Individual (A-Z, 299 scheme, by person)

Seychelles
5890	Periodicals
5891	Bibliographies
5892	Pamphlet volumes
5893	Collected source materials
5894	Government and administration
5895	General history

History by periods
5896.1-.99	Before 1810
5896.100-.299	1810-1900
5896.300-	1900-
5897	Geography, description, travel, etc.
5898	Local

Seychelles (cont.)

Biographies
5899.1-.99	Collected (A-Z, 99 scheme, by author)
5899.101-.399	Individual (A-Z, 299 scheme, by person)

Spanish Africa in general
[Include Spanish West Africa in general]
5900	Periodicals
5901	Bibliographies
5903	Pamphlet volumes
5905	Collected source materials
5906	Historiography
5907	Government and administration
5910	General politics; political parties
5912	General history
5914	General special

History by periods
5915	Before 1800
5916	1800-1900
5917	1900-
5920	Geography, description, etc.
5921	Economic and financial conditions
5922	Races
5923	Special customs, etc.

Biographies
5924.1-.99	Collected (A-Z, 99 scheme, by author)
5924.101-.399	Individual (A-Z, 299 scheme, by person)

Rio de Oro
[Include Spanish Sahara]
5925	Periodicals
5927	Bibliographies
5929	Pamphlet volumes
5931	Collected source materials
5933	Government and administration
5935	General politics; political parties
5937	General history
5938	General special

History by periods
5939	Before 1800
5940	1800-1900
5941	1900-
5944	Geography, description, etc.
5945	Economic and financial conditions
5946	Races
5947	Local
	Biographies. See Afr 5924

5949	**Ifni**

Spanish Guinea
5950	Periodicals
5951.1-.99	Bibliographies
5951.100-	Collected source materials
5952	Historiography
5953	Government and administration
5954	General politics; political parties
5955	General history
5956	General special

History by periods
5957.1-.99	Before 1800
5957.100-.299	1800-1900
5957.300-	1900-
5960	Geography, description, etc.
5962	Economic conditions
5963	Finance
5965	Special customs
5967	Religion; missions
5968	Races

Biographies
5969.1-.99	Collected (A-Z, 99 scheme, by author)
5969.100-.899	Individual (A-Z, 800 scheme, by person)

Spanish Guinea (cont.)

Local
  Muni or Rio Muni (Mainland)
    Periodicals. See Afr 5950
5970.1-.99   Bibliographies
5970.100-   Collected source materials
5971   Government and administration
5972   History
5973   Geography, economic conditions, religion, etc.
    Races. See Afr 5968
5974   Local (Cities, towns, etc.)
    Biographies. See Afr 5969

Elobey
  Periodicals. See Afr 5950
5975.1-.99 Bibliographies
5975.100- Collected source materials
5976 Government and administration
5977 History
5978 Geography, economic conditions, religion, etc.
  Races. See Afr 5968
5979 Local (Cities, towns, etc.)
  Biographies. See Afr 5969

Corisco
  Periodicals. See Afr 5950
5980.1-.99 Bibliographies
5980.100- Collected source materials
5981 Government and administration
5982 History
5983 Geography, economic conditions, religion, etc.
  Races. See Afr 5968
5984 Local (Cities, towns, etc.)
  Biographies. See Afr 5969

Annobon
  Periodicals. See Afr 5950
5985.1-.99 Bibliographies
5985.100- Collected source materials
5986 Government and administration
5987 History
5988 Geography, economic conditions, religion, etc.
  Races. See Afr 5968
5989 Local (Cities, towns, etc.)
  Biographies. See Afr 5969

Fernando Po
  Periodicals. See Afr 5950
5990.1-.99 Bibliographies
5990.100- Collected source materials
5991 Government and administration
5992 History
5993 Geography, economic conditions, religion, etc.
  Races. See Afr 5968
5994 Local (Cities, towns, etc.)
  Biographies. See Afr 5969
5998 Other local

Canary Islands. See Span

British Africa in general
6000 Periodicals
6003 Bibliographies
6005 Pamphlet volumes
6007 Collected source materials
6009 Historiography
6010 Government and administration
6012 General politics; political parties
6014-6020 General history (By date)
6025 General special

  History by periods
6030 Before 1800
6032 1800-1900
6034 1900-1960
6036 1960-
6045 Geography, description, etc.
6046 Economic and financial conditions
6047 Religion; missions

British Africa in general (cont.)
6048 Races
6049 Collected biographies

British West Africa in general
6050 Periodicals
6053 Bibliographies
6055 Pamphlet volumes
6057 Collected source materials
6059 Historiography
6060 Government and administration
6062 General politics; political parties
6064-6070 General history (By date)
6075 General special

  History by periods
6080 Before 1800
6082 1800-1900
6084 1900-1960
6086 1960-
6095 Geography, description, etc.
6096 Economic and financial conditions
6097 Religion; missions
6098 Races
6099 Collected biographies

Gambia
6100 Periodicals
6103 Bibliographies
6105 Pamphlet volumes
6107 Collected source materials
6108 Historiography
6109 Government and administration
6111 General politics; political parties
6113 General history
6114 General special

  History by periods
6115.1-.199 Before 1800
6115.200-.499 1800-1888
6115.500- 1888-1960
6116 1960-
6118 Geography, description, etc.
6119 Economic and financial conditions
6120 Races
6121 Religion; missions
6122 Local

  Biographies
6124.1-.99 Collected (A-Z, 99 scheme, by author)
6124.101-.399 Individual (A-Z, 299 scheme, by person)

Sierra Leone
6125 Periodicals
6128 Bibliographies
6130 Pamphlet volumes
6132 Collected source materials
6133 Historiography
6134 Government and administration
6136 General politics; political parties
6138 General history
6139 General special

  History by periods
6140.1-.199 Before 1800
6140.200-.499 1800-1895
6140.500- 1895-1960
6141 1960-
6143 Geography, description, etc.
6144 Economic and financial conditions
6145 Races
6146 Religion; missions
6147 Local

  Biographies
6149.1-.99 Collected (A-Z, 99 scheme, by author)
6149.101-.399 Individual (A-Z, 299 scheme, by person)

Ghana; Gold Coast

6150	Periodicals
6153	Bibliographies
6155	Pamphlet volumes
6157	Collected source materials
6159	Historiography
6160	Government and administration
6162	General politics; political parties
6164	General history
6166	General special

History by periods

6168	Before 1870
6170	First native war (1873-1874)
6172	Second native war (1895-1896)
6174	Third native war (1900)
6176	1900-1960
6178	1960-
6192	Geography, description, etc.
6193	Economic and financial conditions
6194	Races
6195	Religion; missions
6196	Local

[For Togo, see Afr 6650-6699]

Biographies

6198.1-.99	Collected (A-Z, 99 scheme, by author)
6198.100-.899	Individual (A-Z, 800 scheme, by person)

Nigeria

6200	Periodicals (A-Z, .1-.26)
6203	Bibliographies
6205	Pamphlet volumes
6208	Collected source materials
6209	Historiography
6210	Government and administration
6212	General politics; political parties
6214	General history
6216	General special

History by periods

6218	Before 1860
6220	1860-1900
6222	1900-1960
6225	1960-
6275	Geography, description, etc.
6276	Special customs
6277	Economic and financial conditions
6280	Races
6282	Religion; missions

Local

6283	General works

Northern Region

6284	General works
6285	Special topics
	Provinces, cities, etc. See Afr 6292-6295

Western Region

6286	General works
6287	Special topics
	Provinces, cities, etc. See Afr 6292-6295

Mid-Western Region

6288	General works
6289	Special topics
	Provinces, cities, etc. See Afr 6292-6295

Eastern Region, Biafra

6290	General works
6291	Special topics
	Provinces, cities, etc. See Afr 6292-6295
6292	Individual provinces
	[See also Cameroons in Afr 6700-6749]

Cities, towns, etc.

6293	Lagos
6294	Ibadan
6295	Others (A-Z, 299 scheme, by place)

Nigeria (cont.)

Biographies

6298.1-.99	Collected (A-Z, 99 scheme, by author)
6298.100-.899	Individual (A-Z, 800 scheme, by person)

British East Africa in general

6300	Periodicals (A-Z, 99 scheme)

East African Community

6301.100	Periodicals issued by
6301.102	Monographs issued by

Works about

6301.104	Bibliographies
6301.105	General works
6301.109	Special topics
6303	Bibliographies
6305	Pamphlet volumes
6308	Collected source materials
6309	Historiography
6310	Government and administration
6312	General politics; political parties
6314	General history
6316	General special

History by periods

6320	Before 1800

19th century

6323	First half
6328	Second half

20th century

6330	General
6333	1900-1962
6335	1962-
[6385]	Missions [Discontinued]
6390	Geography, description, etc.
6391	Special customs
6392	Economic and financial conditions
6395	Races
6397	Religion; missions
6398	Collected biographies

Kenya

6400	Periodicals (A-Z, 99 scheme)
6403	Bibliographies
6405	Pamphlet volumes
6408	Collected source materials
6409	Historiography
6410	Government and administration
6412	General politics; political parties
6415	General history
6420	General special

History by periods

6425	Before 1800
6427	1800-1885
6430	1885-1963
6435	1963-
6455	Geography, description, etc.
6456	Special customs
6457	Economic and financial conditions
6460	Races
6463	Religion; missions
6465	Local

Biographies

6470.1-.99	Collected (A-Z, 99 scheme, by author)
6470.101-.399	Individual (A-Z, 299 scheme, by person)

Uganda

6475	Periodicals
6478	Bibliographies
6480	Pamphlet volumes
6482	Collected source materials
6483	Historiography
6484	Government and administration
6486	General politics; political parties

Uganda (cont.)
6488   General history
6490   General special

    History by periods
6495   Before 1500
6496   1500-1850
6497   1850-1900
6498   1900-1962
6500   1962-
6535   Geography, description, etc.
6536   Special customs
6538   Economic and financial conditions
6540   Races
6541   Religion; missions
6542   Local

    Biographies
6549.1-.99   Collected (A-Z, 99 scheme, by author)
6549.101-.399   Individual (A-Z, 299 scheme, by person)

Zanzibar
6550   Periodicals
6553   Bibliographies
6555   Pamphlet volumes
6558   Collected source materials
6559   Historiography
6560   Government and administration
6562   General politics; political parties
6565   General history
6566   General special

    History by periods
6568   Before 1800
6570   1800-1890
6572   1890-1963
6575   1963-
6585   Geography, description, etc.
6586   Special customs
6588   Economic and financial conditions
6590   Races
6591   Religion; missions

    Local
6592   Pemba
6595   Others

    Biographies
6598   Collected
6599   Individual (A-Z, 99 scheme, by person)

Tanganyika; Tanzania. See Afr 6750-6898

German Africa in general
6600   Periodicals
6603   Bibliographies
6605   Pamphlet volumes
6608   Collected source materials
6609   Historiography
6610   Government and administration
6612   General politics; political parties
6615   General history
6616   General special

    History by periods
6618   Before 1850
6619   1850-1914
6620   1914-
[6640] History - Special [Discontinued]
6645   Geography, description, etc.
6646   Economic and financial conditions
6647   Religion; missions
6648   Races
6649   Collected biographies

Togo
    [Include the former German colony, the British and French mandates, the Togoland section of Ghana, and the independent republic of Togo]
6650   Periodicals
6653   Bibliographies
6655   Pamphlet volumes
6657   Collected source materials
6659   Historiography
6660   Government and administration
6662   General politics, political parties
6664   General history
6666   General special

    History by periods
6668   Before 1880
6669   1880-1914
6670   1914-1957
6675   1957-
6685   Geography, description, etc.
6686   Economic and financial conditions
6688   Races
6689   Religion; missions
6690   Special customs
6692   Local

    Biographies
6698   Collected
6699   Individual (A-Z, 99 scheme)

Cameroons
    [Include the former German colony, the British and French mandates, the Cameroons province of Nigeria, and the independent republic of Cameroun]
6700   Periodicals (A-Z, 99 scheme)
6703   Bibliographies
6705   Pamphlet volumes
6708   Collected source materials
6709   Historiography
6710   Government and administration
6712   General politics; political parties
6715   General history
6716   General special

    History by periods
6718   Before 1880
6719   1880-1914
6720   1914-1960
6725   1960-
6738   Geography, description, etc.
6739   Economic and financial conditions
6740   Races
6741   Religion; missions
6742   Special customs
6743   Local

    Biographies
6748   Collected
6749   Individual (A-Z, 99 scheme, by person)

Tanganyika; Tanzania
6750   Periodicals
6753   Bibliographies
6755   Pamphlet volumes
6757   Collected source materials
6759   Historiography
6760   Government and administration
6762   General politics; political parties
6767-6770   General history (By date)
6772   General special

    History by periods
6775   Before 1800
6776   1800-1850
6777   1850-1900
6778   1900-1914
6780   1914-1960
6785   1960-
[6850] History - Special [Discontinued]
6875-6880   Geography, description, etc. (By date)

	Tanganyika; Tanzania (cont.)
6881	Economic and financial conditions
6882	Special customs
6883	Races
6885	Religion; missions
	Local
6886	Dar es Salaam
6887	Kilimanjaro
6888	Tanga
6889	Victoria Nyanza
6890	Others
	Biographies
6898	Collected
6899	Individual (A-Z, 99 scheme, by person)
	Southwest Africa
6900	Periodicals
6903	Bibliographies
6905	Pamphlet volumes
6907	Collected source materials
6909	Historiography
6910	Government and adminstration
6912	General politics; political parties
6917-6920	General history (By date)
6922	General special
	History by periods
6925	To 1892
	1892-1914
6926	General works
6927	1897-1907
6930	1914-
6975-6980	Geography, description, etc. (By date)
6981	Economic and financial conditions
6984	Religion; missions
6985	Races
6987	Special customs
6988	Local (A-Z, 99 scheme, by place)
	Biographies
6989	Collected
6990	Individual (A-Z, 99 scheme, by person)
	Portuguese Africa in general
7000	Periodicals
7003	Bibliographies
7005	Pamphlet volumes
7008	Collected source materials
7009	Historiography
7010	Government and administration
7012	General politics; political parties
7015	General history
7018	General special
	History by periods
7020	Before 1800
7022	1800-1900
7025	1900-
7045	Geography, description, etc.
7046	Economic and financial conditions
7047	Religion; missions
7048	Races
7049	Collected biographies
	Portuguese Guinea
7050	Periodicals
7051	Bibliographies
7053	Pamphlet volumes
7055	Collected source materials
7056	Historiography
7057	Government and administration
7060	General politics; political parties
7062	General history
7064	General special

	Portuguese Guinea (cont.)
	History by periods
7065.1-.199	Before 1800
7065.200-.499	1800-1900
7065.500-	1900-
7068	Geography, description, etc.
7069	Economic and financial conditions
7070	Races
7071	Religion; missions
7072	Special customs
7073	Local
	Biographies
7074.1-.99	Collected (A-Z, 99 scheme)
7074.101-.399	Individual (A-Z, 299 scheme, by person)
	Cabinda
7075	Periodicals
7076	Bibliographies
7078	Pamphlet volumes
7080	Collected source materials
7081	Historiography
7082	Government and administration
7085	General politics; political parties
7087	General history
7089	General special
	History by periods
7090.1-.199	Before 1800
7090.200-.499	1800-1886
7090.500-	1886-
7093	Geography, description, etc.
7094	Economic and financial conditions
7095	Races
7096	Religion; missions
7098	Local
	Biographies
7099.1-.99	Collected (A-Z, 99 scheme)
7099.101-.399	Individual (A-Z, 299 scheme, by person)
	Angola; Portuguese West Africa
7100	Periodicals
7103	Bibliographies
7105	Pamphlet volumes
7108	Collected source materials
7109	Historiography
7110	Government and administration
7112	General politics; political parties
7114-7120	General history (By date)
7122	General special
	History by periods
7125	Before 1800
7127	1800-1886
7130	1886-1934
7135	1934-
7175	Geography, description, etc.
7176	Economic and financial conditions
7179	Special customs
7180	Races
7182	Religion; missions
	Local
7183	Regions, etc.
7185	San Salvador
7187	Others
	Biographies
7188.1-.99	Collected
7188.101-.399	Individual (A-Z, 299 scheme, by person)
7190	**Other Portuguese West Africa**
	[Include here Sao Tome e Principe, etc. For Azores, Madeira, and Cape Verde Islands, see Port.]

	Mozambique; Portuguese East Africa			Congo Republic (Leopoldville); Belgian Congo (cont.)
7200	Periodicals (A-Z, .1-.26)	7545-7550		General history (By date)
7203	Bibliographies	7555		General special
7205	Pamphlet volumes			
7208	Collected source materials			History by periods
7209	Historiography	7560		Early to 1882
7210	Government and administration	7565		1882-1890
7212	General politics; political parties			
7214-7220	General history (By date)			1891-1960
7222	General special	7567		General works
		7568		Questions of misgovernment
	History by periods	7570		European War (1914-1918)
7225	Before 1800	7575		1945-1960
7230	1800-1907			
7235	1907-1942			1960-
7240	1942-	7580		General works
7304-7310	Geography, description, etc. (By date)	7582		Special topics
7312	Economic and financial conditions	[7803]		Religion; missions [Discontinued]
7314	Special customs	7805-7810		Geography, description, etc. (By date)
7315	Races	7812		Economic and financial conditions (By date, e.g.
7318	Religion; missions			.260 for 1960)
		7814		Maps
	Local	7815		Races
	Districts	7817		Religion; missions
7320	Mozambique	7818		Special customs
7322	Zambezia			
7324	Lourenço Marques			Local
7326	Inhambane	7820		Indefinite regions and districts
7328	Gaza Region			
7330	Tete			Provinces
7332	Manica and Sofala	7835		Eastern province
7333	Cabo Delgado	7840		Equator province
7334	Niassa	7845		Kasai province
7335	Cities, towns, etc.	7850		Katanga province
		7855		Kivu province
	Biographies	7858		Kwilu province
7349.1-.99	Collected (A-Z, 99 scheme, by author)	7860		Leopoldville province
7349.101-.399	Individual (A-Z, 299 scheme, by person)	7865		Others
	Liberia			Cities and towns
7350	Periodicals	7870		Leopoldville
7353	Bibliographies	7871-7896		Others (A-Z)
7355	Pamphlet volumes			
7357	Collected source materials			Biographies
7359	Historiography	7900		Collected
7360	Government and administration	7901-7926		Individual (A-Z, by person)
7362	General politics; poliitcal parties			
7367-7370	General history (By date)			Ruanda-Urundi
7372	General special			[Include Rwanda and Burundi]
		7930		Periodicals
	History by periods	7931		Bibliographies
7373	Before 1822	7932		Collected source materials
7375	Settlement and early history (1822-1847)	7932.500-		Historiography
		7933		Government and administration
	Independent state (1847-)	7934		General politics; political parties
7377	1847-1911	7935		General history
7380	1911-1960	7936		General special
7385	1960-			
7455-7460	Geography, description, etc. (By date)			History by periods
7461	Economic and financial conditions	7937.1-.199		Before 1850
7465	Races	7937.200-.499		1850-1919
7468	Religion; missions	7937.500-		1919-1962
7469	Special customs	7938		1962-
		7940		Geography, description, etc.
	Local	7942		Economic conditions
7480	Monrovia	7943		Finance
7485	Others	7945		Races
		7946		Religion; missions
	Biographies	7947		Special customs
7488	Collected	7948		Local
7489	Individual (A-Z, 99 scheme, by person)			
				Biographies
	Congo Republic (Leopoldville); Belgian Congo	7949.1-.99		Collected (A-Z, 99 scheme, by author)
7501-7526	Periodicals (A-Z)	7949.101-.399		Individual (A-Z, 299 scheme, by person)
7530	Bibliographies			
7533	Pamphlet volumes			
7535	Collected source materials			
7538	Historiography			
7540	Government and administration			
7543	General politics; political parties			

South Africa in general

8001-8026	Periodicals (A-Z)
8028	Bibliographies
8029	Pamphlet volumes
	Collected source materials
8030	General
8032	Statutes
8033	Treaties
8035	Other
8037	Yearbooks and almanacs
8038	Dictionaries and encyclopedias
	Government and administration
8040	General works
8045	Special topics
8050	General politics; political parties
8055	Collected political biographies
8057	Historiography
	Military history
8060	General works
8063	Special topics
	Naval history
8065	General works
8068	Special topics
8084-8090	General history (By date)
8095	General special
	History by periods
8100	Early history (1487-1652)
	Dutch period (1652-1814)
8105	General works
8110	Special topics
8115	Huguenots
8125	British conquest (1795-1803, 1806-1814)
	British period (1814-1909)
8135	General works
8140	Special topics
8145	Church history (incl. missions)
	Native wars
8148	General works
	Kaffirs (1779-1877)
8150	General works
8152	Special wars
	Zulus (1822-1887)
8155	General works
8157	Special troubles to 1879
8160	War of 1879 (Cetewayo)
8163	Later history (1879-1887)
	Basutos (1851-1880)
8165	General works
8167	Special wars
8169	Annexation (1868)
	1814-1865
	[See also Afr 8175]
8170	General works
8172	Special topics
	The Dutch and their relations with the British during 1814-1899
8175	General works
8177	Slaagters Nek (1815)
8180	Great Trek (1836-1842) and Boer emigration (1834-1854)
	Natal
8190	Foundation and early history (1824-1843)
	[See also Afr 8157]
8195	British conquest (1842-1843)
	1843- . See Afr 8950-9075
	Orange River Colony
8200	Foundation and early history (1810-1854)
8205	British sovereignty (1848-1854)
	1854- . See Afr 9200-9299
	Transvaal (To War of 1899)
8210	General works
8215	Foundation and early history (1836-1877)
8220	Annexation by British (1877-1881)

South Africa in general (cont.)

	History by periods (cont.)
	British period (1814-1909) (cont.)
	The Dutch and their relations with the... (cont.)
	Transvaal (To War of 1899) (cont.)
8225	War of 1880-1881
8227	1881-1899
	[See also Afr 8283-8285]
8230	Biographies of Dutch in Transvaal
	[Include Kruger, etc.]
	1865-1899
	[See also Afr 8277-8285]
8235	General works
8238	Special topics
	Political biographies
8248	Collected
	Individual
8250	Cecil Rhodes
8252	Others (A-Z, 299 scheme, by person)
	Causes leading up to War of 1899
8277	Pamphlet volumes
8278-8280	General works (By date)
8283	Jameson Raid (Dec. 29-Jan. 2, 1895-1896) and Johannesburg Revolt (1896)
8285	Later developments (1896-1899)
	South African War (1899-1902)
8288-8290	General works (By date)
8292	Regiments and colonial troops
8295	Early operations (Oct. to Dec., 1899)
8300	Siege of Ladysmith and Buller's campaigns
8305	Siege of Kimberly and Relief expeditions
8310	Siege of Mafeking
8315	Campaign of Roberts to Pretoria
8320	Campaigns of Botha, DeWet and Delary (Sept. 1900-May 31, 1902)
8325	Other special
8330	Peace terms
	Reconstruction, 1902-1909. See Afr 8340
	Union of South Africa (Commonwealth, 1909-1961)
8331	Bibliographies
8333	Collected source materials
8335	General works
	Political biographies
8338.1-.99	Collected (A-Z, 99 scheme, by author)
8338.101-.399	Individual (A-Z, 299 scheme, by person)
	Special periods, etc.
8340	Reconstruction and early years, 1902-1913
8350	Chinese question
8355	Indian question
8360	1914-1919
	[Include Insurrection of 1914]
8369	1919-1961 (By date)
	Republic of South Africa (Independent, 1961-)
8371	Bibliographies
8373	Collected source materials
8375	General works [Prefer Afr 8380 now]
8377	Special topics
	Political biographies
8378.1-.99	Collected (A-Z, 99 scheme, by author)
8378.101-.399	Individual (A-Z, 299 scheme, by person)
	Special periods, etc.
8380	Early years, 1961-
	Geography, description, etc.
8654-8660	General works (By date)
8667	Civilization
8668	Special customs
8670	Guidebooks
8673	Views
8675	Maps
8676	Economic conditions (By date, e.g. .60 for 1960)
8677	Finance
	Races
	Indigenous races in general
8678	[Include race question in general, Bantus in general, etc. Special races go with the provinces in Afr 8700-9424, as far as possible. See also Afr 8148-8169]

South Africa in general (cont.)
Races (cont.)

Europeans, Asians, etc.
8680	General works
8685	Special
8686	Religion; missions

Biographies
[See also Afr 8055, 8230, 8250-8252, 8338, 8378, etc.; also with the provinces in Afr 8700-9424]
8687.1-.99	Collected (A-Z, 99 scheme, by author)
8687.101-.399	Individual (A-Z, 299 scheme, by person)
8688	Heraldry and genealogy
8690	Local, indefinite
	[Include only special regions, rivers, etc. which cannot be placed with one of the provinces in Afr 8700-9424]

8695	**British trust territories in South Africa in general**
	[See also Basutoland, Bechuanaland, Swaziland]

Cape Colony
8700	Periodicals
8703	Bibliographies
8705	Pamphlet volumes
8707	Collected source materials
8709	Historiography
8710	Government and administration
8712	General politics; political parties
8714-8720	General history (By date)
8722	General special

History by periods
Early to 1814. See Afr 8100-8125
Kaffir wars, 1779-1877. See Afr 8150-8152
8735	1814-1853
8740	1853-1872
8745	1872-1910
8750	1910-

Geography, description, etc.
8808-8810	General works (By date)
	[Early travels, to about 1820, go with general South Africa]
8813	Special customs
8815	Guidebooks
8817	Views
8819	Maps
8820	Economic and financial conditions

Races
8823	General works
8825	Special
8828	Religion; missions

Local
8830	Districts (Karoo, etc.)
8835	Cape Town
8838	Jansenville
8840	Kimberly
8844	Pondoland
8845	Port Elizabeth
8846	Transkeian Territory
8847	Other local (A-Z, 99 scheme, by place)
8848	Heraldry and genealogy

Biographies
8849.1-.99	Collected (A-Z, 99 scheme, by author)
8849.101-.399	Individual (A-Z, 299 scheme, by person)

Basutoland; Lesotho
8850	Periodicals (A-Z, 99 scheme)
8853	Bibliographies
8855	Pamphlet volumes
8857	Collected source materials
8859	Historiography
8860	Government and administration
8862	General politics; political parties
8865	General history

Basutoland; Lesotho (cont.)
8868	General special

History by periods
8870	Before 1843
8872	1843-1884
	[See also Afr 8165-8169]
8875	1884-1966
8880	1966-

Geography, description, etc.
8918-8920	General works (By date)
8922	Special customs
8923	Economic and financial conditions
8925	Races
8928	Religion; missions
8930	Local
[8931]	Biographies [Discontinued]

Biographies
8934.1-.99	Collected (A-Z, 99 scheme, by author)
8934.101-.399	Individual (A-Z, 299 scheme, by person)

Natal
8950	Periodicals (A-Z, .1-.26)
8953	Bibliographies
8955	Pamphlet volumes
8957	Collected source materials
8959	Historiography
8960	Government and administration
8962	General politics; political parties
8964-8970	General history (By date)
8972	General special

History by periods
8975	Before 1820
	1820-1843. See Afr 8190-8195
	Zulu wars, 1822-1887. See Afr 8155-8163
8980	Conquest to separation from Cape Colony (1843-1856)
8983	Separation to Boer War (1856-1900)
8985	Later history (1900-)

Geography, description, etc.
9028-9030	General works
9038	Special customs
9040	Guidebooks
9042	Views
9043	Maps
9044	Economic and financial conditions

Races
9045	General works
9047	Special
9049	Religion; missions

Local
9050	General works
9060	Durban
9065	Ladysmith
9070	Pietermaritzburg
9071	Others (A-Z, 99 scheme, by place)
9072	Heraldry and genealogy

Biographies
9073.1-.99	Collected
9073.100-.899	Individual (A-Z, 800 scheme, by person)

Transvaal
9075	Periodicals (A-Z, 99 scheme)
9078	Bibliographies
9080	Pamphlet volumes
9083	Collected source materials
9085	Historiography
9086	Government and administration
9087	General politics; political parties
9088-9090	General history (By date)
9092	General special

Transvaal (cont.)

	History by periods
9093	Before 1836
	1836-1899. See Afr 8210-8230
9095	History since War (1902-)

	Geography, description, etc.
9148-9150	General works (By date)
9153	Special customs
9155	Guidebooks
9158	Views
9159	Maps
9160	Economic and financial conditions
9161	Races
9164	Religion; missions
9165	Local (A-Z, 99 scheme, by place)
9168	Heraldry and genealogy

	Biographies
9170.1-.99	Collected (A-Z, 99 scheme, by author)
9170.101-.399	Individual (A-Z, 299 scheme, by person)

Swaziland

9175	Periodicals (A-Z, 99 scheme)
9176	Bibliographies
9177	Pmaphlet volumes
9178	Collected source materials
9179	Historiography
9180	Government and administration
9181	General politics; political parties
9182	General history
9183	General special

	History by periods
9184	Before 1843
9185	1843-1906
9186	1906-

	Geography, description, etc.
9190	General works
9191	Special customs
9193	Economic and financial conditions
9195	Races
9196	Religion; missions
9197	Local

	Biographies
9199.1-.99	Collected (A-Z, 99 scheme, by author)
9199.101-.399	Individual (A-Z, 299 scheme, by person)

Orange Free State

9200	Periodicals
9203	Bibliographies
9205	Pamphlet volumes
9208	Collected source materials
9209	Historiography
9210	Government and administration
9212	General politics; political parties
9218-9220	General history (By date)
9222	General special

	History by periods
9223	Before 1810
	1810-1854. See Afr 8200-8205
9225	Orange Free State (1854-1900)
9230	History since Annexation (1900-)

	Geography, description, etc.
9278-9280	General works (By date)
9283	Special customs
9285	Guidebooks
9286	Views
9287	Maps
9288	Economic and financial conditions
9289	Races
9290	Religion; missions
9291	Local
9293	Heraldry and genealogy

Orange Free State (cont.)

	Biographies
9295.1-.99	Collected (A-Z, 99 scheme, by author)
9295.100-.899	Individual (A-Z, 800 scheme, by person)

Bechuanaland; Botswana

9325	Periodicals (A-Z, .1-.26)
9327	Bibliographies
9330	Pamphlet volumes
9332	Collected source materials
9334	Historiography
9335	Government and administration
9337	General politcs; political parties
9338-9340	General history (By date)
9342	General special

	History by periods
9343	Before 1885
9345	1885-1966
9350	1966-

	Geography, description, etc.
9388-9390	General works (By date)
9393	Special customs
9395	Guidebooks
9396	Views
9397	Maps
9398	Economic and financial conditions
9400	Races
9404	Religion; missions
9405	Local

	Biographies
9424.1-.99	Collected (A-Z, 9. scheme, by author)
9424.101-.399	Individual (A-Z, 299 scheme, by person)

Southern Rhodesia

9425	Periodicals
9428	Bibliographies
9430	Pamphlet volumes
9432	Collected source materials
9434	Historiography
9435	Government and administration
9436	General politics; political parties
9438-9440	General history (By date)
9442	General special

	History by periods
9445	Before 1893
9446	Matabele campaign (1893-1896)
9447	1896-1950
9448	1950-1966
9450	1966-

	Geography, description, etc.
9488-9490	General works (By date)
9493	Special customs
9495	Guidebooks
9497	Views
9498	Maps
9499	Economic and financial conditions

	Races
	Indigenous races
9500	General
9502	Special
9505	Others
9506	Religion; missions

	Local
9510	Regions, etc.
9515	Salisbury
9520	Others (A-Z, 99 scheme, by place)
9523	Heraldry and genealogy

	Biographies
9525.1-.99	Collected (A-Z, 99 scheme, by author)
9525.100-.899	Individual (A-Z, 800 scheme, by person)

British Central Africa
[Include here works dealing with Southern and
Northern Rhodesia together, Northern Rhodesia
and Nyasaland together and the Federation of
Rhodesia and Nyasaland in general]
9535	Periodicals (A-Z, 99 scheme)
9538	Bibliographies
9540	Pamphlet volumes
9542	Collected source materials
9544	Historiography
9545	Government and administration
9547	General politics; political parties
9548-9550	General history (By date)
9552	General special

History by periods
9555	Before 1850
9558	Livingstone
9558.500-	Other early explorers
9560	1850-1950
9563	1950-1963
9565	1963-

Geography, description, etc.
9598-9600	General works (By date)
9603	Special customs
9605	Guidebooks
9606	Views
9607	Maps
9609	Economic and financial conditions
9610	Races
9614	Religion; missions
9619	Collected biographies

Northern Rhodesia; Zambia
9625	Periodicals
9627	Bibliographies
9630	Pamphlet volumes
9632	Collected source materials
9634	Historiography
9635	Government and administration
9636	General politics; political parties
9638-9640	General history (By date)
9642	General special

History by periods
9643	Before 1889
9645	1889-1963
9650	1963-

Geography, description, etc.
9688-9690	General works (By date)
9693	Special customs
9695	Guidebooks
9696	Views
9697	Maps
9699	Economic and financial conditions
9700	Races
9704	Religion; missions

Local
9705	Regions, etc.
9710	Barotseland
9715	Others (A-Z, 99 scheme, by place)
9746	Heraldry and genealogy

Biographies
9748.1-.99	Collected (A-Z, 99 scheme, by author)
9748.100-.899	Individual (A-Z, 800 scheme, by person)

Nyasaland; Malawi
9750	Periodicals
9753	Bibliographies
9755	Pamphlet volumes
9757	Collected source materials
9759	Historiography
9760	Government and administration
9763	General politics; political parties
9768-9770	General history (By date)
9772	General special

Nyasaland; Malawi (cont.)

History by periods
9775	Before 1892
9780	1892-1963
9785	1963-
[9795]	History - special [Discontinued]

Geography, description, etc.
9838-9840	General works (By date)
9845	Special customs
9847	Guidebooks
9848	Views
9849	Maps
9850	Economic and financial conditions
9853	Races
9854	Religion; missions

Local
9855	Regions, etc.
9858	Blantyre
9859	Others (A-Z, 99 scheme, by place)

Biographies
9860.1-.99	Collected (A-Z, 99 scheme, by author)
9860.100-.899	Individual (A-Z, 800 scheme, by person)

10000-10019	**African literature in general (Table A)**
	[Use only for very general works which deal collectively with the literatures written in both the European and indigenous languages. See also Afr 10050-10069 and 20000-20019]

10050-10069	**African literature written originally in the European languages in general (Table A)**
	[Use only for works which deal with the European languages collectively]

African literature written originally in English
[Use Table A for each unless otherwise indicated]
10100-10119	General works
10150-10197	Egypt
10200-10247	Sudan (former Anglo-Egyptian)
10250-10297	British Somaliland

British East Africa
10300-10347	General (incl. Zanzibar)
10350-10397	Uganda
10400-10447	Kenya
10450-10497	Tanganyika

British West Africa
10500-10547	General (incl. Gambia)
10550-10597	Sierra Leone
10600-10647	Ghana (incl. British Togo)
10650-10697	Nigeria (incl. British Cameroons)
10700-10747	Liberia
10750-10797	Southwest Africa

Rhodesia and Nyasaland
10800-10847	General (incl. Nyasaland)
10850-10897	Northern Rhodesia
10900-10947	Southern Rhodesia
10950-10997	Bechuanaland

South Africa
11000-11068	History and collections (Table C)
11100-11899	Individual authors, (A-Z, 800 scheme)
11900-11999	Others (Islands, etc.)
	[Develop as needed, using Table B]

African literature written originally in French
[Use Table A for each unless otherwise indicated]
12000-12019	General works
	[Include French North Africa in general]
12050-12097	French Somaliland
12100-12147	Egypt
12200-12247	Libya
12250-12297	Tunisia
12300-12397	Algeria (Table C)

African literature written originally in French (cont.)

12400-12497	Morocco (Table C)

French West Africa
12500-12519	General
12550-12597	Mauritania
12600-12647	Senegal
12650-12697	Sudan, Mali
12700-12747	Niger
12750-12797	Upper Volta
12800-12847	Guinea
12850-12897	Ivory Coast
12900-12947	Dahomey
12950-12997	French Togo

French Equatorial Africa
13000-13019	General
13050-13097	Chad
13100-13147	Central African Republic
13150-13197	Gabon
13200-13247	Congo (Brazzaville)
13250-13297	French Cameroons
13300-13347	Congo (Leopoldville)
13350-13397	Ruanda-Urundi
13400-13447	Madagascar
13450-13699	Other islands, etc.
	[Develop as needed, using Table B]

African literature written originally in Italian
[Use Table A for each unless otherwise indicated]
13700-13719	General works
13750-13797	Tripoli
13800-13847	Eritrea
13850-13897	Italian Somaliland
13900-13999	Others
	[Develop as needed, using Table B]

African literature written originally in Spanish
[Use Table A for each unless otherwise indicated]
14000-14019	General works
14050-14097	Spanish Morocco

Spanish West Africa
14100-14119	General
14150-14197	Spanish Sahara
14200-14247	Ifni
14250-14297	Canary Islands
14300-14347	Spanish Guinea
14400-14499	Others
	[Develop as needed, using Table B]

African literature written originally in Portuguese
[Use Table A for each unless otehrwise indicated]
14500-14519	General works
14550-14597	Portuguese Guinea
14600-14647	Cabinda
14650-14697	Angola
14700-14747	Mozambique
14800-14899	Others
	[Develop as needed, using Table B]

African literature in other European languages
[15000-15499]	Afrikaans. See Neth
[15500-15699]	German. See GerL
[15700-15999]	Others. See with the literature

African literature in Semitic languages
[16000-16999]	Arabic. See OL 19000-25269
	Ethiopian. See OL 17000-17999
	[Include Geez, Amharic, Tigrina, etc.]

African literature in Hamitic languages
[18000-18099]	Egyptian. See Eg
[18100-18399]	Coptic. See OL 5700-5899
[18400-18999]	Berber. See OL 4000-6999
	[Include ancient Libyan, Kabyle, Rif, Shilha, Tamashek, etc.]
[19000-19999]	Cushitic. See OL 7000-9999
	[Include Afar, Agau, Beja, Galla, Sidama, Somali, etc.]

African literatures written in indigenous languages
[Use Table A for each unless otherwise indicated]
20000-20019	General works

Special countries, etc.
[These numbers are to be used only for works dealing collectively with the various literatures in a particular area. Wherever possible, prefer to class with the language families or special languages below in Afr 23000-49999 or in OL 4000-9999 and 17000]
[20020-20039]	Northern Africa in general. See OL
20040-20059	Subsaharan Africa in general
[20100-20119]	Egypt. See OL
20120-20139	Sudan
	[See also Afr 22340-22359 and 40800-40899]
[20140-20159]	Ethiopia. See OL
[20160-20179]	Eritrea. See OL

	Somalia
[20200-20219]	General works. See OL
[20220-20239]	Somaliland. See OL
[20240-20259]	British Somaliland. See OL
[20260-20279]	French Somaliland. See OL
[20300-20319]	Libya. See OL
[20320-20339]	Tripoli. See OL
[20340-20359]	Tunisia. See OL
[20360-20379]	Algeria. See OL
[20380-20399]	Morocco. See OL
[20400-20419]	Spanish Morocco. See OL

	Spanish West Africa
[20420-20439]	General works. See OL
[20440-20459]	Spanish Sahara. See OL
[20460-20479]	Ifni. See OL
[20480-20499]	Canary Islands. See OL

	French West Africa
20500-20519	General works
20520-20539	Mauritania
20540-20559	Senegal
20560-20579	Sudan, Mali
	[See also Afr 22500-22519]
20580-20599	Niger
20600-20619	Guinea
20620-20639	Ivory Coast
20640-20659	Upper Volta
20660-20679	Dahomey
	[See also Afr 27100-27199]
20680-20699	Cameroons

	British West Africa
20700-20719	General works (incl. Gambia)
20720-20739	Sierra Leone
20740-20759	Ghana
20760-20779	Nigeria
20780-20799	Liberia

	French Equatorial Africa
20800-20819	General works
20820-20839	Chad
20840-20859	Central African Republic
20860-20879	Gabon
20880-20899	Congo (Brazzaville)
20900-20919	Congo (Leopoldville)
	[See also Afr 26700-26799]
20920-20939	Ruanda-Urundi
	[See also Afr 42700-42899]
20940-20959	Spanish Guinea
20960-20979	Portuguese Guinea

	Portuguese West Africa
21000-21019	General
21020-21039	Cabinda
	[See also Afr 26000-26099]
21040-21059	Angola
	[See also Afr 34200-34299]
21060-21079	Southwest Africa
21080-21099	Bechuanaland, Botswana
	[See also Afr 43300-43399]

African literatures written in indigenous... (cont.)
    Special countries, etc. (cont.)

21100-21119	South Africa
21120-21139	Basutoland, Lesotho
21140-21159	Swaziland
	[See also Afr 44800-44899]
21160-21179	Mozambique
21180-21199	Madagascar
	Rhodesia and Nyasaland
21200-21219	General works
21220-21239	Southern Rhodesia
21240-21259	Northern Rhodesia, Zambia
21260-21279	Nyasaland, Malawi
	British East Africa
21300-21319	General works
21320-21339	Tanganyika, Tanzania
21340-21359	Kenya
21360-21379	Uganda
21400-21999	Island groups, etc. [Develop as needed]

    Special language families in general
       [Use Table A for each unless otherwise indicated]

22020-22039	Bantu
[22060-22079]	Berber. See OL 4100-4119
22100-22119	Bushman
[22140-22159]	Cushitic. See OL 7000-7019
22200-22219	Gur
[22240-22259]	Hamitic. See OL 4000-4019
22300-22319	Mande
22340-22359	Nilotic
[22400-22419]	Semitic. See OL 1-699, 17000-17019, etc.
22500-22519	Sudanian
22600-22999	Others [Develop as needed]

    Special languages (Table A)
       [Use Table A for each unless otherwise indicated]

	Accra. See Ga
23100-23199	Acholi (Acoli)
23200-23299	Aduma
	Afar. See OL 7100-7299
	Agau. See OL 7300-7999
23300-23399	Agni
23400-23499	Akan
23500-23599	Akarimojong
	Akra. See Ga
	Akwapim. See Tshi
	Amharic. See OL 17600-17699
23700-23799	Angas
	Angolese. See Kimbundu
	Arabic. See OL 19000-29999
	Ashanti. See Tshi
	Audila. See OL 6100-6199
23900-23999	Other A (Develop as needed, using Table B]
	Bakele. See Kele
	Bambala. See Sidama in OL 9100-9600
24000-24099	Bambara
24100-24199	Banda
24200-24299	Bangala
24300-24399	Barea
24400-24499	Bari
	Barraretta. See Galla in OL 8600-8999
24500-24599	Basa
	Bechuana. See Sechuana
	Beja. See OL 8000-8499
24600-24699	Bemba (Wemba)
24700-24799	Benga
	Beni Amer. See Beja in OL 8100-8499
	Bilin. See Agau in OL 7400-7999
24800-24899	Bini (Edo)
24900-24999	Bisa
	Bishari. See Beja in OL 8100-8499
25000-25099	Bobangi
	Bogos. See Agau in OL 7400-7999
25100-25199	Bondei
25200-25299	Bongo
	Borana. See Galla in OL 8600-8999

African literatures written in indigenous... (cont.)
    Special languages (Table A) (cont.)

	Bornu. See Kanuri
25300-25399	Brissa
25500-25599	Bube (Fernandian)
25600-25699	Bulom (Bullom, Sherbro)
25700-25799	Bulu
25800-25899	Bulu-Bun
	Buluba-Lulua. See Luba
	Bunda. See Kimbundu
	Burji. See Sidama in OL 9100-9699
25900-25999	Other B [Develop as needed, using Table B]
26000-26099	Cabinda (Kabinda, Kokongo)
	Caga. See Chaga
26100-26199	Chaga (Chagga, Caga, Jagga)
26200-26299	Chassu
	Chenoua. See OL 6600-6999
26300-26399	Chewa
	Chi-Tonga. See Tonga of Lake Nyasa
	Chikaranga. See Shona
26400-26499	Chindau
	Chinyanja. See Nyanja
	Chiswina. See Shona
	Chitonga. See Tonga of Lake Nyasa
26500-26599	Chokwe
26600-26699	Chopi
	Ci-Tonga. See Tonga of Rhodesia
26700-26799	Congo (Kongo)
	Coptic. See OL 5700-5899
	Cuanhama. See Kuanyama
26900-26999	Other C [Develop as needed, using Table B]
27000-27099	Dagbane
27100-27199	Dahoman
	Dankali. See Afar in OL 7100-7199
	Daresa. See Sidama in OL 9100-9699
27200-27299	Daza
	Dikele. See Kele
27400-27499	Dinka
27500-27599	Diola
27700-27799	Duala
27800-27899	Dyur
27900-27999	Other D [Develop as needed, using Table B]
	Edo. See Bini
28100-28199	Efik
	Ethiopic. See OL 17200-17399
28200-28299	Ewe
28400-28499	Other E [Develop as needed, using Table B]
28500-28599	Fan
28600-28699	Fanti (See also Tshi)
	Fernandian. See Bube
28700-28799	Fulah (Ful, Fulani, Fulbe, Fulfulde)
	Fyote. See Cabinda or Congo
28900-28999	Other F [Develop as needed, using Table B]
29000-29099	Ga (Accra, Akra, Incran)
	Gafat. See OL 17900-17999
	Galla. See OL 8500-8599
29100-29199	Ganda (Luganda)
29200-29299	Ganguela
29300-29399	Gbandi
29400-29499	Gbea
	Geez. See OL 17200-17399
	Geleba. See OL 9900-9999
	Ghadames. See OL 6200-6299
	Gi-Tonga. See Tonga of Inhambane
	Gimirra. See Sidama in OL 9100-9699
29500-29599	Gogo
29600-29699	Gola
	Gonga. See Sidama in OL 9100-9699
29700-29799	Grebo
	Gudella. See Sidama in OL 9100-9699
	Gurage. See OL 17900-17999
29800-29899	Gusii (Kisii)
	Gwamba. See Thonga
	Gweabo. See Jabo
29900-29999	Other G [Develop as needed, using Table B]

African literatures written in indigenous... (cont.)
Special languages (Table A) (cont.)

	Hadendoa. See Beja in OL 8100-8499
	Hadya. See Sidama in OL 9100-9699
	Hallenga. See Beja in OL 8100-8499
	Harari. See OL 17900-17999
30100-30199	Hausa
30300-30399	Herero
30500-30599	Hottentot (See also Nama)
30700-30799	Humba (Kumbi)
30900-30999	Other H [Develop as needed, using Table B]
31000-31099	Ibo
31100-31199	Idoma
31200-31299	Idzo
31300-31399	Ifumu
31400-31499	Ila
	Incran. See Ga
31600-31699	Iraqw
	Isaq. See Somali in OL 9700-9799
31900-31999	Other I [Develop as needed, using Table B]
32000-32099	Jabo (Gweabo)
	Jagga. See Chaga
32200-32299	Jaunde
	Jenjero. See Sidama in OL 9100-9699
32500-32599	Jita
32700-32799	Junkun
32900-32999	Other J [Develop as needed, using Table B]
	Kabinda. See Cabinda
	Kabyla. See OL 4300-4399
	Kafa. See Sidama in OL 9100-9699
33000-33099	Kafir (Xosa)
33200-33299	Kaguru
	Kakongo. See Cabinda
33300-33399	Kamba
	Kambatta. See Sidama in OL 9100-9699
33400-33499	Kanuri (Bornu)
33500-33599	Kaonde
33600-33699	Kavirondo
	Kavirondo Bantu. See Wanga
33700-33799	Kele (Bakele, Dikele)
	Khamir. See Agau in OL 7400-7999
33900-33999	Khan
34000-34099	Kikuyu
34100-34199	Kilega
34200-34299	Kimbundu (Angolese, Bunda, Mbundu)
34300-34399	Kinga
34400-34499	Kingwana
	Kinyaruanda. See Ruanda
34500-34599	Kioko
	Kirundi. See Rundi
	Kisii. See Gusii
34600-34699	Kitabwa
34700-34799	Kombe
	Konde. See Makonde, Ngonde
	Kongo. See Congo
34800-34899	Kono
	Konso. See OL 9900-9999
34900-34999	Korano
35000-35099	Kpelle
35100-35199	Krej
35200-35299	Kru
35300-35399	Kuanyama (Cuanhama, Ovambo)
	Kulla. See Sidama in OL 9100-9699
	Kumbi. See Humba
35500-35599	Kunama
35600-35699	Kussassi (Kusa, Kusase)
35700-35799	Kwafi
35800-35899	Kwangali
	Kwanyama. See Kuanyama
35900-35999	Other K [Develop as needed, using Table B]
36000-36099	Lamba
	Lamongo. See Mongo
36100-36199	Lango
36300-36399	Lele
36400-36499	Lenje
36600-36699	Lilima

African literatures written in indigenous... (cont.)
Special languages (Table A) (cont.)

36700-36799	Limba
37000-37099	Logbara
	Lomongo. See Mongo
37300-37399	Luba (Buluba-Lulua)
	Luganda. See Ganda
37500-37599	Lunda
37600-37699	Lunkundu
37700-37799	Luragoli
37800-37899	Luvale
37900-37999	Other L [Develop as needed, using Table B]
38000-38099	Maba
38100-38199	Madschame
38200-38299	Makonde (Konde)
38300-38399	Makua
	Mananja. See Nyanja
38400-38499	Mandara
38500-38599	Mandingo
38600-38699	Mandjok
38800-38899	Masai
	Mashona. See Shona
	Mbundu. See Kimbundu
	Megi. See Sagara
39000-39099	Mende
	Michi. See Tivi
	Mole. See Mossi
39200-39299	Mongo (Lomongo)
39300-39399	Mossi (Mole)
39400-39499	Mpongwe
	Munshi. See Tivi
39500-39599	Musgu
39700-39799	Mwamba
39800-39899	Mwera
39900-39999	Other M [Develop as needed, using Table B]
40000-40099	Nama
40100-40199	Nande
40200-40299	Ndonga
	Ng'ange. See Nyanja
40300-40399	Ngonde (Konde)
40400-40499	Nika
40500-40599	Nkosi
40700-40799	Ntomba
40800-40899	Nubian
41000-41099	Nuer
41100-41199	Nupe
	Nyai. See Tete
41200-41299	Nyakyusa
	Nyam-Nyam. See Zande
41300-41399	Nyamwezi
41400-41499	Nyanja (Nyassa, Chinyanja)
41600-41699	Nyankole
41700-41799	Nyoro
41800-41899	Nzima
41900-41909	Nsakkara [Table B]
41910-41999	Other N (Develop as needed, using Table B)
	Oji. See Tshi
	Ometo. See OL 9900-9999
	Oromo. See Galla in OL 8500-8599
42100-42199	Ouengu
	Ovambo. See Kuanyama
42200-42299	Other O (Develop as needed, using Table B)
42300-42399	Pogoro
42400-42499	Punu
42500-42599	Other P [Develop as needed, using Table B]
	Quara. See Agau in OL 7400-7999
42600-42699	Other Q [Develop as needed, using Table B]
	Rif. See OL 4400-4499
	Ronga. See Thonga
42700-42799	Ruanda (Kinyaruanda)
42800-42899	Rundi (Kirundi)
42900-42999	Other R [Develop as needed, using Table B]
43000-43099	Sagara (Megi)

African literatures written in indigenous... (cont.)
Special languages (Table A) (cont.)

	Saho. See Afar in OL 7200-7299
43100-43199	Sandawe
43200-43299	Sango
43300-43399	Sechuana (Bechuana)
43500-43599	Sena
43600-43699	Senga
	Sesuto. See Sotho
43700-43799	Shambala
	Shawia. See OL 6600 6999
	Sherbro. See Bulom
	Shi-Tonga. See Tonga of Shangani
	Shilha. See OL 4500-4599
43800-43899	Shilluk
43900-43999	Shira
	Shironga. See Thonga
44000-44099	Shona (Shuna, Chikaranga, Chiswina, Mashona)
	Sidama. See OL 9000-9099
	Siwah. See OL 6300-6399
	Socna. See OL 6400-6499
	Somali. See OL 9700-9899
44200-44299	Songhai
44300-44399	Sotho (Sesuto)
44500-44599	Susu
44600-44699	Swahili
44800-44899	Swazi
44900-44999	Other S [Develop as needed, using Table B]
45000-45099	Taita
	Tamashek. See OL 4600-4699
	Tamboka. See Tumbuka
45100-45199	Taveta
45200-45299	Tebele
45300-45399	Teda
45400-45499	Teke
	Temissa. See OL 6500-6599
	Temne. See Timne
45500-45599	Teso
45600-45699	Tete
45700-45799	Thonga (Gwamba, Ronga, Shironga)
	Tigrai. See OL 17400-17499
	Tigre. See OL 17500-17599
	Tigrina. See OL 17400-17499
45800-45899	Timne (Temne)
45900-45999	Tivi (Tiwi, Michi, Munshi)
46000-46099	Tonga of Inhambane (Gi-tonga)
46100-46199	Tonga of Lake Nyasa (Chi-Tonga)
46200-46299	Tonga of Rhodesia and Zambesi (Ci-Tonga)
46300-46399	Tonga of Shangani (Tsonga, Shi-Tonga)
46500-46599	Tshi (Akwapim, Ashanti, Oji)
	Tsonga. See Tonga of Shangani
	Tuareg. See OL 4600-4699
	Tulama. See Galla in OL 8600-8999
46700-46799	Tumbuka (Tamboka)
46900-46999	Other T [Develop as needed, using Table B]
47100-47199	Umbundu
47300-47399	Uwana
47400-47499	Other U [Develop as needed, using Table B]
47500-47599	Vei (Vai)
47600-47699	Venda
47700-47799	Vili
47900-47999	Other V [Develop as needed, using Table B]
48000-48099	Wanga (Kavirondo Bantu)
	Wemba. See Bemba
48100-48199	Wolof
48200-48299	Wute
48300-48399	Other W [Develop as needed, using Table B]
	Xosa. See Kafir
48400-48499	Other X [Develop as needed, using Table B]
48500-48599	Yao
48700-48799	Yebu
48900-48999	Yombe
49000-49099	Yoruba
49300-49399	Other Y [Develop as needed, using Table B]

African literatures written in indigenous... (cont.)
Special languages (Table A) (cont.)

49400-49499	Zande (Nyam-Nyam)
49500-49599	Zeguha (Zigula)
	Zenaga. See OL 4700-4799
	Zendjero. See Sidama in OL 9100-9699
49600-49699	Ziba
	Zigula. See Zeguha
49700-49799	Zulu
49900-49999	Other Z [Develop as needed, using Table B]

A	B	Tables for African Literatures
		Bibliographies
0	0	General
2	0	Special
3	0	Dictionaries
4	1	Periodicals
		History of the literature
5	2	General works
7	3	General special
9	3	Local
		Special forms
10	4	Poetry
11	4	Drama
12	4	Fiction
13	4	Journalism
14	4	Other special
		Collections of texts, anthologies
15	5	General
		Special forms
16	6	Poetry
17	6	Drama
18	6	Fiction
19	6	Other special
21-46	7	Individual authors (A-Z)
47	8	Anonymous works (Bible, etc.)
49	9.0	Uncatalogued material

[Use only as a temporary number for books in the native African languages which cannot be catalogued, i.e. no cards made. Make explanatory entries in the shelflist. In Table A, give successive dot numbers. In Table B, use 0 dot numbers (.01, .02, .03, etc.)]

| 50-99 | 9.1- | Texts in original language on special subjects |

[Translations of these will usually be put where they would normally come in the regular classes. In Table B, use .1- for texts on special subjects -- an ad hoc arrangement, but similar to the topics listed in 50-99 of Table A.]

A (cont.)   Tables for African Literatures

Texts in original language on special subjects
Bibliographies [See also 0]

50	General
51	Special
52	Reference works (encyclopedias, etc.)
53	Periodicals (See also 4)
54	General miscellany (incl. pamphlet volumes)

Literature [See also 5-14]

| 55 | General and comparative |
| 56 | Foreign literatures |

Linguistics

57	General and comparative
58	The language of the texts
59	Other languages [Develop as needed]

Art and archaeology

60	General
61	Special
62	Music
63	Other cultural topics
64	Books and writing (incl. paleography, printing and publishing)
65	Libraries and library science
66	Education

Religion

| 67 | General and comparative |
| 68 | Prevailing religion of the country |

[Put sacred and liturgical books with Anonymous works in 47]

| 69 | Other religions |
| 70 | Philosophy |

Tables for African Literatures (cont.)
Texts in original language on special subjects (cont.)

71	Psychology
72	Sciences
73	Technical arts
	Law
74	General
75	Special
76	Political science (theory)
	Government and administration [See also 94 and 99]
77	General
78	Special
79	Geography [See also 93 and 99]
	Economics [See also 95 and 99]
80	General (incl. theory, statistics, etc.)
81	Agriculture and land
82	Industries
83	Commerce and communications
84	Finance (incl. taxation, money, banking)
	Sociology [See also 96 and 99]
85	General (incl. theory, public welfare, etc.)
86	Labor
87	Crime, etc.
88	Social customs (incl. family and marriage, women and children, social classes, etc.)
89	Ethnology [See also 96 and 99]
	History
	Universal
90	General (incl. special periods) [See also 74-89]
91	Biography, genealogy, heraldry
	The country of the language
92	Documents
93	General works (incl. description and special periods)
94	General special (incl. military affairs, foreign relations, government)
95	Economic conditions (cf. topics listed in 81-84)
96	Social conditions and customs (cf. topics listed in 86-89)
97	Local
98	Biography, genealogy, heraldry
99	Other countries

C	**Tables for African Literatures**
	Bibliographies
0	General
1	Special periods
3	Local
5	Special forms
7	Dictionaries
8	Periodicals
	History of the literature
10	General works
12	General special (technique, themes, etc.)
	Special periods
14	19th century
15	20th century
18	Local
	Special forms
	Poetry
21	General works
22	General special
23	Local
	Drama
24	General works
25	General special
26	Local
	Fiction
27	General works
28	General special
29	Local
	Journalism
31	General works
32	General special
33	Local
38	Others
	Collections of texts, anthologies
40	General works
42	General special (technique, themes, etc.)
	Special periods
44	19th century
45	20th century
48	Local
	Special forms
	Poetry
51	General works
52	General special
53	Local
	Drama
54	General works
55	General special
56	Local
	Fiction
57	General works
58	General special
59	Local
	Journalism
61	General works
62	General special
63	Local
68	Others
71-96	Individual authors (A-Z)
97	Anonymous works (Bibles, etc.)

[N.B. Use the appended special table for each
country, except where indicated for Nigeria.]

1-68	**Africa in general**
101-168	**German Africa in general**
	[See also individual colonies below]
301-396	**Ethiopia**
	Italian Africa
501-568	General
601-696	Eritrea
701-796	Somalia, Somaliland
801-896	Libya, Tripoli
	British Africa
1001-1068	General
1201-1296	British Somaliland
1301-1396	Sudan (Anglo-Egyptian)
1401-1496	Egypt
	British West Africa
1501-1568	General
1601-1696	Gambia
1701-1796	Sierra Leone
1801-1896	Ghana, Gold Coast
1901-1996	British Togoland
	[See also Afr Doc 6701-6796]
2001-2096	Ascension Island
2101-2196	St. Helena Island
2200-2299	Other islands off the west coast (Develop as needed)
	Nigeria
2301-2368	General
2401-2496	Northern Nigeria
2500-2509	Southern Nigeria (General Table B)
2520-2529	Western Nigeria (General Table B)
2540-2549	Midwest Nigeria (General Table B)
2560-2569	Eastern Nigeria (General Table B)
2601-2696	British Cameroons
	[See also Afr Doc 7501-7596]
	British islands off the east coast
2701-2796	Seychelles
2801-2896	Mauritius
2900-2999	Other islands (Develop as needed)
	British East Africa
3001-3068	General
3101-3196	Zanzibar
3201-3296	Kenya
3301-3396	Uganda
3401-3496	Tanganyika and Tanzania
	British Central Africa
3501-3568	General; Federation of Rhodesia and Nyasaland
3601-3696	Nyasaland, Malawi
3701-3796	Northern Rhodesia, Zambia
3801-3896	Southern Rhodesia
4001-4096	Bechuanaland Protectorate, Botswana
4101-4196	Swaziland
4201-4296	Basutoland, Lesotho
	South Africa
4301-4368	General, Union of South Africa
4401-4496	Cape Colony, Cape of Good Hope
4501-4596	Natal
4601-4696	Transvaal
4701-4796	Orange Free State
4801-4896	Transkeian Territories
4901-4996	Southwest Africa

	French Africa
5001-5068	General
	French North Africa
5101-5168	General
5201-5296	Morocco
5301-5396	Algeria
5401-5496	Tunisia
5501-5596	French Somaliland
5601-5696	Madagascar, Malagasy Republic
5701-5796	Comores Islands
5801-5896	Reunion
5900-5999	Other islands (Develop as needed)
	French West Africa
6001-6068	General
6101-6196	Mauritania
6201-6296	Senegal
6301-6396	French Guinea
6401-6496	Ivory Coast
6501-6596	Upper Volta
6601-6696	Dahomey
6701-6796	French Togo
6801-6896	French Sudan, Mali
6901-6996	Niger
	French Equatorial Africa
7001-7068	General
7101-7196	Chad
7201-7296	Central African Republic, Ubangi-Chari
7301-7396	French Congo, Middle Congo, Congo (Brazzaville)
7401-7496	Gabon
7501-7596	French Cameroons
	[Include East Cameroon and West Cameroon after 1961]
	Belgian Africa
7601-7668	General
7701-7796	Congo
7801-7896	Ruanda-Urundi, Rwanda
7901-7996	Burundi
	Spanish Africa
8001-8068	General
8101-8196	Spanish Morocco
	Canary Islands. See Span Doc
	Spanish West Africa
8301-8368	General
8401-8496	Ifni
8501-8596	Southern Protectorate of Morocco
8601-8696	Spanish Sahara, Rio de Oro
8701-8796	Spanish Guinea, Rio Muni
8801-8896	Fernando Poo
8900-8999	Other islands (Develop as needed)
	Portuguese Africa
9001-9068	General
	Madeira and Azores Islands. See Port Doc
9101-9196	Cape Verde Islands
9201-9296	Mozambique
9301-9396	Angola
9401-9496	Portuguese Guinea
9501-9596	São Tomé e Principe
9600-9699	Other islands (Develop as needed)
9901-9996	**Liberia**

Special Table for Afr Doc

      General collections
1   Pamphlet volumes
2   Bibliographies, catalogs, etc.
          [See also B, etc.]
3   Blue books, government manuals, directories
5   Annual reports
6   Other

      Statistics
7.1-.199   General compilations (incl. abstracts)
7.200-.999   Census (i.e. general, decennial, etc.)
8.1-.299   Vital, population, etc.
8.300-.499   Labor
8.500-.699   Industry, manufactures
8.700-.999   Trade
9.1-.299   Budget
9.300-.499   National income and accounts, surveys
9.500-.999   Other

      Local. See with local documents in 71-96

      Legislative documents
10   Pamphlet volumes
12   General (incl. a one-house legislature, legislative
          council, etc.)
14   House Journal, etc.
16   Senate Journal, etc.
18   Statutes, etc.
          [See also Afr]
19   Others (incl. constitution, treaties, etc.)

      Executive documents
20   Pamphlet volumes
22   General
24   President (incl. High Commissioner)
26   Special
31-56   Departments, Bureaus, etc. (A-Z, by catchword)
          [30-55 has been used for Egypt, Ghana, Nigeria,
          Mozambique, and South Africa]

      Judicial documents
          [See also Afr. Offer to Law School?]
60   Pamphlet volumes
62   General
68   Special

      Local documents
70   Pamphlet volumes
71-96   Provinces, cities, etc. (A-Z, by place)

WIDENER LIBRARY SHELFLIST, 34

AFRICAN HISTORY
AND
LITERATURES

CLASSIFIED LISTING BY CALL NUMBER

Afr	1 - 24	**Africa in general - Periodicals (A-Z)**

NEDL Afr 1.2   Afrique explorée et civilisée. Genève. 1,1879+   13v.
Afr 1.3F   African colonizer. London. 1,1840+
Afr 1.4   Afrikanische Gesellschaft in Deutschland. Mittheilungen. Berlin. 1,1878+   5v.
Afr 1.4.5   Afrikanische Gesellschaft in Deutschland. Correspondenzblatt. Berlin. 1,1873+
Afr 1.5   Archivio bibliografico coloniale. Libia. 1,1915+
Afr 1.6F   Association Internationale Africaine. Compte rendu. Bruxelles. 1877+
Afr 1.6.7F   Association Internationale Africaine. Comité Naional. Belge. Séance. Bruxelles.
Afr 1.7F   African comrade. Dar-es-Salaam.
NEDL Afr 1.8F   African world and Cape Cairo express. London.
Afr 1.9   Africa. London. 1,1928+   37v.
Afr 1.10   Annuaire de Madagascar et dépendances. Tananarive. 1898+   6v.
Afr 1.11   African observer. Bulawayo, Rhodesia. 1,1934+   7v.
Afr 1.12   African news. Philadelphia.
Afr 1.13   African transcripts. Philadelphia. 1,1945+   2v.
Afr 1.14F   Africa. Madrid. 5,1946+   26v.
Afr 1.15F   African world. London. 1948+   22v.
Afr 1.15.3F   African world annual. London. 1905+   4v.
Afr 1.16   Africa; a reference volume on the African continent. Paris. 1,1968+
Afr 1.17   African home library. London. 109,1948+   2v.
Afr 1.18   Africa's own library. London.
Afr 1.19   African abstracts. London. 1,1950+   11v.
Afr 1.20   Afrique et l'Asie. Paris. 1952+   14v.
Afr 1.22   African and colonial world, a political, cultural and trade review. London. 1,1953+   4v.
Afr 1.25   Africa digest. London. 1,1953+   11v.
Afr 1.25.10   Africa Bureau, London. News. London. 1-5
Afr 1.27   Africa today, bulletin of the American Committee on Africa. N.Y. 3,1956+   10v.
Afr 1.27.5   Africa today pamphlets. N.Y.
Afr 1.28   Africa special report, bulletin of the Institute of African-American Relations. Washington, D.C. 1,1956+   8v.
Afr 1.29   Actualités d'Afrique noire. Paris.
Afr 1.30F   Afrique en marche. Paris. 1,1957+   2v.
Afr 1.31   Afrika - heute. Bonn. 1957+   4v.
Afr 1.32   African studies bulletin. N.Y. 1,1958+   3v.
Afr 1.32.5   African studies bulletin. Index, v.1-10 (1958-1967). Boston, 1968.
Afr 1.33F   Africa, rivista bimestrale di studi e documentazione. Roma. 14,1959+   9v.
Afr 1.34F   Afrika. München. 1-7,1959-1965+   4v.
Afr 1.35   African handbooks. Philadelphia. 1,1943+   4v.
Afr 1.36   Afro-Asian quarterly. Cairo.
Afr 1.37   Afro-Asian bulletin. Cairo. 2,1960+   3v.
Afr 1.38   Afrika Rundschau, Politik, Wirtschaft, Wissenschaft, Forschung, Überseedeutschtum. Hamburg. 1,1935+   7v.
Afr 1.39A   African affairs. London. 1+
Afr 1.39B   African affairs. London. 1+
Afr 1.40   Afrique documents. Dakar. 1961+   7v.
Afr 1.41   Africa for Africans. Cairo.
Afr 1.42   Afrika-Institut, Pretoria. Bulletin. Pretoria. 2,1962+   7v.
Afr 1.42.3   Afrika-Institut, Pretoria. Communications. Pretoria.
Afr 1.42.3
094Afric
Afr 1.44   Africa Bureau, London. Annual report. London.
Afr 1.45   Africa quarterly. New Delhi. 1,1961+   7v.
Afr 1.46   Afrika. Rotterdam. 16,1962+   13v.
Afr 1.47   Africana newsletter. Stanford, Calif.
Afr 1.48   Afrique contemporaine. Paris. 1,1962+   4v.
Afr 1.50F   Afrique. Paris. 1-69, 1961-1967//   9v.
Afr 1.50.5   Afrique. Supplément. 1-9, 1965-1967//
Afr 1.52   Administration et diplomatie d'Afrique Noire et de Madagascar. Paris. 1962+
Afr 1.54   Annuaire des états d'Afrique Noire. Paris. 1961+
Afr 1.56   Africa annual. London. 3v.
Afr 1.58F   African notes. Ibadan. 1,1963+
Afr 1.60   African student. Jerusalem.
Afr 1.62   African Association. Review. Cairo.
Afr 1.64   Afrika-Studien. Berlin. 1,1964+   16v.
Afr 1.64.5   Afrika-Studien. Sonderreihe. Berlin. 1,1968+
Afr 1.66   Afrika heute. Bonn. 1964+   5v.
Afr 1.68   African forum. N.Y. 1-4,1965-1968//   4v.
Afr 1.68.5   American Society of Africa Culture. AMSAC newsletter. N.Y. 8,1965+
Afr 1.70   Africana bulletin. Warszawa. 1,1964+
Afr 1.72   African review. Accra. 1,1965+
Afr 1.73   African scholar. Washington. 1,1968+
Afr 1.75   Africa and the world. London. 1,1964+   2v.
Afr 1.75.5   Report from Africa and the world. London. 1969+
Afr 1.78   Africa's illustrated news. London. 1,1966+
Afr 1.80   Africa-Verein, Hamburg. Afrika-Bericht. Hamburg. 1963+
Afr 1.82   African social research. Lusaka. 1,1966+   2v.
Afr 1.83   Africanist news and views. Cairo. 1,1966+
Afr 1.83.10F   The Africanist. Maseru. 1966+
Afr 1.84F   African Studies Association. Papers of annual meeting. Philadelphia. 8,1965+   9v.
Afr 1.85   African urban notes. Milwaukee. 1,1966+
Afr 1.85.5   African urban notes. Bibliographical supplement. 1,1966+
Afr 1.86   African statesman. Lagos. 1,1965+
Afr 1.87   The African historian. Ibadan. 1,1965+
Afr 1.88   Aberdeen. University. African Studies Group. Bulletin. Aberdeen. 1,1967+
Afr 1.89   L'année politique africaine. Dakar. 1965+
Afr 1.90   African historical studies. Boston. 1,1968+
Afr 1.91   African administrative studies. Tangier. 1966+
Afr 1.92   African Training and Research Centre in Administration for Development. Nouvelles du CAFRAD. Tanger. 1,1967+
Afr 1.93F   Azania news. Lusaka. 1,1966+
Afr 1.94   African studies newsletter. N.Y. 1,1968+
Afr 1.94.5   African Studies Association. Committee of Fine Arts and the Humanities. Occasional papers. Bloomington, Ind. 1,1966+
Afr 1.95   Année africaine. Paris. 1,1963+   5v.
Afr 1.96   Afrika Spectrum. Hamburg. 1,1966+
Afr 1.98   Afro-Asia; publicação semestral do Centro de Estudos Afro-Orientais da Universidade da Bahia. Salvador, Brazil. 1,1965+
Afr 1.99   Afrique et culture. Paris. 8,1968+

Afr	1 - 24	**Africa in general - Periodicals (A-Z) - cont.**

Afr 1.100   Atlas des structures agraires au Sud du Sahara. Paris. 1,1967+   2v.
Afr 1.102   African arts. Los Angeles. 1,1967+   2v.
Afr 1.104   L'Afrique littéraire et artistique. Paris. 1,1968+
Afr 1.106F   L'Afrique urbaine. Yaounde. 4,1963+
Afr 1.108   Associazione degli Africanisti Italiani. Bollettino. Paria. 1,1968+
RRC Afr 1.110   Africa in Soviet studies. Moscow. 1,1968+
Afr 2.1   Bulletin du Comite de l'Afrique française. Paris. 1891+   47v.
NEDL Afr 2.2   Africa italiana. Napoli. 1,1882+   18v.
Afr 2.3F   British Africa monthly. Johannesburg.
Afr 2.4F   Bulletin on African affairs. Accra. 2+   4v.
Afr 2.5   Boston University papers in African history. Boston. 1,1964+   3v.
Afr 3.2   Spain. Consejo Superior de Investigaciones. Archivos. Madrid. 1,1947+   16v.
Afr 3.5   Congo mission news. Bolenge.
Afr 3.7F   Comité Spéciale du Katanga. Rapports et balans. Bruxelles.
Afr 3.8   Cuadernos de estudios africanos. Madrid. 1,1946+   11v.
Afr 3.9   Cahiers de l'Afrique et l'Asie. Paris. 1+   4v.
Afr 3.10   Collana di studi di storia e politica africana. Roma. 1+   4v.
Afr 3.11   Collection le colonialisme. Paris.
Afr 3.12   Collection connaissance de l'Afrique française. Oran, Algeria.
Afr 3.15   Legum, Colin. Bandung, Cairo and Accra. London, 1958.
Afr 3.17   Canadian journal of African studies. Montreal. 1,1967+
Afr 3.20   Conference of Independent African States, 1st, Accra, 1958. Konferenz der unabhängigen Staaten Afrikas, April 15-22, 1958. London, 1958.
Afr 3.22   Cahiers d'études africaines. Paris. 1,1960+   19v.
Afr 3.25   Pamphlet vol. Conference of Independent African States, Accra, 1958. 6 pam.
Afr 3.28   Classiques africains. Aalter.
Afr 3.30F   Cahiers économiques et de liaison des comités eurafrique. Paris. 1,1959+   2v.
Afr 3.32   Cahiers africains. Paris. 1+   4v.
Afr 3.34   Chronologie politique africaine. Paris. 2,1961+   7v.
Afr 3.36   Crisis and change. London. 1,1965+
Afr 3.38   California. University. University at Los Angeles. African Studies Center. Occasional paper. Los Angeles. 1,1965+
Afr 3.40   Cultural events in Africa. London. 1,1964+
Afr 3.42   Cape Town. University. School of African Studies. Communications. Cape Town. 2,1942+   4v.
Afr 3.44   Connaissance de l'Afrique. Paris. 13,1965+
Afr 3.46F   Centre de Recherche et d'Information Socio-Politiques. Travaux africains. Dossier documentaire. Bruxelles. 1,1964+
Afr 3.48   Coleccion monografica africana. Madrid. 1,1967+
Afr 3.50   Centre d'Analyse et de Recherche Documentaires pour l'Afrique Noire. Recherche, enseignement, documentation africanistes francophones. Paris. 1,1969+
Afr 4.5   Deutsche Africa-Gesellschaft, Bonn. Schriftenreihe. Bonn. 1+
Afr 4.7   Dossiers africains. Dakar. 1,1959+   2v.
Afr 4.10   Duquesne University, Pittsburgh. Institute of African Affairs. Publications. Pittsburgh.
Afr 4.12   Documentation pédagogique africaine. Paris. 3v.
Afr 5.5PF   Essor colonial et maritime. Bruxelles. 3v.
Afr 6.1   Friend of Africa. ondon. 1,1841+
Afr 7.1   Guida amministrativa e delle attività economiche dell'impero Africa orientale italiana. Torino. 1938+
Afr 7.2   Ghent. International Fair. International days for African studies. Ghent. 1952+   4v.
Afr 7.5   Genève - Afrique. Genève. 1,1962+   3v.
Afr 7.7   Ghana. University, Legon. Institute of African Studies. Research review. Legon. 1,1965+
Afr 8.1   Harvard African studies. Cambridge. 1,1917+   10v.
Afr 8.2   Historical Association of Tanzania. Paper. Nairobi. 1,1966+
Afr 8.3   Historia, journal of the University of Ibadan Historical Society. Ibadon. 3,1966+
Afr 9.2   International Institute of African Languages and Cultures. Report on progress of work. London.
Afr 9.3   Institute for the Study of Man in Africa. Publication. Johannesburg. 1,1965+
Afr 9.4   Institut Français d'Afrique Noire. Bulletin. Paris. 1,1939+   12v.
Afr 9.4.2   Institut Français d'Afrique Noire. Bulletin. Sér. A. Sciences naturelles. Paris. 16,1954+   28v.
Afr 9.4.3   Institut Français d'Afrique Noire. Bulletin. Sér. B. Sciences humaines. Paris. 16,1954+   16v.
Afr 9.4.4   Institut Français d'Afrique Noire. Bulletin. Tables. Dakar. 1,1952+
Afr 9.4.5   Institut Français d'Afrique Noire. Mémoires. Paris. 1,1939+   58v.
Afr 9.4.8   Institut Français d'Afrique Noire. Catalogues. Dakar. 5+   34v.
Afr 9.5   Institute for the Study of Man in Africa. Report on the progress. 1,1960+
Afr 9.6   International African Service Bureau. Publications. London.
Afr 9.7   International West African Conference, 1st, Dakar, 1945. Comptes rendus. Paris. 1+   2v.
Afr 9.7.3   International West African Conference. Proceedings of the third International West African Conference. Lagos, 1956.
Afr 9.8   Inter-African Conference on Social Sciences. Meeting. London.
Afr 9.10   Ibadan, Nigeria. University. Geographical Society. The university geographer. Ibadan.
Afr 9.12   International Congress of Africanists. Proceedings. Evanston, Ill. 1,1962+
Afr 9.13   United States. Department of State. Office of External Research. Report on the Second International Congress of Africanists, Dakar, Senegal, Dec. 11-20, 1967. Washington, 1968.
Afr 9.14F   Internationales Afrika Forum. München. 1,1965+   4v.
Afr 9.16   Insight and opinion. Cape Coast. 1,1966+   2v.
Afr 9.17   Indian Council for Africa. Annual report. New Delhi. 1963+
Afr 9.18   Institut d'Enseignement Supérieur du Bénin, Lomé. Bulletin. Lomé. 8,1969+
Afr 10.1   African Society. Journal. London. 1901+   65v.
Afr 10.4   Journal of African history. London. 1,1960+   6v.
Afr 10.6   Journal of modern African studies. Cambridge, Eng. 1,1963+   5v.

Afr 1 - 24   Africa in general - Periodicals (A-Z) - cont.

Afr 10.8	Journées africaines. Louvain.
Afr 10.10	Journal of African administration. London. 1,1949+ 7v.
Afr 10.12	Journal of African and Asian studies. Delhi. 1,1967+
Afr 12.5	Länder Afrikas. Bonn. 1+ 35v.
Afr 12.8	Liberator. N.Y. 3,1963+
Afr 12.10	Library materials on Africa. London. 3v.
Afr 12.15	Leeds African studies bulletin. Leeds. 2,1965+ 6v.
Afr 12.20	Leopoldville. Université Lovanium. Institut de Recherches Economiques et Sociales. Collection d'études économiques. Léopoldville. 1,1965+
Afr 12.25	Lagos, Nigeria (City). University. African Studies Division. Proceedings at the staff seminars. Lagos. 1966+
Afr 12.30	Liste de livres, brochures et articles consacrés à l'Afrique, publiés en U.R.S.S. Moscou. 1963+
Afr 12.35	Lincoln University African Centre quarterly review. Lincoln University, Pa. 1,1968+
Afr 12.40	Lagos notes and records. Lagos. 1,1967+
Afr 13.5	Le mois en Afrique. Dakar. 2,1966+
Afr 13.10	Melville, J. Herskovits memorial lecture. Evanston, Ill. 1,1965+
Afr 14.5	New Africa. N.Y.
Afr 14.8	New African. Cape Town. 1,1962+ 4v.
Afr 14.10	Notes on Africa. Brooklyn Heights.
Afr 14.11	Nkanga editions. Kampala. 1,1968+
Afr 14.12	Nordiska Afrikainstitutet, Upsala. Newsletter. Upsala.
Afr 14.14	New Africa. London. 8,1966+
Afr 14.16	Narysy derzhavno-politychnsho rozvytku afrykans'kykh kraïn. Kyïv. 1,1967+
Afr 15.5	Organization of African Unity. OAU review. Asmara, Ethiopia. 1,1964+ 2v.
Afr 15.10	Ohio. University, Athens. Center for Internatiorial Studies. Papers in international studies. Africa series. Athens. 1,1968+
Afr 16.5	Paris. Université. Centre de Hautes Etudes Administratives sur l'Afrique et l'Asie Modernes. Recherches et documents. Série Afrique Noire. Paris. 2v.
Afr 16.8	Permanent Organization for Afro-Asian Peoples' Solidarity. Publications afro-asiatiques. Le Caire. 2v.
Afr 16.10	Permanent Organization for Afro-Asian Peoples' Solidarity. Dokumenty. V.F. Moskva, 1962. 3v.
Afr 16.12F	Pan-Africa. Nairobi. 27,1964+
Afr 16.12	Pan-Africa. Nairobi. 22,1964+
Afr 16.13	Pan-African Cultural Festival. News bulletin. Algiers. 1,1969+
Afr 16.14	Pan-African journal. N.Y. 1,1968+
Afr 16.16	The Pan-Africanist review. Accra. 15,,1964+
Afr 16.18	Pount. Djibouti. 1,1966+
Afr 18.5	Rhodes-Livingstone journal. Cape Town. 1,1944+ 2v.
Afr 18.5.5	Rhodes-Livingstone Journal. Index, v.1-30. Manchester, 1962.
Afr 18.7	Riv-Afrique, magazine africain des cadres et des responsables. Le Havre. 2,1968+
Afr 18.10F	Encyclopédie mensuelle de l'Afrique. Paris. 1958+
Afr 18.11F	Revue encyclopédique de l'Afrique. Abidjan. 1,1960+
Afr 18.14	Renaissance of Africa. Cairo.
Afr 18.16	Rural Africana. East Lansing. 5,1968+
Afr 19.5	Studien zur Auslandskunde. Afrika. Berlin.
Afr 19.8F	Spearhead. Dar es Salaam.
Afr 19.10	Studies in African history. The Hague. 1,1963+ 5v.
Afr 19.12	Salvador, Brazil. Universidade. Centro de Estudos Afro-Orientais. Publicações.
Afr 19.14	Société des Africanistes, Paris. Journal. Paris. 1,1931+ 16v.
Afr 19.16	Société des Africanistes, Paris. Centre de Documentation et d'Information. Bulletin d'information. Paris. 1-6,1964-1965//
Afr 19.18	Studia Africana. Praha. 1,1966+
Afr 19.20	Society for African Church History. Bulletin. London. 2,1965+
Afr 20.5	Tam-tam. Paris. 1961+ ?v
Afr 20.10	Tarikh. Ikeja. 1,1965+
Afr 21.5	United States. Department of State. Office of Public Services. African series. Washington.
Afr 21.10	Union Eurafricaine de Documentation. Informations Eurafdoc. 1+ 3v.
Afr 23.5	Washington notes on Africa. Washington. 1,1969+
Afr 24.5	Yearbook and guide to East Africa. 1950+ 13v.

Afr 25.104   Africa in general - Special organizations, etc. - Organization of African Unity - Publications of the whole body - Others

Afr 25.104.5	Organization of African Unity. OAU perspective, Third Regular Assembly, 1966. Addis Ababa, 1966.

Afr 25.108   Africa in general - Special organizations, etc. - Organization of African Unity - Works about the whole body - General works

Afr 25.108.2	Červenka, Zdenek. The Organization of African Unity and its charter. 2d ed. London, 1969.

Afr 25.160 - .169   Africa in general - Special organizations, etc. - Organization of African Unity - Special organs, etc. - Economic and Social Commission

Afr 25.160F	Organization of African Unity. Economic and Social Commission. Proceedings and report. Addis Ababa. 1,1963+

Afr 26   Africa in general - Portfolios [Discontinued]

Htn	Afr 26.5PF*	Pamphlet box. Miscellaneous broadsides.

Afr 28   Africa in general - Bibliographies

Afr 28.1A	Harvard University. Library. Widener Library shelflist. No.2. Africa. Cambridge, 1965.
Afr 28.1B	Harvard University. Library. Widener Library shelflist. No.2. Africa. Cambridge, 1965.
Afr 28.1.5	Centre de Documentation Economique et Sociale Africaine. Enquêtes bibliographiques. 7-15 2v.
Afr 28.2	Paulitschke, P. Die Afrika-Literatur in der Zeit von 1500 bis 1750 N. Ch. Wien, 1882.
Afr 28.3	Kayser, G. Bibliographie de l'Afrique. Bruxelles, 1887.
Afr 28.4.2	Gay, Jean. Bibliographie de l'Afrique. San Remo, 1875.
Afr 28.4.5	Gay, Jean. Bibliographie des ouvrages relatifs à l'Afrique et à l'Arabie. Amsterdam, 1961.
Afr 28.4.10	Boston Public Library. List of works on Africa. Boston, 1894.
Afr 28.5	Schweinfurth, G. Veröffentliche Briefe, Aufsätze und Werke. Berlin, 1907.

Afr 28   Africa in general - Bibliographies - cont.

Afr 28.6	Carroll, R.F. Selected bibliography of Africana for 1915. Cambridge, 1917.
Afr 28.7	Library of Congress. European Affairs Division. Introduction to Africa. Washington, 1952.
Afr 28.7.5	Library of Congress. European Affairs Division. Continuing sources for research on Africa. Washington, 1952.
Afr 28.8F	Johannesburg. University of the Witwatersrand. Gubbins Library. Preliminary list of Africana, mainly from the Gubbins Library. Johannesburg, 1930.
Afr 28.9	Kelly, Douglas C. Africa in paperbacks. East Lansing, Michigan, 1960.
Afr 28.10	Howard University, Washington, D.C. Library. Moorland Foundation. Catalogue of the African collection in the Moorland Foundation. Washington, 1958.
Afr 28.20	Hache, J. Bibliographie africaine de périodiques. Bruxelles, 1934.
Afr 28.25	Ragatz, L.J. A bibliography for the study of African history in the 19th and 20th centuries. Washington, 1943.
Afr 28.30	Fontan Lobé, Juan de. Bibliografia colonial. Madrid, 1946.
Afr 28.35	Robinson, A. A bibliography of African bibliographies. Cape Town, 1948.
Afr 28.37	Sommer, John W. Bibliography of African geography, 1940-1964. Hanover, N.H., 1965
Afr 28.40	International Social Science Council. International Research Office on Social Implications of Technological Change. Conséquences sociales de l'industrialisation et problèmes urbains en Afrique. Paris, 1954.
Afr 28.45F	Lavanaux, Maurice. A selected annotated bibliography on Africa. n.p., 1959.
Afr 28.50	Geographical Association. Library of the Geographical Association. Sheffield, 1957.
Afr 28.52	Spain. Dirección General de Plazas. Catalogo de autores y obras anonimas. Madrid, 1945.
Afr 28.55	Loewenthal, R. Russian materials on Africa. Washington, 1958.
Afr 28.56	Holdsworth, M. Soviet African studies. pt.1-2. Oxford, 1961.
Afr 28.58	Joint Secretariat C.C.T.A./C.S.A. Inventory of economic studies concerning Africa South of the Sahara. London, 1965.
Afr 28.60	United States and Canadian publications on Africa. Stanford. 1963+ 4v.
Afr 28.65	Moscow. Gosudarstvennaia Biblioteka SSSR imeni V.I. Lenina. Strany Afriki. Moscow, 1961.
Afr 28.68	Italiaander, Rolf. Africana. Holland, Michigan, 1961.
Afr 28.70	Library of Congress. African newspapers currently received in selected American libraries. Washington, 1956.
Afr 28.70.5	Library of Congress. Serial Division. African newspapers in selected American libraries. 2d ed. Washington, 1962.
Afr 28.71F	Nordiska Afrikainstitutet, Upsala. Bibliotek. Periodica i Nordiska Afrikainstitutets. Uppsala, 1966.
Afr 28.72	Northern Rhodesia and Nyasaland. Publications Bureau. A descriptive and classified list of books published by or in association with the Northern Rhodesia and Nyasaland Publication Bureau. n.p., 1961.
Afr 28.73	South African Public Library, Cape Town. A bibliography of african bibliographies. 3d ed. Cape Town, 1955.
Afr 28.74	South African Public Library, Cape Town. A bibliography of African bibliographies covering territories South of the Sahara. 4th ed. Cape Town, 1961.
Afr 28.76	Koehler, Jochen. Deutsche Dissertationen über Afrika. Bonn, 1962.
Afr 28.78	Guides to materials for West African history in European archives. London.
Afr 28.80	Library of Congress. A list of American doctoral dissertations on Africa. Washington, 1962.
Afr 28.82	Coisel. L'Afrique à travers les publications. Paris, 1961.
Afr 28.83	Central Asian Research Centre, London. Soviet writing of Africa, 1959-61. Oxford, 1963.
Afr 28.84	United States. Department of the Army. Africa, its problems and prospects. Washington, 1962.
Afr 28.85	Rio de Janeiro. Biblioteca Nacionale Bibliografia afro-asiatica. Rio de Janeiro, 1962.
Afr 28.86	Padmore Research Library on African Affairs, Accra. Bibliography series. Special subject bibliography. Accra. 2-5,1963-1965//?
Afr 28.86.5F	Accra. Research Library on African Affairs. Bibliography Series. Ghana: a current bibliography. Accra. 1,1967+
Afr 28.87	Padmore Research Library on African Affairs, Accra. Bibliography series. Acquisitions lists. Accra. 1-11,1962-1965//?
Afr 28.88	Tenri Central Library, Tanba City, Japan. Africana. Tenri, 1960. 2v.
Afr 28.89	Library of Congress. General Reference and Bibliography Division. Africa South of the Sahara. Washington, 1957.
Afr 28.89.2	Library of Congress. Africa South of the Sahara. Washington, 1963.
Afr 28.90	Glazier, K.M. Africa South of the Sahara. Stanford, Calif., 1964-69. 2v.
Afr 28.91	Royal Commonwealth Society, London. Annotated bibliography of recent publications on Africa. London, 1943.
Afr 28.92	Akaemiia Nauk SSSR. Institut Afriki. Bibliografiia Afriki, do revoliutsionnaia i liberatura na russkom Iazyke. Moscow, 1964.
Afr 28.93	Scotland. Record Office. Material relating to Africa. Edinburgh, 1962-65.
Afr 28.95	Hanna, W.J. Politics in Black Africa. East Lansing, Michigan, 1964.
Afr 28.96	Copenhagen. Kongelige Bibliotek. Nyere Africa-litteratur. København, 1962.
Afr 28.97	L'Afrique. Paris, 196-
Afr 28.98	Axelson, Eric Victor. African history, books and research. Cape Town. 1964.
Afr 28.99	Lystad, Robert A. The African world. London, 1965.
Afr 28.100	Boston University. Library. Catalog of African government documents and African area index. Boston, 1960.
Afr 28.101	Englborghs-Bertels, Marthe. Les pays de l'est et la décolonisation particulièrement en Afrique. Bruxelles, 1963.
Afr 28.102	Bibliographie éthnographique de l'Afrique Sud-Saharienne. Tervuren, 1963.
Afr 28.103	Ustav pro Mezinarodni Politiku a Ekonomii. Bibliograficke prameny the studiv problematiky africkych zemi. Praha, 1965.

Afr 28	**Africa in general - Bibliographies - cont.**	
Afr 28.104	Afrika-Bibliographie, Verzeichnis der wissenschaftlichen Schrifttum in deutscher Sprache. Bonn. 1,1960+ 2v.	
Afr 28.105	African Bibliographic Center. Special bibliographic series. Washington. 1,1963+ 4v.	
Afr 28.106	United Kingdom publications and theses on Africa. Cambridge, Eng. 1963+	
Afr 28.110	Boston University. African Studies Center. A list of films on Africa. Boston, 1966.	
Afr 28.112	Ghana. University. Library. Union list of Africana and related journals, in the Balme Africana Library, Legon, Institute of African Studies Library, Legon, and the Padmore Research Library on African Affairs, Accra. Legon, 1965.	
Afr 28.114F	Delhi. University. Library. Documentation list, Africa. Delhi. 5,1966+	
Afr 28.118F	Great Britain. Commonwealth Relations Office. Library. African military coups. London, 1966.	
Afr 28.120.2	Standing Conference on Library Materials on Africa. The SCOLMA directory of libraries and special collections on Africa. 2nd ed. London, 1967.	
Afr 28.124	Afrika-Schrifttum. Wiesbaden. 1,1966+	
Afr 28.126	Garling, Arthea. Bibliography of African bibliographies. Cambridge, Eng., 1968.	
Afr 28.128	Handlist of sub-Saharan Africana. Darien, Conn. 1,1968+	
Afr 28.130	Michigan. State University, East Lansing. Library. Research sources for African studies. East Lansing, 1969.	

Afr 29   Africa in general - Pamphlet volumes

Afr 29   Pamphlet box. Africa.
Afr 29.2   Pamphlet vol. Geography of Africa. 35 pam.
Afr 29.3   Pamphlet vol. Geography of Africa. 26 pam.
Afr 29.4   Pamphlet vol. Africa. 32 pam.
Afr 29.5   Pamphlet vol. Africa. 7 pam.
Afr 29.6   Pamphlet vol. Africa. 9 pam.
Afr 29.7   Pamphlet vol. Africa. Reprints.
Afr 29.8   Pamphlet vol. Africa. Reprints.
Afr 29.9   Pamphlet vol. Africa. 2 pam.
Afr 29.10   Pamphlet vol. Africa. Reprints.
Afr 29.11   Pamphlet vol. Africa. 3 pam.
Afr 29.12   Pamphlet vol. Africa. 2 pam.
Afr 29.13   Pamphlet box. Africa.
Afr 29.14   Pamphlet vol. Africa.
Afr 29.15   Pamphlet vol. Afrika. 3 pam.
Afr 29.16   Pamphlet vol. Africa. 5 pam.
Afr 29.17   Pamphlet vol. Africa 6 pam.
Afr 29.18   Pamphlet vol. Africa. Economic conditions. (Russian). 6 pam.
Afr 29.19   Pamphlet vol. Africa (Russian). 6 pam.
Afr 29.20   Pamphlet vol. Africa (Russian). 4 pam.
Afr 29.21   Pamphlet vol. Africa (Russian). 4 pam.
Afr 29.22   Pamphlet vol. Africa. (Russian). 4 pam.
Afr 29.23   Pamphlet vol. Africa. (Russian). 4 pam.
Afr 29.24   Pamphlet vol. Africa. (Russian). 5 pam.
Afr 29.25   Pamphlet vol. Archives - Africa. 3 pam.
Afr 29.26   Pamphlet vol. Africa. (Russian). 5 pam.

Afr 30   Africa in general - Dictionaries

Afr 30.4   Balandier, Georges. Dictionnaire des civilisations africaines. Paris, 1968.
Afr 30.5   Heichen, Paul. Afrika Hand-Lexicon. Leipzig, 1885-86.
Afr 30.6   Rosenthal, E. Encyclopaedia of Southern Africa. London, 1961
Afr 30.6.1   Rosenthal, Eric. Encyclopaedia of Southern Africa. 2nd ed. London, 1964.
Afr 30.6.3   Rosenthal, Eric. Encyclopaedia of Southern Africa. 3d ed. London, 1965.
Afr 30.8   Meyer's Handbuch über Afrika. Mannheim, 1962.
Afr 30.10   Sovetskaia Entsiklopediia. Afrika. Moscow, 1963. 2v.
Afr 30.12   Encyclopédie africaine et malgache. Paris, 1964.
Afr 30.14   Brummelkamp, Jacob. Modern Africa. Utrecht, 1966.

Afr 31   Africa in general - Collected source materials - General

Afr 31.5   Ibn Batuta. Textes et documents relatifs a l'histoire de l'Afrique. Dakar, 1966.
Afr 31.10   Bauer Landauer, I. Papeles de mi archivo, relaciones de Africa. Madrid, 1922-23. 4v.
Afr 31.12   Cordero Torres, J.M. Textos basicos de Africa. v.1-2. Madrid, 1962. 2v.

Afr 32   Africa in general - Collected source materials - Statutes

Afr 32.2   Lavroff, D.G. Les constitutions africaines. v.1-2. Paris, 1961-64. 2v.
Afr 32.3   Akademiia Nauk SSSR. Institut Gosudarstva i Prava. Konstitutsii gosudarstv Afriki. Moskva, 1966. 2v.

Afr 33   Africa in general - Collected source materials - Treaties

Afr 33.10F   France. Ministère des Affaires Etrangères. Documents diplomatiques. Paris, 1890. 16 pam.

Afr 35   Africa in general - Collected source materials - Others

Afr 35.5   Akademiia Nauk SSSR. Institut Afriki. Afrikanskii sbornik. v.1-2. Moscow, 1963. 2v.

Afr 36   Africa in general - Historiography

Afr 36.2   Abel, Herbert. Deutsche Afrikawissenschaft. Stand und Aufgaben. Köln, 1962.
Afr 36.4   Conference on the Position and Problems of the American Scholar in Africa, White Sulphur Springs, West Va., 1966. Summary report. N.Y., 1966?
Afr 36.6   Reconstructing African culture and history. Boston, 1967.
Afr 36.8   International Congress of African Historians, University College, Dar-es-Salaam, 1965. Emerging themes of African history; proceedings. Nairobi, 1968.

Afr 38   Africa in general - Archives

Afr 38.2F   Baxter, T.W. Archival facilities in sub-Saharan Africa. n.p., 1959.
Afr 38.4   Grieken, Emil. Les archives inventoriées au Ministère des colonies. Bruxelles, 1956.

Afr 40   Africa in general - Government and administration - General works

Afr 40.44   Council on African Affairs, Inc. Proceedings of the Conference on Africa. N.Y. 1944.
Afr 40.45   Batten, T.R. Thoughts on African citizenship. London, 1945.
Afr 40.61   Elias, T.O. Government and politics in Africa. N.Y. 1961.

Afr 40   Africa in general - Government and administration - General works - cont.

Afr 40.61.2   Elias, T.O. Government and politics in Africa. 2.ed. N.Y. 1963.
Afr 40.61.3   Elias, T.O. Government and politics in Africa. 2nd ed. Bombay, 1963.
Afr 40.61.5   Feireira, Oliverio. Ordem publica e liberdades politicas na Africa negra. Belo Horizonte, 1961.
Afr 40.62   Deschamps, Hubert. Les institutions politiques de l'Afrique Noire. Paris, 1962.
Afr 40.62.5   Egyptian Society of International Law. Constitutions of the new African states. n.p., 1962.
Afr 40.63   Akademiia Nauk SSSR. Institut Gosudarstva i Prava. Stanovlenie natsionalnoi gosudarstv v nezavisimykh stranakh Afriki. Moscow, 1963.
Afr 40.63.5   Chodak, S. Systemy polityczne czarnej Afryki. Warszawa, 1963.
Afr 40.63.10 Summit Conference of Independent African States. Summit conference of independent African states, Addis Ababa, 22-25 May1963. Cairo, 1963.
Afr 40.64   Foreign Affairs, N.Y. Africa. A Foreign Affairs reader. 1st ed. N.Y., 1964.
Afr 40.64.5   Alderfer, Harold Freed. A bibliography of African government, 1950-1966. 2d ed. Lincoln University, 1967.
Afr 40.65   Tuzmukhamedov, Rais A. Organizatsiia afrikanskogo edinstva. Moskva, 1965.
Afr 40.65.5   California. University. University at Los Angeles. African Studies Center. African law, adaptation and development. Berkeley, 1965.
Afr 40.67   Busia, Kofi Abrefa. Africa in search of democracy. N.Y., 1967.
Afr 40.67.5   Oyebola, Areoye. A textbook of government for West Africa. Ibadan, 1967.
Afr 40.67.10 Nekapitalisticheskii put' razvitiia stran Afriki. Moskva, 1967.

Afr 45   Africa in general - Government and administration - Special topics

Afr 45.29   Fidel, Camille. Les conseils représentatifs. Bruxelles, 1929.
Afr 45.59   Vanderlinden, Jacques. Essai sur les juridictions de droit coutumier. Bruxelles, 1959.
Afr 45.60.5   Diop, Cheikh Anta. Les fondements culturels, techniques et industriels d'un futur état fédéral d'Afrique noire. Paris, 1960.
Afr 45.60.10 Conference on the Future of Law in Africa. The future of law in Africa. London, 1960.
Afr 45.61   African Conference on the Rule of Law, Lagos, Nigeria. A report on the proceedings of the conference. Genève, 1961.
Afr 45.61.5   Constitutions des états africains d'expression française. Paris, 1961.
Afr 45.61.10 Arboussier, Gabriel. L'Afrique vers l'unité. Issy, 1961.
Afr 45.62   Summer Conference on Local Government in Africa. Summer conference on local government in Africa, 28 Aug.-9 Sept., 1961. Cambridge, 1962.
Afr 45.62.5   Buchmann, J. L'Afrique noire indépendante. Paris, 1962.
Afr 45.62.10 Allott, Anthony N. Judicial and legal systems in Africa. London, 1962.
Afr 45.63   Decottignier, R. Les nationalités africaines. Paris, 1963.
Afr 45.63.5   Jeol, M. La reforme de la justice en Afrique noire. Paris, 1963.
Afr 45.63.10 Baade, Hans Wolfgang. African law, new law for new nations. N.Y., 1963.
Afr 45.65   Adu, A.L. The civil service in new African states. London, 1965.
Afr 45.65.5   Payne, Denis. African independence and Christian freedom. London, 1965.
Afr 45.65.10 Allott, Anthony N. Law and language. London, 1965.
Afr 45.66   Gonidec, Pierre François. Cours d'institutions publiques africaines et malgaches. Paris, 1966.
Afr 45.66.5   Masseron, Jean Paul. Le pouvoir et la justice en Afrique noire francophone et à Madagascar. Paris, 1966.
Afr 45.66.10 Conference on African Local Government since Independence, Lincoln University, Pennsylvania, 1966. Proceedings of the Conference on African Local Government since Independence held at Lincoln University, Feb. 3rd and 4th, 1966. Lincoln, 1966.
Afr 45.66.15 International African Seminar. Ideas and prodedures in African customary law. London, 1969.
Afr 45.67   Le Vine, Victor T. Political leadership in Africa. Stanford, 1967.
Afr 45.68   Hutchison, Thomas W. Africa and law. Madison, 1968.
Afr 45.68.5   Andreski, Stanislav. The African predicament. London, 1968.
Afr 45.68.10 Gonidec, Pierre François. Les droits africains. Paris, 1968.

Afr 50   Africa in general - General politics; political parties

Afr 50.5   Fortes, Meyer. African political systems. London, 1940.
Afr 50.7   Fortes, Meyer. African political systems. London, 1958.
Afr 50.8   Diagné, Patné. Pouvoir politique traditionnel en Afrique occidentale. Paris, 1967.
Afr 50.10   Middleton, John. Tribes without rulers. London, 1958.
Afr 50.15A   Mackenzie, William. Five elections in Africa. Oxford, 1960.
Afr 50.15B   Mackenzie, William. Five elections in Africa. Oxford, 1960.
Afr 50.20   Prasad, Bisheshwar. Contemporary Africa. N.Y., 1960.
Afr 50.25   Hodgkin, Thomas. African political parties. Harmondsworth, 1961.
Afr 50.30   Carter, G. African one-party states. Ithaca, 1962.
Afr 50.30.2   Carter, G. African one-party states. Ithaca, 1964.
Afr 50.31   Carter, G. National unity and regionalism in eight African states. Ithaca, 1966.
Afr 50.35   Shepherd, George. The politics of African nationalism. N.Y., 1962.
Afr 50.40   Busia, Kafi A. The challenge of Africa. N.Y., 1962.
Afr 50.41   Gluckman, M. Order and rebellion in tribal Africa. London, 1963.
Afr 50.41B   Gluckman, Max. Order and rebellion in tribal Africa. London, 1963.
Afr 50.42   Pedersen, O.K. Afrikansk nationalisme. København, 1963.
Afr 50.43   Adam, Thomas R. Government and politics in Africa. 3d ed. N.Y., 1963.
Afr 50.44   Hanna, W.J. Independent black Africa. Chicago, 1964.
Afr 50.45   Scipio. Emergent Africa. Boston, 1965.
Afr 50.46   Bustin, Edouard. Guide des partis politiques africains. Bruxelles, 1962.

Afr 50 Africa in general - General politics; political parties - cont.

Afr 50.47	Dodge, Dorothy Rae. African politics in perspective. Princeton, N.J., 1966.
Afr 50.50	Mair, Lucy Philip. The new Africa. London, 1967.
Afr 50.51	Entin, Lev M. Natsional'naia gosudarstvennost' narodov Zapadnoi i Tsentral'noi Afriki. Moskva, 1966.
Afr 50.52	Moscow. Universitet Druzhby Narodov. Kafedra Inczhdunarodnogo Prava. Nezavisimaia Afrika v dokumentakh. Moskva, 1965.
Afr 50.53	Taylor, Don. Africa, the portrait of power. London, 1967.
Afr 50.55	Cunha, Joaquim Moreira da Silva. Politische Aspekte des neuen Afrika. Hamburg, 1965.
Afr 50.58	Mahiou, Ahmed. L'Avènement du parti unique en Afrique noire. Paris, 1969.
Afr 50.60	Bénot, Yvès. Idéologies des indépendances africaines. Paris, 1969.

Afr 55 Africa in general - Collected political biographies

Afr 55.5	Anglo-African who's who. London. 1905 2v.
Afr 55.10	Peters, Karl. Afrikanische Köpfe, Charakterskizzen. Berlin, 1915.
Afr 55.13	Oeste, Sven. Afrikas ansikte. Stockholm, 1962.
Afr 55.15	Italiaander, Rolf. Die neuen Männer Afrikas. Düsseldorf, 1960.
Afr 55.16	Italiaander, Rolf. The new leaders of Africa. Englewood Cliffs, 1961.
Afr 55.17	Italiaander, Rolf. Die neuen Männer Afrikas. Düsseldorf, 1963.
Afr 55.20	Melady, T.P. Profiles of African leaders. N.Y., 1961.
Afr 55.25	Segal, Ronald. African profiles. Baltimore, 1962.
Afr 55.30	Central and East African who's who. Salisbury.
Afr 55.32	Niven, Cecil R. Nine great Africans. London, 1964.
Afr 55.32.2	Niven, Cecil R. Nine great Africans. N.Y., 1965.
Afr 55.33	Kaula, Edna Mason. Leaders of the new Africa. Cleveland, 1966.
Afr 55.34	Gollock, Georgina Anne. Sons of Africa. London, 1928.
Afr 55.36	African yearly register. 1st ed. Johannesburg, 1932.
Afr 55.36.3	The African who's who. Johannesburg. 3,1966
Afr 55.40	Woodson, Carter Godwin. African heroes and heroines. Washington, 1939.
Afr 55.42	The new Africans. 1st American ed. N.Y., 1967.
Afr 55.44	Friedrich-Ebert-Stiftung. Afrika Biographien. Hannover, 1967- 3v.
Afr 55.46	Gollock, Georgina Anne. Lives of eminent Africans. N.Y., 1969.

Afr 104 - 110 Africa in general - General history (By date)

Afr 108.14	Geoffroy, R. L'Afrique ou Histoire, moeurs, usages et coutumes des Africans; le Sénégal. Paris, 1814. 4v.
Afr 108.80	Paulitschke, P. Die geographisch Erforschung der afrikanischen Continents. Wien, 1880.
Afr 108.82	Hahn, T. Early African exploration up to the 16th century. Cape Town, 1882.
NEDL Afr 108.89	Buel, J.W. Heroes of the dark continent and How Stanley found Erwin Pasha. Philadelphia, 1889.
Afr 108.93.2	Keltie, J.S. The partition of Africa. 2d ed. Photoreproduction. London, 1895. 2v.
X Cg Afr 108.93.2	Keltie, J.S. The partition of Africa. 2d ed. London, 1895. (changed to XP 9198)
Afr 108.93.3	Keltie, J.S. Africa. Philadelphia, 1907.
Afr 108.98	Taylor, W. The flaming torch in darkest Africa. N.Y., 1898.
Afr 108.99	Johnston, H.H. A history of the colonization of Africa. Cambridge, 1899.
Afr 108.99.4A	Johnston, H.H. A history of the colonization of Africa. Cambridge, 1905.
Afr 108.99.4B	Johnston, H.H. A history of the colonization of Africa. Cambridge, 1905.
Afr 108.99.6	Johnston, H.H. A history of the colonization of Africa. Cambridge, 1913.
Afr 109.05	Hartig, D. Altere Entdeckungsgeschichte und Kartographie Afrikas. Wien, 1905.
Afr 109.11	Johnston, H.H. The opening up of Africa. London, n.d.
Afr 109.11.5	Johnston, H.H. The opening up of Africa. N.Y., 1911.
Afr 109.13	Darmstaedter, P. Geschichte der Aufteilung und Kolonisation Afrikas. Berlin, 1913-20. 2v.
Afr 109.20	Moulin, Alfred. L'Afrique à travers les ages. Paris, 1920.
Afr 109.20.10	Salkin, Paul. Etudes africaines. Bruxelles, 1920.
Afr 109.22	Hardy, Georges. Vue générale de l'histoire d'Afrique. Paris, 1922.
Afr 109.32	Berger, A. Afrika, schwarz oder weiss. Berlin, 1932.
Afr 109.36A	Woodson, C.G. The African background outlined, or Handbook for the study of the Negro. Washington, 1936.
Afr 109.36B	Woodson, C.G. The African background outlined, or Handbook for the study of the Negro. Washington, 1936.
Afr 109.38	Berger, Arthur. Kampf um Afrika. Berlin, 1938.
Afr 109.44	Bidou, Henry. L'Afrique. Paris, 1944.
Afr 109.46	Monod, Theodore. L'hippopotame et le philosophe. Paris, 1946.
Afr 109.46.5	Labouret, H. Africa before the white man. N.Y., 1963.
Afr 109.46.10	Labouret, H. L'Afrique précoloniale. Paris, 1959.
Afr 109.52	Westermann, Diedrich. Geschichte Afrikas. Köln, 1952.
Afr 109.54	Degraff Johnson, J.C. African glory. London, 1954.
Afr 109.55	Istituto Italiano per l'Africa. L'Africa nei suoi aspetti geografici. Roma, 1955.
Afr 109.57	Hunton, William A. Decision in Africa. N.Y., 1957.
Afr 109.57.3	Hunton, William A. Decision in Africa, sources of current conflict. N.Y., 1960.
Afr 109.58	Italiaander, Rolf. Der ruhelose Kontinent. 1. Aufl. Düsseldorf, 1958.
Afr 109.59	Zierer, Otto. Geschichte Afrikas. v.1-2. Murnau, 1959. 2v.
Afr 109.59.5	Scott, John. Africa, world's last frontier. N.Y., 1959.
Afr 109.59.10	Hatch, John C. Everyman's Africa. London, 1959.
Afr 109.59.12	Hatch, John C. Africa today and tomorrow. 2nd ed. London, 1965.
Afr 109.59.15	Healy, A.M. The map approach to African history. London, 1959.
Afr 109.59.18	Healy, A.M. The map approach to African history. 4th ed. London, 1967.
Afr 109.59.20	Arbeitstagung über Neuere und Neueste Geschichte. Geschichte und Geschichtsbild Afrikas. Berlin, 1960.
Afr 109.59.25	Diop, Cheikh A. Etude comparée des systèmes politiques et sociaux de l'Europe et de l'Afrique, de l'antiquité à la formation des états modernes. Paris 1959.
Afr 109.60	Diop, Cheikh A. L'unité culturelle de l'Afrique. Paris, 1959.

Afr 104 - 110 Africa in general - General history (By date) - cont.

Afr 109.60.3	Diop, Cheikh A. L'Afrique noire pré-coloniale. Paris, 1960.
Afr 109.60.5	Cornevin, Robert. Histoire des peuples de l'Afrique Noire. Paris, 1960.
Afr 109.60.5.2	Cornevin, Robert. Histoire des peuples de l'Afrique Noire. Paris, 1960.
Afr 109.60.10	Ward, William. A history of Africa. London, 1960. 2v.
Afr 109.60.10.3	Ward, William. A history of Africa. v.1-2. London, 1966.
Afr 109.60.15	Dia, Mamadou. Nations africaines et solidarité mondiale. Paris, 1960.
Afr 109.60.15.2	Dia, Mamadou. Nations africaines et solidarité mondiale. Paris, 1963.
Afr 109.60.20	Drachoussoff, V. L'Afrique decolonisée. Bruxelles, 1960.
Afr 109.60.25F	Lenerhulme Inter-Collegiate History Conference, 1960. Historians in tropical Africa. Salisbury, 1962.
Afr 109.61	Cameron, James. The African revolution. London, 1961.
Afr 109.61.1	Cameron, James. The African revolution. N.Y., 1961.
Afr 109.61.5	Oliver, Roland A. The dawn of African history. London, 1961.
Afr 109.61.7	Oliver, Roland A. The dawn of African history. 2d ed. London, 1968.
Afr 109.61.10	Tillion, Germaine. L'Afrique bascule vers l'avenir. Paris, 1961.
Afr 109.61.15	Cardot, Vera. Belles pages de l'histoire africaine. Paris, 1961.
Afr 109.61.20	Favrod, Ch.H. L'Afrique seule. Paris, 1961.
Afr 109.61.25	Sik, Endre. Histoire de l'Afrique noire. v.1- Budapest, 1961. 2v.
Afr 109.61.25.5	Sik, Endre. Histoire de l'Afrique noire. Budapest, 1968. 2v.
Afr 109.61.26	Sik, Endre. The history of black Africa. Budapest, 1966. 2v.
Afr 109.61.30	Adiko, A. Histoire des peuples noirs. Abidjan, 1961.
Afr 109.61.31	Adiko, A. Histoire des peuples noirs. Abidjan, 1963.
Afr 109.61.35	Joos, L.C.D. Brève histoire à l'Afrique noire. v.1-2. Issy-les-Moulineaux, 1961-64. 2v.
Afr 109.61.40	Mukarovsky, H. Afrika. Wien, 1961.
Afr 109.61.41	Mukarovsky, H. Afrique d'hier et d'aujourd'hui. Tournai, 1964.
Afr 109.61.45	Tunis. Secretariat d'Etat à l'Information. New Africa. Tunis, 1961.
Afr 109.61.50	Portella, Eduardo. Africa, colonos e cumplices. Rio de Janeiro, 1961.
Afr 109.61.57	Legum, Colin. Africa, a handbook. 2d ed. London, 1965.
Afr 109.62	Kingsnorth, G.W. Africa south of the Sahara. Cambridge, 1962.
Afr 109.62.5	Wiedner, Donald. A history of Africa. N.Y., 1962.
Afr 109.62.10	Herskovits, Melville. The human factor in changing Africa. 1st ed. N.Y., 1962.
Afr 109.62.15	Oliver, Roland Anthony. A short history of Africa. Harmondsworth, 1962.
Afr 109.62.20	Cornevin, Robert. Histoire de l'Afrique. Paris, 1962. 2v.
Afr 109.62.22	Cornevin, Robert. Histoire de l'Afrique des origines à nos jours. Paris, 1966.
Afr 109.62.25	Svoboda, J. Pet stoleti boju o jizm Afriku. Praha, 1962.
Afr 109.62.30	Calle Iturrino, E. De Tutankamen a Nasser. Bilbao, 1962.
Afr 109.62.35	Pirone, Michele. Appunti di storia dell'Africa. Milano, 1962.
Afr 109.62.41	Ansprenger, Franz. Afrika. Eine politische Länderkunde. 6. Aufl. Berlin, 1969.
Afr 109.63	Pamphlet vol. Africa. 3 pam.
Afr 109.63.5	Anders, Robert. L'Afrique africaine. Paris, 1963.
Afr 109.63.10	Lewicki, Tadeusz. Dzieje Afryki od czasow najdawnicjszych do XIV w. Wyd.1. Warszawa, 1963.
Afr 109.63.15	Brentjes, Burchard. Uraltes junges Afrika; 5000 Jahre afrikanischer Geschichte nach zeitgenössischen Quellen. Berlin, 1963.
Afr 109.64	Davidson, B. The African past. 1st ed. Boston, 1964.
Afr 109.64.5	Bohannan, P. Africa and Africans. 1st ed. Garden City, 1964.
Afr 109.64.6	Bohannan, P. African outline, a general introduction. Harmondsworth, Middlesex, Eng., 1966.
Afr 109.64.10	Wallbank, T.W. Documents on modern Africa. Princeton, N.J., 1964.
Afr 109.64.15	Africa report. A handbook of African affairs. N.Y., 1964.
Afr 109.64.20	Nicol, D. Africa - a subjective view. London, 1964.
Afr 109.64.25	Currie, D.P. Federalism and the new nations. Chicago, 1964.
Afr 109.64.33	Filesi, Teobaldo. Evoluzione storico-politica dell'Africa. 3. ed. Como, 1967.
Afr 109.65.5	Ciba Foundation. Man and Africa. London, 1965.
Afr 109.65.10	Davidson, Basil. A guide to African history. 1st ed. Garden City, N.Y., 1965.
Afr 109.65.15	Fordham, Paul. The geography of African affairs. Baltimore, 1965.
Afr 109.65.16	Fordham, Paul. The geography of African affairs. 2d ed. Harmondsworth, 1968.
Afr 109.65.20	Liubimov, Nikolai N. Afrika v mirovoi ekonomike i politike. Moskva, 1965.
Afr 109.65.25	Chu, Daniel. A glorious age in Africa, the story of three great African empires. 1st ed. Garden City, 1965.
Afr 109.66F	Davidson, Basil. Africa, history of a continent. London, 1966.
Afr 109.66.2	Davidson, Basil. Africa in history, themes and outlines. London, 1968.
Afr 109.66.5	Howe, Russell Warren. Black Africa, Africa south of the Sahara from prehistory to independence. London, 1966. 2v.
Afr 109.66.10	Jacob, Ernest Gerhard. Grundzüge der Geschichte Afrikas. Darmstadt, 1966.
Afr 109.66.15	Howe, Russell Warren. Black Africa, Africa south of the Sahara from pre-history to independence. N.Y., 1966. 2v.
VAfr 109.66.20	Hrbek, Ivan. Dějiny Afriky. Vyd. 1. Praha, 1966. 2v.
Afr 109.66.25	Rainero, Romain. Storia dell'Africa dall'epoca coloniale ad oggi. Torino, 1966.
Afr 109.66.30	Bertaux, Pierre. Afrika. Frankfurt, 1966.
Afr 109.67	Hodder, Bramwell William. Africa in transition, geographical essays. London, 1967.
Afr 109.67.5	Oliver, Roland Anthony. The middle age of African history. London, 1967.
Afr 109.67.10	Hatch, John C. Africa; the rebirth of self-rule. London, 1967.
Afr 109.67.15	Hatch, John C. Africa in the wider world, the inter-relationship of area and comparative studies. Oxford, 1967.
Afr 109.67.20	Singleton, F. Seth. Africa in perspective. N.Y., 1967.
Afr 109.67.25	Davidson, Basil. The growth of African civilization: East and Central Africa to the late nineteenth century. London, 1967.

Afr 104 - 110 Africa in general - General history (By date) - cont.

Afr 109.67.26   Davidson, Basil. A history of East and Central Africa to the late nineteenth century. Garden City, N.Y., 1969.

Afr 109.67.30   Cornevin, Robert. Histoire de l'Afrique. Paris, 1967-

Afr 109.67.35   Sicard, Maurice Ivan. La contre-révolution africaine. Paris, 1967.

Afr 109.67.40   Farelly, Maurice. Africains d'hier et de demain. Neuchâtel, 1967.

Afr 109.68   MacGregor-Hastie, Roy. Africa, background for today. London, 1968.

Afr 109.68.5   McEwan, Peter J.M. Readings in African history. London, 1968. 3v.

Afr 109.68.10   The making of modern Africa. N.Y., 1968-

Afr 109.68.15   Zaghi, Carlo. L'Europa devanti all'Africa dai tempi piu antichi alle soglie dell'Ottocento. Napoli, 1968.

Afr 109.68.20   Colloquium on Institution-Building and the African Development Process, University of California at Los Angeles, 1967. Nations by design; institution-building in Africa. 1st ed. Garden City, 1968.

Afr 109.69   Henries, A. Doris. Africa, our history. London, 1969.

Afr 109.70   July, Robert William. A history of the African people. N.Y., 1970.

Afr 109.70.5   Hallett, Robin. Africa to 1875; a modern history. Ann Arbor, 1970.

Afr 109.70.10   Gailey, Harry A. History of Africa, from the earliest times to 1800. N.Y., 1970.

Afr 115   Africa in general - General special

Afr 115.1   Santarem, M.F. de B. Memoria sobre a prioridade dos descobrimentos portugueses. Porto, 1841.

Afr 115.2   Dujarday, H. Resumé des voyages des portugais. Paris, 1839. 2v.

Afr 115.3   Cardeiro, L. Ed. Viagens explorações dos portugueses. Lisboa, 1881.

Afr 115.3.5   Ribeiro, M.F. Homenagem aôs heróes que precederam. Lisboa, 1885.

Afr 115.3.10   Memoria sobre a prioridade dos descobrimentos dos portugueses. Porto, 1842.

Afr 115.3.25F   Canti, Cesare. L'incivilimento dell Africa, memoria. n.p., 18- .

Afr 115.4   Carrie, F. Thoughts upon present and future of South Africa. London, 1877.

Afr 115.5   Maisel, A.Q. Africa, facts and forecasts. N.Y., 1943. 2v.

Afr 115.6   Louwers, Octave. Le Congrès Volta de 1938 et ses travaux sur l'Afrique. Bruxelles, 1949.

Afr 115.7F   Brunet, P. Les explorateurs de l'Afrique. Tours, 1889.

Afr 115.9.2   Dubois, William E. The world and Africa. N.Y., 1965.

Afr 115.10   South Africa. Institute on International Affairs. Africa south of the Sahara. Cape Town, 1951.

Afr 115.15   Ly, A. Les masses africaines. Paris, 1956.

Afr 115.17   McCall, D.F. Africa in time-perspective. Boston, 1964.

Afr 115.20   Schiffers, H. Wilder Ersteil Afrika. Bonn, 1954.

Afr 115.20.5   Schiffers, H. The quest for Africa. London, 1957.

Afr 115.20.10   Schiffers, Heinrich. Afrika, als die Weissen kamen. Düsseldorf, 1967.

Afr 115.25   Padmore, G. Africa and world peace. London, 1937.

Afr 115.30   Sithole, N. African nationalism. Cape Town, 1959.

Afr 115.30.2   Sithhole, Ndabaningi. African nationalism. 2d ed. London, 1968.

Afr 115.40   Symposium on Africa, Wellesley College. 1960 symposium on Africa. Wellesley, 1960.

Afr 115.42   International West African Conference, 4th, Santa Isabel. Conferencia internacional de africanistas occident. v.2. Madrid, 1954.

Afr 115.45   Conference on the Legal, Economic and Social Aspects of African Refugee Problems. Final report. Uppsala, 1968.

Afr 115.50   Langenhove, F. Consciences tribales et nationales en Afrique noire. Bruxelles, 1960.

Afr 115.55   Wauthier, Claude. L'Afrique des africains. Paris, 1964.

Afr 115.55.2   Wauthier, Claude. The literature and thought of modern Africa, a survey. London, 1966.

Afr 115.60   Des africanistes russes parlent de l'Afrique. Paris, 1960.

Afr 115.70   Jones, Ch. H. Famous explorers and adventures in Africa. v.1-2. N.Y., 1881. 2v.

Afr 115.80   Study Congress on International Cooperation in Africa. La cooperazione internazionale in Africa. Milano, 1960.

Afr 115.85   Vedovato, Giuseppe. Studi africani e asiatici. Firenze, 1964. 3v.

Afr 115.90   Conference on History and Archaeology. History and archaeology in Africa. London, 1959.

Afr 115.91   Heidelberg, Wolfgang. Grundzüge des Niederlassungsrechts in den afrikanischen Staaten. Hamburg, 1965. 2v.

Afr 115.100   Jensen, Johannes V. Afrika, opdagelsesrejserne. København, 1949.

Afr 115.101   Savage, K. The history of Africa south of the Sahara. London, 1961.

Afr 115.102   Okoye, M. African responses. Ilfracombe, 1964.

Afr 115.105   Lion, J. Od Limpopa k Vltave. Praha, 1963.

Afr 115.106   Social Sciences Research Conference. Problems of transition. Pietermaritzburg, Natal, 1964.

Afr 115.107   Bertola, Arnaldo. Storia e istituzioni dei paesi afro-asiatici. Torino, 1964.

Afr 115.108   Shinnie, Margaret. Ancient African kingdoms. London, 1965.

Afr 115.109   Vazquez-Figueros, Alberto. Africa encadenada. 1. ed. Barcelona, 1965.

Afr 115.110   Jones, Arthur M. Africa and Indonesia. Leiden, 1964.

Afr 115.111   Heinrich Barth zum Gedenken. Hamburg, 1965.

Afr 115.112   Homann, Hermann. Wisser Mann auf heissen Pfaden. Stuttgart, 1963.

Afr 115.113   Subbotin, Vaterii A. Problemy istorii Afriki. Moskva, 1966.

Afr 115.114   Melikian, Ovanes N. Neitralizm gosudarstv Afrikii. Moskva, 1966.

Afr 115.115   Amedeo, Duke of Aosta. Studi africani. Bologna, 1942.

Afr 115.116   Nekotorye voprosy istorii Afriki. Moskva, 1968.

Afr 115.117   Izuchenie Afriki v Svetskom Soiuze. Photocopy. Moskva, 1966.

Afr 115.120   Pedrals, Denis Pierre. Manuel scientifique de l'Afrique noire. Paris, 1949.

Afr 115.121   Zarubezhnye tsentry afrikanistiki. Moskva, 1968.

Afr 115.122   African boundary problems. Stockholm, 1969.

Afr 115.123   Prothero, Ralph Mansell. A geography of Africa; regional essays on fundamental characteristics, issues and problems. London, 1969.

Afr 115   Africa in general - General special - cont.

Afr 115.124   Davidson, Basil. The African genius; an introduction to African cultural and social history. 1st American ed. Boston, 1969.

Afr 115.126.2   Awosika, V.O. An African meditation. 2nd ed. N.Y., 1969.

Afr 115.128.2   Huggins, Willis Nathaniel. An introduction to African civilizations. N.Y., 1969.

Afr 115.130   Expanding horizons in African studies. Evanston, Ill., 1969.

Afr 125   Africa in general - History by periods - Ancient to Arab Invasion (To 7th century)

Afr 125.5   Berlioux, E.F. La terre habitable vers l'équator. Paris, 1884.

Afr 125.6F   Morcelli, S.A. Africa christiana. Brixiae, 1816. 3v.

Afr 125.10   Avezac, A. D. Afrique. Paris, 1844.

Afr 125.15   Thompson, Lloyd Arthur. Africa in classical antiquity. Ibadan, Nigeria, 1969.

Afr 150   Africa in general - History by periods - Medieval (7th to 16th centuries)

Afr 150.1   Brasio, A.D. A acção missionaria no periodo henriquino. Lisboa, 1958.

Afr 150.2   Kunstmann, F. Afrika vor den Entdeckungen der Portugiesen. München, 1853.

Afr 150.2.3   Lepitre, J.M.A. De iis qui ante Vascum A Gama Africam legere tentaverunt. Thesis. Parisis, 1880.

Afr 150.2.5F   Castilho, A.M. De. Os padrões dos descobrimentos portuguezes em Africa. 2a memoria. Lisboa, 1871.

Afr 150.2.10   Pamphlet box. Prince Henry the Navigator.

Afr 150.2.15   Soares, Ernesto. Iconografia do Infante Dom Henrique. Lisboa, 1959.

Afr 150.2.20   Nemesio, Vitorino. Vida e obra do Infante Dom Henrique. Lisboa, 1959. 2v.

Afr 150.2.25   Aveiro, Portugal. Museu. Iconografia do Infante Dom Henrique. Aveiro, 1960.

Afr 150.2.30F   Reis-Santos, Luiz. Iconografia henriquina. Coimbra, 1960.

Afr 150.2.35   Diaz de Villegas, José. La epopeya de Enrique el Navegante. Madrid, 1961.

Afr 150.2.40   Moura, J.J.N. O Infante Dom Henrique na conquista das Canarias. Villa Real de Santo Antonio, 1960.

Afr 150.2.45   Selvagem, Carlos (pseud.) Infante Dom Henrique. Lisboa, 1960.

Afr 150.2.50   Camacho Pereira, João. O Infante Dom Henrique do 5. centenario da sua morte. Lisboa, 1960.

Afr 150.2.55   Godinho, Vitoriano de Magalhaes. A economia dos descobrimentos henriquinos. Lisboa, 1962.

Afr 150.2.60   Tavares, Luis C. O Infante Dom Henrique e os descobrimentos. Braga, 1960.

Afr 150.2.65   Portugal. Comissão Executiva das Comemorações do V Centenario da Morte do Infante Dom Henrique. Henri le Navigateur. Lisboa, 1960.

Afr 150.2.66   Portugal. Comissão Executiva das Comemorações do V Centenario da Morte do Infante Dom Henrique. Comemoracoe do V centenario da morte do Infante Dom Henrique. Lisboa, 1961-1963. 4v.

Afr 150.2.70   Estailleur-Chanteraine, Philippe. L'infant de la mer. Paris, 1960.

Afr 150.2.75   Guerreiro, Amaro D. Panorama economico dos descobrimentos henriquinos. Lisboa, 1961.

Afr 150.2.80   Portugal. Comissão Executiva das Comemorações do V Centenario da Morte do Infante Dom Henrique. Programa das comemorações. Lisboa, 1960.

Afr 150.2.85   Azevedo, A.J. da Silva D. Americas, un corolario de sagres. Lisboa, 1964.

Afr 150.2.90   Rio de Janeiro. Cabinete Portugues de Leitura. Catálogo henriquino do Real Cabinete Português de Leitura do Rio de Janeiro. Lisboa, 1960.

X Cg   Afr 150.3   Major, R.H. Life of Prince Henry of Portugal. London, 1868.

Afr 150.3.1   Major, R.H. The life of Prince Henry of Portugal. 1st ed. London, 1967.

Afr 150.3.2   Major, R.H. The discoveries of Prince Henry. London, 1877.

Afr 150.3.5   Major, R.H. Vida do Infante Dom Henrique de Portugal. Lisboa, 1876.

Afr 150.4   Beazley, C.R. Prince Henry the Navigator. N.Y., 1895.

Afr 150.4.5   Beazley, C.R. Prince Henry the Navigator. London, 1923.

Afr 150.4.10   Russell, Peter E. Prince Henry the Navigator. London, 1960.

Afr 150.5   Sanctos Firmo, M. Noticia sobre a vida e escriptos do Infante Dom Henrique. Lisboa, 1866.

Afr 150.6   Mees, Jules. Henri le Navigateur. Bruxelles, 1901.

Afr 150.7.4   Oliveira Martins, J.P. The golden age of Henry the Navigator. London, 1914.

Afr 150.8   Wappaens, J.E. Untersuchungen üeber die geographischen Entdeckungen der Portugiesen unter Heinrich dem Seefahrer. Göttingen, 1842.

Afr 150.9   Freire, F.J. Vida do Infante Dom Henrique. Lisboa, 1758.

Afr 150.9.6   Freire, F.J. Vie de l'Infant Dom Henri de Portugal. Lisbonne, 1781.

Htn   Afr 150.10F*   Zuental, Anthero de. O Infante Dom Henrique. Lisboa, 1894.

Afr 150.11   Almeida, Fortunato. O Infante de Sagres. Porto, 1894.

Afr 150.12   Macedo, Lino da. A obra do Infante. Villafranca de Xira, 1894.

Afr 150.13   Wauwermans, Henri. Henri le Navigateur et l'Académie Portugaise de Sagres. Bruxelles, 1890.

Afr 150.14   Bensaude, J. A cruzada do Infante Dom Henrique. Lisboa, 1942.

Afr 150.15   Mendes de Brito, Francisco. O infante Dom Henrique, 1394-1460. Lisboa, 1942.

Afr 150.15.2   Mendes de Brito, Francisco. O Infante Dom Henrique e a civilização ocidental. Santarém, 1942.

Afr 150.15.5   Mendes De Brito, Francisco. Nota carminativa, uma resposta ão Sr. Dr. Duarte Leite. Lisboa, 1944.

Afr 150.16   Costa, Brochado. Infante Dom Henrique. Lisboa, 1942.

Afr 150.17   Sanceau, Elaine. Henry the Navigator. London, 194-.

Afr 150.17.5   Sanceau, Elaine. Henry the Navigator. N.Y., 1947.

Afr 150.18   Rumbucher, K. Heinrich der Seefahrer. München, 1954.

Afr 150.19   Domingues, Mario. O Infante Dom Henrique. Lisboa, 1957.

Afr 150.20   Henrique, o Navegador, Infante of Portugal. Conselho do Infante Dom Henrique a seu sobrinho El-Rei Dom Afonso V. Lisboa, 1958.

Afr 150.25   Simões Mueller, Adolfo. O principe do mar. Porto, 1959.

Afr 150.27   Ibn Al Hatib. El Africa del Norte en El a mal ol a lam de Ibn al Jatib. Madrid, 1958.

Afr 150 Africa in general - History by periods - Medieval (7th to 16th centuries) - cont.

Afr 150.31 Lopes, F.F. A figura e a obra do Infante Dom Henrique. Lisboa, 1960.
Afr 150.32 Principe, S. Rectificação historica a memoria do Infante Dom Henrique. Lobito, 1961.
Afr 150.35 British Museum. Prince Henry the Navigator. London, 1960.
Afr 150.37 Paris. Musée National du Louvre. Musée de Marine. Henri le navigateur et les decouvreurs portugais. Paris, 1960.
Afr 150.40 Bradford, Ernle. A wind from the north. N.Y., 1960.
Afr 150.40.5 Bradford, Ernle. Southward the caravels. London, 1961.
Afr 150.42 Kake, Baba Ibrahima. Glossaire critique des expressions geographiques concernant le pays des noirs. Paris, 1965.
Afr 150.45 Infante Dom Henrique. Lisboa, 1960.
Afr 150.50 Passos, Vergilio. A projecção do infante no mundo. Lisboa, 1960.
Afr 150.55 Dias, A. Infante de Sagres. Porto, 1960.
Afr 150.60 Vasconcellos, Joaquim de. Taboas da pintura portugueza no seculo XV. Lisboa, 1960.
Afr 150.62 Portugal. Comissão Executiva das Comemorações do V Centenario da Morte do Infante Dom Henrique. Bibliografia Henriquino. Lisboa, 1960. 2v.
Afr 150.64 Portugal. Comissão Executiva das Comemorações do V. Centenario da Morte do Infante Dom Henrique. Monumenta Henricina. Coimbra, 1960. 9v.
Afr 150.66 Cortesão, Jaime. A expansão dos Portugueses no periodo Henriquino. Lisboa, 1965.
Afr 150.68 Moreira de Sa, Artur. O Infante D. Henrique e a universidade. Lisboa, 1960.
Afr 150.70 Portugal. Comissão Executiva das Comemorações do V. Centenario da Morte do Infante Dom Henrique. Exposição Henriquina. Lisboa, 1960.
Afr 150.72 Dias Dinis, Antonio J. Estudos henriquinos. Coimbra, 1960.

Afr 175 Africa in general - History by periods - 16th century to ca. 1850

Afr 175.5 Matep, Benjamin. Heurts et malheurs des rapports Europe-Afrique. Paris, 1959.
Afr 175.6 Deschamps, Hubert Jules. L'Afrique tropicale aux XVIIe-XVIIIe siècles. Paris, 1964.
Afr 175.8 Ward, William Ernest Frank. Emergent Africa. London, 1967.

Afr 200 Africa in general - History by periods - Nineteenth century (1850-1900)

Afr 200.2 Banning, E. Le partage politique de l'Afrique. Bruxelles, 1888.
Afr 200.3A Latimer, E.W. Europe in Africa in the 19th century. Chicago, 1895.
Afr 200.3B Latimer, E.W. Europe in Africa in the 19th century. Chicago, 1895.
Afr 200.4 Darcy, Jean. France et Angleterre: cent années. Paris, 1904.
Afr 200.4.3F France. Ministère des Affaires Etrangères. Documents diplomatiques. Paris, 1898.
Afr 200.5 Sevin-Deplaces, L. Afrique et africains. Paris, 1892.
Afr 200.6 Deville, V. Partage de l'Afrique. Paris, 1898.
Afr 200.7 Chatelain, C. L'Afrique et l'expansion coloniale. Paris, 1901.
Afr 200.8 Darcy, Jean. La conquête de l'Afrique. Paris, 1900.
Afr 200.9 Sanderson, E. Africa in the 19th century. N.Y., 1898.
Afr 200.9.5 Sanderson, E. Africa in the 19th century. London, 1898.
NEDL Afr 200.10 Bonnefon, E.L. L'Afrique politique en 1900. Paris, 1900.
Afr 200.12 Kaltbrunner, David. L'Afrique en 1890. Paris, 1890.
Afr 200.13.5 Septans, Albert. Les expéditions anglaises en Afrique, Ashantel 1873-1874. Paris, 1896.
Afr 200.14 Molto y Campo-Redondo, P. Situación politica de Africa en 1892. Madrid, 1892.
Afr 200.15 Pesenti, Gustavo. Le guerre coloniali. Bologna, 1947.
Afr 200.16 Santa-Rita, José. A Africa nas relações. Lisboa, 1959.
Afr 200.17 Brunschwig, H. L'avénement de l'Afrique noire du XIX siècle à nos jours. Paris, 1963.
Afr 200.18 Rooney, Douglas David. The building of modern Africa. London, 1966.
Afr 200.18.2 Rooney, Douglas David. The building of modern Africa. 2nd ed. London, 1967.

Afr 210 Africa in general - History by periods - Twentieth century - General works and 1900-1960

Afr 210.01 Pamphlet box. Africa in the twentieth century.
Afr 210.3 Pamphlet vol. Africa, twentieth century. 10 pam.
Afr 210.4 Pamphlet vol. Pan-Africanism. 8 pam.
Afr 210.10 Brawley, B.G. Africa and the war. N.Y., 1918.
Afr 210.28A Buell, Raymond Lesley. The native problem in Africa. N.Y., 1928. 2v.
Afr 210.28B Buell, Raymond Lesley. The native problem in Africa. N.Y., 1928. 2v.
Afr 210.28.2 Buell, Raymond Leslie. The native problem in Africa. London, 1965. 2v.
Afr 210.30 Smuts, J.C. Africa and some world problems. Oxford, 1930.
Afr 210.30.10 Oldham, J.H. White and black in Africa. London, 1930.
Afr 210.32 Dix, Arthur. Weltkrise und Kolonialpolitik. Berlin, 1932.
Afr 210.36 Mathews, Basil. Consider Africa. N.Y., 1936.
Afr 210.38 Hailey, W.M.H. An African survey. London, 1938.
Afr 210.38.2 Hailey, W.M.H. An African survey. 2d ed. London, 1945.
Afr 210.38.5A Hailey, W.M.H. An African survey. London, 1957.
Afr 210.38.5B Hailey, W.M.H. An African survey. London, 1957.
Afr 210.41 Cary, Joyce. The case for African freedom. London, 1941.
Afr 210.41.10A Cary, Joyce. The case for African freedom. Austin, 1962.
Afr 210.41.10B Cary, Joyce. The case for African freedom. Austin, 1962.
Afr 210.43 Selwyn, James. South of the Congo. N.Y., 1943.
Afr 210.44 Orizu, A.A.N. Without bitterness. N.Y., 1944.
Afr 210.45 Garcia Figueras, Thomas. La puesta en valor del continente africano. Barcelona, 1945.
Afr 210.47.2 Padmore, G. History of the Pan-African Congress. 2d ed. London, 1963.
Afr 210.53.2 Paulme, Denise. Les civilisations africaines. 2. ed. Paris, 1959.
Afr 210.55A Haines, C.G. Africa today. Baltimore, 1955.
Afr 210.55B Haines, C.G. Africa today. Baltimore, 1955.
Afr 210.55.10 Stillman, Calvin W. Africa in the modern world. Chicago, 1956.
Afr 210.55.12 Stillman, Calvin W. Africa in the modern world. Chicago, 1963.
Afr 210.56 Hodgkin, Thomas. Nationalism in colonial Africa. London, 1956.
Afr 210.56.2 Hodgkin, Thomas. Nationalism in colonial Africa. London, 1962.

Afr 210 Africa in general - History by periods - Twentieth century - General works and 1900-1960 - cont.

Afr 210.56.5 Wallbank, T.W. Contemporary Africa. Princeton, 1956.
Afr 210.56.10 American Academy of Political and Social Sciences. Africa and the Western world. Philadelphia, 1956.
Afr 210.56.15 Lovato, Antonio. Le ultime colonie. Roma, 1956.
Afr 210.58A American Assembly. The United States and Africa. N.Y., 1958.
Afr 210.58B American Assembly. The United States and Africa. N.Y., 1958.
Afr 210.58.5 Tevoedjre, Albert. L'Afrique revoltée. Paris, 1958.
Afr 210.58.10 Diop, Majhemout. Contribution à l'étude des problèmes politiques en Afrique noire. Paris, 1958.
Afr 210.58.15 Van Nguen. Les carnets d'un diplomate. Paris, 1958.
Afr 210.58.22 American Assembly. The United States and Africa. N.Y., 1963.
Afr 210.58.25 Pamphlet vol. Nkrumah, Kwame. All African People's Conferences, 1958. 3 pam.
Afr 210.59A Decraene, Philippe. Le panafricanisme. Paris, 1959.
Afr 210.59B Decraene, Philippe. Le panafricanisme. Paris, 1959.
Afr 210.59.11 Lengyel, Emil. Africa in ferment. N.Y., 1961.
Afr 210.60 Ritner, Peter. The death of Africa. N.Y., 1960.
Afr 210.60.5 Sampson, Anthony. Common sense about Africa. London, 1960.
Afr 210.60.10 Carter, G.M. Independence for Africa. N.Y., 1960.
Afr 210.60.15 Datlin, S.V. Afrika sbrasyvaet tsepi. Moscow, 1960.
Afr 210.60.20 Kummernuss, Adolph. Wohin geht Afrika. Frankfurt a.M., 1960.
Afr 210.60.25 Dekiewiet, C. Can Africa come of age? Johannesburg, 1960.
Afr 210.60.30 Woddis, Jack. Africa, the roots of revolt. London, 1960.
Afr 210.60.35 Afrika 1960. Moscow, 1960.
Afr 210.60.40 Abranches, Esther. Afrique. Luanda, 1960.
Afr 210.60.45 Andrianov, B.V. Naselenie Afriki. Moscow, 1960.
Afr 210.60.50 Sundstroem, Erland. Afrika spronger hojorna. Stockholm, 1960.
Afr 210.60.55 Conférence de l'Action Positive pour la Paix et la Sécurité. Conférence de l action positive pour la paix. Accra, 1960.
Afr 210.60.60 Rhodes-Livingstone Institute, Lusaka, Northern Rhodesia. Conference, 14th, Lusaka, 1960. Myth in modern Africa. Lusaka, 1960.
Afr 210.60.65 Rainero, Romain. Il risveglio dell'Africa nera. Bari, 1960.
Afr 210.61 Duffy, James. Africa speaks. Princeton, N.J., 1961.
Afr 210.61.5 Oakes, John B. The edge of freedom. 1st ed. N.Y., 1961.
Afr 210.61.10 Dessarre, Eve. Que sera le destin de l'Afrique? Paris, 1961.
Afr 210.61.15 Hempstone, Smith. The new Africa. London, 1961.
Afr 210.61.20 Munger, E. African field report. Cape Town, 1961.
Afr 210.61.25 Woddis, J. Africa. London, 1961.
Afr 210.61.30 Hughes, John. The new face of Africa south of the Sahara. 1st ed. N.Y., 1961.
Afr 210.61.35 Bryan, G. McLeod. Whither Africa. Richmond, 1961.
Afr 210.61.40 Pomikkar, Kavalam M. Revolution in Africa. London, 1961.
Afr 210.61.45 Goss, H.P. The political future of the independent nations of Africa. Santa Barbara, Calif., 1961.
Afr 210.61.50 Wallerstein, I. Africa. N.Y., 1961.
Afr 210.61.55A Fanon, Franz. Les damnés de la terre. Paris, 1961.
Afr 210.61.55B Fanon, Franz. Les damnés de la terre. Paris, 1961.
Afr 210.61.56A Fanon, Franz. The damned. Paris, 1963.
Afr 210.61.56B Fanon, Franz. The damned. Paris, 1963.
Afr 210.61.60 United States. National Commission for UNESCO. Africa and the U.S. Washington, 1961.
Afr 210.61.65 Akademiia Nauk SSSR. Institut Afriki. Afrika, 1956-1961. Moscow, 1961.
Afr 210.61.66 Akademiia Nauk SSSR. Institut Afriki. Afrika, 1961-1965gg. Moskva, 1967.
Afr 210.61.70 Schatten, Fritz. Afrika. München, 1961.
Afr 210.61.75 Pierson-Mathy, P. Evolution politique de l'Afrique. Bruxelles, 1961.
Afr 210.61.80 Houart, Pierre. L'Afrique aux trois visages. Bruxelles, 1961.
Afr 210.61.85 Royal African Society. The Africa of 1961. London, 1961.
Afr 210.61.90 Vianney, J.J. The new states of Africa. 1st ed. n.p. 1961.
Afr 210.61.95 Pamphlet vol. Tropical Africa. 2 pam.
Afr 210.61.100 Sutton, Francis Xavier. Africa today; lecture at Cornell University, Nov. 2, 1961. Ithaca? 1961.
Afr 210.62 Perham, M.F. The colonial reckoning. N.Y., 1962.
Afr 210.62.2 Perham, M.F. The colonial reckoning. London, 1961.
Afr 210.62.3 Perham, M.F. The colonial reckoning. London, 1963.
Afr 210.62.5 Spiro, Herbert John. Politics in Africa. Englewood Cliffs, N.J., 1962.
Afr 210.62.10 American Society of African Culture. Pan-Africanism reconsidered. Berkeley, 1962.
Afr 210.62.15 Georgetown Colloquium on Africa. New forces in Africa. Washington, 1962.
Afr 210.62.17 Georgetown Colloquium on Africa. Emerging Africa. Washington, 1963.
Afr 210.62.20 British Commonwealth Relations. The Commonwealth in Africa. London, 1962.
Afr 210.62.25 Robinson, James H. Africa at the crossroads. Philadelphia, 1962.
Afr 210.62.30 Legum, Colin. Pan-Africanism. N.Y., 1962.
Afr 210.62.35 Bow Group Pamphlet. The new Africa. London, 1962.
Afr 210.62.40 Problemy Mira i Sotsializma. Za natsionalniiu nezavisimost. Praha, 1962.
Afr 210.62.42 Braginskii, M.I. Osoobozhdenie Afriki. Moscow, 1962.
Afr 210.62.43 Braginskii, M.I. Africa wins freedom. Moscow, 196-.
Afr 210.62.45 Judd, P. African independence. N.Y., 1963.
Afr 210.62.50 Boyd, Andrew Kirk Henry. An atlas of African affairs. N.Y., 1962.
Afr 210.63 McKay, Vernon. Africa in world politics. N.Y., 1963.
Afr 210.63.5 Padelford, Norman J. Africa and world order. N.Y., 1963.
Afr 210.63.10 Quaison-Sackey, A. Africa unbound. N.Y., 1963.
Afr 210.63.15 Nkrumah, Kwame. Africa must unite. London, 1963.
Afr 210.63.16 Nkrumah, Kwame. Africa must unite. N.Y., 1963.
Afr 210.63.20 Thiam, Doudou. La politique étrangère des états africains. Paris, 1963.
Afr 210.63.23 Thiam, Doudou. The foreign policy of African states. London, 1965.
Afr 210.63.25A Brzezinski, Z.K. Africa and the communist world. Stanford, Calif., 1963.
Afr 210.63.25B Brzezinski, Z.K. Africa and the communist world. Stanford, Calif., 1963.
Afr 210.63.30 Jennings, W. Democracy in Africa. Cambridge, Eng., 1963.
Afr 210.63.35 Mboya, T. Freedom and after. 1. ed. Boston, 1963.

Afr 210 Africa in general - History by periods - Twentieth century - General works and 1900-1960 - cont.

Afr 210.63.40 Hodgson, R.D. The changing map of Africa. Princeton, 1963.
Afr 210.63.45 Woddis, J. Africa, the way ahead. London, 1963.
Afr 210.63.50 Rivkin, A. The African presence in world affairs. N.Y., 1963.
Afr 210.63.55 Carter, G.M. Five African states. Ithaca, 1963.
Afr 210.63.60 Ethiopia. Ministry of Information. Addis Ababa summit. Addis Ababa, 1963.
Afr 210.63.65 Passin, H. Africa. Ibadan, 1963.
Afr 210.63.70 Ziegler, Jean. La contre-révolution en Afrique. Paris, 1963.
Afr 210.63.75 Falcão, F. de S. Quo vadis, Africa. Lisboa, 1963.
Afr 210.63.80 Rainero, Romain. Il nuovo volto dell Africa. Firenze, 1963.
Afr 210.63.85 Fanon, Franz. The wretched of the earth. N.Y., 1963.
Afr 210.63.90 Paul, Edouard C. Afrique: perspectives, politiques. Port-au-Prince, Haiti, 1963.
Afr 210.64 Woddis, J. Africa, the way ahead. N.Y., 1964.
Afr 210.64.2 Woddis, J. L'avenir de l'Afrique. Paris, 1964.
Afr 210.64.5 Burke, Fred. Africa's quest for order. Englewood Cliffs, 1964.
Afr 210.64.10 Davidson, Basil. Which way Africa. Harmondsworth, 1964.
Afr 210.64.12 Davidson, Basil. Which way Africa? The search for a new society. Harmondsworth, 1967.
Afr 210.64.15 Thomas, C.M. African national developments. Maxwell, Ala., 1964.
Afr 210.64.20 Fanon, Frantz. Pour la révolution africaine. Paris, 1964.
Afr 210.64.22 Fanon, Frantz. Toward the African revolution. N.Y., 1967.
Afr 210.64.25 Organization of African Unity. Basic documents and resolutions. Addis Ababa, 1964.
Afr 210.64.30 Organization of African Unity. Assembly of the heads of state and government of O.A.U. Cairo, 1964.
Afr 210.64.35 Wallbank, T.W. Contemporary Africa. Princeton, N.J., 1964.
Afr 210.64.40 Hughes, L. The first book of Africa. N.Y., 1964.
Afr 210.64.45 Africa's freedom. London, 1964.
Afr 210.64.50 Cox, R.H.F. Pan-Africanism in practice. London, 1964.
Afr 210.64.55 Afrika, Colloquium. Afrikas Gegenwart und Zukunft. Hannover, 1964.
Afr 210.64.60 Coleman, J.S. Political parties and national integration in tropical Africa. Berkeley, 1964.
Afr 210.64.60B Coleman, J.S. Political parties and national integration in tropical Africa. Berkeley, 1964.
Afr 210.64.65 Strauch, H. Panafrika. Zürich, 1964.
Afr 210.64.70 American Academy of Political and Social Science. Africa in motion. Philadelphia, 1964.
Afr 210.64.75 Larsen, Peter. Young Africa. London, 1964.
Afr 210.64.80 Ziegler, Jean. Sociologie de la nouvelle Afrique. Paris, 1964.
Afr 210.65 Moraas, Francis Robert. The importance of being black. N.Y., 1965.
Afr 210.65.5 Hatch, J.C. A history of postwar Africa. London, 1965.
Afr 210.65.10 Pepy, Daniel. Les états africains et leurs problèmes. Paris, 1965. 2v.
Afr 210.65.15 Kollmannsperger, Franz. Von Afrika nach Afrika. Mainz, 1965.
Afr 210.65.20 Thomas, Charles Marion. Pan-Africanism. Maxwell Air Force Base, Ala., 1965.
Afr 210.65.25 Prokopczuk, Jerzy. Zarys nowozytnej historii Afryki. Warszawa, 1965.
Afr 210.65.30 Cook, Arthur Norton. Africa, past and present. Ottowa, 1965.
Afr 210.65.35 Chataslnski, Jozef. Blizej afryki. Warszawa, 1965.
Afr 210.65.40 Austin, Dennis. Inter-state relations in Africa. 1st ed. Freiburg, 1965.
Afr 210.65.45 Odede, Simon. Nigerian position in the intra-African situation up to May, 1963. The Hague, 1965.
Afr 210.65.50A Kohn, Hans. African nationalism in the 20th century. Princeton, 1965.
Afr 210.65.50B Kohn, Hans. African nationalism in the 20th century. Princeton, 1965.
Afr 210.65.55 Afro-Asian Peoples' Solidarity Conference, 4th, Winneba, Ghana. The Winneba Conference, Ghana, May 1965. Cairo, 1966.
Afr 210.66 Ferkiss, Victor. Africa's search for identity. N.Y., 1966.
Afr 210.66.5 McKay, Vernon. African diplomacy. N.Y., 1966.
Afr 210.66.10 Welch, Claude Emerson. Dream of unity. Ithaca, N.Y., 1966.
Afr 210.66.15 Ganiage, Jean. L'Afrique au XXe siècle. Paris, 1966.
Afr 210.66.20 Bauw, Jean Anatole de. Politique et révolution africaine. Bruxelles, 1966.
Afr 210.67 Rivkin, Arnold. The new states of Africa. N.Y., 1967.
Afr 210.67.5 Seminar Africa. National and Social Revolution, Cairo, 1966. Seminar Africa, National and Social Revolution, October 24th-29th, 1966, Cairo. Cairo, 1967. 4v.
Afr 210.67.10 East-West confrontation in Africa. Interdoc conference. Cambridge, 22nd and 23rd September 1966. The Hague, 1967.
Afr 210.67.15 Castro, Luis Filipe de Oliveira e. A nova Africa, ensaio sociopolitico. Lisboa, 1967.
Afr 210.67.20 Lantier, Jacques. L'Afrique déchirée, de l'anarchie à la dictature, de la magic à la technologie. Paris, 1967.
Afr 210.67.25 Antiimperialisticheskaia revoliutsiia v Afrike. Moskva, 1967.
Afr 210.67.30 Rooke, Patrick J. The wind of change in Africa. Glasgow, 1967.
Afr 210.67.35 Calchi Novati, Giampado. Le rivoluzioni nell'Africa nera. Milano, 1967.
Afr 210.68 Santos, Eduardo dos. Ideologias politicas africanas. Lisboa, 1968.
Afr 210.68.5 Santos, Eduardo dos. Pan-africanismo de ontem e de hoje. Lisboa, 1968.
Afr 210.68.10 Diallo, Demba. L'Afrique en question. Paris, 1968.
Afr 210.68.15 Geiss, Imanuel. Panafrikanismus. Frankfurt am Main, 1968.
Afr 210.69 Barnes, Leonard. African renaissance. London, 1969.

Afr 212 Africa in general - History by periods - Twentieth century - 1960-

Afr 212.2 Cowan, Laing Gray. The dilemmas of African independence. N.Y., 1964.
Afr 212.3 Harrigan, Anthony. Red star over Africa. Cape Town, 1964.
Afr 212.4 Marais, B.J. The two faces of Africa. Pietermaritzburg, 1964.
Afr 212.5 Hapgood, D. Africa, from independence to tomorrow. 1st ed. N.Y., 1965.

Afr 212 Africa in general - History by periods - Twentieth century - 1960- - cont.

Afr 212.6 Marvin, D.K. Emerging Africa in world affairs. San Francisco, 1965.
Afr 212.7 Molnar, T.S. Africa, a political travelogue. N.Y., 1965.
Afr 212.8 Passos, Inacio de. A grande noite africana. Lisboa, 1964.
Afr 212.9 Lewis, William Hubert. French-speaking Africa. N.Y., 1965.
Afr 212.10 Emerson, Rupert. The political awakening of Africa. Englewood Cliffs, N.J., 1965.
Afr 212.11 Hugent, John Pear. Call Africa 999. N.Y., 1965.
Afr 212.12 Carvalho, Castro. Africa contemporanea. 2. ed. São Paulo, 1963.
Afr 212.14 Matthews, Ronald. African powder keg. London, 1966.
Afr 212.16 Baardseth, Magne. Afrika. 3. Opl. Oslo, 1964.
Afr 212.18 Armah, Kivesi. Africa's golden road. Kenyatta, 1965.
Afr 212.20 Zartman, I. William. International relations in the new Africa. Englewood Cliffs, 1966.
Afr 212.22 Merwe, H.J.J. Black Africa. Johannesburg, 1963.
Afr 212.24 African Conference on Progress through Cooperation. Africa. N.Y., 1966.
Afr 212.25 Carter, Gwendolen Margaret. Politics in Africa. N.Y., 1966.
Afr 212.25.9 Akademiia Nauk SSSR. Institut Afriki. Istoriia Afriki v XIX nachale XX v. Moskva, 1967.
Afr 212.26 Akademiia Nauk SSSR. Institut Afriki. Noveishaia istoriia Afriki. Moskva, 1964.
Afr 212.26.1 Noveishaia istoriia Afriki. 2. izd. Moskva, 1968.
Afr 212.26.2 Akademiia Nauk SSSR. Institut Afriki. A history of Africa, 1918-1967. Moscow, 1968.
Afr 212.28 Spiro, Herbert John. Africa. N.Y., 1966.
Afr 212.28.5 Spiro, Herbert John. Patterns of African development, five comparisons. Englewood Cliffs, N.J., 1967.
Afr 212.30 Barcata, Louis. Schreie aus dem Dschungel. Stuttgart, 1962.
Afr 212.32 Calchi Novati, Giampaolo. L'Africa nera non e indipendente. Milano, 1964.
Afr 212.34 Mezu, Sebastian Okeckukure. The philosophy of Pan-Africanism. Washington, 1965.
Afr 212.36 Mazrui, Ali Al'amin. Towards a Pax Africana, a study of ideology and ambition. London, 1967.
Afr 212.36.5 Mazrui, Ali Al'Amin. On heroes and Uhuru worship. London, 1967.
Afr 212.38 Wallerstein, Immanuel Maurice. Africa, the politics of unity. N.Y., 1967.
Afr 212.40 Europa-Haus, Marienberg (Westerwald) Ger. Partner Afrika. Hangelar bei Bonn, 1962?
Afr 212.42 Italiaander, Rolf. Schwarze Haut im roten Griff. Düsseldorf, 1962.
Afr 212.44 Meyer, Frank S. The African nettle, dilemmas of an emerging continent. N.Y., 1965.
Afr 212.46 Guiton, Raymond. Afrika im Widerspruch. Köln, 1967-
Afr 212.48 Ewandé, Daniel. Vive le Président. La fête africaine. Paris, 1968.
Afr 212.50 Said, Abd al-Aziz. The African phenomenon. Boston, 1968.
Afr 212.52 Etinger, Iakov Ia. Politicheskie problemy afrikanskogo edinstva. Moskva, 1967.
Afr 212.54 Nord, Erik. Militärkupper i Afrika. Uppsala, 1967.
Afr 212.56 Afrikanische Gegenwartsfragen. Berlin, 1960.
Afr 212.58 Hydén, Göran. Politik och samhälle i Afrika. Stockholm, 1967.
Afr 212.60 Dumoga, John. Africa between East and West. London, 1969.
Afr 212.61 Fokeev, German V. Vneshniaia politika stran Afriki. Moskva, 1968.
Afr 212.62 Mungai, Njorge. The independent nations of Africa. Nairobi, 1967.
Afr 212.64 Howe, Russell Warren. The African revolution. Croydon, Eng., 1969.
Afr 212.66 Nationale und soziale Revolution in Afrika. 1. Aufl. n.p., 1967.
Afr 212.68 Ideinye techeniia v tropicheskoi Afrika. Moskva, 1969.
Afr 212.70 Nielsen, Waldemar A. The great powers and Africa. N.Y., 1969.
Afr 212.72 Rivkin, A. Nation-building in Africa; problems and prospects. New Brunswick, N.J., 1969.
Afr 212.74 Williams, G. Mennen. Africa for the Africans. Grand Rapids, 1969.
Afr 212.76 Thompson, Vincent Bakpetu. Africa and unity: the evolution of Pan-Africanism. N.Y., 1970.

Afr 500 Africa in general - Shares of foreign powers and their exploitations - General works

Afr 500.01 Pamphlet box. Partition of Africa.
Afr 500.2 Pamphlet vol. African foreign relations. 4 pam.
Afr 500.3 Biblioteca di studi coloniale. Firenze. 1,1936+ 11v.
Afr 500.5 De Leon, D. The West African question. n.p., 1886.
Afr 500.7 Hertslet, E. Map of Africa by treaty. London, 1896. 3v.
NEDL Afr 500.7.3 Hertslet, E. Map of Africa by treaty. London, 1909. 3v.
Afr 500.7.3 Hertslet, E. Map of Africa by treaty. v.4. London, 1909.
Afr 500.7.4 Hertslet, E. The map of Africa by treaty. 3rd ed. London, 1967. 3v.
Afr 500.8 Ortray, F. van. Conventions internationales. Bruxelles, 1898.
Afr 500.9 Alzola, Pablo de. Africa, su reparto y colonización. Bilbao, 1891.
Afr 500.10.3 Kinsky, Karl. Vade mecum für Diplomatische Arbeit auf dem Afrikanischen Continent. 3. Aufl. Leipzig, 1900.
Afr 500.11A Harris, N.D. Intervention and colonization in Africa. Boston, 1914.
Afr 500.11B Harris, N.D. Intervention and colonization in Africa. Boston, 1914.
Afr 500.11.5 Harris, N.D. Europe and Africa. Boston, 1927.
Afr 500.13A Gibbons, H.A. The new map of Africa, 1900-16. N.Y., 1916.
Afr 500.13B Gibbons, H.A. The new map of Africa, 1900-16. N.Y., 1916.
Afr 500.13.5 Gibbons, H.A. The new map of Africa, 1900-16. N.Y., 1918.
Afr 500.14 Ronze, Raymond. La question d'Afrique. Paris, 1918.
Afr 500.16 Beyens, N.E.L. La question africaine. Bruxelles, 1918.
Afr 500.18 Italy. Direzione Centrale degli Affari Coloniali. Trattati, convenzioni, accordi. v.1,2-3. Roma, 1906. 2v.
Afr 500.18.2 Italy. Direzione Centrale degli Affari Coloniali. Trattati, convenzioni, accordi. Supplemento alla raccolta. Roma, 1909.
Afr 500.19 Morel, Edmund D. Africa and the peace of Europe. Photoreproduction. London, 1917.
Afr 500.19.5 Morel, Edmund D. The black man's burden. N.Y., 1920.
Afr 500.19.10 Morel, Edmund D. The black man's burden. N.Y., 1969.
Afr 500.20 Woolf, Leonard S. Empire and commerce in Africa. Westminster, 1919.

Afr 500 Africa in general - Shares of foreign powers and their exploitations - General works - cont.

Afr 500.20.2	Woolf, Leonard S. Empire and commerce in Africa. N.Y., 1919.
Afr 500.20.5	Woolf, Leonard S. Empire and commerce in Africa. N.Y., 1968.
Afr 500.21	Yanguas Messia, José. Apuntes sobre la expansion colonial en Africa. Madrid, 1915.
Afr 500.25	Antonelli, Etienne. L'Afrique et la Paix de Versailles. Paris, 1921.
Afr 500.25.10	Antonelli, Etienne. L'Afrique et la Paix de Versailles. 4th ed. Paris, 1921.
Afr 500.30	Lucas, C.P. The partition and colonization of Africa. Oxford, 1922.
Afr 500.35	Beer, George Louis. African questions at the Paris Peace Conference. N.Y., 1923.
Afr 500.35.2	Beer, George Louis. African questions at the Paris Peace Conference. 1st ed. London, 1968.
Afr 500.38	Hoskins, Halford Lancaster. European imperialism in Africa. N.Y., 1930.
Afr 500.38.2	Hoskins, Halford Lancaster. European imperialism in Africa. N.Y., 1967.
Afr 500.40	Salvador, M. La penetrazione demografica europea in Africa. Torino, 1932.
Afr 500.43	Middleton, Lamar. The rape of Africa. London, 1936.
Afr 500.44	Mazzucconi, R. Storia della conquista dell Africa. Milano, 1937.
Afr 500.46	Rohrbach, P. Afrika heute und morgen. Berlin, 1939.
Afr 500.48	Italian Library of Information, N.Y. Colonialism in Africa. N.Y., 1940.
Afr 500.50	Mendelssohn-Bartholdy, A. Europäische Mandatgemeinschaft in Mittelafrika. Roma, 1933.
Afr 500.52	Mbadiwe, K.O. British and Axis aims in Africa. N.Y., 1942.
Afr 500.53	Assac, Jacques Ploncard d'. L'erreur africaine. Paris, 1964.
Afr 500.55	Borba za svero-vostochnuice, Afrika. Moscow, 1936.
Afr 500.57	Crocker, Walter R. On governing colonies. London, 1947.
Afr 500.60	Gunzert, T. Kolonialprobleme der Gegenwart in Beitragen. Berlin, 1939.
Afr 500.62	Pesenti, G. Euraffrica. Borgo S. Dalmazzo, 1953.
Afr 500.65	Datlin, S. Afrika unter dem Joch des Imperialismus. Berlin, 1953.
Afr 500.67	Bowles, Chester. Africa's challenge to America. Berkeley, 1956.
Afr 500.69	Zusmanovich, A.Z. Imperialisticheskii razdel Afriki. Moscow, 1959.
Afr 500.70F	Conférence des Institutions Européennes, Rome, 1958. Documentation des travaux de la première conférence. Rome, 1959.
Afr 500.75	Dekiewiet, Cornelis W. America's role in Africa. v. 1-2. Durban, 1960.
Afr 500.80	Chinese-African People's Friendship Association. The Chinese people resolutely support the just struggle of the African people. Peking, 1961.
Afr 500.81	Barboux, H.M. Opinion. Paris, 1903.
Afr 500.82	Hanna, Alexander John. European rule in Africa. London, 1965.
Afr 500.83	Benitez Cabrera, José. Africa, biografia del colonialismo. Habana, 1964.
Afr 500.84	Betts, Raymond F. The scramble of Africa, causes and dimensions of empire. Boston, 1966.
Afr 500.85	Neokolonializm v Afrike. Moskva, 1967.
Afr 500.86	Britain and Germany in Africa; imperial rivalry and colonial rule. New Haven, 1967.
Afr 500.88	Zaghi, Carlo. La spartizione dell'Africa. Napoli, 1968.
Afr 500.90	Collins, Robert O. The partition of Africa: illusion or necessity? N.Y., 1969.
Afr 500.92	Osei, Gabriel Kingsley. Europe's gift to Africa. London, 1968.
Afr 500.94	Colonialism in Africa, 1870-1960. Cambridge, Eng., 1969-

Afr 505 Africa in general - Shares of foreign powers and their exploitations - England

Afr 505.2	Rouard de Card, E. Les territoires africaines. Paris, 1901.
Afr 505.3.5	British empire series. v.2. 2d ed. London, 1901.
Afr 505.3.10	British Africa. 2d ed. N.Y., 1969.
Afr 505.4	Sanderson, E. Great Britain in modern Africa. London, 1907.
Afr 505.5	Johnston, H. Britain across the seas - Africa. London, 1911.
Afr 505.7	Macmillan, W.M. Africa emergent, a survey of social trends in British Africa. London, 1938.
Afr 505.7.5	Macmillan, W.M. Africa emergent, a survey of social, political and economic trends in British Africa. Harmondsworth, 1949.
Afr 505.9	Newman, E.W.P. Britain and North-east Africa. London, 1940.
Afr 505.10	Trofimov, V.A. Politika Anglii i Italii v severo-vostochnoi Afrike. Moscow, 1962.
Afr 505.13	Batten, T.R. Problems of African development. London, 1948.
Afr 505.13.3	Batten, T.R. Problems of African development. 3d ed. London, 1960.
Afr 505.15	Hailey, W.M.H. Native administration in the British African territories. v.1-5. London, 1950-51. 5v.
Afr 505.17	Attitude to Africa. Middlesex, Eng., 1951.
Afr 505.20	Kartun, D. Africa, Africa. N.Y., 1954.
Afr 505.25	Hatch, J.C. New from Africa. London, 1956.
Afr 505.30	Cohen, Andrew. British policy in changing Africa. Evanston, 1959.
Afr 505.35	Bradley, K. Britain's purpose in Africa. N.Y., 1959.
Afr 505.40	Melland, Frank Hulme. African dilemma. London, 1937.
Afr 505.42	Taylor, Don. The British in Africa. London, 1962.
Afr 505.43	Padmore, George. Afrika unter dem Joch der Weissen. Zürich, 193-.
Afr 505.44	Library of Congress. Division of Bibliography. The British empire in Africa. Washington, 1942-43.
Afr 505.45	Kirkwood, Kenneth. Britain and Africa. London, 1965.
Afr 505.46	Padmore, George. Africa, Britain's third empire. London, 1949.
Afr 505.47	Fokeev, German V. Oni ne khotiat ukhodit. Moskva, 1965.
Afr 505.48	Akademiia Nauk SSSR. Institut Narodov Azii. Politika Anglii v Afrike. Moskva, 1967.
Afr 505.50	Hatch, John C. The history of Britain in Africa. London, 1969.

Afr 510 Africa in general - Shares of foreign powers and their exploitations - France

Afr 510.2	Rouard de Card, E. Les traités de protectorat. Paris, 1897.
Afr 510.4	Dumas, P. Les français d'Afrique. Paris, 1889.
Afr 510.5	Ferry, E. La France en Afrique. Paris, 1905.
Afr 510.6	Sarzeau, J. Les français aux colonies. Paris, 1897.
Afr 510.7	Hubert, L. Politique africaine. Paris, 1904.
Afr 510.8	Reclus, O. Lachons l'Asie, prenons l'Afrique. Paris, 1904.
Afr 510.9	Rouard de Card, E. La France...en Afrique. Paris, 1903.
Afr 510.9.10	Rouard de Card, E. Le prince de Bismarck et l'expansion de la France en Afrique. Paris, 1918.
Afr 510.10	Hanotaux, G. Le partage de l'Afrique - Fachoda. Paris, n.d.
Afr 510.10.5	Hanotaux, G. Pour l'empire colonial français. Paris, 1933.
Afr 510.11	Rouard de Card, E. Traités de délimitation concernant l'Afrique française. Paris, 1910.
Afr 510.11.2	Rouard de Card, E. Traités de délimitation concernant l'Afrique franç,aise. Supplément 1910-13. Paris, 1913.
Afr 510.11.10	Rouard de Card, E. Traités de la France avec les pays de l'Afrique du Nord. Paris, 1906.
Afr 510.12	Reibell, Le Commandant. Le commandant Lamy. Paris, 1903.
Afr 510.14	Wahl, M. La France aux colonies. Paris, 1896.
Afr 510.15	Gaffarel, P.L.J. Notre expansion colonial...1870 à nos jours. Paris, 1918.
Afr 510.17	Homet, M. Afrique noire, terre inquiète. Paris, 1939.
Afr 510.20	Mangin, J.E. Regards sur la France d'Afrique. Paris, 1924.
Afr 510.23	Coty, F. Sauvons nos colonies. Paris, 1931.
Afr 510.25F	Burthe d'Annelet, Anarie. A travers l'Afrique française. Paris, 1932. 2v.
Afr 510.26F	Burthe d'Annelet, Anarie. A travers l'Afrique française. Paris, 1939. 2v.
Afr 510.27	Mangin, C.M.E. Souvenirs d'Afrique. Paris, 1936.
Afr 510.30A	Library of Congress. Division of Bibliography. French colonies in Africa. Washington, 1942.
Afr 510.30B	Library of Congress. Division of Bibliography. French colonies in Africa. Washington, 1942.
Afr 510.35	Guy, M., of Tours. Batisseurs d'empire. Paris, 1945.
Afr 510.40A	Despois, J. L'Afrique blanche française. Paris, 1949. 2v.
Afr 510.40B	Despois, J. L'Afrique blanche franéaise. v.1. Paris, 1949.
Afr 510.50F	Encyclopédie Mensuelle d'Outre-Mer. Le tourisme en Afrique française. Paris, 1955.
Afr 510.55	Benazet, H. L'Afrique française en danger. Paris, 1947.
Afr 510.60	Lavergne, B. Afrique du Nord et Afrique Noire. Paris, 1956.
Afr 510.65	Monmarson, R. L'Afrique franco-africaine. Paris, 1956.
Afr 510.70	Durand, Huguette. Essai sur la conjoncture de l'Afrique noire. Paris, 1957.
Afr 510.75A	Nord, Pierre. L'Eurafrique. Paris, 1955.
Afr 510.75B	Nord, Pierre. L'Eurafrique. Paris, 1955.
Afr 510.80	Harmand, Jack. L'Afrique à l'heure française. Paris, 1958.
Afr 510.85	Ehrhard, Jean. Le destin du colonialisme. Paris, 1957.
Afr 510.90	Delaporte, Maurice. La vie coloniale. Paris, 1944.
Afr 510.95	Leger, Jean M. Afrique française. Montréal, 1958.
Afr 510.100	Marchard, Jean Paul. Vérités sur l'Afrique noire. Paris, 1959.
Afr 510.102	France. Ministère de la Coopération. Guide pratique sur les républiques. Paris, 1964.
Afr 510.105	Delavignette, Robert Louis. Les vrais chefs de l'empire. 7. ed. Paris, 1939.
Afr 510.110	Gukasian-Gandzaketsi, L.J. Frantsuzskii imperializm i Afrika. Moscow, 1962.
Afr 510.111	Subbotin, V.A. Frantsuzskaia kolonialnaia ekspansiia v kontse XIX v. Ekuatorialnaia Afrika i Idiiskogo Okeana. Moscow, 1962.
Afr 510.112	Oplustil, Vaclav. O francouzsko-africkem spolecenstvi. Praha, 1963.

Afr 520 Africa in general - Shares of foreign powers and their exploitations - Spain

Afr 520.01	Pamphlet box. Spain in Africa.
Afr 520.2F	Spain. Ministerio de Estado. Documentos diplomaticos. Madrid, 1888.
Afr 520.3	Reparaz, G. España en Africa. Madrid, 1891.
Afr 520.9	Aveilza, J.M.De. Reivindicaciones de espana. 2.Ed. Madrid, 1941.
Afr 520.12	Borras, T. La España completa. Madrid, 1950.
Afr 520.14	Spain. Servicio Historico Militar. Acción de España en Africa. Madrid, 1935. 3v.

Afr 530.1 - .19 Africa in general - Shares of foreign powers and their exploitations - Others - Germany

Afr 530.3	Germany. Kolonialamt. Veröffentlichungen. Jena. 6v.
Afr 530.4	Westermann, D. Beiträge zur deutschen Kolonialfrage. Essen, 1937.
Afr 530.5	Soyaux, H. Deutsche Arbeit in Afrika. Leipzig, 1888.
Afr 530.6	Lewin, Evans. The Germans and Africa. London, 1915.
Afr 530.6.5	Lewin, Evans. The Germans and Africa. London, 1939.
Afr 530.7	Sorela, Luis. Alemania en Africa. Berlin, 1884.
Afr 530.8A	Zimmermann, E. The German empire of Central Africa. N.Y., 1918.
Afr 530.8B	Zimmermann, E. The German empire of Central Africa. N.Y., 1918.
Afr 530.8.5	Zimmermann, E. The German Empire of Central Africa as the basis of a new German world-policy. London, 1918.
Afr 530.9	Caroselli, F.S. L'Africa nella guerra e nella pace d'Europa. Milano, 1918.
Afr 530.10	Zimmermann, E. Bedeutung Afrikas für die deutsche Weltpolitik. Berlin, 1917.
Afr 530.12	Weidmann, C. Deutsche Männer in Afrika. Lübeck, 1894.
Afr 530.12.5	Welk, E. Die schwarze Sonne. Berlin, 1933.
Afr 530.13	Buettner, Kurt. Die Anfänge der deutschen Kolonial-Politik in Ostafrika. Berlin, 1961.
Afr 530.15	Etinger, J. Bonn greift nach Afrika. Berlin, 1961.

Afr 530.20 - .30 Africa in general - Shares of foreign powers and their exploitations - Others - Italy

Afr 530.20	Bassi, Ugo. Note sui diritti dell'Italia in Africa. Modena, 1930.
Afr 530.20.15	Pedrazzi, O. L'Africa dopo la guerra e l'Italia. Firenze, 1917.

Afr 530.20 - .30   Africa in general - Shares of foreign powers and their
exploitations - Others - Italy - cont.

Afr 530.22	Italy. Ufficio Studi e Propaganda. Voyageurs italiens en Afrique. Roma, 1931.
Afr 530.24	Pittaluga, Rosetta. Rievocazioni africane. Brescia, 1935.
Afr 530.26	Plebano, A. I possedimenti italiani in Africa. Roma, 1889.
Afr 530.28.5	Banse, Ewald. Unsere grossen Afrikaner. Berlin, 1943.
Afr 530.28.10	Lancellatti, A. Pionieri italiane in Africa. Brescia, 1951.
Afr 530.30	Premesse al lavoro italiano in Africa. Roma, 1958.

Afr 530.31 - .39   Africa in general - Shares of foreign powers and their
exploitations - Others - Portugal, etc.

Afr 530.32	Pattee, Richard. Portugal na Africa contemporanea. Coimbra, 1959.
Afr 530.33	Duffy, James. Portugal in Africa. Harmondsworth, 1962.
Afr 530.34	Mayor, D.R.W. De rebus Africanis. London, 1886
Afr 530.35.3	Caetano, Marcello. Portugal e a internacionalização dos problemas africanos. 3. ed. Lisboa, 1965.
Afr 530.36	Belges dans l'Afrique centrale. Bruxelles, 1886. 3v.

Afr 530.50 -   Africa in general - Shares of foreign powers and their
exploitations - Others - U.S.

Afr 530.50	Rosenthal, Eric. Stars and stripes in Africa. London, 1938.
Afr 530.50.1	Rosenthal, Eric. Stars and stripes in Africa. Cape Town, 1968.
Afr 530.50.5	Fetov, V.P. Amerikanskii imperializm v Afrike. Moscow, 1962.
Afr 530.50.10	Collins, Robert O. Americans in Africa. Stanford, Calif., 1963.
Afr 530.50.15	Clendenen, C.C. Americans in black Africa up to 1865. Stanford, California, 1964.
Afr 530.50.20	Clendenen, C.C. Americans in Africa, 1865-1900. Stanford, Calif., 1966.
Afr 530.51	Sablier, E. De l'Oural à l'Atlantique. Paris, 1963.
Afr 530.52	Instituto Italiano per l'Africa. Permesse al lavoro italiano in Africa. Roma, 1959.

Afr 545   Africa in general - Religion - General works

Afr 545.2	Mitchell, Robert C. A comprehensive bibliography of modern African religious movements. Evanston, 1966.
Afr 545.5	Smith, E.W. African ideas of God. London, 1950.
Afr 545.10A	Schlosser, Katesa. Propheten in Afrika. Braunschweig, 1949.
Afr 545.10B	Schlosser, Katesa. Propheten in Afrika. Braunschweig, 1949.
Afr 545.15	Wilson, M.H. Divine kings and the breath of men. Cambridge, Eng., 1959.
Afr 545.20	Deschamps, H.J. Les religions de l'Afrique noire. 2. éd. Paris, 1960.
Afr 545.21	Buhlman, Walbert. Afrika. Mainz, 1963.
Afr 545.25	Mendelsohn, J. God, Allah, and Ju Ju. N.Y., 1962.
Afr 545.26	Denis, L. Gas de conscience, à l'usage surtout des pays africains. Bruges, 1962-63. 2v.
Afr 545.27	Sharevskaia, Berta I. Starye i novye religii tropicheskoi i iuzhnoi Afriki. Moscow, 1964.
Afr 545.28	International African Seminar, 3d, Salisbury, Southern Rhodesia, 1960. African systems of thought. London, 1965.
Afr 545.28.2	International African Seminar, 3rd, Salisbury, Southern Rhodesia, 1960. African systems of thought. London, 1966.
Afr 545.29	Holas, Bohumil. L'Afrique noire. Paris, 1964.
Afr 545.30	Colloque sur les Religions, Abidjan. Colloque sur les religions, Abidjan, 5-12 avril, 1961. Paris, 1962.
Afr 545.32	Bernardi, Bernardo. Le religioni in Africa. Torino, 1961.
Afr 545.33	Zajaczkowski, Andrzej. Pierwotne religie czarnej Afryki. Warszawa, 1965. 10v.
Afr 545.34	Benz, Ernst. Messianische Kirchen, Sekten und Bewegungen im heutigen Afrika. Leiden, 1965.
Afr 545.35	Edinburgh. University. Centre Of African Studies. Religion in Africa. Edinburgh, 1964.
Afr 545.36	Zwernemann, Jürgen. Die Erde in Vorstellungswelt und Kultpraktiken der sudanischen Völker. Berlin, 1968.
Afr 545.37	Pettersson, Olof. Afrikas religioner. Stockholm, 1966.
Afr 545.38	Rencontres Internationales, Bouake, Ivory Coast, Oct. 1962. Les religions africaines traditionelles. Paris, 1965.
Afr 545.39	The journal of religion in Africa. Leiden. 1,1967+
Afr 545.42	Parrinder, E.G. African mythology. London, 1967.
Afr 545.44	Shparhnikov, Genrikh A. Religii stran Afriki. Moskva, 1967.
Afr 545.46	All-Africa Church Conference, Kampala, Uganda. La conférence de Kampala, 1963. Kitwe, 1963.
Afr 545.48	Oosthuizen, Gerhardus Cornelis. Post-Christianity in Africa: a theological and anthropological study. London, 1968.
Afr 545.50	Parrinder, E.G. Religion in Africa. Harmondsworth, 1969.
Afr 545.52	Holas, Bohumil. Les dieux d'Afrique noire. Paris, 1968.
Afr 545.54	Bibical revelation and African beliefs. London, 1969.
Afr 545.56	Thomas, Louis Vincent. Les religions d'Afrique noire. Paris, 1969.

Afr 550   Africa in general - Religion - Christian missions - General works

Afr 550.01	Pamphlet box. African missions.
Afr 550.1.5	Pamphlet vol. African missions. 5 pam.
Afr 550.2	Bowen, T.J. Missionary labors in the interior of Africa. Charleston, 1857.
Afr 550.2.5	Bowen, T.J. Missionary labors in the interior of Africa. N.Y., 1857.
Afr 550.2.12	Bowen, T.J. Adventures and missonary labors in several countries in the interior of Africa. 2d ed. London, 1968.
Afr 550.3	Blyden, E.W. Christianity, Islam and the Negro race. London, 1887.
Afr 550.4	Cust, R.N. L'occupation de l'Afrique. Genève, 1891.
Afr 550.4.5	Cust, R.N. Africa rediviva. London, 1891.
Afr 550.5	Noble, F.P. The redemption of Africa. Chicago, 1899. 2v.
Afr 550.6	Bonet-Maury, G. L'islamisme et le christianisme en Afrique. Paris, 1906.
Afr 550.7	Clarke, R.F. Cardinal Lavigerie and African slave trade. London, 1889.
Afr 550.7.10	Bouniol, Joseph. The White Fathers and their missions. London, 1929.
Afr 550.8	Klein, F. Le Cardinal Lavigerie et ses oeuvres africaines. Paris, 1890.
Afr 550.8.3	Klein, F. Le Cardinal Lavigerie et ses oeuvres africaines. 3e éd. Paris, 1893.

Afr 550   Africa in general - Religion - Christian missions - General works - cont.

Afr 550.8.5	Tournier, M.J. Bibliographie du Cardinal Lavigerie. Paris, 1913.
Afr 550.8.10	Baunard, Louis. Le Cardinal Lavigerie. Paris, 1912. 2v.
Afr 550.8.12	Baunard, Louis. Léon XIII et le toast d'Alger. Paris, 1914.
Afr 550.8.15	Pizzoli, D. Per i funeri del Cardinal Lavigerie. Palermo, 1892.
Afr 550.8.20	Perraud, A. Le Cardinal Lavigerie. Paris, 1893.
Afr 550.8.25	Rance-Bourrey, A.J. Les obsèques du Cardinal Lavigerie. Paris, 1893.
Afr 550.8.30	Philippe, A. Le Cardinal Lavigerie, 1825-1892. Dijon, 1923.
Afr 550.8.35	Jammes, F. Lavigerie. Paris, 1927.
Afr 550.8.40	Renard, E. Lavigerie. Paris, 1926.
Afr 550.8.45	Burridge, William. Destiny Africa, Cardinal Lavigerie and the making of the White Fathers. London, 1966.
Afr 550.8.50	Montclos, Xavier de. Lavigerie, le saint-siège et l'Église, de l'avènement de Pié IX à l'avènement de Léon XIII, 1846-1878. Paris, 1965.
Afr 550.8.500	Lavigerie, Charles M.A. Ecrits d'Afrique. Paris, 1966.
Afr 550.9	Scott, A.M. Day dawn in Africa. N.Y., 1858.
Afr 550.10	Tetu, H. Le R.P. Bouchard. Québec, 1897.
Afr 550.11	Apostolat en Afrique. Québec, 1911.
Afr 550.12	Kumm, H.K.W. African missionary heroes and heroines. N.Y., 1917.
Afr 550.13	Fraser, Donald. The future of Africa. London, 1911.
Afr 550.14	Parsons, E. C. Christus liberator. N.Y., 1905.
Afr 550.15	Fraser, Donald. The new Africa. London, 1927.
Afr 550.16	Smith, Edwin W. The Christian mission in Africa. London, 1926.
Afr 550.17	Roome, W.J.W. Can Africa be won? London, 1927.
Afr 550.18	Smith, Edwin. Aggrey of Africa. N.Y., 1930.
Afr 550.18.1	Smith, Edwin. Aggrey of Africa. N.Y., 1929.
Afr 550.19	Taylor, S.E. The price of Africa. Cincinnati, 1902.
Afr 550.20	Boavida, A.J. Missões e missionarios portuguezes...17 de abril 1893. Lisboa, 1893.
Afr 550.21	Farãnha, A.L. A espansao da fe na Africa e no Brasil. v.1-3. Lisboa, 1942-46. 3v.
Afr 550.22	Appeal to the churches in behalf of Africa. N.Y., 1834.
Afr 550.25	Callaway, Godfrey. The soul of an African padré. London, 1932.
Afr 550.27	Thornton, D.M. Africa waiting, or The problem of Africa's evangelization. N.Y., 1898.
Afr 550.29	Sociéte des Missions Evangéliques, Paris. Nos champs de mission. 3e éd. Paris, 1922.
Afr 550.31	Rowling, F. Bibliography of Christian literature. London, 1923.
Afr 550.33.5	Naylor, W.S. Daybreak in the dark continent. 2d ed. Boston, 1905.
Afr 550.35	Mackenzie, J.K. African adventurers. N.Y., 1922.
Afr 550.37	Church Conference on African Affairs. Christian action in Africa. N.Y., 1942.
Afr 550.40	Thompson, G. Africa in a nutshell for the millions. Oberlin, 1886.
Afr 550.42F	Leri, Primo. Missione nell'Africa settentrionale. Roma, 1908.
Afr 550.44	Wrong, Margaret. Five points for Africa. London, 1942.
Afr 550.50	Trew, J.M. Africa wasted by Britain and restored by native agency. London, 1843.
Afr 550.55	Mackenzie, J.K. Friends of Africa. Cambridge, Mass., 1928.
Afr 550.57	Weeks, Nan F. Builders of a new Africa. Nashville, 1944.
Afr 550.59	Floyd, Olive B. Partners in Africa. N.Y., 1945.
Afr 550.63	West Central Africa Regional Conference, Leopoldville, 1946. Abundant life in changing Africa. N.Y., 1946.
Afr 550.68	Groves, C.P. The planting of Christianity in Africa. London, 1948. 4v.
Afr 550.70	Brasio, A.D. Monumenta missionaria africana. Lisboa, 1954. 10v.
Afr 550.70.2	Brasio, A.D. Monumenta missionaria africana. 2d serie. Lisboa, 1958-64. 4v.
Afr 550.72	Sandoval, Alonso de. De instauranda Aethiopum salute. Bogatà, 1956.
Afr 550.75	Taylor, John Vernon. Christianity and politics in Africa. Harmondsworth, 1957.
Afr 550.80	Guilcher, René F. La société des missions africaines. 2. éd. Lyon, 1956.
Afr 550.85	Toppenberg, Valdemar E. Africa has my heart. Mountain View, 1958.
Afr 550.90	Patton, Cornelius H. The lure of Africa. N.Y., 1917.
Afr 550.95	Lory, Marie Joseph. Hacia el futuro. Andorra, 1958.
Afr 550.100	Sundklur, Bengt. The Christian ministry in Africa. Uppsala, 1960.
Afr 550.105	Doell, E.W. A mission doctor sees the wind of change. London, 1960.
Afr 550.110	Hatton, Desmond J. Missionlogy in Africa today. Dublin, 1961.
Afr 550.115	Silva Rego, Antonio da. Alguns problemas sociologicos missionarios da Africa negra. Lisboa, 1960.
Afr 550.120	Mosmans, G. L'Église à l'heure de l'Afrique. Tournai, 1961.
Afr 550.125	Rathe, G. Mud and mosaics. Westminster, Md., 1962.
Afr 550.130	Desai, Ram. Christianity in Africa as seen by Africans. Denver, 1962.
Afr 550.131	Hayward, Victor Evelyn William. African independent church movements. London, 1963.
Afr 550.132	Gonçalves, José. Protestantismo em Africa. Lisboa, 1960. 2v.
Afr 550.133	Wieland, Robert Julius. For a better Africa. South Africa, 1964.
Afr 550.134	Storme, Marcel. Evangelisatiepogingen. Bruxelles, 1951.
Afr 550.135	Afrique chrétienne. Christliches Afrika. Lezay, 1958-1961. 2v.
Afr 550.136	Newington, D. The shape of personality in African Christian leadership. Nelspruit, 1962.
Afr 550.136.5	Newington, D. The shape of power in Africa. Nelspruit, 1962.
Afr 550.137	Personalité africaine. Paris, 1963.
Afr 550.138	Verwimp, E. Thirty years in the African wilds. London, 1938.
Afr 550.139	Darlon, T.H. God's image in ebony. London, 1912.
Afr 550.140	Hertlein, Siegfried. Christentum und Mission im Urteil der neoafrikanischen Prosaliteratur. Münster, 1962.
Afr 550.141	Mullin, Joseph. The Catholic Church in modern Africa. London, 1965.
Afr 550.142	Kaufmann, Robert. Millenarisme et acculturation. Bruxelles, 1964.

Afr 550.143 Dougall, James Watson Cunningham. Christians in the African revolution. Edinburgh, 1963.
Afr 550.144 Parsons, Ellen. A life for Africa. Edinburgh, 1899.
Afr 550.145 Walker, Frank Deaville. The call of the dark continent. London, 1911.
Afr 550.146 Dehoney, Wayne. African diary. Nashville, 1961.
Afr 550.148 Dodge, Ralph Edward. The unpopular missionary. Westwood, N.J., 1964.
Afr 550.150 Beetham, Thomas Allan. Christianity and the new Africa. London, 1967.
Afr 550.155 Hastings, Adrian. Church and mission in modern Africa. London, 1967.
Afr 550.160 Fuller, William Harold. Run while the sun is hot. N.Y., 1966.
Afr 550.165 Barrett, David B. Schism and renewal in Africa. Nairobi, 1968.
Afr 550.170 Dammann, Ernst. Das Christentum in Afrika. München, 1968.
Afr 550.175 Hughes, W. Dark Africa and the way out. N.Y., 1969.

Afr 555.2 Thompson, George. Thompson in Africa. N.Y., 1854.
Afr 555.2.50 Cunha, A. Jornadas e outros trabalhos do missionario Barroso. Lisboa, 1938.
Afr 555.2.101 Socété des Missions Evangéliques, Paris. Un siècle en Afrique et en Océanie. Paris, 1923.
Afr 555.3 Thompson, George. The palm land. Cincinnati, 1859.
Afr 555.3.2 Thompson, George. The palm land. 2nd ed. London, 1969.
Afr 555.3.5 Medbery, R.B. Memoir of William G. Crocker...missionary in South Africa. Boston, 1848.
Afr 555.3.8 Caswall, Henry. The martyr of the Pongas. London, 1857.
Afr 555.3.10 East, D.J. Western Africa, its conditions. London, 1844.
Afr 555.3.11 Walker, S.A. Missions in Western Africa, among Soosoos. Dublin, 1845.
Afr 555.3.12 Cooksey, J.J. Religion and civilization in West Africa. London, 1931.
Afr 555.3.14 Hening, E.F. History of the African mission of the Protestant Episcopal Church. N.Y., 1850.
Afr 555.3.17 Fox, George T. A memoir of the...missionary to Cape Palmas. N.Y., 1868.
Afr 555.3.22 Goyan, George. Mère Javouhey, apôtre des Noirs. Paris, 1929.
Afr 555.3.27 Missionaires en Afrique française. Paris, 1933.
Afr 555.4 Culte protestante en Algérie. Alger, 1867.
Afr 555.4.2 Mettetal, A. Le péril du protestantisme en Algérie. Paris, 1883.
Afr 555.4.4 Pamphlet vol. Pavy, L.A.A. Christian Church in Algeria. 3 pam.
Afr 555.4.5 Ribolet. Un gand évêque, ou Vingt ans d'église d'Afrique sous l'administration de M. Pavy. Alger, 1902. 3v.
Afr 555.4.10 Algiers (Diocese). Statuts synodaux du diocése d'Alger. Alger, 1853.
Afr 555.5 Bazin, René. Charles de Foucauld. Paris, 1921.
Afr 555.5.3 Bazin, René. Charles de Foucauld, hermit. London, 1943.
Afr 555.5.5 Bazin, René. Charles de Foucauld. N.Y., 1923.
Afr 555.5.6 Foucauld, Charles de. Lettres è Henry de Castries. 10. éd. Paris, 1938.
Afr 555.5.9 Gorrée, Georges. Les amitiés sahariennes du Père de Foucauld. Grenoble, 1946. 2v.
Afr 555.6 Ryan, V.W. Mauritius and Madagascar. London, 1864.
Afr 555.6.8 Matthews, T.T. Thirty years in Madagascar. 2d ed. London, 1904.
Afr 555.7 Lloyd, Mrs. Christian work in zulae land. 2d ed. N.Y., 1870.
Afr 555.7.5 Taylor, William. Christian adventures in South Africa. London, 1868.
Afr 555.7.9 Carlyle, J.E. South Africa and its mission fields. London, 1878.
Afr 555.7.10 Davies, Horton. Great South African Christians. Cape Town, 1951.
Afr 555.7.12 Davidson, H. Frances. South and South Central Africa. Elgin, 1915.
Afr 555.8 Paiva Manso, L.M.J. Historia ecclesiastica ultramarina. Lisboa, 1872.
Afr 555.9 Arnot, Frederick Stanley. Garenganze, or Seven years in Central Africe. London, n.d.
Afr 555.9.1 Arnot, Frederick Stanley. Bihe and Garenaganze, or, Four years' further work and travel in Central Africa. London, 1893.
Afr 555.9.2 Arnot, Frederick Stanley. Garenganze, or Seven years in Central Africa. 2d ed. London, 1889.
Afr 555.9.3 Arnot, Frederick Stanley. Missionary travels in Central Africa. Bath, 1914.
Afr 555.9.4 Baker, Ernest. The life and exploration of Frederick Stanley Arnot. London, 1921.
Afr 555.9.5 Means, J.O. The proposed mission in Central Africa. Cambridge, 1879.
Afr 555.9.7 Arnot, Frederick Stanley. Garenganze; or, Seven years' pioneer mission work in Central Africa. London, 1969.
Afr 555.9.10 Rowley, Henry. Twenty years in Central Africa. 3d ed. London, 1883.
Afr 555.9.13 Goodwin, Harvey. Memoir of Bishop Mackenzie. 2d ed. Cambridge, 1865.
Afr 555.9.16 Guinness, Fanny E. The new world of Central Africa. London, 1890.
Afr 555.9.19 Tozer, William G. Letters of Bishop Tozer and his sister. London, 1902.
Afr 555.9.23 Morshead, A.E. The history of the Universities Mission to Central Africa. London, 1897.
Afr 555.9.24 Morshead, A.E. The history of the Universities Mission to Central Africa. London, 1909.
Afr 555.9.25 Morshead, A.E. The history of the Universities' Mission to Central Africa. London, 1955-62. 3v.
Afr 555.9.28 Rankine, W.H. A hero of the dark continent, Rev. William A. Scott. Edinburgh, 1897.
Afr 555.9.33 Duplessis, Johannes. A thousand miles in the heart of Africa. Edinburgh, 1905.
Afr 555.9.36 Duplessis, Johannes. The evangelisation of pagan Africa. Cape Town, 1930.
Afr 555.9.45 Botha Vlok, T.C. Elf jaren in Midden Afrika. Neerbosch, 1901.
Afr 555.9.50 Beltrame, G. Il sennaar e lo sciangallah. Verona, 1879. 2v.
Afr 555.9.55 Hotchkiss, W.R. Sketches from the dark continent. 2d ed. Cleveland, 1901.
Afr 555.9.57 Hotchkiss, W.R. Sketches from the dark continent. London, 1903.
Afr 555.9.60A Davis, John Merle. Modern industry and the African. London, 1933.

Afr 555.9.60B Davis, John Merle. Modern industry and the African. London, 1933.
Afr 555.9.61 Davis, John Merle. Modern industry and the African. 2nd ed. London, 1967.
Afr 555.9.65 Jones, David Picton. After Livingstone. The work of a pioneer missionary in Central Africa. London, 1968.
Afr 555.10 Barges, Jean Joseph Léandre. Aperçu historique sur l'église d'Afrique. Paris, 1848.
Afr 555.11 Guerin, V. La France catholique en Tunisie. Tours, 1886.
Afr 555.12 Sainte-Marie, E. de. La Tunisie chrétienne. Lyon, 1878.
Htn Afr 555.12.5* Memoriale per li missionarii apostolici de Tunis. Manuscript. n.p. 16- .
Afr 555.12.10 Vanlande, René. Chez les pères blancs, Tunisie, Kabylie Sahara. Paris, 1929.
Afr 555.12.15 Philippe, A. Missions des pères blancs en Tunisie. Paris, 1931.
Afr 555.12.20 Excoffon, Ariste. Les pères blancs en Afrique. Paris, 1893.
Afr 555.13 Foster, L.R. Historical sketch - African mission. N.Y., 1884.
Afr 555.14 Hawker, G. The life of George Grenfell. London, 1909.
Afr 555.15 Adger, J.B. Christian missions and African colonization. Columbia, 1857.
Afr 555.15.10 Brownlee, M. The lives and work of South African missionaries. Cape Town, 1952.
Afr 555.16 Dubose, H.C. Memoirs of Rev. John Leighton Wilson, D.D. Richmond, 1895.
Afr 555.17 Castellanos, M.P. Apostolado serafico en Marruecos. Madrid, 1896.
Afr 555.17.10 Copia d huma carta escrita pelo Padre Guardiam do Real Convento de Maquinés. Lisboa, 1756.
Afr 555.17.15 Koehler, Henry. L'église chrétienne du Maroc et la mission franciscaine, 1221-1790. Paris, 1934.
Afr 555.18 Hawker, G. An English woman's twenty-five-years in tropical Africa. London, 1911.
Afr 555.19 Campbell, John. The life of Africaner. Philadelphia, 1827.
Afr 555.20 Crowthers, S.A. Niger mission, report of overland journey. London, 1877.
Afr 555.20.5 Livingstone, W.P. Mary Slessor of Calabar. 9th ed. London, 1917.
Afr 555.20.7 Maxwell, J. Lowry. Nigeria, the land, the people and Christian progress. London, 1927.
Afr 555.20.9 Marwick, William. William and Louisa Anderson. Edinburgh, 1897.
Afr 555.20.10 Naw, Henry. We move into Africa. Saint Louis, Mo., 1945.
Afr 555.21 Crawford, D. Thinking black. 2d ed. London, 1914.
Afr 555.21.15 Crawford, D. Back to the long grass. N.Y., n.d.
Afr 555.22 Mackintosh, C.W. Coillard of the Zambesi. South Africa. 2d ed. London, 1907.
Afr 555.22.3 Depelchin, H. Trois ans dans l'Afrique australe. Bruxelles, 1883.
Afr 555.22.5 Beijer, J. Journal gehouden van Port Elisabeth (Algoabaai) naar Reddersburg. Kaapstad, 1862. 2 pam.
Afr 555.22.7 Calderwood, H. Caffres and Caffres missions. London, 1858.
Afr 555.22.9 Gray, R., bishop of Cape Town. Three months visitation by the Bishop of Cape Town, in...1855. London, 1856.
Afr 555.22.12 Freeman, Joseph J. Tour in South Africa, with notices of Natal. London, 1851.
Afr 555.22.14 Rivett, A.W.L. Ten years' church work in Natal. London, 1890.
Afr 555.22.16 Duplessis, J. A history of Christian missions in South Africa. London, 1911.
Afr 555.22.17 Duplessis, J. A history of Christian missions in South Africa. Cape Town, 1965.
Afr 555.22.19 Callaway, Godfrey. A shepherd of the Veld, Bransly Lewis Key, Africa. London, 1912.
Afr 555.22.22 Merensky, A. Erinnerungen aus dem Missionsleben in Transvaal, 1859-1882. Berlin, 1899.
Afr 555.22.25 Boyce, William B. Memoir of the Rev. William Shaw. London, 1874.
Afr 555.22.28 Smith, Edwin W. The way of the white fields in Rhodesia. London, 1928.
Afr 555.22.89 Livingston Inland Mission. Manual of the principles and practice. London, 1882.
Afr 555.23 London. Baptist Mission Society. Rise and progress of work on Congo river. London, 1884.
Afr 555.23.5 Nassau, Robert H. My Ogowe being a narrative of daily incidents during sixteen years in West Africa. N.Y., 1914.
Afr 555.23.7 Au Congo et aux Indes. Bruxelles, 1906.
Afr 555.23.10 Bentley, H.M. (Mrs.). W. Holman Bentley, the life and adventures of a Congo pioneer. London, 1907.
Afr 555.23.12 Laveille, E. L'évangile au centre de l'Afrique. Louvain, 1926.
Afr 555.23.15 Angola (Diocese). Visitas pastorães em 1910. Loanda, 1911.
Afr 555.23.20 Hensey, Andrew F. My children of the forest. N.Y., 1924.
Afr 555.23.25 Congo Missionary Conference. Reports. 7,1918 2v.
Afr 555.23.30 Annuaire des missions catholiques au Congo Belge.
Afr 555.23.51 Boucher, A. Au Congo français. Les missions catholiques. Paris, 1928.
Afr 555.23.55 Stonedake, A.R. Congo, past and present. London, 1937.
Afr 555.23.63 Grubb, N.P. Alfred Buxton of Abyssinia and Congo. London, 1943.
Afr 555.23.65 Chilson, E. H. Ambassador of the king. Wichita, Kan., 1943.
Afr 555.24.2 Price, William S. My third campaign in East Africa. London, 1891.
Afr 555.24.6 Wakefield, E.S. Thomas Wakefield...in East Africa. 2d ed. London, 1904.
Afr 555.24.9 Light and darkness in East Africa. London, 1927.
Afr 555.24.12 Paul, Carl. Die Mission in unsern Kolonien. Heft 2. Leipzig, 1900.
Afr 555.25 Merensky, A. Deutsche Arbeit am Njassa, Deutsch-Ostafrika. Berlin, 1894.
Afr 555.26.3 Charlesworth, M.L. Africa's mountain valley.
Afr 555.27 Bickersteth, E. Memoirs of S. Wilhelm, a native of West Africa. New Haven, 1819.
Afr 555.27.8 Moister, William. Memorials of missionary labours in West Africa. 3d ed. London, 1866.
Htn Afr 555.28* Stiles, Ezra. On a mission to Guinea. Newport, 1776.
Afr 555.29 Keable, Robert. A city of the dawn. Uganda. London, 1915.
Afr 555.29.5 Fahs, Sophia L. Uganda's white man of work. Boston, 1907.

Afr 555 Africa in general - Religion - Christian missions - Sectional - cont.

Afr 555.29.20 A.M. MacKay, pioneer missionary of the Church Missionary Society to Uganda. N.Y., 1896.
Afr 555.29.22 A.M. MacKay, pioneer missionary of the Church Missionary Society to Uganda. N.Y., 1904.
Afr 555.29.24 Padwick, Constance Evelyn. MacKay of the great lake. London, 1928.
Afr 555.30 Shepherd, A. Tucker of Uganda. London, 1929.
Afr 555.30.10 Thoonen, J.P. Black martyrs. N.Y., 1941.
Afr 555.35 Marin, Eugène. Algérie, Sahara, Soudan. Vie travaux, voyages de Mgr. Hacquard. Paris, 1905.
Afr 555.37 Geyer, F.X. Durch Sand, Sumpf und Wald. München, 1902.
Afr 555.38 Escande, Benj. Souvenirs intimes. Genève, 1898.
Afr 555.39 Witte, Jehan. Un explorateur et un apôtre du Congo français. Paris, 1924.
Afr 555.39.10 Bestier, G.G. L'apôtre du Congo, Monseigneur Augouard. Paris, 1926.
Afr 555.39.15 Goyan, Georges. Monseigneur Augouard. Paris, 1926.
Afr 555.39.20 Augouard, Prosper P. Vingt-huit années au Congo. Vienne, 1905.
Afr 555.40 Lecomte, E. Plan alto do sul de Angola. Lisboa, 1897.
Afr 555.40.5 Tucker, J.T. Angola, the land of the blacksmith prince. London, 1933.
Afr 555.45 Christol, Frank. Quatre ans au Cameroun. Paris, 1922.
Afr 555.50 Cooksey, J.J. The land of the vanished church. London, 1926.
Afr 555.55 Roome, William J.W. London, 1926.
Afr 555.60 Sierra Leone. Native Church. Jubilee Committee. The jubilee volume of the Sierra Leone Native Church. London, 1917.
Afr 555.65 Richter, Julius. Tanganyika and its future. London, 1934.
Afr 555.65.5 Schappi, F.S. Die katholischen Missionsschulen des Tanganyika-Gebietes. Inaug. Diss. Obergniningen, 1935.
Afr 555.70 Marie-Germaine, Soeur. Le Christ au Gabon. Louvain, 1931.
Afr 555.73 Rognes, Louis. Le pionnier du Gabon. Paris, 1957.
Afr 555.75 Philip, H.R.A. The new day in Kenya. London, 1936.
Afr 555.77 Billy, E. de. En Côte d'Ivoire, mission protestante d'A.O.F. Paris, 1931.
Afr 555.81 Callaway, Godfrey. Godfrey Callaway, missionary in Kaffraria, 1892-1942, his life and writings. London, 1945.
Afr 555.83 Dekorne, J.C. To who I now send thee, mission work of the Christian Reformed Church in Nigeria. Grand Rapids, Mich., 1945.
Afr 555.84 Benham, Phyllis. In Livingstone's trail, the quest of the mighty. Westminster, 1939.
Afr 555.85 Therol, J. Sous l'armure de laine blanche. Paris, 1943.
Afr 555.90 MacLean, Norman. Africa in transformation. London, 1914.
Afr 555.95 Baudu, Paul. Vieil empire. Paris, 1957.
Afr 555.100 Keys, Clara E. We pioneered in Portuguese East Africa. 1st ed. N.Y., 1959.
Afr 555.105 Wilson, George H. The history of the Universities Mission to Central Africa. Westminster, 1936.
Afr 555.110 Steinmetz, T. Cinquante ans d'apostolat au Dahomey. Lyon, 1937.
Afr 555.115 Skolaster, Hermann. Die Pallottiner in Kamerun. Limburg an der Lahn, 1924.
Afr 555.120 Beach, Peter. Benedictine and Moor. N.Y., 1959.
Afr 555.125 Barker, Anthony. The man next to me. N.Y., 1959.
Afr 555.130 Lawman, Tony. From the hands of the wicked. London, 1960.
Afr 555.132 Jenkins, David E. They led the way. Cape Town, 1966.
Afr 555.135 Desallues, Elisabeth. Toumliline. Paris, 1961.
Afr 555.136 The Church in Africa. Maryknoll, 1967.
Afr 555.137 Ijlst, Wim. A present for cold mornings. Dublin, 1968.
Afr 555.138 Soras, Alfred de. Relations de l'église et de l'état dans les pays d'Afrique francophone. Paris, 1963.
Afr 555.140 Todd, John Murray. African mission. London, 1962.
Afr 555.141 Welbourn, F.B. East African Christian. London, 1965.
Afr 555.144 Greschat, Hans-Jürgen. Kitawala. Marburg, 1967.
Afr 555.145 Maples, C. Journals and papers. London, 1899.
Afr 555.146 Fraser, A.R. Donald Fraser of Livingstonia. London, 1934.
Afr 555.147 Sanita, Giuseppe. La Barberia e la Sacra Congregazione. Cairo, 1963.
Afr 555.148 Borra, Edoardo. Un meschino di Allah. Torino, 1963.
Afr 555.149 Favre, Edouard. François Coillard. Paris, 1908-13. 3v.
Afr 555.149.5 Bertrand, Alfred. En Afrique avec le missionnaire Coillard. Genève, 1899.
Afr 555.149.10 Fauré, Edouard. Les vingt-cinq ans de Coillard au Lessouto. Paris, 1931.
Afr 555.150 Roome, William John Waterman. Through Central Africa for the Bible. London, 1929.
Afr 555.150.5 Roome, William John Waterman. Through the lands of Nyanka, Central Africa. London, 1930.
Afr 555.151 International African Seminar, 7th, University of Ghana. Christianity in tropical Africa. London, 1968.
Afr 555.152 F.S. Arnot Jubilee Conference, Muchacha, 1931. A Central African jubilee. London, 1932.
Afr 555.153 Bergner, Gerhard. Heiden, Christen und Politiker. Breklum, 1963.
Afr 555.154 Richardson, Kenneth. Garden of miracles; a history of the African Inland Mission. London, 1968.
Afr 555.155 Gallesio, Lydia. Un cuore irlandese in Africa. Torino, 1967.

Afr 575 Africa in general - Religion - Islam in Africa

Afr 575.01 Pamphlet box. Islam in Africa.
Afr 575.5 Barnes, L.C. Shall Islam rule Africa? Boston, 1890.
NEDL Afr 575.6 Lechatelier, A. L'islam dans l'Afrique occidentale. Paris, 1899.
Afr 575.7 Atterbury, Anson Phelps. Islam in Africa. N.Y., 1899.
Afr 575.7.2 Atterbury, Anson Phelps. Islam in Africa. N.Y., 1969.
Afr 575.8 Doutte, E. L'islam algérien en l'an 1900. Alger, 1900.
Afr 575.9 Davis, N. A voice from North Africa. Edinburgh, 1844.
Afr 575.9.10 Faugere, A.P. De la propagande musulmane en Afrique et dans les Indes. Paris, 1851.
Afr 575.10 Quellien, A. La politique musulmane dans l'Afrique occidentale française. Paris, 1910.
Afr 575.11 Simian, M. Les confréries islamiques. Alger, 1910.
Afr 575.12 Rinn, Louis. Marabouts et Khorean. Alger, 1884.
Afr 575.13 Forget, D.A. L'islam et le christianisme. Paris, 1900.
Afr 575.14 Schweinfurth, G. Die Wiedergeburt Agnptens. Berlin, 1895.
Afr 575.15 Agabiti, A. Per la Tripolitania. Roma, 1912.
Afr 575.16 Malrezzi, A. L'Italia e l'islam in Libia. Firenze, 1913.
Afr 575.16.10 Sabetta, Guido. Politica di penetrazione in Africa. Roma, 1913.
Afr 575.17 Servier, A. Le péril de l'avenir. Le nationalisme musulman. Constantine, 1913.

Afr 575 Africa in general - Religion - Islam in Africa - cont.

Afr 575.17.25 Ruini, M. L'islam e le nostre colonie. Città di Castello, 1922.
Afr 575.18 Korei, Aly. Condition juridique des sujets musulmans. Thèse. Paris, 1913.
Afr 575.19 Bel, Alfred. Coup d'oeil sur l'islam en Berberie. Paris, 1917.
Afr 575.19.25 Bel, Alfred. La religion musulmane en Berberie. Paris, 1938.
Afr 575.20 Carles, Fernand. La France et l'islam en Afrique occidentale. Thèse. Toulouse, 1915.
Afr 575.21 Andre, Pierre J. L'islam noir. Paris, 1924.
Afr 575.22 Brunel, René. Essai sur la confrérie religieuse des Aissaoua au Maroc. Thèse. Paris, 1926.
Afr 575.22.5 Sangroniz, José A. Modalidades del islamismo marroqui. Madrid, 1950.
Afr 575.23 Jung, Eugène. L'islam et les musulmans dans l'Afrique du Nord. Paris, 1930.
Afr 575.24 Cardaire, M.P. Contribution à l'étude de l'islam noir. Donala, 1949.
Afr 575.25 Algeria. Direction de l'Intérieur et des Beaux-Arts. Mélanges d'histoire et d'archéologie de l'Occident musulman. v.1-2. Alger, 1957.
Afr 575.27 Ahmad, Mubarak. Islam in Africa. Rabwah, 1962.
Afr 575.30 Hurries, Lyndon. Islam in East Africa. London, 1954.
Afr 575.32 Froelich, Jean Claude. Les musulmans d'Afrique Noire. Paris, 1962.
Afr 575.35 Trimingham, J.S. Islam in West Africa. Oxford, 1959.
Afr 575.35.2 Trimingham, J.S. Islam in West Africa. 2nd ed. Oxford, 1961.
Afr 575.36 Trimingham, J.S. A history of Islam in West Africa. London, 1962.
Afr 575.36.10 Trimingham, J.S. Islam in East Africa. Oxford, 1964.
Afr 575.37 International African Seminar, 5th, London, 1966. Islam in tropical Africa, studies presented and discussed at the fifth International African Seminar. London, 1966.
Afr 575.38 Layer, E. Confréries religieuses musulmanes et marabouts. Rouen, 1916.
Afr 575.40 Monteil, V. L'islam noir. Paris, 1964.
Afr 575.45 Brelvi, Mahmud. Islam in Africa. Lahore, 1964.
Afr 575.47 Reusch, Richard. Der Islam in Ost-Afrika. Leipzig, 1931.
Afr 575.50 Giglio, Carlo. La confraternità senussita dalle sue origini ad oggi. Padova, 1932.
Afr 575.52 L'Afrique islamique. Lezay, 1966.
Afr 575.55 Ibadan, Nigeria. University College. Center of Arabic Documentation. Research bulletin. 1,1944
Afr 575.56 Tarverdova, Ekaterina A. Rasprostranenie islama v zapadnoi Afrike, XI-XVI vv. Moskva, 1967.
Afr 575.58 Leutzion, Nehemia. Muslims and chiefs in West Africa. Oxford, 1968.
Afr 575.60 Trimingham, John S. The influence of Islam upon Africa. Beirut, 1968.

Afr 580 Africa in general - Religion - Jews in Africa

Afr 580.5 Mendelssohn, S. The Jews of Africa. London, 1920.
Afr 580.10 Williams, Joseph J. Hebrewisms of West Africa, from Nile to Niger with the Jews. London, 1930.
Afr 580.10.3 Williams, Joseph J. Hebrewisms of West Africa. N.Y., 1930.
Afr 580.10.4 Williams, Joseph J. Hebrewisms of West Africa, from Nile to Niger with the Jews. N.Y., 1967.

Afr 590 Africa in general - Slavery in Africa

Afr 590.01 Pamphlet box. Slavery.
Afr 590.02 Pamphlet box. Slavery.
Afr 590.2 Lavigerie, Charles Martial Allemand. Slavery in Africa, a speech. Boston, 1888.
Afr 590.3 Lavigerie, Charles Martial Allemand. Documents sur la fond de l'oeuvre antiésclavagiste. Saint-Cloud, 1889.
Afr 590.4 Sumner, Charles. White slavery in Barbary states. Boston, 1853.
X Cg Afr 590.5 Sulivan, G.L. Dhow chasing in Zanzibar waters. London, 1873. (changed to XP 9127)
Afr 590.5.8 Newman, Henry S. Banani, the transition of slavery. London, 1898.
Afr 590.6 Christy, D. Lecture on African civilization. Cincinnati, 1850.
Afr 590.7 Cooper, J. The lost continent. London, 1875.
Afr 590.8 Carstensen, E. Propositions sur l'organisation d'une emigration. v.1-2. Paris, 1869.
Afr 590.9 Forbes, R.N. Six months service in the African blockade. London, 1849.
Afr 590.10 Dias de Carvalho, H.A. L'influence de la civilisation latine et surtout portugais en Afrique. Lisbonne, 1889.
Afr 590.11F Substance of the evidence...on the slave trade. London, 1789.
Afr 590.12 Nevinson, H.W. A modern slavery. London, 1906.
Afr 590.13 Banning, E. La Conférence de Bruxelles. Bruxelles, 1890.
Afr 590.13.5F France. Ministère des Affaires Estrangères. Conférence international de Bruxelles, 18 nov. 1889-2 juil. 1890. v.1-3. Bruxelles, 1890.
Afr 590.14 Barnard, R.N. Three years cruise...for suppression of slave trade. London, 1848.
Afr 590.15 Wilson, J.L. The British squadron on the coast of Africa. London, 1851.
Afr 590.16 Colomb, Philip Howard. Slave catching in the Indian Ocean. London, 1873.
Afr 590.16.2 Colomb, John Charles Ready. Slave-catching in the Indian Ocean. N.Y., 1969.
Afr 590.17 Stanfield, J.F. The Guinea voyage. Edinburgh, 1807.
Afr 590.18 Moore, S. Biography of Mahommah G. Baquaqua. Detroit, 1854.
Afr 590.19 Stevenson, J. Arabs in Central Africa and at Lake Nyassa. Glasgow, 1888.
Afr 590.20 Read, Hollis. The Negro problem solved. N.Y., 1864.
Afr 590.20.2 Read, Hollis. The Negro problem solved. N.Y., 1969.
Afr 590.21 Michiels, A. Le Capitaine Firmin, ou La vie des Nègres en Afrique. Paris, 1853.
Afr 590.22 Swann, A.J. Fighting the slave-hunters in Central Africa. London, 1910.
Afr 590.22.5 Swann, A.J. Fighting the slave-hunters in Central Africa. London, 1914.
Afr 590.23F Portugal. Ministerio dos Negocios Estrangeiros. Documentos relativos ao apresamento. Lisboa, 1858.
Afr 590.24 Huntley, H. Seven year s service on slave coast of Western Africa. London, 1850. 2v.

Afr 590 Africa in general - Slavery in Africa - cont.

Afr 590.24.5 Foote, Andrew H. Africa and the American flag. N.Y., 1862.
Afr 590.25 Harris, John H. Portuguese slavery, Britain's dilemma. London, 1913.
Afr 590.26 Johnston, H.H. The history of a slave. London, 1889.
Afr 590.27 Owen, Nicholas. Journal of a slave-dealer. London, 1930.
Afr 590.28 Bouche, P.B. Sept ans en Afrique occidentale, la côte des esclaves. Paris, 1885.
Afr 590.30 African Institution. Report of the committee of the Institution. London, 1811.
Afr 590.30.5 African Institution. Extracts from 18th and 19th reports...May 1824, and May 1825. Philadelphia, 1826.
Afr 590.30.15 Institut d'Afrique. Annales. Paris.
Afr 590.32 Noyant. Les horreurs de l'esclavage, de la sorcellerie, des sacrifices humains et du cannibalisme en Afrique. Paris, 1891.
Afr 590.34 Abbadie, A. Sur l'abolition de l'esclavage en Afrique. Paris, 1896.
Afr 590.36 Kessel, Joseph. Marchés d'esclaves. Paris, 1933.
Afr 590.38 Cicognani, D. La questione della schiavetà coloniale dal Congresso di Vienna a oggi. Firenze, 1935.
Afr 590.40 Mercier, René. Le travail obligatoire dans les colonies africaines. Vesoul, 1933.
Afr 590.42 Society for Abolishing Slavery All over the World, Newcastle-Upon-Tyne. Declaration of the objects. Newcastle, 1836.
Htn Afr 590.44* Benezet, A. Eine kurtze Vorstellung des Theils von Africa. Ephrata, 1763.
Afr 590.45.2 Benezet, Anthony. Some historical account of Guinea, its situation, produce, and the general disposition of its inhabitants. 2nd ed. London, 1968.
Afr 590.46.3 Brougham And Vaux, H. Brougham, 1st Baron. A concise statement of the question regarding the abolition of the slave trade. 2d ed. London, 1804.
Afr 590.48 Martin, Gaston. Negriers et bois d'ébène. Grenoble, 1934.
Afr 590.52 Edinburg Society for Effecting the Abolition of African Slave Trade. Two of the petitions form Scotland, presented to last Parliament, praying abolition of African slave trade. Edinburg, 1790.
Afr 590.54 Stanley, H.M. Slavery and the slave trade in Africa. N.Y., 1893.
Afr 590.56 Hutchinson, E. The slave trade of East Africa. London, 1874.
Afr 590.56.5 Rinchon, Dieudonne. Les armements negriers au XVIIIe siècle. Bruxelles, 1956.
Afr 590.58 Verhoeven, J.C.M. Jacques de Dixmude. Bruxelles, 1929.
Afr 590.60 Edwards, I.E. Towards emancipation, a study in South African slavery. Cardiff, 1942.
Afr 590.65 Rinchon, D. Le trafic negrier. Bruxelles, 1938.
Afr 590.66 Curtin, Philip de Armond. Africa remembered. Madison, 1967.
Afr 590.70 Xavier Botelho, S. Escravatura, beneficios que podem provir as nossas possessoes. Lisboa, 1840.
Afr 590.73 Birmingham, David. Trade and conflict in Angola, the Mbundu and their neighbours under the influence of the Portuguese, 1483-1790. Oxford, 1966.
Afr 590.75 Davidson, B. Black mother. Boston, 1961.
Afr 590.75.5 Davidson, Basil. Vom Sklavenhandel zur Kolonialisierung, afrikanisch-europäische Beziehungen zwischen 1500 und 1900. Reinbeck bei Hamburg, 1966.
Afr 590.76 Mannix, Daniel. Black cargoes, a history...1518-1865. N.Y., 1962.
Afr 590.77 Neuton, John. The journal of a slave trader, John Neuton, 1750-1754. London, 1962.
Afr 590.78 Mbotela, J.J. The freeing of the slaves in Eat Africa. London, 1956.
Afr 590.79 Edressen, Halfdan. Solgt som slave. Oslo, 1965.
Afr 590.80 Verger, Pierre. Bahia and the West Africa trade, 1549-1851. Ibadan, 1964.
Afr 590.80.5 Verger, Pierre. Flux et reflux de la traité des Nègres entre le Golfe de Boain et Bahia de Todos os Santos de XVIIe au XIXe siècle. Paris, 1968.
Afr 590.81 Edinburgh. University. The transatlantic slave trade from West Africa. Edinburgh, 1965.
Afr 590.82 Abramova, Svetlana I. Istoriia rabotorgovli na verkhne-gvineiskom poberezh'e. Moskva, 1966.
Afr 590.83 Kay, Frederick George. The shameful trade. London, 1967.
Afr 590.85 Sierra Leone. Liberated African Department. Notes from Liberated African Department. Uppsala, 1967.
Afr 590.88 Hansen, Thorkild. Slavernes skibe. København, 1968.
Afr 590.90 Asiegbu, Johnson U.J. Slavery and the politics of liberation, 1787-1861. N.Y., 1969.

Afr 603 - 610 Africa in general - Geography, description, etc. - General works (By date)

Afr 603.23.10 Deherain, Henri. Quid Schems Eddin el dimashqui geographus de Africa cognitum habuerit. Thesis. Paris, 1897.
Htn Afr 605.56F* Leo Africanus, J. Historiale description de l'Afrique. Lyon, 1556. 2v.
Htn Afr 605.56.3* Leo Africanus, J. Descriptione libri IX. Liguri, 1559.
Htn Afr 605.56.4* Leo Africanus, J. A geographical historie of Africa. Londini, 1600.
Htn Afr 605.56.5* Leo Africanus, J. Ioannis Leonis Africani Africae descriptio IX lib. Absoluta. 2 pt. Lugdunum Batavorum, 1632.
Afr 605.56.7 Ramusio, G.B. Il viaggio di Giovan Leone e le navigazioni. Venezia, 1837.
Afr 605.56.10 Leo Africanus, J. De la descripción de Africa. n.p., 1940.
Afr 605.56.11 Leo Africanus, J. De la descripción de Africa y de las cosas notables que ella se encuentran. n.p., 1952.
Afr 605.56.12 Leo Africanus, J. Description de l'Afrique. Paris, 1956. 2v.
Htn Afr 605.73F* Marmol Carvajal, L. del. Descripción géneral de Africa. Pt.1, 1-2, pt.II. Granada, 1573. 3v.
Afr 605.73.5F Marmol Carvajal, L. del. Descripción general de Africa. Madrid, 1953.
Htn Afr 605.73.6* Marmol Carvajal, L. del. L'Afrique de Marmol. Paris, 1667. 3v.
Afr 606.24.1 Braun, Samuel. Schiffahrten. Facsimile-Ausgabe. Basel, 1947.
Htn Afr 606.31* Geraldinus a Merini, A. Itinerarium ad regiones sub aequinoctrali. Romae, 1631.
Htn Afr 606.70F* Ogilby, John. Africa, accurate description...regions, Aegypt, Barbary. London, 1670.
Afr 606.86F Dapper, D.O. Description de l'Afrique. Amsterdam, 1686.
Htn Afr 606.95* Lemaire. Les voyages du Sieur Lemaire. Paris, 1695.

Afr 603 - 610 Africa in general - Geography, description, etc. - General works (By date) - cont.

Afr 606.95.2 Lemaire. Les voyages du Sieur Lemaire. Edinburgh, 1887.
Afr 606.95.2.1 Lemaire. Voyages to the Canaries, Cape Verd and the coast of Africa. Edinburgh, 1887.
Afr 607.48 Lajardière. Reise-Beschreibung nach Africa. Frankfurt, 1748.
Afr 607.80.5 Damberger, C.F. Travels through the interior of Africa. Charlestown, Mass., 1801.
Afr 607.90 Cuhn, E.W. Sammlung merkwüdiger Reisen in dem Innre von Afrika. Leipzig, 1790. 3v.
Afr 607.96 Edrisi, A.A.H.I. el. Africa. Gottingae, 1796.
Afr 608.18 Murray, H. Historical account of discoveries and travels in Africa. Edinburgh, 1818. 2v.
Afr 608.19 Hutton, C. The tour of Africa. London, 1819-21. 3v.
Afr 608.21.2 Taylor, I. Scenes in Africa. London, 1821.
Afr 608.25 Hulbert, Charles. Museum Africanum. London, 1825.
Afr 608.26 Walckenaer, C.A. Histoire générale des voyages...par mer et par terre. Paris, 1826-31. 11v.
Afr 608.30 Jameson, R. Narrative of discovery and adventure in Africa. Edinburgh 1830.
Afr 608.30.2 Jameson, R. Narrative of discovery and adventure in Africa. N.Y., 1836.
Afr 608.30.3 Murray, H. Narrative of discovery and adventure in Africa. Edinburgh, 1832.
Afr 608.30.5 Murray, H. Narrative of discovery and adventure in Africa. 4th ed. Edinburgh, 1844.
Afr 608.37 D'Avezac-Macaya, Marie A.P. Esquisse générale de l'Afrique. Paris, 1837.
Afr 608.40 McQueen, J. A geographical survey of Africa. London, 1840.
Afr 608.41 Kuelb, P.H. Geschichte der Entdeckungsreisen. Mainz, 1841.
Afr 608.41.5A Cooley, William Desborough. The Negroland of the Arabs examined and explained. 2nd ed. London, 1966.
Afr 608.41.5B Cooley, William Desborough. The Negroland of the Arabs examined and explained. 2nd ed. London, 1966.
Afr 608.46.5 Silva Porto, Antonio Francisco Ferreira da. Viagems e apontamentos de um Portuense ém Africa. Lisboa, 1942.
Afr 608.46.7 Silva Porto, Antonio Francisco Ferreira da. Silva Porto e a travessia do continente africano. Lisboa, 1938.
Afr 608.47 Tardieu, E.A. Sénégambie, Guinée, Nubie. Paris, 1847.
Afr 608.48 Frost, John. The book of travels in Africa. N.Y., 1848.
Afr 608.48.2 Hoefer, J.C.F. Afrique australe, orientale. Paris, 1848.
Afr 608.53 Murray, H. The African continent. London, 1853.
Afr 608.53.3 Gumprecht, J.E. Handbuch der Geographie...von Afrika. Leipzig, 1853.
NEDL Afr 608.57 Barth, H. Reisen und Entdeckungen in Nord- und Central-Afrika. Gotha, 1857-58. 5v.
NEDL Afr 608.57.3 Barth, H. Travels and discoveries in North and Central Africa. N.Y., 1857-59. 3v.
Afr 608.57.5 Barth, H. Travels and discoveries in north and central africa. London, 1965. 3v.
Afr 608.60 Committee of General Literature and Education. Sketches of the African kingdoms and peoples. London, 1860.
Afr 608.61 MacBrair, R.M. The Africans at home. London, 1861.
Afr 608.61.2 MacBrair, R.M. The Africans at home. London, 1864.
Afr 608.62 Jacobs, A. L'Afrique nouvelle. Paris, 1862.
Afr 608.73 Kiepert, H. Beiträge zur Entdeckungsgeschichte Afrikas. v.1-4. Berlin, 1873-81. 2v.
Afr 608.74 Forbes, A.G. Africa, geographical exploration. London, 1874.
Afr 608.75 Jones, C.H. Africa, the history of exploration. N.Y., 1875.
Afr 608.76 Day, George T. African adventure and adventures. Boston, 1876.
Afr 608.77 Banning, E. L'Afrique et la Conférence géographique de Bruxelles. Bruxelles, 1877.
Afr 608.78 Bainier, P.F. La géographie appliquée à la marine, au commerce. Paris, 1878.
Afr 608.81 Chavanne, J. Afrika im Lichte unserer Tage. Wien, 1881.
Afr 608.81.3 American Colonization Society. Annual papers on condition of Africa by the Secretary of the American Colonization Society. Washington. 1881+
Afr 608.81.7 Moister, W. Africa, past and present. N.Y., 1881.
Afr 608.84 Johnston, K. Africa. 3d ed. London, 1884.
Afr 608.86 Rohlfs, G. Quid novi ex Africa. Cassel, 1886.
Afr 608.87 Lanier, L. L'Afrique, choix de lectures. 4th ed. Paris, 1887.
Afr 608.88 Hubbard, G.G. Africa, its past and future. n.p., 1888.
Afr 608.89 Benko, J.F.V. Reise S.M. Schiffes. Albatros...Süd-Amerika dem Caplande und West Afrika, 1885-1886. Pola, 1889.
Afr 608.89.4 Junker, Wilhelm. Reisen in Afrika, 1875-1878. Wien, 1889.
Afr 608.90 Junker, W. Travels in Africa. London, 1890-92. 3v.
Afr 608.91 Sievers, W. Afrika. Eine allgemeine Landeskunde. Leipzig, 1891.
Afr 608.91.2 Sievers, W. Afrika. 2. Aufl. Leipzig, 1901.
Afr 608.91.3 Jaeger, F. Afrika. 3. Aufl. Leipzig, 1928.
Afr 608.91.4 Africa and its exploration. Leipzig, 1891. 2v.
Afr 608.91.10 Velten, Carl. Schilderungen Suaheli. Göttingen, 1901.
Afr 608.92 White, A.S. The development of Africa. London, 1890.
Afr 608.92.2 White, A.S. The development of Africa. 2d ed. London, 1892.
Afr 608.93 Colvile, Zelie. Round the black man's garden. Edinburgh, 1893.
Afr 608.94 Reclus, E. Nouvelle géographie universelle Morocco. Maps of Alger. Paris, 1830-94.
Afr 608.95 Vincent, F. Actual Africa. N.Y., 1895.
Afr 608.95.3 Keane, A.H. Africa. London, 1895. 2v.
Afr 608.95.4 Keane, A.H. Africa. v.2. 2nd ed. London, 1904.
Afr 608.96 Heawood, E. Geography of Africa. London, 1896.
Afr 608.97 Schulz, A. The new Africa. London, 1897.
Afr 608.98F Independent. Africa number. May 5, 1898. N.Y., 1898.
Afr 609.00 Schanz, M. Streifzüge der Ost- und Süd-Afrika. Berlin, 1900.
Afr 609.02F Pease, A.E. Travel and sport in America. London, 1902. 3v.
Afr 609.04 Deherain, H. Etudes sur l'Afrique. Paris, 1904.
Afr 609.07 Lowensbach, Lothaire. Promenade autour de l'Afrique, 1907. Paris, 1908.
Afr 609.07.12 Albertis, Enrico Alberto d'. Periplo dell'Africa. 2d ed. Genova, 1925.
Afr 609.10 Forbes, E.A. The land of the white helmet. N.Y., 1910.
Afr 609.12 Goodrich, Joseph K. Africa of to-day. Chicago, 1912.
Afr 609.13 Powell, E.A. The last frontier. London, 1913.
Afr 609.13.2 Powell, E.A. The last frontier. N.Y., 1914.
Afr 609.13.7 Powell, E.A. The last frontier. N.Y., 1919.
Afr 609.16 Gilligan, Edmund. One lives to tell the tale. N.Y., 1931.

Afr 603 - 610 Africa in general - Geography, description, etc. - General works (By date) - cont.

Afr 609.18 Roussel, Raymond. Pages choisies d'impressions d'Afrique et de Locus Solus. Paris, 1918.
Afr 609.20 Anderson, William A. South of Suez. N.Y., 1920.
Afr 609.21 Sharpe, Alfred. The backbone of Africa. London, 1921.
Afr 609.23 Akeley, Carl E. In brightest Africa. Garden City, 1923. 2v.
Afr 609.23.2 Akeley, Carl E. In brightest Africa. Garden City, 1923.
Afr 609.23.5 Lyell, Denis D. Memories of an African hunter. London, 1923.
Afr 609.23.10 Frobenius, Leo. Das unbekannte Afrika. München, 1923.
Afr 609.25 Akeley, Carl E. In brightest Africa. Garden City, N.Y., 1925.
Afr 609.25.5 Boyce, W.D. Illustrated Africa. Chicago, 1925.
Afr 609.26 Smith, Edwin. The golden stool, some aspects of the conflict of cultures in modern Africa. London, 1926.
Afr 609.26.4 Smith, Edwin. The golden stool, some aspects of the conflict of cultures in modern Africa. Garden City, N.Y., 1928.
Afr 609.26.10 Akeley, Carl E. Adventures in the African jungle. N.Y., 1930.
Afr 609.26.15 Court Treatt, S. Cape to Cairo. Boston, 1927.
Afr 609.27 Bernard, Marc. En hydravion au-dessus du continent noir. Paris, 1927.
Afr 609.28 Ross, C. Mit Kamera, Kind und Kegel durch Afrika. Leipzig, 1928.
Afr 609.28.5 Monson, R.A. Across Africa on foot. N.Y., 1931.
Afr 609.28.10 Gray, Frank. My two African journeys. London, 1928.
Afr 609.28.15 Appel, Joseph Herbert. Africa's white magic. N.Y., 1928.
Afr 609.29 Humphrey, Seth. Loafing through Africa. Philadelphia, 1929.
Afr 609.29.5 Vonhoffman, Carl. Jungle gods. London, 1929.
Afr 609.29.10 Willis, Bailey. Living Africa. N.Y., 1930.
Afr 609.29.15 Edschmid, Kasimir. Afrika nackt und Angezogen. Frankfurt a.M., 1934.
Afr 609.29.20 Anderson, I. Circling Africa. Boston, 1929.
Afr 609.29.25.5 Suggate, L.S. Africa. 4th ed. London, 1951.
Afr 609.30 Mott-Smith, M. Africa from port to port. N.Y., 1930.
Afr 609.30.5 Roome, William J.W. Tramping through Africa. N.Y., 1930.
Afr 609.30.10 Akeley, D.J. Jungle portraits. N.Y., 1930.
Afr 609.30.15 Buckley, W. Big game hunting in Central Africa. London, 1930.
Afr 609.30.20 Fort, T. A vacation in Africa. Boston, 1931.
Afr 609.30.25 Court Treatt, Chaplin. Out of the beaten track. London, 1930.
Afr 609.31 Weulersse, Jacques. Noirs et blancs. Paris, 1931.
Afr 609.32 Maydon, H.C. Big game shooting in Africa. London, 1932.
Afr 609.33 Gatti, Attilio. Hidden Africa. London, 1933.
Afr 609.33.5 African Safaris, N.Y. A new motor route through Africa. N.Y., 1933.
Afr 609.33.10 Anstein, H. Afrika, wie ich es erlebte. Stuttgart, 1933.
Afr 609.33.15 Behn, Fritz. Kwa heri Afrika. Stuttgart, 1933.
Afr 609.34.2 Fitzgerald, Walter. Africa. 2d ed. London, 1936.
Afr 609.34.3 Fitzgerald, Walter. Africa. N.Y., 1942.
Afr 609.34.5 Gatti, Attilio. Black mist. London, 1934.
Afr 609.34.10 Weulersse, Jacques. L'Afrique noire. Paris, 1934.
Afr 609.34.11 Fitzgerald, Walter. Africa; a social, economic, and political geography of its major regions. 10th ed. n.p., 1968.
Afr 609.35 Desmond, Shaw. African log. London, 1935.
Afr 609.35.9 Johnson, Martin. Over African jungles. N.Y., 1935.
Afr 609.36 Birch-Reynardson, H. High street, Africa. Edinburgh, 1936.
Afr 609.36.5 Nebel, Heinrich C. Ein Journalist erzählt. Stuttgart, 1936.
Afr 609.36.10 Boehmer, H. Mit 14 ps durch Afrika. Wien, 1936.
Afr 609.36.15 Wilson, James C. Three-wheeling through Africa. N.Y., 1938.
Afr 609.37 Azikiwe, Nnamdi. Renascent Africa. Accra, 1937.
Afr 609.37.2 Azikiwe, Nnamdi. Renascent Africa. N.Y., 1969.
Afr 609.37.5 Daly, Marcus. Big game hunting and adventure, 1897-1936. London, 1937.
Afr 609.38 Tilman, H.W. Show on the equator. N.Y., 1938.
Afr 609.38.5 Sieburg, F. Afrikanischer Frühling, eine Reise. Frankfurt, 1938.
Afr 609.39 Wollschlaeger, Alfred. Gross ist Afrika. Berlin, 1939.
Afr 609.39.2 Wallschläger, Alfred. Afrika gestern und heute. 10. Aufl. Gütersloh, 1963.
Afr 609.39.5 Gedat, Gustav A. Wunderwege durch ein Wunderland. 2. Aufl. Stuttgart, 1939.
Afr 609.40 Rainier, P.W. African hazard. London, 1940.
Afr 609.40.10A Farson, Negley. Behind God's back. N.Y., 1941.
Afr 609.40.10B Farson, Negley. Behind God's back. N.Y., 1941.
Afr 609.41 Childers, J.S. Mumbo Jumbo, esquire. N.Y., 1941.
Afr 609.41.5 Kearton, Cherry. Cherry Kearton's travels. London, 1941.
Afr 609.41.10 Light, Richard V. Focus on Africa. N.Y., 1941
Afr 609.41.15 Bohner, Theodor. Africa. Leipzig, 1941.
Afr 609.42 Perham, M.F. African discovery, an anthology of exploration. London, 1942.
Afr 609.42.5 Viera, Josef. Ein Kontinent rückt näher. München, 1942.
Afr 609.42.10 Bonacelli, B. L'Africa nella concezione geografica degli antichi. Verbania, 1942.
Afr 609.43 Gatti, E.M. Here is Africa. N.Y., 1943.
Afr 609.44 Wells, Carveth. Introducing Africa. N.Y., 1944.
Afr 609.44.5 Campbell, Alexander. Empire in Africa. London, 1944.
Afr 609.45 Robeson, Eslanda G. African journey. N.Y., 1945.
Afr 609.45.5 Estailleur-Chanteraine, P. Ciels d'Afrique, 1931-1945. Paris, 1945.
Afr 609.46 Ojike, Nbonu. My Africa. N.Y., 1940.
Afr 609.46.5 Waldeck, T.J. On safari. London, 1946.
Afr 609.46.10 Lefebvre-Despeaux, Maxime. Croquis d'Afrique; voyages. Paris, 1946.
Afr 609.48 Bolinder, Gustaf. Nykypaivan Afrikka. Helsinki, 1948.
Afr 609.50 Vansinderen, A. Africa, land of many lands. 3d ed. Syracuse, N.Y., 1950.
Afr 609.50.5A Haynes, G.E. Africa. N.Y., 1950.
Afr 609.50.5B Haynes, G.E. Africa. N.Y., 1950.
Afr 609.52A Hunter, J.A. Hunter. 1st ed. N.Y., 1952.
Afr 609.52B Hunter, J.A. Hunter. 1st ed. N.Y., 1952.
Afr 609.52.5 Guernier, E.L. L'apport de l'Afrique à la pensée humaine. Paris, 1952.
Afr 609.52.10 Hanzelka, Jiri. Africa. 1st ed. Prague, 1952. 3v.
Afr 609.52.15 Agundis, T. Campamentos en Africa. México, 1959.
Afr 609.53 Marie André du Sacre Coeur, Sister. La condition humaine en Afrique noire. Paris, 1953.
Afr 609.54 Meeker, Oden. Report on Africa. N.Y., 1954.

Afr 603 - 610 Africa in general - Geography, description, etc. - General works (By date) - cont.

Afr 609.54.5 Thompson, E.B. Africa, land of my fathers. Garden City, 1954.
Afr 609.54.10 Considine, J.J. Africa, world of new men. N.Y., 1954.
Afr 609.54.15 Cintas, Pierre. Contribution à l'étude de l'expansion carthagenoise au Maroc. Paris, 1954.
Afr 609.54.30 Cecchi, Emilio. Appunti per un periplo dell'Africa. Milano, 1954.
Afr 609.55 Reynolds, Reginald. Cairo to Cape Town. 1st ed. Garden City, N.Y., 1955.
Afr 609.55.5 Cloete, Stuart. The African giant. Boston, 1955.
Afr 609.55.10A Gunther, John. Inside Africa. 1st ed. N.Y., 1955.
Afr 609.55.10B Gunther, John. Inside Africa. 1st ed. N.Y., 1955.
Afr 609.55.15 American Academy of Political and Social Science, Philadelphia. Contemporary Africa. Philadelphia, 1955.
Afr 609.55.20 Seymour, John. One man's Africa. London, 1955.
Afr 609.55.25 Brockway, A.F. African journeys. London, 1955.
Afr 609.55.30 Migliorini, Elio. L'Africa. Torino, 1955.
Afr 609.56 Jones, Schuyler. Under the African sun. London, 1956.
Afr 609.56.5 Vergani, Orio. Quarantacinque gradi all'ombra, attraverso l'Africa, dalla Città del Capo al Cairo. Torino, 1964.
Afr 609.56.10 Dutton, Geoffrey. Africa in black and white. London, 1956.
Afr 609.57 Schiffers, Heinrich. Afrika. 4. Aufl. Frankfurt, 1957.
Afr 609.57.2 Schiffers, Heinrich. Afrika. 8. Aufl. München, 1967.
Afr 609.57.5 Schomburgk, Hans Hermann. Zelte in Afrika. 1. Aufl. Berlin, 1957.
Afr 609.57.10 Baumann, Hermann. Les peuples et les civilisations de l'Afrique. Paris, 1957.
Afr 609.57.16 Brom, John L. African odyssey. 1st ed. N.Y., 1966.
Afr 609.58 Gasset, Pierre. L'Afrique, les Africains. v.1-2. Paris, 1958.
Afr 609.58.5 Sholomir, Jack. Beachcombers of the African jungle. 1st ed. N.Y., 1959.
Afr 609.58.10 Jahn, Janheinz. Muntu. Düsseldorf, 1958.
Afr 609.58.12 Jahn, Janheinz. Muntu. London, 1961.
Afr 609.58.15 Goss, Hilton P. Africa, present and potential. Santa Barbara, 1958.
Afr 609.58.20 Favrod, Charles. Le poids de l'Afrique. Paris, 1958.
Afr 609.58.25 François, Charles. Eléments du problème africain. Buhavu, 1958.
Afr 609.58.30 Damme, Fred van. Kaapstad-Kairo per auto-stop. Antwerpen, 1958.
Afr 609.58.35 Hornman, W. Sabonjo de onstuimige. Leiden, 1958.
Afr 609.58.36 Hornman, W. De gesel van angst. Leiden, 1959.
Afr 609.58.37 Hornman, W. Het masker af. Leiden, 1957.
Afr 609.58.40 Africa seen by American Negroes. Paris, 1958.
Afr 609.58.45 Summer, Roger. Inyanga. Cambridge, 1958.
Afr 609.58.50 Laidley, Fernando. Roteiro africano; primeira volta a Africa en automovel. 3. ed. Lisboa, 1958.
Afr 609.59 Carpenter, G.W. The way in Africa. N.Y., 1959.
Afr 609.59.5 Davidson, Basil. The lost cities of Africa. 1st ed. Boston, 1959.
Afr 609.59.10 Ross, Emory. Africa distributed. N.Y., 1959.
Afr 609.59.15 Gribaudi, Dino. Profilo geografico dell'Africa. Torino, 1967.
Afr 609.60 Moorehead, Alan. No room in the ark. N.Y., 1959.
Afr 609.60.5 Gatti, Ellen. The new Africa. N.Y., 1960.
Afr 609.60.10 Dainelli, Giotto. Gli esploratori italiani in Africa. Torino, 1960.
Afr 609.60.15 Vaulx, Bernard de. En Afrique. Paris, 1960.
Afr 609.60.20 Haller, Albert. Die Welt des Afrikaners. Düsseldorf, 1960.
Afr 609.60.25 Lenenberger, Hans. Die Stunde des schwarzen Mannes. München, 1960.
Afr 609.60.30 Bensted-Smith, Richard. Turn left for Tangier. Coventry, 1960.
Afr 609.60.35 Westphal, Clarence. African heritage. Minneapolis, 1960.
Afr 609.60.40 Harcourt, François. L'Afrique à l'heure. Paris, 1960.
Afr 609.60.45 Storey, H.R. The continent of Africa. London, 1960.
Afr 609.60.50 Ehrenfels, O.R. The light continent. London, 1960.
Afr 609.60.55 Jones, H.W. Africa in perspective. London, 1960.
Afr 609.60.60 Forrest, Alfred C. Not tomorrow, now. Toronto, 1960.
Afr 609.60.65 Chatterji, Suniti. Africanism. Calcutta, 1960.
Afr 609.60.70 Ottenberg, Simon. Cultures and societies of Africa. N.Y., 1960.
Afr 609.60.75 Torres, Joaquin. Viaje por Africa. Buenos Aires, 1960.
Afr 609.60.80 Ragusin Righi, Livio. Viaggio nell Africa nera in fermento. Trieste, 1960.
Afr 609.60.85 Potekhin, I.I. Afrika smotrit v budushchee. Moscow, 1960.
Afr 609.61 Smith, Anthony. High street, Africa. London, 1961.
Afr 609.61.5 Eskelund, Karl. While God slept. London, 1961.
Afr 609.61.10 National Research Council. Human environments in middle Africa. Washington, 1961. 2v.
Afr 609.61.15 Money, David Charles. Africa. 2d ed. London, 1961.
Afr 609.61.20 Franck, F. African sketchbook. 1. ed. N.Y., 1961.
Afr 609.61.25 Rakhmatov, M. Afrika idet k svoboda. Moscow, 1961.
Afr 609.61.30 Stillery, A. Africa. London, 1961.
Afr 609.61.35 Williams, C. The rebirth of African civilization. Washington, 1961.
Afr 609.61.40 Green, Lawrence G. Great north road. Capetown, 1961.
Afr 609.61.45 Gauld, Peter. Africa, continent of change. Belmont, 1961.
Afr 609.61.50 Ligne, Eugene. Africa. Bruxelles, 1961.
Afr 609.61.55 Stumbuk, Zdenko. Zapiski iz Afrike. Zagreb, 1961.
Afr 609.61.60 Legum, Colin. Africa, a handbook. London, 1961.
Afr 609.62 Merriam, Alan P. A prologue to the study of the African arts. Yellow Springs, Ohio, 1962.
Afr 609.62.5 Afrika segodnia. Moscow, 1962.
Afr 609.62.10 Deblij, Harm. Africa south. Evanston, 1962.
Afr 609.62.15 Abraham, W. The mind of Africa. London, 1962.
Afr 609.62.20 Fox, Frederic. Fourteen Africans vs. one American. N.Y., 1962.
Afr 609.62.25 Maquet, Jacques. Afrique. Paris, 1962.
Afr 609.62.30 Sousa, Daniel. Perspectivas da actualidade africana. n.p., 1962.
Afr 609.62.35 Byford-Jones, N. Africa, journey out of darkness. London, 1962.
Afr 609.62.40 Dumont, René. L'Afrique noire est mal partie. Paris, 1962.
Afr 609.62.41 Dumont, René. False start in Africa. London, 1966.
Afr 609.62.41.5 Dumont, René. False start in Africa. N.Y., 1966.
Afr 609.62.45 Mphahlele, E. The African image. N.Y., 1962.
Afr 609.62.50 Batson, E. Contemporary dimensions of Africa. Cape Town, 1962.
Afr 609.62.55 Rycroft, W.S. A factual study of sub-Saharan Africa. N.Y., 1962.

54

Afr 626.62	France. Centre National du Commerce Extérieur. Memento commercial. Paris, 1959.
Afr 626.64	International Bank for Reconstruction and Development. The economic development of Libya. Baltimore, 1960.
Afr 626.65	International Bank for Reconstruction and Development. The World Bank in Africa. Washington, 1961.
Afr 626.66	East Africa High Commission. Domestic income and product in Kenya. Nairobi, 1959.
Afr 626.68	Marcus, Edward. Investment and development possibilities in tropical Africa. N.Y., 1960.
Afr 626.70	Shpirt, A.I. Afrika vo Vtoroi Mirovoi Voine. Moscow, 1959.
Afr 626.71	Shpirt, A.I. Ekonomika stran Afriki. Moscow, 1963.
Afr 626.72	Shpirt, A.I. Syrevye resursy Afriki. Moscow, 1961.
Afr 626.75	Stanford Research Institute. African development. Menlo Park, Calif., 1960.
Afr 626.80	Ady, Peter. System of national accounts in Africa. Paris, 1960.
Afr 626.85	Inter-African Labour Institute. The human factors of productivity in Africa. 2d ed. Brazzaville, 1960.
Afr 626.85.3	Inter-African Labour Institute. Les facteurs humains de la productivité. Bumako, 1956.
Afr 626.90	Hesse, Kurt. Wirtschaftliche Entwecklungstendenzen in West-, Mittel- und Ostafrika. Bad Homburg, 1960.
Afr 626.95	Black, Eugene Robert. Tales of two continents. Athens, Ga., 1961.
Afr 626.98	Rivkin, Arnold. Africa and the West. N.Y., 1962.
Afr 626.98.5	Rivkin, Arnold. Africa and the European Common Market. Denver, 1964.
Afr 626.98.6	Rivkin, Arnold. Africa and the European Common Market. 2nd ed. Denver, 1966.
Afr 626.100	Hazlewood, Arthur. The economy of Africa. London, 1961.
Afr 626.100.5	Hazlewood, Arthur. African integration and disintegration. London, 1967.
Afr 626.102	Hunter, Guy. The new societies of tropical Africa. London, 1962.
Afr 626.103A	Green, L. Development in Africa, a study in regional analysis with special reference to southern Africa. Johannesburg, 1962.
Afr 626.103B	Green, L. Development in Africa, a study in regional analysis with special reference to southern Africa. Johannesburg, 1962.
Afr 626.104	Benveneste, Guy. Handbook of African economic development. N.Y., 1962.
Afr 626.105	Ekonomicheskoe i politicheskoe polozhenie stran Afriki. Moskva. 1962+
Afr 626.106	Charbonneau, J. Marches et marchands d'Afrique noire. Paris, 1961.
Afr 626.108	Bohannan, Paul. Markets in Africa. Evanston, Ill., 1962.
Afr 626.110	Food and Agriculture Organization of the United Nations. FAO African survey. Rome, 1962.
Afr 626.112	Mendes, C.B. do Quental. A cooperação em Africa. Lisboa, 1961.
Afr 626.114	United States. Bureau of International Commerce. Africa, sales frontier for U.S. business. Washington, 1963.
Afr 626.116	International Association for Research in Income and Wealth. African studies in income and wealth. Chicago, 1963.
Afr 626.117	Royal Institue of International Affairs. The African economy. Oxford, 1962.
Afr 626.118F	United Kingdom aid to Africa. London, 1959.
Afr 626.119	Special Commonwealth African Assistance Plan. Report. London.
Afr 626.120	Agostino Orsini, P. I problemi economici dell'Africa e l'Europa. Roma, 1961.
Afr 626.121	Morgaut, M.E. Cinq années de psychologies africaines. Paris, 1962.
Afr 626.122	Afrika v tsifrakh. Moscow, 1963.
Afr 626.124	Due, J.F. Taxation and economic development. Cambridge, 1963.
Afr 626.125	Council of Europe. Europe and Africa. Strasbourg, 1960.
Afr 626.126	Neumark, S.D. Foreign trade and economic development in Africa. Stanford, Calif., 1964.
Afr 626.127	Kreinin, M.E. Israel and Africa. N.Y., 1964.
Afr 626.128	Conference On Economic Development for Africa. Economic development for Africa south of the Sahara. London, 1964.
Afr 626.129	Herskovitz, Melville J. Economic transition in Africa. Evanston, 1964.
Afr 626.129.5	Massell, Benton F. African studies and economic analysis. Santa Monica, 1964.
Afr 626.130	Steinfield, Jacques. Pour une cooperation économique africaine, vues et perspectives. Bruxelles, 1964.
Afr 626.131	Bauer, G. Die Wirtschaft Afrikas. Frankfurt a.M., 1963.
Afr 626.132	Little, Ian. Aid to Africa. Oxford, 1964.
Afr 626.133	Lazic, Branko M. L'Afrique et les leçons de l'expérience communiste. Paris, 1961.
Afr 626.134	Amin Samir. Quelques expériences de décolonisation et de développement économique. v.1-2. Dakar, 1964.
Afr 626.135	Suslin, P.N. Ekonomika i vneshniaia torgovlia stran Afriki. Moscow, 1964.
Afr 626.136	International Conference on the Organization of Research and Training in Africa in Relation to the Study, Conservation and Utilization of Natural Resources, Lagos, 1964. Final report of the Lagos conference. Lagos, 1964.
Afr 626.136.2	International Conference on the Organization of Research and Training in Africa in Relation to the Study, Conservation and Utilization of Natural Resources, Lagos, 1964. Lagos Conference, 28 July to 6 Aug. 1964. Paris, 1965.
Afr 626.136.4	International Conference on the Organization of Research and Training in Africa in Relation to the Study, Conservation and Utilization of Natural Resources, Lagos, 1964. Scientific research in Africa. Lagos, 1964.
Afr 626.136.6	International Conference on the Organization of Research and Training in African in Relation to the Study, Conservation and Utilization of Natural Resources, Lagos, 1964. Outline of a plan for scientific research and training in Africa. Paris, 1964.
Afr 626.137	Africa economic digest. Exeter, Eng. 1-2,1965-1966// 3v.
Afr 626.138	Bourgaignie, G.E. Jeune Afrique mobilisable. Paris, 1964.
Afr 626.139	Cambridge Conference on Development Planning. African development planning. Cambridge, England, 1964.
Afr 626.140	Pelletier, R.A. Mineral resources of South-Central Africa. Capetown, 1964.
Afr 626.141	Sousa, Alfredo de. Economia e sociedade em Africa. Lisboa, 1965.

	Afr 626.142	Blair, Thomas Lucien Vincent. Africa, a market profile. N.Y., 1965.
	Afr 626.143	Brokensha, David. Ecology and economic development in tropical Africa. Berkeley, 1965.
	Afr 626.143.5	Brokensha, David W. The anthropology of development in Sub-Saharan Africa. Lexington, Ky., 1969.
	Afr 626.144	Farer, Tom J. Financing African development. Cambridge, Mass., 1965.
	Afr 626.145	Taufer, Otakar. Vyznam hospodarske spoluprace socialistickych statu s africkymi zememi. Praha, 1964.
	Afr 626.146	Nkrumah, Kwame. Neo-colonialism. London, 1965.
	Afr 626.147	Strasbourg. Université. Centre Universitaire des Hautes Etudes Européennes. L'Europe et l'Afrique noire. Strasbourg, 1962.
	Afr 626.148	Akademiia Nauk SSSR. Institut Afrikii. Nezavisimye strany Afriki. Moskva, 1965.
	Afr 626.149	Svenska Handelsdelegationen 1963 till Sudan, Ethiopien, Uganda och Tanganyika. Etiopien, Sudan, Tanganyika, Uganda. Stockholm, 1964.
	Afr 626.150	Giedwidz, Jan. Afryka. Warszawa, 1962.
	Afr 626.152	Nyasaland Economic Symposium. Economic development in Africa. Oxford, 1965.
	Afr 626.153	Akademiia Nauk SSSR. Institut Afriki. Ekonomika Afriki. Moskva, 1965.
	Afr 626.153.5	Akademiia Nauk SSSR. Institut Afriki. Ekonomicheskaia istoriia Afriki. Moskva, 1966.
	Afr 626.154	Massachusetts Institue of Technology. Fellows in Africa Program. Managing economic development in Africa. Cambridge, Mass., 1963.
	Afr 626.155	Dobrska, Zofia. Problemy gospodarcze Afryki. Wyd.1. Warszawa, 1965.
	Afr 626.156	Prague. Vysoka Skola Ekonomicka. Katedra Ekonomiky Rozvojovych Zemi. Africka Sekce. Nastin ekonomiky rozvojovych zemi Afriky. Praha, 1964.
	Afr 626.157F	Halpern, Jan. Wybrane zagadnienia z historii gospodarczej Afryki. Warszawa, 1963.
	Afr 626.157.5	Halpern, Jan. Planowanie w niektorych krajach Afryki. Warszawa, 1963.
	Afr 626.158	Anguile, André G. L'Afrique sans frontières. Monaco, 1965.
	Afr 626.159	Stroitel'stvo natsional'noi ekonomiki v stranakh Afriki. Moskva, 1968.
	Afr 626.160	Tevoedjre, Albert. Contribution à une synthèse sur le problème de la formation des cadres africains en vue de la croissance économique. Paris, 1965.
	Afr 626.161	Kamarck, Andrew Martin. The economics of African development. N.Y., 1967.
	Afr 626.162F	Etheredge, D.A. Economic development in the newly independent states of Africa. Johannesburg, 1963.
Htn	Afr 626.163*	Pamphlet vol. African economic conditions. (German). 7 pam.
Htn	Afr 626.164*	Pamphlet vol. African economic conditions. (German). 8 pam.
	Afr 626.165	Green, Reginald Herbold. Economic co-operation in Africa, retrospect and prospect. Nairobi, 1967.
	Afr 626.165.5	Green, Reginald Herbold. Unity or poverty? The economics of Pan-Africanism. Harmondsworth, 1968.
	Afr 626.166	Symposium of Industrial Development in Africa, Cairo. Report, Cairo, 27 Jan. to 10 Feb. 1966. N.Y., 1966.
	Afr 626.167	Clark, Paul Gordon. Development planning in East Africa. Nairobi, 1965.
	Afr 626.168	Semin, Nikolai S. Strany SEV i Afrika. Moskva, 1968.
	Afr 626.170	Popov, Iurii Nikolaevich. Political economy and African reality. Moscow, 1967.
	Afr 626.172	Whetham, Edith Holt. Readings in the applied economics of Africa. Cambridge, 1967.
	Afr 626.172.1	Whetham, Edith Holt. The economics of African countries. London, 1969.
	Afr 626.174	Okigbo, Pius Nwabufo. Africa and the Common Market. London, 1967.
	Afr 626.176	Stokke, Baard Richard. Soviet and Eastern European trade in Africa. N.Y., 1967.
	Afr 626.178	Ewing, A.F. Industry in Africa. London, 1968.
	Afr 626.180	Timmler, Markus. Die Gemeinsame Afrikanisch-Madegassische Organisation. Köln, 1966.
	Afr 626.185	European Economic Community. Possibilités d'industrialisation des états africains et malgache associés. Paris, 1966. 7v.
	Afr 626.186	Entin, Lev M. Natsional'no-demokraticheskoe ekonomicheskii progress. Moskva, 1968.
	Afr 626.190	Gand, Michel. Les premières expériences de planification en Afrique noire. Paris, 1967.
	Afr 626.195	International Monetary Fund. Surveys of African economics. Washington, 1968. 2v.
	Afr 626.196	Lipets, Iulii G. Strany iugo-vostochne i Afriki. Moskva, 1968.
	Afr 626.200	Robson, Peter. Economic integration in Africa. London, 1968.
	Afr 626.200.5	Robson, Peter. The economics of Africa. London, 1969.
	Afr 626.202	Mars, John. Afrikanische Wirtschaftsintegration. Wien, 1967.
	Afr 626.204	Tevoedjre, Albert. Africa and international co-operation: ILO in Africa. n.p., n.d.
	Afr 626.206	Vinay, Bernard. L'Afrique commence avec l'Afrique. 1. éd. Paris, 1968.
	Afr 626.208	Aromolaran, Adekunie. West African economics today. 1st ed. Ibadan, 1968.
	Afr 626.209	Ekonomicheskoe sotrudnichestvo SSSR so stranami Afriki. Moskva, 1968.
	Afr 626.210	Tamuno, Olufunmilayo Grace Esho. Co-operation for development. Ibadan, 1969.
	Afr 626.212	Martin, Jane. A bibliography on African regionalism. Boston, 1969.
	Afr 626.213	Korendiasov, Evgenii N. Kollektivnyi kolonializm v deistvii. Moskva, 1967.
	Afr 626.214	Seminar on Local Government Finance in Africa, Addis Ababa, 1966. Local government finance in Africa. Berlin, 1967.
	Afr 626.215	Ekonomicheskie i politicheskie problemy Afriki. Moskva, 1968.
	Afr 626.218	African development and Europe. 1st ed. Oxford, 1970.
	Afr 626.220	Rowe, David Nelson. The new diplomacy; international technical cooperation projects of the Republic of China in African countries. New Haven, 1969.

Afr 628 Africa in general - The negro race in general, especially "The world over" (By date, e.g. .258 for 1958)

	Afr 628.2.251	League of Coloured Peoples. The keys. London.
	Afr 628.2.256	League of Coloured Peoples. News letter. London.
	Afr 628.2.257	League Of Coloured Peoples. Annual report. London.
	Afr 628.5	Mills, C.H. Selective annotated bibliography on the Negro and foreign languages. n.p., 1939.
	Afr 628.5.10	Spingarn, A.B. Collecting a library of Negro literature. n.p., 1938.
	Afr 628.6	Présence africaine. Paris. 1,1947+ 23v.
	Afr 628.7	Présence africaine. English edition. Paris. 1,1960+ 6v.
	Afr 628.9	The black scholar. San Francisco. 1,1969+
	Afr 628.10	American Society of African Culture. Summary report, annual conference. N.Y.
	Afr 628.15	Freedomways, a quarterly of the Negro freedom movement. N.Y. 1,1961+ [illegible]v.
	Afr 628.20	Flamingo. London. 1961+ 4v.
	Afr 628.25	Liberator. N.Y. 3,1963+ 7v.
	Afr 628.30	Harvard journal of Negro affairs. Cambridge, Mass. 1,1965+
	Afr 628.108	Gregoire, Henri. De la littérature des Nègres. Paris, 1808.
	Afr 628.108.7	Gregoire, Henri. De la noblesse de la peau. Paris, 1826.
	Afr 628.108.10	Tussac, R. de. Cri des colons contre un ouvrage de M. L'Evêque. Paris, 1810.
Htn	Afr 628.110*	Grégoire, Henri. An enquiry concerning the intellectual and moral faculties...of Negroes. Brooklyn, 1810.
	Afr 628.110.1	Grégoire, Henri. An enquiry concerning the intellectual and moral faculties and literature of Negroes. College Park, 1967.
	Afr 628.141	Pennington, James W.C. A text book of the origin and history, (Hartford, 1841). Detroit, 1969?
	Afr 628.148	Armistead, W. A tribute for the Negro. Manchester, 1848.
	Afr 628.168	Helper, H.R. The Negroes in Negroland. N.Y., 1868.
	Afr 628.210	Johnston, H.H. The Negro in the new world. London, 1910.
	Afr 628.213A	Ferris, William H. The African abroad. New Haven, 1913. 2v.
	Afr 628.213B	Ferris, William H. The African abroad. New Haven, 1913. 2v.
	Afr 628.213C	Ferris, William H. The African abroad. New Haven, 1913. 2v.
	Afr 628.213D	Ferris, William H. The African abroad. New Haven, 1913. 2v.
	Afr 628.215A	Dubois, W.E.B. The Negro. N.Y., 1915.
	Afr 628.215B	Dubois, W.E.B. The Negro. N.Y., 1915.
	Afr 628.215.10	Francke, E. Die geistige Entwicklung der Neger-Kinder. Inaug. Diss. Leipzig, 1915.
	Afr 628.223	Garvey, Marcus. Philosophy and opinions of Marcus Garvey. 1st ed. N.Y., 1923.
	Afr 628.225.10	Garvey, Marcus. Philosophy and opinions, or Africa for the Africans. v.2. 2d ed. N.Y., 1926.
	Afr 628.225.12	Garvey, Marcus. Philosophy and opinions of Marcus Garvey, or Africa for the Africans. 2nd ed. London, 1967.
	Afr 628.225.15	Price, W. The Negro around the world. N.Y., 1925.
	Afr 628.229	Montenegro, Alvaro de. A raça negra perante a civilisação. Lisboa, 1929.
	Afr 628.229.5	Cameron, Norman E. The evolution of the Negro. Georgetown, 1929-34. 2v.
	Afr 628.229.12	Guggisberg, Frederick Gordon. The future of the Negro. N.Y., 1969.
	Afr 628.231	Padmore, George. The life and struggles of Negro toilers. London, 1931.
	Afr 628.234	Rogers, J.A. Hundred amazing facts about the Negro with complete proof. N.Y., 1934.
	Afr 628.238	James, C.L.R. A history of Negro revolt. London, 1938.
	Afr 628.239	Dubois, W.E.B. Black folk, then and now. N.Y., 1939.
	Afr 628.240	Sell, Manfred. Die schwarze Völkerwanderung. Wien, 1940.
	Afr 628.245	Logan, Rayford W. The Negro and the post-war world. Washington, 1945.
	Afr 628.246	Fleming, Beatrice (Jackson.) Distinguished Negroes abroad. Washington, 1946.
	Afr 628.246.5	Rogers, Joel Augustus. World's great men of color. 1st ed. N.Y., 1946-47. 2v.
	Afr 628.248	Burns, A. Colour prejudice. London, 1948.
	Afr 628.252	Fannon, F. Peau noire. Paris, 1952.
	Afr 628.252.5	Fannon, F. Black skin, white masks. N.Y., 1967.
	Afr 628.253	Caruthers, J.C. The African mind in health and disease. Geneva, 1953.
	Afr 628.256	Bartah, Ernst. Neger, Jazz und tiefer Süden. Leipzig, 1956.
	Afr 628.257	Wright, Richard. White man, listen. 1st ed. Garden City, 1957.
	Afr 628.258	Piguion, René. Reveil de culture. Port au Prince, 1958.
	Afr 628.258.5	Aspects de la culture noire. Paris, 1958.
	Afr 628.259	Betancourt, J.R. El Negro. La Habana, 1959.
	Afr 628.262	Mars, Jean. De la préhistoire d'Afrique. Port-au-Prince, 1962.
	Afr 628.264.2	Fernandes, Florestan. Die Integratión des Negers in die Klassengesellschaft. Bad Homburg, 1969.
	Afr 628.264.5	Fernandes, Florestan. A integrafão do negro na sociedade de classes. v.1-2. São Paulo, 1965.
	Afr 628.265	Diop, Cheikh Anta. Nations nègres et culture. 2. éd. Paris, 1955.
	Afr 628.265.5	Osei, Gabriel Kingsley. Forgotten great Africans. London, 1965.
	Afr 628.266	Efimov, Aleksei V. Protiv rasizma. Moskva, 1966.
	Afr 628.266.5	Herskovits, Melville Jean. The new world Negro. Bloomington, 1966.
	Afr 628.267	Diop, Cheikh A. Antériorité des civilisations nègres. Paris, 1967.
	Afr 628.267.5	Colloque sur l'Art Nègre, Dakar. Colloque: fonction et signification de l'art nègre dans la vie du peuple et pour le peuple. Paris, 1967.
	Afr 628.268	Garvey, Marcus. Speech presenting the case of the Negro for international racial adjustment. London?, 1968?
	Afr 628.269	Toledo. University. Library. The Black experience; the Negro in America, Africa, and the world. Toledo, Ohio, 1969.

Afr 630 Africa in general - Races - General works (i.e. the negro race in Africa)

Afr 630.01	Pamphlet box. Races of Africa.
Afr 630.2	Bantu studies. Johannesburg. 2,1923+ 8v.
Afr 630.2.5	Bantu studies, monograph series. Johannesburg.
Afr 630.3	African studies. Johannesburg. 5,1946+ 13v.
Afr 630.5	Vogt, E.F. Les poisons de flèches et les poisons d'épreuve des indigènes de l'Afrique. Lons-le-Saunier, 1912.
Afr 630.6	Hartmann, R. Die Nigritier. Berlin, 1876.
Afr 630.6.5	Hartmann, R. Die Völker Afrikas. Leipzig, 1879.
Afr 630.7	Waller, N. Ivory, apes, and peacocks. London, 1891.
Afr 630.8	Delafosse, Maurice. Les Noires de l'Afrique. Paris, 1922.

Afr 630 Africa in general - Races - General works (i.e. the negro race in Africa) - cont.

Afr 630.8.5	Delafosse, Maurice. The Negroes of Africa. Washington, 1931.
Afr 630.8.10	Delafosse, Maurice. Les Nègres. Paris, 1927.
Afr 630.9	Harris, John H. Africa, slave or free. London, 1919.
Afr 630.9.5	Harris, John H. Africa: slave or free? N.Y., 1969.
Afr 630.10A	Willoughby, W.C. Race problems in the new Africa. Oxford, 1923.
Afr 630.10B	Willoughby, W.C. Race problems in the new Africa. Oxford, 1923.
Afr 630.12	Hambly, Wilfrid D. Ethnology of Africa. Chicago, 1930.
Afr 630.13	Société de Géographie d'Egypte. Cataloque of the Ethnographical Museum of the Royal Geographical Society of Egypt. Le Caire, 1924.
Afr 630.14	Seligman, C.G. Races of Africa. London, 1930.
Afr 630.14.3	Seligman, C.G. Races of Africa. 3d ed. London, 1957.
Afr 630.14.4	Seligman, C.G. Races of Africa. 4th ed. London, 1966.
Afr 630.31	Buxton, Charles R. The race problem in Africa. London, 1931.
Afr 630.34	Westermann, D. The African to-day. London, 1934.
Afr 630.36	Thwaite, Daniel. The seething African pot. London, 1936.
Afr 630.36.5	Mair, L.P. Native policies in Africa. London, 1936.
Afr 630.38	Frazer, J.G. The native races of Africa and Madagascar. London, 1938.
Afr 630.38.5	Abercrombie, Hugh R. Africa's peril. London, 1938.
Afr 630.40	Bigland, Eileen. Pattern in black and white. London, 1940.
Afr 630.41	Tritonj, Romolo. Politica indigena africana. Milano, 1941.
Afr 630.43	Briault, Maurice. Les sauvages d'Afrique. Paris, 1943.
Afr 630.43.5F	Koloniale Völkerkunde. Berlin, 1943.
Afr 630.44	Negro types, 65 pictures. London, 1944.
Afr 630.46	Mason, Philip. Race relations in Africa. London, 1960.
Afr 630.48	Turner, Walter L. Under the skin of the African. Birmingham, Ala., 1948.
Afr 630.50	Labouret, Henri. Histoire des Noirs d'Afrique. 2. éd. Paris, 1950.
Afr 630.52	Mylius, N. Afrika Bibliographie. Wien, 1952.
Afr 630.52.5	Ghurye, G.S. Race relations in Negro Africa. Bombay, 1952.
Afr 630.53	Bartlett, V. Struggle for Africa. London, 1953.
Afr 630.54	Forde, C.D. African worlds. London, 1954.
Afr 630.54.2	Forde, C.D. African worlds. London, 1963.
Afr 630.54.5	Hafter, Rudolf. Schwarz und Weiss in Afrika. Zürich, 1954.
Afr 630.55	Vanderpost, Laurens. The dark eye in Africa. N.Y., 1955.
Afr 630.55.2	Vanderpost, Laurens. The dark eye in Africa. N.Y., 1961.
Afr 630.56	Padmore, George. Pan-Africanism or Communism. N.Y., 1956.
Afr 630.56.5	Pidoux, Edmond. L'Afrique à l'âge ingrat. Neuchâtel, 1956.
Afr 630.56.10	Spinola, Francisco Elias de Tejada. Sociologia del Africa negra. Madrid, 1956.
Afr 630.58	Paraf, Pierre. L'ascension des peuples noirs. Paris, 1958.
Afr 630.58.5	Grobler, Jan H. Africa's destiny. 2. ed. Johannesburg, 1958.
Afr 630.58.10	Traore, Bakary. Le théâtre négro-africain. Paris, 1958.
Afr 630.59	Murdock, George. Africa. N.Y., 1959.
Afr 630.59.5	Stephens, Richard W. Population pressures in Africa, south of the Sahara. Washington, 1958.
Afr 630.60	Lomax, Louis. The reluctant African. 1st ed. N.Y., 1960.
Afr 630.60.5	Diderot, Toussaint. A la recherche de la personnalité négro-africaine. Monte-Carlo, 1960.
Afr 630.61	Isaacs, H.R. Emergent Americans. N.Y., 1961.
Afr 630.62	Pieto, I. Causas de los conflictos en el Africa del sur. Berriz, 1962.
Afr 630.62.5	Melady, T.P. The white man's future in black Africa. N.Y., 1962.
Afr 630.62.10	Seminar on Racialism, Kampala, Uganda. Report. Leiden, 1962.
Afr 630.63	Bryant, A.T. Bantu origins. Cape Town, 1963.
Afr 630.63.5	Borer, M.C. Africa. London, 1963.
Afr 630.65	Gibbs, J.L. Peoples of Africa. N.Y., 1965.
Afr 630.65.5	West, Richard. The white tribes of Africa. London, 1965.
Afr 630.65.10	De Negro-Afrikaanse mens en zijn cultuur. Brugge, 1965.
Afr 630.66	Millin, Sarah Gertrude. White Africans are also people. Cape Town, 1966.
Afr 630.66.5	Belchior, Manual. Fundamentos para uma politica multicultural em Africa. Lisboa, 1966.
Afr 630.66.10	Gayre, George Robert. Ethnological elements of Africa. Edinburgh, 1966.
Afr 630.66.15	Andor, L. Aptitudes and abilities of the black man in sub-Saharan Africa, 1784-1963. Johannesburg, 1966.
Afr 630.69	Man in Africa. London, 1969.
Afr 630.69.5	Santos, Eduardo dos. Elementos de etnologia africana. Lisboa, 1969.
Afr 630.69.10	Bettany, George Thomas. The dark peoples of the land of sunshine. Miami, Fla., 1969.

Afr 632 Africa in general - Races - Sociological aspects

Afr 632.9	Preville, A. de. Les sociétés africaines. Paris, 1894.
Afr 632.10	Frobenius, L.V. Ursprung der Kultur. Berlin, 1898.
Afr 632.11F	Schachtgabel, A. Die Siedelungsverhältnisse der Bantu-Niger. Leiden, 1911.
Afr 632.15	Hartland, Sidney E. The evolution of kinship. Oxford, 1922.
Afr 632.17	Foucart, George. Questionnaire préliminaire d'ethnologie africaine. Le Caire, 1919.
Afr 632.18	Spannaus, Gunther. Züge aus der politischen Organisation afrikanischer Staaten und Völker. Leipzig, 1929.
Afr 632.20	Malinowski, B. The dynamics of culture change. New Haven, 1945.
Afr 632.20.5	Malinowski, B. The dynamics of culture change. New Haven, 1961.
Afr 632.25	Akademiia Nauk SSSR. Institut Narodov Azii. Rasovaia diskriminatsiia v stranakh Afriki. Moscow, 1960.
Afr 632.30	International African Seminar. Social change in modern Africa. London, 1961.
Afr 632.35	Mitchell, J.C. Tribalism and the plural society. London, 1960.
Afr 632.40	Mair, Lucy Philip. Studies in applied anthropology. London, 1961.
Afr 632.45	Deutsche Arbeitsfront. Sozialpolitik im afrikanischen Kolonialraum. Berlin, 1938.
Afr 632.48	Stevenson, Robert F. Population and political systems in tropical Africa. N.Y., 1968.

Afr 632   Africa in general - Races - Sociological aspects - cont.
Afr 632.50   Carlston, Kenneth Smith. Social theory and African tribal organization. Urbana, 1968.
Afr 632.52   Pluralism in Africa. Berkeley, 1969.
Afr 632.54   N'Diaye, Jean Pierre. Elites africaines et culture occidentale, assimilation ou resistance? Paris, 1969.

Afr 635   Africa in general - Races - Other special aspects
Afr 635.1A   Dowd, J. The Negro races, a sociological study. N.Y., 1907. 2v.
Afr 635.1B   Dowd, J. The Negro races, a sociological study. N.Y., 1907.
Afr 635.2   Ellis, A.B. The Ewe-speaking peoples of the Slave Coast of West Africa. London, 1890.
Afr 635.4   Chaneel, A. de. Cham et Zaphet. 2e éd. Paris, 186-.
Afr 635.4.5   Sergi, Giuseppe. Africa, antropologia della stirpe camitica. Torino, 1897.
Afr 635.5F   Tessmann, Günter. Die Pangew. Berlin, 1913-
Afr 635.6   Clemente d'Assis, F. Estudos indianos e africanos. Lisboa, 1889.
Afr 635.7F   Heydrich, Martin. Afrikanische Ornamentik. Inaug. Diss. Leiden, 1914.
Afr 635.7.5   Christol, Frederic. L'art dans l'Afrique australe. Paris, 1911.
Afr 635.7.6   Clouzot, Henri. L'art nègre et l'art océanien. Paris, 1919.
Afr 635.7.10   Markov, Vlats. Iskusstvo negrov. Sankt Peterburg, 1919.
Afr 635.7.15F   Stow, G. William. Rock-paintings in South Africa. London, 1930.
Afr 635.7.20   Sadler, M.E. Arts of West Africa, excluding music. London, 1935.
Afr 635.20   Kroll, Hubert. Die Haustiere der Bantu. Inaug. Diss. Berlin, 1929.
Afr 635.30.15   Seligman, C.G. Egypt and Negro Africa. London, 1934.
Afr 635.35   Jackson, John G. Ethiopia and the origin of civilization. N.Y., 1939.
Afr 635.45   Gluckman, Max. Custom and conflict in Africa. Glencoe, 1955.
Afr 635.50   King-Hall, Stephen. Letters from Africa. London, 1957.
Afr 635.55   Maistriaux, Robert. L'intélligence noire et son destin. Bruxelles, 1957.
Afr 635.60   Muthesius, A. Die Afrikanerin. Düsseldorf, 1959.
Afr 635.61   Smirnova, Raisà M. Polozhenre zhenshchin v stranakh Afriki. Moskva, 1967.
Afr 635.62   Paulme, D. Femmes d'Afrique noire. Paris, 1960.
Afr 635.62.5   Paulme, D. Women of tropical Africa. Berkeley, 1963.
Afr 635.62.10   Plisnier-Ladame, F. La condition de l'Africaine en Afrique noire. Bruxelles, 1961.
Afr 635.65   Hollingworth, L.W. The Asians of East Africa. London, 1960.
Afr 635.65.5   Tandberg, Olof G. Brun mans Africa. Stockholm, 1968.
Afr 635.70   Beart, Charles. Recherche des éléments d'une sociologie des peuples africains. Paris, 1960.
Afr 635.75F   C.S.A. Meeting of Specialists on the Basic Psychology of African and Madagascan Populations, Tannarvio, Madagascar, 1959. Recommendations and reports. London, 1959.
Afr 635.80   Mphahlele, Ezekiel. The African image. London, 1962.
Afr 635.85   Turnbull, Colin. The lonely African. N.Y., 1962.
Afr 635.86   Marie André du Sacre Coeur, Sister. La femme noire en Afrique occidentale. Paris, 1939.
Afr 635.87   Barbe, R. Les classes sociales en Afrique noire. Paris, 1964.
Afr 635.88   Haselberger, Herta. Bautraditionen der westafrikanischen Negerkulturen. Wien, 1964.
Afr 635.89   Fani-Kazode, Remi. Blackism. Lagos, 1965.
Afr 635.90   Boute, Joseph. La démographie de la branche indo-pakistanaise d'Afrique. Louvain, 1965.
Afr 635.92   Doherty, Mary A. The role of the African woman, a report. London, 1962.
Afr 635.94   Szyfelbejn-Sokolewicz, Zofia. Tradycyjne zajecia gospodarcze ludow Afryki. Warszawa, 1963.
Afr 635.95   Refugee problems in Africa. Uppsala, 1967.
Afr 635.98   Klineberg, Otto. Nationalism and tribalism among African students. Paris, 1969.

Afr 640   Africa in general - Races - Pygmies
Afr 640.01   Pamphlet box. Dwarfs.
Afr 640.5   Quatrefages de Bréau, Armand de. Les Pygmées. Paris, 1887.
Afr 640.5.5   Quatrefrages de Bréau, Armand de. The Pygmies. Paris, 1895.
Afr 640.5.35   Trilled, H. Le Pygmées de la forêt équatoriale. Paris, 1932.
Afr 640.6   Haliburton, R.G. Dwarfs of Mount Atlas. London, 1891.
Afr 640.6.3   Haliburton, R.G. Holy land of Punt, racial dwarfs in the Atlas and the Pyrenees. London, 1893.
Afr 640.6.5   Haliburton, R.G. How a race of Pigmies was found. Toronto, 1897.
Afr 640.7   Walendowska-Zapedowska, Barbara. Problem pigmejow afrykanskich w etnografii europejskiej XIX-XX w. Poznan, 1965.

Afr 650   Africa in general - Local in general
Afr 650.2F   C.S.A. Meeting of Specialists on Urbanisation and Its Social Aspects Abidjan, Ivory Coast, 1961. Reports and recommendations. London, 1961.
Afr 650.3   Denis, Jacques. Le phénomène urbain en Afrique Centrale. Namur, 1958.
Afr 650.4   Edinburgh. University. African urbanization. London, 1965.
Afr 650.5   Denis, Jacques. Le phénomène urbain en Afrique Centrale. Bruxelles, 1958.
Afr 650.6   Oram, Nigel. Towns in Africa. London, 1965.
Afr 650.8   Hanna, William John. Urban dynamics in Black Africa. Washington, 1969.

Afr 655 - 660   Africa in general - Local divisions - The North (i.e. Egypt plus the Barbary States) (By date)
Afr 657.88   Association for Promoting the Discovery of the Interior Parts of Africa. Records of the African Association, 1788-1831. London, 1964.
Afr 657.90F   Association for Promoting the Discovery of the Interior Parts of Africa. Proceedings. London, 1790.
Afr 657.90.5   Association for Promoting the Discovery of the Interior Parts of Africa. Proceedings of the Association for Promoting the Discovery of the Interior Parts of Africa. London, 1810. 2v.

Afr 655 - 660   Africa in general - Local divisions - The North (i.e. Egypt plus the Barbary States) (By date) - cont.
Afr 658.21   Walckenaer, C.A. Recherches géographiques sur l'intérieur de l'Afrique. Paris, 1821.
Afr 658.39   Macbrair, R.M. Sketches of a missionary's travels in Egypt, Syria, Western Africa. London, 1839.
Afr 658.61   Guenther, Konrad. Gerhard Rohlfs Lebensbild eines Afrikaforschers. Freiburg, 1912.
Afr 658.74   Ludwig, Salvator. Yacht-Reise in den Syrten, 1873. Prag, 1874.
Afr 658.79   Nachtigal, S. Sahara und Sudan. Berlin, 1879-89.
Afr 659.05   Loyson, H. To Jerusalem through lands of Islam. Chicago, 1905.
Afr 659.11   Douel, Martial. Au pays de Salammbo. Paris, 1911.
Afr 659.13   Bernard, A. L'Afrique du nord. Paris, 1913.
Afr 659.24F   North Africa, Tripoli, Tunis. N.Y., 1924.
Afr 659.42   Jackson, Mabel V. European powers and south-east Africa. London, 1942.
Afr 659.42.2   Haight, Mabel V. Jackson. European powers and south-east Africa. 2nd ed. N.Y., 1967.
Afr 659.45   Dumaine, J. D'Ulysse à Eisenhower. Alger, 1945.
Afr 659.48A   Alal al Fasi. The independence movements in Arab North Africa. Washington, 1954.
Afr 659.48B   Alal al Fasi. The independence movements in Arab North Africa. Washington, 1954.
Afr 659.49A   Welch, Galbraith. North African prelude. N.Y., 1949.
Afr 659.49B   Welch, Galbraith. North African prelude. N.Y., 1949.
Afr 659.55   Albertini, Eugène. L'Afrique du Nord française dans l'histoire. Lyon, 1955.
Afr 659.64   Winid, Bogdan. Geografia gospodarcza Afryki, Afryka potnocna. Warszawa, 1964.
Afr 659.65   Toynbee, Arnold Joseph. Between Niger and Nile. London, 1965.
Afr 659.66   Julien, Charles André. Histoire de l'Afrique blanche. Paris, 1966.
Afr 659.66.7   Zwischen Mittelmeer und Tschadsee: Reisen deutscher Forscher des 19. 2. Aufl. Berlin, 1967.
Afr 659.66.10   Cavallaro, Emanuele. Lo e l'Africa. Palermo, 1966.
Afr 659.67   Landa, Robert G. U arabov Afriki. Moskva, 1967.
Afr 659.67.5   Plum, Werner. Sozialer Wandel im Maghreb i Voraussetzungen und Erfahrungen der genossenschaftlichen Entwicklung. Hannover, 1967.
Afr 659.68   Danasuri, Jamal A.A. Studies in the geography of the Arab world in Africa. Cairo, 1968.

Afr 674 - 680   Africa in general - Local divisions - The West coast (By date)
Afr 674.93F   Eannes de Azurara, G. Chronica do descobrimento e conquista de Guiné. Paris, 1841.
Afr 674.93.2   Eannes de Azurara, G. Chronica de descobrimento e conquista de Guiné. Paris, 1841.
Afr 674.93.9   Eannes de Azurara, G. Conquests and discoveries of Henry the Navigator. London, 1906.
Afr 674.93.12   Eannes de Azurara, G. Cronica dos feitos de Guiné. Lisboa, 1942.
Htn   Afr 674.93.14*   Eannes de Azurara, G. Cronica do descobrimento da Guiné. Porto, 1937. 2v.
Afr 674.93.25   Leite, D. A cerca da cronica dos feitos de Guiné. Lisboa, 1941.
Afr 674.93.30   Eannes de Azurara, G. Vida e obras de Gomes Eanes de Zurara. Lisboa, 1949. 2v.
Afr 675.07.5   Fernandes, V. Description de la côte d'Afrique de Ceuta au Sénégal...1506-1507. Paris, 1938.
Afr 675.07.10F   Fernandes, V. O manuscrito Valentim Fernandes. Lisboa, 1940.
Afr 676.63.20   Feng, C. Glimpses of West Africa. Peking, 1963.
Afr 676.66   Villault, N. Relation des côtes d'Afrique, appellées Guinée. Paris, 1669.
Afr 676.66.5   Villault, N. Relation des côtes d'Afrique, appellées Guinée. Photocopy. Paris, 1669.
Afr 677.28   Labot, J.B. Nouvelles relations de l'Afrique occidentale. Paris, 1728. 5v.
Htn   Afr 677.71*   Benezet, Anthony. Some historical account of Guinea. Philadelphia, 1771. 2 pam.
Htn   Afr 677.71.5*   Benezet, Anthony. Some historical account of Guinea. London, 1772.
Afr 677.71.10   Benezet, Anthony. Some historical account of Guinea: its situation. 2nd ed. London, 1968.
Afr 678.26   Hulbert, C. African fragments. Shrewsbury, 1826.
Afr 678.30   Crow, Hugh. Memoirs of the late Captain Hugh Crow. London, 1830.
Afr 678.33   The western coast of Africa. Philadelphia, 1833.
Afr 678.33.5   Leonard, Peter. Records of a voyage to the western coast of Africa in his Majesty's ship Dryad. Edinburgh, 1833.
Afr 678.34.2   Holman, James. Travels in Madeira. 2d ed. London, 1840.
Afr 678.40.2   Alexander, J.E. Excursions in western Africa. 2d ed. London, 1840. 2v.
Afr 678.43.5   Bridge, Horatio. Journal of an African cruiser. London, 1968.
Afr 678.44   Perry, M.C. Colonial settlements, western coast of Africa. Washington, 1844.
Htn   Afr 678.45*   Bridge, H. Journal of an African cruiser. N.Y., 1845. 2 pam.
Htn   Afr 678.45.3*   Bridge, H. Journal of an African cruiser. London, 1845.
Htn   Afr 678.45.5*   Bridge, H. Journal of an African cruiser. London, 1848.
Afr 678.46   Bouet-Willaumez, Edouard, Comte. Des nautiques des côtes de l'Afrique. Paris, 1846.
Afr 678.49   Hecquard, Hyacinthe. Voyage sur la côte et dans l'intérieur de l'Afrique occidentale. Paris, 1853.
Afr 678.49.5   Hecquard, Hyacinthe. Reise an die Küste und in das Innere von West-Africa. Leipzig, 1854.
Afr 678.51   Smith, J. Trade and travels in the Gulph of Guinea. London, 1851.
Afr 678.53   Carnes, J.A. Journal of a voyage from Boston to the west coast of Africa. London, 1853.
Afr 678.56A   Wilson, T.L. Western Africa. N.Y., 1856.
Afr 678.56B   Wilson, T.L. Western Africa. N.Y., 1856.
Afr 678.60   Thomas, C.W. Adventures...on west coast of Africa. N.Y., 1860.
Afr 678.61   Travassos Valdez, Franciso. Six years of a traveller's life in western Africa. London, 1861. 2v.
Afr 678.61.3   Hutchinson, T.J. Ten years wanderings among the Ethiopians. London, 1861.
Afr 678.61.4   Hutchinson, T.J. Ten years' wanderings among the Ethiopians. London, 1967.
Afr 678.61.5   Travassos Valder, Francisco. Africa occidental. Lisboa, 1864.

Afr 674 - 680 Africa in general - Local divisions - The West coast (By date) - cont.

Afr 678.61.6 Travassos Valdez, Francisco. Africa occidental. Lisboa, 1864.
Afr 678.62 Hewett, J.F.N. European settlements on west coast of Africa. London, 1862.
Afr 678.62.5 Hewett, J.F.N. European settlements on the west coast of Africa. N.Y., 1969.
Afr 678.63 Burton, R.F. Wanderings in West Africa from Liverpool. London, 1863.
Afr 678.66 Castilho, A.M. de. Descripção...costa occidental de Africa. v.1-2. Lisboa, 1866.
Afr 678.69 Cox, John George. Cox and the Juju Coast. St. Helier, 1968.
Afr 678.74 Oberlaender, R. Westafrika von Senegal bis Benquela. Leipzig, 1874.
Afr 678.76 Laffitte, J. Le pays des Nègres et la Côte des esclaves. Tours, 1876.
Afr 678.77 Whitford, J.F.R.G.S. Trading life in Western and Central Africa. Liverpool, 1877.
Afr 678.77.2 Whitford, J.F.R.G.S. Trading life in Western and Central Africa. 2nd ed. London, 1967.
Afr 678.78 Gravier, G. Recherches sur les navigations européennes. Paris, 1878.
Afr 678.79 Lenz, O. Skizzen aus Westafrika. Berlin, 1879.
Afr 678.80 Buchholz, R. Reisen in West Afrika. Leipzig, 1880.
Afr 678.81 Canale, M.G. Memoria. Genova, 1881.
Afr 678.85F Roskoschny, H. Europas Kolonien, West Afrika vom Senegal zum Kamerun. 3. Aufl. Leipzig, n.d.
Afr 678.86 Donacuige. Aventuras de un piloto en el Golfo de Guinea. Madrid, 1886.
Afr 678.89 Crouch, A.P. Glimpses of Feverland. London, 1889.
Afr 678.95 Cadamosto, A. de. Voyages à la côte occidentale d'Afrique. Paris, 1895.
Afr 678.97 Kingsley, M.H. Travels in West Africa. London, 1897.
Afr 678.97.5 Kingsley, M.H. Travels in West Africa. London, 1900.
Afr 678.97.10 Kingsley, M.H. Travels in West Africa. 3d ed. N.Y., 1965.
Afr 679.00 Henning, G. Samuel Braun. Basel, 1900.
Afr 679.00.5 Paris. Exposition Universelle de 1900. Afrique occidentale. Paris, 1900.
Afr 679.00.10 Barrow, Alfred Henry. Fifty years in Western Africa. London, 1900.
Afr 679.08 Milligan, R.H. Jungle folk of Africa. N.Y., 1908.
Afr 679.09 Guggisberg, Decima (Moore). We two in West Africa. London, 1909.
Afr 679.10 Lang, John. The land of the golden trade, West Africa. N.Y., 1969.
Afr 679.12 Nassau, Robert Hamill. In an elephant corral, and other tales of West African experiences. N.Y., 1969.
Afr 679.13.5 Grimm, Hans. Afrikafahrt West. Frankfurt, 1913.
Afr 679.17 Kirsch, M. Der Fremdenlegionär. N.Y., 1917.
Afr 679.20 Psichari, Ernest. Les voix qui crient dans le désert. Paris, 1920.
Afr 679.27 Larsen, K. Krøniker fra Guines. Hellerup, 1927.
Afr 679.27.6 Solanke, Ladipo. United West Africa, or Africa, at the bar of the family of nations. London, 1969.
Afr 679.29 Mills, D.R.M. The golden land. London, 1929.
Afr 679.29.5F Singer, Caroline. White Africans and black. N.Y., 1929.
Afr 679.34 Rossi, V.G. Tropici Senegal all Angola. Milano, 1934.
Afr 679.36 Jones, G.H. The earth goddess. London, 1936.
Afr 679.40 Demaison, A. The new Noah' s ark. N.Y., 1940.
Afr 679.40.5 Meek, Charles K. Europe and West Africa, some problems and adjustments. London, 1940.
Afr 679.40.10 Ca da Mosto, A. Viagens. Lisboa, 194-.
Afr 679.46 Blanchod, F.G. La randonnée africaine. Lausanne, 1946.
Afr 679.47 Psichari, Ernest. Terres de soleil, et de sommeil. Paris, 1947.
Afr 679.51 Pedler, F.J. West Africa. London, 1951.
Afr 679.51.5 Howard, C. West African explorers. London, 1951.
Afr 679.52 Agyeman, N.Y.T.D. West Africa on the march. N.Y., 1952.
Afr 679.53 Davidson, Basil. The new West Africa. London, 1953.
Afr 679.54 Huxley, E.G. Four Guineas. London, 1954.
Afr 679.54.5 Bowen, E.S. Return to laughter. N.Y., 1954.
Afr 679.54.10 Green, Lawrence G. Under a sky like a flame. 2d ed. Cape Town, 1958.
Afr 679.55.5 Fage, J.D. An introduction to the history of West Africa. 3rd ed. Cambridge, Eng., 1962.
Afr 679.55.6 Fage, J.D. A history of West Africa. 4th ed. Cambridge, Eng., 1969.
Afr 679.58 Mosley, Nicholas. African switchback. London, 1958.
Afr 679.58.5 Howe, R.W. Black star rising. London, 1958.
Afr 679.58.10 Richard Molard, Jacques. Problèmes humains en Afrique occidentale. 2. éd. Paris, 1958.
Afr 679.58.15 Santarem, Manuel Francisco de B. Memoria sobre a prioridade dos descobrimentos. Lisboa, 1958.
Afr 679.61 Linkhovoin, L.L. Po stranam Afriki. Ulan-Ude, 1961.
Afr 679.61.5 Niane, D.T. Histoire de l'Afrique occidentale. Paris, 1961.
Afr 679.61.10 Halpern, Jan. Na potudnie od Sahary. Warsawa, 1961.
Afr 679.62 Jahn, Janheinz. Through African doors. N.Y., 1962.
Afr 679.63 Church, Ronald J.H. Environment and policies in West Africa. Princeton, 1963.
Afr 679.63.5 Hargreaves, J.D. Prelude to the partition of West Africa. London, 1963.
Afr 679.63.10 Lawrence, A.W. Trade castles and forts of West Africa. London, 1963.
Afr 679.63.15 Panikkar, K.M. The serpent and the crescent. London, 1963.
Afr 679.63.20 Gardiner, Robert Kweku Atta. The development of social administration. 2nd ed. London, 1963.
Afr 679.63.25 Feng, Chi'h-Tan. Glimpses of West Africa. Peking, 1963.
Afr 679.63.32 Bennett, Nicholas. Zigzag to Timbuktu. N.Y., 1966.
Afr 679.64 Post, K.W.J. The new states of West Africa. Harmondsworth, 1964.
Afr 679.64.2 Post, K.W.J. The new states of West Africa. Harmondsworth, 1968.
Afr 679.64.5 Latham, Norah. The heritage of West Africa. London, 1964.
Afr 679.65 Simms, R.P. Urbanization in West Africa. Evanston, 1965.
Afr 679.65.5A California. University. University at Los Angeles. African Studies Center. Urbanization and migration in West Africa. Berkeley, 1965.
Afr 679.65.5B California. University. University at Los Angeles. African Studies Center. Urbanization and migration in West Africa. Berkeley, 1965.
Afr 679.65.10 Little, Kenneth Lindsay. West African urbanization. Cambridge, Eng., 1965.
Afr 679.65.15 Lewis, William A. Politics in West Africa. London, 1965.

Afr 674 - 680 Africa in general - Local divisions - The West coast (By date) - cont.

Afr 679.65.20 Agbodeka, F. The rise of the nation states. London, 1965.
Afr 679.65.25 Ajayi, J.F. Ade. A thousand years of West African history. London, 1965.
Afr 679.65.30 Davidson, Basil. The growth of African civilisation, West Africa, 1000-1800. London, 1965.
Afr 679.65.30.1 Davidson, Basil. The growth of African civilisation. London, 1967.
Afr 679.65.30.2 Davidson, Basil. A history of West Africa to the nineteenth century. Garden City, N.Y., 1966. 2v.
VAfr 679.65.35 Fenrych, Wiktor. Zapiski z Afriyki Zachodniej. Szczecin, 1965.
Afr 679.65.40 Coquery, Catherine. La découverte de l'Afrique. Paris, 1965.
Afr 679.66 Hallett, Robin. People and progress in West Africa. Oxford, 1966.
Afr 679.66.5 Conton, William F. West Africa in history. London, 1966.
Afr 679.66.10 Bochen, Albert Adu. Topics inWest African history. London, 1966.
Afr 679.66.15 Kubbel', Lev E. Strana zolota. Moskva, 1966.
Afr 679.66.20 Toulat, Jean. Français d'aujourd'hui en Afrique noire. Paris, 1966.
VAfr 679.66.25 Cissoko, Sébéné M. Histoire de l'Afrique occidentale. v.1- Paris, 1966-
Afr 679.66.30 Halpern, Jan. Studia nad gospodarką przedkapitalistyczna no Afryee Gachoancej wieku XIX i XX. Wyd.1. Warszawa, 1966.
Afr 679.66.35 A history of West Africa: A.D. 1,000 to to the present day. 2. ed. Ibadan, 1969.
Afr 679.67 Forde, Cyril Daryll. West African kingdom in the nineteenth century. London, 1967.
Afr 679.67.5 Seck, Assane. L'Afrique occidentale. Paris, 1967.
Afr 679.67.10 Rosenthal, Ricky. The splendor that was Africa. Dobbs Ferry, 1967.
Afr 679.67.15 Grohs, Gerhard. Stufen afrikanischer Emanzipation. Stuttgart, 1967.
Afr 679.67.20 International Conference on South West Africa, Oxford, 1966. South West Africa: travesty of trust. London, 1967.
Afr 679.67.25 Davies, Oliver. West Africa before the Europeans: archaeology and prehistory. London, 1967.
Afr 679.67.30 Price, Joseph Henry. Political institutions of West Africa. London, 1967.
Afr 679.67.35 Croce-Spinelli, Michel. Les Enfants de Poto-Poto. Paris, 1967.
Afr 679.67.40 Deschamps, Hubert Jules. L'Europe découvre l'Afrique. Paris, 1967.
Afr 679.68 July, Robert William. The origins of modern African thought. London, 1968.
Afr 679.68.5 Osqe, T.A. A short history of West Africa. London, 1968.
Afr 679.68.10 Crowder, Michael. West Africa under colonial rule. London, 1968.
Afr 679.68.15 Iordanskii, Vladimir B. Opnennye ieroglify. Moskva, 1968.
Afr 679.68.20 Plessz, Nicolas G. Problems and prospects of economic integration in West Africa. Montreal, 1968.
Afr 679.68.25 Olowokure, Olvsanya. An outline of West African history. Ilesha, 1968.
Afr 679.69 Morgan, William Basil. West Africa. London, 1969.
Afr 679.69.5 Małowist, Marian. Europa a Afryka Zachodnia w dobie wezesnej ekspansji kolonialnej. Wyd. 1. Warszawa, 1969.

Afr 695 - 700 Africa in general - Local divisions - The East coast (By date)

Afr 695.12 Roscher, A. Ptolemaeus und die Handelsstrassen in Central-Africa. Gotha, 1857.
Afr 698.19 Prior, James. Voyage along the eastern coast of Africa. London, 1819.
Afr 698.38 Brun, C. De redding des bemanning van het...nijverheid. Rotterdam, 1838.
Afr 698.50 Guillain, Charles. Exploration de la côte orientale d'Afrique. Paris, 1850.
Afr 698.56 Guillain, Charles. Documents sur l'histoire, la géographie et la commerce de l'Afrique orientale. Paris, 1856. 4v.
Afr 698.56PF Guillain, Charles. Documents sur l'histoire, la géographie et la commerce de l'Afrique orientale. Atlas. Paris, 1856. 4v.
Afr 698.58 Krapf, J.L. Reisen in Ostafrika. Stuttgart, 1964.
Afr 698.60 Krapf, J.L. Travels, researches...eastern Africa. Boston, 1860.
Afr 698.60.2 Krapf, J.L. Travels, researches...eastern Africa. Boston, 1860.
Afr 698.60.3 Krapf, Ludwig. Travels, researches...Eastern Africa. 2. ed. London, 1968.
Afr 698.64 Grant, J.A. A walk across Africa. Edinburgh, 1864.
NEDL Afr 698.66 Horner. Voyage à la côte orientale, 1866. Paris, 1872.
Afr 698.68 Broomfield, S.S. Kachalola, or The early life and adventures of Sidney Spencer Broomfield. London, 1930.
Afr 698.69 Devereux, William Cope. A cruise in the "Gorgon". Reprint of 1869 1. ed. London, 1968.
Afr 698.83 Devic, L. Marcel. Le pays des Zendjs. Paris, 1883.
Afr 698.86 Keller, Konrad. Reisebilder aus Ost-Afrika. Leipzig, 1887.
Afr 698.88 Durand, E. Une exploration française au Zambèze. Paris, 1888.
Afr 699.05 Schillings, C.G. Flashlights in the jungle. N.Y., 1905.
Afr 699.07 Hall, Mary. A woman's trek from the Cape to Cairo. London, 1907.
Afr 699.08 Kirkland, Caroline. Some African highways, journey of two American women to Uganda and the Transvaal. London, 1908.
Htn Afr 699.08.4* Churchill, Winston S. My African journey. London, 1908.
Afr 699.08.4.5 Churchill, Winston S. My African journey. N.Y., 1909.
Afr 699.12 Melland, F.H. Through the heart of Africa. London, 1912.
Afr 699.12.5 Congrés de l'Afrique Orientale, Paris, 1911. Congrés de l'Afrique Orientale. Paris, 1912.
Afr 699.13 Elena, Duchess of Aosta. Viaggi in Africa. Milano, 1913.
Afr 699.28 Jaelson, F.S. Eastern Africa to-day. London, 1928.
Afr 699.28.5 Edward, Duke of Windsor. Sport and travel in East Africa, an account of two visits, 1928 and 1930. N.Y., 1935.
Afr 699.31.3 Waugh, E. They were still dancing. N.Y., 1952.
Afr 699.31.6 Waugh, E. Remote people. London, 1934.
Afr 699.37F Peiner, Werner. Das Gesicht Ostafrikas. Frankfurt, 1937.
Afr 699.40 Courtney, R. A greenhorn in Africa. London, 1940.
Afr 699.53 Fontaine, Pierre. Alger-Tunis-Rabat. Paris, 1953.
Afr 699.54 Hunter, J.A. Tales of the African frontier. 1st ed. N.Y., 1954.
Afr 699.54.5 Reusch, Richard. History of East Africa. Stuttgart, 1954.

Afr 695 - 700 Africa in general - Local divisions - The East coast (By date) - cont.

Afr 699.57A Marsh, Zoe. An introduction to the history of East Africa. Cambridge, Eng., 1957.
Afr 699.57B Marsh, Zoe. An introduction to the history of East Africa. Cambridge, Eng., 1957.
Afr 699.57.2 Marsh, Zoe. An introduction to the history of East Africa. 2. ed. Cambridge, Eng., 1961.
Afr 699.57.3 Marsh, Zoe. An introduction to the history of East Africa. 3. ed. Cambridge, Eng., 1965.
Afr 699.59 Randles, W.G. L'image du sud-est Africain dans la littérature. Lisboa, 1959.
Afr 699.61 Cornet, Jacques. Pharaons d'hier et Fellahs d'aujourd'hui. Lyon, 1961.
Afr 699.62 Miller, Stefan. Vom Nilzum Sambesi. 1. Aufl. Berlin, 1962.
Afr 699.65 Hollingsworth, Lawrence H. A short history of the east coast of Africa. 2nd ed. London, 1965.
Afr 699.67 Pollard, John. The long safari. London, 1967.
Afr 699.68 Ogot, Bethwell Allen. Zamani; a survey of East African history. Nairobi, 1968.
Afr 699.68.5 Laman Trip-de Beaufort, Henriette. Ruimte en zonlicht. Den Haag, 1968.
Afr 699.68.10 Milley, Jacques. L'Afrique orientale, terre des safaris. Paris, 1968.
Afr 699.69 Richards, Audrey. The multicultural states of East Africa. Montreal, 1969.

Afr 710 Africa in general - Local divisions - Tropical Africa

Afr 710.10 Campbell, D. In the heart of Bantuland. London, 1922.
Afr 710.15 Deschamps, H.J. L'éveil politique africain. 1 ed. Paris, 1952.
Afr 710.16 Morán Lopez, Fernando. El nuevo reino. Madrid, 1967.
Afr 710.20 Davidson, B. The African awakening. London, 1955.
Afr 710.20.2 Egerton, F. Clement C. Angola without prejudice. Lisbon, 1955.
Afr 710.22 Gunther, John. Meet central Africa. London, 1959.
Afr 710.23 Hallet, Jean Pierre. Congo kitabu. N.Y., 1966.
Afr 710.25 Oldham, J.H. New hope in Africa. London, 1955.
Afr 710.30 London. University. School of Oriental and African Studies. History and archaeology in Africa. London, 1955.
Afr 710.32 International African Seminar. The historian in tropical Africa. London, 1964.
Afr 710.32.6A International African Seminar, 6th, Ibadan, Nigeria, 1964. The new elites of tropical Africa. London, 1966.
Afr 710.32.6B International African Seminar, 6th, Ibadan, Nigeria, 1964. The new elites of tropical Africa. London, 1966.
Afr 710.32.10 African Population Conference, 1st, University of Ibadan, 1966. The population of tropical Africa; conference held Jan. 3-7, 1966. N.Y., 1968.
Afr 710.35 Booth, Newall S. This is Africa south of the Sahara. N.Y., 1959.
Afr 710.40 Kittler, Glenn D. Equatorial Africa. N.Y., 1959.
Afr 710.45 Soret, Marcel. Les Kongo nord-occidentaux. Paris, 1959.
Afr 710.50 Kimble, George. Tropical Africa. N.Y., 1960. 2v.
Afr 710.55 Belandier, Georges. Afrique ambigue. Paris, 1957.
Afr 710.55.5 Balandier, Georges. Afrique ambigue. Paris, 1962.
Afr 710.55.6 Balandier, Georges. Ambiguous Africa, cultures in collision. London, 1966.
Afr 710.60 Rotborg, Robert Irwin. A political history of tropical Africa. N.Y., 1965.
Afr 710.63 Hunter, Guy. The best of both worlds? A challenge on development policies in Africa. London, 1967.
Afr 710.65 Vansina, Jan. Les anciens royaumes de la savane. Leopoldville, 1965.
Afr 710.68 Barasiola, Carlo. Sulle orme di Roma. Milano, 1934.
Afr 710.70 Vansina, Jan. Kingdom of the savanna. Madison, 1966.
Afr 710.72 Gann, Lewis H. Burden of empire. N.Y., 1967.
Afr 710.74 Aspects of Central African history. London, 1968.
Afr 710.76 South African Broadcasting Corporation. Ons Buurstate op die Afrikaanse vasteland. Johannesburg, 1959.

Afr 715 Africa in general - Local divisions - Journeys across the interior - General works

Afr 715.2 Schweinfurth, G. Im Herzen von Afrika. Leipzig, 1874. 2v.
Afr 715.3 Schweinfurth, G. The heart of Africa. London, 1873. 2v.
Afr 715.3.3 Schweinfurth, G. The heart of Africa. N.Y., 1874. 2v.
Afr 715.3.25 Schweinfurth, G. Afrikanisches Skizzenbuch. Berlin, 1925.
Afr 715.3.30 Schweinfurth, G. Georg Schweinfurth. Stuttgart, 1954.
Afr 715.5 Drummond, Henry. Tropical Africa. N.Y., 1888.
Afr 715.6 Maistre, C. A travers l'Afrique centrale. Paris, 1895.
Afr 715.7 Laveleye, E. de. L'Afrique centrale. Paris, 1878.
Afr 715.9 Trivier, E. Mon voyage au continent noir, "La Gironde" en Afrique. Paris, 1891.
Afr 715.10 Wissenschaftliche Ergebnisse der Deutschen Zentral-Afrika-Expedition. Leipzig. 5v.
Afr 715.11 Drummond, Henry. Tropical Africa. 3rd ed. London, 1889.
Afr 715.12 Cooley, William Desborough. Inner Africa laid open. N.Y., 1969.
Afr 715.15 Haardt, G.M. The black journey across central Africa. N.Y., 1927.
Afr 715.15.5 Haardt, G.M. La croisière noire, expédition citroen central-Afrique. Paris, 1927.
Afr 715.20 Flaudrau, G.C. Then I saw the Congo. N.Y., 1929.
Afr 715.22 Balfour, P. Lords of the equator, an African journey. London, 1937.
Afr 715.25A Wilson, Godfrey. The analysis of social change, based on observations in central Africa. Cambridge, Eng., 1945.
Afr 715.25B Wilson, Godfrey. The analysis of social change, based on observations in central Africa. Cambridge, Eng., 1945.
Afr 715.26 Hallett, Robin. The penetration of Africa. N.Y., 1965.
Afr 715.28 Pares, Eugene. Les explorateurs français en Afrique. Limoges, 1881.
Afr 715.30 Heinrich Barth. Ein Forscher in Afrika. Eine Sammlung von Beiträgen zum 100. Todestag am 25. Nov. 1965. Wiesbaden, 1967.

Afr 718 Africa in general - Local divisions - Journeys across the interior - East to West

Afr 718.1.25 Foran, W.R. African odyssey, the life of Verney Lovett Cameron. London, 1937.
Afr 718.2A Stanley, H.M. Through the dark continent. N.Y., 1878.
Afr 718.2B Stanley, H.M. Through the dark continent. N.Y., 1878.
Afr 718.2.10 Stanley, H.M. Lettres inédites. Bruxelles, 1955.
Afr 718.2.12 Stanley, H.M. Unpublished letters. N.Y., 1957.
Afr 718.2.30 Stanley, H.M. The exploration diaries of H.M. Stanley. London, 1961.

Afr 718 Africa in general - Local divisions - Journeys across the interior - East to West - cont.

Afr 718.2.35 Stanley, H.M. La découverte du Congo. Paris, 18- .
Afr 718.2.40 Stanley, Henry Morton. Stanley's despatches to the New York Herald, 1871-1872, 1874-1877. Boston, 1970.
Afr 718.2.80F Grant, J.H. On Stanley's exploration of S. Victoria. n.p. 1875.
Afr 718.2.81A Grant, J.H. Autobiography of Henry Morton Stanley. Boston, 1909.
Afr 718.2.81B Grant, J.H. Autobiography of Henry Morton Stanley. Boston, 1909.
Afr 718.2.81C Grant, J.H. Autobiography of Henry Morton Stanley. Boston, 1909.
Afr 718.2.81D Grant, J.H. Autobiography of Henry Morton Stanley. Boston, 1909.
Afr 718.2.81E Grant, J.H. Autobiography of Henry Morton Stanley. Boston, 1909.
Afr 718.2.85 Montefiore, A. H.M. Stanley, the African explorer. London, 1889.
Afr 718.2.90 Stanley testimonial shield. n.p., n.d.
Afr 718.2.93 Burdo, Adolphe. Stanley, sa vie, ses voyages et ses aventures. Paris, 1889.
Afr 718.2.95 White, Stanhope. Lost empire on the Nile: H.M. Stanley, Emin Pasha and the imperialists. London, 1969.
Afr 718.2.99 Headley, J.T. Stanley's adventures in the wilds of Africa. Philadelphia, 1890.
Afr 718.2.101 Symons, A.J.A. H.M. Stanley. London, 1933.
Afr 718.2.106 Hird, Frank. H.M. Stanley. London, 1935.
Afr 718.2.110 Malcorps, A. De reus van Kongo. Brugge, 1934.
Afr 718.2.115 Wassermann, J. Bula Matari, Stanley, conqueror of a continent. N.Y., 1933.
Afr 718.2.120 Wassermann, J. Bula Matari. Berlin, 1932.
Afr 718.2.125 Farwell, Byron. The man who presumed. 1st ed. N.Y., 1957.
Afr 718.2.130 Anstruther, Ian. Dr. Livingstone, I presume. 1st American ed. N.Y., 1957.
Afr 718.2.135 Sterling, Thomas. Stanley's way. 1st Amer. ed. N.Y., 1960.
Afr 718.2.140 Castries, R. de la Croix. Les rencontres de Stanley. Paris, 1960.
Afr 718.4 Serpa Pinto, Alexander de. How I crossed Africa. Philadelphia, 1881. 2v.
Afr 718.4.3 Serpa Pinto, Alexander de. Wandering quer durch Afrika. Leipzig, 1881. 2v.
Afr 718.4.6 Serpa Pinto, Alexander de. Como eu atravessei Africa. vol.1-2. Londres, 1881. 2v.
Afr 718.4.10 Ribeiro, M.F. As conferencias e o itinerario do viajante Serpa Pinto. Lisboa, 1879.
Afr 718.4.15 Serpa Pinto, Carlota de. A vida breve e ardente de Serpa Pinto. Lisboa, 1937.
Afr 718.4.80 Cunha, Amadeu. Serpa Pinto e o apelo de Africa. Lisboa, 1946.
Afr 718.5 Wissmann, H. Unter Deutsche Flagge quer durch Afrika. Berlin, 1889.
Afr 718.6 Wissmann, H. Meine zweite Durchquerung Afrikas. Frankfurt a.M., 1891.
Afr 718.7 Wissmann, H. My second journey through Africa. London, 1891.
Afr 718.8F Goetzen, G.A.V. Durch Afrika von Ost nach West. Berlin, 1899.
Afr 718.9 Lacerda e Almeida, F.J.M. de. Journey to Cazembe. London, 1873.
Afr 718.9.10 Royal Geographical Society. The lands of Cazembe: Lacerda's journey to Cazembe in 1798. N.Y., 1969.
Afr 718.10A Stanley, H.M. In darkest Africa. N.Y., 1890. 2v.
Afr 718.10B Stanley, H.M. In darkest Africa. N.Y., 1890. 2v.
Afr 718.10.1 Stanley, H.M. In darkest Africa. N.Y., 1891. 2v.
Afr 718.10.2 Stanley, H.M. In darkest Africa. London, 1904.
Afr 718.11 Jameson, J.S. Story of the rear column. London, 1890.
Afr 718.12 Jameson, J.S. Forschungen und Erlebnisse im dunkelsten Africa. Hamburg, 1891.
Afr 718.13 Troup, J.R. With Stanley's rear column. London, 1890.
Afr 718.14 Barttelot, E.M. Life of E.M. Barttelot. London, 1890.
Afr 718.15 Werner, J.R. Visit to stanley s rear guard. Edinburg, 1889.
Afr 718.16 Parke, T.H. My personal experience in equatorial Africa. London, 1891.
Afr 718.16.3 Parke, T.H. My personal experience in equatorial Africa. 3d ed. London, 1891.
Afr 718.17 Wauters, A.J. Stanley's Emin Pascha expedition. Philadelphia, 1890.
Afr 718.17.2 Wauters, A.J. Stanley's Emin Pascha expedition. London, 1890.
Afr 718.18 Stanley, H.M. The story of Emin's rescue as told in Stanley's letters. N.Y., 1890.
Afr 718.18.3 Stanley, H.M. The story of Emin's rescue as told in Stanley's letters. Boston, 1890.
Afr 718.18.6 Stanley, H.M. Dans les ténébres de l'Afrique. 3 ed. v.1-2. Paris, 1890. 2v.
Afr 718.18.50F Belgium. Ministére des Affaires Africaines. Document notte. Bruxelles, 1960.
Afr 718.19 Brode, H. Tippoo Tib; story of his career in Central Africa. London, 1907.
Afr 718.20 Bourne, H.R.F. The other side of Emin Pasha relief expedition. London, 1891.
Afr 718.21 Kumm, H.K.W. From Hausaland to Egypt. London, 1910.
Afr 718.22 Kumm, H.K.W. Khont-Hon-Nofer, lands of Ethiopia. London, 1910.
Afr 718.25 Adolf, Friedrich. Ins innerste Afrika. Leipzig, 1909.
Afr 718.25.3 Adolf, Friedrich. In the heart of Africa. London, 1910.
Afr 718.25.4 Adolf, Friedrich. From the Congo to the Niger and the Nile. Philadelphia, 1914. 2v.
Afr 718.25.5 Adolf, Friedrich. From the Congo to the Niger and the Nile. V.1-2. London, 1913. 2v.
Afr 718.25.10 Adolf, Friedrich. Vom Kongo zum Niger und Nil. 3e Aufl. Leipzig, 1921. 2v.
Afr 718.25.12 Lukas, J. Zentralsudanische Studien, Wörterverzeichnisse der Deutschen Zentral-Afrika-Expedition 1910-11. Hamburg, 1937.
Afr 718.25.15 Czekanowski, Jan. W głab lasów Aruwimi. Wrocław, 1958.
Afr 718.27 Alexander, Boyd. From the Niger to the Nile. London, 1907.
Afr 718.27.3 Alexander, Boyd. Last journey...memoir by H. Alexander. London, 1912.
Afr 718.28 Durand. Les voyages des Portugais...XVI et XVII siècles. Meaux, 1879.
Afr 718.29 Foa, Edouard. De l'océan Indien à l'océan Atlantique, la traversée de l'Afrique. Paris, 1900.

Afr 718 **Africa in general - Local divisions - Journeys across the interior -**
East to West - cont.

Afr 718.30 Frobenius, L. The voice of Africa. V.1-2. London, 1913. 2v.
Afr 718.30.1 Frobenius, Leo. The voice of Africa. N.Y., 1968. 2v.
Afr 718.31 Johnston, J. Reality versus romance in south central Africa. London, 1893.
Afr 718.31.2 Johnston, J. Reality versus romance in South Central Africa. 2nd ed. London, 1969.
Afr 718.32 Kearton, Cherry. Through central Africa from east to west. London, 1915.
Afr 718.34 Foa, Edouard. Chasses aux grandes fauves pendant la traversée du continent noir. Paris, 1899.
Afr 718.35 Dubourg de Bozas, P.M.R. Mission scientifique. De la mer Rouge. Paris, 1906.
Afr 718.36 Duplessis, J. Thrice through the dark continent. London, 1917.
Afr 718.37 Migeod, F.W.H. Across equatorial Africa. London, 1923.
Afr 718.38 Berg, Gertrud Wilhelmson. Pori. Stockholm, 1964.
Afr 718.39 Powell, E.A. The map that is half unrolled. N.Y., 1925.
Afr 718.40 Barnes, James. Through central Africa from coast to coast. N.Y., 1915.
Afr 718.42 Capello, H. Da Angola a Contra-Costa. v.I,II. Lisboa, 1886. 2v.
Afr 718.43 Lemboum, Hans Jorgen. Hvide mand-hvad nu. København, 1955.
Afr 718.44 Tweedy, Owen. By way of the Sahara. London, 1930.
Afr 718.45 Rogers, M. When rivers meet. London, 1960.
Afr 718.46 Pedroso Gamitto, Antonio Candido. O muata cazembe e os povos Maraves. Lisboa, 1937. 2v.
Afr 718.46.5 Pedroso Gamitto, Antonio Candido. King Kazembe and the Marave, Cheva, Bisa, Bemba,Lundo. v.1-2. Lisboa, 1960.
Afr 718.47 Cameron, Verney Lovett. In savage Africa. London, 1889.
Afr 718.48 Littell, Blaine. South of the moon. 1st ed. N.Y., 1966.
Afr 718.50 Nils-Magnus. Afrikanska strövtåg. Solna, 1968.

Afr 724 **Africa in general - Local divisions - Journeys across the interior -**
Cape to Cairo

Afr 724.2 Farde, P. Voyages et aventures. Gand, 1878.
Afr 724.3A Grogan, E.S. From the Cape to Cairo. London, 1900.
Afr 724.3B Grogan, E.S. From the Cape to Cairo. London, 1900.
Afr 724.4 Kassner, Theo. My journey from Rhodesia to Egypt. London, 1911.
Afr 724.6 Cipriani, Lidio. In Africa dal Capo al Cairo. Firenze, 1932.
Afr 724.8 Gibbons, A. St.H. Africa from south to north. London, 1904. 2v.
Afr 724.9 Taylor, Henry James. Capetown to Kafue. London, 1916.
Afr 724.10.2 Ludwig, Emil. Die Reise nach Afrika. Berlin, 1913.
Afr 724.15 Rosen, Eric von Greve. Traeskfolket. Stockholm, 1916.
Afr 724.15.5 Rosen, Eric von Greve. Vom Kap nach Kairo. Stuttgart, 1924.
Afr 724.20 Hoyningen-Huene, G. African mirage. London, 1938.
Afr 724.22 Wymer, Norman. The man from the Cape. London, 1959.
Afr 724.24 Douglass, Lillie B. Cape Town to Cairo. Caldwell, 1964.

Afr 725 **Africa in general - Local divisions - Region of the great lakes**

Afr 725.2 Burton, R.F. The lake regions of central Africa. London, 1860. 2v.
NEDL Afr 725.4 Thomson, J. To the central African lakes and back. v.1-2. London, 1881. 2v.
Afr 725.4.2 Thomson, J. To the central African lakes and back. 2d ed. Boston, 1881. 2v.
Afr 725.4.3 Thomson, J. To the Central African lakes and back: the narrative of the Royal Geographical Society's East Central African Expedition, 1878-1880. 2nd ed. London, 1968. 2v.
Afr 725.4.5 Thomson, James B. Joseph Thomson, African explorer. London, 1896.
Afr 725.6 Elton, J.F. Lakes and mountains of eastern and central Africa. London, 1879.
Afr 725.6.5 Elton, J.F. Elton and the East African coast slave-trade. London, 1958.
Afr 725.6.10 Elton, J.F. Travels and researches among the lakes and mountains of eastern and central Africa. 1st ed. London, 1968.
Afr 725.8 Moore, J.E.S. To the Mountains of the Moon. London, 1901.
Afr 725.9 Johnson, J.B. Tramp around the Mountains of the Moon and through the back gate of the Congo state. London, 1908.
Afr 725.10A Livingstone, David. The last journals. London, 1874. 2v.
Afr 725.10B Livingstone, David. The last journals. London, 1874. 2v.
X Cg Afr 725.10.5 Livingstone, David. The last journals. N.Y, 1875. (Changed to XP 3656)
Afr 725.10.10 Livingstone, David. Private journals. London, 1960.
Afr 725.10.15 Livingstone, David. African journal, 1853-1856. v.1-2. London, 1963. 2v.
Afr 725.11 Geddie, J.F.R.G. The lake regions of central Africa. London, 1881.
Afr 725.12 Decle, Lionel. Three years in savage Africa. London, 1898.
Afr 725.13 Elliot, G.F.S. A naturalist in mid-Africa. London, 1896.
Afr 725.14 Caddick, Helen. A white woman in central Africa. London, 1900.
Afr 725.15 Geil, William Edgar. A Yankee in Pigmyland. London, 1905.
Afr 725.15.5 Geil, William Edgar. Adventures in the African jungle hunting Pigmies. Garden City, 1917.
Afr 725.16 Taylor, Bayard. The lake regions of central Africa. N.Y., 1881.
Afr 725.17.3F Heudebert, Lucien. Vers les grands lacs de l'Afrique orientale, d'après les notes de l'explorateur. 3. ed. Paris, 19- .
Afr 725.18 Langenmaier, Theo. Alte Kenntnis und Kartographie der zentralafrikanischen Seenregion. Inaug. Diss. Erlangen, 1916.
Afr 725.20A Roscoe, John. The soul of central Africa. London, 1922.
Afr 725.20B Roscoe, John. The soul of central Africa. London, 1922.
Afr 725.22 Moorehead, Alan. The White Nile. N.Y., 1961.

Afr 730 **Africa in general - Local divisions - Circumnavigation of Africa**

Afr 730.2 Illing, K.E. Der Periplus des Hanno. Dresden, 1899.
Afr 730.4 Mueller, W. Die Umsegelung Afrikas. Rathenau, 1889.
Afr 730.10 Smith, C.F. All the way round, sea roads to Africa. London, 1938.

Afr 755 **Africa in general - Local divisions - Lakes - Chad**

Afr 755.2 France. Ministère des Colonies. Documentation scientifique de la mission Tilho. Paris, 1910. 4v.
Afr 755.5 Meynier, O.F. La mission Joalland-Meynier. Paris, 1947.

Afr 765 **Africa in general - Local divisions - Lakes - Victoria**

Afr 765.3 Perthes, Joachim. Der Victoria-Njansa. Göttingen, 1913.
Afr 765.4 Werther, Waldemar. Zum Victoria Nyanza. Berlin, 1894.

Afr 770 **Africa in general - Local divisions - Lakes - Tanganyika**

Afr 770.3 Hore, Edw.C. Lake Tanganyika. Photoreproduction. n.p., 1889.
Afr 770.3.5 Hore, Edw.C. Tanganyika. Eleven years...Central Africa. 2nd ed. Photoreproduction. n.p., 1892.

Afr 775 **Africa in general - Local divisions - Lakes - Nyassa**

Afr 775.5 Bellingham, W. The diary of a working man in central Africa. London, n.d.
Afr 775.10 Johnson, W.P. Nyasa, the great water. London, 1922.

Afr 810 **Africa in general - Local divisions - Rivers - Niger**

Afr 810.1 Lander, R. Journal of an expedition to explore the Niger. London, 1832. 3v.
Afr 810.2 Lander, R. Journal of an expedition to explore the Niger. N.Y., 1837. 2v.
Afr 810.2.5 Lander, R. The Niger journal of Richard and John Lander. N.Y., 1965.
Afr 810.3 Lander, R. Journal of an expedition to explore the Niger. N.Y., 1839. 2v.
Afr 810.3.3 Laird, M. Narrative of expedition into Africa by the river Niger. v.1-2. London, 1837. 2v.
Afr 810.4 Crowther, S. Journal of an expedition up the Niger. London, 1855.
Afr 810.4.5 Crowther, S. The gospel on the banks of the Niger. London, 1968.
Afr 810.5 Mockler-Ferryman, A.F. Up the Niger. London, 1892.
Afr 810.6 Lanoye, F. de. Le Niger et les explorations de l'Afrique centrale. Paris, 1858.
Afr 810.7 Jaime, G. De Koulikoro à Tombouctou. Paris, 1894.
Afr 810.8 Jamieson, R. An appeal...Niger expedition and sequel. London, 1840-43.
Afr 810.8.10 Stephen, George. A letter to the Rt. Hon. Lord John Russell...Niger expedition. London, 1840.
Afr 810.9 Allen, W. Narrative of expedition...river Niger. London, 1848. 2v.
Afr 810.10 Simpson, W. Private journal kept during the Niger expedition. London, 1843.
Afr 810.11F Allen, W. Picturesque views on the river Niger. London, 1840.
Afr 810.12 Jannequin, C. Voyage de Lybie. Paris, 1643.
Afr 810.13 Schoen, J.F. Journals of Schoen and S. Crowther...expedition up Niger. London, 1842.
Afr 810.14 Hutchinson, T.J. Narrative of the Niger, Tshadda and Binue exploration. London, 1855. 2 pam.
Afr 810.15 Lenfant, E.H. Le Niger, voie ouverte à notre empire africain. Paris, 1903.
Afr 810.17 Owen, Richard. Saga of the Niger. London, 1961.
Afr 810.19 Burdo, Adolphe. The Niger and the Benueh. London, 1880.
Afr 810.20 Donkin, Rufane. A dissertation on the course and probable termination of the Niger. London, 1829.
Afr 810.25 Mattei, Antonio. Bas-Niger, Benoue, Dahomey. Grenoble, 1890.
Afr 810.30 Borill, Edward W. The Niger explored. London, 1968.
Afr 810.35.2 Baikie, William B. Narrative of an exploring voyage up the rivers Kwóra and Bínue, commonly known as the Niger and Tsádda in 1854. Facsimile. London, 1966.

Afr 820 **Africa in general - Local divisions - Rivers - Zambesi**

Afr 820.1 Sherlock, Jill. The Zambesi. Cape Town, 1963.
Afr 820.3.3 Coillard, F. On the threshold of central Africa. London, 1897.
Afr 820.3.6 Coillard, F. Sur le Haut-Zambèze. Paris, 1898.
Afr 820.4 Mcdonald, J.F. Zambesi river. London, 1955.
Afr 820.5 Robertson, W. Zambezi days. London, 1936.
Afr 820.15 Luigi, Duke of the Abruzzi. La esplorazione dello Uabi Uebi Scebeli. Milano, 1932.
Afr 820.15.12 Basile, C. Uebi-Scebeli nella spedizione di S.A.R. Luigi di Savoia. Bologna, 1935.

Afr 825 **Africa in general - Local divisions - Rivers - Others**

Afr 825.4 Cat, E. Notice sur la carte de l'Ogooue. Paris, 1890.
Afr 825.5 Bruel, Georges. Notes géographiques sur le bassin de l'Ogooue. Paris, 1911.
Afr 825.10 Sinclair, J.H. Dodging hippopotami and crocodiles in Africa. Rochester, 193- .

Afr 850 **Africa in general - Local divisions - Islands - General works**

Afr 850.2 Avezac-Macayo, M.A.P. Iles de l'Afrique. Paris, 1848.
Afr 850.5 Deherain, Henri. Dans l'Atlantique. Paris, 1912.
Afr 850.6 Green, L.G. Islands time forgot. London, 1962.

Afr 852 **Africa in general - Local divisions - Islands - West coast in general**

Afr 852.2 Ellis, A.B. West African islands. London, 1885.
Afr 852.3 Boudyck Bastiaanse, J. Voyage à la côte de Guinée. La Haye, 1853.
Afr 852.5 Lloyd, Peter Gutt. Africa in social change. Harmondsworth, 1967.

Afr 854 **Africa in general - Local divisions - Islands - East coast in general**

Afr 854.2 Keller, C. Die östafrikanischen Inseln. v.2. Berlin, 1898.
Afr 854.10 Unzueta y Yuste, A. de. Islas del Golfo de Guinea. Madrid, 1945.

Afr 855 **Africa in general - Local divisions - Islands - St. Helena**

Afr 855.2F St. Helena Guardian. St. Helena.
Afr 855.3 Grant, B. A few notes on St. Helena. St. Helena, 1883.
Afr 855.4 Great Britain. Colonial Office. Report on St. Helena. 3v.
Afr 855.5 Jackson, E.L. St. Helena, the historic island. N.Y., 1905.
Afr 855.8 Brooke, T.H. History..island of St. Helena...1823. London, 1824.
Afr 855.9 Description of island of St. Helena. London, 1805.
Afr 855.10 Melliss, J.C. St. Helena. London, 1875.
Afr 855.11 Beatson, A. Tracts relative to the island of St. Helena. London, 1816.
Afr 855.12 St. Helena. Extracts from the St. Helena records. St. Helena, 1885.
Afr 855.12.5 St. Helena. Extracts from the St. Helena records. 2 ed. St. Helena, 1908.
Afr 855.14 Gosse, P. St. Helena, 1502-1938. London, 1938.
Afr 855.16 Souvenir of Saint Helena. St. Helena, 19- .

Afr 855 **Africa in general - Local divisions - Islands - St. Helena - cont.**
Afr 855.18 Blakeston, O. Isle of St. Helena. London, 1957.
Afr 855.20 St. Helena News Review. Jamestown, St. Helena. 5v.
Afr 855.22 St. Helena Wirebird. Jamestown. 2v.
Afr 855.24 Taylor, Margaret Stewart. St. Helens, ocean roadhouse. London, 1969.

Afr 860 **Africa in general - Local divisions - Islands - Ascension**
Afr 860.2 Gill, D. Six months in Ascension. London, 1878.

Afr 861 **Africa in general - Local divisions - Islands - Tristan da Cunha**
Afr 861.1 Barrow, K.M. Three years in Tristan da Cunha. London, 1910.
Afr 861.10 Rogers, Rose A. The lonely island. London, 1926.
Afr 861.10.2 Rogers, Rose A. The lonely island. London, 1927.
Afr 861.15.5 Christophersen, E. Tristan da Cunha. London, 1940.
Afr 861.20 Brander, J. Tristan da Cunha, 1506-1902. London, 1940.
Afr 861.21 Crawford, A.B. I went to Tristan. London, 1941.
Afr 861.25 Boay, D.M. Rock of exile. London, 1957.
Afr 861.30 Gane, Douglas M. Tristan da Cunha. London, 1932.
Afr 861.31 Mackay, M.M. Angry island. London, 1963.
Afr 861.35 Roenne, Arne Falk. Back to Tristan. London, 1967.

Afr 870 **Africa in general - Local divisions - Islands - Others**
Afr 870.3 Honey, William. Narrative of the captivity...of William Honey...on the island of Arguin on the west coast of Africa. London, 1845.
Afr 870.15 Lionnet, J.G. L'ile d'Agalega. Paris, 1924.
Afr 870.20 Holdgate, M.W. Mountains in the sea. N.Y., 1958.

Afr 1001 - 1024 **Barbary States in general - Periodicals (A-Z)**
Afr 1001.2 Archives berbères. Rabat. 1,1915+ 3v.
Afr 1001.3 Afrique latine. Alger. 1,1921+ 2v.
Afr 1001.5 Armée d'Afrique. Alger.
Afr 1001.10 Annuaire de l'Afrique du Nord. Paris. 1,1962+ 6v.
Afr 1002.5 Bibliothèque des questions nord-africaines. Paris. 1,1937+ 2v.
Afr 1003.5 Cahiers Charles de Foucauld. Grenoble. 2,1946+ 13v.
Afr 1005.5 E.S.N.A. Cahiers nord-africaines. Paris. 11,1951+ 11v.
Afr 1013.5 Mediterranean survey. N.Y.
Afr 1013.10 Maghreb digest. Los Angeles. 1,1963+ 7v.
Afr 1013.15 Maghreb. Paris. 1964+ 2v.
Afr 1017.1 Questions nord-africaines. Paris. 1,1934+
Afr 1018.1 Revue africaine. Algiers. 1,1856+ 75v.
Afr 1018.1.5 Revue africaine. Table générale 1856-1881, 1882-1921. Algiers, 1885-1924. 2v.
Afr 1018.2 Société de Géographie de la Province d'Oran. Bulletin trimestriel. Paris. 7,1887+ 55v.
Afr 1018.2.3 Revue de l'Afrique française et des antiquités africaines. Paris. 1-6,1882-1888 3v.
Afr 1018.2.5 Société de Géographie de la Province d'Oran. Journal des travaux, 1878-1927. (Table générale). Oran, 1898-1930. 3v.
Afr 1018.3 Revue africaine. Paris. 1,1836+ 2v.
Afr 1018.4 Revue nord-africaine illustrée. v.1-4. Alger, 1902-05. 4v.
Afr 1018.5 Revue de l'Afrique du Nord. Alger. 1,1921+ 2v.
Afr 1018.6 Revue d'histoire et de civilisation du Malghreb. Alger. 2,1967+
Afr 1018.7 Revue de l'Occident musulman et de la Méditerranee. Aix-en-Provence. 1,1966+
Afr 1019.5 Studi magrebini. Napoli. 1,1966+ 2v.
Afr 1020.5F International African Institute. North-east Africa. London, 1959.

Afr 1025 **Barbary States in general - Folios [Discontinued]**
Afr 1025.1F Fournel, H. Etude sur la conquête de l'Afrique par les Arabes. v.1-2. Paris, 1857.

Afr 1026 **Barbary States in general - Bibliographies**
Afr 1026.4 Jacqueton, G. Les archives espagnoles du gouvernement de l'Algérie. Alger, 1894.
Afr 1026.5 Minutilli, F. Bibliografia della Libia. Torino, 1903.
Afr 1026.5.15 Ceccherini, Ugo. Bibliografia della Libia. Roma, 1915.
Afr 1026.6 Rouard de Card, E. Livres français des XVIIe et XVIIIe siècles concernant les états Barbaresques. Paris, 1911.
Afr 1026.6.2 Rouard de Card, E. Livres français des XVIIe et XVIIIe siècle. Etats Barbaresques. Supplément. Paris, 1917.
Afr 1026.10 France. Etat-Major de l'Armée. Service Historique. L'Afrique français du Nord. T.1-4. Paris, 1930-35. 4v.
Afr 1026.15 Library of Congress. General Reference and Bibliography Division. North and Northeast Africa. Washington, 1957.

Afr 1028 **Barbary States in general - Pamphlet volumes**
Afr 1028 Pamphlet box. North Africa.
Afr 1028.1 Follie. Voyage dans les déserts du Sahara. Paris, 1792. 4 pam.
Afr 1028.2 Pamphlet box. North Africa.
Afr 1028.3 Pamphlet box. North Africa.
Afr 1028.4 Pamphlet volume. Morocco, Tunisia. 6 pam.

Afr 1030 **Barbary States in general - Collected source materials - General**
Afr 1030.20 Textes relatifs à l'histoire de l'Afrique du Nord. Alger. 1,1916+ 2v.

Afr 1033 **Barbary States in general - Collected source materials - Treaties**
Afr 1033.3F Mas Latrie, M.L. de. Traités de paix et de commerce et documents diverses...de l'Afrique septentrionale au Moyen Age. Paris, 1865.
Afr 1033.4 Strupp, K. Urkunden zur Geschichte des völkerrechts. Erg. 1. Gotha, 1912.

Afr 1035 **Barbary States in general - Collected source materials - Others**
Afr 1035.5 Institut des Hautes Etudes Marocaines. Memorial Henri Basset. v.1-2. Paris, 1928. 2v.

Afr 1040 **Barbary States in general - Government and administration - Special topics**
Afr 1040.5 Vassenhove, Leon van. Une solution fédéraliste du problème nord-africain. Neuchâtel, 1957.
Afr 1040.10F Centre des Hautes Etudes. Six conférences d'initiation à la politique musulmane de la France en Afrique du Nord. n.p., 1943.
Afr 1040.15 Ashford, Douglas E. National development and local reform. Princeton, 1967.
Afr 1040.20 Étienne, Bruno. Les Problémes juridiques des minorities européennes au Maghreb. Paris, 1968.

Afr 1047 **Barbary States in general - Military affairs - Special topics**
Afr 1047.15 Azan, Paul. L'armée indigène nord-africaine. Paris, 1925.

Afr 1065 - 1070 **Barbary States in general - General history (By date)**
Afr 1068.17 Jackson, G.A. Algiers...a complete picture of the Barbary states. London, 1817.
Afr 1068.35.2 Russell, M. History of the Barbary states. 2d ed. Edinburgh, 1835.
Afr 1068.35.5 Russell, M. History of the Barbary states. 2d ed. N.Y., 1837.
Afr 1068.88 Mercier, E. Histoire de l'Afrique septentrionale. Paris, 1888-91. 3v.
Afr 1069.09 Piquet, V. Les civilisations de l'Afrique du Nord. Paris, 1909.
Afr 1069.09.3 Piquet, V. Les civilisations de l'Afrique du Nord. 2d ed. Paris, 1917.
Afr 1069.12 Mariam, V. Il fato di Tripoli e il fato latino. Roma, 1912.
Afr 1069.12.5A Coolidge, A.C. The European reconquest of North Africa. n.p., 1912.
Afr 1069.12.5B Coolidge, A.C. The European reconquest of North Africa. n.p., 1912.
Afr 1069.12.5C Coolidge, A.C. The European reconquest of North Africa. n.p., 1912.
Afr 1069.12.5D Coolidge, A.C. The European reconquest of North Africa. n.p., 1912.
Afr 1069.23 Hamet, I. Histoire du Maghreb. Paris, 1923.
Afr 1069.31 Julien, Charles A. Histoire de l'Afrique du Nord. Paris, 1931.
Afr 1069.31.5 Julien, Charles A. Histoire de l'Afrique du Nord. v.1-2. 2. ed. Paris, 1951. 2v.
Afr 1069.31.10 Julien, Charles A. Histoire de l'Afrique du Nord. v.1-2. Paris, 1961.
Afr 1069.31.12 Julien, Charles A. Histoire de l'Afrique du Nord: Tunisie, Algérie, Maroc. 2e éd. Paris, 1966- 2v.
Afr 1069.36 Luigi, G. de. La Francia nord-africana. Padova, 1936.
Afr 1069.37 Albertini, E. L'Afrique du Nord française dans l'histoire. Lyon, 1937.
Afr 1069.37.5 Gautier, Emile F. Le passé de l'Afrique du Nord. Paris, 1952.
Afr 1069.37.7 Gautier, Emile F. Le passé de l'Afrique du Nord. Paris, 1964.
Afr 1069.38 Soames, Jane. The coast of Barbary. London, 1938.
Afr 1069.38.5 Berenson, Mary. A vicarious trip to the Barbary coast. London, 1938.
Afr 1069.42 Ghirelli, Angelo. El pais berebere. Madrid, 1942.
Afr 1069.43 Garcia, F.T. Presencia de España en Berberia central y oriental. Madrid, 1943.
Afr 1069.53 Schaefer, Rene. Drame et chances de l'Afrique du Nord. Paris, 1953.
Afr 1069.55 Naci, Hikmet. Tarih hoyunca kujey Afrika. Istanbul, 1955?
Afr 1069.56 Ricard, Robert. Etudes hispano-africaines. Tetuan, 1956.
Afr 1069.57 Leone, Enrico de. La colonizzazione dell'Africa del Nord. Padova, 1957.
Afr 1069.57.5 Caro Baroja, Julio Estudios mogrebies. Madrid, 1957.
Afr 1069.59 Barbour, Nevill. A survey of North-west Africa. London, 1959.
Afr 1069.59.2 Barbour, Nevill. A survey of North-west Africa. 2nd ed. London, 1962.
Afr 1069.61 Nickerson, J.S. A short history of North Africa. N.Y., 1961.
Afr 1069.63 Gallagher, C.F. The United States and North Africa. Cambridge, 1963.
Afr 1069.64 Brace, R.M. Morocco, Algeria, Tunisia. Englewood Cliffs, N.J., 1964.
Afr 1069.64.5 Monlau, J. Les états barbaresques. Paris, 1964.
Afr 1069.64.10 Etudes maghrébines. Paris, 1964.
Afr 1069.65 Sahli, Mohamed C. Décoloniser l'histoire. Paris, 1965.
Afr 1069.66 Peyrouton, Bernard Marcel. Histoire générale du Maghreb, Algérie, Maroc, Tunisie. Paris, 1966.

Afr 1075 **Barbary States in general - General special**
Afr 1075.5 Duclos, Louis Jean. Les nationalismes maghrébins. Paris, 1966.

Afr 1080 **Barbary States in general - History by periods - Moorish conquest to 16th century - General works**
Afr 1080.1 Ibn Khaldun. Histoire des Berbère. Algiers, 1852-56. 4v.
X Cg Afr 1080.1.5 Ibn Khaldun. Histoire des Berbéres et des dynasties musulmanes. Paris, 1925-27. 4v.
NEDL Afr 1080.3 Faure-Biguet, G. Histoire de l'Afrique septentrionale. Paris, 1905.
Afr 1080.4 Mercier, E. Histoire des Arabes dans l'Afrique septentrionale. Alger, 1875.
Afr 1080.5 Ximenez de Sandovel, C. Guerras de Africa en la antigüdad. Madrid, 1881.
Afr 1080.10 Gautier, Emile F. L'islamisation de l'Afrique du Nord. Les siècles obscures du Maghreb. Paris, 1927.
Afr 1080.15 Marcais, Georges. La Berbérie musulmane et l'Orient au moyen age. Paris, 1946.
Afr 1080.20 Fagnan, Edmond. Extraits inédits rélatifs au Maghreb. Alger, 1924.
Afr 1080.25 Hopkins, J.F.P. Medieval Muslim government in Barbary. London, 1958.

Afr 1082 **Barbary States in general - History by periods - Moorish conquest to 16th century - Arab conquest to 800**
Afr 1082.1 Deslane, M.G. Sur les premiers expéditions. n.p., 1844.

Afr 1083 **Barbary States in general - History by periods - Moorish conquest to 16th century - Aglabite dynasty (800-909)**
Afr 1083.10 Vonderheyden, M. La Berbérie orientale sous la dynastie des Benou'l-Arlab (800-909). Thèse. Paris, 1927.
Afr 1083.15 Talabi, Muhammad. L'Émirat aghlabide. Paris, 1966[1967].

Afr 1084 **Barbary States in general - History by periods - Moorish conquest to 16th century - Fatimite dynasty (903-975)**
Afr 1084.1 Birago, G.B. Historia africana della divisione dell'imperi degli Arabi. Venetia, 1650.

Afr 1085 **Barbary States in general - History by periods - Moorish conquest to 16th century - Ziride dynasty (972-1148)**
Afr 1085.2 Idris, Hady R. La Berbérie orientale sous les Zirides, Xe-XIIe siècles. v.1-2. Paris, 1962.
Afr 1085.3 Idris, Hady R. LaBerbérie orientale sous les Zirides, Xe-XIIe siècles. v.1-2. Paris, 1959.

Afr 1088 Barbary States in general - History by periods - Moorish conquest to 16th century - Almohade dynasty (1130-1275)

Afr 1088.5 Fagnan, E. Histoire des Almohades. Alger, 1893.
Afr 1088.5.6 Fagnan, E. L'Afrique septentrionale au XIIe siècle de notre ère. Constantine, 1900.
Afr 1088.6 Bel, A. Les Benou Ghanya. Paris, 1903.
Afr 1088.7 Levi-Provencal, E. Un recueil de lettres officielles almohades. Paris, 1942.
Afr 1088.10 Huici Miranda, Ambrosio. Historia politica del imperio almohade. v.1. Tetuan, 1955.
Afr 1088.12 Tourneau, Roger. The Almohad movement in North Africa in the twelfth and thirteenth centuries. Princeton, N.J., 1969.

Afr 1089 Barbary States in general - History by periods - Moorish conquest to 16th century - Other special

Afr 1089.3 Thieling, W. Der Hellenismus in Kleinafrika. Leipzig, 1911.
Afr 1089.5 Marcais, Georges. Les Arabes en Berbérie du XIe au XIVe siècle. Constantine, 1913.

Afr 1095 Barbary States in general - History by periods - History since 16th century - General works

Afr 1095.5 Julien, C.A. L'Afrique du Nord en marche. Paris, 1952.
Afr 1095.10A Stevens, E. North African powder keg. N.Y., 1955.
Afr 1095.10B Stevens, E. North African powder keg. N.Y., 1955.
Afr 1095.15 Juin, A.P. Le Maghreb en feu. Paris, 1957.
Afr 1095.20 Fontaine, Pierre. Dossier secret de l'Afrique du Nord. Paris, 1957.
Afr 1095.25 Ilter Aziz Samih. Şimalî Afrikada Türkler. Istanbul, 1934-37.

Afr 1100 Barbary States in general - History by periods - History since 16th century - Barbary Piracy (1500-1830) - General works

Afr 1100.1 Vignols, L. La piraterie sur l'Atlantique. Rennes, 1890.
Afr 1100.2 Currey, E.H. Sea-wolves of the Mediterranean. London, 1910.
Afr 1100.2.5 Currey, E.H. Sea wolves of the Mediterranean. N.Y., 1929.
Afr 1100.3 Carranza, F. de. La guerra santa por mar de los corsarios berberiscos. Ceuta, 1931.
Afr 1100.5 Laprimandaie, F.E. Documents inédits sur l'histoire de l'occupation espagnole en Afrique. Alger, 1875.
Afr 1100.6 Bono, Salvatore. I corsari barbareschi. Torino, 1964.

Afr 1103 Barbary States in general - History by periods - History since 16th century - Barbary Piracy (1500-1830) - Special topics

Htn Afr 1103.4.20* Relación de la traza y modo con que los soldados de Tarifa... cogieron dos barcos de Moros. Malaga, 1623.
Htn Afr 1103.4.30* Relación verdadera de una insigni victoria. Lisboa, 1636.
Afr 1103.5 Verdadeira noticia da grande esquadra que do reino de Napoles sahio em corso contra os Mouros de Argel. Lisboa, 1757.
Afr 1103.6 Nova relaçam e curiosa noticia do combate, que tiveram tres caravellas de Vianna de Caminha com os corsarios dos Mouros. Lisboa, 1754.
Afr 1103.7 Noticia da grande preza, que duas naos de Roma, que andavam de guarda costa fizerão aos mouros em as costas de Sicilia. Lisboa, 175-.
Afr 1103.8 Cunha, Jorge da. Relaçam do successo, que no dia do prezenre mez de julho tiverao os navios. Lisbon, 17- .
Afr 1103.9 Nova, e curiosa relaçao, do fatal combate que teve o capitão de mare guerra espanhol D. Joze Ponce de Leon, com huma nao de Mouros argelinos. Lisbon, 1757.
Afr 1103.10 Freire de Monterroyo Mascarenhas, José. Relaçam summaria de hum combate, sucedido nos mares de Alicante entre hum galeão de Biscainhos que andava de guarda costa. Lisbon, 1755.
Htn Afr 1103.12* Relação do combate, que teve o capitão de navio Dom Pedro Stuart e Portugal. Lisboa, 1752.
Afr 1103.15 Barbareschi e i cristiani. Ginevra, 1822.

Afr 1105 Barbary States in general - History by periods - History since 16th century - 19th and 20th centuries together

Afr 1105.5 Meinicke-Kleint, Heinz. Algerien, Marokko, Tunesien. Berlin, 1965.
Afr 1105.10 Arene, Joseph C. Africa in the nineteenth and twentieth centuries. Ibadan, 1966.

Afr 1110 Barbary States in general - History by periods - History since 16th century - 20th century

Afr 1110.5 Ziadek, Nicola A. Whither North Africa. 1st ed. Aligarh, 1957.
Afr 1110.10 Boyer de Latour, Pierre. Vérités sur l'Afrique du Nord. Paris, 1956.
Afr 1110.15 Hahn, Lora. North Africa. Washington, 1960.
Afr 1110.20 Fernan, F.W. Arabischer Westen. 1. Aufl. Stuttgart, 1959.
Afr 1110.25 Near East Conference. Current problems in North Africa. Princeton, 1960.
Afr 1110.30A Le Tourneau, Roger. Evolution politique de l'Afrique du Nord musulmane 1920-1961. Paris, 1962.
Afr 1110.30B Le Tourneau, Roger. Evolution politique de l'Afrique du Nord musulmane 1920-1961. Paris, 1962.
Afr 1110.35 Baulin, Jacques. The Arab role in Africa. Baltimore, 1962.
Afr 1110.40 Berque, Jacques. Le Maghreb entre deux guerres. Paris, 1962.
Afr 1110.40.5 Berque, Jacques. French North Africa. N.Y., 1967.
Afr 1110.41A Gordon, David. North Africa's French legacy, 1954-1962. Cambridge, 1962.
Afr 1110.41B Gordon, David. North Africa's French legacy, 1954-1962. Cambridge, 1962.
Afr 1110.42 Zartman, I. Government and politics in northern Africa. N.Y., 1963.
Afr 1110.44 Drame de l'Afrique du Nord et la conscience chrétienne. Paris, 1963.

Afr 1200 Barbary States in general - General relations with foreign powers

Afr 1200.5.2 Mémoire concernant le système de paix et de guerre que les puissances européennes pratiquent à l'égard des régences barbaresques. Venise, 1788.
NEDL Afr 1200.50 Boutin, Abel. Anciennes relations de la France avec la Barbarie, 1515-1830. Paris, 1902.
Afr 1200.55 Balch, T.W. France in North Africa, 1906. Philadelphia, 1906.
Afr 1200.58 Reclus, Onesime. L'Atlantide, pays de l'Atlas. Paris, 1918.

Afr 1200 Barbary States in general - General relations with foreign powers - cont.

Afr 1200.60 Perreau Pradier, P. L'Afrique du Nord et la guerre. Paris, 1918.
Afr 1200.62 Deslinieres, L. La France nord-africaine. Paris, 1920.
Afr 1200.63 Serres, Jean. La politique turque en Afrique du Nord sous la Monarchie de Juillet. Paris, 1925.
Afr 1200.63.2 Serres, Jean. La politique turque en Afrique du Nord sous le Monarchie de Juillet. Thèse. Paris, 1925.
Afr 1200.65 Fribourg, Andre. L'Afrique latine. Paris, 1922.
Afr 1200.67 Gasser, J. Role social de la France dans l'Afrique du Nord. Paris, 1924.
Afr 1200.70 Steeg, Theodore. La paix française en Afrique du Nord, en Algérie, au Maroc. Paris, 1926.
Afr 1200.75.4 Benoist, Charles. La question méditerranéenne. Paris, 1928.
Afr 1200.80 Carpentier, J.A. Les problèmes nord-africains. Paris, 1953.
Afr 1200.90 Guernier, E.L. La Berberie. v.1-2. Paris, 1950. 2v.
Afr 1200.100 Chotin, A.G. Histoire des expéditions maritimes de Charles-Quint en Barbarie. Bruxelles, 1849.
Afr 1200.110 Fisher, G. Barbary legend. Oxford, 1957.
Afr 1200.120 Hart, W. Annet. Poker om Noord-Afrika. Den Haag, 1959.

Afr 1254 - 1260 Barbary States in general - Geography, description, etc. - General works (By date)

Afr 1254.62 Abd al-Busit ibn Khalil. Douze récits de voyage inédits en Afrique du nord au XVe siècle. Paris, 1936.
X Cg Afr 1256.49F Dan, Pierre. Histoire de Barbarie et de ses corsaires. Paris, 1649. (Changed to XP 9049)
Afr 1257.04 Etat des royaumes de Barbarie. La Haye, 1704.
Afr 1257.89 Poiret, J.L.M. Voyage en Barbarie. Paris, 1789. 2v.
Afr 1257.89.3 Poiret, J.L.M. Travels through Barbary...1785-1786. London, 1790.
Afr 1258.02 Hornemanns, Fr. Tagebuch seiner Reise. Weimar, 1802.
Afr 1258.16 Badia y Leyblick. Travels of Ali Bey in Morocco, Tripoli. Philadelphia, 1816. 2v.
Afr 1258.16.5 Janson, William. A view of the present condition of the states of Barbary. London, 1816.
Afr 1258.17 Riley, J. Loss of the American brig Commerce. London, 1817.
Afr 1258.17.2 Riley, J. An authentic narrative of the loss of the American brig Commerce. Hartford, 1817.
Afr 1258.17.5 Riley, J. An authentic narrative of the loss of the American brig Commerce. Hartford, 1833.
Afr 1258.17.6 Riley, J. Sequel to Riley's narrative. Columbus, 1851.
Afr 1258.17.8 Riley, J. An authentic narrative of the loss of the American brig Commerce. Hartford, 1844.
Afr 1258.17.10 Riley, J. An authentic narrative of the loss of the American brig Commerce. Hartford, 1847.
Afr 1258.17.15 Riley, J. Sufferings in Africa; Captain Riley's narrative. N.Y., 1965.
Afr 1258.18 Robbins, A. A journal comprising an account of the loss of the brig Commerce. 7 ed. Hartford, 1818.
Afr 1258.18.2 Robbins, A. A journal comprising an account of the loss of the brig Commerce. 8 ed. Hartford, 1818.
Afr 1258.18.3 Robbins, A. A journal comprising an account of the loss of the brig Commerce. 10 ed. Hartford, 1819.
Afr 1258.18.8 Robbins, A. A journal comprising an account of the loss of the brig Commerce. Hartford, 1833.
Htn Afr 1258.18.31* Robbins, A. Robbins journal, comprising an account of the loss of the brig Commerce of Hartford, Conn. Greenwich, 1931.
Afr 1258.26.5 Ebn-el-Dyn El-Aghouathy. Etudes de géographie critique. Paris, 1836.
NEDL Afr 1258.45 London, F.H. Die Berberei. Frankfurt, 1845.
Afr 1258.47 Bodichon. Etudes sur l'Algérie et l'Afrique. Alger, 1847.
Afr 1258.50 Rozet. Algérie, Etats Tripolitains et Tunis. Paris, 1850.
Afr 1258.64 Faidherbe, L.L.C. Chapitres de géographie sur le nord-ouest de l'Afrique. Paris, 1864.
Afr 1258.70 Rohlfs, G. Land und Volk in Afrika, 1865-1870. Bremen, 1870.
Afr 1258.80 Brunialti, A. Algeria, Tunisia e Tripolitania. Milan, 1881.
Afr 1258.80.5 Kostenko, L.Th. Puteshestvie v severnuiu Afriku. Izd 2. Sankt Peterburg, 1880.
Afr 1258.83 Algarate, I.A. Memoria sobre nuestro poder militar. Madrid, 1883.
Afr 1258.87 Fallot, Ernest. Par dela la Méditerranée. Paris, 1887.
Afr 1258.93 Field, Henry M. The Barbary coast. N.Y, 1893.
Afr 1258.93.2 Field, Henry M. The Barbary coast. 2nd ed. N.Y., 1894.
Afr 1258.94 Rogh, J. Från orientens förgårdar. Stockholm, 1894.
Afr 1258.94.5 Lamartiniere, Maximilien Poisson de. Documents pour servir à l'étude du nord-ouest African. v.1-4 and atlas. Alger, 1894-97. 5v.
Afr 1258.96 Drouet, F. Au nord de l'Afrique. Nice, 1896.
Afr 1259.04 Eberhardt, I. Dans l'ombre chaude de l'islam. Paris, 1923.
Afr 1259.04.5 Eberhardt, I. Notes de route, Maroc-Algérie-Tunisie. Paris, 1923.
Afr 1259.08 Lorin, H. L'Afrique du Nord. Paris, 1908.
Afr 1259.10 Shoemaker, M.M. Islam lands, Nubia, the Sudan, Tunisia, and Algeria. N.Y., 1910.
Afr 1259.11 Fraser, J.F. The land of veiled women. London, 1911.
Afr 1259.11.5 Grant, Cyril F. Twixt sand and sea. London, 1911.
Afr 1259.11.7 Grant, Cyril F. Studies in North Africa. N.Y., 1923.
Afr 1259.13A Bullard, A. The Barbary coast. N.Y., 1913.
Afr 1259.13B Bullard, A. The Barbary coast. N.Y., 1913.
Afr 1259.13.5 Martin, A.G.P. Précis de sociologie nord-africaine. Paris, 1913.
Afr 1259.14 Woodberry, G.E. North Africa and the desert. N.Y., 1914.
Afr 1259.14.3 Rondet-Saint, M. En France africaine. Paris, 1914.
Afr 1259.21 Scott, A. Maccallum. Barbary. London, 1921.
Afr 1259.21.2 Scott, A. Maccallum. Barbary. N.Y., 1921.
Afr 1259.21.10 Couperus, Louis. Met Louis Couperus in Afrika. Amsterdam, 1921.
Afr 1259.23 Carpenter, F.G. From Tangier to Tripoli. 1st ed. Garden City, 1923.
Afr 1259.24F Ricard, Prosper. Les merveilles de l'autre France. Paris, 1924.
Afr 1259.24.5F Nordafrika, Tripolis, Tunis, Algier, Marokko. Berlin, 1924.
Afr 1259.25.10 Powell, E.A. In Barbary, Tunisia, Algeria, Morocco, and the Sahara. N.Y., 1926.
Afr 1259.26 Hawkes, C.P. Mauresques, with some Basque and Spanish cameos. London, 1926.
Afr 1259.27 Anderson, I. From Corsair to Riffian. Boston, 1927.
Afr 1259.27.5 McLaurin, Hamish. What about North Africa. N.Y., 1927.

Afr 1254 - 1260 Barbary States in general - Geography, description, etc. - General works (By date) - cont.

Afr 1259.27.10F Afrique du Nord, Algérie, Tunisie, Maroc. Paris, 1927.
Afr 1259.27.20A Erskine, Beatrice. Vanished cities of northern Africa. Boston, 1927.
Afr 1259.27.20B Erskine, Beatrice. Vanished cities of northern Africa. Boston, 1927.
Afr 1259.27.25 Vernon, M. Sands, palms and minarets. London, 1927.
Afr 1259.30 Foster, Harry L. A vagabond in Barbary. N.Y., 1930.
Afr 1259.30.5 Hulme, K.C. Arab interlude. Philadelphia, 1930.
Afr 1259.30.10 Maunier, R. Mélanges de sociologie nord-africaine. Paris, 1930.
Afr 1259.35 Khum de Prorok, B. In quest of lost worlds. N.Y., 1935.
Afr 1259.36 Adrian, W. Friedliches Afrika. Bern, 1936.
Afr 1259.38 Sorrel, J. Pages africaines, l'Afrique du Nord vue par les littérateurs. Paris, 1938.
Afr 1259.39 Gautier, E.F. L'Afrique blanche. Paris, 1939.
Afr 1259.40 Sitwell, S. Mauretania, warrior, man and woman. London, 1940.
Afr 1259.40.5 Sitwell, S. Mauretania. London, 1951.
Afr 1259.42 Bremond, Edouard. Berbères et Arabes. Paris, 1942.
Afr 1259.43 Brodrick, A.H. North Africa. London, 1943.
Afr 1259.43.5 Brodrick, A.H. Parts of Barbary. London, 1943.
Afr 1259.43.10 Ragatz, L.J. Introduction to French North Africa. N.Y., 1943.
Afr 1259.43.15F Wrage, W. Nordafrika. Leipzig, 1943.
Afr 1259.44 Elderkin, K.D. (McKnight). From Tripoli to Marrakesh. Springfield, Mass., 1944.
Afr 1259.44.5 Campbell, D. With the bible in North Africa. Kilmarnock, 1944.
Afr 1259.44.10 Costa Leite, P. da. Africa do Norte, impressões de viagem. Rio de Janeiro, 1944.
Afr 1259.44.15 Tefri (Pseud.) Sonnen-Bilder aus Nord-Afrika. Bulle, 1944.
Afr 1259.49 Maugham, R.C.R. North African notebook. N.Y., 1949.
Afr 1259.49.7 Despois, Jean. L'Afrique blanche. 3. ed. Paris, 1964.
Afr 1259.52 France. Président Du Conseil. Facts and figures about French North Africa. Paris, 1952.
Afr 1259.54 Monnink, G. Gastvriend van vrije volken. Amsterdam, 1954.
Afr 1259.55 Newman, B. North African journey. London, 1955.
Afr 1259.55.5 Wohlfahrt, M. Nordafrika. Berlin, 1955.
Afr 1259.56F Dans la lumière des cités africaines. v.1. Paris, 1956.
Afr 1259.58 Fielding, Xan. Corsair country. London, 1958.
Afr 1259.63 Bowles, Paul. Their heads are green. London, 1963.
Afr 1259.63.5 Liska, Jiri. The greater Maghreb. Washington, 1963.
Afr 1259.66 Isnard, Hildebert. Le Maghreb. Paris, 1966.
Afr 1259.67 Wellard, James. Lost worlds of Africa. 1st ed. N.Y., 1967.
Afr 1259.67.5 Despois, Jean. Géographie de l'Afrique du Nord-Ouest. Paris, 1967.

Afr 1268 Barbary States in general - Geography, description, etc. - Special customs

Afr 1268.5 Centre d'Accueil Nord-Africain de Saint-Louis, Marseilles. Eléments d'introduction à la vie moderne. Paris, 1960.
Afr 1268.6 Denti Di Pirajno, Alberto. A cure for serpents. London, 1955.
Afr 1268.8 Mutations culturelles et coopération au Maghreb. Paris, 1969.

Afr 1270 Barbary States in general - Geography, description, etc. - Guidebooks

Afr 1270.2 United States. Department of Defense. A pocket guide to North Africa. Washington, 1958.
Afr 1270.3 Ortega, M.L. Guia del norte de Africa y sur de España. Cadiz, 1917.
Afr 1270.5 Broutz, Charles. Victory across French North Africa. Alger, 1943.
Afr 1270.10 Schramm, Josef. Nordafrika. 2. Aufl. Buchenhain von München, 1967.

Afr 1271 Barbary States in general - Geography, description, etc. - Views

Afr 1271.5 Bories, H. Avenir de l'Afrique du Nord. Paris, 1938.
Afr 1271.10F Bargone, Chas. L'Afrique du Nord, Tunisie, Algérie, Maroc. Paris, 1924.

Afr 1273.1 - .199 Barbary States in general - Economic history and conditions - Historical works

Afr 1273.2 Bernard, Paul. Les anciens impôts de l'Afrique du Nord. St. Raphael, 1925.
Afr 1273.5F Monde Economique. North Africa, a world in fusion. Tunis, 1952.

Afr 1273.500 - .999 Barbary States in general - Economic history and conditions - Contemporary works (By date)

Afr 1273.922 Cosnier, Henri. L'Afrique du Nord. Paris, 1922.
Afr 1273.926 Bernard, A. L'Afrique du Nord pendant la guerre. Paris, 1926.
Afr 1273.954 France. Commission d'Etude. Deuxième plan de modernisation. n.p., 1954. 2 pam.
Afr 1273.958 Avakov, R.M. Frantsuzskii monopolisticheskii kapital v severnoi Afrike. Moscow, 1958.
Afr 1273.961 Gallissot, Rene. L'économie de l'Afrique du Nord. Paris, 1961.
Afr 1273.961.2 Gallissot, Rene. L'economie de l'Afrique du Nord. Paris, 1964.
Afr 1273.963A Union Nationale des Etudiants du Maroc à Alger. Industrialisation au Maghreb. Paris, 1963.
Afr 1273.963B Union Nationale des Etudiants du Maroc a Alger. Industrialisation au Maghreb. Paris, 1963.
Afr 1273.966 Amin, Samir. L'économie du Maghreb. Paris, 1966.
Afr 1273.966.5 Brown, Leon Carl. State and society in independent North Africa. Washington, 1966.
Afr 1273.967 Tiano, André. Le Maghreb entre les mythes, l'économie nord-africaine. Paris, 1967.
Afr 1273.967.5 Benyoussef, Amor. Populations du Maghreb et communauté économique à quatre. Paris, 1967.
Afr 1273.968 Muzikář, Joseph. Les Perspectives de l'intégration des pays maghrébins et leur attitude vis-à-vis du Marché commun. Nancy, 1968.

Afr 1280 Barbary States in general - Races

Afr 1280.2 Tauxier, Henri. Etude sur les migrations des nations berbères avant l'islamisme. Paris, 1863.
Afr 1280.3 Weisgerber, H. Les blancs d'Afrique. Paris, 1910.
Afr 1280.10 Giesa de Camps, Santiago. Las Kabilas de Bocoya, Beniburiaga y Flemsamana. Barcelona, 1903.

Afr 1280 Barbary States in general - Races - cont.

Afr 1280.15 Duprat, Pascal. Les races anciennes et modernes de l'Afrique septentrionale. Paris, 1845.
Afr 1280.25F Bertholon, Lucien. Recherches anthropologiques dans la Berbérie orientale. Lyon, 1913. 2v.
Afr 1280.30 Chouraqui, A. Marche vers l'Occident. 1. ed. Paris, 1952.
Afr 1280.30.5 Chouraqui, A. Les Juifs d'Afrique du Nord entre l'Orient et l'Occident. Paris, 1965.
Afr 1280.50 Slouschz, Nahum. Travels in North Africa. Philadelphia, 1927.
Afr 1280.60 Bousquet, G.H. Les Berbères. 1st ed. Paris, 1957.

Afr 1285 Barbary States in general - Religion

Afr 1285.5 Cooley, John Kent. Baal, Christ, and Mohammed. London, 1967.

Afr 1301 - 1324 Morocco - Periodicals (A-Z)

Afr 1301.1 Archives marocaines. Paris. 1,1904+ 31v.
Afr 1301.2 Annuaire du Maroc. Paris. 1905+ 12v.
Afr 1301.3 Anuario español de Marruecos. Madrid. 1913+
Afr 1301.4 Annuaire général du Maroc. Casablanca. 1917+ 5v.
Afr 1301.5 Morocco. Annuaire économique et financier. Casablanca. 1917+ 4v.
Afr 1301.6 Africa española. Madrid. 1,1913+ 9v.
Afr 1302.1 Boletin oficial de la zona de influencia española en Marruecos. Madrid. 1913+ 6v.
Afr 1302.1.5 Boletin oficial de la zona de influencia española en Marruecos. Anexo. Madrid. 1,1914+
Afr 1302.2F Bulletin économique du Maroc. Rabat. 1,1934+ 4v.
NEDL Afr 1303.2 Committee for Moroccan Studies and Survey. Newsletter. Rabat.
Afr 1303.5 Confluent, revue marocaine. Rabat. 1,1956+ 13v.
Afr 1306.1F France-Maroc, revue mensuelle. Paris. 1916+ 8v.
Afr 1308.2 Hesperis. Paris. 1,1921+ 34v.
Afr 1308.4 Hesperis-Tamuda. Rabat. 1,1961+ 5v.
Afr 1309.1 Institut des Hautes Études Marocaines. Bulletin. Paris. 1,1920+
Afr 1309.2 Institut des Hautes Études Marocaines. Collection Hesperis. Paris. 1+ 4v.
Afr 1309.3 Institut des Hautes Études Marocaines. Publications (1915-1935). Tables et index. Rochefort-sur-Mer, 1936. 2v.
Afr 1309.5 Institut des Hautes Études Marocaines. Actes du Congrès de l'Institut. Rabat. 1928+ 2v.
Afr 1313.1F Morocco. Service Général de l'Information. Bulletin d'information et de documentation. Rabat.
Afr 1313.2 Morocco. Service Général de l'Information. Bulletin d'information du Maroc. Rabat.
Afr 1313.3 Maroc-documents. Rabat. 5,1958+ 3v.
Afr 1313.4 Maroc, revue du Ministère des Affaires Etrangères. Rabat. 1,1962+
Afr 1313.6 Morocco tourism. Rabat. 42,1966+ 3v.
Afr 1318.6F Réalités marocaines, revue semestrielle. Casablanca. 6,1954+
Afr 1318.10 Revue de géographie du Maroc. Rabat. 7,1965+
Afr 1320.5 Tamuda, revistas de investigaciones marroquies. Tetuan. 1,1953+ 7v.
Afr 1320.6 Ketama, supplemento literario de Tamuda. Tetuan. 1953+

Afr 1325 Morocco - Folios [Discontinued]

Afr 1325.1F Foucauld, Charles de. Reconnaissance au Maroc. Paris, 1888. 2v.
Afr 1325.2F Canal, J. Géographie générale du Maroc. Paris, 1902.
Afr 1325.3F Boletin de la Sociedad Union Hispano-Mauritanica 1894. Granada, 1894. 2v.
Afr 1325.4F Francisco Jesus Maria de San Juan del Puerto, Mission historial de Marruecos. Sevilla, 1708.
Afr 1325.4.5PF Menendez Pidal, Juan. Misiones catolicas de Marruecos. Barcelona, 1897.
Afr 1325.5F Italy. Ministero degli Affari Esteri. Documenti diplomatici. Successione sceriffiana (Marrocco). Roma, 1895.
Afr 1325.6F Keatinge, M. Travels through France and Spain to Morocco. London, 1817.
Afr 1325.7F France. Question de la protection diplomatique au Maroc. Paris, 1880.
Afr 1325.8F France. Ministère des Affaires Etrangères. Accords conclus...entre France et l'Angleterre. Paris, 1904.
Afr 1325.9F Conférence Internationale d'Algeciras. Acte général. La Haye, 1906.
Afr 1325.9.5F Conférence Internationale d'Algeciras. Despatches from British delegate. London, 1906.
Afr 1325.10F Spain. Ministerio de Estado. Documentos presentados a las Cortes en la legislatura. Madrid, 1911.

Afr 1326 Morocco - Bibliographies

Afr 1326.1 Playfair, L. Bibliography of Morocco. London, 1892.
Afr 1326.2 Kampffmeyer, Georg. Studien und Mitteilungen der deutschen Marokko-bibliothek. Berlin, 1911.
Afr 1326.3 Bauer y Landauer, I. Apuntes para una bibliografia de Marruecos. Madrid, 1922.
Afr 1326.5 Levi Provencal, E. Les historiens des Chorfa. Thèse. Paris, 1922.
Afr 1326.5.2 Levi Provencal, E. Les historiens des Chorfa. Paris, 1922.
Afr 1326.7 Lebel, Roland. Les voyageurs français du Maroc. Paris, 1936.
Afr 1326.10 Lebel, Roland. Le Maroc chez les auteurs anglais du XVIe au XIXe siècle. Paris, 1939.
Afr 1326.12 Cenival, Pierre de. Bibliographie marocaine, 1923-33. Paris, 1937.
Afr 1326.14 Bibliografia marroque. Tetuan.
Afr 1326.16 Bibliographie nationale marocaine. Rabat. 1,1962+
Afr 1326.18 Rabat. Université. Centre Universitaire de la Recherche Scientifique. Bulletin signalétique. Rabat. 1,1963+
Afr 1326.20 Bennett, Norman Robert. A study guide for Morocco. Boston, 1968.

Afr 1328 Morocco - Pamphlet volumes

Afr 1328 Pamphlet box. Morocco.
Afr 1328.2 Pamphlet vol. Morocco. 10 pam.
Afr 1328.3 Pamphlet box. Morocco-description.
Afr 1328.4 Pamphlet box. Morocco-history.

Afr 1330 Morocco - Collected source materials - General works

Afr 1330.5 Castries, H. de. Les sources inédites de l'histoire du Maroc. Dynastie saadienne. Paris, 1905-26. 4v.

Afr 1330.5.3 Castries, H. de. Les sources inédites de l'histoire du Maroc. Dynastie saadienne. (Pays-bas, t.1-6). Paris, 1906-23. 6v.

Afr 1330.5.7 Castries, H. de. Les sources inédites de l'histoire du Maroc. Dynastie Saadienne. (Espagne, t.1-3). Paris, 1921. 3v.

Afr 1330.5.9 Castries, H. de. Archives et bibliothèques d'Angleterre, 1661-1757. (France, t.1-3). Paris, 1918-1925. 3v.

Afr 1330.5.12 Archives et bibliothèques de Portugal. 1,1939+ 6v.

Afr 1330.6 Castries, H. de. Les sources inédites de l'histoire du Maroc. Dynastie filalienne. v.1-6. Paris, 1922-31. 6v.

Afr 1333 Morocco - Collected source materials - Treaties

Afr 1333.1 Decard, R. Les traités de commerce conclus par le Maroc. Paris, 1907.

Afr 1333.5.5 Morocco. Laws, statutes, etc. Treaties, codes...Supplément pour 1937. Paris, 1937.

Afr 1333.10 Caille, Jacques. Les accords internationaux du sultan Sidi Mohammed ben Abdallah (1757-1790). Tanger, 1960.

Afr 1333.15 Cagigas, I. Tratados y convenios referentes a Marruecos. Madrid, 1952.

Afr 1335 Morocco - Collected source materials - Others

Afr 1335.5 Actas y memorias del primer Congreso Español de Africanistas. Granada, 1894.

Afr 1335.6 Segundo congreso africanista. Barcelona, 1908.

Afr 1335.7 Documents d'histoire et de géographie marocaines. Paris. 1,1929+ 4v.

Afr 1335.8 Turin. Museo Civico d'Arte Antica. Il medagliere delle raccolte numismatiche torinesi. Torino, 1964.

Afr 1335.20 Milliot, Louis. Recueil de jurisprudence chérifienne. v.1-4. Paris, 1920-24. 4v.

Afr 1338 Morocco - Government and administration - General works

Afr 1338.10 Goulven, Jos. Traité d'économie et de législation marocaines. v.1-2. Paris, 1921. 2v.

Afr 1338.12 Reynal, Raoul. Les particularités du droit fiscal par rapport au droit privé. Rabat, 1962.

Afr 1338.13 Zartman, I. William. Destiny of dynasty. Columbia, 1964.

Afr 1338.15 Bonjean, Jacques. L'unité de l'empire chérifien. Paris, 1955.

Afr 1338.17 Taraki, Muhammad Insan. Les institutions politiques du Maroc depuis l'indépendance. Thèse. Lyon, 1965.

Afr 1338.20 Laubadere, A. de. Les réformes des pouvoirs publics au Maroc. Paris, 1949.

Afr 1338.22 Bourely, Michel. Droit public marocain. v.1-2. Rabat, 1965.

Afr 1340 Morocco - Government and administration - Special topics

Afr 1340.5 Revilliod, M. L'organisation intérieur des pays de protectorat. Paris, 1913.

Afr 1340.6 France. Ministère des Affaires Etrangères. Rapport général sur...le protectorat du Maroc. Rabat, 192- .

Afr 1340.9 Maestacci, Noel. Le Maroc contemporain. Paris, 1928.

Afr 1340.10 Prat, Jean. La responsabilité de la puissance publique au Maroc. Rabat, 1963.

Afr 1340.15 Crouzet-Rayssac, A. de. Le régime des capitulations et la condition des étrangers au Maroc. Thèse. Paris, 1921.

Afr 1340.17 Decroux, Paul. La vie municipale au Maroc. Thèse. Lyon, 1931.

Afr 1340.20 Michel, Andre. Traité du contentieux administratif au Maroc. Thèse. Paris, 1932.

Afr 1340.20.10 Monier, R. Le contentieux administratif au Maroc. Paris, 1935.

Afr 1340.25 Grillet, M. Les alignements en droit marocain. Thèse. Paris, 1935.

Afr 1340.30 Stefani, P. Les libertés publiques au Maroc. Paris, 1938.

Afr 1340.35 Bremard, F. L'organisation régionale du Maroc. Paris, 1949.

Afr 1340.37 Robert, Jacques. La monarchie marocaine. Paris, 1963.

Afr 1340.40 Filizzola, Sabine. L'organisation de l'état civil au Maroc. Paris, 1958.

Afr 1340.41 Mrejen, Nissim. L'office national marocain du tourisme. Rabat, 1963.

Afr 1340.42 Morocco. Ministère de l'Information et du Tourisme. Documents sur la constitution. Rabat, 1960.

Afr 1346 Morocco - Military affairs - General works

Afr 1346.2 Huebner, Max. Militarische und militärgeographische Betrachtungen. Berlin, 1905.

Afr 1347 Morocco - Military affairs - Special topics

Afr 1347.1 Mordacq, J.J.H. La guerre au Maroc. Paris, 1904.

Afr 1347.1.2 Mordacq, J.J.H. La guerre au Maroc. 2e ed. Paris, 1907.

Afr 1347.2.3 Torcy, General de. Les espagnols au Maroc en 1909. 2 ed. Paris, 1911.

Afr 1347.3 Alvarez Cabrera, J. La guerra en Africa. Madrid, 1893.

Afr 1347.3.8 Alvarez Cabrera, J. Accion militar...imperio de Marruecos. Madrid, 1898.

Afr 1347.4 Nido y Torres, M. del. Historial de la Mehal-la Xeriffiana. Melilla-Tetuan, 1913.

Afr 1347.5 Guillaume, A. Les Berberes marocains et la pacification de l'Atlas central (1912-1933). Paris, 1946.

Afr 1365 - 1370 Morocco - General history (By date)

Afr 1367.64 Sagarra, J. de. Compendio de la historia de la España. v.1-2. Barcelona, 1764. 2v.

Afr 1367.87 Chenier, L.S. de. Recherches historiques sur les Maures. Paris, 1787. 3v.

Htn Afr 1368.60* Canovas del Castello, A. de. Apuntes para la historia de Marruecos. Madrid, 1860.

Afr 1368.60.6 Canovas del Castello, A. de. Apuntes para la historia de Marruecos. Madrid, 1913.

Afr 1368.78 Castellanos, M.P. Descripcion historica de Marruecos. Santiago, 1878.

Afr 1368.78.3 Castellanos, M.P. Historia de Marruecos. Tanger, 1898.

Afr 1368.78.5 Castellanos, M.P. Historia de Marruecos. Madrid, 1946. 2v.

Afr 1368.99 Meakin, B. The Moorish empire. London, 1899.

Afr 1369.15 Becker, Jeronimo. Historia de Marruecos. Madrid, 1915.

Afr 1369.21 Hardy, Georges. Les grandes étapes de l'histoire du Maroc. Paris, 1921.

Afr 1369.23 Martin, Alfred G.P. Quatre siècles d'histoire marocaine. Paris, 1923.

Afr 1369.31 Coissac de Chavrebiere. Histoire du Maroc. Paris, 1931.

Afr 1369.39 Garcia Figueras, T. Marruecos. Barcelona, 1939.

Afr 1365 - 1370 Morocco - General history (By date) - cont.

Afr 1369.49 Terrasse, Henri. Histoire du Maroc des origines a l'établissement du protectorat français. Casablanca, 1949-50. 2v.

Afr 1369.49.3 Terrasse, Henri. Histoire du Maroc. Casablanca, 1952.

Afr 1369.49.5 Garcia Figueras, T. Miscelanea de estudios historicos sobre Marruecos. Larache, 1949.

Afr 1369.50 Caille, Jacques. La petite histoire du Maroc. Casablanca, 1950. 2v.

Afr 1369.52 Cambon, H. Histoire du Maroc. Paris, 1952.

Afr 1369.53 American Committee for Moroccan Independence. The case for Morocco. Washington, 1953.

Afr 1369.53.5 Montagne, Robert. Révolution au Maroc. Paris, 1953.

Afr 1369.56A Ayache, Albert. Le Maroc. Paris, 1956.

Afr 1369.56B Ayache, Albert. Le Maroc. Paris, 1956.

Afr 1369.60 Husson, Philippe. La question des frontières terrestres du Maroc. Paris, 1960.

Afr 1369.61A Ashford, Douglas. Political change in Morocco. Princeton, 1961.

Afr 1369.61B Ashford, Douglas. Political change in Morocco. Princeton, 1961.

Afr 1369.61.5 Avakov, R.M. Marokko. Moscow, 1961.

Afr 1369.65 Barbour, N. Morocco. London, 1965.

Afr 1369.65.5 Hoffmann, E. Realm of the evening star. Philadelphia, 1965.

Afr 1369.67 Histoire du Maroc, par Jean Brignon. Paris, 1967.

Afr 1380 Morocco - History by periods - Mohammedan conquest (690-788) - General works

Afr 1380.5 Ibn Azzuz, M. Historia de Marruecos hasta la dominacion almoravide. Madrid, 1955.

Afr 1380.8 Vernet Gines, Juan. Historia de Marruecos, la islamizacion. Tetuan, 1957.

Afr 1390 Morocco - History by periods - Medieval history (788-1550) - General works

Afr 1390.1 Annales regum Mauritaniae. v.1-2. Upsaliae, 1843.

Afr 1390.1.5 Roudh el-Kartas. Histoire des souverains du Maghreb. Paris, 1860.

Afr 1390.2 Moura, J. de S.A. Historia dos Soberanos Mohametanos. Lisboa, 1828.

Afr 1390.3 Fagnan, E. Al-bayano'l-mogrib. Alger, 1901. 2v.

Afr 1390.4 Ibn al-Atir. Annales du Maghreb et de l'Espagne. Alger, 1898.

Afr 1390.5 Cour, Auguste. La dynastie marocaine des Beni Wattas (1420-1554). Constantine, 1920.

Afr 1390.6 Millet, Rene. Les Almohades, histoire dune dynastie berbère. Paris, 1923.

Afr 1390.7.5F Jimenez de la Espada, Marcos. La guerra del Moro a fines del siglo XV. Ceuta, 1940.

Afr 1390.8 Bosch Vila, Jacinto. Los Almoravidas. Tetuan, 1956.

Afr 1395 Morocco - History by periods - Medieval history (788-1550) - Merinide dynasty (1195-1551) - Special topics

Htn Afr 1395.25* Tratado da vida e martirio dos cinco martires de Marrocos. Coimbra, 1928.

Afr 1398 Morocco - History by periods - Medieval history (788-1550) - Merinide dynasty (1195-1551) - Portuguese wars

Htn Afr 1398.5* Faria e Sousa, Manuel de. Africa portuguesa por su autor Manuel de Faria. Lisboa, 1681.

Afr 1400 Morocco - History by periods - Piratical period (1529-1795) - General works

Afr 1400.1 Muhammed al-Segir. Nozhet-Elhadi, histoire de la dynastie saadienne au Maroc, (1511-1670). Paris, 1889.

Afr 1400.2 Aljaiyani. Le Maroc de 1631 à 1812. Paris, 1886.

Afr 1400.3 Boulet. Histoire de l'empire des chérifs en Afrique. Paris, 1733.

Afr 1400.4 Dombay, F. von. Geschichte der Scherifen. Agram, 1801.

Afr 1400.5 Weir, T.H. The shaikhs of Morocco in the XVI century. Edinburgh, 1904.

Afr 1400.6 Cour, Auguste. L'établissement des dynasties des chérif au Maroc. Paris, 1904.

Afr 1401 Morocco - History by periods - Piratical period (1529-1795) - Rise of Sherif dynasty

Htn Afr 1401.1* Torres, D. de. Relation de l'origine et succez des cherifs. Paris, 1636.

Htn Afr 1401.5* Torres, D. de. Relacion del origen y sucesso de los karifes. Sevilla, 1586.

Htn Afr 1401.7* True historicall discourse of Muley-Hamets rising. London, 1609.

Afr 1401.80 Caro Baroja, Julio. Una vision de Marruecos a mediados del siglo XVI. Madrid, 1956.

Afr 1403 Morocco - History by periods - Piratical period (1529-1795) - Battle of El Kasar (1578)

Htn Afr 1403.1* Histoiria de bello Africano. Noribergae, 1580.

Htn Afr 1403.2* Coppia d'una litera venuta di Spagna. Mantova, 1578.

Afr 1403.3 Mesa, S. de. Jornada de Africa por el rey Don Sebastian. Barcelona, 1630.

Afr 1403.4 Baena Parada, J. Epitome de la vida y hechos de Don Sebastian. Madrid, 1692.

Afr 1403.5 Mendonca, Jeronymo de. Jornada de Africa. Lisboa, 1785.

Htn Afr 1403.5.5* Mendonca, Jeronymo de. Jornada de Africa. Lisboa, 1607.

Afr 1403.6 Esaguy, Jose de. O minuto vitorioso de Alacer-Quibir. Lisboa, 1944.

Afr 1406 Morocco - History by periods - Piratical period (1529-1795) - Sherif dynasty (1580-1672)

Htn Afr 1406.1* Cortende waerachlich verhail...1607. Hague, 1607.

Htn Afr 1406.2* Wilkins, George. Three miseries of Barbary. London, 1606.

Afr 1406.3 Francois d'Angers. L'histoire de la mission des pères capucins...à Maroc, 1624-1636. Rabat, 1888.

Afr 1406.5 Nader tractaet van oredeende vrundtschap...22 marti 1657. Hague, 1659.

Htn Afr 1406.7* Short and strange relation of some part of the life of Tafiletta. London, 1669.

Afr 1406.8 Waerachtigh verhael van Tafilette. n.p., 1669.

Afr 1406.9 Fernandez Alvarez, Manuel. Felipe II, Isabel de Inglaterra y Marruecos. Madrid, 1951.

Afr 1406.13 Tractaat susschen Marocco en de Nederlanden. 's-Gravenhage, 1777.

Afr 1406.14 Translaat susschen Marocco en de Nederlanden n.p., 1791.

Afr 1406.16 Castries, H. de. Agents et voyageurs français au Maroc, 1530-1660. Paris, 1911.

Afr 1407 Morocco - History by periods - Piratical period (1529-1795) - Stories of piracy and captivity

Afr 1407.1 Pellow, J. History of long captivity. London, 1736.
Afr 1407.1.2 Pellow, J. History of long captivity. 2 ed. London, 1740.
Afr 1407.1.5 Pellow, J. Adventures. London, 1890.
Htn Afr 1407.2* Dunton, J. True iournall of the Sally Fleet. London, 1637.
Htn Afr 1407.2.5* Carteret, George. The Barbary voyage of 1638. Philadelphia, 1929.
Htn Afr 1407.3* Brooks, F. Barbarian cruelty. London, 1693.
Afr 1407.4 Lafaye, J. de. Relation en forme de journal...des captifs. Paris, 1726.
Afr 1407.5 Kort...verhaal...slavernye onder de Mooren. Amsterdam, 1753.
Htn Afr 1407.6* Monette, G. Relation de la captivité dans les royaumes de Fez. Paris, 1683.
Afr 1407.7 Savine, A. Dans les fers du Moghreb. Paris, n.d.

Afr 1408 Morocco - History by periods - Piratical period (1529-1795) - Ismail (1672-1727)

Afr 1408.1 Braithwaite, Capt. History of revolution upon death of Ishmail. London, 1729.
Afr 1408.1.5 Braithwaite, Capt. Histoire des révolutions de l'empire de Maroc. Amsterdam, 1731.
Afr 1408.2.5 Busnot, F.D. Histoire du regne de mouley Ismael. Rouen, 1714.
Afr 1408.2.10 Busnot, F.D. Récits d'aventures au temps de Louis XIV. Paris, 1928.
Afr 1408.3 Mouette, G. Histoire des conquestes de Mouley Archy. Paris, 1783.
Afr 1408.4 Plantet, E. Mouley Ismael. Paris, 1893.
Afr 1408.5 Guidotti, P. Storia dei Mori. Firenze, 1775.
Afr 1408.6 Castries, H. de. Moulay Ismail et Jacques II. Paris, 1903.
Afr 1408.7 Blunt, Wilfrid. Black sunrise. London, 1951.
Afr 1408.8 Colin, E.R. Le grand Ismail. Paris, 1929.

Afr 1409 Morocco - History by periods - Piratical period (1529-1795) - Other special (1529-1795)

Afr 1409.1 Mairault, A.M. Relation...de Maroc, 1727-1737. Paris, 1742.
Afr 1409.2.5 Relacao verdadeira da implacavel peste. Lisboa, 1756.
Afr 1409.3 Relation de l'affaire de Larache. Amsterdam, 1775.
Afr 1409.4 Marchesi, V. Le relazioni tra la repubblica Veneta ed il Marocco dal 1750 al 1797. Torino, 1886.
Afr 1409.9 Spain. Sovereigns. Carlos III. El rei. Madrid, 1774.
Afr 1409.10 Spain. Sovereigns. Carlos IV. Real cedula en que S.M. declara la guerra al rey de Marruecos. Madrid, 1791.
Afr 1409.15 Oliver Asin, J. Vida de Don Felipe de Africa. Madrid, 1955.
Afr 1409.17 Garcia Figueras, T. Apoyo de España a Mawlay Hisam. Tetuan, 1953.
Afr 1409.18 Arribas Palau, Mariano. Cartas arabes de Marruecos en tiempo de Mawlay al Yazid, 1790-1792. Tetuan, 1959.
Afr 1409.18.2 Arribas Palau, Mariano. Cartas arabes de Marruecos en tiempo de Mawlay al Yazid, 1790-1792. Tetuan, 1961.
Afr 1409.20 Caillé, Jacques. Une Corse sultane du Maroc, Davia Franceschini et sa famille. Paris, 1968.

Afr 1410 Morocco - History by periods - Nineteenth century - General works

Afr 1410.2 Oliver, Roland. Africa since 1800. London, 1967.

Afr 1415 Morocco - History by periods - Nineteenth century - Sulaiman) 1795-1822 - General works

Afr 1415.01 Pamphlet box. Sulaiman.

Afr 1422 Morocco - History by periods - Nineteenth century - Abd'er Rahman II (1822-1859) - Relations and war with France (1844)

Afr 1422.3 Chais, G. De la convention de Tangier. n.p., 1845.
Afr 1422.5 Duprat, P. Peuples anciens et modernes de Maroc. n.p., n.d.
Afr 1422.6 Warnier, A.H. Campagne du Maroc (1844). Paris, 1899.
Afr 1422.7 Latreille, A. La campagne de 1844 au Maroc. La bataille d'Isly. Paris, 1912.
Afr 1422.10 Cosse Brissac, P. de. Les rapports de la France et du Maroc pendant la conquête de l'Algérie (1830-1847). Paris, 1931.

Afr 1425 Morocco - History by periods - Nineteenth century - Abd'er Rahman II (1822-1859) - Other special topics

Afr 1425.5 Caille, Jacques. Une mission de Leon Roches à Rabat en 1845. Thèse. Casablanca, 1947.

Afr 1430 Morocco - History by periods - Nineteenth century - Sidi Mohammed (1859-1873) - General works

Afr 1430.2 Arnaud, L. Au temps de Mehallas. Casablanca, 1952.

Afr 1432 Morocco - History by periods - Nineteenth century - Sidi Mohammed (1859-1873) - War with Spain (1859-1860)

Afr 1432.1 Alarcon, P.A. Diario de la guerra de Africa. Madrid, 1880. 3v.
Afr 1432.1.2F Alarcon, P.A. Diario de la guerra de Africa. Madrid, 1860.
Afr 1432.2 Baudoz, A. Histoire de la guerre de l'Espagne. Paris, 1860.
Afr 1432.3 Hardman, F. The Spanish campaign in Morocco. Edinburgh, 1860.
Afr 1432.4 Fillias, A. L'Espagne et le Maroc en 1860. Paris, 1860.
Afr 1432.5 Yriarte, C. Sous la tente: souvenirs du Maroc. Paris, 1863.
Afr 1432.6 Schlagintweit, E. Der spanisch-marokkanische Krieg...1859-60. Leipzig, 1863.
Afr 1432.7F Castelar, E. Cronica de la guerra de Africa. Madrid, 1859.
Afr 1432.8F Album de la guerra de Africa. Madrid, 1860.
Afr 1432.9 Boudot, P. Une mission militaire prussienne. Paris, 1908.
Afr 1432.10 Alvarez, J.A. de. Biografia y retratos de los generales jefes de los cuerpos. Barcelona, 1860.
Afr 1432.11 Chronica de la guerra de Africa. Madrid, 1860.
Afr 1432.12 Castillo, R. del. España y Marruecos, historia de la guerra de Africa. Cadiz, 1859.
Afr 1432.13 Beltran, F.C. Historia de la guerra de Africa. T.1. Madrid, 1860.
Afr 1432.14 Martin Arrue, F. Guerra hispano-marroqui, 1859-60. Madrid, 1915.
Afr 1432.15 Monedero Ordoñez, Dionisio. Episodios militares del ejercito de Africa. 2a ed. Burgos, 1893.

Afr 1432 Morocco - History by periods - Nineteenth century - Sidi Mohammed (1859-1873) - War with Spain (1859-1860) - cont.

Afr 1432.16 Pamphlet vol. Poesias a la guerra de Africa. 6 pam.
Afr 1432.17 Joly, A. Historia critica de la guerra...en 1859-60. Madrid, 1910.
Afr 1432.18 Spain. Ministerio de Estado. Correspondencia..Guerra de Africa. Madrid, 1860.
Afr 1432.19 Ameller, V. de. Juicio critico de la guerra de Africa. Madrid, 1861.
Afr 1432.20 Poblacion y Fernandez, A. Historia medica de la guerra de Africa. Madrid, 1860.
Afr 1432.21.2 Navarrete, José. Desde Vad-Ras a Sevilla: Acuarelas de la campaña de Africa. 2a ed. Madrid, 1880.
Afr 1432.22 Perez Calvo, Juan. Siete dias en el campamento de Africa. Madrid, 1860.
Afr 1432.23 Landa, Nicasio de. La campaña de Marruecos. Madrid, 1860.
Afr 1432.24 Baeumen, A. von. Nach Marokko. Berlin, 1861.
Afr 1432.25 Spain. Comision del Tesoro. Relato de las gestiones para el cumplimiento de la clausula de indemnizacion del tratado de paz con el Imperio de Marruecos (1860). Madrid, 1950.
Afr 1432.26 Garcia Figueras, T. Recuerdos centenarios de una guerra romantica. Madrid, 1961.
Afr 1432.28 Ventosa, E. Españoles y Marroquies. Barcelona, 1860.

Afr 1435 Morocco - History by periods - Nineteenth century - Sidi Mohammed (1859-1873) - Other special topics

Afr 1435.3 Amaudru, N. Sultane française du Maroc. Paris, 1906.
Afr 1435.5 Baule y Landauer. Consecuencias de la campana de 1860. Madrid, 1923. 4v.
Afr 1438.1 Pamphlet box. War with Spain (1859-60).

Afr 1442 Morocco - History by periods - Nineteenth century - El Hasan III (1873-1894) - Troubles with Spain (1894)

Afr 1442.1 Pamphlet box. Troubles with Spain (about 1894).
Afr 1442.5 Taviel de Andrade, E. Cuestion de Marruecos. Madrid, 1888.
Afr 1442.10F Spain. Ministerio de Estado. Documentos presentados a las Cortes. Madrid, 1894.

Afr 1445 Morocco - History by periods - Nineteenth century - El Hasan III (1873-1894) - Other special topics

Afr 1445.5F Spain. Ministerio de Estado. Documents diplomatiques. Conférences de Madrid. Supplément. Madrid, 1880. 2 pam.
Afr 1445.6F Spain. Ministerio de Estado. Documentos presentados a las Cortes. Madrid, 1889.
Afr 1445.10 Cruikshank, E.F. Morocco at the parting of the ways. Diss. Philadelphia, 1935.
Afr 1445.10.5 Cruikshank, E.F. Morocco at the parting of the ways. Philadelphia, 1935.

Afr 1450 Morocco - History by periods - Nineteenth century - Abd el Aziz (1894-1907) - General works

Afr 1450.1 Veyre, Gabriel. Au Maroc dans l'intimité du sultan. Paris, n.d.
Afr 1450.2 Sabran, J. de. Le Maroc rouge. Paris, n.d.
Afr 1450.3 Sarnette, F. Aventures d'un français au Maroc. Paris, 1905.
Afr 1450.6 Karow, K.L. Neun Jahre in marokkanischen Diensten. Berlin, 1909.
Afr 1450.9 Diaz Moreu, E. Problema de actualidad: la cuestion de Marruecos. Madrid, 1909.

Afr 1453 Morocco - History by periods - Nineteenth century - Abd el Aziz (1894-1907) - Tourmaline Expedition (1897-1898)

Afr 1453.1 Grey, H.M. In Moorish captivity. London, 1899.
Afr 1453.7 Salmon, Albert. Le Maroc. Paris, 1908.
Afr 1453.8 Schanz, Moritz. Nordafrika, Marokko. Halle, 1905.
Afr 1453.10 Harris, Walter B. Morocco that was. Edinburgh, 1921.
Afr 1453.11 Weisgerber, F. Au seuil du Maroc moderne. Rabat, 1947.

Afr 1470 Morocco - History by periods - Nineteenth century - Abd el Aziz (1894-1907) - Diplomatic negotiations concerning Morocco

Afr 1470.3 Aflalo, M. The truth about Morocco. London, 1904.
Afr 1470.5 Anderson, Eugene Newton. The first Moroccan crisis, 1904-1906. Chicago, 1930.
Afr 1470.5.2 Anderson, Eugene Newton. The first Moroccan crisis, 1904-1906. Hamden, Conn., 1966.

Afr 1485 Morocco - History by periods - Nineteenth century - Abd el Aziz (1894-1907) - Other special topics (incl. Casablanca)

Afr 1485.2 Rankin, R. In Morocco with General d'Amade. London, 1908.
Afr 1485.3 Perez, D. El ocaso de un sultan. Zaragoza, 1909.
Afr 1485.4 Morote, L. La conquista del Mogreb. Valencia, n.d.
Afr 1485.5 Grasset, Capitaine. A travers la Chaouia. Paris, 1911.
Afr 1485.6 Bourdon, G. Les journees de Casablanca. Paris, 1908.
Afr 1485.7 Guillaume. Sur la frontière marocaine. Paris, 1913.
Afr 1485.8 Marietti, Giovanni. Politica ed armi al Marocco. Torino, 1909.
Afr 1485.9 Espinosa de los Monteros, R. España en Africa 1903. Madrid, 1903.

Afr 1487 Morocco - History by periods - 20th century - General works

Afr 1487.5 Landau, Rom. Moroccan drama, 1900-1955. San Francisco, 1956.
Afr 1487.10 Taillard, Fulbert, Le nationalisme marocain. Paris, 1947.
Afr 1487.15 Larteguy, Jean. La tragédie du Maroc interdit. Paris, 1957.
Afr 1487.20 Lutskaia, N.S. Marokko vnovobretaet nezavisimost'. Moscow, 1958.
Afr 1487.22 Ortega y Gasset, Eduardo. Annual. Madrid, 1922.
Afr 1487.25 Maestre, Pedro. Divulgacion y orientacion. Granada, 1923.
Afr 1487.28 Garcia Figueras, T. Del Marruecos feudal, episodios de la vida del cherif Raisuri. Madrid, 1930.
Afr 1487.32 Sermaye, J. L'oeuvre française en terre marocaine. Casablanca, 1938.
Afr 1487.36 Cohen, Mark I. Morocco, old land, new nation. N.Y., 1966.
Afr 1487.40 Spillmann, Georges. Du protectorat à l'indépendance, Maroc, 1912-1955. Paris, 1967.

Afr 1490 Morocco - History by periods - 20th century - Mulai Hafid (1907-1912)

Afr 1490.2 Ashmead-Bartlett, E. Passing of the shereefian empire. Edinburgh, 1910.
Afr 1490.2.5 Ashmead-Bartlett, E. Passing of the shereefian empire. N.Y., 1910.
Afr 1490.3 Harris, Lawrence. With Mulai Hafid at Fez. London, 1909.
Afr 1490.3.5 Harris, Lawrence. With Mulai Hafid at Fez. Boston, 1910.
Afr 1490.4.7 Riera, A. España en Marruecos. 7a ed. Barcelona, 1911.

Afr 1490   Morocco - History by periods - 20th century - Mulai Hafid (1907-1912) - cont.
Afr 1490.5   Kreuter, A. Marokko: wirtschaftliche und soziale Studien in Marokko 1911. Berlin, 1911.
Afr 1490.6   Rene-Leclerc, C. Situation économique du Maroc 1908-09. Oran, 1910.
Afr 1490.9   Mohr, P. Marokko, eine politisch-wirtschaftliche Studie. Berlin, 1902.
Afr 1490.10   D'Amade, Général. Campagne de 1908-1909 en Chaouia. Rapport. Paris, 1911.
Afr 1490.11   Capperon, L. Au secours de Fès. Paris, 1912.
Afr 1490.11.9   Hubert-Jacques. Journées sanglantes de Fez. 4 ed. Paris, 1913.
Afr 1490.11.15 Azan, Paul. L'expédition de Fez. Paris, 1924.
Afr 1490.12   Ceccaldi, C. Au pays de la poudre. Paris, 1914.
Afr 1490.13   Khorat, P. En colonne au Maroc. Paris, 1913.
Afr 1490.14   Azan, Paul. Souvenirs de Casablanca. Paris, 1911.
Afr 1490.15   Feline, M.H. L'artillerie au Maroc, campagnes en Chaouia. Paris, 1912.
Afr 1490.16   Clement-Grandcourt, A. Croquis marocains, sur la Moulouya. Paris, 1912.
Afr 1490.17   Pierrat, J. Vingt-six mois au Maroc. Paris, 1916.
Afr 1490.18   Serra Orts, A. Recuerdos de la guerra del Kert de 1911-12. Barcelona, 1914.
Afr 1490.19   Lechartier, G.G. La colonne du Haut-Guir en Sept. 1908. Paris, 1908.
Afr 1490.20   Berenguer. La guerra en Marruecos. Madrid, 1918.
Afr 1490.21   Camarasa, M. de. La cuestion de Marruecos y su solucion...1911. Barcelona, 1911.
Afr 1490.22   Hildebrand, Gerhard. Sozialistische Auslandspolitik. Jena, 1911.

Afr 1493   Morocco - History by periods - 20th century - Mulai Yusoef (1912-1927) (incl. Abd-el Krim)
Afr 1493.5   Cornet. A la conquête du Maroc sud, 1912-13. Paris, 1914.
Afr 1493.6   Bernard, Francois. Le Maroc économique et agricole. Paris, 1917.
Afr 1493.7   Dugard, Henry. Le Maroc de 1918. Paris, 1918.
Afr 1493.7.5   Dugard, Henry. Le Maroc de 1917. Paris, 1917.
Afr 1493.7.10   Dugard, Henry. Le Maroc de 1919. Paris, 1919.
Afr 1493.8   Lareveliere, Comte de. Les énergies françaises au Maroc. Paris, 1917.
Afr 1493.9   Lichtenberger, A. Un coin de la guerre, la France au Maroc. Paris, 1918.
Afr 1493.10   Stichel, Bernhard. Die Zukunft in Marokko. Berlin, 1917.
Afr 1493.20   Gomez Hidalgo, F. Marruecos. Madrid, 1921.
Afr 1493.25   Franco, Francisco. Marruecos, diario de una bandera, 1922. Sevilla, 1939.
Afr 1493.30   Mellor, F.H. Morocco awakes. London, 1939.
Afr 1493.35   Loustaunau-Lacau, G. Au Maroc français en 1925. Paris, 1928.
Afr 1493.40   Bermudo-Soriano, E. El Raisuni (caudillo de Yebala). Madrid, 1941.
Afr 1493.45   Vial, Jean. Le Maroc héroique. Paris, 1938.
Afr 1493.50   Gabrielli, L. Abd-el-Krim et les événements du Rif. Casablanca, 1953.
Afr 1493.50.5   Fontaine, Pierre. Abd-el-Krim. Paris, 1958.
Afr 1493.50.10 Furneaux, Rupert. Abdel Krim: Emir of the Rif. London, 1967.
Afr 1493.50.15 Woolman, David J. Rebels in the RF; Abd el Krim and the Rif rebellion. Stanford, 1968.
Afr 1493.55   Goulven, Joseph. La France au Maroc. Paris, 1937.
Afr 1493.60   Maridalyn, H. Présence française au Maroc. Monte carlo, 1952.
Afr 1493.65   Leyris de Campredon. Lyautey. Paris, 1955.
Afr 1493.70   Rebellon Dominguez, G. Seis meses en Yebala. Madrid, 1925.
Afr 1493.71   Osuna Servent, Arturo. Frente a Abd-el-Krim. Madrid, 1922.
Afr 1493.72   Goded, M. Marruecos, las etapas de la pacificacion. Madrid, 1932.
Afr 1493.74   Hernandez Mir, F. Del desastre al fracaso. Madrid, 1922.
Afr 1493.76   Garcia Figueras, Tomás. Recuerdos de la campaña. Jeréz, 1925.
Afr 1493.78A   Halstead, John Preston. Rebirth of a nation;...Moroccan nationalism, 1912-1944. Cambridge, 1967.
Afr 1493.78B   Halstead, John Preston. Rebirth of a nation;...Moroccan nationalism, 1912-1944. Cambridge, 1967.

Afr 1494   Morocco - History by periods - 20th century - Mulai Mohammad (Nov. 1929-1961)
Afr 1494.5   Comité d'Action Marocaine. Plan de réformes marocaines. n.p., 1934.
Afr 1494.5.2   Comité d'Action Marocaine. Annexes au plan de réformes marocaines. n.p., 1934.
Afr 1494.6   Landau, Rom. The Sultan of Morocco. London, 1951.
Afr 1494.6.5   Landau, Rom. Mohammed V. Rabat, 1957.
Afr 1494.7   Moroccan Office of Information and Documentation, N.Y. Morocco under the protectorate. N.Y., 1953.
Afr 1494.10   Barrat, Robert. Justice pour le Maroc. Paris, 1953.
Afr 1494.12   Parent, P. The truth about Morocco. N.Y., 1953.
Afr 1494.15   Hure, A.J.J. La pacification du Maroc. Paris, 1952.
Afr 1494.20   Bridel, T. Le Maroc. Lausanne, 1954.
Afr 1494.25   Howe, Marvine. The prince and I. N.Y., 1955.
Afr 1494.30F   Quarante ans de présence française au Maroc. Casablanca, 1953.
Afr 1494.35   Conférence Nationale pour la Solution du Problème Franco-Marocain. Compte-rendu. v.1. Paris, 1956.
Afr 1494.37   Barbau, Muslim. Tempête sur le Maroc. Paris, 1931.
Afr 1494.40   Muhammad V, Sultan of Morocco. Le Maroc à l'heure de l'indépendance. v.1. Rabat, 1958.
Afr 1494.45   Dehedin, Charles. Adieu Maroc. Paris, 1959.
Afr 1494.50   Ben Barka el Mehdi. Problèmes d'édification du Maroc et du Moghreb. Paris, 1959.
Afr 1494.55F   Diplomatist. In memoriam, His Majesty King Mohammed V. London, 1961.
Afr 1494.60   Session d'études administratives. Rabat, 1959.
Afr 1494.61   Bernard, S. Le conflit franco-marocain, 1943-56. v.1-2, 3. Bruxelles, 1963. 2v.
Afr 1494.61.5   Bernard, S. The Franco-Moroccan conflict, 1943-1956. New Haven, 1968.
Afr 1494.62   Ashford, D.E. Perspectives of a Moroccan nationalist. Totowa, N.J., 1964.
Afr 1494.63   Cerych, Ladislav. Europeens et Marocains. Bruges, 1964.
Afr 1494.64   Communist Party of Morocco. Le parti communiste marocain. Paris, 1958.
Afr 1494.65   Manaserian, Levon P. Marokko v bor'be za nezavisimost'. Erevan, 1969.

Afr 1495   Morocco - History by periods - 20th century - Hassan II (1961-   )
Afr 1495.2   Landau, Rom. Hassan II, King of Morocco. London, 1962.
Afr 1495.3   Vaucher, G. Sous les cèdres d'Ifrane. Paris, 1962.
Afr 1495.4   Zartman, I.W. Morocco, problems of new power. N.Y., 1964.
Afr 1495.5   Cassaigne, Jean. La situation des Français au Maroc depuis l'indépendance, 1956-1964. Paris, 1965.
Afr 1495.6   Benbarka, El Mehdi. Option révolutionnaire au Maroc. Paris, 1966.
Afr 1495.6.5   Marec, Jean Paul. La Ténébreuse affaire Ben Barka. Paris, 1966.
Afr 1495.6.10   Mali, Tidiane. Une Philosophie sur l'affaire Ben Barka. Lyon, 1966.
Afr 1495.6.15   Ben Barka, Abdelkader. El Mehdi Ben Barka, mon frère. Paris, 1966.
Afr 1495.6.20   Sarne, Daniel. L'affaire Ben Barka. Paris, 1966.
Afr 1495.6.25   Caviglioli, François. Ben Barka chez les juges. Paris, 1967.
Afr 1495.6.30   Muratet, Roger. On a tué Ben Barka. Paris, 1967.
Afr 1495.6.35   Ben Barka, el Mehdi. The political thought of Ben Barka. Havana, 1968.

Afr 1550   Morocco - General relations with foreign powers - The Morocco question - General works
Afr 1550   Pamphlet box. Morocco question.
Afr 1550.01   Pamphlet box. Morocco question.
Afr 1550.1   Kerdec Cheny, A. Un boulevard de l'islam. Tanger, 1895.
Afr 1550.2   Mohr, P. Marokko, eine politische-wirtschaftliche Studie. Berlin, 1902.
Afr 1550.3   Maura y Gamazo, Gabriel. La cuestion de Marruecos. Madrid, 1905.
Afr 1550.3.5   Maura y Gamazo, Gabriel. La question du Maroc. Paris, 1911.
Afr 1550.4   Berard, V. L'affaire marocaine. Paris, 1906.
Afr 1550.5   Mantegazza, V. Il Marocco e l'Europa. Milano, 1906.
Afr 1550.6   Immanuel. Marokko. Berlin, 1903.
Afr 1550.7   Ferry, E. La réorganisation marocaine. Paris, 1905.
Afr 1550.8   Betegon, T. La conferencia de Algeciras. Madrid, 1906.
Afr 1550.9   Lapradelle, A. de. La condition du Maroc d'après l'accord de 1904. Paris, 1905.
Afr 1550.10   Diercks, Gustav. Die Marokkofrage und die Konferenz von Algeciras. Berlin, 1906.
Afr 1550.11   Tardier, J. La conférence d'Algésiras. Paris, 1908.
Afr 1550.12   Peyreigne, C. Les influences européennes au Maroc. n.p., n.d.
Afr 1550.13   Paquot, G. La question marocaine. Paris, 1908.
Afr 1550.14   Rouard de Card, E. Documents diplomatiques pour servir a l'étude de la question marocaine. n.p., 1911.
Afr 1550.15   Rouard de Card, E. Négociation franco-espagnole de 1902. Paris, 1912.
Afr 1550.16   Morel, E.D. Morocco in diplomacy. London, 1912.
NEDL Afr 1550.16.5 Morel, E.D. Ten years of secret diplomacy. 3d ed. London, 1915.
Afr 1550.17   Grand-Carteret, J. Une victoire sans guerre. Paris, 1911.
Afr 1550.18   Bretschger, J. Die Marokko-Konferenz. Zürich, 1913.
Afr 1550.19   Collection of magazine articles on...Morocco's relations with foreign countries. Zürich, 1904.
Afr 1550.20   Wirth, A. Marokko. Frankfurt, 1908.
Afr 1550.21   Barclay, T. El acta de Algeciras y el porvenir de Espana en Marruecos. Madrid, 1907.
Afr 1550.22   Algeciras. International Conference on Moroccan Affairs, 1906. Acta general. Madrid, 1906.
Afr 1550.22.5F Spain. Ministerio de Estado. Documentos presentados a las Cortes. Madrid, 1906.
Afr 1550.23   Gomez Gonzalez, M. La penetracion en Marruecos. Zaragoza, 1909.
Afr 1550.24   Camarasa, M. de. La cuestion de Marruecos y su honrada solucion. Madrid, 1911.
Afr 1550.27   Neumann, K. Die Internationalität Marokkos. Berlin, 1919.
Afr 1550.28   Ruediger, Georg von. Die Bedeutung der Algeciras-Konferenz. München, 1920.
Afr 1550.28.5   Ruediger, Georg von. Die Bedeutung der Algeciras-Konferenz Inaug.-Diss. Hamburg, 1917.
Afr 1550.30   Alengry, Jean. Les relations franco-espagnoles et l'affaire du Maroc. Paris, 1920.
Afr 1550.33   Semard, Pierre. Marokko. Hamburg, 1925.
Afr 1550.35   Martin, Alfred G.P. Le Maroc et l'Europe. Paris, 1928.
Afr 1550.37   Felix, Lucien. Le statut international du Maroc d'après les traités. Thèse. Paris, 1928.
Afr 1550.38   Schoettle, Hermann. Die Times in der ersten Marokkokrise. Vaduz, 1965.
Afr 1550.39A   Enthoven, Henri Emile. Van Tanger tot Agadir. Utrecht, 1929.
Afr 1550.39B   Enthoven, Henri Emile. Van Tanger tot Agadir. Utrecht, 1929.
Afr 1550.41   Schaettle, Hermann. Die Times in der ersten Marokkokrise mit besonderer Berücksichtigung der englisch-deutschen Beziehungen. Berlin, 1930.
Afr 1550.43   Rheinlaender, G. Deutschland, England und die Marokkokrise. Inaug. Diss. Bochum-Langendreer, 1931.
Afr 1550.45   Brenning, H.E. Die grossen Mächte und Marokko in den Jahren vor demMarokko-Abkommen von 8. Apr. 1904 (1898-1904). Berlin, 1934.
Afr 1550.50   Usborne, C.V. The conquest of Morocco. London, 1936.
Afr 1550.52   Guernier, E.L. Pour une politique d'empire. Paris, 1938.
Afr 1550.54   El-Hajoui, M.O. Histoire diplomatique du Maroc (1900-1912). Paris, 1937.
Afr 1550.56   Vieleux, Christian. Aspects marocains. La Rochelle, 1957.
Afr 1550.58   Miege, J.L. Le Maroc et l'Europe. v.1-4. Paris, 1961. 4v.

Afr 1555   Morocco - General relations with foreign powers - The Morocco question - Special topics
Afr 1555.3   Albin, P. Le coup d'Agadir. Paris, 1912.
Afr 1555.3.5   Ferrail, Gabriel. La chronique de l'an 1911. Paris, 1912.
Afr 1555.3.10   Caillaux, J. Agadir. Paris, 1919.
Afr 1555.3.15   Brugmans, H. Pantersprong. 's-Gravenhage, 1933.
Afr 1555.3.25   Mann, Walter. Die Agadirkrisis des Jahres 1911. Inaug. Diss. Giessen, 1934.
Afr 1555.3.30   Kleinknecht, W. Die englische Politik in der Agadirkrise (1911). Berlin, 1937.
Afr 1555.3.35   Barlow, I.C. The Agadir crisis. Chapel Hill, 1940.
Afr 1555.5   Melzer, F. Die Bedeutung der Marokkofrage für die englisch-französischen Beziehungen vor 1901. Inaug.-Diss. Dresden, 1937.
Afr 1555.7   Regendanz, W. Searchlight on German Africa. London, 1939.
Afr 1555.10   Campoamor, J.M. La actitud de España ante la cuestion de Marruecos. Madrid, 1951.

Afr 1555 Morocco - General relations with foreign powers - The Morocco question - Special topics - cont.

Afr 1555.12 Trout, Frank Emanuel. Morocco's Saharan frontiers. Geneva, 1969.

Afr 1567 Morocco - General relations with foreign powers - United States - Special topics

Afr 1567.3 Pericaris, I. American claims and the protection of native subjects in Morocco. n.p., n.d.

Afr 1568 Morocco - General relations with foreign powers - Great Britain - General works

Afr 1568.1 Presse anglaise et le Maroc. n.p., n.d.
Afr 1568.3 Flournoy, F.R. Political relations of Great Britain with Morocco from 1830 to 1841. N.Y., 1932.
Afr 1568.5 Flournoy, F.R. British policy towards Morocco in the age of Palmerston (1830-1865). London, 1935.

Afr 1570 Morocco - General relations with foreign powers - France - General works

Afr 1570.01 Pamphlet box. France and Morocco.
Afr 1570.1 Thomassy, R. Le Maroc et ses caravanes. Paris, 1845.
Afr 1570.2 Rouard de Card, E. Les traités. La France et le Maroc. Paris, 1898.
Afr 1570.3 Hess, J. La question du Maroc. Paris, 1903.
Afr 1570.4 Luzeux. Notre politique au Maroc. Paris, n.d.
Afr 1570.5 Pinon, Rene. L'empire de la Méditerranée. Paris, 1904.
Afr 1570.6 Dubois, M. Le Maroc et l'intérêt français. Rouen, 1904.
Afr 1570.7 Bourassin, R. La question du Maroc. Paris, 1904.
Afr 1570.8 Vaulx, A. de. La France et le Maroc. Paris, 1903.
Afr 1570.9 Fallot, E. La solution française de la question du Maroc. Paris, 1904.
Afr 1570.10F France. Ministère des Affaires Etrangères. Documents diplomatiques. Affaires du Maroc. v.1-6. Paris, 1904. 6v.
Afr 1570.11 Fidel, C. Les intérêts français...au Maroc. Paris, 1905.
Afr 1570.12 Conférence d'Algésiras. Paris, 1906.
Afr 1570.13 Polignac. La France, vassale de l'Angleterre. Alger, 1894.
Afr 1570.14 Lechatelier, A. Note sur les affaires marocaines. n.p., n.d.
Afr 1570.15 Rouard de Card, E. Protectorat de la France sur le Maroc. Toulouse, 1905.
Afr 1570.16 Ternant, V. de. La question marocaine. Paris, 1894.
Afr 1570.17 Castellane. Maroc. Paris, 1907.
Afr 1570.18 Rolland-Chevillon. La France, l'Allemagne au Maroc. Paris, 1907.
Afr 1570.19 Moulin, H.A. La question marocaine. Paris, 1906.
Afr 1570.20 Daunay. Le Maroc: que devons-nous faire. Paris, 1903.
Afr 1570.21 Palacios, C.M. De Marruecos. Badajoz, 1908.
Afr 1570.22 Romagny, J. Le role de la France au Maroc. Oran, 1908.
Afr 1570.23 Cimbali, E. L'Europa fa opera di civilta nel Marocco. Roma, 1907.
Afr 1570.24 Jacquin, P. L'action française au Maroc. Paris, 1911.
Afr 1570.25 Dupuy, E. Comment nous avons conquis le Maroc. Paris, n.d.
Afr 1570.26 Chastaud, P. Les conditions d'établissement du protectorat français au Maroc. Paris, 1913.
Afr 1570.27 Gourdin, A. La politique française au Maroc. Paris, 1906.
Afr 1570.28 Lecussan, J. de. Notre droit historique au Maroc. Paris, 1912.
Afr 1570.29 Millet, R. La conquête du Maroc. Paris, 1913.
Afr 1570.30 Jary, G. Les intérêts de la France au Maroc. Paris, 1911.
Afr 1570.31 Sainte-Chapelle, A.M.G. La conquête du Maroc (mai 1911-mars 1913). Paris, 1913.
Afr 1570.32 Couillieaux. Le programme de la France au Maroc. Paris, 1912.
Afr 1570.33 Besnard, R. L'oeuvre française au Maroc. Paris, 1914.
Afr 1570.34 Cochin, D. Affaires marocaines...1902-1911. Paris, 1912.
Afr 1570.35 Babin, G. Au Maroc par les camps et par les villes. Paris, 1912.
Afr 1570.36 Lebre, G. De l'établissement du protectorat de la France au Maroc. Paris, 1914.
Afr 1570.37.2 Torcy, L.V.F.J. de. L'Espagne et la France au Maroc...1911. 2e ed. Paris, 1911.
Afr 1570.38 Gonzalez Hontoria, M. El protectorado frances en Marruecos. Madrid, 1915.
Afr 1570.39 Saint-Rene-Taillaudier, Georges. Les origines du Maroc français. Paris, 1930.
Afr 1570.40 Rouard de Card, E. Traités et accords concernant le protectorat de la France au Maroc. Paris, 1914.
Afr 1570.41 Rouard de Card, E. Accords secrets entre la France et l'Italie concernant le Maroc et la Lybie. Paris, 1921.
Afr 1570.42 Maura y Gamazo, Gabriel. El convenio entre España by francia relativo a Marruecos. Madrid, 1912.
Afr 1570.43 Alengry, Jean. Les relations franco-espagnoles et l'affaire du Maroc. Thèse. Paris, 1920.
Afr 1570.44 Barthou, Louis. La bataille du Maroc. 3e ed. Paris, 1919.
Afr 1570.47 Caussin. Vers Taza. Paris, 1922.
Afr 1570.48 Renaissance du Maroc. Poitiers, 1922.
Afr 1570.49 Touron, Max. Notre protectorat marocain. Thèse. Poitiers, 1923.
Afr 1570.50 Raynaud, Robert. En marge du livre jaune. Le Maroc. Paris, 1923.
Afr 1570.52 Dutaillis, J. Le nouveau Maroc. Paris, 1923.
Afr 1570.54 Begue, Leon. Le secret d'une conquête. Paris, 1929.
Afr 1570.55 Colliez, A. Notre protectorat marocain. Paris, 1930.
Afr 1570.58 Sloane, Wm.M. Greater France in Africa. N.Y., 1924.
Afr 1570.61 Berard, Victor. L'affaire marocaine. Paris, 1906.
Afr 1570.65 Sabin, Mony. La paix au Maroc. Paris, 1933.
Afr 1570.67 Charbonneau, J. Maroc, vingt-troisième heure. Paris, 1938.
Afr 1570.70 Charles-Roux, François. Missions diplomatiques françaises a Fès. Paris, 1955.
Afr 1570.75 Corval, Pierre. Le Maroc en révolution. Paris, 1956.

Afr 1571 Morocco - General relations with foreign powers - France - Special topics

Afr 1571.1 Lechatelier, A. Sud-Oranais et Maroc. Paris, 1903.
Afr 1571.1.10 Messal, R. La genèse de notre victoire marocaine. Paris, 1931.
Afr 1571.2 Rouard de Card, E. La frontière franco-marocaine...20 july 1901. Toulouse, 1902.
Afr 1571.3 Hess, Jean. Une Algérie nouvelle. Paris, 1909.
Afr 1571.4 Bernard, A. Les confins algéro-marocains. Paris, 1911.
Afr 1571.4.8 Bernard, A. La France au Maroc. Paris, 1917.
Afr 1571.5A Tardieu, A. Le mystère d'Agadir. Paris, 1912.
Afr 1571.5B Tardieu, A. Le mystère d'Agadir. Paris, 1912.
Afr 1571.8 Peyris, G. Randonnées au Maroc, 1911-1913. Paris, 1924.

Afr 1571 Morocco - General relations with foreign powers - France - Special topics - cont.

Afr 1571.14 Georges-Gaulis, B. La France au Maroc. Paris, 1919.
Afr 1571.15 Leglay, M. Chronique marocaine. Paris, 1933.
Afr 1571.16 Lyautey, L.H.G. Vers le Maroc, lettres du Sud-Oranais, 1903-1906. Paris, 1937.
Afr 1571.17.2 Lyautey, L.H.G. Paroles d'action. Paris, 1927.
Afr 1571.17.3 Lyautey, L.H.G. Lyautey l'Africain. v.1-4. Paris, 1953. 4v.
Afr 1571.17.6 Maurois, A. Lyautey. Paris, 1931.
Afr 1571.17.8 Maurois, A. Lyautey. Paris, 1931.
Afr 1571.17.9 Maurois, A. Lyautey. Paris, 1932.
Afr 1571.17.10A Maurois, A. Lyautey. N.Y., 1931.
Afr 1571.17.10B Maurois, A. Lyautey. N.Y., 1931.
Afr 1571.17.11 Maurois, A. Lyautey. Paris, 1934.
Afr 1571.17.12A Maurois, A. Lyautey. N.Y., 1932.
Afr 1571.17.12B Maurois, A. Lyautey. N.Y., 1932.
Afr 1571.17.13 Dubly, H.L. Lyautey-le-magicien. Lille, 1931.
Afr 1571.17.18 Esperandieu, Pierre. Lyautey et le protectorat. Paris, 1947.
Afr 1571.17.22 Franchet Desperey, L.F.M.F. Discours de réception. 2e ed. Paris, 1935.
Afr 1571.17.25 Willette, H. Au Maroc avec Lyautey. Paris, 1931.
Afr 1571.17.27 Figueras, Andre. Lyautey assassine. Paris, 1958.
Afr 1571.17.30 Barthou, Louis. Lyautey et le Maroc. Paris, 1931.
Afr 1571.17.35 Georges-Gaulis, B. Lyautey, intime. Paris, 1938.
Afr 1571.17.40 Ormesson, W. Adieux, souvenirs sur Lyautey. Paris, 1937.
Afr 1571.17.42 Ormesson, W. Auprès de Lyautey. Paris, 1963.
Afr 1571.17.45 Borely, J. Le tombeau de Lyautey. Paris, 1937.
Afr 1571.17.50 Howe, S.E. Lyautey du Tonkin au Maroc par Madagascar et le Sud-Oranais. Paris, 1938.
Afr 1571.17.55 Gouraud, H.J.E. Lyautey. Paris, 1938.
Afr 1571.17.57 Lyautey, L.H.G. Rayonnement de Lyautey. Paris, 1941.
Afr 1571.17.60 Heidsieck, P. Rayonnement de Lyautey. Paris, 1944.
Afr 1571.17.62 Lyautey, L.H.G. Rayonnement de Lyautey. Paris, 1947.
Afr 1571.17.65 Lyautey, L.H.G. Les plus belles lettres de Lyautey. Paris, 1962.
Afr 1571.17.70 Garrick, Robert. Le message de Lyautey. Paris, 1944.
Afr 1571.17.75 Hardy, G. Portrait de Lyautey. Paris, 1949.
Afr 1571.17.80 Postal, R. Présence de Lyautey. Paris, 1938.
Afr 1571.17.85 Catroux, G. Lyautey. Paris, 1952.
Afr 1571.17.90 Roux, F. de. La jeunesse de Lyautey. Paris, 1952.
Afr 1571.17.95 Boisboissel, Y. de. Dans l'ombre de Lyautey. Paris, 1954.
Afr 1571.17.100 Cahiers Charles de Foucauld. Lyautey Grenoble, 1954.
Afr 1571.17.105 Madras, Didier. Dans l'ombre du maréchal Lyautey. Rabat, 1953.
Afr 1571.17.110 Durasoy, M. Lyautey. Paris, 1956.
Afr 1571.17.115 Farrere, Claude. Lyautey. Paris, 1955.
Afr 1571.17.120 Deloncle, Pierre. Lyautey. Paris, 1955.
Afr 1571.17.125 Proust, L. Le maréchal Lyautey tel que je l'ai connu. Vichy, 1954.
Afr 1571.17.130 Maroc-Medical, Publishers, Casablanca. Lydutey et le médecin. Casablanca, 1954.
Afr 1571.17.135 Benoist-Méchin, Jacques. Lyautey l'Africain, ou Le rêve immolé. Lausanne, 1966.
Afr 1571.18 Leclerc, Max. Au Maroc avec Lyautey. Paris, 1927.
Afr 1571.19 Perrot, Raymond de. The golden road. London, 1926.
Afr 1571.22 Babin, Gustave. La mystérieuse Ouaouizert. Casablanca, 1923.
Afr 1571.27 Bordeaux, Henry. Le miracle du Maroc. Paris, 1934.
Afr 1571.29 Pinon, Rene. Au Maroc, fin des temps héroiques. Paris, 1935.
Afr 1571.31 Deschamps, Jean L. Souvenirs des premiers temps du Maroc français (1912-1915). Paris, 1935.
Afr 1571.33 Vallerie, Pierre. Conquérants et conquis au Maroc. Thèse. Paris, 1934.
Afr 1571.35A Knight, M.M. Morocco as a French economic venture. N.Y., 1937.
Afr 1571.35B Knight, M.M. Morocco as a French economic venture. N.Y., 1937.
Afr 1571.37 Ladreit Delacharriere, J. La pacification du Maroc, 1907-1934. Paris, 1936.
Afr 1571.39 Simon, H.J. Un officer d'Afrique, le commandant Verlet-Hanus. Paris, 1930.
Afr 1571.41 Gorrée, Georges. Au service du Maroc: Charles de Foucauld. Paris, 1939.
Afr 1571.43 Paluel-Marmont, A.P.H.J. Le général Gouraud. Paris, 1937.
Afr 1571.45 France. Journal du consulat général de France à Maroc. Casablanca, 1943.
Afr 1571.48 Parent, Pierre. The truth about Morocco. N.Y., 1952.
Afr 1571.50 Caille, Jacques. La représentation diplomatique de la France au Maroc. Paris, 1951.
Afr 1571.50.5 Caillé, Jacques. Le consulat de Tanger; des origines à 1830. Paris, 1967.
Afr 1571.52 Selous, G.H. Appointment to Fez. London, 1956.
Afr 1571.55 Grandval, G. Ma mission au Maroc. Paris, 1956.

Afr 1573 Morocco - General relations with foreign powers - Spain - General works

Afr 1573.1 Pamphlet box. Spain and Morocco.
Afr 1573.5 Pezzi, Rafael. La influencia española en el Rif. Madrid, 1893.
Afr 1573.7 Carvajal, Jose de. España y Marruecos. Madrid, 1884.
Afr 1573.8 Becker, J. España y Marruecos. Madrid, 1903.
Afr 1573.9 Gutierrez Sobral, J. Marruecos. Madrid, 1905.
Afr 1573.10 Reparaz, G. de. Politica de España en Africa. Barcelona, 1907.
Afr 1573.10.5 Reparaz, G. de. Lo que pudo hacer España en Marruecos. Barcelona, 1937.
Afr 1573.11 Caballero de Puga. Marruecos, politica e interes de España en este imperio. Madrid, 1907.
Afr 1573.12 Marenco, S. La dominacion de España en Tanger. Madrid, 1911.
Afr 1573.13 Coello y Quesada, Francisco. Intereses de España en Marruecos. Madrid, 1884.
Afr 1573.14 Lopez Pinto, V. Memoria sobre intereses generales del pais y especiales de las colonias africanas. Ceuta, 1877.
Afr 1573.16 Larios de Medrano, Justo. España en Marruecos, historia secreta de la campaña. Madrid, 1916.
Afr 1573.17 Bande, Nicasio. La cuestion del dia: desenlace del problema norte-africano y el porvenir de España. Barcelona, 1909.
Afr 1573.18 Pita, Federico. La accion militar y politica de España en Africa a traves de los tiempos. Madrid, 1915.
Afr 1573.19 Liga Africanista Española. Tratados, convenios y acuerdos referentes a Marruecos. Madrid, 1918.
Afr 1573.20 Alvarez, Melquiades. El problema de Marruecos. Madrid, 1914.

Afr 1573   Morocco - General relations with foreign powers - Spain - General works - cont.

Afr 1573.21   Ortega, Manuel L. España en Marruecos. El Raisuni. Madrid, 1917.
Afr 1573.22   Martin Peinador, L. El suelo de Marruecos y sus primeros habitantes. Madrid, 1920.
Afr 1573.23   Merino Alvarez, A. Marruecos. Madrid, 1921.
Afr 1573.24   España, Juan de. La actuacion de España en Marruecos. Madrid, 1926.
Afr 1573.25   Ruiz Albeniz, V. Tanger y la colaboracion franco-española en Marruecos. Madrid, 1927.
Afr 1573.26   Hernandez Mir, Francisco. La dictadura en Marruecos. Madrid, 1930.
Afr 1573.27   Armiñan, J.M. Francia, el dictador y el moro. Madrid, 1930.
Afr 1573.28   Reparaz, G. de. Alfonso XIII y sus complices. Madrid, 1931.
Afr 1573.29F   Hernandez de Herrera, C. Accion de España en Marruecos. v.1-2. Madrid, 1929-30. 2v.
Afr 1573.30   Donnadieu, M. Les relations diplomatiques de l'Espagne et du Maroc de janvier 1592 a juillet 1926. Montpellier, 1931.
Afr 1573.31   Laget, Paul de. Au Maroc espagnol. Marseille, 1935.
Afr 1573.32   Maturana Vargas, C. La tragica realidad: Marruecos, 1921. Barcelona, 1921.
Afr 1573.33   Guastavino Gallant, Guillermo. De ambos lados del estrecho. Tetuan, 1955.
Afr 1573.34   Millas y Vallicrosa, J.M. España y Marruecos. Barcelona, 1945.
Afr 1573.35   Fernandez Arias, Adelardo. Visperas de sangre en Marruecos. Madrid, 1933.
Afr 1573.36   Problema de Marruecos. Madrid, 1914.

Afr 1574   Morocco - General relations with foreign powers - Spain - Special topics

Afr 1574.1   Perez del Torro, F. España en el noroeste de Africa. Madrid, 1892.
Afr 1574.5   Embaxada de la Corte de España al Rey de Marruecos en el año de 1799. Madrid, 1800.
Afr 1574.7   Rouard de Card, E. Les relations de l'Espagne et du Maroc. Paris, 1905.
Afr 1574.8   Gutierrez, F.L. España y las demas naciones. Madrid, 1906.
Afr 1574.9   Cordero Torres, J.M. Organizacion del protectorado español en Marruecos. v.1-2. Madrid, 1942-43.
Afr 1574.10   Spain. Treaties. Morocco. Coleccion completa de tratados y convenios entre Espana y Marruecos, 1799 a 1895. Melilla, 1904.
Afr 1574.12   Romanones, Alvaro Figueroa y Torres. Conferencia del Excmo. Sr. conde de Romanones sobre el problema de Marruecos, Pronunciada en al Teatro de San Fernando de Sevilla el 26 de abril de 1922. Sevilla, 1922.

Afr 1575   Morocco - General relations with foreign powers - Portugal - General works

Afr 1575.2F   Azevedo, Pedro de. Documentos das chancelarias reais anteriores a 1531. v.1-2. Lisboa, 1915. 2v.
Afr 1575.2.10F   Baiao, Antonio. Documentos do corpo chronologico relativo a Marrocos, 1488 a 1514. Coimbra, 1925.
Afr 1575.5   Castonnet Des Fosses, H. Les Portugais au Maroc. Paris, 1886.
Afr 1575.10   Testa, Carlos. Portugal e Marrocos perante a historia e a politica europea. Lisboa, 1888.
Afr 1575.12   Ricard, Robert. Etudes sur l'histoire des Portugals au Maroc. Coimbra, 1955.
Afr 1575.14   Periale, Marise. Maroc lusitanien, 1415-1769. Paris, 1938.
Afr 1575.15   Souto, A. Meyselles do. Portugal e Marrocos; fostos e noticias. Lisboa, 1967.

Afr 1576   Morocco - General relations with foreign powers - Portugal - Special topics

Afr 1576.3F   Vieira da S. y Guimaraes. Marrocos e tres mestres da ordem de cristo, memória publicada por ordem da academia das sciências de Lisboa. Lisboa, 1916.
Afr 1576.5   Carvalho, V. de. La domination portugaise au Maroc du XVeme au XVIIIeme siècle. Lisbonne, 1942.
Afr 1576.5.2   Carvalho, V. de. La domination portugaise au Maroc du XV. Lisbonne, 1936.

Afr 1579   Morocco - General relations with foreign powers - Italy - Special topics

Afr 1579.5   Ricard, R. Contribution a l'étude du commerce genois au Maroc durant la periode portugaise, 1415-1550. Paris, 1937.

Afr 1581   Morocco - General relations with foreign powers - Belgium - General works

Afr 1581.5   Collin, V. Le maroc et les intérêts belges. Louvain, 1900.

Afr 1583   Morocco - General relations with foreign powers - Germany - General works

Afr 1583.1   Pamphlet box. Germany and Morocco.
Afr 1583.2F   Aktenstuecke über Marokko der Reichstage...8. I. 1906. Berlin, 1906.
Afr 1583.3F   Aktenstuecke über Marokko. Berlin, 1908.
Afr 1583.5   Werle. Deutschlands beziehungen zu marokko. Coburg, 1902.
Afr 1583.7   Adam, Paul. Affaires du Maroc, livre blanc allemand. Paris, 1910.
Afr 1583.8   Wirth, A. Die Entscheidung über Marokko. Stuttgart, 1911.
Afr 1583.9   Buelow, J. von. Marocco Deutsch. Berlin, 1911.
Afr 1583.10   Haruisch, J. Marokko rückzug. Berlin, 1911.
Afr 1583.11   Pamphlet vol. Germany's relations with Morocco. Berlin, 1908. 9 pam.
Afr 1583.12   Maurus, Pseud. Ave caesar. Deutsche Luftschiffe...Marokko. Leipzig, 1909.
Afr 1583.14   Osman, H.A. Die Mannesmann-Rechte und den Weissbuch. Berlin, 1910.
Afr 1583.14.15   Mannesmann, C.H. Die unternehmungen des brüder mannesmann in Marokko. Würzburg, 1931.
Afr 1583.15   Maurice, Louis. La politique marocaine de l'allemagne. Paris, 1916.
Afr 1583.16   Richet, Etienne. La politique allemand. Paris, 1917.
Afr 1583.17   Bartels, Albert. Auf eigene Faust meine Erlebnisse vor und während des Weltkrieges in Marokko. Leipzig, 1925.
Afr 1583.18   Guillen, Pierre. L'Allemagne et le Maroc de 1870-1905. Thèse. Paris, 1967.

Afr 1584   Morocco - General relations with foreign powers - Germany - Special topics

Afr 1584.5   Fischer, A. Das marokkanische Berggesetz. Berlin, 1910.
Afr 1584.6   Arning, W. Marokko-Kongo. Leipzig, 1912.
Afr 1584.7F   Bethmann, H. Denkschrift über deutsche bergwerksinteressen in Marokko. Berlin, 1910.
Afr 1584.9   Williamson, F.T. Germany and Morocco before 1905. Baltimore, 1937.
Afr 1584.9.2   Williamson, F.T. Germany and Morocco before 1905. Diss. Baltimore, 1937.

Afr 1585   Morocco - General relations with foreign powers - Austria

Afr 1585.3F   Austro-Hungarian Monarchy. Ministerium des Aüssern. Diplomatische Aktenstücken über die Internationale Konferenz von Algeciras, 1905-06. Wien, 1906.
Afr 1585.5   Caille, Jacques. Une ambassade autrichienne au Maroc en 1805. Paris, 1957.

Afr 1590   Morocco - General relations with foreign powers - Other Christian

Afr 1603.80   Abu Al-Feda. Description du pays du Magreb. Alger, 1839.

Afr 1605 - 1610   Morocco - Geography, description, etc. - General works (By date)

Afr 1605.50   Massignon, L. Le Maroc dans les premières années du XVIe siècle. Alger, 1906.
Afr 1605.96   Castries, H. de. Une description du Maroc. Paris, 1909.
Htn   Afr 1606.31*   Jean Armand, Called Mustapha. Voyages d'Afrique faicts par le commandement du roy. Paris, 1631.
Afr 1606.40   Nathaim, D.A. Voyage au Maroc (1640-41). La Have, 1866.
Htn   Afr 1606.44*   San Francisco, Matias de. Relacion del viage espiritual. Madrid, 1644.
Htn   Afr 1606.70*   Letter from a gentleman of Lt. Howard's retinue. London, 1670.
Htn   Afr 1606.71*   Addison, L. West Barbary. Oxford, 1671.
Htn   Afr 1606.71.3*   Frejus, R. Relation of a voyage made into Mauritania. London, 1671.
Htn   Afr 1606.94*   St. Olon, P. Etat present de l'empire de Maroc. Paris, 1694.
Htn   Afr 1606.94.3*   St. Olon, P. Relation de l'empire de Maroc. Paris, 1695.
Htn   Afr 1606.94.5*   St. Olon, P. Present state of Morocco. London, 1695.
Htn   Afr 1606.96*   St. Amant. Voyage de St. Amant. Lyon, 1698.
Htn   Afr 1607.13*   Ockley, S. An account of south-west Barbary. London, 1713.
Afr 1607.24   Relation de ce qui s'est passe...1704-12. Paris, 1724.
Afr 1607.24.3F   Francisco de Jesus Maria, de San Juan Del Puerto. Primera parte de las chronicas de la provincia de San Diego. Sevilla, 1724.
Htn   Afr 1607.25*   Windus, J. A journey to Mequinez. London, 1725. (Changed to EC7.W7255.725j, 30/6/69)
Afr 1607.51   Riese, Otto. Harck Olufs aus der Insul amron im stifte ripen in Juetland. Flensburg, 1751.
Afr 1607.53.4   Journaal Wegens de Rampspoedige Reys-Tocht van H.C. Steenis. Amsterdam, n.d.
Afr 1607.81   Hoest, G. Nachrichten von Morokos und Fes. Kopenhagen, 1781.
Afr 1607.87.5   Chenier, L.S. Present state of Morocco. London, 1788. 2v.
Afr 1607.91.2   Lempriere, W. Tour to Tangier and Morocco. 2nd ed. London, 1793.
Afr 1607.91.3   Lempriere, W. Tour to Tangier and Morocco. 3rd ed. Newport, 1813.
Afr 1607.91.5   Lempriere, G. Voyage dans l'empire de Maroc. Paris, 1801.
Afr 1607.91.7   Lempriere, W. Le Maroc, il y a cent ans. Paris, 1911.
Afr 1607.91.9   Marruecos hace cien anos. Paris, 1911.
Afr 1608.03   Haringman, H. Beknopt dag-journaal van Marocco. Haag, 1803.
Afr 1608.08   Burel, Antoine. La mission du capitaine Burel au Maroc en 1808. Paris, 1953.
Afr 1608.09.2   Jackson, J.G. An account...empire of Morocco. 2d ed. London, 1811.
Afr 1608.09.3   Jackson, J.G. An account...empire of Morocco. Philadelphia, 1810.
Afr 1608.10   Buffa, J. Travels through the empire of Morocco. London, 1810.
Afr 1608.16   Cock, S. The narrative of Robert Adams. London, 1816.
Afr 1608.16.20   Adams, Robert. Nouveau voyage dans l'interieur de l'Afrique. Paris, 1817.
Afr 1608.18   Paddock, J. A narrative...shipwreck of the ship Oswego. N.Y., 1818.
Afr 1608.20   Jackson, J.G. An account of Timbuctoo and Housa. London, 1820.
Afr 1608.21   Cochelet, C. Naufrage du brick français la sophie. v.1-2. Paris, 1821. 2v.
Afr 1608.22   Comyn, T. De. Ligera ojeada o breve idea...de Marruecos en 1822. Barcelona, 1825.
Afr 1608.34   Graaback Fraan Hemso. Speccio...dell impero di Marocco. Genova, 1834.
Afr 1608.38   Augustin, F. von. Erinnerungen aus Marokko. Wien, 1838.
Afr 1608.39   Davidson, J. Notes taken during travels in Africa. London, 1839.
Afr 1608.44   Calderon, S.E. Manual del oficial en Marruecos. Madrid, 1844.
Afr 1608.44.3   Didier, C. Promenade au Maroc. Paris, 1844.
Afr 1608.44.6   Hay, J.H.D. Morocco and the Moors. London, 1861.
Afr 1608.44.7   Hay, J. Le Maroc et ses tribus nomades. Paris, 1844.
Afr 1608.46   Löwenstein, W. Zu. Ausflug von Lissabon nach Andalusien und...Marokko. Dresden, 1846.
Afr 1608.46.5   Hay, J.H.D. Journal of an expedition to court of Morocco in year 1846. Cambridge, Eng., 1848.
Afr 1608.54   Durrieu, X. Present state of Morocco. 2 in 1. London, 1854. 2 pam.
Afr 1608.59   Murray, J. Sixteen years in Morocco. London, 1859. 2v.
Afr 1608.59.3   Gomez de Arteche y Moro, José. Descripcion y mapas de Marruecos. Madrid, 1859.
Afr 1608.59.5   Torrijos, Manuel. El imperio de Marruecos, su historia etc. Madrid, 1859.
Afr 1608.60   Richardson, J. Travels in Morocco. v.1-2. London, 1860.
Afr 1608.60.3   Godard, L. Description et histoire du Maroc. v.1-2. Paris, 1860.
Afr 1608.60.4   Godard, L. Le Maroc, notes d'un voyageur. Alger, 1860.
Afr 1608.60.5   Cotte, N. Le Maroc contemporain. Paris, 1860.
Afr 1608.60.7   Breve escursion por el imperio de Marruecos. Malaga, 1860.
Afr 1608.60.9   Ferreiro, Martin. Descripcion del imperio de Marruecos. Madrid, 1860.
Afr 1608.64   Rohlfs, G. Reise durch Marokko. Norden, 1884.
Afr 1608.64.3   Merry y Colom, F. Relacion del viaje a la ciudad de Marruecos. Madrid, 1864.

Afr 1605 - 1610 date) - cont. **Morocco - Geography, description, etc. - General works (By**

Afr 1608.64.6	Merry y Colom, F. Mi embajada extraordinaria a Marruecos en 1863. Madrid, 1894.
Afr 1608.66	Hodgkin, T. Narrative of a journey to Morocco. London, 1866.
Afr 1608.68	Murga, Jose Maria de. Recuerdos marroquies. Madrid, 1906.
Afr 1608.68.5	Murga, José Maria de. Recuerdos marroquies del moro vizcaino. Barcelona, 1913.
Afr 1608.72.3	Rohlfs, G. Mein ersten aufenthalt in Morokko. Norden, 1885.
Afr 1608.72.8	Rohlfs, G. Adventures in Morocco. London, 1874.
Afr 1608.73	Perrier, A. A winter in Morocco. London, 1873.
Afr 1608.75	Urrestarazu, D.T. de A. de. Viajes por Marruecos. Madrid, 18- .
Afr 1608.77	Fernandez Duro, Cesareo. Apuntes biograficas de el hach mohamed el Bagdady, Don José Maria de Murqa, segui dos de otros varios para idea de los usas. Madrid, 1877.
Afr 1608.78	Hooker, J.D. Journal of a tour in Marocco. London, 1878.
Afr 1608.78.3	Pietsch, L. Marokko-brief von der Deutschen gesand 1877. Leipzig, 1878.
Afr 1608.78.6	Gatell, Joaquin. Viajes por Marruecos. Madrid, 1878-79.
Afr 1608.79	M. y Rodriganez, T. El imperio de Marruecos. Madrid, 1879.
Afr 1608.79.4	Leared, Arthur. A visit to the court of Morocco. London, 1879.
Afr 1608.80	Conring, A. von. Marroco, das Land und die Leute. Berlin, 1880.
Afr 1608.80.05	Conring, A. von. Marroco, das Land und die Leute. Berlin, 1884.
Afr 1608.80.1	Conring, A. von. Marroco, el pais y los habitantes. 2e ed. Madrid, 1881.
Afr 1608.80.2	Colvile, H.E. A ride in petticoats and slippers. London, 1880.
Afr 1608.81	Trotter, P.D. Our mission to Marocco. Edinburg, 1881.
Afr 1608.81.3	Durier, C. Une excursion au Maroc. Paris, 1882.
Afr 1608.81.5	Ovilo y Canales, F. La mujer Marroqui, estudio social. 2e ed. Madrid, 1881.
Afr 1608.82	Amicis, E. de. Morocco. N.Y., 1882.
Afr 1608.82.2	Amicis, E. de. Morocco. N.Y., 1882.
Afr 1608.82.2.5	Amicis, E. de. Morocco. 9 ed. Milano, 1882.
Afr 1608.82.3	Amicis, E. de. Morocco. Milano, 1890.
Afr 1608.82.4F	Amicis, E. de. Marruecos. Barcelona, 1892.
Afr 1608.82.5	Bonelli, E. El imperio de Marruecos y su constitucion. Madrid, 1882.
Afr 1608.82.10	Lamartiniere, Henri P. De. Souvenirs du Maroc. Paris, 1919.
Afr 1608.85	Erckmann, J. Le Maroc moderne. Paris, 1895.
Afr 1608.85.3	Mercet, A. Le Maroc. Paris, 1895.
Afr 1608.85.5	Mercet, A. Marruecos. Madrid, 1887.
Afr 1608.85.8	Cervera Baviera, J. Expedicion geografico-militar...Marruecos. Barcelona, 1885.
Afr 1608.86	Duveyrier, H. De Tanger a fas et meknas en 1885. Paris, 1886.
Afr 1608.86.3	Stutfield, H.E.M. El Maghreb, 1200 miles ride through Marocco. London, 1886.
Afr 1608.86.5	Campos, L. de. Un empire qui croule. Paris, 1886.
Afr 1608.86.8	Mackenzie, Don. Report on the condition...empire of Morocco. London, 1886.
Afr 1608.86.10	Ovilo y Canales, D.F. La mujer marroqui. Nueva edicion. Madrid, 1886.
Afr 1608.87	Charmes, G. Une ambassade au Maroc. Paris, 1887.
Afr 1608.87.3	Horowitz, V.J. Marokko. Leipzig, 1886.
Afr 1608.89	Harris, W.B. The land of an african sultan. London, 1889.
Afr 1608.89.3	Lamartiniere, H.M.P. de. Morocco. London, 1889.
Afr 1608.89.5	Sestri, J.A. de. Por todo marruecos descripcion del imperio. Barcelona, 1889.
Afr 1608.89.20	Viaud, J. Into Morocco. Chicago, n.d.
Afr 1608.90	Viaud, J. Au Maroc. Paris, 1890.
Afr 1608.91A	Leared, A. Morocco and the Moors. London, 1891.
Afr 1608.91B	Leared, A. Morocco and the Moors. London, 1891.
Afr 1608.93	Bonsal, S. Jr. Morocco as it is. London, 1893.
Afr 1608.93.5	Olivie, M. Marruecos. Barcelona, 1893.
Afr 1608.93.6	Picard, E. El Maghreb al aksa. Bruxelles, 1893.
Afr 1608.93.7	Villaescusa, M.H. La cuestion de Marruecos y el conflicto de melilla. Barcelona, 1893.
Afr 1608.94	Montbard, G. Among the Moors. London, 1894.
Afr 1608.94.1	Montbard, G. Among the Moors. N.Y., 1894.
Afr 1608.94.2	Montbard, G. A travers le Maroc. Paris, 1894.
Afr 1608.94.3	Kerr, Robert. Pioneering in Morocco. London, 1894.
Afr 1608.94.4	Soriano, Rodrigo. Moros y cristianos. Madrid, 1894.
Afr 1608.94.5	Ganniers, A. de. Le Maroc d'aujourd hui, d'hier et de demain. Nouvelle ed. Paris, 1894.
Afr 1608.94.6	Ganniers, A. de. Le Maroc d'aujourd hui, d'hier et de demain. Paris, n.d.
Afr 1608.94.8	Reina, T.B. Geografia de Marruecos. Barcelona, 1894.
Afr 1608.94.10	Diercks, G. Marokko...Kenntnis und Beurteilung des Scherifreiches. Berlin, 1894.
Afr 1608.94.14	Salmon. Les français au Maroc, mort du sultan. Paris, 1894.
Afr 1608.95	Moulieras, A. Le Maroc inconnu. v.1-2. Paris, 1895. 2v.
Afr 1608.95.3	Frisch, R.J. Le Maroc géoraphie Organisation politique. Paris, 1895.
Afr 1608.95.5	Boada y Romeu, J. Allende el estrecho, viajes por Marruecos (1889-94). Barcelona, 1895.
Afr 1608.95.7	Canizares y Moyano, ed. Apuntes sobre Marruecos. Madrid, 1895.
Afr 1608.96	Hay, J.D. A memoir of Sir John Hay Drummond Hay. London, 1896.
Afr 1608.96.3	Schabelsky, E. von. Harem und Moschee. Reiseskizzen aus Marokko. Berlin, 1896.
Afr 1608.97	Martiniere, H.M.P. de la. Notice sur le Maroc. Paris, 1897.
Afr 1608.97.5	Campbell, A. A ride in Morocco. Toronto, 1897.
Afr 1608.98	Graham, R.B.C. Mogreb-el-Acksa, a journey in Morocco. London, 1898.
Afr 1608.98.5	Graham, R.B.C. Mogreb-el-Acksa, a journey in Morocco. London, 1921.
Afr 1608.98.10	Graham, R.B.C. Mogreb-el-Acksa. London, 1928.
Afr 1608.99.3	Verneau, R. Le Maroc et les Canaries. Paris, 1899.
Afr 1609.00	Arnold, R.S. Studien zur wirthschaftsgeographie von Marokko. Marburg, 1900.
Afr 1609.01	Meakin, B. The land of the Moors. London, 1901.
Afr 1609.01.3	Niessel, A. Le Maroc. Paris, 1901.
Afr 1609.01.5	Bacheracht, Mme A. de. Une mission à la cour cherifienne. Genève, 1901.
Afr 1609.01.8	Hamet, Ismael. Cinq mois au Maroc. Alger, 1901.

Afr 1605 - 1610 date) - cont. **Morocco - Geography, description, etc. - General works (By**

Afr 1609.02	Meakin, B. The Moors. London, 1902.
Afr 1609.02.3	Grove, Lady. Seventy-one days camping in Morocco. London, 1902.
Afr 1609.02.5	Macnab, Frances. A ride in Morocco. London, 1902.
Afr 1609.02.7	Pfeil, J.V. Geographische Beobachtungen in Marokko. Jena, 1902.
Afr 1609.03	Savory, Isabel. In the tail of the peacock. London, 1903.
Afr 1609.03.3	Segonzac, de. Voyages au Maroc (1899-1901). Paris, 1903.
Afr 1609.03.5	Kampffmeyer, G. Marokko. Halle, 1903.
Afr 1609.03.6	Adelmann, S. 13 monate in Marokko. Sigmaring, 1903.
Afr 1609.03.7	Sid el Hach Abd-el-Nabi Ben Ramos. Perlas negras. Madrid, 1903.
Afr 1609.03.9	Irabien Larranaga, E. de. Africa, apuntes de Marruecos. San Sebastian, 1903.
Afr 1609.03.12	Aubin, Eugene. Morocco of today. London, 1906.
Afr 1609.04	Aubin, Eugene. Le Maroc d'aujourd hui. Paris, 1904.
Afr 1609.04.3	Girard. Etude sur le Maroc. Paris, 1904.
Afr 1609.04.5	Weisgerber, F. Trois mois de campagne au Maroc. Paris, 1904.
Afr 1609.04.9	Dawson, A.J. Things seen in Morocco. London, 1904.
Afr 1609.04.10A	Bensusan, S.L. Morocco. London, 1904.
Afr 1609.04.10B	Bensusan, S.L. Morocco. London, 1904.
Afr 1609.05	Meakin, B. Life in Morocco and glimpses beyond. London, 1905.
Afr 1609.05.3	Dutaillis, J. Le Maroc pittoresque. Paris, n.d.
Afr 1609.05.4	Rene-Leclerc, C. Le Maroc septentrional...(Ete 1904). Alger, 1905.
Afr 1609.05.5	Hübner, M. Unbekannte gebiete Marokkos. Berlin, 1905.
Afr 1609.05.8	Lemoine, Paul. Mission dans le Maroc occidental. Paris, 1905.
Afr 1609.05.10	Cousin, A. Le Maroc. Paris, 1905.
Afr 1609.05.11	Zabel, R. Im muhammendanischen abendlande. Altenburg, 1905.
Afr 1609.06	Genthe, S. Marokko reiseschilderungen. Berlin, 1906.
Afr 1609.06.3	Minguez Y Vicente, M. Descripcion geografica del imperio de Marruecos. Madrid, 1906.
Afr 1609.06.5	Gentil, L. Explorations au Maroc. Paris, 1906.
Afr 1609.06.6	Diez De Tejada, V. Cosas de los moros. Barcelona, 1906.
Afr 1609.06.7	Auer, Grethe. Marokkanische sittenbilder. Bern, 1906.
Afr 1609.06.9	Mitjana, R. En el Magreb-el-Aksa. Valencia, 1906.
Afr 1609.06.10	Wolfrom, G. Le Maroc. Paris, 1906.
Afr 1609.07	Pleydell, K.M. Sketches of life in Morocco. London, 1907.
Afr 1609.07.2	Jeannot, G. Etude sociale...sur le Maroc. Dijon, 1907.
Afr 1609.07.3	Abou-Djebel. Tres meses en Marruecos. Madrid, 1907.
Afr 1609.08	Moore, Frederick. The passing of Morocco. Boston, 1908.
Afr 1609.08.3	Sternberg, Adalb. Die barbaren von Marokko. Wien, 1908.
Afr 1609.08.4	Zeys, Mathilde. Une française au Maroc. Paris, 1908.
Afr 1609.08.5	Leon Y Ramos, E. Marruecos. Madrid, 1908.
Afr 1609.08.5.4	Leon Y Ramos, E. Marruecos. Novisima ed. Madrid, 1915.
Afr 1609.08.6	Campo Angulo, G. Geografia de Marruecos. Madrid, 1908.
Afr 1609.08.7	Finnemore, J. Peeps at many lands, Morocco. London, 1910.
Afr 1609.09	Metour, E.P. In the wake of the green banner. N.Y., 1909.
Afr 1609.09.3	Mauran. Le maroc d'aujourd hui et de demain. Paris, 1909.
Afr 1609.09.5	Brines, A. Voyages au Maroc (1901-1907). Alger, 1909.
Afr 1609.10	Segonzac, M. De. Itineraires au Maroc. (Maps). Paris, 1910.
Afr 1609.11	Mackenzie, D. The khalifate of the west. London, 1911.
Afr 1609.11.4	Artbauer, O.C. Ein ritt durch Marokko. 2 ed. Regensberg, 1912.
Afr 1609.11.6	Artbauer, O.C. Kreuz und qür durch Marokko. Stuttgart, 1911.
Afr 1609.12	Kerr, Robert. Morocco after twenty-five years. London, 1912.
Afr 1609.12.3	Haillot. Le Maroc. Vincennes, 1912.
Afr 1609.12.4	Munoz, I. La agonia del Mogreb. Madrid, 1912.
Afr 1609.12.5	Rousselet, L. Sur les confins du Maroc. Paris, 1912.
Afr 1609.12.7	Nieto, P.E. En Marruecos. Barcelona, 1912.
Afr 1609.12.9	Mauran. La societe marocaine. Paris, 1912.
Afr 1609.12.11	Bourote, M. Pour coloniser au Maroc. Paris, 1912.
Afr 1609.12.13	Gentil, L. Le Maroc physique. 2e ed. Paris, 1912.
Afr 1609.12.15	Richet, E. Voyage au Maroc. Nouvelle ed. Paris, 1912.
Afr 1609.12.18	Detanger, Emile. Gens de guerre au Maroc. Paris, 1912.
Afr 1609.13	Bernard, A. Le Maroc. Paris, 1913.
Afr 1609.13.2	Bernard, A. Le Maroc. 4. ed. Paris, 1916.
Afr 1609.13.2.3	Bernard, A. Le Maroc. 7. ed. Paris, 1931.
Afr 1609.13.2.5	Bernard, A. Le Maroc. 8e ed. Paris, 1932.
Afr 1609.13.3	Douoso-Cortes, R. Estudio geográfica politico-militar sobre las zonas Españolas. Madrid, 1913.
Afr 1609.13.4	Zabel, R. Zu unruhiger Zeit in Marokko. Cöln am Rhein, 1913.
Afr 1609.13.5	Van Wincxtenhoven. Le Maroc, rapport général. Bruxelles, 1913.
Afr 1609.13.6	Munoz, I. En el pais de los cherifes. Madrid, 1913.
Afr 1609.13.7	Cros, L. Le Maroc pour tous. Paris, 1913.
Afr 1609.13.8	Botte, L. Au coeur du Maroc. Paris, 1913.
Afr 1609.13.10	Desroches, G. Le Maroc, son passe, son present, son avenir. Paris, 1913.
Afr 1609.13.12	Ladreit de Lacharriere, R. Voyage au Maroc, 1910-11. Paris, 1913.
Afr 1609.13.15	Chevrillon, A. Marrakech dans les palmes. Paris, 1919.
Afr 1609.14	Holt, G.E. Morocco the piquant. London, 1914.
Afr 1609.14.3	Doutte, E. Missions au Maroc, en tribu. Paris, 1914.
Afr 1609.14.5	Dantin Cereceda, J. Una expedicion cientifica por la zona de influencia española en Marruecos. Barcelona, 1914.
Afr 1609.15	Roulleaux Dugage, G. Lettres du Maroc, illustrations de E. Stoeckel. Paris, 1915.
Afr 1609.15.3	Mission Scientifique du Maroc. Villes et tribus du Maroc. v.1-11. Paris, 1915-32. 11v.
Afr 1609.16	Vera Salas, Antonio. Porvenir de Espana en Marruecos. Toledo, 1916.
Afr 1609.17	Ajalbert, Jean. Le Maroc sans les boches. Paris, 1917.
Afr 1609.17.3	Koechlin, Raymond. Le Maroc en paix. Paris, 1917.
Afr 1609.17.5	Piquet, Victor. Le Maroc, geographie, histoire, mise en valeur. Paris, 1917.
Afr 1609.17.7	Piquet, Victor. Le Maroc, geographie, histoire, mise en valeur. 3 éd. Paris, 1920.
Afr 1609.19A	Wharton, Edith. In Morocco. N.Y, 1920.
Afr 1609.19B	Wharton, Edith. In Morocco. N.Y, 1920.
Afr 1609.19.5	Goulven, J. Le Maroc. Paris, 1919.
Afr 1609.20	Tharaud, Jerome. Marrakech. Paris, 1920.
Afr 1609.20.5	Amic, Henri. Le Maroc, hier et aujourd hui. Paris, 1925.
Afr 1609.21.5	Kann, Reginald. Le protectorat marocain. Nancy, 1921.
Afr 1609.22	Andrews, C. E. Old Morocco and the forbidden atlas. N.Y., 1922.
Afr 1609.22.5	Rabbe, P. Au Maroc. Sur les rives. Paris, 1922.

Afr 1605 - 1610 Morocco - Geography, description, etc. - General works (By date) - cont.

Afr 1609.22.10 Hardy, Georges. Les grandes lignes de la geographie du Maroc. Paris, 1922.
Afr 1609.23 Tarde, Alfred de. Le Maroc, ecole d'energie. Paris, 1923.
Afr 1609.23.5 Oconnor, V.C.S. A vision of Morocco. London, 1923.
Afr 1609.23.10 Tharaud, J. Le Maroc. Paris, 1923.
Afr 1609.23.15 Celarie, H. Un mois au Maroc. Paris, 1923.
Afr 1609.23.20 Cansino-Roldan, Luis. Recuerdos de Marruecos. Malaga, 1923.
Afr 1609.23.25 Sadler, Georges. A travers le Maghreb. Paris, 1923.
Afr 1609.24 Tranchant de Lunel, M. Au pays du paradoxe, Maroc. Paris, 1924.
Afr 1609.24.5 Champion, P. Tanger, fes et meknes. Paris, 1924.
Afr 1609.24.10 Cabrera Lattore. Magreb-el-aksai. Madrid, 1924.
Afr 1609.25 Sheean, V. Adventures among the Riffi. London, 1926.
Afr 1609.25.3A Sheean, V. An american among the Riffi. N.Y., 1926.
Afr 1609.25.3B Sheean, V. An american among the Riffi. N.Y., 1926.
Afr 1609.25.5 Magrini, L. Marocco. Milano, 1926.
Afr 1609.25.10 Horne, John. Many days in Morocco. London, 1925.
Afr 1609.25.12 Horne, John. Many days in Morocco. 2d ed. Rev. London, 1936.
Afr 1609.26.5 Terhorst, Bernd. With the Riff Kabyles. London, 1926.
Afr 1609.26.10 Ossendowski, F. The fire of desert folk. London, 1926.
Afr 1609.26.15 Odinot, Paul. Le monde marocain. Paris, 1926.
Afr 1609.27 Vernon, Paul E. Morocco from a motor. London, 1927.
Afr 1609.27.5F Celarie, H. Behind moroccan walls. N.Y., 1931.
Afr 1609.28 Elsner, Eleanor. The magic of Morocco. London, 1928.
Afr 1609.29 Lowth, Alys. A wayfarer in Morocco. London, 1929.
Afr 1609.29.2 Lowth, Alys. A wayfarer in Morocco. Boston, 1929.
Afr 1609.29.5 Bickerstaffe, Lovelyn Elaine. Things seen in Morocco. N.Y., 1929.
Afr 1609.30 Assher, Ben. A nomad in Morocco. London, n.d.
Afr 1609.30.5 Hardy, Georges. Le Maroc. Paris, 1930.
Afr 1609.30.10 Willette, H. Au Maroc. Paris, 1930.
Afr 1609.30.15 Manue, G. R. Sur les marches du Maroc insoumis. 3e ed. Paris, 1930.
Afr 1609.30.20 Berthel, J. Impressions marocaines. Paris, 1930.
Afr 1609.30.25 Nahon, Moise. Propos d'un vieux marocain. Paris, 1930.
Afr 1609.30.30 Desvallieres, Jean. Le Maroc. Paris, 1930.
Afr 1609.31 Celerier, Jean. Le Maroc. Paris, 1931.
Afr 1609.31.5 Vicuna, Alejandro. Bajo cielo africano. Paris, 1931.
Afr 1609.31.10 Gadala, M.T. La feerie marocaine. Grenoble, 1931.
Afr 1609.31.15 Terrier, A. Le Maroc. Paris, 1931.
Afr 1609.31.20 Dumas, P. Le Maroc. Grenoble, 1931.
Afr 1609.31.30 Hall, Leland. Salah and his American. N.Y., 1935.
Afr 1609.32F Ladreit de Lacharrière, J. Au Maroc en suivant Foucauld. Paris, 1932.
Afr 1609.32.5 Rabat, Maroc. Institut des Hautes Études Marocaines. Initiation au Maroc. Rabat, 1932.
Afr 1609.32.7 Rabat. Maroc. Institut des Hautes Études Marocaines. Initiation au Maroc. Paris, 1937.
Afr 1609.32.9 Rabat. Maroc. Institut des Hautes Études Marocaines. Initiation au Maroc. Nouvelle ed. Paris, 1945.
Afr 1609.33F Chevrillon, A. Visions du Maroc. Marseille, 1933.
Afr 1609.34 Wattenavyl, R. Von. Ein land, menschen in Marokko. Zürich, 1934.
Afr 1609.35 Rigo Derighi, E. Holiday in Morocco. London, 1935.
Afr 1609.36.5 Thornton, P. The voice of atlas, in search of music in Morocco. London, 1936.
Afr 1609.36.10 Capriles, Georges. La promenade marocaine. Paris, 1936.
Afr 1609.37 Ciarlantine, T. Il marocco com e. Milano, 1937.
Afr 1609.38 Orano, E. A traverso il Marocco. Napoli, 1938.
Afr 1609.38.5 Turnbull, P. Black barbary. London, 1938.
Afr 1609.38.10 Arques, Enrique. Tierra de moros, estampas de folklore. v.1-2. Ceuta, 1938-53. 2v.
Afr 1609.42 Morocco. Casablanca, 1942.
Afr 1609.48 Celerier, Jean. Maroc. 2. ed. Paris, 1954.
Afr 1609.48.5 Joly, Fernand. Geographie du Maroc. Paris, 1949.
Afr 1609.49 Coindreau, R. Le Maroc. Paris, 1949.
Afr 1609.50 Bonn, G. Marokko. 1. Aufl. Stuttgart, 1950.
Afr 1609.50.5 Landau, R. Invitation to Morocco. London, 1950.
Afr 1609.50.10 Miege, Jean L. Le Maroc. 1. ed. Paris, 1950.
Afr 1609.50.12 Miege, Jean L. Morocco. Paris, 1952.
Afr 1609.52 Landau, R. Moroccan journal. London, 1952.
Afr 1609.52.5 Durham, Eng. University. Exploration society expedition to French Morocco. Report of the expedition to French Morocco. Durham, 1956.
Afr 1609.53 Newman, B. Morocco today. London, 1953.
Afr 1609.54 Honel, C. Mes aventures marocaines. Casablanca, 1954.
Afr 1609.54.5 Encyclopedie Mensuelle d'Outre-Mer. Morocco 54. Paris, 1954.
Afr 1609.55 Mensching, Horst. Zwischen rif und draa. Leipzig, 1955.
Afr 1609.55.5 Buttin, Paul. Le drame du Maroc. Paris, 1955.
Afr 1609.57 Nebel, Gerhard. An den Saulen des Herakles. Hamburg, 1957.
Afr 1609.58 Epton, Nina C. Saints and sorcerers. London, 1958.
Afr 1609.58.5F Morocco. Ministere des Affaires Étrangeres. Morocco. Rabat, 1958.
Afr 1609.58.10 Miazgowski, Brouirlew. Merakko-Krasnaie zemlia. Moskva, 1963.
Afr 1609.59 Bourgeois, Paul. L'univers de l'ecolier marocain. v.1-5. Rabat, 1959-60.
Afr 1609.60 Heinemeijir, W.F. Marokko. Meppel, 1960.
Afr 1609.61 Mikesell, M.W. Northern Morocco, a cultural geography. Berkeley, 1961.
Afr 1609.61.5 Simoes, Antonio. Marruecos, ayer-hoy. Buenos Aires, 1961.
Afr 1609.62 Rouze, Michel. Maroc. Lausanne, 1962.
Afr 1609.63 Morin-Barde, M. Le Maroc etincelant. Casablanca, 1963.
Afr 1609.64 Chalyi, Bohdan I. Marokko, svitanok. Kyiv, 1964.
Afr 1609.64.5 Geographie du Maroc. Paris, 1964.
Afr 1609.65 American University, Washington D.C. Foreign Area Studies Division. Area handbook for Morocco. Washington, 1965.
Afr 1609.66 Garrique, Francois. Maroc enchante. Paris, 1966.
Afr 1609.66.5 Herault, Andre. Le Maroc a visage decouvert. Paris, 1966.
Afr 1609.66.10 Gornung, Mikhail B. Marokko. Moskva, 1966.
Afr 1609.67 Dominicus, Johannes. Portret van Marokko. s'Hertogenbosch, 1967.

Afr 1618 Morocco - Geography, description, etc. - Special customs

Afr 1618.5F Rackow, Ernst. Beiträge zur kenntnis der Materiellen kultur nordwest-marokkos. Wiesbaden, 1958.
Afr 1618.10 Dolinger, Jane. Behind harem walls. London, 1960.
Afr 1618.15 Cola Alberich, Julio. Cultos primitivos de Marruecos. Madrid, 1954.
Afr 1618.20 Guillaume, A. La propriété collective au Maroc. Rabat, 1960.

Afr 1618 Morocco - Geography, description, etc. - Special customs - cont.

Afr 1618.22 Duran Pulis, Guillermo. La caza en Marruecos. Las Palmas de Gran Canaria, 1955.
Afr 1618.24 Albarracin de Martinez Ruiz, Joaquina. Vestido y adorno de la mujer musulmana de Vêbala (Marruecos). Madrid, 1964.
Afr 1618.26 Hoffman, Bernard G. The structure of traditional Morroccan rural society. The Hague, 1967.
Afr 1618.28 Bonjean, François. L'ame marocaine, une à travers les croyances et la politesse. Paris, 1948.

Afr 1620 Morocco - Geography, description, etc. - Guidebooks

Afr 1620.10 Monmarche, Marcel. Le Maroc. Paris, 1919.
Afr 1620.15 Ricard, Prosper. Le Maroc. 3e ed. Paris, 1925.
Afr 1620.15.5 Heywood, C. Morocco. Paris, 1924.
Afr 1620.15.10 Ricard, Prosper. Maroc. 7. ed. Paris, 1950.
Afr 1620.25 Nagel, Publishers. Morocco. Paris, 1953.
Afr 1620.25.5 Nagel, Publishers. Maroc. Geneve, 1966.
Afr 1620.28.9 Maroc. 9.ed. Paris, 1966.
Afr 1620.28.12 Maroc. Paris, 1969.
Afr 1620.30 U.S. Office of Armed Forces Information and Education. A pocket guide to French Morocco. Washington, 1956.
Afr 1620.35 Fodor, Eugene. Morocco, 1965-66. N.Y., 1966.
Afr 1620.40 Dennis-Jones, Harold. Your guide to Morrocco. London, 1965.
Afr 1620.42 Morocco. Paris, 1966.

Afr 1621 Morocco - Geography, description, etc. - Views

Afr 1621.5 Echague, F. Marruecos...en 1894, fotografias. Madrid, 1906.
Afr 1621.10 Beaurieux, Remy. Le Maroc. Marseille, 1930.

Afr 1622 Morocco - Geography, description, etc. - Maps

Afr 1622.5F Levi-Provencal, E. Maroc, atlas historique, geographique et économique. Paris, 1935.

Afr 1623.1 - .199 Morocco - Economic history and conditions - Historical works

Afr 1623.5F Situation économique du Maroc. Rabat.
Afr 1623.25 Lareveliere, J. Les energies françaises auMaroc. Paris, 1917.
Afr 1623.30 Bouissi, R. Etude sur la colonisation capitaliste au Maroc. Thèse. Paris, 1921.

Afr 1623.500 - .999 Morocco - Economic history and conditions - Contemporary works (By date)

Afr 1623.899 Schwegel, H. Marokko. Wien, 1899.
Afr 1623.919 Ancey, Cesar. Nos interets économiques du Maroc. Paris, 1919.
Afr 1623.927 Lucien-Graux. Le Maroc économique. Paris, 1928.
Afr 1623.932 Pourquier, Rene. L'impôt sur les plus-values immobilieres au Maroc. Thèse. Paris, 1932.
Afr 1623.932.5 Hoffher, René. L'économie marocaine. Paris, 1932.
Afr 1623.932.10 Desfeuilles, Paul. Les colonies françaises, le Maroc. Paris, 1932.
Afr 1623.933.5 Evin, Guy. L'industrie au Maroc et ses problemes. Thèse. Paris, 1933.
Afr 1623.934 Romanus, H. Eine wirtschaftsgeographische darstellung...Marokkos und Tunesiens. Inaug. Diss. Königsberg, 1934.
Afr 1623.934.5 Hoffherr, Rene. Revenus et niveaux de vie indigenes au Maroc. Paris, 1934.
Afr 1623.934.10 Ecorcheville, C. Production et protection au Maroc. Paris, 1934.
Afr 1623.935 Tomas Perez, V. Marruecos. Barcelona, 1935.
Afr 1623.937 Garcin, Pierre. La politique des contingents dans les relations franco-marocaines. Thèse. Lyon, 1937.
Afr 1623.942 Massa, Jose L. Economia marroqui. Tetuan, 1942.
Afr 1623.942.5 Piersius. Etude sur les communautés rurales en Beni-Ahsen. Rabat, 1942.
Afr 1623.954F Ripoche, Paul. Problemes économiques au Maroc. Rabat, 1954.
Afr 1623.954.5 Morocco. Division du Commerce et de la Marine Marchande. Maroc, cinq ans de realisation du programme d'equipement. Rabat, 1954.
Afr 1623.955 Guillaume, Albert. L'evolution economique de la societe rurale marocaine. Paris, 1955.
Afr 1623.956F Ripoche, Paul. Problemes économiques au Maroc. 2. ed. Rabat, 1956.
Afr 1623.957 France. Institut National de la Statistique et des Études Économiques. Dix ans d'économie marocaine, 1945-1955. Paris, 1957.
Afr 1623.958 Lacouture, Jean. Le Maroc a l'epreuve. Paris, 1958.
Afr 1623.958.5 Morocco. L'evolution économique du Maroc dans le cadre du deuxieme plan quadriennal. Casablanca, 1958.
Afr 1623.958.10 Cowan, Laing. The economic development of Morocco. Santa Monica, 1958.
Afr 1623.958.15F Maroc. Division de la Coordination Économique et du Plan. Plan biennal d'equipement, 1958-1959. Rabat, 1958.
Afr 1623.960 Morocco. Division de la Coordination Economique et du Plan. Tableaux économiques du Maroc. Rabat, 1960.
Afr 1623.960.5 Morocco. Division de la Coordination Économique et du Plan. Plan quinquennal, 1960-1964. Rabat, 1960.
Afr 1623.960.6 Morocco. Division de la Coordination Économique et du Plan. Plan quinquennal, 1960-1964. Rabat, 1961.
Afr 1623.961 Lahaye, R. Les entreprises publiques au Maroc. Rabat, 1961.
Afr 1623.961.5 Middle East Research Association. Washington, D.C. Morocco, a politico-economic analysis, 1956-60. Washington, 1961.
Afr 1623.961.10 Hauet, Daniel. La formation professionnelle par ses propres moyens dans les pays en voie. Rabat, 1961.
Afr 1623.962 Waterston, A. Planning in Morocco. Washington, 1962.
Afr 1623.963 Tiano, A. La politique économique et financiere du Maroc independant. Paris, 1963.
Afr 1623.963.5 Morocco. Delegation Generale a la Promotion Nationale et au Plan. Promotion nationale au Maroc. Casa, 196-.
Afr 1623.963.10 Italy. Instituto Nazionale per il Commercio Estero. Marocco. Roma, 1963.
Afr 1623.963.15 Zerilli Marimó, Guido. Maroc économique. Milan, 1963.
Afr 1623.964 Stewart, C.F. The economy of Morocco, 1912-1962. Cambridge, 1964. 2v.
Afr 1623.964.5 United States. Bureau of International Commerce. A market for United States products in Morocco. Washington, 1964.
Afr 1623.964.10 Gallissot, Rene. Le patronat europeen au Maroc. Rabat, 1964.
Afr 1623.964.15 Kratz, Achim. Untersuchung der morokkanischen Industriestruktur. Hamburg, 1964.

tions -

Tunisia. 1st ed.

-ekonomicheskoe
Moskva, 1965.
on Economique et du Plan.
bat, 1965.
on Economique et du Plan.
Rabat, 1965? 3v.
on and Development. The
cco. Baltimore, 1966.

orks (By date)
financiere de l'empire

du Maroc. Paris, 1914.
engagements de depenses

est Marocain.

ribus de Marruecos.

entaires au Maroc.

hie marocaine.

ocaine. Rabat, 1961.

s. v.1-2. Tunis, 1898.
u zenete...Au Maroc.

res. Paris, 1912.
Makhzen dans le sud du

. N.Y., 1927.
res berberes. Thèse.

in. Paris, 1925.
ere les ait oumalon et le

. Rabat, 1934.
roupement berbere.

berberes. Paris, 1930.
e berbere. Paris, 1954.
s en Marruecos.
Madrid, 1954.

Afr 1635.27	Koller Angelus, Father. Essai sur l'esprit du berbere marocain. 2 ed. Fribourg, 1949.
Afr 1635.30	Dobo, Nicolas. J'étais le médecin de cent mille Berbères. Paris, 1964.
Afr 1635.35	Carim, Fuat. Yusuf Taşfin; yer yüzünün en Büyük devletlerinden birini kuran Berber imparatoru. Istanbul, 1966.
Afr 1635.40	Gellner, Ernest. Saints of the Atlas. London, 1969.

Afr 1640   Morocco - Races - Others

Afr 1640.1	Hess, Jean. Israel au Maroc. Paris, 1907.
Afr 1640.3	Ortega, Manuel L. Los hebreos en Marruecos. Madrid, 1919.
Afr 1640.5	Goulven, J. Les Mellah de Rabat-Sale. Paris, 1927.
Afr 1640.10	Lachapelle, F. Les Tekna du sud Marocain. Paris, 1934.
Afr 1640.10.5	Monteil, Vincent. Notes sur les Tekna. Paris, 1948.
Afr 1640.15	Vainot, L. Pelerinages judeo-musulmans du Maroc. Paris, 1948.

Afr 1645   Morocco - Religion

Afr 1645.5	García Barriuso, Patrocinio. Los derechos del gobierno español en la misión de Marruecos. Madrid, 1968.

Afr 1655   Morocco - Provinces of French Morocco - Fez - General works

Afr 1655.1	Chevrillon, Andre. Un crepuscule d'islam-Maroc. Paris, 1906.
Afr 1655.4	Tharaud, J. Fez, ou les bourgeois de l'islam. Paris, 1930.

Afr 1658   Morocco - Provinces of French Morocco - Fez - Riff

Afr 1658.4	Artbauer, O.C. Die rifpiraten und ihre heimat. Stuttgart, 1911.
Afr 1658.5	Duveyrier, H. La derniere partie...Littoral de la mediterranee-le Rif. Paris, 1888.
Afr 1658.6	Calvo, G. Espana en Marruecos (1910-1913). Barcelona, 1914.
Afr 1658.7	Ruiz Albeniz, R. El riff, el riff en paz, la guerra del riff. Madrid, 1912.
Afr 1658.7.2	Ruiz Albeniz, Victor. Espana en el rif. 2a ed. Madrid, 1921.
Afr 1658.8	Delbrel, G. Geografia general de la provincia del Rif. Melilla, 1911.
Afr 1658.9	Diana, M.J. Un prisionero en el riff, memorias del ayudante alvarez. Madrid, 1859.
Afr 1658.10	Avenia Taure, I. Memorias sobre el riff, su conquista y colonizacion. Zaragoza, 1859.
Afr 1658.11	Zuhueta Y Gomis, J. Impresiones del Rif. Barcelona, 1916.
Afr 1658.12	Becker, Jeronimo. El Rif. Madrid, 1909.
Afr 1658.13	Fernandez De Castro, Rafael. El Rif. Malaga, 1911.
Afr 1658.15	Vera Salas, A. El Rif oriental. Melilla, 1918.
Afr 1658.16	Basallo, Francisco. Memorias del sargento Basallo. Madrid, 1923?
Afr 1658.17	Guardiola Cardellach, E. El Rif en Espana. Barcelona, 1923.
Afr 1658.18	Michaux-Bellaire, Ed. Apuntes para la historia del Rif. Madrid, 1926.
Afr 1658.23	Thyen, Maurice. Trois mois de colonne sur le front riffian, juin a sept. 1925. Paris, 1926.
Afr 1658.25	Laure, August M.E. La victoire franco-espagnole dans le Rif. Paris, 1927.
Afr 1658.27	Hubert, Jacques. L'aventure riffaine et ses dessous politiques. Paris, 1927.
Afr 1658.28	Hernandez Mir, F. Del desastre à la victoria 1921-1926. v.1-4. Madrid, 1926-27. 4v.
Afr 1658.29	Pech Soff, Zinovi. La legion étrangere au Maroc. Paris, 1927.
Afr 1658.30	Damidaux, C. Combats au Maroc 1925-1926. Paris, 1928.

Afr   1658   Morocco - Provinces of French Morocco - Fez - Riff - cont.

Afr 1658.31	Bordes, Pierre. Dans le Rif (Cornet de route d'un marsouin). Orne de gravures et de cartes. Lyon, 1929.
Afr 1658.32	Queipo De Llano, G. El general. 7a ed. Madrid, 1930.
Afr 1658.35	Vazquez Sastre, C. En tierras del rif. Melilla, 1913.
Afr 1658.37	Reguert, P.T. L'agression riffaine en 1925. Paris, 1933.
Afr 1658.39	Nearing, Scott. Stopping at war. N.Y., 1926.
Afr 1658.40	Sanchez, J.G. Nuestro protectorado. Madrid, 1930.
Afr 1658.42	Sanchez Javaloy, Roque. El Manco de Tikun. Murcia, 1935.
Afr 1658.45	Lutskaia, N.S. Respublika rif. Moscow, 1959.
Afr 1658.47	Gaudio, A. Rif, terre marocaine d'epopee et de legende. Paris, 1962.
Afr 1658.48	Lopez Rienda, R. Abd-el-krim contra francia. Madrid, 1925.
Afr 1658.49	Santiago Guerrero, M. La columna saro en la campana de alhucemas. Barcelona, 1926.
Afr 1658.50	Harris, W.B. France, Spain and the rif. London, 1927.
Afr 1658.52	Vivero, Augusto. El derrumbamiento. Madrid, 1922.
Afr 1658.54	Ramos Charco-Villasenor, Aniceto. El Rif. Toledo, 1930.
Afr 1658.56	Guixé, Juan. El Rif en sombras lo que yo he visto en Melilla. Madrid, 1922.

Afr   1660   Morocco - Provinces of French Morocco - Fez - Other districts

Afr 1660.1	Doutte, E. Les djebala du Maroc. Oran, 1899.

Afr   1665   Morocco - Provinces of French Morocco - Sus

Afr 1665.5	Boron De Segonzac, R. De. Excursion au sous. Paris, 1901.
Afr 1665.7	Dugard, Henry. La colonne du sous, janvier-juin, 1917. Paris, 1918.

Afr   1675   Morocco - Provinces of French Morocco - Marrakesh

Afr 1675.1	Doutte, Edmond. Merrakech. Paris, 1905.
Afr 1675.2	Perigny, Maurice. Au Maroc, marrakech et les ports du sud. Paris, 1918.

Afr   1680   Morocco - Provinces of French Morocco - Atlas and Transatlas - General works

Afr 1680.1	Thomson, J. Travels in the atlas and southern Morocco. London, 1889.
Afr 1680.2.5	Schnell, P. L'atlas marocain d'apres les documents originaux. Paris, 1898.
Afr 1680.3	Fischer, T. Meine dritte forschungsreise im atlas-vorlande von Marokko im Jahre 1901. Hamburg, 1902.
Afr 1680.4	Ichmann, G. Der hohe Atlas. Marburg, 1891.
Afr 1680.5	Segonzac, De. Au coeur de l'atlas. Paris, 1910.
Afr 1680.6	Thomas, L. Voyage au goundafa et au sous. Paris, 1918.
Afr 1680.7	Chatinieres, P. Dans le grand atlas marocain. Paris, 1919.
Afr 1680.9	Felze, Jacques. Au Maroc inconnu dans le haut-atlas et le sud Marocain. Grenoble, 1935.
Afr 1680.10	Berque, Jacques. Structures sociales du haut-atlas. 1 ed. Paris, 1955.
Afr 1680.12	Clarke, Bryan. Berber village. London, 1959.
Afr 1680.14	Dresch, Jean. Commentaire des cartes sur les genres de vie de montagne dans le massif central du grand atlas. Tours, 1941.
Afr 1680.16	Monreal Agustí, Luis. La montaña de los guerrilleros; relato. Barcelona, 1967.
Afr 1680.50	Montagne, Robert. Un magasin collectif de l'anti-atlas. Thèse. Paris, 1930.

Afr   1685   Morocco - Provinces of French Morocco - Atlas and Transatlas - Tafilelt

Afr 1685.1	Harris, W.B. Tafilet. Edinburg, 1895.

Afr   1688   Morocco - Provinces of French Morocco - Atlas and Transatlas - Figig

Afr 1688.5	Castries, H. De. Notes sur figuig. Paris, 1882.

Afr   1700   Morocco - Cities, towns, etc. of French Morocco - General works

Afr 1700.5	Lechatelier, A. Notes sur les villes et tribus du Maroc. Angers, 1902.

Afr   1703   Morocco - Cities, towns, etc. of French Morocco - A

Afr 1703.2	Cortocero Hanares, H.F. Alcazarquiver 1950. Tetuan, 1953.
Afr 1703.3F	Rodrigues, Bernardo. Anais de arzila, cronica inedita do seculo XVI. Lisboa, 1915-20. 2v.
Afr 1703.3.10	Lopes, David. Historia de arzila durante o dominio portugues (1471-1550 e 1577-1589). Coimbra, 1924.
Afr 1703.3.15	Ladron De Guevara, A. Arcila durante la ocupacion portuguesa. Tanger, 1940.
Afr 1703.5.7	Figanier, Joaquim. Historia de Santa Cruz do cabo de gue (Agadir). Lisboa, 1945.
Afr 1703.5.10	Cappe, Willy. Agadir, 29 février 1960, histoire et leçons d'une catastrophe. Marseille, 1967.
Afr 1703.6	Peres, Damiao. Conquista de azamor pelo duque de braganca don jaime. Lisboa, 1951.

Afr   1705   Morocco - Cities, towns, etc. of French Morocco - B

Afr 1705.5	Thouvenot, R. Une colonie romaine de Mauretanie Tingitane. Paris, 1941.

Afr   1706   Morocco - Cities, towns, etc. of French Morocco - C

Afr 1706.2	Lapeyre. Casablanca. Paris, 1918.
Afr 1706.5	Miege, Jean L. Les Européens à Casablanca au XIXe siècle. Paris, 1954.
Afr 1706.8	Adam, André. Casablanca. Thèse. Paris, 1968. 2v.

Afr   1709   Morocco - Cities, towns, etc. of French Morocco - D (Others)

Afr 1709.5	Flamand, P. Demnate, un mellah en pays berbere. Paris, 1952.

Afr   1713   Morocco - Cities, towns, etc. of French Morocco - Fez

Afr 1713.4	Letourneau, Roger. Fez in the age of marinides. 1st ed. Norman, 1961.
Afr 1713.4.5	Letourneau, Roger. Fez avant le protectorat. Casablanca, 1949.
Afr 1713.4.10	Letourneau, Roger. La vie quotidienne à Fes en 1900. Paris, 1965.
Afr 1713.5	Moulieras, A. Fez. Paris, 1902.
Afr 1713.6	Gaillard, H. Une ville d'islam, fes. Paris, 1905.
Afr 1713.7	Cisotti-Ferrara, M. Nel marocco. Milano, 1912.
Afr 1713.8	Dieulefils, P. Maroc occidental. Paris, 1916.
Afr 1713.9	Erigny, Maurice. Au Maroc. Fes la capitale du nord. Paris, 191- .
Afr 1713.10	Terrasse, Henri. La mosquee des andalous à Fes. Text and atlas. v.1-2. Paris, 1942. 2v.
Afr 1713.11	Lucas, Georges. Fes dans la Maroc moderne. Paris, 1937.
Afr 1713.12F	Burckhardt, Titus. Fes, Stadt des Islam. Alten, 1960.

Afr 1713 Morocco - Cities, towns, etc. of French Morocco - Fez - cont.

Afr 1713.14 Al-Tazi, Abd Al- Hali. Eleven centuries in the university of al-qarawiyyin. Mohammedia, 1960.
Afr 1713.15 Tharaud, Jerome. La nuit de Fes. Paris, 1932.

Afr 1719 Morocco - Cities, towns, etc. of French Morocco - J

Afr 1719.2 Story of Cape Juby. London, 1894.

Afr 1721 Morocco - Cities, towns, etc. of French Morocco - Laraiche

Afr 1721.3 Narvaez Pacheco, J. Sitio de San Antonio de alareche en 1689. Madrid, 1893.
Afr 1721.5 Cabanas, Rafael. Rasgos fisiograficos y geologicos. Madrid, 1955.
Afr 1721.7 Moreno Gilabert, Andres. La Ciudad Dormida. Madrid, 1923.
Afr 1721.9 Garcia Figueras, T. Temas de protectorado. Ceuta, 1926.

Afr 1723 Morocco - Cities, towns, etc. of French Morocco - Marrakesh

Afr 1723.5 Canetti, Elias. Die Stimmen von Marrakesch. München, 1968.
Afr 1723.10 Dupac, J. Le sud marocain. Marrakech. Safi et Mogador. Paris, 192- .
Afr 1723.15 Mayne, Peter. The alleys of Marrakesh. 1st ed. Boston, 1953.
Afr 1723.20 Deverdun, G. Marrakech, des origines à 1912. Rabat, 1959. 2v.

Afr 1724 Morocco - Cities, towns, etc. of French Morocco - Mazagan

Afr 1724.1 Coutinho, Goncalo. Discurso da jornada de D. Goncalo Coutinho. Lisboa, 1629.
Afr 1724.1.2 Coutinho, Goncalo. Discurso da jornada de D. Goncalo Coutinho. (Another issue). Lisboa, 1629.
Afr 1724.2 Goulven, J. La place de mazagan. Paris, 1917.
Afr 1724.3F Portugal. Sovereigns, 1688-1706 (Peter Ii). Regimento da praca de mazagam. Lisboa, 1692.
Afr 1724.5 Relacao do grande terremoto. Lisboa, 1756.
Afr 1724.7 Ricard, Robert. Un document portugais sur la place de Mazagrn au début du XVIIe siècle. Thèse. Paris, 1932.

Afr 1727 Morocco - Cities, towns, etc. of French Morocco - M (Others)

Afr 1727.2 Servando Marenco, D. La conquista de la Mehedia. Madrid, 1908.
Afr 1727.5 Raynal, R. Plaines et piedmonts du bassin de la Moulouya. Rabat, 1961.
Afr 1727.8 Ibn Talha, Abd al-Wahid. Moulay-Idriss du Zerhoun. Rabat, 1965.

Afr 1731 Morocco - Cities, towns, etc. of French Morocco - P

Afr 1731.1 Rouard De Card, E. L'isle de Perecil. Toulouse, 1903.

Afr 1733 Morocco - Cities, towns, etc. of French Morocco - R

Afr 1733.5 Tharaud, Jerome. Rabat. Paris, 1918.
Afr 1733.5.10 Brunot, Louis. La mer dans les traditions et les industries indigenes a Rabat et Sale. Paris, 1920.
Afr 1733.5.15 Mauclair, Camille. Rabat et Sale. Paris, 1934.
Afr 1733.5.20 Caille, Jacques. La petite histoire de Rabat. Casablanca, 1950.
Afr 1733.5.25 Caille, Jacques. La ville de Rabat. Vanoest, 1949. 3v.
Afr 1733.6 Lecoz, J. Le Rharb, fellahs et colons. Rabat, 1964. 2v.
Afr 1733.6.1 Lecoz, J. Le Rharb. Rabat, 1964. 2v.

Afr 1734 Morocco - Cities, towns, etc. of French Morocco - Saffi

Afr 1734.5 Lopes, David. Textas em aljamia portuguesa. Lisboa, 1897.

Afr 1735 Morocco - Cities, towns, etc. of French Morocco - Sale

Afr 1735.5 Coindreau, Roger. Corsaires de Sale. Paris, 1948.

Afr 1736 Morocco - Cities, towns, etc. of French Morocco - S (others)

Afr 1736.3 Alcala galiano, pelayo. Memoria sobre la situación de Santa Cruz de Mar Pegueña. 3 in 1. Madrid, 1878. 3 pam.
Afr 1736.4 Alcala Galiano, Pelayo. Santa Cruz de Mar Pequeña. Madrid, 1900.

Afr 1738 Morocco - Cities, towns, etc. of French Morocco - Tangier

Afr 1738.01 Hudson, Manley O. The international mixed court of Tangier. n.p., 1927.
Afr 1738.1 Rouard de Card, E. La defaite des Anglais à Tanger, 1664. n.p., 1912.
Htn Afr 1738.2* Present state of Tangier. London, 1676.
Htn Afr 1738.3.5* Ross, John. Tanger's rescue. London, 1681.
Afr 1738.4 Howard-Vyse, L. A winter in Tangier. London, 1882.
Afr 1738.5 Cousin, A. Tanger. 1st ed. Paris, 1902.
Afr 1738.5.3 Cousin, A. Tanger. 3d ed. Paris, 1903.
Afr 1738.6 Conditions d'existence à Tanger. Paris, 1906.
Afr 1738.7 Escribano del Pino, E. Tanger y sus alrededores. Madrid, 1903.
Afr 1738.8 Furlong, C.W. At the strait's mouth. N.Y., 1904.
Afr 1738.9F Menezes, D.F. De. Historia de Tangere. Lisboa, 1732.
Htn Afr 1738.10* Particular narrative of a great engagement. Savoy, 1680.
Afr 1738.11 Routh, E.M.G. Tangier. London, 1912.
Afr 1738.12 Views of tangier. n.p., n.d.
Htn Afr 1738.13* Addison, L. The Moores baffled. London, 1681.
Afr 1738.15 Garcia, S.F. Color. Madrid, 1919.
Afr 1738.20F Tangier, Africa. Registos paroquiais da se de Tanger. Lisboa, 1922.
Afr 1738.21 Lilius, Aleko E. Tapahtui tangerissa. Helsingissa, 1955.
Afr 1738.22 Luke, John. Tangier at high tide. Geneva, 1958.
Afr 1738.23F Rouard De Card, E. Le statut de Tanger d'après la convention du 18 decembre 1923. Paris, 1925.
Afr 1738.24 Raymond, Chas. Le statut de Tanger. Alger, 1927.
Afr 1738.25 Graevenitz, K.F.H.A.R. Die Tanger-Frage. Berlin, 1925.
Afr 1738.26 Durand, Raphael. Le probleme de Tanger. Thèse. Aix-en-provence, 1926.
Afr 1738.27 Sibieude, Jean. La question de Tanger. Thèse. Montpellier, 1927.
Afr 1738.29 Comite de Propagande et de Tourisme, Paris. Tanger. Paris, 1929.
Afr 1738.30 Stuart, G.H. The international city of Tanger. Stanford, calif., 1931.
Afr 1738.30.2 Stuart, G.H. The international city of Tanger. 2d ed. Stanford, calif., 1955.
Afr 1738.35 Vernier, Victor. La singuliere zone de Tanger. Paris, 1955.
Afr 1738.38.4 Petzet, H.W. Tanger und die britische Reichsbildung. Inaug. Diss. Berlin, 1938.
Afr 1738.38.5 Petzet, H.W. Tanger und die britische Reichsbildung. Berlin, 1938.

Afr 1738 Morocco - Cities, towns, etc. of French Morocco - Tangier - cont.

Afr 1738.40 Abbey, W.B.T. Tangier under british rule, 1661-1684. Jersey, Channel Islands, British Isles, 1940.
Afr 1738.45 Bonjean, Jacques. Tanger. Paris, 1967.
Afr 1738.50 Castellani Pastorio, Giovanni. Sviluppi e conclusione della questione di Tangeri. Roma, 1964.
Afr 1738.55 Un folleto inglés del siglo XVII referente a Tánger. Larache, 1939.

Afr 1739 Morocco - Cities, towns, etc. of French Morocco - Tetuan

Afr 1739.3 Munoz, I. La corte de Tetuan. Madrid, 1913.
Afr 1739.3.5 Al-Rahuni, A. Ben M. Historia de Tetuan. Tetuan, 1953.
Afr 1739.3.10 Ruiz De Cuevas, T. Apuntes para la historia de Tetuan. Tetuan, 1951.
Afr 1739.5 Valderrama Martinez, P. El palacio califal de Tetuan. Tetuan, 1961.

Afr 1742 Morocco - Cities, towns, etc. of French Morocco - U

Afr 1742.1 Voinot, L. Oudjds et l'Amalat (Maroc). Oran, 1912.

Afr 1745 Morocco - Cities, towns, etc. of French Morocco - Wazzan

Afr 1745.1 Watson, R.S. A visit to Wazan. London, 1880.

Afr 1750 Morocco - Spanish possessions in Morocco and environs - General works

Afr 1750.1 Galindo y de Vera. Historia vicisitudes y politica...respecto de sus posesiones en las costas de Africa. Madrid, 1884.
Afr 1750.2 Martin Y Peinador. Marruecos y plazas españolas. Madrid, 1908.
Afr 1750.3F Spain. Ministerio de Estado. Documentos presentados a las cortes en la legislatura de 1891 por el Ministro de Estado. Madrid, 1891. 3v.
Afr 1750.4.3 Congreso Africanista. Tercer congreso africanista. Barcelona, 1909.
Afr 1750.4.4 Congreso Africanista. Cuarto congreso africanista. IVth. Barcelona, 1910.
Afr 1750.5 Et-Tabyi. Miscelanea marroqui. Ceuta, 1953.
Afr 1750.6 Garcia Perez, A. Zona española del norte de Marruecos. Toledo, 1913.
Afr 1750.6.5 Garcia Pérez, Antonio. Heroicos infantes en Marruecos. Madrid, 1926.
Afr 1750.7 Spain. Dirección General de Estadistica. Annuario estadistico. Zona de protectorado y de los territorios de soberania de España en el norte de Africa. 1,1941+ 3v.
Afr 1750.8 Vieuchange, M. Smara, the forbidden city. N.Y., 1932.
Afr 1750.9 Alfaro y Zarabozo, S. de. Geografia de Marruecos y posesiones españolas de Africa. Toledo, 1920.
Afr 1750.10 Azpeitua, Antonio. Marruecos, la mala semilla. Madrid, 1921.
Afr 1750.11.6 Domenech Lafuente, A. Apuntes sobre geografia de la zona norte del protectorado de Espana en Marruegos. 3. ed. Madrid, 1942.
Afr 1750.12 Trivino Valdura, F. Del Marruecos español. Melilla, 1920.
Afr 1750.13 Arques, Enrique. El momento de Espana en Marruecos. Madrid, 1942.
Afr 1750.14 Gimenez, S. Espana en el Africa septentrional. Madrid, 1885.
Afr 1750.15 Silveira, L. Documentos portugueses sobre la accion de Espana en Africa. Madrid, 1954.
Afr 1750.20 Garcia Figueras, Tomas. Espana y su protectorado en Marruecos. Madrid, 1957.
Afr 1750.21 Garcia Figueras, Tomas. España en Marruecos. Madrid, 1947.
Afr 1750.21.5 Garcia Figueras, Tomes. La accion africana de Espana en torno al 98 (1860-1912). Madrid, 1966. 2v.
Afr 1750.22 Sangroniz, Jose Antonio De. Marruecos, sus condiciones fisicas. 2 ed. Madrid, 1926.
Afr 1750.25 Mensua Fernandez, Salvador. Bibliografia geografica de Marruecos español y zona internacional de Tanger. Aragoza, 1955.
Afr 1750.28 Pita, F. Del protectorado español en Marruecos. Melilla, 1933.
Afr 1750.28.5 Pita, F. Marruecos. Melilla, 1925.
Afr 1750.30 Bauer Y Landauer, Ignacio. Papeles de mi archivo. Madrid, 1923.
Afr 1750.32 Ghirelli, A. El norte de Marruecos. Melilla, 1926.
Afr 1750.33 Miranda Diaz, Mario. Espana en el continente africano. Madrid, 1963.
Afr 1750.34 Morocco (Spanish Zone). Seleccion de conferencias y trabajos realizados por la Academia de Interventores. Tetuan. 1949+
Afr 1750.35 Gomez, Vitaliano. En la hora de la paz, Marruecos, 1924-29. Tetuan, 1928.
Afr 1750.38 Arques, Enrique. Las adelantadas de España. Madrid, 1966.
Afr 1750.40 Ciges Aparicio, Manuel. Entre la paz y la guerra: Marruecos. Madrid, 1912.
Afr 1750.42 Ruiz Albéniz, Victor. Ecce homo: las responsabilidades del desastre. Madrid, 1922.
Afr 1750.44 Triviño Valdivia, Francisco. Cinco años en Marruecos. Madrid, 1903.
Afr 1750.47 Guanner, Vicente. El Sahara y Sur Marroqui españoles. Toledo, 1931.

Afr 1753 Morocco - Spanish possessions in Morocco and environs - Ceuta

Afr 1753.1 Pamphlet box. Ceuta.
Afr 1753.1.10 Academia das Sciencias de Lisboa. Centenarios de Ceuta e de Afonso de Albuquerque. Lisboa, 1916.
Afr 1753.2FA Eannes de Zurara, G. Cronica da tomada de Ceuta. Coimbra, 1915.
Afr 1753.2FB Eannes de Zurara, G. Cronica da tomada de Ceuta. Coimbra, 1915.
Afr 1753.3F Mascarenhas, J. Historia de la ciudad de Ceuta. Lisboa, 1918.
Afr 1753.4F Mateus de Pisano. Livro de guerra de Ceuta. Lisboa, 1915.
Afr 1753.4.5 Breve noticia da gloriosa Vitoria...1732. Lisboa, 1732.
Afr 1753.5 Relosillas, J.J. Catorce meses enCeuta. Malaga, 1886.
Afr 1753.6 Alvarez Cabrera, J. Columnas de operaciones en Marruecos. Tanger, 1909.
Afr 1753.7 Marquez De Prado, J.A. Recuerdos de Africa, historia de la plaza de Ceuta. Madrid, 1859.
Afr 1753.8 Tello Amondareyn, M. Ceuta llave principal del Estrecho. Madrid, 1897.
Afr 1753.9 Coleccion Ceuta. Ceuta. 1,1961+ 4v.
Afr 1753.10 Dornellas, Affonso De. Santissima virgem d'Africa, padroeira de Ceuta. Lisboa, 1924.
Afr 1753.10.2 Dornellas, Affonso De. Alleo, gloriosa epopeia portuguezaum Ceuta. Lisboa, 1924.

Afr 1753 Morocco - Spanish possessions in Morocco and environs - Ceuta - cont.

Afr 1753.10.3 Dornellas, Affonso de. O tercio de extranjeros do exercito espanhol. Lisboa, 1924.
Afr 1753.10.4 Dornellas, Affonso de. Os jogos floraes de 1923 em Ceuta. Lisboa, 1924.
Afr 1753.10.8 Dornellas, Affonso de. De Ceuta a alacacer kibir em 1923. Lisboa, 1925.
Afr 1753.10.12 Dornellas, Affonso de. As armas de Ceuta. Lisboa, 1925.
Afr 1753.12 Leria, C. Don Francisco y don dionisio. Tetuan, 1953.
Afr 1753.13 Sureda Blanes, F. Aby la herculana. Calpe, 1925.
Afr 1753.14 Leria, Manuel. Un siglo medieval en la historia de Ceuta, 931-1031. Ceuta, 1961.
Afr 1753.16 Paiva Manso, Levy Maria Jordão. Memoria historica sobre os bispados de Ceuta e Tanger. Lisboa, 1858.

Afr 1755 Morocco - Spanish possessions in Morocco and environs - Melilla

Afr 1755.01 Pamphlet box. Melilla.
Afr 1755.4 Guerra del rif. Paris, 1894.
Afr 1755.5 Morales, G. de. Datos para la historia de Melilla. Melilla, 1909.
Afr 1755.6 Corral Caballe, M. del. Cronica de la guerra de Africa en 1909. Barcelona, 1909.
X Cg Afr 1755.7 Fernandez, M.B. Notas referente a la tribu de Kelaia. Madrid, 1909. (Changed to XP 3964)
Afr 1755.8 Urquijo, F. De. La Campana del rif en 1909. Madrid, n.d.
Afr 1755.9 Noel, E. Notas de un voluntario. Madrid, 1910.
Afr 1755.10 Gallego Ramos, E. La Campana del rif. Madrid, 1909.
Afr 1755.11 Llanos Y Alcaraz, A. Melilla. Madrid, 1894.
Afr 1755.12 Albeniz, R. La Campana del rif, la Verdad de la guerra. n.p., n.d.
Afr 1755.13 Lopez Alarcon, E. Melilla 1909, diario de la guerra. Madrid, 1913.
Afr 1755.14 Spain. Cuerpo de Estado Mayor del Ejercito. Ensenanzas de la Campana del rif en 1909. Madrid, 1911.
Afr 1755.15 Marenco, Servando. Una solucion a los conflictos de Melilla. Madrid, 1894.
Afr 1755.16 Garcialavin, R. La guerra en africa. Madrid, 1911.
Afr 1755.17 Cronica artillera...Campana de Melilla. Text and plates. Madrid, 1911.
Afr 1755.19 Sablotny, R. Legionnaire in Morocco. Los Angeles, 1940.
Afr 1755.45 Ansart, F.B. El desastre de annual. Barcelona, 1921.
Afr 1755.47 Martinez de Campos, Arsenio. Melilla, 1921. Ciudad Real, 1922.
Afr 1755.49 Berenguer, Damaso. Campanas en el rif y Yebala 1921-1922. Madrid, 1923.
Afr 1755.55 Maldonado, E. El rogui. Tetuan, 1952.
Afr 1755.60 Fernández de la Reguera, Ricardo. El desastre de Annual. Barcelona, 1968.

Afr 1757 Morocco - Spanish possessions in Morocco and environs - Peñon de Velez (Gomera, Peñon de la)

Afr 1757.1 Feliu De La Pena, F. Leyenda historica...del penon de velez de la Gomera. Valencia, 1846.

Afr 1769.1 - .26 Morocco - Biographies - Individual (A-Z)

Afr 1769.1 Abd El-Krim. Memoires d'Abd-el-Krim. 5e ed. Paris, 1927.
Afr 1769.1.5 Abd Al-Karim. Memoiren. Dresden, 1927.
Afr 1769.1.80 Ladreit de Lacharriere, Jacques. Le reve d'Aabd el Kerim. Paris, 1925.
Afr 1769.5 Dewazan, Emily. My life story. London, 1911.
Afr 1769.7 Santamaria Quesada, R. Quien es el glani. Tetuan, 1955.
Afr 1769.7.10 Maxwell, Gavin. Lords of the atlas, the rise and fall of the house of Glaoua, 1893-1956. London, 1966.
Afr 1769.18 Forbes, Rosita. El Raisuni, the sultan of the mountains. London, 1924.
Afr 1769.18.5 Lopez Rienda, R. Frente al fracaso, Raisuni. De silvestre a burguete. Madrid, 1923.
Afr 1769.20 Jalade, Max. Mohammed ben Youssef. Paris, 1956.

Afr 1801 - 1824 Algeria - Periodicals (A-Z)

Afr 1801.2F Algeria, revue mensuelle illustrée. Alger. 1,1933+
Afr 1801.3 L'Afrique française. Paris. 1,1837
Afr 1801.5 Almanach de l'Algerie. Alger. 1900+
Afr 1801.8 Algérie dans le monde. Alger.
Afr 1801.10 Algeria. Direction Général de l'Information. Actualité et documents. 45,1964+
Afr 1801.12 Annales algériennes de géographie. Alger. 1,1966+
Afr 1803.1 Congrés National des Sciences Historiques. Proceedings. Alger. 2,1930+
Afr 1803.5 Centre d'Information pour les Problèmes de l'Algérie et du Sahara. Publications. Paris. 1+
Afr 1807.1 Guides Thiolier. Paris. 1+
Afr 1814.5 Nouvelles realités algériennes. Alger. 1,1955+ 3v.
Afr 1814.6 Nouvelles Realites Algériennes. Bulletin d'information NRA. Alger. 1,1958+
Afr 1814.10 Novembre. Alger. 3v.
Afr 1818.2 Réunion d'Etudes Algériennes. Bulletin. Paris.
Afr 1818.5 Revue algérienne des sciences juridiques. Alger. 1964 5v.
Afr 1819.1 Société de Géographie d'Alger et de l'Afrique du Nord. Bulletin. Alger. 1,1896+ 32v.
Afr 1819.3 Algiers. Ecole Supérieure des Lettres d'Alger. Bulletin de correspondance africaine. Alger. 1882+ 4v.
Afr 1819.4 Societe Archéologique de Constantine. Recueil des notices et mémoires. Constantine. 1,1953+ 7v.
Afr 1819.4.6 Société Archéologique, Historique et Géographique du Département de Constantine. Bulletin mensuel. Constantine. 35,1930+
Afr 1822.2PF Vérité, liberté, cahier d'information sur la guerre d'Algérie. Paris. 2+

Afr 1825 Algeria - Folios [Discontinued]

Afr 1825.1F Histoire de l'Algerie. Paris, 1900.
Afr 1825.2 Ludwig, Salvator. Bougie, die perle nord afrikas. Leipzig, 1900.
Afr 1825.3PF Berbrugger. Algerie historique, pittoresque. Paris, 1843. 3v.

Afr 1826 Algeria - Bibliographies

Afr 1826.1 Playfair, R.L. Bibliography of Algeria and supplement. London, 1888.
Afr 1826.5 Taillart, C. L'Algerie dans la litterature française. Thèse. Paris, 1925.
Afr 1826.5.5 Taillart, C. L'Algerie dans la litterature française. Thèse. Paris, 1925.
Afr 1826.5.7 Taillart, C. L'Algerie dans la litterature française. Paris, 1925.

Afr 1826 Algeria - Bibliographies - cont.

Afr 1826.5.9 Taillart, C. L'Algerie dans la litterature française, essai de bibliog. Paris, 1925.
Afr 1826.6 Fiori, H. Bibliographie des ouvrages imprimes à Alger. Alger, 1938.
Afr 1826.25 Franc, Julien. L'histoire de la colonie de l'Algérie, sources d'archives. Thèse. Alger, 1928.
Afr 1826.27 Société Historique Algerienne. Vingt cinq ans d'histoire algerienne. 4 in 1. Alger, 1856.
Afr 1826.30 Constantine, Algeria. Archives Départmentals. Répertoire de documentation nord-africaine. v.1-2. Constantine, 1954.
Afr 1826.33 France. Ministère d'Etat Chargé des Affaires Algériennes. Bulletin de documentation. Paris. 11-44,1961-1965

Afr 1828 Algeria - Pamphlet volumes

Afr 1828.01 Pamphlet box. Algeria.
Afr 1828.1 Pamphlet vol. Algeria. Bibliography. 7 pam.
Afr 1828.2 Pamphlet vol. Coup d'oeil rapide sur bougie. 9 pam.

Afr 1830 Algeria - Collected source materials - General

Afr 1830.10.1 Milliot, Louis. L'oeuvre legislative de la France en Algérie. Paris, 1930.
Afr 1830.10.2 Donec, Martial. Un siècle de finances coloniales. Paris, 1930.
Afr 1830.10.3 Nores, Edmond. L'oeuvre de la france en Algerie, la justice. Paris, 1931.
Afr 1830.20.1 Savornin, J. La géologie algérienne et nord-africaine depuis 1830. Paris, 1931.
Afr 1830.20.2F Pouget. Agrologie du Sahel. Paris, 1930.
Afr 1830.20.5 Maire, Rene. Les progres des connaissances botaniques en Algerie depuis 1830. Paris, 1931.
Afr 1830.20.6 Seurat, L.G. Exploration zoologique de l'Algerie. Paris, 1930.
Afr 1830.20.7 Dalloni, Marius. Geologie appliquee de l'Algerie. Paris, 1939.
Afr 1830.20.8 Petitjean, L. Le temps et la prevision du temps en Algerie et auSahara. Paris, 1930.
Afr 1830.20.40 Fraynaud, Lucien. Hygiène et pathologie nord-africaines. v.1-2. Paris, 1932. 2v.
Afr 1830.20.51 Billiard, Louis. Les ports et la navigation de l'Agérie. Paris, 1930.
Afr 1830.20.52 Poggi, Jacques. Les chemins de fer...de l'Algérie. Paris, 1931.
Afr 1830.20.53 Algeria. Service des Postes, Télégraphes. Exposé du développement des services postaux. Alger, 1930.
Afr 1830.20.56 Demontes, Victor. L'Algérie agricole. Paris, 1930.
Afr 1830.20.57 Demontes, Victor. L'Algerie industrielle et commercante. Paris, 1930.
Afr 1830.20.58 Marc, H. Notes sur les forets de l'Algeria. Paris, 1930.
Afr 1830.20.61 Ernest-Picard, P. La monnaie et le crédit en Algérie depuis 1830. Alger, 1930.
Afr 1830.20.80 Lacoste, Louis. La colonisation maritime en Algerie. Paris, 1931.
Afr 1830.20.85 Dussert, D. Les mines et les carrieres en Algerie. Paris, 1931.
Afr 1830.30.2 Lespes, René. Alger, étude de géographie et d'histoire urbaines. Paris, 1930.
Afr 1830.30.4 Franc, Julien. La colonisation de la Mitidja. Paris, 1928.
Afr 1830.30.5 Lespes, Rene. Oran. Paris, 1938.
Afr 1830.40.5 Schefer, Christian. La politique coloniale de la monarchie de juillet. Paris, 1928.
Afr 1830.40.10F Broussard, M.E.A. Les carreaux de faience peints dans l'Afrique du nord. Paris, 1930.
Afr 1830.40.11 Marcais, Georges. Le costume musulman d'Alger. Paris, 1930.
Afr 1830.40.13 Gautier, E.F. Un siècle de colonisation, études au microscope. Paris, 1930.
Afr 1830.40.15 Alazard, J. Histoire et historiens de l'Algérie. Paris, 1931.
Afr 1830.40.20 Charles-Roux, François. France et Afrique du nord avant 1830, les precurseurs de la conquete. Paris, 1932.
Afr 1830.50.4 Basset, André. La langue berbère. Paris, 1929.
Afr 1830.50.5 Alazard, Jean. L'orient et la peinture française au XIXe siècle. Paris, 1930.
Afr 1830.50.15 Giacobetti, R.P. Les tapis et tissages du Djebel-amour. Paris, 1932.
Afr 1830.105 Algeria. Commissariat General du Centenaire. Le centenaire de l'Algerie. Alger, 1931. 2v.
Afr 1830.110 Algeria. Commissariat General du Centenaire. Les parcs nationaux en Algérie. Alger, 1930.

Afr 1835 Algeria - Collected source materials - Others

Afr 1835.1 Carette, E. Etudes des routes suivies par les Arabes. Paris, 1844.
Afr 1835.1.2 Carette, E. Recherches sur la géographie de l'Algérie. Paris, 1844.
Afr 1835.1.3 Carette, E. Recherches sur l'origine et les migrations. Paris, 1853.
Afr 1835.1.4 Carette, E. Etudes sur la kabilie proprement dite. Paris, 1849.
Afr 1835.1.5 Carette, E. Etudes sur la kabilie. v.2. Paris, 1848.
Afr 1835.1.6 Pellissier, E. Memoires...sur l'Algerie. Paris, 1844.
Afr 1835.1.7A Kairuani, Al. Histoire de l'Afrique. Paris, 1845.
Afr 1835.1.7B Kairuani, Al. Histoire de l'Afrique. Paris, 1845.
Afr 1835.1.8 Renou, E. Description...de l'empire de Maroc. Paris, 1846.
Afr 1835.1.9 Abu Salem, Called Al-Aiasi. Voyages dans le sud de l'Algérie. Paris, 1846.
Afr 1835.1.10 Hatil Ibn-Ishah. Précis de jurisprudence musulmane. Paris, 1848. 6v.
Afr 1835.1.11 Hatil Ibn-Ishah. Table analytique de juridisprudence musulmane. Paris, 1854.
Afr 1835.1.12 Pellissier de Reynaud, E. Description de la régence de Tunis. Paris, 1853.
Afr 1835.2 Perier, J.A.N. De l'hygiene en Algerie. v.1-2. Paris, 1847. 2v.
Afr 1835.4 Collection de documents inédits sur l'histoire de l'Algérie après 1830. 1. Serie. Paris. 1-6,1914-1954 7v.
Afr 1835.4.2 Collection de documents inédits...après 1830. Sér.2. Paris. 1,1912+ 5v.
Afr 1835.4.3 Collection de documents inédits sur l'histoire de l'Algérie. Sér.3. Paris.

Afr 1838 Algeria - Government and administration - General works
Afr 1838.1   Bugeaud. L'Algérie, des moyens de conserver cette conquête. Paris, 1842.
Afr 1838.2   Bavoux, E. Alger, voyage politique. v.1-2. Paris, 1841.
Afr 1838.3   Leroy, L. Etat...du royaume et de la ville d'Alger. La Haye, 1750.
Afr 1838.4   Gmelin, H. Die verfassungsentwicklung von Algerien. Hamburg, 1911.
Afr 1838.5   Cambon, Jules. Le gouvernement general de l'Algerie. Paris, 1918.
Afr 1838.7   Ferry, J. Le gouvernement de l'Algérie. Paris, 1892.
Afr 1838.8   Paillard, Jean. Faut-il faire de l'Algérie un dominion. Paris, 1938.
Afr 1838.9   Algeria. Constitution. La constitution. Alger, 1963.

Afr 1840 Algeria - Government and administration - Special topics
Afr 1840.1   Algeria. Gouvernement General. Exposé de l'état...du gouvernement. Algiers, 1844.
Afr 1840.2   Rouard de Card, E. La réprésentation des indigènes musulmans dans les conseils de l'Algérie. Paris, 1909.
Afr 1840.3   Hugues, A. La nationalite française. Paris, 1899.
Afr 1840.3.15   Lazard, Claude. L'accession des indigènes algériens à la citoyenneté française. Thèse. Paris, 1938.
Afr 1840.5   Mary, P. Influence de la conversion...sur la condition...en Algérie. Thèse. Paris, 1910.
Afr 1840.6   Bounichon, A. La conversion au christianisme de l'indigène musulman algérien. Thèse. Paris, 1931.
Afr 1840.7   Marneur, F. L'indigenat en Algerie. Thèse. Paris, 1914.
Afr 1840.9   Gentil, M. Administration de la justice musulmane en Algerie. Thèse. Paris, 1895.
Afr 1840.12   Piquet, Victor. Les reformes en Algerie et le statut des indigenes. Paris, 1919.
Afr 1840.15   Elie-Edmond, A. De la condition politique des indigenes musulmans d'Algerie. Thèse. Alger, 1921.
Afr 1840.17   Duclos, Marcel. Contribution a l'étude de la réforme administrative de l'Algérie. Thèse. Alger, 1921.
Afr 1840.19   Riols De Fonclare, F. de. Les diverses politiques coloniales. Thèse. Toulouse, 1919.
Afr 1840.22   Maunier, R. Loi française et coutume indigene en Algerie. Paris, 1932.
Afr 1840.23   Algeria. Service de l'Information. Elections cantonales en Algérie. Alger, 1960.
Afr 1840.24   Purtschet, Christian. Sociologie électorale en Afrique du Nord. Paris, 1966.
Afr 1840.26   Lapassat, Etienne Jean. La justice en Algérie, 1962-1968. Paris, 1968.

Afr 1844 Algeria - Collected political biographies
Afr 1844.5   Azan, Paul. Les grands soldats de l'Algerie. Paris, 1931.

Afr 1846 Algeria - Military history
Afr 1846.6F   Duruy, V. Le 1er regiment de tirailleurs algeriens. Paris, 1899.
Afr 1846.7   Sibe, A. La conscription des indigenes d'Algérie. Paris, 1912.
Afr 1846.8   Ferand, L.C. Les interprètes de l'armée d'Afrique. Alger, 1876.
Afr 1846.9   Wolf, Christian. Der fremdenlegionaer in Krieg und Frieden. Berlin, 1913.
Afr 1846.11   Arnaud, Ed. Nos confins sahariens, étude d'organisation militaire. Paris, 1908.
Afr 1846.13   Azan, Paul. L'armee d'Afrique de 1830 à 1852. Paris, 1936.

Afr 1848 Algeria - Naval history
Afr 1848.5   Lacoste, L. La marine algerienne sous les Turcs. Paris, 1931.
Afr 1848.7   Braibant, Chas. Inventaire des archives de l'amiraute d'Alger. Alger, 1922.

Afr 1865 - 1870 Algeria - General history (By date)
Afr 1867.28   Morgan, John. Complete history of Algiers. London, 1728. 2v.
Afr 1867.97.2   Stevens, J.W. Historical and geographical account of Algiers. Brooklyn, 1800.
Afr 1868.05   Short history of Algiers. 3rd ed. N.Y., 1805.
Afr 1868.43   Clausolles, M.P. Algerie pittoresque. Toulouse, 1845.
Afr 1868.43.5   Estry, Stephen D'. Histoire d'Alger. Tours, 1843.
Afr 1868.44   Galibert, L. L'Algérie ancienne et moderne. Paris, 1844.
Afr 1868.47   Brunet, Jean B. La question algerienne. Paris, 1847.
Afr 1868.53   Ximenez de Sandoval, C. Memorias sobre la Argelia. Madrid, 1853.
Afr 1868.59   Roy, J.J.E. Histoire de l'Algerie. Tours, 1859.
Afr 1868.59.5   Galibert, L. La Argelia, antigua y moderna. v.1-2,3. Madrid, 1859-60. 2v.
Afr 1868.60   Fillias, A. L'Algerie ancienne et moderne. 2e ed. Alger, 1875.
Afr 1868.60.3   Lefloch, L. Mahomet, al Koran, Algerie. Paris, 1860.
Afr 1868.85   Mohammed Abou Ras. Voyages extraordinaires. Alger, 1885.
Afr 1868.86   Bardon, Xavier. Histoire nationale de l'Algérie. Paris, 1886.
Afr 1868.88   Cat, Edouard. Petite histoire de l'Algérie, Tunisie, Maroc. v.1-2. Alger, 1888-91. 2v.
Afr 1869.10   Garrot, Henri. Histoire generale de l'Algerie. Alger, 1910.
Afr 1869.27   Gsell, S. Histoire d'Algerie. Paris, 1927.
Afr 1869.29   Bernard, Augustin. L'Algerie. Paris, 1929.
Afr 1869.29.5   Paris. Ecole Libre des Sciences Politiques. Société des Anciens Elèves. Une oeuvre française d'Algérie. Paris, 1929.
Afr 1869.30   France. Comite National. Cahiers du centenaire de l'Algerie. Alger, 1930. 2v.
Afr 1869.51   Berthier, A. L'Algérie et son passé. Paris, 1951.
Afr 1869.57   Egretaud, Marcel. Réalité de la nation algérienne. Paris, 1957.
Afr 1869.57.2   Egretaud, Marcel. Réalité de la nation algérienne. Paris, 1961.
Afr 1869.57.7   Esquer, Gabriel. Histoire de l'Algerie. 2. ed. Paris, 1957.
Afr 1869.57.10   Amrouche, Marcel. Terres et hommes d'Algérie. v.1. Alger, 1957.
Afr 1869.58   Question algerienne. Paris, 1958.
Afr 1869.59   Rainero, Romain. Storia dell Algeria. Firenze, 1959.
Afr 1869.60   Lacoste, Yves. L'Algérie. Paris, 1960.
Afr 1869.62   Mouilleseaux, L. Histoire de l'Algerie. Paris, 1962.
Afr 1869.63   Juin, A.P. Histoire parallele. Paris, 1963.
Afr 1869.64   Moncade, Noel. Les français d'Algerie. Paris, 1964.

Afr 1865 - 1870 Algeria - General history (By date) - cont.
Afr 1869.65   American University, Washington, D.C. Foreign Area Studies Division. Area handbook for Algeria. Washington, 1965.
Afr 1869.67   Pečar, Zdravko. Alžir do nezavisnosti. Beograd, 1967.

Afr 1878 Algeria - General special
Afr 1878.1   Laprimaudie, F.E. de. Le commerce...de l'Algerie. Paris, 1861.
Afr 1878.5   Gallico, Augusto. Tunisi i berberi e l'Italia nei secoli. Ancona, 1928.
Afr 1878.8   Lespes, Rene. Alger, étude de geographie et d'histoire urbaines. Paris, 1930.
Afr 1878.10   Marchika, Jean. La peste en Afrique septentrionale. Alger, 1927.
Afr 1878.15   Cornaton, Michel. Les regroupements de la décolonisation en Algérie. Thèse. Paris, 1967.

Afr 1880 Algeria - History by periods - 7th to 16th centuries - General works
Afr 1880.5   Esterhazy, W. De la domination turque. Paris, 1840.
Afr 1880.10   Lewicki, J. Etudes ibadites nord-africaines. v.1. Warszawa, 1955.

Afr 1885 Algeria - History by periods - 7th to 16th centuries - Zeianide dynasty (1239-1554)
Afr 1885.1   Muhammed Al-Tunisi. Histoire des Beni Zeiyan. Paris, 1852.
Afr 1885.2   Barges, J.J.L. Complement de l'histoire des Beni-Zeiyan. Paris, 1887.
Afr 1885.3   Blum, N. La croisade de XImenes en Afrique. Oran, 1898.

Afr 1900 Algeria - History by periods - 16th century to 1830 - General works
Afr 1900.1   Grammont, H.D. Histoire d'Alger. Paris, 1887.
Afr 1900.2   Grammont, H.D. Histoire des rois d'Alger. Alger, 1881.
Afr 1900.3   Plantet, E. Correspondance des deys d'Alger, 1579-1833. Paris, 1889.
Htn   Afr 1900.4*   Carey, M. Short account of Algiers...wars. Philadelphia, 1794.

Afr 1903 Algeria - History by periods - 16th century to 1830 - Relations and wars with Spain (1515-1830) - General works
Afr 1903.1   Cat, E. Mission bibliog. En Espagne. Paris, 1891.
Afr 1903.5   Froelicher, E. La domination espagnôle en Algeria. Paris, 1904.
Afr 1903.6   Lettere istoriche...d'Africa, e d'America. Venezia, 1775.
Afr 1903.7   Guerras de los españoles en Africa 1542, 43 y 1632. Madrid, 1881.

Afr 1905 Algeria - History by periods - 16th century to 1830 - Relations and wars with Spain (1515-1830) - Special topics
Afr 1905.1   Ruff, Paul. La domination espagnôle a Oran. Paris, 1900.
Afr 1905.2   Fey, H.L. Histoire d'Oran, avant, pendant et après la domination espagnole. Oran, 1858.
Afr 1905.3   Continorazione del diario e relazione. Firenze, 1733.
Htn   Afr 1905.4F*   Nuevo blason de los cardenas y elogios del Duque de Maqueda en Oran. Madrid, 1624.

Afr 1910 Algeria - History by periods - 16th century to 1830 - Foreign relations and Piracy (1515-1830) - General works
Afr 1910.10   Schwarzenberg, F. Rueckblicke auf Algier. Wien, 1837.

Afr 1915 Algeria - History by periods - 16th century to 1830 - Foreign relations and Piracy (1515-1830) - France - General works
Afr 1915.1   Grammont, H.D. Relation entre la France et la regime d'Alger au XVIIe siècle. 4 in 1. Algier, 1879.
Afr 1915.2   Devoulx, A. Les archives du consulat général de France. Alger, 1865.
Afr 1915.3   Frousseaux. Aventures de dona ines de la Cisternas. Utrecht, 1737.
Afr 1915.4   Stein, H. Un dessein français sur Alger et Tunis. n.p., 1883.
Afr 1915.5   Heinrich, P. L'alliance franco-algérienne. Lyon, 1898.
Afr 1915.6   Wahl, Maurice. L'Algérie et alliance française. Bordeaux, 1887.
Afr 1915.8   Lavigerie, C.M. L'armée et la mission de la France en Afrique. Alger, 1875.
Afr 1915.9   Plantet, Eugène. Les consuls de France à Alger avant la conquête, 1579-1830. Paris, 1930.
Afr 1915.11   Hutin, Paul. La doctrine de l'Association des indigènes et des Français en Algérie. Thèse. Paris, 1933.
Afr 1915.13   Orient, N. La question algérienne. Paris, 1936.
Afr 1915.14   Meningaud, Jean. La France à l'heure algérienne. Paris, 1956.

Afr 1920 Algeria - History by periods - 16th century to 1830 - Foreign relations and Piracy (1515-1830) - France - Duquesne
Afr 1920.25   Mismont, L. Le double bombardement d'Alger par Duquesne. Paris, 1905.

Afr 1922 Algeria - History by periods - 16th century to 1830 - Foreign relations and Piracy (1515-1830) - France - Others
Afr 1922.5   Pièces curieuses, ou Alger en 1802. Paris, 1830.
Afr 1922.10   Celarie, H. La prise d'Alger. Paris, 1929.
Afr 1922.15   Julien, A. La question d'Alger devant les Chambres sous la Restauration. Paris, 1922.

Afr 1925 Algeria - History by periods - 16th century to 1830 - Foreign relations and Piracy (1515-1830) - England - General works
Htn   Afr 1925.1*   Robinson, H. Libertas or reliefe to English captives in Algeria. London, 1642.
Afr 1925.5   Playfair, R.L. The scourge of Christendom. London, 1884.
Afr 1925.5.5   Playfair, R.L. Episodes de l'histoire des relations de Grande Bretagne. Alger, 1879.

Afr 1930 Algeria - History by periods - 16th century to 1830 - Foreign relations and Piracy (1515-1830) - England - Exmouth
Afr 1930.1   Salame, A. Narrative of the expedition to Algiers in 1816. London, 1819.
Afr 1930.2   Private journal...from Portsmouth. Exeter, 1817.

Afr 1935 Algeria - History by periods - 16th century to 1830 - Foreign relations and Piracy (1515-1830) - Holland
Htn   Afr 1935.1*   Algiers. Dey. Letter written by the governour...law-counteys. London, 1679.

Afr 1940 Algeria - History by periods - 16th century to 1830 - Foreign relations and Piracy (1515-1830) - Portugal

Afr 1940.5	Ferreira Lobo, R.J. Deducção das votas no Supremo Conselho provizorio. Londres, 1817.
Afr 1940.10	American University, Wahington D.C. Foreign Area Studies. Area handbook for Burundi. Washington, 1969.

Afr 1942 Algeria - History by periods - 16th century to 1830 - Foreign relations and Piracy (1515-1830) - United States

Afr 1942.5	Ross, F.E. The mission of Joseph Donaldson, Jr. to Algiers, 1795-97. n.p., 1935.
Afr 1942.6	Barnly, Henry George. The prisoners of Algiers. London, 1966.

Afr 1947 Algeria - History by periods - 16th century to 1830 - Foreign relations and Piracy (1515-1830) - Stories of piracy and captivity

	Afr 1947.1	Cathcart, J.L. The captives. La Porte, 1902.
	Afr 1947.2	Aranda, E.D. Relation de la captivité...esclave à Alger. Bruxelles, 1662.
	Afr 1947.2.3	Aranda, E.D. Relation de la captivité...esclave à Alger. Paris, 1657.
Htn	Afr 1947.3*	Comelin, F. Voyage pour la rédemption des captives...1720. Paris, 1721.
	Afr 1947.4	Lomon, A. Captivité de l'Amiral Bonard. Paris, n.d.
	Afr 1947.5	Laranda, V. Neapolitan captive, interesting narrative of the captivity and sufferings of V. Laranda. N.Y., 1830.
	Afr 1947.6	Victoires de la charité. Paris, 1846.
	Afr 1947.7	Pfeiffer, G.S.F. Voyages and five years captivity in Algiers. Harrisburg, 1836.
Htn	Afr 1947.8*	Martin, M. History of the captivity and sufferings in Algiers. Boston, 1807.
	Afr 1947.9	Amiet, J.J. Lorenz Arregger, Sklave in Algier. Bern, 1874.
	Afr 1947.9.5	Amiet, J.J. Geschichte des Lorenz Arregger von Solothurn. Bern, 1920.
	Afr 1947.10	Dumont, P.J. Histoire de l'esclavage de Dumont. Paris, 1819.
	Afr 1947.11	Bologna. Arciconfraternità di Santa Maria. Ragguaglio della schiavitù in Algeri di Giuseppe Giovanni Nicola Albertazzi. Bologna, 1772.
	Afr 1947.13	Registre des prises maritimes. Alger, 1872.
	Afr 1947.14	Cruelties of the Algerine pirates shewing the present dreadful state of the English slaves. 4th ed. London, 1816.
	Afr 1947.15	Contremoulins, C. Souvenirs d'un officier français. Paris, 1830.

Afr 1955 Algeria - History by periods - French conquest (1830-1860) - General works

Afr 1955.1	Fillias, Achille. Histoire de la congrès de l'Algérie (1830-60). Paris, 1860.
Afr 1955.2	Roches, Léon. Trente-deux ans à travers l'islam (1832-64). Paris, 1884.
Afr 1955.3	Cooke, G.W. Conquest and colonization in North Africa. Edinburgh, 1860.
Afr 1955.4	Gerard, J. L'Afrique du nord. Paris, 1861.
Afr 1955.4.5	Gerard, J. L'Afrique du nord. Paris, 1860.
Afr 1955.5	Christian, P. L'Afrique française. Paris, 1845.
Afr 1955.5.5	Christian, P. L'Affrica francese. Firenze, 1849. 2v.
Afr 1955.6	Rousset, C. La conquête d'Alger. Paris, 1880.
Afr 1955.6.2	Rousset, C. Les commencements d'une conquête. Paris, 1900. 2v.
Afr 1955.6.3	Rousset, C. La conquête de l'Algérie. v.1,2 and atlas. Paris, 1904. 3v.
Afr 1955.6.4	Rousset, C. La conquête d'Alger. Paris, 1899.
Afr 1955.6.5	Rousset, C. Les commencements d'une conquête. Paris, 1887. 2v.
Afr 1955.7	Trumelet, C. Le général Yusuf. Paris, 1890. 2v.
Afr 1955.7.5	Constantin-Weyer, M. La vie du général Yusuf. 10e éd. Paris, 1930.
Afr 1955.8	Dieuzaide, V.A. Histoire de l'Algérie, 1830-1878. v.1-2. Oran, 1880-83.
Afr 1955.9	Perret, E. Récits algériens. Paris, n.d. 2v.
Afr 1955.10	Hennequin, A. La conquête de l'Algérie. Paris, 1857.
Afr 1955.11	Bonnafont, Jean Pierre. Douze ans en Algérie, 1830-1842. Paris, 1880.
Afr 1955.12	Berteuil, A. L'Algérie française, histoire. Paris, 1856. 2v.
Afr 1955.13	Leynadier. Histoire de l'Algérie française. Paris, 1846. 2 pam.
Afr 1955.14	Grieu, R. de. Le duc d'Aumale et l'Algérie. Paris, 1884.
Afr 1955.15	Esterhazy, W. Notice historique sur le Maghzen d'Oran. Oran, 1849.
Afr 1955.16	Baudicour, L. de. La guerre et le gouvernement de l'Algérie. Paris, 1853.
Afr 1955.17	Castellane, P. de. Military life in Algeria. London, 1853. 2v.
Afr 1955.17.5	Castellane, P. de. Souvenirs de la vie militaire en Afrique. Paris, 1852.
Afr 1955.18	Hugonnet, F. Français et Arabes en Algérie. Paris, 1860.
Afr 1955.19	Cornulier-Lucinière, Comte de. La prise de Bône et Bougie...1832-33. Paris, 1895.
Afr 1955.20	Hatin, Eugene. Malerische Beschreibung der Regenschaft Algier. Karlsruhe, 1841.
Afr 1955.21	Laurie, G.B. The French conquest of Algeria. London, 1909.
Afr 1955.22	Pélissier, A.J.J. Mémoire sur les opérations de l'armée française. Alger, 1863.
Afr 1955.22.5	Maréchal Pélissier. Tours, 1892.
Afr 1955.23	Denniée. Précis historique et administrative de la campagne d'Afrique. Paris, 1830.
Afr 1955.24	Général Lapasset. Algérie 1817-1864. Paris, 1897. 2v.
Afr 1955.25	Journal d'un officier de l'armée d'Afrique. Paris, 1831.
Afr 1955.26	Barehou-Penhoen. Souvenirs de l'expédition d'Afrique. Paris, 1832.
Afr 1955.27	Randon, J.L.C.A. Mémoires du maréchal Randon. Paris, 1875. 2v.
Afr 1955.27.5	Randon, J.L.C.A. Mémoires du maréchal Randon. 2e éd. Paris, 1875-77. 2v.
Afr 1955.28	Clauzel, M. Explications. Paris, 1837.
Afr 1955.30	Piquet, V. Campagnes d'Afrique, 1830-1910. Paris, 1912.
Afr 1955.31	Marchaud, E.C. L'Europe et la conquête d'Alger. Paris, 1913.
Afr 1955.32	Aus Africa und Spanien. Jena, 1870.
Afr 1955.34	Ferrand, G. La colonisation militaire du maréchal Bugeaud, 1841-47. Thèse. Paris, 1909.
Afr 1955.35	Mont-Rond, P. Histoire de la conquête de l'Algérie de 1830 à 1847. Paris, 1847. 2v.

Afr 1955 Algeria - History by periods - French conquest (1830-1860) - General works - cont.

	Afr 1955.36	Pellissier de Reynaud, E. Annales algériennes. Paris, 1854. 3v.
	Afr 1955.40	Esquer, G. La prise d'Alger, 1830. Alger, 1923.
	Afr 1955.40.2	Esquer, G. La prise d'Alger, 1830. Paris, 1929.
X Cg	Afr 1955.42	Valet, René. L'Afrique du nord devant le Parlement au XIXme siècle. Alger, 1924.
	Afr 1955.46	Gautherat, Gustave. La conquête de l'Alger. Paris, 1929.
	Afr 1955.47	Esquer, G. Les commencements d'un empire. Paris, 1929.
	Afr 1955.48	Esquer, G. Histoire de l'Algérie. 1. ed. Paris, 1950.
	Afr 1955.49	Maze, Jules. La conquête de l'Algérie. Tours, 1930.
	Afr 1955.51	Changarnier, N.A.T. Campagnes d'Afrique, 1830-1848. Paris, 1930.
	Afr 1955.57	Rasteil, M. Le calvaire des colons de 48. Paris, 1930.
	Afr 1955.61	Algiers. Université. Faculté de Droit. Recherches sur la colonisation de l'Algérie au XIXe siècle. Alger, 1960.
	Afr 1955.62	Lamurière, Marc. Histoire de l'Algérie illustrée de 1830 à nos jours. Paris, 1962.
	Afr 1955.63	Bloch, P. Algérie, terre des occasions perdues. Paris, 1961.

Afr 1957 Algeria - History by periods - French conquest (1830-1860) - Expedition against Algiers (1830)

Afr 1957.1	Nettement, A. Histoire de la conquête d'Alger. Paris, 1867.
Afr 1957.2	Ault-Dumesnil, E.D. De l'expédition d'Afrique en 1830. Paris, 1832.
Afr 1957.3	Perrot, A.M. La conquête d'Alger. Paris, 1830.
Afr 1957.4	Dopigez. Souvenirs de l'Algérie. Douai, 1840.
Afr 1957.5	Berthezene. Dix-huit mois à Alger. Montpellier, 1834.
Afr 1957.6	Juchereau de St. Denis, A. Considerations sur la régence d'Alger. Paris, 1831.
Afr 1957.6.10	Loverdo, N. Extrait du journal d'un officier supérieur attaché à la deuxième division de l'armée d'Afrique. Paris, 1831.
Afr 1957.7	Sixte, Prince of Bourbon-Parma. La dernière conquête du roi, Alger, 1830. V.1-2. Paris, 1930. 2v.
Afr 1957.8	Azan, Paul. L'expédition d'Alger. Paris, 1929.
Afr 1957.9	Chaudau de Raynal, P. L'expédition d'Alger, 1830. Paris, 1930.
Afr 1957.11	Douin, Georges. Mohamed Aly et l'expédition d'Alger (1829-1830). Aire, 1930.
Afr 1957.15	Debu-Bridel, J. La guerre qui paye, Alger, 1830. Paris, 1930.
Afr 1957.20.5	Merle, J.T. La prise d'Alger. Paris, 1930.
Afr 1957.25	Dufestre, Henri. Les conquérants de l'Algérie (1830-1857). Paris, 1930.
Afr 1957.27	Bianchi, Thomas. Relation de l'arrivée dans la rade d'Alger du vaisseau. Paris, 1830.
Afr 1957.28	Lauvergne, Hubert. Histoire de l'expédition d'Afrique en 1830. Paris, 1831.
Afr 1957.29	Noguères, H. L'expédition d'Alger, 1830. Paris, 1962.
Afr 1957.30	Matterer, Amable. Journal de la prise d'Alger. Paris, 1960.
Afr 1957.31	Serval, Pierre. Alger fut à lui. Paris, 1965.
Afr 1957.32	Barchou de Penhoen, Auguste Theodore Hitaire, Baron. Mémoires d'un officier d'état-major. Paris, 1835.

Afr 1960 Algeria - History by periods - French conquest (1830-1860) - Earlier military operations in the interior

Afr 1960.1	Blondel, L. Nouvel aperçu sur l'Algérie. Paris, 1838.
Afr 1960.2	Grand, E. Défence et occupation de la colonie d'Alger. Toulon, 1837.
Afr 1960.5	Gaffarel, Paul. La conquête de l'Algérie jusqu'à la prise de Constantine. Paris, 1887.

Afr 1965 Algeria - History by periods - French conquest (1830-1860) - Abd-el-Kadar (1847)

	Afr 1965.1	Dupuch, A.A. Abd-el-Kader. Bordeaux, 1860.
	Afr 1965.2	Orleans, F.P.L.C.H., Duc. Récits de campagne 1833-41. Paris, 1890.
	Afr 1965.2.10	Orleans, F.P.L.C.H., Duc. Campagnes de l'armée d'Afrique, 1835-1839. 2e éd. Paris, 1870.
	Afr 1965.2.25	Claye, A. Essai bibliographique sur le "Journal de l'expédition au portes de fer" (Paris, 1844). Paris, 1902.
	Afr 1965.3	Raasloeff, W. Rückblick auf Algerie (1840-41). Altona, 1845.
	Afr 1965.4	Christian, P. Souvenirs du maréchal Bugeaud. Bruxelles, 1845.
	Afr 1965.4.5	Demontes, Victor. La colonisation militaire sous Bugeaud. Thèse. Paris, 1916.
	Afr 1965.4.10	Azan, Paul. Bugeaud et l'Algérie. Paris, 1930.
	Afr 1965.5	Scott. Journal of a residence in the Esmailla of Abd-el-Kader. London, 1842.
	Afr 1965.5.15F	Batsalle. Album militaire d'Afrique. Paris, 1846.
	Afr 1965.6	Richard, C. Etude sur l'insurrection du Dhara. Alger, 1846.
	Afr 1965.7	Pichon, J. Abd el-Kader. Tlemcen, n.d.
	Afr 1965.7.5	Legras, J. Abd el-Kader. Paris, 1929.
	Afr 1965.8	Gheel Gildemeester. Reis naar Algiers en verblyf by het fransche leger in 1845. Gouda, 1847.
	Afr 1965.9	Notice sur...la prise de la lmahia d'Abd el-Kader. n.p., n.d.
	Afr 1965.10	Derrecagaix, V.B. Yusuf. Paris, 1907.
	Afr 1965.10.5	Yusuf. De la guerra en Africa...en 1851. Madrid, 1859.
	Afr 1965.12	Azan, Paul. Récits d'Afrique Sidi-Brahim. Paris, 1905.
	Afr 1965.12.5	Azan, Paul. Sidi-Brahim. Paris, 1930.
	Afr 1965.12.10	Azan, Paul. L'émir Abd el-Kader, 1808-1883. Paris, 1925.
	Afr 1965.13	Lamping, Clemens. The French in Algiers. N.Y., 1845.
	Afr 1965.20	Cockenpot, C. Le traité Desmichels. Paris, 1924.
	Afr 1965.22	Montagnac, L.F. Lettres d'un soldat. Paris, 1885.
	Afr 1965.23	Bellemare, Alex. Abd-el-Kader. Paris, 1863.
	Afr 1965.25	Estailleur-Chanteraine, Phillippe d'. Abd-el-Kader. Paris, 1947.
	Afr 1965.25.5	Estailleur-Chanteraine, Phillippe d'. L'émir magnanime. Paris, 1959.
	Afr 1965.27	Berbrugger, L.A. Négociation entre monseigneur l'évêque d'Alger et Abd el-qader. Paris, 1844.
	Afr 1965.30	Churchill, Charles Henry. The life of Abdel Kader. London, 1867.

Afr 1973 Algeria - History by periods - French conquest (1830-1860) - Two sieges of Constantine (1836, 1837)

Afr 1973.1 Devoisins, V. Expéditions de Constantine. Paris, 1840.
Afr 1973.1.5 Devoisins, V. Recueil de documents sur l'expédition et la prise de Constantine. Text and atlas. Paris, 1838. 2v.
Afr 1973.2 Sur l'expédition et le siège de Constantine. Paris, 1838.
Afr 1973.3 Watbled, E. Souvenirs de l'armée d'Afrique. Paris, 1877.
Afr 1973.4 Wagner, M. Lettres sur l'expédition de Constantine. n.p., 1838.
Afr 1973.5 Caraman, V.L.C. de R. Relation...de la part que le Feu duc de Caraman a prise à la première expédition de Constantine en 1836. Toulouse, 1843.

Afr 1975 Algeria - History by periods - French conquest (1830-1860) - Conquest of Khabyla

Afr 1975.1 Carrey, E. Récits de Kabylie, campagne de 1857. Paris, 1858.
Afr 1975.2 Daumas. La grande Kabylie, études historiques. Paris, 1847.
Afr 1975.3 Delorme, A. Sous la chéchia. Paris, 1901.
Afr 1975.4 Booms, P.G. Veldtogt van het fransch-afrikaansche leger tegen Klein-Kabylie in 1851. Hertogenbosch, 1852.
Afr 1975.5 Walmsley, H.M. Sketches of Algeria during Kabyle war. London, 1858.
Afr 1975.6 Borrer, D. Narrative of a campaign against Kabailes of Algeria. London, 1848.

Afr 1990 Algeria - History by periods - French conquest (1830-1860) - Other special topics

Afr 1990.1 Lamping, C. The French in Algiers. N.Y., 1845.
Afr 1990.2 De la domination française en Afrique. Paris, 1832.
Afr 1990.3 Rozey, A.G. Cris de conscience de l'Algérie. Paris, 1840.
Afr 1990.4 Ribourt, F. Le gouvernement de l'Algérie, 1852-1858. Paris, 1859.
Afr 1990.4.10 Moulis, R.F. Le ministère de l'Algérie (24 juin 1858-24 nov. 1860). Thèse. Alger, 1926.
Afr 1990.5 Feullide, C. de. L'Algérie française. Paris, 1856.
Afr 1990.6 Desjobert, A. La question d'Alger. Paris, 1837.
Afr 1990.7 Letang, B. Des moyens d'assurer la domination française en Algérie. Paris, 1840-46. 4 pam.
Afr 1990.8 Genty de Bussy, P. De l'établissement des Français. 2e éd. Paris, 1839. 2v.
Afr 1990.9 Lingau. La France et Afrique. Paris, 1846.
Afr 1990.10 Buret, Eugène. Question d'Afrique. Paris, 1842.
Afr 1990.11 Baillet, Noël Bernard. Nécessité de la colonisation de l'Algerie. Paris, 1857.
Afr 1990.11.5 Baillet, Noël Bernard. Rapport...sur son voyage de 1852 en Algérie. Rouen, 1852.
Afr 1990.12 Duvivier. Solution de la question de l'Algérie. Paris, 1841.
Afr 1990.13 Broglie, A. de. Une réforme administrative en Afrique. Paris, 1860.
Afr 1990.14 Pamphlet vol. Algeria. History, 1830-1860. 9 pam.
Afr 1990.15 Fabar, Paul. L'Algérie et l'opinion. Paris, 1847.
Afr 1990.16 Javary, A. Etudes sur le gouvernement. Paris, 1855.
Afr 1990.17 Pamphlet vol. Algeria. History, 1830-1860. 11 pam.
Afr 1990.18 Pamphlet vol. Algeria. History, 1830-1860. 10 pam.
Afr 1990.19 Pamphlet vol. Algeria. History, 1830-1860. 10 pam.
Afr 1990.20 Pamphlet vol. Algeria. History, 1830-1860. 11 pam.
Afr 1990.21 Alby, E. Histoire des prisonniers français en Afrique. Paris, 1849.
Afr 1990.21.5 Alby, E. Les vêpres marocaines. v.1-2. Paris, 1853.
Afr 1990.22 Boulle, L. La France et les Beni-Snassen. Paris, n.d.
Afr 1990.24 Mordacq, J.J.H. La guerre en Afrique. Paris, 1908.
Afr 1990.25 Demontes, Victor. Les préventions du général Berthezène. Paris, 1918.
Afr 1990.25.5 Demontes, Victor. Papiers du général Berthezène...colonisation de l'Algérie. Paris, n.d.
Afr 1990.26 Annales de la colonisation algérienne. Paris. 1-14,1852-1858 14v.
Afr 1990.27 Touchard-Lafosse, T. Histoire de la gendarmerie d'Afrique. Alger, 1860.
Afr 1990.30 Bugeaud de la Piconnerie, T.R. Le peuplement français de l'Algérie. Tunis, 1934.
Afr 1990.32 Emerit, Marcel. La révolution de 1848 en Algérie. Paris, 1949.

Afr 2000 Algeria - History by periods - History from the Conquest to independence - General works

Afr 2000.01 Pamphlet box. Tunis and Algiers.
Afr 2000.3 Ajam, Maurice. Problèmes algériens. Paris, 1913.
Afr 2000.5 Benhabiles, Cherif. L''Algérie française vue par un indigène. Alger, 1914.
Afr 2000.6 Camus, Albert. Actuelles, III. Paris, 1958.
Afr 2000.7 Martin, C. Histoire de l'Algérie française, 1830-1962. Paris, 1963.
Afr 2000.8 Uzighan, 'Ammar. Le meilleur combat. Paris, 1958.
Afr 2000.10 Piquet, V. L'Algérie française. Paris, 1930.
Afr 2000.11 Boyer, Pierre. L'évolution de l'Algérie mediane. Paris, 1960.
Afr 2000.12 Margueritte, V. Un grand Français, le général Margueritte. Paris, 1930.
Afr 2000.13 Wisner, S. L'Algérie dans l'impasse. Paris, 1949.
Afr 2000.14 Viollette, M. L'Algérie vivra-t-elle? Paris, 1931.
Afr 2000.15 Abbas, Ferhat. Guerre et révolution d'Algérie. Paris, 1962.
Afr 2000.16 Nouschi, André. La naissance du nationalisme algérien. Paris, 1962.
Afr 2000.17 Julien, Charles A. Histoire de l'Algérie contemporaine. v.1- Paris, 1964-
Afr 2000.18 Ageron, Charles R. Histoire de l'Algérie contemporaine, 1830-1964. Paris, 1964.
Afr 2000.19 Lacheraf, Mostafa. L'Algérie, nation et société. Paris, 1965.
Afr 2000.20 Khaldi, Abd al-Aziz. Le problème algérien devant la conscience démocratique. Alger, 1946.

Afr 2005 Algeria - History by periods - History from the Conquest to independence - Wars with Arabs in the south

Afr 2005.1 Oget, Jules. Une expédition algérienne; épisode de l'insurrection de 1864. Bastia, 1872.
Afr 2005.3 Trumelet, C. Histoire de l'insurrection dans le sud de la province d'Alger, 1864-69. Alger, 1879-84.

Afr 2010 Algeria - History by periods - History from the Conquest to independence - Rising of 1871

Afr 2010.1 Beauvois, E. En colonne dans la Grande Kabylie...1871. Paris, 1872.
Afr 2010.3 Rinn, L. Histoire de l'insurrection de 1871. Alger, 1891.
Afr 2010.4 Robin. L'insurrection de la Grande Kabylie en 1871. Paris, n.d.
Afr 2010.5 Voission, Louis. Si-el-Hadj-Mokrani et la révolte de 1871. Paris, 1905.
Afr 2010.6 Bletterie, A. Le 9me régiment des mobiles de l'Allier. 1870-71. Lapalisse, 1900.
Afr 2010.7 Basset, R. L'insurrection algérienne de 1871. Louvain, 1892.

Afr 2020 Algeria - History by periods - History from the Conquest to independence - Other risings

Afr 2020.1 Le Chatelier, A. Les Medaganat. Alger, 1888
Afr 2020.2 Lohan, Guillo. Un contre-rezzou au Hoggar. Paris, 1903.

Afr 2025 Algeria - History by periods - History from the Conquest to independence - Speical topics (1860-1914)

Afr 2025.1 Gourgeot, F. Les sept plaies d'Algérie. Alger, 1891.
Afr 2025.1.5 Gourgeot, F. Situation politique de l'Algérie. Paris, 1881.
Afr 2025.2 Marial, W. La France d'Afrique et ses destinées. Paris, 1883.
Afr 2025.3 Casteran, A. L'Algérie française. Paris, 1900.
Afr 2025.4 Warnier, A. L'Algérie devant l'empereur. Paris, 1865.
Afr 2025.5 Duval, Jules. Réflexions sur la politique de l'empereur. Paris, 1866.
Afr 2025.6 Hess, Jean. La vérité sur l'Algérie. Paris, 1905.
Afr 2025.6.3 Hess, Jean. La vérité sur l'Algérie. Paris, 19- .
Afr 2025.7A Napoleon III, Empereur. Lettre sur la politique de la France en Algérie. Paris, 1865. 2 pam.
Afr 2025.7B Napoleon III, Empereur. Lettre sur la politique de la France en Algérie. Paris, 1865.
Afr 2025.8 Pamphlet vol. Algeria. History, 1860- 14 pam.
Afr 2025.9 Pamphlet vol. Algeria. History, 1860- 13 pam.
Afr 2025.10 Pamphlet vol. Algeria. History, 1860- 12 pam.
Afr 2025.11 Pamphlet vol. Algeria. History, 1860- 7 pam.
Afr 2025.11.15 Vignes, Kenneth. Le gouverneur général Tirman. Paris, 1958. 2v.
Afr 2025.12 Pamphlet vol. Algeria. History, 1860- 9 pam.
Afr 2025.13 Lasicotière. Rapport...sur les actes du gouvernement. Versailles, 1874.
Afr 2025.13.10 Martin, Claude. La commune d'Alger, 1870-1871. Paris, 1936.
Afr 2025.13.12 Martin, Claude. La commune d'Alger, 1870-1871. Thèse. Paris, 1936.
Afr 2025.14 Benoist, Charles. Enquête algérienne. Paris, 1892.
Afr 2025.15 Ferriol, M. Demain en Algérie. Paris, n.d.
Afr 2025.16 Colin, M. Quelques questions algériennes. Paris, 1899.
Afr 2025.17 Pommerol, J. Chez ceux qui guettent. Islam saharien. Paris, 1902.
Afr 2025.19 Dominique, L.C. Gouverneur général de l'Algérie. Alger, 1908.
Afr 2025.21 Algeria. Gouverneur Général. Etat de l'Algérie au 31 dec. 1882. Alger, 1883.
Afr 2025.23 Aynard, R. L'oeuvre française en Algérie. Paris, 1912.
Afr 2025.23.10 Cordier, E.W. Napoleon III et l'Algérie. Thèse. Alger, 1937.
Afr 2025.25 Melia, Jean. La France et l'Algérie. Paris, 1919.
Afr 2025.27 Gautier, Emile F. L'Algérie et la métropole. Paris, 1920.
Afr 2025.29 Abbas, F. Le jeune Algérien. Paris, 1931.
Afr 2025.30 Joesten, Joachim. The red hand. London, 1962.
Afr 2025.31.5 Depont, O. L'Algerie du centenaire. Paris, 1928.
Afr 2025.32 Landa, R.G. Natsionalno-osvoboditelnoe dvizhenie v Alzhire. Moscow, 1962.
Afr 2025.34 Confer, Vincent. France and Algeria. 1st ed. N.Y., 1966.
Afr 2025.36 Montclos, Xavier de. Le toast d'Alger, documents, 1890-1891. Paris, 1966.
Afr 2025.38 Ageron, Charles Robert. Les Algériens musulmans et la France, 1871-1919. Paris, 1968. 2v.

Afr 2026 Algeria - History by periods - History from the Conquest to independence - 1914-1945

Afr 2026.1 Melia, Jean. L'Algérie et la guerre (1914-18). Paris, 1918.
Afr 2026.5 Sarrasin, P.C. La crise algérienne. Paris, 1949.
Afr 2026.7 Davan, Y.M. La vie politique à Alger de 1940 à 1944. Paris, 1963.
Afr 2026.9 Ohneck, Wolfgang. Die französische Algerienpolitik von 1919-1939. Köln, 1967.
Afr 2026.10 Mirad, Ali. Le réformisme musulman en Algérie de 1925 à 1940. Paris, 1967.

Afr 2030 Algeria - History by periods - History from the Conquest to independence - 1945-1962

Afr 2030.5 Algeria. Gouverneur Général, 1951-55. Quatre ans en Algérie. Alger, 1955.
Afr 2030.10 Soustelle, Jacques. Aimée et souffrante Algérie. Paris, 1956.
Afr 2030.10.5 Soustelle, Jacques. Le drame algérien et la décadence française. Paris, 1957.
Afr 2030.15 Schaefer, René. Révolution en Algérie. Paris, 1956.
Afr 2030.20 Massenet, Michel. Contrepoison, ou la morale en Algérie. Paris, 1957.
Afr 2030.25A Aron, Raymond. La tragédie algérienne. Paris, 1957.
Afr 2030.25B Aron, Raymond. La tragédie algérienne. Paris, 1957.
Afr 2030.30 Barberot, Roger. Malaventure en Algérie avec le général Paris de Ballardière. Paris, 1957.
Afr 2030.35 Servan-Schreiber, Jean Jacques. Lieutenant in Algeria. 1st Amer. ed. N.Y., 1957.
Afr 2030.35.2 Servan-Schreiber, Jean Jacques. Lieutenant en Algérie. Paris, 1957.
Afr 2030.40 Vialet, Georges. L'Algérie restera française. Paris, 1957.
Afr 2030.45 Lavie, Louis. Le drame algérien. 3 ed. Alger, 1956.
Afr 2030.50 Tillion, G. L'Algérie en 1957. Paris, 1957.
Afr 2030.50.5 Tillion, G. Algeria. 1st Amer. ed. N.Y., 1958.
Afr 2030.50.10 Tillion, G. France and Algeria. 1st Amer. ed. N.Y., 1961.
Afr 2030.50.15 Tillion, G. Les ennemis complémentaires. Paris, 1960.
Afr 2030.55 Fabre-Luce, Alfred. Demain en Algérie. Paris, 1958.
Afr 2030.60 Alleg, Henri. The question. N.Y., 1958.
Afr 2030.60.2 Alleg, Henri. Texte intégral du livre "La question." Paris, 1958.
Afr 2030.60.5 Alleg, Henri. La question. Paris, 1965.

Afr 2030 Algeria - History by periods - History from the Conquest to e independence - 1945-1962 - cont.

Afr 2030.65 Beau de Lomenie, Emmanuel. L'Algérie trahie par l'argent. Paris, 1957.
Afr 2030.70.5 Faucher, Jean André. Les barricades d'Alger. Paris, 1960.
Afr 2030.75 Leprevost, Jacques. La bataille d'Alger. Alger, 1957.
Afr 2030.77 Leprevost, Jacques. Défense de l'Algérie. Alger, 1957.
Afr 2030.80 Mezerik, Avrahn G. The Algerian-French conflict. N.Y., 1958.
Afr 2030.85 Fournier, Christiane. Nous avons encore des héros. Paris, 1957.
Afr 2030.90 Dronne, Raymond. La révolution d'Alger. Paris, 1958.
Afr 2030.95 Aron, Raymond. L'Algérie et la République. Paris, 1958.
Afr 2030.100 Bromberger, Serge. Les rébelles algériens. Paris, 1958.
Afr 2030.105 Serigny, Alain de. La révolution du 13 mai. Paris, 1958.
Afr 2030.106 Serigny, Alain de. Un procés. Paris, 1961.
Afr 2030.110 Duquesne, Jacques. L'Algérie. Bruges, 1958.
Afr 2030.115 Kernmayr, Erich. Algerien in Flammen. 2.Aufl. Göttingen, 1958.
Afr 2030.120 Michelet, Edmond. Contre la guerre civile. Paris, 1957.
Afr 2030.125 Ceux d'Algérie, lettres de rappelés. Paris, 1957.
Afr 2030.130 Alquier, Jean Yves. Nous avons pacifié Tazalt. Paris, 1957.
Afr 2030.135 Candas, Maurice F.M. Plaidoyer pour l'Algérie. Paris, 1957.
Afr 2030.140 Girard, Henri Georges. Pour Djamila Bouhired. Paris, 1958.
Afr 2030.145 Lentin, Albert Paul. L'Algérie des colonels. Paris, 1958.
Afr 2030.147 Lentin, Albert Paul. L'Algérie des colonels. Paris, 1959.
Afr 2030.150 Lombard, Pierre. Crise algérienne vue d'Alger. Alger, 1958.
Afr 2030.155 Montpeyroux, André Brousse de. Autour d'une erreur politique. Alger, 1958.
Afr 2030.160 Servier, Jean. Adieu Djebels. Paris, 1958.
Afr 2030.165 Mainguy, M. Le pétrole et l'Algérie. Paris, 1958.
Afr 2030.170 Rosfelder, André. L'Algérie à bâtir. Alger, 1959.
Afr 2030.175 Jeanson, Colette. L'Algérie hors la loi. Paris, 1955.
Afr 2030.180 Dion, Michel. Armée d'Algérie et la pacification. Paris, 1959.
Afr 2030.190 Favrod, Charles. La révolution algérienne. Paris, 1959.
Afr 2030.200 Folliet, Joseph. Guerre et paix en Algérie. Lyon, 1958.
Afr 2030.205 Gerin, Paul. L'Algérie du 13 mai. Paris, 1958.
Afr 2030.210 Clark, Michael. Algeria in turmoil. N.Y., 1959.
Afr 2030.211 Clark, Michael. Algeria in turmoil. N.Y., 1960.
Afr 2030.215 Beuchard, Georges. L'équivoque algérienne. Paris, 1959.
Afr 2030.220 Darboy, Marcel. Jeunesse de France en Algérie. Paris, 1959.
Afr 2030.225 Vidal-Naquet, Pierre. L'affaire Audin. Paris, 1958.
Afr 2030.230 Alwan, Mohamed. Algeria before the United Nations. N.Y., 1959.
Afr 2030.235 Sneider, Bertrand. La Cinquième République et l'Algérie. Paris, 1959.
Afr 2030.240 Rispy, Franz. Sie klagen an. Zürich, 1958.
Afr 2030.245 Rahmani, Abd el-Kader. L'affaire des officiers algériens. Paris, 1959.
Afr 2030.250 Oppermann, Thomas. Die algerische Frage. Stuttgart, 1959.
Afr 2030.252 Oppermann, Thomas. Le problème algérien. Paris, 1961.
Afr 2030.255 Mezerik, Avrahm G. Algerian developments, 1959. N.Y., 1960.
Afr 2030.260 Savary, Alain. Nationalisme algérien et grandeur française. Paris, 1960.
Afr 2030.265F Flament, Marc. Aucune bête au monde. Paris, 1959.
Afr 2030.270 Franza, Angelo. La rivoluzione algerina. Milano, 1959.
Afr 2030.275 Algeria. Programme et action du gouvernement en Algérie. Alger, 1956.
Afr 2030.276 Algeria. Cabinet du Gouverneur Général. Action du gouvernement en Algérie. Alger, 1957.
Afr 2030.280 Houart, Pierre. L attitude de l eglise dans la guerre d algerie. Bruxelles, 1960.
Afr 2030.285 Eulage, André. L'envers des barricades. Paris, 1960.
Afr 2030.290 Pamphlet box. Algeria. History, 1945- .
Afr 2030.291 Pamphlet box. Ageria. History, 1945- .
Afr 2030.292 Pamphlet vol. Algeria. History, 1945 . 6 pam.
Afr 2030.295 Gangrène. Paris, 1959.
Afr 2030.300 Verges, Jacques. Les disparus. Lausanne, 1959.
Afr 2030.305 Ribaud, Paul. Barricades pour un drapeau. Paris, 1960.
Afr 2030.310 Algeria. Délégation Générale. Algeria's development. Algiers, 1959.
Afr 2030.315 Priester, Eva. In Algerien sprechen die Gewehrc. 1. Aufl. Berlin, 1959.
Afr 2030.320 Fanon, Frantz. L'an cinq de la révolution algérienne. Paris, 1959.
Afr 2030.320.2 Fanon, Frantz. Studies in a dying colonialism. N.Y., 1955.
Afr 2030.325 Manevy, Alain. L'Algérie à vingt ans. Paris, 1960.
Afr 2030.330 Gillespie, Joan. Algeria. London, 1960.
Afr 2030.335 Centre d'Etudes Régionales de Kabylie. Publication. Mémoires et travaux. Alger.
Afr 2030.340 Algerian Front of National Liberation. Algeria. N.Y., 1960.
Afr 2030.340.5 Algerian Front of National Liberation. Miscellaneous papers. n.p., 1959-1961. 43 pam.
Afr 2030.340.10 Algerian Front of National Liberation. La révolution algérienne par les textes. Paris, 1961.
Afr 2030.340.10.5 Algerian Front of National Liberation. La révolution algérienne par les textes. 3. ed. Paris, 1962.
Afr 2030.345 Brace, Richard M. Ordeal in Algeria. Princeton, 1960.
Afr 2030.346 Brace, Richard M. Algerian voices. Princeton, N.J., 1965.
Afr 2030.350 Roy, Jules. La guerre d'Algérie. Paris, 1960.
Afr 2030.350.2 Roy, Jules. The war in Algeria. N.Y., 1961.
Afr 2030.352 Roy, Jules. Autour du drame. Paris, 1961.
Afr 2030.355 Debatty, Andre. Le treize mai et la presse. Paris, 1960.
Afr 2030.360 Reygasse, René. Témoinage d'un ultra sur le drame algérien. Paris, 1960.
Afr 2030.365 Barricades et colonels, 24 janvier 1960 par Bromberger. Paris, 1960.
Afr 2030.370 Moureau, Maurice. Des Algériens accusent. Paris, 1959.
Afr 2030.375 Maschino, Maurice. Le refus. Paris, 1960.
Afr 2030.376 Maschino, Maurice. L'engagement. Paris, 1961.
Afr 2030.380 Darboise, Jean M. Officiers en Algérie. Paris, 1960.
Afr 2030.385 Gaschet-Veyret de la Tour, E. L'erreur du siècle et l'homme des civilisations agricoles. Paris, 1956.
Afr 2030.390 Servier, Jean. Demain en Algérie. Paris, 1959.
Afr 2030.395 Hermans, Fons. Algerije. Amsterdam, 1960.
Afr 2030.400 Pajaud, Henri. La révolution d'Alger. Paris, 1958.
Afr 2030.405 Noureddine, Meziane. Un Algérien raconte. Paris, 1960.

Afr 2030 Algeria - History by periods - History from the Conquest to e independence - 1945-1962 - cont.

Afr 2030.410 Union Nationale des Étudiants de France. Le syndicalisme étudiant et le problème algérien. Paris, 1960.
Afr 2030.415 Boisson, Jean. Essai sur le probléme algérien. Paris, 1960.
Afr 2030.420 Boudot, Pierre. L'Algérie mal enchaînée. Paris, 1961.
Afr 2030.425 Habart, Michel. Histoire d'un parjure. Paris, 1960.
Afr 2030.430 Pamphlet vol. Algeria. History, 1945- 8 pam.
Afr 2030.449 Bennabi, Malek. Discours sur les conditions de la renaissance algérienne. Alger, 1949.
Afr 2030.456 Douxey, Jean. S.O.S. Algérie. Paris, 1956.
Afr 2030.458 Chevallier, Jacques. Nous. Paris, 1958.
Afr 2030.459 Scheer, Maximillian. Algerien. 1. Aufl. Berlin, 1959.
Afr 2030.459.5 Aumeran, Adolphe. Paix en Algérie. Paris, 1959.
Afr 2030.460 Mustapha G. Barberousse. Paris, 1960.
Afr 2030.460.5 Lauriol, M. Au service de l'Algérie française nouvelle. Alger, 1960.
Afr 2030.460.10 Keramane, Hadif. La pacification. Lausanne, 1960.
Afr 2030.460.15 Larteguy, J. Les dieux meurent en Algérie. Paris, 1960.
Afr 2030.460.20 Cercle d'Études Algériennes. Lettres à un métropolitain. Alger, 1960.
Afr 2030.460.25A Algeria. White paper on the application of the Geneva Convention of 1949. N.Y., 1960.
Afr 2030.460.25B Algeria. White paper on the application of the Geneva Convention of 1949. N.Y., 1960.
Afr 2030.460.30 Comité pour la Paix en Algérie. La Belgique devant le problème algérien. Chênée, 1961.
Afr 2030.460.35 Buy, François. La République algérienne. Paris, 1965.
Afr 2030.461 Moch, J.S. En 1961, paix en Algérie. Paris, 1961.
Afr 2030.461.5 Bedjaoui, Mohammed. La révolution algérienne et le droit. Bruxelles, 1961.
Afr 2030.461.10 Dufresnay, Claude. Des officiers parlent. Paris, 1961.
Afr 2030.461.15 Alleg, Henri. Prisionniers de guerre. Paris, 1961.
Afr 2030.461.20 Davezies, Robert. Le temps de la justice. Lausanne, 1961.
Afr 2030.461.25 Darbois, Dominique. Les Algériens en guerre. Milano, 1961.
Afr 2030.461.30 Mansell, G. Tragedy in Algeria. London, 1961.
Afr 2030.461.35 Charby, J. L'Algérie en prison. Paris, 1961.
Afr 2030.461.40 Maspero, Francois. Le droit à l'insoumission. Paris, 1961.
Afr 2030.461.45 Behr, Edward. The Algerian problem. London, 1961.
Afr 2030.461.45.2 Behr, Edward. The Algerian problem. N.Y., 1962.
Afr 2030.461.46 Behr, Edward. Dramatique Algérie. Paris, 1962.
Afr 2030.461.50 Kraft, Joseph. The struggle for Algeria. 1st ed. Garden City, 1961.
Afr 2030.461.55 Mus, Paul. Guerre sans visage. Paris, 1961.
Afr 2030.461.60 Paillat, Claude. Dossier secret de l'Algérie. Paris, 1961. 2v.
Afr 2030.461.65 Fauvet, J. La Fronde des généraux. Paris, 1961.
Afr 2030.461.70 Landa, R.G. Alzhir sbrasyvaet okovy. Moscow, 1961.
Afr 2030.461.75 Martin-Chauffier, L. L'examen des consciences. Paris, 1961.
Afr 2030.461.80 Nazoun, Amar. Ferhat Abbas. Paris, 1961.
Afr 2030.461.85 Legaillarde, Pierre. On a triché avec l'honneur. Paris, 1961.
Afr 2030.461.90 Algerian Front of National Liberation. Documents. N.Y. 1961-62
Afr 2030.461.95 Extraditions d'Algériens, ou le chemin de la guillotine. Bruxelles, 1961.
Afr 2030.462 Matthews, T.S. War in Algeria. N.Y., 1962.
Afr 2030.462.5 Peyrefitte, Alain. Faut-il partager l'Algérie? Paris, 1962.
Afr 2030.462.10 Greer, Herb. A scattering of dust. London, 1962.
Afr 2030.462.15 Colloque Internationale sur l'Algérie. Les conditions de l'indépendance. Bruxelles, 1962.
Afr 2030.462.20 Azeau, Henri. Révolte militaire, Alger, 22 avril 1961. Paris, 1962.
Afr 2030.462.25 Denoyer, François. Quatre ans de guerre en Algérie. Paris, 1962.
Afr 2030.462.30 Naegelen, Marcel. Mission en Algérie. Paris, 1962.
Afr 2030.462.35 Club Jean-Moulin. Deux pièces du dossier Algérie. Paris, 1962.
Afr 2030.462.40 Potemkin, Iu. V. Alzhirskii narod v borbe za nezavisimosti. Moscow, 1962.
Afr 2030.462.45 Kessel, Patrick. Le peuple algérien et la guerre. Paris, 1962.
Afr 2030.462.50 Thorez, Maurice. Textes choisis sur l'Algérie. Paris, 1962.
Afr 2030.462.55 Allais, Maurice. Les accords d'Evian. Paris, 1962.
Afr 2030.462.60 Michel, F. Christ et croissant pour l'Algérie nouvelle. Paris, 1962.
Afr 2030.462.65 Boualam, B. Mon pays, la France. Paris, 1962.
Afr 2030.462.70 Duchemin, Jacques. Histoire du F.L.N. Paris, 1962.
Afr 2030.462.75 Perroux, Francois. L'Algérie de demain. Paris, 1962.
Afr 2030.462.80 Aron, Robert. Les origines de la guerre d'Algérie. Paris, 1962.
Afr 2030.462.85 Periot, Gerard. Deuxième. Paris, 1962.
Afr 2030.462.90 Khelifa, L. Manuel du militant algérien. Lausanne, 1962.
Afr 2030.462.95 Favrod, C.H. Le F.L.N. et l'Algérie. Paris, 1962.
Afr 2030.462.100 Benzine, A. Le camp. Paris, 1962.
Afr 2030.462.110 Algeria. Treaties, etc. Les accords d'Evian. Paris, 1962.
Afr 2030.462.112 Algeria. Treaties, etc. Texts of declarations drawn up in common agreement at Evian. N.Y., 1962.
Afr 2030.462.115 Vidal-Naquet, P. La raison d'état. Paris, 1962.
Afr 2030.462.120 Enfants d'Algérie. Paris, 1962.
Afr 2030.462.125 Algérie nouvelle et la presse française. Paris, 1962.
Afr 2030.462.130A Feraoun, M. Journal, 1955-62. Paris, 1962.
Afr 2030.462.130B Feraoun, M. Journal, 1955-62. Paris, 1962.
Afr 2030.462.135 Trinquier, R. Le coup d'état du 13 mai. Paris, 1962.
Afr 2030.462.140 Bonnaud, R. Itinéraire. Paris, 1962.
Afr 2030.462.145 Nicol, A. La bataille de l'O.A.S. Paris, 1962.
Afr 2030.462.150 Moureaux, S. Les accords d 'Evian et l'avenir de la révolution algérienne. Paris, 1962.
Afr 2030.462.155 Girardet, R. Pour le tombeau d'un capitaine. Paris, 1962.
Afr 2030.462.160 Grall, Xavier. La génération du Djebel. Paris, 1962.
Afr 2030.463 Pickles, D.M. Algeria and France. N.Y., 1963.
Afr 2030.463.5 Vidal-Naquet, P. Torture, cancer of democracy. Harmondsworth, 1963.
Afr 2030.463.10 Lancelot, Marie-Thérèse. L'Organisation armée secrète. v.1-2. Paris, 1963.
Afr 2030.463.15 Buchard, R. Organisation armée secrète, fév. 14-déc. 1961. Paris, 1963.
Afr 2030.463.20 Boualam, B. Les Harkis au service de la France. Paris, 1963.
Afr 2030.463.25 Cretin-Vercel, Michel. Nouvelle Algérie. Paris, 1963.
Afr 2030.463.30 Jacob, A. D'une Algérie à l'autre. Paris, 1963.

Afr 2030 Algeria - History by periods - History from the Conquest to independence - 1945-1962 - cont.

Afr 2030.463.35 Loiseau, J. Pied-noir, mon frère. Paris, 1963.
Afr 2030.463.40 Kessel, P. Lettere della rivoluzione algerina. Torino, 1963.
Afr 2030.463.45 Susini, J.J. Histoire de l'O.A.S. Paris, 1963.
Afr 2030.463.50 Yacef, Saadi. Souvenirs de la bataille d'Alger déc. 1956-sept. 1957. Paris, 1963.
Afr 2030.463.55 Aguirre, Carlos. Argelia. Año 8. Buenos Aires, 1963.
Afr 2030.464 Lentin, Albert. L'Algérie entre deux mondes. Paris, 1964.
Afr 2030.464.5 Ortiz, Joseph. Mes combats. Paris, 1964.
Afr 2030.464.10 Algerian Front of National Liberation. La charte d'Alger, ensemble des textes adoptés par le premier congrés du Parti de Front de libération nationale. Alger, 1964.
Afr 2030.464.15 Joesten, Joachim. The new Algeria. Chicago, 1964.
Afr 2030.464.20 Bergleaud, Edmond. Le premier quart d'heure. Paris, 1964.
Afr 2030.464.25 Boualam, Bachaga. L'Algérie sans la France. Paris, 1964.
Afr 2030.464.30 Boudiaf, M. Notre révolution. Paris, 196-.
Afr 2030.464.35 Leulliette, P. St. Michael and the dragon. London, 1964.
Afr 2030.464.40 Scherb, J.D. Le soleil ne chauffe que les vivants. Paris, 1964.
Afr 2030.464.44 Merle, Robert. Ahmed Ben Bella. Paris, 1965.
Afr 2030.464.45 Ben Bella, Ahmed. Discours, année 1963. Alger, 1964.
Afr 2030.464.50 Terrenoire, Louis. De Gaulle et l'Algérie. Paris, 1964.
Afr 2030.464.55 Estier, Claude. Pour l'Algérie. Paris, 1964.
Afr 2030.464.60 Pravda, Moscow. Nerushimaia druzhba i bratstvo. Moscow, 1964.
Afr 2030.464.65 Algeria. Treaties, etc. Accords passés entre la France et l'Algérie de juillet 1962 au 31 décembre 1963. Paris, 1964.
Afr 2030.464.70 Douence, J.C. La mise en place des institutions algériennes. Paris, 1964.
Afr 2030.464.75 Laparre, M. de. Journal d'un prêtre en Algérie. Paris, 1964.
Afr 2030.464.80 Morland. HistoireDe l'organisation de l'armée secréte. Paris, 1964.
Afr 2030.464.85 OAS parle. Paris, 1964.
Afr 2030.465 Buron, Robert. Carnets politiques de la guerre d'Algérie. Paris, 1965.
Afr 2030.465.5 Moinet, Bernard. Journal d'une agonie. Paris, 1965.
Afr 2030.466 Humbaraci, Arslan. Algeria, a revolution that failed. London, 1966.
Afr 2030.466.5 Poerner, Arthur J. Argélia: o caminho da independência. Rio de Janeiro, 1966.
Afr 2030.467 O'Ballance, Edgar. The Algerian insurrection, 1954-62. London, 1967.
Afr 2030.467.5 Frolkin, Nikolai M. Krest'ianstvo v alzhirskoi revoliutsii, 1954-1962. Kiev, 1967.
Afr 2030.467.10 Merle, Robert. Ahmed Ben Bella. N.Y., 1967.
Afr 2030.467.15 Carréras, Fernand. L'Accord F.L.N.-O.A.S. Paris, 1967.
Afr 2030.467.20 Fontaine, Pierre. L'Aventure algérienne continue. Paris, 1967.
Afr 2030.467.25 Comité pour la Défense de Ben Bella et des Autres Victimes de la Répression en Algérie. Qu'est devenu Ben Bella? Paris, 1967.
Afr 2030.468 Bocca, Geoffrey. The secret army. Englewood Cliffs, 1968.
Afr 2030.468.5 Courrière, Yves. La guerre d'Algérie. Paris, 1968. 2v.
Afr 2030.468.10 Beyssade, Pierre. La guerre d'Algérie, 1954-1962. Paris, 1968.
Afr 2030.469 Jouhaud, Edmond. O mon pays perdu. Paris, 1969.
Afr 2030.469.5 Quandt, William B. Revolution and political leadership: Algeria, 1954-1968. Cambridge, 1969.

Afr 2035 Algeria - History by periods - History since Independence (1962-) - General works

Afr 2035.5 Chaliand, Gérard. L'Algérie est-elle socialiste? Paris, 1964.
Afr 2035.6 Gordon, David. The passing of French Algeria. London, 1966.
Afr 2035.7 Naegelen, Marcel. Une route plus large que longue. Paris, 1965.
Afr 2035.9 Guerin, Daniel. L'Algérie caporalisée. Paris, 1965.
Afr 2035.9.5 Guérin, Daniel. L'Algérie qui se cherche. Paris, 1964.
Afr 2035.11 Bergheaud, Edmond. Le premier quart d'heure. Paris, 1964.
Afr 2035.15 Bourges, Hervé. L'Algérie à l'épreuve du pouvoir (1962-1967). Paris, 1967.
Afr 2035.20 Rogati, Elio. La seconda rivoluzione algeriana. Roma, 1965.

Afr 2037 Algeria - History by periods - History since Independence (1962-) - Special topics

Afr 2037.2 Comité pour la Défense de Ben Bella et des Autres Victimes de la Répression en Algérie. Les torturés d'El Harrach. Paris, 1966.
Afr 2037.5 Algeria. Ministère de l'Orientation Nationale. Une année de révolution socialiste, 1962 - 5 juillet - 1963. Alger, 1963?
Afr 2037.5.5 Algeria. Ministère de l'Orientation Nationale. Algérie, an II, 1962-1964. Alger, 1965?
Afr 2037.8 Palacio, Léo. Les Pieds-Noirs dans le monde. Paris, 1968.

Afr 2205 - 2210 Algeria - Geography, description, etc. - General works (by date)

Htn Afr 2206.44* Okeley, W. Ebenezer, or A small monument of great mercy. London, 1676.
Afr 2206.75 Rocqueville. Relation des moeurs...des Turcs d'Alger. Paris, 1675.
Afr 2207.25 Laugier de Tassy, N. Histoire du royaume d'Alger. Amsterdam, 1725.
Afr 2207.25.3 Laugier de Tassy, N. Compleat history of the piratical states of Barbary. London, 1750.
Afr 2207.25.5 Laugier de Tassy, N. Histoire des Etats Barbaresques. Paris, 1757. 2v.
Afr 2207.38.10 Shaw, Thomas. Voyage dans la régence d'Alger. Paris, 1830.
Afr 2207.38.15 Shaw, Thomas. Voyage dans la régence d'Alger. Paris, 1830.
Afr 2207.38.16 Shaw, Thomas. Voyage dans la régence d'Alger. Cover 1831. Paris, 1830.
Afr 2208.17 Pananti, F. Aventure e osservazioni. Firenze, 1817. 2v.
Afr 2208.17.3 Pananti, F. Narrative of a residence in Algiers. London, 1818.
Afr 2208.26 Shaler, William. Sketches of Algiers. Boston, 1826.
Afr 2208.26.5 Shaler, William. Esquisse de l'état d'Alger. Paris, 1830.
Afr 2208.30 Aperçu...sur l'état d'Alger. 2e ed. Paris, 1830.
Afr 2208.30.3 Perrot, A.M. Alger, esquisse topographique et historique. Paris, 1830.

Afr 2205 - 2210 Algeria - Geography, description, etc. - General works (by date) - cont.

Afr 2208.30.8 Renaudot. Alger, tableau du royaume. Paris, 1830.
Afr 2208.32.3 Pfeiffer, S.F. Meine Reisen und Gefangenschaft in Algier. 3rd ed. Giessen, 1834.
Afr 2208.32.5 Malo de Molina, M. Viaje a la Argelia. Valencia, 1852.
Afr 2208.33 Rozet. Voyage dans la régence d'Alger. 3 vols. and atlas. Paris, 1833. 4v.
Afr 2208.34 Schimper, W. Reise nach Algier in den Jahren 1831-32. Stuttgart, 1834.
Afr 2208.35 Temple, G.T. Excursions...Algiers and Tunis. London, 1835. 2v.
Afr 2208.35.2 Lord, P.B. Algiers, notices of neighboring states of Barbary. London, 1835. 2v.
Afr 2208.35.10 Algier wie es ist. Stuttgart, 1835.
Afr 2208.36 Campbell, Thomas. Letters from the south, written during a journey to Algiers. Philadelphia, 1836.
Afr 2208.36.5 Campbell, Thomas. Letters from the south. London, 1837. 2v.
Afr 2208.38 Dureau de la Malle. Peyssonnel et Desfontaines voyages...d'Alger. Paris, 1838. 2v.
Afr 2208.40 Suchet. Lettres...sur l'Algérie. Tours, 1840.
Afr 2208.45 Veuillot, L. Les Français en Algérie. 3e ed. Tours, 1863.
Afr 2208.46 Pamphlet vol. Algeria. Geography, travels. 6 pam.
Afr 2208.46.3 Kennedy, J.C. Algeria and Tunis in 1845. London, 1846. 2v.
Afr 2208.46.4 Saint-Marie, Count. A visit to Algeria in 1845. London, 1846.
Afr 2208.46.8 Texier, C. Les grandes chasses d'Afrique. n.p., n.d.
Afr 2208.47 Marmier, X. Lettres sur l'Algérie. Paris, 1847.
Afr 2208.47.3 Lumsden, William. Journal of a trip to the Algerine territory, 1837. Glasgow, 1847.
Afr 2208.48.10 Dumas, Alexandre. Tales of Algeria, or Life among the Arabs. Philadelphia, 1868.
Afr 2208.50 Joanne, A. Voyage en Afrique. Ixelles, 1850.
Afr 2208.52 Prus. A residence in Algeria. London, 1852.
Afr 2208.53 France. Ministére de la Guerre. Rapport sur la situation de l'Algérie en 1853. Paris, 1854.
Afr 2208.53.5 Daumas, E. Moeurs et coutumes de l'Algérie. 2e ed. Paris, 1854.
Afr 2208.54 Morell, J.R. Algeria. London, 1854.
Afr 2208.54.3 Pulszky, F. The tricolor on the atlas. London, 1854.
Afr 2208.55 Buvry, L. Algerien und seine Zukunft unter französischer Herrschaft. Berlin, 1855.
Afr 2208.55.6 Marcotte de Quivieres, C. Deux ans en Afrique. Paris, 1856.
Afr 2208.56 Gerard, Cecile J.B. The adventures of Gerard, the Lion Killer. N.Y., 1856.
Afr 2208.56.5F Gerard, Jules. Le tueur de lions. Paris, 1892.
Afr 2208.56.10 Mornaud, F. La vie arabe. Paris, 1856.
Afr 2208.57 Duveyrier, H. Journal d'un voyage dans la province. Paris, 1900.
Afr 2208.58 MacCarthy, O. Géographie de l'Algérie. Algiers, 1858.
Afr 2208.58.3 Duvernois, C. L'Algérie, ce qu'elle est. Alger, 1858.
Afr 2208.59 Ditson, G.L. The crescent and French crusaders. N.Y., 1859.
Afr 2208.59.2 Ditson, G.L. The crescent and French crusaders. N.Y., 1860.
Afr 2208.59.5 Blakesley, J.W. Four months in Algeria. Cambridge, 1859.
Afr 2208.62 Hirsch, M. Reise in das Innere von Algerien. Berlin, 1862.
Afr 2208.62.4 Thierry-Mieg, C. Six semaines en Afrique. 2e ed. Paris, 1862.
Afr 2208.65 Behaghel, A. L'Algérie. Alger, 1865.
Afr 2208.65.3 Zaccone, J. De batna à Tuggurt et au Souf. Paris, 1865.
Afr 2208.65.4 Schneider, O. Tagebuch aus Algier. Dresden, n.d.
Afr 2208.65.5 Hartevelt, D. Herinneringen uit Algiers. Arnhem, 1865.
Afr 2208.65.6 Rogers, P.A. A winter in Algeria. London, 1865.
Afr 2208.65.9 Peissier, Octave. Napoleon III en Algérie. Paris, 1865.
Afr 2208.66.3 Rasch, Gustav. Nach den Oasen von Siban. Berlin, 1866.
Afr 2208.66.5 Rasch, Gustav. Nach Algier. Dresden, 1875.
Afr 2208.66.8 Sala, George A. A trip to Barbary. London, 1866.
Afr 2208.67 Edwards, M.B. A winter with the swallows. London, 1867.
Afr 2208.68 Naphegyi, G. Among the Arabs. Philadelphia, 1868.
Afr 2208.68.5 Evans, H.L. Last winter in Algeria. London, 1868.
Afr 2208.68.8 Wingfield, L. Under the palms in Algeria and Tunis. London, 1868.
Afr 2208.71.5 Villot, E. Moeurs, coutumes, de l'Algérie. 3e ed. Alger, 1888.
Afr 2208.72 Herbert, Lady. A search after sunshine, or Algeria in 1871. London, 1872.
Afr 2208.72.3 Dubouzet, Charles. Algérie. n.p., 1872. 2 pam.
Afr 2208.74 Blackburn, H. Artists and Arabs. Boston, 1874.
Afr 2208.77 Wattenwyl, M. von. Zwei Jahre in Algerien. Bern, 1877.
Afr 2208.78 Beijerman, H. Drie maanden in Algerie. 's-Gravenhage, 1878.
Afr 2208.79 Fontanes, J. de. Deux touristes en Algérie. Paris, 1879.
Afr 2208.79.3 Bourde, P. A travers l'Algérie. Paris, 1880.
Afr 2208.80 Tchihatchef, P. Espagne,Algérie et Tunisie. Paris, 1880.
Afr 2208.80.3 Philippe, F. Etapes sahariennes. Alger, 1880.
Afr 2208.80.5 Mercier, E. L'Algérie en 1880. Paris, 1880.
Afr 2208.80.6 Lubomirski, J. Côte barbaresque et le Sahara. Paris, 1880.
Afr 2208.81 Schwarz, B. Algerien. Leipzig, 1881.
Afr 2208.81.3 Pulligny, F.A. de. Six semaines en Algérie. Paris, 1881.
Afr 2208.81.5 Notices...surAlger et l'Algérie. Alger, 1881.
Afr 2208.81.7 Bourquelot, E. En Algérie. Paris, 1881.
Afr 2208.81.9 Knox, A.A. The new playground...Algeria. London, 1881.
Afr 2208.81.11 Lelu, P. En Algérie. Paris, 1881.
Afr 2208.81.13 Girault, A. En Algérie. Paris, 1881.
Afr 2208.81.15 Mouchez, E. La côte et les ports de l'Algérie. Paris, 1881.
Afr 2208.82 Wahl, M. L'Algérie. Paris, 1882.
Afr 2208.82.4 Wahl, M. L'Algérie. 4e ed. Paris, 1903.
Afr 2208.82.5 Wahl, M. L'Algérie. 5e ed. Paris, 1908.
Afr 2208.83 Gaffarel, P. L'Algérie. Paris, 1883.
Afr 2208.83.5 Mercier, E. L'Algérie. Paris, 1883.
Afr 2208.83.7 Niel, O. Algérie, géographie générale. 3e ed. Paris, 1883.
Afr 2208.83.9 Clamageran, J.J. L'Algérie, impressions de voyage. 2e ed. Paris, 1883.
Afr 2208.84 Niox, G.L. Algérie. Paris, 1884.
Afr 2208.84.2 Reuss, L.M. A travers l'Algérie. Paris, 1884.
Afr 2208.85 Quesnoy, F. L'Algérie. 2e ed. Paris, 1890.
Afr 2208.87 Baudel, J. Un an à Alger. Paris, 1887.
Afr 2208.87.2 Leroy-Beaulieu. L'Algérie et la Tunis. Paris, 1897.
Afr 2208.88 Vignon, L. La France dans l'Afrique du nord. Paris, 1888.
Afr 2208.88.3 Gaffarel, Paul. Lectures...sur l'Algérie. Paris, 1888.
Afr 2208.88.5 Deporter, Victor. A propos du Transsaharien. Alger, 1890.

Afr 2205 - 2210 Algeria - Geography, description, etc. - General works (by date) - cont.

Afr 2208.90 Bergot, Raoul. L'Algérie telle qu'elle est. Paris, 1890.
Afr 2208.90.3 Bridgman, F.A. Winters in Algeria. London, 1890.
Afr 2208.92 Burdeau, A. L'Algérie en 1891. Paris, 1892.
Afr 2208.93 Baraudon, A. Algérie et Tunisie. Paris, 1893.
Afr 2208.93.3 Chatrieux, E. Etudes algériennes. Paris, 1893.
Afr 2208.93.4 Boutroue, A. L'Algérie et la Tunisie à travers les ages. Paris, 1893.
Afr 2208.93.6 Bernard, Marius. De Tunis à Alger. Paris, 1893.
Afr 2208.93.10 Bruun, Daniel. Algier og Sahara. Billeder fra nomade- og krigerlivet. Kjøbenhavn, 1893.
Afr 2208.94 Greville-Nugent. A land of mosques and marabouts. London, 1894.
Afr 2208.94.3 Pensa, Henri. L'Algérie. Paris, 1894.
Afr 2208.95.3A Leroux, H. Je deviens colon. Paris, 1895.
Afr 2208.95.3B Leroux, H. Je deviens colon. Paris, 1895.
Afr 2208.95.5 Leroux, H. Je deviens colon. 4e ed. Paris, 1895.
Afr 2208.95.9 Workman, F.B. Algerian memories. London, 1895.
Afr 2208.97 Grandin. A pied, le tour de la terre...à travers le sud-algérien. Paris, 1897.
Afr 2208.98 Battandier. L'Algérie. Paris, 1898.
Afr 2208.98.3 Barbet, Charles. Au pays des Burnous. Alger, 1898.
Afr 2208.98.8 Leroux, H. Je deviens colon. 2e ed. Paris, 1895.
Afr 2208.99 Duval, P. Heures d'Afrique. Paris, 1899.
Afr 2208.99.11 Hyam, Joseph C. The illustrated guide to Algiers. 6th ed. Algiers, 1908.
Afr 2209.00 Galland, C. de. Les petits cahiers algériens. Alger, 1900.
Afr 2209.00.5 Eberhardt, I. Mes journaliers. Paris, 1923.
Afr 2209.02.2 Gay, E. L'Algérie d'aujourd'hui. Paris, 1907.
Afr 2209.04 Bourdonnaye. Dans le Bled. Paris, 1904.
Afr 2209.05 Richardot, H. Sept semaines en Tunisie et en Algérie. Paris, 1905.
Afr 2209.05.2 Phillips, L.M. In the desert. London, 1905.
Afr 2209.05.5 Phillips, L.M. In the desert. London, 1909.
Afr 2209.06 Hilton-Simpson, M.W. Algiers and beyond. London, 1906.
Afr 2209.06.2 Belloc, H. Esto perpetua. London, 1906.
Afr 2209.06.3 Crouse, M.E. Algiers. N.Y., 1906.
Afr 2209.06.10 Bernard, P. Histoire, colonization, géographie et administration de l'Algérie. 2e ed. Alger, 1906.
Afr 2209.06.15 Nesbitt, Frances E. Algeria and Tunis. London, 1906.
Afr 2209.08 Bruchard, H. de. La France au soleil, notes sur l'Algérie. Paris, 1908.
Afr 2209.08.2 Donop. Lettres sur l'Algérie, 1907-08. Paris, 1908.
Afr 2209.08.3 Miltoun, F. In the land of mosques and minarets. Boston, 1908.
Afr 2209.08.5 Kuehnel, Ernst. Algerien. Leipzig, 1908.
Afr 2209.09 Congrès de l'Afrique du nord. Paris, 1909. 2v.
Afr 2209.10 Hyam, Joseph C. Biskra, Sidi-Okba and the desert. 1st ed. Algiers, 1910.
Afr 2209.11 Colliez, A. La frontière algéro-marocaine. Paris, 1911.
Afr 2209.11.3 Mueller, Charles. Fünf Jahre Fremdenlegionär in Algier. Stuttgart, 1911.
Afr 2209.11.5 Thomas-Stanford, C. About Algeria, Algiers. London, 1912.
Afr 2209.11.7 Roy, R. Au pays des mirages. Paris, 1911.
Afr 2209.12 Devereux, R. Aspects of Algeria historical. London, 1912.
Afr 2209.12.3 Bonand, R. de. La France de l'Afrique du nord. Paris, 1912.
Afr 2209.12.7 Betham-Edwards, M. In French-Africa. Scenes and memories. London, 1912.
Afr 2209.12.9 Brieux, E. Algérie. Vincennes, 1912.
Afr 2209.12.15 Schmitthenner, H. Tunisien und Algerien. Stuttgart, 1924.
Afr 2209.13 Lara, Juan F. de. De Madrid a Uxda. Madrid, 1913.
Afr 2209.14 Gennep, A. van. En Algérie. Paris, 1914.
Afr 2209.14.3 Lavion, H. L'Algérie musulmane. Paris, 1914.
Afr 2209.14.5 Stott, M.D. The real Algeria. London, 1914.
Afr 2209.14.10 Gennep, A. van. En Algérie. Paris, 1914.
Afr 2209.20F Bovet, Marie A. L'Algérie. Paris, 1920.
Afr 2209.20.5 Ward, Emily. Three travellers in North Africa. London, 1921.
Afr 2209.21 Warren, Lady. Through Algeria and Tunisia on a motor-bicycle. Boston, 1923.
Afr 2209.22.10 Casserly, Gordon. Algeria to-day. London, 1922.
Afr 2209.26 Wilson, Albert. Rambles in North Africa. Boston, 1926.
Afr 2209.27 Gajon, Edmond. En Algérie avec la France. Paris, 1927.
Afr 2209.27.5 Hafsa. Desert winds. N.Y., 1927.
Afr 2209.27.10 Bodley, R.V.C. Algeria from within. London, 1927.
Afr 2209.27.34 Ossendowski, F.A. Oasis and simoon. N.Y., 1927.
Afr 2209.27.35 Chevrillon, A. Les puritains du désert. Paris, 1927.
Afr 2209.27.40 Algerian State Railways. The mountain, the sea, Roman ruins, the desert. Algiers, 1927.
Afr 2209.28 Kerr, Alfred. Die Allgier trieb nach Algier...Ausflug nach Afrika. 1.Aufl. Berlin, 1929.
Afr 2209.31 Malo, Pierre. Palmes et burnous. Paris, 1931.
Afr 2209.31.5 Dumas, Pierre. L'Algérie. Grenoble, 1931.
Afr 2209.31.10 Bernard, A. L'Algérie. Paris, 1931.
Afr 2209.31.15 Bernard, A. L'Algérie. Paris, 1931.
Afr 2209.33 Arnaud, R. Les compagnons du jardin. Paris, 1933.
Afr 2209.34F Horizons de France, Paris. Algérie. Paris, 1934.
Afr 2209.35.4 Henriot, Emile. Vers l'oasis, en Algérie. Paris, 1935.
Afr 2209.35.10 Berenson, Mary. Across the Mediterranean. Prato, 1935.
Afr 2209.36 Faci, S. L'Algérie sous l'égide de la France contre la féodalité algérienne. Toulouse, 1936.
Afr 2209.36.5 Sheridan, C.F. Arab interlude. London, 1936.
Afr 2209.36.10 Stuart, B. Adventure in Algeria. London, 1936.
Afr 2209.37F Algeria. Les arts et la technique moderne. Algérie, 1937.
Afr 2209.37.5 Berque, A. L'Algérie, terre d'art et d'histoire. Alger, 1937.
Afr 2209.37.10 Lespes, René. Pour comprendre l'Algérie. Alger, 1937.
Afr 2209.44 Collier, Joy. Algerian adventure. London, 1944.
Afr 2209.44.5 Great Britain. Naval Intelligence Division. Algeria. v.2. London, 1944.
Afr 2209.48 Blottière, J.E. L'Algérie. Paris, 1948.
Afr 2209.54 Encyclopédie Mensuelle d'Outre-Mer. Algérie 54. Paris, 1954.
Afr 2209.55 Blottière, J.E. L'Algérie. 2. ed. Paris, 1955.
Afr 2209.55.5 Charbonneau, Jean. Des Africains s'interrogent. Paris, 1955.
Afr 2209.56 Service de Propagande, d'Edition et d'Information, Paris. A survey of Algeria. Paris, 1956.
Afr 2209.57 Marcais, Georges. Algérie médiévale. Paris, 1957.
Afr 2209.57.5 Algeria. Cabinet du Gouverneur Général. Algérie. Alger, 1957.
Afr 2209.57.10 Initiation à l'Algérie. Paris, 1957.
Afr 2209.58 Olivier, Claude. Institutrice en Algérie. Paris, 1958.

Afr 2205 - 2210 Algeria - Geography, description, etc. - General works (by date) - cont.

Afr 2209.58.5 France. Délégation Générale en Algérie. Documents algériens. Paris, 1958.
Afr 2209.58.10 Laurent, Jacques. L'Algérie. Paris, 1958.
Afr 2209.59 Davezies, Robert. Le front. Paris, 1959.
Afr 2209.60 Algeria. Délégation Générale du Gouvernement en Algérie. Algerian documents, 1960. Paris, 1960.
Afr 2209.60.5 Muslim Students Federation. Life in Algeria. 3 ed. London, 1960.
Afr 2209.61 Secrétariat Social d'Alger. De l'Algérie originelle à l'Algérie moderne. Alger, 1961.
Afr 2209.61.5 Descloitres, R. L'Algérie des Bidonvilles. Paris, 1961.
Afr 2209.61.10 Saadia. L'aliénation colonialiste et la résistance de la famille algérienne. Lausanne, 1961.
Afr 2209.61.20 Algeria. Conseil Supérieur de la Promotion Sociale en Algérie. Compte rendu analytique de la troisième session. Alger, 1961.
Afr 2209.62 Servier, J. Les poètes de l'année, rites et symboles. Paris, 1962.
Afr 2209.63 Boyer, P. La vie quotidienne à Alger à la veille de l'intervention française. Paris, 1963.
Afr 2209.65 Castel, Robert. Inoubliable Algérie. Paris, 1965.
Afr 2209.66 Gohier, Jacques. Instructeur en Algérie. Rodez, 1966.
Afr 2209.66.5 Joret, Madeleine. L'Afrique en flânant, de Paris à Tamanrasset. Paris, 1966.

Afr 2218 Algeria - Geography, description, etc. - Special customs

Afr 2218.5 Gaudefroy-Demombynes, M. Notes de sociologie maghrébine. Paris, 1901.
Afr 2218.6 Gaudry, Mathéa. La société féminine au Djebel amour et au Ksel. Alger, 1961.
Afr 2218.6.10 Mrabet, F. La femme algérienne. Paris, 1964.
Afr 2218.6.15A Gordon, David C. Women of Algeria; an essay on change. Cambridge, 1968.
Afr 2218.6.15B Gordon, David C. Women of Algeria; an essay on change. Cambridge, 1968.
Afr 2218.6.20 M'rabet, Fadéla. Les Algériennes. Paris, 1967.
Afr 2218.8 Frère, Suzanne. Sons et images dans le bled algérien. Alger, 1961.
Afr 2218.9 Bouteméne, Yahia. La Zaouia des Ouled Sidi Bénamar près de Nédroma. Tlemcen, 1950.
Afr 2218.10 Neveu, Edouard. Les Khouan. 3. ed. Alger, 1913.
Afr 2218.11 Charnay, Jean Paul. La vie musulmane en Algérie d'aprés la jurisprudence de la premiére moitié du XXe siècle. Paris, 1965.
Afr 2218.12 Desparment, Joseph. Coutumes, institutions, croyances, des indigénes de l'Algérie. Alger, 1939.

Afr 2220 Algeria - Geography, description, etc. - Guidebooks

Afr 2220.1 Quetin. Guide du voyage en Algérie. Paris, 1847.
Afr 2220.2 Bodichon, E. Guide book. London, 1858.
Afr 2220.3 Piesse, L. Itinéraire de l'Algérie. Paris, 1862.
Afr 2220.4 Barbier, J. Itinéraire...de l'Algérie. Paris, 1855.
Afr 2220.5 Piesse, L. Itinéraire de l'Algérie. Paris, 1881.
Afr 2220.6 Piesse, L. Itinéraire de l'Algérie. Paris, 1885.
Afr 2220.7 Joanne, P. Algérie et Tunisie. Paris, 1911.
Afr 2220.10 Celarie, Henriette. Un mois en Algérie et en Tunisie. Paris, 1924.
Afr 2220.12 Monmarche, Marcel. Algérie, Tunisie. Paris, 1923.
Afr 2220.12.3 Monmarche, Marcel. Algérie, Tunisie. Paris, 1930.
Afr 2220.12.5 Heywood, C. Algeria and Tunisia. Paris, 1926.
Afr 2220.14 Algérie, Tunisie. Paris, 1955.

Afr 2221 Algeria - Geography, description, etc. - Views

Afr 2221.2 Algeria, a synthesis of civilizations. n.p., 1961.
Afr 2221.3F Algeria. Service de l'Information. Direction de la Documentation Générale. Aspects of Algeria. Algiers. 196-.

Afr 2223.1 - .199 Algeria - Economic history and conditions - General works

Afr 2223.5 Algeria. Service de la Statistique Générale. Tableaux de l'économie algérienne. 1960+
Afr 2223.10 Caisse d'Equipement pour le Développement de l'Algérie. Programme d'équipement. Alger. 1960+
Afr 2223.25 Dessoliers, F.L. L'Algérie libre, étude économique sur l'Algérie. Alger, 1895.
Afr 2223.35 Schanz, M. Algerien, Tunesien, Tripolitanien. Halle, 1905.
Afr 2223.36 Macquart, E. Les réalités algériennes. Blida, 1906.
Afr 2223.38 France. Chambre des Députés (1908). Rapport fait...budget spécial de l'Algérie. v.1-2. Paris, 1908.
Afr 2223.52 Demontes, V. Renseignements sur l'Algérie économique. Paris, 1922.
Afr 2223.55 Société des Fermes Françaises de Tunisie. Vingt-cinq ans de colonisation nord-africaine. Paris, 1925.
Afr 2223.57 Société des Fermes Françaises de Tunisie. Trente-deux ans de colonisation nord-africaine. Paris, 1931.
Afr 2223.60 Dobrenn, Rene. L'apport économique de l'Algérie pendant la guerre. Thèse. Oran, 1925.
Afr 2223.65 Algeria. Direction de l'Agriculture, du Commerce et de l'Industrie. Notes sur la vie commerciale et industrielle de l'Algérie en 1923-1924. Alger, 1924.

Afr 2223.500 - .999 Algeria - Economic history and conditions - Contemporary works (By date)

Afr 2223.916 Desroches, G. Pour s'enrichir en Algérie. Paris, 1916.
Afr 2223.922 Falck, Felix. Guide économique de l'Algérie. Paris, 1922.
Afr 2223.922.5 Algeria. Direction de l agriculture du commerce et de la colonisation. Miscellaneous publications.
Afr 2223.924.5 Juving, Alex. Le socialisme en Algérie. Thèse. Alger, 1924.
Afr 2223.925 Jones, C.L. Algeria, a commercial handbook. Washington, 1925.
Afr 2223.930 Selnet, F.P.V. Colonisation officielle et crédit agricole en Algérie. Thèse. Alger, 1930.
Afr 2223.930.5 Falck, Felix. L'Algérie, un siécle de colonisation française. Paris, 1930.
Afr 2223.931 Desfeuilles, P. L'Algérie. Paris, 1931.
Afr 2223.933 Münnich, H. Der Verkehr Algeriens-Tunesiens mit Frankreich. Inaug. Diss. Leipzig, 1933.
Afr 2223.938 Pasquier Bronde, P.M.E. La coopération et les fellahs algériens. Thèse. Alger, 1938.
Afr 2223.940 Apiotti, Angelo. Sei milioni di affamati. Milan, 1940.
Afr 2223.950 Saint Germes, Jean. Economie algérienne. Alger, 1950.
Afr 2223.950.2 Saint Germes, Jean. Economie algérienne. Alger, 1955. 2 pam.

Afr 2223.500 - .999   Algeria - Economic history and conditions -
Contemporary works (By date) - cont.

Afr 2223.954   France. Commission d'Etude et de Coordination des Plans. Deuxiéme plan de modernisation. n.p., 1954.

Afr 2223.957   Dalmulder, J.J.J. De economische problematiek van Algerije. Leiden, 1957.

Afr 2223.957.5   France. Embassy. Algeria at work. N.Y., 1957.

Afr 2223.958   Algérie française. Sidi-bel-Abbès, 1958.

Afr 2223.958.5   Algeria. Perspectives décennales de développement économique de l'Algérie. Alger, 1958.

Afr 2223.959   Secrétariat Social d'Alger. Le sous-développement en Algérie. Alger, 1959.

Afr 2223.959.2   Secrétariat Social d'Alger. La micro-industrie. Alger, 1959.

Afr 2223.959.5   Dumoulin, Roger. La structure asymétrique de l'économie algérienne. Paris, 1959.

Afr 2223.960   Algeria. Conseil Supérieur de la Promotion Sociale en Algérie. Pour une promotion dans la coopération. Alger, 1960.

Afr 2223.960.5   Banque Nationale pour le Commerce et l'Industrie, Algiers. Les entreprises industrielles en Algérie et au Sahara. Alger, 1960.

Afr 2223.960.10   Algeria. Secrétariat Général Adjoint pour les Affaires Economiques. Leé comptes économiques de l'Algérie et du Sahara pour les années 1957 et 1958. Alger, 1960.

Afr 2223.960.15   Algeria. Caisse D'Equipement pour Le Développement de l'Algérie. Rapport sur l'exécution du programme d'équipement de l'Algérie en 1960. Alger, 1961.

Afr 2223.960.20   Algeria. Direction du Plan et des Etudes Economiques. Plan de Constantine, 1959-1963. Alger, 1960.

Afr 2223.961   Secretariat Social d'Alger. Les commissaires du développement. Alger, 1961.

Afr 2223.961.5   Association pour la Recherche. La consommation des familles d'Algérie. Paris, 1961.

Afr 2223.961.10   Vaucher, G. Le plan de Constantine et la République Algérienne de demain. Neuchâtel, 1961.

Afr 2223.961.15   France. Embassy. United States. The Constantine plan for Algeria, opening new frontiers in development. N.Y., 1961.

Afr 2223.962   Cercle Taleb-Moumié. Fidel Castro ou tshombe? Paris, 1962.

Afr 2223.962.5   Jeanson, F. La révolution algérienne. Milano, 1962.

Afr 2223.963   Launay, M. Paysans algériens. Paris, 1963.

Afr 2223.963.5   Paris. Université. Institut d'Etudes du Développement, etc. Problèmes de l'Algérie indépendante. Paris, 1963.

Afr 2223.964   Pawera, J.C. Algeria's infrastruture. N.Y., 1964.

Afr 2223.965   Arcy, François d'. Essais sur l'économie de l'Algérie nouvelle. Paris, 1965.

VAfr 2223.966   Alžir. Beograd, 1966.

Afr 2224.1 - .199   Algeria - Finance - General works

Afr 2224.20   Delmonte, Fabien R.S. Les pouvoirs financiers des assemblées algériennes et le contrôle de la métropole. Thèse. Alger, 1923.

Afr 2224.25   Common, Jacques. Le budget et le fisc algériens. Thèse. Paris, 1929.

Afr 2224.30   Peraldi, Geo. L'organisation financiére de l'Algérie du nord. Thèse. Alger, 1930.

Afr 2224.500 - .999   Algeria - Finance - Contemporary works (By date)

Afr 2224.862   Algeria. Commission à l'Exposition Universelle de Londres. L'Algérie à l'Exposition universelle de Londres, 1862. Alger, 1862. 2v.

Afr 2224.865   Leblanc de Prebois, F. Bilan de l'Algérie à la fin de l'an 1864 ou de la crise financiére commerciale et agricole. Alger, 1865.

Afr 2224.899   Bonzom, Lucien. Du régime fiscal en Algérie. Paris, 1899.

Afr 2224.922   Capot de Quissac. Le budget spécial de l'Algérie. Thèse. Paris, 1922.

Afr 2224.922.2   Capot de Quissac. Le budget spécial de l'Algérie. Paris, 1922.

Afr 2224.929   Lejeune, André. Le role du crédit dans le développement économique de l'Algérie depuis la fin de la guerre. Thèse. Paris, 1930.

Afr 2224.939   Houdiard, Y. Les problèmes financiers du Protectorat tunisien. Thèse. Paris, 1939.

Afr 2224.961   Cumunel, G. Guide administratif. Paris, 1961.

Afr 2224.961.2   Cumunel, G. Guide administratif. Mise à jour au 15. juin 1961. Paris, 1961.

Afr 2224.962   Lubell, Harold. A note on the national accounts of Algeria, 1950-1959 and 1964. Santa Monica, Calif., 1962.

Afr 2225   Algeria - Races - General works

Afr 2225.1   Pamphlet vol. Algeria. Races. General. 9 pam.

Afr 2225.2   Houdas, O. Ethnographie de l'Algérie. Paris, 1886.

Afr 2225.3   Drapier, H. La condition sociale des indigènes algériens. Paris, 1899.

Afr 2225.4   Lacroix, Bernardo. L'évolution du nomadisme en Algérie. Alger, 1906.

Afr 2225.5   Hamet, I. Les Musulmans français du nord de l'Afrique. Paris, 1906.

Afr 2225.9   Mercier, E. La question indigène en Algérie au commencement du XXe siècle. Paris, 1901.

Afr 2225.11   Azan, Paul J.L. Recherche d'une solution de la question indigène en Algérie. Paris, 1903.

Afr 2225.14   Bourdieu, Pierre. Sociologie de l'Algérie. 1. ed. Paris, 1958.

Afr 2225.14.5   Bourdieu, Pierre. The Algerians. Boston, 1962.

Afr 2225.16   Roger, J.J. Les Musulmans algériens en France et dans les pays islamiques. Paris, 1950.

Afr 2225.18   Muracciole, Luc. L'émigration algérienne. Alger, 1950.

Afr 2225.20   Pautard, André. Mohammed, l'Algérien mon ami. Paris, 1962.

Afr 2225.22   Mazuni, Abd Allah. Culture et enseignement en Algérie et au Maghreb. Paris, 1969.

Afr 2228   Algeria - Races - African and Asiatic elements - Arabs

Afr 2228.2.3   Richard, C. Scénes de moeurs arabes. 3e ed. Paris, 1876.

Afr 2228.3   Hugonnet, F. Souvenirs d'un chef de bureau arabe. Paris, 1858.

Afr 2228.4   Caix de St. Aymour, A. de. Arabes et Kabyles. Paris, 1891.

Afr 2228.5   Mule, A. Chez les Moumenins. Paris, 1906.

Afr 2228.6   Guimet, E. Arabes et Kabyles. Lyon, 1873.

Afr 2228.7   Robert, A. L'arabe tel qu'il est. Alger, 1900.

Afr 2228.8   Daumas, E. La vie arabe et la société musulmane. Paris, 1869.

Afr 2228.9   Auclert, Hubertine. Les femmes arabes. Paris, 1900.

Afr 2228   Algeria - Races - African and Asiatic elements - Arabs - cont.

Afr 2228.10   Marchand, Henri. La musulmane algérienne. Rodez, 1960.

Afr 2230   Algeria - Races - African and Asiatic elements - Berbers and Kabyles

Afr 2230.1   Excursion dans la Haute Kabylie. Alger, 1859.

Afr 2230.2   Hanoteau, A. La Kabylie et les coutumes kabyles. Paris, 1873. 3v.

Afr 2230.3   Lionel, J. Kabylie du Jurjura. Paris, 1892.

Afr 2230.4   Devaux, C. Les Kebailes du Djerdjera. Marseille, 1859.

Afr 2230.5   Wilkin, A. Among the Berbers of Algeria. London, 1900.

Afr 2230.6   Colonization de la Kabylie. Alger, 1871.

Afr 2230.7   Aucapitaine, H. Les Kabyles. Paris, 1864.

Afr 2230.8   Vilbort, J. En Kabylie. Paris, 1875.

Afr 2230.9   Pamphlet vol. Algeria. Races. 8 pam.

Afr 2230.9.5   Monglave, E. de. La Kabylie. n.p., n.d.

Afr 2230.10   Hun, F. Promenades...chez les Kabyles. Alger, 1860.

Afr 2230.11   Farine, Charles. Kabyles et Kroumirs. Paris, 1882.

Afr 2230.12   Berbrugger, A. Les époques militaires de la Grande Kabilie. Paris, 1857.

Afr 2230.13   Kabylie. Paris, 1846.

Afr 2230.14   Aucapitaine, H. Les confins militaires de la Grande Kabylie. Paris, 1857.

Afr 2230.15   Fabre, C. Grand Kabylie, légendes and souvenirs. Paris, 1901.

Afr 2230.16   Violard, Emile. Le banditisme en Kabylie. Paris, 1895.

Afr 2230.17   Barclay, E. Mountain life in Algeria. London, 1882.

Afr 2230.18   Drouet, F. Grande-Kabylie. Les Beni Yenni. Rouen, 1887.

Afr 2230.19F   Charveriat, F. A travers la Kabylie. n.p., n.d.

Afr 2230.20   Leroy, J. Deux ans de séjour en Petite Kabilie. Paris, 1911.

Afr 2230.21   Geniaux, Charles. Sous les figuiers de Kabylie. Paris, 1917.

Afr 2230.22F   Randall-MacIver, D. Libyan notes. London, 1901.

Afr 2230.23   Pharaon, J. Les Cabiles et Boudjie. Alger, 1835.

Afr 2230.30   Hilton-Simpson, M.W. Among the hill-folk of Algeria. London, 1921.

Afr 2230.35   Gaudry, Mathéa. La femme Chaouia de l'Aurès. Thèse. Paris, 1928.

Afr 2230.38   Ait Ahmed, Hocine. La guerre et l'après-guerre. Paris, 1964.

Afr 2230.40   Remond, Martial. Au coeur du pays kabyle. Alger, 1933.

Afr 2230.41   Lacoste, Camille. Bibliographie ethnologique de la Grande Kabylie. Paris, 1962.

Afr 2230.42   Sas, Pierre. Vie d'un peuple mort. Paris, 1961.

Afr 2230.43   Wysner, Glora May. The Kabyle people. N.Y., 1945.

Afr 2230.44   Feraoun, Mouloud. Jours de Kabylie. (Dessins de Brouty). Paris, 1968.

Afr 2232   Algeria - Races - African and Asiatic elements - The Mzab

Afr 2232.1   Robin. Le Mzab et son annexion. Alger, 1884.

Afr 2232.2   Amat, C. Le Mzab et les Mzabites. Paris, 1888.

Afr 2232.3A   Coyne, A. Le Mzab. Alger, 1879.

Afr 2232.3B   Coyne, A. Le Mzab. Alger, 1879.

Afr 2232.4   Mercier, Marcel. La civilisation urbaine au Mzab. Alger, 1922.

Afr 2232.8   Goichon, A. La vie féminine au Mzab. Paris, 1927. 2v.

Afr 2235   Algeria - Races - African and Asiatic elements - Moors in towns

Afr 2235.1   Morelet. Les Maures de Constantine. Dijon, 1876.

Afr 2235.42   Brauner, Siegmund. Lohrbuch der Hausa-Sprache. München, 1966.

Afr 2248   Algeria - Races - African and Asiatic elements - Others

Afr 2248.5   Cauneille, A. Les Chaanba (leur nomadisme). Paris, 1968.

Afr 2248.10   Regnier, Yves. Les Chaamba sous le régime français, leure transformation. Thèse. Paris, 1938.

Afr 2248.15   Centre d'Etudes et d'Informations des Problèmes Humaines dans les Zones Arides. Les Mekhadma. Paris, 1960.

Afr 2250   Algeria - Races - European elements and colonization - General works

Afr 2250.01   Pamphlet box. Colonization in Algeria.

Afr 2250.1   Baudicour, L. Histoire de la colonization de l'Agérie. Paris, 1860.

Afr 2250.2   Lenormand, J. Le peril étranger. 2e ed. Paris, 1899.

Afr 2250.3   Demontes, V. Le peuple algérien. Alger, 1906.

Afr 2250.5   Yacono, Xavier. La colonisation des plaines du Chélif. Alger, 1955-56. 2v.

Afr 2250.6   Millet, Jean. La coexistence des communautés en Algérie. Aix-en-Provence, 1962.

Afr 2260   Algeria - Races - European elements and colonization - French

Afr 2260.1   Cazenave, J. La colonization en Algérie. Alger, 1900.

Afr 2260.2   Cosentino. L'Algérie en 1865. Paris, 1865.

Afr 2260.3   Lamoriciére. Projets de colonization. Paris, 1847.

Afr 2260.4   Preaux. Réflexions sur la colonization. Paris, 1832.

Afr 2260.5   Pamphlet vol. Algeria. Races. 8 pam.

Afr 2260.6   Pamphlet vol. Algeria. Races. 10 pam.

Afr 2260.7   Bugeaud, M. De l'établissement de légions de colons. Paris, 1838.

Afr 2260.8   Lasnavères. De l'impossibilité de fonder des colonies...en Algérie. Paris, 1866.

Afr 2260.9   Clauzel, B. Observations...sur quelques actes. Paris, 1831.

Afr 2260.10   Vian, L. L'Algérie contemporaine. Paris, 1863.

Afr 2260.11   Mohr, P. Algerien, eine Studie über die Französische Land- und Siedelungspolitik. Berlin, 1907.

Afr 2260.12   Booms, P.G. Studien over Algerie. 's-Gravenhage, 1878.

Afr 2260.13   Piquet, V. La colonisation française dans l'Afrique du nord. Paris, 1912.

Afr 2260.13.3   Piquet, V. La colonisation française dans l'Afrique du nord. Paris, 1914.

Afr 2260.15   Vignon, L. La France en Algérie. Paris, 1893.

Afr 2260.16   René-Eugène, P. Les grandes sociétés et la colonisation dans l'Afrique du Nord. Thèse. Alger, 1925.

Afr 2260.17   Pieds-noirs et la presse française. Paris, 1962.

Afr 2260.18   Tiquet, J.E.P. Une expérience de petite colonisation indigène en Algérie. Thèse. Maison-Carrée, 1936.

Afr 2260.20   Nora, Pierre. Les français d'Algérie. Paris, 1961.

Afr 2260.22   Suffert, Georges. Les perspectives d'emploi des européens en Algérie. Paris, 1961.

Afr 2260.24   Ducrocq, Michel. Notre Algérie. Paris, 1962.

Afr 2260.25   Figueras, André. Les pieds noirs dans le plat. Paris, 1962.

Afr 2260.26   Dessaigne, Francine. Déraciné. Paris, 1964.

Afr 2260.27   Le droit à indemnisation des Français d'Algérie atteints par des mesures de dépossession. Paris, 1965.

Afr 2268   Algeria - Races - European elements and colonization - Italian
    Afr 2268.1   Loth, Gaston. Le peuplement italien en Tunisie et en
        Algérie. Paris, 1905.
    Afr 2268.3   Michel, E. Esuli italiani in Algeria, 1815-1861.
        Bologna, 1935.

Afr 2274   Algeria - Races - European elements and colonization - Others
    Afr 2274.1   Aumerat, J.F. L'anti-sémitisme à Alger. Alger, 1885.
    Afr 2274.3   Meynie, G. L'Algérie juive. Paris, 1887.
    Afr 2274.5   Martin, Claude. Les israélites algériens de 1830 à 1902.
        Thèse. Paris, 1936.

Afr 2280   Algeria - Provinces, etc. - Description by regions - The Tell and
Littoral
    Afr 2280.3   Fromentin, E. Une année dans le Sahel. 2d ed.
        Paris, 1859.
    Afr 2280.5   Fromentin, E. Une année dans le Sahel. 6th ed.
        Paris, 1884.
    Afr 2280.8   Martino, P. Les descriptions de Fromentin. Alger, 1910.
    Afr 2280.10   Franc, Julien. La colonisation de la Milidja. Thèse.
        Paris, 1928.
    Afr 2280.12   Roudaire, F.E. La mer intérieure africaine. Paris, 1883.

Afr 2283   Algeria - Provinces, etc. - Description by regions - The Plateau (incl.
Aures Mts.)
    Afr 2283.1   Lartigue, R. de. Monographie de l'Aurés.
        Constantine, 1904.
    Afr 2283.2   Stuhlmann, F. Ein kulturgeschichtlicher Ausflug in den
        Aures. Hamburg, 1912.
    Afr 2283.3   Keun, Odette. Les oasis dans la montagne. Paris, 1919.
    Afr 2283.4   Servier, Jean. Dans l'Aurès sur les pas des rébelles.
        Paris, 1955.

Afr 2285   Algeria - Provinces, etc. - Description by regions - The Desert
    Afr 2285.1   Sabatier, C. La question du sud-ouest. Alger, 1881.
    Afr 2285.2   Trumelet, C. Les français dans le désert. Paris, 1865.
    Afr 2285.3   Choisy, A. Le Sahara, souvenirs d'une mission à Goléah.
        Paris, 1881.
    Afr 2285.4   Soleillet, Paul. L'Afrique occidentale. Paris, 1877.
    Afr 2285.5   Daumas, E. Le Sahara algérien. Paris, 1845.
    Afr 2285.6   Largeau, V. Le pays de Rirha Quargla. Paris, 1879.
    Afr 2285.7   Champeaux, G. A travers les oasis sahariennes.
        Paris, 1903.
    Afr 2285.8   Watson, G. The voice of the south (Algeria).
        London, 1905.
    Afr 2285.9   Orpen, A.E. The chronicles of the Sid. N.Y., n.d.
    Afr 2285.10   Goblet D'Alviella. Sahara et Laponie. Paris, 1873.
    Afr 2285.12   Mackworth, C. The destiny of Isabelle Eberhardt.
        London, 1951.
    Afr 2285.12.5   Noel, Jean. Isabelle Eberhardt. Algers, 1961.
    Afr 2285.20   Hull, E.M. Camping in the Sahara. London, 1926.
    Afr 2285.21   The Paris Lyons and Mediterranean Railway Co.
        Algeria...season 1927-28. Algiers, 1927.
    Afr 2285.22   Kenny, H.T. In lightest Africa. London, 1935.
    Afr 2285.23   Gardi, René. Blue veils, red tents. London, 1953.
    Afr 2285.25   Skolle, John. Azalai. 1st ed. N.Y., 1956.
    Afr 2285.30   Dermenghem, Emile. Le pays d'Abel. Paris, 1960.
    Afr 2285.31   Vanney, Jean-René. Pluie et crue dans le Sahara
        nord-occidental. Alger, 1960.

Afr 2287   Algeria - Provinces, etc. - Administrative divisions - Northern
Territory
    Afr 2287.5   Brenot, H.E.L. Le douar. Alger, 1938.

Afr 2288   Algeria - Provinces, etc. - Administrative divisions - Southern
Territory
    Afr 2288.5   Algérie. Direction des Territoires du Sud. Les territoires
        du sud. Exposé de leur situation. (Extrait) Description
        géographique par E.-F. Gautier. Alger, 1922.
    Afr 2288.10   Thinières, A.F.C. Le régime de la répression dans les
        territoires du sud de l'Algérie. Thèse. Alger, 1928.
    Afr 2288.15   Algérie. Direction des Territoires du Sud. Les territoires
        du sud. Exposé de leur situation. Pt.1. Alger, 1922.
    Afr 2288.15.3   Algeria. Direction des Territoires du Sud. Les territoires
        du sud de l'Algérie. Alger, 1954.
    Afr 2288.15.5   Algeria. Commissariat Général du Centenaire. Les
        territoires du sud de l'Algérie. 2d ed. Pt.1-3,5 et cartes.
        Alger, 1929-30. 5v.

Afr 2290   Algeria - Provinces, etc. - Administrative divisions - Oran
    Afr 2290.1   Lacretelle, L. Etudes sur la province d'Oran.
        Marseille, 1865.
    Afr 2290.2   Association Française pour l'Avancement des Sciences. Oran
        et l'Algérie en 1887. Oran, 1888. 2v.
    Afr 2290.3   Leclerc, L. Les oasis de la province d'Oran. Alger, 1858.
    Afr 2290.4   Bourdonnaye. Le moral algérien. Paris, n.d.
    Afr 2290.5   Pimodan. Oran Tlemcen sud-oranais (1899-1900).
        Paris, 1903.
    Afr 2290.6   Barges, l'Abbé. Excursion à Sebdon. Paris, 1849.
    Afr 2290.8   Lambert, E. L'Algérie...deux mois dans province d'Oran.
        Paris, 1877.
    Afr 2290.10   Guillaume. Conquête du sud-oranais; la colonne d'Igli en
        1900. Paris, 1910.
    Afr 2290.12   Thurin, Guy. Le rôle agricole des espagnols en Oranie.
        Thèse. Lyon, 1937.

Afr 2295   Algeria - Provinces, etc. - Administrative divisions - Constantine
    Afr 2295.1   Lamalle, D. de. Province de Constantine. Paris, 1837.
    Afr 2295.2   Guyon. Voyage d'Alger aux Ziban (Text and atlas).
        Alger, 1852. 2v.
    Afr 2295.3   Duvivieu. Recherches...sur la portion de l'Algérie au sud
        de Guelnia. Paris, 1841.
    Afr 2295.5   Ragot, W. Le Sahara de la province de Constantine.
        Constantine, 1874-75.
    Afr 2295.7.3   Oasis de l'Oued Rir' en 1856 et 1880. 3e ed. Paris, 1881.
    Afr 2295.8   Bonnafont, Jean Pierre. Réflexions sur l'Algérie.
        Paris, 1846.

Afr 2300   Algeria - Cities, towns, etc. - General works
    Afr 2300.2   Davis, N. Ruined cities within Numidian and Carthaginian
        territories. London, 1862.
    Afr 2300.4   Masqueray, E. Formation des cités chez les populations
        sédentaires de l'Algérie. Paris, 1886.
    Afr 2300.6   Merlo, Manuel. Les personnels des communes algériennes.
        Blida, 1957.
    Afr 2300.8   Planhol, Xavier de. Nouveaux villages algérois.
        Paris, 1961.

Afr 2305   Algeria - Cities, towns, etc. - Adrar
    Afr 2305.1   Lapalud, P. Le douar Aghbal: monographie économique.
        Thèse. Alger, 1934.

Afr 2308   Algeria - Cities, towns, etc. - Algiers
    Afr 2308.1   Feydeau, E. Alger. Paris, 1862.
    Afr 2308.2   Seguin, L.G. Walks in Algiers. London, 1878.
    Afr 2308.3   Piesse, L. Alger et ses environs. Paris, 1901.
    Afr 2308.4   Pichon. Alger...son état présent et son avenir.
        Paris, 1833.
    Afr 2308.5   Montagne, D.J. Physiologie morale et physique d'Alger.
        Marseille, 1834.
    Afr 2308.6   Guiauchain, G. Alger. Alger-Mustapha, 1905.
    Afr 2308.7   Gifford, R. Relazione. Firenze, 1604.
    Afr 2308.8   Davies, E.W.L. Algiers in 1857. London, 1858.
    Afr 2308.9   Souvenir d'Alger...24 vues choisies. n.p., n.d.
    Afr 2308.10   Vieil Alger. n.p., n.d.
    Afr 2308.11   Gubb, A.S. Algiers as a winter resort. London, n.d.
    Afr 2308.12   Broughton. Six years residence in Algiers. London, 1839.
    Afr 2308.15   Melia, Jean. La ville blanche, Alger et son département.
        Paris, 1921.
    Afr 2308.16   Espel, Françoise. Alger. Paris, 1959.
    Afr 2308.17   Delvert, C.L. Le port d'Alger. Paris, 1923.
    Afr 2308.19   Baeza, H.L. Le rôle économique du port d'Alger. Thèse.
        Alger, 1924.
    Afr 2308.20   Laye, Yves. Le port d'Alger. Alger, 1951.
    Afr 2308.21   Algiers. Chambre de Commerce. Le port d'Alger,1930.
        Alger, 1930.
    Afr 2308.22   Janon, R. Hommes de peine et filles de joie. Alger, 1936.
    Afr 2308.23   Palais d'Eté, résidence du gouverneur général de l'Algérie.
        Alger, 194-

Afr 2310   Algeria - Cities, towns, etc. - A (Others)
    Afr 2310.1   Melix. Le stèle d'Abisae. n.p., n.d.
    Afr 2310.3   Despois, Jean. Le djebel amour. Paris, 1957.

Afr 2312   Algeria - Cities, towns, etc. - Biskra
    Afr 2312.1   Seriziat. Etudes sur l'oasis de Biskra. 2d ed.
        Paris, 1875.
    Afr 2312.2   Leeder, S.H. The desert gateway. London, 1910.
    Afr 2312.4   Hautfort, Felix. Au pays des palmes, Biskra. Paris, 1897.
    Afr 2312.4.2   Hautfort, Felix. Au pays des palmes, Biskra. 2e ed.
        Paris, 1897.
    Afr 2312.5   Heinke, Kurt. Monographie der algerischen Oase Biskra.
        Inaug. Diss. Halle, 1914.

Afr 2313   Algeria - Cities, towns, etc. - Blidah
    Afr 2313.1   Trumelet, C. Blida. v.1-2. Alger, 1887.
    Afr 2313.5   Ferrendier, M. La population musulmane de Blida. Thèse.
        Blois, 1928.

Afr 2315   Algeria - Cities, towns, etc. - Boufarik
    Afr 2315.1   Trumelet, C. Bou-Farik. 2e ed. Alger, 1887.
    Afr 2315.5   Gojon, Edmond. Cent ans d'effort français en Algérie.
        Paris, 1930.

Afr 2318   Algeria - Cities, towns, etc. - Constantine
    Afr 2318.1   Mercier, E. Constantine avant la conquête française.
        Constantine, 1879.
    Afr 2318.1.5   Mercier, E. Histoire de Constantine. Constantine, 1903.
    Afr 2318.1.10   Vaysseties, E. Histoire de Constantine.
        Constantine, 1869.
    Afr 2318.1.15   Antoine, L.F. Constantine, centre économique. Thèse.
        Toulouse, 1930.
    Afr 2318.1.20   Berthier, Andre. Constantine. Toulouse, 1965.

Afr 2326   Algeria - Cities, towns, etc. - F
    Afr 2326.5   Bresson, Gilbert. Histoire d'un centre rural algérien.
        Alger, 1957.

Afr 2331   Algeria - Cities, towns, etc. - Gourara
    Afr 2331.1   Motylinski, A. de C. Guerara depuis sa fondation.
        Alger, 1885.

Afr 2336   Algeria - Cities, towns, etc. - H
    Afr 2336.5   Dennis, H.V.M. Hippo Regius from the earliest times to the
        Arab conquest. Diss. Princeton, 1924.
    Afr 2336.5.5   Papier, Alexander. Lettres sur Hippone. Bone, 1887.
    Afr 2336.10   Despais, J. Le Hodna. 1. ed. Paris, 1953.

Afr 2344   Algeria - Cities, towns, etc. - Laghouat
    Afr 2344.10   Mangin, J.E. Notes sur l'histoire de Laghouat.
        Alger, 1895.

Afr 2345   Algeria - Cities, towns, etc. - L (Others)
    Afr 2345.5   Féraud, Charles. Histoire des villes de la province de
        Constantine. La Calle. Alger, 1877.
    Afr 2345.6   Notice...sur l'ancienne ville de Lamboese. Paris, 1860.

Afr 2352   Algeria - Cities, towns, etc. - M (Others)
    Afr 2352.1   Robert, M.A. La Kalaa et Tihamamine. Constantine, 1903.

Afr 2355   Algeria - Cities, towns, etc. - N (Others)
    Afr 2355.5   Basset, René. Nedromah et les Traras. Paris, 1901.

Afr 2357   Algeria - Cities, towns, etc. - Oran
    Afr 2357.5   Offrey, R. Oran-Mers-el-Kebir. Thèse. Bourg, 1938.
    Afr 2357.10   Villot, Roland. Jules Du Pré de Saint Maur. 2. ed.
        Oran, 1955.
    Afr 2357.15   Marchand, Max. Guide touristique de l'Oranie agréé par la
        municipalité. Oran, 1958.
    Afr 2357.20   Basset, René. Fastes chronologiques de la ville d'Oran.
        Paris, 1892.
    Afr 2357.25   Desmichels, L.A. Oran sous le commandement du général
        Desmichels. Paris, 1835.
    Afr 2357.26   Vulliez, Albert. Mers-el-Kebir. Paris, 1964.

Afr 2358   Algeria - Cities, towns, etc. - Orleansville
    Afr 2358.5   Debia, René Yves. Orléansville. Alger, 1955.

Afr 2360   Algeria - Cities, towns, etc. - O (Others)
    Afr 2360.1   Féraud, L. Monographie des Oulad-Ab-en-Nour.
        Constantine, 1864.

Afr	2362	**Algeria - Cities, towns, etc. - Philippeville**
	Afr 2362.5	Solal, Edouard. Philippeville et sa région. Alger, 1957.
Afr	2368	**Algeria - Cities, towns, etc. - S**
	Afr 2368.1	Bastide, L. Sidi-bel-Abbés et son arrondissement. Oran, 1881.
	Afr 2368.5	Société Historique et Géographique de la Région de Sétif. Bulletin. Sétif.
	Afr 2368.5.10	Février, Paul Albert. Fouilles de Sétif, les basiliques chrétiennes du quartier Nord-Ouest. Paris, 1965.
Afr	2370	**Algeria - Cities, towns, etc. - Tebessa**
	Afr 2370.1	Castel, P. Tébessa, histoire et description d'un territoireAlgérien. Paris, 1905. 2v.
Afr	2373	**Algeria - Cities, towns, etc. - Tlemcen**
	Afr 2373.1	Barbet, Charles. La perle du Maghreb (Tlemeen). Alger, n.d.
X Cg	Afr 2373.3	Piesse, Louis. Les villes de l'Algérie, Tlemcen. Paris, 1889. (Changed to XP 3867)
	Afr 2373.4	Marcais, Georges. Tlemcen. Paris, 1950.
	Afr 2373.5	Barges, J.J.L. Tlemcen, ancienne capitale du royaume. Paris, 1859.
	Afr 2373.10.2	Bel, Alfred. Tlemcen et ses environs. 2e ed. Toulouse, 192-
Afr	2374	**Algeria - Cities, towns, etc. - Touat**
	Afr 2374.1	Vivarez, M. Au sujet du Touat. Alger, 1896.
	Afr 2374.2	Martin, A.G.P. Les oasis sahariennes. Alger, 1908.
Afr	2376	**Algeria - Cities, towns, etc. - T (Others)**
	Afr 2376.1	Pein, T. Lettres familières sur l'Algérie (Tougourt). 2e ed. Alger, 1893.
	Afr 2376.2	Baader, Walter. Nach der Oase Tugurt in der Wüste Sahara. Basel, 1903.
	Afr 2376.5	Champault, Francine Dominique. Une oasis du Sahara nord-occidental: Tabelbala. Paris, 1969.
Afr	2386	**Algeria - Cities, towns, etc. - Z**
	Afr 2386.1	Harbillon, M. Relation du siège de Zaatcha. Paris, 1863.
Afr	2396	**Algeria - Biographies - Collected**
	Afr 2396.1	Trumelet, C. L'Algérie légendaire. Alger, 1892.
	Afr 2396.2	Algérie biographique. Sidi-bel-Abbès, 1956.
Afr	2397	**Algeria - Biographies - Individual**
	Afr 2397.1	Berbrugger, A. Geronimo. Alger, 1854.
	Afr 2397.2	Amrani, Djamal. Le témoin. Paris, 1960.
	Afr 2397.3	Beauvoir, Simone de. Djamila Boupacha. Paris, 1962.
	Afr 2397.3.2	Beauvoir, Simone de. Djamila Boupacha. 1st American ed. N.Y., 1962.
	Afr 2397.5	Dessagne, F. Journal d'une mère de famille pied-noir. Paris, 1962.
	Afr 2397.6	Bittari, Zoubeida. O mes soeurs musulmanes, pleurez Paris, 1964.
	Afr 2397.7	Pignal, Jacques. Maurice Cochard, mon ami. Toulouse, 1964.
	Afr 2397.8	Amrouche, Fadhma Aïth Mansour. Histoire de ma vie. Paris, 1968.
	Afr 2397.36	Hadj Ali, Bachir. L'Arbitraire. Paris, 1966.
Afr	2401 - 2424	**Tunisia - Periodicals (A-Z)**
	Afr 2403.5	Cahiers de Tunisie, revue de sciences humaines. Tunis. 5,1957+ 9v.
	Afr 2405.5	Ecole Nationale d'Administration, Tunis. Centre de Recherches et d'Etudes Administratives. Etudes et documents. Tunis. 2,1968+
	Afr 2409.5	I.B.L.A., revue de l'Institut des Belles Lettres Arabes. Tunis. 5,1942+ 28v.
	Afr 2418.1	Revue tunisienne. Tunis. 1,1894+ 36v.
	Afr 2418.2	Revue tunisienne de sciences sociales. Tunis. 3,1966+
	Afr 2418.2.2	Revue Tunisienne de Sciences Sociales. Index bibliographique. Tunis. 1964-1968
	Afr 2420.5	Tunis (City). Université. Faculté des Lettres et des Sciences Humaines. Publications. Histoire. 1,1961+ 6v.
	Afr 2420.10	Tunis (City). Université. Faculté des Lettres et des Sciences Humaines. Publications. Sources de l'histoire de la Tunisie. 3+ 3v.
	Afr 2420.15	Tunisia. Secrétariat d'Etat à l'Information. Etudes et documents. Tunis. 1,1959+
	Afr 2420.20	Tunisia. Secrétariat d'Etat à l'Information. Surveys and documents. Tunis. 1,1959+
	Afr 2420.25	Tunis (City). Université. Centre d'Etudes et de Recherches Economiques et Sociales. Cahiers du C.E.R.E.S. Série économique. Tunis. 1966+
	Afr 2420.26	Tunis (City). Université. Centre d'Etudes et de Recherches Economiques et Sociales. Cahiers du C.E.R.E.S. Série démographique. Tunis. 1,1967+
	Afr 2420.27	Tunis (City). Université. Centre d'Etudes et de Recherches Economiques et Sociales. Cahiers du C.E.R.E.S. Série sociologique. Tunis. 1,1968+
	Afr 2420.28	Tunis (City). Université. Centre d'Etudes et de Recherches Economiques et Sociales. Cahiers du C.E.R.E.S. Série géographique. Tunis. 1,1968+
	Afr 2420.30	Tunis (City). Université. Centre d'Etudes et de Recherches Economiques et Sociales. Cahiers du C.E.R.E.S. Série linguistique. Tunis. 1,1968+
Afr	2425	**Tunisia - Folios [Discontinued]**
	Afr 2425.1F	Lallemand, C. Tunis et ses environs. Paris, 1890.
Afr	2426	**Tunisia - Bibliographies**
	Afr 2426.5	Ashbee, H.S. A bibliography of Tunisia...to 1888. London, 1889.
	Afr 2426.10	Bennett, Norman Robert. A study guide for Tunisia. Boston, 1968.
Afr	2428	**Tunisia - Pamphlet volumes**
	Afr 2428	Pamphlet box. Tunis.
Afr	2430	**Tunisia - Collected source materials**
	Afr 2430.1F	France. Ministère des Affaires Etrangéres. Documents diplomatiques. Affaires de Tunisie, 1870-81, et supplément. Paris, 1881. 2v.
	Afr 2430.5F	Tunisia. Secrétariat d'Etat à l'Information. La documentation tunisienne. 1957+

Afr	2438	**Tunisia - Government and administration**
	Afr 2438.1	Fitoussi, Elie. L'état tunisien...1525-1901. Tunis, 1901.
	Afr 2438.1.25	Fitoussi, Elie. L'état tunisien et le protectorat français. Paris, 1931. 2v.
	Afr 2438.5	Tunis. Conférences sur les administrations tunisiennes, 1902. 2.ed. Sousse, 1902.
	Afr 2438.7	Demay, Jules. L'organisation des communes en Tunisie. Tunis, 1915.
	Afr 2438.8	Richon, Jean. Le contentieux administratif en Tunisie. Paris, 1916.
	Afr 2438.10	Genet, Jean. Etude comparative du protectorat tunisien et du protectorat marocain. Thèse. Paris, 1920.
	Afr 2438.12	Bismut, Victor. Essai sur la dualité législative et judiciaire en Tunisie. Dijon, 1922.
	Afr 2438.15	Winkler, Pierre. Essai sur la nationalité dans les protectorats de Tunisie et du Maroc. Thèse. Paris, 1926.
	Afr 2438.17	Aguesse, L.C.P. Le problème de la nationalité en Tunisie. Thèse. Paris, 1930.
	Afr 2438.19	Scemama, A. De l'influence du mariage sur la nationalité tunisienne. Thèse. Paris, 1931.
	Afr 2438.21	Jung, Eugene. Les réformes en Tunisie. Paris, 1926.
	Afr 2438.23	Guiga, Bahri. Essai sur l'évolution du Charaa et son application judiciaire en Tunisie. Thèse. Paris, 1930.
	Afr 2438.25	Pinon, J.P.M. Les attributions des contrôleurs civils en Tunisie. Thèse. Tunis, 1931.
	Afr 2438.30	Saada, Raoul. Essai sur l'oeuvre de la justice française en Tunisie. Paris, 1928.
	Afr 2438.32	Snoussi, Mohamed. Les collectivités locales en Tunisie. Paris, 1958.
	Afr 2438.35	Tunisia. Constitution. Constitution of the Tunisian Republic. Tunis, 1959.
Afr	2442	**Tunisia - General politics, political parties**
	Afr 2442.2	Tunisia. Secrétariat d'Etat à l'Information. Les congrès du Néo-Destour. Tunis, 1959.
	Afr 2442.5	Néo-Destour Congrès, 7th, Bizerte. Septième congrès. Tunis, 1965.
Afr	2446	**Tunisia - Military affairs**
	Afr 2446.5	Varloud. La Tunisie d'il y a cinquante ans. Paris, 1932.
Afr	2448	**Tunisia - Naval affairs**
	Afr 2448.5	Grandchamp, P. Documents relatifs aux corsaires tunisiens (2 octobre 1777-4 mai 1824). Tunis, 1925.
Afr	2455 - 2460	**Tunisia - General history (By date)**
	Afr 2458.38	Niculy, G. Documenti sulla storia di Tunis. Livorno, 1863.
	Afr 2458.83	Clarin de la Rive, Abel. Histoire générale de la Tunisie. Tunis, 1883.
	Afr 2458.93	Faucon, N. La Tunisie. Paris, 1893. 2v.
	Afr 2458.94	Pavy, A. Histoire de Tunis. Tours, 1894.
	Afr 2458.98	Loth, Gaston. Histoire de la Tunisie. Paris, 1898.
	Afr 2459.38	Pellegrin, A. Histoire de la Tunisie depuis les origines jusqu'à nos jours. Paris, 1938.
	Afr 2459.48	Cambon, H. Histoire de la régence de Tunis. Paris, 1948.
	Afr 2459.52F	Encyclopédie Mensuelle d'Outre-Mer. Tunisie 53. Paris, 1952.
	Afr 2459.53F	Encyclopédie Mensuelle d'Outre-Mer. Tunisie 54. Paris, 1953.
	Afr 2459.60	Histoire de la Tunisie. Tunis, 196-?
	Afr 2459.62	Ziadeh, N.A. Origins of nationalism in Tunisia. Beirut, 1962.
	Afr 2459.69	Sylvester, Anthony. Tunisia. London, 1969.
Afr	2475	**Tunisia - History by periods - To 16th century - Hafside dynasty (1236-1574) - General works**
	Afr 2475.5	Cusson, C. Histoire du royaume de Tunis. Oran, 1863.
Afr	2480	**Tunisia - History by periods - To 16th century - Hafside dynasty (1236-1574) - English siege of Mahdiya (1390)**
	Afr 2480.5	Mirot, Leon. Une expédition française en Tunisie au XIVe siècle. Paris, 1932.
Afr	2482	**Tunisia - History by periods - To 16th century - Hafside dynasty (1236-1574) - Other special topics**
	Afr 2482.5	Marengo, E. Genova e Tunisi, 1388-1515. Roma, 1901.
	Afr 2482.10	Brunschvig, R. La Berbèrie orientale sous les Hafsides. Paris, 1940-47. 2v.
	Afr 2484.4	Breve, ma distintissima relatione della conversione alla Santa Fede del primogenito del re di Tunisi, Mamet Celebi hoggi detto D. Filippo Dai. Roma, 1646.
Afr	2485	**Tunisia - History by periods - 16th century to 1819 - General works**
	Afr 2485.1	Rousseau, A. Anales tunisiennes. Alger, 1864.
	Afr 2485.5	Grandchamp, P. La France en Tunisie. Tunis, 1920-33. 10v.
Afr	2489	**Tunisia - History by periods - 16th century to 1819 - Turkish conquest (1573)**
	Afr 2489.1	Serbellone, G. Serbellone a Tunisi. Sierra, 1880.
Htn	Afr 2489.2*	Floriani, Pompeo. Discorso della Goletta. Macerata, 1574.
	Afr 2489.3	Garzia, G.D. Vera relazione copia di lettera scritta. Venezia, 1677.
	Afr 2489.4	Relation de la prise de Tunis et de La Goulette par les troupes ottomanes en 981 de l'Hégire. Alger, 1845.
Afr	2494	**Tunisia - History by periods - 16th century to 1819 - 1580-1705 - General works**
Htn	Afr 2494.5*	Great Britain and Tunis. Articles of peace betwixt Charles II and Mahamet of Tunis and Osman. Tripoli. 5 october, 1662. n.p., 1662.
	Afr 2494.7	Generoso corsario. Lisboa, 1821.
	Afr 2494.10	Grandchamp, P. La France en Tunisie à la fin du XVIe siècle. Tunis, 1920.
Afr	2498	**Tunisia - History by periods - 16th century to 1819 - 1702-1819 (Decadence of piracy) - General works**
	Afr 2498.1	Arnoldo Soler...et sa correspondance. Tunis, 1905.
	Afr 2498.15	Noticia da festividade que na ilha de Malta se celebrou no baptismo do rey de Tunes. Lisboa, 1757.
	Afr 2498.16	Relaçam da tragica morte do novo rey de Tunes. Lisboa, 1757.

Afr 2500 **Tunisia - History by periods - 16th century to 1819 - 1702-1819 (Decadence of piracy) - Relations with France**
Afr 2500.1 Plantet, E. Correspondance des beys de Tunis. Paris, 1893-4. 3v.
Afr 2500.10 Poiron, M. Mémoires concernants l'état présent du Royaume de Tunis. Thèse complémentaire présentée par Jean Serres. Paris, 1925.
Afr 2500.10.2 Poiron, M. Mémoires concernants l'état présent du Royaume de Tunis. Paris, 1925.
Afr 2500.15 Fiennes, J.B. Une mission tunisienne à Paris en 1743. Tunis, 1931.
Afr 2500.20 Pleville-le-Pelley, G.R. La mission de Pleville-le-Pelley à Tunis, 1793-1794. Tunis, 1921.
Afr 2500.22 Gerin-Ricard, H. de. Etienne Famin et son vrai rôle diplomatique à Tunis,1795-1802. Tunis, 1905.

Afr 2505 **Tunisia - History by periods - 1819-1881 - General works**
Afr 2505.1 Carta, F. La questione tunisina e l'Europa. Roma, 1879.
Afr 2505.2 Prevost, F. La Tunisie devant l'Europe. Paris, 1862.
Afr 2505.5A Chiala, L. Tunisi. Torino, 1895.
Afr 2505.5B Chiala, L. Tunisi. Torino, 1895.
Afr 2505.10 Monchicourt, C. Relations inédites de Nyssen. Paris, 1929.
Afr 2505.18 Slama, Bice. L'insurrection de 1864 en Tunisie. Tunis, 1967.

Afr 2508 **Tunisia - History by periods - 1819-1881 - Relations with France**
Afr 2508.1 Estourneller de Constant, Paul. La politique française en Tunisie. Paris, 1891.
Afr 2508.2 Rouard de Card, E. La politique de la France. Toulouse, 1906.
Afr 2508.3 Hofstetter, Balthasar. Vorgeschichte des französischen Protektorats in Tunis. Bern, 1914.
Afr 2508.5 Foucher, Louis. De l'évolution du protectorat de la France sur la Tunisie. Thése. Paris, 1897.
Afr 2508.6 Desfosses, Edmond. Affaires d'orient, la question tunisienne. Paris, 1881.
Afr 2508.10 Langer, W.L. The European power and the French occupation of Tunis, 1878-1881. n.p., 1926.
Afr 2508.15 Mallon, Jean. L'influence française dans la régence de Tunis. Paris, 1931.
Afr 2508.20 Ganiage, Jean. Les origines du protectorat français en Tunisie, 1861-1881. 2ème éd. Tunis, 1968.

Afr 2510 **Tunisia - History by periods - 1819-1881 - Relations with Italy**
Afr 2510.1 Santi, F.L. Italia e Tunisi. Milano, 1881.
Afr 2510.5 Italy. Ministero degli Affari Esteri. Intorno ai provvedimenti relativi alla giurisdizione consolare italiana in Tunisia. Roma, 1884.
Afr 2510.10 Gallico, A. Tunisi e i consoli Sardi, 1816-1834. Bologna, 1935.
Afr 2510.15 Piano, Lorenzo del. La penetrazione italiana in Tunisia, 1861-1881. Padova, 1964.

Afr 2514 **Tunisia - History by periods - 1819-1881 - Relations with other powers**
Afr 2514.5 Grandchamp, P. Les différends de 1832-1833 entre la régence de Tunis et les royaumes de Sardaigne et des Deus-Siciles. Tunis, 1931.

Afr 2525 **Tunisia - History by periods - 1881-1956 - General works**
Afr 2525.2 Rouard de Card, E. La Turquie et le protectorat français. Paris, 1916.
Afr 2525.5 Giaccardi, A. La conquista di Tunisi. Milano, 1940.
Afr 2525.10 Huc, Paul. L'oeuvre politique et économique du protectorat français en Tunisie. Thèse. Toulouse, 1924.
Afr 2525.13 Ardenne de Tizao. Notre Tunisie. Paris, 1939.
Afr 2525.15 Marpurgo, G. Italia, Francia, Tunisia. Livorno, 1938.
Afr 2525.20 Villiers, G. Derriére le rideau tunisien. Paris, 1955.
Afr 2525.21 Nicaud, C.A. Tunisia. N.Y., 1964.

Afr 2527 **Tunisia - History by periods - 1881-1956 - French invasion (1881)**
NEDL Afr 2527.1 Broadley, A.M. Tunis, past and present. Edinburgh, 1882. 2v.
Afr 2527.2 Cealis, E. De Sousse à Gafsa. Lettres, 1881-84. Paris, n.d.
Afr 2527.3 Expédition militaire en Tunisia, 1881-82. Paris, n.d.
Afr 2527.5 Bois, M. Expédition française en Tunisie (1881-82). Paris, 1886.
Afr 2527.7 Benoyts, F. de. Au pays de Kroumers et au Maroc. Lille, 1913.

Afr 2530 **Tunisia - History by periods - 1881-1956 - 1882-1945 - General works**
Afr 2530.1 Bahar, J. Le protectorat tunisien. Paris, 1904.
Afr 2530.2 Parker, M. Les pêcheurs bretons en Tunisie. Paris, 1904.
Afr 2530.3 Tunisia. Secrétariat d'Etat à l'Information. Six mois de gouvernement Bourguiba. 4 pts. Tunis, 1956.
Afr 2530.5F France. Ministère des Affaires Etrangères. Documents diplomatiques. Paris, 1897.
Afr 2530.10 Dauphin, M. La conférence consultative tunisienne. Thèse. Paris, 1919.
Afr 2530.15 Tumedei, C. La questione tunisina e l'Italia. Bologna, 1922.
Afr 2530.17 Caniglia, R. Il dramma di Tunisi. Napoli, 1930.
Afr 2530.19 Gray, E.M. Noi e Tunisi. 4a ed. Milano, 1939.
Afr 2530.19.10 Gray, E.M. Italy and the question of Tunis. Milano, 1939.
Afr 2530.21 Occhipinti, D. Tunisi oggi. Roma, 1939.
Afr 2530.23 Cataluccio, F. Italia e Francia in Tunisia, 1878-1939. Roma, 1939.
Afr 2530.25 Question italienne en Tunisie (1868-1938). Paris, 1939.
Afr 2530.40FA Monde Economique. Tunisia faces the future. Tunis, 1956.
Afr 2530.40FB Monde Economique. Tunisia faces the future. Tunis, 1956.
Afr 2530.71A Raymond, André. La Tunisie. Paris, 1961.
Afr 2530.71B Raymond, André. La Tunisie. Paris, 1961.

Afr 2532 **Tunisia - History by periods - 1881-1956 - 1882-1945 - Speical topics**
Afr 2532.2 Droulers, C. Le marquis de Mores, 1858-1896. Paris, 1932.
Afr 2532.4 Pavy, A. L'expédition de Mores. Paris, 1899.
Afr 2532.6 Duran-Angliviel, André. Ce que la Tunisie demande à la France. Paris, 1921.
Afr 2532.7 Livre blanc tunisien des évènements qui amenèrent la déposition. Tunis, 1946.
Afr 2532.10 Le Néo-Destour face à la première épreuve, 1934-36. Tunis, 1969.

Afr 2533 **Tunisia - History by periods - 1881-1956 - 1945-1956**
Afr 2533.1 Rous, Jean. Tunisie...attention. Paris, 1952.
Afr 2533.2 Laitman, L. Tunisia today. N.Y., 1954.
Afr 2533.4 Aymard, C.E. Tragédie française en Afrique du nord. Paris, 1958.
Afr 2533.6 Gros, Simone. La politique de Carthage. Paris, 1958.
Afr 2533.8 Tunisian Office for National Liberation. An account of the Tunisian question and its most recent developments. N.Y., 1952.
Afr 2533.10 Day, Georges. Les affaires de la Tunisie et du Maroc devant les Nations Unies. Paris, 1953.
Afr 2533.11 Szymanski, E. Le problème de l'indépendance de la Tunisie. Warszawa, 1962.

Afr 2535 **Tunisia - History by periods - 1956- (Independence) - General works**
Afr 2535.2 Ivanov, N.A. Sovremennyi Tunis. Moscow, 1959.
Afr 2535.4 Mezerik, A. Tunisian-French dispute. N.Y., 1961.
Afr 2535.6 Debbasch, C. La République Tunisienne. Paris, 1962.
Afr 2535.7 Vokrouhlicky, Zbynck. Napric Tuniskem. Praha, 1962.
Afr 2535.8 Moore, Clement Henry. Tunisia since independence. Berkeley, 1965.
Afr 2535.10 Rossi, Pierre. La Tunisie de Bourguiba. Tunis, 1967.

Afr 2536 **Tunisia - History by periods - 1956- (Independence) - Biographies**
Afr 2536.10 Garas, Felix. Bourguiba et la naissance d'une nation. Paris, 1956.
Afr 2536.10.5 Stephane, R. La Tunisie de Bourguiba. Paris, 1958.
Afr 2536.10.10 Bourguiba, H. La Tunisie et la France. Paris, 1954.
Afr 2536.10.15 Bourguiba, H. La bataille de l'évacuation, 17 avril 1956-17 février 1959. Tunis, 1959.
Afr 2536.10.20 Pamphlet vol. Bourguiba, Habib. Collection of speeches, 1963-64. 12 pam.
Afr 2536.10.25 Bourguiba, Habib. Les procès Bourguiba, 9 avril, 1938. Tunis, 1967. 2v.
Afr 2536.10.30 Bourguiba, Habib. Articles de presse, 1929-1934. Tunis, 1967.

Afr 2539 **Tunisia - History by periods - 1956- (Independence) - Special topics**
Afr 2539.2 Montety, H. Femmes de Tunisie. Paris, 1958.

Afr 2605 - 2610 **Tunisia - Geography, description, etc. - General works (By date)**
Afr 2607.36 Saint-Gervais, M. Memoires, historiques qui concernent le gouvernement...de Tunis. 1736.
Afr 2608.11 MacGill, Thomas. An account of Tunis. Glasgow, 1811.
Afr 2608.11.5 MacGill, Thomas. Neue Reise nach Tunis. Weimar, 1816. 2 pam.
Afr 2608.54 Davis, N. Evenings in my tent. London, 1854. 2v.
Afr 2608.58 Dunant, J.H. Notice sur la régence de Tunis. Genève, 1858.
Afr 2608.61 Flaux, A. de. La régence de Tunis au dix-neuvième siècle. Paris, 1865.
Afr 2608.67.5 Gubernatis, E. de. Lettere sulla Tunisia. Firenze, 1867.
NEDL Afr 2608.69 Perry, Amos. Carthage and Tunis. Providence, 1869.
Afr 2608.70 Maltzan, Heinrich. Reise in den Regentschaften Tunis und Tripolis. Leipzig, 1870. 3v.
Afr 2608.72 Schneider, O. Von Algier nach Tunis und Constantine. Dresden, 1872.
Afr 2608.75 Zaccone, P. Notes sur la régence de Tunis. Paris, 1875.
Afr 2608.77 Rae, Edward. The country of the Moors. London, 1877.
Afr 2608.80 Desgodins de Souhesmes, G. Tunis. Paris, 1880.
Afr 2608.81 Duveyrier, Henri. La Tunisie. Paris, 1881.
Afr 2608.82 Hesse-Wartegg, E. Tunis. N.Y., 1882.
Afr 2608.82.10F Itinéraires en Tunisie, 1881-82. Pt.1-2 and tables. Paris, 1882.
Afr 2608.83 Michel, L. Tunis. Paris, 1883.
Afr 2608.84.2 Mayet, Valery. Voyage dans le sud de la Tunisie. 2e ed. Paris, 1887.
Afr 2608.85 Boddy, A.A. To Kairwan the Holy. London, 1885.
Afr 2608.85.7 Cambon, Victor. De Bone à Tunis. Lyon, 1885.
Afr 2608.86 Fournel, M. La Tunisie. Paris, 1886.
Afr 2608.87 Baraban, L. A travers la Tunisie. Paris, 1887.
Afr 2608.88 Kleist, H. Tunis und seine Umgebung. Leipzig, 1888.
Afr 2608.92 Bernard, M. De Tripoli à Tunis. Paris, 1892.
Afr 2608.92.3 Poire, Eugene. La Tunisie française. Paris, 1892.
Afr 2608.92.10 Lafitte, Fernand. Contribution à l'étude médicale de la Tunisie. Bordeaux, 1892.
Afr 2608.94 Cagnat. Voyage en Tunisie. Paris, 1894.
Afr 2608.95.2 Fitzner. Die Regentschaft Tunis. Berlin, 1895.
Afr 2608.95.8 Bruun, D. Cave dwellers of southern Tunisia. London, 1898.
Afr 2608.99 Vivian, H. Tunisia. N.Y., 1899.
Afr 2608.99.3 Zolla, D. La colonisation agricole en Tunisie. Paris, 1899.
Afr 2609.00 Vitry, Alexis. L'oeuvre française en Tunisie. Compiegne, 1900.
Afr 2609.00.3 Rey, R. Voyage d'études en Tunisie. Paris, n.d.
Afr 2609.01 Claretie, G. De Syracuse à Tripoli. Paris, 1901.
Afr 2609.03 Tunis. Notice sur la Tunisie. Tunis, 1903.
Afr 2609.03.2 Pensa, H. L'avenir de la Tunisie. Paris, 1903.
Afr 2609.04 Tunisie au début du XXme siècle. Paris, 1904.
Afr 2609.04.5 Saint-Paul, Georges. Souvenirs de Tunisie et d'Algérie. Tunis, 1909.
Afr 2609.06 Sladin, D. Carthage and Tunis. London, 1906. 2v.
Afr 2609.06.3 Tunis. Comité. D'Hivernage. La Tunisie. Tunis, 1906.
Afr 2609.06.6 Lorimer, Norma. By the waters of Carthage. London, 1906.
Afr 2609.07 Loth, G. La Tunisie et l'oeuvre du protectorat français. Paris, 1907.
Afr 2609.11 Castellini, G. Tunisi, e Tripoli. Torino, 1911.
Afr 2609.12 Harry, M. Tunis la blanche. Paris, 1910.
Afr 2609.12.3 Douglas, N. Fountains in the sand...oases of Tunisia. N.Y., n.d.
Afr 2609.13 Monchicourt, C. La région du Haut Tell en Tunisie. Paris, 1913.
Afr 2609.21 Ferdinand-Lop, S. La Tunisie et ses richesses. Paris, 1921.
Afr 2609.22 Voligny, R.B. de. Behind Tunisian walls by L.E. Douglas. London, 1922.
Afr 2609.30 Warsfold, W.B. France in Tunis and Algeria. N.Y., 1930.
Afr 2609.30.5 Mori, Attilio. La Tunisia. Roma, 1930.
Afr 2609.30.10F Thomas, Jean. A travers le sud Tunisie. Paris, 1930.
Afr 2609.30.15 Despois, Jean. La Tunisie. Paris, 1930.
Afr 2609.34 Bonniard, F. La Tunisie du nord. Paris, 1934. 2v.
Afr 2609.34.5 Bonniard, F. Le tell septentrional en Tunisie. Thèse. Paris, 1934.
Afr 2609.34.10 Geniaux, C. L'âme musulmane en Tunisie. Paris, 1934.
Afr 2609.37 Margueritte, L.P. Tunisiennes. Paris, 1937.
Afr 2609.39 Steer, G.L. Date in the desert. London, 1939.

Afr 2605 - 2610		Tunisia - Geography, description, etc. - General works (By date) - cont.
	Afr 2609.39.5	Stephens, E. En Tunisie. Paris, 1939.
	Afr 2609.40	Despois, Jean. La Tunisie orientale, Sahel et Basse Steppe, étude géographique. Paris, 1940.
	Afr 2609.40.5	Despois, Jean. La Tunisie orientale. 2.ed. Paris, 1955.
	Afr 2609.45	Great Britain. Naval Intelligence Division. Tunisia. London, 1945.
	Afr 2609.46	Eparvier, Jean. Tunisie vivante. Paris, 1946.
	Afr 2609.50	Initiation à la Tunisie. Paris, 1950.
	Afr 2609.52	Hoppenot, Hélène. Tunisie. Lausanne, 1952.
	Afr 2609.55	Zeraffa, Michel. Tunisie. Paris, 1955.
	Afr 2609.60	Schleinitz, E.G. Tunisien. Frankfurt a.M., 1960.
	Afr 2609.61	Despois, Jean. La Tunisie. Paris, 1961.
	Afr 2609.61.5	Roy, Claude. Tunisie. Paris, 1961.
	Afr 2609.62	Coque, R. La Tunisie présaharienne. Paris, 1962.
	Afr 2609.62.5	Tunisia, yesterday and today. Tunis, 1962.
	Afr 2609.63	Schuman, L.O. Tunesië. Meppel, 1963.
	Afr 2609.65	Duvignaud, Jean. Tunisie. Lausanne, 1965.
	Afr 2609.65.5	Zeraffa, Michel. Tunisia. N.Y., 1965.
	Afr 2609.68	Olivier, Pierre. Tunisie, ma mie. Tunis, 1968.

Afr 2618		Tunisia - Geography, description, etc. - Special customs
	Afr 2618.10	Darmon, Raoul. La situation des cultes en Tunisie. Thèse. Paris, 1928.
	Afr 2618.15	Demeerseman, A. Tunisie: sève nouvelle. Tournai, 1957.
	Afr 2618.20	Chatelain, Yves. La vie littéraire et intellectuelle en Tunisie de 1900 à 1937. Paris, 1937.
	Afr 2618.25	Hammerton, Thomas. Tunisia unveiled. London, 1959.
	Afr 2618.26	Demeerseman, A. Soixante ans de pensée tunisienne à travers les revues. Tunis, 1955.
	Afr 2618.26.5	Demeerseman, A. Vocation culturelle de la Tunisie. Tunis, 1953.
	Afr 2618.28	Bernard, Augustin. Enquête sur l'habitation rurale des indigènes de la Tunisie. Tunis, 1924.

Afr 2620		Tunisia - Geography, description, etc. - Guidebooks
	Afr 2620.2	Tunisie. Paris, 1965.

Afr 2622		Tunisia - Geography, description, etc. - Maps
	Afr 2622.1	Mager, Henri. Atlas de Tunisie. Paris, n.d.
	Afr 2623.01	Pamphlet box. Tunis. Economic resources.

Afr 2623.1 - .199		Tunisia - Economic history and conditions - General works
	Afr 2623.3	Pennec, Pierre. Les transformations des corps de métiers de Tunis. Tunis, 1964.
	Afr 2623.10	Economic yearbook of Tunisia. Tunis. 1964+
	Afr 2623.15	Tunis. Welt-Ausstellung 1873 in Wien. Wien, 1873.

Afr 2623.500 - .999		Tunisia - Economic history and conditions - Contemporary works (By date)
	Afr 2623.938	Sccmama, R. La Tunisie agricole ct rurale ct l'ocuvre dc la France. Thèse. Paris, 1938.
	Afr 2623.938.3	Scemama, R. La Tunisie agricole et rurale. Paris, 1938.
	Afr 2623.938.10	Housset, L. Le statut des terres collectives et la fixation au sol des indigènes en Tunisie. Thèse. Paris, 1938.
	Afr 2623.956	Colloque international sur les niveaux de vie en Tunisie. Travaux du colloque international les niveaux de vie en Tunisie. Paris, 1956-58. 3 pam.
	Afr 2623.957	Tlatli, S.E. Tunisie nouvelle. Tunis, 1957.
	Afr 2623.958	Marini, Fr. Population et production en Tunisie. Auch, 1958.
	Afr 2623.960F	Tunisia. Secrétariat d'Etat à l'Information. Tunisia works. Tunis, 1960.
	Afr 2623.960.5	Cuisenier, Jean. L'Ansarine; contribution à la sociologie du développement. Paris, 1960.
	Afr 2623.961	Guen, Moncef. La Tunisie indépendante face à son économie. Paris, 1961.
	Afr 2623.961.5	Ardant, G. La Tunisie d'aujourd'hui et de demain. Paris, 1961.
	Afr 2623.962	Poucet, J. La colonisation et l'agriculture européennes en Tunisie depuis 1881. Paris, 1962.
	Afr 2623.962.5F	Tunisia. Secretariat. Tunisian development. Tunis, 1962.
	Afr 2623.962.10	Tunisia. Secrétariat d'Etat au Plan et aux Finances. Perspectives décennales de développement, 1962-1971. Tunis, 1962.
	Afr 2623.964	Mission de Productivité en Tunisie. Actions de productivité en Tunisie. Paris, 1964.
	Afr 2623.965	Tunisia. Secrétariat d'Etat au Plan et à l'Economie Nationale. Plan guadriennal, 1965-1968. Tunis, 1965?
	Afr 2623.966	Kratz, Achim. Voraussetzungen und Möglichkeiten einer industriellen Entwicklung in Tunesien. Hamburg, 1966.
	Afr 2623.967	Duwaji, Ghazi. Economic development in Tunisia. N.Y., 1967.

Afr 2624.500 - .999		Tunisia - Finance - Contemporary works (By date)
	Afr 2624.912	Sala, R. Le budget tunisien. Paris, 1912.
	Afr 2624.932	Guenee, Georges. Les finances tunisiennes. Thèse. Tunis, 1932.

Afr 2625		Tunisia - Races - General works
	Afr 2625.5	Schwab, M. Mémoire sur l'ethnographie de la Tunisie. Paris, 1868.
	Afr 2625.6	Lapie, P. Les civilisations tunisiennes. Paris, 1898.
	Afr 2625.7F	Tunisia. Secrétaire Général du Gouvernement. Nomenclature et répartition des tribus de Tunisie. Chelons-Saône, 1900.

Afr 2628		Tunisia - Races - Natives
	Afr 2628.1	Stuhlmann, F. Die Mazigh-Völker. Hamburg, 1914.
	Afr 2628.2	Antichan, P.H. Le pays des Khroumirs. Paris, 1883.

Afr 2630		Tunisia - Races - French
	Afr 2630.1	Lorin, H. Le peuplement français de la Tunisie. Paris, 1904.
	Afr 2630.2	Poublon, G. La terre, projet de petite colonisation. Tunis, 1901.
	Afr 2630.5	Galinier, P. La France tunisienne. Tunis, 1940.
	Afr 2630.7	Debbasch, Yvan. La nation française en Tunisie, 1577-1835. Paris, 1957.

Afr 2632		Tunisia - Races - Italians
	Afr 2632.2	Saurin, J. L'invasion sicilienne. Paris, 1900.
	Afr 2632.4	Fidel, Camille. Les intérêts italiens en Tunisie. Paris, 1911.
	Afr 2632.6	Sarfatti, M.G. Tunisiaca. Milano, 1924.

Afr 2632		Tunisia - Races - Italians - cont.
	Afr 2632.8	Ficaya, P. Le peuplement italien en Tunisie. Thèse. Paris, 1931.
	Afr 2632.9	Maggio, G. di. Gli Italiani e le professioni liberali in Tunisia. Tunis, 1934.
	Afr 2632.11	Sulla questione tunisina. Roma, 1933.

Afr 2636		Tunisia - Races - Other European
	Afr 2636.2	Smaja, M. L'extension de la juridiction et de la nationalité française en Tunisie. Tunis, 1900.

Afr 2640		Tunisia - Religion
	Afr 2640.1	Couche, L. Pourquoi devenir propriétaire en Tunisie. Lille, 1900.

Afr 2650		Tunisia - Provinces, regions, etc.
	Afr 2650.1	Perry, Amos. An official tour of eastern Tunis. Providence, 1891.
	Afr 2650.2	Rouire, A.M.F. La découverte du bassin hydrographique de la Tunisie centrale. Paris, 1887.
	Afr 2650.3	Bardin, Pierre. La vie d'un douar. Paris, 1965.
	Afr 2650.4	Moreau, Pierre. Le pays des Nefezaouas. Tunis, 1947.
	Afr 2650.5	Tunisia. Secrétariat d'Etat à l'Information. Land development in the Medjerda valley. n.p., 1959.

Afr 2662		Tunisia - Cities, towns, etc. - Bizerta
	Afr 2662.1	Ludwig Salvator. Bizerta und seine Zukunft. Prag, 1881.
	Afr 2662.1.5F	Ludwig Salvator. Benzert. Prag, 1897.
	Afr 2662.5	Lepotier, Adolphe Auguste Marie. Bizerte. Paris, 1965.

Afr 2665		Tunisia - Cities, towns, etc. - C (Others)
	Afr 2665.5	Mabille de Poncheville, A. Carthage. Paris, 1931.

Afr 2669		Tunisia - Cities, towns, etc. - Gafsa
	Afr 2669.1	Bodereau, P. La Capsa ancienne, la Gafsa moderne. Paris, 1907.
	Afr 2669.5	Bordin, P. Les populations arabes du contrôle civil de Gafsa et leurs genres de vie. Tunis, 1944.

Afr 2670		Tunisia - Cities, towns, etc. - G (Others)
	Afr 2670.5	Servonnet, Jean. En Tunisie, le golfe de Gabès en 1888. Paris, 1888.

Afr 2674		Tunisia - Cities, towns, etc. - J
	Afr 2674.2	Naceur. Description et histoire de l'île de Djerba. Tunis, 1884.

Afr 2675		Tunisia - Cities, towns, etc. - Kairwan
	Afr 2675.1.5	Martin, D.B. I know Tunisia. N.Y., 1943.

Afr 2676		Tunisia - Cities, towns, etc. - K (Others)
	Afr 2676.2	Louis, André. Documents ethnographiques et linguistiques sur les îles Gerkena. Alger, 1962.

Afr 2680		Tunisia - Cities, towns, etc. - N
	Afr 2680.5	Coque, Roger. Nabeul et ses environs, étude d'une population tunisienne. Paris, 1965?

Afr 2681		Tunisia - Cities, towns, etc. - O
	Afr 2681.2	Territoire des Ouled Ali ben-Aoun. 1. ed. Paris, 1956.

Afr 2685		Tunisia - Cities, towns, etc. - Sfax
	Afr 2685.1	Dupaty de Clam, A. Fastes chronologiques de la ville de Sfaks. Paris, 1890.

Afr 2687		Tunisia - Cities, towns, etc. - S (Others)
	Afr 2687.1	Sebag, Paul. Un faubourg de Tunis, Saida Manoubia. Paris, 1960.
	Afr 2687.4	Duvignaud, Jean. Chebika; mutations dans un village du Maghreb. Paris, 1968.
	Afr 2687.4.2	Duvignaud, Jean. Changes at Shebika. 1st American ed. N.Y., 1970.

Afr 2688		Tunisia - Cities, towns, etc. - Tunis
	Afr 2688.2	Saladin, H. Tunis et Kairouan. Paris, 1908.
	Afr 2688.5F	Turki, Zubayr. Tunis, naguère et aujourd'hui. Tunis, 1967.

Afr 2689		Tunisia - Cities, towns, etc. - T (Others)
	Afr 2689.1	Dupaty de Clam, A. Fastes chronologiques de Tozeur. Paris, 1890.

Afr 2696		Tunisia - Heraldry
	Afr 2696.2F	Hugon, Henri. Les emblèmes des beys de Tunis. Paris, 1913.

Afr 2698		Tunisia - Biographies - Collected
	Afr 2698.5	Zmerli, Sadok. Les successeurs. Tunis, 1967.

Afr 2700		Sahara - Periodicals (A-Z)
	Afr 2700.3	Perspectives sahariennes. Tanger.
	Afr 2700.5F	Revue du Sahara. Alger. 5,1959+
	Afr 2700.7	Bulletin de liaison saharienne. Alger. 33,1959+ 2v.
	Afr 2700.8F	Nouvelle Revue du Sahara. Noisy-le-Sec. (Seine). 1960+
	Afr 2700.10	Algiers. Université. Institut de Recherches Sahariennes. Documents pour servir à la connaissance du Sahara. 1,1961+

Afr 2702		Sahara - Folios [Discontinued]
	Afr 2702.1F	Monteil, P.L. De Saint-Louis à Tripoli. Paris, 1895.
	Afr 2702.2F	France. Ministère des Travaux Publiques. Documents rel. à ... par Flatters. Paris, 1884.

Afr 2704		Sahara - Bibliographies
	Afr 2704.5	Blaudin de The, Bernard M.S. Essai de bibliographie du Sahara. Paris, 1960- 2v.

Afr 2705		Sahara - Pamphlet volumes
	Afr 2705	Pamphlet box. Sahara.

Afr 2710		Sahara - General politics
	Afr 2710.1	Mercier, E. La France dans le Sahara. Paris, 1889.
	Afr 2710.2	Lechatelier, A. Lettre...sur la politique saharienne. n.p., 1900.
	Afr 2710.2.3	Lechatelier, A. Sahara-Touat et frontière marocaine. n.p., 1901.

Afr 2710 Sahara - General politics - cont.

Afr 2710.3 Rouard de Card, E. La France et la Turquie dans le Sahara oriental. Paris, 1910.
Afr 2710.4 Bissuel, H. Le Sahara français. Alger, 1891.
Afr 2710.6 Salvati, Cesare. Italia e Francia nel Sahara orientale. Milano, 1929.
Afr 2710.10 Vermale, Paul. Au Sahara pendant la guerre européenne. Alger, 1926.
Afr 2710.12 Benedetti, Achille. Dal Sahara al Ciad. Milano, 1935.

Afr 2714 2720 Sahara - General history (By date)

Afr 2719.06 Bernard, A. La pénétration saharienne, 1830-1906. Alger, 1906.
Afr 2719.23 Martin, A.G.P. Quatre siècles d'histoire marocaine. Paris, 1923.
Afr 2719.36 Schiffers-Davringhausen, H. Stumme Front. Leipzig, 1936.
Afr 2719.47 Pottier, René. Histoire du Sahara. Paris, 1947.
Afr 2719.54 Lecler, René. Sahara. 1st ed. Garden City, 1954.
Afr 2719.55 Banque Dambert-Blitz. L'avenir du Sahara. Paris, 1955.
Afr 2719.56 Lefevre, Georges. Notre Sahara. Paris, 1956.
Afr 2719.56.5 Strasser, Daniel. Réalités et promesses sahariennes. Paris, 1956.
Afr 2719.60 Thomas, Marc-Robert. Sahara et communauté. Paris, 1960.
Afr 2719.62 Genin, I. A. Imperialisticheskaia bor'ba za Sakharu. Moscow, 1962.
Afr 2719.64 Boahen, A.A. Britain, the Sahara. Oxford, 1964.
Afr 2719.64.5 Wellard, J.H. The great Sahara. London, 1964.
Afr 2719.68 Bodley, Ronald V.C. The soundless Sahara. London, 1968.

Afr 2730 Sahara - History by periods - Flooding of the Sahara Railway

Afr 2730.1 Mackenzie, D. The flooding of the Sahara. London, 1877.

Afr 2731 Sahara - History by periods - 20th century

Afr 2731.1 Abadie, F. Lettres sur le Trans-saharien. Constantine, 1880.
Afr 2731.3 Esquer, G. Un saharien, le colonel Ludovic de Polignac, 1827-1904. Paris, 1930.
Afr 2731.4 Société d'Etudes du Chemin de Fer Transafricain. Mission du Transafricain. v.1-2 and atlas. Paris, 1924-25. 3v.
Afr 2731.5 Becker, Georges. La pénétration française au Sahara. Un transsaharien? Paris, 1928.
Afr 2731.7 Leroy-Beaulieu, P. Le Sahara. Paris, 1904.
Afr 2731.10 Lehuraux, L.J. Au Sahara avec le commandant Charlet. Paris, 1932.
Afr 2731.12 Howe, S.E. Les héros du Sahara. Paris, 1931.
Afr 2731.12.5 Gautier, E.F. Figures de conquêtes coloniales. Paris, 1931.
Afr 2731.13 Drouilly, J.G. Le général Laperrine, grand saharien. Paris, 1922.
Afr 2731.14 Pottier, René. Laperrine, conquérant pacifique du Sahara. Paris, 1943.
Afr 2731.15.3 Herisson, R. Avec le père de Foucauld et le général Laperrine, 1909-11. Paris, 1937.
Afr 2731.15.6 Foucauld, Charles, Vicomte de. Lettres inédites au général Laperrine. Paris, 1954.
Afr 2731.15.7 Foucauld, Charles. Lettres à Mme. de Bondy, de la Trappe à Tamanrasset. Paris, 1966.
Afr 2731.15.8 Foucauld, Charles, Vicomte de. Memories of Charles de Foucauld. London, 1938.
Afr 2731.15.10 Gorrée, Georges. Sur les traces de Charles de Foucauld. Paris, 1936.
Afr 2731.15.15 Robert, C.M. L'ermite du Hoggar...Charles de Foucauld. Alger, 1938.
Afr 2731.15.20 Pottier, René. La vocation saharienne du père de Foucauld. Paris, 1939.
Afr 2731.15.25 Fremantle, A.J. Desert calling. N.Y., 1949.
Afr 2731.15.26 Fremantle, A.J. Desert calling. London, 1950.
Afr 2731.15.30 Bodley, R.V.C. The warrior saint. 1st ed. Boston, 1953.
Afr 2731.15.34 Carrouges, Michel. Charles de Foucauld. 3 ed. Paris, 1958.
Afr 2731.15.35 Carrouges, Michel. Soldier of the spirit. N.Y., 1956.
Afr 2731.15.40 Federici, Emidio. L'eremità del Sahara. Roma, 1954.
Afr 2731.15.45 Vignaud, Jean. Frère Charles. Paris, 1947.
Afr 2731.15.50 Nord, Pierre. Le père de Foucauld. Paris, 1957.
Afr 2731.15.52 Nord, Pierre. Charles de Foucauld. Paris, 1959.
Afr 2731.15.55 Foucauld, Charles de. Oeuvres spirituelles. Paris, 1958.
Afr 2731.15.58 Foucauld, Charles de. Père de Foucauld, Abbé Huvelin. Correspondance inédite. Tournai, 1957.
Afr 2731.15.60 Charbonneau, Jean. La destinée paradoxale de Charles de Foucauld. Paris, 1958.
Afr 2731.15.65 Six, Jean F. Itinéraire spirituel de Charles de Foucauld. Paris, 1958.
Afr 2731.15.67 Foucauld, Charles, Vicomte de. Spiritual autobiography of Charles de Foucauld. N.Y., 1964.
Afr 2731.15.70 Carrouges, Michel. Foucauld devant l'Afrique du nord. Paris, 1961.
Afr 2731.15.75 Cristiani, L. Pèlerin de l'absolu. Paris, 1960.
Afr 2731.15.80 Six, Jean F. Witness in the desert, the life of Charles de Foucauld. N.Y., 1965.
Afr 2731.15.85 Roche, Aimé. Charles de Foucauld. Lyon, 1964.
Afr 2731.15.90 Quesnel, Roger. Charles de Foucauld, les étapes d'une recherche. Tours, 1966.
Afr 2731.15.95 Lyautey, Pierre. Charles de Foucauld. Paris, 1966.
Afr 2731.15.100 Gorrée, Georges. Charles de Foucauld. Paris, 1965.
Afr 2731.15.105 Foucauld, Charles. Schriften. Einsiedeln, 1961.
Afr 2731.15.110 Hamilton, Elizabeth. The desert my dwelling place: a study of Charles de Foucauld, 1858-1916. London, 1968.
Afr 2731.17.3 Pottier, René. Un prince saharien méconnu, Henri Duveyrier. Paris, 1938.
Afr 2731.19 Dervil, Guy. Trois grands Africains. Paris, 1945.
Afr 2731.21 Pagés, Louis. Jacques Faugère le Saharien. Nérac, 1967.

Afr 2745 - 2750 Sahara - Geography, description, etc. - General works (By date)

Afr 2748.26 Denham. Narration of travels...in central Africa. Boston, 1826.
Afr 2748.26.2 Denham. Narration of travels...in central Africa. London, 1826.
Afr 2748.26.3 Denham, Dixon. Narration of travels and discoveries in Northern and Central Africa in the years 1822, 1823 and 1824. 3. ed. London, 1828.
Afr 2748.26.4 Williams, Harry. Quest beyond the Sahara. London, 1965.
Afr 2748.32 Bargagli-Petrucci, O. Nel Fezzan, aprile, maggio 1932. Firenze, 1934.
Afr 2748.47 Jacquot, Felix. Expédition du général Cavaignac dans le Sahara algérien en avril et mai 1847. Paris, 1849.
Afr 2748.48 Richardson, J. Travels in the...Sahara. London, 1848. 2v.

Afr 2745 - 2750 Sahara - Geography, description, etc. - General works (By date) - cont.

Afr 2748.48.3 Daumas, E. Le grand désert. Paris, 1848.
Afr 2748.53 Richardson, J. Narrative of mission to central Africa (1850-51). London, 1853. 2v.
Afr 2748.54PF Petermann, August. Account of progress of expedition to central Africa, 1850-53. London, 1854.
Afr 2748.57 Fromentin, E. Un été dans le Sahara. Paris, 1857.
Afr 2748.57.5 Fromentin, E. Un été dans le Sahara. Paris, 1922.
Afr 2748.57.20 Assollant, Georges. Eugène Fromentin, un été dans le Sahara. Paris, 1931.
Afr 2748.59 Laurent, C. Mémoire sur le Sahara oriental. Paris, 1859.
Afr 2748.60 Tristram, H.B. The great Sahara. London, 1860.
NEDL Afr 2748.74 Rohlfs, G. Quer durch Afrika. Leipzig, 1874. 2v.
Afr 2748.79 Chavanne, J. Die Sahara. Vienna, 1879.
Afr 2748.81 Soleillet, P. Les voyages...dans le Sahara. Paris, 1881.
Afr 2748.82 Algeria. Service Central des Affaires Indigènes. Deuxième mission Flatters. Algiers, 1882.
Afr 2748.82.3 Patorni, F. Récits faits par 3 survivants de la mission Flatters. Constantine, 1884.
Afr 2748.82.4 Brosselard-Faidherbe, H. Voyage de la mission Flatters au pays des Touareg Azdjers. Paris, 1883.
Afr 2748.82.5 Brosselard-Faidherbe, H. Les deux missions Flatters. 2e ed. Paris, 1889.
Afr 2748.82.6 Barbier, J.V. A travers le Sahara, les missions du colonel Flatters. Paris, 1895.
Afr 2748.82.7 Rabourdin, L. Algérie et Sahara. Paris, 1882.
Afr 2748.84 Trip to the great Sahara. London, 1884.
Afr 2748.85 Lagarde, Charles. Une promenade dans le Sahara. Paris, 1885.
Afr 2748.87 Bonelli, D.E. El Sahara. Madrid, 1887.
Afr 2748.88 Lara, Juan F. de. De la Peña al Sahara. Madrid, 1888.
Afr 2748.89 Philebert, C. La conquête pacifique de l'intérieur africain. Paris, 1889.
Afr 2748.90 Foureau, F. Une mission au Tademayt. Paris, 1890.
Afr 2748.91 Sabatier, Camille. Touat, Sahara et Soudan. Paris, 1891.
Afr 2748.93 Schirmer, H. Le Sahara. Paris, 1893.
Afr 2748.95 Foureau, F. Mission chez les Touareg. Paris, 1895.
Afr 2748.98 Foureau, F. Mon neuvième voyage au Sahara. Paris, 1898.
Afr 2748.98.5 Basset, R. Documents géographiques sur l'Afrique septentrional. Paris, 1898.
Afr 2749.00 Pommeret, J. Une femme chez les sahariennes. Paris, 1900.
Afr 2749.02 Foureau, F. D'Alger au Congo par le Tchad. Paris, 1902.
Afr 2749.02.2F Foureau, F. Documents scientifiques de la mission saharienne. Paris, 1903.
Afr 2749.04 Guilleux, Charles. Journal de route d'un caporal de tirailleurs de la mission saharienne. Belfort, 1904.
Afr 2749.05 Comité du Maroc. Dans l'ouest de la Saoura. Paris, 1905.
Afr 2749.05.5 Duveyrier, Henri. Sahara algérien et tunisien. Paris, 1905.
Afr 2749.06 Vischer, H. Across the Sahara. London, 1910.
Afr 2749.08 Cortier, M. D'une rive à l'autre du Sahara. Paris, 1908.
Afr 2749.08.3 Gautier, E.F. Missions du Sahara. Paris, 1908-09. 2v.
Afr 2749.10 Gautier, E.F. La conquête du Sahara. Paris, 1910.
Afr 2749.13 Angieras, E.M. Le Sahara occidental. Paris, 1919.
Afr 2749.15 Gordan, H.C. Woman in the Sahara. London, 1915.
Afr 2749.22 Haardt, G.M. Le raid Citroen. Paris, 1923.
Afr 2749.22.5 Killian, Conrad. Au Hoggar, mission de 1922. Paris, 1925.
Afr 2749.22.10 Buchanan, Angus. Sahara. London, 1926.
Afr 2749.23 Gautier, E.F. Le Sahara. Paris, 1923.
Afr 2749.23.5 Gautier, E.F. Sahara avec 10 figures et 26 illustrations hors texte. Paris, 1928.
Afr 2749.23.10A Gautier, E.F. Sahara. N.Y., 1935.
Afr 2749.23.10B Gautier, E.F. Sahara. N.Y., 1935.
Afr 2749.25.10 Kerillis, Henri de. De l'Algérie au Dahomey en automobile. Paris, 1925.
Afr 2749.27 Cameron, Donald R. A Saharan venture. London, 1928.
Afr 2749.27.5 Deloncle, P.E.M.J. La caravane aux éperons verts (Mission Alger-Niger). Paris, 1927.
Afr 2749.29.5 Khun de Prorok, B. Mysterious Sahara, the land of gold, of sand, and of ruin. London, 1930.
Afr 2749.30 Augieras, Ernest M. Chronique de l'ouest saharien (1900-1930). Paris, 1930.
Afr 2749.32 Sanchez, J.G.R. El Sahara occidental. 1. ed. Madrid, 1930.
Afr 2749.34 Paris. Musée d'Ethnographie du Trocadero. Exposition du Sahara, 15 mai-28 oct. 1934. Paris, 1934.
Afr 2749.39.5 Symons, H.E. Two roads to Africa. London, 1939.
Afr 2749.40 Turnbull, P. Sahara unveiled, a great story of French colonial conquest. London, 1940.
Afr 2749.44 Bodley, R.V.C. Wind in the Sahara. N.Y., 1944.
Afr 2749.45.5 Lelong, Maurice H., Père. Le Sahara aux cent visages. Paris, 1945.
Afr 2749.48 Etherton, P.T. Across the great deserts. N.Y., 1948.
Afr 2749.50 Schiffers, H. Die Sahara und die Syrten-Länder. 1. Aufl. Stuttgart, 1950.
Afr 2749.54 MacArthur, D.W. The desert watches. 1st Amer. ed. Indianapolis, 1954.
Afr 2749.54.5 Stuart, B. Desert adventure. London, 1954.
Afr 2749.54.10 Carl, Louis. Tefedest. London, 1954.
Afr 2749.56 Britsch, Jacques. Perspectives sahariennes. Limoges, 1956.
Afr 2749.57 Bowles, Paul Frederic. Yallah. N.Y., 1957.
Afr 2749.57.5 Christopher, Robert. Ocean of fire. London, 1957.
Afr 2749.57.10 Cornet, Pierre. Sahara. Paris, 1957.
Afr 2749.57.15 Kollmannsperger, Fr. Drohende Wüste. Wiesbaden, 1957.
Afr 2749.57.20 Normand, S. Sahara. Paris, 1957.
Afr 2749.58 Furon, Raymond. Le Sahara. Paris, 1957.
Afr 2749.58.5 Favrod, Charles F. Sahara. Lausanne, 1958.
Afr 2749.58.13 Verlet, Bruno. Le Sahara. Paris, 1958.
Afr 2749.60 Heseltine, Nigel. From Libyan sands to Chad. London, 1960.
Afr 2749.60.5 Gerster, Georg. Sahara. London, 1960.
Afr 2749.60.10 Gaudio, Attilio. Le Sahara des Africaines. Paris, 1960.
Afr 2749.60.15 Lerumeur, Guy. Le Sahara avant le pétrole. Paris, 1960.
Afr 2749.61 Joos, Louis D. Through the Sahara to the Congo. London, 1961.
Afr 2749.61.5 Bodington, Nicolas. The awakening Sahara. London, 1961.
Afr 2749.61.10 Frison-Roche, Roger. Sahara de l'aventure. Paris, 1961.
Afr 2749.61.15 Migliorini, Elio. L'esplorazione del Sahara. Torino, 1961.
Afr 2749.64 Toy, Barbara. The way of the chariots. London, 1964.
Afr 2749.65 Besson, Ferny. Sahara, terre de vérité. Paris, 1965.
Afr 2749.66 Baker, Richard Saint Barbe. Sahara conquest. London, 1966.
Afr 2749.68 Norwich, John Julius Cooper. Sahara. London, 1968.

86

Afr 2745 - 2750   Sahara - Geography, description, etc. - General works (By date) - cont.
Afr 2749.68.5   Nau, Christian. La première traversée du Sahara en char a voile. Condé-sur-l'Escaut, 1968.
Afr 2749.69   Stevens, Jon. The Sahara is yours; a handbook for desert travellers. London, 1969.

Afr 2753   Sahara - Geography, description, etc. - Special customs
Afr 2753.1   Daumas, E. Les chevaux du Sahara. Paris, 1858.
Afr 2753.2   Wolff, H. Les régiments de dromadaires. Paris, 1884.
Afr 2753.3   Problèmes humains posés. Paris, 1961.
Afr 2753.4   Unesco. Nomades et nomadisme au Sahara. Paris, 1963.

Afr 2755   Sahara - Geography, description, etc. - Guidebooks
Afr 2755.2   Foucaucourt, J. de. De l'Algérie au Soudan par le Sahara. 5000 kilomètres en automobile dans le désert et la brousse. Paris, 1928.

Afr 2760   Sahara - Races - General works
Afr 2760.5   Briggs, Lloyd C. Tribes of the Sahara. Cambridge, 1960.

Afr 2762   Sahara - Races - Tuareg
Afr 2762.2   Bissuel, H. Les Touareg de l'ouest. Algiers, 1888.
Afr 2762.3   Koehler, A. Verfassung der Tuareg. Gotha, 1903.
Afr 2762.4   Benhazera, M. Six Mois chez Les touaregDu Ahaggar. Alger, 1908.
Afr 2762.5   Jean, C. Les Touareg du sud-est l'Air. Leur rôle dans la politique saharienne. Paris, 1909.
Afr 2762.6   Aymard, C. Les Touareg. Paris, 1911.
Afr 2762.7   King, W.J.H. Search for the masked Tuwareks. London, 1903.
Afr 2762.9   Bernard, F. Deux missions françaises chez les Touareg en 1880-81. Alger, 1896.
Afr 2762.10   Richer, A. Les Touareg du Niger. Paris, 1924.
Afr 2762.12   Rodd, Francis R. People of the veil. London, 1926.
Afr 2762.15   The white Tuareg by operator 1384. London, 1936.
Afr 2762.17   Fuchs, Peter. The land of veiled men. London, 1955.
Afr 2762.20   Lede, Marie Louise. Seule avec les Touareg du Hoggar. Paris, 1954.
Afr 2762.22   Hama, Boubou. Recherches sur l'histoire des Touareg sahariens et soudanais. Paris, 1967.

Afr 2780   Sahara - Cities, towns, etc. - Air
Afr 2780.5   Buchanan, Angus. Exploration of Air. London, 1921.

Afr 2798   Sahara - Cities, towns, etc. - Others
Afr 2798.3   Eu, Clement Celestin. In-Salah et le Tidikelt. Paris, 1903.
Afr 2798.5   Perret, Robert. Itinéraire d'In-Salah au Tahat à travers l'Ahaggar. Paris, 1932.
Afr 2798.5.5   Grevin, Emmanuel. Voyage au Hoggar. Paris, 1936.
Afr 2798.5.10   Couvert, Léon. Contact avec l'Afrique noire par le Hoggar. Paris, 1953.
Afr 2798.5.15   Couvert, Léon. Tourisme en zigzag vers le Hoggar. Bourg, 1951.

Afr 2800   Libya - Periodicals (A-Z)
Afr 2800.12   Libya. Roma. 1924-1927 3v.

Afr 2802   Libya - Folios [Discontinued]
Afr 2802.5   Beechey, F.W. Proceedings of the expedition to explore the northern coast of Africa, from Tripoly eastward. London, 1828.
Afr 2802.6F   Vattier de Bourville, T. Coup d'oeil sur la Cyrénaique. n.p., n.d.

Afr 2804   Libya - Bibliographies
Afr 2804.1   Playfair, R.L. Bibliography of the Barbary states. Pt.1. Tripoli and the Cyrenaica. London, 1889.
Afr 2804.5   Murabet, Mohammed. A bibliography of Libya. Valetta, 1959.

Afr 2808   Libya - Government and administration
Afr 2808.5A   Khalidi, I.R. Constitutional development in Libya. Beirut, 1956.
Afr 2808.5B   Khalidi, I.R. Constitutional development in Libya. Beirut, 1956.
Afr 2808.6   Libya. Constitution. Constitution of the Kingdom of Libya as modified by Law No.1 of 1963. Benghazi, 1964.

Afr 2815 - 2820   Libya - General history (By date)
Afr 2818.35   Greenhow, R. The history of Tripoli. Richmond, 1835.
Afr 2819.12   Manfroni, C. Tripoli nella storia marinara d'Italia. Padova, 1912.
Afr 2819.12.3   Longo, G. La Sicilia e Tripoli. Catania, 1912.
Afr 2819.25   Bergna, C. Tripoli dal 1510 al 1850. Tripoli, 1925.
Afr 2819.27   Firaud, L.C. Annales tripolitaines. Tunis, 1927.
Afr 2819.28   Ghisleri, A. La Libia nella storia e nei viaggiatori dai tempi omerici all'occupazione italiana. Torino, 1928.
Afr 2819.30   Aleo, G.M. Turchi, senussi e italiani in Libia. Bengasi, 1930.
Afr 2819.32   Taraschi, T.M. La Libia italiana, nella preparazione diplomatica e nella conquista. Napoli, 1932.
Afr 2819.60   Murabet, Mohammed. Some facts about Libya. Malta, 1960.
Afr 2819.60.5   Karasapan, Celâ Tevfik. Libya; trablusgarp, bingazi ve fizan. Ankara, 1960.
Afr 2819.64   Murabet, Mohammed. Facts about Libya. 3rd ed. Malta, 1964.
Afr 2819.65   Bodianskii, Vadim. Sovremennaia Liviia. Moskva, 1965.
Afr 2819.65.5   Asal, Muhammad Sami. Die Entstehung Libyens als souveräner Staat. Inaug.-Diss. Berlin, 1965?
Afr 2819.69   Wright, John L. Libya. London, 1969.

Afr 2840   Libya - History by periods - Period of the Deys (1815-1833)
Afr 2840.5   Micacchi, Rodolfo. La Tripolitania sotto il dominio dei Caramànli. Intra, 1936.

Afr 2845   Libya - History by periods - Second Turkish period (1833-1911) - General works
Afr 2845.5   Coro, F. Settantasei anni di dominazione turca in Libia, 1835-1911. Tripoli, 1937.

Afr 2850   Libya - History by periods - Second Turkish period (1833-1911) - Relations with foreign powers - Italy
Afr 2850.1   Riccheri, G. La Tripolitania e l'Italia. Milan, 1902.
Afr 2850.2   Italy. Parlamento. La Libia. Milano, 1912. 2v.
Afr 2850.3   Vecchi, B. Italy's civilizing mission in africa. N.Y., 1912.
Afr 2850.5   Rouard de Card, E. La France et l'Italie et l'article 13 du Pacte de Londres. Paris, 1922.
Afr 2850.8   Pisani, F. Un esperimento di colonizzazione nella Tripolitania. Messina, 1904.
Afr 2850.10F   Gonni, G. Nel centenario della spedizione navale di Tripoli. Genova, 1925.
Htn   Afr 2850.12.5*   Italy. Ministero della Marina. Le condizioni militari della Tripolitania. Rome, 1885.
Htn   Afr 2850.12.10*   Italy. Ministero della Marina. Relazione sulla visita fatta alla R. Corvetta Vettor Pisani alla baia di Tobruch e Dernah. Rome, 1885.

Afr 2862   Libya - History by periods - Second Turkish period (1833-1911) - Relations with foreign powers - Other powers
Afr 2862.5   Mehemed Emin Efendi (Pseud.). Der Kampf um Tripolis. Leipzig, 1912.

Afr 2870   Libya - History by periods - Italian period (1912-1951) - General works
Afr 2870.01   Pamphlet box. Tripolitan affairs, 1911-
Afr 2870.5   Corradini, E. La conquista di Tripoli. Milano, 1912.
Afr 2870.6   Lapworth, Charles. Tripoli and young Italy. London, 1912.
Afr 2870.7   Coen, G. L'Italia a Tripoli. Livorno, 1912.
Afr 2870.7.35   Provenzal, G. La missione politica dell'Italia nell'Africa mediterranea. Roma, 1913.
Afr 2870.8   Cottafari, V. Nella Libia italiana. Bologna, 1912.
Afr 2870.9   Mantegazza, V. Tripoli e i diritti della civiltà. Milano, 1912.
Afr 2870.10   Mosca, G. Italia e Libia. Milano, 1912.
Afr 2870.10.50   Come siamo andati in Libia. Firenze, 1914.
Afr 2870.10.65   Barzilai, Salvatore. La impresa libica e la situazione parlamentare esaurita. Roma, 1914. 3 pam.
Afr 2870.11   Rinascita della Tripolitania. Milano, 1926.
Afr 2870.12   Ravizza, A. La Libia nel suo ordinamento giuridico. Padova, 1931.
Afr 2870.14   Sillani, T. La Libia in venti anni di occupazione italiana. Roma, 1932.
Afr 2870.15   Federzoni, Luigi. Rinascita dell'Africa romana. Bologna, 1929.
Afr 2870.16   Piccioli, A. Tripolitania scuola di energia. Roma, 1932.
Afr 2870.18   Sandri, S. Il generale Rodolfo Groziani. Roma, 19-
Afr 2870.20   Despois, Jean. La colonisation italienne en Libye. Thèse. Paris, 1935.
Afr 2870.25.5   Gaziani, R. Pace romana in Libia. Milano, 1937.
Afr 2870.25.10   Graziani, R. Libia redenta. Napoli, 1948.
Afr 2870.30   Moore, M. Fourth shore, Italy's mass colonization of Libya. London, 1940.
Afr 2870.32   Grothe, Hugo. Libyen. Leipzig, 1941.
Afr 2870.35A   Italian Library of Information, N.Y. The Italian empire: Libya. N.Y., 1940.
Afr 2870.35B   Italian Library of Information, N.Y. The Italian empire: Libya. N.Y., 1940.
Afr 2870.40   Pichon, Jean. La question de Libye dans le règlement de la paix. Paris, 1945.

Afr 2875   Libya - History by periods - Italian period (1912-1951) - Turco-Italian War
Afr 2875.3F   Turco-Italian war concerning Tripoli. n.p., 1911.
Afr 2875.5   Bechler, W.H. The history of the Italian war. Annapolis, 1913.
Afr 2875.6   Abbott, G.F. The holy war in Tripoli. London, 1912.
Afr 2875.7   Irace, T. With the Italians in Tripoli. London, 1912.
Afr 2875.8   Barclay, T. The Turco-Italian war and its problems. London, 1912.
Afr 2875.9   Pasetti, P. Note ed episodi della guerra in Tripolitania. Roma, 1912.
Afr 2875.10   Bevione, G. Come siamo andati a Tripoli. Torino, 1912.
Afr 2875.11   Facchinetti, P.V. Ai caduti nella guerra italo-turca n.p., 1912.
Afr 2875.12   Gray, E.M. La bella guerra. Firenze, 1912.
Afr 2875.13   Piazza, G. Come conquistammo Tripoli. Roma, 1912.
Afr 2875.14   Bennett, E.N. With the Turks in Tripoli. London, 1912.
Afr 2875.15   Ostler, A. The Arabs in Tripoli. London, 1912.
Afr 2875.16   Castellini, G. Nelle trincee di Tripoli. Bologna, 1912.
Afr 2875.17   Sorbi, R. In Libia. Firenze, n.d.
Afr 2875.18   Remond, G. Aux camps turco-arabes. Paris, 1913.
Afr 2875.19   Theilhaber, F.A. Beim roten Halbmond vor Tripolis. Cöln, 1912.
Afr 2875.20   Wright, H.C.S. Two years under the crescent. London, 1913.
Afr 2875.21   McCullagh, F. Italy's war for a desert (Experiences of war correspondent with Italians in Tripoli). Chicago, 1913.
Afr 2875.22   Roncagli, Giovanni. Guerra italo-turca, 1911-12. Milano, 1918. 2v.
Afr 2875.23   In memoriam du pacifisme contre la guerre déclarée par l'Italie à la Turquie. Berne, 1912.
Afr 2875.24   Zoppi, Ottavio. La spedizione Ameglio su Rodi nel maggio 1912. Novara, 1913.
Afr 2875.25   Cicerone, G. La terza colonia italiana. Roma, 1913.
Afr 2875.30   Enver. UmTripolis. München, 1918.
Afr 2875.35   Italy. Esercito. Corpo di Stato Maggiore. Ufficio Storico. Campagna di Libia. Roma, 1922-27. 5v.
Afr 2875.37   Melli, B. La guerra italo-turca. Roma, 1914.
Afr 2875.39   Album-portfolio della guerra italo-turca, 1911-12, per la conquista della Libia. Milano, 1913.
Afr 2875.41   Dietrich, Richard. Die Tripolis-Krise, 1911-12, und die erneuerung des Dreibundes 1912. Würzburg, 193-
Afr 2875.43   Kalbskopf, W. Die Aussenpolitik der Mittelmächte im Tripoliskrieg...1911-1912. Erlangen, 1932.
Afr 2875.45   Meyer, Paul. Die Neutralität Deutschlands und Österreich-Ungarns im italienischer Krieg, 1911-1912. Inaug. Diss. Göttingen, 1932.
Afr 2875.47   Spellanzon, C. L'Africa nemica alla guerra. Venezia, 1912.
Afr 2875.50   Tancredi, L. Dopo Tripoli. Lugano, 1913.
Afr 2875.53   Labriola, Arturo. La guerra di Tripoli e l'opinione socialista. Napoli, 1912.
Afr 2875.56   Fovel, Natale M. Tripoli e i problemi della democrazia. Firenze, 1914.
Afr 2875.58   Marinette, F.T. La battaglia di Tripoli (26 ottobre 1911). Milano, 1912.
Afr 2875.60   Askew, W.C. Europe and Italy's acquisition of Libya, 1911-1912. Durham, N.C., 1942.

Afr 2875   Libya - History by periods - Italian period (1912-1951) - Turco-Italian War - cont.

Afr 2875.62	Volpe, Grocchino. L'impresa de Tripoli, 1911-12. Roma, 1946.
Afr 2875.64	McClare, William K. Italy in north Africa. London, 1913.
Afr 2875.65	Kutay, Cemal. Trablus-garbde bir avuc. Istanbul, 1963.
Afr 2875.66	Iakhimovich, Zinaida P. Italo-turetskaia voina, 1911-1912 gg. Moskva, 1967.
Afr 2875.67	Maltese, Paolo. La terra promessa. Milano, 1968.

Afr 2880   Libya - History by periods - Italian period (1912-1951) - Other special topics

Afr 2880.5	Scaglione, Emilio. Tripoli e la guerra. Napoli, 1918.
Afr 2880.10	Zoli, C. Le operazioni libiche sul 29 parallelo nord. Roma, 1928.
Afr 2880.15	Bignami, Paolo. Tra i colonizzatori in Tripolitania. Bologna, 1931.
Afr 2880.20	Caselli, F. Restauratio libyca. Roma, 1935.
Afr 2880.22	Gray, E.M. Il Duce in Libia. Milano, 1937.

Afr 2885   Libya - History by periods - Period of Independence (1951-   ) - General works

Afr 2885.5	Villard, H.S. Libya. Ithaca, 1956.
Afr 2885.10	Owen, Roger. Libya, a brief political and economic survey. London, 1961.
Afr 2885.11A	Khadduri, M. Modern Libya, a study in political development. Baltimore, 1963.
Afr 2885.11B	Khadduri, M. Modern Libya, a study in political development. Baltimore, 1963.

Afr 2925 - 2930   Libya - Geography, description, etc. - General works (By date)

Htn	Afr 2928.18*	Tully, R. Narrative of a ten years'Residence in Tripoli. London, 1816.
	Afr 2928.18.2	Tully, R. Narrative of a ten years' residence in Tripoli. 2d ed. London, 1817.
Htn	Afr 2928.18.3*	Lyon, G.F. Narrative of travels in North Africa, 1818, 1819 and 1820. London, 1821.
	Afr 2928.18.5	Tully, R. Letters written during a ten years' residence at the court of Tripoli. London, 1957.
	Afr 2928.18.8	Tully, R. Letters written during a ten years' residence at the court of Tripoli. 3rd ed. London, 1819. 2v.
	Afr 2928.19	Cella, Paolo della. Viaggio da Tripoli di Barberia. Genova, 1819.
	Afr 2928.19.2	Cella, Paolo della. Viaggio da Tripoli di Barberia. 3e ed. Città di Castello, 1912.
	Afr 2928.56	Testa, C.E. le. Notice statistique et commerciale. La Haye, 1856.
	Afr 2928.62	Mission de Ghadamès. Rapports officiels. Alger, 1863.
	Afr 2928.78	Medina, G. La reggenza di Tripoli. Cagliari, 1878.
	Afr 2928.85	Rohlfs, G. Von Tripolis nach Alexandrien. Norden, 1885.
	Afr 2928.87	Fournel, M. La Tripolitaine. Paris, 1887.
	Afr 2928.94	Thompson, G.E. Life in Tripoli. Liverpool, 1894.
	Afr 2929.01	Mehier de Mathuisieulx, H. A travers la Tripolitaine. Paris, 1903.
	Afr 2929.01.3	Mehier de Mathuisieulx, H. A travers la Tripolitaine. 3e ed. Paris, 1912.
	Afr 2929.02	Minutilli, F. La Tripolitania. Torino, 1902.
	Afr 2929.02.2	Minutilli, F. La Tripolitania. 2 ed. Torino, 1912.
	Afr 2929.09	Furlong, C.W. Gateway to the Sahara...Tripoli. N.Y., 1909.
	Afr 2929.11	Corradini, E. L'ora di Tripoli. Milano, 1911.
	Afr 2929.11.2	Corradini, E. Ora di tripoli. Milano, 1911.
	Afr 2929.11.5	Piazza, G. La nostra terra promessa. 2 ed. Madre, 1911.
	Afr 2929.11.7	Tumiati, D. Tripolitania. Milano, 1911.
	Afr 2929.11.9	Tragni. Tripolitania e Cirenaica. Bologna, 1911.
	Afr 2929.11.11	Vatter, E. Die Grundzüge einer Landeskunde von Tripolitanien. Marburg, 1912.
	Afr 2929.11.12	Vatter, E. Tripolitanien: Grundzüge zu einer Landeskunde. Strassburg, 1912.
	Afr 2929.12.5	Martino, G. de. Tripoli, Cirene e Cartagine. 2 ed. Bologna, 1912.
	Afr 2929.12.7	Ghisleri, A. Tripolitania e Cirenaica. Milano, 1912.
	Afr 2929.12.9	Mehier de Mathuisieulx, H. La Tripolitaine. Paris, 1912.
	Afr 2929.12.11	Nazari, V. Tripolitania. 2 ed. Roma, 1912.
	Afr 2929.12.13	Podrecca, G. Libia. Roma, 1912.
	Afr 2929.12.15	Darkling, L. La Libia romana e l'impresa italiana. Roma, 1912.
	Afr 2929.12.17	Franzoni, A. Colonizzazione e proprietà fondiaria in Libia. Roma, 1912.
	Afr 2929.12.20	Beltramelli, A. Paesi di conquista. Ferrara, 1915.
	Afr 2929.12.25	Cavazza, F. La Libia italiana e il campo che offre a ricerche scientifiche. Bologna, 1912.
	Afr 2929.13	Vivassa de Regny, P. Libya italica. Milano, 1913.
	Afr 2929.13.5	Ricchieri, Giuseppe. La Libia. Milano, 1913.
	Afr 2929.14	Braun, Ethel. The new Tripoli. London, 1914.
	Afr 2929.17	Great Britain. Admiralty. A handbook of Libya. Sept. 1917. Naval Staff. n.p., 1917.
	Afr 2929.25	King, William Joseph Harding. Mysteries of the Libyan desert. London, 1925.
	Afr 2929.26	Traglia, Gustavo. Il Duce libico. Bari, 1926.
	Afr 2929.26.5F	Calzini, R. Da Leptis Magna a Gadames. Milano, 1926.
	Afr 2929.27	Mori, Attilio. L'esplorazione geografica della Libia. Firenze, 1927.
	Afr 2929.29	Mandosio, Mario. Tripolitania d'oggi. Milano, 1929.
	Afr 2929.30A	Fatuzzo, Giacomo. Notiziario geografico del Sud-Tripolitano. Tripoli, 1930.
	Afr 2929.30B	Fatuzzo, Giacomo. Notiziario geografico del Sud-Tripolitano. Tripoli, 1930.
	Afr 2929.34	Siciliani, D. Paesaggi libici. Tripolitania. Tripoli, 1934.
	Afr 2929.34.5	Paris. Musée d'Ethnographie du Trocadéro. Exposition du Sahara, Paris. Le Sahara italien. Rome, 1934.
	Afr 2929.35.3	Piccioli, Angelo. The magic gate of the Sahara. London, 1935.
	Afr 2929.35.15	Campbell, D. Camels through Libya. Philadelphia, 1935.
	Afr 2929.36.5	Rava, C.E. Ai margini del Sahara. Bologna, 1936.
	Afr 2929.37	Società Geografica Italiana, Rome. Il Sahara italiano. Pt.1. Rome, 1937.
	Afr 2929.37.5	Pottier, R. La Tripolitaine vue par un Français. Paris, 1937.
	Afr 2929.43	Casairey, G. Tripolitania. London, 1943.
	Afr 2929.53	Epton, N.C. Oasis kingdom. N.Y., 1953.
	Afr 2929.56	Royal Institute of International Affairs. Libya. London, 1956.
	Afr 2929.60	Willimot, St. G. Field studies in Libya. Durham, Eng., 1960.

Afr 2925 - 2930   Libya - Geography, description, etc. - General works (By date) - cont.

Afr 2929.64	Jongmans, D.G. Libie, land van de dorst. Meppel, 1964.
Afr 2929.66	Keith, Agnes Newton. Children of Allah. 1st ed. Boston, 1966.
Afr 2929.67	Ward, Philip. Touring Libya. London, 1967.
Afr 2929.68	Ward, Philip. Touring Libya. London, 1968.

Afr 2938   Libya - Economic history and conditions

Afr 2938.5	The African economist. Tripoli. 1,1967+
Afr 2938.15	Persellini, Mario. La Tripolitania: il presente e l'avvenire. Milano, 1924.
Afr 2938.20.2	Coletti, Francesco. La Tripolitania settentrionale e la sua vita sociale, studiate dal vero. 2a ed. Bologna, 1923.
Afr 2938.25	Simonetti, R. Le opere pubbliche della Tripolitania e della Cirenaica. Roma, 1914.
Afr 2938.30	Tripolitania. Ufficio Studi e Propaganda. Vigor di vita in Tripolitania (anno 1928). Tripoli, 1928.
Afr 2938.32	Hilli, Abbas Hilmi. Grundlagen. Köln, 1961.
Afr 2938.34	Libya. Ministry of Planning and Development. Five-year economic and social development plan, 1963-1968. Tripoli, 1964.
Afr 2938.34.5	Libya. Ministry of Planning and Development. A summary of the evolution of planning institutions in Libya. Tripoli, 1965.
Afr 2938.35	Ortner-Heun, Irene. Das Entwicklungsland Libyen. Köln, 1965.
Afr 2938.38	Bank of Libya. Economic Research Department. The development of public finance in Libya, 1944-1963. Tripoli, 1965.
VAfr 2938.39	Libija. Beograd, 1966.

Afr 2940   Libya - Races

Afr 2940.10	Cohen, M. Gli Ebrei in Libia. Roma, 1930.
Afr 2940.15.2	al-Hashayishi, Muhammad ibn Uthman. Voyage au pays des Senoussia a travers à Tripolitaine et les pays touareg. 2.ed. Paris, 1912.

Afr 2945   Libya - Provinces, etc. - Cyrenaica (Barca)

Afr 2945.1	Haimann, G. Cirenaica. Roma, 1882.
Afr 2945.1.2	Haimann, G. Cirenaica. 2a ed. Milan, 1886.
Afr 2945.2	Rainaud, A. La pentapole cyrénéenne. Paris, 1895.
Afr 2945.2.3	Rainaud, A. Quid de natura...Cyrenaicae pentapolis. Paris, 1894.
Afr 2945.3	Hildebrand, G. Cyrenaika als Gebiet künftiger Besiedlung. Bonn, 1904.
Afr 2945.4	Pedretti, A. Un escursione in Cirenaica. Rome, 1901.
Afr 2945.5	Borsari, F. Geografia etnologica e storica della Tripolitania, Cirenaica e Fezzan. Naples, 1888.
Afr 2945.6	Hamilton, J. Wanderings in North Africa. London, 1856.
Afr 2945.7	Sanctis, E. de. Dalla Canea a Tripoli. Roma, 1912.
Afr 2945.8	Almagia, R. Cirenaica. Milano, 1912.
Afr 2945.9	Checchi, S. Attraverso la Cirenaica. Roma, 1912.
Afr 2945.10	Goretti, L. In Cirenaica ed in Arabia. Roma, 1912.
Afr 2945.12	Pezant, J. Voyage en Afrique au royaume de Barcah et dans la Cyrénaique à travers le désert. Paris, 1840.
Afr 2945.13	Delaporte. Relations inédites de la Cyrénaique. Paris, 1825.
Afr 2945.15	Marinelli, O. La Cirenaica. Milano, 1923.
Afr 2945.17	Williams, Gwyn. Green mountain, an informal guide to Cyrenaica. London, 1963.
Afr 2945.20	Mura, Nicolo. La terra delle donne tenebrose. Bologna, 1930.
Afr 2945.22	Salvadori, Alessandro. La Cirenaica ed i suoi servizi civile. Roma, 1914.
Afr 2945.24	Teruzzi, Attilio. Cirenaica verde. Milano, 1931.
Afr 2945.26	Serra, F. Italia e Senussia. Milano, 1933.
Afr 2945.26.10	Gaslini, Mario dei. Col generale Cantore alla caccia del Gran Senusso. Milano, 1928.
Afr 2945.26.15	Bourbon del Monte Santa Maria, G. L'islamismo e la Confraternità dei Senussi. Città di Castello, 1912.
Afr 2945.26.20	Evans-Pritchard, Edward Evan. The Sanusi of Cyrenaica. Oxford, 1949.
Afr 2945.26.25	Ziadeh, N. Abdo. Sanusiyah. Leiden, 1958.
Afr 2945.28	Graziani, Rodolfo. Cirenaica pacificata. Milano, 1932.
Afr 2945.30	Agostini, E. de. Le populazioni della Cirenaica. Bengasi, 1922-23.
Afr 2945.33	Fritz, Egon. Romantische Cyrenaika. Hamburg, 1941.
Afr 2945.35	Cyrenaica. Camera di Commercio, Industria ed Agricultura. La Cirenaica. Bengasi, 1928.
Afr 2945.40	Narducci, G. La colonizzazione della Cirenaica nell antichita e nel presente. Bengasi, 1934.

Afr 2948   Libya - Provinces, etc. - Fessan

Afr 2948.9	Subtil, E. Histoire d'Abd-el-Gelil. n.p., 18- .
Afr 2948.10	Petragnani, Enrico. Il Sahara tripolitano. Roma, 1928.
Afr 2948.12	Scarin, Emilio. Le oasi del Fezzan. v.1-2. Bologna, 1934.
Afr 2948.13	Lethielleux, J. Le Fezzan. Tunis, 1948.
Afr 2948.14	Graziani, Rodolfo. La riconquista del Fezzan. Milano, 1934.
Afr 2948.16	Zoli, Corrado. Nel Fezzan. Milano, 1926.
Afr 2948.18	Fontaine, Pierre. La mort étrange de C. Kilian. Paris, 1959.

Afr 2949   Libya - Provinces, etc. - Gebel

Afr 2949.5	Società Italiana per lo Studio della Libia. Missione Franchetti in Tripolitania (Il Gebel). Firenze, 1914.
Afr 2949.7	Despois, Jean. Le djebel Nefousa (Tripolitaine). Paris, 1935.
Afr 2949.7.3	Despois, Jean. Le djebel Nefousa (Tripolitaine). Thèse. Paris, 1935.

Afr 2950   Libya - Provinces, etc. - Sirte

Afr 2950.15	Cerrata, L. Sirtis, studio geografico-storico. Avellino, 1933.

Afr 2970   Libya - Cities, towns, etc. - G

Afr 2970.5	Bary, Erica de. Ghadames, Ghadames. München, 1961.

Afr 2974   Libya - Cities, towns, etc. - J

Afr 2974.5	Meriano, F. La questione di Giarabub. Bologna, 1925.

Afr 2975   Libya - Cities, towns, etc. - Kupfra

Afr 2975.1	Rohlfs, G. Kufra. Leipzig, 1881.
Afr 2975.2	al-Hashayishi, Muhammad ibn Uthman. Voyage au pays des Senoussia. Paris, 1903.

88

Afr 3074 - 3080   Egypt - General special (By date) - cont.

Afr 3078.63	Paton, A.A. History of the Egyptian revolution. London, 1863. 2v.
Afr 3078.63.3	Paton, A.A. History of the Egyptian revolution. London, 1870. 2v.
Afr 3078.77	Marcel, J.J. Egypte depuis la conquête des Arabes. Paris, 1877.
Afr 3079.03	Gruenan, W.V. Die staats- und völkerrechtliche Stellung Ägyptens. Leipzig, 1903.
Afr 3079.36	Zananiri, Gaston. Egypte et léquilibre du Levant. Marseille, 1936.
Afr 3079.54	al-Muwaylihi, Ibrahim. Le paysan d'Egypte à travers l'histoire. Le Caire, 1954.
Afr 3079.59	Lutskii, V.B. Ocherki po istorii arabskikh stran. Moscow, 1959.
Afr 3079.64	Hurst, Harold. A short account of the Nile basin. Cairo, 1964.
Afr 3079.66	Semenova, Lidiia Andreevna. Salakh-ad-Din i Mamliuki v Egipte. Moskva, 1966.
Afr 3079.68	Ziadeh, Farhat Jacob. Lawyers. Stanford, 1968.
Afr 3079.68.7	Morenz, Siegfried. Die Begegnung Europas mit Ägypten. 2. Aufl. Zürich, 1969.
Afr 3079.69	Hopkins, Harry. Egypt, the crucible: the unfinished revolution of the Arab world. London, 1969.

Afr 3125   Egypt - History by periods - Arab conquest to 1250 (or to 1517) - Arab Conquest (638)

Afr 3125.5	Butler, A.J. The Arab conquest of Egypt. Oxford, 1902.

Afr 3128   Egypt - History by periods - Arab conquest to 1250 (or to 1517) - First period (638-972) - General works

Afr 3128.15	Hassan, Z.M. Les Tulunides, étude de l'Egypte musulmane à fin du IXe siècle 868-905. Thèse. Paris, 1933.

Afr 3132   Egypt - History by periods - Arab conquest to 1250 (or to 1517) - First period (638-972) - Special topics

Afr 3132.5	Becker, C.H. Beiträge zur Geschichte Ägyptens unter den Islam. Strassburg, 1902. 2v.
Afr 3132.6F	Becker, C.H. Papyri Schott-Reinhardt I. Heidelberg, 1906.

Afr 3135   Egypt - History by periods - Arab conquest to 1250 (or to 1517) - Fatimite dynasty (972-1171) - General works

Afr 3135.5	Al-Hamdani, Abbas H. The Fatimids. Karachi, 1962.

Afr 3138   Egypt - History by periods - Arab conquest to 1250 (or to 1517) - Fatimite dynasty (972-1171) - Special topics

Afr 3138.5	Solomon Ben Joseph, Ha-Kohen. The Turcoman defeat at Cairo. Chicago, 1906.
Afr 3138.10	Mamour, P.H. Polemics on the origin of the Fatimi caliphs. London, 1934.
Afr 3138.10.5	O'Leary, De Lacy. A short history of the Fatimid khalifate. London, 1923.
Afr 3138.10.10	Vatikiotis, P.J. The Fatimid theory of state. Lahore, 1957.

Afr 3143   Egypt - History by periods - Arab conquest to 1250 (or to 1517) - Ayubite dynasty (1171-1250) - Special topics

Afr 3143.5	Helbig, Adolph H. Al-Qadi al-Fadil, der Wezir Saladins. Inaug.-Diss. Berlin, 1908.
Afr 3143.10	Gottschalk, Hans L. Al-Malik al-Kamil von Egypten und seine Zeit. Wiesbaden, 1958.
Afr 3143.15	Schregle, Goetz. Die Sultanin Sagarat ad-Durr. Inaug.-Diss. Erlangen, 1960.
Afr 3143.18	Schregle, Goetz. Die Sultanin von Ägypten. Wiesbaden, 1961.

Afr 3150   Egypt - History by periods - Mameluke dynasties (1250-1517) - General works

Afr 3150.5A	Muir, William. The Mameluke or slave dynasty of Egypt. London, 1896.
Afr 3150.5B	Muir, William. The Mameluke or slave dynasty of Egypt. London, 1896.
Afr 3150.7	Niemeyer, W. Agypten zur Zeit der Mamluken. Berlin, 1936.
Afr 3150.9	Poliak, A.N. Les revoltes populaires en Egypte à l'époque des Mamelouks. Paris, 1935.

Afr 3155   Egypt - History by periods - Mameluke dynasties (1250-1517) - First Mameluke dynasty (Tartar, 1250-1382) - General works

Afr 3155.1F	Makrizi. Histoire des sultans mamlouks. Paris, 1837-42. 2v.
Afr 3155.2F	Amari, M. De titoli che usava la cancelleria di sultani di Egitto. Roma, 1886.
Afr 3155.5	Sadeque, Syedah. Baybars I of Egypt. 1st ed. Dacca, 1956.
Afr 3155.10	Khawli, Amir. Sviazi mezhdu Nilom i Volgoi v XIII-XIV vv. Moscow, 1962.

Afr 3158   Egypt - History by periods - Mameluke dynasties (1250-1517) - First Mameluke dynasty (Tartar, 1250-1382) - Special topics

Afr 3158.5	Wiet, Gaston. Les marchands d'épices sous les sultans mamlouks. Le Caire, 1955.

Afr 3160   Egypt - History by periods - Mameluke dynasties (1250-1517) - Second Mameluke dynasty (Circassian, 1382-1517) - General works

Afr 3160.5	Ibn Tagribardi. History of Egypt. Berkeley, 1954. 2v.

Afr 3163   Egypt - History by periods - Mameluke dynasties (1250-1517) - Second Mameluke dynasty (Circassian, 1382-1517) - Special topics

Afr 3163.8	Pagani, Z. Viaggio di Domenico Trevisan, 1512. Venice, 1875.
Afr 3163.10	Tekindaÿ, M.C. Şehabeddin. Berkuk devrinde Memluk Sultanhgi. Istanbul, 1961.
Afr 3163.15	Darrag, Ahmad. L'Egypte sous le règne de Barsbay. Thèse. Paris, 195-. 2v.
Afr 3163.15.5	Darrag, Ahmad. L'Egypte sous le règne de Barsbay. Damas, 1961.
Afr 3163.20A	Ibn Iyas. Journal d'un bourgeois du Caire. Paris, 1955. 2v.
Afr 3163.20B	Ibn Iyas. Journal d'un bourgeois du Caire. Paris, 1955. 2v.
Afr 3163.20.10	Ibn Iyas. Histoire des Mamlouks circassiens. v.2. Le Caire, 1945.

Afr 3180   Egypt - History by periods - Period of Turkish rule (1517-1798) - 1650-1798 - General works

Afr 3180.5	Abd-el-Rahman, Cheikh. Merveilles biographiques et historiques ou chroniques. Paris 1888. 8v.
X Cg Afr 3180.5	Abd-el-Rahman, Cheikh. Merveilles biographiques et historiques ou chroniques. v.9. Paris, 1888.
Afr 3180.5.5	Jabarti, Abd Al-Rahman. Egipet v period ekspeditsii Bonaparta (1798-1801). Moscow, 1962.

Afr 3180   Egypt - History by periods - Period of Turkish rule (1517-1798) - 1650-1798 - General works - cont.

Afr 3180.6	Baldwin, G. Political recollections related to Egypt. London, 1801.
Afr 3180.7A	Cezzar, Ahmed. Ottoman Egypt in the eighteenth century. Cambridge, 1962.
Afr 3180.7B	Cezzar, Ahmed. Ottoman Egypt in the eighteenth century. Cambridge, 1962.

Afr 3183   Egypt - History by periods - Period of Turkish rule (1517-1798) - 1650-1798 - Special topics

Afr 3183.7	Relaçao do tumulto popular que succedeo em de dezembro do auno passado de 1754. n.p., 1755. 2 pam.
Afr 3183.8A	Lusignan, S. History of the revolt of Ali Bey. London, 1783.
Afr 3183.8B	Lusignan, S. History of the revolt of Ali Bey. London, 1783.
Afr 3183.15	Charles-Roux, François. Autour d'une route. Paris, 1922.
Afr 3183.20	Leibniz, G.W. Consilium Aegyptiacum. Paris, 1842.
Afr 3183.25	Charles-Roux, François. France, Egypte et mer Rouge, de 1715 à 1798. Le Caire, 1951.

Afr 3193   Egypt - History by periods - Period after French expedition (1801-1806) - Special topics

Afr 3193.5	Guemard, Gabriel. Bibliographie critique de la Commission des sciences et arts et de l'Institut d'Egypte. Thèse complémentaire. Le Caire, 1936.
Afr 3193.10	Edmonds, J. L'Egypte indépendante. Projet de 1801. Caire, 1924.
Afr 3193.15	Ghorbal, Shafik. The beginnings of the Egyptian question and the rise of Mehemet Ali. London, 1928.
Afr 3193.20	Douin, Georges. L'Angleterre et l'Egypte. Caire, 1929-30. 2v.
Afr 3193.25	Douin, Georges. L'Egypte de 1802 à 1804. Caire, 1925.

Afr 3198 - 3200   Egypt - History by periods - Nineteenth century - General works (By date)

Afr 3198.64	Merruan, P. L'Egypte contemporaine. Paris, 1864.
Afr 3198.82	DeLeon, E. Egypt under its khedives. London, 1882.
Afr 3198.83	Malortie, Karl. Egypt: native rulers and foreign interference. 2nd ed. London, 1883.
Afr 3198.86	Vingtrinier, A. Solimar-Pacha...guerres de l'Egypte. Paris, 1886.
Afr 3198.87	Bowen, J.E. Conflict of East and West in Egypt. N.Y., 1887.
Afr 3198.95	Pensa, Henri. L'Egypte et le Soudan égyptien. Paris, 1895.
Afr 3198.98	Cameron, D.A. Egypt in the nineteenth century. London, 1898.
Afr 3198.98.5	Notovich, Nikolai. L'Europe et l'Egypte. Paris, 1898.
Afr 3198.99	Penfield, F.C. Present-day Egypt. N.Y., 1899.
Afr 3199.01	Brehier, L. L'Egypte de 1798 à 1900. Paris, 1901.
Afr 3199.02B	Dicey, E. The story of the khedivate. London, 1902.
Afr 3199.05	Freycinet, C. de. La question d'Egypte. Paris, 1905.
Afr 3199.06	Balboni, L.A. Gl'Italiani nella civiltà egiziana del secolo XIX. Alessandria, 1906. 3v.
Afr 3199.11	Duse Muhammad. In the land of the pharaohs. N.Y., 1911.
Afr 3199.11.2	Duse Muhammad. In the land of the Pharaohs. 2nd ed. London, 1968.
Afr 3199.15	Weigall, Arthur E.P. Brome. History of events in Egypt from 1798 to 1914. Edinburgh, 1915.
Afr 3199.15.5	Steindorff, Georg. Agypten in Vergangenheit und Gegenwart. Berlin, 1915.
Afr 3199.17	Hasenclever, A. Geschichte Ägyptens im 19 Jahrhundert, 1798-1914. Halle a.S., 1917.
Afr 3199.20	Sabry, Mohammed. La question d'Egypte depuis Bonaparte jusqu'à la révolution de 1919. Paris, 1920.
NEDL Afr 3199.27	Young, George. Egypt. N.Y., 1927.
Afr 3199.37	Sammarco, Angelo. Histoire de l'Egypte moderne depuis Mohammed Ali jusqu'à l'occupation britannique. Le Caire, 1937.
Afr 3199.38	Amad, E.S. La question d'Egypte, 1841-1938. Thèse. Paris, 1938.
Afr 3199.47	Rifaat, M. The awakening of modern Egypt. London, 1947.
Afr 3199.47.2	Rifaat, M. The awakening of modern Egypt. Lahore, 1964.
Afr 3199.54	Marlowe, J. A history of modern Egypt and Anglo-Egyptian relations. N.Y., 1954.
Afr 3199.54.2	Marlowe, J. A history of modern Egypt and Anglo-Egyptian relations. 2d ed. Hamden, 1965.
Afr 3199.54.10	Marlowe, J. Anglo-Egyptian relations, 1800-1953. London, 1954.
Afr 3199.58	Stewart, D.S. Young Egypt. London, 1958.
Afr 3199.60	Ahmed Jamal, M. The intellectual origins of Egyptian nationalism. London, 1960.
Afr 3199.61A	Safran, N. Egypt in search of political community. Cambridge, 1961.
Afr 3199.61B	Safran, N. Egypt in search of political community. Cambridge, 1961.
Afr 3199.61.5	Mommsen, Wolfgang. Imperialismus in Ägypten. München, 1961.
Afr 3199.67	Waterfield, Gordon. Egypt. London, 1967.
Afr 3199.69	Vatikiotis, Panayiotis Jerasimof. The modern history of Egypt. London, 1969.

Afr 3204   Egypt - History by periods - Nineteenth century - Special topics

Afr 3204.10	Auriant, L. L'Egypte. Paris, 1920.
Afr 3204.15	Munier, Jules. La presse en Egypte, 1799-1900. Le Caire, 1930.
Afr 3204.17	Ahmed, Chafik Bey. L'Egypte moderne et les influences étrangères. Le Caire, 1931.
Afr 3204.18	Guenard, Gabriel. Aventuriers mameluks d'Egypte. Toulouse, 1928.
Afr 3204.20	Tarman, E.E. Egypt and its betrayal. N.Y., 1908.
X Cg Afr 3204.22	Question of Egypt in Anglo-French relations. Edinburgh, 1917.
Afr 3204.24	Briffauet, Robert. L'Angleterre et l'Egypte. Paris, 194-.
Afr 3204.26	Blayland, Gregory. Objective: Egypt. London, 1966.
Afr 3204.28	Abdel-Malek, Anouar. Idéologie et renaissance nationale; l'Egypte moderne. Paris, 1969.

Afr 3205   Egypt - History by periods - Nineteenth century - Mehemet Ali (1806-1849) - General works

Afr 3205.1	Mengin, Felix. Histoire de l'Egypte sous le gouvernement de Mohammed-Aly. v.1-2 and atlas. Paris, 1823. 3v.
Afr 3205.1.5	Mengin, Felix. Histoire sommaire de l'Egypte. Paris, 1839.

Afr 3205 **Egypt - History by periods - Nineteenth century - Mehemet Ali (1806-1849) - General works - cont.**

Afr 3205.2	Gouin, Edouard. L'Egypte au XIXe siècle, histoire militaire et politique. Paris, 1847.
Afr 3205.3	Prokesch-Osten, A. Mehmed-Ali. Wien, 1877.
Afr 3205.4	Mouriez, Paul. Histoire de Mehemet-Ali. v.1-5. Paris, 1858. 4v.
Afr 3205.5	Hamont, P.N. L'Egypte sous Mehemet-Ali. Paris, 1843. 2v.
Afr 3205.6	Madden, R.R. Egypt and Mohammed Ali. 2d ed. London, 1841.
Afr 3205.7	Sabry, Mohammed. L'empire égyptien sous Mohamed-Ali et la question d'Orient, 1811-1849. Paris, 1930.
Afr 3205.8	Cattaui, Joseph E. Histoire des rapports de l'Egypte avec la Sublime Porte. Thèse. Paris, 1919.
Afr 3205.10	Finati, Giovanni. Narrative of the life and adventures of Giovanni Finati. London, 1830. 2v.
X Cg Afr 3205.13	Dodwell, Henry. The founder of modern Egypt. Cambridge, Eng., 1931.
Afr 3205.15	Cattaui, René. Le règne de Mohamed Aly d'après les archives russes en Egypte. v.1-3. Caire, 1931-1936. 4v.
Afr 3205.16	Cattaui, René. Mohamed-Aly et l'Europe. Paris, 1950.
Afr 3205.17	Sammarco, Angelo. Il regno di Mohammed Ali nei documenti diplomatici italiani inediti. v.1,8,9,10. Caire, 1930-32. 4v.
Afr 3205.19	Guemard, G. Les réformes en Egypte. Thèse. Le Caire, 1936.
Afr 3205.20	Tagher, Jacques. Mohamed Ali jugé par les Européens de son temps. Le Caire, 1942.

Afr 3207 **Egypt - History by periods - Nineteenth century - Mehemet Ali (1806-1849) - Early years**

Afr 3207.1	Wilson, R.J. History of the British expedition to Egypt. London, 1803.
Afr 3207.2	Walsh, T. Journey of the late campaign in Egypt. London, 1803.
Afr 3207.13	Douin, Georges. Mohamed Aly, pacha du Caire, 1805-1807. Caire, 1926.
Afr 3207.15	Driault, E. Mohamed Aly et Napoléon, 1807-1814. Le Caire, 1925.
Afr 3207.17	Douin, Georges. L'Angleterre et l'Egypte. Paris, 1928.
Afr 3207.20	Thedenet-Duvent, P.P. L'Egypte sous Mehemed-Ali. Paris, 1822.

Afr 3215 **Egypt - History by periods - Nineteenth century - Mehemet Ali (1806-1849) - Other special**

Afr 3215.2	Driault, E. La formation de l'empire de Mohamed Aly de l'Arabie au Sudan (1814-1823). Paris, 1927.
Afr 3215.3	Douin, Georges. Une mission militaire française auprès de Mohamed Aly. Caire, 1923.
Afr 3215.3.5	Douin, Georges. Les premières frégates de Mohamed Aly (1824-27). Caire, 1926.
Afr 3215.3.10	Douin, Georges. La maison du baron de Boislecomte. Caire, 1927.
Afr 3215.3.15	Driault, E. L'Egypte et l'Europe. Caire, 1930-31. 3v.
Afr 3215.3.20	Douin, Georges. L'Egypte de 1828 à 1930. Roma, 1935.
Afr 3215.3.25	Charles-Roux, François. Thiers et Méhémet-Ali. Paris, 1951.
Afr 3215.3.30	Durand-Viel, G.C. Les campagnes navales de Mohammed Aly et d'Ibrahim. Paris, 1935. 2v.
Afr 3215.5	Jomard, E.F. Coup-d'oeil...sur l'état présent de l'Egypte. Paris, 1836.
Afr 3215.15	Roy, H. La vie héroïque et romantique du docteur Charles Cuny. Paris, 1930.
Afr 3215.20	Politeș, Athanasios G. Les rapports de la Grèce et de l'Egypte pendant le regne de Mohamed Aly, 1833-1849. Roma, 1935.

Afr 3217 **Egypt - History by periods - Nineteenth century - Mehemet Ali (1806-1849) - Ibrahim (Regent 1841-1848)**

Afr 3217.15	Crabitès, Pierre. Ibrahim of Egypt. London, 1935.

Afr 3223 **Egypt - History by periods - Nineteenth century - Abbas I (Regent 1848; Pasha, 1849-1854) - Special topics**

Afr 3223.5	Perron, A. Lettres du Dr. Perron du Caire et l'Alexandrie à M. Jules Mohl, à Paris, 1838-54. Le Caire, 1911.

Afr 3230 **Egypt - History by periods - Nineteenth century - Ismail (1863-1879) - General works**

Afr 3230.5	Jerrold, W.B. Egypt under Ismail Pacha. London, 1879.
X Cg Afr 3230.6	Loring, W.W. A Confederate soldier in Egypt. N.Y., 1884.
Afr 3230.7	Peabody, F.G. Egypt and the powers. n.p., 1879.
Afr 3230.8	Bordeano, N. L'Egypte d'après les traités de 1840-41. Constantine, 1869.
Afr 3230.9	Kusel, S.S. de. An Englishman's recollections of Egypt. London, 1915.
Afr 3230.12	Sabry, Mohammed. La genèse de l'esprit national égyptien (1863-1882). Thèse. Paris, 1924.
Afr 3230.12.5	Sabry, Mohammed. L'empire égyptien sous Ismail et l'ingérence anglo-française (1863-1879). Paris, 1933.
Afr 3230.15	Zananiri, G. Le khedive Ismail et l'Egypte, 1830-1894. Alexandrie, 1923.
Afr 3230.17	Crabitès, Pierre. Ismail, the maligned khedive. London, 1933.
Afr 3230.20A	Douin, Georges. Histoire du règne du khedive Ismail. Roma, 1933-34. 5v.
Afr 3230.20B	Douin, Georges. Histoire du règne du khedive Ismail. v.3, pt.3. Roma, 1933-34.
Afr 3230.25	Khedive Ismail and slavery in the Sudan. Cairo, 1937.
Afr 3230.26	Hesseltine, W.B. The Blue and the Gray on the Nile. Chicago, 1961.

Afr 3240 **Egypt - History by periods - Nineteenth century - Ismail (1863-1879) - Foreign influence and control - General works**

Afr 3240.3	Bemmelen, P.V. L'Egypte et l'Europe. Leiden, 1882. 2v.

Afr 3243 **Egypt - History by periods - Nineteenth century - Ismail (1863-1879) - Foreign influence and control - England to 1882**

X Cg Afr 3243.3	Dicey, E. England and Egypt. London, 1881.
Afr 3243.4.2	Keay, J.S. Spoiling the Egyptians. N.Y., 1882.
Afr 3243.5	Wallace, D.M. Egypt and the Egyptian question. London, 1883.
Afr 3243.6	Hennebert, E. Les Anglais en Egypte. Paris, 1884.
Afr 3243.7	Lesage, C. L'achat des actions de Suez. Paris, 1906.
Afr 3243.8	Malet, E.B. Egypt 1879-1883. London, 1909.
Afr 3243.10	Kilberg, K.I. Vosstanie Arabi-Pashi v Egipte. Moscow, 1937.

Afr 3245 **Egypt - History by periods - Nineteenth century - Ismail (1863-1879) - Foreign influence and control - France to 1904**

Afr 3245.3	Guillon, E. L'Egypte contemporaine et intérêts français. Grenoble, 1885.
Afr 3245.5	Giffard, Pierre. Les Français en Egypte. 2. ed. Paris, 1883.

Afr 3248 **Egypt - History by periods - Nineteenth century - Ismail (1863-1879) - Foreign influence and control - Dual control (1876-1883)**

Afr 3248.3	Bourguet, A. La France et l'Angleterre en Egypte. Paris, 1897.
Afr 3248.6	Bioves, Achille. Français et Anglais en Egypte, 1881-1882. Paris, 1910.

Afr 3252 **Egypt - History by periods - Nineteenth century - Ismail (1863-1879) - Other special topics**

Afr 3252.1	La destitution de Lapenna et la reforme judiciaire en Egypte. Geneva, 1878.
Afr 3252.5	Holynski, A. Nubar-Pacha devant l'histoire. Paris, 1886.
Afr 3252.10	Politis, A.G. Un projet d'alliance entre l'Egypte et la Grèce en 1867. Caire, 1931.
Afr 3252.20	Lenghi, N. Considerazioni sul discorso da Layard...Riforma giudiziaria in Egitto. Alexandria, 1868.
Afr 3252.22	Crabitès, Pierre. Americans in the Egyptian army. London, 1938.

Afr 3255 **Egypt - History by periods - Nineteenth century - Tewfik (1879-1892) - General works**

Afr 3255.3	Bell, C.F.M. Khedives and pashas. London, 1884.
Afr 3255.5	Long, C.C. The three prophets. N.Y., 1884.
Afr 3255.6	Kamel, S. La conférence de Constantinople et la question égyptienne 1882. Paris, 1913.
Afr 3255.7	Rowlatt, Mary. Founders of modern Egypt. London, 1962.

Afr 3258 **Egypt - History by periods - Nineteenth century - Tewfik (1879-1892) - Revolt of Arabi (1882) - General works**

Afr 3258.3	Retrospect of the war in Egypt. London, 1882.
Afr 3258.4	Vogt, H. The Egyptian war of 1882. London, 1883.
Afr 3258.5	Royle, C. The Egyptian campaigns, 1882-85. London, 1886. 2v.
Afr 3258.5.2	Royle, C. The Egyptian campaigns, 1882-85. London, 1900.
Afr 3258.6	Archer, T. War in Egypt and the Soudan. London, 1887. 2v.
Afr 3258.7	Vizetelly, F. From Cyprus to Zanzibar. London, 1901.
Afr 3258.8.3A	Blunt, W.S. Secret history of the English occupation of Egypt. N.Y., 1922.
Afr 3258.8.3B	Blunt, W.S. Secret history of the English occupation of Egypt. N.Y., 1922.
Afr 3258.8.5	Blunt, W.S. Gordon at Khartoum. London, 1911.
Afr 3258.8.10	Shukri, M.F. Gordon at Khartoum. Cairo, 1951.
Afr 3258.11	Sandes, E.W.C. The Royal Engineer in Egypt and the Sudan. Chatham, 1937.
Afr 3258.16F	Illustriret Familie-Journals. Krigen i Aegypten. Pt.1-3. Kjøbenhavn, 1882.
Afr 3258.20	Ata, M.M. Egypt between two revolutions. Cairo, 1956.

Afr 3265 **Egypt - History by periods - Nineteenth century - Tewfik (1879-1892) - Revolt of Arabi (1882) - Other special events**

Afr 3265.2	Stone, Fanny. Diary of an American girl in Cairo, 1882. N.Y., 1884.
Afr 3265.5	Baynes, K.S. Narrative of the part taken by the 79th Queen's Own Cameron Highlanders, in the Egyptian campaign, 1882. London, 1883.

Afr 3267 **Egypt - History by periods - Nineteenth century - Tewfik (1879-1892) - Revolt of Arabi (1882) - Trial of Arabi and settlement**

X Cg Afr 3267.1	Broadley, S.M. How we defended Arabi. London, 1884.
Afr 3267.5	Arabi, Ahmed. Memoire d'Arabi-Pacha à ses avocats. Thèse. Photoreproduction. Paris, 1924.

Afr 3269 **Egypt - History by periods - Nineteenth century - Tewfik (1879-1892) - Other special topics**

Afr 3269.05F	France. Ministère des Affaires Etrangères. Documents diplomatiques. Paris, 1881.
Afr 3269.08F	France. Ministère des Affaires Etrangères. Documents diplomatiques. Paris, 1883.
Afr 3269.1F	France. Ministère des Affaires Etrangères. Affaires d'Egypte 1884. Paris, 1884.
Afr 3269.2F	France. Ministère des Affaires Etrangères. Documents diplomatiques. Paris, 1893.
Afr 3269.3F	France. Ministère des Affaires Etrangères. Documents diplomatiques. Paris, 1885. 5 pam.
Afr 3269.4F	France. Ministère des Affaires Etrangères. Documents diplomatiques. Paris, 1881. 4 pam.
Afr 3269.10	Italy. Ministero degli Affari Esteriore. Documenti diplomatici relativi alle indennità per danni sofferti. Roma, 1883.
Afr 3269.15	Kleine, Mathilde. Deutschland und die ägyptische Frage. Greifswald, 1927.

Afr 3275 **Egypt - History by periods - Nineteenth century - England in Egypt (1882-1904)**

Afr 3275.1	Pamphlet box. England in Egypt.
Afr 3275.3	Harrison, F. The crisis in Egypt, a letter to Mr. Gladstone. London, 1882.
Afr 3275.4	Wood, H.F. Egypt under the British. London, 1896.
Afr 3275.5	Faris, Selim. Decline of British prestige in the East. London, 1887.
Afr 3275.6	Britain's work in Egypt. Edinburgh, 1892.
Afr 3275.7	Resener, Hans. Agypten unter englischer Okkupation. Berlin, 1896.
Afr 3275.8A	White, A.S. The expansion of Egypt. London, 1899.
Afr 3275.8B	White, A.S. The expansion of Egypt. London, 1899.
Afr 3275.9	Traill, H.D. England, Egypt and the Sudan. Westminster, 1900.
Afr 3275.10	Pensa, Henri. L'Egypte et l'Europe. Paris, 1896.
Afr 3275.11	Fuller, F.W. Egypt and the hinterland. London, 1901.
Afr 3275.12	Traill, H.D. LordCromer. London, 1897.
Afr 3275.12.5	al-Sayyid, Afaf Lutfi. Egypt and Cromer; a study in Anglo-Egyptian relations. London, 1968.
Afr 3275.12.5.2	al-Sayyid, Afaf Lutfi. Egypt and Cromer; a study in Anglo-Egyptian relations. N.Y., 1969.
Afr 3275.12.100	Boyle, C.A. A servant of the Empire, a memoir of Harry Boyle. London, 1938.
Afr 3275.12.110	Boyle, C.A. Boyle of Cairo, a diplomatist's adventures in the Middle East. Kendal, 1965.
Afr 3275.13	Aubin, E. Les Anglais aux Indes et en Egypte. Paris, 1899.

Afr 3275 Egypt - History by periods - Nineteenth century - England in Egypt (1882-1904) - cont.

Afr 3275.13.2 Aubin, E. Les Anglais aux Indes et en Egypte. Paris, 1900.
Afr 3275.14 Milner, A. England in Egypt. London, 1892.
Afr 3275.14.5 Milner, A. England in Egypt. London, 1894.
Afr 3275.15A Colvin, A. The making of modern Egypt. 3d ed. London, 1906.
Afr 3275.15B Colvin, A. The making of modern Egypt. 3d ed. London, 1906.
Afr 3275.16 Blunt, W.S. Atrocities of justice under British rule in Egypt. London, 1906.
Afr 3275.16.2 Rifat, M.M. Lest we forget. n.p., 1915.
Afr 3275.17A Cromer, E.B. Modern Egypt. N.Y., 1908. 2v.
Afr 3275.17B Cromer, E.B. Modern Egypt. N.Y., 1908. 2v.
Afr 3275.17.2A Cromer, E.B. Modern Egypt. London, 1908. 2v.
Afr 3275.17.2B Cromer, E.B. Modern Egypt. London, 1908. 2v.
Afr 3275.17.4A Cromer, E.B. Modern Egypt. N.Y., 1908. 2v.
Afr 3275.17.4B Cromer, E.B. Modern Egypt. N.Y., 1908. 2v.
Afr 3275.17.4.5 Cromer, E.B. Modern Egypt. London, 1911.
Afr 3275.17.4.10 Cromer, E.B. Modern Egypt. N.Y., 1916.
Afr 3275.17.5 Rotshtein, F.A. Zakhvat i zakabalenie Egipta. Moscow, 1925.
Afr 3275.17.5.2 Rotshtein, F.A. Zakhvat i zakabalenie Egipta. Moscow, 1959.
Afr 3275.17.85 Lloyd, G.A.L. Egypt since Cromer. London, 1933-34. 2v.
Afr 3275.18 Noailles, G. de. Les Anglais en Egypte. Paris, 1898.
Afr 3275.19 Adams, F. The new Egypt. London, 1893.
Afr 3275.20 Letters from an Egyptian...upon the affairs of Egypt. London, 1908.
Afr 3275.21 Rotshtein, F.A. Egypt's ruin. London, 1910.
Afr 3275.22 Alexander, J. The truth about Egypt. London, 1911.
Afr 3275.23 Mikhail, K. Copts and Moslems under British control. London, 1911.
Afr 3275.24 Pierre l'Ermite. Brigands in Egypt. London, 1882.
Afr 3275.25 Méra. Une page de politique coloniale. Paris, 1913.
Afr 3275.26 Cressaty. L'Egypte d'aujourd'hui. Paris, 1912.
Afr 3275.27 Browne, A. Bonaparte in Egypt. London, 1907.
Afr 3275.28 Sladen, D.B.W. Egypt and the English. London, 1908.
Afr 3275.29 Willmore, J.S. The Welfare of Egypt. London, 1917.
Afr 3275.30 Mosely, Sydney R. With Kitchener in Cairo. London, 1917.
Afr 3275.31A Worsfold, William B. The future of Egypt. London, 1914.
Afr 3275.31B Worsfold, William B. The future of Egypt. London, 1914.
Afr 3275.32 Coles, Charles E. Recollections and reflections. London, 1918.
Afr 3275.35 Adam, Juliette. L'Angleterre en Egypte. Paris, 1922.
Afr 3275.38 Tignor, Robert L. Modernization and British colonial rule in Egypt, 1882-1914. Princeton, 1966.
Afr 3275.39 Marshall, J.E. The Egyptian enigma, 1890-1928. London, 1928.
Afr 3275.41 Elgood, P.G. The transit of Egypt. London, 1928.
Afr 3275.42 Kamil, Mustafa. Egyptiens et Anglais. Paris, 1906.
NEDL Afr 3275.43 Regatz, L.J. The question of Egypt in Anglo-French relations, 1875-1904. Edinburgh, 1922.
Afr 3275.45 To see with others' eyes. Cairo, 1907.
Afr 3275.47 Ambrosini, G. La situazione internazionale dell'Egitto. Firenze, 1937.
Afr 3275.49 Halassie, S. Democracy on the Nile. Scotch Plains, N.J., 1940.
Afr 3275.55 Egyptian Information Bureau. The Egyptian question. Washington, 1951.
Afr 3275.60 Cromer, E.B. The situation in Egypt. London, 1908.

Afr 3280 Egypt - History by periods - Nineteenth century - Abbas II (1892-1914) - General works

Afr 3280.5 Ghali, Ibrahim Amin. L'Egypte nationaliste et libérale. La Haye, 1969.
Afr 3280.10 Beaman, Ardern H. The dethronement of the khedive. London, 1929.

Afr 3285 Egypt - History by periods - Nineteenth century - Abbas II (1892-1914) - Special topics

Afr 3285.2 Saint-Martin, H. de. La question égyptienne et l'Italie. Florence, 1884.
Htn Afr 3285.3F* Egyptian Delegation. Speeches and statements, 1908. n.p., n.d. 3 pam.
Afr 3285.3.5 Egypt. Delegation, 1908. Report submitted by the Egyptian delegation to Foreign Secretary of Great Britain. Alexandria, 1909.
Afr 3285.4 Cromer, E.B. Abbas II. London, 1915.
Afr 3285.5 Harrison, T.S. The homely diary of a diplomat in the East. Boston, 1917.
Afr 3285.7 Cecil, E. The leisure of an Egyptian official. London, 1921.
Afr 3285.7.5 Cecil, E. The leisure of an Egyptian official. 2d ed. London, 1921.
Afr 3285.10 Chirol, Valentine. The Egyptian problem. London, 1920.
Afr 3285.15A Richter, Erhard. Lord Cromer, Ägypten und die Entstehung der französisch-englischer Entente von 1904. Inaug. Diss. Leipzig, 1931.
Afr 3285.15B Richter, Erhard. Lord Cromer, Ägypten und die Entstehung der französisch-englischer Entente von 1904. Inaug.-Diss. Leipzig, 1931.
Afr 3285.15.4 Mathews, J.J. Egypt and the formation of the Anglo-French entente of 1904. Thesis. Philadelphia, 1939.
Afr 3285.20 Adams, Charles C. Islam and modernism in Egypt. London, 1933.
Afr 3285.21 Kerr, Malcolm H. Islamic reform. Berkeley, 1966.
Afr 3285.22 Yeghen, Foulad. Saad Zaghloul. Paris, 1927.

Afr 3290 Egypt - History by periods - 20th century - General works

Afr 3290.5 Berque, Jacques. L'Egypte, imperialisme et revolution. Paris, 1967.
Afr 3290.10 Wilber, Donald Newton. United Arab Republic: Egypt. New Haven, 1968.

Afr 3295 Egypt - History by periods - 20th century - Special topics

Afr 3295.4 Hayter, William Goodenough. Recent constitutional developments in Egypt. Cambridge, Eng., 1924.
Afr 3295.5 Atiyah, S. Razvitie natsionalno-osvoboditelnogo dvizheniia v Egipte. Moscow, 1961.
Afr 3295.6 Gallini, Fahmy. Choses d'Egypte. Le Caire, 1917.

Afr 3300 Egypt - History by periods - 20th century - 1914-1952 - General works

Afr 3300.01 Pamphlet box. Egyptian history, 1919- .
Afr 3300.1 Himaya, Latif. La condition internationale de l'Egypte depuis 1914. Thèse. Paris, 1922.
Afr 3300.10 Sabry, Mohammed. La révolution égyptienne. Paris, 1919. 2v.
Afr 3300.15 Elgood, P.G. Egypt and the army. London, 1924.
Afr 3300.17 Harris, Murray G. Egypt under the Egyptians. London, 1925.
Afr 3300.20 Howell, Joseph M. Egypt's past, present and future. Dayton, O., 1929.
Afr 3300.22 Abbas II Hilmi, Khedive of Egypt. A few words on the Anglo-Egyptian settlement. London, 1930.
Afr 3300.25 Vandenbosch, F. Vingt années d'Egypte. Paris, 1932.
Afr 3300.32 Centre d'Etudes de Politique Etrangère, Paris. L'Egypte indépendante. Paris, 1938.
Afr 3300.39.5 Sammarco, Angelo. Egitto moderno. Roma, 193-.
Afr 3300.41 Youssef Bey, A. Independent Egypt. London, 1940.
Afr 3300.45 Times, London. The Times book of Egypt... 26 Jan. 1937. London, 1937.
Afr 3300.48F Great Britain. Special Mission to Egypt. Report of the Special Mission to Egypt. London, 1921.
Afr 3300.50A Issawi, Charles. Egypt. London, 1947.
Afr 3300.50B Issawi, Charles. Egypt. London, 1947.
Afr 3300.51 Issawi, Charles. Egypt at mid-century. London, 1954.
Afr 3300.55 Hussein, Ahmad. The story of Egypt and Anglo-Egyptian relations. N.Y., 1947.
Afr 3300.60 Egypt. Ministry of Foreign Affairs. Records of conversation, notes and papers. Cairo, 1951.
Afr 3300.70 Kamil, M. Tomorrow's Egypt. 1st English ed. Cairo, 1953.
Afr 3300.75 Ghali, M.B. The policy of tomorrow. Washington, 1953.
Afr 3300.80 Moore, A.L. Farewell Farouk. Chicago, 1954.
Afr 3300.85 Lacouture, Jean. L'Egypte en mouvement. Paris, 1956.
Afr 3300.85.2A Lacouture, Jean. Egypt in transition. London, 1958.
Afr 3300.85.2B Lacouture, Jean. Egypt in transition. London, 1958.
Afr 3300.85.3 Lacouture, Jean. L'Egypte en mouvement. Paris 1962.
Afr 3300.90 Zayid, Mahmud Yusuf. Egypt's struggle for independence. 1st ed. Beirut, 1965.

Afr 3305 Egypt - History by periods - 20th century - 1914-1952 - Special topics

Afr 3305.3 Awad, Fawzi Tadrus. La souveraineté égyptienne et la déclaration du 28 février 1922. Paris, 1935.
Afr 3305.5 Moussa, F. Les négociations anglo-égyptiennes de 1950-1951 sur Suez et le Soudan. Genève, 1955.
Afr 3305.8 Royal Institute of International Affairs. Great Britain and Egypt, 1914-1951. London, 1952.
Afr 3305.10 Sadat, Anwar. Revolt on the Nile. London, 1957.
Afr 3305.10.1 Sadat, Anwar. Geheimtagebuch der ägyptischen Revolution. Düsseldorf, 1957.
Afr 3305.12 Grant, C. Nationalism and revolution in Egypt. The Hague, 1964.
Afr 3305.12.5 Heyworth-Dunne, James. Religious and political trends in modern Egypt. Washington, 1950.
Afr 3305.12.10 Mitchell, Richard Paul. The society of the Muslim Brothers. London, 1969.
Afr 3305.15 Goldobin, A. M. Egipetskaia revoliutsiia 1919 goda. Leningrad, 1958.
Afr 3305.16 Shah, Ikbal Ali. Fuad, king of Egypt. London, 1936.
Afr 3305.18 McBride, Barrie St. Clair. Farouk of Egypt; a biography. 1st American ed. South Brunswick, N.J., 1968.
Afr 3305.18.5 McLeave, Hugh. The last Pharaoh: the ten faces of Farouk. London, 1969.
Afr 3305.20 Makarius, R. La jeunesse intellectuelle d'Egypte. Paris, 1960.
Afr 3305.25 Politi, Elie I. L'Egypte de 1914 à Suez. Paris, 1965.

Afr 3310 Egypt - History by periods - 20th century - 1952-1958 - General works

Afr 3310.5 Neguib, M. Egypt's destiny. London, 1955.
Afr 3310.5.2 Neguib, M. Egypt's destiny. 1st American ed. Garden City, 1955.
Afr 3310.7 Abdel-Malek, Anouar. Egypte, société militaire. Paris, 1962.
Afr 3310.10 Nasser, G.A. Egypt's liberation. Washington, 1955.
Afr 3310.10.5 Nasser, G.A. The philosophy of the revolution. Cairo, 195-.
Afr 3310.10.5.5 Nasser, G.A. The philosophy of the revolution. Buffalo, 1959.
Afr 3310.10.5.10 Nasser, G.A. Historical address on occasion of 4th anniversary of the Union, Feb. 22, 1962. Cairo, 1962.
Afr 3310.10.5.25 Nasser, G.A. The philosophy of the revolution. Cairo, 196-.
Afr 3310.10.10 Nasser, G.A. Speeches delivered. Cairo, 1961.
Afr 3310.10.15 International Studies Association, Cairo. Afro-Asian solidarity. Cairo, 1960.
Afr 3310.10.20 Nasser, G.A. On peace. (Cairo I.S.A.). Cairo, 1960. 2 pam.
Afr 3310.10.22 Egypt. President. Address by the President of the Republic of Egypt. Cairo, 1957.
Afr 3310.10.25 Nasser, G.A. Speeches and press-interviews. Cairo. 1958+ 2v.
Afr 3310.10.30 Nasser, G.A. Collection of addresses. Cairo, 1962. 8 pam.
Afr 3310.10.32 Nasser, G.A. Speech delivered on the occasion of the 10th anniversary of the revolution. n.p., n.d.
Afr 3310.10.35 Nasser, G.A. Nasser. Miscellaneous speeches. n.p., n.d. 7 pam.
Afr 3310.10.40 Nasser, G.A. Pre-election speeches in Assiut, March 8, 1965. Cairo, 1965.
Afr 3310.10.45 Nasser, G.A. President Gamal Abdel Nasser on Palestine. Cairo, 1964.
Afr 3310.10.50 La voie égyptienne vers le socialisme. Le Caire, 1966.
Afr 3310.10.55 Nasser, G.A. President Gamal Abdel Nasser on consolidation of the cause of world peace. Cairo, 1968?
Afr 3310.10.80 Taylor, Edmond. The real case against Nasser. n.p., 1956.
Afr 3310.10.85 Mansfield, Peter. Nasser's Egypt. Harmondsworth, 1965.
Afr 3310.10.85.5 Mansfield, Peter. Nasser's Egypt. Harmondsworth, 1969.
Afr 3310.10.85.10 Mansfield, Peter. Nasser. London, 1969.
Afr 3310.10.90 Pamphlet vol. G.A. Nasser, a collection of addresses, November 25, 1961 to May 31, 1965. 10 pam.
Afr 3310.10.95 Saber, Ali. Nasser en procès face à la nation arabe. Paris, 1968.
Afr 3310.15 Egyptian Information Bureau. Egypt in two years. Washington, 1954.
Afr 3310.20 India. Information Services. The Suez Canal crisis and India. New Delhi, 1956.
Afr 3310.25 Laqueur, W.Z. Nasser's Egypt. London, 1956.
Afr 3310.30 Manchester Guardian, Manchester, Eng. The record on Suez. Manchester, 1956.
Afr 3310.35 Lengyel, Emil. Egypt's role in world affairs. Washington, 1957.

Afr 3310   Egypt - History by periods - 20th century - 1952-1958 - General works - cont.

Afr 3310.40	Hasan Abd al-Razik Muhammad. Krizis ekonomiki Egipta. Moscow, 1955.
Afr 3310.45	Wynn, Wilton. Nasser of Egypt. Cambridge, Mass., 1959.
Afr 3310.50	Barawi, Rashid. The military coup in Egypt. Cairo, 1952.
Afr 3310.55	Vauchu, Georges. General Abdel Nasser. Paris, 1959. 2v.
Afr 3310.60A	Wheelock, K. Nasser's new Egypt. N.Y., 1960.
Afr 3310.60B	Wheelock, K. Nasser's new Egypt. N.Y., 1960.
Afr 3310.65	Joesten, Joachim. Nasser. London, 1960.
Afr 3310.70	Jassen, Raul. Nasser. Buenos Aires, 1961.
Afr 3310.75	International Studies Association. Nasser. Cairo, 1960.
Afr 3310.85A	Abul-Fath, A. L'affaire Nasser. Paris, 1962.
Afr 3310.85B	Abul-Fath, A. L'affaire Nasser. Paris, 1962.
Afr 3310.86PF	Egyptian Gazette. Eleven years of achievement. Cairo, 1963.
Afr 3310.87	Kerr, M.H. Egypt under Nasser. N.Y., 1963.
Afr 3310.88	Riad, H. L'Egypte nassérienne. Paris, 1964.
Afr 3310.90	United Arab Republic. The Revolution in thirteen years, 1952-1965. Cairo, 1965.
Afr 3310.92	United Arab Republic. Diary of the Revolution, 1952-1965. Cairo, 1965.
Afr 3310.93	Estier, Claude. L'Egypte en révolution. Paris, 1965.
Afr 3310.94	Karanjia, Rustom Khurshedji. How Nasser did it. Bombay, 1964.
Afr 3310.95	Kurdgelashvili, Shota N. Revoliutsiia 1952 g. i krakh britanskogo gospodstva v Egipte. Moskva, 1966.
Afr 3310.100	Vatikiotis, Panayiotis Jerasimof. Egypt since the revolution. London, 1968.

Afr 3315   Egypt - History by periods - 20th century - 1952-1958 - Special topics

Afr 3315.5	Henriques, R.D.Q. A hundred hours to Suez. N.Y., 1957.
Afr 3315.10	United States. Department of State. The Suez Canal problem. Washington, 1956.
Afr 3315.15	Bromberger, M. Secrets of Suez. London, 1957.
Afr 3315.15.5	Bromberger, M. Les secrets de l'expédition d'Egypte. Paris, 1957.
Afr 3315.20	Robertson, J.H. The most important country. London, 1957.
Afr 3315.25	Watt, Donald C. Documents on the Suez crisis. London, 1957.
Afr 3315.35	Port Said, nouveau Stalingrad. Paris, 1956.
Afr 3315.45	Soviet News. Suez. London, 1956.
Afr 3315.50	Byford-Jones, Wilfred. Oil on troubled waters. London, 1957.
Afr 3315.55	International Review Service. The Suez Canal. N.Y., 1957.
Afr 3315.60	Amir, Adil. Le complot continué. Caire, 1957.
Afr 3315.65	Dzelepy, E.N. Le complot de Suez. Bruxelles, 1957.
Afr 3315.68	Pearson, Lester B. The crisis in the Middle East. Ottawa, 1957.
Afr 3315.70	Camille, Paul. Suez. Paris, 1957.
Afr 3315.75	Gallean, Georges. Des deux côtés du Canal. Paris, 1958.
Afr 3315.80	Marshall, S.L.A. Sinai victory. N.Y., 1958.
Afr 3315.81	Dayan, Moshe. Diary of the Sinai campaign. London, 1966.
Afr 3315.85	Johnson, Paul. Suez war. London, 1957.
Afr 3315.90	Foot, Michael. Guilty men. N.Y., 1957.
Afr 3315.95	Lauterpacht, E. The Suez Canal settlement. London, 1960.
Afr 3315.100	Barer, Schlomo. The weekend war. N.Y., 1960.
Afr 3315.105	United Arab Republic on the seventh anniversary. n.p., 1959.
Afr 3315.110	Primakov, E.M. Pouchitelnyi urok. Moscow, 1957.
Afr 3315.115	India. Parliament. Hok Sabha. Suez Canal. New Delhi, 1956.
Afr 3315.120A	Childers, E.B. The road to Suez. London, 1962.
Afr 3315.120B	Childers, E.B. The road to Suez. London, 1962.
Afr 3315.121	Eayrs, James. The Commonwealth and Suez. London, 1964.
Afr 3315.122	Clark, D.M.J. Suez touchdown. London, 1964.
Afr 3315.124	Barker, A.J. Suez, the seven-day war. London, 1964.
Afr 3315.125	Robertson, Terence. Crisis, the inside story of the Suez conspiracy. 1st ed. N.Y., 1965.
Afr 3315.125.2	Robertson, Terence. Crisis, the inside story of the Suez conspiracy. London, 1965.
Afr 3315.126	Azeau, Henri. Le siège de Suez. Paris, 1964.
Afr 3315.127	Cavenagh, Sandy. Airborne to Suez. London, 1965.
Afr 3315.128	Soviet News. Suez and the Middle East; documents. London, 1956.
Afr 3315.130	Meyer-Ranke, Peter. Der rote Pharao. Hamburg, 1964.
Afr 3315.132	Thomas, Hugh. The Suez affair. London, 1967.
Afr 3315.132.7	Thomas, Hugh. Suez. N.Y., 1967.
Afr 3315.133	Nutting, Anthony. No end of a lesson. London, 1967.
Afr 3315.136	Calvocoressi, Peter. Suez ten years after: broadcasts from the BBC. London, 1967.
Afr 3315.138	Yanguas Messia, José de. El clima politico de ayer y de hoy en Africa. Escorial, 1959.
Afr 3315.140	Bar-Zohar, Michel. Suez: ultra-secret. Paris, 1964.
Afr 3315.142	Beaufre, Andre. L'Expédition de Suez. Paris, 1967.
Afr 3315.144	United Arab Republic. Information Department. Secrets of the Suez War. Cairo, 1966.
Afr 3315.145	Akademiia Nauk SSSR. Institut Mirovoi Ekonomiki i Mezhdunarodnykh Otnoshenii. Suetskii vopros i imperialisticheskaia agressiia protiv Egipta. Moskva, 1957.
Afr 3315.146	Protopopov, Anatolii S. Sovetskii Soiuz i Suetskii krizis 1956 goda (iiul'-noiabr'). Moskva, 1969.
Afr 3315.148	Love, Kenneth. Souez: the twice-fought war; a history. 1st ed. N.Y., 1969.
Afr 3315.150	Mezerik, Avrahm G. The Suez Canal: 1956 crisis - 1967 war. N.Y., 1969.
Afr 3315.152	Kipping, Norman Victor. The Suez contractors. Havant, Hampshire, 1969.
Afr 3315.154.1	Beaufre, André. The Suez expedition 1956. N.Y., 1969.

Afr 3320   Egypt - History by periods - Egypt, 1958-   ; United Arab Republic - Periodicals

Afr 3320.10F	Arab review. Cairo. 1,1960+ 5v.
Afr 3320.46	Fédération Egyptienne de l'Industrie. Yearbook. Cairo. 1960+ 6v.
Afr 3320.143	United Arab Republic. State Tourist Administration. Tourisme in Egypt. n.p., n.d.
Afr 3320.143	United Arab Republic. Information Department. Pocket book.
Afr 3320.143.5F	U.A.R. today. Cairo. 1963+
Afr 3320.143.10	United Arab Republic. Ministry of Culture and National Guidance. The cultural yearbook. Cairo. 1959+ 2v.

Afr 3322   Egypt - History by periods - Egypt, 1958-   ; United Arab Republic - Collected source materials

Afr 3322.2	Nasser, G.A. A draft of the Charter. Cairo, 1962.
Afr 3322.4	Arab political encyclopedia. Cairo. 10,1961+ 2v.
Afr 3322.6	Gazette fiscale. Alexandrie.

Afr 3325   Egypt - History by periods - Egypt, 1958-   ; United Arab Republic - General works

| Afr 3325.5 | United Arab Republic. Information Department. The United Arab Republic, nine years. Cairo, 1961. |
| Afr 3325.10 | Powell, Ivor. Disillusion by the Nile: what Nasser has done to Egypt. London, 1967. |

Afr 3326   Egypt - History by periods - Egypt, 1958-   ; United Arab Republic - Government and administration

Afr 3326.2	United Arab Republic. Declaration of the Union accord. Cairo, 1963.
Afr 3326.3	Cairo. Institute of National Planning. Institute of National Planning. Cairo, 1961.
Afr 3326.3.10	Cairo. Institute of National Planning. National Planning Institute. Cairo, 1962.
Afr 3326.4	Nasser, G.A. The Charter. Cairo, 1962.
Afr 3326.5	United Arab Republic. The Revolution in eleven years. Cairo, 1963.
Afr 3326.6	United Arab Republic. Information Department. The Revolution in twelve years. Cairo, 1964.
Afr 3326.7	United Arab Republic. Information Service. Ministry of Social Affairs in eleven years from July 23rd, 1952 to July 23rd, 1963. Cairo, 1963.
Afr 3326.8	Gulick, Luther Halsey. Government reorganization in the United Arab Republic. Cairo, 1962.

Afr 3329.1 - .99   Egypt - History by periods - Egypt, 1958-   ; United Arab Republic - Political biographies - Collected (A-Z, 99 scheme)

| Afr 3329.18 | Directory of United Arab Republic personages. Cairo. 1966+ |

Afr 3329.101 - .899   Egypt - History by periods - Egypt, 1958-   ; United Arab Republic - Political biographies - Individual (A-Z, 800 scheme)

| Afr 3329.598 | Daumal, Jack. Gamal Abd-el-Nasser. Paris, 1967. |

Afr 3330   Egypt - History by periods - Egypt, 1958-   ; United Arab Republic - Military affairs

| Afr 3330.5 | Vatikiotis, P.J. Egyptian army in politics. Bloomington, 1961. |

Afr 3335   Egypt - History by periods - Egypt, 1958-   ; United Arab Republic - Foreign relations

Afr 3335.5	United States Trade Mission to the United Arab Republic. Seven Americans in theUnited Arab Republic. Washington, 1960.
Afr 3335.10	United Arab Republic. Information Department. The United Arab Republic in world public opinion. Cairo, 1959.
Afr 3335.12	Egypt. Ministry of Education. Cultural Relations Department. Cultural agreements between Egypt and other countries. Cairo, 1956.
Afr 3335.15	United Arab Republic. Ministry of National Guidance. The U.A.R. and the policy of non-alignment. Cairo, 1966?
Afr 3335.20	Copeland, Miles. The game of nations: the amorality of power politics. London, 1970.

Afr 3339   Egypt - History by periods - Egypt, 1958-   ; United Arab Republic - Other special topics

Afr 3339.2	Pamphlet box. United Arab Republic. 6 pam.
Afr 3339.3	Pamphlet box. United Arab Republic.
Afr 3339.4	Pamphlet box. United Arab Republic.
Afr 3339.10	Hatim, Muhammad Abdal-Quadir. Culture and national guidance in twelve years. Cairo, 1964.
Afr 3339.12	United Arab Republic. Laws, statutes, etc. Une authentique promotion démocratique. Le Caire, 1964.
Afr 3339.14	Hussein, Mahmoud. La Lutte de classes en Égypte de 1945 à 1968. Paris, 1969.

Afr 3340   Egypt - History by periods - Egypt, 1958-   ; United Arab Republic - 1958- - General works

Afr 3340.5	Sedar, Irving. Behind the Egyptian sphinx. Philadelphia. 1960.
Afr 3340.8.2	Terra Viera, Blanca. Egipto en blanco y negro. 2. ed. Madrid, 1965.
Afr 3340.10	United Arab Republic. The United Arab Republic. Cairo, 1960.
Afr 3340.12	United Arab Republic. Information Department. The French spy ring in the UAR. Cairo, 1962.
Afr 3340.13	Robinson, Nehemiah. Nasser's Egypt. N.Y., 1963.
Afr 3340.14	United Arab Republic. Information report, ten years. Cairo, 1962.
Afr 3340.15	Pamphlet vol. United Arab Republic. 9 pam.
Afr 3340.20	Abdel Malek, Anouar. Egypt: military society; social change under Nasser. 1st American ed. N.Y., 1968.
Afr 3340.25	Assassa, Sami. Die Entstehung der Vereinigten Arabischen Republik und die Entwicklung. Diss. Berlin, 1965.

Afr 3669   Egypt - Egyptian Sudan; Sudan Republic - Bibliographies

| Afr 3669.5 | Santandrea, S. Bibliografia di studi africani. Verona, 1948. |
| Afr 3669.6 | Nasri, Abdel R. A bibliography of the Sudan, 1938-1958. London, 1962. |

Afr 3670   Egypt - Egyptian Sudan; Sudan Republic - Pamphlet volumes

| Afr 3670.01 | Pamphlet vol. Egyptian Sudan. |

Afr 3671   Egypt - Egyptian Sudan; Sudan Republic - Periodicals

Afr 3671.5	Diplomatic press directory of the Republic of the Sudan, including trade index and biographical section. London. 1957+ 6v.
Afr 3671.10	Sudan almanac. Khartoum. 1958+ 4v.
Afr 3671.15	Sudan society. Khartoum.
Afr 3671.20	Sudan research information bulletin. Khartoum. 1,1965+
Afr 3671.25	Sudan. Ministry of Finance and Economics. Sudan economic and financial review. Khartoum. 1,1961+
Afr 3671.26	Sudan. Ministry of Finance and Economics. Sudan economic and financial review. A special issue. 1,1962+

Afr 3673 Egypt - Egyptian Sudan; Sudan Republic - Historiography
Afr 3673.5 Hill, R.L. A bibliography of the Anglo-Egyptian Sudan, from the earliest times to 1937. London, 1939.

Afr 3674 Egypt - Egyptian Sudan; Sudan Republic - Government and administration
Afr 3674.2 Sudan. The sub-mamur's handbook. Khartoum, 1926.

Afr 3675 Egypt - Egyptian Sudan; Sudan Republic - General history
Afr 3675.2 Syndham, Q. The Soudan. London, 1884.
Afr 3675.3 Buchta, R. Der Sudan. Leipzig, 1888.
Afr 3675.4 Budge, E.A.W. The Egyptian Sudan. London, 1907. 2v.
Afr 3675.5 Sarkissian, G. Le Soudan égyptien. Paris, 1913.
Afr 3675.7 Dal Verme, L. I Dervisci nel Sudan egiziano. Roma, 1894.
Afr 3675.9 Mustafa, O.M. Le Soudan égyptien. Thèse. Neuville-sur-Saone, 1931.
Afr 3675.11 Crabitès, Pierre. The winning of the Sudan. London, 1934.
Afr 3675.15 MacMichael, H. The Anglo-Egyptian Sudan. London, 1934.
Afr 3675.15.5 MacMichael, H. The Sudan. London, 1954.
Afr 3675.17 Kraemer, W. Die koloniale Entwicklung des Anglo-Ägyptischen Sudans. Berlin, 1938.
Afr 3675.19 Anchiere, E. Storia della politica inglese nel Sudan, 1882-1938. Milano, 1939.
Afr 3675.20 Theobald, A.B. The Mahdiya. London, 1951.
Afr 3675.21 Abbas, Mekki. The Sudan question. London, 1952.
Afr 3675.22 Duncan, J.S.R. The Sudan. Edinburgh, 1952.
Afr 3675.22.5 Duncan, J.S.R. The Sudan's path to independence. Edinburgh, 1957.
Afr 3675.25 Jackson, H.C. The fighting Sudanese. London, 1954.
Afr 3675.28 Arkell, A.J. A history of the Sudan. London, 1955.
Afr 3675.28.2 Arkell, A.J. A history of the Sudan. 2.ed. London, 1961.
Afr 3675.30 Shibeika, Mekki. The independent Sudan. N.Y., 1959.
Afr 3675.35 Baddur, Abd al-Fattah Ibrahim al-Sayid. Sudanese-Egyptian relations. The Hague, 1960.
Afr 3675.40 Fabunmi, L.A. The Sudan in Anglo-Egyptian relations. London, 1960.
Afr 3675.45 Hill, R.L. Egypt in the Sudan. London, 1959.
Afr 3675.50 Sabry, Mohammed. Le Soudan égyptien. Le Caire, 1947.
Afr 3675.55 Holt, P.M. A modern history of the Sudan. London, 1961.
Afr 3675.60 Wharton, William M. The Sudan in pre-history and history. Khartoum, 1960.
Afr 3675.64 Smirnov, Sergei R. Istoriia Sudana (1821-1956). Moskva, 1968.
Afr 3675.65 Timbukti, Mahmud. Tariks el-Jettoch, ou Chronique du chercheur pour servir a l'histoire des villes, des armées et des principaux personnages du Tekrour. Paris, 1913.
Afr 3675.66 Trimingham, J.S. Islam in the Sudan. London, 1949.
Afr 3675.67 Al-Mahdi, Mandur. A short history of the Sudan. London, 1965.
Afr 3675.68 Henderson, Kenneth David Driutt. Sudan Republic. London, 1965.
VAfr 3675.69 Skuratowicz, Witold. Sudan. Warszawa, 1965.
Afr 3675.70 Douin, Georges. Histoire du Soudan égyptien. Le Caire, 1944.

Afr 3685 Egypt - Egyptian Sudan; Sudan Republic - History by periods - Egyptian conquest (1820-1823)
Afr 3685.5 Deherain, H. Le Soudan égyptien sous Mehemet Ali. Paris, 1898.
Afr 3685.6 English, G.B. Narrative of the expedition to Dongola and Senvaar. Boston, 1823.
Afr 3685.9 Gray, Richard. A history of the southern Sudan. London, 1961.

Afr 3695 Egypt - Egyptian Sudan; Sudan Republic - History by periods - First Governorship of Gordon (1874-1880)
Afr 3695.3A Gessi Pasha, R. Seven years in the Soudan. London, 1892.
Afr 3695.3B Gessi Pasha, R. Seven years in the Soudan. London, 1892.
Afr 3695.3.81 Zanaboni, G. Gessi, l'eroe del Bahr-el-Ghazal. Roma, 1934.
Afr 3695.3.83 Stocchetti, F. Romolo Gessi. Milano, 1952.
Afr 3695.3.85 Zaghi, Carlo. Vita di Romolo Gessi. Milano, 1939.
Afr 3695.3.86 Zaghi, Carlo. Gordon, Gessi e la riconquista del Sudan, 1874-1881. Firenze, 1947.
Afr 3695.4 Gordon, C.G. Provinces of the equator. Cairo, 1877.
Afr 3695.5 Hill, G.B. Gordon in Central Africa. London, 1881.
Afr 3695.6 Gordon, C.G. Equatoria under Egyptian rule. Cairo, 1953.
Afr 3695.7A Allen, B.M. Gordon and the Sudan. London, 1931.
Afr 3695.7B Allen, B.M. Gordon and the Sudan. London, 1931.

Afr 3700 Egypt - Egyptian Sudan; Sudan Republic - History by periods - Revolt of Mahdi (1881-1885) - General works
NEDL Afr 3700.2 Wylde, A.B. Eighty-three to eighty-seven in the Soudan. London, 1888. 2v.
Afr 3700.3 Wingate, F.R. Mahdiism and the Egyptian Sudan. London, 1891.
Afr 3700.3.2 Wingate, F.R. Mahdiism and the Egyptian Sudan. 2nd ed. London, 1891.
Afr 3700.4 Russell, Henry. The ruin of the Soudan. London, 1892.
NEDL Afr 3700.5 Slatin, R.C. Fire and sword in the Sudan. London, 1896.
Afr 3700.5.2 Slatin, R.C. Fire and sword in the Sudan. London, 1896.
Afr 3700.5.3 Slatin, R.C. Fire and sword in the Sudan. Leipzig, 1896.
Afr 3700.5.7 Slatin, R.C. Fire and sword in the Sudan. London, 1898.
Afr 3700.5.10 Slatin, R.C. Fer et feu au Soudan. Le Caire, 1898. 2v.
Afr 3700.5.15 Slatin, R.C. Ferro e fuoco nel Sudan. Roma, 1898.
Afr 3700.6 Bujac, E. Précis de quelques campagnes contemporaines. Pt. III - Egypte et Soudan. Paris, 1899.
Afr 3700.7 Duyarric, G. L'Etat Mahdiste au Soudan. Paris, 1901.
Afr 3700.8 Gordon, John. My six years with the Black Watch, 1881-1887. Boston, 1929.
Afr 3700.9 Haggard, A.C. Under crescent and star. Edinburgh, 1895.
Afr 3700.10 Grant, James. Cassell's history of the war in the Soudan. v.1-6. London, n.d. 2v.
Afr 3700.11 Bermann, R.A. Mahdi of Allah. London, 1931.
Afr 3700.12 Haultain, T.A. The war in the Soudan. Toronto, 1885.
Afr 3700.14 Galloway, W. The battle of Tofrek fought near Suakin. London, 1887.
Afr 3700.16 Holt, P.M. The Mahdist state in the Sudan, 1881-1898. Oxford, 1958.
Afr 3700.18 Collins, R.O. The southern Sudan. New Haven, 1962.
Afr 3700.20 Pimblett, W. Melville. Story of the Soudan war. London, 1885.
Afr 3700.22 Short, Thomas. The wars in Egypt. Bristol, 19- .
Afr 3700.24 Farwell, Byron. Prisoners of the Mahdi. London, 1967.

Afr 3705 Egypt - Egyptian Sudan; Sudan Republic - History by periods - Revolt of Mahdi (1881-1885) - Siege of Khartum (1884-1885)
Afr 3705.3A Gordon, C.G. Journals at Khartoum. Boston, 1885.
Afr 3705.3B Gordon, C.G. Journals at Khartoum. Boston, 1885.
Afr 3705.3C Gordon, C.G. Journals at Khartoum. Boston, 1885.
Afr 3705.3.5 Gordon, C.G. The journals of Major General Gordon. London, 1885.
Afr 3705.3.10F Gordon, C.G. General Gordon's last journal. London, 1885.
Afr 3705.3.15 Gordon, C.G. General Gordon's Khartoum journal. London, 1961.
Afr 3705.3.16 Gordon, C.G. General Gordon's Khartoum journal. N.Y., 1961.
Afr 3705.4 Pall Mall Gazette, London. Who is to have the Soudan? London, 1884.
Afr 3705.5 Macdonald, A. Too late for Gordon and Khartoum. London, 1887.
Afr 3705.7 Power, Frank. Letters from Khartoum. London, 1885.
Afr 3705.7.2 Power, Frank. Letters from Khartoum. 3d ed. London, 1885.
Afr 3705.9 Macdonald, A. Why Gordon perished...Political causes which led to Sudan disasters. London, 1896.
Afr 3705.12 Buchan, John. Gordon at Khartoum. Edinburgh, 1934.
Afr 3705.14 Delebecque, J. Gordon et le drame de Khartoum. Paris, 1935.
Afr 3705.16 Egyptian red book. Edinburgh, 1884.

Afr 3708 Egypt - Egyptian Sudan; Sudan Republic - History by periods - Revolt of Mahdi (1881-1885) - Expedition of Wolseley (1884-1885)
Afr 3708.3 Wilson, C.W. From Korti to Khartum. Edinburgh, 1886.
Afr 3708.3.2 Wilson, C.W. From Korti to Khartum. Edinburgh, 1885.
Afr 3708.4 Butler, W.F. The campaign of the Cataracts. London, 1887.
Afr 3708.5 Burleigh, B. Desert warfare, being the chronicle of the Eastern Soudan campaign. London, 1884.
Afr 3708.6 Colvile, H.E. History of the Sudan campaign. London, 1889. 3v.
Afr 3708.7 Gleichen, C. With the Camel Corps up the Nile. London, 1888.
Afr 3708.8 Brackenbury, H. The river column. Edinburgh, 1885.
Afr 3708.10 Labat, G.P. Les voyageurs canadiens à l'expédition du Soudan. Québec, 1886.
Afr 3708.12F Verner, Willoughby. Sketches in the Soudan. 2d ed. London, 1886.
Afr 3708.14 Jackson, Louis. Our Caughnawagas in Egypt. Montreal, 1885.
Afr 3708.16 Symons, Julian. England's pride. London, 1965.
Afr 3708.20 Wolseley, Garnet Joseph Wolseley. In relief of Gordon; Lord Wolseley's campaign journal of the Khartoum Relief Expedition, 1884-1885. London, 1967.

Afr 3710 Egypt - Egyptian Sudan; Sudan Republic - History by periods - Revolt of Mahdi (1881-1885) - Other special topics
Afr 3710.3.2 Colborne, J. With Hicks Pasha in the Soudan. 2d ed. London, 1885.
Afr 3710.13.5 Messedaglia, Luigi. Uomini d'Africa. Bologna, 1935.
Afr 3710.15 Stacey, Charles. Records of the Nile voyageurs. Toronto, 1959.
Afr 3710.16 Hill, R.L. Slatin Pasha. London, 1965.

Afr 3715 Egypt - Egyptian Sudan; Sudan Republic - History by periods - History from Evacuation (1885-1899) - General works
Afr 3715.3F Sudan intelligence reports. Cairo. 1-111,1892-1903
Afr 3715.5A Shibeika, Mekki. British policy in the Sudan, 1882-1902. London, 1952.
Afr 3715.5B Shibeika, Mekki. British policy in the Sudan, 1882-1902. London, 1952.
Afr 3715.10 Nigumi, M.A. A great trusteeship. London, 1957.
Afr 3715.10.2 Nigumi, M.A. A great trusteeship. 2d ed. London, 1958.
Afr 3715.12 Sanderson, George Neville. England, Europe and the upper Nile, 1882-1899. Edinburgh, 1965.

Afr 3718 Egypt - Egyptian Sudan; Sudan Republic - History by periods - History from Evacuation (1885-1899) - Special topics
Afr 3718.15 Jackson, H.C. Osman Digna. London, 1926.

Afr 3725 Egypt - Egyptian Sudan; Sudan Republic - History by periods - History from Evacuation (1885-1899) - Emin Pasha in Equatoria (1878-1889)
Afr 3725.2 Emin Pasha. Emin Pasha, his life and work. N.Y., 1969. 2v.
Afr 3725.3 Schnitzer, E. Emin Pasha in Central Africa. London, 1888.
Afr 3725.3.25 Jephson, A.J.M. Emin Pasha and the rebellion at the equator. N.Y., 1891.
X Cg Afr 3725.4 Casati, G. Ten years in Equatoria. London, 1891. (Changed to XP 3865) 2v.
Afr 3725.4.5 Casati, G. Zehn Jahre in Äquatoria. Hamburg, 1891. 3v.
Afr 3725.5 Ghisleri, A. Gl'Italiani nell'Equatoria. Bergamo, 1893.
Afr 3725.6 Stuhlmann, F. Mit EminPasha in Herz von Africa. Berlin, 1894.
Afr 3725.7 Emin Pasha. Emin Pasha. Berlin, 1898.
Afr 3725.7.5 Schweitzer, G. Von Khartum zum Kongo. Berlin, 1932.
Afr 3725.8 Emin Pascha. Tagebücher. Bd.1-4, 6. Hamburg, 1916-1927. 5v.
Afr 3725.9 Symons, A.J.A. Emin, the governor of Equatoria. London, 1928.
Afr 3725.10 Reichard, Paul. Dr. Emin Pascha. Leipzig, 1891.
Afr 3725.11 Prout, H.G. Where Emin is. n.p., 1889.
Afr 3725.12.5 Manning, Olivia. The remarkable expedition. London, 1947.
Afr 3725.12.10 Manning, Olivia. The reluctant rescue. 1st ed. Garden City, N.Y., 1947.
Afr 3725.13 Little, H.W. One man's power. The life and work of Emin Pasha in Equatorial Africa. London, 1889.
Afr 3725.14 Ade, H.C. Pioniere im Osten. Stuttgart, 1923.

Afr 3730 Egypt - Egyptian Sudan; Sudan Republic - History by periods - History from Evacuation (1885-1899) - Stories of captivities
Afr 3730.2 Ohrwalder, J. Ten years' captivity in the Mahdi's camp. 7th ed. London, 1892.
Afr 3730.2.5 Ohrwalder, J. Ten years' captivity in the Mahdi's camp. 10th ed. Leipzig, 1893.
Afr 3730.3 Ohrwalder, J. Ten years' captivity in the Mahdi's camp. London, 1893.
Afr 3730.3.5 Ohrwalder, J. Ten years' captivity in the Mahdi's camp. N.Y., 1893.
Afr 3730.4 Cuzzi, G. Fünfzehn Jahre Gefangener des falschen Propheten. Leipzig, 1900.
Afr 3730.5 Neufeld, C. A prisoner of the Khaleefa. N.Y., 1899.
Afr 3730.5.10 Neufeld, C. A prisoner of the Khaleefa. 3d ed. N.Y., 1899.

Afr 3735   **Egypt - Egyptian Sudan; Sudan Republic - History by periods - History from Evacuation (1885-1899) - Reconquest of the Sudan (1898-1899)**

Afr 3735.2   Burleigh, B. Sirdar and Khalifa. London, 1898.
Afr 3735.2.5   Burleigh, B. Sirdar and Khalifa. 3rd ed. London, 1898.
Afr 3735.3   Burleigh, B. Khartoum campaign, 1898. London, 1899.
Afr 3735.4   Steevens, G.W. With Kitchener to Khartum. Edinburgh, 1898.
Afr 3735.4.1   Steevens, G.W. With Kitchener to Khartum. N.Y., 1898.
Afr 3735.4.2   Steevens, G.W. With Kitchener to Khartum. 12th ed. Edinburgh, 1898.
Afr 3735.4.3   Steevens, G.W. With Kitchener to Khartum. N.Y., 1899.
Afr 3735.4.6   Steevens, G.W. With Kitchener to Khartum. London, 1909.
Afr 3735.5   Alford, H.S.L. The Egyptian Soudan. London, 1898.
Afr 3735.6   Bennett, E.N. The downfall of the Dervishes. London, 1898.
Htn   Afr 3735.7*   Churchill, Winston S. The river war. London, 1899. 2v.
Afr 3735.7.5   Churchill, Winston S. The river war. London, 1902?
Afr 3735.8   Atteridge, A.H. Towards Khartoum. ondon, 1897.
Afr 3735.9   Knight, E.F. Letters from the Sudan. London, 1897.
Afr 3735.10   Sudan campaign 1896-99. London, 1899.
Afr 3735.11   Egerton, G. With the Seventy-Second Highlanders in the Sudan campaign. London, 1909.

Afr 3740   **Egypt - Egyptian Sudan; Sudan Republic - History by periods - History from Evacuation (1885-1899) - Fashoda question (1898-1899)**

Afr 3740.1F   France. Ministère des Affaires Etrangères. Affaires du Haut-Nil 1897-98. Paris, 1898.
Afr 3740.2F   Great Britain. Parliament. Correspondence with the French government. London, 1898.
Afr 3740.3   Barre, P. Fachoda. Paris, n.d.
NEDL   Afr 3740.4   Caix, R. de. Fachoda. Paris, 1899.
Afr 3740.5   Castellani, C. Marchand l'africain. Paris, n.d.
Afr 3740.6.2   Emily, J. Mission Marchand journal. 2d ed. Paris, 1913.
Afr 3740.6.25   Bobichon, H. Contribution a l'histoire de la mission Marchand. Paris, 1937.
Afr 3740.6.30   Delebecque, J. Vie du Général Marchand. Paris, 1936.
Afr 3740.6.35   Delebecque, J. Vie du Général Marchand. Paris, 1936.
Afr 3740.7   Guetant, L. Marchand-Fashoda. Paris, 1899.
Afr 3740.8   Giffen, Morrison B. Fashoda, the incident and its diplomatic setting. Chicago, 1930.
Afr 3740.9   Wauters, A.J. Souvenirs de Fashoda et de l'expedition Dhanis. Bruxelles, 1910.
Afr 3740.10   Labatut, Guy de. Fachoda. 4e ed. Paris, 1932.
Afr 3740.12   Yatin, Fernand. Une mise au point, la vérité sur Fachoda. Chaumont, 1923.
Afr 3740.14   Kossatz, Heinz. Untersuchungen über den französisch-englischen Weltgegensatz im Faschodajahr (1898). Breslau, 1934.
Afr 3740.16   Riker, T.W. A survey of British policy in the Fashoda crisis. N.Y., 1929.
Afr 3740.18   Treves, P. Il dramma di Fascioda. Milano, 1937.

Afr 3745   **Egypt - Egyptian Sudan; Sudan Republic - History by periods - The Sudan since the conquest (1900-1956)**

NEDL   Afr 3745.5   Great Britain. Foreign Office. Report on the finances, administration and condition of the Sudan. London. 1908
Afr 3745.5   Great Britain. Foreign Office. Report on the finances, administration and condition of the Sudan. London. 1,1932
Afr 3745.10A   Martin, Percy F. The Sudan in evolution. London, 1921.
Afr 3745.10B   Martin, Percy F. The Sudan in evolution. London, 1921.
Afr 3745.20   Cheibany, A.K. La situation administrative et économique du Soudan anglo-égyptien. These. Paris, 1926.
Afr 3745.25   Keun, Odette. Foreigner looks at the British Sudan. London, 1930.
Afr 3745.30   Yardley, J. Parengon, or eddies in Equatoria. London, 1931.
Afr 3745.35   Colin, Hugues. La condition internationale du Soudan anglo-égyptien et du Haut-Nil. Thèse. Paris, 1936.
Afr 3745.40A   Henderson, K.D.D. Survey of the Anglo-Egyptian Sudan, 1898-1944. N.Y., 1946.
Afr 3745.40B   Henderson, K.D.D. Survey of the Anglo-Egyptian Sudan, 1898-1944. N.Y., 1946.
Afr 3745.45   Sudan, Egyptian. The Sudan. Khartoum, 1947.
Afr 3745.50   Newbold, D. The making of modern Sudan. London, 1953.
Afr 3745.55   British Information Service. The Sudan, 1899-1953. N.Y., 1953.
Afr 3745.60   Jackson, H.C. Behind the modern Sudan. London, 1955.
Afr 3745.65   Kiselev, V.I. Put sudana v nezavisimosti. Moscow, 1958.
Afr 3745.70   British Information Services. The Anglo-Egyptian Sudan. N.Y., 1951.
Afr 3745.71   Sudan. Central Office of Information. Basic facts about the southern provinces of the Sudan. Khartoum, 1964.
Afr 3745.73   Bashir, Muhammad Umar. The Southern Sudan. London, 1968.
Afr 3745.75   Collins, Robert O. King Leopold, England and the Upper Nile, 1899-1909. New Haven, 1968.
Afr 3745.80   Abd al-Rahim, Muddathir. Imperialism and nationalism in the Sudan. Oxford, 1969.

Afr 3750   **Egypt - Egyptian Sudan; Sudan Republic - History by periods - History since independence (1956-) - General works**

Afr 3750.1   Griadunov, Iurii S. Novye gorizonty Sudana. Moskva, 1969.

Afr 3805 - 3810   **Egypt - Egyptian Sudan; Sudan Republic - Geography, description, etc. - General works (By date)**

Afr 3808.81.5   Ensor, F. Sidney. Incidents on a journey through Nubia to Darfoor. London, 1881.
Afr 3809.33   Roulet, Edouard. La mission Roulet. Paris, 1933.

Afr 3811   **Egypt - Egyptian Sudan; Sudan Republic - Geography, description, etc. - Special customs**

Afr 3811.5   Nordenstam, Tore. Sudanese ethics. Uppsala, 1968.

Afr 3812   **Egypt - Egyptian Sudan; Sudan Republic - Geography, description, etc. - Guidebooks, gazetteers, etc.**

Afr 3812.5   Guide - annuaire d'Egypte. Le Caire. 1872-1873

Afr 3813   **Egypt - Egyptian Sudan; Sudan Republic - Economic history and conditions**

Afr 3813.5   Kleve, Jacob Geert. Capital formation and increase in national income in Sudan in 1955-1959. Rotterdam, 1961.
Afr 3813.8   Italy. Instituto Nazionale per il Commercio Estero. Sudan. Roma, 1960.
Afr 3813.10   Sudan. Ministry of Finance and Economics. The ten year plan of economic and social development, 1962-1971. Khartoum, 1963.

Afr 3813   **Egypt - Egyptian Sudan; Sudan Republic - Economic history and conditions - cont.**

Afr 3813.15   Sudan. Treaties, etc. 1961. Administration agreement (Roseires irrigation project) between the Republic of the Sudan and Kreditanstalt für Wiederaufbau and International Development Association and International Bank for Reconstruction and Development dated as of June 14, 1961. n.p., 1961.
Afr 3813.18   al-Kammash, Majdi M. Economic development and planning in Egypt. N.Y., 1968.
Afr 3813.20   Massow, Heinrich von. Die Industrie den Republik Sudan. Hamburg, 1964.
Afr 3813.22   Sudan. Treaties, etc. Kuwait Fund for Arab Economic Development. Loan agreement between the Republic for Sudan and the Kuwait Fund for Arab Economic Development dated March 25th, 1962. Kuwait, 1962?

Afr 3814   **Egypt - Egyptian Sudan; Sudan Republic - Finance**

Afr 3814.5   Fedorov, T. Finansy i kredit sudana. Moskva, 1962.

Afr 3816   **Egypt - Egyptian Sudan; Sudan Republic - Races - General works**

Afr 3816.2   Frobenius, Herman. Die Heiden-Neger des ägyptischen Sudan. Berlin, 1893.
Afr 3816.4   Santandrea, Stefano. A tribal history. Bologna, 1964.
Afr 3816.7   McLoughlin, Peter F. Language-switching as an index of socialization. Berkeley, 1964.

Afr 3817   **Egypt - Egyptian Sudan; Sudan Republic - Races - Special**

Afr 3817.5   MacMichael, Harold Alfred. The tribes of northern and central Kordofan. Cambridge, 1912.
Afr 3817.6   Westermann, Diedrich. The Shilluk people. Philadelphia, 1912.
Afr 3817.6.5   Hofmayr, Wilhelm. Die Schilluk. St. Gabriel, 1925.
Afr 3817.8   Evans-Pritchard, Edward Evan. The Nuer. Oxford, 1940.
Afr 3817.10   Lienharot, Godfrey. Divinity and experience, the religion of the Dinka. Oxford, 1961.
Afr 3817.12   American Jewish Congress. Committee on International Affairs and on Israel. The black record, Nasser's persecution. N.Y., 1957.
Afr 3817.14   Cunnison, Ivan George. Baggara Arabs, power and the lineage in a Sudanese nomad tribe. Oxford, 1966.
Afr 3817.16   De Giorgi, Luigi. Culto dei gemelli nel Sudan meridionale. Bologna, 1966.

Afr 3818   **Egypt - Egyptian Sudan; Sudan Republic - Religion; missions**

Afr 3818.2   Elder, Earl. Vindicating a vision. Philadelphia, 1958.
Afr 3818.4   Veenstra, Johanna. Pioneering for Christ in the Sudan. London, 1928.
Afr 3818.7   Trimingham, John Spencer. The Christian approach to Islam in the Sudan. London, 1948.
Afr 3818.10   Allison, Oliver Claude. A pilgrim church's progress. London, 1966.
Afr 3818.12.2   Bonfanti, Adriano. Espulsi dal Sudan. 2. ed. Bologna, 1964.
Afr 3818.14   Vandevort, Eleanor. A leopard tamed; the story of an African pastor, his people, and his problems. N.Y., 1968.

Afr 3821   **Egypt - Egyptian Sudan; Sudan Republic - Provinces - Kordofan**

Afr 3821.2   Meinhof, Carl. Eine Studienfahrt nach Kordofan. Hamburg, 1916.
Afr 3821.5   Prout, Henri Goslee. General report on the province of Kordofan. Cairo, 1877.

Afr 3822   **Egypt - Egyptian Sudan; Sudan Republic - Provinces - Darfur**

Afr 3822.2   Henriques, Robert. Death by moonlight. London, 1938.
Afr 3822.5   Theobald, Alan B. Ali Dinar, last sultan of Darfor, 1895-1916. London, 1965.
Afr 3822.8   Al-Tunisi, Muhammad Ibn Umar. Voyage au Darfour. Paris, 1845.
Afr 3822.11   Jomard, Edme Francois. Observations sur le voyage au Darfour. Paris, 1845.

Afr 3823   **Egypt - Egyptian Sudan; Sudan Republic - Provinces - Bahr el Ghazal**

Afr 3823.2   Wyndham, Richard. The gentle savage. London, 1936.
Afr 3823.4   Lupton, Frank. Geographical observations in the Bahr-el-Ghazal region. London, 1884.
Afr 3823.6   Lemaire, Charles. Journal de route de Charles Lemaire. Bruxelles, 1953.

Afr 3826   **Egypt - Egyptian Sudan; Sudan Republic - Provinces - Blue Nile, Gezira**

Afr 3826.2   Gaitskell, Arthur. Gezira. London, 1959.
Afr 3826.5   Sudan. Gezira Board. The Gezira scheme from within. Khartoum, 1954.

Afr 3834   **Egypt - Egyptian Sudan; Sudan Republic - Cities, towns, etc. - Khartoum**

Afr 3834.2   Sudan. Khartoum, capital. Khartoum, 1963.

Afr 3843   **Egypt - Egyptian Sudan; Sudan Republic - Cities, towns, etc. - Others**

X Cg   Afr 3843.5   Khartum. University. Department of Architecture. El Kereiba village. Khartoum, 1963. (Changed to XP 223)
Afr 3843.8   Reining, Conrad C. The Zande scheme; an anthropological case study of economic development in Africa. Evanston, 1966.

Afr 3974 - 3980   **Egypt - Geography, description, etc. of Egypt - General works (By date)**

Afr 3974.00   Abd-Al-Latif. Relation de l'Egypte (XIVe siècle). Paris, 1810.
Afr 3974.00.5   Wahl, G.F.G. Abdallatifs Denkwürdigkeiten Egyptens. Halle, 1790.
Afr 3974.83.9   Breydenbach, B. von. Les saintes pérégrinations... Texte ... Par F. Larrinaz. Le Caire, 1904.
Afr 3976.17   Scortia, J.B. De natura et incremento nili. Lugduni, 1617.
Htn   Afr 3976.78*   Vansleb, F. The present state of Egypt. London, 1678.
Afr 3976.86   Giacomo d'Albano, Father. Historia della missione francescana in alto Egitto-Fungi-Etiopia, 1686-1720. Cairo, 1961.
Afr 3976.92   Maillet, B. de. Description de l'Egypte. Paris, 1735.
Afr 3977.19   Ildefonso da Palermo, Father. Cronaca della missione francescana dell'Alto Egitto, 1719-1739. Cairo, 1962.
Afr 3977.30   Granger, called Tourtechot. Relation du voyage fait en Egypte... En l'annee 1730. Paris, 1745.
Afr 3977.37.10F   Norden, Frederik L. The antiquities, natural history, ruins... of Egypt, Nubia and Thebes. London, 1780.
Htn   Afr 3977.49PF*   Dalton, Richard. A series of prints relative to the manner, customs, etc, of the present inhabitants of Egypt. London, 1752.

Afr 3974 - 3980 Egypt - Geography, description, etc. of Egypt - General works (By date) - cont.

Afr 3977.57F Norden, F.L. Travels in Egypt and Nubia. London, 1757. 2v.
Afr 3977.73 Pauw, C.V. Recherches philosophiques sur les égyptiens. Berlin, 1773. 2v.
Afr 3977.76 Abu-l-Feda. Descriptio aegypti. Göttingen, 1776.
Afr 3977.86 Savary, C. Lettres sur l'Egypte. Paris, 1786. 3v.
Afr 3977.86.5 Savary, C. Letters on Egypt. vol.1. Dublin, 1787.
Afr 3977.91 Trecourt, Jean Baptiste. Memoires sur l'Egypte. Le Caire, 1942.
Afr 3977.98 Geoffroy Saint Hilaire, E. Lettres ecrites d'Egypte. Paris, 1901.
Afr 3977.98.5 Browne, W.G. Travels in Africa, Egypt, and Syria. London, 1799.
Afr 3977.98.6 Browne, W.G. Travels in Africa, Egypt, and Syria, 1792-98. London, 1806.
Afr 3977.99 Sonnini, C.S. Voyage dans ... Egypte. v.1-3 + atlas. Paris, 1799. 4v.
Htn Afr 3977.99.3* Remmey, John. An account of the present state of Egypt. N.Y., 1799.
Afr 3978.00 Institut d'Egypte, Cairo. Memoires sur l'Egypte. Paris, 1800.
Afr 3978.00.3 Institut d'Egypte, Cairo. Mémoires sur l'Egypte publiés pendant les campagnes de Général Bonaparte dans les annees VI et VII. Paris, 1801.
Afr 3978.00.10 Antes, J. Beobachtungen über die Sitten und Gebräuche der Ägypter. Gera, 1801.
Afr 3978.02PF Mayer, Ludwig. Vues en Egypte. Londres, 1802.
Afr 3978.02.1PF Mayer, L. Views in Egypt, from the original drawings in the possession of Sir Robert Ainslie. London, 1801.
Afr 3978.02.5PF Mayer, Ludwig. Views in Egypt. London, 1804.
Afr 3978.03A Denon, V.D. Travels in upper and lower Egypt. N.Y., 1803. 2v.
Afr 3978.03B Denon, V.D. Travels in upper and lower Egypt. N.Y., 1803. 2v.
Afr 3978.03.3 Non-military journal, or Observations made in Egypt. London, 1803.
Afr 3978.14 Breton, M. L'Egypte et la Syrie. v.1-6. Paris, 1814. 3v.
Afr 3978.17 Legh, T. Narrative of a journey in Egypt. Philadelphia, 1817.
Afr 3978.17.2 Legh, T. Narrative of a journey in Egypt. 2d. ed. London, 1817.
NEDL Afr 3978.17.3 Legh, T. Narrative of a journey in Egypt. London, 1817.
Afr 3978.18 Light, Henry. Travels in Egypt, Nubia, Holy Land, Mount Lebanon and Cyprus, in the year 1814. London, 1818.
Afr 3978.22 Waddington, G. Journal of a visit to some parts of Ethiopia. London, 1822.
Afr 3978.24 Fruits of enterprize, travels in Egypt. Boston, 1824.
Afr 3978.24.5 Fruits of enterprize, travels in Egypt. New ed. N.Y., 1843.
Afr 3978.25 Sherer, M. Scenes and impressions in Egypt and Italy. London, 1825.
Afr 3978.27 Minutoli. Recollections of Egypt. Philadelphia, 1827.
Afr 3978.30F Burckhardt, J.L. Manners and customs of modern Egyptians. London, 1830.
Afr 3978.30.3 Webster, James. Travels through Egypt. London, 1830. 2v.
Afr 3978.31 Ferrario, G. Il costume antico e moderno. Livorno, 1831. 3 pam.
Afr 3978.34 Saint John, J.A. Egypt, and Mohammed Ali. vol.1-2. London, 1834. 2v.
Afr 3978.35 Wilkinson, J.G. Topography of Thebes. London, 1835.
NEDL Afr 3978.37 Lane, E.W. Manners and customs of the modern Egyptians. London, 1837.
Afr 3978.37.8 Lane, E.W. An account of the manners and customs of the modern Egyptians. v.1-2. London, 1837. 2v.
Afr 3978.37.15 Scott, C.R. Rambles in Egypt and Candia. v.1-2. London, 1837. 2v.
Afr 3978.38.5 Sammarco, A. Il viaggio di Mohammed Ali al Sudan. Caire, 1929.
Afr 3978.39 Dumas, A. Impressions of travel in Egypt. N.Y., 1839.
Afr 3978.40 Clat-Bey, A. Aperçu général sur l'Egypte. Bruxelles, 1840. 2v.
Afr 3978.40.2 Clat-Bey, A. Aperçu général sur l'Egypte. v.1-2. Paris, 1840.
Afr 3978.40.5 Ravioli, C. Viaggio della spedizione romana in Egitto. v.1. Roma, 1870.
Afr 3978.42 Cooley, J.E. The American in Egypt. N.Y., 1842.
Afr 3978.42.3 Gliddon, G.R. Appendix to the American in Egypt. Philadelphia, 1842.
Afr 3978.43 Millard, D. Journal of travels in Egypt. N.Y., 1843.
Afr 3978.43.3 Wilkinson, J.G. Modern Egypt. London, 1843. 2v.
Afr 3978.43.5 Yates, W.H. Modern history and condition of Egypt. London, 1843. 2v.
Afr 3978.44 Pueckler-Muskau. Aus Mehemed Alis Reich. Stuttgart, 1844.
Afr 3978.44.5 Ampere, J.J. Voyage en Egypte et en Nubie. Paris, 1868.
Afr 3978.45 Saint John, J.A. Egypt and Nubia. London, 1845.
Afr 3978.45.3 Poole, Sophia L. The Englishwoman in Egypt. London, 1845.
Afr 3978.45.5 Saint John, J.A. Egypt and Nubia. London, n.d.
Afr 3978.46 Schoelcher, V. L'Egypte en 1845. Paris, 1846.
Afr 3978.46.3 Combes, Edmond. Voyage en Egypte. Paris, 1846.
Afr 3978.49 Gliddon, Geo. R. Hand-book to the American panorama of the Nile. London, 1849.
Afr 3978.49.5 Bartlett, W.H. The Nile boat. London, 1849.
Afr 3978.49.6 Bartlett, W.H. The Nile boat, glimpses of Egypt. 2d ed. London, 1850.
Afr 3978.49.8 Bartlett, W.H. The Nile boat. 4th ed. London, 1861.
Afr 3978.49.20 Bevan, Samuel. Sand and canvas, a narrative of adventures in Egypt. London, 1849.
Afr 3978.50.5 Furniss, William. Waraga, or The charms of the Nile. N.Y., 1850.
Afr 3978.51 Bartlett, W.H. The Nile boat. N.Y., 1851.
Htn Afr 3978.51.4* Curtis, G.W. Nile notes of a howadji. N.Y., 1851.
Afr 3978.51.5 Curtis, G.W. Nile notes. N.Y., 1851.
Afr 3978.51.6 Curtis, G.W. Nile notes. N.Y., 1852.
Afr 3978.51.9 Melly, George. Khartoum, and the blue and white Niles. London, 1851. 2v.
Afr 3978.51.11 Journal of a voyage up the Nile. Buffalo, 1851.
Afr 3978.52 Smith, J.V.C. A pilgrimage to Egypt. Boston, 1852.
Afr 3978.52.5 Wainwright, J.M. The land of bondage..a tour in Egypt. N.Y., 1852.
Afr 3978.53 Saint John, Bayle. Village life in Egypt. Boston, 1853. 2v.
Afr 3978.53.3 Lepsius, R. Letters from Egypt. London, 1853.
Afr 3978.53.6 Gentz, W. Briefe aus Ägypten und Nubien. Berlin, 1853.
Afr 3978.53.8 Churi, J.H. Sea Nile, the desert, and Nigritia, travels. London, 1853.
Afr 3978.53.10 Norov, Avraam S. Puteshestvie po Egiptu i Nubii, v 1834-1835. Izd.2. Sankt Peterburg, 1853. 2v.

Afr 3974 - 3980 Egypt - Geography, description, etc. of Egypt - General works (By date) - cont.

Afr 3978.54 Thompson, J.P. Photographic views of Egypt. Glasgow, n.d.
Afr 3978.54.2 Thompson, J.P. Photographic views of Egypt. Boston, 1854.
Afr 3978.54.5 Thompson, J.P. Photographic views of Egypt. Boston, 1856.
Afr 3978.55 Brugsch-Bey, H. Reiseberichte aus Ägypten. Leipzig, 1855.
Afr 3978.56 Borthelemy Saint-Hilaire. Lettres sur l'Egypte. Paris, 1856.
Afr 3978.56.5 Saint John, B. Two years residence in a Levantine family. London, 1856.
Afr 3978.57 Prime, W.C. Boat life in Egypt and Nubia. N.Y., 1857.
Afr 3978.57.2 Prime, W.C. Boat life in Egypt and Nubia. N.Y., 1868.
Afr 3978.57.3 Tomard, E.F. Fragments. (Mainly Egypt). Paris, 1857.
Afr 3978.57.5 Saint Hilaire, J.B. Egypt and the great Suez Canal. London, 1857.
Afr 3978.58 Ditson, G.L. The Para papers on France, Egypt and Ethiopia. Paris, 1858.
Afr 3978.59 Paine, Caroline. Tent and harem. N.Y., 1859.
Afr 3978.59.2 Gregory, W.H. Egypt 1855-56. Tunis 1857-58. London, 1859. 2v.
Afr 3978.60 Beamont, William. To Sinai and Syene and back in 1860 and 1861. 2nd ed. London, 1871.
Afr 3978.61 Petherick, J. Egypt, the Soudan and Central Africa. Edinburgh, 1861.
Afr 3978.63 Carey, M.L.M. Four months in a dahabeeh. London, 1863.
Afr 3978.63.5 Whately, M.L. Ragged life in Egypt. London, 1863.
Afr 3978.63.8 Whately, M.L. Child life in Egypt. Philadelphia, 1866.
Afr 3978.63.10 Hoskins, G.A. A winter in upper and lower Egypt. London, 1863.
Afr 3978.63.15 Kremer, Alfred, Freiherr von. Aegypten. Leipzig, 1863.
Afr 3978.64 Brugsch, H.K.F. Aus dem Orient. (Mainly Egypt). Berlin, 1864.
Afr 3978.65 Duff-Gordon, Lucie Austin. Letters from Egypt 1863-65. London, 1865.
Afr 3978.65.3 Duff-Gordon, Lucie Austin. Last letters from Egypt. London, 1875.
Afr 3978.65.4 Duff-Gordon, Lucie Austin. Last letters from Egypt. 2d ed. London, 1876.
Afr 3978.65.5 Duff-Gordon, Lucie Austin. Letters from Egypt. London, 1902.
Afr 3978.65.6 Duff-Gordon, Lucie Austin. Letters from Egypt. N.Y., 1902.
Afr 3978.65.7 Duff-Gordon, Lucie Austin. Letters from Egypt. N.Y., 1904.
Afr 3978.65.8 Duff-Gordon, Lucie Austin. Letters from Egypt, (1862-1869). London, 1969.
Afr 3978.65.9 Wace, A.T. Palm leaves from the Nile. Shrewsbury, 1865.
Afr 3978.66 Kraemer, R. von. En vinter Orienten. Reseanteckingar fraan Egypten. Stockholm, 1866.
Afr 3978.67 Billard, F.L. Les moeurs et le gouvernemnt de l'egypte. Milan, 1867.
Afr 3978.67.3 Warren, W.W. Life on the Nile. Paris, 1867.
Afr 3978.67.4 Warren, W.W. Life on the Nile. 2d ed. Boston, 1873.
Afr 3978.67.5F Gottberg, E. de. Des cataractes du Nil..Hannek...Kaybar. Paris, 1867.
Afr 3978.68 Irby, C.L. Travels in Nubia. London, 1868.
Afr 3978.68.5 Frankl, L.A. Aus Egypten. Wien, 1868.
Afr 3978.69 Bolgiani, V.M.V. Pharaonernas land. Resebilder fraan egypten. Stockholm, 1869.
Afr 3978.69.1 Bolgiani, V.M.V. Im Lande der Pharaonen. Wien, 1869.
Afr 3978.69.2 Wachenhusen, H. Vom armen egyptischen Mann. Bd.1-2. Berlin, 1871.
Afr 3978.69.5 About, E. Le fellah: souvenirs d'Egypte. Paris, 1869.
Afr 3978.69.5.2 About, E. Le fellah: souvenirs d'Egypte. 2e ed. Paris, 1870.
Afr 3978.69.5.4 About, E. Le fellah: souvenirs d'Egypte. 3e ed. Paris, 1873.
Afr 3978.69.5.6 About, E. Le fellah: souvenirs d'Egypte. 6e ed. Paris, 1896.
Afr 3978.69.6 Grey, W. Journal...visit to Egypt, Constantinople. London, 1869.
Afr 3978.69.15 Eca de Queiroz, J.M. O Egypto, notas de viagem. Porto, 1926.
Afr 3978.69.25 Fromentin, E. Voyage en Egypte (1869). Paris, 1935.
Afr 3978.70 Lacour, Raoul. L'Egypte d'Alexandrie a la Seconde Cataracte. Paris, 1871.
Afr 3978.70.5 Castro y Serrano, Jose de. La novela del Egipto. Madrid, 1870.
Afr 3978.70.10 Watt, Robert. Fra aegypternes land. Kjøbenhavn, 1870.
Afr 3978.70.15 Couvidou, Henri. Etude sur l'Egypte contemporaine. Le Caire, 187-.
Afr 3978.71 Zincke, F.B. Egypt of the pharaohs and of the kedive. London, 1871.
Afr 3978.71.2 Lane, E.W. An account of manners and customs of modern Egyptians. London, 1846. 2v.
Afr 3978.71.3 Lane, E.W. Account of manners and customs of modern Egyptians. London, 1871. 2v.
Afr 3978.71.4 Lane, E.W. The manners and customs of modern Egyptians. London, 1923.
Afr 3978.71.5 Hamley, W.G. New sea and an old land..visit to Egypt. Edinburgh, 1871.
Afr 3978.71.8 Whately, Mary L. Among the huts in Egypt. London, 1871.
Afr 3978.72 Stephan, H. Das heutige Agypten. Leipzig, 1872.
Afr 3978.73 Knorring, O.V. Tvaa maanader i egypten. Stockholm, 1873.
Afr 3978.73.5 Lenoir, Paul. The Fayoum, or Artists in Egypt. London, 1873.
Afr 3978.74 Leland, C.G. The Egyptian sketch book. N.Y., 1874.
Afr 3978.74.5F Hoppin, Augustus. On the Nile. Boston, 1874.
NEDL Afr 3978.75 Southworth, A.S. Four thousand miles of African travel. N.Y., 1875.
Afr 3978.76 Appleton, T.G. A Nile journal. Boston, 1876.
Afr 3978.76.3 Warner, C.D. My winter on the Nile. Hartford, 1876.
Afr 3978.76.4 Warner, C.D. My winter on the Nile. Boston, 1876.
Afr 3978.76.4.5 Warner, C.D. My winter on the Nile. Boston, 1881.
Afr 3978.76.5 Warner, C.D. My winter on the Nile. v.1-2. Leipzig, 1891.
Afr 3978.76.6 Warner, C.D. Mummies and Moslems. Hartford, 1876.
Afr 3978.76.7 Gellion-Dangler, Eugène. Lettres sur l'Egypte. Paris, 1876.
Afr 3978.76.9F Manning, S. The land of the pharaohs. London, 1876.
Afr 3978.76.10 Manning, S. The land of the pharaohs. N.Y., 1924.
Afr 3978.76.11 Lund, Fr. Taflor fraan orienten af hother tolderlund. Stockholm, 1876.
Afr 3978.77 McCoan, J.G. Egypt as it is. London, n.d.
Afr 3978.77.2 McCoan, J.C. Egypt as it is. London, n.d.
Afr 3978.77.3 McCoan, J.C. Egypt as it is. N.Y., 1877.
Afr 3978.77.8A Edwards, A.B. A thousand miles up the Nile. Leipzig, 1878.

Afr 3974 - 3980 Egypt - Geography, description, etc. of Egypt - General works (By date) - cont.

Afr 3978.77.8B Edwards, A.B. A thousand miles up the Nile. Leipzig, 1878.
Afr 3978.77.10 Edwards, A.B. A thousand miles up the Nile. 2d. ed. London, 1889.
Afr 3978.77.11 Edwards, A.B. A thousand miles up the Nile. London, 1890.
Afr 3978.77.13 Edwards, A.B. A thousand miles up the Nile. London, 1891.
Afr 3978.77.15 Edwards, A.B. A thousand miles up the Nile. London, 1899.
Afr 3978.78 Deleon, E. The khedives Egypt. N.Y., 1878.
Afr 3978.79F Ebers, G. Agypten. Stuttgart, 1880. 2v.
Afr 3978.79.3 Delchevalerie, G. L'Egypte. Paris, 1879.
Afr 3978.80 Hunt, Sarah K. On the Nile. London, 1880.
Afr 3978.80.5 Denis de Rivoyre, B.L. Mer Rouge et Abyssinie. Paris, 1880.
Afr 3978.81 Lane-Poole, S. Egypt. London, 1881.
Afr 3978.81.5F Ebers, G. Egypt, descriptive, historical. London, 1881. 2v.
Afr 3978.81.6F Ebers, G. Egypt, descriptive, historical, and picturesque. London, 1881-82. 2v.
Afr 3978.82 Senior, N.W. Conversations and journals in Egypt. London, 1882. 2v.
Afr 3978.82.5 Girard, B. Souvenirs d'une campagne dans le Heraut. Paris, 1883.
Afr 3978.82.10 Knox, T.W. The boy travellers in the Far East. Pt. 4 - Egypt and the Holy Land. N.Y., 1883.
Afr 3978.82.15 Arnold, J.T.B. Palms and temples. London, 1882.
Afr 3978.83 Stuart, H.V. Egypt after the war. London, 1883.
Afr 3978.83.3 Stuart, H.V. Egypt after the war. London, 1883.
Afr 3978.83.4 James, F.L. The wild tribes of the Soudan. London, 1883.
Afr 3978.83.7 Malanco, Luis. Viaje a oriente. Mexico, 1883. 2v.
Afr 3978.83.10 Vaujany, H. Le Caire et ses environs. Paris, 1883.
Afr 3978.84F Lane-Poole, S. Social life in Egypt. London, 1884.
Afr 3978.86 Ebers, G. Cicerone durch das Süd und Nord Agypten. Stuttgart, 1886.
Afr 3978.87.5 Sebah, P. Catalogue of views in Egypt and Nubia. Caire, 1887.
Afr 3978.88 Taylor, Isaac. Leaves from an Egyptian note-book. London, 1888.
Afr 3978.92 Rae, W.F. Egypt to-day. London, 1892.
Afr 3978.92.2 Rawnsley, H.D. Notes for the Nile. Leipzig, 1892.
Afr 3978.92.5 Pretynian, H.E. Journal, Kittar mountains, 1891. London, 1892.
Afr 3978.93 Budge, E.A.W. The Nile. London, 1893.
Afr 3978.93.15 Budge, E.A.W. The Nile. 7th. ed. London, 1901.
Afr 3978.93.20 Harcourt, François. L'Egypte et les Egyptiens. Paris, 1893.
Afr 3978.95 Attfield, D.H. Private journal in Egypt. London, 1895.
Afr 3978.96 Delmas, E. Egypte et Palestine. Paris, 1896.
Afr 3978.97 Budge, E.A.W. The Nile. 5th ed. London, 1897.
Afr 3978.98 Steevens, G.W. Egypt in 1898. N.Y., 1898.
Afr 3978.98.5 Pollard, Joseph. The land of the monuments. 2nd ed. London, 1898.
Afr 3978.99 Worsfold, W.B. The redemption of Egypt. London, 1899.
Afr 3979.00 Cook, J. Programme for visiting Egypt. London, 1900.
Afr 3979.00.3 Tillet, J. du. En Egypte. Paris, 1900.
Afr 3979.01.2 Bacon, Lee. Our houseboat on the Nile. Boston, 1901.
Afr 3979.01.5A Bacon, Lee. Our houseboat on the Nile. Boston, 1901.
Afr 3979.01.5B Bacon, Lee. Our houseboat on the Nile. Boston, 1901.
Afr 3979.01.10 Page, Thomas Nelson. On the Nile in 1901. Miami, 1970.
Afr 3979.02.3 Kelly, R.J. Egypt painted and described. London, 1903.
Afr 3979.02.4 Kelly, R. Talbot. Egypt painted and described. London, 1906.
Afr 3979.02.5 Kelly, R. Talbot. Egypt painted and described. London, 1910.
Afr 3979.02.15 Babcock, M.D. Letters from Egypt and Palestine. N.Y., 1902.
Afr 3979.03 Henze, H. Der Nil... Hydrographie und seiner Wirt. Halle, 1903.
Afr 3979.03.3 Metin, A. La transformation de l'Egypte. Paris, 1903.
Afr 3979.04.5 Kandt, Richard. Caput Nili, eine Empfindsarne. Berlin, 1905.
Afr 3979.05 Gayet, A. Coins d'Egypte ignorés. Paris, 1905.
Afr 3979.05.2 Deguerville, A.B. New Egypt. London, 1905.
Afr 3979.05.5 Curtis, W.E. Egypt, Burma and British Malaysia. Chicago, 1905.
Afr 3979.05.10A Dunning, H.W. Today on the Nile. N.Y., 1905.
Afr 3979.05.10B Dunning, H.W. Today on the Nile. N.Y., 1905.
Afr 3979.06 Brianchaninov, N. Skitaniia, Nubiia, Sudan. Moscow, 1908.
Afr 3979.07 Tyndale, W. Below the Cataracts. Philadelphia, 1907.
Afr 3979.08.5 Holland, Clive. Things seen in Egypt. N.Y., 1908.
Afr 3979.08.10 Albertis, E.A.D. Une croisière sur le Nil, Khartoum-Goudokoro. Le Caire, 1908.
Afr 3979.09 Banse, E. Agypten. Halle, 1909.
Afr 3979.09.5 Weigall, A.E.P. Travels in the Upper Egyptian deserts. Edinburgh, 1909.
Afr 3979.09.10 Lorimer, Norma. By the waters of Egypt. N.Y., 1909.
Afr 3979.10 Sladen, D. Queer things about Egypt. London, 1910.
Afr 3979.10.5 Maspero, Gaston. Ruines et paysages d'Egypte. Paris, 1910.
Afr 3979.10.8A Budge, E.A.W. The Nile. 11th ed. London, 1910.
Afr 3979.10.8B Budge, E.A.W. The Nile. 11th ed. London, 1910.
Afr 3979.10.9 Budge, E.A.W. The Nile. 12th ed. London, 1912.
Afr 3979.10.20 Butcher, E.L. Things seen in Egypt. London, 1923.
Afr 3979.11 Butcher, E.L. Egypt as we knew it. London, 1911.
Afr 3979.11.3 Fyfe, H.H. The new spirit in Egypt. Edinburgh, 1911.
Afr 3979.11.10 Lamoriniere de la Rochecautin. Promenades au pays des pharaons. Paris, 1913.
Afr 3979.11.15 L'vov, A.N. V strane Amon-Ra. Sankt Peterburg, 1911.
Afr 3979.12 Humphreys, R. Algiers, the Sahara and the Nile. London, 1912.
Afr 3979.12.2 Tyndale, W. An artist inEgypt. N.Y., 1912.
Afr 3979.12.3 Parkhurst, L. A vacation on the Nile. Boston, 1913.
Afr 3979.12.5 Mielert, Fritz. Im Lande des Khedive. Regensburg, 1916.
Afr 3979.12.7 Marden, P.S. Egyptian days. London, 1912.
Htn Afr 3979.13* Blackburne, D. Journals of my African travels. Maidstone, 1913.
Afr 3979.13.5 Gomez Carrillo, E. La sonrisa de la esfinge. Madrid, 1913.
Afr 3979.13.8 Crossland, Cyril. Desert and water gardens of the Red Sea. Cambridge, 1913.
Afr 3979.13.12 Todd, J.A. The banks of the Nile. London, 1913.
Afr 3979.13.15 Cooper, Clayton Sedwick. The man of Egypt. London, 1913.
Afr 3979.14 Low, S. Egypt in transition. London, 1914.
Afr 3979.14.2 Low, S. Egypt in transition. N.Y., 1914.
Afr 3979.15 Balls, W.L. Egypt of the Egyptians. London, 1915.
Afr 3979.15.5 Salmon, P.R. The wonderland of Egypt. N.Y., 1915.

Afr 3974 - 3980 Egypt - Geography, description, etc. of Egypt - General works (By date) - cont.

Afr 3979.16 Walther, J. Zum Kampf in der Wüste am Sinai und Nil. Leipzig, 1916.
Afr 3979.18A Leeder, S.H. Modern sons of the pharaohs. London, 1918.
Afr 3979.18B Leeder, S.H. Modern sons of the pharaohs. London, 1918.
Afr 3979.18.5 Briggs, Martin. Through Egypt in war time. London, 1918.
Afr 3979.23 Carpenter, F.G. Cairo to Kisumu. Garden City, 1923.
Afr 3979.23.5A Martin, P.F. Egypt old and new. London, 1923.
Afr 3979.23.5B Martin, P.F. Egypt old and new. London, 1923.
Afr 3979.23.10 Edgar, H.M. Dahaheah days, an Egyptian winter holiday. Toronto, 1923.
Afr 3979.24 Powers, H.H. Egypt. N.Y., 1924.
Afr 3979.25 LeCarpentier, Georges. L'Egypte moderne. Paris, 1925.
Afr 3979.25.20 Harry, Myriam. La vallée des rois et des reines. Paris, 1925.
Afr 3979.26 Lorin, Henri. L'Egypte d'aujourd hui, le pays et les hommes. Cairo, 1926.
Afr 3979.26.5 Quibell, Annie. A wayfarer in Egypt. Boston, 1926.
Afr 3979.26.12 Traz, Robert de. Le depaysement oriental. 7.ed. Paris, 1926.
Afr 3979.27 Rydh, H. Solskivans land. Stockholm, 1927.
Afr 3979.28A Hall, Trowbridge. Egypt in silhouette. N.Y., 1928.
Afr 3979.28B Hall, Trowbridge. Egypt in silhouette. N.Y., 1928.
Afr 3979.29 Hanotaux, G. Regards sur l'Egypte et la Palestine. Paris, 1929.
Afr 3979.29.5 Borchardt, Ludwig. Agypten. Berlin, 1929.
Afr 3979.31 Vandyke, J.C. In Egypt, studies and sketches along the Nile. N.Y., 1931.
Afr 3979.31.5 Egypt. Survey Department. Views of typical desert scenery in Egypt. Giza, 1931.
Afr 3979.33 Géographie du bassin du Nil. Paris, 1933.
Afr 3979.33.3 Oliver, Mildred Alice. Letters from Egypt. London, 1933.
Afr 3979.33.5 Carre, Jean Marie. Voyageurs et ecrivains français en Egypte. 2. éd. Le Caire, 1956. 2v.
Afr 3979.34 Aveline, Claude. La promenade égyptienne. Paris, 1934.
Afr 3979.36.5A Ludwig, Emil. The Nile, the life story of a river. N.Y., 1937.
Afr 3979.36.5B Ludwig, Emil. The Nile, the life story of a river. N.Y., 1937.
Afr 3979.36.5C Ludwig, Emil. The Nile, the life story of a river. N.Y., 1937.
Afr 3979.37 Rameses (pseud.). Oriental spotlight. London, 1937.
Afr 3979.38 Jarvis, C.S. Desert and delta. London, 1938.
Afr 3979.38.5 Herriot, E. Sanctuaires. Roma, 1938.
Afr 3979.38.10 Ayrout, H.H. Moeurs et coutumes des fellahs. Thèse. Paris, 1938.
Afr 3979.38.11 Ayrout, H.H. Fellahs d'Egypte. 6. ed. Le Caire, 1952.
Afr 3979.38.11.2 Ayrout, H.H. Fellahs. 2. ed. Le Caire, 1942.
Afr 3979.38.12 Ayrout, H.H. The fellaheen. 7th ed. Cairo, 1954.
Afr 3979.38.14 Ayrout, H.H. The Egyptian peasant. Boston, 1963.
Afr 3979.39F Temps. Numéro special. L'Egypte. Paris, 1939.
Afr 3979.39.5 Fedden, H.R. The land of Egypt. N.Y., 1939.
Afr 3979.39.10 Leprette, Fernand. Egypte, terre du Nil. Paris, 1939.
Afr 3979.42 Florence, L.S. My goodness. My passport. London, 1942.
Afr 3979.42.5 Bowman, H.E. Middle east window. London, 1942.
Afr 3979.42.13 Jarvis, C.S. Scattered shots. London, 1949.
Afr 3979.46 Spring, Frieda. Hell-dunkel Agyptenfahrt. Bern, 1946.
Afr 3979.46.5 Choudhary, M.L. Roy. Egypt in 1945. Calcutta, 1946.
Afr 3979.46.10 Bordeaux, Henri. Le sphinx sans visage. Marseille, 1946.
Afr 3979.47 Mosharrafa, M. Cultural survey of modern Egypt. v.1-2. London, 1947.
Afr 3979.48 Bigland, E. Journey to Egypt. London, 1948.
Afr 3979.49 Hughes, Pennethorne. While Shepheard's watched. London, 1949.
Afr 3979.50 Bilainkin, G. Cairo to Riyadh diary. London, 1950.
Afr 3979.50.5 Egypt. Cairo, 1950.
Afr 3979.52.5 United Arab Republic. Information Department. Eleven years of progress and development. Cairo, 1963.
Afr 3979.53 Khalid, K.M. From here we start. 3d. ed. Washington, 1953.
Afr 3979.55F Kusch, E. Ägypten im Bild. Nürnberg, 1955.
Afr 3979.55.5 Aafjes, Bertus. Morgen bloeien de abrikozen. Amsterdam, 1954.
Afr 3979.55.10 Robichon, C. Eternal Egypt. Reprinted. London, 1956.
Afr 3979.56F Viollet, Roger. Regards sur l'Egypte. Paris, 1956.
Afr 3979.56.5 Cordan, Wolfgang. DerNil. Düsseldorf, 1956.
Afr 3979.56.10F Viollet, Roger. Egypt. N.Y., 1957.
Afr 3979.57 Harris, G.L. Egypt. New Haven, 1957.
Afr 3979.57.5 Besancon, Jacques. L'homme et le Nil. Paris, 1957.
Afr 3979.57.10 Abreu, Paradela De. Reportagens no Egipto. Lisboa, 1957.
Afr 3979.58 Tregenza, L.A. Egyptian years. London, 1958.
Afr 3979.58.5 Kondrashov, S.N. Na beregakh Nila. Moscow, 1958.
Afr 3979.58.10 Davy, Andre. Four thousand miles of adventure. London, 1958.
Afr 3979.59 Carrington, R. The tears of Isis. London, 1959.
Afr 3979.59.5 Laporte, Jean. Première descente du Nil de l'Equateur à la Méditerranée. Paris, 1959.
Afr 3979.59.10 Mahmond, Zaki Naguib. The land and people of Egypt. Rev.Ed. Philadelphia, 1965.
Afr 3979.60 Dynkin, A.V. Na drevnei zemle. Stalingrad, 1960.
Afr 3979.60.5 Egypt. State Tourist Administration. Trends of the travel movement. Cairo, 1960. 2 pam.
Afr 3979.60.10 United Arab Republic. State Tourist Administration. Bases of tourist statistics. Cairo, 1960?
Afr 3979.61 Scheer, M. Von Afrika nach Kuba. Berlin, 1961.
Afr 3979.62 Moorehead, Alan. The Blue Nile. 1st ed. N.Y., 1962.
Afr 3979.62.5 Kaesser, Hans. Einiges ägypten. Baden-Baden, 1962.
Afr 3979.62.10 Wohlfahrt, M. Das neue Agypten. Berlin, 1962.
Afr 3979.63 United Arab Republic. Information Department. Tourism in the U.A.R. Cairo, 1963.
Afr 3979.63.5 United Arab Republic. Information Department. United Arab Republic. Cairo, 1963.
Afr 3979.63.6F United Arab Republic. Information Department. United Arab Republic. Cairo, 1964.
Afr 3979.63.8 United Arab Republic. Information Department. U.A.R., United Arab Republic. Cairo, 1963.
Afr 3979.63.10F Gary, D.H. Sun, stones and silence. N.Y., 1963.
Afr 3979.63.15 Einmann, E. Pueramiidide maal. Tallinn, 1963.
Afr 3979.63.20 Stevens, G.G. Egypt, yesterday and today. N.Y., 1963.
Afr 3979.64A Husayn, Efendi. Ottoman Egypt in the age of French revolution. Cambridge, 1964.
Afr 3979.64B Husayn, Efendi. Ottoman Egypt in the age of French revolution. Cambridge, 1964.
Afr 3979.64.5F United Arab Republic. Information Department. Culture and arts. Cairo, 1964.

Afr 3974 - 3980   Egypt - Geography, description, etc. of Egypt - General
works (By date) - cont.

Afr 3979.64.10   Mikhaelides, Gaby. La terre qui berça l'histoire.
Bomas-sur-Ourthe, 1964.
Afr 3979.64.15   American University. Foreign Area Studies Division. Area
handbook for the United Arab Republic. Washington, 1964.
Afr 3979.66   Marlowe, John. Four aspects of Egypt. London, 1966.
Afr 3979.66.5   Ivanov, Boris V. 40 vekov i 4 goda. Moskva, 1966.
Afr 3979.66.10   Owen, Robert. Egypt, United Arab Republic, the country and
its people. London, 1966.
Afr 3979.66.15   Cottrell, Leonard. Egypt. N.Y., 1966.
Afr 3979.66.20   Kinross, Patrick. Portrait of Egypt. N.Y., 1966.
Afr 3979.66.25   Kinross, Patrick. Portrait of Egypt. London, 1966.
Afr 3979.66.30   Laurent-Täckholm, Vivi. Egyptisk vardag. Stockholm, 1966.
Afr 3979.67   Andres, Stefan Paul. Agyptisches tagebuch. München, 1967.
Afr 3979.68   Ob'edinennaia Arabskaia Respublika. Moskva, 1968.
Afr 3979.69   Sykes, John. Down into Egypt, a revolution observed.
London, 1969.

Afr 3982   Egypt - Geography, description, etc. of Egypt - History of travel
Afr 3982.2F   Lumbroso, Giacomo. Descrittori italiani dell'Egitto e di
Alessandria. Roma, 1879.

Afr 3986   Egypt - Geography, description, etc. of Egypt - Economic history and
conditions [Discontinued]

Afr 3986.1   Nahas, Joseph F. Situation économique et sociale du fellah
égyptien. Paris, 1901.
Afr 3986.5   Bank Misr. Economic bulletin. Cairo. 3,1959
Afr 3986.7   Garzonzi, Eva. Old ills and new remedies in Egypt.
Cairo, 1958.
Afr 3986.9   United Arab Republic. The economy of the U.A.R.
Cairo, 1960.
Afr 3986.11   United Arab Republic. Overall five year plan for economic
and social development. n.p., 1960.
Afr 3986.12F   United Arab Republic. Cadre du plan quinquennal général.
Le Caire, 1960.
Afr 3986.13   Pamphlet vol. Egypt. Economic and social conditions. 12 pam.
Afr 3986.14   Pamphlet vol. U.A.R. Pams. 6 pam.
Afr 3986.15   Pamphlet vol. Egypt. Economic and social conditions. 6 pam.
Afr 3986.33   Naldoni, Nardo. L'Egitto economico e le sue relazioni con
l'Italia. Genova, 1933.
Afr 3986.931PF   Manchester Guardian Commercial, March 19, 1931. Egypt.
London, 1931.
Afr 3986.938A   Crouchley, A.E. The economic development of modern Egypt.
London, 1938.
Afr 3986.938B   Crouchley, A.E. The economic development of modern Egypt.
London, 1938.
Afr 3986.939   Raja'i, Nur al-Din. De la condition légale des sociétés
anonymes étrangères en Egypte. Thèse. Paris, 1938.
Afr 3986.954   Fahmy, M. La révolution de l'industrie en Egypte et ses
conséquences sociales au 19. siècle. Leiden, 1954.
Afr 3986.955   Little, Arthur D. Opportunities for industrial development
in Egypt. Cairo, 1955.
Afr 3986.956A   Cooke, M.L. Nasser's High Aswan Dam. Washington, 1956.
Afr 3986.956B   Cooke, M.L. Nasser's High Aswan Dam. Washington, 1956.
Afr 3986.958   Landes, David S. Bankers and pashas. Cambridge, 1958.
Afr 3986.958.2   Landes, David S. Bankers and pashas. London, 1958.
Afr 3986.958.5   Platt, Raye R. Egypt, a compendium. N.Y., 1958.
Afr 3986.958.10   Sultanov, A.F. Polozhenie egipetskogo krestianstva pered
zemelskoi reformoi 1952 goda. Moscow, 1958.
Afr 3986.958.15A   Harbison, F.H. Human resources for Egyptian enterprise.
N.Y., 1958.
Afr 3986.958.15B   Harbison, F.H. Human resources for Egyptian enterprise.
N.Y., 1958.
Afr 3986.959   Addison, Herbert. Sun and shadow at Aswan. London, 1959.
Afr 3986.959.5   Register of Egyptian economy. v.1. n.p., 195-.
Afr 3986.959.10   Nour, Mustafa M. Les rapports entre l'évolution économique
en Egypte. Fribourg, 1959.
Afr 3986.960A   Austry, J. Structure économique et civilisation.
Paris, 1960.
Afr 3986.960B   Austry, J. Structure économique et civilisation.
Paris, 1960.
Afr 3986.960.5   International Studies Association, Cairo. Progress in
United Arab Republic. Cairo, 1960.
Afr 3986.960.10   Bughdadi, A. Address on the five year plan. Cairo, 1960.
Afr 3986.960.15   Egypt. Ministry of Economy. A statistical portrait.
Cairo, 1960.
Afr 3986.960.20   Egypt. Ministry of Economy. Economic progress in the
U.A.R. Cairo, 1960.
Afr 3986.960.25   United Arab Republic. National Planning Committee. General
frame of the five year plan. Cairo, 1960.
Afr 3986.961   Warriner, D. Agrarian reform and community development in
U.A.R. Cairo, 1961.
Afr 3986.961.5   United Arab Republic. Economic Research Department.
Indicators of economic development. Cairo, 1961.
Afr 3986.961.10   Bahig, A.F. Selected passages for students of commerce.
4th ed. Alexandria, 1961.
Afr 3986.961.15   Egypt. Information Administration. Assouan. Le
Caire, 1961.
Afr 3986.962   Vatolina, L.N. Ekonomika Obedinenie Arabskoi Respubliki.
Moscow, 1962.
Afr 3986.962.5   Johne, Alfred. Die Industrialisierungspolitik des Ägypten
unter besonderer Berücksichtigung. Berlin, 1962.
Afr 3986.962.10   Messayer, Mohamed Zaki. Le développement économique de
l'Egypte. Lausanne, 1962.
Afr 3986.962.15   Bahig, A.F. Readings for students of commerce.
Alexandria, 1962.
Afr 3986.962.20   United Arab Republic. Information Department. Ten years of
progress...1952-62. Cairo, 1962.
Afr 3986.963   Issawi, C.P. Egypt in revolution. London, 1963.
Afr 3986.963.5   Fridman, L.A. Kapitalisticheskoe razvitie Egipta,
1882-1939. Moscow, 1963.
Afr 3986.963.10   Dlin, Nikolai A. Obedinennaia Arabskaia Respublika.
Moscow, 1963.
Afr 3986.964   United States. Department of Agriculture. Economic Research
Service. Development and Trade Analysis Division. Public
Law 480 and other economic assistance to United Arab
Republic. Washington, 1964.
Afr 3986.964.5   United Arab Republic. The High Aswan Dam. Cairo, 1964.
Afr 3986.964.6   United Arab Republic. Information Department. The High
Dam. Cairo, 1964.
Afr 3986.964.10   United Arab Republic. Ministry of Industry. Twelve years
of industrial development, 1952-1964. Cairo, 1964.
Afr 3986.964.15   Weiss, Dieter. Wirtschaftliche Entwicklungsplanung in der
Vereinigten Arabischen Republik. Koeln, 1964.
Afr 3986.964.20   Komzin, Ivan V. Svet Asuana. Moscow, 1964.

Afr 3988   Egypt - Geography, description, etc. of Egypt - Special customs
Afr 3988.3   McPherson, Joseph Williams. The Moulids of Egypt.
Cairo, 1941.
Afr 3988.4   Winkler, Hans Alexander. Baueren zwischen Wasser und
Wüste. Stuttgart, 1934.
Afr 3988.5A   Blackman, Winifred Susan. The fellahin of Upper Egypt.
London, 1927.
Afr 3988.5B   Blackman, Winifred Susan. The fellahin of Upper Egypt.
London, 1927.
Afr 3988.5.5   Blackman, Winifred Susan. Les fellahs de la Haute-Egypte.
Paris, 1948.
Afr 3988.6   Chabral de Volvic. Essai sur les mours des habitans
modernes de l'Egypte. Paris, 1826.
Afr 3988.8   Poinsenet, Marie Dominque. Rien n'est impossible à
l'amour. Paris, 1968.
Afr 3988.10   Cooper, Elizabeth. The women of Egypt. London, 1914.

Afr 3990   Egypt - Geography, description, etc. of Egypt - Guidebooks
Afr 3990.1   Budge, E.A.W. Cook's handbook. Egypt and the sudan.
London, 1906.
Afr 3990.1.7   Budge, E.A.W. Cook's handbook. Egypt and the sudan. 4th
ed. Suppl. 1925. London, 1921-25.
Afr 3990.2   Baedeker, K. Egypt. 5th ed. Leipzig, 1902.
Afr 3990.3   Egypt and how to see it. N.Y., 1908.
Afr 3990.4.2   Busch, M. Ägypten, Reisenhandbuch. 2.Aufl. Triest, 1870.
Afr 3990.5   Benedite, G. Aaron. Egypte. Paris, 1900.
Afr 3990.15   Macmillan, firm, London. Guide to Egypt and Sudan. 3d ed.
London, 1905.
Afr 3990.15.5   Macmillan, firm, London. Guide to Egypt and Sudan. 6th ed.
London, 1911.
Afr 3990.20   Band, Marcelle. Egypte. Paris, 1956.
Afr 3990.22   Cairo, Alexandria, and environs. Paris, 1963.
Afr 3990.24   Guide hotelier et touristique d'Egypte. Cairo. 1962
Afr 3990.25   Saad, Zaki Yusef. Pharaonic egypt, quick visit.
Cairo, 1964.
Afr 3990.26   United Arab Republic. Information Department. Guide book
for U.A.R. Cairo, 1964.
Afr 3990.27   Abd Allah, Hasan. The handbook of Egypt. Cairo, 1966.
Afr 3990.28   United Arab Republic. State Tourist Administration.
Tourist information, U.A.R. Egypt. Cairo, 1963.
Afr 3990.29   Luxor; how to see it. Cairo. 14,1965

Afr 3991   Egypt - Geography, description, etc. of Egypt - Gazetteers
Afr 3991.2   Boinet, Bey, A. Dictionnaire géographique de l'Egypte. Le
Caire, 1899.
Afr 3991.5   Egypt. Direction Générale de la Statistique de l'Egypte.
Dictionnaire des villes, villages, hameaux. Caire, 1881.

Afr 3993.1 - .199   Egypt - Economic history and conditions - General
works
Afr 3993.1   Crouchley, Arthur Edwin. The investment of foreign capital
in Egyptian companies and public debt. Cairo, 1936.
Afr 3993.5   Pravda, Moskva. Asuan, simvol sovetsko-arabskoi druzhby.
Moskva, 1964.
Afr 3993.5.5   United Arab Republic. Ministry of the High Dam. Aswan High
Dam, diversion of Nile. Aswan, 1964.
Afr 3993.8   Jiritli, Ali. The structure of modern industry in Egypt.
Cairo, 1948.
Afr 3993.10   United Arab Republic. Mining, food, and textile industries
in the second five-year industrial plan. Cairo, 196-. 2 pam.
Afr 3993.15   Little, Thomas. High dam at Aswan. London, 1945.
Afr 3993.18   The scientific industrial record. Cairo. 1,1966+

Afr 3993.500 - .999   Egypt - Economic history and conditions -
Contemporary works (By date)
Afr 3993.538   Mboria, L. La population de l'Egypte. Thèse. Le
Caire, 1938.
Afr 3993.563   United Arab Republic. Ministry of the High Aswan Dam. The
High Aswan Dam begins its fourth year of construction.
Cairo, 1963.
Afr 3993.903   Socolis, Georges. Notes sur l'Egypte et son histoire
économique depuis 30 ans. Paris, 1903.
Afr 3993.904   Fenn, George Manville. The khedive's country.
London, 1904.
Afr 3993.932   Sulayman, Ali. L'industrialisation de l'Egypte.
London, 1932.
Afr 3993.963   United Arab Republic. Information Department. Handbook on
U.A.R. economy. Cairo, 1963.
Afr 3993.965   Hansen, Bent. Development and economic policy in the
U.A.R. (Egypt). Amsterdam, 1965.
Afr 3993.965.5   Issawi, Charles Philip. Egypt in revolution.
London, 1965.
Afr 3993.966   Matiukhin, Ivan S. Ob'edinennaia Arabskaia Respublika.
Moskva, 1966.
Afr 3993.966.5   O'brien, Patrick Karl. The revolution in Egypt's economic
system, from private enterprise to socialism, 1952-1965.
London, 1966.
Afr 3993.966.10   Gataullin, Maliuta F. Ekonomika OAR na novom puti.
Moskva, 1966.
Afr 3993.967.2   Kornrumpf, Hans-Jurgen. Vereinigte Arabische Republik.
Opladen, 1967.
Afr 3993.967.10   Mead, Donald C. Growth and structural change in the
Egyptian economy. Homewood, 1967.

Afr 3994.1 - .199   Egypt - Finance - General works
Afr 3994.2   Kamil, Ali. Les conséquences financières de l'occupation
de l'Egypte par l'Angleterre. Bruxelles, 1911.

Afr 3994.500 - .999   Egypt - Finance - Contemporary works (By date)
Afr 3994.876   Histoire financière de l'Egypte. Paris, 1878.
Afr 3994.876.5F   Pamphlet vol. Egypt. Guidebooks and maps. 11 pam.
Afr 3994.880   Egypt for the Egyptians. London, 1880.
Afr 3994.880.5F   France. Ministère des Affaires Etrangères. Documents
diplomatiques. Affaires d'Egypte. Paris, 1880.
Afr 3994.891F   Egypt. Ministère des Finances. Budget du gouvernement
égyptien. Le Caire. 1909+
Afr 3994.891.3F   Egypt. Ministère des Finances. Compte général. Le Caire.
1922/23- 2v.
Afr 3994.891.5   Kaufmann, Wilhelm. Das internationale Recht der
egyptischen Staatsschuld. Berlin, 1891.
Afr 3994.895F   Gavillot, J.C. Aristide. L'Angleterre ruine l'Egypte.
Paris, 1895.
Afr 3994.912   Haekal, M.H. La dette publique égyptienne. Paris, 1912.
Afr 3994.932   Michel, Bernard. L'évolution du budget égyptien.
n.p., 1932.
Afr 3994.934   Yunus, Muhammed Tawfig. The preparation of the Egyptian
budget. Cairo, 1934.

Afr 3994.500 - .999 Egypt - Finance - Contemporary works (By date) - cont.
Afr 3994.938   Casson, L. Nine papyrus texts in the New York University collection. Diss. N.Y., 1939.
Afr 3994.967   Kardouche, George K. The U.A.R. in development, a study in expansionary finance. N.Y., 1967.

Afr 3998   Egypt - Registers, directories, etc.
Afr 3998.5   Egyptian directory of the United Arab Republic. Le Caire. 1961-1962+
Afr 3998.10   Commercial directory of Egypt. Cairo. 1964+ 2v.
Afr 3998.15   Egyptian exports and industries. Cairo. 1,1969+

Afr 4000   Egypt - Races - General works
Afr 4000.10F   Chantre, E. Recherches anthropologiques dans l'Afrique orientale. Lyon, 1904.
Afr 4000.15   Seligman, C.G. Pagan tribes of the Nilotic Sudan. London, 1932.

Afr 4008   Egypt - Races - Copts
Afr 4008.1   Worrell, William H. A short account of the Copts. Ann Arbor, 1945.
Afr 4008.2   Kammerer, M. A Coptic bibliography. Ann Arbor, 1950.
Afr 4008.5   Cramer, Maria. Das christlich-koptische Ägypten einst und heute. Wiesbaden, 1959.
Afr 4008.8   Chauleur, S. Histoire des Coptes d'Egypte. Paris, 1960.
Afr 4008.10   Kamil, Murad. Aspects de l'Égypte copte. Berlin, 1965.
Afr 4008.12   Laurent-Taeckholm, Vivi. Faraos barn. Stockholm, 1965.
Afr 4008.14   Koptologische Arbeitskonferenz, Halle, 1964. Koptologische Studien in der DDR. Halle, 1965.

Afr 4010   Egypt - Races - Arabs
Afr 4010.1   Macmichael, H.A. A history of the Arabs in Sudan. v.1-2. Cambridge, 1922.

Afr 4012   Egypt - Races - Ishmaelites
Afr 4012.1   Murray, G.W. Sons of Ishmael. London, 1935.

Afr 4015   Egypt - Races - Bejas
Afr 4015.5   Paul, Andrew. A history of the Beja tribes of the Sudan. Cambridge, 1954.

Afr 4025   Egypt - Races - European elements
Afr 4025.10   Carnoy, Norbert. La colonie française du Caire. These. Paris, 1928.
Afr 4025.15   Polites, Athanasios G. L'hellénisme et l'Egypte moderne. T.1-2. Paris, 1929-30.
Afr 4025.15.5   Polites, Athanasios G. O hellynismos kai i neotera Aigyptos. Alexandreia, 1928. 2v.
Afr 4025.15.10   Gialourakès, Manolès. E Egyptos ton Ellenon. Athens, 1967.
Afr 4025.18   Lachanokardes, E. Palaia kai nea Alexandreia. Alexandreia, 1927.
Afr 4025.20.5   Italy. Ministero degli Affari Esteri. Sulla tutela degli interessi italiani in Egitto. Rome, 1880.
Afr 4025.20.10   Italy. Ministero degli Affari Esteri. Sulla politica italiana in Egitto. Roma, 1882.
Afr 4025.20.15   Sterlich, R. de. Sugli italiani d'Egitto. Cairo, 1888.
Afr 4025.20.20   Oddi, F.F. Gl italiani in Egitto. Alessandria, 1895.
Afr 4025.20.25   Sammarco, Angelo. Gli italiani in Egitto. Alessandria, 1937.

Afr 4040   Egypt - Religion
Afr 4040.5   Watson, Charles R. In the valley of the Nile. N.Y., 1908.

Afr 4045   Egypt - Districts, etc. - Isthmus of Suez
Afr 4045.1   Berchere, N. Le desert de Suez. Paris, n.d.
Afr 4045.2   Schleiden, M.J. Die Landenge von Suez. Leipzig, 1858.
Afr 4045.3   Juromenha, J.A. de R.P. de Lacerda. O Isthmo de Suez e as portuguezes. Lisboa, 1870.
Afr 4045.5   Bernard, H. Itinéraire pour l'isthme de Suez et les grandes villes d'Egypte. Paris, 1869.
Afr 4045.10   Societe d'Études Historiques et Géographiques de l'Isthme de Suez. Cahiers. Le Caire. 1,1955
Afr 4045.12   Kienitz, Ernst. Der Suezkanal. Berlin, 1957.
Afr 4045.14   Cervani, Giulio. Il voyage en Egypte, 1861-1862, di Pasquale Revoltella. Trieste, 1962.

Afr 4050   Egypt - Districts, etc. - Libyan Desert
Afr 4050.1   Horneman, F.K. Journal from Cairo to Mourzouk. London, 1802.
Afr 4050.2   Minutoli, H.V. Reise zum Tempel der Jupiter Ammon. Berlin, 1825.
Afr 4050.3   Saint John, B. Adventures in the Libyan desert. N.Y., 1849.
Afr 4050.4   Ehrenburg, C.G. Naturgeschichtliche Reisen durch Nord-Afrika undWest-Asien. Berlin, 1828.
Afr 4050.5   Rohlfs, G. Drei Monate in der libyschen Wüste. Cassel, 1875.
Afr 4050.7   White, A.S. From sphinx to oracle. London, 1899.
Afr 4050.8   Steindorff, G. Durch die Libysche. Leipzig, 1904.
Afr 4050.9   Cobbold, E. Wayfarers in the Libyan desert. London, 1912.
Afr 4050.9.5   Alexander, F.G. Wayfarers in the Libyan desert. N.Y., 1912.
Afr 4050.10   Falls, J.C.E. Three years in the Libyan desert. London, 1913.
Afr 4050.10.5   Falls, J.C.E. Drei Jahre in der libyschen Wüste. Freiburg, 1911.
Afr 4050.11   Sforza, Ascanio M. Esplorazioni e prigionia in Libia. Milano, 1919.
Afr 4050.15   Hassanein, A.M. The lost oases. London, 1925.
Afr 4050.15.5   Hassanein, A.M. The lost oases. N.Y., 1925.
Afr 4050.16   Edmonstone, A. A journey to two of the oases of Upper Egypt. London, 1822.
Afr 4050.20   Dumreicher, A. von. Trackers and smugglers in the deserts of Egypt. London, 1931.
Afr 4050.35   Bagnold, R.A. Libyan sands, travel in a dead world. London, 1935.
Afr 4050.36   Mason, M.H. The paradise of fools. London, 1936.
Afr 4050.36.5   Jarvis, C.S. Three deserts. London, 1936.

Afr 4055   Egypt - Districts, etc. - Arabian Desert
Afr 4055.5   Tregenza, L.A. The Red Sea mountains of Egypt. London, 1955.

Afr 4060   Egypt - Districts, etc. - Nubia
Afr 4060.2   Rueppell, E. Reisen im Nubien, Kordofan. Text and atlas. Frankfurt, 1829.
Afr 4060.3   Heuglin, Th. von. Reise in Nordost Afrika. Braunschweig, 1877. 2v.
Afr 4060.4   Burckhardt, J.L. Travels in Nubia. London, 1819.
Afr 4060.4.2   Burckhardt, J.L. Travels in Nubia. 2d ed. London, 1822.
Afr 4060.5   Rossi, Elia. La Nubia e il Sudan. Constantinopoli, 1858.
Afr 4060.6F   Monneret de Villard, U. I vescovi giacobiti della Nubia. Le Caire, 1934.
Afr 4060.8   Curt, Silvio. Nubia, storia di una civilta favolosa. Novara, 1965.
Afr 4060.15   Kraus, J. Die Anfänge des Christentums in Nubien. Inaug. Diss. Mödling, 1930.
Afr 4060.20   Greener, Leslie. High Dam over Nubia. N.Y., 1962.
Afr 4060.25   Fairservis, W.A. The ancient kingdoms of the Nile and the doomed monuments of Nubia. N.Y., 1962.
Afr 4060.30   Keating, Rex. Nubian twilight. N.Y., 1963.
Afr 4060.35   Emery, Walter Bryan. Egypt in Nubia. London, 1965.
Afr 4060.36   Geroter, Georg. Nubien. Zurich, 1964.
Afr 4060.37   Nicholls, W. The shaikiya. Dublin, 1913.

Afr 4070   Egypt - Districts, etc. - Egyptian Sudan - Geography, description, etc. [Discontinued]
Afr 4070.2   Escayrac de Lauture, S. Mémoire sur le Soudan. Paris, 1855.
Afr 4070.3   Heuglin, M.T. Reise in das Gebiet des Weissen Nil. Leipzig, 1869.
Afr 4070.4   Marno, E. Reisen im Gebiete des Blauen und Weissen Nil, im egyptischen Sudan. Wien, 1874.
Afr 4070.5   Great Britain. Intelligence. Report on Sudan. London, 1884.
Afr 4070.6   Klunzinger, C.B. Upper Egypt. N.Y., 1878.
Afr 4070.7   Williams, J. Life in the Soudan. London, 1884.
Afr 4070.8   Fothergill, E. Five years in the Sudan. London, 1910.
Afr 4070.9   Peel, Sidney. The binding of the Nile and the new Soudan. London, 1904.
Afr 4070.9.5   Policy for the eastern Soudan. Biarritz, 1885.
Afr 4070.10PF   Hartmann, Robert. Reise des Freiherrn Adalbert von Barnim durch Nord-Ost-Afrika 1859-60. Berlin, 1863. 2v.
Afr 4070.12   Gleichen, Count. The Anglo-Egyptian Sudan. London, 1905. 2v.
Afr 4070.13   Munzinger, W. Ostafrikanische Studien. Basle, 1883.
Afr 4070.14   Johnson, W. Fliegende blätter...Reise in Nord-Ost-Afrika...1847-49. Stuttgart, 1851.
Afr 4070.15   Tangye, H.S. In the torrid Sudan. Boston, 1910.
Afr 4070.16.3   Artin, Y.P. England in the Sudan. London, 1911.
Afr 4070.17   Klun, V.F. Reise auf dem Weissen Nil. Laibach, 1851. 3 pam.
Afr 4070.18   Bulpett, C.W.L. A picnic party in wildest Africa. London, 1907.
Afr 4070.19   Speedy, C.M. My wanderings in the Soudan. London, 1884. 2v.
Afr 4070.20   Myers, A.B.R. Life with the Hamran Arabs. London, 1876.
Afr 4070.21   Kumm, H.K.W. The Sudan. 2d ed. London, 1909.
Afr 4070.23   Cailliaud, F. Voyage à Meroe, au Fleuve Blanc. Paris, 1823-27. 5v.
Afr 4070.24   Cuny, Charles. Journal de voyage...de Siout à El-Obeid. Paris, 1863.
Afr 4070.25   Escayrac de Lauture, S. Le desert et le Soudan. Paris, 1853.
Afr 4070.25.2   Escayrac de Lauture, S. Die afrikanische Wüste und das Land der Schwarzen am obern Nil. Leipzig, 1867.
Afr 4070.27   Tremaux, P. Voyage en Ethiopie au Soudan oriental et dans la Nigritie. v.1- Paris, 1862. 2v.
Afr 4070.28   Stevens, E.S. My Sudan year. London, 1912.
Afr 4070.29   Comyn, D.C.E. Service and sport in the Sudan. London, 1911.
Afr 4070.30   Rivoyre, D. De. Aux pays du Soudan, Bagos, Mensah, Souakim. Paris, 1885.
Afr 4070.35   Dugmore, A.R. The vast Sudan. London, 1924.
Afr 4070.35.5   Dugmore, A.R. The vast Sudan. N.Y., 1925.
Afr 4070.36   Millais, John Guille. Far away up the Nile. London, 1924.
Afr 4070.37.2   Streeter, D.W. Camels. N.Y., 1927.
Afr 4070.38   Streeter, D.W. Camels. N.Y., 1927.
Afr 4070.39   Domville Fife, C.W. Savage life in the dark Sudan. London, 1927.
Afr 4070.41   Matteucci, P. Sudan e Gallas. Milano, 1879.
Afr 4070.43   Chapman, Abel. Savage Sudan. London, 1921.
Afr 4070.43.5   Chapman, Abel. Savage Sudan. N.Y., 1922.
Afr 4070.45   Howard-Williams, E.G. Something new out of Africa. London, 1934.
Afr 4070.47   Worsley, A. Land of the blue veil. Sudan. Birmingham, 1940.
Afr 4070.49   Assher, B. A nomad in the south Sudan. London, 1928.
Afr 4070.51   Langley, M. No woman's country. London, 1950.
Afr 4070.53A   Hamilton, J.A. de C. The Anglo-Egyptian Sudan from within. London, 1935.
Afr 4070.53B   Hamilton, J.A. de C. The Anglo-Egyptian Sudan from within. London, 1935.
Afr 4070.55   Davies, R.T. The camel's back. London, 1957.
Afr 4070.57   Jackson, Henry Cecil. Sudan days and ways. N.Y., 1954.
Afr 4070.59.2   American University, Washington D.C. Foreign Areas Studies Division. Area handbook for the Republic of the Sudan. 2. ed. Washington, 1964.
Afr 4070.62   Barbour, K.M. The Republic of the Sudan. London, 1961.
Afr 4070.64   Odu, Joseph. The problem of the southern Sudan. London, 1963.
Afr 4070.65   Barclay, Harold. Buurri al Lamaab. Ithaca, 1964.
Afr 4070.65.5   Said, Beshir Mohammed. The Sudan. London, 1965.

Afr 4080   Egypt - Districts, etc. - Egyptian Sudan - Local - Kordofan [Discontinued]
NEDL Afr 4080.4   Pallme, J. Travels in Kordofan. London, 1844.

Afr 4093   Egypt - Districts, etc. - Egyptian Sudan - Races [Discontinued]
Afr 4093.62   Huffman, Ray. Nuer customs and folk-lore. London, 1931.

Afr 4095   Egypt - Districts, etc. - Equatorial Egypt
Afr 4095.2   Cooley, W.D. Claudius Ptolemy and the Nile. London, 1854.
Afr 4095.3.2   Taylor, G.B. A journey to central Africa. N.Y., 1854.
Afr 4095.3.3   Taylor, G.B. A journey to central Africa. N.Y., 1854.
Afr 4095.3.4   Taylor, G.B. Eine Reise nach Centralafrika. Leipzig, 1855.
Afr 4095.4   Beke, C.T. Enquiry into N.D. Abbadie's journey to Kaffa. London, 1851.
Afr 4095.5   Werne, Ferd. Expedition to sources of White Nile. London, 1849.
Afr 4095.5.5   Werne, Ferd. Expedition zur Entdeckung der Quellen des Weissen Nil. Berlin, 1848.

Afr 4095 Egypt - Districts, etc. - Equatorial Egypt - cont.

Afr 4095.6 Speke, J.H. Journal of discovery of source of the Nile. Edinburgh, 1863.
Afr 4095.6.3 Speke, J.H. Journal of discovery of source of the Nile. N.Y., 1864.
Afr 4095.6.10 Speke, J.H. Journal of discovery of source of the Nile. N.Y., 1868.
NEDL Afr 4095.7 Burton, R.F. The Nile basin. London, 1864.
Afr 4095.8 Baker, S.W. The Albert Nyanza. London, 1867. 2v.
Afr 4095.8.2 Baker, S.W. The Albert Nyanza. London, 1866.
Afr 4095.8.2.5 Baker, S.W. The Albert Nyanza. New ed. London, 1870.
Afr 4095.8.2.10 Baker, S.W. The Albert Nyanza. London, 1907.
NEDL Afr 4095.8.3 Baker, S.W. Ismailia. N.Y., 1875.
Afr 4095.8.3.5 Baker, S.W. Ismailia; a narrative of the expedition to Central Africa for the suppression of the slave trade. N.Y., 1969. 2v.
Afr 4095.8.4 Rubakin, N.A. Prikliucheniia v strane rabstva. Moscow, 1918.
Afr 4095.8.5 Murray, T.D. Sir S.W. Baker, a memoir. London, 1895.
Afr 4095.8.6 Middleton, D. Baker of the Nile. London, 1949.
Afr 4095.9 Marno, Ernst. Reise in der egyptischen Aequatorial-Provinz. Wien, 1879.
Afr 4095.9.5 Marno, Ernst. Reise in der egyptischen Aequatorial-Provinz. Wien, 1878.
Afr 4095.10F Torelli-Viollier, E. Ricerca delle sorgenti del Nilo. Milano, 1878.
NEDL Afr 4095.11 Long, C.C. Central Africa. N.Y., 1877.
Afr 4095.12 Beke, C.T. The sources of the Nile. London, 1860.
Afr 4095.12.5 Beke, C.T. A lecture on the sources of the Nile. London, 1864.
Afr 4095.13 Speke, John Hanning. What led to the discovery of the source of the Nile. London, 1967.
Afr 4095.18 Johnston, H. The Nile quest. N.Y., 1903.
Afr 4095.18.15 Omar Toussoun, Prince. Mémoire sur l'histoire du Nil. Le Caire, 1925.
Afr 4095.19 Chaille-Long, C. My life in four continents. v.1-2. London, 1912. 2v.
Afr 4095.21 Piva, Gino. Un pioniere italiano delle scoperte del Nilo, Giovanni Miani, il Leone Bianco. Firenze, 1930.
Afr 4095.25 Stigand, C.H. Equatoria, the Lado Enclave. London, 1923.
Afr 4095.28 Bradham, Frederick. The long walks, journeys to the sources of the White Nile. London, 1969.

Afr 4098 Egypt - Cities, towns, etc. of Egypt - Egyptian cities in general

Afr 4098.2 Poole, R.S. The cities of Egypt. London, 1882.

Afr 4105 Egypt - Cities, towns, etc. of Egypt - Alexandria

Afr 4105.1 Saint John, B. Two years residence in a Levantine family. Paris, 1850.
Afr 4105.3 Pamphlet vol. Egypt, local. 3 pam.
Afr 4105.8 Thuile, H. Commentaires sur l'atlas historique d'Alexandrie. Le Caire, 1922.
Afr 4105.10 Forster, E.M. Alexandria. 3d ed. Garden City, 1961.
Afr 4105.15 Cahiers d'Alexandrie. Alexandrie. 2,1964+

Afr 4108 Egypt - Cities, towns, etc. of Egypt - A (Others)

Afr 4108.2 Habachi, Labib. Aswan. Le Caire, 1959.
Afr 4108.5 United Arab Republic. Aswan. Cairo, 196-.
Afr 4108.5.2 United Arab Republic. Information Department. Aswan. Cairo, 1964.
Afr 4108.10F United Arab Republic. Information Department. Le Haut-Barrage d'Assouan. Aswan High Dam. Cairo, 1964?

Afr 4115 Egypt - Cities, towns, etc. of Egypt - Cairo

Afr 4115.3 Indicateur égyptien administratif et commercial. Alexandrie, 1907.
Afr 4115.4PF Hay, Robert. Illustrations of Cairo. London, 1840.
Afr 4115.5 Fullerton, W.M. In Cairo. London, 1891.
NEDL Afr 4115.6 Lane-Poole, S. Cairo. London, 1892.
Afr 4115.6.3 Lane-Poole, S. Cairo. 3d ed. London, 1898.
Afr 4115.6.5 Lane-Poole, S. The story of Cairo. London, 1902.
Afr 4115.6.8A Lane-Poole, S. The story of Cairo. London, 1906.
Afr 4115.6.8B Lane-Poole, S. The story of Cairo. London, 1906.
Afr 4115.6.15 Lane-Poole, S. The story of Cairo. London, 1924.
Afr 4115.7 Reclus, E. Nouvelle géographie. Cairo. Paris, 1885.
Afr 4115.8 Ball, E.A. Reynold. The city of the caliphs. London, 1898.
Afr 4115.9 Sladen, D. Oriental Cairo. London, 1911.
Afr 4115.9.5 Sladen, D. Oriental Cairo. Philadelphia, 1911.
Afr 4115.11 Bassi, Alessandro. Santuario della sacra famiglia in Cairo vecchio. Torino, 1862.
Afr 4115.12 Lamplough, A.O. Cairo and its environs. London, 1909.
Afr 4115.14A Margoliouth, D.S. Cairo, Jerusalem, and Damascus. N.Y., 1907.
Afr 4115.14B Margoliouth, D.S. Cairo, Jerusalem, and Damascus. N.Y., 1907.
Afr 4115.16F Artin, Yakub, Pasha. Essai sur les causes du renchérissement de la vie matérielle au Caire dans le courant du XIXe siècle (1800-1907). Le Caire, 1907.
Afr 4115.17 Nelson, Nina. Shepheard's hotel. London, 1960.
Afr 4115.18 Clerget, Marcel. Le Caire. v.1-2. Le Caire, 1934. 2v.
Afr 4115.20.7 Devonshire, H.C. Rambles in Cairo. 3d ed. Cairo, 1947.
Afr 4115.20.10 Cairo; a life-story of 1000 years, 969-1969. Cairo, 1969.
Afr 4115.22 Cairo, Egypt. Coptic Museum. A brief guide to the Coptic Museum. Cairo, 1938.
Afr 4115.24 Russell, Dorothea. Medieval Cairo and the monasteries of the Wadi Natrun. London, 1962.
Afr 4115.25 Wiet, Gaston. Cairo, city of art and commerce. 1st ed. Norman, 1964.
Afr 4115.26 Devonshire, Henrietta Caroline. Some Cairo mosques. London, 1921.
Afr 4115.30 Stewart, Desmond Stirling. Cairo, 5500 years. N.Y., 1968.
Afr 4115.30.1 Stewart, Desmond Stirling. Great Cairo; the world. London, 1969.
Afr 4115.31 Khodzhash, Jvettana I. Kair. Moskva, 1967.

Afr 4128 Egypt - Cities, towns, etc. of Egypt - E

Afr 4128.9 Caccia Dominioni di Sillavengo, Paolo. Alamein, 1933-1962. 9. ed. Milano, 1965.

Afr 4150 Egypt - Cities, towns, etc. of Egypt - K

Afr 4150.2 Beadnell, H.J.L. An Egyptian oasis. London, 1909.
Afr 4150.2.5F Caton-Thompson, G. Kharga Oasis in prehistory. London, 1952.

Afr 4155 Egypt - Cities, towns, etc. of Egypt - M

Afr 4155.5 Decosson, A. Mareotis. London, 1935.
Afr 4155.10 Barque, Jacques. Histoire sociale d'un village égyptien au XXème siècle. Paris, 1957.
Afr 4155.15 Lackany, Radames Sany. Mersa Matruh and its environments. 2nd ed. Alexandria, 1960.

Afr 4158 Egypt - Cities, towns, etc. of Egypt - N

Afr 4158.5 Burmester, O.H.E. A guide to the monasteries of the Wadi Natrun. Le Caire, 1954.

Afr 4178 Egypt - Cities, towns, etc. of Egypt - Suez

Afr 4178.5 Sammarco, Angelo. Suez, storia e problemi. Milano, 1943.
Afr 4178.10 Hueber, Reinhard. Der Suezkanal einst und heute. Berlin, 1941.
Afr 4178.15 Gaslini, Mario. Suez. Milano, 1957.
Afr 4178.20 Istituto Italiano per l'Africa. Il Congresso di Trento per il centenario del progetto italiano per il taglio dell istmo di Suez. Roma, 1956.
Afr 4178.25 Compagnie Universlle du Canal Maritime de Suez. La Compagnie Universelle du Canal Maritime de Suez et la décision. v.1-2. Paris, 1956.

Afr 4180 Egypt - Cities, towns, etc. of Egypt - S Others

Afr 4180.3 Falls, J.C.E. Siwah. Mainz, 1910.
Afr 4180.3.3 Bates, O. Siwan superstitions. Alexandria, 1911.
Afr 4180.3.5 Stanley, C.V.B. A report on the Oasis of Siwa. Cairo, 1911.
Afr 4180.3.10A Belgrave, C.D. Siwa. London, 1923.
Afr 4180.3.10B Belgrave, C.D. Siwa. London, 1923.
Afr 4180.3.15 Simpson, G.E. The heart of Libya, the Siwa Oasis, its people, customs and sport. London, 1929.
Afr 4180.3.20 Maugham, R.C.R. Journey to Siwa. N.Y., 1950.
Afr 4180.3.25F Fakhry, Ahmed. Siwa Oasis. Cairo, 1944.
Afr 4180.4 Crawford, O.G.S. The Fung Kingdom of Sennar. Gloucester, 1951.
Afr 4180.4.5 Jackson, H.C. Tooth of fire. Oxford, 1912.
Afr 4180.5 Ammar, H. Growing up in an Egyptian village. London, 1954.
Afr 4180.6 Lackany, Radames Sany. Sollum and its environments. Alexandria, 1962.

Afr 4198 Egypt - Biographies - Collected

Afr 4198.5 Hill, Richard Leslie. A biographical dictionary of the Anglo-Egyptian Sudan. Oxford, 1951.
Afr 4198.5.2 Hill, Richard Leslie. A biographical dictionary of the Anglo-Egyptian Sudan. 2nd ed. London, 1967.

Afr 4199 Egypt - Biographies - Individual (A-Z, 800 scheme, by person)

Afr 4199.5 Keller-Zschokke, J.V. Werner Munzinger-Pascha. Aarau, 1891.
Afr 4199.5.5 Lemandowski, H. Ein Leben für Afrika. Zürich, 1954.
Afr 4199.10.5 Hussain, Tacha. Kindheitstage in Ägypten. München, 1957.
Afr 4199.15 Bland, J. Prince Ahmad of Egypt. London, 1939.
Afr 4199.20 Ibn Tagribandi. Les biographies du Manhal Safi. Le Caire, 1932.
Afr 4199.25 Russell, T.W. Egyptian service. 1st ed. London, 1949.
Afr 4199.37 Fergusson, V.H. The story of Fergie Bey. London, 1930.
Afr 4199.66 Mohamed Ali, Prince. Souvenirs d'enfance. Pts.1-3. Le Caire, 1946.
Afr 4199.90A Bird, Michael. Samuel Shepheard of Cairo. London, 1957.
Afr 4199.90B Bird, Michael. Samuel Shepheard of Cairo. London, 1957.
Afr 4199.100 Bahay, Muhammad. Muhammed Abduh. Hamburg, 1936.
Afr 4199.105 Amin, Osman. Muhammad Abduh. Le Caire, 1944.
Afr 4199.105.5 Amin, Osman. MuhammadAbduh. Washington, 1953.
Afr 4199.759 Seth, Ronald. Russell pasha. London, 1966.

Afr 4201 - 4224 Ethiopia - Periodicals (A-Z)

Afr 4205.5 Ethiopia observer. Addis Ababa. 1,1956+ 11v.
Afr 4205.10F Ethiopie d'aujourd'hui. Addis-Ababa. 1962 2v.
Afr 4205.15 Ethiopia. Paris.
Afr 4205.16 Ethiopie. Paris. 38,1965+
Afr 4205.20 Ethiopian geographical journal. Addis Ababa. 1-2,1963-1964
Afr 4205.25 Ethiopia. Chamber of Commerce. Trade directory and guide book to Ethiopia. Addis Abada, 1967.
Afr 4205.30F Etiopia ilustrata. Asmara. 3,1964+
Afr 4208.5 Haile Selassie I University. Department of History. Historical studies. Addis Ababa. 1,1964+
Afr 4210.4 University college review. Addis Ababa. 1,1961
Afr 4210.5 Journal of Ethiopian studies. Addis Ababa. 1,1963+ 2v.
Afr 4214.5 Notes for anthropologists and other field workers in Ethiopia. Addis Ababa. 1,1965+
Afr 4220.5F Tarik; gazette d'information archéologique, historique et littéraire. Addis Ababa. 2,1963+
Afr 4222.5 Rassegna di studi etiopici. Roma. 1,1941+ 8v.

Afr 4225 Ethiopia - Folios [Discontinued]

Afr 4225.5F Holland, T.J. Record of the expedition to Abyssinia. v.1-2 and maps. London, 1870. 3v.

Afr 4226 Ethiopia - Bibliographies

Afr 4226.1 Fumagalli, G. Bibliografia etiopica. Milan, 1893.
Afr 4226.1.10 Zanutto, Silvio. Bibliografia etiopica. v.1-2. Roma, 1929. 2v.
Afr 4226.3 Manetti, C. Il contributo italiano all esplorazione ed allo studio dell Etiopia. Roma, 1936.
Afr 4226.4 Chojnacki, S. List of current periodical publications in Ethiopia. Addis Ababa, 1964.
Afr 4226.5 Register of current research on Ethiopia and the horn of Africa. Addis Ababa.
Afr 4226.6.2 Baylor, Jim. Ethiopia. 2nd ed. Berkeley, 1967.
Afr 4226.7 Ethiopia. Press and Information Office. Bibliography of Ethiopia. Addis Ababa, 1968.
Afr 4226.8 Sommer, John W. A study guide for Ethiopia and the Horn of Africa. Boston, 1969.

Afr 4228 Ethiopia - Pamphlet volumes

Afr 4228 Pamphlet box. Abyssinia.
Afr 4228.01 Pamphlet box. Abyssinia.

Afr 4230 Ethiopia - Collected source materials - General

Afr 4230.4 Beccari, C. Rerum aethiopicarum scriptores occidentales. Introductio generalis. Roma, 1903.
NEDL Afr 4230.4.2 Paez, P. Historia Aethiopiae. v.1-4. Roma, 1905-06. 2v.
Afr 4230.4.3 Paez, P. Historia de Etiopia. Livro 1-3. Porto, 1945. 3v.

Afr 4230 Ethiopia - Collected source materials - General - cont.
Afr 4230.4.4 Barradas, M. Tractatus tres historico-geographico. Porto, 1906.
Afr 4230.4.5 Almeida, M. De. Historia Aethiopiae. Liber 1-10. Romae, 1907. 3v.
Afr 4230.4.6 Mendez S.I., P.A. Expeditiones Aethiopicae. v.1-4. Roma, 1909. 2v.
Afr 4230.4.7 Relationes et epistolae variorum. v.1-2. Romae, 1910-14. 3v.
Afr 4230.4.10 Relationes et epistolae variorum. Index analyticus totius operis. Romae, 1917.
Afr 4230.4.15 Pankhurst, Richard Keir Pethick. The Ethiopian royal chronicles. Addis Ababa, 1967.

Afr 4232 Ethiopia - Collected source materials - Statutes
Afr 4232.1F Corpus juris abessinorum. Berlin, 1889.

Afr 4234 Ethiopia - Collected source materials - Other
Afr 4234.2 Almagia, R. Contributi alla storia della conscenza dell Etiopia. Padova, 1941.

Afr 4236 Ethiopia - Church history in general
Afr 4236.928 Symons, R. What Christianity has done for Abyssinia. London, 1928.
Afr 4236.936 Sottochiesa, G. La religione in Etiopia. Torino, 1936.
Afr 4236.936.5 Barsotti, G. Etiopia cristiana. Milano, 1939.
Afr 4236.957 Cleret, Maxime. Ethiopie. Paris, 1957.
Afr 4236.963 Hammerschmidt, E. Stellung und Bedeutung des Sabbats. Stuttgart, 1963.
Afr 4236.965F Davis, Asa J. A note on ideological basis of union of church and state in Ethopia. Ibadan, 1965.
Afr 4236.965.5 Ethiopia. Ministry of Information. Religious freedom in Ethiopia. Addis Ababa, 1965.

Afr 4238 Ethiopia - Government and administration - General works
Afr 4238.5 Ghersi, E. L'organizzazione politica dell Etiopia. Padova, 1936.
Afr 4238.10 Perham, M.F. The government of Ethiopia. London, 1948.
Afr 4238.10.2 Perham, M.F. The government of Ethiopia. 2nd ed. London, 1969.
Afr 4238.15 Howard, W.E.H. Public administration in Ethiopia. Groningen, 1956.

Afr 4240 Ethiopia - Government and administration - Special topics
Afr 4240.5 Giannini, A. La costituzione etiopica. 2. ed. Roma, 1936.

Afr 4255 - 4260 Ethiopia - General history (By date)
Htn Afr 4256.10* Urreta, L. Historia eclesiastica, politica, natural, y moral de los grandes y remotos reynos de la Etiopia. Pt.1. Valencia, 1610.
Afr 4258.65 Lesseps, F. Principaux faits de l'histoire d'Abyssinie. Paris, 1865.
Afr 4258.67 Peacock, Geo. Hand-book of Abyssinia. London, 1867.
Afr 4258.90 Sapeto, Giuseppe. Etiopia, notizie racolte. Roma, 1890.
Afr 4258.97 Castonnet des Fosses. L'Abyssinie et les Italiens. Paris, 1897.
Afr 4259.04 Morie, L.J. Les civilisations africaines. Paris, 1904. 2v.
Afr 4259.17 Leroux, Hughes. Chez la reine de Saba. Paris, 1917.
Afr 4259.25 Pierre-Alype, L.M. Sous la couronne de Salomon. L'empire des Negus. Paris, 1925.
Afr 4259.28 Budge, E.A. A history of Ethiopia, Nubia and Abyssinia. London, 1928. 2v.
Afr 4259.28.5F Conti Rossini, Carlo. Storia d'Etiopia. Pt.1. Milano, 1928.
Afr 4259.29 Coulbeaux, J.B. Histoire politique et religieuse d'Abyssinie depuis les temps les plus reculés jusqu'à l'avènement. T.1-3. Paris, 1929. 3v.
Afr 4259.31 Gabre-Hiot, A. La vérité sur l'Ethiopie révélée après le couronnement du roi des rois. Lausanne, 1931.
Afr 4259.35F Istituto della Enciclopedia Italiana. L'Etiopia. Roma, 1935.
Afr 4259.35.7 Arcuno, Irma. Abissinia ieri ed oggi. 2a ed. Napoli, 1935.
Afr 4259.35.15 Nomado, R. Abissinia. Napoli, 1935.
Afr 4259.35.21 Jones, A.H. A history of Ethiopia. Oxford, 1955.
Afr 4259.35.23 Jones, A.H. A history of Ethiopia. Oxford, 1960.
Afr 4259.35.30 Rossi, Corrado. Abissinia. Milano, 1935.
NEDL Afr 4259.36 Markoff, A. Los siete mil anos de Etiopia. Barcelona, 1936.
Afr 4259.36.5 Sabelli, L. Storia di Abissinia. v.1-4. Livorno, 1936-38. 4v.
Afr 4259.47A Mathew, David. Ethiopia, the study of a polity, 1540-1935. London, 1947.
Afr 4259.47B Mathew, David. Ethiopia, the study of a polity, 1540-1935. London, 1947.
Afr 4259.49 Mikael, K. Ethiopia and Western civilization. n.p., 1949.
Afr 4259.55 Pankhurst, E.S. Ethiopia. Essex, 1955.
Afr 4259.57 Doresse, Jean. L'empire du Prêtre-Jean. v.1-2. Paris, 1957. 2v.
Afr 4259.59 Neubacher, Hermann. Die Festung der Löwen. Olten, 1959.
Afr 4259.63 Jesman, Czeslaw. The Ethiopian paradox. London, 1963.
Afr 4259.65 Greenfield, Richard. Ethiopia, a new political history. London, 1965.
Afr 4259.67 Hammerschmidt, Ernst. Äthiopien, christliches Reich zwisches Gestern und Morgen. Wiesbaden, 1968.

Afr 4280 Ethiopia - History by periods - Ancient Ethiopia to 4th century - General works
Afr 4280.15 Kammerer, A. Essai sur l'histoire antique d'Abyssinie. Paris, 1926.

Afr 4285 Ethiopia - History by periods - Ancient Ethiopia to 4th century - Special topics
Afr 4285.3 Dillmann, A. Über die Anfänge des axumitischen Reiches. Berlin, 1879.
Afr 4285.5 Varenbergh, Joseph. Studien zur äthiopischen Reichsordnung. Strassbourg, 1915.
Afr 4285.6 Hable-Selassie, Sergew. Beziehungen Äthiopiens zur griechisch-römischen Welt. Bonn, 1964.

Afr 4290 Ethiopia - History by periods - Christianization (4th to 6th centuries - General works
Afr 4290.5 Kobishchanov, Iurii M. Aksum. Moskva, 1966.

Afr 4295 Ethiopia - History by periods - Christianization (4th to 6th centuries - Special topics
Afr 4295.1 Pereira, F.M.E. Historia dos martyres de Nagran. Lisbon, 1899.
Afr 4295.2 Almeida, M. de. Vida de Takla Haymanot. Lisboa, 1899.

Afr 4300 Ethiopia - History by periods - 6th to 16th centuries - General works
Afr 4300.1 Conti Rossini, C. Note etiopiche. Una guerra fra la Nubia. Roma, 1897.

Afr 4306 Ethiopia - History by periods - 6th to 16th centuries - 12th century
Afr 4306.1 Perruchon, J. Vie de Lalibala. Paris, 1892.

Afr 4308 Ethiopia - History by periods - 6th to 16th centuries - 14th century
Afr 4308.5 The glorious victories of 'Amda Seyon. Oxford, 1965.

Afr 4309 Ethiopia - History by periods - 6th to 16th centuries - 15th century
Afr 4309.1 Perruchon, J. Les chroniques de Zara Yaeqob. Paris, 1893.

Afr 4313 Ethiopia - History by periods - 16th century - Lebna Dengel (1508-1540)
Afr 4313.1 Sarsa, Dengel. Storia di Lebna Dengel re d'Etiopia. Rome, 1894.
Afr 4313.2 Lebna Dengel. Legatio ad Sanctissimum D.N. Clementem Papam VII. Bononiae, 1533.
Afr 4313.3 Schleicher, A.W. Geschichte der Galla. Berlin, 1893.
Afr 4313.5F Sequeira, D.L. The discovery of Abyssinia by the Portuguese in 1520. London, 1938.
Afr 4313.6 Sequeira, D.L. Carta das novas que vieram. Lisboa, 1938.

Afr 4315 Ethiopia - History by periods - 16th century - Mohammedan conflicts and conquest
Afr 4315.01 Pamphlet box. Mohammedan conquest of Abyssinia.
Afr 4315.1 Shihab al-Din Ahmad Ibn Abd al-Kadir. La conquista mussulmana dell'Etiopia. Rome, 1891.
Afr 4315.2 Shihab al-Din Ahmad ibn 'Abd al-Kadir. Futuh al-Habashah. Pt.1. London, 1894.
Afr 4315.3 Shihab al-Din Ahmad Ibn 'Abd al-Kadir. Histoire de la conquête de l'Abyssinie. Texte arabe v.1, française v.2. Paris, 1897-1909. 2v.

Afr 4317 Ethiopia - History by periods - 16th century - Mohammed Gragne
Afr 4317.1 Shihab al-Din Ahmad Ibn Abd al-Kadir. Futuh el-Habacha. Paris, 1898.

Afr 4320 Ethiopia - History by periods - 16th century - Relations with the Portuguese in general
Afr 4320.3 Krause, K. Die Portugiesen in Abessinien. Dresden, 1912.
Afr 4320.7 Rey, Charles. The romance of the Portuguese in Abyssinia. London, 1929.
Afr 4320.10 Sanceau, Elaine. Portugal in quest of Prester John. London, 1943.
Afr 4320.10.5 Sanceau, Elaine. The land of Prester John. 1st American ed. N.Y., 1944.
Htn Afr 4320.25* Urreta, Luis de. Historia de la Sagrada Orden de Predicadores. Valencia, 1611.

Afr 4335 Ethiopia - History by periods - 16th century - Galawdewos (1540-1559) - Expedition of Da Gama
Afr 4335.1 Castanhoso, M. de. Dos feitos de D. Christovam da Gama. Lisboa, 1898.
Afr 4335.2 Castanhoso, M. de. Die Heldentaten des Dom Christoph da Gama. Berlin, 1907.
Afr 4335.3 Castanhoso, M. de. Historia das cousas que o muy esforçado Christovam da Gama. Lisboa, 1855.

Afr 4338 Ethiopia - History by periods - 16th century - Galawdewos (1540-1559) - Other special
Afr 4338.301 Saineanu, M. L'Abyssinie dans la seconde moitié du XVI siècle. Inaug. Diss. Leipzig, 1892.

Afr 4339 Ethiopia - History by periods - 16th century - Minas
Afr 4339.5 Esteves Pereira, F.M. Historia de Minás, Además Sagad, rei de Ethiopia. Lisboa, 1888.

Afr 4340 Ethiopia - History by periods - Later Portuguese expeditions
Afr 4340.5 Ferreira, F. Palyart Pinto. Os Portugueses na Ethiópia. Lisboa, 1935.

Afr 4349 Ethiopia - History by periods - 17th century - Susemyos (1606-1632)
Afr 4349.1 Esteves Pereira, F.M. Chronica de Susenyos, rei de Ethiopia. Lisbon, 1892. 2v.
Htn Afr 4349.3* Jesuits. Letters from Missions. (Abyssinia). Histoire d'Ethiopie, en l'année 1626. Paris, 1629.
Htn Afr 4349.3.5F* Fernandez, A. Copia de una del padre A. Fernandez. Madrid, 1627.

Afr 4350 Ethiopia - History by periods - 17th century - Facilidas and end of Catholic missions (1633-1665) - General works
Afr 4350.2.3 Jesuits. Letters from Missions. (Abyssinia). Relaçam geral do estado da Christandade de Ethiopia. Lisboa, 1628.
Afr 4350.2.5 Jesuits. Letters from Missions. (Abyssinia). Carta do patriarcha de Ethiopia. Lisboa, 1631.
Htn Afr 4350.2.6* Jesuits. Letters from Missions. (Abyssinia). Carta do patriarcha de Ethiopia. Lisboa, 1631.

Afr 4357 Ethiopia - History by periods - Christianity in the 18th century
Afr 4357.5 Freire de Monterroyo Mascarenhas, José. Novo triunfo da religiam serafica, ou noticia summaria do martyrio...3 de marco de 1716. Lisboa, 1718.

Afr 4360 Ethiopia - History by periods - 18th century to rise of Theodore (to 1855) - General works
Afr 4360.3 Cronaca reale Abissinia dall'anno 1800 all'anno 1840. Rome, 1916.
Afr 4360.5 Conti Rossini, C. La cronaca reale Abissinia dall'anno 1800 all'anno 1840. Roma, 1917.
Afr 4360.7 Royal Chronicle of Abyssinia. The Royal Chronicle of Abyssinia, 1769-1840. Cambridge, Eng., 1922.
Afr 4360.10 Abir, Mordechai. Ethiopia: the era of the princes. London, 1968.

Afr 4365 Ethiopia - History by periods - 18th century to rise of Theodore (to 1855) - Special topics
Afr 4365.1 Demimuid, M. Vie...Justin de Jacobis. 2 ed. Paris, 1906.
Afr 4365.2 Duchesne, Albert. Le consul Blondeel en Abyssinie. Bruxelles, 1953.

Afr 4368   Ethiopia - History by periods - Missions in the 19th century
Afr 4368.5F   Massaja, E.G. Missione nell'alta Etiopia. Roma, 1885. 6v.
Afr 4368.5.3   Cenni biografici dell'eminentissimo Cardinale Guglielmo Massaja. Milano, 1889.
Afr 4368.5.5   Gianozza, E. Guglielmo Massaia. Torino, 1932.
Afr 4368.5.20   Gentile, Lorenzo. L'apostolo dei Galla. 3 ed. Torino, 1931.
Afr 4368.5.25   Massaja, G. I miei trentacinque anni di missione. Torino, 1932.
Afr 4368.5.30   Massaja, G. Lettere del Cardinale Massaia dal 1846 al 1886. Torino, 1937.
Afr 4368.10   Coulbeaux, J.B. Vers la lumière. 2e ed. Paris, 1926.
Afr 4368.12   Cassinari, E. Il beato Ghebre-Michael. Roma, 1926.
Afr 4368.12.5   Catholic Church. Litterae apostolicae quibus venerabilis dei Fain Abba Ghebec Michael. Romae, 1926.
Afr 4368.16   Constantin, Jean R. L'archimandrite Paisi et l'ataman Achinoff. Paris, 1891.
Afr 4368.17   Constantin, N. Une expédition religieuse en Abyssinie. Paris, 1891.
Afr 4368.20   Giselsson, Emanuel. Med frälsningens budskap; några bilder från den svenskamissionen. Stockholm, 1967.

Afr 4370   Ethiopia - History by periods - Theodore (1855-1868) - General works
Afr 4370.2   Theodoros II. Chronique. Paris, 1905.
Afr 4370.5   Alaqa Walda Maryam. History of King Theodore. London, 1906.
Afr 4370.7   Lejean, G. Theodore II, le nouvel empire d'Abyssinie et les intérêts français dans le sud de la Mer Rouge. Paris, 1865.

Afr 4375   Ethiopia - History by periods - Theodore (1855-1868) - English expedition (1867-1868)
Afr 4375.1   Hozier, H.M. British expedition to Abyssinia. London, 1869.
Afr 4375.3   Bussidon, C. Abyssinie et Angleterre (Theodoros). Paris, 1888.
Afr 4375.4   Blanc, H. Ma captivité en Abyssinie. Paris, 1870.
Afr 4375.4.5   Blanc, H. A narrative of captivity in Abyssinia. London, 1868.
Afr 4375.5   Shepherd, A.F. The campaign in Abyssinia. Bombay, 1868.
Afr 4375.6   Henty, G.A. The march to Magdala. London, 1868.
Afr 4375.7   Bechtinger, J. Ost Afrika. Wien, 1870.
Afr 4375.8F   Holland, T.J. Record of the expedition to Abyssinia. v.1-2, and atlas. London, 1870. 3v.
Afr 4375.9PF   Acton, Roger. The Abyssinian expedition and the life and the reign of King Theodore. London, 1868.
Afr 4375.15   Wilkins, H. St.C. Reconnoitring in Abyssinia. London, 1870.
Afr 4375.17   Fanton, A. L'Abyssinie lors de l'expedition anglaise, 1867-1868. Paris, 1936.
Afr 4375.19   Urquehart, David. The Abyssinian war. London, 1868.

Afr 4378   Ethiopia - History by periods - Theodore (1855-1868) - Other special topics
Afr 4378.1   Apel, F.H. Drei Monate en Abyssinien. Zürich, 1866.
NEDL Afr 4378.2   Stern, H.A. The captive missionary, account of country and people of Abyssinia. London, 1869.

Afr 4382   Ethiopia - History by periods - John (1871-1889) - War with Egypt (1875-1876)
Afr 4382.1   Dye, W.M. Moslem Egypt and Christian Abyssinia. N.Y., 1880.

Afr 4384   Ethiopia - History by periods - John (1871-1889) - Wars with Italy in general
Afr 4384.1   Pamphlet vol. Italia in Africa, 1887-97. 11 pam.
Afr 4384.2   Chiala, L. Discorso sul credito di 20 milioni per l'azione militare in Africa. Roma, 1887.
Afr 4384.10   Traversi, L. Let-Marefia. Milano, 1931.

Afr 4386   Ethiopia - History by periods - John (1871-1889) - Battles of Saati and Dogali (1887)
Afr 4386.5   Frassinesi, M.A. Primo anniversairio dei combattimenti di Saati e Dogali. Casale, 1888.
Afr 4386.8   Antona-Traversi, Camillo. Sahati e Dogali. Roma, 1887.

Afr 4388   Ethiopia - History by periods - John (1871-1889) - Other special topics
Afr 4388.5   Mitchell, L.H. Report on seizure by Abyssinians of geological expedition. Cairo, 1878.
Afr 4388.12   Mancini, P.S. Dichiarazioni...intorno all'eccidio di G. Bianchi. Roma, 1885.
Afr 4388.15   Pankhurst, Richard Keir Patrick. The great Ethiopian famine of 1888-1892, a new assessment. Addis Ababa, 1964.

Afr 4389   Ethiopia - History by periods - 20th century - General works
Afr 4389.11.20   Cipolla, A. In Etiopia. 4a ed. Torino, 1933.
Afr 4389.12   Mancini, P.S. Dichiarazioni...all'eccedio del viaggiatore Gustavo Bianchi. Roma, 1885.
Afr 4389.35   Zischka, A. Abessinien, das letzte ungelöste Problem Afrikas. Bern, 1935.
Afr 4389.35.3   Zischka, A. Abissinia, l'ultimo problema insoluto dell'Africa. Firenze, 1936.
Afr 4389.35.7   Lahse, Erich. Abessinien. 2e Aufl. Leipzig, 1935.
Afr 4389.35.10   Sperduti, G. Aspetti della questione etiopica. Roma, 1935.
Afr 4389.35.18   Zoli, Corrado. Etiopia d'oggi. 3a ed. Roma, 1935.
Afr 4389.36A   Newman, E.W.P. Ethiopian realities. London, 1936.
Afr 4389.36B   Newman, E.W.P. Ethiopian realities. London, 1936.
Afr 4389.36.5   Shaw, John H. Ethiopia. N.Y., 1936.
Afr 4389.36.10   Levin, I.D. Sovremennaia Abissinia. Moscow, 1936.
Afr 4389.43A   Lambie, T.A. Boot and saddle in Africa. Philadelphia, 1943.
Afr 4389.43B   Lambie, T.A. Boot and saddle in Africa. Philadelphia, 1943.
Afr 4389.54   Stradal, Otto. Der Weg zum letzten Pharao. Wien, 1954.
Afr 4389.58   Luther, E.W. Ethiopia today. Stanford, Calif., 1958.
Afr 4389.61   Voblikov, D.R. Efiopiia v borbe za sokhranenie nezavisimosti. Moscow, 1961.

Afr 4390   Ethiopia - History by periods - 20th century - Menelek II (1889-1913) - General works
Afr 4390.10   Guebre Sellassie. Chronique du règne de Menelik II, roi des rois d'Ethiopie. Paris, 1930-31. 2v.
Afr 4390.15   Keller, Konrad. Alfred Ilg. Frauenfeld, 1918.
Afr 4390.20   Piozza, G. Alla corte di Menelik. Ancona, 1912.
Afr 4390.25   Mantegazza, Vico. La guerra in Africa. 3a ed. Firenze, 1896.

Afr 4390   Ethiopia - History by periods - 20th century - Menelek II (1889-1913) - General works - cont.
Afr 4390.30   Zintgraff, Alfred. Der Tod des Löwen von Juda. Berlin, 1932.
Afr 4390.35   Yaltsasamma. Les amis de Menelik II, roi des rois d'Ethiopie. Paris, 1899.
Afr 4390.40   Scarforglio, E. Abissinia (1888-1896). v.1. Roma, 1936.
Afr 4390.45   Lauribar, Paul de. Douze ans en Abyssinie. Paris, 1898.
Afr 4390.47   Pariset, Dante. Al tempo di Menelik. Milano, 1937.
Afr 4390.50   Monfreid, H. de. Menelik. 7. ed. Paris, 1954.
Afr 4390.55   Salimbeni, A., Conte. Crispi e Menelick nel diario inedito del Conte Augusto Salimbeni. Torino, 1956.
Afr 4390.60   Fanelli, Armando. Taitù e Manelik. Milano, 1935.

Afr 4392   Ethiopia - History by periods - 20th century - Menelek II (1889-1913) - War with Italy (1895-1896)
Afr 4392.1   Eletz, Yu. Imperator Menelik. St. Petersburg, 1898.
Afr 4392.2   Bulatovitch, A.K. S voiskami Menelika II. St. Petersburg, 1900.
Afr 4392.3   Baratieri, O. Memorie d'Africa (1892-1896). Torino, 1898.
Afr 4392.3.5   Baratieri, O. Mémoires d'Afrique (1892-1896). Paris, 1897.
NEDL Afr 4392.4   Berkeley, G.F.H. The campaign of Adowa and the rise of Menelik. Westminster, 1902.
Afr 4392.4.5   Berkeley, G.F.H. The campaign of Adowa and the rise of Menelik. New ed. London, 1930.
Afr 4392.4.10   Berkeley, G.F.H. The campaign of Adowa and the rise of Menelik. N.Y., 1969.
Afr 4392.6   Pellenc, A.J.J. Les Italiens en Afrique (1880-1896). Paris, 1897.
Afr 4392.7   Red Cross, Italy (Croce Rossa). Asunto delle relazione sul servizio sanitario...in occasione delle campagna d'Africa, 1895-1896. Roma, 1899.
Afr 4392.8.5   Canuti, Giuseppe. L'Italia in Africa e le guerre con l'Abissinia. Firenze, 1911.
Afr 4392.9   Gaibi, A. La guerra d'Africa (1895-96). Roma, 1930.
Afr 4392.15F   Treves, Firm, Publisher, Milan. La guerra italo-abissinia, 1895-96. Milano, 1896.
Afr 4392.20   Navarotto, Adriano. Il contegno della Santa Sede nel conflitto italo-etiopico. Vicenza, 1936.
Afr 4392.25   Bono, Giulio del. Da Assab ad Adua. Roma, 1937.
Afr 4392.30   Tedone, Giovanni. Angerà. Milano, 1964.

Afr 4393   Ethiopia - History by periods - 20th century - Menelek II (1889-1913) - Siege of Nakalleh (8 Dec.-2 Jan. 1895-1896)
Afr 4393.5   L'Assedio di Macallè. Milano, 1935.

Afr 4394   Ethiopia - History by periods - 20th century - Menelek II (1889-1913) - Battle of Adua (March 1896)
Afr 4394.1   Ximenes, E. Sul campo di Adua. Milan, 1897.
Afr 4394.2   Chiala, Valentino. Il Generale Dabormida nella giornata del 1 marzo 1896. Roma, 1897.
Afr 4394.3.5   Guarniere, L. La battaglia di Adua e il popola italiano. 2a ed. Torino, 1897.
Afr 4394.3.8   Pollera, Alberto. La battaglia di Adua del 1 marzo 1896. Firenze, 1928.
Afr 4394.3.11   Pini, Cesare G. Adua, brevi cenni sulla guerra italo-etiopica mahdista degli anni 1895-96. Torino, 1926.
Afr 4394.3.14   Bellavita, E. Adua, i precedenti, la battaglia. Genova, 1931.
Afr 4394.5   Bronzuoli, A. Adua. Roma, 1935.
Afr 4394.7   Mansueti, C. Le due Adue, 1896-1936. Milano, 1937.
Afr 4394.9.5   Oriani, A. L'Ora d'Africa. 2a ed. Bologna, 1935.
Afr 4394.11   Conti Rossini, C. La battaglia di Adua. Roma, 1939.
Afr 4394.13   Gamerra, Giovanni. Ricordi di un prigioniero di guerra nello Scioa, marzo 1896-gennaio 1897. 2a ed. Firenze, 1897.
Afr 4394.14   Bourelly, G. La battaglia di Abba Garima. Milano, 1901.
Afr 4394.15   Petrides, Saint Pierre. Le héros d'Adoua. Paris, 1963.

Afr 4396   Ethiopia - History by periods - 20th century - Menelek II (1889-1913) - Policy of the Powers
Afr 4396.10   Rossetti, Carlo. Storia diplomatica dell'Etiopia durante il regno di Menelik II. Torino, 1910.
Afr 4396.15   Jesman, Czesław. The Russians in Ethiopia. London, 1958.

Afr 4420   Ethiopia - History by periods - 20th century - Zauditu (1916-1928)
Afr 4420.5   Arce, L. L'Abyssinie. Avignon, 1925.

Afr 4430   Ethiopia - History by periods - 20th century - Haile Selassie I (1928-) - General works
Afr 4430.5   Pamphlet vol. Italo-Ethiopian conflict. 24 pam.
Afr 4430.25   Zoli, Corrado. Cronache etiopiche. Roma, 1930.
Afr 4430.27   Jacoby, C.M. On special mission to Abyssinia. N.Y., 1933.
Afr 4430.35   Harmsworth, G. Abyssinian adventure. London, 1935.
Afr 4430.35.5   Prochazka, R. von. Abessinien, die schwarze Gefahr. Wien, 1935.
Afr 4430.35.8   Prochazka, R. von. Abissinia pericolo nero. Milano, 1935.
Afr 4430.35.19   Africanus. (Pseud.). Etiopia, 1935. 4 ed. Roma, 1935.
Afr 4430.35.25   Collombet, E. L'Ethiopie moderne et son avènement à la communauté internationale. Thèse. Dijon, 1936.
Afr 4430.36   Asfa Yilma, Princess. Haile Selassie. London, 1936.
Afr 4430.36.5   MacLean, R. John Hay ofEthiopia. N.Y., 1936.
Afr 4430.36.10   Virgin. The Abyssinia I knew. London, 1936.
Afr 4430.36.20   Tharaud, J. Le passant d'Ethiopie. Paris, 1936.
Afr 4430.40.5   Monfreid, H. de. Masque d'or, ou, Le dernier Negus. 11e éd. Paris, 1936.
Afr 4430.46A   Pankhurst, Estelle S. Ethiopia and Eritrea. Woodford, 1953.
Afr 4430.46B   Sandford, C.L. Ethiopia under Haile Selassie. London, 1946.
Afr 4430.48   Sandford, C.L. Ethiopia under Haile Selassie. London, 1946.
Afr 4430.55   Haile Selassie. The eighteenth anniversary of the coronation of His Imperial Majesty Haile Selassie I. Addis Ababa, 1948.
Afr 4430.55.5   Talbot, D.A. Haile Selassie I. The Hague, 1955.
Afr 4430.55.6   Sandford, C.L. The Lion of Judah hath prevailed. N.Y., 1955.
Afr 4430.55.10   Sandford, C.L. The Lion of Judah hath prevailed. London, 1955.
Afr 4430.55.15   Gorham, Charles Orson. The Lion of Judah. N.Y., 1966.
Afr 4430.61   Gingold Duprey, A. De l'invasion à la libération de l'Ethiopie. Paris, 1955.
Afr 4430.61.2   Pignatelli, L. La guerra dei sette mesi. Napoli, 1961.
          Pignatelli, L. La guerra dei sette mesi. Milano, 1965.

Afr 4430 Ethiopia - History by periods - 20th century - Haile Selassie I (1928-) - General works - cont.

Afr 4430.64 Mosley, Leonard O. Haile Selassie, the conquering Lion. London, 1964.
Afr 4430.66 Clapham, Christopher S. Haílde-Selassie's government. London, 1969.

Afr 4431 Ethiopia - History by periods - 20th century - Haile Selassie I (1928-) - War with Italy (1934-1935)

Afr 4431.5 Baer, George Webster. The coming of the Italian-Ethiopian war. Cambridge, 1967.
Afr 4431.10 Gallo, Max. L'Affaire d'Ethiopie aux origines de la guerre mondiale. Paris, 1967.
Afr 4431.15 Borra, Eduardo. Prologo di un conflitto. Milano, 1965.
Afr 4431.20 Barker, Arthur J. The civilizing minion; a history of the Italo-Ethiopian War of 1935-1936. N.Y., 1968.
Afr 4431.25 Boca, Angelo del. La guerra d'Abissinia, 1935-1941. Milano, 1965.
Afr 4431.25.1 Boca, Angelo del. The Ethiopian War, 1935-1941. Chicago, 1969.
Afr 4431.30 Mussolini, Vittorio. Voli sulle ambe. Firenze, 1937.

Afr 4433 Ethiopia - History by periods - 20th century - Haile Selassie I (1928-) - 1941-

Afr 4433.1 Iag'ia, Vatamiar S. Efiopiia v 1941-1954 gg. Moskva, 1969.

Afr 4434 Ethiopia - History by periods - 20th century - Haile Selassie I (1928-) - Other special topics

Afr 4434.5 Wilsson, Wils Gunnar. Det är ju människor det gäller. Stockholm, 1966.
Afr 4454.10 Davis, Raymond J. Fire on the mountains, the church in Ethiopia. London, 1967.

Afr 4500 Ethiopia - General relations with foreign powers - General works

Afr 4500.1 Pierre-Alype, L. L'Ethiopie et les convoitises allemandes. Paris, 1917.
Afr 4500.5 Pigli, Mario. L'Etiopia moderna nelle sue relazioni internazionali, 1859-1931. Padova, 1933.
Afr 4500.5.5 Pigli, Mario. L'Etiopia, l'incognita africana. 2a ed. Padova, 1935.
Afr 4500.10 Work, Ernest. Ethiopia, a pawn in European diplomacy. New Concord, 1935.
Afr 4500.15 MacCallum, Elizabeth P. Rivalries in Ethiopia. Boston, 1935.
Afr 4500.20 Rouard de Card, E. L'Ethiopie auPoint de vue du droit international. Paris, 1928.
Afr 4500.22 Reischies, S. Abessinien als Kampfobjekt der grossen Mächte von 1880-1916. Bleicherode am Harz, 1937.
Afr 4500.24 Schwarz, H. Die Entwicklung der völkerrechtlichen Beziehungen äthiopiens zu den Mächten seit 1885. Breslau, 1937.

Afr 4509 Ethiopia - General relations with foreign powers - England - Special topics

Afr 4509.15.3 Beke, Charles F. The British captives in Abyssinia. 2nd ed. London, 1867.
Afr 4509.17 Portal, G.H. An account of the English mission to King Johannis of Abyssinia in 1887. Winchester, 1888.
Afr 4509.19 Cito de Bitetto, Carlo. Méditerranée, Mer Rouge. Paris, 1937.

Afr 4512 Ethiopia - General relations with foreign powers - Italy - General works

Afr 4512.10.3 Marotta, Renato. L'Abissinia nelle questioni internazionali. 3a ed. Torino, 1936.
Afr 4512.15 Agostino Orsini, P. D. Perche andiamo in Etiopia. Roma, 1936.
Afr 4512.18 Faraci, Giuseppe. Etiopia, guerra epace. Torino, 1965.
Afr 4512.20 Caioli, Aldo. L'Italia di Fronte a Gineura, aspetti del conflitto italo-etiopico dalle origini alla conquista dell Impero. Roma, 1965.

Afr 4513 Ethiopia - General relations with foreign powers - Italy - Special topics

Afr 4513.05 Pamphlet box. Abyssinia. Foreign relations with Italy.
Afr 4513.07 Pamphlet box. Abyssinia. Foreign relations with Italy.
Afr 4513.09F Pamphlet box. Abyssinia. Foreign relations.
Htn Afr 4513.2PF* Pamphlet box. Abyssinia. Foreign relations with Italy.
Afr 4513.5 Haskell, D.C. Ethiopia, and the Italo-Ethiopian conflict, 1928-1936. N.Y., 1936.
Afr 4513.15 Micaletti, K. Sangue italiano in Etiopia. Firenze, 1933.
Afr 4513.17 Sapelli, A. Memorie d'Africa 1883-1906. Bologna, 1935.
Afr 4513.19 Conti Rossini, C. Italia ed Etiopia dal trattato d'Uccialli alla battaglia di Adua. Roma, 1935.
Afr 4513.20 Royal Institute of International Affairs. Abyssinia and Italy. N.Y., 1935.
Afr 4513.25 Varanini, Varo. L'Abissinia attuale sotto tutti i suoi aspetti. Torino, 1935.
Afr 4513.35 Rowan-Robinson, H. England, Italy, Abyssinia. London, 1935.
Afr 4513.35.5 White, F. The Abyssinian dispute. London, 1935.
Afr 4513.35.10 Legionarius (pseud.). The grounds for the serious charges brought by Italy against Abyssinia. Roma, 1935.
Afr 4513.35.10.2 Legionarius (pseud.). The grounds for the serious charges brought by Italy against Abyssinia. Rome, 1935.
Afr 4513.35.15 Italo-Ethiopian dispute. Roma, 1935.
Afr 4513.35.16 Italy. Italo-Ethiopian dispute. Roma, 1935.
Afr 4513.35.17 Italy. Il conflitto italo-etiopico. Roma, 1935.
Afr 4513.35.20 Carnegie Endowment for International Peace. Division of Intercourse and Education. The Abyssinian dispute. N.Y., 1935.
Afr 4513.35.25 Italy. Historical Society. The Italo-Ethiopian controversy. n.p., 1935.
Afr 4513.35.27 Italy. Historical Society. The Italo-Ethiopian controversy. N.Y., 1935.
Afr 4513.35.30 Carter, Boak. Black shirt, black skin. Harrisburg, 1935.
Afr 4513.35.33 Carter, Boak. Black shirt, black skin. London, 1935.
Afr 4513.35.41 Vare, Daniele. Italy, Great Britain and the League in the Italo-Ethiopian conflict. N.Y., 1935.
Afr 4513.35.44 Vare, Daniele. Italy, Great Britain and the League in the Italo-Ethiopian conflict. N.Y., 1935.
Afr 4513.35.50 Makin, W.J. War over Ethiopia. London, 1935.
Afr 4513.35.55 Burns, Emile. Abyssinia and Italy. London, 1935.
Afr 4513.35.60F Aloise, P. Speech of Baron Aloise, head of the Italian delegation to the League of Nations. n.p., 1935.
Afr 4513.35.65F Italy. Memoria del governo italiano circa la situazione in Etiopia. II. n.p., 1935.

Afr 4513 Ethiopia - General relations with foreign powers - Italy - Special topics - cont.

Afr 4513.35.70F Italy. Memorandum of the Italian government on the situation in Abyssinia. n.p., 1935.
Afr 4513.35.78 Wencker-Wiedberg, F. Abessinien, das Pulverfass Afrikas. 3e Aufl. Düsseldorf, 1935.
Afr 4513.35.83 Bonardi, Pierre. Brassard amarante. Paris, 1935.
Afr 4513.35.90 Ridley, F.A. Mussolini over Africa. London, 1935.
Afr 4513.35.100 Lachin, M. L'Ethiopie et son destin. 5e ed. Paris, 1935.
Afr 4513.35.105 Malizia, N. L'Africa orientale italiana e l'Abissinia. Napoli, 1935.
Afr 4513.35.110 Marino, A. Italia ed Abissinia. Bengasi, 1935.
Afr 4513.35.115 Klein, Fritz. Warum Krieg um Abessinien. Leipzig, 1935.
Afr 4513.35.120 Hernandez Alfonso, L. Abisinia. Madrid, 1935.
Afr 4513.35.125 Abissinia, problema italiano. Roma, 1935.
Afr 4513.35.130 Traversi, L. L'Italia e l'Etiopia. Bologna, 1935.
Afr 4513.35.135 Ortega y Gasset, E. Etiopia, el conflicto italo-abisinio. Madrid, 1935.
Afr 4513.35.145 Cipolla, A. Da Baldissera a Badoglio. 4a ed. Firenze, 1936.
Afr 4513.35.150 Nenni, P. Il delitto africano del fascismo. Paris, 1935.
Afr 4513.35.155 West, J. War and the workers. N.Y., 1935.
Afr 4513.35.160 Ford, J.W. War in Africa. N.Y., 1935.
Afr 4513.35.165 Coppola, Francesco. La vittoria bifronte. Milano, 1936.
Afr 4513.36 Canada. Department of External Affairs. Documents relating to the Italo-Ethiopian conflict. Ottawa, 1936.
Afr 4513.36.5 Lapradelle, A.G. Le conflit italo-ethiopien. Paris, 1936.
Afr 4513.36.10 Hubbard, W.D. Fiasco in Ethiopia. N.Y., 1936.
Afr 4513.36.15 Villari, Luigi. Italy, Abyssinia and the League. Rome, 1936.
Afr 4513.36.20 Chaplin, W.W. Blood and ink. N.Y., 1936.
Afr 4513.36.25 Currey, M. A woman at the Abyssinian war. London, 1936.
Afr 4513.36.30 Istituto per gli Studi di Politica Internazionale, Milan. Il conflitto italo-etiopico. Milano, 1936. 2v.
Afr 4513.36.33 Istituto per gli Studi di Politica Internazionale, Milan. Breve storia del conflitto italo-etiopico. Milano, 1936.
Afr 4513.36.34 Istituto per gli Studi di Politica Internazionale, Milan. The Italian empire in Africa, present and future. Milano, 1936.
Afr 4513.36.35 Bourcier, E. L'aventure abyssine. Paris, 1936.
Afr 4513.36.40 Vecchi, B.V. La conquista del Tigrai. Milano, 1936.
Afr 4513.36.45 Salvemini, G. Can Italy live at home. N.Y., 1936.
Afr 4513.36.50 Abbati, A.H. Italy and the Abyssinian war. London, 1936.
Afr 4513.36.55 Ciccarelli, Socrate. L'Italia fascista e l'Abissinia. Torino, 1935.
Afr 4513.36.60 Gentizon, Paul. La conquête de l'Ethiopie. Paris, 1936.
Afr 4513.36.68 Badoglio, P. La guerra d'Etiopia. Milano, 1936.
Afr 4513.36.69 Badoglio, P. War in Abyssinia. London, 1937.
Afr 4513.36.69.5 Badoglio, P. War in Abyssinia. N.Y., 1937.
Afr 4513.36.70 Cimmaruta, R. Ual ual. Milano, 1936.
Afr 4513.36.75 Lauro, R. Tre anni a Gondar. Milano, 1936.
Afr 4513.36.83 Bono, E. La preparazione e le primi operazioni. 3a ed. Roma, 1937.
Afr 4513.36.84 Bono, E. de. Anno XIIII, the conquest of an empire. London, 1937.
Afr 4513.36.85 Fasci Italiani all'Estero. L'Abissinia e noi. Roma, 1935.
Afr 4513.36.95 Cabiati, A. La conquista dell impero. Milano, 1936.
Afr 4513.36.100 Salemi, L. Politica estera. Palermo, 1936.
Afr 4513.36.105 Societa Editrice de Novissima, Roma. Facts Geneva refuses to see. Roma, 1936.
Afr 4513.36.110 Po di posto al sole. Milano, 1936.
Afr 4513.36.115 Frusci, L. In Somalia sul fronte meridionale. Bologna, 1936.
Afr 4513.36.120 Fuller, J.F.C. The first of the League wars. London, 1936.
Afr 4513.36.130 Montfreid, Henri de. Les guerriers de l'Ogaden. Paris, 1936.
Afr 4513.36.135 Ultima barbarie, come Tafari lascio Addis Abeba. n.p., 1936.
Afr 4513.36.145 Volta, Sandro. Graziani a Neghelli. 2 ed. Firenze, 1936.
Afr 4513.36.150 Pinti, Luigi. Le vie dell'impero. Roma, 1936.
Afr 4513.37.5 Steer, G. Caesar in Abyssinia. Boston, 1937
Afr 4513.37.10 Farfaglio, S. Le bande autocarrate dei fedelissimi da Roma ad Addis Ababa. Paris, 1937.
Afr 4513.37.15 Konovalov, T.E. Con le armate del Negus. Bologna, 1937.
Afr 4513.37.22 Xylander, R. von. La conquista dell Abissinia. Milano, 1937.
Afr 4513.37.25 Pesenti, G. Storia della prima divisione Eritrea, (8 aprile 1935-XIII - 1 maggio XIV). Milano, 1937.
Afr 4513.37.30 Bastin, J. L'affaire d'Ethiopie et les diplomates, 1934-1937. Bruxelles, 1937.
Afr 4513.37.37 Simon, Yves. La campagne d'Ethiopie et la pensée politique française. 2e éd. Lille, 1937.
Afr 4513.37.42A Martelli, G. Italy against the world. N.Y., 1938.
Afr 4513.37.42B Martelli, G. Italy against the world. N.Y., 1938.
Afr 4513.37.47 Newman, E.W.P. Italy's conquest of Abyssinia. London, 1937.
Afr 4513.37.55 Appelius, M. Il crollo dell'impero dei Negus. Milano, 1937.
Afr 4513.37.60 Luongo, G. L'Etiopia, dalla vigilia di sangue alla conquista dell'impero. Napoli, 1937.
Afr 4513.37.65 Benedetti, A. La guerra equatoriale. Milano, 1937.
Afr 4513.37.70 Armellini, Quirino. Con Badoglio in Ethiopia. Milano, 1937.
Afr 4513.37.75 Franchini, M. Ogadèn dal II parallelo al cuore dell'Impero. Bologna, 1937.
Afr 4513.37.80 Italy. Comando delle Forze Armate della Somalia. La guerra italo-etiopica. Addis Abeba, 1937.
Afr 4513.38A Matthews, H.L. Two wars and more to come. N.Y., 1938.
Afr 4513.38B Matthews, H.L. Two wars and more to come. N.Y., 1938.
Afr 4513.38.5 Wienholt, A. The African's last stronghold in Nabath's vineyard. London, 1938.
Afr 4513.38.12 Graziani, R. Il fronte sud. 2a ed. Milano, 1938.
Afr 4513.38.20A Società Editrice di Novissima, Rome. The social and economic system of Italian East Africa. Roma, 1938.
Afr 4513.38.20B Società Editrice di Novissima, Rome. The social and economic system of Italian East Africa. Roma, 1938.
Afr 4513.38.25 Poggiali, Ciro. Albori dell'impero; l'Etiopia come è e come sarà. Milano, 1938.
Afr 4513.38.30 Bollati, Ambrogio. La campagne italo-etiopica. Roma, 1938.
Afr 4513.38.35 Marchese, Aldo. G.M. Giulietti. Milano, 1938.
Afr 4513.39 Lessona, A. Verso l'impero. Firenze, 1939.
Afr 4513.39.10 Neri, Italo. La questione del Nilo. Roma, 1939.
Afr 4513.39.15A Quaranta, F. Ethiopia. London, 1939.
Afr 4513.39.15B Quaranta, F. Ethiopia. London, 1939.

Afr 4513 Ethiopia - General relations with foreign powers - Italy - Special topics - cont.

Afr 4513.39.20 Marabini, A. La barbarie dell'imperialismo fascista nelle colonie italiane. Parigi, 1939.
Afr 4513.39.25 Diel, Louise. Behold our new empire, Mussolini. London, 1939.
Afr 4513.39.30 Brown, S.H. Für das Rote Kreuz in äthiopien. Zürich, 1939.
Afr 4513.39.35 Mattioli, Guido. L'aviazione fascista e la conquista dell'impero. Roma, 1939.
Afr 4513.39.40 Italy. Esercito. Corpo di stato maggiore. Ufficio storico. La campagna 1935-46 in Africa oriental. Roma, 1939.
Afr 4513.40A Delvalle, P.A. Roman eagles over Ethiopia. Harrisburg, 1940.
Afr 4513.40B Delvalle, P.A. Roman eagles over Ethiopia. Harrisburg, 1940.
Afr 4513.41 Rodeno, Franz. Frankreichs Stellung im Abessinienkonflikt. Berlin, 1941.
Afr 4513.43 Villani, Luigi. Storia diplomatica del conflitto italo-etiopico. Bologna, 1943.
Afr 4513.46 Pankhurst, E.S. The Ethiopian people. Woodford, 1946.
Afr 4513.49 Gandar Dower, K. Abyssinian patchwork. London, 1949.
Afr 4513.59 Caffo, Aventino. Il genio militare nella campagna in Africa orientale. Roma, 1959.
Afr 4513.60 Cohen, Armand. La Société des Nations devant le conflit italo-éthiopien. Genève, 1960.
Afr 4513.61 Schaefer, Ludwig F. The Ethiopian crisis, touchstone of appeasement. Boston, 1961.

Afr 4515 Ethiopia - General relations with foreign powers - France - General works

Afr 4515.1 Caix de St. Aymour. Histoire des relations de la France avec abyssinie. Paris, 1886.
Afr 4515.1.2 Caix de St. Aymour. Histoire des relations de la France avec l'Abyssinie. Paris, 1892.
Afr 4515.5F Italy. Ministero degli Affairi Esteri. Documenti diplomatici presentati al parliamento italiano. Roma, 1890.

Afr 4523 Ethiopia - General relations with foreign powers - Other powers - Special topics

Afr 4523.5 Hasan ibn Ahmad al Haimi. Zur Geschichte Abessiniens im 17. Jahrhundert. Berlin, 1898.

Afr 4555 - 4560 Ethiopia - Geography, description, etc. - General works (By date)

Afr 4555.00 Ficalho. Viagens de Pedro da Covilhan. Lisboa, 1898.
Afr 4555.00.5 Brandao, Zephyrino. Pero da Borilhan. Lisboa, 1897.
Afr 4555.31 Pearce, N. Life and adventures of N. Pearce during residence. London, 1831. 2v.
Htn Afr 4555.40* Alvares, Francisco. Ho Preste Joam das Indias. Verdadeira informaçam. Lisbon, 1540.
Afr 4555.40.3F Alvares, Francisco. Verdadeiro informação das terras do Preste João das Indias. Lisboa, 1889.
Afr 4555.40.3.5 Alvares, Francisco. Verdadeira informação das terras do Preste João das Indias. Lisboa, 1943.
Htn Afr 4555.40.4* Alvares, Francisco. Historia de las cosas de Ethiopia. Çragoça, 1561.
Htn Afr 4555.40.5* Alvares, Francisco. Historia de las cosas de Ethiopia. Toledo, 1588.
Htn Afr 4555.40.8* Alvares, Francisco. Historiale description de l'Ethiopie. Anvers, 1558.
Afr 4555.40.22 Alvares, Francisco. Kurtze und wahrhafftige Beschreibung der Ethiopie. Eiszlebe, 1567.
Htn Afr 4555.40.71* Goes, D. Fides, religio moresque Aethiopum. Paris, 1541.
Afr 4555.86A Waldmeier, T. Autobiography, account of ten years' life in Abyssinia. London, 1886.
Afr 4555.86B Waldmeier, T. Autobiography, account of ten years' life in Abyssinia. London, 1886.
Afr 4556.34 Le Blanc, Vincent. Histoire géographique et mémorable de l'Assiete de la terre universelle. Aix, 1634.
Afr 4556.59.12 Lobo, J. Voyage historique d'Abyssinie. Paris, 1728.
Afr 4556.59.13 Lobo, J. Relation historique d'Abissinie. Paris, 1728.
Htn Afr 4556.59.23* Lobo, J. Voyage to Abyssinia. London, 1735.
Afr 4556.59.39 Lobo, J. A voyage to Abyssinia. London, 1789.
Htn Afr 4556.60F* Almeida, Manoel. Historia geral de Ethiopia. Coimbra, 1660.
Htn Afr 4556.60.2* Tellez, B. Historia geral de Ethiopia. (Earlier issue). Coimbra, 1660.
Afr 4556.60.10 Tellez, B. Historia geral de Ethiopia. Porto, 1936.
Htn Afr 4556.81F* Ludolf, H. Historia aethiopica. Francofurti ad Moenum, 1681.
Afr 4556.81.2F Ludolf, H. Historia aethiopica. Francofurti ad Moenum, 1691.
Afr 4556.81.11 Ludolf, H. A new history of Ethiopia. London, 1682.
Afr 4556.81.21 Ludolf, H. Nouvelle histoire d'Abissinie. Paris, 1684.
Afr 4556.81.31 Ludolf, H. Historie van Abissinien. Utrecht, 1687.
Afr 4557.90F Bruce, J. Travels. Edinburgh, 1790. 5v.
Afr 4557.90.2F Bruce, J. Travels to discover source of the Nile. 2nd ed. v.1-8. Plates and maps. Edinburgh, 1805. 8v.
Afr 4557.90.12 Bruce, J. Travels to discover the source of the Nile. Abridged. Boston, 1798.
Afr 4557.90.14 Bruce, J. Travels, between the years 1765 and 1773. London, 1822?
Afr 4557.90.25 Head, F.B. The life of Bruce. London, 1830.
Afr 4557.90.30 Drohojowska, Antoinette Joséphine Françoise Anne. L'Abyssinie d'après James Bruce et les voyageurs contemporains. Lille, 1886.
Afr 4557.97 Pacelli, M. Viaggi in Etiopia. Napoli, 1797.
Afr 4558.14.2 Salt, Henry. Voyage to Abyssinia. Philadelphia, 1816.
Afr 4558.14.5 Salt, Henry. A voyage to Abyssinia, and travels into the interior of that country. 1st ed. London, 1967.
Afr 4558.33.2 Russell, M. Nubia and Abyssinia. N.Y., 1837.
Afr 4558.33.3 Russell, M. Nubia and Abyssinia. 2d ed. Edinburgh, 1833.
Afr 4558.33.5 Russell, M. Nubia and Abyssinia. N.Y., 1840.
Afr 4558.34 Gobat, Samuel. Journal of a three years' residence in Abyssinia. London, 1834.
Afr 4558.35 Hoskins, G.A. Travels in Ethiopia. London, 1835.
Afr 4558.35.5 Gobat, Samuel. Journal d'un séjour en Abyssinia. Paris, 1835.
Afr 4558.37.2 Combes, Edmond. Voyage en Abyssinie...1835-37. Paris, 1839. 4v.
Afr 4558.38 Rueppell, Edward. Reise in Abyssinien. Frankfurt, 1838. 2v.
Afr 4558.43 Journals of Messers Isenberg and Krape. London, 1843.
Afr 4558.43.5 Isenberg, Karl Wilhelm. The journals of C.W. Isenberg and J.L. Krapt. London, 1968.
Afr 4558.44 Johnston, C. Travels in southern Abyssinia. London, 1844. 2v.

Afr 4555 - 4560 Ethiopia - Geography, description, etc. - General works (By date) - cont.

Afr 4558.44.2 Harris, W.C. The highlands of Ethiopia. N.Y., n.d.
Afr 4558.44.2.1 Harris, W.C. The highlands of Ethiopia. 1st ed. London, 1968.
Afr 4558.44.3 Harris, W.C. Adventures in Africa. Philadelphia, n.d.
Afr 4558.44.11 Lefebvre, Theophile. Voyage en Abyssinie. Paris, 1844.
Htn Afr 4558.45* Lefebvre, Theophile. Voyage en Abyssinie. v.1-. Paris, 1845. 8v.
Htn Afr 4558.45.2PF* Lefebvre, Theophile. Voyage en Abyssinie. Paris, 1845-51. 3v.
Afr 4558.47 Ferret, A. Voyage en Abyssinie dans les provinces. Paris, 1847-48. 2v.
Afr 4558.47PF Ferret, A. Voyage en Abyssinie dans les provinces. Atlas. Paris, 1847-48.
Afr 4558.52 Heughlin, T. Reisen in Nord-Ost-Afrika. Gotha, 1857.
Afr 4558.53 Parkyns, M. Life in Abyssinia. London, 1853. 2v.
Afr 4558.53.2 Parkyns, M. Life inAbyssinia. London, 1868.
Afr 4558.54 Parkyns, M. Life in Abyssinia. v.1-2. N.Y., 1854.
Afr 4558.55F Fenzl, E. Bericht über C. Reitz und seine Reise. Vienna, 1855.
Afr 4558.59 Munzinger, W. Über die Sitten und das Recht der Bogos. Winterthur, 1859.
Afr 4558.64F Lejean, G. Voyage en Abyssinie executé de 1862 à 1864. Text and atlas. Paris, 1873. 2v.
Afr 4558.67.3 Baker, S.W. The Nile tributaries of Abyssinia. 3rd ed. London, 1868.
Afr 4558.67.4 Baker, S.W. The Nile tributaries of Abyssinia. Hartford, 1868.
Afr 4558.67.5A Baker, S.W. The Nile tributaries of Abyssinia. 4th ed. Philadelphia, 1868.
Afr 4558.67.5B Baker, S.W. The Nile tributaries of Abyssinia. 4th ed. Philadelphia, 1868.
Afr 4558.67.5.4 Baker, S.W. The Nile tributaries of Abyssinia. 4th ed. London, 1871.
Afr 4558.67.6 Baker, S.W. The Nile tributaries of Abyssinia. London, 1883.
Afr 4558.67.7 Baker, S.W. The Nile tributaries of Abyssinia. London, 1886.
Afr 4558.67.9 Dufton, H. Narrative of a journey through Abyssinia. London, 1867.
Afr 4558.68 Hotten, J.C. Abyssinia. London, 1868.
Afr 4558.68.3 Plowden, W.C. Travels in Abyssinia. London, 1868.
Afr 4558.68.7 Heuglin, T. von. Reise nach Abessinien. Jena, 1868.
Afr 4558.69 Rassam, H. Narrative of British mission to Theodore. London, 1869. 2v.
Afr 4558.69.5 Andree, Richard. Abessinien, das Alpenland unter den Tropen. Leipzig, 1869.
Afr 4558.75 Raffray, A. Voyage en Abyssinie, à Zanzibar et aux pays des Ouanika. n.p., 1875.
Afr 4558.76 Raffray, A. Abyssinie. Paris, 1876.
Afr 4558.77 Decosson, E.A. The cradle of the Blue Nile. London, 1877. 2v.
Afr 4558.80 Matteucci, P. In Abissinia, viaggio. Milano, 1880.
Afr 4558.80.20 Pesci, Dino. Esplorazioni in Africa di Gustavo Bianchi. Milano, 1886.
Afr 4558.80.25 Bianchi, G. In Abissinia. Milano, 1896.
Afr 4558.81 Winstanley, W. A visit to Abyssinia. London, 1861. 2v.
Afr 4558.81.5 Vigoni, Pippo. Abissinia, giornale di un viaggio. Milano, 1881.
Afr 4558.83 Rohlfs, G. Meine Mission nach Abessinien. Leipzig, 1883.
Afr 4558.83.2 Rohlfs, G. L'Abissinia. Milano, 1885.
Afr 4558.83.3 Hartmann, R. Abyssinien und die übrigen Gebiete des Afrikas. Leipzig, 1883.
Afr 4558.83.5 Abargues de Sosten, J.V. Notas del viaje por Etiopia. Madrid, 1883.
Afr 4558.84 Russel, S. Une mission en Abyssinie. Paris, 1884.
Afr 4558.84.5 Soleillet, Paul. Voyages en Ethiopie jan. 1882-oct. 1884. Rouen, 1886.
Afr 4558.85 Simon, Gabriel. Voyage en Abyssinie et chez les Gallas-Raias. Paris, 1885.
Afr 4558.87 Cecchi, A. L'Abissinia settentrionale. Photoreproduction. Milano, 1887.
Afr 4558.88.5 Parises, N. L'Abissinia. Milan, 1888.
Afr 4558.90 Smith, F.H. Through Abyssinia. London, 1890.
Afr 4558.90.5 Pasini, L. Usi e costumi. Milano, n.d.
Afr 4558.92 Villiers, F. Negus negusti. N.Y., 1892.
Afr 4558.92.5 Muenzenberger, E.F.A. Abessinien. Freiberg, 1892.
Afr 4558.92.9 Portal, G.H. My mission to Abyssinia. London, 1892.
Afr 4558.96 Comber, P. L'Abyssinie en 1896. Paris, 1896.
Afr 4558.97 Vigneras, S. Une mission française en Abyssinie. Paris, 1897.
Afr 4558.97.5 Dorleans, H. Une visite à l'empereur Menelick. Paris, 1897.
Afr 4558.98A Gleichen, A.E.W. With the mission to Menelik 1897. London, 1898.
Afr 4558.98B Gleichen, A.E.W. With the mission to Menelik 1897. London, 1898.
Afr 4559.01 Wellby, M.S. Twixt Sirdar and Menelik. London, 1901.
Afr 4559.01.5 Vivian, H. Abyssinia. N.Y., 1901.
Afr 4559.01.9 Leroux, H. Menelik et nous. Paris, 1901.
Afr 4559.01.15 Wylde, A.B. Modern Abyssinia. London, 1901.
Afr 4559.03 Leroux, H. Chasses et gens d'Abyssinie. Paris, 1903.
Afr 4559.05A Hayes, A.J. The source of the Blue Nile. London, 1905.
Afr 4559.05B Hayes, A.J. The source of the Blue Nile. London, 1905.
Afr 4559.06 Skinner, R.P. Abyssinia of to-day. London, 1906.
Afr 4559.06.5 Skinner R.P. Abyssinia of to-day, an account of the first mission sent by the Americam Government to the court of King of Kings, 1903-1904. N.Y., 1969.
Afr 4559.07 Kulmer, F. Im Reiche Kaiser Meneliks. Leipzig, 1910.
Afr 4559.07.10 Rosen, Felix. Eine deutsche Gesandtschaft in Abessinien. Leipzig, 1907.
Afr 4559.08 Holts, A. Im Auto zu Kaiser Menelik. Berlin, 1908.
Afr 4559.09 Duchesne-Fournet, J. Mission en Ethiopie (1901-1903). v.1-2 and atlas. Paris, 1909. 3v.
Afr 4559.09.5 Escherich, G. Im Lande des Negus. Berlin, 1912.
Afr 4559.10 Faitlovitch, J. Quer durch Abessinien. Berlin, 1910.
Afr 4559.11 Rathjens, Carl. Beiträge zur Landeskunde von Abessinien. These. Erlangen, 1911.
Afr 4559.13 Citerni, Carlo. Ai confini meridionali dell'Etiopia. Milano, 1913.
Afr 4559.13.5 Halle, C. To Menelek in a motor car. London, 1913.
Afr 4559.14 Kolmodin, J. Traditions de Tsazzega et Hazzega. Annales. Uppsala, 1914.
Afr 4559.14.10 Merab. Impressions d'Ethiopie. Paris, 1921-29. 3v.
Afr 4559.15 Castro, Lincoln de. Nella terra dei negies. Milano, 1915. 2v.

Afr 4559.18   Rein, G.K. Abessinien, eine Landeskunde. Berlin, 1918-20. 3v.
Afr 4559.20   Tedesco Zammarano, V. Alle sorgenti del Nilo azzurro. Roma, 1920.
Afr 4559.23   Rey, Charles F. Unconquered Abyssinia as it is today. London, 1923.
Afr 4559.23.10   Maydon, H.C. Simen, its heights and abysses. London, 1925.
Afr 4559.24.9   Civimini, G. Ricordi di carovana. 2 ed. Milano, 1933.
Afr 4559.25   Powell, E.A. Beyond the utmost purple rim. N.Y., 1925.
Afr 4559.25.3   Forbes, R.T. From Red Sea to blue Nile. N.Y., 1925.
Afr 4559.25.5   Forbes, R.T. From Red Sea to blue Nile. N.Y., 1935.
Afr 4559.26   Darley, Henry. Slaves and ivory. London, 1926.
Afr 4559.26.3   Darley, Henry. Slaves and ivory. London, 1935.
Afr 4559.26.4   Darley, Henry. Slaves and ivory in Abyssinia. N.Y., 1935.
Afr 4559.26.5   Pollera, Alberto. Lo stato etiopico e la sua chiesa. Roma, 1926.
Afr 4559.26.13   Simertz, S. En färd tell Abessinien. 2a upp. Stockholm, 1926.
Afr 4559.27   Rey, Charles F. In the country of the blue Nile. London, 1927.
Afr 4559.27.5   Hodson, A.W. Seven years in southern Abyssinia. London, 1927.
Afr 4559.27.10   Mueller, Otto. Rings um den Tschertischer. Hannover, 1927.
Afr 4559.28.3   MacCreagh, Gordon. The last of free Africa. 2d ed. N.Y., 1935.
Afr 4559.28.5   Baum, James E. Savage Abyssinia. London, 1928.
Afr 4559.28.10   Cerulli, E. Etiopia occidentale. Roma, 1928. 2v.
Afr 4559.28.15   Schrenzel, E.H. Abessinien. Berlin, 1928.
Afr 4559.28.20   Hentze, W. Volldampf unter Palmen. Leipzig, 1928.
Afr 4559.29   Conti Rossini, C. L'Abissinia. Roma, 1929.
Afr 4559.29.5   Sander, Erich. Das Hochland von Abessinien, Habesch. Heidelberg, 1929.
Afr 4559.29.10   Liano, A. Ethiopie, empire des nègres blancs. Paris, 1929.
Afr 4559.29.15   Lubinski, Kurt. Hochzeitreise nach Abessinien. Leipzig, 1929.
Afr 4559.30   Norden, Hermann. Africa's last empire. London, 1930.
Afr 4559.30.5   Ciravegna, G. Nell impero del negus neghest. Torino, 1930.
Afr 4559.30.10   Fulgenzio da Vecchieto, Padre. Il contributo alla geografia dell'Abissinia nelle memorie del cardinale Guglielmo Massaia. Tivoli, 1930.
Afr 4559.30.15   Jannasch, Hans. Im Schatten des Negus. Berlin, 1930.
Afr 4559.30.20   Civinini, G. Sotto le pioggie equatoriali. Roma, 1930.
Afr 4559.30.25   Armandy, A. La désagréable partie de campagne. Paris, 1930.
Afr 4559.30.30   Roth-Roesthof, A. von. Ba Menelik. Leipzig, 1930.
Afr 4559.32.5   Gruehl, Max. The citadel of Ethiopia. London, 1932.
Afr 4559.32.10   Bergsma, S. Rainbow empire, Ethiopia stretches out her hands. Grand Rapids, 1932.
Afr 4559.33   Monfried, Henri de. Vers les terres hostiles de l'Ethiopie. Paris, 1933.
Afr 4559.34   Mittelholzer, W. Abessinienflug. Zürich, 1934.
Afr 4559.34.5   Rebeaud, Henri. Chez le roi des rois d'Ethiopie. Neuchâtel, 1934.
Afr 4559.34.10   Griaule, M. Les flambeurs d'hommes. Paris, 1934.
Afr 4559.34.15   Griaule, M. Abyssinian journal. London, 1935.
Afr 4559.34.20   Griaule, M. Burners of men, modern Ethiopia. Philadelphia, 1935.
Afr 4559.34.25   Celarie, H. Ethiopie XXe siècle. Paris, 1934.
Afr 4559.34.30   Pucci, Generoso. Coi 'Negadi' in Etiopia. Firenze, 1934.
Afr 4559.34.35   Bartleet, Eustace John. In the land of Sheda. Birmingham, 1934.
Afr 4559.35   Gruehl, Max. Abessinien, ahoi. Berlin, 1935.
Afr 4559.35.3   Gruehl, Max. L'impero del Negus Neghesti. Milano, 1935.
Afr 4559.35.5   Lieberenz, P.K. Das Rätsel Abessinien. Berlin, 1935.
Afr 4559.35.18   Jansen, P.G. Abissinia di oggi. 8a ed. Milano, 1935.
Afr 4559.35.30   Farago, L. Abyssinia on the eve. London, 1935.
Afr 4559.35.35   Nanni, Ugo. Che cosa è l'Etiopia. Milano, 1935.
Afr 4559.35.40   Rocchi, A. Etiopia ed etiopia. Milano, 1935.
Afr 4559.35.45   Rey, C.F. The real Abyssinia. London, 1935.
Afr 4559.35.50   Coon, C.S. Measuring Ethiopia and flight into Arabia. Boston, 1935.
Afr 4559.35.55   Goldmann, Wilhelm. Das ist Abessinien. Bern, 1935.
Afr 4559.35.58   Baravelli, G.C. L'ultimo baluardo della schiavitù, l'Abyssinia. Roma, 1935.
Afr 4559.35.60   Baravelli, G.C. The last stronghold of slavery, what Abyssinia is. Roma, 1935.
Afr 4559.35.60.5   Baravelli, G.C. The last stronghold of slavery, what Abyssinia is. Roma, 1935.
Afr 4559.35.62   Baravelli, G.C. The last stronghold of slavery. London, 1936.
Afr 4559.35.65   Gruehl, Max. Abessinien. Berlin, 1935.
Afr 4559.35.70   Herrmann, Gerhard. Abessinien; Raum als Schicksal. Leipzig, 1935.
Afr 4559.35.75   Dunckley, F.C. Eight years in Abyssinia. London, 1935.
Afr 4559.35.80   Comyn-Platt, Thomas. The Abyssinian storm. London, 1935.
Afr 4559.35.85   Caimpenta, U. L'impero abissino. 10. ed. Milano, 1935.
Afr 4559.35.87   Muehlen, Leo. Im Banne des äthiopischen Hochlandes. 2e Aufl. Berlin, 1935.
Afr 4559.35.92   Monfried, H. de. Le drame éthiopien. Paris, 1935.
Afr 4559.35.95   Hayter, Frank Edward. The quest of Sheba's mines. London, 1935.
Afr 4559.35.102   Frangipani, A. L'equivoco abissino. 2a ed. Milano, 1936.
Afr 4559.35.107   Huyn, Ludwig. Abessinien, Afrikas Unruhe-Herd. Salzburg, 1935.
Afr 4559.35.110   Stuessy, J. Mit dem Faltboot nach Abessinien. Frauenfeld, 1935.
Afr 4559.35.117   Rebeaud, Henri. Au service du négus. 2e ed. Paris, 1935.
Afr 4559.35.125   Manzini, Luigi. Panorama etiopico. Milano, 1935.
Afr 4559.35.130   Littmann, Enno. Abessinien. Hamburg, 1935.
Afr 4559.36   Leichner, G. Gefahrvolles Abessinien. Leipzig, 1936.
Afr 4559.36.5   Roussan, S.M. Seule en Ethiopie. Paris, 1936.
Afr 4559.36.10   Hayter, Frank Edward. Gold of Ethiopia. London, 1936.
Afr 4559.36.15F   Zervos, A. L'empire d'Ethiopie. Athens, 1936.
Afr 4559.36.20   Brusati, G.C. Etiopia, studio geografico-economico. Milano, 1936.
Afr 4559.36.25   Castro, Lincoln de. Etiopia terra, uomini e cose. 2. ed. Milano, 1936.
Afr 4559.38   Newman, E.W.P. The new Abyssinia. London, 1938.
Afr 4559.38.10   Papini, I. La produzione dell'Etiopia. Roma, 1938.
Afr 4559.39   Hayter, Frank Edward. African adventurer. London, 1939.

Afr 4559.40A   Shortridge, G.C. A gazetteer of Abyssinia. Pts.1-3. n.p., 1940.
Afr 4559.40B   Shortridge, G.C. A gazetteer of Abyssinia. Pts.1-3. n.p., 1940.
Afr 4559.42A   Khun de Prorok, Byron. Dead men do tell tales. N.Y., 1942.
Afr 4559.42B   Khun de Prorok, Byron. Dead men do tell tales. N.Y., 1942.
Afr 4559.48   Philip, H. Abyssinian memories. Santa Barbara, Calif., 1948.
Afr 4559.49   Buxton, D.R. Travels in Ethiopia. London, 1949.
Afr 4559.49.5   Buxton, D.R. Travels in Ethiopia. N.Y., 1950.
Afr 4559.49.6   Buxton, D.R. Travels in Ethiopia. N.Y., 1967.
Afr 4559.52   Talbot, D.A. Contemporary Ethiopia. N.Y., 1952.
Afr 4559.53   Kamil, M. Das Land der Negus. Innsbruck, 1953.
Afr 4559.55   Rittlinger, H. Ethiopian adventure. London, 1959.
Afr 4559.56F   Doresse, Jean. Au pays de la ruine de Saba. Paris, 1956.
Afr 4559.56.2   Doresse, Jean. Ethiopia. London, 1959.
Afr 4559.57   Busk, Douglas L. The fountain of the sun. London, 1957.
Afr 4559.57.5   Jenny, Hans. Athiopien, Land im Aufbruch. Stuttgart, 1957.
Afr 4559.59   Pakenham, T. The mountains of Rasselas. N.Y., 1959.
Afr 4559.60   Ullendorff, Edward. The Ethiopians. London, 1960.
Afr 4559.60.1   Ullendorff, Edward. The Ethiopians. London, 1961.
Afr 4559.61   Abu al-Hajjaj, Y. A contribution to the physiography of northern Ethiopia. London, 1961.
Afr 4559.62   Lipsky, George A. Ethiopia. New Haven, 1962.
Afr 4559.62.5   Ouannou, J. L'Ethiopie, pilote de l'Afrique. Paris, 1962.
Afr 4559.63   Ethiopia. Ministry of Information. Ethiopia, a brief sketch. Addis Ababa, 1963.
Afr 4559.64   American University, Washington, D.C. Area handbook for Ethiopia. 2. ed. Washington, D.C., 1964.
Afr 4559.64.5   Bush och lustgaard. Stockholm, 1964.
Afr 4559.65   Levine, Donald Nathan. Wax and gold. Chicago, 1965.
Afr 4559.65.5   Greim, Armin. Im Reich des Negus. Leipzig, 1965.
Afr 4559.65.10   Choleva, Emil. Etiopska dobrodruzstvi. Praha, 1965.
Afr 4559.66   Ethiopia. Ministry Of Information. Ethiopia, Liberation Silver Jubilee, 1941-1966. Addis Ababa, 1966.
VAfr 4559.67   Ogrin, Miran. Od Nila de Kartagine. Ljubljana, 1967.
Afr 4559.68   Gal'perin, Georgii L. Ekvatoe riadom. Moskva, 1968.
Afr 4559.68.5   Murphy, Dervla. In Ethiopia with a mule. London, 1968.

Afr 4568   Ethiopia - Geography, description, etc. - Special customs
Afr 4568.15   Baravelli, G.C. The last stronghold of slavery. Roma, 1922.
Afr 4568.17   Pollera, A. La donna in Etiopia. Roma, 1922.
Afr 4568.19B   Trimingham, J.S. Islam in Ethiopia. London, 1952.
Afr 4568.19.2   Trimingham, J.S. Islam in Ethiopia. London, 1965.
Afr 4568.20   Conti Rossini, C. Studi etiopici. Roma, 1945.

Afr 4570   Ethiopia - Geography, description, etc. - Guidebooks
Afr 4570.5   Ethiopia. Chamber of Commerce. Guide book of Ethiopia. Addis Ababa, 1954.

Afr 4571   Ethiopia - Geography, description, etc. - Views
Afr 4571.1   Views in central Abyssinia. London, 1868.
Afr 4571.3   Schneiders, Toni. L'Ethiopie. Paris, 1958.
Afr 4571.5   Ethiopia. Ministry of Information. Twenty years of work, 1941-1961. Addis Ababa, 1962.
Afr 4571.8F   Ethiopia. Ministry of Information. Notre terre. Addis Ababa, 196-.

Afr 4572   Ethiopia - Geography, description, etc. - Maps
Afr 4572.15   Padoan, G. L'Abissinia nella geografia dell'Africa orientale. Milano, 1935.

Afr 4573   Ethiopia - Economic history and conditions
Afr 4573.2   Ouannou, J. L'Ethiopie et son économie. 2. ed. Paris, 1961.
Afr 4573.4   Pankhurst, R.K.P. An introduction to the economic history of Ethiopia from early times to 1800. London, 1961.
Afr 4573.6   Ethiopia. Second five year development plan, 1955-1959. Addis Ababa, 1962.
Afr 4573.7   Ethiopia. Third five year development plan, 1961-1965 E-C (1968/69-1972/73 G-c). v.1-4. Addis Ababa, 1969.
Afr 4573.8   Ethiopian economic review. Addis Ababa. 1-5,1959-1960
Afr 4573.10   Ethiopia. Ministry of Commerce and Industry. Economic progress of Ethiopia. Addis Ababa, 1955.
Afr 4573.12   Economic journal. Addis Ababa. 1,1964+
Afr 4573.13   El'ianov, Aratolu Ia. Efiopiia. Moskva, 1967.
Afr 4573.15   Wohlgemuth, Lennart. Etiopiens ekonomi. Uppsala, 1967.
Afr 4573.20   Pankhurst, Richard Keir Pethick. Economic history of Ethiopia, 1800-1935. 1st ed. Addis Ababa, 1968.
Afr 4573.25   Zerom, Kifle-Mariam. The resources and economy of Ethiopia. Menlo Park, Calif., 1969.
Afr 4573.30   Schwarz, William L.K. Industrial investment climate in Ethiopia. Menlo Park, Calif., 1968.
Afr 4573.35F   Ethiopia. Ministry of Planning and Development. Memorandum on the establishment of appropriate machinery at the central government level for preparation of the third five-year development plan. Addis-Ababa, 1967.

Afr 4574   Ethiopia - Finance
Afr 4574.2   Pischke, J.D. The public sector. Addis Ababa, 1966.

Afr 4575   Ethiopia - Races - General works
Afr 4575.5   Conti Rossini, C. Popoli dell'Ethiopia occidentale. Roma, 1919.
Afr 4575.6   Simoons, Frederick. Northwest Ethiopia. Madison, 1960.
Afr 4575.7   Rait, Mariia V. Narody Efiopii. Moskva, 1965.

Afr 4580   Ethiopia - Races - Abyssinians Proper
Afr 4580.1   Glaser, E. Die Abessinier in Arabien und Afrika. München, 1895.

Afr 4582   Ethiopia - Races - Afars (Danakil)
Afr 4582.5   Jousseaume, F. Impressions de voyage en Apharras. Paris, 1914. 2v.
Afr 4582.10   Franchetti, R. Nella Dancalia etiopica. Milano, 1930.
Afr 4582.15   Nesbitt, L.M. La Dancalia esplorata. Firenze, 1930.
Afr 4582.15.5   Nesbitt, L.M. Hell-hole of creation. N.Y., 1935.
Afr 4582.20   Vinassa de Regny, P. Dancalia. Roma, 1923.

Afr 4585   Ethiopia - Races - Falasha (i.e. Jews)
Afr 4585.1   Stern, H.A. Wanderings among the Falashas. London, 1862.
Afr 4585.1.2   Stern, H.A. Wanderings among the Falashas in Abyssinia. 2d ed. London, 1968.
Afr 4585.2   Flad, M. Kurze Schilderung...abessinischen Juden. Basel, 1869.

Afr 4590   Ethiopia - Races - Gallas
Afr 4590.1   Martial de Salviac, R.P. Les Galla, grande nation africaine. Cahors, 1900.
Afr 4590.1.2   Martial de Salviac, R.P. Les Galla, grande nation africaine. Paris, 1901.
Afr 4590.2   Lewis, Herbert Samuel. A Galla monarchy. Madison, Wisconsin, 1965.

Afr 4591   Ethiopia - Races - Gurages
Afr 4591.2   Shack, William A. The Gurage. London, 1966.

Afr 4592   Ethiopia - Races - Konsos
Afr 4592.1   Nowack, Ernst. Land und Volk der Konso. Bonn, 1954.

Afr 4593   Ethiopia - Races - Mensa
Afr 4593.1.3   Roden, K.G. Le tribu dei Mensa. Stockholm, 1913.

Afr 4598   Ethiopia - Races - Others
Afr 4598.5   Gamst, Frederick C. The Qemant. N.Y., 1969.

Afr 4605   Ethiopia - Provinces - Amhara
Afr 4605.1F   Borelli, Jules. Ethiopie meridionale, Amhara. Paris, 1890.

Afr 4610   Ethiopia - Provinces - Shoa
Afr 4610.2   Rochet d'Héricourt, C.E. Second voyage dans...le royaume de Choa. Paris, 1846.
Afr 4610.3   Cecchi, A. Da Zeila alle frontiere del Caffa. Roma, 1886-87. 3v.
Afr 4610.4F   Bremond, L.A. Expedition scientifique et commerciale au...Choa...Gallas. Paris, 1883.
Afr 4610.6   Rochet d'Héricourt, C.E. Voyage sur la côte orientale de la Mer Rouge et...de Choa. Paris, 1841.

Afr 4612   Ethiopia - Provinces - Harrar
Afr 4612.1   Burton, R.F. First-footsteps...or Exploration of Harrar. London, 1856.
Afr 4612.1.5   Burton, R.F. First footsteps in East Africa. Memorial ed. London, 1894. 2v.
Afr 4612.1.6   Burton, R.F. First footsteps in East Africa. N.Y., 1966.
Afr 4612.1.7   Burton, R.F. First footsteps in East Africa. London, 1966.
Afr 4612.2   Paulitschke, P. Harrar. Leipzig, 1888.

Afr 4615   Ethiopia - Provinces - Nile
Afr 4615.1   Michel, C. Vers Fachoda. Paris, 1901.

Afr 4618   Ethiopia - Provinces - Kaffa
Afr 4618.5   Bieber, Friedrich J. Kaffa. Münster, 1920-23. 2v.

Afr 4620   Ethiopia - Provinces - Equatorial
Afr 4620.3   Leontieff. Provinces équatoriales d'Abyssinie. n.p., n.d.

Afr 4640   Ethiopia - Cities, towns, etc. - Addis Ababa
Afr 4640.2   Berlan, E. Addis-Abeba. Grenoble, 1963.
Afr 4640.3   Haile Selassie I University. Social survey of Addis Ababa, 1960. Addis Ababa, 1960.
Afr 4640.5   Comhaire-Sylvain, Suzanne. Considerations of migration in Addis Ababa. Addis Ababa, 1962.
Afr 4640.7   Ethiopia. Ministry of Information. Africa Hall. Addis Ababa, 1968.

Afr 4642   Ethiopia - Cities, towns, etc. - Aksum
Afr 4642.1   Bent, J.J. The sacred city of the Ethiopians. London, 1893.

Afr 4658   Ethiopia - Cities, towns, etc. - Gondar
Afr 4658.5   Monti della Corte, A.A. I castelli di Gondar. Roma, 1938.

Afr 4660   Ethiopia - Cities, towns, etc. - H
Afr 4660.5   Santagata, Fernando. L'Harar. Milano, 1940.

Afr 4688   Ethiopia - Cities, towns, etc. - T
Afr 4688.15   Rava, M. Al Lago Tsana. Roma, 1913.
Afr 4688.15.5   Cheesman, R.E. Lake Tana and the blue Nile. London, 1936.
Afr 4688.15.10   Marchi, Giulio de. Il Lago Tana e le sue possibilità di sfruttamento. Milano, 1936.
Afr 4688.15.15   Lauro, R. di. Le terre del Lago Tana. Roma, 1936.
Afr 4688.15.20   Dainelli, G. La regione del Lago Tana. Milano, 1939.

Afr 4700   Italian Africa in general (By date, e.g. .40 for 1940)
Afr 4700.1   Africa italiana. Bergamo. 1927+ 2v.
Afr 4700.1.7   Annali dell'Africa italiana. Roma. 1,1938+ 20v.
Afr 4700.1.74   Rassegna sociale dell'Africa italiana. Roma. 1,1938+
Afr 4700.2   Marson, Luigi. Commemorazione dell'esploratore africano. Mantova, 1902.
Afr 4700.3.5   Italy. Comitato per la documentazione dell'opera dell'Italia in Africa. L'Italia in Africa. Roma, 1955.
Afr 4700.4.5   Italy. Comitato per la Documentazione dell'Opera dell'Italia in Africa, le scoperte archeologiche Tripolitania. Roma, 1962. 2v.
Afr 4700.4.10   Panetta, Ester. Studi italiani di etnografia e di folklore della Libia. Roma, 1963.
Afr 4700.4.15   Girolami, Mario. Contributo dell'Italia alla conoscenza della nosografia dell'Africa. Roma, 1963.
Afr 4700.4.20   Traversi, Carlo. Storia della cartografia coloniale italiana. Roma, 1964.
Afr 4700.5.5   Perticone, Giacomo. La politica coloniale dell'Italia. Roma, 1965.
Afr 4700.5.10   Giglio, Carlo. Etiopia Mar rosso. Roma, 1958. 3v.
Afr 4700.6   Italy. Comitato per la Documentazione dell'Opera dell'Italia in Africa. L'Italia in Africa; serie civile. Roma, 1965. 2v.
Afr 4700.13   Pollera, Alberto. Piccola bibliografia dell'Africa orientale con speciale riguardo all'Eritrea e paesi confinanti. Asmara, 1933.
Afr 4700.13.5   Italy. Direzione Centrale degli Affari Coloniali. Raccolta di pubblicazioni coloniali italiane. Roma, 1911.
Afr 4700.13.10   Royal Empire Society. London. A bibliography of Italian colonisation in Africa...Abyssinia. London, 1936.

Afr 4700   Italian Africa in general (By date, e.g. .40 for 1940) - cont.
Afr 4700.13.15   Gorresio, V. Paesi e problemi africani. Milano, 1937.
Afr 4700.14   Colajanni, N. Politica coloniale. Palermo, 1891.
Afr 4700.14.20   Colonia italiana in Africa e Francesco Crispi; il parlamento ed il paese per un Italiano. Roma, 1896.
Afr 4700.14.25   Botarelli, A. Compendio di storia coloniale italiana. Roma, 1914.
Afr 4700.15F   Italy. Direzione Centrale degli Affari Coloniali. L'Africa italiana al Parlamento nazionale, 1882-1905. Roma, 1907.
Afr 4700.17   Congresso Coloniale Italiano, Asmara. Atti. v.1. Roma, 1906.
Afr 4700.20   Governo fascista nelle colonie (Somalia-Eritrea-Libia). Milano, 1925.
Afr 4700.23   Agostino Orsini, P.D. Espansionismo italiano odierno. Salerno, 1923.
Afr 4700.24   Capra, G. L'Africa centro-australe e l'emigrazione italiana. Torino, 1924.
Afr 4700.25   Cantalupe, R. L'Italia musulmana. Roma, 1928.
Afr 4700.26   Federzoni, L. Venti mesi di azione coloniale. Milano, 1926.
Afr 4700.26.5   Gibello Socca, G. Colonie d italia e colonie ex-germaniche d'Africa. Milano, 1926.
Afr 4700.26.10   Italy. Ministero delle Colonie. Notizia generali sulla colonie italiane. Roma, 1926.
Afr 4700.26.18   Italy. Comitato per la Documentazione dell'Opera dell'Italia in Africa. L'Italia in Africa. T.1-5. Roma, 1960- 8v.
Afr 4700.26.20   Italy. Comitato per la Documentazione dell'Opera dell'Italia in Africa. L'Itali in Africa. Roma, 1963.
Afr 4700.27   Virgilli, Filippo. Le colonie italiane. Milano, 1927.
Afr 4700.27.5   Istituto Agricolo Coloniale Italiano. Per le nostre colonie. Firenze, 1927.
Afr 4700.27.10   Guyot, Georges. L'Italie devant le problème colonial. Roma, 1927.
Afr 4700.27.15   Angelini, A. La politica coloniale italiana dalle sue origini ad oggi. Messina, 1927.
Afr 4700.27.20   Vecchi, B.V. Satto il soffio del monsone. Milano, 1927.
Afr 4700.28   Beguinot, F. La nostra aurora coloniale. Imperia, 1928.
Afr 4700.28.5   Stefanini, G. Le colonie. Torino, 1928.
Afr 4700.28.10   Cesari, Cesare. I nostri precursori coloniale. Roma, 1928.
Afr 4700.28.15   Italy. Ministero delle Colonie. Ordinamento amministrativo-contabile per l'Eritrea e per la Somalia. Roma, 1928.
Afr 4700.29   Stefanini, Giuseppe. I possedimenti italiani in Africa. 2 ed. Firenze, 1929.
Afr 4700.29.5   Italy. Ufficio Studi e Propaganda. Le colonie italiane de diretto dominio. Roma, 1929.
Afr 4700.29.10   Ciarlantini, F. Antologia coloniale. Roma, 1929.
Afr 4700.30   Battistelle, V. Africa italiana. Firenze, 1930.
Afr 4700.30.5   Giaccone, E. Le colonie d'Italia. Torino, 1930.
Afr 4700.30.10   Cesari, Cesare. L'evoluzione della coscienza e dell'attività coloniale italiana. Roma, 1930.
Afr 4700.31   Della Valle, Carlo. I pionieri italiani nelle nostre colonie. Roma, 1931.
Afr 4700.31.5   Gaslini, Mario dei. L'oltremare d'Italia in terra d'Africa. Bergamo, 1931.
Afr 4700.31.8   Holmboe, Knud. Desert encounter. London, 1936.
Afr 4700.32   Agostino Orsini, P. Le colonie italiane. Roma, 1932.
Afr 4700.33   Cesari, Cesare. Gli italiani nella conoscenza dell'Africa. Roma, 1933.
Afr 4700.33.5   Cesari, Cesare. Pionieri italiani in Africa. Rome, 1933.
Afr 4700.33.10   Piccioli, A. La nuova Italia d'oltremare. Verona, 1933. 2v.
Afr 4700.33.12   Piccioli, A. La nuova Italia d'oltremare. Milano, 1934. 2v.
Afr 4700.33.15   Gravelli, A. Africa. Roma, 1933.
Afr 4700.34   Giaccardi, A. Dieci anni di fascismo nelle colonie italiane. Verona, 1934.
Afr 4700.34.5   Castelbarco, G. L'ordinamento sindacale-corporativo nell organizzazione delle colonie italiane. Milano, 1934.
Afr 4700.35   Canevari, E. Il generale Tommaso Salsa e le sue campagne coloniali. Milano, 1935.
Afr 4700.35.5   Vecchi, B.V. L'Italia ai margini d'Etiopia. Milano, 1935.
Afr 4700.35.10   Bermasconi, G. Le guerre e la politica dell'Italia nell'Africa orientale. Milano, 1935.
Afr 4700.35.15   Societa Geografica Italiana, Roma. L'Africa orientale. Bologna, 1935.
Afr 4700.35.20   Italia in Africa. Torino, 1935.
Afr 4700.35.25   Giglio, V. Le guerre coloniali d'Italia. Milano, 1935.
Afr 4700.35.30   Dotti, Ernesto. Aspetti attuoli dell'economia delle colonie italiane dell'Africa orientale. Roma, 1935.
Afr 4700.36   Federzoni, L. A.O., Africa orientale, il posto al sole. Bologna, 1936.
Afr 4700.36.5   Bollati, A. Enciclopedia dei nostri combattenti coloniali fino al 2 ottobre 1935. Torino, 1936.
Afr 4700.36.10   Sangiorgi, G.M. L'impero italiano nell'Africa orientale. Bologna, 1936.
Afr 4700.36.17   Istituto per gli Studi di Politica Internazionale, Milan. L'Africa orientale. 2e ed. Milano, 1936. 2v.
Afr 4700.36.20   Giardini, C. Italiani in Africa orientale, pagine di pionieri. Milano, 1936.
Afr 4700.36.25   Bardi, Pietro M. Pionieri e soldati d'Africa orientale dall'acquisto di Assab all'impero romano d'Etiopia. Milano, 1936.
Afr 4700.36.30   Laccetti, B. Le nostre colonie e cenni geografici generali. Napoli, 1936.
Afr 4700.36.35   Vademecum per l'Africa orientale. Milano, 1936.
Afr 4700.37   Silbani, T. L'impero (A.O.I.). Roma, 1937.
Afr 4700.37.5   Pistolese, G.E. L'economia dell'impero. Roma, 1937.
Afr 4700.37.12   Lischi, D. Nell'impero liberato. 2a ed. Pisa, 1938.
Afr 4700.37.15   Fornaciari, J. Nel piano dell'impero. Bologna, 1937.
Afr 4700.37.20   Vecchi, B.V. Nel sud dell'impero. Milano, 1937.
Afr 4700.38   Pesenti del Thei, F. Clima, acqua, terreno, dove e cosa si produce e si alleva in A.O.I. Venezia, 1938.
Afr 4700.38.5   Giaccardi, A. L'opera del fascismo in Africa. Milano, 1938-39. 2v.
Afr 4700.38.10   Jaeger, N. Diritto di Roma nelle terre africane. Padova, 1938.
Afr 4700.38.15   Gaslini, M. L'Italia sul Mar Rosso. Milano, 1938.
Afr 4700.38.20   Cobolli Gigli, G. Strade imperiali. Milano, 1938.
Afr 4700.38.25   Touring Club italiano...Africa orientale italiana. Milano, 1938.
Afr 4700.40   Italian Library of Information. Development of Italian East Africa. N.Y., 1940.
Afr 4700.41.5   Hollis, Christopher. Italy in Africa. London, 1941.
Afr 4700.42   Borelli, Gioranni. Albori coloniali d'Italia (1891-1895). Modena, 1942.

Afr 4700   **Italian Africa in general (By date, e.g. .40 for 1940) - cont.**
Afr 4700.48   Fabian Society. Colonial Bureau. The fate of Italy's colonies. London, 1948.
Afr 4700.62   Ivanitskii, M.N. Put k nezavisimosti. Kiev, 1962.

Afr 4703   **Eritrea - Pamphlet volumes**
Afr 4703.01   Pamphlet box. Eritrea.

Afr 4707   **Eritrea - Historiography**
Afr 4708.5   Eritrea economica. Novara, 1913.

Afr 4710   **Eritrea - Government and administration**
Afr 4710.5   Mondaini, G. L organisation de la colonie de l'Erythrée. Bruxelles, 1912.
Afr 4710.7   Pollera, A. Le popolazioni indigene dell'Eritrea. Bologna, 1935.

Afr 4712   **Eritrea - General politics; political parties**
Afr 4712.1   Franchetti, L. L'Italia e la sua colonia africana. Città de Castello, 1891.

Afr 4715 - 4720   **Eritrea - General history (By date)**
Afr 4718.91.20   Martini, Ferdinando. Nell'Africa italiana. Milano, 1895.
Afr 4718.97   Jaffanel, C. de. Les Italiens en Erythrie. Paris, 1897.
Afr 4718.97.5F   Bizzoni, A. L'Eritrea nel passato e nel presente. Milano, 1897.
Afr 4718.99   Melli, T.B. La colonia Eritrea. Parma, 1899.
Afr 4718.99.2   Melli, T.B. La colonia Eritrea. Parma, 1900.
Afr 4719.02   Melli, Beniamino. L'Eritrea dalle sue origini a tutto l'anno 1901. Milano, 1902.
Afr 4719.14   Palarnenghi-Crispi, Tommaso. Francesco Crispi, la prima guerra d'Africa. Milano, 1914.
Afr 4719.29   Italy. Marina Stato Maggiore. Officio Storico. L'opera della marina in Eritrea e Somalia dalla occupazione...1928. Roma, 1929.
Afr 4719.32   Pantano, G. Ventitre anni di vita africana. Firenze, 1932.
Afr 4719.34   Cortese, Guido. Eritrea. Roma, 1934.
Afr 4719.35   Italy. Escrito. Corpo di stato maggiore. Officio Storico. Storia militare della colonia Eritrea. v.1-2, 2 bis. Roma, 1935-36. 3v.
Afr 4719.45   Longrigg, S.H. A short history of Eritrea. Oxford, 1945.
Afr 4719.47   Martini, Ferdinando. Il diario eritreo. Firenze, 1947. 4v.
Afr 4719.52   Pankhurst, E.S. Eritrea on the eve. Essex, 1952.

Afr 4730   **Eritrea - History by periods - 1869-1890**
Afr 4730.1   Geullot, M.E. La Mer Rouge et l'Abyssinie. Lille, 1890.
Afr 4730.2   Rawson, R.W. European territorial claims on the Red Sea. London, 1885.
Afr 4730.3   Italy. Ministero di Affari Esteri. La colonia italiana di Assab. Roma, 1882.
Htn   Afr 4730.4F*   Italy. Ministero di Affari Esteri. Beilul-Zula-Massaua-Sudan. Rome, 1885.
Afr 4730.5   Chicala, L. La spedizione di Massaua. Torino, 1888.
Afr 4730.10   Da Assab al Mareb. Roma, 1891.
Afr 4730.15A   Zaghi, Carlo. Le origini della colonia Eritrea. Bologna, 1934.
Afr 4730.15B   Zaghi, Carlo. Le origini della colonia Eritrea. Bologna, 1934.
Afr 4730.20   Passamonti, E. Dall'eccidio di Beilul alla questione di Raheita. Roma, 1937.

Afr 4731   **Eritrea - History by periods - Wars with Dervishes (1890-   )**
Afr 4731.5   Baldissera. Rapport...de la campagne d'Afrique (1895-96). Paris, n.d.
Afr 4731.6   Italy. Commissione d'Inchiesta sulla Colonia Eritrea. Relazione generale. Roma, 1891.

Afr 4732   **Eritrea - History by periods - 1890-1952**
Afr 4732.2   Martini, F. Cose africane, da Saati ad Abba Carima. Milano, 1897.
Afr 4732.5   Penne, G.B. Per l'Italia africana. Roma, 1906.
Afr 4732.10F   Italy. Ministero delle Colonie. Relazione sulla colonia Eritrea del R. Commissario civile deputato. Ferdinando Martini per gli esercizi 1902-07. v.1-4. Roma, 1913. 2v.
Afr 4732.15   Petazzi, E. Egitto e Sudan nei loro rapporti economici con la colonia Eritrea. Roma, 1923.
Afr 4732.17   Sillani, Tomaso. L'Affrica orientale italiana. Roma, 1933.
Afr 4732.17.3   Sillani, Tomaso. L'Affrica orientale italiana. Roma, 1936.
Afr 4732.20   Trevaskis, G.K.N. Eritrea. London, 1960.
Afr 4732.21   Rainero, R. I primi tentativi di colonizzazione agricola. Milano, 1960.

Afr 4742   **Eritrea - Geography, description, etc. - General works**
Afr 4742.3   Societa Italiana per il Progresso delle Scienze, Rome. La colonia Eritrea. Fasc.1 Roma, 1913.
Afr 4742.4   Mulazzani, A. Geografia della colonia Eritrea. Firenze, 1930.
Afr 4742.5   Dainelli, Giotto. Risultati scientifici di un viaggio nella colonia Eritrea. Firenze, 1912.
Afr 4742.5.5   Dainelli, Giotto. In Africa, lettere dall'Eritrea. v.1. Bergamo, 1908.
Afr 4742.10   Corni, Guido. Tra Gasc e Setit. Roma, 1930.
Afr 4742.15   Martinelli, Renzo. Sud. Firenze, 1930.
Afr 4742.17.3   Paoli, Renato. Nella colonia Eritrea. Milano, 1908.
Afr 4742.20   Issel, A. Viaggio nel Mar Rosso e tra i Bogos (1870). Milano, 1872.
Afr 4742.22   Baralta, M. Atlante delle colonie italiane. Novara, 1928.
Htn   Afr 4742.24*   Conti Rossini, C. Ricordi di un soggiorno in Eritrea. Fasc.1. Asmara, 1903.
Afr 4742.26   Santagata, F. La colonia Eritrea. Napoli, 1935.
Afr 4742.28   Pollera, Alberto. I Baria e i Cunama. Roma, 1913.

Afr 4743   **Eritrea - Geography, description, etc. - Special customs**
Afr 4743.5   Bartolommei-Gioli, G. Le attitudini della colonia Eritrea all'agricoltura. Firenze, 1902.
Afr 4743.10   Metodio da Nembro. La missione dei Minori Cappuccini in Eritrea (1894-1952). Rome, 1953.

Afr 4745   **Eritrea - Economic history and conditions**
Afr 4745.5   Società di Studi Geografici e Coloniali. L'Eritrea economica. Novara, 1913.

Afr 4746   **Eritrea - Provinces, cities, towns, etc. - Assab**
Afr 4746.10F   Italy. Assab et les limites de la souveraineté turco-égyptienne dans la Mer Rouge. Rome, 1882.
Afr 4746.15   Sapeto, G. Assab e i suoi critici. Genova, 1879.

Afr 4747   **Eritrea - Provinces, cities, towns, etc. - Others**
Afr 4747.1   Calciatti, C. Nel paese dei Cunama, 1922-23. Milano, 1927.
Afr 4747.7   Ericksen, E.G. Africa company town. Dubuque, 1964.

Afr 4750   **Italian Somaliland; Somalia - Periodicals**
Afr 4750.5F   National review. Mogadishu. 2,1964+
Afr 4750.10   Directory of Somalia. London. 1,1968+

Afr 4753   **Italian Somaliland; Somalia - Bibliographies**
Afr 4753.5   Palieri, M. Contributo alla bibliografia e cartografia della Somalia Italiana. Roma, 193 .
Afr 4753.10   Somaliland, Italian. Camera di commercio, industria ed agricoltura. Bibliografia somala. Mogadiscio, 1958.
Afr 4753.15   United States. Operations Mission to the Somali Republic. Inter-river economic exploration. Washington, 1961.

Afr 4760   **Italian Somaliland; Somalia - Government and administration**
Afr 4760.3   Italy. Ministero degli Affari Esteri. Rapport du gouvernement italien à l'Assemblée générale des Nations Unies. 1950+ 5v.
Afr 4760.5   Somaliland, Italian. Manuale per la Somalia italiana, 1912. Roma, 1912.
Afr 4760.10   Meregazzi, R. L'amministrazione fiduciaria italiana della Somalia. Milano, 1954.
Afr 4760.12   Angeloni, Renato. Diritto costituzionale somalo. Milano, 1964.
Afr 4760.14   Nigam, Shyam Behari Lal. Utilisation of manpower in the public service in Somalia. Mogadiscio, 1964.

Afr 4764   **Italian Somaliland; Somalia - General history**
Afr 4764.934   Cesari, Cesare. La Somalia italiana. Roma, 1934-35.
Afr 4764.938   Italy. Esercito. Corpo di Stato Maggiore. Ufficio Storico. Somalia. Roma, 1938. 2v.
Afr 4764.957   Cerulli, Enrico. Somalia. v.1-2. Roma, 1957-64. 3v.

Afr 4766   **Italian Somaliland; Somalia - General special**
Afr 4766.5   Caroselli, F.S. Ferro e fuoco in Somalia. Roma, 1931.
Afr 4766.10   Italy. Treaties. Great Britain. 1933. Agreement concerning claims of certain British and Italian protected persons. London, 1933.
Afr 4766.10.15   Lefebvre, R. Politica somala. Bologna, 1933.
Afr 4766.15.4   Vecchi, Bernardo V. Somalia. 4a ed. Milano, 1936.
Afr 4766.20   Vecchi di Val Cismon, C.M. Orizzonti d'impero. Milano, 1935.
Afr 4766.23   Finkelstein, L.S. Somaliland under Italian administration. N.Y., 1955.
Afr 4766.25   Gasparro, A. La Somalia italiana nell'antichità classica. Palermo, 1910.
Afr 4766.27   Mantegazza, Vico. Il Benadir. Milano, 1908.
Afr 4766.30   Pankhurst, E. Ex-Italian Somaliland. London, 1951.
Afr 4766.31A   Pankhurst, E. Ex-Italian Somaliland. N.Y., 1951.
Afr 4766.31B   Pankhurst, E. Ex-Italian Somaliland. N.Y., 1951.
Afr 4766.33A   Wettmann, S. Somali nationalism. Cambridge, 1963.
Afr 4766.33B   Wettmann, S. Somali nationalism. Cambridge, 1963.
Afr 4766.34   Drysdale, J.G.S. The Somali dispute. London, 1964.
Afr 4766.35   Lewis, I.M. The modern history of Somaliland. London, 1965.
Afr 4766.36   Somalia. Consiglio dei Ministri. L'attività del governo dall'indipendenza ad oggi. Mogadiscio, 1964.
Afr 4766.38   Hess, Robert L. Italian colonialism in Somalia. Chicago, 1966.
Afr 4766.40   Mariam, Mesfin Wolde. The background of the Ethio-Somalia boundary dispute. Addis Ababa, 1964.

Afr 4770   **Italian Somaliland; Somalia - History by periods - 1889-1960**
Afr 4770.5   Bollati, Ambiogio. Somalia italiana. Roma, 1938.

Afr 4772   **Italian Somaliland; Somalia - History by periods - 1960-**
Afr 4772.5F   Somalia. Prime Minister. Statement of programme by Abdirizak Hagi Hussen, Prime Minister and President of the Council of Ministers. Mogadiscio, 1964.
Afr 4772.10   Somalia. Council of Ministers. Government activities from independence until today. Mogadiscio, 1964.

Afr 4785   **Italian Somaliland; Somalia - Geography, description, etc.**
Afr 4785.3   Revoil, G. Voyage au Cap des Aromates (Africa orientale). Paris, 1880.
Afr 4785.4   Ferrandi, U. Lugh, emporio commerciale sul Giuba. Roma, 1903.
Afr 4785.6   Mocchi, A. La Somalia italiana. Napoli, 1896.
Afr 4785.7   Wolverton, Frederick Glyn, 4th Baron. Five months sport in Somaliland. London, 1894.
Afr 4785.10   Vannutelli, L. L'Omo. Viaggio d'esplorazione nell'Africa orientale. Milano, 1899.
Afr 4785.12   Revoil, G.E.J. La vallé du Darrar. Paris, 1882.
Afr 4785.13PF   Potocki, Jozef. Notatki mysLiwskie z Afryki. Warszawa, 1897.
Afr 4785.14   Sorrentino, G. Ricordi del Benadir. Napoli, 1912.
Afr 4785.15   Albertio, Enrico Alberto d'. In Africa, Victoria Nyaza e Benadir. Bergamo, 1906.
Afr 4785.16   Piazza, G. Il Benadir...con 16 fotografie originali. Roma, 1913.
Afr 4785.20   Lavagetto, A. La vita eroica del Capitano Bottego (1893-1897). Milano, 1934.
Afr 4785.25   Vecchi, B.V. Migiurtinia. Torino, 1933.
Afr 4785.27   Pomilio, Marco. Un giornalista all'equatore. Firenze, 1933.
Afr 4785.29   Monile, F. Somalia (ricordi e visioni). Bologna, 1932.
Afr 4785.35   Zammarano, V. Tedesco. Impressioni di caccia in Somalia italiana. 3a ed. Milano, 1932.
Afr 4785.37   Vecchi, B.V. Vecchio Benadir. Milano, 1933.
Afr 4785.39   Corni, G. Somalia italiana. Milano, 1937. 2v.
Afr 4785.933.5   Monile, F. Africa orientale. Bologna, 1933.
Afr 4785.934.5   Neuhaus, V. Nella piu lontana terra dell'impero. Bologna, 1937.
Afr 4785.935   Perricone, A. Ricordi somali. Bologna, 1935.
Afr 4785.961   Prozhogin, N.P. Dobrogo utra, Afrika. Moscow, 1961.
Afr 4785.965   Sergeeva, Irina S. Somaliiskaia Respublika. Moskva, 1965.
Afr 4785.965.5   Balsan, Francois. A pied au Nord Somali. Paris, 1965.
Afr 4785.967   Travis, William. The voice of the turtle. London, 1967.

Afr 4787   Italian Somaliland; Somalia - Economic history and conditions
Afr 4787.5   Karp, Mark. The economics of trusteeship in Somalia. Boston, 1960.
Afr 4787.6   Italy. Ministero degli Affari Esteri. L'amministrazione fiduciaria della Somalia. Roma, 1961.
Afr 4787.8   Orthner-Heun, Irene. Das Entwicklungsland Somalia. Köln, 1963.
Afr 4787.10   Carusoglu, T. Mid-term appraisal of the first five-year plan of Somalia. 1st draft. Mogadiscio, 1966.
Afr 4787.12   Somalia. Planning Commission. Short term development programme, 1968-1970. Mogadiscio, 1968.

Afr 4788   Italian Somaliland; Somalia - Races
Afr 4788.2   Lewis, I.M. A pastoral democracy. London, 1961.
Afr 4788.4   Puccioni, Nello. Le popolazioni indigene della Somalia italiana. Bologna, 1937.

Afr 4789   Italian Somaliland; Somalia - Religion; missions
Afr 4789.2   Eby, Omar. Sense and license. Scottsdale, 1965.
Afr 4789.4   Eby, Omar. A whisper in a dry land. Scottdale, 1968.

Afr 4790   Italian Somaliland; Somalia - Local
Afr 4790.10   Dracopoli, I.N. Through Jubaland to the Lorian Swamp. London, 1914.
Afr 4790.10.15   Haywood, C.W. To the mysterious Lorian Swamp. London, 1927.
Afr 4790.10.25   Zoli, C. Oltre Giuba. Roma, 1927.
Afr 4790.10.26   Zoli, C. Oltre Giuba. Supplemento. Roma, 1927.
Afr 4790.10.27   Zoli, C. Oltre Giuba. Roma, 1927.
Afr 4790.10.30F   Somaliland, Italian. Monografia delle regioni della Somalia. v.1-3 and plates. Torino, 1926-27.

Afr 4798   Italian Somaliland; Somalia - Biographies - Collected
Afr 4798.5   United States. Mission to the Somali Republic. Training Office. A listing of Somalis who participated in a technical assistance training program in the U.S. Mogadiscio, 1968.

Afr 4815 - 4820   French Somaliland - General history (By date)
Afr 4818.99   Rouard de Card, E. Les possessions françaises de la côte orientale. Paris, 1899.
Afr 4819.68   Thompson, Virginia M. Djibonti and the Horn of Africa. Stanford, Calif., 1968.

Afr 4835   French Somaliland - History by periods - 1881-1946 - Building of railway
Afr 4835.1   Ilg, Alfred. Über die Verkehrsentwicklung in Athiopien. Zürich, 1900.

Afr 4865 - 4870   French Somaliland - Geography, description, etc. - General works (By date)
Afr 4868.79   Comptoirs français de l'Afrique orientale. Paris, 1879.
Afr 4869.00   Vigneras, S. Notice sur la côte française des Somalis. Paris, 1900.
Afr 4869.01   Heudebert, L. Au pays des Somalis et des Comoriens. Paris, 1901.
Afr 4869.35   Monfried, H. de. Le lepreux. Paris, 1935.
Afr 4869.39.12   Aubert de la Rue, E. La Somalie française. Paris, 1939.

Afr 4875   French Somaliland - Geography, description, etc. - Special customs
Afr 4875.5   Lippmann, A. Guerriers et sorciers en Somalie. Paris, 1953.

Afr 4886   French Somaliland - Cities, towns, etc. - Obock
Afr 4886.5   Salma, L. de. Obock. Paris, 1893.
Afr 4886.7   Denis de Rivoyre, B.L. Obock, Mascate, Bouchire, Bassorah. Paris, 1883.

Afr 4892   French Somaliland - Cities, towns, etc. - Djibuti
Afr 4892.5   Angoulvant, G. Djibout, Mer Rouge, Abyssinie. Paris, 1902.
Afr 4892.8   Hachette, R. Djibouti, au seuil de l'Orient. Paris, 1931.
Afr 4892.9   Francolini, B. Djibuti. Rome, 1939.
Afr 4892.11   Salata, F. Il nodo di Gibuti, storia diplomatica su documenti inediti. Milano, 1939.
Afr 4892.12   Poinsot, Jean Paul. Djibouti et la côte française des Somalis. Paris, 1964.
Afr 4892.15   Djibonti, son port, son arrière-pays. Paris, 1965.

Afr 4905   British Somaliland - Collected source materials
Afr 4905.5   Great Britain. Colonial Office. Report on the Somaliland Protectorate. 1948+ 2v.

Afr 4935   British Somaliland - History by periods - 1894-1960 - General works
Afr 4935.5   Great Britain. War Office. Official history of operations in Somaliland, 1901-04. London, 1907. 2v.
Afr 4935.6   Hamilton, Angus. Somaliland. London, 1911.

Afr 4937   British Somaliland - History by periods - 1894-1960 - The Mad Mulla
Afr 4937.1   Jennings, J.W. With the Abyssinians in Somaliland. London, 1905.
Afr 4937.2   Battersby, H.F.P. Richard Corfield of Somaliland. London, 1914.
Afr 4937.10   Jardine, D. The Mad Mullah of Somaliland. London, 1923.
Afr 4937.11   McNeill, M. In pursuit of the Mad Mullah. London, 1902.

Afr 4965 - 4970   British Somaliland - Geography, description, etc. - General works (By date)
Afr 4968.85   James, F.L. Journey through the Somali country. London, 1885.
Afr 4968.88   James, F.L. The unknown hour of Africa. London, 1888.
Afr 4968.95   Francis, J.C. Three months leave in Somaliland. London, 1895.
Afr 4968.95.4   Swayne, H. Seventeen trips through Somaliland. London, 1895.
Afr 4968.95.5   Swayne, H. Seventeen trips through Somaliland and a visit to Abyssinia. 2d ed. London, 1900.
Afr 4969.00   Peel, C.V.A. Somaliland. London, 1900.
Afr 4969.07.3   Herbert, A. Two dianas in Somaliland. 2d ed. London, 1908.
Afr 4969.13   Mosse, A.H.E. My Somali book. London, 1913.
Afr 4969.21   Rayne, H.A. Sun, sand and Somalis. London, 1921.
Afr 4969.51F   Hurt, John A. A general survey of the Somaliland Protectorate, 1944-1950. Harquisa, 1951.
Afr 4969.59   Buchholzer, John. The Horn of Africa. London, 1959.
Afr 4969.63   Laurence, M. The prophet's camel bell. London, 1963.
Afr 4969.63.5   Laurence, M. New wind in a dry land. 1. American ed. N.Y., 1964.

Afr 4975   British Somaliland - Geography, description, etc. - Special customs
Afr 4975.5PF   Potocki, Jozef. Sport in Somaliland. London, 1900.

Afr 5000   French Africa in general - Periodicals
Afr 5000.1.5   Annuaire politique d'Afrique noire et de Madagascar. Paris. 2,1958+
Afr 5000.5   French West Africa. Comité d'Etudes Historiques et Scientifiques. Annuaire et mémoires. Gorée. 1916+ 2v.
Afr 5000.5.3   French West Africa. Comité d'Etudes Historiques et Scientifiques. Bulletin. 1919+ 19v.
Afr 5000.10   Annales africaines. Paris. 1958+ 7v.
Afr 5000.11   Annales africaines. Tables quinquennales, 1954-58. Dakar, 1960.
Afr 5000.15   Développement africain. Alger. 1,1958+ 2v.
Afr 5000.20   Noria. Edition africaine. Limoges. 1960+ 2v.
Afr 5000.25   Centre de Documentation et de Diffusion des Industries, des Mines et de l'Energie Outre-Mer. Colloques. Paris. 1,1963+ 4v.
Afr 5000.29   Memento statistique de l'économie africaine. Paris. 1969+
Afr 5000.31   La politique africaine. Paris. 1968+

Afr 5001.100   French Africa in general - Special organizations, etc. - Union Africaine et Malgache; Organization Commune Africaine et Malgache (1965-   ) - Periodicals issued by
Afr 5001.100   Organisation Commune Africaine et Malgache. Departement des Affaires Economiques, Financieres et des Transports. Bulletin statistique. Yaounde. 2,1966+

Afr 5001.107   French Africa in general - Special organizations, etc. - Union Africaine et Malgache; Organization Commune Africaine et Malgache (1965-   ) - Works about - General works
Afr 5001.107   Union africaine et malgache. Documentation: OAMCE (Organisation africaine et malgache de coopération économique). Paris, 1963.

Afr 5001.109   French Africa in general - Special organizations, etc. - Union Africaine et Malgache; Organization Commune Africaine et Malgache (1965-   ) - Works about - Special topics
Afr 5001.109   Verin, V.P. Prezidentskie respubliki v Afrike. Moscow, 1963.

Afr 5001.110 - .119   French Africa in general - Special organizations, etc. - Union Africaine et Malgache; Organization Commune Africaine et Malgache (1965-   ) - Specialized agencies of UAM - Organization africaine et malgache de coopération économique
Afr 5001.110   Organisation Africaine et Malgache de Coopération Economique. Revue trimestrielle. Yaounde.
Afr 5001.110.5   Nations nouvelles. Yaounde. 1,1964+

Afr 5003   French Africa in general - Bibliographies
Afr 5003.1   Joucla, E. Bibliographie de l'Afrique occidentale française. Paris, 1912.
Afr 5003.1.5   Grandidier, G. Bibliographie de l'Afrique occidentale française. Paris, 1937.
Afr 5003.2   Tuaillon, J.L. Bibliographie critique de l'Afrique occidentale française. Paris, 1936.
Afr 5003.2.3   Tuaillon, J.L. Bibliographie critique de l'Afrique occidentale française. Thèse. Paris, 1936.

Afr 5005   French Africa in general - Pamphlet volumes
Afr 5005.1   Pamphlet box. French Tropical Africa.

Afr 5010   French Africa in general - Government and administration
Afr 5010.2   Hubert, L. L'éveil d'un monde. Paris, 1909.
Afr 5010.3   Poirier, Jean. Etudes de droit africain et de droit malgache. Paris, 1965.
Afr 5010.5   Lamput, Pierre. Les constitutions des états. Paris, 1962.
Afr 5010.10   Sy, Seydou Madani. Recherches sur l'exercice du pouvoir politique en Afrique noire. Paris, 1965.
Afr 5010.12   Etats africains d'expression française et République Malgache. Paris, 1962.

Afr 5012   French Africa in general - General politics; political parties
Afr 5012.4   Hamon, Leo. Les partis politiques africains. Paris, 1962.

Afr 5014 - 5020   French Africa in general - General history (By date)
Afr 5019.58   Suret-Canale, Jean. Afrique noire, occidentale et centrale. Paris, 1958. 2v.
Afr 5019.58.2   Suret-Canale, Jean. Afrique noire occidentale et centrale. 2 ed. v.1. Paris, 1961.
Afr 5019.58.3   Suret-Canale, Jean. Afrique noire occidentale et centrale. 3e éd. Paris, 1968.
Afr 5019.58.4   Suret-Canale, Jean. Schwarzafrika i Geographie, Bevölkerung. Berlin, 1966. 2v.
Afr 5019.58.5   Africanus. L'Afrique noire devant l'indépendance. Paris, 1958.
Afr 5019.58.10   Blanchet, Andre. L'itinéraire des partis africains depuis Bamoko. Paris, 1958.
Afr 5019.61   Boubacar, Diabete. Porte ouverte sur la communauté franco-africaine. Bruxelles, 1961.

Afr 5023   French Africa in general - General special
Afr 5023.5   Bouche, Denise. Les villages de liberté en Afrique noire française, 1887-1910. Paris, 1968.

Afr 5035   French Africa in general - History by periods - 19th century
Afr 5035.5   Monteil, P.L. Souvenirs vécus. Quelques feuillets de l'histoire coloniale. Paris, 1924.
Afr 5035.5.10   Labouret, H. Monteil, explorateur et soldat. Paris, 1937.

Afr 5040   French Africa in general - History by periods - 20th century
Afr 5040.2   Ansprenger, Franz. Politik im schwarzen Afrika. Köln, 1961.
Afr 5040.5   Monmarson, R. L'Afrique noire et son destin. Paris, 1950.
Afr 5040.6   Delavignette, R.L. L'Afrique noire française et son destin. Paris, 1962.
Afr 5040.8   Lusignan, Guy de. French-speaking Africa since independence. London, 1969.
Afr 5040.10   Mortimer, Edward. France and the Africans, 1944-1960: a political history. London, 1969.
Afr 5040.12   Scherk, Nikolaus. Dekolonisation und Souveränität. Wien, 1969.

Afr 5045   French Africa in general - Geography, description, etc.

Afr 5045.2   Demanet, Abbé. Nouvelle histoire de l'Afrique française. Paris, 1767. 2v.

Afr 5045.5   Deherme, G. L'Afrique occidentale française. Paris, 1908.

Afr 5045.7   Crouch, Archer P. On a surf-bound coast. London, 1887.

Afr 5045.9   Gaffarel, Paul. Comptoirs de l'Afrique française occidentale. Dijon, 1910.

Afr 5045.11   Demaison, Andre. La vie des noirs d'Afrique. 4. ed. Paris, 1956.

Afr 5045.15   Londres, Albert. A very naked people. N.Y., 1929.

NEDL Afr 5045.17.5   Martin du Gard, M. Courrier d'Afrique. Paris, 1931.

Afr 5045.20   Clerisse, Henry. Trente mille kilomètres à travers l'Afrique française. Paris, 1934.

Afr 5045.22   Baratier, A.E.A. A travers l'Afrique. Paris, 1910.

Afr 5045.24   Ossendowski, F.A. Slaves of the sun. London, 1928.

Afr 5045.27   Rondet-Saint, Maurice. Dans notre empire noir. Paris, 1912.

Afr 5045.28   Abensour, Leon. La France noire, ses peuples. Paris, 1931.

Afr 5045.30   Delafosse, M. Enquête coloniale dans l'Afrique française occidentale et équatoriale. Paris, 1930.

Afr 5045.38.5   Bordeaux, H. Nos Indes noires. Paris, 1936.

Afr 5045.40   Morand, Paul. Paris, Tombouctou, documentaire. Paris, 1928.

Afr 5045.42   Société d'Editions Géographiques. Afrique française. Paris, 1931.

Afr 5045.44   France. Agence de la France d'Outre-Mer. France d'outre-mer. Paris, 1950. 6 pam.

Afr 5045.46   Lerumeur, Guy. L'imprévu dans les dunes. Paris, 1963.

Afr 5046   French Africa in general - Economic and financial conditions

Afr 5046.2   France. Direction des Affaires Economiques et Financières. Planification en Afrique. v.2- Paris, 1962- 3v.

Afr 5046.5   France. Ministère de la Coopération. Problemes de planification. Paris, 1964. 11v.

Afr 5046.6   Leduc, Michel. Les institutions monétaire africaines, pays francophones. Paris, 1965.

Afr 5046.8   France. Ministère de la Coopération. Rapport sur la coopération franco-africaine. Paris, 1964.

Afr 5046.9   Fock, Andreas. Algérie, Sahara, Tchad, réponse à M. Camille Sabatier. Paris, 1891.

Afr 5046.10   Delavignette, Robert Louis. Du bon usage de la décolonisation. Paris, 1968.

Afr 5046.12   Duverger, Daniel. La croissance des quantités globales en Afrique de l'ouest de 1947 à 1964. Paris, 1967.

Afr 5048   French Africa in general - Races

Afr 5048.5   Burdo, A. Les Arabs dans l'Afrique centrale. Paris, 1885.

NEDL Afr 5048.7   Mangin, C. La force noire. Paris, 1910.

Afr 5048.10   Bascom, W.R. Continuity and change in African cultures. Chicago, 1958.

Afr 5048.15   Chapelle, Jean. Nomades noirs du Sahara. Paris, 1957.

Afr 5049   French Africa in general - Religion

Afr 5049.5   Louveau, E. Essai sur l'influence sociale et économique des religions de l'Afrique occidental française. Thèse. Paris, 1920.

Afr 5049.100   Masseguin, Christiane. A l'ombre des palmes, l'oeuvre familiale et missionaire des soeurs du Saint-Esprit. Paris, 1942.

Afr 5049.100.7   Ponet, Marthe Bordeaux. Hyacinthe Jalabert. 2.éd. Paris, 1924.

Afr 5050   French West Africa in general - Periodicals

Afr 5050.3   Guid'ouest africain. Paris. 1965+

Afr 5050.5   French West Africa. Agence Economique. Bulletin mensuel. Paris. 5,1924+ 4y.

Afr 5050.6   Banque Centrale des Etats de l'Afrique de l'Ouest. Etudes économiques ouest africaines. Paris. 3,1961+ 2v.

Afr 5050.10   Semaine en Afrique occidentale française. Dakar. 1,1958+ 6v.

Afr 5050.15   Dakar. Université. Département de Géographie. Travaux.

Afr 5050.20   Construire ensemble. Bobo-Dioulasso. 1966+

Afr 5051   French West Africa in general - Bibliographies

Afr 5051.10   French West Africa. Archives. Répertoire des archives. Rufisque, 1957. 2v.

Afr 5051.15   Lebel, A.R. L'Afrique occidentale dans la littérature française depuis 1870. Thèse. Paris, 1925.

Afr 5051.15.2   Lebel, A.R. L'Afrique occidentale dans la littérature française depuis 1870. Paris, 1925.

Afr 5051.25   Martonne, E. de. Inventaire méthodique des cartes et croquis...relatifs á l'Afrique occidentale. Laval, 1926.

Afr 5051.30   Clozel, M.F.J. Bibliographie des ouvrages relatifs à la Sénégambie au au Soudan occidental. Paris, 1891.

Afr 5052   French West Africa in general - Collected source materials

Afr 5052.2   Hargreaves, J.D. France and West Africa. London, 1969.

Afr 5053   French West Africa in general - Government and administration

Afr 5053.5   Labouret, Henri. A la recherche d'une politique indigène dans l'Ouest africain. Paris, 1931.

Afr 5053.7   Delavignette, R. Freedom and authority in French West Africa. London, 1969.

Afr 5053.10   Forgeron, J.B. Le protectorat en Afrique occidentale française et les chefs indigènes. Thèse. Bordeaux, 1920.

Afr 5053.12   Schefer, Christian. Instructions générales données de 1763 à 1870. Paris, 1921. 2v.

Afr 5053.15   Senghor, Leopold. Congrès constitutif de P.F.A. Paris, 1959.

Afr 5053.20   Gandolfi, Alain. L'administration territoriale en Afrique noire de langue française. Aix-en-Provence, 1959.

Afr 5053.25   Cowan, Laing G. Local government in West Africa. N.Y., 1958.

Afr 5053.30   Bourcart, Robert. Le grand conseil de l'Afrique occidentale. Paris, 1955.

Afr 5053.30.2   Bourcart, Robert. Le grand conseil de l'Afrique occidentale. 2. ed. Paris, 1956.

Afr 5053.32   Morgenthau, R.S. Political parties in French-speaking West Africa. Oxford, 1964.

Afr 5053.34   Foltz, William J. From French West Africa to the Mali federation. New Haven, 1965.

Afr 5053.36   Zolberg, Aristide R. Creating political order. Chicago, 1966.

Afr 5053.38   Campbell, Michael J. The structure of local government in West Africa. The Hague, 1965.

Afr 5053.40   La succession d'état en Afrique du Nord. Paris, 1968.

Afr 5054   French West Africa in general - General history

Afr 5054.02   Dreyfus, Camille. La France dans l'Afrique occidentale. Paris, 1902.

Afr 5054.10.2   Lebrun-Renaud, C.G.N. Les possessions françaises de l'Afrique occidentale. 2e éd. Paris, 1886.

Afr 5054.10.5   Ancelle, Jules. Les explorations au Sénégal et dans les contrées voisines. Paris, 1886.

Afr 5054.25   Delafosse, M. Histoire de l'Afrique occidentale française. Paris, 1926.

Afr 5054.29   Lassalle-Séré, R. Le recrutement de l'armée noire. Thèse. Paris, 1929.

Afr 5054.29.5   Lassalle-Séré, R. Le recrutement de l'armée noire. Paris, 1929.

Afr 5054.33   Bovill, E.W. Caravans of the old Sahara. London, 1933.

Afr 5054.34   Davis, S.C. Reservoirs of men, a history of the black troops of French West Africa. Thèse. Chambéry, 1934.

Afr 5054.36.3   Tuaillon, J.L.G. L'Afrique occidentale française par l'Atlantique ou par le Sahara. Thèse. Paris, 1936.

Afr 5054.36.5   Tuaillon, J.L.G. L'Afrique occidentale française par l'Atlantique ou par le Sahara. Paris, 1936.

Afr 5054.36.10   Bordeaux, W. L'épopée noire. Paris, 1936.

Afr 5054.37   Hardy, Georges. L'Afrique occidentale française. Paris, 1937.

Afr 5054.37.5   Mary, Gaston. Précis historique de la colonisation française. Paris, 1937.

Afr 5054.58   Bovill, E.W. The golden trade of the Moors. London, 1958.

Afr 5054.58.2   Bovill, E.W. The golden trade of the Moors. 2nd ed. London, 1968.

Afr 5054.62   Neres, Philip. French-speaking West Africa. London, 1962.

Afr 5054.67   Hargreaves, John. West Africa. Englewood Cliffs, 1967.

Afr 5054.68   Chailley, Marcel. Histoire de l'Afrique occidentale française, 1638-1959. Paris, 1968.

Afr 5055.1 - .99   French West Africa in general - General special

Afr 5055.6   Duboc, E. L'épopée coloniale en Afrique occidentale française. Paris, 1938.

Afr 5055.10   Mangin, Charles. La mission des troupes noires. Paris, 1911.

Afr 5055.50   Baratier, A.E.A. Epopées africaines, ouvrage inédit. Paris, 1912.

Afr 5055.57   Laroche, Jean de. Le gouverneur général Felix Ebane. Paris, 1957.

Afr 5055.58A   Milcent, Ernest. L'A.O.F. entre en scène. Paris, 1958.

Afr 5055.58B   Milcent, Ernest. L'A.O.F. entre en scène. Paris, 1958.

Afr 5055.59   Ehrhard, Jean. Communauté ou sécession. Paris, 1959.

Afr 5055.59.5   Subbotin, V.A. Kolonialnaia politika Frantsii v Zapadnoi Afrike, 1880-1900. Moscow, 1959.

Afr 5055.59.10   Senghor, Leopold. African socialism. N.Y., 1959.

Afr 5055.61   Schnapper, Bernard. La politique et le commerce français dans le Golfe de Guinée. Paris, 1961.

Afr 5055.62   Debay, Jean. Evolutions en Afrique noire. Paris, 1962.

Afr 5055.65   Gavrilov, Nikolai Ivanovich. National liberation movement in West Africa. Moscow, 1965.

Afr 5055.65.5   Jore, Leonce Alphonse Noel Henri. Les établissements français, sur la côte occidentale d'Afrique de 1758 à 1809. Paris, 1965.

Afr 5055.66   Kouassigan, Guy Adjéte. L'homme et la terre. Paris, 1966.

Afr 5055.67   Webster, James B. The revolutionary years: West Africa since 1800. London, 1967.

Afr 5056   French West Africa in general - Geography, description, etc. (By date, e.g. .131 for 1931)

Afr 5056.9   Pruneau de Pommegorge, Antoine Edmé. Description de la Nigritie. Amsterdam, 1789.

Afr 5056.12   Saugnier. Voyages to the coast of Africa. London, 1792.

Afr 5056.21   Macqueen, James. A geographical and commercial view of northern Central Africa. Edinburgh, 1821.

Afr 5056.83   Veistroffer, Albert. Vingt ans dans la brousse africaine. Lille, 1931.

Afr 5056.99   Benitez, Cristobal. Mi viaje por el interior del Africa. Tangier, 1899.

Afr 5056.107   French West Africa. La Maurétanie. Corseil, 1907.

Afr 5056.108   Cheran, Georges. La société noire de l'Afrique occidentale française. Paris, 1908.

Afr 5056.110   Frobenius, Leo. Auf dem Wege nach Atlantis. Berlin, 1911.

Afr 5056.113   Afrique occidentale française. Paris, 1913.

Afr 5056.122   French West Africa. Dispositions cartographiques relatives aux cartes et plans de l'A.O.F. Laval, 1922.

Afr 5056.122.5   Petit, André. Mon voyage au Soudan français de Dakar...à Conakry...par Bamako. Paris, 1922.

Afr 5056.123   French West Africa. Catalogue des positions géographiques provisoirement admises par le Service géographique de l'A.O.F. Laval, 1923-24.

Afr 5056.123.5   French West Africa. Supplément au Catalogue des positions géographiques de l'A.O.F. Laval, 1925.

Afr 5056.124   French West Africa. Service Géographique. Rapport annuel, technique et administratif. Laval. 1922+

Afr 5056.125   Proust, Louis. Visions d'Afrique. Paris, 1925.

Afr 5056.130   Campbell, Dugald. Wanderings in widest Africa. London, 1930.

Afr 5056.130.5   Rondet-Saint, M. Un voyage en A.O.F. Paris, 1930.

Afr 5056.130.10   Semaines Sociales de France. Le problème social aux colonies. Lyon, 1930.

Afr 5056.131   Seabrook, W.B. Jungle ways. London, 1931.

Afr 5056.131.5   Societe de Géographie, Paris. D'Algérie au Sénégal, mission Augieras-Draper, 1927-1928. Texte et plates. Paris, 1931. 2v.

Afr 5056.131.10   Delavignette, R. Afrique occidentale française. Paris, 1931.

Afr 5056.131.20   Seabrook, W.B. Jungle ways. N.Y., 1931.

Afr 5056.134.7   Martet, Jean. Les batisseurs de royaumes. Paris, 1934.

Afr 5056.135   Gorer, G. Africa dances, West African Negroes. London, 1935.

Afr 5056.139   Perrot, Emile. Où en est l'Afrique occidentale française. Paris, 1939.

Afr 5056.143.5   Great Britain. Naval Intelligence Division. French West Africa. v.1-2. London, 1943.

Afr 5056.146   Gentil, P. Confins libyens, lac Tchad, fleuve Niger. Paris, 1946.

Afr 5056.149   Richard Malard, J. Afrique occidentale française. Paris, 1949.

Afr 5056.151   Gautier Walter, André. Afrique noire. Paris, 1951.

Afr 5056.154   Du Puigaudeau, Odette. La piste Maroc-Sénégal. Paris, 1954.

Afr 5056.157   Legras, Paul. Voyages et aventures en Afrique française. Nancy, 1957.

Afr 5056.157.5   Thompson, V.M. French West Africa. Stanford, Calif., 1957.

Afr 5056   **French West Africa in general - Geography, description, etc. (By date, e.g. .131 for 1931) - cont.**

Afr 5056.157.10	Siriex, Paul. Une nouvelle Afrique. Paris, 1957.
Afr 5056.158	Pouquet, Jean. L'Afrique occidentale française. 2.ed. Paris, 1958.
Afr 5056.158.5	Afrique occidentale française. Togo. Paris, 1958.
Afr 5056.159	Balez, Eugene. Vagabondage en Afrique noire. Toulouse, 1959.
Afr 5056.164	Adloff, Richard. West Africa. N.Y., 1964.
Afr 5056.165	Binet, Jacques. Afrique en question, de la tribu à la nation. Tours, 1965.
Afr 5056.168	Goure, Claude. Les inconnus d'Afrique. Paris, 1968.

Afr 5057   **French West Africa in general - Economic and financial conditions**

X Cg Afr 5057.8	Cosmier, Henri. L'Ouest africain français. Paris, 1921. (Changed to XP 9038).
Afr 5057.10	Bressolles, H. Organisation financière locale de l'Afrique. Thèse. Bordeaux, 1922.
Afr 5057.11	Wade, Abdoulaye. Economie de l'Ouest africain. Paris, 1964.
Afr 5057.12	Lenoir, Robert. Les concessions foncières en Afrique occidentale française et équatoriale. Thèse. Paris, 1936.
Afr 5057.14.5	Labouret, Henri. Paysans d'Afrique occidentale. Paris, 1941.
Afr 5057.16	France. Direction de la Documentation. French West Africa. Rennes, 1954.
Afr 5057.20	Hoffherr, Rene. Coopération économique franco-africaine. Paris, 1958.
Afr 5057.22F	French West Africa. Direction Générale des Services Economiques et du Plan. Le financement du plan. Paris, 1957.
Afr 5057.24	Capet, Marcel F. Traité d'économie tropicale. Paris, 1958.
Afr 5057.25	Gavrilov, N.I. Zapadnaia Afrika pod gnetom Frantsii. Moscow, 1961.
Afr 5057.26	France. Embassy. U.S. French Africa. N.Y., 1958.
Afr 5057.27	French West Africa. L'équipement de l'A.O.F. Paris, 1950.
Afr 5057.28	Poquin, Jean. Les relations économiques extérieures des pays d'Afrique. Paris, 1957.
Afr 5057.30	Lacroix, Alain. Les conditions de la mise en valeur de l'Afrique occidentale française. Paris, 1959.
Afr 5057.32	Afana, Osende. L'économie de l'Ouest-africain. Paris, 1966.

Afr 5058.1   **French West Africa in general - Races**

Afr 5058.5	Dim Delobsom, A.A. L'empire du Mogho-Naba. Paris, 1932.
Afr 5058.6	Hovelacque, Abel. Les Nègres de l'Afrique sus-équatoriale. Paris, 1889.
Afr 5058.7	Desbordes, J.G. L'immigration libano-syrienne en Afrique occidentale française. Thèse. Poitiers, 1938.
Afr 5058.10	Gouilly, A. L'islam dans l'Afrique occidentale française. Paris, 1952.
Afr 5058.11	Roseberry, R.S. The Niger vision. Harrisburg, 1934.
Afr 5058.13	Gessain, Monique. Les migrations des Coniagui et Bassari. Paris, 1967.

Afr 5070   **Mauritania - Government and administration**

Afr 5070.5	Jeol, Michel. Cours de droit administratif mauritanien. Bordeaux, 1964.
Afr 5070.10	Ould Daddah, Marie Thérèse. Cours de droit constitutionnel mauritanien. Bordeaux, 1964.

Afr 5074   **Mauritania - General history**

Afr 5074.20	Du Puigaudeau, Odette. Le passé maghrébin de la Mauritanie. Rabat, 1962.
Afr 5074.25	Gillier, L. La pénétration en Mauritanie. Paris, 1926.
Afr 5074.30	Otton Loyewski, S.W.C. Rezzons sur l'Adrar. Rufisque, 1942.
Afr 5074.35	Garnier, C. Désert fertile. Paris, 1960.
Afr 5074.36	Hamet, Ismael. Chroniques de la Mauritanie sénégalaise. Paris, 1911.
Afr 5074.37	Morocco. Ministère des Affaires Etrangères. Livre blanc sur la Mauritanie. Rabat, 1960.

Afr 5078   **Mauritania - History by periods - Before 1800**

Afr 5078.18	Dandin, Georges. Journal historique de Georges Dandin, 1777-1812. Tananarive, 1939.
Afr 5078.20	Desire-Vuillemin, G. Contribution à l'histoire de la Mauritanie. Dakar, 1962.
Afr 5078.22	Morocco. Ministère de l'Information et du Tourisme. La libération de la province mauritanienne et l'opinion international. Rabat, 1961.

Afr 5090   **Mauritania - Geography, description, etc.**

Afr 5090.3	Gerteiny, Alfred G. Mauritania. N.Y., 1967.
Afr 5090.6	Brisson, P.R. de. Histoire du naufrage et de la captivité. Genève, 1789.
Afr 5090.10	France. Embassy. U.S. The Islamic Republic of Mauritania. N.Y., 1960.
Afr 5090.12	Mauritania. La République islamique de Mauritanie. Paris, 1960.
Afr 5090.14	Du Puigaudeau, Odette. Barefoot through Mauritania. London, 1937.
Afr 5090.16	Gruvel, Abel. A travers la Mauritanie occidentale. Paris, 1909.

Afr 5091   **Mauritania - Economic and financial conditions**

Afr 5091.5	Pujos, Jerome. Croissance économique. Paris, 1964.
Afr 5091.10	Société d'Etudes pour le Développement Economique et Social, Paris. Analyse de l'économie de la République islamique de Mauritanie en 1959. Paris, 1961.
Afr 5091.12	France. Ministère de la Coopération. Economie et plan de développement, République islamique de Mauritanie. 2.éd. Paris, 1963.
Afr 5091.14	Mauritania. Ministère des Affaires Etrangères et du Plan. Service de la statistique plan quadriennal, 1963-1966. Nouakchott, 1967.
Afr 5091.15	International Bank for Reconstruction and Development. Mauritania; guidelines for a four-year development program. Washington, D.C.?, 1968.

Afr 5093   **Mauritania - Races**

Afr 5093.2	Poulet, G. Les Maures de l'Afrique occidentale française. Paris, 1904.

Afr 5094   **Mauritania - Religion; missions**

Afr 5094.2	Marty, Paul. Etudes sur l'islam et les tribus maures. Paris, 1921.

Afr 5096   **Mauritania - Local - Adrar**

Afr 5096.2	Gravier, Gabriel. Voyage de Paul Soleillet à l'Adrar. Rouen, 1881.

Afr 5100   **Senegal - Periodicals**

Afr 5100.1	Annuaire du Sénégal et dépendances. St.-Louis, 1869.
Afr 5100.2	Etudes senegalaises. Saint-Louis, Senegal. 2-6,1952-1955
Afr 5100.3F	Mali, organe central du P.F.A. Dakar.
Afr 5100.5F	Senegal magazine. Dakar. 1960+
Afr 5100.7PF	L'unité africaine. Dakar. 250,1967+
Afr 5100.9	Senegal d'aujourd'hui. Dakar. 1966+

Afr 5103   **Senegal - Bibliographies**

Afr 5103.1	Sénégal. Archives Nationales. Centre de Documentation. Eléments de bibliographie sénégalaise. Dakar, 1964.

Afr 5105   **Senegal - Pamphlet volumes**

Afr 5105	Pamphlet box. Senegal.

Afr 5110   **Senegal - Government and administration**

Afr 5110.20	Gueye, L. De la situation politique des sénégalais. Paris, 1922.
Afr 5110.25	Gonidec, Pierre François. La République du Sénégal. Paris, 1968.

Afr 5112   **Senegal - General politics; political parties**

Afr 5112.5	Traore, Bakary. Forces politiques en Afrique noire. Paris, 1966.
Afr 5112.10	Doll, Peter. Der senegalesische Weg zum afrikanischen Sozialismus. Hamburg, 1966.

Afr 5114 - 5120   **Senegal - General history (By date)**

Afr 5118.89	Faidherbe, L.L.C. Le Sénégal. Paris, 1889.
Afr 5119.07	Olivier, M. Le Sénégal. Paris, 1907.
Afr 5119.10	Cultru, P. Histoire du Sénégal du XV siècle à 1870. Paris, 1910.
Afr 5119.25	Sabatie, A. Le Sénégal. Saint-Louis, 1925.
Afr 5119.35	Beslier, G.G. Le Sénégal. Paris, 1935.
Afr 5119.64	Deschamps, H.J. Le Sénégal et la Gambie. Paris, 1964.
Afr 5119.64.2	Deschamps, H.J. Le Sénégal et la Gambie. 2e éd. Paris, 1964.
Afr 5119.64.5	Brigaud, Felix. Histoire du Sénégal. Dakar, 1964.
Afr 5119.65	Milcent, Ernest. Au carrefour des options africaines, le Sénégal. Paris, 1965.
Afr 5119.68	Klien, Martin A. Islam and imperialism in Senegal; Sine-Saloum, 1847-1914. Stanford, 1968.

Afr 5130   **Senegal - History by periods - 1800-1900**

Afr 5130.2	Berlioux, E.F. André Brue, ou L'Origine. Paris, 1874.
NEDL Afr 5130.3F	Monet, H. Le siège de Médine, 1857. Paris, n.d.
Afr 5130.5	Machat, J. Documents sur les établissements français. Paris, 1906.
Htn Afr 5130.6*	Postlethwayt, M. The importance of the African expedition considered. London, 1758.
Afr 5130.15	Hardy, Georges. La mise en valeur du Sénégal de 1817 à 1854. Thèse. Paris, 1921.
Afr 5130.15.5	Hardy, Georges. La mise en valeur du Sénégal de 1817 à 1854. Paris, 1921.
Afr 5130.20	Gaffarel, P. Administration du général Faidherbe au Sénégal. Dijon, 188-.
Afr 5130.20.5	Demaison, A. Faidherbe. Paris, 1932.
Afr 5130.20.10	Hardy, Georges. Faidherbe. Paris, 1947.
Afr 5130.22	Peter, G. L'effort français au Sénégal. Thèse. Paris, 1933.
Afr 5130.22.3	Peter, G. L'effort français au Sénégal. Paris, 1933.
Afr 5130.25	Ly, Abdoulaye. La compagnie du Sénégal. Paris, 1958.
Afr 5130.30	Saint-Martin, Yves. L'empire toucouleur et la France un demi-siècle de relation diplomatiques, 1846-1893. Dakar, 1967.

Afr 5135   **Senegal - History by periods - 1900-1946**

Afr 5135.5	Gueve, Lamine. Itinéraire africain par Lamine Gueve. Paris, 1966.

Afr 5180   **Senegal - Geography, description, etc.**

Afr 5180.2	Adanson, M. A voyage to Senegal. London, 1759.
Afr 5180.3	Marche, A. Trois voyages dans l'Afrique. Paris, 1879.
Afr 5180.4	Noirot, E. A travers le Fouta-Diallon et le Bambouc. Paris, n.d.
Afr 5180.5	Rancon, A. Dans la Haute-Gambie. Paris, 1894.
Afr 5180.8	Lasnet. Une mission au Sénégal. Paris, 1900.
Afr 5180.9	Saugnier. Relation des voyages. Paris, 1799.
Afr 5180.10	Golberry, S.M.X. Reise durch das westliche Afrika...1785-87. Leipzig, 1803. 2v.
Afr 5180.10.5	Golberry, S.M.X. Fragmens d'un voyage en Afrique. Paris, 1802. 2v.
Afr 5180.11	Mitchinson, A.W. The expiring continent. London, 1881.
Htn Afr 5180.12*	Durand, J.B.L. Voyage au Sénégal. v.1-2 and atlas. Paris, 1802. 3v.
Afr 5180.12.5	Durand, J.B.L. Voyage au Sénégal. v.1-2. Paris, 1807.
Afr 5180.13	Correard, A. Naufrage de la frigate La Méduse. Paris, 1818.
Afr 5180.13.3	Savigny, J.B.H. Schipbreuk van het fregat Medusa. Haarlem, 1818.
Afr 5180.13.5	Dard, C.A.P. Perils and captivity, Medusa shipwreck. Edinburgh, 1827.
Afr 5180.13.8	Savigny, J.B.H. Narrative of a voyage to Senegal in 1816. London, 1818.
Afr 5180.14	Alvares d'Almada, Andre. Rios de Guine do Cabo-Verde. Porto, 1841.
Afr 5180.14.2	Alvares d'Almada, Andre. Relação e descrpção de Guiné. Lisboa, 1733.
Afr 5180.14.10	Santarem, M.F. de B. Notice sur Andre Alvares d'Almada et sa description de la Guinée. Paris, 1842.
Afr 5180.15	Colonies françaises, Sénégal-Soudan. Paris, 1900.
Afr 5180.16	Boilat, P.D. Esquisses sénégalaises. Paris, 1853.
Afr 5180.17	Mavidal, J. Le Sénégal. Paris, 1863.
Afr 5180.18	Raffenel, A. Voyage dans l'Afrique occidentale. Text and atlas. Paris, 1846. 2v.
Afr 5180.19.4	Lacourbe, M.J. de. Premier voyage...fait à la côte d'Afrique...1865. Paris, 1913.
Afr 5180.20	Mollien, G.T. Voyage...aux sources du Sénégal et de la Gambie, 1818. Paris, 1820.

Afr 5180   Senegal - Geography, description, etc. - cont.

Afr 5180.20.5   Mollien, G.T. Travels in the interior of Africa. 1st ed. London, 1967.

Afr 5180.21   Labarthe, P. Voyage au Sénégal pendant les années 1784 et 1785. Paris, 1802.

Afr 5180.22   Saintlo, A. de. Relation du voyage du Cap-Verd. Paris, 1637.

Afr 5180.24   Anfreville de la Salle. Notre vieux Sénégal, son histoire. Paris, 1909.

Afr 5180.25   Raffenel, Anne. Nouveau voyage dans le pays des Nègres. Paris, 1856. 2v.

Afr 5180.26   Gaffarel, Paul. La Sénégal et le Soudan français. Paris, 1890.

Afr 5180.28   Foret, Auguste. Un voyage dans le Haut-Sénégal. Paris, 1888.

Afr 5180.29   Ricard, F. Le Sénégal Paris, 1865,

Afr 5180.31   Rouch, J. Sur les côtes du Sénégal et de la Guinée. Paris, 1925.

Afr 5180.33   Sere de Rivières, E. Le Sénégal. Paris, 1953.

Afr 5180.37.6   Bosshard, J.M. Ces routes qui ne menent à rien. 6e éd. Paris, 1937.

Afr 5180.40   Gaby, Jean B. Relation de la Nigritie. Paris, 1689.

Afr 5180.42   France. Embassy. U.S. The Republic of Senegal. N.Y., 1960.

Afr 5180.44   Garnier, C. Sénégal, porte de l'Afrique. Paris, 1962.

Afr 5180.46   Liubeckis, M. Karsta afrikos saule. Vilnius, 1963.

Afr 5180.48   Lavroff, Dimitri Georges. La République du Sénégal. Paris, 1966.

Afr 5180.50   Sénégal. Ministère du Développement. Cartes pour servir à l'aménagement du territoire. Dakar, 1965.

Afr 5180.52   Carrére, Frédéric. De la Sénégambie française. Paris, 1855.

Afr 5183.1 - .199   Senegal - Economic conditions - General works

Afr 5183.2   Ly, Abdoulays. L'état et la production paysanne. Paris, 1958.

Afr 5183.500 - .999   Senegal - Economic conditions - Contemporary works
(By date)

Afr 5183.900   Paris. Exposition Universelle de 1900. Sénégal-Soudan, agriculture, industrie, commerce. Paris, 1900.

Afr 5183.951   Fouquet, Joseph. La traite des Arachides dans le pays de Kaolack. Montpelier, 1951.

Afr 5183.957   Mersadier, Yvon. Budgets familiaux africains. St. Louis du Sénégal, 1957.

Afr 5183.958   Fouquet, Joseph. La traite des Arachides dans le pays de Kaolack. St. Louis du Sénégal, 1958.

Afr 5183.958.5   Touze, R.L. Mieux vivre dans notre village; lettres a Seydon. Dakar?, 1958.

Afr 5183.960.3   France. Ministère de la Coopération. Economie et plan de développement. 3. éd. Paris, 1964.

Afr 5183.960.8   Compagnie d'Etudes Industrielles et d'Aménagement du Territoire. Rapport général sur les perspectives de développement du Sénégal. 3. éd. Dakar, 1963.

Afr 5183.961   Ndiaye, M. Le Sénégal à l'heure de l'indépendance. Doullens, 1961.

Afr 5183.961.5   Senegal. Plan quadriennal de développement, 1961-1964. Dakar, 1961.

Afr 5183.961.10   Touze, R.L. Nouvelles lettres à Seydon. Dakar, 1961.

Afr 5183.962   Moyenne vallée du Sénégal. Paris, 1962.

Afr 5183.962.5   Zajadski, Paul. Probleme und Möglichkeiten der industriellen Entwicklung im Senegal. Köln, 1962.

Afr 5183.964   Senegal. Plan réorienté. n.p., n.d.

Afr 5183.964.5   Senegal. Ministère du Développement, et du Plan et l'Economie Génerale. Bilan d'execution materielle et financière des investissements publics au 31 dec. 1963. Dakar, 1964.

Afr 5183.965   Dakar. Chambre de Commerce. L'économie du Sénégal. 2. éd. Dakar, 1965.

Afr 5183.965.5   Dakar. Chambre de Commerce d'Agriculture et d'Industrie. Catalogue des principales productions industrielles du Sénégal. Dakar, 1965.

Afr 5183.965.10   Senegal. Deuxième plan quadriennal de développement économique et social, 1965-1969. v.1-3. Dakar?, 1965.

Afr 5183.968   Brochier, Jacques. La diffusion du progrès technique en milieu rural sénégalais. Paris, 1968.

Afr 5184.1 - .199   Senegal - Finance - General works

Afr 5184.20   Faulong, L. Les rapports financiers de la métropole et de l'Afrique occidentale française. Paris, 1910.

Afr 5184.25   Sénégal. Ministère du Développement du Plan et Economie Générale. Deuxième plan quadriennal. Pts. 1-2. Dakar?, 1965.

Afr 5185   Senegal - Races

Afr 5185.4   Tautain, L. Sur l'ethnologie...du Sénégal. Paris, 1885.

Afr 5185.5   Faidherbe, L.L.C. Le Zenaga des tribus sénégalaises. Paris, 1877.

Afr 5185.6   Berenger-Ferand, L.J.B. Les peuples de la Sénégambie. Paris, 1879.

Afr 5185.7   Schobel, Fred. The world in miniature, Africa. v.2-3. London, n.d. 2v.

Afr 5185.8   Thomas, L.V. Les Diola. Macon, 1959. 2v.

Afr 5185.9   Crowder, Michael. Senegal. London, 1962.

Afr 5185.9.2   Crowder, Michael. Senegal; a study of French assimilation policy. London, 1967.

Afr 5185.10   Reverdy, Jean Claude. Une société rurale au Senegal. Aix-en-Provence, 1968?

Afr 5185.12   Diop, Abdoulaye. Société toucouleur et migration. Dakar, 1965.

Afr 5187   Senegal - Religion; missions

Afr 5187.5   Marty, Paul. Etudes sur l'islam au Sénégal. v.2-3, pt.1-2. Paris, 1917. 2v.

Afr 5187.10   Martin, V. Notes d'introduction à une étude socio-religieuse des populations de Dakar et du Sénégal. Dakar, 1964.

Afr 5187.15   Martin, V. La chrétienté africaine de Dakar. Dakar, 1964. 3 pam.

Afr 5187.16   Gravrand, Henri. Visage africain de l'Eglise. Paris, 1961.

Afr 5187.20   Behrman, Lucy C. Muslim brotherhoods and politics in Senegal. Cambridge, 1970.

Afr 5188   Senegal - Special customs

Afr 5188.5   Fougeyrollas, Pierre. Modernisation des hommes, l'exemple du Sénégal. Paris, 1967.

Afr 5190   Senegal - Local

Afr 5190.2   Brosselard-Faidherbe, H. Casamance et Mellacorée. Paris, 1892.

Afr 5190.3   Verneuil, V. Mes aventures au Sénégal. Paris, 1858.

Afr 5190.10   Faure, Claude. Histoire de la presqu'île du Cap Vert et des origines de Dakar. Paris, 1914.

Afr 5190.10.5   French West Africa. Notice sur le plan de Dakar et environs d'après photo-aérienne. Gorée, 1923.

Afr 5190.10.9   Lengyel, Emil. Dakar, outpost of two hemispheres. N.Y., 1941.

Afr 5190.10.12   Lengyel, Emil. Dakar avant-poste de deux hémisphères. N.Y., 1943.

Afr 5190.10.13   Vaillande, René. Dakar. Paris, 1941.

Afr 5190.10.20   Garnier, C. Dakar. Paris, 1961.

Afr 5190.12   Gaffiot, R. Gorée, capitale déchue. Paris, 1933.

Afr 5190.14   Leca, N. Les pêcheurs de Guet N'Dar. Paris, 1935.

Afr 5190.15   Savonnet, G. Le ville de Thiès. Paris, 1955.

Afr 5190.16   Charpy, Jacques. La fondation de Dakar. Paris, 1958.

Afr 5190.18   Duchemin, G. Saint-Louis du Sénégal. Saint-Louis, 1955.

Afr 5190.20   Delmas, Robert. Des origines de Dakar et ses relations avec l'Europe. Dakar, 1957.

Afr 5190.22   Siré-Abbâs-Soh. Chroniques du Foûta senegalais. Traduit. Paris, 1913.

Afr 5190.24   Peterec, Richard J. Dakar and West African economic development. N.Y., 1967.

Afr 5190.25   Dessertine, A. Un port secondaire de la côte occidentale d'Afrique, Kaolack; étude historique, juridique et économique des origines à 1958. Kaolack, Sénégal, 1967?

Afr 5190.26   Groope d'Etudes Dakaroises. Dakar en devenir. Paris, 1968.

Afr 5199.101 - .399   Senegal - Biographies - Individual (A-Z, 299 scheme,
by person)

Afr 5199.337   Markovitz, Irving Leonard. Léopold Sédar Senghor and the politics of Negritude. 1st ed. N.Y., 1969.

Afr 5199.337.5   Milcent, Ernest. Léopold Sédar Senghor et la naissance de l'Afrique moderne. Paris, 1969.

Afr 5200   Sudan; Mali - Periodicals

Afr 5200.24   Etudes soudaniennes. Koulouba. 3+

Afr 5200.29   France. Ministère de la France d'Outre-Mer. Service des Statistiques. Mission Socio-Economique du Soudan. Rapport provisoire. 2-3,1957-1958

Afr 5203   Sudan; Mali - Bibliographies

Afr 5203.3   Clozel, M. Bibliographie des ouvrages relatifs à la Sénégambie. Paris, 1891.

Afr 5205   Sudan; Mali - Pamphlet volumes

Afr 5205   Pamphlet box. French Sudan.

Afr 5205.1   Pamphlet box. French Sudan.

Afr 5210   Sudan; Mali - Government and administration

Afr 5210.5   Merzliakov, Nikolai S. Stanovlenie natsional'noi gosudarstvennosti Respubliki Mali. Moskva, 1966.

Afr 5212   Sudan; Mali - General politics; political parties

Afr 5212.2   Union Soudanaise. Congrès extraordinaire de l'U.S.R.D.A. le 22 septembre 1960, le Mali continue. Bamako? 1960?

Afr 5217 - 5220   Sudan; Mali - General history (By date)

Afr 5218.83   Hontay, J. Le Soudan française. Lille, 1881-83. 2v.

Afr 5218.88   Frey, H. Campagne dans le haut Sénégal et dans le haut Niger, 1885-86. Paris, 1888.

Afr 5219.02   Dujarris, G. La vie du sultan Rabah. Paris, 1902.

Afr 5219.02.2   Oppenheim, M.F. von. Rabeh und das Tschadseegebiet. Berlin, 1902.

Afr 5219.02.5   Gentil, E. La chute de l'empire du Rabah. Paris, 1902.

Afr 5219.05   Decorse, J. Rabah et les Arabes du Chari. Paris, 1905.

Afr 5219.10   Terrier, A. L'expansion française et la formation territoriale. Paris, 1910.

Afr 5219.12   Pasquier, G. L'organisation des troupes indigènes. Paris, 1912.

Afr 5219.12.3   Pasquier, G. L'organisation des troupes indigènes en Afrique occidentale française. Paris, 1912.

Afr 5219.20   Marty, Paul. Etudes sur l'islam et les tribus du Soudan. Paris, 1920-21. 4v.

Afr 5219.28   Palmer, H.R. Sudanese memoirs. Lagos, 1928. 3v.

Afr 5219.28.5   Palmer, H.R. Sudanese memoirs. v.1-3. London, 1967.

Afr 5219.36   Urvoy, Yves François Marie Aimé. Histoire des populations du Soudan central (colonie du Niger). Paris, 1936.

Afr 5219.60   Niane, D.T. Soundjata. Paris, 1960.

Afr 5219.60.5   Niane, D.T. Sundiata. London, 1965.

Afr 5219.63   Vasianin, A.J. Respublika Mali. Moscow, 1963.

Afr 5225   Sudan; Mali - History by periods - To 1870

Afr 5225.5   Abd al-Rahman ibn Abdallah al-Tonbukti. Tedzkiret en-nisian fi akhbar molouk es-Soudan. Paris, 1901.

VAfr 5225.6   Clair, Andrée. Le fabuleur empire du Mali. Paris, 1959.

Afr 5225.7   Ba, Amadou H. L'empire Peul du Macina. Paris, 1962.

Afr 5225.8   Niane, D.T. Recherches sur l'empire du Mali au Moyen Age. Conakry, 1962.

Afr 5225.10   Hasan, Yûsuf Fadl. The Arabs and the Sundan: from the seventh to the early sixteenth century. Edinburgh, 1967.

Afr 5225.12   Monteil, Charles Victor. Les Empires du Mali. Paris, 1968.

Afr 5227   Sudan; Mali - History by periods - French conquest

Afr 5227.5   Gatelet, A.L.C. Histoire de la conquête du Soudan français. Paris, 1901.

Afr 5227.10   Joffre, J.J.C. My march to Timbuctoo. N.Y., 1915.

Afr 5227.10.5   Joffre, J.J.C. My march to Timbuctoo. London, 1915.

Afr 5227.15   Meniaud, Jacques. Les pionniers du Soudan. Paris, 1931. 2v.

Afr 5227.20   Lecert, Paul Edmond. Lettres du Soudan. Paris, 1895.

Afr 5227.25   Gallieni, Joseph Simon. Deux campagnes au Soudan français, 1886-1888. Paris, 1891.

Afr 5227.28   Kanya-Forstner, Alexander Sidney. The conquest of the Western Sedan. Cambridge, Eng., 1969.

Afr 5228 **Sudan; Mali - History by periods - 1900-1960 (French rule)**
Afr 5228.2 Caioli, Aldo. Esperienza politiche africane; la Federazione del Mali. Milano, 1966.

Afr 5230 **Sudan; Mali - History by periods - 1960-   (Republic)**
Afr 5230.7 Mali. Embassy. United Arab Republic. Mars 1961-mars 1962. Les relations Mali - République Arabe Unie. Cairo, 1962.
Afr 5230.8 Snyder, Frank Gregory. One-party government in Mali. New Haven, 1965.

Afr 5235 **Sudan; Mali - Geography, description, etc. (By date, e.g. .250 for 1950)**
Afr 5235.51 Park, Mungo. The life and travels of Mungo Park. N.Y., 1840.
Afr 5235.51.5 Park, Mungo. Travels in the interior of Africa. Edinburgh, 1860.
Afr 5235.51.10 Park, Mungo. Travels in the interior districts of Africa. London, 1815. 2v.
Afr 5235.52 Park, Mungo. Travels in the interior districts of Africa...1795-1797. 1st ed. London, 1799.
Afr 5235.52.5 Park, Mungo. Mungo Parks Reise in das Innere von Afrika in den Jahren 1795, 96, und 97. Hamburg, 1799.
Afr 5235.52.10 Park, Mungo. Travels in the interior districts of Africa...1795, 1796 and 1797. N.Y., 1800.
Afr 5235.52.15 Park, Mungo. Travels in the interior districts of Africa. N.Y., 1813.
Afr 5235.54 Park, Mungo. The journal of a mission to the interior of Africa...1805. Philadelphia, 1815.
Afr 5235.55 MacLachlan, T. Banks. Mungo Park. London, 1898.
Afr 5235.55.5 Hewitt, William Henry. Mungo Park. London, 1923.
Afr 5235.55.10 Gwynn, Stephen. Mungo Park and the quest of the Niger. N.Y., 1935.
Afr 5235.55.15 Thomson, Joseph. Mungo Park and the Niger. London, 1890.
Afr 5235.121 Gray, William. Travels in western Africa. London, 1825.
Afr 5235.128 Caillié, René. Journal d'un voyage à Tembouctou. Paris, 1830. 3v.
Afr 5235.128.2 Caillié, René. Journal d'un voyage à Tembouctou et à Jenne, dans l'Afrique centrale. Paris, 1965?
Afr 5235.128.5 Caillié, René. Travels through central Africa to Timbuctoo. London, 1830. 2v.
Afr 5235.128.10 Caillié, René. Le voyage de René Caillié à Tombouctou. Paris, 1937.
Afr 5235.128.25 Lamande, André. La vie de René Caillié. Paris, 1928.
Afr 5235.128.30 Welch, Galbraith. The unveiling of Timbuctoo. N.Y., 1939.
Afr 5235.179 Gravier, Gabriel. Paul Soleillet. Paris, 1887.
Afr 5235.180 Sanderval, A.O., vicomte de. De l'Atlantique au Niger par le Foutah-Djallon. Paris, 1882.
Afr 5235.180.2 Sanderval, A.O., vicomte de. De l'Atlantique au Niger. Paris, 1883.
Afr 5235.181 Gallieni, J.S. Mission d'exploration du Haut-Niger. Paris, 1885.
Afr 5235.186 Mage, Eugène. Voyage dans le Soudan occidental. Paris, 1868.
Afr 5235.189 Peroz, Etienne. Au Soudan français. Paris, 1889.
Afr 5235.189.5 Binger, Gustave. Du Niger au golfe de Guinée par le pays de Konge le Mossi. Paris, 1892. 2v.
Afr 5235.189.10 Bechet, Eugène. Cinq ans de séjour au Soudan français. Paris, 1889.
Afr 5235.191 Caran, Edmond. De Saint-Louis au port de Temboctou. Paris, 1891.
Afr 5235.194 Bonnetain, Raymonde. Une française au Soudan. Paris, 1894.
Afr 5235.194.5 Triviet, E. Au Soudan français. Paris, 1932.
Afr 5235.212 Clozel, F.J. Haut-Sénégal-Niger (Soudan français). Paris, 1912. 5v.
Afr 5235.212.5 Haywood, A.H.W. Through Timbuctu and across the great Sahara. London, 1912.
Afr 5235.235 Delavignette, R.L. Soudan, Paris, Boulogne. Paris, 1935.
Afr 5235.255 Spitz, Georges. Le Soudan français. Paris, 1955.
Afr 5235.261 Bamako. Chambre de Commerce, d'Agriculture et d'Industrie. Mali. Bamako, 1961.
Afr 5235.263 Hemmo, Klaus. Zwischen Sahara und Elfenbeinküste. Leipzig, 1963.
Afr 5235.269 Radchenko, Galina F. Respublika Mali. Moskva, 1969.

Afr 5240 **Sudan; Mali - Economic conditions**
Afr 5240.2 Bris, Alexis. Sénégal et Soudan. Paris, 1887.
Afr 5240.3 Amin, Samir. Trois expériences africaines de développement. Paris, 1965.
Afr 5240.4F Bamako. Chambre de Commerce, d'Agriculture et d'Industrie. Répertoire des entreprises financières. Bamako, 1964.
Afr 5240.5F Bamako. Chambre de Commerce, d'Agriculture et d'Industrie. Eléments du bilan économique. 1962+ 2v.
Afr 5240.6 Mali. Ministère du Plan. Rapport sur le plan quinquennal de développement économique. Paris, 1961.
Afr 5240.7 Mali. Ministère du Plan et de l'Economie Rurale. Données économiques. Bamako, 1962.
Afr 5240.8 Italy. Instituto Nazionale per il Commercio Estero. Mali. Roma, 1964.
Afr 5240.10F Bamako. Chambre de Commerce, d'Agriculture et d'Industrie. Répertoire des représentations exclusives assurées au Mali. Bamako, 1962.
Afr 5240.12 Bureau pour le Développement de la Production Agricole Outre-Mer. La modernisation rurale dans la haute-vallée du Niger. Paris, 1961? 3v.
Afr 5240.14 France. Ministère de la Coopération. Direction des affaires économiques et financières. 2. éd. Paris, 1965.

Afr 5243 **Sudan; Mali - Races (299 scheme, by race)**
Afr 5243.10 Urvoy, Y.F.M.A. Petit atlas ethno-démographique du Soudan. Paris, 1942.
Afr 5243.12 Tauxier, Louis. Le Noir du Soudan. Paris, 1912.
Afr 5243.122 Thuriaux-Hennebert, Arlette. Les Zande dans l'histoire du Bahr el-Ghazal et de l'Equatoria. Bruxelles, 1964.
Afr 5243.122.5 Giorgetti, Filiberto. La superstizione Zande. Bologna, 1966.
Afr 5243.125 Henry, Joseph. L'âme d'un peuple africain...les Bambara. Münster, 1910.
Afr 5243.125.5 Monteil, Charles. Les Bambara du Ségou et du Kaarta. Paris, 1924.
Afr 5243.125.10 Lebarbier, Louis. Les Bambaras. Paris, 1918.
Afr 5243.125.15 Tauxier, Louis. La religion bambara. Paris, 1927.
Afr 5243.125.20 Pageard, Robert. Notes sur l'histoire des Bambaras de Ségou. Paris, 1957.
Afr 5243.125.25 Zahan, Dominique. Sociétés d'initiation bambara. v.1. Paris, 1960.
Afr 5243.125.30 Benchelt, Eno. Kulturawandel bei den Bambara von Segou. Bonn, 1962.

Afr 5243 **Sudan; Mali - Races (299 scheme, by race) - cont.**
Afr 5243.125.35 Tauxier, Louis. Histoire des Bambara. Paris, 1942.
Afr 5243.174 Griaule, Marcel. Masques dogons. Thèse. Paris, 1938.
Afr 5243.174.5 Griaule, Marcel. Jeux dogons. Thèse complementaire. Paris, 1938.
Afr 5243.174.10 Ganay, Solange de. Le Binou Yébéné. Paris, 1942.
Afr 5243.174.15 Parin, Paul. Die Weissen denken zuviel. Zürich, 1963.
Afr 5243.174.20 Griaule, Marcel. Conversations with Ogotemmeli. London, 1965.
Afr 5243.174.25 Calame-Griaule, Geneviève. Ethnologie et langage, la parole chez les Dogon. Paris, 1965.
Afr 5243.174.30 Zahan, Dominique. La Viande et la graine, mythologie dogon. Paris, 1969.
Afr 5243.207 Ba, A.H. Koumen. Paris, 1961.
Afr 5243.207.5 Suret-Canale, Jean. Essai sur la signification sociale et historique des hégémonies peules. Paris, 1968.
Afr 5243.207.10 Hama, Boubou. Contribution à la connaissance de l'histoire des Peul. Paris, 1968.
Afr 5243.250 Monteil, Charles. Les Khassonke. Paris, 1915.
Afr 5243.337.2 Holas, Bohumil. Les Senoufo (y compris les minianka). 2nd ed. Paris, 1966.
Afr 5243.343 Sadi, Abd al-Rahman. Tarikh es-Soudan. Paris, 1900.
Afr 5243.343.5 Berand-Villars, J.M.E. L'empire de Gao. Paris, 1946.
Afr 5243.343.10 Boulnois, Jean. L'empire de Gao. Paris, 1954.
Afr 5243.343.15 Ronch, Jean. La religion et la magie songhay. Paris, 1960.
Afr 5243.343.20 Hama, Boubou. Histoire des Songhay. Paris, 1968.
Afr 5243.343.20.5 Hama, Boubou. L'Histoire traditionnelle d'un peuple: les Zarma-Songhay. Paris, 1967.

Afr 5245 **Sudan; Mali - Religion; missions**
Afr 5245.5 Ouane, Ibrahima Mamadou. L'islam et la civilisation française. Avignon, 1957.
Afr 5245.10 Brevie, J. Islamisme contre naturisme au Soudan français. Paris, 1923.

Afr 5247 **Sudan; Mali - Local - Timbuctu**
Afr 5247.5 Hacquard, Augustin. Monographie de Tombouctou. Paris, 1900.
Afr 5247.10 Dubois, Felix. Tombouctou la mystérieuse. Paris, 1897.
Afr 5247.10.5 Dubois, Felix. Timbuctoo the mysterious. N.Y., 1896.
Afr 5247.15 Lenz, Oscar. Timboctou. Paris, 1886-87. 2v.
Afr 5247.17 Bonnel de Méziéres, Albert. Le Major A. Gordon Laing, Tomboucton (1826). Paris, 1912.
Afr 5247.20A Hall, Leland. Timbuctoo. N.Y., 1927.
Afr 5247.20B Hall, Leland. Timbuctoo. N.Y., 1927.
Afr 5247.25 Bonnier, Gaetan. L'occupation de Tombouctou. Paris, 1926.
Afr 5247.30 Maugham, R. The slaves of Timbuktu. 1.Am.ed. N.Y., 1961.
Afr 5247.35 Miner, H.M. The primitive city of Timbuctoo. Garden City, 1965.
Afr 5247.38 Gardner, Brian. The quest for Timbuctoo. London, 1968.
Afr 5247.40 Miner, Horace Mitchell. The primitive city of Timbuctoo. Princeton, 1953.

Afr 5248 **Sudan; Mali - Local - Others**
Afr 5248.5 Desplagnes, Louis. Le plateau central nigérien. Paris, 1907.
Afr 5248.10 Monteil, Charles. Une cité soudanaise, Djénné. Paris, 1932.
Afr 5248.15 Kaufmann, Herbert. Reiten durch Iforas. Munich, 1958.
Afr 5248.16 Małowist, M. Wielkie państwa sudanu zachodniego w późnym średniowieczu. Warszawa, 1964.
Afr 5248.20 Meillassoux, Claude. Urbanization of an African community. Seattle, 1968.

Afr 5249.1 - .99 **Sudan; Mali - Biographies - Collected (A-Z, 99 scheme, by author)**
Afr 5249.5 Seabrook, William Buehler. The white monk of Timbuctoo. N.Y., 1934.
Afr 5249.6 Gologo, M. Le rescapé de l'Ethylos. Paris, 1963.
Afr 5249.7 Briault, Maurice. La prodigieuse vie de René Caillié. Paris, 1930.

Afr 5249.101 - .399 **Sudan; Mali - Biographies - Individual (A-Z, 299 scheme, by person)**
Afr 5249.123 Badri, Babakr. The memoiris of Babiker Bedu. London, 1969.

Afr 5250 **Niger - Periodicals**
Afr 5250.5 Perspectives nigériennes. Paris. 1,1966 ׀

Afr 5252 **Niger - Collected source materials**
Afr 5252.5 Niger. Constitution. Constitution. Paris, 1959.

Afr 5255 **Niger - General history**
Afr 5255.65 Séré de Rivières, Edmond. Histoire du Niger. Paris, 1965.

Afr 5257.1 - .99 **Niger - History by periods - Before 1900**
Afr 5257.5 Joalland. Le drame de Dankori. Paris, 1930.
Afr 5257.5.5 Klobb. Un drame colonial. Paris, 1931.
Afr 5257.10 Herbart, Pierre. La chancre du Niger. Paris, 1939.
Afr 5257.15 Bonardi, Pierre. La république du Niger. Paris, 1960.

Afr 5260 **Niger - Geography, description, etc.**
Afr 5260.5 Toutée, Georges Joseph. Dahomé, Niger, Touareg. Paris, 1897.
Afr 5260.10 Toutée, Georges Joseph. Du Dahomé au Sahara. Paris, 1899.
Afr 5260.20 Abadie, Maurice. La colonie du Niger. Paris, 1927.
Afr 5260.25 Séré de Rivières, Edmond. Le Niger. Paris, 1952.
Afr 5260.30 France. Embassy. U.S. The Republic of the Niger. N.Y., 1960.
Afr 5260.32 Clair, Andrée. Le Niger, pays à découvrir. Paris, 1965.
Afr 5260.35 Hinkmann, Ulrich. Niger. München, 1968.

Afr 5262 **Niger - Economic conditions**
Afr 5262.1 Agency for International Development. Review of co-operative programme for economic development in Nigeria. Lagos, 1964.

Afr 5265 **Niger - Races**
Afr 5265.5 Ligers, Ziedonis. Les Sorko (Bozo), maîtres du Niger. Paris, 1964-1967. 3v.

Afr 5266   Niger - Religion; missions
Afr 5266.3   Epelle, Emanuel Tobiah. The church in the Niger Delta. Aba, Nigeria, 1955.
Afr 5266.5   Ploussard, Jean. Carnet de route de Jean Ploussard. Paris, 1964.

Afr 5269.1 - .99   Niger - Biographies - Collected (A-Z, 99 scheme, by author)
Afr 5269.24   Epelle, Emanuel Tobiah. Bishops in the Niger Delta. Aba, Nigeria, 1964.

Afr 5270   Upper Volta - Periodicals
Afr 5270.18   Recherches voltaïques; collection de travaux des sciences humaines sur la Haute-Volta. Paris. 3,1966+

Afr 5272   Upper Volta - Collected source materials
Afr 5272.2   Upper Volta. Laws, statutes, etc. Le drame de la Haute-Volta. Paris, 1960.

Afr 5275   Upper Volta - General history
Afr 5275.5   Bassolet, François Djoby. Evolution de la Haute-Volta de 1898 au 3 janvier 1966. Ouagadougou, 1968.

Afr 5280   Upper Volta - Geography, description, etc.
Afr 5280.5   France. Embassy. U.S. The Republic of the Upper Volta. N.Y., 1960.

Afr 5282   Upper Volta - Economic conditions
Afr 5282.2   Upper Volta. Ministère des Finances, des Affaires Economiques et du Plan. Rapport économique, 1959. Ouagadougou, 1960.
Afr 5282.3   Société d'Etudes pour le Développement Economique et Social, Paris. Développement économique en Haute-Volta. Paris, 1963. 2v.
Afr 5282.4   Italy. Istituto Nazionale per il Commercio Estero. Alto volta. Roma, 1964.
Afr 5282.5   Centre d'Etudes Economiques et Sociales d'Afrique Occidentale. Fonctionnaire et développement. Bobo-Dioulasso, 1966.
Afr 5282.8   Société d'Aide Technique et de Cooperation. Données critiques sur la campagne depuits villageois encadrée par la SATEC en Haute-Volta. Paris, 1965.
Afr 5282.10   Upper Volta. Service du Plan. Données actuelles de l'économie voltaïque. Paris, 1962.

Afr 5285   Upper Volta - Races (299 scheme, by race)
Afr 5285.260   France. Institut National de la Statistique et des Etudes Economiques. Une enquête de ménage en pays Lobi. Paris, 1961.
Afr 5285.277   Marc, Lucien. Le pays Mossi. Paris, 1909.
Afr 5285.277.5   Tauxier, Louis. Le noir du Yatenga-Mossi. Paris, 1917.
Afr 5285.277.7   Tauxier, Louis. Nouvelles notes sur le Mossi et le Gourounsi. Paris, 1924.
Afr 5285.277.10   Leroy Ladurie, Marie. Pâques africaines. Paris, 1965.
Afr 5285.277.15   Tiendrebeogo, Yamba. Histoire et coutumes royales des Mossi de Ouagadougou. Ouagadougou, 1964.
Afr 5285.277.20   Hammond, Peter B. Yatenga. N.Y., 1966.
Afr 5285.277.25   Skinner, Elliott Percival. The Mossi of the Upper Volta. Stanford, 1964.
Afr 5285.277.30   Deniel, Raymond. De la savane à la ville. Aix-en-Provence, 1967.
Afr 5285.277.35   Kassoum, Congo. Conséquences de la colonisation sur la vie coutumière en pays mossi. Thèse. Montepellier, 1955.

Afr 5300   French Guinea - Periodicals
Afr 5300.5   Recherches africaines. 1,1960+ 4v.

Afr 5303   French Guinea - Bibliographies
Afr 5303.2   Guinea. Archive Nationale. Répertoire des archives nationales. v.1. Conakry, 1962.
Afr 5303.4   Organization for Economic Cooperation and Development. Development Center. Bibliographie sur la Guinee. Paris, 1965.

Afr 5305   French Guinea - Pamphlet volumes
Afr 5305   Pamphlet box. French Guinea.
Afr 5305.1   Pamphlet box. French Guinea.

Afr 5312   French Guinea - General politics; political parties
Afr 5312.5A   Guinée. Paris, 1959.
Afr 5312.5B   Guinée. Paris, 1959.
Afr 5312.10   Solonitskii, A.S. Gvineiskaia Respublika. Moscow, 1961.
Afr 5312.10.5   Solonitskii, A.S. Republik Guinea. Berlin, 1962.
Afr 5312.15   Parti Démocratique de Guinée. L'action politique du P.D.G. Conakry. 1,1961+ 6v.
Afr 5312.18   Toré, Sékou. The doctrine and methods of the Democratic Party of Guinea. v.1-2. Conakry, 196-.

Afr 5314   French Guinea - General history
Afr 5314.3   Hardy, Jules. Les Dieppois en Guinée en 1364. Dieppe, 1864.
Afr 5314.5   Arcin, André. Histoire de la Guinée française. Paris, 1911.
Afr 5314.10   Touré, Sékou. Expérience guinéenne et unité africaine. Paris, 1959.
Afr 5314.10.2   Touré, Sékou. Expérience guinéenne et unité africaine. Paris, 1961.

Afr 5316.1 - .99   French Guinea - History by periods - Before 1860
Afr 5316.5   Gigon, Fernand. Guinée, état pilote. Paris, 1959.
Afr 5316.10   Touré, Sékou. L'action politique du parti démocratique de guinée. Paris, 1959.
Afr 5316.10.5   Toure, Sekou. Guinean revolution and social progress. Cairo, 1963.
Afr 5316.12   Ameillon, B. La Guinée. Paris, 1964.
Afr 5316.14   Attwood, William. The reds and the blacks, a personal adventure. 1st ed. N.Y., 1967.

Afr 5316.500 - .699   French Guinea - History by periods - 1946-1958
Afr 5316.501   Iordanskii, Vladimir B. Strategiia bor'by za nezavisimost? Moskva, 1968.

Afr 5316.700 -   French Guinea - History by periods - 1958-
Afr 5316.705   Morrow, John H. First American ambassador to Guinea. New Brunswick, 1967[1968].
Afr 5316.710   Pamphlet vol. Guinea. Language: French. 3 pam.

Afr 5318   French Guinea - Geography, description, etc.
Htn   Afr 5318.2*   Snelgrave, W. A new account of parts of Guinea. London, 1734.
Afr 5318.2.89   Bosman, W. A new accurate description of the coast of Guinea. London, 1705.
Afr 5318.2.89.2   Bosman, W. A new and accurate description of the coast of Guinea. London, 1967.
Afr 5318.3   Guinea (Republic). Secretariat d'Etat à l'Information et au Tourisme. La Guinée et son peuple. Conakry, 1965.
Afr 5318.3.5   Bosman, W. Neuwkeurige beschryning van de Guinese. Amsterdam, 1737.
Afr 5318.3.9   Bosman, W. Voyage de Guinée. Utrecht, 1705.
Htn   Afr 5318.5*   Hawkins, J. History of a voyage to the coast of Africa. Troy, 1797.
Afr 5318.7   Guinée française. Rapport d'ensemble. Paris, 1900.
Afr 5318.8   Famechon. Notice sur la Guinée française. Paris, 1900.
Afr 5318.9   Machat, J. Les Rivières du Sud et le Fouta-Diallon. Paris, 1906.
Afr 5318.10   Sanderval, C. de. Soudan français...Kahel. Paris, 1893.
Afr 5318.11   Arcin, A. La Guinée française. Paris, 1907.
Afr 5318.12   Baudin, P.N. Fetichism and fetich worshipers. N.Y., 1885.
Afr 5318.14   Aspe-Fleurimont, L. La Guinée française. Paris, 1900.
Afr 5318.16   Lebarbier, L. Dans la Haute-Guinée (journal de route). Paris, 1904.
Afr 5318.17   Laumann, E.M. A la côte occidentale d'Afrique. Paris, 1890.
Afr 5318.18.2   Doelter, C. Uber die Capverden nach dem Rio Grande. Leipzig, 1888.
Afr 5318.20   Lecoeur, C. Le culte de la génération. Paris, 1932.
Afr 5318.30   Hovis, Maurice. La Guinée française. Paris, 1953.
Afr 5318.35   Gavrilov, N.I. Gvineiskaia Respublika. Moscow, 1960.
Afr 5318.40   Bochkarev, I.A. Gvineia segodnia. Moscow, 1961.
Afr 5318.45   Youla, Nabi. Mussa; ein Kind aus Guinea. Regensburg, 1964.

Afr 5319   French Guinea - Economic and financial conditions
Afr 5319.5   Toure, Ismael. Parti Dée de Guinée, R.D.A. Le développement économique de la république de Guinée. n.p., 1966.

Afr 5320   French Guinea - Races
Afr 5320.5   Gaisseau, P.D. The sacred forest. 1st Amer.ed. N.Y., 1954.
Afr 5320.10   Laye, Camara. The dark child. N.Y., 1954.
Afr 5320.15   Modupe, Prince. I was a savage. N.Y., 1957.
Afr 5320.15.1   Modupe, Prince. A royal African. N.Y., 1969.
Afr 5320.16   Paulme, Denise. Le gens du riz. Paris, 1954.

Afr 5321   French Guinea - Religion; missions
Afr 5321.5   Tchidimbo, Raymond-M. L'homme noir dans l'Eglise. Paris, 1963.

Afr 5322   French Guinea - Special customs
Afr 5322.5   Vieillard, G. Notes sur les coutumes des Peuls au Fouta Djallon. Paris, 1939.
Afr 5322.10   Decker, Henry de. Nation et développement communautaire en Guinée et au Sénégal. Paris, 1968.
Afr 5322.10.5   Decker, Henry de. Le développement communautaire, une stratégie d'édification de la nation. Paris, 1968.

Afr 5324.1 - .99   French Guinea - Biographies - Collected (A-Z, 99 scheme, by author)
Afr 5324.3   Koeler, H. Einige Notizen über Bonny. Göttingen, 1848.

Afr 5325   Ivory Coast - Periodicals
Afr 5325.5F   Ivory Coast. Abidjan. 25,1966+
Afr 5325.8   Realités ivoiriennes. Paris. 16,1966+

Afr 5326   Ivory Coast - Bibliographies
Afr 5326.5   Organization for Economic Cooperation and Development. Development Centre. Essai d'une bibliographie sur la Côte-d'Ivoire. Paris, 1964.

Afr 5329   Ivory Coast - Pamphlet volumes
Afr 5329.1   Pamphlet box. French Ivory Coast.

Afr 5333   Ivory Coast - Government and administration
Htn   Afr 5333.2*   Clozel, F.J. Coutumes indigènes de la Côte-d'Ivoire. Paris, 1902.
Afr 5333.4   Villamur, R. Les coutumes Agni. Paris, 1904.

Afr 5335   Ivory Coast - General politics; political parties
Afr 5335.2A   Zolberg, Aristide R. One-party government in the Ivory Coast. Princeton, N.J., 1964.
Afr 5335.2B   Zolberg, Aristide R. One-party government in the Ivory Coast. Princeton, N.J., 1964.
Afr 5335.2.1   Zolberg, Aristide R. One party government in the Ivory Coast. Princeton, N.J., 1969.

Afr 5337   Ivory Coast - General history
Afr 5337.3   Amon d'Aby, F. La Côte-d'Ivoire dans la cité africaine. Paris, 1951.
Afr 5337.5   Ivory Coast. Ministère de l'Education Nationale. Nation, société, travail. Abidjan, 1960.

Afr 5340.1 - .99   Ivory Coast - History by periods - Before 1840
Afr 5340.5   Monteil, P.L. Un page d'histoire militaire coloniale, la colonne de Kong. Paris, n.d.
Afr 5340.10   Binger, G. Une vie d'explorateur. Paris, 1938.
Afr 5340.20   Angoulvant, G.L. La pacification de la Côte-d'Ivoire. Paris, 1916.
Afr 5340.21   Atger, Paul. La France en Côte-d'Ivoire de 1843 à 1893. Dakar, 1962.
Afr 5340.25   Houphouet-Boigny, Felix. Discours à l'assemblée nationale. Abidjan, 1962.

Afr 5340.500 - .699   Ivory Coast - History by periods - 1946-1958
Afr 5340.505   Zeller, Claus. Elfenbeinküste. 1. Aufl. Freiburg im Breisgau, 1969.

Afr 5342   Ivory Coast - Geography, description etc.
Afr 5342.2   Villamur, R. Notre colonie de la Côte-d'Ivoire. Paris, 1903.
Afr 5342.3   Mille, P. Notice sur la Côte-d'Ivoire. n.p., 1900.
X Cg   Afr 5342.4   Monnier, M. France noire (Côte-d'Ivoire et Soudan). Paris, 1894.
Afr 5342.6   Clozel, F.J. Dix ans à la Côte-d'Ivoire. Paris, 1906.

Afr 5342   Ivory Coast - Geography, description etc. - cont.

Afr 5342.7	Gaston, Joseph. La Côte-d'Ivoire. Paris, 1917.
Afr 5342.8.3	Ollone, C.A. De la Côte-d'Ivoire au Soudan. 3e éd. Paris, 1901.
Afr 5342.10	Jacolliot, L. La Côte-d'Ivoire, l'homme des deserts. Paris, 1877.
Afr 5342.12	Dupire, Marguerite. Le pays Adioukrou et sa palmeraie. Paris, 1958.
Afr 5342.15	Neveux, M. Religion des noirs...fétiches de la Côte-d'Ivoire. Alencon, 1923.
Afr 5342.20	Chivas-Baron, C. Côte-d'Ivoire. Paris, 1939.
Afr 5342.25	Avice, E. La Côte-d'Ivoire. Paris, 1951.
Afr 5342.30	France. Service de Documentation Economique. Côte-d'Ivoire, 1954. Paris, 1954.
Afr 5342.40	Holas, Bohumil. Cultures matérielles de la Côte-d'Ivoire. Paris, 1960.
Afr 5342.50	Lebarbier, Louis. La Côte-d'Ivoire. Paris, 1916.
Afr 5342.55	France. Embassy. U.S. The Republic of the Ivory Coast. N.Y., 1960.
Afr 5342.60	Holas, Bohumil. Changements sociaux en Côte-d'Ivoire. Paris, 1961.
Afr 5342.60.5	Holas, Bohumil. Côte-d'Ivoire. Paris, 1963.
Afr 5342.60.6	Holas, Bohumil. La Côte-d'Ivoire. Paris, 1964.
Afr 5342.62	Young, T. Rex. West African agent. London, 1943.
Afr 5342.63	Rougerie, Gabriel. La Côte-d'Ivoire. Paris, 1964.
Afr 5342.64	Ivory Coast. Embassy. U.S. General data on the Republic of the Ivory Coast. Washington, D.C., 1963.
Afr 5342.65	Holas, Bohumil. Industries et cultures en Côte-d'Ivoire. Abidjan, 1965.
Afr 5342.65.2	Holas, Bohumil. Craft and culture in the Ivory Coast. Paris, 1968.
Afr 5342.66	Brétignère, Amédée. Aux temps héroïques de la Côte-d'Ivoire. Paris, 1931.
Afr 5342.67	Grzimek, Bernhard. He and I and the elephants. London, 1967.
Afr 5342.68.2	Cadel, Georges. Noirs et Blances, la lutte contre le racism et le transformation des coutumes africaines. Confances, 1967?

Afr 5343   Ivory Coast - Economic and financial conditions

Afr 5343.2	Ivory Coast. Conseil Economique et Social. Rapport sur l'évolution économique et sociale de la Côte-d'Ivoire, 1960-1969. Abidjan, 1965.
Afr 5343.3	France. Ministère de la Coopération. Direction des Affaires Economiques. Economie et plan de développement. Paris, 196-.
Afr 5343.4F	Mission d'Etude des Groupements. Mission d'étude des groupements immigrés en Côte-d'Ivoire. Paris, 1957.
Afr 5343.5	Ivory Coast. Service de la Statistique Générale et de la Mécanographie. Les budgets familiaux des salariés africains en Abidjan. Paris, 1958.
Afr 5343.6	Ivory Coast. Service de la Statistique Générale et de la Mécanographie. Inventaire économique de la Côte-d'Ivoire. Abidjan, 1958.
Afr 5343.6.3	Ivory Coast. Inventaire économique et social de la Côte-d'Ivoire, 1958. Abidjan, 1960.
Afr 5343.7	Ivory Coast. Ministère du Plan. Troisieme plan quadriennal de développement économique et social. Abidjan, 1958.
Afr 5343.7.5	Ivory Coast. Ministère du Plan. Perspectives decennales de développement èconomic, social et cultural, 1960-1970. Abidjan, 1967.
Afr 5343.7.6	Ivory Coast. Ministère du Plan. Perspectives decennales...Annexes. Abidjan?, 1967?
Afr 5343.7.10	Ivory Coast. Ministère du Plan. Première esquisse du plan quinquennal de développement. Paris, 1968.
Afr 5343.7.15	Ivory Coast. Loi plan de développement économique, social et culturel pour les années, 1967-1968, 1969-1970. Abidjan, 1967.
Afr 5343.8	Strasbourg. Université. Centre de Géographie Appliquée. Etude géographique des problèmes de transports en Côte-d'Ivoire. Paris, 1963.
Afr 5343.9	United States. Bureau of International Commerce. A market for U.S. products in the Ivory cOast. Washington, 1966.
Afr 5343.10	Société d'Etudes pour le Développement Economique et Social. Le sud-est frontalier. Paris, 1963. 2v.
Afr 5343.10.2	Société d'Etudes pour le Développement Economique et Social. Rapport de synthèse. Paris, 1963.
Afr 5343.10.5	Société d'Etudes pour le Développement Economique et Social, Paris. Etudes de petites industries en Côte-d'Ivoire. Paris, 1966.
Afr 5343.12	Marche ivoirien. Paris. 1,1967+
Afr 5343.13	Blokhin, Leonid F. Bereg Slonovoi Kosti. Moskva, 1967.
Afr 5343.14	Amin, Samir. Le Développement du capitalisme en Côte d'Ivoire. Paris, 1967.
Afr 5343.20	Italy. Istituto nazionale per il commercio estero Costa d'Avorio. Roma, 1963.
Afr 5343.25.2	Obermaier, Heinrich. Die Elfenbeinküste als Wirtschaftspartner. 2. Aufl. Köln, 1965.
Afr 5343.30	Bureau pour le Development de la Production Agricole outre-mer. Étude générale de la région de Man. Paris, 196-? 6v.
Afr 5343.35	La Côte-d'Ivoire. Chances et risques. Session d'étude 20 juillet-11 août 1966. Bruxelles, 1967. 2v.
Afr 5343.40	Development and Resources Corporation. A development plan for the Southwest Region. N.Y., 1968. 4v.

Afr 5344   Ivory Coast - Races

NEDL Afr 5344.5	Tauxier, Louis. Le noir de Bondoukou. Paris, 1921.
Afr 5344.7	Boulnois, Jean. Gnon-Sua, dieu du Guéré. Paris, 1933.
Afr 5344.8	Meillassoux, Claude. Anthropologie économique des Gouro de Côte-d'Ivoire. Paris, 1964.
Afr 5344.9	Holas, Bohumil. Les Toura. Paris, 1962.
Afr 5344.10	Paulme, Denise. Une société de Côte-d'Ivoire. Paris, 1962.
Afr 5344.11	Holas, Bonumil. L'Image du monde Bété. Paris, 1968.

Afr 5345   Ivory Coast - Religion; missions

Afr 5345.5	Marty, Paul. Etudes sur l'islam en Côte-d'Ivoire. Paris, 1922.
Afr 5345.10	Holas, Bohumil. Le séparatisme religieux en Afrique noire. Paris, 1965.
Afr 5345.17	Gorju, Joseph. La Côte-d'Ivoire chrétienne. 2. éd. Lyon, 1915.
Afr 5345.20	Niangoran-Bauah, Georges. La division du temps et le calendrier rituel des peuples lagunaires de Côte-d'Ivoire. Paris, 1964.

Afr 5346   Ivory Coast - Local

Afr 5346.5	Loyer, G. Relation du voyage du royaume d'Issyny. Paris, 1714.
Afr 5346.5.5	Roussier, Paul. L'établissement d'Issiny, 1687-1702. Paris, 1935.
Afr 5346.5.10	Mouezy, Henri. Histoire et coutumes du pays d'Assinie et du royaume de Krinjabo (fondation de la Côte-d'Ivoire). Paris, 1942.
Afr 5346.5.15	Mouezy, Henri. Assinie et le royaume de Krinjabo. 2. éd. Paris, 1953.
Afr 5346.6	Société d'Etudes pour le Développement Economique et Social. Région de Korhogo. T.1-8. Paris, 1965. 3v.
Afr 5346.11	Bouys, P. Le bas Cavally (Afrique occidentale française) et son avenir. Thèse. Montpellier, 1933.
Afr 5346.15	Boutillier, J.L. Bongouanou. Paris, 1960.

Afr 5350   Dahomey; Slave Coast - Periodicals (A-Z)

Afr 5350.3	Etudes dahoméennes. Porto-Noro, Dahomey. 2,1964+

Afr 5360   Dahomey; Slave Coast - Government and administration

Afr 5360.5	Glélé, Maurice A. Naissance d'un état noir, l'évolution politique et constitutionelle du Dahomey, de la colonisation à nos jours. Paris, 1969.

Afr 5365   Dahomey; Slave Coast - General history

Htn Afr 5365.2*	Dalzel, A. The history of Dahomy. London, 1793.
Afr 5365.2.2	Dalzel, A. The history of Dahomey, an inland kingdom of Africa. 1st ed. London, 1967.
Afr 5365.3	Heudebert, L. Promenades au Dahomey. Paris, 1902.
Afr 5365.4	Aublet, E. La guerre au Dahomey. Paris, 1894.
Afr 5365.5	Salinis, A. Le protectorat français sur la Côte des Esclaves. Paris, 1908.
Afr 5365.6	Cornevin, R. Histoire du Dahomey. Paris, 1962.

Afr 5368   Dahomey; Slave Coast - History by periods - Early to 1818

Afr 5368.3	Palau Marti, Montserrat. Le roi-dieu au Bénin. Paris, 1964.
Afr 5368.5	Norris, Robert. Memoirs of the reign of Bossa Ahadee, king of Dahomey...country of Guiney. London, 1789.
Afr 5368.8	Argyle, William Johnson. The Fon of Dahomey, a history and ethnography of the Old Kingdom. Oxford, 1966.
Afr 5368.10	Akinjogbin, I.A. Dahomey and its neighbours, 1708-1818. Cambridge, Eng., 1967.
Afr 5368.15	Verger, Pierre. Le Fort St. Jean-Baptiste d'Ajuda. n.p., 1966.

Afr 5385   Dahomey; Slave Coast - Geography, description, etc.

Afr 5385.1	Burton, R.F. A mission to Gelele, king of Dahome, with notices. v.1-2. London, 1864. 2v.
Afr 5385.2	Burton, R.F. Mission to Gelele, king of Dahome. v.1. 2d ed. London, 1864.
Afr 5385.2.5	Burton, R.F. A mission to Gelele. London, 1893. 2v.
Afr 5385.2.10	Burton, R.F. A mission to Gelele. London, 1966. 2v.
Afr 5385.3	Forbes, F.E. Dahomey and the Dahomans. London, 1851. 2v.
Afr 5385.3.5	Forbes, F.E. Dahomey and the Dahomans. Paris, 1857.
Afr 5385.5	Macleod, John. A voyage to Africa. London, 1820.
Afr 5385.7	Brunet, L. Dahomey et dépendances. Paris, 1901.
Afr 5385.8	Fonssagrives, J. Notice sur le Dahomey. Paris, 1900.
Afr 5385.9	François, G. Notre colonie du Dahomey. Paris, 1906.
Afr 5385.10	Cornevin, R. Le Dahomey. Paris, 1965.
Afr 5385.11	Leherisse, R. Voyage au Dahomey et à la Côte-d'Ivoire. Paris, 1903.
Afr 5385.12	Albeca, A.L. Les établissements français du Golfe de Bénin. Paris, 1889.
Afr 5385.13	Besolow, T.E. From the darkness of Africa to light of America. Boston, 1891.
Afr 5385.14	Laffitte, J. Le Dahomé - souvenirs de voyage et de mission. 4 ed. Tours, 1876.
Afr 5385.14.2	Laffitte, J. Le Dahomé - souvenirs de voyage et de mission. Tours, 1873.
Afr 5385.15	Skertchly, J.A. Dahomey as it is. London, 1874.
Afr 5385.16	Dubarry, A. Voyage au Dahomey. Paris, n.d.
NEDL Afr 5385.17	Duncan, John. Travels in western africa...through Dahomey. London, 1847. (Changed to KPE 9015) 2v.
NEDL Afr 5385.17.2	Duncan, John. Travels in western africa in 1845 and 1846. London, 1847. (Changed to KPE 9014) 2v.
Afr 5385.17.5	Duncan, John. Travels in western African in 1845 and 1846. 1st ed. London, 1968.
Afr 5385.19	Foa, Edouard. Le Dahomey, histoire, géographie, moeurs (1891-94). Paris, 1895.
Afr 5385.21	Chaudoin, E. Trois mois de captivité au Dahomey. Paris, 1891.
Afr 5385.23	Guillevin. Voyage dans l'intérieur du royaume de Dahomey. Paris, 1862.
Afr 5385.24	Grivot, René. Réactions dahoméennes. Paris, 1954.
Afr 5385.25	Herskovits, M.J. Dahomey, an ancient West African kingdom. N.Y., 1938. 2v.
Afr 5385.27.2	Quenum, M. Au pays des Fons. 2me éd. Paris, 1938.
Afr 5385.30	Akindele, Adolphe. Le Dahomey. Paris, 1955.
Afr 5385.32	Pires, Vicente F. Viagem de Africa em o reino de Dahome. São Paulo, 1957.
Afr 5385.36	France. Embassy. U.S. The Republic of Dahomey. N.Y., 1960.
Afr 5385.37	Simon, Marc. Souvenirs de brousse, 1905-1910. Paris, 1965.
VAfr 5385.38	Hentsch, Henry. Deux années au Dahomey, 1903-1905. Nancy, 1916.

Afr 5387   Dahomey; Slave Coast - Economic conditions

Afr 5387.5	Hurault, Jean. Mission d'étude des structures agraires dans le sud Dahomey (février à Nov.1961). Rapport annexe. Paris, 1963.
Afr 5387.8	Polanyi, Karl. Dahomey and the slave trade; an analysis of an archaic economy. Seattle, 1966.
Afr 5387.10	Cheminault, R. L'artisanat. Paris, 1965. 2v.
Afr 5387.12	Serreau, Jean. Le développement à la base au Dahomey et au Sénégal. Paris, 1966.
Afr 5387.14	Dahomey. Plan de développement économique et social, 1966-1970. Cotohou, 1966.

Afr 5388   Dahomey; Slave Coast - Finance

Afr 5388.5F	Dahomey. Budget national.

Afr 5390 Dahomey; Slave Coast - Races

Afr 5390.2 Lombard, Jacques. Structures de type féodal en Afrique noire. Paris, 1965.
Afr 5390.4 Mercier, Paul. Tradition, changement, histoire, les "Somba" du Dahomey septentrional. Paris, 1968.

Afr 5392 Dahomey; Slave Coast - Religion; missions

Afr 5392.2 Marty, Paul. Etudes sur l'islam au Dahomey. Paris, 1926.
Afr 5392.3 Hardy, Georges. Un apôtre d'aujourd'hui. Paris, 1949.
Afr 5392.4 Desribes, Emmanuel. L'évangile au Dahomey et à la Côte des Esclaves. Clermont-Ferrand, 1877.

Afr 5394 Dahomey; Slave Coast - Special customs

Afr 5394.2 Adandé, A. Les récades des rois du Dahomey. Dakar, 1962.

Afr 5396 Dahomey; Slave Coast - Local

Afr 5396.2 Tardits, C. Porto Novo. Paris, 1958.
Afr 5396.2.5 Ballard, J.A. The Porto Novo incidents of 1923, politics in the colonial era. Ibadan, 1965.

Afr 5400 French Equatorial Africa in general - Periodicals

Afr 5400.5 Congo, revue générale de la colonie belge. Bruxelles. 1,1920+ 41v.
Afr 5400.5.5 Congo, revue générale de la colonie belge. Tables de Congo. Bruxelles. 1920+
Afr 5400.6 Liaison, organe des cercles culturels de l'A.E.F. (Afrique équatoriale française). Brazzaville. 51,1956+ 3v.
Afr 5400.7F Union Douanière et Economique de l'Afrique Centrale. Journal officiel. Brazzaville. 1,1966+
Afr 5400.8 Union Douanière et Economique de l'Afrique Centrale. Annuaire. Douala. 1,1968+

Afr 5401 French Equatorial Africa in general - Bibliographies

Afr 5401.5 Bruel, Georges. Bibliographie de l'Afrique équatoriale française. Paris, 1914.

Afr 5402 French Equatorial Africa in general - Collected source materials

Afr 5402.5F French Equatorial Africa. Direction des Finances. Budget général. 1948+ 2v.
Afr 5402.10F France. Ministère des Affaires Etrangères. Documents diplomatiques. Paris, 1885.

Afr 5403 French Equatorial Africa in general - Government and administration

Afr 5403.10 Demetz, Henri. Le régime foncier en Afrique équatoriale française. Annecy, 1939.
Afr 5403.20 Dairiam, Emmanuel. La subdivision en Afrique équatoriale française. Lyon, 1931.
Afr 5403.30 Massion, Jacques. Les grandes concessions au Congo français. Paris, 1920.

Afr 5404 French Equatorial Africa in general - General history

Afr 5404.5 Ronget, Fernand. L'expansion coloniale au Congo français. Paris, 1906.
Afr 5404.10 Thompson, V.M. The emerging states of French Equatorial Africa. Stanford, Calif., 1960.
Afr 5404.15 Gamache, Pierre. Géographie et histoire de l'Afrique équatoriale française. Paris, 1949.
Afr 5404.20 France. Agence de la France d'Outre-mer. Afrique équatoriale française. v.1-4. Paris, 1950.
Afr 5404.25 Dreux-Brézé, Joachim de. Le Probléme du regroupement en Afrique équatoriale, du régime colonial à l'union douamière et économique de l'Afrique centrale. Thèsis. Paris, 1968.

Afr 5405.100 - .199 French Equatorial Africa in general - History by periods - 1840-1910

Afr 5405.109 Drohojowska, Antoinette J.F.A. M. Savorgnan de Brazza. Lille, 1884.
Afr 5405.109.5 Brousseau, G. Souvenirs de la mission Savorgnan de Brazza. Paris, 1925.
Afr 5405.109.10 Chambrun, J.A. de P. Brazza. Paris, 1930.
Afr 5405.109.15 Froment-Guieysse, G. Brazza. Paris, 1945.
Afr 5405.109.20 Maran, René. Savorgnan de Brazza. Paris, 1951.
Afr 5405.109.25 Croidys, Pierre. Brazza. Paris, 1947.
Afr 5405.109.30 Savorgnan de Brazza, Pierre. Conférences et lettres sur ses trois explorations dans l'ouest africain de 1875 à 1886. Paris, 1887.
Afr 5405.109.35 Cerbelaud-Salagnac, Georges. Savorgnan de Brazza. Paris, 1960.
Afr 5405.112 Chavannes, Charles de. Avec Brazza. Paris, 1936.
Afr 5405.112.2 Chavannes, Charles de. Le Congo français. Paris, 1937.
Afr 5405.112.5 Challaye, Felicien. Le Congo français. Paris, 1909.
Afr 5405.179 Saintoyant, J.F. L'affaire du Congo 1905. Paris, 1960.
Afr 5405.190 Violette, M. La N'Goko-Sangha. Paris, 1914.

Afr 5405.200 - .399 French Equatorial Africa in general - History by periods - 1910-1946

Afr 5405.270 Homet, Marcel. Congo, terre de souffrances. Paris, 1934.
Afr 5405.285 Saurat, Denis. Watch over Africa. London, 1941.
Afr 5405.300 Maurice, Albert. Félix Eboué, sa vie et son oeuvre. Bruxelles, 1954.

Afr 5406 French Equatorial Africa in general - Geography, description, etc. (By date, e.g. .231 for 1931)

Afr 5406.50 Duchaillu, Paul Belloni. Adventures in the great forest of Equatorial Africa. N.Y., 1890.
Afr 5406.51 Duchaillu, Paul Belloni. Explorations and adventures in Equatorial Africa. N.Y., 1861.
Afr 5406.51.5 Duchaillu, Paul Belloni. Explorations and adventures in Equatorial Africa. N.Y., 1871.
Afr 5406.51.10 Duchaillu, Paul Belloni. Explorations and adventures in Equatorial Africa. N.Y., 1861.
Afr 5406.51.12 Duchaillu, Paul Belloni. Explorations and adventures in Equatorial Africa. London, 1945.
Afr 5406.52 Duchaillu, Paul Belloni. A journey to Ashango-land. N.Y., 1871.
Afr 5406.52.5 Duchaillu, Paul Belloni. A journey to Ashango-land. N.Y., 1867.
Afr 5406.53 Duchaillu, Paul Belloni. Lost in the jungle. N.Y., 1873.
Afr 5406.54 Duchaillu, Paul Belloni. Wild life under the equator. N.Y., 1869.
Afr 5406.54.5 Duchaillu, Paul Belloni. Wild life under the equator. N.Y., 1871.
Afr 5406.55 Duchaillu, Paul Belloni. Stories of the gorilla country. N.Y., 1874.
Afr 5406.56 Duchaillu, Paul Belloni. My Apingi kingdom. N.Y., 1874.
Afr 5406.57 Duchaillu, Paul Belloni. The country of the dwarfs. N.Y., 1874.

Afr 5406 French Equatorial Africa in general - Geography, description, etc. (By date, e.g. .231 for 1931) - cont.

Afr 5406.58 Duchaillu, Paul Belloni. King Mombo. N.Y., 1902.
Afr 5406.60 Vaucaire, Michel. Paul Duchaillu. N.Y., 1930.
Afr 5406.176 Burton, Richard F. Two trips to gorilla land. London, 1876. 4v.
Afr 5406.181 Dietz, Emile. Un explorateur africain, Auguste Stahl. Paris, 1884.
Afr 5406.185 Franche, Lucien. Les possessions françaises du...Congo. Paris, 1885.
Afr 5406.186 Jeannest, Charles. Quatre années au Congo. Paris, 1886.
Afr 5406.189 Guiral, Léon. Le Congo français du Gabon à Brazzaville. Paris, 1889.
Afr 5406.191 Dybowski, Jean. La route du Tchad. Paris, 1903.
Afr 5406.198 Castellani, Charles. Vers le Nil français. Paris, 1898.
Afr 5406.201 Guillemot, Marcel. Notice sur le Congo français. (2e. série). Paris, 1901.
Afr 5406.204 Renouard, G. L'ouest africain. Paris, 1904.
Afr 5406.209 Riemer, Otto. Das französische Congogebiet. Mörs, 1909.
Afr 5406.211 Deschamps, Jean Leopold. De Bordeaux au Tchad par Brazzaville. Paris, 1911.
Afr 5406.211.5 Thouin, Marcel. Etude sur la délimitation de frontière du Congo-Cameroun. Thesis. Paris, 1911.
Afr 5406.211.10 Cottes, A. La mission Cottes au Sud-Cameroun. Paris, 1911.
Afr 5406.211.15.2 Rondet-Saint, Maurice. L'Afrique equatoriale française. 2. ed. Paris, 1911.
Afr 5406.213 Ranget, Fernand. L'Afrique équatoriale illustrée. Paris, 1913.
Afr 5406.218 Bruel, Georges. L'Afrique équatoriale française. Paris, 1918.
Afr 5406.218.5 Bruel, Georges. La France équatoriale africaine. Paris, 1935.
Afr 5406.225 Grossard, Jacques H. Mission de délimitation de l'Afrique. Text and plates. Paris, 1925. 2v.
Afr 5406.225.5 Vassal, Gabrielle M. Life in French Congo. London, 1925.
Afr 5406.230 Bruel, Georges. L'Afrique équatoriale française (A.E.F.). Paris, 1930.
Afr 5406.231 Maigret, Julien. Afrique équatoriale française. Paris, 1931.
Afr 5406.242 Great Britain. Naval Intelligence Division. French Equatorial Africa and Cameroons. London, 1942.
Afr 5406.250.3 Trezenem, Edouard. L'Afrique équatoriale française. Paris, 1955.
Afr 5406.250.5 France. Direction de la Documentation. French Equatorial Africa. Levallois, 195-.
Afr 5406.252 Ziegle, Henri. Afrique équatoriale française. Paris, 1952.
Afr 5406.253F Encyclopédie Mensuelle d'Outre-Mer. AEF 53. Paris, 1953.
Afr 5406.257 Fieret, Jeannette. L'enfant blanc de l'Afrique noire. Paris, 1957.
Afr 5406.259 Motley, Mary. Devils in waiting. London, 1959.
Afr 5406.262 Afrique centrale, les républiques d'expression française. Paris, 1962.
Afr 5406.264 Gardi, René. Kiligei. Heitere und ernste Erlebnisse in Afrika. Aarau, 1964.
Afr 5406.266 Sautter, Gilles. De l'Atlantique au fleuve Congo. Paris, 1966. 2v.

Afr 5407 French Equatorial Africa in general - Economic and financial conditions

Afr 5407.5 Marel, Edmund D. The British case in French Congo. London, 1903.
Afr 5407.8 French Equatorial Africa. Service de Coordination des Affaires Economiques. L'A.E.F. économique et sociale, 1947-1958. Paris, 1959.
Afr 5407.10 Voss, Harald. Kooperation in Afrika. Hamburg, 1965.
Afr 5407.12F Réalités africaines. La mise en valeur de l'A.E.F. Casablanca, 1956.
Afr 5407.14 Economist Intelligence Unit, Ltd., London. The states of Equatorial Africa: Gabon, Congo. London, 1964.

Afr 5408 French Equatorial Africa in general - Special customs, etc.

Afr 5408.5 Cureau, Adolphe L. Les sociétés primitives de l'Afrique. Paris, 1912.
Afr 5408.5.5 Cureau, Adolphe L. Savage man in Central Africa. London, 1915.
Afr 5408.10 Castellani, Charles. Das Weib am Kongo. Minden, 1902.
Afr 5408.15 Balandier, Georges. Sociologie actuelle de l'Afrique noire. Paris, 1955.
Afr 5408.15.2 Balandier, Georges. Sociologie actuelle de l'Afrique noire, changements sociaux au Gabon et au Congo. Paris, 1955.
Afr 5408.15.5 Balandier, Georges. Sociologie actuelle de l'Afrique noire. Paris, 1963.
Afr 5408.16 Muraz, Gaston. Satyres illustrées de l'Afrique noire. Paris, 1947.
Afr 5408.105 Witte, Jehan. Les deux Congo, trente-cinq ans d'apostolat. Paris, 1913.

Afr 5410 Gabon - Periodicals

Afr 5410.5F Gabon d'aujourd'hui. Libreville. 66-84,1965-1966
Afr 5410.10 Gabon. Institut Pédagogique National. Arts et lettres. Libreville. 1,1966+
Afr 5410.15 Réalités gabonaises. 26,1965+

Afr 5415 Gabon - General history

Afr 5415.5 Walker, A.R. Notes d'histoire du Gabon. Montpellier, 1960.
Afr 5415.8 Darlington, Charles F. African betrayal. N.Y., 1968.

Afr 5417.1 - .99 Gabon - History by periods - Before 1840

Afr 5417.2 Mba, Léon. Discours, messages. Libreville, 1965.
Afr 5417.70.2 Weinstein, Brian. Gabon; nation-building on the Ogooue. Cambridge, Mass., 1966.

Afr 5417.100 - .299 Gabon - History by periods - 1840-1910

Afr 5417.100 Deschamps, Hubert. Quinze ans de Gabon;...1839-1853. Paris, 1965.

Afr 5417.700 - Gabon - History by periods - 1958-

Afr 5417.702 Gabon. Ministère de l'Information et du Tourisme. Gabon an 5.cinq années de progrès. Libreville, 1965.

Afr 5420 Gabon - Geography, description, etc.
Afr 5420.175   Compiegne, Victor D. L'Afrique équatoriale. Paris, 1875.
Afr 5420.222   Grebert, F. Au Gabon, Afrique. Paris, 1922.
Afr 5420.257   Charbonnier, François. Gabon, terre d'avenir.
     Paris, 1957.
Afr 5420.261   France. Embassy. U.S. The Gabon Republic. N.Y., 1961.

Afr 5422 Gabon - Economic conditions
Afr 5422.2F   Gabon. Laws, statutes, etc. Loi no. 11-63 du 12/1/63
     portant approbation du programme intérimaire de
     développement. Libreville, 1965.
Afr 5422.5   Gabon. Ministère d'Etat Chargé de l'Economie Nationale du
     Plan et des Mines. Commissariat au Plan. Résumé du plan de
     développement économique et social, période 1966-1971.
     Monaco, 1966.
Afr 5422.7   Gabon. Plan de développement économique et social,
     1966-1970. Paris, 1967?

Afr 5425 Gabon - Races
Afr 5425.5   Alexandre, Pierre. Le groupe dit Pahouin. Paris, 1958.
Afr 5425.10   Trilles, H. Le totémisme chez les Fan. Münster, 1912.
Afr 5425.15   France, Louis. De l'origine des Pahouins. Paris, 1905.
Afr 5425.18   Deschamps, H. Traditions orales et archives au Gabon.
     Paris, 1962.
Afr 5425.20   Trujeda Incerna, Luis. Los pámues de nuestra Guin.
     Madrid, 1946.

Afr 5426 Gabon - Religion; missions
Afr 5426.100   Schweitzer, Albert. On the edge of the primeval forest.
     London, 1922.
Afr 5426.100.5   Schweitzer, Albert. On the edge of the primeval forest.
     London, 1928.
Afr 5426.100.10   Schweitzer, Albert. From my African note-book.
     London, 1938.
Afr 5426.100.12   Schweitzer, Albert. Zwischen Wasser und Urwald.
     München, 1949.
Afr 5426.100.15   Schweitzer, Albert. The forest hospital at Lambaréné.
     N.Y., 1931.
Afr 5426.100.20   Schweitzer, Albert. A l'orée de la forêt vierge.
     Paris, 1929.
Afr 5426.100.25   Woyott-Secretan, Marie. Albert Schweitzer. Munich, 1949.
Afr 5426.100.30   Monestier, Marianne. Le grand docteur blanc. Paris, 1952.
Afr 5426.100.35   Urquhart, Clara. With Dr. Schweitzer in Lambaréné.
     London, 1957.
Afr 5426.100.40   Joy, Charles Rhind. The Africa of Albert Schweitzer.
     N.Y., 1948.
Afr 5426.100.45   Gollomb, Joseph. Albert Schweitzer. London, 1951.
Afr 5426.100.50   Franck, Frederick. Days with Albert Schweitzer.
     N.Y., 1959.
Afr 5426.100.60   McKnight, G. Verdict on Schweitzer. London, 1964.
Afr 5426.100.65   Pamphlet vol. Schweitzer, Albert. 3 pam.
Afr 5426.100.70   Bessuges, Jacques. Lambaróné à l'ombre de Schweitzer.
     Limoges, 1968.
Afr 5426.110   Milligan, Robert H. The fetish folk of West Africa.
     N.Y., 1912.
Afr 5426.115   Briault, Maurice. Sur les pistes de l'AEF. Paris, 1945.
Afr 5426.120   Bonzon, Charles. A Lambaréné. Nancy, 1897.
Afr 5426.125   Raponda-Walker, A. Rites et croyances des peuples du
     Gabon. Paris, 1962.

Afr 5430 Congo Republic (Brazzaville); Middle or Lower Congo - Periodicals
Afr 5430.5   United Nations. Delegation from the Congo (Brazzaville).
     Bulletin d'information.
Afr 5430.10   Congo (Brazzaville). Plan interimaire de développement
     économique et social. Paris. 1964-1968

Afr 5432 Congo Republic (Brazzaville); Middle or Lower Congo - Collected source materials
Afr 5432.5   Documents pour servir à l'histoire de l'Afrique équatoriale
     française. Série 2. Brazza et la fondation du Congo
     français. Paris. 1,1966+

Afr 5435 Congo Republic (Brazzaville); Middle or Lower Congo - General history
Afr 5435.2   Wagret, Jean Michel. Histoire et sociologie politiques de
     la République du Congo. Paris, 1963.

Afr 5437.1 - .99 Congo Republic (Brazzaville); Middle or Lower Congo - History by periods - Before 1840
Afr 5437.5   Martynov, V.A. Zagovor protiv Kongo. Moscow, 1960.
Afr 5437.74   Randles, W.G.L. L'ancien royaume du Congo des origines à
     la fin du XIXE siècle. Paris, 1968.

Afr 5440 Congo Republic (Brazzaville); Middle or Lower Congo - Geography, description, etc.
Afr 5440.5   Wauters, Alphonse Jules. Les bassins de l'Ubangi.
     Brussels, 1902.
Afr 5440.10   France. Embassy. U.S. The Republic of Congo. N.Y., 1961.
Afr 5440.15   Vennetier, Pierre. Les hommes et leur activités dans le
     Nord du Congo-Brazzaville. Paris, 1965.
Afr 5440.20.5   Soedergren, Sigfried. Sweet smell of mangoes.
     London, 1968.

Afr 5442 Congo Republic (Brazzaville); Middle or Lower Congo - Economic conditions
Afr 5442.5   Vennetier, Pierre. Geographie du Congo-Brazzaville.
     Paris, 1966.
Afr 5442.13   France. Ministère de la Coopération. Direction des Affaires
     Economiques et Financières. Sous-Direction des Etudes
     Générales. Economie et plan de développement: Republique
     du Congo-Brazzaville. 3. éd. Paris, 1965.
Afr 5442.15   Tollet, Marcel. Initiation sociologique à l'Afrique
     centrale. Anvers, 1966.

Afr 5445 Congo Republic (Brazzaville); Middle or Lower Congo - Races
Afr 5445.5   Dennett, R.E. At the back of the black man's mind.
     London, 1906.
Afr 5445.10   Macleod, Olive. Chiefs and cities of Central Africa.
     Edinburgh, 1912.

Afr 5446 Congo Republic (Brazzaville); Middle or Lower Congo - Religion; missions
Afr 5446.5   Andersson, Efraim. Churches at the grass-roots.
     London, 1968.

Afr 5447 Congo Republic (Brazzaville); Middle or Lower Congo - Special customs
Afr 5447.5   Vincent, Jeanne Françoise. Femmes africaines en milieu
     urbain. Paris, 1966.

Afr 5448 Congo Republic (Brazzaville); Middle or Lower Congo - Local
Afr 5448.5A   Bastian, Adolf. Die deutsche Expedition an der
     Loango-Küste. Jena, 1874.
Afr 5448.5B   Bastian, Adolf. Die deutsche Expedition an der
     Loango-Küste. Jena, 1874.
Afr 5448.7   Pechuel-Loesche, E. Volkskunde von Loango.
     Stuttgart, 1907.
Afr 5448.10   Devauges, Roland. Le chômage à Brazzaville en 1957.
     Paris, 1958.
Afr 5448.12F   Devauges, Roland. Les conditions sociologiques d'une
     politique d'urbanisme à Brazzaville. Paris, 1959.
Afr 5448.13   Augouard, Prosper Philippe. Notes historiques sur la
     fondation de Brazzaville. Paris, 1917.
Afr 5448.14   Le chômage à Brazzaville. Paris, 1963. 2v.
Afr 5448.15   Devauges, Roland. Les chômeurs de Brazzaville et les
     perspectives du barrage du Kouilou. Paris, 1963.
Afr 5448.15.5   Devauges, Roland. Les dépenses exceptionnelles dans les
     budgets de ménage à Pointe-Noire en 1958. Paris, 1963.
Afr 5448.15.10   France. Ministère de la Coopération. Les budgets des
     ménages africains a Pointe-Noire, 1958-1959. Paris, 1962.
Afr 5448.16   Préclin, Louis. Pointe-Noire sous la croix de Lorraine.
     Paris, 1967.
Afr 5448.18   Quinze ans de travaux et de recherches dans les pays du
     Niari. Monaco, 1966-1968.

Afr 5460 Central African Republic; Ubangi-Shari - Geography, description, etc.
Afr 5460.5   Bonnel de Mezières, A. Rapport sur le Haut-Oubangui.
     Paris, 1901.
Afr 5460.10   Kalck, Pierre. Réalités oubanguiennes. Paris, 1959.
Afr 5460.15   France. Embassy. U.S. The Central African Republic.
     N.Y., 1960.

Afr 5465 Central African Republic; Ubangi-Shari - Races
Afr 5465.2   Thomas, Jacqueline M.C. Les Ngbaka de la Lobaye.
     Paris, 1963.
Afr 5465.3   Jean, S. Les Langbas, population d'Oubangui-Chari.
     Paris, 1961.
Afr 5465.5   Dampierre, Eric de. Un ancien royaume bandia de Haut
     Oubanqui. Paris, 1967.
Afr 5465.6   Retel-Laurention, Anne. Oracles et ordalies chez les
     Nzakara. Paris, 1969.

Afr 5466 Central African Republic; Ubangi-Shari - Religion; missions
Afr 5466.5   Remy. Le catholicisme et la vapeur au centre de l'Afrique.
     Poitiers, 1901.

Afr 5470 Chad - Periodicals
Afr 5470.5   Cahiers de l'unité. Fort-Lamy. 1,1966+
Afr 5470.10   France. Centre National de la Recherche Scientifique.
     Dossiers de la Recherche cooperative sur programme.
     Paris. 2,1968

Afr 5476 Chad - General special
Afr 5476.5   Boisson, Jacques. L'histoire du Tchad et de Fort
     Archambault. Besançon, 1966.

Afr 5477.500 - .699 Chad - History by periods - 1946-1958
Afr 5477.505   Diguimbaye, Georges. L'essor du Tchad. Paris, 1969.

Afr 5477.700 - Chad - History by periods - 1958-
Afr 5477.930   Ferrandi, Jean. Le Centre-africain français. Paris, 1930.
Afr 5477.963   Lecornec, J. Histoire politique du Tchad de 1900 à 1962.
     Paris, 1963.

Afr 5480 Chad - Geography, description, etc.
Afr 5480.194   Brunache, Paul. Le centre de l'Afrique. Paris, 1894.
Afr 5480.205   L'Enfant, Eugène A. La grande route du Tchad.
     Paris, 1905.
Afr 5480.207   Chevalier, Auguste. Mission Chari, lac Tchad, 1902-1904.
     Paris, 1907.
Afr 5480.208   Freydenberg, Henri. Le Tchad et le bassin du Chari. Thèse.
     Paris, 1908.
Afr 5480.211   Cornel, Charles J.H. Au Tchad. Paris, 1911.
Afr 5480.231   Maran, René. Le Tchad de sable et d'or. Paris, 1931.
Afr 5480.243   Lapie, Pierre O. Mes tournées au tchad. London, 1943.
Afr 5480.243.3   Lapie, Pierre O. My travels through Chad. London, 1943.
Afr 5480.260   Scheid, T. Journal d'un safari au Tchad. Bruxelles, 1960.
Afr 5480.261   France. Embassy. U.S. The Republic of Chad. N.Y., 1961.
Afr 5480.262F   Gentil, Pierre. Les treize préfectures de la République du
     Tchad. Fort-Lamy, 1962.
Afr 5480.265   Hugot, Pierre. Le Tchad. Paris, 1965.
Afr 5480.267   Chad, President. Terre tchadienne. Paris, 1967.

Afr 5482 Chad - Economic conditions
Afr 5482.5   France. Ministère de la Coopération. Direction des Affaires
     Economiques. Economie et plan de développement.
     Paris, 1963.
Afr 5482.10   Chambre de Commerce d'Agriculture et d'Industrie du Tchad.
     Situation économique de la Republique du Tchad.
     Fort-Lamy, 1965.
Afr 5482.15   Chad. Ministère du Plan et de la Coopération. Premier plan
     quinquennal de développement économique et social,
     1966-1970. Fort Lamy?, 1967.
Afr 5482.20   Italy. Instituto Nazionale per il Commercio Estero. Tchad.
     Romo, 1963.

Afr 5485 Chad - Races
Afr 5485.5   Lebeuf, Annie M.D. Les populations du Tchad. Paris, 1959.
Afr 5485.10   Lerouvreur, A. Saheliens et Sahariens du Tchad.
     Paris, 1962.
Afr 5485.15   Jaulin, Robert. La Mort sara, l'ordre de la vie ou la
     pensée de la mort au Tchad. Paris, 1967.

Afr 5488 Chad - Local
Afr 5488.5   Muhammad Ibn Omar. Voyage au Ouadaï. Paris, 1851.
Afr 5488.10   Carbou, Henri. La region du Tchad et du Ouadaï. V.1-2.
     Paris, 1912. 2v.
Afr 5488.12   Capot-Rey, R. Borkou et Ouninga. Alger, 1961.
Afr 5488.14   Laigret-Pascault, Denyse E. Fort-lamy. Fort-Lamy, 1961.
Afr 5488.16F   Société d'Études pour le Développement Economique et
     Social. Etude socio-économique de la ville d'Abéché.
     Paris, 1965.

Afr 5488 Chad - Local - cont.
Afr 5488.20 Cabot, Jean. Le bassin du moyen Logone. Thèse. Paris, 1965.
Afr 5488.22 Pairault, Claude. Boum-le-Grand, village d'Iro. Paris, 1966.

Afr 5501 - 5526 Madagascar - Periodicals (A-Z)
Afr 5501.2 Antananarivo annual. Antananarivo. 1,1885+ 4v.
Afr 5501.2.5 Antananarivo annual and Madagascar magazine. Antananarivo. 2,1876+ 2v.
Afr 5501.3 Academie Malgache. Bulletin. Tananarivo. 1,1902+ 20v.
Afr 5501.3.6 Academie...Tananarivo. Academie Malgache, Tananarivo. Memoires. 1,1926+ 14v.
Afr 5501.3.10 Poisson, Henri. Le cinquantenaire de l'Academie malgache. Tananarive, 1952.
Afr 5501.5 Annales malgaches. Droit. Paris. 2v.
Afr 5501.6 Annales malgaches. Lettres. Paris. 3v.
Afr 5502.2 Madagascar. Bulletin economique. Tananarive. 1923+ 2v.
Afr 5502.2.5 Madagascar. Bulletin economique mensuel. Tananarive. 1,1926+
Afr 5513.2 Madagascar. Revue de geographie. Toulouse. 1,1962+ 5v.
NEDL Afr 5514.1 Madagascar. Notes, reconnaissances et explorations. Tananarive. 1,1897+ 5v.
Afr 5514.2F Madagascar news. Antananarivo.
Afr 5518.1F Revue de Madagascar. Tananarive. 1-27,1933-1939// 14v.
Afr 5518.4F Revue de Madagascar. Tananarive. 30,1965+
Afr 5520.1 Trait d'union. Tananarive.

Afr 5530 Madagascar - Bibliographies
Afr 5530.1 Sibree, J. A Madagascar bibliography. Antananarivo, 1885.
Afr 5530.1.5 Sibree, J. A Madagascar bibliography. Mss. Additions and corrections. Antananarivo, 1885.
Afr 5530.2 Grandidier, G. Bibliographie de Madagascar. Paris, 1905. 4v.
Afr 5530.4 Duignan, Peter. Madagascar. Stanford, Calif., 1962.
Afr 5530.5 Bibliotheque Nationale, Paris. Periodiques malgaches. Paris, 1964.
Afr 5530.6 Bibliographie annuelle de Madagascar. Tananarive. 1,1964+
Afr 5530.7 Malagasy Republic. Service des Archives et de la Documentation. Inventaire de la serié Mi des Archives de la République Malgache. Tananariva, 1963.

Afr 5533 Madagascar - Pamphlet volumes
Afr 5533.01 Pamphlet box. Madagascar.
Afr 5533.02F Pamphlet box. Madagascar.
Afr 5533.5 Pamphlet vol. Madagascar. 7 pam.

Afr 5538 Madagascar - Collected source materials - Others
X Cg Afr 5538.2 Grandidier, A. Collection des ouvrages anciens concernant Madagascar. v.1-9. Paris, 1903-20. (Changed to XP 3889) 9v.
Afr 5538.3 Cremazy, P. Notice bibliographique sur Madagascar. St. Denis, 1884.
Afr 5538.10 Guillain, C. Documents sur l'histoire, la géographie...de la partie occidentale de Madagascar. Paris, 1845.

Afr 5540 Madagascar - Government and administration
Afr 5540.1 Lejamble, George. Le fokonolona et le pouvoir. Tananarive, 1963.
Afr 5540.3 Julien, G. Institutions politiques et socials de Madagascar. V.1-2. Paris, 1908. 2v.
Afr 5540.4 Spas, L. Etude sur l'organisation de Madagascar. Paris, 1912.
Afr 5540.6F Madagascar, gouvernement générale. Tananarive, 1903.
Afr 5540.8 Barrel, G.P. Le code des 305 articles de Madagascar. Thèse. Paris, 1931.
Afr 5540.10 Delteil, Pierre. Le fokon'olona (commune malgache) et les conventions de fokon'olona. Thèse. Paris, 1931.
Afr 5540.11 Madagascar. Constitution. Constitution et lois organiques de la République Malgache et accords franco-malgaches. Tananarive, 1962.
Afr 5540.12 Bilbao, Rene. Le droit malgache de la nationalité. Paris, 1965.
Afr 5540.14 Comte, Jean. Les communes malgaches. Tananarive, 1963.
Afr 5540.16 Malagusy Republic Institute National de la Statistique et de la Recherche Economique. Des ordinateurs dans l'administration Malgache! Tananarive?, 1966?

Afr 5544 - 5550 Madagascar - General history (By date)
Afr 5548.22 Copland, Samuel. A history of the island of Madagascar. London, 1822.
Afr 5548.33 Ackerman. Histoire des revolutions de Madagascar. Paris, 1833.
Afr 5548.38 Ellis, W. History of Madagascar. London, 1838. 2v.
Afr 5548.44 Laverdant, D. Colonisation de Madagascar. Paris, 1844.
Afr 5548.46 Descartes, M. Histoire et geographie de Madagascar. Paris, 1846.
Afr 5548.59 Barbie du Bocage, V.A. Madagascar, possession française depuis 1642. Paris, 1859.
Afr 5548.63 Lacaille, L.P. Connaissance de Madagascar. Paris, 1863.
Afr 5548.65 Mcleod, Lyons. Madagascar and its people. London, 1865.
Afr 5548.84 Lavaissiere, C. De. Histoire de Madagascar. Paris, 1884.
Afr 5548.84.5 Escamps, H. D. Histoire et geographie de Madagascar. Paris, 1884.
Afr 5548.84.10 Castonnet des Fosses, H. Madagascar. Paris, 1884. 2 pam.
Afr 5548.84.15 Pauliat, Louis. Madagascar. Paris, 1884.
Afr 5548.85 Shaw, George A. Madagascar and France. London, 1885.
Afr 5548.86 Oliver, S.P. Madagascar. London, 1886. 2v.
Afr 5548.86.5 Hartmann, R. Madagascar und die Inseln Seychellen. Leipzig, 1886.
Afr 5548.87 Hue, Fernand. Le Français à Madagascar. Paris, 1887.
Afr 5548.88 Guet, M.I. Les origines de l'Ile Bourbon. Paris, 1888.
Afr 5548.95 Cousins, W.E. Madagascar of to-day. London, 1895.
Afr 5548.95.3 Brunet, L. La France à Madagascar. 2e ed. Paris, 1895.
Afr 5548.95.5 Joubert, J. La question de Madagascar. Paris, 1895.
Afr 5549.08 Darcy, J. France et Angleterre, cent années de rivalité coloniale. Paris, 1908.
Afr 5549.08.12 Callet, F. Histoire des rois. V.1-3. Tananarive, 1953. 2v.
Afr 5549.09 Suau, Pierre. La France à Madagascar. Paris, 1909.
Afr 5549.12 Villars, E.J. Madagascar, 1638-1894, établissement des Français dans l'île. Paris, 1912.
Afr 5549.12.5 Malzac, V. Histoire du royaume Hova depuis ses origines jusqu'à sa fin. Tananarive, 1912.
Afr 5549.38 Howe, Sonia Elizabeth. The drama of Madagascar. London, 1938.
Afr 5549.43 Haenel, Karl. Madagaskar. Leipzig, 1943.
Afr 5549.52 Rabemananjara, R.W. Madagascar. Paris, 1952.
Afr 5549.52.5 Damantsoha. Histoire politique et religieuse des Malgaches. Tananarive?, 1952.

Afr 5544 - 5550 Madagascar - General history (By date) - cont.
Afr 5549.55 Isnard, Hildebert. Madagascar. Paris, 1955.
Afr 5549.58F Grandidier, G. Histoire politique et coloniale. V.3. Tananarive, 1958.
Afr 5549.60 Deschamps, H.J. Histoire de Madagascar. Paris, 1960.
Afr 5549.60.5 Tananarive. Bibliotheque Universitaire. Madagasihara, regards vers le passe. Tananarive, 1960.
Afr 5549.61 Chapus, Georges. Manuel d'histoire de Madagascar. Paris, 1961.
Afr 5549.62 Kent, R.K. From Madagascar to the Malagasy Republic. N.Y., 1962.
Afr 5549.65.5 Pascal, Roger. La République Malgache. Paris, 1965.
Afr 5549.65.10 Ralaimihoatra, Edouard. Histoire de Madagascar. Tananarive, 1965. 2v.
Afr 5549.67 Rajemisa-Raolison, Regis. Dictionnaire historique et geographique de Madagascar. Fianarantsoa, 1966.

Afr 5555 Madagascar - General special
Afr 5555.2 Decary, Raymond. Coutumes guerrieres et organisation militaire chez les anciens Malgaches. Paris, 1966. 2v.

Afr 5565 Madagascar - History by periods - Early to 1600
Afr 5565.2 Kammerer, A. La decouverte de Madagascar. n.p., n.d.
Afr 5565.2.2 Kammerer, A. La decouverte de Madagascar. Lisboa, 1950.

Afr 5570 Madagascar - History by periods - 1600-1700 - General works
Afr 5570.1 Pauliat, L. Louis XIV et la campagnie des Indes Orient de 1664. Paris, 1886.

Afr 5573 Madagascar - History by periods - 1600-1700 - Early colonization
Afr 5573.5 Malotet, A. Les origines de la colonisation française à Madagascar, 1648-1661. Paris, 1898.
Afr 5573.10 Froidevaux, H. Un mémoire inédit de La Haye sur Madagascar. Paris, 1897. 4 pam.
Afr 5573.10.5 Froidevaux, H. La France à Madagascar au XVIIe siècle. Paris, 1901.

Afr 5575 Madagascar - History by periods - 1600-1700 - Pirates
Afr 5575.10 Broke, A. van. Aller neueste Nachricht von Madagascar und dem Leben des jetzigen Beherrschers dieses Insul. Frankfurt, 1748.

Afr 5580 Madagascar - History by periods - 1700-1808
Afr 5580.2 Ponget de St. Andre. La colonisation de Madagascar sous Louis XV. Paris, 1886.
Afr 5580.3 Cultru, P. De colonia in...Madagascar. Paris, 1901.
Afr 5580.3.5 Cultru, P. Un empereur de Madagascar au XVIIIe siècle, Benyowszky. Paris, 1906.
Afr 5580.3.9 Lepecki, M.B. Maurycy August Beniowski. Lwow, 1938.
Afr 5580.3.10 Lepecky, M.B. Maurycy August Beniowski, zdob. Madagaskaru. Warszawa, 1959.
Afr 5580.3.15 Ortowski, Leon. Maurycy August Beniowski. Warszawa, 1961.
Afr 5580.3.20 Beniowski, M.A. Memoirs and travels of Mauritius Augustus. London, 1790. 2v.
VAfr 5580.3.25 Beniowski, M.A. Denník Mórica A. Beňovského. Bratislava, 1966.
Afr 5580.3.30 Beniowski, M.A. Pamigtniki. Wyd. 1. Warszawa, 1967.
Afr 5580.4 Foury, B. Mandove et la colonisation de Madagascar. Paris, 1956.

Afr 5585 Madagascar - History by periods - 19th century - General works
Afr 5585.3 Précis sur les établissements français formés à Madagascar. Paris, 1836.
Afr 5585.8 Hue, Fernand. La France et l'Angleterre à Madagascar. Paris, 1885. 2 pam.
Afr 5585.10 Saillens, R. Nos droits sur Madagascar. Paris, 1885.
Afr 5585.15 Brunet, Louis. La France à Madagascar, 1815-1895. Paris, 1895.
Afr 5585.20 Grandidier, G. Le Myre de Vilers. Paris, 1923.
Afr 5585.25 Launois, Pierre. L'Etat Malgache et ses transformations avant le régime français. Thèse. Paris, 1932.
Afr 5585.30 Chapus, G.S. Rainilaiarivony, un homme d'Etat Malgache. Paris, 1953.
Afr 5585.35 Lyall, R. Le journal de Robert Lyall. Tananarive, 1954.

Afr 5590 Madagascar - History by periods - 19th century - Radama I (1808-1828) - General works
Afr 5590.10 Carayon, U. Histoire de l'établissement français de Madagascar pendant la restauration. Paris, 1845. 3 pam.
Afr 5590.12 Valette, J. Etudes sur le regne de Radama Uer. Tananarive, 1962.

Afr 5593 Madagascar - History by periods - 19th century - Radama I (1808-1828) - Introduction of Christianity
Afr 5593.2 Froidevaux, H. Les Lazaristes à Madagascar au XVIII siècle. Paris, 1904.

Afr 5600 Madagascar - History by periods - 19th century - Ranavalona I (1828-1861)
Afr 5600.3 Warnier de Wailly, L.M.A.A. Campagne de Madagascar (1829-1830). Paris, 1895.
Afr 5600.4 Madagascar, combat livre à Tananarive. n.p., 1846.
Afr 5600.5 Madagascar, past and present. London, 1847.
Afr 5600.6 Chauvot, H. Madagascar et la France. Paris, 1848.
Afr 5600.7 Boudon, A. Le complot de 1857. Tananarive, 1943.

Afr 5605 Madagascar - History by periods - 19th century - Radama II (1861-1868)
Afr 5605.3 Regnon, Henry de. Madagascar et le roi Radama II. Paris, 1863.
Afr 5605.5 Desbassayns de Richemont, P. Documents sur la compagnie de Madagascar. Paris, 1867.

Afr 5615 Madagascar - History by periods - 19th century - Ranavalona II (1868-1883)
Afr 5615.5 Brenier, J. La question de Madagascar. Paris, 1882.

Afr 5620 Madagascar - History by periods - 19th century - Ranavalona III (1883-1897) - General works
Afr 5620.2F France. Ministère des Affaires Etrangeres. Documents diplomatiques. Paris, 1883. 4 pam.
Afr 5620.3F France. Ministère des Affaires Etrangeres. Documents diplomatiques. Paris, 1895.
Afr 5620.4 Bonnemaison, J. Historique de Madagascar. Tarbes, 1894.
Afr 5620.5 Martineau, A. Madagascar en 1894, étude de politique. Paris, 1894.
Afr 5620.6 Shervinton, Kathleen. The Shervintons, soldiers of fortune. London, 1899.

Afr 5620 Madagascar - History by periods - 19th century - Ranavalona III (1883-1897) - General works - cont.

Afr 5620.8 Mignard, E. Etude sur l'établissement de la domination française a Madagascar. Paris, 1900.
Afr 5620.9 Courand, Charles J. Madagascar, son avenir colonial. La Rochelle, 1895.
Afr 5620.10 Lux. La verité sur Madagascar. Paris, 1896.
Afr 5620.15 Durand, Alfred. Les derniers jours de la cour hova. Paris, 1933.

Afr 5625 Madagascar - History by periods - 19th century - Ranavalona III (1883-1897) - War with France, 1882-1884

Afr 5625.2 Oliver, S. Pasfield. True story of the French dispute in Madagascar. London, 1885.
Afr 5625.2.5 Oliver, S. Pasfield. French operations in Madagascar, 1883-1885. London, 1885-86. 2 pam.
Afr 5625.4 Marield, J. La France à Madagascar. Paris, 1887.
Afr 5625.6 Pamphlet vol. Madagascar. 5 pam.
Afr 5625.8 Pamphlet vol. Madagascar, 1868-97. 8 pam.

Afr 5635 Madagascar - History by periods - 19th century - Ranavalona III (1883-1897) - French expedition, 1895

Afr 5635.1 Hanotaux, G. L'affaire de Madagascar. 3e ed. Paris, 1896.
Afr 5635.2 Knight, E.F. Madagascar in war time. London, 1896.
Afr 5635.3 Orleans, H.P.D. A Madagascar. Paris, 1895.
Afr 5635.4 Ortus, C. Madagascar. Paris, 1895.
Afr 5635.5 Brunet, L. L'oeuvre de la France à Madagascar. Paris, 1903.
Afr 5635.6 Galli, H. La guerre a Madagascar. Paris, n.d. 2v.
Afr 5635.7 Bienaime. L'expedition de Madagascar de 1895. n.p., n.d. 4 pam.
Afr 5635.8 Duchesne, C. L'expedition de Madagascar...1896. Paris, n.d.
Afr 5635.8.5 Duchesne, C. Rapport sur l'expedition de Madagascar. Text and atlas. Paris, 1897. 2v.
Afr 5635.10 Lenure, Jean. Madagascar, l'expedition au point de vue medical. Paris, 1896.
Afr 5635.10.5 Verité sur la guerre de Madagascar par le colonel XXX. Toulouse, 1896.
Afr 5635.12F Hocquard, C.E. L'expedition de Madagascar. Paris, 1897.
Afr 5635.13 Burleigh, B. Two campaigns, Madagascar and Ashantee. London, 1896.
Afr 5635.14 Gallieni, J.S. Madagascar, la vie du soldat. Paris, 1905.
Afr 5635.16 Poirier, Jules. Conquete de Madagascar (1895-1896). Paris, 1902.
Afr 5635.17 Darricarrere, J. Au pays de la fièvre. Paris, 1904.
Afr 5635.18 Anthouard, Albert. L'expedition de Madagascar en 1895. Paris, 1930.
Afr 5635.20 Reibell, Emile. Le calvaire de Madagascar. Paris, 1935.
Afr 5635.22 David Bernard, Eugene. La conquête de Madagascar. Paris, 1944.

Afr 5640 Madagascar - History by periods - French colony (1896-1958)

Afr 5640.2 Hellot, F. La pacification de Madagascar. Paris, 1900.
Afr 5640.3 Gravier, G. Madagascar, les Malgaches. Paris, 1904.
Afr 5640.4 Lyautey, L.H.G. Dans le sud de Madagascar. Paris, 1903.
Afr 5640.4.51 Lyautey, L.H.G. Lettres du sud de Madagascar, 1900-1902. Paris, 1935.
Afr 5640.6 Basset, Charles. Madagascar et l'oeuvre du Général Gallieni. Thèse. Paris, 1903.
Afr 5640.7 Charbonneau, Jean. Gallieni à Madagascar. Paris, 1950.
Afr 5640.8 Gheuse, P.B. Gallieni et Madagascar. Paris, 1931.
Afr 5640.9 Lebon, A. La pacification de Madagascar, 1896-98. Paris, 1928.
Afr 5640.10 Peill, J. Social conditions...in Madagascar. n.p., n.d.
Afr 5640.12 Lyautey, Pierre. Gallieni. 6. ed. Paris, 1959.
Afr 5640.14 Ellie, Paul. Le Général Gallieni. Paris, 1900.
Afr 5640.14.5 Gallieni, J.S. Rapport d'ensemble du Général Gallieni sur la situation général de Madagascar. Paris, 1899. 2v.
Afr 5640.14.10 Grandidier, Guillaume. Gallieni. Paris, 1931.
Afr 5640.15 Gallieni, J.S. Neuf ans a Madagascar. Paris, 1908.
Afr 5640.15.5 Gallieni, J.S. Lettres de Madagascar, 1896-1905. Paris, 1928.
Afr 5640.15.10 Esmenard, Jeand D', Vicomte. Gallieni. Paris, 1965.
Afr 5640.15.20 Charbonnel, Henry. De Madagascar à Verdun. Paris, 1962.
Afr 5640.20 Delelee-Desloges, J.G. Madagascar et dependances. Paris, 1931.
Afr 5640.25 Olivier, Marcel. Six ans de politique sociale a Madagascar. Paris, 1931.
Afr 5640.27 Leblond, M. Madagascar, creation française. Paris, 1934.
Afr 5640.30 Rabemananjara, R.W. Madagascar sous la revolution Malgache. Paris, 1953.
Afr 5640.35 Stibbe, Pierre. Justice pour les Malgaches. Paris, 1954.
Afr 5640.40 Boiteau, Pierre. Contribution à l'histoire de la nation Malgache. Paris, 1958.
Afr 5640.45 Rabemananjara, Jacques. Nationalisme et problemes Malgaches. Paris, 1959.

Afr 5645 Madagascar - History by periods - Malagasy Republic (1958-) - General works

Afr 5645.5 France. Embassy. U.S. Madagascar, birth of a new republic. N.Y., 1960.
Afr 5645.10 Datlin, S.V. Malgashskaia respublika. Moscow, 1961.
Afr 5645.11 Korneev, L.A. Obrazovanie Malgashskoi respubliki. Moscow, 1963.
Afr 5645.12 Ordre National de la République Malgache. Le grand livre de l'Ordre national de la République Malgache. Tananarive, 1964.

Afr 5744 - 5750 Madagascar - Geography, description, etc. - General works (By date)

Afr 5746.09 Megiserum, H. Beschreibung...insul Madagascar. Altenburg, 1609.
Afr 5746.38 Morizot, C.B. Relations véritables et curieuses de l'isle de Madagascar. Paris, 1651.
Afr 5746.43 Hamond, W. Madagascar, the richest and most fruitful island in the world. London, 1643.
Afr 5746.50 Chavanon, J. Une ancienne relation sur Madagascar (1650). Paris, 1897.
Afr 5746.61 Flacourt, E. de. Histoire de la grande isle Madagascar. Paris, 1661.
Afr 5746.63 Carpeau du Saussay. Voyage de Madagascar. Paris, 1722.
Afr 5747.31.10 Marcel, G. Memoire inédit de Grossin sur Madagascar. Paris, 1883.
Afr 5747.91 Rochon, A.M. Voyage à Madagascar. Paris, 1791.
Afr 5748.40 Lequevel de Lacombe, B.F. Voyage à Madagascar...Camores (1825-30). Paris, 1840. 2v.

Afr 5744 - 5750 Madagascar - Geography, description, etc. - General works (By date) - cont.

Afr 5748.57.10 Pfeiffer, Ida R. Voyage à Madagascar. Paris, 1881.
NEDL Afr 5748.58 Ellis, William. Three visits to Madagascar during the years 1853-1854-1856. London, 1858.
Afr 5748.59 Ellis, William. Three visits to Madagascar. N.Y., 1859.
Afr 5748.59.3 Ellis, William. Three visits to Madagascar. Philadelphia, 1859.
Afr 5748.61 Pfeiffer, Ida R. Last travels of Ida Pfeiffer. N.Y., 1861.
Afr 5748.63 Dupre, Jules. Trois mois de sejour à Madagascar. Paris, 1863.
Afr 5748.65 Vinson, A. Voyage à Madagascar au couronnement de Radama II. Paris, 1865.
Afr 5748.66 Oliver, S. Pasfield. Madagascar and the Malagasy. London, 1866.
Afr 5748.66.5 Pamphlet vol. Madagascar. Geography. 4 pam.
Afr 5748.67 Ellis, William. Madagascar revisited. London, 1867.
Afr 5748.67.4 Pollen, F.P.L. Een blik in Madagaskar. Leyden, 1867.
Afr 5748.70 Sibree, James. Madagascar and its people. London, 1870.
Afr 5748.70.5 Sibree, James. Madagascar et ses habitants. Toulouse, 1873.
Afr 5748.72 Blanchard, Emile. L'ile de Madagascar. Paris, 1872.
Afr 5748.75 Mullens, J. Twelve months in Madagascar. London, 1875.
Afr 5748.80 Sibree, James. The great African islands. London, 1880.
Afr 5748.81 Lacaze, H. Souvenirs de Madagascar. Paris, 1881.
Afr 5748.83 Audebert, J. Madagaskar und das Hovareich. Berlin, 1883.
Afr 5748.83.5 Cremazy, L. Notes sur Madagascar. Pt.1-3. Paris, 1883-84.
Afr 5748.83.10 Buet, Charles. Madagascar, la reine des iles africaines. Paris, 1883.
Afr 5748.84 Leroy, L. Les Français à Madagascar. Paris, 1884.
Afr 5748.84.5 Little, H. William. Madagascar, its history and people. Edinburgh, 1884.
Afr 5748.84.7 Macquarie, J.L. Voyage à Madagascar. Paris, 1884.
Afr 5748.84.10 Buet, Charles. Six mois à Madagascar. Paris, 1884.
Afr 5748.85 Lavaissiere, C. de. Vingt ans à Madagascar. Paris, 1885.
Afr 5748.85.5F Grandidier, Alfred. Histoire de la geographie. Text and atlas. Paris, 1892. 2v.
Afr 5748.86 Pastel, R. Madagascar. Paris, 1886.
Afr 5748.86.5 Genin, E. Madagascar. Paris, 1886.
Afr 5748.87 Standing, H.F. The children of Madagascar. London, 1887.
Afr 5748.87.5 Duverge. Madagascar et peuplades independantes abandonnées par la France. Paris, 1887.
Afr 5748.87.10 Cortese, Emilio. Sei mesi al Madagascar. Roma, 1888.
Afr 5748.88 Lechartier, H. Madagascar depuis sa decouverte jusqu'a nos jours. Paris, 1888.
Afr 5748.92 Mandat-Grancey, Edmond. Souvenirs de la côte d'Afrique, Madagascar. Paris, 1892.
Afr 5748.94 Martineau, A. Madagascar. Paris, 1894.
Afr 5748.94.5 Pamphlet vol. Madagascar. 2 pam.
Afr 5748.95 Maude, F.C. Five years in Madagascar. London, 1895.
Afr 5748.95.3F Catat, Louis. Voyage à Madagascar (1889-1890). Paris, 1895.
Afr 5748.95.5 Gautier, Emile F. Guide pratique du colon et du soldat à Madagascar. Paris, 1895.
Afr 5748.95.10 Humbert, G. Madagascar. Paris, 1895.
Afr 5748.95.12 Pamphlet vol. Madagascar. 3 pam.
Afr 5748.95.15 Piolet, J.B. Madagascar et les Hova. Paris, 1895.
Afr 5748.95.20 Beylie, Leon De. Itineraire de Majunga à Tananarive. Paris, 1895.
Afr 5748.95.25 Benoit, Felix. Madagascar, étude economique, geographique et ethnographique. Dijon, 1895.
Afr 5748.95.30 Paisant, M. Madagascar. 2e ed. Paris, 1895.
Afr 5748.96 Sibree, J. Madagascar before the conquest. London, 1896.
Afr 5748.96.5 Cazeneuve, M. A la cour de Madagascar. Paris, 1896.
Afr 5748.96.7 Locamus, P. Madagascar et ses richesses. Paris, 1896.
Afr 5748.96.8 Locamus, P. Madagascar et l'alimentation européenne. Paris, 1896.
Afr 5748.96.9 Blavet, Emile. Au pays Malgache de Paris à Tananarive et retour. 2e ed. Paris, 1897.
Afr 5748.96.10 Blavet, Emile. Au pays Malgache. Paris, 1897.
Afr 5748.98 Grosclaude, E. Un Parisien à Madagascar. Paris, 1898.
Afr 5748.98.3 Escande, E. A Madagascar, hier et aujourd'hui. Paris, 1898.
Afr 5748.98.5 Piolet, J.B. Douze leçons à la Sorbonne sur Madagascar. Paris, 1898.
Afr 5748.98.10 Mager, Henri. La vie à Madagascar. Paris, 1898.
Afr 5748.99 Madagascar. Guide de l'immigrant à Madagascar. V.1-3 and plates. Paris, 1899. 4v.
Afr 5749.00F Piolet, J.B. Madagascar. Paris, 1900.
Afr 5749.00.5 Paris. Exposition Universelle (1900). Madagascar. Paris, 1900.
Afr 5749.00.10 Grandidier, G. Voyage dans le sud-ouest. Paris, 1900.
Afr 5749.00.15 Fournier, René. Notice sur Madagascar. Paris, 1900.
Afr 5749.02 Danfreville de la Salle. A Madagascar. Paris, 1902.
Afr 5749.02.5 Madagascar au debut du XXe siècle. Paris, 1902.
Afr 5749.05 You, Andre. Madagascar, histoire, organisation, colonisation. Paris, 1905.
Afr 5749.07 Leblond, M.A. La grande ile de Madagascar. Paris, 1907.
Afr 5749.09 Gallois, E. La France dans l'ocean Indien. Paris, 1909.
Afr 5749.14 Marcuse, W.D. Through western Madagascar in quest of the golden bean. London, 1914.
Afr 5749.15.5 Guilloteaux, E. Madagascar et la côte de Somalie. Paris, 1922.
Afr 5749.16 Galy-Ache, P. Horizons malgaches, de Fort-Dauphin à Andovorante. Paris, 1916.
Afr 5749.22 Dandouau, A. Geographie de Madagascar. Paris, 1922.
Afr 5749.23 Cros, Louis. Madagascar pour tous. Paris, 1923.
Afr 5749.24 Osborn, C.S. Madagascar, land of the man-eating tree. N.Y., 1924.
Afr 5749.28 Camo, Pierre A. Peinture de Madagascar. Paris, 1928.
Afr 5749.28.5 Esmenard, J. L'ile rouge. Paris, 1928.
Afr 5749.29 Dandouau, A. Manuel de geographie de Madagascar. 2e ed. Paris, 1929.
Afr 5749.31 You, André. Madagascar, colonie française, 1896-1930. Paris, 1931.
Afr 5749.31.5 Paris, Pierre. Madagascar. Paris, 1931.
Afr 5749.33 Rusillon, H. Un petit continent, Madagascar. Paris, 1933.
Afr 5749.33.5 Laurence, A. Madagascar. Paris, 1933.
Afr 5749.33.10 Petit, G. Madagascar. Paris, 1933.
Afr 5749.43 Chapman, O.M. Across Madagascar. London, 1942.
Afr 5749.44 Fiedler, Arkady. Zarliwa wispa Beniowskiego. Letchworth, 1944.
Afr 5749.46 Fiedler, Arkady. The Madagascar I love. London, 1946.
Afr 5749.47 Launois, Pierre. Madagascar, hier et aujourd'hui. Paris, 1947.
Afr 5749.47.5 Deschamps, H. Madagascar. Paris, 1947.

Afr 5744 - 5750   Madagascar - Geography, description, etc. - General works
(By date) - cont.

Afr 5749.52	France de l'ocean Indien. Paris, 1952.
Afr 5749.54	Madagascar à travers ses provinces. Paris, 1954.
Afr 5749.55	Bastian, Georges. Madagascar. Tananarive, 1955.
Afr 5749.58F	Robequain, Chas. Madagascar et les bases dispersees de l'union française. Paris, 1958. 2v.
Afr 5749.58.5F	Battistini, R. Population et économie paysanne du Bas-Mangoky. Paris, n.d.
Afr 5749.60	France. Institut Geographique National. Service Geographique a Tananarive. Expose des travaux exécutes en 1959 sur le territoire de la Republique Malgache. Paris, 1960.
Afr 5749.60.5	Dandouau, André. Manuel de geographie de Madagascar. Paris, 1960.
Afr 5749.61	Thiout, Michel. Madagascar et l'ame malgache. Paris, 1961.
Afr 5749.62	Pidoux, Edmond. Madagascar, maître à son bord. Lausanne, 1962.
Afr 5749.62.5	Joubert, Elsa. Suid van die wind. Kaapstad, 1962.
Afr 5749.64	Stratton, A. The great red island. N.Y., 1964.
Afr 5749.64.5	Battestini, René. Etude geomorphologique de l'Extreme Sud de Madagascar. Paris, 1964.
Afr 5749.64.10	Battistini, René. Géographie humaine de la plaine côtière Mahafaly. Thèse. Paris, 1964.
Afr 5749.64.15	Madagascar. Tananarive, 1964.
Afr 5749.65	Thompson, Virginia McLean. The Malagasy Republic. Stanford, 1965.
Afr 5749.65.5	Madagascar. v.1-2. Chambéry (Savoie), 1965-1966.
Afr 5749.66	France. Institut Geographique National. Annexe de Tananarive. Expose des travaux executes en 1965 sur le territoire de la Republique Malgache. Paris, 1966.
Afr 5749.67	Dubrau, Louis (pseud.). Les îles du Capricorne: Maurice, La Réunion, Madagascar. Bruxelles, 1967.

Afr 5753   Madagascar - Geography, description, etc. - Special customs

Afr 5753.3	Andre, C. De l'esclavage à Madagascar. Paris, 1899.
Afr 5753.4	Rusillon, H. Un culte dynast. Avec évocation des morts. Paris, 1912.
Afr 5753.5	Cournot, M. La famille à Madagascar. Angers, 1842.
Afr 5753.7	Mondain, G. Raketaka, tableau de moeurs féminines malgaches dressé à l'aide de proverbes et de Fady. Paris, 1925.
Afr 5753.9	Andoiamanjato, Richard. Le Tsiny et le Tody dans la pensée malgache. Paris, 1957.
Afr 5753.12	Molet, Louis. Le bain royal à Madagascar. Tananarive, 1956.
Afr 5753.15	Ruud, Joergen. Taboo. Oslo, 1960.
Afr 5753.20	Decary, Raymond. Les ordalies et sacrifices rituels chez les Anains Malgaches. Pau, 1959.
Afr 5753.22	Decary, Raymond. La mort et les coutumes funeraires à Madagascar. Paris, 1962.

Afr 5755   Madagascar - Geography, description, etc. - Guidebooks

Afr 5755.2	Madagascar. Camores, Reunion, ile Maurice. Paris, 1955.

Afr 5757   Madagascar - Geography, description, etc. - Maps

Afr 5757.5	Gravier, Gabriel. La cartographie de Madagascar. Rouen, 1896.

Afr 5758   Madagascar - Economic and financial conditions

Afr 5758.1	Guides d'initiation active au développement. Tananarive. 1,1966+
Afr 5758.2	Bonnavoy De Premoti, F.H. Rapport a l'empereur sur la question malgache. Paris, 1856.
Afr 5758.4	Roux, Jules C. Les voies de communication et les moyens de transport à Madagascar. Paris, 1898.
Afr 5758.5	Jully, M.A. Madagascar. Marseille, 1900.
Afr 5758.14	Loisy, F.X. Madagascar, étude économique. Paris, 1914.
Afr 5758.25	Tananarive, 1923, Madagascar économique. Tananarive, 1923.
Afr 5758.25F	Paulin, H. Madagascar. Paris, 1925.
Afr 5758.27	Thorel, Jean. La mise en valeur des richesses économiques de Madagascar. Thèse. Paris, 1927.
Afr 5758.30	Nemours, C.P. Madagascar et ses richesses. Paris, 1930.
Afr 5758.34	Prunieres, A. Madagascar et la crise. Paris, 1934.
Afr 5758.37	Lebel, Charles. La standardisation à Madagascar. Paris, 1937.
Afr 5758.38	Martin, A. Les delegations économiques et financieres de Madagascar. Thèse. Paris, 1938.
Afr 5758.57F	Madagascar. Haut Commissariat. Plan de developpement économique et social, programme, 1958-1962. Tananarive, 1957.
Afr 5758.58	Madagascar. Plan de developpement economique et social. Tananarive. 1947+ 4v.
Afr 5758.60	Italy. Istituto Nazionale per il Commercio Estero. Madagascar. Roma, 1963.
Afr 5758.60.4	Italy. Istituto Nazionale per il Commercio Estero. Madagascar. Roma, 1964-[1965].
Afr 5758.60.5	Gendarme, René. L'économie de Madagascar. Paris, 1960.
Afr 5758.60.10	Malagasy Republic. Commissariat Général au Plan. The economy of Madagascar. Tananarive, 196-.
Afr 5758.61	Madagascar, birth of a new republic. N.Y., 1961.
Afr 5758.63	Ottino, Paul. Les économies paysannes malgaches du Bas Mangoky. Paris, 1963.
Afr 5758.63.3	France. Ministère de la Coopération. Direction des Affaires Economiques et Financières. Sous-Direction des Etudes Générales. Economie et plan de développement. 3. éd. Paris, 1963.
Afr 5758.64F	Madagascar. Commissariat Général au Plan. Plan quinquennal, 1964-1968. Tananarive, 1964.
Afr 5758.66	Sala, G. Les travaux au ras du sol; l'investissement humain à Madagascar. Tananarive, 1966.
Afr 5758.66.5	Clairmonte, Frédéric F. Analysis of the Madagascar Plan, 1964-1968. Addis Ababa, 1966.
Afr 5758.67	Bostian, Georges. Madagascar, étude géographique et économique. Paris, 1967.
Afr 5758.67.5	Paproth, Klaus. Voraussetzungen und Möglichkeiten für Industriegründungen in Madagaskar. Hamburg, 1967.

Afr 5760   Madagascar - Races

Afr 5760.2	Schnackenberg, H. Beitrag zur ethnographie Madagaskars. Strassburg, 1888.
Afr 5760.3	Leclerc, Max. Les peuplades de Madagascar. Paris, 1887.
Afr 5760.5F	Grandidier, A. L'origine des Malgaches. Paris, 1901.
Afr 5760.6	Carol, Jean. Chez les Hovas (au pays rouge). Paris, 1898.
Afr 5760.6.2	Carol, Jean. Chez les Hovas (au pays rouge). 2e ed. Paris, 1898.

Afr 5760   Madagascar - Races - cont.

Afr 5760.7	Cailliet, E. Essai sur la psychologie du Hovas. Thèse. Paris, 1926.
Afr 5760.10	Besson, L. Voyage au pays des Tanala indépendants. n.p., n.d.
Afr 5760.11	Mondain, C. L'histoire des tribus de l'Imoro au XVIIe siècle. Paris, 1910.
Afr 5760.12F	Grandidier, Alfred. Ethnographie de Madagascar. v.1-4. Paris, 1908-1928. 4v.
Afr 5760.14	Molet, Louis. Demographie de l'Ankaizinana. Paris, 1955.
Afr 5760.16	Peuple malgache. Monographies ethnologiques. Paris. 1,1959+
Afr 5760.18	Deschamps, H.J. Les migrations. Paris, 1959.
Afr 5760.20	Vianes, S. Contribution à l'étude des migrations antesaka. Paris, 1959.

Afr 5765   Madagascar - Religion - General works, Christian missions

Afr 5765.1	Missionary reviews. Antananarivo, 1871-80. 4 pam.
Afr 5765.2	Freeman, J.J. A narrative of the persecution of the Christians in Madagascar. London, 1840.
Afr 5765.2.10	Griffiths, D. The persecuted Christians of Madagascar. London, 1841.
Afr 5765.3	Ellis, John E. Life of William Ellis, missionary. London, 1873.
Afr 5765.3.5	Ellis, William. Faithful unto death. London, 1876.
Afr 5765.4.2	Madagascar, its missions and its martyrs. London, 1863.
Afr 5765.5	Ellis, William. The martyr church. Boston, 1870.
Afr 5765.5.2	Ellis, William. The martyr church...Christianity in Madagascar. London, n.d.
Afr 5765.5.10	Gospel in Madagascar. London, 1863.
Afr 5765.6	Bianquis, J. L'oeuvre des missions protestantes à Madagascar. Paris, 1907.
Afr 5765.6.10	Escande, Benjamin. Neuf mois à Madagascar. Paris, 1898.
Afr 5765.7	Malotet, A. Saint Vincent de Paul et les missions de Madagascar. Paris, 1900.
Afr 5765.7.5	Histoire de la mission fondée à Madagascar par Saint Vincent de Paul. Paris, 1895.
Afr 5765.7.10	Congregation of Priests of the Mission. Memoires. v.9. Paris, 1866.
Afr 5765.7.20	Maupoint, A.R. Madagascar et ses deux premiers évêques. v.1-2. 3. ed. Paris, 1864.
Afr 5765.7.25	Lamaigniere. Le R.P. Barbe de la compagnie de Jesus. Poitiers, 1885.
Afr 5765.8	Cameron, James. Recollections of mission life in Madagascar. Antananarivo, 1874.
Afr 5765.8.5	Jordaan, Bee. Splintered cruicifix; early pioneers for Christendom on Madagascar and the Cape of Good Hope. Cape Town, 1969.
Afr 5765.9	Matthews, T.T. Notes of nine years mission work in the province of Vonizongo, N.W., Madagascar. London, 1881.
Afr 5765.10	Colin, E. Madagascar et la mission catholique. Paris, 1895.
Afr 5765.11	Richardson, James. Lights and shadows. Antananarivo, 1877.
Afr 5765.12	London Missionary Society. Ten years review of mission work in Madagascar, 1870-80. Antananarivo, 1880.
Afr 5765.13	Townsend, William J. Madagascar, its missionaries and martyrs. 2d ed. London, 1892.
Afr 5765.15	Sibree, James. Fifty years in Madagascar. London, 1924.
Afr 5765.15.5	Sibree, James. Madagascar, country, people, missions. London, 1880.
X Cg Afr 5765.16	Pamphlet vol. Madagascar. (Changed to XP 3993) 7 pam.
Afr 5765.17	Keck, Daniel. Histoire des origines du christianisme à Madagascar. Thèse. Paris, 1898.
Afr 5765.20	Derville, Leon. Ils ne sont que quarante...les jésuites chez les Betsileos. Paris, 1931.
Afr 5765.20.5	Mission de Madagascar betsileo. Lille, 1925.
Afr 5765.22	Mondain, G. Un siècle de mission protestante à Madagascar. Paris, 1920.
Afr 5765.24	Lhande, P. Madagascar, 1832-1932. Paris, 1932.
Afr 5765.26	Goyau, G. Les grands desseins missionnaires d'Henri de Solages (1786-1832). Paris, 1933.
Afr 5765.28	Gale, William K. Church planting in Madagascar. London, 1937.
Afr 5765.30	Boudou, Adrien. Les Jesuites à Madagascar au XIXe siècle. v.1-2. Paris, 1940. 2v.
Afr 5765.31	Dailliez, André. A la découverte d'un diocèse Malgache, Fianarantsoa. Bar-le-Duc, 1966.
Afr 5765.32	McMahon, Edward Oliver. Christian missions in Madagascar. Westminster, 1914.
Afr 5765.34	Malagasy. Republic Service des Archives et de la Documentation. Fampisehaana. Fampisehaana. Tananarive, 1964.
Afr 5765.36	Doncaster, Phebe. Faithful unto death;...life...of William and Lucy S. Johnson. London, 1896.

Afr 5767   Madagascar - Religion - Islam in Madagascar

Afr 5767.2	Ferrand, G. Les Musulmans à Madagascar. v.1-3. Paris, 1891-1902. 2v.

Afr 5780   Madagascar - Cities, towns, etc. - General

Afr 5780.5	Decary, Raymond. L'Androy, extrem sud de Madagascar. Paris, 1933. 2v.
Afr 5780.88	Deschamps, N. Les Antaisaka. Thèse. Tananarivé, 1936. 2 pam.

Afr 5781   Madagascar - Cities, towns, etc. - Tamatave

Afr 5781.5	Pooka. Cinq jours à Tamatave. Maurice, 1888.

Afr 5783   Madagascar - Cities, towns, etc. - Tananarive

Afr 5783.5	Madagascar. Tananarive. Tananarive, 1952.

Afr 5787   Madagascar - Cities, towns, etc. - Others

Afr 5787.5	Lavondes, Henri. Problemes humains dans la region de la Sakay. Tananarive, 1961.
Afr 5787.5.5	Lavondes, Henri. Bekoropoka quelques aspects de la vie familiale et sociale d'un village Malgache. Paris, 1967.
Afr 5787.6	Trouchaud, J.P. La basse plaine du Mangoky. Paris, 1965.

Afr 5792   Islands near Madagascar - Sainte Marie

Afr 5792.2	Valette, Jean. Sainte-Marie et la côte est de Madagascar en 1818. Tananarive, 1962.
Afr 5792.3	Decary, Raymond. L'établissement de Sainte-Marie de Madagascar. Paris, 1937.

Afr 5794 Islands near Madagascar - Nosi Be
Afr 5794.5 Decary, Raymond. L'ile Nosy-Bé de Madagascar. Paris, 1960.
Afr 5794.6 Deblenne, Paul. Essai de géographie medicale de Nosi-Bé. Thèse. Paris, 1883.

Afr 5796 Islands near Madagascar - Comoro Islands - General
Afr 5796.5 Gevrey, Alfred. Essai sur les Comores. Pondichery, 1870.
Afr 5796.5.5 Vienne, Emile. Notice sur Mayotte et les Comores. Paris, 1900.
Afr 5796.5.10 Gorse, Jean. Territoire des Comores; bibliographie. Paris, 1964?

Afr 5798 Islands near Madagascar - Comoro Islands - Special islands
Afr 5798.5 A letter from a gentleman giving an account of Joanna. London, 1789.

Afr 5805 Mascarenes in general - General history
Afr 5805.5 Toussaint, Auguste. La Route des îles, coutribution à l'histoire maritime des Mascareignes. Paris, 1967.

Afr 5806.1 - .99 Mascarenes in general - History by periods - Before 1800
Afr 5806.5 Visdelou-Guimbeau, G. La découverte des Iles Mascareignes par les Portugais. N.Y., 1940.

Afr 5810 Mauritius; Isle de France - Periodicals
NEDL Afr 5810.5 Revue historique et litteraire de l'ile Maurice. Archives coloniales. Port-Louis. 1,1887+ 6v.
NEDL Afr 5810.6 Revue historique et litteraire de l'ile Maurice. Variétés et romans. Port Louis. 1,1887+ 6v.
Afr 5810.12 Mauritius register. Mauritius, 1859.

Afr 5813 Mauritius; Isle de France - Bibliographies
Afr 5813.5 Toussaint, Auguste. Select bibliography of Mauritius. Port Louis, 1951.
Afr 5813.10 Mauritius. Archives Department. Bibliography of Mauritius. Port Louis, 1956.
Afr 5813.12 Toussaint, Auguste. Répertoire des archives de l'Ile de France. Nerac, 1956.
Afr 5813.12.5 Toussaint, Auguste. L'administration française de l'île Maurice et ses archives, 1721-1810. Fort Luis, 1965.
Afr 5813.14 Hahn, Lorna. Mauritius; a study and annotated bibliography. Washington, 1969.

Afr 5815 Mauritius; Isle de France - Pamphlet volumes
Afr 5815.1 Pamphlet box. Mauritius.
Afr 5815.2F Mauritius. Letters, patent, 1879-1894. n.p., n.d.

Afr 5817 Mauritius; Isle de France - Collected source materials
Afr 5817.5 Great Britain. Colonial Office. Report on Mauritius. 1946+ 5v.

Afr 5820 Mauritius; Isle de France - Government and administration
Afr 5820.15 Mauritius. Mauritius, Mr. Jeremie's case. London, 1834.

Afr 5824 - 5830 Mauritius; Isle de France - General history (By date)
Afr 5828.01 Grant, Charles. The history of Mauritius. London, 1801.
Afr 5829.08.5 Herve de Rauville. L'Ile de France contemporaine. Paris, 1908.
Afr 5829.10 Deburgh Edwardes, S.B. L'histoire de l'ile Maurice d'après les documents les plus authentiques, 1507-1895. Paris, 1910.
Afr 5829.10.7 Deburgh Edwardes, S.B. The history of Mauritius (1507-1914). London, 1921.
Afr 5829.49 Unienville, N. L'ile Maurice et sa civilisation. Paris, 1949.
Afr 5829.49.5 Barnwell, P.J. A short history of Mauritius. London, 1949.
Afr 5829.58 Babaju, Esno. A concise history of Mauritius. Bombay, 1958.
Afr 5829.65 Rassool, S. Hassam A. Il Maurice; creuset de l'Ocean Indien. Paris, 1965.

Afr 5832 Mauritius; Isle de France - History by periods - To 1800
Afr 5832.3 Bonaparte, R. Le premier établissement des Neerlandais à Maurice. Paris, 1890.
Afr 5832.5 Grant, Charles. Letters from Mauritius in 18th century. Mauritius, 1886
Afr 5832.5.5 Roubaud, L. La Bourdonnais. Paris, 1932.
Afr 5832.7 Epinay, A.D. Renseignements pour servir l'histoire de l'Ile de France jusqu'à l'année 1810. Ile Maurice, 1890.
Afr 5832.9 Averbeck, Franz. Geschichte und Physiographie der Kolonie Mauritius. Metz, 1905.
Afr 5832.10 Pitot, Albert. L'Ile de France. Port-Louis, 1899.
Afr 5832.10.3 Pitot, Albert. T'eylandt Mauritius. Port-Louis, 1905.
Afr 5832.10.5 Pitot, Albert. L'ile de Maurice. V.1-2. Port-Louis, 1910-12.
Afr 5832.12 Ly-Tio-Fane, Madeleine. Mauritius and the spice trade. Port Louis, 1958. 2v.
Afr 5832.15.2F Austen, H.C.M. Sea fights and corsairs of the Indian Ocean. Port Louis, 1935.

Afr 5833 Mauritius; Isle de France - History by periods - 1800-1900
Afr 5833.1 Huet de Froberville, B. Ephemerides mauriciennes, 1827-1834. Port Louis, 1906.
Afr 5833.2 Prentout, H. L'Ile de France sous Decaen. Paris, 1901.
Afr 5833.4 Archer, Edward. A letterTo the right honourable Lord John Russell. London, 1840.

Afr 5840 Mauritius; Isle de France - Religion; missions
Afr 5840.10 Anderson, J.F. Esquisse de l'histoire du protestantisme à l'Ile Mauurice et aux Iles Mascarègnes, 1505 à 1902. Paris, 1903.
Afr 5840.15 Chassagnon, H., Abbé. Le frère Scubilion de l'Institut des frères des écoles chrétiennes. Paris, 1902.
Afr 5840.20 Lagesse, Lois. Le père Laval. Port-Louis, 1955.

Afr 5842 Mauritius; Isle de France - Geography, description, etc.
Afr 5842.2 Leclercq, J. Au pays de Paul et Virginie. Paris, 1895.
Afr 5842.4 Saint-Pierre, J.H.B. de. Voyage à l'Isle de France. Amsterdam, 1773. 2v.
Afr 5842.4.5 Saint-Pierre, J.H.B. de. Viaggi al Madagascar, alle isole Comore ed allIsola di Francia. Prato, 1844.
Afr 5842.6 Pike, N. Sub-tropical rambles. London, 1873.
Afr 5842.8 Account of the island of Mauritius. London, 1842.
Afr 5842.9 Billiard, A. Voyage aux colonies orientales. Paris, 1822.

Afr 5842 Mauritius; Isle de France - Geography, description, etc. - cont.
Afr 5842.10 Beaton, P. Creoles and coolies. London, 1859.
Afr 5842.11F Bradshaw, T. Views in the Mauritius, or Isle of France. London, 1832.
Afr 5842.12 Stirling, E. Cursory notes on the Isle of France. Calcutta, 1833.
Afr 5842.14 Boyle, C.J. Far away, scenery and society in Mauritius. London, 1867.
Afr 5842.16.2 Anderson, John. Descriptive account of Mauritius. Mauritius, 1858.
Afr 5842.18 Herve de Rauville. L'Ile de France légendaire. Paris, 1889.
Afr 5842.19 Great Britain. Central Office of Information. Mauritius and Seychelles. N.Y., 1964.
Afr 5842.20 Titmuss, R.M. Social policies and population growth in Mauritius. London, 1961.
Afr 5842.22 Benedict, Burton. Mauritius. London, 1965.
Afr 5842.24 Bartram, Alfred, Lady. Recollections of seven years' residence at the Mauritius. London, 1830.
Afr 5842.26 Bissoondoyal, Basdeo. The truth about Mauritius. 1. ed. Bombay, 1968.

Afr 5843 Mauritius; Isle de France - Economic and financial conditions
Afr 5843.2 Meade, James E. The economic and social structure of Mauritius. London, 1961.
Afr 5843.5 Mauritius. Ministry of Industry. Commerce and industry in Mauritius. Port Louis, 1964.
Afr 5843.6 Mauritius. Commission of Enquiry into the Disturbances Which Occurred in the North of Mauritius in 1943. Report. London, 1943.

Afr 5844 Mauritius; Isle de France - Races
Afr 5844.2 Benedict, B. Indians in a plural society. London, 1961.
Afr 5844.5 Mukherji, S.B. The indenture system in Mauritius, 1837-1915. 1. ed. Calcutta, 1962.

Afr 5845 Mauritius; Isle de France - Special customs
Afr 5845.5 Gay, Francois. Ile Maurice, régulation des naissances et action familiale. Lyon, 1968.

Afr 5846 Mauritius; Isle de France - Local Mauritius
Afr 5846.2 Great Britain. Imperial Shipping Commission. Report on the harbour of Port Louis. London, 1931.
Afr 5846.3 Toussaint, Auguste. Port-Louis, deux siècles d'histoire, 1735-1935. Port-Louis, 1936.
Afr 5846.3.5 Toussaint, Auguste. Une cite tropicale, Port-Louis de L'île Maurice. Paris, 1966.

Afr 5847 Mauritius; Isle de France - Dependencies of Mauritius collectively
Afr 5847.5 Scott, Robert. Limuria, the lesser dependencies of Mauritius. London, 1961.

Afr 5849.1 - .99 Mauritius; Isle de France - Biographies - Collected (A-Z, 99 scheme, by author)
Afr 5849.2 Hollingworth, Derek. They came to Mauritius. London, 1965.
Afr 5849.82 Société de l'Histoire de l'Ile Maurice. Dictionnaire de biographie mauricienne. Dictionary of Mauritian biography. v.1-30- Saint Louis, 1941- 5v.

Afr 5853 Réunion - Bibliographies
Afr 5853.2 Réunion. Archives Departementales. Documents concernant les iles de Bourbon et de France. Nerac, 1953.

Afr 5857 Réunion - Collected source materials
Afr 5857.2 Lougnon, Albert. Classement et inventaire du fonds de la Compagnie des Indes des archives. Thèse. Nerac, 1956.
Afr 5857.5 Réunion. Archives Départementales. Recueil de documents et travaux inédits pour servir à l'histoire de la Réunion. Nerac. 1,1954+ 3v.
Afr 5857.10 Réunion. Archives Departementales. Classement et inventaire du fonds de la Compagnie des Indes (Série C.), 1665-1767. Nerac, 1956.
Afr 5857.15 Réunion. Archives Départementales. Répertoire numérique de la série L; Révolution, Empire, régime anglais, 1789-1815. Nérac, 1954.
Afr 5857.20 Réunion. Archives Départementales. Répertoire des registres paroissiaux et d'état civil antérieurs à 1849. Nérac, 1963.

Afr 5860 Réunion - Government and administration
Afr 5860.15 Cornu, Henri. Une expérience législative à la Réunion. Thèse. Paris, 1935.

Afr 5864 - 5870 Réunion - General history (By date)
Afr 5868.59 Azema, Georges. Histoire de l'Ile Bourbon depuis 1643 jusqu'au 20 décembre 1848. Paris, 1859.
Afr 5868.59.5 Azema, Georges. Histoire de l'Ile Bourbon depuis 1643 jusqu'au 20 décembre 1848. Paris, 1859.
Afr 5868.81 Crestien, G.F. Causeries historiques. Paris, 1881.
Afr 5868.87 Pajot, Elie. Simples renseignements sur l'Ile Bourbon. Paris, 1887.
Afr 5869.23 Foucque, Hippolyte. L'Ile de la Réunion. Paris, 1923.
Afr 5869.54 Souris, Eugène. Histoire abrégée de l'Ile de la Réunion. Saint-Denis, 1954.
Afr 5869.65 Scherer, André. Histoire de la Réunion. Paris, 1965.
Afr 5869.67 Prosset, Alfred. Les Premiers colons de l'Ile Bourbon. 2. ed. Paris, n.d.

Afr 5871 Réunion - History by periods - Before 1700
Afr 5871.53 Barassin, Jean. Naissance d'une chrétienté. Saint-Denis, 1953.

Afr 5872 Réunion - History by periods - 1700-
Afr 5872.5 Trouette, E. L'Ile Bourbon de 1789 à 1803. Paris, 1888.
Afr 5872.7 Réunion. Conseil Supérieur. Correspondance du conseil supérieur de Bourbon et de la Compagnie des Indes...1724-1741. V.1-3. Saint-Denis, 1934-37. 4v.
Afr 5872.10 Freon, L.S. Un ardennais conseiller du roi. Verviers, 1953.
Afr 5872.12 Lougnon, Albert. L'Ile Bourbon pendant la régence. Paris, 1956.

Afr 5874   **Réunion - Geography, description, etc.**
Afr 5874.5   Gassault, A.G. Notice sur la Réunion. Paris, 1900.
Afr 5874.7   Jacob de Cordemoy, H. Etude sur l'Ile de la Réunion.
                    Marseille, 1904.
Afr 5874.8   Mahy, F. de. Autour de l'Ile Bourbon et de Madagascar.
                    Paris, 1891.
Afr 5874.9   Textor de Rairsi. Etudes sur...des palmistes....l'Ile de
                    la Réunion. Saint-Denis, 1848.
Afr 5874.10   Dubois. Voyages made to Dauphine and Bourbon.
                    London, 1897.
Afr 5874.10.5   Dubois. Les voyages faits...aux isles Dauphine ou
                    Madagascar. Paris, 1674.
Afr 5874.11   Compagnie des Indes Orientales. Isle de Bourbon (Réunion);
                    documents, 1701-1710. N.Y., 1909.
Afr 5874.12   Beaton, P. Six months in Réunion. London, 1860. 2v.
Afr 5874.15   Lebband, M. Ile de la Réunion...côte française des
                    Oumolis. Paris, 1931.
Afr 5874.16   Leblond, Marius. Les îles soeurs ou Le paradis retrouvé.
                    Paris, 1946.
Afr 5874.18   Defos du Rau, J. L'Ile de la Réunion. Bordeaux, 1960.
Afr 5874.19   Vailland, Roger. La Réunion. Lausanne, 1964.
Afr 5874.20   Besant, Walter. Bourbon journal, August, 1863.
                    London, 1933.
Afr 5874.21   Ravat, Yves. La Réunion, terre française. Port
                    Louis, 1967.
Afr 5874.22   Leloutre, Jean Claude. La Réunion, departement français.
                    Paris, 1968.

Afr 5876   **Réunion - Local**
Afr 5876.1   Macauliffe, J.M. Ile de la Réunion, Cilaos. Saint
                    Denis, 1902.

Afr 5887   **Rodriguez - Geography, description, etc.**
Afr 5887.5   Leguat, F. Voyages et aventures de François Leguat et de
                    ses compagnons en deux îles désertes 1690-1698.
                    Paris, 1934.

Afr 5890   **Seychelles - Periodicals**
Afr 5890.5   Seychelles Society. Journal. Victoria. 5,1966+

Afr 5892   **Seychelles - Pamphlet volumes**
Afr 5892.2   Pamphlet volume. Seychelles Peoples' United Party. 3 pam.
Afr 5892.5   Seychelles. A plan for Seychelles. Victoria, 1960? 5 pam.

Afr 5893   **Seychelles - Collected source materials**
Afr 5893.10   Great Britain. Colonial Office. Report on Seychelles.
                    1946+ 2v.
Afr 5893.15   Seychelles annual. Victoria.

Afr 5895   **Seychelles - General history**
Afr 5895.5.2   Benedict, Burton. People of the Seychelles. 2nd ed.
                    London, 1968.

Afr 5897   **Seychelles - Geography, description, travel, etc.**
Afr 5897.2   Barkly, Fanny Alexandra. From the tropics to the North
                    Sea. London, 1897.
Afr 5897.5   Thomas, Athol. Forgotten Eden. London, 1968.

Afr 5900   **Spanish Africa in general - Periodicals**
Afr 5900.5   Rumeu de Armas, Antonio. España en el Africa atlantica.
                    V.1-2. Madrid, 1956-57.

Afr 5903   **Spanish Africa in general - Pamphlet volumes**
Afr 5903.1   Pamphlet box. Spanish Africa.
Afr 5903.5   Spain. Curso de conferencias sobre la politica africana de
                    los reyes catolicos. V.1-6. Madrid, 1951-53. 3v.

Afr 5905   **Spanish Africa in general - Collected source materials**
Afr 5905.5   Spain. Dirección General de Plazas y Provincias Africanas.
                    Resumen estadistico de Africa española. 1947+ 2v.

Afr 5907   **Spanish Africa in general - Government and administration**
Afr 5907.5F   Spain. Ministerio de Estado. Memoria que presenta a las
                    cortes...posesiones españolas del Africa occidental.
                    Madrid. 1902+
Afr 5907.5   Spain. Ministerio de Estado. Memoria que presenta a las
                    cortes...posesiones españolas del Africa occidental.
                    Madrid. 1910+
Afr 5907.6F   Spain. Comisario Regio en las Posesiones Españoles del
                    Africa Occidental. Memoria. Madrid. 1907+

Afr 5912   **Spanish Africa in general - General history**
Afr 5912.2   Gonzalez Jimenez, E. Territorios del sur de Marruecos y
                    Sahara occidental. Toledo, 1930.
Afr 5912.3   Otto, Archduke of Austria. Européens et Africains.
                    Paris, 1963.
Afr 5912.5   Pelissier, René. Los territorios españoles de Africa.
                    Madrid, 1964.

Afr 5915   **Spanish Africa in general - History by periods - Before 1800**
Afr 5915.5   Prieto y Llovera, P. Politica aragonesa en Africa hasta la
                    muerte de Fernando el Catolico. Madrid, 1952.

Afr 5920   **Spanish Africa in general - Geography, description, etc.**
Afr 5920.1.3   Iradier, Manuel. Africa. Madrid, 1878.
Afr 5920.1.5   Iradier, Manuel. Africa. Vitoria, 1887. 2v.
Afr 5920.1.15   Cordero Torres, J.M. Iradier. Madrid, 1944.
Afr 5920.2   Iradier, Manuel. Africa, viajes y trabajos de la
                    asociación. Bilbao, 1901. 2v.
Afr 5920.3   Navarro, J.J. Apuntes sobre el estado de la costa
                    occidental. Madrid, 1859.
Afr 5920.4   Saavedra y Magdalena, D. España en el Africa occidental.
                    Madrid, 1910.
Afr 5920.5   Posesiones españolas en el Africa occidental.
                    Madrid, 1900.
Afr 5920.6   Moros y Morellon, J. de. Memorias sobre las islas
                    africanas de España. Madrid, 1844.
Afr 5920.7   Rio Joan, F. del. Africa occidental española.
                    Madrid, 1915.
Afr 5920.7.3   Rio Joan, F. del. Atlas icono-geografico-estadistico del
                    Africa occidental española. Madrid, 1915.
Afr 5920.9   Dalmonte, Enrique. Ensayo de una breve descripción del
                    Sahara. Madrid, 1914.
Afr 5920.11   Arambilet, S. Posesiones españolas del Africa occidental.
                    Madrid, 1903.

Afr 5920   **Spanish Africa in general - Geography, description, etc. - cont.**
Afr 5920.12   Spain. Consejo Superior de Investigaciones Científicas.
                    Instituto de Estudios Africanos. Manuales del Africa
                    española. Madrid, 1955- 2v.
Afr 5920.13   Ortega Canadell, Rosa. Provincias africanas espanolas.
                    1.ed. Barcelona, 1962.
Afr 5920.14   Diaz de Villegas, José. Africa septentrional: Marruecos,
                    el nexo del Estrecho. Madrid, 1961.

Afr 5921   **Spanish Africa in general - Economic and financial conditions**
Afr 5921.64   Spain. Servicio Informativo Español. España en el Africa
                    ecuatorial. Madrid, 1964.

Afr 5924.101 - .399   **Spanish Africa in general - Biographies - Individual**
(A-Z, 299 scheme, by person)
Afr 5924.240   Spain. Consejo Superior de Investigaciones. Iradier.
                    Madrid, 1956.

Afr 5933   **Rio de Oro - Government and administration**
Afr 5933.2   Yanguas Mirarete, José. Antecedentes históricos. Sidi
                    Infi, 1960.

Afr 5944   **Rio de Oro - Geography, description, etc.**
Afr 5944.5   Lodwick, John. The forbidden coast. London, 1956.
Afr 5944.10   Carnero Ruiz, Ismael. Vocabulario geográfico-saharico.
                    Madrid, 1955.
Afr 5944.15   Domenech Lafuente, A. Algo sobre Rio de Oro.
                    Madrid, 1946.
Afr 5944.20   Hernandez-Pacheco, Francisco. El Sahara español.
                    Madrid, 1962.
Afr 5944.22   Spain. Consejo Superior de Investigaciones Cientificas.
                    Instituto de Estudios Africancos. Sahara, provincia
                    española. Madrid, 1966.
Afr 5944.24   España en el Sahara. Madrid, 1968.

Afr 5947   **Rio de Oro - Local**
Afr 5947.10   Coll, A. Villa-cisneros. Madrid, 1933.

Afr 5949   **Ifni**
Afr 5949.5   Monteil, Vincent. Notes sur Ifni et les Ait Ba-e Amran.
                    Paris, 1948.

Afr 5950   **Spanish Guinea - Periodicals**
Afr 5950.5   La Guinea Ecuatorial. Santa Isabel. 1621,1968+

Afr 5953   **Spanish Guinea - Government and administration**
Afr 5953.2   Spain. Consejo Superior de Investigaciones Cientificas. La
                    Guinea ecuatorial y su regimen de Autonomia. Madrid, 1964.

Afr 5955   **Spanish Guinea - General history**
Afr 5955.2   Moreno Moreno, José A. Reseña histórica de la presencia de
                    España en el Golfo de Guinea. Madrid, 1952.
Afr 5955.4   Bravo Carbonell, J. Territorios españoles del Golfo de
                    Guinea. Madrid, 1929.
Afr 5955.5   Madrid, F. La Guinea incognita. Madrid, 1933.

Afr 5957.100 - .299   **Spanish Guinea - History by periods - 1800-1900**
Afr 5957.105   Cervera Pery, José. La marina española en Guinea
                    Ecuatorial, sentido y grandeza de una aportacion historica.
                    Santa Isabel, 1968.

Afr 5960   **Spanish Guinea - Geography, description, etc.**
Afr 5960.2   Bravo Carbonell, J. Fernando Poo y el Muni. Madrid, 1917.
Afr 5960.2.5   Bravo Carbonell, J. En la selva virgen del Muni.
                    Madrid, 1925.
Afr 5960.4   Barrera y Luyando. Lo que son y lo que deben ser las
                    posesiones. Madrid, 1907.
Afr 5960.6   Sorela, Luis. Les possessions espagñoles du Golfe de
                    Guinée, leur présent et leur avenir. Paris, 1884.
Afr 5960.8   Najera y Angulo. La Guinea española y su riqueza forestal.
                    Madrid, 1930.
Afr 5960.9   Rios, Mateos. La Guinea ignorada. Barcelona, 1959.
Afr 5960.10   Ramos Izquierdo Y Vivar, L. Descripción geografica y
                    gobierno. Madrid, 1912.
Afr 5960.12   Bonelli Rubio, J.M. Notas sobra la geográfica humana.
                    Madrid, 1944-45.
Afr 5960.13   Beltran y Rozpide, Ricardo. La Guinea española.
                    Barcelona, 1901.
Afr 5960.14   Miranda, Agustin. Cartas de la Guinea. Madrid, 1940.

Afr 5962   **Spanish Guinea - Economic conditions**
Afr 5962.2   Banciella y Barcena, José Cesar. Rutas de imperio.
                    Madrid, 1940.
Afr 5962.4   Perpina Grau, Ramon. De colonización y economia en la
                    Guinea española. Barcelona, 1945.
Afr 5962.6   Arija, Julio. La Guinea española y sus riquezas.
                    Madrid, 1930.
Afr 5962.8   Clairmonte, Frédéric F. Analysis of Spanish Equatorial
                    Guinea Plan, 1964-1967. Addis Ababa, 1966.

Afr 5967   **Spanish Guinea - Religion; missions**
Afr 5967.2   Veciana Vilaldach, Antonio de. La secta del Bwiti en la
                    Guinea española. Madrid, 1958.

Afr 5968   **Spanish Guinea - Races**
Afr 5968.2   Veciana Vilaldach, Antonio de. Los Bujeba. Madrid, 1956.

Afr 5969.1 - .99   **Spanish Guinea - Biographies - Collected (A-Z, 99**
scheme, by author)
Afr 5969.8   Guinea Lopez, Emilio. En el pais de los Bubis.
                    Madrid, 1949.

Afr 5969.100 - .899   **Spanish Guinea - Biographies - Individual (A-Z, 800**
scheme, by person)
Afr 5969.157   Cencillo de Pineda, Manuel. El brigadier Conde de
                    Argelejo. Madrid, 1948.
Afr 5969.462   Majo Framis, R. Las generosas y primitivas empresas de
                    Manuel Iradier Bulfy en la Guinea española. Madrid, 1954.

Afr 5973   **Spanish Guinea - Local - Muni or Rio Muni (Mainland) - Geography,**
economic conditions, religion, etc.
Afr 5973.2   Granador, Gregorio. España en el Muni. Madrid, 1907.

Afr 5992 Spanish Guinea - Local - Fernando Po - History

Afr 5992.2 Usera y Alarcon, Gerónimo M. Observaciones al Llamado Opusculo. Madrid, 1852.
Afr 5992.4 Guillermar de Aragon, Adolfo. Opusculo sobre la colonización de Fernando Poo. Madrid, 1852.

Afr 5993 Spanish Guinea - Local - Fernando Po - Geography, economic conditions, religion, etc.

Afr 5993.2 Coll, Armengol. Segunda memoria de las misiones. Madrid, 1899.
Afr 5993.6 Janikowski, L. L'île de Fernando Poo. Paris, 1886.
Afr 5993.8 Ferrer Piera, P. Fernando Poo y sus dependencias. Barcelona, 1900.
Afr 5993.10 Williamson, David. A true narrative of the sufferings of David Williamson. London, 1771.
Afr 5993.12 Baumann, O. Eine afrikanische Tropeninsel. Wien, 1888.
Afr 5993.14 San Javier. Tres años en Fernando Poo. Madrid, 1875.
Afr 5993.15 Usera y Alarcon, Gerónimo M. Memoria de la isla de Fernando Poo. Madrid, 1848.
Afr 5993.16 Martinez y Sanz, M. Breves apuntes sobre la isla de Fernando Poo en el Golfo de Guinea. Madrid, 1859.
Afr 5993.17 Jeran, Manuel de. Sintesis geografica de Fernando Poo. Madrid, 1962.
Afr 5993.20 Ceruti, Frorencio. Africa la virgen. Santander, 1928.

Afr 6003 British Africa in general - Bibliographies

Afr 6003.5 National Book League, London. Commonwealth in Africa. London, 1969.

Afr 6010 British Africa in general - Government and administration

Afr 6010.3 Hailey, William Malcolm H. Native administration and political development in British tropical Africa. London, 1944.
Afr 6010.5 Stigand, C.H. Administration in tropical Africa. London, 1914.
Afr 6010.10 Lugard, F.D. The dual mandate in British Tropical Africa. 2d ed. Edinburgh, 1923.
Afr 6010.10.1 Lugard, F.D. The dual mandate in British Tropical Africa. 5th ed. Hamden, Conn., 1965.
Afr 6010.10.2 Lugard, F.D. The dual mandate in British Tropical Africa. 5th ed. London, 1965.
Afr 6010.13 Padmore, George. How Britain rules Africa. London, 1936.
Afr 6010.14 Akpan, N.U. Epitaph to indirect rule. London, 1956.
Afr 6010.16 Carter, G.M. Transition in Africa. Boston, 1958.
Afr 6010.20 Gower, Laurence Cecil Bartlett. Independent Africa. Cambridge, 1967.
Afr 6010.22 Adu, Amishadai Lawson. The civil service in Commonwealth Africa. London, 1969.

Afr 6014 - 6020 British Africa in general - General history (By date)

Afr 6018.98 Vandeleur, S. Campaigning on the upper Nile. London, 1898.
Afr 6019.29 Evans, Ifor Leslie. British in tropical Africa. Cambridge, Eng., 1929.
Afr 6019.38 Batten, T.R. Tropical Africa in world history. London, 1938. 4v.
Afr 6019.41 Perham, Margery. Africans and British rule. London, 1941.
Afr 6019.46 Kam, Josephine. African challenge, story of the British in tropical Africa. London, 1946.
Afr 6019.54 Legum, Colin. Must we lose Africa. London, 1954.
Afr 6019.60 Rothchild, Donald. Toward unity in Africa. Washington, 1960.

Afr 6025 British Africa in general - General special

Afr 6025.2 Pollet, Maurice. L'Afrique du Commonwealth. Paris, 1963.
Afr 6025.5 Mazrui, Ali Al'Amin. The Anglo-African Commonwealth. 1st ed. Oxford, 1967.

Afr 6034 British Africa in general - History by periods - 1900-1960

Afr 6034.2 Perham, Margery Freda. Colonial sequence, 1930 to 1949. London, 1967.

Afr 6048 British Africa in general - Races

Afr 6048.2 Broomfield, Gerald Webb. Colour conflict; race relations in Africa. London, 1943.

Afr 6049 British Africa in general - Collected biographies

Afr 6049.63.2 Perham, M.F. Ten Africans. 2. ed. London, 1963.

Afr 6050 British West Africa in general - Periodicals

NEDL Afr 6050.3.5 Comet. Lagos, Nigeria.
Afr 6050.5F West Africa, a weekly news paper. London. 1956+ 23v.
Afr 6050.10 West African review. London. 33,1962+
Afr 6050.15 West Africa annual. London. 1962+ 4v.

Afr 6053 British West Africa in general - Bibliographies

Afr 6053.5 Library of Congress. Division of Bibliography. British West Africa, a selected list of references. Washington. 1942+ 2v.

Afr 6055 British West Africa in general - Pamphlet volumes

Afr 6055.1 Pamphlet box. British West Africa.
Afr 6055.5 Crowder, Michael. Pagans and politicians. London, 1959.

Afr 6057 British West Africa in general - Collected source materials

Afr 6057.65 Newbury, C.W. British policy towards West Africa. Oxford, 1965.
Afr 6057.69 Wilson, Henry S. Origins of West African nationalism. N.Y., 1969.

Afr 6060 British West Africa in general - Government and administration

Afr 6060.4 Law in Africa. London. 35v.
Afr 6060.20F Gold Coast (Colony). Memorandum on the revision of salaries and other conditions...West Africa. Accra, 1935.
Afr 6060.56 Kimble, David. The machinery of self government. London, 1956.
Afr 6060.56.5 Wraith, R.E. Local government. London, 1956.
Afr 6060.58 Hansard Society for Parliamentary Government. What are the problems of parliamentary government in West Africa. London, 1958.
Afr 6060.64 Wraith, R.E. Local government in West Africa. London, 1964.
Afr 6060.64.2 Wraith, R.E. Local government in West Africa. N.Y., 1964.
Afr 6060.65 Ward, William Ernest Frank. Government in West Africa. London, 1965.
Afr 6060.69 Jordan, Robert Smith. Government and power in West Africa. London, 1969.

Afr 6064 - 6070 British West Africa in general - General history (By date)

Afr 6069.04 George, C. Rise of British West Africa. London, 1904.
Afr 6069.12 Bailland, E. La politique indigène de l'Angleterre en Afrique occidentale. Paris, 1912.
Afr 6069.46 Cary, Joyce. Britain and West Africa. London, 1946.
NEDL Afr 6069.46 Cary, Joyce. Britain and West Africa. London, 1946.
Afr 6069.64 Curtin, P.D. The image of Africa. Madison, 1964.
Afr 6069.68 Harris, John Hobbis. Dawn in darkest Africa. 1st ed. London, 1968.
Afr 6069.69 Horton, James Africanus Beale. West African countries and peoples. Edinburgh, 1969.

Afr 6075 British West Africa in general - General special

Afr 6075.10 Belshan, H. Facing the future in West Africa. London, 1951.
Afr 6075.15 Newbury, C.W. The western Slave Coast and its rulers. Oxford, 1961.
Afr 6075.16 Newbury, C.W. The West African commonwealth. Durham, N.C., 1964.
Afr 6075.17 Pamphlet vol. British West Africa. History. 10 pam.

Afr 6095 British West Africa in general - Geography, description, etc.

Afr 6095.2 Morel, E.D. Affairs of West Africa. London, 1902.
Afr 6095.3 Mockler-Ferryman, A.F. Imperial Africa; the rise, progress and future in British...Africa. London, 1898.
Afr 6095.4 Kingsley, Mary Henrietta. West African studies. London, 1899.
Afr 6095.4.3 Kingsley, Mary Henrietta. West African studies. 3d ed. London, 1964.
Afr 6095.5 West African sketches...G.R. Collier. London, 1824.
Afr 6095.6 Atkins, J. Voyage to Guinea, Brasil. London, 1735.
Afr 6095.6.2 Atkins, J. Voyage to Guinea, Brasil. 2nd ed. London, 1737.
Afr 6095.7 Nassau, R.H. Fetichism in West Africa. N.Y., 1904.
Afr 6095.8 Gaunt, M. Alone in West Africa. London, n.d.
Afr 6095.9 Tremearne, A.J.U. The Niger and the West Sudan. London, n.d.
Afr 6095.10 Reading, J.H. The Ogowe band. Philadelphia, 1890.
Afr 6095.11 Reade, W.W. Savage Africa. 2. ed. London, 1864.
Afr 6095.12 Adams, J. Remarks on the country...Cape Palmas to the river Congo. London, 1823.
Afr 6095.13 Hutchinson, T.J. Impressions of western Africa. London, 1858.
Afr 6095.14 Labarthe, P. Voyage à la côte de Guinée. Paris, 1805.
Afr 6095.14.5 Labarthe, P. Reise nach der Küste von Guinea. Weimar, 1803.
Afr 6095.15.5 Tracy, J. Colonization and missions, historical examination of the state of society in western Africa. 5th ed. Boston, 1846.
Afr 6095.16 Tremearne, A.J. Some Austral-African notes and anecdotes. London, 1913.
Afr 6095.18 Barret, P.M.V. Sénégambie et Guinée...l'Afrique occidentale. Paris, 1888. 2v.
Afr 6095.19 Reade, Winwood. The African sketch-book. London, 1873. 2v.
Afr 6095.20 Flickinger, D.K. Off-hand sketches of men and things in western Africa. Dayton, 1857.
Afr 6095.21 Johnston, Harry. Pioneers in West Africa. London, 1912.
Afr 6095.22 Smith, William. A new voyage to Guinea. London, 1744.
Afr 6095.22.5 Smith, William. Nouveau voyage de Guinée. Paris, 1751.
Afr 6095.22.10 Smith, William. A new voyage to Guinea: describing the customs. 1st ed. London, 1967.
Afr 6095.23 British Information Service. Introducing West Africa. N.Y., 1944.
Afr 6095.30 Clifford, Elizabeth de la P. Our days on the Gold Coast, in Ashanti, in the northern territories, and...in Togoland. Accra, 1918.
Afr 6095.38 Henry, Warren. The confessions of a tenderfoot coaster, a trader's chronicle of life on the west African coast. London, 1927.
Afr 6095.322 Newland, M.O. West Africa. London, 1922.
Afr 6095.343A Graves, A.M. Benvenuto Cellini had no prejudice against bronze, letters from West Africans. Baltimore, 1943.
Afr 6095.343B Graves, A.M. Benvenuto Cellini had no prejudice against bronze, letters from West Africans. Baltimore, 1943.
Afr 6095.351 Wills, Colin. White traveller in black Africa. London, 1951.
Afr 6095.357 Church, R.J.H. West Africa. N.Y., 1957.
Afr 6095.357.2 Church, R.J.H. West Africa. 2. ed. London, 1960.
Afr 6095.357.5 Church, R.J.H. West Africa, a study of the environment and of man's use of it. 5th ed. London, 1966.
Afr 6095.357.6 Church, R.J.H. West Africa. 6th ed. N.Y., 1968.
Afr 6095.358 Niven, C.R. The land and people of West Africa. London, 1958.
Afr 6095.360 Fax, Elton C. West Africa vignettes. N.Y., 1960.
Afr 6095.360.2 Fax, Elton C. West Africa vignettes. 2 ed. N.Y., 1963.
Afr 6095.360.5 Jahn, Janheinz. Durch afrikanische Türen. 1.Aufl. Düsseldorf, 1960.
Afr 6095.361 Oboli, H.O.N. An outline geography of West Africa. New ed. rev. London, 1961.
Afr 6095.361.5 Oboli, H.O.N. An outline geography of West Africa. 5th ed. London, 1967.
Afr 6095.362 Braithwaite, E.R. A kind of homecoming. Englewood, N.J., 1962.
Afr 6095.362.5F Lander, H. Westafrikanische Impressionen. Darmstadt, 1962.
Afr 6095.365 Hennessy, M.N. Africa under my heart. N.Y., 1965.
Afr 6095.365.5 Rosenberger, Homer Tope. Letters from Africa. Washington, 1965.
Afr 6095.366 Church, R.J.H. Some geographical aspects of West African development. London, 1966.
Afr 6095.369 Johnston, Harry Hamilton. Pioneers in West Africa. N.Y., 1969.

Afr 6096 British West Africa in general - Economic and financial conditions

Afr 6096.5 Pedler, F.J. Economic geography of West Africa. London, 1955.
Afr 6096.6.2 Economics of West Africa. 2. ed. Ibadan, 1966.
Afr 6096.8 Ajayi, G.B. Introduction to the economics of West Africa. Rev. ed. Ibadan, 1965. 2v.
Afr 6096.10 Carney, David E. Government and economy in British West Africa. N.Y., 1961.
Afr 6096.12 Forrest, Ona B. Financing development plans in West Africa. Cambridge, 1965.
Afr 6096.15 Conference on Educational and Occupational Selection in West Africa. Educational and occupational selection in West Africa. London, 1962.

Afr 6096   **British West Africa in general - Economic and financial conditions - cont.**

Afr 6096.16   Carlson, Sune. International finance and development planning in West Africa. Stockholm, 1964.
Afr 6096.17   Runov, Boris B. Iunaited Afrika kompani. Moskva, 1966.
Afr 6096.20   Edinburgh. University. Centre of African Studies. Markets and marketing in West Africa. Edinburgh, 1966.
Afr 6096.22   West Africa Committee. Foreign investment. London, 1968.
Afr 6096.24   Hodder, Bramwell William. Markets in West Africa. Ibadan, 1969.

Afr 6097   **British West Africa in general - Religion; missions**

Afr 6097.5   Fox, William. A brief history of the Wesleyan missions on the western coast of Africa. London, 1851.
Afr 6097.6   Faulkner, Rose E. Joseph Sidney Hill, first bishop in western Equatorial Africa. London, 1895.
Afr 6097.7   Platt, William James. From fetish to faith. London, 1935.
Afr 6097.8   Froelich, Jean Claude. Animismes, les religions païennes de l'Afrique de l'ouest. Paris, 1964.
Afr 6097.10   West African Congress on Evangelism, Ibadan, Nigeria, 1968. West African Congress on Evangelism. n.p., 1969.

Afr 6098   **British West Africa in general - Races**

Afr 6098.5   Fortes, Meyer. Oedipus and Job in West African religion. Cambridge, Eng., 1959.
Afr 6098.10   Parrinder, E.G. West African religion. London, 1961.

Afr 6099   **British West Africa in general - Collected biographies**

Afr 6099.2   Ahuma, S.R.B. Attoh. Memoirs of West African celebrities. Liverpool, 1905.
Afr 6099.5.2   Macmillan, Allister. The red book of West Africa. London, 1968.

Afr 6103   **Gambia - Bibliographies**

Afr 6103.5F   Gamble, David P. Bibliography of the Gambia. Bathurst, 1967.

Afr 6107   **Gambia - Collected source materials**

Afr 6107.10   Great Britain. Colonial Office. Report on the Gambia. 1948+

Afr 6109   **Gambia - Government and administration**

Afr 6109.10   Gambia. Laws, statutes, etc. A revised edition of the ordinances of the colony of Gambia. London, 1926. 2v.
Afr 6109.15   Cameron, Ian Donald. The West African councillor. 2d ed. London, 1961.

Afr 6113   **Gambia - General history**

Afr 6113.5   Archer, F.B. Gambia colony and protectorate. London, 1906.
Afr 6113.5.2   Archer, F.B. The Gambia colony and protectorate and official handbooks. 1st ed. London, 1967.
Afr 6113.10   Gray, J.M. A history of the Gambia. Cambridge, Eng., 1940.
Afr 6113.10.2   Gray, J.M. A history of the Gambia. N.Y., 1966.
Afr 6113.15   Southorn, B.S.W. The Gambia. London, 1952.
Afr 6113.20   Gailey, Harry A. A history of the Gambia. London, 1964.
Afr 6113.21   Gailey, Harry A. A history of the Gambia. N.Y., 1965.

Afr 6118   **Gambia - Geography, description, etc.**

Htn   Afr 6118.2*   Jobson, R. The golden trade. London, 1623.
Afr 6118.2.7   Jobson, R. The golden trade, 1620-21. London, 1933.
Afr 6118.5   Moore, F. Travels into the inland parts of Africa. London, 1738.
Afr 6118.6   Reeve, H.F. The Gambia, its history. London, 1912.
Afr 6118.7   Hardinge, Rex. Gambia and beyond. London, 1934.
Afr 6118.10   Rice, Berkeley. Enter Gambia; the birth of and improbable nation. Boston, 1969.

Afr 6119   **Gambia - Economic and financial conditions**

Afr 6119.2   Petch, G.A. Economic development and modern West Africa. London, 1961.

Afr 6122   **Gambia - Local**

Afr 6122.5F   Haswell, Margaret Rosary. Economics of agriculture in a savannah village. London, 1953.

Afr 6124.101 - .399   **Gambia - Biographies - Individual (A-Z, 299 scheme, by person)**

Afr 6124.248   Grant, Douglas. The fortunate slave. London, 1968.

Afr 6125   **Sierra Leone - Periodicals**

Afr 6125.5   Sierra Leone studies. Freetown. 5,1922+ 7v.
Afr 6125.7F   Royal gazette. Freetown. 3,1821+
Afr 6125.9   Sierra Leone bulletin of religion. Freetown. 2,1960+
Afr 6125.12   Bulletin, the journal of the Sierra Leone Geographical Association. Freetown. 9,1965+
Afr 6125.13   Sierra Leone Geographical Association. Occasional paper. Freetown. 1,1965+

Afr 6128   **Sierra Leone - Bibliographies**

X Cg   Afr 6128.3   Lukach, H.C. A bibliography of Sierra Leone. Oxford, 1910. (Changed to XP 3869)
Afr 6128.3.2   Luke, H.C. A bibliography of Sierra Leone. 2d ed. London, 1925.
Afr 6128.4   Library of Congress. African Section. Official publications of Sierra Leone and Gambia. Washington, 1963.
Afr 6128.5   Zell, Hans M. A bibliography of non-periodical literature on Sierra Leone, 1925-1966. Freetown, 1967?

Afr 6132   **Sierra Leone - Collected source materials**

Afr 6132.10   Great Britain. Colonial Office. Report on Sierra Leone. 1952+
Afr 6132.12   Fyfe, Christopher. Sierra Leone inheritance. London, 1964.

Afr 6134   **Sierra Leone - Government and administration**

Afr 6134.2   Sierra Leone. Collected statements of constitutional proposals. Freetown, 1955.
Afr 6134.3F   Sierra Leone. Report, 1957. Sierra Leone, 1957.
Afr 6134.5   Kilson, Martin Luther. Political change in a West African state. Cambridge, 1966.
Afr 6134.8   Sierra Leone. Constitutional Conference, London, 1960. Report. Freetown, 1960.

Afr 6138   **Sierra Leone - General history**

Htn   Afr 6138.2*   Sierra Leone Company. Substance of the report delivered by the Court of directors of the Sierra Leone Company. Philadelphia, 1795.
Afr 6138.2.01   Thorpe, Robert. A letter to William Wilberforce, Esq. London, 1815.
Afr 6138.5   Crooks, John J. A history of the colony of Sierra Leone. Dublin, 1903.
Afr 6138.26   Butt-Thompson, F.W. Sierra Leone in history and tradition. London, 1926.
Afr 6138.31   Utting, F.A.J. The story of Sierra Leone. London, 1931.
Afr 6138.54   Lewis, Roy. Sierra Leone. London, 1954.
Afr 6138.61   Great Britain. Central Office of Information. Sierra Leone. London, 1961.
Afr 6138.61.5   Mador, Iulii P. Sierra-Leone vchera i segodnia. Moscow, 1961.
Afr 6138.62   Fyfe, Christopher. A history of Sierra Leone. London, 1962.
Afr 6138.62.2   Fyfe, Christopher. A short history of Sierra Leone. London, 1967.
Afr 6138.64   Kup, A.P. The story of Sierra Leone. Cambridge, Eng., 1964.

Afr 6139   **Sierra Leone - General special**

Afr 6139.5   Sierra Leone trade journal. Freetown. 1,1961+ 2v.

Afr 6140.1 - .199   **Sierra Leone - History by periods - Before 1800**

Afr 6140.5   Macaulay, K. The colony of Sierra Leone. London, 1827.
Afr 6140.10   Kup, A.P. A history of Sierra Leone. Cambridge, Eng., 1961.
Afr 6140.15   British Information Services. Sierra Leone. N.Y., 1960.

Afr 6140.200 - .499   **Sierra Leone - History by periods - 1800-1895**

Afr 6140.201   Peterson, John. Province of freedom; a history of Sierra Leone, 1787-1870. London, 1969.

Afr 6140.500 -   **Sierra Leone - History by periods - 1895-1960**

Afr 6140.501   Wallis, Charles Braithwaite. The advance of our West African empire. London, 1903.

Afr 6141   **Sierra Leone - History by periods - 1960-**

Afr 6141.2F   Sierra Leone. Commission of Inquiry into the Conduct of the 1967 General Elections in Sierra Leone. Report of the Dove-Edwin Commission of inquiry into the conduct of the 1967 general election in Sierra Leone and the government statement thereon. Freetown, 1967.

Afr 6143   **Sierra Leone - Geography, description, etc.**

Afr 6143.1.5   Falconbridge, Anna Maria. Narrative of two voyages to the River Sierra Leone during the years 1791-1793. Facsimile of 2. ed. London, 1967.
Afr 6143.2   Norton. Residence at Sierra Leone. London, 1849.
Afr 6143.3   Alldrige, T.J. The Sherbro and its hinterland. London, 1901.
Afr 6143.5   Laing, A.G. Travels in...western Africa. London, 1825.
Afr 6143.6   Church, Mary. Sierra Leone, or The liberated Africans. London, 1835.
Afr 6143.7   Rankin, F.H. The white man's grave. London, 1836. 2v.
Afr 6143.8   Corry, J. Observations upon the windward coast of Africa. London, 1807.
Htn   Afr 6143.9.2*   Matthews, J. Voyage to the river Sierra-Leone. London, 1788.
Afr 6143.9.5   Matthews, J. Voyage to the river Sierra-Leone. London, 1966.
Afr 6143.10   Clarke, R. Sierra Leone. London, n.d.
Afr 6143.11   Walker, S.A. Church of England mission in Sierra Leone. London, 1847.
Afr 6143.12   Alldridge, T.J. A transformed colony. London, 1910.
Afr 6143.14   Caswall, H. The martyr of the Pongas. N.Y., 1857.
Afr 6143.15   Poole, T.E. Life...in Sierra Leone and the Gambia. London, 1850. 2v.
Afr 6143.16   Winterbottom, T. An account of native Africans...in Sierra Leone. London, 1803. 2v.
Afr 6143.16.2A   Winterbottom, T. An account of the native African in the neighborhood of Sierra Leone. 2nd ed. London, 1969.
Afr 6143.16.2B   Winterbottom, T. An account of the native African in the neighborhood of Sierra Leone. 2nd ed. London, 1969.
Afr 6143.16.5   Winterbottom, T. Nachrichten von der Sierra Leona Kuste. Weimar, 1805.
Afr 6143.17   Padenheim, D.W. Bref innehaallande beskrifning oefver Sierra Leona. Stockholm, 1801.
Afr 6143.18   Banbury, G.A.L. Sierra Leone, or The white man's grave. London, 1888.
Afr 6143.19   Trotter, James Keith. The Niger sources and the borders of the new Sierra Leone protectorate. London, 1898.
Afr 6143.20   Beatty, K.J. Human leopards...with note on Sierra Leone. London, 1915.
Afr 6143.21   Newland, H. Sierra Leone, its people, products, and secret societies. London, 1916.
Afr 6143.23   Michell, Harold. An introduction to the geography of Sierra Leone. London, 1919.
Afr 6143.25   Goddard, T.N. The handbook of Sierra Leone. London, 1925.
Afr 6143.26   Migeod, Frederick W. A view of Sierra Leone. London, 1926.
Afr 6143.27   Eberl-Elber, Ralph. Westafrikas letztes Rätsel. Salzburg, 1936.
Afr 6143.38   Fowler-Lunn, K. The gold missus. N.Y., 1938.
Afr 6143.44   Hargrave, C.G. African primitive life as I saw it in Sierra Leone. Wilmington, N.C., 1944.
Afr 6143.54   Jarrett, H.R. A geography of Sierra Leone and Gambia. London, 1954.
Afr 6143.54.2   Jarrett, H.R. A geography of Sierra Leone and Gambia. Rev. ed. London, 1964.
Afr 6143.65   Dalton, Kenneth Godfrey. A geography of Sierra Leone. Cambridge, Eng., 1965. 2v.
Afr 6143.66   Clark, John Innes. Sierra Leone in maps. London, 1966.
Afr 6143.68   Ingham, Ernest Graham. Sierra Leone after a hundred years. 1st ed. London, 1968.

Afr 6144   **Sierra Leone - Economic and financial conditions**

Afr 6144.2F   Sierra Leone. Education and economic development in Sierra Leone. Sierra Leone, 1962.
Afr 6144.5A   Cox-George, N.A. Finance and development in West Africa. London, 1961.
Afr 6144.5B   Cox-George, N.A. Finance and development in West Africa. London, 1961.

Afr 6144 Sierra Leone - Economic and financial conditions - cont.

Afr 6144.6F — Sierra Leone. Ten-year plan of economic and social development, 1962/63-1971/72. Freetown, 1962.
Afr 6144.8F — Sierra Leone. Commission to Enquire into and Report on the Matters Contained in the Director of Audit's Report on the Accounts of Sierra Leone for the Year 1960-1961. Report of the commission and the government statement thereon. Freetown, 1963.
Afr 6144.10 — Saylor, Ralph Gerald. The economic system of Sierra Leone. Durham, 1967.

Afr 6145 Sierra Leone - Races

Afr 6145.2 — Parsons, R.T. Religion in an African society. Leiden, 1964.
Afr 6145.3F — Sierra Leone. Commissioners of Enquiry into the Conduct of Certain Chiefs. Reports of the commissioners of enquiry into the conduct of certain chiefs and the government statement thereon. Freetown, 1957.
Afr 6145.3.5F — Sierra Leone. Commission of Enquiry into the Conduct of Certain Chiefs. Further reports of the commissioners of enquiry into the conduct of certain chiefs and the government statement thereon. Sierra Leone, 1957.
Afr 6145.4F — Great Britain. Commissioners of Inquiry into the Subject of Emigration from Sierra Leone to the West Indies. Copy of the reports made in 1844-1845. London, 1948.
Afr 6145.6.2 — Little, Kenneth. The Mende of Sierra Leone. London, 1967.
Afr 6145.6.5 — Harris, William Thomas. The springs of Mende belief and conduct. Freetown, 1968.

Afr 6146 Sierra Leone - Religion; missions

Afr 6146.5 — Johnson, T.S. The story of a mission, the Sierra Leone church. London, 1953.
Afr 6146.8 — Pierson, Arthur. Seven years in Sierra Leone. N.Y., 1897.
Afr 6146.10 — Coke, Thomas. An interesting narrative of a mission sent to Sierra Leone. Paris, 1812.
Afr 6146.12 — Olson, Gilbert W. Church growth in Sierra Leone. Grand Rapids, 1969.

Afr 6147 Sierra Leone - Local

Afr 6147.5 — Banton, M.P. West African city. London, 1957.
Afr 6147.5.3 — Clark, William R.E. The morning star of Africa. London, 1960.
Afr 6147.5.10 — Porter, A.T. Creoledom. London, 1963.
Afr 6147.8 — Sierra Leone. Commission of Inquiry into the Strike and Riots in Freetown, Sierra Leone. Report. Freetown, 1955.
Afr 6147.8.5 — Freetown; a symposium. Freetown, 1968.
Afr 6147.8.10 — Kreutzinger, Helga. The picture of Krio life, Freetown, 1900-1920. Wien, 1968.

Afr 6149.1 - .99 Sierra Leone - Biographies - Collected (A-Z, 99 scheme, by author)

Afr 6149.99.5 — Eminent Sierra Leoneans in the nineteenth century. Freetown, 1961.

Afr 6149.101 - .399 Sierra Leone - Biographies - Individual (A-Z, 299 scheme, by person)

Afr 6149.162.5 — Cole, R.W. Kossoh town boy. Cambridge, Eng., 1960.
Afr 6149.257.5 — Hargreaves, J.D. A life of Sir Samuel Lewis. London, 1958.

Afr 6150 Ghana; Gold Coast - Periodicals

Afr 6150.18 — Diplomatic press directory of the Republic of Ghana, including trade index and biographical section. London. 1959+ 3v.
Afr 6150.21.5 — Economic bulletin. Accra. 4,1960+ 4v.
Afr 6150.32 — Ghana today. London. 1,1957+ 5v.
Afr 6150.32.10 — Ghana. Accra.
Afr 6150.32.15 — Ghana Geographical Association. Bulletin. Kumasi.
Afr 6150.32.20 — Ghana notes and queries. Kumasi.
Afr 6150.32.25F — Ghana reconstructs. Accra. 1,1961+ 2v.
Afr 6150.32.30F — Ghana. Central Bureau of Statistics. Directory of industrial enterprises and establishments. Accra. 1963+
Afr 6150.32.35F — Legon observer. Legon. 1,1966+
Afr 6150.34F — Gold Coast independent. Accra. 10,1926+
NEDL Afr 6150.34.4F — Gold Coast leader. Cape Coast. 1926+
Afr 6150.34.10 — Gold Coast review. London. 1,1925+ 2v.
Afr 6150.34.15 — Gold Coast and Togoland Historical Society. Transactions. Achimotu. 1,1956+ 3v.
Afr 6150.35 — Ghana. University. Institute of African Studies. Ashanti Research Project; progress report. Legon. 1,1963+
Afr 6150.36 — Ghana; an objective summary. Accra. 1966+

Afr 6153 Ghana; Gold Coast - Bibliographies

Afr 6153.5 — Cardinall, A.W. A bibliography of the Gold Coast. Accra, 1931.
Afr 6153.10 — Johnson, A.F. Books about Ghana. Accra, 1961.
Afr 6153.15 — Bibliography of Ghana, 1957-60. Kumasi, 1962.
Afr 6153.20F — Ghana. Bureau of Ghana Languages. Bibliography of works in Ghana languages. Accra, 1967.
Afr 6153.25 — Adams, Cynthia. A study guide for Ghina. Boston, 1967.

Afr 6155 Ghana; Gold Coast - Pamphlet volumes

Afr 6155 — Pamphlet box. Gold Coast.
Afr 6155.1 — Codrington, W.J. Lecture on...defence of...Gold Coast. n.p., n.d.
Afr 6155.2 — Pamphlet vol. Ghana. 8 pam.
Afr 6155.3 — Gold Coast (Colony). The Volta River project. Accra, 195-? 4v.
Afr 6155.4 — Gold Coast (Colony). Report. Accra, 1955.

Afr 6157 Ghana; Gold Coast - Collected source materials

Afr 6157.5 — Great Britain. Colonial Office. Report on the Gold Coast. 1948+
Afr 6157.12 — Metcalfe, George E. Great Britain and Ghana. London, 1964.

Afr 6160 Ghana; Gold Coast - Government and administration

Afr 6160.5 — Hayford, Casely. Gold Coast native institutions. London, 1903.
Afr 6160.7 — Carbon Ferrière, J. L'organisation politique, administratif et financière de la colonie britannique de la Gold Coast. Thèse. Paris, 1936.
Afr 6160.8 — Nsarkoh, J.K. Local government in Ghana. Accra, 1964.
Afr 6160.10 — Wight, M. The Gold Coast legislative council. London, 1947.
Afr 6160.15 — Bernard, Jane. Black mistress. London, 1957.

Afr 6160 Ghana; Gold Coast - Government and administration - cont.

Afr 6160.20 — Hansard Society for Parliamentary Government. The parliament of Ghana. London, 1959.
Afr 6160.22 — Gold Coast (Colony). Government proposals in regard to the future constitution and control of statutory boards and corporations in the Gold Coast. Accra, 1956.
Afr 6160.23 — Gold Coast (Colony). Legislative Assembly. Select Committee on Federal System. Report, and an appendix. Accra, 1955.
Afr 6160.25 — Rubin, L. The constitution and government of Ghana. London, 1961.
Afr 6160.26 — Bennion, Francis. The constitutional law of Ghana. London, 1962.
Afr 6160.27 — Harvey, William Burnett. Law and social change in Ghana. Princeton, 1966.
Afr 6160.28 — Ghana. Commission Appointed to Enquire into Salaries and Wages of the Civil Service and Non-Government Teaching Service. Report. Accra, 1957.
Afr 6160.29 — Ghana. Commission Appointed to Enquire into the Circumstances which Led to the Payment of 28,545 Pounds to James Colledge (Cocoa) Ltd. Report. Accra, 1963.
Afr 6160.30 — Ghana. Regional Constitutional Commission. Regional assemblies. Accra, 1958.
Afr 6160.32 — Ghana. Delimitation Commission. Revised report, 1964. Accra, 1965.
Afr 6160.35 — Tixier, Gilbert. Le Ghana. Paris, 1965.
Afr 6160.36 — Ghana. Commissioner for Local Government Enquiries. Report, June, 1957. Accra, 1960.
Afr 6160.37 — Ghana. Commission of Enquiry on the Commercial Activities. Report. Accra-Tema, 1967?
Afr 6160.40F — Ghana. Public Services Structure and Salaries Commission. Report of the commission on the structure and renumeration of the public services in Ghana. Accra, 1967.
Afr 6160.45 — Busia, Kofi A. The position of the chief in the modern political system of Ashanti. 1st ed. London, 1968.

Afr 6162 Ghana; Gold Coast - General politics; political parties

Afr 6162.5 — Gold Coast (Colony). The government's proposals for constitutional reform. Accra, 1953.
Afr 6162.10A — Apter, D.E. The Gold Coast in transition. Princeton, 1955.
Afr 6162.10B — Apter, D.E. The Gold Coast in transition. Princeton, 1955.
Afr 6162.10.2 — Apter, D.E. Ghana in transition. N.Y., 1963.
Afr 6162.14 — Austin, Dennis. Politics in Ghana, 1946-1960. N.Y., 1964.
Afr 6162.15 — Cudjoe, S.D. Aids to African autonomy. London, 1949.
Afr 6162.20 — Dowse, Robert Edward. Modernization in Ghana and the U.S.S.R., a comparative study. London, 1969.

Afr 6164 Ghana; Gold Coast - General history

Afr 6164.2 — Ellis, A.B. History of Gold Coast of West Africa. London, 1893.
Afr 6164.2.5 — Ellis, A.B. A history of the Gold Coast of West Africa. N.Y., 1969.
Afr 6164.3.5 — Beecham, John. Ashantee and the Gold Coast. London, 1874.
Afr 6164.4 — Hay, J.D. Ashanti and the Gold Coast. London, 1874.
Afr 6164.5 — Claridge, W.W. History of the Gold Coast and Ashanti. London, 1915. 2v.
Afr 6164.5.2 — Claridge, W.W. A history of the Gold Coast. London, 1964. 2v.
Htn Afr 6164.6F* — Specimens of letters written by applicants for mercantiles employment. n.p., n.d.
Afr 6164.7 — Fuller, F. A vanished dynasty. London, 1921.
Afr 6164.7.2 — Fuller, F. A vanished dynasty. 2. ed. London, 1968.
Afr 6164.9 — Ward, W.E.F. A history of the Gold Coast. London, 1948.
Afr 6164.9.2 — Ward, W.E.F. A history of Ghana. 2d ed. London, 1958.
Afr 6164.9.3 — Ward, W.E.F. A history of Ghana. N.Y., 1963.
Afr 6164.9.4 — Ward, W.E.F. A history of Ghana. 3rd ed. London, 1966.
Afr 6164.9.5 — Ward, W.E.F. A history of Ghana. 4th ed. London, 1967.
Afr 6164.9.7 — Ward, W.E.F. A short history of Ghana. 7th ed. London, 1957.
Afr 6164.10 — Bourret, F.M. The Gold Coast, 1919-46. Stanford, 1949.
Afr 6164.10.2 — Bourret, F.M. The Gold Coast. 2d ed. Stanford, 1952.
Afr 6164.10.5 — Bourret, F.M. Ghana. Rev. ed. Stanford, 1960.
Afr 6164.11 — Padmore, G. The Gold Coast revolution. London, 1953.
Afr 6164.12 — Fage, J. Ghana. Madison, Wis., 1959.
Afr 6164.15 — Diplomatic Bulletin. Ghana. London, 1957.
Afr 6164.17 — Royal Institute of International Affairs. Ghana. London, 1957.
Afr 6164.18 — Wallenstein, Immanuel. The road to independence. La Haye, 1964.
Afr 6164.19 — Brown, G.N. An active history of Ghana. London, 1961. 2v.
Afr 6164.20 — Kimble, D. A political history of Ghana. Oxford, 1963.
Afr 6164.21 — Dei-Anang, Michael. Ghana resurgent. Accra, 1964.
Afr 6164.22 — Potekhin, Ivan I. Stanovlenie novoi Gany. Moskva, 1965.
Afr 6164.25 — Ghana. Information Services Department. Ghana reborn. N.Y., 1966.
Afr 6164.30 — Welman, Charles Wellesley. The native states of the Gold Coast. London, 1969.

Afr 6166 Ghana; Gold Coast - General special

Afr 6166.2 — Noerregaard, Georg. Danish settlements in West Africa, 1658-1850. Boston, 1966.
Afr 6166.2.5 — Hansen, Thorkild. Slavernes kyst. København, 1967.

Afr 6168 Ghana; Gold Coast - History by periods - Before 1870

Afr 6168.4 — Kyereteire, K.O. Bonsu Ashanti heroes. Accra, 1964.
Afr 6168.5 — Bowdich, E.T. Mission from Cape Coast Castle to Ashanti. London, 1873.
Afr 6168.6 — Lloyd, A. The drums of Kumasi. London, 1964.
Afr 6168.7 — Dupuis, J. Journal of a residence in Ashanti. London, 1824.
Afr 6168.7.2 — Dupuis, J. Journal of a residence in Ashanti. 2d. ed. London, 1966.
Afr 6168.8F — Hill, S.J. Gold Coast. 2 pts. n.p., 1853.
Afr 6168.9 — Ricketts, H. D. Narrative of the Ashantee war. London, 1831.
Afr 6168.10 — Brandenburg-Preussen auf der West-Küste von Afrika. Leipzig, 1912.
Afr 6168.15 — Coombs, D. The Gold Coast. London, 1963.
Afr 6168.20 — Reindorf, Carl Christian. The history of the Gold Coast and Asante. 2d. ed. Basel, 1951.
Afr 6168.25 — Torodoff, William. Ashanti under the Prempehs, 1888-1935. London, 1965.
Afr 6168.30 — Bowdich, Thomas Edward. Voyage dans le pays d'Aschantie. Paris, 1819.

124

Afr 6170 Ghana; Gold Coast - History by periods - First native war (1873-1874)
Afr 6170.1F   Pamphlet box. First Ashanti war.
Afr 6170.5   Rogers, E. Campaigning in West Africa and the Ashantee invasion. London, 1874.
Afr 6170.6   Boyle, F. Through Fanteeland to Coomassie. London, 1874.
Afr 6170.7   Reade, W. Story of the Ashantee campaign. London, 1874.
Afr 6170.8.2   Henty, G.A. The march to Coomassie. 2nd ed. London, 1874.
Afr 6170.9   Butler, W.F. Akim-foo, the history of a failure. London, 1876.
Afr 6170.11   Brackenbury, H. The Ashanti war. Edinburgh, 1874. 2v.
Afr 6170.11.1   Brackenbury, H. The Ashanti War: a narrative. 1st ed. London, 1968.
NEDL Afr 6170.13   Stanley, H.M. Coomassie and Magdala. London, 1874.
Afr 6170.15   Brackenbury, H. Fanti and Ashanti. Edinburgh, 1873.
Afr 6170.16   Maurice, J.F. The Ashantee war. London, 1874.
Afr 6170.17   Snape, Thomas. The Ashantee war, causes and results, lecture. Manchester, 1874.

Afr 6172 Ghana; Gold Coast - History by periods - Second native war (1895-1896)
Afr 6172.1   Baden-Powell, R. The downfall of Prempeh. London, 1898.

Afr 6174 Ghana; Gold Coast - History by periods - Third native war (1900)
Afr 6174.2   Hodgson, M. The siege of Kumassi. N.Y., 1901.
Afr 6174.3   Haylings, D.M. Letters from a bush campaign. London, 1902.
Afr 6174.4   Armitage, C.H. The Ashanti campaign of 1900. London, 1901.
Afr 6174.5   Willcocks, J. From Kabul to Kumassi. London, 1904.
Afr 6174.6   Ramseyer, F.A. Dark and stormy days at Kumassi, 1900. London, 1901.
Afr 6174.7   Great Britain. Central Office of Information. Reference Division. The making of Ghana. London, 1956.
Afr 6174.8   Nkrumah, Kwame. Ghana. N.Y., 1957.
Afr 6174.9   Biss, Harold C. The relief of Kumasi. London, 1901.
Afr 6174.10F   Great Britain. Colonial Office. Gold Coast. London, 1901.
Afr 6174.11   Myatt, Fred. The golden stool. London, 1966.

Afr 6176 Ghana; Gold Coast - History by periods - 1900-1960
Afr 6176.5   Timothy, B. Kwame Nkrumah. London, 1955.
Afr 6176.10   Amamoo, J.G. The new Ghana. London, 1958.
Afr 6176.15   Ghana. Information Service Department. Ghana is born, 6th March 1957. London, 1958.
Afr 6176.20   Phillips, John F. Kwame Nkrumah and the future of Africa. London, 1960.
Afr 6176.25   Orestov, O.L. V Respublike Gana. Moscow, 1961.
Afr 6176.30   Nkrumah, Kwame. I speak of freedom. N.Y., 1961.
Afr 6176.30.5   Nkrumah, Kwame. Hands off Africa. Accra, 1960.
Afr 6176.30.10   Pamphlet vol. Nkrumah, Kwame. Miscellaneous collection of speeches. 26 pam.
Afr 6176.30.15A   Nkrumah, Kwame. Consciencism. N.Y., 1965.
Afr 6176.30.15B   Nkrumah, Kwame. Consciencism. N.Y., 1965.
Afr 6176.30.20   Nkrumah, Kwame. Le consciencisme. Paris, 1965.
Afr 6176.30.25   Bretton, Henry L. The rise and fall of Kwame Nkrumah; a study of personal rule in Africa. N.Y., 1966.
Afr 6176.30.30   Nkrumah, Kwame. Axioms of Kwame Nkrumah. London, 1967.
Afr 6176.30.31   Nkrumah, Kwame. Axioms of Kwame Nkrumah. London, 1967.
Afr 6176.30.35   Nkrumah, Kwame. Towards colonial freedom. London, 1962.
Afr 6176.30.40   Nkrumah, Kwame. Handbook of revolutionary warfare. London, 1968.
Afr 6176.30.80   Jones, Peter. Kwame Nkrumah and Africa. London, 1965.
Afr 6176.35   Ghana. Statement by the government on the recent conspiracy. Accra, 1961.
Afr 6176.37   Bing, Geoffrey. Reap the whirlwind: an account of Kwame Nkrumah's Ghana farm 1950 to 1966. London, 1968.
Afr 6176.39   Grammens, Mark. Kwame Nkrumah, leider van Afrika. Tielt, 1961.
Afr 6176.40   Dzirasa, Stephen. Political thought of Dr. Kwame Nkrumah. Accra, 1962.
Afr 6176.40.10   Ghana. Commission Enquire into the Kwame Nkrumah Properties. Report of the comission, appointed under the Commission of Enquiry Act, 1964. Accra, 1967.
Afr 6176.41   Balogum, K. Mission to Ghana. 1st ed. N.Y., 1963.
Afr 6176.42   Alexander, Henry Templer. African tightrope. London, 1965.
Afr 6176.42.5   Alexander, Henry Templer. African tightrope. N.Y., 1966.
Afr 6176.43   Jopp, Keith. Ghana, 1957. Accra, 1957.
Afr 6176.44F   Ghana. Commission Appointed to Enquire into the Matters Disclosed at the Trial of Captain Benjamin Awhaitey, before a Court Martial, and the Surrounding Circumstances. Proceedings and report, with minutes of evidence taken before the commission, January-March, 1959. Accra, 1959.
Afr 6176.45F   Gold Coast (Colony). Commission of Enquiry into Mr. Braimah's Resignation and Allegations Arising therefrom. Report. Accra, 1954.
Afr 6176.46   Fitch, Robert Beck. Ghana; end of an illusion. N.Y., 1966.
Afr 6176.50   Bediako, K.A. The downfall of Kwame Nkrumah. Accra, 1966?
Afr 6176.52   Hayford, Casely. West African leadership. 1st ed. London, 1969.

Afr 6178 Ghana; Gold Coast - History by periods - 1960-
Afr 6178.3   Afrifa, A.R. The Ghana coup, 24th February, 1966. London, 1966.
Afr 6178.4   Ghana. Ministry of Information and Broadcasting. Nkrumah's subversion in Africa. Accra, 1966.
Afr 6178.6   Nkrumah, Kwame. Voice from Conakry. London, 1967.
Afr 6178.10   Nkrumah, Kwame. Dark days in Ghana. London, 1968.
Afr 6178.10.2   Nkrumah, Kwame. Dark days in Ghana. London, 1968.
Afr 6178.15   Thompson, William Scott. Ghana's foreign policy, 1957-1966. Princeton, N.J., 1969.
Afr 6178.20   Ocran, A.K. A myth is broken. Harlow, 1968.

Afr 6192 Ghana; Gold Coast - Geography, description, etc.
Htn Afr 6192.1F*   Marees, Pieter de. Description et récit historique du riche royaume d'or de Guinea. Amsterdamme, 1605.
Afr 6192.2   Macdonald, G. The Gold Coast, past and present. London, 1898.
Afr 6192.3   Kemp, Dennis. Nine years at the Gold Coast. London, 1898.
Afr 6192.4   Ramseyer, F.A. Four years in Ashante. London, 1875.
Afr 6192.4.3   Gundert, H. Vier Jahre in Asante-Tagebücher der Missionäre Ramseyer und Kühne. Basel, 1875.
Afr 6192.5   Cruickshank, B. Eighteen years on the Gold Coast of Africa. London, 1853. 2v.
Afr 6192.5.2   Cruickshank, B. Eighteen years on the Gold Coast of Africa. 2nd ed. London, 1966. 2v.
Afr 6192.6   Hutton, W. A voyage to Africa. London, 1821.

Afr 6192 Ghana; Gold Coast - Geography, description, etc. - cont.
Afr 6192.7   Meredith, H. Account of the Gold Coast of Africa. London, 1812.
Afr 6192.8   Freeman, T.B. Journal of...visits to...Ashanti, Aku, and Dahomi. London, 1844.
Afr 6192.8.3   Freeman, T.B. Journal of various visits to the Kingdoms of Ashanti, Aku, and Dahomi in Western Africa. 3rd ed. London, 1968.
Afr 6192.9   Isert, P.E. Voyages en Guinée. Paris, 1793.
Afr 6192.9.2   Isert, P.E. Reise nach Guinea. Kopenhagen, 1788.
Afr 6192.11   Hart, F. The Gold Coast, its wealth and health. London, 1904.
Afr 6192.12   Clarke, R. Remarks on the topography and diseases of the Gold Coast. n.p., n.d.
Afr 6192.13   Burton, R.F. To the Gold Coast for gold. London, 1883. 2v.
Afr 6192.14F   Bowdich, T.E. Mission from Cape Coast Castle to Ashantee. London, 1819.
Afr 6192.15   Marrée, J.A. de. Reizen op en beschrijving van de Goudkust van Guinea. v.1-2. 's-Gravenhage, 1817-18.
Afr 6192.16   Bowler, Louis P. Gold Coast palaver. London, 1911.
Afr 6192.17   Gros, Jules. Voyages, aventures et captivité de J. Bonnat chez les Achantis. Paris, 1884.
Afr 6192.18   Freeman, Richard A. Travels and life in Ashanti and Jaman. Westminster, 1898.
Afr 6192.20   Clifford, Elizabeth. Our days on the Gold Coast. London, 1919.
Afr 6192.22   Cardinall, Alan W. The natives of northern territories of Gold Coast. London, 1920.
Afr 6192.23   Cardinall, Allan W. In Ashanti and beyond. London, 1927.
Afr 6192.24   Gold Coast (Colony). Public Relations Department. Achievement in the Gold Coast. Accra, 1951.
Afr 6192.25   Gold Coast handbook. 2d. ed. Accra, 1924.
Afr 6192.25.5   Gold Coast handbook, 1928. London, 1928.
Afr 6192.25.19   Gold Coast handbook. London, 1937.
Afr 6192.27   Warner, Douglas. Ghana and the new Africa. London, 1961.
Afr 6192.28   Antubam, K. Ghana's heritage of culture. Leipzig, 1963.
Afr 6192.30   Wright, R. Black power. 1st ed. N.Y., 1954.
Afr 6192.32   Marie Louise, Princess. Letters from the Gold Coast. London, 1926.
Afr 6192.35   Great Britain. Central Office of Information. Britain and the Gold Coast. London, 1957.
Afr 6192.40   Redmayne, P. Gold Coast to Ghana. London, 1957.
Afr 6192.45   Wolfson, Freda. Pageant of Ghana. London, 1958.
Afr 6192.50   Mitchison, Naomi (Haldane). Other peoples' worlds. London, 1958.
Afr 6192.55   Varley, W.J. The geography of Ghana. London, 1958.
Afr 6192.57   Cone, Virginia. Africa, a world in progress. 1st ed. N.Y., 1960.
Afr 6192.60   Ryan, Isobel. Black man's town. London, 1953.
Afr 6192.65   Eskelund, Karl. Black man's country. London, 1958.
Afr 6192.70   Boateng, E.A. A geography of Ghana. Cambridge, Eng., 1959.
Afr 6192.70.2   Boateng, E.A. A geography of Ghana. 2nd ed. Cambridge, 1966.
Afr 6192.71   Sliwka-Szczerbic, W. Harmattan i wielki deszcz. Wyd. 1. Warszawa, 1965.
Afr 6192.72   Pfeffer, Karl Heinz. Ghana. 2. Aufl. Bonn, 1964.
Afr 6192.75   Joslin, Mike. Im Tempel der bösen Geister. Wiesbaden, 1959.
Afr 6192.80   Balk, Theodor. Unter dem schwarzen Stern. Berlin, 1960.
Afr 6192.85   Bell, Willis. The roadmakers. Accra, 1961.
Afr 6192.90   Mozheiko, I.V. Eto, Gana. Moscow, 1962.
Afr 6192.92   Rouch, Jane. Ghana. Lausanne, 1964.
Afr 6192.95   Morgan, Clyde. Background to Ghana. 1st ed. London, 1965.
Afr 6192.95.5   Kuzvart, Milos. Ghanska cesta. Praha, 1962.
Afr 6192.96   Bowdich, Thomas Edward. Mission der englisch-afrikanischen Compagnie von Cape Coast Castle nach Ashantee. Weimar, 1820.
Afr 6192.96.5   Bowdich, Thomas Edward. Mission from Cape Coast Castle to Ashantee. 3d ed. London, 1966.
Afr 6192.97   Zeitlin, Arnold. To the Peace Corps, with love. 1st ed. Garden City, 1965.
VAfr 6192.98   Pundik, Herbert. Ghana, 20 stammer-én stat. København, 1965.
Afr 6192.100   Smith, Edward. Where to, black man? Chicago, 1967.
Afr 6192.102.2   Mayer, Emerico Somassa. Ghana: past and present. 2nd ed. The Hague, n.d.

Afr 6193 Ghana; Gold Coast - Economic and financial conditions
Afr 6193.5   Tete-Ansa, W. Africa at work. N.Y., 1930.
Afr 6193.7   Akwawuah, Kwadwo A. Prelude to Ghana's industrialization. London, 1959.
Afr 6193.10   Dusantoy, Peter. Community development in Ghana. London, 1958.
Afr 6193.15   Wittman, G.H. The Ghana report. N.Y., 1959.
Afr 6193.17   Birmingham, Walter Barr. A study of contemporary Ghana. London, 1966.
Afr 6193.19   Ghana. Planning Commission. Seven year development plan; a brief outline. Accra? 1963?
Afr 6193.19.5   Ghana. Planning Commission. Seven-year plan for national reconstruction and development. Accra, 1964.
Afr 6193.20   Ghana. Second development plans. Accra, 1959.
Afr 6193.21F   Gold Coast (Colony). The development plan, 1951. Accra, 1951.
Afr 6193.40   Akwawuah, Kwadwo A. Preludes to Ghana's industrialisation. London, 1960.
Afr 6193.45   Italy. Istituto Nazionale per il Commercio Estero. Ghana. Roma, 1960.
Afr 6193.46   Manshard, W. Die geographischen Grundlagen der Wirtschaft Ghanas. Wiesbaden, 1961
Afr 6193.47   Szcreszewski, R. Structural changes in the economy of Ghana, 1891-1911. London, 1965.
Afr 6193.48F   Lewis, William Arthur. Report on industrialisation and the Gold Coast. Accra, 1963.
Afr 6193.50   Volta Resettlement Symposium. Volta Resettlement Symposium papers read at Volta Resettlement Symposium held in Kumasi. Accra, 1965.
Afr 6193.52   Ayatey, Siegfried B.Y. Central banking, international law, and economic development. Dubugre, 1968.
Afr 6193.54   Jevoch, Michael. Voraussetzungen und Möglichkeiten einer industriellen Entwichlung in Ghana. Hamburg, 1907.
Afr 6193.56   Dutta Roy, D.K. Household budget survey in Ghana. Legon, 1966.
Afr 6193.58F   Ghana. Central Bureau of Statistics. Directory of distributive establishments. Accra, 1968.
Afr 6193.60   International Bank for Reconstruction and Development. Stabilization and development in Ghana. N.Y.?, 1967.

Afr 6193 Ghana; Gold Coast - Economic and financial conditions - cont.

Afr 6193.62 Dickson, Kwamina. A historical geography of Ghana. Cambridge, 1969.
Afr 6193.64 Ghana. Ministry of Economic Affairs. Two-year development plan: from stabilisation to development. Accra, 1968.
Afr 6193.66 Halbach, Axel J. Ghana als Wirtschaftspartner. Köln, 1969.

Afr 6194 Ghana; Gold Coast - Races

Afr 6194.3 Ellis, A.B. The Tshi-speaking peoples of the Gold Coast. London, 1887.
Afr 6194.4 Perregaux, E. Chez les Ashanti. n.p., n.d.
Afr 6194.10 Rattray, R.S. Ashanti. Oxford, 1923.
Afr 6194.10.1 Rattray, Robert Sutherland. Ashanti. N.Y., 1969.
Afr 6194.10.5 Rattray, R.S. Religion and art in Ashanti. Oxford, 1927.
Afr 6194.10.6 Rattray, R.S. Religion and art in Ashanti. London, 1959.
Afr 6194.10.11 Lystad, Robert A. The Ashanti; a proud people. N.Y., 1968.
Afr 6194.20 Danquah, J.B. Gold Coast, Akan laws and customs. London, 1928.
Afr 6194.20.5 Danquah, J.B. The Akan doctrine of God, a fragment of Gold Coast ethics and religion. London, 1944.
Afr 6194.20.5.2 Danquah, J.B. The Akan doctrine of God: a fragment of Gold Coast ethics and religion. 2nd ed. London, 1968.
Afr 6194.20.10 Balmer, W.T. A history of the Akan peoples of the Gold Coast.' London, 1925.
Afr 6194.20.15 Meyerowitz, Eva. The Akan of Ghana. London, 1958.
Afr 6194.20.16 Meyerowitz, Eva. The divine kingship in Ghana. London, 1960.
Afr 6194.20.20 Rouch, Jean. Migrations au Ghana (Gold Coast). Paris, 1956.
Afr 6194.22 Jahoda, Gustav. White man. London, 1961.
Afr 6194.25 Tamakloe, E.F. A brief history of the Daybamba people. Accra, 1931.
Afr 6194.27 Field, Margaret Joyce. Social organization of the Ga people. London, 1940.
Afr 6194.28 Field, Margaret Joyce. Religion and medicine of the Ga people. Accra, 1961.
Afr 6194.30 Fortes, Meyer. The dynamics of clanship among the Tallensi. London, 1945.
Afr 6194.32 Goody, J.R. The social organization of the Lo Wiili. London, 1956.
Afr 6194.32.2 Goody, J.R. The social organization of the Lo Wiili. 2nd ed. London, 1967.
Afr 6194.36 Tait, David. The Konkomba of northern Ghana. London, 1961.
Afr 6194.37 Gil, B. Tribes in Ghana. Accra, 1964.
Afr 6194.38 Wieke, Ivor. The northern factor in Ashanti history. Achimotu, 1961.
Afr 6194.39 Zajaczkowski, A. Aszanti, kraj Złotego Tronu. Warszawa, 1963.
Afr 6194.40F Gold Coast (Colony). Committee on Asanteman-Brong Dispute. Report. Accra, 1955.
Afr 6194.41.2 Sarban, John Mensah. Fanti national constitution; a short treatise. London, 1968.

Afr 6195 Ghana; Gold Coast - Religion; missions

Afr 6195.5 Wiltgen, R.M. Gold Coast mission history, 1471-1880. Techny, Ill., 1956.
Afr 6195.7 Bartels, Francis Lodovic. The roots of Ghana Methodism. Cambridge, 1965.
Afr 6195.10 Braun, Richard. Letters from Ghana. Philadelphia, 1959.
Afr 6195.15 Oelschner, Walter. Landung in Osu. Stuttgart, 1959.
Afr 6195.16 Baeta, C.G. Prophetism in Ghana. London, 1962.
Afr 6195.17 Parsons, R.T. The churches and Ghana society, 1918-1955. Leiden, 1963.
Afr 6195.18 Williamson, Sydney George. Akan religion and the Christian faith. Accra, 1965.
Afr 6195.19 Smith, Noel. The Presbyterian Church of Ghana, 1835-1960. Accra, 1966.
VAfr 6195.20 Chodak, Szymon. Kaplani, czarownicy, wiedźmy. Wyd. 1. Warszawa, 1967.
Afr 6195.22 Dearunner, Hans Werner. A history of Christianity in Ghana. Accra, 1967.
Afr 6195.24 Pamphlet vol. Christians in Ghana. 5 pam.

Afr 6196 Ghana; Gold Coast - Local

Afr 6196.3 Adjaye, Annor. Nzima land. London, 193-?
Afr 6196.5 Welman, C.W. The native states of the Gold Coast. London, 1930.
Afr 6196.7 Ghana. Town and Country Planning Division. Accra, a plan for the town. Accra, 1958.
Afr 6196.10 Danquah, J.B. The Akim Abwakwa handbook. London, 1928.
Afr 6196.12 Musgrave, George Clarke. To Kumassi with Scott. London, 1896.
Afr 6196.13 Amarteifio, Godfrey William. Tema Manhean; a study of resettlement. Kumasi, 1966.
Afr 6196.14 Braiman, Joseph Adam. The two Isanwurfos. London, 1967.
Afr 6196.14.5 Braiman, Joseph Adam. Salaga: the struggle for power. London, 1967.
Afr 6196.15 Acquah, Ioné. Accra survey. London, 1958.
Afr 6196.20 Ansah, J.K. The centenary history of the Larteh Presbyterian Church, 1853-1953. Larteh, 1955.
Afr 6196.20.5 Brokensha, David W. Social change at Larteh, Ghana. Oxford, 1966.
Afr 6196.25 Arthur, John. Brong Ahafo handbook. Accra, 1960.
Afr 6196.26 Meyerowitz, Eva. At the court of an African king. London, 1962.
Afr 6196.27 Hall, Wynyard Montagu. The great drama of Kumasi. London, 1939.
Afr 6196.28 Trans-Volta Togoland. Trans-Volta Togoland handbook, 1955. Accra, 1955.
Afr 6196.29 Johnson, M. The Salaga papers. v.1-2. Legen, 1967-

Afr 6198.1 - .99 Ghana; Gold Coast - Biographies - Collected (A-Z, 99 scheme, by author)

Afr 6198.71 Priestley, Margaret. West African trade and coast society; a family study. London, 1969.
Afr 6198.79.1 Sampson, Magnus John. Makers of modern Ghana. Accra, 1969.

Afr 6198.100 - .899 Ghana; Gold Coast - Biographies - Individual (A-Z, 800 scheme, by person)

Afr 6198.231 Boyle, Laura. Diary of a colonial officer's wife. Oxford, 1968.
Afr 6198.405 Birtwhistle, Allen. Thomas Birch Freeman. London, 1950.

Afr 6198.100 - .899 Ghana; Gold Coast - Biographies - Individual (A-Z, 800 scheme, by person) - cont.

Afr 6198.405.5 Walker, Frank Diaville. Thomas Birch Freeman. London, 1929.
Afr 6198.436 Griffith, William Brandford. The far horizon. Devon, 1951.
Afr 6198.440 Wraith, Ronald E. Guggisberg. London, 1967.
Afr 6198.546 Metcalfe, George. MacLean of the Gold Coast. London, 1962.
Afr 6198.670 Hooker, James R. Black revolutionary; George Padmore. London, 1967.

Afr 6200 Nigeria - Periodicals (A-Z, .1-.26)

Afr 6200.1F Africa. Lagos. 11,1961+
Afr 6200.1.5 Ahmadu Bello University, Zaria, Nigeria. Institute of Administration. Information memo. Zaria. 4,1963+
Afr 6200.1.8 Ahmadu Bello University, Zaria, Nigeria. Northern history research scheme. Interim report. Zaria. 1,1966
Afr 6200.1.10 American Committee on Africa. ACOA Nigeria-Biafra relief memo. N.Y. 1,1968+
Afr 6200.1.12 Administration. Ibadan. 2,1968+
Afr 6200.1.14 ANSWA publication. Ibadan. 1,1968+
Afr 6200.2 Bulletin of rural economics and sociology. Ibadan. 2,1966+
Afr 6200.2.5 Biafra newsletter. Enugu. 2,1968+
Afr 6200.2.10 Biafra; le journal des damnés. Paris. 1,1968+
Afr 6200.3 Consortium for the Study of Nigerian Rural Development. Report. East Lansing, Michigan. 1,1965+ 10v.
Afr 6200.4 Diplomatic press directory of the Federation of Nigeria. London. 1960+ 2v.
Afr 6200.8 Historical Society of Nigeria. Journal. Ibadan. 1,1956+ 3v.
Afr 6200.9 Ibadan, Nigeria. University. Institute of Education. Occasional publication. Ibadan. 1,u960+
Afr 6200.12 Living in Nigeria series. Ibadan. 1,1966+
Afr 6200.12.5F Lagos, Nigeria (City). University. Continuing Education Center. Conference and seminar reports. Lagos. 1,1968+
Afr 6200.13 Materials for the study of Nigerian church history. Nsukka. 1,1964+
Afr 6200.13.5 Markpress News Feature Service. Biafran Overseas Press Division. Press actions. Geneva. 1968+ 2v.
Afr 6200.14 Nigeria, a quarterly magazine of general interest. Lagos. 5v.
Afr 6200.14.5 Nigerian field. London. 7,1938+ 3v.
Afr 6200.14.10 Ibadan, Nigeria. University. Department of Geography. Research notes. 1,1952+
Afr 6200.14.15 Nigerian geographical journal. Ibadan. 3v.
Afr 6200.14.30 Nigerian journal of economics and social studies. Ibadan. 1,1959+ 4v.
Afr 6200.14.35 Nigerian social and economics studies. London. 1+ 3v.
Afr 6200.14.40 Nigerian opinion. Ibadan. 1,1965+
Afr 6200.14.45F Nigerian Institute of Social and Economic Research, Ibadan, Nigeria. Conference proceedings. Ibadan. 1,1952+ 3v.
Afr 6200.14.46 Nigerian Institute of Social and Economic Research, Ibadan, Nigeria. Publications. Ibadan. 1963+
Afr 6200.14.50F Nigerian newsletter. Cairo. 7,1965+
Afr 6200.14.55 Nigerian students voice. Baltimore. 3,1965+
Afr 6200.14.60 Nigeria year book. Apapa. 1963+
Afr 6200.14.65F New perspectives. Nsukka, Nigeria. 1,1967+
Afr 6200.14.70F Nigerian socialist. Ibadan. 1,1967+
Afr 6200.14.75 Nigerian record; background notes on the events in the Federal Republic of Nigeria. Washington. 1968+
Afr 6200.14.80 Nigeria/Biafra conflict. N.Y. 1,1968
Afr 6200.15 Odu. Ibadan. 1,1955+ 2v.
Afr 6200.15.5 Odu; University of Ife journal of African studies. Ibadan. 1,1964+
Afr 6200.19F Spear. Lagos. 1966+
Afr 6200.19.5 Spectator. Aba, Nigeria. 1,1965+
Afr 6200.20 Nigerian Institute of Social and Economic Research, Ibadan, Nigeria. Information bulletin. Ibadan. 1,1965+
Afr 6200.23 The West Coast directory. Lagos. 1968+

Afr 6203 Nigeria - Bibliographies

Afr 6203.2 Amosu, Margaret. Nigerian theses. Ibadan, 1965.
Afr 6203.4 Harris, John. Books about Nigeria. 2. ed. Nigeria, 1960.
Afr 6203.4.4 Harris, John. Books about Nigeria. 4th ed. Ibadan, 1963.
Afr 6203.4.5 Harris, John. Books about Nigeria. Nigeria, 1962.
Afr 6203.5 Ibadan, Nigeria. University. Library. Nigerian periodicals and newspapers, 1950-1955. Ibadan, 1956.
Afr 6203.6 Kaduna, Nigeria. Regional Library. An author catalogue of books about Nigeria in the regional library. Kaduna, 1962.
Afr 6203.7 Nigeria. National Archives. A special list of records in chieftaincy matters. Ibadan, 1962.
Afr 6203.7.5 Nigeria. National Archives. An index to organisation and reorganisation reports in record group CS0.26. Ibadan, 1961.
Afr 6203.7.10F Nigeria. National Archives. A special list of annual, half-yearly and quarterly reports. Ibadan, 1963.
Afr 6203.7.15 Nigeria. National Archives. Kaduna Branch. An inventory of the records of the Secretariat. Kaduna, 1963.
Afr 6203.8 Nigerian Institute of Social and Economic Research, Ibadan, Nigeria. A list of books, articles and government publications on the economy of Nigeria. Ibadan. 1,1960+ 2v.
Afr 6203.9 Wolpe, Howard. A study guide for Nigeria. Boston, 1966.
Afr 6203.10 Dipeolu, J.O. Bibliographical sources for Nigerian studies. Evanston, Ill., 1966.
Afr 6203.12F Ibadan, Nigeria. University. Library. Africana pamphlets; microfilm record. n.p., n.d.
Afr 6203.13 Nigerian Institute of Social and Economic Research, Ibadan, Nigeria. Research for national development. Ibadan. 1965+
Afr 6203.15 London. Commonwealth Institute. Nigeria. London, 1967.
Afr 6203.18 McLoughlin, Peter F.M. Eastern region of Nigeria. Santa Clara, Calif., 1966.
Afr 6203.20 Nigeria. National Library. Index to selected Nigerian periodicals. Lagos. 1,1965+

Afr 6205 Nigeria - Pamphlet volumes

Afr 6205.1 Pamphlet box. Lagos and Nigeria.
Afr 6205.2 Pamphlet vol. Nigeria. 6 pam.
Afr 6205.5 Pamphlet vol. Binder's title. Nigeria. 4 pam.

Afr 6208 Nigeria - Collected source materials

Afr 6208.5F Lagos. Blue book 1904, 1905. Lagos, 1905.
Afr 6208.8F Nigeria. National Archives. Annual report.
Afr 6208.10 Great Britain. Colonial Office. Report on Nigeria. 1952+
Afr 6208.20 Nigeria. Federal Information Service. Federal Nigeria, annual report. London, 1957.

Afr 6210 Nigeria - Government and administration

Afr 6210.1 Lugard, Frederick Dealtry. Instructions to political and other officers. London, 1966.
Afr 6210.1.5 Lugard, Frederick Dealtry. Lugard and the amalgamation of Nigeria. London, 1968.
Afr 6210.5 Crocker, W.R. Nigeria, a critique of British colonial administration. London, 1936.
Afr 6210.7 Perham, M. Native administration in Nigeria. London, 1937.
Afr 6210.8 Nigeria. Legislative Council. Review of the constitution. Lagos, 1949.
Afr 6210.8.10 Nigeria. General Conference. Proceedings of the General conference on review of the constitution. Lagos, 1950.
Afr 6210.9 Awolowo, Olafemi. Path to Nigerian freedom. London, 1947.
Afr 6210.9.5 Awolowo, Olafemi. Thoughts on Nigerian constitution. Ibadan, 1966.
Afr 6210.10 Kirk-Greene, A.H.M. The principles of native administration in Nigeria. London, 1965.
Afr 6210.11 Launders, J. Report to the Muffidd Foundation on a visit to Nigeria. London, 1946.
Afr 6210.12 Wheare, J. The Nigerian legislative council. London, 1950.
Afr 6210.13F Nigeria Ad Hoc Conference on the Nigerian Constitution. The ad hoc conference on the Nigerian constitution. Enugu, 1966.
Afr 6210.14 Aluko, S.A. The problems of self-government for Nigeria. Ilfracombe, 1955.
Afr 6210.15 Harris, Philip. Local government in southern Nigeria. Cambridge, 1960.
Afr 6210.20 Elias, Taslim O. Groundwork of Nigerian law. London, 1954.
Afr 6210.21 Elias, Taslim O. The Nigerian legal system. 2nd ed. London, 1963.
Afr 6210.25 Ezera, Kalu. Constitutional development in Nigeria. Cambridge, 1960.
Afr 6210.25.2 Ezera, Kalu. Constitutional development in Nigeria. 2d ed. Cambridge, Eng., 1964.
Afr 6210.28 North and constitutional developments in Nigeria. Enugu, 1966.
Afr 6210.30 Nigeria. Constitution. n.p., 196-.
Afr 6210.31 Nigeria. Constitution. The Constitution of the Federal Republic of Nigeria. Lagos, 1963.
Afr 6210.32 Berelt, Lionel. Constitutional problems of federalism in Nigeria. Lagos, 1961.
Afr 6210.34 Nigeria. Electoral Committee. Report on the Nigeria federal election. Lagos, 1960.
Afr 6210.35F Nigeria, Western. Executive and Higher Technical Grading Team. Western region executive and higher technical grading team report. Ibadan, 1956.
Afr 6210.36 Odumosu, O.I. The Nigerian constitution. London, 1963.
Afr 6210.36.5 Odumosu, O.I. Constitutional crisis: legality and the president's conscience. Ibadan, Nigeria, 1963.
Afr 6210.37 Campbell, M.J. Law and practice of local government in northern Nigeria. Lagos, 1963.
Afr 6210.38 Nigeria. Governor-General, 1920. Address delivered at the 7th meeting of Nigeria council held at Lagos. Lagos, 1920.
Afr 6210.39 Nigeria. Commission on the Public Services of the Governments in the Federation of Nigeria. Report of the Commission on public services of the governments of Nigeria, 1954-1955. Lagos, 1955.
Afr 6210.40 Awa, Eme O. Federal government in Nigeria. Berkeley, 1964.
Afr 6210.41 Derrett, John Duncan Martin. Studies in the laws of succession in Nigeria. London, 1965.
Afr 6210.42 Blitz, L. Franklin. The politics and administration of Nigerian government. N.Y., 1965.
Afr 6210.43 Palau Marti, Montserrat. Essai sur la notion de roi chez les Yoraba et les Aja-fon. Paris, 1960.
Afr 6210.44F Mackintosh, John P. Nigerian government and politics. London, 1966.
Afr 6210.45F Nigeria. Delimitation Commission. Report of the Constituency Delimitation Commission, 1964. Lagos, 1964.
Afr 6210.46 Nigeria, Midwestern. Ministry of Information. Planting the vineyard. Benin City, 1964.
Afr 6210.48 Nigeria. Northern Legislature. Report of the Joint Select Committee of the Northern Regional Council, 20th and 21st July, and Northern legislature, 7th, 8th and 9th, August, 1951. Kaduna, 1952.
Afr 6210.50F Maddocks, K.P. Report on local government in the Northern provinces of Nigeria. Kaduna, 1951.
Afr 6210.52 Dada, Paul O.A. Evaluation of local government courses in relation to careers of staff trained in Zaria, 1954-1964. Zaria, 1966.
Afr 6210.54 Ohonbamu, Obarogie. The Nigerian constitution and its review. Onitsha, 1965.
Afr 6210.56 Nigeria. Supreme Military Council. The meeting of the Supreme Military Council at Aburi, Accra, Ghana 4-5 January 1967. Enugu, 1967.
Afr 6210.56.5 Nigeria. Supreme Military Council. Meeting of the Nigerian military leaders held at Peduase Lodge. Lagos, 1967.
Afr 6210.57 Ad hoc Conference on Constitutional Proposals, Lagos, 1966. Memoranda submitted by the delegations to the Ad hoc Conference on Constitutional proposals for Nigeria. Apapa, 1967.
Afr 6210.58 Nigeria. Nigerianisation Office. Guide to careers in the federal public service of Nigeria. Lagos, 1961.
Afr 6210.60 Adedeji, Adebayo. Nigerian administration and its political setting. London, 1968.
Afr 6210.62 Fairholm, Gilbert Wayne. Urban government organization in Northern Nigeria. Zaria?, 1964?
Afr 6210.64 Murray, David John. The progress of Nigerian public administration: a report on research. Ibadan, 1968.

Afr 6210 Nigeria - Government and administration cont.

Afr 6210.64.5 Murray, D.J. The work of administration in Nigeria; case studies. London, 1969.
Afr 6210.66 Sharwood Smith, Bryan. Recollections of British administration in the Cameroons and Northern Nigeria, 1921-1957. Durham, N.C., 1969.
Afr 6210.68 Nicolson, I.F. The administration of Nigeria, 1900-1960: men, methods, and myths. Oxford, 1969.

Afr 6212 Nigeria - General politics; political parties

Afr 6212.5 Azihiwe, Nrandi. The development of political parties in Nigeria. London, 1957.
Afr 6212.10 Mitchison, Lois. Nigeria. London, 1960.
Afr 6212.15 Royal Institute of International Affairs. Nigeria. Oxford, 1960.
Afr 6212.16 Pamphlet vol. Azikiwe addresses. 4 pam.
Afr 6212.20 Azikiwe, N. Zik. Cambridge, 1961.
Afr 6212.20.5 Azikiwe, Nnamdi. Sélection de discours de Nnamdi Azikiwe. Paris, 1968.
Afr 6212.25 Gaskiya Corporation, Zaria, Nigeria. Federation of Nigeria. Zaria, 1959.
Afr 6212.35 British Information Service. Nigeria, the making of a nation. N.Y., 1960.
Afr 6212.40 Bretton, Henry. Power and stability in Nigeria. N.Y., 1962.
Afr 6212.42 Sklar, R.L. Nigerian political parties. Princeton, 1963.
Afr 6212.42B Sklar, R.L. Nigerian political parties. Princeton, 1963.
Afr 6212.44 Tamsino, Tekena N. Nigeria and elective representation, 1923-1947. London, 1966.
Afr 6212.46 Williams, Balatunde A. Political trends in Nigeria, 1960-1964. Ibadan, 1965.

Afr 6214 Nigeria - General history

Afr 6214.1 Shaw, F.A. A tropical dependency. London, 1906.
Afr 6214.1.5 Lugard, Flora Louisa. A tropical dependency. N.Y., 1965.
Afr 6214.3 Orr, Charles William James. The making of Northern Nigeria. 9 maps. London, 1911.
Afr 6214.3.2 Orr, Charles William James. The making of Northern Nigeria. 2nd ed. London, 1965.
Afr 6214.5 Historical Society of Nigeria. Memorandum and articles of associations. n.p., 1955.
Afr 6214.8 Burns, Alan C. History of Nigeria. London, 1929.
Afr 6214.8.10 Burns, Alan C. History of Nigeria. 4th ed. London, 1948.
Afr 6214.8.15 Burns, Alan C. History of Nigeria. 5th ed. London, 1955.
Afr 6214.8.18 Burns, Alan C. History of Nigeria. London, 1958.
Afr 6214.8.19 Burns, Alan C. History of Nigeria. 6th ed. London, 1964.
Afr 6214.8.20 Burns, Alan C. History of Nigeria. 7th ed. London, 1969.
Afr 6214.10 Hoghen, S.J. The Muhammadan emigrants of Nigeria. London, 1930.
Afr 6214.10.5 Hoghen, S.J. The emirates of Northern Nigeria. London, 1966.
Afr 6214.10.10 Hoghen, S.J. An introduction to the history of the Islamic states of Northern Nigeria. Ibadan, 1967.
Afr 6214.12 Niven, C.R. A short history of Nigeria. London, 1937.
Afr 6214.12.5A Niven, C.R. Nigeria, outline of a colony. London, 1946.
Afr 6214.12.5B Niven, C.R. Nigeria, outline of a colony. London, 1946.
Afr 6214.15 Miller, W.R.S. Have we failed in Nigeria? London, 1947.
Afr 6214.17 Thorp, Ellen. Ladder of bones. London, 1966.
Afr 6214.20 Coleman, J.S. Nigeria. Berkeley, 1958.
Afr 6214.23 Schwarz, Walter. Nigeria. London, 1968.
Afr 6214.25 Hodgkin, Thomas. Nigerian perspectives. London, 1960.
Afr 6214.30 Crowder, M. The story of Nigeria. London, 1962.
Afr 6214.30.2 Crowder, M. A short history of Nigeria. N.Y., 1966.
Afr 6214.31 Ottonkwo, D.O. History of Nigeria in a new setting. Onitsha, 1962.
Afr 6214.32 Schwarz, Frederick August Otto. Nigeria; the tribes, the nation, or the race. Cambridge, 1965.
Afr 6214.33 Flint, John E. Nigeria and Ghana. Englewood Cliffs, N.J., 1966.
Afr 6214.34 Awdowo Obateni. The people's republic. Ibadan, 1968.
Afr 6214.36 Fajana, A. Nigeria in history. Pkeja, 1969.
Afr 6214.38 Renard, Alain. Biafra, naissance d'une nation? Paris, 1969.

Afr 6218 Nigeria - History by periods - Before 1860

Afr 6218.1 Johnson, Samuel. The history of the Yorubas from the earliest times to the beginning of the British protectorate. London, 1921.
Afr 6218.1.5 Johnson, Samuel. The history of the Yorubas; from the earliest times to the beginning of the British protectorate. 1st ed. London, 1966.
Afr 6218.5.2 Geary, Nevill. Nigeria under British rule. N.Y., 1965.
Afr 6218.7 Crozier, F.P. Five years hard. N.Y., 1932.
Afr 6218.8 Anyiam, F.U. Men and matters in Nigerian politics 1934-58. Yaba, 1959.
Afr 6218.9 Wellesley, D.A. Sir George Goldie, founder of Nigeria. London, 1934.
Afr 6218.10A Dike, K.O. Trade and politics in the Niger Delta. Oxford, 1956.
Afr 6218.10B Dike, K.O. Trade and politics in the Niger Delta. Oxford, 1956.
Afr 6218.10.1 Dike, K.O. Trade and politics in the Niger Delta. Oxford, 1966.
Afr 6218.11 Cook, Arthur. British enterprise in Nigeria. Philadelphia, 1943.
Afr 6218.12 Davies, H.O. Nigeria. London, 1961.
Afr 6218.13 Gordon Lennox, Esme Charles. With the West African frontier force in Southern Nigeria. London, 1905.
Afr 6218.14 Obi, Chike. Our struggle. V.1-2. Yaba, 1962.
Afr 6218.15 Azikiwe, Nnamdi. The evolution of federal government in Nigeria. Orlu, 195-. 4 pam.
Afr 6218.16 Ademoyega, Wale. The federation of Nigeria from earliest times to independence. London, 1962.
Afr 6218.17 Post, K.W.J. The Nigerian federal election of 1959. Oxford, 1963.
Afr 6218.18 Jones, G.I. The trading states of the oil rivers. London, 1963.
Afr 6218.19 Muffett, D.J.M. Concerning brave captains. London, 1964.
Afr 6218.20 Kopytoff, Jean Herskovits. A preface to modern Nigeria. Madison, 1965.
Afr 6218.22 Anene, Joseph Christopher. Southern Nigeria in transition, 1885-1906. Cambridge, Eng., 1966.

Afr 6222 Nigeria - History by periods - 1900-1960

Afr 6222.1 Pribytkavskii, L.N. Nigeriia v bor'be za nezqvisimost'. Moskva, 1961.
Afr 6222.2 Pamphlet volume. Nigerian modern history. 4 pam.

Afr 6225 Nigeria - History by periods - 1960-

Afr 6225.3 Independent Nigeria. Yaba, 1960.
Afr 6225.5 Tilman, Robert O. The Nigerian political scene. Durham, 1962.
Afr 6225.7 Koriavin, L.A. Probudivshaisia Nigeriia. Moscow, 1962.
Afr 6225.8 Phillips, C.S. The development of Nigerian foreign policy. Evanston, 1964.
Afr 6225.10 Nigeria, Eastern. Ministry of Information. Nigerian crisis, 1966. Enugu, 1966.
Afr 6225.10.5 Nigeria, Eastern. Ministry of Information. The problem of Nigerian unity. Enugu, 1966?
Afr 6225.12 Current Issues Society, Kaduna, Nigeria. The Nigerian situation; facts and background. Zaria, 1966.
Afr 6225.14 Nigeria, Eastern. Ministry of Information. Nigerian pogrom; the organized massacre of eastern Nigerians. Enugu, 1966.
Afr 6225.16 Nigeria, Eastern. Ministry of Information. January 15, before and after. Enugu, 1966.
Afr 6225.20 Orbit Publications. Events; a diary of important happenings in Nigeria from 1960-1966. Ebute-Metta, 1967.
Afr 6225.22 Pamphlet vol. Nigeria - Political crisis, 1966-1967. 16 pam.
Afr 6225.25 Ohonbamu, Obarogie. Whither Nigeria? Lagos, 1967.
Afr 6225.30 Nigeria 1965; crisis and criticism. Ibadan, 1966.
Afr 6225.35 Toyo, Eskar. The working class and the Nigerian crisis. Ibadan, 1967.
Afr 6225.40 Great Britain. Parliament. House of Commons. Extracts from British parliamentary debates on the Nigerian situation in the House of Commons, London, Tuesday, 27th August, 1968. Washington, 1968.
Afr 6225.45 Unongo, Paul Iyorpuu. The case for Nigeria. Lagos, 1968.
Afr 6225.50 Pourguoi le Nigéria. Paris, 1968.
Afr 6225.55 Ohonbamu, Obarogie. The psychology of the Nigerian revolution. Ilfracombe, 1969.

Afr 6275 Nigeria - Geography, description, etc.

Afr 6275.3 Clapperton, Hugh. Journal of second expedition into interior of Africa. London, 1829.
Afr 6275.4 Lander, R.L. Records of Captain Clapperton's last expedition to Africa. London, 1830. 2v.
Afr 6275.4.5 Lander, R.L. Journal of an expedition to explore the course and termination of theNiger. N.Y., 1839.
Afr 6275.5 Mockler-Ferryman, A.F. British Nigeria. London, 1902.
Afr 6275.6 Hastings, A.C.G. The voyage of the Dayspring. London, 1926.
NEDL Afr 6275.7 Robinson, C.H. Hausaland. London, 1896.
Afr 6275.7.8 Robinson, C.H. Nigeria, our latest protectorate. London, 1900.
Afr 6275.8 Standinger, P. Im Herzen der Haussaländer. 2. Aufl. Oldenburg, 1891.
Afr 6275.9 Bindloss, H. In the Niger country. Edinburgh, 1898.
Afr 6275.10 Flegel, C. Vom Niger-Benue. Leipzig, 1890.
Afr 6275.11 Viard, E. Au Bas-Niger. 3. ed. Paris, 1886.
Afr 6275.12 Burda, A. Am Niger und Benue. Leipzig, 1886.
Afr 6275.16 Delevoye. En Afrique centrale. Paris, 1906.
Afr 6275.17 Hinderer, A. Seventeen years in the Yoruba country. London, 1873.
NEDL Afr 6275.18 Tucker, Charlotte Maria. Abbeokuta, or Sunrise within the tropics. London, 1853.
Afr 6275.18.2 Tucker, Charlotte Maria. Abbeokuta, or Sunrise within the tropics. N.Y., 1853.
Afr 6275.18.3 Tucker, Charlotte Maria. Abbeokuta, or Sunrise within the tropics. 5th ed. London, 1856.
Afr 6275.18.5 Tucker, Charlotte Maria. Abbeokuta, or Sunrise within the tropics. N.Y., 1859.
NEDL Afr 6275.19 Campbell, R. A pilgrimage to my mother land (Central Africa). London, 1861.
Afr 6275.19.3 Campbell, R. A pilgrimage to my mother land (Central Africa). N.Y., 1861.
Afr 6275.19.10 Campbell, R. A few facts, relating to Lagos...Africa. Philadelphia, 1860.
Afr 6275.20 Kisch, M.S. Letters and sketches from northern Nigeria. London, 1910.
Afr 6275.21 Falconer, J.D. On horseback through Nigeria. London, 1911.
Afr 6275.22 McKeown, R.L. Twenty-five years in Qua Iboe. London, 1912.
Afr 6275.23 Raphael, J.R. Through unknown Nigeria. London, 191-.
Afr 6275.24 Carnegie, David W. Letters from Nigeria...1899-1900. Brechin, 1902.
Afr 6275.25 Tremlett, Horace. With the tin gods. London, 1915.
Afr 6275.26 Hazzledine, George D. The white man in Nigeria. London, 1904.
Afr 6275.26.5 Hazzledine, George D. The white man in Nigeria. N.Y., 1969.
Afr 6275.27 Hermon-Hodge, H.B. Up against it in Nigeria. London, 1922.
Afr 6275.28 Fraser, Douglas C. Impressions - Nigeria 1925. London, 1926.
Afr 6275.29 Hayward, A.H.W. Sport and service in Africa. Philadelphia, 1927.
Afr 6275.30 Nigeria handbook. Lagos. 6,1925+ 2v.
Htn Afr 6275.32.5* Hives, Frank. Ju-Ju and justice in Nigeria. London, 1933.
Afr 6275.33 Dickson, Mora. New Nigerians. London, 1960.
Afr 6275.34 Anderson, David. Surveyors trek. London, 1940.
Afr 6275.35 Hanny, Erich Robert. Vom Sudan zum Mittelmeer. St. Gallen, 1944.
Afr 6275.36 Oakley, R.R. Treks and palavers. London, 1938.
Afr 6275.38 Quinn-Young, C.T. Geography of Nigeria. London, 1946.
Afr 6275.39 Grant, James. A geography of Western Nigeria. Cambridge, 1960.
Afr 6275.42 Calvert, A.F. Nigeria and its tin fields. London, 1912.
Afr 6275.46 Ryan, Isobel. Black man's palaver. London, 1958.
Afr 6275.50 Great Britain. Central Office of Information. Nigeria today. London, 1960.
Afr 6275.55 Ardener, Edwin. Plantation and village in the Cameroons. London, 1960.
Afr 6275.60 Smythe, Hugh. The new Nigerian elite. Stanford, 1960.
Afr 6275.65 Harrison, Godfrey. To the new Nigeria. London, 1960.

Afr 6275 Nigeria - Geography, description, etc.
cont.

Afr 6275.70 Great Britain. Central Office of Information. Nigeria. London, 1960.
Afr 6275.75 Nigeria, Eastern. Ministry of Information. Eastern Nigeria. Enugu, 1960.
Afr 6275.80 Collis, Robert. African encounter. N.Y., 1961.
Afr 6275.85 Taylor Woodrow, ltd. Building for the future in Nigeria. London, 1960.
Afr 6275.90 Marris, P. Family and social change in an African city. London, 1961.
Afr 6275.90.5 Marris, P. Family and social change in an African city. Evanston, Ill., 1962.
Afr 6275.95 Barth, H. Travels in Nigeria. London, 1962.
Afr 6275.100 Miller, E.P. Change here for Kano. Zaria, 1959.
Afr 6275.102 Williams, Harry. Nigeria free. N.Y., 1963.
Afr 6275.103 Laroche, H. La Nigeria. Paris, 1962.
Afr 6275.104 London. Commonwealth Institute. The federation of Nigeria. London, 1963.
Afr 6275.105 Institute for International Social Research. The attitudes, hopes and fears of Nigerians. Princeton, 1964.
Afr 6275.106 Okakor-Omali, Dilim. A Nigerian villager in two worlds. London, 1965.
Afr 6275.107 Miller, W.R.S. Yesterday and tomorrow in Northern Nigeria. London, 1938.
Afr 6275.107.5 Miller, W.R.S. Success in Nigeria; assets and possibilities. London, 1948.
Afr 6275.108 Larymore, Constance. A resident's wife in Nigeria. London, 1911.
Afr 6275.109 Hastings, Archibald Charles Gardner. Nigerian days. London, 1925.
Afr 6275.110 Ariwoola, Olagoke. The African wife. London, 1965.
Afr 6275.112 Jennings, J.H. A geography of the eastern provinces of Nigeria. Cambridge, 1966.
Afr 6275.114 Leith Ross, Sylvia. Beyond the Niger. London, 1951.
Afr 6275.116 White, Stanhope. Dan Bana; the memoirs. London, 1966.
Afr 6275.117 Nigeria. Federal Ministry of Research and Information. Nigeria, 1966. Apapa, 1966.
Afr 6275.119.3 Perkins, William Alfred. Nigeria; a descriptive geography. 3rd ed. Ibadan, 1966.
Afr 6275.120 Brook, Ian. The one eyed man is king. N.Y., 1967.
Afr 6275.122 Niven, Cecil Rex. Nigeria. London, 1967.
Afr 6275.124 Arikpo, Okoi. The development of modern Nigeria. Harmondsworth, 1967.
Afr 6275.126 Nigeria. Federal Information Service. Nigeria 1960. Lagos, 196-.
Afr 6275.127 Miller, Stefan. Nigeria zwischen Wüste und Lagune. Berlin, 1966.
Afr 6275.130 Okin, Theophilus Adelodum. The urbanized Nigerian. 1st ed. N.Y., 1968.
Afr 6275.132 Sowande, Fela. Come now Nigeria. Ibadan, 1968.
Afr 6275.134 Iloeje, Nwadilibe P. A new geography of Nigeria. London, 1969.
Afr 6275.136 Watson, George Derek. A human geography of Nigeria. London, 1960.

Afr 6276 Nigeria - Special customs

Afr 6276.2 Schmoelder, Konstanz. Nigeria, von der traditionnellen Gemeinschaft zur angepassten Sozialpolitik. Stuttgart, 1966.
Afr 6276.4 Beier, Vlli. A year of sacred festivals in one Yoruba town. Marina, 1959.

Afr 6277 Nigeria - Economic and financial conditions

Afr 6277.2F Nigeria. University. Economic Development Institute. EDI working papers. Enugu. 1,1965+
Afr 6277.3 Nigeria. National Manpower Board. Manpower studies. Lagos. 1,1963+
Afr 6277.5 Meniru, G.U. African-American cooperation. Glen Gardner, N.J., 1954.
Afr 6277.10 Handbook of commerce and industry in Nigeria. Lagos. 2,1954+ 3v.
Afr 6277.15 Buchanan, K.M. Land and people in Nigeria. London, 1955.
Afr 6277.20 Stapleton, G.B. The wealth of Nigeria. London, 1958.
Afr 6277.20.2 Stapleton, G.B. The wealth of Nigeria. 2nd ed. Ibadan, 1967.
Afr 6277.25 Prest, A.R. The national income of Nigeria. London, 1953.
Afr 6277.27 Okigbo, Pius N.C. Nigerian national accounts 1950-57. Nigeria, 1962.
Afr 6277.27.5 Okigbo, Pius N.C. Nigerian public finance. Evanston, 1965.
Afr 6277.30 International Bank for Reconstruction and Development. The economic development of Nigeria. Baltimore, 1955.
Afr 6277.35 Nigeria. Economic Council. Economic survey of Nigeria, 1959. Lagos, 1959.
Afr 6277.45 Chukwuemeka, N. Industrialization of Nigeria. N.Y., 1952.
Afr 6277.45.5 Chukwuemeka, N. African dependencies, a challenge to Western democracy. N.Y., 1950.
Afr 6277.46 Onyemelukwe, Clement Chukwukadibia. Problems of industrial planning and management in Nigeria. London, 1966.
Afr 6277.47 Aboyade, O. Foundations of an African economy. N.Y., 1966.
Afr 6277.50 Nigeria trade journal, Lagos. Special independence issue, 1960. Lagos, 1960.
Afr 6277.52 Ike, Adelimpe O. Economic development of Nigeria, 1950-1964. Nsukka, 1966.
Afr 6277.55 Industrial Development Conference, Lagos, 1961. Nigeria. London, 1961.
Afr 6277.58 Pamphlet vol. Rural development in eastern Nigeria.
Afr 6277.60 Italy. Istituto Nazionale per il Commercio Estero. Nigeria. Roma, 1960.
Afr 6277.63 Italy. Embassy. Nigeria. Italiens in Nigeria; a story of successful international co-operation. Lagos, 1967?
Afr 6277.64 Conference on Attitudes in Development Planning in Local Government, Ahmadu Bello University, 1963. Report. Zaria, Northern Nigeria, 1964.
Afr 6277.68 Wells, Frederick A. Studies in industrialization, Nigeria and the Cameroons. London, 1962.
Afr 6277.70 Nigeria. Cocoa Marketing Board. Nigerian cocoa farmers. London, 1956.
Afr 6277.71 Onitiri, H.M.A. A preliminary report on the possibilities of price control in Nigeria. Ibadan, 1966.
Afr 6277.73 Okechuku, Ikechuku. Nigeria, socialism or capitalism. Port Harcourt, 1965.
Afr 6277.74 Nigeria. Federal Ministry of Economic Development. National development plan, 1962-68. Lagos, 1962.

128

Afr 6282   Nigeria - Religion; missions
cont.

Afr 6282.15   Ajayi, J.F. Aoe. Christian missions in Nigeria, 1841-1891. London, 1965.

Afr 6282.16   Grimley, John. Church growth in central and southern Nigeria. Grand Rapids, 1966.

Afr 6282.17F   Nigeria. Commission Appointed to Enquire into the Owegbe Cult. Report. Benin City, 1966.

Afr 6282.20   Epelle, E.T. Writing a local church history, a short guide. Nsukka, Eastern Nigeria, 1965.

Afr 6282.22   Amu, Josiah Wel-Lean Omo. The rise of Christianity in mid-western Nigeria. Lagos, 1965.

Afr 6282.25   Anderson, Susan. May Perry of Africa. Nashville, 1966.

Afr 6282.27   Fletcher, Jesse C. The Wimpy Harper story. Nashville, 1966.

Afr 6282.27.2   Fletcher, Jesse C. Wimpy Harper of Africa. Nashville, 1967.

Afr 6282.30   Det nye Nigeria. Adrhus, 1966.

Afr 6282.35   Davis, Raymond J. Swords in the desert. 5th ed. London, 1966.

Afr 6282.37   Nigeria. National Archives. Index for history of Yoruba Mission (CM.S) 1844-1915, in the National Archives at the University of Ibadan, Western Nigeria. Ibadan, 1965? 5v.

Afr 6282.40   Walker, Frank Deaville. The romance of the Black River. London, 1930.

Afr 6282.42   Peel, John David Yeadon. Aladura: a religious among the Yoruba. London, 1968.

Afr 6282.44   Rubingh, Eugene. Sons of Tiv; a study of the rise of the church among the Tiv of Central Nigeria. Grand Rapids, Michigan, 1969.

Afr 6282.46   Waddell, Hope Masterton. Twenty-nine years in the West Indies and Central Africa. London, 1863.

Afr 6282.46.2   Waddell, Hope Masterton. Twenty-nine years in the West Indies and Central Africa. 2nd ed. London, 1970.

Afr 6283   Nigeria - Local - General works

Afr 6283.2   Sandolphe, J.F. Memoires. Paris, 1823. 2v.

Afr 6283.3   Boisragon, A. The Benin massacre. London, 1897.

X Cg Afr 6283.5   Roth, H.L. Great Benin. Halifax, 1903.

Afr 6283.7   Fawckner, J. Narrative of travels on the coast of Benin. London, 1837.

Afr 6283.9   Bacon, R.H. Benin, the city of blood. London, 1897.

Afr 6283.11   Jackson, I.C. Advance in Africa. London, 1956.

Afr 6283.12   Bryan, K.J. Nigeria, guidebooks. Zaria, 1960. 3 pam.

Afr 6283.13   Nigeria, Northern. Gazetteer. London, 1920. 2v.

Afr 6284   Nigeria - Local - Northern Region - General works

Afr 6284.5   Heussler, Robert. The British in Northern Nigeria. London, 1968.

Afr 6284.8   Smith, John Hilary. Colonial cadet in Nigeria. Durham, N.C., 1968.

Afr 6284.10   Whitaker, C. Sylvester. The politics of tradition; continuity and change in Northern Nigeria, 1946-1966. Princeton, N.J., 1970.

Afr 6285   Nigeria - Local - Northern Region - Special topics

Afr 6285.5A   Dudley, Billy J. Parties and politics in Northern Nigeria. London, 1968.

Afr 6285.5B   Dudley, Billy J. Parties and politics in Northern Nigeria. London, 1968.

Afr 6286   Nigeria - Local - Western Region - General works

Afr 6286.2   Adedeji, Adebayo. An introduction to Western Nigeria. Ibadan?, 1966?

Afr 6287   Nigeria - Local - Western Region - Special topics

Afr 6287.2   Nigeria, Western. Ministry of Economic Planning and Social Development. Statistics Division. Directory of industrial establishments in Western Nigeria. Ibadan, 1966.

Afr 6287.4   Search for a place: black separatism and Africa, 1860. Ann Arbor, 1969.

Afr 6291   Nigeria - Local - Eastern Region, Biafra - Special topics

Afr 6291.5   Kingsley, John Donald. Staff development; Eastern Nigeria public service. Enugu, 1961.

Afr 6291.10   Nigeria, Eastern. Distribution of amenities [in Eastern Nigeria] data and statistics. Enugu, 1963.

Afr 6291.15   Nigeria, Eastern. Economic Mission. Report of the Economic Mission, 1961. Enugu, 1962.

Afr 6291.20F   Nigeria. Federal Ministry of Information. The collapse of Ojukwu's rebellion and prospects for lasting peace in Nigeria. Lagos, 1968.

Afr 6291.22   Pamphlet vol. Nigeria civil war. 9 pam.

Afr 6291.24   Pamphlet vol. Nigeria civil war. 14 pam.

Afr 6291.25   Pamphlet vol. Biafa. Miscellaneous pamphlets. 5 pam.

Afr 6291.28   Pamphlet vol. A collection of speeches. 2 pam.

Afr 6291.30A   Mok, Michael. Biafra journal. N.Y., 1969.

Afr 6291.30B   Mok, Michael. Biafra journal. N.Y., 1969.

Afr 6291.32   Buhler, Jean. Tuez-les tous. Paris, 1968.

Afr 6291.34   Bonneville, Floris de. La mort du Biafra. Paris, 1968.

Afr 6291.36   Goodell, Charles Ellsworth. Goodell report on the Biafra study mission. Denver, 1969.

Afr 6291.38   International observer team in Nigeria. Washington, 1968.

Afr 6291.40   Debré, François. Biafra, an II. Paris, 1968.

Afr 6291.42   Beijbom, Anders. Rapport fran Biafra. Stockholm, 1968.

Afr 6291.44   Sullivan, John R. Breadless Biafra. Dayton, Ohio, 1969.

Afr 6291.46   Yu, Mok Chiu. Nigeria-Biafra; a reading into the problems and peculiarities of the conflict. Adelaide, 1968.

Afr 6291.48   Nwankwo, Arthur Agwuncha. The making of a nation: Biafra. London, 1969.

Afr 6291.50   Conference on the Nigeria-Biafra Conflict, Washington. The Nigeria-Biafra conflict; report of a one day conference. Washington, 1969.

Afr 6291.52   Uwechue, Raph. Reflections on the Nigerian civil war; a call for realism. London, 1969.

Afr 6291.54   Floyd, Barry. Eastern Nigeria. London, 1969.

Afr 6291.56   Wolf, Jean. La guerre des rapaces, la vérité sur la guerre du Biafra. Paris, 1969.

Afr 6291   Nigeria - Local - Eastern Region, Biafra - Special topics
cont.

Afr 6291.58F   Nigeria, South-Eastern. Ministry of Home Affairs and Information. Information Division. Fact sheets on South-Eastern state of Nigeria. Calabar, 1969.

Afr 6291.60   Ojukwu, Chukwuemeka Odumeywu. Biafra; selected speeches and random thoughts of C.O. Ojukwu. 1st ed. N.Y., 1969.

Afr 6291.62   Waugh, Auberon. Biafra; Britain's shame. London, 1969.

Afr 6291.64   Hilton, Bruce. Highly irregular. N.Y., 1969.

Afr 6291.66   Santos, Eduardo dos. A questão de Biafra. Porto, 1968.

Afr 6291.68   Metrowich, Frederick Redvers. Nigeria: the Biafran War. Pretoria, 1969.

Afr 6292   Nigeria - Local - Individual provinces

Afr 6292.1   Kirk-Greene, Anthony. Adamawa, past and present. London, 1958.

Afr 6292.9   Stenning, Derrick J. Savannah nomads...the Wodaabe pastural Fulani. London, 1959.

Afr 6292.9.5   Ahmed ibn Fartua. History of the first twelve years of the reign of Mai Idris Alooma of Bornu. Lagos, 1926.

Afr 6292.9.10   Palmer, Herbert Richmond. Bornu Sahara and Sudan. London, 1936.

Afr 6292.9.15   Schultze, Arnold. The sultanate of Bornu. London, 1913.

Afr 6292.41   Hermon-Hodge, Harry Baldwin. Gazetteer of Ilarin Province. London, 1929.

Afr 6292.82   Johnston, Hugh Anthony St. The Fulani Empire of Sokoto. London, 1967.

Afr 6292.82.5   Last, Murray. The Sokoto Caliphate. London, 1967.

Afr 6292.82.10   Backwell, H.F. The occupation of Hausaland, 1900-1904. Lagos, 1927.

Afr 6292.82.12A   Backwell, H.F. The occupation of Hausaland, 1900-1904. London, 1969.

Afr 6292.82.12B   Backwell, H.F. The occupation of Hausaland, 1900-1904. London, 1969.

Afr 6293   Nigeria - Local - Cities, towns, etc. - Lagos

Afr 6293.2   Lagos. City Council. Tribunal of Inquiry. Report of the Tribunal ofInquiry into the affairs of the Lagos City Council for the period Oct. 15, 1962 to Apr. 18, 1966. Lagos, 1966.

Afr 6293.2.5   Nigeria. Comments of the federal military government on the report of the Tribunal of Inquiry into the affairs of the Lagos City Council for the period Oct. 15, 1962 to Apr. 18, 1966. Lagos, 1966.

Afr 6293.2.10   Nigeria. Lagos Executive Development Board Tribunal of Inquiry. Report of the tribunal of inquiry into the affairs of the Lagos Executive Development Board for the period 1st October, 1960 to 31st December, 1965. Lagos, 1968.

Afr 6293.4   SES Publishers. Your ABC of Lagos and suburbs including guide maps of Benin, Enugu, Ibadan and Kaduna. Lagos, 1967.

Afr 6293.5   Williams, Babatunde A. Urban government for metropolitan Lagos. N.Y., 1968.

Afr 6293.7.2   Losi, John B. History of Lagos. Lagos, 1967.

Afr 6294   Nigeria - Local - Cities, towns, etc. - Ibadan

Afr 6294.2   Parrinder, Edward Geoffrey. Religion in an African city. London, 1953.

Afr 6294.5   The City of Ibadan; series of papers presented to a seminar organized early in 1964 by the Institute of African Studies, University of Ibadan. London, 1967.

Afr 6295   Nigeria - Local - Cities, towns, etc. - Others (A-Z, 299 scheme, by place)

Afr 6295.5F   Davies, J.G. The Biu book, a collection and reference book on Biu division (Northern Nigeria). Norla, 1954-56.

Afr 6295.44   Leith-Ross, Sylvia. African conversation piece. London, 1944.

Afr 6295.60   Pedraza, Howard. Dirrioboola-Gha. London, 1960.

Afr 6295.60.5   Smith, Michael. Government in Zazzau, 1800-1950. London, 1960.

Afr 6295.60.10   Egharevba, Jacob. A short history of Benin. 3rd ed. Ibadan, 1960.

Afr 6295.60.15   Nigeria, Eastern. Ministry of Economic Planning. Speech by G.E. Ohehe on the presentation of Eastern Nigeria development. Enugu, 196-.

Afr 6295.61F   Nigeria. National Archives. An inventory of the administrative records. Ibadan, 1961.

Afr 6295.61.5F   Nigeria. National Archives. An inventory of the administrative records. Ibadan, 1961.

Afr 6295.62   Mercier, Paul. Civilisation du Benin. Paris, 1962.

Afr 6295.62.5   Maboganj, A. Yoruba towns. Ibadan, 1962.

Afr 6295.63   Gervis, P. Of emirs and pagans. London, 1963.

Afr 6295.63.5F   Nigeria. National Archives. A preliminary inventory of the administrative records assembled from Endo province. Ibadan, 1963.

Afr 6295.64   Alagoa, E.J. The small brave city-state. Ibadan, 1964.

Afr 6295.64.5   Fox, A.J. Uzuakoli. London, 1964.

Afr 6295.65   Gilles, H.M. Akufo, an environmental study of a Nigerian village community. Ibadan, 1965.

Afr 6295.66   Old Calabar. Provincial union Oshogbo constitution. Oshogbo, 1961.

Afr 6295.66.5   Shell Company Of Nigeria. Uboma, a socio-economic and nutritional survey. Bude, Eng., 1966.

Afr 6295.66.10   Osogo, John. A history of the Baluyia. Nairobi, 1966.

Afr 6295.66.15   Barber, C.R. Igbo-Ora; a town in transition. Ibadan, 1966.

Afr 6295.101   Hassan, Alhajl. A chronicle of Abuja. Lagos, 1962.

Afr 6295.130   Ryder, Alan Frederick Charles. Benin and the Europeans, 1485-1897. London, 1969.

Afr 6295.185   Nigeria, Eastern. Commission of Inquiry into the Administration of the Affairs of the Enugu Municipal Council. Report of the inquiry into the administration of the affairs of the Enugu Municipal Council. v.1-2. Enugu, 1960.

Afr 6295.221   Hama, Boubou. Histoire du Gobir et de Sokoto. Paris, 1967.

Afr 6295.248   Plotnicov, Leonard. Strangers to the city; urban man in Jos, Nigeria. Pittsburgh, 1967.

Afr 6295.250   Mortimore, M.J. Land and people in the Kano close-settled zone. Zaria, 1967.

Afr 6295.250.200F   Lock, Max. Kabuna, 1917-1967, 2017. London, 1967.

Afr 6298.1 - .99		**Nigeria - Biographies - Collected (A-Z, 99 scheme, by author)**
	Afr 6298.3	Anyiam, F.U. Among Nigerian celebrities. Yaba, 1960.
	Afr 6298.60A	Nigeria Broadcasting Corporation. Eminent Nigerians of the nineteenth century. Cambridge, 1960.
	Afr 6298.60B	Nigeria Broadcasting Corporation. Eminent Nigerians of the nineteenth century. Cambridge, 1960.
Afr 6298.100 - .899		**Nigeria - Biographies - Individual (A-Z, 800 scheme, by person)**
	Afr 6298.110	Balewa, Abubakar Tafawa. Nigeria speaks. Ikeja, 1964.
	Afr 6298.110.5	Balewa, Abubakar Tafawa. Mr. Prime Minister. Lagos, Nigeria, 1964.
	Afr 6298.181	Awolowo, Obaf. Awo. Cambridge, 1960.
	Afr 6298.181.2	Awolowo, Obaf. My early life. Lagos, 1968.
	Afr 6298.181.5	Takunda, Latif Kayode. The trial of Obafemi Awolowo. Lagos, 1966.
	Afr 6298.181.80	Otubushin, Christopher. The exodus and the return of Chief Obafemi Awolowo. Yala, Nigeria, 1966.
	Afr 6298.183	Jones-Quarley, K.A.B. A life of Azikiwe. Baltimore, Maryland, 1965.
	Afr 6298.202	Bello, Ahmadu. My life. Cambridge, 1962.
	Afr 6298.363	Enahoro, Anthony. Fugitive offender. London, 1965.
	Afr 6298.432	Flint, John E. Sir George Goldie and the making of Nigeria. London, 1960.
	Afr 6298.646	Ikime, Obaro. Merchant prince of the Niger Delta; the rise and fall of Nana Olomu. London, 1968.
	Afr 6298.785	Jordan, John P. Bishop Shanahan of Southern Nigeria. Dublin, 1949.
Afr 6300		**British East Africa in general - Periodicals (A-Z, 99 scheme)**
	Afr 6300.2F	Africana. Nairobi.
	Afr 6300.9	British Institute of History and Archaeology in East Africa. Report. London.
	Afr 6300.10	British Institute of History and Archaeology in East Africa. Memoir. Nairobi. 1,1966+
	Afr 6300.10.5	Business and economy of Central and East Africa. Ndola. 1-2,1966-1967// 2v.
	Afr 6300.14.5	Contemporary African monograph series. Nairobi. 1,1965+
	Afr 6300.21F	East African annual. Nairobi.
	Afr 6300.21.3	East African Literature Bureau. Occasional papers on community development. Kampala. 1,1962+
	Afr 6300.21.5	East African studies. Nairobi. 1+ 4v.
	Afr 6300.21.7	East African rural development studies. Nairobi. 1,1968+
	Afr 6300.21.10	East African trade and industry. Nairobi. 1,1954+ 26v.
	Afr 6300.21.15F	East Africa and Rhodesia, a weekly journal. London. 34,1958+ 16v.
	Afr 6300.21.20	East African economic review. Nairobi. 6v.
	Afr 6300.21.25	East Africa journal. Nairobi. 5v.
	Afr 6300.21.30	East African geographical review. 1,1963+
	Afr 6300.21.35	East African Institute of Social Research. A report on three years' work, 1950-1953. Kampala, 1955.
	Afr 6300.21.40	East African Institue of Social Research. Occasional paper. Nairobi. 1,1967+
	Afr 6300.44	Kenya Institute of Administration. K.I.A. occasional papers. Lower Kakete. 1,1968+
	Afr 6300.58F	Nairobi. University College. Institute for Development Studies. Discussion paper. Nairobi. 1,1964+
	Afr 6300.75	Reporter. Nairobi. 1963+ 6v.
	Afr 6300.79	Safari. Nairobi. 1,1969+
	Afr 6300.83	Syracuse University. Program of Eastern African Studies. Occasional paper. 1,1964+ 10v.
	Afr 6300.87F	Transition. Kampala. 5v.
	Afr 6300.98	Year book of East Africa. Nairobi. 1953+
Afr 6303		**British East Africa in general - Bibliographies**
	Afr 6303.3F	East African Research Information Centre. EARIC information circular. Nairobi. 1,1968+
	Afr 6303.5	Library of Congress. Division of Bibliography. British East and Central Africa, a selected list of references. Washington, 1942.
	Afr 6303.7	Kuria, Lucas. A bibliography on anthropology and sociology in Tanzania and East Africa. Syracuse, 1966.
Afr 6308		**British East Africa in general - Collected source materials**
	Afr 6308.5	East Africa High Commission. Annual report. Nairobi. 1957+ 2v.
	Afr 6308.10	Great Britain. Colonial Office. Annual report on the East Africa High Commission. 1948+
Afr 6310		**British East Africa in general - Government and administration**
	Afr 6310.5	Driberg, J.H. The East African problem. London, 1930.
	Afr 6310.8	Great Britain. Colonial Office. Statement of the conclusions of His Majesty's government in the United Kingdom...East Africa. London, 1930.
	Afr 6310.9	Great Britain. Colonial Office. The future of East Africa High Commission Services: reports of the London discussions. London, 1961.
	Afr 6310.10F	Great Britain. Colonial Office. Papers relating to the question of the closer union of Kenya. London, 1931.
	Afr 6310.12	Great Britain. Colonial Office. Correspondence (1931-1932) arising from the report of the Joint Select Commission on East Africa. London, 1932.
	Afr 6310.34F	Great Britain. Commission. Administration of Justice in Kenya. Commission of inquiry into the administration of justice in Kenya, Uganda...in criminal matters, May, 1933. London, 1934.
	Afr 6310.35	Thurnwald, R. Black and white in East Africa. London, 1935.
	Afr 6310.36	Richards, Audrey. East African chiefs. London, 1960.
	Afr 6310.38	Schrader, R. Die Zwangsarbeit in Ostafrika nach deutschen und britischen Kolonialrecht. Hamburg, 1919.
	Afr 6310.39	Bustin, Edouard. La décentralisation administrative et l'évolution des structures. Liège, 1958.
	Afr 6310.42	British Information Services. Regional cooperation in British East Africa. N.Y., 1959.

Afr 6310 cont.		**British East Africa in general - Government and administration**
	Afr 6310.44	Great Britain. Commissions. Civil Services of the East African Territories. Report, 1953-54. London, 1954.
	Afr 6310.47	Great Britain. Commissions. Public Services of the East African Territories and the East Africa High Commission. Report. Entebbe, 1960.
	Afr 6310.49	Uganda. Proposals for the implementation of the recommendations contained in the report of the Commission on the Civil Services of the East African territories and the East Africa High Commission, 1953-1954. Entebbe, 1954.
Afr 6314		**British East Africa in general - General history**
	Afr 6314.25	Lloyd-Jones, W. K.A.R.; being an unofficial account of...the King's African Rifles. London, 1926.
	Afr 6314.27	Great Britain. Foreign Office. History Section. Kenya Uganda and Zanzibar. London, 1920.
	Afr 6314.29	Great Britain. Colonial Office. The British territories in East and Central Africa. London, 1950.
	Afr 6314.31	Marsh, Zoe. East Africa through contemporary records. Cambridge, Eng., 1961.
	Afr 6314.33	Ingham, K. A history of East Africa. London, 1962.
	Afr 6314.33.2	Ingham, K. A history of East Africa. 2. ed. London, 1963.
	Afr 6314.33.3	Ingham, K. A history of East Africa. 3. ed. London, 1965.
	Afr 6314.34	Oliver, R.A. History of East Africa. Oxford, 1963. 2v.
	Afr 6314.36	Bourde, André. L'Afrique orientale. Paris, 1968.
Afr 6316		**British East Africa in general - General special**
	Afr 6316.5	Diamond, Stanley. The transformation of East Africa. N.Y., 1967.
	Afr 6316.10	Ngano; studies in traditional and modern East African history. Nairobi, 1969.
Afr 6320		**British East Africa in general - History by periods - Before 1800**
	Afr 6320.2	Strandes, J. Die Portugiesenzeit von Deutsch- und Englisch-Ostafrika. Berlin, 1899.
	Afr 6320.2.5	Strandes, J. The Portuguese period in East Africa. Nairobi, 1961.
	Afr 6320.4A	Coupland, R. East Africa and its invaders. Oxford, 1938.
	Afr 6320.4B	Coupland, R. East Africa and its invaders. Oxford, 1938.
	Afr 6320.5	Freeman-Grenville, G. The East-Africa coast, selected documents. Oxford, 1962.
Afr 6328		**British East Africa in general - History by periods - 19th century - Second half**
	Afr 6328.1	McDermott, P.L. British East Africa. London, 1893.
	Afr 6328.2	McDermott, P.L. British East Africa, or Ibea. New ed. London, 1895.
	Afr 6328.3	Collister, Peter. The last days of slavery, England and the East African slave trade, 1870-1900. Dar es Salaam, 1961.
Afr 6333		**British East Africa in general - History by periods - 20th century - 1900-1962**
	Afr 6333.02	Buxton, Edward North. Two African trips, with notes and suggestions. London, 1902.
	Afr 6333.2	Brode, Heinrich. British and German East Africa. N.Y., 1911.
	Afr 6333.27	Church, Archibald. East Africa, a new dominion. London, 1927.
	Afr 6333.28	Buell, R.L. The destiny of East Africa. N.Y., 1928.
	Afr 6333.29	East Africa in transition, being a review of the principles and proposals of the Commission on closer union...Eastern and Central Africa. London, 1929.
	Afr 6333.54	Mitchell, Philip Euen. African afterthoughts. London, 1954.
	Afr 6333.55	Dundas, Charles C.F. African crossroads. London, 1955.
	Afr 6333.55.5	Mason, Philip. A new deal in East Africa. London, 1955.
	Afr 6333.56	Moyse-Bartlett, Hubert. The King's African Rifles. Aldershot, 1956.
	Afr 6333.56.5	Africa Bureau, London. Reflections on the report of the Royal Commission on East Africa. London, 1956.
	Afr 6333.61A	Chidzero, B.T.G. Tanganyika and international trusteeship. London, 1961.
	Afr 6333.61B	Chidzero, B.T.G. Tanganyika and international trusteeship. London, 1961.
	Afr 6333.62	Gregory, Robert. Sidney Webb and East Africa. Berkeley, 1962.
	Afr 6333.62.5	Glukhov, A.M. Britanskii imperializm v Vostochnoi Afrike. Moscow, 1962.
	Afr 6333.62.10	Khazanov, A.M. Osvoboditel'naia bor'ba narodov Vostochnoi Afriki. Moscow, 1962.
	Afr 6333.63	Hughes, Anthony. East Africa. Harmondsworth, 1963.
	Afr 6333.64	Kirkman, James S. Men and monuments on the East African coast. London, 1964.
	Afr 6333.65	Nye, Joseph Samuel. Pan-Africanism and East African integration. Cambridge, 1965.
	Afr 6333.66	Lytton, Noel. The stolen desert. London, 1966.
	Afr 6333.68	Rothchild, Donald S. Politics of integration. Nairobi, 1968.
Afr 6335		**British East Africa in general - History by periods - 20th century - 1962-**
	Afr 6335.2	Tanzania. Ministry of Information and Tourism. Meetings and discussions on the proposed East Africa Federation. Dar es Salaam, 1964.
Afr 6385		**British East Africa in general - Missions [Discontinued]**
	Afr 6385.5	Oliver, R. The missionary factor in East Africa. London, 1952.
	Afr 6385.10	McFarlan, D.M. Calabar. Rev. ed. London, 1957.
	Afr 6385.15	Welbourn, Frederick B. East African rebels. London, 1961.
	Afr 6385.16	Mondini, A.G. Africa or death. Boston, 1964.
Afr 6390		**British East Africa in general - Geography, description, etc.**
	Afr 6390.4	Schoeller, M. Mitteilungen über Aquatorial-Ost-Afrika, 1896-97. v.1-2. and plates. Berlin, 1901. 3v.
	Afr 6390.5	Austin, H.H. Among swamps and giants in Equatorial Africa. London, 1902.
Htn	Afr 6390.7*	Dickinson, F.A. Lake Victoria to Khartoum with rifle and camera. London, 1910.
	Afr 6390.8	Handbook for East Africa, Uganda and Zanzibar, 1906. Mombasa, 1906.
	Afr 6390.10	Frere, H.B.E. Eastern Africa as a field for missionary labour. London, 1874.

Afr 6390 British East Africa in general - Geography, description, etc.
cont.

Afr 6390.10.59 Great Britain. War Office. Intelligence Division. Precis of information concerning the British East Africa Protectorate and Zanzibar. London, 1901.
Afr 6390.11.3 Ward, H.F. Handbook of British East Africa. London, 1912.
Afr 6390.11.10 East African red book. Nairobi. 1925+
Afr 6390.11.15 Great Britain. Admiralty. A handbook of Kenya colony (British East Africa). n.p., 1920.
Afr 6390.12 Younghusband, E. Glimpses of East Africa and Zanzibar. London, 1910.
Afr 6390.13 Wason, J.C. East Africa and Uganda. London, 1905.
Afr 6390.14 Powell-Cotton, P.H.G. In unknown Africa. London, 1904.
Afr 6390.15 Wilson, H.A. A British borderland, service and sport in Equatoria. London, 1913.
Afr 6390.16 Tjader, Richard. The big game of Africa. N.Y, 1910.
Afr 6390.18A Huxley, Julian S. Africa view. N.Y., 1931.
Afr 6390.18B Huxley, Julian S. Africa view. N.Y., 1931.
Afr 6390.20 Jackson, F.J. Early days in East Africa. London, 1930.
Afr 6390.21 Great Britain. Colonial Office. Introducing East Africa. London, 1950.
Afr 6390.22 Wilson, H.A. A British borderland. London, 1913.
Afr 6390.23 Young, T.C. African ways and wisdom. London, 1937.
Afr 6390.24.3 Leigh, W.R. Frontiers of enchantment. N.Y., 1938.
Afr 6390.25 Huxley, Elspeth J.G. The sorcerer's apprentice, a journey through East Africa. London, 1948.
Afr 6390.26 Akeley, Mary L. The wilderness lives again, Carl Akeley and the great adventure. N.Y., 1940.
Afr 6390.26.10 Akeley, Mary L. Carl Akeley's Africa. N.Y., 1929.
Afr 6390.28A Markham, B.C. West with the night; autobiography. Boston, 1942.
Afr 6390.28B Markham, B.C. West with the night; autobiography. Boston, 1942.
Afr 6390.29 Ruark, R.C. Harm of the hunter. 1st ed. Garden City, 1953.
Afr 6390.30 Gontard, E.P.U. Other people. Hollywood, 1942.
Afr 6390.32 Czernin, Ottokar G. Mein afrikanisches Tagebuch. Zürich, 1927.
Afr 6390.35 McDougall, Jan. African turmoil. London, 1954.
Afr 6390.36F Gillsaeter, Sven. Pias safari. Stockholm, 1964.
Afr 6390.37 Waugh, Evelyn. A tourist in Africa. London, 1960.
Afr 6390.40 Cameron, R.W. Equator farm. N.Y., 1956.
Afr 6390.43 Pulitzer, Ralph. Diary of two safaris. N.Y., 1927.
Afr 6390.44 Huxley, Elspeth Grant. Forks and hope. London, 1964.
Afr 6390.44.2 Huxley, Elspeth Grant. With forks and hope. N.Y., 1964.
Afr 6390.45 Great Britain. East Africa Royal Commission. Report. London, 1955.
Afr 6390.47 Barker-Benfield, M.A. The lands and peoples of East Africa. London, 1960.
Afr 6390.50F Bulpin, T.V. East Africa and the islands. Cape Town, 1956.
Afr 6390.53 Burger, John F. My forty years in Africa. London, 1960.
Afr 6390.55 Trawell, M. African tapestry. London, 1957.
Afr 6390.58 Foster, Paul. White to move. London, 1961.
Afr 6390.60 Roux, Louis. L'Est Africain britannique. Paris, 1950.
Afr 6390.63 Zwilling, Ernst. Tierparadies Ostafrika. Mödling, 1959.
Afr 6390.64 Meister, Albert. L'Afrique peut-elle partir? Paris, 1966.
Afr 6390.64.2 Meister, Albert. East Africa; the past in chains, the future in pawn. N.Y., 1968.
Afr 6390.65 Richards, C.G. East African explorers. London, 1960.
Afr 6390.65.5 Richards, C.G. Some historic journeys in East Africa. London, 1961.
Afr 6390.65.10 Richards, C.G. East African explorers. Nairobi, 1967.
Afr 6390.70 Pritchard, J.M. A geography of East Africa. London, 1962.
Afr 6390.72 Hickman, G.M. The lands and peoples of East Africa. London, 1961.
Afr 6390.73 Johnson, Asa Helen. Four years in paradise. London, 1941.
Afr 6390.74 Ostrowski, W. Safari przez czarny lad. Londyn, 1947.
Afr 6390.75.2 Korabiewicz, Waclaw. Safari mingi. Wyd.2. Warszawa, 1963.
Afr 6390.76 Lorimer, Norma Octavia. By the waters of Africa. London, 1917.
Afr 6390.77 Meikle, R.S. After big game. London, 1917.
Afr 6390.78 Travellers guide to East Africa. Oxford, 1966.
Afr 6390.79 Truepeney, Charlotte. Our African farm. London, 1965.
Afr 6390.80 Castle, Edgar Bradshaw. Growing up in East Africa. London, 1966.
Afr 6390.81 Petrov, Valeri. Afrikanski belezhnik. Sofiia, 1965.
Afr 6390.85 Walmsley, Leo. Flying and sport in East Africa. Edinburgh, 1920.
Afr 6390.86 Browne, Robert. Beyond the Cape of Hope. London, 1965.
Afr 6390.87 East Africa, past and present. Paris, 1964.
Afr 6390.90 Grahame, Iain. Jambo effendi: seven years with the King's African Rifles. London, 1966.
Afr 6390.92 Spencer, Hope Rockefeller. The way to Rehema's house. N.Y., 1967.
Afr 6390.93 Kirby, C.P. East Africa: Kenya, Uganda and Tanzania. London, 1968.
Afr 6390.96 Cloudsley-Thompson, John. Animal twilight. Chester Springs, 1967.
Afr 6390.98 Morgan, Gordon Daniel. African vignettes. Jefferson City, 1967.
Afr 6390.100 Ames, Evelyn (Perkins). A glimpse of Eden. Boston, 1967.
Afr 6390.102 Townsend, Derek. Wild Africa's silent call. London, 1969.

Afr 6391 British East Africa in general - Special customs

Afr 6391.5 Fox, Lorene Kimball. East African childhood. Nairobi, 1967.

Afr 6392 British East Africa in general - Economic and financial conditions

Afr 6392.2 Mezger, Dorothea. Wirtschaftswissenschaftliche Veröffentlichungen über Ostafrika in englischer Sprache. v.1-3. München, 1967. 2v.
Afr 6392.5 East Africa High Commission. Some notes on industrial development in East Africa. Nairobi, 1956.
Afr 6392.8 Symposium on East African Range Problems, Lake Como, Italy, 1968. Report of a symposium on East African range problems held at Villa Serbellani, Lake Como. N.Y.? 1968?
Afr 6392.10 Joelson, F.S. Rhodesia and East Africa. London, 1958.
Afr 6392.15 East Africa High Commission. Some notes on industrial development in East Africa. 2nd ed. Nairobi, 1959.
Afr 6392.17 Leys, Colin. Federation in East Africa, opportunities. Oxford, 1966.
Afr 6392.18 O'Connor, Anthony Michael. An economic geography of East Africa. N.Y., 1966.
Afr 6392.20 Wraith, Ronald E. East African citizen. London, 1959.

Afr 6392 British East Africa in general - Economic and financial conditions
cont.

Afr 6392.25 Meister, Albert. Le development economique de l'Afrique orientale. Paris, 1966.
Afr 6392.30 International Bank for Reconstruction and Development. The economic development of Tanganyika. Baltimore, 1961.
Afr 6392.31 Conference on Education, Employment and Rural Development, Kericho, Kenya, 1966. Education employment and rural development. Nairobi, 1967.
Afr 6392.32 Robinson, Edward A.G. Report on the needs for economic research and investigation in East Africa. Entebbe, Uganda, 1955.
Afr 6392.33 Cherniavsky, Mark. Development prospects in East-Africa: Kenya, Tanzania and Uganda. Bergen, 1965.
Afr 6392.34 Great Britain. Colonial Office. East Africa Economic and Financial Commission. East Africa. London, 1961.
Afr 6392.35 Walker, David. Economic growth in East Africa. Exeter, 1964.
Afr 6392.36 Massell, B.F. East African economic union. Santa Monica, Calif., 1963.
Afr 6392.36.5 Massell, B.F. The distribution of gains in a common market. Santa Monica, Calif., 1964.
Afr 6392.37 Weigt, Ernest. Beiträge zur Entwicklungspolitik in Afrika. Köln, 1964.
Afr 6392.38 United States. Bureau of International Commerce. A market for U.S. products in East Africa. Washington, 1966.
Afr 6392.39F Nairobi. University College. Institute for Development Studies. Social Science Division. Bulletin. Nairobi. 1,1966+
Afr 6392.40 Nairobi. University College. Institute for Development Studies. Occasional paper. 1,1967+
Afr 6392.45 Conseil National du Patronat Français. Mission industrielle française en Afrique orientale et centrale britannique. Paris, 1965.

Afr 6395 British East Africa in general - Races

Afr 6395.1 Hinde, S.L. Last of the Masai. London, 1901.
Afr 6395.2 Routledge, W.S. With a prehistoric people, the Akikuyu of British East Africa. London, 1910.
Afr 6395.2.5 Boyes, John. A white king of East Africa. N.Y., 1912.
Afr 6395.2.10 Leakey, L.S.B. Mau Mau and the Kikuyu. London, 1953.
Afr 6395.2.12 Leakey, L.S.B. Mau Mau and the Kikuyu. 1. American ed. N.Y., 1954.
Afr 6395.2.14A Leakey, L.S.B. Defeating Mau Mau. London, 1954.
Afr 6395.2.14B Leakey, L.S.B. Defeating Mau Mau. London, 1954.
Afr 6395.2.15 Kenyatta, Jona. Facing Mt. Kenya. London, 1953.
Afr 6395.2.16 Kenyatta, Jona. Au pied du Mont Kenya. Paris, 1960.
Afr 6395.2.20 Baker, R.St.B. Kabongo. 1st ed. Wheatley, Eng., 1955.
Afr 6395.2.25 Brom, John L. Mau-Mau. Paris, 1956.
Afr 6395.2.30 Corfield, F.D. Historical survey of the origins and growth of Mau Mau. London, 1960.
Afr 6395.2.35 Makorere College, Kampala, Uganda. Round Mount Kenya. Kampala, 1960.
Afr 6395.2.40 Garothers, John C. The psychology of Mau Mau. Nairobi, 1954.
Afr 6395.3 Beech, M.W.H. The Suk, their language and folklore. Oxford, 1911.
Afr 6395.3.2 Beech, M.W.H. The Suk, their language and folklore. N.Y., 1969.
Afr 6395.4 Hobley, C.W. Ethnology of A-kamba and other East African tribes. Cambridge, 1910.
Afr 6395.4.5 Lindblom, Gerhard. The Akamba in British East Africa. Pt.1-3. Inaug. Diss. Uppsala, 1916.
Afr 6395.6 Leys, N.M. The colour bar in East Africa. London, 1941.
Afr 6395.8 Gulliver, P.H. The family herds. London, 1955.
Afr 6395.10 Stoneham, C.T. Mau Mau. London, 1953.
Afr 6395.12 Grubbe, Peter. Die Trommeln verstummen. Wiesbaden, 1957.
Afr 6395.14 Goldthorpe, J.E. Outlines of East African society. Kampala, 1958.
Afr 6395.16 Mair, L.P. Primitive government. Harmondsworth, 1962.
Afr 6395.18 Gann, L.H. White settlers in tropical Africa. Harmondsworth, 1962.
Afr 6395.20 Delf, George. Asians in East Africa. London, 1963.
Afr 6395.22 Ghai, Dharam P. Portrait of a minority, Asians in East Africa. London, 1965.
Afr 6395.25 Good, Charles M. Dimensions of East African cultures. East Lansing, 1966.
Afr 6395.28 Mangat, J.S. A history of the Asians in East Africa, 1886 to 1945. Oxford, 1969.
Afr 6395.30 Gulliver, Phillip Hugh. Tradition and transition in East Africa. Berkeley, 1969.

Afr 6397 British East Africa in general - Religion; missions

Afr 6397.2 Matheson, Elizabeth Mary. An enterprise so perilous. London, 1959.
Afr 6397.5 Catrice, Paul. Un audacieux pionnier de l'église au Afrique. Lyon, 1964.
Afr 6397.10 Crawford, E.M. By the equator's snowy peak. London, 1913.
Afr 6397.11 Crawford, E.M. By the equator's snowy peak. 2d ed. London, 1914.
Afr 6397.15 Frank, Cedric N. The life of Bishop Steere. Dar es Salaam, 1953.
Afr 6397.17 Walker, Frank Deaville. A hundred years in Nigeria: the story of the Methodist Mission in the Western Nigeria district, 1842-1942. London, 1942.

Afr 6398 British East Africa in general - Collected biographies

Afr 6398.5 Who's who in East Africa. Nairobi. 1963+ 2v.
Afr 6398.10 Bennett, Norman R. Leadership in eastern Africa. Boston, 1968.

Afr 6400 Kenya - Periodicals (A-Z, 99 scheme)

Afr 6400.1 Administration in Kenya. Lower Kabete. 1,1965+
Afr 6400.36 Hadith; proceedings of the annual conference of the Historical Association of Kenya. Nairobi. 1,1967+ 2v.
Afr 6400.44 Kenya today. Nairobi.
Afr 6400.93 West Kenya annual. Kisumu. 1967+

Afr 6403 Kenya - Bibliographies

Afr 6403.2 Moses, Larry. Kenya, Uganda, Tanganyika, 1960-1964, a bibliography. Washington, 1964.
Afr 6403.5 Webster, John B. A bibliography on Kenya. Syracuse, 1967.
Afr 6403.6 Hakes, Jay E. A study guide for Kenya. Boston, 1969.

Afr 6405   **Kenya - Pamphlet volumes**
Afr 6405   Pamphlet box. Kenya.
Afr 6405.2   Pamphlet vol. Kenya. Social and economic conditions, 1965.
   2 pam.
Afr 6405.3   Pamphlet vol. Kenya.
   6 pam.
Afr 6405.4   Pamphlet vol. Kenya.
   11 pam.

Afr 6408   **Kenya - Collected source materials**
Afr 6408.5   British Indian Colony. Merchants Association, Bombay. The Kenya decision. Bombay, 1923.
Afr 6408.10   Kenya Colony and Protectorate. Planning Committee. Report.
Afr 6408.25   Kenya. Kenya Regiment. Annual report. Nairobi. 1957-58

Afr 6410   **Kenya - Government and administration**
Afr 6410.2F   Great Britain. Colonial Office. Political and social aspects of the development of municipal government in Kenya with special reference to Nairobi. Nairobi, 1949.
Afr 6410.5   Carson, J.B. The administration of Kenya Colony and Protectorate. Rev. ed. Nairobi, 1951.
Afr 6410.6   Dilley, Marjorie Ruth. British policy in Kenya colony. N.Y., 1937.
Afr 6410.6.2   Dilley, Marjorie Ruth. British policy in Kenya colony. 2. ed. London, 1966.
Afr 6410.7   Kenya Independence Conference, London, 1963. Report presented to Parliament. London, 1963.
Afr 6410.8   Kenya. Committee of Review into the Kenya Institute of Administration. Report, 30th Nov., 1964. Nairobi, 1965.
Afr 6410.10   Kenya. Constitutional Conference, London, 1962. Report presented to Parliament by the Secretary of State for the colonies. London, 1962.
Afr 6410.12   Parker, Mary. How Kenya is governed. Nairobi, 1951.
Afr 6410.14   Kenya. Commission on the Law of Sucession. Report. Nairobi, 1968.
Afr 6410.14.2   Slade, Humphrey. The Parliament of Kenya. 2nd ed. Nairobi, 1969.

Afr 6412   **Kenya - General politics; political parties**
Afr 6412.5   British Information Services. Kenya, progress and problems. N.Y., 1960.
Afr 6412.6   Kenyatta, J. Harambee. Nairobi, 1964.
Afr 6412.7   Rosberg, Carl Gustav. The myth of Mau Mau. Stanford, Calif., 1966.

Afr 6415   **Kenya - General history**
Afr 6415.5   Gregory, J.W. Foundation of British East Africa. London, 1901.
Afr 6415.10   Hobley, C.W. Kenya, from chartered company to crown colony. London, 1929.
Afr 6415.15   Pankhurst, R.K.P. Kenya. London, 1954.
Afr 6415.20   Stoneham, C.T. Out of barbarism. London, 1955.
Afr 6415.25   Altrimcham, E.G. Kenya's opportunity. London, 1955.
Afr 6415.30   Huxley, Elspeth. Grant. Kenya today. London, 1954.
Afr 6415.35   Koinange, M. The people of Kenya speak for themselves. Detroit, 1955.
Afr 6415.40   Askwith, Tom G. The story of Kenya's progress. Nairobi, 1953.
Afr 6415.40.2   Askwirth, Tom G. Kenya's progress. 2nd ed. Kampala, 1958.
Afr 6415.42   MacPhee, Archibald Marshall. Kenya. London, 1968.
Afr 6415.42.2   MacPhee, Archibald Marshall. Kenya. N.Y., 1968.

Afr 6420   **Kenya - General special**
Afr 6420.5   Ross, W.M. Kenya from within. London, 1927.
   2v.
Afr 6420.10   Robertson, J.W. The Kenya coastal strip. London, 1961.
Afr 6420.20   Commission Regarding the Boundary Between Kenya and Italian Somaliland. Agreement recording the decisions of the commission appointed and treaty between the United Kingdom and Italy of July 15, 1924. London, 1933.
Afr 6420.20.5   Commission Regarding the Boundary Between Kenya and Italian Somaliland. Agreement between the local commission appointed to settle certain points...boundary...Kenya and Italian Somaliland. London, 1933.
Afr 6420.25   Wood, Susan B. Kenya. London, 1960.
Afr 6420.26   Wood, Susan B. Kenya. London, 1962.
Afr 6420.30   Weigt, Ernst. Die Kolonisation Kenias. Inaug. Diss. Leipzig, 1932.
Afr 6420.30.5   Salvadori, M. La colonisation européenne au Kenya. Paris, 1938.
Afr 6420.35.3   Huxley, Elspeth. White man's country. London, 1953.
   2v.
Afr 6420.35.7   Huxley, E. Grant. Race and politics in Kenya. London, 1956.
Afr 6420.36   Huxley, Elspeth. A new earth. London, 1960.
Afr 6420.37   Great Britain. East Africa Commission. East Africa. London, 1925.
Afr 6420.40A   Aaronovitch, S. Crisis in Kenya. London, 1947.
Afr 6420.40B   Aaronovitch, S. Crisis in Kenya. London, 1947.
Afr 6420.45   Wills, Colin. Who killed Kenya. N.Y., 1953.
Afr 6420.50   Rancliffe, D.H. The struggle for Kenya. London, 1954.
Afr 6420.55   Leigh, Ione. In the shadow of the Mau Mau. London, 1954.
Afr 6420.57   Kitson, Frank. Gangs and counter-gangs. London, 1960.
Afr 6420.60   Baldwin, W.W. Mau Mau man-hunt. 1st ed. N.Y., 1957.
Afr 6420.65   Evans, Peter. Law and disorder. London, 1956.
Afr 6420.70   Cole, Keith. Kenya. London, 1959.
Afr 6420.72   Bennett, G. The Kenyatta election. London, 1961.
Afr 6420.72.5   Bennett, G. Kenya, a political history. London, 1963.
Afr 6420.73   Majdalany, F. State of emergency, the full story of Mau Mau. London, 1962.
Afr 6420.74   Kariuki, Josiah M. Mau Mau detainee. London, 1963.
Afr 6420.75   Pamphlet vol. Kenya.
   3 pam.
Afr 6420.76   Blundell, M. So rough a wind. London, 1964.
Afr 6420.77   Holman, D. Bwana drum. London, 1964.
Afr 6420.78   Cox, Richard. Kenyatta's country. London, 1965.
Afr 6420.80   Davis, Alexander. Chronicles of Kenya. London, 1928.
Afr 6420.82   Wilson, Christopher James. Before the dawn in Kenya. London, 1953.

Afr 6430   **Kenya - History by periods - 1885-1963**
Afr 6430.3   Barnett, Donald L. Mau Mau from within, autobiography and analysis of Kenya's peasant revolt. London, 1966.
Afr 6430.3.1   Barnett, Donald L. Mau Mau from within. N.Y., 1966.
Afr 6430.5   Mungeam, Gordon Hudson. British rule in Kenya, 1895-1912. Oxford, 1966.

Afr 6430   **Kenya - History by periods - 1885-1963**
cont.
Afr 6430.10   Kenyatta, Jouro. Suffering without bitterness. Nairobi, 1968.
Afr 6430.15   Lipscomb, J.F. We built a country. London, 1956.

Afr 6435   **Kenya - History by periods - 1963-**
Afr 6435.5   Huxley, Elspeth Grant. Race and politics in Kenya. London, 1944.
Afr 6435.6   Kenya. Kenya-Somalia relations. Nairobi, 1967.
Afr 6435.8   Roberts, John S. A land full of people: Kenya today. London, 1967.
Afr 6438.30   Uganda. The first five-year development plan, 1961-62 to 1965-66. Entebbe, 1964.
Afr 6454.26   Kenya. Committee on African Wages. Report. Nairobi, 1954.

Afr 6455   **Kenya - Geography, description, etc.**
Afr 6455.2   Hardwick, A.A. An ivory trader in North Kenia. London, 1903.
Afr 6455.3   Thomson, J. Through Masai land. Photoreproduction. London, 1895.
Afr 6455.3.5   Thomson, J. Through Masai land. London, 1885.
Afr 6455.3.10   Thomson, Joseph. Au pays des Massai. Paris, 1886.
Afr 6455.3.15   Thomson, Joseph. Through Masai land with Joseph Thomson. Evanston, Ill., 1962.
Afr 6455.3.21   Thomson, Joseph. Through Masai land. London, 1968.
Afr 6455.4   Chanler, W.A. Through jungle and desert. 1 vol. and maps. N.Y., 1896.
   2v.
Afr 6455.6   Smith, A.D. Through unknown African countries. London, 1897.
Afr 6455.7   Price, Roger. Private journal. Photoreproduction. n.p., 1877.
Afr 6455.8   Peters, Carl. New light on dark Africa. London, 1891.
Afr 6455.8.2   Peters, Karl. Die deutsche Emin Pascha Expedition. München, 1891.
Afr 6455.8.3   Arendt, Otto. Die Streit um die deutsche Emin Pascha Expedition. Berlin, 1889.
Afr 6455.8.4   Rust. Die deutsche Emin Pascha Expedition. Berlin, 1890.
Afr 6455.9   Allsopp, Charles. Sport and travel, Abyssinia and British East Africa. London, 1906.
Afr 6455.10   Pruen, S.R. The Arab and the African. London, 1891.
Afr 6455.11   Eliot, C. The East Africa Protectorate. London, 1905.
Afr 6455.12   Hoehnel, Ludwig. Discovery of Lakes Rudolf and Stefanie. London, 1894.
   2v.
Afr 6455.12.2   Hoehnel, Ludwig Ritter von. Zum Rudolph-See und Stephanie-See. Wien, 1892.
Afr 6455.12.5   Hoehnel, Ludwig. Discovery of Lakes Rudolf and Stefanie. 1st English ed. London, 1968.
   2v.
Afr 6455.13   Patterson, J.H. The man-eaters of Travo. London, 1907.
Afr 6455.14   Patterson, J.H. In the grip of Nyika. London, 1909.
Afr 6455.16   Dugmore, A.R. Camera adventures in the African wilds. N.Y., 1910.
Afr 6455.17   Roosevelt, T. African game trails. N.Y., 1910.
Afr 6455.17.20   Roosevelt, K. A sentimental safari. N.Y., 1963.
Afr 6455.18   Stigand, C.H. To Abyssinia through an unknown land. London, 1910.
Afr 6455.19   MacQueen, P. In wildest Africa. London, 1910.
Afr 6455.20   Scull, G.H. Lassoing wild animals in Africa. N.Y., 1911.
Afr 6455.21   Cranworth, B.F.G. A colony in the making. London, 1912.
Afr 6455.21.5   Cranworth, B.F.G. Kenya chronicles. London, 1939.
Afr 6455.22   Fitzgerald, W.W.A. Travels in...British East Africa...Zanzibar and Pemba. London, 1898.
Afr 6455.23   Stigand, C.H. The land of Zinj. London, 1913.
Afr 6455.24   From Natal to Zanzibar. Durban, 1873.
Afr 6455.25   British East Africa. The Uganda railway. London, 1911.
Afr 6455.26   White, Stewart E. African camp fires. London, 1914.
NEDL Afr 6455.27   New, Charles. Life, wanderings, and labours in eastern Africa. London, 1873.
NEDL Afr 6455.28   Neumann, A.H. Elephant hunting in East Equatorial Africa. London, 1898.
Afr 6455.30   Oswald, Felix. Alone in the sleeping-sickness country. London, 1915.
Afr 6455.31   White, Stewart E. Land of foot prints. Garden City, 1912.
Afr 6455.33   Bennet, Edward. Shots and snapshots in British East Africa. London, 1914.
Afr 6455.34   Bronson, Edgar B. In closed territory. Chicago, 1910.
Afr 6455.35   Purvis, J.B. Through Uganda to Mt. Elgon. London, 1909.
Afr 6455.36   Watt, Rachel. In the heart of savagedom. 2d ed. London, 1920.
Afr 6455.37   Roscoe, John. Twenty-five years in East Africa. Cambridge, 1921.
Afr 6455.38   Preston, R.O. The genesis of Kenya colony. Nairobi, 1935.
Afr 6455.39   Johnson, M. Camera trails in Africa. N.Y., 1924.
Afr 6455.39.5   Johnson, M. Safari. N.Y., 1928.
Afr 6455.40   Curtis, Charles. P. Hunting in Africa east and west. Boston, 1925.
Afr 6455.42   Powys, L. Black laughter. N.Y., 1924.
Afr 6455.43.5   Percival, A.B. A game ranger's note book. N.Y., 1924.
Afr 6455.44   Streeter, D.W. Denatured Africa. N.Y., 1926.
Afr 6455.44.5   Streeter, D.W. Denatured Africa. N.Y., 1927.
Afr 6455.44.10   Streeter, D.W. Denatured Africa. Garden City, 1927.
Afr 6455.45.2   Leys, Norman MacLean. Kenya. 2d ed. London, 1925.
Afr 6455.45.3   Leys, Norman MacLean. Kenya. 3d ed. London, 1926.
Afr 6455.45.5   Leys, Norman MacLean. A last chance in Kenya. London, 1931.
Afr 6455.45.10   Eastman, G. Chronicles of an African trip. Rochester, 1927.
Afr 6455.46   Buxton, Mary Aline B. Kenya days. London, 1927.
Afr 6455.47   Carnegie, V.M. A Kenyan farm diary. Edinburgh, 1930.
Afr 6455.49   Great Britain. Oversea Settlement Department. Kenya Colony and Protectorate. London, 1930.
Afr 6455.50   Kenya Colony and Protectorate. Kenya. 3d ed. London, 1959.
Afr 6455.55   Kenya and Uganda Rail Road and Harbours. Travel guide to Kenya and Uganda. London, 1931.
Afr 6455.59.7   Szechenyi, Z. Land of elephants, Kenya. London, 1935.
Afr 6455.61   Leakey, L.S.B. Kenya. London, 1936.
Afr 6455.65.5A   Blixen Finecke, K. Out of Africa. N.Y., 1938.
Afr 6455.65.5B   Blixen Finecke, K. Out of Africa. N.Y., 1938.
Afr 6455.66   Blixen Finecke, K. Den afrikanske farm. København, 1943.
Afr 6455.67   Dower, K.G. The spotted lion, in Kenya. Boston, 1937.
Afr 6455.69   Smeaton-Stuart, J.A. Safari for gold. London, 1942.
Afr 6455.71   Baker, R.St.B. Africa drums. London, 1942.

Afr 6455   Kenya - Geography, description, etc.
cont.

Afr 6455.73.5	Schwarzenberg, A. A Kenya farmer looks at his colony. N.Y., 1946.
Afr 6455.75	Farson, N. Last chance in Africa. London, 1949.
Afr 6455.77	Hennings, R.O. African morning. London, 1951.
Afr 6455.79	Wilson, C.J. Kenya's warning. Nairobi, 1954.
Afr 6455.80	Simpson, Alyse. Red dust of Africa. London, 1952.
Afr 6455.82	Brodhurst-Hill, Evelyn. So this is Kenya. London, 1936.
Afr 6455.85	Scott, R.L. Between the elephant's eyes. N.Y., 1954.
Afr 6455.86	Simonen, Seppo. Mau Mau iskee. Helsinki, 1954.
Afr 6455.90	Meinertzhagen, R. Kenya diary. Edinburg, 1957.
Afr 6455.95	Pickering, Elsa. When the windows were opened. London, 1957.
Afr 6455.100	Keller, W.P. Africa's wild glory. London, 1959.
Afr 6455.105	Benzon, Boeje. Mine afrikanshe udfingter. København, 1948.
Afr 6455.110	Great Britain. Central Office of Information. Kenya. London, 1960
Afr 6455.115	Bell, W.D.M. Karamojo safari. 1st ed. N.Y., 1949.
Afr 6455.120	Gatti, Attilio. Africa is adventure. London, 1960.
Afr 6455.122	Carey Jones, N.S. The anatomy of Uhuru, an essay on Kenya's independence. Manchester, 1966.
Afr 6455.125	Hepburn, Alonzo Barton. The story of an outing. N.Y., 1913.
Afr 6455.130	Lander, Cherry. My Kenya acres. London, 1957.
Afr 6455.135	Lloyd-Jones, William. Havash. London, 1925.
Afr 6455.140	Shaposhnikova, Vera D. Bol'shoe safari. Moskva, 1966.
Afr 6455.142	Leakey, Louis S.B. Kenya; contrasts and problems. Cambridge, Mass., 1966.
Afr 6455.145	Reece, Alys. To my wife, 50 camels. Leicester, 1963.
Afr 6455.150	Heland, Erik von. Mina Afrikaar. Stockholm, 1966.
Afr 6455.152	American University, Washington, D.C. Foreign Areas Studies Division. Area handbook for Kenya. Washington, 1967.
Afr 6455.154	Seaton, Henry. Lion in the morning. London, 1963.
Afr 6455.157	Soja, Edward W. The geography of modernization in Kenya. Syracuse, N.Y., 1968.
Afr 6455.160	Denis, Michaela. At home with Michaela. London, 1965.

Afr 6456   Kenya - Special customs

Afr 6456.5	Osogo, John. Life in Kenya in the olden days, the Baluyia. Nairobi, 1965.

Afr 6457   Kenya - Economic and financial conditions

Afr 6457.3	Kenya. Ministry of Economic Planning and Development. High-level manpower. Nairobi, 1965.
Afr 6457.5	Fearn, Hugh. An African economy. London, 1961.
Afr 6457.8	United Nations. United Nations mission to Kenya on housing. N.Y., 1965.
Afr 6457.10	East Africa High Commission. Capital formation in Kenya, 1954-1960. Nairobi, 1961. 2 pam.
Afr 6457.15	East Africa High Commission. Reported employment and wages in Kenya. Nairobi, 1961.
Afr 6457.20	Forrester, M. Kenya today, social prerequisite for economic development. Monton, 1962.
Afr 6457.21	Kenya. Laws, statutes, etc. The Foreign Investments Protection Act, 1964 and rules of procedure. Nairobi, 1964.
Afr 6457.22	International Bank for Reconstruction and Development. The economic development of Kenya. Baltimore, 1963.
Afr 6457.22.2	International Bank for Reconstruction and Development. The economic development of Kenya. Nairobi, 1962.
Afr 6457.23	Kenya. Development plan for the period from 1st July, 1964, to 30th June, 1970. Nairobi, 1964.
Afr 6457.23.5	Kenya. Development plan for the period 1965-1966 to 1966-1970. Nairobi, 1966.
Afr 6457.24	Njuguna Wa Gakuo, E. Bedeutung und Möglichkeiten. Freiburg, 1960.
Afr 6457.25	Kenya. Africa socialism and its application to planning in Kenya. Nairobi, 1965.
Afr 6457.27	Great Britain. Financial Commissioner to Kenya. Report by the Financial commissioner. n.p., 1932.
Afr 6457.28	Great Britain. Fiscal Commission for Kenya. Report of the Fiscal Commission. Nairobi, 1963.
Afr 6457.29F	Kenya Tea Development Authority. The operations and development plans of the Kenya Tea Development Authority. Nairobi, 1964.
Afr 6457.30	Italy. Instituto Nationale Per Il Commercio Estero. Kenya Roma, 1964.
Afr 6457.32	Sorrenson, M.P.K. Land reform in the Kikuyu country. Nairobi, 1967.
Afr 6457.34	Ominde, Simeon H. Land and population movements in Kenya. London, 1968.
Afr 6457.36	Oser, Jacob. Promoting economie development with illustrations from Kenya. Nairobi, 1967.
Afr 6457.38	Faaland, Just. The economy of Kenya. Bergen, 1967.
Afr 6457.40	Waller, Peter P. Grundzüge der Raumplanung in der Region Kisumu (Kenia). Berlin, 1968.
Afr 6457.42	Who controls industry in Kenya? Report of a working party. Nairobi, 1968.
Afr 6457.46	International Research Associates. A survey of the Kenyan participant training program. N.Y., 1967.

Afr 6460   Kenya - Races

Afr 6460.1	Freitag, C. Beiträge zur Völkerkunde von Östafrika. n.p., 1908.
Afr 6460.5	Vanden Bergh, L.J. On the trail of the Pigmies. N.Y., 1921.
Afr 6460.10	Mallet, M. A white woman among the Masai. London, 1923.
Afr 6460.15A	Orde-Browne, G.S. The vanishing tribes of Kenya. Philadelphia, 1925.
Afr 6460.15B	Orde-Browne, G.S. The vanishing tribes of Kenya. Philadelphia, 1925.
Afr 6460.15.2	Orde-Browne, G.S. The vanishing tribes of Kenya. London, 1925.
Afr 6460.20	Massam, J.A. The cliff dwellers of Kenya. London, 1927.
Afr 6460.25	Wilson, C.J. One African colony, the native races of Kenya. London, 1945.
Afr 6460.30	Lipscomb, J.F. White Africans. London, 1955.
Afr 6460.35F	Mayer, Philip. Two studies in applied anthropology in Kenya. London, 1951.
Afr 6460.40F	Huntingford, G.W.B. Nandi work and culture. London, 1950.
Afr 6460.45	Gicaru, Muga. Land of sunshine. London, 1958.
Afr 6460.50	Wagner, Guenter. The Bantu of North Kavirondo. London, 1949-56. 2v.

Afr 6460   Kenya - Races
cont.

Afr 6460.55	Koenig, Oskar. The Maisai story. London, 1956.
Afr 6460.58F	Sandford, G.R. An administrative and political history. London, 1919.
Afr 6460.60	Henderson, Ian. The hunt for Kimathi. London, 1958.
Afr 6460.65	Cloete, Stuart. Storm over Africa. Cape Town, 1956.
Afr 6460.70	Carothers, John C. The psychology of Mau Mau. Nairobi, 1955.
Afr 6460.72	Sangree, Walter H. Age, prayer, and politics Ineriki, Kenya. N.Y., 1966.
Afr 6460.75	Lambert, H.E. Kikuyu social and political institutions. London, 1965.
Afr 6460.80	Wilson, Gordon. Luo customary law and marriage laws customs. Nairobi, 1961.
Afr 6460.80.5	Whisson, Michael. Change and challenge (A study of the social and economic changes among the Kenya Luo). Nairobi, 1964.
Afr 6460.80.10	Crazzolara, J. Pasquale. The Lwoo. Verona, 1950-54. 3v.
Afr 6460.80.15	Ogot, Bethwell Allan. History of the southern Luo. Nairobi, 1967.
Afr 6460.85	Great Britain. Colonial Office. Indians in Kenya. London, 1967.
Afr 6460.87	Were, Gideon S. A history of the Abaluyia of western Kenia. Nairobi, 1967.
Afr 6460.87.5	Were, Gideon S. Western Kenya historical texts: Abaluyia, Teso, and Elgon Kalenjin. Nairobi, 1967.
Afr 6460.90	Adamson, Joy. The peoples of Kenya. London, 1967.
Afr 6460.92	Holman, Dennis. The elephant people. London, 1967.
Afr 6460.94	Goldschmidt, Walter Rochs. Kambvya's cattle. Berkeley, 1967.

Afr 6463   Kenya - Religion; missions

Afr 6463.3	Welbourn, Frederick B. A place to feel at home, a study of two independent churches in western Kenya. London, 1966.
Afr 6463.5	Blakeslee, H. Beyond the Kikuyu curtain. Chicago, 1956.
Afr 6463.6	Kenya. Commission of Inquiry into the Affray at Kolloa, Baringo. Report. Nairobi, 1950.
Afr 6463.7	Conference on the Role of the Church in Independent Kenya Limuru. Report of the conference held at Limuru Conference Centre, Kenya. Nairobi, 196- .
Afr 6463.10	Olivotti, Guiseppe. Verde Kenya. Con presentazione di Giovanni Urbani. Venezia, 1967.

Afr 6465   Kenya - Local

Afr 6465.5	Dutton, E.H.T. Kenya mountain. London, 1929.
Afr 6465.56	Bellingham, B.L. Mombasa. Nairobi, 1933.
Afr 6465.56.5	Gray, J.M. The British in Mombasa, 1824-1826. London, 1957.
Afr 6465.56.9	Boxer, Charles R. A fortaleza de Jesus e os portugueses em Mombaça. Lisboa, 1960.
Afr 6465.56.10	Boxer, Charles R. Fort Jesus and the Portuguese in Mombasa. London, 1960.
Afr 6465.56.15	De Blij, Harm J. Membasa; an African city. Evanston, Ill., 1968.
Afr 6465.58F	White, L.W.T. Nairobi, master plan for a colonial capital. London, 1948.
Afr 6465.58.5	Walmsley, Ronald W. Nairobi. Kampala, 1957.
Afr 6465.58.10	Morgan, W.T.W. Nairobi, city and region. Nairobi, 1967.
Afr 6465.59	Prins, Adriaan Hendrik Johan. Sailing from Lamu. Assen, 1965.
Afr 6465.60F	Kenya. Economics and Statistics Division. Economic survey of Central Province, 1963-1964. Nairobi, 1968.

Afr 6470.101 - .399   Kenya - Biographies - Individual (A-Z, 299 scheme, by person)

Afr 6470.103	Adamson, George. A lifetime with lions. Garden City, 1968.
Afr 6470.106	Ainsworth, J.D. John Ainsworth. London, 1959.
Afr 6470.113	Archer, G.F. Personal and historical memoirs. Edinburgh, 1963.
Afr 6470.135	Binks, H.K. African rainbow. London, 1959.
Afr 6470.145	Gregory, J.R. Under the sun. Nairobi, 1952.
Afr 6470.211	Gatheru, R.M. Child of two worlds. London, 1964.
Afr 6470.231	Huxley, Elspeth Grant. The flame trees of Thika. London, 1959.
Afr 6470.231.5	Huxley, Elspeth Grant. On the edge of the rift, memories of Kenya. N.Y., 1962.
Afr 6470.231.6	Huxley, Elspeth Grant. The mottled lizard. London, 1962.
Afr 6470.242	Hurd, David. Kidnap at Kiunga. London, 1965.
Afr 6470.250	Itote, Warohiu. "Mau Mau" general. Nairobi, 1967.
Afr 6470.250	Delf, George. Jomo Kenyatta. London, 1961.
Afr 6470.250.5	Slater, Montagu. The trial of Jomo Kenyatta. 2d ed. London, 1966.
Afr 6470.250.10	Delf, George. Jomo Kenyatta. 1st ed. Garden City, 1961.
Afr 6470.250.15F	Howarth, Anthony. Kenyatta, a photographic biography. Nairobi, 1967.
Afr 6470.250.20	Patel, Anubu H. Struggle for Release Jomo and his colleagues. 1st ed. Nairobi, 1963.
Afr 6470.269	Rake, Alan. Tom Mboya. 1st ed. Garden City, N.Y., 1962.
Afr 6470.278	Osogo, John. Nabongo Mumia of the Baluyia. Nairobi, 1965?
Afr 6470.289	Odinga, Ajuma Oginga. Not yet Uhuru, an autobiography. London, 1967.

Afr 6475   Uganda - Periodicals

Afr 6475.5	Crane. Kampala.
Afr 6475.8	Uganda journal. Kampala. 10v.
Afr 6475.8.2	Uganda journal. Index, v.1-20, 1934-56. Kampala, n.d.
Afr 6475.10	Uganda Museum, Kampala, Uganda. Occasional paper. Kampala. 1,1956+
Afr 6475.15	Uganda. Entebbe. 1,1962+ 2v.

Afr 6478   Uganda - Bibliographies

Afr 6478.2	Kuria, Lucas. A bibliography on politics and government in Uganda. Syracuse, 1965.
Afr 6478.3	Syracuse. University. A bibliography on anthropology and sociology in Uganda. Syracuse, 1965.
Afr 6478.5	Hopkins, Terence K. A study guide for Uganda. Boston, 1969.

Afr 6480	**Uganda - Pamphlet volumes**	
Afr 6480		Pamphlet box. Uganda.
Afr 6480.5		Pamphlet vol. Uganda government, pamphlets on local matters. 8 pam.
Afr 6480.6		Pamphlet vol. Pamphlets on disturbances in Uganda. 3 pam.
Afr 6480.7		Pamphlet vol. Uganda government publications, 1945-1965. 9 pam.

Afr 6482   Uganda - Collected source materials

Afr 6482.5   Great Britain. Colonial Office. Uganda, report for the year. 1948+ 3v.

Afr 6484   Uganda - Government and administration

Afr 6484.4   Great Britain. Commissions. Uganda Relationship. Report, 1961. Entebbe, 1961.
Afr 6484.5   Uganda. Constitutional Committee. Report of the constitutional committee, 1957. Entebbe, 1959.
Afr 6484.6   Bentley, E.L. British East Africa and Uganda. London, 1892.
Afr 6484.8   Namirembe Conference. Agreed recommendations of the Namirembe Conference. Entebbe, 1959? 2 pam.
Afr 6484.10   Wild, John V. The story of the Uganda Agreement. London, 1957.
Afr 6484.15   Uganda Independence Conference. Report of the Uganda Independence Conference, 1962. London, 1962.
Afr 6484.20   Uganda. Commissioners for Africanisation. Report. Entebbe, 1962.
Afr 6484.21   Wallis, C.A.G. Report of an inquiry into African local government in the protectorate of Uganda. Uganda, 1953.
Afr 6484.22   Uganda. Board of Inquiry into a Claim for a Rise in Salaries of "E" Scale Public Officers. Report. Entebbe, 1966. 2 pam.

Afr 6486   Uganda - General politics; political parties

Afr 6486.5   Ingrams, William. Uganda. London, 1960.

Afr 6488   Uganda - General history

Afr 6488.5   Brendel, Horst. Die Kolonisation Ugandas. Inaug. Diss. Grossenhain, 1934.
Afr 6488.10   Ingham, Kenneth. The making of modern Uganda. London, 1958.
Afr 6489.12F   Uganda. Local Government Committee. Report, 1930. Entebbe, 1930.

Afr 6490   Uganda - General special

Afr 6490.5   Barber, James P. Imperial frontier. Nairobi, 1968.

Afr 6497   Uganda - History by periods - 1850-1900

Afr 6497.5   Ashe, R.P. Chronicles of Uganda. N.Y., 1895.
Afr 6497.8A   Lugard, F.D. The rise of our East African empire. Edinburgh, 1893. 2v.
Afr 6497.8B   Lugard, F.D. The rise of our East African Empire. Edinburgh, 1893. 2v.
Afr 6497.9   Catholic Union of Great Britain. Memorandum on war in Uganda, 1892. London, 1894.
Afr 6497.10   Colvile, H. The land of the Nile springs. London, 1895.
Afr 6497.12   MacDonald, J.R.L. Soldiering and surveying in British East Africa. London, 1897.
Afr 6497.13   Thruston, A.B. African incidents...Egypt and Unyoro. London, 1900.
Afr 6497.14   Portal, Gerald H. The British mission to Uganda, 1893. London, 1894.
Afr 6497.16   Wild, John Vernon. The Uganda mutiny. London, 1954.
Afr 6497.18A   Low, D.A. Buganda and British overrule. London, 1960.
Afr 6497.18B   Low, D.A. Buganda and British overrule. London, 1960.
Afr 6497.18C   Low, D.A. Buganda and British overrule. London, 1960.

Afr 6498   Uganda - History by periods - 1900-1962

Afr 6498.30   Jones, Herbert G. Uganda in transformation, 1876-1926. London, 1926.
Afr 6498.32   Uganda. President, 1963-1966 (Mutesa). His Exellency the President's speech from the chair of the National Assembly on 15th Dec., 1965. Uganda, 1965.
Afr 6498.35   Thomas, H.B. Uganda. London, 1935.
Afr 6498.47   Postlethwaite, John R. I look back. London, 1947.
Afr 6498.61A   Apter, David E. The political kingdom in Uganda. Princeton, N.J., 1961.
Afr 6498.61B   Apter, David E. The political kingdom in Uganda. Princeton, N.J., 1961.
Afr 6498.61.7   Apter, David E. The political kingdom in Uganda; a study in bureaucratic nationalism. 2nd ed. Princeton, 1967.
Afr 6498.65   Stacey, T. Summons to Ruwenzori. London, 1965.
Afr 6498.65.5   Welbourn, Frederick Burkewood. Religion and politics in Uganda. Nairobi, 1965.

Afr 6535   Uganda - Geography, description, etc.

Afr 6535.3   Wilson, C.F. Uganda and Eyptian Sudan. London, 1882. 2v.
Afr 6535.4   Ansorge, W.J. Under the African sun. N.Y., 1899.
Afr 6535.5A   Johnston, H. The Uganda Protectorate. N.Y., 1902. 2v.
Afr 6535.5B   Johnston, H. The Uganda Protectorate. N.Y., 1902.
Afr 6535.5.2   Johnston, H. The Uganda Protectorate. London, 1902. 2v.
Afr 6535.6   Lloyd, A.B. Uganda to Khartoum. N.Y., 1906.
Afr 6535.7   Filippi, F. de. Ruwenzori, an account of the expedition of L. Arredo. London, 1908.
Afr 6535.7.5   Filippi, F. de. Ruwenzori, an account of the expedition of L. Arredo. N.Y., 1908.
Afr 6535.7.51   Synge, P.M. Mountains of the moon. London, 1937.
Afr 6535.8   Tucker, A.R. Eighteen years in Uganda and East Africa. London, 1908. 2v.
Afr 6535.9   Harford-Battersby, P.F. Pilkington of Uganda. London, n.d.
Afr 6535.10   Wollaston, A.F.R. From Ruwenzore to the Congo. London, 1908.
Afr 6535.10.3   Wollaston, A.F.R. From Ruwenzore to the Congo. N.Y., 1908.
Afr 6535.11   Austin, H.H. MacDonald in Uganda. London, 1903.

Afr 6535   Uganda - Geography, description, etc.
cont.

Afr 6535.12   Wallis, H.R. The handbook of Uganda. London, 1913.
Afr 6535.12.2   Wallis, H.R. Uganda, the handbook of Uganda. London, 1920.
Afr 6535.13   Treves, Fred. Uganda for a holiday. London, 1910.
Afr 6535.14   Jack, E.M. On the Congo frontier. London, 1914.
Afr 6535.15   Fisher, R.B. On the borders of Pigmy land. London, 1905.
Afr 6535.16   Lardner, E.S.D. Soldiering and sport in Uganda. London, 1912.
Afr 6535.16.20   Great Britain. Admiralty. A handbook of the Uganda Protectorate. Oxford, 1920.
Afr 6535.17   Bland-Sutton, J. Men and creatures in Uganda. London, 1933.
Afr 6535.18   Uganda. Department of Information. A guide to Uganda. Entebbe, 1954.
Afr 6535.19   Great Britain. War Office. Intelligence Division. Precis of information concerning the Uganda Protectorate. London, 1902.
Afr 6535.20   Cott, Hugh B. Uganda in black and white. London, 1959.
Afr 6535.33   Worthington, S. Inland waters of Africa. London, 1933.
Afr 6535.36   Nyabongo, A.K. Africa answers back. London, 1936.
Afr 6535.40   Beaufaere, Abel. Ouganda. Paris, 1942.
Afr 6535.45   Cook, Albert R. Uganda memories, 1897-1940. Kampala, 1945.
Afr 6535.61   Harwick, Christopher. Red dust. London, 1961.
Afr 6535.62   McMaster, D.N. A subsistence agricultural geography of Uganda. Bude, 1962.
Afr 6535.62.5   British Information Service. Uganda. N.Y., 1962.
Afr 6535.62.10   British Information Service. Uganda. N.Y., 1962.
Afr 6535.63   Zwilling, Ernst Alexander. Wildes Karamoja. Mödling bei Wien, 1965.
Afr 6535.64   London. Commonwealth Institute. Uganda. London, 1964.
Afr 6535.65   Uganda. National Parks Trustees. Uganda national parks handbook. 24th ed. Kampala, 1965.
Afr 6535.66   Julsrud, Harald G. Jambo Uganda. Oslo, 1966.
Afr 6535.68   Uganda. Ministry of Information. Broadcasting and Tourism. Facts about Uganda. Entebbe, 1968.
Afr 6535.69   American University, Washington, D.C. Foreign Area Studies Division. Area handbook for Uganda. Washington, 1969.

Afr 6538   Uganda - Economic and financial conditions

Afr 6538.3F   Uganda. Development Commission. Report, 1920. Entebbe, 1920.
Afr 6538.5   Uganda. Agricultural Department. Agriculture in Uganda. London, 1940.
Afr 6538.10   Economist (London). Power in Uganda, 1957-1970. London, 1957.
Afr 6538.15   East Africa High Commission. East African Statistical Department. Uganda Unit. The geographical income of Uganda. Summary.
Afr 6538.16   East Africa High Commission. East African Statistical Department. Uganda Unit. The geographical income of Uganda. Annual.
Afr 6538.20   International Bank for Reconstruction and Development. The economic development of Uganda. Baltimore, 1962.
Afr 6538.25   Elkan, Walter. The economic development of Uganda. London, 1961.
Afr 6538.34   Uganda. Government white paper on the report of the Commonwealth Development Corporation's tea survey team. Uganda, 1964.
Afr 6538.35   Commonwealth Development Corporation. Uganda tea survey, 1964. London, 1964.
Afr 6538.36   Uganda. Ministry of Planning and Community Development. Statistics Division. The real growth of the economy of Uganda. Entebbe, 1964.
Afr 6538.37   Overseas Development Institute. Aid in Uganda. London, 1966. 3v.
Afr 6538.38   Uganda. Standing Finance Committee. Joint report of the Standing Finance Committee and the Development and Welfare Committee on post-war development. 2d ed. Entebbe, 1945.
Afr 6538.40F   Uganda. Fiscal Commission. Report. Entebbe, 1962.
Afr 6538.45   Uganda. A five year capital development plan, 1955-1960. Uganda, 1954.
Afr 6538.47   Uganda. Work for progress, the second five-year plan, 1966-1971. Entebbe, 1966.
Afr 6538.50   Italy. Istituto Nazionale per il Commercio Estero. Uganda. Roma, 1964.
Afr 6538.55   Uganda. Ministry of Planning and Economic Development. Work for progress. Entebbe, 1967.
Afr 6538.60   Milton Obote Foundation. The challenge of Uganda's second five year development plan. Kampala, 1967.
Afr 6538.65   Foster, Phillips Wayne. Population growth and rural development in Buganda. College Park, Md., 1968.
Afr 6538.70   Kade, Gunnar. Die Stellung der zentralen Orte in der Kulturlandschaftlichen Entwicklung Bugandas (Uganda). Frankfurt, 1969.

Afr 6540   Uganda - Races

Afr 6540.1   Cunningham, J.F. Uganda and its peoples. London, 1905.
Afr 6540.2   Hattersley, C.W. The Beganda at home. London, 1908.
Afr 6540.3   Kitching, A.L. On the backwaters of the Nile. London, 1912.
Afr 6540.4.5   Roscoe, John. The northern Bantu. Cambridge, 1915.
Afr 6540.4.7   Roscoe, John. Immigrants and their influence. Cambridge, Eng., 1924.
Afr 6540.4.10A   Fallers, Lloyd A. Bantu bureaucracy. Cambridge, Eng., 195-.
Afr 6540.4.11   Fallers, Lloyd A. Bantu bureaucracy. Chicago, 1965.
Afr 6540.4.15   Fallers, Lloyd A. Law without precedent. Chicago, 1969.
X Cg Afr 6540.6A Roscoe, John. The Baganda, account of their customs. London, 1911.
Afr 6540.6B   Roscoe, John. The Baganda, account of their customs. London, 1911.
Afr 6540.6.5   Mair, L.P. An African people in the twentieth century. London, 1934.
Afr 6540.6.10   Kagwa, Apolo. The customs of the Baganoa. N.Y., 1969.
Afr 6540.6.12   Roscoe, John. The Baganda, an account of their native customs and beliefs. 2d ed. N.Y., 1966.
Afr 6540.6.15   Fisher, Ruth Hurditch. Twilight tales of the black Baganda. London, 1911.
Afr 6540.7   Middleton, J. Lugbara religion. London, 1960.
Afr 6540.7.5   Middleton, J. The Lugbara of Uganda. N.Y., 1965.
Afr 6540.8   Hobley, C.W. Eastern Uganda. London, 1902.
Afr 6540.9   Gurling, F.K. The Acholi of Uganda. London, 1960.
Afr 6540.10   Driberg, J.H. The Lango. London, n.d.

Afr 6540   Uganda - Races
cont.

Afr 6540.12	Roscoe, John. The Bakitara or Banyoro. Cambridge, 1923.
Afr 6540.13	Roscoe, John. The Banyankole. Cambridge, 1923.
Afr 6540.14	Roscoe, John. The Bagesu and other tribes of the Uganda protectorate. Cambridge, Eng., 1924.
Afr 6540.15	Hayley, T.T.S. The anatomy of Lango religion and groups. Cambridge, Eng., 1947.
Afr 6540.16	Beattie, John. Bunyord, an African kingdom. N.Y., 1960.
Afr 6540.16.2	Beattie, John. Bunyord, an African kingdom. N.Y., 1964.
Afr 6540.20	Southall, A.W. Alur society. Cambridge, Eng., 1956.
Afr 6540.21	Winter, Edward. Beyond the mountains of the moon. London, 1959.
Afr 6540.23	Thomas, Elizabeth Marshall. Warrior herdsmen. 1st ed. N.Y., 1965.
Afr 6540.24	Richards, Audrey Isabel. Economic development and tribal change, a study of immigrant labour in Baganda. Cambridge, Eng., 1954.
Afr 6540.25	Morris, H.S. The Indians in Uganda. London, 1968.
Afr 6540.30	Edel, May Mandelbaum. The Chiga of western Uganda. London, 1969.

Afr 6541   Uganda - Religion; missions

Afr 6541.3	Michael, Charles D. James Hannington, bishop and martyr; the story of a noble life. London, 1910.
Afr 6541.5	Gale, Hubert Philip. Uganda and Mill Hill fathers. London, 1959.
Afr 6541.10	Faupel, John. African holocaust. London, 1962.
Afr 6541.10.2	Faupel, John. African holocaust. 2nd ed. London, 1962.
Afr 6541.11	Marie André du Sacre Coeur. Uganda. 2.ed. Tournai, 1964.
Afr 6541.12	Willis, John Jameson. An African church in building. London, 1925.
Afr 6541.16	Richards, A.I. Economic development and tribal change. Cambridge, Eng., 1954.
Afr 6541.17	Shephard, G.W. They wait in darkness. N.Y., 1955.
Afr 6541.23	Wilson, C.J. Uganda in the days of Bishop Tucker. London, n.d.
Afr 6541.24	Mullins, Joseph Dennis. The wonderful story of Uganda. London, 1904.
Afr 6541.25	Stock, Sarah Geraldina. The story of Uganda and the Victoria Nyanza Mission. London, 1892.
Afr 6541.27	Philippe, Antony. Au coeur de l'Afrique. Paris, 1929.
Afr 6541.28	Russel, John Keith. Men without god. London, 1966.
Afr 6541.30	Taylor, John Vernon. The growth of the church in Buganda. London, 1958.

Afr 6542   Uganda - Local

Afr 6542.3	Uganda. Commission Appointed to Review the Boundary Between the Districts of Bugisu and Bukedi. Report. Entebbe, 1962.
Afr 6542.4	Uganda. Commission of Inquiry into Disturbances in the Eastern Province, 1960. Report. Entebbe, 1960.
Afr 6542.5	Munger, E.S. Relational patterns of Kampala. Chicago, 1951.
Afr 6542.5.10	Gutkind, Peter. The royal capital of Buganda. The Hague, 1963.
Afr 6542.5.15	Mutesa II, King of Buganda. Desecration of my kingdom. London, 1967.
Afr 6542.10	Larimore, Ann Evans. The alien town. Chicago, 1958.
Afr 6542.15	Morris, H.F. A history of Ankole. Nairobi, 1962.
Afr 6542.16	Fallers, Lloyd A. The king's men. London, 1964.
Afr 6542.16.10	Buganda. Planning Commission. The economic development of kingdom of Buganda. Kampala, 1965.
Afr 6542.17	Burke, Fred. Local government and politics in Uganda. Syracuse, 1964.
Afr 6542.18	Great Britain. Commission. Dispute Between Buganda and Bunyoro. Uganda. Report of a commission of privy counselors on a dispute between Buganda and Bunyoro presented to Parliament. London, 1962.
Afr 6542.20	Bere, Rennie Montague. The way to the mountains of the moon. London, 1966.
Afr 6542.22	Leys, Colin. Politicians and policies. Nairobi, 1967.
Afr 6542.43	Dyson-Hudson, Neville. Karimojong politics. Oxford, 1966.
Afr 6542.45	Farina, Felice. Nel paese dei bevitori di sangue; genti nuove alla ribalta: il popolo Karimojòng. Bologna, 1965.
Afr 6542.50	Vorlaufer, Karl. Physiognomie, Struktur und Funktion Gross Kampalas. Frankfurt, 1967. 2v.
Afr 6542.52	Kreuer, Werner. Der Wandel der sozialen Struktur in den drei ostafrikanischen Königreichen Ankole, Bunyoro und Buganda. Thesis. Bonn, 1966.

Afr 6549.101 - .399   Uganda - Biographies - Individual (A-Z, 299 scheme, by person)

Afr 6549.251	Luck, Anne. African saint. London, 1963.
Afr 6549.251.5	Lloyd, Albert B. Apolo of the Pygmy forest. London, 1936.

Afr 6550   Zanzibar - Periodicals

Afr 6550.5	Dawn in Zanzibar. Cairo.

Afr 6555   Zanzibar - Pamphlet volumes

Afr 6555.01	Pamphlet box. Zanzibar.

Afr 6558   Zanzibar - Collected source materials

Afr 6558.5	Great Britain. Colonial Office. Report on Zanzibar. 1946+ 4v.
Afr 6558.10F	Reports on Zanzibar. Zanzibar, 1936. 3 pam.

Afr 6560   Zanzibar - Government and administration

Afr 6560.2	Zanzibar Constitutional Conference, 1962. Report of the Zanzibar Constitutional Conference, 1962. London, 1962.

Afr 6562   Zanzibar - General politics; political parties

Afr 6562.2	Zanzibar National Party. Whither Zanzibar. Cairo, 1960.

Afr 6565   Zanzibar - General history

Afr 6565.5.2	Pearce, Francis B. Zanzibar. London, 1920.
Afr 6565.24	British Empire Exhibition, Wembley, 1924. Zanzibar, an account of its people. Zanzibar, 1924.
Afr 6565.25	Ingrams, W.H. A school history of Zanzibar. London, 1925.
Afr 6565.31.2	Ingrams, W.H. Zanzibar. London, 1931.
Afr 6565.35	Hollingsworth, L.W. Zanzibar under the Foreign Office. London, 1953.
Afr 6565.40	Gray, John. History of Zanzibar. London, 1962.

Afr 6565   Zanzibar - General history
cont.

Afr 6565.42	Bennett, N.R. Studies in East African history. Boston, 1963.
Afr 6565.44A	Loschie, Michael F. Zanzibar, background to revolution. Princeton, N.J., 1965.
Afr 6565.44B	Loschie, Michael F. Zanzibar, background to revolution. Princeton, N.J., 1965.

Afr 6570   Zanzibar - History by periods - 1800-1890

Afr 6570.3	Russell, L.M.R. General Rigby, Zanzibar and the slave trade. London, 1935.
Afr 6570.3.15	Pease, J.A. How we countenance slavery. London, 1895.
Afr 6570.5	Lyne, Robert Nunez. Zanzibar in contemporary times. N.Y., 1969.
Afr 6570.7A	Coupland, R. The exploitation of East Africa, 1856-1890. London, 1939.
Afr 6570.7B	Coupland, R. The exploitation of East Africa, 1856-1890. London, 1939.
Afr 6570.7.2	Coupland, R. The exploitation of East Africa, 1856-1890. 2nd ed. London, 1968.
Afr 6570.10	Crafton, R.H. Zanzibar affairs, 1914-1933. London, 1953.
Afr 6570.12	Hamilton, Genesta. Princes of Zinj. London, 1957.
Afr 6570.14	Zanzibar. Commission of Inquiry into Disturbances in Zanzibar during June 1961. Report. London, 1961.

Afr 6575   Zanzibar - History by periods - 1963-

Afr 6575.2	Okello, John. Revolution in Zanzibar. Nairobi, 1967.

Afr 6585   Zanzibar - Geography, description, etc.

Afr 6585.1	Middleton, John. Zanzibar. London, 1965.
Afr 6585.2	Schmidt, K.W. Zanzibar. Leipzig, 1888.
Afr 6585.4	Burton, Richard Francis. Zanzibar; city, island, and coast. N.Y., 1967. 2v.
Afr 6585.6	Ruete, E. Memoirs of an Arabian princess. N.Y., 1888.
Afr 6585.7	Ommanney, F.D. Isle of Cloves. Philadelphia, 1956.
Afr 6585.8	Great Britain. Central Office Of Information. Zanzibar. Harrow, 1963.
Afr 6585.9	Shelswell-White, Geoffrey Henry. A guide to Zanzibar. Zanzibar, 1949.

Afr 6588   Zanzibar - Economic and financial conditions

Afr 6588.2	Bartlett, C. Statistics of the Zanzibar Protectorate. 8th ed. Zanzibar, 1936.
Afr 6588.4	East African Common Services Organization. The pattern of income expenditure and consumption of unskilled workers in Zanzibar. Nairobie, 1963. 2 pam.

Afr 6590   Zanzibar - Races

Afr 6590.5	Saleh, Ibuni. A short history of the Comorians in Zanzibar. Tanganyika, 1936.
Afr 6590.10	Dale, Godfrey. The peoples of Zanzibar. Westminster, 1920.

Afr 6592   Zanzibar - Local - Pemba

Afr 6592.1	Craster, J.E.E. Pemba, the spice island of Zanzibar. London, 1913.

Afr 6595   Zanzibar - Local - Others

Afr 6595.5	Harkema, Roelof Cornelius. De stad Zanzibar in de tweede helft van de negentiende eeuw en enkele oudere Oostafrikaanse Kuststeden. Loenen aan de Vecht, 1967.

Afr 6599   Zanzibar - Biographies - Individual (A-Z, 99 scheme, by person)

Afr 6599.2	Smith, Herbert Maynard. Frank, bishop of Zanzibar. London, 1926.

Afr 6603   German Africa in general - Bibliographies

Afr 6603.2	Bridgman, Jon. German Africa. Stanford, 1965.

Afr 6605   German Africa in general - Pamphlet volumes

Afr 6605.3	Pamphlet box. German Africa.

Afr 6612   German Africa in general - General politics; political parties

Afr 6612.5	Zamengof, M. Kolonialnye Pritiazanie germanskogo fashizma v Afrike. Moscow, 1937.

Afr 6615   German Africa in general - General history

Afr 6615.5	Africanus. The Prussian lash in Africa. London, 1918.
Afr 6615.10	Calvert, Albert Frederick. The German African empire. London, 1916.

Afr 6620   German Africa in general - History by periods - 1914-

Afr 6620.50	O'Neill, H.C. The war in Africa, 1914-1917. London, 1919.
Afr 6620.51	Dane, Edmond. British campaigns in Africa and...Pacific. London, 1919.
Afr 6620.52	Through swamp and forest. London, 1917.
Afr 6620.55	Gorges, E.H. The great war in West Africa. London, 1930.
Afr 6620.60	Charbonneau, J. On se bat sous l'équateur. Paris, 1933.
Afr 6620.65	Steer, G.L. Judgment on German Africa. London, 1939.
Afr 6620.70	Reitz, Deneys. Africander. N.Y., 1933.
Afr 6620.75.5	Reitz, Deneys. Trekking on. London, 1933.

Afr 6640   German Africa in general - History - Special [Discontinued]

Afr 6640.3	Luecke, J.H. Bevölkerung und Aufenthaltsrecht in den Department schutzgebieten Afrikas. Hamburg, 1913.
Afr 6640.4	Luecke, J.H. Bevölkerung und Aufenthaltsrecht in den Department schutzgebieten Afrikas. Inaug. Diss. Hamburg, 1913.
Afr 6640.10	Grosclaude, P. Menaces Allemandes sur l'Afrique. Paris, 1938.
Afr 6640.12	Ritchie, E.M. The unfinished war, the drama of Anglo-German conflict in Africa. London, 1940.
Afr 6640.17	Freytagh Loringhoven, Axel F. Das Mandatsrecht in den Deutschen Kolonien. München, 1938.
Afr 6640.19	Perbandt, C. von. Hermann von Wissmann. Berlin, 1906.
Afr 6640.20	Becker, A. Hermann von Wissmann. Berlin, 1914.
Afr 6640.22	Mueller, F.F. Kolonien unter der Peitsche. Berlin, 1962.

Afr 6645   German Africa in general - Geography, description, etc.

Afr 6645.5	Bongard, Oscar. Wie wandere ich nach Deutschen Kolonien aus. 3. Aufl. Berlin, 1910.
Afr 6645.10	Zoeller, Hugo. Als Jurnalist und Forscher in Deutschlands grosser Kolonialzeit. Leipzig, 1930.

Afr 6645   German Africa in general - Geography, description, etc.
cont.
Afr 6645.15   Langheld, Wilhelm. Zwanzig Jahre in deutschen Kolonien.
Berlin, 1909.
Afr 6645.17   Zoeller, Hugo. Die deutschen Besitzungen an der
westafricanischen Küste. v.1-4. Berlin, 1885.
2v.

Afr 6648   German Africa in general - Races
Afr 6648.3F   Luschan, F. Von. Beitraege zur Völkerkunde. Berlin, 1897.

Afr 6650   Togo - Periodicals
Afr 6650.5   Centre d'Études et de Recherches de Kara. Documents.
Lama-Kara, Togo. 1,1967+

Afr 6664   Togo - General history
Afr 6664.5   Alcandre, Sylvine. La république autonome du Togo.
Paris, 1957.
Afr 6664.10   Cornevin, Robert. Histoire du Togo. Paris, 1959.
Afr 6664.10.2   Cornevin, Robert. Histoire du Togo. Paris, 1962.
Afr 6664.10.3   Cornevin, Robert. Histoire du Togo. 3e ed. Paris, 1969.
Afr 6664.10.5   Cornevin, Robert. Le Togo, nation-pilote. Paris, 1963.
Afr 6664.12   Wuelker, Gabriele. Togo: Tradition und Entwicklung.
Stuttgart, 1966.
Afr 6664.15   Tokareva, Z.I. Togolezskaia respublika. Moscow, 1962.
Afr 6664.16   Togo. Bühl-boden, 1961.

Afr 6670   Togo - History by periods - 1914-1957
Afr 6670.25   Maroix, J.E.P. Le Togo. Paris, 1938.
Afr 6670.928   Luce, Edmond P. L'acte de naissance d'une république
africaine autonome. Paris, 1928.
Afr 6670.939   Pechoux, L. Le mandat français sur le Togo. Paris, 1939.
Afr 6670.957   Luchaire, Fr. Le Togo français. Paris, 1957.

Afr 6685   Togo - Geography, description, etc.
Afr 6685.2   Henrici, Ernst. Das deutsche Togogebiet und meine
Afrikareise, 1887. Leipzig, 1888.
Afr 6685.3   Klose, Heinrich. Togo unter deutschen Flagge.
Berlin, 1899.
Afr 6685.5   Calvert, Albert F. Togoland. London, 1918.
Afr 6685.7   Full, August. Fünfzig Jahre Togo. Berlin, 1935.
Afr 6685.8   Chazelas, V. Territoires africains sous mandat de la
France. Paris, 1931.
Afr 6685.9   Armattoe, R.E.G. The golden age of West African
civilization. Londonderry, 1946.
Afr 6685.10   France. Commissariat au Togo. Guide de la colonisation au
Togo. Paris, 1924.
Afr 6685.11   Banque Centrale des Etats de l'Afrique de l'Ouest. Togo,
1960. Paris, 1960.
Afr 6685.12   Kueas, Richard. Togo-Erinnerungen. Berlin, 1939.

Afr 6686   Togo - Economic and financial conditions
Afr 6686.20   Checchi and Company. A development company for Togo.
Washington, 1963.
Afr 6686.25   Samuel, Ferjus. La muse en valeur du Togo sous le mandat
français. Thèse. Paris, 1926.
Afr 6686.30   Och, Helmut. Die wirtschaftsgeographische
Entwicklung...Togo und Kamerun. Königsberg, 1931.
Afr 6686.35   Metzger, O.F. Unsere alte Kolonie Togo. Neudamm, 1941.
Afr 6686.40.2   France. Ministère de la Coopération. Economie et plan de
développement, Republique Togolaise. 2. ed. Paris, 1965.
Afr 6686.48   Togo. Plan quinquennal de développement, 1966-1970.
Paris, 1965.
Afr 6686.48.2   Togo. Five year development plan, 1966-1970. Paris, 1965.
Afr 6686.48.5F   Togo. Plan de développement économique et social,
1966-1970: annexes techniques, développement rural.
Paris, 1965.
Afr 6686.48.10   Togo. Plan de développement économique et social,
1966-1970. Annexes techniques: industrie. Paris, 1965.
Afr 6686.48.15F   Müller, Julius Otto. Enquête sociologique "Le paysan face
au développement". Munich, 1965.
Afr 6686.48.20F   Munich. Institut für Wirtschaftsforschung. Plan de
développement économique et social, 1966-1970; l'artisanat
togolais. Munich, 1965.
Afr 6686.48.25F   Société d'Études pour le Développement Économique et
Social, Paris. Plan de développement, 1966-1970:
organization administrative et développement. Paris, 1965.
Afr 6686.48.30F   Munich. Institut für Wirtschaftsforschung. Plan de
développement économique et social, 1966-1970; le commerce
au Togo. Munich, 1965.
Afr 6686.48.35F   Société d'Études pour le Développement Économique et
Social, Paris. Plan de développement économique et social,
1966-1970: scolarisation. Paris, 1965.
Afr 6686.48.40F   Munich. Institut für Wirtschaftsforschung. Les finances
publiques du Togo, budget-fiscalité; situation,
1965-perspectives, 1970. München, 1965.
Afr 6686.48.45F   Société d'Études pour le Développement Économique et
Social, Paris. Plan de développement économique et social,
1966-1970. Paris, 1965.
Afr 6686.201   Kuczynski, R.R. The Cameroons and Togoland. London, 1939.

Afr 6688   Togo - Races
Afr 6688.2   Phehn, R. Beitraege zur Völkerkunde des Togogebietes.
Halle, 1898.
Afr 6688.4   Puig, F. Etude sur les coutumes des Cabrais (Togo). Thèse.
Toulouse, 1934.
Afr 6688.5   Froelich, J.C. Les populations du Nord-Togo. Paris, 1963.

Afr 6689   Togo - Religion; missions
Afr 6689.1   Church between colonial powers. London, 1965.
Afr 6689.5   Faure, Jean. Togo; champ de mission. Paris, 1943.
Afr 6689.10   Nelle, Albrecht. Aufbruch vom Götterberg.
Stuttgart, 1968.

Afr 6700   Cameroons - Periodicals (A-Z, 99 scheme)
Afr 6700.1   Abbia. Yaoundé. 1,1963+
2v.
Afr 6700.2F   Afri-Cam. Yaoundé. 6,1969+
Afr 6700.4   Association Française pour les Recherches et Études
Camerounaises. Bulletin. Bordeaux. 1,1965+
Afr 6700.34   Good news from over the sea. Naperville, Illinois. 1920
Afr 6700.75   Recherches et études camerounaises. Yaounde.
2v.
Afr 6700.91   Voice of Kamerun. Cairo. 1958
Afr 6700.91.2   Voix du Kamerun. Caire. 1958

Afr 6703   Cameroons - Bibliographies
Afr 6703   Pamphlet box. Cameroon.

Afr 6705   Cameroons - Pamphlet volumes
Afr 6705.1   Pamphlet box. Cameroon.
Afr 6705.5   Cameroon, West. Constitution. West Cameroon Constitution,
1961. Buea, 1961.

Afr 6708   Cameroons - Collected source materials
Afr 6708.5   Cameroons, Southern. Development Agency. Report. 1,1957+

Afr 6710   Cameroons - Government and administration
Afr 6710.3   Cameroon. Laws, statutes, etc. Die Landesgesetzgebung für
das Schutzgebiet Kamerun. Berlin, 1912.
Afr 6710.5   Kwayeb, E.K. Les institutions de droit public du pays
Bamileke. Paris, 1960.
Afr 6710.6   Cameroon. Constitution. Constitution. Buea, 1963.

Afr 6715   Cameroons - General history
Afr 6715.1   Mveny, Engelbert. Histoire du Cameroun. Paris, 1963.
Afr 6715.10   Drews, Max. Frankreich versagt in Kamerun. Berlin, 1940.
Afr 6715.15   Froelich, Jean Claude. Cameroun, Togo. Paris, 1956.
Afr 6715.20   Lembezat, Bertrand. Le Cameroun. Paris, 1954.
Afr 6715.21   Gardinier, D.E. Cameroon, United Nations challenge to
French policy. London, 1963.
Afr 6715.25   El Kamerun. n.p., 1957?

Afr 6719   Cameroons - History by periods - 1880-1914
Afr 6719.5   Pultkamer, Jesko. Gouverneursjahre in Kamerun.
Berlin, 1912.

Afr 6720   Cameroons - History by periods - 1914-1960
Afr 6720.2   Zimmermann, Oscar. Durch Busch und Steppe vom Camps.
Berlin, 1909.
Afr 6720.3   Rudin, H.R. Germans in the Cameroons, 1814-1914.
London, 1938.
Afr 6720.10   Seitz, Theodor. Vom Aufstieg und Niederbruck deutscher
Kolonialmacht. Karlsruhe, 1927-29.
3v.
Afr 6720.15   Zimmermann, Emil. Meine Kriegsfahrt von Kamerun zur
Heimat. Berlin, 1915.
Afr 6720.25   Franceschi, Roger. Le mandat français au Cameroun. Thèse.
Paris, 1929.
Afr 6720.25.5   Sholaster, H. Bischof Heinrich Vieter. Limburg, 1925.
Afr 6720.28   Ferrandi, Jean. Conquête du Cameroun-Nord, 1914-1915.
Paris, 1928.
Afr 6720.28.3   Ferrandi, Jean. De la Benoue à l'Atlantique à la poursuite
des allemands. Paris, 1931.
Afr 6720.28.10   Mentzel, H. Die Kämpfe in Kamerun, 1914-1916. Vorbereitung
und Verlauf. Inaug. Diss. Berlin, 1936.
Afr 6720.28.15   Aymerich, J.G. La conquête du Camcroun. Paris, 1936.
Afr 6720.30   Costedoat, René. Le français et la réorganisation des
territoires du Cameroun. Thèse. Besançon, 1930.
Afr 6720.37   Kemner, W. Kamerun. Berlin, 1937.
Afr 6720.56   Nguini, Marcel. La valeur politique et sociale de la
tutelle française au Cameroun. Thèse.
Aix-en-Provence, 1956.
Afr 6720.59   Cameroons, French. Cameroun. Paris, 1959.
Afr 6720.60   Stoecker, Helmuth. Kamerun unter deutscher
Kolonialherrschaft. v.1- Berlin, 1960-
2v.
Afr 6720.60.5   Union des Peuples Camerounais. Memoire soumis à la
Conférence des états africains indépandants. Le
Caire, 1960.
Afr 6720.62   Kuoh Mukouri, J. Doigts noirs. Montreal, 1963.
Afr 6720.64   Levini, V.T. The Cameroons, from mandate to independence.
Berkeley, 1964.
Afr 6720.65.2   Cameroon. Ministère de l'Information et du Tourisme. Les
grandes dates du Cameroun. 2. éd. Yaoundé, 1965.

Afr 6725   Cameroons - History by periods - 1960-
Afr 6725.5   Ahidjo, Ahmado. Contribution à la construction nationale.
Paris, 1964.

Afr 6738   Cameroons - Geography, description, etc.
Afr 6738.2A   Burton, R.F. Abeokuta and the Camaroons mountains.
London, 1863.
Afr 6738.2B   Burton, R.F. Abeokuta and the Camaroons mountains.
London, 1863.
Afr 6738.3   Seidel, A. Deutsch-Kamerun wie es ist. Berlin, 1906.
Afr 6738.4   Hutter, F. Wanderungen und Forschungen im nordhinterland
von Kamerun. Braunschweig, 1902.
Afr 6738.4.9   Morgen, C. Von. Durch Kamerun von sued nach nord.
Leipzig, 1893.
Afr 6738.5   Zintgraff, E. Nord-Kamerun. Berlin, 1895.
Afr 6738.6F   Thorbecke, F. Das Maneuguba-Hochland. Berlin, 1911.
Afr 6738.6.5   Thorbecke, F. Im Hochland von Mittel-Kamerun.
Hamburg, 1914-16.
4v.
Afr 6738.8.5   Schwarz, B. Kamerun, Reise in die Hinterlande der Kolonie.
2e Ausgabe. Leipzig, 1888.
Afr 6738.9   Sembritzki, Emil. Kamerun. Berlin, 1909.
Afr 6738.10   Haase, Lene. Durchs unbekannte Kamerun. Berlin, 1915.
Afr 6738.11   Calvert, A.F. The Cameroons. London, 1917.
Afr 6738.12   Marabail, H.J.J. Etude sur les territoires du Cameroun
occupés par les troupes françaises. Paris, 1919.
Afr 6738.13   France. Commissariat de la République Française au
Cameroun. Guide de la colonisation au Cameroun.
Paris, 1923.
Afr 6738.15A   Mackenzie, J.K. African clearings. Boston, 1924.
Afr 6738.15B   Mackenzie, J.K. African clearings. Boston, 1924.
Afr 6738.15C   Mackenzie, J.K. African clearings. Boston, 1924.
Afr 6738.17   Dominik, Hans. Vom Atlantik zum Tschadsee. Berlin, 1908.
Afr 6738.20   Masson, Georges. La mise en valeur des territoires des
Cameroun placés sous le mandat français. Thèse.
Paris, 1928.
Afr 6738.22   Mueller, Arno. Die kameruner Waldländer. Inaug. Diss.
Ohlau in Schlesien, 1930.
Afr 6738.23   Chazelas, Victor. Territoires africains sous mandat de la
France. Paris, 1931.
Afr 6738.25   Weiler, Carlos. Wirtschaftsgeographie des britischen
Mandats Kamerun. Inaug. Diss. Berlin, 1933.
Afr 6738.30   Wilbois, J. La Cameroun. Paris, 1934.
Afr 6738.35   Vereet, E.P.A. Het zwarte leven van Mabumba. n.p., 1935.
Afr 6738.40   Schmidt, Agathe. Kamerun. Berlin, 1955.
Afr 6738.41   Reicheon, Anton. Die deutsche Kolonie Kamerun.
Berlin, 1884.

Afr 6738   Cameroons - Geography, description, etc.
cont.

Afr 6738.42   Mackenzie, Jean Kenyon. Black sheep. New ed.
Boston, 1925.

Afr 6738.43   Cameroun. 1966, bilan de cinq années d'indépendance.
Monaco, 1966.

Afr 6738.44   Vaast, Pierre. La République fédérale du Cameroun.
Paris, 1962.

Afr 6738.46   L'oeuvre de la France au Cameroun. Yaoundé, 1936.

Afr 6738.48   Brendl, Oskar. Die Bundes-Republik Kamerun. Hagen, 1965.

Afr 6738.50   Billard, Pierre. Le Cameroun fédéral. Lyon, 1968.
2v.

Afr 6738.52   Haeberle, Wilhelm. Kamerun. Stuttgart, 1967.

Afr 6738.54   Cameroon. Ministère de l'Information et du Tourisme.
Cameroun. Paris, 1970.

Afr 6739   Cameroons - Economic and financial conditions

Afr 6739.5   Cameroon. Ministère des Finances et du Plan. Direction du
Plan et de la Coopération Technique. Bulletin trimestriel
d'information. Yaounde. 4,1964+

Afr 6739.236   Lawless, L.G. Le principe de l'égalité économique au
Cameroun. Paris, 1936.

Afr 6739.236.5   Lawless, L.G. Le principe de l'égalité économique au
Cameroun. Paris, 1937.

Afr 6739.256   Binet, Jacques. Budgets familiaux des planteurs de Cacao
au Cameroun. Paris, 1956.

Afr 6739.260   Societe d'Etudes pour le Developpement. Rapport sur les
possibilités de développement industriél. Paris, 1960.

Afr 6739.260.5F   Société Générale d'Etudes et de Planification, Paris.
Cameroun. Paris, 1960.
2v.

Afr 6739.261F   Cameroon. Ministère des Finances et du Plan. Premier plan
quinquennal économique. Yaounde, 1961.

Afr 6739.262.2   France. Ministère de la Coopération. Direction des Affaires
Économiques et Financières. Sous-Direction des Études
Générales. Economie et plan de développement, République
fédérale du Cameroun. 2. éd. Paris, 1965.

Afr 6739.263   Italy. Istituto Nazionale per il Commercio Estero.
Cameroun. Roma, 1963.

Afr 6739.264F   Cameroon. Ministère des Finances et du Plan. Rapport
général du premier plan quinquennal. Yaounde, 1964.

Afr 6739.265   Société d'Etudes pour le Développement Economique et
social. Développement industriel au Cameroun.
Paris, 1965.

Afr 6739.265.5   Kratz, Achim. Voraussetzungen und Möglichkeiten einer
industriellen Entwicklung in Kamerun. Hamburg, 1965.

Afr 6739.268   Bederman, Sanford Harold. The Cameroons Development
Corporation. Bota, 1968.

Afr 6739.268.5   Golubchik, Mark M. Federativnaia Respublika Kamerun.
Moskva, 1968.

Afr 6739.268.10   Hugon, Philippe. Analyse du sous-développement en Afrique
noire. Paris, 1968.

Afr 6739.268.15   Loginova, Valentina P. Federativnaia Respublika Kamerun.
Moskva, 1968.

Afr 6740   Cameroons - Races

Afr 6740.5   Mansfield, Alfred. Verwald-Dokumente. Berlin, 1908.

Afr 6740.10   Nicol, Yves. La tribu des Bakoko. Thèse. Paris, 1929.

Afr 6740.15   Tardits, Claude. Contribution à l'étude des populations
Bamileke de l'Ouest Cameroun. Paris, 1960.

Afr 6740.15.5   Hurault, Jean. La structure sociale des Bamileke.
Paris, 1962.

Afr 6740.15.10   Lecoq, Raymond. Les Bamileke. Paris, 1953.

Afr 6740.18   Garine, Igor de. Les Massa du Cameroun. Paris, 1964.

Afr 6740.20   Duisbung, Adolf von. In Lande des Cheghu von Bornu.
Berlin, 1942.

Afr 6740.25   "It's like this" essays. Bali, Cameroon. 2,1964+

Afr 6740.30   Lembezat, Bertrand. Les populations paiennes.
Paris, 1961.

Afr 6740.35   Lebeuf, J.P. L'habitation des Fati. Paris, 1961.

Afr 6740.40   Podlewski, André Michel. La dynamique des principales
populations du Nord Cameroun. Paris, 1966.

Afr 6740.45   Koch, Henri. Magie et chasse dans la forêt camerounaise.
Paris, 1968.

Afr 6741   Cameroons - Religion; missions

Afr 6741.2   Emonts, Johannes. Ins Steppen- und Bergland Innerkameruns.
Aachen, 1922.

Afr 6741.4   Bahoken, Jean Calvin. Clairières métaphysiques africaines,
essai sur la philosophie et la religion chez les Bantu du
Sud-Caméroun. Paris, 1967.

Afr 6741.6   Häberle, Wilhelm. Trommeln, Mächte und ein Ruf.
Stuttgart, 1966.

Afr 6741.10   Reyburn, William David. Out of the African night. 1st ed.
N.Y., 1968.

Afr 6741.12   Grob, Francis. Témoins camerounais de l'Évangile.
Yaoundé, 1967.

Afr 6742   Cameroons - Special customs

Afr 6742.5   Endresen, Halfdan. Als Sklave verkauft; Sklaverei und
Sklavenhandel im heutigen Afrika und Arabien. Basel, 1966.

Afr 6742.8   Libère, Mahend Betind Pierre. Rites et croyances relatifs
à l'enfance chez les Banen du Cameroun. Paris, 1967.

Afr 6743   Cameroons - Local

Afr 6743.3   Passarge, S. Adamana. Berlin, 1895.

Afr 6743.5   Ardener, Edwin. Historical notes on the scheduled
monuments of West Cameroon. Buea, 1965.

Afr 6743.50   Egerton, F.C.C. African majesty, a record of refuge at the
court of the king of Bangangte in the French Cameroons.
London, 1938.

Afr 6743.55   Guillard, Joanny. Galenpoui. Paris, 1965.

Afr 6743.60   Lestringant, Jacques. Les pays de guider au Cameroun.
Versailles, 1964.

Afr 6743.65   Mohamadou, Eldridge. L'histoire de Tibati, chefferie
Foulbé du Cameroun. Yaoundé, 1965.

Afr 6750   Tanganyika; Tanzania - Periodicals

Afr 6750.2   Mambo Leo (Tanganyika territory). Dar es Salaam. 55,1925+
2v.

Afr 6750.3F   Settler, a weekly journal. Dar es Salaam.

Afr 6750.4   Handbook of Tanganyika. London, n.d.

Afr 6750.4.2   Handbook of Tanganyika. 2d ed. Dar es Salaam, 1958.

Afr 6750.5   Tanganyika trade bulletin. Dar es Salaam. 6,1957+

Afr 6750.6   Tanganyika notes and records. Dar es Salaam. 34,1953+
6v.

Afr 6750.7   Mbioni. Dar es Salaam. 2,1965+
12v.

Afr 6750   Tanganyika; Tanzania - Periodicals
cont.

Afr 6750.8   Dar es Salaam. University College. Institute of Public
Administration. IPA study. Dar es Salaam. 1,1965+
2v.

Afr 6750.10   Mwenge. Dar es Salaam. 2,1962+

Afr 6750.12   Tanzania. National Museum. Annual report. Dar es Salaam.
1966+

Afr 6750.14   Dar-es-Salaam. University College. Bureau of Resource
Assessment and Land Use Planning. Research papers.
1,1968+

Afr 6750.15   Dar-es-Salaam. University College. Bureau of Resource
Assessment and Land Use Planning. Research notes.
Dar-es-Salaam. 2,1967+

Afr 6750.16F   Tanzania zamani. Dar-es-Salaam. 1,1967+

Afr 6753   Tanganyika; Tanzania - Bibliographies

Afr 6753.5   Bibliografi over Tanzania. København, 1967.

Afr 6753.10   Decalo, Samuel. Tanzania: an introductory bibliography.
Kingston?, 1968.

Afr 6753.15   Bates, Margaret L. A study guide for Tanzania.
Boston, 1969.

Afr 6755   Tanganyika; Tanzania - Pamphlet volumes

Afr 6755   Pamphlet box. German East Africa.

Afr 6755.01   Pamphlet box. German East Africa.

Afr 6755.1   Pamphlet box. German East Africa.

Afr 6757   Tanganyika; Tanzania - Collected source materials

Afr 6757.2   Tanganyika. Department of Antiquities. Annual report.

Afr 6757.4   Tanganyika. Public Work Department. Annual report.

Afr 6757.10   Tanganyika. National Assembly. Assembly debates, official
report. 27,1952+
12v.

Afr 6760   Tanganyika; Tanzania - Government and administration

Afr 6760.5   MacKenzie, William James Millar. Report of the Special
Commissioner appointed to examine matters arising out of
the report of the Committee on Constitutional Development.
Dar es Salaam, 1953.

Afr 6760.7   Fabri, F. Deutsch-Ostafrica. Köln, 1886.

Afr 6760.10   Datta, A.K. Tanganyika. n.p., 1955.

Afr 6760.15   Tanzania. Presidential Commission on the Establishment of a
Democratic One Party State. Report. Dar es Salaam, 1965.

Afr 6760.20F   Tanganyika. Africanisation Commission. Report of the
Africanisation Commission, 1962. Dar es Salaam, 1950.

Afr 6760.22A   Bienen, Henry. Tanzania; party transformation.
Princeton, 1967.

Afr 6760.22B   Bienen, Henry. Tanzania; party transformation.
Princeton, 1967.

Afr 6760.25   Meienberg, Hildebrand. Tanzanian citizen: a civics
textbook. Nairobi, 1966[1967].

Afr 6760.30   Tanganyika. Local government memoranda. Dar-es-Salaam.
2,1957

Afr 6767 - 6770   Tanganyika; Tanzania - General history (By date)

Afr 6769.60   Clarke, P.H.C. A short history of Tanganyika.
London, 1960.

Afr 6769.60.2   Clarke, P.H.C. A short history of Tanganyika. 2nd ed.
Nairobi, 1963.

Afr 6769.63   Taylor, J.C. The political development of Tanganyika.
Stanford, 1963.

Afr 6769.65   Listowel, Judith. The making of Tanganyika. London, 1965.

Afr 6769.68   Austen, Ralph Albert. Northwest Tanzania under German and
British rule. New Haven, 1968.

Afr 6769.68.5   Roberts, Andrew. Tanzania before 1900. Nairobi, 1968.

Afr 6775   Tanganyika; Tanzania - History by periods - Before 1800

Afr 6775.5   Robinson, A.E. Some historical notes on East Africa.
n.p., 1936.

Afr 6775.6F   Freeman-Grenville, G.S. The medieval history of the coast
of Tanganyika. Berlin, 1962.

Afr 6776   Tanganyika; Tanzania - History by periods - 1800-1850

Afr 6776.5   Fouquer, Roger. Mirambo, un chief de guerre dans l'Est
Africain vers 1830-1884. Paris, 1967.

Afr 6777   Tanganyika; Tanzania - History by periods - 1850-1900

Afr 6777.2   Behr, H.F. von. Kriegsbilder aus dem Araberaupland.
Leif, 1891.

Afr 6777.3   Schmidt, R. Geschichte des Araberaufstandes in Ost-Afrika.
Frankfurt, n.d.

Afr 6777.4   Wagner, J. Deutsch-Ostafrika. 2. ed. Berlin, 1888.

Afr 6777.5   Plumon, E. La colonie allemande de l'Afrique Orientale.
Heidelberg, 1906.

Afr 6777.6   Peters, Karl. Die Gründung von Deutsch-Ostafrika.
Berlin, 1906.

Afr 6777.7   Peters, Karl. Die Deutsche-Ostafrikanische Kolonie.
Berlin, 1889.

Afr 6777.7.5   Peters, Karl. Wie Deutsch-Ostafrika entstand.
Leipzig, 1912.

Afr 6777.7.8   Peters, Karl. Wie Deutsch-Ostafrika entstand.
Leipzig, 1940.

Afr 6777.8   Peters, Karl. Deutsch-national. Berlin, 1887.

Afr 6777.9   Peters, Karl. Gesammelte Schriften. München, 1943-44.
3v.

Afr 6777.10   Nigmann, Ernst. Geschichte der kaiserlichen Schutztruppe
für Deutsch-Ostafrika. Berlin, 1911.

Afr 6778   Tanganyika; Tanzania - History by periods - 1900-1914

Afr 6778.1   Goetzen, Gustave Adolf, Graf von. Deutsche-Ostafrika im
Aufstand, 1905-06. Berlin, 1909.

Afr 6778.2   Iliffe, John. Tanganyika under German rule, 1905-1912.
London, 1969.

Afr 6780   Tanganyika; Tanzania - History by periods - 1914-1960

Afr 6780.01   Pamphlet box. German East Africa.

Afr 6780.5   Young, F.B. Marching on Tanga. London, 1917.

Afr 6780.6   Crowe, J.H. General Smuts campaign in East Africa.
London, 1918.

Afr 6780.7   Stienon, Charles. La campagne anglo-belge. Paris, 1917.

Afr 6780.8   Dolbey, R.V. Sketches of the East Africa campaign.
London, 1918.

Afr 6780.9   Schnee, A. Meine Erlebnisse Während der Kriegszeit in
Deutsch-Ostafrika. Leipzig, 1918.

Afr 6780.10A   Lettow-Vorbeck, P.E. von. Meine Erinnerungen aus
Ostafrika. Leipzig, 1920.

Afr 6780 **Tanganyika; Tanzania - History by periods - 1914-1960**
cont.

Afr 6780.10B	Lettow-Vorbeck, P.E. von. Meine Erinnerungen aus Ostafrika. Leipzig, 1920.
Afr 6780.10.5	Lettow-Vorbeck, P.E. von. My reminiscences of East Africa. London, 1920.
Afr 6780.10.7	Lettow-Vorbeck, P.E. von. East African campaigns. N.Y., 1957.
Afr 6780.10.20	Lettow-Vorbeck, P.E. von. Um Vaterland und Kolonies. Berlin, 1919.
Afr 6780.10.23	Lettow-Vorbeck, P.E. von. Mein Leben. Biberach an der Riss, 1957.
Afr 6780.10.25	Goebel, J. Afrika zu unsern Füssen. Leipzig, 1925.
Afr 6780.10.30	Gardner, B. German east, the story of the First World War in East Africa. London, 1963.
Afr 6780.10.31	Gardner, B. On to Kilimanjaro. Philadelphia, 1963.
Afr 6780.11	Arning, W. Vier Jahre Weltkrieg in Deutsch-Ostafrika. Hannover, 1919.
Afr 6780.12	Deppe, L. Mit Lettow-Vorbeck durch Afrika. Berlin, 1919.
Afr 6780.13	Downes, Walter D. With the Nigerians in German East Africa. London, 1919.
Afr 6780.14	Schnee, Heinrich. Deutsch-ostafrika Während des Weltkrieges. Berlin, 1919.
Afr 6780.15	Buchanan, A. Three years of war in East Africa. London, 1919.
Afr 6780.16	Fendall, C.P. The East African force, 1915-1919. London, 1921.
Afr 6780.18	Buhrer, J. L'Afrique orientale allemande et la guerre. Paris, 1922.
Afr 6780.20	Daye, P. Avec les Vainqueures de Tahora. 2. ed. Paris, 1918.
Afr 6780.22	Clifford, H. The Gold Coast regiment in the East African campaign. London, 1920.
Afr 6780.24	Letcher, O. Cohort of the tropics. London, 1930.
Afr 6780.26	Moulaert, Georges. La campagne du Tanganika (1916-1917). Bruxelles, 1934.
Afr 6780.28	Cameron, D. My Tanganyika service and some Nigeria. London, 1939.
Afr 6780.30	Kock, Nis. Blockade and jungle. London, 1940.
Afr 6780.32	Weston, F. The black slaves of Prussia. Boston, 1918.
Afr 6780.35	Regendanz, W.C. Die Giraffe und der König von England. n.p., n.d.
Afr 6780.37	Pienaar, M.J.P. Baanbrekers in die maalstroom. Kaapstad, 1942.
Afr 6780.40	United Nations Review. Tanganyika. N.Y., 1955.
Afr 6780.42	Leubuscher, Charlotte. Tanganyika territory. Oxford, 1944.
Afr 6780.43	Mustafa, Sophia. The Tanganyika way. London, 1962.
Afr 6780.46	Katsman, V.I. Tanganika, 1946-61. Moscow, 1962.
Afr 6780.68	Stephens, Hugh W. The political transformation of Tanganyika, 1920-1967. N.Y., 1968.

Afr 6785 **Tanganyika; Tanzania - History by periods - 1960-**

Afr 6785.2	Tanzania. President. President's address to the National assembly, June 8, 1965. Dar es Salaam, 1965.
Afr 6785.5	Tordoff, William. Government and politics in Tanzania. Nairobi, 1967.
Afr 6785.8	Cliffe, Lionel. One party democracy; the 1965 Tanzania general elections. Nairobi, 1967.

Afr 6850 **Tanganyika; Tanzania - History - Special [Discontinued]**

Afr 6850.3	Stuhlmann, F. Handwerk und Industrie in Ostafrika. Hamburg, 1910.
Afr 6850.7	Koch, Ludwig. Ostafrika in der Geschichte der Weltwirtschaft. Berlin, 1930.
Afr 6850.9F	Tanganyika Territory. Secretariat. Census of the native population of Tanganyika territory, 1931. Dar es Salaam, 1932.
Afr 6850.11	Redeker, D. Die Geschichte der Tagespresse Deutsch-Ostafrikas, 1899-1916. Inaug. Diss. Berlin, 1937.
Afr 6850.13	Vitzthum von Eckstaedt, B. Tanganjikas wirtschaftliche Bedeutung für Deutschland. Abhandlung. München, 1937.
Afr 6850.15	Wood, Alan. The groundnut affair. London, 1950.

Afr 6875 - 6880 **Tanganyika; Tanzania - Geography, description, etc. (By date)**

Afr 6878.59	Decken, Carl Claus, Baron von der. Baron Carl Claus von der Decken's Reisen in Ost Afrika in den Jahren 1859 bis 1865. Leipzig, 1869-79. 6v.
Afr 6878.72.2	Stanley, H.M. How I found Livingstone. N.Y., 1872.
NEDL Afr 6878.73	Stanley, H.M. How I found Livingstone. London, 1873. (Changed to KPE 2829)
Afr 6878.73.2	Stanley, H.M. How I found Livingstone: travels, adventures, and discoveries in Central Africa. London, 1890.
Afr 6878.73.3	Stanley, H.M. How I found Livingstone. N.Y., 1902.
Afr 6878.73.5	Stanley, H.M. My Kalulu, prince, king and slave. London, 1873.
Afr 6878.73.10	Stanley, H.M. My Kalulu, prince, king and slave. N.Y., 1874.
Afr 6878.73.15	Stanley, H.M. My Kalulu, prince, king and slave. N.Y., 1969.
Afr 6878.77	Dodgshun, Arthur W. From Zanzibar to Ujiji. Boston, 1969.
Afr 6878.79	Association Internationale Africaine. Rapports sur les marchés de la premiére expédition. v.1-4. Bruxelles, 1879-80.
Afr 6878.86	Hore, Annie B. To Lake Tanganyika in a bath chair. London, 1886.
Afr 6878.88	Pfeil, J.G. Vorschläge zur praktischen Kolonisation in Ost-Afrika. Berlin, 1888.
Afr 6878.88.5PF	Hellgrewe, Rudolf. Aus Deutsch-Ost-Afrika. Berlin, 1888.
Afr 6878.88.10	Boehm, Richard. Von Sansibar zum Tanganjika. Leipzig, 1888.
Afr 6878.89	Hessel, Heinrich. Deutsche Kolonisation in Ostafrika. Bonn, 1889.
Afr 6878.90	Foerster, Brix. Deutsch-Ostafrika. Leipzig, 1890.
Afr 6878.90.5	Schynse, August. Mit Stanley und Emin Pascha durch deutsch Ost-Afrika. Köln, 1890.
Afr 6878.91	Coelln, Daniel. Bilder aus Ostafrika. Berlin, 1891.
Afr 6878.92	Reichard, Paul. Deutsch-Ostafrika. Leipzig, 1892.
Afr 6878.92.5	Denkschrift betreffend Deutsch-Ostafrika. Berlin, n.d.
Afr 6878.93	Moloney, J.A. With Captain Stairs to Katanga. London, 1893.
Afr 6878.94	Baumann, Oscar. Durch Massailand zur Nilquelle. Berlin, 1894.

Afr 6875 - 6880 **Tanganyika; Tanzania - Geography, description, etc. (By date)**
cont.

Afr 6878.95	Peters, Karl. Das Deutsch-Ostafrikanische Schutzgebiet. München, 1895.
Afr 6879.02	Johnson, Harry. Night and morning in dark Africa. London, 1902.
Afr 6879.06	Fuellebon, F. Das Deutsche Njassa- und Ruwuma-Gebiet. Text. Berlin, 1906.
Afr 6879.06F	Fuellebom, F. Das Deutsche Njassa- und Ruwuma-Gebiet. Atlas. Berlin, 1906.
Afr 6879.07F	Jaeger, Fritz. Das Hochland der Riesenkrater...Deutsch-Ostafrika. Berlin, 1911.
Afr 6879.10	Fonck, Heinrich. Deutsch-Ost-Afrika. Berlin, 1910.
Afr 6879.12	Sutherland, J. The adventures of an elephant hunter. London, 1912.
Afr 6879.13	White, Stewart E. Rediscovered country. Garden City, 1915.
Afr 6879.15.5	Werth, Emil. Das Deutsch-Ostafrikanische Küstenland. Berlin, 1915. 2v.
Afr 6879.16	Great Britain. Admiralty. A handbook of German East Africa. n.p., 1916.
Afr 6879.16.3	Great Britain. Naval Intelligence Division. A handbook of German East Africa. N.Y., 1969.
Afr 6879.20	Joelson, F.S. The Tanganyika territory. London, 1920.
Afr 6879.24	British Empire Exhibition, Wembley, 1924. Central commission of Tanganyika exhibition handbook. London, 1924.
Afr 6879.24.9	Dundas, A.L.H. Beneath African glaciers. London, 1924.
Afr 6879.25.6	Dugmore, Arthur R. The wonderland of big game, being an account of two trips through Tanganyika and Kenya. London, 1933.
Afr 6879.26	White, Stewart E. Lions in the path. Garden City, 1926.
Afr 6879.28	Wells, Carveth. In coldest Africa. Garden City, 1929.
Afr 6879.29A	Johnson, M.E. Lion, African adventure with the king of beasts. N.Y., 1929.
Afr 6879.29B	Johnson, M.E. Lion, African adventure with the king of beasts. N.Y., 1929.
Afr 6879.31	Tanganyika Railways and Harbours. Travel guide to Tanganyika and Central Africa. London, 1931.
Afr 6879.36	Bent, Newell. Jungle giants. Norwood, Mass., 1936.
Afr 6879.36.5	Tanganyika guide. 2d ed. Dar es Salaam, 1948.
Afr 6879.39	Braun, Hans. Die Reise nach Ostafrika. Berlin, 1939.
Afr 6879.59	Cairns, John C. Bush and boma. London, 1959.
Afr 6879.61	British Information Services. Tanganyika. N.Y., 1961.
Afr 6879.61.5	Varma, Shanti Narayan. Tanganyika. 1st. ed. New Delhi, 1961.
Afr 6879.61.10	British Information Services. Tanganyika. N.Y., 1961.
Afr 6879.64	Imperato, Pascal James. Doctor in the land of the lion. 1st ed. N.Y., 1964.
Afr 6879.65	Dibble, James Birney. In this land of Eve. N.Y., 1965.
Afr 6879.66	Macdonald, Alexander. Tanzania, young nation in a hurry. 1st ed. N.Y., 1966.
Afr 6879.67	Levitt, Leonard. An African season. N.Y., 1967.
Afr 6879.67.5	Svendsen, Knud Erik. Tanzania vil selv. København, 1967.
Afr 6879.68	American University, Washington, D.C. Foreign Area Studies Division. Area handbook for Tanzania. Washington, 1968.
Afr 6879.68.5	University Press of Africa. Tanzania today. Nairobi, 1968.
Afr 6879.68.10	University Press of Africa. Kilimanjaro country. Nairobi, 1968.

Afr 6881 **Tanganyika; Tanzania - Economic and financial conditions**

Afr 6881.1	Wright, Fergus C. African consumers in Nyasaland and Tanganyika. London, 1955.
Afr 6881.255	Tanganyika Territory. Tanganyika. n.p., n.d.,
Afr 6881.257	Tanganyika Territory. Department of Commerce and Industry. Commerce and industry in Tanganyika. Dar es Salaam, 1957.
Afr 6881.259	East Africa High Commission. East Africa Statistical Division. Tanganyika Office. The gross domestic product of Tanganyika. v.1-2. Dar es Salaam, 1959.
Afr 6881.261	Tanganyika. Development plan for Tanganyika, 1961/62-1963/64. Dar es Salaam, 1961.
Afr 6881.264	Tanzania. Tanganyika five-year plan for economic and social development, 1st July, 1964-30th June, 1969. Dar es Salaam, 1964.
Afr 6881.264.5	Tanzania. Ministry of Economic Affairs and Development Planning. First year progress report on the implementation of the Five-year Development Plan. Dar-es-Salaam, 1965?
Afr 6881.265	Burke, Fred George. Tanganyika. 1st ed. Syracuse, N.Y., 1965.
Afr 6881.266	Tanzania. Presidential Special Committee of Enquiry into the Cooperative Movement and Marketing Boards. Report. Dar-es-Salaam, 1966.
Afr 6881.267	International Research Associates. A survey of the Tanzanian participant training program. N.Y., 1967.
Afr 6881.268	Rutman, Gilbert. The economy of Tanganyika. N.Y., 1968.

Afr 6882 **Tanganyika; Tanzania - Special customs**

Afr 6882.2	Hauer, Albert. Ali Moçambique; Bilder aus dem Leben eines schwarzen Fabeldichters. Berlin, 1922.

Afr 6883 **Tanganyika; Tanzania - Races**

Afr 6883.1	Merker, M. Die Masai. Berlin, 1904.
Afr 6883.2	Vander Burgt. Un grand peuple de l'Afrique équatoriale. Bois le Duc, 1903.
Afr 6883.2.5	Meyer, Hans. Die Barundi. Leipzig, 1916.
Afr 6883.3	Weiss, Max. Die Völkerstämme in nord Deutsch-Ostafrika. Berlin, 1910.
Afr 6883.4	Reche, O. Zur Ethnographie der abflusslosen Gebietes Deutsch-Ostafrikas. Hamburg, 1914.
Afr 6883.5.3	Weule, Karl. Native life in East Africa. London, 1909.
Afr 6883.6	Dempwolff, Otto. Die Sandawe...Material aus deutsch Ostafrika. Hamburg, 1916.
Afr 6883.7	Ried, H.A. Zur Anthropologie des abflusslosen Rumpfschollenlandes im nordöstlichen Deutsch-Ostafrika. Hamburg, 1915.
Afr 6883.8	Wohlab, Karl. Die Christliche Missionspredigt unter den Schambala. Inaug. Diss. Tübingen, 1929.
Afr 6883.9	Boesch, F. Les Banyamwezi, peuple de l'Afrique orientale. Münster, 1930.
Afr 6883.10	Kjellberg, Eva. The Ismailis in Tanzania. Photoreproduction. Dar-es-Salaam, 1967.
Afr 6883.11	Culwick, A.F. Ubena of the rivers. London, 1935.
Afr 6883.13	Cory, Hans. Customary law of the Haya tribe. London, 1945.

Afr 6883   Tanganyika; Tanzania - Races
cont.
Afr 6883.13.5	Cory, Hans. Sukuma law and customs. London, 1954.
Afr 6883.15A	Malcolm, D.W. Sukumaland. London, 1953.
Afr 6883.15B	Malcolm, D.W. Sukumaland. London, 1953.
Afr 6883.15.5	Tanner, Ralph E.S. Transition in African beliefs. Maryknoll, 1967.
Afr 6883.18	Nelson, Anton. The freemen of Meru. Nairobi, 1967.
Afr 6883.20	Boehrenz, Wolfgang. Beiträge zur materiellen Kultur der Nyamwezi. Hamburg, 1940.
Afr 6883.20.10	Abrahams, R.G. The political organization of Unyamwezi. Cambridge, 1967.
Afr 6883.25	Molohan, M.J.B. Detribalization. Dar es Salaam, 1959.
Afr 6883.26	Fouquet, Roger. Irakou. Paris, 1955.
Afr 6883.30	Winnus, Edgar. Shambala. Berkeley, 1962.
Afr 6883.31	Gulliver, P.H. Social control in an African society, a study of the Arusha, agricultural Masai of northern Tanganyika. Boston, 1963.
Afr 6883.31.2	Gulliver, P.H. Social control in an African society. London, 1963.
Afr 6883.32	Komba, J.J. God and man. Rome, 1961.
Afr 6883.33	Nigmann, Ernst. Schwärze. Berlin, 1922.
Afr 6883.34	Carnochan, Frederic Grosvenor. Out of Africa. London, 1937.
Afr 6883.35	Robert, J.M. Croyances et coutumes magico-religieuses des Wafipa païens. Tabora, 1949.
Afr 6883.40	Klima, George J. The Barabaig; East African cattle-herders. N.Y., 1970.

Afr 6885   Tanganyika; Tanzania - Religion; missions
Afr 6885.5	Gutmann, Bruno. Afrikaner-Europäer in nächstenschaftlicher Entsprechung. Stuttgart, 1966.
Afr 6885.6	Heremans, Roger. Les établissements de l'Association Internationale Africaine au lac Tanganika et les pères blancs, Mpala et Karema, 1877-1885. Tervuren, 1966.
Afr 6885.10	Mowinza, Joseph. The human soul. Thesis. Tabora, 1967?
Afr 6885.15	Pesce, Geremia. Vitie missionaria nel Tanganika. Bologna, 1963.
Afr 6885.20	Sibtain, Nancy de S.P. Dare to look up. Sydney, 1968.

Afr 6886   Tanganyika; Tanzania - Local - Dar es Salaam
Afr 6886.2	Leslie, J.A.K. A survey of Dar es Salaam. London, 1963.
Afr 6886.3	Schneider, Karl-Günther. Dar es Salaam. Wiesbaden, 1965.

Afr 6887   Tanganyika; Tanzania - Local - Kilimanjaro
Afr 6887.1F	Meyer, H. Zum Schneedom des Kilmandscharo. Berlin, 1888.
Afr 6887.2	Leroy, A. Au Kilima-ndjaro. Paris, 1893.
Afr 6887.3	Johnston, H.H. The Kilima-njaro expedition. London, 1885.
Afr 6887.4	Meyer, H. Der Kilimandjaro. Berlin, 1900.
Afr 6887.5	Meyer, H. Across East African glaciers. London, 1891.
Afr 6887.6	Volkens, G. Der Kilimandscharo. Berlin, 1897.
Afr 6887.7	Sheldon, M.F. Sultan to sultan. London, 1892.
Afr 6887.8	Jaeger, Fritz. Forschungen in den Hochregionen des Kilimand. Berlin, 1909.
Afr 6887.10	Dundas, C. Kilimanjaro and its people. London, 1924.
Afr 6887.11	Gutmann, B. Das Recht der Dschagga. München, 1926.
Afr 6887.11.9	Gutmann, B. Die Stammeslehren der Dschagga. München, 1932. 3v.
Afr 6887.11.15	Gutmann, B. Dichten und Denken der Dschagganeger. Leipzig, 1909.
Afr 6887.12.5	Young, Roland A. Land and politics among the Luguru of Tanganyika. London, 1960.
Afr 6887.12.10	Young, Roland A. Smoke in the hills. Evanston, 1960.

Afr 6888   Tanganyika; Tanzania - Local - Tanga
Afr 6888.2	Baumann, O. Usambara und seine Nachbargebiete. Berlin, 1891.
Afr 6888.3	Baumann, Oscar. In Deutsch-Ostafrika wahrend Aufstandes. Wien, 1890.
Afr 6888.5	University Press of Africa. Tanga, the central port for East Africa. Nairobi, 1968.

Afr 6889   Tanganyika; Tanzania - Local - Victoria Nyanza
Afr 6889.3	Kollmann, P. The Victoria Nyanza. London, 1899.

Afr 6890   Tanganyika; Tanzania - Local - Others
Afr 6890.1	Freeman-Grenville, G.S.P. The French at Kilwa Island. Oxford, 1965.
Afr 6890.2	Jacobsen, Axel. Paa Afrikas vilkaar. København, 1951.
Afr 6890.4	Wenner, Kate. Shamba letu. Boston, 1970.

Afr 6898   Tanganyika; Tanzania - Biographies - Collected
Afr 6898.2	Roegels, Fritz Carl. Mit Carl Peters in Afrika. Berlin, 1933.

Afr 6899   Tanganyika; Tanzania - Biographies - Individual (A-Z, 99 scheme, by person)
Afr 6899.62	Nyerere, Julius Kambarage. Freedom and socialism. Dar-es-Salaam, 1968.

Afr 6900   Southwest Africa - Periodicals
Afr 6900.5	Solidarity. Cairo.
Afr 6900.8F	South West Africa People's Organisation. News bulletin. Cairo. 4,1965+
Afr 6900.15	Freedom. Cairo.
Afr 6900.20	Perspective. London. 2,1965+ 5v.
Afr 6900.25	Muschel. Swakopmund. 1961+
Afr 6900.30	South West Africa. Handbook. Windhoek. 1964+
Afr 6900.35	South West Africa. Annual. Windhoek. 1965+

Afr 6903   Southwest Africa - Bibliographies
Afr 6903.5F	Welch, F.J. South-west Africa. Cape Town, 1946.
Afr 6903.8	Poller, Robert Manfred. Swakopmund and Walvis Bay. Cape Town, 1964.
Afr 6903.10	Loening, L.S.E. A bibliography of the states of South-west Africa. Rondebosch, 1951.
Afr 6903.12	Jager, J. de. South-west Africa. Pretoria, 1964.
Afr 6903.15	Roukens de Lange, E. South-west Africa, 1946-1960. Bibliography. Cape Town, 1961.
Afr 6903.17	Voigts, B. South African imprints. Cape Town, 1963.

Afr 6905   Southwest Africa - Pamphlet volumes
Afr 6905	Pamphlet box. German Southwest Africa.
Afr 6905.01	Pamphlet box. German Southwest Africa.

Afr 6910   Southwest Africa - Government and adminstration
Afr 6910.3	Goldblatt, Israel. The mandated territory of Southwest Africa in relation to the United States. CapeTown, 1961.
Afr 6910.5	Goldblatt, Israel. The conflict between the United Nations and the Union of South Africa in regard to Southwest Africa. Windhoek, 1960.
Afr 6910.8	South Africa. Parliament. Decisions by the government on the financial and administrative relations between the Republic and South West Africa. Cape Town, 1968.

Afr 6917 - 6920   Southwest Africa - General history (By date)
Afr 6919.06	Leutwein, T. Elf Jahre Gouverneur in deutsch Südwestafrika. Berlin, 1906.
Afr 6919.12	Sauder, L. Geschichte der deutsch Kolonial-Gesellschaft für Südwest-Afrika. Berlin, 1912. 2v.
Afr 6919.15	Eveleigh, William. South-west Africa. London, 1915.
Afr 6919.34.5	Vedder, H. South-west Africa in early times. London, 1938.
Afr 6919.34.6	Vedder, H. South-west Africa in early times. London, 1966.
Afr 6919.41	Preller, G.S. Voortrekkers van suidwes. Kaapstad, 1941.
Afr 6919.41.5	Vedden, H. Inleiding tot die geskiedenis van Suidwes-Afrika. Kaapstad, 1941.
Afr 6919.61	Levinson, O. The ageless land. Capetown, 1961.
Afr 6919.63	First, Ruth. South West Africa. Baltimore, 1963.
Afr 6919.66	Bruwer, Johannes Petrus. South West Africa, the disputed land. Capetown, 1966.
Afr 6919.66.8	Jenny, Hans. Südwestafrika. 3. Aufl. Stuttgart, 1968.
Afr 6919.67	Wellington, John Harold. South West Africa and its human issues. Oxford, 1967.
Afr 6919.67.5	Carroll, Faye. South West Africa and the United Nations. Lexington, 1967.
Afr 6919.67.10	Rhoodie, Eschel Mostert. South West: the last frontier in Africa. Johannesburg, 1967.

Afr 6925   Southwest Africa - History by periods - To 1892
Afr 6925.5A	Aydelotte, W.O. Bismarck and British colonial policy, the problem of South West Africa, 1883-1885. Philadelphia, 1937.
Afr 6925.5B	Aydelotte, W.O. Bismarck and British colonial policy, the problem of South West Africa, 1883-1885. Philadelphia, 1937.
Afr 6925.5C	Aydelotte, W.O. Bismarck and British colonial policy, the problem of South West Africa, 1883-1885. Philadelphia, 1937.
Afr 6925.10	Schuessler, W. Adolf Luederitz, ein deutscher Kanipf um Südafrika 1883-1886. Bremen, 1936.
Afr 6925.15	Francois, K. von. Deutsch Sudwest-Afrika. Berlin, 1899.
Afr 6925.20	Esterhuyse, J.H. South West Africa, 1880-1894; the establishment of German authority in South West Africa. Cape Town, 1968.

Afr 6926   Southwest Africa - History by periods - 1892-1914 - General works
Afr 6926.1	Frenssen, G. Peter Moors fahrt nach Südwest. Berlin, 1907.
Afr 6926.1.2	Frenssen, G. Peter Moor's journey to Southwest Africa. London, 1908.
Afr 6926.2	Schwabe, K. In deutschen Diamantenlande, Deutsch-Südwest-Afrika, 1884-1910. Berlin, 1909.
Afr 6926.3	Leutwein, T. Die Kämpfe mit Hendrik Witboi 1894 und Witbois Ende. Leipzig, 1912.
Afr 6926.4	Prussia. Grosser Generalität. Die Kämpfe der deutschen Truppen in Südwest Afrika. Berlin, 1906-08. 2v.
Afr 6926.5	Calvert, A.F. South-west Africa during German occupation. London, 1915.
Afr 6926.7	Close, P.L. Prisoner of the Germans in South-west Africa. London, 1916.
Afr 6926.9	Robinson, J.P.K. With Botha's army. London, 1916.
Afr 6926.11	Ritchie, Moore. With Botha in the field. London, 1915.
Afr 6926.11.5	Whittall, W. With Botha and Smuts in Africa. London, 1917.
Afr 6926.11.10	Trew, H.F. Botha treks. London, 1936.
Afr 6926.12F	Great Britain. Parliament. Papers relating to certain trials in German Southwest Africa. London, 1916.
Afr 6926.13F	Great Britain. Parliament. Papers relating to German atrocities. London, 1916. 2v.
Afr 6926.14F	Great Britain. Parliament, 1918. Report on the natives of South-west Africa. London, 1918.
Afr 6926.15	Weck, Ruediger. In Deutsche-Südwestafrika, 1913-15. Berlin, 1919.
Afr 6926.16	Hennig, Richard. Deutsch-Südwest im Weltkriege. Berlin, 1920.
Afr 6926.17	Bayer, M.G.S. Mit dem Hauptquartier in Südwestafrika. Berlin, 1909.
Afr 6926.18	Blumhagen, H. Entscheidungsjahre in Deutsch-Südwestafrika. Berlin, 1939.
Afr 6926.20	Germany. Reichs-Kolonialamt. The treatment of native and other populations in the colonial possessions of Germany and England. Berlin, 1919.
Afr 6926.21F	South Africa. Government Information Office. Southwest Africa and Union of South Africa, history of a mandate. N.Y., 1946.
Afr 6926.22	Bennett, Benjamin. Hitler over Africa. London, 1939.
Afr 6926.23	O'Connor, J.K. The Hun in our Hinterland. Cape Town, 1914?
Afr 6926.24	Dincklage-Campe, F. Deutsche reiber in Südwest. Berlin, 1908.
Afr 6926.25	Rohrbach, P. Dernburg und die Südwestafrikaner. Berlin, 1911.
Afr 6926.26	Visser, P.G. Herinneringe van suidwes-voortrekkers. Kaapstad, 1940.
Afr 6926.27	Steward, A. The sacred trust. Johannesburg, 1963.
Afr 6926.28	Drechsler, Horst. Südwestafrika unter deutscher Kolonialherrschaft. Berlin, 1966.
Afr 6926.30	Bley, Helmut. Kolonialherrschaft und Sozialstruktur in Deutsch-Südwestafrika, 1894-1914. Hamburg, 1968.
Afr 6926.32	Jenssen, H.E. Chronik von Deutsch-Südwestafrika. Windhoek, 1966.

Afr 6927 Southwest Africa - History by periods - 1892-1914 - 1897-1907

Afr 6927.5 Hintrager, O. Südwestafrika in der deutschen Zeit. München, 1955.
Afr 6927.8 Lowenstein, Allard K. Brutal mandate. N.Y., 1962.

Afr 6930 Southwest Africa - History by periods - 1914-

Afr 6930.5 Freislich, Richard. The last tribal war. Cape Town, 1964.
Afr 6930.10 Sweden. Utrikesdepartementet. Faktasamling angaende Sydvaestatrikafra'gan i foerenta nationenna. Stockholm, 1965.
Afr 6930.12 Imeshve, R.W. South West Africa. London, 1965.
Afr 6930.20.2 Hague. International Court of Justice. Ethiopia and Liberia versus South Africa. 2d ed. Pretoria, 1966.
Afr 6930.25 Hidayatullah, M. The South-West Africa case. Bombay, 1967.

Afr 6973 - 6980 Southwest Africa - Geography, description, etc. (By date)

Afr 6978.61 Andersson, Carl J. The Okavango River: a narrative of travel, exploration, and adventure. N.Y., 1861.
Afr 6978.61.2 Andersson, Carl J. The Okavango River: a narrative of travel, exploration and adventure. Facsimile. Cape Town, 1968.
Afr 6978.64 Baines, T. Exploration in South-west Africa. London, 1864.
Afr 6978.91 Sching, H. Deutsch-Südwest-Afrika. Oldenburg, 1891.
Afr 6978.99 Schwabe, K. Mit Schwert inDeutsch-Südwestafrika. Berlin, 1899.
Afr 6979.03 Done, K. Deutsch-Südwest-Afrika. Berlin, 1903.
Afr 6979.03.2 Done, K. Deutsch-Südwest-Afrika. 2e Aufl. Berlin, 1913.
Afr 6979.04 Seiner, F. Bergtouren und Steppenfahrten in Kererolande. Berlin, 1904.
Afr 6979.20 Pimienta, R. L'ancienne colonie allemande en Sud-ouest Afrique. Paris, 1920.
Afr 6979.29.5 Grimm, H. Das deutsche Südwester-buch. Muenchen, 1937.
Afr 6979.34 Beumhagen, H., O Südwestafrika Einst und Jetzt. Berlin, 1934.
Afr 6979.37 Hardinge, Rex. South African cinderella, a trip through ex-German West Africa. London, 1937.
Afr 6979.44 Marsh, John H. Skeleton coast. London, 1944.
Afr 6979.53 Green, Laurence G. Lords of the last frontier. London, 1953.
Afr 6979.53.2 Green, Laurence G. Lords of the last frontier. Cape Town, 1962.
Afr 6979.59 Carnegie, Sacha. Red dust of Africa. London, 1959.
Afr 6979.61 Bruwer, Johannes Petrus. Ons mandaat: Suidwes-Afrika. Johannesburg, 1961.
Afr 6979.62 Klerk, W.A. Drie swerwers oor die einders. 3. verb. uitg. Kaapstad, 1962.
Afr 6979.65 South Africa. Department of Information. South West Africa, the land, its peoples and their future. Pretoria, 1965.
Afr 6979.65.5 Jaeger, Friedrich Robert. Geographische Landschaften Südwestafrikas. Windhoek, 1965.
Afr 6979.66 Mertens, Alice. South West Africa and its indigenous peoples. London, 1966.
Afr 6979.66.5 Giniewski, Paul. Livre noir, livre blanc. Paris, 1966.
Afr 6979.67 South Africa. Department of Foreign Affairs. South West Africa survey, 1967. Pretoria, 1967.
Afr 6979.67.5 Green, Lawrence George. On wings of fire. Cape Town, 1967.
Afr 6979.69.2 White, Jon Manchip. The land God made in anger: reflections on a journey through South West Africa. London, 1970.

Afr 6981 Southwest Africa - Economic and financial conditions

Afr 6981.120 Great Britain. Report on the conditions and prospects of trade in the protectorate of South West Africa. London, 1920.

Afr 6984 Southwest Africa - Religion; missions

Afr 6984.5 Haythornthwaite, Frank. All the way to Abenab. London, 1956.
Afr 6984.10 Simon, J.M. Bishop for the Hottentots. N.Y., 1959.
Afr 6984.11 Loth, H. Die Christliche Mission in Südwestafrika. Berlin, 1963.

Afr 6985 Southwest Africa - Races

Afr 6985.1 Native tribes of Southwest Africa. Cape Town, 1928.
Afr 6985.2 Dannert, E. Zum Rechte der Herero. Berlin, 1906.
Afr 6985.3F Range, Paul. Beiträge...zur Landskunde des deutschen Namalandes. Hamburg, 1914.
Afr 6985.4 Troup, Freda. In face of fear. London, 1950.
Afr 6985.5 Loeb, Edwin. In feudal Africa. Bloomington, 1962.
Afr 6985.6F South Africa. Commission of Enquiry into South West African Affairs. Report, 1962-1963. Pretoria, 1964.
Afr 6985.7 Scheer, Maximillian. Schwarz und weiss am Waterberg. Schwerin, 1961.
Afr 6985.10 Molnar, Thomas Steven. South West Africa. N.Y., 1966.
Afr 6985.12 Kahn, Carl Hugo Linsingen. The native tribes of South West Africa. 1st ed. London, 1966.
Afr 6985.14 Giniewski, Paul. Die stryd om Suidwes-Afrika. Kaapstad, 1966.

Afr 6988 Southwest Africa - Local (A-Z, 99 scheme, by place)

Afr 6988.16.114 Anderson, Charles J. Notes of travel in South Africa. London, 1875.
NEDL Afr 6988.16.116 Anderson, Charles J. Notes of travel in South Africa. N.Y., 1875.
Afr 6988.16.120 Wallis, J.P.R. Fortune may fall, the story of Charles John Anderson, African explorer, 1827-1867. London, 1936.
Afr 6988.16.209 Galton, F. Narrative of an explorer in tropical South Africa. London, 1889.
Afr 6988.16.385 Walker, H.F.B. A doctor's diary in Damaraland. London, 1917.
Afr 6988.52.230 Hodge, A.L. Angra Pequeña. Inaug. Diss. München, 1936.
Afr 6988.58.260 Logan, R.F. The central Namib Desert. Washington, 1960.
Afr 6988.58.268 Martin, H. The sheltering desert. London, 1957.
Afr 6988.66.205 Freyer, E.P.W. Chronik von Otavi und einer Karte. Otavi, 1966.
Afr 6988.94.256 Lempp, Ferdinand. Windhoek. 1st ed. Windhoek, 1964.
Afr 6988.94.277 Mossolow, Nicolai. Windhoek heute. Windhoek to-day. Windhoek, 1967.

Afr 6990 Southwest Africa - Biographies - Individual (A-Z, 99 scheme, by person)

Afr 6990.6 Naude, C.P. Ongebaande wee. Kaapstad, 1931.
Afr 6990.21.5 Eckenbrecher, M. Was Afrika nur gab und nahm. 3. Aufl. Berlin, 1908.
Afr 6990.79 Scholl, Carl. Nach Kamerun. Leipzig, 1886.
Afr 6990.90 Leben für Südwestafrika. Windhoek, 1961.
Afr 6990.90.10 Baumann, Julius. Mission und Ökumene in Südwestafrika, Dargestellt am Lebenswerk. Leiden, 1965.
Afr 6990.90.20 Vedder, Heinrich. Kort verhale uit 'n lang lewe. Kaapstad, 1957.

Afr 7000 Portuguese Africa in general - Periodicals

Afr 7000.15 Portugal em Africa. Lisboa. 22,1965+ 3v.
X Cg Afr 7000.15 Portugal em Africa. Lisboa. 1-17,1894-1910 18v.
X Cg Afr 7000.15.2 Portugal em Africa. Supplemento colonial. Lisboa. 169-235 3v.

Afr 7003 Portuguese Africa in general - Bibliographies

Afr 7003.2 Chilcote, Ronald H. Emerging nationalism in Portuguese Africa. Stanford, 1969.

Afr 7005 Portuguese Africa in general - Pamphlet volumes

Afr 7005.2 Pamphlet vol. Portuguese Tropical Africa. 6 pam.

Afr 7010 Portuguese Africa in general - Government and administration

Afr 7010.2 Portugal. Ministère de la Marine et des Colonies. Droits de patronage du Portugal en Afrique. Lisbonne, 1883.
Afr 7010.3 Portugal et la France au Congo. Paris, 1884.
Afr 7010.4 Lisbon. Sociedade Geografica. La question du Zaire, droits de Portugal. Lisbonne. 1883+
Afr 7010.6 Portugal. Ministério da Marinha e Ultramar. Direitos de padroado de Portugal em Africa; memoranda. Lisboa, 1883.
Afr 7010.8 Visita do Chefe do Estado Almirante Américo Thomaz às províncias da Guiné de Cabo Verde. Lisboa, 1968.

Afr 7012 Portuguese Africa in general - General politics; political parties

Afr 7012.5 Lobiano do Rego. Patria Morena da vista da maior epopeia lusiada. Macierra de Cambra, 1959.

Afr 7015 Portuguese Africa in general - General history

Afr 7015.2 Cavazzi, G.A. Relation historique de l'Ethiopie occidentale. Paris, 1732. 5v.
Afr 7015.2.1 Cavazzi, G.A. Istorica descrizione de tre regni Congo, Matamba. Bologna, 1687.
Htn Afr 7015.2.2* Cavazzi, G.A. Istorica descrittione de tre regni Congo, Matamba. n.p., 1690.
Afr 7015.8 Politica portugueza na Africa. Lisboa, 1889.
Afr 7015.10 Academia das Sciencias de Lisboa. Conferencias celebradas na Academia Real das Sciencias de Lisboa. Lisboa, 1892.
Afr 7015.15 Republica Portuguesa. Aires de Ornelas. Lisboa, 1934. 3v.
Afr 7015.20A Duffy, James Edward. Portuguese Africa. Cambridge, 1959.
Afr 7015.20B Duffy, James Edward. Portuguese Africa. Cambridge, 1959.
Afr 7015.25 Axelson, Eric V. Portuguese in South East Africa. Johannesburg, 1960.
Afr 7015.30 Lupi, Luis C. Quem incendion o Congo. Lisboa, 1960.
Afr 7015.35 Duffy, James Edward. Portugal in Africa. Cambridge, 1962.
Afr 7015.40 Bondarevskii, G.L. Portugalskie kolonizatory, vragi narodov Afriki. Moscow, 1962.
Afr 7015.42 Evangelista, J. A queixa do Ghana e a conjura contra Portugal. Lisboa, 1963.
Afr 7015.45 Matos, R.J. da Cunha. Compendio historico das possesões de Portugal na Africa. Rio de Janeiro, 1963.
Afr 7015.46 Chilcote, Ronald H. Portuguese Africa. Englewood Cliffs, N.J., 1967.
Afr 7015.50 Bosgra, Sietse Jan. Angola, Mozambique, Guinee. Amsterdam, 1969.
Afr 7015.55 Abshire, David M. Portuguese Africa; a handbook. N.Y., 1969.

Afr 7018 Portuguese Africa in general - General special

Afr 7018.5 Felgas, Hélio Augusto Estevez. Os movimentos terroristos de Angola, Guiné, Moçambique. Lisboa, 1966.
Afr 7018.10 Matos, José Mendes Ribeiro Norton de. Africa nossa. Porto, 1953.

Afr 7020 Portuguese Africa in general - History by periods - Before 1800

Afr 7020.15 Lavradio, Marques do. Portugal em Africa depois de 1851. Lisboa, 1936.
Afr 7020.20 Blake, J.W. European beginnings in West Africa, 1454-1578. London, 1937.
Afr 7020.25 Oliviera Martins, J.P. Portugal em Africa. Porto, 1891.
Afr 7020.30 Ayres d'Ornellas. Viagem do principe real julho-setembro 1907. Lisboa, 1928.
Afr 7020.35 Sociedade de Geografia de Lisboa. Boletim. Numero comemorativo da entrega a S. Ex. a Presidente da republica. Lisboa, 1938.
Afr 7020.40 Welsch, S.R. South Africa under John III. Capetown, 1949.

Afr 7022 Portuguese Africa in general - History by periods - 1800-1900

Afr 7022.2 Hammond, Richard. Portugal and Africa, 1815-1910. Stanford, 1966.
Afr 7022.4 Axelson, Eric. Portugal and the scramble for Africa, 1875-1891. Johannesburg, 1967.

Afr 7025 Portuguese Africa in general - History by periods - 1900-

Afr 7025.5 Chaliand, Gérard. Lutte armée en Afrique. Paris, 1967.
Afr 7025.8 Simões, Martinho. Nos três frentes durante três messes. Lisboa?, 1966.
Afr 7025.10 Cunha, Manuel. Aquelas longas horas. Lisboa, 1968.
Afr 7025.12 Goemaere, Pierre. Le Portugal restera-t-il en Afrique? Bruxelles, 1968.

Afr 7045 Portuguese Africa in general - Geography, description, etc.

Afr 7045.2 Bowdich, T.E. An account of the discoveries of the Portuguese in the interior of Angola and Mozambique. London, 1824.
NEDL Afr 7045.5.2 Cadbury, W.A. Labour in Portuguese West Africa. 2d ed. N.Y., 1910.
Afr 7045.20 Rates, J. Carlos. Angola, Moçambique, San Tome. Edição do autor. Lisboa, 1929.
Afr 7045.25 Pattec, Richard. Portugal em Africa. Lisboa, 1959.

Afr 7045   Portuguese Africa in general - Geography, description, etc.
cont.
Afr 7045.26F   Galvao, Henrique. Ronda de Africa. Porto, 1950.
2v.

Afr 7046   Portuguese Africa in general - Economic and financial conditions
Afr 7046.2   Gersdorff, R. von. Wirtschaftsprobleme
Portugisisch-Afrikas. Bielefeld, 1962.

Afr 7048   Portuguese Africa in general - Races
Afr 7048.10   Nogueira, A.F. A raça negra sob o ponto de vista da
civilisação da Africa. Lisboa, 1880.
Afr 7048.15   Ferreira, Vincente. Colonização etnica da Africa
portuguesa. Lisboa, 1944.
Afr 7048.20   Durieux, Andre. Essai sur le statut. Bruxelles, 1955.

Afr 7050   Portuguese Guinea - Periodicals
Afr 7050.5   Boletim cultural da Guiné Portuguesa. Bissau. 3,1948+
18v.
Afr 7050.10   Centro de Estudos da Guiné Portuguesa. Publicações.
1,1947+
9v.
Afr 7050.15PF   Bolamense, orgao de propaganda regional de cultura e de
turismo. Bolama.
Afr 7050.20   Guiné; anuário turístico. Bissau. 1,1963+

Afr 7053   Portuguese Guinea - Pamphlet volumes
Afr 7053.1   Pamphlet box. Guinea.

Afr 7062   Portuguese Guinea - General history
Afr 7062.5   Barreto, João. Historia da Guiné, 1418-1918.
Lisboa, 1938.
Afr 7062.10   Viegas, Luis A.C. Guiné portuguesa. Lisboa, 1936.
2v.

Afr 7065.1   - .199   Portuguese Guinea - History by periods - Before 1800
Afr 7065.5   Dias Dinis, A.J. O quinto centenario do descobrimento da
Guiné portuguesa a luz da critica historica. Braga, 1946.
Afr 7065.7   Sociedade de Geografia de Lisboa. Congresso comemorativo
do quinto centenario do descobrimento da Guinea.
Lisboa, 1946.
2v.
Afr 7065.10   Terra, Branco da. Guiné do século XV. Lisboa?, 196-.

Afr 7065.500 -   Portuguese Guinea - History by periods - 1900-
Afr 7065.500   Ignat'ev, Oleg K. Pepel i plamia kafina. Moskva, 1966.
Afr 7065.510   Chagas, Frederico Pinheiro. Na Guiné, 1907-1908.
Lisboa, 1910.
Afr 7065.515   Pinto, João Teixeira. A ocupação militar da Guiné.
Lisboa, 1936.
Afr 7065.520   Davidson, Basil. The liberation of Guiné.
Harmondsworth, 1969.
Afr 7065.526   Chaliand, Gérard. Armed struggle in Africa. N.Y., 1969.
Afr 7065.526.5   Cabral, Amilcar. Revolution in Guinea: an African people's
struggle. London, 1969.
Afr 7065.526.10   Davidson, Basil. Révolution en Afrique; la libération de
la Guinée portugaise. Paris, 1969.

Afr 7068   Portuguese Guinea - Geography, description, etc.
Afr 7068.3   Zucchelli, A. Merckwurdige Missions und Reise-Beschreibung
nach Congo in Ethiopien. Frankfurt, 1715.
Afr 7068.4   Cesar, Amandio. Guine 1965, contra-atorque. Braga, 1965.
Afr 7068.5   Coelho, F. de L. Duas descrições seiscentistas da Guiné.
Lisbon, 1953.
Afr 7068.7   Guerra, M. dos S. Terras da Guiné e Cabo Verde.
Lisboa, 1956.
Afr 7068.9   Mota, Avelino Teixeira da. Guiné portuguesa. v.2.
Lisboa, 1954.
Afr 7068.11   Dias de Carvalho. Guiné. Lisboa, 1944.
Afr 7068.12   Aquiar, Armando de. Guiné, minha terra. Lisboa, 1964.
Afr 7068.14   César, Amândio. Em "Chão papel" na terra da Guiné.
Lisboa, 1967.

Afr 7069   Portuguese Guinea - Economic and financial conditions
Afr 7069.5   Guinea, Portuguese. Governor. Relatório da provincia da
Guiné Portugueza referido ao anno econômico de 1888-1889.
Lisboa, 1890.

Afr 7071   Portuguese Guinea - Religion; missions
Afr 7071.5   Gonçalves, J.J. O islamismo na Guiné portuguesa.
Lisboa, 1961.

Afr 7072   Portuguese Guinea - Special customs
Afr 7072.5   Barbosa, Alexandre. Guinéus; contos, narrativas, crónicas.
Lisboa, 1967.

Afr 7073   Portuguese Guinea - Local
Afr 7073.2   Bulam Association. Report of the institution...Dec. 11,
1792. London, 1792.
Afr 7073.3   Bernatzik, Hugo. Geheimnisvolle Inseln Tropen-Afrikas.
Berlin, 1933.
Afr 7073.4   Beaver, Philip. African memoranda. London, 1805.
Afr 7073.6F   Great Britain. Case in support of the claim of Great
Britain to the Island of Bulama. London, 1869.
Afr 7073.8F   Portugal. Resposta do governo portuguez a exposição a
favor dos direitos que a Gran-Bretanha. Lisboa, 1869.

Afr 7093   Cabinda - Geography, description, etc.
Afr 7093.3   Proyart, L.B. Histoire de Loango, Kakongo. Paris, 1819.
Afr 7093.3.5   Proyart, L.B. Histoire de Loango, Kakongo. Paris, 1776.
Afr 7093.4F   Falkenstein. Die Loango Kuste. Berlin, 1876.
Afr 7093.5   Dennett, R.C. Seven years among the Fjort. London, 1887.

Afr 7100   Angola; Portuguese West Africa - Periodicals
Afr 7100.5   Anuario de Angola. Lisboa. 1,1923+
Afr 7100.6   Arquivos de Angola. Luanda. 1-2,1943-1945
2v.
Afr 7100.10   Angola. Instituto de Angola. Boletim. Luanda. 3,1954
3v.
Afr 7100.12   Angola. Instituto de Angola. Boletim informativo.
61,1964+
Afr 7100.15   Sociedade Cultural De Angola. Cadernos culturais. Luanda.
Afr 7100.18   Angola; revista de doctrina e propaganda educativa.
Luanda. 24,1956+

Afr 7103   Angola; Portuguese West Africa - Bibliographies
Afr 7103.5   Borchardt, P. Bibliographie de l'Angola. Bruxelles, n.d.
Afr 7103.10   Luanda. Instituto de Investigação Cientifica de Angola.
Archivo Histórico. Roteiro topográfico dos códices.
Angola, 1966.
Afr 7103.15   Greenwood, Margaret Joan. Angola; a bibliography. Cape
Town, 1967.
Afr 7103.20   Angola; catálogo do documentário coligido pela Comissão de
Luanda. Luanda, 1937.
Afr 7103.25   Granado, António Coxito. Dicionário corográfico comercial
de Angola Atonito. 2. ed. Luanda, 1948.

Afr 7105   Angola; Portuguese West Africa - Pamphlet volumes
Afr 7105.1   Pamphlet box. Angola.
Afr 7105.4   Pamphlet vol. Higher education in Angola. Portuguese.
3 pam.

Afr 7108   Angola; Portuguese West Africa - Collected source materials
Afr 7108.10   Paiva Manso, L.M.J. Historia do Congo. Lisboa, 1877.
Afr 7108.15   Miralles de Imperial y Gomez, C. Angola en tiempos de
Felipe II y de Felipe III. Madrid, 1951.
Afr 7108.20   Angolana. Luanda, 1968.

Afr 7110   Angola; Portuguese West Africa - Government and administration
Afr 7110.5   Abreu e Brito, D. de. Um inquerito a vida administrativa e
economica de Angola e doBrasil. Coimbra, 1931.
Afr 7110.10   Matos, J.M.R.N. A nação una. Lisboa, 1953.

Afr 7114 - 7120   Angola; Portuguese West Africa - General history (By date)
Afr 7118.25   Feo Cardoza de Castellobranco e Torres, J.C. Memorias
contendo a biographia do vice almirante Huiz da Motta a Feo
e Torres. Paris, 1825.
Afr 7119.5   Freitas Morna, A. de. Angola, um ano no governo geral
(1942-43). Lisboa, 1944.
Afr 7119.20   Trancoso, Francisco. Angola; memoria. Lisboa, 1920.
Afr 7119.32   Lemos, A. de. Historia de Angola. Lisboa, 1932.
Afr 7119.34   Teixeira, Alberto de Almeida. Angola intangivel.
Pôrto, 1934.
Afr 7119.37   Correa, E.A. da Silva. Historia de Angola. Lisboa, 1937.
2v.
Afr 7119.40   Cruz, José Ribeiro da. Resumo da história de Angola.
Lisboa, 1940.
Afr 7119.47   Lefebvre, G. L'Angola. Liège, 1947.
Afr 7119.48   Delgado, Ralph. História de Angola. Bereguela, 1948-53.
4v.
Afr 7119.56   Chela, João da. Africa lusiada. Alges-Lisboa, 1956.
Afr 7119.56.5   Machado, Ernesto. No sul de Angola. Lisboa, 1956.
Afr 7119.57   Egerton, F.C.C. Angola in perspective. London, 1957.
Afr 7119.57.5   Sarmento, Alexandre. Temas angolanos. Lisboa, 1957.
Afr 7119.58   Felgas, Helio A. Historia do Congo (Esteres) portugues.
Carmona, 1958.
Afr 7119.59   Sousa Dias, G. Portugueses em Angola. Lisboa, 1959.
Afr 7119.62   Panikkar Kavalam Madhusudan. Angola in flames.
N.Y., 1962.
Afr 7119.62.5   Angola atraves dos textos. São Paulo, 1962.
Afr 7119.62.10   Vinhos, Manuel. Para um dialogo sobre Angola.
Lisboa, 1962.
Afr 7119.63   Maciel, A. Angola heroica. 2.ed. Lisboa, 1963.
Afr 7119.63.5   Maciel, A. Angola heroica. Lisboa, 1963.
Afr 7119.63.10   Archer, Maria. Brasil, fronteirada Africa. Sao
Paulo, 1963.
Afr 7119.63.15   Hermans, Fons. Angola in opstand. 1. druk. Den
Haag, 1963.
Afr 7119.65   Birmingham, D. The Portuguese conquest of Angola.
London, 1965.
Afr 7119.69   Gonzaga, Norberto. História de Angola, 1482-1963.
Luanda, 1969.

Afr 7122   Angola; Portuguese West Africa - General special
Htn   Afr 7122.5*   Andrade Leitão, F. de. Copia das proposições e secunda
allegaçam. Lisboa, 1642.
Htn   Afr 7122.5.5*   Andrade Leitão, F. de. Copia primae allegationis.
n.p., 1642.
Htn   Afr 7122.10*   Cruz, L.F. da. Manifesto das ostillidades que a gente.
Lisboa, 1651.
Afr 7122.12   Albuquerque Felner, A. De. Angola. Coimbra, 1933.
Htn   Afr 7122.15*   Relaçam do felice successo. Lisboa, 1671[1672?]
Afr 7122.20   Sa da Bandeira, B. de S.N. de F da. Facts and statistics
concerning the right of the crown of Portugal to the
territory of Molembo Cabinda, Ambriz. London, 1877.
Afr 7122.20.2   Sa da Bandeira, B. de S.N. de F. da. Factos e consideraçõs
relativas aos direitos de Portugal. Lisboa, 1855.
Afr 7122.35   Casimiro, Augusto. Angola e o futuro. Lisboa, 1958.
Afr 7122.38   Galvao, Henrique. Historia de nosso tempo. Lisboa, 1931.
Afr 7122.39   Galvao, H. Por Angola. Lisboa, 1949.
Afr 7122.40   Paiva Couceiro, H.M. de. Angola (Dous annos de governo
junho 1907 - junho 1909). Lisboa, 1910.
Afr 7122.41   Oliveira de Cadonnega, A. Historia geral das guerras
angolanas. Lisboa, 1940-42.
3v.
Afr 7122.45   Vinhas, Manuel. Aspectos actuais de Angola. Lisboa, 1961.
Afr 7122.48   Felgas, Hélio. Guerra em Angola. Lisboa, 1961.
Afr 7122.48.5   Felgas, Hélio. Guerra em Angola. 5. ed. Lisboa, 1968.
Afr 7122.50   Cruz, D. da. A crise de Angola. Lisboa, 1928.
Afr 7122.52   Cesar, A. Angola, 1961. 3. ed. Verbo, 1961.
Afr 7122.54   Caio, H. Angola. 3.ed. Lisboa, 1961.
Afr 7122.56   Sidenko, V.P. Angola v ogne. Moscow, 1961.
Afr 7122.58A   Okuma, T. Angola in ferment. Boston, 1962.
Afr 7122.58B   Okuma, T. Angola in ferment. Boston, 1962.
Afr 7122.60   Angola. Governo. Despachas do governador geral de Angola.
Luanda, 1947.
Afr 7122.61   Angola. Govêrno Geral, 1943-1947 (Alves). Discursos do
governador geral de Angola, capitão de mar e guerra Vasco
Lopes Alves, 1943-1946. Luanda, 1946.
Afr 7122.62   Angola, a symposium. London, 1962.
Afr 7122.64   Addicott, Len. Cry Angola. London, 1962.
Afr 7122.66   Nogueira, Jofre A. Angola na epoca pombalina.
Lisboa, 1960.
Afr 7122.68   Telo, Alencastre. Angola, terra nossa. Lisbon, 1962.
Afr 7122.70   Cotta, Goncalves. Grito de Angola. Luanda, 1961.
Afr 7122.72   Ehnmark, Anders. Angola and Mozambique, the case against
Portugal. London, 1963.
Afr 7122.74   Waring, R. The war in Angola, 1961. Lisbon, 1962.
Afr 7122.75   Front Revolutionnaire Africain pour l'Indépendence
Nationale des Colonies Portugaises. La repression
colonialiste en Angola. 2d ed. Anvers, 1960.
Afr 7122.76   Pires, P. Braseiro da morte. Viseu, Portugal, 1963.

Afr 7122 Angola; Portuguese West Africa - General special
cont.

Afr 7122.77   Teixeira, Bernardo. The fabric of terror, three days in Angola. N.Y., 1965.

Afr 7122.78   Santos, Eduardo dos. Maza. Lisboa, 1965.

Afr 7122.79   Ventura, Reis. O caso de Angola. Braga, 1964.

Afr 7122.80   Barreiros, Americo. A verdade sobre os acontecimentos de Angola. T.1-2. 2.ed. Angola, 1961.

Afr 7122.82   Laidley, Fernando. Missoes de guerra e de paz no norte de Angola. Lisboa, 1964.

Afr 7122.83   Duffy, James Edward. A question of slavery. Cambridge, 1967.

Afr 7122.85   Davezies, Robert. Les Angolais. Paris, 1965.

Afr 7122.90   Diogo, Alfredo. O Brasil na restauração de Angola. Luanda, 1965.

Afr 7122.90.5   Pamphlet vol. Angola. 2 pam.

Afr 7122.95   Boavida, Américo. Angola; cinco séculos de exploracão portuguesa. Rio de Janeiro, 1967.

Afr 7122.100   Gilchrist, Sid. Angola awake. Toronto, 1968.

Afr 7122.102   Pereira, Alberto Feliciano Marques. Quadros chronologicos dos governadores geraes da provincia d'Angola. Loanda, 1889.

Afr 7125 Angola; Portuguese West Africa - History by periods - Before 1800

Afr 7125.2   Jesuits. Relações de Angola. Coimbra, 1934.

Afr 7127 Angola; Portuguese West Africa - History by periods - 1800-1886

Afr 7127.5   Paxeco, Fran. Angola e os Alemãis. Marahão, 1916.

Afr 7130 Angola; Portuguese West Africa - History by periods - 1886-1934

Afr 7130.5   Eça, Antonio Julio da Costa Pereira de. Campanha do sul de Angola em 1915. Lisboa, 1921.

Afr 7130.10   Santos, Ernesto Moreira dos. Combate de Naulila; cobiça de Angola. Cuimarães, 1957.

Afr 7130.15.2   Almeida, João de. Sul de Angola, relatório de um govêrno de distrito, 1908-1910. 2. ed. Lisboa, 1936.

Afr 7135 Angola; Portuguese West Africa - History by periods - 1934-

Afr 7135.1   Oganis'ian, Iulii S. Natsional'naia revoliutsiia v Angole. (1961-1965gg.). Moskva, 1968.

Afr 7135.4   Marcum, John. The Angolan revolution. Cambridge, 1969.

Afr 7135.10   Venter, Al Johannes. The terror fighters: a profile of guerilla warfare in southern Africa. Cape Town, 1969.

Afr 7135.12   Gauzes, Anne. Angola, 1961-1963. Luanda? 196-.

Afr 7135.14   Costa, Pereira da. Um mês de terrorismo; Angola, março-abril de 1961. Lisboa, 1969. ?

Afr 7175 Angola; Portuguese West Africa - Geography, description, etc.

Afr 7175.2   Capello, H. From Benguella to the territory of Yacca. London, 1882. 2v.

Afr 7175.2.5   Capello, H. De Benguella as terras de Iacca. Lisboa, 1881. 2v.

Afr 7175.3   Guessfeldt, P. Die Loango. Expedition 1873-76. London, 1879. 2v.

Afr 7175.5   Monteiro, J.J. Angola and the river Congo. London, 1875. 2v.

Afr 7175.5.3   Monteiro, J.J. Angola and the river Congo. v.1-2. N.Y., 1876.

Afr 7175.5.5   Monteiro, J.J. Angola and the River Congo. 1st ed. London, 1968. 2v.

Afr 7175.6   Marques, A.S. Os clinas e as producções...Malenge a Lunda. Lisboa, 1889.

Afr 7175.6.2   Dias de Carvalho, H.A. Descripção da viagem a Mussumba do Muatianvua. v.1-4. Lisboa, 1890.

Afr 7175.6.3   Dias de Carvalho, H.A. Ethnographia e historia tradicional dos povos da Lunda. Lisboa, 1890.

Afr 7175.6.4   Dias de Carvalho, H.A. Meteorologia, climalogia e colonisação. Lisboa, 1892.

Afr 7175.7   Grandpre, S. de. Voyage à la côte occidentale d'Afrique. Paris, 1801. 2v.

Afr 7175.8   Veth, Pieter J. Daniel Veths reizer in Angola. Haarlem, 1887.

Afr 7175.9   Paiva Conceiro, H.M. de. Relatorio de viagem entre Bailundo e as terras do Mususso. Lisboa, 1892.

Afr 7175.12   Lina Vidal, João Avangelista. Por terras d'Angola. Coimbra, 1916.

Afr 7175.13   Marguardsen, H. Angola. Berlin, 1920.

Afr 7175.15   Statham, J.C.B. Through Angola, a coming colony. Edinburgh, 1922.

Afr 7175.15.10   Statham, J.C.B. With my wife across Africa by canoe and caravan. 2d ed. London, 1926.

Afr 7175.16   Schachtzabel, A. Im Hochland von Angola. Dresden, 1923.

Afr 7175.17   Ferreira Pinto, J. Angola. Lisboa, 1926.

Afr 7175.18   Morton de Matas. A provincia de Angola. Porto, 1926.

Afr 7175.20   Barns, T. Alexander. Angolian sketches. London, 1928.

Afr 7175.22F   Associação Comercial de Lajistas de Lisboa. Alguns aspectos psicologicos de nossa colonização en Angola. Lisboa, 1930.

Afr 7175.23   Jaspert, Willem. Through unknown Africa. London, 1929.

Afr 7175.25   Carvalho e Menezes, A. Memoria geografica. Lisboa, 1834.

Afr 7175.27   Burr, Malcolm. A fossicker in Angola. London, 1933.

Afr 7175.28   Cruz, José Ribeiro da. Geografia de Angola. Lisboa, 1940.

Afr 7175.30   Santos, Afonso C.V.T. dos. Angola coração do imperio. Lisboa, 1945.

Afr 7175.33   Delachaux, T. Pays et peuples d'Angola. Neuchatel, 1934.

Afr 7175.35   Costa, Ferreira da. Na pista do marfim e da morte. Porto, 1944.

Afr 7175.36   Jessen, O. Reisen und Forschungen in Angola. Berlin, 1936.

Afr 7175.37   Costa, Ferreira da. Pedro do feitico. Porto, 1945.

Afr 7175.39   Galvao, H. Outras terras, outras gentes. Lisboa, 1941. 2v.

Afr 7175.39.5F   Galvao, H. Outras terras, outras gentes (viagens em Africa). v.1-. Porto, 1944-.

Afr 7175.40   Cardoso, A.J.A. Angola. Johannesburg, 1950.

Afr 7175.42   Pinto, F.A. Angola e Congo. Lisboa, 1888.

Afr 7175.45   Zwilling, Ernst. Angola-safari. 2.Aufl. Mödling, 1957.

Afr 7175.47   Borchert, Günter. Südost-Angola. Hamburg, 1963.

Afr 7175.50   Rebelo, Horacio de la Viara. Angola na Africa deste tempo. Lisboa, 1961.

Afr 7175.52   Falcato, J. Angola do meu coração. Lisboa, 1961.

Afr 7175 Angola; Portuguese West Africa - Geography, description, etc.
cont.

Afr 7175.54   Tams, Georg. Visita as possessões portugueses. Porto, 1850.

Afr 7175.54.5   Tams, Georg. Die portugiesischen Besitzungen in Süd-West-Afrika. Hamburg, 1845.

Afr 7175.54.10   Tams, Georg. Visit to the Portuguese possessions in South-Western Africa. N.Y., 1969.

Afr 7175.60   Granado, Antonio C. Mucandos, ou cartos de Angola. Lisboa, 1940.

Afr 7175.70F   Marjay, Frederico Pedro. Angola. Lisbon, 1961.

Afr 7175.72   Amaral, I. do. Ensaio de um estudo geografico da rede urbana de Angola. Lisboa, 1962.

Afr 7175.74   Rodrigues, J. Angola, terra de Portugal. Lourenço Marques, 1964.

Afr 7175.75   Huibregtse, Pieter Kornelius. Angola is anders. Den Huag, 1965.

Afr 7175.76   Iglesias, Luis. A verdade sobre Angola. Rio de Janeiro, 1961.

Afr 7175.77   Hanu, Jose. Quand le vent souffle en Angola. Bruxelles, 1965.

Afr 7175.78   American University, Washington, D.C. Foreign Affairs Studies Division. Area handbook for Angola. Washington, 1967.

Afr 7175.79   Válahu, Mugur. Angola, chave de Africa. Lisboa, 1968.

Afr 7175.80   Gonzaga, Norberto. Angola, a brief survey. Lisbon, 1967.

Afr 7176 Angola; Portuguese West Africa - Economic and financial conditions

Afr 7176.5   Oliveira Boleo, Jose de. Ensaio sobre geografia agraria. Lisboa, 1958.

Afr 7176.6   Pires, Antonio. Angola. Luanda, 1964.

Afr 7176.7   Angola. Direcção dos Serviços de Economia. Angola. Luanda, 1953.

Afr 7176.7.10   Angola. Governor General, 1923-1927 (Ferreira). A situação de Angola. Luanda, 1927.

Afr 7176.9   Azevedo, João M.C. de. Angola. Luanda, 1958.

Afr 7176.12   Ferreira, Eugenio. Sob o signo do real. Luanda, 1961.

Afr 7176.14   Soares, Amaden. Politica de bem e estoi rival en Angola. Lisbon, 1961.

Afr 7176.16   Santos, A.L.F. dos. Estrutura do comercio externo de Angola. Lisboa, 1959.

Afr 7176.18   Lima. Manuela. Contribuição para o estudo do comercio externo angolano. Lisboa, 1963.

Afr 7176.20   Banco de Angola, Lisbon. Economic and financial survey of Angola, 1960-1965. Lisboa, 1966.

Afr 7176.22   Pössinger, Hermann. Angola als Wirtschaftspartner. Köln, 1966.

Afr 7176.24   Freitas Morna, Alvaro de. Problemas económicos da colónia. Luanda, 1943.

Afr 7176.26.2   Graça, Joaquim José da. Projecto de uma companhia agricola e comercial africana. 2. ed. Lisboa, 1879.

Afr 7176.27   Galvão, Henrique. Informação económia sobre Angola. Lisboa, 1932.

Afr 7176.28   Informação económica sôbre o Império e alguns elementos de informação geral. Pôrto, 1934.

Afr 7176.30   Borchert, Günter. Die Wirtschafsräume Angolas. Pfaffenhofen/Ilm, 1967.

Afr 7176.32   Araujo, A. Correia de. Apectos do desenvolvimento económico e social de Angola. Lisboa, 1964.

Afr 7176.34   Ventura, Reis. O após-guerra em Angola. Luanda, 1954.

Afr 7176.36   Ventura, Reis. Os problemas de Angola, no Primeiro Congresso dos Economistas Portugueses. Lisboa, 1956.

Afr 7179 Angola; Portuguese West Africa - Special customs

Afr 7179.5   Sousa, Gabriel de. A portugalização do suesto de Angola. Lisboa, 1967.

Afr 7179.10   Vacchi, Dante. Penteados de Angola. Lisbonne, 1965.

Afr 7180 Angola; Portuguese West Africa - Races

Afr 7180.5   Questionario ethnographico acerca dos populações indigenas de Angola e Congo. Luanda, 1912.

Afr 7180.10   Claridge, G.C. Wild bush tribes of tropical Africa. Philadelphia, 1922.

Afr 7180.15   Jaspert, Fritz. Die Völkerstämme Mittel-Angolas. Frankfurt a.M., 1930.

Afr 7180.20   Sarmento, Alexandre. O negro de Menongue, notas antropologicas e etnograficas. Lisboa, 1945.

Afr 7180.25   Amaral, I. do. Aspectos do povoamento branco de Angola. Lisboa, 1960.

Afr 7180.30   Childs, Gladwyn Murray. Umbundu kinship and character. London, 1949.

Afr 7180.35   Edwards, Adrian. The Ovimbundu under two sovereignties. London, 1962.

Afr 7180.36.2   Milheiros, Mario. Notas de etnografia angolana. 2. ed. Luanda, 1967.

Afr 7180.38.2   Felgas, Hélio. As populacões nativas do norte de Angola. 2. ed. Lisboa, 1965.

Afr 7180.40   Cruz, José Ribeiro da. Notas de etnografia angolana. Lisboa, 1940.

Afr 7180.45   Semana do Ultramar, 1st, Luanda, 1965. Migrações e povoamento. Luanda, 1966.

Afr 7182 Angola; Portuguese West Africa - Religion; missions

Afr 7182.3   Freyre, Gilberto. Em torno de alguns tumulos afro-cristaos. Bahia, 1960.

Afr 7182.5   Cushman, W.S. Missionary doctor, the story of twenty years in Africa. 1st ed. N.Y., 1944.

Afr 7182.8   Sociedade de Geographia de Lisboa. Commissão africana missões de Angola. Lisboa, 1892.

Afr 7182.10   Ruiz de Arcaute, H. Por tierras de Angola. Victoria, 1961.

Afr 7182.15   Graham, Robert Haldane Carson. Under seven Congo kings. London, 1931.

Afr 7182.17   Wilson, Thomas E. Angola beloved. Neptune, N.J., 1967.

Afr 7182.20   Santos, Eduardo dos. Sobre a religião dos Quiocos. Lisboa, 1962.

Afr 7183 Angola; Portuguese West Africa - Local - Regions, etc.

Afr 7183.5   Andrade, Alfredo de. Relatorio da viagem de exploração...de Benguella e Novo Redondo. Lisboa, 1902.

Afr 7183.10   Angola. Repartição do Gabinete. Relatorio da missao de colonisação no planalto de Benguella em 1909. Loanda, 1910.

Afr 7183.15   Pires, Rui. Luanda. Porto, 195-.

Afr 7183.18   Lopes, Francisco Xavier. Tres fortalezas de Luanda em 1846. Luanda, 1954.

Afr 7183 Angola; Portuguese West Africa - Local - Regions, etc.
cont.

Afr 7183.20   Felgas, H.A. As populações nativas do Congo portugues. Luanda, 1960.
Afr 7183.22   António, Mário. Luanda, "ilha" crioula. Lisboa, 1968.
Afr 7183.25   Companhia de Diamantes de Angola. Breve noticia sobre o Museu do Dundo. Lisbon, 1959.
Afr 7183.26   Arriaga, Noel de. Luanda. Lisboa, 1964.
Afr 7183.27   Neto, Jose Pereira. O baixo cunene. Lisboa, 1963.
Afr 7183.28   Urquhart, Alvin W. Patterns of settlement and subsistence in Southwestern Angola. Washington, 1963.
Afr 7183.33   Cardoso, Manuel da Costa Lobo. Subsidios para a historia de Luanda. Luanda, 1954.
Afr 7183.34   Santos, Eduardo dos. A questão da Lunda, 1885-1894. Lisboa, 1964.
Afr 7183.35   Dias de Carvalho, Henrique Augusto. Memoria: A. Lunda; ou, Os estados do Muatiânvua. Lisboa, 1890.
Afr 7183.40   Galvão, Henrique. Huíla; relatório de govêrno. Vila Nova de Famalicão? 1929[1930].

Afr 7185 Angola; Portuguese West Africa - Local - San Salvador
Afr 7185.3   Bastian, A. Ein Besuch in San Salvador. Bremen, 1859.

Afr 7187 Angola; Portuguese West Africa - Local - Others
Afr 7187.2   Santos, Nuno Beja Valdez Thomaz dos. A fortaleza de S. Miguel. Luanda, 1967.
Afr 7187.5   Moncada, Francisco C. A campanha do Bailundo em 1902. Lisboa, 1903.
Afr 7187.10   Roma Machado de Faria e Maria, Carlos. A cidade do Huambo. Lisboa, 1913.

Afr 7188.1 - .99 Angola; Portuguese West Africa - Biographies - Collected
Afr 7188.5   Dias, Gastão Sousa. Julgareis qual e mas excelente. Lisboa, 1948[1949].
Afr 7188.79   Santos Martins dos. A história de Angola através dos seus personagens principais. Lisboa, 1967.

Afr 7188.101 - .399 Angola; Portuguese West Africa - Biographies - Individual (A-Z, 299 scheme, by person)
Afr 7188.109   O coronel João de Almeida. Lisboa, 1927.
Afr 7188.150   Pereira, Henrique Antonio. Silva Carvalho na provincia portuguêsa de Angola. Montijo, 1966.
Afr 7188.269   Cunha Leal, Francisco Pinto da. Caligula em Brazil. Lisboa, 1924.
Afr 7188.301.800   Lopo, Júlio de Castro. Paiva Couceiro, uma grande figura de Angola. Lisboa, 1968.

Afr 7190 Other Portuguese West Africa
Afr 7190.15   Cunha Mattos, R.J. da. Corographia historica das ilhas de San Thome, Anno Bom, e Fernando Po. Porto, 1842.
Afr 7190.16   Portugal. Agencia Geral do Ultramar. San Tome e principe. Lisboa, 1964.
Afr 7190.18F   O cacau de S. Thomé. Lisboa, 1907.
Afr 7190.25   Almada Negreiros, A.D. Colonies portugaises, ile de San-Thome. Paris, 1901.
Afr 7190.27   Almada Negreiros, A.D. Historia ethnographica da ilha de San Thome. Lisboa, 1895.
Afr 7190.30   Nogueira, A.F. A ilha de San Thome. Lisboa, 1893.
Afr 7190.32   Cadbury, William A. Os serviçaes de S. Thomé. Lisboa, 1910.
Afr 7190.35   Viagem de Lisboa a ilha de San Tome,...tradução da lingua italiana para a portugues (Seculo XVI). Lisboa, 194-.
Afr 7190.40   San Thome, Africa. Direcção dos Portos e Viação. Missão geodesica. Porto, 1917.
Afr 7190.45   Mantero Velarde, A. de. L'espansione politica e coloniale portoghese. Roma, 1924.
Afr 7190.50   Mantero, F. Portuguese planters and British humanitarians. Lisbon, 1911.

Afr 7200 Mozambique; Portuguese East Africa - Periodicals (A-Z, .1-.26)
Afr 7200.3   Combate. Cairo. 2v.
Afr 7200.6   Frente de Libertação de Moçambique. War communiqué. Cairo. 2,1966+
Afr 7200.13   Moçambique, documentario trimestral. Lourenço Marques. 3,1935+ 31v.
Afr 7200.13.5   Moçambique, Documentario Trimestral. Index. Lourenço Marques. 1,1935+
Afr 7200.16   Paginas de doutrinação moçambicana. Lisboa.

Afr 7203 Mozambique; Portuguese East Africa - Bibliographies
Afr 7203.5   Costa, Mario A. do. Bibliografia geral de Moçambique. Lisboa, 1946-
Afr 7203.10   Almeida de Eca, F.G. Achegas para a bibliografia de Moçambique. Lisboa, 1949.

Afr 7205 Mozambique; Portuguese East Africa - Pamphlet volumes
Afr 7205.01   Pamphlet vol. Mozambique.

Afr 7208 Mozambique; Portuguese East Africa - Collected source materials
Afr 7208.2   Documentos sobre os portugueses em Mozambique en na Africa central, 1497-1840. v.1- Lisboa, 1962- 5v.
Afr 7208.8   Portugal. Ministério do Ultramar. Providências legislativas ministeriasis, tomadas em Moçambique em 22 outubro 1966. Lisboa, 1966.

Afr 7210 Mozambique; Portuguese East Africa - Government and administration
Afr 7210.5F   Termos de vassallagem nos territorios de machona, etc., 1858 a 1889. Lisboa, 1890.
Afr 7210.10   Lobato, Alexandre. Evolução administrativa e economica de Moçambique, 1752-1763. v.1-. Lisboa, 1957.
Afr 7210.15   Companhia de Moçambique. Decretos. Lisboa, 1891.

Afr 7212 Mozambique; Portuguese East Africa - General politics; political parties
Afr 7212.3   Pamphlet vol. Frente de Libertação de Moçambique. Spanish. 2 pam.

Afr 7214 - 7220 Mozambique; Portuguese East Africa - General history (By date)
Htn   Afr 7216.09*   Santos, João dos. Ethiopia oriental. v.1-2. Evora, 1609.
Afr 7216.09.5   Santos, João Dos. Histoire de l'Ethiopie orientale. Paris, 1688.
Afr 7216.09.10   Santos, João dos. Ethiopia oriental. v.1-2. Lisboa, 1891.

Afr 7214 - 7220 Mozambique; Portuguese East Africa - General history (By date)
cont.

Afr 7218.93.5   Ennes, Antonio. Moçambique, relatorio apresentado ao governo. Lisboa, 1946.
Afr 7218.96   Theal, George McCall. The Portuguese in South Africa. Cape Town, 1896.
Afr 7218.96.2   Theal, George McCall. The Portuguese in South Africa. N.Y., 1969.
Afr 7219.28   Silva, J. Guides. Colonização. Lourenço Marques, 1928.
Afr 7219.42   Alberto, Manuel Simoes. O oriente africano portugues. Lourenç Marques, 1942.
Afr 7219.51   Hamilton, G. In the wake of Da Gama. London, 1951.
Afr 7219.63   Mano, M.L. Entre jente remota. Lourenço Marques, 1963.
Afr 7219.63.10   Spence, C.F. Moçambique. London, 1963.
Afr 7219.64   Portugal. Archivo Ultramarino. Historico documentação avulsa moçambicana do arquivo historico ultramarino. Lisboa, 1964. 2v
Afr 7219.65   Lisbon. Universidade Tecnica. Instituto Superior de Ciências Sociais e Politica Ultramarina. Moçambique; curso de Extensão Universitária, ano lectivo de 1964-1965. Lisboa, 1965.
Afr 7219.67   Lobato, Alexandre. Ilha de Moçambique; panorama histórico. Lisboa, 1967.
Afr 7219.69   Mondlane, Eduardo. The struggle for Mozambique. Harmondsworth, 1969.

Afr 7222 Mozambique; Portuguese East Africa - General special
Htn   Afr 7222.5*   Durao, Antonio. Cercos de Moçambique. Madrid, 1633.
Afr 7222.5.10   Durao, Antonio. Cercos de Moçambique. Lisboa, 1937.
Afr 7222.15F   Moçambique. Modus-vivendi entre a provincia de Moçambique e o Transvaal...1901. Lisboa, 1905.
Afr 7222.30   Ornellas, Ayres D. Campanha do Gungunhana, 1895. Lisboa, 1930.
Afr 7222.40   Axelson, E.V. South-east Africa, 1488-1530. London, 1940.
Afr 7222.50   Almeida de Eca, O.G. De degredado a governado. Lisboa, 1950.
Afr 7222.60   Lobato, A. A expansão portuguesa em Moçambique de 1498 a 1530. Lisboa, 1960. 3v.
Afr 7222.70   Mousinha de Albuquerque. Mousinho de Albuquerque. Lisboa, 1935. 2v.
Afr 7222.72   Sarmento Rodrigues, M.M. Presença de Moçambique na vida da nação. Lisboa, 1964. 3v.
Afr 7222.80   Faria, Dutra. Portugal do capricornio. Lisboa, 1965.
Afr 7222.82   Lobato, Alexandre. Colonização senhorial da Zambezia. Lisboa, 1962.
Afr 7222.90   Saldanha, Eduardo d'Almeida. Moçambique perante genébra. Porto, 1931.

Afr 7225 Mozambique; Portuguese East Africa - History by periods - Before 1800
Afr 7225.5   Hoppe, Fritz. Portugiesisch-Ostafrika in der Zeit des Marquês de Pombal, 1750-1777. Berlin, 1965.
Afr 7225.8   Oliveira Boléo, José de. A campanha de 1783 contra o Vtigulo. Lourenço Marques, 1964.

Afr 7230 Mozambique; Portuguese East Africa - History by periods - 1800-1907
Afr 7230.5   Santos, Ernesto Moreira dos. Combate de Negomano. Guimarães, 1961.

Afr 7304 - 7310 Mozambique; Portuguese East Africa - Geography, description, etc. (By date)
Afr 7306.69   Gioja, Francesco Maria. Maravigliosa conversione alla Santa Fede. Napoli, 1669.
Afr 7307.98.10   Fonseca, Q. Vulgarização de episodios coloniais. Famalição, 1936.
Afr 7308.34   Botelho, S.X. Resumo para servir de introdução a memoria estatistica sobre os domintos portuguezes na Africa oriental. Lisboa, 1834.
Afr 7308.35   Botelho, S.X. Memoria estatistica portuguezes na Africa oriental. Lisboa, 1835-37. 2v.
Afr 7308.60   McLeod, L. Travels in Eastern Africa. London, 1860. 2v.
Afr 7308.66   Rowley, Henry. Story of the universities' missions to Central Africa. London, 1866.
Afr 7308.66.2   Rowley, Henry. The story of the universities' mission to Central Africa. 2nd ed. N.Y., 1969.
Afr 7308.80   Wauters, Alphonse Jules. Voyage au pays de l'ivoire. Bruxelles, 190-.
Afr 7308.89   Lapa, Joaquim J. Elementos para um diccionario chorographico da provincia de Moçambique. Lisboa, 1889.
Afr 7308.99   Worsfold, W.B. Portuguese Nyassaland. London, 1899.
Afr 7309.02   Peters, C. Im Goldland des Altertums. München, 1902.
Afr 7309.02.4   Peters, C. The eldorado of the ancients. London, 1902.
Afr 7309.02.5   Ferraz, Guilherme Ivens. Descripção da costa de Moçambique de Lourenço Marques ao Bazaruto. Lisboa, 1902.
Afr 7309.04   Negreiros, A. Le Mozambique. Paris, 1904.
Afr 7309.20   Great Britain. Admiralty. A manual of Portuguese East Africa. London, 1920.
Afr 7309.23   Chamberlain, G.A. African hunting among the Thongas. N.Y., 1923.
Afr 7309.29F   Santos Rufino, Jose dos. Albuns fotograficos e descritivos da...colonia de Mozambique. v.1-10. Hamburgo, 1929. 5v.
Afr 7309.30   Paes Mamede. Nas costas d'Africa. Lisboa, 1930.
Afr 7309.34   Hubbard, M.C. No one to blame. N.Y., 1934.
Afr 7309.36   Lacerda e Almeida, Francisco José de. Travessia da Africa. Lisboa, 1936.
Afr 7309.38   Mozambique. Repartição Teenica de Estatistica. The ports and lighthouses of Moçambique. Lourenço Marques, 1938.
Afr 7309.38.5   Mozambique. Repartição Teenica de Estatistica. Game hunting in Mozambique. Lourenço Marques, 1938.
Afr 7309.38.10   Mozambique. Repartição Teenica de Estatistica. The roads of Moçambique. Lourenço Marques, 1938.
Afr 7309.51   Oliveira Boléo, José de. Moçambique. Lisboa, 1951.
Afr 7309.55   Fonseca, M. da. Na fogueira do jornalismo. Lourenço Marques, 1955.
Afr 7309.57   Almeida, Eugenio Ferreira de. Governo do distrito de Moçambique. Lisboa, 1957.
Afr 7309.59   Barreiros, Pinho. Africa, mae e madrasta. Coimbra, 1959.
Afr 7309.60.5   Overseas Companies of Portugal. Mozambique. N.Y., 196-.
Afr 7309.61   Oliveira Bolio, Jose de. Moçambique. Lisboa, 1961.

Afr 7304 - 7310 Mozambique; Portuguese East Africa - Geography, description, etc. (By date)
cont.

Afr 7309.61.2   Oliveira Boléo, José de. Mozambique; petite monographie. 2. éd. Lisbonne, 1967.

Afr 7309.63F   Marjay, Frederico. Moçambique. Lisboa, 1963.

Afr 7309.64   União Democratica Nacional de Moçambique. Memorandum to 2nd non-aligned conference. Cairo, 1964.

Afr 7309.64.5   Joubert, Elsa (pseud.). Die staf van Monomotapa. Kaapstad, 1964.

Afr 7309.65   Rodrigues Júnior, José. Moçambique. Lisboa, 1965.

Afr 7309.66   Lobato, Alexandre. Ilha de Moçambique: panorama estético. Lisboa, 1966.

Afr 7309.66.5   Karlsson, Elis. Cruising off Mozambique. London, 1969.

Afr 7309.68   Huibregtse, Pieter Kornelis. Zó is Mozambique. Den Haag, 1968.

Afr 7309.69   American University, Washington, D.C. Foreign Areas Studies Division. Area handbook for Mozambique. Washington, 1969.

Afr 7312 Mozambique; Portuguese East Africa - Economic and financial conditions

Afr 7312.5   Costa, D. Moçambique, nossa terra. Lisboa, 1942.

Afr 7312.15   Spence, C.F. The Portuguese colony of Moçambique. Cape Town, 1951.

Afr 7312.20   Italy. Istituto Nazionale per il Commercio Estero. Mozambico. Roma, 1959.

Afr 7312.25   Grupo de Trabalho de Promoção Social. Promoção social en Moçambique. Lisboa, 1964.

Afr 7312.30   Baptista, J. do Amparo. Moçambique, província portuguesa. Vila Nova de Famalicão, 1962.

Afr 7315 Mozambique; Portuguese East Africa - Races

Afr 7315.2   Ornellas, A.D. Raças e linguas indigenas en Moçambique. n.p., 1905.

Afr 7315.3   Junod, H.A. Les Ba-ronga. Neuchatel, 1898.

Afr 7315.4   White, William. Journal of a voyage performed in the Lion Extra Indiaman. London, 1800.

Afr 7315.5   Pires de Lima, A. Contribuição para o estudo antropologico indigenas de Moçambique. Porto, 1918.

Afr 7315.20.5   Junod, H.A. The life of a South African tribe. 2d ed. London, 1927. 2v.

Afr 7315.20.6   Junod, H.A. The life of a South African tribe. New Hyde Park, N.Y., 1962. 2v.

Afr 7315.20.10   Junod, H.A. A vida d'uma tribu sul-africana. Famalição, 1917.

Afr 7315.25   Belchior, M.D. Comprendamos os negros. Lisboa, 1951.

Afr 7315.26.1   Earthy, Emily D. Valenge women; an ethnographic study. London, 1968.

Afr 7315.30   Feio, Manuel Moreira. Estudos sociologicos; indigenas de Moçambique. Lisboa, 1900.

Afr 7318 Mozambique; Portuguese East Africa - Religion; missions

Afr 7318.5   Arcangelo da Barletta. Sulle rive dello Zambesi. Palo del Calle, 1964.

Afr 7320 Mozambique; Portuguese East Africa - Local - Districts - Mozambique

Afr 7320.1.3   Pamphlet vol. A collection of pamphlets on Mozambique published by the colonial exposition at Paris, 1931. 26 pam.

Afr 7320.2   Ayres de Carvalho Soveral. Breve estudio,--ilha de Moçambique. Porto, 1887.

Afr 7320.4   Castilho, S. de. La province portugaise de Mosambique. n.p., 1890.

Afr 7320.4.5   Moreira, E. Portuguese East Africa. London, 1936.

Afr 7320.5   Lyne, Robert N. Mozambique. London, 1913.

Afr 7320.6   Azevedo Coutinho, João de. Do Nyassa a Pemba. Lisboa, 1931.

Afr 7320.8   Andrade, Antonio Alberto de. Relações de Moçambique setecentista. Lisboa, 1955.

Afr 7320.10   Portugal. Ministerio dos Negocios da Marinha e Ultramar. Regimento. Lisboa, 1867.

Afr 7320.15   Romero, J. Memoria acerca do districto de Cabo Delgado. Lisboa, 1856.

Afr 7320.17   Saldanha, Eduardo d'Almeida. O Sul do Save. Lisboa, 1928-31. 2v.

Afr 7320.20   Pires de Lima, Americo. Explorações em Moçambique. Lisboa, 1943.

Afr 7320.25   Gomes de Amorim, F. Colonizacao. Lisboa, 1945.

Afr 7320.27F   Eca de Queiroz, J.M.D. Santuario bravio. Lisboa, 1964.

Afr 7322 Mozambique; Portuguese East Africa - Local - Districts - Zambezia

Afr 7322.2   Muller, H.P.N. Land und Volk zwischen Zambesi und Limpopo. Giessen, 1894.

Afr 7322.3   Maugham, R.C.F. Zambezia. London, 1910.

Afr 7322.4   Caldas Xavier, A. Estudos coloniais. Lisboa, 1889.

Afr 7322.5   Lacerda, F.G. de. Figuras e episodios da Zambezia. 2.ed. Lisboa, 1943.

Afr 7322.6   Almeida de Eca, Felipe Gastão. Historia das guerras no Zambeze. Lisboa, 1953-54. 2v.

Afr 7322.8   Santos, Joaquim Rodriques dos. Alguns muzimos da Zambezia e o culto dos mortos. Lisboa, 1940.

Afr 7322.10   Castilho Barreto e Noronha, Augusto de. Relatorio da guerra da Zambezia em 1888. Lisboa, 1891.

Afr 7322.12   Sampaio, Matheus Augusto Ribeiro de. Cartas, officios, ordens de serviço lavrada a 23 de dezembro de 1897 e alguns documentos. Lisboa, 1898.

Afr 7324 Mozambique; Portuguese East Africa - Local - Districts - Lourenço Marques

Afr 7324.2   Monteiro, R. Delagoa Bay. London, 1891.

Afr 7324.4   Jessett, M.G. Key to South Africa, Delagoa Bay. London, 1899.

Afr 7324.5   Pawa Manso. Memoria sobre Lourenço Marques (Delagoa Bay). Lisboa, 1870.

Afr 7324.6F   Noronha, E. de. O districto de Lourenço Marques e a Africa do sul. Lisboa, 1895.

Afr 7324.7   Delagoa directory, a year book of information. Lourenço Marques. 1917+ 4v.

Afr 7324.7.2   Anuaria de Lourenço Marques. Lourenço Marques. 18,1931+ 3v.

Afr 7324.8   Circumscripções de Lourenço Marques. Lourenço Marques, 1909.

Afr 7324.9   Resumo historico dos melhoramentos pedidos. Lisboa, 1902.

Afr 7324 Mozambique; Portuguese East Africa - Local - Districts - Lourenço Marques
cont.

Afr 7324.10   Freire d'Andrade, Alfredo. Colonisação de Lourenço Marques. Porto, 1897.

Afr 7324.17   Official correspondence on the Lourenço Marques-Delagoa Bay question. London, 1874.

Afr 7324.19   Lobato, A. Historia do presidio de Lourenço. Lisboa, 1949-60. 2v.

Afr 7324.19.5   Lobato, A. Quatro estudos e uma evocação para a historia de Lourenço Marques. Lisboa, 1961.

Afr 7324.20   Portugal. Comissão de Limitação da Fronteira de Lourenço Marques. Explorações portuguezas em Lourenço Marques e Inhambane. Lisboa, 1894.

Afr 7324.21   Araujo, Antonio José de. Os acontecimentos de Lourenço Marques. Lisbon, 1890.

Afr 7326 Mozambique; Portuguese East Africa - Local - Districts - Inhambane

Afr 7326.4   Garrett, T. de A. Um governo em Africa. Lisboa, 1907.

Afr 7326.5   Cabral, Augusto. Racas, usos e costumes dos indigenas do districto de Inhambane. Lourenço Marques, 1910.

Afr 7328 Mozambique; Portuguese East Africa - Local - Districts - Gaza Region

Afr 7328.2   Gillmore, P. Through Gasa land. London, 1890.

Afr 7330 Mozambique; Portuguese East Africa - Local - Districts - Tete

Afr 7330.10   Sousa e Silva, Pedro. Distrito de Tete. Lisboa, 1927.

Afr 7332 Mozambique; Portuguese East Africa - Local - Districts - Manica and Sofala

Afr 7332.1   Maugham, R.C.F. Portuguese East Africa. London, 1906.

Afr 7332.5   Brandao Cro de Castro Ferreri, Alfredo. Apontamentos de um ex-governador de Sofalla. Lisboa, 1886.

Afr 7332.10   Documentos relativos aos acontecimentos de manica. Lisboa, 1891.

Afr 7332.12   Pedro, E.R. Resenha geografica do distrito da Beira. Lisboa, 1950.

Afr 7332.15   Bonnefont de Varinay, P. de. La compagnie de Mozambique. Lisboa, 1899.

Afr 7335 Mozambique; Portuguese East Africa - Local - Cities, towns, etc.

Afr 7335.2   Bermudes, F. A cidade da Beira. Lisboa, 1964.

Afr 7335.5   Silva, Julia. Tavares de Almeida de Sousa e Lupata. Lisboa, 1966.

Afr 7349.101 - .399 Mozambique; Portuguese East Africa - Biographies - Individual (A-Z, 299 scheme, by person)

Afr 7349.327   Almeida de Eça, Felipe Gastão de. O capitão César Maria de Serpa Rosa. Lisboa, 1969.

Afr 7350 Liberia - Periodicals

Afr 7350.1   African repository and colonial journal. Washington. 1-68,1825-1892 28v.

Afr 7350.2   Colonizationist and journal of freedom. Boston. 1834+

NEDL Afr 7350.3   American Colonization Society. Annual report. Washington. 1,1818+ 9v.

Afr 7350.3.3   American Colonization Society. Bulletins - Liberia. Washington. 5,1894+

Afr 7350.3.7   Ladies Association, Auxiliary to the American Colonization Society. Annual report. Philadelphia. 2,1934+

Afr 7350.3.9   Garrison, W.L. Thoughts on African colonization. Boston, 1832.

Afr 7350.3.10   Garrison, W.L. Thoughts on African colonization. Boston, 1832.

Afr 7350.3.11   Hopkins, E. Objections...report of the African Colonization Society. Philadelphia, 1833. 2 pam.

Afr 7350.3.12   Hodgkin, T. Inquiry into merits of the American Colonization Society. London, 1833.

Afr 7350.3.13   Gurley, R.R. Mission to England...American Colonization Society. Washington, 1841.

Afr 7350.3.14   Gurley, R.R. Letter to Hon. H. Clay, president of the American Colonization Society. London, 1841.

Afr 7350.3.15   Stebbins, G.B. Facts and opinions touching the real origin, chracter...American Colonization Society. Cleveland, 1853.

NEDL Afr 7350.3.16   American Colonization Society. Memorial of the semi-centennial anniversary. Washington, 1867.

Afr 7350.3.18   Thomasson, W.P. To the citizens of Jefferson County. n.p., 1849.

Afr 7350.3.20   Fox, Early L. The American Colonization Society. Baltimore, 1919.

Afr 7350.3.21   Fox, Early L. The American Colonization Society, 1817-40. Diss. Baltimore, 1919.

Htn Afr 7350.3.23*   Burgess, E. Address to the American Society for Colonizing the Free People of Colour of the U.S. Washington, 1818.

Afr 7350.3.25   Colonization herald and general register. Philadelphia. 1839+

Afr 7350.3.30   Fruits of colonizationism. n.p., 1833.

Afr 7350.3.35   Smith, G. Facts designed to exhibit the real character and tendency of the American Colonizaton Society. Liverpool, 1833.

Afr 7350.4   New York Colonization Society (Founded 1823). Report. N.Y. 1,1823+

Afr 7350.4.10   New York State Colonization Society (Founded 1829). African Colonization. Proceedings...of the society. Albany. 1,1829+

Afr 7350.4.20   New York State Colonization Society (Founded 1832). Annual report. N.Y.

Afr 7350.4.23   New York State Colonization Society (Founded 1832). Miscellaneous pamphlets. N.Y.

Afr 7350.4.25   New York State Colonization Society (Founded 1832). Report to board of managers...by O.F.Cook. N.Y.

Afr 7350.5   Pennsylvania Young Men's Colonization Society. Annual report. Philadelphia. 1830+

Afr 7350.5.3   Pennsylvania Colonization Society. Report of the managers. Appendix. Philadelphia, 1830.

Afr 7350.5.5   Pennsylvania Colonization Society. Annual meeting.

Afr 7350.5.8   Ingersoll, J.R. Address...at the annual meeting of the Pennsylvania Colonization Society, Oct. 25, 1838. Philadelphia, 1838.

Afr 7350.5.10   Allen, W.H. Address before Pennsylvania Colonization Society, Oct. 25. Philadelphia, 1863.

Afr 7350   Liberia - Periodicals
cont.

Afr 7350.5.12	Tyson, J.R. A discourse before the Young Men's Colonization Society of Pennsylvania. Philadelphia, 1834.
Afr 7350.5.20	Whedon, D.D. An address delivered before the Middletown Colonization Society at their annual meeting, July 4, 1834. Middletown, 1834.
Afr 7350.6	Maryland colonization journal. Baltimore. 2,1843+
Afr 7350.6.3	Maryland State Colonization Society. Annual report. Baltimore. 3,1835+ 2v.
Afr 7350.6.10	Harper, C.C. An address delivered...annual meeting of Maryland State Colonization Society...Annapolis, Jan. 23, 1835. Baltimore, 1835.
Afr 7350.7	Worcester County. Auxiliary Colonization Society. Report. Worcester. 1832+
Afr 7350.8	New Hampshire Colonization Society. Report of the board of managers. Concord, N.H.
Afr 7350.10	Massachusetts Colonization Society. Annual report. Boston.
Afr 7350.12	Vermont Colonization Society. Annual report. Montpelier. 40,1859+
Afr 7350.14	Liberian letter. Washington.
Afr 7350.16	Liberian year book. London. 1956+
Afr 7350.18	Liberian studies journal. Greencastle, Ind. 1,1968+

Afr 7353   Liberia - Bibliographies

Afr 7353.1	Pamphlet box. Colonization of Negroes.
Afr 7353.5	Library Of Congress. Division of Bibliography. Liberia, a selected list of references. Photostat. Washington, 1942.
Afr 7353.6	Solomon, Marian D. A general bibliography of the Republic of Liberia. Evanston, 1962.
Afr 7353.10	Holsoe, Svend. A study guide for Liberia. Boston, 1967.

Afr 7355   Liberia - Pamphlet volumes

Afr 7355	Pamphlet box. Liberia.
Afr 7355.1	Pamphlet box. Liberia.
Afr 7355.2	Pamphlet vol. Tracts on colonization and slavery. 17 pam.
Afr 7355.3	Pamphlet vol. Liberia and colonization. 7 pam.
Afr 7355.4	Pamphlet vol. Liberia. 6 pam.
Afr 7355.5	Pamphlet vol. Liberia. 4 pam.
Afr 7355.6	Pamphlet vol. Colonization 1837-62. 3 pam.
Afr 7355.7F	Pamphlet box. Liberia.

Afr 7357   Liberia - Collected source materials

Afr 7357.2	Liberia. Laws, statutes, etc. The statute laws of the Republic of Liberia. Monrovia, 1856.

Afr 7360   Liberia - Government and administration

	Afr 7360.5	Independent Republic of Liberia. Philadelphia, 1848.
	Afr 7360.10	Liberia. Attorney General. Report of L.A. Grimes, submitted to the 4th session of the 34th legislature of the Republic of Liberia. n.p., 1922.
Htn	Afr 7360.15*	Liberia. Constitution. Constitution, government and digest of the laws of Liberia. Washington, 1825.

Afr 7367 - 7370   Liberia - General history (By date)

Afr 7368.32	Maryland State Colonization Society. Colonization Society of Free Colored Population. Maryland. Baltimore, 1852.
Afr 7368.33	Wright, E. The sin of slavery and its remedy. N.Y., 1833.
Afr 7368.36	Freeman, F. Yaradee, plea for Africa. Philadelphia, 1836.
Afr 7368.36.5	Freeman, F. Yaradee, a plea for Africa. N.Y., 1969.
Afr 7368.45	Tables showing the number of emigrants and recaptured Africans sent to the Colony of Liberia. Washington, 1845.
Afr 7368.50	United States. Congress. House. Committee on Naval Affairs. Report of the Naval Committee. Washington, 1850.
Afr 7368.52	Pettit, W.V. Addresses...of the House of Representatives. Harrisburg, Pa. Philadelphia, 1852.
Afr 7368.55	Slaughter, P. Virginian history of African colonization. Richmond, 1855.
Afr 7368.56	Blyden, E.W. Brief account...retirement of President J.J. Roberts. Liberia, 1856.
Afr 7368.56.5	Crummell, A. The duty of a rising Christian state. Boston, 1857. 3 pam.
Afr 7368.57	Christy, David. Ethiopia. Cincinnati, 1857.
Afr 7368.57.5	Christy, David. Ethiopia: her gloom and glory. N.Y., 1969.
Afr 7368.62	Crummell, A. The future of Africa. N.Y., 1862.
Afr 7368.62.2	Crummell, A. The future of Africa. N.Y., 1969.
Afr 7368.65	Blyden, E.W. Our origin, dangers, and duties. N.Y., 1865.
Afr 7368.68	Stockwell, G.S. The Republic of Liberia. N.Y., 1868.
Afr 7368.85	Wauwermans, H. Les premices de l'oeuvre d'émancipation africaine. Liberia. Bruxelles, 1885.
Afr 7368.87	Bourzeix, R.P.P. La république de Liberia. Paris, 1887.
Afr 7368.88	Hodge, J.A. America and Africa. Washington, 1888.
Afr 7368.91	McPherson, J.H.T. History of Liberia. Baltimore, 1891.
Afr 7369.09	Karnga, A.W. The Negro Republic on West Africa. Monrovia, 1909.
Afr 7369.13	Starr, F. Liberia, description, history, problems. Chicago, 1913.
Afr 7369.20.5	Walker, T.H.B. History of Liberia. Boston, 1921.
Afr 7369.29	Boone, C.C. Liberia as I know it. Richmond, Va., 1929.
Afr 7369.34	Yancy, E.J. Historical lights of Liberia's yesterday and today. Xenia, 1934.
Afr 7369.43	Hayman, A.I. Lighting up Liberia. N.Y., 1943.
Afr 7369.46	Phillips, H.A. Liberia's place in Africa's sun. N.Y., 1946.
Afr 7369.47	Huberich, Charles Henry. The political and legislative history of Liberia. N.Y., 1947. 2v.
Afr 7369.47.5A	Wilson, Charles M. Liberia. N.Y., 1947.
Afr 7369.47.5B	Wilson, Charles M. Liberia. N.Y., 1947.
Afr 7369.52	Anderson, R.E. Liberia. Chapel Hill, 1952.
Afr 7369.53	Davis, S.A. This is Liberia. N.Y., 1953.
Afr 7369.57	Bixler, R.W. The foreign policy of the United States in Liberia. 1st ed. N.Y., 1957.
Afr 7369.59	Yancy, Ernest Jerome. The Republic of Liberia. London, 1959.
Afr 7369.59.2	Yancy, Ernest Jerome. The Republic of Liberia. Cairo, 1961.

Afr 7367 - 7370   Liberia - General history (By date)
cont.

Afr 7369.59.5	Richardson, N.R. Liberia's past and present. London, 1959.
Afr 7369.60	Welch, Galbraith. The jet lighthouse. London, 1960.
Afr 7369.61	Khodosh, I.A. Liberiia. Moscow, 1961.
Afr 7369.63	Egorov, V.V. Liberiia posle Vtoroi Mirovoi Voiny. Moscow, 1963.
Afr 7369.64	Frenkel, Matrei I. SShA i Liberiia. Moscow, 1964.
Afr 7369.69	Liebenow, J. Gus. Liberia; the evolution of privilege. Ithaca, 1969.

Afr 7375   Liberia - History by periods - Settlement and early history (1822-1847)

Afr 7375.4	Ashmun, J. History of the American colony in Liberia. Washington, 1826.
Afr 7375.5	Alexander, A. History of colonization on the western coast. Philadelphia, 1846.
Afr 7375.6	Roberts, J.T. The Republic of Liberia. Washington, 1899.
Afr 7375.7	Gurley, R.R. Life of Jehudi Ashmun. Washington, 1835.
Afr 7375.7.2	Gurley, R.R. Life of Jehudi Ashmun. 2d. ed. N.Y., 1839.
Afr 7375.8	Taylor, J.B. Biography of Elder Lott Cary. Baltimore, 1837.
Afr 7375.9.2	Knight, H.C. Africa redeemed. London, 1851.
Afr 7375.9.5	Knight, H.C. The new republic. 2d ed. Boston, 1851.
Afr 7375.11	President Roberts - the Republic of Liberia. N.Y., 1854.
Afr 7375.12	Wilkeson, Samuel. A concise history of...the American colonies in Liberia. Washington, 1839.
Afr 7375.13	Christy, David. A lecture on African colonization. Cincinnati, 1849.
Afr 7375.14.5	Innes, William. Liberia. 2d ed. Edinburgh, 1833.

Afr 7377   Liberia - History by periods - Independent state (1847-   ) - 1847-1911

Afr 7377.5	Mitchell, James. Letters...white and African races. Washington, 1860.
Afr 7377.5.5	Colonization Society of the State of Indiana. Answer of the agent of the Indiana Colonization Society. Indianapolis, 1852.
Afr 7377.6	Hammond, J.H. Regina coeli. Correspondence of J.H.B. Latrobe. Baltimore, 1858.
Afr 7377.25	Allen, Gardner M. The trustees of donations for education in Liberia. Boston, 1923.
Afr 7377.30	Young, James C. Liberia rediscovered. Garden City, 1934.
Afr 7377.34	Azikiwe, Nnamdi. Liberia in world politics. London, 1934.
Afr 7377.34.5	Koren, W. Liberia, the league and the United States. N.Y., 1934.
Afr 7377.59	Tubman, William. President Tubman of Liberia speaks. London, 1959.
Afr 7377.61	Simpson, C.L. The memoirs of C.L. Simpson. London, 1961.
Afr 7377.64	Marinelli, L.A. The new Liberia. N.Y., 1964. 2v.

Afr 7380   Liberia - History by periods - Independent state (1847-   ) - 1911-1960

Afr 7380.5	Smith, Robert A. The emancipation of the hinterland. Monrovia, 1964.

Afr 7385   Liberia - History by periods - Independent state (1847-   ) - 1960-

Afr 7385.5	Tubman, William. President William V.S. Tubman on African unity. Monrovia, 1964.

Afr 7455 - 7460   Liberia - Geography, description, etc. (By date)

Afr 7458.22	Bacon, E. Abstract of a journal...to Afrika. Philadelphia, 1822.
Afr 7458.32	News from Africa. Collection of facts. Baltimore, 1832.
Afr 7458.50	United States. Department of State. Report of Secretary of State...in respect to Liberia. Washington, 1850.
Afr 7458.51	Latrobe, J.H.B. Colonization. Notice of V. Hugo's views of slavery. Baltimore, 1851.
Afr 7458.51.3	Latrobe, J.H.B. Colonization and abolition. Baltimore, 1851.
Afr 7458.51.7	Fuller, T. Journal of voyage to Liberia. Baltimore, 1851.
Afr 7458.52	American Colonization Society. Information about emigration to Liberia. Washington, 1852. 2 pam.
Afr 7458.53	Hale, Sarah J. Liberia. N.Y., 1853.
Afr 7458.54	Foote, A.H. Africa and the American flag. N.Y., 1854.
Afr 7458.57	Williams, S. Four years in Liberia. Philadelphia, 1857.
Afr 7458.60	Payne, J.S. Prize essay on political economy of Liberia. Monrovia, 1860.
Afr 7458.61	Crummell, A. Relations and duties of free colored men in America. Hartford, 1861.
Afr 7458.62	Ralston, Gerard. On the Republic of Liberia, its products and resources. London, 1862.
Afr 7458.62.5	Blyden, E.W. Liberia's offering. N.Y., 1862.
Afr 7458.66	Fitzgerald, J.J. Seven years in Africa. Columbus, 1866.
Afr 7458.68	Merriam, M.B. Home life in Africa. Boston, 1868.
Afr 7458.70	Anderson, B. Narrative of a journey to Musardu. N.Y., 1870.
Afr 7458.79	Dyer, A.S. Christian Liberia. London, 1879.
Afr 7458.80	Latrobe, J.H.B. Liberia...an address delivered before American Colonization Society. Washington, 1880.
Afr 7458.81A	Stetson, G.R. The Liberian Republic as it is. Photoreproduction. Boston, 1881.
Afr 7458.81B	Stetson, G.R. The Liberian Republic as it is. Photoreproduction. Boston, 1881.
Afr 7458.90	Buettikofer, J. Reisebilder aus Liberia. Leiden, 1890. 2v.
NEDL Afr 7458.92	Durham, F.A. Lone star of Liberia. London, 1892.
Afr 7458.98	Heard, William Henry. The bright side of African life. N.Y., 1969.
Afr 7459.06	Johnston, H. Liberia. London, 1906. 2v.
Afr 7459.10	Toepfer, R. Liberia. Berlin, 1910.
Afr 7459.12	Jore, L. La république de Liberia. Paris, 1912.
Afr 7459.20A	Maugham, R.C.F. The Republic of Liberia. London, 1920.
Afr 7459.20B	Maugham, R.C.F. The Republic of Liberia. London, 1920.
Afr 7459.23	Reeve, H.F. The Black Republic, Liberia. London, 1923.
Afr 7459.26	Mills, Dorothy. Through Liberia. London, 1926.
Afr 7459.28	Sibley, James L. Liberia, old and new. London, 1928.
Afr 7459.30	Delarue, S. The land of the pepper bird. N.Y., 1930.
Afr 7459.30.10A	Harvard African Expedition, 1926-1927. The African republic of Liberia and the Belgian Congo. N.Y., 1969. 2v.
Afr 7459.30.10B	Harvard African Expedition, 1926-1927. The African republic of Liberia and the Belgian Congo. N.Y., 1969. 2v.

Afr 7540 Congo Republic (Leopoldville); Belgian Congo - Government and administration cont.

Afr 7540.29	Delvaux, Roger. L'organisation administrative du Congo belge. Anvers, 1945.
Afr 7540.30	Perin, François. Les institutions politiques du Congo...30 juin 1960. Bruxelles, 1960.
Afr 7540.34	Poupart, R. Première esquisse de l'évolution du syndicalisme au Congo. Bruxelles, 1960.
Afr 7540.36	Brausch, G. Belgian administration in the Congo. London, 1961.
Afr 7540.38	Lippens, Maurice. Notes sur le gouvernement du Congo, 1921-22. Gand, 1923.
Afr 7540.39	Congo. Laws, statutes, etc. Les circonscriptions indigènes. Bruxelles, 1938.
Afr 7540.40A	Janssens, E. J'étais le général Janssens. Bruxelles, 1961.
Afr 7540.40B	Janssens, E. J'étais le général Janssens. Bruxelles, 1961.
Afr 7540.41	Paulus, Jean Pierre. Droit public du Congo belge. Bruxelles, 1959.
Afr 7540.42	Sohier, Jean. Essai sur les transformations des coutumes. Bruxelles, 1956.
Afr 7540.43	Durieux, André. Souveraineté et communauté belgo-congolaise. Bruxelles, 1959.
Afr 7540.44	Piron, Pierre. L'indépendance de la magistrature et la statut des magistrats. Bruxelles, 1956.

Afr 7543 Congo Republic (Leopoldville); Belgian Congo - General politics; political parties

Afr 7543.5	Centre de Recherche et d'Information Socio-Politiques. Documents, 1950-1960. Bruxelles, 1962.
Afr 7543.10	Parti Solidaire Africain. Parti solidaire africain (P.S.A.). Bruxelles, 1963.
Afr 7543.12	Weiss, Herbert F. Political protest in the Congo. Princeton, 1967.

Afr 7545 - 7550 Congo Republic (Leopoldville); Belgian Congo - General history (By date)

Afr 7548.85	Patzig, Carl Albrecht. Die afrikanische Konferenz und der Kongostaat. Heidelberg, 1885.
Afr 7548.90	Desoer, F. Le Congo belge. Liège, 1890.
Afr 7548.94	Reeves, J.S. International beginnings of the Congo Free State. Baltimore, 1894.
Afr 7548.94.5	Chapaux, Albert. Le Congo historique. Bruxelles, 1894.
Afr 7548.98	Boulger, D.C. The Congo state. London, 1898.
Afr 7549.00	Jozon, L. L'état indépendant du Congo. Paris, 1900.
Afr 7549.09	Claparède, René. L'évolution d'un état philanthropique. Genève, 1909.
Afr 7549.11	Vandervelde, E. La Belgique et le Congo. Paris, 1911.
Afr 7549.11.3	Wauters, A.J. Histoire politique du Congo belge. Bruxelles, 1911.
Afr 7549.11.7	Anton, G.K. Kongostaat und Kongoreform. Leipzig, 1911.
Afr 7549.13	Nasoin, Fritz. Histoire de l'état indépandant du Congo. Namur, 1912-13. 2v.
Afr 7549.19A	Keith, Arthur B. The Belgian Congo and the Berlin Act. Oxford, 1919.
Afr 7549.19B	Keith, Arthur B. The Belgian Congo and the Berlin Act. Oxford, 1919.
Afr 7549.21	Pirenne, Jacques. Coup d'oeil sur l'histoire du Congo. Bruxelles, 1921.
Afr 7549.28	Monheim, A. Le Congo et les livres. Bruxelles, 1928.
Afr 7549.37	Jentgen, Pierre. La terre belge du Congo. Bruxelles, 1937.
Afr 7549.39	Bollati, A. Il Congo belga. Milano, 1939.
Afr 7549.48	Marvel, T. The new Congo. N.Y., 1948.
Afr 7549.48.3	Marvel, T. The new Congo. 1st British ed. London, 1949.
Afr 7549.48.10	Cornet, Rene Jules. Sommaire de l'histoire du Congo belge. Bruxelles, 1948.
Afr 7549.50	Encyclopédie du Congo belge. Bruxelles, 1950. 3v.
Afr 7549.50.5	Bevel, M.L. Le dictionnaire colonial (Encyclopédie). Bruxelles, 1950-51. 2v.
Afr 7549.52	Belgium. Force Publique. Etat-Major. Le force publique de sa naissance à 1914. Bruxelles, 1952.
Afr 7549.53	Ydewalle, Charles D. Le Congo du fétiche à l'uranium. Bruxelles, 1953.
Afr 7549.54	Dellicour, Fernand. Les propos d'un colonial belge. Bruxelles, 1954.
Afr 7549.54.5	Hostelet, Georges. L'oeuvre civilisatrice de la Belgique au Congo. Bruxelles, 1954. 2v.
Afr 7549.59	Zuylen, Pierre van. L'échequier congolais. Bruxelles, 1959.
Afr 7549.59.5	Lévèque, Robert J. Le Congo belge. Bruxelles, 1959.
Afr 7549.59.10	Ranieri, Liane. Les relations entre l'état indépendant du Congo et l'Italie. Bruxelles, 1959.
Afr 7549.59.15	Lacger, L. de. Ruanda. Kabgayi, 1959.
Afr 7549.61	Merriam, Alan P. Congo, background of conflict. Evanston, Ill., n.d.
Afr 7549.61.5	Hennessy, Maurice N. The Congo. London, 1961.
Afr 7549.62	Zusmanovich, A.Z. Imperialisticheskii razdel basseina Kongo. Moscow, 1962.
Afr 7549.62.5	Maurice, Albert. Belgique, gouvernante du Congo. Bruxelles, 1962.
Afr 7549.62.10	Martelli, George. Leopold to Lumumba. London, 1962.
Afr 7549.62.15	Schuyler, Philippa. Who killed the Congo? N.Y., 1962.
Afr 7549.63	Cornevin, R. Histoire du Congo (Leopoldville). Paris, 1963.
Afr 7549.63.2	Cornevin, Robert. Histoire du Congo: Léopoldville-Kinshassa. 2. éd. Paris, 1966.
Afr 7549.64	Meyers, Joseph. Le prix d'un empire. 3.ed. Bruxelles, 1964.
Afr 7549.65	Loth, Heinrich. Kongo, heisses Herz Afrikas. Geschichte des Landes bis auf unsere Tage. Berlin, 1965.
Afr 7549.66	Giovannini, Giovanni. Congo. 2.ed. Milano, 1966.

Afr 7555 Congo Republic (Leopoldville); Belgian Congo - General special

Afr 7555.51	Lederer, Andre. Histoire de la navigation au Congo. Tervuren, 1965.

Afr 7560 Congo Republic (Leopoldville); Belgian Congo - History by periods - Early to 1882

Htn Afr 7560.2*	Lopes, D. Relazione del reame del Congo et del circonvisine contrade. Roma, 1591.
Afr 7560.3	Pigafetta, F. A report on the kingdom of Congo. London, 1881.
Afr 7560.3.2	Lopes, D. Le Congo. Bruxelles, 1883.
Afr 7560.3.10	Simar, T. Le Congo au XVIe siècle d'aprés la relation de Lopez-Pigafetta. Bruxelles, 1919.
Afr 7560.4	Moynier, G. La fondation de l'état indépandant du Congo. Paris, 1887.
Afr 7560.5	Bal, W. Le royaume du Congo aux XVe et XVIe siècle. Léopoldville, 1963.
Afr 7560.10	Ihle, Alexander. Das Alte Königreich Kongo. Inaug. Diss. Leipzig, 1929.
Afr 7560.12	Cuvelier, Jean. L'ancien royaume de Congo. Bruges, 1946.
Afr 7560.14	Roeykens, A. Le dessein africain de Léopold II. Bruxelles, 1956.
Afr 7560.14.5	Roeykens, A. Léopold II et l'Afrique, 1855-1880. Bruxelles, 1958.
Afr 7560.14.10	Roeykens, A. La période initiale de l'oeuvre africaine de Lépold II. Bruxelles, 1957.
Afr 7560.14.15	Roeykens, A. Les débuts de l'oeuvre de Léopold II, 1875-1876. Bruxelles, 1955.
Afr 7560.15	Balandier, Georges. La vie quotidienne au royaume de Kongo du XVI au XVIII siècle. Paris, 1965.
Afr 7560.15.5	Balandier, Georges. Daily life in the Kingdom of the Kongo from the sixteenth to the eighteenth century. London, 1968.
Afr 7560.18	Lopes, Duarte. Description du royaume de Congo et des contrées environnantes. Louvain, 1963.
Afr 7560.18.2	Lopes, Duarte. Description du royaume de Congo et des contrées environnantes parFilippo Pigafetta et Duarte Lopes (1951). 2.ed. Louvain, 1965.
Afr 7560.18.10	Lopes, Duarte. A report of the Kingdom of Congo and of the surrounding countries. N.Y., 1969.
Afr 7560.19	Orlova, Antonina S. Istoriia gosudarstva Kongo (XVI-XVII vv.). Moskva, 1968.
Afr 7561.5	McLaughlin, Russell U. Foreign investment and development in Liberia. N.Y., 1966.

Afr 7565 Congo Republic (Leopoldville); Belgian Congo - History by periods - 1882-1890

Afr 7565.5	Kassai, Pierre. La civilisation africaine, 1876-1888. Bruxelles, 1888.
Afr 7565.8	Thomson, R.S. Fondation de l'état indépendant du Congo. Bruxelles, 1933.
Afr 7565.9	Stengers, J. Belgique et Congo. Bruxelles, 1963.
Afr 7565.10F	Italy. Ministero degli Affari Esteri. Documenti diplomatici presentati al senato. Roma, 1885.
Afr 7565.12	Jooris, J. L'acte général de la Conférence de Berlin. Bruxelles, 1885.
Afr 7565.12.5F	Berlin. Conference, 1884-85. Protocoles et acte général de la Conférence de Berlin, 1884-85. n.p., (1885).
Afr 7565.12.15	Yarnall, H.E. The great powers and the Congo Conference in the year 1884 and 1885. Inaug. Diss. Göttingen, 1934.
Afr 7565.12.20	Courcel, G. de. L'influence de la Conférence de Berlin de 1885. Paris, 1936.
Afr 7565.12.25	Koenigk, G. Die Berliner Kongo-Konferenz, 1884-1885. Essen, 1938.
Afr 7565.12.30	Crowe, S.E. The Berlin West African Conference, 1884-1885. London, 1942.
Afr 7565.14	Banning, Emile. Mémoires politiques et diplomatiques. Paris, 1927.
Afr 7565.14.5	Banning, E. Textes inédits. Bruxelles, 1955.
Afr 7565.16	Twiss, Travers. An international protectorate of the Congo River. London, 1883.
Afr 7565.17	Mendiaux, E. Histoire du Congo. Bruxelles, 1961.
Afr 7565.18	Descamps, E. L'Afrique nouvelle. Paris, 1903.
Afr 7565.19	Ruytjens, E. Historisch ontstaan der grens van de onafhankelijke. Bruxelles, 1958.
Afr 7565.20	Cannart d'Hamale, Art. Quelques pages sur le Congo. Bruxelles, 1908.
Afr 7565.22	Loth, Heinrich. Kolonialismus und Humanitätsintervention. Berlin, 1966.

Afr 7567 Congo Republic (Leopoldville); Belgian Congo - History by periods - 1891-1960 - General works

Afr 7567.4	Hinde, S.L. The fall of the Congo Arabs. London, 1897.
Afr 7567.4.5	Hinde, Sidney L. The fall of the Congo Arabs. N.Y., 1897.
Afr 7567.6	Gochet, J.B. Soldats et missionnaires au Congo de 1891 à 1894. Bruxelles, 1896.
Afr 7567.8	Blanc, J. Le droit de préférence de la France sur le Congo belge (1884-1911). Thèse. Paris, 1921.
Afr 7567.10	Payen, Edouard. Belgique et Congo (Une carte itinéraire). Paris, 1917.
Afr 7567.12	Landbeck, P. Kongoerinnerungen. Berlin, 1923.
Afr 7567.13	Cola Alberich, Julio. El Congo, 1885-1963. Madrid, 1964.
Afr 7567.14	Mountmorres, W.S.B. de M. The Congo Independent State. London, 1906.
Afr 7567.15	Luwel, Marcel. De limburgers in Congo. Hasselt, 1952.
Afr 7567.19	Cornet, Rene. Katanga. 3 ed. Bruxelles, 1946.
Afr 7567.20	Habran, Louis. Coup d'oeil sur le problème politique et militaire du Congo belge. Bruxelles, 1925.
Afr 7567.22	Flechet, Ferdinand. L'annexion du Congo devant Parlement belge. 2d ed. Liège, 1909.
Afr 7567.24	Ryckmans, Pierre. Etapes et jalons. Bruxelles, 1946.
Afr 7567.25	Anstey, Roger. Britain and the Congo in the 19th century. Oxford, 1962.
Afr 7567.26	Merlier, Michel. Le Congo de la colonisation belge à l'indépendance. Paris, 1962.
Afr 7567.28	Daye, Pierre. Problèmes congolais. Bruxelles, 1943.
Afr 7567.30	Okumu, Washington A. Lumumba's Congo. N.Y., 1963.
Afr 7567.32	Willequet, I. Le Congo belge et Weltpolitik. Bruxelles, 1962.
Afr 7567.34	Lemarchand, Rene. Political awakening in the Belgian Congo. Berkeley, 1964.
Afr 7567.36	Anstey, Roger. King Leopold's legacy. London, 1966.
Afr 7567.38	Liebrechts, Charles. Notre colonie. Bruxelles, 1922.
Afr 7567.40	Bricusse, Georges Henri A. Les carnets de campagne. Bruxelles, 1966.
VAfr 7567.41	Ratajski, Lech. Konge Kinszasa. Wyd. 1. Warszawa, 1967.
Afr 7567.42	Cookey, Sylvanus John Sodienye. Britain and the Congo question, 1885-1913. London, 1968.
Afr 7567.44	Dettes de guerre. Elisabethville, 1945.

Afr 7568   Congo Republic (Leopoldville); Belgian Congo - History by periods -
1891-1960 - Questions of misgovernment

	Afr 7568F	Pamphlet box. Congo Free State.
	Afr 7568.3	Stengel, K.F. von. Der Kongostaat. München, 1903.
	Afr 7568.5	Burrows, G. The curse of Central Africa. London, 1903.
	Afr 7568.7	Bourne, H.R.F. Civilisation in Congoland. London, 1903.
	Afr 7568.9	Truth about civilisation in Congoland. Brussels, 1903.
	Afr 7568.11	Congo. Vice-Governor General. Report to Secretary of State. Brussels, 1904.
Htn	Afr 7568.13*	Clemens, S.L. King Leopold's soliloquy. Boston, 1905.
	Afr 7568.15	Morel, E.D. King Leopold's rule in Africa. N.Y., 1905.
	Afr 7568.15.2	Morel, E.D. King Leopold's rule in Africa. London, 1904.
	Afr 7568.15.5	Morel, E.D. The future of the Congo. London, 1909.
	Afr 7568.15.10	Morel, Edmund D. Morel's history of the Congo reform movement. Oxford, 1968.
	Afr 7568.15.15	Morel, Edmund D. Red rubber. N.Y., 1969.
	Afr 7568.16	Congo Reform Association. Memorial concerning conditions...in Kongo. Washington, 1904.
	Afr 7568.18	Wack, H.W. The story of the Congo Free State. N.Y., 1905.
	Afr 7568.20F	New Africa. Edinburgh, 1904.
	Afr 7568.23	Dorman, M.R.P. Journal...tour in the Congo Free State. Brussels, 1905.
	Afr 7568.25	Belguim. Commission Chargée de Faire une Enquête dans les Territoires de l'Etat du Congo. The Congo. N.Y., 1906.
	Afr 7568.25.5	Belgium. Commission Chargée de Faire une Enquête dans les Territoires de l'Etat du Congo. Abstract of the report of the Commission enquiry into a administration of Congo Free State. London, 1906.
	Afr 7568.26	Bowdoin-Clark Debate. The Bowdoin argument in the Bowdoin-Clark debate. n.p., 1906.
	Afr 7568.27	Pamphlet box. Alleged conditions in Kongo Free State.
	Afr 7568.28	Cattier, F. Etude sur la situation de l'état...Congo. Bruxelles, 1906.
	Afr 7568.29	Doyle, A.C. The crime of the Congo. N.Y., 1909.
	Afr 7568.30	Tisdel, W.P. Kongo. Leipzig, 1886.
	Afr 7568.31	Williams, G.W. An open letter to His Serene Majesty Leopold II. n.p., n.d. 2 pam.
	Afr 7568.33	Starr, F. The truth about the Congo. Chicago, 1907.
	Afr 7568.35	Castelein, A. The Congo State; its origin, rights, and duties, the charges of its accusers. N.Y., 1969.

Afr 7570   Congo Republic (Leopoldville); Belgian Congo - History by periods -
1891-1960 - European War (1914-1918)

	Afr 7570.15	Belgium. Ministère de la Défense Nationale. Etat-Major Général de l'Armée. Les campagnes coloniales belges, 1914-1918. Bruxelles, 1927-1929. 2v.
	Afr 7570.20	Segairt, Henri. Un terme au Congo belge. Bruxelles, 1919.

Afr 7575   Congo Republic (Leopoldville); Belgian Congo - History by periods -
1891-1960 - 1945-1960

	Afr 7575.4	Legum, Cohn. Congo disaster. Harmondsworth, 1961.
	Afr 7575.5A	Bilsen, Antoine. Vers l'indépendance du Congo et du Ruanda-Urundi. Kraainem, 1958.
	Afr 7575.5B	Bilsen, Antoine. Vers l'indépendance du Congo et du Ruanda-Urundi. Kraainem, 1958.
	Afr 7575.6	Bilsen, Antoine. L'indépendance du Congo. Tournai, 1962.
	Afr 7575.10	Morres, Jacques. L'équinoxe de janvier. Bruxelles, 1959.
	Afr 7575.12	Niedergang, M. Tempête sur le Congo. Paris, 1960.
	Afr 7575.15A	Hostelet, Georges. Le problème politique capital au Congo et en Afrique noire. Burxelles, 1959.
	Afr 7575.15B	Hostelet, Georges. Le problème politique capital au Congo et en Afrique noire. Bruxelles, 1959.
	Afr 7575.17	Hostelet, Georges. Pour éviter l'anarchie puis là. Bruxelles, 1959.
	Afr 7575.20	Mendiaux, Edouard. Moscou, Accra et le Congo. Bruxelles, 1960.
	Afr 7575.25	Mezerik, A.G. Congo and the United Nations. N.Y., 1960. 3v.
	Afr 7575.30	Calder, Ritchie. Agony of the Congo. London, 1961.
	Afr 7575.35	Houart, P. La pénétration communiste au Congo. Bruxelles, 1960.
	Afr 7575.36	Bartlet, R.E. Communist penetration and subversion of the Belgian Congo, 1946-1960. 1st. ed. Berkeley, 1962.
	Afr 7575.40	Ribeaud, P. Adieu Congo. Paris, 1961.
	Afr 7575.45	Dessart, C. Le Congo à tombeau ouvert. Bruxelles, 1959.
	Afr 7575.50	Khokhlov, N.P. Tragediia Kongo. Moscow, 1961. 2 pam.
	Afr 7575.55	Scholl-Latour, Peter. Matata am Kongo. Stuttgart, 1961.
	Afr 7575.60	Houart, Pierre. Les évènements du Congo. Bruxelles, 1961.
	Afr 7575.65	Belgo-Congolese Round Table Conference, Brussels, 1960. De historische dagen von februari 1960. Brussels, 1960.
	Afr 7575.66	Dumont, G.H. La table ronde belgo-congolaise. Paris, 1961.
	Afr 7575.67	Demany, Fernand. S.O.S. Congo. Bruxelles, 1959.
	Afr 7575.75	Slade, R. The Belgian Congo. 2. ed. London, 1961.
	Afr 7575.80	Lumumba, Patrice. Le Congo. Bruxelles, 1961.
	Afr 7575.80.5	Chome, Jules. A propos d'un livre posthume de Patrice Lumumba. Bruxelles, 1961.
	Afr 7575.80.10	Lumumba, Patrice. Congo, my country. London, 1962.
	Afr 7575.80.11	Lumumba, Patrice. Congo, my country. N.Y., 1962.
	Afr 7575.80.12	Lumumba, Patrice. Congo, my country. London, 1969.
	Afr 7575.85	Volodin, L.D. Trudnye dni Kongo. Moscow, 1961.
	Afr 7575.90	Parti Socialiste Belge. Congo. Brussels, 1961.
	Afr 7575.95	Netherlands. Department van Buitenlandse Zaken. Kongo en de Verenigde Naties. 's-Gravenhage, 1961- 2v.
	Afr 7575.96	Wauters, A. Le norde communiste et la crise du Congo belge. Brussels, 1961.
	Afr 7575.97	Paulus, J.P. Congo, 1956-1960. Bruxelles, 1961.
	Afr 7575.98	Bouvier, Paule. L'accession du Congo belge à l'indépendance. Bruxelles, 1965.
	Afr 7575.99	Vinokurov, Iurii N. Kongo. Moskva, 1967.

Afr 7580   Congo Republic (Leopoldville); Belgian Congo - History by periods -
1960- - General works

	Afr 7580.2	Duyzings, Martin. Mensen en machten in Congo. Amsterdam, 1960.
	Afr 7580.3	Institut Royal des Relations Internationales. La crise congolaise. Brussels, 1960.
	Afr 7580.4	Institut Royal des Relations Internationales. Evolution de la crise congolaise de septembre 1960 à avril 1961. Brussels, 1961.
	Afr 7580.5	Stenmans, Alain. Les premiers mois de la République du Congo. Bruxelles, 1961.
	Afr 7580.6	Roberts, John. My Congo adventure. London, 1963.

Afr 7580   Congo Republic (Leopoldville); Belgian Congo - History by periods -
1960- - General works
cont.

	Afr 7580.7	Borri, M. Nous, ces affreux, dossier secret de l'ex-Congo belge. Paris, 1962.
	Afr 7580.8A	Ganshof van der Meersch, W.J. Fin de la souveraineté belge au Congo. Bruxelles, 1963.
	Afr 7580.8B	Ganshof van der Meersch, W.J. Fin de la souveraineté belge au Congo. Bruxelles, 1963.
	Afr 7580.9	Congo. The Adoula-Tshombe talks. Leopoldville, 1962.
	Afr 7580.10	Tournaire, H. Le livre noir du Congo. Paris, 1963.
	Afr 7580.11	Tran-Minh Tiet. Congo ex-belge entre l'est et l'ouest. Paris, 1962.
	Afr 7580.12F	Trinquier, R. Notre guerre au Katanga. Paris, 1963.
	Afr 7580.13	Valahu, M. The Katanga circus. 1st ed. N.Y., 1964.
	Afr 7580.14	Buccianto, G. Il Congo. Milano, 1963.
	Afr 7580.15	Cabanes, Bernard. Du Congo belge au Katanga. Paris, 1963.
	Afr 7580.16	Gilis, Charles A. Kasa-Vubu, au coeur du drame congolais. Bruxelles, 1964.
	Afr 7580.17	Hoskyns, Catherine. The Congo since independence. London, 1965.
	Afr 7580.18	Sturdza, Michel. World government and international assassination. Belmont, Mass., 1963.
	Afr 7580.19	Lafever, E.W. Crisis in the Congo. Washington, 1965.
	Afr 7580.20	Young, Crawford. Politics in the Congo. Princeton, N.J., 1965.
	Afr 7580.21	Kestergat, Jean. Congo Congo. Paris, 1965.
	Afr 7580.22	Epstein, Howard M. Revolt in the Congo, 1960-64. N.Y., 1965.
	Afr 7580.23	La rébellion au Congo. Leopoldville, Congo, 1964.
	Afr 7580.24	Truby, David William. Congo saga. London, 1965.
	Afr 7580.25	Jarschel, Fritz. Lumumba. Kreuzweingarten/Rhld., 1965.
	Afr 7580.26	Nkrumah, Kwame. Challenge of the Congo. London, 1967.
	Afr 7580.28	Union des Jeunesses Revolutionaires Congolaises. Memorandum; l'agression armée de l'impérialisme Americano-Belge à Stanleyville et Paulis. Bruxelles, 1966.
	Afr 7580.30	Kitchen, Helen A. Footnotes to the Congo story. N.Y., 1967.
	Afr 7580.32	Topuzoglu. Kongo kurtuluş, sowosi. 1. baski. Istanbul, 1965.
	Afr 7580.35	Rétillon, Leon A.M. Témoignage et réflexions. Bruxelles, 1967.
VAfr	7580.36	Bin'kowski, Andrzej. Drugi cień mojzesza Czombe. Wyd.1. Warszawa, 1967.
	Afr 7580.38	Scott, Ian. Tumbled house: the Congo at independence. London, 1969.

Afr 7582   Congo Republic (Leopoldville); Belgian Congo - History by periods -
1960- - Special topics

	Afr 7582.3	Lawson, Richard G. Strange soldiering. London, 1963.
	Afr 7582.4	Liège. Université. Fondation pour les Recherches Scientifiques en Afrique Central. Recherches sur le développement rural en Afrique central. Liège, 1965.
	Afr 7582.5	Verhaegen, Benoit. Rébellions au Congo. Leopoldville, 1966.
	Afr 7582.6	Germani, Hans. White soldiers in black Africa. Cape Town, 1967.
	Afr 7582.8	Martelli, George. Experiment in world government, an account of the United Nations operation in the Congo, 1960-1964. London, 1966.
	Afr 7582.10.4	Hoare, Michael. Congo mercenary. London, 1967.
	Afr 7582.15	Brookings Institute, Washington, D.C. Foreign Policy Studies Division. United Nations peacekeeping in the Congo: 1960-1964. v.1-4. Washington, 1966. 2v.

Afr 7803   Congo Republic (Leopoldville); Belgian Congo - Religion; missions
[Discontinued]

	Afr 7803.5	Kellersberger, Julia L.S. A life for the Congo. N.Y., 1947.
	Afr 7803.10	Abel, Armand. Les Musulmans noirs du Maniema. Bruxelles, 1960.
	Afr 7803.15	Nelson, Robert G. Congo crisis and Christian mission. St. Louis, 1961.
	Afr 7803.20	Hildebrand. Le martyr Georges de Geel et les débuts de la mission du Congo. Anvers, 1940.
	Afr 7803.25	Slade, Ruth. English-speaking missions in the Congo Independent State (1878-1908). Bruxelles, 1959.
	Afr 7803.26	Richardson, Kenneth. Freedom in Congo. London, 1962.
	Afr 7803.28	Lorenzo da Lucca. Relations sur le Congo du père Lament de Lucques. Bruxelles, 1953.
	Afr 7803.30	Cuvelier, J. Documents sur une mission française au Kakongo 1766-1776. Bruxelles, 1953.
	Afr 7803.32	Thibaut, Emile. Les jésuites et les fermes-chapelles, à propos d'un débat récent. Bruxelles 1911.
	Afr 7803.33	Meeus, F. de. Les missions religieuses au Congo belge. Anvers, 1947.
	Afr 7803.34	Laridan, P. Les martyrs noirs de l'Ouganda. Tournai, 1962.
	Afr 7803.36	Heyse, T. Associations religieuses au Congo belge. Bruxelles, 1948.
	Afr 7803.38	Carpenter, G.W. Les chemins du seigneur du Congo. Leopoldville, 1953.
	Afr 7803.40	Storme, Marcel. Rapports du père Planque. Bruxelles, 1957.
	Afr 7803.40.5	Storme, Marcel. Het ontstaan van de Kasai-missie. Brussels, 1961.
	Afr 7803.41	Hege, Ruth. We two alone. N.Y., 1965.
	Afr 7803.42	Dowdy, Homer E. Out of the jaws of the lion. 1st ed. N.Y., 1965.
	Afr 7803.43	Italiaander, Rolf. Im Namen des Herrn im Kongo. Kassel, 1965.
	Afr 7803.44	Anciaux, Leon. Le problème musulman dans l'Afrique belge. Bruxelles, 1949.
	Afr 7803.45	Bittremieux, Leo. La société secrète des Bakhimba au Mayombe. Bruxelles, 1936.
	Afr 7803.46	Cazlson, Lois. Monganga Paul. N.Y., 1966.
	Afr 7803.48	Jeanroy, V. Vingt-cinq ans de mission au Congo. Bruxelles, 1923.

Afr 7805 - 7810   Congo Republic (Leopoldville); Belgian Congo - Geography,
description, etc. (By date)

	Afr 7806.66.5	Guattini, M.A. Viaggio del P. Michael Angelo de Guattini da Reggio. Reggio, 1672.
	Afr 7806.66.10F	Guattini, M.A. A curious and exact account of a voyage to Congo...1666 and 1667. London, 1704. 2 pam.

Afr 7806.92	Merolla da Sorrento. Breve e succinta relazione del viaggio nel regno. Napoli, 1692.
Afr 7808.18.2	Tuckey, J.K. Narrative of an expedition to explore the River Zaire. N.Y., 1818.
Afr 7808.18.3	Tuckey, J.K. Narrative of an expedition to explore the River Zaire. London, 1818.
Afr 7808.32	Douville, J.B. Voyage au Congo, 1828-1830. Paris, 1832. 4v.
Afr 7808.32.2	Douville, J.B. Voyage au Congo, 1829-1830. Stuttgart, 1832. 3v.
Afr 7808.74	Delcommune, A. Vingt années de vie africaine. Bruxelles, 1922. 2v.
Afr 7808.76	Rocykens, Aug. Leopold II et la conférence géographique. Bruxelles, 1956.
Afr 7808.84	Johnston, H.H. The river Congo. London, 1884.
NEDL Afr 7808.85	Stanley, H.M. The Congo. London, 1885. 2v.
Afr 7808.85.5	Stanley, H.M. The Congo. v.1-2. N.Y., 1885.
Afr 7808.86	Conférences sur le Congo. Bruxelles, 1886.
Afr 7808.86.2F	Dewinton, F.W. The Congo Free State. London, 1886.
Afr 7808.87	Bentley, William Holman. Life on the Congo. London, 1887.
Afr 7808.88.3	Wissmann, H.V. Im innern Afrikas. Leipzig, 1891.
Afr 7808.88.5	Coquilhat, Camille. Sur le Haut-Congo. Paris, 1888.
Afr 7808.89	Dupont, C.F. Lettres sur le Congo. Paris, 1889.
Afr 7808.89.2	Wolff, W. Von Banana zum Kiammo. Oldenburg, 1889.
Afr 7808.89.3	Schynse, P.A. Zwei Jahre am Congo. Köln, 1889.
Afr 7808.89.5	Phillips, Henry. Account of the Congo Independent State. n.p., 1889.
Afr 7808.89.7	Bateman, C.S.L. The first ascent of the Kasai. London, 1889.
Afr 7808.89.9	Michaux, Oscar. Au Congo. Namur, 1913.
Afr 7808.90	Ward, Herbert. Life among the Congo savages. N.Y., 1890.
Afr 7808.90.2	Ward, Herbert. Five years with Congo cannibals. London, 1890.
Afr 7808.90.4	Ward, Herbert. Five years with the Congo cannibals. n.p., 1890.
Afr 7808.90.7	Ward, Herbert. Five years with the Congo cannibals. 3rd ed. N.Y., 1969.
Afr 7808.92	Ramaix, M.M. de. Le Congo. Anvers, 1892.
Afr 7808.93	Glave, E.J. Six years of adventure in Congo-land. London, 1893.
Afr 7808.94	Bailey, Henry. Travel and adventures in Congo Free State. London, 1894.
Afr 7808.95	Wincxtenhoven. Les colonies et l'état indépendant du Congo. Bruxelles, 1895.
Afr 7808.97	Guide de la section de l'Etat Indépendant du Congo, la Bruxelles exposition. Bruxelles, 1897.
Afr 7808.98	Burrows, G. The land of the pigmies. London, 1898.
Afr 7808.98.2	Burrows, G. The land of the pigmies. N.Y., 1898.
Afr 7808.99	Wauters, A.J. L'Etat Indépendant du Congo. Bruxelles, 1899.
Afr 7808.99.3	Mille, P. Au Congo belge. Paris, 1899.
Afr 7808.99.5	Buls, Charles. Croquis congolais. Bruxelles, 1899.
Afr 7809.00	Lloyd, A.B. In dwarf land and cannibal country. London, 1899.
Afr 7809.00.3	Lloyd, A.B. In dwarf land and cannibal country. London, 1907.
Afr 7809.00.5	Bentley, W.H. Pioneering on the Congo. N.Y., 1900. 2v.
Afr 7809.00.10	Carton de Wiart, H. Mes vacances au Congo. Bruges, 19- .
Afr 7809.01	Svambera, V. Kongo. Praha, 1901.
Afr 7809.03	Verner, S.P. Pioneering in Central Africa. Richmond, 1903.
Afr 7809.04	Frobenius, L. Im Schatten des Kongostaates. Berlin, 1907.
Afr 7809.04.5	Boillat-Robert, I. Léopold II et le Congo. Neuchâtel, 1904.
Afr 7809.08	Johnston, H. George Grenfell and the Congo. London, 1908. 2v.
Afr 7809.08.5	Davis, R.H. The Congo and coasts of Africa. London, 1908.
Afr 7809.09	Delhaise, C.G.F.F. Les Warega (Congo belge) par le commandant Delhaise. Bruxelles, 1909.
Afr 7809.09.05	Lilbrechts, C. Souvenirs d'Afrique. Congo. Bruxelles, 1909.
Afr 7809.09.10	Vandervelde, Emile. Les derniers jours de l'Etat du Congo. Mons, 1909.
Afr 7809.10	Ward, H. A voice from the Congo. London, 1910.
Afr 7809.11	Roby, Marguerite. My adventures in the Congo. London, 1911.
Afr 7809.13	Torday, Emil. Camp and tramp in African wilds. Philadelphia, 1913.
Afr 7809.14	Bratier, Albert Ernest Augustin. Souvenirs de la mission marchande. Paris, 1914.
Afr 7809.14.5	Wauters, Alphones Jules. Voyages en Afrique. Bruxelles, 1914.
Afr 7809.15	Thornhill, J.B. Adventures in Africa under the British, Belgian and Portuguese flags. N.Y., 1915.
Afr 7809.17	Briey, Renaud de. Le sphinx noir. Paris, 1926.
Afr 7809.20	Great Britain. Admiralty. A manual of Belgian Congo. London, 1920.
Afr 7809.21	Delcommune, A. L'avenir du Congo belge menacé. 2e ed. Bruxelles, 1921. 2v.
Afr 7809.21.5	Leger, L.T. Du Tanganika à l'Atlantique. Bruxelles, 1921.
Afr 7809.21.10	Bradley, Mary. On the gorilla trail. N.Y., 1923.
Afr 7809.22	Daye, Pierre. L'empire colonial belge. Bruxelles, 1923.
Afr 7809.22.5	Barns, T.A. The wonderland of the eastern Congo. London, 1922.
Afr 7809.23	Verlaine, Louis. Notre colonie, contribution à la recherche de la méthode de colonisation. Bruxelles, 1923.
Afr 7809.23.5	Robert, M. Le Congo physique. Bruxelles, 1923.
Afr 7809.24.5	Bradley, M.H. Caravans and cannibals. N.Y., 1927.
Afr 7809.24.10	Norden, H. Fresh tracks in the Belgian Congo. London, 1924.
Afr 7809.24.15	Wauters, Joseph. Le Congo au travail. Bruxelles, 1924.
Afr 7809.26	Barns, T.A. An African eldorado, the Belgian Congo. London, 1926.
Afr 7809.26.5	Strickland, Diana. Through the Belgian Congo. London, 1926.
Afr 7809.27	Fraser, D.C. Through the Congo basin. London, 1927.
Afr 7809.28	Auric, Henri. L'avenir du Congo et du Congo-océan. Thèse. Paris, 1928.
Afr 7809.28.5	Franck, Louis. Le Congo belge. Bruxelles, 1928. 2v.

Afr 7809.29	Crokaert, J. Boula-matari. Bruxelles, 1929.
Afr 7809.29.5	Wauters, Arthur. D'Anvers à Bruxelles via le Lac Kivu. Bruxelles, 1929.
Afr 7809.30	Landbeck, Paul. Malu Malu; Erlebnisse aus der Sturm- und Drangperiode du Kongostaates. Berlin, 1930.
Afr 7809.31	Miller, Janet. Jungles preferred. Boston, 1931.
Afr 7809.31.5	Johnson, Martin. Congorilla. N.Y., 1931.
Afr 7809.34	Belgium. Commission du Parc National Albert. Parc National Albert. Bruxelles, 1934.
Afr 7809.34.5	Fondation pour favoriser l'étude scientifique des parcs nationaux du Congo belge. Brussels, 1934.
Afr 7809.35	Belgian Luxembourg Touring Office. Travel in the Belgian Congo. Brussels, 1935.
Afr 7809.37	Gatti, A. Great mother forest. N.Y., 1937.
Afr 7809.38	Institut des Parcs Nationaux du Congo Belge. National parks in the Belgian Congo. Brussels, 1938.
Afr 7809.38.5	Davis, W.E. Ten years in the Congo. N.Y., 1940.
Afr 7809.41.5	Kellersberger, J.L.S. God's ravens. N.Y., 1941.
Afr 7809.42F	Belgian Information Center. Belgian Congo at war. N.Y., 194-.
Afr 7809.42.5	Comeliau, Marie. Blancs et noirs. Paris, 1942.
Afr 7809.43	Banks, Emily. White woman on the Congo. N.Y., 1943.
Afr 7809.43.5	Franssen, F. La vie du noir. Liège, 1943.
Afr 7809.43.10	Hove, Julien van. Regards sur notre Congo. Bruxelles, 1943.
Afr 7809.44	Gatti, Ellen M. (Woddill). Exploring we would go. N.Y., 1944.
Afr 7809.44.5	Great Britain. Naval Intelligence Division. The Belgian Congo. London, 1944.
Afr 7809.45	Latouche, J.T. Congo. N.Y., 1945.
Afr 7809.46	Michiels, A. Notre colonie. 14.ed. Bruxelles, 1946.
Afr 7809.48	Moulaert, George. Souvenirs d'Alfrique, 1902-1919. Bruxelles, 1948.
Afr 7809.49	Congo, Belgian. Guide de voyageur au Congo belge et au Ruanda-Urundi. 1.ed. Bruxelles, 1949.
Afr 7809.50	Verleyen, E.J.B. Congo. Bruxelles, 1950.
Afr 7809.51	Tourist Bureau for the Belgian Congo and Ruanda-Urundi. Travelers guide to the Belgian Congo and Ruanda-Urundi. 1st ed. Brussels, 1951.
Afr 7809.51.2	Tourist Bureau for the Belgian Congo and Ruanda-Urundi. Travellers guide to the Belgian Congo and Ruanda-Urundi. 2d ed. Brussels, 1956.
Afr 7809.51.5	Sinderen, A. van. The country of the mountains of the moon. N.Y., 1951.
Afr 7809.52	Severn, M. Congo pilgrim. London, 1952.
Afr 7809.52.5	Belgian Information Services. The Belgian Congo appraised. N.Y., 1952.
Afr 7809.52.10	Jentgen, P. Les frontières du Congo belge. Bruxelles, 1952.
Afr 7809.53	Thibaut, J. Sous l'ombre des volcans africains. Bruxelles, 1953.
Afr 7809.54	Putnam, A.E. Madami. N.Y., 1954.
Afr 7809.54.5	Sion, Georges. Voyages aux quartre coins du Congo, 1949-1952. 3.ed. Bruxelles, 1954.
Afr 7809.55F	Derhinderen, G. Atlas du Congo belge et du Ruanda-Urundi. Paris, 1955.
Afr 7809.55.5	Vallotton, Henry. Voyage au Congo et au Ruanda-Urundi. Bruxelles, 1955.
Afr 7809.55.10	Congo. Service de l'Information. Congo: Belgique d'outre-mer. Léopoldville, 1955?
Afr 7809.56	Ahl, Frances Norene. Wings over the Congo. Boston, 1956.
Afr 7809.57.5	Jonchleere, K. Kongo, met het blote oog. Amsterdam, 1959.
Afr 7809.58	Meyer, Roger. Introducing the Belgian Congo and the Ruanda-Urundi. Bruxelles, 1958.
Afr 7809.59	Congo belge. Genève, 1958.
Afr 7809.59.5	Delooz, Eugenus. Zwarte handen en blank kapitaal. Antwerpen, 1959.
Afr 7809.59.10	Belgium. Office de l'Information et des Relations. Belgian Congo. Brussels, 1959.
Afr 7809.59.15	Rhodius, Georges. Congo 1959. Bruxelles, 1959.
Afr 7809.60	Gruenebaum, Kurt. Kongo im Umbruch. Bruxelles, 1960.
Afr 7809.60.10	Cuypers, J.P. Alphonse Vangele (1848-1939). Bruxelles, 1960.
Afr 7809.60.15	Verbung, C. Afscheid van Kongo. Antwerpen, 1960.
Afr 7809.61	Dugauquier, D.P. Congo cauldron. London, 1961.
Afr 7809.62	Knapen, Marie Thérèse. L'enfant Mukongo. Louvain, 1962.
Afr 7809.62.5	Académie Royale des Sciences d'Outre-Mer. Apport scientifique de la Belgique au développement de l'Afrique centrale. Bruxelles, 1962. 3v.
Afr 7809.62.10	Liveing, Edward G.D. Across the Congo. London, 1962.
Afr 7809.64	Thurn, Max. Afrika. Wien, 1964.
Afr 7809.65	Verbeck, Roger. Le Congo en question. Paris, 1965.
Afr 7809.65.5	Peeters, Leo. Les limites forêt-savane dans le nord du Congo en relation avec le milieu géographique. Bruxelles, 1965.
Afr 7809.66	Ohm, Sven. Svart folk bygger. Stockholm, 1966.
Afr 7809.68	Scotti, Pietro. Il Congo. Ieri, oggi, domani. Genova, 1968.

Afr 7812   Congo Republic (Leopoldville); Belgian Congo - Economic and financial conditions (By date, e.g. .260 for 1960)

Afr 7812.4	Belgium. Ministère des Affaires Africaines. Firmes, établissements particuliers d'activité économique.
Afr 7812.6F	Belgium. Ministère des Affaires Africaines. Secretariat du Plan Décennal. Rapport sur l'execution du plan décennal pour le développment...du Congo belge, 1956-1958. n.p., n.d.
Afr 7812.224	Congrès Colonial National. La politique économique au Congo belge. Bruxelles, 1924.
Afr 7812.233	Louwers, Octave. Le problème financier et le problème économique au Congo belge en 1932. Bruxelles, 1933.
Afr 7812.236	Velde, M.W. Economie belge et Congo belge. Thèse. Nancy, 1936.
Afr 7812.236.10	Moulaert, G. Problèmes coloniaux d'hier et d'aujourd'hui. Bruxelles, 1939.
Afr 7812.246	Dehoux, Emile. Le problème de demain. Bruxelles, 1946.
Afr 7812.249	Belgium. Ministère des Colonies. Plan décennal pour le développement économique et social du Congo belge. Bruxelles, 1949.
Afr 7812.251F	Belgium. Plan décennal pour le développement. Bruxelles, 1949.
Afr 7812.255	Lefebvre, J. Structures économiques du Congo belge et du Ruanda-Urundi. Bruxelles, 1955.

Afr 7812   Congo Republic (Leopoldville); Belgian Congo - Economic and financial conditions (By date, e.g. .260 for 1960) cont.

Afr 7812.255.5   Belgium. Office de l'Information et des Relations Publiques pour le Congo Belge. L'économie du Congo belge et du Ruanda-Urundi. Bruxelles, 1955.
Afr 7812.256   Sion, Georges. Soixante-quinze ans de Congo. Gand, 1956.
Afr 7812.256.5   Brussels. Université Libre. Vers la promotion de l'économie indigène. Bruxelles, 1956.
Afr 7812.257   Bezy, Fernand. Problèmes structurels de l'économie congolaise. Louvain, 1957.
Afr 7812.257.5F   Hauzeur de Fooz, C. Un demi-siècle avec l'économie du Congo belge. Bruxelles, 1957.
Afr 7812.257.10   Stengers, Jean. Combien le Congo a-t-il coûté à la Belgique? Bruxelles, 1957.
Afr 7812.258   Journées d'Etudes Coloniales, Institut Universitaire des Territoires d'Outre Mer, Antwerp, 1957. Promotion de la société rurale du Congo belge et du Ruanda-Urundi. Bruxelles, 1958.
Afr 7812.259   Baeck, Louis. Economische ontwikkeling en sociale structuur in Belgisch-Kongo. Leuven, 1959.
Afr 7812.259.5   Martynov, Vladimir A. Kongo pod gnetom imperializma. Moskva, 1959.
Afr 7812.260   Leurquin, Philippe. Le niveau de vie des populations rurales du Ruanda-Urundi. Louvain, 1960.
Afr 7812.260.2   Leurquin, Philippe. Le niveau de vie des populations rurales du Ruanda-Urundi. Louvain, 1960.
Afr 7812.260.10   Congo, Belgian. Commissariat au Plan Décennal. Le plan décennal pour le développement économique et social du Congo belge. Bruxelles, 1960.
Afr 7812.260.15   Fédération des Enterprises Congolaises. The Congolese economy on the eve of independence. Brussels, 1960.
Afr 7812.260.20   Parisis, A. Les finances communales et urbaines au Congo belge. Bruxelles, 1960.
Afr 7812.261.5   Joye, Pierre. Les trusts au Congo. Bruxelles, 1961.
Afr 7812.261.10   Carbonnelle, C. L'économie des deux Ueles. Bruxelles, 1961.
Afr 7812.262   Katanga. Livre blanc du gouvernement katangais sur les évènements. Elisabethville, 1962.
Afr 7812.263   Brussels. Université Libre. Centre d'Étude des Questions Economiques Africaines. Le revenu des populations indigènes (du Congo-Léopoldville). Bruxelles, 1963.
Afr 7812.263.1   Brussels. Université Libre. Centre d'Etudes des Questions Economiques Africaines. Le revenu des populations indigènes du Congo-Léopoldville. Etude élaborée par le Groupe de l'économie africaine. Bruxelles, 1963.
Afr 7812.264   Fonds du Bien-Etre Indigène. A work of cooperation in development. Brussels, 1964.
Afr 7812.266   Leopoldville. Université Lovanium. Institut de Recherche Economiques et Sociales. Étude d'orientation pour le plan de développement et de diversification industrielle. Kinshasa, 1966.
Afr 7812.267   Romaniuk, Anatole. La fécondité des populations congolaises. Paris, 1967.
Afr 7812.267.5   Lacroix, Jan Louis. Industrialisation au Congo. Paris, 1967.
Afr 7812.269   Comeliau, Christian. Conditions de la planification du développement; l'exemple du Congo. Paris, 1969.

Afr 7814   Congo Republic (Leopoldville); Belgian Congo - Maps
Afr 7814.1   Congo Free State (1887). Carte de l'Etat. Bruxelles, 1887.

Afr 7815   Congo Republic (Leopoldville); Belgian Congo - Races
Afr 7815.1F   Schmeltz, J.D.E. Album...ethnography...Congo-basin. Leyden, n.d.
Afr 7815.2   Overbergh, C. van. Les Bangala. 1. Bruxelles, 1907.
Afr 7815.3   Overbergh, C. van. Les Mayombe. 2. Bruxelles, 1907.
Afr 7815.4   Overbergh, C. van. Les Basonge. 3. Bruxelles, 1908.
Afr 7815.5   Overbergh, C. van. Les Mangbetu (Congo belge). 4. Bruxelles, 1909.
Afr 7815.5.5   Delhaise, C.G. Les Warega (Congo belge) 5 Bruxelles, 1909.
Afr 7815.5.6   Plas, J.V. Les Kuku. 6. Bruxelles, 1910.
Afr 7815.5.7   Halkin, Joseph. Les Abatua. 7. Bruxelles, 1911.
Afr 7815.5.8   Gaud, Fernand. Les Mandja. 8. Bruxelles, 1911.
Afr 7815.5.9   Schmitz, Robert. Les Baholoholo. 9. Bruxelles, 1912.
Afr 7815.5.10   Colle, R.P. Les Baluta. 10-11. Bruxelles, 1913. 2v.
Afr 7815.6   Smith, H.S. Yakusu. London, 1911.
Afr 7815.7   Boyd, F.R. Les races indigènes du Congo belge. Paris, 1913.
Afr 7815.8   Weeks, J.H. Among Congo cannibals. London, 1913.
Afr 7815.8.5   Weeks, J.H. Among the primitive Bakongo. London, 1914.
Afr 7815.9   Hilton-Simpson, M.W. Land and peoples of the Kasai. London, 1911.
Afr 7815.10   Weeks, John H. Congo life and folklore. London, 1911.
Afr 7815.11   Hutereau, Armand. Histoire des peuplades de l'Uele et de l'Ubangi. Bruxelles, 1912.
Afr 7815.12   Piscelli, M. Nel paese dei Bango-bango. Napoli, 1909.
Afr 7815.13   Colonne-Beaufaict, A. de. Azande, introduction à une ethnographie générale des bassins de l'Ubangi-Uele et de l'Arvwimi. Bruxelles, 1921.
Afr 7815.13.15   Evans-Pritchard, E.E. Witchcraft, oracles and magic among the Azande. Oxford, 1937.
Afr 7815.13.20   Giorgetti, Filiberto. Note di musica zande. Verona, 1951.
Afr 7815.14   Torday, Emil. On the trail of the Bushongo. London, 1925.
Afr 7815.15   Kerken, Georges van der. Les sociétés bantoues du Congo belge. Bruxelles, 1919.
Afr 7815.15.5   Moeller, Alfred. Les grandes lignes des migrations des Bantous de la province orientale du Congo belge. Bruxelles, 1936.
Afr 7815.16   Slade, Ruth. The Belgian Congo, some recent changes. London, 1960.
Afr 7815.17   Maes, J. Volkenkunde van Belgisch Kongo. Antwerpen, 1935.
Afr 7815.18   Wuig, J. Van. Etudes Bakongo. 2.ed. Bruges, 1959.
Afr 7815.19   Association des Intérêts Coloniaux Belges. Des relations de travail entre européens et africains. Bruxelles, 1956.
Afr 7815.20   Cleene, Natal de. Introduction à l'ethnographie du Congo belge et du Ruanda-Burundi. 2.éd. Anvers, 1957.
Afr 7815.22   Dooent, Jean. Elite noire. Bruxelles, 1957.
Afr 7815.23   Kanza, Thomas. Tot ou tard. Bruxelles, 1959.
Afr 7815.24   Mertens, Joseph. Les Ba Dzing de la Kamtsha. Bruxelles, 1935-39.
Afr 7815.25   Fédération des Associations de Colons du Congo. L'opinion publique coloniale devant l'assimilation des indigènes. Bruxelles, 1951.

Afr 7815   Congo Republic (Leopoldville); Belgian Congo - Races cont.
Afr 7815.26   Ceulemans, P. La question arabe et le Congo, 1883-1892. Bruxelles, 1959.
Afr 7815.27   Wolfe, A.W. In the Ngombe tradition. Evanston, Ill., 1961.
Afr 7815.28   Schebesta, Paul. Baba wa Bambuti. Moedling, 1951.
Afr 7815.28.5   Turnbull, Colin M. Wayward servants. 1st ed. Garden City, N.Y., 1965.
Afr 7815.28.10   Turnbull, Colin M. The forest people. N.Y., 1961.
Afr 7815.29   Dauer, Alfonsus. Studien zur Ethnogenese bei den Mangbetu. Mainz, 1961.
Afr 7815.30   Slade, Ruth. King Leopold's Congo. London, 1962.
Afr 7815.32   Verbeken, A. La révolte des Batetela en 1895. Bruxelles, 1958.
Afr 7815.34   Benoit, J. La population africaine à Elisabethville. Elisabethville, 193-.
Afr 7815.35   Danois, Jacques. Mon frère bantu. Bruxelles, 1965.
Afr 7815.36   Lelong, M.H. Mes frères du Congo. Alger, 1946. 2v.
Afr 7815.37   Plancquaert, M. Les Jaga et les Bayaka du Kwango. Bruxelles, 1932.
Afr 7815.38   Mueller, Ernst Wilhelm. Le droit de propriété chez les Mongo-bokote. Bruxelles, 1958.
Afr 7815.39   Bulck, Gaston van. Orthographie des noms ethniques au Congo belge. Bruxelles, 1954.
Afr 7815.40   Sousberghe, Léon de. Les danses rituelles mungonge et kela des Ba-pende. Bruxelles, 1956.
Afr 7815.41   Caeneghem, R. La notion de Dieu chez les Baluba du Kasai. Bruxelles, 1956.
Afr 7815.42   Haveaux, O.L. La tradition historique des Bapende orientaux. Bruxelles, 1954.
Afr 7815.43   Lamal. Essai d'étude démographique d'une population de Kwango. Bruxelles, 1949.
Afr 7815.44   Domont, Jean Marie. La prise de conscience de l'individu en milieu rural Kongo. Bruxelles, 1957.
Afr 7815.46   Vansina, Jan. Introduction à l'ethnographie du Congo. Kinshasa, 1966.
Afr 7815.48   Doutreloux, Albert. L'ombre des fétiches; société et culture yombe. Louvain, 1967.
Afr 7815.50   Martins, Manuel Alfredo de Morais. Contacto de culturas no Congo Português. Lisboa, 1958.
Afr 7815.52   Pamphlet vol. Leyder, Jean. Pamphlet on Belgian Congo and Libya. 4 pam.
Afr 7815.54   Onze Kongo. Leuven. 1,1910-1911

Afr 7817   Congo Republic (Leopoldville); Belgian Congo - Religion; missions
Afr 7817.2   Law, Virginia W. Appointment Congo. Chicago, 1966.
Afr 7817.3   McKinnon, Arch C. Kapitene of the Congo steamship Lapsley. Boston, 1968.
Afr 7817.5   Bormann, Martin. Zwischen Kreuz und Fetisch. Bayreuth, 1965.
Afr 7817.10   Petersen, William J. Another hand on mine; the story of Dr. Carl K. Becker of the Africa Inland Mission. 1st ed. N.Y., 1967.
Afr 7817.15   Agwala, Marie Jean. Evènements du Congo à Wamba, 15 août-29 décembre 1964. Clermont-Ferrand, 1966.
Afr 7817.20   Davies, David Michael. The captivity and triumph of Winnie Davies. London, 1968.
Afr 7817.25   Roelens, Victor. Notre vieux Congo, 1891-1917. v.1-2. Namur, 1948.
Afr 7817.30   Tielemans, H. Gijzelaars in Congo. Tilburg, 1967?

Afr 7818   Congo Republic (Leopoldville); Belgian Congo - Special customs
Afr 7818.5   Comhaire-Sylvain, Suzanne. Femmes de Kinshasa hier et aujourd'hui. Paris, 1968.
Afr 7818.5.5   Leblanc, Maria. Personnalité de la femme katangaise. Louvain, 1960.

Afr 7820   Congo Republic (Leopoldville); Belgian Congo - Local - Indefinite regions and districts
Afr 7820.5   Droogmans, Hubert. Notices sur le Bas-Congo. Bruxelles, 1901.
Afr 7820.6   Devroey, E. Le Bas-Congo, artère vitale de notre colonie. Bruxelles, 1938.
Afr 7820.7F   Meessen, J.M.T. Monographie de l'Ituri (nord-est du Congo belge) histoire. Bruxelles, 1951.
Afr 7820.8   Verstraeten, E. Six années d'action sociale au Maniema, 1948-1953. Bruxelles, 1954.

Afr 7835   Congo Republic (Leopoldville); Belgian Congo - Local - Provinces - Eastern province
Afr 7835.2   Tucker, Angeline. He is in heaven. 1st ed. N.Y., 1965.
Afr 7835.3   Hayes, Margaret. Missing - believed killed. London, 1967.
Afr 7835.4   Reed, David E. One hundred and eleven days in Stanleyville. 1st ed. N.Y., 1965.
Afr 7835.5   Bayly, Joseph T. Congo crisis. Grand Rapids, 1966.
Afr 7835.8   Roseveare, Helen. Doctor among Congo rebels. London, 1966.

Afr 7850   Congo Republic (Leopoldville); Belgian Congo - Local - Provinces - Katanga province
Afr 7850.2   Walraet, Marcel. Bibliographie du Katanga. Bruxelles, 1954.
Afr 7850.3   Cornet, R.J. Terre katangaise. Bruxelles, 1950.
Afr 7850.5   Verdick, E. Les premiers jours au Katanga. Bruxelles, 1952.
Afr 7850.10   Whyms. Léopoldville, son histoire, 1881-1956. Bruxelles, 1956.
Afr 7850.15   Thier, Franz M. Le centre extra-coutumier de Coquilhatville. Bruxelles, 1956.
Afr 7850.20   Caprasse, P. Leaders africains en milieu urbain. Bruxelles, 1959.
Afr 7850.25   Sauvy, Jean. Le Katanga, cinquante ans décisifs. Paris, 1961.
Afr 7850.30   Hempstone, Smith. Rebels, mercenaries, and dividends. N.Y., 1962.
Afr 7850.35   Davister, P. Croisettes et casques bleus, récits. Bruxelles, 1962.
Afr 7850.40   Musini, P. Kantanga, pelli di fuoco. Parma, 1961.
Afr 7850.42   Lekime, Fernand. Katanga, pays du cuirre. Verviers, 1965.
Afr 7850.45   Forty-six angry men, the forty-six civilian doctors of Elisabethville denounce U.N. violations in Katanga. Bruxelles, 1962.
Afr 7850.45.5   Cuarenta y seis hombres en colera. Bruselas, 1962.
Afr 7850.50   Vandenhang, E. The war in Katanga. N.Y., 1962.

Afr 7850   Congo Republic (Leopoldville); Belgian Congo - Local - Provinces -
Katanga province
cont.

Afr 7850.52F   Belgium. Chambre des Représentants. Commission
parlamentaire chargée de faire une enquête.
Bruxelles, 1959.
Afr 7850.53   Verbeken, A. La première traversée du Katanga en 1806.
Bruxelles, 1953.
Afr 7850.54   Gerard Libois, J. Secession au Katanga. Bruxelles, 1963.
Afr 7850.54.2   Gerard Libois, J. Katanga secession. Madison, 1966.
Afr 7850.55F   Comité Spécial du Katanga. Comité spécial du Katanga,
1900-1950. Bruxelles, 1950.
Afr 7850.56   Nagy, Laszló. Katanga. Lausanne, 1965.
Afr 7850.60   Hederén, Olle. Afrikanskt mellanspeli om berättelse om
händelserna på Kaminabasen, 1960-1964. Östra Ryd, 1965.
Afr 7850.62   Muller, Emmanuel. Les troupes du Katange et les campagnes
d'Afrique 1914-1918. v.1-2. Bruxelles, 1937.
Afr 7851.3   Droogmans, H. Notices sur le Bas-Congo. Bruxelles, 1901.
Afr 7851.58   Wilmet, Jules. La répartition de la population dans la
dépression des rivières Mufuvya et Lufira.
Bruxelles, 1963.

Afr 7855   Congo Republic (Leopoldville); Belgian Congo - Local - Provinces - Kivu
province
Afr 7855.1   Cornet, René Jules. Maniema. 2.ed. Bruxelles, 1955.
Afr 7855.4   Hecq, J. Agriculture et structures économiques d'un
société traditionnelle au Kivu. Bruxelles, 1963.

Afr 7858   Congo Republic (Leopoldville); Belgian Congo - Local - Provinces - Kwilu
province
Afr 7858.2F   Nicolai, Henri. Le Kwilu. Bruxelles, 1963.

Afr 7870   Congo Republic (Leopoldville); Belgian Congo - Local - Cities and
towns - Leopoldville
Afr 7870.5   Whyms. Leopoldville, son histoire, 1881-1956.
Bruxelles, 1956.
Afr 7870.6   Raymaekers, P. L'organisation des zones de squatting.
Leopoldville, 1963.
Afr 7870.7   Capelle, Emmanuel. La cité indigène de Léopoldville.
Léopoldville, 1948.

Afr 7871 - 7896   Congo Republic (Leopoldville); Belgian Congo - Local -
Cities and towns - Others (A-Z)
Afr 7873.5   Thier, Franz M. de. Le centre extra-coutumier de
Coquilhatville. Bruxelles, 1956.
Afr 7875.5   Caprasse, Pierre. Leaders africains en milieu urbain,
Elisabethville. Bruxelles, 1959.
Afr 7875.5.5   Chapelier, Alice. Elisabethville. Bruxelles, 1951.
Afr 7875.5.10   Kuitenbrouwer, Joost B.W. Le camp des Balula.
Bruxelles, 1963.
Afr 7881.2   Moulaert, G. Vingt années à Kilo-Moto, 1920-40.
Bruxelles, 1950.
Afr 7886.5   Choprix, Guy. La naissance d'une ville; étude géographique
de Paulis, 1934-1957. Bruxelles, 1961.
Afr 7889.2   Thier, F.M. Singhitini, la Stanleyville musulmane.
Bruxelles, 1961.
Afr 7889.5   Pous, Valdo. Stanleyville: an African urban community
under Belgian administration. London, 1969.

Afr 7900   Congo Republic (Leopoldville); Belgian Congo - Biographies - Collected
Afr 7900.5   Brussels. Institut Royal Colonial Belge. Biographie
coloniale belge. 1,1948+
5v.

Afr 7901 - 7926   Congo Republic (Leopoldville); Belgian Congo -
Biographies - Individual (A-Z, by person)
Afr 7903.3   Myers, John Brown. Thomas J. Comber, missionary pioneer to
the Congo. London, 1888.
Afr 7911.5   Chome, Jules. La passion de Simon Kimbangu. 2. ed.
Bruxelles, 1959.
Afr 7911.5.5   Gilis, Charles A. Kimbangu, fondateur d'église.
Bruxelles, 1960.
Afr 7912.5   Soiuz Zhurnalistov SSSR. Patris Lumumba. Moscow, 1961.
Afr 7912.5.5   Michel, Serge. Uhuru Lumumba. Paris, 1962.
Afr 7912.5.10   Lumumba, Patrice. Patrice Lumumba. Moscou, 1964.
Afr 7912.5.100   Lumumba, Patrice. La pensée politique. Paris, 1963.
Afr 7912.10   Rouch, Jane. En cage avec Lumumba. Paris, 1961.
Afr 7912.15   Vos, Pierre de. Vie et mort de Lumumba. Paris, 1961.
Afr 7912.15.5   Vos, Pierre de. Vida y muerte de Lumumba. Mexico, 1962.
Afr 7912.15.10   Monheim, Francis. Réponse à père De Vos au
sujet...Lumumba. Anvers, 1961.
Afr 7912.15.20   Lopez Alvarez, Luis. Lumumba ou l'Afrique frustrée.
Paris, 1964.
Afr 7912.15.25   Turski, Marian. Lumumba i jego kraj. Warszawa, 1962.
Afr 7912.15.30   Kashamura, Anicet. De Lumumba aux colonels. Paris, 1966.
Afr 7912.15.35   Maquet-Tombu, Jeanne. Le siècle marche; vie du chef
congolais Lutunu. 2. éd. Bruxelles, 1952?
Afr 7912.15.40   Heinz, G. Lumumba Patrice: les cinquante derniers jours de
sa vie. Bruxelles, 1966.
Afr 7912.15.45   McKown, Robin. Lumumba; a biography. 1st ed. Garden
City, 1969.
Afr 7912.15.50   Skurnik, W.A.E. African political thought: Lumumba,
Nkrumah and Toure. Denver, 1968.
Afr 7912.20   Semenov, M.G. Ubiitsa s Ist-river. Moscow, 1961.
Afr 7913.2   Monheim, F. Mobutu, l'homme seul. Paris, 1962.
Afr 7913.2.5   Chomé, Jules. Mobutu et la contre-révolution en Afrique.
Waterloo, 1967.
Afr 7913.5   Verbeken, A. Msiri. Bruxelles, 1956.
Afr 7918.5   Kestergat, Jean. Andre Ryckmans. Paris, 1961.
Afr 7920.3   Chome, Jules. Moise Tshombe et l'escroquerie katangaise.
Bruxelles, 1966.
Afr 7920.3.5   Tshombe, Moise. Quinze mois de gouvernement du Congo.
Paris, 1966.
Afr 7920.3.10   Colvin, Ian Goodhope. The rise and fall of Moise Tshombe:
a biography. London, 1968.
Afr 7920.3.15   Tshombe, Moise. My fifteen months in government. Plano,
Tex., 1967.
Afr 7923.5   Luwel, Marcel. Sir Francis de Winton, administrateur
général du Congo, 1884-1886. Tervuren, 1964.

Afr 7930   Ruanda-Urundi - Periodicals
Afr 7930.5   Eglise et développement. Bujumbura. 1967+

Afr 7933   Ruanda-Urundi - Government and administration
Afr 7933.2   Jentgen, P. Les frontiéres du Ruanda-Urundi et le régime
international de Tutelle. Bruxelles, 1957.
Afr 7933.3   Maquet, J.J. Elections en société féodale.
Bruxelles, 1959.

Afr 7935   Ruanda-Urundi - General history
Afr 7935.1   Afrianoff, A. Histoire des Bagesera. Bruxelles, 1952.

Afr 7937.1 - .199   Ruanda-Urundi - History by periods - Before 1850
Afr 7937.2   Belgium. Centre de Recherche et d'Information. Rwanda
politique (1958-1960). Bruxelles, 1961.
Afr 7937.4   Ryckmans, P. Une page d'histoire coloniale.
Bruxelles, 1953.
Afr 7937.6   Dansina, Jan. L'évolution du royaume Rwanda des origines
à 1900. Bruxelles, 1962.
Afr 7937.7   Papadopoullos, T. Poésie, dynastique du Ruanda et épopée
akritique. Paris, 1963.
Afr 7937.8   Louis, W.R. Ruanda-Urundi, 1884-1919. Oxford, 1963.
Afr 7937.9   Kagame, Alexis. Le code des institutions politiques du
Rwanda précolonial. Bruxelles, 1952.

Afr 7940   Ruanda-Urundi - Geography, description, etc.
Afr 7940.5   Lyr, Claude. Ruanda Urundi. Brussels, 195-.
Afr 7940.10   American University, Washington, D.C. Foreign Area Studies.
Area handbook for Burundi. Washington, 1969.
Afr 7940.15   American University, Washington, D.C. Foreign Area Studies.
Area handbook for Rwanda. Washington, 1969.

Afr 7942   Ruanda-Urundi - Economic conditions
Afr 7942.2   Gourou, Pierre. La densité de la population au
Ruanda-Urundi. Bruxelles, 1953.
Afr 7942.5   Masera, Francesco. Rwanda e Burundi; problemi e
prospettive di sviluppo economico. Milano, 1963.

Afr 7945   Ruanda-Urundi - Races
Afr 7945.2   Kagame, Alexis. La philosophie bantu-rwandaise de être.
Bruxelles, 1955.
Afr 7945.3   Makarakiza, André. La dialectique des Barundi.
Bruxelles, 1959.
Afr 7945.5   Heusch, Luc de. Le Rwanda et la civilisation
interlacustre. Bruxelles, 1966.

Afr 7946   Ruanda-Urundi - Religion; missions
Afr 7946.5   Pauwels, M. Imana et le culte des Manes au Rwanda.
Bruxelles, 1958.
Afr 7946.10   Mulago, Vicent. Un visage africain du christianisme.
Paris, 1965.
Afr 7946.12   Kjellberg, Alice. Missionsarbetets börgan i Burundi.
Orebro, 1966.

Afr 7947   Ruanda-Urundi - Special customs
Afr 7947.2   Maquet, J.J. The premise of inequality in Ruanda.
London, 1961.
Afr 7947.4   Klemke, O. Die Erziehung bei Eingeborenengruppen in
Ruanda-Urundi. Bonn, 1962.
Afr 7947.6   Kagame, A. Les milices du Rwanda précolonial.
Bruxelles, 1963.
Afr 7947.7   Lestrade, A. La médecine indigène au Ruanda et lexique des
termes médicaux français-urunyarwanda. Bruxelles, 1955.
Afr 7947.8   Kagame, Alexis. L'histoire des armées-bovines dans
l'ancien Rwanda. Bruxelles, 1961.
Afr 7947.9   Lacroix, Benoît. Le Rwanda: mille heures au pays des mille
collines. Montréal, 1966.

Afr 7948   Ruanda-Urundi - Local
Afr 7948.5   Baeck, Louis. Etude socio-économique du centre
extra-coutumier d'Usumbura. Bruxelles, n.d.

Afr 7949.101 - .399   Ruanda-Urundi - Biographies - Individual (A-Z, 299
scheme, by person)
Afr 7949.250   Church, John Edward. Forgive them: the story of an African
martyr. London, 1966.

Afr 8001 - 8026   South Africa in general - Periodicals (A-Z)
Afr 8001.5   Argief jaarboek vir suid-afrikaanse geskiedenis. 1,1938+
33v.
Afr 8001.10   Africa south. Cape Town. 2,1957+
2v.
Afr 8001.15   Africana notes and news. Johannesburg. 1,1943+
9v.
Afr 8001.16   Africana notes and news. Index v.1-10. (1943-53).
Johannesburg, n.d.
Afr 8001.17   Africana Museum, Johannesburg. Annual report.
Johannesburg.
Afr 8001.20   Asaagou. London. 1,1963+
Afr 8001.25   Afrika-post. Pretoria. 12,1966+
5v.
VAfr 8001.30PF   The anti-apartheid news. London. 1,1964
Afr 8002.2F   Blythswood review. Butterworth, South Africa. 3,1926+
2v.
Afr 8003.2   Civil rights. Cape Town. 1958+
3v.
Afr 8003.2.5   Civil Rights League, Cape Town. Annual report.
Afr 8003.3F   Contact; for united non-racial action. Cape Town. 1958+
4v.
Afr 8003.4   Contact pamphlet. Cape Town.
Afr 8003.5   Common sense. Johannesburg.
Afr 8003.10F   Citizen annual. Claremont, South Africa.
Afr 8006.5F   Fleur, verbeeld die fleur van ons land en sy volk.
Johannesburg.
Afr 8006.10   Forum, South Africa's independent journal of opinion.
Johannesburg. 8,1959+
5v.
Afr 8008.10   Historia. Germiston. 3,1958+
17v.
Afr 8009.5   Industrial profile of South Africa. Johannesburg.
1963-1966
2v.
Afr 8010.5   Johannesburg. University of the Witwatersrand. African
Studies Programme. Occasional paper. 2,1967+
Afr 8012.3   Lantern, journal of knowledge and culture. Pretoria.
1,1949+
11v.
Afr 8012.5   Liberal opinion. Pietermaritzburg. 2-6,1963-1968//
Afr 8013.3   Mens en gemeenskap. Pretoria. 1,1960+
Afr 8015.5   Optima. Johannesburg. 1-2,1951-1952
8v.

Afr 8001 - 8026   South Africa in general - Periodicals (A-Z)
cont.

Afr 8015.10	Onward. Johannesburg. 1,1965+
Afr 8018.6	Reality; a journal of liberal opinion. Pietermaritzburg. 1,1969+
Afr 8018.8	Republic in a changing world. Johannesburg.
Afr 8019.1	South Africa. 39+ 21v.
Afr 8019.1.3	South Africa. Alphabetic index to biographical notices, 1892-1928. Johannesburg, 1963.
Afr 8019.1.5	South Africa (Weekly). The story of South Africa newspaper. London, 1903.
Afr 8019.3	South African National Union. Annual report. Johannesburg.
Afr 8019.4	Suid-Afrikaanse Buro vir Raase-Aanngeleenthede. Nuusbrief. Stellenbosch. 10,1954+ 2v.
Afr 8019.4.5	Triomf, jaarboek van die Suid-afrikaanse Buro vir Raase-aangeleenthede. Pretoria. 1,1966+
Afr 8019.6	Saint Benedicts booklets. Johannesburg. 2+
Afr 8019.8F	South African panorama. Pretoria. 6,1961+ 9v.
Afr 8019.10	South African digest. Pretoria. 6v.
Afr 8019.12	South Africa speaks. Cairo.
Afr 8019.14F	Spotlight on South Africa. Dar es Salaam. 1,1966+ 5v.
Afr 8019.15	Sechaba; official organ of the African National Congress of South Africa. London. 1,1967+
Afr 8019.17F	South Africa; information and analysis. Paris. 51,1967+
Afr 8020.2F	Trek. Cape Town. 6,1941+ 6v.
Afr 8020.2	Trek. Cape Town. 12,1948+ 4v.
Afr 8020.3	Tydskrif vir raase-aangeleenthede. Stellenbosch. 3,1951+ 10v.
NEDL Afr 8021.2F	Umteteli wa bantu. Johannesburg. 1926+
Afr 8021.2F	Umteteli wa bantu. Johannesburg. 1941+
Afr 8021.5	Commentary on politics today. Pretoria.
Afr 8021.6	United Party (South Africa). Election news. Johannesburg.
Afr 8022.5	Van Riebeeck Society. Publications. Cape Town. 2,1919+ 52v.
Afr 8023.5	What's happening in South Africa. London.

Afr 8028   South Africa in general - Bibliographies

Afr 8028.1	Theal, G.M. Notes upon books referring to South Africa. Cape Town, 1882.
Afr 8028.1.3	Theal, G.M. Catalogues of books and pamphlets. Cape Town, 1912.
Afr 8028.2	Suhnnke Hollnay, H.C. Bibliography related to South Africa. Cape Town, 1898.
Afr 8028.3	Library of Congress. Division of Bibliography. The British empire in Africa. v.9. Washington, 1942-43.
Afr 8028.4	Wagner, Mary Saint Clair. The 1st British occupation of the Cape of Good Hope, 1795-1803; a bibliography. Cape Town, 1946.
Afr 8028.5	Mendelssohn, S. Mendelssohn's South African bibliography. London, 1910. 2v.
Afr 8028.6	Besselaar, G. Zuid-Afrika in de letterkunde. Amsterdam, 1914.
Afr 8028.7F	Roberts, E.S. Preliminary finding-list of Southern African pamphlets. Cape Town, 1959.
Afr 8028.15	Towert, A.M.F. Constitutional development in South Africa. Cape Town, 1959.
Afr 8028.20	Amyat, D.L. Background material for the tercentenary of the landing of Jan van Riebeeck. Cape Town, 1950.
Afr 8028.25	Heerden, J. van. Closer union movement. Cape Town, 1952.
Afr 8028.26	Taetemeyer, Gerhard. Suedafrika, Suedwestafrika, eine Bibliographie. Freiburg, 1964.
Afr 8028.30F	Macdonald, A.M. A contribution to a bibliography on university apartheid. Cape Town, 1959.
Afr 8028.35	Nicholson, G. German settlers in South Africa. Cape Town, 1953.
Afr 8028.40	Musiker, R. Guide to South African reference books. 3d ed. Grahamstown, 1963.
Afr 8028.42	Spohr, Otto. Catalogue of books. Cape Town, 1950.
Afr 8028.43F	Pamphlet vol. German Africana. 2 pam.
Afr 8028.45	Olivier, Le Roux. Versamelde Suid-Afrikaanse biografieë. Kaapstad, 1963.
Afr 8028.100	South Africa. Parliament. Library. Afrikaanse publikasies. Kaapstad, 1931.
Afr 8028.101	South Africa. Parliament. Library. Afrikanse publikasies. 2. uitg. Pretoria, 1934.
Afr 8028.102	South Africa. Parliament. Library. Annual list of Africana added to the Mendelssohn collection. Cape Town. 1-9,1938-1946 2v.
Afr 8028.110	Nederlandsch-Zuid-Afrikansche Vereeniging. Bibliothek. Catalogues. Amsterdam, 1939.
Afr 8028.111	Nederlandsch-Zuid-Afrikansche Vereeniging. Bibliothek. Supplements. 1939+
Afr 8028.115	Brett, E.A. Tentative list of books and pamphlets on South Africa. Johannesburg, 1959.
Afr 8028.125	Cape Town. Van Riebeek Festival Book Exhibition. South Africa in print. Cape Town, 1952.
Afr 8028.128	Goldman, F. An index to the colour-plate relating to South Africa appearing in books published before 1850. Johannesburg, 1962.
Afr 8028.128.5	Goldman, Freda Y. An index to South African colour-plates in books, 1851-1899. Johannesburg, 1963.
Afr 8028.130	Coke, R.M. South Africa as seen by the French, 1610-1850. Cape Town, 1957.
Afr 8028.132F	Wilkoy, A. Some English writings by non-Europeans in South Africa, 1944-1960. Johannesburg, 1962.
Afr 8028.133F	Richards, Margaret Patricia. Mountaineering in Southern Africa. Johannesburg, 1966.
Afr 8028.135	Ashpol, M. A select bibliography of South African auto-biographies. Cape Town, 1958.
Afr 8028.140	South Africa. Department of Colored Affairs. Consolidated general bibliography. Cape Town, 1960.
Afr 8028.145F	Johannesburg. Public Library. Index to South African periodicals. Johannesburg. 1,1940+ 7v.

Afr 8028   South Africa in general - Bibliographies
cont.

Afr 8028.148	Cape Town. University. Consolidated list, 1941-1966. Cape Town, 1966.
Afr 8028.149	Beckerling, Joan Letitia. The medical history of the Anglo-Boer war. Cape Town, 1967.
Afr 8028.150	Kesting, J.G. The Anglo-Boer war, 1899-1902. Cape Town, 1956.
Afr 8028.151	Varley, D.H. Adventures in Africana. Cape Town, 1949.
Afr 8028.152	Muller, Christoffel Frederik Jakobus. A select bibliography of South African history; a guide for historical research. Pretoria, 1966.
Afr 8028.153	Archibald, Jane Erica. The works of Isaac Schapera; a selective bibliography. Johannesburg, 1969.
Afr 8028.154	New York (City) Public Library. Works relating to South Africa in the New York Public Library. N.Y., 1899.
Afr 8028.156	Kuper, B. A bibliography of native law in South Africa, 1941-1961. Johannesburg, 1962.
Afr 8028.160	Grivainis, Ilze. Material published after 1925 on the Great Trek until 1854. Thesis. Cape Town, 1967.
Afr 8028.162	Evans, Margaret Jane. Index to pictures of South African interest in the Graphic, 1875-1895. Johannesburg, 1966.
Afr 8028.164	Matton, Carol Ann. Pictures of South African interest in the Graphic, 1896-1899, a list. Thesis. Johannesburg, 1967.
Afr 8028.200	Botha, C.G. The public archives of South Africa, 1652-1910. Cape Town, 1928.
Afr 8028.200.5	Botha, C.G. The science of archives in South Africa. Johannesburg, 1937.
Afr 8028.200.10	Botha, C.G. A brief guide to the various classes of documents in the Cape archives for 1652-1806. Cape Town, 1918.
Afr 8028.200.15	Botha, Carol. A catalogue of manuscripts and papers in the Killie Campbell African collection relating to the African peoples. Johannesburg, 1967.
Afr 8028.205	Both, Ellen Lisa Marianne. Catalogue of books and pamphlets published in German relating to South Africa and South West Africa as found in the South African Public Library. Cape Town, 1969.

Afr 8029   South Africa in general - Pamphlet volumes

Afr 8029	Pamphlet box. South Africa.
Afr 8029.1	Pamphlet box. South Africa.
Afr 8029.2	Pamphlet vol. Africa bureau. 9 pam.
Afr 8029.3F	Pamphlet vol. South African Institute of Race Relations. Miscellaneous publications. 5 pam.

Afr 8030   South Africa in general - Collected source materials - General

Afr 8030.05F	Pamphlet box. South Africa. Documents.
Afr 8030.5	Cape of Good Hope. Archives. Precis. Cape Town. 1,1896+ 13v.
Afr 8030.7	Cape of Good Hope. Archives. Kaapse archiefstukken, lopende over het jaar 1778- Cape Town. 1926+ 6v.
Afr 8030.10	Theal, G.M. Records of South-eastern Africa. v.1- London, 1898- 9v.
Afr 8030.12	Pretorius, H.S. Voortrekker-argiefstukke, 1829-1849. Pretoria, 1937.
Afr 8030.15	Suid-afrikaanse argiefstukke. v.1- Cape Town, 1949. 7v.
Afr 8030.15.5	Suid-afrikaanse argiefstukke. v.1- Oranje-Vrystaat. 1952+ 4v.
Afr 8030.15.10	Suid-afrikaanse argiefstukke. v.1- Parow, 1958. 5v.
Afr 8030.15.15	Suid-afrikaanse argiefstukke. v.1- Kaapstad, 1957- 6v.
Afr 8030.16	Preller, Gustav Schoeman. Voortrek Kermense. Kaapstad, 1920- 5v.

Afr 8032   South Africa in general - Collected source materials - Statutes

Afr 8032.15F	Pamphlet vol. South Africa. Documents. 5 pam.

Afr 8035   South Africa in general - Collected source materials - Other

Afr 8035.5	Silver, S.W. S.W. Silver and Company's handbook to South Africa. London, 1880. 2v.
Afr 8035.10	South African Native Affairs Commission. Report of the commission. Cape Town, 1904-05. 5v.
Afr 8035.20F	South Africa. Native Affairs Commission. Report.
Afr 8035.35	South Africa. Native Affairs Department. Report.

Afr 8037   South Africa in general - Yearbooks and almanacs

Afr 8037.5	State of the Union, year book for the Union of South Africa. Cape Town. 1957+ 4v.
Afr 8037.10	South Africa, a chronicle. Cape Town. 1960+
Afr 8037.15	South African review. Durban. 1962+ 2v.
Afr 8037.20	South African year-book. London. 1914+ 5v.
Afr 8037.25	South Africa today. Johannesburg.
Afr 8037.30	Mockford, Julian. Overseas reference book of the Union of South Africa. London, 1945.

Afr 8038   South Africa in general - Dictionaries and encyclopedias

Afr 8038.5	Afrikaanse kinderensiklopedi. Kaapstad, 1963. 10v.
Afr 8038.10	Afrikaanse kernensiklopedie. Kaapstad, 1965.

Afr 8040   South Africa in general - Government and administration - General works

Afr 8040.3	Government of South Africa. Cape Town, 1908. 2v.
Afr 8040.5F	South African constitution bill. n.p., n.d.
Afr 8040.8	Cowen, D.V. The foundations of freedom. Cape Town, 1961.
Afr 8040.10	Nathan, Manfred. The South African commonwealth. Johannesburg, 1919.
Afr 8040.12	Kennedy, W.P.M. The law and custom of the South African constitution. London, 1935.
Afr 8040.15	Kayser, H. Demokratie und Föderalismus in der südafrikanischen Union. Düsseldorf, 1934.

Afr 8040.20   Steyn, J.H. Ein Beitrag zu der Geschichte des Föderalismus. Inaug. Diss. Würzburg, 1936.

Afr 8040.22   Cloete, Jacobus J.N. Sentrale, provinsiale en munisipale instellings van Suid-Afrika. Pretoria, 1964.

Afr 8045   South Africa in general - Government and administration - Special topics

Afr 8045.3   South Africa. Department of Information. Progress through separate development, South Africa in peaceful transition. N.Y., 1965.

Afr 8045.5   South Africa. Parliament. The parliament of the Republic of South Africa. Cape Town, 1962.

Afr 8045.7   South Africa. Parliament. House of Assembly. Report of the Select Committee on the subject of the constitution amendment bill. Cape Town, 1965.

Afr 8045.10   Winship, Thomas. Law and practice of arbitration in South Africa. Durban, 1925.

Afr 8045.12   Perham, M. The protectorates of South Africa. London, 1935.

Afr 8045.14   Jabavu, D.D.T. Native disabilities in South Africa. Lovedale, 1932.

Afr 8045.16   Edelman, H. Vorming en ontvoogding van de Unie van Zuid-Africa. Proefschrift. Rotterdam, 1935.

Afr 8045.18   Bodenstein, H.D.J. Engelse invloeden op het gemeenrecht van Zuid Afrika. Amsterdam, 1912.

Afr 8045.20   Lewin, Julius. Studies in African native law. Cape Town, 1947.

Afr 8045.22.5   May, Henry John. The South African constitution. 2d. ed. Cape Town, 1949.

Afr 8045.22.6   May, Henry John. The South African constitution. 3d ed. Cape Town, 1955.

Afr 8045.24   Kilpin, R.P. Parliamentary procedure in South Africa. 2d. ed. Juta, 1950.

Afr 8045.26   Royal Institute of International Affairs. The high commission territories and the Union of South Africa. London, 1956.

Afr 8045.30   Green, L.P. History of local government in South Africa. Cape Town, 1957.

Afr 8045.32   Schapera, Isaac. Government and politics in tribal societies. London, 1956.

Afr 8045.34   Cowen, D.V. Parliamentary sovereignty and the entrenched sections of the South Africa act. Cape Town, 1951.

Afr 8045.36   Rogers, Mirabel. The black sash. Johannesburg, 1956.

Afr 8045.38   Brookes, Edgar H. Civil liberty in South Africa. Cape Town, 1958.

Afr 8045.40   Kirkwood, Kenneth. The group areas act. Johannesburg, 195-.

Afr 8045.42   Dodd, Anthony D. South African citizenship. Cape Town, 1958.

Afr 8045.45   Coetzee, G.A. The Republic. Johannesburg, 1960.

Afr 8045.50   Schoor, M.C.E. Republieke en republikeine. Kaapstad, 1960.

Afr 8045.52   Kahn, Ellison. The new constitution. London, 1962.

Afr 8045.53   Hailey, W.M.H. The Republic of South Africa. London, 1963.

Afr 8045.54   Progressive Party of South Africa. Molteno report. Johannesburg, 1960-62.

Afr 8045.55   Wessels, F.J. Die republeinse grondwet. Kaapstad, 1962.

Afr 8045.56   Iuzhnoafrikanskii blok Kolonizatorov. Moskva, 1968.

Afr 8050   South Africa in general - General politics; political parties

Afr 8050.5   Worsfold, W.B. The problem of South African unity. London, 1900.

Afr 8050.8   Vrugte van die nasionale bewind, 1948-1966. Bloemfontein, 1966.

Afr 8050.8.2   Fruit of the national regime, 1948-1966. Bloemfontein, 1966.

Afr 8050.8.5   Malan, Maarten Petrus Albertus. Die nasionale party van Suid-Afrika, 1914-1964. Pretoria, 1964.

Afr 8050.10   Coetzee, Jan A. Politieke groepering in die wording van die afrikanernasie. Thesis. Johannesburg, 1941.

Afr 8050.12   Malan, Daniel Francois. Glo in u volk. D.F. Malan as redenaar, 1908-1954. Kaapstad, 1964.

Afr 8050.15   Krueger, Daniel. South African parties and policies. Cape Town, 1960.

Afr 8050.15.5   Krueger, Daniel. South African parties and policies, 1910-1960. London, 1960.

Afr 8050.18   Scholtz, Gert Daniel. Die bedreiging van die liberalisme. Pretoria, 1966.

Afr 8050.20   Feit, Edward. South Africa. London, 1962.

Afr 8050.21   Potchefstroom. University for Christian Higher Education. Republiek en koninkryk. Potchefstroom, 1964.

Afr 8050.22   Johns, S.W. Marxism-Leninism in a multiracial environment. Thesis. Cambridge, 1965.

Afr 8050.24   Davenport, T.R.H. The Afrikaner bond. Cape Town, 1966.

Afr 8050.26   Thompson, Leonard Monteath. Politics in the Republic of South Africa. Boston, 1966.

Afr 8050.28   Vermaak, Christopher Johann. The red trap: Communism and violence in South Africa. Johannesburg, 1966.

Afr 8055   South Africa in general - Collected political biographies

Afr 8055.5   Boonzaier, D.C. Owlographs, a collection of South African celebrities in caricature. Cape Town, 1901.

Afr 8055.10   South Africa who's who, 1911. Johannesburg. 1911-1967 12v.

Afr 8055.12   Wie is wie in Suid-Afrika. Johannesburg. 1958+ 6v.

Afr 8055.13   South African woman's who's who. v.1. Johannesburg, 1938.

Afr 8055.15   Nienaber, P.J. Afrikaanse biografiese woordeboek. Johannesburg, 1947.

Afr 8055.20   Brett, B.L.W. Makers of South Africa. London, 1944.

Afr 8055.25   Emden, P.H. Randlords. London, 1935.

Afr 8055.30   Neame, L.E. Some South African politicians. Cape Town, 1929.

Afr 8055.35   Cartwright, A.P. South Africa's hall of fame. Cape Town, 1958.

Afr 8055.38F   Men of the times. Johannesburg, 1906.

Afr 8055.40F   Cape Town. University. Library. Biographical index to men of the times. Cape Town, 1960.

Afr 8055.45   Hattersley, Alan H. Oliver the spy. Cape Town, 1959.

Afr 8057   South Africa in general - Historiography

Afr 8057.5   Jaarsveld, F.A. van. Die afrikaner en sy geskiedenis. Kaapstad, 1959.

Afr 8057.5.5   Jaarsveld, F.A. van. Lewende verlede. Johannesburg, 1962.

Afr 8057.6   Jaarsveld, F.A. van. The Afrikaners interpretation. Cape Town, 1964.

Afr 8057.10   Cronjé, Geoffrey. Aspekte van die Suid-Afrikaanse historiografie. Pretoria, 1967.

Afr 8060   South Africa in general - Military history - General works

Afr 8060.5   Tylden, G. The armed forces of South Africa. Johannesburg, 1954.

Afr 8063   South Africa in general - Military history - Special topics

Afr 8063.5   Woon, Harry V. Twenty-five years soldiering in South Africa. London, 1909.

Afr 8063.10   Birkby, C. The saga of the Transval Scottish Regiment. Cape Town, 1950.

Afr 8063.15   Young, P.J. Boot and saddle. Cape Town, 1955.

Afr 8063.20   Perridge, Frank. The history of Prince Alfred's Guard. Port Elizabeth, 1939.

Afr 8063.20.10   Orpen, Neil. Prince Alfred's guard, 1856-1966. Port Elizabeth, 1967.

Afr 8063.25   Vrdoljak, M.K. The history of South African regiments. Cape Town, 1957.

Afr 8063.30   South Africa. Martial Law Inquiry Judicial Commission. Report. Pretoria, 1922.

Afr 8063.32   Anderson, Ken. Nine flames. Cape Town, 1964.

Afr 8084 - 8090   South Africa in general - General history (By date)

Afr 8088.55.2   Holden, William Clifford. History of the colony of Natal. Cape Town, 1963.

Afr 8088.77   Noble, John. South Africa. London, 1877.

Afr 8088.77.5   Theal, G.M. Compendium of South African history and geography. 3d ed. Lovedale, 1877.

Afr 8088.85   Greswell, W. Our South African empire. London, 1885. 2v.

Afr 8088.85.5   Boon, Martin J. The immortal history of South Africa. London, 1885.

NEDL Afr 8088.88   Theal, G.M. History of South Africa. London, 1888- 5v.

NEDL Afr 8088.88.5   Theal, G.M. History and ethnography of Africa Zambesi. London, 1907. 3v.

Afr 8088.88.7   Theal, G.M. History of South Africa since Sept. 1795. v.1- London, 1908- 3v.

Afr 8088.88.8   Theal, G.M. Geschiedenis van Zuid-Afrika. 's-Gravenhage, 1897.

Afr 8088.88.9   Theal, G.M. History of South Africa from 1795-1872. London, 1915. 2v.

Afr 8088.88.10   Theal, G.M. History of South Africa from 1873-1884. London, 1919. 2v.

Afr 8088.88.14   Moodie, Duncan C.F. The history of the battles and adventures of the British. Cape Town, 1888. 2v.

Afr 8088.90   Lelu, Paul. Histoire de la colonie anglaise du Cap de Bonne-Espérance. Paris, 1890.

Afr 8088.91   Murray, R.W. South Africa from Arab domination to British rule. London, 1891.

Afr 8088.91.5   Spohr, Otto. Indexes to Limner (R.W. Murray), pen and ink sketches. Cape Town, 1965.

Afr 8088.92.2   Aitton, D. Geschiedenis van Zuid Afrika. 2e druk. Amsterdam, 1897.

Afr 8088.94   Wilmot, Alex. History of the expansion of South Africa. London, 1894.

Afr 8088.94.3   Theal, G.M. South Africa. N.Y., 1894.

Afr 8088.94.15   Theal, G.M. South Africa. 8th ed. London, 1917.

Afr 8088.95   Worsfold, W.B. South Africa. London, 1895.

Afr 8088.97A   Bryce, James. Impressions of South Africa. N.Y., 1897.

Afr 8088.97B   Bryce, James. Impressions of South Africa. N.Y., 1897.

Afr 8088.97.2   Bryce, James. Impressions of South Africa. N.Y., 1898.

Afr 8088.97.3   Bryce, James. Impressions of South Africa. London, 1899.

Afr 8088.97.4A   Bryce, James. Impressions of South Africa. N.Y., 1900.

Afr 8088.97.4B   Bryce, James. Impressions of South Africa. N.Y., 1900.

Afr 8088.97.6   Wirth, A. Geschichte Südafrikas. Bonn, 1897.

Afr 8088.99   Little, W.J.K. Sketches and studies in South Africa. London, 1899.

Afr 8088.99.5   Mackenzie, W.D. South Africa, its history. Chicago, 1899.

Afr 8089.00   South Africa handbooks. London, 1903.

Afr 8089.00.3A   Worsfold, W.B. A history of South Africa. London, 1900.

Afr 8089.00.3B   Worsfold, W.B. A history of South Africa. London, 1900.

Afr 8089.00.8   Pratt, E.A. Leading points in South African history, 1486 to March 30, 1900. London, 1900.

Afr 8089.01   Wilmot, Alex. The history of South Africa. London, 1901.

Afr 8089.01.3   Hesteren, J.P. van. Het land van kruger en steijn. Utrecht, 1901.

Afr 8089.01.5   Klok, J. De boeren-republieken in Zuid-Afrika, hun ontstaan. Utrecht, 1901.

Afr 8089.02   Theal, G.M. Progress of South Africa. Toronto, 1902.

Afr 8089.04   Bryden, H.A. A history of South Africa. Edinburgh, 1904.

Afr 8089.06   Beck, Henry. History of South Africa and the Boer-British war. Philadelphia, 1900.

Afr 8089.09   Colvin, Ian Duncan. South Africa. London, 19- .

Afr 8089.10   Cory, G.E. The rise of South Africa. v.1- London, 1910- 6v.

Afr 8089.13   Merimee, P. La politique anglaise au Transvaal. Toulouse, 1913.

Afr 8089.13.3A   Worsfold, W.B. The reconstruction of the new colonies under Lord Milner. London, 1913. 2v.

Afr 8089.13.3B   Worsfold, W.B. The reconstruction of the new colonies under Lord Milner. London, 1913. 2v.

Afr 8089.14.5   Tilby, A.W. South Africa, 1486-1913. Boston, 1916.

Afr 8089.15   Scully, W.C. History of South Africa, from earliest days to union. London, 1915.

Afr 8089.18A   Fairbridge, D. A history of South Africa. London, 1918.

Afr 8089.18B   Fairbridge, D. A history of South Africa. London, 1918.

Afr 8089.27.5   Gie, S.F.N. Geskiedenis van Suid Afrika af ons verlede. Stellenbosch, 1942. 2v.

Afr 8089.28A   Walker, E.A. A history of South Africa. London, 1928.

Afr 8089.28B   Walker, E.A. A history of South Africa. London, 1928.

Afr 8089.28.15   Walker, E.A. A history of Southern Africa. 3rd ed. London, 1957.

Afr 8089.31   Hofmeyer, J.H. South Africa. London, 1931.

Afr 8110   South Africa in general - History by periods - Dutch period
(1652-1814) - Special topics
cont.

Afr 8110.25.5	Vos, Michiel Christiaan. Merkwaardig verhaal, aangaande het leven en de lotgevallen van Michiel Christiaan Vos. 2. druk. Amsterdam, 1850.
Afr 8110.28	Milo, Taco H. De geheime onderhandelingen tusschen de Bataafshe en Fransche Republieken. Den Helder, 1942.
Afr 8110.30	Welch, Sidney R. Portuguese and Dutch in South Africa. Cape Town, 1951.
Afr 8110.32F	Botha, Colin G. Three hundred years. Johannesburg, 1952.

Afr 8115   South Africa in general - History by periods - Dutch period
(1652-1814) - Huguenots

Afr 8115.10	Botha, Colin G. The French refugees at the Cape. Cape Town, 1919.
Afr 8115.12	Nathan, M. The Huguenots in South Africa. Johannesburg, 1939.

Afr 8125   South Africa in general - History by periods - Dutch period
(1652-1814) - British conquest (1795-1803, 1806-1814)

Afr 8125.5	Heeres, Jan E. Heeft Nederland de Kaap verkocht. Amsterdam, 1914.
Afr 8125.10	Fairbridge, D. Lady Anne Barnard at the Cape of Good Hope, 1797-1802. Oxford, 1924.
Afr 8125.15	Mueller, C.F.J. Johannes Frederick Kirsten oor die toestand van die Kaapkolonie in 1795. Pretoria, 1960.

Afr 8135   South Africa in general - History by periods - British period
(1814-1909) - General works

Afr 8135.5	Cana, F.R. South Africa from the great trek to the union. London, 1909.
Afr 8135.6	Hart-Synnot, F. Letters. London, 1912.
Afr 8135.7	Eybers, G.W. Select constitutional documents...South African history 1795-1910. London, 1918.
Afr 8135.8	Reitz, F.W. Ein Jahrhundert voller Unrecht. Berlin, 1900.
Afr 8135.10	Colquhoun, Archibald. The Africander land. London, 1906.
Afr 8135.15	Brookes, E.H. The history of native policy in South Africa from 1830 to the present day. Cape Town, 1924.
Afr 8135.17	Agar-Hamilton, J.A.I. South Africa. London, 1934.
Afr 8135.21	Walker, E.A. Britain and South Africa. London, 1941.
Afr 8135.23	Williams, Basil. Botha, Smuts and South Africa. London, 1946.
Afr 8135.23.5	Williams, Basil. Botha. N.Y., 1962.
Afr 8135.25	Kuit, Albert. Transvaalse verskeidenheid. Pretoria, 1940.
Afr 8135.25.5	Kuit, Albert. Transvaalse terugblikke. Pretoria, 1945.
Afr 8135.27	Preller, Gustav S. Ekelse en opstelle. Pretoria, 1928.
Afr 8135.29	Kemp, J.C.G. Die pad van die veroweraar. 2. druk. Kaapstad, 1946.
Afr 8135.29.10	Kemp, J.C.G. Vir vryheid en vir reg. 3 druk. Kaapstad, 1946.

Afr 8140   South Africa in general - History by periods - British period
(1814-1909) - Special topics

Afr 8140.5	King, E. On advantages of triform...colonization in South Africa. Bicester, 1844.
Afr 8140.6F	Committee of Observation on All Matters Connected with Attainment of Independence of British Kaffraria. British Kaffaria, the people's blue book. King Williams Town, 1863.
Afr 8140.15	Brookes, E.H. The history of native policy in South Africa. 2d ed. Pretoria, 1927.
Afr 8140.16	Brookes, E.H. The colour problems of South Africa. Lovedale, 1934.
Afr 8140.17	Kiewiet, C.W. de. British colonial policy and the South African republics. London, 1929.
Afr 8140.19	Brookes, E.H. The political future of South Africa. Pretoria, 1927.
Afr 8140.21	Rogers, Howard. Native administration in the Union of South Africa. Johannesburg, 1933.
Afr 8140.23	Evans, I.L. Native policy in Southern Africa. Cambridge, Eng., 1934.
Afr 8140.25	Uys, C.J. In the era of Shepstone, being a study of British expansion in South Africa (1842-1877). Lovedale, 1933.
Afr 8140.27	Kiewiet, C.W. The imperial factor in South Africa, a study of politics and economics. Cambridge, Eng., 1937.
Afr 8140.29	Blackwell, L. African occasions, reminiscences of thirty years of bar, bench and politics in South Africa. London, 1938.
Afr 8140.29.5	Blackwell, L. Farewell to parliament. Pietermaritzburg, 1946.
Afr 8140.31	Sauer, H. Ex Africa. London, 1937.
Afr 8140.33	Malan, D.F. Foreign policy of the Union of South Africa. Pretoria, 1950.
Afr 8140.35	Braak, K. Zuid-Afrika en Engeland. Utrecht, 1933.
Afr 8140.40	Hattersley, Alan Frederick. The convict crisis and the growth of unity. Pietermaritzburg, 1965.

Afr 8145   South Africa in general - History by periods - British period
(1814-1909) - Church history (incl. missions)

Afr 8145.5	Wirgman, A.T. The history of the English Church in South Africa. London, 1895.
Afr 8145.5.5	Wirgman, A.T. The history of the English church and people in South Africa. N.Y., 1969.
Afr 8145.6	Ebner, J.S. Reise nach Süd-Afrika und Darstellung. Berlin, 1839.
Afr 8145.7	Wirgman, A.T. Life of James Green...dean of Maritzburg, Natal, 1849-1906. London, 1909. 2v.
Afr 8145.9	Merriman, N.J. The Kafir, the Hottentot, and the frontier farmer...missionary life. London, 1854.
Afr 8145.10	Edwards, John. Reminiscences of the early life and missionary labours of John Edwards. Grahamstown, 1883.
Afr 8145.12	Mother Cecile. South Africa, 1883-1906. London, 1930.
Afr 8145.14	Shepherd, R.H.W. Lovedale, South Africa. Lovedale, 1940.
Afr 8145.16	Davies, H. South African missions. London, 1954.
Afr 8145.18	Lewis, Cecil. Historical records of the Church of the province of South Africa. London, 1934.
Afr 8145.20	Inter-Racial Conference of Church Leaders, Johannesburg. God's kingdom in multi-racial South Africa. Johannesburg, 1955.
Afr 8145.22F	Turnbull, C.E.P. The work of the missionaries of Die Nederduits Gereformeerde Kerk van Suid-Afrika up to the year 1910. Johannesburg, 1965.
Afr 8145.25	Pauw, Barthold. Religion in a Tswana chiefdom. London, 1960.

Afr 8145   South Africa in general - History by periods - British period
(1814-1909) - Church history (incl. missions)
cont.

Afr 8145.28	Gerdener, Gustav S.A. Studies in the evangelisation of South Africa. London, 1911.
Afr 8145.30	Pellissier, S.H. Jean Pierre Pellissier van Bethulie. Pretoria, 1956.
Afr 8145.32A	Geyser, A.S. Delayed action. Pretoria, 1960.
Afr 8145.32B	Geyser, A.S. Delayed action. Pretoria, 1960.
Afr 8145.34	Victor, Osmund. The salient of South Africa. London, 1931.
Afr 8145.35	Knietoch, Clemens M. Nur einer von Vielen, aus dem Leben eines Missionsarztes. Frankfurt, 1961.
Afr 8145.38	Anderson, Theophilus. The story of Pacaltsdorp. Port Elizabeth, 1957.
Afr 8145.40	Hinchliff, P.B. The Anglican Church in South Africa. London, 1963.
Afr 8145.42	Church of England in South Africa. Constitution and canons of the Church of the province of South Africa. Cape Town, 1962.
Afr 8145.44	Deblank, J. Out of Africa. London, 1964.
Afr 8145.45	Ervin, Spencer. The polity of the Church of the province of South Africa. Ambler, Pa., 1964.
Afr 8145.46	Martin, Marie L. The biblical concept of Messianism and Messianism in Southern Africa. Morija, 1964.
Afr 8145.47	Shaw, William, Rector of Chelvey. The story of my mission among the native tribes of South Eastern Africa. London, 1872.

Afr 8152   South Africa in general - History by periods - British period
(1814-1909) - Native wars - Kaffirs (1779-1877) - Special wars

Afr 8152.72	Ward, H. The Cape and the Kaffirs. London, 1851.
Afr 8152.72.5	Ward, H. Five years in Kaffirland. London, 1848. 2v.
Afr 8152.73.2	King, W.R. Campaigning in Kaffirland...1851-52. 2d ed. London, 1855.
Afr 8152.73.5	Johannesburg. Public Library. General index of the first edition of King's Campaigning in Kaffirland. Johannesburg, 1958.
Afr 8152.74	McKay, James. Reminiscences of the last Kaffir war. Grahamstown, 1871.
Afr 8152.74.2	McKay, James. Reminiscences of the last Kaffir war. General index, excluding appendices. Johannesburg, 1962.
Afr 8152.75	Hudson, M.B. Feature in South African frontier life...embracing complete record of Kafir war 1850-51. Port Elizabeth, 1852.
Afr 8152.76	Godlonton, Robert. Narrative of the Kaffir war, 1850-1851-1852. Cape Town, 1962.
Afr 8152.76.05	Godlonton, Robert. A narrative of the irruption of the Kaffir hordes into the eastern province of the Cape of Good Hope. Cape Town, 1965.
Afr 8152.76.2	Johannesburg. Public Library. General index to Narrative of the Kaffir war. Johannesburg, 1960.
Afr 8152.81	Cathcart, G. Correspondence. 2nd ed. London, 1857.
Afr 8152.90	Aylward, A. The Transvaal of to-day. Edinburgh, 1878.
Afr 8152.91	Cunynghame, A.T. My command in South Africa 1874-8. London, 1879.
Afr 8152.92	Lucas, T.J. Camp life in South Africa. London, 1878.
Afr 8152.92.5	Lucas, T.J. Pen and pencil reminiscences of campaign in South Africa. London, 1861.
Afr 8152.93	Molyneux, W.C.F. Campaigning in South Africa and Egypt. London, 1896.
Afr 8152.94	Streatfield, F.M. Kafirland, a ten months campaign. London, 1879.
Afr 8152.95	Fenn, T.E. How I volunteered for the Cape. London, 1879.
Afr 8152.96	Prichard, A.M. Friends and foes in the Transkei. London, 1880.
Afr 8152.98	Browning, F.G. Fighting and farming in South Africa. London, 1880.
Afr 8152.99	Napier, Elers. Excursions in Southern Africa. London, 1850. 2v.

Afr 8155   South Africa in general - History by periods - British period
(1814-1909) - Native wars - Zulus (1822-1887) - General works

Afr 8155.5.2	Gibson, J.Y. The story of the Zulus. London, 1911.
Afr 8155.7	Jenkinson, T.B. Amazulu. The Zulus, their history. London, 1882.
Afr 8155.9	Lucas, T.J. The Zulus and the British frontiers. London, 1879.
Afr 8155.10	Bulpin, J. Victor. Shakas country. 3d ed. Cape Town, 1956. 2v.
Afr 8155.11	Becker, Peter. Rule of fear. London, 1964.
Afr 8155.11.2	Becker, Peter. Dingane, King of the Zulu, 1828-1840. N.Y., 1965.
Afr 8155.12	Samuelson, Robert Charles Azariah. Long, long ago. Durban, 1929.

Afr 8160   South Africa in general - History by periods - British period
(1814-1909) - Native wars - Zulus (1822-1887) - War of 1879 (Cetewayo)

Afr 8160.3	Dixie, Florence Douglas. A defence of Zululand and its king. London, 188-
Afr 8160.4	Parr, H.H. A sketch of the Kafir and Zulu wars. London, 1880.
Afr 8160.5	Montague, W.E. Campaigning in South Africa. Edinburgh, 1880.
Afr 8160.6	Vijn, Cornelius. Cetshwayo's Dutchman. London, 1880.
Afr 8160.7	Dunn, John. Cetywayo and the three generals. Pietermaritzburg, 1886.
Afr 8160.8	Norris-Newman, C.L. In Zululand with the British. London, 1880.
Afr 8160.9F	Mackinnon, J.P. The South African campaign 1879. London, 1880.
Afr 8160.10	Wilmot, A. History of the Zulu war. London, 1880.
Afr 8160.11	Colenso, F.E. History of the Zulu war and its origin. London, 1880.
Afr 8160.12	McToy, E.D. Brief history of the 13th Regiment...1877-78-79. Devonport, 1880.
Afr 8160.13	Laurence, W.M. Selected writings. Grahamstown, 1882.
Afr 8160.14	Norbury, H.F. Naval brigade in South Africa during...1877-78-79. London, 1880.
Afr 8160.15	Hamilton-Browne, G. A lost legionary in South Africa. London, 1912.
Afr 8160.16	Ewart, J.S. British foreign policy and the next war. The Zulu war. Ottawa, 1927.

Afr 8160 South Africa in general - History by periods - British period
(1814-1909) - Native wars - Zulus (1822-1887) - War of 1879 (Cetewayo)
cont.

Afr 8160.18	Coupland, R. Zulu battle piece, Isandhlwana. London, 1948.
Afr 8160.19	Clements, W.H. The glamour and tragedy of the Zulu war. London, 1936.
Afr 8160.20	French, G. Lord Chelmsford and the Zulu war. London, 1939.
Afr 8160.22	Ashe, Major. The story of the Zulu campaign. London, 1880.
Afr 8160.24	Furneaux, Rupert. The Zulu war. 1st ed. Philadelphia, 1963.
Afr 8160.25	Morris, Donald R. The washing of the spears. N.Y., 1965.
Afr 8160.26F	Smail, J.L. Historical monuments and battlefields in Natal. Cape Town, 1965.

Afr 8163 South Africa in general - History by periods - British period
(1814-1909) - Native wars - Zulus (1822-1887) - Later history
(1879-1887)

Afr 8163.2	Colenso, Frances Ellen. The ruin of Zululand, an account of British doings in Zululand since the invasion of 1879. London, 1884-85. 2v.

Afr 8167 South Africa in general - History by periods - British period
(1814-1909) - Native wars - Basutos (1851-1880) - Special wars

Afr 8167.5	Brownlee, Charles. A chapter on the Basuto war, a lecture. Lovedale, 1889.

Afr 8175 South Africa in general - History by periods - British period
(1814-1909) - The Dutch and their relations with the British during
1814-1899 - General works

Afr 8175.5	Theal, G.M. History of the Boers in South Africa. London, 1887.
Afr 8175.5.1	Theal, G.M. History of the Boers in South Africa. N.Y., 1969.
Afr 8175.6	Voigt, J.C. Fifty years of the history of republic in South Africa, 1795-1845. London, 1899. 2v.
Afr 8175.7	Cachet, F.L. De worstelstrijd der transvalers. Amsterdam, 1900.
Afr 8175.8	Fisher, W.E.G. The Transvaal and the Boers. London, 1900.
Afr 8175.9	Keane, A.H. The Boer states. London, 1900.
Afr 8175.10	Deherain, H. L'expansion des Boers au XIXe siècle. Paris, 1905.
Afr 8175.12	Wormser, J.A. Drie en zestig jaren in dienst der vrijheid. Amsterdam, 1900.
Afr 8175.13	Schreiner, O. Thoughts on South Africa. N.Y., 1923.
Afr 8175.15	England and the Boers. Leeds, 1899.
Afr 8175.17	Imperial South African Association. The British case against the Boer republics. Westminster, 1900.
Afr 8175.19	Mansvelt, Nicolas. De betrekkingen tusschen Nederland en Zuid-Africa sedert de verovering van de Kaapkolonie door de Engelschen. Utrecht, 1902.
Afr 8175.20	Jaarsveld, F.A. van. Die ontwaking van die afrikaanse nasionale bewussyn. Johannesburg, 1957.
Afr 8175.20.4	Jaarsveld, F.A. van. The awakening of Afrikaner nationalism, 1868-1881. Cape Town, 1961.
Afr 8175.22	Galbraith, J.S. Reluctant empire. Berkeley, 1963.
Afr 8175.24	Chilvers, Hedley A. The yellow man looks on, being the story of the Anglo-Dutch conflict in Southern Africa. London, 1933.

Afr 8177 South Africa in general - History by periods - British period
(1814-1909) - The Dutch and their relations with the British during
1814-1899 - Slaagters Nek (1815)

Afr 8177.5	Cape of Good Hope. Archives. The rebellion of 1815. Cape Town, 1902.

Afr 8180 South Africa in general - History by periods - British period
(1814-1909) - The Dutch and their relations with the British during
1814-1899 - Great Trek (1836-1842) and Boer emigration (1834-1854)

Afr 8180.5	Cloete, Henry. The history of the great Boer trek. London, 1899.
Afr 8180.5.3	Cloete, Henry. The history of the great Boer trek. N.Y., 1899.
Afr 8180.5.4	Cloete, Henry. Vijf voorlezingen over de landverhuizing der hollandsche Boeren. Kaapstad, 1856.
Afr 8180.10	Walker, E.A. The great trek. London, 1934.
Afr 8180.10.3	Walker, E.A. The great trek. 3d ed. London, 1948.
Afr 8180.10.4	Walker, E.A. The great trek. 4th ed. London, 1960.
Afr 8180.20A	Agar-Hamilton, J.A. von. The native policy of the Voortrekkers. Cape Town, 1928.
Afr 8180.20B	Agar-Hamilton, J.A. von. The native policy of the Voortrekkers. Cape Town, 1928.
Afr 8180.22	Merwe, P.J. Die noordwaartse beweging van die Boere voor die groot trek, 1770-1842. Den Haag, 1937.
Afr 8180.22.3	Merwe, P.J. Die noordwaartse beweging van die Boere voor die groot trek, 1770-1842. Proefschrift. Den Haag, 1937.
Afr 8180.23	Merwe, P.J. Nog verder noord. Kaapstad, 1962.
Afr 8180.24	Merwe, P.J. Trek. Kaapstad, 1945.
Afr 8180.26	Muller, Christoffel Frederik Jakobus. Die Britse owerheid en die groot trek. Thesis. Kaapstad, 1949.
Afr 8180.26.5	Muller, Christoffel Frederik Jakobus. Die Britse owerheid en die groot trek. 2. uitg. Johannesburg, 1963.
Afr 8180.28	Thom, H.B. Die geloftekerk. Kaapstad, 1949.
Afr 8180.30	Franken, J.L.M. Piet retief. Kaapstad, 1949.
Afr 8180.31	Preller, G.S. Piet retief. Pretoria, 1912.
Afr 8180.32	Rooseboom, H. The romance of the great trek. Johannesburg, 1949.
Afr 8180.34	Trigerdt, L. Dagboek. Bloemfontein, 1917.
Afr 8180.35	Hugo, M. Piet retief. Johannesburg, 1961.

Afr 8190 South Africa in general - History by periods - British period
(1814-1909) - The Dutch and their relations with the British during
1814-1899 - Natal - Foundation and early history (1824-1843)

Afr 8190.5	Bird, John. Annals of Natal 1495-1845. v.1 and index. Pietermaritzburg, 1888. 2v.
Afr 8190.5.2	Bird, John. The annals of Natal, 1495 to 1845. Capetown, 1965. 2v.
Afr 8190.10	Mackeurtan, G. The cradle days of Natal, 1497-1845. London, 1930.
Afr 8190.15	Watt, E.P. Febana. London, 1962.

Afr 8190 South Africa in general - History by periods - British period
(1814-1909) - The Dutch and their relations with the British during
1814-1899 - Natal - Foundation and early history (1824-1843)
cont.

Afr 8190.20	Brookes, Edgar Harry. A history of Natal. Pietermaritzburg, 1965.

Afr 8210 South Africa in general - History by periods - British period
(1814-1909) - The Dutch and their relations with the British during
1814-1899 - Transvaal (To War of 1899) - General works

Afr 8210.3	Nixon, John. The complete story of the Transvaal. London, 1885.
Afr 8210.5	Haggard, H.R. A history of the Transvaal. N.Y., 1899.
Afr 8210.5.5	Haggard, H.R. A history of the Transvaal. N.Y., 1900.
Afr 8210.6	Africanus. The Transvaal Boers. London, 1899.
Afr 8210.7	Poirier, Jules. Le Transvaal. Paris, 1900.
Afr 8210.8	Vallentin, W. Die Geschichte der Süd-Afrikanischen Republiken. Berlin, 1901.
Afr 8210.9	Oordt, J.F.V. Paul Kruger en de opkomst der Zuid Afrikaansche Republiek. Amsterdam, 1898.
Afr 8210.10	Kloessel, M.H. Die Südafrikanischen Republiken. Leipzig, 1888.
Afr 8210.11	Jeppe, Carl. The kaleidoscopic Transvaal. London, 1906.
Afr 8210.12	Botha, P.R. Die staatkundige ontwikkeling van den Zuid Afrikanse Republiek onder Krueger en Leyds. Amsterdam, 1925.
Afr 8210.14	Leyds, W.J. Kruger days, reminiscences of Dr. W.J. Leyds. London, 1939.
Afr 8210.16	Gey van Pittius, E.F.W. Staatsopvattings van die voortrekkers en die Boere. Pretoria, 1941.
Afr 8210.18	Cowan, L.G. Local government in West Africa. N.Y., 1958.
Afr 8210.20	Bulpin, Thomas Victor. Lost rails of the Transvaal. Johannesburg, 1965.

Afr 8215 South Africa in general - History by periods - British period
(1814-1909) - The Dutch and their relations with the British during
1814-1899 - Transvaal (To War of 1899) - Foundation and early history
(1836-1877)

Afr 8215.1	Leyds, W.J. The first annexation of the Transvaal. London, 1906.
Afr 8215.1.3	Leyds, W.J. De eerste annexatie van de Transvaal. v.1. Amsterdam, 1906.
Afr 8215.1.8	Leyds, W.J. The Transvaal surrounded. London, 1919.
Afr 8215.5	Chesson, Frederick William. The Dutch Boers and slavery. London, 1869.
Afr 8215.6	Chesson, Frederick William. The Dutch Republic of South Africa. London, 1871.
Afr 8215.7	Huet, P. Het lot der zwarten in Transvaal. Utrecht, 1869.

Afr 8220 South Africa in general - History by periods - British period
(1814-1909) - The Dutch and their relations with the British during
1814-1899 - Transvaal (To War of 1899) - Annexation by British
(1877-1881)

Afr 8220.5	Tromp, Theo M. Herinneringen uit Zuid Africa. Leiden, 1879.

Afr 8225 South Africa in general - History by periods - British period
(1814-1909) - The Dutch and their relations with the British during
1814-1899 - Transvaal (To War of 1899) - War of 1880-1881

Afr 8225.4.2	Carter, T.F. A narrative of the Boer war. London, 1896.
Afr 8225.5	Bellairs, Blanche St. John. The Transvaal war 1880-81. Edinburg, 1885.
Afr 8225.6	Newman, C.L.N. With the Boers in the Transvaal 1880-1. London, 1896.
Afr 8225.7	Butler, W.F. Life of Sir George Pomeroy-Colley. London, 1899.
Afr 8225.8	Haggard, H.R. The last Boer war. London, 1900.
Afr 8225.10	Jordan, Robert Alan. The Transvaal War, 1808-1881; a bibliography. Johannesburg, 1969.
Afr 8225.15	Ransford, Oliver. The battle of Majuba Hill, the first Boer war. London, 1967.
Afr 8225.20	Schreuder, Deryck Marshall. Gladstone and Kruger: liberal government and colonial "home rule". London, 1969.

Afr 8230 South Africa in general - History by periods - British period
(1814-1909) - The Dutch and their relations with the British during
1814-1899 - Transvaal (To War of 1899) - Biographies of Dutch in
Transvaal

Afr 8230.3	Kruger, S.J.P. Paul Kruger amptelike briewe, 1851-1877. Pretoria, 1925.
Afr 8230.5A	Statham, F.R. Paul Kruger and his times. London, 1898.
Afr 8230.5B	Statham, F.R. Paul Kruger and his times. London, 1898.
Afr 8230.6A	Kruger, Paul. Memoirs. N.Y., 1902.
Afr 8230.6B	Kruger, Paul. Memoirs. N.Y., 1902.
Afr 8230.6.5	Kruger, Paul. Memoirs. v.1-2. London, 1902.
Afr 8230.6.10	Vys, C.J. Paul Kruger. Kaapstad, 1955.
Afr 8230.6.15	Krueger, D.W. Paul Kruger. Johannesburg, 1961. 2v.
Afr 8230.6.20	Rademeyer, J.I. Paul Kruger. Johannesburg, 1962.
Afr 8230.7	Brouwer, W. Paul Kruger. Amsterdam, 1900.
Afr 8230.9	Gluckstein, S.M. Queen or president. London, 1900.
Afr 8230.10	Bruce, C.T. The real Kruger and the Transvaal. N.Y., 1900.
Afr 8230.10.10	Juta, M. The pace of the ox, the life of Paul Kruger. London, 1937.
Afr 8230.10.12	Cloete, Stuart. Against these three, a biography of Paul Kruger. Boston, 1945.
Afr 8230.10.13	Cloete, Stuart. African portraits. London, 1946.
Afr 8230.10.13.2	Cloete, Stuart. African portraits: a biography of Paul Kruger, Cecil Rhodes and Lobengula. Cape Town, 1969.
Afr 8230.10.15	Postma, F. Paul Kruger. Stellenbosch, 1944.
Afr 8230.10.20	Nathan, Manfred. Paul Kruger, his life and times. 5. ed. Durban, 1946.
Afr 8230.25.5	Preller, G.S. Andries pretorius. 2. verb. uitg. Johannesburg, 1940.
Afr 8230.30	Engelbrecht, S.P. Thomas François Burgers, a biography. Pretoria, 1946.
Afr 8230.33	Kruger's secret service. London, 1900.
Afr 8230.34F	Huldeblad van nederlandsche letterkundigen. Rotterdam, 1900.
Afr 8230.35	Boey, Marcel. Paul Kruger. Tielt, 194-.
Afr 8230.38	Potgieter, C. Kommandant-generaal Hendrik Potgieter. Johannesburg, 1938.

Afr 8235 South Africa in general - History by periods - British period (1814-1909) - The Dutch and their relations with the British during 1814-1899 - 1865-1899 - General works

Afr 8235.5	Wilmot, A. History of our own times in South Africa 1872-1898. Cape Town, 1897. 3v.
Afr 8235.6	Matthews, J.W. Incwadi Yami, twenty years in South Africa. London, 1887.
Afr 8235.7	Haggard, H.R. Cetywayo and his white neighbours. London, 1888.
Afr 8235.8	Statham, F.R. Blacks, Boers and British. London, 1881.
Afr 8235.8.5	Statham, F.R. Blacks, Boers, and British. N.Y., 1969.
Afr 8235.9	Froude, J.A. Two lectures on South Africa. London, 1900.
Afr 8235.10	Weale, J.P.M. The truth about the Portuguese in Africa. London, 1891.
Afr 8235.11	Boyle, Frederick. To the Cape for diamonds. London, 1873.
Afr 8235.13	Molteno, Percy A. A federal in South Africa. London, 1896.
Afr 8235.14	Wued, Johannes Andreas. Die Rolle der Biurenrepubliken in der auswaertigen und kolonialen Politik des deutschen Reiches, 1883-1900. Nürnberg, 1927.
Afr 8235.15	Bixler, R.W. Anglo-German imperialism in South Africa 1880-1900. Diss. Columbus, Ohio, 1932.
Afr 8235.16	Bixler, R.W. Anglo-German imperialism in South Africa, 1880-1900. Baltimore, 1932.
Afr 8235.17A	Lovell, R.I. The struggle for South Africa, 1875-1899. N.Y., 1934.
Afr 8235.17B	Lovell, R.I. The struggle for South Africa, 1875-1899. N.Y., 1934.
Afr 8235.19	Leonard, C. Papers on the political situation in South Africa, 1885-1895. London, 1903.
Afr 8235.20	Holmberg, Ake. African tribes and European agencies. Göteborg, 1966.

Afr 8238 South Africa in general - History by periods - British period (1814-1909) - The Dutch and their relations with the British during 1814-1899 - 1865-1899 - Special topics

Afr 8238.2	Goodfellow, Clement Francis. Great Britain and South African confederation, 1870-1881. Cape Town, 1966.
Afr 8238.4	Williams, Alpheus Fuller. Some dreams come true. Cape Town, 1949.
Afr 8238.6	McNish, James Thomas. The road to El Dorado. Cape Town, 1968.

Afr 8250 South Africa in general - History by periods - British period (1814-1909) - The Dutch and their relations with the British during 1814-1899 - Political biographies - Individual - Cecil Rhodes

Afr 8250.1	Pamphlet box. Cecil Rhodes.
Afr 8250.2	Thomson, D.W. Cecil John Rhodes. Cape Town, 1947.
Afr 8250.3	Cecil Rhodes. London, 1897.
Afr 8250.5	Hensman, H. Cecil Rhodes. Edinburg, 1901.
Afr 8250.6	Michell, L. Life and times of C.J. Rhodes. N.Y., 1910. 2v.
Afr 8250.7	Fuller, T.E. Right Honourable Cecil J. Rhodes. London, 1910.
Afr 8250.8	Jourdan, P. Cecil Rhodes. London, 1911.
Afr 8250.8.2	Jourdan, P. Cecil Rhodes. London, 1911.
Afr 8250.8.5	Jourdan, P. Cecil Rhodes. London, 19- .
Afr 8250.9A	Lesueur, G. Cecil Rhodes, the man and his work. London, 1913.
Afr 8250.9B	Lesueur, G. Cecil Rhodes, the man and his work. London, 1913.
Afr 8250.9.5	Lesueur, G. Cecil Rhodes, the man and his work. N.Y., 1914.
Afr 8250.10	Verschoyle, F. Cecil Rhodes, his political life and speeches 1881-1900. London, 1900.
Afr 8250.12	Radziwill, E. Cecil Rhodes, man and empire-maker. London, 1918.
Afr 8250.15	Waal, D.C. Reizen met Cecil Rhodes door de wilde wereld van Zuid-Afrika. Amsterdam, 1896.
Afr 8250.16	Waal, David C. With Rhodes in Mashonaland. Cape Town, 1896.
Afr 8250.17A	Williams, B. Cecil Rhodes. London, 1921.
Afr 8250.17B	Williams, B. Cecil Rhodes. London, 1921.
Afr 8250.17.2	Williams, B. Cecil Rhodes. (Makers of the 19th century). N.Y., 1921.
Afr 8250.19	Stent, Vere. A personal record of some incidents in the life of Cecil Rhodes. Cape Town, 1924.
Afr 8250.21	McDonald, J.G. Rhodes, a life. London, 1927.
Afr 8250.21.5	McDonald, J.G. Rhodes, a heritage. London, 1943.
Afr 8250.23	Watts-Danton, T. The Rhodes memorial at Oxford. London, 1910.
Afr 8250.25	Millin, S.G. Rhodes. London, 1933.
Afr 8250.25.10	Millin, S.G. Rhodes. London, 1952.
Afr 8250.27	Plomer, W. Cecil Rhodes. London, 1933.
Afr 8250.29	Lockhart, J.G. Cecil Rhodes. London, 1933.
Afr 8250.29.5	Lockhart, J.G. Cecil Rhodes, the colossus of Southern Africa. N.Y., 1963.
Afr 8250.29.6	Lockhart, J.G. Rhodes. London, 1963.
Afr 8250.31	Baker, H. Cecil Rhodes. London, 1934.
Afr 8250.33	Oudard, G. Cecil Rhodes. Paris, 1939.
Afr 8250.35	Maurois, Andre. Cecil Rhodes. N.Y., 1953.
Afr 8250.35.2	Maurois, Andre. Cecil Rhodes. London, 1953.
Afr 8250.35.5	Maurois, André. Cecil Rhodes. Hamden, Conn., 1968.
Afr 8250.37	Gross, Felix. Rhodes of Africa. London, 1956.
Afr 8250.40	Bulawayo, South Africa. Central African Rhodes Centenary Exhibition. The story of Cecil Rhodes. Bulawayo, 1953.
Afr 8250.42	Brookner, Anita. An iconography of Cecil Rhodes. n.p., 1956.
Afr 8250.43	Cape Town. University. Libraries. Pictorial material of Cecil J. Rhodes. Cape Town, 1964.
Afr 8250.44	Green, Jolin Eric Sidney. Rhodes goes north. London, 1936.
Afr 8250.45	Roberts, Brian. Cecil Rhodes and the princess. London, 1969.

Afr 8252 South Africa in general - History by periods - British period (1814-1909) - The Dutch and their relations with the British during 1814-1899 - Political biographies - Individual - Others (A-Z, 299 scheme, by person)

Afr 8252.1	Boreherds, P.B. An autobiographical memoir. Cape Town, 1861.
Afr 8252.1.5	Borcherds, P.B. An autobiographical memoir. Facsimile reproduction. Cape Town, 1963.
Afr 8252.3	Cowen, Charles. The honorable Lt. Col. Frederick Schermbrucker, M.L.C., at the Cape of Good Hope. Wynberg, 1884.

Afr 8252 South Africa in general - History by periods - British period (1814-1909) - The Dutch and their relations with the British during 1814-1899 - Political biographies - Individual - Others (A-Z, 299 scheme, by person) cont.

Afr 8252.4	Cowen, Charles. Charles Tennant Jones, M.L.A., and our government. Wynberg, 1884.
Afr 8252.5A	Molteno, P.A. Life and times of Sir J.C. Molteno. London, 1900. 2v.
Afr 8252.5B	Molteno, P.A. Life and times of Sir J.C. Molteno. London, 1900. 2v.
Afr 8252.5.10	Molteno, J.T. The dominion of Afrikanderdom. London, 1923.
Afr 8252.5.15	Molteno, J.T. Further South African recollections. London, 1926.
Afr 8252.6	Mackenzie, W.D. John Mackenzie. N.Y., 1902.
Afr 8252.7	Raymond, H. B.I. Barnato. London, 1897.
Afr 8252.7.7	Lewinsohn, R. Barney Barnato, from Whitechapel clown to diamond king. London, 1937.
Afr 8252.8	Mueller, E.B.I. Lord Milner and South Africa. London, 1902.
Afr 8252.8.5	Worsfold, W.B. Lord Milner's work in South Africa. London, 1906.
Afr 8252.8.10	Milner, A.M. The Milner papers...1897-1905. London, 1931-33. 2v.
Afr 8252.8.15	Walker, E.A. Lord Milner and South Africa. London, 1942.
Afr 8252.8.20	Crankshaw, E. The forsaken idea. London, 1952.
Afr 8252.8.25	Wrench, Evelyn. Alfred Lord Milner. London, 1958.
Afr 8252.9	Cox, G.W. Life of John William Colenso. London, 1888. 2v.
Afr 8252.9.5	Gray, R. A statement...in connexion with the consecration of the Right Rev. Dr. Colenso. London, 1867.
Afr 8252.9.10	Colenso, F.B. Colenso letters from Natal. Pietermaritzburg, 1958.
Afr 8252.9.15	Hinchliff, Peter Bingham. John William Colenso. London, 1964.
Afr 8252.9.20	Fraser, Barbara Davidson. John William Colenso. Cape Town, 1952.
Afr 8252.10	Martineau, John. The life and correspondence of Sir Bartle Frere. London, 1895. 2v.
Afr 8252.10.5	Worsfold, B. Sir Bartle Frere. London, 1923.
Afr 8252.11	Wilmot, Alex. The life and times of Sir Richard Southey. London, 1904.
Afr 8252.12	Durnford, E. A soldiers life and work in South Africa 1872-1879. London, 1882.
Afr 8252.13	Streatfeild, F.N. Reminiscences of an old 'un. London, 1911.
Afr 8252.14	Afrikaander. Amsterdam, 1883.
Afr 8252.14.10	Cronwright-Schreiner, S.C. Her South African ancestors. London, 1930.
Afr 8252.15	Millais, J.G. Life of Frederick Courtenay Selous. N.Y., 1919.
Afr 8252.16	Hofmeyr, Jan. The life of Jan Hendrik Hofmeyr. Cape Town, 1913.
Afr 8252.17	Ronan, B. Forty South African years. London, 1923.
Afr 8252.17.10	Kestell, J.D. Christiaan de wet'n lewensbeskrywing. Beperkt, 1920.
Afr 8252.18	Flemming, L. The call of the Veld. 2d. ed. London, 1924.
Afr 8252.19	Phillips, L. Some reminiscences. London, 1924.
Afr 8252.20	Walker, E.A. Lord de Villiers and his times. London, 1925.
Afr 8252.21	Sampson, Victor. My reminiscences. London, 1926.
Afr 8252.25	Buxton, Earl. General Botha. London, 1924.
Afr 8252.25.5	Engelenburg, Frans V. General Louis Botha. London, 1929.
Afr 8252.25.10	Clark, E.M. Louis Botha, a bibliography. Cape Town, 1956.
Afr 8252.30	Fraser, J. Episodes in my life. Cape Town, 1922.
Afr 8252.36	Harris, D. Pioneer, soldier and politician. London, 1931.
Afr 8252.37	Neame, L.E. General Hertzog, Prime Minister of the Union of South Africa since 1924. London, 1930.
Afr 8252.54	Laurence, P.M. The life of John Xavier Merriman. London, 1930.
Afr 8252.56	Fort, G.S. Alfred Beit. London, 1932.
Afr 8252.77	Rowbotham, A.F. Perilous moments, a true story. London, 1930.
Afr 8252.80	Fitzpatrick, J.P. South African memories. London, 1932.
Afr 8252.124	Wallis, J.P.R. Thomas Baines of Kings Lynn. London, 1941.
Afr 8252.144	Swart, Marius. Hendrik Teodor Buehrmann. Kaapstad, 1963.
Afr 8252.155	Binns, C.T. The last Zulu king. London, 1963.
Afr 8252.156	Long, B.K. Drummond chaplin. London, 1941.
Afr 8252.172	Rosenthal, Eric. General De Wet, a biography. Cape Town, 1946.
Afr 8252.172.2	Rosenthal, Eric. General De Wet; a biography. 2. ed. Cape Town, 1968.
Afr 8252.172.10	Wet, Izak J.C. de. Met general De Wet op kommando. Johannesburg, 1954.
Afr 8252.172.16.2	Schoor, Marthinus Cornelius Ellnarius van. Christiaan Rudolph de Wet, 1854-1922. 2. uitg. Bloemfontein, 1964.
Afr 8252.188.5	Preller, Gustav S. Talana, die drie generaals-slag. Kaapstad, 1942.
Afr 8252.194	Fairbridge, K. The autobiography of Kingsley Fairbridge. London, 1927.
Afr 8252.227	Harding, C. Far bugles. London, 1933.
Afr 8252.227.15	Halle, G. Mayfair to Maritzburg. London, 1933.
Afr 8252.228	Heever, Christiaan. General J.B.M. Hertzog. Johannesburg, 1946.
Afr 8252.228.2	Heever, Christiaan. General J.B.M. Hertzog. Johannesburg, 1943.
Afr 8252.228.5	Burger, M.J. General J.B.M. Hertzog in Batilio. Kaapstad, 1953.
Afr 8252.228.6	Burger, M.J. General J.B.M. Hertzog. Kaapstad, 1950.
Afr 8252.228.10	Pirow, Oswald. James Barry Munnik Hertzog. London, 1958.
Afr 8252.248	Johnson, F. Great days, the autobiography of an empire pioneer. London, 1940.
Afr 8252.251.5	Kotze, J.G. Biographical memoirs and reminiscences. v.1. Cape Town, 193-
Afr 8252.257	Huninsohn, Richard. Barney Barnato. 1st ed. N.Y., 1938.
Afr 8252.267.2	Thom, Hendrik Bernardus. Die lewe van Gert maritz. 2.druk. Kaapstad, 1965.
Afr 8252.322	Rainier, P.W. My vanished Africa. New Haven, 1940.
Afr 8252.323	Meintjes, Johannes. De la Rey, lion of the west, a biography. Johannesburg, 1966.
Afr 8252.326	Weinthal, Leo. Memories. London, 1929.

Afr 8252 South Africa in general - History by periods - British period (1814-1909) - The Dutch and their relations with the British during 1814-1899 - Political biographies - Individual - Others (A-Z, 299 scheme, by person)
cont.

	Afr 8252.335.5	Walker, E.A. W.P. Schreiner, a South African. London, 1937.
	Afr 8252.341.5	Millin, S.G.L. General Smuts. Boston, 1936.
	Afr 8252.341.10	Armstrong, H.C. Grey steel, J.C. Smuts, a study in arrogance. London, 1937.
	Afr 8252.341.15	Levi, N. Jan Smuts. London, 1917.
	Afr 8252.341.18	Smuts, J.C. The thoughts of General Smuts. Cape Town, 1951.
	Afr 8252.341.20	Crafford, F.S. Jan Smuts, a biography. 1st ed. N.Y., 1943.
	Afr 8252.341.21	Crafford, F. Jan Smuts, a biography. Garden City, 1944.
	Afr 8252.341.25A	Kraus, Rene. Old master, the life of Jan Christian Smuts. 1st ed. N.Y., 1944.
	Afr 8252.341.25B	Kraus, Rene. Old master, the life of Jan Christian Smuts. 1st ed. N.Y., 1944.
	Afr 8252.341.30	Kiernan, R.H. General Smuts. London, 1944.
	Afr 8252.341.35	Wilson, Dorothy F. Smuts of South Africa. London, 1946.
	Afr 8252.341.40	Burbidge, W. Frank. Field Marshal Smuts. Bognor Regis, 1943.
	Afr 8252.341.45	Smuts, J.C. Jan Christian Smuts. London, 1952.
	Afr 8252.341.47	Smuts, J.C. Jan Christian Smuts. N.Y., 1952.
	Afr 8252.341.48	Smuts, J.C. Selections from the Smuts papers. Cambridge, 1966.
	Afr 8252.341.50	Scott, J.A.S. Jan Christian Smuts. Cape Town, 1955.
	Afr 8252.341.60	Macdonald, Tom. Ouma Smuts. London, 1946.
	Afr 8252.341.65	Hancock, William Keith. The Smuts papers. London, 1956.
	Afr 8252.341.68	Lean, Phyllis Scannell. One man in his time. Johannesburg, 1964.
	Afr 8252.341.70	Smuts, J.C. Greater South Africa. Johannesburg, 1940.
	Afr 8252.341.75	Millin, S.G.L. General Smuts. London, 1936. 2v.
	Afr 8252.341.80A	Hancock, William Keith. Smuts. Cambridge, 1962. 2v.
	Afr 8252.341.80B	Hancock, William Keith. Smuts. Cambridge, 1962.
	Afr 8252.341.82	Hancock, William Keith. Smuts and the shift of world power. London, 1964.
	Afr 8252.341.83	Hancock, William Keith. Smuts; study for a portrait. London, 1965.
	Afr 8252.341.85	Mincher, Kathleen. I lived in his shadow. Capetown, 1965.
	Afr 8252.342.5	Smithers, E.D. March hare. London, 1935.
	Afr 8252.348	Struben, Charles. Vein of gold. Cape Town, 1957.
	Afr 8252.354	Bosman, J.D. Dr. George McCall theal as die geskiedskrywer van Suid-Afrika. Amsterdam, 1931.
	Afr 8252.354.20	Thompson, F.R. Matabele Thompson. London, 1936.
	Afr 8252.354.25	Thompson, F.R. Matabele Thompson. Johannesburg, 1953.

Afr 8277 South Africa in general - History by periods - British period (1814-1909) - The Dutch and their relations with the British during 1814-1899 - Causes leading up to War of 1899 - Pamphlet volumes

	Afr 8277.1	Pamphlet vol. Boer war. Causes. 7 pam.
	Afr 8277.2	Pamphlet vol. Boer war. Causes. 5 pam.
	Afr 8277.3	Pamphlet vol. Boer war. Causes. 60 pam.
	Afr 8277.4	Pamphlet vol. Boer war. 17 pam.
	Afr 8277.5	Pamphlet vol. Boer war. Causes. 9 pam.
	Afr 8277.6	Pamphlet box. Boer war. Causes.

Afr 8278 - 8280 South Africa in general - History by periods - British period (1814-1909) - The Dutch and their relations with the British during 1814-1899 - Causes leading up to War of 1899 - General works (By date)

	Afr 8278.96	Spruyt, C.B. Africaners en Nederlanders. Amsterdam, 1896.
	Afr 8278.96.3	Regan, W.F. Boer and Uitlander. London, 1896.
	Afr 8278.96.5	Withers, H. English and Dutch in South Africa. London, 1896.
	Afr 8278.97	Procter, John. Boers and little Englanders. London, 1897.
	Afr 8278.97.3	Hofmeyr, N.J. Die Buren und Jamesons Einfall. Bremen, 1897.
	Afr 8278.97.5	Jorissen, E.J.P. Transvaalische herinneringen 1876-96. Amsterdam, 1897.
	Afr 8278.98A	Younghusband, F.E. South Africa of to-day. London, 1898.
	Afr 8278.98B	Younghusband, F.E. South Africa of to-day. London, 1898.
	Afr 8278.98.3	Kotze, J.G. Documents relating to judicial crisis in Transvaal. London, 1898.
	Afr 8278.98.5	Duplessis, C.N.J. Uit de geschiedenis van de Zuid-Afrikanische Republiek en de afrikaanders. Amsterdam, 1898.
	Afr 8278.99F	Schreiner, Olive. An English-South African's view of the situation. London, 1899.
	Afr 8278.99.03	Schreiner, Olive. An English-South African's view of the situation. London, 1899.
	Afr 8278.99.1	Fitzpatrick, J.P. The Transvaal from within. N.Y., 1899.
X Cg	Afr 8278.99.2	Fitzpatrick, J.P. The Transvaal from within. London, 1900.
	Afr 8278.99.3A	Fitzpatrick, J.P. The Transvaal from within. London, 1899.
	Afr 8278.99.3B	Fitzpatrick, J.P. The Transvaal from within. London, 1899.
X Cg	Afr 8278.99.4	Fitzpatrick, J.P. The Transvaal from within. London, 1900.
	Afr 8278.99.4.5A	Fitzpatrick, J.P. The Transvaal from within. N.Y., 1900.
	Afr 8278.99.4.5B	Fitzpatrick, J.P. The Transvaal from within. N.Y., 1900.
	Afr 8278.99.5	Phillips, F. Some South African recollections. London, 1899.
	Afr 8278.99.7	Stead, W.T. Shall I slay my brother Boer. London, 1899.
	Afr 8278.99.9	Martineau, J. The Transvaal trouble. London, 1899.
	Afr 8278.99.11	Duplessis, C.N.J. The Transvaal Boer speaking for himself. London, 1899.
	Afr 8278.99.13	Hillegas, H.C. Oom Paul's people. N.Y., 1899.
	Afr 8278.99.15	Wilkinson, S. British policy in South Africa. London, 1899.
	Afr 8278.99.17	Meysey-Thompson, H. The Transvaal crisis. London, 1899.
	Afr 8278.99.19	Bigger, E.B. The Boer war, its causes. Toronto, 1899.
	Afr 8278.99.21F	Hollandia, special Transvaal number. The Hague, 1899.
	Afr 8278.99.23	Demolins, E. Boers et Anglais. Paris, 1899.
	Afr 8278.99.25	Morning leader leaflets. v.1- London, 1899-1900.
	Afr 8278.99.27	Appleton, L. Britain and the Boers. London, 1899.

Afr 8278 - 8280 South Africa in general - History by periods - British period (1814-1909) - The Dutch and their relations with the British during 1814-1899 - Causes leading up to War of 1899 - General works (By date)
cont.

	Afr 8278.99.29	Schreiner, Olive. The South African question. Chicago, 1899.
	Afr 8278.99.33	Leyds, W.J. Eenige correspondentie uit 1899. 2e druk. Amsterdam, 1938.
	Afr 8278.99.35	Leyds, W.J. Tweede verzameling (Correspondentie 1899-1900 . v.1-2. Dordrecht, 1930. 3v.
	Afr 8278.99.36	Leyds, W.J. Derde verzameling. Deel 1-21. Dordrecht, 1931.
	Afr 8278.99.37	Leyds, W.J. Vierde verzameling (Correspondentie 1900-1902 . Deel 1-2. 's-Gravenhage, 1934. 3v.
	Afr 8278.99.45	Engelenburg, F.V. A Transvaal view of the South African question. Pretoria, 1899.
	Afr 8278.99.50	Britain and the Boers. Both sides of the South African question. v.2. N.Y., 1899-1900.
	Afr 8278.101	Vulliamy, C.E. Outlanders, a study of imperial expansion in South Africa, 1877-1902. London, 1938.
	Afr 8279.00A	Bryce, J. Briton and Boer. N.Y., 1900.
	Afr 8279.00B	Bryce, J. Briton and Boer. N.Y., 1900.
	Afr 8279.00.2	Bryce, J. Briton and Boer. New ed. N.Y., 1900.
	Afr 8279.00.3	Ireland, A. The Anglo-Boer conflict. Boston, 1900.
	Afr 8279.00.5	MacVane, S.M. The South African question. Boston, 1900.
	Afr 8279.00.7	Vanderhoogt, C.V. The story of the Boers. N.Y., 1900.
	Afr 8279.00.9	Hammond, J.H. The Transvaal trouble. N.Y., 1900.
	Afr 8279.00.11	Scoble, J. The rise and fall of Krugerism. London, 1900.
	Afr 8279.00.13	Bell, F.W. The South African conspiracy. London, 1900.
	Afr 8279.00.15	Kuyper, A. La crise sud-africaine. Paris, 1900.
	Afr 8279.00.17	Droit des Anglais dans la guerre de Transvaal. Genève, 1900.
	Afr 8279.00.19	Stead, W.J. The candidates of Cain. London, 1900.
	Afr 8279.00.21	Farrelly, M.J. The settlement after the war. London, 1900.
	Afr 8279.00.23	Cecil, Evelyn. On the eve of the war. London, 1900.
	Afr 8279.00.25	Guyot, Yves. Boer politics. London, 1900.
	Afr 8279.00.26	Boissevain, Charles. The struggle of the Dutch republics, open letter to an American lady. Amsterdam, 1900.
	Afr 8279.00.27	Buttery, J.A. Why Kruger made war. London, 1900.
	Afr 8279.00.29	Zuid-afrikaansche vlugschriften. Dordrecht. 1,1899+
	Afr 8279.00.31	Wormser, J.A. De oorlog in Zuid-Afrika. Amsterdam, 1900.
	Afr 8279.00.32	Hobson, J.A. The war in South Africa. London, 1900.
	Afr 8279.00.33	Hobson, J.A. The war in South Africa. N.Y., 1900.
	Afr 8279.00.33.1	Hobson, J.A. The war in South Africa. N.Y., 1969.
	Afr 8279.00.34	Hobson, J.A. The war in South Africa. London, 1900.
	Afr 8279.00.35	Hillier, A.P. South African studies. London, 1900.
	Afr 8279.00.37F	Achilles, Kort. Aanleiding tot den engelsch-transvaal oorlog. 's-Gravenhage, n.d.
	Afr 8279.00.39	Thomas, C.H. Origin of the Anglo-Boer war revealed. London, 1900.
Htn	Afr 8279.00.41*	Reitz, Francois W. A century of wrong. London, 1900.
	Afr 8279.00.44	Eisenhart, Karl. Die Abrechnung mit England. 2. Aufl. München, 1900.
	Afr 8279.00.47	Volkonskii, G.M. Pour les Boers contre l'impérialisme. Genève, 1900.
	Afr 8279.00.52	Clark, G.B. The official correspondence between the governments of Great Britain, the South African Republic. London, 1900.
	Afr 8279.00.54	Hooker, Leroy. The Africanders, a century of Dutch-English feud in South Africa. Chicago, 1900.
	Afr 8279.00.56	Naville, Edouard. L'indépendance des républiques sud-africaines et l'Angleterre. Genève, 1900.
	Afr 8279.01	Davis, W. John Bull's crime. N.Y., 1901.
	Afr 8279.01.2	Methuen, A.M.M. Peace or war in South Africa. 4th ed. London, 1901.
	Afr 8279.01.3	Methuen, A.M.M. Peace or war in South Africa. London, 1901.
	Afr 8279.01.4	Methuen, A.M.M. Peace or war in South Africa. London, 1901.
	Afr 8279.01.5F	Great Britain. Report on the Transvaal Concession Commission. London, 1901.
	Afr 8279.01.8	Cook, Edward T. Rights and wrongs of the Transvaal war. London, 1902.
	Afr 8279.01.15	Bellows, J. The truth about the Transvaal war and the truth about war. 2d. ed. London, 1901.
	Afr 8279.01.20	Elout, Cornelis. Der Kulturkampf in Süd Afrika. Leipzig, 1901.
	Afr 8279.02	Smith, Goldwin. In the court of history. Toronto, 1902.
	Afr 8279.02.5	Smith, Goldwin. Devant le tribunal de l'histoire. Montreal, 1903.
	Afr 8279.40.5A	Vroom, E. The hapless Boers. Scotch Plains, N.J., 1940.
	Afr 8279.40.5B	Vroom, E. The hapless Boers. Scotch Plains, N.J., 1940.
	Afr 8279.48	Scholtz, Gert D. Die oorsake van die tweede vryheids-oorlog. Johannesburg, 1948-49. 2v.
	Afr 8279.61	Marais, Johannes. The fall of Kruger's republic. Oxford, 1961.

Afr 8283 South Africa in general - History by periods - British period (1814-1909) - The Dutch and their relations with the British during 1814-1899 - Causes leading up to War of 1899 - Jameson Raid (Dec. 29-Jan. 2, 1895-1896) and Johannesburg Revolt (1896)

Htn	Afr 8283.1*	Pamphlet box. South Africa. Jameson raid.
	Afr 8283.5F	South Africa. Stukken betrekking hebbende op den inval van de troepen der British South Africa Company. Pretoria, 1896.
	Afr 8283.6F	Great Britain. Colonial Office. Correspondence related to South Africa Republic. London, 1896.
	Afr 8283.7	Mann, A.M. The truth from Johannesburg. London, 1897.
	Afr 8283.8	Stead, W.J. The scandal of the South African committee. London, 1899.
	Afr 8283.8.5	Stead, W.J. Joseph Chamberlain, conspirator of statesman. London, 1900.
	Afr 8283.9.2	Davis, R.H. Dr. Jameson's raiders. N.Y., 1897.
	Afr 8283.10	Hammond, J.H. A woman's part in a revolution. N.Y., 1897.
	Afr 8283.11	Garrett, Fydell Edmund. The story of an African crisis. Westminster, 1897.
	Afr 8283.12	Terrail, G. Le Transvaal et la chartered. Paris, 1897.
	Afr 8283.13	Hillier, A.P. Raid and reform. London, 1898.
	Afr 8283.14	Thomas, C.G. Johannesburg in arms, 1895-96. London, 1896.
	Afr 8283.15A	Hammond, J.H. The truth about the Jameson raid. Boston, 1918.

Afr 8283   South Africa in general - History by periods - British period (1814-1909) - The Dutch and their relations with the British during 1814-1899 - Causes leading up to War of 1899 - Jameson Raid (Dec. 29-Jan. 2, 1895-1896) and Johannesburg Revolt (1896) cont.

Afr 8283.15B	Hammond, J.H. The truth about the Jameson raid. Boston, 1918.
Afr 8283.16	Hofmeyr, N.J. De Afrikaner-Boer en de Jameson-inval. Kaapstad, 1896.
Afr 8283.17	King, James. Dr. Jameson's raid. London, 1896.
Afr 8283.18	Fort, G. Seymour. Dr. Jameson. London, 1918.
Afr 8283.19	Colvin, Ian D. The life of Jameson. London, 1922. 2v.
Afr 8283.20	Hale, Hugh M. The Jameson raid. London, 1930.
Afr 8283.21	Van der Poel, Jean. The Jameson raid. Cape Town, 1951.
Afr 8283.22	Jameson's heroic charge. Johannesburg, 1896.
Afr 8283.23	Pakenham, E.H.P. Jameson's raid. London, 1960.
Afr 8283.24	Moggridge, Ann. The Jameson raid. Cape Town, 1960.
Afr 8283.25F	Cape of Good Hope. Parliament. House of Commons. Report of the Select Committee of the Cape of Good Hope. London, 1897.
Afr 8283.26F	Great Britain. Parliament. House of Commons. Second report. London, 1897.
Afr 8283.28	Butler, Jeffrey. The Liberal Party and the Jameson Raid. Oxford, 1968.

Afr 8285   South Africa in general - History by periods - British period (1814-1909) - The Dutch and their relations with the British during 1814-1899 - Causes leading up to War of 1899 - Later developments (1896-1899)

Afr 8285.5F	Great Britain. Foreign Office. Further correspondence relating to political affairs in the South African Republic. London, 1899.
Afr 8285.10	Alderson, E.A.H. With the mounted infantry and the Mashona-landfield force, 1896. London, 1898.
Afr 8285.15	Barthold, U. Studien zur englischen Vorbereitung des Burenkriegs. Inaug. Diss. Köln, 1936.
Afr 8285.20	Kieser, A. President Steijn in die krisesjare. Kaapstad, 1951.
Afr 8285.20.5	Rompel, Frederik. Marthinus Theunis Steijn. Amsterdam, 1902.
Afr 8285.20.10	Merwe, N.J. Marthinus Theunis Steijn. Kaapstad, 1921. 2v.

Afr 8288 - 8290   South Africa in general - History by periods - South African War (1899-1902) - General works (By date)

Afr 8288.1	Pamphlet vol. The Boer war. 26 pam.
Afr 8288.2	Pamphlet vol. The Boer war. 12 pam.
Afr 8288.3	Pamphlet box. South African war, 1899-1902.
Afr 8288.4F	Pamphlet vol. South African war, 1899-1902. 9 pam.
Afr 8288.99F	Buitengewone staat-courant 1899-00. Pretoria, 1899-00.
Htn Afr 8288.99.3F*	Scrapbook of miscellaneous cuttings, but largely concerned with affairs of South Africa, 1899-1900. n.p., n.d.
Afr 8288.99.4F	Great Britain. Colonial Office. South African Republic. Correspondence. London, 1899-03.
Afr 8288.99.5F	Great Britain. Colonial Office. South African Republic. Correspondence. London, 1899-03.
Afr 8288.99.6F	Great Britain. Colonial Office. South African Republic. Correspondence. London, 1899-03.
Afr 8288.99.7F	Great Britain. Commissions. South African War. Report...war in South Africa. London, 1903.
Afr 8288.99.9F	Great Britain. Commissions. South African War. Minutes of evidence on war in South Africa. London, 1903. 2v.
Afr 8288.99.10F	Great Britain. Commissions. South African War. Appendices evidence on war in South Africa. London, 1903.
Afr 8288.99.11F	Pamphlet vol. South African war, 1899-1902. 18 pam.
Afr 8288.99.12F	Pamphlet vol. South African war, 1899-1902. 18 pam.
Afr 8288.99.13F	Pamphlet vol. South Africa. Military despatches, 1900-02. 25 pam.
Afr 8288.99.14F	Pamphlet vol. South African war, 1899-1902. 11 pam.
Afr 8288.99.15F	Great Britain. War Department. True history of the war, official despatches. v.1-5. London, 1900.
Afr 8288.99.18	War against war in South Africa. London, 1899-00.
Afr 8288.99.20	Penning, L. De oorlog in Zuid-Afrika. Rotterdam, 1899-03. 3v.
NEDL Afr 8288.99.23	Birch, J.H. History of the war in South Africa. London, Ont., 1899.
Afr 8288.99.25	Harding, William. War in South Africa and the dark continent from savagery to civilization. Chicago, 1899.
Afr 8289.00A	Times, London. The Times history of the war in South Africa. London, 1900-6. 7v.
Afr 8289.00B	Times, London. The Times history of the war in South Africa. London, 1900-6. 7v.
Afr 8289.00.3	Absent minded war. London, 1900.
Afr 8289.00.5	Hillegas, H.C. The Boers in war. N.Y., 1900.
Afr 8289.00.7	Davis, R.H. With both armies in South Africa. N.Y., 1900.
Afr 8289.00.9	Wilkinson, S. Lessons of the war. Westminster, 1900.
Afr 8289.00.11	Mahan, A.T. Story of the war in South Africa. London, 1900.
Afr 8289.00.13	Rosslyn, James. Twice captured. Edinburg, 1900.
Afr 8289.00.15	Doyle, A.C. The great Boer war. London, 1900.
Afr 8289.00.19A	Doyle, A.C. The great Boer war. N.Y., 1902.
Afr 8289.00.19B	Doyle, A.C. The great Boer war. N.Y., 1902.
Afr 8289.00.19.5	Doyle, A.C. The great Boer war. London, 1903.
Afr 8289.00.20	Creswicke, L. South Africa and the Transvaal war. London, n.d. 4v.
Afr 8289.00.21	Childers, E. In the ranks of the C.I.V. London, 1901.
Afr 8289.00.24F	Wilson, H.W. With the flag to Pretoria, history, Boer war 1899-1900. London, 1900-01. 2v.
Afr 8289.00.25F	Wilson, H.W. After Pretoria, the guerilla war. London, 1902. 2v.
Afr 8289.00.28F	Edwards Dennis and Co. The Anglo-Boer war 1899-1900, an album. Cape Town, 190-
Afr 8289.00.30	Johnson, H. With our soldiers at the front. London, 1907.
Afr 8289.00.35F	Kepper, G.L. De zuid-afrikaansche oorlog. Leiden, 1900.

Afr 8288 - 8290   South Africa in general - History by periods - South African War (1899-1902) - General works (By date) cont.

Afr 8289.00.38	Peinlich, Fuerchtgots. Gedanken und Erinnerungen an den Krieg Englands gegen die Burenstaaten. Berlin, 1900.
Afr 8289.00.40	Hales, A.G. Campaign pictures of the war in South Afrique (1899-1900). London, 1900.
Afr 8289.00.42	Stickney, Albert. The Transvaal outlook. N.Y., 1900.
Afr 8289.00.47	Mueller, A. von. Der Krieg in Süd-afrika, 1899-1900. v.1-5. Berlin, 1900.
Afr 8289.00.50	Kings handbook of the war. London, 1900.
Afr 8289.00.52	Hudleston, W.H. The war in South Africa, 1899-1900. London, 1900.
Afr 8289.00.55F	South African War. Scrapbook of newspaper clippings, chiefly maps, of campaigns in the South African War, Jan. 7, 1900 - June 10, 1900. n.p., n.d.
NEDL Afr 8289.01	Boer version of the Transvaal war. London, 1901.
Afr 8289.01.3	Wisser, J.P. The second Boer war 1899-1900. Kansas City, 1901. 2v.
Afr 8289.01.5	Sternberg, A. My experiences of the Boer war. London, 1901. 2v.
Afr 8289.01.7	Bujac, E. Precis de...campagnes contemporaines d'Afrique centrale. Paris, 1901.
Afr 8289.01.8	Villebois Mareuil. War notes, diary. London, 1901.
Afr 8289.01.9	Villebois Mareuil. Dix mois de campagne chez les Boers. Paris, 1901.
Afr 8289.01.10	Warmelo, D.S. Mijn commando en guerilla commando-leven. Amsterdam, 1901.
Afr 8289.01.10.5	Warmelo, D.S. On commando. London, 1902.
Afr 8289.01.11	Mempes, M. War impressions. London, n.d.
Afr 8289.01.14	Dickson, W.K.L. The biograph in battle. London, 1901.
Afr 8289.01.17	Ogden, H.J. The war against the Dutch republics in South Africa. Manchester, 1901.
Afr 8289.01.20	Brooke-Hunt, V. A woman's memories of the war in South Africa. London, 1901.
Afr 8289.01.23	Rolleston, Maud. Yeoman service. London, 1901.
Afr 8289.01.25	Fremantle, F.E. Impressions of a doctor in Khaki. London, 1901.
Afr 8289.01.27	Rose-Innes, C. With Paget's horse to the front. London, 1901.
Afr 8289.01.29	Wallace, E. Unofficial dispatches. London, 1901.
Afr 8289.01.31	Maydon, J.G. French's calvary campaign. 2d ed. London, 1902.
Afr 8289.01.33	Ross, P.T. A yeoman's letters. London, 1901.
Afr 8289.01.35F	Veber, Jean. Die boeren-kampen. Amsterdam, 1901.
Afr 8289.01.37	Mueller, Alfred von. Kritische Betrachtungen über den Burenkrieg. Berlin, 1901.
Afr 8289.01.39	Robertson, J.M. Wrecking the empire. London, 1901.
Afr 8289.01.42	Premier livre de l'épopée boer. Paris, 1901.
Afr 8289.02	Roany, J.H. La guerre anglo-boer. Paris, 1902.
Afr 8289.02.3	Pienaar, P. With Steijn and De Wet. London, 1902.
Afr 8289.02.6	Phillipps, L.M. With Rimmington. London, 1902.
Afr 8289.02.8	Davitt, Michael. The Boer fight for freedom. N.Y., 1902.
Afr 8289.02.10	Hiley, Alan R.I. The mobile Boer. N.Y., 1902.
Afr 8289.02.12A	Dewet, C.R. Three years war. N.Y., 1902.
Afr 8289.02.12B	Dewet, C.R. Three years war. N.Y., 1902.
Afr 8289.02.14	Fournier, P.V. La guerre sud-africaine. Paris, 1902. 3v.
Afr 8289.02.16	Gilbert, G. La guerre sud-africaine. Paris, 1902.
Afr 8289.02.18A	Doyle, A.C. The war in South Africa. London, 1902.
Afr 8289.02.18B	Doyle, A.C. The war in South Africa. London, 1902.
Afr 8289.02.20	Louter, Jan de. La guerre sud-africaine. Bruxelles, 1902.
Afr 8289.02.21	Goldmann, C.S. With General French and the cavalry in Africa. London, 1902.
Afr 8289.02.22	Viljoen, B.J. Mijne herinneringen...anglo-boeren-oorlog. Amsterdam, 1902.
Afr 8289.02.22.2	Viljoen, B.J. My reminiscences of Anglo-Boer war. London, 1902.
Afr 8289.02.23	Kestell, J.D. Met de boeren-commandos. Amsterdam, 1902.
Afr 8289.02.24	Everdingen, W. De oorlog in Zuid-Afrika. Delft, 1902.
Afr 8289.02.27	Rompel, F. Präsident Steijn. München, 1902.
Afr 8289.02.28	Schowalter, A. Die Buren in der Kap Kolonie im Kriege mit England. München, 1902.
Afr 8289.02.29	Villebois-Mareuil. Carnet de campagne. Paris, 1902.
Afr 8289.02.32	Milne, J. The epistles of Atkins. London, 1902.
Afr 8289.02.35	Raoul-Duval, R. Au Transvaal, et dans le Sud-Afrique avec les attachés militaires. Paris, 1902.
Afr 8289.02.37	Thomson, Ada. Memorials of C.D. Kimber. London, 1902.
Afr 8289.02.39	Klinck-Luetetsburg, F. Christian de Wet, de held van Zuid-Afrika. Zutphen, 1902.
Afr 8289.02.45	Stevens, F.T. Complete history of the South African war in 1899-1902. London, 1902.
Afr 8289.03	Loren van Thernaat, H. Twee jaren in de Boerenoorlog. Haarlem, 1902.
Afr 8289.03.2	Vallentin, W. Der burenkrieg. Wald-Solingen, 1903. 2v.
Afr 8289.03.4	Lynch, G. Impressions of a war correspondent. London, 1903.
Afr 8289.03.7	Stirling, J. Our regiments in South Africa, 1899-1902. Edinburgh, 1913.
Afr 8289.03.9	Crowe, George. Commission of H.M.S. Terrible. London, 1903.
Afr 8289.03.12	Saint Leger, S.E. War sketches in colour. London, 1903.
Afr 8289.03.15	Kestell, J.D. Through shot and flame. London, 1903.
Afr 8289.03.20	Blake, J.Y.D. A West Pointer with the Boers. Boston, 1903.
Afr 8289.04	Prussia-Grosser. The war in South Africa. London, 1904. 2v.
Afr 8289.04.5	Prussia. Grosser Generalstab. Kriegsgeschichtliche Abteilung. The war in South Africa. N.Y., 1969.
Afr 8289.06	Maurice, F. History of the war in South Africa 1899-02. v.1-4. London, 1906. 8v.
Afr 8289.07	Larey, M. de. Herinneringen. Amsterdam, 1907.
Afr 8289.09	Wilson, S. South African memories. London, 1909.
Afr 8289.13	Jackson, M.C. A soldier's diary, South Africa 1899-1901. London, 1913.
Afr 8289.14	Miller, David S. A captain of the Gordon's Service experience. London, 1914.
Afr 8289.14.2	Miller, David S. A captain of the Gordon's Service experience. London, 1914.
Afr 8289.29	Reitz, Deneys. Commando. London, 1929.
Afr 8289.29.3	Reitz, Deneys. Commando. N.Y., 1930.
Afr 8289.29.4	Reitz, Deneys. Commando. London, 1933.
Afr 8289.29.5	Reitz, Deneys. La guerre des Boers. Paris, 1930.

160

Afr 8325 South Africa in general - History by periods - South African War (1899-1902) - Other special cont.

Htn Afr 8325.35.10* Pamphlet vol. A collection of forty-one stereopticon views of the Boer war.
Afr 8325.36 Haldane, A. How we escaped from Pretoria. Edinburg, 1901.
Afr 8325.37F Thoma, Ludwig. Der Burenkrieg. München, 1900.
Afr 8325.38 Swinton, Ernest. The defence of Duffer's Drift. London, 1911.
Afr 8325.40 Treves, Frederick. The tale of a field hospital. London, 1900.
Afr 8325.45 Pilcher, T.D. Some lessons from the Boer War. London, 1903.
Afr 8325.50 Evans, W.S. The Canadian contingents and Canadian imperialism. Toronto, 1901.
Afr 8325.52F Royal Engineering Institute, Chatham. Detailed history of railways in South African War. Chatham, 1904. 2v.
Afr 8325.55 Burdett-Coretts, W. The sick and wounded in South Africa. London, 1900.
Afr 8325.56 Bennett, E.N. With Methuen's column on an ambulance train. London, 1900.
Afr 8325.58F Transvaal war album, the British forces in South Africa. London, 190-.
Afr 8325.60 Cleaver, M.M. A young South African. Johannesburg, 1913.
Afr 8325.62 American Hospital Ship Fund for South Africa. The concert. Souvenir programme. n.p., n.d.
Afr 8325.64 Notes on reconnoitering in South Africa. Boer War, 1899-1900. London, 1901.
Afr 8325.66 Preller, G.S. Ons parool. 2. druk. Kaapstad, 1943.
Afr 8325.66.5 Preller, G.S. Kaptein Hindon. 2nd ed. Kaapstad, 1921.
Afr 8325.68.5 Mostert, D. Slegtkamp van Spioenkap. 2. druk. Kaapstad, 1938.
Afr 8325.68.10 Ransford, Oliver. The battle of Spion Kop. London, 1969.
Afr 8325.70 Kotzé, C.R. My bollingskap (St. Helena). Bloemfontein, 1942.
Afr 8325.75 Hillegas, H.C. With the Boer forces. London, 1900.

Afr 8330 South Africa in general - History by periods - South African War (1899-1902) - Peace terms

Afr 8330.5 Kestell, J.D. De vredesonderhandelingen. Pretoria, 1909.

Afr 8331 South Africa in general - History by periods - Union of South Africa (Commonwealth, 1909-1961) - Bibliographies

Afr 8331.10 Hutton, James. The constitution of the Union of South Africa. Cape Town, 1946.
Afr 8331.15 Hodge, Gillian M.M. South African politics, 1933-1939. Cape Town, 1955.
Afr 8331.20F Johannesburg. Public Library. Southern African municipal publications. Johannesburg, 1965.

Afr 8333 South Africa in general - History by periods - Union of South Africa (Commonwealth, 1909-1961) - Collected source materials

Afr 8333.6 South Africa. Parliament. House of Assembly. Index to the manuscript annexures and printed papers. Cape Town, 1963.

Afr 8335 South Africa in general - History by periods - Union of South Africa (Commonwealth, 1909-1961) - General works

Afr 8335.2 Mansergh, N. South Africa, 1906-1961. N.Y., 1962.
Afr 8335.5 Vatcher, William Henry. White laager. London, 1965.
Afr 8335.8F Halfeen van afrikaner-prestasie, 1900-1950. Johannesburg, 1950.
Afr 8335.10 Ballinger, Margaret Livingstone. From union to apartheid; a trek to isolation. Bailey, 1969.

Afr 8338.101 - .399 South Africa in general - History by periods - Union of South Africa (Commonwealth, 1909-1961) - Political biographies - Individual (A-Z, 299 scheme, by person)

Afr 8338.230 Paton, Alan. South African tragedy. N.Y., 1965.
Afr 8338.230.5 Paton, Alan. Hofmeyr. London, 1964.
Afr 8338.284 Hopkins, Henry Charles. Maar één soos hy. Kaapstad, 1963.
Afr 8338.326 Kock, Willem J. de. Jacob de Villiers Roos, 1869-1940. Kaapstad, 1958.

Afr 8340 South Africa in general - History by periods - Union of South Africa (Commonwealth, 1909-1961) - Special periods, etc. - Reconstruction and early years, 1902-1913

Afr 8340.3 Walton, E.H. The inner history of the national convention of South Africa. Cape Town, 1912.
Afr 8340.3.5 Newton, A.P. Select documents relating to the unification of South Africa. London, 1924. 2v.
Afr 8340.4F Pamphlet vol. South Africa, 1903. 7 pam.
Afr 8340.4.3F Great Britain. Papers on finances of Transvaal and Orange River colony. London, 1903.
Afr 8340.4.5F Great Britain. Papers on criminal procedure code of the Transvaal. London, 1903.
Afr 8340.5 Buchan, J. The African colony. Edinburgh, 1903.
Afr 8340.6 Letters from an uitlander, 1899-02. London, 1903.
Afr 8340.7 Bleloch, W. The new South Africa. N.Y., 1901.
Afr 8340.8 Fremantle, H.E.S. The new nation. A survey of the condition and prospects of South Africa. London, 1909.
Afr 8340.9A Brand, R.H. The Union of South Africa. Oxford, 1909.
Afr 8340.9B Brand, R.H. The Union of South Africa. Oxford, 1909.
Afr 8340.11 Dormer, F.J. Vengeance as a policy in Afrikanderland. London, 1901.
Afr 8340.12A Phillips, Lionel. Transvaal problems. London, 1905.
Afr 8340.12B Phillips, Lionel. Transvaal problems. London, 1905.
Afr 8340.14 Spender, H. General Botha, the career and the man. London, 1916.
Afr 8340.14.2A Spender, H. General Botha, the career and the man. Boston, 1916.
Afr 8340.14.2B Spender, H. General Botha, the career and the man. Boston, 1916.
Afr 8340.15 Plaatje, S.T. Native life in South Africa. London, 1916.
Afr 8340.18.5 Selborne, W.W.P. The Selborne memorandum. London, 1925.
Afr 8340.20F Great Britain. Commission. War Stores in South Africa. Report of the Royal Commission on War Stores in South Africa. London, 1906.
Afr 8340.25 Pyrah, G.B. Imperial policy and South Africa, 1902-10. Oxford, 1955.
Afr 8340.30 Thompson, Leonard. The unification of South Africa. Oxford, 1960.
Afr 8340.40 Mukherji, S.B. Indian minority in South Africa. New Delhi, 1959.

Afr 8350 South Africa in general - History by periods - Union of South Africa (Commonwealth, 1909-1961) - Special periods, etc. - Chinese question

Afr 8350.5 Payne, E.G. An experiment in alien labor. Chicago, 1912.
Afr 8350.25 Kuper, Leo. Passive resistance in South Africa. London, 1956.
Afr 8350.30 Markham, Violet Rosa. The new era in South Africa. London, 1904.

Afr 8355 South Africa in general - History by periods - Union of South Africa (Commonwealth, 1909-1961) - Special periods, etc. - Indian question

Afr 8355.10 Doke, Joseph J. An Indian patriot in South Africa. London, 1909.
Afr 8355.20 Gandhi, Mohandas K. Satyagraha in South Africa. Madras, 1928.
Afr 8355.20.5A Gandhi, Mohandas K. Satyagraha in South Africa. 2. ed. Ahmedabad, 1950.
Afr 8355.20.5B Gandhi, Mohandas K. Satyagraha in South Africa. 2. ed. Ahmedabad, 1950.
Afr 8355.30 Ferguson-Davie, C.J. The early history of Indians in Natal. Johannesburg, 1957.
Afr 8355.35 South African Institute of Race Relations. The Indian as a South African. Johannesburg, 1956.
Afr 8355.40 Mukherji, S.B. Indian minority in South Africa. New Delhi, 1959.
Afr 8355.42 Currie, J.C. A bibliography of material published during the period 1946-56. Cape Town, 1957.
Afr 8355.45 Shastitko, P.M. Sto let bespraviia. Moscow, 1963.

Afr 8360 South Africa in general - History by periods - Union of South Africa (Commonwealth, 1909-1961) - Special periods, etc. - 1914-1919

Afr 8360.01 Pamphlet box. South Africa. Insurrection of 1914.
Afr 8360.5 Sampson, P.J. The capture of De Wet. The South African rebellion, 1914. London, 1915.
Afr 8360.6F South Africa. Report on the outbreak of the rebellion. Pretoria, 1915.
Afr 8360.7.89 Standaert, E.H.G. A Belgian mission to the Boers. London, 1917.
Afr 8360.8 Standaert, E.H.G. A Belgian mission to the Boers. N.Y., 1917.
Afr 8360.10 Scholtz, G.D. Die rebellie, 1914-15. Johannesburg, 1942.
Afr 8360.11 Quinn, Gerald D. The rebellion of 1914-15, a bibliography. Cape Town, 1957.

Afr 8369 South Africa in general - History by periods - Union of South Africa (Commonwealth, 1909-1961) - Special periods, etc. - 1919-1961 (By date)

Afr 8369.38 Webster, W.A. Real union in South Africa. Cape Town, 1938.
Afr 8369.42.1 Smuts, J.C. Investing in friendship. London, 1942.
Afr 8369.42.2 Smuts, J.C. Plans for a better world. London, 1942.
Afr 8369.42.10A Smuts, J.C. Toward a better world. N.Y., 1944.
Afr 8369.42.10B Smuts, J.C. Toward a better world. N.Y., 1944.
Afr 8369.42.20 Malherbe, D.Y. Afrikaner-volkseeheid. Bloemfontein, 1942.
Afr 8369.43 Sowden, L. The Union of South Africa. Garden City, N.Y., 1943.
Afr 8369.43.7 Campbell, Alex. Smuts and swastika. London, 1943.
Afr 8369.43.15 Reitz, Deneys. No outspan. London, 1943.
Afr 8369.43.20 Sowden, Lewis. The South African Union. London, 1945.
Afr 8369.44 Coulter, C.W.A. Empire unity. Cape Town, 1944.
Afr 8369.44.5 South African affairs pamphlets. Johannesburg.
Afr 8369.45 Long, Basil K. In Smuts's camp. London, 1945.
Afr 8369.47.2 Keppel-Jones, A.M. When Smuts goes. London, 1947.
Afr 8369.47.5 Roberts, Michael. The South African opposition, 1939-1945. London, 1947.
Afr 8369.52 Sachs, E.S. The choice before South Africa. London, 1952.
Afr 8369.53 Joekoms, Jan. When Malan goes. Johannesburg, 1953.
Afr 8369.53.5 Goosen, D.P. Die triomf van nasionalisme in Suid-Afrika, 1910-1953. Johannesburg, 1953.
Afr 8369.54 Saint John, Robert. Through Malan's Africa. London, 1954.
Afr 8369.54.5 United Party, South Africa. The native policy of the United Party. Johannesburg, 1955.
Afr 8369.56 Bate, H.M. South Africa without prejudice. London, 1956.
Afr 8369.57 Robertson, H.M. South Africa. Durham, N.C., 1957.
Afr 8369.58 Carter, G.M. The politics of inequality. N.Y., 1958.
Afr 8369.58.3 Carter, G.M. The politics of inequality, South Africa since 1948. 3rd ed. London, 1962.
Afr 8369.58.5 Forman, Lionel. The South African treason trial. N.Y., 1958.
Afr 8369.58.10A Sampson, Anthony. The treason cage. London, 1958.
Afr 8369.58.10B Sampson, Anthony. The treason cage. London, 1958.
Afr 8369.58.15 Paver, Bertram G. His own oppressor. London, 1958.
Afr 8369.60 Barlow, A.G. That we may tread safely. Cape Town, 1960.
Afr 8369.60.5 Holm, Erik. Erik Holm, man en standpunt. Potgietersrus, 1960.
Afr 8369.61A Calvocoressi, P. South Africa and world opinion. London, 1961.
Afr 8369.61B Calvocoressi, P. South Africa and world opinion. London, 1961.
Afr 8369.61.5 Broughton, M. Press and politics of South Africa. Cape Town, 1961.
Afr 8369.61.10 Sachs, Bernard. The road from Sharpeville. London, 1961.
Afr 8369.61.15 Natal Convention. University of Natal. Proceedings. Natal, 1961.
Afr 8369.61.20 Malan, Daniel François. Afrikaner-volkseenheid en my ervarings op die pad daarheen. 3. druk. Kaapstad, 1961.
Afr 8369.63 Joseph, Helen. If this be treason. London, 1963.
Afr 8369.64 Bunting, B.P. The rise of the South African Reich. Harmondsworth, 1964.
Afr 8369.64.1 Bunting, B.P. The rise of the South African Reich. Harmondsworth, 1969.
Afr 8369.65 Karis, Thomas. The treason trial in South Africa. Stanford, Calif., 1965.
Afr 8369.65.5 Dawie (pseud.). Dawie, 1946-1964; 'n bloemlesing uit die geskrifte van Die Burger se politieke kommentator. Kaapstad, 1965.

Afr 8371 South Africa in general - History by periods - Republic of South Africa (Independent, 1961-) - Bibliographies

Afr 8371.5 Lurie, Angela Shulmith. Urban Africans in the Republic of South Africa, 1950-1966. Johannesburg, 1969.

Afr 8377 South Africa in general - History by periods - Republic of South Africa (Independent, 1961-) - Special topics

Afr 8377.1 Munger, Edwin S. Notes on the formation of South African foreign policy. Pasadena, 1965.
Afr 8377.2 Schreiner, Oliver Deneys. The nettle. Johannesburg, 1964.
Afr 8377.3 Brokensha, Miles. The Fourth of July raids. Cape Town, 1965.

Afr 8377   South Africa in general - History by periods - Republic of South Africa (Independent, 1961-) - Special topics
cont.

Afr 8377.4F	Afro-Asian Solidarity Committee. Memorandum on cooperation between the West German Federal Republic and the Republic of South Africa in the military and atomic fields. Berlin, 1964.
Afr 8377.5	Nicol, Margaret. South African protocol, and other formalities. Cape Town, 1964.
Afr 8377.6	Degenaar, Johannes Jacobus. Op weg na 'n nuwe politieke lewenshouding. Kaapstad, 1963.
Afr 8377.8	Bogaerde, Frans van den. Suid-Afrika in die politiek-ekonomiese proses. Pretoria, 1966.
Afr 8377.10	Villiers, Hans Heinrich Wicht de. Rivonia, operation Mayibuye. Johannesburg, 1964.
Afr 8377.10.5	Villiers, Hans Heinrich Wicht de. Danger en Afrique du Sud. Paris, 1966.
Afr 8377.10.10	Strydom, Lauritz. Rivonia unmasked. Johannesburg, 1965.
Afr 8377.12	Orpen, Neil. Total defence. 1st ed. Cape Town, 1967.

Afr 8378.101 - .399   South Africa in general - History by periods - Republic of South Africa (Independent, 1961-) - Political biographies - Individual (A-Z, 299 scheme, by person)

Afr 8378.200	First, Ruth. One hundred and seventeen days. N.Y., 1965.
Afr 8378.200.10	Ludi, Gerard. The amazing Mr. Fischer. Cape Town, 1966.
Afr 8378.200.11	Vermaak, Christopher J. Braam Fischer. Johannesburg, 1966.
Afr 8378.331	Sachs, Albert. The jail diary of Albie Sachs. London, 1966.
Afr 8378.331.30	Sachs, Albert. Stephanie on trial. London, 1968.
Afr 8378.337	Segal, Ronald. Into exile. London, 1963.
Afr 8378.349	Kruger, J.J. President C.R. Swart. Kaapstad, 1961.
Afr 8378.379	Verwoerd, Hendrik Frensch. Verwoerd aan die woord. 3. druk. Johannesburg, 1966.
Afr 8378.379.5	Allighan, Garry. Verwoerd - the end, a look-back from the future. London, 1961.
Afr 8378.379.10	Grobbelaar, Pieter Willem. This was a man. Cape Town, 1967.
Afr 8378.379.15	Verwoerd, fotobiografie, pictorial biography, 1901-1966. Johannesburg, 1966.
Afr 8378.379.20	Botha, Jan. Verwoerd is dead. Cape Town, 1967.
Afr 8378.379.25	Hepple, Alexander. Verwoerd. Harmondsworth, 1967.
Afr 8378.379.30.3	Barnard, Fred. Dertien jaar in die skadu. 3. druk. Johannesburg, 1967.
Afr 8378.379.35F	South Africa. Commission of Enquiry Into the Circumstances of the Death of the Late Dr. the Honourable Hendrik Frensch Verwoerd. Report. Pretoria, 1967.

Afr 8380   South Africa in general - History by periods - Republic of South Africa (Independent, 1961-) - Special periods, etc. - Early years, 1961-

Afr 8380.2	Scholtz, Gert. Die Republiek van Suid-Afrika. Johannesburg, 1962.
Afr 8380.3	South Africa. South African Information Service. South Africa source books. v.1-4. N.Y., 1964.
Afr 8380.4	South African Communist Party. The road to South African freedom. London, 1964.
Afr 8380.5	Merwe, Hendrik Johannes Jan Matthijs van der. Gebeure in Afrika. Johannesburg, 1964.
Afr 8380.10	Adstin, Dennis. Britain and South Africa. London, 1966.
Afr 8380.15	Bringolf, Walther. Gespräche in Südafrika. Zürich, 1968.
Afr 8380.20	Rupert, Anton. Progress through partnership. Cape Town, 1967.

Afr 8654 - 8660   South Africa in general - Geography, description, etc. - General works (By date)

	Afr 8656.85	Stel, Simon van der. Journal of his expedition to Namaqualand. London, 1932.
	Afr 8656.85.2	Stel, Simon van der. Simon van der Stel's journal. Supplement. Dublin, 1953.
	Afr 8657.1	Colvin, Ian D. The cape of adventure. London, 1912.
	Afr 8657.10	Natal. Town and Regional Planning Commission. Tugela basin, a regional survey. Pietermaritzburg, 1953.
	Afr 8657.11F	Buetner, Johan Daniel. Beschrijving van Cabo de Goede Hoop en Rio de la Goa. Pietermaritzburg, 1960.
	Afr 8657.19F	Kolbe, Peter. Caput Bonae Spei hodiernum. Nurnberg, 1719.
	Afr 8657.19.3F	Kolbe, Peter. Naaukeurige en uitvoerige beschryving van de Kaap de Goede Hoop. Amsterdam, 1727. 2v.
	Afr 8657.19.5	Kolbe, Peter. Present state of the Cape of Good Hope. London, 1731. 2v.
	Afr 8657.19.7	Kolbe, Peter. Description du cap de Bonne-Espérance. Amsterdam, 1741. 3v.
	Afr 8657.67	Hemmy, Gysbert. De Promontorio Bonae Spei, a Latin oration. Cape Town, 1959.
	Afr 8657.77.4	Neue Kurzgefasste Beschreibung des Vorgebirges der guten Hoffnung. Leipzig, 1779.
	Afr 8657.79.5	Paterson, W. A narrative of four journeys into the country of the Hottentots and Caffraria. 2d ed. London, 1790.
Htn	Afr 8657.85*	Mentzel, O. Beschreibung des Vorgebirges der Guten Hoffnung. Glogau, 1885-87. 2v.
	Afr 8657.90	Le Vaillant, F. Voyage...dans l'intérieur de l'Afrique. Lausanne, 1790. 2v.
	Afr 8657.90.5	Johannesburg. Public Library. Bibliography of Le Vaillant's "Voyages" and "Oiseaux d'Afrique." Johannesburg, 1962.
	Afr 8657.90.6	Le Vaillant, F. Reise in das Innere von Afrika. v.1, 3-5. Frankfurt, 1799. 4v.
	Afr 8657.90.11	Le Vaillant, F. New travels into the interior parts of Africa. London, 1796. 3v.
	Afr 8657.90.12	Le Vaillant, F. Neue Reise in das Innere von Afrika. Berlin, 1796. 2v.
	Afr 8657.90.17	Le Vaillant, F. Travels into the interior parts of Africa. 2nd ed. London, 1796. 2v.
	Afr 8657.90.51	Le Vaillant, F. Voyages de F. Le Vaillant dans l'intérieur de l'Afrique, 1781-1785. v.1-2. Paris, 1932.
Htn	Afr 8658.00*	Stout, Benjamin. Narrative of the loss of the ship Hercules. New Bedford, 1800.
	Afr 8658.01	Barrow, J. An account of travels into...South Africa. London, 1801.

Afr 8654 - 8660   South Africa in general - Geography, description, etc. - General works (By date)
cont.

	Afr 8658.01.2	Barrow, J. An account of travels into...South Africa. N.Y., 1802.
	Afr 8658.01.3	Barrow, J. Travels into the interior of South Africa. London, 1806. 2v.
	Afr 8658.01.4	Barrow, J. An account of travels into the interior of Southern Africa, in the years 1797 and 1798. N.Y., 1968.
	Afr 8658.01.5	Barnard, Anne. South Africa a century ago. London, 1901.
	Afr 8658.01.8	Barnard, Anne. South Africa a century ago. London, 1901.
	Afr 8658.02	Mist, Augusta Uitenhage de. Diary of a journey to the Cape of Good Hope and the interior of Africa in 1802 and 1803. Capetown, 1954.
	Afr 8658.03	Semple, Robert. Walks and sketches at the Cape of Good Hope. London, 1803.
	Afr 8658.04	Percival, R. An account of the Cape of Good Hope. London, 1804.
Htn	Afr 8658.06*	Gleanings in Africa. London, 1806.
	Afr 8658.06.5	Gleanings in Africa; exhibiting a faithful and correct view of the manners and customs of the inhabitants of the Cape of Good Hope, and surrounding country. N.Y., 1969.
	Afr 8658.11.3	Lichtenstein, H. Reisen im südlichen Africa...1803-06. Berlin, 1811. 2v.
	Afr 8658.11.5	Lichtenstein, H. Travels in southern Africa. London, 1812. 2v.
	Afr 8658.11.6	Lichtenstein, H. Reisen im südlichen Afrika...1803, 1804, 1805, und 1806. Stuttgart, 1967. 2v.
	Afr 8658.15	Campbell, J. Travels in South Africa. London, 1815.
	Afr 8658.15.5	Latrole, Christian Ignatius. Journal of a visit to South Africa in 1815 and 1816. Cape Town, 1969.
	Afr 8658.16	Campbell, J. Travels in South Africa. Andover, 1816.
	Afr 8658.20	Stout, Benjamin. Cape of Good Hope. London, 1820.
	Afr 8658.22	Burchell, W.J. Travels in...southern Africa. London, 1822. 2v.
	Afr 8658.22.5	Burchell, W.J. Travels in the interior of southern Africa. London, 1953. 2v.
	Afr 8658.27	Thompson, George. Travels and adventures in southern Africa. London, 1827.
	Afr 8658.27.3	Thompson, George. Travels and adventures in Southern Africa. 2d ed. London, 1827. 2v.
	Afr 8658.27.4F	Thompson, George. Travels and adventures in southern Africa. Cape Town, 1962.
	Afr 8658.34	Pringle, Thomas. African sketches. London, 1834.
	Afr 8658.34.2	Pringle, Thomas. Narrative of a residence in South Africa. London, 1840.
	Afr 8658.34.5	Pringle, Thomas. Narrative of a residence in South Africa. London, 1835.
	Afr 8658.34.10	Pringle, Thomas. Narrative of a residence in South Africa. Cape Town, 1966.
	Afr 8658.35	Steedman, A. Wanderings and adventures...of South Africa. London, 1835.
	Afr 8658.35.5	Steedman, A. Wanderings and adventures in the interior of southern Africa. Cape Town, 1966. 2v.
	Afr 8658.36	Martin, R.M. History of southern Africa. London, 1836.
	Afr 8658.36.3	Martin, R.M. History of southern Africa. 2nd ed. London, 1843.
	Afr 8658.36.6	Harris, W.C. Wild sports of southern Africa. 4 ed. London, 1844.
	Afr 8658.36.7	Harris, W.C. The wild sports of southern Africa. Cape Town, 1963.
	Afr 8658.38	Alexander, James E. An expedition of discovery into the interior of Africa. London, 1835. 2v.
	Afr 8658.38.5	Alexander, James E. An expedition of discovery into the interior of Africa. Cape Town, 1967. 2v.
	Afr 8658.42	Arbousset, Thomas. Relation d'un voyage...au cap de Bonne-Espérance. Paris, 1842.
	Afr 8658.42.3	Weyermueller, F. Die Völker Südafrikas. Strassburg, 1842.
	Afr 8658.44	Backhouse, J. Visit to the Mauritius and South Africa. London, 1844.
NEDL	Afr 8658.46.2	Methuen, H.H. Life in the wilderness. 2d ed. London, 1848.
	Afr 8658.46.5	Arbousset, Thomas. Narrative of an exploratory tour to the North-East of the Colony of the Cape of Good Hope. Facsimile. Cape Town, 1968.
	Afr 8658.47	Delegorgue, A. Voyage dans l'Afrique australe...1838-44. Paris, 1847. 2v.
	Afr 8658.49	Dolman, Alfred. In the footsteps of Livingstone, being...our travel notes. London, 1924.
	Afr 8658.50	Gordon Cumming, R. Five years of a hunter's life in the far interior of South Africa. London, 1850. 2v.
	Afr 8658.53	Kretzschmar, E. Südafrikanische Skizzen. Leipzig, 1853.
	Afr 8658.55	Brown, G. Personal adventure in South Africa. London, 1855.
	Afr 8658.58	Cortambert, M.E. Esquisse...d'une partie de l'Afrique australe. Paris, 1858.
	Afr 8658.58.5	Draipon, A.W. Sporting scenes amongst the Kaffirs of South Africa. London, 1858.
	Afr 8658.61	Meidinger, H. Die südafrikanischen Colonien Englands. Frankfurt, 1861.
	Afr 8658.63	Baldwin, William C. African hunting from Natal to the Zambesi. N.Y., 1863.
	Afr 8658.63.4	Baldwin, William C. African hunting and adventure. Facsimile of 3rd ed. Capetown, 1967.
NEDL	Afr 8658.66	Moodie, J.W.D. Scenes and adventures as a soldier and settler. Montreal, 1866. (Changed to KPC 2144)
	Afr 8658.66.5	Leyland, J. Adventures in the far interior of South Africa. London, 1866.
NEDL	Afr 8658.68	Chapman, J. Travels in the interior of South Africa. London, 1868. 2v.
	Afr 8658.68.5	Fritsch, G. Drei Jahre in Süd-Afrika. Breslau, 1868.
	Afr 8658.69	Mauch, Karl. The journals of Carl Mauch; his travels in the Transvaal and Rhodesia, 1869-1872. Salisbury, 1969.

Afr 8658.71   Mackenzie, J. Ten years north of the Orange River. Edinburgh, 1871.
Afr 8658.72   Thomas, T.M. Eleven years in central South Africa. London, 1872.
Afr 8658.72.5   Taylor, Bayard. Travels in South Africa. N.Y., 1872.
Afr 8658.72.10   Taylor, Bayard. Travels in South Africa. N.Y., 1881.
Afr 8658.73   Koerner, F. Süd Afrika. Breslau, 1873.
Afr 8658.75   Bisset, John J. Sport and war...1834-1867. London, 1875.
Afr 8658.75.5   Drummond, William Henry. The large game and natural history of South and South-East Africa. Edinburgh, 1875.
Afr 8658.76   Mohr, Edward. To the Victoria Falls of the Zambesi. London, 1876.
Afr 8658.76.3   Lacaille, N.L. Journal historique du voyage fait au cap de Bonne-Espérance. Paris, 1776.
Afr 8658.78   Gillmore, Parker. The great thirst land. London, 1878.
Afr 8658.79   Kennedy, D. Kennedy at the Cape. Edinburgh, 1879.
Afr 8658.79.5   Deleage, Paul. Trois mois chez les Zoulous et les derniers jours du prince impérial. Paris, 1879.
Afr 8658.80   Sandeman, E.F. Eight months in an ox-wagon. London, 1880.
Afr 8658.80.4   Gillmore, Parker. On duty, a ride through hostile Africa. London, 1880.
Afr 8658.80.6   Leyland, Ralph W. A holiday in South Africa. London, 1882.
Afr 8658.81   Holub, Emil. Seven years in South Africa. London, 1881. 2v.
Afr 8658.82   Duval, C. With a show through southern Africa. London, 1882. 2v.
Afr 8658.82.4   Dixie, Florence. In the land of misfortune. London, 1882.
Afr 8658.84.2   Little, James S. South Africa. 2d ed. London, 1887.
Afr 8658.86   Kerr, W.M. The far interior. London, 1886. 2v.
Afr 8658.86.5   Gillmore, Parker. The hunter's arcadia. London, 1886.
Afr 8658.87   Mackinnon, J. South African traits. Edinburgh, 1887.
Afr 8658.87.4   Matthews, J.W. Incwadi Yami, or twenty years' personal experience in South Africa. N.Y., 1887.
Afr 8658.87.7   Anderson, Andrew Arthur. Twenty-five years in the gold regions of Africa. London, 1887. 2v.
Afr 8658.87.8   Anderson, Andrew Arthur. Twenty-five years in a waggon. London, 1888.
Afr 8658.87.15   Bethell, Alfred J. Notes on South African hunting and notes on a ride to the Victoria Falls of the Zambesi. York, 1887.
Afr 8658.88   Sheldon, L.V. Yankee girls in Zulu land. N.Y., 1888.
Afr 8658.89   Blink, Hendrik. Transvaal en omliggende landen. Amsterdam, 1889.
Afr 8658.89.5   Young, Frederick. A winter tour in South Africa. London, 1890.
Afr 8658.90   Blink, Hendrik. De Zuid-Afrikaansche Republiek en hare bewoners. Amsterdam, 1890.
Afr 8658.91   South Africa and its future. Cape Town, 1890.
Afr 8658.91.7   Foà, Édouard. A travers l'Afrique centrale du Cap au lac Nyassa. 2. éd. Paris, 1901.
Afr 8658.92   Churchill, R.S. Men, mines and animals in South Africa. London, 1892.
Afr 8658.92.3   Greswall, W.P. Geography of Africa south of Zambesi. Oxford, 1892.
Afr 8658.92.5   Ritchie, James Ewing. Brighter South Africa. London, 1892.
Afr 8658.93   Letters from South Africa. London, 1893.
Afr 8658.94   Cooper-Chadwick, J. Three years with Lobengula. London, 1894.
Afr 8658.95   Balfour, A.B. Twelve hundred miles in a waggon. London, 1895.
Afr 8658.95.5   Leclercq, Jules. Aux chutes du Zambèze. Paris, 19-.
Afr 8658.96   Brownlee, Chas. Reminiscences of Kaffir life. Lovedale, 1896.
Afr 8658.96.3   Cumberland, S. What I think of South Africa. London, 1896.
Afr 8658.96.5   Tangye, H. Lincoln. In new South Africa. London, 1896.
Afr 8658.97   MacNab, J. On veldt and farm. London, 1897.
Afr 8658.97.7   Bigelow, P. White man's Africa. N.Y., 1898.
Afr 8658.97.10   Bigelow, P. White man's Africa. N.Y., 1900.
Afr 8658.98   Stanley, H.M. Through South Africa. N.Y., 1898.
Afr 8658.98.2   Stanley, H.M. Through South Africa. London, 1898.
Afr 8658.98.5   Aubert, Georges. L'Afrique du Sud. Paris, 1898.
Afr 8658.98.7   Wormser, J.A. Van Amsterdam naar Pretoria. Amsterdam, 1898.
Afr 8658.99   Devereux, Roy. Side lights on South Africa. London, 1899.
Afr 8658.99.3F   Wormser, J.A. De Zuster-Republieken in Zuid-Afrika. Amsterdam, 1899.
Afr 8658.99.5   Laurence, Percival M. Collectanea. London, 1899.
Afr 8659.00.5   Schreiner, O. Losse gedachten over Zuid-Afrika. Haarlem, 1900.
Afr 8659.00.8   Sykes, Jessica. Side lights on the war in South Africa. London, 1900.
Afr 8659.00.11   Mann, Arthur M. The Boer in peace and war. London, 1900.
Afr 8659.00.15   Markham, Violet Rosa. South Africa, past and present. London, 1900.
Afr 8659.01   Reclus, E. L'Afrique australe. Paris, 1901.
Afr 8659.02   Warren, Charles. On the veldt in the seventies. London, 1902.
Afr 8659.02.4   Luck, R.A. A visit to Lewanika, king of the Barotse. London, 1902.
Afr 8659.02.6   Orléans-Brangance, L. Tour d'Afrique. Paris, 1902.
Afr 8659.03   Braun, D.E. Auf und ab in Süd-Afrika. Berlin, 1903.
Afr 8659.03.5   Scott, Edward Daniel. Some letters from South Africa, 1894-1902. Manchester, Eng., 1903.
Afr 8659.04   Lucas, C.P. Geography of South Africa. Oxford, 1904.
Afr 8659.05   Hutchinson, G.T. From the Cape to the Zambesi. London, 1905.
Afr 8659.05.5   Samassa, Paul. Das neue Südafrika. Berlin, 1905.
Afr 8659.05.8   Browne, J.H. Balfour. South Africa. London, 1905.
Afr 8659.08   Fuller, R.H. South Africa at home. London, n.d.
Afr 8659.09   Maturin, Edith. Petticoat pilgrims on trek. London, 1909.
Afr 8659.10   Hyatt, S.P. Diary of a soldier of fortune. London, 1910.
Afr 8659.10.3   Southey, Rosamond. Storm and sunshine in South Africa. London, 1910.
Afr 8659.10.5   Angore, John. In the early days. Kimberley, 1910.
Afr 8659.11   Fyfe, H.H. South Africa to-day. London, 1911.
Afr 8659.11.2   Fyfe, H.H. South Africa today. London, 1911.
Afr 8659.11.3   Blackburn, D. Secret service in South Africa. London, 1911.

Afr 8659.11.5   Durand, H.M. A holiday in South Africa. Edinburgh, 1911.
Afr 8659.11.7   Streitwolf. Der Caprivizipfel. Berlin, 1911.
Afr 8659.12   Worsfold, W.B. Union of South Africa. London, 1912.
Afr 8659.12.5F   Kock, J.H.M. De Kaap als een nieuw land. 2. druk. Kaapstad, 1912.
Afr 8659.12.10   Agate, W. Diary of a tour in South Africa. Paisley, 1912.
Afr 8659.13   Scully, Wm. C. Reminiscences of a South African pioneer. London, 1913.
Afr 8659.13.3   Scully, Wm. C. Further reminiscences of a South African pioneer. London, 1913.
Afr 8659.13.5   Williams, R. How I became a governor. London, 1913.
Afr 8659.13.9   Pratt, A. The real South Africa. Indianapolis, 1913.
Afr 8659.13.12   Maturin, E. Adventures beyond the Zambesi. London, 1913.
Afr 8659.13.15   Markham, Violet R. The South African scene. London, 1913.
Afr 8659.14   Johnston, H.H. Pioneers in South Africa. London, 1914.
Afr 8659.14.5   Hyatt, Stanley P. The old transport road. London, 1914.
Afr 8659.16   Alston, Madeline. From the heart of the veld. London, 1916.
Afr 8659.25   Dawson, Wm. South Africa, people, places, problems. N.Y., 1925.
Afr 8659.25.8   Zachariah, O. Travel in South Africa. 3d ed. Johannesburg, 1927.
Afr 8659.26   Nathan, M. South Africa from within. London, 1926.
Afr 8659.26.5   Millin, S.G. The South Africans. London, 1926.
Afr 8659.26.5.5   Millin, S.G. The people of South Africa. London, 1951.
Afr 8659.28   Fairbridge, D. The pilgrims' way in South Africa. London, 1928.
Afr 8659.28.5   Lowth, Alys. South Africa calling. 1st ed. London, 1928.
Afr 8659.29   Alston, M. From an old Cape homestead. London, 1929.
Afr 8659.29.5   Chelvers, H.A. The seven wonders of southern Africa. Johannesburg, 1929.
Afr 8659.30   Camacho, Brito. Gente Bóer, aspectos d'Africa. Lisboa, 1930.
Afr 8659.30.5   Butterfield, Fred. Passing notes of a visit to the Cape (1930). London, 1930.
Afr 8659.30.10   Narath, R. Die Union von Südafrika und ihre Bevölkerung. Leipzig, 1930.
Afr 8659.30.15   Chilvers, H.A. The seven lost trails of Africa. London, 1930.
Afr 8659.30.20   Jannasch, Hans. Unter Buren, Briten, Bantus. Berlin, 193-.
Afr 8659.31   Leubuscher, C. Der südafrikanische Eingeborne als Industriearbeiter und als Stadtherrscher. Jena, 1931.
Afr 8659.32   Trevor, Tudor Gruffydd. Forty years in Africa. London, 1932.
Afr 8659.33   Stackpole, E.J. South Africa, impressions of an American, 1933. Harrisburg, 1933.
Afr 8659.35   South Africa. Railways and Harbours Administration, Johannesburg. The sunshine route. London, 1935.
Afr 8659.36   Rippmann, Ernst. Weisses und schwarzes Südafrika heute und morgen. Gotha, 1936.
Afr 8659.36.3   Birkby, Carel. Thirstland treks. London, 1936.
Afr 8659.36.5   Lea, Henry. A veld farmer's adventures. London, 1936.
Afr 8659.38   Trew, H.F. African man hunts. London, 1938.
Afr 8659.39.15   Wells, Arthur W. South Africa. London, 1947.
Afr 8659.39.20   Wells, Arthur W. Southern Africa. London, 1956.
Afr 8659.40   Green, Lawrence George. To the river's end. Cape Town, 194-.
Afr 8659.43.5   James, S. South of the Congo. London, 1944.
Afr 8659.43.10   Marquard, Leopold. The black man's burden. London, 1943.
Afr 8659.43.15   Pamphlet vol. South Africa - description. 10 pam.
Afr 8659.44   Malherbe, J.A. Complex country. London, 1944.
Afr 8659.45   South Africa. Government Information Office. This is South Africa. N.Y., 1945.
Afr 8659.45.2   South Africa. Government Information Office. This is South Africa. N.Y., 1952.
Afr 8659.47   Blackwell, L. This is South Africa. Pietermaritzburg, 1947.
Afr 8659.47.5   Delius, Anthony. The young traveller in South Africa. London, 1947.
Afr 8659.47.10   Shepherd, Robert H.W. African contrasts. Cape Town, 1947.
Afr 8659.49   Siegfried, A. Afrique du Sud. Paris, 1949.
Afr 8659.49.5   Mockford, Julian. The golden land. London, 1949.
Afr 8659.49.10   South Africa. Commission for the Preservation of Natural and Historical Monuments, Relics and Antiques. The monuments of South Africa. 2d ed. Johannesburg, 1949.
Afr 8659.50   Flavin, Martin. Black and white. 1st ed. N.Y., 1950.
Afr 8659.50.5   Brady, Cyrus T. Africa astir. Melbourne, 1950.
Afr 8659.50.10   Reed, D. Somewhere south of Suez. London, 1950.
Afr 8659.50.10.2   Reed, D. Somewhere south of Suez. N.Y., 1951.
Afr 8659.50.15   South Africa. State Information Office. South African scene. Pretoria, 195-.
Afr 8659.50.20   Sledzinski, Waclaw. Rzeka Limpopo wpada do Tamizy. Warszawa, 1958.
Afr 8659.52   Davidson, B. Report on southern Africa. London, 1952.
Afr 8659.52.5   Young, F.B. In South Africa. London, 1952.
Afr 8659.52.15   Kaptein, A. De Unie van Zuid-Afrika. Amsterdam, 1952.
Afr 8659.53   Deguingand, F.W. African assignment. London, 1953.
Afr 8659.53.5   Coetzee, Abel. Die Afrikaanse volkskultuur. Kaapstad, 1953.
Afr 8659.53.5.2   Coetzee, Abel. Die Afrikaanse volkskultuur. 2. druk. Amsterdam, 1960.
Afr 8659.54   Campbell, A. The heart of Africa. 1st ed. N.Y., 1954.
Afr 8659.54.5   Brown, John. The thirsty land. London, 1954.
Afr 8659.54.10   South Africa. State Information Office. South African quiz. Pretoria, 1954.
Afr 8659.54.15   South Africa. South Africa. Pretoria, 1954.
Afr 8659.55   Carter, G.M. South Africa. N.Y., 1955.
Afr 8659.55.5   Wellington, J.H. Southern Africa. Cambridge, Eng., 1955. 2v.
Afr 8659.58   Morris, James. South African winter. N.Y., 1958.
Afr 8659.58.5   Kirby, Percival Robson. Jacob van Reenen and the Grosvenor expedition of 1790-1791. Johannesburg, 1958.
Afr 8659.58.10   Friend, M.L. Without fear or favour. Cape Town, 1958.
Afr 8659.58.15   Green, Lawrence George. South Africa beachcomber. 1st ed. Cape Town, 1958.
Afr 8659.59.3   Boydell, T. My beloved country. Cape Town, 1960.
Afr 8659.60   Our first half-century, 1910-1960. Johannesburg, 1960.
Afr 8659.60.5   Savoy, Alan. Thunder in the air. London, 1960.
Afr 8659.60.10   Albertyn, J.R. Land en stad. Kaapstad, 1960.
Afr 8659.60.15   Kirby, Percival Robson. The true story of the Grosvenor. N.Y., 1960.

Afr 8654 - 8660   South Africa in general - Geography, description, etc. - General works (By date) cont.

Afr 8659.60.20   Varley, Douglas. South African reading in earlier days. Johannesburg, 1960.
Afr 8659.60.25F   Friend, Bloemfontein. Union jubilee, 1910-1960. Bloemfontein, 1960.
Afr 8659.61   Stanton, Hannah. Go well. London, 1961.
Afr 8659.61.5   Jenny, H. Afrika ist nicht nur schwarz. Düsseldorf, 1961.
Afr 8659.62   Nel, Andries. Stad en dorp. Stellenbosch, 1962.
Afr 8659.62.5   Blumberg, Myrna. White madam. London, 1962.
Afr 8659.63   Serton, P. Zuid-Afrika, land van goede hoop. 3. druk. Meppel, 1963.
Afr 8659.63.5   South Africa. National Parks Board of Trustees. Ons nasionale parke. Pretoria, 1963.
Afr 8659.64   Boom, M.J. Reis door Zuid-Afrika. Meppel, 1964.
Afr 8659.64.5   Hopkinson, T. South Africa. N.Y., 1964.
Afr 8659.65   Newman, Bernard. South African journey. London, 1965.
Afr 8659.65.5   Fournier, Gilles. Vérité pour l'Afrique du Sud. Paris, 1965.
Afr 8659.66   Harrigan, Anthony. The new republic, South Africa's role in the world. Pretoria, 1966.
Afr 8659.66.5   Molnar, Thomas Steven. L'Afrique du Sud. Paris, 1966.
Afr 8659.66.10   Lehmann, Emily. Pretoria, Skinnerstraat 295. Wuppertal, 1966.
Afr 8659.66.17   Rittershaus, Wilhelm. Südafrika, eine Bastion Europas? Tagebuch einer Seereise mit Betrachtung des Rossenproblems. 2. Aufl. Klagenfurt, 1966.
Afr 8659.66.20   Rip, Colin Melville. Contemporary social pathology. Pretoria, 1966.
Afr 8659.66.25   Green, Lawrence George. Thunder on the Blaauwberg. 1st ed. Cape Town, 1966.
Afr 8659.67   Drury, Allen. A very strange society. N.Y., 1967.
Afr 8659.67.5   Somoy, A.G. Paspoort voor Zuid-Afrika. Lier, 1967.
Afr 8659.67.10   Leenen, Guillaume A.H. Suid Afrikamoe nie huil nie. Melle, 1967.
Afr 8659.68   Paton, Alan. The long view. London, 1968.
Afr 8659.68.5   Klooster, Willem Simon Brand. Zuid-Africa. Baarn, 1968.
Afr 8659.68.10F   Smail, John Lees. Monuments and trails of the Voortrekkers. Cape Town, 1968.

Afr 8667   South Africa in general - Geography, description, etc. - Civilization

Afr 8667.5   Heever, C.M. van den. Die stryjd om ewewig. Kaapstad, 1941.
Afr 8667.5.10   Heever, C.M. van der. Kultur geskiedenis van die Afrikaner. Kaapstad, 1945. 3v.
Afr 8667.20   Calpin, G.H. The South African way of life. London, 1953.
Afr 8667.30   Jackmann, S.B. The numbered day. London, 1954.
Afr 8667.40   Paton, Alan. South Africa and her people. London, 1957.
Afr 8667.45   Gerard, Francis. Springbok rampant. London, 1951.
Afr 8667.55   Spoelstra, B. Ons volkslewe. Pretoria, 1922.
Afr 8667.60   Alberts, Andries. Die Afrikaanse wêreldbeskouing. Kaapstad, 1956.
Afr 8667.65   Meyer, P.J. Trek verder. Kaapstad, 1959.
Afr 8667.66   Grense, 'n simposium oor rasse- en ander verhoudinge. Stellenbosch, 1961.
Afr 8667.68   Cronjé, Geoffrey. Die Westerse kultuur in Suid-Afrika. Pretoria, 1963.
Afr 8667.70   Caltex (Africa). South Africa's heritage. Cape Town, 1960.
Afr 8667.71   South Africa. South African Information Service. The South African tradition, a brief survey. N.Y., 1960.
Afr 8667.72   Idenburg, Petrus Johannes. The Cape of Good Hope. Leiden, 1963.
Afr 8667.75   Schapera, Isaac. Western civilization and the natives of South Africa, studies in culture contrast. 1st ed. London, 1967.
Afr 8667.80   Hancock, William Keith. Are there South Africans? Johannesburg, 1966.
Afr 8667.85   Junius, J.H. Het leven in Zuid-Afrika. Amsterdam, 1896.
Afr 8667.90   Meyer, Pieter Johannes. Nog nie die einde nie. Kaapstad, 1954.
Afr 8667.97   Calpin, George Harold. At last we have got our country back. 2nd ed. Cape Town, 1969.

Afr 8668   South Africa in general - Geography, description, etc. - Special customs

Afr 8668.5   Lake, Alexander. Hunter's choice. 1st ed. Garden City, 1954.
Afr 8668.8   Dubow, Rhona. The status of women in South Africa. Cape Town, 1965.
Afr 8668.10   Brandel-Syrier, Mia. Black woman in search of God. London, 1962.
Afr 8668.12   Burman, José. A peak to climb;...mountaineering. Cape Town, 1966.
Afr 8668.14   Hattersley, Alan. An illustrated social history of South Africa. Cape Town, 1969.

Afr 8670   South Africa in general - Geography, description, etc. - Guidebooks

Afr 8670.5   Brown, A.S. South Africa. London. 1893 + 48v.
Afr 8670.6   Argus annual and South African gazetteer. Johannesburg. 28,1895 +
Afr 8670.7.11   Union Steam Ship Company, Ltd. The emigrant's guide to South Africa including Cape Colony. 11th ed. London, 1896.
Afr 8670.9   Royal Automobile Club Of South Africa. In and out of town. Cape Town, 1929.
Afr 8670.10.2   Lewis, David. Let's stop here; the pictorial guide to hotels in South Africa, South West Africa, Rhodesia and Moçambique. 2. ed. Durban, 1967.

Afr 8673   South Africa in general - Geography, description, etc. - Views

Afr 8673.5F   Daniell, W. Sketches representing the native tribes...South Africa. London, 1820.
Afr 8673.10   South Africa. South African Information Service. South Africa, 1910-1960. Pretoria, 1960.
Afr 8673.15   Bensusan, A.D. South Africa. Cape Town, 1960.
Afr 8673.17F   Souvenir of South Africa. Two hundred thirty-one photographs in full colour. Johannesburg, 1960.
Afr 8673.18   Elionson, Sima. This is South Africa. Cape Town, 1962.
Afr 8673.19   Johannesburg. Public Library. Some Africana coloured prints and the originals from which they may have been made. Johannesburg, 1963.

Afr 8675   South Africa in general - Geography, description, etc. - Maps
Afr 8675.5   Conseil Scientifique pour l'Afrique au Sud du Sahara. Cartographie de l'Afrique au sud du Sahara. Bukavu, 1953.

Afr 8676   South Africa in general - Economic conditions (By date, e.g. .60 for 1960)

Afr 8676.02   Pamphlet box. South Africa. Economic conditions.
Afr 8676.2   South Africa. University, Pretoria. Bureau of Market Research. Research report. 3 + 9v.
Afr 8676.3   South Africa. University, Pretoria. Bureau of Market Research. Buro vir marknavorsing. Pretoria, 1963.
Afr 8676.25   Lehfeldt, R.A. The national resources of South Africa. Johannesburg, 1922.
Afr 8676.32   Barnes, L. The new Boer war. London, 1932.
Afr 8676.34   Ballinger, W.G. Race and economics in South Africa. London, 1934.
Afr 8676.35   Werle, G. Landwirtschaft und Industrie in der Südafrikanischen Union unter Berücksichtigung der deutschen Pionierarbeit. Inaug. Diss. Eisfeld, 1935.
Afr 8676.36   Kock, M.H. The economic development of South Africa. London, 1936.
Afr 8676.37   Gerich, K.H.A. Aussenhandel und Handelspolitik der Südafrikanischen Union unter besonderer Berücksichtigung der Wirtschafts der Union. Düsseldorf, 1937.
Afr 8676.40F   South Africa. Rural Industries Commission. Report of the Rural Industries Commission. Pretoria, 1940.
Afr 8676.42   Vanderhorst, S.T. Native labor in South Africa. London, 1942.
Afr 8676.42.5   Tinley, J.M. The native labor problem of South Africa. Chapel Hill, 1942.
Afr 8676.44   Spino, Richard B. Rationalisation of South African industry. Durban, 1944.
Afr 8676.45   Bruwer, A.J. South Africa. Johannesburg, 1945.
Afr 8676.46   Horwitz, Ralph. South Africa's business. Cape Town, 1946.
Afr 8676.47   Campbell, Alexander. South Africa, what now? Cape Town, 1947.
Afr 8676.48   Franklin, N.N. Economics in South Africa. Cape Town, 1948.
Afr 8676.48.2   Franklin, N.N. Economics in South Africa. 2d ed. Cape Town, 1954.
Afr 8676.48.2.1   Franklin, N.N. Economics in South Africa. 2nd ed. N.Y., 1969.
Afr 8676.50   Duplessis, J.C. Economic fluctuations in South Africa, 1910-1949. Stellenbosch, 1950.
Afr 8676.50.5   Routh, Guy. Industrial relations and race relations. Johannesburg, 195-.
Afr 8676.53   Eck, H.J. van. Some aspects of the South African industrial revolution. 2d ed. Johannesburg, 1953.
Afr 8676.54   United States. Bureau of Foreign Commerce. Investment in Union of South Africa. Washington, 1954.
Afr 8676.54.5   Hesse, K. Wirtschaftswunder Südafrika. Düsseldorf, 1954.
Afr 8676.54.10F   Economic survey of South Africa. London. 1954 +
Afr 8676.55   Strand, D. The financial and statistical digest of South Africa. Cape Town, 1955.
Afr 8676.55.5   South African Institute of Race Relations. South Africa's changing economy. Johannesburg, 1955.
Afr 8676.57   Neumark, S.D. Economic influences of the South African frontier. Stanford, 1957.
Afr 8676.59   Rabie, Zacharias Johannes. Der Staat als Unternehmer in der Union von Südafrika. Köln, 1959.
Afr 8676.60   South African Council for Scientific and Industrial Research. A survey of rent paying capacity of urban natives in South Africa. Pretoria, 1960.
Afr 8676.60.5   Sporner, F.P. South African predicament. London, 1960.
Afr 8676.60.10   Franzsen, David G. Die ekonomiese lewe van Suid-Africa. Pretoria, 1960.
Afr 8676.60.13   Franzsen, D.G. Die ekonomiese lewe van Suid-Africa, onder redaksie van D.G. Franzsen en H.J.J. Reynders. 3. uitg. Pretoria, 1966.
Afr 8676.60.17   Wijnholds, Heiko. Gren, goud en goedere. Pretoria, 1960.
Afr 8676.60.20   Serton, P. Suid-Afrika en Brasilie. Kaapstad, 1960.
Afr 8676.60.25   Franzsen, David G. Economic growth and stability in a developing economy. Pretoria, 1960.
Afr 8676.60.30   Standard Bank of South Africa. Union of South Africa national income and production. Johannesburg, 1960.
Afr 8676.61   Cole, M.M. South Africa. London, 1961.
Afr 8676.61.2   Cole, M.M. South Africa. 2nd ed. London, 1966.
Afr 8676.61.5F   Denys, A. Land of apartheid, an introduction to the word "apartheid." Natal, 1961.
Afr 8676.62   Princeton University. Enterprise and politics in South Africa. Princeton, N.J., 1962.
Afr 8676.62.5   Norval, A. A quarter of a century of industrial progress in South Africa. Cape Town, 1962.
Afr 8676.62.10   South Africa Foundation. South Africa in the sixties. Johannesburg, 1962.
Afr 8676.62.12   South Africa Foundation. South Africa in the sixties. 2nd ed. Johannesburg, 1965.
Afr 8676.62.15   Hurwitz, N. Economic framework of South Africa. Pietermaritzburg, 1962.
Afr 8676.63   Rosenthal, E. Manne en maatskappye. Kaapstad, 1963.
Afr 8676.63.10   Hupkes, G.J. A survey of contemporary economic conditions and prospects for 1964. Stellenbosch, 1963.
Afr 8676.64   Houghton, D. Hobart. The South African economy. Cape Town, 1964.
Afr 8676.64.2   Houghton, D. Hobart. The South African economy. 2. ed. Capetown, 1967.
Afr 8676.64.5   Svermann, Josef. Die weltwirtschaftliche Bedeutung der Südafrikanischen Republik. Göttingen, 1964.
Afr 8676.64.6   Hamer, Eberhard. Die Industrialisierung Südafrikas seit dem Zweiten Weltkrieg. Stuttgart, 1964.
Afr 8676.64.10   Katzen, Leo. Implications of economic and other boycotts for South Africa. Cape Town, 1964.
Afr 8676.64.15   Du Plessis, Eduard Petrus. 'N volk staan op. Kaapstad, 1964.
Afr 8676.66   Moiseeva, Galina M. Iuzhno-Afrikanskaia Respublika. Moskva, 1964.
Afr 8676.67   Croizat, Victor J. The economic development of South Africa in its political context. Santa Monica, 1967.
Afr 8676.67.5   Hupkes, G.J. A reappraisal of economic prospects for 1967. Stellenbosch, 1967.
Afr 8676.67.10   Horwitz, Ralph. The political economy of South Africa. London, 1967.
Afr 8676.67.15   Lombard, Johannes Anthonie. Die ekonomiese stelsel van Suid-Afrika. Kaapstad, 1967.
Afr 8676.67.20   Lombard, Johannes Anthonie. Die ekonomiese politiek van Suid-Afrika. Kaapstad, 1967.

Afr 8677 South Africa in general - Finance

Afr 8677.02F Pamphlet box. Finances, Union of South Africa.
Afr 8677.15 Union of South Africa. Financial regulations. Pretoria, 1915.
Afr 8677.25 Koch, M.H. An analysis of the finances of the Union of South Africa. Cape Town, 1922.
Afr 8677.25.5 Koch, M.H. An analysis of the finances of the Union of South Africa. Cape Town, 1927.
Afr 8677.30 South Africa. Parliament. House of Assembly. Select Committee on Public Accounts. 1924. Report. Cape Town, 1924. 2v.
Afr 8677.35 Steyn, Daniel. Inleiding tot die Suid-Afrikaanse Staatsfinansies. Pretoria, 1961.
Afr 8677.36 Waasdijk, Tom van. Public expenditure in South Africa. Johannesburg, 1964.

Afr 8678 South Africa in general - Races - Indigenous races in general

Afr 8678.1 Schapera, I. Select bibliography of South African native life and problems. London, 1941.
Afr 8678.1.5 Schapera, I. Select bibliography of South African native life and problems. Supplement. Cape Town, 1950.
Afr 8678.1.10F Schapera, I. Select bibliography of South African native life and problems. 2nd supplement. Cape Town, 1958.
Afr 8678.3 Sutherland. Original matter...in Sutherland's memoir...of South Africa. Cape Town, 1847.
Afr 8678.4 Survey of race relations in South Africa. Johannesburg. 1957+ 6v.
Afr 8678.5 Fritsch, G. Die Eingeborenen Süd-Afrikas. Atlas und Text. Breslau, 1872.
Afr 8678.6 Clarence, W. The aborigines of South Africa. Boston, 1860.
Afr 8678.7 South African Native Races Comittee. The natives of South Africa. London, 1901.
Afr 8678.7.5 South African Native Races Committee. The South African natives. Paris, 1909.
Afr 8678.8 Stow, G.W. The native races of South Africa. London, 1905.
Afr 8678.8.1 Stow, G.W. The native races of South Africa. London, 1905.
Afr 8678.8.10 Fagan, H.A. Co-existence in South Africa. Cape Town, 1963.
Afr 8678.9F Duggan-Cronin, A.M. The Bantu tribes of South Africa. Cambridge, Eng., 1928- 3v.
Afr 8678.9.50 Sonnabend, E.H. Il fattore demografico nell'organizzazione sociale del Bantu. Roma, 1935.
Afr 8678.9.65 Junod, H.A. Moeurs et coutumes des Bantous. Paris, 1936. 2v.
Afr 8678.9.75 Shropshire, D.W.T. The church and primitive peoples...southern Bantu. London, 1938.
Afr 8678.9.80 Schapera, I. The Bantu-speaking tribes of South Africa. London, 1956-
Afr 8678.9.85 Shepherd, Robert Henry Wishart. Literature for the South African Bantu. Pretoria, 1936.
Afr 8678.10 Kidd, D. Savage childhood...Kafir children. London, 1906.
Afr 8678.10.5 Kidd, D. Essential Kafir. London, 1904.
Afr 8678.10.7 Kidd, D. Kafir socialism. London, 1908.
Afr 8678.10.8 Kidd, D. South Africa. London, 1908.
Afr 8678.10.15 Gavicho de Lacerda, T. Os Cafres, seus usos e costumes. Lisboa, 1944.
Afr 8678.10.20 Walker, Oliver. Kaffirs are livelier. London, 1964.
Afr 8678.12 Schultze, L. Aus Namaland und Kalahari. Jena, 1907.
NEDL Afr 8678.13 Theal, G.M. The yellow and dark skinned people...Zambesi. London, 1910.
Afr 8678.13.3 Theal, G.M. The yellow and dark-skinned people of Africa south of the Zambesi. N.Y., 1969.
Afr 8678.13.5 Molema, S.M. The Bantu, past and present. Edinburgh, 1920.
Afr 8678.13.6 Molema, S.M. The Bantu. Cape Town, 1963.
Afr 8678.13.10 Phillips, Ray E. The Bantu in the city; a study of...cultural adjustment on the Witwatersrand. Diss. Lovedale, 1938.
Afr 8678.13.15 Shepherd, R.H.W. Children of the Veld, Bantu vignettes. London, 1937.
Afr 8678.13.20 Soga, J.H. The south-eastern Bantu Abe-Nguni, Aba-Mbo, Ama-Lala. Johannesburg, 1930.
Afr 8678.13.30 Stayt, H.A. The Bavenda. London, 1931.
Afr 8678.13.40 Richards, A.I. Hunger and work in a savage tribe. London, 1932.
Afr 8678.13.41A Richards, A.I. Hunger and work in a savage tribe. Glencoe, Ill., 1948.
Afr 8678.13.41B Richards, A.I. Hunger and work in a savage tribe. Glencoe, Ill., 1948.
Afr 8678.13.45 Natal. University. A study of the social circumstances and characteristics of Bantu in the Durban region. Durban, 1965. 2v.
Afr 8678.14 Alberti, L. Description physique et historique des Cafres. Amsterdam, 1811.
Afr 8678.15 Holden, W.C. The past and future of Kaffir races. London, 1866.
Afr 8678.15.2 Holden, W.C. The past and future of the Kaffir races. Cape Town, 1963.
Afr 8678.17 Macdonald, J. Light in Africa. London, 1890.
Afr 8678.18 Kay, S. Travels and researches in Caffraria. London, 1833.
Afr 8678.19 Davis, A. The native problem in South Africa. London, 1903.
Afr 8678.20 Indicus. Labour and other questions in South Africa. London, 1903.
Afr 8678.21 Stevens, E.J.C. White and black. London, 1914.
Afr 8678.23 Question of colour, study of South Africa. Edinburgh, 1906.
Afr 8678.24.2 Jabavu, D.D.T. The black problem. 2d ed. Lovedale, 1921.
Afr 8678.24.7 Jabavu, Davidson Don Tengo. The black problem. N.Y., 1969.
Afr 8678.25 Nielsen, P. The black man's place in South Africa. Cape Town, 1922.
Afr 8678.26 Gibson, J.Y. The evolution of South African native policy. Pietermaritzburg, 1919.
Afr 8678.28 Olivier, S.H.O. The anatomy of African misery. London, 1927.
Afr 8678.30 Silburn, P.A. South Africa, white and black or brown. London, 1927.

Afr 8678 South Africa in general - Races - Indigenous races in general cont.

Afr 8678.31 Marais, J.S. The Cape coloured people, 1652-1937. London, 1939.
Afr 8678.31.5 Marais, J.S. The Cape coloured people, 1652-1937. Johannesburg, 1957.
Afr 8678.32 MacMillan, W.M. The Cape colour question, a historical survey. London, 1927.
Afr 8678.32.2 Macmillan, W.M. The Cape colour question. Facsimile. Cape Town, 1968.
Afr 8678.32.3 MacMillan, W.M. Bantu, Boer, and Briton, the making of the South African native problem. London, 1929.
Afr 8678.32.4 MacMillan, W.M. Bantu, Boer, and Briton. Oxford, 1963.
Afr 8678.32.5 MacMillan, W.M. Complex South Africa, an economic foot-note to history. London, 1930.
Afr 8678.33F South Africa. Native Economic Committee. Report of Native Economic Committee 1930-1932. Pretoria, 1932.
Afr 8678.34 Kirk, J. The economic aspects of native segregation in South Africa. London, 1929.
Afr 8678.35 Barnes, L. Caliban in Africa. London, 1930.
Afr 8678.36 South Africa. Department of Information. The progress of the Bantu peoples towards nationhood. Pretoria, 1965?
Afr 8678.37 South Africa. Parliament. House of Assembly. Select Committee on Native Affairs. First and second (third and fourth [final]) reports of the Select Committee on Native Affairs. Cape Town, 1924.
Afr 8678.39 Schapera, I. The Khoisan peoples of South Africa. London, 1930.
Afr 8678.40.5 Marquand, Leopold. The native in South Africa. 2. ed. Johannesburg, 1944.
Afr 8678.41 Hoernle, R.F.A. South African native policy and the liberal spirit. Cape Town, 1939.
Afr 8678.41.5 Hoernle, R.F.A. South African native policy and the liberal spirit. Johannesburg, 1945.
Afr 8678.42 Krieger, Heinrich. Das Rassenrecht in Südafrika. Berlin, 1944.
Afr 8678.43 Studies and types of South African native life. Durban, 1934.
Afr 8678.44 Peattie, R. Struggle on the Veld. N.Y., 1947.
Afr 8678.45 Hoernle, R.F.A. Race and reason. Johannesburg, 1945.
Afr 8678.47 Cronje, G. 'N truiste vir die nageslag. Johannesburg, 1945.
Afr 8678.47.5 Cronje, G. Regverdige rasse-apartheid. Stellenbosch, 1947.
Afr 8678.49 Cotton, W.A. Racial segregation in South Africa. London, 1931.
Afr 8678.49.7 Cotton, Walter Aidan. The race problem in South Africa. N.Y., 1969.
Afr 8678.51 Rey, Charles F. The Union of South Africa and some of its problems. N.Y., 1947.
Afr 8678.53.2 Roux, Edward. Time longer than rope. 2. ed. Madison, 1964.
Afr 8678.55 Malherbe, E. Race attitudes and education. Johannesburg, 1946.
Afr 8678.57 Hellmann, E. Handbook on race relations in South Africa. Cape Town, 1949.
Afr 8678.57.5 Hellmann, E. In defence of a shared society. Johannesburg, 1956.
Afr 8678.57.10 Hellmann, E. Racial laws versus economic and social forces. Johannesburg, 1955.
Afr 8678.59 Adamastor, (pseud.). White man boss. Boston, 1951.
Afr 8678.60 Dvorin, E.P. Racial separation in South Africa. Chicago, 1952.
Afr 8678.62 Marquard, L. The peoples and policies of South Africa. London, 1952.
Afr 8678.62.2 Marquard, L. The peoples and policies of South Africa. 2d. ed. London, 1960.
Afr 8678.64 Manuel, G. The coloured people. Cape Town, 1943.
Afr 8678.66 India. Information Service. World opinion on apartheid. New Delhi, 1952.
Afr 8678.68 Rhoodie, N.J. Die apartheidsgedougte. Kaapstad, 1960.
Afr 8678.68.5 Rhoodie, N.J. Apartheid. Cape Town, 1960.
Afr 8678.68.12 Rhoodie, N.J. Apartheid en partnership. 2. uitg. Pretoria, 1968.
Afr 8678.68.15 Rhoodie, N.J. Apartheid and racial partnership in Southern Africa. Pretoria, 1969.
Afr 8678.69 Prins, Jan. De beknelde kleurling Zuid-Afrika's vierstromenbeld. Assen, 1967.
Afr 8678.70 Huddleston, T. Naught for your comfort. Garden City, 1956.
Afr 8678.70.10 Steward, Alex. You are wrong. 1. ed. London, 1956.
Afr 8678.71A South Africa. Commission for the Socio-Economic Development of the Bantu Areas. Summary of the report. Pretoria, 1955.
Afr 8678.71B South Africa. Commission for the Socio-Economic Development of the Bantu Areas. Summary of the report. Pretoria, 1955.
Afr 8678.72 Sampson, Anthony. Drum. London, 1956.
Afr 8678.74 Holloway, J.E. The problems of race relations in South Africa. N.Y., 1956.
Afr 8678.76 Dekiewiet, C.W. The anatomy of South African misery. London, 1956.
Afr 8678.78 Keet, B.B. Whither South Africa. Stellenbosch, 1956.
Afr 8678.80 Horrell, Muriel. South Africa's non-white workers. Johannesburg, 1956.
Afr 8678.82 Ziervogel, C. Brown South Africa. Cape Town, 1938.
Afr 8678.84 Houghton, D. Hobart. Life in the Ciskei. Johannesburg, 1955.
Afr 8678.86 Buskes, Johannes Jacobus. South Africa's apartheid policy - unacceptable. Heidelberg, 1956.
Afr 8678.88 Smuts, Jan Christian. The basis of trusteeship in African native policy. Johannesburg, 1942.
Afr 8678.90 Paton, D.M. Church and race in South Africa. London, 1958.
Afr 8678.92 Suid-Afrikaanse Buro vir Rasse-Angeleenthede. Referate geleiver op die jaarvergadering. Stellenbosch. 1,1950+ 6v.
Afr 8678.94 Scott, Michael. A time to speak. London, 1958.
Afr 8678.96F South Africa. Commission of Enquiry on Separate Training Facilities for Non-Europeans at Universities. Report. Pretoria, 1954.
Afr 8678.98 Hogarth, Paul. People like us. London, 1958.
Afr 8678.100 Paton, Alan. Hope for South Africa. London, 1958.
Afr 8678.102 Joshi, Pranshankar Someshwar. Unrest in South Africa. Bombay, 1958.
Afr 8678.104 Duplessis, W.C. Highway to harmony. N.Y., 1958.
Afr 8678.106 Thomas, E.M. The harmless people. 1st ed. N.Y., 1959.

Afr 8678.108	Brayshaw, E. Russell. The racial problems of South Africa. London, 1953.
Afr 8678.110	Jurgens, Isabel. Why cry beloved country. Ilfracombe, 1958.
Afr 8678.115	Hahn, Theophilus. Beitrage zur Kunde der Hottentotten. Durban, 19- .
Afr 8678.120	Brown, William O. Race relations in the American South and in South Africa. Boston, 1959.
Afr 8678.125	Hutchinson, Alfred. Road to Ghana. London, 1960.
Afr 8678.125.5	Hutchinson, Alfred. Road to Ghana. 1st Amer. ed. N.Y., 1960.
Afr 8678.130	Pienaar, S. South Africa. London, 1960.
Afr 8678.135	Fagan, Henry Allan. Our responsibility. Stellenbosch, 1960.
Afr 8678.140	Roskam, Karel Lodewijk. Apartheid and discrimination. Leyden, 1960.
Afr 8678.140.5	Roskam, Karel Lodewijk. Alleen voor blanken. Amsterdam, 1961.
Afr 8678.142F	Russell, Margo. A study of a South African interracial neighbourhood. Durban, 1961.
Afr 8678.143	Mueren, K. van der. Apartheid zonder vooroordelen. Antwerpen, 1958.
Afr 8678.145	Mezerik, Avrahm G. Apartheid in the Union of South Africa. N.Y., 1960.
Afr 8678.147	Merwe, Hendrik J.J.M. Segregeer of Sterf. Johannesburg, 1961.
Afr 8678.150	Brentz, Paul Lenert. Die politischen und gesellschaftlichen Verhältnisse der Sotho-Tswana in Transvaal und Betschauanaland. Hamburg, 1941.
Afr 8678.155	Bruwer, J.P. Die Bantö van Suid-Africa. Johannesburg, 1957.
Afr 8678.155.2	Bruwer, J.P. Die Bantoe van Suid-Africa. Johannesburg, 1963.
Afr 8678.160	Crijns, Arthur. Race relations and race attitudes in South Africa. Nijmegen, 1957.
Afr 8678.165	Phillips, Norman. The tragedy of apartheid. N.Y., 1960.
Afr 8678.167	Phillips, Norman. La tragedia del apartheid. Mexico, 1962.
Afr 8678.170	Joshi, Pranshankar. Apartheid in South Africa. Kimberley, 1950.
Afr 8678.175	Burger, Jan. The gulf between. Cape Town, 1960.
Afr 8678.180	International Commission of Jurists. South Africa and the rule of law. Geneva, 1960.
Afr 8678.185	Reeves, Ambrose. Shooting at Sharpville. London, 1960.
Afr 8678.186	Reeves, Ambrose. South Africa, yesterday and tomorrow. London, 1962.
Afr 8678.190	Sabloniere, Margrit. Apartheid. Amsterdam, 1960.
Afr 8678.195	South African Institute of Race Relations. Monograph series. Johannesburg.
Afr 8678.196F	South African Institute of Race Relations. Fact paper. Johannesburg. 3+ 4v.
Afr 8678.197	South African Institute of Race Relations. Presidential address. Johannesburg.
Afr 8678.200	Dupreez, Andries B. Inside the South African crucible. Kaapstad, 1959.
Afr 8678.205	Moodie, Donald. The record. Amsterdam, 1960.
Afr 8678.210	Doxey, G.V. The industrial colour bar in South Africa. London, 1961.
Afr 8678.215	Spottiswoode, Hildegarde. South Africa. 2. ed. Cape Town, 1960.
Afr 8678.218	Race Relations Journal. Johannesburg. 24,1957+ 2v.
Afr 8678.220	Dison, L.R. Group areas and their development. Durban, 1960.
Afr 8678.222	Forman, L. From the notebooks of Lionel Forman, black and white in South African history. Cape Town, 1960.
Afr 8678.223	Mandela, Nelson Rolihlahla. L'apartheid. Paris, 1965.
Afr 8678.225	South Africa. Inter-Departmental Committee on the Native Pass Law. Report, 1920. Cape Town, 1922.
Afr 8678.230	South Africa. Commission on Rebellion of the Bondelzwarts. Report, 1923. Cape Town, 1923.
Afr 8678.235	South Africa. Commissioner on Native Grievances Inquiry. Report, 1913-1914. Cape Town, 1914.
Afr 8678.240	Debeer, Zacharias Johannes. Multi-racial South Africa. London, 1961.
Afr 8678.245	Deridder, J.C. The personality of the urban African in South Africa. London, 1961.
Afr 8678.250	Knoob, Willi. Die afrikanisch-christlichen Bewegungen unter den Bantu. Köln, 1961.
Afr 8678.250.10	Roumeguère-Eberhardt, Jacqueline. Pensée et société africaines. Paris, 1963.
Afr 8678.255	Krishna Mevor, Vengalil Kreshnan. Question of race conflict resulting from the policies of apartheid. New Delhi, 1959.
Afr 8678.260	Neame, L.E. The history of apartheid. London, 1962.
Afr 8678.265	Vanrensburg, P. Guilty land. London, 1962.
Afr 8678.270	Lardon, Naphail. Noirs et blancs. Paris, 1961.
Afr 8678.275	Giniewski, P. Bantustans. Cape Town, 1961.
Afr 8678.280	Pamphlet vol. South Africa. Races. 5 pam.
Afr 8678.281	Tatz, C. Shadow and substance in South Africa. Pietermaritzburg, 1962.
Afr 8678.282	Cilliers, Stephanus Petrus. The coloureds of South Africa. Cape Town, 1963.
Afr 8678.283	Brown, Douglas. Against the world. London, 1966.
Afr 8678.284	Freeland, Sydney Percy. The Christian gospel and the doctrine of separate development. Pretoria, 1961.
Afr 8678.285	Giniewski, P. Une autre Afrique du Sud. Paris, 1962.
Afr 8678.288	Churchill, Rhona. White man's god. N.Y., 1962.
Afr 8678.289	Steward, Alex. The challenge of change. Cape Town, 1962.
Afr 8678.290	Badertscher, Jean. La segregation raciale en Afrique du Sud. Lausanne, 1962.
Afr 8678.291	Waetberg, Per. På svarta listan. Stockholm, 1960.
Afr 8678.292	Lewin, Jilius. Politics and law in South Africa. London, 1963.
Afr 8678.294	Koos Vorrink Instituut. Zuid-Afrika en de apartheid. Amsterdam, 1962.
Afr 8678.295	Apartheid, feiten en commentaren. Amsterdam, 1966.
Afr 8678.296	South Africa. Commission for the Social Economic Development. The Tomlinson report. Johannesburg, 1956.
Afr 8678.298	Kotze, J.C.G. Principle and practice in race relations. Stellenbosch, 1962.
Afr 8678.299	Brookes, E.H. Power, law, right and love. Durham, 1963.
Afr 8678.300	Haigh, Alan. South African tragedy. London, 1962.

Afr 8678.301	Friedmann, M.V. I will still be moved. Chicago, 1963.
Afr 8678.302	Louw, E.H. The case of South Africa. N.Y., 1963.
Afr 8678.303	Holloway, John Edward. Apartheid, a challenge. Johannesburg, 1964.
Afr 8678.304	Niekerk, R. Ons uis jon Suid-Afrika. Pretoria, 1962.
Afr 8678.305	Gereformeerde Kerke in Suid-Afrika. Algemene Sinode. Uit een bloed. Potchefstroom, 1961.
Afr 8678.306	Botha, David P. Die opkoms van ons derde stand. Kaapstad, 1960.
Afr 8678.307	Duncan, P.B. South Africa's rule of violence. London, 1964.
Afr 8678.308	Snethlage, J.L. Meer begrip voor Suid-Afrika. Amsterdam, 1964.
Afr 8678.309	Horrell, Muriel. Action, reaction and counteraction. Johannesburg, 1963.
Afr 8678.310	Mezerik, A.G. Apartheid in the Republic of South Africa. N.Y., 1964.
Afr 8678.310.5	Mezerik, A.G. Apartheid in the Republic of South Africa. N.Y., 1967.
Afr 8678.311	Abrahams, Peter. Return to Goli. London, 1953.
Afr 8678.312	Brookes, E.H. The city of God and the city of man in Africa. Lexington, 1964.
Afr 8678.313	Pamphlet vol. South African race relations. 5 pam.
Afr 8678.314	Hutt, W.H. The economics of the colour bar. London, 1964.
Afr 8678.315	Magidi, D.T. Black background. N.Y., 1964.
Afr 8678.316	South African Digest. Pretoria. The pattern of race policy in South Africa. Pretoria, 1956.
Afr 8678.317	Pamphlet vol. South Africa. Race question. 8 pam.
Afr 8678.318	United Nations. Secretary-General. A new course in South Africa. N.Y., 1964.
Afr 8678.319	Mbeki, G.A.M. South Africa. Harmondsworth, 1964.
Afr 8678.320	Hill, C.R. Bantustans. London, 1964.
Afr 8678.320.5	Mbata, J.C.M. Urban Bantu councils. Johannesburg, 1965.
Afr 8678.320.10	Ellis, Barbaralyn. Religion among the Bantu in South Africa. Johannesburg, 1968.
Afr 8678.321	Pamphlet vol. South Africa. Race question. 15 pam.
Afr 8678.321.3	Pamphlet vol. South African race question. 11 pam.
Afr 8678.321.5	Mandela, Nelson Rolihlahla. No easy walk to freedom. London, 1965.
Afr 8678.321.10	Pamphlet vol. South Africa. Race question. 8 pam.
Afr 8678.321.15	Pamphlet vol. South African race question. 13 pam.
Afr 8678.321.16	Pamphlet vol. South African race question. 4 pam.
Afr 8678.321.20	Feit, Edward. African opposition in South Africa. Stanford, 1967.
Afr 8678.322	Laurence, John. The seeds of disaster: a guide to the realities, race politics and world-wide propaganda campaigns of the Republic of South Africa. London, 1968.
Afr 8678.323	Legum, Colin. South Africa, crisis for the West. London, 1964.
Afr 8678.324	Cawood, Lesley. The churches and race relations in South Africa. Johannesburg, 1964.
Afr 8678.325	Kuper, Leo. An African bourgeoisie. New Haven, 1965.
Afr 8678.326	Hudson, William. Anatomy of South Africa. Cape Town, 1966.
Afr 8678.327	Namgalies, Ursula. Südafrika Zwischen weiss und schwarz. Stuttgart, 1963.
Afr 8678.328	Eyo, B.E. Apartheid. Jerusalem, 1964.
Afr 8678.329	Nielsen, Waldemar A. African battle line. 1st ed. N.Y., 1965.
Afr 8678.330	British Council of Churches. The future of South Africa. London, 1965.
Afr 8678.331	Katzew, Henry. Apartheid and survival. Cape Town, 1965.
Afr 8678.332	Dominicus, Foort Comelius. Apartheid een wijze voorzorg. Utrecht, 1965.
Afr 8678.333	Schuette, H.G. Weisse ismen, schwarze fakten. Vaterstetten, 1963.
Afr 8678.334	Black, Margaret. No room for tourists. London, 1965.
Afr 8678.335	Pamphlet vol. Bantus. 4 pam.
Afr 8678.336	Kuper, Leo. Passive resistance in South Africa. New Haven, 1957.
Afr 8678.337	Harrell, Muriel. Reserves and reservations. Johannesburg, 1965.
Afr 8678.337.5	Horrell, Muriel. Legislation and race relations. Johannesburg, 1966.
Afr 8678.338	Shepstone, Theophilus. The native question. n.p., n.d.
Afr 8678.339	Campbell, Dugald. Blazing trails in Bantu land. London, 1933.
Afr 8678.340	Rainero, Romain. La segregazione razziale nel Sud Africa. Milano, 1965.
Afr 8678.341	Marof, Achkar. Racism in South Africa. N.Y., 1965.
Afr 8678.342	Levinson, Deirdre. Five years. London, 1966.
Afr 8678.343	Joseph, Helen. Tomorrow's sun. London, 1966.
Afr 8678.343.1	Joseph, Helen. Tomorrow's sun. 1. ed. London, 1968.
Afr 8678.345	Nederduits Gereformeerde Kerk in Suid Afrika. Statements on race relations. Johannesburg. 1,1960//?
Afr 8678.350	Leiss, Amelia Catherine. Apartheid and United Nations collective measures. N.Y., 1965.
Afr 8678.351F	Carter, G.M. South Africa's international position. Cape Town, 1964.
Afr 8678.352	Nienaber, Gabriel Stefanus. Hottentots. Pretoria, 1963.
Afr 8678.353	Manning, Charles Anthony Woodward. The British churches and South Africa. London, 1965.
Afr 8678.354	Mahabahe, Zaccheus R. The good fight. Evanston, 196-.
Afr 8678.355	United Party (South Africa). Handbook for better race relations. Johannesburg, 1963.
Afr 8678.356	Sachs, Emil Solomon. The anatomy of apartheid. London, 1965.
Afr 8678.357	Fuller, Basil. South Africa - not guilty. London, 1957.
Afr 8678.360	Francos, Ania. L'Afrique des Afrikaaners. Paris, 1966.
Afr 8678.362	Savage, R.B. A study of Bantu retail traders in certain areas of the eastern Cape. Grahamstown, 1966.
Afr 8678.363	Blaxall, Arthur William. Wake up South Africa, an essay. Johannesburg, 1966.
Afr 8678.364	Brinkman, H.J. Zuidafrikaans samenleven. Zaandijk, 1964.
Afr 8678.365	Sampson, Harold Fehrsan. The principle of apartheid. Johannesburg, 1966.

Afr 8678   **South Africa in general - Races - Indigenous races in general**
cont.

Afr 8678.366	National Catholic Federation of Students. Moral conflict in South Africa. Johannesburg, 1963.
Afr 8678.367	Hawarden, Eleanor. Prejudice in the classroom. Johannesburg, 1967.
Afr 8678.368	Sacks, Benjamin. South Africa, an imperial dilemma, non-Europeans and the British nation, 1902-1914. 1st ed. Albuquerque, 1967.
Afr 8678.370	Munger, Edwin S. Afrikaner and African nationalism. London, 1967.
Afr 8678.375	Sweden. Utrikesdepartementet. Apartheidfragan i förenta nationerna. Stockholm, 1967.
Afr 8678.376	Bernstein, Hilda. The world that was ours. London, 1967.
Afr 8678.378	Kantor, James. A healthy grave. London, 1967.
Afr 8678.380	India. Ministry of External Affairs. Disabilities of the non-white peoples in the Union of South Africa. Delhi, 1953.
Afr 8678.381	Cole, Ernest. House of bondage. N.Y., 1967.
Afr 8678.382	UNESCO. Apartheid; its effects on education, science, culture and information. Paris, 1967.
Afr 8678.383	Strydom, Christiaan Johannes Scheepers. Black and white Africans. 1st ed. Cape Town, 1967.
Afr 8678.386	Kahn, Ely Jacques. The separated people; a look at contemporary South Africa. 1st ed. N.Y., 1968.
Afr 8678.388	Lever, Henry. Ethnic attitudes of Johannesburg youth. Johannesburg, 1968.
Afr 8678.390	Institute of Administrators of Non-European Affairs. The tightrope dancers; report on the 7th Annual Conference, Institute of Administrators of Non-European Affairs. Durban, 1958.
Afr 8678.392	Brown, Douglas. Against the world. 1st ed. Garden City, 1968.
Afr 8678.395	Kap ohne Hoffnung; oder, Die Politik der Apartheid. Reinbek bei Hamburg, 1965.
Afr 8678.400	Laurence, John. The seeds of disaster; a guide to the realities, race politics and world-wide propaganda campaigns of the Republic of South Africa. N.Y., 1968.
Afr 8678.405	Booth, Joseph. Africa for the African. Photoreproduction. n.p., 1897?
Afr 8678.410	Frye, William R. In whitest Africa; the dynamics of apartheid. Englewood Cliffs, 1968.
Afr 8678.415	Brookes, Edgar Harry. Apartheid. London, 1968.
Afr 8678.420	Whitehead, Sylvia. The story of Sarah. London, 1965.
Afr 8678.425	Glashagen, Ulrich H. Probleme der räumlich getrennten Einbeziehung der Bantu-Bevölkerung Südafrikas in den Wirtschaftsprozes des Landes. Pretoria, 1966.
Afr 8678.428	Ngubane, Jordan K. An African explains apartheid. N.Y., 1963.
Afr 8678.429	Tairov, Tair F. Apartkheid - prestuplenie veka. Moskva, 1968.
Afr 8678.430	Volkskongres oon die toekoms van Bantoe, referate en besluite. Stellenbosch, 1956.
Afr 8678.432	Hirsch, M.I. For whom the land? Salisbury, 1967.
Afr 8678.434	Evans, Maurice Smethurst. Black and white in South East Africa. N.Y., 1969.
Afr 8678.436	Thion, Serge. Le pouvoir pâle. Paris, 1969.
Afr 8678.438	Simons, Harold. Class and colour in South Africa, 1850-1950. Harmondsworth, 1969.
Afr 8678.440	Sachs, Albert. South Africa. London, 1969.
Afr 8678.442	Gorodnov, Valentin P. Iuzhno-afrikanskii rabochii klass v bor'be protiv reaktsii i rasizma. Moskva, 1969.
Afr 8678.444	Ballinger, Margaret. From union to apartheid. N.Y., 1969.
Afr 8678.446	Innes, Duncan. Our country, our responsibility. London, 1969.
Afr 8678.448	Beckers, Gerhard. Religiöse Faktoren in der Entwicklung der südafrikanischen Rassenfrage. München, 1969.
Afr 8678.450	African societies in Southern Africa; historical studies. London, 1969.

Afr 8680   **South Africa in general - Races - Europeans, Asians, etc. - General works**

Afr 8680.5	Eloff, Gerhardus. Rasse en rassevermenging. Bloemfontein, 1942.
Afr 8680.10	Hettema, H.H. De Nederlandse stam in Zuid-Afrika. Zutphen, 1949.
Afr 8680.15	Tingsten, Herbert. The problem of South Africa. London, 1955.
Afr 8680.20	Meihuizen, Jan. Dat vrije volk. Amsterdam, 1941.
Afr 8680.22	Loedolff, J.F. Nederlandse immigrante. Kaapstad, 1960.
Afr 8680.25	MacCrone, Ian Douglas. Race attitudes in South Africa. Johannesburg, 1957.
Afr 8680.30	Dutch Reformed Conference of Church Leaders, Pretoria, 1953. Christian principles in multiracial South Africa. Pretoria, 1954.
Afr 8680.35	Horwitz, Ralph. Expand or explode. Cape Town, 1957.
Afr 8680.40	Neame, Lawrence Elvin. White man's Africa. Cape Town, 1952.
Afr 8680.45	Katzew, Henry. Solution for South Africa. Cape Town, 1955.
Afr 8680.47	Bantu. An informal publication of the Department of Native Affairs of the Union of South Africa. Pretoria, 1954.
Afr 8680.50	Nielsen, Erik W. Afrikanska rasproblem. Stockholm, 1963.
Afr 8680.53	Indian Opinion, Phoenix, Natal. Souvenir of the passive resistance movement in South Africa, 1906-1914. Phoenix, 1914.

Afr 8685   **South Africa in general - Races - Europeans, Asians, etc. - Special**

Afr 8685.1	Hampson, Ruth M. Islam in South Africa. Cape Town, 1964.
Afr 8685.3	Samuelson, L.H. Some Zulu customs and folk-lore. London, n.d.
Afr 8685.5	Bleek, W.H.I. Zulu legends. 1st ed. Pretoria, 1952.
Afr 8685.10F	Jacobson, Evelyn. The cape coloured. Rondebosch, 1945.
Afr 8685.15	Dickie-Clark, H.F. The marginal situation. London, 1966.
Afr 8685.20	Morris, G.R. A bibliography of the Indian question in South Africa. Cape Town, 1946.
Afr 8685.22F	Mann, John William. The problem of the marginal personality. Durban, 1957.
Afr 8685.25	Chatterjee, M.N. Auswanderung aus Indien. I. Inaug. Diss. Leipzig, 1931.
Afr 8685.26	Chatterjee, Santosh Kumar. Indians in South Africa. Calcutta, 1944.
Afr 8685.27	Wetherell, V. The Indian question in South Africa. Cape Town, 1946.
Afr 8685.27.5	Joshi, Pranshankar S. Verdict on South Africa. Bombay, 1945.

Afr 8685   **South Africa in general - Races - Europeans, Asians, etc. - Special**
cont.

Afr 8685.27.7A	Joshi, Pranshankar S. The struggle for equality. Bombay, 1951.
Afr 8685.27.7B	Joshi, Pranshankar S. The struggle for equality. Bombay, 1951.
Afr 8685.27.10	Khan, Shafa At A. The Indian in South Africa. Allahabad, 1946.
Afr 8685.27.15	Narain, I. The politics of racialism. 1. ed. Agra, 1962.
Afr 8685.27.20	Mukhamedova, Dil'bar. Iz istorii rasovoi diskriminatsii inditsev v Iuzhnoi Afrike. Tashkent, 1965.
Afr 8685.27.25	The Indian South African. Durban, 1967.
Afr 8685.30	Herman, L. A history of the Jews in South Africa. London, 1930.
Afr 8685.30.2	Herman, L. A history of the Jews in South Africa from the earliest times to 1895. Johannesburg, 1935.
Afr 8685.35	Cronje, Geoffrey. Afrika soder die asiaat. Johannesburg, 1946.
Afr 8685.40	Joshi, Pranshankar S. The tyranny of colour. Durban, 1942.
Afr 8685.45	Lenk, Heinrich von. Die Geschichte der Buren. Leipzig, 1901-3.
Afr 8685.46	Anjar, P.L. Conflict of races in South Africa. Durban, 1946.
Afr 8685.50	Calpin, G.H. Indians in South Africa. Pietermaritzburg, 1949.
Afr 8685.50.5	Calpin, G.H. There are no South Africans. London, 1944.
Afr 8685.55	Patterson, S. Colour and culture in South Africa. London, 1953.
Afr 8685.55.1	Patterson, S. Colour and culture in South Africa. N.Y., 1953.
Afr 8685.55.5	Patterson, S. The last trek. London, 1957.
Afr 8685.60	Schnell, E.L.G. For men must work. Capetown, 1954.
Afr 8685.61	Carstens, W. Peter. The social structure of a cape coloured reserve. Cape Town, 1966.
Afr 8685.65	Schaltz, Gert D. Het die afrikaanse volk n toekoms. 3. druk. Johannesburg, 1954.
Afr 8685.70	Schmidt-Pretoria, W. Deutsche Wanderung nach Südafrika im 19. Jahrhundert. Berlin, 1955.
Afr 8685.70.5	Schwaer, J. Deutsche in Kaffraria. King Williams Town, 1958.
Afr 8685.75	Horrell, Muriel. The group areas act. Johannesburg, 1956.
Afr 8685.80	Sen, Dhirendra Kumar. The position of Indians in South Africa. Calcutta, 1950.
Afr 8685.82	Theron, Erika. Die kleurlingbevolking van Suid-Afrika, Stellenbosch. Grahamstad, 1964.
Afr 8685.85	Reeves, Ambrose. The pass laws and slavery. London, 1961.
Afr 8685.89	Benson, Mary. South Africa, the struggle for a birthright. London, 1966.
Afr 8685.90	Benson, Mary. The African patriots. London, 1963.
Afr 8685.95	South Africa. Department of Bantu Administration and Development. Summary of the report of the Committee on Foreign Affairs. Johannesburg, 1964.
Afr 8685.96	Holm, Erik. Tier und Gott. Basel, 1965.
Afr 8685.98	Verner, Beryl Anne. Huguenots in South Africa; a bibliography. Cape Town, 1967.
Afr 8685.100	Fiat Lux. Durban. 2,1967+
Afr 8685.102	Fisher, John. The Afrikaners. London, 1969.
Afr 8685.104	Meer, Fatima. Portrait of Indian South Africans. Durban, 1969.
Afr 8685.327	Rousseau, Francois. Handbook on the Group Areas Act. Cape Town, 1960.

Afr 8686   **South Africa in general - Religion; missions**

Afr 8686.2	Arnot, Frederick Stanley. From Natal to the Upper Zambesi. 2. ed. Glasgow, 1883.
Afr 8686.3	Chirgwin, Arthur Mitchell. An African pilgrimage. London, 1932.
Afr 8686.4	Kellermann, Abraham Gerhardus. Profetisme in Suid-Afrika in akkulturasie perspektief. Proefschrift. Voorburg, 1964.
Afr 8686.5	Clavier, Henri. Thomas Arbousset. Paris, 1965.
Afr 8686.8	Stewart, James. Lovedale, South Africa. Edinburgh, 1894.
Afr 8686.10	Hance, Gertrude Rachel. The Zulu yesterday and today; twenty-nine years in South Africa. N.Y., 1916.
Afr 8686.12	Weber, Karl Friedrich. Kreuz zwischen Weiss und Schwarz. Breklum, 1965.
Afr 8686.14	Krueger, Bernhard. The pear tree blossoms; a history of the Moravian mission stations in South Africa, 1737-1869. Thesis. Genadendal, 1966.
Afr 8686.16	Wiberg, Erik. Hundra dagar i Afrika. Jönköping, 1967.
Afr 8686.18	Christofersen, Arthur Fridtjof. Adventuring with God. Durban, 1967.
Afr 8686.20	Champion, George. Journal of the Reverend George Champion. Cape Town, 1967.
Afr 8686.22	Ive, Anthony. The Church of England in South Africa. Cape Town, 1966.
Afr 8686.24F	Engelbrecht, Stephanus P. Album vir die geskiedenis van die Nederduitsch Hervormde Kerk van Afrika. Pretoria, 1965.
Afr 8686.26	Cowie, Margaret J. South African missionary bibliography. n.p., n.d. 2 pam.
Afr 8686.28	Strassberger, Elfriede. The Rhenish Mission Society in South Africa. Cape Town, 1969.

Afr 8687.1 - .99   **South Africa in general - Biographies - Collected (A-Z, 99 scheme, by author)**

Afr 8687.7	Bell, Nancy R.E. (Mevgens). Heroes of discovery in South Africa. London, 1899.
Afr 8687.42	Jaff, Fay. They came to South Africa. Cape Town, 1963.

Afr 8687.101 - .399   **South Africa in general - Biographies - Individual (A-Z, 299 scheme, by person)**

Afr 8687.101	Abercrombie, H.R. The secret history of South Africa. 2. ed. Johannesburg, 1952.
Afr 8687.105	Paton, Alan. The people wept. Kloop, 1959.
Afr 8687.109	Altmann, Hendrik. Overdrafts and overwork. Cape Town, 1959.
Afr 8687.111	Anderson, Kenneth. Heroes of South Africa. Cape Town, 1955.
Afr 8687.124	Udeman, Elsa. The published works of Margaret Livingstone Ballinger; a bibliography. Johannesburg, 1968.
Afr 8687.126	Barlow, Arthur G. Almost in confidence. Cape Town, 1952.
Afr 8687.128	Scully, W.C. Sir J.H. Meiring Beck. Cape Town, 1921.
Afr 8687.131	Berger, Lucy Gough. Where's the madam? Cape Town, 1966.
Afr 8687.132	Besselaar, Gerrit. Sestig jaar belewenis van dietse kultuur. Pretoria, 1941.

Afr 8687.101 - .399   South Africa in general - Biographies - Individual
(A-Z, 299 scheme, by person)
cont.

Afr 8687.137	Spohr, Otto H. Wilhelm Heinrich Immanuel Bleek. Cape Town, 1962.
Afr 8687.137.5	Blaxall, Arthur. Suspended sentence. London, 1965.
Afr 8687.137.10	Bleek, Wilhelm Heinrich Immanuel. The Natal diaries of Dr. W.H.I. Bleek, 1855-1856. Cape Town, 1965.
Afr 8687.141	Bowker, John. Speeches. Cape Town, 1962.
Afr 8687.142	Bresler, Casparus Philippus. Tilt the sack. Pretoria, 1965.
Afr 8687.143	Broome, F.N. Not the whole truth. Pietermaritzburg, 1962.
Afr 8687.144	Roux, Edward. S.P. Bunting. Cape Town, 1944.
Afr 8687.150	Carr, Barbara Comyns. Cherries on my plate. Cape Town, 1965.
Afr 8687.166	Cranwell, Margaret. An epoch of the political history of South Africa. Cape Town, 195-.
Afr 8687.174	Boreham, Frank W. The man who saved Gandhi, John Joseph Doke. London, 1948.
Afr 8687.174.5	Cursons, William E. Joseph Doke. Johannesburg, 1929.
Afr 8687.175	Rose, Walter. Bushman, whale and dinosaur. Cape Town, 1961.
Afr 8687.200A	Wallis, John P.R. Fitz. London, 1955.
Afr 8687.200B	Wallis, John P.R. Fitz. London, 1955.
Afr 8687.200.20	Fischer, Maria Adriana. Kampdagboek. Kaapstad, 1964.
Afr 8687.202	Livingstone, William. Christina Forsyth of Fingoland. London, 1918.
Afr 8687.221	Metrowich, F.C. Scotty Smith. Cape Town, 1962.
Afr 8687.225	Guthrie, F.H. Frontier magistrate. Cape Town, 1946.
Afr 8687.228	Heerden, Petronella van. Kerssnutsels. Kaapstad, 1962.
Afr 8687.228.5	Heerden, Petronella van. Die sestiende koppie. Kaapstad, 1965.
Afr 8687.230	Macdonald, Tom. Jan Hofmeyer. London, 1948.
Afr 8687.238	Innes, James Rose. Autobiography. Cape Town, 1949.
Afr 8687.245	Jabavu, N. Drawn in colour. London, 1960.
Afr 8687.245.5	Jabavu, N. The Ochre people. N.Y., 1963.
Afr 8687.245.10	Jackson, Albert. Trader on the veld. Cape Town, 1958.
Afr 8687.248	Barnes, Bertram Herbert. Johnson of Nyasaland. Westminster, 1933.
Afr 8687.250	Kentridge, Morris. I recall. Johannesburg, 1959.
Afr 8687.251	Kohler, C.W.H. The memoirs of Kohler of the K.W.V. London, 1946.
Afr 8687.258	Smith, E.W. The life and times of Daniel Lindley. N.Y., 1952.
Afr 8687.258.5	Lister, Georgina. Reminiscences. Johannesburg, 1960.
Afr 8687.262	Louw, Abraham F. My eerste neentig jaar. Kaapstad, 1958.
Afr 8687.262.5	Louw, Andries Andriaan. Andrew Louw van Morgenster. Kaapstad, 1965.
Afr 8687.263	Luthuli, A. Let my people go. N.Y., 1962.
Afr 8687.263.5	Callan, Edward. Albert John Luthuli and the South African race conflict. Kalamazoo, 1962.
Afr 8687.263.10	Benson, M. Chief Albert Lutuli of South Africa. London, 1963.
Afr 8687.265	Walker, O. Sailor Malan. London, 1953.
Afr 8687.265.5	Robins, Eric. This man Malan. Cape Town, 1953.
Afr 8687.265.10	Pretorius, Gert. Die Malans van Môrewag. Kaapstad, 1965.
Afr 8687.271	Lehmann, Olga. Look beyond the wind; the life of Hans Merensky. Capetown, 1955?
Afr 8687.271.5	Lehmann, Olga. Hans Merensky. Göttingen, 1965.
Afr 8687.273	Cowley, Cecil. Kwa Zulu. Cape Town, 1966.
Afr 8687.274	Modisane, B. Blame me on history. London, 1963.
Afr 8687.275	Molema, S.M. Montshiwa, 1815-1896. Cape Town, 1966.
Afr 8687.278	Spies, F.J. du T. N Nederlander in diens van-die Oranjevrystaat. (Mueller, H.P.N.). Amsterdam, 1946.
Afr 8687.281	Gutsche, Thelma. Selective index to Not heaven itself; an autobiography. 2. ed. Johannesburg, 1968.
Afr 8687.284	Nicholls, G.H. South Africa in my time. London, 1961.
Afr 8687.294	Gregory, T.E.G. Ernest Oppenheimer and the economic development of southern Africa. Cape Town, 1962.
Afr 8687.308	Huenermann, Wilhelm. Der gehorsame Rebell. Innsbruck, 1959.
Afr 8687.308.5	Huenermann, G. Le rebelle obéissant. 2. ed. Mulhouse, 1960.
Afr 8687.309	Philipps, T. Philipps, 1820 settler. Pietermaritzburg, 1960.
Afr 8687.309.5	Gutsche, Thelma. No ordinary woman. Cape Town, 1966.
Afr 8687.320	Mcfall, J.L. Trust betrayed, the murder of Sister Mary Aidan. Cape Town, 1963.
Afr 8687.322	Ralls, Alice M. Glory which is yours. Pietermaritzburg, 1949.
Afr 8687.323	Reitz, Hjalmar. The conversion of a South African nationalist. Cape Town, 1946.
Afr 8687.323.5	Reitz, Conrad Hjalmar. The Reitz family. Cape Town, 1964.
Afr 8687.323.25	Metelerkamp, Sanni. George Rex of Knysna. London, 1963.
Afr 8687.335	Schiel, Adolf. Drei-und-zwanzig Jahre Sturm und Sonnenschein in Südafrika. Leipzig, 1902.
Afr 8687.335.5	Schonegevel, Bernardo. This much I'll tell. Cape Town, 1959.
Afr 8687.339	Shaw, William. Never a young man: extracts from the letters and journals of the Reverend William Shaw. Cape Town, 1967.
Afr 8687.342	Solomon, W.E. Saul Solomon, the member for Cape Town. Cape Town, 1948.
Afr 8687.345	Spulhaus, Karl Antonio. From Lisbon via Lübeck to Cape Town. Cape Town, 1960.
Afr 8687.347	Boeeseken, Anna J. Simon van der Stel en sy kinders. Kaapstad, 1964.
Afr 8687.354	Cheeseman, Thomas. The story of William Threlfall. Cape Town, 1910.
Afr 8687.359	Tremlett, Rex. Road to Ophir. London, 1956.
Afr 8687.375	Van der Spuy, Kenneth R. Chasing the wind. Cape Town, 1966.
Afr 8687.380	Pretorius, G. Man van die daad. Kaapstad, 1959.
Afr 8687.386	Wilder, George Albert. The white African. Bloomfield, 1933.

Afr 8688   South Africa in general - Heraldry and genealogy

Afr 8688.5	Pama, C. Die wapens van die ou afrikaanse families. Kaapstad, 1959.
Afr 8688.5.5	Pama, C. Simbole van die Unie. Kaapstad, 1960.
Afr 8688.5.10	Pama, C. Heraldiek in Suid-Afrika. Kaapstad, 1956.
Afr 8688.5.15	Pama, C. Die unievlag. Kaapstad, 1957.
Afr 8688.5.20	Pama, C. Lions and virgins. Cape Town, 1965.
Afr 8688.5.25	Partridge, A.C. The story of our South African flag. Cape Town, 1966.
Afr 8688.6	Villiers, Daniel P. A history of the de Villiers family. Cape Town, 1960.

Afr 8688   South Africa in general - Heraldry and genealogy
cont.

Afr 8688.7	Hoge, J. Bydraes tot die genealogie van ou afrikaanse families. Amsterdam, 1958.
Afr 8688.7.10	Villiers, Christoffel Coetzee de. Geslagsregisters van die ou Kaapse families. Kaapstad, 1966.
Afr 8688.10F	Morkel, Philip William. The Morkels; family history and family tree. Cape Town, 1961. 2v.
Afr 8688.12	Joûbert, Joseph. Les armoiries de la République Sud-africaine. Paris, 1903.
Afr 8688.14.3	Malherbe, Daniel François du Toit. Stamregister van die Suid-Afrikaanse volk. 3. uitg. Stellenbosch, 1966.
Afr 8688.230	Hopkins, Henry Charles. Die Smalberger familieregister. Wynberg, 1962.

Afr 8690   South Africa in general - Local, indefinite

Afr 8690.5	Muller, D.J. The Orange river. Cape Town, 1953.
Afr 8690.15	Rosenthal, E. River of diamonds. Cape Town, 1957.
Afr 8690.20	Birkby, Carel. In the sun I'm rich. Cape Town, 1953.
Afr 8690.25	Ridsdale, Benjamin. Scenes and adventures in great Namaqualand. London, 1883.

Afr 8695   British trust territories in South Africa in general

Afr 8695.5	Dundas, Charles C.F. Problem territories of southern Africa. Cape Town, 1952.
Afr 8695.10	Royal Institute of International Affairs. The high commission territories. London, 1963.
Afr 8695.11	Halpern, Jack. South Africa's hostages. Harmondsworth, Eng., 1965.

Afr 8700   Cape Colony - Periodicals

Afr 8700.3	Wackrill, Jill D. Index to the Cape Illustrated Magazine. Johannesburg, 1963.
Afr 8700.5	Cape Town mirror. Cape Town. 1,1848+
Afr 8700.10F	Rhodes University, Grahamstown, South Africa. Institute of Social and Economic Research. Report.

Afr 8703   Cape Colony - Bibliographies

Afr 8703.5	Barker, Mary. Sir Benjamin d'Urbans administration. Cape Town, 1946.
Afr 8703.10	Southery, N. Monica. Kimberley and the diamond fields of Griqualand West. Cape Town, 1946.

Afr 8705   Cape Colony - Pamphlet volumes

Afr 8705.1	Pamphlet box. South Africa. Cape colony.

Afr 8707   Cape Colony - Collected source materials

Afr 8707.5	Theal, G.M. Records of Cape colony. v.1-35 and index. London, 1897-1905. 36v.
Afr 8707.10	Cape of Good Hope civil service list. Cape Town. 1888+ 3v.
Afr 8707.12	Cape of Good Hope almanac and register. Cape Town. 1849+ 5v.

Afr 8710   Cape Colony - Government and administration

Afr 8710.10	Kilpin, Ralph. The romance of a colonial parliament. London, 1930.
Afr 8710.10.5	Kilpin, Ralph. The parliament of the Cape. London, 1938.
Afr 8710.15	Botha, C.G. An eighteenth century law library. Cape Town, 1935.
Afr 8710.17	Vanlille, A.J. The native council system with special reference to the Transvaal local councils. Pretoria, 1938.
Afr 8710.19	Rosenthal, Eric. The changing years. Cape Town, 1957.
Afr 8710.20	Cape of Good Hope. Die administrasie van Kaapland, 1910-1960. Kaapstad, 1960.
Afr 8710.22	McCracken, John Leslie. The Cape parliament, 1854-1910. Oxford, 1967.

Afr 8714 - 8720   Cape Colony - General history (By date)

Htn	Afr 8718.42*	Cannon, R. History of Cape Mounted Riflemen. London, 1842.
	Afr 8718.66	Haussmann, A. Souvenirs du Cap de Bonne-Espérance. Paris, 1866.
	Afr 8718.69	Wilmot, A. History of the colony of the Cape of Good Hope. Cape Town, 1869.
	Afr 8719.01	Cappon, James. Britain's title in South Africa. London, 1901.
	Afr 8719.37	Nathan, M. The Voortrekkers of South Africa. Johannesburg, 1937.
	Afr 8719.62	Botha, C.G. Collected works. Cape Town, 1962. 3v.

Afr 8722   Cape Colony - General special

Afr 8722.2.1	Wright, William. Slavery at the Cape of Good Hope. N.Y., 1969.

Afr 8735   Cape Colony - History by periods - 1814-1853

Afr 8735.3	Newman, W.A. Biographical memoir of John Montagu. London, 1855.
Afr 8735.4	Botha, Andries. Trial of Andries Botha for high treason. Cape Town, 1852.
Afr 8735.4.5	Botha, Andries. Trial of Andries Botha. Cape Town, 1969.
Afr 8735.5	Notes on the Cape of Good Hope...1820. London, 1821.
Afr 8735.5.5	Sheffield, T. The story of the settlement with a sketch of Grahamstown as it was. 2d ed. Grahamstown, 1884.
Afr 8735.5.10	Edwards, I.E. Eighteen-twenty settlers in South Africa. London, 1934.
Afr 8735.5.15A	Hockly, H.E. The story of the British settlers of 1820 in South Africa. Cape Town, 1948.
Afr 8735.5.15B	Hockly, H.E. The story of the British settlers of 1820 in South Africa. Cape Town, 1948.
Afr 8735.5.15.2	Hockly, H.E. The story of the British settlers of 1820 in South Africa. 2. ed. Cape Town, 1957.
Afr 8735.5.20	Rivett-Carnac, D. Thus came the English in 1820. 2. ed. Cape Town, 1946.
Afr 8735.10	Dracopoli, J.L. Sir Andries Stockenstrom, 1792-1864; the origin of the racial conflict in South Africa. Cape Town,

Afr 8740   Cape Colony - History by periods - 1853-1872

Afr 8740.5	Lindley, A.E. Adamantia. London, 1873.

Afr 8745   Cape Colony - History by periods - 1872-1910
Afr 8745.10   Schriener, O. The political situation. London, 1896.
Afr 8745.15   Strydom, C.J.S. Kaapland en die Tweede Vryheidsoorlog. Kaapstad, 1937.
Afr 8745.20   Krueger, D.W. The age of the generals. Johannesburg, 1958.

Afr 8750   Cape Colony - History by periods - 1910-
Afr 8805   Pamphlet box. South Africa. Cape colony.

Afr 8808 - 8810   Cape Colony - Geography, description, etc. - General works (By date)
Htn   Afr 8808.18*   Latrobe, C.I. Journal of a visit to South Africa 1815-1816. London, 1818.
Afr 8808.23   State of the Cape of Good Hope in 1822. London, 1823.
Afr 8808.23.5   Bird, William Wilberforce. State of the Cape of Good Hope in 1822. Cape Town, 1966.
Afr 8808.24   Rose, C. Four years in southern Africa. London, 1829.
Afr 8808.35   Moodie, John W.D. Ten years in South Africa. London, 1835. 2v.
Afr 8808.41   Shaw, B. Memorials of South Africa. London, 1841.
Afr 8808.41.3   Shaw, B. Memorials of South Africa. N.Y., 1841.
Afr 8808.42   Moffatt, Robert. Missionary labours...in southern Africa. London, 1842.
Afr 8808.42.9   Moffatt, Robert. Missionary labours...in southern Africa. 9. ed. N.Y., 1846.
Afr 8808.42.11   Moffatt, Robert. Missionary labours...in southern Africa. 11. ed. N.Y., 1850.
Afr 8808.43   Chase, John C. The Cape of Good Hope...Algoa bay. London, 1843.
Afr 8808.43.5   Chase, John C. The Cape of Good Hope and the Eastern Province of Algoa Bay. Facsimile. Cape Town, 1967.
Afr 8808.48   Bunbury, C.J.F. Journal of a residence at Cape of Good Hope. London, 1848.
Afr 8808.52   Hatfield, E.F. Saint Helena and the Cape of Good Hope. N.Y., 1852.
Afr 8808.52.2   Cole, A.W. The Cape and the Kafirs. London, 1852.
Afr 8808.61   Duff-Gordon, Lucie. Letters from the Cape. London, 1921.
Afr 8808.61.5   Duff-Gordon, Lucie. Letters from the Cape. London, 1927.
Afr 8808.61.10   Life at the Cape a hundred years ago. Cape Town, 1963.
Afr 8808.65   Drayson, A.W. Tales at the outspan, or adventures in South Africa. London, 1865.
Afr 8808.69   Noble, R. The Cape and its people, and other essays. Cape Town, 1869.
Afr 8808.72   Chapman, Charles. A voyage from Southhampton to Cape Town. London, 1872.
Afr 8808.75   Noble, John. Descriptive handbook of the Cape colony. Cape Town, 1875.
Afr 8808.79   Ballantyne, R.M. Six months at the Cape. London, 1879.
Afr 8808.86   Noble, John. History, productions and resources of Cape of Good Hope. Cape Town, 1886.
NEDL   Afr 8808.86.2   Noble, John. History, productions and resources of the Cape of Good Hope. Cape Town, 1886.
Afr 8808.87   Ellis, A.B. South African sketches. London, 1887.
Afr 8808.89   Bryden, H.A. Kloof and Karoo...in Cape colony. London, 1889.
Afr 8809.10   Juta, Rene. The Cape peninsula. Cape Town, 1910.
Afr 8809.15   Scully, W.C. Lodges in the wilderness. London, 1915.
Afr 8809.27   Mossop, E.E. Old Cape highways. Cape Town, 1927.
Afr 8809.41   Merwe, Petrus J. van der. Pioniers van die Dorsland. Kaapstad, 1941.
Afr 8809.46   Middlemiss, E. Cape country. Cape Town, 1946.
Afr 8809.51   Luckhoff, C.A. Table mountain. Cape Town, 1951.
Afr 8809.52   Hondius, J. Klare besgryving van Cabo de Bona Esperança. Kaapstad, 1952.
Afr 8809.60   Meintzis, Johannes. Complex canvas. Johannesburg, 1960.
Afr 8809.61   Rosenthal, Eric. The story of Table mountain. Cape Town, 1961.
Afr 8809.61.5   Vanonsden, L. Trekboer. Cape Town, 1961.
Afr 8809.62   Board, Chr. The border region, natural environment and land use in the eastern Cape. Cape Town, 1962. 2v.
Afr 8809.62.5   Burman, Jose. Safe to the sea. Kaapstad, 1962.
Afr 8809.63   Burman, Jose. So high the road, mountain passes of the western Cape. Cape Town, 1963.
Afr 8809.65   South African heritage, from van Riebeeck to nineteenth century times. Cape Town, 1965.

Afr 8813   Cape Colony - Geography, description, etc. - Special customs
Afr 8813.2   Bouws, Jan. Die musieklewe van Kaapstad, 1800-1850. Thesis. Kaapstadt, 1966.

Afr 8815   Cape Colony - Geography, description, etc. - Guidebooks
Afr 8815.2   Guide to the Cape province of South Africa. Cape Town. 3,1960+
Afr 8815.4   Irons, H. The settler's guide to the Cape of Good Hope and colony of Natal. London, 1858.
Afr 8815.5   General directory and guide book, to Cape of Good Hope. Cape Town, 1872.
Afr 8815.8   Port Elizabeth directory and guide. Port Elizabeth, 1877.
Afr 8815.10   East London, Cape of Good Hope. City Council. The city of East London. Cape Town, 1950.

Afr 8817   Cape Colony - Geography, description, etc. - Views
Afr 8817.2   Bulpin, Thomas V. The Cape province. Cape Town, 1960.

Afr 8820   Cape Colony - Economic and financial conditions
Afr 8820.5   Houghton, D. Hobart. Economic development in a plural society. Cape Town, 1960.
Afr 8820.6   Illiers, Stephanus. Wes-Kaapland. Stellenbosch, 1964.

Afr 8825   Cape Colony - Races - Special
Afr 8825.3   Hahn, T. Tsuni-Goam, the supreme being. London, 1881.
Afr 8825.4   Beverley, R.M. The wrongs of the Caffre nation. London, 1837.
Afr 8825.4.3   Maclean, J. A compendium of Kafir laws and customs. Mount Cape, 1858. 2 pam.
Afr 8825.4.5   Callaway, Godfrey. Sketches of Kafir life. Oxford, 1905.
Afr 8825.6   Cook, R.A.W. Social organisation and ceremonial institutions of the Bomvana. Cape Town, 19- .
Afr 8825.8   Schonken, F.T. De oorsprong der kaapsch-hollandsche volksoveringen. Amsterdam, 1914.
Afr 8825.10   Halford, S.J. The Griquas of Griqualand. Cape Town, 1949.
Afr 8825.15   Duplessis, I.D. The Cape Malays. Cape Town, 1944.
Afr 8825.20   United Party. The Cape coloured vote. Cape Town, 1954.

Afr 8825   Cape Colony - Races - Special
cont.
Afr 8825.25   Kock, V. de. Those in bondage. Cape Town, 1950.
Afr 8825.30   Mayer, Philip. Xhosa in town. Cape Town, 1961-63. 3v.
Afr 8825.35   Hammond-Tooke, W.D. Bhaca society. Cape Town, 1962.
Afr 8825.40   South Africa. Department of Coloured Affairs. Opportunities for the coloureds. Pretoria, 1963.
Afr 8825.45   Banch, Kurt. Deutsche Kultur am Kap. 1st ed. Capetown, 1964.

Afr 8828   Cape Colony - Religion; missions
Afr 8828.5   Hinchliff, Peter Brigham. Calendar of Cape missionary correspondence, 1800-1850. Pretoria, 1967.

Afr 8830   Cape Colony - Local - Districts (Karoo, etc.)
Afr 8830.5   Martin, A. Home life on an ostrich farm. London, 1890.
Afr 8830.6   Hallbeck, H.P. Narrative of visit made in 1819 to...Erron. London, 1820.
Afr 8830.7   Fleming, F. Kaffraria, and its inhabitants. London, 1853.
Afr 8830.8   Alberti, J.C.L. Die Kaffern auf der Südküste von Afrika. Gotha, 1815.
Afr 8830.9   King Williams Town, Cape of Good Hope. King Williams Town, Cape province. Cape Town, 1836.
Afr 8830.10   Green, L.G. Beyond the city lights. Cape Town, 1957.
Afr 8830.12   Green, Lawrence George. Karoo, the story of the Karoos of South Africa - the great Karoo. Cape Town, 1955.

Afr 8835   Cape Colony - Local - Cape Town
Afr 8835.3   Cape Town. The Cape of Good Hope. Cape Town, 1911.
Afr 8835.5   Cape Town. The Cape of Good Hope. 4. ed. Cape Town, 1926.
Afr 8835.10   Cape Town. Foreshore Joint Technical Committee. The Cape Town Foreshore plan. Cape Town, 1948.
Afr 8835.15   Duplessis, I.D. The Malay quarter and its people. Cape Town, 1953.
Afr 8835.20   Tonder, I.W. Van Riebeecksestad. 1. uitg. Kaapstad, 1950.
Afr 8835.21   Burman, Jose. Peninsula profile, a guide to the fairest cape. Johannesburg, 1963.
Afr 8835.25   Lewis, C. Cape Town. Cape Town, 1934.
Afr 8835.25.2   Lewis, C. Cape Town. Cape Town, 1927.
Afr 8835.26   Honikman, Alfred Harold. Cape Town, city of Good Hope. Cape Town, 1966.
Afr 8835.30   Wagner, O.J.M. Poverty and dependency in Cape Town. Cape Town, 1936.
Afr 8835.35   Laidler, Percy Ward. A tavern of the ocean. Cape Town, 1926.
Afr 8835.36   Shorten, John R. Cape Town, a record of the mother city from the earliest days to the present. Cape Town, 1963.
Afr 8835.40F   Varley, Vera. Index to the growth and government of Cape Town. Cape Town, 1961.
Afr 8835.41   Laidler, Percy Ward. The growth and government of Cape Town. Cape Town, 1939.
Afr 8835.43F   Bowler, Thomas William. Pictorial album of Cape Town. Cape Town, 1966.
Afr 8835.46   Bax, Dirk. Argitektoniese shoonheid in Kaapstadse kompanjiestuin, 1777-1805. Kaapstad, 1963.
Afr 8835.47   Merkens, Alice. Cape Town, Kaapstad, Kapstadt. 2. ed. Cape Town, 1962.
Afr 8835.48   Orpen, Neil. Gunners of the Cape. Cape Town, 1965.
Afr 8835.49   Rosenthal, Eric. Three hundred years of the castle at Cape Town. Capetown, 1966.
Afr 8835.50   Manuel, George. District Six. Cape Town, 1967.
Afr 8835.55   Green, Lawrence George. Tavern of the seas. Cape Town, 1966.
Afr 8835.58   Williams, Roger. Cape Town Africans today. Johannesburg, 1965.
Afr 8835.60   Cape directory. Cape Town, 1800.

Afr 8838   Cape Colony - Local - Jansenville
Afr 8838.2   Fourie, S. Jansenville yesterday and today. Jansenville, 1956.

Afr 8840   Cape Colony - Local - Kimberly
Afr 8840.5   Cohen, L. Reminiscences of Kimberley. London, 1911.
Afr 8840.10   Kimberley, South Africa. The city of Kimberley. Cape Town, 1952.

Afr 8844   Cape Colony - Local - Pondoland
Afr 8844.5   Wilson, M. Hunter. Reaction to conquest. London, 1936.
Afr 8844.5.2   Wilson, M. Hunter. Reaction to conquest. London, 1961.
Afr 8844.10   Callaway, G. Pioneers in Pondoland. Lovedale, 1939.

Afr 8845   Cape Colony - Local - Port Elizabeth
Afr 8845.5   Price, G.N. Port Elizabeth, a bibliography. Cape Town, 1949.
Afr 8845.8   Leigh, Ramon Lewis. The city of Port Elizabeth. Johannesburg, 1966.
Afr 8845.10   Redgrave, J.J. Port Elizabeth in bygone days. Wynberg, 1947.
Afr 8845.15   Port Elizabeth Publicity Association. Port Elizabeth municipal centenary. Port Elizabeth, 1960.
Afr 8845.16   Port Elizabeth Publicity Association. This is Port Elizabeth. Port Elizabeth, 1963.

Afr 8846   Cape Colony - Local - Transkeian Territory
Afr 8846.10   Transkeian Territories. Native Appeal Court. Reports of cases decided in the native appeal courts of the Transkeian territories, 1914. Cape Town, 1912.
Afr 8846.15   Kenyon, J.T. An address delivered at the University of Stellenbosch on 12th, 13th, 14th Oct. 1932. n.p., 1932.
Afr 8846.15.5   Kenyon, J.T. An address on the general council administration system of the Transkeian territories, rev. 1939. n.p., 1939.
Afr 8846.16   Mbeki, Govan Archibald Mrunyelwa. Transkei in the making. n.p., 1939.
Afr 8846.17   Brownlee, F. The Transkeian native territories. n.p., 1923.
Afr 8846.19   Pim, H. A Transkei enquiry, 1933. Lovedale, 1934.
Afr 8846.20   National Union of South African Students. The Transkei survey. Cape Town, 1951.
Afr 8846.25   Schroth, H. Die Transkei-Territorien, ihre Entstehung. Inaug. Diss. Bottropi, 1936.
Afr 8846.26   Bellwood, W. Whither the Transkei. London, 1964.
Afr 8846.30   Carter, Gwendolen Margaret. South Africa's Transkei, the politics of domestic colonialism. Evanston, 1967.
Afr 8846.30.5   Carter, Gwendolen Margaret. Separate development. Johannesburg, 1966.

Afr 8846   **Cape Colony - Local - Transkeian Territory**
cont.

Afr 8846.32	Broster, Joan A. Red blanket valley. Johannesburg, 1967.
Afr 8846.34	South Africa. Department of Information. The Transkei; emancipation without chaos. Pretoria, 1966?

Afr 8847   **Cape Colony - Local - Other local (A-Z, 99 scheme, by place)**

Afr 8847.21	Barker, John P. Industrial development in a border area. Grahamstown, 1964.
Afr 8847.32	Staes, E.L.P. George, die verhaal van die dorp en distrik. George, 1961.
Afr 8847.34	Collier, Joy. Frontier post, the story of Grahamstown. Grahamstown, 1961.
Afr 8847.34.50	Murray, Marischal. Under lion's head. 2. ed. Cape Town, 1964.
Afr 8847.34.75	Records of a pioneer family. Capetown, 1966
Afr 8847.34.100	Shaw, R.C. Graaff-Reinet, a bibliography. Cape Town, 1964.
Afr 8847.37	Tredgold, Ardeme. Village of the sea. Cape Town, 1965.
Afr 8847.45.2	Tapson, Winifred. Timber and tides; the story of Knysna and Plettenberg Bay. 2. ed. Johannesburg, 1963.
Afr 8847.48	Wilson, M. Langa. Cape Town, 1963.
Afr 8847.53F	Irving, James. Macleantown. Grahamstown, 1959.
Afr 8847.56	Lomax, Ambrose. Portret van'n Suid-Afrikaanse dorp. Molteno, 1964.
Afr 8847.77	Pamphlet vol. Rondebosch, South Africa. 2 pam.
Afr 8847.81	Jones, S.M. Personal accounts of visitors to Simon's Town, 1770-1899. Cape Town, 1964.
Afr 8847.83	Stellenbosch. Stadsraad. Stellenbosch, 1679-1929. Stellenbosch, 1929.
Afr 8847.83.5	Collier, Joy. Stellenbosch revisited. Stellenbosch, 1959.
Afr 8847.83.10	Rothmann, M.E. The drostdy at Swellendam. Swellendam, 1960.
Afr 8847.89	Smit, Mattheus Theodoros Rehuel. The romance of the village Ugie. Cape Town, 1964.
Afr 8847.90	Rosenthal, Eric. One hundred years of Victoria West, 1859-1959. Victoria West, 1959.

Afr 8848   **Cape Colony - Heraldry and genealogy**

Afr 8848.3	Meintjes, J. Frontier family. n.p., 1956.
Afr 8848.5	Efolliott, Pamela. From Moscow to the Cape, the story of the Wienands of Waldeck. Cape Town, 1963.

Afr 8849.1 - .99   **Cape Colony - Biographies - Collected (A-Z, 99 scheme, by author)**

Afr 8849.3	Sachs, W. Black anger. Boston, 1947.
Afr 8849.6	Gray, C.N. Life of Robert Gray. London, 1876. 2v.
Afr 8849.7	Gray, C.N. Life of Robert Gray. London, 1883.
Afr 8849.7.5	Brooke, A. Robert Gray. Cape Town, 1947.
Afr 8849.8	Benham, M.S. Henry Callaway. London, 1896.
Afr 8849.10	Mphahlele, E. Down Second avenue. London, 1959.
Afr 8849.12	Murray, Andrew. The political philosophy of J.A. de Mist. Cape Town, 1959.
Afr 8849.16	Folliott, Pamela. One titan at a time. Cape Town, 1960.

Afr 8849.101 - .399   **Cape Colony - Biographies - Individual (A-Z, 299 scheme, by person)**

Afr 8849.141	Bosman di Ravelli, Vere. Saint Theodore and the crocodile. Cape Town, 1964.
Afr 8849.169	Dale, Emmé Ross. Mrs. Dale's diary, 1857-1872. Cape Town, 1966.
Afr 8849.212	Gearing, Gladys. This was my world. Cape Town, 1966.
Afr 8849.229	Herschel, John Frederick William. Herschel at the Cape: diaries and correspondence of Sir John Herschel, 1834-1838. Cape Town, 1969.
Afr 8849.295	Orpen, Joseph Millerd. Reminiscences of life in South Africa from 1846 to the present day. Cape Town, 1964.
Afr 8849.347	Stockenstroom, Andries. The autobiography of the late Sir Andries Stockenstroem. Cape Town, 1964. 2v.

Afr 8850   **Basutoland; Lesotho - Periodicals (A-Z, 99 scheme)**

Afr 8850.6F	Basutoland newsletter. Cairo. 1,1963+
Afr 8850.49	Lesotho. Morija. 1,1959+
Afr 8850.49.5	Lesotho quarterly. Morija. 2,1967+

Afr 8853   **Basutoland; Lesotho - Bibliographies**

Afr 8853.2F	Groen, Julie. Bibliography of Basutoland. Cape Town, 1946.
Afr 8853.3F	Basutoland. Government Archives. Catalogue. n.p., 1962.

Afr 8857   **Basutoland; Lesotho - Collected source materials**

Afr 8857.5	Basutoland records. Cape Town, 1883. 3v.
Afr 8857.10	Basutoland. Basutoland records. v.1-3. Facsimile. Cape Town, 1964. 4v.

Afr 8860   **Basutoland; Lesotho - Government and administration**

Afr 8860.5	Ballinger, M.L. Basutoland. Lovedale, 1931.
Afr 8860.10	Brockway, Tenner. British protectorates. London, 1957.
Afr 8860.15	Basutoland. Council. Report on constitutional reform. Maseru, 1958.
Afr 8860.16	Basutoland Constitutional Conference, London, 1964. Basutoland constitutional conference, report. London, 1964.

Afr 8862   **Basutoland; Lesotho - General politics; political parties**

Afr 8862.5F	Pamphlet vol. Memorandums, petition, and statements issued by the Basutoland Congress Party and the Marematlou Freedom Party. 5 pam.

Afr 8865   **Basutoland; Lesotho - General history**

Afr 8865.5	Lagden, G. The Basutos. N.Y., 1910. 2v.
Afr 8865.7	Ellenberger, D.F. History of the Basuto, ancient, and modern. London, 1912.
Afr 8865.10	Tylden, G. The rise of the Basuto. Cape Town, 1950.
Afr 8865.12	Great Britain. Commonwealth Relations Office. Annual report on Basutoland. 1947+ 3v.
Afr 8865.14	Stevens, Richard P. Lesotho, Botswana, and Swaziland: the former High Commission territoris in Southern Africa. London, 1967.

Afr 8865   **Basutoland; Lesotho - General history**
cont.

Afr 8865.16	Spence, John Edward. Lesotho: the politics of dependence. London, 1968.
Afr 8865.18	Chakela, Koenyama S. The past and present Lesotho (Basutoland). Cairo, 1962.

Afr 8868   **Basutoland; Lesotho - General special**

Afr 8868.5	Theal, G.M. A fragment of Basuto history. Cape Town, 1886.
Afr 8868.10	Wallman, Sandra. Take out hunger; two case studies of rural development in Basutoland. London, 1969.

Afr 8918 - 8920   **Basutoland; Lesotho - Geography, description, etc. - General works (By date)**

Afr 8918.59	Casalis, E. Le Bassoutos. Paris, 1859.
Afr 8918.59.5	Casalis, E. The Basutos. London, 1861.
Afr 8918.59.10	Casalis, E. The Basutos, or, Twenty-three years in South Africa. Cape Town, 1965.
Afr 8918.91	Widdicombe, John. Fourteen years in Basutoland. London, 1891.
Afr 8919.08	Bertrand, Alfred. Dans le Sud-Africain et au serial de l'Afrique centrale. Genève, 1911.
Afr 8919.49	Rosenthal, Eric. African Switzerland, Basutoland of today. London, 1949.
Afr 8919.49.5	Rosenthal, Eric. African Switzerland. Cape Town, 1948.
Afr 8919.57	Walton, James. Historic buildings of Basutoland. Morija, 1957.
Afr 8919.66	Coates, Austin. Basutoland. London, 1966.

Afr 8923   **Basutoland; Lesotho - Economic and financial conditions**

Afr 8923.2	Great Britain. High Commissioner for Basutoland, the Bechuanaland Protectorate and Swaziland. Basutoland, Bechuanaland protectorate and Swaziland, report of an economic survey mission. London, 1960.

Afr 8925   **Basutoland; Lesotho - Races**

Afr 8925.2	MacGregor, J.C. Basuto traditions. n.p., n.d.
Afr 8925.10	Ashton, H. The Basuto. London, 1952.
Afr 8925.15	Orpen, Joseph M. History of the Basutur of South Africa. Cape Town, 1857.
Afr 8925.20	Auin, P.J. Foods and feeding habits of the Pedi. Johannesburg, 1959.
Afr 8925.25	How, Marion Wulsham. The mountain bushmen of Basutoland. Pretoria, 1962.

Afr 8928   **Basutoland; Lesotho - Religion; missions**

Afr 8928.2	Ellenberger, Victor. A century of mission work in Basutoland, 1833-1933. Morija, 1938.
Afr 8928.5	Germond, Robert Charles. Chronicles of Basutoland. Morija, 1967.

Afr 8931   **Basutoland; Lesotho - Biographies [Discontinued]**

Afr 8931.29	Forssman, Alric. Chevalier Oscar Wilhelm Alric Forssman. Pretoria, 1961.
Afr 8931.53	Smith, E.W. The Mabilles of Basutoland. London, 1939.
Afr 8931.53.5	Dieterlen, H. Adolphe Mabile. Paris, 1930.

Afr 8934.101 - .399   **Basutoland; Lesotho - Biographies - Individual (A-Z, 299 scheme, by person)**

Afr 8934.123	Baker, Jeff. African flying journal. London, 1968.
Afr 8934.277.2	Williams, John Grenfell. Moshesh, the man on the mountain. 2nd ed. London, 1959.
Afr 8934.277.5	Becker, Peter. Hill of destiny. London, 1969.

Afr 8950   **Natal - Periodicals (A-Z, .1-.26)**

Afr 8950.22	Vietzen, Colleen. The Natal almanac and yearly register, 1863-1906. Cape Town, 1963.

Afr 8953   **Natal - Bibliographies**

Afr 8953.2	Pamphlet vol. Natal. 2 pam.
Afr 8953.5	Simmonds, Heather A. European immigration into Natal, 1824-1910. Cape Town, 1964.

Afr 8955   **Natal - Pamphlet volumes**

Afr 8955.01	Pamphlet box. Natal government railways.
Afr 8955.10	Pamphlet vol. Natal. 12 pam.

Afr 8957   **Natal - Collected source materials**

Afr 8957.5	Natal regional survey. Cape Town. 1,1951+ 11v.
Afr 8957.5.5	Natal Regional Survey. Report. Cape town. 3+ 3v.
Afr 8957.6	Natal Regional Survey. Additional report. Pietermaritzburg. 1,1951+ 5v.
Afr 8957.10	Natal town and regional planning reports. Pietermaritzburg. 1,1953+ 10v.

Afr 8964 - 8970   **Natal - General history (By date)**

Afr 8968.76	Brooks, Henry. Natal, a history and description of the colony. London, 1876.
Afr 8968.79	Farrer, J.A. Zululand and the Zulus. 3rd ed. London, 1879.
Afr 8969.13	Holt, H.P. Mounted police of Natal. London, 1913.
Afr 8969.24	Natal. Volksraad. Voortrekker wetgewing, notule van die natalse Volksraad, 1839-1845. Pretoria, 1924.
Afr 8969.50	Hattersley, A. The British settlement of Natal. Cambridge, Eng., 1950.
Afr 8969.66	Bulpin, Thomas Victor. Natal and the Zulu country. Cape Town, 1966.
Afr 8969.67	Brookes, Edgar Harry. A history of Natal. Pietermaritzburg, 1967.

Afr 8980   **Natal - History by periods - Conquest to separation from Cape Colony (1843-1856)**

Afr 8980.3	Bannister, S. Humane policy. 2. ed. London, n.d.
Afr 8980.3.5	Bannister, S. Humane policy; or, Justice to the aborigines of new settlements. 1st ed. London, 1968.
Afr 8980.5	Colenso, J.W. Defence of Langalibalele. n.p., 187-.
Afr 8980.6	Shuter, C.F. Englishman's inn, 'engelsche logie'. Cape Town, 1963.
Afr 8980.10	Hattersley, Alan Frederick. The Natal settlers, 1849-1951. Pietermaritzburg, 1949.

Afr 8983 Natal - History by periods - Separation to Boer War (1856-1900)
Afr 8983.5 Robinson, J. A life time in South Africa. London, 1900.
Afr 8983.8.5 Hattersley, A.F. More annals of Natal. London, 1936.
Afr 8983.8.10 Hattersley, A.F. The Natalians, further annals of Natal. Pietermaritzburg, 1940.
Afr 8983.10 Hattersley, A.F. Later annals of Natal. London, 1938.

Afr 8985 Natal - History by periods - Later history (1900-)
Afr 8985.2 Bosman, W. The Natal rebellion of 1906. London, 1907.
Afr 8985.4 Stuart, J. A history of the Zulu rebellion 1906. London, 1913.
Afr 8985.6 Binns, C.T. Dinuzuln: the death of the House of Shaka. London, 1968.

Afr 9028 - 9030 Natal - Geography, description, etc. - General works
Afr 9028.36 Gardiner, A.F. Narrative of a journey to the Zoolu country. London, 1836.
Afr 9028.36.5 Gardiner, A.F. Narrative of a journey to the Zoolu country in South Africa. Cape Town, 1966.
Afr 9028.52 Barter, Charles. The dorp and the veld or Six months in Natal. London, 1852.
Afr 9028.55 Colenso, J.W. Ten weeks in Natal. Cambridge, 1855.
Afr 9028.55.4 Mason, G.H. Life with the Zulus of Natal, South Africa. London, 1855.
Afr 9028.59 Mann, R.J. The colony of Natal. London, 1859.
Afr 9028.64A Grout, Lewis. Zulu-land. Philadelphia, 1864.
Afr 9028.64B Grout, Lewis. Zulu-land. Philadelphia, 1864.
Afr 9028.64.5 Grout, Lewis. Autobiography. Brattleboro, 1905.
Afr 9028.65 Ireland, W. Historical sketch of the Zulu mission. Boston, n.d.
Afr 9028.72.1 Robinson, J. Notes on Natal. Pretoria, 1967.
Afr 9028.75 Leslie, D. Among the Zulus and Amatongas. 2. ed. Edinburgh, 1875.
Afr 9028.80 Wylde, A. My chief and I, or Six months in Natal. London, 1880.
Afr 9028.83 Peace, Walter. Our colony of Natal. London, 1883.
Afr 9028.85.5 Great Britain. War Office. Intelligence Division. Precis of information concerning Zululand. London, 1895.
Afr 9028.87 Blink, H. Door Natal in het hart van Zuid-Afrika. Amsterdam, 1887.
Afr 9028.94 Thomas, E. Neumann. How thankful should we be. Cape Town, 1894.
Afr 9028.95 Ingram, J.F. The colony of Natal. London, 1895.
Afr 9029.11 Tatlow, A.H. Natal province, descriptive guide. Durban, 1911.
Afr 9029.40 Hattersley, A.F. Portrait of a colony, the story of Natal. Cambridge, 1940.
Afr 9029.49 Braatvedt, H. Roaming Zululand with a native commissioner. Pietermaritzburg, 1949.
Afr 9029.59 Cowles, Raymond Bridgman. Zulu journal. Berkeley, 1959.
Afr 9029.62 Gatti, Attilio. Sangoma. London, 1962.

Afr 9038 Natal - Geography, description, etc. - Special customs
Afr 9038.2 Vandenberghe, P.L. Caneville. 1st. ed. Middletown, Conn., 1964.
Afr 9038.5 Barker, Anthony. Giving and receiving. London, 1959.

Afr 9040 Natal - Geography, description, etc. - Guidebooks
Afr 9040.5 Natal. General Commission. Glimpses in Natal. Durban, 1905.
Afr 9040.6 Harrison, C.W.F. Natal. London, 1903.
Afr 9040.7 Natal. Natal official guide. Cape Town, 1959.

Afr 9044 Natal - Economic and financial conditions
Afr 9044.5F Leverton, Basil James Trewin. Government finance and political development in Natal, 1843 to 1893. Thesis. Pretoria, 1968.

Afr 9045 Natal - Races - General works
Afr 9045.10 Bryant, Alfred T. Olden times in Zululand and Natal. London, 1929.
Afr 9045.10.1 Bryant, Alfred T. Olden times in Zululand and Natal. Capetown, 1965.
Afr 9045.15 Krige, E.J. The social system of the Zulus. London, 1936.

Afr 9047 Natal - Races - Special
Afr 9047.5 Shooter, J. The Kafirs of Natal and Zulu country. London, 1857.
Afr 9047.5.40 Neilson, Agnes J. An index to Joseph Shooter: the Kafirs of Natal and the Zulu country. Johannesburg, 1967.
Afr 9047.10 Reyher, R.H. Zulu woman. N.Y., 1948.
Afr 9047.15 Ritter, E.A. Shaka Zulu. London, 1955.
Afr 9047.16 Rademeyer, J.I. Shaka. Johannesburg, 1963.
Afr 9047.20 Kuper, Hilda. Indian people in Natal. Natal, 1960.
Afr 9047.21 Russel, Margo. Unemployment among Indians in Durban, 1962. Durban, 1962.
Afr 9047.25 Thompson, Leonard Monteath. Indian immigration into Natal. Pretoria, 1938.
Afr 9047.27 Shropshire, Denys William Tinniswood. The Bantu woman under the Natal code of native law. Lovedale, 1941.
Afr 9047.30 Hey, Peter D. The rise of the Natal Indian elite. Pietermaritzburg, 1962.
Afr 9047.35 Vilakazi, A. Zulu transformations. Pietermaritzburg, 1962.
Afr 9047.36 Bryant, A.T. A history of the Zulu and neighboring tribes. Cape Town, 1964.
Afr 9047.37 Bryant, Alfred T. Zulu medicine and medicine-men. Cape Town, 1966.
Afr 9047.38 Reader, Desmond Harold. Zulu tribe in transition. Manchester, 1966.
Afr 9047.39 Mutwa, Vusamazulu Credo. My people, my Africa. 1st American ed. N.Y., 1969.

Afr 9049 Natal - Religion; missions
Afr 9049.5 Sundkler, Bengt. Bantu prophets in South Africa. 2. ed. London, 1964.
Afr 9049.7 Sturges, Stanley G. In the valley of seven cities. Washington, D.C., 1965.
Afr 9049.8 Wilkinson. A lady's life and travels in Zululand. London, 1882.

Afr 9050 Natal - Local - General works
Afr 9050.7 Paton, A. The Charlestown story. Pietermaritzburg, 1961.
Afr 9050.10 Watson, R.G.T. Tongaati. London, 1960.
Afr 9050.15 Schimlek, Francis. Mariannhill. Mariannhill, 1953.
Afr 9050.54 Keiskammahoek rural survey. Pietermaritzburg, 1952.

Afr 9060 Natal - Local - Durban
Afr 9060.2F Bee, Barbara M. Historical bibliography of the city of Durban, or Port Natal. Cape Town, 1946.
Afr 9060.5 Russell, George. The history of old Durban and reminiscences of an emigrant of 1850. Durban, 1899.
Afr 9060.10A Kuper, Leo. Durban. London, 1958.
Afr 9060.10B Kuper, Leo. Durban. London, 1958.
Afr 9060.10C Kuper, Leo. Durban. London, 1958.
Afr 9060.15 Frost, R.K. No other foundation. Durban, 1960.
Afr 9060.20 Praechter, Vallmar. Durban. Hamburg, 1961.
Afr 9060.25 Durban, Natal. Durban. Johannesburg, 1961.
Afr 9060.26 Durban, Natal. Saint Andrew's Presbyterian Church. The story of Saint Andrew's Presbyterian church. Durban, 1962.
Afr 9060.27 Malherbe, Janie. Port Natal. Cape Town, 1965.
Afr 9060.28 Rosenthal, Eric. Schooners and sky scrapers. Cape Town, 1963.

Afr 9070 Natal - Local - Pietermaritzburg
Afr 9070.5 Pietermaritzburg. Corporation. Pietermaritzburg, Natal, South Africa. Pietermaritzburg, 193-.
Afr 9070.7 Hattersley, A.F. Pietermaritzburg panorama. Pietermaritzburg, 1938.
Afr 9070.9 Karlson, Esme D. Pattern of wings. Pietermaritzburg, 1946.
Afr 9070.10F Vowles, Margaret. The city of Pietermaritzburg. Capetown, 1946.

Afr 9071 Natal - Local - Others (A-Z, 99 scheme, by place)
Afr 9071.41 Slayter, Eric. Isipingo, village in the sun. Durban, 1961.

Afr 9072 Natal - Heraldry and genealogy
Afr 9072.5 St. Leger-Gordon, Ruth E. Shepstone: the role of the family in the history of South Africa, 1820-1900. Cape Town, 1968.

Afr 9073.1 - .99 Natal - Biographies - Collected
Afr 9073.5 Who's who in Natal. 1933. Durban, South Africa.

Afr 9073.100 - .899 Natal - Biographies - Individual (A-Z, 800 scheme, by person)
Afr 9073.252 Byron, Lewis. Recollections of an octogenarian. Kloof, 1964.
Afr 9073.263 Goetzsche, Eric. The father of a city, the life and times of George Cato. Pietermaritzburg, 1967.
Afr 9073.413 Fynn, Henry Francis. Diary. Malcolm, 1950.
Afr 9073.451 Hey, Peter Drummond. One kind of Phoenix and the story of Peter Hey. Pietermaritzburg, 1967.
Afr 9073.467 Lee, Albert William. Charles Johnson of Zululand. Westminster, Eng., 1930.
Afr 9073.687 Phipson, Thomas. Letters and other writings of a Natal sheriff. Cape Town, 1968.
Afr 9073.797 Osborn, Robert F. C.G., a great Natalian; biography of Charles George Smith. Durban, 1966.

Afr 9078 Transvaal - Bibliographies
Afr 9078.50 Goldman, P.L.A. Transvaal Archief. Pretoria, 1927.

Afr 9080 Transvaal - Pamphlet volumes
Afr 9080.1 Pamphlet box. Transvaal.

Afr 9086 Transvaal - Government and administration
Afr 9086.5 South Africa. Constitution. London, 1899.
Afr 9086.10 South Africa. Political laws. London, 1896.
Afr 9086.15 Transvaal civil service list, 1905. Pretoria, 1905.
Afr 9086.16 Huessen, F. Verfassungsentwickelung Transvaals. Karlsruhe, 1909.
Afr 9086.17 Roels, E. Boers et Anglais. Autours des mines d'or. Paris, 1897.
Afr 9086.20 De Villiers, John. The Transvaal. London, 1896.

Afr 9087 Transvaal - General politics; political parties
Afr 9087.5 Valter, M.P.C. Duitschland en de Hollandsche Republieken in Zuid-Afrika. Amsterdam, 1918.
Afr 9087.8 Mulder, Cornelius Petrus. Die eerste skof van die Nasionale Party in Transvaal, 1914-1964. Johannesburg, 1964.

Afr 9088 - 9090 Transvaal - General history (By date)
Afr 9088.5 Oordt, J.W.G. van. De Transvaalsche Gebeurtenissen en... Suid-Africa. 's-Gravenhage, 1881.
Afr 9088.8 Loo, C.J. van der. De... Zuid-Afrikaansche Republiek. Zwolle, 1896.
Afr 9089.38 Coetzee, A. Die opkoms van die Afrikaanse Kultuurgedagte aan die rand. Johannesburg, 1938.
Afr 9089.42 Kuit, Albent. Transvaalse gister. Pretoria, 1942.

Afr 9092 Transvaal - General special
Afr 9092.5 Swart, Marius Johannes. Geloftedag. Kaapstad, 1961.

Afr 9093 Transvaal - History by periods - Before 1836
Afr 9093.5 Rae, C. Malaboch. London, 1898.
Afr 9093.10 Jaarsveld, F.A. van. Die eenheidstrewe van die republikeinse Afrikaners. Johannesburg, 1951.
Afr 9093.15 Weilbach, J.D. Geschiedenis van de emigranten-boeren en van den vrijheids-oorlog. Kaapstad, 1882.
Afr 9093.20 Bulpin, T.V. The golden republic. Cape Town, 1953.
Afr 9093.20.5 Bulpin, T.V. Storm over the Transvaal. 2. ed. Cape Town, 1955.
Afr 9093.22 Sandberg, Christoph Georg. Twintig jaren onder Kugers Boeren in voor-en tegenspoed. Amsterdam, 1944.
Afr 9093.25 Mason, Rivil. Prehistory of the Transvaal. Johannesburg, 1962.
Afr 9093.27 Wangemann, H. Maleo und Sekukuni. Berlin, 1868.

Afr 9095 Transvaal - History by periods - History since War (1902-)
Afr 9095.25F Transvaal (Colony). Volunteers Commission. Reports of Transvaal Volunteers Commission. Pretoria, 1906.

Afr 9148 - 9150 Transvaal - Geography, description, etc. - General works (By date)
Afr 9148.43 Bennie, John. An account of a journey into Transorangia and the Potchefstroom-Winburg Trekker Republic in 1843. Cape Town, 1956.
Afr 9148.77 Baines, Thomas. The gold regions of southeast Africa. London, 1877.

Afr 9148 - 9150   Transvaal - Geography, description, etc. - General works
   (By date)
      cont.
   Afr 9148.77.5   Baines, Thomas. The gold regions of south eastern Africa. Bulawayo, 1968.
   Afr 9148.78   Roche, H.A. On trek in the Transvaal. London, 1878.
   Afr 9148.82   Heckford, S. A lady trader in the Transvaal. London, 1882.
   Afr 9148.88   Gillmore, Parker. Days and nights by the desert. London, 1888.
   Afr 9148.98   Seidel, A. Transvaal. Berlin, 1898.
NEDL Afr 9148.99   Davis, Nathaniel Newnham. The Transvaal under the Queen. London, 1899.
   Afr 9148.99.3   Kalff, S. Onder een worsteland volk. Haarlem, 1899.
   Afr 9148.99.5F   Harpen, N. van. Nederland-Zuid-Afrika. Amsterdam, 1899.
   Afr 9149.00   Edwards, Neville. The Transvaal in war and peace. London, 1900.
   Afr 9149.01   Wilson, D.M. Behind the scenes in the Transvaal. London, 1901.
   Afr 9149.28   Figulus, Jiri V. J.V. Figulus a jeho Africka dobrodruzstvi. Praha, 1928. 2 pam.
   Afr 9149.32   Stevenson-Hamilton, James. The Kruger national park. Johannesburg, South Africa, 1932.
   Afr 9149.34   South Africa. National Parks Board of Trustees. A brief description of the Union's national parks. Pretoria, 1934.
   Afr 9149.39   Birkley, C. Limpopo journey. London, 1939.
   Afr 9149.53   Middelberg, Gerrit Adrian Arnold. Briewe uit Transvaal. Pretoria, 1953.
   Afr 9149.56   Cole, Monica M. Land use studies in the Transvaal Lowveld. London, 1956.
   Afr 9149.61   Helbling, Margrit. Tshakhuma. Zürich, 1961.
   Afr 9149.61.5   MacDonald, Tom. Transvaal story. Cape Town, 1961.
   Afr 9149.61.10   Bigalke, Rudolph. Let's visit the Kruger park. Johannesburg, 1961.
   Afr 9149.62   Cartwright, Alan. Valley of gold. Cape Town, 1962.
   Afr 9149.65F   Battiss, Walter W. Limpopo. 1. ed. Pretoria, 1965.

Afr 9155   Transvaal - Geography, description, etc. - Guidebooks
   Afr 9155.5   Bell, H.T.M. A guide to the Transvaal and map. Johannesburg, 1905. 2v.
   Afr 9155.10   Transvaal. Provincial Council. Official guide. Cape Town, 1960.

Afr 9160   Transvaal - Economic and financial conditions
   Afr 9160.5   Lowveld Regional Development Association. A survey of the resources and development of the southern region of the eastern Transvaal. Barberton, 1954.

Afr 9161   Transvaal - Races
   Afr 9161.5   Bovill, J.H. Natives under the Transvaal flag. London, 1900.
   Afr 9161.6   Werrmann, R. The Bawenda of the Spelonken. London, 1908.
   Afr 9161.7   Butler, J.E. Native races and the war. London, 1900.
   Afr 9161.8F   Asiatic land tenure (amendement) bill, commonly known as the Transvaal Asiatic bill, 1930. Johannesburg, 1930.
   Afr 9161.10   Krige, E. (Jensen). The realm of a rain-queen. London, 1943.
   Afr 9161.15   Munro, A. The Transvaal (Chinese) labour problem. London, 1906.
   Afr 9161.20   Hooper, Charles. Brief authority. N.Y., 1961.
   Afr 9161.21   Hooper, Charles. Brief authority. London, 1960.
   Afr 9161.21.20   Wall, M.A. The Dominee and the Dom-Pas. Cape Town, 1961.
   Afr 9161.23   Potgieter, E.F. The disappearing Bushmen of Lake Clirissie. Pretoria, 1955.
   Afr 9161.24   Horrell, Muriel. Visit to Bantu areas of the northern Transvaal. Johannesburg, 1965.
   Afr 9161.24.5   Horrell, Muriel. Group areas; the emerging pattern with illustrative examples from Transvaal. Johannesburg, 1966.

Afr 9165   Transvaal - Local (A-Z, 99 scheme, by place)
   Afr 9165.5   Engelbrecht, S.P. Die nederduitsch hervormde gemeente zurust (Marico). n.p., 1946.
   Afr 9165.7   Mathewson, J. Edw. The establishment of an urban Bantu township. Pretoria, 1957.
   Afr 9165.7.5   Humphriss, Deryck. Benoni, son of my sorrow. Benoni, 1968.
   Afr 9165.42   Johannesburg Publicity Association. Johannesburg's 40th birthday, Sept. 22, 1926. Johannesburg, 1926.
   Afr 9165.42.10F   Johannesburg Publicity Association. Johannesburg, city of achievement. Johannesburg, 1936.
   Afr 9165.42.15   Rosenthal, E. Gold bricks and mortar, 60 years of Johannesburg history. Johannesburg, 1946.
   Afr 9165.42.20   Chilvers, Hedley A. Out of the crucible. Johannesburg, 1948.
   Afr 9165.42.25F   Smith, Anna H. Pictorial history of Johannesburg. Johannesburg, 1956.
   Afr 9165.42.30   Maud, J.P.R. Johannesburg and the art of self-government. Johannesburg, 1937.
   Afr 9165.42.35   Erasmus, J.L.P. Die rand en sy goud. Pretoria, 1944.
   Afr 9165.42.40   Macmillan, Allister. The golden city. London, 193-.
   Afr 9165.42.41   Macmillan, Allister. Environs of the golden city and Pretoria. Capetown, 193-.
   Afr 9165.42.45   Neame, Lawrence. City built on gold. Johannesburg, 1960.
   Afr 9165.42.50   Picton-Seymour, Desirée. Transvaal republican. Cape Town, 1956.
   Afr 9165.42.55   Johannesburg. City Council. The city of Johannesburg. 2. ed. Cape Town, 1956.
   Afr 9165.42.57   Shaw, T.R. The growth of Johannesburg from 1886-1939. Johannesburg, 1963.
   Afr 9165.42.60   Market Research Africa. An African day. Johannesburg, 1962.
   Afr 9165.42.65   Crisp, Robert. The outlanders. London, 1964.
   Afr 9165.42.70   Leyds, Gerard A. A history of Johannesburg, the early years. Cape Town, 1964.
   Afr 9165.42.75   Cartwright, Alan Patrick. The corner house. Capetown, 1965.
   Afr 9165.42.80   Gutsche, Thelma. Old gold, the history of the Wanderers club. Cape Town, 1966.
   Afr 9165.42.85F   Johannesburg. Non-European Affairs Department. Report of the manager. Johannesburg. 1957+
   Afr 9165.42.90   Winter, James Sydney. First-hand accounts of Johannesburg in English-language periodicals, 1886-1895, a list. Johannesburg, 1967.

Afr 9165   Transvaal - Local (A-Z, 99 scheme, by place)
   cont.
   Afr 9165.42.95   Hughes, Blanche. Personal reminiscences of early Johannesburg in printed books, 1884-1895. Johannesburg, 1966.
   Afr 9165.70   Davidson, Elizabeth. Pietersburg Magisterial District; a bibliography. Johannesburg, 1968.
   Afr 9165.71   Cross, K.G. Bibliography of Pretoria. Pretoria, 1948.
   Afr 9165.71.5   Rex, H.M. Pretoria van kerkplaas tot regeringsetel. Kaapstad, 1960.
   Afr 9165.71.10   Collier, Joy. The purple and the gold. Cape Town, 1965.
   Afr 9165.71.15   Ploeger, Jan. Over-Vaal; the history of an official residence. Pretoria, 1963.
   Afr 9165.82   Johannesburg. Non-European Affairs Department. Cultural change in Soweto. Johannesburg, 1965.
   Afr 9165.94   Scully, W.C. The ridge of the white waters. London, 1912.

Afr 9170.1 - .99   Transvaal - Biographies - Collected (A-Z, 99 scheme, by author)
   Afr 9170.7   Behrman, F. My fifty-odd years in Johannesburg. Johannesburg, 1961.
   Afr 9170.11   Carr, W.S. Pioneers' path. Cape Town, 1953.
   Afr 9170.20   Wood, Clement. The man who killed Kitchener, the life of Fritz Joubert Duquesne, 1879. N.Y., 1932.
   Afr 9170.25   Siwundhla, Alice Princess. Alice Princess. Omaha, 1965.
   Afr 9170.34   Goosen, Willem. On the run. Cape Town, 1964.

Afr 9170.101 - .399   Transvaal - Biographies - Individual (A-Z, 299 scheme, by person)
   Afr 9170.126.2   Bulpin, Thomas Victor. The ivory trail. 2nd ed. Capetown, 1967.

Afr 9176   Swaziland - Bibliographies
   Afr 9176.5   Wallace, Charles S. Swaziland; a bibliography. Johannesburg, 1967.

Afr 9180   Swaziland - Government and administration
   Afr 9180.2   Great Britain. Colonial Office. Swaziland, constitutional proposals. London, 1966.

Afr 9190   Swaziland - Geography, description, etc. - General works
   Afr 9190.3   Scutt, Joan F. The story of Swaziland. Mbabane, 1965?
   Afr 9190.5   Swaziland recorder. Johannesburg.
   Afr 9190.10   Swaziland newsletter. Cairo. 1965+

Afr 9191   Swaziland - Geography, description, etc. - Special customs
   Afr 9191.5   Arnheim, J. Swaziland. Cape Town, 1950.
   Afr 9191.7   Warwick, Brian Allan. The Swazi, an ethnographic account of the natives of the Swaziland protectorate. London, 1966.
   Afr 9192.5F   Great Britain. Colonial Office. Affairs of Swaziland. London, 1899.
   Afr 9192.10   Great Britain. Commonwealth Relations Office. Annual report on Swaziland. n.p. 1946+ 6v.
   Afr 9192.15F   Swaziland. Treasury. Revenue and expenditure, 1947-1957. Mababane, 1958.

Afr 9193   Swaziland - Economic and financial conditions
   Afr 9193.2   Cowen, D.V. Swaziland, report on constitutional reform. n.p., 1961.
   Afr 9193.3F   Swaziland. Development plan. Mababane, 1966.
   Afr 9193.3.5   Fair, Thomas J.D. Development in Swaziland: a regional analysis. Johannesburg, 1969.

Afr 9195   Swaziland - Races
   Afr 9195.10   Oneil, Owen Rowe. Adventures in Swaziland. N.Y., 1921.
   Afr 9195.15   Miller, A.M. Mamisa, the Swazi warrior. Pietermaritzburg, 1953.
   Afr 9195.15.5   Miller, Allister Mitchell. Swazieland and the Swazieland corporation. London, 1900.

Afr 9196   Swaziland - Religion; missions
   Afr 9196.5   South African Institute of Race Relations. Swaziland. Johannesburg, 1955.
   Afr 9196.6   Barker, Dudley. Swaziland. London, 1965.

Afr 9197   Swaziland - Local
   Afr 9197.2   Natal. University. Institute for Social Research. Experiment in Swaziland. Cape Town, 1964.
   Afr 9198.2   Kuper, H. The Swazi, a South African kingdom. N.Y., 1963.
   Afr 9198.5   Kuper, H. The uniform of color... Swaziland. Johannesburg, 1947.
   Afr 9198.10   Kuper, H. An African aristocracy. London, 1961.

Afr 9200   Orange Free State - Periodicals
   Afr 9200.5   Vrijstaatsch jaarboek en almanak, 1894. Bloemfontein, 1893.

Afr 9203   Orange Free State - Bibliographies
   Afr 9203.5   Sinclair, Dorothy Mary. The Orange Free State goldfields; a bibliography. Cape Town, 1967.

Afr 9205   Orange Free State - Pamphlet volumes
   Afr 9205.1   Pamphlet box. Orange River cop.

Afr 9218 - 9220   Orange Free State - General history (By date)
   Afr 9218.54   Molesworth, William. Materials for a speech in defense of the policy of abandoning the Orange River Territory, May 1854. London, 1854.
   Afr 9218.93   Orange Free State (Republic). South Africa. Chicago, 1893.

Afr 9225   Orange Free State - History by periods - Orange Free State (1854-1900)
   Afr 9225.10   Boon, M.J. The history of the Orange Free State. London, 1885.
   Afr 9225.15   Brauer, A. Der Oranje-Freistaat, 1854-1888. Emsdetten, 1931.
   Afr 9225.20   Scholtz, G.D. Die konstitusie en die staatsinstellings van die Oranje-Vrystaat, 1854-1902. Amsterdam, 1936.
   Afr 9225.20.5   Scholtz, G.D. President Johannes Henricus Brand, 1823-1888. Johannesburg, 1957.
   Afr 9225.25   Spies, François Jacobus du Toit. Hamelberg en die Oranje-Vrystaat. Amsterdam, 1941.
   Afr 9225.28   Muller, Hendrik Pieter Nicolaas. Oude tyden in den Oranje-Vrystaat. Leiden, 1907.

Afr 9230   Orange Free State - History by periods - History since Annexation (1900-
)
Afr 9230.2   Beak, George B. The aftermath of war. London, 1906.

Afr 9285   Orange Free State - Geography, description, etc. - Guidebooks
Afr 9285.5   Orange Free State. The Orange Free State. Cape Town, 1956.

Afr 9289   Orange Free State - Races
Afr 9289.5   Engelbrecht, J.A. The Korana. Cape Town, 1936.
Afr 9289.6   Molema, S. Chief Moroka. Cape Town, 195-.

Afr 9290   Orange Free State - Religion; missions
Afr 9290.5   Gunn, Hugh. The language question in the Orange River Colony. Johannesburg, 1910.

Afr 9291   Orange Free State - Local
Afr 9291.5   Murray, Emma (Rutherford). Young Mrs. Murray goes to Bloemfontein, 1856-1869. Cape Town, 1954.
Afr 9291.10   Prinsloo, A. Die geskiedenis van Smithfield en die Caledonrivierdistrik. Bloemfontein, 1955.
Afr 9291.15   Bloemfontein. City Council. The city of Bloemfontein. Cape Town, 1950.
Afr 9291.15.2   Bloemfontein. City Council. The city of Bloemfontein. Cape Town, 1960.
Afr 9291.18   Schoor, Marthinus. Edenburg. Edenburg, 1963.
Afr 9291.20   Uys, Cornelis Janse. Rouxville, 1863-1963. Bloemfontein, 1966.

Afr 9293   Orange Free State - Heraldry and genealogy
Afr 9293.2   Walton, J. Vroeë plase en nedersettings in die Oranje Vrystaat. Amsterdam, 1955.

Afr 9295.1 - .99   Orange Free State - Biographies - Collected (A-Z, 99 scheme, by author)
Afr 9295.5   Collins, William W. Free statia. Cape Town, 1965.

Afr 9295.100 - .899   Orange Free State - Biographies - Individual (A-Z, 800 scheme, by person)
Afr 9295.452   Hill, Caroline. Orange days. Pietermaritzburg, 1965.

Afr 9325   Bechuanaland; Botswana - Periodicals (A-Z, .1-.26)
Afr 9325.2F   Bechuanaland newsletter. Cairo. 2,1965+
Afr 9325.11   Kutlwano. Botswana. 4,1965+
5v.
Afr 9325.13   Masa. Cairo. 1,1964+

Afr 9327   Bechuanaland; Botswana - Bibliographies
Afr 9327.47F   Stevens, Pamela. Bibliography of Bechuanaland. Cape Town, 1947.
Afr 9327.65   Middleton, Coral. Bechuanaland. Cape Town, 1965.
Afr 9327.66F   Mohome, Paulus. A bibliography on Bechuanaland. Syracuse, 1966.

Afr 9332   Bechuanaland; Botswana - Collected source materials
Afr 9332.5   Great Britain. Commonwealth Relations Office. Bechuanaland protectorate, report for the year. 1946+
6v.

Afr 9335   Bechuanaland; Botswana - Government and administration
Afr 9335.5F   Bechuanaland Independence Conference. Report, signed at Marlborough house. n.p., 1966.
Afr 9335.10   Bechuanaland. Commissioner to Consider Localization of Civil Service. Report on localisation and training. Mafeking, 1966.

Afr 9338 - 9340   Bechuanaland; Botswana - General history (By date)
Afr 9339.57   Gabatshwane, S.M. Introduction to the Bechuanaland protectorate history and administration. Kanye, 1957.
Afr 9339.65   Munger, Edwin S. Bechuanaland. London, 1965.

Afr 9345   Bechuanaland; Botswana - History by periods - 1885-1966
Afr 9345.5   Lloyd, E. Three great African chiefs. London, 1895.
Afr 9345.10   Mockford, J. Khama, king of the Bamangwato. London, 1931.
Afr 9345.10.8   Harris, J.C. Khama, the great African chief. 4. ed. London, 1923.
Afr 9345.10.10   Redfern, John. Ruth and Seretse. London, 1955.
Afr 9345.20   Mockford, J. Seretse Khama and the Bamongwato. London, 1950.
Afr 9345.50   Great Britain. Commission on the Financial Position of Bechuanaland Protectorate. Financial and economic position of Bechuanaland protectorate. London, 1933.
Afr 9345.50.5   Ballinger, M.L. Bechuanaland protectorate. Lovedale, 1931.
Afr 9345.55   Sillery, A. The Bechuanaland protectorate. Cape Town, 1952.
Afr 9345.60   Sillery, A. Sechele. Oxford, 1954.
Afr 9345.65   Smith, E.W. Great lion of Bechuanaland. London, 1957.
Afr 9345.70   Gabatshwane, S.M. Seretse Khama and Botswana. Kanye? 1966.
Afr 9345.72   Robins, Eric. White Queen in Africa. London, 1967.

Afr 9350   Bechuanaland; Botswana - History by periods - 1966-
Afr 9350.66   Bechuanaland Independence Conference, London, 1966. Report. London, 1966.

Afr 9388 - 9390   Bechuanaland; Botswana - Geography, description, etc. - General works (By date)
Afr 9388.57   Anderson, C.J. Lake Ngami. N.Y., 1857.
Afr 9388.57.5   Anderson, C.J. Lake Ngami, or Explorations and discovery during four years of wanderings in wilds of South Western Africa. Cape Town, 1967.
Afr 9388.76F   Orange Free State Commission. Sketch of the Orange Free State. Philadelphia, 1876.
Afr 9388.84   Mackenzie, John. Day dawn in dark places. London, 1884.
X Cg   Afr 9388.86   Farini, G.A. Through the Kalahari desert. London, 1886. (Changed to XP 3879)
Afr 9388.87   Mackenzie, J. Austral Africa. London, 1887. 2v.
Afr 9388.93.3   Bryden, H.A. Gun and camera in South Africa. London, 1893.
Afr 9388.95   Hepburn, J.D. Twenty years in Khamas country. London, 1895.
Afr 9389.13   Hodson, A.W. Trekking the great thirst. 2. ed. London, 1913.
Afr 9389.13.5   Hodson, A.W. Trekking the great thirst. London, 1914.
Afr 9389.53   Debenham, F. Kalahari sand. London, 1953.

Afr 9388 - 9390   Bechuanaland; Botswana - Geography, description, etc. - General works (By date) cont.
Afr 9389.57   Tshekedi Khama. Bechuanaland. Johannesburg, 1957.
Afr 9389.58   Kantor, Cyril. The big thirst. London, 1958.
Afr 9389.59   Balsan, Francois. Nouvelles aventures au Kalahari. Paris, 1959.
Afr 9389.60   Bjerre, Jens. Kalahari. London, 1960.
Afr 9389.63   Goldie, F. Lost city of the Kalahari. Cape Town, 1963.
Afr 9389.66   Young, Bertram Alfred. Bechuanaland. London, 1966.
Afr 9389.67   Clement, A. John. The Kalahari and its lost city. Cape Town, 1967.

Afr 9398   Bechuanaland; Botswana - Economic and financial conditions
Afr 9398.2   Botswana. Economic Planning Unit. Transitional plan for social and economic development. Gaberones, 1966.
Afr 9398.4   Botswana. Republic of Botswana. Ministry of Development Planning. National development plan, 1968-1973. Gaberones, 1968.

Afr 9400   Bechuanaland; Botswana - Races
Afr 9400.3   Crisp, W. The Bechuana of South Africa. London, 1896.
Afr 9400.3.5   Schapera, J. Migrant labour and tribal life. London, 1947.
Afr 9400.5   Brown, John. Among the Bantu nomads. London, 1926.
Afr 9400.10   Passarge, S. Die Buschmänner der Kalahari. Berlin, 1907.
Afr 9400.10.5   Dornan, S.S. Pygmies and bushmen of the Kalahari. London, 1925.
Afr 9400.10.10   Bleek, D.F. The Naron, a bushman tribe of central Kalahari. Cambridge, 1928.
Afr 9400.10.15   Schwarz, E.H.L. The Kalahari and its native races. London, 1928.
Afr 9400.10.20   Schapera, I. Married life in an African tribe. London, 1940.
Afr 9400.10.22   Schapera, I. Married life in an African tribe. Evanston, 1966.
Afr 9400.10.25   Vanderpost, Laurens. The lost world of the Kalahari. N.Y., 1958.
Afr 9400.11   Mitchison, Naomi. Return to the fairy hill. London, 1966.
Afr 9400.12   Cowley, Olive. Fabled tribe; a voyage to discover the River Bushmen of the Okavango Swamps. 1st ed. N.Y., 1968.

Afr 9404   Bechuanaland; Botswana - Religion; missions
Afr 9404.2   Merriweather, Alfred Musgrave. Desert doctor: medicine and evangelism in the Kalahan Desert. London, 1969.

Afr 9405   Bechuanaland; Botswana - Local
Afr 9405.5   Randall, D. Factors and economic development and the Okovanggo Delta. Chicago, 1957.
Afr 9405.6   Wesleyan Methodist Missionary Society. Affairs of Bechuanaland. London, 1887.

Afr 9424.101 - .399   Bechuanaland; Botswana - Biographies - Individual (A-Z, 299 scheme, by person)
Afr 9424.250   Knight-Bruce, Louise (Torr). The story of an African chief. London, 1893.
Afr 9424.360   Benson, Mary. Tshekedi Khama. London, 1960.
Afr 9424.360.5   Gabatshwane, S.M. Tshekedi Khama of Bechuanaland. Cape Town, 1961.

Afr 9425   Southern Rhodesia - Periodicals
Afr 9425.5F   Rhodesian annual. Bulawayo. 1927+
Afr 9425.10   Concord, the journal of the interracial association of Southern Rhodesia. Salisbury, Southern Rhodesia. 13+
Afr 9425.15   Central African examiner. Salisbury, Southern Rhodesia. 1,1957+
10v.
Afr 9425.20   Rhodesia and Nyasaland. Salisbury. 1960+
Afr 9425.25   Salisbury, Rhodesia. University College of Rhodesia and Nyasaland. Department of African Studies. Occasional paper. 1+
Afr 9425.30   Chapupu, independent Southern Rhodesia. Salisbury. 1,1962+
Afr 9425.35   Zimbabgive review. Cairo.
Afr 9425.35.10F   Zimbabwe to-day. Cairo. 1,1964+
Afr 9425.36F   Zimbabgive review. Supplement. Cairo. 1,1965+
Afr 9425.40   Rhodesiana. Salisbury. 2,1957+
2v.
Afr 9425.45   Rhodesia (British Colony). National development plan. Salisbury. 1965+
Afr 9425.50   Zimbabwe review. London. 2,1967+
Afr 9425.55F   Zimbabwe news. Lusaka. 2,1967+
Afr 9425.60   The Rhodesian community development review. Causeway. 1,1966+
Afr 9425.65   Rhodesian commentary. Salisbury, Rhodesia. 1,1966+

Afr 9428   Southern Rhodesia - Bibliographies
Afr 9428.3F   Carpenter, Olive. The development of Southern Rhodesia from the earliest times to the year 1900. Rondebosch, 1946.
Afr 9428.5F   Rhodes-Livingstone Institute, Lusaka, Northern Rhodesia. A selected bibliography of the federation of Rhodesia and Nyasaland. Lusaka, 1957.
Afr 9428.8   Bean, Elizabeth Ann. Political development in Southern Rhodesia. Cape Town, 1969.

Afr 9430   Southern Rhodesia - Pamphlet volumes
Afr 9430   Pamphlet box. Southern Rhodesia.
Afr 9430.01   Pamphlet box. Southern Rhodesia.
Afr 9430.2   Pamphlet vol. Rhodesia and Nyasaland. 4 pam.
Afr 9430.3   Pamphlet vol. Rhodesia and Nyasaland. 9 pam.

Afr 9432   Southern Rhodesia - Collected source materials
Afr 9432.5   Rhodesia, Southern. Central African Archives. A guide to the public records of Southern Rhodesia under the regime of the British South Africa Company. Cape Town, 1956.
Afr 9432.7   Rhodesia, Southern. Central African Archives. Central African Archives in retrospect and prospect. Salisbury, 1947.
Afr 9432.15   Great Britain. Commonwealth Relations Office. Southern Rhodesia constitution. London, 1961. 2 pam.
Afr 9432.25   Rhodesia, Southern. Legislative Assembly. Select Committee on Resettlement of Natives. Report. Salisbury.

174

Afr 9432   Southern Rhodesia - Collected source materials
cont.

Afr 9432.26	Rhodesia and Nyasaland. Archives in a growing society. Salisbury, 1963.

Afr 9435   Southern Rhodesia - Government and administration

Afr 9435.5	British South Africa Company. Reports. London. 1896+
Afr 9435.5.5	British South Africa Company. Director's report and accounts. London. 1896+
Afr 9435.5.10	British South Africa Company. Report of general meeting. London.
Afr 9435.6F	Martin, R.E.R. Report on native administration of British South Africa Company. London, 1897.
Afr 9435.7	Great Britain. Advisory Commission on the Review of Constitution. Report. (With appendix 1-5, appendix 6-8). London 1960.
Afr 9435.8	Hickman, A.S. Men who made Rhodesia. Salisbury, 1960.
Afr 9435.9	Passmore, Gloria. Source book of parliamentary elections and referenda in Rhodesia, 1892-1962. Salisbury, 1963.
Afr 9435.9.5	Passmore, Gloria C. Local government legislation in Southern Rhodesia up to Sept. 30th, 1963. Salisbury, 1966.
Afr 9435.10	Scott, L. The struggle for native rights in Rhodesia. London, 1918.
Afr 9435.11	Southern Rhodesia Constitutional Conference, London, 1961. Report. London, 1961.
Afr 9435.12	Africa Bureau, London. Central Africa and the British Parliament. London, 1957.
Afr 9435.12.5	Africa Bureau, London. Central Africa and the franchise. London, 1958.
Afr 9435.13	Central African Conference. Report. London, 1963.
Afr 9435.14	Rhodesia and Nyasaland. Commission Appointed to Divide the Territory of Nyasaland into Electoral Districts. Report. Salisbury, 1958..
Afr 9435.14.5	Rhodesia and Nyasaland. Commission Appointed to Divide the Territory of Northern Rhodesia into Electoral Districts. Report. Salisbury, 1958.
Afr 9435.14.10	Rhodesia and Nyasaland. Commission Appointed to Divide the Territory of Southern Rhodesia into Electoral Districts. Report. Salisbury, 1958.
Afr 9435.14.15	Rhodesia and Nyasaland. Report to the federal assembly. Salisbury, 1954. 2 pam.
Afr 9435.15	Rhodesia and Nyasaland. The constitution of the federation of Rhodesia and Nyasaland. Salisbury, 1959.
Afr 9435.16	Palley, Claire. The constitutional history and law of Southern Rhodesia, 1888-1965. Oxford, 1966.
Afr 9435.17F	Local Government Association of Rhodesia. Report of proceedings of the annual conference. Salisbury. 1966+ 2v.
Afr 9435.18	Day, John. International nationalism. N.Y., 1967.
Afr 9435.20	Marshall, Charles Burton. Crisis over Rhodesia: a skeptical view. Baltimore, 1967.
Afr 9435.22	Holleman, Johan Frederik. Chief, council and commissioner: some problems of government in Rhodesia. Assen, 1969.

Afr 9436   Southern Rhodesia - General politics; political parties

Afr 9436.5	Leys, Colin. European politics in Southern Rhodesia. Oxford, 1959.
Afr 9436.6	Leys, Colin. A new deal in central Africa. London, 1960.
Afr 9436.10	Stonehouse, John. Prohibited immigrant. London, 1960.
Afr 9436.12	Rhodesia and Nyasaland. The franchise for federal elections in Rhodesia and Nyasaland. Salisbury, 1957.
Afr 9436.12.5	Rhodesia, Southern. Franchise Commission. Report. Salisbury, 1957.
Afr 9436.13	Zimbabwe African Peoples' Union. Zimbabwe. Cairo, 1964.
Afr 9436.14	Peck, A.J.A. Rhodesia accuses. Salisbury, 1966.
Afr 9436.15	Spurling, Basil G. Reluctant rebel. Johannesburg, 1966.

Afr 9438 - 9440   Southern Rhodesia - General history (By date)

Afr 9438.96	Muller, H.P.N. De Zuid-Afrikaansche Republiek en Rhodesia. 's-Gravenhage, 1896.
Afr 9438.98	Thomson, H.C. Rhodesia and its government. London, 1898.
Afr 9438.165	Hanna, A.J. The story of the Rhodesias and Nyasaland. 2nd ed. London, 1965.
Afr 9439.00	Hensman, H. A history of Rhodesia. Edinburgh, 1900.
Afr 9439.10	Southern Rhodesia. Government Archives. Oppenheimer scrics. 1,1945	13v.
Afr 9439.35	Standing, T.G. A short history of Rhodesia and her neighbours. London, 1935.
Afr 9439.35.5	Gale, W.D. One man's vision. London, 1935.
Afr 9439.40.2	Boggie, Jeannie M. First steps in civilizing Rhodesia. Bulawayo, 1953.
Afr 9439.50	Gale, W.D. Heritage of Rhodes. Cape Town, 1950.
Afr 9439.53	Bate, Henry M. Report from the Rhodesias. London, 1953.
Afr 9439.53.5	Jones, Neville. Rhodesian genesis. Bulawayo, 1953.
Afr 9439.54	Kane, N.S. The world's view. London, 1954.
Afr 9439.54.5	Lumb, Sybil Victoria. Central and southern Africa. 2. ed. Cambridge, 1962.
Afr 9439.58	Gale, W.D. Zambezi sunrise. Cape Town, 1958.
Afr 9439.60	Clegg, E.M. Race and politics. London, 1960.
Afr 9439.60.5	Loveday, A.F. Three stages of history in Rhodesia. Cape Town, 1960.
Afr 9439.60.10	Gale, W.D. Deserve to be great. Bulawayo, 1960.
Afr 9439.60.15	Hanna, A.J. The story of the Rhodesias and Nyasaland. London, 1960.
Afr 9439.61	Black, Colin. The lands and peoples of Rhodesia and Nyasaland. London, 1961.
Afr 9439.63	Rhodesia and Nyasaland. Legacy of progress. Salisbury, 1963.
Afr 9439.64	Wills, Alfred John. An introduction to the history of central Africa. London, 1964.
Afr 9439.64.2	Wills, Alfred John. An introduction to the history of central Africa. 2. ed. London, 1967.
Afr 9439.65	Gann, Lewis H. A history of Southern Rhodesia. London, 1965.
Afr 9439.65.5	Bulpin, Thomas Victor. To the banks of the Zambezi. Johannesburg, 1965.
Afr 9439.65.10	Eeden, Guy Van. The crime of being white. Cape Town, 1965.
Afr 9439.65.11	Eeden, Guy van. Die vuur brand nader. Kaapstad, 1964.
Afr 9439.66	Baxter, J.W. Rhodesian epic. Cape Town, 1966.
Afr 9439.67	Bull, Theodore. Rhodesian perspective. London, 1967.
Afr 9439.67.5	Bull, Theodore. Rhodesia: crisis of color. Chicago, 1968.
Afr 9439.68	Ransford, Oliver. The rulers of Rhodesia from earliest times to the referendum. London, 1968.

Afr 9438 - 9440   Southern Rhodesia - General history (By date)
cont.

Afr 9439.68.5	Samkange, Stanlake John Thompson. Origins of Rhodesia. London, 1968.
Afr 9439.69	Clements, Frank. Rhodesia: the course to collision. London, 1969.

Afr 9445   Southern Rhodesia - History by periods - Before 1893

Afr 9445.5	Colquhoun, A.R. Matabeleland, the war, and our position in South Africa. London, 1894.
Afr 9445.10	Harris, John H. The chartered millions. London, 1920.
Afr 9445.15	Hole, Hugh Marshall. The making of Rhodesia. London, 1926.
Afr 9445.20	Wallis, J.P.R. One man's hand. London, 1950.
Afr 9445.25	Tabler, Edward C. The far interior. Cape Town, 1955.
Afr 9445.30	Olivier, C.P. Many treks made Rhodesia. Cape Town, 1957.
Afr 9445.35	Dunn, Cyril. Central African witness. London, 1959.
Afr 9445.40	Mason, Philip. Year of decision. London, 1960.
Afr 9445.45	Gelfand, M. Northern Rhodesia. Oxford, 1961.
Afr 9445.50	Summers, Roger. The warriors. Cape Town, 1970.

Afr 9446   Southern Rhodesia - History by periods - Matabele campaign (1893-1896)

Afr 9446.20	Chalmers, James. Fighting the Matabele. London, 1898.
Afr 9446.24	Selous, Frederick Courteney. Sunshine and storm in Rhodesia. N.Y., 1969.
Afr 9446.25	Laing, D.J. The Matabele rebellion, 1896. London, 1897.
Afr 9446.26	Baden-Powell. The Matabele campaign, 1896. London, 1897.
Afr 9446.27	Selous, F.C. Sunshine and storm in Rhodesia. London, 1896.
Afr 9446.28	Plumer, Herbert C. An irregular corps in Matabeleland. London, 1897.
Afr 9446.29	Hale, H.M. Lobengula. London, 1929.
Afr 9446.30	Grey, A.H.G. Hubert Hervey. London, 1899.
Afr 9446.32	Davidson, A.B. Matabele i Mashona v bor'be protiv angliiskoi kolonizatsii, 1888-1897. Moscow, 1958.
Afr 9446.33	Mziki. 'Mlimo. Pietermaritzburg, 1926.
Afr 9446.34	Donovan, Charles Henry Wynne. With Wilson in Matabeleland. London, 1894.
Afr 9446.35	Wills, William Arthur. The downfall of Lobengula. London, 1894.
Afr 9446.36	Sykes, Frank W. With Plumer in Matabeleland, an account of the operations of the Matabeleland relief force during the rebellion of 1896. Westminster, 1897.
Afr 9446.37	Ranger, Terence O. Revolt in Southern Rhodesia, 1896-1897. London, 1967.
Afr 9446.38	Glass, Stafford. The Matabele War. Harlow, 1968.
Afr 9446.40	Ranger, Terence Osborn. Revolt in Southern Rhodesia, 1896-97. Evanston, Ill., 1967.
Afr 9446.47	Cary, Robert. A time to die. 2nd ed. Cape Town, 1969.

Afr 9448   Southern Rhodesia - History by periods - 1950-1966

Afr 9448.50	Sanger, Clyde. Central African emergency. London, 1960.
Afr 9448.51	Young, Kenneth. Rhodesia and independence, a study in British colonial policy. London, 1967.
Afr 9448.55	Blake, W.T. Central African survey. London, 1961.
Afr 9448.56	Rhodesia (British Colony). The demand for independence in Rhodesia. Salisbury, 1965.
Afr 9448.60	Creighton, P.R. The anatomy of partnership. London, 1960.
Afr 9448.65	Phillips, Cecil E.L. The vision splendid. London, 1960.
Afr 9448.70	Africa Bureau, London. Britains dilemma in central Africa. London, 1960.
Afr 9448.72	Keatley, Patrick. The politics of partnership. Harmondsworth, Middlesex, 1963.
Afr 9448.73	Rhodesia and Nyasaland. Prime Minister. The break-up. Salisbury, 1963.
Afr 9448.74	Franklin, H. Unholy wedlock. London, 1963.
Afr 9448.75	Welensky, Roy. Welensky's four thousand days. London, 1965.
Afr 9448.76A	Great Britain. Prime Minister. Southern Rhodesia. London, 1965.
Afr 9448.76B	Great Britain. Prime Minister. Southern Rhodesia. London, 1965.
Afr 9448.77	Alport, Cuthbert James McCall. The sudden assignment. London, 1965.
Afr 9448.78	Shamugawia, Nathan M. Crisis in Rhodesia. London, 1965.
Afr 9448.79	Skeen, Andrew. Prelude to independence, Skeen's 115 days. Cape Town, 1966.

Afr 9450   Southern Rhodesia - History by periods - 1966-

Afr 9450.3F	Great Britain. Commonwealth Office. Library. Southern Rhodesia illegal declaration of independence. London, 1966?
Afr 9450.5	Lardner-Burke, Desmond. Rhodesia, the story of the crisis. London, 1966.
Afr 9450.8	Peck, A.J.A. Rhodesia condemns. Salisbury, Rhodesia, 1967.
Afr 9450.10	Edwards, Hilton. Rhodesian independence justified. Queenstown, South Africa, 1966.
Afr 9450.15	Sparrow, Gerald. Rhodesia in 'rebellion'. London, 1967.
Afr 9450.20	Barber, James. Rhodesia: the road to rebellion. London, 1967.
Afr 9450.25	Bolze, Louis W. Life with Udi; a cartoon history of independant Rhodesia. v.1-2. Bulawayo, 1966.
Afr 9450.30	Great Britain. Foreign and Commonwealth Office. Rhodesia; report on the discussions held on board H.M.S. Fearless. London, 1968.
Afr 9450.35	Smith, Donald. Rhodesia: the problem. London, 1969.
Afr 9450.40	Metrowich, Frederick Redvers. Rhodesia; birth of a nation. Pretoria, 1969.

Afr 9488 - 9490   Southern Rhodesia - Geography, description, etc. - General works (By date)

Afr 9488.75	Stabb, Henry. To the Victoria Falls via Matabeleland. Cape Town, 1967.
Afr 9488.81	Oates, Frank. Matabele land. London, 1881.
Afr 9488.89	Vaughan-Williams, H. A visit to Lobengula in 1889. Pietermaritzburg, 1947.
Afr 9488.90	Holub, E. Von der Capstadt ins land der Maschukulunbe. Vienna, 1890. 2v.
Afr 9488.91	Lippert, Marie. The Matabeleland travel letters of Marie Lippert. Cape Town, 1960.
Afr 9488.92	Knight-Bruce. Journals of the Mashonaland mission. London, 1892.
Afr 9488.93	Selous, F.C. Travel and adventure in south-east Africa. London, 1893.
Afr 9488.93.2	Blennerhassett. Adventures in Mashonaland. London, 1893.

Afr 9488 - 9490 Southern Rhodesia - Geography, description, etc. - General works (By date) cont.

Afr 9488.94.2 Carnegie, D. Among the Matabele. 2. ed. London, 1894.
Afr 9488.94.5 Nadellaic, Jean François Albert du Pouget Marquis de. Le Mashonaland. Paris, 1894.
Afr 9488.95 Knight-Bruce. Memories of Mashonaland. London, 1895.
Afr 9488.95.3 Selous, F.C. A hunter's wanderings in Africa. London, 1895.
Afr 9488.95.5 Knight, E.F. Rhodesia of to-day. London, 1895.
Afr 9488.95.7 Mathers, E.P. Zambesia, England's El Dorado in Africa. London, 1895.
Afr 9488.95.8.3 Finlason, C.E. A nobody in Mashonaland. 3. ed. London, 1895.
Afr 9488.96.2 Leonard, A.G. How we made Rhodesia. 2. ed. London, 1896.
Afr 9488.97 Dutoit, Stephanus Jacobus. Rhodesia. London, 1897.
Afr 9488.99 Brown, W.H. On the South African frontier. N.Y., 1899.
Afr 9488.99.3 Dawkins, C.T. Precis of information concerning Southern Rhodesia. London, 1899.
Afr 9489.00 Bordeaux, A. Rhodesia et Transvaal. Paris, 1900.
Afr 9489.04 Wright, E.H.S. Railways in Rhodesia. London, 1904.
Afr 9489.05 British South Africa Company. Southern Rhodesia. London, 1905.
Afr 9489.07 Ferguson, F.W. Southern Rhodesia...past history. London, 1907.
Afr 9489.08 Selous, F.C. African nature notes and reminiscences. London, 1908.
Afr 9489.09 Hone, P.F. Southern Rhodesia. London, 1909.
Afr 9489.11 Mansfield, C. Via Rhodesia. London, 1911.
Afr 9489.11.3 Hyatt, S.P. Off the main track. London, 1911.
Afr 9489.11.6 Woods, M.L. Pastels under the Southern Cross. London, 1911.
Afr 9489.24 Colquhoun, E.C. The real Rhodesia. London, 1924.
Afr 9489.26 Rhodesia, Southern. Department of Agriculture and Lands. Southern Rhodesia. Salisbury, 1926.
Afr 9489.28 Hole, Hugh Marshall. Old Rhodesian days. London, 1928.
Afr 9489.35 Hemans, H.N. The log of a native commissioner. London, 1935.
Afr 9489.36 Rhodesia, Southern. Bureau of Publicity. Southern Rhodesia. 4. ed. Salisbury, 1936.
Afr 9489.37 Windram, Foster. Night over Africa. London, 1937.
Afr 9489.47 Wadio, A.S.N. The romance of Rhodesia. London, 1947.
Afr 9489.54 Federation of Rhodesia and Nyasaland. Federal Information Services. The new federation of Rhodesia and Nyasaland. Salisbury, 1954.
Afr 9489.57 Lessing, Doris M. Going home. London, 1957.
Afr 9489.57.2 Lessing, Doris M. Going home. London, 1968.
Afr 9489.60 Blake, W.T. Rhodesia and Nyasaland journey. London, 1960.
Afr 9489.60.5 Barber, F.H. Zambezia andMatabeleland in the seventies. London, 1960.
Afr 9489.63 Rotishauser, Josef. Mann in der Mitte. Immensee, 1963.
Afr 9489.65 Symonds, Jane. Southern Rhodesia. Oxford, 1966.
Afr 9489.65.5 Lloyd, Frank. Rhodesian patrol. Ilfracombe, 1965.
Afr 9489.66 Haw, Richard Claude. Rhodesia. Salisbury, 1966.
Afr 9489.66.5 Reed, Douglas. The battle for Rhodesia. Cape Town, 1966.
Afr 9489.66.6 Reed, Douglas. Insanity fair '67. London, 1967.
Afr 9489.66.10 Orcival, Francois d'. Rhodésie, pays des lions fidèles. Paris, 1966.
Afr 9489.67 Berlyn, Phillippa. Rhodesia, beleaguered country. London, 1967.
Afr 9489.67.5 Mohn, Albert Henrik. Rhodesia. Oslo, 1967.
Afr 9489.67.10 National Federation of Women's Institutes (Rhodesia). Great spaces washed with sun: Rhodesia. Salisbury, 1967.
Afr 9489.68 Stonier, George Walter. Rhodesian spring. London, 1968.
Afr 9489.68.5 Tredgold, Robert Clarkson. The Rhodesia that was my life. London, 1968.
Afr 9489.69 Strauss, Frances. My Rhodesia. Boston, 1969.

Afr 9493 Southern Rhodesia - Geography, description, etc. - Special customs

Afr 9493.38 Boggie, Jeannie M. Experiences of rHodesia's pioneer women. Bulawayo, 1938.
Afr 9493.58 Griffiths, James. Livingstone's Africa. London, 1958.
Afr 9493.67 Gelfand, Michael. The African witch: with particular reference to...Shona of Rhodesia. Edinburgh, 1967.

Afr 9497 Southern Rhodesia - Geography, description, etc. - Views

Afr 9497.5F King, Ralph W. The Rhodesias and Nyasaland. 2. ed. Cape Town, 1956.
Afr 9497.10 La Rhodésie. Paris, 1968.

Afr 9499 Southern Rhodesia - Economic and financial conditions

Afr 9499.5 Rhodesia, Southern. Progress of southern Rhodesia, 1920-27. Salisbury, 1928.
Afr 9499.10 Rhodesia, Southern. Public Relations Department. Southern Rhodesia, a field for investment. n.p., 1950.
Afr 9499.15 Federation of Rhodesia and Nyasaland. Federal Information Services. Opportunity in Rhodesia and Nyasaland. Salisbury, 1955.
Afr 9499.20 Mai, Erwin. Die Wirtschaft von Britisch-Zentral Afrika. Köln, 1953.
Afr 9499.25A United States. Bureau of Foreign Commerce (1953-). Investment in Federation of Rhodesia and Nyasaland. Washington, 1956.
Afr 9499.25B United States. Bureau of Foreign Commerce (1953-). Investment in Federation of Rhodesia and Nyasaland. Washington, 1956.
Afr 9499.27 Tow, Leonard. The manufacturing economy of Southern Rhodesia, problems and prospects. Washington, 1960.
Afr 9499.28 Cherkasov, Iurii N. Ekonomicheskie problemy Iuzhnoi Rodezii. Moskva, 1966.
Afr 9499.30 United States. Trade Mission to the Federation of Rhodesia and Nyasaland. Report. Washington, 1960.
Afr 9499.35 Rhodesia and Nyasaland. Report. Salisbury, 1960.
Afr 9499.37 Italy. Istituto Nazionale per il Commercio Estero. Federazione delle Rodesia e del Niassaland. Roma, 1962.
Afr 9499.40 Haglewood, Arthur. Nyasaland. Oxford, 1960.
Afr 9499.50 Barber, W.J. The economy of British Central Africa. Stanford, 1961.
Afr 9499.60F Rhodesia and Nyasaland. Central Statistical Office. National accounts of the Federation of Rhodesia and Nyasaland. Salisbury, 1961.
Afr 9499.70 Rhodesia, Southern. Advisory Committee on the Development of the Economic Resources of Southern Rhodesia. The development of the economic resources of Southern Rhodesia. Salisbury, 1962.
Afr 9499.74 Phoenix Group. Planning the development of the wealth of three nations. Salisbury, 1960.

Afr 9499 Southern Rhodesia - Economic and financial conditions cont.

Afr 9499.75F Central African Statistical Office. Report on Southern Rhodesia family expenditure survey. Salisbury, 1952.
Afr 9499.76 Guides and Handbooks of Africa. Resources and opportunities in the Rhodesias and Nyasaland. Nairobi, 1963.
Afr 9499.78 Sowelem, R.A. Towards financial independance in a developing economy. London, 1967.
Afr 9499.80 Gedamu, T. Country study on Southern Rhodesia. Addis Ababa? 1963.

Afr 9500 Southern Rhodesia - Races - Indigenous races - General

Afr 9500.5 Cripps, A.S. An Africa for Africans. London, 1927.
Afr 9500.10 Unyanda, B.J. In search of truth. Bombay, 1954.
Afr 9500.15 Franck, Thomas M. Race and nationalism. N.Y., 1960.
Afr 9500.20 Parker, Franklin. African development and education in Southern Rhodesia. Columbus, 1960.
Afr 9500.25 Gray, Richard. The two nations. Oxford, 1960.
Afr 9500.30 Haw, Richard C. No other home. Bulawayo, 1960.
Afr 9500.35 Rhodesian Institute of African Affairs, Bulawayo, South Africa. The progress of Africans in Southern Rhodesia. Bulawayo, 1958.
Afr 9500.38 Harrigan, Anthony. One against the mob. Arlington, 1966.
Afr 9500.40 Rayner, W. The tribe and its successors. London, 1962.
Afr 9500.45 Rogers, Cyril A. Racial themes in Southern Rhodesia. New Haven, 1962.
Afr 9500.46 Gussman, Boris. Out in the mid-day sun. London, 1962.
Afr 9500.50 Sonius, H.W.J. Rhodesia, een dilemma van ras en grond. Leiden, 1966.

Afr 9502 Southern Rhodesia - Races - Indigenous races - Special

Afr 9502.10 Bullock, Charles. The Mashona. Cape Town, 1928.
Afr 9502.12 Plaatje, S.T. Uhudi. Kimberley, 1930.
Afr 9502.13 Gelfand, M. Shona religion. Cape Town, 1962.
Afr 9502.13.5 Gelfand, M. African background. Cape Town, 1965.
Afr 9502.13.10 Gelfand, M. An African's religion, the spirit of Nyajena. Cape Town, 1966.
Afr 9502.13.15 Gelfand, M. African crucible. Cape Town, 1968.
Afr 9502.14 Bullock, C. The Mashona and Matabele. Cape Town, 1950.
Afr 9502.15 Holleman, J.F. African interlude. Cape Town, 1958.
Afr 9502.18 Howarth, David. The shadow of the dam. N.Y., 1961.
Afr 9502.22 Mitchell, J.C. An outline of the sociological background to African labour. Salisbury, 1961.
Afr 9502.24 Nielsen, Peter. The Matabele at home. Bulawayo, 1913.
Afr 9502.25 Bullock, Charles. Mashona laws and customs. Salisbury, 1913.
Afr 9502.26 Dotson, Floyd. The Indian minority of Zambia, Rhodesia and Malawi. New Haven, 1968.

Afr 9505 Southern Rhodesia - Races - Others

Afr 9505.2 Todd, Judith. Rhodesia. London, 1966.

Afr 9506 Southern Rhodesia - Religion; missions

Afr 9506.1 Gray, S. Douglas. Frontiers of the kingdom. London, 1930.
Afr 9506.2 Chater, Patricia. Grass roots. London, 1962.
Afr 9506.4 Clinton, Iris. 'These vessels' the story of Inyati, 1859-1959. Bulawayo, 1959.
Afr 9506.6 Gelfand, Michael. Mother Patrick and her nursing sister. Capetown, 1964.
Afr 9506.7 King, Paul. Mission in Southern Rhodesia. Inyati, 1959.
Afr 9506.8 In god's white-robed army. Cape Town, 1951.
Afr 9506.10 Elliott, William Allan. Gold from the quartz. London, 1910.

Afr 9510 Southern Rhodesia - Local - Regions, etc.

Afr 9510.5PF Baines, Thomas. The Victoria Falls, Zambesi River. London, 1865.
Afr 9510.5.5 Clark, John Desmond. The Victoria Falls. Lusaka, 1952.
Afr 9510.5.10 Fagan, Brian M. The Victoria Falls, a handbook to the Victoria Falls, the Batoka Gorge and part of the upper Zambesi River. 2. ed. Lusaka, 1964.
Afr 9510.7 Goy, M.K. Dans les solitudes de l'Afrique. Genève, 1901.
Afr 9510.9 Maie, B. Voortrekkerslawe in donker Afrika. 2. druk. Pretoria, 1928.
Afr 9510.10.5 Kariba studies. Manchester, Eng. 1,1960+ 3v.
Afr 9510.10.10 Kariba. Kariba. Bloemfontein, 1959.
Afr 9510.11 Nobles, E.A. Guide to the Matapos. Cape Town, 1924.
Afr 9510.11.5 Tredgold, Robert Clarksen. The Matapos. Salisbury, 1956.
Afr 9510.12 Bulawayo, Southern Rhodesia. City Council. The city of Bulawayo. 2. ed. Cape Town, 1957.
Afr 9510.12.5F Rhodesia and Nyasaland. Report on urban African budget survey in Bulawayo, 1958/59. Salisbury, 1960.

Afr 9515 Southern Rhodesia - Local - Salisbury

Afr 9515.5.2 Salisbury. The city ofSalisbury. 2. ed. Cape Town, 1957.
Afr 9515.5.5F Rhodesia and Nyasaland. Report on urban African budget survey in Salisbury, 1957/58. Salisbury, 1958. 2v.
Afr 9515.6 Tanser, George Henry. A scantling of time. Salisbury, 1965.
Afr 9515.7 Rixom, Frank. History of the Salisbury club. Salisbury, 1953.

Afr 9520 Southern Rhodesia - Local - Others (A-Z, 99 scheme, by place)

Afr 9520.10 Ransford, Oliver. Bulawayo: historic battleground of Rhodesia. Cape Town, 1968.

Afr 9523 Southern Rhodesia - Heraldry and genealogy

Afr 9523.275 Burrows, Edmund Hartford. The moodies of Melsetter. Cape Town, 1954.

Afr 9525.100 - .899 Southern Rhodesia - Biographies - Individual (A-Z, 800 scheme, by person)

Afr 9525.201 Beit, Alfred. The will and the way. London, 1957.
Afr 9525.224 Boggie, Jeannie. A husband and a farm in Rhodesia. Gwelo, S.R., 1959.
Afr 9525.288 Clark, Percy M. The autobiography of an old drifter. London, 1936.
Afr 9525.393.2 Finaughty, William. The recollections of William Finaughty, elephant hunter. 2nd ed. Cape Town, 1957.
Afr 9525.435 Some account of George Gray and his work in Africa. London, 1914.
Afr 9525.457 Gann, L.H. Huggins of Rhodesia. London, 1964.
Afr 9525.529 Posselt, Friedrich Wilhelm Traugott. Uppengula the scatterer. Bulawayo, 1945.

Afr 9525.100 - .899 Southern Rhodesia - Biographies - Individual (A-Z, 800 scheme, by person) cont.

Afr 9525.529.25   Preller, Gustav Schoeman. Lobengula, the tragedy of a Matabele king. Johannesburg, 1963.
Afr 9525.575   Farrant, Jean. Mashonaland martyr. Cape Town, 1966.
Afr 9525.578   Northcott, C. Robert Moffat. London, 1961.
Afr 9525.578.5   Moffat, Robert. A life's labours in South Africa. London, 1871.
Afr 9525.578.10   Moffat, Robert. Scenes and services in South Africa. London, 1876.
Afr 9525.593   Becker, Peter. Path of blood. London, 1962.
Afr 9525.875   Taylor, Don. The Rhodesian, the life of Sir Roy Welensky. London, 1955.
Afr 9525.875.10   Allighan, Garry. The Welensky story. Cape Town, 1962.
Afr 9525.877   Andrews, Charles. John White of Mashonaland. London, 1935.

Afr 9535   British Central Africa - Periodicals (A-Z, 99 scheme)
Afr 9535.12F   Central Africa Historical Association. Local series pamphlet. Salisbury, Rhodesia. 2,1960+
Afr 9535.12.5   Central Africa research bulletin. London. 1,1968+
Afr 9535.75   Rhodesia and Nyasaland. National Archives. Occasional papers. Salisbury. 1,1963//
Afr 9535.75.5   Rhodesia (British Colony). National Archives. Occasional papers. Salisbury. 1,1965+
Afr 9535.98   Zambezia; a journal of social studies in southern and central Africa. Salisbury. 1,1969+

Afr 9538   British Central Africa - Bibliographies
Afr 9538.5   Cox, D.L. A bibliography of the Federation of the Rhodesias and Nyasaland. Cape Town, 1949.
Afr 9538.10F   International African Institute, London. South-east central Africa and Madagascar. London, 1961.
Afr 9538.12   Rhodesia and Nyasaland. National Archives. A select bibliography of recent publications. Salisbury, 1960.

Afr 9540   British Central Africa - Pamphlet volumes
Afr 9540.1   Pamphlet box. Central Africa.

Afr 9542   British Central Africa - Collected source materials
Afr 9542.5   Northern Rhodesia and Nyasaland. Publication Bureau. Annual report. Lusaka. 1950+
Afr 9542.8   Central Bantu historical texts. Lusaka. 1+

Afr 9545   British Central Africa - Government and administration
Afr 9545.5   Rhodes-Livingston Institute, Lusaka. From tribal rule to modern government. Lusaka, 1959.
Afr 9545.10   Coissoró, Narana. The customary laws of succession in Central Africa. Thesis. Lisboa, 1966.

Afr 9548 - 9550   British Central Africa - General history (By date)
Afr 9548.3   Johnston, H.H. British central Africa. N.Y., 1897.
Afr 9548.5   Johnston, H.H. British central Africa. 2. ed. London, 1898.
Afr 9548.7   Robert, Maurice. L'Afrique centrale. Paris, 1934.
Afr 9549.32   Letcher, Owen. South central Africa. Johannesburg, 1932.
Afr 9549.60   Raven, Faith. Central Africa. London, 1960.
Afr 9549.61   Cerulli, Ernesta. Nel paese dei Bantu. Torino, 1961.
Afr 9549.65   Cairns, H. Alan C. The clash of cultures. N.Y., 1965.
Afr 9549.65.5   Cairns, H. Alan C. Prelude to imperialism; British reactions to Central African society, 1840-1890. London, 1965.
Afr 9549.66   Stokes, Eric. The Zambesian past. Manchester, 1966.
Afr 9549.67   Mtshali, B. Valindlela. Rhodesia: background to conflict. N.Y., 1967.
Afr 9549.68   Tindall, P.E.N. A history of Central Africa. London, 1968.

Afr 9555   British Central Africa - History by periods - Before 1850
Afr 9555.5   Akademiia Nauk SSSR. Institut Etnografii. Arabskie istochniki VII-X vekov. Moscow, 1960. 2v.

Afr 9558   British Central Africa - History by periods - Livingstone
Afr 9558.5A   Livingstone, D. Travels ans researches in South Africa. Philadelphia, 1858.
Afr 9558.5B   Livingstone, D. Travels and researches in South Africa. Philadelphia, 1858.
Afr 9558.6   Livingstone, D. Missionary travels in South Africa. N.Y., 1858.
Afr 9558.6.3   Livingstone, D. Missionary travels and researches in South Africa. 25 ed. London, 1859.
Afr 9558.6.10   Livingstone, D. Missionary travels and researches in South Africa. N.Y., 1870.
Afr 9558.6.15   Livingstone, D. Missionary travels and researches in South Africa. London, 1899.
Afr 9558.7   Livingstone, D. Livingstone's travels. London, 1955.
Afr 9558.8   Livingstone, D. Cambridge lectures. London, 1860.
Afr 9558.8.5   Livingstone, David. Dr. Livingstone's Cambridge lectures. Farnborough, Hants., Eng., 1968.
Afr 9558.9   Livingstone, D. Travels and researches in South Africa. Philadelphia, 1860.
NEDL Afr 9558.10   Livingstone, D. Narrative of an expedition to the Zambesi. London, 1865.
Afr 9558.10.5   Livingstone, D. Narrative of an expedition to the Zambesi. N.Y., 1866.
Afr 9558.11   Livingstone, D. Explorations dans l'Afrique australe. 2. ed. Paris, 1869.
Afr 9558.12   Livingstone, D. Dreissig Jahre Afrika. Leipzig, 191-.
Afr 9558.14   Livingstone, D. Some letters from Livingstone, 1840-1872. London, 1940.
Afr 9558.14.5   Livingstone, D. Family letters, 1841-1856. London, 1959. 2v.
Afr 9558.14.10   Livingstone, D. Livingstone's missionary correspondence. London, 1961.
Afr 9558.14.15   Livingstone, D. The Zambesi doctors. Edinburgh, 1964.
Afr 9558.15   Appleyard, M.E. Doctor David Livingstone. Cape Town, 1949.
Afr 9558.16.3   Paumier, H. L'Afrique ouverte... du Docteur Livingstone. 3. ed. Paris, 1868.
Afr 9558.20   Lacerda, F.J. de. Exams das viagens do Doutor Livingstone. Lisbon, 1867.
Afr 9558.23   Pamphlet box. Livingstone.
Afr 9558.25   Life and explorations of Dr. Livingstone. London, 187-.
Afr 9558.26   Roberts, J.S. Life and explorations of Dr. Livingstone. Boston, 1875.

Afr 9558   British Central Africa - History by periods - Livingstone cont.

Afr 9558.27   Caranti, B. Notizie biografiche sul dottore David Livingstone. Torino, 1876.
Afr 9558.29   Vattemare, H. David Livingstone. Paris, 1879.
Afr 9558.30   Blaikie, W.G. Personal life of David Livingstone. London, 1880.
Afr 9558.30.2A   Blaikie, W.G. Personal life of David Livingstone. N.Y., 1881.
Afr 9558.30.2B   Blaikie, W.G. Personal life of David Livingstone. N.Y., 1881.
Afr 9558.30.15   Blaikie, W.G. Personal life of David Livingstone. N.Y., 1895.
Afr 9558.30.20   Blaikie, W.G. The personal life of David Livingstone. N.Y., 1969.
Afr 9558.32   Chambliss, J.E. The lives and travels of Livingstone and Stanley. Boston, 1881.
Afr 9558.35   Johnston, H.H. Livingstone and exploration of central Africa. London, 1891.
Afr 9558.36   Charles, Elizabeth. Three martyrs of the nineteenth century... Livingstone, Gordon, and Patteson. N.Y., 1886.
Afr 9558.38A   Hughes, T. David Livingstone. London, 1889.
Afr 9558.38B   Hughes, T. David Livingstone. London, 1889.
Afr 9558.43   MacLachlan, T.B. David Livingstone. Edinburgh, 1901.
Afr 9558.48   Young, E.D. The search after Livingstone. (A diary). London, 1868.
Afr 9558.51A   Fraser, A.Z. Livingstone and Newstead. London, 1913.
Afr 9558.51B   Fraser, A.Z. Livingstone and Newstead. London, 1913.
Afr 9558.55   Finger, Charles J. David Livingstone, explorer and prophet. Garden City, N.Y., 1928.
Afr 9558.57   Campbell, R.J. Livingstone. London, 1929.
Afr 9558.59   Somervell, D.C. Livingstone. London, 1936.
Afr 9558.61   MacNair, James I. Livingstone the liberator. London, 1940.
Afr 9558.65   Horne, C.S. David Livingstone. N.Y., 1913.
Afr 9558.75   Oswell, W.E. William C. Oswell, hunter and explorer. N.Y., 1900. 2v.
Afr 9558.85   Coupland, R. Kirk on the Zambesi. Oxford, 1928.
Afr 9558.85.2   Coupland, R. Kirk on the Zambesi; a chapter of African history. Oxford, 1968.
Afr 9558.86   Coupland, R. Livingstone's last journey. London, 1945.
Afr 9558.90   Debenham, F. The way to Ilala. London, 1955.
Afr 9558.95   Seaver, George. David Livingstone. N.Y., 1957.
Afr 9558.100   Sharp, J.A. David Livingstone. London, 1920.
Afr 9558.110   Livingstone, David. David Livingstone and the Rovuma. Edinburgh, 1965.

Afr 9558.500 -   British Central Africa - History by periods - Other early explorers
Afr 9558.500   Thornton, Richard. The Zambezi papers of Richard Thornton. London, 1963. 2v.
Afr 9558.510   Kirk, John. The Zambesi journal and letters of Dr. John Kirk, 1858-63. Edinburgh, 1965. 2v.
Afr 9558.520   Simmons, Jack. Livingstone and Africa. London, 1966.

Afr 9560   British Central Africa - History by periods - 1850-1950
Afr 9560.5   Moir, F.L.M. After Livingstone. London, 19-.
Afr 9560.15   Belgium. Treaties. Great Britain, 1933. Exchange of notes between His Majesty's government in the United Kingdon...Belgian government. London, 1933.
Afr 9560.18   Warhurst, P.R. Anglo-Portuguese relations in South-Central Africa. London, 1962.
Afr 9560.20A   Rotberg, Robert Irwin. The rise of nationalism in central Africa. Cambridge, 1965.
Afr 9560.20B   Rotberg, Robert Irwin. The rise of nationalism in central Africa. Cambridge, 1965.

Afr 9565   British Central Africa - History by periods - 1963-
Afr 9565.2   Pitch, Anthony. Inside Zambia - and out. Cape Town, 1967.
Afr 9565.5   Rhodesia: the moral issue. Gwelo, 1968.

Afr 9598 - 9600   British Central Africa - Geography, description, etc. - General works (By date)
Afr 9598.58   Malte-Brun, V.A. Resume histoire de l'exploration faite dans l'Afrique centrale. Paris, 1858.
Afr 9598.82   Macdonald, D. Africana or the heart of heathen Africa. London, 1882. 2v.
Afr 9598.84   Maps. Africa, South (1884). Notes on geography of south central Africa. London, 1884.
Afr 9598.84.5   Knox, T.W. The boy travellers in the Far East. N.Y., 1884.
Afr 9598.91   Moir, J.F. A lady's letter from central Africa. Glasgow, 1891.
Afr 9598.93   Rankin, D.J. The Zambesi basin and Nyassaland. Edinburgh, 1893.
Afr 9599.07   Landor, A.H.S. Across widest Africa. London, 1907. 2v.
Afr 9599.07.5   Schillings, C.G. In wildest Africa. N.Y., 1907.
Afr 9599.11   Colville, A. One thousand miles in a Machilla. London, 1911.
Afr 9599.12   Moubray, John M. In south central Africa. London, 1912.
Afr 9599.14   Morrison, J.H. Streams in the desert. London, 1919.
Afr 9599.24   Christy, C. Big game and Pygmies. London, 1924.
Afr 9599.24.5   Savile, F. The high grass trail. London, 1924.
Afr 9599.28   Haefler, P.L. Africa speaks, a story of adventure. London, 1931.
Afr 9599.29   Maugham, R.C.F. Africa as I have known it. London, 1929.
Afr 9599.32   Duff, Hector Livingstone. A small chop. London, 1932.
Afr 9599.34   Wood and iron, a story of Africa written in memory of H.U.C. Wood. London, 1929.
Afr 9599.45   Gatti, Attilio. South of the Sahara. N.Y., 1945.
Afr 9599.54   Verbeken, Auguste. Contribution à la géographie historique du Katanga et de régions voisines. Bruxelles, 1954.
Afr 9599.55   Ingerman, Karel J.J. Een slavenband als ereteken. 2. druk. Amsterdam, 1955.
Afr 9599.56   Ingerman, Karel J.J. Dreigend drennen de tam-tams. Amsterdam, 1956.
Afr 9599.59   Ingerman, Karel J.J. Sluimerend paradijs. Amsterdam, 1959.
Afr 9599.61   Gibbs, Peter. Avalanche in central Africa. London, 1961.

Afr 9603   British Central Africa - Geography, description, etc. - Special customs
    Afr 9603.5   Rhodes-Livingstone Institute, Lusaka, Northern Rhodesia. 11th Conference, Lusaka, 1958. Present interrelations in Central African rural and urban life. Lusaka, 1958.
    Afr 9603.10   Nyabongo, Akiki K. The story of an African chief. N.Y., 1935.
    Afr 9603.15   Mitchell, J.C. Social networks in urban situations. Manchester, 1969.

Afr 9606   British Central Africa - Geography, description, etc. - Views
    Afr 9606.2   Bulpin, Thomas Victor. Rhodesia and Nyasaland. Cape Town, 1960.

Afr 9609   British Central Africa - Economic and financial conditions
    Afr 9609.5   Deane, Phyllis. Colonial social accounting. Cambridge, England, 1953.
    Afr 9609.10   Thompson, C.H. Economic development in Rhodesia and Nyassaland. London, 1954.
    Afr 9609.15F   Rhodesia and Nyasaland. Report on a economic survey of Nyasaland. Salisbury, 1959.
    Afr 9609.20F   Rhodesia and Nyasaland. National accounts of the federation. Salisbury, 1960.
    Afr 9609.25   Arrighi, G. The political economy of Rhodesia. The Hague, 1967.

Afr 9610   British Central Africa - Races
    Afr 9610.1   Aucapitaine, L.B.H. Les Yem-Yem tribu anthropophage de l'Afrique centrale. Paris, 1857.
    Afr 9610.5   Mackenzie, D.R. The spirit-ridden Konde. Philadelphia, 1925.
    Afr 9610.10   Taylor, Don. Rainbow on the Zambezi. London, 1953.
    Afr 9610.15   Colson, Elizabeth. Seven tribes of BritishCentral Afrika. Manchester, 1959.
    Afr 9610.16   Marwick, Maxwell Gay. Sorcery in its social setting. Manchester, 1965.

Afr 9614   British Central Africa - Religion; missions
    Afr 9614.2.3   Dale, Godfrey. Darkness or light. 3rd ed. London, 1925.
    Afr 9614.4   Hine, John Edward. Days gone by. London, 1924.
    Afr 9614.10   Bulley, Mary Winifred. Kabanza; a story of Africa. Westminster, 1927.

Afr 9619   British Central Africa - Collected biographies
    Afr 9619.2   Tabler, Edward C. Pioneers of Rhodesia. Cape Town, 1966.

Afr 9625   Northern Rhodesia; Zambia - Periodicals
    Afr 9625.5   Northern Rhodesia journal. Livingston. 3,1956+ 6v.
    Afr 9625.10F   Rhodesia, Northern. Central Race Relations Advisory And Conciliation Committee. Annual report. n.p.
    Afr 9625.10.5F   Rhodesia, Northern. Central Race Relations Advisory Committee. Annual report. Lusaka. 1-2,1960-1961//
    Afr 9625.15   Voice of Northern Rhodesia. Cairo.
    Afr 9625.16   United National Independence Party (Zambia). Proceedings of the annual general conference. Luska. 1967
    Afr 9625.20   Zambia. Lusaka. 1965-1969// 3v.
    Afr 9625.22   Z; international edition. Lusaka. 1,1969+
    Afr 9625.25   Zambia. University. Institute for Social Research. Communication. Lusaka. 1,1966+
    Afr 9625.30   Horizon. Nodola, Zambia. 9,1967+ 2v.
    Afr 9625.35   Zambian papers. Manchester, England. 1,1967+
    Afr 9625.40   Zambia. University. Institute of Social Research. Bulletin. 1,1966+
    Afr 9625.45   Lusaka. Livingstone Museum. Annual report. Lusaka. 1966

Afr 9630   Northern Rhodesia; Zambia - Pamphlet volumes
    Afr 9630   Pamphlet box. Northern Rhodesia.

Afr 9632   Northern Rhodesia; Zambia - Collected source materials
    Afr 9632.5F   Maugham, F.H. North Charterland concession inquiry. Report, July, 1932. London, 1932.
    Afr 9632.5.5F   Maugham, F.H. North charterland concession inquiry. Report, May 30, 1933. London, 1933.
    Afr 9632.10   Great Britain. Colonial Office. Report on northern Rhodesia. 4v.
    Afr 9632.15F   Rhodesia, Northern. Department of Water Affairs. Annual report.

Afr 9635   Northern Rhodesia; Zambia - Government and administration
    Afr 9635.5   Davidson, J.W. The Northern Rhodesian legislative council. London, 1948.
    Afr 9635.10F   Epstein, A.L. The administration of justice and the urban African. London, 1953.
    Afr 9635.15   Rhodesia, Northern. Commission to Inquire into the Participation of Africans in Local Government. Report. Lusaka, 1960.
    Afr 9635.20   Rhodesia, Northern. Northern Rhodesia proposal for constitutional change. London, 1961.
    Afr 9635.22A   Morris, Colin. Colin Morris and Kenneth Haunda. London, 1960.
    Afr 9635.22B   Morris, Colin. Colin Morris and Kenneth Haunda. London, 1960.
    Afr 9635.25   Great Britain. Colonial Office. Northern Rhodesia. London, 1961.
    Afr 9635.26   Rhodesia, Northern. Commission Appointed to Review the Salaries and Conditions of Service. Report. Lusaka, 1964.

Afr 9636   Northern Rhodesia; Zambia - General politics; political parties
    Afr 9636.5   Mulford, David C. Zambia: the politics of independence, 1957-1964. London, 1967.
    Afr 9636.8   Kaunda, Kenneth David. Humanism in Zambia and a guide to its implementation. Lusaka, 1967.

Afr 9638 - 9640   Northern Rhodesia; Zambia - General history (By date)
    Afr 9639.64   Gann, L.H. A history of Northern Rhodesia. London, 1964.
    Afr 9639.65   Kay, George. Changing patterns of settlement and land use in the eastern province of Northern Rhodesia. Hull, 1965.

Afr 9643   Northern Rhodesia; Zambia - History by periods - Before 1889
    Afr 9643.5   Fagan, Brian M. A short history of Zambia. Nairobi, 1966.

Afr 9645   Northern Rhodesia; Zambia - History by periods - 1889-1963
    Afr 9645.5   Gann, L.H. The birth of a plural society. Manchester, 1958.
    Afr 9645.10   Mason, Philip. The birth of a dilemma. London, 1958.
    Afr 9645.15   Morris, Colin M. The hour after midnight. London, 1961.
    Afr 9645.17   Mulford, D.C. The Northern Rhodesia general election, 1962. Nairobi, 1964.

Afr 9650   Northern Rhodesia; Zambia - History by periods - 1963-
    Afr 9650.5   Zambia. Tribunal on Detainees. Report. Lusaka, 1967.
    Afr 9650.10   Hall, Richard Seymour. The high price of principles. London, 1969.

Afr 9688 - 9690   Northern Rhodesia; Zambia - Geography, description, etc. - General works (By date)
    Afr 9689.8   Butt, G.E. My travels in north west Rhodesia. London, 1908.
    Afr 9689.11   Gouldsbury, C. Great plateau of Northern Rhodesia. London, 1911.
    Afr 9689.11.1   Gouldsbury, C. The great plateau of Northern Rhodesia. N.Y., 1969.
    Afr 9689.11.5   Gouldsbury, C. An African year. London, 1912.
    Afr 9689.22   Mackintosh, Catharine Winkworth. The new Zambesi trail. London, 1922.
    Afr 9689.33   Hughes, Joseph Edward. Eighteen years on Lake Bangweulu. London, 1933.
    Afr 9689.34   Letcher, Owen. When life was rusted through. Johannesburg, 1934.
    Afr 9689.38   Bradley, K. The diary of district officer. London, 1943.
    Afr 9689.38.4   Bradley, K. The diary of a district officer. 4th ed. London, 1966.
    Afr 9689.40   Cullen, Lucy P. Beyond the smoke that thunders. N.Y., 1940.
    Afr 9689.57   Tapson, Winifred (Haw). Old timer. Cape Town, 1957.
    Afr 9689.60   Duffy, Kevin. Black elephant hunter. London, 1960.
    Afr 9689.61   Wood, Anthony Saint John. Northern Rhodesia. London, 1961.
    Afr 9689.61.5   Rhodes-Livingstone Institute, Lusaka, Northern Rhodesia. Social research and community development. Lusaka, 1961.
    Afr 9689.63   Hock, E. Know your home: Zambia. Chensali? 1963?
    Afr 9689.65   Hall, Richard Seymour. Zambia. London, 1965.
    Afr 9689.65.5   Hall, Richard Seymour. Zambia. London, 1968.
    Afr 9689.68   Zambia, Rpresident (Kaunda). Zambia's guideline for the next decade. Lusaka, 1968.
    Afr 9689.69   American University, Washington, D.C. Foreign Area Studies. Area handbook for Zambia. Washington, 1969.

Afr 9693   Northern Rhodesia; Zambia - Geography, description, etc. - Special customs
    Afr 9693.3   Josephine (pseud.). Tell me, Josephine. London, 1964.
    Afr 9693.5   Epstein, A.L. Politics in an urban African community. Manchester, 1958.
    Afr 9693.7   Morris, Colin. The end of the missionary. London, 1962.
    Afr 9693.8   Rhodes-Livingstone Institute. The multitribal society. Lusaka, 1962.
    Afr 9693.10   Long, Norman. Social change and the individual: a study of the social and religious responses to innovation in a Zambian rural community. Manchester, 1968.

Afr 9699   Northern Rhodesia; Zambia - Economic and financial conditions
    Afr 9699.3   Zambia. Republic of Zambia. Lusaka, 1965.
    Afr 9699.41   Hinden, Rita. Plan for Africa, a report prepared for the colonial bureau of the Fabian Society. London, 1941.
    Afr 9699.47   Brelsford, W.V. Copperbelt markets. Lusaka, 1947.
    Afr 9699.59   Rhodesia, Northern. Special Commissioner for the Western Province. First report on a regional survey of the copperbelt, 1959. Lusaka, 1960.
    Afr 9699.65   Wallstorm, Tord. Grying, en bok om Zambia. Stockholm, 1965.
    Afr 9699.66   Baldwin, Robert Edward. Economic development and export growth. Berkeley, 1966.
    Afr 9699.66.5F   Zambia. Office of National Development and Planning. First national development plan, 1966-1970. Lusaka, 1966.
    Afr 9699.66.10   Zambia. Office of National Development and Planning. The building industry and the First National Development·Plan. Lusaka, 1967.
    Afr 9699.66.15   Clairmonte, Frédéric. Rhodesia: National Development Plan, 1965-1968. Addis Abbaba, 1966.
    Afr 9699.67   Kay, George. A social geography of Zambia; a survey of population. London, 1967.
    Afr 9699.68   Clausen, Lars. Industrialisierung in Schwarzafrika. Bielefeld, 1968.

Afr 9700   Northern Rhodesia; Zambia - Races
    Afr 9700.3   Cannison, Ian. The Luapula people of Northern Rhodesia. Manchester, 1959.
X Cg Afr 9700.5   Smith, E. Pla-speaking people of Northern Rhodesia. London, 1920. 2v.
    Afr 9700.5.5   Smith, Edwin William. The Ila-speaking peoples of Northern Rhodesia. New Hyde Park, 1968. 2v.
    Afr 9700.10   Melland, F.H. In witch-bound Africa. London, 1923.
    Afr 9700.10.2   Melland, F.H. In witch-bound Africa. Philadelphia, 1923.
    Afr 9700.13   Keith, Grace. The fading colour bar. London, 1966.
    Afr 9700.15   Dake, C.M. The Lambas of Northern Rhodesia. London, 1931.
    Afr 9700.16   Poole, Edward Humphry Lane. The native tribes of the eastern province of Northern Rhodesia. 2nd ed. Lusaka, 1938.
    Afr 9700.17   Richards, A.I. Land labour and diet in Northern Rhodesia. London, 1939.
    Afr 9700.20   Barnes, J.A. Politics in changing society. Cape Town, 1954.
    Afr 9700.20.5.2   Barnes, J.A. Politics in a changing society. 2nd ed. Manchester, 1967.
    Afr 9700.25   Gluckman, Max. The judicial process among the Barotse. Manchester, 1955.
    Afr 9700.25.5.2   Gluckman, Max. The judicial process among the Barotse of Northern Rhodesia. 2. ed. Manchester, 1967.
    Afr 9700.30   Watson, W. Tribal cohesion in a money economy. Manchester, 1958.
    Afr 9700.32   Turner, Victor Witter. The drums of affliction. Oxford, 1968.
    Afr 9700.32.5   Turner, Victor Witter. The forest of symbols; aspects of Ndembu ritual. Ithaca, 1967.
    Afr 9700.35   Colson, Elizabeth. The plateau Tonga of Northern Rhodesia. Manchester, 1962.

Afr 9700   Northern Rhodesia; Zambia - Races
cont.

Afr 9700.40   Bigland, Eileen. The lake of the royal crocodiles. London, 1939.

Afr 9700.41   Brelsford, William Vernon. Generation of men. Salisbury, 1965.

Afr 9700.41.5.2   Brelsford, William Vernon. The tribes of Zambia. 2nd ed. Lusaka, 1965?

Afr 9700.45F   Rhodesia. Northern. Committee Appointed to Investigate the Extent to which Racial Discrimination is Practised in Shops and in Other Similar Business Premises. Report. Lusaka, 1956.

Afr 9700.50   Stefaniszyn, Bronislaw. Social and ritual life of the Ambo of Northern Rhodesia. London, 1964.

Afr 9704   Northern Rhodesia; Zambia - Religion; missions

Afr 9704.1   Jamieson, Gladys. Zambia contrasts. London, 1965.

Afr 9704.2   Rotberg, Robert Irwin. Christian missionaries and the creation of Northern Rhodesia, 1880-1924. Princeton, N.J., 1965.

Afr 9704.3   Chapman, William. A pathfinder in south Central Africa. London, 1909.

Afr 9704.6   Zambia. Commission of Inquiry into the Former Lumpa Church. Report. Lusaka, 1965.

Afr 9704.8   Smith, Julia A. Sunshine and shade in Central Africa. London, 1911.

Afr 9704.10   Bolink, Peter. Towards church union in Zambia. Akademisch Proefschrift. Franeker, 1967.

Afr 9704.12   Gelfland, Michael. Gubulawayo and beyond: letters and journals of the early Jesuit missionaires to Zambesia. London, 1968.

Afr 9705   Northern Rhodesia; Zambia - Local - Regions, etc.

Afr 9705.5   Lusaka, the new capital of Northern Rhodesia, opened Jubilee Week, 1935. London, 1935.

Afr 9705.10A   Turner, O.W. Schism and continuity in African society. Manchester, 1957.

Afr 9705.10B   Turner, O.W. Schism and continuity in African society. Manchester, 1957.

Afr 9705.15   Powdermaker, Hortense. Copper town. 1st ed. N.Y., 1962.

Afr 9710   Northern Rhodesia; Zambia - Local - Barotseland

Afr 9710.5   Bertrand, Alfred. The kingdom of the Barotsi. London, 1899.

Afr 9710.5.7   Bertrand, Alfred. Au pays des Barotsi, Haut-Zambèze. Paris, 1898.

Afr 9710.6   Beguin, E. Les Barotse. Lausanne, 1903.

Afr 9710.7   Harding, C. In remotest Barotseland. London, 1905.

Afr 9710.8   Stirke, D.E.C.R. Barotseland. London, 1922.

Afr 9710.12   Fintan. Life and laughter in darkest Africa. Dublin, 1943.

Afr 9710.13   Westbeach, George. Trade and travel in early Barotseland. London, 1963.

Afr 9710.14   Gluckman, Max. The ideas in Barotse jurisprudence. New Haven, 1965.

Afr 9710.15F   Selwyn, P. Report on the economy of Barotseland. n.p., 1964?

Afr 9710.17   Clay, Gervas. Your friend, Lewanika. London, 1968.

Afr 9748.100 - .899   Northern Rhodesia; Zambia - Biographies - Individual
(A-Z, 800 scheme, by person)

Afr 9748.193   Bulpin, Thomas Victor. Trail of the copper king. Cape Town, 1959.

Afr 9748.475   Kaunda, Kenneth David. Zambia shall be free. London, 1962.

Afr 9748.475.5   Hall, Richard. Kaunda, founder of Zambia. London, 1965.

Afr 9748.475.10   Kaunda, Kenneth David. A humanist in Africa. London, 1967.

Afr 9748.475.15   Kaunda, Kenneth David. Zambia, independence and beyond, the speeches of Kenneth Kaunda. London, 1966.

Afr 9748.580   Charlton, Leslie. Spark in the stubble: Colin Morris of Zambia. London, 1969.

Afr 9748.582   Fraser, D. The autobiography of an African. London, 1925.

Afr 9748.807   Rukavina, Kathleen (Stevens). Jungle pathfinder. London, 1951.

Afr 9750   Nyasaland; Malawi - Periodicals

Afr 9750.3   Tsopano, Nyasaland monthly. Salisbury, Southern Rhodesia. 1,1959+

Afr 9750.5   Nyasaland journal. Blantyre. 4,1951+ 5v.

Afr 9753   Nyasaland; Malawi - Bibliographies

Afr 9753.2   Syracuse University. A bibliography of Malawi. Syracuse, N.Y., 1965.

Afr 9755   Nyasaland; Malawi - Pamphlet volumes

Afr 9755.2   Pamphlet vol. Nyasaland government documents. 4 pam.

Afr 9757   Nyasaland; Malawi - Collected source materials

Afr 9757.5   Great Britain. Colonial Office. Nyasaland protectorate, report for the year. 1946+ 4v.

Afr 9757.20   Nyasaland Constitutional Conference. Report of the Nyasaland Constitutional Conference held in London in Nov. 1962. London, 1962.

Afr 9760   Nyasaland; Malawi - Government and administration

Afr 9760.5F   Mair, L.P. Native administration in central Nyasaland. London, 1952.

Afr 9760.15   Nyasaland Constitutional Conference, London, 1960. Report. London, 1960.

Afr 9768 - 9770   Nyasaland; Malawi - General history (By date)

Afr 9769.39   Schwerin, W. Nyassaland. Neudamm, 1939.

Afr 9769.60   Tanser, George Henry. A history of Nyasaland. Capetown, 1960.

Afr 9769.64   Jones, G. Britain and Nyasaland. London, 1964.

Afr 9769.66   Ransford, Oliver. Livingstone's lake, the drama of Nyasa. London, 1966.

Afr 9769.68   Pike, John G. Malawi; a political and economic history. London, 1968.

Afr 9769.68.2   Pike, John G. Malawi; a political and economic history. N.Y., 1968.

Afr 9775   Nyasaland; Malawi - History by periods - Before 1892

Afr 9775.2   Hanna, Alexander John. The beginnings of Nyasaland and north-eastern Rhodesia. Oxford, 1956.

Afr 9780   Nyasaland; Malawi - History by periods - 1892-1963

Afr 9780.2   Rhodesia and Nyasaland. The issue of Nyasaland's secession. Salisbury, 1962.

Afr 9795   Nyasaland; Malawi - History - Special [Discontinued]

Afr 9795.15   Cluston-Brock, Guy. Down in Nyasaland. London, 1959.

Afr 9838 - 9840   Nyasaland; Malawi - Geography, description, etc. - General
works (By date)

Afr 9838.77   Young, Edward Daniel. Nyassa. London, 1877.

Afr 9838.84.2   Pringle, M. A journey in East Africa. Edinburgh, 1886.

Afr 9838.85   Buchanan, J. The Shire Highlands. Edinburgh, 1885.

Afr 9838.89   Botelho Reis, Jayme. Os portuguezes na região do Nyassa. Lisboa, 1889.

Afr 9838.91   Fotheringham, L.M. Adventures in Nyassaland. London, 1891.

Afr 9838.99   Elmslie, W.A. Among the wild Ngoni. N.Y., 1899.

Afr 9838.99.3   Elmslie, Walter Angus. Among the wild Ngoni. 3rd ed. London, 1970.

Afr 9838.99.5   Great Britain. War Office. Intelligence Division. Precis of information concerning the British Central Africa protectorate. London, 1899.

Afr 9839.03   Duff, H.L. Nyasaland under the Foreign Office. London, 1903.

Afr 9839.05   Duff, H.L. Nyasaland under the Foreign Office. 2. ed. London, 1906.

Afr 9839.12   Lyell, D.D. Nyasaland for the hunter and settler. London, 1912.

Afr 9839.20   Great Britain. Admiralty. A handbook of Portuguese Nyasaland. Oxford, 1920.

Afr 9839.22.5   Murray, S.S. A handbook of Nyasaland. London, 1932.

Afr 9839.34.5   Ntara, S.Y. Man of Africa. London, 1934.

Afr 9839.51A   Vanderpost, L. Venture to the interior. N.Y., 1951.

Afr 9839.51B   Vanderpost, L. Venture to the interior. N.Y., 1951.

Afr 9839.55   Debenham, F. Nyasaland. London, 1955.

Afr 9839.64   Young, Anthony. A geography of Malawi. London, 1964.

Afr 9839.64.5   Gandu, Madeleine. Matilda, fille du Nyassaland. Paris, 1964.

Afr 9839.64.10   Portrait of Malawi. Zomba, 1964.

Afr 9839.65   Pike, John G. Malawi, a geographical study. London, 1965.

Afr 9839.66   Malawi. Department of Information. Facts from Malawi. Zomba, 1966.

Afr 9839.67   Reed, Frank E. Malawi, land of promise. Blantyre, 1967.

Afr 9850   Nyasaland; Malawi - Economic and financial conditions

Afr 9850.3F   Malawi. Ministry of Natural Resources. Development policies and plans, 1965-1969. Zomba, 1965?

Afr 9850.5   Malawi - development plan. Zomba, 1964.

Afr 9850.7   Nyasaland development plan, 1962-1965. Zomba, 1962.

Afr 9850.10   Nyasaland. Capital development plan, 1957-1961. Zomba, 1957.

Afr 9853   Nyasaland; Malawi - Races

Afr 9853.1A   Werner, A. Natives of British Central Africa. London, 1906.

Afr 9853.1B   Werner, A. Natives of British Central Africa. London, 1906.

Afr 9853.5   Read, Margaret. The Ngoni of Nyasaland. London, 1956.

Afr 9853.5.5   Read, Margaret. Children of their fathers...Ngoni of Malawi. N.Y., 1968.

Afr 9853.6A   Vanvelsen, J. The politics of kinship. Manchester, 1964. 2v.

Afr 9853.6B   Vanvelsen, J. The politics of kinship. Manchester, 1964. 2v.

Afr 9853.8   Mitchell, James Clyde. The Yao village, a study in the social structure of a Nyasaland tribe. 1st ed. Manchester, 1966.

Afr 9854   Nyasaland; Malawi - Religion; missions

Afr 9854.2   Wishlade, Robert Leonard. Modern sectarian movements in Nyasaland. Durham, 1961.

Afr 9854.2.5   Wishlade, Robert Leonard. Sectarianism in southern Nyasaland. London, 1965.

Afr 9854.3   Tilsley, George E. Dan Crawford, missionary and pioneer in Central Africa. London, 1929.

Afr 9854.5   Ward, Gertrude. Life of Charles Alan Smythies, bishop of the university mission to Central Africa. London, 1898.

Afr 9854.10   Johnson, William Percival. My African reminiscences. Westminster, 1926.

Afr 9854.12   Laws, Robert. Reminiscences of Livingstonia. Edinburgh, 1934.

Afr 9854.14   Mills, Dora S. What we do in Nyasaland. London, 1911.

Afr 9854.16   Langworthy, Emily (Booth). This Africa was mine. Stirling, Scotland, 1952.

Afr 9854.18   Retief, Malcolm. William Murray of Nyasaland. Lovedale, 1958.

Afr 9854.20   Douglas, Arthur. Arthur Douglas, missionary on Lake Nyasa. Westminster, 1912.

Afr 9854.22   Pineau, Henry. Evêque roi des brigands. Paris, 1938.

Afr 9855   Nyasaland; Malawi - Local - Regions, etc.

Afr 9855.2F   Nyasaland. Commission of Inquiry into Disturbances at Mangunda Estate. Report. Zomba, 1953.

Afr 9858   Nyasaland; Malawi - Local - Blantyre

Afr 9858.5   Nyasaland. Southworth Commission. Report on the incident which took place outside Ryalls Hotel. Zomba, 1960.

Afr 9858.10   Hetherwick, Alexander. The romance of Blantyre. London, 1931.

Afr 9860.100 - .899   Nyasaland; Malawi - Biographies - Individual (A-Z,
800 scheme, by person)

Afr 9860.276   Mwase, George Simeon. Strike a blow and die. Cambridge, 1967.

Afr 9860.276.5   Shepperson, George. Independent African; John Chilembwe and the origins, setting and significance of the Nyasaland native rising of 1915. Edinburgh, 1958.

Afr 9860.475   Kayira, Regson. I will try. 1st ed. Garden City, N.Y., 1965.

Afr 10002 African literature in general - Bibliographies - Special
Afr 10002.1   Jahn, Janheinz. A bibliography of Neo-African literature from Africa, America and the Carribean. London, 1965.
Afr 10002.2   Moscow. Vsesoiuznaia Gosudarstvennaia Biblioteka Inostrannoi Literatury. Khudozhestvennaia literatura stran Afriki v sovetskoi pechati. Moskva, 1967.
Afr 10002.5   Tanzania. Ministry of Information and Tourism. United Republic press directory. Dar es Salaam. 1965+

Afr 10003 African literature in general - Dictionaries
Afr 10003.4   Conference of Writers, Publishers, Editors, and University Teachers of English. Proceedings. Johannesburg, 1957.
Afr 10003.5   Johannesburg. Public Library. A list of theatre performances in Johannesburg, 1887-1897. Johannesburg, 1964.

Afr 10004 African literature in general - Periodicals
Afr 10004.5   Journal of the new African literature. Stanford, Calif. 1966+
Afr 10004.10   The Afro-Asian writer; journal of the Permanent Bureau of Afro-Asian Writers. Cairo. 1,1966+
Afr 10004.15   Afro-Asian writings. Cairo. 1,1968+
Afr 10004.20   The conch. Paris. 1,1969+
Afr 10004.25   L'écrivain africain. Kitwe. 11,1968?+
Afr 10004.30   Studies in black literature. Fredericksburg, Va. 1,1970+

Afr 10005 African literature in general - History of the literature - General works
Afr 10005.2A   Approaches to African literature. Ibadan, 1959.
Afr 10005.2B   Approaches to African literature. Ibadan, 1959.
Afr 10005.3   Jahn, Janheinz. Geschichte der neoafrikanischen Literatur. Düsseldorf, 1966.
Afr 10005.3.1   Jahn, Janheinz. Neo-African literature. N.Y., 1969.
Afr 10005.4   Ramsaran, J.A. New approaches to African literature. Ibadan, 1965.
Afr 10005.5   Akademiia Nauk SSSR. Institut Afriki. Literatura stran Afriki. Moskva, 1964-66. 2v.
Afr 10005.6   Eliet, Edouard. Panorama de la littérature négro-africaine, 1921-62. Paris, 1965.
Afr 10005.7   Bol, Victor P. Littérateurs et poètes noirs. Léopoldville, 196-.
Afr 10005.10   Beier, Ulli. Introduction to Africa literature. Evanston, 1967.
Afr 10005.15   Morán López, Fernando. Natión y alienación en la literatura negro-africana. Madrid, 1964.
Afr 10005.20   Cartey, Wilfred. Whispers from a continent; the literature of contemporary black Africa. N.Y., 1969.

Afr 10007 African literature in general - History of the literature - General special
Afr 10007.2   Melone, Thomas. De la négritude dans la littérature négro-africaine. Paris, 1962.
Afr 10007.2.5   Berrian, Albert H. Négritude; essays and studies. Hampton, 1967.
Afr 10007.4   Protest and conflict in African literature. London, 1969.

Afr 10009 African literature in general - History of the literature - Local
Afr 10009.5   Taiwo, Oladele. An introduction to West African literature. London, 1967.
Afr 10009.10   Pantůček, Svetozár. La litterature algérienne moderne. Prague, 1969.

Afr 10013 African literature in general - History of the literature - Special forms - Journalism
Afr 10013.2   Ainslie, Rosalynde. The press in Africa. London, 1966.
Afr 10013.2.5   Ainslie, Rosalynde. The press in Africa: communications past and present. N.Y., 1968.
Afr 10013.5   Münster. Universität. Institut für Publizistik. Publizist und Publikum in Afrika. Köln, 1962.
Afr 10013.6   Barton, Frank. The press in Africa. Nairobi, 1966.
Afr 10013.8   Behn, Hans Ulrich. Die Presse in Westafrika. Hamburg, 1968.

Afr 10015 African literature in general - Collections of texts, anthologies - General
Afr 10015.1   Zuka; a journal of East African creative writing. Nairobi. 1,1967+
Afr 10015.2   Drachler, J. African heritage. N.Y., 1963.
Afr 10015.3   Sulzer, Peter. Christ erscheint am Kongo. Heilbronn, 1958.
Afr 10015.4   Whiteley, Wilfred H. A selection of African prose. Oxford, 1964. 2v.
Afr 10015.5   Kesteloot, Lilyan. Anthologie négro-africaine. Verviers, 1967.
Afr 10015.6   Pamphlet vol. African literature. 4 pam.
Afr 10015.7   Edwards, Paul Geoffrey. Through African eyes. Cambridge, 1966-
Afr 10015.8   Dathorne, Oscar Ronald. Africa in prose. Harmondsworth, 1969.
Afr 10015.10   Mphahlele, Ezekiel. African writing today. Harmondsworth, 1967.

Afr 10016 African literature in general - Collections of texts, anthologies - Special forms - Poetry
Afr 10016.2   Hughes, L. Poems from Black Africa. Bloomington, Ind., 1963.
Afr 10016.10   Reed, John. A book of African verse. London, 1965.
Afr 10016.12   Doob, Leonard William. Ants will not eat your fingers. N.Y., 1966.
Afr 10016.15   Kurgantsev, Mikhail. Iz afrikanskoi liriki. Moskva, 1967.

Afr 10017 African literature in general - Collections of texts, anthologies - Special forms - Drama
Afr 10017.5   Pamphlet vol. African plays. English and Citonega. 8 pam.

Afr 10018 African literature in general - Collections of texts, anthologies - Special forms - Fiction
Afr 10018.2   Jahn, Janheinz. Das junge Afrika. Wien, 1963.
Afr 10018.3   Sainville, L. Anthologie de la littérature nègro-africaine. Paris, 1963- 2v.
Afr 10018.4   Black Orpheus. Black Orpheus. N.Y., 1965.
Afr 10018.5   Brambilla, Cristina. Narrativa africana. Bologna, 1965.

Afr 10018 African literature in general - Collections of texts, anthologies - Special forms - Fiction cont.
Afr 10018.8   Beier, Ulli. Political spider. London, 1969.

Afr 10050 African literature written originally in the European languages in general - Bibliographies - General
Afr 10050.3   Amosu, Margaret. A preliminary bibliography of creative African writing in the European languages. Ibadan, 1964.

Afr 10052 African literature written originally in the European languages in general - Bibliographies - Special
Afr 10052.5   Rolf, Pamela Gail. An index to the programmes of the Johannesburg repertory players from 1928 to 1959. Johannesburg, 1968.

Afr 10055 African literature written originally in the European languages in general - History of the literature - General works
Afr 10055.5   Moore, Gerald. African literature and the universities. Ibadan, 1965.

Afr 10060 African literature written originally in the European languages in general - Special forms - Poetry
Afr 10060.2   Sartre, Jean Paul. Black Orpheus. Paris, 1963.

Afr 10062 African literature written originally in the European languages in general - Special forms - Fiction
Afr 10062.2   Gleason, Judith Illsley. This Africa, novels by West Africans in English and French. Evanston, 1965.
Afr 10062.3   Irasheva, Valentina V. Literatura stran Zapadnoi Afriki; proza. Moskva, 1967.

Afr 10065 African literature written originally in the European languages in general - Collections of texts, anthologies - General
Afr 10065.2   Waestberg, Per. Afrika beraettar. Malmoe, 1961.
Afr 10065.5   Shelton, Austin J. The African assertion. N.Y., 1968.

Afr 10066 African literature written originally in the European languages in general - Collections of texts, anthologies - Special forms - Poetry
Afr 10066.2A   Moore, Gerald. Modern poetry from Africa. Harmondsworth, 1963.
Afr 10066.2B   Moore, Gerald. Modern poetry from Africa. Harmondsworth, 1963.
Afr 10066.2.2   Moore, Gerald. Modern poetry from Africa. Harmondsworth, 1966.
Afr 10066.2.15   Balogun, Samuel Idown. Notes and exercises on Modern poetry from Africa. Ibadan, 1967.
Afr 10066.3   Kaminski-Durocher, B. Poezja czarnej Afryki. Warszawa, 1962.
Afr 10066.4   Présence Africaine. Nouvelle somme de poésie du monde noir. Paris, 1966.
Afr 10066.5   Ophir, an independent magazine. Pretoria. 4,1968+

Afr 10100 African literature written originally in English - General works - Bibliographies - General
Afr 10100.5   Abrash, Barbara. Black African literature in English since 1952; works and criticism. N.Y., 1967.

Afr 10104 African literature written originally in English - General works - Periodicals
Afr 10104.5F   Association for African Literature in English. Bulletin. Freetown. 2,1965+
Afr 10104.7   African literature today. London. 1,1968+

Afr 10105 African literature written originally in English - General works - History of the literature - General works
Afr 10105.65   Tibble, Anne (Northgrave). African-English literature. London, 1965.
Afr 10105.67   Tucker, Martin. Africa in modern literature. N.Y., 1967.

Afr 10115 African literature written originally in English - General works - Collections of texts, anthologies - General
Afr 10115.2   Rutherfoord, Peggy. Darkness and light. London, 1958.
Afr 10115.2.2   Rutherfoord, Peggy. African voices. N.Y., 1960.
Afr 10115.5   Pamphlet vol. African literature. 5 pam.

Afr 10116 African literature written originally in English - General works - Collections of texts, anthologies - Special forms - Poetry
Afr 10116.5   Sergeant, Howard. Poetry from Africa. Oxford, 1968.

Afr 10117 African literature written originally in English - General works - Collections of texts, anthologies - Special forms - Drama
Afr 10117.5   Pietense, Cosmo. Ten one-act plays. London, 1968.
Afr 10117.10   Litto, Fredric M. Plays from black Africa. 1st ed. N.Y., 1968.

Afr 10118 African literature written originally in English - General works - Collections of texts, anthologies - Special forms - Fiction
Afr 10118.2A   Young, T. Cullen. African new writing. London, 1947.
Afr 10118.2B   Young, T. Cullen. African new writing. London, 1947.
Afr 10118.3   Komey, Ellis A. Modern African stories. London, 1964.
Afr 10118.4   Rive, Richard. Modern African prose. London, 1964.
Afr 10118.5   Edwards, Paul. Modern African narrative, an anthology. London, 1966.

Afr 10215 African literature written originally in English - Sudan - Collections of texts, anthologies - General
Afr 10215.5F   Committee for Inter-African Relations, Ibadan, Nigeria. Report on the press in West Africa. Ibadan, 1960.

Afr 10304 African literature written originally in English - British East Africa - General - Periodicals
Afr 10304.4   Nexus. Nairobi. 1-2,1967-1968//
Afr 10304.5   Busara. Nairobi. 1,1968+

Afr 10309 African literature written originally in English - British East Africa - General - History of the literature - Local
Afr 10309.60   Hughes, Langston. An African treasury. N.Y., 1960.

Afr 10315 African literature written originally in English - British East Africa - General - Collections of texts, anthologies - General
Afr 10315.5   Cook, David. Origin East Africa. London, 1965.
Afr 10315.10   East African readers library. Nairobi. 24,1969+

Afr 10316 African literature written originally in English - British East Africa - General - Collections of texts, anthologies - Special forms - Poetry

Afr 10316.5 — Okola, Lennard. Drum beat; East African poems. Nairobi, 1967.

Afr 10317 African literature written originally in English - British East Africa - General - Collections of texts, anthologies - Special forms - Drama

Afr 10317.5 — Cook, David. Short East African plays in English: ten plays in English. Nairobi, 1968.

Afr 10361 African literature written originally in English - British East Africa - Uganda - History of the literature - Special forms - Drama

Afr 10361.5F — Makerere University College, Kampala, Uganda. Makerere Travelling Theatre. Report. Kampala, Uganda. 1965+

Afr 10365 African literature written originally in English - British East Africa - Uganda - Collections of texts, anthologies - General

Afr 10365.5 — Penpoint. Kampala, Uganda. 10,1961+

Afr 10371 - 10396 African literature written originally in English - British East Africa - Uganda - Individual authors (A-Z)

Afr 10381.2 — Kimenye, Barbara. Kalasanda. London, 1965.
Afr 10385.15.100 — Oculi, Okello. Prostitute. Nairobi, 1968.

Afr 10397 African literature written originally in English - British East Africa - Uganda - Anonymous works (Bible, etc.)

Afr 10397.2 — Passion in Africa. 1st ed. London, 1957.

Afr 10419 African literature written originally in English - British East Africa - Kenya - Collections of texts, anthologies - Special forms - Other special

Afr 10419.2 — Njururi, Ngumbu. Agikuyu folk tales. London, 1966.

Afr 10421 - 10446 African literature written originally in English - British East Africa - Kenya - Individual authors (A-Z)

Afr 10421.79.100 — Asalache, Khadambi. A calabash of life. London, 1967.
Afr 10431.41.100 — Kibera, Leonard. Potent ash. Nairobi, n.d.
Afr 10434.127.100 — Ngugi, James. Weep not, child. London, 1964.
Afr 10434.127.110 — Ngugi, James. The river between. London, 1965.
Afr 10434.127.120 — Ngugi, James. A grain of wheat. London, 1967.
Afr 10435.34.100 — Ogot, Grace Akinyi. The promised land. Nairobi, 1966.
Afr 10435.34.102 — Ogot, Grace Akinyi. Land without thunder; short stories. Nairobi, 1968.
Afr 10443.1.41 — Waciuma, Charity. Daughter of Mumbi. Nairobi, 1969.
Afr 10443.12.100 — Wachira, Godwin. Ordeal in the forest. Nairobi, 1968.

Afr 10465 African literature written originally in English - British East Africa - Tanganyika - Collections of texts, anthologies - General

Afr 10465.5 — Darlite. Dar es Salaam. 1,1966+

Afr 10516 African literature written originally in English - British West Africa - General - Collections of texts, anthologies - Special forms - Poetry

Afr 10516.2 — Bassir, O. An anthology of West African verse. Nigeria, 1957.
Afr 10516.5 — Nwoga, Donatus Ibe. West African verse; an anthology. London, 1967.

Afr 10521 - 10546 African literature written originally in English - British West Africa - General - Individual authors (A-Z)

Afr 10528.36.100 — Hayford, Casely. Ethiopia unbound; studies in race emancipation. 2nd ed. London, 1969.
Afr 10531.61.100 — Kinteh, Ramatoulie. Rebellion; a play in three acts. N.Y., 1968.
Afr 10536.69.100 — Peters, Lenrie. Poems. Ibadan, 1964.
Afr 10536.69.110 — Peters, Lenrie. Satellites. London, 1967.

Afr 10571 - 10596 African literature written originally in English - British West Africa - Sierra Leone - Individual authors (A-Z)

Afr 10575.82.100 — Easmon, R. Sarif. The new patriots. London, 1965.
Afr 10575.82.110 — Easmon, R. Sarif. The burnt-out marriage. London, 1967.
Afr 10575.82.120 — Easmon, R. Sarif. Dear parent and ogre. London, 1964.
Afr 10584.14.100 — Nicol, Davidson. The truly married woman. London, 1965.
Afr 10584.14.110 — Nicol, Davidson. Two African tales. Cambridge, Eng., 1965.

Afr 10604 African literature written originally in English - British West Africa - Ghana - Periodicals

Afr 10604.5 — Okyeame. Accra, n.d.

Afr 10615 African literature written originally in English - British West Africa - Ghana - Collections of texts, anthologies - General

Afr 10615.2 — Ghana. Ministry of Information and Broadcasting. Voices of Ghana. Accra, 1958.
Afr 10615.5 — The new generation: prose and verse from the secondary schools and training colleges of Ghana. Accra, 1967.
Afr 10615.7 — Talent for tomorrow; an anthology of creative writing from the training colleges of Ghana. Accra. 1,1966+
Afr 10615.10 — Pamphlet vol. Ghanaian literature in English. Miscellaneous publications. 8 pam.

Afr 10621 - 10646 African literature written originally in English - British West Africa - Ghana - Individual authors (A-Z)

Afr 10621.9.100 — Abruquah, Joseph W. The catechist. London, 1965.
Afr 10621.41.100A — Aidoo, C.A.A. The dilemma of a ghost. Accra, 1965.
Afr 10621.41.100B — Aidoo, C.A.A. The dilemma of a ghost. Accra, 1965.
Afr 10621.53.100 — Armah, Ayi Kwei. The beautyful ones are not yet born. Boston, 1968.
Afr 10621.53.110 — Armah, Ayi Kwei. Fragments. Boston, 1970[c1969].
Afr 10621.71.100 — Appiah, Peggy. The children of Anause. London, 1968.
Afr 10621.76.100 — Armattoe, Raphael E.G. Deep down the blackman's mind. Ilfracombe, 1954.
Afr 10622.18.100 — Bediako, K.A. A husband for Esi Ellua. Ghana, 1967.
Afr 10622.76.100 — Brew, Kwesi. The shadows of laughter: poems. London, 1968.
Afr 10624.2.100 — Dei-Anang, M. Africa speaks. 2d ed. Accra, 1960.
Afr 10624.2.110 — Dei-Anang, M. Ghana glory. London, 1965.
Afr 10624.2.120 — Dei-Anang, M. Okomfo Anakye's golden stool. Accra, 1963.
Afr 10624.2.700 — Dei-Anang, M. Ghana spricht, Gedichte. Herrenalb, 1962.
Afr 10624.3.100 — Danqush, Joseph B. The third woman. London, 1943.
Afr 10624.42.100 — Djoleto, Amu. The strange man. London, 1967.
Afr 10624.63.100 — Duodu, Cameron. The gab boys. London, 1967.
Afr 10628.37.100 — Hihetah, Robert Kofi. Painful road to Kadjebi. Accra, 1966.
Afr 10631.58.100 — Konadu, Asare. The wizard of Osamang. Accra, 1964.
Afr 10631.58.110 — Konadu, Asare. Come back Dora, a husband's confession and ritual. Accra, 1966.

Afr 10621 - 10646 African literature written originally in English - British West Africa - Ghana - Individual authors (A-Z) cont.

Afr 10631.58.120 — Konadu, Asare. Shadow of wealth. Accra, 1966.
Afr 10631.58.130 — Konadu, Asare. A woman in her prime. London, 1967.
Afr 10631.58.140 — Konadu, Asare. Ordained by the oracle. London, 1969.
Afr 10633.13.100 — Mickson, E.K. When the heart decides. Who killed Lucy? v.1-2. Accra, 1966?
Afr 10636.4.100 — Parkes, Frank K. Songs from the wilderness. London, 1965.
Afr 10639.23.100 — Selormey, Francis. The narrow path. London, 1966.

Afr 10657 African literature written originally in English - British West Africa - Nigeria - History of the literature - General special

Afr 10657.5 — Laurence, Margaret. Long drums and cannons. London, 1968.

Afr 10662 African literature written originally in English - British West Africa - Nigeria - History of the literature - Special forms - Fiction

Afr 10662.5 — Klima, Vladimir. Modern Nigerian novels. Prague, 1969.

Afr 10663 African literature written originally in English - British West Africa - Nigeria - History of the literature - Special forms - Journalism

Afr 10663.5 — Chick, John D. An exploratory investigation of press readership among selected students in Zaria. Zaria, 1966.
Afr 10663.10 — Elias, Taslim O. Nigerian press law. Lagos, 1969.

Afr 10665 African literature written originally in English - British West Africa - Nigeria - Collections of texts, anthologies - General

Afr 10665.05 — Pamphlet vol. Onitsha market literature. 12 pam.
Afr 10665.08 — Pamphlet vol. Onitsha market literature. 13 pam.
Afr 10665.2 — Ademola, F. Reflections, Nigerian prose and verse. Lagos, 1962.
Afr 10665.5 — African reader's library. Lagos. 1,1962+

Afr 10671 - 10696 African literature written originally in English - British West Africa - Nigeria - Individual authors (A-Z)

Afr 10671.12.100 — Achebe, Chinua. A man of the people. London, 1966.
Afr 10671.12.110 — Achebe, Chinua. No longer at ease. N.Y., 1961.
Afr 10671.12.120 — Achebe, Chinua. Things fall apart. London, 1966.
Afr 10671.12.121 — Achebe, Chinua. Things fall apart. London, 1968.
Afr 10671.12.130 — Achebe, Chinua. Arrow of God. London, 1964.
Afr 10671.12.800 — Adejumo, Matthew S. Notes and essays on Chinua Achebe's Things fall apart. Ibadan, 1966.
Afr 10671.12.805 — Ravenscroft, Arthur. Chinua Achebe. Burnt Mill, 1969.
Afr 10671.12.810 — Killam, Gordon Douglas. The novels of Chinua Achebe. N.Y., 1969.
Afr 10671.12.815 — Carroll, David. Chinua Achebe. N.Y., 1970.
Afr 10671.35.100 — Agunwa, Clement. More than once. London, 1967.
Afr 10671.46.100 — Akpan, Ntieyong Udo. The wooden gong. London, 1965.
Afr 10671.52.100 — Aluko, Timothy Mofolorunso. One man, one matchet. London, 1964.
Afr 10671.52.110 — Aluko, Timothy Mofolorunso. One man, one wife. Lagos, 1959.
Afr 10671.52.120 — Aluko, Timothy Mofolorunso. Kinsman and foreman. London, 1966.
Afr 10671.53.100 — Amadi, Elechi. The concubine. London, 1966.
Afr 10671.53.110 — Amadi, Elechi. The great ponds. London, 1969.
Afr 10671.53.1100 — Amali, Samson Onyilokwu Onche. The downfall of Ọgbúu; a play. Ibadan, 1968?
Afr 10673.48.100 — Clark, John Pepper. Song of a goat. Ibadan, 1961.
Afr 10673.48.110 — Clark, John Pepper. America, their America. London, 1964.
Afr 10673.48.120 — Clark, John Pepper. Three plays, song of a goat. London, 1964.
Afr 10673.48.130 — Clark, John Pepper. Poems. Ibadan, 1962.
Afr 10673.48.140 — Clark, John Pepper. A reed in the tide. London, 1965.
Afr 10673.48.160 — Clark, John Pepper. Ozidii. London, 1966.
Afr 10674.71.100 — Dipoko, Mbella Sonne. A few nights and days. London, 1966.
Afr 10674.71.110 — Dipoko, Mbella Sonne. Because of women. London, 1969.
Afr 10675.10.100 — Egbuna, Obi Benue. Wind versus polygamy. London, 1964.
Afr 10675.10.110 — Egbuna, Obi Benue. The anthill. London, 1965.
Afr 10675.37.100 — Echeruo, Michael J.C. Mortality. London, 1968.
Afr 10675.47.100 — Ekwensi, Cyprian. Burning grass. London, 1962.
Afr 10675.47.110 — Ekwensi, Cyprian. Beautiful feathers. London, 1963.
Afr 10675.47.140 — Ekwensi, Cyprian. People of the city. London, 1954.
Afr 10675.47.141 — Ekwensi, Cyprian. People of the city. Greenwich, Conn., 1969.
Afr 10675.47.150 — Ekwensi, Cyprian. Lokotown and other stories. London, 1966.
Afr 10675.47.160 — Ekwensi, Cyprian. Jagua Nana. London, 1961.
Afr 10675.47.170 — Ekwensi, Cyprian. The great elephant-bird. London, 1965.
Afr 10675.47.171 — Ekwensi, Cyprian. Jagua Nana; a novel. Greenwich, Conn., 1969.
Afr 10675.47.180 — Ekwensi, Cyprian. Iska. London, 1966.
Afr 10675.47.190 — Pamphlet vol. Ekwensi, Cyprian. Works. 4 pam.
Afr 10678.61.100 — Henshaw, James Ene. Children of the goddess, and other plays. London, 1964.
Afr 10678.61.110 — Henshaw, James Ene. Dinner for promotion; a comedy in three acts. London, 1967.
Afr 10679.44.100 — Ike, Vincent Chukwuemeka. Toads for supper. London, 1965.
Afr 10679.96.100 — Iwunze, Godwin Egejuruka. The sting that cures. Enugu, 1966.
Afr 10684.92.100 — Nwankwo, Nkem. Danda. London, 1964.
Afr 10684.92.1100 — Nwanodi, Okogbule Glory. Icheke and other poems. Ibadan, 1964.
Afr 10684.92.2100 — Nwapa, Flora. Efuru. London, 1966.
Afr 10684.99.100 — Nzekwu, Onuora. High life for lizards. London, 1965.
Afr 10684.99.110 — Nzekwu, Onuora. Blade among the boys. London, 1962.
Afr 10684.99.120 — Nzekwu, Onuora. Wand of noble wood. London, 1961.
Afr 10685.43.100 — Okara, Gabriel. The voice. London, 1964.
Afr 10685.45.100 — Okigbo, Christopher. Heaven's gate. Ibadan, 1962.
Afr 10685.67.100 — Okoye, Mokwugo. African cameos. Onitsha, 1956.
Afr 10685.67.110 — Okoye, Mokwugo. The rebel line. Onitsha, 1962.
Afr 10685.67.120 — Okoye, Mokwugo. Some men and women. Onitsha, 195-.
Afr 10685.67.130 — Okoye, Mokwugo. Vistas of life. Enugu, 1961.
Afr 10685.67.140 — Okoye, Mokwugo. The beard of Prometheus. Ilfracombe, 1966.
Afr 10689.67.21 — Soyinka, W. Idanre, and other poems. London, 1967.
Afr 10689.67.100 — Soyinka, W. Three plays. Nigeria, 1963.
Afr 10689.67.110 — Soyinka, W. A dance of the forests. London, 1963.
Afr 10689.67.120 — Soyinka, W. The lion and the jewel. London, 1963.
Afr 10689.67.130 — Soyinka, W. Five plays. London, 1964.
Afr 10689.67.140 — Soyinka, W. The interpreters. London, 1965.
Afr 10689.67.150 — Soyinka, W. The road. London, 1965.
Afr 10689.67.160 — Soyinka, W. Kongi's harvest. London, 1967.

Afr 10671 - 10696 African literature written originally in English - British West Africa - Nigeria - Individual authors (A-Z) cont.

Afr 10689.67.170	Soyinka, W. The forest of a thousand demons: a hunter's saga. London, 1968.
Afr 10689.68.100	Solarin, Tai. Thinking with you. Iheja, 1965.
Afr 10690.89.100	Tutuola, Amos. My life in the bush of ghosts. London, 1954.
Afr 10690.89.110	Tutuola, Amos. The brave African huntress. London, 1958.
Afr 10690.89.120	Tutuola, Amos. Feather woman of the jungle. London, 1962.
Afr 10690.89.130	Tutuola, Amos. Ajaiyi and his inherited poverty. London, 1967.
Afr 10690.89.800	Collins, Harold R. Amos Tutuola. N.Y., 1969.
Afr 10691.99.100	Uzodinma, Edmund. Our dead speak. London, 1967.
Afr 10693.53.21	Pamphlet vol. Wimbush, Dorothy. African stories. 2 pam.

Afr 10721 - 10746 African literature written originally in English - Liberia - Individual authors (A-Z)

Afr 10733.66.100	Moore, Bai T. Ebony dust. Liberia, 1965.

Afr 10821 - 10846 African literature written originally in English - Rhodesia and Nyasaland - General - Individual authors (A-Z)

Afr 10822.3.100	Ballinger, W.A. Call it Rhodesia. London, 1967.
Afr 10831.1.100	Kachingwe, A. No easy task. London, 1966.
Afr 10831.5.100	Kayira, Legson. The looming shadow. Garden City, 1967.
Afr 10831.5.110	Kayira, Legson. Jingala. Harlow, 1969.
Afr 10838.89.100	Rubadiri, David. No bride price. Nairobi, 1967.
Afr 10839.55.100	Smith, Wilbur Addison. When the lion feeds. N.Y., 1964.
Afr 10839.55.110	Smith, Wilbur Addison. Iets moet sterf. Johannesburg, 1965.

Afr 10865 African literature written originally in English - Rhodesia and Nyasaland - Northern Rhodesia - Collections of texts, anthologies - General

Afr 10865.5	New writing from Zambia. Lusaka. 1,1966+

Afr 10871 - 10896 African literature written originally in English - Rhodesia and Nyasaland - Northern Rhodesia - Individual authors (A-Z)

Afr 10882.41.100	Livingstone, Douglas. Sjambok, and other poems from Africa. London, 1964.
Afr 10883.89.100	Mulikita, Fwanyanga Matale. A point of no return. London, 1968.

Afr 10904 African literature written originally in English - Rhodesia and Nyasaland - Southern Rhodesia - Periodicals

Afr 10904.5	Chirimo. Salisbury. 1,1968+

Afr 10911 African literature written originally in English - Rhodesia and Nyasaland - Southern Rhodesia - History of the literature - Special forms - Drama

Afr 10911.2	Taylor, Charles T.C. The history of Rhodesian entertainment, 1890-1930. Salisbury, 1968.

Afr 10913 African literature written originally in English - Rhodesia and Nyasaland - Southern Rhodesia - History of the literature - Special forms - Journalism

Afr 10913.2	Gale, W.I. The Rhodesian press. Salisbury, 1962.

Afr 10916 African literature written originally in English - Rhodesia and Nyasaland - Southern Rhodesia - Collections of texts, anthologies - Special forms - Poetry

Afr 10916.2	Snelling, John. Fifty years of Rhodesian verse. Oxford, 1939.
Afr 10916.3	Snelling, John. A new anthology of Rhodesian verse. Oxford, 1950.
Afr 10916.5	Two tone. Salisbury, Rhodesia. 5,1969+

Afr 10921 - 10946 African literature written originally in English - Rhodesia and Nyasaland - Southern Rhodesia - Individual authors (A-Z)

Afr 10924.5	Davis, John Gordon. Hold my hand, I'm dying. 1st ed. N.Y., 1968.
Afr 10933.5	McIntosh, John. The thorn trees. 1st ed. N.Y., 1967.
Afr 10939.2	Samkange, Stanlake. On trial for my country. London, 1966.

Afr 10971 - 10996 African literature written originally in English - Bechuanaland - Individual authors (A-Z)

Afr 10978.5	Head, Bessie. When rain clouds gather. N.Y., 1969.

Afr 11005 African literature written originally in English - South Africa - History and collections - Bibliographies - Special forms

Afr 11005.2	Kiersen, S. English and Afrikaans novels on South African history. Cape Town, 1958.
Afr 11005.3	South African Public Library, Cape Town. Union list of South African newspapers, Nov. 1949. Cape Town, 1950.
Afr 11005.4	Silbert, Rachel. Southern African drama in English, 1900-1964. Johannesburg, 1965.
Afr 11005.5F	Snyman, J.P.L. A bibliography of South African novels in English. Potchefstroom, 1951.
Afr 11005.6	Astrinsky, Aviva. A bibliography of South African English novels, 1930-1960. Cape Town, 1965.

Afr 11008 African literature written originally in English - South Africa - History and collections - Periodicals

Afr 11008.5	South African P.E.N. year book. Johannesburg. 1954-1960// 2v.
Afr 11008.8	Contrast. Cape Town. 1,1960+ 4v.
Afr 11008.10	Black Orpheus. Ibadan. 5v.

Afr 11010 African literature written originally in English - South Africa - History and collections - History of the literature - General works

Afr 11010.2	Nathan, Manfred. South African literature. Cape Town, 1925.

Afr 11021 African literature written originally in English - South Africa - History and collections - History of the literature - Special forms - Poetry - General works

Afr 11021.2	Miller, G.M. A critical survey of South African poetry in English. Cape Town, 1957.

Afr 11025 African literature written originally in English - South Africa - History and collections - History of the literature - Special forms - Drama - General special

Afr 11025.2	Sowden, Lewis. Both sides of the mask. Cape Town, 1964.

Afr 11026 African literature written originally in English - South Africa - History and collections - History of the literature - Special forms - Drama - Local

Afr 11026.2	Raester, Olga. Curtain up. Cape Town, 1951.
Afr 11026.5	Hatfield, Denis. Cape theatre in the 1940's. Cape Town, 1967.

Afr 11027 African literature written originally in English - South Africa - History and collections - History of the literature - Special forms - Fiction - General works

Afr 11027.5	Booysen, C. Murray. More tales of South Africa. Cape Town, 1967.

Afr 11031 African literature written originally in English - South Africa - History and collections - History of the literature - Special forms - Journalism - General works

Afr 11031.2	Meurant, L.H. Sixty years ago. Cape Town, 1963.

Afr 11033 African literature written originally in English - South Africa - History and collections - History of the literature - Special forms - Journalism - Local

Afr 11033.2	Robinson, A.M.L. None daring to make us afraid. Cape Town, 1962.

Afr 11040 African literature written originally in English - South Africa - History and collections - Collections of texts, anthologies - General works

Afr 11040.2	Rosenthal, E. The South African Saturday book. Cape Town, 1948.
Afr 11040.3	Partridge, A.C. Readings in South African English prose. Pretoria, 1941.

Afr 11045 African literature written originally in English - South Africa - History and collections - Collections of texts, anthologies - Special periods - 20th century

Afr 11045.2	Booysen, C. Footprints. Johannesburg, 1956.
Afr 11045.4	New South African writing. Cape Town. 1,1964+ 5v.

Afr 11048 African literature written originally in English - South Africa - History and collections - Collections of texts, anthologies - Local

Afr 11050.2	MacNab, R.M. Towards the sun. London, 1950.

Afr 11051 African literature written originally in English - South Africa - History and collections - Collections of texts, anthologies - Special forms - Poetry - General works

Afr 11051.2	Klaas Gezwint en zijn paert and other songs and rijmpjes of South Africa. Cape Town, 1884.
Afr 11051.3	Songs of the veld, and other poems. London, 1902.
Afr 11051.4	Crouch, E.H. Gold dust. London, 1917.
Afr 11051.5	Crouch, E.H. A treasury of South African poetry and verse. 2. ed. London, 1909.
Afr 11051.6	MacNab, R.M. Poets in South Africa. Cape Town, 1958.
Afr 11051.7	Butler, G. A book of South African verse. London, 1959.
Afr 11051.8	Cope, Jack. The Penguin book of South African verse. Harmondsworth, 1968.

Afr 11052 African literature written originally in English - South Africa - History and collections - Collections of texts, anthologies - Special forms - Poetry - General special

Afr 11052.2	Petrie, A. Poems of South African history. London, 1919.
Afr 11052.3	Crouch, E.H. Sonnets of South Africa. London, 1911.

Afr 11053 African literature written originally in English - South Africa - History and collections - Collections of texts, anthologies - Special forms - Poetry - Local

Afr 11053.2	Johannesburg. University of the Witwatersrand. Songs and war cries. Johannesburg, 1936.
Afr 11053.4	Desmond, Nerine. Candlelight poets of the Cape. Cape Town, 1967.

Afr 11055 African literature written originally in English - South Africa - History and collections - Collections of texts, anthologies - Special forms - Drama - General special

Afr 11055.5	Gordimer, Nadine. South African writing today. Harmondsworth, 1967.

Afr 11057 African literature written originally in English - South Africa - History and collections - Collections of texts, anthologies - Special forms - Fiction - General works

Afr 11057.2	Moore, G. Seven African writers. London, 1962.
Afr 11057.3	Leary, E.N. South African short stories. Capetown, 1947.
Afr 11057.4	Rive, Richard. Quartet. N.Y., 1963.
Afr 11057.5	Hooper, A.G. Short stories from Southern Africa. Cape Town, 1963.
Afr 11057.6	Millar, Clive. Sixteen stories by South African writers. Cape Town, 1964.
Afr 11057.7	Wright, David. South African stories. London, 1960.
Afr 11057.8	Shore, Herbert L. Come back, Africa! N.Y., 1968.
Afr 11057.10	Lennox-Short, Alan. Stories, South African. Johannesburg, 1969.

Afr 11058 African literature written originally in English - South Africa - History and collections - Collections of texts, anthologies - Special forms - Fiction - Geneal special

Afr 11058.2	Dodd, A.D. Anthology of short stories. Cape Town, 1958.

Afr 11100 - 11899 African literature written originally in English - South Africa - Individual authors (A-Z, 800 scheme)

Afr 11108.74.100A	Abrahams, Peter. A wreath for Udomo. 1st American ed. N.Y., 1956.
Afr 11108.74.100B	Abrahams, Peter. A wreath for Udomo. 1st American ed. N.Y., 1956.
Afr 11108.74.110	Abrahams, Peter. A night of their own. London, 1965.
Afr 11108.74.120	Abrahams, Peter. Tell freedom. 1st American ed. N.Y., 1954.
Afr 11119.4.100	Adams, Perseus. The land at my door. Cape Town, 1965.
Afr 11193.74.100	Baragwanath, Paul. The brave remain. Cape Town, 1965.
Afr 11197.5.100	Beaumont, John H. Poems. Cape Town, 1957.
Afr 11200.21.100	Bee, David. Curse of Magira. 1st ed. N.Y., 1965.
Afr 11203.59.100	Bennett, J. Mister fisherman. 1st American ed. Boston, 1965.

Afr 11100 - 11899 African literature written originally in English - South Africa - Individual authors (A-Z, 800 scheme) cont.

Afr 11211.5	Achebe, Chinua. Things fall apart. N.Y., 1959.
Afr 11211.5.15	Achebe, Chinua. Arrow of God. London, 1964.
Afr 11216.5	Bley, J. Benibengor. Thoughts of youth. Aboso, 1961.
Afr 11216.10	Blackburn, Douglas. Prinsloo of Prinsloosdorp. London, 1899.
Afr 11219.66.100	Bloom, Harry. Transvaal episode. Berlin, 1959.
Afr 11219.66.110	Bloom, Harry. King Kong. London, 1961.
Afr 11219.66.120	Bloom, Harry. Whittaker's wife. London, 1964.
Afr 11229.5	Bosman, Herman. Mafeking road. Johannesburg, 1947.
Afr 11229.10	Bosman, Herman. A cask of jerepigo. Johannesburg, 1957.
Afr 11229.81.21	Bosman, Herman. Bosman at his best. Cape Town, 1967.
Afr 11229.81.100	Bosman, Herman. Unto dust, stories. 2d ed. Cape Town, 1964.
Afr 11230.92.100	Bowditch, L. Peter, a tale of the Greek trek. Pretoria, 1933.
Afr 11237.67.100	Brown, J.A. Seven against the sun. Johannesburg, 1962.
Afr 11239.67.110	Brown, J.A. The assassins. Johannesburg, 1965.
Afr 11240.5	Brutus, Dennis. Sirens, knuckles, boots. Ibadan, 1963.
Afr 11240.89.100	Brutus, Dennis. Letters to Martha, and other poems from a South African prison. London, 1969.
Afr 11246.51.100	Bulpin, Thomas U. The white whirlwind. Johannesburg, 1961.
Afr 11248.76.100	Burke, Colin. Elephant across border: a novel. London, 1968.
Afr 11249.86.100	Butler, Guy. Stranger to Europe; poems, 1939-1949. Capetown, 1952.
Afr 11249.86.110	Butler, Guy. Stranger to Europe, with additional poems. Capetown, 1960.
Afr 11249.86.120	Butler, Guy. South of the Zambesi, poems from South Africa. N.Y., 1966.
Afr 11249.86.130	Butler, Guy. Cape Charade. Cape Town, 1968. 2v.
Afr 11249.86.140	Butler, Guy. The dam. Cape Town, 1953.
Afr 11249.86.800	Muller, G. A bibliography of the poetical works of Guy Butler, Anthony Delius and Roy MacNab. Johannesburg, 1962. 2v.
Afr 11298.5	Conton, William. The African. Boston, 1960.
Afr 11299.69.21	Cope, Jack. The man who doubted, and other stories. London, 1967.
Afr 11299.69.100	Cope, Jack. The fair house. London, 1955.
Afr 11299.69.110	Cope, Jack. The golden oriole. London, 1958.
Afr 11299.69.120	Cope, Jack. The tame ox. London, 1960.
Afr 11300.83.21	Coster, Vera. Here Everest, and other poems. Grahamstown, 1963.
Afr 11302.89.100	Couper, J.K. Mixed humanity. Cape Colony, 1892.
Afr 11303.2.100	Crafford, Frederick Simon. The place of dragons. Cape Town, 1964.
Afr 11310.52.100	Culwick, Arthur Theodore. Back to the trees. Cape Town, 1965.
Afr 11317.76.100	Darks, D. Offei. Friends today, enemies tomorrow. Akropong, 1961.
Afr 11319.9.100	Debruyn, Phillip. The secret place, jazz verse. Cape Town, 1964.
Afr 11319.76.1100	Darlow, David John. Paths of peace in Africa. Lovedale, 1960.
Afr 11319.76.1120	Darlow, David John. In remembrance. Lovedale, 1965.
Afr 11319.76.1130	Darlow, David John. African heroes. Lovedale, 1958.
Afr 11320.41.100	Dei-Anang, Michael. Africa speaks. 2. ed. Accra, 1960.
Afr 11320.50.100	Delius, Anthony. The last division. Cape Town, 1959.
Afr 11320.50.110	Delius, Anthony. The fall. Cape Town, 1960.
Afr 11320.50.120	Delius, Anthony. The day Natal took off. Cape Town, 1963.
Afr 11320.50.130	Delius, Anthony. The day Natal took off. London, 1963.
Afr 11320.50.140	Delius, Anthony. A corner of the world. Cape Town, 1962.
Afr 11320.50.150	Delius, Anthony. An unknown border; poems. Cape Town, 1954.
Afr 11327.90.100	Divine, David. The golden fool. 1st ed. London, 1954.
Afr 11327.90.2100A	Divine, Arthur D. Wine of good hope. N.Y., 1939.
Afr 11327.90.2100B	Divine, Arthur D. Wine of good hope. N.Y., 1939.
Afr 11336.41.100	Drin, Michael. Signpost to fear. Cape Town, 1964.
Afr 11336.41.110	Drin, Michael. McKilty's bride. Cape Town, 1965.
Afr 11347.82.100	Eastwood, C. The estranged face. London, 1956.
Afr 11394.88.100	Fitzroy, V.M. Dark bright land. Cape Town, 1955.
Afr 11397.50.100	Collin-Smiths, J. Locusts and wild honey. London, 1953.
Afr 11406.41.100	Friedmann, M.V. The slap. London, 1961.
Afr 11410.31.100	Fugard, Athol. Hello and goodbye; a play in two acts. Cape Town, 1966.
Afr 11410.51.100	Fulton, Anthony. The dark side of mercy. Cape Town, 1968.
Afr 11433.64.100	Goodwin, Harold. Songs from the settler city. Grahamstown, 1963.
Afr 11433.74.100	Gordimer, N. The lying days. N.Y., 1953.
Afr 11433.74.110	Gordimer, N. The soft voice of the serpent. N.Y., 1952.
Afr 11433.74.115	Gordimer, N. Six feet of the country. London, 1956.
Afr 11433.74.120	Gordimer, N. A world of strangers. N.Y., 1958.
Afr 11433.74.125	Gordimer, N. Face to face. Johannesburg, 1949.
Afr 11433.74.130	Gordimer, N. Friday's footprint. London, 1960.
Afr 11433.74.140	Gordimer, N. Occasion for loving. N.Y., 1963.
Afr 11433.74.150	Gordimer, N. Not for publication, and other stories. N.Y., 1965.
Afr 11433.74.160	Gordimer, N. The late bourgeois world. London, 1966.
Afr 11433.74.800	Nell, Racilla Jilian. Nadine Gordimer. Johannesburg, 1964.
Afr 11433.75.100	Gordon, Gerald. Let the day perish. London, 1952.
Afr 11433.75.110	Gordon, Gerald. Four people, a novel of South Africa. London, 1964.
Afr 11435.3.100	Granger, Vivian Hector. Sacred is the breed. Cape Town, 1967.
Afr 11435.22.100	Green, George L. Where men still dream. Cape Town, 1950.
Afr 11435.22.110	Green, George L. Eight bells at Salamander. 2d ed. Cape Town, 1961.
Afr 11435.22.120	Green, George L. Almost forgotten, never told. Cape Town, 1965.
Afr 11435.22.130	Green, George L. I heard the old men say, secrets of the Cape that has vanished. 2nd ed. Cape Town, 1965.
Afr 11448.77.100	Harris, Peter. Some small compassion. Cape Town, 1964.
Afr 11456.14.1	Yudelman, Myra. Dan Jacobson, a bibliography. Johannesburg, 1967.
Afr 11456.77.800	Horn, Alfred A. Trader horn. N.Y., 1928.
Afr 11456.77.805	Horn, Alfred A. Trader Horn. v.2. "Harold the Webbed." N.Y., 1928.
Afr 11456.77.810A	Horn, Alfred A. Trader Horn. N.Y., 1927.
Afr 11456.77.810B	Horn, Alfred A. Trader Horn. N.Y., 1927.
Afr 11456.77.810C	Horn, Alfred A. Trader Horn. N.Y., 1927.

Afr 11100 - 11899 African literature written originally in English - South Africa - Individual authors (A-Z, 800 scheme) cont.

Afr 11456.77.810D	Horn, Alfred A. Trader Horn. N.Y., 1927.
Afr 11456.77.812	Horn, Alfred A. Trader Horn. N.Y., 1927.
Afr 11456.77.814	Horn, Alfred A. Life and works of Alfred A. Horn. London, 1927. 5v.
Afr 11465.14.21	Jacobson, Dan. Through the wilderness, and other stories. N.Y., 1968.
Afr 11465.14.100	Jacobson, Dan. The price of diamonds. London, 1957.
Afr 11465.14.100.2	Jacobson, Dan. The price of diamonds. 1st ed. N.Y., 1958.
Afr 11465.14.110	Jacobson, Dan. A long way from London. London, 1958.
Afr 11465.14.120	Jacobson, Dan. The Zulu and the zeide. 1st ed. Boston, 1959.
Afr 11465.14.130	Jacobson, Dan. Evidence of love, a novel. 1st ed. Boston, 1960.
Afr 11465.14.140	Jacobson, Dan. Time of arrival, and other essays. London, 1962.
Afr 11465.14.150	Jacobson, Dan. Beggar my neighbour, short stories. London, 1964.
Afr 11465.14.160	Jacobson, Dan. The beginners. N.Y., 1966.
Afr 11501.89.100	Kruger, Rayne. The spectacle. London, 1953.
Afr 11501.89.110	Kruger, Rayne. Young villain with wings. London, 1953.
Afr 11505.69.100	Kuper, Leo. The college brew. Durban, 1960.
Afr 11509.35.100	LaGuma, Alex. The stone country. Berlin, 1967.
Afr 11509.35.110	LaGuma, Alex. A walk in the night. Ibadan, 196-?
Afr 11509.35.120	LaGuma, Alex. And a threefold cord. Berlin, 1964.
Afr 11510.60.100	Lanham, Peter. Blanket boy's moon. London, 1953.
Afr 11517.76.100	Lerner, Laurence. Domestic interior. London, 1959.
Afr 11517.76.110	Lerner, Laurence. The Englishmen. London, 1959.
Afr 11517.76.120	Lerner, Laurence. The directions of memory. London, 1963.
Afr 11517.76.130	Lerner, Laurence. A free man. London, 1968.
Afr 11517.84.100	Letscher, O. Africa unveiled. London, 1931.
Afr 11523.32.100	Lighton, R.E. Out of the strong. London, 1957.
Afr 11534.18.100	Ludi, Gerard. Operation Atlantis. Cape Town, 1967.
Afr 11542.87	Lytton, David. The goddam white man. N.Y., 1961.
Afr 11542.87.110	Lytton, David. A place apart. London, 1961.
Afr 11542.87.120	Lytton, David. The paradise people. London, 1962.
Afr 11542.87.130	Lytton, David. The freedom of the cage. London, 1966.
Afr 11546.13.60	McNeile, Michael. This Africa of ours. Johannesburg, 1957.
Afr 11546.58.100	MacNab, Roy M. The man of grass. London, 1960.
Afr 11555.61.65	Manson, H.W.D. The noose-knot ballad, a play. Cape Town, 1962.
Afr 11555.61.100	Manson, H.W.D. The magnolia tree. Cape Town, 1963.
Afr 11555.61.110	Manson, H.W.D. Pat Mulholland's day. Cape Town, 1964.
Afr 11555.61.120	Manson, H.W.D. Captain Smith. Cape Town, 1966.
Afr 11558.76.100	Markowitz, A. Market street. Johannesburg, 1959.
Afr 11558.78.100	Martins, Harper. Nongalazi of the Bemba. Ilfrawmbe, 1965.
Afr 11560.85.100	Matheson, G.E. From veld and street. London, 1899.
Afr 11563.49.100	Miller, Ruth. Floating island, poems. Cape Town, 1965.
Afr 11563.98.100	Mayne, Frederick. The slaughter of an innocent. Johannesburg, 1955.
Afr 11572.50.5	Whyte, Moray. Bibliography of the works of Sarah Gertrude Millin. Cape Town, 1952.
Afr 11572.50.100	Millin, S.G.(L.). The night is long. London, 1941.
Afr 11572.50.110	Millin, S.G.(L). Mary Glenn. N.Y., 1925.
Afr 11572.50.120	Millin, S.G.(L). King of the bastards. N.Y., 1949.
Afr 11572.50.130	Millin, S.G.(L). What hath a man. 1st ed. N.Y., 1938.
Afr 11572.50.140	Millin, S.G.(L). The burning man. London, 1952.
Afr 11572.50.150	Millin, S.G.(L). The coming of the Lord. N.Y., 1928.
Afr 11572.50.160	Millin, S.G.(L). The dark gods. 1st ed. N.Y., 1941.
Afr 11572.50.170	Millin, S.G.(L). The fiddler. N.Y., 1929.
Afr 11572.50.180	Millin, S.G.(L). God's stepchildren. N.Y., 1925.
Afr 11572.50.190	Millin, S.G.(L). The measure of my days. London, 1955.
Afr 11572.50.200	Millin, S.G.(L). Two bucks without hair. London, 1957.
Afr 11572.50.210	Millin, S.G.(L). The wizard bird. London, 1962.
Afr 11572.50.800	Snyman, J.P.L. The works of Sarah Gertrude Millin. South Africa, 1955.
Afr 11580.75.100	Morgan, Robert. The winds blow red. Ilfracombe, 1962.
Afr 11580.77.100	Morris, Michael. The sweetness and the sadness. Cape Town, 1964.
Afr 11582.70.21	Mphahlele, Ezekiel. In corner b; short stories. Nairobi, 1967.
Afr 11586.77.100	Murray, M. The fire-raisers. London, 1953.
Afr 11598.85.100	Nathan, Manfred. Sarie Marais. London, 1938.
Afr 11598.89.100	Naude, Adele. Only a setting forth, poems. Cape Town, 1965.
Afr 11611.66.100	Nkosi, Lewis. The rhythm of violence. London, 1964.
Afr 11611.66.110	Nkosi, Lewis. Home and exile. London, 1965.
Afr 11612.100	Noble, Alex. Boy with a flute. London, 1962.
Afr 11626.23.110	Nzekwu, Onuora. Blade among the boys. London, 1962.
Afr 11669.13	Packer, Joy (P). Valley of the vines. Philadelphia, 1956.
Afr 11669.13.5	Packer, Joy (P). The high roof. 1st ed. Philadelphia, 1959.
Afr 11669.13.10	Packer, Joy (P). Home from sea. London, 1963.
Afr 11675.87.2	Bentel, Lea. Alan Paton. Johannesburg, 1969.
Afr 11675.87.100A	Paton, Alan. Too late the phalarope. N.Y., 1953.
Afr 11675.87.100B	Paton, Alan. Too late the phalarope. N.Y., 1953.
Afr 11675.87.110A	Paton, Alan. Cry, the beloved country. N.Y., 1948.
Afr 11675.87.110B	Paton, Alan. Cry, the beloved country. N.Y., 1948.
Afr 11675.87.112	Paton, Alan. Cry, the beloved country. N.Y., 1960.
Afr 11675.87.120	Paton, Alan. Tales from a troubled land. N.Y., 1961.
Afr 11675.87.130	Paton, Alan. Debbie go home. London, 1961.
Afr 11675.87.140	Paton, Alan. For you departed. N.Y., 1969.
Afr 11675.87.150	Paton, Alan. Kontakion for you departed. London, 1969.
Afr 11675.87.800	Callan, Edward. Alan Paton. N.Y., 1968.
Afr 11683.88.100	Petrie, A. Saint Andrew's day, 1919-61. Pietermaritzburg, 1962.
Afr 11705.39.641	Pohl, V. The down and after. London, 1964.
Afr 11705.39.645	Pohl, V. Land of distant horizons. Johannesburg, 1946.
Afr 11728.41.100	Raik, Lea. Redeemed. 1st ed. Johannesburg, 1964.
Afr 11747.90.100	Rive, Richard. Emergency. London, 1964.
Afr 11749.7.100	Robertson, Olive. The mighty turtle and other poems. Cape Town, 1966.
Afr 11750.21.100	Roebuck, M.F.C. Nyitso, a novel of West Africa. Cape Town, 1964.
Afr 11752.65.1	Camberg, Helen. Daphne Rooke; her works and selected literary criticism. Johannesburg, 1969.
Afr 11752.65.100	Rooke, Daphne. A grove of fever trees. London, 1951.
Afr 11752.65.110	Rooke, Daphne. The Greyling. London, 1962.
Afr 11752.65.120	Rooke, Daphne. Mittee. Boston, 1952.
Afr 11757.58.100	Runcie, John. Songs by the stoep. London, 1905.
Afr 11764.12.100	Sachs, Bernard. South African personalities and places. Johannesburg, 1959.

Afr 11100 - 11899 African literature written originally in English - South Africa - Individual authors (A-Z, 800 scheme) cont.

Afr 11764.12.102 Sachs, Bernard. Personalities and places. 2nd series. Johannesburg, 1965.
Afr 11774.39.100 Scholefield, Alan. A view of vultures. London, 1966.
Afr 11774.39.110 Scholefield, Alan. Great elephant. London, 1967.
Afr 11774.39.120 Scholefield, Alan. The eagles of malice. N.Y., 1968.
Afr 11780.31.100 Segal, A. Johannesburg Friday. N.Y., 1954.
Afr 11780.51.100 Sellier, Richard. Twin-brother hell. London, 1960.
Afr 11790.58.100 Sinclair, F.D. Lovers and hermits. Cape Town, 1957.
Afr 11790.58.110 Sinclair, F.D. The cold veld. Wynberg, 1946.
Afr 11790.59.100 Singh, A.R. Behold the earth mourns. Johannesburg, 1961.
Afr 11795.4.100 Slatter, Eve Mary. My leaves are green. Cape Town, 1967.
Afr 11796.41.100 Smit, Lillian. The wind's wing. Bloemfontein, 1961.
Afr 11797.41.100A Smith, Pauline. The little karoo. N.Y., 1925.
Afr 11797.41.100B Smith, Pauline. The little karoo. N.Y., 1925.
Afr 11797.41.102 Smith, Pauline. The little karoo. N.Y., 1952.
Afr 11797.41.111 Smith, Pauline. The beadle. Cape Town, 1956.
Afr 11797.41.800 Haresnape, Geoffrey. Pauline Smith. N.Y., 1969.
Afr 11802.92.100 Sowden, Lewis. The land of afternoon. London, 1968.
Afr 11802.92.110 Sowden, Lewis. Poems with flute. London, 1955.
Afr 11802.92.120 Sowden, Lewis. Lady of Coventry. London, 1950.
Afr 11802.92.130 Sowden, Lewis. The crooked bluegum. London, 1955.
Afr 11803.21.100 Spears, D. No common day. Cape Town, 1962.
Afr 11807.24.100 Stern, Rhona. The bird flies blind. London, 1965.
Afr 11848.87.100 Trotter, W.M. Radiance of the veld. Ilfracombe, 1960.
Afr 11853.88.100 Tutuola, Amos. My life in the bush of ghosts. N.Y., 1954.
Afr 11853.88.110 Tutuola, Amos. The palm-wine drinkard and his dead palm-wine tapster. London, 1952.
Afr 11853.88.120 Tutuola, Amos. Simbi and the satyr of the dark jungle. London, 1955.
Afr 11865.59.100 Vanderpost, Laurens. The face beside the fire. N.Y., 1953.
Afr 11865.59.110 Vanderpost, Laurens. In a province. London, 1953.
Afr 11865.59.120 Vanderpost, Laurens. Flamingo feather. N.Y., 1955.
Afr 11865.59.140 Vanderpost, Laurens. The seed and the sower. London, 1963.
Afr 11865.59.150 Vanderpost, Laurens. A bar of shadow. N.Y., 1956.
Afr 11865.59.160 Vanderpost, Laurens. The hunter and the whale: a story. London, 1967.
Afr 11865.59.800 Carpenter, Frederic Ives. Laurens Van der Post. N.Y., 1969.
Afr 11874.86.100 Watling, Cyril. Ink in my blood. Cape Town, 1966.
Afr 11874.87.100 Watson, J.C. Shadow over the Rand. Johannesburg, 1955.
Afr 11878.12.21 Wicht, Hein. The mountain; selected short stories. Cape Town, 1966.
Afr 11878.24.100 Wiesmar, Chriss. The lowly and the worldly. South Africa, 1957.
Afr 11878.49.100 Wiles, John. The moon to play with. 1st American ed. N.Y., 1955.
Afr 11899.98.100 Zyl, Tania. Shadow and wall. Cape Town, 1958.

Afr 11900 - 11999 African literature written originally in English - Others (Islands, etc.)

Afr 11907.9.100 Gabre-Medhin, Tsegaye Oda. Oak oracle. London, 1965.

Afr 12002 African literature written originally in French - General works - Bibliographies - Special

Afr 12002.1 Gras, Jacqueline. Situation de la presse dans les états de l'Union Africaine et Malgache, en Guinée, au Mali, au Togo. Paris, 1963.
Afr 12002.2 Baratte, Thérèse. Bibliographie, auteurs africains et malgaches de langue française. Paris, 1965.
Afr 12002.5 Memmi, Albert. Bibliographie de la littérature nord-africaine d'expression française, 1945-1962. Paris, 1965.

Afr 12004 African literature written originally in French - General works - Periodicals

Afr 12004.5 Littérature africaine. Paris. 4,1964+ 3v.

Afr 12005 African literature written originally in French - General works - History of the literature - General works

Afr 12005.2 Colloque sur la littérature africaine d'expression française, actes. Dakar, 1965.
Afr 12005.5 Pageard, Robert. Littérature négro-africaine. Paris, 1966.
Afr 12005.8 Groos, Almuth. Die Gegenwartsliteratur des Maghreb in französischer Sprache. Frankfurt, 1963.

Afr 12007 African literature written originally in French - General works - History of the literature - General special

Afr 12007.1 Prozhogina, S.V. Literatura Marokko i Tunisa. Moskva, 1968.

Afr 12012 African literature written originally in French - General works - History of the literature - Special forms - Fiction

Afr 12012.3 Brench, Anthony Cecil. The novelists' inheritance in French Africa. London, 1967.
Afr 12012.6 Khatibi, Abdelkabir. Le roman maghrébin, essai. Paris, 1968.

Afr 12015 African literature written originally in French - General works - Collections of texts, anthologies - General

Afr 12015.2 Hughes, L. Anthologie africaine et malgache. Paris, 1962.
Afr 12015.10 Memmi, Albert. Anthologie des écrivains maghrébins d'expression française. Paris, 1964.
Afr 12015.15 Vezinet, Paul. Pages africaines. Paris, 1963-[1966-]. 5v.

Afr 12016 African literature written originally in French - General works - Collections of texts, anthologies - Special forms - Poetry

Afr 12016.2 Senghor, L.S. Anthologie de la nouvelle poésie nègre. 1st ed. Paris, 1948.
Afr 12016.3 Clive, Wake. An anthology of African and Malagasy poetry in French. London, 1965.

Afr 12018 African literature written originally in French - General works - Collections of texts, anthologies - Special forms - Fiction

Afr 12018.5 Brench, Anthony Cecil. Writing in French from Senegal to Cameroon. London, 1967.
Afr 12018.8 Irele, Abiola. Lectures africaines. London, 1969.

Afr 12121 - 12146 African literature written originally in French - Egypt - Individual authors (A-Z)

NEDL Afr 12131.5.100 Khayat, Georges. Riad. Caire, 1934.

Afr 12271 - 12296 African literature written originally in French - Tunisia - Individual authors (A-Z)

Afr 12288.63.100 Robert, Georges. Incidences 50. Tunis, 1950.

Afr 12321 African literature written originally in French - Algeria - History of the literature - Special forms - Poetry - General works

Afr 12321.2 Memmi, Albert. La poésie algérienne de 1830 à nos jours. Paris, 1963.

Afr 12351 African literature written originally in French - Algeria - Collections of texts, anthologies - Special forms - Poetry - General works

Afr 12351.63 Barrat, D. Espoir et parole. Paris, 1963.

Afr 12371 - 12396 African literature written originally in French - Algeria - Individual authors (A-Z)

Afr 12371.1.100 Aba, Noureddine. La Toussaint des énigmes. Paris, 1963.
Afr 12372.67.100 Boukman, Daniel. Chants pour hâter la mort du temps des Orphée ou Madinina île esclave. Honfleur, 1967.
Afr 12377.23.100 Greki, Anna. Temps forts, poèmes. Paris, 1966.

Afr 12421 African literature written originally in French - Morocco - History of the literature - Special forms - Poetry - General works

Afr 12421.2 Lebel, Roland. Les poètes français du Maroc. Tanger, 1956.

Afr 12431 African literature written originally in French - Morocco - History of the literature - Special forms - Journalism - General works

Afr 12431.2 Mollard, P.J. Le régime juridique de la presse au Maroc. Rabat, 1963.

Afr 12505 African literature written originally in French - French West Africa - General - History of the literature - General works

Afr 12505.1 Potekhina, Gena I. Ocherki sovremennoi literatury Zapadnoi Afriki. Moskva, 1968.

Afr 12571 - 12596 African literature written originally in French - French West Africa - Mauritania - Individual authors (A-Z)

Afr 12574.5 Diallo, Assane Y. Leyd'am, poémes. Honfleur, 1967.

Afr 12621 - 12646 African literature written originally in French - French West Africa - Senegal - Individual authors (A-Z)

Afr 12622.3.100 Balogun, Ola. Shango, suivi de Le roi-éléphant. Honfleur, 1968.
Afr 12624.4.100 Diop, Birago. Contes et lavanes. Paris, 1963.
Afr 12624.41.20 Diop, Birago. Leurres et lueurs, poèmes. Photoreproduction. Paris, 1960.
Afr 12624.41.25 Diop, Birago. Contes choisis. Cambridge, Eng. 1967.
Afr 12624.41.30 Diop, Birago. Les nouveaux contes d'Amadou Koumba. Paris, 1962.
Afr 12624.41.33 Diop, Birago. Les nouveaux contes d'Amadou Koumba. 3. ed. Paris, 1967.
Afr 12624.41.35 Diop, Birago. Les contes d'Amadou-Koumba. Paris, 1960.
Afr 12624.41.1100 Diakhaté, Lamine. Primordiale du sixième jour. Paris, 1963.
Afr 12624.41.1110 Diakhaté, Lamine. Temps de mémoire. Paris, 1967.
Afr 12628.64.100 Hoffmane, Simone. Envoûtement. Dakar, 1967?
Afr 12634.16.100 Ndao, H. Alion. L'Exil d'Albouri. Suivi de La décision. Honfleur, 1967.
Afr 12639.18.100 Sadji, Abdoulaye. Nini, mulâtresse du Sénégal. 2. éd. Paris, 1965.
Afr 12639.18.110 Sadji, Abdoulaye. Tounka, nouvelle. Paris, 1965.
Afr 12639.24.21 Senghor, L.S. Selected poems. London, 1964.
Afr 12639.24.25 Senghor, L.S. Liberté. Paris, 1964.
Afr 12639.24.29 Senghor, L.S. Prose and poetry. London, 1965.
Afr 12639.24.100 Senghor, L.S. Ethiopiques, poèmes. Paris, 1956.
Afr 12639.24.110 Senghor, L.S. Chants pour Naëtt. Paris, 1949.
Afr 12639.24.120A Senghor, L.S. Nocturnes. Paris, 1961.
Afr 12639.24.120B Senghor, L.S. Nocturnes. Paris, 1961.
Afr 12639.24.130 Senghor, L.S. Poèmes. Paris, 1964.
Afr 12639.24.700 Senghor, Leopold Sédar. Nocturnes. London, 1969.
Afr 12639.24.800 Guibert, A. Léopold Sédar Senghor. Paris, 1962.
Afr 12639.24.805 Leusse, Hubert de. Léopold Sédar Senghor, l'Africain. Paris, 1967.
Afr 12639.24.810 Bonn, Gisela. Léopold Sédar Senghor. Düsseldorf, 1968.
Afr 12639.24.815 Mezu, Sebastian Okechukwu. Léopold Sédar Senghor et la défense et illustration de la civilisation noire. Paris, 1968.

Afr 12671 - 12696 African literature written originally in French - French West Africa - Sudan, Mali - Individual authors (A-Z)

Afr 12672.3.100 Badian, S. Sous l'orage (Kany). Paris, 1963.
Afr 12672.3.110 Badian, S. La mort de Chaka. Paris, 1965.
Afr 12673.41.100 Cissoko, Siriman. Ressac de nous-mêmes, poèmes. Paris, 1967.
Afr 12674.1.100 Dia, Amadou Cissé. Les derniers jours de Lat Dior. Paris, 1965.
Afr 12684.41.100 Niger, Paul. Les grenouilles du mont Kimbo. Paris, 1964.
Afr 12686.17.100 Owologuem Yambo. Le devoir de violence, roman. Paris, 1968.

Afr 12771 - 12796 African literature written originally in French - French West Africa - Upper Volta - Individual authors (A-Z)

Afr 12785.89.100 Ousmane, Sembene. Voltaique; nouvelles. Paris, 1962.
Afr 12785.89.110 Ousmane, Sembene. L'harmattan. Paris, 1965.
Afr 12785.89.120 Ousmane, Sembene. O pays, mon beau peuple; roman. Paris, 1957.
Afr 12785.89.130 Ousmane, Sembene. Les bouts de bois de Dieu, Banty Mam Yall. Photoreproduction. Paris, 1960.
Afr 12785.89.140 Ousmane, Sembene. Vehi-ciosane, ou Blanche-genèse, suivi du Mandat. Paris, 1965.

Afr 12821 - 12846 African literature written originally in French - French West Africa - Guinea - Individual authors (A-Z)

Afr 12832.5.100 Laye, Camara. Dramouss. Paris, 1966.
Afr 12832.5.110 Laye, Camara. L'enfant noir. Paris, 1953.
Afr 12832.5.112 Laye, Camara. L'enfant noir. Cambridge, 1966.
Afr 12832.5.120 Laye, Camara. Le regard du roi. Paris, 1954.
Afr 12832.5.700 Laye, Camara. The radiance of the King. London, 1956.
Afr 12832.5.705 Laye, Camara. A dream of Africa. London, 1968.

Afr 12871 - 12896   **African literature written originally in French - French West Africa - Ivory Coast - Individual authors (A-Z)**
Afr 12871.56.100	Amoi, Fatho. Mon beau pays d'Ivoire. Saint-Genix-sur-Guiers, Savoie, 1967.
Afr 12881.67.100	Kourouma, Ahmadou. Les soleils des indépendances. Montréal, 1968.
Afr 12884.65.100	Nokan, Charles. Violent était le vent. Paris, 1966.
Afr 12884.65.110	Nokan, Charles. Le soleil noir point. Paris, 1962.
Afr 12884.65.120	Nokan, Charles. Les malheurs de Tchakô. Honfleur, 1968.

Afr 12921 - 12946   **African literature written originally in French - French West Africa - Dahomey - Individual authors (A-Z)**
Afr 12922.7.100	Bhely-Quenum, Olympe. Un piège sans fin. Paris, 1960.
Afr 12922.7.110	Bhely-Quenum, Olympe. Le chant du lac. Paris, 1965.
Afr 12928.3.100	Hazoumé, Paul. Doguicimi. Paris, 1938.
Afr 12936.50.102	Pliya, Jean. Kondo le requin; drame historique en trois actes. 2. éd. Porto-Novo, 1966?

Afr 12966   **African literature written originally in French - French West Africa - French Togo - Collections of texts, anthologies - Special forms - Poetry**
Afr 12966.2	Lagneau, Lilyan. Neuf poètes camerounais. Yaounde, 1965.

Afr 12971 - 12996   **African literature written originally in French - French West Africa - French Togo - Individual authors (A-Z)**
Afr 12972.41.100	Biyidi, Alexandre. Ville cruelle. Paris, 195-.
Afr 12972.41.110	Biyidi, Alexandre. King Lazarus. London, 1960.
Afr 12972.41.120	Biyidi, Alexandre. Le pauvre Christ de Bomba. Paris, 1956.
Afr 12972.41.130	Biyidi, Alexandre. Le roi miraculé. Paris, 1958.
Afr 12972.41.700	Biyidi, Alexandre. Mission accomplished. N.Y., 1958.
Afr 12972.41.705	Biyidi, Alexandre. Mission to Kala. London, 1964.
Afr 12974.51.100	Almeida, Modeste d'. Kétéyouli, l'étudiant noir. Lomé, 1965.
Afr 12979.44.100	Ikelle-Matiba, J. Cette Afrique-là. Paris, 1963.
Afr 12985.65.100	Oyono, Ferdinand. Chemin d'Europe. Paris, 1960.
Afr 12985.65.110	Oyono, Ferdinand. Le vieux Nègre et la médaille. Paris, 1956.
Afr 12985.65.120	Oyono, Ferdinand. Une vie de boy, roman. Paris, 1956.
Afr 12985.65.700	Oyono, Ferdinand. House boy. London, 1966.
Afr 12985.65.701	Oyono, Ferdinand. House boy. London, 1967.
Afr 12985.65.705	Oyono, Ferdinand. The old man and the medal. London, 1967.

Afr 13221 - 13246   **African literature written originally in French - French Equatorial Africa - Congo (Brazzaville) - Individual authors (A-Z)**
Afr 13240.39.100	Thsinday Lukumbi, Etienne. Marche, pays des espoirs. Paris, 1967.

Afr 13271 - 13296   **African literature written originally in French - French Equatorial Africa - French Cameroons - Individual authors (A-Z)**
Afr 13272.21.100	Bebey, Francis. Le fils d'Agatha Moudio. Yaoundé, 1967.
Afr 13272.21.110	Bebey, Francis. Embarras et Cie; nouvelles et poèmes. Yaoundé, 1968.
Afr 13275.90.100	Evembe, François Borgia Marie. Sur la terre en passant. Paris, 1966.
Afr 13284.99.100	Nzouankeu, Jacques Mariel. Le souffle des ancêtres; nouvelles. Yaoundé, 1965.
Afr 13285.98.700	Oyono, Guillaume. Three suitors: one husband. London, 1968.
Afr 13286.38.100	Philombe, René. Sola ma chérie. Yaoundé, 1966.

Afr 13305   **African literature written originally in French - Congo (Leopoldville) - History of the literature - General works**
Afr 13305.5	Jadot, Joseph. Les écrivains africains du Congo belge et du Ruanda-Urundi. Bruxelles, 1959.

Afr 13315   **African literature written originally in French - Congo (Leopoldville) - Collections of texts, anthologies - General**
Afr 13315.5	Editions belles-lettres. Kinshasa. 1,196-?+

Afr 13321 - 13346   **African literature written originally in French - Congo (Leopoldville) - Individual authors (A-Z)**
Afr 13324.7.100	Debertry, Leon. Kitawala. Elisabethville, 1953.
Afr 13332.53.100	Lomami-Tshibamba, Paul. Ngando (Le crocodile). Bruxelles, 1948.
Afr 13333.51.100	Malonga, Jean. La légende de MiPfoumou Ma Mazono. Paris, 1954.
Afr 13340.12.100	Tchicaya U Tamsi, Gerald Felix. Feu de brousse. Paris, 1957.
Afr 13340.13.100	Tchicaya U Tamsi, Gerald Felix. Epitome. Tunis, 1962.
Afr 13340.13.110	Tchicaya U Tamsi, Gerald Felix. Le ventre. Paris, 1964.
Afr 13340.13.120	Tchichaya U Tamsi, Gerald Felix. Le mauvais sang, poèmes. Paris, 1955.
Afr 13340.13.700	Tchicaya U Tamsi, Gerald Felix. Brush fire. Ibadan, 1964.

Afr 13421 - 13446   **African literature written originally in French - Madagascar - Individual authors (A-Z)**
Afr 13438.1.100	Rabemananjara, Jacques. Agapes des dieux ou Tritriva. Paris, 1962.
Afr 13438.1.110	Rabemananjara, Jacques. Antidote. Paris, 1961.
Afr 13438.1.120	Rabemananjara, Jacques. Antsa. Paris, 1956.
Afr 13438.1.132	Rabemananjara, Jacques. Lamba. 2. éd. Paris, 1961.
Afr 13438.1.140	Rabemananjara, Jacques. Les boutriers de l'aurore. Paris, 1957.
Afr 13438.1.150	Rabemananjara, Jacques. Rites millénaires. Photocopy. Paris, 1955.
Afr 13438.1.775	Rabemananjara, Jacques. Insel mit Flammensilben. Herranalb, 1962.

Afr 13450 - 13699   **African literature written originally in French - Other islands, etc.**
Afr 13467.53.100	Maunick, Edouard. Mascaret ou Le livre de la mer et de la mort. Paris, 1966.

Afr 14505   **African literature written originally in Portuguese - General works - History of the literature - General works**
Afr 14505.5	Rodrigues Junior, Manuel. Literatura ultramarina. Lourenço, 1962.
Afr 14505.10	César, Amândio. Parágrafos de literatura ultramarina. Lisboa, 1967.

Afr 14518   **African literature written originally in Portuguese - General works - Collections of texts, anthologies - Special forms - Fiction**
Afr 14518.2	Neves, João Alves das. Poetas e contistas africanos de expressão portuguesa. São Paulo, 1963.
Afr 14518.5	César, Amândio. Contos portugueses do ultramar; antologia. Porto, 1969.

Afr 14654   **African literature written originally in Portuguese - Angola - Periodicals**
Afr 14654.5	Colecção imbondeiro. Angola. 3v.

Afr 14663   **African literature written originally in Portuguese - Angola - History of the literature - Special forms - Journalism**
Afr 14663.5	Lopo, Júlio de Castro. Jornalismo de Angola. Luanda, 1964.

Afr 14665   **African literature written originally in Portuguese - Angola - Collections of texts, anthologies - General**
Afr 14665.5	Guerra, Mario Lopes. Dumba e a bangala. 1a cancão. Sá da Bandeira, 1956.

Afr 14671 - 14696   **African literature written originally in Portuguese - Angola - Individual authors (A-Z)**
Afr 14692.41.100	Victor, Geraldo Bessa. Cubata abandonada. Lisboa, 1958.
Afr 14692.41.110	Victor, Geraldo Bessa. Mucanda. Braga, 1964.
Afr 14692.41.120	Victor, Geraldo Bessa. Sanzala sem batuque. Braga, 1967.
Afr 14692.41.1100	Vieira, Luandino. Luuanda. Luanda, 1963.
Afr 14692.41.1110	Vieira, Luandino. A cidade e a infância. Lisboa, 1957?

Afr 14721 - 14746   **African literature written originally in Portuguese - Mozambique - Individual authors (A-Z)**
Afr 14722.5	Beira, Maria da. Luz no túnel; romane. Porto, 1966.
Afr 14723.1	Craveirinha, José. Chigubo. Lisboa, 1964.
Afr 14728.1	Honwana, Luís. Nós matámos o Cão-Tinhoso! Lourenço Marques, 1964.
Afr 14740.76.100	Trindade, Francisco Alberto Cartaxo e. Chinanga, poemas. Lisboa, 1969.

Afr 14800 - 14899   **African literature written originally in Portuguese - Others**
Afr 14805.1	Reis, Fernando. Soiá. Braga, 1965.

Afr 20002   **African literatures written in indigenous languages - General works - Bibliographies - Special**
Afr 20002.5	Coldham, Geraldine Elizabeth. A bibliography of Scriptures in African languages. London, 1966. 2v.

Afr 20015   **African literatures written in indigenous languages - General works - Collections of texts, anthologies - General**
Afr 20015.5	Annotated African texts. London. 1,1952+ 5v.

Afr 20016   **African literatures written in indigenous languages - General works - Collections of texts, anthologies - Special forms - Poetry**
Afr 20016.5	Beier, Ulli. African poetry. Cambridge, Eng., 1966.

Afr 20059   **African literatures written in indigenous languages - Special countries, etc. - Subsaharan Africa in general - Collections of texts, anthologies - Special forms - Other special**
Afr 20059.5	Dieterlen, Germaine. Textes sacrés d'Afrique noire. Paris, 1965.

Afr 20136   **African literatures written in indigenous languages - Special countries, etc. - Sudan - Collections of texts, anthologies - Special forms - Poetry**
Afr 20136.2	Tescaroli, Livio. Poesia sudanese. Bologna, 1961.

Afr 20756   **African literatures written in indigenous languages - Special countries, etc. - British West Africa - Ghana - Collections of texts, anthologies - Special forms - Poetry**
Afr 20756.2	Pawelzik, Fritz. I lie on my mat and pray. N.Y., 1964.

Afr 21059   **African literatures written in indigenous languages - Special countries, etc. - Portuguese West Africa - Angola - Collections of texts, anthologies - Special forms - Other special**
Afr 21059.5.2	Hinos escolhidos. 2. ed. Bela Vista, Angola, 1943.
Afr 21059.5.3	Hinos escolhidos. 3. ed. Bela Vista, Angola, 1948.

Afr 21107   **African literatures written in indigenous languages - Special countries, etc. - South Africa - History of the literature - General special**
Afr 21107.5	Kunene, Daniel P. The beginning of South African vernacular literature. Los Angeles, 1967.

Afr 21205   **African literatures written in indigenous languages - Special countries, etc. - Rhodesia and Nyasaland - General works - History of the literature - General works**
Afr 21205.5	National Creative Writers Conference, Salisbury, 1966. African literature in Rhodesia. Rhodesia, 1966.

Afr 22025   **African literatures written in indigenous languages - Special language families in general - Bantu - History of the literature - General works**
Afr 22025.5F	Witahnkenge, E. Panorama de la littérature ntu. Kinshase, 1968.

Afr 23121 - 23146   **African literatures written in indigenous languages - Special languages - Acholi (Acoli) - Individual authors (A-Z)**
Afr 23135.46.30	p'Bitek, Okot. SongOf Lawino. Nairobi, 1966.

Afr 26700 - 26799   **African literatures written in indigenous languages - Special languages - Congo (Kongo)**
Afr 26719.24.21	Lepoutre, Paul. Contes congolais. Limete, 1964. 2 pam.

Afr 28200 - 28299   **African literatures written in indigenous languages - Special languages - Ewe**
Afr 28226.41.100	Fiawoo, F. Kwasi. The fifth landing stage. London, 1943.

Afr 28715   **African literatures written in indigenous languages - Special languages - Fulah (Ful, Fulani, Fulbe, Fulfulde) - Collections of texts, anthologies - General**
Afr 28715.2	Mohamadou, Eldridge. Contes et poèmes foulbé de la Bénoué-Nord-Cameroun. Yaounde, 1965.
Afr 28715.4	Sow, Alfâ Ibrâhîm. La Femme, la vache, la foi. Paris, 1966.
Afr 28715.6.2	East, Rupert Moultrie. Stories of old Adamawa: a collection of historical texts in the Adamawa dialect of Fulani. Farnborough, 1967.

Afr 28716   African literatures written in indigenous languages - Special
languages - Fulah (Ful, Fulani, Fulbe, Fulfulde) - Collections of texts,
anthologies - Special forms - Poetry
    Afr 28716.2   Lacroix, Pierre Francis. Poésie peule de l'Adamawa.
                    Paris, 1965.
                    2v.

Afr 28747   African literatures written in indigenous languages - Special
languages - Fulah (Ful, Fulani, Fulbe, Fulfulde) - Anonymous works
(Bible, etc.)
    Afr 28747.5   Ba, Amadou Hampâté. Kaidara. Paris, 1969.

Afr 30100 - 30199   African literatures written in indigenous languages -
Special languages - Hausa
    Afr 30115.2   Johnston, H.A.S. A selection of Hausa stories.
                    Oxford, 1966.

Afr 33300 - 33399   African literatures written in indigenous languages -
Special languages - Kamba
    Afr 33319.2   Mbiti, John. Akamba stories. Oxford, 1966.

Afr 39900 - 39999   African literatures written in indigenous languages -
Special languages - Other M
    Afr 39906.5   Le mythe et les contes de sou en pays Mbaï-Moïssala.
                    Paris, 1967.

Afr 41600 - 41699   African literatures written in indigenous languages -
Special languages - Nyankole
    Afr 41610.2   Morris, H.F. The heroic recitation of the Bahima of
                    Ankole. Oxford, 1964.

Afr 41900 - 41909   African literatures written in indigenous languages -
Special languages - Nsakkara
    Afr 41906.2   Dampierre, Eric de. Poètes nzakara. Paris, 1963.

Afr 41910 - 41999   African literatures written in indigenous languages -
Special languages - Other N
    Afr 41918.5   Mwindo (Nyanga Folk Epic). English and Nyanga. The Mwindo
                    epic from the Banyanga (Congo Republic). Berkeley, 1969.

Afr 42200 - 42299   African literatures written in indigenous languages -
Special languages - Other O
    Afr 42208.5   Ward, Philip. The Okefani song of Nij Zitru.
                    London, 1969.

Afr 42700 - 42799   African literatures written in indigenous languages -
Special languages - Ruanda (Kinyaruanda)
    Afr 42715.22   Hurel, Eugène. La poésie chez les primitifs, ou Contes,
                    fables, récits et proverbes du Rwanda (Lac Kivu).
                    Bruxelles, 1922.
    Afr 42731.2.700   Kagame, A. La divine pastorale. Bruxelles, 1952.

Afr 43300 - 43399   African literatures written in indigenous languages -
Special languages - Sechuana (Bechuana)
    Afr 43316.21   Schapera, Isaac. Praise-poems of Tswana chiefs.
                    Oxford, 1965.
    Afr 43393.2   Schapera, I. Ditirafalô tsa merafe ya BaTswana ba lefatshe
                    la Tshireletsô. Tswana, 1954.

Afr 44610   African literatures written in indigenous languages - Special
languages - Swahili - History of the literature - Special forms - Poetry
    Afr 44610.5   Knappert, Jan. Traditional Swahili poetry. Leiden, 1967.

Afr 44615   African literatures written in indigenous languages - Special
languages - Swahili - Collections of texts, anthologies - General
    Afr 44615.2   Velton, Carl. Swahili prose texts. London, 1965.

Afr 44616   African literatures written in indigenous languages - Special
languages - Swahili - Collections of texts, anthologies - Special
forms - Poetry
    Afr 44616.2   Harries, L. Swahili poetry. Oxford, 1962.

Afr 44619   African literatures written in indigenous languages - Special
languages - Swahili - Collections of texts, anthologies - Special
forms - Other special
    Afr 44619.5   Madan, Arthur Cornwallis. Kiungani, or Story and history
                    from Central Africa written by boys in the schools.
                    London, 1887.

Afr 44621 - 44646   African literatures written in indigenous languages -
Special languages - Swahili - Individual authors (A-Z)
    Afr 44622.89.100   al-Buhry, Hemed Abdallah. Utenzi wa AbdirRahmani na
                    Sufiyani. Dar es Salaam, 1961.
    Afr 44622.89.112   al-Buhry, Hemed Abdallah. Utenzi wa vita vya wadachi
                    kutamalaki mrima 1307 A.H. 2. ed. Dar es Salaam, 1960.
    Afr 44622.89.120   al-Buhry, Hemed Abdallah. Utenzi wa Seyyidna Huseni bin
                    Ali. Dar es Salaam, 1965.
    Afr 44622.89.122   al-Buhry, Hemed Abdallah. Utenzi wa Seyyidna Huseni bin
                    Ali. Dar es Salaam, 1965.
    Afr 44622.89.124A Bhalo, Ahmad Nassir Bin Juma. Poems from Kenya.
                    Madison, 1966.
    Afr 44622.89.124B Bhalo, Ahmad Nassir Bin Juma. Poems from Kenya.
                    Madison, 1966.
    Afr 44623.40.100   Chum, Haji. Atenji wa vita vya Uhud. Dar es Salaam, 1962.
    Afr 44628.5.700   Hasani Bin Ismail. The medicine man. Swifa ya ngurumali.
                    Oxford, 1968.

Afr 47600 - 47699   African literatures written in indigenous languages -
Special languages - Venda
    Afr 47619.5   Blacking, John. Venda children's songs.
                    Johannesburg, 1967.

Afr 49000   African literatures written in indigenous languages - Special
languages - Yoruba - Bibliographies - General
    Afr 49000.89.79F   Ogunsheye, F. Adetowun. A preliminary bibliography of the
                    Yoruba language. Ibadan, 1963.

Afr 49016   African literatures written in indigenous languages - Special
languages - Yoruba - Collections of texts, anthologies - Special forms -
Poetry
    Afr 49016.5   Gbadamosi, Bakare. Yoruba poetry. Ibadan, 1959.

Afr 49017   African literatures written in indigenous languages - Special
languages - Yoruba - Collections of texts, anthologies - Special forms -
Drama
    Afr 49017.2   Beier, Ulli. Three Nigerian plays. London, 1967.

Afr 49019   African literatures written in indigenous languages - Special
languages - Yoruba - Collections of texts, anthologies - Special forms -
Other special
    Afr 49019.2   Babalola, S.A. The content and form of Yoruba ijala.
                  Oxford, 1966.

Afr 49021 - 49046   African literatures written in indigenous languages -
Special languages - Yoruba - Individual authors (A-Z)
    Afr 49029.41.700   Ljimere, Obotunde. The imprisonment of Obatala, and other
                    plays. London, 1966.
    Afr 49032.1.100   Ladipo, Duro. Three Yoruba plays. Ibadan, 1964.

Afr 49400 - 49499   African literatures written in indigenous languages -
Special languages - Zande (Nyam-Nyam)
    Afr 49419.4.100   Evans-Pritchard, Edward Evan. The Zande trickster.
                    Oxford, 1967.

Afr 49716   African literatures written in indigenous languages - Special
languages - Zulu - Collections of texts, anthologies - Special forms -
Poetry
    Afr 49716.5   Stuart, James. Izibongo; Zulu praise-poems. Oxford, 1968.

Afr 49721 - 49746   African literatures written in indigenous languages -
Special languages - Zulu - Individual authors (A-Z)
    Afr 49724.100   Dube, John. Jeqe, the bodyservant of King Tshaka (Insila
                    Ka Tshaka). Lovedale, 1951.
    Afr 49742.41.100   Vilakazi, B.W. Udingiswayo kajobe. London, 1939.
    Afr 49742.41.700   Vilakazi, B.W. Zulu horizons. Cape Town, 1962.

AFRICAN DOCUMENTS

CLASSIFIED LISTING BY CALL NUMBER

Afr Doc 5 Africa in general - General Collections - Annual reports

Afr Doc 5.2 — Boston University. Library. Catalog of African government documents and African area index. 2d ed. Boston, 1964.
Afr Doc 5.8 — Landskron, William A. Official serial publications relating to economic development in Africa South of the Sahara. Cambridge, 1961.
Afr Doc 5.10 — Michigan. State University, East Lansing. Library. Research sources for African studies. East Lansing, 1969.

Afr Doc 303 Ethiopia - General Collections - Blue books, government manuals, directories

Afr Doc 303.5F — Ethiopia. Ministry of Interior. Administrative sub-divisions of Ethiopia, as of the end of Sené 1956 e.c. or July 7th, 1964. Addis Ababa, 1964.
Afr Doc 303.7 — Addis Ababa. Imperial Ethiopian Institute of Public Administration. Administrative directory of the Ethiopian government. Addis Ababa. 5,1965+

Afr Doc 307.1 - .199 Ethiopia - Statistics - General compilations

Afr Doc 307.5 — Ethiopia. Central Statistical Office. Statistical abstract. Addis Ababa. 1964+
Afr Doc 307.10F — Ethiopia. Central Statistical Office. Report on a survey. Addis Ababa, 1966. 3 pam.
Afr Doc 307.15F — Ethiopia. Central Statistical Office. Report on a survey. Addis Ababa, 1966.
Afr Doc 307.20 — Ethiopia. Ministry of Commerce and Industry. Economic handbook of Ethiopia. Addis Ababa, 1951,

Afr Doc 308.700 - .999 Ethiopia - Statistics - Trade

Afr Doc 308.700F — Ethiopia. Central Statistical Office. Summary report on Ethiopia's external trade, 1953-1963. Addis Ababa, 1963.
Afr Doc 308.705F — Ethiopia. Customs Head Office. Annual import and export trade statistics. Addis Ababa. 1962+

Afr Doc 309.500 - .999 Ethiopia - Statistics - Other

Afr Doc 309.502 — Ethiopia. Ministry of Education and Fine Arts Government, mission, private, community and church schools, 1959-1960. Addis Ababa, 1961?
Afr Doc 309.505 — School census for Ethiopia. Addis Ababa. 1961+

Afr Doc 603 Italian Africa - Eritrea - General collections - Blue books, government manuals, directories

Afr Doc 603.5 — Ethiopia. Governorate General of Evitrea. Official list. Asmara. 1967+

Afr Doc 707.1 - .199 Italian Africa - Somalia, Somaliland - Statistics - General compilations

Afr Doc 707.5 — Somalia. Planning Directorate. Statistical Department. Compendio statistico. Mogadiscio. 2,1965+
Afr Doc 707.10F — Pamphlet vol. Statistical survey of Solali towns. 9 pam.
Afr Doc 707.10.2F — Somalia. Ministry of Planning and Coordination. Statistical Department. A multipurpose survey of Afgoi municipality. Mogadiscio, 1966.
Afr Doc 707.15F — Somalia. Ministry of Planning and Coordination. Statistical Department. Bollettino trimestralle di statistica. Mogadiscio. 1,1966+

Afr Doc 707.200 - .999 Italian Africa - Somalia, Somaliland - Statistics - Census

Afr Doc 707.353 — Italy. Istituto Centrali di Statistica. Censimento della popolazione Italiana e straniera della Somalia 4 novembre 1953. Roma, 1958.

Afr Doc 708.700 - .999 Italian Africa - Somalia, Somaliland - Statistics - Trade

Afr Doc 708.731F — Somalia. Customs and Excise Department. Annual trade report of Northern Region. Mogadisco. 1960+
Afr Doc 708.732F — Somalia. Statistical Service. Statistica del commercio con l'estero (delle Regioni Meridionali). Mogadisco. 1961+
Afr Doc 708.733F — Somalia. Planning Directorate. Statistical Department. Statistica del commercio con l'estero. Mogadisco. 1964+

Afr Doc 709.1 - .299 Italian Africa - Somalia, Somaliland - Statistics - Budget

Afr Doc 709.5 — Somalia. Bilancio di previsione per l'esercizio finanziario. Mogadiscio. 1962+

Afr Doc 719 Italian Africa - Somalia, Somaliland - Legislative documents - Others

Afr Doc 719.12 — Somalia. Constitution. The Constitution. Mogadiscio, 1964?

Afr Doc 807.1 - .199 Italian Africa - Libya, Tripoli - Statistics - General compilations

Afr Doc 807.5 — Libya. Census and Statistical Department. Statistical abstract. 1,1958+

Afr Doc 807.200 - .999 Italian Africa - Libya, Tripoli - Statistics - Census

Afr Doc 807.354 — Libya. Census and Statistical Department. General population census of Libya, 1954; report and tables. Tripoli, 1959.
Afr Doc 807.364F — Libya. Census and Statistical Department. General population census, 1964. Tripoli, 1964?
Afr Doc 807.364.10 — Libya. Census and Statistical Department. Preliminary results of the general population census 1964. Tripoli, 1964.

Afr Doc 808.500 - .699 Italian Africa - Libya, Tripoli - Statistics - Industry, manufactures

Afr Doc 808.510 — Libya. Census and Statistical Department. Report of the annual survey of large manufacturing establishments. Tripoli. 1,1965+

Afr Doc 808.700 - .999 Italian Africa - Libya, Tripoli - Statistics - Trade

Afr Doc 808.705 — Libya. Census and Statistical Department. External trade statistics. 1959+ 3v.
Afr Doc 808.710 — Libya. Census and Statistical Department. Summary of external trade statistics. 1962+
Afr Doc 808.715 — Libya. Census and Statistical Department. Balance of payments. 1956+
Afr Doc 808.720 — Libya. Census and Statistical Department. External trade indices. Tripoli. 1962+

Afr Doc 809.300 - .499 Italian Africa - Libya, Tripoli - Statistics - National income and accounts, surveys

Afr Doc 809.305 — Libya. Central Statistics Office. National income estimates. Benghazi. 1958+

Afr Doc 831 - 856 Italian Africa - Libya, Tripoli - Executive documents - Depts., Bureaus, etc., A-Z (by catchword)

Afr Doc 844.5 — Libya. National Planning Council. Annual report on development activities. Tripoli. 1,1963+

Afr Doc 871 - 896 Italian Africa - Libya, Tripoli - Local documents - Provinces, cities, etc., A-Z

Afr Doc 890.5 — Libya. Census and Statistical Department. Monthly cost of living index for Tripoli town.

Afr Doc 1305 British Africa - Sudan (Anglo-Egyptian) - General collections - Annual reports

Afr Doc 1305.5 — Sudan. Central Office of Information. Progress. Anniversary of the Sudan revolution. Khartoum. 1963+

Afr Doc 1307.1 - .199 British Africa - Sudan (Anglo-Egyptian) - Statistics - General compilations

Afr Doc 1307.5F — Sudan. Department of Statistics. Internal statistics. 1,1960+

Afr Doc 1307.200 - .999 British Africa - Sudan (Anglo-Egyptian) - statistics - Census

Afr Doc 1307.353 — Sudan. Department of Statistics. The 1953 pilot population census for the first population census in Sudan. Khartoum, 1955.
Afr Doc 1307.356.10 — Sudan. Population Census Office. First population census of Sudan, 1955-56. Interim report. Khartoum, 1957.
Afr Doc 1307.356.11 — Sudan. Population Census Office. First population census of Sudan, 1955-56. Supplement. Khartoum, 1956.
Afr Doc 1307.356.15 — Sudan. Population Census Office. 21 facts about the Sudanese. First population census of Sudan, 1955-56. Khartoum? 1958.
Afr Doc 1307.356.20 — Sudan. Department of Statistics. First population census of Sudan 1955-56; methods report. Khartoum, 1960.
Afr Doc 1307.365 — Sudan. Department of Statistics. Population and housing survey, 1964-65. Khartoum, 1965. 11v.

Afr Doc 1308.700 - .999 British Africa - Sudan (Anglo-Egyptian) - statistics - Trade

Afr Doc 1308.705 — Sudan. Department of Statistics. Foreign trade statistics. 1962+

Afr Doc 1309.1 - .299 British Africa - Sudan (Anglo-Egyptian) - Statistics - Budget

Afr Doc 1309.5 — Sudan. Memorandum on the budget estimates. Khartoum. 1966+
Afr Doc 1309.10F — Sudan. Ten year plan of economic and social development, 1961/62-1970/71. Development budget. Khartoum. 1965+
Afr Doc 1309.10.5 — Sudan. Ten year plan of economic and social development. Explanatory memorandum on development budgets. Khartoum. 1965+
Afr Doc 1309.15 — Sudan. The central budget; estimates of revenue and expenditure. Khartoum? 1966+

Afr Doc 1309.300 - .499 British Africa - Sudan (Anglo-Egyptian) - statistics - National income and accounts, surveys

Afr Doc 1309.305 — Sudan. Ministry of Finance and Economics. Economic survey. Khartoum. 1959
Afr Doc 1309.310 — Sudan. Department of Statistics. The national income of Sudan. 1,1955+

Afr Doc 1309.500 - .999 British Africa - Sudan (Anglo-Egyptian) - s statistics - Other

Afr Doc 1309.505 — Sudan. Bureau of Education Statistics. Education statistics. Khartoum. 1959+

Afr Doc 1319 British Africa - Sudan (Anglo-Egyptian) - Legislative documents - Others

Afr Doc 1319.58 — Sudan. The National Charter of the Coalition Government. n.p., 1965?

Afr Doc 1331 - 1356 British Africa - Sudan (Anglo-Egyptian) - Executive documents - Depts., Bureaus, etc., A-Z (by catchword)

Afr Doc 1342.5 — Sudan. Department of Land Use and Rural Water Development. Annual report. 1962+

Afr Doc 1371 - 1396 British Africa - Sudan (Anglo-Egyptian) - Local documents - Provinces, cities, etc., A-Z

Afr Doc 1385.5F — Sudan. Department of Statistics. Ordurman household budget survey. Khartoum, 1965.

Afr Doc 1403 British Africa - Egypt - General collections - Blue books, government manuals, directories

Afr Doc 1403.6 — Egypt. Government Press. Almanac. Cairo. 1933-1949
Afr Doc 1403.10 — United Arab Republic. Ministry of Foreign Affairs. Liste du corps diplomatique au Caire. Cairo. 1964+

Afr Doc 1405 British Africa - Egypt - General collections - Annual reports

Afr Doc 1405.5 — United Arab Republic. Ministry of National Guidance. The yearbook. Cairo. 1959+

Afr Doc 1406 British Africa - Egypt - General collections - Other

Afr Doc 1406.5 — Journal official du gouvernement egyptien. Cairo, 1909. 2v.

Afr Doc 1407.1 - .199 British Africa - Egypt - Statistics - General compilations

Afr Doc 1407.5 — United Arab Republic. Central Agency for Public Mobilisation and Statistics. Statistical handbook of the UAR. Cairo. 1952+
Afr Doc 1407.8 — United Arab Republic. Department of Statistics and Census. Statistical pocket year-book. Cairo. 1945+
Afr Doc 1407.10 — United Arab Republic. Department of Statistics and Census. Annuaire statistique. Cairo. 1909+
Afr Doc 1407.12 — United Arab Republic. Central Agency for Public Mobilisation and Statistics. Basic statistics. Cairo. 1964+
Afr Doc 1407.20F — United Arab Republic. Central Agency for Public Mobilization and Statistics. United Arab Republic statistical atlas, 1952-1966. Cairo, 1968.

Afr Doc 1407.200 - .999   British Africa - Egypt - Statistics - Census
Afr Doc 1407.307   Egypt. Department of Statistics and Census. The census of Egypt taken in 1907. Cairo, 1909.
Afr Doc 1407.317   Egypt. Department of Statistics and Census. The census of Egypt taken in 1917. Cairo, 1920-21. 2v.
Afr Doc 1407.344.10   Egypt. Department of Statistics and Census. Census of industrial production, 1944. Cairo, 1947.

Afr Doc 1408.700 - .999   British Africa - Egypt - Statistics - Trade
Afr Doc 1408.700   United Arab Republic. Central Agency for Public Mobilisation and Statistics. U.A.R. foreign trade according to standard international trade classification revised. Cairo. 1944+
Afr Doc 1408.705   Egypt. Customs Administration. Commerce extérieur de l'Egypte. Statistique comparée. Roma. 1884-1903 2v.
Afr Doc 1408.710   Egypt. Customs Administration. Rapport sur le commerce extérieur de l'Egypte. 1923-1938
Afr Doc 1408.715   United Arab Republic. Central Agency for Public Mobilisation and Statistics. Annual bulletin of foreign trade. Cairo. 1918
Afr Doc 1408.720   United Arab Republic. Central Agency for Public Mobilisation and Statistics. Monthly bulletin of foreign trade. Caire. 1918+
Afr Doc 1408.725   Egypt. Customs Administration. Bulletin mensuel du commerce extérieur de l'Egypte. 1899+

Afr Doc 1409.1 - .299   British Africa - Egypt - Statistics - Budget
Afr Doc 1409.3F   United Arab Republic. Ministry of Treasury. Budget report. Cairo. 1961+
Afr Doc 1409.5F   United Arab Republic. Ministry of Treasury. Statement on the draft budget. Cairo. 1962+

Afr Doc 1409.300 - .499   British Africa - Egypt - Statistics - National income and accounts, surveys
Afr Doc 1409.300   United Arab Republic. Department of Statistics and Census. Monthly bulletin of agricultural and economic statistics. Cairo. 10-50,1921-1961 23v.

Afr Doc 1409.500 - .999   British Africa - Egypt - Statistics - Other
Afr Doc 1409.500   United Arab Republic. State Tourist Administration. Annual statistical report. Cairo. 1960+
Afr Doc 1409.505F   United Arab Republic. Ministry of War. Civil Aviation Department. Civil aviation statistics. Cairo? 1966+

Afr Doc 1419   British Africa - Egypt - Legislative documents - Others
Afr Doc 1419.2   United Arab Republic. Constitution. La consitution, 25 mars, 1964. Le Caire, 1964.

Afr Doc 1430 - 1455   British Africa - Egypt - Executive documents - Depts., Bureaus, etc., A-Z (by catchword)
Afr Doc 1437.5   United Arab Republic. Ministry of the High Dam. Sadd-el-Aali project. n.p., n.d.
Afr Doc 1439.3F   Egypt. Ministry of Justice. Reports. Cairo. 1898-1907 3v.
Afr Doc 1439.3.5   Egypt. Ministry of Justice. Annuaire du Ministère de la justice. Le Caire. 1909
Afr Doc 1448.5   United Arab Republic. Science Council. Annual report.

Afr Doc 1603   British Africa - British West Africa - Gambia - General collections - Blue books, government manuals, directories
Afr Doc 1603.5   Gambia. Blue book. London. 1904-1914
Afr Doc 1603.10   Gambia. Staff list. Bathurst. 1965+
Afr Doc 1603.11   Gambia. Diplomatic and consular list and office directory. Bathurst. 1966+

Afr Doc 1609.1 - .299   British Africa - British West Africa - Gambia - Statistics - Budget
Afr Doc 1609.72   Gambia. Development fund estimates. Bathurst. 1964+
Afr Doc 1609.89   Gambia. Estimates. Bathurst. 1964+

Afr Doc 1612   British Africa - British West Africa - Gambia - Legislative documents - General
Afr Doc 1612.5   Gambia. Legislative Council. Sessional paper. Bathurst. 1961+

Afr Doc 1631 - 1656   British Africa - British West Africa - Gambia - Executive documents - Depts., Bureaus, etc., A-Z (by catchword)
Afr Doc 1633.5   Gambia. Currency Board. Report. Bathurst. 2,1965+

Afr Doc 1702   British Africa - British West Africa - Sierra Leone - General collections - Bibliographies, catalogs, etc.
Afr Doc 1702.5   Sierra Leone. Library Board. Sierra Leone publications. Freetown. 1962+
Afr Doc 1702.8   Library of Congress. African Section. Official publications of Sierra Leone and Gambia. Washington, 1963.

Afr Doc 1703   British Africa - British West Africa - Sierra Leone - General collections - Blue books, government manuals, directories
Afr Doc 1703.5F   Sierra Leone. Blue book. 7v.
Afr Doc 1703.7   Sierra Leone. Clerical staff list. Freetown. 1963+
Afr Doc 1703.7.5   Sierra Leone. The staff list. Freetown. 1960+
Afr Doc 1703.10   Sierra Leone. Department of External Affairs. Diplomatic and consular list, and list of Sierra Leone Commonwealth and Foreign Service postings. Freetown. 1967+

Afr Doc 1705   British Africa - British West Africa - Sierra Leone - General collections - Annual reports
Afr Doc 1705.5   Sierra Leone. Review of governement departments. Freetown. 1960+

Afr Doc 1707.1 - .199   British Africa - British West Africa - Sierra Leone - Statistics - General compilations
Afr Doc 1707.5   Sierra Leone. Central Statistical Office. Quarterly statistical bulletin. Freetown. 1,1963+

Afr Doc 1707.200 - .999   British Africa - British West Africa - Sierra Leone - Statistics - Census
Afr Doc 1707.363   Sierra Leone. Central Statistics Office. 1963 population census Sierra Leone. Freetown, 1965.

Afr Doc 1708.700 - .999   British Africa - British West Africa - Sierra Leone - Statistics - Trade
Afr Doc 1708.705   Sierra Leone. Quarterly trade statistics. Freetown. 41,1962+
Afr Doc 1708.710   Sierra Leone. Trade report. Freetown. 1960+

Afr Doc 1709.1 - .299   British Africa - British West Africa - Sierra Leone - Statistics - Budget
Afr Doc 1709.5   Sierra Leone. Budget speech. Freetown. 1962+
Afr Doc 1709.89   Sierra Leone. Estimates of revenue and expenditure. Freetown. 1959+
Afr Doc 1709.92   Sierra Leone. Development estimates. Freetown. 1962+

Afr Doc 1709.300 - .499   British Africa - British West Africa - Sierra Leone - Statistics - National income and accounts, surveys
Afr Doc 1709.300   Sierra Leone. Treasury Department. Financial report. Freetown. 1957+
Afr Doc 1709.320F   Sierra Leone. Central Statistical Office. National accounts. Freetown. 2,1963+

Afr Doc 1712   British Africa - British West Africa - Sierra Leone - Legislative documents - General
Afr Doc 1712.5F   Sierra Leone. Legislative Council. Minutes. 1922-1925 3v.
Afr Doc 1712.10F   Sierra Leone. Legislative Council. Sessional paper.
Afr Doc 1712.15   Sierra Leone. Legislative Council. Debates. 3v.

Afr Doc 1714   British Africa - British West Africa - Sierra Leone - Legislative documents - House Journal, etc.
Afr Doc 1714.5   Sierra Leone. House of Representatives. Debates. 1958+

Afr Doc 1719   British Africa - British West Africa - Sierra Leone - Legislative documents - Others
Afr Doc 1719.5   Sierra Leone. Constitution. The Sierra Leone Constitution, Order in Council, 1961. Freetown, 1961.

Afr Doc 1724   British Africa - British West Africa - Sierra Leone - Executive documents - President
Afr Doc 1724.5F   Sierra Leone. Governor. Address by His Excellency the Governor on the occasion of the opening of the Legislative Council.

Afr Doc 1731 - 1756   British Africa - British West Africa - Sierra Leone - Executive documents - Depts., Bureaus, etc., A-Z (by catchword)
Afr Doc 1731.5   Sierra Leone. Audit Department. Report of the Director of Audit on the accounts of Sierra Leone. Freetown. 1956+
Afr Doc 1735.5   Sierra Leone. Ministry of Education. Report. Freetown. 1962+
Afr Doc 1739.5   Sierra Leone. Department of Information. Report. Freetown. 1959+
Afr Doc 1743.5   Sierra Leone. Monuments and Relics Commission. Report. Freetown. 1955+
Afr Doc 1746.5   Sierra Leone. Public Service Commission. Report. Freetown. 1955+
Afr Doc 1746.10   Sierra Leone. Posts and Telecommunications Deparment. Report. Freetown. 1959+
Afr Doc 1746.15   Sierra Leone. Public Works Department. Report. Freetown. 1958+
Afr Doc 1748.5   Sierra Leone. Road Transport Department. Report. Freetown. 1955+
Afr Doc 1749.5   Sierra Leone. Surveys and Lands Department. Annual report. Freetown. 1963+

Afr Doc 1802   British Africa - British West Africa - Ghana, Gold Coast - General collections - Bibliographies, catalogs, etc.
Afr Doc 1802.10   Ghana. State Publishing Corporation. Publications price list. Accra. 1958+
Afr Doc 1802.15   Witherell, Julian W. Ghana; a guide to official publications, 1872-1968. Washington, 1969.

Afr Doc 1803   British Africa - British West Africa - Ghana, Gold Coast - General collections - Blue books, government manuals, directories
Afr Doc 1803.5   Gold Coast (Colony). Blue book. Accra. 1910-1913 4v.

Afr Doc 1805   British Africa - British West Africa - Ghana, Gold Coast - General collections - Annual reports
Afr Doc 1805.5   Gold Coast (Colony). Development progress report. Accra. 1951-1953
Afr Doc 1805.10F   Gold Coast (Colony). Departmental reports. 1909+ 9v.

Afr Doc 1806   British Africa - British West Africa - Ghana, Gold Coast - General collections - Other
Afr Doc 1806.5F   Gold Coast Gazette. Accra. 1925-1932
Afr Doc 1806.5.10F   Gold Coast Gazette. Supplement (trade). Accra. 1924-1931 5v.

Afr Doc 1807.1 - .199   British Africa - British West Africa - Ghana, Gold Coast - Statistics - General compilations
Afr Doc 1807.5   Ghana. Central Bureau of Statistics. Statistical yearbook. Accra. 1961+
Afr Doc 1807.10   Statistical handbook of the Republic of Ghana. Accra. 1967+
Afr Doc 1807.15   Ghana. Central Bureau of Statistics. Statistical and economic papers. Accra. 1,1957+
Afr Doc 1807.20   Ghana. Central Bureau of Statistics. Quarterly digest of statistics. Accra. 1,1952+
Afr Doc 1807.25   Gold Coast (Colony). Office of the Government Statistician. Statistical abstracts. 1,1956

Afr Doc 1807.200 - .999   British Africa - British West Africa - Ghana, Gold Coast - Statistics - Census
Afr Doc 1807.321   Gold Coast (Colony). Census Office. Census report, 1921, for the Gold Coast and Colony. Accra, 1923.
Afr Doc 1807.331   Gold Coast (Colony). Census Office. The Gold Coast 1931. A review of conditions in the Gold Coast in 1931 as compared with those of 1921. Accra, 1932. 4v.
Afr Doc 1807.348   Gold Coast (Colony). Census Office. Census of populations 1948. Report and tables. London, 1950.
Afr Doc 1807.360   Ghana. Census Office. Ghana. 1960 population census. Accra. 3,1960+
Afr Doc 1807.360.5   Ghana. Census Office. 1960 population census of Ghana. Special report. Accra, 1964.
Afr Doc 1807.360.10   Ghana. Central Bureau of Statistics. Summary of procedures in the 1960 population census of Ghana. Accra, 1968.
Afr Doc 1807.362   Ghana. Central Bureau of Statistics. 1962 industrial census report. Accra, 1965.

Afr Doc 1808.1 - .299 British Africa - British West Africa - Ghana, Gold Coast - Statistics - Vital, population, etc.

Afr Doc 1808.5   Ghana. Central Bureau of Statistics. Migration statistics. Accra. 1953+

Afr Doc 1808.500 - .699 British Africa - British West Africa - Ghana, Gold Coast - Statistics - Industry, manufactures

Afr Doc 1808.505   Ghana. Central Bureau of Statistics. Industrial statistics. Accra. 1958+

Afr Doc 1808.510   Ghana. Central Bureau of Statistics. Area sample survey of small manufacturing establishments, 1963. Accra, 1965.

Afr Doc 1808.700 - .999 British Africa - British West Africa - Ghana, Gold Coast - Statistics - Trade

Afr Doc 1808.700   Ghana. Central Bureau of Statistics. Trade report. Accra. 1952+

Afr Doc 1808.705   Ghana. Central Bureau of Statistics. External trade statistics of Ghana. 13,1963+

Afr Doc 1808.715F   Ghana. Central Bureau of Statistics. Balance of payments estimates. 1,1950+

Afr Doc 1808.715.5F   Ghana. Central Bureau of Statistics. Balance of payments estimates. v.2. Definitions, sources and methods of estimation. 1,1950+

Afr Doc 1809.1 - .299 British Africa - British West Africa - Ghana, Gold Coast - Statistics - Budget

Afr Doc 1809.5   Ghana. Ministry of France. The financial statement presented to the National Assembly on budget day. Accra. 1953+

Afr Doc 1809.10   Ghana. Ministry of Finance. Budget. Accra. 1963+

Afr Doc 1809.15   Ghana. Ministry of Finance. Budget statement. Accra. 1963+

Afr Doc 1809.20F   Gold Coast (Colony). Gold Coast estimates. Accra. 1926+

Afr Doc 1809.25F   Gold Coast (Colony). Memorandum on the draft estimates. Accra. 1930+

Afr Doc 1809.30   Gold Coast (Colony). Estimates of expenditure from development funds. Accra. 1956+

Afr Doc 1809.35   Ghana. The consolidation development plan. Accra. 1,1957+

Afr Doc 1809.40   Ghana. Annual estimates. Accra. 1960+

Afr Doc 1809.45   Ghana. Estimates of statutory boards, corporations, institutions, etc. Accra. 1962+

Afr Doc 1809.50   Ghana. Estimates of charged expenditure. Accra. 1963+

Afr Doc 1809.55   Ghana. Estimates of financial service. Accra. 1966+

Afr Doc 1809.300 - .499 British Africa - British West Africa - Ghana, Gold Coast - Statistics - National income and accounts, surveys

Afr Doc 1809.300   Ghana. Auditor-General. Report on the accounts of Ghana. Accra. 1958+

Afr Doc 1809.305   Ghana. Accountant general. Report and financial statements. Accra. 1958+

Afr Doc 1809.310   Gold Coast (Colony). Accountant General's Department. Report on the finances and accounts of the Gold Coast. 1949-1955

Afr Doc 1809.315   Ghana. Central Bureau of Statistics. Economic survey. Accra. 1955+

Afr Doc 1809.500 - .999 British Africa - British West Africa - Ghana, Gold Coast - Statistics - Other

Afr Doc 1809.500   Ghana. Central Bureau of Statistics. Motor vehicle statistics. Accra. 1956+

Afr Doc 1809.505   Ghana. Central Bureau of Statistics. Education statistics. Accra. 1962+

Afr Doc 1809.510F   Ghana. Central Bureau of Statistics. Civil aviation statistics. Accra. 1954+

Afr Doc 1812 British Africa - British West Africa - Ghana, Gold Coast - Legislative documents - General

Afr Doc 1812.5   Gold Coast (Colony). Legislative Council. Debates. 1925-1928 3v.

Afr Doc 1812.6   Gold Coast (Colony). Legislative Assembly. Debates. 1953-1958 8v.

Afr Doc 1812.7   Ghana. Constituent Assembly. Proceedings of the Constituent assembly. Accra, 1960.

Afr Doc 1812.202   Ghana. Commission of Enquiry into Electoral and Local Government Reform. Report. Accra, 1967.

Afr Doc 1814 British Africa - British West Africa - Ghana, Gold Coast - Legislative documents - House Journal, etc.

Afr Doc 1814.205   Ghana. National Assembly. Public Accounts Committee. Report. 1959+

Afr Doc 1814.215   Ghana. National Assembly. Finance Committee. Report. Accra. 1957+

Afr Doc 1819 British Africa - British West Africa - Ghana, Gold Coast - Legislative documents - Others

Afr Doc 1819.5   Ghana. Constitutional Commission. Memorandum on the proposals for a constitution for Ghana. Accra, 1968.

Afr Doc 1822 British Africa - British West Africa - Ghana, Gold Coast - Executive documents - General

Afr Doc 1822.5   Ghana. White paper. Accra. 1,1958+

Afr Doc 1826 British Africa - British West Africa - Ghana, Gold Coast - Executive documents - Special

Afr Doc 1826.5F   Gold Coast (Colony). Documents. Accra. 1926-1930 4v.

Afr Doc 1826.10   Gold Coast (Colony). Proclamations, orders-in-council. Accra. 1928-1936 10v.

Afr Doc 1830 - 1855 British Africa - British West Africa - Ghana, Gold Coast - Executive documents - Depts., Bureaus, etc., A-Z (by catchword)

Afr Doc 1830.5   Ghana. National Archives. Annual report. Accra. 1957

Afr Doc 1830.10   Ghana. Agricultural Produce Marketing Board. Annual report and accounts. Accra. 1947-1956

Afr Doc 1830.15   Ghana. Auditor-General. Report on the account of the Ghana railway and Harbours Administration. Accra. 1956-1957

Afr Doc 1830.20F   Ghana. Department of Agriculture. Annual report. Accra. 1924-1957

Afr Doc 1832.5   Ghana. Department of Cooperation. Annual report. Accra. 1949-1950

Afr Doc 1832.10   Gold Coast (Colony). Department of Cocoa Rehabilitation. Report. Accra. 1949-1950

Afr Doc 1832.15   Ghana. Registrar of Cooperative Societies. Report. Accra. 1959-1960

Afr Doc 1832.20   Ghana. State Cocoa Marketing Board. Annual report and accounts. Accra. 1964+

Afr Doc 1830 - 1855 British Africa - British West Africa - Ghana, Gold Coast - Executive documents - Depts., Bureaus, etc., A-Z (by catchword) - cont.

Afr Doc 1834.5   Ghana. Ministry of Education. Education report. Accra. 1957+

Afr Doc 1835.15   Ghana foreign affairs. Accra. 1,1961+

Afr Doc 1845.5   Ghana. Public Works Department. Annual report. Accra. 1953+

Afr Doc 1845.10   Ghana. Police Service. Annual report. Accra. 1959+

Afr Doc 1848.5   Ghana. Department of Social Welfare and Community Development. Annual report. Accra. 1946+

Afr Doc 1849.5   Ghana. Tema Corporation. Report and accounts. Accra. 1953+

Afr Doc 2302 British Africa - British West Africa - Nigeria - General - General collections - Bibliographies, catalogs, etc.

Afr Doc 2302.5   Library of Congress. General Reference and Bibliography Division. Nigeria; a guide to official publications. Washington, 1966.

Afr Doc 2303 British Africa - British West Africa - Nigeria - General - General collections - Blue books, government manuals, directories

Afr Doc 2303.5   Nigeria. Blue book. Lagos. 1914-1924

Afr Doc 2303.10   Nigeria. Federal staff list. Lagos. 10,1962+

Afr Doc 2303.15   The Nigeria civil service list. Lagos. 1927

Afr Doc 2305 British Africa - British West Africa - Nigeria - General - General collections - Annual reports

Afr Doc 2305.5   Nigeria. Annual report on the social and economic progress of the people of Nigeria. Lagos.

Afr Doc 2305.10F   Nigeria. Commissioner. Annual report on the colony. Lagos.

Afr Doc 2305.15   Nigeria. Commissioner. Annual reports for the western, northern, eastern provinces and the colony. Lagos.

Afr Doc 2307.1 - .199 British Africa - British West Africa - Nigeria - General - Statistics - General compilations

Afr Doc 2307.5   Nigeria. Federal Office of Statistics. Annual abstract of statistics. 1960+

Afr Doc 2307.7   Nigeria. Federal Office of Statistics. Digest of statistics. 11,1962+

Afr Doc 2307.200 - .999 British Africa - British West Africa - Nigeria - General - Statistics - Census

Afr Doc 2307.353   Nigeria. Department of Statistics. Population census of Nigeria. Lagos. 1952-1953

Afr Doc 2307.363.2F   Nigeria. Regional Census Office. Population census of Nigeria, Nov., 1963. 2d ed. Ibadan, 1963.

Afr Doc 2307.363.10F   Nigeria. Federal Census Office. Population census of Nigeria, 1963. Northern region. Lagos, 1965. 5v.

Afr Doc 2308.300 - .499 British Africa - British West Africa - Nigeria - General - Statistics - Labor

Afr Doc 2308.300F   Nigeria. Federal Office of Statistics. Report on employment and ear-nings inquiry, Sept., 1959. Lagos, 1959?

Afr Doc 2308.500 - .699 British Africa - British West Africa - Nigeria - General - Statistics - Industry, manufactures

Afr Doc 2308.524F   Nigeria. Federal Ministry of Research and Information. Estimates. 1962+

Afr Doc 2308.530F   Nigeria. Federal Office of Statistics. Industrial survey. Lagos. 1963+

Afr Doc 2308.700 - .999 British Africa - British West Africa - Nigeria - General - Statistics - Trade

Afr Doc 2308.705   Nigeria. Federal Office of Statistics. Trade report. Lagos. 1958+

Afr Doc 2308.710   Nigeria. Customs Department. Trade statistical abstract. Lagos. 1-7,1911-1915

Afr Doc 2308.715   Nigeria trade summary. Lagos. 1964+

Afr Doc 2308.720   Nigeria. Federal Office of Statistics. Review of external trade. Lagos. 1964

Afr Doc 2309.1 - .299 British Africa - British West Africa - Nigeria - General - Statistics - Budget

Afr Doc 2309.223   Nigeria. Federal Ministry of Finance. Report of the accountant-general. Lagos. 1964+

Afr Doc 2309.300 - .499 British Africa - British West Africa - Nigeria - General - Statistics - National income and accounts, surveys

Afr Doc 2309.300   Nigeria. Federal Office of Statistics. Economic and functional analysis of government accounts. Lagos. 1958+

Afr Doc 2309.305F   Nigeria. Depaartment of Statistics. Urban consumer surveys in Nigeria. Lagos, 1957.

Afr Doc 2309.305.5F   Nigeria. Federal Office of Statistics. Urban Consumer surveys in Nigeria. Lagos, 1963.

Afr Doc 2309.305.10F   Nigeria. Federal Office of Statistics. Urban consumer surveys. Lagos, 1966. 3v.

Afr Doc 2309.310   Nigeria. Federal Audit Depaartment. Report of the Director of Federal Audit on the accounts of the government. Lagos. 1960

Afr Doc 2309.500 - .999 British Africa - British West Africa - Nigeria - General - Statistics - Other

Afr Doc 2309.500   Nigeria. Federal Ministry of Education. Statistics of education in Nigeria. Lagos. 1,1961+

Afr Doc 2309.503   Nigeria. Federal Ministry of Education. Digest of education statistics. Lagos. 1959

Afr Doc 2309.505F   Nigeria. Federal Office of Statistics. Rural economic survey of Nigeria. Lagos. 1966+

Afr Doc 2310 British Africa - British West Africa - Nigeria - General - Legislative documents - Pamphlet volumes

Afr Doc 2310.5   Pamphlet box. Nigeria. Legislative documents.

Afr Doc 2312 British Africa - British West Africa - Nigeria - General - Legislative documents - General

Afr Doc 2312.5F   Nigeria. Legislative Council. Debates. Lagos.

Afr Doc 2312.10   Nigeria. Legislative Council. Sessional paper. 1944-1948

Afr Doc 2312.15   Nigeria. Parliament. Sessional paper. Lagos. 1958+

Afr Doc 2314   British Africa - British West Africa - Nigeria - General - Legislative
documents - House Journal, etc.
    Afr Doc 2314.5   Nigeria. Parliament. House of Representatives. Debates.
        Official report.
    Afr Doc 2314.7   Nigeria. Parliament. House of Representatives.
        Parliamentary debates.
    Afr Doc 2314.205   Nigeria. Parliament. House of Representatives. Public
        Accounts Committee. Minutes of evidence. Lagos. 1960+
    Afr Doc 2314.215   Nigeria. Parliament. House of Representatives. Public
        Accounts Committee. Report. 2,1961+

Afr Doc 2319   British Africa - British West Africa - Nigeria - General - Legislative
documents - Others
    Afr Doc 2319.5   Nigeria. Constitution. The consitution of the Federal
        Republic of Nigeria. Lagos, 1963.
    Afr Doc 2319.15   Nigeria. Federal Ministry of Finance. Budget speech.
        Lagos? 1962+

Afr Doc 2324   British Africa - British West Africa - Nigeria - General - Executive
documents - President
    Afr Doc 2324.5   Nigeria. Governor General. Address by the Governor the the
        Nigerian council. 6,1919+
    Afr Doc 2324.8   Nigeria. Governor General. Address by the Governor to the
        Legislative Council. 1924+

Afr Doc 2330 - 2355   British Africa - British West Africa - Nigeria - General -
Executive documents - Depts., Bureaus, etc., A-Z (by catchword)
    Afr Doc 2330.5   Nigeria. Department of Antiquities. Annual report. Apapa.
        1,1958+
    Afr Doc 2332.5F   Nigeria. Customs Department. Annual report. Lagos.
        1925-1926
    Afr Doc 2332.10F   Nigeria. Federal Ministry of Commerce and Industry. Annual
        report. Lagos. 1959+
    Afr Doc 2332.15F   Nigeria. Federal Ministry of Commerce and Industry. Annual
        report. Lagos. 1958
    Afr Doc 2341.15   Nigeria. Federal Ministry of Labour and Welfare. Social
        Welfare Division. Annual report. Lagos. 1961+
    Afr Doc 2342.5   Nigeria. National Manpower Board. Annual report. Lagos.
        1962+
    Afr Doc 2343.5   Nigeria. Nigerianisation Office. Annual report of the
        Nigerianisation Office. Lagos, 1957.
    Afr Doc 2343.10   Niger Delta Development Board. Annual report. Port
        Harcourt. 1961+
    Afr Doc 2343.20   Nigeria. Petroleum Division. Annual report. Lagos.
        1,1962+
    Afr Doc 2345.10   Nigeria. Federal Public Service Commission. Report.
        Lagos. 1959+
    Afr Doc 2352.3   Nigeria. Federal Ministry of Works and Surveys. Works
        Division. Report. Lagos. 1960+

Afr Doc 2402   British Africa - British West Africa - Nigeria - Northern Nigeria -
General collections - Bibliographies, catalogs, etc.
    Afr Doc 2402.2F   Yakuba, Stephen. Publications of the government of the
        northern region of Nigeria, 1960-1962. Zaria, 1963.

Afr Doc 2403   British Africa - British West Africa - Nigeria - Northern Nigeria -
General collections - Blue books, government manuals, directories
    Afr Doc 2403.5F   Nigeria, Northern. Blue book, 1908-1913. Lagos, 1909.
    Afr Doc 2403.7   Nigeria, Northern. Staff list. Kaduna. 9,1961+

Afr Doc 2405   British Africa - British West Africa - Nigeria - Northern Nigeria -
General collections - Annual reports
    Afr Doc 2405.5   Nigeria, Northern. Provincial annual reports. Kaduna.
        1952+

Afr Doc 2406   British Africa - British West Africa - Nigeria - Northern Nigeria -
General collections - Other
    Afr Doc 2406.5   Northern Nigeria local government yearbook. Zavia.
        2,1964+

Afr Doc 2407.1 - .199   British Africa - British West Africa - Nigeria -
Northern Nigeria - Statistics - General compilations
    Afr Doc 2407.5   Nigeria, Northern. Ministry of Economic Planning.
        Statistical yearbook. Kaduna. 1965+

Afr Doc 2407.200 - .999   British Africa - British West Africa - Nigeria -
Northern Nigeria - Statistics Census
    Afr Doc 2407.352.105
        Nigeria. Department of Statistics. Population census of
        the Northern Region of Nigeria, 1952 Bulletins.
        Lagos, 1954.

Afr Doc 2409.1 - .299   British Africa - British West Africa - Nigeria -
Northern Nigeria - Statistics - Budget
    Afr Doc 2409.5F   Nigeria, Northern. First supplementary estimates of the
        government. Kaduna. 1962+
    Afr Doc 2409.8F   Nigeria, Northern. Estimates of the government. Kaduna.
        1967+

Afr Doc 2409.300 - .499   British Africa - British West Africa - Nigeria -
Northern Nigeria - Statistics - National income and accounts, surveys
    Afr Doc 2409.300   Nigeria, Northern. Accountant General. Report with
        financial statements. Kaduna. 1964+
    Afr Doc 2409.305   Nigeria, Northern. Audit Department. Report of the
        Director of Audit on the accounts of the government.
        1954+

Afr Doc 2409.500 - .999   British Africa - British West Africa - Nigeria -
Northern Nigeria - Statistics - Other
    Afr Doc 2409.505F   Nigeria, Northern. Ministry of Education. Planning and
        Development Division. Classes, enrollments and teachers in
        the primary schools of Northern Nigeria. Kaduna. 2,1965+
    Afr Doc 2409.510F   Nigeria, Northern. Ministry of Education. Planning and
        Development Division. Classes, enrollments and teachers in
        schools and colleges of Northern Nigeria. Kaduna. 1967+

Afr Doc 2412   British Africa - British West Africa - Nigeria - Northern Nigeria -
Legislative documents - General
    Afr Doc 2412.205   Nigeria, Northern. Legislature. Public Accounts Joint
        Committee. Minutes of evidence. Kaduna. 1963+

Afr Doc 2414   British Africa - British West Africa - Nigeria - Northern Nigeria -
Legislative documents - House Journal, etc.
    Afr Doc 2414.5   Nigeria, Northern. Legislature. House of Assembly.
        Parliamentary debates; official report. Kaduna. 1954+

Afr Doc 2416   British Africa - British West Africa - Nigeria - Northern Nigeria -
Legislative documents - Senate Journal, etc.
    Afr Doc 2416.5   Nigeria, Western. House of Chiefs. Debates. Official
        report.
    Afr Doc 2416.10   Nigeria, Northern. Legislature. House of Chiefs.
        Parliamentary debates. Kaduna. 1961+

Afr Doc 2431 - 2456   British Africa - British West Africa - Nigeria - Northern
Nigeria - Executive documents - Depts., Bureaus, etc., A-Z (by catchword)
    Afr Doc 2434.5   Northern Nigeria. Development Corporation. Annual report.
        Kaduna. 10,1964+
    Afr Doc 2434.10   Nigeria. Committee on the Grading of Duty Posts in
        Voluntary Agency Educational Institutions. Report.
        Lagos, 1967.
    Afr Doc 2434.15F   Nigeria, Northern. Delimitation Authority. Report.
        Kaduna. 1965
    Afr Doc 2436.5   Nigeria, Northern. Ministry of Finance. Revenue Division.
        Report by the Commissioner of Revenue. Kaduna. 1962+
    Afr Doc 2438.5   Nigeria, Northern. Ministry of Health. Rural health
        report. Kaduna. 1963+
    Afr Doc 2446.5   Nigeria, Northern. Public Service Commission. Report.
        Kaduna. 1963+
    Afr Doc 2449.5   Nigera, Northern. Ministry of Social Welfare and
        Cooperatives. Annual report on the social welfare
        services. Kaduna. 1961+
    Afr Doc 2453.5   Nigeria, Northern. Ministry of Works. Annual report.
        Kaduna. 1960+

Afr Doc 2500.500 - .599   British Africa - British West Africa - Nigeria -
Southern Nigeria (General Table B) - General documents, etc. - General
annual report
    Afr Doc 2500.505   Nigeria, Southern. Annual reports. Lagos. 1906

Afr Doc 2500.600 - .699   British Africa - British West Africa - Nigeria -
Southern Nigeria (General Table B) - General documents, etc. -
Government manual, handbook, etc.
    Afr Doc 2500.605   Nigeria, Southern. Blue book. Calabar. 1905-1913 9v.

Afr Doc 2501.1 - .199   British Africa - British West Africa - Nigeria -
Southern Nigeria (General Table B) - Legislative documents - General
works
    Afr Doc 2501.5   Nigeria, Southern. Legislative Council. Council papers.
        Lagos. 1909-1911 3v.

Afr Doc 2520.600 - .699   British Africa - British West Africa - Nigeria -
Western Nigeria (General Table B) - General documents, etc. - Government
manual, handbook, etc.
    Afr Doc 2520.605   Nigeria, Western. Stafflist. Ibadan. 1964+

Afr Doc 2520.700 - .719   British Africa - British West Africa - Nigeria -
Western Nigeria (General Table B) - Statistics - General compilations
    Afr Doc 2520.703   Nigeria, Western. Ministry of Economic Planning and Social
        Development. Statistics Division. Abstract of local
        government statistics. Ibadan. 1,1966+
    Afr Doc 2520.705   Nigeria, Western. Ministry of Economic Planning and Social
        Development. Statistics Division. Statistical bulletin.
        Ibadan. 1,1959+

Afr Doc 2520.720 - .799   British Africa - British West Africa - Nigeria -
Western Nigeria (General Table B) - Statistics - Census
    Afr Doc 2520.725   Nigeria. Department of Statistics. Population census of
        the Western region of Nigeria, 1952. Lagos, 1956.
    Afr Doc 2520.725.5
        Nigeria. Department of Statistics. Population census of
        the Western region of Nigeria, 1952. Bulletins.
        Lagos, 1955.

Afr Doc 2520.900 - .929   British Africa - British West Africa - Nigeria -
Western Nigeria (General Table B) - Statistics - Budget
    Afr Doc 2520.905   Nigeria, Western. Estimates (including memorandum).
        1961+

Afr Doc 2520.950 - .999   British Africa - British West Africa - Nigeria -
Western Nigeria (General Table B) - Statistics - Other
    Afr Doc 2520.950F   Nigeria, Western. Ministry of Economic Planning and Social
        Development. Statistics Division. Development plan
        statistics of western group of provinces of Nigeria.
        Ibadan, 1966.
    Afr Doc 2520.955   Nigeria, Western. Ministry of Economic Planning and
        Community Development. Statistics Division. Annual
        abstract of education statistics. 1953+

Afr Doc 2521.1 - .199   British Africa - British West Africa - Nigeria -
Western Nigeria (General Table B) - Legislative documents - General
works
    Afr Doc 2521.5   Nigeria, Western. House of Chiefs. Joint sitting of the
        House of Chiefs and House of Assembly debates. Official
        report. Ibadan. 1,1960+
    Afr Doc 2521.10F   Nigeria, Western. House of Chiefs. Report of the Joint
        Standing Committee on Finance of the Western House of
        Chiefs and of the Western House of Assembly. Ibadan.
        1957+
    Afr Doc 2521.15   Nigeria, Western. Legislature. Sessional paper. Ibadan.
        1955+

Afr Doc 2522.1 - .199   British Africa - British West Africa - Nigeria -
Western Nigeria (General Table B) - Legislative documents - Upper
chamber, Senate, etc. - Journals, debates, etc.
    Afr Doc 2522.5   Nigeria, Western. House of Chiefs. Debates. 1,1952+

Afr Doc 2523.1 - .199   British Africa - British West Africa - Nigeria -
Western Nigeria (General Table B) - Legislative documents - Lower
chamber, House, etc. - Journals, debates, etc.
    Afr Doc 2523.5   Nigeria, Western. House of Assembly. Debates. 1956+

Afr Doc 2524.1 - .499   British Africa - British West Africa - Nigeria -
Western Nigeria (General Table B) - Legislative documents - Statutes,
laws, etc.
    Afr Doc 2524.5   Nigeria, Western. Laws, statutes, etc. Local government
        manual incorporating the Local government law, cop.68, the
        chiefs law, cop.19 staff regulations. Ibadan, 196-.

Afr Doc 2525.1 - .199   British Africa - British West Africa - Nigeria -
Western Nigeria (General Table B) - Executive documents - General works
    Afr Doc 2525.5   Nigeria, Western. Official document. Ibadan. 1962+

Afr Doc 2527.1 - .999   British Africa - British West Africa - Nigeria -
Western Nigeria (General Table B) - Executive documents - Departments,
Bureaus, etc.
    Afr Doc 2527.5   Western Region Housing Corporation. Annual report and
        accounts. Ibadan. 2,1959+
    Afr Doc 2527.10   Nigeria, Western. Marketing Board. Annual report. Ibadan.
        1,1954+

Afr Doc 2540.900 - .929   British Africa - British West Africa - Nigeria -
Midwest Nigeria (General Table B) - Statistics - Budget
    Afr Doc 2540.905   Nigeria, Mid-Western. Estimates (including memorandum and
        budget speech). Benin City. 1964+

Afr Doc 2541.1 - .199   British Africa - British West Africa - Nigeria -
Midwest Nigeria (General Table B) - Legislative documents - General
works
    Afr Doc 2541.5   Nigeria, Mid-Western. Legislature. Joint Sitting of the
        Houses of Chiefs and Assembly. Parliamentary debates.
        Benin City. 1,1964+

Afr Doc 2542.1 - .199   British Africa - British West Africa - Nigeria -
Midwest Nigeria (General Table B) - Legislative documents - Upper
chamber, Senate, etc. - Journals, debates, etc.
    Afr Doc 2542.5   Nigeria, Mid-Western. Legislature. House of Chiefs.
        Parliamentary debates. Benin City. 1,1964+

Afr Doc 2543.1 - .199   British Africa - British West Africa - Nigeria -
Midwest Nigeria (General Table B) - Legislative documents - Lower
chamber, House, etc. - Journals, debates, etc.
    Afr Doc 2543.5   Nigeria, Mid-Western. Legislature. House of Assembly.
        Parliamentary debates. Benin City. 1,1964+

Afr Doc 2547.1 - .999   British Africa - British West Africa - Nigeria -
Midwest Nigeria (General Table B) - Executive documents - Departments,
Bureaus, etc.
    Afr Doc 2547.5   Nigeria, Mid-Western. Housing Corporation. Annual report
        and accounts. Benin City. 1,1963+

Afr Doc 2560.600 - .699   British Africa - British West Africa - Nigeria -
Eastern Nigeria (General Table B) - General documents, etc. - Government
manual, handbook, etc.
    Afr Doc 2560.600   Nigeria, Eastern. Ministry of Information. Know your
        legislators; biographical notes. Enugu, 1963.
    Afr Doc 2560.602   Ajuluchukee, M.C.K. Profiles of the ministers of Eastern
        Nigeria. Enugu, 1960.

Afr Doc 2560.720 - .799   British Africa - British West Africa - Nigeria -
Eastern Nigeria (General Table B) - Statistics - Census
    Afr Doc 2560.725.5
        Nigeria. Department of Statistics. Population census of
        the Eastern Region of Nigeria, 1953. Bulletins.
        Lagos, 1955.

Afr Doc 2560.900 - .929   British Africa - British West Africa - Nigeria -
Eastern Nigeria (General Table B) - Statistics - Budget
    Afr Doc 2560.903F   Nigeria, Eastern. Local government estimates. 1960+
    Afr Doc 2560.905F   Nigeria, Eastern. Memorandum on local government
        estimates. 1957+

Afr Doc 2562.1 - .199   British Africa - British West Africa - Nigeria -
Eastern Nigeria (General Table B) - Legislative documents - Upper
chamber, Senate, etc. - Journals, debates, etc.
    Afr Doc 2562.5   Nigeria, Eastern. House of Chiefs. Parliamentary debates.
        1,1959+

Afr Doc 2563.1 - .199   British Africa - British West Africa - Nigeria -
Eastern Nigeria (General Table B) - Legislative documents - Lower
chamber, House, etc. - Journals, debates, etc.
    Afr Doc 2563.5   Nigeria, Eastern. House of Assembly. Debates. 1,1956+

Afr Doc 2565.1 - .199   British Africa - British West Africa - Nigeria -
Eastern Nigeria (General Table B) - Executive documents - General works
    Afr Doc 2565.5   Nigeria, Eastern. Official document. 1958+

Afr Doc 2614   British Africa - British West Africa - British Cameroons - Legislative
documents - House Journal, etc.
    Afr Doc 2614.5   Cameroons, Southern. House of Assembly. Debates. Buea.
        1931-1959

Afr Doc 2631 - 2656   British Africa - British West Africa - British Cameroons -
Executive documents - Depts., Bureaus, etc., A-Z (by catchword)
    Afr Doc 2643.5   Cameroons, Southern. Marketing Board. Annual report.
        Lagos, Nigeria. 1959+

Afr Doc 2703   British Africa - British West Africa - Seychelles - General
collections - Blue books, government manuals, directories
    Afr Doc 2703.5F   Seychelles. Blue book. 10v.

Afr Doc 2707.200 - .999   British Africa - British West Africa - Seychelles -
Statistics - Census
    Afr Doc 2707.360   Seychelles. Population census of the Seychelles Colony.
        Victoria? 1961?

Afr Doc 2708.700 - .999   British Africa - British West Africa - Seychelles -
Statistics - Trade
    Afr Doc 2708.700   Seychelles. Trade report. Victoria. 1963+

Afr Doc 2709.1 - .299   British Africa - British West Africa - Seychelles -
Statistics - Budget
    Afr Doc 2709.10   Seychelles. Approved estimates of expenditure. Victoria.
        1964+
    Afr Doc 2709.15   Seychelles. Approved estimates of revenue. Victoria.
        1964+

Afr Doc 2709.300 - .499   British Africa - British West Africa - Seychelles -
Statistics - National income and accounts, surveys
    Afr Doc 2709.300   Seychelles. Treasury. Annual report by the Accountant
        General. 1963+

Afr Doc 2731 - 2756   British Africa - British West Africa - Seychelles -
Executive documents - Depts., Bureaus, etc., A-Z (by catchword)
    Afr Doc 2731.5   Seychelles. Department of Agriculture. Annual report.
        Victoria. 1964+
    Afr Doc 2731.10   Seychelles. Audit Department. Report on the accounts of
        the Colony of Seychelles. Victoria. 1960+
    Afr Doc 2733.5   Seychelles. Department of Cooperative Development. Annual
        report. Victoria. 1965+
    Afr Doc 2733.10   Seychelles. Registry of Deeds and Civil Status Department.
        Annual report. Victoria. 1965+
    Afr Doc 2735.5   Seychelles. Department of Education. Report. Victoria.
        1958+
    Afr Doc 2739.5   Seychelles. Income Tax Department. Annual report.
        Victoria. 1957+
    Afr Doc 2742.5F   Seychelles. Labour and Welfare Department. Report.
        Victoria. 1961-1966
    Afr Doc 2742.10   Seychelles. Labour Department. Report. Mahe. 1,1967+
    Afr Doc 2743.5F   Seychelles. Medical Department. Report. Victoria. 1964+
    Afr Doc 2746.5   Seychelles. Port and Marine Department. Triennial report.
        Victoria. 1961+
    Afr Doc 2746.10F   Seychelles. Public Works Department. Annual report.
        Victoria. 1966+
    Afr Doc 2746.15   Seychelles. Police Force. Annual report. Victoria. 1966+
    Afr Doc 2750.5F   Seychelles. Department of Tourism, Information, and
        Broadcasting. Report. Victoria. 1960+
    Afr Doc 2750.7F   Seychelles. Department of Tourism, Information, and
        Broadcasting. Annual report. Victoria. 1966+
    Afr Doc 2753.5   Seychelles. Welfare Department. Report. Victoria. 1968+

Afr Doc 2803   British Africa - British West Africa - Mauritius - General collections -
Blue books, government manuals, directories
    Afr Doc 2803.5F   Mauritius. Blue book. 8v.

Afr Doc 2805   British Africa - British West Africa - Mauritius - General collections -
Annual reports
    Afr Doc 2805.5   Great Britain. Colonial Office. Census Commissioner.
        Mauritius. London. 1964

Afr Doc 2806   British Africa - British West Africa - Mauritius - General collections -
Other
    Afr Doc 2806.5   The Mauritius almanac and commercial handbook. Port Louis.
        1923-1941 10v.

Afr Doc 2807.1 - .199   British Africa - British West Africa - Mauritius -
Statistics - General compilations
    Afr Doc 2807.5   Mauritius. Central Statistical Office. Year book of
        statistics. 13,1958+
    Afr Doc 2807.10   Mauritius. Central Statistical Office. Quarterly digest of
        statistics. 1-6,1961-1966

Afr Doc 2807.200 - .999   British Africa - British West Africa - Mauritius -
Statistics - Census
    Afr Doc 2807.344F   Mauritius. Final report on the census enumeration made in
        the colony of Mauritius. Port Louis, 1948.
    Afr Doc 2807.352F   Mauritius. Census 1952 of Mauritius and of its
        dependencies. Port Louis, 1953. 3 pam.
    Afr Doc 2807.362F   Mauritius. 1962 population census of Mauritius and its
        dependencies. Port Louis, 1964.
    Afr Doc 2807.364F   Mauritius. Central Statistical Office. The census of
        industrial production, 1964. Port Louis, 1965.

Afr Doc 2808.1 - .299   British Africa - British West Africa - Mauritius -
Statistics - Vital, population, etc.
    Afr Doc 2808.5   Mauritius. Central Statistical Office. Natality and
        fertility in Mauritius. Port Louis? 1956?

Afr Doc 2808.300 - .499   British Africa - British West Africa - Mauritius -
Statistics - Labor
    Afr Doc 2808.305F   Mauritius. Central Statistical Office. Survey of
        employment and earnings in large establishments. Rose
        Hill. 1,1966

Afr Doc 2809.1 - .299   British Africa - British West Africa - Mauritius -
Statistics - Budget
    Afr Doc 2809.89   Mauritius. Estimates as passed by the Legislative
        Assembly. Port Louis. 1963+
    Afr Doc 2809.90   Mauritius. Memorandum on estimates. Port Louis. 1965+
    Afr Doc 2809.95   Mauritius. Draft capital estimates. Port Louis. 1960+
    Afr Doc 2809.99   Mauritius. Financial report for the year. Port Louis.
        1962+
    Afr Doc 2809.100   Mauritius. Draft estimates. Port Louis. 1959+
    Afr Doc 2809.100.5
        Mauritius. Memorandum on draft estimates. Port Louis.
    Afr Doc 2809.115   Mauritius. Capital budget. Port Louis. 1966+

Afr Doc 2809.300 - .499   British Africa - British West Africa - Mauritius -
Statistics - National income and accounts, surveys
    Afr Doc 2809.300   Mauritius. Central Statistical Office. Abstract of
        economic statistics. Port Louis? 1965?
    Afr Doc 2809.305   Mauritius. Central Statistical Office. The national income
        and national accounts of Mauritius, 1948-1954. Port
        Louis, 1956.

Afr Doc 2812   British Africa - British West Africa - Mauritius - Legislative   s
ocuments - General
    Afr Doc 2812.10   Mauritius. Legislative Council. Debates. Port Louis.
        2-4,1957-1963
    Afr Doc 2812.12   Mauritius. Legislative Assembly. Debates. Port Louis.
        1,1964+

Afr Doc 2822   British Africa - British West Africa - Mauritius - Executive documents -
General
    Afr Doc 2822.5   Mauritius. Annual departmental reports. Port Louis.
        1951+

Afr Doc 2826   British Africa - British West Africa - Mauritius - Executive documents -
Special
    Afr Doc 2826.5   Mauritius. Report on district administration in Mauritius.
        Port Louis. 1949

Afr Doc 2831 - 2856   British Africa - British West Africa - Mauritius -
Executive documents - Depts., Bureaus, etc., A-Z (by catchword)
    Afr Doc 2831.5   Mauritius. Colonial Audit Department. Report of the
        Principal Auditor on the accounts of the Colony of
        Mauritius and the Mauritius government railways. Port
        Louis. 1946-1949

Afr Doc 2831 - 2856   **British Africa - British West Africa - Mauritius -**
Executive documents - Depts., Bureaus, etc., A-Z (by catchword) - cont.

Afr Doc 2833.5	Mauritius. Registrar of Co-operative Credit Societies. Annual report of the cooperative credit societies.
Afr Doc 2835.5	Mauritius. Education Department. Annual report. Port Louis. 1945-1946
Afr Doc 2835.5.5	Mauritius. Education Department. Triennial survey of education in Mauritius. Port Louis. 1958+
Afr Doc 2838.5	Mauritius. Central Housing Authority. Report on the activities. Rose Hill. 1,1960+
Afr Doc 2846.5	Mauritius. Public Relations Office. Annual report. Port Louis. 1947-1948
Afr Doc 2846.10	Mauritius. Public Assistance Department. Annual report. Port Louis. 1948-1949
Afr Doc 2846.15	Mauritius. Public Works and Surveys Department. Annual report for the financial year. Port Louis. 1946-1948
Afr Doc 2848.5	Mauritius. Reabsorption Office. Report on the activities. Port Louis. 1947-1949
Afr Doc 2850.5	Mauritius. Transport Control Board. Annual report. 1949

Afr Doc 3002   **British Africa - British East Africa - General - General collections -**
Bibliographies, catalogs, etc.

Afr Doc 3002.5	Library of Congress. African Section. Official publications of British East Africa. Washington, 1960-1963.

Afr Doc 3005   **British Africa - British East Africa - General - General collections -**
Annual reports

Afr Doc 3005.5	East African Common Services Organization. Annual report. London. 1961+

Afr Doc 3007.1 - .199   **British Africa - British East Africa - General -**
Statistics - General compilations

Afr Doc 3007.4	East Africa High Commission. East African Statistical Department. Quarterly economic and statistical bulletin. 3-52,1949-1961 3v.
Afr Doc 3007.5	East African Common Services Organization. East African Statistical Department. Economic and statistical review. 1,1961+

Afr Doc 3008.700 - .999   **British Africa - British East Africa - General -**
Statistics - Trade

Afr Doc 3008.700	East African Common Services Organization. East African Customs and Excise Department. Annual trade report of Tanganyika, Uganda and Kenya. Mombasa. 1962+ 2v.

Afr Doc 3009.500 - .999   **British Africa - British East Africa - General -**
Statistics - Other

Afr Doc 3009.500	East African Common Services Organization. East African Statistical Department. East Africa insurance statistics. Nairobi. 1963+

Afr Doc 3012   **British Africa - British East Africa - General - Legislative documents -**
General

Afr Doc 3012.5	East African Common Services Organization. Central Legislative Assembly. Proceedings of the debates. 1,1962+

Afr Doc 3019   **British Africa - British East Africa - General - Legislative documents -**
Others

Afr Doc 3019.5	Kenya. Treaties. Treaty for East African co-operation. Nairobi, 1967.

Afr Doc 3031 - 3056   **British Africa - British East Africa - General - Executive**
documents - Depts., Bureaus, etc., A-Z (by catchword)

Afr Doc 3039.5	East African Industrial Research Organization. Annual report. Nairobi. 1959+
Afr Doc 3049.5	East Africa High Commission. East African Statistical Department. Annual report. Nairobi. 1950+

Afr Doc 3103   **British Africa - British East Africa - Zanzibar - General collections -**
Blue books, government manuals, directories

Afr Doc 3103.5F	Zanzibar. Blue book. 4v.

Afr Doc 3105   **British Africa - British East Africa - Zanzibar - General collections -**
Annual reports

Afr Doc 3105.5	Zanzibar. District Administration. Biennial report. Zanzibar. 1,1961+

Afr Doc 3109.1 - .299   **British Africa - British East Africa - Zanzibar -**
Statistics - Budget

Afr Doc 3109.4F	Zanzibar. Estimates of revenue and expenditure of the Zanzibar Protectorate. Zanzibar. 1961-1964
Afr Doc 3109.5	Tanzania. Revised approved estimates of the revenue and expenditure for Zanzibar. Zanzibar. 1,1964+

Afr Doc 3109.300 - .499   **British Africa - British East Africa - Zanzibar -**
Statistics - National income and accounts, surveys

Afr Doc 3109.300	Zanzibar. Report on the accounts of the Zanzibar Protectorate. Zanzibar. 1953-1957

Afr Doc 3112   **British Africa - British East Africa - Zanzibar - Legislative**
documents - General

Afr Doc 3112.5F	Zanzibar. Papers laid before the Legislative Council.

Afr Doc 3131 - 3156   **British Africa - British East Africa - Zanzibar - Executive**
documents - Depts., Bureaus, etc., A-Z (by catchword)

Afr Doc 3149.5	Zanibar. Social Welfare Department. Annual report. Zanibar. 1961+

Afr Doc 3202   **British Africa - British East Africa - Kenya - General collections -**
Bibliographies, catalogs, etc.

Afr Doc 3202.64F	Kenya. Archives. Archives microfilming programme. Nairobi, 1964.

Afr Doc 3203   **British Africa - British East Africa - Kenya - General collections -**
Blue books, government manuals, directories

Afr Doc 3203.3F	Kenya. Blue book.
Afr Doc 3203.10F	Kenya. Directory of the govenment. Nairobi. 1965+
Afr Doc 3203.15	Kenya. Stafflist. Nairobi. 1957-1962
Afr Doc 3203.20	Kenya directory of the diplomatic corps. Nairobi. 1966

Afr Doc 3205   **British Africa - British East Africa - Kenya - General collections -**
Annual reports

Afr Doc 3205.5	Kenya; report for the year. London. 1947-1962 4v.

Afr Doc 3207.1 - .199   **British Africa - British East Africa - Kenya -**
Statistics - General compilations

Afr Doc 3207.4	East Africa High Commission. East Africa Statistical Department. Kenya Unit. Statistical abstract. Nairobi.
Afr Doc 3207.5	Kenya. Ministry of Economic Planning and Development. Statistics Division. Statistical abstract. Nairobi. 1,1961
Afr Doc 3207.10	Kenya statistical digest. Nairobi. 1,1963+

Afr Doc 3207.200 - .999   **British Africa - British East Africa - Kenya -**
Statistics - Census

Afr Doc 3207.331	Kenya. Census Office. Report on the non-native census enumeration made in the colony and protectorate of Kenya. Nairobi, 1932.
Afr Doc 3207.359.10	East Africa. High Commission. East Africa Statistical Department. Kenya Unit. Agricultural census 1959 (non African). Nairobi? 1960.
Afr Doc 3207.360	Kenya. Economics and Statistics Division. Kenya African agricultural sample census, 1960-1961. Nairobi, 1962.
Afr Doc 3207.361	Kenya. Economics and Statistics Division. Agriculture census, 1961. Nairobi, 1961.
Afr Doc 3207.362	Kenya. Ministry of Finance and Economic Planning Kenya Population Census, 1962. Nairobi? 1964.
Afr Doc 3207.362.5F	Kenya. Economics and Statistics Division. Population census, 1962. Nairobi? 1964.
Afr Doc 3207.362.5.5F	Kenya. Economics and Statistics Division. Kenya agricultural census, 1962, schedualed areas and coastal strip. n.p., 1963.
Afr Doc 3207.362.10	Morgan, W.T.W. Population of Kenya; density and distribution; a geographical introduction to the Kenya population census, 1962. Nairobi, 1966.
Afr Doc 3207.363	Kenya. Economics and Statistics Division. Census of industrial production, 1963. Nairobi, 1965.
Afr Doc 3207.364	Kenya. Economics and Statistics Division. Agriculture census, 1964; IV, large farm areas. Nairobi, 1965?

Afr Doc 3208.300 - .499   **British Africa - British East Africa - Kenya -**
Statistics - Labor

Afr Doc 3208.375	Kenya. Economis and Statistics Division. Reported employment and earnings in Kenya.
Afr Doc 3208.468F	Kenya. Directorate of Planning. The pattern of income. Nairobi, 1964.

Afr Doc 3208.700 - .999   **British Africa - British East Africa - Kenya -**
Statistics - Trade

Afr Doc 3208.700	Kenya. Economics and Statistics Division. Survey of distribution, 1960. Nairobi. 1963
Afr Doc 3208.705	Kenya. Customs Department. Trade report of Kenya and Uganda. 1928-1948

Afr Doc 3209.1 - .299   **British Africa - British East Africa - Kenya -**
Statistics - Budget

Afr Doc 3209.1	Kenya. Development estimates. 1958+
Afr Doc 3209.5	Kenya. Ministry for Finance and Development. Budget. Nairobi. 1959+
Afr Doc 3209.10	Kenya. Estimates of revenue. Nairobi. 1,1958+
Afr Doc 3209.15	Kenya. Estimates of expenditure. Nairobi. 1,1958+
Afr Doc 3209.20	Kenya. Estimates of recurrent expenditure. Nairobi? 1963+
Afr Doc 3209.30	Kenya. African District Councils. Approved estimates of revenue and expenditure. Nairobi. 1962+
Afr Doc 3209.112	Kenya. The appropriation accounts. Nairobi. 1957+

Afr Doc 3209.300 - .499   **British Africa - British East Africa - Kenya -**
Statistics - National income and accounts, surveys

Afr Doc 3209.300	Kenya. Economics and Statistics Division. Economic survey. 1961+

Afr Doc 3209.500 - .999   **British Africa - British East Africa - Kenya -**
Statistics - Other

Afr Doc 3209.505	Kenya. Department of Agriculture. Agricultural census. Annual report. Nairobi. 6-15,1925-1934 2v.

Afr Doc 3212   **British Africa - British East Africa - Kenya - Legislative documents -**
General

Afr Doc 3212.2	Kenya. Legislative Council. Debates; official report. Nairobi. 28-91,1947-1963 51v.
Afr Doc 3212.15	Kenya. Council of State. Annual report. Nairobi. 1958+
Afr Doc 3212.20	Kenya. Public Accounts Committee. Epitome of reports and the treasury memoranda thereon and an index. Nairobi. 1947-1954
Afr Doc 3212.25F	Kenya. Legislative Council. Minutes of the proceedings. 1920-1923
Afr Doc 3212.30F	Kenya. Legislative Council. Record of the proceedings. 1923
Afr Doc 3212.35	Kenya. Legislative Council. Sessional paper. 1947+
Afr Doc 3212.205	Kenya. Public Accounts Committee. Report on the governmetn of Kenya accounts. Nairobi. 1947+
Afr Doc 3212.210	Kenya. Public Accounts Committee. Evidence on the report of the Public Accounts Committee on the Government of Kenya accounts. Nairobi. 1965+

Afr Doc 3214   **British Africa - British East Africa - Kenya - Legislative documents -**
House Journal, etc.

Afr Doc 3214.2	Kenya. National Assembly. House of Representatives. Official report. Nairobi. 1,1963+ 11v.

Afr Doc 3216   **British Africa - British East Africa - Kenya - Legislative documents -**
Senate Journal, etc.

Afr Doc 3216.2	Kenya. National Assembly. Senate. Official report. Nairobi. 1,1963+

Afr Doc 3219   **British Africa - British East Africa - Kenya - Legislative documents -**
Others

Afr Doc 3219.5	Kenya. Constitution. The Constitution of Kenya. Nairobi, 1969.

Afr Doc 3224 British Africa - British East Africa - Kenya - Executive documents - President
Afr Doc 3224.5 Kenya. President. President's circular. Nairobi. 1967+

Afr Doc 3226 British Africa - British East Africa - Kenya - Executive documents - Special
Afr Doc 3226.5 Kenya. Social development report. Nairobi. 1956-1957

Afr Doc 3231 - 3256 British Africa - British East Africa - Kenya - Executive documents - Depts., Bureaus, etc., A-Z (by catchword)
Afr Doc 3231.5F Kenya. Native Affairs Department. Annual report. 3v.
Afr Doc 3231.10 Kenya. Report on native affairs.
Afr Doc 3231.15 Kenya. African Affairs Department. Annual report.
Afr Doc 3231.20 Kenya. Ministry of Agriculture, Animal Husbandry and Water Resources. Three-year report. Nairobi. 1958+
Afr Doc 3233.5 Kenya. Civil Service Commission. Report on the working of the Civil Service Commission.
Afr Doc 3233.10 Kenya. Department of Co-operative Development. Annual report.
Afr Doc 3233.15 Kenya. Central Land Board. A review of the activities of the Land Development and Settlement Board. Nairobi. 1961+
Afr Doc 3233.20 Kenya. Central Land Board. Annual report. Nairobi. 1963+
Afr Doc 3233.25 Kenya. Registrar of Co-operation Societies. Annual report. Nairobi. 1953-1957
Afr Doc 3233.30 Kenya. Ministry of Community Development. Annual report. Nairobi. 1957+
Afr Doc 3233.35 Kenya. Department of Community Development and Rehabilitation. Annual report. Nairobi. 1951-1955
Afr Doc 3234.5 Kenya. Development and Reconstruction Authority. Annual report.
Afr Doc 3234.10 Kenya. Development and Reconstruction Authority. Quarterly report.
Afr Doc 3236.5 Kenya. Ministry of Finance and Development. Report on the progress of development projects.
Afr Doc 3236.10 Kenya. Forest Department. Annual report. 1964+
Afr Doc 3237.5 Kenya. Game Department. Annual report. 1953-1954
Afr Doc 3238.5 Kenya. Ministry of Health and Social Affairs. Annual report. 1960+
Afr Doc 3238.15 Kenya. Ministry of Housing. Annual report. Nairobi. 1,1958+
Afr Doc 3238.20 Kenya. Central Housing Board. Annual report. 1964+
Afr Doc 3239.3 Kenya. Department of Information. Annual report. Nairobi. 1955+
Afr Doc 3239.5 Kenya. Information Services. Annual report. 1960+
Afr Doc 3239.10 Kenya. Ministry of Information, Broadcasting and Tourism. Annual report.
Afr Doc 3239.15 Kenya. Department of Immigration. Annual report.
Afr Doc 3239.30 Kenya. Inland Revenue Department. Annual report. Nairobi. 1953-1954
Afr Doc 3242.5 Kenya. Lands Department. Annual report.
Afr Doc 3242.5.10 Kenya. Department of Lands. Annual report. Nairobi. 1926
Afr Doc 3242.5.15 Kenya. Ministry of Lands and Settlement. Annual report of the Commissioner. Nairobi. 1938
Afr Doc 3242.5.20 Kenya. Department of Lands, Mines and Surveys. Annual report. Nairobi. 1945
Afr Doc 3242.7 Kenya. Department of Local Government, Lands and Settlement. Annual report of the commissioner. Nairobi. 1930-1934
Afr Doc 3242.10 Kenya. Ministry of Local Government. Report of the Permanent Secretary for Local Government. 1948-1950
Afr Doc 3242.15 Kenya. Ministry of Local Government. Report of Nairobi Standing Committee. Nairobi. 1964
Afr Doc 3242.20 Kenya. Local Government. Loans Authority. Annual report. 1964+
Afr Doc 3242.25 Kenya. Ministry of Labour. Annual report. Nairobi. 1965+
Afr Doc 3242.30 Kenya. Ministry of Labour and Housing. Housing Section. Annual report. Nairobi? 1961
Afr Doc 3246.5 Kenya. Printing and Stationery Department. Annual report.
Afr Doc 3246.8 Kenya. Public Service Commission. Report on the working of the Public Service Commission. Nairobi. 1,1963+
Afr Doc 3246.15 Kenya. Public Works Department. Report. Nairobi. 1935-1956
Afr Doc 3248.5 Kenya. Department of the Registrar-General. Annual report of the Registrar-General.
Afr Doc 3248.10F Kenya. Road Authority. Annual report. Nairobi. 1955+
Afr Doc 3249.5 Kenya. Survey of Kenya. Administration report.
Afr Doc 3249.10 Kenya. Department of Settlement. Annual report.
Afr Doc 3250.5 Kenya. Tea Development Authority. Annual report and accounts. Nairobi. 1965+
Afr Doc 3253.5F Kenya. Water Development Department. Annual report. Nairobi. 1965+

Afr Doc 3271 - 3296 British Africa - British East Africa - Kenya - Local documents - Provinces, cities, etc., A-Z
Afr Doc 3284.1.73 East Africa High Commission. Kenya; sample population census of Nairobi, 1957-1958, an experiment on sampling methods. Nairobi, 1958.
Afr Doc 3284.1.75 East Africa High Commission. East African Statistical Department. Kenya Unit. The patterns of income, expenditure and consumption of Africans in Nairobi, 1957-1958. Nairobi, 1959.

Afr Doc 3302 British Africa - British East Africa - Uganda - General collections - Bibliographies, catalogs, etc.
Afr Doc 3302.5 Uganda. Catalogue of government publications published prior to 1st January, 1965. Entebbe, 1966?

Afr Doc 3303 British Africa - British East Africa - Uganda - General collections - Blue books, government manuals, directories
Afr Doc 3303.5F Uganda. Blue book. 9v.
Afr Doc 3303.10 Uganda government directory. Entebbe. 27,1965+
Afr Doc 3303.15 Uganda. Ministry of Foreign Affairs. List of diplomatic missions and other foreign and Commonwealth representatives in Uganda. Entebbe. 1965+

Afr Doc 3305 British Africa - British East Africa - Uganda - General collections - Annual reports
Afr Doc 3305.5 Uganda. Annual reports on the Kingdom of Buganda, Eastern Province, Western Province and Northern Province. Entebbe. 1947+

Afr Doc 3307.1 - .199 British Africa - British East Africa - Uganda - Statistics - General compilations
Afr Doc 3307.5 Uganda. Ministry of Planning and Economic Development. Statistics Division. Statistical abstract. Entebbe. 1957+ 2v.
Afr Doc 3307.10 Uganda quarterly digest of statistics. Entebbe. 1,1965+

Afr Doc 3307.200 - .999 British Africa - British East Africa - Uganda - Statistics - Census
Afr Doc 3307.321 Uganda. Census returns, 1921. Uganda, 1921.
Afr Doc 3307.348 Uganda. Report on the census of the non-native population of Uganda Protectorate. Nairobi, 1953.
Afr Doc 3307.348.10 East Africa High Commission. East African Statistical Department. African population of Uganda Protectorate; geographical and tribal studies. Nairobi, 1950.
Afr Doc 3307.359 East Africa High Commission. East African Statistical Department. Uganda census, 1959; non-African population. Nairobi, 1960.
Afr Doc 3307.359.5 East Africa High Commission. East African Statistical Department. Uganda census, 1959; African population. Entebbe, 1961.
Afr Doc 3307.359.10 East Africa High Commission. East African Statistical Department. Uganda: General African Census, 1959. Nairobi, 1960. 2v.
Afr Doc 3307.362 Uganda. Ministry of Agriculture and Co-operatives. Report on Uganda census of agriculture. Entebbe. 1966

Afr Doc 3308.300 - .499 British Africa - British East Africa - Uganda - Statistics - Labor
Afr Doc 3308.305F Uganda. Ministry of Planning and Economic Development. Statistics Division. Enumeration of employees. Entebbe. 1964+

Afr Doc 3308.500 - .699 British Africa - British East Africa - Uganda - Statistics - Industry, manufactures
Afr Doc 3308.510 Uganda. Ministry of Planning and Community Development. Statistics Division. Survey of industrial production. Entebbe. 1963+
Afr Doc 3308.512 Uganda. Ministry of Planning and Economic Development. Statistics Division. Survey of industrial production. Building and construction. Entebbe. 1964

Afr Doc 3308.700 - .999 British Africa - British East Africa - Uganda - Statistics - Trade
Afr Doc 3308.705F Uganda. Ministry of Economic Development. Statistics Branch. The external trade of Uganda, 1950-1960. Entebbe, 1962.

Afr Doc 3309.1 - .299 British Africa - British East Africa - Uganda - Statistics - Budget
Afr Doc 3309.5 Uganda. Ministry of Finance. Budget speech delivered in the National Assembly by the Minister of Finance. Entebbe. 1963+
Afr Doc 3309.7 Uganda. Ministry of Finance. Background to the budget. 1955+
Afr Doc 3309.10 Uganda. Estimates of recurrent expenditure. Entebbe. 1964+
Afr Doc 3309.15 Uganda. Estimates of development expenditure. Entebbe. 1964+
Afr Doc 3309.189 Uganda. National Assembly. Estimates of expenditure. Entebbe. 1956+ 2v.
Afr Doc 3309.189.5 Uganda. Financial summary and revenue estimates. Entebbe. 1961+
Afr Doc 3309.227 Harris, Douglas Gordon. Development in Uganda, 1947 to 1956. Wisbech?, Eng., 1956.

Afr Doc 3309.300 - .499 British Africa - British East Africa - Uganda - Statistics - National income and accounts, surveys
Afr Doc 3309.305 Uganda. Controller and Auditor General. The public accounts of the government of Uganda together with the report thereon by the Controller and Auditor General. Entebbe. 1963+
Afr Doc 3309.310 Uganda. Controller and Auditor General. Report on the accounts. Entebbe. 1947+
Afr Doc 3309.315F Uganda. Ministry of planning and Economic Development. Statistics Division. The government accounts of Uganda. Entebbe. 1,1959+

Afr Doc 3312 British Africa - British East Africa - Uganda - Legislative documents - General
Afr Doc 3312.20 Uganda. National Assembly. Proceedings. Official report. 1951+ 31v.
Afr Doc 3312.25 Uganda. National Assembly. Parliamentary debates. Official report. 1,1962+ 6v.
Afr Doc 3312.30 Uganda. National Assembly. Sessional paper. Entebbe. 1948+

Afr Doc 3319 British Africa - British East Africa - Uganda - Legislative documents - Others
Afr Doc 3319.5 Uganda. Constitution. The Constitution of Uganda, 15th April, 1966. Entebbe, 1966.
Afr Doc 3319.6 Urganda. Constitutional Committe. Report, 1959 and Supplementary Report 1960. n.p., n.d. 2 pam.
Afr Doc 3319.10 Uganda. Constitution. The govenment proposals for a new Constitution, 9th June, 1967. Entebbe, 1967.
Afr Doc 3319.15 Uganda. Constitution. The constitution of the Republic of Uganda. Entebbe, 1967?

Afr Doc 3326 British Africa - British East Africa - Uganda - Executive documents - Special
Afr Doc 3326.5 Uganda. Annual development report. Entebbe. 1947

Afr Doc 3331 - 3356 British Africa - British East Africa - Uganda - Executive documents - Depts., Bureaus, etc., A-Z (by catchword)
Afr Doc 3331.5 Uganda. Department of the Administrator General. Annual report. Entebbe. 1947+
Afr Doc 3331.10 Uganda. Agriculture Department. Annual report. Entebbe. 1947-1956
Afr Doc 3331.15 Uganda. Controller and Auditor General. Report. Entebbe. 1947+
Afr Doc 3333.5 Uganda. Department of Community Development. Annual report. Entebbe. 1952+

Afr Doc 3331 - 3356 **British Africa - British East Africa - Uganda - Executive documents - Depts., Bureaus, etc., A-Z (by catchword) - cont.**

Afr Doc 3333.10   Uganda. Civil reabsorption. Progress report. Entebbe. 1947-1948

Afr Doc 3333.15   Uganda. Ministry of Commerce and Industry. Annual report. Entebbe. 1960+

Afr Doc 3335.5   Uganda. Economic Development Commission. Report. 1956+

Afr Doc 3339.5   Uganda. Department of Information. Annual report. Entebbe. 1953+

Afr Doc 3343.5   Uganda. Department of Geological Survey and Mines. Mines Division. Annual report. Entebbe. 1961+

Afr Doc 3346.5   Uganda. Printing Department. Annual report. Entebbe. 1939-1947

Afr Doc 3346.10   Uganda. Department of Public Relations and Social Welfare. Annual report. Entebbe. 1947-1948

Afr Doc 3346.15   Uganda. Public Accounts Committee. Report on the protectorate's accounts. Entebbe. 1951

Afr Doc 3349.3   Tanganyika. Social Development Department. Annual report. 1959+

Afr Doc 3349.5   Uganda. Ministry of Social Development. Annual report. Entebbe. 1959+

Afr Doc 3371 - 3396 **British Africa - British East Africa - Uganda - Local documents - Provinces, cities, etc., A-Z**

Afr Doc 3376.5F   East Africa High Commission. East African Statistical Department. Uganda Unit. The patterns of income, expenditure...of workers in Fort Portal, February 1960. Entebbe, 1960.

Afr Doc 3377.5F   Uganda. Ministry of Economic Development. Statistics Branch. The patterns of income, expenditure and consumption of African unskilled workers in Gulu, February 1961. Entebbe, 1961.

Afr Doc 3380.5F   Uganda. Ministry of Planning and Economic Development. Statistics Division. The patterns of income expenditure and consumption of African unskilled workers in Jinga. Entebbe. 1,1952+

Afr Doc 3381.5F   East Africa High Commission. East African Statistical Department. Uganda Unit. The patterns of income, expenditure, unskilled workers in Kampala. 1950+

Afr Doc 3383.5F   East Africa High Commission. East African Statistical Department. Uganda Unit. The patterns of income, expenditure and consumption of African unskilled workers in Mbale, February 1958. Entebbe. 1958

Afr Doc 3402 **British Africa - British East Africa - Tanganyika and Tanzania - General collections - Bibliographies, catalogs, etc.**

Afr Doc 3402.5   Tanzania. Government publications. Dar es Salaam. 1961+

Afr Doc 3403 **British Africa - British East Africa - Tanganyika and Tanzania - General collections - Blue books, government manuals, directories**

Afr Doc 3403.5   Tanzania. Staff list. Dar es Salaam. 1965+

Afr Doc 3407.1 - .199 **British Africa - British East Africa - Tanganyika and Tanzania - Statistics - General compilations**

Afr Doc 3407.5   Tanganyika. Treasury. Central Statistical Bureau. Statistical abstract. 1959+

Afr Doc 3407.10   Tanzania. Central Statistical Bureau. Statistical abstract. Dar es Salaam. 1,1964+

Afr Doc 3407.200 - .999 **British Africa - British East Africa - Tanganyika and Tanzania - Statistics - Census**

Afr Doc 3407.321   Tanganyika. Non-native census, 1921, report. Report on the native census, 1921. Dar es Salaam, 1921. 2 pam.

Afr Doc 3407.331F   Tanganyika. Secretariat. Census of the native population of Tanganyika territory, 1931. Dar es Salaam, 1932.

Afr Doc 3407.348.10   East Africa High Commission. East African Statistical Department. African population of Tanganyika Territory; geographical and tribal studies. Source: East African population census, 1948. Nairobi, 1950.

Afr Doc 3407.352   East Africa High Commission. East African Statistical Department. Report on the census of the non-African population taken on the night of 13 february 1952. Dar es Salaam, 1954.

Afr Doc 3407.357   East African High Commission. East African Statistical Department. Report on the census of the non-African population taken 20-21 February 1957. Dar es Salaam, 1958.

Afr Doc 3407.357.5   Tanganyika. Treasury. Central Statistical Bureau. African Census report, 1957. Dar es Salaam, 1963.

Afr Doc 3407.357.10   East Africa High Commission. East African Statistical Department. General African census August 1957. Tribal analysis. Nairobi, 1958.

Afr Doc 3407.357.15   East Africa High Commission. East African Statistical Department. Tanganyika population census, 1957. Dar es Salaam, 1958. 2 pam.

Afr Doc 3407.361.10   Tanzania. Central Statistical Bureau. Census of industrial production in Tanganyika. Tanganiyika, 1961.

Afr Doc 3407.362F   Tanganyika. Treasury. Central Statistical Bureau. Census of large scale commercial farming in Tanganyika, October 1962. Dar es Salaam, 1963.

Afr Doc 3407.367   Tanzania. Central Census Office. Summary of procedures in the 1967 Tanzania population census. Dar es Salaam, 1968.

Afr Doc 3408.300 - .499 **British Africa - British East Africa - Tanganyika and Tanzania - Statistics - Labor**

Afr Doc 3408.300   Tanganyika. Tresury. Economics and Statistics Division. Employment and earnings in Tanganyika. Dar es Salaam, 1961-1963.

Afr Doc 3408.700 - .999 **British Africa - British East Africa - Tanganyika and Tanzania - Statistics - Trade**

Afr Doc 3408.705   Tanganyika trade bulletin. Dar es Salaam. 6,1957+

Afr Doc 3409.1 - .299 **British Africa - British East Africa - Tanganyika and Tanzania - Statistics - Budget**

Afr Doc 3409.40   Tanzania. Estimates of the expenditure of the United Republic of Tanganyika and Zanzibar. Dar es Salaam. 1964+

Afr Doc 3409.44   Tanganyika. Budget survey. 1956-1957

Afr Doc 3409.300 - .499 **British Africa - British East Africa - Tanganyika and Tanzania - Statistics - National income and accounts, surveys**

Afr Doc 3409.300   Tanganyika. Treasury. Central Statistical Bureau. Village economic surveys. Dar es Salaam. 1961-1962

Afr Doc 3409.305F   Tanganyika. Treasury. Report on the accounts and finances. Dar es Salaam. 1924-1954

Afr Doc 3409.310F   Tanzania. The appropriation accounts, revenue statements, accounts of the funds and other public accounts together with the report thereon by the Controller and Auditor-General. Dar es Salaam. 1966+

Afr Doc 3412 **British Africa - British East Africa - Tanganyika and Tanzania - Legislative documents - General**

Afr Doc 3412.5   Tanganyika. National Assembly. Government paper. Dar es Salaam. 7,1958

Afr Doc 3412.7   Tanzania. Government paper. Dar es Salaam. 2,1966+

Afr Doc 3414 **British Africa - British East Africa - Tanganyika and Tanzania - Legislative documents - House Journal, etc.**

Afr Doc 3414.5   Tanganyika. Parliament. National Assembly. Parliamentry debates. 1,1961+ 3v.

Afr Doc 3414.10   Tanganyika. National Assembly. Assembly debates; official report. 27,1952+ 13v.

Afr Doc 3419 **British Africa - British East Africa - Tanganyika and Tanzania - Legislative documents - Others**

Afr Doc 3419.5   Tanganyika. Constitution. An act to declare the Constitution of Tanganyika. Dar es Salaam, 1962?

Afr Doc 3431 - 3456 **British Africa - British East Africa - Tanganyika and Tanzania - Executive documents - Depts., Bureaus, etc., A-Z (by catchword)**

Afr Doc 3431.5   Tanganyika. Audit Department. Annual report. Dar es Salaam. 1955-1956

Afr Doc 3431.10   Tanzania. Administrator General's Department. Annual report. Dar es Salaam. 1964+

Afr Doc 3433.5   Tanganyika. Co-operative Development Department. Annual report on co-operative development. Dar es Salaam. 1956-63

Afr Doc 3433.10   Tanzania. Ministry of Commerce and Co-operatives. Annual report. Dar es Salaam. 1964

Afr Doc 3435.5   Tanzania. Ministry of Education. Annual report. Dar es Salaam. 1964+

Afr Doc 3436.5   Tanzania. Ministry of Foreign Affairs. Foreign affairs bulletin. Dar es Salaam. 2,1966+

Afr Doc 3439.5   Tanganyika. Immigration and Passport Department. Annual report. Dar es Salaam. 1955

Afr Doc 3439.10   Tanzania. Ministry of Industries, Mineral Resources and Power. Annual report. Dar es Salaam. 1,1964+

Afr Doc 3442.5   Tanganyika. Labour Department. Annual report.

Afr Doc 3444.5   Tanzania. National Archives. Annual report. Dar es Salaam. 1,1964+

Afr Doc 3446.5   Tanganyika. Public Works Department. Annual report. 1957+

Afr Doc 3450.5   Tanzania. Town Planning Division. Annual report. Dar es Salaam. 1964+

Afr Doc 3453.5   Tanganyika. Department of Water Development and Irrigation. Annual report. 1959+

Afr Doc 3502 **British Africa - British Central Africa - General; Federation of Rhodesia and Nyasaland - General collections - Bibliographies, catalogs, etc.**

Afr Doc 3502.5   Library of Congress. African Section. The Rhodesias and Nyasaland. Washington, 1965.

Afr Doc 3507.200 - .999 **British Africa - British Central Africa - General; Federation of Rhodesia and Nyasaland - Statistics - Census**

Afr Doc 3507.356   Rhodesia and Nyasaland. Central Statistical Office. Census of population, 1956. Salisbury, 1960.

Afr Doc 3507.356.15   Rhodesia and Nyasaland. Central Statistical Office. Report on the census of Africans in employment. Salisbury, 1956.

Afr Doc 3507.359.10   Rhodesia and Nyasaland. Central Statistical Office. The censuses of production of the Federation of Rhodesia and Nyasaland, 1958-1959. Salisbury, 1961.

Afr Doc 3507.360F   Rhodesia and Nyasaland. The census of production in 1960 and 1961: mining, manufacturing, electricity and water supply. Salisbury, 1963.

Afr Doc 3507.361   Rhodesia and Nyasaland. Central Statistical Office. Preliminary results of federal censuses of population and of employees, September, 1961. Salisbury, 1962.

Afr Doc 3508.1 - .299 **British Africa - British Central Africa - General; Federation of Rhodesia and Nyasaland - Statistics - Vital, population, etc.**

Afr Doc 3508.255   Rhodesia and Nyasaland. Central Statistical Office. Migration report. Salisbury. 1963

Afr Doc 3508.700 - .999 **British Africa - British Central Africa - General; Federation of Rhodesia and Nyasaland - Statistics - Trade**

Afr Doc 3508.705   Rhodesia and Nyasaland. Central Statistical Office. Balance of payments. Salisbury. 1954+

Afr Doc 3508.707F   Rhodesia and Nyasaland. Central Statistical Office. Annual statement of external trade. Salisbury. 1954+ 4v.

Afr Doc 3509.1 - .299 **British Africa - British Central Africa - General; Federation of Rhodesia and Nyasaland - Statistics - Budget**

Afr Doc 3509.5   Rhodesia and Nyasaland. Central Statistical Office. Quarterly bulletin of financial statistics. Salisbury. 1963

Afr Doc 3509.10   Rhodesia. Southern. Central Statistical Office. Quarterly bulletin of financial statistics. Salisbury. 1964

Afr Doc 3509.15   Rhodesia and Nyasaland. Auditor-General. Report on the finance accounts, appropriation accounts and accounts of miscellaneous funds. Salisbury. 1953+

Afr Doc 3509.20   Rhodesia and Nyasaland. Financial statements. 1953-1964

Afr Doc 3509.25   Rhodesia and Nyasaland. Estimates of expenditure to be defrayed from revenue funds and loan funds. 1957+ 2v.

Afr Doc 3509.300 - .499 **British Africa - British Central Africa - General; Federation of Rhodesia and Nyasaland - Statistics - National income and accounts, surveys**

Afr Doc 3509.300   Rhodesia and Nyasaland. Ministry of Economic Affairs. Economic report. Salisbury. 1954+

Afr Doc 3509.300 - .499   British Africa - British Central Africa - General;
Federation of Rhodesia and Nyasaland - Statistics - National income and
accounts, surveys - cont.
Afr Doc 3509.305F   Rhodesia (British Colony). Central Statistical Office.
Report on the results of the national income and balance
of payments questionaire sent to companies operating in
Malaur. v.1. Salisbury, 1964.

Afr Doc 3509.500 - .999   British Africa - British Central Africa - General;
Federation of Rhodesia and Nyasaland - Statistics - Other
Afr Doc 3509.505   Rhodesia and Nyasaland. Central Statistical Office.
Insurance statistics. Salisbury. 1957+
Afr Doc 3509.510   Rhodesia and Nyasaland. Central Statistical Office. Income
tax statistics. v.2. Salisbury, 1961.
Afr Doc 3509.515F   Rhodesia and Nyasaland. Central Statistical Office.
Preliminary report on the federal European family
expenditure survey, October 1960. Salisbury, 1963.
Afr Doc 3509.520F   Rhodesia and Nyasaland. Central Statistical Office. Report
on the agricultural production of Southern Rhodesia,
Northern Rhodesia and Nyasaland. Salisbury. 1960+

Afr Doc 3514   British Africa - British Central Africa - General; Federation of
Rhodesia and Nyasaland - Legislative documents - House Journal, etc.
Afr Doc 3514.5   Rhodesia and Nyasaland. Assembly. Debates. 20v.
Afr Doc 3514.10   Rhodesia and Nyasaland. Assembly. Votes and proceedings.
1954-1963 10v.

Afr Doc 3531 - 3556   British Africa - British Central Africa - General;
Federation of Rhodesia and Nyasaland - Executive documents - Depts.,
Bureaus, etc., A-Z (by catchword)
Afr Doc 3531.5   Rhodesia and Nyasaland. Ministry of Agriculture. Report of
the Secretary to the Federal Ministry of Agriculture.
Salisbury. 1954+
Afr Doc 3533.3   Rhodesia and Nyasaland. Ministry of Commerce and Industry.
Report of the secretary. 1961-1963
Afr Doc 3533.6   Rhodesia and Nyasaland. Department of Civil Aviation.
Report of the Director. Salisbury. 1954+
Afr Doc 3533.10   Rhodesia and Nyasaland. Department of Customs and Excise.
Report of the Controller of Customs and Excise.
Salisbury. 1954+
Afr Doc 3533.13F   Rhodesia and Nyasaland. Central Africa Command. Annual
report of the general officer commanding, Central Africa
Command. Salisbury. 1,1954
Afr Doc 3534.5   Rhodesia and Nyasaland. Ministry of Defense. Annual report
of the Secretary for Defence and the Chief of Air Staff.
Salisbury. 1955+
Afr Doc 3535.5   Rhodesia and Nyasaland. Ministry of Education. Annual
report on education, 1954-1963.
Afr Doc 3535.10F   Rhodesia and Nyasaland. Ministry of External Affairs.
Report of the secretary. Salisbury. 1955-1957
Afr Doc 3538.5F   Rhodesia and Nyasaland. Ministry of Health. Annual report
of the public health. Zomba. 1,1954+
Afr Doc 3539.5   Rhodesia and Nyasaland. Registrar of Insurance. Report.
Afr Doc 3542.5   Rhodesia and Nyasaland. Ministry of Law. Report of the
secretary to the Ministry of Law. Salisbury. 1,1955+
Afr Doc 3543.5   Rhodesia and Nyasaland. Department of Meteorological
Services. Report of the director. 1954-1955
Afr Doc 3546.5   Rhodesia and Nyasaland. Pension Fund Board. Annual report
on the operation and financial position of the Federal
Pension Fund. Salisbury. 1956+
Afr Doc 3546.10   Rhodesia and Nyasaland. Pension Fund Board. Annual report
on the operation and financial position of the Federal
Provident Fund. Salisbury. 1961+
Afr Doc 3546.15   Rhodesia and Nyasaland. Ministry of Power. Report of the
Secretary for Power. Salisbury. 1955+
Afr Doc 3546.20   Rhodesia and Nyasaland. Ministry of Posts. Annual report
on the Post Office Savings Bank and Savings Certificates.
Salisbury. 1954+
Afr Doc 3546.25   Rhodesia and Nyasaland. Ministry of Posts. Annual report
of the Postmaster-General. Salisbury. 1954+
Afr Doc 3546.30F   Rhodesia and Nyasaland. Public Works Department. Annual
report. Salisbury. 1955+
Afr Doc 3550.5   Rhodesia and Nyasaland. Department of Taxes. Report of the
Commissioner of Tades. 1954+
Afr Doc 3553.5   Rhodesia and Nyasaland. Ministry of Works. Annual report
of the Under Secretary.

Afr Doc 3603   British Africa - British Central Africa - Nyasaland, Malawi - General
collections - Blue books, government manuals, directories
Afr Doc 3603.5F   Nyasaland. Blue book. 11v.
Afr Doc 3603.10   The Malawi government directory. Zomba. 1965+
Afr Doc 3603.15   Malawi. Ministry of External Affairs. Diplomatic and
consular. Zomba. 1965

Afr Doc 3607.1 - .199   British Africa - British Central Africa - Nyasaland,
Malawi - Statistics - General compilations
Afr Doc 3607.5   Malawi. National Statistical Office. Quarterly digest of
statistics. Zomba. 1,1966+
Afr Doc 3607.6   Malawi. National Statistical Office. Monthly bulletin of
key economics indicators. Zomba. 17,1966+
Afr Doc 3607.8F   Malawi. National Statistical Office. Compendium of
statistics for Malawi. Zomba. 1965+

Afr Doc 3607.200 - .999   British Africa - British Central Africa - Nyasaland,
Malawi - Statistics - Census
Afr Doc 3607.366F   Malawi. National Statistical Office. Malawi population
census, 1966; provisional report. Zomba, 1966?

Afr Doc 3608.500 - .699   British Africa - British Central Africa - Nyasaland,
Malawi - Statistics - Industry, manufactures
Afr Doc 3608.505   Malawi. National Statistical Office. Census of industrial
production. Zomba. 1962+

Afr Doc 3608.700 - .999   British Africa - British Central Africa - Nyasaland,
Malawi - Statistics - Trade
Afr Doc 3608.700   Malawi. Ministry of Finance. Preliminary report on the
balance of payments 1964. Zomba.
Afr Doc 3608.705   Malawi. National Statistical Office. Annual statement of
external trade. Zomba. 1,1964+

Afr Doc 3609.1 - .299   British Africa - British Central Africa - Nyasaland,
Malawi - Statistics - Budget
Afr Doc 3609.5   Malawi. National Statistical Office. Budget; background
information. Zomba. 1966
Afr Doc 3609.10   Malawi. Estimates of revenue and expenditure on revenue
account. Zomba. 1966+

Afr Doc 3609.1 - .299   British Africa - British Central Africa - Nyasaland,
Malawi - Statistics - Budget - cont.
Afr Doc 3609.15   Malawi. Estimates of resources and expenditure on
development account. Zomba. 1965+
Afr Doc 3609.20   Malawi. Ministry of Finance. Budget statement. Zomba.
3,1967+
Afr Doc 3609.25   Malawi. Supplementary estimates of expenditure on revenue
and development account. Zomba. 1,1965+

Afr Doc 3609.300 - .499   British Africa - British Central Africa - Nyasaland,
Malawi - Statistics - National income and accounts, surveys
Afr Doc 3609.300   Nyasaland. Auditor-General Department. Report on the
accounts. Zomba. 1956-1957
Afr Doc 3609.305   Financial statements and reports thereon by the accountant
general and the auditor general. Zomba. 1957+
Afr Doc 3609.310F   Malawi. The appropriation accounts; revenue statements and
other public accounts. Zomba. 1967+

Afr Doc 3612   British Africa - British Central Africa - Nyasaland, Malawi -
Legislative documents - General
Afr Doc 3612.5   Malawi. Parliament. Official verbatim report of the
debates. Zomba. 1,1964+
Afr Doc 3612.10   Nyasaland. Legislative Council. Proceedings.
Afr Doc 3612.205   Malawi. Parliament. Public Accounts Committee. Report.
Zomba. 1962+

Afr Doc 3631 - 3656   British Africa - British Central Africa - Nyasaland,   i
malawi - Executive documents - Depts., Bureaus, etc., A-Z (by catchword)
Afr Doc 3631.5   Malawi. Department of Agriculture. Annual report. Zomba.
1957+
Afr Doc 3631.10   Nyasaland. Secretary for African Affairs. Annual report.
1958
Afr Doc 3633.5   Malawi. Department of Customs and Excise. Annual report of
the Controller. Zomba. 1964
Afr Doc 3634.5   Malawi Development Corporation. Annual report and
statement of accounts. Blantyre. 1967+
Afr Doc 3636.5   Malawi. Farmers Marketing Board. Annual report. Limbe.
1965+
Afr Doc 3638.5   Malawi. Ministry of Home Affairs. Annual report. Zomba.
1965+
Afr Doc 3640.5   Malawi. Ministry of Justice. Annual report of the Ministry
of Justice including the Department of the Registrar
General. Zomba. 1966+
Afr Doc 3646.5   Malawi. Public Service Commission. Annual report. Zomba.
1963+
Afr Doc 3648.5   Malawi. Department of the Registrar General. Annual
report. Zomba. 1959+
Afr Doc 3648.10   Malawi. Road Traffic Department. Annual report of the Road
Traffic Commissioner. Zomba. 1965+
Afr Doc 3649.5   Malawi. Department of Surveys. Annual report. Zomba.
1965+
Afr Doc 3653.5   Malawi. Ministry of Works. Annual report. Zomba. 1958+
Afr Doc 3653.10   Malawi. Water Development Department. Annual report.
Zomba. 1962+

Afr Doc 3702   British Africa - British Central Africa - Northern Rhodesia, Zambia -
General collections - Bibliographies, catalogs, etc.
Afr Doc 3702.5   Zambia. List of publications. 1954+

Afr Doc 3703   British Africa - British Central Africa - Northern Rhodesia, Zambia -
General collections - Blue books, government manuals, directories
Afr Doc 3703.2   Zambia. Ministry of Foreign Affaires. List of Diplomatic
Missions and other Foreign Representatives. Lusaka, 1965.
Afr Doc 3703.5   Rhodesia, Northern. General list of chiefs. Lusaka.
1960+
Afr Doc 3703.10   Zambia. General list of chiefs. Lusaka, 1966.

Afr Doc 3705   British Africa - British Central Africa - Northern Rhodesia, Zambia -
General collections - Annual reports
Afr Doc 3705.5   Zambia. Government paper. Lusaka. 1966+

Afr Doc 3707.1 - .199   British Africa - British Central Africa - Northern
Rhodesia, Zambia - Statistics - General compilations
Afr Doc 3707.56   Zambia. Central Statistical Office. Monthly digest of
statistics. 1,1964+

Afr Doc 3707.200 - .999   British Africa - British Central Africa - Northern
Rhodesia, Zambia - Statistics - Census
Afr Doc 3707.346   Rhodesia, Northern. Census. Census, 1946. Lusaka, 1947.
Afr Doc 3707.351   Rhodesia and Nyasaland. Central Statistical Office. Report
on the census of population, 1951. Lusaka, 1954.
Afr Doc 3707.361   Zambia. Central Statistical Office. Final report of the
Sept. 1961 censuses of non-Africans and employees.
Lusaka, 1965.
Afr Doc 3707.362F   Zambia. Central Statistical Office. Census of distribution
in 1962; wholesale, retail trade and selected services.
Lusaka, 1965.
Afr Doc 3707.363F   Zambia. Central Statistical Office. May/June 1963 census
of Africans: v.1 village population. Lusaka, 1965.
Afr Doc 3707.363.2F   Zambia. Second report of the May/June 1963 census of
Africans. Lusaka, 1964.
Afr Doc 3707.363.5   Zambia. Central Statistical Office. The census of
production in 1963. Lusaka, 1965.

Afr Doc 3708.1 - .299   British Africa - British Central Africa - Northern
Rhodesia, Zambia - Statistics - Vital, population, etc.
Afr Doc 3708.5   Zambia. Central Statistical Office. Recorded megration.
Lusaka, 1,1964+
Afr Doc 3708.7F   Rhodesia and Nyasaland. Central Statistical Office. Report
on Northern Rhodesia. Salisbury. 1961+
Afr Doc 3708.9F   Zambia. Central Statistical Office. Vital statistics.
Lusaka. 1965+

Afr Doc 3708.300 - .499   British Africa - British Central Africa - Northern
Rhodesia, Zambia - Statistics - Labor
Afr Doc 3708.315   Zambia. Cabinet Office. Manpower report. Lusaka, 1966.

Afr Doc 3708.700 - .999   British Africa - British Central Africa - Northern
Rhodesia, Zambia - Statistics - Trade
Afr Doc 3708.700   Zambia. Central Statistical Office. Annual statement of
external trade. Lusaka. 1,1964+
Afr Doc 3708.705F   Zambia. Central Statistical Office. External trade
statistics. Lusaka. 1965+
Afr Doc 3708.710F   Zambia. Central Statistical Office. Balance of payments.
Lusaka. 1,1964+

Afr Doc 3709.1 - .299 British Africa - British Central Africa - Northern Rhodesia, Zambia - Statistics - Budget

Afr Doc 3709.5   Zambia. Audit Office. Report of the Auditor-General on the public accounts. Lusaka. 1964+

Afr Doc 3709.10F   Zambia. Estimates of revenue and expenditure. Lusaka. 1,1964+

Afr Doc 3709.300 - .499 British Africa - British Central Africa - Northern Rhodesia, Zambia - Statistics - National income and accounts, surveys

Afr Doc 3709.300   Zambia. Ministry of Finance. Economic report. Lusaka. 2,1965+

Afr Doc 3709.305   Zambia. Central Statistical Office. National accounts and balance of payments of Zambia, 1954-1964. Lusaka, 1964.

Afr Doc 3709.310   Zambia. Ministry of Finance. Financial report. Lusaka. 1964+

Afr Doc 3709.315F   Zambia. Central Statistical Office. National accounts and input-output table. Lusaka. 1964+

Afr Doc 3709.500 - .999 British Africa - British Central Africa - Northern Rhodesia, Zambia - Statistics - Other

Afr Doc 3709.505   Zambia. Central Statistical Office. Agriculture production in Zambia. Lusaka. 1963+

Afr Doc 3709.510F   Zambia. Central Statistical Office. Agriculture production statistics. Lusaka. 1964+

Afr Doc 3709.515F   Zambia. Ministry of Agriculture. Monthly economic bulletin. Lusaka. 1964-1968

Afr Doc 3709.516F   Zambia. Ministry of Rural Development. Bulletin of agricultural statistics. Lusaka. 1969+

Afr Doc 3709.520F   Zambia. Central Statistical Office. Agricultural and pastoral production statistics (For commercial farms only). Lusaka. 1966+

Afr Doc 3709.525F   Zambia. Central Statistical Office. Registration of motor vehicles in Zambia. Lusaka. 1965+

Afr Doc 3709.530F   Zambia. Central Statistical Office. Income tax statistics. Lusaka. 1,1962+

Afr Doc 3709.535F   Zambia. Central Statistical Office. Insurance statistics. Lusaka. 1,1964+

Afr Doc 3709.540F   Zambia. Central Statistical Office. Transport statistics. Lusaka. 1965+

Afr Doc 3709.550F   Rhodesia and Nyasaland. Central Statistical Office. First report on Urban African budget surveys held in Northern Rhodesia, May to Aug., 1960. Salisbury, 1965. 2 pam.

Afr Doc 3712 British Africa - British Central Africa - Northern Rhodesia, Zambia - Legislative documents - General

Afr Doc 3712.5   Rhodesia, Northern. Legislative Council. Debates. 15v.

Afr Doc 3712.15   Rhodesia, Northern. African Representative Council. Proceedings. 1,1946 4v.

Afr Doc 3714 British Africa - British Central Africa - Northern Rhodesia, Zambia - Legislative documents - House Journal, etc.

Afr Doc 3714.5   Rhodesia, Northern. Legislative Assembly. Debates. 1,1964+

Afr Doc 3714.10   Zambia. National Assembly. Debates. 1,1964+

Afr Doc 3731 - 3756 British Africa - British Central Africa - Northern Rhodesia, Zambia - Executive documents - Depts., Bureaus, etc., A-Z (by catchword)

Afr Doc 3731.4F   Rhodesia, Northern. Department of Agriculture. Annual report. Lusaka. 1956-1959

Afr Doc 3731.5   Rhodesia, Northern. Ministry of African Agriculture. Annual report. Lusaka. 1963+

Afr Doc 3731.6F   Zambia. Ministry of Agriculture. Annual report. Lusaka. 2,1965+

Afr Doc 3731.10   Rhodesia, Northern. Agricultural Marketing Committee. Review of the general economic condition of the agricultural industry. Lusaka. 1963+

Afr Doc 3731.15   Zambia. Agricultural Marketing Committee. Review of the operations. Lusaka. 1964+

Afr Doc 3731.20   Zambia. Department of the Administrator-General and Official Receiver. Annual report. Lusaka. 1964+

Afr Doc 3731.25   Zambia. National Archives. Annual report. Lusaka. 1964+

Afr Doc 3732.5   Zambia. Registrar of Building Societies. Annual report. Lusaka. 1959+

Afr Doc 3732.10   Zambia. Registrar of Banks. Annual report. Lusaka. 1965+

Afr Doc 3733.5   Rhodesia, Northern. Department of Cooperative Societies. Annual report. Lusaka. 1952+

Afr Doc 3733.10   Rhodesia, Northern. Department of Community Development. Annual report. Lusaka. 1961+

Afr Doc 3733.12   Zambia. Department of Community Development. Annual report. Lusaka. 1964+

Afr Doc 3733.15   Zambia. Ministry of Commerce and Industry. Annual report. Lusaka. 1964+

Afr Doc 3733.20   Zambia. Department of Customs and Excise. Report of the controller of customs and excise. Lusaka. 1965+

Afr Doc 3733.25F   Zambia. Department of Zambia Cultural Services. Annual report. Lusaka. 1,1966+

Afr Doc 3735.5   Zambia. Ministry of Education. Annual report. Lusaka. 1964+

Afr Doc 3737.5   Rhodesia, Northern. Department of Game and Fisheries. Annual report. Lusaka. 1960+

Afr Doc 3737.10   Zambia. Game and Fisheries Department. Annual report. Lusaka. 1964+

Afr Doc 3739.5   Rhodesia, Northern. Advisory Committee on Industrial Development. Report. 1,1946+

Afr Doc 3739.10   Rhodesia, Northern. Information Department. Annual report. Lusaka. 1963+

Afr Doc 3739.15   Zambia. Immigration Department. Annual report. Lusaka. 1964+

Afr Doc 3739.20   Zambia. Information Services. Annual report. Lusaka. 1964+

Afr Doc 3739.25   Zambia. Registrar of Insurance. Report. Lusaka. 1964+

Afr Doc 3739.30   Rhodesia, Northern. Income Tax Department. Report. Lusaka. 1953-1954

Afr Doc 3742.5   Rhodesia, Northern. Department of Lands. Annual report. Lusaka. 1963+

Afr Doc 3742.7   Zambia. Department of Lands. Annual report. Lusaka. 1963+

Afr Doc 3742.10   Zambia. Ministry of Local Government. Annual report. Lusaka. 1963+

Afr Doc 3742.15   Land and Agricultural Bank of Northern Rhodesia. Report. 1957-1963

Afr Doc 3743.5   Zambia. Mines Department. Annual report. Lusaka. 1964+

Afr Doc 3743.10   Zambia. National Museums Board. Annual report. Lusaka. 1,1967+

Afr Doc 3744.5   Rhodesia, Northern. Natural Resources Board. Annual report. 1959+

Afr Doc 3731 - 3756 British Africa - British Central Africa - Northern Rhodesia, Zambia - Executive documents - Depts., Bureaus, etc., A-Z (by catchword) - cont.

Afr Doc 3744.10   Rhodesia, Northern. Ministry of Native Affairs. African affairs annual report. Lusaka. 1961+

Afr Doc 3746.5   Zambia. General Post Office. Annual report of the Postmaster-General. Lusaka. 1963+

Afr Doc 3746.10   Rhodesia, Northern. Printing and Stationery Department. Annual report. Lusaka. 1963+

Afr Doc 3746.15   Zambia. Public Service Commission. Annual report. Lusaka. 1964+

Afr Doc 3746.20   Zambia. Provincial and District Government. Annual report. Lusaka. 1964+

Afr Doc 3746.25   Zambia. Printing and Stationery Department. Annual report. Lusaka. 1964+

Afr Doc 3746.30   Zambia. Commission for the Preservation of Natural and Historical Monuments and Relics. Annual report. Lusaka. 1964+

Afr Doc 3748.5   Rhodesia, Northern. Roads Department. Annual report. Lusaka. 1963

Afr Doc 3749.3F   Rhodesia, Northern. Department of Social Welfare. Annual report. Lusaka. 1962-1963 3v.

Afr Doc 3749.5   Zambia. Department of Social Welfare. Annual report. Lusaka. 1964+

Afr Doc 3749.10   Rhodesia, Northern. Survey Department. Annual report. Lusaka. 1962-1963

Afr Doc 3749.12   Zambia. Survey Department. Annual report. Lusaka. 1964+

Afr Doc 3749.14F   Rhodesia, Northern. Department of Welfare and Probation Services. Social welfare; annual report. Lusaka. 1,1952

Afr Doc 3749.16F   Zambia. Central Statistical Office. Annual report. Lusaka. 1965+

Afr Doc 3750.10   Rhodesia, Northern. Town and Country Planning Service. Annual report. Lusaka. 1961+

Afr Doc 3750.15   Zambia. Town and Country Planning Service. Annual report. Lusaka. 1964+

Afr Doc 3750.20   Zambia. Ministry of Transport and Works. Annual report. Lusaka. 1964+

Afr Doc 3750.25   Rhodesia, Northern. Teaching Service Commission. Annual report. Lusaka. 1963

Afr Doc 3750.30   Zambia. Teaching Service Commission. Annual report. Lusaka. 1964+

Afr Doc 3750.35   Zambia. Department of Taxes. Annual report. Lusaka. 1964+

Afr Doc 3753.5   Rhodesia, Northern. Workmen's Compensation Commissioner. Annual report. Lusaka. 1960+

Afr Doc 3753.10F   Zambia. Ministry of Works. Report. Lusaka. 1966+

Afr Doc 3802 British Africa - British Central Africa - Southern Rhodesia - General collections - Bibliographies, catalogs, etc.

Afr Doc 3802.2   Willson, Francis Michael Glenn. Catalogue of the parliamentary papers of Southern Rhodesia, 1899-1953. Salisbury, 1965.

Afr Doc 3803 British Africa - British Central Africa - Southern Rhodesia - General collections - Blue books, government manuals, directories

Afr Doc 3803.2   Willson, Francis Michael Glenn. Holders of administrative and ministerial office, 1894-1964. Salisbury, 1966.

Afr Doc 3807.1 - .199 British Africa - British Central Africa - Southern Rhodesia - Statistics - General compilations

Afr Doc 3807.5   Official yearbook of the Colony of Southern Rhodesia. Salisbury. 1-3,1924-1932 3v.

Afr Doc 3807.8   Statistical handbook of Southern Rhodesia. Salisbury. 1939-1945

Afr Doc 3807.10   Statistical yearbook of Southern Rhodesia. Salisbury. 1947

Afr Doc 3807.13   Rhodesia. Central Statistical Office. Monthly digest of statistics. Salisbury. 1964+

Afr Doc 3807.15   Rhodesia. Central Statistical Office. Quarterly statistical summary. Salisbury. 1,1967+

Afr Doc 3807.200 - .999 British Africa - British Central Africa - Southern Rhodesia - Statistics - Census

Afr Doc 3807.311.5   Rhodesia, Southern. Census Office. Preliminary returns of a census taken on May 1911, together with comparative figures from the census of 1907 and 1904 Salisbury, 1911. 2 pam.

Afr Doc 3807.321.10   Rhodesia, Southern. Census Office. Second and final report of the director of census regarding the census taken on 3rd May 1921. Salisbury, 1922.

Afr Doc 3807.326.5   Rhodesia, Southern. Census Office. Report of the director of Census regarding the Census taken on the 4th May 1926. Salisbury, 1927.

Afr Doc 3807.351   Central African Statistical Office. Census of population 1951. Salisbury, 1954.

Afr Doc 3807.359F   Rhodesia and Nyasaland. Report on Umtali and Gwelo African demographic surveys held in August and September, 1959. Salisbury, 1960.

Afr Doc 3807.361F   Rhodesia (British Colony). Central Statistical Office. Final report on the September 1961 census of employees. Salisbury, 1965.

Afr Doc 3807.361.5F   Rhodesia (British Colony). Central Statistical Office. 1961 census of the European, Asian coloured population. Salisbury, 1965?

Afr Doc 3807.362F   Rhodesia, Southern. Central Statistical Office. Final report of the April/May 1962 census of Africans in Southern Rhodesia. Salisbury, 1964.

Afr Doc 3807.362.5F   Rhodesia (British Colony). Central Statistical Office. The census of distribution in 1962 wholesale and retail trade and selected services. Salisbury, 1965.

Afr Doc 3808.1 - .299 British Africa - British Central Africa - Southern Rhodesia - Statistics - Vital, population, etc.

Afr Doc 3808.5   Rhodesia, Southern. Central Statistical Office. Migration report. Salisbury. 1964+

Afr Doc 3808.7F   Rhodesia and Nyasaland. Central Statistical Office. The 1953-55 demographic sample survey of the indigenous African population of Southern Rhodesia. Salisbury, 1959.

Afr Doc 3808.10   Rhodesia (British Colony). Central Statistical Office. Migration report. Salisbury. 1965+

Afr Doc 3808.12   Rhodesia (British Colony). European life table no. 2 and Analysis of deaths by causes, 1961-63. Salisbury, 196-.

Afr Doc 3808.500 - .699   British Africa - British Central Africa - Southern Rhodesia - Statistics - Industry, manufactures
Afr Doc 3808.502F   Rhodesia (British Colony). Central Statistical Office. An analysis of company accounts. Salisbury. 1960+
Afr Doc 3808.505   Rhodesia (British Colony). Central Statistical office. The association of commodities with industries in Rhodesia. Salisbury, 1966.
Afr Doc 3808.510F   Rhodesia (British Colony). Central Statistical Office. The census of production mining manufacturing construction, electricity, and water supply. Salisbury. 1962+

Afr Doc 3808.700 - .999   British Africa - British Central Africa - Southern Rhodesia - Statistics - Trade
Afr Doc 3808.705   Rhodesia (British Colony). Central Statistical Office. Annual statement of external trade. Salisbury. 1964+
Afr Doc 3808.710   Central African Statistical Office. Annual statement of the trade of Southern Rhodesia with British countries and foreign countries. Salisbury. 22-24,1951-1953

Afr Doc 3809.1 - .299   British Africa - British Central Africa - Southern Rhodesia - Statistics - Budget
Afr Doc 3809.5   Rhodesia (British Colony). Central Statistical Office. Quarterly bulletin of financial statistics. Salisbury. 1965+
Afr Doc 3809.10   Rhodesia, Southern. Estimates of expenditure to be defrayed from revenue funds and from loan funds. Salisbury. 1964+
Afr Doc 3809.15F   Rhodesia, Southern. Budget statements by the minister of Finance. Salisbury? 1964+

Afr Doc 3809.300 - .499   British Africa - British Central Africa - Southern Rhodesia - Statistics - National income and accounts, surveys
Afr Doc 3809.304   Rhodesia (British Colony). Central Statistical Office. National accounts and balance of payments. Salisbury. 1954+

Afr Doc 3809.500 - .999   British Africa - British Central Africa - Southern Rhodesia - Statistics - Other
Afr Doc 3809.505   Rhodesia (British Colony). Central Statistical Office. Insurance statistics. Salisbury. 1964+
Afr Doc 3809.510   Rhodesia (British Colony). Central Statistical Office. Income tax statistics: income years 1953/54-1962/63. Salisbury, 1965.
Afr Doc 3809.515   Rhodesia and Nyasaland. Central Statistical Office. Sample survey of African agriculture, Southern Rhodesia, 1959/60. Salisbury, 1962.
Afr Doc 3809.524F   Rhodesia (Southern). Central Statistical Office. Registrations of motor vehicles in Southern Rhodesia. Salisbury. 1964+
Afr Doc 3809.525F   Rhodesia (British Colony). Central Statistical Office. Registrations of motor vehicles in Rhodesia. Salisbury. 1964+
Afr Doc 3809.530F   Rhodesia (British Colony). Central Statistical Office. Agricultural production in Rhodesia. Salisbury. 1965+

Afr Doc 3812   British Africa - British Central Africa - Southern Rhodesia - Legislative documents - General
Afr Doc 3812.5   Rhodesia (British Colony). Parliament. Parliamentary debates. Salisbury. 3,1925+ 13v.

Afr Doc 3814   British Africa - British Central Africa - Southern Rhodesia - Legislative documents - House Journal, etc.
Afr Doc 3814.10F   Rhodesia, Southern. Legislative Assembly. Votes and proceedings. 41v.
Afr Doc 3814.15F   Rhodesia (British Colony). Parliament. C.S.R. [papers]. Salisbury. 1901+

Afr Doc 3819   British Africa - British Central Africa - Southern Rhodesia - Legislative documents - Others
Afr Doc 3819.5   Rhodesia (British Colony). Constitution. The Constitution of Rhodesia, 1965. Salisbury, 1965.
Afr Doc 3819.10   Rhodesia (British Colony). Constitutional Commission. Report of the Constitutional Commission, 1968. Salisbury, 1968.

Afr Doc 3831 - 3856   British Africa - British Central Africa - Southern rhodesia - Executive documents - Depts., Bureaus, etc., A-Z (by catchword)
Afr Doc 3835.5   Rhodesia, Southern. Secretary for African Education. Annaul report. Salisbury. 1964+
Afr Doc 3842.5F   Land and Agricultural Bank of Southern Rhodesia. Report. Salisbury. 1957+
Afr Doc 3842.10   Rhodesia, Southern. Ministry of Lands and Natural Resources. Report of the Secretary. Salisbury. 1963+
Afr Doc 3843.5   Rhodesia (British Colony). Ministry of Mines and Lands. Report of the Secretary for Mines and Lands. Salisbury. 1964+
Afr Doc 3853.5   Rhodesia, Southern. Ministry of Water Development. Report of the Director. Salisbury. 1963+
Afr Doc 3853.10   Rhodesia (British Colony). Ministry of Water Development. Report of the Director. Salisbury. 1964+

Afr Doc 3871 - 3896   British Africa - British Central Africa - Southern rhodesia - Local documents - Provinces, cities, etc., A-Z
Afr Doc 3872.2   Rhodesia and Nyasaland. Report on Bulawayo African demographic survey, held in May 1959. Salisbury, 1960.
Afr Doc 3889.5F   Salisbury, Rodesia. City Council. African Administration Department. Annual report. Salisbury. 1964+
Afr Doc 3889.358   Rhodesia and Nyasaland. Central Statistical Office. Preliminary report on the Salisbury African Demographic survey, August/September, 1958. Salisbury, 1958.
Afr Doc 3889.363F   Rhodesia (British Colony). Central Statistical Office. Report on urban African budget survey in Salisbury, 1963/64. Salisbury, 1965.
Afr Doc 3891.363F   Rhodesia (British Colony). Central Statistical Office. Report on the urban African budget survey in Umtali, 1963. Salisbury, 1965.
Afr Doc 3893.361F   Rhodesia and Nyasaland. Report on Wankie urban African budget survey held in April/May 1960. Salisbury, 1961.

Afr Doc 4003   British Africa - Bechuanaland Protectorate, Botswana - General collections - Blue books, government manuals, directories
Afr Doc 4003.5F   Botswana. Central government organization chart. Gaberones. 1968+

Afr Doc 4007.1 - .199   British Africa - Bechuanaland Protectorate, Botswana - Statistics - General compilations
Afr Doc 4007.5F   Botswana. Central Statistical Office. Statistical abstract. Gaberones. 2,1967+

Afr Doc 4007.200 - .999   British Africa - Bechuanaland Protectorate, botswana - Statistics - Census
Afr Doc 4007.364   Bechuanaland (Protectorate). Report on the census of the Bechuanaland Protectorate, 1964. Mafeking, South Africa? 1965?

Afr Doc 4009.1 - .299   British Africa - Bechuanaland Protectorate, Botswana - Statistics - Budget
Afr Doc 4009.5F   Botswana. Estimates for the development fund. Gaberones. 1966+
Afr Doc 4009.10F   Botswana. Estimates of revenue and expenditures. Gaberones. 1967+

Afr Doc 4009.300 - .499   British Africa - Bechuanaland Protectorate, botswana - Statistics - National income and accounts, surveys
Afr Doc 4009.305F   Bechuanaland (Protectorate). Annual statements of account. Gaberones? 1964+

Afr Doc 4012   British Africa - Bechuanaland Protectorate, Botswana - Legislative documents - General
Afr Doc 4012.5F   Bechuanaland (Protectorate). Legislative Council. Official report of the debates. 1,1961+

Afr Doc 4014   British Africa - Bechuanaland Protectorate, Botswana - Legislative documents - House Journal, etc.
Afr Doc 4014.5   Bechuanaland (Protectorate). Legislative Assembly. Official report of the debates. Lobatsi. 1,1965+
Afr Doc 4014.6F   Botswana. National Assembly. Official report of the debates. Gaberones. 1,1966+
Afr Doc 4014.7   Bechuanaland (Protectorate). Legislative Assembly. Papers. Lobatsi. 21,1965+
Afr Doc 4014.205   Botswana. National Assembly. Public Accounts Committee. Report. Gaberones. 1966+

Afr Doc 4031 - 4056   British Africa - Bechuanaland Protectorate, Botswana - Executive documents - Depts., Bureaus, etc., A-Z (by catchword)
Afr Doc 4031.5   Botswana. Department of Agriculture. Annual report. Gaberones. 1962+
Afr Doc 4046.5   Bechuanaland. Public Works Department. Annual report. Gaberones. 1956+

Afr Doc 4107.200 - .999   British Africa - Swaziland - Statistics - Census
Afr Doc 4107.356   Swaziland. Census, 1956. Mbabane, 1956?
Afr Doc 4107.362F   Swaziland. Census Office. Population census, 1962. n.p., n.d.
Afr Doc 4107.366F   Swaziland. Census Office. Swaziland population census, 1966. Mbabane, 1966.
Afr Doc 4107.366.5   Swaziland. Census Office. Report on the 1966 Swaziland population census. Mbabane, 1968.
Afr Doc 4107.366.6   Distribution and density maps. Mbabane, 1968.

Afr Doc 4108.700 - .999   British Africa - Swaziland - Statistics - Trade
Afr Doc 4108.705F   Swaziland. Commerce report. 1955+

Afr Doc 4109.1 - .299   British Africa - Swaziland - Statistics - Budget
Afr Doc 4109.5F   Swaziland. Treasury. Estimates of revenue and expenditure for the financial year.
Afr Doc 4109.20   Swaziland. Colonial development and welfare schemes. Estimates. 1954+

Afr Doc 4109.300 - .499   British Africa - Swaziland - Statistics - National income and accounts, surveys
Afr Doc 4109.305F   Swaziland. Treasury. Report on the finance and accounts. 1958+

Afr Doc 4112   British Africa - Swaziland - Legislative documents - General
Afr Doc 4112.5F   Swaziland. European Advisory Council. Minutes of the 4th Reconstituted European Advisory Council. 3v.
Afr Doc 4112.10F   Swaziland. Legislative Council. Official report of the debates.
Afr Doc 4112.205F   Swaziland. Legislative Council. Public Accounts Committee. Report. 1,1964+
Afr Doc 4112.207F   Swaziland. Parliament. Public Accounts Committee. Report. 1,1965+

Afr Doc 4114   British Africa - Swaziland - Legislative documents - House Journal, etc.
Afr Doc 4114.5F   Swaziland. House of Assembly. Official report of the debates. 1967+

Afr Doc 4116   British Africa - Swaziland - Legislative documents - Senate Journal, etc.
Afr Doc 4116.5F   Swaziland. Senate. Official report of the debates. 1,1967+

Afr Doc 4119   British Africa - Swaziland - Legislative documents - Others
Afr Doc 4119.5   Swaziland. Constitutional Committee. Report, 24th March, 1966. Mbabane, 1966.

Afr Doc 4131 - 4156   British Africa - Swaziland - Executive documents - Depts., Bureaus, etc., A-Z (by catchword)
Afr Doc 4131.5   Swaziland. Director of Audit. Report on the audit of the accounts. 1964+
Afr Doc 4131.10   Swaziland. Department of Agriculture. Annual report. Mbabane. 1963+
Afr Doc 4139.5   Swaziland. Income Tax Department. Annual report. Mbabane. 1965+
Afr Doc 4142.5F   Swaziland. Department of Land Utilization. Annual report.
Afr Doc 4146.5F   Swaziland. Public Works Department. Annual report by the Director of Public Works.

Afr Doc 4205   British Africa - Basutoland, Lesotho - General collections - Annual reports
Afr Doc 4205.5   Basutoland; report for the years 1947-1965. London, n.d.
Afr Doc 4205.10   Lesotho; report. Maseru. 1967+

Afr Doc 4207.1 - .199 British Africa - Basutoland, Lesotho - Statistics - General compilations

Afr Doc 4207.5 Lesotho. Bureau of Statistics. Annual statistical bulletin. Maseru. 1965+

Afr Doc 4207.200 - .999 British Africa - Basutoland, Lesotho - Statistics - Census

Afr Doc 4207.356 Basutoland. Census Office. 1956 population census, 8th April 1956. Maseru, 1958.
Afr Doc 4207.360 Basutoland. Department of Agriculture. 1960 agricultural census. v.1-6. Maseru, 1963.
Afr Doc 4207.360F Basutoland. Department of Agriculture. 1960 agricultural census. v.7. Maseru, 1963.
Afr Doc 4207.365F Lesotho. Bureau of Statistics. Lesotho census of production, 1965. Maseru, 1966?

Afr Doc 4209.1 - .299 British Africa - Basutoland, Lesotho - Statistics - Budget

Afr Doc 4209.5F Basutoland. Treasury. Report of the finances and accounts for the financial year. Maseru. 1962+
Afr Doc 4209.10F Lesotho. Estimates of development fund revenue and expenditure. 1966+
Afr Doc 4209.11F Lesotho. Memorandum on the Estimates of development fund revenue. 1966+
Afr Doc 4209.12F Basutoland. Estimates of revenue and expenditure. 1967+
Afr Doc 4209.13F Basutoland. Memorandum on the estimates of revenue and expenditure. 1967+

Afr Doc 4209.300 - .499 British Africa - Basutoland, Lesotho - Statistics - National income and accounts, surveys

Afr Doc 4209.305F Lesotho. Bureau of Statistics. National accounts, 1964/5 and 1965/6. Maseru, 1967.

Afr Doc 4209.500 - .999 British Africa - Basutoland, Lesotho - Statistics - Other

Afr Doc 4209.500 Basutoland. Supervisor of Elections. A report on the first general election in Basutoland, 1960. Maseru, 1963.

Afr Doc 4212 British Africa - Basutoland, Lesotho - Legislative documents - General

Afr Doc 4212.5 Basutoland. National Council. Legislative Council. Debates. 1,1960+

Afr Doc 4218 British Africa - Basutoland, Lesotho - Legislative documents - Statutes, etc.

Afr Doc 4218.5 Basutoland constitutional handbook. Maseru, 1960.

Afr Doc 4219 British Africa - Basutoland, Lesotho - Legislative documents - Others

Afr Doc 4219.5 Basutoland. Constitutional Commission. Report of the Basutoland Constitutional Commission. Maseru, 1963.

Afr Doc 4224 British Africa - Basutoland, Lesotho - Executive documents - President

Afr Doc 4224.5 Basutoland. High Commissioner. Basutoland proclamations and notices.

Afr Doc 4231 - 4256 British Africa - Basutoland, Lesotho - Executive documents - Depts., Bureaus, etc., A-Z (by catchword)

Afr Doc 4231.5F Basutoland. Department of Agriculture. Annual report. 1958+
Afr Doc 4231.10F Lesotho. Ministry of Agriculture, Co-ops, and Marketing. Annual report. 1,1966+

Afr Doc 4302 British Africa - South Africa - General, Union of South Africa - General collections - Bibliographies, catalogs, etc.

Afr Doc 4302.10 Yale Univeristy. Library. South African official publications held by Yale University. New Haven, 1966.

Afr Doc 4303 British Africa - South Africa - General, Union of South Africa - General collections - Blue books, government manuals, directories

Afr Doc 4303.5 South Africa. Department of Foreigh Affairs. Department of Foreign Affairs list. Pretoria. 1966+

Afr Doc 4305 British Africa - South Africa - General, Union of South Africa - General collections - Annual reports

Afr Doc 4305.5 South Africa. Bureau of Statistics. Official yearbook of the Union. Pretoria. 2,1918+

Afr Doc 4306 British Africa - South Africa - General, Union of South Africa - General collections - Other

Afr Doc 4306.5 South Africa. Staats-almanak voor de Zuidafrikaansche republiek. Pretoria. 1898-1899 2v.
Afr Doc 4306.7F South Africa. Questions affecting South Africa at the United Nations. Pretoria. 1965+

Afr Doc 4307.1 - .199 British Africa - South Africa - General, Union of South Africa - Statistics - General compilations

Afr Doc 4307.2 South Africa. Bureau of Statistics. Statistical yearbook. Pretoria. 1964+
Afr Doc 4307.4 South Africa. Bureau of Statistics. Statistical year book of the Union of South Africa. Pretoria. 1,1913+
Afr Doc 4307.6F South Africa. Bureau of Statistics. Short term economic indicators. Pretoria. 1,1967+
Afr Doc 4307.8 South Africa. Bureau of Statistics. Uniestatistieke, oor vyftig jaar. Jubileumuitgawe. Pretoria, 1960.
Afr Doc 4307.10F South Africa. Bureau of Statistics. Report. Pretoria. 1,1923+
Afr Doc 4307.15 South African Bureau of Statistics. Bulletin of statistics. Pretoria. 1,1967+
Afr Doc 4307.20 South Africa. Bureau of Statistics. South African statistics. Pretoria. 1,1968+

Afr Doc 4307.200 - .999 British Africa - South Africa - General, Union of South Africa - Statistics - Census

Afr Doc 4307.311 South Africa. Office of Census and Statistics. Census of the Union of South Africa, 1911. Pretoria, 1913. 2v.
Afr Doc 4307.318 South Africa. Office of Census and Statistics. Census of the European or White races of the Union of South Africa, 1918 . Cape Town, 1919-1920.
Afr Doc 4307.318.5
South Africa. Office of Census and Statistics. Census of the European or white races of the Union of South Africa 1918. Final report and supplementary tables. Cape Town, 1920.
Afr Doc 4307.321.10F
Pamphlet vol. South Africa. Census, 1921. 9 pam.
Afr Doc 4307.326.5F
Pamphlet vol. South Africa. Census, 1926.

Afr Doc 4307.200 - .999 British Africa - South Africa - General, Union of South Africa - Statistics - Census - cont.

Afr Doc 4307.331F South Africa. Report with summaries and analysis, number, sex, geographical distribution and ages of the European population. Pretoria, 1933.
Afr Doc 4307.336 South Africa. Bureau of Statistics. Sixth census of the population of the Union of South Africa, 1936. v.1-10. Pretoria, 1938- 12v.
Afr Doc 4307.341F South Africa. Bureau of Statistics. Census of Europeans, 6th May, 1941: report on the wages of domestic servants. Pretoria, 1946.
Afr Doc 4307.341.5F
South Africa. Bureau of Statistics. Census of Europeans, 6 May, 1941: report on dwellings. Pretoria, 1945.
Afr Doc 4307.341.10F
South Africa. Bureau of Statistics. Census of Europeans, 6th May, 1941: report on structure and income on families. Pretoria, 1945.
Afr Doc 4307.346 South Africa. Office of Census and Statistics. Population census 7th May 1946. Bevolkinsensus, 7 Mai 1946. Pretoria, 1949. 2v.
Afr Doc 4307.351 South Africa. Bureau of Statistics. Population census, 8th May 1951. Pretoria, 1955. 2v.
Afr Doc 4307.360 South Africa. Office of Census and Statistics. Population census, 1960. Pretoria, 1962-65. 2v.
Afr Doc 4307.360.5F
South Africa. Bureau of Statistics. Bevolkingsensus, 6 september 1960. Pretoria, 1963. 8v.
Afr Doc 4307.360.10
South Africa. Bureau of Statistics. Sensus van groot en kleindistribusiehandel, 1960-61. Pretoria, 1966. 2v.

Afr Doc 4308.1 - .299 British Africa - South Africa - General, Union of South Africa - Statistics - Vital, population, etc.

Afr Doc 4308.5F South Africa. Bureau of Statistics. Report on deaths: South Africa and South West Africa. Pretoria. 1958+
Afr Doc 4308.10 South Africa. Bureau of Statistics. Report on the vital statistics. 1930-1934
Afr Doc 4308.145 South Africa. Bureau of Statistics. Verslag oor geboortes Suid-Afrikaen suidwes-Afrika, 1958 tot 1963. Report on births. Pretoria, 1965.
Afr Doc 4308.282F South Africa. Office of Census and Statistics. Statistics of migration. 1927-1934

Afr Doc 4308.500 - .699 British Africa - South Africa - General, Union of South Africa - Statistics - Industry, manufactures

Afr Doc 4308.500 South Africa. Bureau of Statistics. Industrial censuses, 1950-51 to 1960-61. Pretoria, 1966.

Afr Doc 4308.700 - .999 British Africa - South Africa - General, Union of South Africa - Statistics - Trade

Afr Doc 4308.705 South Africa. Department of Customs and Excise. Monthly abstract of trade statistics. Pretoria. 1964+
Afr Doc 4308.710F South Africa. Department of Customs and Excise. Foreign trade statistics. Pretoria. 3-51,1909-1959 9v.
Afr Doc 4308.715F South Africa. Department of Customs and Excise. Trade of the Union of South Africa, Southern and Northern Rhodesia, British South Africa and the territory of Southwest Africa. Cape Town. 1909+ 21v.

Afr Doc 4309.1 - .299 British Africa - South Africa - General, Union of South Africa - Statistics - Budget

Afr Doc 4309.5 South Africa. Finance Department. Begroting van die addisionele uitgawes wat bestry moet word uit in komste en leningsrekemings. Pretoria. 1965+
Afr Doc 4309.7F South Africa. Finance Department. Estimates of the expenditure to be defrayed from loan funds. 1930-1931
Afr Doc 4309.10 South Africa. Finance Department. White paper in connection with the budget statement. 1957+
Afr Doc 4309.12F South Africa. Finance Department. Estimate of the expenditure to be defrayed from revenue accounts. 1912+ 6v.
Afr Doc 4309.15F South Africa. South African railways and harbours. Estimates of the additional expenditure to be defrayed from revenue funds. Pretoria. 1966+
Afr Doc 4309.18F South Africa. South African railways and harbours. Estimates of additional expenditure on capital and betterment works. Pretoria. 1966+
Afr Doc 4309.20F South Africa. Estimate of the revenue. 1930+
Afr Doc 4309.22F South Africa. Finance Department. Estimate of the expenditure to be defrayed from Bantu education account. 1967+

Afr Doc 4309.500 - .999 British Africa - South Africa - General, Union of South Africa - Statistics - Other

Afr Doc 4309.500 South Africa. Office of Census and Statistics. Agricultural census. Cape Town, 1918.

Afr Doc 4312 British Africa - South Africa - General, Union of South Africa - Legislative documents - General

Afr Doc 4312.125 South Africa. Parliament. Official language of the Union Bill. Cape Town, 1925.
Afr Doc 4312.126 South Africa. Parliament. Mines and work act. Cape Town, 1926.
Afr Doc 4312.127 South Africa. Parliament. Precious stones bill. Cape Town, 1927.
Afr Doc 4312.129 South Africa. Parliament. Natives parliamentary representation bill. Cape Town, 1929.
Afr Doc 4312.130 South Africa. Parliament. Natives Parliamentary Representation Bill. Cape Town, 1930.
Afr Doc 4312.153 South Africa. Parliament. South Africa Act Amendment Act. v.1-2. Cape Town, 1953.
Afr Doc 4312.154 South Africa. Parliament. Separate representation of voters act validation and amendment bill, 1954. Cape Town, 1954.
Afr Doc 4312.156 South Africa. Parliament. South Africa Act Amendment Bill. v.1-2. Cape Town, 1956.

Afr Doc 4314 British Africa - South Africa - General, Union of South Africa - Legislative documents - House Journal, etc.

Afr Doc 4314.4 South Africa. Parliament. House of Assembly. Debates. 1,1936+
Afr Doc 4314.5F South Africa. Parliament. House of Assembly. Minutes of proceedings. 3v.
Afr Doc 4314.6 South Africa. Parliament. House of Assembly. Debates. 1962+

Afr Doc 4314 **British Africa - South Africa - General, Union of South Africa -**
Legislative documents - House Journal, etc. - cont.
    Afr Doc 4314.8F   South Africa. Parliament. House of Assembly. Debates of
        the House of Assembly of the Union of South Africa as
        reported in the Cape Times. Pretoria, 1966. 8v.
    Afr Doc 4314.205   South Africa. Parliament. House of Assembly. Select
        Committee on Public Accounts. Report. Cape Town. 1966+

Afr Doc 4316 **British Africa - South Africa - General, Union of South Africa -**
Legislative documents - Senate Journal, etc.
    Afr Doc 4316.5F   South Africa. Parliament. Senate. Minutes of proceedings.

Afr Doc 4320 **British Africa - South Africa - General, Union of South Africa -**
Executive documents - Pamphlet volumes
    Afr Doc 4320.5F   Union of South Africa. Miscellaneous collection of reports
        of government departments. n.p., n.d.

Afr Doc 4322 **British Africa - South Africa - General, Union of South Africa -**
Executive documents - General
    Afr Doc 4322.5   South Africa. Bureau of Statistics. Annual departmental
        reports. Pretoria. 1,1920+

Afr Doc 4324 **British Africa - South Africa - General, Union of South Africa -**
Executive documents - President
    Afr Doc 4324.5F   South Africa. High Commissioner. Official gazette.
        Pretoria. 115,1931+ 14v.

Afr Doc 4330 - 4355 **British Africa - South Africa - General, Union of South**
Africa - Executive documents - Depts., Bureaus, etc., A-Z (by catchword)
    Afr Doc 4330.5F   South Africa. Central Road Transportation Board. Report.
        2v.
    Afr Doc 4330.10   South Africa. Department of Agricultural Economics and
        Marketing. Annual report of the secretary for agricultural
        economics and marketing. Pretoria. 1959+
    Afr Doc 4331.5F   South Africa. Bantu Affairs Commission. Report.
    Afr Doc 4331.6   South Africa. Department of Bantu Administration and
        Development. Report. Pretoria. 1963+
    Afr Doc 4331.10   South Africa. Department of Bantu Education. Annual
        report. Pretoria. 1966+
    Afr Doc 4332.5F   South Africa. Control and Audit Office. Finance accounts,
        appropriation accounts, loan funds and miscellaneous
        funds...with report of the controller and auditor-general.
        Pretoria. 10,1919+
    Afr Doc 4332.10F   South Africa. Department of Community Development. Report
        on the activities. 1961+
    Afr Doc 4332.15F   South Africa. Office of Census and Statistics. Annual
        report of the Statistics council. 1951+
    Afr Doc 4332.20F   South Africa. Registrar of Building Societies. Annual
        report. Pretoria. 1964+
    Afr Doc 4332.25F   South Africa. Department of Coloured Affairs. Report.
        1955+
    Afr Doc 4333.5F   South Africa. Directorate of Demobilization. Annual
        report. Pretoria.
    Afr Doc 4336.5   South Africa. Group Areas Development Board. Report on the
        activities. 1959+
    Afr Doc 4338.5F   South Africa. Inland Revenue Department. Report for the
        Secretary for Inland Revenue. Pretoria. 1959+
    Afr Doc 4342.5F   South Africa. Department of Lands. Report. Pretoria.
        1958+
    Afr Doc 4343.5F   South Africa. Natives Resettlement Board. Annual report.
        1954+
    Afr Doc 4343.10F   South Africa. Natural Resources Development Council.
        Annual report. Pretoria. 1,1948+
    Afr Doc 4345.10F   South Africa. Department of Planning. Report on the
        activities. Pretoria. 1,1964+
    Afr Doc 4345.15F   South Africa. Department of Planning. Economic development
        programme for the Republic of South Africa. Pretoria.
        1964+
    Afr Doc 4345.20   South Africa. Department of Public Works. Report. Cape
        Town. 1966+
    Afr Doc 4348.3   South Africa. Social and Economic Planning Council. Annual
        report.
    Afr Doc 4348.5F   South Africa. Social and Economic Planning Council.
        Report. 1-10,1943-1947
    Afr Doc 4353.5   South Africa. National Welfare Board. Welfare organisation
        act no. 40 of 1947 quinquennial report. 1,1957+
    Afr Doc 4353.7   South Africa. National Welfare Board. Welfare
        organizations act no. 40 of 1947. Report on the operation
        and administration of the act [annual]. 4,1951+

Afr Doc 4407.1 - .199 **British Africa - South Africa - Cape Colony, Cape of**
Good Hope - Statistics - General compilations
    Afr Doc 4407.5   Cape of Good Hope. Statistical register. Cape Town.
        1886-1909
        23v.

Afr Doc 4407.200 - .999 **British Africa - South Africa - Cape Colony, Cape of**
Good Hope - Statistics - Census
    Afr Doc 4407.291F   Cape of Good Hope. Results of a census of the colony of
        the Cape of Good Hope. Cape Town, 1892.

Afr Doc 4409.1 - .299 **British Africa - South Africa - Cape Colony, Cape of**
Good Hope - Statistics - Budget
    Afr Doc 4409.5F   Cape of Good Hope. Department of Treasurer. Begrooting van
        uitgaaf te worden gedekt gedurende net jaar. 1890-1910
        27v.
    Afr Doc 4409.6F   Cape of Good Hope. Department of Treasurer. Estimates of
        the expenditure to be defrayed during the year 1899/1900.

Afr Doc 4502 **British Africa - South Africa - Natal - General collections -**
Bibliographies, catalogs, etc.
    Afr Doc 4502.2   Webb, C. de B. A guide to the official records of the
        Colony of Natal. Pietermaritzburg, 1965.

Afr Doc 4507.1 - .199 **British Africa - South Africa - Natal - Statistics -**
General compilations
    Afr Doc 4507.5   Natal, Africa. Statistical yearbook. 1904-1909
        6v.

Afr Doc 4531 - 4556 **British Africa - South Africa - Natal - Executive** s
ocuments - Depts., Bureaus, etc., A-Z (by catchword)
    Afr Doc 4535.5F   Natal. Education Department. Report of the Director of
        Education. 1899-1929
        4v.

Afr Doc 4707.200 - .999 **British Africa - South Africa - Orange Free State -**
Statistics - Census
    Afr Doc 4707.304F   Orange Free State. Census report of the Orange River
        Colony. Bloemfontein, 1904.

Afr Doc 4806 **British Africa - South Africa - Transkeian Territories - General**
collections - Other
    Afr Doc 4806.5   Transkeian Territories. Transkei official gazette.
        Umtata. 1,1964+
        2v.

Afr Doc 4809.1 - .299 **British Africa - South Africa - Transkeian**
territories - Statistics - Budget
    Afr Doc 4809.5   South Africa. Transkei. Estimates of expenditure to be
        defrayed from the Transkeian revenue fund. 1965+

Afr Doc 4812 **British Africa - South Africa - Transkeian Territories - Legislative**
documents - General
    Afr Doc 4812.5F   Transkeian Territories. General Council. Proceedings and
        report of select committees. 1928+
    Afr Doc 4812.5.10   Transkeian Territories. General Council. Prodeedings of a
        special session of the United Transkeian Territories
        General Council held on 23rd and 24th Nov., 1955.
        Umtata, 1955.

Afr Doc 4814 **British Africa - South Africa - Transkeian Territories - Legislative**
documents - House Journal, etc.
    Afr Doc 4814.5   Transkeian Territories. Legislative Assembly. Debates.
        Umtata. 1,1963+

Afr Doc 4831 - 4856 **British Africa - South Africa - Transkeian Territories -**
Executive documents - Depts., Bureaus, etc., A-Z (by catchword)
    Afr Doc 4832.5F   South Africa. Control and Audit Office. Report of the
        Controller and Auditor-General. Pretoria. 1964+
    Afr Doc 4839.5F   Transkeian Territories. Department of the Interior. Annual
        report. 3,1966+

Afr Doc 5002 **French Africa - General - General collections - Bibliographies,**
catalogs, etc.
    Afr Doc 5002.5   France. Institut National de la Statistique et des Etudes
        Economiques. Situation des enquêtes statistiques et
        socio-économiques dans les états africains et malgaches.
        Paris. 1964+

Afr Doc 5008.1 - .299 **French Africa - General - Statistics - Vital,**
population, etc.
    Afr Doc 5008.5   France. Institut National de la Statistique et des Etudes
        Economiques. Service de Cooperation. Afrique noire,
        Madagascar, Comores; démographie comparée. v.1-5,7,9-10.
        Paris, 1965-67.
        3v.
    Afr Doc 5008.207   France. Ministère de la Cooperation. Perspectives de
        population dans les pays africains et malgache d'expression
        française. Paris, 1963.

Afr Doc 5008.700 - .999 **French Africa - General - Statistics - Trade**
    Afr Doc 5008.700   France. Institut National de la Statistique et des Etudes
        Economique. Service de Coopération. Commerce extérieur des
        états d'Afrique et de Madagascar. Paris. 1949+
    Afr Doc 5008.705   France. Institut National de la Statistique et des Etudes
        Economiques. Compendium des statistiques du commerce
        extérieur de pays africains et Malgache. 1960+

Afr Doc 5009.500 - .999 **French Africa - General - Statistics - Other**
    Afr Doc 5009.505   France. Secrétariat d'Etat aux affaires étrangères, Charge
        de la Cooperation. Données statistiques sur l'enseignement
        dans les etats africains et malgache d'expression
        française. Paris. 1965+

Afr Doc 5031 - 5056 **French Africa - General - Executive documents - Depts.,**
Bureaus, etc., A-Z (by catchword)
    Afr Doc 5033.5   France. Direction de la coopération culturelle et
        technique. Rapport d'activité. Paris. 1961+

Afr Doc 5207.1 - .199 **French Africa - French North Africa - Morocco -**
Statistics - General compilations
    Afr Doc 5207.5   Morocco. Service Central des Statistiques. Annuaire
        statistique du Maroc. 1959+
    Afr Doc 5207.10   Morocco. Service Central des Statistiques. Bulletin
        mensuel de statistique. 1,1957+
    Afr Doc 5207.11   Morocco. Service Central des Statistiques. Bulletin
        mensuel de statistique. Supplement. 1958+

Afr Doc 5207.200 - .999 **French Africa - French North Africa - Morocco -**
Statistics - Census
    Afr Doc 5207.360   Morocco. Service Central des Statistiques. Recensement
        demographique juin 1960. Population legale du Maroc.
        Rabat, 1961-62.
        2v.
    Afr Doc 5207.360.5   Morocco. Service Central des Statistiques. Résultats du
        recensement de 1960. Rabat, 1964-65.
    Afr Doc 5207.361   Morocco. Service Central des Statistiques. Résultats de
        l'enquête à objectifs multiples, 1961-1963. Rabat? 1964.

Afr Doc 5208.500 - .699 **French Africa - French North Africa - Morocco -**
Statistics - Industry, manufactures
    Afr Doc 5208.500F   Etude de conjoncture; situation et perspectives de
        l'industrie. Rabat. 13,1968+

Afr Doc 5208.700 - .999 **French Africa - French North Africa - Morocco -**
Statistics - Trade
    Afr Doc 5208.705   Morocco. Ministere du Commerce et de l'Artisanat.
        Statistiques du mouvement commercial et maritime du Maroc.
        Maroc. 1960+

**Afr Doc   5306   French Africa - French North Africa - Algeria - General collections -
Other**
    Afr Doc 5306.3F   Moniteur algérien, journal official de la colonie. Alger.
        12-13,1843-1844

**Afr Doc   5307.1   -   .199   French Africa - French North Africa - Algeria -
Statistics - General compilations**
    Afr Doc 5307.5   Algeria. Service de la Statistique Génerale. Bulletin de
        statistique generale. Statistiques industrielles.   8,1956 +
    Afr Doc 5307.10   Algeria. Direction générale du plan et des études
        économiques. Bulletin mensuel de statistiques générales.
        Alger. 1956-1965
    Afr Doc 5307.15   Algeria. Direction générale du plan et des études
        économiques. Bulletin de statistiques générales. Alger.
        1967+

**Afr Doc   5307.200   -   .999   French Africa - French North Africa - Algeria -
Statistics - Census**
    Afr Doc 5307.348   Algeria. Service de la Statistique Générale. Resultats
        statistique du dénombrement de la population effective le
        31 octobre 1948. Alger, 1950?
        2v.
    Afr Doc 5307.354   Algeria. Service de la Statistique Générale. Resultats
        statistiques du denombrement de la population effective le
        31 octobre 1954. Alger, 1957.
        3v.
    Afr Doc 5307.354.5
        Algeria. Service de la Statistique Générale. Résultats
        statistiques du denombrement de la population effective le
        31 octobre, 1954. Alger, 1958.

**Afr Doc   5402   French Africa - French North Africa - Tunisia - General collections -
Bibliographies, catalogs, etc.**
    Afr Doc 5402.5   Pilipenko, Helene. Recapitulation des periodiques
        officiels parus en Tunisie de 1881 à 1955. Tunis, 1956.

**Afr Doc   5405   French Africa - French North Africa - Tunisia - General collections -
Annual reports**
    Afr Doc 5405.5   Evénements du mois en Tunisie. Tunis. 1,1967+

**Afr Doc   5407.1   -   .199   French Africa - French North Africa - Tunisia -
Statistics - General compilations**
    Afr Doc 5407.5   Tunisia. Service des Statistiques. Annuaire statistique de
        Tunisie. 1955+
        2v.

**Afr Doc   5408.700   -   .999   French Africa - French North Africa - Tunisia -
Statistics - Trade**
    Afr Doc 5408.705   Tunisia. Secretariat d'Etat au Plan et à l'Economie
        Nationale. Statistiques du commerce exterieur. Tunisia.
        1965+

**Afr Doc   5409.1   -   .299   French Africa - French North Africa - Tunisia -
Statistics - Budget**
    Afr Doc 5409.5   Tunisia. Secretariat d'Etat au Plan et à l'Economie
        Nationale. Rapport sur le budget économique. Tunis.
        1967+
    Afr Doc 5409.6   Tunisia. Secretariat d'Etat au Plan et à l'Economie
        Nationale. Annexe statistique au rapport sur le budget
        économique. Tunis. 1967+

**Afr Doc   5409.300   -   .499   French Africa - French North Africa - Tunisia -
Statistics - National income and accounts, surveys**
    Afr Doc 5409.305   Tunisia. Service des Statistiques. Les comptes économiques
        de la Tunisie. 1,1953

**Afr Doc   5507.200   -   .999   French Africa - French Somaliland - Statistics -
Census**
    Afr Doc 5507.356   France. Institut National de la Statistique et des Etudes
        Economiques. Recensement de la population de la Cote
        française des Somalis, population non originaire, 1956.
        Paris, 1961.

**Afr Doc   5508.500   -   .699   French Africa - French Somaliland - Statistics -
Industry, manufactures**
    Afr Doc 5508.614   France. Institut National de la Statistique et des Etudes
        Economiques. Comptes économiques de la Cote française des
        Somalis. Paris. 1959+

**Afr Doc   5602   French Africa - Madagascar, Malagasy Republic - General collections -
Bibliographies, catalogs, etc.**
    Afr Doc 5602.5   Library of Congress. African Section. Madagascar and
        adjacent islands; a guide to official publications.
        Washington, 1965.

**Afr Doc   5605   French Africa - Madagascar, Malagasy Republic - General collections -
Annual reports**
    Afr Doc 5605.5   Malagasy Republic. Rapport sur l'activité du gouvernement.
        Tananarive. 1,1963+

**Afr Doc   5607.1   -   .199   French Africa - Madagascar, Malagasy Republic -
Statistics - General compilations**
    Afr Doc 5607.5   Madagascar. Service de Statistique Generale. Annuaire
        statistique. Tananarive. 1,1938+
    Afr Doc 5607.10   Malagasy Republic. Institut National de la Statistique et
        de la Recherche Economique. Bulletin mensuel de
        statistique. Tananarive. 64,1961+
    Afr Doc 5607.15F   Madagascar. Statistiques générales. 1906-1908

**Afr Doc   5607.200   -   .999   French Africa - Madagascar, Malagasy Republic -
Statistics - Census**
    Afr Doc 5607.362   Malagasy Republic. Institut National de la Statistique et
        de la Recherche Economique. Recensements urbains.
        Tananarive, 1965-
        2v.

**Afr Doc   5608.1   -   .299   French Africa - Madagascar, Malagasy Republic -
Statistics - Vital, population, etc.**
    Afr Doc 5608.41.5   Malagasy Republic. Institut National de la Statistique et
        de la Recherche Economique. Etat civil, année 1965.
        Tananarive? 1966?
    Afr Doc 5608.105F   Malagasy Republic. Institut National de la Statistique et
        de la Recherche Economique. Population de Madagascar.
        Tananarive. 1962+

**Afr Doc   5608.700   -   .999   French Africa - Madagascar, Malagasy Republic -
Statistics - Trade**
    Afr Doc 5608.700   Madagascar. Institut National de la Statistique et de la
        Recherche Economique. Statistiques du commerce exterieur.
        1964+
    Afr Doc 5608.700.5   Madagascar. Institut National de la Statistique et de la
        Recherche Economique. Series retrospectives, 1949-1961.
        n.p., n.d.

**Afr Doc   5609.1   -   .299   French Africa - Madagascar, Malagasy Republic -
Statistics - Budget**
    Afr Doc 5609.5   Malagasy Republic. Ministère des Finances et du Commerce.
        Budget général de l'état. Tananarive. 1964+

**Afr Doc   5609.300   -   .499   French Africa - Madagascar, Malagasy Republic -
Statistics - National income and accounts, surveys**
    Afr Doc 5609.300   Madagascar. Institut National de la Statistique et de la
        Recherche Economique. Situation économique. Tananarive.
        1961+
    Afr Doc 5609.305   Malagasy. Republic National de la Statistique et de la
        Recherche Economique. Series chronologiques et graphiques
        relatifs a l'économie malgache. Madagascar, 1963.

**Afr Doc   5609.500   -   .999   French Africa - Madagascar, Malagasy Republic -
Statistics - Other**
    Afr Doc 5609.500   Madagascar. Notice sur les impôts, droits et taxes.
        Tananarive. 1964+

**Afr Doc   5622   French Africa - Madagascar, Malagasy Republic - Executive documents -
General**
    Afr Doc 5622.5   Madagascar. Rapport sur la situation générale de la
        colonie. n.p., n.d.
    Afr Doc 5622.10   Madagascar. Gouvernement Général de Madagascar et
        Dépendences. Madagascar de 1896 à 1905. n.p., n.d.
        2v.

**Afr Doc   5631   -   5656   French Africa - Madagascar, Malagasy Republic - Executive
documents - Depts., Bureaus, etc., A-Z (by catchword)**
    Afr Doc 5635.5   Malagasy Republic. Ministere de l'Equipement et des
        Communications. Bulletin d'information. Tananarive.
        8,1963+

**Afr Doc   5709.300   -   .499   French Africa - Comores Islands - Statistics -
National income and accounts, surveys**
    Afr Doc 5709.303   France. Institut National de la Statistique et des Etudes
        Economiques. Comptes économiques du territoire des
        Comores. Paris. 1959+

**Afr Doc   5807.1   -   .199   French Africa - Reunion - Statistics - General
compilations**
    Afr Doc 5807.5   France. Institut National de la Statistique et des Etudes
        Economiques. Annuaire statistique de la Reunion. Paris.
        1952-1955

**Afr Doc   6002   French Africa - French West Africa - General - General collections -
Bibliographies, catalogs, etc.**
    Afr Doc 6002.2   Library of Congress. African Section. French-speaking West
        Africa; a guide to official publications.
        Washington, 1967.

**Afr Doc   6003   French Africa - French West Africa - General - General collections -
Blue books, government manuals, directories**
    Afr Doc 6003.5   French West Africa. Annuaire du gouvernement général de
        l'Afrique occidentale française. n.p., n.d.

**Afr Doc   6007.1   -   .199   French Africa - French West Africa - General -
Statistics - General compilations**
    Afr Doc 6007.2   French West Africa. Service des Etudes et Coordination
        Statistique et Mécanographiques. Annuaire statistique.
        Dakar. 3-6,1936-1957
        2v.
    Afr Doc 6007.5   French West Africa. Service des Etudes et Coordination
        Statistiques et Mécanographiques. Bulletin statistique et
        economique mensuel. 1955-1959
        8v.

**Afr Doc   6107.1   -   .199   French Africa - French West Africa - Mauritania -
Statistics - General compilations**
    Afr Doc 6107.5   Maurtiania. Service de la Statistique. Bulletin
        statistique et economique. Nouakchott. 2,1964+
    Afr Doc 6107.10   Mauritania. Ministere de la Planification et du
        Developpement Rural. Direction de la Statistique. Bulletin
        mensuel statistique. Nouakchott. 1968

**Afr Doc   6108.700   -   .999   French Africa - French West Africa - Mauritania -
Statistics - Trade**
    Afr Doc 6108.705   European Communities. Statistical Office. Republique
        Islamique de Mauritanie. Statistiques du commerce
        extérieur. Nouakchott. 1966+

**Afr Doc   6109.500   -   .999   French Africa - French West Africa - Mauritania -
Statistics - Other**
    Afr Doc 6109.504   Mauritania. Ministère de L'Education Nationale.
        Statistiques de l'enseignement du premier degré. 1967+
    Afr Doc 6109.505   Mauritania. Ministère de l'Education Nationale.
        Statistiques de l'enseignement du second degré. 1967+

**Afr Doc   6207.1   -   .199   French Africa - French West Africa - Senegal -
Statistics - General compilations**
    Afr Doc 6207.5   Sénégal. Service de la Statistique Generale. Bulletin
        statistique bimestriel. 3,1959+
    Afr Doc 6207.10   Sénégal. Service de la Statistique et de la Mécanographie.
        Bulletin statistique et économique mensuel. 1,1960+

**Afr Doc   6208.500   -   .699   French Africa - French West Africa - Senegal -
Statistics - Industry, manufactures**
    Afr Doc 6208.505   Bernard, Jean. Les industries du Sénégal. Paris, 1965.

**Afr Doc   6208.700   -   .999   French Africa - French West Africa - Senegal -
Statistics - Trade**
    Afr Doc 6208.705PF
        Sénégal. Service de la Statistique Generale. Commerce
        extérieur du Sénégal. Commerce special. 1966+

Afr Doc 6209.300 - .499 French Africa - French West Africa - Senegal - Statistics - National income and accounts, surveys
Afr Doc 6209.300   Sénégal. Service de la Statistique Generale. Situation économique du Sénégal. Dakar. 1962+
Afr Doc 6209.305   Sénégal. Ministère du Développement du Plan et de l'Economie. Comptes économiques. Paris. 1959+

Afr Doc 6219   French Africa - French West Africa - Senegal - Legislative documents - Others
Afr Doc 6219.14   Sénégal. Constitution. Constitution de la République du Sénégal. Dakar? 1963

Afr Doc 6271 - 6296   French Africa - French West Africa - Senegal - Local documents - Provinces, cities, etc., A-Z
Afr Doc 6274.4.73   French West Africa. Service des Etudes et Coordination Statistiques et Mécanographiques. Recensement, démographique de Dakar, 1955: résultats définitifs. Paris, 1958-62.
2v.

Afr Doc 6307.200 - .999   French Africa - French West Africa - French Guinea - Statistics - Census
Afr Doc 6307.355   France. Ministère de la France d'Outre-Mer. Service des Statistiques. Mission démographique de Guinée. Etude démographique par sondage, Guinée, 1954-1955. Paris, 1956.

Afr Doc 6407.1 - .199 French Africa - French West Africa - Ivory Coast - Statistics - General compilations
Afr Doc 6407.3   Ivory Coast. Direction de la Statistique et des Etudes Economiques et Démographiques. Bulletin mensuel de statistique. 12,1959+
3v.
Afr Doc 6407.3.2   Ivory Coast. Direction de la Statistique et des Etudes Economiques et Démographiques. Bulletin mensuel de statistique. Supplement trimestriel. Etudes et rapports.
5v.

Afr Doc 6408.700 - .999   French Africa - French West Africa - Ivory Coast - Statistics - Trade
Afr Doc 6408.705   Ivory Coast. Direction de la Statistique et des Etudes Economiques et Démographiques. Statistiques du commerce extérieur de la Côte d'Ivoire. 1961+
Afr Doc 6408.707   Ivory Coast. Direction du Commerce Extérieur. Commerce exterieur et balance commerciale. Abidjan. 1964+
Afr Doc 6408.709   Ivory Coast. Direction du Commerce Extérieur. Memento économique. Abidijan. 1964+

Afr Doc 6409.300 - .499   French Africa - French West Africa - Ivory Coast - Statistics - National income and accounts, surveys
Afr Doc 6409.305   Ivory Coast. Direction de la Statistique et des Etudes Economiques et Démographiques. Situation économique de la Côte d'Ivoire. 1960+
3v.
Afr Doc 6409.307   Ivory Coast. Direction de la Statistique et des Etudes Economiques et Démographiques. Les comptes économiques. 1958+
Afr Doc 6409.310   Ivory Coast. Caisse Autonome d'Amortissement. Gestion de la dette publique. Gestion des depôts. Abidjan. 1960+
Afr Doc 6409.315   Leblan, Pierre Jean. Les comptes de la nation, 1966-1967 (provisoire). Abidjan, 1968.

Afr Doc 6431 - 6456   French Africa - French West Africa - Ivory Coast - Executive documents - Depts., Bureaus, etc., A-Z (by catchword)
Afr Doc 6443.5   Ivory Coast. Direction des Mines et de la Geologie. Rapport annuel. Abidjan. 1966+

Afr Doc 6471 - 6496   French Africa - French West Africa - Ivory Coast - Local documents - Provinces, cities, etc., A-Z
Afr Doc 6471.1.73   Ivory Coast. Direction de la Statistique et des Etudes economiques et démographiques. Recensement d'Abidjan 1955. Paris, 1960.
Afr Doc 6471.5   Ivory Coast. Ministère des Travaux Publics et des Transports. Port d'Abidjan; rapport annuel. Abidjan. 1966+
Afr Doc 6471.10   Ivory Coast. Direction de la Statistique et des Etudes Economiques et Démographiques. Recensement des centres urbains d'Abengoonon, Aghoville, Dunboko et Man, 1956, 1957. Résultats définitif. Paris, 1960.
Afr Doc 6472.5   Ivory Coast. Direction de la Statistique et des Etudes Economiques et Démographiques. Recensement démographique de Bruehe, 1958. Résultats définitifs. Paris, 1961.

Afr Doc 6507.1 - .199   French Africa - French West Africa - Upper Volta - Statistics - General compilations
Afr Doc 6507.5   Upper Volta. Ministère du Developpement et du Tourisme. Bulletin mensuel de statistique. Ouagadougou. 7,1966+

Afr Doc 6507.200 - .999   French Africa - French West Africa - Upper Volta - Statistics - Census
Afr Doc 6507.361.10   Upper Volta. Service de Statistique. La situation démographique en Haute-Volta; résultats partiels de l'énquête démographique, 1960-1961. Paris, 1962.

Afr Doc 6508.700 - .999   French Africa - French West Africa - Upper Volta - Statistics - Trade
Afr Doc 6508.705   Upper Volta. Ministère de l'Economie Nationale. Commerce extérieur de la Haute-Volta. Ouagadougou. 1961+

Afr Doc 6509.300 - .499   French Africa - French West Africa - Upper Volta - Statistics - National income and accounts, surveys
Afr Doc 6509.305   Upper Volta. Service de la Statistique. Comptes économiques de la Haute-Volta. Paris. 1964+

Afr Doc 6571 - 6596   French Africa - French West Africa - Upper Volta - Local documents - Provinces, cities, etc., A-Z
Afr Doc 6585.1.73   Upper Volta. Service de la Statistique. Recensement démographique Ouagadougou, 1961-1962. Paris, 1964.

Afr Doc 6607.1 - .199   French Africa - French West Africa - Dahomey - Statistics - General compilations
Afr Doc 6607.5   Dahomey. Haut Commissariat au Plan et au Tourisme. Annuaire statistique. Cotonou. 1965
Afr Doc 6607.10   Dahomey. Service Central de la Statistique et de la Mécanographie. Bulletin de statistique. Cotonou. 2,1965+
Afr Doc 6607.15   Dahomey. Direction des Affaires Economiques. Bulletin économique et statistique. 1961+
3v.

Afr Doc 6607.1 - .199   French Africa - French West Africa - Dahomey - Statistics - General compilations cont.
Afr Doc 6607.20   Dahomey. Ministère des Finances et des Affaires Economiques. Aspects éonomiques. Cotonou. 1962+

Afr Doc 6607.200 - .999   French Africa - French West Africa - Dahomey - Statistics - Census
Afr Doc 6607.361   France. Institut National de la Statistiqe et des Etudes Economique. Service de Cooperation. Données de base sur la situation démographique au Dahomey en 1961. Paris, 1962.

Afr Doc 6609.1 - .299   French Africa - French West Africa - Dahomey - Statistics - Budget
Afr Doc 6609.5F   Dahomey. Budget national. 1960+

Afr Doc 6631 - 6656   French Africa - French West Africa - Dahomey - Executive documents - Depts., Bureaus, etc., A-Z (by catchword)
Afr Doc 6634.5   Dahomey. Service du Développement Rural. Rapport annuel. Porto-Novo. 1962+

Afr Doc 6705   French Africa - French West Africa - French Togo - General collections - Annual reports
Afr Doc 6705.5   L'annuaire du Togo. Lomé, Togo. 1963+

Afr Doc 6707.1 - .199   French Africa - French West Africa - French Togo - Statistics - General compilations
Afr Doc 6707.2   Togoland. Service de la Statistique Générale. Bulletin de statistique. Lomé 7,1964+

Afr Doc 6707.200 - .999   French Africa - French West Africa - French Togo - Statistics - Census
Afr Doc 6707.358   Togo. Service de la Statistique Général. Recensement général de la population du Togo, 1958-1960. Lomé, 1962?
Afr Doc 6707.361   Togo. Service de la Statistique Général. Enquête démographique, 1961. Lomé. 1962

Afr Doc 6708.700 - .999   French Africa - French West Africa - French Togo - Statistics - Trade
Afr Doc 6708.702   Togo. Service de la Statistique Générale. Annuaire retrospectif du commerce special du Togo, 1937-1964. Lomé, 1964.

Afr Doc 6709.300 - .499   French Africa - French West Africa - French Togo - Statistics - National income and accounts, surveys
Afr Doc 6709.300   Togoland. Service de la Statistique Générale. Inventaire économique du Togo. Lomé. 1959+
Afr Doc 6709.305   Togo. Haut Commissariat au Plan. Comptes nationaux. Lomé. 1963+

Afr Doc 6771 - 6796   French Africa - French West Africa - French Togo - Local documents - Provinces, cities, etc., A-Z
Afr Doc 6781.735   Togo. Service de la Statistique Général. Etude démographique du pays Kabre, 1957. Paris, 1960.

Afr Doc 6803   French Africa - French West Africa - French Sudan, Mali - General collections - Blue books, government manuals, directories
Afr Doc 6803.5   Mali. Gouvernement, assemblée nationale et representations diverses de la République du Mali. Bamalco, 1963.

Afr Doc 6807.1 - .199   French Africa - French West Africa - French Sudan, Mali - Statistics - General compilations
Afr Doc 6807.5   Mali. Direction de la Statistique. Annuaire statistique. Bamako. 1963+
Afr Doc 6807.10   Mali. Service de la Statistique Générale et de la Comptabilité Economique Nationale. Bulletin mensuel de statistique. Bamako. 1964+

Afr Doc 6807.200 - .999   French Africa - French West Africa - French Sudan, Mali - Statistics - Census
Afr Doc 6807.360   Mali. Enquête agricole au Mali, 1960.
Afr Doc 6807.364   Mali. Service de la Statistique de la Coruptabilité Nationale et de la Mécanographie. Rapport définitif de l'enquête agricole, 1964. Mali, 196 .

Afr Doc 6808.1 - .299   French Africa - French West Africa - French Sudan, Mali - Statistics - Vital, population, etc.
Afr Doc 6808.90   France. Ministère de la France d'Outre-Mer. Etude démographique du delta vif du Niger. pt.1. v.2. Paris. 1962

Afr Doc 6809.1 - .299   French Africa - French West Africa - French Sudan, Mali - Statistics - Budget
Afr Doc 6809.2F   Mali. Ministère des Finances et du Commerce. Budget d'état. Bamako. 1962+

Afr Doc 6812   French Africa - French West Africa - French Sudan, Mali - Legislative documents - General
Afr Doc 6812.5F   Mali. Fédération. Assemblée Fédérale. Journal officiel. Debats parlementaires.

Afr Doc 6907.1 - .199   French Africa - French West Africa - Niger - Statistics - General compilations
Afr Doc 6907.5   France. Ministère de la Coopération. Mission Economique et Pastorale, 1963. Etude démographique et économique en milieu homade. Paris, 1966.
Afr Doc 6907.10   Niger. Service de la Statistique. Bulletin de statistique. Niamey. 8,1966+

Afr Doc 6907.200 - .999   French Africa - French West Africa - Niger - Statistics - Census
Afr Doc 6907.360   France. Institut National de la Statistique et des Etudes Economiques. Service de Coopération. Etude démographique du Niger. Paris, 1962-1963.
2v.

Afr Doc 6931 - 6956   French Africa - French West Africa - Niger - Executive documents - Depts., Bureaus, etc., A-Z (by catchword)
Afr Doc 6931.5   Niger. Service de l'Agriculture. Rapport. Niamey. 1964+

Afr Doc 7002   French Africa - French Equatorial Africa - General - General ollections - Bibliographies, catalogs, etc.
Afr Doc 7002.5   Library of Congress. African Section. Official publications of French Equatorial Africa, French Cameroons, and Togo, 1946-1958. Washington, 1964.

Afr Doc 7007.1 - .199   French Africa - French Equatorial Africa - General -
Statistics - General compilations
    Afr Doc 7007.5   French Equatorial Africa. Service de la Statistique
        Générale. Bulletin mensuel de statistique de l'Afrique
        equatoriale française. 4-11,1950-1957
        3v.

Afr Doc 7103   French Africa - French Equatorial Africa - Chad - General collections -
Blue books, government manuals, directories
    Afr Doc 7103.7   United States. Embassy. Chad. Diplomatic list, Fort Lamy.
        Chad. Fort Lamy? 1966.

Afr Doc 7107.1 - .199   French Africa - French Equatorial Africa - Chad -
Statistics - General compilations
    Afr Doc 7107.5   Chad. Service de la Statistique Générale. Bulletin mensuel
        de la statistique. Fort-Lamy. 127,1965+
    Afr Doc 7107.10   Chad. Service de la Statistique Générale. Annuaire
        statistique du Tchad. Fort Lamy? 2,1968+

Afr Doc 7107.200 - .999   French Africa - French Equatorial Africa - Chad -
Statistics - Census
    Afr Doc 7107.364   Chad. Service de la Statistique Générale. Enquête
        démographique ou Tchad, 1964 résultats définitifs. v.1-2.
        Paris, 1966.

Afr Doc 7108.1 - .299   French Africa - French Equatorial Africa - Chad -
Statistics - Vital, population, etc.
    Afr Doc 7108.5   France. Institut National de la Statistique et des Etudes
        Economique. La situation démographique au Tchad, résultats
        provisoires. Paris, 196-.

Afr Doc 7109.1 - .299   French Africa - French Equatorial Africa - Chad -
Statistics - Budget
    Afr Doc 7109.5F   French Equatorial Africa. Territoire du Tchad; budget
        local. Fort Lamy. 1952-1953

Afr Doc 7109.300 - .499   French Africa - French Equatorial Africa - Chad -
Statistics - National income and accounts, surveys
    Afr Doc 7109.305   Chad. Comptes économiques. Paris. 1961-1963

Afr Doc 7114   French Africa - French Equatorial Africa - Chad - Legislative
documents - House Journal, etc.
    Afr Doc 7114.5F   Chad. Assemblée Territoriale. Procès-verbaux, etc.
        1951-1953

Afr Doc 7131 - 7156   French Africa - French Equatorial Africa - Chad - Executive
documents - Depts., Bureaus, etc., A-Z (by catchword)
    Afr Doc 7135.5   Chad. Ministère de l'Economie et des Transports. Rapport
        annuel. 1965+

Afr Doc 7171 - 7196   French Africa - French Equatorial Africa - Chad - Local
documents - Provinces, cities, etc., A-Z
    Afr Doc 7176.5   Chad. Service de la Statistique Générale. Recensement
        démographique de Fort Lamy. Paris. 1965

Afr Doc 7207.1 - .199   French Africa - French Equatorial Africa - Central
African Republic, Ubangi-Chari - Statistics - General compilations
    Afr Doc 7207.5   Central African Republic. Service de la Statistique et de
        la Conjoncture. Bulletin mensuel de statistique. Bangui.
        14,1965+
    Afr Doc 7207.10   Central African Republic. Direction de la Statistique et de
        la Conjoncture. Annuaire statistique. Paris. 1964

Afr Doc 7207.200 - .999   French Africa - French Equatorial Africa - Central
African Republic, Ubangi-Chari - Statistics - Census
    Afr Doc 7207.359   Mission Socioéconomique Centre Oubanqui. Enquête
        démographique Centre-Oubanqui 1959; méthodologie, résultats
        provisoires. Paris, 1960.
    Afr Doc 7207.360   Central African Republic. Service de la Statistique
        Generale. Enquête démographique. n.p., 1959-60.
    Afr Doc 7207.361   Central African Republic. Service de la Statistique
        Générale. Enquête agricole en République centrafricaine.
        n.p., 1960-61.

Afr Doc 7209.1 - .299   French Africa - French Equatorial Africa - Central
African Republic, Ubangi-Chari - Statistics - Budget
    Afr Doc 7209.44   Central African Republic. Budget de l'état. 1959 |
        8v.

Afr Doc 7209.500 - .999   French Africa - French Equatorial Africa - Central
African Republic, Ubangi-Chari - Statistics - Other
    Afr Doc 7209.505   Central African Republic. Ministère l'Education Nationale,
        de la Jeunesse et des Sports. Statistiques scolaires.
        Bangui. 1964+

Afr Doc 7307.1 - .199   French Africa - French Equatorial Africa - French
Congo, Middle Congo, Congo (Brazzaville) - Statistics - General
compilations
    Afr Doc 7307.5   Congo (Brazzaville). Direction du Service National de la
        Statistique, des Etudes Démographiques et Economiques.
        Bulletin mensuel des statistiques. Brazzaville. 1962+

Afr Doc 7307.200 - .999   French Africa - French Equatorial Africa -
French Congo, Middle Congo, Congo (Brazzaville) - Statistics - Census
    Afr Doc 7307.361   Congo (Brazzaville). Direction du Service National de la
        Statistique, des Etudes Démographiques et Economiques.
        Enquête démographique, 1960-1961. Résultats définitifs.
        n.p., n.d.

Afr Doc 7312   French Africa - French Equatorial Africa - French Congo, Middle Congo,
Congo (Brazzaville) - Legislative documents - General
    Afr Doc 7312.5F   Congo (Brazzaville). Assemblée Nationale. Journal des
        debats.

Afr Doc 7331 - 7356   French Africa - French Equatorial Africa - French Congo,
Middle Congo, Congo (Brazzaville) - Executive documents - Depts.,
Bureaus, etc., A-Z (by catchword)
    Afr Doc 7335.5   Congo (Brazzaville). Conseil Economique et Social. Rapport
        annuel. 1964+

Afr Doc 7371 - 7396   French Africa - French Equatorial Africa - French Congo,
Middle Congo, Congo (Brazzaville) - Local documents - Provinces, cities,
etc., A-Z
    Afr Doc 7372.361   Congo (Brazzaville). Service de Statistique. Recensement
        de Brazzaville, 1961; résultats définitifs. Paris, 1965.
    Afr Doc 7386.5.73   Congo (Brazzaville). Statistique Générale. Recensement
        démographique de Pointe-Noire, 1958. Paris, 1961.

Afr Doc 7403   French Africa - French Equatorial Africa - Gabon - General collections -
Blue books, government manuals, directories
    Afr Doc 7403.3   Le Gabon. Monte-Carlo. 1964

Afr Doc 7405   French Africa - French Equatorial Africa - Gabon - General collections -
Annual reports
    Afr Doc 7405.5   Gabon. Ministère de l'Information. Annuaire national.
        Paris. 1967+

Afr Doc 7407.1 - .199   French Africa - French Equatorial Africa - Gabon -
Statistics - General compilations
    Afr Doc 7407.5   Gabon. Service National de la Statistique. Annuaire
        statistique. 1964+
    Afr Doc 7407.10   Gabon. Service National de la Statistique. Bulletin
        mensuel de statistique. 5,1963+
        4v.
    Afr Doc 7407.10.2   Gabon. Service National de la Statistique. Bulletin
        mensuel de statistique. Supplement. 5,1962+
        2v.

Afr Doc 7407.200 - .999   French Africa - French Equatorial Africa - Gabon -
Statistics - Census
    Afr Doc 7407.361   Gabon. Service de Statistiques. Recensement et enquête
        démographiques, 1960-1961; résutats provisionelles.
        Paris, 1963.
    Afr Doc 7407.361.10   Gabon. Service National de la Statistique. Recensement et
        enquête démographiques, 1960-1961: Résultats pour
        Libreville. Paris, 1962.
    Afr Doc 7407.361.15   Gabon. Service Nat+onal de la Statistique. Recensement et
        enquête demographiques, 1960-1961: ensemble du Gabon.
        Paris, 1965.

Afr Doc 7409.1 - .299   French Africa - French Equatorial Africa - Gabon -
Statistics - Budget
    Afr Doc 7409.5   Gabon. Ministère d'état chargé de l'économie nationale, du
        plan et des mines. Budget de développement. 1964+

Afr Doc 7409.300 - .499   French Africa - French Equatorial Africa - Gabon -
Statistics - National income and accounts, surveys
    Afr Doc 7409.305   Gabon. Commissariat au Plan. Comptes economicas.
        Libreville. 1964+

Afr Doc 7409.500 - .999   French Africa - French Equatorial Africa - Gabon -
Statistics - Other
    Afr Doc 7409.505F   Gabon. Ministère de l'Education Nationale. Statistiques de
        l'enseignement au Gabon. Libreville. 1965+

Afr Doc 7505   French Africa - French Cameroons - General collections - Annual reports
    Afr Doc 7505.5   Cameroon. Annuaire national. Yaoundé. 1964+

Afr Doc 7506   French Africa - French Cameroons - General collections - Other
    Afr Doc 7506.2   Cameroon. Commissariat Général á l'Information.
        Institutions et Constitution de la République Fédérale du
        Cameroun. Yaoundé, 1962?

Afr Doc 7507.1 - .199   French Africa - French Cameroons - Statistics -
General compilations
    Afr Doc 7507.2   Cameroon. Service de la Statistique Générale et de la
        Mécanographie. Resumé des statistiques du Cameroun
        oriental. Yaoundé. 3,1965+
    Afr Doc 7507.5.2   Cameroon. Service de la Statistique Générale et de la
        Mécanographie. Bulletin de la statistique general.
        Supplement. 1,1958+
    Afr Doc 7507.7   Cameroon. Service de la Statistique Générale et de la
        Mécanographie. Note trimestrielle sur la situation
        économique. 2,1963+
    Afr Doc 7507.9   Cameroon. Direction de la Statistique et de la
        Comptabilité Nationale. Bulletin mensuel de statistique.
        5,1967+

Afr Doc 7508.1 - .299   French Africa - French Cameroons - Statistics - Vital,
population, etc.
    Afr Doc 7508.5   Cameroon. Service de la Statistique Général et la
        Mécanographie. Enquête démographique sur la zone Centre et
        l'Est. Yaoundé, 1963.
    Afr Doc 7508.6   Cameroon. Service de la Statistique Générale et la
        Mécanographie. The population of West Cameroon; main
        findings. Paris, 1966.

Afr Doc 7509.1 - .299   French Africa - French Cameroons - Statistics - Budget
    Afr Doc 7509.5   Cameroon. Budget. Yaoundé. 1961+
        2v.
    Afr Doc 7509.89   West Cameroon. Estimates. Buea. 1964+

Afr Doc 7509.300 - .499   French Africa - French Cameroons - Statistics -
National income and accounts, surveys
    Afr Doc 7509.300   Cameroon. Ministère des Finances du Plan et de l'Equipement
        National. Données essentielles de l'économie. Yaoundé.
        1951+
    Afr Doc 7509.305F   West Cameroon. The accounts of the government together
        with a report of the Controller of Accounts. Buea. 1960+
    Afr Doc 7509.310   Cameroon. Service de la Statistique Générales et de la
        Mécanographie. Etude de l'économie Cameroonaise. 1957+
        2v.

Afr Doc 7509.500 - .999   French Africa - French Cameroons - Statistics -
Other
    Afr Doc 7509.500   Cameroon. Service de la Statistique Générale et de la
        Mécanographie. Le niveau de vie des populations de
        l'Adamaoua. Ircam, 1964.
        2v.
    Afr Doc 7509.505   West Cameroon. Department of Education. Education
        department statistics. Buea. 1962+
    Afr Doc 7509.510F   Cameroon. Ministère de l'Education, de la Jeunesse et de la
        Culture. Annuaire statistique. Enseignement: sécondaire
        (général et technique), superior, éducation des adultes.
        Yaoundé. 1964+

Afr Doc 7516   French Africa - French Cameroons - Legislative documents - Senate
Journal, etc.
    Afr Doc 7516.5   West Cameroon. House of Chiefs. Debates. Buea. 2,1962+
    Afr Doc 7516.8   West Cameroon. House of Assembly. Debates; official
        report. Buea. 1963+
    Afr Doc 7516.10   West Cameroon. House of Chiefs. Standing orders. Buea.
        1962+

Afr Doc 7531 - 7556   French Africa - French Cameroons - Executive documents -
Depts., Bureaus, etc., A-Z (by catchword)
Afr Doc 7533.5   Cameroon. Conseil Economique et Social. Rapport annuel.
     1962+
Afr Doc 7533.10   Cameroon. Conseil National de Credit. Rapport. Paris.
     1962+
Afr Doc 7535.5   Cameroun. Direction de l'Elevage et des Industries
     Animales. Rapport annuel. Yaoundé 1,1966+

Afr Doc 7607.1 - .199   Belgian Africa - General - Statistics - General
compilations
Afr Doc 7607.3   Congo. Direction de la Statistique. Bulletin mensuel des
     statistiques générales du Congo belge et du Ruanda-Urundi.
     Série speciale. Leopoldville. 1,1959+

Afr Doc 7705   Belgian Africa - Congo - General collections - Annual reports
Afr Doc 7705.5F   Belgium. Ministère des Affaires Africaines. Rapport annuel
     sur l'administration de la colonie du Congo Belge.
     1921-1956
     6v.

Afr Doc 7707.1 - .199   Belgian Africa - Congo - Statistics - General
compilations
Afr Doc 7707.10   Congo. Statistiques relatives à l'année. 1957-1958
Afr Doc 7707.15   Congo (Brazzaville). Direction du Service National de la
     Statistique des Etudes Démographiques et Economiques.
     Annuaire statistique. 1,1958+

Afr Doc 7708.1 - .299   Belgian Africa - Congo - Statistics - Vital,
population, etc.
Afr Doc 7708.5   Congo. Secretariat Général. La population congolaise en
     1953. n.p., 195-?

Afr Doc 7708.700 - .999   Belgian Africa - Congo - Statistics - Trade
Afr Doc 7708.705   Congo. Diréction de la Statistique et des Etudes
     Economiques. Annuaire des statistiques du commerce
     extérieur. Leopoldville. 1963+

Afr Doc 7709.1 - .299   Belgian Africa - Congo - Statistics - Budget
Afr Doc 7709.3F   Congo. Service du Budget-Contrôle. Budget ordinaire.
     1966+

Afr Doc 7709.300 - .499   Belgian Africa - Congo - Statistics - National
income and accounts, surveys
Afr Doc 7709.305F   Banque Nationale du Congo. Bulletin. Kinhasa. 7,1968+

Afr Doc 7714   Belgian Africa - Congo - Legislative documents - House Journal, etc.
Afr Doc 7714.5   Congo. Chambre des Representants. Compte rendu analytique.
     Leopoldville. 1962+
     5v.
Afr Doc 7714.10   Congo. Chambre des Députés. Compte rendu analytique
     officiel. Leopoldville. 1966+

Afr Doc 7716   Belgian Africa - Congo - Legislative documents - Senate Journal, etc.
Afr Doc 7716.5F   Congo. Parlement. Senat. Compte rendu officiel.
     Leopoldville. 1965+

Afr Doc 7724   Belgian Africa - Congo - Executive documents - President
Afr Doc 7724.5   Congo. Gouverneur Général. Discours. 1949-1959
     4v.

Afr Doc 7806   Belgian Africa - Ruanda-Urundi, Rwanda - General collections - Other
Afr Doc 7806.5   Rwanda. Embassy. United States. Information bulletin.
     Washington. 1,1966+

Afr Doc 7807.1 - .199   Belgian Africa - Ruanda-Urundi, Rwanda - Statistics -
General compilations
Afr Doc 7807.5   Rwanda. Direction de l'Office Général des Statistiques.
     Bulletin de statistique. Kigali. 1,1964+
     2v.

Afr Doc 7819   Belgian Africa - Ruanda-Urundi, Rwanda - Legislative documents - Others
Afr Doc 7819.5   Rwanda. Constitution. Constitution de la République
     Rwandaise. Kigali, 1963?

Afr Doc 7907.1 - .199   Belgian Africa - Burundi - Statistics - General
compilations
Afr Doc 7907.5   Burundi. Institut Rundi des Statistiques. Bulletin de
     statistique. Bujumbura. 1,1966+
Afr Doc 7907.5.5   Burundi. Institut Rundi des Statistiques. Bulletin de
     statistique. Supplement. 1,1966+

Afr Doc 7909.500 - .999   Belgian Africa - Burundi - Statistics - Other
Afr Doc 7909.505F   Burundi. Service des Statistiques et de la Planification.
     Statistiques de l'enseignement. 1966+

Afr Doc 8707.1 - .199   Spanish Africa - Spanish West Africa - Spanish Guinea,
Rio Muni - Statistics - General compilations
Afr Doc 8707.3   Spain. Delegacion de Estadistica del Gobierna General de la
     Region Equatorial. Resumenes estadisticos. 1948+
     2v.

Afr Doc 8707.200 - .999   Spanish Africa - Spanish West Africa - Spanish
Guinea, Rio Muni - Statistics - Census
Afr Doc 8707.350   Guinea, Spanish. Delegacion Colonial de Estadistica.
     Resúmenes estadisticos del anso general de poblacion del
     Gobcerno General de los Españoles del Golfo de Guinea al 31
     de diciembre de 1950. Madrid, 1952.

Afr Doc 9002   Portuguese Africa - General - General collections - Bibliographies,
catalogs, etc.
Afr Doc 9002.5   Gibson, Mary Jane. Portuguese Africa; a guide to official
     publications. Washington, 1967.

Afr Doc 9018   Portuguese Africa - General - Legislative documents - Statutes, etc.
Afr Doc 9018.5   Portugal. Laws, statutes, etc. Collecção de legeslação
     relativa ás colonias portuguezas em Africa.
     2v.

Afr Doc 9202   Portuguese Africa - Mozambique - General collections - Bibliographies,
catalogs, etc.
Afr Doc 9202.15.3   Mozambique. Relatorios e informações. Lourenço Marques.
     1909
Afr Doc 9202.15.5   Mozambique. Repertorio alphabetica des Boletins officiaes
     da provincia. Lourenço Marques. 1910
Afr Doc 9202.15.8   Mozambique. Synopse dos diplomas officiaes de caracter
     permanente. Lourenço Marques. 1908-1915

Afr Doc 9207.1 - .199   Portuguese Africa - Mozambique - Statistics - General
compilations
Afr Doc 9207.5   Mozambique. Repartição Tecnica de Estatistica. Amerário
     estatistico da colónia de Moçambique. Lourenço Marques.
     12,1939+
     13v.
Afr Doc 9207.10   Mozambique. Repartição Tecnica de Estatistica. Boletim
     trimestral de estatistica. 16-23,1940-1947
Afr Doc 9207.15   Mozambique. Orçamento geral.
Afr Doc 9207.20   Mozambique. Direcção Provincial dos Serviços de Estatistica
     Geral. Boletim mensal. 5,1964+
     5v.

Afr Doc 9207.200 - .999   Portuguese Africa - Mozambique - Statistics - Census
Afr Doc 9207.340   Mozambique. Repartição Tecnica de Estatistica. Censo da
     população em 1940. Lourenço Marques, 1942.
     4v.
Afr Doc 9207.345   Mozambique. Repartição Tecnica de Estatistica.
     Recenseamento da população mão indigena, em 12 de junho de
     1945. Lourenço Marques, 1947.
Afr Doc 9207.350   Mozambique. Repartição Tecnica de Estatistica.
     Recenseamento geral da população em 1950. Lourenço
     Marques, 1953-1955.
     2v.
Afr Doc 9207.355   Mozambique. Direcção dos Serviços de Economica e de
     Estatistica Gerel. Recenseamento geral da população
     civilanada em 1955. Lourenço Marques. 1,1950+

Afr Doc 9208.500 - .699   Portuguese Africa - Mozambique - Statistics -
Industry, manufactures
Afr Doc 9208.505   Mozambique. Direcção Provincial dos Serviços de Estatistica
     Geral. Estatistica industrial. Lourenço Marques. 1,1947+
     2v.

Afr Doc 9208.700 - .999   Portuguese Africa - Mozambique - Statistics - Trade
Afr Doc 9208.700   Mozambique. Direcção Provincial dos Serviços de Estatistica
     Geral. Cabotagem. Laurenço Marques. 35,1962+
Afr Doc 9208.705   Mozambique. Direcção dos Serviços Aduaneiros. Estatistica
     do comercio e navegação. Lourenço Marques. 1904-1930
Afr Doc 9208.710   Mozambique. Direcção Provincial dos Serviços de Estatistica
     Geral. Comercio externo. 1951+
     2v.

Afr Doc 9209.1 - .299   Portuguese Africa - Mozambique - Statistics - Budget
Afr Doc 9209.5F   Mozambique. Orçamento geral para o ano economico. 1945
Afr Doc 9209.10   Mozambique. Orçamentos das câmaras municipais, edilidades
     e comissões. Louvenço. 1917

Afr Doc 9209.300 - .499   Portuguese Africa - Mozambique - Statistics -
National income and accounts, surveys
Afr Doc 9209.300   Mozambqiue. Direcção Provincial des Serviços de Estatistica
     Geral. Estatistica das contribuições e impostos. Lourenço
     Marques. 1,1960+

Afr Doc 9209.500 - .999   Portuguese Africa - Mozambique - Statistics - Other
Afr Doc 9209.500   Mozambique. Direcção Provincial dos Serviços de Estatistica
     Geral. Estatistica do ensino. Lourenço Marques. 1,1963+
Afr Doc 9209.505   Mozambique. Direcção Provincial dos Serviços de
     Estatistica. Estatistica agricola. Lourenço Marques.
     1941+
Afr Doc 9209.510   Mozambique. Reparticão Superior dos Correios. Estatistica
     geral dos correios da provencia de Moçambique. Lourenço
     Marques. 1908

Afr Doc 9224   Portuguese Africa - Mozambique - Executive documents - President
Afr Doc 9224.5   Mozambique. Governado. Relatorio. Lourenço Marques.
     1940-1942
     2v.

Afr Doc 9226   Portuguese Africa - Mozambique - Executive documents - Special
Afr Doc 9226.3   Mozambique. Relatorios. Louvenço. 1915-1916

Afr Doc 9230 - 9255   Portuguese Africa - Mozambique - Executive documents -
Depts., Bureaus, etc., A-Z (by catchword)
Afr Doc 9233.5   Portugal. Curadoria dos Indigenas Portugueses no Transvaal.
     Relatório do curador. Lourenço Marques.
Afr Doc 9244.5   Mozambique. Inspecção dos Obras Publicas. Relatorio.
     1910-1911
Afr Doc 9245.5F   Portugal. Procuradoria. Relatorio da Procuradoria.
     1915-1916

Afr Doc 9271 - 9296   Portuguese Africa - Mozambique - Local documents -
Provinces, cities, etc., A-Z
Afr Doc 9271.5   Amorim, Massano de. Relatorio sobre a occupação de
     Angoche. Lourenço Marques, 1911.
Afr Doc 9272.5   Beira. Intendente do Governo. Relatorio. Lourenço
     Marques. 1908
Afr Doc 9279.5   Inhambane. Governador. Relatorio. Lourenço Marques.
     1907-1917
Afr Doc 9279.10F   Inhambane. Projecto de orçamento. 1917-1918
Afr Doc 9282.4   Lourenço Marques (District). Inspecção das Circunscrições.
     Relatorio. 1909-1915
Afr Doc 9282.10F   Mozambique. Repartição de Agricultura. Reconhecimento
     agricola-económico do distrito de Lourenço Marques.
     1916-1917
Afr Doc 9282.12F   Mozambique. Secretaria Geral. Recenseamentos
     população...de Lourenço Marques. n.p., 1913.
Afr Doc 9282.15F   Mozambique. Relatorios do distrito de Lourenço Marques.
     Laurenço Marques. 1915-1918
Afr Doc 9283.5F   Mozambique. Projecto de orçamonto. 1917-1918
Afr Doc 9287.5   Quelimane. Governador. Relatorio. Louvenço Marques.
     1907-1915
Afr Doc 9290.5F   Tete. Projecto de orçamento. 1917-1918
Afr Doc 9290.10   Tete. Governador. Relatorio. Lourenço Marques. 1908-1912

Afr Doc 9307.1 - .199   Portuguese Africa - Angola - Statistics - General
compilations
Afr Doc 9307.5   Angola. Repartição de Estatistica Geral. Boletim mensal de
     estatistica. Luanda. 22,1966+
Afr Doc 9307.10   Angola. Repartição de Estatistica Geral. Annuario
     estatistico. Luanda. 1962+

Afr Doc 9307.200 - .999   Portuguese Africa - Angola - Statistics - Census
Afr Doc 9307.350   Angola. Segundo recenseamento geral da população, 1950.
     Luanda, 1953-1956.
     5v.

Afr Doc 9307.200 - .999   Portuguese Africa - Angola - Statistics - Census
cont.
     Afr Doc 9307.360   Angola. Reparticão de Estatistica Geral. Terceiro
recenseamento geral da população, 1960. v.1-5.
Luanda, 1964-1969.

Afr Doc 9308.700 - .999   Portuguese Africa - Angola - Statistics - Trade
     Afr Doc 9308.703   Angola. Repartição de Estatistica Geral. Comercio
exterior. Luanda. 1961+

Afr Doc 9309.500 - .999   Portuguese Africa - Angola - Statistics - Other
     Afr Doc 9309.505   Angola. Repartição de Estatistica Geral. Estatistica da
educação. Luanda. 1951+

Afr Doc 9331 - 9356   Portuguese Africa - Angola - Executive documents - Depts.,
Bureaus, etc., A-Z (by catchword)
     Afr Doc 9336.5   Angola. Secretaria Provincial de Formento Rural. Sintese
da actividade dos organismos e serviços. Luanda. 1963+
     Afr Doc 9345.5   Angola. Secretaria Provincial de Obras Publicas e
Comunicações. Sintese da actividade dos serviços. Luanda.
1964+

Afr Doc 9405   Portuguese Africa - Portuguese Guinea - General collections - Annual
reports
     Afr Doc 9405.5   Guinea. Portuguese. Anuário. Lisbon. 1-2,1946-1948
2v.

Afr Doc 9407.200 - .999   Portuguese Africa - Portuguese Guinea - Statistics -
Census
     Afr Doc 9407.350   Guinea. Portuguese. Secção Tecnica de Estatistica. Censo
da população de 1950. Lisboa, 1952?
2v.
     Afr Doc 9407.360   Portugal. Missão de Inquerito Agrícola de Cabo Verte,
Guiné S. Tomé Principe. Recenseamento agrícola da Guiné,
1960-1961. Lisboa, 1963.

Afr Doc 9524   Portuguese Africa - São Tomé e Principe - Executive documents -
President
     Afr Doc 9524.5   São Tomé Island. Governor. Relatorio.

Afr Doc 9600 - 9699   Portuguese Africa - Other islands (Develop as needed)
     Afr Doc 9625.5F   Zambia. Geographical Association. ZGA newsletter. Lusaka.
1,1967+

Afr Doc 9907.200 - .999   Liberia - Statistics - Census
     Afr Doc 9907.362   Liberia. Office of National Planning. Bureau of Statistics.
1962 population census of Liberia: population
characteristics of major areas. Monrovia, 1964?
13v.

Afr Doc 9908.700 - .999   Liberia - Statistics - Trade
     Afr Doc 9908.705   Liberia. Department of Agriculture and Commerce. Bureau of
Statistics. Foreign trade supplement. Monrovia.
1955-1957

Afr Doc 9919   Liberia - Legislative documents - Others
     Afr Doc 9919.5   Liberia. The Declaration of Independence and the
Constitution of the Republic of Liberia as amended through
May, 1955. Monrovia, 196-?

Afr Doc 9924   Liberia - Executive documents - President
     Afr Doc 9924.5F   Liberia. President. Inaugural address.
     Afr Doc 9924.10F   Liberia. President. Annual message.

Afr Doc 9931 - 9956   Liberia - Executive documents - Depts., Bureaus, etc., A-Z
(by catchword)
     Afr Doc 9931.5   Liberia. Department of Agriculture. Annual report.
Monrovia. 1964+
     Afr Doc 9933.5   Liberia. Department of Commerce and Industry. Annual
report. Monorovia. 1965+
     Afr Doc 9935.5   Liberia. Department of Education. Annual report.
Monrovia. 3,1961+
     Afr Doc 9939.5   Liberia. Department of Information and Cultural Affairs.
Annual report. Monrovia. 1964+
     Afr Doc 9939.10   Liberia. Interior Department. Annual report on the
operation. Monrovia. 1961+
     Afr Doc 9939.15   Liberia. Information Service. Annual report. Monrovia.
1962+
     Afr Doc 9944.5   Liberia. Bureau of Natural Resources and Surveys. Annual
report. Monrovia. 1965+
     Afr Doc 9946.5   Liberia. Office of National Planning. Annual report.
Monrovia. 1961+
     Afr Doc 9946.8   Liberia. Department of Planning and Economic Affairs.
Annual report. Monrovia. 1966+
     Afr Doc 9946.10F   Liberia. Postmaster General. Annual report of Postmaster
General on the operation of the Liberian Postal
Administration. Monrovia. 1961+
     Afr Doc 9946.15   Liberia. Department of Public Works and Utilities. Annual
report. Monrovia. 1966+
     Afr Doc 9949.5F   Liberia. Department of State. Annual report. Monrovia.
1963+
     Afr Doc 9950.5   Liberia. Department of the Treasury. Annual report.
Monrovia. 1965+

Afr Doc 9971 - 9996   Liberia - Local documents - Provinces, cities, etc., A-Z
     Afr Doc 9983.1.73   Liberia. Department of Agriculture and Commerce. Bureau of
Statistics. Census of population of Monrovia 1956; general
characteristics. Report. Monrovia, 1956.

WIDENER LIBRARY SHELFLIST, 34

AFRICAN HISTORY
AND
LITERATURES

CHRONOLOGICAL LISTING

	Afr 8279.00.37F	Achilles, Kort. Aanleiding tot den engelsch-transvaal oorlog. 's-Gravenhage, n.d.
	Afr 8001.16	Africana notes and news. Index v.1-10. (1943-53). Johannesburg, n.d.
	Afr 1755.12	Albeniz, R. La Campana del rif, la Verdad de la guerra. n.p., n.d.
	Afr 8325.62	American Hospital Ship Fund for South Africa. The concert. Souvenir programme. n.p., n.d.
	Afr 555.9	Arnot, Frederick Stanley. Garenganze, or Seven years in Central Africa. London, n.d.
	Afr 1609.30	Assher, Ben. A nomad in Morocco. London, n.d.
	Afr 7948.5	Baeck, Louis. Etude socio-économique du centre extra-coutumier d'Usumbura. Bruxelles, n.d.
	Afr 4731.5	Baldissera. Rapport...de la campagne d'Afrique (1895-96). Paris, n.d.
	Afr 8980.3	Bannister, S. Humane policy. 2. ed. London, n.d.
	Afr 2373.1	Barbet, Charles. La perle du Maghreb (Tlemeen). Alger, n.d.
	Afr 3740.3	Barre, P. Fachoda. Paris, n.d.
	Afr 5749.58.5F	Battistini, R. Population et économie paysanne du Bas-Mangoky. Paris, n.d.
	Afr 7812.6F	Belgium. Ministère des Affaires Africaines. Secretariat du Plan Décennal. Rapport sur l'execution du plan décennal pour le développment...du Congo Belge, 1956-1958. n.p., n.d.
	Afr 775.5	Bellingham, W. The diary of a working man in central Africa. London, n.d.
	Afr 4045.1	Berchere, N. Le desert de Suez. Paris, n.d.
	Afr 5760.10	Besson, L. Voyage au pays des Tanala indépendants. n.p., n.d.
	Afr 5635.7	Bienaime. L'expedition de Madagascar de 1895. n.p., n.d. 4 pam.
	Afr 7103.5	Borchardt, P. Bibliographie de l'Angola. Bruxelles, n.d.
	Afr 1990.22	Boulle, L. La France et les Beni-Snassen. Paris, n.d.
	Afr 2290.4	Bourdonnaye. Le moral algérien. Paris, n.d.
	Afr 3740.5	Castellani, C. Marchand l'africain. Paris, n.d.
	Afr 2527.2	Cealis, E. De Sousse à Gafsa. Lettres, 1881-84. Paris, n.d.
	Afr 2230.19F	Charveriat, F. A travers la Kabylie. n.p., n.d.
	Afr 6192.12	Clarke, R. Remarks on the topography and diseases of the Gold Coast. n.p., n.d.
	Afr 6143.10	Clarke, R. Sierra Leone. London, n.d.
	Afr 6155.1	Codrington, W.J. Lecture on...defence of...Gold Coast. n.p., n.d.
	Afr Doc 7307.361	Congo (Brazzaville). Direction du Service National de la Statistique, des Etudes Démographiques et Economiques. Enquête démographique, 1960-1961. Résultats définitifs. n.p., n.d.
	Afr 8686.26	Cowie, Margaret J. South African missionary bibliography. n.p., n.d. 2 pam.
	Afr 555.21.15	Crawford, D. Back to the long grass. N.Y., n.d.
	Afr 8289.00.20	Creswicke, L. South Africa and the Transvaal war. London, n.d. 4v.
	Afr 1990.25.5	Demontes, Victor. Papiers du général Berthezène...colonisation de l'Algérie. Paris, n.d.
	Afr 6878.92.5	Denkschrift betreffend Deutsch-Ostafrika. Berlin, n.d.
	Afr 2609.12.3	Douglas, N. Fountains in the sand...oases of Tunisia. N.Y., n.d.
	Afr 6540.10	Driberg, J.H. The Lango. London, n.d.
	Afr 5385.16	Dubarry, A. Voyage au Dahomey. Paris, n.d.
	Afr 5635.8	Duchesne, C. L'expedition de Madagascar...1896. Paris, n.d.
	Afr 1422.5	Duprat, P. Peuples anciens et modernes de Maroc. n.p., n.d.
	Afr 1570.25	Dupuy, E. Comment nous avons conquis le Maroc. Paris, n.d.
	Afr 1609.05.3	Dutaillis, J. Le Maroc pittoresque. Paris, n.d.
Htn	Afr 3285.3F*	Egyptian Delegation. Speeches and statements, 1908. n.p., n.d. 3 pam.
	Afr 5765.5.2	Ellis, William. The martyr church...Christianity in Madagascar. London, n.d.
	Afr 2527.3	Expédition militaire en Tunisia, 1881-82. Paris, n.d.
	Afr 2025.15	Ferriol, M. Demain en Algérie. Paris, n.d.
	Afr Doc 6003.5	French West Africa. Annuaire du gouvernment général de l'Afrique occidentale française. n.p., n.d.
	Afr 8659.08	Fuller, R.H. South Africa at home. London, n.d.
	Afr 5635.6	Galli, H. La guerre a Madagascar. Paris, n.d. 2v.
	Afr 6108.94.6	Ganniers, A. de. Le Maroc d'aujoud hui, d'hier et de demain. Paris, n.d.
	Afr 6095.8	Gaunt, M. Alone in West Africa. London, n.d.
	Afr 3700.10	Grant, James. Cassell's history of the war in the Soudan. v.1-6. London, n.d. 2v.
	Afr 2308.11	Gubb, A.S. Algiers as a winter resort. London, n.d.
	Afr 6750.4	Handbook of Tanganyika. London, n.d.
	Afr 510.10	Hanotaux, G. Le partage de l'Afrique - Fachoda. Paris, n.d.
	Afr 6535.9	Harford-Battersby, P.F. Pilkington of Uganda. London, n.d.
	Afr 4558.44.3	Harris, W.C. Adventures in Africa. Philadelphia, n.d.
	Afr 4558.44.2	Harris, W.C. The highlands of Ethiopia. N.Y., n.d.
	Afr 2609.12	Harry, M. Tunis la blanche. Paris, n.d.
	Afr 6203.12F	Ibadan, Nigeria. University. Library. Africana pamphlets; microfilm record. n.p., n.d.
	Afr 9028.65	Ireland, W. Historical sketch of the Zulu mission. Boston, n.d.
	Afr 8325.30	Ives, Herbert. Britons and Boers. London, n.d.
	Afr 505.5	Johnston, H. Britain across the seas - Africa.
	Afr 109.11	Johnston, H.H. The opening up of Africa. London, n.d.
	Afr 1607.53.4	Journaal Wegens de Rampspoedige Reys-Tocht van H.C. Steenis. Amsterdam, n.d.
	Afr 5565.2	Kammerer, A. La decouverte de Madagascar. n.p., n.d.
	Afr 10431.41.100	Kibera, Leonard. Potent ash. Nairobi, n.d.
	Afr 1570.14	Lechatelier, A. Note sur les affaires marocaines.
	Afr 4620.3	Leontieff. Provinces équatoriales d'Abyssinie. n.p., n.d.
	Afr 1947.4	Lomon, A. Captivité de l'Amiral Bonard. Paris, n.d.
	Afr 1570.4	Luzeux. Notre politique au Maroc. Paris, n.d.
	Afr 3978.77.2	McCoan, J.C. Egypt as it is. London, n.d.
	Afr 3978.77	McCoan, J.C. Egypt as it is. London, n.d.
	Afr 8925.2	MacGregor, J.C. Basuto traditions. n.p., n.d.
	Afr Doc 5622.5	Madagascar. Rapport sur la situation générale de la colonie. n.p., n.d.
	Afr Doc 5622.10	Madagascar. Gouvernement Général de Madagascar et Dépendances. Madagascar de 1896 à 1905. n.p., n.d. 2v.

	Afr Doc 5608.700.5	Madagascar. Institut National de la Statistique et de la Recherche Economique. Series retrospectives, 1949-1961. n.p., n.d.
Htn	Afr 8310.7F*	Mafeking Mail. Special siege edition. Nov. 1, 1899 to May 31, 1900. n.p., n.d.
	Afr 2622.1	Mager, Henri. Atlas de Tunisie. Paris, n.d.
	Afr 5815.2F	Mauritius. Letters, patent, 1879-1894. n.p., n.d.
	Afr 6192.102.2	Mayer, Emerico Somassa. Ghana: past and present. 2nd ed. The Hague, n.d.
	Afr 2310.1	Melix. Le stèle d'Abisae. n.p., n.d.
	Afr 8289.01.11	Mempes, M. War impressions. London, n.d.
	Afr 7549.61	Merriam, Alan P. Congo, background of conflict. Evanston, Ill., n.d.
NEDL	Afr 5130.3F	Monet, H. Le siège de Médine, 1857. Paris, n.d.
	Afr 2230.9.5	Monglave, E. de. La Kabylie. n.p., n.d.
	Afr 5340.5	Monteil, P.L. Un page d'histoire militaire coloniale, la colonne de Kong. Paris, n.d.
	Afr 1485.4	Morote, L. La conquista del Mogreb. Valencia, n.d.
	Afr 3310.10.35	Nasser, G.A. Nasser. Miscellaneous speeches. n.p., n.d. 7 pam.
	Afr 3310.10.32	Nasser, G.A. Speech delivered on the occasion of the 10th anniversary of the revolution. n.p., n.d.
	Afr 8320.10	Naude, J.F. Vechten en vluchten van beyers en kemp. Rotterdam, n.d.
	Afr 5180.4	Noirot, E. A travers le Fouta-Diallon et le Bambouc. Paris, n.d.
	Afr 1965.9	Notice sur...la prise de la Imahla d'Abd el-Kader. n.p., n.d.
	Afr 10604.5	Okyeame. Accra, n.d.
	Afr 2285.9	Orpen, A.E. The chronicles of the Sid. N.Y., n.d.
	Afr 4558.90.5	Pasini, L. Usi e costumi. Milano, n.d.
	Afr 5640.10	Peill, J. Social conditions...in Madagascar. n.p., n.d.
	Afr 1567.3	Pericaris, I. American claims and the protection of native subjects in Morocco. n.p., n.d.
	Afr 6194.4	Perregaux, E. Chez les Ashanti. n.p., n.d.
	Afr 1955.9	Perret, E. Récits algériens. Paris, n.d. 2v.
	Afr 1550.12	Peyreigne, C. Les influences européennes au Maroc. n.p., n.d.
	Afr 1965.7	Pichon, J. Abd el-Kader. Tlemcen, n.d.
	Afr 1568.1	Presse anglaise et le Maroc. n.p., n.d.
	Afr 7503.3.4	Problèmes sociaux congolais. Sommaire des bulletins parus 1946-1966. n.p., n.d.
	Afr 5869.67	Prosset, Alfred. Les Premiers colons de l'Ile Bourbon. 2. ed. Paris, n.d.
	Afr 6780.35	Regendanz, W.C. Die Giraffe und der König von England. n.p., n.d.
	Afr 2609.00.3	Rey, R. Voyage d'études en Tunisie. Paris, n.d.
	Afr 2010.4	Robin. L'insurrection de la Grande Kabylie en 1871. Paris, n.d.
	Afr 678.85F	Roskoschny, H. Europas Kolonien, West Afrika vom Senegal zum Kamerun. 3. Aufl. Leipzig, n.d.
	Afr 1450.2	Sabran, J. de. Le Maroc rouge. Paris, n.d.
	Afr 3978.45.5	Saint John, J.A. Egypt and Nubia. London, n.d.
	Afr 8685.3	Samuelson, L.H. Some Zulu customs and folk-lore. London, n.d.
	Afr 1407.7	Savine, A. Dans les fers du Moghreb. Paris, n.d.
	Afr 7815.1F	Schmeltz, J.D.E. Album...ethnography...Congo-basin. Leyden, n.d.
	Afr 6777.3	Schmidt, R. Geschichte des Araberaufstandes in Ost-Afrika. Frankfurt, n.d.
	Afr 2208.65.4	Schneider, O. Tagebuch aus Algier. Dresden, n.d.
	Afr 5185.7	Schobel, Fred. The world in miniature, Africa. v.2-3. London, n.d. 2v.
Htn	Afr 8288.99.3F*	Scrapbook of miscellaneous cuttings, but largely concerned with affairs of South Africa, 1899-1900. n.p., n.d.
	Afr 5183.964	Senegal. Plan réorienté. n.p., n.d.
	Afr 8678.338	Shepstone, Theophilus. The native question. n.p., n.d.
	Afr 2875.17	Sorbi, R. In Libia. Firenze, n.d.
	Afr 8040.5F	South African constitution bill. n.p., n.d.
	Afr 8289.00.55F	South African War. Scrapbook of newspaper clippings, chiefly maps, of campaigns in the South African War, Jan. 7, 1900 - June 10, 1900. n.p., n.d.
	Afr 2308.9	Souvenir d'Alger...24 vues choisies. n.p., n.d.
Htn	Afr 6164.6F*	Specimens of letters written by applicants for mercantiles employment. n.p., n.d.
	Afr 718.2.90	Stanley testimonial shield. n.p., n.d.
	Afr Doc 4107.362F	Swaziland. Census Office. Population census, 1962. n.p., n.d.
	Afr 6881.255	Tanganyika Territory. Tanganyika. n.p., n.d.,
	Afr 626.204	Tevoedjre, Albert. Africa and international co-operation: ILO in Africa. n.p., n.d.
	Afr 2208.46.8	Texier, C. Les grandes chasses d'Afrique. n.p., n.d.
	Afr 3978.54	Thompson, J.P. Photographic views of Egypt. Glasgow, n.d.
	Afr 6095.9	Tremearne, A.J.U. The Niger and the West Sudan. London, n.d.
	Afr 6475.8.2	Uganda journal. Index, v.1-20, 1934-56. Kampala, n.d.
	Afr Doc 4320.5F	Union of South Africa. Miscellaneous collection of reports of government departments. n.p., n.d.
	Afr Doc 1437.5	United Arab Republic. Ministry of the High Dam. Sadd-el-Aali project. n.p., n.d.
	Afr 3320.142	United Arab Republic. State Tourist Administration. Tourisme in Egypt. n.p., n.d.
	Afr Doc 3319.6	Urganda. Constitutional Committe. Report, 1959 and Supplementary Report 1960. n.p., n.d. 2 pam.
	Afr 1755.8	Urquijo, F. De. La Campana del rif en 1909. Madrid, n.d.
	Afr 2802.6F	Vattier de Bourville, T. Coup d'oeil sur la Cyrénaique. n.p., n.d.
	Afr 1450.1	Veyre, Gabriel. Au Maroc dans l'intimité du sultan. Paris, n.d.
	Afr 1608.89.20	Viaud, J. Into Morocco. Chicago, n.d.
	Afr 2308.10	Vieil Alger. n.p., n.d.
	Afr 1738.12	Views of tangier. n.p., n.d.
	Afr 7568.31	Williams, G.W. An open letter to His Serene Majesty Leopold II. n.p., n.d. 2 pam.
	Afr 6541.23	Wilson, C.J. Uganda in the days of Bishop Tucker. London, n.d.

1530-1539

	Afr 4313.2	Lebna Dengel. Legatio ad Sanctissimum D.N. Clementem Papam VII. Bononiae, 1533.

1540-1549

Htn	Afr 4555.40*	Alvares, Francisco. Ho Preste Joam das Indias. Verdadeira informaçam. Lisbon, 1540.
Htn	Afr 4555.40.71*	Goes, D. Fides, religio moresque Aethiopum. Paris, 1541.

1550-1559

Htn	Afr 605.56F*	Leo Africanus, J. Historiale description de l'Afrique. Lyon, 1556. 2v.
Htn	Afr 4555.40.8*	Alvares, Francisco. Historiale description de l'Ethiopie. Anvers, 1558.
Htn	Afr 605.56.3*	Leo Africanus, J. Descriptione libri IX. Liguri, 1559.

1560-1569

Htn	Afr 4555.40.1*	Alvares, Francisco. Historia de las cosas de Ethiopia. Çragoça, 1561.
	Afr 4555.40.22	Alvares, Francisco. Kurtze und wahrhafftige Beschreibung der Ethiopie. Eiszlebe, 1567.

1570-1579

Htn	Afr 605.73F*	Marmol Carvajal, L. del. Descripción général de Africa. Pt.1, 1-2, pt.II. Granada, 1573. 3v.
Htn	Afr 2489.2*	Floriani, Pompeo. Discurso della Goletta. Macerata, 1574.
Htn	Afr 1403.2*	Coppia d'una litera venuta di Spagna. Mantova, 1578.

1580-1589

Htn	Afr 1403.1*	Histoiria de bello Africano. Noribergae, 1580.
Htn	Afr 1401.5*	Torres, D. de. Relacion del origen y sucesso de los karifes. Sevilla, 1586.
Htn	Afr 4555.40.5*	Alvares, Francisco. Historia de las cosas de Ethiopia. Toledo, 1588.

1590-1599

Htn	Afr 7560.2*	Lopes, D. Relazione del reame del Congo et del circonvisine contrade. Roma, 1591.

16-

Htn	Afr 555.12.5*	Memoriale per li missionarii apostolici de Tunis. Manuscript. n.p. 16- .

1600-1609

Htn	Afr 605.56.4*	Leo Africanus, J. A geographical historie of Africa. Londini, 1600.
	Afr 2308.7	Gifford, R. Relazione. Firenze, 1604.
Htn	Afr 6192.1F*	Marees, Pieter de. Description et récit historique du riche royaume d'or de Guinea. Amsterdamme, 1605.
Htn	Afr 1406.2*	Wilkins, George. Three miseries of Barbary. London, 1606.
Htn	Afr 1406.1*	Cortende waerachlich verhail...1607. Hague, 1607.
Htn	Afr 1403.5.5*	Mendonca, Jeronymo de. Jornada de Africa. Lisboa, 1607.
	Afr 5746.09	Megiserum, H. Beschreibung...insul Madagascar. Altenburg, 1609.
Htn	Afr 7216.09*	Santos, João dos. Ethiopia oriental. v.1-2. Evora, 1609.
Htn	Afr 1401.7*	True historicall discourse of Muley-Hamets rising. London, 1609.

1610-1619

Htn	Afr 4256.10*	Urreta, L. Historia eclesiastica, politica, natural, y moral de los grandes y remotos reynos de la Etiopia. Pt.1. Valencia, 1610.
Htn	Afr 4320.25*	Urreta, Luis de. Historia de la Sagrada Orden de Predicadores. Valencia, 1611.
	Afr 3976.17	Scortia, J.B. De natura et incremento nili. Lugduni, 1617.

1620-1629

Htn	Afr 6118.2*	Jobson, R. The golden trade. London, 1623.
Htn	Afr 1103.4.20*	Relación de la traza y modo con que los soldados de Tarifa... cogieron dos barcos de Moros. Malaga, 1623.
Htn	Afr 1905.4F*	Nuevo blason de los cardenas y elogios del Duque de Maqueda en Oran. Madrid, 1624.
Htn	Afr 4349.3.5F*	Fernandez, A. Copia de una del padre A. Fernandez. Madrid, 1627.
	Afr 4350.2.3	Jesuits. Letters from Missions. (Abyssinia). Relaçam geral do estado da Christandade de Ethiopia. Lisboa, 1628.
	Afr 1724.1.2	Coutinho, Goncalo. Discurso da jornada de D. Goncalo Coutinho. (Another issue). Lisboa, 1629.
	Afr 1724.1	Coutinho, Goncalo. Discurso da jornada de D. Goncalo Coutinho. Lisboa, 1629.
	Afr 4349.3*	Jesuits. Letters from Missions. (Abyssinia). Histoire d'Ethiopie, en l'année 1626. Paris, 1629.

1630-1639

	Afr 1403.3	Mesa, S. de. Jornada de Africa por el rey Don Sebastian. Barcelona, 1630.
Htn	Afr 606.31*	Geraldinus a Merini, A. Itinerarium ad regiones sub aequinoctrali. Romae, 1631.
Htn	Afr 1606.31*	Jean Armand, Called Mustapha. Voyages d'Afrique faicts par le commandement du roy. Paris, 1631.
	Afr 4350.2.5	Jesuits. Letters from Missions. (Abyssinia). Carta do patriarcha de Ethiopia. Lisboa, 1631.
Htn	Afr 4350.2.6*	Jesuits. Letters from Missions. (Abyssinia). Carta do patriarcha de Ethiopia. Lisboa, 1631.
Htn	Afr 605.56.5*	Leo Africanus, J. Ioannis Leonis Africani Africae descriptio IX lib. Absoluta. 2 pt. Lugdunum Batavorum, 1632.
Htn	Afr 7222.5*	Durao, Antonio. Cercos de Moçambique. Madrid, 1633.
	Afr 4556.34	Le Blanc, Vincent. Histoire géographique et mémorable de l'Assiete de la terre universelle. Aix, 1634.
Htn	Afr 1103.4.30*	Relación verdadera de una insigni victoria. Lisboa, 1636.
Htn	Afr 1401.1*	Torres, D. de. Relation de l'origine et succez des cherifs. Paris, 1636.
Htn	Afr 1407.2*	Dunton, J. True iournall of the Sally Fleet. London, 1637.
	Afr 5180.22	Saintlo, A. de. Relation du voyage du Cap-Verd. Paris, 1637.

1640-1649

Htn	Afr 7122.5*	Andrade Leitão, F. de. Copia das proposições e secunda allegaçam. Lisboa, 1642.
Htn	Afr 7122.5.5*	Andrade Leitão, F. de. Copia primae allegationis. n.p., 1642.
Htn	Afr 1925.1*	Robinson, H. Libertas or reliefe to English captives in Algeria. London, 1642.
	Afr 5746.43	Hamond, W. Madagascar, the richest and most fruitful island in the world. London, 1643.
	Afr 810.12	Jannequin, C. Voyage de Lybie. Paris, 1643.
Htn	Afr 1606.44*	San Francisco, Matias de. Relacion del viage espiritual. Madrid, 1644.
	Afr 2484.4	Breve, ma distintissima relatione della conversione alla Santa Fede del primogenito del re di Tunisi, Mamet Celebi hoggi detto D. Filippo Dai. Roma, 1646.
X Cg	Afr 1236.49F*	Dan, Pierre. Histoire de Barbarie et de ses corsaires. Paris, 1649. (Changed to XP 9049)

1650-1659

	Afr 1084.1	Birago, G.B. Historia africana della divisione dell'imperi degli Arabi. Venetia, 1650.
Htn	Afr 7122.10*	Cruz, L.F. da. Manifesto das ostillidades que a gente. Lisboa, 1651.
	Afr 5746.38	Morizot, C.B. Relations véritables et curieuses de l'isle de Madagascar. Paris, 1651.
	Afr 1947.2.3	Aranda, E.D. Relation de la captivité...esclave à Alger. Paris, 1657.
	Afr 1406.5	Nader tractaet van oredeende vrundtschap...22 marti 1657. Hague, 1659.

1660-1669

Htn	Afr 4556.60F*	Almeida, Manoel. Historia geral de Ethiopia. Coimbra, 1660.
Htn	Afr 4556.60.2*	Tellez, B. Historia geral de Ethiopia. (Earlier issue). Coimbra, 1660.
	Afr 5746.61	Flacourt, E. de. Histoire de la grande isle Madagascar. Paris, 1661.
	Afr 1947.2	Aranda, E.D. Relation de la captivité...esclave à Alger. Bruxelles, 1662.
Htn	Afr 2494.5*	Great Britain and Tunis. Articles of peace betwixt Charles II and Mahamet of Tunis and Osman. Tripoli. 5 october, 1662. n.p., 1662.
Htn	Afr 605.73.6*	Marmol Carvajal, L. del. L'Afrique de Marmol. Paris, 1667. 3v.
	Afr 7306.69	Gioja, Francesco Maria. Maravigliosa conversione alla Santa Fede. Napoli, 1669.
Htn	Afr 1406.7*	Short and strange relation of some part of the life of Tafiletta. London, 1669.
	Afr 676.66	Villault, N. Relation des côtes d'Afrique, appellées Guinée. Paris, 1669.
	Afr 676.66.5	Villault, N. Relation des côtes d'Afrique, appellées Guinée. Photocopy. Paris, 1669.
	Afr 1406.8	Waerachtigh verhael van Tafilette. n.p., 1669.

1670-1679

Htn	Afr 1606.70*	Letter from a gentleman of Lt. Howard's retinue. London, 1670.
Htn	Afr 606.70F*	Ogilby, John. Africa, accurate description...regions, Aegypt, Barbary. London, 1670.
Htn	Afr 1606.71*	Addison, L. West Barbary. Oxford, 1671.
Htn	Afr 1606.71.3*	Frejus, R. Relation of a voyage made into Mauritania. London, 1671.
Htn	Afr 7122.15*	Relaçam do felice successo. Lisboa, 1671[1672?]
	Afr 7806.66.5	Guattini, M.A. Viaggio del P. Michael Angelo de Guattini da Reggio. Reggio, 1672.
	Afr 5874.10.5	Dubois. Les voyages faits...aux isles Dauphine ou Madagascar. Paris, 1674.
	Afr 2206.75	Rocqueville. Relation des moeurs...des Turcs d'Alger. Paris, 1675.
Htn	Afr 2206.44*	Okeley, W. Ebenezer, or A small monument of great mercy. London, 1676.
Htn	Afr 1738.2*	Present state of Tangier. London, 1676.
	Afr 2489.3	Garzia, G.D. Vera relazione copia di lettera scritta. Venezia, 1677.
Htn	Afr 3976.78*	Vansleb, W. The present state of Egypt. London, 1678.
Htn	Afr 1935.1*	Algiers. Dey. Letter written by the governour...law-counteys. London, 1679.

1680-1689

Htn	Afr 1738.10*	Particular narrative of a great engagement. Savoy, 1680.
Htn	Afr 1738.13*	Addison, L. The Moores baffled. London, 1681.
Htn	Afr 1398.5*	Faria e Sousa, Manuel de. Africa portuguesa por su autor Manuel de Faria. Lisboa, 1681.
Htn	Afr 4556.81F*	Ludolf, H. Historia aethiopica. Francofurti ad Moenum, 1681.
Htn	Afr 1738.3.5*	Ross, John. Tanger's rescue. London, 1681.
	Afr 4556.81.11	Ludolf, H. A new history of Ethiopia. London, 1682.
Htn	Afr 1407.6*	Monette, G. Relation de la captivité dans les royaumes de Fez. Paris, 1683.
	Afr 4556.81.21	Ludolf, H. Nouvelle histoire d'Abissinie. Paris, 1684.
	Afr 606.86F	Dapper, D.O. Description de l'Afrique. Amsterdam, 1686.
	Afr 7015.2.1	Cavazzi, G.A. Istorica descrizione di tre regni Congo, Matamba. Bologna, 1687.
	Afr 4556.81.31	Ludolf, H. Historie van Abissinien. Utrecht, 1687.
	Afr 7216.09.5	Santos, João Dos. Histoire de l'Ethiopie orientale. Paris, 1688.
	Afr 5180.40	Gaby, Jean B. Relation de la Nigritie. Paris, 1689.

1690-1699

Htn	Afr 7015.2.2*	Cavazzi, G.A. Istorica descrittione de tre regni Congo, Matamba. n.p., 1690.
	Afr 4556.81.2F	Ludolf, H. Historia aethiopica. Francofurti ad Moenum, 1691.
	Afr 1403.4	Baena Parada, J. Epitome de la vida y hechos de Don Sebastian. Madrid, 1692.
	Afr 7806.92	Merolla da Sorrento. Breve e succinta relatione del viaggio nel regno. Napoli, 1692.
	Afr 1724.3F	Portugal. Sovereigns, 1688-1706 (Peter Ii). Regimento da praca de mazagam. Lisboa, 1692.

1690-1699 - cont.

Htn	Afr 1407.3*	Brooks, F. Barbarian cruelty. London, 1693.
Htn	Afr 1606.94*	St. Olon, P. Etat present de l'empire de Maroc. Paris, 1694.
Htn	Afr 606.95*	Lemaire. Les voyages du Sieur Lemaire. Paris, 1695.
Htn	Afr 1606.94.5*	St. Olon, P. Present state of Morocco. London, 1695.
Htn	Afr 1606.94.3*	St. Olon, P. Relation de l'empire de Maroc. Paris, 1695.
Htn	Afr 1606.96*	St. Amant. Voyage de St. Amant. Lyon, 1698.

17-

	Afr 1103.8	Cunha, Jorge da. Relaçam do successo, que no dia do prezenre mez de julho tiverao os navios. Lisbon, 17- .

1700-1709

	Afr 1257.04	Etat des royaumes de Barbarie. La Haye, 1704.
	Afr 7806.66.10F	Guattini, M.A. A curious and exact account of a voyage to Congo...1666 and 1667. London, 1704. 2 pam.
	Afr 5318.2.89	Bosman, W. A new accurate description of the coast of Guinea. London, 1705.
	Afr 5318.3.9	Bosman, W. Voyage de Guinée. Utrecht, 1705.
	Afr 1325.4F	Francisco Jesus Maria de San Juan del Puerto, Mission historial de Marruecos. Sevilla, 1708.

1710-1719

Htn	Afr 1607.13*	Ockley, S. An account of south-west Barbary. London, 1713.
	Afr 1408.2.5	Busnot, F.D. Histoire du regne de mouley Ismael. Rouen, 1714.
	Afr 5346.5	Loyer, G. Relation du voyage du royaume d'Issyny. Paris, 1714.
	Afr 7068.3	Zucchelli, A. Merckwurdige Missions und Reise-Beschreibung nach Congo in Ethiopien. Frankfurt, 1715.
	Afr 4357.5	Freire de Monterroyo Mascarenhas, José. Novo triunfo da religiam serafica, ou noticia summaria do martyrio...3 de marco de 1716. Lisboa, 1718.
	Afr 8657.19F	Kolbe, Peter. Caput Bonae Spei hodiernum. Nurnberg, 1719.

1720-1729

Htn	Afr 1947.3*	Comelin, F. Voyage pour la rédemption des captives...1720. Paris, 1721.
	Afr 5746.63	Carpeau du Saussay. Voyage de Madagascar. Paris, 1722.
	Afr 1607.24.3F	Francisco de Jesus Maria, de San Juan Del Puerto. Primera parte de las chronicas de la provincia de San Diego. Sevilla, 1724.
	Afr 1607.24	Relation de ce qui s'est passe...1704-12. Paris, 1724.
	Afr 2207.25	Laugier de Tassy, N. Histoire du royaume d'Alger. Amsterdam, 1725.
Htn	Afr 1607.25*	Windus, J. A journey to Mequinez. London, 1725. (Changed to EC7.W7255.725j, 30/6/69)
	Afr 1407.4	Lafaye, P.J. de. Relation en forme de journal...des captifs. Paris, 1726.
	Afr 8657.19.3F	Kolbe, Peter. Naaukeurige en uitvoerige beschryving van de Kaap de Goede Hoop. Amsterdam, 1727. 2v.
	Afr 677.28	Labot, J. Nouvelles relations de l'Afrique occidentale. Paris, 1728. 5v.
	Afr 4556.59.13	Lobo, J. Relation historique d'Abissinie. Paris, 1728.
	Afr 4556.59.12	Lobo, J. Voyage historique d'Abyssinie. Paris, 1728.
	Afr 1867.28	Morgan, John. Complete history of Algiers. London, 1728. 2v.
	Afr 1408.1	Braithwaite, Capt. History of revolution upon death of Ishmail. London, 1729.

1730-1739

	Afr 1408.1.5	Braithwaite, Capt. Histoire des révolutions de l'empire de Maroc. Amsterdam, 1731.
	Afr 8657.19.5	Kolbe, Peter. Present state of the Cape of Good Hope. London, 1731. 2v.
	Afr 1753.4.5	Breve noticia da gloriosa Vitoria...1732. Lisboa, 1732.
	Afr 7015.2	Cavazzi, G.A. Relation historique de l'Ethiopie occidentale. Paris, 1732. 5v.
	Afr 1738.9F	Menezes, D.F. De. Historia de Tangere. Lisboa, 1732.
	Afr 5180.14.2	Alvares d'Almada, Andre. Relação e descripção de Guiné. Lisboa, 1733.
	Afr 1400.3	Boulet. Histoire de l'empire des chérifs en Afrique. Paris, 1733.
	Afr 1905.3	Continorazione del diario e relazione. Firenze, 1733.
Htn	Afr 5318.2*	Snelgrave, W. A new account of parts of Guinea. London, 1734.
	Afr 6095.6	Atkins, J. Voyage to Guinea, Brasil. London, 1735.
Htn	Afr 4556.59.23*	Lobo, J. Voyage to Abyssinia. London, 1735.
	Afr 3976.92	Maillet, B. de. Description de l'Egypte. Paris, 1735.
	Afr 1407.1	Pellow, J. History of long captivity. London, 1736.
	Afr 2607.36	Saint-Gervais, M. Memoires, historiques qui concernent le gouvernement...de Tunis. Paris, 1736.
	Afr 6095.6.2	Atkins, J. Voyage to Guinea, Brasil. 2nd ed. London, 1737.
	Afr 5318.3.5	Bosman, W. Neuwkeurige beschryning de de Guinese. Amsterdam, 1737.
	Afr 1915.3	Frousseaux. Aventures de dona ines de la Cisternas. Utrecht, 1737.
	Afr 6118.5	Moore, F. Travels into the inland parts of Africa. London, 1738.

1740-1749

	Afr 1407.1.2	Pellow, J. History of long captivity. 2 ed. London, 1740.
	Afr 8657.19.7	Kolbe, Peter. Description du cap de Bonne-Espérance. Amsterdam, 1741. 3v.
	Afr 1409.1	Mairault, A.M. Relation...de Maroc, 1727-1737. Paris, 1742.
	Afr 6095.22	Smith, William. A new voyage to Guinea. London, 1744.
	Afr 3977.30	Granger, called Tourtechot. Relation du voyage fait en Egypte...En l'annee 1730. Paris, 1745.
	Afr 5575.10	Broke, A. van. Aller neueste Nachricht von Madagascar und dem Leben des jetzigen Beherrschers dieses Insul. Frankfurt, 1748.
	Afr 607.48	Lajardière. Reise-Beschreibung nach Africa. Frankfurt, 1748.

	Afr 1103.7	Noticia da grande preza, que duas naos de Roma, que andavam de guarda costa fizerãos aos mouros em as costas de Sicilia. Lisboa, 175-.

1750-1759

	Afr 2207.25.3	Laugier de Tassy, N. Compleat history of the piratical states of Barbary. London, 1750.
	Afr 1838.3	Leroy, L. Etat...du royaume et de la ville d'Alger. La Haye, 1750.
	Afr 1607.51	Riese, Otto. Harck Olufs aus der Insul amron im stifte ripen in Juetland. Flensburg, 1751.
	Afr 6095.22.5	Smith, William. Nouveau voyage de Guinée. Paris, 1751.
Htn	Afr 3977.49PF*	Dalton, Richard. A series of prints relative to the manner, customs, etc, of the present inhabitants of Egypt. London, 1752.
Htn	Afr 1103.12*	Relação do combate, que teve o capitão de navio Dom Pedro Stuart e Portugal. Lisboa, 1752.
	Afr 1407.5	Kort...verhaal...slavernye onder de Mooren. Amsterdam, 1753.
	Afr 1103.9	Nova, e curiosa relação, do fatal combate que teve o capitão de mare guerra espanhol D. Joze Ponce de Leon, com huma nao de Mouros argelinos. Lisbon, 1753.
	Afr 1103.6	Nova relaçam e curiosa noticia do combate, que tiveram tres caravellas de Vianna de Caminha com os corsarios dos Mouros. Lisboa, 1754.
	Afr 1103.10	Freire de Monterroyo Mascarenhas, José. Relaçam summaria de hum combate, sucedido nos mares de Alicante entre hum galeão de Biscainhos que andava de guarda costa. Lisbon, 1755.
	Afr 3183.7	Relaçao do tumulto popular que succedeo em de dezembro do auno passado de 1754. n.p., 1755. 2 pam.
	Afr 555.17.10	Copia d huma carta escrita pelo Padre Guardiam do Real Convento de Maquinés. Lisboa, 1756.
	Afr 1724.5	Relacao do grande terremoto. Lisboa, 1756.
	Afr 1409.2.5	Relacao verdadeira da implacavel peste. Lisboa, 1756.
	Afr 2207.25.5	Laugier de Tassy, N. Histoire des Etats Barbaresques. Paris, 1757. 2v.
	Afr 3977.57F	Norden, F.L. Travels in Egypt and Nubia. London, 1757. 2v.
	Afr 2498.15	Noticia da festividade que na ilha de Malta se celebrou no baptismo do rey de Tunes. Lisboa, 1757.
	Afr 2498.16	Relaçam da tragica morte do novo rey de Tunes. Lisboa, 1757.
	Afr 1103.5	Verdadeira noticia da grande esquadra que do reino de Napoles sahio em corso contra os Mouros de Argel. Lisboa, 1757.
	Afr 150.9	Freire, F.J. Vie de l'Infante Dom Henrique. Lisboa, 1758.
Htn	Afr 5130.6*	Postlethwayt, M. The importance of the African expedition considered. London, 1758.
	Afr 5180.2	Adanson, M. A voyage to Senegal. London, 1759.

1760-1769

Htn	Afr 590.44*	Benezet, A. Eine kurtze Vorstellung des Theils von Africa. Ephrata, 1763.
	Afr 1367.64	Sagarra, J. de. Compendio de la historia de la España. v.1-2. Barcelona, 1764. 2v.
	Afr 5045.2	Demanet, Abbé. Nouvelle histoire de l'Afrique française. Paris, 1767. 2v.

1770-1779

Htn	Afr 677.71*	Benezet, Anthony. Some historical account of Guinea. Philadelphia, 1771. 2 pam.
	Afr 5993.10	Williamson, David. A true narrative of the sufferings of David Williamson. London, 1771.
Htn	Afr 677.71.5*	Benezet, Anthony. Some historical account of Guinea. London, 1772.
	Afr 1947.11	Bologna. Arciconfraternità di Santa Maria. Ragguaglio della schiavitù in Algeri di Giuseppe Giovanni Nicola Albertazzi. Bologna, 1772.
	Afr 3977.73	Pauw, C.V. Recherches philosophiques sur les égyptiens. Berlin, 1773. 2v.
	Afr 5842.4	Saint-Pierre, J.H.B. de. Voyage à l'Isle de France. Amsterdam, 1773. 2v.
	Afr 1409.9	Spain. Sovereigns. Carlos III. El rei. Madrid, 1774.
	Afr 1408.5	Guidotti. Storia dei Mori. Firenze, 1775.
	Afr 1903.6	Lettere istoriche...d'Africa, e d'America. Venezia, 1775.
	Afr 1409.3	Relation de l'affaire de Larache. Amsterdam, 1775.
	Afr 3977.76	Abul-Feda. Descriptio aegypti. Göttingen, 1776.
	Afr 8658.76.3	Lacaille, N.L. Journal historique du voyage fait au cap de Bonne-Espérance. Paris, 1776.
	Afr 7093.3.5	Proyart, L.B. Histoire de Loango, Kakongo. Paris, 1776.
Htn	Afr 555.28*	Stiles, Ezra. On a mission to Guinea. Newport, 1776.
	Afr 1406.13	Tractaat susschen Marocco en de Nederlanden. 's-Gravenhage, 1777.
	Afr 8657.77.4	Neue Kurzgefasste Beschreibung des Vorgebirges der guten Hoffnung. Leipzig, 1779.

1780-1789

	Afr 3977.37.10F	Norden, Frederik L. The antiquities, natural history, ruins...of Egypt, Nubia and Thebes. London, 1780.
	Afr 150.9.6	Freire, F.J. Vie de l'Infant Dom Henri de Portugal. Lisbonne, 1781.
	Afr 1607.81	Hoest, G. Nachrichten von Morokos und Fes. Kopenhagen, 1781.
	Afr 3183.8A	Lusignan, S. History of the revolt of Ali Bey. London, 1783.
	Afr 1408.3	Mouette, G. Histoire des conquestes de Mouley Archy. Paris, 1783.
	Afr 1403.5	Mendonca, Jeronymo de. Jornada de Africa. Lisboa, 1785.
	Afr 3977.86	Savary, C. Lettres sur l'Egypte. Paris, 1786. 3v.
	Afr 1367.87	Chenier, L.S. de. Recherches historiques sur les Maures. Paris, 1787.
	Afr 3977.86.5	Savary, C. Letters on Egypt. vol.1. Dublin, 1787.
	Afr 1607.87.5	Chenier, L.S. Present state of Morocco. London, 1788. 2v.
	Afr 6192.9.2	Isert, P.E. Reise nach Guinea. Kopenhagen, 1788.
Htn	Afr 6143.9.2*	Matthews, J. Voyage to the river Sierra-Leone. London, 1788.

1780-1789 - cont.

Afr 1200.5.2   Mémoire concernant le système de paix et de guerre que les puissances européennes pratiquent à l'égard des régences barbaresques. Venise, 1788.

Afr 5090.6   Brisson, P.R. de. Histoire du naufrage et de la captivité. Genève, 1789.

Afr 5798.5   A letter from a gentleman giving an account of Joanna. London, 1789.

Afr 4556.59.39   Lobo, J. A voyage to Abyssinia. London, 1789.

Afr 5368.5   Norris, Robert. Memoirs of the reign of Bossa Ahadee, king of Dahomey...country of Guiney. London, 1789.

Afr 1257.89   Poiret, J.L.M. Voyage en Barbarie. Paris, 1789. 2v.

Afr 5056.9   Pruneau de Pommegorge, Antoine Edmé. Description de la Nigritie. Amsterdam, 1789.

Afr 590.11F   Substance of the evidence...on the slave trade. London, 1789.

1790-1799

Afr 657.90F   Association for Promoting the Discovery of the Interior Parts of Africa. Proceedings. London, 1790.

Afr 5580.3.20   Beniowski, M.A. Memoirs and travels of Mauritius Augustus. London, 1790. 2v.

Afr 4557.90F   Bruce, J. Travels. Edinburgh, 1790. 5v.

Afr 607.90   Cuhn, E.W. Sammlung merkwüdiger Reisen in dem Innre von Afrika. Leipzig, 1790. 3v.

Afr 590.52   Edinburg Society for Effecting the Abolition of African Slave Trade. Two of the petitions form Scotland, presented to last Parliament, praying abolition of African slave trade. Edinburgh, 1790.

Afr 8657.90   Le Vaillant, F. Voyage...dans l'intérieur de l'Afrique. Lausanne, 1790. 2v.

Afr 8657.79.5   Paterson, W. A narrative of four journeys into the country of the Hottentots and Caffraria. 2d ed. London, 1790.

Afr 1257.89.3   Poiret, J.L.M. Travels through Barbary...1785-1786. London, 1790.

Afr 3974.00.5   Wahl, G.F.G. Abdallatifs Denkwürdigkeiten Egyptens. Halle, 1790.

Afr 5747.91   Rochon, A.M. Voyage à Madagascar. Paris, 1791.

Afr 1409.10   Spain. Sovereigns. Carlos IV. Real cedula en que S.M. declara la guerra al rey de Marruecos. Madrid, 1791.

Afr 1406.14   Translaat susschen Marocco en de Nederlanden n.p., 1791.

Afr 7073.2   Bulam Association. Report of the institution...Dec. 11, 1792. London, 1792.

Afr 1028.1   Follie. Voyage dans les déserts du Sahara. Paris, 1792. 4 pam.

Afr 5056.12   Saugnier. Voyages to the coast of Africa. London, 1792.

Htn   Afr 5365.2*   Dalzel, A. The history of Dahomy. London, 1793.

Afr 6192.9   Isert, P.E. Voyages en Guinée. Paris, 1793.

Afr 1607.91.2   Lempriere, W. Tour to Tangier and Morocco. 2nd ed. London, 1793.

Htn   Afr 1900.4*   Carey, M. Short account of Algiers...wars. Philadelphia, 1794.

Htn   Afr 6138.2*   Sierra Leone Company. Substance of the report delivered by the Court of directors of the Sierra Leone Company. Philadelphia, 1795.

Afr 607.96   Edrisi, A.A.H.I. el. Africa. Gottingae, 1796.

Afr 8657.90.12   Le Vaillant, F. Neue Reise in das Innere von Afrika. Berlin, 1796. 2v.

Afr 8657.90.11   Le Vaillant, F. New travels into the interior parts of Africa. London, 1796. 3v.

Afr 8657.90.17   Le Vaillant, F. Travels into the interior parts of Africa. 2nd ed. London, 1796. 2v.

Htn   Afr 5318.5*   Hawkins, J. History of a voyage to the coast of Africa. Troy, 1797.

Afr 4557.97   Pacelli, M. Viaggi in Etiopia. Napoli, 1797.

Afr 4557.90.12   Bruce, J. Travels to discover the source of the Nile. Abridged. Boston, 1798.

Afr 3977.98.5   Browne, W.G. Travels in Africa, Egypt, and Syria. London, 1799.

Afr 8657.90.6   Le Vaillant, F. Reise in das Innere von Afrika v 1, 3-5 Frankfurt, 1799. 4v.

Afr 5235.52.5   Park, Mungo. Mungo Parks Reise in das Innere von Afrika in den Jahren 1795, 96, und 97. Hamburg, 1799.

Afr 5235.52   Park, Mungo. Travels in the interior districts of Africa...1795-1797. 1st ed. London, 1799.

Htn   Afr 3977.99.3*   Remmey, John. An account of the present state of Egypt. N.Y., 1799.

Afr 5180.9   Saugnier. Relation des voyages. Paris, 1799.

Afr 3977.99   Sonnini, C.S. Voyage dans ... Egypte. v.1-3 + atlas. Paris, 1799. 4v.

18-

Afr 115.3.25F   Canti, Cesare. L'incivilimento dell Africa, memoria. n.p., 18- .

Afr 718.2.35   Stanley, H.M. La découverte du Congo. Paris, 18- .

Afr 2948.9   Subtil, E. Histoire d'Abd-el-Gelil. n.p., 18- .

Afr 1608.75   Urrestarazu, D.T. de A. de. Viajes por Marruecos. Madrid, 18- .

1800-1809

Afr 8835.60   Cape directory. Cape Town, 1800.

Afr 1574.5   Embaxada de la Corte de España al Rey de Marruecos en el año de 1799. Madrid, 1800.

Afr 3978.00   Institut d'Egypte, Cairo. Memoires sur l'Egypte. Paris, 1800.

Afr 5235.52.10   Park, Mungo. Travels in the interior districts of Africa...1795, 1796 and 1797. N.Y., 1800.

Afr 1867.97.2   Stevens, J.W. Historical and geographical account of Algiers. Brooklyn, 1800.

Htn   Afr 8658.00*   Stout, Benjamin. Narrative of the loss of the ship Hercules. New Bedford, 1800.

Afr 7315.4   White, William. Journal of a voyage performed in the Lion Extra Indiaman. London, 1800.

Afr 3978.00.10   Antes, J. Beobachtungen über die Sitten und Gebräuche der Agypter. Gera, 1801.

Afr 3180.6   Baldwin, G. Political recollections related to Egypt. London, 1801.

Afr 8658.01   Barrow, J. An account of travels into...South Africa. London, 1801.

Afr 607.80.5   Damberger, C.F. Travels through the interior of Africa. Charlestown, Mass., 1801.

Afr 1400.4   Dombay, F. von. Geschichte der Scherifen. Agram, 1801.

1800-1809 - cont.

Afr 7175.7   Grandpre, S. de. Voyage à la côte occidentale d'Afrique. Paris, 1801. 2v.

Afr 5828.01   Grant, Charles. The history of Mauritius. London, 1801.

Afr 3978.00.3   Institut d'Egypte, Cairo. Mémoires sur l'Egypte publiés pendant les campagnes de Général Bonaparte dans les annees VI et VII. Paris, 1801.

Afr 1607.91.5   Lempriere, G. Voyage dans l'empire de Maroc. Paris, 1801.

Afr 3978.02.1PF   Mayer, L. Views in Egypt, from the original drawings in the possession of Sir Robert Ainslie. London, 1801.

Afr 6143.17   Padenheim, D.W. Bref innehaallande beskrifning oefver Sierra Leona. Stockholm, 1801.

Afr 8658.01.2   Barrow, J. An account of travels into...South Africa. N.Y., 1802.

Htn   Afr 5180.12*   Durand, J.B.L. Voyage au Sénégal. v.1-2 and atlas. Paris, 1802. 3v.

Afr 5180.10.5   Golberry, S.M.X. Fragmens d'un voyage en Afrique. Paris, 1802. 2v.

Afr 4050.1   Horneman, F.K. Journal from Cairo to Mourzouk. London, 1802.

Afr 1258.02   Hornemanns, Fr. Tagebuch seiner Reise. Weimar, 1802.

Afr 5180.21   Labarthe, P. Voyage au Sénégal pendant les années 1784 et 1785. Paris, 1802.

Afr 3978.02PF   Mayer, Ludwig. Vues en Egypte. Londres, 1802.

Afr 3978.03A   Denon, V.D. Travels in upper and lower Egypt. N.Y., 1803. 2v.

Afr 5180.10   Golberry, S.M.X. Reise durch das westliche Afrika...1785-87. Leipzig, 1803. 2v.

Afr 1608.03   Haringman, H. Beknopt dag-journaal van Marocco. Haag, 1803.

Afr 6095.14.5   Labarthe, P. Reise nach der Küste von Guinea. Weimar, 1803.

Afr 8110.7   Nederburgh, S.C. Echte stukken. Haage, 1803.

Afr 3978.03.3   Non-military journal, or Observations made in Egypt. London, 1803.

Afr 8658.03   Semple, Robert. Walks and sketches at the Cape of Good Hope. London, 1803.

Afr 3207.2   Walsh, T. Journey of the late campaign in Egypt. London, 1803.

Afr 3207.1   Wilson, R.J. History of the British expedition to Egypt. London, 1803.

Afr 6143.16   Winterbottom, T. An account of native Africans...in Sierra Leone. London, 1803. 2v.

Afr 590.46.3   Brougham And Vaux, H. Brougham, 1st Baron. A concise statement of the question regarding the abolition of the slave trade. 2d ed. London, 1804.

Afr 3978.02.5PF   Mayer, Ludwig. Views in Egypt. London, 1804.

Afr 8658.04   Percival, R. An account of the Cape of Good Hope. London, 1804.

Afr 7073.4   Beaver, Philip. African memoranda. London, 1805.

Afr 4557.90.2F   Bruce, J. Travels to discover source of the Nile. 2nd ed. v.1-8. Plates and maps. Edinburgh, 1805. 8v.

Afr 855.9   Description of island of St. Helena. London, 1805.

Afr 8110.5   Kicheren. Extract from the narrative of his mission, 1803. Wiscasset, 1805.

Afr 6095.14   Labarthe, P. Voyage à la côte de Guinée. Paris, 1805.

Afr 1868.05   Short history of Algiers. 3rd ed. N.Y., 1805.

Afr 6143.16.5   Winterbottom, T. Nachrichten von der Sierra Leona Küste. Weimar, 1805.

Afr 8658.01.3   Barrow, J. Travels into the interior of South Africa. London, 1806. 2v.

Afr 3977.98.6   Browne, W.G. Travels in Africa, Egypt, and Syria, 1792-98. London, 1806.

Htn   Afr 8658.06*   Gleanings in Africa. London, 1806.

Afr 6143.8   Corry, J. Observations upon the windward coast of Africa. London, 1807.

Afr 5180.12.5   Durand, J.B.L. Voyage au Sénégal. v.1-2. Paris, 1807.

Htn   Afr 1947.8*   Martin, M. History of the captivity and sufferings in Algiers. Boston, 1807.

Afr 590.17   Stanfield, J.F. The Guinea voyage. Edinburgh, 1807.

Afr 628.108   Gregoire, Henri. De la littérature des Nègres. Paris, 1808.

1810-1819

Afr 3974.00   Abd-Al-Latif. Relation de l'Egypte (XIVe siècle). Paris, 1810.

Afr 657.90.5   Association for Promoting the Discovery of the Interior Parts of Africa. Proceedings of the Association for Promoting the Discovery of the Interior Parts of Africa. London, 1810. 2v.

Afr 1608.10   Buffa, J. Travels through the empire of Morocco. London, 1810.

Htn   Afr 628.110*   Grégoire, Henri. An enquiry concerning the intellectual and moral faculties...of Negroes. Brooklyn, 1810.

Afr 1608.09.3   Jackson, J.G. An account...empire of Morocco. Philadelphia, 1810.

Afr 628.108.10   Tussac, R. de. Cri des colons contre un ouvrage de M. L'Evêque. Paris, 1810.

Afr 590.30   African Institution. Report of the committee of the Institution. London, 1811.

Afr 8678.14   Alberti, L. Description physique et historique des Cafres. Amsterdam, 1811.

Afr 1608.09.2   Jackson, J.G. An account...empire of Morocco. 2d ed. London, 1811.

Afr 8658.11.3   Lichtenstein, H. Reisen im südlichen Africa...1803-06. Berlin, 1811. 2v.

Afr 2608.11   MacGill, Thomas. An account of Tunis. Glasgow, 1811.

Afr 3078.11   Quatremère, Etienne Marc. Mémoires géographiques et historiques sur l'Egypte. Paris, 1811. 2v.

Afr 6146.10   Coke, Thomas. An interesting narrative of a mission sent to Sierra Leone. Paris, 1812.

Afr 8658.11.5   Lichtenstein, H. Travels in southern Africa. London, 1812. 2v.

Afr 6192.7   Meredith, H. Account of the Gold Coast of Africa. London, 1812.

Afr 3078.11.1   Quatremère, Etienne Marc. Observations sur quelques points de la géographie de l'Egypte. Paris, 1812.

Afr 1607.91.3   Lempriere, W. Tour to Tangier and Morocco. 3rd ed. Newport, 1813.

Afr 5235.52.15   Park, Mungo. Travels in the interior districts of Africa. N.Y., 1813.

Afr 623.5   Scenery of Africa. London, 1813.

Afr 3978.14   Breton, M. L'Egypte et la Syrie. v.1-6. Paris, 1814. 3v.

Afr 108.14   Geoffroy, R. L'Afrique ou Histoire, moeurs, usages et coutumes des Africans; le Sénégal. Paris, 1814. 4v.

1810-1819 - cont.

	Afr 8830.8	Alberti, J.C.L. Die Kaffern auf der Südküste von Afrika. Gotha, 1815.
	Afr 8658.15	Campbell, J. Travels in South Africa. London, 1815.
	Afr 5235.54	Park, Mungo. The journal of a mission to the interior of Africa...1805. Philadelphia, 1815.
	Afr 5235.51.10	Park, Mungo. Travels in the interior districts of Africa. London, 1815. 2v.
	Afr 6138.2.01	Thorpe, Robert. A letter to William Wilberforce, Esq. London, 1815.
	Afr 1258.16	Badia y Leyblick. Travels of Ali Bey in Morocco, Tripoli. Philadelphia, 1816. 2v.
	Afr 855.11	Beatson, A. Tracts relative to the island of St. Helena. London, 1816.
	Afr 8658.16	Campbell, J. Travels in South Africa. Andover, 1816.
	Afr 1608.16	Cock, S. The narrative of Robert Adams. London, 1816.
	Afr 1947.14	Cruelties of the Algerine pirates shewing the present dreadful state of the English slaves. 4th ed. London, 1816.
	Afr 1258.16.5	Janson, William. A view of the present condition of the states of Barbary. London, 1816.
	Afr 2608.11.5	MacGill, Thomas. Neue Reise nach Tunis. Weimar, 1816. 2 pam.
	Afr 125.6F	Morcelli, S.A. Africa christiana. Brixiae, 1816. 3v.
	Afr 4558.14.2	Salt, Henry. Voyage to Abyssinia. Philadelphia, 1816.
Htn	Afr 2928.18*	Tully, R. Narrative of a ten years'Residence in Tripoli. London, 1816.
	Afr 1608.16.20	Adams, Robert. Nouveau voyage dans l'interieur de l'Afrique. Paris, 1817.
	Afr 1940.5	Ferreira Lobo, R.J. Deducção das votas no Supremo Conselho provizorio. Londres, 1817.
	Afr 1068.17	Jackson, G.A. Algiers...a complete picture of the Barbary states. London, 1817.
	Afr 1325.6F	Keatinge, M. Travels through France and Spain to Morocco. London, 1817.
NEDL	Afr 3978.17.3	Legh, T. Narrative of a journey in Egypt. London, 1817.
	Afr 3978.17	Legh, T. Narrative of a journey in Egypt. Philadelphia, 1817.
	Afr 3978.17.2	Legh, T. Narrative of a journey in Egypt. 2d. ed. London, 1817.
	Afr 6192.15	Marrée, J.A. de. Reizen op en beschrijving van de Goudkust van Guinea. v.1-2. 's-Gravenhage, 1817-18.
	Afr 2208.17	Pananti, F. Aventure e osservazioni. Firenze, 1817. 2v.
	Afr 1930.2	Private journal...from Portsmouth. Exeter, 1817.
	Afr 1258.17.2	Riley, J. An authentic narrative of the loss of the American brig Commerce. Hartford, 1817.
	Afr 1258.17	Riley, J. Loss of the American brig Commerce. London, 1817.
	Afr 2928.18.2	Tully, R. Narrative of a ten years' residence in Tripoli. 2d ed. London, 1817.
Htn	Afr 7350.3.23*	Burgess, E. Address to the American Society for Colonizing the Free People of Colour of the U.S. Washington, 1818.
	Afr 5180.13	Correard, A. Naufrage de la frigate La Méduse. Paris, 1818.
Htn	Afr 8808.18*	Latrobe, C.I. Journal of a visit to South Africa 1815-1816. London, 1818.
	Afr 3978.18	Light, Henry. Travels in Egypt, Nubia, Holy Land, Mount Lebanon and Cyprus, in the year 1814. London, 1818.
	Afr 608.18	Murray, H. Historical account of discoveries and travels in Africa. Edinburgh, 1818. 2v.
	Afr 1608.18	Paddock, J. A narrative...shipwreck of the ship Oswego. N.Y., 1818.
	Afr 2208.17.3	Pananti, F. Narrative of a residence in Algiers. London, 1818.
	Afr 1258.18	Robbins, A. A journal comprising an account of the loss of the brig Commerce. 7 ed. Hartford, 1818.
	Afr 1258.18.2	Robbins, A. A journal comprising an account of the loss of the brig Commerce. 8 ed. Hartford, 1818.
	Afr 5180.13.8	Savigny, J.B.H. Narrative of a voyage to Senegal in 1816. London, 1818.
	Afr 5180.13.3	Savigny, J.B.H. Schipbreuk van het fregat Medusa. Haarlem, 1818.
	Afr 7808.18.3	Tuckey, J.K. Narrative of an expedition to explore the River Zaire. London, 1818.
	Afr 7808.18.2	Tuckey, J.K. Narrative of an expedition to explore the River Zaire. N.Y., 1818.
	Afr 555.27	Bickersteth, E. Memoirs of S. Wilhelm, a native of West Africa. New Haven, 1819.
	Afr 6192.14F	Bowdich, T.E. Mission from Cape Coast Castle to Ashantee. London, 1819.
	Afr 6168.30	Bowdich, Thomas Edward. Voyage dans le pays d'Aschantie. Paris, 1819.
	Afr 4060.4	Burckhardt, J.L. Travels in Nubia. London, 1819.
	Afr 2928.19	Cella, Paolo della. Viaggio da Tripoli di Barberia. Genova, 1819.
	Afr 1947.10	Dumont, P.J. Histoire de l'esclavage de Dumont. Paris, 1819.
	Afr 608.19	Hutton, C. The tour of Africa. London, 1819-21. 3v.
	Afr 698.19	Prior, James. Voyage along the eastern coast of Africa. London, 1819.
	Afr 7093.3	Proyart, L.B. Histoire de Loango, Kakongo. Paris, 1819.
	Afr 1258.18.3	Robbins, A. A journal comprising an account of the loss of the brig Commerce. 10 ed. Hartford, 1819.
	Afr 1930.1	Salame, A. Narrative of the expedition to Algiers in 1816. London, 1819.
	Afr 2928.18.8	Tully, R. Letters written during a ten years' residence at the court of Tripoli. 3rd ed. London, 1819. 2v.

1820

	Afr 6192.96	Bowdich, Thomas Edward. Mission der englisch-afrikanischen Compagnie von Cape Coast Castle nach Ashantee. Weimar, 1820.
	Afr 8673.5F	Daniell, W. Sketches representing the native tribes...South Africa. London, 1820.
	Afr 8830.6	Hallbeck, H.P. Narrative of visit made in 1819 to...Erron. London, 1820.
	Afr 1608.20	Jackson, J.G. An account of Timbuctoo and Housa. London, 1820.
	Afr 5385.5	Macleod, John. A voyage to Africa. London, 1820.
	Afr 5180.20	Mollien, G.T. Voyage...aux sources du Sénégal et de la Gambie. 1818. Paris, 1820.
	Afr 8658.20	Stout, Benjamin. Cape of Good Hope. London, 1820.

1821

	Afr 1608.21	Cochelet, C. Naufrage du brick français la sophie. v.1-2. Paris, 1821. 2v.
	Afr 2494.7	Generoso corsario. Lisboa, 1821.
	Afr 6192.6	Hutton, W. A voyage to Africa. London, 1821.
Htn	Afr 2928.18.3*	Lyon, G.F. Narrative of travels in North Africa, 1818, 1819 and 1820. London, 1821.
	Afr 5056.21	Macqueen, James. A geographical and commercial view of northern Central Africa. Edinburgh, 1821.
	Afr 8735.5	Notes on the Cape of Good Hope...1820. London, 1821.
	Afr 608.21.2	Taylor, I. Scenes in Africa. London, 1821.
	Afr 658.21	Walckenaer, C.A. Recherches géographiques sur l'intérieur de l'Afrique. Paris, 1821.

1822

	Afr 7458.22	Bacon, E. Abstract of a journal...to Afrika. Philadelphia, 1822.
	Afr 1103.15	Barbareschi e i cristiani. Ginevra, 1822.
	Afr 5842.9	Billiard, A. Voyage aux colonies orientales. Paris, 1822.
	Afr 4557.90.14	Bruce, J. Travels, between the years 1765 and 1773. London, 1822?
	Afr 8658.22	Burchell, W.J. Travels in...southern Africa. London, 1822. 2v.
	Afr 4060.4.2	Burckhardt, J.L. Travels in Nubia. 2d ed. London, 1822.
	Afr 5548.22	Copland, Samuel. A history of the island of Madagascar. London, 1822.
	Afr 4050.16	Edmonstone, A. A journey to two of the oases of Upper Egypt. London, 1822.
	Afr 3207.20	Thedenat-Duvent, P.P. L'Egypte sous Mehemed-Ali. Paris, 1822.
	Afr 3978.22	Waddington, G. Journal of a visit to some parts of Ethiopia. London, 1822.

1823

	Afr 6095.12	Adams, J. Remarks on the country...Cape Palmas to the river Congo. London, 1823.
	Afr 4070.23	Cailliaud, F. Voyage à Meroe, au Fleuve Blanc. Paris, 1823-27. 5v.
	Afr 3685.6	English, G.B. Narrative of the expedition to Dongola and Senvaar. Boston, 1823.
	Afr 3205.1	Mengin, Felix. Histoire de l'Egypte sous le gouvernement de Mohammed-Aly. v.1-2 and atlas. Paris, 1823. 3v.
	Afr 6283.2	Sandolphe, J.F. Memoires. Paris, 1823. 2v.
	Afr 8808.23	State of the Cape of Good Hope in 1822. London, 1823.

1824

	Afr 7045.2	Bowdich, T.E. An account of the discoveries of the Portuguese in the interior of Angola and Mozambique. London, 1824.
	Afr 855.8	Brooke, T.H. History..island of St. Helena...1823. London, 1824.
	Afr 6168.7	Dupuis, J. Journal of a residence in Ashanti. London, 1824.
	Afr 3978.24	Fruits of enterprize, travels in Egypt. Boston, 1824.
	Afr 6095.5	West African sketches...G.R. Collier. London, 1824.

1825

	Afr 1608.22	Comyn, T. De. Ligera ojeada o breve idea...de Marruecos en 1822. Barcelona, 1825.
	Afr 2945.13	Delaporte. Relations inédites de la Cyrénaique. Paris, 1825.
	Afr 7118.25	Feo Cardoza de Castellobranco e Torres, J.C. Memorias contendo a biographia do vice almirante Huiz da Motta a Feo e Torres. Paris, 1825.
	Afr 5235.121	Gray, William. Travels in western Africa. London, 1825.
	Afr 608.25	Hulbert, Charles. Museum Africanum. London, 1825.
	Afr 6143.5	Laing, A.G. Travels in...western Africa. London, 1825.
Htn	Afr 7360.15*	Liberia. Constitution. Constitution, government and digest of the laws of Liberia. Washington, 1825.
	Afr 4050.2	Minutoli, H.V. Reise zum Tempel der Jupiter Ammon. Berlin, 1825.
	Afr 3978.25	Sherer, M. Scenes and impressions in Egypt and Italy. London, 1825.

1826

	Afr 590.30.5	African Institution. Extracts from 18th and 19th reports...May 1824, and May 1825. Philadelphia, 1826.
	Afr 7375.4	Ashmun, J. History of the American colony in Liberia. Washington, 1826.
	Afr 3988.6	Chabral de Volvic. Essai sur les mours des habitans modernes de l'Egypte. Paris, 1826.
	Afr 2748.26	Denham. Narration of travels...in central Africa. Boston, 1826.
	Afr 2748.26.2	Denham. Narration of travels...in central Africa. London, 1826.
	Afr 628.108.7	Gregoire, Henri. De la noblesse de la peau. Paris, 1826.
	Afr 678.26	Hulbert, C. African fragments. Shrewsbury, 1826.
	Afr 2208.26	Shaler, William. Sketches of Algiers. Boston, 1826.
	Afr 608.26	Walckenaer, C.A. Histoire générale des voyages...par mer et par terre. Paris, 1826-31. 11v.

1827

	Afr 555.19	Campbell, John. The life of Africaner. Philadelphia, 1827.
	Afr 5180.13.5	Dard, C.A.P. Perils and captivity, Medusa shipwreck. Edinburgh, 1827.
	Afr 6140.5	Macaulay, K. The colony of Sierra Leone. London, 1827.
	Afr 3978.27	Minutoli. Recollections of Egypt. Philadelphia, 1827.
	Afr 8658.27	Thompson, George. Travels and adventures in southern Africa. London, 1827.
	Afr 8658.27.3	Thompson, George. Travels and adventures in Southern Africa. 2d ed. London, 1827. 2v.

1828

	Afr 2802.5	Beechey, F.W. Proceedings of the expedition to explore the northern coast of Africa, from Tripoly eastward. London, 1828.

1828 - cont.

Afr 2748.26.3   Denham, Dixon. Narration of travels and discoveries in Northern and Central Africa in the years 1822, 1823 and 1824. 3. ed. London, 1828.

Afr 4050.4   Ehrenburg, C.G. Naturgeschichtliche Reisen durch Nord-Afrika undWest-Asien. Berlin, 1828.

Afr 1390.2   Moura, J. de S.A. Historia dos Soberanos Mohametanos. Lisboa, 1828.

1829

Afr 6275.3   Clapperton, Hugh. Journal of second expedition into interior of Africa. London, 1829.

Afr 810.20   Donkin, Rufane. A dissertation on the course and probable termination of the Niger. London, 1829.

Afr 8808.24   Rose, C. Four years in southern Africa. London, 1829.

Afr 4060.2   Rueppell, E. Reisen im Nubien, Kordofan. Text and atlas. Frankfurt, 1829.

1830

Afr 2208.30   Aperçu...sur l'état d'Alger. 2e ed. Paris, 1830.

Afr 5842.24   Bartram, Alfred, Lady. Recollections of seven years' residence at the Mauritius. London, 1830.

Afr 1957.27   Bianchi, Thomas. Relation de l'arrivée dans la rade d'Alger du vaisseau. Paris, 1830.

Afr 3978.30F   Burckhardt, J.L. Manners and customs of modern Egyptians. London, 1830.

Afr 5235.128   Caillié, René. Journal d'un voyage à Tembouctou. Paris, 1830. 3v.

Afr 5235.128.5   Caillié, René. Travels through central Africa to Timbuctoo. London, 1830. 2v.

Afr 1947.15   Contremoulins, C. Souvenirs d'un officier français. Paris, 1830.

Afr 678.30   Crow, Hugh. Memoirs of the late Captain Hugh Crow. London, 1830.

Afr 1955.23   Denniée. Précis historique et administrative de la campagne d'Afrique. Paris, 1830.

Afr 3205.10   Finati, Giovanni. Narrative of the life and adventures of Giovanni Finati. London, 1830. 2v.

Afr 4557.90.25   Head, F.B. The life of Bruce. London, 1830.

Afr 608.30   Jameson, R. Narrative of discovery and adventure in Africa. Edinburgh 1830.

Afr 6275.4   Lander, R.L. Records of Captain Clapperton's last expedition to Africa. London, 1830. 2v.

Afr 1947.5   Laranda, V. Neapolitan captive, interesting narrative of the captivity and sufferings of V. Laranda. N.Y., 1830.

Afr 7350.5.3   Pennsylvania Colonization Society. Report of the managers. Appendix. Philadelphia, 1830.

Afr 2208.30.3   Perrot, A.M. Alger, esquisse topographique et historique. Paris, 1830.

Afr 1957.3   Perrot, A.M. La conquête d'Alger. Paris, 1830.

Afr 1922.5   Pièces curieuses, ou Alger en 1802. Paris, 1830.

Afr 608.94   Reclus, E. Nouvelle géographie universelle Morocco. Maps of Alger. Paris, 1830-94.

Afr 2208.30.8   Renaudot. Alger, tableau du royaume. Paris, 1830.

Afr 2208.26.5   Shaler, William. Esquisse de l'état d'Alger. Paris, 1830.

Afr 2207.38.15   Shaw, Thomas. Voyage dans la régence d'Alger. Paris, 1830.

Afr 2207.38.10   Shaw, Thomas. Voyage dans la régence d'Alger. Paris, 1830.

Afr 2207.38.16   Shaw, Thomas. Voyage dans la régence d'Alger. Cover 1831. Paris, 1830.

Afr 3978.30.3   Webster, James. Travels through Egypt. London, 1830. 2v.

1831

Afr 2260.9   Clauzel, B. Observations...sur quelques actes. Paris, 1831.

Afr 3978.31   Ferrario, G. Il costume antico e moderno. Livorno, 1831. 3 pam.

Afr 1955.25   Journal d'un officier de l'armée d'Afrique. Paris, 1831.

Afr 1957.6   Juchereau de St. Denis, A. Considerations sur la régence d'Alger. Paris, 1831.

Afr 1957.28   Lauvergne, Hubert. Histoire de l'expédition d'Afrique en 1830. Paris, 1831.

Afr 1957.6.10   Loverdo, N. Extrait du journal d'un officier supérieur attaché à la deuxième division de l'armée d'Afrique. Paris, 1831.

Afr 4555.31   Pearce, N. Life and adventures of N. Pearce during residence. London, 1831. 2v.

Afr 6168.9   Ricketts, H.D. Narrative of the Ashantee war. London, 1831.

Afr 3068.31   Russell, M. View of ancient and modern Egypt. Edinburgh, 1831.

1832

Afr 1957.2   Ault-Dumesnil, E.D. De l'expédition d'Afrique en 1830. Paris, 1832.

Afr 1955.26   Barchou-Penhoen. Souvenirs de l'expédition d'Afrique. Paris, 1832.

Afr 5842.11F   Bradshaw, T. Views in the Mauritius, or Isle of France. London, 1832.

Afr 1990.2   De la domination française en Afrique. Paris, 1832.

Afr 7808.32   Douville, J.B. Voyage au Congo, 1828-1830. Paris, 1832. 4v.

Afr 7808.32.2   Douville, J.B. Voyage au Congo, 1829-1830. Stuttgart, 1832. 3v.

Afr 7350.3.9   Garrison, W.L. Thoughts on African colonization. Boston, 1832.

Afr 7350.3.10   Garrison, W.L. Thoughts on African colonization. Boston, 1832.

Afr 810.1   Lander, R. Journal of an expedition to explore the Niger. London, 1832. 3v.

Afr 608.30.3   Murray, H. Narrative of discovery and adventure in Africa. Edinburgh, 1832.

Afr 7458.32   News from Africa. Collection of facts. Baltimore, 1832.

Afr 2260.4   Preaux. Réflexions sur la colonization. Paris, 1832.

1833

Afr 5548.33   Ackerman. Histoire des revolutions de Madagascar. Paris, 1833.

Afr 7350.3.30   Fruits of colonizationism. n.p., 1833.

Afr 7350.3.12   Hodgkin, T. Inquiry into merits of the American Colonization Society. London, 1833.

1833 - cont.

Afr 7350.3.11   Hopkins, E. Objections...report of the African Colonization Society. Philadelphia, 1833. 2 pam.

Afr 7375.14.5   Innes, William. Liberia. 2d ed. Edinburgh, 1833.

Afr 8678.18   Kay, S. Travels and researches in Caffraria. London, 1833.

Afr 678.33.5   Leonard, Peter. Records of a voyage to the western coast of Africa in his Majesty's ship Dryad. Edinburgh, 1833.

Afr 2308.4   Pichon. Alger...son état présent et son avenir. Paris, 1833.

Afr 1258.17.5   Riley, J. An authentic narrative of the loss of the American brig Commerce. Hartford, 1833.

Afr 1258.18.8   Robbins, A. A journal comprising an account of the loss of the brig Commerce. Hartford, 1833.

Afr 2208.33   Rozet. Voyage dans la régence d'Alger. 3 vols. and atlas. Paris, 1833. 4v.

Afr 4558.33.3   Russell, M. Nubia and Abyssinia. 2d ed. Edinburgh, 1833.

Afr 7350.3.35   Smith, G. Facts designed to exhibit the real character and tendency of the American Colonizaton Society. Liverpool, 1833.

Afr 5842.12   Stirling, E. Cursory notes on the Isle of France. Calcutta, 1833.

Afr 678.33   The western coast of Africa. Philadelphia, 1833.

Afr 7368.33   Wright, E. The sin of slavery and its remedy. N.Y., 1833.

1834

Afr 550.22   Appeal to the churches in behalf of Africa. N.Y., 1834.

Afr 1957.5   Berthezene. Dix-huit mois à Alger. Montpellier, 1834.

Afr 7308.34   Botelho, S.X. Resumo para servir de introdução a memoria estatistica sobre os dominios portuguezes na Africa oriental. Lisboa, 1834.

Afr 7175.25   Carvalho e Menezes, A. Memoria geografica. Lisboa, 1834.

Afr 4558.34   Gobat, Samuel. Journal of a three years' residence in Abyssinia. London, 1834.

Afr 1608.34   Graaberg Fraan Hemso. Speccio...dell impero di Marocco. Genova, 1834.

Afr 5820.15   Mauritius; Mr. Jeremie's case. London, 1834.

Afr 2308.5   Montagne, D.J. Physiologie morale et physique d'Alger. Marseille, 1834.

Afr 2208.32.3   Pfeiffer, S.F. Meine Reisen und Gefangenschaft in Algier. 3rd ed. Giessen, 1834.

Afr 8658.34   Pringle, Thomas. African sketches. London, 1834.

Afr 3978.34   Saint John, J.A. Egypt, and Mohammed Ali. vol.1-2. London, 1834. 2v.

Afr 2208.34   Schimper, W. Reise nach Algier in den Jahren 1831-32. Stuttgart, 1834.

Afr 7350.5.12   Tyson, J.R. A discourse before the Young Men's Colonization Society of Pennsylvania. Philadelphia, 1834.

Afr 7350.5.20   Whedon, D.D. An address delivered before the Middletown Colonization Society at their annual meeting, July 4, 1834. Middletown, 1834.

1835

Afr 8658.38   Alexander, James E. An expedition of discovery into the interior of Africa. London, 1835. 2v.

Afr 2208.35.10   Algier wie es ist. Stuttgart, 1835.

Afr 1957.32   Barchou de Penhoen, Auguste Theodore Hitaire, Baron. Mémoires d'un officier d'état-major. Paris, 1835.

Afr 7308.35   Botelho, S.X. Memoria estatistica portuguezes na Africa oriental. Lisboa, 1835-37. 2v.

Afr 6143.6   Church, Mary. Sierra Leone, or The liberated Africans. London, 1835.

Afr 2357.25   Desmichels, L.A. Oran sous le commandement du général Desmichels. Paris, 1835.

Afr 4558.35.5   Gobat, Samuel. Journal d'un séjour en Abyssinia. Paris, 1835.

Afr 2818.35   Greenhow, R. The history of Tripoli. Richmond, 1835.

Afr 7375.7   Gurley, R.R. Life of Jehudi Ashmun. Washington, 1835.

Afr 7350.6.10   Harper, C.C. An address delivered...annual meeting of Maryland State Colonization Society. Annapolis, Jan. 23, 1835. Baltimore, 1835.

Afr 4558.35   Hoskins, G.A. Travels in Ethiopia. London, 1835.

Afr 2208.35.2   Lord, P.B. Algiers, notices of neighboring states of Barbary. London, 1835. 2v.

Afr 8100.25   Loureiro, Manoel José Gomes. Memorias dos estabelecimentos portuguezes a l'este. Lisboa, 1835.

Afr 8808.35   Moodie, John W.D. Ten years in South Africa. London, 1835. 2v.

Afr 2230.23   Pharaon, J. Les Cabiles et Boudgie. Alger, 1835.

Afr 8658.34.5   Pringle, Thomas. Narrative of a residence in South Africa. London, 1835.

Afr 1068.35.2   Russell, M. History of the Barbary states. 2d ed. Edinburgh, 1835.

Afr 8658.35   Steedman, A. Wanderings and adventures...of South Africa. London, 1835. 2v.

Afr 2208.35   Temple, G.T. Excursions...Algiers and Tunis. London, 1835. 2v.

Afr 3978.35   Wilkinson, J.G. Topography of Thebes. London, 1835.

1836

Afr 2208.36   Campbell, Thomas. Letters from the south, written during a journey to Algiers. Philadelphia, 1836.

Afr 1258.26.5   Ebn-el-Dyn El-Aghouathy. Etudes de géographie critique. Paris, 1836.

Afr 7368.36   Freeman, F. Yaradee, plea for Africa. Philadelphia, 1836.

Afr 9028.36   Gardiner, A.F. Narrative of a journey to the Zoolu country. London, 1836.

Afr 608.30.2   Jameson, R. Narrative of discovery and adventure in Africa. N.Y., 1836.

Afr 3215.5   Jomard, E.F. Coup-d'oeil...sur l'état présent de l'Egypte. Paris, 1836.

Afr 8830.9   King Williams Town, Cape of Good Hope. King Williams Town, Cape province. Cape Town, 1836.

Afr 8658.36   Martin, R.M. History of southern Africa. London, 1836.

Afr 1947.36   Pfeiffer, G.S.F. Voyages and five years captivity in Algiers. Harrisburg, 1836.

Afr 5585.3   Précis sur les établissements français formés à Madagascar. Paris, 1836.

Afr 6143.7   Rankin, F.H. The white man's grave. London, 1836. 2v.

Afr 3068.31.2   Russell, M. View of ancient and modern Egypt. N.Y., 1836.

Afr 590.42   Society for Abolishing Slavery All over the World, Newcastle-Upon-Tyne. Declaration of the objects. Newcastle, 1836.

1837

	Afr 8825.4	Beverley, R.M. The wrongs of the Caffre nation. London, 1837.
	Afr 2208.36.5	Campbell, Thomas. Letters from the south. London, 1837. 2v.
	Afr 1955.28	Clauzel, M. Explications. Paris, 1837.
	Afr 608.37	D'Avezac-Macaya, Marie A.P. Esquisse générale de l'Afrique. Paris, 1837.
	Afr 1990.6	Desjobert, A. La question d'Alger. Paris, 1837.
	Afr 6283.7	Fawckner, J. Narrative of travels on the coast of Benin. London, 1837.
	Afr 1960.2	Grand, E. Défence et occupation de la colonie d'Alger. Toulon, 1837.
	Afr 810.3.3	Laird, M. Narrative of expedition into Africa by the river Niger. v.1-2. London, 1837. 2v.
	Afr 2295.1	Lamalle, D. de. Province de Constantine. Paris, 1837.
	Afr 810.2	Lander, R. Journal of an expedition to explore the Niger. N.Y., 1837. 2v.
	Afr 3978.37.8	Lane, E.W. An account of the manners and customs of the modern Egyptians. v.1-2. London, 1837. 2v.
NEDL	Afr 3978.37	Lane, E.W. Manners and customs of the modern Egyptians. London, 1837.
	Afr 3155.1F	Makrizi. Histoire des sultans mamlouks. Paris, 1837-42. 2v.
	Afr 605.56.7	Ramusio, G.B. Il viaggio di Giovan Leone e le navigazioni. Venezia, 1837.
	Afr 1068.35.5	Russell, M. History of the Barbary states. 2d ed. N.Y., 1837.
	Afr 4558.33.2	Russell, M. Nubia and Abyssinia. N.Y., 1837.
	Afr 1910.10	Schwarzenberg, F. Rueckblicke auf Algier. Wien, 1837.
	Afr 3978.37.15	Scott, C.R. Rambles in Egypt and Candia. v.1-2. London, 1837. 2v.
	Afr 7375.8	Taylor, J.B. Biography of Elder Lott Cary. Baltimore, 1837.

1838

	Afr 1608.38	Augustin, F. von. Erinnerungen aus Marokko. Wien, 1838.
	Afr 1960.1	Blondel, L. Nouvel aperçu sur l'Algérie. Paris, 1838.
	Afr 698.38	Brun, C. De redding des bemanning van het...nijverheid. Rotterdam, 1838.
	Afr 2260.7	Bugeaud, M. De l'établissement de légions de colons. Paris, 1838.
	Afr 1973.1.5	Devoisins, V. Recueil de documents sur l'expédition et la prise de Constantine. Text and atlas. Paris, 1838. 2v.
	Afr 2208.38	Dureau de la Malle. Peyssonnel et Desfontaines voyages...d'Alger. Paris, 1838. 2v.
	Afr 5548.38	Ellis, W. History of Madagascar. London, 1838. 2v.
	Afr 7350.5.8	Ingersoll, J.R. Address...at the annual meeting of the Pennsylvania Colonization Society, Oct. 25, 1838. Philadelphia, 1838.
	Afr 2458.38	Niculy, G. Documenti sulla storia di Tunis. Livorno, 1838.
	Afr 4558.38	Rueppell, Edward. Reise in Abyssinien. Frankfurt, 1838. 2v.
	Afr 3068.31.4	Russell, M. View of ancient and modern Egypt. Edinburgh, 1838.
	Afr 1973.2	Sur l'expédition et le siège de Constantine. Paris, 1838.
	Afr 1973.4	Wagner, M. Lettres sur l'expédition de Constantine. n.p., 1838.

1839

	Afr 1603.80	Abu Al-Feda. Description du pays du Magreb. Alger, 1839.
	Afr 2308.12	Broughton. Six years residence in Algiers. London, 1839.
	Afr 4558.37.2	Combes, Edmond. Voyage en Abyssinie...1835-37. Paris, 1839. 4v.
	Afr 1608.39	Davidson, J. Notes taken during travels in Africa. London, 1839.
	Afr 115.2	Dujarday, H. Resumé des voyages des portugais. Paris, 1839.
	Afr 3978.39	Dumas, A. Impressions of travel in Egypt. N.Y., 1839.
	Afr 8145.6	Ebner, J.S. Reise nach Süd-Afrika und Darstellung. Berlin, 1839.
	Afr 1990.8	Genty de Bussy, P. De l'établissement des Français. 2e éd. Paris, 1839. v.
	Afr 7375.7.2	Gurley, R.R. Life of Jehudi Ashmun. 2d. ed. N.Y., 1839.
	Afr 810.3	Lander, R. Journal of an expedition to explore the Niger. N.Y., 1839. 2v.
	Afr 6275.4.5	Lander, R.L. Journal of an expedition to explore the course and termination of theNiger. N.Y., 1839.
	Afr 658.39	Macbrair, R.M. Sketches of a missionary's travels in Egypt, Syria, Western Africa. London, 1839.
	Afr 3205.1.5	Mengin, Felix. Histoire sommaire de l'Egypte. Paris, 1839.
	Afr 7375.12	Wilkeson, Samuel. A concise history of...the American colonies in Liberia. Washington, 1839.

1840

	Afr 678.40.2	Alexander, J.E. Excursions in western Africa. 2d ed. London, 1840. 2v.
	Afr 810.11F	Allen, W. Picturesque views on the river Niger. London, 1840.
	Afr 5833.4	Archer, Edward. A letterTo the right honourable Lord John Russell. London, 1840.
	Afr 3978.40	Clat-Bey, A. Aperçu général sur l'Egypte. Bruxelles, 1840. 2v.
	Afr 3978.40.2	Clat-Bey, A. Aperçu général sur l'Egypte. v.1-2. Paris, 1840.
	Afr 1973.1	Devoisins, V. Expéditions de Constantine. Paris, 1840.
	Afr 1957.4	Dopigez. Souvenirs de l'Algérie. Douai, 1840.
	Afr 1880.5	Esterhazy, W. De la domination turque. Paris, 1840.
	Afr 5765.2	Freeman, J.J. A narrative of the persecution of the Christians in Madagascar. London, 1840.
	Afr 4115.4PF	Hay, Robert. Illustrations of Cairo. London, 1840.
	Afr 678.34.2	Holman, James. Travels in Madeira. 2d ed. London, 1840.
	Afr 810.8	Jamieson, R. An appeal...Niger expedition and sequel. London, 1840-43.
	Afr 5748.40	Lequevel de Lacombe, B.F. Voyage à Madagascar...Camores (1825-30). Paris, 1840. 2v.
	Afr 1990.7	Letang, B. Des moyens d'assurer la domination française en Algérie. Paris, 1840-46. 4 pam.
	Afr 608.40	McQueen, J. A geographical survey of Africa. London, 1840.
	Afr 5235.51	Park, Mungo. The life and travels of Mungo Park. N.Y., 1840.

1840 - cont.

	Afr 2945.12	Pezant, A. Voyage en Afrique au royaume de Barcah et dans la Cyrénaique à travers le désert. Paris, 1840.
	Afr 8658.34.2	Pringle, Thomas. Narrative of a residence in South Africa. London, 1840.
	Afr 1990.3	Rozey, A.G. Cris de conscience de l'Algérie. Paris, 1840.
	Afr 4558.33.5	Russell, M. Nubia and Abyssinia. N.Y., 1840.
	Afr 810.8.10	Stephen, George. A letter to the Rt. Hon. Lord John Russell...Niger expedition. London, 1840.
	Afr 2208.40	Suchet. Lettres...sur l'Algérie. Tours, 1840.
	Afr 590.70	Xavier Botelho, S. Escravatura, beneficios que podem provir as nossas possessoes. Lisboa, 1840.

1841

	Afr 5180.14	Alvares d'Almada, Andre. Rios de Guine do Cabo-Verde. Porto, 1841.
	Afr 6280.14	Anezac, A.D. Notice sur le pays et le peuple des Yebous en Afrique. Paris, 1841.
	Afr 1838.2	Bavoux, E. Alger, voyage politique. v.1-2. Paris, 1841.
	Afr 1990.12	Duvivier. Solution de la question de l'Algérie. Paris, 1841.
	Afr 2295.3	Duvivieu. Recherches...sur la portion de l'Algérie au sud de Guelnia. Paris, 1841.
	Afr 674.93.2	Eannes de Azurara, G. Chronica de descobrimento e conquista de Guiné. Paris, 1841.
	Afr 674.93F	Eannes de Azurara, G. Chronica do descobrimento e conquista de Guiné. Paris, 1841.
	Afr 5765.2.10	Griffiths, D. The persecuted Christians of Madagascar. London, 1841.
	Afr 7350.3.14	Gurley, R.R. Letter to Hon. H. Clay, president of the American Colonization Society. London, 1841.
	Afr 7350.3.13	Gurley, R.R. Mission to England...American Colonization Society. Washington, 1841.
	Afr 1955.20	Hatin, Eugene. Malerische Beschreibung der Regenschaft Algier. Karlsruhe, 1841.
	Afr 608.41	Kuelb, P.H. Geschichte der Entdeckungsreisen. Mainz, 1841.
	Afr 3205.6	Madden, R.R. Egypt and Mohammed Ali. 2d ed. London, 1841.
	Afr 4610.6	Rochet d'Héricourt, C.E. Voyage sur la côte orientale de la Mer Rouge et...de Choa. Paris, 1841.
	Afr 115.1	Santarem, M.F. de B. Memoria sobre a prioridade dos descobrimentos portugueses. Porto, 1841.
	Afr 8808.41	Shaw, B. Memorials of South Africa. London, 1841.
	Afr 8808.41.3	Shaw, B. Memorials of South Africa. N.Y., 1841.

1842

	Afr 5842.8	Account of the island of Mauritius. London, 1842.
	Afr 8658.42	Arbousset, Thomas. Relation d'un voyage...au cap de Bonne-Espérance. Paris, 1842.
	Afr 1838.1	Bugeaud. L'Algérie, des moyens de conserver cette conquête. Paris, 1842.
	Afr 1990.10	Buret, Eugène. Question d'Afrique. Paris, 1842.
Htn	Afr 8718.42*	Cannon, R. History of Cape Mounted Riflemen. London, 1842.
	Afr 3978.42	Cooley, J.E. The American in Egypt. N.Y., 1842.
	Afr 7190.15	Cunha Mattos, R.J. da. Corographia historica das ilhas de San Thome, Anno Bom, e Fernando Po. Porto, 1842.
	Afr 3978.42.3	Gliddon, G.R. Appendix to the American in Egypt. Philadelphia, 1842.
	Afr 3183.20	Leibniz, G.W. Consilium Aegyptiacum. Paris, 1842.
	Afr 115.3.10	Memoria sobre a prioridade dos descobrimentos dos portugueses. Porto, 1842.
	Afr 8808.42	Moffatt, Robert. Missionary labours...in southern Africa. London, 1842.
	Afr 5180.14.10	Santarem, M.F. de B. Notice sur Andre Alvares d'Almada et sa description de la Guinée. Paris, 1842.
	Afr 810.13	Schoen, J.F. Journals of Schoen and S. Crowther...expedition up Niger. London, 1842.
	Afr 1965.5	Scott. Journal of a residence in the Esmailla of Abd-el-Kader. London, 1842.
	Afr 150.8	Wappaens, J.E. Untersuchungen üeber die geographischen Entdeckungen der Portugiesen unter Heinrich dem Seefahrer. Göttingen, 1842.
	Afr 8658.42.3	Weyermueller, F. Die Völker Südafrikas. Strassburg, 1842.

1843

	Afr 1390.1	Annales regum Mauritaniae. v.1-2. Upsaliae, 1843.
	Afr 1825.3PF	Berbrugger. Algerie historique, pittoresque. Paris, 1843. 3v.
	Afr 1973.5	Caraman, V.L.C. de R. Relation...de la part que le Feu duc de Caraman a prise à la première expédition de Constantine en 1836. Toulouse, 1843.
	Afr 8808.43	Chase, John C. The Cape of Good Hope...Algoa bay. London, 1843.
	Afr 1868.43.5	Estry, Stephen D'. Histoire d'Alger. Tours, 1843.
	Afr 3978.24.5	Fruits of enterprize, travels in Egypt. New ed. N.Y., 1843.
	Afr 3205.5	Hamont, P.N. L'Egypte sous Mehemet-Ali. Paris, 1843. 2v.
	Afr 4558.43	Journals of Messers Isenberg and Krape. London, 1843.
	Afr 8658.36.3	Martin, R.M. History of southern Africa. 2nd ed. London, 1843.
	Afr 3978.43	Millard, D. Journal of travels in Egypt. N.Y., 1843.
	Afr 810.10	Simpson, W. Private journal kept during the Niger expedition. London, 1843.
	Afr 550.50	Trew, J.M. Africa wasted by Britain and restored by native agency. London, 1843.
	Afr 3978.43.3	Wilkinson, J.G. Modern Egypt. London, 1843. 2v.
	Afr 3978.43.5	Yates, W.H. Modern history and condition of Egypt. London, 1843. 2v.

1844

	Afr 1840.1	Algeria. Gouvernement Général. Exposé de l'état...du gouvernement. Algiers, 1844.
	Afr 125.10	Avezac, A. D. Afrique. Paris, 1844.
	Afr 8658.44	Backhouse, J. Visit to the Mauritius and South Africa. London, 1844.
	Afr 1965.27	Berbrugger, L.A. Négociation entre monseigneur l'évêque d'Alger et Abd el-qader. Paris, 1844.
	Afr 1608.44	Calderon, S.E. Manual del oficial en Marruecos. Madrid, 1844.
	Afr 1835.1	Carette, E. Etudes des routes suivies par les Arabes. Paris, 1844.

1849 - cont.

Afr 4095.5	Werne, Ferd. Expedition to sources of White Nile. London, 1849.

1850

Afr 3978.49.6	Bartlett, W.H. The Nile boat, glimpses of Egypt. 2d ed. London, 1850.
Afr 590.6	Christy, D. Lecture on African civilization. Cincinnati, 1850.
Afr 3978.50.5	Furniss, William. Waraga, or The charms of the Nile. N.Y., 1850.
Afr 8658.50	Gordon Cumming, R. Five years of a hunter's life in the far interior of South Africa. London, 1850. 2v.
Afr 698.50	Guillain, Charles. Exploration de la côte orientale d'Afrique. Paris, 1850.
Afr 555.3.14	Hening, E.F. History of the African mission of the Protestant Episcopal Church. N.Y., 1850.
Afr 590.24	Huntley, H. Seven year s service on slave coast of Western Africa. London, 1850. 2v.
Afr 2208.50	Joanne, A. Voyage en Afrique. Ixelles, 1850.
Afr 8808.42.11	Moffatt, Robert. Missionary labours...in southern Africa. 11. ed. N.Y., 1850.
Afr 8152.99	Napier, Elers. Excursions in Southern Africa. London, 1850. 2v.
Afr 6143.15	Poole, T.E. Life...in Sierra Leone and the Gambia. London, 1850. 2v.
Afr 1258.50	Rozet. Algérie, Etats Tripolitains et Tunis. Paris, 1850.
Afr 4105.1	Saint John, B. Two years residence in a Levantine family. Paris, 1850.
Afr 7175.54	Tams, Georg. Visita as possessões portugueses. Porto, 1850.
Afr 7368.50	United States. Congress. House. Committee on Naval Affairs. Report of the Naval Committee. Washington, 1850.
Afr 7458.50	United States. Dept. of State. Report of Secretary of State...in respect to Liberia. Washington, 1850.
Afr 8110.25.5	Vos, Michiel Christiaan. Merkwaardig verhaal, aangaande het leven en de lotgevallen van Michiel Christiaan Vos. 2. druk. Amsterdam, 1850.

1851

Afr 3978.51	Bartlett, W.H. The Nile boat. N.Y., 1851.
Afr 4095.4	Beke, C.T. Enquiry into N.D. Abbadie's journey to Kaffa. London, 1851.
Afr 3978.51.5	Curtis, G.W. Nile notes. N.Y., 1851.
Htn Afr 3978.51.4*	Curtis, G.W. Nile notes of a howadji. N.Y., 1851.
Afr 575.9.10	Faugere, A.P. De la propagande musulmane en Afrique et dans les Indes. Paris, 1851.
Afr 5385.3	Forbes, F.E. Dahomey and the Dahomans. London, 1851. 2v.
Afr 6097.5	Fox, William. A brief history of the Wesleyan missions on the western coast of Africa. London, 1851.
Afr 555.22.12	Freeman, Joseph J. Tour in South Africa, with notices of Natal. London, 1851.
Afr 7458.51.7	Fuller, T. Journal of voyage to Liberia. Baltimore, 1851.
Afr 4070.14	Johnson, W. Fliegende blätter...Reise in Nord-Ost-Afrika...1847-49. Stuttgart, 1851.
Afr 3978.51.11	Journal of a voyage up the Nile. Buffalo, 1851.
Afr 4070.17	Klun, V.F. Reise auf dem Weissen Nil. Laibach, 1851. 3 pam.
Afr 7375.9.2	Knight, H.C. Africa redeemed. London, 1851.
Afr 7375.9.5	Knight, H.C. The new republic. 2d ed. Boston, 1851.
Afr 7458.51	Latrobe, J.H.B. Colonization. Notice of V. Hugo's views of slavery. Baltimore, 1851.
Afr 3978.51.9	Melly, George. Khartoum, and the blue and white Niles. London, 1851. 2v.
Afr 5488.5	Muhammad Ibn Omar. Voyage au Ouadaï. Paris, 1851.
Afr 1258.17.6	Riley, J. Sequel to Riley's narrative. Columbus, 1851.
Afr 678.51	Smith, J. Trade and travels in the Gulph of Guinea. London, 1851.
Afr 8152.72	Ward, H. The Cape and the Kaffirs. London, 1851.
Afr 590.15	Wilson, J.L. The British squadron on the coast of Africa. London, 1851.

1852

Afr 7458.52	American Colonization Society. Information about emigration to Liberia. Washington, 1852. 2 pam.
Afr 1990.11.5	Baillet, Noël Bernard. Rapport...sur son voyage de 1852 en Algérie. Rouen, 1852.
Afr 9028.52	Barter, Charles. The dorp and the veld or Six months in Natal. London, 1852.
Afr 1975.4	Booms, P.G. Veldtogt van het fransch-afrikaansche leger tegen Klein-Kabylie in 1851. Hertogenbosch, 1852.
Afr 8735.4	Botha, Andries. Trial of Andries Botha for high treason. Cape Town, 1852.
Afr 1955.17.5	Castellane, P. de. Souvenirs de la vie militaire en Afrique. Paris, 1852.
Afr 8808.52.2	Cole, A.W. The Cape and the Kafirs. London, 1852.
Afr 7377.5.5	Colonization Society of the State of Indiana. Answer of the agent of the Indiana Colonization Society. Indianapolis, 1852.
Afr 3978.51.6	Curtis, G.W. Nile notes. N.Y., 1852.
Afr 5992.4	Guillermar de Aragon, Adolfo. Opusculo sobre la colonización de Fernando Poo. Madrid, 1852.
Afr 2295.2	Guyon. Voyage d'Alger aux Ziban (Text and atlas). Alger, 1852. 2v.
Afr 8808.52	Hatfield, E.F. Saint Helena and the Cape of Good Hope. N.Y., 1852.
Afr 8152.75	Hudson, M.B. Feature in South African frontier life...embracing complete record of Kafir war 1850-51. Port Elizabeth, 1852.
Afr 1080.1	Ibn Khaldun. Histoire des Berbère. Algiers, 1852-56. 4v.
Afr 7458.51.3	Latrobe, J.H.B. Colonization and abolition. Baltimore, 1852.
Afr 2208.32.5	Malo de Molina, M. Viaje a la Argelia. Valencia, 1852.
Afr 7368.32	Maryland State Colonization Society. Colonization Society of Free Colored Population. Maryland. Baltimore, 1852.
Afr 1885.1	Muhammed Al-Tunisi. Histoire des Beni Zeiyan. Paris, 1852.
Afr 7368.52	Pettit, W.V. Addresses...of the House of Representatives. Harrisburg, Pa. Philadelphia, 1852.
Afr 2208.52	Prus. A residence in Algeria. London, 1852.
Afr 3978.52	Smith, J.V.C. A pilgrimage to Egypt. Boston, 1852.
Afr 5992.2	Usera y Alarcon, Gerónimo M. Observaciones al Llamado Opusculo. Madrid, 1852.

1852 - cont.

Afr 3978.52.5	Wainwright, J.M. The land of bondage..a tour in Egypt. N.Y., 1852.

1853

Afr 1990.21.5	Alby, E. Les vêpres marocaines. v.1-2. Paris, 1853.
Afr 555.4.10	Algiers (Diocese). Statuts synodaux du diocése d'Alger. Alger, 1853.
Afr 1955.16	Baudicour, L. de. La guerre et le gouvernement de l'Algérie. Paris, 1853.
Afr 5180.16	Boilat, P.D. Esquisses sénégalaises. Paris, 1853.
Afr 852.3	Boudyck Bastiaanse, J. Voyage à la côte de Guinée. La Haye, 1853.
Afr 1835.1.3	Carette, E. Recherches sur l'origine et les migrations. Paris, 1853.
Afr 678.53	Carnes, J.A. Journal of a voyage from Boston to the west coast of Africa. London, 1853.
Afr 1955.17	Castellane, P. de. Military life in Algeria. London, 1853. 2v.
Afr 3978.53.8	Churi, J.H. Sea Nile, the desert, and Nigritia, travels. London, 1853.
Afr 6192.5	Cruickshank, B. Eighteen years on the Gold Coast of Africa. London, 1853. 2v.
Afr 4070.25	Escayrac de Lauture, S. Le desert et le Soudan. Paris, 1853.
Afr 8830.7	Fleming, F. Kaffraria, and its inhabitants. London, 1853.
Afr 3978.53.6	Gentz, W. Briefe aus Aegypten und Nubien. Berlin, 1853.
Afr 608.53.3	Gumprecht, J.E. Handbuch der Geographie...von Afrika. Leipzig, 1853.
Afr 7458.53	Hale, Sarah J. Liberia. N.Y., 1853.
Afr 678.49	Hecquard, Hyacinthe. Voyage sur la côte et dans l'intérieur de l'Afrique occidentale. Paris, 1853.
Afr 6168.8F	Hill, S.J. Gold Coast. 2 pts. n.p., 1853.
Afr 8658.53	Kretzschmar, E. Südafrikanische Skizzen. Leipzig, 1853.
Afr 150.2	Kunstmann, F. Afrika vor den Entdeckungen der Portugiesen. München, 1853.
Afr 3978.53.3	Lepsius, R. Letters from Egypt. London, 1853.
Afr 590.21	Michiels, A. Le Capitaine Firmin, ou La vie des Nègres en Afrique. Paris, 1853.
Afr 608.53	Murray, H. The African continent. London, 1853.
Afr 3978.53.10	Norov, Avraam S. Puteshestvie po Egiptu i Nubii, v 1834-1835. Izd.2. Sankt Peterburg, 1853. 2v.
Afr 4558.53	Parkyns, M. Life in Abyssinia. London, 1853. 2v.
Afr 1835.1.12	Pellissier de Reynaud, E. Description de la régence de Tunis. Paris, 1853.
Afr 2748.53	Richardson, J. Narrative of mission to central Africa (1850-51). London, 1853. 2v.
Afr 3978.53	Saint John, Bayle. Village life in Egypt. Boston, 1853. 2v.
Afr 7350.3.15	Stebbins, G.B. Facts and opinions touching the real origin, character...American Colonization Society. Cleveland, 1853.
Afr 590.4	Sumner, Charles. White slavery in Barbary states. Boston, 1853.
NEDL Afr 6275.18	Tucker, Charlotte Maria. Abbeokuta, or Sunrise within the tropics. London, 1853.
Afr 6275.18.2	Tucker, Charlotte Maria. Abbeokuta, or Sunrise within the tropics. N.Y., 1853.
Afr 1868.53	Ximenez de Sandoval, C. Memorias sobre la Argelia. Madrid, 1853.

1854

Afr 2397.1	Berbrugger, A. Geronimo. Alger, 1854.
Afr 4095.2	Cooley, W.D. Claudius Ptolemy and the Nile. London, 1854.
Afr 2208.53.5	Daumas, E. Moeurs et coutumes de l'Algérie. 2e ed. Paris, 1854.
Afr 2608.54	Davis, N. Evenings in my tent. London, 1854. 2v.
Afr 1608.54	Durrieu, X. Present state of Morocco. 2 in 1. London, 1854. 2 pam.
Afr 7458.54	Foote, A.H. Africa and the American flag. N.Y., 1854.
Afr 2208.53	France. Ministére de la Guerre. Rapport sur la situation de l'Algérie en 1853. Paris, 1854.
Afr 1835.1.11	Hatil Ibn-Ishah. Table analytique de juridisprudence musulmane. Paris, 1854.
Afr 678.49.5	Hecquard, Hyacinthe. Reise an die Küste und in das Innere von West-Africa. Leipzig, 1854.
Afr 8145.9	Merriman, N.J. The Kafir, the Hottentot, and the frontier farmer...missionary life. London, 1854.
Afr 9218.54	Molesworth, William. Materials for a speech in defense of the policy of abandoning the Orange River Territory, May 1854. London, 1854.
Afr 590.18	Moore, S. Biography of Mahommah G. Baquaqua. Detroit, 1854.
Afr 2208.54	Morell, J.R. Algeria. London, 1854.
Afr 4558.54	Parkyns, M. Life in Abyssinia. v.1-2. N.Y., 1854.
Afr 1955.36	Pellissier de Reynaud, E. Annales algériennes. Paris, 1854. 3v.
Afr 2748.54PF	Petermann, August. Account of progress of expedition to central Africa, 1850-53. London, 1854.
Afr 7375.11	President Roberts - the Republic of Liberia. N.Y., 1854.
Afr 2208.54.3	Pulszky, F. The tricolor on the atlas. London, 1854.
Afr 4095.3.3	Taylor, G.B. A journey to central Africa. N.Y., 1854.
Afr 4095.3.2	Taylor, G.B. A journey to central Africa. N.Y., 1854.
Afr 555.2	Thompson, George. Thompson in Africa. N.Y., 1854.
Afr 3978.54.2	Thompson, J.P. Photographic views of Egypt. Boston, 1854.

1855

Afr 2220.4	Barbier, J. Itinéraire...de l'Algérie. Paris, 1855.
Afr 8658.55	Brown, G. Personal adventure in South Africa. London, 1855.
Afr 3978.55	Brugsch-Bey, H. Reiseberichte aus Ägypten. Leipzig, 1855.
Afr 2208.55	Buvry, L. Algerien und seine Zukunft unter französischer Herrschaft. Berlin, 1855.
Afr 5180.52	Carrére, Frédéric. De la Sénégambie française. Paris, 1855.
Afr 4335.3	Castanhoso, M. de. Historia das cousas que o muy esforçado Christovam da Gama. Lisboa, 1855.
Afr 9028.55	Colenso, J.W. Ten weeks in Natal. Cambridge, 1855.
Afr 810.4	Crowther, S. Journal of an expedition up the Niger. London, 1855.
Afr 4070.2	Escayrac de Lauture, S. Mémoire sur le Soudan. Paris, 1855-56.
Afr 4558.55F	Fenzl, E. Bericht über C. Reitz und seine Reise. Vienna, 1855.

1855 - cont.

Afr 810.14	Hutchinson, T.J. Narrative of the Niger, Tshadda and Binue exploration. London, 1855. 2 pam.
Afr 1990.16	Javary, A. Etudes sur le gouvernement. Paris, 1855.
Afr 8152.73.2	King, W.R. Campaigning in Kaffirland...1851-52. 2d ed. London, 1855.
Afr 9028.55.4	Mason, G.H. Life with the Zulus of Natal, South Africa. London, 1855.
Afr 8735.3	Newman, W.A. Biographical memoir of John Montagu. London, 1855.
Afr 7122.20.2	Sa da Bandeira, B. de S.N. de F. da. Factos e consideraçõs relativas aos direitos de Portugal. Lisboa, 1855.
Afr 7368.55	Slaughter, P. Virginian history of African colonization. Richmond, 1855.
Afr 4095.3.4	Taylor, G.B. Eine Reise nach Centralafrika. Leipzig, 1855.

1856

Afr 1955.12	Berteuil, A. L'Algérie française, histoire. Paris, 1856. 2v.
Afr 7368.56	Blyden, E.W. Brief account...retirement of President J.J. Roberts. Liberia, 1856.
Afr 5758.2	Bonnavoy De Premoti, F.H. Rapport a l'empereur sur la question malgache. Paris, 1856.
Afr 3978.56	Borthelemy Saint-Hilaire. Lettres sur l'Egypte. Paris, 1856.
Afr 4612.1	Burton, R.F. First-footsteps...or Exploration of Harrar. London, 1856.
Afr 8180.5.4	Cloete, Henry. Vijf voorlezingen over de landverhuizing der hollandsche Boeren. Kaapstad, 1856.
Afr 1990.5	Feullide, C. de. L'Algérie française. Paris, 1856.
Afr 2208.56	Gerard, Cecile J.B. The adventures of Gerard, the Lion Killer. N.Y., 1856.
Afr 555.22.9	Gray, R., bishop of Cape Town. Three months visitation by the bishop of Cape Town, in...1855. London, 1856.
Afr 698.56	Guillain, Charles. Documents sur l'histoire, la géographie et la commerce de l'Afrique orientale. Paris, 1856. 4v.
Afr 698.56PF	Guillain, Charles. Documents sur l'histoire, la géographie et la commerce de l'Afrique orientale. Atlas. Paris, 1856. 4v.
Afr 2945.6	Hamilton, J. Wanderings in North Africa. London, 1856.
Afr 7357.2	Liberia. Laws, statutes, etc. The statute laws of the Republic of Liberia. Monrovia, 1856.
Afr 2208.55.6	Marcotte de Quivieres, C. Deux ans en Afrique. Paris, 1856.
Afr 2208.56.10	Mornaud, F. La vie arabe. Paris, 1856.
Afr 5180.25	Raffenel, Anne. Nouveau voyage dans le pays des Nègres. Paris, 1856. 2v.
Afr 7320.15	Romero, J. Memoria acerca do districto de Cabo Delgado. Lisboa, 1856.
Afr 3978.56.5	Saint John, B. Two years residence in a Levantine family. London, 1856.
Afr 1826.27	Société Historique Algerienne. Vingt cinq ans d'histoire algerienne. 4 in 1. Alger, 1856.
Afr 2928.56	Testa, C.E. le. Notice statistique et commerciale. La Haye, 1856.
Afr 3978.54.5	Thompson, J.P. Photographic views of Egypt. Boston, 1856.
Afr 6275.18.3	Tucker, Charlotte Maria. Abbeokuta, or Sunrise within the tropics. 5th ed. London, 1856.
Afr 678.56A	Wilson, T.L. Western Africa. N.Y., 1856.

1857

Afr 555.15	Adger, J.B. Christian missions and African colonization. Columbia, 1857.
Afr 9388.57	Anderson, C.J. Lake Ngami. N.Y., 1857.
Afr 2230.14	Aucapitaine, H. Les confins militaires de la Grande Kabylie. Paris, 1857.
Afr 9610.1	Aucapitaine, L.B.H. Les Yem-Yem tribu anthropophage de l'Afrique centrale. Paris, 1857.
Afr 1990.11	Baillet, Noël Bernard. Nécessité de la colonisation de l'Algerie. Paris, 1857.
NEDL Afr 608.57	Barth, H. Reisen und Entdeckungen in Nord- und Central-Afrika. Gotha, 1857-58. 5v.
NEDL Afr 608.57.3	Barth, H. Travels and discoveries in North and Central Africa. N.Y., 1857-59. 3v.
Afr 2230.12	Berbrugger, A. Les époques militaires de la Grande Kabilie. Alger, 1857.
Afr 550.2	Bowen, T.J. Missionary labors in the interior of Africa. Charleston, 1857.
Afr 550.2.5	Bowen, T.J. Missionary labors in the interior of Africa. N.Y., 1857.
Afr 6143.14	Caswall, H. The martyr of the Pongas. N.Y., 1857.
Afr 555.3.8	Caswall, Henry. The martyr of the Pongas. London, 1857.
Afr 8152.81	Cathcart, G. Correspondence. 2nd ed. London, 1857.
Afr 555.26.3	Charlesworth, M.L. Africa's mountain valley. London, 1857.
Afr 7368.57	Christy, David. Ethiopia. Cincinnati, 1857.
Afr 7368.56.5	Crummell, A. The duty of a rising Christian state. Boston, 1857. 3 pam.
Afr 6095.20	Flickinger, D.K. Off-hand sketches of men and things in western Africa. Dayton, 1857.
Afr 5385.3.5	Forbes, F.E. Dahomey and the Dahomans. Paris, 1857.
Afr 1025.1F	Fournel, H. Etude sur la conquête de l'Afrique par les Arabes. v.1-2. Paris, 1857.
Afr 2748.57	Fromentin, E. Un été dans le Sahara. Paris, 1857.
Afr 1955.10	Hennequin, A. La conquête de l'Algérie. Paris, 1857.
Afr 4558.52	Heughlin, T. Reisen in Nord-Ost-Afrika. Gotha, 1857.
Afr 8925.15	Orpen, Joseph M. History of the Basutur of South Africa. Cape Town, 1857.
Afr 3978.57	Prime, W.C. Boat life in Egypt and Nubia. N.Y., 1857.
Afr 695.12	Roscher, A. Ptolemaeus und die Handelsstrassen in Central-Afrika. Gotha, 1857.
Afr 3978.57.5	Saint Hilaire, J.B. Egypt and the great Suez Canal. London, 1857.
Afr 9047.5	Shooter, J. The Kafirs of Natal and Zulu country. London, 1857.
Afr 3978.57.3	Tomard, E.F. Fragments. (Mainly Egypt). Paris, 1857.
Afr 7458.57	Williams, S. Four years in Liberia. Philadelphia, 1857.

1858

Afr 5842.16.2	Anderson, John. Descriptive account of Mauritius. Mauritius, 1858.
Afr 2220.2	Bodichon, E. Guide book. London, 1858.

1858 - cont.

Afr 555.22.7	Calderwood, H. Caffres and Caffres missions. London, 1858.
Afr 1975.1	Carrey, E. Récits de Kabylie, campagne de 1857. Paris, 1858.
Afr 8658.58	Cortambert, M.E. Esquisse...d'une partie de l'Afrique australe. Paris, 1858.
Afr 2753.1	Daumas, E. Les chevaux du Sahara. Paris, 1858.
Afr 2308.8	Davies, E.W.L. Algiers in 1857. London, 1858.
Afr 3978.58	Ditson, G.L. The Para papers on France, Egypt and Ethiopia. Paris, 1858.
Afr 8658.58.5	Draipon, A.W. Sporting scenes amongst the Kaffirs of South Africa. London, 1858.
Afr 2608.58	Dunant, J.H. Notice sur la régence de Tunis. Genève, 1858.
Afr 2208.38.3	Duvernois, C. L'Algérie, ce qu'elle est. Alger, 1858.
NEDL Afr 5748.58	Ellis, William. Three visits to Madagascar during the years 1853-1854-1856. London, 1858.
Afr 1905.2	Fey, H.L. Histoire d'Oran, avant, pendant et après la domination espagnole. Oran, 1858.
Afr 7377.6	Hammond, J.H. Regina coeli. Correspondence of J.H.B. Latrobe. Baltimore, 1858.
Afr 2228.3	Hugonnet, F. Souvenirs d'un chef de bureau arabe. Paris, 1858.
Afr 6095.13	Hutchinson, T.J. Impressions of western Africa. London, 1858.
Afr 8815.4	Irons, H. The settler's guide to the Cape of Good Hope and colony of Natal. London, 1858.
Afr 3026.3	Jolowicz, Hermann. Bibliotheca Agyptiaca. Leipzig, 1858.
Afr 810.6	Lanoye, F. de. Le Niger et les explorations de l'Afrique centrale. Paris, 1858.
Afr 2290.3	Leclerc, L. Les oasis de la province d'Oran. Alger, 1858.
Afr 9558.6	Livingstone, D. Missionary travels in South Africa. N.Y., 1858.
Afr 9558.5A	Livingstone, D. Travels ans researches in South Africa. Philadelphia, 1858.
Afr 2208.58	MacCarthy, O. Géographie de l'Algérie. Algiers, 1858.
Afr 8825.4.3	Maclean, J. A compendium of Kafir laws and customs. Mount Cape, 1858. 2 pam.
Afr 9598.58	Malte-Brun, V.A. Resume histoire de l'exploration faite dans l'Afrique centrale. Paris, 1858.
Afr 3205.4	Mouriez, Paul. Histoire de Mehemet-Ali. v.1-5. Paris, 1858. 4v.
Afr 1753.16	Paiva Manso, Levy Maria Jordão. Memoria historica sobre os bispados de Ceuta e Tanger. Lisboa, 1858.
Afr 590.23F	Portugal. Ministerio dos Negocios Estrangeiros. Documentos relativos ao apresamento. Lisboa, 1858.
Afr 4060.5	Rossi, Elia. La Nubia e il Sudan. Constantinopoli, 1858.
Afr 4045.2	Schleiden, M.J. Die Landenge von Suez. Leipzig, 1858.
Afr 550.9	Scott, A.M. Day dawn in Africa. N.Y., 1858.
Afr 5190.3	Verneuil, V. Mes aventures au Sénégal. Paris, 1858.
Afr 1975.5	Walmsley, H.M. Sketches of Algeria during Kabyle war. London, 1858.
Afr 8105.5.3	Watermeyer, E.B. Drie voorlezingen over de Kaap de Goede Hoop. Kaapstad, 1858.

1859

Afr 1658.10	Avenia Taure, I. Memorias sobre el riff, su conquista y colonizacion. Zaragoza, 1859.
Afr 5868.59	Azema, Georges. Histoire de l'Ile Bourbon depuis 1643 jusqu'au 20 décembre 1848. Paris, 1859.
Afr 5868.59.5	Azema, Georges. Histoire de l'Ile Bourbon depuis 1643 jusqu'au 20 décembre 1848. Paris, 1859.
Afr 5548.59	Barbie du Bocage, V.A. Madagascar, possession française depuis 1642. Paris, 1859.
Afr 2373.5	Barges, J.J.L. Tlemcen, ancienne capitale du royaume. Paris, 1859.
Afr 7185.3	Bastian, A. Ein Besuch in San Salvador. Bremen, 1859.
Afr 5842.10	Beaton, P. Creoles and coolies. London, 1859.
Afr 2208.9.5	Blakesley, J.W. Four months in Algeria. Cambridge, 1859.
Afr 8918.59	Casalis, E. Le Bassoutos. Paris, 1859.
Afr 1432.7F	Castelar, E. Cronica de la guerra de Africa. Madrid, 1859.
Afr 1432.12	Castillo, R. del. España y Marruecos, historia de la guerra de Africa. Cadiz, 1859.
Afr 2230.4	Devaux, C. Les Kebailes du Djerdjera. Marseille, 1859.
Afr 1658.19	Diana, M.J. Un prisionero en el riff, memorias del ayudante alvarez. Madrid, 1859.
Afr 2208.59	Ditson, G.L. The crescent and French crusaders. N.Y., 1859.
Afr 5748.59	Ellis, William. Three visits to Madagascar. N.Y., 1859.
Afr 5748.59.3	Ellis, William. Three visits to Madagascar. Philadelphia, 1859.
Afr 2230.1	Excursion dans la Haute Kabylie. Alger, 1859.
Afr 2280.3	Fromentin, E. Une année dans le Sahel. 2d ed. Paris, 1859.
Afr 1868.59.5	Galibert, L. La Argelia, antigua y moderna. v.1-2,3. Madrid, 1859-60. 2v.
Afr 1608.59.3	Gomez de Arteche y Moro, José. Descripcion y mapas de Marruecos. Madrid, 1859.
Afr 3978.59.2	Gregory, W.H. Egypt 1855-56. Tunis 1857-58. London, 1859. 2v.
Afr 2748.59	Laurent, C. Mémoire sur le Sahara oriental. Paris, 1859.
Afr 9558.6.3	Livingstone, D. Missionary travels and researches in South Africa. 25 ed. N.Y., 1859.
Afr 9028.59	Mann, R.J. The colony of Natal. London, 1859.
Afr 1753.7	Marquez De Prado, J.A. Recuerdos de Africa, historia de la plaza de Ceuta. Madrid, 1859.
Afr 5993.16	Martinez y Sanz, M. Breves apuntes sobre la isla de Fernando Poo en el Golfo de Guinea. Madrid, 1859.
Afr 5810.12	Mauritius register. Mauritius, 1859.
Afr 4558.59	Munzinger, W. Über die Sitten und das Recht der Bogos. Winterthur, 1859.
Afr 1608.59	Murray, E. Sixteen years in Morocco. London, 1859. 2v.
Afr 5920.3	Navarro, J.J. Apuntes sobre el estado de la costa occidental. Madrid, 1859.
Afr 3978.59	Paine, Caroline. Tent and harem. N.Y., 1859.
Afr 1990.4	Ribourt, F. Le gouvernement de l'Algérie, 1852-1858. Paris, 1859.
Afr 1868.59	Roy, J.J.E. Histoire de l'Algerie. Tours, 1859.
Afr 555.3	Thompson, George. The palm land. Cincinnati, 1859.
Afr 1608.59.5	Torrijos, Manuel. El imperio de Marruecos, su historia etc. Madrid, 1859.
Afr 6275.18.5	Tucker, Charlotte Maria. Abbeokuta, or Sunrise within the tropics. N.Y., 1859.

1859 - cont.

Afr 1965.10.5   Yusuf. De la guerra en Africa...en 1851. Madrid, 1859.

186-

Afr 635.4   Chaneel, A. de. Cham et Zaphet. 2e éd. Paris, 186-.

1860

Afr 1432.1.2F   Alarcon, P.A. Diario de la guerra de Africa. Madrid, 1860.
Afr 1432.8F   Album de la guerra de Africa. Madrid, 1860.
Afr 1432.10   Alvarez, J.A. de. Biografia y retratos de los generales jefes de los cuerpos. Barcelona, 1860.
Afr 2250.1   Baudicour, L. Histoire de la colonization de l'Agérie. Paris, 1860.
Afr 1432.2   Baudoz, A. Histoire de la guerre de l'Espagne. Paris, 1860.
Afr 5874.12   Beaton, P. Six months in Réunion. London, 1860. 2v.
Afr 4095.12   Beke, C.T. The sources of the Nile. London, 1860.
Afr 1432.13   Beltran, F.C. Historia de la guerra de Africa. T.1. Madrid, 1860.
Afr 1608.60.7   Breve escursion por el imperio de Marruecos. Malaga, 1860.
Afr 1990.13   Broglie, A. de. Une réforme administrative en Afrique. Paris, 1860.
Afr 725.2   Burton, R.F. The lake regions of central Africa. London, 1860. 2v.
Afr 6275.19.10   Campbell, R. A few facts, relating to Lagos...Africa. Philadelphia, 1860.
Htn   Afr 1368.60*   Canovas del Castello, A. de. Apuntes para la historia de Marruecos. Madrid, 1860.
Afr 1432.11   Chronica de la guerra de Africa. Madrid, 1860.
Afr 8678.6   Clarence, W. The aborigines of South Africa. Boston, 1860.
Afr 608.60   Committee of General Literature and Education. Sketches of the African kingdoms and peoples. London, 1860.
Afr 1955.3   Cooke, G.W. Conquest and colonization in North Africa. Edinburgh, 1860.
Afr 1608.60.5   Cotte, N. Le Maroc contemporain. Paris, 1860.
Afr 2208.59.2   Ditson, G.L. The crescent and French crusaders. N.Y., 1860.
Afr 1965.1   Dupuch, A.A. Abd-el-Kader. Bordeaux, 1860.
Afr 1608.60.9   Ferreiro, Martin. Descripcion del imperio de Marruecos. Madrid, 1860.
Afr 1432.4   Fillias, A. L'Espagne et le Maroc en 1860. Paris, 1860.
Afr 1955.1   Fillias, Achille. Histoire de la congrès de l'Algérie (1830-60). Paris, 1860.
Afr 1955.4.5   Gerard, J. L'Afrique du nord. Paris, 1860.
Afr 1608.60.3   Godard, L. Description et histoire du Maroc. v.1-2. Paris, 1860.
Afr 1608.60.4   Godard, L. Le Maroc, notes d'un voyageur. Alger, 1860.
Afr 1432.3   Hardman, F. The Spanish campaign in Morocco. Edinburgh, 1860.
Afr 1955.18   Hugonnet, F. Français et Arabes en Algérie. Paris, 1860.
Afr 2230.10   Hun, F. Promenades...chez les Kabyles. Alger, 1860.
Afr 698.60   Krapf, J.L. Travels, researches...eastern Africa. Boston, 1860.
Afr 698.60.2   Krapf, J.L. Travels, researches...eastern Africa. Boston, 1860.
Afr 1432.23   Landa, Nicasio de. La campaña de Marruecos. Madrid, 1860.
Afr 1868.60.3   Lefloch, J. Mahomet, al Koran, Algerie. Paris, 1860.
Afr 9558.8   Livingstone, D. Cambridge lectures. London, 1860.
Afr 9558.9   Livingstone, D. Travels and researches in South Africa. Philadelphia, 1860.
Afr 7308.60   McLeod, L. Travels in Eastern Africa. London, 1860. 2v.
Afr 7377.5   Mitchell, James. Letters...white and African races. Washington, 1860.
Afr 2345.6   Notice...sur l'ancienne ville de Lamboese. Paris, 1860.
Afr 5235.51.5   Park, Mungo. Travels in the interior of Africa. Edinburgh, 1860.
Afr 7458.60   Payne, J.S. Prize essay on political economy of Liberia. Monrovia, 1860.
Afr 1432.22   Perez Calvo, Juan. Siete dias en el campamento de Africa. Madrid, 1860.
Afr 1432.20   Poblacion y Fernandez, A. Historia medica de la guerra de Africa. Madrid, 1860.
Afr 1608.60   Richardson, J. Travels in Morocco. v.1-2. London, 1860.
Afr 1390.1.5   Roudh el-Kartas. Histoire des souverains du Maghreb. Paris, 1860.
Afr 1432.18   Spain. Ministerio de Estado. Correspondencia..Guerra de Africa. Madrid, 1860.
Afr 678.60   Thomas, C.W. Adventures...on west coast of Africa. N.Y., 1860.
Afr 1990.27   Touchard-Lafosse, T. Histoire de la gendarmerie d'Afrique. Alger, 1860.
Afr 2748.60   Tristram, H.B. The great Sahara. London, 1860.
Afr 1432.28   Ventosa, E. Españoles y Marroquies. Barcelona, 1860.

1861

Afr 1432.19   Ameller, V. de. Juicio critico de la guerra de Africa. Madrid, 1861.
Afr 6978.61   Andersson, Carl J. The Okavango River: a narrative of travel, exploration, and adventure. N.Y., 1861.
Afr 1432.24   Baeumen, A. von. Nach Marokko. Berlin, 1861.
Afr 3978.49.8   Bartlett, W.H. The Nile boat. 4th ed. London, 1861.
Afr 8252.1   Boreherds, P.B. An autobiographical memoir. Cape Town, 1861.
NEDL   Afr 6275.19   Campbell, R. A pilgrimage to my mother land (Central Africa). London, 1861.
Afr 6275.19.3   Campbell, R. A pilgrimage to my mother land (Central Africa). N.Y., 1861.
Afr 8918.59.5   Casalis, E. The Basutos. London, 1861.
Afr 7458.61   Crummell, A. Relations and duties of free colored men in America. Hartford, 1861.
Afr 5406.51   Duchaillu, Paul Belloni. Explorations and adventures in Equatorial Africa. N.Y., 1861.
Afr 5406.51.10   Duchaillu, Paul Belloni. Explorations and adventures in Equatorial Africa. N.Y., 1861.
Afr 1955.4   Gerard, J. L'Afrique du nord. Paris, 1861.
Afr 1608.44.6   Hay, J.H.D. Morocco and the Moors. London, 1861.
Afr 678.61.3   Hutchinson, T.J. Ten years wanderings among the Ethiopians. London, 1861.
Afr 3026.4   Jolowicz, Hermann. Bibliotheca Ägyptiaca. Supplement I. Leipzig, 1861.

1861 - cont.

Afr 1878.1   Laprimaudie, F.E. de. Le commerce...de l'Algerie. Paris, 1861.
Afr 8152.92.5   Lucas, T.J. Pen and pencil reminiscences of campaign in South Africa. London, 1861.
Afr 608.61   MacBrair, R.M. The Africans at home. London, 1861.
Afr 8658.61   Meidinger, H. Die südafrikanischen Colonien Englands. Frankfurt, 1861.
Afr 3978.61   Petherick, J. Egypt, the Soudan and Central Africa. Edinburgh, 1861.
Afr 5748.61   Pfeiffer, Ida R. Last travels of Ida Pfeiffer. N.Y., 1861.
Afr 678.61   Travassos Valdez, Franciso. Six years of a traveller's life in western Africa. London, 1861. 2v.
Afr 4558.81   Winstanley, W. A visit to Abyssinia. London, 1861. 2v.

1862

Afr 2224.862   Algeria. Commission à l'Exposition Universelle de Londres. L'Algérie à l'Exposition universelle de Londres, 1862. Alger, 1862. 2v.
Afr 4115.11   Bassi, Alessandro. Santuario della sacra famiglia in Cairo vecchio. Torino, 1862.
Afr 555.22.5   Beijer, J. Journal gehouden van Port Elisabeth (Algoabaai) naar Reddersburg. Kaapstad, 1862. 2 pam.
Afr 7458.62.5   Blyden, E.W. Liberia's offering. N.Y., 1862.
Afr 7368.62   Crummell, A. The future of Africa. N.Y., 1862.
Afr 2300.2   Davis, N. Ruined cities within Numidian and Carthaginian territories. London, 1862.
Afr 2308.1   Feydeau, E. Alger. Paris, 1862.
Afr 590.24.5   Foote, Andrew H. Africa and the American flag. N.Y., 1862.
Afr 5385.23   Guillevin. Voyage dans l'intérieur du royaume de Dahomey. Paris, 1862.
Afr 678.62   Hewett, J.F.N. European settlements on west coast of Africa. London, 1862.
Afr 2208.62   Hirsch, M. Reise in das Innere von Algerien. Berlin, 1862.
Afr 608.62   Jacobs, A. L'Afrique nouvelle. Paris, 1862.
Afr 2220.3   Piesse, L. Itinéraire de l'Algérie. Paris, 1862.
Afr 2505.2   Prevost, F. La Tunisie devant l'Europe. Paris, 1862.
Afr 7458.62   Ralston, Gerard. On the Republic of Liberia, its products and resources. London, 1862.
Afr 4585.1   Stern, H.A. Wanderings among the Falashas. London, 1862.
Afr 2208.62.4   Thierry-Mieg, C. Six semaines en Afrique. 2e ed. Paris, 1862.
Afr 4070.27   Tremaux, P. Voyage en Ethiopie au Soudan oriental et dans la Nigritie. v.1- Paris, 1862. 2v.

1863

Afr 7350.5.10   Allen, W.H. Address before Pennsylvania Colonization Society, Oct. 25. Philadelphia, 1863.
Afr 8658.63   Baldwin, William C. African hunting from Natal to the Zambesi. N.Y., 1863.
Afr 1965.23   Bellemare, Alex. Abd-el-Kader. Paris, 1863.
Afr 6738.2A   Burton, R.F. Abeokuta and the Camaroons mountains. London, 1863.
Afr 678.63   Burton, R.F. Wanderings in West Africa from Liverpool. London, 1863.
Afr 3978.63   Carey, M.L.M. Four months in a dahabeek. London, 1863.
Afr 8140.6F   Committee of Observation on All Matters Connected with Attainment of Independence of British Kaffraria. British Kaffaria, the people's blue book. King Williams Town, 1863.
Afr 4070.24   Cuny, Charles. Journal de voyage...de Siout à El-Obeid. Paris, 1863.
Afr 2475.5   Cusson, C. Histoire du royaume de Tunis. Oran, 1863.
Afr 5748.63   Dupre, Jules. Trois mois de sejour à Madagascar. Paris, 1863.
Afr 5765.5.10   Gospel in Madagascar. London, 1863.
Afr 2386.1   Harbillon, M. Relation du siège de Zaatcha. Paris, 1863.
Afr 4070.10PF   Hartmann, Robert. Reise des Freiherrn Adalbert von Barnim durch Nord-Ost-Afrika 1859-60. Berlin, 1863. 2v.
Afr 3978.63.10   Hoskins, G.A. A winter in upper and lower Egypt. London, 1863.
Afr 3978.63.15   Kremer, Alfred, Freiherr von. Aegypten. Leipzig, 1863.
Afr 5548.63   Lacaille, L.P. Connaissance de Madagascar. Paris, 1863.
Afr 5765.4.2   Madagascar, its missions and its martyrs. London, 1863.
Afr 5180.17   Mavidal, J. Le Sénégal. Paris, 1863.
Afr 2928.60   Mission de Ghadamès. Rapports officiels. Alger, 1863.
Afr 7461.35   Morris, E.D. An address before the Liberia Union Agricultural Enterprise Co. Philadelphia, 1863.
Afr 3078.63   Paton, A.A. History of the Egyptian revolution. London, 1863. 2v.
Afr 1955.22   Pélissier, A.J.J. Mémoire sur les opérations de l'armée française. Alger, 1863.
Afr 5605.3   Regnon, Henry de. Madagascar et le roi Radama II. Paris, 1863.
Afr 1432.6   Schlagintweit, E. Der spanisch-marokkanische Krieg...1859-60. Leipzig, 1863.
Afr 4095.6   Speke, J.H. Journal of discovery of source of the Nile. Edinburgh, 1863.
Afr 1280.2   Tauxier, Henri. Etude sur les migrations des nations berbères avant l'islamisme. Paris, 1863.
Afr 2208.45   Veuillot, L. Les Français en Algérie. 3e ed. Tours, 1863.
Afr 2260.10   Vian, L. L'Algérie contemporaine. Paris, 1863.
Afr 6282.46   Waddell, Hope Masterton. Twenty-nine years in the West Indies and Central Africa. London, 1863.
Afr 3978.63.5   Whately, M.L. Ragged life in Egypt. London, 1863.
Afr 1432.5   Yriarte, C. Sous la tente: souvenirs du Maroc. Paris, 1863.

1864

Afr 2230.7   Aucapitaine, H. Les Kabyles. Paris, 1864.
Afr 6978.64   Baines, T. Exploration in South-west Africa. London, 1864.
Afr 4095.12.5   Beke, C.T. A lecture on the sources of the Nile. London, 1864.
Afr 3978.64   Brugsch, H.K.F. Aus dem Orient. (Mainly Egypt). Berlin, 1864.
Afr 5385.1   Burton, R.F. A mission to Gelele, king of Dahome, with notices. v.1-2. London, 1864. 2v.
Afr 5385.2   Burton, R.F. Mission to Gelele, king of Dahome. v.1. 2d ed. London, 1864.

1864 - cont.

NEDL Afr 4095.7   Burton, R.F. The Nile basin. London, 1864.
Afr 1258.64   Faidherbe, L.L.C. Chapitres de géographie sur le nord-ouest de l'Afrique. Paris, 1864.
Afr 2360.1   Féraud, L. Monographie des Oulad-Ab-en-Nour. Constantine, 1864.
Afr 698.64   Grant, J.A. A walk across Africa. Edinburgh, 1864.
Afr 9028.64A   Grout, Lewis. Zulu-land. Philadelphia, 1864.
Afr 5314.3   Hardy, Jules. Les Dieppois en Guinée en 1364. Dieppe, 1864.
Afr 608.61.2   MacBrair, R.M. The Africans at home. London, 1864.
Afr 5765.7.20   Maupoint, A.R. Madagascar et ses deux premiers évêques. v.1-2. 3. ed. Paris, 1864.
Afr 3198.64   Merruan, P. L'Egypte contemporaine. Paris, 1864.
Afr 1608.64.3   Merry y Colom, F. Relacion del viaje a la ciudad de Marruecos. Madrid, 1864.
Afr 590.20   Read, Hollis. The Negro problem solved. N.Y., 1864.
Afr 6095.11   Reade, W.W. Savage Africa. 2. ed. London, 1864.
Afr 2485.1   Rousseau, A. Anales tunisiennes. Alger, 1864.
Afr 555.6   Ryan, V.W. Mauritius and Madagascar. London, 1864.
Afr 4095.6.3   Speke, J.H. Journal of discovery of source of the Nile. N.Y., 1864.
Afr 678.61.5   Travassos Valder, Francisco. Africa occidental. Lisboa, 1864.
Afr 678.61.6   Travassos Valdez, Francisco. Africa occidental. Lisboa, 1864.

1865

Afr 9510.5PF   Baines, Thomas. The Victoria Falls, Zambesi River. London, 1865.
Afr 2208.65   Behaghel, A. L'Algérie. Alger, 1865.
Afr 7368.65   Blyden, E.W. Our origin, dangers, and duties. N.Y., 1865.
Afr 2260.2   Cosentino. L'Algérie en 1865. Turin, 1865.
Afr 1915.2   Devoulx, A. Les archives du consulat général de France. Alger, 1865.
Afr 8808.65   Drayson, A.W. Tales at the outspan, or adventures in South Africa. London, 1865.
Afr 3978.65   Duff-Gordon, Lucie Austin. Letters from Egypt 1863-65. London, 1865.
Afr 2608.61   Flaux, A. de. La régence de Tunis au dix-neuvième siècle. Paris, 1865.
Afr 555.9.13   Goodwin, Harvey. Memoir of Bishop Mackenzie. 2d ed. Cambridge, 1865.
Afr 2208.65.5   Hartevelt, D. Herinneringen uit Algiers. Arnhem, 1865.
Afr 2290.1   Lacretelle, L. Etudes sur la province d'Oran. Marseille, 1865.
Afr 2224.865   Leblanc de Prebois, F. Bilan de l'Algérie à la fin de l'an 1864 ou de la crise financiére commerciale et agricole. Alger, 1865.
Afr 4370.7   Lejean, G. Theodore II, le nouvel empire d'Abyssinie et les intérêts français dans le sud de la Mer Rouge. Paris, 1865.
Afr 4258.65   Lesseps, F. Principaux faits de l'histoire d'Abyssinie. Paris, 1865.
NEDL Afr 9558.10   Livingstone, D. Narrative of an expedition to the Zambesi. London, 1865.
Afr 5548.65   Mcleod, Lyons. Madagascar and its people. London, 1865.
Afr 1033.3F   Mas Latrie, M.L. de. Traités de paix et de commerce et documents diverses...de l'Afrique septentrionale au Moyen Age. Paris, 1865.
Afr 2025.7A   Napoleon III, Empereur. Lettre sur la politique de la France en Algérie. Paris, 1865. 2 pam.
Afr 2208.65.9   Peissier, Octave. Napoleon III en Algérie. Paris, 1865.
Afr 5180.29   Ricard, F. Le Sénégal. Paris, 1865.
Afr 2208.65.6   Rogers, P.A. A winter in Algeria. London, 1865.
Afr 2285.2   Trumelet, C. Les français dans le désert. Paris, 1865.
Afr 5748.65   Vinson, A. Voyage à Madagascar au couronnement de Radama II. Paris, 1865.
Afr 3978.65.9   Wace, A.T. Palm leaves from the Nile. Shrewsbury, 1865.
Afr 2025.4   Warnier, A. L'Algérie devant l'empereur. Paris, 1865.
Afr 2208.65.3   Zaccone, J. De batna à Tuggurt et au Souf. Paris, 1865.

1866

Afr 4378.1   Apel, F.H. Drei Monate en Abyssinien. Zürich, 1866.
Afr 4095.8.2   Baker, S.W. The Albert Nyanza. London, 1866.
Afr 678.66   Castilho, A.M. de. Descripção...costa occidental de Africa. v.1-2. Lisboa, 1866.
Afr 5765.7.10   Congregation of Priests of the Mission. Memoires. v.9. Paris, 1866.
Afr 2025.5   Duval, Jules. Réflexions sur la politique de l'empereur. Paris, 1866.
Afr 7458.66   Fitzgerald, J.J. Seven years in Africa. Columbus, 1866.
Afr 8718.66   Haussmann, A. Souvenirs du Cap de Bonne-Espérance. Paris, 1866.
Afr 1608.66   Hodgkin, T. Narrative of a journey to Morocco. London, 1866.
Afr 8678.15   Holden, W.C. The past and future of Kaffir races. London, 1866.
Afr 3978.66   Kraemer, R. von. En vinter Orienten. Reseanteckningar fraan Egypten. Stockholm, 1866.
Afr 2260.8   Lasnavères. De l'impossibilité de fonder des colonies...en Algerie. Paris, 1866.
Afr 8658.66.5   Leyland, J. Adventures in the far interior of South Africa. London, 1866.
Afr 9558.10.5   Livingstone, D. Narrative of an expedition to the Zambesi. N.Y., 1866.
Afr 555.27.8   Moister, William. Memorials of missionary labours in West Africa. 3d ed. London, 1866.
NEDL Afr 8658.66   Moodie, J.W.D. Scenes and adventures as a soldier and settler. Montreal, 1866. (Changed to KPC 2144)
Afr 1606.40   Nathaim, D.A. Voyage au Maroc (1640-41). La Have, 1866.
Afr 5748.66   Oliver, S. Pasfield. Madagascar and the Malagasy. London, 1866.
Afr 2208.66.3   Rasch, Gustav. Nach den Oasen von Siban. Berlin, 1866.
Afr 7308.66   Rowley, Henry. Story of the universities' missions to Central Africa. London, 1866.
Afr 2208.66.8   Sala, George A. A trip to Barbary. London, 1866.
Afr 150.5   Sanctos Firmo, M. Noticia sobre a vida e escriptos do Infante Dom Henrique. Lisboa, 1866.
Afr 3978.63.8   Whately, M.L. Child life in Egypt. Philadelphia, 1866.

1867

NEDL Afr 7350.3.16   American Colonization Society. Memorial of the semi-centennial anniversary. Washington, 1867.
Afr 4095.8   Baker, S.W. The Albert Nyanza. London, 1867. 2v.
Afr 4509.15.3   Beke, Charles F. The British captives in Abyssinia. 2nd ed. London, 1867.
Afr 3978.67   Billard, F.L. Les moeurs et le gouvernemnt de l'egypte. Milan, 1867.
Afr 5842.14   Boyle, C.J. Far away, scenery and society in Mauritius. London, 1867.
Afr 1965.30   Churchill, Charles Henry. The life of Abdel Kader. London, 1867.
Afr 555.4   Culte protestante en Algérie. Alger, 1867.
Afr 5605.5   Desbassayns de Richemont, P. Documents sur la compagnie de Madagascar. Paris, 1867.
Afr 5406.52.5   Duchaillu, Paul Belloni. A journey to Ashango-land. N.Y., 1867.
Afr 4558.67.9   Dufton, H. Narrative of a journey through Abyssinia. London, 1867.
Afr 2208.67   Edwards, A.B. A winter with the swallows. London, 1867.
Afr 5748.67   Ellis, William. Madagascar revisited. London, 1867.
Afr 4070.25.2   Escayrac de Lauture, S. Die afrikanische Wüste und das Land der Schwarzen am obern Nil. Leipzig, 1867.
Afr 3978.67.5F   Gottberg, E. de. Des cataractes du Nil..Hannek...Kaybar. Paris, 1867.
Afr 8252.9.5   Gray, R. A statement...in connexion with the consecration of the Right Rev. Dr. Colenso. London, 1867.
Afr 2608.67.5   Gubernatis, E. de. Lettere sulla Tunisia. Firenze, 1867.
Afr 9558.20   Lacerda, F.J. de. Exams das viagens do Doutor Livingstone. Lisbon, 1867.
Afr 1957.1   Nettement, A. Histoire de la conquête d'Alger. Paris, 1867.
Afr 4258.67   Peacock, Geo. Hand-book of Abyssinia. London, 1867.
Afr 5748.67.4   Pollen, F.P.L. Een blik in Madagaskar. Leyden, 1867.
Afr 7320.10   Portugal. Ministerio dos Negocios da Marinha e Ultramar. Regimento. Lisboa, 1867.
Afr 3978.67.3   Warren, W.W. Life on the Nile. Paris, 1867.

1868

Afr 4375.9PF   Acton, Roger. The Abyssinian expedition and the life and the reign of King Theodore. London, 1868.
Afr 3978.44.5   Ampere, J.J. Voyage en Egypte et en Nubie. Paris, 1868.
Afr 4558.67.4   Baker, S.W. The Nile tributaries of Abyssinia. Hartford, 1868.
Afr 4558.67.3   Baker, S.W. The Nile tributaries of Abyssinia. 3rd ed. London, 1868.
Afr 4558.67.5A   Baker, S.W. The Nile tributaries of Abyssinia. 4th ed. Philadelphia, 1868.
Afr 4375.4.5   Blanc, H. A narrative of captivity in Abyssinia. London, 1868.
NEDL Afr 8658.68   Chapman, J. Travels in the interior of South Africa. London, 1868. 2v.
Afr 2208.48.10   Dumas, Alexandre. Tales of Algeria, or Life among the Arabs. Philadelphia, 1868.
Afr 2208.68.5   Evans, H.L. Last winter in Algeria. London, 1868.
Afr 555.3.17   Fox, George T. A memoir of the...missionary to Cape Palmas. N.Y., 1868.
Afr 3978.68.5   Frankl, L.A. Aus Aegypten. Wien, 1868.
Afr 8658.68.5   Fritsch, G. Drei Jahre in Süd-Afrika. Breslau, 1868.
Afr 628.168   Helper, H.R. The Negroes in Negroland. N.Y., 1868.
Afr 4375.6   Henty, G.A. The march to Magdala. London, 1868.
Afr 4558.68.7   Heuglin, T. von. Reise nach Abessinien. Jena, 1868.
Afr 4558.68   Hotten, J.C. Abyssinia. London, 1868.
Afr 3978.68   Irby, C.L. Travels in Nubia. London, 1868.
Afr 3252.20   Lenghi, N. Considerazioni sul discorso da Layard...Riforma giudiziaria in Egitto. Alexandria, 1868.
Afr 5235.186   Mage, Eugène. Voyage dans le Soudan occidental. Paris, 1868.
X Cg Afr 150.3   Major, R.H. Life of Prince Henry of Portugal. London, 1868.
Atr 7458.68   Merriam, M.B. Home life in Africa. Boston, 1868.
Afr 2208.68   Naphegyi, G. Among the Arabs. Philadelphia, 1868.
Afr 4558.53.2   Parkyns, M. Life in Abyssinia. London, 1868.
Afr 9558.16.3   Paumier, H. L'Afrique ouverte... du Docteur Livingstone. 3. ed. Paris, 1868.
Afr 4558.68.3   Plowden, W.C. Travels in Abyssinia. London, 1868.
Afr 3978.57.2   Prime, W.C. Boat life in Egypt and Nubia. N.Y., 1868.
Afr 2625.5   Schwab, M. Mémoire sur l'ethnographie de la Tunisie. Paris, 1868.
Afr 4375.5   Shepherd, A.F. The campaign in Abyssinia. Bombay, 1868.
Afr 4095.6.10   Speke, J.H. Journal of discovery of source of the Nile. N.Y., 1868.
Afr 7368.68   Stockwell, G.S. The Republic of Liberia. N.Y., 1868.
Afr 555.7.5   Taylor, William. Christian adventures in South Africa. London, 1868.
Afr 4375.19   Urquehart, David. The Abyssinian war. London, 1868.
Afr 4571.1   Views in central Abyssinia. London, 1868.
Afr 9093.27   Wangemann, H. Maleo und Sekukuni. Berlin, 1868.
Afr 2208.68.8   Wingfield, L. Under the palms in Algeria and Tunis. London, 1868.
Afr 9558.48   Young, E.D. The search after Livingstone. (A diary). London, 1868.

1869

Afr 3978.69.5   About, E. Le fellah: souvenirs d'Egypte. Paris, 1869.
Afr 4558.69.5   Andree, Richard. Abessinien, das Alpenland unter den Tropen. Leipzig, 1869.
Afr 5100.1   Annuaire du Sénégal et dépendances. St.-Louis, 1869.
Afr 4045.5   Bernard, F. Itinéraire pour l'isthme de Suez et les grandes villes d'Egypte. Paris, 1869.
Afr 3978.69.1   Bolgiani, V.M.V. Im Lande der Pharaonen. Wien, 1869.
Afr 3978.69   Bolgiani, V.M.V. Pharaonernas land. Resebilder fraan egypten. Stockholm, 1869.
Afr 3230.8   Bordeano, N. L'Egypte d'après les traités de 1840-41. Constantine, 1869.
Afr 590.8   Carstensen, E. Propositions sur l'organisation d'une emigration. v.1-2. Paris, 1869.
Afr 8215.5   Chesson, Frederick William. The Dutch Boers and slavery. London, 1869.
Afr 2228.8   Daumas, E. La vie arabe et la société musulmane. Paris, 1869.

1869 - cont.

Afr 6878.59	Decken, Carl Claus, Baron von der. Baron Carl Claus von der Decken's Reisen in Ost Afrika in den Jahren 1859 bis 1865. Leipzig, 1869-79. 6v.
Afr 5406.54	Duchaillu, Paul Belloni. Wild life under the equator. N.Y., 1869.
Afr 4585.2	Flad, M. Kurze Schilderung...abessinischen Juden. Basel, 1869.
Afr 7073.6F	Great Britain. Case in support of the claim of Great Britain to the Island of Bulama. London, 1869.
Afr 3978.69.6	Grey, W. Journal...visit to Egypt, Constantinople. London, 1869.
Afr 4070.3	Heuglin, M.T. Reise in das Gebiet des Weissen Nil. Leipzig, 1869.
Afr 4375.1	Hozier, H.M. British expedition to Abyssinia. London, 1869.
Afr 8215.7	Huet, P. Het lot der zwarten in Transvaal. Utrecht, 1869.
Afr 3068.69	Lanoye, F. de. Le Nil, son bassin et ses sources. Paris, 1869.
Afr 9558.11	Livingstone, D. Explorations dans l'Afrique australe. 2. ed. Paris, 1869.
Afr 8808.69	Noble, R. The Cape and its people, and other essays. Cape Town, 1869.
NEDL Afr 2608.69	Perry, Amos. Carthage and Tunis. Providence, 1869.
Afr 7073.8F	Portugal. Resposta do governo portuguez a exposição a favor dos direitos que a Gran-Bretanha. Lisboa, 1869.
Afr 4558.69	Rassam, H. Narrative of British mission to Theodore. London, 1869. 2v.
NEDL Afr 4378.2	Stern, H.A. The captive missionary, account of country and people of Abyssinia. London, 1869.
Afr 2318.1.10	Vaysseties, E. Histoire de Constantine. Constantine, 1869.
Afr 8718.69	Wilmot, A. History of the colony of the Cape of Good Hope. Cape Town, 1869.

187-

Afr 8980.5	Colenso, J.W. Defence of Langalibalele. n.p., 187-.
Afr 3978.70.15	Couvidou, Henri. Etude sur l'Egypte contemporaine. Le Caire, 187-.
Afr 9558.25	Life and explorations of Dr. Livingstone. London, 187-.

1870

Afr 3978.69.5.2	About, E. Le fellah: souvenirs d'Egypte. 2e ed. Paris, 1870.
Afr 7458.70	Anderson, B. Narrative of a journey to Musardu. N.Y., 1870.
Afr 1955.32	Aus Africa und Spanien. Jena, 1870.
Afr 4095.8.2.5	Baker, S.W. The Albert Nyanza. New ed. London, 1870.
Afr 4375.7	Bechtinger, J. Ost Afrika. Wien, 1870.
Afr 4375.4	Blanc, H. Ma captivité en Abyssinie. Paris, 1870.
Afr 3990.4.2	Busch, M. Agypten, Reisenhandbuch. 2.Aufl. Triest, 1870.
Afr 3978.70.5	Castro y Serrano, Jose de. La novela del Egipto. Madrid, 1870.
Afr 3040.60F	Commission Internationale pour l'Examen des Réformes, Egypte. Rapport de la Commission internationale réunie au Caire pour l'examen des réformes proposées...dans l'administration de la justice en Egypte. Alexandrie, 1870.
Afr 5765.5	Ellis, William. The martyr church. Boston, 1870.
Afr 5796.5	Gevrey, Alfred. Essai sur les Comores. Pondichery, 1870.
Afr 4375.8F	Holland, T.J. Record of the expedition to Abyssinia. v.1-2, and atlas. London, 1870. 3v.
Afr 4225.5F	Holland, T.J. Record of the expedition to Abyssinia. v.1-2 and maps. London, 1870. 3v.
Afr 4045.3	Juromenha, J.A. de R.P. de Lacerda. O Isthmo de Suez e as portuguezes. Lisboa, 1870.
Afr 9558.6.10	Livingstone, D. Missionary travels and researches in South Africa. N.Y., 1870.
Afr 555.7	Lloyd, Mrs. Christian work in zulae land. 2d ed. N.Y., 1870.
Afr 2608.70	Maltzan, Heinrich. Reise in den Regentschaften Tunis und Tripolis. Leipzig, 1870. 3v.
Afr 1965.2.10	Orleans, F.P.L.C.H., Duc. Campagnes de l'armée d'Afrique, 1835-1839. 2e éd. Paris, 1870.
Afr 3078.63.3	Paton, A.A. History of the Egyptian revolution. London, 1870. 2v.
Afr 7324.5	Pawa Manso. Memoria sobre Lourenço Marques (Delagoa Bay). Lisboa, 1870.
Afr 3978.40.5	Ravioli, C. Viaggio della spedizione romana in Egitto. v.1. Roma, 1870.
Afr 1258.70	Rohlfs, G. Land und Volk in Afrika, 1865-1870. Bremen, 1870.
Afr 5748.70	Sibree, James. Madagascar and its people. London, 1870.
Afr 3978.70.10	Watt, Robert. Fra aegypternes land. Kjøbenhavn, 1870.
Afr 4375.15	Wilkins, H. St.C. Reconnoitring in Abyssinia. London, 1870.

1871

Afr 4558.67.5.4	Baker, S.W. The Nile tributaries of Abyssinia. 4th ed. London, 1871.
Afr 3978.60	Beamont, William. To Sinai and Syene and back in 1860 and 1861. 2nd ed. London, 1871.
Afr 150.2.5F	Castilho, A.M. De. Os padrões dos descobrimentos portuguezes em Africa. 2a memoria. Lisboa, 1871.
Afr 8215.6	Chesson, Frederick William. The Dutch Republic of South Africa. London, 1871.
Afr 2230.6	Colonization de la Kabylie. Alger, 1871.
Afr 5406.51.5	Duchaillu, Paul Belloni. Explorations and adventures in Equatorial Africa. N.Y., 1871.
Afr 5406.52	Duchaillu, Paul Belloni. A journey to Ashango-land. N.Y., 1871.
Afr 5406.54.5	Duchaillu, Paul Belloni. Wild life under the equator. N.Y., 1871.
Afr 3978.71.5	Hamley, W.G. New sea and an old land..visit to Egypt. Edinburgh, 1871.
Afr 3978.70	Lacour, Raoul. L'Egypte d'Alexandrie a la Seconde Cataracte. Paris, 1871.
Afr 3978.71.3	Lane, E.W. Account of manners and customs of modern Egyptians. London, 1871. 2v.
Afr 8152.74	McKay, James. Reminiscences of the last Kaffir war. Grahamstown, 1871.
Afr 8658.71	Mackenzie, J. Ten years north of the Orange River. Edinburgh, 1871.

1871 - cont.

Afr 5765.1	Missionary reviews. Antananarivo, 1871-80. 4 pam.
Afr 9525.578.5	Moffat, Robert. A life's labours in South Africa. London, 1871.
Afr 3978.69.2	Wachenhusen, H. Vom armen egyptischen Mann. Bd.1-2. Berlin, 1871.
Afr 3978.71.8	Whately, Mary L. Among the huts in Egypt. London, 1871.
Afr 3978.71	Zincke, F.B. Egypt of the pharaohs and of the kedive. London, 1871.

1872

Afr 2010.1	Beauvois, E. En colonne dans la Grande Kabylie...1871. Paris, 1872.
Afr 5748.72	Blanchard, Emile. L'ile de Madagascar. Paris, 1872.
Afr 8808.72	Chapman, Charles. A voyage from Southhampton to Cape Town. London, 1872.
Afr 555.20	Crowthers, S.A. Niger mission, report of overland journey. London, 1872.
Afr 2208.72.3	Dubouzet, Charles. Algérie. n.p., 1872. 2 pam.
Afr 8678.5	Fritsch, G. Die Eingeborenen Süd-Afrikas. Atlas und Text. Breslau, 1872.
Afr 8815.5	General directory and guide book, to Cape of Good Hope. Cape Town, 1872.
Afr 2208.72	Herbert, Lady. A search after sunshine, or Algeria in 1871. London, 1872.
NEDL Afr 698.66	Horner. Voyage à la côte orientale, 1866. Paris, 1872.
Afr 4742.20	Issel, A. Viaggio nel Mar Rosso e tra i Bogos (1870). Milano, 1872.
Afr 2005.1	Oget, Jules. Une expédition algérienne; épisode de l'insurrection de 1864. Bastia, 1872.
Afr 555.8	Paiva Manso, L.M.J. Historia ecclesiastica ultramarina. Lisboa, 1872.
Afr 1947.13	Registre des prises maritimes. Alger, 1872.
Afr 2608.72	Schneider, O. Von Algier nach Tunis und Constantine. Dresden, 1872.
Afr 8145.47	Shaw, William, Rector of Chelvey. The story of my mission among the native tribes of South Eastern Africa. London, 1872.
Afr 6878.72.2	Stanley, H.M. How I found Livingstone. N.Y., 1872.
Afr 3978.72	Stephan, H. Das heutige Agypten. Leipzig, 1872.
Afr 8658.72.5	Taylor, Bayard. Travels in South Africa. N.Y., 1872.
Afr 8658.72	Thomas, T.M. Eleven years in central South Africa. London, 1872.

1873

Afr 3978.69.5.4	About, E. Le fellah: souvenirs d'Egypte. 3e ed. Paris, 1873.
Afr 6168.5	Bowdich, E.T. Mission from Cape Coast Castle to Ashanti. London, 1873.
Afr 8235.11	Boyle, Frederick. To the Cape for diamonds. London, 1873.
Afr 6170.15	Brackenbury, H. Fanti and Ashanti. Edinburgh, 1873.
Afr 590.16	Colomb, Philip Howard. Slave catching in the Indian Ocean. London, 1873.
Afr 5406.53	Duchaillu, Paul Belloni. Lost in the jungle. N.Y., 1873.
Afr 5765.3	Ellis, John E. Life of William Ellis, missionary. London, 1873.
Afr 6455.24	From Natal to Zanzibar. Durban, 1873.
Afr 2285.10	Goblet D'Alviella. Sahara et Laponie. Paris, 1873.
Afr 2228.6	Guimet, E. Arabes et Kabyles. Lyon, 1873.
Afr 2230.2	Hanoteau, A. La Kabylie et les coutumes kabyles. Paris, 1873. 3v.
Afr 6275.17	Hinderer, A. Seventeen years in the Yoruba country. London, 1873.
Afr 608.73	Kiepert, H. Beiträge zur Entdeckungsgeschichte Afrikas. v.1-4. Berlin, 1873-81. 2v.
Afr 3978.73	Knorring, O.V. Tvaa maanader i egypten. Stockholm, 1873.
Afr 8658.73	Koerner, F. Süd Afrika. Breslau, 1873.
Afr 718.9	Lacerda e Almeida, F.J.M. de. Journey to Cazembe. London, 1873.
Afr 5385.14.2	Laffitte, J. Le Dahomé - souvenirs de voyage et de mission. Tours, 1873.
Afr 4558.64F	Lejean, G. Voyage en Abyssinie executé de 1862 à 1864. Text and atlas. Paris, 1873. 2v.
Afr 3978.73.5	Lenoir, Paul. The Fayoum, or Artists in Egypt. London, 1873.
Afr 8740.5	Lindley, A.E. Adamantia. London, 1873.
NEDL Afr 6455.27	New, Charles. Life, wanderings, and labours in eastern Africa. London, 1873.
Afr 1608.73	Perrier, A. A winter in Morocco. London, 1873.
Afr 5842.6	Pike, N. Sub-tropical rambles. London, 1873.
Afr 6095.19	Reade, Winwood. The African sketch-book. London, 1873. 2v.
Afr 715.3	Schweinfurth, G. The heart of Africa. London, 1873. 2v.
Afr 5748.70.5	Sibree, James. Madagascar et ses habitants. Toulouse, 1873.
NEDL Afr 6878.73	Stanley, H.M. How I found Livingstone. London, 1873. (Changed to KPE 2829)
Afr 6878.73.5	Stanley, H.M. My Kalulu, prince, king and slave. London, 1873.
X Cg Afr 590.5	Sulivan, G.L. Dhow chasing in Zanzibar waters. London, 1873. (changed to XP 9127)
Afr 2623.15	Tunis. Welt-Ausstellung 1873 in Wien. Wien, 1873.
Afr 3978.67.4	Warren, W.W. Life on the Nile. 2d ed. Boston, 1873.

1874

Afr 1947.9	Amiet, J.J. Lorenz Arregger, Sklave in Algier. Bern, 1874.
Afr 5448.5A	Bastian, Adolf. Die deutsche Expedition an der Loango-Küste. Jena, 1874.
Afr 6164.3.5	Beecham, John. Ashantee and the Gold Coast. London, 1874.
Afr 5130.2	Berlioux, E.F. André Brue, ou L'Origine. Paris, 1874.
Afr 2208.74	Blackburn, H. Artists and Arabs. London, 1874.
Afr 555.22.25	Boyce, William B. Memoir of the Rev. William Shaw. London, 1874.
Afr 6164.3.5	Boyle, F. Through Fanteeland to Coomassie. London, 1874.
Afr 6170.11	Brackenbury, H. The Ashanti war. London, 1874. 2v.
Afr 5765.8	Cameron, James. Recollections of mission life in Madagascar. Antananarivo, 1874.
Afr 5406.57	Duchaillu, Paul Belloni. The country of the dwarfs. N.Y., 1874.
Afr 5406.56	Duchaillu, Paul Belloni. My Apingi kingdom. N.Y., 1874.
Afr 5406.55	Duchaillu, Paul Belloni. Stories of the gorilla country. N.Y., 1874.

222

1874 - cont.

Afr 608.74	Forbes, A.G. Africa, geographical exploration. London, 1874.
Afr 6390.10	Frere, H.B.E. Eastern Africa as a field for missionary labour. London, 1874.
Afr 6164.4	Hay, J.D. Ashanti and the Gold Coast. London, 1874.
Afr 6170.8.2	Henty, G.A. The march to Coomassie. 2nd ed. London, 1874.
Afr 3978.74.5F	Hoppin, Augustus. On the Nile. Boston, 1874.
Afr 590.56	Hutchinson, E. The slave trade of East Africa. London, 1874.
Afr 2025.13	Lasicotière. Rapport...sur les actes du gouvernement. Versailles, 1874.
Afr 3978.74	Leland, C.G. The Egyptian sketch book. N.Y., 1874.
Afr 725.10A	Livingstone, David. The last journals. London, 1874. 2v.
Afr 658.74	Ludwig, Salvator. Yacht-Reise in den Syrten, 1873. Prag, 1874.
Afr 4070.4	Marno, E. Reisen im Gebiete des Blauen und Weissen Nil, im egyptischen Sudan. Wien, 1874.
Afr 6170.16	Maurice, J.F. The Ashantee war. London, 1874.
Afr 3068.74	Notizie di viaggiatori italiani in Egitto. Torino, 1874.
Afr 678.74	Oberlaender, R. Westafrika von Senegal bis Benquela. Leipzig, 1874.
Afr 7324.17	Official correspondence on the Lourenço Marques-Delagoa Bay question. London, 1874.
Afr 2295.5	Ragot, W. Le Sahara de la province de Constantine. Constantine, 1874-75.
Afr 6170.7	Reade, W. Story of the Ashantee campaign. London, 1874.
Afr 6170.5	Rogers, E. Campaigning in West Africa and the Ashantee invasion. London, 1874.
Afr 1608.72.8	Rohlfs, G. Adventures in Morocco. London, 1874.
NEDL Afr 2748.74	Rohlfs, G. Quer durch Afrika. Leipzig, 1874. 2v.
Afr 715.3.3	Schweinfurth, G. The heart of Africa. N.Y., 1874. 2v.
Afr 715.2	Schweinfurth, G. Im Herzen von Afrika. Leipzig, 1874. 2v.
Afr 5385.15	Skertchly, J.A. Dahomey as it is. London, 1874.
Afr 6170.17	Snape, Thomas. The Ashantee war, causes and results...lecture. Manchester, 1874.
NEDL Afr 6170.13	Stanley, H.M. Coomassie and Magdala. London, 1874.
Afr 6878.73.10	Stanley, H.M. My Kalulu, prince, king and slave. N.Y., 1874.

1875

Afr 6988.16.114	Anderson, Charles J. Notes of travel in South Africa. London, 1875.
NEDL Afr 6988.16.116	Anderson, Charles J. Notes of travel in South Africa. N.Y., 1875.
NEDL Afr 4095.8.3	Baker, S.W. Ismailia. N.Y., 1875.
Afr 8658.75	Bisset, John J. Sport and war...1834-1867. London, 1875.
Afr 5420.175	Compiegne, Victor D. L'Afrique équatoriale. Paris, 1875.
Afr 590.7	Cooper, J. The lost continent. London, 1875.
Afr 8658.75.5	Drummond, William Henry. The large game and natural history of South and South-East Africa. Edinburgh, 1875.
Afr 3978.65.3	Duff-Gordon, Lucie Austin. Last letters from Egypt. London, 1875.
Afr 1868.60	Fillias, A. L'Algerie ancienne et moderne. 2e ed. Alger, 1875.
Afr 28.4.2	Gay, Jean. Bibliographie de l'Afrique. San Remo, 1875.
Afr 718.2.80F	Grant, J.H. On Stanley's exploration of S. Victoria. n.p. 1875.
Afr 6192.4.3	Gundert, H. Vier Jahre in Asante-Tagebücher der Missionäre Ramseyer und Kühne. Basel, 1875.
Afr 608.75	Jones, C.H. Africa, the history of exploration. N.Y., 1875.
Afr 1100.5	Laprimandaie, F.E. Documents inédits sur l'histoire de l'occupation espagnole en Afrique. Alger, 1875.
Afr 1915.8	Lavigerie, C.M. L'armée et la mission de la France en Afrique. Alger, 1875.
Afr 9028.75	Leslie, D. Among the Zulus and Amatongas. 2. ed. Edinburgh, 1875.
X Cg Afr 725.10.5	Livingstone, David. The last journals. N.Y, 1875. (Changed to XP 3656)
Afr 855.10	Meliss, J.C. St. Helena. London, 1875.
Afr 1080.4	Mercier, E. Histoire des Arabes dans l'Afrique septentrionale. Alger, 1875.
Afr 7175.5	Monteiro, J.J. Angola and the river Congo. London, 1875. 2v.
Afr 5748.75	Mullens, J. Twelve months in Madagascar. London, 1875.
Afr 8808.75	Noble, John. Descriptive handbook of the Cape colony. Cape Town, 1875.
Afr 3163.8	Pagani, Z. Viaggio di Domenico Trevisan, 1512. Venice, 1875.
Afr 4558.75	Raffray, A. Voyage en Abyssinie, à Zanzibar et aux pays des Ouanika. n.p., 1875.
Afr 6192.4	Ramseyer, F.A. Four years in Ashante. London, 1875.
Afr 1955.27	Randon, J.L.C.A. Mémoires du maréchal Randon. Paris, 1875. 2v.
Afr 1955.27.5	Randon, J.L.C.A. Mémoires du maréchal Randon. 2e éd. Paris, 1875-77. 2v.
Afr 2208.66.5	Rasch, Gustav. Nach Algier. Dresden, 1875.
Afr 9558.26	Roberts, J.S. Life and explorations of Dr. Livingstone. Boston, 1875.
Afr 4050.5	Rohlfs, G. Drei Monate in der libyschen Wüste. Cassel, 1875.
Afr 5993.14	San Javier. Tres años en Fernando Poo. Madrid, 1875.
Afr 2312.1	Seriziat. Etudes sur l'oasis de Biskra. 2d ed. Paris, 1875.
NEDL Afr 3978.75	Southworth, A.S. Four thousand miles of African travel. N.Y., 1875.
Afr 2230.8	Vilbort, J. En Kabylie. Paris, 1875.
Afr 2608.75	Zaccone, P. Notes sur la régence de Tunis. Paris, 1875.

1876

Afr 3978.76	Appleton, T.G. A Nile journal. Boston, 1876.
Afr 8968.76	Brooks, Henry. Natal, a history and description of the colony. London, 1876.
Afr 5406.176	Burton, Richard F. Two trips to gorilla land. London, 1876. 4v.
Afr 6170.9	Butler, W.F. Akim-foo, the history of a failure. London, 1876.
Afr 9558.27	Caranti, B. Notizie biografiche sul dottore David Livingstone. Torino, 1876.
Afr 608.76	Day, George T. African adventure and adventures. Boston, 1876.
Afr 3978.65.4	Duff-Gordon, Lucie Austin. Last letters from Egypt. 2d ed. London, 1876.
Afr 5765.3.5	Ellis, William. Faithful unto death. London, 1876.

1876 - cont.

Afr 7093.4F	Falkenstein. Die Loango Kuste. Berlin, 1876.
Afr 1846.8	Ferand, L.C. Les interprètes de l'armée d'Afrique. Alger, 1876.
Afr 3978.76.7	Gellion-Dangler, Eugène. Lettres sur l'Egypte. Paris, 1876.
Afr 8849.6	Gray, C.N. Life of Robert Gray. London, 1876. 2v.
Afr 630.6	Hartmann, R. Die Nigritier. Berlin, 1876.
Afr 5385.14	Laffitte, J. Le Dahomé - souvenirs de voyage et de mission. 4 ed. Tours, 1876.
Afr 678.76	Laffitte, J. Le pays des Nègres et la Côte des esclaves. Tours, 1876.
Afr 3978.76.11	Lund, Fr. Taflor fraan orienten af hother tolderlund. Stockholm, 1876.
Afr 150.3.5	Major, R.H. Vida do Infante Dom Henrique de Portugal. Lisboa, 1876.
Afr 3978.76.9F	Manning, S. The land of the pharaohs. London, 1876.
Afr 9525.578.10	Moffat, Robert. Scenes and services in South Africa. London, 1876.
Afr 8658.76	Mohr, Edward. To the Victoria Falls of the Zambesi. London, 1876.
Afr 7175.5.3	Monteiro, J.J. Angola and the river Congo. v.1-2. N.Y., 1876.
Afr 2235.1	Morelet. Les Maures de Constantine. Dijon, 1876.
Afr 4070.20	Myers, A.B.R. Life with the Hamran Arabs. London, 1876.
Afr 9388.76F	Orange Free State Commission. Sketch of the Orange Free State. Philadelphia, 1876.
Afr 4558.76	Raffray, A. Abyssinie. Paris, 1876.
Afr 2228.2.3	Richard, C. Scénes de moeurs arabes. 3e ed. Paris, 1876.
Afr 3978.76.6	Warner, C.D. Mummies and Moslems. Hartford, 1876.
Afr 3978.76.4	Warner, C.D. My winter on the Nile. Boston, 1876.
Afr 3978.76.3	Warner, C.D. My winter on the Nile. Hartford, 1876.

1877

Afr 9148.77	Baines, Thomas. The gold regions of southeast Africa. London, 1877.
Afr 608.77	Banning, E. L'Afrique et la Conférence géographique de Bruxelles. Bruxelles, 1877.
Afr 115.4	Carrie, F. Thoughts upon present and future of South Africa. London, 1877.
Afr 4558.77	Decosson, E.A. The cradle of the Blue Nile. London, 1877. 2v.
Afr 5392.4	Desribes, Emmanuel. L'évangile au Dahomey et à la Côte des Esclaves. Clermont-Ferrand, 1877.
Afr 5185.5	Faidherbe, L.L.C. Le Zenaga des tribus sénégalaises. Paris, 1877.
Afr 2345.5	Féraud, Charles. Histoire des villes de la province de Constantine. La Calle. Alger, 1877.
Afr 1608.77	Fernandez Duro, Cesareo. Apuntes biograficas de el hach mohamed el Bagdady, Don José Maria de Murga, segui de otros varios para idea de los usas. Madrid, 1877.
Afr 3695.4	Gordon, C.G. Provinces of the equator. Cairo, 1877.
Afr 4060.3	Heuglin, Th. von. Reise in Nordost Afrika. Braunschweig, 1877. 2v.
Afr 5342.10	Jacolliot, L. La Côte-d'Ivoire, l'homme des deserts. Paris, 1877.
Afr 2290.8	Lambert, E. L'Algérie...deux mois dans province d'Oran. Paris, 1877.
NEDL Afr 4095.11	Long, C.C. Central Africa. N.Y., 1877.
Afr 1573.14	Lopez Pinto, V. Memoria sobre intereses generales del pais y especiales de las colonias africanas. Ceuta, 1877.
Afr 3978.77.3	McCoan, J.C. Egypt as it is. N.Y., 1877.
Afr 2730.1	Mackenzie, D. The flooding of the Sahara. London, 1877.
Afr 150.3.2	Major, R.H. The discoveries of Prince Henry. London, 1877.
Afr 3078.77	Marcel, J.J. Egypte depuis la conquête des Arabes. Paris, 1877.
Afr 8088.77	Noble, John. South Africa. London, 1877.
Afr 7108.10	Paiva Manso, L.M.J. Historia do Congo. Lisboa, 1877.
Afr 8815.8	Port Elizabeth directory and guide. Port Elizabeth, 1877.
Afr 6455.7	Price, Roger. Private journal. Photoreproduction. n.p., 1877.
Afr 3205.3	Prokesch-Osten, A. Mehmed-Ali. Wien, 1877.
Afr 3821.5	Prout, Henri Goslee. General report on the province of Kordofan. Cairo, 1877.
Afr 2608.77	Rae, Edward. The country of the Moors. London, 1877.
Afr 5765.11	Richardson, James. Lights and shadows. Antananarivo, 1877.
Afr 7122.20	Sa da Bandeira, B. de S.N. de F. da. Facts and statistics concerning the right of the crown of Portugal to the territory of Molembo Cabinda, Ambriz. London, 1877.
Afr 2285.4	Soleillet, Paul. L'Afrique occidentale. Paris, 1877.
Afr 8088.77.5	Theal, G.M. Compendium of South African history and geography. 3d ed. Lovedale, 1877.
Afr 1973.3	Watbled, E. Souvenirs de l'armée d'Afrique. Paris, 1877.
Afr 2208.77	Wattenwyl, M. von. Zwei Jahre in Algerien. Bern, 1877.
Afr 678.77	Whitford, J.F.R.G.S. Trading life in Western and Central Africa. Liverpool, 1877.
Afr 9838.77	Young, Edward Daniel. Nyassa. London, 1877.

1878

Afr 1736.3	Alcala galiano, pelayo. Memoria sobre la situación de Santa Cruz de Mar Pegueña. 3 in 1. Madrid, 1878. 3 pam.
Afr 8152.90	Aylward, A. The Transvaal of to-day. Edinburgh, 1878.
Afr 608.78	Bainier, P.F. La géographie appliquée à la marine, au commerce. Paris, 1878.
Afr 2208.78	Beijerman, H. Drie maanden in Algerie. 's-Gravenhage, 1878.
Afr 2260.12	Booms, P.G. Studien over Algerie. 's-Gravenhage, 1878.
Afr 555.7.9	Carlyle, J.E. South Africa and its mission fields. London, 1878.
Afr 1368.78	Castellanos, M.P. Descripcion historica de Marruecos. Santiago, 1878.
Afr 3978.78	Deleon, E. The khedives Egypt. N.Y., 1878.
Afr 3252.1	La destitution de Lapenna et la reforme judiciaire en Egypte. Geneva, 1878.
Afr 3978.77.8A	Edwards, A.B. A thousand miles up the Nile. Leipzig, 1878.
Afr 724.2	Farde, P. Voyages et aventures. Gand, 1878.
Afr 1608.78.6	Gatell, Joaquin. Viajes por Marruecos. Madrid, 1878-79.
Afr 860.2	Gill, D. Six months in Ascension. London, 1878.
Afr 8658.78	Gillmore, Parker. The great thirst land. London, 1878.
Afr 678.78	Gravier, G. Recherches sur les navigations européennes. Paris, 1878.

1878 - cont.

Afr 3994.876	Histoire financière de l'Egypte. Paris, 1878.
Afr 1608.78	Hooker, J.D. Journal of a tour in Marocco. London, 1878.
Afr 5920.1.3	Iradier, Manuel. Africa. Madrid, 1878.
Afr 4070.6	Klunzinger, C.B. Upper Egypt. N.Y., 1878.
Afr 715.7	Laveleye, E. de. L'Afrique centrale. Paris, 1878.
Afr 8152.92	Lucas, T.J. Camp life in South Africa. London, 1878.
Afr 4095.9.5	Marno, Ernst. Reise in der egyptischen Aequatorial-Provinz. Wien, 1878.
Afr 2928.78	Medina, G. La reggenza di Tripoli. Cagliari, 1878.
Afr 4388.5	Mitchell, L.H. Report on seizure by Abyssinians of geological expedition. Cairo, 1878.
Afr 1608.78.3	Pietsch, W. Marokko-brief von der Deutschen gesand 1877. Leipzig, 1878.
Afr 9148.78	Roche, H.A. On trek in the Transvaal. London, 1878.
Afr 555.12	Sainte-Marie, E. de. La Tunisie chrétienne. Lyon, 1878.
Afr 2308.2	Seguin, L.G. Walks in Algiers. London, 1878.
Afr 718.2A	Stanley, H.M. Through the dark continent. N.Y., 1878
Afr 4095.10F	Torelli-Viollier, E. Ricerca delle sorgenti del Nilo. Milano, 1878.

1879

Afr 6878.79	Association Internationale Africaine. Rapports sur les marchés de la première éxpedition. v.1-4. Bruxelles, 1879-80.
Afr 8808.79	Ballantyne, R.M. Six months at the Cape. London, 1879.
Afr 555.9.50	Beltrame, G. Il sennaar e lo sciangallah. Verona, 1879. 2v.
Afr 5185.6	Berenger-Ferand, L.J.B. Les peuples de la Sénégambie. Paris, 1879.
Afr 2505.1	Carta, F. La questione tunisina e l'Europa. Roma, 1879.
Afr 2748.79	Chavanne, J. Die Sahara. Vienna, 1879.
Afr 4868.79	Comptoirs français de l'Afrique orientale. Paris, 1879.
Afr 2232.3A	Coyne, A. Le Mzab. Alger, 1879.
Afr 8152.91	Cunynghame, A.T. My command in South Africa 1874-8. London, 1879.
Afr 3978.79.3	Delchevalerie, G. L'Egypte. Paris, 1879.
Afr 8658.79.5	Deleage, Paul. Trois mois chez les Zoulous et les derniers jours du prince impérial. Paris, 1879.
Afr 4285.3	Dillmann, A. Uber die Anfänge des axumitischen Reiches. Berlin, 1879.
Afr 718.28	Durand. Les voyages des Portugais...XVI et XVII siècles. Meaux, 1879.
Afr 7458.79	Dyer, A.S. Christian Liberia. London, 1879.
Afr 725.6	Elton, J.F. Lakes and mountains of eastern and central Africa. London, 1879.
Afr 8968.79	Farrer, J.A. Zululand and the Zulus. 3rd ed. London, 1879.
Afr 8152.95	Fenn, T.E. How I volunteered for the Cape. London, 1879.
Afr 2208.79	Fontanes, J. de. Deux touristes en Algérie. Paris, 1879.
Afr 7176.26.2	Graça, Joaquim José da. Projecto de uma companhia agricola e comercial africana. 2. ed. Lisboa, 1879.
Afr 1915.1	Grammont, H.D. Relation entre la France et la regime d'Alger au XVIIe siècle. 4 in 1. Algier, 1879.
Afr 7175.3	Guessfeldt, P. Die Loango. Expedition 1873-76. London, 1879. 2v.
Afr 630.6.5	Hartmann, R. Die Völker Afrikas. Leipzig, 1879.
Afr 3230.5	Jerrold, W.B. Egypt under Ismail Pacha. London, 1879.
Afr 8658.79	Kennedy, D. Kennedy at the Cape. Edinburgh, 1879.
Afr 2285.6	Largeau, V. Le pays de Rirha Quargla. Paris, 1879.
Afr 1608.79.4	Leared, Arthur. A visit to the court of Morocco. London, 1879.
Afr 678.79	Lenz, O. Skizzen aus Westafrika. Berlin, 1879.
Afr 8155.9	Lucas, T.J. The Zulus and the British frontiers. London, 1879.
Afr 3982.2F	Lumbroso, Giacomo. Descrittori italiani dell'Egitto e di Alessandria. Roma, 1879.
Afr 1608.79	M. y Rodriguez, T. El imperio de Marruecos. Madrid, 1879.
Afr 5180.3	Marche, A. Trois voyages dans l'Afrique. Paris, 1879.
Afr 4095.9	Marno, Ernst. Reise in der egyptischen Aequatorial-Provinz. Wien, 1879.
Afr 4070.41	Matteucci, P. Sudan e Gallas. Milano, 1879.
Afr 555.9.5	Means, J.O. The proposed mission in Central Africa. Cambridge, 1879.
Afr 2318.1	Mercier, E. Constantine avant la conquête française. Constantine, 1879.
Afr 658.79	Nachtigal, S. Sahara und Sudan. Berlin, 1879-89.
Afr 3230.7	Peabody, F.G. Egypt and the powers. n.p., 1879.
Afr 1925.5.5	Playfair, R.L. Episodes de l'histoire des relations de Grande Bretagne. Alger, 1879.
Afr 718.4.10	Ribeiro, M.F. As conferencias e o itinerario do viajante Serpa Pinto. Lisboa, 1879.
Afr 4746.15	Sapeto, G. Assab e i suoi critici. Genova, 1879.
Afr 8152.94	Streatfield, F.M. Kafirland, a ten months campaign. London, 1879.
Afr 8220.5	Tromp, Theo M. Herinneringen uit Zuid Africa. Leiden, 1879.
Afr 2005.3	Trumelet, C. Histoire de l'insurrection dans le sud de la province d'Alger, 1864-69. Alger, 1879-84.
Afr 9558.29	Vattemare, H. David Livingstone. Paris, 1879.

188-

Afr 8160.3	Dixie, Florence Douglas. A defence of Zululand and its king. London, 188-
Afr 5130.20	Gaffarel, P. Administration du général Faidherbe au Sénégal. Dijon, 188-.

1880

Afr 2731.1	Abadie, F. Lettres sur le Trans-saharien. Constantine, 1880.
Afr 1432.1	Alarcon, P.A. Diario de la guerra de Africa. Madrid, 1880. 3v.
Afr 8160.22	Ashe, Major. The story of the Zulu campaign. London, 1880.
Afr 9558.30	Blaikie, W.G. Personal life of David Livingstone. London, 1880.
Afr 1955.11	Bonnafont, Jean Pierre. Douze ans en Algérie, 1830-1842. Paris, 1880.
Afr 2208.79.3	Bourde, P. A travers l'Algérie. Paris, 1880.
Afr 8152.98	Browning, F.G. Fighting and farming in South Africa. London, 1880.
Afr 678.80	Buchholz, R. Reisen in West Afrika. Leipzig, 1880.
Afr 810.19	Burdo, Adolphe. The Niger and the Benueh. London, 1880.

1880 - cont.

Afr 8160.11	Colenso, F.E. History of the Zulu war and its origin. London, 1880.
Afr 1608.80.2	Colvile, H.E. A ride in petticoats and slippers. London, 1880.
Afr 1608.80	Conring, A. von. Marroco, das Land und die Leute. Berlin, 1880.
Afr 3978.80.5	Denis de Rivoyre, B.L. Mer Rouge et Abyssinie. Paris, 1880.
Afr 2608.80	Desgodins de Souhesmes, G. Tunis. Paris, 1880.
Afr 1955.8	Dieuzaide, V.A. Histoire de l'Algérie, 1830-1878. v.1-2. Oran, 1880-83.
Afr 4382.1	Dye, W.M. Moslem Egypt and Christian Abyssinia. N.Y., 1880.
Afr 3978.79F	Ebers, G. Agypten. Stuttgart, 1880. 2v.
Afr 3994.880	Egypt for the Egyptians. London, 1880.
Afr 1325.7F	France. Question de la protection diplomatique au Maroc. Paris, 1880.
Afr 3994.880.5F	France. Ministère des Affaires Etrangères. Documents diplomatiques. Affaires d'Egypte. Paris, 1880.
Afr 8658.80.4	Gillmore, Parker. On duty, a ride through hostile Africa. London, 1880.
Afr 3978.80	Hunt, Sarah K. On the Nile. London, 1880.
Afr 4025.20.5	Italy. Ministero degli Affari Esteri. Sulla tutela degli interessi italiani in Egitto. Rome, 1880.
Afr 1258.80.5	Kostenko, L.Th. Puteshestvie v severnuiu Afriku. Izd 2. Sankt Peterburg, 1880.
Afr 7458.80	Latrobe, J.H.B. Liberia...an address delivered before American Colonization Society. Washington, 1880.
Afr 150.2.3	Lepitre, J.M.A. De iis qui ante Vascum A Gama Africam legere tentaverunt. Thesis. Parisis, 1880.
Afr 5765.12	London Missionary Society. Ten years review of mission work in Madagascar, 1870-80. Antananarivo, 1880.
Afr 2208.80.6	Lubomirski, J. Côte barbaresque et le Sahara. Paris, 1880.
Afr 8160.9F	Mackinnon, J.P. The South African campaign 1879. London, 1880.
Afr 8160.12	McToy, E.D. Brief history of the 13th Regiment...1877-78-79. Devonport, 1880.
Afr 4558.80	Matteucci, P. In Abissinia, viaggio. Milano, 1880.
Afr 2208.80.5	Mercier, E. L'Algérie en 1880. Paris, 1880.
Afr 8160.5	Montague, W.E. Campaigning in South Africa. Edinburgh, 1880.
Afr 1432.21.2	Navarrete, José. Desde Vad-Ras a Sevilla: Acuarelas de la campaña de Africa. 2a ed. Madrid, 1880.
Afr 7048.10	Nogueira, A.F. A raça negra sob o ponto de vista da civilisação da Africa. Lisboa, 1880.
Afr 8160.14	Norbury, H.F. Naval brigade in South Africa during...1877-78-79. London, 1880.
Afr 8160.8	Norris-Newman, C.L. In Zululand with the British. London, 1880.
Afr 8160.4	Parr, H.H. A sketch of the Kafir and Zulu wars. London, 1880.
Afr 108.80	Paulitschke, P. Die geographisch Erforschung der afrikanischen Continents. Wien, 1880.
Afr 2208.80.3	Philippe, F. Etapes sahariennes. Alger, 1880.
Afr 8152.96	Prichard, A.M. Friends and foes in the Transkei. London, 1880.
Afr 4785.3	Revoil, G. Voyage au Cap des Aromates (Africa orientale). Paris, 1880.
Afr 1955.6	Rousset, C. La conquête d'Alger. Paris, 1880.
Afr 8658.80	Sandeman, E.F. Eight months in an ox-wagon. London, 1880.
Afr 2489.1	Serbellone, G. Serbellone a Tunisi. Sierra, 1880.
Afr 5748.80	Sibree, James. The great African islands. London, 1880.
Afr 5765.15.5	Sibree, James. Madagascar, country, people, missions. London, 1880.
Afr 8035.5	Silver, S.W. S.W. Silver and Company's handbook to South Africa. London, 1880. 2v.
Afr 1445.5F	Spain. Ministerio de Estado. Documents diplomatiques. Conférences de Madrid. Supplément. Madrid, 1880. 2 pam.
Afr 2208.80	Tchihatchef, P. Espagne,Algérie et Tunisie. Paris, 1880.
Afr 8160.6	Vijn, Cornelius. Cetshwayo's Dutchman. London, 1880.
Afr 1745.1	Watson, R.S. A visit to Wazan. London, 1880.
Afr 8160.10	Wilmot, A. History of the Zulu war. London, 1880.
Afr 9028.80	Wylde, A. My chief and I, or Six months in Natal. London, 1880.

1881

Afr 2368.1	Bastide, L. Sidi-bel-Abbés et son arrondissement. Oran, 1881.
Afr 9558.30.2A	Blaikie, W.G. Personal life of David Livingstone. N.Y., 1881.
Afr 2208.81.7	Bourquelot, E. En Algérie. Paris, 1881.
Afr 1258.80	Brunialti, A. Algeria, Tunisia e Tripolitania. Milan, 1881.
Afr 678.81	Canale, M.G. Memoria. Genova, 1881.
Afr 7175.2.5	Capello, H. De Benguella as terras de Iacca. Lisboa, 1881. 2v.
Afr 115.3	Cardeiro, L. Ed. Viagens explorações dos portugueses. Lisboa, 1881.
Afr 9558.32	Chambliss, J.E. The lives and travels of Livingstone and Stanley. Boston, 1881.
Afr 608.81	Chavanne, J. Afrika im Lichte unserer Tage. Wien, 1881.
Afr 2285.3	Choisy, A. Le Sahara, souvenirs d'une mission à Goléah. Paris, 1881.
Afr 1608.80.1	Conring, A. von. Marroco, el pais y los habitantes. 2e ed. Madrid, 1881.
Afr 5868.81	Crestien, G.F. Causeries historiques. Paris, 1881.
Afr 2508.6	Desfosses, Edmond. Affaires d'orient, la question tunisienne. Paris, 1881.
X Cg Afr 3243.3	Dicey, E. England and Egypt. London, 1881.
Afr 2608.81	Duveyrier, Henri. La Tunisie. Paris, 1881.
Afr 3978.81.6F	Ebers, G. Egypt, descriptive, historical, and picturesque. London, 1881-82. 2v.
Afr 3978.81.5F	Ebers, G. Egypt, descriptive, historical. London, 1881. 2v.
Afr 3991.5	Egypt. Direction Générale de la Statistique de l'Egypte. Dictionnaire des villes, villages, hameaux. Caire, 1881.
Afr 3808.81.5	Ensor, F. Sidney. Incidents on a journey through Nubia to Darfoor. London, 1881.
Afr 3269.05F	France. Ministère des Affaires Etrangères. Documents diplomatiques. Paris, 1881.
Afr 3269.4F	France. Ministère des Affaires Etrangères. Documents diplomatiques. Paris, 1881. 4 pam.

1881 - cont.

Afr 2430.1F France. Ministère des Affaires Etrangéres. Documents diplomatiques. Affaires de Tunisie, 1870-81, et supplément. Paris, 1881. 2v.
Afr 725.11 Geddie, J.F.R.G. The lake regions of central Africa. London, 1881.
Afr 2208.81.13 Girault, A. En Algérie. Paris, 1881.
Afr 2025.1.5 Gourgeot, F. Situation politique de l'Algérie. Paris, 1881.
Afr 1900.2 Grammont, H.D. Histoire des rois d'Alger. Alger, 1881.
Afr 5096.2 Gravier, Gabriel. Voyage de Paul Soleillet à l'Adrar. Rouen, 1881.
Afr 1903.7 Guerras de los españoles en Africa 1542, 43 y 1632. Madrid, 1881.
Afr 8825.3 Hahn, T. Tsuni-Goam, the supreme being. London, 1881.
Afr 3695.5 Hill, G.B. Gordon in Central Africa. London, 1881.
Afr 8658.81 Holub, Emil. Seven years in South Africa. London, 1881. 2v.
Afr 5218.83 Hontay, J. Le Soudan française. Lille, 1881-83. 2v.
Afr 115.70 Jones, Ch. H. Famous explorers and adventures in Africa. v.1-2. N.Y., 1881. 2v.
Afr 2208.81.9 Knox, A.A. The new playground...Algeria. London, 1881.
Afr 5748.81 Lacaze, H. Souvenirs de Madagascar. Paris, 1881.
Afr 3978.81 Lane-Poole, S. Egypt. London, 1881.
Afr 2208.81.11 Lelu, P. En Algérie. Paris, 1881.
Afr 2662.1 Ludwig Salvator. Bizerta und seine Zukunft. Prag, 1881.
Afr 5765.9 Matthews, T.T. Notes of nine years mission work in the province of Vonizongo, N.W., Madagascar. London, 1881.
Afr 5180.11 Mitchinson, A.W. The expiring continent. London, 1881.
Afr 608.81.7 Moister, W. Africa, past and present. N.Y., 1881.
Afr 2208.81.15 Mouchez, E. La côte et les ports de l'Algérie. Paris, 1881.
Afr 2208.81.5 Notices...surAlger et l'Algérie. Alger, 1881.
Afr 2295.7.3 Oasis de l'Oued Rir' en 1856 et 1880. 3e ed. Paris, 1881.
Afr 9488.81 Oates, Frank. Matabele land. London, 1881.
Afr 9088.5 Oordt, J.W.G. van. De Transvaalsche Gebeurtenissen en... Suid-Africa. 's-Gravenhage, 1881.
Afr 1608.81.5 Ovilo y Canales, F. La mujer Marroqui, estudio social. 2e ed. Madrid, 1881.
Afr 715.28 Pares, Eugene. Les explorateurs français en Afrique. Limoges, 1881.
Afr 5748.57.10 Pfeiffer, Ida R. Voyage à Madagascar. Paris, 1881.
Afr 2220.5 Piesse, L. Itinéraire de l'Algérie. Paris, 1881.
Afr 7560.3 Pigafetta, F. A report on the kingdom of Congo. London, 1881.
Afr 2208.81.3 Pulligny, F.A. de. Six semaines en Algérie. Paris, 1881.
Afr 2975.1 Rohlfs, G. Kufra. Leipzig, 1881.
Afr 2285.1 Sabatier, C. La question du sud-ouest. Alger, 1881.
Afr 2510.1 Santi, F.L. Italia e Tunisi. Milano, 1881.
Afr 2208.81 Schwarz, B. Algerien. Leipzig, 1881.
Afr 718.4.6 Serpa Pinto, Alexander de. Como eu atravessei Africa. vol.1-2. Londres, 1881. 2v.
Afr 718.4 Serpa Pinto, Alexander de. How I crossed Africa. Philadelphia, 1881. 2v.
Afr 718.4.3 Serpa Pinto, Alexander de. Wandering quer durch Afrika. Leipzig, 1881. 2v.
Afr 2748.81 Soleillet, P. Les voyages...dans le Sahara. Paris, 1881.
Afr 8235.8 Statham, F.R. Blacks, Boers and British. London, 1881.
Afr 7458.81A Stetson, G.R. The Liberian Republic as it is. Photoreproduction. Boston, 1881.
Afr 725.16 Taylor, Bayard. The lake regions of central Africa. N.Y., 1881.
Afr 8658.72.10 Taylor, Bayard. Travels in South Africa. N.Y., 1881.
NEDL Afr 725.4 Thomson, J. To the central African lakes and back. v.1-2. London, 1881. 2v.
Afr 725.4.2 Thomson, J. To the central African lakes and back. 2d ed. Boston, 1881. 2v.
Afr 1608.81 Trotter, P.D. Our mission to Marocco. Edinburg, 1881.
Afr 3068.81 Vaujany, H.. Histoire de l'Egypte, depuis les temps les plus reculés jusqu'à nos jours. Le Caire, 1881.
Afr 4558.81.5 Vigoni, Pippo. Abissinia, giornale di un viaggio. Milano, 1881.
Afr 3978.76.4.5 Warner, C.D. My winter on the Nile. Boston, 1881.
Afr 3068.81.5 Waters, C.E.C. Egypt. Boston, 1881.
Afr 1080.5 Ximenez de Sandovel, C. Guerras de Africa en la antigüdad. Madrid, 1881.

1882

Afr 2748.82 Algeria. Service Central des Affaires Indigènes. Deuxième mission Flatters. Algiers, 1882.
Afr 1608.82.2 Amicis, E. de. Morocco. N.Y., 1882.
Afr 1608.82 Amicis, E. de. Morocco. N.Y., 1882.
Afr 1608.82.2.5 Amicis, E. de. Morocco. 9 ed. Milano, 1882.
Afr 3978.82.15 Arnold, J.T.B. Palms and temples. London, 1882.
Afr 2230.17 Barclay, E. Mountain life in Algeria. London, 1882.
Afr 3240.3 Bemmelen, P.V. L'Egypte et l'Europe. Leiden, 1882. 2v.
Afr 1608.82.5 Bonelli, E. El imperio de Marruecos y su constitucion. Madrid, 1882.
Afr 5615.5 Brenier, J. La question de Madagascar. Paris, 1882.
NEDL Afr 2527.1 Broadley, A.M. Tunis, past and present. Edinburgh, 1882. 2v.
Afr 7175.2 Capello, H. From Benguella to the territory of Yacca. London, 1882. 2v.
Afr 1688.5 Castries, H. De. Notes sur figuig. Paris, 1882.
Afr 625.10 Chavanne, J. Erleuterungen zur Wandkarte von Afrika. Wien, 1882.
Afr 3198.82 DeLeon, E. Egypt under its khedives. London, 1882.
Afr 8658.82.4 Dixie, Florence. In the land of misfortune. London, 1882.
Afr 1608.81.3 Durier, C. Une excursion au Maroc. Paris, 1882.
Afr 8252.12 Durnford, E. A soldiers life and work in South Africa 1872-1879. London, 1882.
Afr 8658.82 Duval, C. With a show through southern Africa. London, 1882. 2v.
Afr 2230.11 Farine, Charles. Kabyles et Kroumirs. Paris, 1882.
Afr 108.82 Hahn, T. Early African exploration up to the 16th century. Cape Town, 1882.
Afr 2945.1 Haimann, G. Cirenaica. Roma, 1882.
Afr 3275.3 Harrison, F. The crisis in Egypt, a letter to Mr. Gladstone. London, 1882.
Afr 9148.82 Heckford, S. A lady trader in the Transvaal. London, 1882.
Afr 2608.82 Hesse-Wartegg, E. Tunis. N.Y., 1882.
Afr 1738.4 Howard-Vyse, L. A winter in Tangier. London, 1882.
Afr 3258.16F Illustriret Familie-Journals. Krigen i Aegypten. Pt.1-3. Kjøbenhavn, 1882.
Afr 4746.10F Italy. Assab et les limites de la souveraineté turco-égyptienne dans la Mer Rouge. Rome, 1882.

1882 - cont.

Afr 4025.20.10 Italy. Ministero degli Affari Esteri. Sulla politica italiana inEgitto. Roma, 1882.
Afr 4730.3 Italy. Ministero di Affari Esteri. La colonia italiana di Assab. Roma, 1882.
Afr 2608.82.10F Itinéraires en Tunisie, 1881-82. Pt.1-2 and tables. Paris, 1882.
Afr 8155.7 Jenkinson, T.B. Amazulu. The Zulus, their history. London, 1882.
Afr 3243.4.2 Keay, J.S. Spoiling the Egyptians. N.Y., 1882.
Afr 8160.13 Laurence, W.M. Selected writings. Grahamstown, 1882.
Afr 8658.80.6 Leyland, Ralph W. A holiday in South Africa. London, 1882.
Afr 555.22.89 Livingston Inland Mission. Manual of the principles and practice. London, 1882.
Afr 9598.82 Macdonald, D. Africana or the heart of heathen Africa. London, 1882. 2v.
Afr 28.2 Paulitschke, P. Die Afrika-Literatur in der Zeit von 1500 bis 1750 N. Ch. Wien, 1882.
Afr 3275.24 Pierre l'Ermite. Brigands in Egypt. London, 1882.
Afr 4098.2 Poole, R.S. The cities of Egypt. London, 1882.
Afr 2748.82.7 Rabourdin, L. Algérie et Sahara. Paris, 1882.
Afr 3258.3 Retrospect of the war in Egypt. London, 1882.
Afr 4785.12 Revoil, G.E.J. La vallé du Darrar. Paris, 1882.
Afr 5235.180 Sanderval, A.O., vicomte de. De l'Atlantique au Niger par le Foutah-Djallon. Paris, 1882.
Afr 3978.82 Senior, N.W. Conversations and journals in Egypt. London, 1882. 2v.
Afr 8028.1 Theal, G.M. Notes upon books referring to South Africa. Cape Town, 1882.
Afr 2208.82 Wahl, M. L'Algérie. Paris, 1882.
Afr 9093.15 Weilbach, J.D. Geschiedenis van de emigranten-boeren en van den vrijheids-oorlog. Kaapstad, 1882.
Afr 9049.8 Wilkinson. A lady's life and travels in Zululand. London, 1882.
Afr 6535.3 Wilson, C.F. Uganda and Eyptian Sudan. London, 1882. 2v.

1883

Afr 4558.83.5 Abargues de Sosten, J.V. Notas del viaje por Etiopia. Madrid, 1883.
Afr 8252.14 Afrikaander. Amsterdam, 1883.
Afr 1258.83 Algarate, I.A. Memoria sobre nuestro poder militar. Madrid, 1883.
Afr 2025.21 Algeria. Gouverneur Général. Etat de l'Algérie au 31 dec. 1882. Alger, 1883.
Afr 2628.2 Antichan, P.H. Le pays des Khroumirs. Paris, 1883.
Afr 8686.2 Arnot, Frederick Stanley. From Natal to the Upper Zambesi. 2. ed. Glasgow, 1883.
Afr 5748.83 Audebert, J. Madagaskar und das Hovareich. Berlin, 1883.
Afr 4558.67.6 Baker, S.W. The Nile tributaries of Abyssinia. London, 1883.
Afr 8857.5 Basutoland records. Cape Town, 1883. 3v.
Afr 3265.5 Baynes, K.S. Narrative of the part taken by the 79th Queen's Own Cameron Highlanders, in the Egyptian campaign, 1882. London, 1883.
Afr 4610.4F Bremond, L.A. Expedition scientifique et commerciale au...Choa...Gallas. Paris, 1883.
Afr 2748.82.4 Brosselard-Faidherbe, H. Voyage de la mission Flatters au pays des Touareg Azdjers. Paris, 1883.
Afr 5748.83.10 Buet, Charles. Madagascar, la reine des iles africaines. Paris, 1883.
Afr 6192.13 Burton, R.F. To the Gold Coast for gold. London, 1883. 2v.
Afr 2208.83.9 Clamageran, J.J. L'Algérie, impressions de voyage. 2e ed. Paris, 1883.
Afr 2458.83 Clarin de la Rive, Abel. Histoire générale de la Tunisie. Tunis, 1883.
Afr 5748.83.5 Cremazy, L. Notes sur Madagascar. Pt.1-3. Paris, 1883-84.
Afr 5794.6 Deblenne, Paul. Essai de géographie medicale de Nosi-Bé. Thèse. Paris, 1883.
Afr 4886.7 Denis de Rivoyre, B.L. Obock, Mascate, Bouchire, Bassorah. Paris, 1883.
Afr 555.22.3 Depelchin, H. Trois ans dans l'Afrique australe. Bruxelles, 1883.
Afr 698.83 Devic, L. Marcel. Le pays des Zendjs. Paris, 1883.
Afr 8145.10 Edwards, John. Reminiscences of the early life and missionary labours of John Edwards. Grahamstown, 1883.
Afr 3269.08F France. Ministère des Affaires Etrangères. Documents diplomatiques. Paris, 1883.
Afr 5620.2F France. Ministère des Affaires Etrangeres. Documents diplomatiques. Paris, 1883. 4 pam.
Afr 2208.83 Gaffarel, P. L'Algérie. Paris, 1883.
Afr 3245.5 Giffard, Pierre. Les Français en Egypte. 2. ed. Paris, 1883.
Afr 3978.82.5 Girard, B. Souvenirs d'une campagne dans le Heraut. Paris, 1883.
Afr 855.3 Grant, B. A few notes on St. Helena. St. Helena, 1883.
Afr 8849.7 Gray, C.N. Life of Robert Gray. London, 1883.
Afr 4558.83.3 Hartmann, R. Abyssinien und die übrigen Gebiete des Afrikas. Leipzig, 1883.
Afr 3269.10 Italy. Ministero degli Affari Esteriore. Documenti diplomatici relativi alle indennità per danni sofferti. Roma, 1883.
Afr 3978.83.4 James, F.L. The wild tribes of the Soudan. London, 1883.
Afr 3978.82.10 Knox, T.W. The boy travellers in the Far East. Pt. 4 - Egypt and the Holy Land. N.Y., 1883.
Afr 7560.3.2 Lopes, D. Le Congo. Bruxelles, 1883.
Afr 3978.83.7 Malanco, Luis. Viaje a oriente. Mexico, 1883. 2v.
Afr 3198.83 Malortie, Karl. Egypt: native rulers and foreign interference. 2nd ed. London, 1883.
Afr 5747.31.10 Marcel, G. Memoire inédit de Grossin sur Madagascar. Paris, 1883.
Afr 2025.2 Marial, W. La France d'Afrique et ses destinées. Paris, 1883.
Afr 2208.83.5 Mercier, E. L'Algérie. Paris, 1883.
Afr 555.4.2 Mettetal, A. Le péril du protestantisme en Algérie. Paris, 1883.
Afr 2608.83 Michel, L. Tunis. Paris, 1883.
Afr 4070.13 Munzinger, W. Ostafrikanische Studien. Basle, 1883.
Afr 2208.83.7 Niel, O. Algérie, géographie générale. 3e ed. Paris, 1883.
Afr 9028.83 Peace, Walter. Our colony of Natal. London, 1883.
Afr 7010.2 Portugal. Ministère de la Marine et des Colonies. Droits de patronage du Portugal en Afrique. Lisbonne, 1883.
Afr 7010.6 Portugal. Ministério da Marinha e Ultramar. Direitos de padroado de Portugal em Africa; memoranda. Lisboa, 1883.

1883 - cont.

	Afr 8690.25	Ridsdale, Benjamin. Scenes and adventures in great Namaqualand. London, 1883.
	Afr 4558.83	Rohlfs, G. Meine Mission nach Abessinien. Leipzig, 1883.
	Afr 2280.12	Roudaire, F.E. La mer intérieure africaine. Paris, 1883.
	Afr 555.9.10	Rowley, Henry. Twenty years in Central Africa. 3d ed. London, 1883.
	Afr 5235.180.2	Sanderval, A.O., vicomte de. De l'Atlantique au Niger. Paris, 1883.
	Afr 1915.4	Stein, H. Un dessein français sur Alger et Tunis. n.p., 1883.
	Afr 3978.83	Stuart, H.V. Egypt after the war. London, 1883.
	Afr 3978.83.3	Stuart, H.V. Egypt after the war. London, 1883.
	Afr 7565.16	Twiss, Travers. An international protectorate of the Congo River. London, 1883.
	Afr 3978.83.10	Vaujany, H. Le Caire et ses environs. Paris, 1883.
	Afr 3258.4	Vogt, H. The Egyptian war of 1882. London, 1883.
	Afr 3243.5	Wallace, D.M. Egypt and the Egyptian question. London, 1883.

1884

	Afr 3255.3	Bell, C.F.M. Khedives and pashas. London, 1884.
	Afr 125.5	Berlioux, E.F. La terre habitable vers l'équator. Paris, 1884.
X Cg	Afr 3267.1	Broadley, S.M. How we defended Arabi. London, 1884.
	Afr 5748.84.10	Buet, Charles. Six mois à Madagascar. Paris, 1884.
	Afr 3708.5	Burleigh, B. Desert warfare, being the chronicle of the Eastern Soudan campaign. London, 1884.
	Afr 1573.7	Carvajal, Jose de. España y Marruecos. Madrid, 1884.
	Afr 5548.84.10	Castonnet des Fosses, H. Madagascar. Paris, 1884. 2 pam.
	Afr 1573.13	Coello y Quesada, Francisco. Intereses de España en Marruecos. Madrid, 1884.
	Afr 8163.2	Colenso, Frances Ellen. The ruin of Zululand, an account of British doings in Zululand since the invasion of 1879. London, 1884-85. 2v.
	Afr 1608.80.05	Conring, A. von. Marroco, das Land und die Leute. Berlin, 1884.
	Afr 8252.4	Cowen, Charles. Charles Tennant Jones, M.L.A., and our government. Wynberg, 1884.
	Afr 8252.3	Cowen, Charles. The honorable Lt. Col. Frederick Schermbrucker, M.L.C., at the Cape of Good Hope. Wynberg, 1884.
	Afr 5538.3	Cremazy, P. Notice bibliographique sur Madagascar. St. Denis, 1884.
	Afr 5406.181	Dietz, Emile. Un explorateur africain, Auguste Stahl. Paris, 1884.
	Afr 5405.109	Drohojowska, Antoinette J.F.A. M. Savorgnan de Brazza. Lille, 1884.
	Afr 3705.16	Egyptian red book. Edinburgh, 1884.
	Afr 5548.84.5	Escamps, H. D. Histoire et geographie de Madagascar. Paris, 1884.
	Afr 555.13	Foster, L.R. Historical sketch - African mission. N.Y., 1884.
	Afr 3269.1F	France. Ministère des Affaires Etrangères. Affaires d'Egypte 1884. Paris, 1884.
	Afr 2702.2F	France. Ministère des Travaux Publiques. Documents rel. à miss. par Flatters. Paris, 1884.
	Afr 2280.5	Fromentin, E. Une année dans le Sahel. 6th ed. Paris, 1884.
	Afr 1750.1	Galindo y de Vera. Historia vicisitudes y politica...respecto de sus posesiones en las costas de Africa. Madrid, 1884.
	Afr 4070.5	Great Britain. Intelligence. Report on Sudan. London, 1884.
	Afr 1955.14	Grieu, R. de. Le duc d'Aumale et l'Algérie. Paris, 1884.
	Afr 6192.17	Gros, Jules. Voyages, aventures et captivité de J. Bonnat chez les Achantis. Paris, 1884.
	Afr 3243.6	Hennebert, E. Les Anglais en Egypte. Paris, 1884.
	Afr 2510.5	Italy. Ministero degli Affari Esteri. Intorno ai provvedimenti relativi alla giurisdizione consolare italiana in Tunisia. Roma, 1884.
	Afr 7808.84	Johnston, H.H. The river Congo. London, 1884.
	Afr 608.84	Johnston, K. Africa. 3d ed. London, 1884.
	Afr 11051.2	Klaas Gezwint en zijn paert and other songs and rijmpjes of South Africa. Cape Town, 1884.
	Afr 9598.84.5	Knox, T.W. The boy travellers in the Far East. N.Y., 1884.
	Afr 3978.84F	Lane-Poole, S. Social life in Egypt. London, 1884.
	Afr 5548.84	Lavaissiere, C. De. Histoire de Madagascar. Paris, 1884.
	Afr 5748.84	Leroy, L. Les Français à Madagascar. Paris, 1884.
	Afr 5748.84.5	Little, H. William. Madagascar, its history and people. Edinburgh, 1884.
	Afr 555.23	London. Baptist Mission Society. Rise and progress of work on Congo river. London, 1884.
	Afr 3255.5	Long, C.C. The three prophets. N.Y., 1884.
X Cg	Afr 3230.6	Loring, W.W. A Confederate soldier in Egypt. N.Y., 1884.
	Afr 3823.4	Lupton, Frank. Geographical observations in the Bahr-el-Ghazal region. London, 1884.
	Afr 9388.84	Mackenzie, John. Day dawn in dark places. London, 1884.
	Afr 5748.84.7	Macquarie, J.L. Voyage à Madagascar. Paris, 1884.
	Afr 9598.84	Maps. Africa, South (1884). Notes on geography of south central Africa. London, 1884.
	Afr 2674.2	Naceur. Description et histoire de l'île de Djerba. Tunis, 1884.
	Afr 2208.84	Niox, G.L. Algérie. Paris, 1884.
	Afr 3705.4	Pall Mall Gazette, London. Who is to have the Soudan? London, 1884.
	Afr 2748.82.3	Patorni, F. Récits faits par 3 survivants de la mission Flatters. Constantine, 1884.
	Afr 5548.84.15	Pauliat, Louis. Madagascar. Paris, 1884.
	Afr 1925.5	Playfair, R.L. The scourge of Christendom. London, 1884.
	Afr 7010.3	Portugal et la France au Congo. Paris, 1884.
	Afr 6738.41	Reicheon, Anton. Die deutsche Kolonie Kamerun. Berlin, 1884.
	Afr 2208.84.2	Reuss, L.M. A travers l'Algérie. Paris, 1884.
	Afr 575.12	Rinn, Louis. Marabouts et Khorean. Alger, 1884.
	Afr 2232.1	Robin. Le Mzab et son annexion. Alger, 1884.
	Afr 1955.2	Roches, Léon. Trente-deux ans à travers l'islam (1832-64). Paris, 1884.
	Afr 1608.64	Rohlfs, G. Reise durch Marokko. Norden, 1884.
	Afr 4558.84	Russel, S. Une mission en Abyssinie. Paris, 1884.
	Afr 3285.2	Saint-Martin, H. de. La question égyptienne et l'Italie. Florence, 1884.
	Afr 8735.5.5	Sheffield, T. The story of the settlement with a sketch of Grahamstown as it was. 2d ed. Grahamstown, 1884.

1884 - cont.

	Afr 530.7	Sorela, Luis. Alemania en Africa. Berlin, 1884.
	Afr 5960.6	Sorela, Luis. Les possessions espagñoles du Golfe de Guinée, leur présent et leur avenir. Paris, 1884.
	Afr 4070.19	Speedy, C.M. My wanderings in the Soudan. London, 1884. 2v.
	Afr 3046.5.3	Stone, Charles. P. Asuntos militares en Egipto. Habana, 1884.
	Afr 3265.2	Stone, Fanny. Diary of an American girl in Cairo, 1882. N.Y., 1884.
	Afr 3675.2	Syndham, Q. The Soudan. London, 1884.
	Afr 2748.84	Trip to the great Sahara. London, 1884.
	Afr 4070.7	Williams, J. Life in the Soudan. London, 1884.
	Afr 2753.2	Wolff, H. Les régiments de dromadaires. Paris, 1884.

1885

	Afr 2274.1	Aumerat, J.F. L'anti-sémitisme à Alger. Alger, 1885.
	Afr 5318.12	Baudin, P.N. Fetichism and fetich worshipers. N.Y., 1885.
	Afr 8225.5	Bellairs, Blanche St. John. The Transvaal war 1880-81. Edinburg, 1885.
	Afr 7565.12.5F	Berlin. Conference, 1884-85. Protocoles et acte général de la Conférence de Berlin, 1884-85. n.p., 1885.
	Afr 2608.85	Boddy, A.A. To Kairwan the Holy. London, 1885.
	Afr 9225.10	Boon, M.J. The history of the Orange Free State. London, 1885.
	Afr 8088.85.5	Boon, Martin J. The immortal history of South Africa. London, 1885.
	Afr 590.28	Bouche, P.B. Sept ans en Afrique occidentale, la côte des esclaves. Paris, 1885.
	Afr 3708.8	Brackenbury, H. The river column. Edinburgh, 1885.
	Afr 9838.85	Buchanan, J. The Shire Highlands. Edinburgh, 1885.
	Afr 5048.5	Burdo, A. Les Arabs dans l'Afrique centrale. Paris, 1885.
	Afr 2608.85.7	Cambon, Victor. De Bone à Tunis. Lyon, 1885.
	Afr 1608.85.8	Cervera Baviera, J. Expedicion geografico-militar...Marruecos. Barcelona, 1885.
	Afr 3710.3.2	Colborne, J. With Hicks Pasha in the Soudan. 2d ed. London, 1885.
	Afr 852.2	Ellis, A.B. West African islands. London, 1885.
	Afr 3269.3F	France. Ministère des Affaires Etrangères. Documents diplomatiques. Paris, 1885. 5 pam.
	Afr 5402.10F	France. Ministère des Affaires Etrangères. Documents diplomatiques. Paris, 1885.
	Afr 5406.185	Franche, Lucien. Les possessions françaises du...Congo. Paris, 1885.
	Afr 5235.181	Gallieni, J.S. Mission d'exploration du Haut-Niger. Paris, 1885.
	Afr 1750.14	Gimenez, S. Espana en el Africa septentrional. Madrid, 1885.
	Afr 3705.3.10F	Gordon, C.G. General Gordon's last journal. London, 1885.
	Afr 3705.3A	Gordon, C.G. Journals at Khartoum. Boston, 1885.
	Afr 3705.3.5	Gordon, C.G. The journals of Major General Gordon. London, 1885.
	Afr 8088.85	Greswell, W. Our South African empire. London, 1885. 2v.
	Afr 3245.3	Guillon, E. L'Egypte contemporaine et intérêts français. Grenoble, 1885.
	Afr 3700.12	Haultain, T.A. The war in the Soudan. Toronto, 1885.
	Afr 30.5	Heichen, Paul. Afrika Hand-Lexicon. Leipzig, 1885-86.
	Afr 5585.8	Hue, Fernand. La France et l'Angleterre à Madagascar. Paris, 1885. 2 pam.
	Afr 7565.10F	Italy. Ministero degli Affari Esteri. Documenti diplomatici presentati al senato. Roma, 1885.
Htn	Afr 2850.12.5*	Italy. Ministero della Marina. Le condizioni militari della Tripolitania. Rome, 1885.
Htn	Afr 2850.12.10*	Italy. Ministero della Marina. Relazione sulla visita fatta dalla R. Corvetta Vettor Pisani alla baia di Tobruch e Dernah. Rome, 1885.
Htn	Afr 4730.4F*	Italy. Ministero di Affari Esteri. Beilul-Zula-Massaua-Sudan. Rome, 1885.
	Afr 3708.14	Jackson, Louis. Our Caughnawagas in Egypt. Montreal, 1885.
	Afr 4968.85	James, F.L. Journey through the Somali country. London, 1885.
	Afr 6887.3	Johnston, H.H. The Kilima-njaro expedition. London, 1885.
	Afr 7565.12	Jooris, J. L'acte général de la Conférence de Berlin. Bruxelles, 1885.
	Afr 2748.85	Lagarde, Charles. Une promenade dans le Sahara. Paris, 1885.
	Afr 5765.7.25	Lamaigniere. Le R.P. Barbe de la compagnie de Jesus. Poitiers, 1885.
	Afr 5748.85	Lavaissiere, C. de. Vingt ans à Madagascar. Paris, 1885.
	Afr 4388.12	Mancini, P.S. Dichiarazioni...intorno all'eccidio di G. Bianchi. Roma, 1885.
	Afr 4389.12	Maneini, P.S. Dichiarazioni...all'eccedio del viaggiatore Gustavo Bianchi. Roma, 1885.
	Afr 4368.5F	Massaja, E.G. Missione nell'alta Etiopia. Roma, 1885. 6v.
Htn	Afr 8657.85*	Mentzel, O. Beschreibung des Vorgebirges der Guten Hoffnung. Glogau, 1885-87. 2v.
	Afr 1868.85	Mohammed Abou Ras. Voyages extraordinaires. Alger, 1885.
	Afr 1965.22	Montagnac, L.F. Lettres d'un soldat. Paris, 1885.
	Afr 2331.1	Motylinski, A. de C. Guerara depuis sa fondation. Alger, 1885.
	Afr 8210.3	Nixon, John. The complete story of the Transvaal. London, 1885.
	Afr 5625.2.5	Oliver, S. Pasfield. French operations in Madagascar, 1883-1885. London, 1885-86. 2 pam.
	Afr 5625.2	Oliver, S. Pasfield. True story of the French dispute in Madagascar. London, 1885.
	Afr 7548.85	Patzig, Carl Albrecht. Die afrikanische Konferenz und der Kongostaat. Heidelberg, 1885.
	Afr 2220.6	Piesse, L. Itinéraire de l'Algérie. Paris, 1885.
	Afr 3700.20	Pimblett, W. Melville. Story of the Soudan war. London, 1885.
	Afr 4070.9.5	Policy for the eastern Soudan. Biarritz, 1885.
	Afr 3705.7	Power, Frank. Letters from Khartoum. London, 1885.
	Afr 3705.7.2	Power, Frank. Letters from Khartoum. 3d ed. London, 1885.
	Afr 4730.2	Rawson, R.W. European territorial claims on the Red Sea. London, 1885.
	Afr 4115.7	Reclus, E. Nouvelle géographie. Cairo. Paris, 1885.
	Afr 1018.1.5	Revue africaine. Table générale 1856-1881, 1882-1921. Algiers, 1885-1924. 2v.
	Afr 115.3.5	Ribeiro, M.F. Homenagem aõs herões que precederam. Lisboa, 1885.
	Afr 4070.30	Rivoyre, D. De. Aux pays du Soudan, Bagos, Mensah, Souakim. Paris, 1885.
	Afr 4558.83.2	Rohlfs, G. L'Abissinia. Milano, 1885.

1885 - cont.

Afr 1608.72.3 Rohlfs, G. Mein ersten aufenthalt in Morokko. Norden, 1885.
Afr 2928.85 Rohlfs, G. Von Tripolis nach Alexandrien. Norden, 1885.
Afr 5585.10 Saillens, R. Nos droits sur Madagascar. Paris, 1885.
Afr 855.12 St. Helena. Extracts from the St. Helena records. St. Helena, 1885.
Afr 5548.85 Shaw, George A. Madagascar and France. London, 1885.
Afr 5530.1 Sibree, J. A Madagascar bibliography. Antananarivo, 1885.
Afr 5530.1.5 Sibree, J. A Madagascar bibliography. Mss. Additions and corrections. Antananarivo, 1885.
Afr 4558.85 Simon, Gabriel. Voyage en Abyssinie et chez les Gallas-Raias. Paris, 1885.
NEDL Afr 7808.85 Stanley, H.M. The Congo. London, 1885. 2v.
Afr 7808.85.5 Stanley, H.M. The Congo. v.1-2. N.Y., 1885.
Afr 5185.4 Tautain, L. Sur l'ethnologie...du Sénégal. Paris, 1885.
Afr 6455.3.5 Thomson, J. Through Masai land. London, 1885.
Afr 7368.85 Wauwermans, H. Les premices de l'oeuvre d'émancipation africaine. Liberia. Bruxelles, 1885.
Afr 3708.3.2 Wilson, C.W. From Korti to Khartum. Edinburgh, 1885.
Afr 6645.17 Zoeller, Hugo. Die deutschen Besitzungen an der westafricanischen Küste. v.1-4. Berlin, 1885. 2v.

1886

Afr 1400.2 Aljaiyani. Le Maroc de 1631 à 1812. Paris, 1886.
Afr 3155.2F Amari, M. De titoli che usava la cancelleria de sultani di Egitto. Roma, 1886.
Afr 5054.10.5 Ancelle, Jules. Les explorations au Sénégal et dans les contrées voisines. Paris, 1886.
Afr 4558.67.7 Baker, S.W. The Nile tributaries of Abyssinia. London, 1886.
Afr 1868.86 Bardon, Xavier. Histoire nationale de l'Algérie. Paris, 1886.
Afr 530.36 Belges dans l'Afrique centrale. Bruxelles, 1886. 3v.
Afr 2527.5 Bois, M. Expédition française en Tunisie (1881-82). Paris, 1886.
Afr 7332.5 Brandao Cro de Castro Ferreri, Alfredo. Apontamentos de um ex-governador de Sofalla. Lisboa, 1886.
Afr 6275.12 Burda, A. Am Niger und Benue. Leipzig, 1886.
Afr 4515.1 Caix de St. Aymour. Histoire des relations de la France avec abyssinie. Paris, 1886.
Afr 1608.86.5 Campos, L. de. Un empire qui croule. Paris, 1886.
Afr 718.42 Capello, H. Da Angola a Contra-Costa. v.I,II. Lisboa, 1886. 2v.
Afr 1575.5 Castonnet Des Fosses, H. Les Portugais au Maroc. Paris, 1886.
Afr 4610.3 Cecchi, A. Da Zeila alle frontiere del Caffa. Roma, 1886-87. 3v.
Afr 9558.36 Charles, Elizabeth. Three martyrs of the nineteenth century... Livingstone, Gordon, and Patteson. N.Y., 1886.
Afr 7808.86 Conférences sur le Congo. Bruxelles, 1886.
Afr 500.5 De Leon, D. The West African question. n.p., 1886.
Afr 7808.86.2F Dewinton, F.W. The Congo Free State. London, 1886.
Afr 678.86 Donacuige. Aventuras de un piloto en el Golfo de Guinea. Madrid, 1886.
Afr 4557.90.30 Drohojowska, Antoinette Joséphine Françoise Anne. L'Abyssinie d'après James Bruce et les voyageurs contemporains. Lille, 1886.
Afr 8160.7 Dunn, John. Cetywayo and the three generals. Pietermaritzburg, 1886.
Afr 1608.86 Duveyrier, H. De Tanger a fas et meknas en 1885. Paris, 1886.
Afr 3978.86 Ebers, G. Cicerone durch das Süd und Nord Agypten. Stuttgart, 1886.
Afr 6760.7 Fabri, F. Deutsch-Ostafrica. Köln, 1886.
X Cg Afr 9388.86 Farini, G.A. Through the Kalahari desert. London, 1886. (Changed to XP 3879)
Afr 2608.86 Fournel, M. La Tunisie. Paris, 1886.
Afr 5748.86.5 Genin, E. Madagascar. Paris, 1886.
Afr 8658.86.5 Gillmore, Parker. The hunter's arcadia. London, 1886.
Afr 5832.5 Grant, Charles. Letters from Mauritius in 18th century. Mauritius, 1886.
Afr 555.11 Guerin, V. La France catholique en Tunisie. Tours, 1886.
Afr 2945.1.2 Haimann, G. Cirenaica. 2a ed. Milan, 1886.
Afr 5548.86.5 Hartmann, R. Madagascar und die Inseln Seychellen. Leipzig, 1886.
Afr 3252.5 Holynski, A. Nubar-Pacha devant l'histoire. Paris, 1886.
Afr 6878.86 Hore, Annie B. To Lake Tanganyika in a bath chair. London, 1886.
Afr 1608.87.3 Horowitz, V.J. Marokko. Leipzig, 1886.
Afr 2225.2 Houdas, O. Ethnographie de l'Algérie. Paris, 1886.
Afr 3026.1 Ibrahim-Hilmy. The literature of Egypt. London, 1886. 2v.
Afr 5993.6 Janikowski, L. L'île de Fernando Poo. Paris, 1886.
Afr 5406.186 Jeannest, Charles. Quatre années au Congo. Paris, 1886.
Afr 8658.86 Kerr, W.M. The far interior. London, 1886. 2v.
Afr 3708.10 Labat, G.P. Les voyageurs canadiens à l'expédition du Soudan. Québec, 1886.
Afr 5054.10.2 Lebrun-Renaud, C.G.N. Les possessions françaises de l'Afrique occidentale. 2e éd. Paris, 1886.
Afr 5247.15 Lenz, Oscar. Timbouctou. Paris, 1886-87. 2v.
Afr 1608.86.8 Mackenzie, Don. Report on the condition...empire of Morocco. London, 1886.
Afr 1409.4 Marchesi, V. Le relazioni tra la repubblica Veneta ed il Marocco dal 1750 al 1797. Torino, 1886.
Afr 2300.4 Masqueray, E. Formation des cités chez les populations sédentaires de l'Algérie. Paris, 1886.
Afr 530.34 Mayor, D.R.W. De rebus Africanis. London, 1886.
Afr 8808.86 Noble, John. History, productions and resources of Cape of Good Hope. Cape Town, 1886.
NEDL Afr 8808.86.2 Noble, John. History, productions and resources of the Cape of Good Hope. Cape Town, 1886.
Afr 5548.86 Oliver, S.P. Madagascar. London, 1886. 2v.
Afr 1608.86.10 Ovilo y Canales, D.F. La mujer marroqui. Nueva edicion. Madrid, 1886.
Afr 5748.86 Pastel, R. Madagascar. Paris, 1886.
Afr 5570.1 Pauliat, L. Louis XIV et la campagnie des Indes Orient de 1664. Paris, 1886.
Afr 4558.80.20 Pesci, Dino. Esplorazioni in Africa di Gustavo Bianchi. Milano, 1886.
Afr 5580.2 Ponget de St. Andre. La colonisation de Madagascar sous Louis XV. Paris, 1886.
Afr 9838.84.2 Pringle, M. A journey in East Africa. Edinburgh, 1886.
Afr 1753.5 Relosillas, J.J. Catorce meses enCeuta. Malaga, 1886.
Afr 608.86 Rohlfs, G. Quid novi ex Africa. Cassel, 1886.
Afr 3258.5 Royle, C. The Egyptian campaigns, 1882-85. London, 1886. 2v.

1886 - cont.

Afr 6990.79 Scholl, Carl. Nach Kamerun. Leipzig, 1886.
Afr 4558.84.5 Soleillet, Paul. Voyages en Ethiopie jan. 1882-oct. 1884. Rouen, 1886.
Afr 1608.86.3 Stutfield, H.E.M. El Maghreb, 1200 miles ride through Marocco. London, 1886.
Afr 8868.5 Theal, G.M. A fragment of Basuto history. Cape Town, 1886.
Afr 550.40 Thompson, G. Africa in a nutshell for the millions. Oberlin, 1886.
Afr 6455.3.10 Thomson, Joseph. Au pays des Massai. Paris, 1886.
Afr 7568.30 Tisdel, W.P. Kongo. Leipzig, 1886.
Afr 3708.12F Verner, Willoughby. Sketches in the Soudan. 2d ed. London, 1886.
Afr 6275.11 Viard, E. Au Bas-Niger. 3. ed. Paris, 1886.
Afr 3198.86 Vingtrinier, A. Soliman-Pacha...guerres de l'Egypte. Paris, 1886.
Afr 4555.86A Waldmeier, T. Autobiography, account of ten years' life in Abyssinia. London, 1886.
Afr 3708.3 Wilson, C.W. From Korti to Khartum. Edinburgh, 1886.

1887

Afr 8658.87.7 Anderson, Andrew Arthur. Twenty-five years in the gold regions of Africa. London, 1887. 2v.
Afr 4386.8 Antona-Traversi, Camillo. Sahati e Dogali. Roma, 1887.
Afr 3258.6 Archer, T. War in Egypt and the Soudan. London, 1887. 2v.
Afr 7320.2 Ayres de Carvalho Soveral. Breve estudio,--ilha de Moçambique. Porto, 1887.
Afr 2608.87 Baraban, L. A travers la Tunisie. Paris, 1887.
Afr 1885.2 Barges, J.J.L. Complement de l'histoire des Beni-Zeiyan. Paris, 1887.
Afr 2208.87 Baudel, J. Un an à Alger. Paris, 1887.
Afr 7808.87 Bentley, William Holman. Life on the Congo. London, 1887.
Afr 8658.87.15 Bethell, Alfred J. Notes on South African hunting and notes on a ride to the Victoria Falls of the Zambesi. York, 1887.
Afr 9028.87 Blink, H. Door Natal in het hart van Zuid-Afrika. Amsterdam, 1887.
Afr 550.3 Blyden, E.W. Christianity, Islam and the Negro race. London, 1887.
Afr 2748.87 Bonelli, D.E. El Sahara. Madrid, 1887.
Afr 7368.87 Bourzeix, R.P.P. La république de Liberia. Paris, 1887.
Afr 3198.87 Bowen, J.E. Conflict of East and West in Egypt. N.Y., 1887.
Afr 5240.2 Bris, Alexis. Sénégal et Soudan. Paris, 1887.
Afr 3708.4 Butler, W.F. The campaign of the Cataracts. London, 1887.
Afr 4558.87 Cecchi, A. L'Abissinia settentrionale. Photoreproduction. Milano, 1887.
Afr 1608.87 Charmes, G. Une ambassade au Maroc. Paris, 1887.
Afr 4384.2 Chiala, L. Discorso sul credito di 20 milioni per l'azione militare in Africa. Roma, 1887.
Afr 7814.1 Congo Free State (1887). Carte de l'Etat. Bruxelles, 1887.
Afr 5045.7 Crouch, Archer P. On a surf-bound coast. London, 1887.
Afr 7093.5 Dennett, R.C. Seven years among the Fjort. London, 1887.
Afr 2230.18 Drouet, F. Grande-Kabylie. Les Beni Yenni. Rouen, 1887.
Afr 5748.87.5 Duverge. Madagascar et peuplades independantes abandonnées par la France. Paris, 1887.
Afr 8808.87 Ellis, A.B. South African sketches. London, 1887.
Afr 6194.3 Ellis, A.B. The Tshi-speaking peoples of the Gold Coast. London, 1887.
Afr 1258.87 Fallot, Ernest. Par dela la Méditerranée. Paris, 1887.
Afr 3275.5 Faris, Selim. Decline of British prestige in the East. London, 1887.
Afr 2928.87 Fournel, M. La Tripolitaine. Paris, 1887.
Afr 1960.5 Gaffarel, Paul. La conquête de l'Algérie jusqu'à la prise de Constantine. Paris, 1887.
Afr 3700.14 Galloway, W. The battle of Tofrek fought near Suakin. London, 1887.
Afr 1900.1 Grammont, H.D. Histoire d'Alger. Paris, 1887.
Afr 5235.179 Gravier, Gabriel. Paul Soleillet. Paris, 1887.
Afr 5548.87 Hue, Fernand. Le Français à Madagascar. Paris, 1887.
Afr 5920.1.5 Iradier, Manuel. Africa. Vitoria, 1887. 2v.
Afr 28.3 Kayser, G. Bibliographie de l'Afrique. Bruxelles, 1887.
Afr 698.86 Keller, Konrad. Reisebilder aus Ost-Afrika. Leipzig, 1887.
Afr 608.87 Lanier, L. L'Afrique, choix de lectures. 4th ed. Paris, 1887.
Afr 5760.3 Leclerc, Max. Les peuplades de Madagascar. Paris, 1887.
Afr 8105.35 Leilebrandt, Hendrik Carel von. Rambles through the archives of the colony of the Cape of Good Hope. Cape Town, 1887.
Afr 606.95.2 Lemaire. Les voyages du Sieur Lemaire. Edinburgh, 1887.
Afr 606.95.2.1 Lemaire. Voyages to the Canaries, Cape Verd and the coast of Africa. Edinburgh, 1887.
Afr 8658.84.2 Little, James S. South Africa. 2d ed. London, 1887.
Afr 3705.5 Macdonald, A. Too late for Gordon and Khartoum. London, 1887.
Afr 9388.87 Mackenzie, J. Austral Africa. London, 1887. 2v.
Afr 8658.87 Mackinnon, J. South African traits. Edinburgh, 1887.
Afr 44619.5 Madan, Arthur Cornwallis. Kiungani, or Story and history from Central Africa written by boys in the schools. London, 1887.
Afr 5625.4 Marield, J. La France à Madagascar. Paris, 1887.
Afr 8658.87.4 Matthews, J.W. Incwadi Yami, or twenty years' personal experience in South Africa. N.Y., 1887.
Afr 8235.6 Matthews, J.W. Incwadi Yami, twenty years in South Africa. London, 1887.
Afr 2608.84.2 Mayet, Valery. Voyage dans le sud de la Tunisie. 2e ed. Paris, 1887.
Afr 1608.85.5 Mercet, A. Marruecos. Madrid, 1887.
Afr 2274.3 Meynie, G. L'Algérie juive. Paris, 1887.
Afr 7560.4 Moynier, G. La fondation de l'état indépendant du Congo. Paris, 1887.
Afr 5868.87 Pajot, Elie. Simples renseignements sur l'Ile Bourbon. Paris, 1887.
Afr 2336.5.5 Papier, Alexander. Lettres sur Hippone. Bone, 1887.
Afr 6777.8 Peters, Karl. Deutsch-national. Berlin, 1887.
Afr 640.5 Quatrefages de Bréau, Armand de. Les Pygmées. Paris, 1887.
Afr 2650.2 Rouire, A.M.F. La découverte du bassin hydrographique de la Tunisie centrale. Paris, 1887.
Afr 1955.6.5 Rousset, C. Les commencements d'une conquête. Paris, 1887. 2v.

1887 - cont.

Afr 5405.109.30 Savorgnan de Brazza, Pierre. Conférences et lettres sur ses trois explorations dans l'ouest africain de 1875 à 1886. Paris, 1887.

Afr 3978.87.5 Sebah, P. Catalogue of views in Egypt and Nubia. Caire, 1887.

Afr 5748.87 Standing, H.F. The children of Madagascar. London, 1887.

Afr 8175.5 Theal, G.M. History of the Boers in South Africa. London, 1887.

Afr 2313.1 Trumelet, C. Blida. v.1-2. Alger, 1887.

Afr 2315.1 Trumelet, C. Bou-Farik. 2e ed. Alger, 1887.

Afr 7175.8 Veth, Pieter J. Daniel Veths reizer in Angola. Haarlem, 1887.

Afr 1915.6 Wahl, Maurice. L'Algérie et alliance française. Bordeaux, 1887.

Afr 9405.6 Wesleyan Methodist Missionary Society. Affairs of Bechuanaland. London, 1887.

1888

Afr 3180.5 Abd-el-Rahman, Cheikh. Merveilles biographiques et historiques ou chroniques. Paris 1888. 8v.

X Cg Afr 3180.5 Abd-el-Rahman, Cheikh. Merveilles biographiques et historiques ou chroniques. v.9. Paris, 1888.

Afr 2232.2 Amat, C. Le Mzab et les Mzabites. Paris, 1888.

Afr 8658.87.8 Anderson, Andrew Arthur. Twenty-five years in a waggon. London, 1888.

Afr 2290.2 Association Française pour l'Avancement des Sciences. Oran et l'Algérie en 1887. Oran, 1888. 2v.

Afr 6143.18 Banbury, G.A.L. Sierra Leone, or The white man's grave. London, 1888.

Afr 200.2 Banning, E. Le partage politique de l'Afrique. Bruxelles, 1888.

Afr 6095.18 Barret, P.M.V. Sénégambie et Guinée...l'Afrique occidentale. Paris, 1888. 2v.

Afr 5993.12 Baumann, O. Eine afrikanische Tropeninsel. Wien, 1888.

Afr 8190.5 Bird, John. Annals of Natal 1495-1845. v.1 and index. Pietermaritzburg, 1888. 2v.

Afr 2762.2 Bissuel, H. Les Touareg de l'ouest. Algiers, 1888.

Afr 6878.88.10 Boehm, Richard. Von Sansibar zum Tanganjika. Leipzig, 1888.

Afr 2945.5 Borsari, F. Geografia etnologica e storica della Tripolitania, Cirenaica e Fezzan. Naples, 1888.

Afr 3675.3 Buchta, R. Der Sudan. Leipzig, 1888.

Afr 4375.3 Bussidon, C. Abyssinie et Angleterre (Theodoros). Paris, 1888.

Afr 1868.88 Cat, Edouard. Petite histoire de l'Algérie, Tunisie, Maroc. v.1-2. Alger, 1888-91. 2v.

Afr 4730.5 Chicala, L. La spedizione di Massaua. Torino, 1888.

Afr 7808.88.5 Coquilhat, Camille. Sur le Haut-Congo. Paris, 1888.

Afr 5748.87.10 Cortese, Emilio. Sei mesi al Madagascar. Roma, 1888.

Afr 8252.9 Cox, G.W. Life of John William Colenso. London, 1888. 2v.

Afr 5318.18.2 Doelter, C. Über die Capverden nach dem Rio Grande. Leipzig, 1888.

Afr 715.5 Drummond, Henry. Tropical Africa. N.Y., 1888.

Afr 698.88 Durand, E. Une exploration française au Zambèze. Paris, 1888.

Afr 1658.5 Duveyrier, H. La derniere partie...Littoral de la mediterranee-le Rif. Paris, 1888.

Afr 4339.5 Esteves Pereira, F.M. Historia de Minás, Además Sagad, rei de Ethiopia. Lisboa, 1888.

Afr 5180.28 Foret, Auguste. Un voyage dans le Haut-Sénégal. Paris, 1888.

Afr 1325.1F Foucauld, Charles de. Reconnaissance au Maroc. Paris, 1888. 2v.

Afr 1406.3 Francois d'Angers. L'histoire de la mission des pères capucins...à Maroc, 1624-1636. Rabat, 1888.

Afr 4386.5 Frassinesi, M.A. Primo anniversairio dei combattimenti di Saati e Dogali. Casale, 1888.

Afr 5218.88 Frey, H. Campagne dans le haut Sénégal et dans le haut Niger, 1885-86. Paris, 1888.

Afr 2208.88.3 Gaffarel, Paul. Lectures...sur l'Algérie. Paris, 1888.

Afr 9148.88 Gillmore, Parker. Days and nights by the desert. London, 1888.

Afr 3708.7 Gleichen, C. With the Camel Corps up the Nile. London, 1888.

Afr 5548.88 Guet, M.I. Les origines de l'Ile Bourbon. Paris, 1888.

Afr 8235.7 Haggard, H.R. Cetywayo and his white neighbours. London, 1888.

Afr 6878.88.5PF Hellgrewe, Rudolf. Aus Deutsch-Ost-Afrika. Berlin, 1888.

Afr 6685.2 Henrici, Ernst. Das deutsche Togogebiet und meine Afrikareise, 1887. Leipzig, 1888.

Afr 7368.88 Hodge, J.A. America and Africa. Washington, 1888.

Afr 608.88 Hubbard, G.G. Africa, its past and future. n.p., 1888.

Afr 4968.88 James, F.L. The unknown hour of Africa. London, 1888.

Afr 7565.5 Kassai, Pierre. La civilisation africaine, 1876-1888. Bruxelles, 1888.

Afr 2608.88 Kleist, H. Tunis und seine Umgebung. Leipzig, 1888.

Afr 8210.10 Kloessel, M.H. Die Südafrikanischen Republiken. Leipzig, 1888.

Afr 2748.88 Lara, Juan F. de. De la Peña al Sahara. Madrid, 1888.

Afr 590.2 Lavigerie, Charles Martial Allemand. Slavery in Africa, a speech. Boston, 1888.

Afr 5748.88 Lechartier, H. Madagascar depuis sa decouverte jusqu'a nos jours. Paris, 1888.

Afr 2020.1 Le Chatelier, A. Les Medaganat. Alger, 1888.

Afr 1068.88 Mercier, E. Histoire de l'Afrique septentrionale. Paris, 1888-91. 3v.

Afr 6887.1F Meyer, H. Zum Schneedom des Kilmandscharo. Berlin, 1888.

Afr 8088.88.14 Moodie, Duncan C.F. The history of the battles and adventures of the British. Cape Town, 1888. 2v.

Afr 7903.3 Myers, John Brown. Thomas J. Comber, missionary pioneer to the Congo. London, 1888.

Afr 4558.88.5 Parises, N. L'Abissinia. Milan, 1888.

Afr 4612.2 Paulitschke, P. Harrar. Leipzig, 1888.

Afr 6878.88 Pfeil, J.G. Vorschläge zur praktischen Kolonisation in Ost-Afrika. Berlin, 1888.

Afr 7175.42 Pinto, F.A. Angola e Congo. Lisboa, 1888.

Afr 1826.1 Playfair, R.L. Bibliography of Algeria and supplement. London, 1888.

Afr 5781.5 Pooka. Cinq jours à Tamatave. Maurice, 1888.

Afr 4509.17 Portal, G.H. An account of the English mission to King Johannis of Abyssinia in 1887. Winchester, 1888.

Afr 6585.6 Ruete, E. Memoirs of an Arabian princess. N.Y., 1888.

Afr 6585.2 Schmidt, K.W. Zanzibar. Leipzig, 1888.

1888 - cont.

Afr 5760.2 Schnackenberg, H. Beitrag zur ethnographie Madagaskars. Strassburg, 1888.

Afr 3725.3 Schnitzer, E. Emin Pasha in Central Africa. London, 1888.

Afr 6738.8.5 Schwarz, B. Kamerun, Reise in die Hinterlande der Kolonie. 2e Ausgabe. Leipzig, 1888.

Afr 2670.5 Servonnet, Jean. En Tunisie, le golfe de Gabès en 1888. Paris, 1888.

Afr 8658.88 Sheldon, L.V. Yankee girls in Zulu land. N.Y., 1888.

Afr 530.5 Soyaux, H. Deutsche Arbeit in Afrika. Leipzig, 1888.

Afr 520.2F Spain. Ministerio de Estado. Documentos diplomaticos. Madrid, 1888.

Afr 4025.20.15 Sterlich, R. de. Sugli italiani d'Egitto. Cairo, 1888.

Afr 590.19 Stevenson, J. Arabs in Central Africa and at Lake Nyassa. Glasgow, 1888.

Afr 1442.5 Taviel de Andrade, E. Cuestion de Marruecos. Madrid, 1888.

Afr 3978.88 Taylor, Isaac. Leaves from an Egyptian note-book. London, 1888.

Afr 1575.10 Testa, Carlos. Portugal e Marrocos perante a historia e a politica europea. Lisboa, 1888.

NEDL Afr 8088.88 Theal, G.M. History of South Africa. London, 1888- 5v.

Afr 5872.5 Trouette, E. L'Ile Bourbon de 1789 à 1803. Paris, 1888.

Afr 2208.88 Vignon, L. La France dans l'Afrique du nord. Paris, 1888.

Afr 2208.71.5 Villot, E. Moeurs, coutumes, de l'Algérie. 3e ed. Alger, 1888.

Afr 6777.4 Wagner, J. Deutsch-Ostafrika. 2. ed. Berlin, 1888.

NEDL Afr 3700.2 Wylde, A.B. Eighty-three to eighty-seven in the Soudan. London, 1888. 2v.

1889

Afr 5385.12 Albeca, A.L. Les établissements français du Golfe de Bénin. Paris, 1889.

Afr 4555.40.3F Alvares, Francisco. Verdadeiro informação das terras do Preste João das Indias. Lisboa, 1889.

Afr 7324.21 Araujo, Antonio José de. Os acontecimentos de Lourenço Marques. Lisboa, 1889.

Afr 6455.8.3 Arendt, Otto. Die Streit um die deutsche Emin Pascha Expedition. Berlin, 1889.

Afr 555.9.2 Arnot, Frederick Stanley. Garenganze, or Seven years in Central Africa. 2d ed. London, 1889.

Afr 2426.5 Ashbee, H.S. A bibliography of Tunisia...to 1888. London, 1889.

Afr 9838.89 Batalha Reis, Jayme. Os portuguezes na região do Nyassa. Lisboa, 1889.

Afr 7808.89.7 Bateman, C.S.L. The first ascent of the Kasai. London, 1889.

Afr 5235.189.10 Bechet, Eugène. Cinq ans de séjour au Soudan français. Paris, 1889.

Afr 608.89 Benko, J.F.V. Reise S.M. Schiffes. Albatros...Süd-Amerika dem Caplande und West Afrika, 1885-1886. Pola, 1889.

Afr 8658.89 Blink, Hendrik. Transvaal en omliggende landen. Amsterdam, 1889.

Afr 2748.82.5 Brosselard-Faidherbe, H. Les deux missions Flatters. 2e ed. Paris, 1889.

Afr 8167.5 Brownlee, Charles. A chapter on the Basuto war, a lecture. Lovedale, 1889.

Afr 115.7F Brunet, P. Les explorateurs de l'Afrique. Tours, 1889.

Afr 8808.89 Bryden, H.A. Kloof and Karoo...in Cape colony. London, 1889.

NEDL Afr 108.89 Buel, J.W. Heroes of the dark continent and How Stanley found Erwin Pasha. Philadelphia, 1889.

Afr 718.2.93 Burdo, Adolphe. Stanley, sa vie, ses voyages et ses aventures. Paris, 1889.

Afr 7322.4 Caldas Xavier, A. Estudos coloniaes. Lisboa, 1889.

Afr 718.47 Cameron, Verney Lovett. In savage Africa. London, 1889.

Afr 4368.5.3 Cenni biografici dell'eminentissimo Cardinale Guglielmo Massaja. Milan, 1889.

Afr 550.7 Clarke, R.F. Cardinal Lavigerie and African slave trade. London, 1889.

Afr 635.6 Clemente d'Assis, F. Estudos indianos e africanos. Lisboa, 1889.

Afr 3708.6 Colvile, H.E. History of the Sudan campaign. London, 1889. 3v.

Afr 4232.1F Corpus juris abessinorum. Berlin, 1889.

Afr 678.89 Crouch, A.P. Glimpses of Feverland. London, 1889.

Afr 590.10 Dias de Carvalho, H.A. L'influence de la civilisation latine et surtout portugais en Afrique. Lisbonne, 1889.

Afr 715.11 Drummond, Henry. Tropical Africa. 3rd ed. London, 1889.

Afr 510.4 Dumas, P. Les français d'Afrique. Paris, 1889.

Afr 7808.89 Dupont, C.F. Lettres sur le Congo. Paris, 1889.

Afr 3978.77.10 Edwards, A.B. A thousand miles up the Nile. 2d ed. London, 1889.

Afr 5118.89 Faidherbe, L.L.C. Le Sénégal. Paris, 1889.

Afr 6988.16.209 Galton, F. Narrative of an explorer in tropical South Africa. London, 1889.

Afr 5406.189 Guiral, Léon. Le Congo français du Gabon à Brazzaville. Paris, 1889.

Afr 1608.89 Harris, W.B. The land of an african sultan. London, 1889.

Afr 5842.18 Herve de Rauville. L'Ile de France légendaire. Paris, 1889.

Afr 6878.89 Hessel, Heinrich. Deutsche Kolonisation in Ostafrika. Bonn, 1889.

Afr 770.3 Hore, Edw.C. Lake Tanganyika. Photoreproduction. n.p., 1889.

Afr 5058.6 Hovelacque, Abel. Les Nègres de l'Afrique sus-équatoriale. Paris, 1889.

Afr 9558.38A Hughes, T. David Livingstone. London, 1889.

Afr 590.26 Johnston, H.H. The history of a slave. London, 1889.

Afr 608.89.4 Junker, Wilhelm. Reisen in Afrika, 1875-1878. Wien, 1889.

Afr 1608.89.3 Lamartiniere, H.M.P. de. Morocco. London, 1889.

Afr 7308.89 Lapa, Joaquim J. Elementos para um diccionario chorographico da provincia de Moçambique. Lisboa, 1889.

Afr 590.3 Lavigerie, Charles Martial Allemand. Documents sur la fond de l'oeuvre antiésclavagiste. Saint-Cloud, 1889.

Afr 3725.13 Little, H.W. One man's power. The life and work of Emin Pasha in Equatorial Africa. London, 1889.

Afr 7175.6 Marques, A.S. Os clinas e as producções...Malenge a Lunda. Lisboa, 1889.

Afr 2710.1 Mercier, E. La France dans le Sahara. Paris, 1889.

Afr 718.2.85 Montefiore, A. H.M. Stanley, the African explorer. London, 1889.

Afr 730.4 Mueller, W. Die Umsegelung Afrikas. Rathenau, 1889.

Afr 1400.1 Muhammed al-Segir. Nozhet-Elhadi, histoire de la dynastie saadienne au Maroc, (1511-1670). Paris, 1889.

1889 - cont.

Afr 7122.102 — Pereira, Alberto Feliciano Marques. Quadros chronologicos dos governadores geraes da provincia d'Angola. Loanda, 1889.

Afr 5235.189 — Peroz, Etienne. Au Soudan français. Paris, 1889.

Afr 6777.7 — Peters, Karl. Die Deutsche-Ostafrikanische Kolonie. Berlin, 1889.

Afr 2748.89 — Philebert, C. La conquête pacifique de l'intérieur africain. Paris, 1889.

Afr 7808.89.5 — Phillips, Henry. Account of the Congo Independent State. n.p., 1889.

X Cg Afr 2373.3 — Piesse, Louis. Les villes de l'Algérie, Tlemcen. Paris, 1889. (Changed to XP 3867)

Afr 1900.3 — Plantet, E. Correspondance des deys d'Alger, 1579-1833. Paris, 1889.

Afr 2804.1 — Playfair, R.L. Bibliography of the Barbary states. Pt.1. Tripoli and the Cyrenaica. London, 1889.

Afr 530.26 — Plebano, A. I possedimenti italiani in Africa. Roma, 1889.

Afr 7015.8 — Politica portugueza na Africa. Lisboa, 1889.

Afr 3725.11 — Prout, H.G. Where Emin is. n.p., 1889.

Afr 8100.20 — Quelques notes sur l'établissement et les travaux des Portugais au Monomotapa. Lisbonne, 1889.

Afr 7808.89.3 — Schynse, P.A. Zwei Jahre am Congo. Köln, 1889.

Afr 1608.89.5 — Sestri, J.A. de. Por todo marruecos descripcion del imperio. Barcelona, 1889.

Afr 1445.6F — Spain. Ministerio de Estado. Documentos presentados a las Cortes. Madrid, 1889.

Afr 1680.1 — Thomson, J. Travels in the atlas and southern Morocco. London, 1889.

Afr 718.15 — Werner, J.R. Visit to stanley s rear guard. Edinburg, 1889.

Afr 718.5 — Wissmann, H. Unter Deutsche Flagge quer durch Afrika. Berlin, 1889.

Afr 7808.89.2 — Wolff, W. Von Banana zum Kiammo. Oldenburg, 1889.

1890

Afr 1608.82.3 — Amicis, E. de. Morocco. Milano, 1890.

Afr 590.13 — Banning, E. La Conférence de Bruxelles. Bruxelles, 1890.

Afr 575.5 — Barnes, L.C. Shall Islam rule Africa? Boston, 1890.

Afr 718.14 — Barttelot, E.M. Life of E.M. Barttelot. London, 1890.

Afr 6888.3 — Baumann, Oscar. In Deutsch-Ostafrika wahrend Aufstandes. Wien, 1890.

Afr 2208.90 — Bergot, Raoul. L'Algérie telle qu'elle est. Paris, 1890.

Afr 8658.90 — Blink, Hendrik. De Zuid-Afrikaansche Republiek en hare bewoners. Amsterdam, 1890.

Afr 5832.3 — Bonaparte, R. Le premier établissement des Neerlandais à Maurice. Paris, 1890.

Afr 4605.1F — Borelli, Jules. Ethiopie meridionale, Amhara. Paris, 1890.

Afr 2208.90.3 — Bridgman, F.A. Winters in Algeria. London, 1890.

Afr 7458.90 — Buettikofer, J. Reisebilder aus Liberia. Leiden, 1890. 2v.

Afr 7320.4 — Castilho, S. de. La province portugaise de Mosambique. n.p., 1890.

Afr 825.4 — Cat, E. Notice sur la carte de l'Ogooue. Paris, 1890.

Afr 2208.88.5 — Deporter, Victor. A propos du Transsaharien. Alger, 1890.

Afr 7548.90 — Desoer, F. Le Congo belge. Liège, 1890.

Afr 7175.6.2 — Dias de Carvalho, H.A. Descripção da viagem a Mussumba do Muatianvua. v.1-4. Lisboa, 1890.

Afr 7175.6.3 — Dias de Carvalho, H.A. Ethnographia e historia tradicional dos povos da Lunda. Lisboa, 1890.

Afr 7183.35 — Dias de Carvalho, Henrique Augusto. Memoria: A. Lunda; ou, Os estados do Muatiânvua. Lisboa, 1890.

Afr 5406.50 — Duchaillu, Paul Belloni. Adventures in the great forest of Equatorial Africa. N.Y., 1890.

Afr 2685.1 — Dupaty de Clam, A. Fastes chronologiques de la ville de Sfaks. Paris, 1890.

Afr 2689.1 — Dupaty de Clam, A. Fastes chronologiques de Tozeur. Paris, 1890.

Afr 3978.77.11 — Edwards, A.B. A thousand miles up the Nile. London, 1890.

Afr 635.2 — Ellis, A.B. The Ewe-speaking peoples of the Slave Coast of West Africa. London, 1890.

Afr 5832.7 — Epinay, A.D. Renseignements pour servir l'histoire de l'Ile de France jusqu'à l'année 1810. Ile Maurice, 1890.

Afr 6275.10 — Flegel, C. Vom Niger-Benue. Leipzig, 1890.

Afr 6878.90 — Foerster, Brix. Deutsch-Ostafrika. Leipzig, 1890.

Afr 2748.90 — Foureau, F. Une mission au Tademayt. Paris, 1890.

Afr 590.13.5F — France. Ministère des Affaires Estrangères. Conférence international de Bruxelles, 18 nov. 1889-2 juil. 1890. v.1-3. Bruxelles, 1890.

Afr 33.10F — France. Ministère des Affaires Etrangères. Documents diplomatiques. Paris, 1890. 16 pam.

Afr 5180.26 — Gaffarel, Paul. La Sénégal et le Soudan français. Paris, 1890.

Afr 4730.1 — Geullot, M.E. La Mer Rouge et l'Abyssinie. Lille, 1890.

Afr 7328.2 — Gillmore, P. Through Gasa land. London, 1890.

Afr 7069.5 — Guinea, Portuguese. Governor. Relatório da provincia da Guiné Portugueza referido ao anno econômico de 1888-1889. Lisboa, 1890.

Afr 555.9.16 — Guinness, Fanny E. The new world of Central Africa. London, 1890.

Afr 718.2.99 — Headley, J.T. Stanley's adventures in the wilds of Africa. Philadelphia, 1890.

Afr 9488.90 — Holub, E. Von der Capstadt ins land der Maschukulunbe. Vienna, 1890. 2v.

Afr 4515.5F — Italy. Ministero degli Affairi Esteri. Documenti diplomatici presentati al parliamento italiano. Roma, 1890.

Afr 718.11 — Jameson, J.S. Story of the rear column. London, 1890.

Afr 608.90 — Junker, W. Travels in Africa. London, 1890-92. 3v.

Afr 200.12 — Kaltbrunner, David. L'Afrique en 1890. Paris, 1890.

Afr 550.8 — Klein, F. Le Cardinal Lavigerie et ses oeuvres africaines. Paris, 1890.

Afr 2425.1F — Lallemand, C. Tunis et ses environs. Paris, 1890.

Afr 5318.17 — Laumann, E.M. A la côte occidentale d'Afrique. Paris, 1890.

Afr 8088.90 — Lelu, Paul. Histoire de la colonie anglaise du Cap de Bonne-Espérance. Paris, 1890.

Afr 8678.17 — Macdonald, J. Light in Africa. London, 1890.

Afr 8830.5 — Martin, A. Home life on an ostrich farm. London, 1890.

Afr 810.25 — Mattei, Antonio. Bas-Niger, Benoue, Dahomey. Grenoble, 1890.

Afr 1965.2 — Orleans, F.P.L.C.H., Duc. Récits de campagne 1833-41. Paris, 1890.

Afr 1407.1.5 — Pellow, J. Adventures. London, 1890.

1890 - cont.

Afr 2208.85 — Quesnoy, F. L'Algérie. 2e ed. Paris, 1890.

Afr 6095.10 — Reading, J.H. The Ogowe band. Philadelphia, 1890.

Afr 555.22.14 — Rivett, A.W.L. Ten years' church work in Natal. London, 1890.

Afr 6455.8.4 — Rust. Die deutsche Emin Pascha Expedition. Berlin, 1890.

Afr 4258.90 — Sapeto, Giuseppe. Etiopia, notizie racolte. Roma, 1890.

Afr 6878.90.5 — Schynse, August. Mit Stanley und Emin Pascha durch deutsch Ost-Afrika. Köln, 1890.

Afr 4558.90 — Smith, F.H. Through Abyssinia. London, 1890.

Afr 8658.91 — South Africa and its future. Cape Town, 1890.

Afr 718.18.6 — Stanley, H.M. Dans les ténébres de l'Afrique. 3 ed. v.1-2. Paris, 1890. 2v.

Afr 6878.73.2 — Stanley, H.M. How I found Livingstone: travels, adventures, and discoveries in Central Africa. London, 1890.

Afr 718.10A — Stanley, H.M. In darkest Africa. N.Y., 1890. 2v.

Afr 718.18.3 — Stanley, H.M. The story of Emin's rescue as told in Stanley's letters. Boston, 1890.

Afr 718.18 — Stanley, H.M. The story of Emin's rescue as told in Stanley's letters. N.Y., 1890.

Afr 7210.5F — Termos de vassallagem nos territorios de machona, etc., 1858 a 1889. Lisboa, 1890.

Afr 5235.55.15 — Thomson, Joseph. Mungo Park and the Niger. London, 1890.

Afr 718.13 — Troup, J.R. With Stanley's rear column. London, 1890.

Afr 1955.7 — Trumelet, C. Le général Yusuf. Paris, 1890. 2v.

Afr 1608.90 — Viaud, J. Au Maroc. Paris, 1890.

Afr 1100.1 — Vignols, L. La piraterie sur l'Atlantique. Rennes, 1890.

Afr 7808.90.2 — Ward, Herbert. Five years with Congo cannibals. London, 1890.

Afr 7808.90.4 — Ward, Herbert. Five years with the Congo cannibals. n.p., 1890.

Afr 7808.90 — Ward, Herbert. Life among the Congo savages. N.Y., 1890.

Afr 718.17.2 — Wauters, A.J. Stanley's Emin Pascha expedition. London, 1890.

Afr 718.17 — Wauters, A.J. Stanley's Emin Pascha expedition. Philadelphia, 1890.

Afr 150.13 — Wauwermans, Henri. Henri le Navigateur et l'Académie Portugaise de Sagres. Bruxelles, 1890.

Afr 608.92 — White, A.S. The development of Africa. London, 1890.

Afr 8658.89.5 — Young, Frederick. A winter tour in South Africa. London, 1890.

1891

Afr 608.91.4 — Africa and its exploration. Leipzig, 1891. 2v.

Afr 500.9 — Alzola, Pablo de. Africa, su reparto y colonización. Bilbao, 1891.

Afr 6888.2 — Baumann, O. Usambara und seine Nachbargebiete. Berlin, 1891.

Afr 6777.2 — Behr, H.F. von. Kriegsbilder aus dem Araberaupland. Leif, 1891.

Afr 5385.13 — Besolow, T.E. From the darkness of Africa to light of America. Boston, 1891.

Afr 2710.4 — Bissuel, H. Le Sahara français. Alger, 1891.

Afr 718.20 — Bourne, H.R.F. The other side of Emin Pasha relief expedition. London, 1891.

Afr 2228.4 — Caix de St. Aymour, A. de. Arabes et Kabyles. Paris, 1891.

Afr 5235.191 — Caran, Edmond. De Saint-Louis au port de Temboctou. Paris, 1891.

X Cg Afr 3725.4 — Casati, G. Ten years in Equatoria. London, 1891. (Changed to XP 3865) 2v.

Afr 3725.4.5 — Casati, G. Zehn Jahre in Aquatoria. Hamburg, 1891. 3v.

Afr 7322.10 — Castilho Barreto e Noronha, Augusto de. Relatorio da guerra da Zambezia em 1888. Lisboa, 1891.

Afr 1903.1 — Cat, E. Mission bibliog. En Espagne. Paris, 1891.

Afr 1625.5 — Chatelier, A. Le. Tribus du sud-ouest Marocain. Paris, 1891.

Afr 5385.21 — Chaudoin, E. Trois mois de captivité au Dahomey. Paris, 1891.

Afr 5203.3 — Clozel, M. Bibliographie des ouvrages relatifs à la Sénégambie. Paris, 1891.

Afr 5051.30 — Clozel, M.F.J. Bibliographie des ouvrages relatifs à la Sénégambie et au Soudan occidental. Paris, 1891.

Afr 6878.91 — Coelln, Daniel. Bilder aus Ostafrika. Berlin, 1891.

Afr 4700.14 — Colajanni, N. Politica coloniale. Palermo, 1891.

Afr 7210.15 — Companhia de Moçambique. Decretos. Lisboa, 1891.

Afr 4368.16 — Constantin, Jean R. L'archimandrite Paisi et l'ataman Achinoff. Paris, 1891.

Afr 4368.17 — Constantin, N. Une expédition religieuse en Abyssinie. Paris, 1891.

Afr 550.4.5 — Cust, R.N. Africa rediviva. London, 1891.

Afr 550.4 — Cust, R.N. L'occupation de l'Afrique. Genève, 1891.

Afr 4730.10 — Da Assab al Mareb. Roma, 1891.

Afr 7332.10 — Documentos relativos aos acontecimentos de manica. Lisboa, 1891.

Afr 3978.77.13 — Edwards, A.B. A thousand miles up the Nile. London, 1891.

Afr 2508.1 — Estourneller de Constant, Paul. La politique française en Tunisie. Paris, 1891.

Afr 5767.2 — Ferrand, G. Les Musulmans à Madagascar. v.1-3. Paris, 1891-1902. 2v.

Afr 5046.9 — Fock, Andreas. Algérie, Sahara, Tchad, réponse à M. Camille Sabatier. Paris, 1891.

Afr 9838.91 — Fotheringham, L.M. Adventures in Nyassaland. London, 1891.

Afr 4712.1 — Franchetti, L. L'Italia e la sua colonia africana. Città de Castello, 1891.

Afr 4115.5 — Fullerton, W.M. In Cairo. London, 1891.

Afr 5227.25 — Gallieni, Joseph Simon. Deux campagnes au Soudan français, 1886-1888. Paris, 1891.

Afr 2025.1 — Gourgeot, F. Les sept plaies d'Algérie. Alger, 1891.

Afr 640.6 — Haliburton, R.G. Dwarfs of Mount Atlas. London, 1891.

Afr 1680.4 — Ichmann, G. Der hohe Atlas. Marburg, 1891.

Afr 4731.6 — Italy. Commissione d'Inchiesta sulla Colonia Eritrea. Relazione generale. Roma, 1891.

Afr 718.12 — Jameson, J.S. Forschungen und Erlebnisse im dunkelsten Africa. Hamburg, 1891.

Afr 3725.3.25 — Jephson, A.J.M. Emin Pasha and the rebellion at the equator. N.Y., 1891.

Afr 9558.35 — Johnston, H.H. Livingstone and exploration of central Africa. London, 1891.

Afr 3994.891.5 — Kaufmann, Wilhelm. Das internationale Recht der egyptischen Staatsschuld. Berlin, 1891.

Afr 4199.5 — Keller-Zschokke, J.V. Werner Munzinger-Pascha. Aarau, 1891.

1891 - cont.

Afr 1608.91A   Leared, A. Morocco and the Moors. London, 1891.
Afr 7368.91   McPherson, J.H.T. History of Liberia. Baltimore, 1891.
Afr 5874.8   Mahy, F. de. Autour de l'Ile Bourbon et de Madagascar. Paris, 1891.
Afr 6887.5   Meyer, H. Across East African glaciers. London, 1891.
Afr 9598.91   Moir, J.F. A lady's letter from central Africa. Glasgow, 1891.
Afr 7324.2   Monteiro, R. Delagoa Bay. London, 1891.
Afr 8088.91   Murray, R.W. South Africa from Arab domination to British rule. London, 1891.
Afr 590.32   Noyant. Les horreurs de l'esclavage, de la sorcellerie, des sacrifices humains et du cannibalisme en Afrique. Paris, 1891.
Afr 7020.25   Oliviera Martins, J.P. Portugal em Africa. Porto, 1891.
Afr 718.16   Parke, T.H. My personal experience in equatorial Africa. London, 1891.
Afr 718.16.3   Parke, T.H. My personal experience in equatorial Africa. 3d ed. London, 1891.
Afr 2650.1   Perry, Amos. An official tour of eastern Tunis. Providence, 1891.
Afr 6455.8   Peters, Carl. New light on dark Africa.London, 1891.
Afr 6455.8.2   Peters, Karl. Die deutsche Emin Pascha Expedition. München, 1891.
Afr 555.24.2   Price, William S. My third campaign in East Africa. London, 1891.
Afr 6455.10   Pruen, S.R. The Arab and the African. London, 1891.
Afr 3725.10   Reichard, Paul. Dr. Emin Pascha. Leipzig, 1891.
Afr 520.3   Reparaz, G. España en Africa. Madrid, 1891.
Afr 2010.3   Rinn, L. Histoire de l'insurrection de 1871. Alger, 1891.
Afr 2748.91   Sabatier, Camille. Touat, Sahara et Soudan. Paris, 1891.
Afr 7216.09.10   Santos, João dos. Ethiopia oriental. v.1-2. Lisboa, 1891.
Afr 6978.91   Sching, H. Deutsch-Südwest-Afrika. Oldenburg, 1891.
Afr 4315.1   Shihab al-Din Ahmad Ibn Abd al-Kadir. La conquista mussulmand dell'Etiopia. Rome, 1891.
Afr 608.91   Sievers, W. Afrika. Eine allgemeine Landeskunde. Leipzig, 1891.
Afr 1750.3F   Spain. Ministerio de Estado. Documentos presentados a las cortes en la legislatura de 1891 por el Ministro de Estado. Madrid, 1891. 3v.
Afr 6275.8   Standinger, P. Im Herzen der Haussaländer. 2. Aufl. Oldenburg, 1891
Afr 718.10.1   Stanley, H.M. In darkest Africa. N.Y., 1891. 2v.
Afr 715.9   Trivier, E. Mon voyage au continent noir, "La Gironde" en Afrique. Paris, 1891.
Afr 630.7   Waller, N. Ivory, apes, and peacocks. London, 1891.
Afr 3978.76.5   Warner, C.D. My winter on the Nile. v.1-2. Leipzig, 1891.
Afr 8235.10   Weale, J.P.M. The truth about the Portuguese in Africa. London, 1891.
Afr 8918.91   Widdicombe, John. Fourteen years in Basutoland. London, 1891.
Afr 3700.3   Wingate, F.R. Mahdiism and the Egyptian Sudan. London, 1891.
Afr 3700.3.2   Wingate, F.R. Mahdiism and the Egyptian Sudan. 2nd ed. London, 1891.
Afr 718.6   Wissmann, H. Meine zweite Durchquerung Afrikas. Frankfurt a.M., 1891.
Afr 718.7   Wissmann, H. My second journey through Africa. London, 1891.
Afr 7808.88.3   Wissmann, H.V. Im innern Afrikas. Leipzig, 1891.

1892

Afr 7015.10   Academia das Sciencias de Lisboa. Conferencias celebradas na Academia Real das Sciencias de Lisboa. Lisboa, 1892.
Afr 1608.82.4F   Amicis, E. de. Marruecos. Barcelona, 1892.
Afr 2010.7   Basset, R. L'insurrection algérienne de 1871. Louvain, 1892.
Afr 2357.20   Basset, René. Fastes chronologiques de la ville d'Oran. Paris, 1892.
Afr 2025.14   Benoist, Charles. Enquête algérienne. Paris, 1892.
Afr 6484.6   Bentley, E.L. British East Africa and Uganda. London, 1892.
Afr 2608.92   Bernard, M. De Tripoli à Tunis. Paris, 1892.
Afr 5235.189.5   Binger, Gustave. Du Niger au golfe de Guinée par le pays de Konge le Mossi. Paris, 1892. 2v.
Afr 3275.6   Britain's work in Egypt. Edinburgh, 1892.
Afr 5190.2   Brosselard-Faidherbe, H. Casamance et Mellacorée. Paris, 1892.
Afr 2208.92   Burdeau, A. L'Algérie en 1891. Paris, 1892.
Afr 4515.1.2   Caix de St. Aymour. Histoire des relations de la France avec l'Abyssinie. Paris, 1892.
Afr Doc 4407.291F   Cape of Good Hope. Results of a census of the colony of the Cape of Good Hope. Cape Town, 1892.
Afr 8658.92   Churchill, R.S. Men, mines and animals in South Africa. London, 1892.
Afr 11302.89.100   Couper, J.K. Mixed humanity. Cape Colony, 1892.
Afr 7175.6.4   Dias de Carvalho, H.A. Meteorologia, climalogia e colonisação. Lisboa, 1892.
NEDL Afr 7458.92   Durham, F.A. Lone star of Liberia. London, 1892.
Afr 4349.1   Esteves Pereira, F.M. Chronica de Susenyos, rei de Ethiopia. Lisbon, 1892. 2v.
Afr 1838.7   Ferry, A. Au gouvernement de l'Algérie. Paris, 1892.
Afr 2208.56.5F   Gerard, Jules. Le tueur de lions. Paris, 1892.
Afr 3695.3A   Gessi Pasha, R. Seven years in the Soudan. London, 1892.
Afr 5748.85.5F   Grandidier, Alfred. Histoire de la geographie. Text and atlas. Paris, 1892. 2v.
Afr 8658.92.3   Greswall, W.P. Geography of Africa south of Zambesi. Oxford, 1892.
Afr 7540.4   Hebette, L. Les codes du Congo. Bruxelles, 1892.
Afr 6455.12.2   Hoehnel, Ludwig Ritter von. Zum Rudolph-See und Stephanie-See. Wien, 1892.
Afr 770.3.5   Hore, Edw.C. Tanganyika. Eleven years...Central Africa. 2nd ed. Photoreproduction. n.p., 1892.
Afr 9488.92   Knight-Bruce. Journals of the Mashonaland mission. London, 1892.
Afr 2608.92.10   Lafitte, Fernand. Contribution à l'étude médicale de la Tunisie. Bordeaux, 1892.
NEDL Afr 4115.6   Lane-Poole, S. Cairo. London, 1892.
Afr 2230.3   Lionel, J. Kabylie du Jurjura. Paris, 1892.
Afr 5748.92   Mandat-Grancey, Edmond. Souvenirs de la côte d'Afrique, Madagascar. Paris, 1892.
Afr 1955.22.5   Maréchal Pélissier. Tours, 1892.
Afr 3275.14   Milner, A. England in Egypt. London, 1892.
Afr 810.5   Mockler-Ferryman, A.F. Up the Niger. London, 1892.

1892 - cont.

Afr 200.14   Molto y Campo-Redondo, P. Situación politica de Africa en 1892. Madrid, 1892.
Afr 4558.92.5   Muenzenberger, E.F.A. Abessinien. Freiberg, 1892.
Afr 3730.2   Ohrwalder, J. Ten years' captivity in the Mahdi's camp. 7th ed. London, 1892.
Afr 7175.9   Paiva Conceiro, H.M. de. Relatorio de viagem entre Bailundo e as terras do Mususso. Lisboa, 1892.
Afr 1574.1   Perez del Torro, F. España en el noroeste de Africa. Madrid, 1892.
Afr 4306.1   Perruchon, J. Vie de Lalibala. Paris, 1892.
Afr 550.8.15   Pizzoli, D. Per i funeri del Cardinal Lavigerie. Palermo, 1892.
Afr 1326.1   Playfair, L. Bibliography of Morocco. London, 1892.
Afr 2608.92.3   Poire, Eugene. La Tunisie française. Paris, 1892.
Afr 4558.92.9   Portal, G.H. My mission to Abyssinia. London, 1892.
Afr 3978.92.5   Pretynian, H.E. Journal, Kittar mountains, 1891. London, 1892.
Afr 3978.92   Rae, W.F. Egypt to-day. London, 1892.
Afr 7808.92   Ramaix, M.M. de. Le Congo. Anvers, 1892.
Afr 3978.92.2   Rawnsley, H.D. Notes for the Nile. Leipzig, 1892.
Afr 6878.92   Reichard, Paul. Deutsch-Ostafrika. Leipzig, 1892.
Afr 8658.92.5   Ritchie, James Ewing. Brighter South Africa. London, 1892.
Afr 3700.4   Russell, Henry. The ruin of the Soudan. London, 1892.
Afr 4338.301   Saineanu, M. L'Abyssinie dans la seconde moitié du XVI siècle. Inaug. Diss. Leipzig, 1892.
Afr 200.5   Sevin-Deplaces, L. Afrique et africains. Paris, 1892.
Afr 6887.7   Sheldon, M. Sultan to sultan. London, 1892.
Afr 7182.8   Sociedade de Geographia de Lisboa. Commissão africana missões de Angola. Lisboa, 1892.
Afr 6541.25   Stock, Sarah Geraldina. The story of Uganda and the Victoria Nyanza Mission. London, 1892.
Afr 5765.13   Townsend, William J. Madagascar, its missionaries and martyrs. 2d ed. London, 1892.
Afr 2396.1   Trumelet, C. L'Algérie légendaire. Alger, 1892.
Afr 4558.92   Villiers, F. Negus negusti. N.Y., 1892.
Afr 608.92.2   White, A.S. The development of Africa. 2d ed. London, 1892.

1893

Afr 3275.19   Adams, F. The new Egypt. London, 1893.
Afr 1347.3   Alvarez Cabrera, J. La guerra en Africa. Madrid, 1893.
Afr 555.9.1   Arnot, Frederick Stanley. Bihe and Garenaganze, or, Four years' further work and travel in Central Africa. London, 1893.
Afr 2208.93   Baraudon, A. Algérie et Tunisie. Paris, 1893.
Afr 4642.1   Bent, J.J. The sacred city of the Ethiopians. London, 1893.
Afr 2208.93.6   Bernard, Marius. De Tunis à Alger. Paris, 1893.
Afr 9488.93.2   Blennerhassett. Adventures in Mashonaland. London, 1893.
Afr 550.20   Boavida, A.J. Missões e missionarios portuguezes...17 de abril 1893. Lisboa, 1893.
Afr 1608.93   Bonsal, S. Jr. Morocco as it is. London, 1893.
Afr 2208.93.4   Boutroue, A. L'Algérie et la Tunisie à travers les ages. Paris, 1893.
Afr 2208.93.10   Bruun, Daniel. Algier og Sahara. Billeder fra nomade- og krigerlivet. Kjøbenhavn, 1893.
Afr 9388.93.3   Bryden, H.A. Gun and camera in South Africa. London, 1893.
Afr 3978.93   Budge, E.A.W. The Nile. London, 1893.
Afr 5385.2.5   Burton, R.F. A mission to Gelele. London, 1893. 2v.
Afr 2208.93.3   Chatrieux, E. Etudes algériennes. Paris, 1893.
Afr 608.93   Colvile, Zelie. Round the black man's garden. Edinburgh, 1893.
Afr 6164.2   Ellis, A.B. History of Gold Coast of West Africa. London, 1893.
Afr 555.12.20   Excoffon, Ariste. Les pères blancs en Afrique. Paris, 1893.
Afr 1088.5   Fagnan, E. Histoire des Almohades. Alger, 1893.
Afr 2458.93   Faucon, N. La Tunisie. Paris, 1893. 2v.
Afr 1258.93   Field, Henry M. The Barbary coast. N.Y., 1893.
Afr 3269.2F   France. Ministère des Affaires Etrangères. Documents diplomatiques. Paris, 1893.
Afr 3816.2   Frobenius, Herman. Die Heiden-Neger des ägyptischen Sudan. Berlin, 1893.
Afr 4226.1   Fumagalli, G. Bibliografia etiopica. Milan, 1893.
Afr 3725.5   Ghisleri, A. Gl'Italiani nell'Equatoria. Bergamo, 1893.
Afr 7808.93   Glave, E.J. Six years of adventure in Congo-land. London, 1893.
Afr 640.6.3   Haliburton, R.G. Holy land of Punt, racial dwarfs in the Atlas and the Pyrenees. London, 1893.
Afr 3978.93.20   Harcourt, François. L'Egypte et les Egyptiens. Paris, 1893.
Afr 718.31   Johnston, J. Reality versus romance in south central Africa. London, 1893.
Afr 550.8.3   Klein, F. Le Cardinal Lavigerie et ses oeuvres africaines. 3e éd. Paris, 1893.
Afr 9424.250   Knight-Bruce, Louise (Torr). The story of an African chief. London, 1893.
Afr 6887.2   Leroy, A. Au Kilima-ndjaro. Paris, 1893.
Afr 8658.93   Letters from South Africa. London, 1893.
Afr 6497.8A   Lugard, F.D. The rise of our East African empire. Edinburgh, 1893. 2v.
Afr 6328.1   McDermott, P.L. British East Africa. London, 1893.
Afr 6878.93   Moloney, J.A. With Captain Stairs to Katanga. London, 1893.
Afr 1432.15   Monedero Ordoñez, Dionisio. Episodios militares del ejercito de Africa. 2a ed. Burgos, 1893.
Afr 6738.4.9   Morgen, C. Von. Durch Kamerun von sued nach nord. Leipzig, 1893.
Afr 1721.3   Narvaez Pacheco, J. Sitio de San Antonio de alareche en 1689. Madrid, 1893.
Afr 7190.30   Nogueira, A.F. A ilha de San Thome. Lisboa, 1893.
Afr 3730.3   Ohrwalder, J. Ten years' captivity in the Mahdi's camp. London, 1893.
Afr 3730.3.5   Ohrwalder, J. Ten years' captivity in the Mahdi's camp. N.Y., 1893.
Afr 3730.2.5   Ohrwalder, J. Ten years' captivity in the Mahdi's camp. 10th ed. Leipzig, 1893.
Afr 1608.93.5   Olivie, M. Marruecos. Barcelona, 1893.
Afr 9218.93   Orange Free State (Republic). South Africa. Chicago, 1893.
Afr 2376.1   Pein, T. Lettres familières sur l'Algérie (Tougourt). 2e ed. Alger, 1893.
Afr 550.8.20   Perraud, A. Le Cardinal Lavigerie. Paris, 1893.

1893 - cont.

Afr 4309.1 Perruchon, J. Les chroniques de Zara Yaeqob. Paris, 1893.
Afr 1573.5 Pezzi, Rafael. La influencia española en el Rif. Madrid, 1893.
Afr 1608.93.6 Picard, E. El Maghreb al aksa. Bruxelles, 1893.
Afr 2500.1 Plantet, E. Correspondance des beys de Tunis. Paris, 1893-4. 3v.
Afr 1408.4 Plantet, E. Mouley Ismael. Paris, 1893.
Afr 550.8.25 Rance-Bourrey, A.J. Les obsèques du Cardinal Lavigerie. Paris, 1893.
Afr 9598.93 Rankin, D.J. The Zambesi basin and Nyassaland. Edinburgh, 1893.
Afr 4886.5 Salma, L. de. Obock. Paris, 1893.
Afr 5318.10 Sanderval, C. de. Soudan français...Kahel. Paris, 1893.
Afr 2748.93 Schirmer, H. Le Sahara. Paris, 1893.
Afr 4313.3 Schleicher, A.W. Geschichte der Galla. Berlin, 1893.
Afr 9488.93 Selous, F.C. Travel and adventure in south-east Africa. London, 1893.
Afr 590.54 Stanley, H.M. Slavery and the slave trade in Africa. N.Y., 1893.
Afr 2260.15 Vignon, L. La France en Algérie. Paris, 1893.
Afr 1608.93.7 Villaescusa, M.H. La cuestion de Marruecos y el conflicto de melilla. Barcelona, 1893.
Afr 9200.5 Vrijstaatsch jaarboek en almanak, 1894. Bloemfontein, 1893.

1894

Afr 1335.5 Actas y memorias del primer Congreso Español de Africanistas. Granada, 1894.
Afr 150.11 Almeida, Fortunato. O Infante de Sagres. Porto, 1894.
Afr 5365.4 Aublet, E. La guerre au Dahomey. Paris, 1894.
Afr 7808.94 Bailey, Henry. Travel and adventures in Congo Free State. London, 1894.
Afr 6878.94 Baumann, Oscar. Durch Massailand zur Nilquelle. Berlin, 1894.
Afr 1325.3F Boletin de la Sociedad Union Hispano-Mauritanica 1894. Granada, 1894. 2v.
Afr 5620.4 Bonnemaison, J. Historique de Madagascar. Tarbes, 1894.
Afr 5235.194 Bonnetain, Raymonde. Une française au Soudan. Paris, 1894.
Afr 28.4.10 Boston Public Library. List of works on Africa. Boston, 1894.
Afr 5480.194 Brunache, Paul. Le centre de l'Afrique. Paris, 1894.
Afr 4612.1.5 Burton, R.F. First footsteps in East Africa. Memorial ed. London, 1894. 2v.
Afr 2608.94 Cagnat. Voyage en Tunisie. Paris, 1894.
Afr 9488.94.2 Carnegie, D. Among the Matabele. 2. ed. London, 1894.
Afr 6497.9 Catholic Union of Great Britain. Memorandum on war in Uganda, 1892. London, 1894.
Afr 7548.94.5 Chapaux, Albert. Le Congo historique. Bruxelles, 1894.
Afr 9445.5 Colquhoun, A.R. Matabeleland, the war, and our position in South Africa. London, 1894.
Afr 8658.94 Cooper-Chadwick, J. Three years with Lobengula. London, 1894.
Afr 3675.7 Dal Verme, L. I Dervisci nel Sudan egiziano. Roma, 1894.
Afr 1608.94.10 Diercks, G. Marokko...Kenntnis und Beurteilung des Scherifreiches. Berlin, 1894.
Afr 9446.34 Donovan, Charles Henry Wynne. With Wilson in Matabeleland. London, 1894.
Afr 6280.2 Ellis, A.B. The Yoruba-speaking peoples of the Slave Coast of West Africa. London, 1894.
Afr 1258.93.2 Field, Henry M. The Barbary coast. 2nd ed. N.Y., 1894.
Afr 1608.94.5 Ganniers, A. de. Le Maroc d'aujoud hui, d'hier et de demain. Nouvelle ed. Paris, 1894.
Afr 2208.94 Greville-Nugent. A land of mosques and marabouts. London, 1894.
Afr 1755.4 Guerra del rif. Paris, 1894.
Afr 6455.12 Hoehnel, Ludwig. Discovery of Lakes Rudolf and Stefanie. London, 1894. 2v.
Afr 1026.4 Jacqueton, G. Les archives espagnoles du gouvernement de l'Algérie. Alger, 1894.
Afr 810.7 Jaime, G. De Koulikoro à Tombouctou. Paris, 1894.
Afr 1608.94.3 Kerr, Robert. Pioneering in Morocco. London, 1894.
Afr 1258.94.5 Lamartiniere, Maximilien Poisson de. Documents pour servir à l'étude du nord-ouest African. v.1-4 and atlas. Alger, 1894-97. 5v.
Afr 1755.11 Llanos Y Alcaraz, A. Melilla. Madrid, 1894.
Afr 150.12 Macedo, Lino de. A obra do Infante. Villafranca de Xira, 1894.
Afr 1755.15 Marenco, Servando. Una solucion a los conflictos de Melilla. Madrid, 1894.
Afr 5748.94 Martineau, A. Madagascar. Paris, 1894.
Afr 5620.5 Martineau, A. Madagascar en 1894, étude de politique. Paris, 1894.
Afr 555.25 Merensky, A. Deutsche Arbeit am Njassa, Deutsch-Ostafrika. Berlin, 1894.
Afr 1608.64.6 Merry y Colom, F. Mi embajada extraordinaria a Marruecos en 1863. Madrid, 1894.
Afr 3275.14.5 Milner, A. England in Egypt. London, 1894.
X Cg Afr 5342.4 Monnier, M. France noire (Côte-d'Ivoire et Soudan). Paris, 1894.
Afr 1608.94.2 Montbard, G. A travers le Maroc. Paris, 1894.
Afr 1608.94 Montbard, G. Among the Moors. London, 1894.
Afr 1608.94.1 Montbard, G. Among the Moors. N.Y., 1894.
Afr 7322.2 Muller, H.P.N. Land und Volk zwischen Zambesi und Limpopo. Giessen, 1894.
Afr 9488.94.5 Nadellaic, Jean François Albert du Pouget Marquis de. Le Mashonaland. Paris, 1894.
Afr 2458.94 Pavy, A. Histoire de Tunis. Tours, 1894.
Afr 2208.94.3 Pensa, Henri. L'Algérie. Paris, 1894.
Afr 1570.13 Polignac. La France, vassale de l'Angleterre. Alger, 1894.
Afr 6497.14 Portal, Gerald H. The British mission to Uganda, 1893. London, 1894.
Afr 7324.20 Portugal. Comissão de Limitação da Fronteira de Lourenço Marques. Explorações portuguezas em Lourenço Marques e Inhambane. Lisboa, 1894.
Afr 632.9 Preville, A. de. Les sociétés africaines. Paris, 1894.
Afr 2945.2.3 Rainaud, A. Quid de natura...Cyrenaicae pentapolis. Paris, 1894.
Afr 5180.5 Rancon, A. Dans la Haute-Gambie. Paris, 1894.
Afr 7548.94 Reeves, J.S. International beginnings of the Congo Free State. Baltimore, 1894.
Afr 1608.94.8 Reina, T.B. Geografia de Marruecos. Barcelona, 1894.
Afr 1258.94 Rogh, J. Från orientens förgårdar. Stockholm, 1894.

1894 - cont.

Afr 1608.94.14 Salmon. Les français au Maroc, mort du sultan. Paris, 1894.
Afr 4313.1 Sarsa, Dengel. Storia di Lebna Dengel re d'Etiopia. Rome, 1894.
Afr 4315.2 Shihab al-Din Ahmad ibn 'Abd al-Kadir. Futuh al-Habashah. Pt.1. London, 1894.
Afr 1608.94.4 Soriano, Rodrigo. Moros y cristianos. Madrid, 1894.
Afr 1442.10F Spain. Ministerio de Estado. Documentos presentados a las Cortes. Madrid, 1894.
Afr 8686.8 Stewart, James. Lovedale, South Africa. Edinburgh, 1894.
Afr 1719.2 Story of Cape Juby. London, 1894.
Afr 3725.6 Stuhlmann, F. Mit EminPasha in Herz von Africa. Berlin, 1894.
Afr 1570.16 Ternant, V. de. La question marocaine. Paris, 1894.
Afr 8088.94.3 Theal, G.M. South Africa. N.Y., 1894.
Afr 9028.94 Thomas, E. Neumann. How thankful should we be. Cape Town, 1894.
Afr 2928.94 Thompson, G.E. Life in Tripoli. Liverpool, 1894.
Afr 530.12 Weidmann, C. Deutsche Männer in Afrika. Lübeck, 1894.
Afr 765.4 Werther, Waldemar. Zum Victoria Nyanza. Berlin, 1894.
Afr 9446.35 Wills, William Arthur. The downfall of Lobengula. London, 1894.
Afr 8088.94 Wilmot, Alex. History of the expansion of South Africa. London, 1894.
Afr 4785.7 Wolverton, Frederick Glyn, 4th Baron. Five months sport in Somaliland. London, 1894.
Htn Afr 150.10F* Zuental, Anthero de. O Infante Dom Henrique. Lisboa, 1894.

1895

Afr 7190.27 Almada Negreiros, A.D. Historia ethnographica da ilha de San Thome. Lisboa, 1895.
Afr 6497.5 Ashe, R.P. Chronicles of Uganda. N.Y., 1895.
Afr 3978.95 Attfield, D.H. Private journal in Egypt. London, 1895.
Afr 8658.95 Balfour, A.B. Twelve hundred miles in a waggon. London, 1895.
Afr 2748.82.6 Barbier, J.V. A travers le Sahara, les missions du colonel Flatters. Paris, 1895.
Afr 150.4 Beazley, C.R. Prince Henry the Navigator. N.Y., 1895.
Afr 5748.95.25 Benoit, Felix. Madagascar, étude economique, geographique et ethnographique. Dijon, 1895.
Afr 5748.95.20 Beylie, Leon De. Itineraire de Majunga à Tananarive. Paris, 1895.
Afr 9558.30.15 Blaikie, W.G. Personal life of David Livingstone. N.Y., 1895.
Afr 1608.95.5 Boada y Romeu, J. Allende el estrecho, viajes por Marruecos (1889-94). Barcelona, 1895.
Afr 5748.95.3 Brunet, L. La France à Madagascar. 2e ed. Paris, 1895.
Afr 5585.15 Brunet, Louis. La France à Madagascar, 1815-1895. Paris, 1895.
Afr 678.95 Cadamosto, A. de. Voyages à la côte occidentale d'Afrique. Paris, 1895.
Afr 1608.95.7 Canizares y Moyano, ed. Apuntes sobre Marruecos. Madrid, 1895.
Afr 5748.95.3F Catat, Louis. Voyage à Madagascar (1889-1890). Paris, 1895.
Afr 2505.5A Chiala, L. Tunisi. Torino, 1895.
Afr 5765.10 Colin, E. Madagascar et la mission catholique. Paris, 1895.
Afr 6497.10 Colvile, H. The land of the Nile springs. London, 1895.
Afr 1955.19 Cornulier-Lucinière, Comte de. La prise de Bône et Bougie...1832-33. Paris, 1895.
Afr 5620.9 Courand, Charles J. Madagascar, son avenir colonial. La Rochelle, 1895.
Afr 5548.95 Cousins, W.E. Madagascar of to-day. London, 1895.
Afr 2223.25 Dessoliers, F.L. L'Algérie libre, étude économique sur l'Algérie. Alger, 1895.
Afr 555.16 Dubose, H.C. Memoirs of Rev. John Leighton Wilson, D.D. Richmond, 1895.
Afr 1608.85 Erckmann, J. Le Maroc moderne. Paris, 1895.
Afr 6097.6 Faulkner, Rose E. Joseph Sidney Hill, first bishop in western Equatorial Africa. London, 1895.
Afr 9488.95.8.3 Finlason, C.E. A nobody in Mashonaland. 3. ed. London, 1895.
Afr 2608.95.2 Fitzner, R. Die Regentschaft Tunis. Berlin, 1895.
Afr 5385.19 Foa, Eduard. Le Dahomey, histoire, géographie, moeurs (1891-94). Paris, 1895.
Afr 2748.95 Foureau, F. Mission chez les Touareg. Paris, 1895.
Afr 5620.3F France. Ministère des Affaires Etrangères. Documents diplomatiques. Paris, 1895.
Afr 4968.95 Francis, J.C. Three months leave in Somaliland. London, 1895.
Afr 1608.95.3 Frisch, R.J. Le Maroc géographie Organisation politique. Paris, 1895.
Afr 5748.95.5 Gautier, Emile F. Guide pratique du colon et du soldat à Madagascar. Paris, 1895.
Afr 3994.895F Gavillot, J.C. Aristide. L'Angleterre ruine l'Egypte. Paris, 1895.
Afr 1840.9 Gentil, M. Administration de la justice musulmane en Algerie. Thèse. Paris, 1895.
Afr 4580.1 Glaser, E. Die Abessinier in Arabien und Afrika. München, 1895.
Afr 9028.85.5 Great Britain. War Office. Intelligence Division. Precis of information concerning Zululand. London, 1895.
Afr 3700.9 Haggard, A.C. Under crescent and star. Edinburgh, 1895.
Afr 1685.1 Harris, W.B. Tafilet. Edinburg, 1895.
Afr 9388.95 Hepburn, J.D. Twenty years in Khamas country. London, 1895.
Afr 5765.7.5 Histoire de la mission fondée à Madagascar par Saint Vincent de Paul. Paris, 1895.
Afr 5748.95.10 Humbert, G. Madagascar. Paris, 1895.
Afr 9028.95 Ingram, J.F. The colony of Natal. London, 1895.
Afr 1325.5F Italy. Ministero degli Affari Esteri. Documenti diplomatici. Successione sceriffiana (Marrocco). Roma, 1895.
Afr 5548.95.5 Joubert, L. La question de Madagascar. Paris, 1895.
Afr 608.95.3 Keane, A.H. Africa. London, 1895. 2v.
X Cg Afr 108.93.2 Keltie, J.S. The partition of Africa. London, 1895. (changed to XP 9198)
Afr 108.93.2 Keltie, J.S. The partition of Africa. 2d ed. Photoreproduction. London, 1895. 2v.
Afr 1550.1 Kerdec Cheny, A. Un boulevard de l'islam. Tanger, 1895.
Afr 9488.95.5 Knight, E.F. Rhodesia of to-day. London, 1895.
Afr 9488.95 Knight-Bruce. Memories of Mashonaland. London, 1895.

1895 - cont.

Afr 200.3A	Latimer, E.W. Europe in Africa in the 19th century. Chicago, 1895.
Afr 5227.20	Lecert, Paul Edmond. Lettres du Soudan. Paris, 1895.
Afr 5842.2	Leclercq, J. Au pays de Paul et Virginie. Paris, 1895.
Afr 2208.95.3A	Leroux, H. Je deviens colon. Paris, 1895.
Afr 2208.98.8	Leroux, H. Je deviens colon. 2e ed. Paris, 1895.
Afr 2208 95.5	Leroux, H. Je deviens colon. 4e ed. Paris, 1895.
Afr 9345.5	Lloyd, E. Three great African chiefs. London, 1895.
Afr 6328.2	McDermott, P.L. British East Africa, or Ibea. New ed. London, 1895.
Afr 715.6	Maistre, C. A travers l'Afrique centrale. Paris, 1895.
Afr 2344.10	Mangin, J.E. Notes sur l'histoire de Laghouat. Alger, 1895.
Afr 8252.10	Martineau, John. The life and correspondence of Sir Bartle Frere. London, 1895. 2v.
Afr 4718.91.20	Martini, Ferdinando. Nell'Africa italiana. Milano, 1895.
Afr 9488.95.7	Mathers, E.P. Zambesia, England's El Dorado in Africa. London, 1895.
Afr 5748.95	Maude, F.C. Five years in Madagascar. London, 1895.
Afr 1608.85.3	Mercet, A. Le Maroc. Paris, 1895.
Afr 2702.1F	Monteil, P.L. De Saint-Louis à Tripoli. Paris, 1895.
Afr 1608.95	Moulieras, A. Le Maroc inconnu. v.1-2. Paris, 1895. 2v.
Afr 4095.8.5	Murray, T.D. Sir S.W. Baker, a memoir. London, 1895.
Afr 7324.6F	Noronha, E. de. O districto de Lourenço Marques e a Africa do sul. Lisboa, 1895.
Afr 4025.20.20	Oddi, F.F. Gl italiani in Egitto. Alessandria, 1895.
Afr 5635.3	Orleans, H.P.D. A Madagascar. Paris, 1895.
Afr 5635.4	Ortus, C. Madagascar. Paris, 1895.
Afr 5748.95.30	Paisant, M. Madagascar. 2e ed. Paris, 1895.
Afr 6743.3	Passarge, S. Adamana. Berlin, 1895.
Afr 6570.3.15	Pease, J.A. How we countenance slavery. London, 1895.
Afr 3198.95	Pensa, Henri. L'Egypte et le Soudan égyptien. Paris, 1895.
Afr 6878.95	Peters, Karl. Das Deutsch-Ostafrikanische Schutzgebiet. München, 1895.
Afr 5748.95.15	Piolet, J.B. Madagascar et les Hova. Paris, 1895.
Afr 640.5.5	Quatrefrages de Bréau, Armand de. The Pygmies. Paris, 1895.
Afr 2945.2	Rainaud, A. La pentapole cyrénéenne. Paris, 1895.
Afr 575.14	Schweinfurth, G. Die Wiedergeburt Agnptens. Berlin, 1895.
Afr 9488.95.3	Selous, F.C. A hunter's wanderings in Africa. London, 1895.
Afr 4968.95.4	Swayne, H. Seventeen trips through Somaliland. London, 1895.
Afr 6455.3	Thomson, J. Through Masai land. Photoreproduction. London, 1895.
Afr 608.95	Vincent, F. Actual Africa. N.Y., 1895.
Afr 2230.16	Violard, Emile. Le banditisme en Kabylie. Paris, 1895.
Afr 5600.3	Warnier de Wailly, L.M.A.A. Campagne de Madagascar (1829-1830). Paris, 1895.
Afr 7530.3	Wauters, A.J. Bibliographie du Congo 1880-1895. Bruxelles, 1895.
Afr 7808.95	Wincxtenhoven. Les colonies et l'état indépendant du Congo. Bruxelles, 1895.
Afr 8145.5	Wirgman, A.T. The history of the English Church in South Africa. London, 1895.
Afr 2208.95.9	Workman, F.B. Algerian memories. London, 1895.
Afr 8088.95	Worsfold, W.B. South Africa. London, 1895.
Afr 6738.5	Zintgraff, E. Nord-Kamerun. Berlin, 1895.

1896

Afr 555.29.20	A.M. MacKay, pioneer missionary of the Church Missionary Society to Uganda. N.Y., 1896.
Afr 590.34	Abbadie, A. Sur l'abolition de l'esclavage en Afrique. Paris, 1896.
Afr 3978.69.5.6	About, E. Le fellah: souvenirs d'Egypte. 6e ed. Paris, 1896.
Afr 8849.8	Benham, M.S. Henry Callaway. London, 1896.
Afr 2762.9	Bernard, F. Deux missions françaises chez les Touareg en 1880-81. Alger, 1896.
Afr 4558.80.25	Bianchi, G. In Abissinia. Milano, 1896.
Afr 8658.96	Brownlee, Chas. Reminiscences of Kaffir life. Lovedale, 1896.
Afr 5635.13	Burleigh, B. Two campaigns, Madagascar and Ashantee. London, 1896.
Afr 8225.4.2	Carter, T.F. A narrative of the Boer war. London, 1896.
Afr 555.17	Castellanos, M.P. Apostolado serafico en Marruecos. Madrid, 1896.
Afr 5748.96.5	Cazeneuve, M. A la cour de Madagascar. Paris, 1896.
Afr 6455.4	Chanler, W.A. Through jungle and desert. 1 vol. and maps. N.Y., 1896. 2v.
Afr 4700.14.20	Colonia italiana in Africa e Francesco Crispi; il parlamento ed il paese per un Italiano. Roma, 1896.
Afr 4558.96	Comber, P. L'Abyssinie en 1896. Paris, 1896.
Afr 9400.3	Crisp, W. The Bechuana of South Africa. London, 1896.
Afr 8658.96.3	Cumberland, S. What I think of South Africa. London, 1896.
Afr 3978.96	Delmas, E. Egypte et Palestine. Paris, 1896.
Afr 9086.20	De Villiers, John. The Transvaal. London, 1896.
Afr 5765.36	Doncaster, L. Faithful unto death;...life...of William and Lucy S. Johnson. London, 1896.
Afr 1258.96	Drouet, F. Au nord de l'Afrique. Nice, 1896.
Afr 5247.10.5	Dubois, Felix. Timbuctoo the mysterious. N.Y., 1896.
Afr 725.13	Elliot, G.F.S. A naturalist in mid-Africa. London, 1896.
Afr 7567.6	Gochet, J.B. Soldats et missionnaires au Congo de 1891 à 1894. Bruxelles, 1896.
Afr 5757.5	Gravier, Gabriel. La cartographie de Madagascar. Rouen, 1896.
Afr 8283.6F	Great Britain. Colonial Office. Correspondence related to South Africa Republic. London, 1896.
Afr 5635.1	Hanotaux, G. L'affaire de Madagascar. 3e ed. Paris, 1896.
Afr 1608.96	Hay, J.D. A memoir of Sir John Hay Drummond Hay. London, 1896.
Afr 608.96	Heawood, E. Geography of Africa. London, 1896.
Afr 500.7	Hertslet, E. Map of Africa by treaty. London, 1896. 3v.
Afr 8283.16	Hofmeyr, N.J. De Afrikaner-Boer en de Jameson-inval. Kaapstad, 1896.
Afr 8283.22	Jameson's heroic charge. Johannesburg, 1896.
Afr 8667.85	Junius, J.H. Het leven in Zuid-Afrika. Amsterdam, 1896.
Afr 8283.17	King, James. Dr. Jameson's raid. London, 1896.
Afr 5635.2	Knight, E.F. Madagascar in war time. London, 1896.
Afr 5635.10	Lenure, Jean. Madagascar, l'expedition au point de vue medical. Paris, 1896.
Afr 9488.96.2	Leonard, A.G. How we made Rhodesia. 2. ed. London, 1896.

1896 - cont.

Afr 5748.96.8	Locamus, P. Madagascar et l'alimentation européenne. Paris, 1896.
Afr 5748.96.7	Locamus, P. Madagascar et ses richesses. Paris, 1896.
Afr 9088.8	Loo, C.J. van der. De... Zuid-Afrikaansche Republiek. Zwolle, 1896.
Afr 5620.10	Lux. La verité sur Madagascar. Paris, 1896.
Afr 3705.9	Macdonald, A. Why Gordon perished...Political causes which led to Sudan disasters. London, 1896.
Afr 4390.25	Mantegazza, Vico. La guerra in Africa. 3a ed. Firenze, 1896.
Afr 4785.6	Mocchi, L. La Somalia italiana. Napoli, 1896.
Afr 8235.13	Molteno, Percy A. A federal in South Africa. London, 1896.
Afr 8152.93	Molyneux, W.C.F. Campaigning in South Africa and Egypt. London, 1896.
Afr 3150.5A	Muir, William. The Mameluke or slave dynasty of Egypt. London, 1896.
Afr 9438.96	Muller, H.P.N. De Zuid-Afrikaansche Republiek en Rhodesia. 's-Gravenhage, 1896.
Afr 6196.12	Musgrave, George Clarke. To Kumassi with Scott. London, 1896.
Afr 8225.6	Newman, C.L.N. With the Boers in the Transvaal 1880-1. London, 1896.
Afr 3275.10	Pensa, Henri. L'Egypte et l'Europe. Paris, 1896.
Afr 8278.96.3	Regan, W.F. Boer and Uitlander. London, 1896.
Afr 3275.7	Resener, Hans. Agypten unter englischer Okkupation. Berlin, 1896.
NEDL Afr 6275.7	Robinson, C.H. Hausaland. London, 1896.
Afr 1608.96.3	Schabelsky, E. von. Harem und Moschee. Reiseskizzen aus Marokko. Berlin, 1896.
Afr 8745.10	Schriener, O. The political situation. London, 1896.
Afr 9446.27	Selous, F.C. Sunshine and storm in Rhodesia. London, 1896.
Afr 200.13.5	Septans, Albert. Les expéditions anglaises en Afrique, Ashantel 1873-1874. Paris, 1896.
Afr 5748.96	Sibree, J. Madagascar before the conquest. London, 1896.
Afr 3700.5.3	Slatin, R.C. Fire and sword in the Sudan. Leipzig, 1896.
Afr 3700.5.2	Slatin, R.C. Fire and sword in the Sudan. London, 1896.
NEDL Afr 3700.5	Slatin, R.C. Fire and sword in the Sudan. London, 1896.
Afr 9086.10	South Africa. Political laws. London, 1896.
Afr 8283.5F	South Africa. Stukken betrekking hebbende op den inval van de troepen der British South Africa Company. Pretoria, 1896.
Afr 8278.96	Spruyt, C.B. Africaners en Nederlanders. Amsterdam, 1896.
Afr 8658.96.5	Tangye, H. Lincoln. In new South Africa. London, 1896.
Afr 7218.96	Theal, George McCall. The Portuguese in South Africa. Cape Town, 1896.
Afr 8283.14	Thomas, C.G. Johannesburg in arms, 1895-96. London, 1896.
Afr 725.4.5	Thomson, James B. Joseph Thomson, African explorer. London, 1896.
Afr 4392.15F	Treves, Firm, Publisher, Milan. La guerra italo-abissinia, 1895-96. Milano, 1896.
Afr 8670.7.11	Union Steam Ship Company, Ltd. The emigrant's guide to South Africa including Cape Colony. 11th ed. London, 1896.
Afr 5635.10.5	Verité sur la guerre de Madagascar par le colonel XXX. Toulouse, 1896.
Afr 2374.1	Vivarez, M. Au sujet du Touat. Alger, 1896.
Afr 8250.15	Waal, D.C. Reizen met Cecil Rhodes door de wilde wereld van Zuid-Afrika. Amsterdam, 1896.
Afr 8250.16	Waal, David C. With Rhodes in Mashonaland. Cape Town, 1896.
Afr 510.14	Wahl, M. La France aux colonies. Paris, 1896.
Afr 8278.96.5	Withers, H. English and Dutch in South Africa. London, 1896.
Afr 3275.4	Wood, H.F. Egypt under the British. London, 1896.

1897

Afr 8088.92.2	Aitton, D. Geschiedenis van Zuid Afrika. 2e druk. Amsterdam, 1897.
Afr 3735.8	Atteridge, A.H. Towards Khartoum. ondon, 1897.
Afr 6283.9	Bacon, R.H. Benin, the city of blood. London, 1897.
Afr 9446.26	Baden-Powell. The Matabele campaign, 1896. London, 1897.
Afr 5897.2	Barkly, Fanny Alexandra. From the tropics to the North Sea. London, 1897.
Afr 4718.97.5F	Bizzoni, A. L'Eritrea nel passato e nel presente. Milano, 1897.
Afr 5748.96.10	Blavet, Emile. Au pays Malgache. Paris, 1897.
Afr 5748.96.9	Blavet, Emile. Au pays Malgache de Paris à Tananarive et retour. 2e ed. Paris, 1897.
Afr 6283.3	Boisragon, A. The Benin massacre. London, 1897.
Afr 5426.120	Bonzon, Charles. A Lambaréné. Nancy, 1897.
Afr 8678.405	Booth, Joseph. Africa for the African. Photoreproduction. n.p., 1897?
Afr 3248.3	Bourguet, A. La France et l'Angleterre en Egypte. Paris, 1897.
Afr 4555.00.5	Brandao, Zephyrino. Pero da Borilhan. Lisboa, 1897.
Afr 8088.97A	Bryce, James. Impressions of South Africa. N.Y., 1897.
Afr 3978.97	Budge, E.A.W. The Nile. 5th ed. London, 1897.
Afr 1608.97.5	Campbell, A. A ride in Morocco. Toronto, 1897.
Afr 8283.25F	Cape of Good Hope. Parliament. House of Commons. Report of the Select Committee of the Cape of Good Hope. London, 1897.
Afr 4258.97	Castonnet des Fosses. L'Abyssinie et les Italiens. Paris, 1897.
Afr 8250.3	Cecil Rhodes. London, 1897.
Afr 5746.50	Chavanon, J. Une ancienne relation sur Madagascar (1650). Paris, 1897.
Afr 4394.2	Chiala, Valentino. Il Generale Dabormida nella giornata del 1 marzo 1896. Roma, 1897.
Afr 820.3.3	Coillard, F. On the threshold of central Africa. London, 1897.
Afr 4300.1	Conti Rossini, C. Note etiopiche. Una guerra fra la Nubia. Roma, 1897.
Afr 5753.5	Cournot, M. La famille à Madagascar. Angers, 1897.
Afr 8283.9.2	Davis, R.H. Dr. Jameson's raiders. N.Y., 1897.
Afr 603.23.10	Deherain, Henri. Quid Schems Eddin el dimashqui geographus de Africa cognitum habuerit. Thesis. Paris, 1897.
Afr 4558.97.5	Dorleans, H. Une visite à l'empereur Menelick. Paris, 1897.
Afr 5247.10	Dubois, Felix. Tombouctou la mystérieuse. Paris, 1897.
Afr 5874.10	Dubois. Voyages made to Dauphine and Bourbon. London, 1897.
Afr 5635.8.5	Duchesne, C. Rapport sur l'expedition de Madagascar. Text and atlas. Paris, 1897. 2v.

1897 - cont.

Afr 9488.97   Dutoit, Stephanus Jacobus. Rhodesia. London, 1897.
Afr 2508.5   Foucher, Louis. De l'évolution du protectorat de la France sur la Tunisie. Thèse. Paris, 1897.
Afr 2530.5F   France. Ministère des Affaires Etrangères. Documents diplomatiques. Paris, 1897.
Afr 7324.10   Freire d'Andrade, Alfredo. Colonisação de Lourenço Marques. Porto, 1897.
Afr 5573.10   Froidevaux, H. Un mémoire inédit de La Haye sur Madagascar. Paris, 1897. 4 pam.
Afr 4394.13   Gamerra, Giovanni. Ricordi di un prigioniero di guerra nello Scioa, marzo 1896-gennaio 1897. 2a ed. Firenze, 1897.
Afr 8283.11   Garrett, Fydell Edmund. The story of an African crisis. Westminster, 1897.
Afr 1955.24   Général Lapasset. Algérie 1817-1864. Paris, 1897. 2v.
Afr 2208.97   Grandin. A pied, le tour de la terre...à travers le sud-algérien. Paris, 1897.
Afr 8283.26F   Great Britain. Parliament. House of Commons. Second report. London, 1897.
Afr 4394.3.5   Guarniere, L. La battaglia di Adua e il popola italiano. 2a ed. Torino, 1897.
Afr 7808.97   Guide de la section de l'Etat Indépendant du Congo, la Bruxelles exposition. Bruxelles, 1897.
Afr 640.6.5   Haliburton, R.G. How a race of Pigmies was found. Toronto, 1897.
Afr 8283.10   Hammond, J.H. A woman's part in a revolution. N.Y., 1897.
Afr 2312.4   Hautfort, Felix. Au pays des palmes, Biskra. Paris, 1897.
Afr 2312.4.2   Hautfort, Felix. Au pays des palmes, Biskra. 2e ed. Paris, 1897.
Afr 7567.4   Hinde, S.L. The fall of the Congo Arabs. London, 1897.
Afr 7567.4.5   Hinde, Sidney L. The fall of the Congo Arabs. N.Y., 1897.
Afr 5635.12F   Hocquard, C.E. L'expedition de Madagascar. Paris, 1897.
Afr 8278.97.3   Hofmeyr, N.J. Die Buren und Jamesons Einfall. Bremen, 1897.
Afr 4718.97   Jaffanel, C. de. Les Italiens en Érythrie. Paris, 1897.
Afr 9548.3   Johnston, H.H. British central Africa. N.Y., 1897.
Afr 8278.97.5   Jorissen, E.J.P. Transvaalische herinneringen 1876-96. Amsterdam, 1897.
Afr 678.97   Kingsley, M.H. Travels in West Africa. London, 1897.
Afr 3735.9   Knight, E.F. Letters from the Sudan. London, 1897.
Afr 9446.25   Laing, D.J. The Matabele rebellion, 1896. London, 1897.
Afr 555.40   Lecomte, E. Plan alto do sul de Angola. Lisboa, 1897.
Afr 2208.87.2   Leroy-Beaulieu. L'Algérie et la Tunis. Paris, 1897.
Afr 1734.5   Lopes, David. Textas em aljamia portuguesa. Lisboa, 1897.
Afr 2662.1.5F   Ludwig Salvator. Benzert. Prag, 1897.
Afr 6648.3F   Luschan, F. Von. Beitraege zur Völkerkunde. Berlin, 1897.
Afr 6497.12   MacDonald, J.R.L. Soldiering and surveying in British East Africa. London, 1897.
Afr 8658.97   MacNab, F. On veldt and farm. London, 1897.
Afr 8283.7   Mann, A.M. The truth from Johannesburg. London, 1897.
Afr 9435.6F   Martin, R.E.R. Report on native administration of British South Africa Company. London, 1897.
Afr 4732.2   Martini, F. Cose africane, da Saati ad Abba Carima. Milano, 1897.
Afr 1608.97   Martiniere, H.M.P. de la. Notice sur le Maroc. Paris, 1897.
Afr 555.20.9   Marwick, William. William and Louisa Anderson. Edinburgh, 1897.
Afr 1325.4.5PF   Menendez Pidal, Juan. Misiones catolicas de Marruecos. Barcelona, 1897.
Afr 555.9.23   Morshead, A.E. The history of the Universities Mission to Central Africa. London, 1897.
Afr 2532.4   Pavy, A. L'expédition de Mores. Paris, 1897.
Afr 4392.6   Pellenc, A.J.J. Les Italiens en Afrique (1880-1896). Paris, 1897.
Afr 6146.8   Pierson, Arthur. Seven years in Sierra Leone. N.Y., 1897.
Afr 9446.28   Plumer, Herbert C. An irregular corps in Matabeleland. London, 1897.
Afr 4785.13PF   Potocki, Jozef. Notatki mysliwskie z Afryki. Warszawa, 1897.
Afr 8278.97   Procter, John. Boers and little Englanders. London, 1897.
Afr 555.9.28   Rankine, W.H. A hero of the dark continent, Rev. William A. Scott. Edinburgh, 1897.
Afr 8252.7   Raymond, H. B.I. Barnato. London, 1897.
Afr 9086.17   Roels, E. Boers et Anglais. Autours des mines d'or. Paris, 1897.
Afr 510.2   Rouard de Card, E. Les traités de protectorat. Paris, 1897.
Afr 510.6   Sarzeau, J. Les français aux colonies. Paris, 1897.
Afr 608.97   Schulz, A. The new Africa. London, 1897.
Afr 635.4.5   Sergi, Giuseppe. Africa, antropologia della stirpe camitica. Torino, 1897.
Afr 4315.3   Shihab al-Din Ahmad Ibn 'Abd al-Kadir. Histoire de la conquête de l'Abyssinie. Texte arabe v.1, française v.2. Paris, 1897-1909. 2v.
Afr 6455.6   Smith, A.D. Through unknown African countries. London, 1897.
Afr 9446.36   Sykes, Frank W. With Plumer in Matabeleland, an account of the operations of the Matabeleland relief force during the rebellion of 1896. Westminster, 1897.
Afr 1753.8   Tello Amondareyn, M. Ceuta llave principal del Estrecho. Madrid, 1897.
Afr 8283.12   Terrail, G. Le Transvaal et la chartered. Paris, 1897.
Afr 550.10   Tetu, H. Le R.P. Bouchard. Québec, 1897.
Afr 8088.88.8   Theal, G.M. Geschiedenis van Zuid-Afrika. 's-Gravenhage, 1897.
Afr 8707.5   Theal, G.M. Records of Cape colony. v.1-35 and index. London, 1897-1905. 36v.
Afr 5260.5   Toutée, Georges Joseph. Dahomé, Niger, Touareg. Paris, 1897.
Afr 3275.12   Traill, H.D. LordCromer. London, 1897.
Afr 4558.97   Vigneras, S. Une mission française en Abyssinie. Paris, 1897.
Afr 6887.6   Volkens, G. Der Kilimandscharo. Berlin, 1897
Afr 8235.5   Wilmot, A. History of our own times in South Africa 1872-1898. Cape Town, 1897. 3v.
Afr 8088.97.6   Wirth, A. Geschichte Südafrikas. Bonn, 1897.
Afr 4394.1   Ximenes, E. Sul campo di Adua. Milan, 1897.

1898

Afr 8285.10   Alderson, E.A.H. With the mounted infantry and the Mashona-landfield force, 1896. London, 1898.
Afr 3735.5   Alford, H.S.L. The Egyptian Soudan. London, 1898.

1898 - cont.

Afr 1347.3.8   Alvarez Cabrera, J. Accion militar...imperio de Marruecos. Madrid, 1898.
Afr 8658.98.5   Aubert, Georges. L'Afrique du Sud. Paris, 1898.
Afr 6172.1   Baden-Powell, R. The downfall of Prempeh. London, 1898.
Afr 4115.8   Ball, E.A. Reynold. The city of the caliphs. London, 1898.
Afr 4392.3   Baratieri, O. Memorie d'Africa (1892-1896). Torino, 1898.
Afr 2208.98.3   Barbet, Charles. Au pays des Burnous. Alger, 1898.
Afr 2748.98.5   Basset, R. Documents géographiques sur l'Afrique septentrional. Paris, 1898.
Afr 2208.98   Battandier. L'Algérie. Paris, 1898.
Afr 3735.6   Bennett, E.N. The downfall of the Dervishes. London, 1898.
Afr 1635.1   Bertholon. Les premiers colons. v.1 2. Tunis, 1898.
Afr 9710.5.7   Bertrand, Alfred. Au pays des Barotsi, Haut-Zambèze. Paris, 1898.
Afr 8658.97.7   Bigelow, P. White man's Africa. N.Y., 1898.
Afr 6275.9   Bindloss, H. In the Niger country. Edinburgh, 1898.
Afr 1885.3   Blum, N. La croisade de XImenes en Afrique. Oran, 1898.
Afr 7548.98   Boulger, D.C. The Congo state. London, 1898.
Afr 2608.95.8   Bruun, D. Cave dwellers of southern Tunisia. London, 1898.
Afr 8088.97.2   Bryce, James. Impressions of South Africa. N.Y., 1898.
Afr 3735.2   Burleigh, B. Sirdar and Khalifa. London, 1898.
Afr 3735.2.5   Burleigh, B. Sirdar and Khalifa. 3rd ed. London, 1898.
Afr 7808.98   Burrows, G. The land of the pigmies. London, 1898.
Afr 7808.98.2   Burrows, G. The land of the pigmies. N.Y., 1898.
Afr 3198.98   Cameron, D.A. Egypt in the nineteenth century. London, 1898.
Afr 5760.6   Carol, Jean. Chez les Hovas (au pays rouge). Paris, 1898.
Afr 5760.6.2   Carol, Jean. Chez les Hovas (au pays rouge). 2e ed. Paris, 1898.
Afr 4335.1   Castanhoso, M. de. Dos feitos de D. Christovam da Gama. Lisboa, 1898.
Afr 5406.198   Castellani, Charles. Vers le Nil français. Paris, 1898.
Afr 1368.78.3   Castellanos, M.P. Historia de Marruecos. Tanger, 1898.
Afr 9446.20   Chalmers, James. Fighting the Matabele. London, 1898.
Afr 820.3.6   Coillard, F. Sur le Haut-Zambèze. Paris, 1898.
Afr 725.12   Decle, Lionel. Three years in savage Africa. London, 1898.
Afr 3685.5   Deherain, H. Le Soudan égyptien sous Mehemet Ali. Paris, 1898.
Afr 200.6   Deville, V. Partage de l'Afrique. Paris, 1898.
Afr 8278.98.5   Duplessis, C.N.J. Uit de geschiedenis van de Zuid-Afrikansche Republiek en de afrikaanders. Amsterdam, 1898.
Afr 4392.1   Eletz, Yu. Imperator Menelik. St. Petersburg, 1898.
Afr 3725.7   Emin Pasha. Emin Pasha. Berlin, 1898.
Afr 555.38   Escande, Benj. Souvenirs intimes. Genève, 1898.
Afr 5765.6.10   Escande, Benjamin. Neuf mois à Madagascar. Paris, 1898.
Afr 5748.98.3   Escande, E. A Madagascar, hier et aujourd'hui. Paris, 1898.
Afr 4555.00   Ficalho. Viagens de Pedro da Covilhan. Lisboa, 1898.
Afr 6455.22   Fitzgerald, W.W.A. Travels in...British East Africa...Zanzibar and Pemba. London, 1898.
Afr 2748.98   Foureau, F. Mon neuvième voyage au Sahara. Paris, 1898.
Afr 3740.1F   France. Ministère des Affaires Étrangères. Affaires du Haut-Nil 1897-98. Paris, 1898.
Afr 200.4.3F   France. Ministère des Affaires Etrangères. Documents diplomatiques. Paris, 1898.
Afr 6192.18   Freeman, Richard A. Travels and life in Ashanti and Jaman. Westminster, 1898.
Afr 632.10   Frobenius, L.V. Ursprung der Kultur. Berlin, 1898.
Afr 4558.98A   Gleichen, A.E.W. With the mission to Menelik 1897. London, 1898.
Afr 1608.98   Graham, R.B.C. Mogreb-el-Acksa, a journey in Morocco. London, 1898.
Afr 3740.2F   Great Britain. Parliament. Correspondence with the French government. London, 1898.
Afr 5748.98   Grosclaude, E. Un Parisien à Madagascar. Paris, 1898.
Afr 4523.5   Hasan ibn Ahmad al Haimi. Zur Geschichte Abessiniens im 17. Jahrhundert. Berlin, 1898.
Afr 1915.2   Heinrich, P. L'alliance franco-algérienne. Lyon, 1898.
Afr 8283.13   Hillier, A.P. Raid and reform. London, 1898.
Afr 1390.4   Ibn al-Atir. Annales du Maghreb et de l'Espagne. Alger, 1898.
Afr 608.98F   Independent. Africa number. May 5, 1898. N.Y., 1898.
Afr 9548.5   Johnston, H.H. British central Africa. 2. ed. London, 1898.
Afr 7315.3   Junod, H.A. Les Ba-ronga. Neuchatel, 1898.
Afr 5765.17   Keck, Daniel. Histoire des origines du christianisme à Madagascar. Thèse. Paris, 1898.
Afr 854.2   Keller, C. Die östafrikanischen Inseln. v.2. Berlin, 1898.
Afr 6192.3   Kemp, Dennis. Nine years at the Gold Coast. London, 1898.
Afr 8278.98.3   Kotze, J.G. Documents relating to judicial crisis in Transvaal. London, 1898.
Afr 4115.6.3   Lane-Poole, S. Cairo. 3d ed. London, 1898.
Afr 2625.6   Lapie, P. Les civilisations tunisiennes. Paris, 1898.
Afr 4390.45   Lauribar, Paul de. Douze ans en Abyssinie. Paris, 1898.
Afr 2458.98   Loth, Gaston. Histoire de la Tunisie. Paris, 1898.
Afr 6192.2   Macdonald, G. The Gold Coast, past and present. London, 1898.
Afr 5235.55   MacLachlan, T. Banks. Mungo Park. London, 1898.
Afr 5748.98.10   Mager, H. La vie à Madagascar. Paris, 1898.
Afr 5573.5   Malotet, A. Les origines de la colonisation française à Madagascar, 1648-1661. Paris, 1898.
Afr 6095.3   Mockler-Ferryman, A.F. Imperial Africa; the rise, progress and future in British...Africa. London, 1898.
NEDL Afr 6455.28   Neumann, A.H. Elephant hunting in East Equatorial Africa. London, 1898.
Afr 590.5.8   Newman, Henry S. Banani, the transition of slavery. London, 1898.
Afr 3275.18   Noailles, G. de. Les Anglais en Egypte. Paris, 1898.
Afr 3198.98.5   Notovich, Nikolai. L'Europe et l'Égypte. Paris, 1898.
Afr 8210.9   Oordt, J.F.V. Paul Kruger en de opkomst van de Zuid Afrikaansche Republiek. Amsterdam, 1898.
Afr 500.8   Ortray, F. van. Conventions internationales. Bruxelles, 1898.
Afr 6688.2   Phehn, R. Beitraege zur Völkerkunde des Togogebietes. Halle, 1898.
Afr 7540.3   Pierantoni, R. Il Trattato di Berlino e lo stato del Congo. Roma, 1898.
Afr 5748.98.5   Piolet, J.B. Douze leçons à la Sorbonne sur Madagascar. Paris, 1898.

1898 - cont.

Afr 3978.98.5 Pollard, Joseph. The land of the monuments. 2nd ed. London, 1898.
Afr 9093.5 Rae, C. Malaboch. London, 1898.
Afr 1570.2 Rouard de Card, E. Les traités. La France et le Maroc. Paris, 1898.
Afr 5758.4 Roux, Jules C. Les voies de communication et les moyens de transport à Madagascar. Paris, 1898.
Afr 7322.12 Sampaio, Matheus Augusto Ribeiro de. Cartas, officios, ordens de serviço lavrada a 23 de dezembro de 1897 e alguns documentos. Lisboa, 1898.
Afr 200.9.5 Sanderson, E. Africa in the 19th century. London, 1898.
Afr 200.9 Sanderson, E. Africa in the 19th century. N.Y., 1898.
Afr 1680.2.5 Schnell, P. L'atlas marocain d'apres les documents originaux. Paris, 1898.
Afr 9148.98 Seidel, A. Transvaal. Berlin, 1898.
Afr 4317.1 Shihab al-Din Ahmad Ibn Abd al-Kadir. Futuh el-Habacha. Paris, 1898.
Afr 3700.5.10 Slatin, R.C. Fer et feu au Soudan. Le Caire, 1898. 2v.
Afr 3700.5.15 Slatin, R.C. Ferro e fuoco nel Sudan. Roma, 1898.
Afr 3700.5.7 Slatin, R.C. Fire and sword in the Sudan. London, 1898.
Afr 1018.2.5 Société de Géographie de la Province d'Oran. Journal des travaux, 1878-1927. (Table générale). Oran, 1898-1930. 3v.
Afr 8658.98.2 Stanley, H.M. ThroughSouth Africa. London, 1898.
Afr 8658.98 Stanley, H.M. ThroughSouth Africa. N.Y., 1898.
Afr 8230.5A Statham, F.R. Paul Kruger and his times. London, 1898.
Afr 3978.98 Steevens, G.W. Egypt in 1898. N.Y., 1898.
Afr 3735.4 Steevens, G.W. With Kitchener to Khartum. Edinburgh, 1898.
Afr 3735.4.1 Steevens, G.W. With Kitchener to Khartum. N.Y., 1898.
Afr 3735.4.2 Steevens, G.W. With Kitchener to Khartum. 12th ed. Edinburgh, 1898.
Afr 8028.2 Suhnnke Hollnay, H.C. Bibliography related to South Africa. Cape Town, 1898.
Afr 108.98 Taylor, W. The flaming torch in darkest Africa. N.Y., 1898.
Afr 8030.10 Theal, G.M. Records of South-eastern Africa. v.1- London, 1898- 9v.
Afr 9438.98 Thomson, H.C. Rhodesia and its government. London, 1898.
Afr 550.27 Thornton, D.M. Africa waiting, or The problem of Africa's evangelization. N.Y., 1898.
Afr 6143.19 Trotter, James Keith. The Niger sources and the borders of the new Sierra Leone protectorate. London, 1898.
Afr 6018.98 Vandeleur, S. Campaigning on the upper Nile. London, 1898.
Afr 9854.5 Ward, Gertrude. Life of Charles Alan Smythies, bishop of the university mission to Central Africa. London, 1898.
Afr 8658.98.7 Wormser, J.A. Van Amsterdam naar Pretoria. Amsterdam, 1898.
Afr 8278.98A Younghusband, F.E. South Africa of to-day. London, 1898.

1899

Afr 8210.6 Africanus. The Transvaal Boers. London, 1899.
Afr 4295.2 Almeida, M. de. Vida de Takla Haymanot. Lisboa, 1899.
Afr 5753.3 Andre, C. De l'esclavage à Madagascar. Paris, 1899.
Afr 6535.4 Ansorge, W.J. Under the African sun. N.Y., 1899.
Afr 8278.99.27 Appleton, L. Britain and the Boers. London, 1899.
Afr 575.7 Atterbury, Anson Phelps. Islam in Africa. N.Y., 1899.
Afr 3275.13 Aubin, E. Les Anglais aux Indes et en Egypte. Paris, 1899.
Afr 4392.3.5 Baratieri, O. Mémoires d'Afrique (1892-1896). Paris, 1899.
Afr 8687.7 Bell, Nancy R.E. (Mevgens). Heroes of discovery in South Africa. London, 1899.
Afr 5056.99 Benitez, Cristobal. Mi viaje por el interior del Africa. Tangier, 1899.
Afr 555.149.5 Bertrand, Alfred. En Afrique avec le missionnaire Coillard. Genève, 1899.
Afr 9710.5 Bertrand, Alfred. The kingdom of the Barotsi. London, 1899.
Afr 8278.99.19 Bigger, E.B. The Boer war, its causes. Toronto, 1899.
NEDL Afr 8288.99.23 Birch, J.H. History of the war in South Africa. London, Ont., 1899.
Afr 11216.10 Blackburn, Douglas. Prinsloo of Prinsloosdorp. London, 1899.
Afr 3991.2 Boinet, Bey, A. Dictionnaire géographique de l'Egypte. Le Caire, 1899.
Afr 7332.15 Bonnefont de Varinay, P. de. La compagnie de Mozambique. Lisboa, 1899.
Afr 2224.899 Bonzom, Lucien. Du régime fiscal en Algérie. Paris, 1899.
Afr 8278.99.50 Britain and the Boers. Both sides of the South African question. v.2. N.Y., 1899-1900.
Afr 9488.99 Brown, W.H. On the South African frontier. N.Y., 1899.
Afr 8088.97.3 Bryce, James. Impressions of South Africa. London, 1899.
Afr 8288.99F Buitengewone staat-courant 1899-00. Pretoria, 1899-00.
Afr 3700.6 Bujac, E. Précis de quelques campagnes contemporaines. Pt. III - Egypte et Soudan. Paris, 1899.
Afr 7808.99.5 Buls, Charles. Croquis congolais. Bruxelles, 1899.
Afr 3735.3 Burleigh, B. Khartoum campaign, 1898. London, 1899.
Afr 8225.7 Butler, W.F. Life of Sir George Pomeroy-Colley. London, 1899.
NEDL Afr 3740.4 Caix, R. de. Fachoda. Paris, 1899.
Htn Afr 3735.7* Churchill, Winston S. The river war. London, 1899. 2v.
Afr 8180.5 Cloete, Henry. The history of the great Boer trek. London, 1899.
Afr 8180.5.3 Cloete, Henry. The history of the great Boer trek. N.Y., 1899.
Afr 2025.16 Colin, M. Quelques questions algériennes. Paris, 1899.
Afr 5993.2 Coll, Armengol. Segunda memoria de las misiones. Madrid, 1899.
NEDL Afr 9148.99 Davis, Nathaniel Newnham. The Transvaal under the Queen. London, 1899.
Afr 9488.99.3 Dawkins, C.T. Precis of information concerning Southern Rhodesia. London, 1899.
Afr 8278.99.23 Demolins, E. Boers et Anglais. Paris, 1899.
Afr 8658.99 Devereux, Roy. Side lights on South Africa. London, 1899.
Afr 1660.1 Doutte, E. Les djebala du Maroc. Oran, 1899.
Afr 2225.3 Drapier, H. La condition sociale des indigènes algériens. Paris, 1899.
Afr 8278.99.11 Duplessis, C.N.J. The Transvaal Boer speaking for himself. London, 1899.
Afr 1846.6F Duruy, V. Le 1er regiment de tirailleurs algeriens. Paris, 1899.
Afr 2208.99 Duval, P. Heures d'Afrique. Paris, 1899.
Afr 3978.77.15 Edwards, A.B. A thousand miles up the Nile. London, 1899.

1899 - cont.

Afr 9838.99 Elmslie, W.A. Among the wild Ngoni. N.Y., 1899.
Afr 8278.99.45 Engelenburg, F.V. A Transvaal view of the South African question. Pretoria, 1899.
Afr 8175.15 England and the Boers. Leeds, 1899.
Afr 8278.99.3A Fitzpatrick, J.P. The Transvaal from within. London, 1899.
Afr 8278.99.1 Fitzpatrick, J.P. The Transvaal from within. N.Y., 1899.
Afr 718.34 Foa, Edouard. Chasses aux grandes fauves pendant la traversée du continent noir. Paris, 1899.
Afr 6925.15 Francois, K. von. Deutsch Sudwest-Afrika. Berlin, 1899.
Afr 5640.14.5 Gallieni, J.S. Rapport d'ensemble du Général Gallieni sur la situation général de Madagascar. Paris, 1899. 2v.
Afr 3025.5F Garstin, W. Note on the Soudan. Cairo, 1899.
Afr 718.8F Goetzen, G.A.V. Durch Afrika von Ost nach West. Berlin, 1899.
Afr 9192.5F Great Britain. Colonial Office. Affairs ofSwaziland. London, 1899.
Afr 8288.99.6F Great Britain. Colonial Office. South African Republic. Correspondence. London, 1899-03.
Afr 8288.99.5F Great Britain. Colonial Office. South African Republic. Correspondence. London, 1899-03.
Afr 8288.99.4F Great Britain. Colonial Office. South African Republic. Correspondence. London, 1899-03.
Afr 8285.5F Great Britain. Foreign Office. Further correspondence relating to political affairs in the South African Republic. London, 1899.
Afr 9838.99.5 Great Britain. War Office. Intelligence Division. Precis of information concerning the British Central Africa protectorate. London, 1899.
Afr 9446.30 Grey, A.H.G. Hubert Hervey. London, 1899.
Afr 1453.1 Grey, H.M. In Moorish captivity. London, 1899.
Afr 3740.7 Guetant, L. Marchand-Fashoda. Paris, 1899.
Afr 8210.5 Haggard, H.R. A history of the Transvaal. N.Y., 1899.
Afr 8288.99.25 Harding, William. War in South Africa and the dark continent from savagery to civilization. Chicago, 1899.
Afr 9148.99.5F Harpen, N. van. Nederland-Zuid-Afrika. Amsterdam, 1899.
Afr 8278.99.13 Hillegas, H.C. Oom Paul's people. N.Y., 1899.
Afr 8278.99.21F Hollandia, special Transvaal number. The Hague, 1899.
Afr 1840.3 Hugues, A. La nationalite française. Paris, 1899.
Afr 730.2 Illing, K.E. Der Periplus des Hanno. Dresden, 1899.
Afr 7324.4 Jessett, M.G. Key to South Africa, Delagoa Bay. London, 1899.
Afr 108.99 Johnston, H.H. A history of the colonization of Africa. Cambridge, 1899.
Afr 9148.99.3 Kalff, S. Onder een worsteland volk. Haarlem, 1899.
Afr 6095.4 Kingsley, Mary Henrietta. West African studies. London, 1899.
Afr 6685.3 Klose, Heinrich. Togo unter deutschen Flagge. Berlin, 1899.
Afr 6889.3 Kollmann, P. The Victoria Nyanza. London, 1899.
Afr 8658.99.5 Laurence, Percival M. Collectanea. London, 1899.
NEDL Afr 575.6 Lechatelier, A. L'islam dans l'Afrique occidentale. Paris, 1899.
Afr 2250.2 Lenormend, J. Le peril étranger. 2e ed. Paris, 1899.
Afr 8088.99 Little, W.J.K. Sketches and studies in South Africa. London, 1899.
Afr 9558.6.15 Livingstone, D. Missionary travels and researches in South Africa. London, 1899.
Afr 7809.00 Lloyd, A.B. In dwarf land and cannibal country. London, 1899.
Afr 8088.99.5 Mackenzie, W.D. South Africa, its history. Chicago, 1899.
Afr 5748.99 Madagascar. Guide de l'immigrant à Madagascar. V.1-3 and plates. Paris, 1899. 4v.
Afr 555.145 Maples, C. Journals and papers. London, 1899.
Afr 8278.99.9 Martineau, J. The Transvaal trouble. London, 1899.
Afr 11560.85.100 Matheson, G.E. From veld and street. London, 1899.
Afr 1368.99 Meakin, B. The Moorish empire. London, 1899.
Afr 4718.99 Melli, T.B. La colonia Eritrea. Parma, 1899.
Afr 555.22.22 Merensky, A. Erinnerungen aus dem Missionsleben in Transvaal, 1859-1882. Berlin, 1899.
Afr 8278.99.17 Meysey-Thompson, H. The Transvaal crisis. London, 1899.
Afr 7808.99.3 Mille, P. Au Congo belge. Paris, 1899.
Afr 8278.99.25 Morning leader leaflets. v.1- London, 1899-1900.
Afr 3730.5 Neufeld, C. A prisoner of the Khaleefa. N.Y., 1899.
Afr 3730.5.10 Neufeld, C. A prisoner of the Khaleefa. 3d ed. N.Y., 1899.
Afr 8028.154 New York (City) Public Library. Works relating to South Africa in the New York Public Library. N.Y., 1899.
Afr 550.5 Noble, F.P. The redemption of Africa. Chicago, 1899. 2v.
Afr 550.144 Parsons, Ellen. A life for Africa. Edinburgh, 1899.
Afr 3198.99 Penfield, F.C. Present-day Egypt. N.Y., 1899.
Afr 8288.99.20 Penning, L. De oorlog in Zuid-Afrika. Rotterdam, 1899-03. 3v.
Afr 4295.1 Pereira, F.M.E. Historia dos martyres de Nagran. Lisbon, 1899.
Afr 8278.99.5 Phillips, F. Some South African recollections. London, 1899.
Afr 5832.10 Pitot, Albert. L'Ile de France. Port-Louis, 1899.
Afr 4392.7 Red Cross, Italy (Croce Rossa). Asunto delle relazione sul servizio sanitario...in occasione delle campagna d'Africa, 1895-1896. Roma, 1899.
Afr 7375.6 Roberts, J.T. The Republic of Liberia. Washington, 1899.
Afr 4818.99 Rouard de Card, E. Les possessions françaises de la côte orientale. Paris, 1899.
Afr 1955.6.4 Rousset, C. La conquête d'Alger. Paris, 1899.
Afr 9060.5 Russell, George. The history of old Durban and reminiscences of an emigrant of 1850. Durban, 1899.
Afr 8278.99F Schreiner, Olive. An English-South African's view of the situation. London, 1899.
Afr 8278.99.03 Schreiner, Olive. An English-South African's view of the situation. London, 1899.
Afr 8278.99.29 Schreiner, Olive. The South African question. Chicago, 1899.
Afr 6978.99 Schwabe, K. Mit Schwert inDeutsch-Südwestafrika. Berlin, 1899.
Afr 1623.899 Schwegel, H. Marokko. Wien, 1899.
Afr 5620.6 Shervinton, Kathleen. The Shervintons, soldiers of fortune. London, 1899.
Afr 9086.5 South Africa. Constitution. London, 1899.
Afr 8283.8 Stead, W.J. The scandal of the South African committee. London, 1899.
Afr 8278.99.7 Stead, W.T. Shall I slay my brother Boer. London, 1899.
Afr 3735.4.3 Steevens, G.W. With Kitchener to Khartum. N.Y., 1899.
Afr 6320.2 Strandes, J. Die Portugiesenzeit von Deutsch- und Englisch-Ostafrika. Berlin, 1899.

1899 - cont.

Afr 3735.10 Sudan campaign 1896-99. London, 1899.
Afr 5260.10 Toutée, Georges Joseph. Du Dahomé au Sahara. Paris, 1899.
Afr 4785.10 Vannutelli, L. L'Omo. Viaggio d'esplorazione nell'Africa orientale. Milano, 1899.
Afr 1608.99.3 Verneau, R. Le Maroc et les Canaries. Paris, 1899.
Afr 2608.99 Vivian, H. Tunisia. N.Y., 1899.
Afr 8175.6 Voigt, J.C. Fifty years of the history of republic in South Africa, 1795-1845. London, 1899. 2v.
Afr 8288.99.18 War against war in South Africa. London, 1899-00.
Afr 1422.6 Warnier, A.H. Campagne du Maroc (1844). Paris, 1899.
Afr 7808.99 Wauters, A.J. L'Etat Indépendant du Congo. Bruxelles, 1899.
Afr 3275.8A White, A.S. The expansion of Egypt. London, 1899.
Afr 4050.7 White, A.S. From sphinx to oracle. London, 1899.
Afr 8278.99.15 Wilkinson, S. British policy in South Africa. London, 1899.
Afr 8658.99.3F Wormser, J.A. De Zuster-Republieken in Zuid-Afrika. Amsterdam, 1899.
Afr 7308.99 Worsfold, W.B. Portuguese Nyassaland. London, 1899.
Afr 3978.99 Worsfold, W.B. The redemption of Egypt. London, 1899.
Afr 4390.35 Yaltsasamma. Les amis de Menelik II, roi des rois d'Ethiopie. Paris, 1899.
Afr 2608.99.3 Zolla, D. La colonisation agricole en Tunisie. Paris, 1899.

19-

Afr 7809.00.10 Carton de Wiart, H. Mes vacances au Congo. Bruges, 19- .
Afr 8089.09 Colvin, Jan Duncan. South Africa. London, 19- .
Afr 8825.6 Cook, R.A.W. Social organisation and ceremonial institutions of the Bomvana. Cape Town, 19- .
Afr 8678.115 Hahn, Theophilus. Beitrage zur Kunde der Hottentotten. Durban, 19- .
Afr 2025.6.3 Hess, Jean. La vérité sur l'Algérie. Paris, 19- .
Afr 725.17.3F Heudebert, Lucien. Vers les grands lacs de l'Afrique orientale, d'après les notes de l'explorateur. 3. ed. Paris, 19- .
Afr 8250.8.5 Jourdan, P. Cecil Rhodes. London, 19- .
Afr 8658.95.5 Leclercq, Jules. Aux chutes du Zambèze. Paris, 19-.
Afr 9560.5 Moir, F.L.M. After Livingstone. London, 19-.
Afr 2870.18 Sandri, S. Il generale Rodolfo Groziani. Roma, 19-
Afr 3700.22 Short, Thomas. The wars in Egypt. Bristol, 19- .
Afr 855.16 Souvenir of Saint Helena. St. Helena, 19- .
Afr 8325.34 Watson, J. Hannan. A trooper's sketch book of Boer War. Glasgow, 19- .

190-

Afr 8289.00.28F Edwards Dennis and Co. The Anglo-Boer war 1899-1900, an album. Cape Town, 190-
Afr 8325.58F Transvaal war album, the British forces in South Africa. London, 190-.
Afr 7308.80 Wauters, Alphonse Jules. Voyage au pays de l'ivoire. Bruxelles, 190-.

1900

Afr 8289.00.3 Absent minded war. London, 1900.
Afr 1736.4 Alcala Galiano, Pelayo. Santa Cruz de Mar Pequeña. Madrid, 1900.
Afr 1609.00 Arnold, R.S. Studien zur wirthschaftsgeographie von Marokko. Marburg, 1900.
Afr 8305.6 Ashe, E.O. Besieged by the Boers. N.Y., 1900.
Afr 5318.14 Aspe-Fleurimont, L. La Guinée française. Paris, 1900.
Afr 8300.8 Atkins, J.B. The relief of Ladysmith. London, 1900.
Afr 3275.13.2 Aubin, E. Les Anglais aux Indes et en Egypte. Paris, 1900.
Afr 2228.9 Auclert, Hubertine. Les femmes arabes. Paris, 1900.
Afr 8325.17 Bagot, Dosia. Shadows of the war. London, 1900.
Afr 8310.5 Baillie, F.D. Mafeking. N.Y., 1900.
Afr 679.00.10 Barrow, Alfred Henry. Fifty years in Western Africa. London, 1900.
Afr 8315.13 Battersby, H.F.P. In the web of a war. London, 1900.
Afr 8089.06 Beck, Henry. History of South Africa and the Boer-British war. Philadelphia, 1900.
Afr 8279.00.13 Bell, F.W. The South African conspiracy. London, 1900.
Afr 3990.5 Benedite, G. Aaron. Egypte. Paris, 1900.
Afr 8325.56 Bennett, E.N. With Methuen's column on an ambulance train. London, 1900.
Afr 7809.00.5 Bentley, W.H. Pioneering on the Congo. N.Y., 1900. 2v.
Afr 8658.97.10 Bigelow, P. White man's Africa. N.Y., 1900.
Afr 2010.6 Bletterie, A. Le 9me régiment des mobiles de l'Allier. 1870-71. Lapalisse, 1900.
Afr 8279.00.26 Boissevain, Charles. The struggle of the Dutch republics, open letter to an American lady. Amsterdam, 1900.
NEDL Afr 200.10 Bonnefon, E.L. L'Afrique politique en 1900. Paris, 1900.
Afr 9489.00 Bordeaux, A. Rhodesia et Transvaal. Paris, 1900.
Afr 9161.5 Bovill, J.H. Natives under the Transvaal flag. London, 1900.
Afr 8230.7 Brouwer, W. Paul Kruger. Amsterdam, 1900.
Afr 8230.10 Bruce, C.T. The real Kruger and the Transvaal. N.Y., 1900.
Afr 8279.00A Bryce, J. Briton and Boer. N.Y., 1900.
Afr 8279.00.2 Bryce, J. Briton and Boer. New ed. N.Y., 1900.
Afr 8088.97.4A Bryce, James. Impressions of South Africa. N.Y., 1900.
Afr 4392.2 Bulatovitch, A.K. S voiskami Menelika II. St. Petersburg, 1900.
Afr 8325.55 Burdett-Coretts, W. The sick and wounded in South Africa. London, 1900.
Afr 8300.6 Burleigh, B. The Natal campaign. London, 1900.
Afr 9161.7 Butler, J.E. Native races and the war. London, 1900.
Afr 8279.00.27 Buttery, J.A. Why Kruger made war. London, 1900.
Afr 8175.7 Cachet, F.L. De worstelstrijd der transvalers. Amsterdam, 1900.
Afr 725.14 Caddick, Helen. A white woman in central Africa. London, 1900.
Afr 2025.3 Casteran, A. L'Algérie française. Paris, 1900.
Afr 2260.1 Cazenave, J. La colonization en Algérie. Alger, 1900.
Afr 8279.00.23 Cecil, Evelyn. On the eve of the war. London, 1900.
Afr 8315.6 Churchill, W.S. Jan Hamilton's march. London, 1900.
Afr 8300.7A Churchill, W.S. London to Ladysmith. London, 1900.
Afr 8300.7.3 Churchill, W.S. London to Ladysmith. Toronto, 1900.
Afr 8300.7.5 Churchill, W.S. London to Ladysmith via Pretoria. London, 1900.

1900 - cont.

Afr 8279.00.52 Clark, G.B. The official correspondence between the governments of Great Britain, the South African Republic. London, 1900.
Afr 1581.5 Collin, V. Le maroc et les intérêts belges. Louvain, 1900.
Afr 5180.15 Colonies françaises, Sénégal-Soudan. Paris, 1900.
Afr 3979.00 Cook, J. Programme for visiting Egypt. London, 1900.
Afr 2640.1 Couche, L. Pourquoi devenir propriétaire en Tunisie. Lille, 1900.
Afr 3730.4 Cuzzi, G. Fünfzehn Jahre Gefangener des falschen Propheten. Leipzig, 1900.
Afr 200.8 Darcy, Jean. La conquête de l'Afrique. Paris, 1900.
Afr 8289.00.7 Davis, R.H. With both armies in South Africa. N.Y., 1900.
Afr 575.8 Doutte, E. L'islam algérien en l'an 1900. Alger, 1900.
Afr 8289.00.15 Doyle, A.C. The great Boer war. London, 1900.
Afr 8279.00.17 Droit des Anglais dans la guerre de Transvaal. Genève, 1900.
Afr 2208.57 Duveyrier, H. Journal d'un voyage dans la province. Paris, 1900.
Afr 9149.00 Edwards, Neville. The Transvaal in war and peace. London, 1900.
Afr 8279.00.44 Eisenhart, Karl. Die Abrechnung mit England. 2. Aufl. München, 1900.
Afr 5640.14 Ellie, Paul. Le Général Gallieni. Paris, 1900.
Afr 1088.5.6 Fagnan, E. L'Afrique septentrionale au XIIe siècle de notre ère. Constantine, 1900.
Afr 5318.8 Famechon. Notice sur la Guinée française. Paris, 1900.
Afr 8279.00.21 Farrelly, M.J. The settlement after the war. London, 1900.
Afr 7315.30 Feio, Manuel Moreira. Estudos sociologicos; indigenas de Moçambique. Lisboa, 1900.
Afr 5993.8 Ferrer Piera, P. Fernando Poo y sus dependencias. Barcelona, 1900.
Afr 8175.8 Fisher, W.E.G. The Transvaal and the Boers. London, 1900.
X Cg Afr 8278.99.4 Fitzpatrick, J.P. The Transvaal from within. London, 1900.
X Cg Afr 8278.99.2 Fitzpatrick, J.P. The Transvaal from within. London, 1900.
Afr 8278.99.4.5A Fitzpatrick, J.P. The Transvaal from within. N.Y., 1900.
Afr 718.29 Foa, Edouard. De l'océan Indien à l'océan Atlantique, la traversée de l'Afrique. Paris, 1900.
Afr 5385.8 Fonssagrives, J. Notice sur le Dahomey. Paris, 1900.
Afr 575.13 Forget, D.A. L'islam et le christianisme. Paris, 1900.
Afr 5749.00.15 Fournier, René. Notice sur Madagascar. Paris, 1900.
Afr 8295.5 Frocard. La guerre au Transvaal. Paris, 1900. 2v.
Afr 8235.9 Froude, J.A. Two lectures on South Africa. London, 1900.
Afr 2209.00 Galland, C. de. Les petits cahiers algériens. Alger, 1900.
Afr 5874.5 Gassault, A.G. Notice sur la Réunion. Paris, 1900.
Afr 8230.9 Gluckstein, S.M. Queen or president. London, 1900.
Afr 5749.00.10 Grandidier, G. Voyage dans le sud-ouest. Paris, 1900.
Afr 8288.99.15F Great Britain. War Department. True history of the war, official despatches. v.1-5. London, 1900.
Afr 724.3A Grogan, E.S. From the Cape to Cairo. London, 1900.
Afr 5318.7 Guinée française. Rapport d'ensemble. Paris, 1900.
Afr 8279.00.25 Guyot, Yves. Boer politics. London, 1900.
Afr 5247.5 Hacquard, Augustin. Monographie de Tombouctou. Paris, 1900.
Afr 8210.5.5 Haggard, H.R. A history of the Transvaal. N.Y., 1900.
Afr 8225.8 Haggard, H.R. The last Boer war. London, 1900.
Afr 8289.00.40 Hales, A.G. Campaign pictures of the war in South Africa (1899-1900). London, 1900.
Afr 8310.8 Hamilton, J.A. Siege of Mafeking. London, 1900.
Afr 8279.00.9 Hammond, J.H. The Transvaal trouble. N.Y., 1900.
Afr 5640.2 Hellot, F. La pacification de Madagascar. Paris, 1900.
Afr 679.00 Henning, G. Samuel Braun. Basel, 1900.
Afr 9439.00 Hensman, H. A history of Rhodesia. Edinburgh, 1900.
Afr 8289.00.5 Hillegas, H.C. The Boers in war. N.Y., 1900.
Afr 8325.75 Hillegas, H.C. With the Boer forces. London, 1900.
Afr 8279.00.35 Hillier, A.P. South African studies. London, 1900.
Afr 1825.1F Histoire de l'Algérie. Paris, 1900.
Afr 8279.00.32 Hobson, J.A. The war in South Africa. London, 1900.
Afr 8279.00.34 Hobson, J.A. The war in South Africa. London, 1900.
Afr 8279.00.33 Hobson, J.A. The war in South Africa. N.Y., 1900.
Afr 8325.10 Hofmeyr, A. The story of my captivity. London, 1900.
Afr 8279.00.54 Hooker, Leroy. The Africanders, a century of Dutch-English feud in South Africa. Chicago, 1900.
Afr 8289.00.52 Hudleston, W.H. The war in South Africa, 1899-1900. London, 1900.
Afr 8230.34F Huldeblad van nederlandsche letterkundigen. Rotterdam, 1900.
Afr 4835.1 Ilg, Alfred. Über die Verkehrsentwicklung in Äthiopien. Zürich, 1900.
Afr 8175.17 Imperial South African Association. The British case against the Boer republics. Westminster, 1900.
Afr 8279.00.3 Ireland, A. The Anglo-Boer conflict. Boston, 1900.
Afr 7549.00 Jozon, L. L'état indépendant du Congo. Paris, 1900.
Afr 5758.5 Jully, M.A. Madagascar. Marseille, 1900.
Afr 8175.9 Keane, A.H. The Boer states. London, 1900.
Afr 8289.00.35F Kepper, G.L. De zuid-afrikaansche oorlog. Leiden, 1900.
Afr 8289.00.50 Kings handbook of the war. London, 1900.
Afr 678.97.5 Kingsley, M.H. Travels in West Africa. London, 1900.
Afr 8305.5 Kinnear, A. To Modder River with Methuen. Bristol, 1900.
Afr 500.10.3 Kinsky, Karl. Vade mecum für Diplomatische Arbeit auf dem Afrikanischen Continent. 3. Aufl. Leipzig, 1900.
Afr 8230.33 Kruger's secret service. London, 1900.
Afr 8279.00.15 Kuyper, A. La crise sud-africaine. Paris, 1900.
Afr 5180.8 Lasnet. Une mission au Sénégal. Paris, 1900.
Afr 2710.2 Lechatelier, A. Lettre...sur la politique saharienne. n.p., 1900.
Afr 1825.2 Ludwig, Salvator. Bougie, die perle nord afrikas. Leipzig, 1900.
Afr 8279.00.5 MacVane, S.M. The South African question. Boston, 1900.
Afr 8289.00.11 Mahan, A.T. Story of the war in South Africa. London, 1900.
Afr 5765.7 Malotet, A. Saint Vincent de Paul et les missions de Madagascar. Paris, 1900.
Afr 8659.00.11 Mann, Arthur M. The Boer in peace and war. London, 1900.
Afr 8659.00.15 Markham, Violet Rosa. South Africa, past and present. London, 1900.
Afr 4590.1 Martial de Salviac, R.P. Les Galla, grande nation africaine. Cahors, 1900.
Afr 4718.99.2 Melli, T.B. La colonia Eritrea. Parma, 1900.
Afr 8292.5 Mellish, A.E. Our boys under fire. Charlottetown, 1900.
Afr 6887.4 Meyer, H. Der Kilimandjaro. Berlin, 1900.

1900 - cont.

Afr 5620.8   Mignard, E. Etude sur l'établissement de la domination française a Madagascar. Paris, 1900.
Afr 5342.3   Mille, P. Notice sur la Côte-d'Ivoire. n.p., 1900.
Afr 9195.15.5   Miller, Allister Mitchell. Swazieland and the Swazieland corporation. London, 1900.
Afr 8252.5A   Molteno, P.A. Life and times of Sir J.C. Molteno. London, 1900. 2v.
Afr 8289.00.47   Mueller, A. von. Der Krieg in Sud-afrika, 1899-1900. v.1-5. Berlin, 1900.
Afr 8279.00.56   Naville, Edouard. L'indépendance des républiques sud-africaines et l'Angleterre. Genève, 1900.
Afr 8310.9   Neilly, J.E. Besieged with Baden-Powell. Record of siege. London, 1900.
Afr 8300.11   Nevinson, H.W. Ladysmith, the diary of a siege. London, 1900.
Afr 9558.75   Oswell, W.E. William C. Oswell, hunter and explorer. N.Y., 1900. 2v.
Afr 5749.00.5   Paris. Exposition Universelle (1900). Madagascar. Paris, 1900.
Afr 679.00.5   Paris. Exposition Universelle de 1900. Afrique occidentale. Paris, 1900.
Afr 5183.900   Paris. Exposition Universelle de 1900. Sénégal-Soudan, agriculture, industrie, commerce. Paris, 1900.
Afr 555.24.12   Paul, Carl. Die Mission in unsern Kolonien. Heft 2. Leipzig, 1900.
Afr 8300.5   Pearse, H.H.S. Four months besieged. Story of Ladysmith. London, 1900.
Afr 4969.00   Peel, C.V.A. Somaliland. London, 1900.
Afr 8289.00.38   Peinlich, Fuerchtgots. Gedanken und Erinnerungen an den Krieg Englands gegen die Burenstaaten. Berlin, 1900.
Afr 5749.00F   Piolet, J.B. Madagascar. Paris, 1900.
Afr 8210.7   Poirier, Jules. Le Transvaal. Paris, 1900.
Afr 2749.00   Pommerot, J. Une femme chez les sahariennes. Paris, 1900.
Afr 5920.5   Posesiones españolas en el Africa occidental. Madrid, 1900.
Afr 4975.5PF   Potocki, Jozef. Sport in Somaliland. London, 1900.
Afr 8089.00.8   Pratt, E.A. Leading points in South African history, 1486 to March 30, 1900. London, 1900.
Afr 8295.6   Ralph, Julian. Towards Pretoria. N.Y., 1900.
Afr 8135.8   Reitz, F.W. Ein Jahrhundert voller Unrecht. Berlin, 1900.
Htn   Afr 8279.00.41*   Reitz, Francois W. A century of wrong. London, 1900.
Afr 2228.7   Robert, A. L'arabe tel qu'il est. Alger, 1900.
Afr 8320.3   Roberts, Lord. Proclamation 15th Sept. 1900. Lourenço Marques, 1900.
Afr 6275.7.8   Robinson, C.H. Nigeria, our latest protectorate. London, 1900.
Afr 8983.5   Robinson, J. A life time in South Africa. London, 1900.
Afr 8289.00.13   Rosslyn, James. Twice captured. Edinburg, 1900.
Afr 1955.6.2   Rousset, C. Les commencements d'une conquête. Paris, 1900. 2v.
Afr 3258.5.2   Royle, C. The Egyptian campaigns, 1882-85. London, 1900.
Afr 1905.1   Ruff, Paul. La domination espagñole a Oran. Paris, 1900.
Afr 5243.343   Sadi, Abd al-Rahman. Tarikh es-Soudan. Paris, 1900.
Afr 2632.2   Saurin, J. L'invasion sicilienne. Paris, 1900.
Afr 609.00   Schanz, M. Streifzüge der Ost- und Süd-Afrika. Berlin, 1900.
Afr 8659.00.5   Schreiner, O. Losse gedachten over Zuid-Afrika. Haarlem, 1900.
Afr 8279.00.11   Scoble, J. The rise and fall of Krugerism. London, 1900.
Afr 2636.2   Smaja, M. L'extension de la juridiction et de la nationalité française en Tunisie. Tunis, 1900.
Afr 8279.00.19   Stead, W.J. The candidates of Cain. London, 1900.
Afr 8283.8.5   Stead, W.J. Joseph Chamberlain, conspirator of statesman. London, 1900.
Afr 8295.7   Steevens, S.W. From Capetown to Ladysmith. N.Y., 1900.
Afr 8289.00.42   Stickney, Albert. The Transvaal outlook. N.Y., 1900.
Afr 6280.2.20   Stone, Richard Henry. In Afric's [Sic] forest and jungle. Edinburgh, 1900.
Afr 4968.95.5   Swayne, H. Seventeen trips through Somaliland and a visit to Abyssinia. 2d ed. London, 1900.
Afr 8659.00.8   Sykes, Jessica. Side lights on the war in South Africa. London, 1900.
Afr 8325.37F   Thoma, Ludwig. Der Burenkrieg. München, 1900.
Afr 8279.00.39   Thomas, C.H. Origin of the Anglo-Boer war revealed. London, 1900.
Afr 6497.13   Thruston, A.B. African incidents...Egypt and Unyoro. London, 1900.
Afr 3979.00.3   Tillet, J. du. En Egypte. Paris, 1900.
Afr 8289.00A   Times, The. Times history of the war in South Africa. London, 1900-6. 7v.
Afr 3275.9   Traill, H.D. England, Egypt and the Sudan. Westminster, 1900.
Afr 8325.40   Treves, Frederick. The tale of a field hospital. London, 1900.
Afr 2625.7F   Tunisia. Secrétaire Général du Gouvernement. Nomenclature et répartition des tribus de Tunisie. Chelons-Saône, 1900.
Afr 8279.00.7   Vanderhoogt, C.V. The story of the Boers. N.Y., 1900.
Afr 8250.10   Verschoyle, F. Cecil Rhodes, his political life and speeches 1881-1900. London, 1900.
Afr 5796.5.5   Vienne, Emile. Notice sur Mayotte et les Comores. Paris, 1900.
Afr 4869.00   Vigneras, S. Notice sur la côte française des Somalis. Paris, 1900.
Afr 2609.00   Vitry, Alexis. L'oeuvre française en Tunisie. Compiegne, 1900.
Afr 8279.00.47   Volkonskii, G.M. Pour les Boers contre l'impérialisme. Genève, 1900.
Afr 2230.5   Wilkin, A. Among the Berbers of Algeria. London, 1900.
Afr 8289.00.9   Wilkinson, S. Lessons of the war. Westminster, 1900.
Afr 8289.00.24F   Wilson, H.W. With the flag to Pretoria, history, Boer war 1899-1900. London, 1900-01 2v.
Afr 8175.12   Wormser, J.A. Drie en zestig jaren in dienst der vrijheid. Amsterdam, 1900.
Afr 8279.00.31   Wormser, J.A. De oorlog in Zuid-Afrika. Amsterdam, 1900.
Afr 8089.00.3A   Worsfold, W.B. A history of South Africa. London, 1900.
Afr 8050.5   Worsfold, W.B. The problem of South African unity. London, 1900.
Afr 8310.6   Young, Filson. The relief of Mafeking. London, 1900.

1901

Afr 5225.5   Abd al-Rahman ibn Abdallah al-Tonbukti. Tedzkiret en-nisian fi akhbar molouk es-Soudan. Paris, 1901.
Afr 6143.3   Alldrige, T.J. The Sherbro and its hinterland. London, 1901.

1901 - cont.

Afr 7190.25   Almada Negreiros, A.D. Colonies portugaises, ile de San-Thome. Paris, 1901.
Afr 6174.4   Armitage, C.H. The Ashanti campaign of 1900. London, 1901.
Afr 1609.01.5   Bacheracht, Mme A. de. Une mission à la cour cherifienne. Genève, 1901.
Afr 3979.01.5A   Bacon, Lee. Our houseboat on the Nile. Boston, 1901.
Afr 3979.01.2   Bacon, Lee. Our houseboat on the Nile. Boston, 1901.
Afr 8658.01.5   Barnard, Anne. South Africa a century ago. London, 1901.
Afr 8658.01.8   Barnard, Anne. South Africa a century ago. London, 1901.
Afr 2355.5   Basset, René. Nedromah et les Traras. Paris, 1901.
Afr 8315.14   Batts, H.J. Pretoria from within...1899-1900. London, 1901.
Afr 8279.01.15   Bellows, J. The truth about the Transvaal war and the truth about war. 2d. ed. London, 1901.
Afr 5960.13   Beltran y Rozpide, Ricardo. La Guinea española. Barcelona, 1901.
Afr 6174.9   Biss, Harold C. The relief of Kumasi. London, 1901.
Afr 8340.7   Bleloch, W. The new South Africa. N.Y., 1901.
NEDL   Afr 8289.01   Boer version of the Transvaal war. London, 1901.
Afr 5460.5   Bonnel de Meziéres, A. Rapport sur le Haut-Oubangui. Paris, 1901.
Afr 8055.5   Boonzaier, D.C. Owlographs, a collection of South African celebrities in caricature. Cape Town, 1901.
Afr 1665.5   Boron De Segonzac, R. De. Excursion au sous. Paris, 1901.
Afr 555.9.45   Botha Vlok, T.C. Elf jaren in Midden Afrika. Neerbosch, 1901.
Afr 4394.14   Bourelly, G. La battaglia di Abba Garima. Milano, 1901.
Afr 3199.01   Brehier, L. L'Egypte de 1798 à 1900. Paris, 1901.
Afr 505.3.5   British empire series. v.2. 2d ed. London, 1901.
Afr 8289.01.20   Brooke-Hunt, V. A woman's memories of the war in South Africa. London, 1901.
Afr 5385.7   Brunet, L. Dahomey et dépendances. Paris, 1901.
Afr 3978.93.15   Budge, E.A.W. The Nile. 7th ed. London, 1901.
Afr 8289.01.7   Bujac, E. Precis de...campagnes contemporaines d'Afrique centrale. Paris, 1901.
Afr 8292.5.10   Canada. Department of Militia and Defence. Organization, equipment, despatch and service of the Canadians during war in South Africa. Ottawa, 1901. 2 pam.
Afr 8719.01   Cappon, James. Britain's title in South Africa. London, 1901.
Afr 200.7   Chatelain, C. L'Afrique et l'expansion coloniale. Paris, 1901.
Afr 8289.00.21   Childers, E. In the ranks of the C.I.V. London, 1901.
Afr 2609.01   Claretie, G. De Syracuse à Tripoli. Paris, 1901.
Afr 8315.8   Colvile, H.E. Work of the Ninth Division. London, 1901.
Afr 5580.3   Cultru, P. De colonia in...Madagascar. Paris, 1901.
Afr 8279.01   Davis, W. John Bull's crime. N.Y., 1901.
Afr 7465.3   Delafosse, M. Les Libériens et les Baoule. Paris, 1901.
Afr 1975.3   Delorme, A. Sous la chéchia. Paris, 1901.
Afr 8289.01.14   Dickson, W.K.L. The biograph in battle. London, 1901.
Afr 8340.11   Dormer, F.J. Vengeance as a policy in Afrikanderland. London, 1901.
Afr 7851.3   Droogmans, H. Notices sur le Bas-Congo. Bruxelles, 1901.
Afr 7820.5   Droogmans, Hubert. Notices sur le Bas-Congo. Bruxelles, 1901.
Afr 3700.7   Duyarric, G. L'Etat Mahdiste au Soudan. Paris, 1901.
Afr 8279.01.20   Elout, Cornelis. Der Kulturkampf in Süd Afrika. Leipzig, 1901.
Afr 8325.50   Evans, W.S. The Canadian contingents and Canadian imperialism. Toronto, 1901.
Afr 2230.15   Fabre, C. Grand Kabylie, légendes and souvenirs. Paris, 1901.
Afr 1390.3   Fagnan, E. Al-bayano'l-mogrib. Alger, 1901. 2v.
Afr 2438.1   Fitoussi, Elie. L'état tunisien...1525-1901. Tunis, 1901.
Afr 8658.91.7   Foà, Edouard. A travers l'Afrique centrale du Cap au lac Nyassa. 2. éd. Paris, 1901.
Afr 8289.01.25   Fremantle, F.E. Impressions of a doctor in Khaki. London, 1901.
Afr 5573.10.5   Froidevaux, H. La France à Madagascar au XVIIe siècle. Paris, 1901.
Afr 3275.11   Fuller, F.W. Egypt and the hinterland. London, 1901.
Afr 5227.5   Gatelet, A.L.C. Histoire de la conquête du Soudan français. Paris, 1901.
Afr 2218.5   Gaudefroy-Demombynes, M. Notes de sociologie maghrébine. Paris, 1901.
Afr 3977.98   Geoffroy Saint Hilaire, E. Lettres ecrites d'Egypte. Paris, 1901.
Afr 8292.37   Gilbert, S.H. Rhodesia - and after. London, 1901.
Afr 9510.7   Goy, M.K. Dans les solitudes de l'Afrique. Genève, 1901.
Afr 5760.5F   Grandidier, A. L'origine des Malgaches. Paris, 1901.
Afr 8279.01.5F   Great Britain. Report on the Transvaal Concession Commission. London, 1901.
Afr 6174.10F   Great Britain. Colonial Office. Gold Coast. London, 1901.
Afr 6390.10.59   Great Britain. War Office. Intelligence Division. Precis of information concerning the British East Africa Protectorate and Zanzibar. London, 1901.
Afr 6415.5   Gregory, J.W. Foundation of British East Africa. London, 1901.
Afr 5406.201   Guillemot, Marcel. Notice sur le Congo français. (2e. série). Paris, 1901.
Afr 8325.36   Haldane, A. How we escaped from Pretoria. Edinburg, 1901.
Afr 1609.01.8   Hamet, Ismael. Cinq mois au Maroc. Alger, 1901.
Afr 8250.5   Hensman, H. Cecil Rhodes. Edinburg, 1901.
Afr 8089.01.3   Hesteren, J.P. van. Het land van kruger en steijn. Utrecht, 1901.
Afr 4869.01   Heudebert, L. Au pays des Somalis et des Comoriens. Paris, 1901.
Afr 6395.1   Hinde, S.L. Last of the Masai. London, 1901.
Afr 6174.2   Hodgson, M. The siege of Kumassi. N.Y., 1901.
Afr 555.9.55   Hotchkiss, W.R. Sketches from the dark continent. 2d ed. Cleveland, 1901.
Afr 8320.7   Howland, F.H. The chase of De Wet. Providence, 1901.
Afr 5920.2   Iradier, Manuel. Africa, viajes y trabajos de la asociación. Bilbao, 1901. 2v.
Afr 8089.01.5   Klok, J. De boeren-republieken in Zuid-Afrika, hun ontstaan. Utrecht, 1901.
Afr 8292.5.15   Labat, G.P. Le livre d'or. Montreal, 1901.
Afr 2710.2.3   Lechatelier, A. Sahara-Touat et frontière marocaine. n.p., 1901.
Afr 8685.45   Lenk, Heinrich von. Die Geschichte der Buren. Leipzig, 1901-3.
Afr 4559.01.9   Leroux, H. Menelik et nous. Paris, 1901.
Afr 8295.9.3   Linesman. Words by an eye witness. Edinburg, 1901.

1901 - cont.

Afr 8292.16.5 Lloyd, J.B. One thousand miles with the C.I.V. London, 1901.
Afr 8315.11 Mackern, H.F. Side lights on the march. London, 1901.
Afr 8292.15 Mackinnon, W.H. The journal of the C.I.V. (City Imperial Volunteers) in South Africa. London, 1901.
Afr 9558.43 MacLachlan, T.B. David Livingstone. Edinburgh, 1901.
Afr 2482.5 Marengo, E. Genova e Tunisi, 1388-1515. Roma, 1901.
Afr 4590.1.2 Martial de Salviac, R.P. Les Galla, grande nation africaine. Paris, 1901.
Afr 8325.13 May, Edward S. A retrospect on the South African war. London, 1901.
Afr 1609.01 Meakin, B. The land of the Moors. London, 1901.
Afr 150.6 Mees, Jules. Henri le Navigateur. Bruxelles, 1901.
Afr 2225.9 Mercier, E. La question indigène en Algérie au commencement du XXe siècle. Paris, 1901.
Afr 8279.01.4 Methuen, A.M.M. Peace or war in South Africa. London, 1901.
Afr 8279.01.3 Methuen, A.M.M. Peace or war in South Africa. London, 1901.
Afr 8279.01.2 Methuen, A.M.M. Peace or war in South Africa. 4th ed. London, 1901.
Afr 4615.1 Michel, C. Vers Fachoda. Paris, 1901.
Afr 725.8 Moore, J.E.S. To the Mountains of the Moon. London, 1901.
Afr 8289.01.37 Mueller, Alfred von. Kritische Betrachtungen über den Burenkrieg. Berlin, 1901.
Afr 3986.1 Nahas, Joseph F. Situation économique et sociale du fellah égyptien. Paris, 1901.
Afr 1609.01.3 Niessel, A. Le Maroc. Paris, 1901.
Afr 8325.64 Notes on reconnoitering in South Africa. Boer War, 1899-1900. London, 1901.
Afr 8289.01.17 Ogden, H.J. The war against the Dutch republics in South Africa. Manchester, 1901.
Afr 5342.8.3 Ollone, C.A. De la Côte-d'Ivoire au Soudan. 3e éd. Paris, 1901.
Afr 2945.4 Pedretti, A. Un escursione in Cirenaica. Rome, 1901.
Afr 2308.3 Piesse, L. Alger et ses environs. Paris, 1901.
Afr 2630.2 Poublon, G. La terre, projet de petite colonisation. Tunis, 1901.
Afr 8289.01.42 Premier livre de l'épopée boer. Paris, 1901.
Afr 5833.2 Prentout, H. L'Ile de France sous Decaen. Paris, 1901.
Afr 8315.5 Ralph, Julian. An American with Lord Roberts. N.Y., 1901.
Afr 8315.5.5A Ralph, Julian. War's brighter side. N.Y., 1901.
Afr 6174.6 Ramseyer, F.A. Dark and stormy days at Kumassi, 1900. London, 1901.
Afr 2230.22F Randall-MacIver, D. Libyan notes. London, 1901.
Afr 8659.01 Reclus, E. L'Afrique australe. Paris, 1901.
Afr 5466.5 Remy. Le catholicisme et la vapeur au centre de l'Afrique. Poitiers, 1901.
Afr 8289.01.39 Robertson, J.M. Wrecking the empire. London, 1901.
Afr 8289.01.23 Rolleston, Maud. Yeoman service. London, 1901.
Afr 8289.01.27 Rose-Innes, C. With Paget's horse to the front. London, 1901.
Afr 8289.01.33 Ross, P.T. A yeoman's letters. London, 1901.
Afr 505.2 Rouard de Card, E. Les territoires africaines. Paris, 1901.
Afr 6390.4 Schoeller, M. Mitteilungen über Äquatorial-Ost-Afrika, 1896-97. v.1-2. and plates. Berlin, 1901. 3v.
Afr 608.91.2 Sievers, W. Afrika. 2. Aufl. Leipzig, 1901.
Afr 8678.7 South African Native Races Comittee. The natives of South Africa. London, 1901.
Afr 8289.01.5 Sternberg, A. My experiences of the Boer war. London, 1901. 2v.
Afr 8315.7 Subaltern's letters to his wife. London, 1901.
Afr 7809.01 Svambera, V. Kongo. Praha, 1901.
Afr 8315.12 Unger, F.W. With Bobs and Kruger. Philadelphia, 1901.
Afr 8210.8 Vallentin, W. Die Geschichte der Süd-Afrikanischen Republiken. Berlin, 1901.
Afr 8289.01.35F Veber, Jean. Die boeren-kampen. Amsterdam, 1901.
Afr 608.91.10 Velten, Carl. Schilderungen Suaheli. Göttingen, 1901.
Afr 8289.01.9 Villebois Mareuil. Dix mois de campagne chez les Boers. Paris, 1901.
Afr 8289.01.8 Villebois Mareuil. War notes, diary. London, 1901.
Afr 4559.01.5 Vivian, H. Abyssinia. N.Y., 1901.
Afr 3258.7 Vizetelly, E. From Cyprus to Zanzibar. London, 1901.
Afr 8289.01.29 Wallace, E. Unofficial dispatches. London, 1901.
Afr 8289.01.10 Warmelo, D.S. Mijn commando en guerilla commando-leven. Amsterdam, 1901.
Afr 4559.01 Wellby, M.S. Twixt Sirdar and Menelik. London, 1901.
Afr 8292.11 Wilkinson, F. Australia at the front, colonial view of Boer war. London, 1901.
Afr 8089.01 Wilmot, Alex. The history of South Africa. London, 1901.
Afr 9149.01 Wilson, D.M. Behind the scenes in the Transvaal. London, 1901.
Afr 8289.01.3 Wisser, J.P. The second Boer war 1899-1900. Kansas City, 1901. 2v.
Afr 3069.01 Worsfold, W.B. Egypt yesterday and to-day. N.Y., 1901.
Afr 4559.01.15 Wylde, A.B. Modern Abyssinia. London, 1901.

1902

Afr 8292.10 Abbott, J.H.M. Tommy Comstalle. (Australian troops). London, 1902.
Afr 7183.5 Andrade, Alfredo de. Relatorio da viagem de exploração...de Benguella e Novo Redondo. Lisboa, 1902.
Afr 4892.5 Angoulvant, G. Djibout, Mer Rouge, Abyssinie. Paris, 1902.
Afr 6390.5 Austin, H.H. Among swamps and giants in Equatorial Africa. London, 1902.
Afr 3979.02.15 Babcock, M.D. Letters from Egypt and Palestine. N.Y., 1902.
Afr 3990.2 Baedeker, K. Egypt. 5th ed. Leipzig, 1902.
Afr 4743.5 Bartolommei-Gioli, G. Le attitudini della colonia Eritrea all'agricoltura. Firenze, 1902.
Afr 3132.5 Becker, C.H. Beiträge zur Geschichte Ägyptens unter den Islam. Strassburg, 1902. 2v.
NEDL Afr 4392.4 Berkeley, G.F.H. The campaign of Adowa and the rise of Menelik. Westminster, 1902.
Afr 8325.18 Boers and the war, from the impartial foreigner's point of view. London, 1902.
NEDL Afr 1200.50 Boutin, Abel. Anciennes relations de la France avec la Barbarie, 1515-1830. Paris, 1902.
Afr 3125.5 Butler, A.J. The Arab conquest of Egypt. Oxford, 1902.
Afr 6333.02 Buxton, Edward North. Two African trips, with notes and suggestions. London, 1902.
Afr 1325.2F Canal, J. Géographie générale du Maroc. Paris, 1902.

1902 - cont.

Afr 8177.5 Cape of Good Hope. Archives. The rebellion of 1815. Cape Town, 1902.
Afr 6275.24 Carnegie, David W. Letters from Nigeria...1899-1900. Brechin, 1902.
Afr 5408.10 Castellani, Charles. Das Weib am Kongo. Minden, 1902.
Afr 1947.1 Cathcart, J.L. The captives. La Porte, 1902.
Afr 8325.25 Chamberlain, J. Defence of the British troops in South Africa. London, 1902.
Afr 5840.15 Chassagnon, H., Abbé. Le frère Scubilion de l'Institut des frères des écoles chrétiennes. Paris, 1902.
Afr 3735.7.5 Churchill, Winston S. The river war. London, 1902.
Afr 1965.2.25 Claye, A. Essai bibliographique sur le "Journal de l'expédition au portes de fer" (Paris, 1844). Paris, 1902.
Htn Afr 5333.2* Clozel, F.J. Coutumes indigènes de la Côte-d'Ivoire. Paris, 1902.
Afr 8095.5 Colenbrander, Herman Theodoor. De afkomst der Boeren. n.p., 1902.
Afr 8279.01.8 Cook, Edward T. Rights and wrongs of the Transvaal war. London, 1902.
Afr 8292.46 Corner, William. The story of the 34th Company. London, 1902.
Afr 1738.5 Cousin, A. Tanger. 1st ed. Paris, 1902.
Afr 5749.02 Danfreville de la Salle. A Madagascar. Paris, 1902.
Afr 8289.02.8 Davitt, Michael. The Boer fight for freedom. N.Y., 1902.
Afr 8300.12 Defender. Sir Charles Warren and Spion Kop, a vindication. London, 1902.
Afr 8320.8 Dewet, C.R. De strijd tusschen boer en brit. Amsterdam, 1902.
Afr 8289.02.12A Dewet, C.R. Three years war. N.Y., 1902.
Afr 8289.00.19A Doyle, A.C. The great Boer war. N.Y., 1902.
Afr 8289.02.18A Doyle, A.C. The war in South Africa. London, 1902.
Afr 5054.02 Dreyfus, Camille. La France dans l'Afrique occidentale. Paris, 1902.
Afr 5406.58 Duchaillu, Paul Belloni. King Mombo. N.Y., 1902.
Afr 3978.65.5 Duff-Gordon, Lucie Austin. Letters from Egypt. London, 1902.
Afr 3978.65.6 Duff-Gordon, Lucie Austin. Letters from Egypt. N.Y., 1902.
Afr 5219.02 Dujarris, G. La vie du sultan Rabah. Paris, 1902.
Afr 8289.02.24 Everdingen, W. De oorlog in Zuid-Afrika. Delft, 1902.
Afr 7309.02.5 Ferraz, Guilherme Ivens. Descripção da costa de Moçambique de Lourenço Marques ao Bazaruto. Lisboa, 1902.
Afr 1680.3 Fischer, T. Meine dritte forschungsreise im atlas-vorlande von Marokko im Jahre 1901. Hamburg, 1902.
Afr 2749.02 Foureau, F. D'Alger au Congo par le Tchad. Paris, 1902.
Afr 8289.02.14 Fournier, P.V. La guerre sud-africaine. Paris, 1902. 3v.
Afr 5219.02.5 Gentil, E. La chute de l'empire du Rabah. Paris, 1902.
Afr 555.37 Geyer, F.X. Durch Sand, Sumpf und Wald. München, 1902.
Afr 8289.02.16 Gilbert, G. La guerre sud-africaine. Paris, 1902.
Afr 8289.02.21 Goldmann, C.S. With General French and the cavalry in Africa. London, 1902.
Afr 6535.19 Great Britain. War Office. Intelligence Division. Precis of information concerning the Uganda Protectorate. London, 1902.
Afr 1609.02.3 Grove, Lady. Seventy-one days camping in Morocco. London, 1902.
Afr 8292.33 Hart-Meltarg, W. From Quebec to Pretoria with...Royal Canadian Regiment. Toronto, 1902.
Afr 6174.3 Haylings, D.M. Letters from a bush campaign. London, 1902.
Afr 5365.3 Heudebert, L. Promenades au Dahomey. Paris, 1902.
Afr 8289.02.10 Hiley, Alan R.I. The mobile Boer. N.Y., 1902.
Afr 8325.15 Hobhouse, Emily. The brunt of the war (refugee camps). London, 1902.
Afr 6540.8 Hobley, C.W. Eastern Uganda. London, 1902.
Afr 8325.20 Hobson, J.A. The psychology of jingoism. London, 1902. 2v.
Afr 6738.4 Hutter, F. Wanderungen und Forschungen im nordhinterland von Kamerun. Braunschweig, 1902.
Afr 6879.02 Johnson, Harry. Night and morning in dark Africa. London, 1902.
Afr 6535.5.2 Johnston, H. The Uganda Protectorate. London, 1902. 2v.
Afr 6535.5A Johnston, H. The Uganda Protectorate. N.Y., 1902. 2v.
Afr 8289.02.23 Kestell, J.D. Met de boeren-commandos. Amsterdam, 1902.
Afr 8289.02.39 Klinck-Luetetsburg, F. Christian de Wet, de held van Zuid-Afrika. Zutphen, 1902.
Afr 8300.9 Knox, E.B. Buller' campaign. London, 1902.
Afr 8230.6A Kruger, Paul. Memoirs. N.Y., 1902.
Afr 8230.6.5 Kruger, Paul. Memoirs. v.1-2. London, 1902.
Afr 4115.6.5 Lane-Poole, S. The story of Cairo. London, 1902.
Afr 1700.5 Lechatelier, A. Notes sur les villes et tribus du Maroc. Angers, 1902.
Afr 8289.02.20 Louter, Jan de. La guerre sud-africaine. Bruxelles, 1902.
Afr 8292.24 Lowry, E.P. With the Guards Brigade. London, 1902.
Afr 8659.02.4 Luck, R.A. A visit to Lewanika, king of the Barotse. London, 1902.
Afr 5876.1 Macauliffe, J.M. Ile de la Réunion, Cilaos. Saint Denis, 1902.
Afr 8252.6 Mackenzie, W.D. John Mackenzie. N.Y., 1902.
Afr 1609.02.5 Macnab, Frances. A ride in Morocco. London, 1902.
Afr 4937.11 McNeill, M. In pursuit of the Mad Mullah. London, 1902.
Afr 5749.02.5 Madagascar au debut du XXe siècle. Paris, 1902.
Afr 8175.19 Mansvelt, Nicolas. De betrekkingen tusschen Nederland en Zuid-Africa sedert de verovering van de Kaapkolonie door de Engelschen. Utrecht, 1902.
Afr 4700.2 Marson, Luigi. Commemorazione dell'esploratore africano. Mantova, 1902.
Afr 8289.01.31 Maydon, J.G. French's calvary campaign. 2d ed. London, 1902.
Afr 1609.02 Meakin, B. The Moors. London, 1902.
Afr 4719.02 Melli, Beniamino. L'Eritrea dalle sue origini a tutto l'anno 1901. Milano, 1902.
Afr 8289.02.32 Milne, J. The epistles of Atkins. London, 1902.
Afr 2929.02 Minutilli, F. La Tripolitania. Torino, 1902.
Afr 6275.5 Mockler-Ferryman, A.F. British Nigeria. London, 1902.
Afr 1490.9 Mohr, P. Marokko, eine politisch-wirtschaftliche Studie. Berlin, 1902.
Afr 1550.2 Mohr, P. Marokko, eine politische-wirtschaftliche Studie. Berlin, 1902.
Afr 6095.2 Morel, E.D. Affairs of West Africa. London, 1902.
Afr 1713.5 Moulieras, A. Fez. Paris, 1902.
Afr 8252.8 Mueller, E.B.I. Lord Milner and South Africa. London, 1902.
Afr 8320.11.4 On the heels of De Wet, by the intelligence officer. Edinburgh, 1902.

1902 - cont.

Afr 5219.02.2 — Oppenheim, M.F. von. Rabeh und das Tschadseegebiet. Berlin, 1902.
Afr 8659.02.6 — Orléans-Bragance, L. Tour d'Afrique. Paris, 1902.
Afr 609.02F — Pease, A.E. Travel and sport in America. London, 1902. 3v.
Afr 7309.02.4 — Peters, C. The eldorado of the ancients. London, 1902.
Afr 7309.02 — Peters, C. Im Goldland des Altertums. München, 1902.
Afr 1609.02.7 — Pfeil, J.V. Geographische Beobachtungen in Marokko. Jena, 1902.
Afr 8289.02.6 — Phillipps, L.M. With Rimmington. London, 1902.
Afr 8289.02.3 — Pienaar, P. With Steijn and De Wet. London, 1902.
Afr 5635.16 — Poirier, Jules. Conquete de Madagascar (1895-1896). Paris, 1902.
Afr 2025.17 — Pommerol, J. Chez ceux qui guettent. Islam saharien. Paris, 1902.
Afr 8289.02.35 — Raoul-Duval, R. Au Transvaal, et dans le Sud-Afrique avec les attachés militaires. Paris, 1902.
Afr 7324.9 — Resumo historico dos melhoramentos pedidos. Lisboa, 1902.
Afr 1018.4 — Revue nord-africaine illustrée. v.1-4. Alger, 1902-05. 4v.
Afr 555.4.5 — Ribolet. Un gand évêque, ou Vingt ans d'église d'Afrique sous l'administration de M. Pavy. Alger, 1902. 3v.
Afr 2850.1 — Riccheri, G. La Tripolitania e l'Italia. Milan, 1902.
Afr 8289.02 — Roany, J.H. La guerre anglo-boer. Paris, 1902.
Afr 8289.02.27 — Rompel, F. Präsident Steijn. München, 1902.
Afr 8285.20.5 — Rompel, Frederik. Marthinus Theunis Steijn. Amsterdam, 1902.
Afr 1571.2 — Rouard de Card, E. La frontière franco-marocaine...20 july 1901. Toulouse, 1902.
Afr 8687.335 — Schiel, Adolf. Drei-und-zwanzig Jahre Sturm und Sonnenschein in Südafrika. Leipzig, 1902.
Afr 8289.02.28 — Schowalter, A. Die Buren in der Kap Kolonie im Kriege mit England. München, 1902.
Afr 8292.16 — Scott, G.H.G. Record of mounted infantry of the City Imperial Volunteers. London, 1902.
Afr 8292.30 — Seton-Kaar, H. The call to arms, 1900-01, mounted sharpshooters. London, 1902.
Afr 8279.02 — Smith, Goldwin. In the court of history. Toronto, 1902.
Afr 11051.3 — Songs of the veld, and other poems. London, 1902.
Afr 6878.73.3 — Stanley, H.M. How I found Livingstone. N.Y., 1902.
Afr 8320.9 — Steijn, de Wet und die Oranje-freistaater. Tübingen, 1902.
Afr 8289.02.45 — Stevens, F.T. Complete history of the South African war in 1899-1902. London, 1902.
Afr 550.19 — Taylor, S.E. The price of Africa. Cincinnati, 1902.
Afr 8100.5 — Theal, G.M. The beginning of South African history. London, 1902.
Afr 8089.02 — Theal, G.M. Progress of South Africa. Toronto, 1902.
Afr 8289.02.37 — Thomson, Ada. Memorials of C.D. Kimber. London, 1902.
Afr 555.9.19 — Tozer, William G. Letters of Bishop Tozer and his sister. London, 1902.
Afr 2438.5 — Tunis. Conférences sur les administrations tunisiennes, 1902. 2.ed. Sousse, 1902.
Afr 8289.02.22 — Viljoen, B.J. Mijne herinneringen...anglo-boeren-oorlog. Amsterdam, 1902.
Afr 8289.02.22.2 — Viljoen, B.J. My reminiscences of Anglo-Boer war. London, 1902.
Afr 8289.02.29 — Villebois-Mareuil. Carnet de campagne. Paris, 1902.
Afr 8289.01.10.5 — Warmelo, D.S. On commando. London, 1902.
Afr 8659.02 — Warren, Charles. On the veldt in the seventies. London, 1902.
Afr 5440.5 — Wauters, Alphonse Jules. Les bassins de l'Ubangi. Brussels, 1902.
Afr 1583.5 — Werle. Deutschlands beziehungen zu marokko. Coburg, 1902.
Afr 8289.00.25F — Wilson, H.W. After Pretoria, the guerilla war. London, 1902. 2v.

1903

Afr 1609.03.6 — Adelmann, S. 13 monate in Marokko. Sigmaring, 1903.
Afr 5840.10 — Anderson, J.F. Esquisse de l'histoire du protestantisme à l'Ile Mauurice et aux Iles Mascarègnes, 1505 à 1902. Paris, 1903.
Afr 1625.6 — Anton Y Ferrandiz, M. Razas y tribus de Marruecos. Madrid, 1903.
Afr 5920.11 — Arambilet, S. Posesiones españolas del Africa occidental. Madrid, 1903.
Afr 6535.11 — Austin, H.H. MacDonald in Uganda. London, 1903.
Afr 2225.11 — Azan, Paul J.L. Recherche d une solution de la question indigène en Algéric. Paris, 1903.
Afr 2376.2 — Baader, Walter. Nach der Oase Tugurt in der Wüste Sahara. Basel, 1903.
Afr 500.81 — Barboux, H.M. Opinion. Paris, 1903.
Afr 5640.6 — Basset, Charles. Madagascar et l'oeuvre du Général Gallieni. Thèse. Paris, 1903.
Afr 4230.4 — Beccari, C. Rerum aethiopicarum scriptores occidentales. Introductio generalis. Roma, 1903.
Afr 1573.8 — Becker, J. España y Marruecos. Madrid, 1903.
Afr 9710.6 — Beguin, E. Les Barotse. Lausanne, 1903.
Afr 1088.6 — Bel, A. Les Benou Ghanya. Paris, 1903.
Afr 8289.03.20 — Blake, J.Y.D. A West Pointer with the Boers. Boston, 1903.
Afr 8320.6 — Boldingh, G. Een hollandsch officier in Zuid-Afrika. Rotterdam, 1903.
Afr 7568.7 — Bourne, H.R.F. Civilisation in Congoland. London, 1903.
Afr 8659.03 — Braun, D.E. Auf und ab in Süd-Afrika. Berlin, 1903.
Afr 5635.5 — Brunet, L. L'oeuvre de la France à Madagascar. Paris, 1903.
Afr 8340.5 — Buchan, J. The African colony. Edinburgh, 1903.
Afr 7568.5 — Burrows, G. The curse of Central Africa. London, 1903.
Afr 1408.6 — Castries, H. de. Moulay Ismail et Jacques II. Paris, 1903.
Afr 2285.7 — Champeaux, G. A travers les oasis sahariennes. Paris, 1903.
Htn Afr 4742.24* — Conti Rossini, C. Ricordi di un soggiorno in Eritrea. Fasc.1. Asmara, 1903.
Afr 1738.5.3 — Cousin, A. Tanger. 3d ed. Paris, 1903.
Afr 6138.5 — Crooks, John J. A history of the colony of Sierra Leone. Dublin, 1903.
Afr 8289.03.9 — Crowe, George. Commission of H.M.S. Terrible. London, 1903.
Afr 1570.20 — Daunay. Le Maroc: que devons-nous faire. Paris, 1903.
Afr 8678.19 — Davis, A. The native problem in South Africa. London, 1903.
Afr 7565.18 — Descamps, E. L'Afrique nouvelle. Paris, 1903.
Afr 6979.03 — Done, K. Deutsch-Südwest-Afrika. Berlin, 1903.
Afr 8289.00.19.5 — Doyle, A.C. The great Boer war. London, 1903.

1903 - cont.

Afr 9839.03 — Duff, H.L. Nyasaland under the Foreign Office. London, 1903.
Afr 5406.191 — Dybowski, Jean. La route du Tchad. Paris, 1903.
Afr 1738.7 — Escribano del Pino, E. Tanger y sus alrededores. Madrid, 1903.
Afr 1485.9 — Espinosa de los Monteros, R. España en Africa 1903. Madrid, 1903.
Afr 2798.3 — Eu, Clement Celestin. In-Salah et le Tidikelt. Paris, 1903.
Afr 4785.4 — Ferrandi, U. Lugh, emporio commerciale sul Giuba. Roma, 1903.
Afr 2749.02.2F — Foureau, F. Documents scientifiques de la mission saharienne. Paris, 1903.
Afr 1280.10 — Giesa de Camps, Santiago. Las Kabilas de Bocoya, Beniburiaga y Flemsamana. Barcelona, 1903.
X Cg Afr 5538.2 — Grandidier, A. Collection des ouvrages anciens concernant Madagascar. v.1-9. Paris, 1903-20. (Changed to XP 3889) 9v.
Afr 8340.4.5F — Great Britain. Papers on criminal procedure code of the Transvaal. London, 1903.
Afr 8340.4.3F — Great Britain. Papers on finances of Transvaal and Orange River colony. London, 1903.
Afr 8288.99.10F — Great Britain. Commissions. South African War. Appendices evidence on war in South Africa. London, 1903.
Afr 8288.99.9F — Great Britain. Commissions. South African War. Minutes of evidence on war in South Africa. London, 1903. 2v.
Afr 8288.99.7F — Great Britain. Commissions. South African War. Report...war in South Africa. London, 1903.
Afr 8292.12 — Green, James. The story of the Australian Bushmen. Sydney, 1903.
Afr 3079.03 — Gruenen, W.V. Die staats- und völkerrechtliche Stellung Ägyptens. Leipzig, 1903.
Afr 6455.2 — Hardwick, A.A. An ivory trader in North Kenia. London, 1903.
Afr 9040.6 — Harrison, C.W.F. Natal. London, 1903.
Afr 2975.2 — al-Hashayishi, Muhammad ibn Uthman. Voyage au pays des Senoussia. Paris, 1903.
Afr 6160.5 — Hayford, Casely. Gold Coast native institutions. London, 1903.
Afr 3979.03 — Henze, H. Der Nil... Hydrographie und seiner Wirt. Halle, 1903.
Afr 1570.3 — Hess, J. La question du Maroc. Paris, 1903.
Afr 8295.8 — Hofmeyr, N. Zes maanden bij de commandos. 's-Gravenhage, 1903.
Afr 555.9.57 — Hotchkiss, W.R. Sketches from the dark continent. London, 1903.
Afr 1550.6 — Immanuel. Marokko. Berlin, 1903.
Afr 8678.20 — Indicus. Labour and other questions in South Africa. London, 1903.
Afr 1609.03.9 — Irabien Larranaga, E. de. Africa, apuntes de Marruecos. San Sebastian, 1903.
Afr 4095.18 — Johnston, H. The Nile quest. N.Y., 1903.
Afr 8688.12 — Joûbert, Joseph. Les armoiries de la République Sud-africaine. Paris, 1903.
Afr 1609.03.5 — Kampffmeyer, G. Marokko. Halle, 1903.
Afr 3979.02.3 — Kelly, R.J. Egypt painted and described. London, 1903.
Afr 8289.03.15 — Kestell, J.D. Through shot and flame. London, 1903.
Afr 2762.7 — King, W.J.H. Search for the masked Tuwareks. London, 1903.
Afr 2762.3 — Koehler, A. Verfassung der Tuareg. Gotha, 1903.
Afr 1571.1 — Lechatelier, A. Sud-Oranais et Maroc. Paris, 1903.
Afr 5385.11 — Leherisse, R. Voyage au Dahomey et à la Côte-d'Ivoire. Paris, 1903.
Afr 810.15 — Lenfant, E.H. Le Niger, voie ouverte à notre empire africain. Paris, 1903.
Afr 8235.19 — Leonard, C. Papers on the political situation in South Africa, 1885-1895. London, 1903.
Afr 4559.03 — Leroux, H. Chasses et gens d'Abyssinie. Paris, 1903.
Afr 8340.6 — Letters from an uitlander, 1899-02. London, 1903.
Afr 2020.2 — Lohan, Guillo. Un contre-rezzou au Hoggar. Paris, 1903.
Afr 8289.03 — Loren van Thernaat, H. Twee jaren in de Boerenoorlog. Haarlem, 1903.
Afr 5640.4 — Lyautey, L.H.G. Dans le sud de Madagascar. Paris, 1903.
Afr 8289.03.4 — Lynch, G. Impressions of a war correspondent. London, 1903.
Afr 5540.6F — Madagascar, gouvernement générale. Tananarive, 1903.
Afr 5407.5 — Marel, Edmund D. The British case in French Congo. London, 1903.
Afr 2929.01 — Mehier de Mathuisieulx, H. A travers la Tripolitaine. Paris, 1903.
Afr 2318.1.5 — Mercier, E. Histoire de Constantine. Constantine, 1903.
Afr 3979.03.3 — Metin, A. La transformation de l'Egypte. Paris, 1903.
Afr 1026.5 — Minutilli, F. Bibliografia della Libia. Torino, 1903.
Afr 8315.10 — Moeller, B. Two years at the front. London, 1903.
Afr 7187.5 — Moncada, Francisco C. A campanha do Bailundo em 1902. Lisboa, 1903.
Afr 8292.58 — Pearse, H.H.S. The history of Lumsden's Horse. London, 1903.
Afr 2609.03.2 — Pensa, H. L'avenir de la Tunisie. Paris, 1903.
Afr 8325.45 — Pilcher, T.D. Some lessons from the Boer War. London, 1903.
Afr 2290.5 — Pimodan. Oran Tlemcen sud-oranais (1899-1900). Paris, 1903.
Afr 510.12 — Reibell, Le Commandant. Le commandant Lamy. Paris, 1903.
Afr 8292.35 — Richardson, W.D. With the Army Service Corps in South Africa. London, 1903.
Afr 2352.1 — Robert, M.A. La Kalaa et Tihamamine. Constantine, 1903.
X Cg Afr 6283.5 — Roth, H.L. Great Benin. Halifax, 1903.
Afr 510.9 — Rouard de Card, E. La France...en Afrique. Paris, 1903.
Afr 1731.1 — Rouard De Card, E. L'isle de Perecil. Toulouse, 1903.
Afr 8289.03.12 — Saint Leger, S.E. War sketches in colour. London, 1903.
Afr 1609.03 — Savory, Isabel. In the tail of the peacock. London, 1903.
Afr 8659.03.5 — Scott, Edward Daniel. Some letters from South Africa, 1894-1902. Manchester, Eng., 1903.
Afr 1609.03.3 — Segonzac. Voyages au Maroc (1899-1901). Paris, 1903.
Afr 1609.03.7 — Sid el Hach Abd-el-Nabi Ben Ramos. Perlas negras. Madrid, 1903.
Afr 8279.02.5 — Smith, Goldwin. Devant le tribunal de l'histoire. Montreal, 1903.
Afr 3993.903 — Socolis, Georges. Notes sur l'Egypte et son histoire économique depuis 30 ans. Paris, 1903.
Afr 8019.1.5 — South Africa (Weekly). The story of South Africa newspaper. London, 1903.
Afr 8089.00 — South Africa handbooks. London, 1903.
Afr 7568.3 — Stengel, K.F. von. Der Kongostaat. München, 1903.

238

1905 - cont.

Afr 1346.2   Huebner, Max. Militarische und militärgeographische Betrachtungen. Berlin, 1905.

Afr 8659.05   Hutchinson, G.T. From the Cape to the Zambesi. London, 1905.

Afr 855.5   Jackson, E.L. St. Helena, the historic island. N.Y., 1905.

Afr 4937.1   Jennings, J.W. With the Abyssinians in Somaliland. London, 1905.

Afr 108.99.4A   Johnston, H.H. A history of the colonization of Africa. Cambridge, 1905.

Afr 3979.04.5   Kandt, Richard. Caput Nili, eine Empfindsarne. Berlin, 1905.

Afr 6208.5F   Lagos. Blue book 1904, 1905. Lagos, 1905.

Afr 1550.9   Lapradelle, A. de. La condition du Maroc d'après l'accord de 1904. Paris, 1905.

Afr 1609.05.8   Lemoine, Paul. Mission dans le Maroc occidental. Paris, 1905.

Afr 5480.205   L'Enfant, Eugène A. La grande route du Tchad. Paris, 1905.

Afr 2268.1   Loth, Gaston. Le peuplement italien en Tunisie et en Algérie. Paris, 1905.

Afr 659.05   Loyson, H. To Jerusalem through lands of Islam. Chicago, 1905.

Afr 3990.15   Macmillan, firm, London. Guide to Egypt and Sudan. 3d ed. London, 1905.

Afr 555.35   Marin, Eugène. Algérie, Sahara, Soudan. Vie travaux, voyages de Mgr. Hacquard. Paris, 1905.

Afr 1550.3   Maura y Gamazo, Gabriel. La cuesticn de Marruecos. Madrid, 1905.

Afr 1609.05   Meakin, B. Life in Morocco and glimpses beyond. London, 1905.

Afr 1920.25   Misermont, L. Le double bombardement d'Alger par Duquesne. Paris, 1905.

Afr 7568.15   Morel, E.D. King Leopold's rule in Africa. N.Y., 1905.

Afr 1635.2   Moulieras, A. Les zkara, une tribu zenete...Au Maroc. Paris, 1905.

Afr 7222.15F   Mozambique. Modus-vivendi entre a provincia de Moçambique e o Transvaal...1901. Lisboa, 1905.

Afr 9040.5   Natal. General Commission. Glimpses in Natal. Durban, 1905.

Afr 550.33.5   Naylor, W.S. Daybreak in the dark continent. 2d ed. Boston, 1905.

Afr 7315.2   Ornellas, A. Raças e linguas indigenas em Moçambique. n.p., 1905.

NEDL Afr 4230.4.2   Paez, P. Historia Aethiopiae. v.1-4. Roma, 1905-06. 2v.

Afr 550.14   Parsons, E. C. Christus liberator. N.Y., 1905.

Afr 6280.3   Partridge, Charles. Cross river natives. London, 1905.

Afr 2209.05.2   Phillips, L.M. In the desert. London, 1905.

Afr 8340.12A   Phillips, Lionel. Transvaal problems. London, 1905.

Afr 5832.10.3   Pitot, Albert. T'eylandt Mauritius. Port-Louis, 1905.

Afr 1609.05.4   Rene-Leclerc, C. Le Maroc septentrional...(Ete 1904). Alger, 1905.

Afr 2209.05   Richardot, H. Sept semaines en Tunisie et en Algérie. Paris, 1905.

Afr 1570.15   Rouard de Card, E. Protectorat de la France sur le Maroc. Toulouse, 1905.

Afr 1574.7   Rouard de Card, E. Les relations de l'Espagne et du Maroc. Paris, 1905.

Afr 11757.58.100   Runcie, John. Songs by the stoep. London, 1905.

Afr 8659.05.5   Samassa, Paul. Das neue Südafrika. Berlin, 1905.

Afr 1450.3   Sarnette, F. Aventures d'un français au Maroc. Paris, 1905.

Afr 2223.35   Schanz, M. Algerien, Tunesien, Tripolitanien. Halle, 1905.

Afr 1453.8   Schanz, Moritz. Nordafrika, Marokko. Halle, 1905.

Afr 699.05   Schillings, C.G. Flashlights in the jungle. N.Y., 1905.

Afr 8678.8   Stow, G.W. The native races of South Africa. London, 1905.

Afr 8678.8.1   Stow, G.W. The native races of South Africa. London, 1905.

Afr 4370.2   Theodoros II. Chronique. Paris, 1905.

Afr 9086.15   Transvaal civil service list, 1905. Pretoria, 1905.

Afr 8315.9   Vane, Francis Patrick Fletcher. Pax britannia in South Africa. London, 1905.

Afr 2010.5   Voission, Louis. Si-el-Hadj-Mokrani et la révolte de 1871. Paris, 1905.

Afr 7568.18   Wack, H.W. The story of the Congo Free State. N.Y., 1905

Afr 8325.33   Warmelo, J.B.V. Het concentratie-kamp van Irene. Amsterdam, 1905.

Afr 6390.13   Wason, J.C. East Africa and Uganda. London, 1905.

Afr 2285.8   Watson, G. The voice of the south (Algeria). London, 1905.

Afr 5749.05   You, Andre. Madagascar, histoire, organisation, colonisation. Paris, 1905.

Afr 1609.05.11   Zabel, R. Im muhammendanischen abendlande. Altenburg, 1905.

1906

Afr 1583.2F   Aktenstuecke über Marokko der Reichstage...8. I. 1906. Berlin, 1906.

Afr 4370.5   Alaqa Walda Maryam. History of King Theodore. London, 1906.

Afr 4785.15   Albertio, Enrico Alberto d'. In Africa, Victoria Nyaza e Benadir. Bergamo, 1906.

Afr 1550.22   Algeciras. International Conference on Moroccan Affairs, 1906. Acta general. Madrid, 1906.

Afr 6455.9   Allsopp, Charles. Sport and travel, Abyssinia and British East Africa. London, 1906.

Afr 1435.3   Amaudru, N. Sultane française du Maroc. Paris, 1906.

Afr 6113.5   Archer, F.B. Gambia colony and protectorate. London, 1906.

Afr 555.23.7   Au Congo et aux Indes. Bruxelles, 1906.

Afr 1609.03.12   Aubin, Eugene. Morocco of today. London, 1906.

Afr 1609.06.7   Auer, Grethe. Marokkanische sittenbilder. Bern, 1906.

Afr 1585.3F   Austro-Hungarian Monarchy. Ministerium des Äussern. Diplomatische Aktenstücken über die Internationale Konferenz von Algeciras, 1905-06. Wien, 1906.

Afr 3199.06   Balboni, L.A. Gl'Italiani nella civiltà egiziana del secolo XIX. Alessandria, 1906. 3v.

Afr 1200.55   Balch, T.W. France in North Africa, 1906. Philadelphia, 1906.

Afr 4230.4.4   Barradas, M. Tractatus tres historico-geographico. Porto, 1906.

Afr 9230.2   Beak, George B. The aftermath of war. London, 1906.

1906 - cont.

Afr 3132.6F   Becker, C.H. Papyri Schott-Reinhardt I. Heidelberg, 1906.

Afr 7568.25.5   Belgium. Commission Chargée de Faire une Enquête dans les Territoires de l'Etat du Congo. Abstract of the report of the Commission enquiry into a administration of Congo Free State. London, 1906.

Afr 7568.25   Belguim. Commission Chargée de Faire une Enquête dans les Territoires de l'Etat du Congo. The Congo. N.Y., 1906.

Afr 2209.06.2   Belloc, H. Esto perpetua. London, 1906.

Afr 1550.4   Berard, V. L'affaire marocaine. Paris, 1906.

Afr 1570.61   Berard, Victor. L'affaire marocaine. Paris, 1906.

Afr 2719.06   Bernard, A. La pénétration saharienne, 1830-1906. Alger, 1906.

Afr 2209.06.10   Bernard, P. Histoire, colonization, géographie et administration de l'Algérie. 2e ed. Alger, 1906.

Afr 1550.8   Betegon, P. La conferencia de Algeciras. Madrid, 1906.

Afr 3275.16   Blunt, W.S. Atrocities of justice under British rule in Egypt. London, 1906.

Afr 550.6   Bonet-Maury, G. L'islamisme et le christianisme en Afrique. Paris, 1906.

Afr 7568.26   Bowdoin-Clark Debate. The Bowdoin argument in the Bowdoin-Clark debate. n.p., 1906.

Afr 3990.1   Budge, E.A.W. Cook's handbook. Egypt and the sudan. London, 1906.

Afr 1330.5.3   Castries, H. de. Les sources inédites de l'histoire du Maroc. Dynastie saadienne. (Pays-bas, t.1-6). Paris, 1906-23. 6v.

Afr 7568.28   Cattier, F. Etude sur la situation de l'état...Congo. Bruxelles, 1906.

Afr 1655.1   Chevrillon, Andre. Un crepuscule d'islam-Maroc. Paris, 1906.

Afr 5342.6   Clozel, F.J. Dix ans à la Côte-d'Ivoire. Paris, 1906.

Afr 8135.10   Colquhoun, Archibald. The Africander land. London, 1906.

Afr 3275.15A   Colvin, A. The making of modern Egypt. 3d ed. London, 1906.

Afr 1738.6   Conditions d'existence à Tanger. Paris, 1906.

Afr 1570.12   Conférence d'Algésiras. Paris, 1906.

Afr 1325.9F   Conférence Internationale d'Algeciras. Acte général. La Haye, 1906.

Afr 1325.9.5F   Conférence Internationale d'Algeciras. Despatches from British delegate. London, 1906.

Afr 4700.17   Congresso Coloniale Italiano, Asmara. Atti. v.1. Roma, 1906.

Afr 2209.06.3   Crouse, M.E. Algiers. N.Y., 1906.

Afr 5580.3.5   Cultru, P. Un empereur de Madagascar au XVIIIe siècle, Benyowszky. Paris, 1906.

Afr 6985.2   Dannert, E. Zum Rechte der Herero. Berlin, 1906.

Afr 6275.16   Delevoye. En Afrique centrale. Paris, 1906.

Afr 4365.1   Demimuid, M. Vie...Justin de Jacobis. 2 ed. Paris, 1906.

Afr 2250.3   Demontes, V. Le peuple algérien. Alger, 1906.

Afr 5445.5   Dennett, R.E. At the back of the black man's mind. London, 1906.

Afr 1550.10   Diercks, Gustav. Die Marokkofrage und die Konferenz von Algeciras. Berlin, 1906.

Afr 1609.06.6   Diez De Tejada, V. Cosas de los moros. Barcelona, 1906.

Afr 718.35   Dubourg de Bozas, P.M.R. Mission scientifique. De la mer Rouge. Paris, 1906.

Afr 9839.05   Duff, H.L. Nyasaland under the Foreign Office. 2. ed. London, 1906.

Afr 674.93.9   Eannes de Azurara, G. Conquests and discoveries of Henry the Navigator. London, 1906.

Afr 1621.5   Echague, F. Marruecos...en 1894, fotografias. Madrid, 1906.

Afr 5385.9   François, G. Notre colonie du Dahomey. Paris, 1906.

Afr 6879.06F   Fuellebom, F. Das Deutsche Njassa- und Ruwuma-Gebiet. Atlas. Berlin, 1906.

Afr 6879.06   Fuellebon, F. Das Deutsche Njassa- und Ruwuma-Gebiet. Text. Berlin, 1906.

Afr 1609.06   Genthe, S. Marokko reiseschilderungen. Berlin, 1906.

Afr 1609.06.5   Gentil, L. Explorations au Maroc. Paris, 1906.

Afr 1570.27   Gourdin, A. La politique française au Maroc. Paris, 1906.

Afr 8340.20F   Great Britain. Commission. War Stores in South Africa. Report of the Royal Commission on War Stores in South Africa. London, 1906.

Afr 1574.8   Gutierrez, F.L. España y las demas naciones. Madrid, 1906.

Afr 2225.5   Hamet, I. Les Musulmans français du nord de l'Afrique. Paris, 1906.

Afr 6390.8   Handbook for East Africa, Uganda and Zanzibar, 1906. Mombasa, 1906.

Afr 2209.06   Hilton-Simpson, M.W. Algiers and beyond. London, 1906.

Afr 5833.1   Huet de Froberville, B. Ephemerides mauriciennes, 1827-1834. Port Louis, 1906.

Afr 500.18   Italy. Direzione Centrale degli Affari Coloniali. Trattati, convenzioni, accordi. v.1,2-3. Roma, 1906. 2v.

Afr 8210.11   Jeppe, Carl. The kaleidoscopic Transvaal. London, 1906.

Afr 7459.06   Johnston, H. Liberia. London, 1906. 2v.

Afr 3275.42   Kamil, Mustafa. Egyptiens et Anglais. Paris, 1906.

Afr 3979.02.4   Kelly, R. Talbot. Egypt painted and described. London, 1906.

Afr 8678.10   Kidd, D. Savage childhood...Kafir children. London, 1906.

Afr 2225.4   Lacroix, Bernardo. L'évolution du nomadisme en Algérie. Alger, 1906.

Afr 4115.6.8A   Lane-Poole, S. The story of Cairo. London, 1906.

Afr 6280.4   Leonard, A.G. Lower Niger and its tribes. London, 1906.

Afr 3243.7   Lesage, C. L'achat des actions de Suez. Paris, 1906.

Afr 6919.06   Leutwein, T. Elf Jahre Gouverneur in deutsch Südwestafrika. Berlin, 1906.

Afr 8215.1.3   Leyds, W.J. De eerste annexatie van de Transvaal. v.1. Amsterdam, 1906.

Afr 8215.1   Leyds, W.J. The first annexation of the Transvaal. London, 1906.

Afr 6535.6   Lloyd, A.B. Uganda to Khartoum. N.Y., 1906.

Afr 2609.06.6   Lorimer, Norma. By the waters of Carthage. London, 1906.

Afr 5130.5   Machat, J. Documents sur les établissements français. Paris, 1906.

Afr 5318.9   Machat, J. Les Rivières du Sud et le Fouta-Diallon. Paris, 1906.

Afr 2223.36   Macquart, E. Les réalités algériennes. Blida, 1906.

Afr 1550.5   Mantegazza, V. Il Marocco e l'Europa. Milano, 1906.

Afr 1605.50   Massignon, L. Le Maroc dans les premières années du XVIe siècle. Alger, 1906.

Afr 7332.1   Maugham, R.C.F. Portuguese East Africa. London, 1906.

Afr 8289.06   Maurice, F. History of the war in South Africa 1899-02. v.1-4. London, 1906. 8v.

Afr 8055.38F   Men of the times. Johannesburg, 1906.

240

1906 - cont.

Afr 1609.06.3	Minguez Y Vicente, M. Descripcion geografica del imperio de Marruecos. Madrid, 1906.
Afr 1609.06.9	Mitjana, R. En el Magreb-el-Aksa. Valencia, 1906.
Afr 1570.19	Moulin, H.A. La question marocaine. Paris, 1906.
Afr 7567.14	Mountmorres, W.S.B. de M. The Congo Independent State. London, 1906.
Afr 2228.5	Mule, A. Chez les Moumenins. Paris, 1906.
Afr 9161.15	Munro, A. The Transvaal (Chinese) labour problem. London, 1906.
Afr 1608.68	Murga, Jose Maria de. Recuerdos marroquies. Madrid, 1906.
Afr 2209.06.15	Nesbitt, Frances E. Algeria and Tunis. London, 1906.
Afr 590.12	Nevinson, H.W. A modern slavery. London, 1906.
Afr 4732.5	Penne, G.B. Per l'Italia africana. Roma, 1906.
Afr 6640.19	Perbandt, C. von. Hermann von Wissmann. Berlin, 1906.
Afr 6777.6	Peters, Karl. Die Gründung von Deutsch-Ostafrika. Berlin, 1906.
Afr 6777.5	Plumon, E. La colonie allemande de l'Afrique Orientale. Heidelberg, 1906.
Afr 6926.4	Prussia. Grosser Generalität. Die Kämpfe der deutschen Truppen in Südwest Afrika. Berlin, 1906-08. 2v.
Afr 8678.23	Question of colour, study of South Africa. Edinburgh, 1906.
Afr 5404.5	Ronget, Fernand. L'expansion coloniale au Congo français. Paris, 1906.
Afr 2508.2	Rouard de Card, E. La politique de la France. Toulouse, 1906.
Afr 510.11.10	Rouard de Card, E. Traités de la France avec les pays de l'Afrique du Nord. Paris, 1906.
Afr 6738.3	Seidel, A. Deutsch-Kamerun wie es ist. Berlin, 1906.
Afr 6214.1	Shaw, F.A. A tropical dependency. London, 1906.
Afr 4559.06	Skinner, R.P. Abyssinia of to-day. London, 1906.
Afr 2609.06	Sladin, D. Carthage and Tunis. London, 1906. 2v.
Afr 3138.5	Solomon Ben Joseph, Ha-Kohen. The Turcoman defeat at Cairo. Chicago, 1906.
Afr 1550.22.5F	Spain. Ministerio de Estado. Documentos presentados a las Cortes. Madrid, 1906.
Afr 9095.25F	Transvaal (Colony). Volunteers Commission. Reports of Transvaal Volunteers Commission. Pretoria, 1906.
Afr 2609.06.3	Tunis. Comité. D'Hivernage. La Tunisie. Tunis, 1906.
Afr 9853.1A	Werner, A. Natives of British Central Africa. London, 1906.
Afr 1609.06.10	Wolfrom, G. Le Maroc. Paris, 1906.
Afr 8252.8.5	Worsfold, W.B. Lord Milner's work in South Africa. London, 1906.

1907

Afr 1609.07.3	Abou-Djebel. Tres meses en Marruecos. Madrid, 1907.
Afr 718.27	Alexander, Boyd. From the Niger to the Nile. London, 1907.
Afr 4230.4.5	Almeida, M. De. Historia Aethiopiae. Liber 1-10. Romae, 1907. 3v.
Afr 5318.11	Arcin, A. La Guinée française. Paris, 1907.
Afr 4115.16F	Artin, Yakub, Pasha. Essai sur les causes du renchérissement de la vie matérielle au Caire dans le courant du XIXe siècle (1800-1907). Le Caire, 1907.
Afr 8310.10F	Baden-Powell, R.S.S. Sketches in Mafeking and East Africa. London, 1907.
Afr 4095.8.2.10	Baker, S.W. The Albert Nyanza. London, 1907.
Afr 1550.21	Barclay, T. El acta de Algeciras y el porvenir de Espana en Africa. Madrid, 1907.
Afr 5960.4	Barrera y Luyando. Lo que son y lo que deben ser las posesiones. Madrid, 1907.
Afr 555.23.10	Bentley, H.M. (Mrs.). W. Holman Bentley, the life and adventures of a Congo pioneer. London, 1907.
Afr 5765.6	Bianquis, J. L'oeuvre des missions protestantes à Madagascar. Paris, 1907.
Afr 2669.1	Bodereau, P. La Capsa ancienne, la Gafsa moderne. Paris, 1907.
Afr 8985.2	Bosman, W. The Natal rebellion of 1906. London, 1907.
Afr 718.19	Brode, H. Tippoo Tib; story of his career in Central Africa. London, 1907.
Afr 3275.27	Browne, A. Bonaparte in Egypt. London, 1907.
Afr 3675.4	Budge, E.A.W. The Egyptian Sudan. London, 1907. 2v.
Afr 4070.18	Bulpett, C.W.L. A picnic party in wildest Africa. London, 1907.
Afr 1573.11	Caballero de Puga. Marruecos, politica e interes de España en este imperio. Madrid, 1907.
Afr 7190.18F	O cacau de S. Thomé. Lisboa, 1907.
Afr 4335.2	Castanhoso, M. de. Die Heldentaten des Dom Christoph da Gama. Berlin, 1907.
Afr 1570.17	Castellane. Maroc. Paris, 1907.
Afr 5480.207	Chevalier, Auguste. Mission Chari, lac Tchad, 1902-1904. Paris, 1907.
Afr 1570.23	Cimbali, E. L'Europa fa opera di civilta nel Marocco. Roma, 1907.
Afr 1333.1	Decard, R. Les traités de commerce conclus par le Maroc. Paris, 1907.
Afr 1965.10	Derrecagaix, V.B. Yusuf. Paris, 1907.
Afr 5248.5	Desplagnes, Louis. Le plateau central nigérien. Paris, 1907.
Afr 635.1A	Dowd, J. The Negro races, a sociological study. N.Y., 1907. 2v.
Afr 8292.22	Dumoulin, L.E. Two years on trek, Royal Sussex Regiment. London, 1907.
Afr 3038.5	Egypt. Ministère de l'Interieur. Législation administrative et criminelle. Cairo, 1907. 3v.
Afr 555.29.5	Fahs, Sophia L. Uganda's white man of work. Boston, 1907.
Afr 9489.07	Ferguson, F.W. Southern Rhodesia...past history. London, 1907.
Afr 5056.107	French West Africa. La Maurétanie. Corseil, 1907.
Afr 6926.1	Frenssen, G. Peter Moors fahrt nach Südwest. Berlin, 1907.
Afr 7809.04	Frobenius, L. Im Schatten des Kongostaates. Berlin, 1907.
Afr 7326.4	Garrett, T. de A. Um governo em Africa. Lisboa, 1907.
Afr 2209.02.2	Gay, E. L'Algérie d'aujourd'hui. Paris, 1907.
Afr 8292.47.5	Gilson, C.J.L. History of the 1st Battalion Sherwood Foresters Boer War. London, 1907.
Afr 5973.2	Granador, Gregorio. España en el Muni. Madrid, 1907.
Afr 4935.5	Great Britain. War Office. Official history of operations in Somaliland, 1901-04. London, 1907. 2v.
Afr 699.07	Hall, Mary. A woman's trek from the Cape to Cairo. London, 1907.
Afr 1640.1	Hess, Jean. Israel au Maroc. Paris, 1907.

1907 - cont.

Afr 4115.3	Indicateur égyptien administratif et commercial. Alexandrie, 1907.
Afr 4700.15F	Italy. Direzione Centrale degli Affari Coloniali. L'Africa italiana al Parlamento nazionale, 1882-1905. Roma, 1907.
Afr 1609.07.2	Jeannot, G. Etude sociale...sur le Maroc. Dijon, 1907.
Afr 6193.54	Jevoch, Michael. Voraussetzungen und Möglichkeiten einer industriellen Entwicklung im Ghana. Hamburg, 1907.
Afr 8289.00.30	Johnson, M. With our soldiers at the front. London, 1907.
Afr 108.93.3	Keltie, J.S. Africa. Philadelphia, 1907.
Afr 9599.07	Landor, A.H.S. Across widest Africa. London, 1907. 2v.
Afr 8289.07	Larey, M. de. Herinneringen. Amsterdam, 1907.
Afr 5749.07	Leblond, M.A. La grande ile de Madagascar. Paris, 1907.
Afr 7809.00.3	Lloyd, A.B. In dwarf land and cannibal country. London, 1907.
Afr 2609.07	Loth, G. La Tunisie et l'oeuvre du protectorat français. Paris, 1907.
Afr 7540.19	Louwers, Octave. Eléments du droit de l'état indépendant du Congo. Bruxelles, 1907.
Afr 555.22	Mackintosh, C.W. Coillard of the Zambesi. South Africa. 2d ed. London, 1907.
Afr 4115.14A	Margoliouth, D.S. Cairo, Jerusalem, and Damascus. N.Y., 1907.
Afr 2260.11	Mohr, P. Algerien, eine Studie über die Französische Land- und Siedelungspolitik. Berlin, 1907.
Afr 1347.1.2	Mordacq, J.J.H. La guerre au Maroc. 2e ed. Paris, 1907.
Afr 9225.28	Muller, Hendrik Pieter Nicolaas. Oude tyden in den Oranje-Vrystaat. Leiden, 1907.
Afr 5119.07	Olivier, M. Le Sénégal. Paris, 1907.
Afr 7815.2	Overbergh, C. van. Les Bangala. 1. Bruxelles, 1907.
Afr 7815.3	Overbergh, C. van. Les Mayombe. 2. Bruxelles, 1907.
Afr 9400.10	Passarge, S. Die Buschmänner der Kalahari. Berlin, 1907.
Afr 6455.13	Patterson, J.H. The man-eaters of Travo. London, 1907.
Afr 5448.7	Pechuel-Loesche, E. Volkskunde von Loango. Stuttgart, 1907.
Afr 1609.07	Pleydell, K.M. Sketches of life in Morocco. London, 1907.
Afr 1573.10	Reparaz, G. de. Politica de España en Africa. Barcelona, 1907.
Afr 1570.18	Rolland-Chevillon. La France, l'Allemagne au Maroc. Paris, 1907.
Afr 4559.07.10	Rosen, Felix. Eine deutsche Gesandtschaft in Abessinien. Leipzig, 1907.
Afr 505.4	Sanderson, E. Great Britain in modern Africa. London, 1907.
Afr 9599.07.5	Schillings, C.G. In wildest Africa. N.Y., 1907.
Afr 8678.12	Schultze, L. Aus Namaland und Kalahari. Jena, 1907.
Afr 28.5	Schweinfurth, G. Veröffentliche Briefe,Aufsätze und Werke. Berlin, 1907.
Afr 3040.1	Scott, G.H. The law affecting foreigners in Egypt. Edinburgh, 1907.
Afr 7568.33	Starr, F. The truth about the Congo. Chicago, 1907.
Afr 8292.3	Stirling, John. The colonials in South Africa 1899-1902. Edinburgh, 1907.
NEDL Afr 8088.88.5	Theal, G.M. History and ethnography of Africa Zambesi. London, 1907. 3v.
Afr 3275.45	To see with others' eyes. Cairo, 1907.
Afr 3979.07	Tyndale, W. Below the Cataracts. Philadelphia, 1907.

1908

Afr 1583.3F	Aktenstuecke über Marokko. Berlin, 1908.
Afr 3979.08.10	Albertis, E.A.D. Une croisière sur le Nil, Khartoum-Goudokoro. Le Caire, 1908.
Afr 1846.11	Arnaud, Ed. Nos confins sahariens, étude d'organisation militaire. Paris, 1908.
Afr 2762.4	Benhazera, M. Six Mois chez Les touaregDu Ahaggar. Alger, 1908.
Afr 1432.9	Boudot, P. Une mission militaire prussienne. Paris, 1908.
Afr 1485.6	Bourdon, G. Les journees de Casablanca. Paris, 1908.
Afr 3979.06	Brianchaninov, N. Skitaniia, Nubiia, Sudan. Moscow, 1908.
Afr 2209.08	Bruchard, H. de. La France au soleil, notes sur l'Algérie. Paris, 1908.
Afr 9689.8	Butt, G.E. My travels in north west Rhodesia. London, 1908.
Afr 1609.08.6	Campo Angulo, G. Geografia de Marruecos. Madrid, 1908.
Afr 7565.20	Cannart d'Hamale, Art. Quelques pages sur le Congo. Bruxelles, 1908.
Afr 5056.108	Cheran, Georges. La société noire de l'Afrique occidentale française. Paris, 1908.
Htn Afr 699.08.4*	Churchill, Winston S. My African journey. London, 1908.
Afr 2749.08	Cortier, M. D'une rive à l'autre du Sahara. Paris, 1908.
Afr 3275.17.2A	Cromer, E.B. Modern Egypt. London, 1908. 2v.
Afr 3275.17.4A	Cromer, E.B. Modern Egypt. N.Y., 1908. 2v.
Afr 3275.17A	Cromer, E.B. Modern Egypt. N.Y., 1908. 2v.
Afr 3275.60	Cromer, E.B. The situation in Egypt. London, 1908.
Afr 4742.5.5	Dainelli, Giotto. In Africa, lettere dall'Eritrea. v.1. Bergamo, 1908.
Afr 5549.08	Darcy, J. France et Angleterre, cent années de rivalité coloniale. Paris, 1908.
Afr 7809.08.5	Davis, R.H. The Congo and coasts of Africa. London, 1908.
Afr 5045.5	Deherme, G. L'Afrique occidentale française. Paris, 1908.
Afr 6926.24	Dincklage-Campe, F. Deutsche reiber in Südwest. Berlin, 1908.
Afr 6738.17	Dominik, Hans. Vom Atlantik zum Tschadsee. Berlin, 1908.
Afr 2025.19	Dominique, L.C. Gouverneur général de l'Algérie. Alger, 1908.
Afr 2209.08.2	Donop, J. Lettres sur l'Algérie, 1907-08. Paris, 1908.
Afr 6990.21.5	Eckenbrecher, M. Was Afrika nur gab und nahm. 3. Aufl. Berlin, 1908.
Afr 3990.3	Egypt and how to see it. N.Y., 1908.
Afr 555.149	Favre, Edouard. François Coillard. Paris, 1908-13. 3v.
Afr 6535.7	Filippi, F. de. Ruwenzori, an account of the expedition of L. Arredo. London, 1908.
Afr 6535.7.5	Filippi, F. de. Ruwenzori, an account of the expedition of L. Arredo. N.Y., 1908.
Afr 2223.38	France. Chambre des Députés (1908). Rapport fait...budget spécial de l'Algérie. v.1-2. Paris, 1908.
Afr 6460.1	Freitag, C. Beiträge zur Völkerkunde von Östafrika. n.p., 1908.
Afr 6926.1.2	Frenssen, G. Peter Moor's journey to Southwest Africa. London, 1908.
Afr 5480.208	Freydenberg, Henri. Le Tchad et le bassin du Chari. Thèse. Paris, 1908.
Afr 5640.15	Gallieni, J.S. Neuf ans a Madagascar. Paris, 1908.
Afr 2749.08.3	Gautier, E.F. Missions du Sahara. Paris, 1908-09. 2v.

1908 - cont.

Afr 1583.11	Pamphlet vol. Germany's relations with Morocco. Berlin, 1908. 9 pam.
Afr 8040.3	Government of South Africa. Cape Town, 1908. 2v.
Afr 5760.12F	Grandidier, Alfred. Ethnographie de Madagascar. v.1-4. Paris, 1908-1928. 4v.
Afr 6540.2	Hattersley, C.W. The Beganda at home. London, 1908.
Afr 3143.5	Helbig, Adolph H. Al-Qadi al-Fadil, der Wezir Saladins. Inaug.-Diss. Leipzig, 1908.
Afr 4969.07.3	Herbert, A. Two dianas in Somaliland. 2d ed. London, 1908.
Afr 5829.08.5	Herve de Rauville. L'Ile de France contemporaine. Paris, 1908.
Afr 3979.08.5	Holland, Clive. Things seen in Egypt. N.Y., 1908.
Afr 4559.08	Holts, A. Im Auto zu Kaiser Menelik. Berlin, 1908.
Afr 2208.99.11	Hyam, Joseph C. The illustrated guide to Algiers. 6th ed. Algiers, 1908.
Afr 8292.55	Jacson, M. The record of a regiment of the line. London, 1908.
Afr 725.9	Johnson, J.B. Tramp around the Mountains of the Moon and through the back gate of the Congo state. London, 1908.
Afr 7809.08	Johnston, H. George Grenfell and the Congo. London, 1908. 2v.
Afr 5540.3	Julien, G. Institutions politiques et socials de Madagascar. V.1-2. Paris, 1908. 2v.
Afr 8678.10.7	Kidd, D. Kafir socialism. London, 1908.
Afr 8678.10.8	Kidd, D. South Africa. London, 1908.
Afr 699.08	Kirkland, Caroline. Some African highways, journey of two American women to Uganda and the Transvaal. London, 1908.
Afr 2209.08.5	Kuehnel, Ernst. Algerien. Leipzig, 1908.
Afr 1490.19	Lechartier, G.G. La colonne du Haut-Guir en Sept. 1908. Paris, 1908.
Afr 1609.08.5	Leon Y Ramos, E. Marruecos. Madrid, 1908.
Afr 550.42F	Leri, Primo. Missione nell'Africa settentrionale. Roma, 1908.
Afr 3275.20	Letters from an Egyptian...upon the affairs of Egypt. London, 1908.
Afr 1259.08	Lorin, H. L'Afrique du Nord. Paris, 1908.
Afr 609.07	Lowensbach, Lothaire. Promenade autour de l'Afrique, 1907. Paris, 1908.
Afr 6740.5	Mansfield, Alfred. Verwald-Dokumente. Berlin, 1908.
Afr 4766.27	Mantegazza, Vico. Il Benadir. Milano, 1908.
Afr 2374.2	Martin, A.G.P. Les oasis sahariennes. Alger, 1908.
Afr 1750.2	Martin Y Peinador. Marruecos y plazas españolas. Madrid, 1908.
Afr 679.08	Milligan, R.H. Jungle folk of Africa. N.Y., 1908.
Afr 2209.08.3	Miltoun, F. In the land of mosques and minarets. Boston, 1908.
Afr 1609.08	Moore, Frederick. The passing of Morocco. Boston, 1908.
Afr 1990.24	Mordacq, J.J.H. La guerre en Afrique. Paris, 1908.
Afr 7815.4	Overbergh, C. van. Les Basonge. 3. Bruxelles, 1908.
Afr 1570.21	Palacios, C.M. De Marruecos. Badajoz, 1908.
Afr 4742.17.3	Paoli, Renato. Nella colonia Eritrea. Milano, 1908.
Afr 1550.13	Paquot, G. La question marocaine. Paris, 1908.
Afr 1485.2	Rankin, R. In Morocco with General d'Amade. London, 1908.
Afr 1570.22	Romagny, J. Le role de la France au Maroc. Oran, 1908.
Afr 8292.20	Romer, C.F. Second Battalion Royal Dublin Fusiliers in South African war. London, 1908.
Afr 855.12.5	St. Helena. Extracts from the St. Helena records. 2 ed. St. Helena, 1908.
Afr 2688.2	Saladin, H. Tunis et Kairouan. Paris, 1908.
Afr 5365.5	Salinis, A. Le protectorat français sur la Côte des Esclaves. Paris, 1908.
Afr 1453.7	Salmon, Albert. Le Maroc. Paris, 1908.
Afr 1335.6	Segundo congreso africanista. Barcelona, 1908.
Afr 9489.08	Selous, F.C. African nature notes and reminiscences. London, 1908.
Afr 1727.2	Servando Marenco, D. La conquista de la Mehedia. Madrid, 1908.
Afr 3275.28	Sladen, D.B.W. Egypt and the English. London, 1908.
Afr 1609.08.3	Sternberg, Adalb. Die barbaren von Marokko. Wien, 1908.
Afr 1550.11	Tardier, A. La conférence d'Algésiras. Paris, 1908.
Afr 3204.20	Tarman, E.E. Egypt and its betrayal. N.Y., 1908.
Afr 8088.88.7	Theal, G.M. History of South Africa since Sept. 1795. v.1- London, 1908- 3v.
Afr 6535.8	Tucker, A.R. Eighteen years in Uganda and East Africa. London, 1908. 2v.
Afr 2208.82.5	Wahl, M. L'Algérie. 5e ed. Paris, 1908.
Afr 4040.5	Watson, Charles R. In the valley of the Nile. N.Y., 1908.
Afr 9161.6	Werrmann, R. The Bawenda of the Spelonken. London, 1908.
Afr 8292.45	Wetton, T.C. Reminiscences of the 34th Battalion, Imperial Yeomanry. London, 1908.
Afr 1550.20	Wirth, A. Marokko. Frankfurt, 1908.
Afr 6535.10	Wollaston, A.F.R. From Ruwenzore to the Congo. London, 1908.
Afr 6535.10.3	Wollaston, A.F.R. From Ruwenzore to the Congo. N.Y., 1908.
Afr 1609.08.4	Zeys, Mathilde. Une française au Maroc. Paris, 1908.

1909

Afr 718.25	Adolf, Friedrich. Ins innerste Afrika. Leipzig, 1909.
Afr 1753.6	Alvarez Cabrera, J. Columnas de operaciones en Marruecos. Tanger, 1909.
Afr 5180.24	Anfreville de la Salle. Notre vieux Sénégal, son histoire. Paris, 1909.
Afr 1573.17	Bande, Nicasio. La cuestion del dia: desenlace del problema norte-africano y el porvenir de España. Barcelona, 1909.
Afr 3979.09	Banse, E. Agypten. Halle, 1909.
Afr 6926.17	Bayer, M.G.S. Mit dem Hauptquartier in Südwestafrika. Berlin, 1909.
Afr 8300.10	Baynes, A.H. My diocese during the war. London, 1909.
Afr 4150.2	Beadnell, H.J.L. An Egyptian oasis. London, 1909.
Afr 1658.12	Becker, Jeronimo. El Rif. Madrid, 1909.
Afr 8340.9A	Brand, R.H. The Union of South Africa. Oxford, 1909.
Afr 1609.09.5	Brines, A. Voyages au Maroc (1901-1907). Alger, 1909.
Afr 8135.5	Cana, F.R. South Africa from the great trek to the union. London, 1909.
Afr 1605.96	Castries, H. de. Une description du Maroc. Paris, 1909.
Afr 5405.112.5	Challaye, Felicien. Le Congo français. Paris, 1909.
Afr 9704.3	Chapman, William. A pathfinder in south Central Africa. London, 1909.
Afr 699.08.4.5	Churchill, Winston S. My African journey. N.Y., 1909.
Afr 7324.8	Circumscripções de Lourenço Marques. Lourenço Marques, 1909.

1909 - cont.

Afr 7549.09	Claparède, René. L'évolution d'un état philanthropique. Genève, 1909.
Afr 5874.11	Compagnie des Indes Orientales. Isle de Bourbon (Réunion); documents, 1701-1710. N.Y., 1909.
Afr 2209.09	Congrès de l'Afrique du nord. Paris, 1909. 2v.
Afr 1750.4.3	Congreso Africanista. Tercer congreso africanista. Barcelona, 1909.
Afr 1755.6	Corral Caballe, M. del. Cronica de la guerra de Africa en 1909. Barcelona, 1909.
Afr 11051.5	Crouch, E.H. A treasury of South African poetry and verse. 2. ed. London, 1909.
Afr 8105.20	Deherain, Henri. Le Cap de Bonne-Espérance au XVIIe siècle. Paris, 1909.
Afr 7815.5.5	Delhaise, C.G. Les Warega (Congo belge). 5. Bruxelles, 1909.
Afr 7809.09	Delhaise, C.G.F.F. Les Warega (Congo belge) par le commandant Delhaise. Bruxelles, 1909.
Afr 1450.9	Diaz Moreu, E. Problema de actualidad: la cuestion de Marruecos. Madrid, 1909.
Afr 8355.10	Doke, Joseph J. An Indian patriot in South Africa. London, 1909.
Afr 7568.29	Doyle, A.C. The crime of the Congo. N.Y., 1909.
Afr 4559.09	Duchesne-Fournet, J. Mission en Ethiopie (1901-1903). v.1-2 and atlas. Paris, 1909. 3v.
Afr 3735.11	Egerton, G. With the Seventy-Second Highlanders in the Sudan campaign. London, 1909.
Afr 3285.3.5	Egypt. Delegation, 1908. Report submitted by the Egyptian delegation to Foreign Secretary of Great Britain. Alexandria, 1909.
Afr Doc 1407.307	Egypt. Department of Statistics and Census. The census of Egypt taken in 1907. Cairo, 1909.
X Cg Afr 1755.7	Fernandez, M.B. Notas referente a la tribu de Kelaia. Madrid, 1909. (Changed to XP 3964)
Afr 1955.34	Ferrand, G. La colonisation militaire du maréchal Bugeaud, 1841-47. Thèse. Paris, 1909.
Afr 7567.22	Flechet, Ferdinand. L'annexion du Congo devant Parlement belge. 2d ed. Liège, 1909.
Afr 8340.8	Fremantle, H.E.S. The new nation. A survey of the condition and prospects of South Africa. London, 1909.
Afr 2929.09	Furlong, C.W. Gateway to the Sahara...Tripoli. N.Y., 1909.
Afr 1755.10	Gallego Ramos, E. La Campana del rif. Madrid, 1909.
Afr 5749.09	Gallois, E. La France dans l'ocean Indien. Paris, 1909.
Afr 6778.1	Goetzen, Gustave Adolf, Graf von. Deutsche-Ostafrika im Aufstand, 1905-06. Berlin, 1909.
Afr 1550.23	Gomez Gonzalez, M. La penetracion en Marruecos. Zaragoza, 1909.
Afr 718.2.81A	Grant, J.H. Autobiography of Henry Morton Stanley. Boston, 1909.
Afr 5090.16	Gruvel, Abel. A travers la Mauritanie occidentale. Paris, 1909.
Afr 679.09	Guggisberg, Decima (Moore). We two in West Africa. London, 1909.
Afr 6887.11.15	Gutmann, B. Dichten und Denken der Dschagganeger. Leipzig, 1909.
Afr 1490.3	Harris, Lawrence. With Mulai Hafid at Fez. London, 1909.
Afr 555.14	Hawker, G. The life of George Grenfell. London, 1909.
NEDL Afr 500.7.3	Hertslet, E. Map of Africa by treaty. London, 1909. 3v.
Afr 500.7.3	Hertslet, E. Map of Africa by treaty. v.4. London, 1909.
Afr 1571.3	Hess, Jean. Une Algérie nouvelle. Paris, 1909.
Afr 9489.09	Hone, P.F. Southern Rhodesia. London, 1909.
Afr 5010.2	Hubert, L. L'éveil d'un monde. Paris, 1909.
Afr 9086.16	Huessen, F. Verfassungsentwickelung Transvaals. Karlsruhe, 1909.
Afr 500.18.2	Italy. Direzione Centrale degli Affari Coloniali. Trattati, convenzioni, accordi. Supplemento alla raccolta. Roma, 1909.
Afr 6887.8	Jaeger, Fritz. Forschungen in den Hochregionen des Kilimand. Berlin, 1909.
Afr 2762.5	Jean, C. Les Touareg du sud-est l'Air. Leur rôle dans la politique saharienne. Paris, 1909.
Afr Doc 1406.5	Journal official du gouvernement egyptien. Cairo, 1909. 2v.
Afr 7369.09	Karnga, A.W. The Negro Republic on West Africa. Monrovia, 1909.
Afr 1450.6	Karow, K.L. Neun Jahre in marokkanischen Diensten. Berlin, 1909.
Afr 8330.5	Kestell, J.D. De vredesonderhandelingen. Pretoria, 1909.
Afr 4070.21	Kumm, H.K.W. The Sudan. 2d ed. London, 1909.
Afr 4115.12	Lamplough, A.O. Cairo and its environs. London, 1909.
Afr 6645.15	Langheld, Wilhelm. Zwanzig Jahre in deutschen Kolonien. Berlin, 1909.
Afr 1955.21	Laurie, G.B. The French conquest of Algeria. London, 1909.
Afr 7809.09.05	Lilbrechts, C. Souvenirs d'Afrique. Congo. Bruxelles, 1909.
Afr 3979.09.10	Lorimer, Norma. By the waters of Egypt. N.Y., 1909.
Afr 3243.8	Malet, E.B. Egypt 1879-1883. London, 1909.
Afr 5285.277	Marc, Lucien. Le pays Mossi. Paris, 1909.
Afr 1485.8	Marietti, Giovanni. Politica ed armi al Marocco. Torino, 1909.
Afr 8659.09	Maturin, Edith. Petticoat pilgrims on trek. London, 1909.
Afr 1609.09.3	Mauran. Le maroc d'aujourd hui et de demain. Paris, 1909.
Afr 1583.12	Maurus, Pseud. Ave caesar. Deutsche Luftschiffe...Marokko. Leipzig, 1909.
Afr 4230.4.6	Mendez S.I., P.A. Expeditiones Aethiopicae. v.1-4. Roma, 1909. 2v.
Afr 1609.09	Metour, E.P. In the wake of the green banner. N.Y., 1909.
Afr 1755.5	Morales, G. de. Datos para la historia de Melilla. Melilla, 1909.
Afr 7568.15.5	Morel, E.D. The future of the Congo. London, 1909.
Afr 555.9.24	Morshead, A.E. The history of the Universities Mission to Central Africa. London, 1909.
Afr Doc 2403.5F	Nigeria, Northern. Blue book, 1908-1913. Lagos, 1909.
Afr 7815.5	Overbergh, C. van. Les Mangbetu (Congo belge). 4. Bruxelles, 1909.
Afr 6455.14	Patterson, J.H. In the grip of Nyika. London, 1909.
Afr 1485.3	Perez, D. El ocaso de un sultan. Zaragoza, 1909.
Afr 2209.05.5	Phillips, L.M. In the desert. London, 1909.
Afr 1069.09	Piquet, V. Les civilisations de l'Afrique du Nord. Paris, 1909.
Afr 7815.12	Piscelli, M. Nel paese dei Bango-bango. Napoli, 1909.
Afr 6455.35	Purvis, J.B. Through Uganda to Mt. Elgon. London, 1909.
Afr 5406.209	Riemer, Otto. Das französische Congogebiet. Mörs, 1909.
Afr 1840.2	Rouard de Card, E. La réprésentation des indigènes musulmans dans les conseils de l'Algérie. Paris, 1909.

1909 - cont.

Afr 2609.04.5   Saint-Paul, Georges. Souvenirs de Tunisie et d'Algérie. Tunis, 1909.

Afr 6926.2   Schwabe, K. In deutschen Diamantenlande, Deutsch-Südwest-Afrika, 1884-1910. Berlin, 1909.

Afr 6738.9   Sembritzki, Emil. Kamerun. Berlin, 1909.

Afr 8678.7.5   South African Native Races Committee. The South African natives. Paris, 1909.

Afr 3735.4.6   Steevens, G.W. With Kitchener to Khartum. London, 1909.

Afr 5549.09   Suau, Pierre. La France à Madagascar. Paris, 1909.

Afr 7809.09.10   Vandervelde, Emile. Les derniers jours de l'Etat du Congo. Mons, 1909.

Afr 3979.09.5   Weigall, A.E.P. Travels in the Upper Egyptian deserts. Edinburgh, 1909.

Afr 6883.5.3   Weule, Karl. Native life in East Africa. London, 1909.

Afr 8289.09   Wilson, S. South African memories. London, 1909.

Afr 8145.7   Wirgman, A.T. Life of James Green...dean of Maritzburg, Natal, 1849-1906. London, 1909. 2v.

Afr 8063.5   Woon, Harry V. Twenty-five years soldiering in South Africa. London, 1909.

Afr 6720.2   Zimmermann, Oscar. Durch Busch und Steppe vom Camps. Berlin, 1909.

191-

Afr 1713.9   Erigny, Maurice. Au Maroc. Fes la capitale du nord. Paris, 191-.

Afr 9558.12   Livingstone, D. Dreissig Jahre Afrika. Leipzig, 191-.

Afr 6275.23   Raphael, J.R. Through unknown Nigeria. London, 191-.

1910

Afr 1583.7   Adam, Paul. Affaires du Maroc, livre blanc allemand. Paris, 1910.

Afr 718.25.3   Adolf, Friedrich. In the heart of Africa. London, 1910.

Afr 6143.12   Alldridge, T.J. A transformed colony. London, 1910.

Afr 7183.10   Angola. Repartição do Gabinete. Relatorio da missao de colonisação no planalto de Benguella em 1909. Loanda, 1910.

Afr 8659.10.5   Angore, John. In the early days. Kimberley, 1910.

Afr 1490.2   Ashmead-Bartlett, E. Passing of the shereefian empire. Edinburgh, 1910.

Afr 1490.2.5   Ashmead-Bartlett, E. Passing of the shereefian empire. N.Y., 1910.

Afr 5045.22   Baratier, A.E.A. A travers l'Afrique. Paris, 1910.

Afr 861 1   Barrow, K.M. Three years in Tristan da Cunha. London, 1910.

Afr 1584.7F   Bethmann, H. Denkschrift über deutsche bergwerksinteressen in Marokko. Berlin, 1910.

Afr 3248.6   Bioves, Achille. Français et Anglais en Egypte, 1881-1882. Paris, 1910.

Afr 6645.5   Bongard, Oscar. Wie wandere ich nach Deutschen Kolonien aus. 3. Aufl. Berlin, 1910.

Afr 6455.34   Bronson, Edgar B. In closed territory. Chicago, 1910.

Afr 3979.10.8A   Budge, E.A.W. The Nile. 11th ed. London, 1910.

Afr 7326.5   Cabral, Augusto. Racas, usos e costumes dos indigenas do districto de Inhambane. Lourenço Marques, 1910.

NEDL   Afr 7045.5.2   Cadbury, W.A. Labour in Portuguese West Africa. 2d ed. N.Y., 1910.

Afr 7190.32   Cadbury, William A. Os serviçaes de S. Thomé. Lisboa, 1910.

Afr 7065.510   Chagas, Frederico Pinheiro. Na Guiné, 1907-1908. Lisboa, 1910.

Afr 8687.354   Cheeseman, Thomas. The story of William Threlfall. Cape Town, 1910.

Afr 1750.4.4   Congreso Africanista. Cuarto congreso africanista. IVth. Barcelona, 1910.

Afr 8089.10   Cory, G.E. The rise of South Africa. v.1- London, 1910- 6v.

Afr 5119.10   Cultru, P. Histoire du Sénégal du XV siècle à 1870. Paris, 1910.

Afr 1100.2   Currey, E.H. Sea-wolves of the Mediterranean. London, 1910.

Afr 5829.10   Deburgh Edwardes, S.B. L'histoire de l'ile Maurice d'après les documents les plus authentiques, 1507-1895. Paris, 1910.

Htn   Afr 6390.7*   Dickinson, F.A. Lake Victoria to Khartoum with rifle and camera. London, 1910.

Afr 6455.16   Dugmore, A.R. Camera adventures in the African wilds. N.Y., 1910.

Afr 9506.10   Elliott, William Allan. Gold from the quartz. London, 1910.

Afr 4559.10   Faitlovitch, J. Quer durch Abessinien. Berlin, 1910.

Afr 4180.3   Falls, J.C.E. Siwah. Mainz, 1910.

Afr 5184.20   Faulong, L. Les rapports financiers de la métropole et de l'Afrique occidentale française. Paris, 1910.

Afr 1609.08.7   Finnemore, J. Peeps at many lands, Morocco. London, 1910.

Afr 1584.3   Fischer, A. Das marokkanische Berggesetz. Berlin, 1910.

Afr 6879.10   Fonck, Heinrich. Deutsch-Ost-Afrika. Berlin, 1910.

Afr 609.10   Forbes, A. The land of the white helmet. N.Y., 1910.

Afr 4070.8   Fothergill, E. Five years in the Sudan. London, 1910.

Afr 755.2   France. Ministère des Colonies. Documentation scientifique de la mission Tilho. Paris, 1910. 4v.

Afr 8250.7   Fuller, T.E. Right Honourable Cecil J. Rhodes. London, 1910.

Afr 5045.9   Gaffarel, Paul. Comptoirs de l'Afrique française occidentale. Dijon, 1910.

Afr 1869.10   Garrot, Henri. Histoire generale de l'Algerie. Alger, 1910.

Afr 4766.25   Gasparro, A. La Somalia italiana nell'antichità classica. Palermo, 1910.

Afr 2749.10   Gautier, E.F. La conquête du Sahara. Paris, 1910.

Afr 7540.6   Gohr, Albrecht. De l'organisation judiciaire et de la compétence en matière civile et commerciale au Congo. Liège, 1910.

Afr 2290.10   Guillaume. Conquête du sud-oranais; la colonne d'Igli en 1900. Paris, 1910.

Afr 9290.5   Gunn, Hugh. The language question in the Orange River Colony. Johannesburg, 1910.

Afr 1490.3.5   Harris, Lawrence. With Mulai Hafid at Fez. Boston, 1910.

Afr 5243.125   Henry, Joseph. L'âme d'un peuple africain...les Bambara. Münster, 1910.

Afr 6395.4   Hobley, C.W. Ethnology of A-kamba and other East African tribes. Cambridge, 1910.

Afr 2209.10   Hyam, Joseph C. Biskra, Sidi-Okba and the desert. 1st ed. Algiers, 1910.

Afr 8659.10   Hyatt, S.P. Diary of a soldier of fortune. London, 1910.

1910 - cont.

Afr 628.210   Johnston, H.H. The Negro in the new world. London, 1910.

Afr 1432.17   Joly, A. Historia critica de la guerra...en 1859-60. Madrid, 1910.

Afr 8809.10   Juta, Rene. The Cape peninsula. Cape Town, 1910.

Afr 3979.02.5   Kelly, R. Talbot. Egypt painted and described. London, 1910.

Afr 6275.20   Kisch, M.S. Letters and sketches from northern Nigeria. London, 1910.

Afr 4559.07   Kulmer, F. Im Reiche Kaiser Meneliks. Leipzig, 1910.

Afr 718.21   Kumm, H.K.W. From Hausaland to Egypt. London, 1910.

Afr 718.22   Kumm, H.K.W. Khont-Hon-Nofer, lands of Ethiopia. London, 1910.

Afr 8865.5   Lagden, G. The Basutos. N.Y., 1910. 2v.

Afr 2312.2   Leeder, S.H. The desert gateway. London, 1910.

X Cg   Afr 6128.3   Lukach, H.C. A bibliography of Sierra Leone. Oxford, 1910. (Changed to XP 3869)

Afr 6455.19   MacQueen, P. In wildest Africa. London, 1910.

NEDL   Afr 5048.7   Mangin, C. La force noire. Paris, 1910.

Afr 2280.8   Martino, P. Les descriptions de Fromentin. Alger, 1910.

Afr 1840.5   Mary, P. Influence de la conversion...sur la condition...en Algérie. Thèse. Paris, 1910.

Afr 3979.10.5   Maspero, Gaston. Ruines et paysages d'Egypte. Paris, 1910.

Afr 7322.3   Maugham, R.C.F. Zambezia. London, 1910.

Afr 8028.5   Mendelssohn, S. Mendelssohn's South African bibliography. London, 1910. 2v.

Afr 6541.3   Michael, Charles D. James Hannington, bishop and martyr; the story of a noble life. London, 1910.

Afr 8250.6   Michell, L. Life and times of C.J. Rhodes. N.Y., 1910. 2v.

Afr 5760.11   Mondain, C. L'histoire des tribus de l'Imoro au XVIIe siècle. Paris, 1910.

Afr 1755.9   Noel, E. Notas de un voluntario. Madrid, 1910.

Afr 1583.14   Osman, H.A. Die Mannesmann-Rechte und den Weissbuch. Berlin, 1910.

Afr 7122.40   Paiva Couceiro, H.M. de. Angola (Dous annos de governo junho 1907 - junho 1909.) Lisboa, 1910.

Afr 5832.10.5   Pitot, Albert. L'ile de Maurice. V.1-2. Port-Louis, 1910-12.

Afr 7815.5.6   Plas, J.V. Les Kuku. 6. Bruxelles, 1910.

Afr 575.10   Quellien, A. La politique musulmane dans l'Afrique occidentale française. Paris, 1910.

Afr 4230.4.7   Relationes et epistolae variorum. v.1-2. Romae, 1910-14. 3v.

Afr 1490.6   Rene-Leclerc, C. Situation économique du Maroc 1908-09. Oran, 1910.

Afr 6455.17   Roosevelt, T. African game trails. N.Y., 1910.

Afr 4396.10   Rossetti, Carlo. Storia diplomatica dell'Etiopia durante il regno di Menelik II. Torino, 1910.

Afr 3275.21   Rotshtein, F.A. Egypt's ruin. London, 1910.

Afr 2710.3   Rouard de Card, E. La France et la Turquie dans le Sahara oriental. Paris, 1910.

Afr 510.11   Rouard de Card, E. Traités de délimitation concernant l'Afrique française. Paris, 1910.

Afr 6395.2   Routledge, W.S. With a prehistoric people, the Akikuyu of British East Africa. London, 1910.

Afr 5920.4   Saavedra y Magdalena, D. España en el Africa occidental. Madrid, 1910.

Afr 1680.5   Segonzac, De. Au coeur de l'atlas. Paris, 1910.

Afr 1609.10   Segonzac, M. De. Itineraires au Maroc. (Maps). Paris, 1910.

Afr 1259.10   Shoemaker, M.M. Islam lands, Nubia, the Sudan, Tunisia, and Algeria. N.Y., 1910.

Afr 575.10   Simian, M. Les confréries islamiques. Alger, 1910.

Afr 3979.10   Sladen, D. Queer things about Egypt. London, 1910.

Afr 8659.10.3   Southey, Rosamond. Storm and sunshine in South Africa. London, 1910.

Afr 6455.18   Stigand, C.H. To Abyssinia through an unknown land. London, 1910.

Afr 6850.3   Stuhlmann, F. Handwerk und Industrie in Ostafrika. Hamburg, 1910.

Afr 590.22   Swann, A.J. Fighting the slave-hunters in Central Africa. London, 1910.

Afr 4070.15   Tangye, H.S. In the torrid Sudan. Boston, 1910.

Afr 5219.10   Terrier, A. L'expansion française et la formation territoriale. Paris, 1910.

NEDL   Afr 8678.13   Theal, G.M. The yellow and dark skinned people...Zambesi. London, 1910.

Afr 6280.12   Thomas, N.W. Anthropological report on...peoples of Nigeria. London, 1910. 2v.

Afr 6390.16   Tjader, Richard. The big game of Africa. N.Y, 1910.

Afr 7459.10   Toepfer, R. Liberia. Berlin, 1910.

Afr 6535.13   Treves, Fred. Uganda for a holiday. London, 1910.

Afr 2749.06   Vischer, H. Across the Sahara. London, 1910.

Afr 7809.10   Ward, H. A voice from the Congo. London, 1910.

Afr 8250.23   Watts-Danton, T. The Rhodes memorial at Oxford. London, 1910.

Afr 3740.9   Wauters, A.J. Souvenirs de Fashoda et de l'expedition Dhanis. Bruxelles, 1910.

Afr 1280.3   Weisgerber, H. Les blancs d'Afrique. Paris, 1910.

Afr 6883.3   Weiss, Max. Die Völkerstämme in nord Deutsch-Ostafrika. Berlin, 1910.

Afr 6390.12   Younghusband, E. Glimpses of East Africa and Zanzibar. London, 1910.

1911

Afr 1624.911   Abdesselem, Faleb. L'organisation financiere de l'empire marocain. Paris, 1911.

Afr 3275.22   Alexander, J. The truth about Egypt. London, 1911.

Afr Doc 9271.5   Amorim, Massano de. Relatorio sobre a occupação de Angoche. Lourenço Marques, 1911.

Afr 7549.11.7   Anton, G.K. Kongostaat und Kongoreform. Leipzig, 1911.

Afr 550.11   Apostolat en Afrique. Québec, 1911.

Afr 5314.5   Arcin, André. Histoire de la Guinée française. Paris, 1911.

Afr 1609.11.6   Artbauer, O.C. Kreuz und qür durch Marokko. Stuttgart, 1911.

Afr 1658.4   Artbauer, O.C. Die rifpiraten und ihre heimat. Stuttgart, 1911.

Afr 4070.16.3   Artin, Y.P. England in the Sudan. London, 1911.

Afr 2762.6   Aymard, C. Les Touareg. Paris, 1911.

Afr 1490.14   Azan, Paul. Souvenirs de Casablanca. Paris, 1911.

Afr 4180.3.3   Bates, O. Siwan superstitions. Alexandria, 1911.

Afr 6395.3   Beech, M.W.H. The Suk, their language and folklore. Oxford, 1911.

Afr 1571.4   Bernard, A. Les confins algéro-marocains. Paris, 1911.

Afr 8919.08   Bertrand, Alfred. Dans le Sud-Africain et au serial de l'Afrique centrale. Genève, 1911.
Afr 8659.11.3 Blackburn, D. Secret service in South Africa. London, 1911.
Afr 3258.8.5   Blunt, W.S. Gordon at Khartoum. London, 1911.
Afr 6192.16   Bowler, Louis P. Gold Coast palaver. London, 1911.
Afr 6455.25   British East Africa. The Uganda railway. London, 1911.
Afr 6333.2   Brode, Heinrich. British and German East Africa. N.Y., 1911.
Afr 825.5   Bruel, Georges. Notes géographiques sur le bassin de l'Ogooue. Paris, 1911.
Afr 1583.9   Buelow, J. von. Marocco Deutsch. Berlin, 1911.
Afr 3979.11   Butcher, E.L. Egypt as we knew it. London, 1911.
Afr 1550.24   Camarasa, M. de. La cuestion de Marruecos y su honrada solucion. Madrid, 1911.
Afr 1490.21   Camarasa, M. de. La cuestion de Marruecos y su solucion...1911. Barcelona, 1911.
Afr 4392.8.5   Canuti, Giuseppe. L'Italia in Africa e le guerre con l'Abissinia. Firenze, 1911.
Afr 8835.3   Cape Town. The Cape of Good Hope. Cape Town, 1911.
Afr 2609.11   Castellini, G. Tunisi, e Tripoli. Torino, 1911.
Afr 1406.16   Castries, H. de. Agents et voyageurs français au Maroc, 1530-1660. Paris, 1911.
Afr 635.7.5   Christol, Frederic. L'art dans l'Afrique australe. Paris, 1911.
Afr 8840.5   Cohen, L. Reminiscences of Kimberley. London, 1911.
Afr 2209.11   Colliez, A. La frontière algéro-marocaine. Paris, 1911.
Afr 9599.11   Colville, A. One thousand miles in a Machilla. London, 1911.
Afr 4070.29   Comyn, D.C.E. Service and sport in the Sudan. London, 1911.
Afr 5480.211   Cornel, Charles J.H. Au Tchad. Paris, 1911.
Afr 2929.11.2 Corradini, E. Ora di tripoli. Milano, 1911.
Afr 2929.11   Corradini, E. L'ora di Tripoli. Milano, 1911.
Afr 5406.211.10 Cottes, A. La mission Cottes au Sud-Cameroun. Paris, 1911.
Afr 3275.17.4.5 Cromer, E.B. Modern Egypt. London, 1911.
Afr 1755.17   Cronica artillera...Campana de Melilla. Text and plates. Madrid, 1911.
Afr 11052.3   Crouch, E.H. Sonnets of South Africa. London, 1911.
Afr 1490.10   D'Amade, Général. Campagne de 1908-1909 en Chaouia. Rapport. Paris, 1911.
Afr 1658.8   Delbrel, G. Geografia general de la provincia del Rif. Melilla, 1911.
Afr 5406.211   Deschamps, Jean Leopold. De Bordeaux au Tchad par Brazzaville. Paris, 1911.
Afr 1769.5   Dewazan, Emily. My life story. London, 1911.
Afr 659.11   Douel, Martial. Au pays de Salammbo. Paris, 1911.
Afr 555.22.16 Duplessis, J. A history of Christian missions in South Africa. London, 1911.
Afr 8659.11.5 Durand, H.M. A holiday in South Africa. Edinburgh, 1911.
Afr 3199.11   Duse Muhammad. In the land of the pharaohs. N.Y., 1911.
Afr 2875.11   Facchinetti, P.V. Ai caduti nella guerra italo-turca. n.p., 1911.
Afr 6275.21   Falconer, J.D. On horseback through Nigeria. London, 1911.
Afr 4050.10.5 Falls, J.C.E. Drei Jahre in der libyschen Wüste. Freiburg, 1911.
Afr 1658.13   Fernandez De Castro, Rafael. El Rif. Malaga, 1911.
Afr 2632.4   Fidel, Camille. Les intérêts italiens en Tunisie. Paris, 1911.
Afr 6540.6.15 Fisher, Ruth Hurditch. Twilight tales of the black Baganda. London, 1911.
Afr 550.13   Fraser, Donald. The future of Africa. London, 1911.
Afr 1259.11   Fraser, J.F. The land of veiled women. London, 1911.
Afr 5056.110   Frobenius, Leo. Auf dem Wege nach Atlantis. Berlin, 1911.
Afr 3979.11.3 Fyfe, H.H. The new spirit in Egypt. Edinburgh, 1911.
Afr 8659.11   Fyfe, H.H. South Africa to-day. London, 1911.
Afr 8659.11.2 Fyfe, H.H. South Africa today. London, 1911.
Afr 1755.16   Garcialavin, R. La guerra en africa. Madrid, 1911.
Afr 7815.5.8   Gaud, Fernand. Les Mandja. 8. Bruxelles, 1911.
Afr 8145.28   Gerdener, Gustav S.A. Studies in the evangelisation of South Africa. London, 1911.
Afr 8155.5.2   Gibson, J.Y. The story of the Zulus. London, 1911.
Afr 1838.4   Gmelin, H. Die verfassungsentwicklung von Algerien. Hamburg, 1911.
Afr 9689.11   Gouldsbury, C. Great plateau of Northern Rhodesia. London, 1911.
Afr 1550.17   Grand-Carteret, J. Une victoire sans guerre. Paris, 1911.
Afr 1259.11.5 Grant, Cyril F. Twixt sand and sea. London, 1911.
Afr 1485.5   Grasset, Capitaine. A travers la Chaouia. Paris, 1911.
Afr 7815.5.7   Halkin, Joseph. Les Abatua. 7. Bruxelles, 1911.
Afr 5074.36   Hamet, Ismael. Chroniques de la Mauritanie sénégalaise. Paris, 1911.
Afr 4935.6   Hamilton, Angus. Somaliland. London, 1911.
Afr 1583.10   Haruisch, J. Marokko rückzug. Berlin, 1911.
Afr 555.18   Hawker, G. An English woman's twenty-five-years in tropical Africa. London, 1911.
Afr 1490.22   Hildebrand, Gerhard. Sozialistische Auslandspolitik. Jena, 1911.
Afr 7815.9   Hilton-Simpson, M.W. Land and peoples of the Kasai. London, 1911.
Afr 9489.11.3 Hyatt, S.P. Off the main track. London, 1911.
Afr 4700.13.5 Italy. Direzione Centrale degli Affari Coloniali. Raccolta di publicazioni coloniali italiane. Roma, 1911.
Afr 1570.24   Jacquin, P. L'action française au Maroc. Paris, 1911.
Afr 6879.07F   Jaeger, Fritz. Das Hochland der Riesenkrater...Deutsch-Ostafrika. Berlin, 1911.
Afr 1570.30   Jary, G. Les intérêts de la France au Maroc. Paris, 1911.
Afr 2220.7   Joanne, P. Algérie et Tunisie. Paris, 1911.
Afr 109.11.5   Johnston, H.H. The opening up of Africa. N.Y., 1911.
Afr 8250.8   Jourdan, P. Cecil Rhodes. London, 1911.
Afr 8250.8.2   Jourdan, P. Cecil Rhodes. London, 1911.
Afr 3994.2   Kamil, Ali. Les conséquences financières de l'occupation de l'Egypte par l'Angleterre. Bruxelles, 1911.
Afr 1326.2   Kampffmeyer, Georg. Studien und Mitteilungen der deutschen Marokko-bibliothek. Berlin, 1911.
Afr 724.4   Kassner, Theo. My journey from Rhodesia to Egypt. London, 1911.
Afr 1490.5   Kreuter, A. Marokko: wirtschaftliche und soziale Studien in Marokko 1911. Berlin, 1911.
Afr 6275.108   Larymore, Constance. A resident's wife in Nigeria. London, 1911.
Afr 1607.91.7 Lempriere, W. Le Maroc, il y a cent ans. Paris, 1911.

Afr 2230.20   Leroy, J. Deux ans de séjour en Petite Kabilie. Paris, 1911.
Afr 3979.11.15 L'vov, A.N. V strane Amon-Ra. Sankt Peterburg, 1911.
Afr 1609.11   Mackenzie, D. The khalifate of the west. London, 1911.
Afr 3990.15.5 Macmillan, firm, London. Guide to Egypt and Sudan. 6th ed. London, 1911.
Afr 5055.10   Mangin, Charles. La mission des troupes noires. Paris, 1911.
Afr 9489.11   Mansfield, C. Via Rhodesia. London, 1911.
Afr 7190.50   Mantero, F. Portuguese planters and British humanitarians. Lisbon, 1911.
Afr 1573.12   Marenco, S. La dominacion de España en Tanger. Madrid, 1911.
Afr 1607.91.9 Marruecos hace cien anos. Paris, 1911.
Afr 1550.3.5   Maura y Gamazo, Gabriel. La question du Maroc. Paris, 1911.
Afr 3275.23   Mikhail, K. Copts and Moslems under British control. London, 1911.
Afr 9854.14   Mills, Dora S. What we do in Nyasaland. London, 1911.
Afr 6280.7   Morel, E.D. Nigeria; its people and its problems. London, 1911.
Afr 2209.11.3 Mueller, Charles. Fünf Jahre Fremdenlegionär in Algier. Stuttgart, 1911.
Afr 6777.10   Nigmann, Ernst. Geschichte der kaiserlichen Schutztruppe für Deutsch-Ostafrika. Berlin, 1911.
Afr 6214.3   Orr, Charles William James. The making of Northern Nigeria. 9 maps. London, 1911.
Afr 3223.5   Perron, A. Lettres du Dr. Perron du Caire et l'Alexandrie à M. Jules Mohl, à Paris, 1838-54. Le Caire, 1911.
Afr 2929.11.5 Piazza, G. La nostra terra promessa. 2 ed. Madre, 1911.
Afr 4559.11   Rathjens, Carl. Beiträge zur Landeskunde von Abessinien. These. Erlangen, 1911.
Afr Doc 3807.311.5 Rhodesia, Southern. Census Office. Preliminary returns of a census taken on May 1911, together with comparative figures from the census of 1907 and 1904. Salisbury, 1911. 2 pam.
Afr 1490.4.7   Riera, A. España en Marruecos. 7a ed. Barcelona, 1911.
Afr 7809.11   Roby, Marguerite. My adventures in the Congo. London, 1911.
Afr 6926.25   Rohrbach, P. Dernburg und die Südwestafrikaner. Berlin, 1911.
Afr 5406.211.15.2 Rondet-Saint, Maurice. L'Afrique equatoriale française. 2. ed. Paris, 1911.
X Cg Afr 6540.6A Roscoe, John. The Baganda, account of their customs. London, 1911.
Afr 1550.14   Rouard de Card, E. Documents diplomatiques pour servir a l'étude de la question marocaine. n.p., 1911.
Afr 1026.6   Rouard de Card, E. Livres français des XVIIe et XVIIIe siècles concernant les états Barbaresques. Paris, 1911.
Afr 2209.11.7 Roy, R. Au pays des mirages. Paris, 1911.
Afr 632.11F   Schachtgabel, A. Die Siedelungsverhältnisse der Bantu-Niger. Leiden, 1911.
Afr 6455.20   Scull, G.H. Lassoing wild animals in Africa. N.Y., 1911.
Afr 4115.9   Sladen, D. Oriental Cairo. London, 1911.
Afr 4115.9.5   Sladen, D. Oriental Cairo. Philadelphia, 1911.
Afr 7815.6   Smith, H.S. Yakusu. London, 1911.
Afr 9704.8   Smith, Julia A. Sunshine and shade in Central Africa. London, 1911.
Afr 1755.14   Spain. Cuerpo de Estado Mayor del Ejercito. Ensenanzas de la Campana del rif en 1909. Madrid, 1911.
Afr 1325.10F   Spain. Ministerio de Estado. Documentos presentados a las Cortes en la legislatura. Madrid, 1911.
Afr 4180.3.5   Stanley, C.V.B. A report on the Oasis of Siwa. Cairo, 1911.
Afr 8252.13   Streatfeild, F.N. Reminiscences of an old 'un. London, 1911.
Afr 8659.11.7 Streitwolf. Der Caprivizipfel. Berlin, 1911.
Afr 8325.38   Swinton, Ernest. The defence of Duffer's Drift. London, 1911.
Afr 9029.11   Tatlow, A.H. Natal province, descriptive guide. Durban, 1911.
Afr 7803.32   Thibaut, Emile. Les jésuites et les fermes-chapelles, à propos d'un débat récent. Bruxelles 1911.
Afr 1089.3   Thieling, W. Der Hellenismus in Kleinafrika. Leipzig, 1911.
Afi 6738.6F   Thorbecke, F. Das Maneuguba-Hochland. Berlin, 1911.
Afr 5406.211.5 Thouin, Marcel. Etude sur la délimitation de frontière du Congo-Cameroun. Thesis. Paris, 1911.
Afr 1347.2.3   Torcy, General de. Les espagnols au Maroc en 1909. 2 ed. Paris, 1911.
Afr 1570.37.2 Torcy, L.V.V.F.J. de. L'Espagne et la France au Maroc...1911. 2e ed. Paris, 1911.
Afr 7540.17   Touchard, G. Jurisprudence de l'état indépendant du Congo. v.2. Bruxelles, 1911.
Afr 2929.11.9 Tragni. Tripolitania e Cirenaica. Bologna, 1911.
Afr 2929.11.7 Tumiati, D. Tripolitania. Milano, 1911.
Afr 2875.3F   Turco-Italian war concerning Tripoli. n.p., 1911.
Afr 7549.11   Vandervelde, E. La Belgique et le Congo. Paris, 1911.
Afr 550.145   Walker, Frank Deaville. The call of the dark continent. London, 1911.
Afr 7549.11.3 Wauters, A.J. Histoire politique du Congo belge. Bruxelles, 1911.
Afr 7815.10   Weeks, John H. Congo life and folklore. London, 1911.
Afr 1583.8   Wirth, A. Die Entscheidung über Marokko. Stuttgart, 1911.
Afr 9489.11.6 Woods, M.L. Pastels under the Southern Cross. London, 1911.

Afr 2875.6   Abbott, G.F. The holy war in Tripoli. London, 1912.
Afr 575.15   Agabiti, A. Per la Tripolitania. Roma, 1912.
Afr 8659.12.10 Agate, W. Diary of a tour in South Africa. Paisley, 1912.
Afr 1555.3   Albin, P. Le coup d'Agadir. Paris, 1912.
Afr 718.27.3   Alexander, Boyd. Last journey...memoir by H. Alexander. London, 1912.
Afr 4050.9.5   Alexander, F.G. Wayfarers in the Libyan desert. N.Y., 1912.
Afr 2945.8   Almagia, R. Cirenaica. Milano, 1912.
Afr 555.23.15 Angola (Diocese). Visitas pastorães em 1910. Loanda, 1912.
Afr 1584.6   Arning, W. Marokko-Kongo. Leipzig, 1912.
Afr 1609.11.4 Artbauer, O.C. Ein ritt durch Marokko. 2 ed. Regensburg, 1912.
Afr 2025.23   Aynard, R. L'oeuvre française en Algérie. Paris, 1912.

1912 - cont.

Afr 1570.35   Babin, G. Au Maroc par les camps et par les villes. Paris, 1912.

Afr 6069.12   Bailland, E. La politique indigène de l'Angleterre en Afrique occidentale. Paris, 1912.

Afr 5055.50   Baratier, A.E.A. Epopées africaines, ouvrage inédit. Paris, 1912.

Afr 2875.8   Barclay, T. The Turco-Italian war and its problems. London, 1912.

Afr 550.8.10   Baunard, Louis. Le Cardinal Lavigerie. Paris, 1912. 2v.

Afr 2990.2   Bause, E. Tripoli. Weimar, 1912.

Afr 2875.14   Bennett, E.N. With the Turks in Tripoli. London, 1912.

Afr 2209.12.7   Betham-Edwards, M. In French-Africa. Scenes and memories. London, 1912.

Afr 2875.10   Bevione, G. Come siamo andati a Tripoli. Torino, 1912.

Afr 8043.18   Bodenstein, H.D.J. Engelsc invloeden op het gemeenrecht van Zuid Afrika. Amsterdam, 1912.

Afr 2209.12.3   Bonand, R. de. La France de l'Afrique du nord. Paris, 1912.

Afr 5247.17   Bonnel de Méziéres, Albert. Le Major A. Gordon Laing, Tomboucton (1826). Paris, 1912.

Afr 2945.26.15   Bourbon del Monte Santa Maria, G. L'islamismo e la Confraternita dei Senussi. Città di Castello, 1912.

Afr 1609.12.11   Bourote, M. Pour coloniser au Maroc. Paris, 1912.

Afr 6395.2.5   Boyes, John. A white king of East Africa. N.Y., 1912.

Afr 6168.10   Brandenburg-Preussen auf der West-Küste von Afrika. Leipzig, 1912.

Afr 2209.12.9   Brieux, E. Algérie. Vincennes, 1912.

Afr 3979.10.9   Budge, E.A.W. The Nile. 12th ed. London, 1912.

Afr 555.22.19   Callaway, Godfrey. A shepherd of the Veld, Bransly Lewis Key, Africa. London, 1912.

Afr 6275.42   Calvert, A.F. Nigeria and its tin fields. London, 1912.

Afr 6710.3   Cameroon. Laws, statutes, etc. Die Landesgesetzgebung für das Schutzgebiet Kamerun. Berlin, 1912.

Afr 1490.11   Capperon, L. Au secours de Fès. Paris, 1912.

Afr 5488.10   Carbou, Henri. La region du Tchad et du Ouadaï. V.1-2. Paris, 1912. 2v.

Afr 2875.16   Castellini, G. Nelle trincee di Tripoli. Bologna, 1912.

Afr 2929.12.25   Cavazza, F. La Libia italiana e il campo che offre a ricerche scientifiche. Bologna, 1912.

Afr 2928.19.2   Cella, Paolo della. Viaggio da Tripoli di Barberia. 3e ed. Città di Castello, 1912.

Afr 4095.19   Chaille-Long, C. My life in four continents. v.1-2. London, 1912. 2v.

Afr 2945.9   Checchi, S. Attraverso la Cirenaica. Roma, 1912.

Afr 1750.40   Ciges Aparicio, Manuel. Entre la paz y la guerra: Marruecos. Madrid, 1912.

Afr 1713.7   Cisotti-Ferrara, M. Nel marocco. Milano, 1912.

Afr 1490.16   Clement-Grandcourt, A. Croquis marocains, sur la Moulouya. Paris, 1912.

Afr 5235.212   Clozel, F.J. Haut-Sénégal-Niger (Soudan français). Paris, 1912. 5v.

Afr 4050.9   Cobbold, E. Wayfarers in the Libyan desert. London, 1912.

Afr 1570.34   Cochin, D. Affaires marocaines...1902-1911. Paris, 1912.

Afr 2870.7   Coen, G. L'Italia a Tripoli. Livorno, 1912.

Afr 8657.1   Colvin, Ian D. The cape of adventure. London, 1912.

Afr 699.12.5   Congrés de l'Afrique Orientale, Paris, 1911. Congrés de l'Afrique Orientale. Paris, 1912.

Afr 1069.12.5A   Coolidge, A.C. The European reconquest of North Africa. n.p., 1912.

Afr 2870.5   Corradini, E. La conquista di Tripoli. Milano, 1912.

Afr 2870.8   Cottafari, V. Nella Libia italiana. Bologna, 1912.

Afr 1570.32   Couillieaux. Le programme de la France au Maroc. Paris, 1912.

Afr 6455.21   Cranworth, B.F.G. A colony in the making. London, 1912.

Afr 3275.26   Cressaty. L'Egypte d'aujourd'hui. Paris, 1912.

Afr 5408.5   Cureau, Adolphe L. Les sociétés primitives de l'Afrique. Paris, 1912.

Afr 4742.5   Dainelli, Giotto. Risultati scientifici di un viaggio nella colonia Eritrea. Firenze, 1912.

Afr 2929.12.15   Darkling, L. La Libia romana e l'impresa italiana. Roma, 1912.

Afr 550.139   Darlon, T.H. God's image in ebony. London, 1912.

Afr 850.5   Deherain, Henri. Dans l'Atlantique. Paris, 1912.

Afr 1609.12.18   Detanger, Emile. Gens de guerre au Maroc. Paris, 1912.

Afr 2209.12   Devereux, R. Aspects of Algeria interior. London, 1912.

Afr 9854.20   Douglas, Arthur. Arthur Douglas, missionary on Lake Nyasa. Westminster, 1912.

Afr 8865.7   Ellenberger, D.F. History of the Basuto, ancient, and modern. London, 1912.

Afr 4559.09.5   Escherich, G. Im Lande des Negus. Berlin, 1912.

Afr 3040.35.3   Fayed, Osman. Tribunaux mixtes d'Egypte. Paris, 1912.

Afr 1490.15   Feline, M.H. L'artillerie au Maroc, campagnes en Chaouia. Paris, 1912.

Afr 1555.3.5   Ferrail, Gabriel. La chronique de l'an 1911. Paris, 1912.

Afr 2929.12.17   Franzoni, A. Colonizzazione e proprietà fondiaria in Libia. Roma, 1912.

Afr 6280.8   Frobenius, L. Und Afrika sprach. Berlin, 1912.

Afr 1609.12.13   Gentil, L. Le Maroc physique. 2e ed. Paris, 1912.

Afr 2929.12.7   Ghisleri, A. Tripolitania e Cirenaica. Milano, 1912.

Afr 609.12   Goodrich, Joseph K. Africa of to-day. Chicago, 1912.

Afr 2945.10   Goretti, L. In Cirenaica ed in Arabia. Roma, 1912.

Afr 9689.11.5   Gouldsbury, C. An African year. London, 1912.

Afr 2875.12   Gray, E.M. La bella guerra. Firenze, 1912.

Afr 658.61   Guenther, Konrad. Gerhard Rohlfs Lebensbild eines Afrikaforschers. Freiburg, 1912.

Afr 3994.912   Haekal, M.H. La dette publique égyptienne. Paris, 1912.

Afr 1609.12.3   Haillot. Le Maroc. Vincennes, 1912.

Afr 8160.15   Hamilton-Browne, G. A lost legionary in South Africa. London, 1912.

Afr 8135.6   Hart-Synnot, F. Letters. London, 1912.

Afr 2940.15.2   al-Hashayishi, Muhammad ibn Uthman. Voyage au pays des Senoussia a travers à Tripolitaine et les pays touareg. 2.ed. Paris, 1912.

Afr 5235.212.5   Haywood, A.H.W. Through Timbuctu and across the great Sahara. London, 1912.

Afr 3979.12   Humphreys, R. Algiers, the Sahara and the Nile. London, 1912.

Afr 7815.11   Hutereau, Armand. Histoire des peuplades de l'Uele et de l'Ubangi. Bruxelles, 1912.

Afr 2875.23   In rei memoriam du pacifisme contre la guerre déclarée par l'Italie à la Turquie. Berne, 1912.

Afr 2875.7   Irace, C.F. With the Italians in Tripoli. London, 1912.

Afr 2850.2   Italy. Parlamento. La Libia. Milano, 1912. 2v.

Afr 4180.4.5   Jackson, H.C. Tooth of fire. Oxford, 1912.

Afr 1635.4   Jary, Georges. Les derniers berberes. Paris, 1912.

1912 - cont.

Afr 6095.21   Johnston, Harry. Pioneers in West Africa. London, 1912.

Afr 7459.12   Jore, L. La république de Liberia. Paris, 1912.

Afr 5003.1   Joucla, E. Bibliographie de l'Afrique occidentale française. Paris, 1912.

Afr 1609.12   Kerr, Robert. Morocco after twenty-five years. London, 1912.

Afr 6540.3   Kitching, A.L. On the backwaters of the Nile. London, 1912.

Afr 8659.12.5F   Kock, J.H.M. De Kaap als een nieuw land. 2. druk. Kaapstad, 1912.

Afr 4320.3   Krause, K. Die Portugiesen in Abessinien. Dresden, 1912.

Afr 2875.53   Labriola, Arturo. La guerra di Tripoli e l'opinione socialista. Napoli, 1912.

Afr 2870.6   Lapworth, Charles. Tripoli and young Italy. London, 1912.

Afr 6535.16   Lardner, E.S.D. Soldiering and sport in Uganda. London, 1912.

Afr 1422.7   Latreille, A. La campagne de 1844 au Maroc. La bataille d'Isly. Paris, 1912.

Afr 1570.28   Lecussan, J. de. Notre droit historique au Maroc. Paris, 1912.

Afr 6926.3   Leutwein, T. Die Kämpfe mit Hendrik Witboi 1894 und Witbois Ende. Leipzig, 1912.

Afr 2819.12.3   Longo, G. La Sicilia e Tripoli. Catania, 1912.

Afr 9839.12   Lyell, D.D. Nyasaland for the hunter and settler. London, 1912.

Afr 6275.22   McKeown, R.L. Twenty-five years in Qua Iboe. London, 1912.

Afr 5445.10   Macleod, Olive. Chiefs and cities of Central Africa. Edinburgh, 1912.

Afr 3817.5   MacMichael, Harold Alfred. The tribes of northern and central Kordofan. Cambridge, 1912.

Afr 5549.12.5   Malzac, V. Histoire du royaume Hova depuis ses origines jusqu'à sa fin. Tananarive, 1912.

Afr 2819.12   Manfroni, C. Tripoli nella storia marinara d'Italia. Padova, 1912.

Afr 2870.9   Mantegazza, V. Tripoli e i diritti della civiltà. Milano, 1912.

Afr 3979.12.7   Marden, P.S. Egyptian days. London, 1912.

Afr 1069.12   Mariam, V. Il fato di Tripoli e il fato latino. Roma, 1912.

Afr 2875.58   Marinette, F.T. La battaglia di Tripoli (26 ottobre 1911). Milano, 1912.

Afr 2929.12.5   Martino, G. de. Tripoli, Cirene e Cartagine. 2 ed. Bologna, 1912.

Afr 1570.42   Maura y Gamazo, Gabriel. El convenio entre España by francia relativo a Marruecos. Madrid, 1912.

Afr 1609.12.9   Mauran. La societe marocaine. Paris, 1912.

Afr 2862.5   Mehemed Emin Efendi (Pseud.). Der Kampf um Tripolis. Leipzig, 1912.

Afr 2929.01.3   Mehier de Mathuisieulx, H. A travers la Tripolitaine. 3e ed. Paris, 1912.

Afr 2929.12.9   Mehier De Mathuisieulx, H. La Tripolitaine. Paris, 1912.

Afr 699.12   Melland, F.H. Through the heart of Africa. London, 1912.

Afr 5426.110   Milligan, Robert H. The fetish folk of West Africa. N.Y., 1912.

Afr 2929.02.2   Minutilli, F. La Tripolitania. 2 ed. Torino, 1912.

Afr 4710.5   Mondaini, G. Il organisation de colonie de l'Erythrée. Bruxelles, 1912.

Afr 1550.16   Morel, E.D. Morocco in diplomacy. London, 1912.

Afr 2870.10   Mosca, G. Italia e Libia. Milano, 1912.

Afr 9599.12   Moubray, John M. In south central Africa. London, 1912.

Afr 1609.12.4   Munoz, I. La agonia del Mogreb. Madrid, 1912.

Afr 7549.13   Nasoin, Fritz. Histoire de l'état indépendant du Congo. Namur, 1912-13. 2v.

Afr 2929.12.11   Nazari, V. Tripolitania. 2 ed. Roma, 1912.

Afr 1609.12.7   Nieto, P.E. En Marruecos. Barcelona, 1912.

Afr 2875.15   Ostler, A. The Arabs in Tripoli. London, 1912.

Afr 2875.9   Pasetti, P. Note ed episodi della guerra in Tripolitania. Roma, 1912.

Afr 5219.12   Pasquier, G. L'organisation des troupes indigènes. Paris, 1912.

Afr 5219.12.3   Pasquier, G. L'organisation des troupes indigènes en Afrique occidentale française. Paris, 1912.

Afr 8350.5   Payne, E.G. An experiment in alien labor. Chicago, 1912.

Afr 2984.1   Pervinquière, L. La Tripolitaine interdite: Ghadames. Paris, 1912.

Afr 6777.7.5   Peters, Karl. Wie Deutsch-Ostafrika entstand. Leipzig, 1912.

Afr 2875.13   Piazza, G. Come conquistammo Tripoli. Roma, 1912.

Afr 4390.20   Piozza, G. Alla corte di Menelik. Ancona, 1912.

Afr 1955.30   Piquet, V. Campagnes d'Afrique, 1830-1910. Paris, 1912.

Afr 2260.13   Piquet, V. La colonisation française dans l'Afrique du nord. Paris, 1912.

Afr 2929.12.13   Podrecca, G. Libia. Roma, 1912.

Afr 8180.31   Preller, G.S. Piet retief. Pretoria, 1912.

Afr 6719.5   Pultkamer, Jesko. Gouverneursjahre in Kamerun. Berlin, 1912.

Afr 7180.5   Questionario ethnographico acerca dos populações indigenas de Angola e Congo. Luanda, 1912.

Afr 5960.10   Ramos Izquierdo Y Vivar, L. Descripción geografica y gobierno. Madrid, 1912.

Afr 6118.6   Reeve, H.F. The Gambia, its history. London, 1912.

Afr 1609.12.15   Richet, E. Voyage au Maroc. Nouvelle ed. Paris, 1912.

Afr 5045.27   Rondet-Saint, Maurice. Dans notre empire noir. Paris, 1912.

Afr 1738.1   Rouard de Card, E. La defaite des Anglais à Tanger, 1664. n.p., 1912.

Afr 1550.15   Rouard de Card, E. Négociation franco-espagnole de 1902. Paris, 1912.

Afr 1609.12.5   Rousselet, L. Sur les confins du Maroc. Paris, 1912.

Afr 1738.11   Routh, E.M.G. Tangier. London, 1912.

Afr 1658.7   Ruiz Albeniz, R. El riff, el riff en paz, la guerra del riff. Madrid, 1912.

Afr 5753.4   Rusillon, H. Un culte dynast. Avec évocation des morts. Paris, 1912.

Afr 2624.912   Sala, R. Le budget tunisien. Paris, 1912.

Afr 2945.7   Sanctis, E. de. Dalla Canea a Tripoli. Roma, 1912.

Afr 6919.12   Sauder, L. Geschichte der deutsch Kolonial-Gesellschaft für Südwest-Afrika. Berlin, 1912. 2v.

Afr 7815.5.9   Schmitz, Robert. Les Baholoholo. 9. Bruxelles, 1912.

Afr 9165.94   Scully, W.C. The ridge of the white waters. London, 1912.

Afr 1846.7   Sibe, A. La conscription des indigenes d'Algerie. Paris, 1912.

Afr 7530.4   Simar, T. Bibliographie congolaise 1895-1910. Uccle, 1912. 2v.

1912 - cont.

Afr 4760.5   Somaliland, Italian. Manuale per la Somalia italiana, 1912. Roma, 1912.
Afr 4785.14   Sorrentino, G. Ricordi del Benadir. Napoli, 1912.
Afr 5540.4   Spas, L. Etude sur l'organisation de Madagascar. Paris, 1912.
Afr 2875.47   Spellanzon, C. L'Africa nemica la guerra. Venezia, 1912.
Afr 4070.28   Stevens, E.S. My Sudan year. London, 1912.
Afr 1033.4   Strupp, K. Urkunden zur Geschichte des völkerrechts. Erg. 1. Gotha, 1912.
Afr 2283.2   Stuhlmann, F. Ein kulturgeschichtlicher Ausflug in den Aures. Hamburg, 1912.
Afr 6879.12   Sutherland, J. The adventures of an elephant hunter. London, 1912.
Afr 6280.11   Talbot, P.A. In the shadow of the bush. London, 1912.
Afr 1571.5A   Tardieu, A. Le mystère d'Agadir. Paris, 1912.
Afr 5243.12   Tauxier, Louis. Le Noir du Soudan. Paris, 1912.
Afr 8028.1.3   Theal, G.M. Catalogues of books and pamphlets. Cape Town, 1912.
Afr 2875.19   Theilhaber, F.A. Beim roten Halbmond vor Tripolis. Cöln, 1912.
Afr 2209.11.5   Thomas-Stanford, C. About Algeria, Algiers. London, 1912.
Afr 2990.1.2   Todd, M.L. Tripoli the mysterious. Boston, 1912.
Afr 2990.1   Todd, M.L. Tripoli the mysterious. London, 1912.
Afr 8846.10   Transkeian Territories. Native Appeal Court. Reports of cases decided in the native appeal courts of the Transkeian territories, 1914. Cape Town, 1912.
Afr 6280.6   Tremearne, A.J.N. The tailed head-hunters of Nigeria. London, 1912.
Afr 5425.10   Trilles, H. Le totémisme chez les Fan. Münster, 1912.
Afr 3979.12.2   Tyndale, W. An artist in Egypt. London, 1912.
Afr 2929.11.11   Vatter, E. Die Grundzüge einer Landeskunde von Tripolitanien. Marburg, 1912.
Afr 2929.11.12   Vatter, E. Tripolitanien: Grundzüge zu einer Landeskunde. Strassburg, 1912.
Afr 2850.3   Vecchi, P. Italy's civilizing mission in africa. N.Y., 1912.
Afr 5549.12   Villars, E.J. Madagascar, 1638-1894, établissement des Français dans l'ile. Paris, 1912.
Afr 630.5   Vogt, E.F. Les poisons de flèches et les poisons d'épreuve des indigènes de l'Afrique. Lons-le-Saunier, 1912.
Afr 1742.1   Voinot, L. Oudjds et l'Amalat (Maroc). Oran, 1912.
Afr 8340.3   Walton, E.H. The inner history of the national convention of South Africa. Cape Town, 1912.
Afr 6390.11.3   Ward, H.F. Handbook of British East Africa. London, 1912.
Afr 3817.6   Westermann, Diedrich. The Shilluk people. Philadelphia, 1912.
Afr 6455.31   White, Stewart E. Land of foot prints. Garden City, 1912.
Afr 8659.12   Worsfold, W.B. Union of South Africa. London, 1912.

1913

Afr 718.25.5   Adolf, Friedrich. From the Congo to the Niger and the Nile. V.1-2. London, 1913. 2v.
Afr 5056.113   Afrique occidentale française. Paris, 1913.
Afr 2000.3   Ajam, Maurice. Problèmes algériens. Paris, 1913.
Afr 2875.39   Album-portfolio della guerra italo-turca, 1911-12, per la conquista della Libia. Milano, 1913.
Afr 2875.5   Bechler, W.H. The history of the Italian war. Annapolis, 1913.
Afr 2527.7   Benoyts, F. de. Au pays de Kroumers et au Maroc. Lille, 1913.
Afr 659.13   Bernard, A. L'Afrique du nord. Paris, 1913.
Afr 1609.13   Bernard, A. Le Maroc. Paris, 1913.
Afr 1280.25F   Bertholon, Lucien. Recherches anthropologiques dans la Berbérie orientale. Lyon, 1913. 2v.
Htn   Afr 3979.13*   Blackburne, D. Journals of my African travels. Maidstone, 1913.
Afr 1609.13.8   Botte, L. Au coeur du Maroc. Paris, 1913.
Afr 7815.7   Boyd, F.R. Les races indigènes du Congo belge. Paris, 1913.
Afr 1550.18   Bretschger, J. Die Marokko-Konferenz. Zürich, 1913.
Afr 1259.13A   Bullard, A. The Barbary coast. N.Y., 1913.
Afr 9502.25   Bullock, Charles. Mashona laws and customs. Salisbury, 1913.
Afr 1368.60.6   Canovas del Castello, A. de. Apuntes para la historia de Marruecos. Madrid, 1913.
Afr 1570.26   Chastaud, P. Les conditions d'établissement du protectorat français au Maroc. Paris, 1913.
Afr 2875.25   Cicerone, G. La terza frontiera italiana. Roma, 1913.
Afr 4559.13   Citerni, Carlo. Ai confini meridionali dell'Etiopia. Milano, 1913.
Afr 8325.60   Cleaver, M.M. A young South African. Johannesburg, 1913.
Afr 7815.5.10   Colle, R.P. Les Baluta. 10-11. Bruxelles, 1913. 2v.
Afr 3979.13.15   Cooper, Clayton Sedwick. The man of Egypt. London, 1913.
Afr 6592.1   Craster, J.E.E. Pemba, the spice island of Zanzibar. London, 1913.
Afr 6397.10   Crawford, E.M. By the equator's snowy peak. London, 1913.
Afr 1609.13.7   Cros, L. Le Maroc pour tous. Paris, 1913.
Afr 3979.13.8   Crossland, Cyril. Desert and water gardens of the Red Sea. Cambridge, 1913.
Afr 109.13   Darmstaedter, P. Geschichte der Aufteilung und Kolonisation Afrikas. Berlin, 1913-20. 2v.
Afr 1609.13.10   Desroches, G. Le Maroc, son passe, son present, son avenir. Paris, 1913.
Afr 6979.03.2   Done, K. Deutsch-Südwest-Afrika. 2e Aufl. Berlin, 1913.
Afr 1609.13.3   Douoso-Cortes, R. Estudio geográfica politico-militar sobre las zonas Españolas. Madrid, 1913.
Afr 699.13   Elena, Duchess of Aosta. Viaggi in Africa. Milano, 1913.
Afr 3740.6.2   Emily, J. Mission Marchand journal. 2d ed. Paris, 1913.
Afr 4708.5   Eritrea economica. Novara, 1913.
Afr 4050.10   Falls, J.C.E. Three years in the Libyan desert. London, 1913.
Afr 628.213A   Ferris, William H. The African abroad. New Haven, 1913. 2v.
Afr 9558.51A   Fraser, A.Z. Livingstone and Newstead. London, 1913.
Afr 718.30   Frobenius, L. The voice of Africa. V.1-2. London, 1913. 2v.
Afr 1750.6   Garcia Perez, A. Zona española del norte de Marruecos. Toledo, 1913.
Afr 8095.45F   Godee Molsbergen, E.C. Zuid-Afrikas geschiedenis in beeld. Amsterdam, 1913.
Afr 3979.13.5   Gomez Carrillo, E. La sonrisa de la esfinge. Madrid, 1913.
Afr 679.13.5   Grimm, Hans. Afrikafahrt West. Frankfurt, 1913.
Afr 1485.7   Guillaume. Sur la frontière marocaine. Paris, 1913.
Afr 4559.13.5   Halle, C. To Menelek in a motor car. London, 1913.

1913 - cont.

Afr 590.25   Harris, John H. Portuguese slavery, Britain's dilemma. London, 1913.
Afr 6455.125   Hepburn, Alonzo Barton. The story of an outing. N.Y., 1913.
Afr 9389.13   Hodson, A.W. Trekking the great thirst. 2. ed. London, 1913.
Afr 8252.16   Hofmeyr, Jan. The life of Jan Hendrik Hofmeyr. Cape Town, 1913.
Afr 8969.13   Holt, H.P. Mounted police of Natal. London, 1913.
Afr 9558.65   Horne, C.S. David Livingstone. N.Y., 1913.
Afr 1490.11.9   Hubert-Jacques. Journées sanglantes de Fez. 4 ed. Paris, 1913.
Afr 2696.2F   Hugon, Henri. Les emblèmes des beys de Tunis. Paris, 1913.
Afr 4732.10F   Italy. Ministero delle Colonie. Relazione sulla colonia Eritrea del R. Commissario civile deputato. Ferdinando Martini per gli esercizi 1902-07. v.1-4. Roma, 1913. 2v.
Afr 8289.13   Jackson, M.C. A soldier's diary, South Africa 1899-1901. London, 1913.
Afr 108.99.6   Johnston, H.H. A history of the colonization of Africa. Cambridge, 1913.
Afr 3255.6   Kamel, S. La conférence de Constantinople et la question égyptienne 1882. Paris, 1913.
Afr 1490.13   Khorat, P. En colonne au Maroc. Paris, 1913.
Afr 575.18   Korei, Aly. Condition juridique des sujets musulmans. Thèse. Paris, 1913.
Afr 5180.19.4   Lacourbe, M.J. de. Premier voyage...fait à la côte d'Afrique...1865. Paris, 1913.
Afr 1609.13.12   Ladreit de Lacharriere, R. Voyage au Maroc, 1910-11. Paris, 1913.
Afr 3979.11.10   Lamoriniere de la Rochecautin. Promenades au pays des pharaons. Paris, 1913.
Afr 2209.13   Lara, Juan F. de. De Madrid a Uxda. Madrid, 1913.
Afr 8250.9A   Lesueur, G. Cecil Rhodes, the man and his work. London, 1913.
Afr 1755.13   Lopez Alarcon, E. Melilla 1909, diario de la guerra. Madrid, 1913.
Afr 724.10.2   Ludwig, Emil. Die Reise nach Afrika. Berlin, 1913.
Afr 6640.3   Luecke, J.H. Bevölkerung und Aufenthaltsrecht in den Department schutzgebieten Afrikas. Hamburg, 1913.
Afr 6640.4   Luecke, J.H. Bevölkerung und Aufenthaltsrecht in den Department schutzgebieten Afrikas. Inaug. Diss. Hamburg, 1913.
Afr 7320.5   Lyne, Robert N. Mozambique. London, 1913.
Afr 2875.64   McClare, William K. Italy in north Africa. London, 1913.
Afr 2875.21   McCullagh, F. Italy's war for a desert (Experiences of war correspondent with Italians in Tripoli). Chicago, 1913.
Afr 575.16   Malrezzi, A. L'Italia e l'islam in Libia. Firenze, 1913.
Afr 1089.5   Marcais, Georges. Les Arabes en Berbérie du XIe au XIVe siècle. Constantine, 1913.
Afr 1955.31   Marchaud, E.C. L'Europe et la conquête d'Alger. Paris, 1913.
Afr 8659.13.15   Markham, Violet R. The South African scene. London, 1913.
Afr 1259.13.5   Martin, A.G.P. Précis de sociologie nord-africaine. Paris, 1913.
Afr 8659.13.12   Maturin, E. Adventures beyond the Zambesi. London, 1913.
Afr 3275.25   Méra. Une page de politique coloniale. Paris, 1913.
Afr 8089.13   Merimee, P. La politique anglaise au Transvaal. Toulouse, 1913.
Afr 7808.89.9   Michaux, Oscar. Au Congo. Namur, 1913.
Afr 1570.29   Millet, R. La conquête du Maroc. Paris, 1913.
Afr 2609.13   Monchicourt, C. La région du Haut Tell en Tunisie. Paris, 1913.
Afr 4969.13   Mosse, A.H.E. My Somali book. London, 1913.
Afr Doc 9282.12F   Mozambique. Secretaria Geral. Recenseamentos população...de Lourenço Marques. n.p., 1913.
Afr 1739.3   Munoz, I. La corte de Tetuan. Madrid, 1913.
Afr 1609.13.6   Munoz, I. En el pais de los cherifes. Madrid, 1913.
Afr 1608.68.5   Murga, José Maria de. Recuerdos marroquies del moro vizcaino. Barcelona, 1913.
Afr 2218.10   Neveu, Edouard. Les Khouan. 3. ed. Alger, 1913.
Afr 4060.37   Nicholls, W. The shaikiya. Dublin, 1913.
Afr 9502.24   Nielsen, Peter. The Matabele at home. Bulawayo, 1913.
Afr 3979.12.3   Parkhurst, L. A vacation on the Nile. Boston, 1913.
Afr 765.3   Perthes, Joachim. Der Victoria-Njansa. Göttingen, 1913.
Afr 4785.16   Piazza, G. Il Benadir...con 16 fotografie originali. Roma, 1913.
Afr 4742.28   Pollera, Alberto. I Baria e i Cunama. Roma, 1913.
Afr 609.13   Powell, E.A. The last frontier. London, 1913.
Afr 8659.13.9   Pratt, A. The real South Africa. Indianapolis, 1913.
Afr 2870.7.35   Provenzal, G. La missione politica dell'Italia nell'Africa mediterranea. Roma, 1913.
Afr 5406.213   Ranget, Fernand. L'Afrique équatoriale illustrée. Paris, 1913.
Afr 4688.15   Rava, M. Al Lago Tsana. Roma, 1913.
Afr 2875.18   Remond, G. Aux camps turco-arabes. Paris, 1913.
Afr 1340.5   Revilliod, M. L'organisation intérieur des pays de protectorat. Paris, 1913.
Afr 2929.13.5   Ricchieri, Giuseppe. La Libia. Milano, 1913.
Afr 4593.1.3   Roden, L. Le tribu dei Mensa. Stockholm, 1913.
Afr 7187.10   Roma Machado de Faria e Maria, Carlos. A cidade do Huambo. Lisboa, 1913.
Afr 510.11.2   Rouard de Card, E. Traités de délimitation concernant l'Afrique franç.aise. Supplément 1910-13. Paris, 1913.
Afr 575.16.10   Sabetta, Guido. Politica di penetrazione in Africa. Roma, 1913.
Afr 1570.31   Sainte-Chapelle, A.M.G. La conquête du Maroc (mai 1911-mars 1913). Paris, 1913.
Afr 3675.5   Sarkissian, G. Le Soudan égyptien. Paris, 1913.
Afr 6292.9.15   Schultze, Arnold. The sultanate of Bornu. London, 1913.
Afr 8659.13.3   Scully, Wm. C. Further reminiscences of a South African pioneer. London, 1913.
Afr 8659.13   Scully, Wm. C. Reminiscences of a South African pioneer. London, 1913.
Afr 575.17   Servier, A. Le péril de l'avenir. Le nationalisme musulman. Constantine, 1913.
Afr 5190.22   Siré-Abbâs-Soh. Chroniques du Foûta senegalais. Traduit. Paris, 1913.
Afr 4745.5   Società di Studi Geografici e Coloniali. L'Eritrea economica. Novara, 1913.
Afr 4742.3   Societa Italiana per il Progresso delle Scienze, Rome. La colonia Eritrea. Fasc.1 Roma, 1913.
Afr Doc 4307.311   South Africa. Office of Census and Statistics. Census of the Union of South Africa, 1911. Pretoria, 1913. 2v.

1913 - cont.

Afr 7369.13	Starr, F. Liberia, description, history, problems. Chicago, 1913.
Afr 6455.23	Stigand, C.H. The land of Zinj. London, 1913.
Afr 8289.03.7	Stirling, J. Our regiments in South Africa, 1899-1902. Edinburgh, 1913.
Afr 8985.4	Stuart, J. A history of the Zulu rebellion 1906. London, 1913.
Afr 2875.50	Tancredi, L. Dopo Tripoli. Lugano, 1913.
Afr 635.5F	Tessmann, Günter. Die Pangwe. Berlin, 1913-
Afr 6280.9	Thomas, N.W. Anthropological report on the Ibo speaking peoples. V.1-6. London, 1913-14.
Afr 3675.65	Timbukti, Mahmud. Tariks el-Jettoch, ou Chronique du chercheur pour servir a l'histoire des villes, des armées et des principaux personnages du Tekrour. Paris, 1913.
Afr 3979.13.12	Todd, J.A. The banks of the Nile. London, 1913.
Afr 7809.13	Torday, Emil. Camp and tramp in African wilds. Philadelphia, 1913.
Afr 550.8.5	Tournier, M.J. Bibliographie du Cardinal Lavigerie. Paris, 1913.
Afr 6095.16	Tremearne, A.J. Some Austral-African notes and anecdotes. London, 1913.
Afr 1609.13.5	Van Wincxtenhoven. Le Maroc, rapport général. Bruxelles, 1913.
Afr 1658.35	Vazquez Sastre, C. En tierras del rif. Melilla, 1913.
Afr 2929.13	Vivassa de Regny, P. Libya italica. Milano, 1913.
Afr 6535.12	Wallis, H.R. The handbook of Uganda. London, 1913.
Afr 7815.8	Weeks, J.H. Among Congo cannibals. London, 1913.
Afr 8659.13.5	Williams, R. How I became a governor. London, 1913.
Afr 6390.15	Wilson, H.A. A British borderland, service and sport in Equatoria. London, 1913.
Afr 6390.22	Wilson, H.A. A British borderland. London, 1913.
Afr 5408.105	Witte, Jehan. Les deux Congo, trente-cinq ans d'apostolat. Paris, 1913.
Afr 1846.9	Wolf, Christian. Der fremdenlegionaer in Krieg und Frieden. Berlin, 1913.
Afr 8089.13.3A	Worsfold, W.B. The reconstruction of the new colonies under Lord Milner. London, 1913. 2v.
Afr 2875.20	Wright, H.C.S. Two years under the crescent. London, 1913.
Afr 1609.13.4	Zabel, R. Zu unruhiger Zeit in Marokko. Cöln am Rhein, 1913.
Afr 2875.24	Zoppi, Ottavio. La spedizione Ameglio su Rodi nel maggio 1912. Novara, 1913.

1914

Afr 718.25.4	Adolf, Friedrich. From the Congo to the Niger and the Nile. Philadelphia, 1914. 2v.
Afr 1573.20	Alvarez, Melquiades. El problema de Marruecos. Madrid, 1914.
Afr 555.9.3	Arnot, Frederick Stanley. Missionary travels in Central Africa. Bath, 1914.
Afr 2870.10.65	Barzilai, Salvatore. La impresa libica e la situazione parlamentare esaurita. Roma, 1914. 3 pam.
Afr 4937.2	Battersby, H.F.P. Richard Corfield of Somaliland. London, 1914.
Afr 550.8.12	Baunard, Louis. Léon XIII et le toast d'Alger. Paris, 1914.
Afr 6640.20	Becker, A. Hermann von Wissmann. Berlin, 1914.
Afr 2000.5	Benhabiles, Cherif. L''Algérie française vue par un indigène. Alger, 1914.
Afr 6455.33	Bennet, Edward. Shots and snapshots in British East Africa. London, 1914.
Afr 1570.33	Besnard, R. L'oeuvre française au Maroc. Paris, 1914.
Afr 8028.6	Besselaar, G. Zuid-Afrika in de letterkunde. Amsterdam, 1914.
Afr 4700.14.25	Botarelli, A. Compendio di storia coloniale italiana. Roma, 1914.
Afr 7809.14	Bratier, Albert Ernest Augustin. Souvenirs de la mission marchande. Paris, 1914
Afr 2929.14	Braun, Ethel. The new Tripoli. London, 1914.
Afr 5401.5	Bruel, Georges. Bibliographie de l'Afrique équatoriale française. Paris, 1914.
Afr 1658.6	Calvo, G. Espana en Marruecos (1910-1913). Barcelona, 1914.
Afr 1490.12	Ceccaldi, C. Au pays de la poudre. Paris, 1914.
Afr 1624.14	Colomb, Jean. Le regime financier du Maroc. Paris, 1914.
Afr 2870.10.50	Come siamo andati in Libia. Firenze, 1914.
Afr 3988.10	Cooper, Elizabeth. The women of Egypt. London, 1914.
Afr 1493.5	Cornet. A la conquête du Maroc sud, 1912-13. Paris, 1914.
Afr 555.21	Crawford, D. Thinking black. 2d ed. London, 1914.
Afr 6397.11	Crawford, E.M. By the equator's snowy peak. 2d ed. London, 1914.
Afr 5920.9	Dalmonte, Enrique. Ensayo de una breve descripción del Sahara. Madrid, 1914.
Afr 1609.14.5	Dantin Cereceda, J. Una expedicion cientifica por la zona de influencia española en Marruecos. Barcelona, 1914.
Afr 1609.14.3	Doutte, E. Missions au Maroc, en tribu. Paris, 1914.
Afr 4790.10	Dracopoli, I.N. Through Jubaland to the Lorian Swamp. London, 1914.
Afr 7465.6	Ellis, G.W. Negro culture in West Africa. N.Y., 1914.
Afr 5190.10	Faure, Claude. Histoire de la presqu'île du Cap Vert et des origines de Dakar. Paris, 1914.
Afr 2875.56	Fovel, Natale M. Tripoli e i problemi della democrazia. Firenze, 1914.
Afr 618.5	Gaul, Wilhelm. Das Geschenk nach Form und Inhalt. Braunschweig, 1914.
Afr 2209.14	Gennep, A. van. En Algérie. Paris, 1914.
Afr 2209.14.10	Gennep, A. van. En Algérie. Paris, 1914.
Afr 500.11A	Harris, N.D. Intervention and colonization in Africa. Boston, 1914.
Afr 8125.5	Heeres, Jan E. Heeft Nederland de Kaap verkocht. Amsterdam, 1914.
Afr 2312.5	Heinke, Kurt. Monographie der algerischen Oase Biskra. Inaug. Diss. Halle, 1914.
Afr 635.7F	Heydrich, Martin. Afrikanische Ornamentik. Inaug. Diss. Leiden, 1914.
Afr 9389.13.5	Hodson, A.W. Trekking the great thirst. London, 1914.
Afr 2508.3	Hofstetter, Balthasar. Vorgeschichte des französischen Protektorats in Tunis. Bern, 1914.
Afr 1609.14	Holt, G.E. Morocco the piquant. London, 1914.
Afr 8659.14.5	Hyatt, Stanley P. The old transport road. London, 1914.
Afr 8680.53	Indian Opinion, Phoenix, Natal. Souvenir of the passive resistance movement in South Africa, 1906-1914. Phoenix, 1914.

1914 - cont.

Afr 6535.14	Jack, E.M. On the Congo frontier. London, 1914.
Afr 8659.14	Johnston, H.H. Pioneers in South Africa. London, 1914.
Afr 4582.5	Jousseaume, F. Impressions de voyage en Apharras. Paris, 1914. 2v.
Afr 4559.14	Kolmodin, J. Traditions de Tsazzega et Hazzega. Annales. Uppsala, 1914.
Afr 2209.14.3	Lavion, H. L'Algérie musulmane. Paris, 1914.
Afr 1570.36	Lebre, G. De l'établissement du protectorat de la France au Maroc. Paris, 1914.
Afr 8250.9.5	Lesueur, G. Cecil Rhodes, the man and his work. N.Y., 1914.
Afr 5758.14	Loisy, F.X. Madagascar, étude économique. Paris, 1914.
Afr 3979.14	Low, S. Egypt in transition. London, 1914.
Afr 3979.14.2	Low, S. Egypt in transition. N.Y., 1914.
Afr 353.90	MacLean, Norman. Africa in transformation. London, 1914
Afr 5765.32	McMahon, Edward Oliver. Christian missions in Madagascar. Westminster, 1914.
Afr 5749.14	Marcuse, W.D. Through western Madagascar in quest of the golden bean. London, 1914.
Afr 1840.7	Marneur, F. L'indigenat en Algerie. Thèse. Paris, 1914.
Afr 2875.37	Melli, B. La guerra italo-turca. Roma, 1914.
Afr 8289.14	Miller, David S. A captain of the Gordon's Service experience. London, 1914.
Afr 8289.14.2	Miller, David S. A captain of the Gordon's Service experience. London, 1914.
Afr 555.23.5	Nassau, Robert H. My Ogowe being a narrative of daily incidents during sixteen years in West Africa. N.Y., 1914.
Afr 6926.23	O'Connor, J.K. The Hun in our Hinterland. Cape Town, 1914?
Afr 150.7.4	Oliveira Martins, J.P. The golden age of Henry the Navigator. London, 1914.
Afr 4719.14	Palarnenghi-Crispi, Tommaso. Francesco Crispi, la prima guerra d'Africa. Milano, 1914.
Afr 2260.13.3	Piquet, V. La colonisation française dans l'Afrique du nord. Paris, 1914.
Afr 609.13.2	Powell, E.A. The last frontier. N.Y., 1914.
Afr 1573.36	Problema de Marruecos. Madrid, 1914.
Afr 6985.3F	Range, Paul. Beiträge...zur Landskunde des deutschen Namalandes. Hamburg, 1914.
Afr 6883.4	Reche, O. Zur Ethnographie der abflusslosen Gebietes Deutsch-Ostafrikas. Hamburg, 1914.
Afr 1259.14.3	Rondet-Saint, M. En France africaine. Paris, 1914.
Afr 1570.40	Rouard de Card, E. Traités et accords concernant le protectorat de la France au Maroc. Paris, 1914.
Afr 2945.22	Salvadori, Alessandro. La Cirenaica ed i suoi servizi civile. Roma, 1914.
Afr 8825.8	Schonken, F.T. De oorsprong der kaapsch-hollandsche volksoveringen. Amsterdam, 1914.
Afr 1490.18	Serra Orts, A. Recuerdos de la guerra del Kert de 1911-12. Barcelona, 1914.
Afr 2938.25	Simonetti, R. Le opere pubbliche della Tripolitania e della Cirenaica. Roma, 1914.
Afr 2949.5	Società Italiana per lo Studio della Libia. Missione Franchetti in Tripolitania (Il Gebel). Firenze, 1914.
Afr 9525.435	Some account of George Gray and his work in Africa. London, 1914.
Afr 8678.235	South Africa. Commissioner on Native Grievances Inquiry. Report, 1913-1914. Cape Town, 1914.
Afr 8678.21	Stevens, E.J.C. White and black. London, 1914.
Afr 6010.5	Stigand, C.H. Administration in tropical Africa. London, 1914.
Afr 2209.14.5	Stott, M.D. The real Algeria. London, 1914.
Afr 2628.1	Stuhlmann, F. Die Mazigh-Völker. Hamburg, 1914.
Afr 590.22.5	Swann, A.J. Fighting the slave-hunters in Central Africa. London, 1914.
Afr 8110.6.5A	Tas, A. Diary. London, 1914.
Afr 6738.6.5	Thorbecke, F. Im Hochland von Mittel-Kamerun. Hamburg, 1914-16. 4v.
Afr 5405.190	Violette, M. La N'Goko-Sangha. Paris, 1914.
Afr 7809.14.5	Wauters, Alphones Jules. Voyages en Afrique. Bruxelles, 1914.
Afr 7815.8.5	Weeks, J.H. Among the primitive Bakongo. London, 1914.
Afr 6455.26	White, Stewart E. African camp fires. London, 1914.
Afr 1259.14	Woodberry, G.E. North Africa and the desert. N.Y., 1914.
Afr 3275.31A	Worsfold, William B. The future of Egypt. London, 1914.

1915

Afr 1575.2F	Azevedo, Pedro de. Documentos das chancelarias reais anteriores a 1531. v.1-2. Lisboa, 1915. 2v.
Afr 3979.15	Balls, W.L. Egypt of the Egyptians. London, 1915.
Afr 718.40	Barnes, James. Through central Africa from coast to coast. N.Y., 1915.
Afr 6143.20	Beatty, K.J. Human leopards...with note on Sierra Leone. London, 1915.
Afr 1369.15	Becker, Jeronimo. Historia de Marruecos. Madrid, 1915.
Afr 2929.12.20	Beltramelli, A. Paesi di conquista. Ferrara, 1915.
Afr 6926.5	Calvert, A.F. South-west Africa during German occupation. London, 1915.
Afr 575.20	Carles, Fernand. La France et l'islam en Afrique occidentale. Thèse. Toulouse, 1915.
Afr 4559.15	Castro, Lincoln de. Nella terra dei negies. Milano, 1915. 2v.
Afr 1026.5.15	Ceccherini, Ugo. Bibliografia della Libia. Roma, 1915.
Afr 6164.5	Claridge, W.W. History of the Gold Coast and Ashanti. London, 1915. 2v.
Afr 3285.4	Cromer, E.B. Abbas II. London, 1915.
Afr 5408.5.5	Cureau, Adolphe L. Savage man in Central Africa. London, 1915.
Afr 555.7.12	Davidson, H. Frances. South and South Central Africa. Elgin, 1915.
Afr 2438.7	Demay, Jules. L'organisation des communes en Tunisie. Tunis, 1915.
Afr 628.215A	Dubois, W.E.B. The Negro. N.Y., 1915.
Afr 1753.2FA	Eannes de Zurara, G. Cronica da tomada de Ceuta. Coimbra, 1915.
Afr 6919.15	Eveleigh, William. South-west Africa. London, 1915.
Afr 628.215.10	Francke, E. Die geistige Entwicklung der Neger-Kinder. Inaug. Diss. Leipzig, 1915.
Afr 1570.38	Gonzalez Hontoria, M. El protectorado frances en Marruecos. Madrid, 1915.
Afr 2749.15	Gordan, H.C. Woman in the Sahara. London, 1915.
Afr 5345.17	Gorju, Joseph. La Côte-d'Ivoire chrétienne. 2. éd. Lyon, 1915.
Afr 6738.10	Haase, Lene. Durchs unbekannte Kamerun. Berlin, 1915.

1915 - cont.

Afr 5227.10.5   Joffre, J.J.C. My march to Timbuctoo. London, 1915.
Afr 5227.10   Joffre, J.J.C. My march to Timbuctoo. N.Y., 1915.
Afr 555.29   Keable, Robert. A city of the dawn. Uganda. London, 1915.
Afr 718.32   Kearton, Cherry. Through central Africa from east to west. London, 1915.
Afr 3230.9   Kusel, S.S. de. An Englishman's recollections of Egypt. London, 1915.
Afr 1609.08.5.4   Leon Y Ramos, E. Marruecos. Novisima ed. Madrid, 1915.
Afr 530.6   Lewin, Evans. The Germans and Africa. London, 1915.
Afr 1432.14   Martin Arrue, F. Guerra hispano-marroqui, 1859-60. Madrid, 1915.
Afr 1753.4F   Mateus de Pisano. Livro de guerra de Ceuta. Lisboa, 1915.
Afr 1609.15.3   Mission Scientifique du Maroc. Villes et tribus du Maroc. v.1-11. Paris, 1915-32. 11v.
Afr 5243.250   Monteil, Charles. Les Khassonke. Paris, 1915.
NEDL   Afr 1550.16.5   Morel, E.D. Ten years of secret diplomacy. 3d ed. London, 1915.
Afr 6455.30   Oswald, Felix. Alone in the sleeping-sickness country. London, 1915.
Afr 55.10   Peters, Karl. Afrikanische Köpfe, Charakterskizzen. Berlin, 1915.
Afr 1573.18   Pita, Federico. La accion militar y politica de España en Africa a traves de los tiempos. Madrid, 1915.
Afr 6883.7   Ried, H.A. Zur Anthropologie des abflusslosen Rumpfschollenlandes im nordöstlichen Deutsch-Ostafrika. Hamburg, 1915.
Afr 3275.16.2   Rifat, M.M. Lest we forget. n.p., 1915.
Afr 5920.7   Rio Joan, F. del. Africa occidental española. Madrid, 1915.
Afr 5920.7.3   Rio Joan, F. del. Atlas icono-geografico-estadistico del Africa occidental española. Madrid, 1915.
Afr 6926.11   Ritchie, Moore. With Botha in the field. London, 1915.
Afr 1703.3F   Rodrigues, Bernardo. Anais de arzila, cronica inedita do seculo XVI. Lisboa, 1915-20. 2v.
Afr 6540.4.5   Roscoe, John. The northern Bantu. Cambridge, 1915.
Afr 1609.15   Roulleaux Dugage, G. Lettres du Maroc, illustrations de E. Stoeckel. Paris, 1915.
Afr 3979.15.5   Salmon, P.R. The wonderland of Egypt. N.Y., 1915.
Afr 8360.5   Sampson, P.J. The capture of De Wet. The South African rebellion, 1914. London, 1915.
Afr 8089.15   Scully, W.C. History of South Africa, from earliest days to union. London, 1915.
Afr 8809.15   Scully, W.C. Lodges in the wilderness. London, 1915.
Afr 8360.6F   South Africa. Report on the outbreak of the rebellion. Pretoria, 1915.
Afr 3199.15.5   Steindorff, Georg. Ägypten in Vergangenheit und Gegenwart. Berlin, 1915.
Afr 6280.10   Talbot, D.A. Woman's mysteries of a primitive people, the Ibibios of Southern Nigeria. London, 1915.
Afr 8088.88.9   Theal, G.M. History of South Africa from 1795-1872. London, 1915. 2v.
Afr 7809.15   Thornhill, J.B. Adventures in Africa under the British, Belgian and Portuguese flags. N.Y., 1915.
Afr 6275.25   Tremlett, Horace. With the tin gods. London, 1915.
Afr 8677.15   Union of South Africa. Financial regulations. Pretoria, 1915.
Afr 4285.5   Varenbergh, Joseph. Studien zur äthiopischen Reichsordnung. Strassbourg, 1915.
Afr 3199.15   Weigall, Arthur E.P. Brome. History of events in Egypt from 1798 to 1914. Edinburgh, 1915.
Afr 6879.15.5   Werth, Emil. Das Deutsch-Ostafrikanische Küstenland. Berlin, 1915. 2v.
Afr 6879.15   White, Stewart E. Rediscovered country. Garden City, 1915.
Afr 3038.7   Winterei, Hermann. Ägypten, seine staats- und völkerrechtliche Stellung. Berlin, 1915.
Afr 500.21   Yanguas Messia, José. Apuntes sobre la expansion colonial en Africa. Madrid, 1915.
Afr 6720.15   Zimmermann, Emil. Meine Kriegsfahrt von Kamerun zur Heimat. Berlin, 1915.

1916

Afr 1753.1.10   Academia das Sciencias de Lisboa. Centenarios de Ceuta e de Afonso de Albuquerque. Lisboa, 1916.
Afr 8659.16   Alston, Madeline. From the heart of the veld. London, 1916.
Afr 5340.20   Angoulvant, G.L. La pacification de la Côte-d'Ivoire. Paris, 1916.
Afr 8095.50   Areyer, A.Ndries. Zuid-afrikaanse monumenten album. Kaapstad, 1916.
Afr 1609.13.2   Bernard, A. Le Maroc. 4ed. Paris, 1916.
Afr 6615.10   Calvert, Albert Frederick. The German African empire. London, 1916.
Afr 6926.7   Close, P.L. Prisoner of the Germans in South-west Africa. London, 1916.
Afr 3275.17.4.10   Cromer, E.B. Modern Egypt. N.Y., 1916.
Afr 4360.3   Cronaca reale Abissinia dall'anno 1800 all'anno 1840. Rome, 1916.
Afr 1965.4.5   Demontes, Victor. La colonisation militaire sous Bugeaud. Thèse. Paris, 1916.
Afr 6883.6   Dempwolff, Otto. Die Sandawe...Material aus deutsch Ostafrika. Hamburg, 1916.
Afr 2223.916   Desroches, G. Pour s'enrichir en Algérie. Paris, 1916.
Afr 1713.8   Dieulefils, P. Maroc occidental. Paris, 1916.
Afr 3725.8   Emin Pascha. Tagebücher. Bd.1-4, 6. Hamburg, 1916-1927. 5v.
Afr 5749.16   Galy-Ache, P. Horizons malgaches, de Fort-Dauphin à Andovorante. Paris, 1916.
Afr 500.13A   Gibbons, H.A. The new map of Africa, 1900-16. N.Y., 1916.
Afr 6879.16   Great Britain. Admiralty. A handbook of German East Africa. n.p., 1916.
Afr 6926.12F   Great Britain. Parliament. Papers relating to certain trials in German Southwest Africa. London, 1916.
Afr 6926.13F   Great Britain. Parliament. Papers relating to German atrocities. London, 1916. 2v.
Afr 8686.10   Hance, Gertrude Rachel. The Zulu yesterday and today; twenty-nine years in South Africa. N.Y., 1916.
VAfr 5385.38   Hentsch, Henry. Deux années au Dahomey, 1903-1905. Nancy, 1916.
Afr 725.18   Langenmaier, Theo. Alte Kenntnis und Kartographie der zentralafrikanischen Seenregion. Inaug. Diss. Erlangen, 1916.
Afr 1573.16   Larios de Medrano, Justo. España en Marruecos, historia secreta de la campaña. Madrid, 1916.

1916 - cont.

Afr 575.38   Layer, E. Confréries religieuses musulmanes et marabouts. Rouen, 1916.
Afr 5342.50   Lebarbier, Louis. La Côte-d'Ivoire. Paris, 1916.
Afr 7175.12   Lina Vidal, João Avangelista. Por terras d'Angola. Coimbra, 1916.
Afr 6395.4.5   Lindblom, Gerhard. The Akamba in British East Africa. Pt.1-3. Inaug. Diss. Uppsala, 1916.
Afr 1583.15   Maurice, Louis. La politique marocaine de l'allemagne. Paris, 1916.
Afr 3821.2   Meinhof, Carl. Eine Studienfahrt nach Kordofan. Hamburg, 1916.
Afr 6883.2.5   Meyer, Hans. Die Barundi. Leipzig, 1916.
Afr 3979.12.5   Mielert, Fritz. Im Lande des Khedive. Regensburg, 1916.
Afr 6143.21   Newland, H. Sierra Leone, its people, products, and secret societies. London, 1916.
Afr 1347.4   Nido y Torres, M. del. Historial de la Mehal-la Xeriffiana. Melilla-Tetuan, 1916.
Afr 7127.5   Paxeco, Fran. Angola e os Alemãis. Marahão, 1916.
Afr 1490.17   Pierrat, J. Vingt-six mois au Maroc. Paris, 1916.
Afr 8340.15   Plaatje, S.T. Native life in South Africa. London, 1916.
Afr 2438.8   Richon, Jean. Le contentieux administratif en Tunisie. Paris, 1916.
Afr 6926.9   Robinson, J.P.K. With Botha's army. London, 1916.
Afr 724.15   Rosen, Eric von Greve. Traeskfolket. Stockholm, 1916.
Afr 2525.2   Rouard de Card, E. La Turquie et le protectorat français. Paris, 1916.
Afr 8340.14.2A   Spender, H. General Botha, the career and the man. Boston, 1916.
Afr 8340.14   Spender, H. General Botha, the career and the man. London, 1916.
Afr 724.9   Taylor, Henry James. Capetown to Kafue. London, 1916.
Afr 8089.14.5   Tilby, A.W. South Africa, 1486-1913. Boston, 1916.
Afr 1609.16   Vera Salas, Antonio. Porvenir de Espana en Marruecos. Toledo, 1916.
Afr 1576.3F   Vieira da S. y Guimaraes. Marrocos e três mestres da ordem de cristo, memória publicada por ordem da academia das sciências de Lisboa. Lisboa, 1916.
Afr 3979.16   Walther, J. Zum Kampf in der Wüste am Sinai und Nil. Leipzig, 1916.
Afr 1658.11   Zuhueta Y Gomis, J. Impresiones del Rif. Barcelona, 1916.

1917

Afr 1609.17   Ajalbert, Jean. Le Maroc sans les boches. Paris, 1917.
Afr 5448.13   Augouard, Prosper Philippe. Notes historiques sur la fondation de Brazzaville. Paris, 1917.
Afr 575.19   Bel, Alfred. Coup d'oeil sur l'islam en Berberie. Paris, 1917.
Afr 1571.4.8   Bernard, A. La France au Maroc. Paris, 1917.
Afr 1493.6   Bernard, Francois. Le Maroc économique et agricole. Paris, 1917.
Afr 5960.2   Bravo Carbonell, J. Fernando Poo y el Muni. Madrid, 1917.
Afr 6738.11   Calvert, A.F. The Cameroons. London, 1917.
Afr 28.6   Carroll, R.F. Selected bibliography of Africana for 1915. Cambridge, 1917.
Afr 4360.5   Conti Rossini, C. La cronaca reale Abissinia dall'anno 1800 all'anno 1840. Roma, 1917.
Afr 11051.4   Crouch, E.H. Gold dust. London, 1917.
Afr 626.5   Dove, Karl. Wirtschaftsgeographie von Afrika. Jena, 1917.
Afr 1493.7.5   Dugard, Henry. Le Maroc de 1917. Paris, 1917.
Afr 718.36   Duplessis, J. Thrice through the dark continent. London, 1917.
Afr 3295.6   Gallini, Fahmy. Choses d'Egypte. Le Caire, 1917.
Afr 5342.7   Gaston, Joseph. La Côte-d'Ivoire. Paris, 1917.
Afr 725.15.5   Geil, William Edgar. Adventures in the African jungle hunting Pigmies. Garden City, 1917.
Afr 2230.21   Geniaux, Charles. Sous les figuiers de Kabylie. Paris, 1917.
Afr 1724.2   Goulven, J. La place de mazagan. Paris, 1917.
Afr 2929.17   Great Britain. Admiralty. A handbook of Libya. Sept. 1917. Naval Staff. n.p., 1917.
Afr 3285.5   Harrison, T.S. The homely diary of a diplomat in the East. Boston, 1917.
Afr 3199.17   Hasenclever, A. Geschichte Ägyptens im 19 Jahrhundert, 1798-1914. Halle a.S., 1917.
Afr 7315.20.10   Junod, H.A. A vida d'uma tribu sul-africana. Famalição, 1917.
Afr 679.17   Kirsch, M. Der Fremdenlegionär. N.Y., 1917.
Afr 1609.17.3   Koechlin, Raymond. Le Maroc en paix. Paris, 1917.
Afr 550.12   Kumm, H.K.W. African missionary heroes and heroines. N.Y., 1917.
Afr 1493.8   Lareveliere, Comte de. Les énergies françaises au Maroc. Paris, 1917.
Afr 1623.25   Lareveliere, J. Les energies françaises auMaroc. Paris, 1917.
Afr 4259.17   Leroux, Hughes. Chez la reine de Saba. Paris, 1917.
Afr 8252.341.15   Levi, N. Jan Smuts. London, 1917.
Afr 555.20.5   Livingstone, W.P. Mary Slessor of Calabar. 9th ed. London, 1917.
Afr 6390.76   Lorimer, Norma Octavia. By the waters of Africa. London, 1917.
Afr 5187.5   Marty, Paul. Etudes sur l'islam au Sénégal. v.2-3, pt.1-2. Paris, 1917. 2v.
Afr 6390.77   Meikle, R.S. After big game. London, 1917.
Afr 500.19   Morel, Edmund D. Africa and the peace of Europe. Photoreproduction. London, 1917.
Afr 3275.30   Mosely, Sydney R. With Kitchener in Cairo. London, 1917.
Afr 1270.3   Ortega, M.L. Guia del norte de Africa y sur de España. Cadiz, 1917.
Afr 1573.21   Ortega, Manuel L. España en Marruecos. El Raisuni. Madrid, 1917.
Afr 550.90   Patton, Cornelius H. The lure of Africa. N.Y., 1917.
Afr 7567.10   Payen, Edouard. Belgique et Congo (Une carte itinéraire). Paris, 1917.
Afr 530.20.15   Pedrazzi, O. L'Africa dopo la guerra e l'Italia. Firenze, 1917.
Afr 4500.1   Pierre-Alype, L. L'Ethiopie et les convoitises allemandes. Paris, 1917.
Afr 1069.09.3   Piquet, V. Les civilisations de l'Afrique du Nord. 2d ed. Paris, 1917.
Afr 1609.17.5   Piquet, Victor. Le Maroc, geographie, histoire, mise en valeur. Paris, 1917.
X Cg   Afr 3204.22   Question of Egypt in Anglo-French relations. Edinburgh, 1917.

1917 - cont.

Afr 4230.4.10 Relationes et epistolae variorum. Index analyticus totius operis. Romae, 1917.
Afr 1583.16 Richet, Etienne. La politique allemand. Paris, 1917.
Afr 1026.6.2 Rouard de Card, E. Livres français des XVIIe et XVIIIe siècle. Etats Barbaresques. Supplément. Paris, 1917.
Afr 1550.28.5 Ruediger, Georg von. Die Bedeutung der Algeciras-Konferenz. Inaug.-Diss. Altenburg, 1917.
Afr 7190.40 San Thome, Africa. Direcção dos Portos e Viação. Missão geodesica. Porto, 1917.
Afr 555.60 Sierra Leone. Native Church. Jubilee Committee. The jubilee volume of the Sierra Leone Native Church. London, 1917.
Afr 8360.7.89 Standaert, E.H.G. A Belgian mission to the Boers. London, 1917.
Afr 8360.8 Standaert, E.H.G. A Belgian mission to the Boers. N.Y., 1917.
Afr 1493.10 Stichel, Bernhard. Die Zukunft in Marokko. Berlin, 1917.
Afr 6780.7 Stienon, Charles. La campagne anglo-belge. Paris, 1917.
Afr 5285.277.5 Tauxier, Louis. Le noir du Yatenga-Mossi. Paris, 1917.
Afr 8088.94.15 Theal, G.M. South Africa. 8th ed. London, 1917.
Afr 6620.52 Through swamp and forest. London, 1917.
Afr 8180.34 Trigerdt, L. Dagboek. Bloemfontein, 1917.
Afr 6988.16.385 Walker, H.F.B. A doctor's diary in Damaraland. London, 1917.
Afr 6926.11.5 Whittall, W. With Botha and Smuts in Africa. London, 1917.
Afr 3275.29 Willmore, J.S. The Welfare of Egypt. London, 1917.
Afr 6780.5 Young, F.B. Marching on Tanga. London, 1917.
Afr 530.10 Zimmermann, E. Bedeutung Afrikas für die deutsche Weltpolitik. Berlin, 1917.

1918

Afr 6615.5 Africanus. The Prussian lash in Africa. London, 1918.
Afr 1490.20 Berenguer. La guerra en Marruecos. Madrid, 1918.
Afr 500.16 Beyens, N.E.L. La question africaine. Bruxelles, 1918.
Afr 8028.200.10 Botha, C.G. A brief guide to the various classes of documents in the Cape archives for 1652-1806. Cape Town, 1918.
Afr 210.10 Brawley, B.G. Africa and the war. N.Y., 1918.
Afr 3979.18.5 Briggs, Martin. Through Egypt in war time. London, 1918.
Afr 5406.218 Bruel, Georges. L'Afrique équatoriale française. Paris, 1918.
Afr 6685.5 Calvert, Albert F. Togoland. London, 1918.
Afr 1838.5 Cambon, Jules. Le gouvernement general de l'Algerie. Paris, 1918.
Afr 530.9 Caroselli, F.S. L'Africa nella guerra e nella pace d'Europa. Milano, 1918.
Afr 1330.5.9 Castries, H. de. Archives et bibliothèques d'Angleterre, 1661-1757. (France, t.1-3). Paris, 1918-1925. 3v.
Afr 6095.30 Clifford, Elizabeth de la P. Our days on the Gold Coast, in Ashanti, in the northern territories, and...in Togoland. Accra, 1918.
Afr 3275.32 Coles, Charles E. Recollections and reflections. London, 1918.
Afr 6780.6 Crowe, J.H. General Smuts campaign in East Africa. London, 1918.
Afr 6780.20 Daye, P. Avec les Vainqueures de Tahora. 2. ed. Paris, 1918.
Afr 1990.25 Demontes, Victor. Les préventions du général Berthezène. Paris, 1918.
Afr 6780.8 Dolbey, R.V. Sketches of the East Africa campaign. London, 1918.
Afr 1665.7 Dugard, Henry. La colonne du sous, janvrier-juin, 1917. Paris, 1918.
Afr 1493.7 Dugard, Henry. Le Maroc de 1918. Paris, 1918.
Afr 2875.30 Enver. UmTripolis. München, 1918.
Afr 8135.7 Eybers, G.W. Select constitutional documents...South African history 1795-1910. London, 1918.
Afr 8089.18A Fairbridge, D. A history of South Africa. London, 1918.
Afr 8283.18 Fort, G. Seymour. Dr. Jameson. London, 1918.
Afr 510.15 Gaffarel, P.L.J. Notre expansion colonial...1870 à nos jours. Paris, 1918.
Afr 500.13.5 Gibbons, H.A. The new map of Africa, 1900-16. N.Y., 1918.
Afr 6926.14F Great Britain. Parliament. Report on the natives of South-west Africa. London, 1918.
Afr 8283.15A Hammond, J.H. The truth about the Jameson raid. Boston, 1918.
Afr 4390.15 Keller, Konrad. Alfred Ilg. Frauenfeld, 1918.
Afr 1706.2 Lapeyre. Casablanca. Paris, 1918.
Afr 5243.125.10 Lebarbier, Louis. Les Bambaras. Paris, 1918.
Afr 3979.18A Leeder, S.H. Modern sons of the pharaohs. London, 1918.
Afr 1493.9 Lichtenberger, A. Un coin de la guerre, la France au Maroc. Paris, 1918.
Afr 1573.19 Liga Africanista Española. Tratados, convenios y acuerdos referentes a Marruecos. Madrid, 1918.
Afr 8687.202 Livingstone, William. Christina Forsyth of Fingoland. London, 1918.
Afr 1753.3F Mascarenhas, J. Historia de la ciudad de Ceuta. Lisboa, 1918.
Afr 3026.10 Maunier, René. Bibliographie économique. Le Caire, 1918.
Afr 2026.1 Melia, Jean. L'Algérie et la guerre (1914-18). Paris, 1918.
Afr 1675.2 Perigny, Maurice. Au Maroc, marrakech et les ports du sud. Paris, 1918.
Afr 1200.60 Perreau Pradier, P. L'Afrique du Nord et la guerre. Paris, 1918.
Afr 7315.5 Pires de Lima, A. Contribução para o estudo antropologico indigenas de Moçambique. Porto, 1918.
Afr 8250.12 Radziwill, E. Cecil Rhodes, man and empire-maker. London, 1918.
Afr 1200.58 Reclus, Onesime. L'Atlantide, pays de l'Atlas. Paris, 1918.
Afr 4559.18 Rein, G.K. Abessinien, eine Landeskunde. Berlin, 1918-20. 3v.
Afr 2875.22 Roncagli, Giovanni. Guerra italo-turca, 1911-12. Milano, 1918. 2v.
Afr 500.14 Ronze, Raymond. La question d'Afrique. Paris, 1918.
Afr 510.9.10 Rouard de Card, E. Le prince de Bismarck et l'expansion de la France en Afrique. Paris, 1918.
Afr 609.18 Roussel, Raymond. Pages choisies d'impressions d'Afrique et de Locus Solus. Paris, 1918.
Afr 4095.8.4 Rubakin, N.A. Prikliucheniia v strane rabstva. Moscow, 1918.
Afr 2880.5 Scaglione, Emilio. Tripoli e la guerra. Napoli, 1918.

1918 - cont.

Afr 6780.9 Schnee, A. Meine Erlebnisse Während der Kriegszeit in Deutsch-Ostafrika. Leipzig, 1918.
Afr 9435.10 Scott, L. The struggle for native rights in Rhodesia. London, 1918.
Afr Doc 4309.500 South Africa. Office of Census and Statistics. Agricultural census. Cape Town, 1918.
Afr 6280.17 Temple, Charles L. Native races and their rulers. London, 1918.
Afr 1733.5 Tharaud, Jerome. Rabat. Paris, 1918.
Afr 1680.6 Thomas, L. Voyage au goundafa et au sous. Paris, 1918.
Afr 9087.5 Valter, M.P.C. Duitschland en de Hollandsche Republieken in Zuid-Afrika. Amsterdam, 1918.
Afr 1658.15 Vera Salas, A. El Rif oriental. Melilla, 1918.
Afr 6780.32 Weston, F. The black slaves of Prussia. Boston, 1918.
Afr 530.8A Zimmermann, E. The German empire of Central Africa. N.Y., 1918.
Afr 530.8.5 Zimmermann, E. The German Empire of Central Africa as the basis of a new German world-policy. London, 1918.

1919

Afr 1623.919 Ancey, Cesar. Nos interets économiques du Maroc. Paris, 1919.
Afr 2749.13 Angieras, E.M. Le Sahara occidental. Paris, 1919.
Afr 6780.11 Arning, W. Vier jahre Weltkrieg in Deutsche-Ostafrika. Hannover, 1919.
Afr 1570.44 Barthou, Louis. La bataille du Maroc. 3e ed. Paris, 1919.
Afr 8115.10 Botha, Colin G. The French refugees at the Cape. Cape Town, 1919.
Afr 6780.15 Buchanan, A. Three years of war in East Africa. London, 1919.
Afr 1555.3.10 Caillaux, J. Agadir. Paris, 1919.
Afr 3205.8 Cattaui, Joseph E. Histoire des rapports de l'Egypte avec la Sublime Porte. Thèse. Paris, 1919.
Afr 1680.7 Chatinieres, P. Dans le grand atlas marocain. Paris, 1919.
Afr 1609.13.15 Chevrillon, A. Marrakech dans les palmes. Paris, 1919.
Afr 6192.20 Clifford, Elizabeth. Our days on the Gold Coast. London, 1919.
Afr 635.7.6 Clouzot, Henri. L'art nègre et l'art océanien. Paris, 1919.
Afr 4575.5 Conti Rossini, C. Popoli dell'Ethiopia occidentale. Roma, 1919.
Afr 6620.51 Dane, Edmond. British campaigns in Africa and...Pacific. London, 1919.
Afr 2530.10 Dauphin, M. La conférence consultative tunisienne. Thèse. Paris, 1919.
Afr 6780.12 Deppe, L. Mit Lettow-Vorbeck durch Afrika. Berlin, 1919.
Afr 8110.8 Dominicus, F.C. Het huiselik en maatschappelik leven van de zuid-afrikaner. 's-Gravenhage, 1919.
Afr 6780.13 Downes, Walter D. With the Nigerians in German East Africa. London, 1919.
Afr 1493.7.10 Dugard, Henry. Le Maroc de 1919. Paris, 1919.
Afr 632.17 Foucart, George. Questionnaire préliminaire d'ethnologie africaine. Le Caire, 1919.
Afr 7350.3.21 Fox, Early L. The American Colonization Society, 1817-40. Diss. Baltimore, 1919.
Afr 7350.3.20 Fox, Early L. The American Colonization Society. Baltimore, 1919.
Afr 1738.15 Garcia, S.F. Color. Madrid, 1919.
Afr 1571.14 Georges-Gaulis, B. La France au Maroc. Paris, 1919.
Afr 6926.20 Germany. Reichs-Kolonialamt. The treatment of native and other populations in the colonial possessions of Germany and England. Berlin, 1919.
Afr 8678.26 Gibson, J.Y. The evolution of South African native policy. Pietermaritzburg, 1919.
Afr 1609.19.5 Goulven, J. Le Maroc. Paris, 1919.
Afr 630.9 Harris, John H. Africa, slave or free. London, 1919.
Afr 7549.19A Keith, Arthur B. The Belgian Congo and the Berlin Act. Oxford, 1919.
Afr 7815.15 Kerken, Georges van der. Les sociétés bantoues du Congo belge. Bruxelles, 1919.
Afr 2283.3 Keun, Odette. Les oasis dans le montagne. Paris, 1919.
Afr 1608.82.10 Lamartiniere, Henri P. De. Souvenirs du Maroc. Paris, 1919.
Afr 6780.10.20 Lettow-Vorbeck, P.E. von. Um Vaterland und Kolonies. Berlin, 1919.
Afr 8215.1.8 Leyds, W.J. The Transvaal surrounded. London, 1919.
Afr 6738.12 Marabail, H.J.J. Etude sur les territoires du Cameroun occupés par les troupes françaises. Paris, 1919.
Afr 635.7.10 Markov, Vlats. Iskusstvo negrov. Sankt Peterburg, 1919.
Afr 2025.25 Melia, Jean. La France et l'Algérie. Paris, 1919.
Afr 6143.23 Michell, Harold. An introduction to the geography of Sierra Leone. London, 1919.
Afr 8252.15 Millais, J.G. Life of Frederick Courtenay Selous. N.Y., 1919.
Afr 1620.10 Monmarche, Marcel. Le Maroc. Paris, 1919.
Afr 9599.14 Morrison, J.H. Streams in the desert. London, 1919.
Afr 8040.10 Nathan, Manfred. The South African commonwealth. Johannesburg, 1919.
Afr 1550.27 Neumann, K. Die Internationalität Marokkos. Berlin, 1919.
Afr 1625.10 Nouvel, Suzanne. Nomades et sedentaires au Maroc. Paris, 1919.
Afr 6620.50 O'Neill, H.C. The war in Africa, 1914-1917. London, 1919.
Afr 1640.3 Ortega, Manuel L. Los hebreos en Marruecos. Madrid, 1919.
Afr 3035.5 Paris. Peace Conference, 1919. Egyptian Delegation. Collection of official correspondence. Paris, 1919.
Afr 11052.2 Petrie, A. Poems of South African history. London, 1919.
Afr 1840.12 Piquet, Victor. Les reformes en Algerie et le statut des indigenes. Paris, 1919.
Afr 609.13.7 Powell, E.A. The last frontier. N.Y., 1919.
Afr 1840.19 Riols de Fonclare, F. de. Les diverses politiques coloniales. Thèse. Toulouse, 1919.
Afr 3300.10 Sabry, Mohammed. La révolution égyptienne. Paris, 1919. 2v.
Afr 6460.58F Sandford, G.R. An administrative and political history. London, 1919.
Afr 6780.14 Schnee, Heinrich. Deutsch-ostafrika Während des Weltkrieges. Berlin, 1919.
Afr 6310.38 Schrader, R. Die Zwangsarbeit in Ostafrika nach deutschen und britischen Kolonialrecht. Hamburg, 1919.
Afr 7570.20 Segairt, Henri. Un terme au Congo belge. Bruxelles, 1919.
Afr 4050.11 Sforza, Ascanio M. Esplorazioni e prigionia in Libia. Milano, 1919.
Afr 7560.3.10 Simar, T. Le Congo au XVIe siècle d'aprés la relation de Lopez-Pigafetta. Bruxelles, 1919.

248

1919 - cont.

Afr Doc 4307.318   South Africa. Office of Census and Statistics. Census of the European or White races of the Union of South Africa, 1918. Cape Town, 1919-1920.

Afr 8100.5.3   Theal, G.M. Ethnography and condition of South Africa. London, 1919.

Afr 8088.88.10   Theal, G.M. History of South Africa from 1873-1884. London, 1919. 2v.

Afr 6926.15   Weck, Ruediger. In Deutsche-Südwestafrika, 1913-15. Berlin, 1919.

Afr 500.20.2   Woolf, Leonard S. Empire and commerce in Africa. N.Y., 1919.

Afr 500.20   Woolf, Leonard S. Empire and commerce in Africa. Westminster, 1919.

192-

Afr 2373.10.2   Bel, Alfred. Tlemcen et ses environs. 2e ed. Toulouse, 192-

Afr 1723.10   Dupac, J. Le sud marocain. Marrakech. Safi et Mogador. Paris, 192- .

Afr 1340.6   France. Ministère des Affaires Etrangères. Rapport général sur...le protectorat du Maroc. Rabat, 192- .

1920

Afr 1550.30   Alengry, Jean. Les relations franco-espagnoles et l'affaire du Maroc. Paris, 1920.

Afr 1570.43   Alengry, Jean. Les relations franco-espagnoles et l'affaire du Maroc. Thèse. Paris, 1920.

Afr 1750.9   Alfaro y Zarabozo, S. de. Geografia de Marruecos y posesiones españolas de Africa. Toledo, 1920.

Afr 1947.9.5   Amiet, J.J. Geschichte des Lorenz Arregger von Solothurn. Bern, 1920.

Afr 609.20   Anderson, William A. South of Suez. N.Y., 1920.

Afr 3204.10   Auriant, L. L'Egypte. Paris, 1920.

Afr 4618.5   Bieber, Friedrich J. Kaffa. Münster, 1920-23. 2v.

Afr 2209.20F   Bovet, Marie A. L'Algérie. Paris, 1920.

Afr 1733.5.10   Brunot, Louis. La mer dans les traditions et les industries indigenes a Rabat et Sale. Paris, 1920.

Afr 6192.22   Cardinall, Alan W. The natives of northern territories of Gold Coast. London, 1920.

Afr 3285.10   Chirol, Valentine. The Egyptian problem. London, 1920.

Afr 6780.22   Clifford, H. The Gold Coast regiment in the East African campaign. London, 1920.

Afr 1390.5   Cour, Auguste. La dynastie marocaine des Beni Wattas (1420-1554). Constantine, 1920.

Afr 6590.10   Dale, Godfrey. The peoples of Zanzibar. Westminster, 1920.

Afr 1200.62   Deslinieres, L. La France nord-africaine. Paris, 1920.

Afr Doc 1407.317   Egypt. Department of Statistics and Census. The census of Egypt taken in 1917. Cairo, 1920-21. 2v.

Afr 5053.10   Forgeron, J.B. Le protectorat en Afrique occidentale française et les chefs indigènes. Thèse. Bordeaux, 1920.

Afr 2025.27   Gautier, Emile F. L'Algérie et la métropole. Paris, 1920.

Afr 2438.10   Genet, Jean. Etude comparative du protectorat tunisien et du protectorat marocain. Thèse. Paris, 1920.

Afr 2485.5   Grandchamp, P. La France en Tunisie. Tunis, 1920-33. 10v.

Afr 2494.10   Grandchamp, P. La France en Tunisie à la fin du XVIe siècle. Tunis, 1920.

Afr 6981.120   Great Britain. Report on the conditions and prospects of trade in the protectorate of South West Africa. London, 1920.

Afr 6390.11.15   Great Britain. Admiralty. A handbook of Kenya colony (British East Africa). n.p., 1920.

Afr 9839.20   Great Britain. Admiralty. A handbook of Portuguese Nyasaland. Oxford, 1920.

Afr 6535.16.20   Great Britain. Admiralty. A handbook of the Uganda Protectorate. Oxford, 1920.

Afr 7809.20   Great Britain. Admiralty. A manual of Belgian Congo. London, 1920.

Afr 7309.20   Great Britain. Admiralty. A manual of Portuguese East Africa. London, 1920.

Afr 6314.27   Great Britain. Foreign Office. History Section. Kenya, Uganda and Zanzibar. London, 1920.

Afr 9445.10   Harris, John H. The chartered millions. London, 1920.

Afr 6926.16   Hennig, Richard. Deutsch-Südwest im Weltkriege. Berlin, 1920.

Afr 6879.20   Joelson, F.S. The Tanganyika territory. London, 1920.

Afr 8252.17.10   Kestell, J.D. Christiaan de wet'n lewensbeskrywing. Beperkt, 1920.

Afr 6780.10A   Lettow-Vorbeck, P.E. von. Meine Erinnerungen aus Ostafrika. Leipzig, 1920.

Afr 6780.10.5   Lettow-Vorbeck, P.E. von. My reminiscences of East Africa. London, 1920.

Afr 7540.15   Liebrechts, C. Congo, suite à mes souvenirs d'Afrique. Bruxelles, 1920.

Afr 5049.5   Louveau, E. Essai sur l'influence sociale et économique des religions de l'Afrique occidentale française. Thèse. Paris, 1920.

Afr 7175.13   Marguardsen, H. Angola. Berlin, 1920.

Afr 1573.22   Martin Peinador, L. El suelo de Marruecos y sus primeros habitantes. Madrid, 1920.

Afr 5219.20   Marty, Paul. Etudes sur l'islam et les tribus du Soudan. Paris, 1920-21. 4v.

Afr 5403.30   Massion, Jacques. Les grandes concessions au Congo français. Paris, 1920.

Afr 7459.20A   Maugham, R.C.F. The Republic of Liberia. London, 1920.

Afr 580.5   Mendelssohn, S. The Jews of Africa. London, 1920.

Afr 1335.20   Milliot, Louis. Recueil de jurisprudence chérifienne. v.1-4. Paris, 1920-24. 4v.

Afr 8678.13.5   Molema, S.M. The Bantu, past and present. Edinburgh, 1920.

Afr 5765.22   Mondain, G. Un siècle de mission protestante à Madagascar. Paris, 1920.

Afr 500.19.5   Morel, Edmund D. The black man's burden. N.Y., 1920.

Afr 109.20   Moulin, Alfred. L'Afrique à travers les ages. Paris, 1920.

Afr 6283.13   Nigeria, Northern. Gazetteer. London, 1920. 2v.

Afr 6210.38   Nigeria. Governor-General, 1920. Address delivered at the 7th meeting of Nigeria council held at Lagos. Lagos, 1920.

Afr 6565.5.2   Pearce, Francis B. Zanzibar. London, 1920.

Afr 6979.20   Pimienta, R. L'ancienne colonie allemande en Sud-ouest Afrique. Paris, 1920.

Afr 1609.17.7   Piquet, Victor. Le Maroc, geographie, histoire, mise en valeur. 3 éd. Paris, 1920.

1920 - cont.

Afr 8030.16   Preller, Gustav Schoeman. Voortrek Kermense. Kaapstad, 1920- 5v.

Afr 679.20   Psichari, Ernest. Les voix qui crient dans le désert. Paris, 1920.

Afr 1550.28   Ruediger, Georg von. Die Bedeutung der Algeciras-Konferenz. München, 1920.

Afr 3199.20   Sabry, Mohammed. La question d'Egypte depuis Bonaparte jusqu'à la révolution de 1919. Paris, 1920.

Afr 109.20.10   Salkin, Paul. Etudes africaines. Bruxelles, 1920.

Afr 9558.100   Sharp, J.A. David Livingstone. London, 1920.

X Cg   Afr 9700.5   Smith, E. Pla-speaking people of Northern Rhodesia. London, 1920. 2v.

Afr Doc 4307.318.5   South Africa. Office of Census and Statistics. Census of the European or white races of the Union of South Africa 1918. Final report and supplementary tables. Cape Town, 1920.

Afr 4559.20   Tedesco Zammarano, V. Alle sorgenti del Nilo azzurro. Roma, 1920.

Afr 1609.20   Tharaud, Jerome. Marrakech. Paris, 1920.

Afr 7119.20   Trancoso, Francisco. Angola; memoria. Lisboa, 1920.

Afr 1750.12   Trivino Valdura, F. Del Marruecos español. Melilla, 1920.

Afr 6538.3F   Uganda. Development Commission. Report, 1920. Entebbe, 1920.

Afr 6535.12.2   Wallis, H.R. Uganda, the handbook of Uganda. London, 1920.

Afr 6390.85   Walmsley, Leo. Flying and sport in East Africa. Edinburgh, 1920.

Afr 6455.36   Watt, Rachel. In the heart of savagedom. 2d ed. London, 1920.

Afr 1609.19A   Wharton, Edith. In Morocco. N.Y, 1920.

1921

Afr 718.25.10   Adolf, Friedrich. Vom Kongo zum Niger und Nil. 3e Aufl. Leipzig, 1921. 2v.

Afr 1755.45   Ansart, F.B. El desastre de annual. Barcelona, 1921.

Afr 500.25   Antonelli, Etienne. L'Afrique et la Paix de Versailles. Paris, 1921.

Afr 500.25.10   Antonelli, Etienne. L'Afrique et la Paix de Versailles. 4th ed. Paris, 1921.

Afr 1750.10   Azpeitua, Antonio. Marruecos, la mala semilla. Madrid, 1921.

Afr 555.9.4   Baker, Ernest. The life and exploration of Frederick Stanley Arnot. London, 1921.

Afr 6280.9.5   Basden, George Thomas. Among the Ibos of Nigeria. London, 1921.

Afr 6280.9.7   Basden, George Thomas. Among the Ibos of Nigeria. Philadelphia, 1921.

Afr 555.5   Bazin, René. Charles de Foucauld. Paris, 1921.

Afr 7567.8   Blanc, J. Le droit de préférence de la France sur le Congo belge (1884-1911). Thèse. Paris, 1921.

Afr 1623.30   Bouissi, R. Etude sur la colonisation capitaliste au Maroc. Thèse. Paris, 1921.

Afr 2780.5   Buchanan, Angus. Exploration of Air. London, 1921.

Afr 3990.1.7   Budge, E.A.W. Cook's handbook. Egypt and the sudan. 4th ed. Suppl. 1925. London, 1921-25.

Afr 1330.5.7   Castries, H. de. Les sources inédites de l'histoire du Maroc. Dynastie Saadienne. (Espagne, t.1-3). Paris, 1921. 3v.

Afr 3285.7   Cecil, E. The leisure of an Egyptian official. London, 1921.

Afr 3285.7.5   Cecil, E. The leisure of an Egyptian official. 2d ed. London, 1921.

Afr 4070.43   Chapman, Abel. Savage Sudan. London, 1921.

Afr 7815.13   Colonne-Beaufaict, A. de. Azande, introduction à une ethnographie générale des bassins de l'Ubangi-Uele et de l'Arvwimi. Bruxelles, 1921.

X Cg   Afr 5057.8   Cosmier, Henri. L'Ouest africain français. Paris, 1921. (Changed to XP 9038).

Afr 1259.21.10   Couperus, Louis. Met Louis Couperus in Afrika. Amsterdam, 1921.

Afr 1340.15   Crouzet-Rayssac, A. de. Le régime des capitulations et la condition des étrangers au Maroc. Thèse. Paris, 1921.

Afr 5829.10.7   Deburgh Edwardes, S.B. The history of Mauritius (1507-1914). London, 1921.

Afr 7809.21   Delcommune, A. L'avenir du Congo belge menacé. 2e ed. Bruxelles, 1921. 2v.

Afr 4115.26   Devonshire, Henrietta Caroline. Some Cairo mosques. London, 1921.

Afr 1840.17   Duclos, Marcel. Contribution a l'étude de la réforme administrative de l'Algérie. Thèse. Alger, 1921.

Afr 8808.61   Duff-Gordon, Lucie. Letters from the Cape. London, 1921.

Afr 2532.6   Duran-Angliviel, André. Ce que la Tunisie demande à la France. Paris, 1921.

Afr 7130.5   Eça, Antonio Julio da Costa Pereira de. Campanha do sul de Angola em 1915. Lisboa, 1921.

Afr 1840.15   Elie-Edmond, A. De la condition politique des indigenes musulmans d'Algerie. Thèse. Alger, 1921.

Afr 6780.16   Fendall, C.P. The East African force, 1915-1919. London, 1921.

Afr 2609.21   Ferdinand-Lop, S. La Tunisie et ses richesses. Paris, 1921.

Afr 2975.3   Forbes, Rosita. The secret of the Sahara, Kufara. London, 1921.

Afr 2975.3.5   Forbes, Rosita. The secret of the Sahara, Kufara. N.Y., 1921.

Afr 6164.7   Fuller, F. A vanished dynasty. London, 1921.

Afr 1493.20   Gomez Hidalgo, F. Marruecos. Madrid, 1921.

Afr 1338.10   Goulven, Jos. Traité d'économie et de législation marocaines. v.1-2. Paris, 1921. 2v.

Afr 1608.98.5   Graham, R.B.C. Mogreb-el-Acksa, a journey in Morocco. London, 1921.

Afr 3300.48F   Great Britain. Special Mission to Egypt. Report of the Special Mission to Egypt. London, 1921.

Afr 1369.21   Hardy, Georges. Les grandes étapes de l'histoire du Maroc. Paris, 1921.

Afr 5130.15.5   Hardy, Georges. La mise en valeur du Sénégal de 1817 à 1854. Paris, 1921.

Afr 5130.15   Hardy, Georges. La mise en valeur du Sénégal de 1817 à 1854. Thèse. Paris, 1921.

Afr 1453.10   Harris, Walter B. Morocco that was. Edinburgh, 1921.

Afr 2230.30   Hilton-Simpson, M.W. Among the hill-folk of Algeria. London, 1921.

Afr 8678.24.2   Jabavu, D.D.T. The black problem. 2d ed. Lovedale, 1921.

1921 - cont.

Afr 6218.1   Johnson, Samuel. The history of the Yorubas from the earliest times to the beginning of the British protectorate. London, 1921.

Afr 1609.21.5   Kann, Reginald. Le protectorat marocain. Nancy, 1921.

Afr 7809.21.5   Leger, L.T. Du Tanganika à l'Atlantique. Bruxelles, 1921.

Afr 3745.10A   Martin, Percy F. The Sudan in evolution. London, 1921.

Afr 5094.2   Marty, Paul. Etudes sur l'islam et les tribus maures. Paris, 1921.

Afr 1573.32   Maturana Vargas, C. La tragica realidad: Marruecos, 1921. Barcelona, 1921.

Afr 2308.15   Melia, Jean. La ville blanche, Alger et son département. Paris, 1921.

Afr 4559.14.10   Merab. Impressions d'Ethiopie. Paris, 1921-29. 3v.

Afr 1573.23   Merino Alvarez, A. Marruecos. Madrid, 1921.

Afr 8285.20.10   Merwe, N.J. Marthinius Theunis Steijn. Kaapstad, 1921. 2v.

Afr 9195.10   Oneil, Owen Rowe. Adventures in Swaziland. N.Y., 1921.

Afr 7549.21   Pirenne, Jacques. Coup d'oeil sur l'histoire du Congo. Bruxelles, 1921.

Afr 2500.20   Pleville-le-Pelley, G.R. La mission de Pleville-le-Pelley à Tunis, 1793-1794. Tunis, 1921.

Afr 8325.66.5   Preller, G.S. Kaptein Hindon. 2nd ed. Kaapstad, 1921.

Afr 4969.21   Rayne, H.A. Sun, sand and Somalis. London, 1921.

Afr 6455.37   Roscoe, John. Twenty-five years in East Africa. Cambridge, 1921.

Afr 1570.41   Rouard de Card, E. Accords secrets entre la France et l'Italie concernant le Maroc et la Lybie. Paris, 1921.

Afr 1658.7.2   Ruiz Albeniz, Victor. Espana en el rif. 2a ed. Madrid, 1921.

Afr 5053.12   Schefer, Christian. Instructions générales données de 1763 à 1870. Paris, 1921. 2v.

Afr 1259.21   Scott, A. Maccallum. Barbary. London, 1921.

Afr 1259.21.2   Scott, A. Maccallum. Barbary. N.Y., 1921.

Afr 8687.128   Scully, W.C. Sir J.H. Meiring Beck. Cape Town, 1921.

Afr 609.21   Sharpe, Alfred. The backbone of Africa. London, 1921.

Afr Doc 3407.321   Tanganyika. Non-native census, 1921, report. Report on the native census, 1921. Dar es Salaam, 1921. 2 pam.

NEDL Afr 5344.5   Tauxier, Louis. Le noir de Bondoukou. Paris, 1921.

Afr Doc 3307.321   Uganda. Census returns, 1921. Uganda, 1921.

Afr 6460.5   Vanden Bergh, L.J. On the trail of the Pigmies. N.Y., 1921.

Afr 7369.20.5   Walker, T.H.B. History of Liberia. Boston, 1921.

Afr 2209.20.5   Ward, Emily. Three travellers in North Africa. London, 1921.

Afr 7465.8   Westermann, D. Die Kpelle. Göttingen, 1921.

Afr 8110.15   Wieringa, P.A.C. De oudste boeren-republieken graaff-reinst en Zwellendam van 1775-1806. 's-Gravenhage, 1921.

Afr 8250.17.2   Williams, B. Cecil Rhodes. (Makers of the 19th century). N.Y., 1921.

Afr 8250.17A   Williams, B. Cecil Rhodes. London, 1921.

1922

Afr 3275.35   Adam, Juliette. L'Angleterre en Egypte. Paris, 1922.

Afr 2945.30   Agostini, E. de. Le populazioni della Cirenaica. Bengasi, 1922-23.

Afr 2288.15   Algérie. Direction des Territoires du Sud. Les territoires du sud. Exposé de leur situation. Pt.1. Alger, 1922.

Afr 2288.5   Algérie. Direction des Territoires du Sud. Les territoires du sud. Exposé de leur situation. (Extrait) Description géographique par E.-F. Gautier. Alger, 1922.

Afr 1609.22   Andrews, C. E. Old Morocco and the forbidden atlas. N.Y., 1922.

Afr 7809.22.5   Barns, T.A. The wonderland of the eastern Congo. London, 1922.

Afr 31.10   Bauer Landauer, I. Papeles de mi archivo, relaciones de Africa. Madrid, 1922-23. 4v.

Afr 1326.3   Bauer y Landauer, I. Apuntes para una bibliografia de Marruecos. Madrid, 1922.

Afr 2438.12   Bismut, Victor. Essai sur la dualité législative et judiciaire en Tunisie. Dijon, 1922.

Afr 3258.8.3A   Blunt, W.S. Secret history of the English occupation of Egypt. N.Y., 1922.

Afr 1848.7   Braibant, Chas. Inventaire des archives de l'amiraute d'Alger. Alger, 1922.

Afr 5057.10   Bressolles, H. Organisation financière locale de l'Afrique. Thèse. Bordeaux, 1922.

Afr 6780.18   Buhrer, J. L'Afrique orientale allemande et la guerre. Paris, 1922.

Afr 710.10   Campbell, D. In the heart of Bantuland. London, 1922.

Afr 2224.922.2   Capot de Quissac. Le budget spécial de l'Algérie. Paris, 1922.

Afr 2224.922   Capot de Quissac. Le budget spécial de l'Algérie. Thèse. Paris, 1922.

Afr 2209.22.10   Casserly, Gordon. Algeria to-day. London, 1922.

Afr 1330.6   Castries, H. de. Les sources inédites de l'histoire du Maroc. Dynastie filalienne. v.1-6. Paris, 1922-31. 6v.

Afr 1570.47   Caussin. Vers Taza. Paris, 1922.

Afr 4070.43.5   Chapman, Abel. Savage Sudan. N.Y., 1922.

Afr 3183.15   Charles-Roux, François. Autour d'une route. Paris, 1922.

Afr 555.45   Christol, Frank. Quatre ans au Cameroun. Paris, 1922.

Afr 7180.10   Claridge, G.C. Wild bush tribes of tropical Africa. Philadelphia, 1922.

Afr 8283.19   Colvin, Ian D. The life of Jameson. London, 1922. 2v.

Afr 1273.922   Cosnier, Henri. L'Afrique du Nord. Paris, 1922.

Afr 5749.22   Dandouau, A. Geographie de Madagascar. Paris, 1922.

Afr 630.8   Delafosse, Maurice. Les Noires de l'Afrique. Paris, 1922.

Afr 7808.74   Delcommune, A. Vingt années de vie africaine. Bruxelles, 1922. 2v.

Afr 2223.52   Demontes, V. Renseignements sur l'Algérie économique. Paris, 1922.

Afr 2731.13   Drouilly, J.G. Le général Laperrine, grand saharien. Paris, 1922.

Afr 6741.2   Emonts, Johannes. Ins Steppen- und Bergland Innerkameruns. Aachen, 1922.

Afr 2223.922   Falck, Felix. Guide économique de l'Algérie. Paris, 1922.

Afr 8252.30   Fraser, J. Episodes in my life. Cape Town, 1922.

Afr 5056.122   French West Africa. Dispositions cartographiques relatives aux cartes et plans de l'A.O.F. Laval, 1922.

Afr 1200.65   Fribourg, Andre. L'Afrique latine. Paris, 1922.

Afr 2748.57.5   Fromentin, E. Un été dans le Sahara. Paris, 1922.

Afr 5420.222   Grebert, F. Au Gabon, Afrique. Paris, 1922.

Afr 5110.20   Gueye, L. De la situation politique des sénégalais. Paris, 1922.

1922 - cont.

Afr 5749.15.5   Guilloteaux, E. Madagascar et la côte de Somalie. Paris, 1922.

Afr 1658.56   Guixé, Juan. El Rif en sombras lo que yo he visto en Melilla. Madrid, 1922.

Afr 1609.22.10   Hardy, Georges. Les grandes lignes de la geographie du Maroc. Paris, 1922.

Afr 109.22   Hardy, Georges. Vue générale de l'histoire d'Afrique. Paris, 1922.

Afr 632.15   Hartland, Sidney E. The evolution of kinship. Oxford, 1922.

Afr 6882.2   Hauer, August. Ali Moçambique; Bilder aus dem Leben eines schwarzen Fabeldichters. Berlin, 1922.

Afr 6275.27   Hermon-Hodge, H.B. Up against it in Nigeria. London, 1922.

Afr 1193.71   Hernandez Mir, F. Del desastre al fracaso. Madrid, 1922.

Afr 3300.1   Himaya, Latif. La condition internationale de l'Egypte depuis 1914. Thèse. Paris, 1922.

Afr 42715.22   Hurel, Eugène. La poésie chez les primitifs, ou Contes, fables, récits et proverbes du Rwanda (Lac Kivu). Bruxelles, 1922.

Afr 2875.35   Italy. Esercito. Corpo di Stato Maggiore. Ufficio Storico. Campagna di Libia. Roma, 1922-27. 5v.

Afr 775.10   Johnson, W.P. Nyasa, the great water. London, 1922.

Afr 1922.15   Julien, A. La question d'Alger devant les Chambres sous la Restauration. Alger, 1922.

Afr 8677.25   Koch, M.H. An analysis of the finances of the Union of South Africa. Cape Town, 1922.

Afr 8676.25   Lehfeldt, R.A. The national resources of South Africa. Johannesburg, 1922.

Afr 1326.5.2   Levi Provencal, E. Les historiens des Chorfa. Paris, 1922.

Afr 1326.5   Levi Provencal, E. Les historiens des Chorfa. Thèse. Paris, 1922.

Afr 7360.10   Liberia. Attorney General. Report of L.A. Grimes, submitted to the 4th session of the 34th legislature of the Republic of Liberia. n.p., 1922.

Afr 7567.38   Liebrechts, Charles. Notre colonie. Bruxelles, 1922.

Afr 500.30   Lucas, C.P. The partition and colonization of Africa. Oxford, 1922.

Afr 550.35   Mackenzie, J.K. African adventurers. N.Y., 1922.

Afr 9689.22   Mackintosh, Catharine Winkworth. The new Zambesi trail. London, 1922.

Afr 4010.1   Macmichael, H.A. A history of the Arabs in Sudan. v.1-2. Cambridge, 1922.

Afr 1755.47   Martínez de Campos, Arsenio. Melilla, 1921. Ciudad Real, 1922.

Afr 5345.5   Marty, Paul. Etudes sur l'islam en Côte-d'Ivoire. Paris, 1922.

Afr 2232.4   Mercier, Marcel. La civilisation urbaine au Mzab. Alger, 1922.

Afr 6095.322   Newland, M.O. West Africa. London, 1922.

Afr 8678.25   Nielsen, P. The black man's place in South Africa. Cape Town, 1922.

Afr 6883.33   Nigmann, Ernst. Schwärze. Berlin, 1922.

Afr 1487.22   Ortega y Gasset, Eduardo. Annual. Madrid, 1922.

Afr 1493.71   Osuna Servent, Arturo. Frente a Abd-el-Krim. Madrid, 1922.

Afr 5056.122.5   Petit, André. Mon voyage au Soudan français de Dakar...à Conakry...par Bamako. Paris, 1922.

Afr 4568.17   Pollera, A. La donna in Etiopia. Roma, 1922.

Afr 1609.22.5   Rabbe, C. Au Maroc. Sur les rives. Paris, 1922.

NEDL Afr 3275.43   Regatz, L.J. The question of Egypt in Anglo-French relations, 1875-1904. Edinburgh, 1922.

Afr 1570.48   Renaissance du Maroc. Poitiers, 1922.

Afr Doc 3807.321.10   Rhodesia, Southern. Census Office. Second and final report of the director of census regarding the census taken on 3rd May 1921. Salisbury, 1922.

Afr 1574.12   Romanones, Alvaro Figueroa y Torres. Conferencia del Excmo. Sr. conde de Romanones sobre el problema de Marruecos. Pronunciada en al Teatro de San Fernando de Sevilla el 26 de abril de 1922. Sevilla, 1922.

Afr 725.20A   Roscoe, John. The soul of central Africa. London, 1922.

Afr 2850.5   Rouard de Card, E. La France et l'Italie et l'article 13 du Pacte de Londres. Paris, 1922.

Afr 4360.7   Royal Chronicle of Abyssinia. The Royal Chronicle of Abyssinia, 1769-1840. Cambridge, Eng., 1922.

Afr 575.17.25   Ruini, M. L'islam e le nostre colonie. Città di Castello, 1922.

Afr 1750.42   Ruiz Albéniz, Victor. Ecce homo: las responsabilidades del desastre. Madrid, 1922.

Afr 5426.100   Schweitzer, Albert. On the edge of the primeval forest. London, 1922.

Afr 550.29   Société des Missions Evangéliques, Paris. Nos champs de mission. 3e éd. Paris, 1922.

Afr 8678.225   South Africa. Inter-Departmental Committee on the Native Pass Law. Report, 1920. Cape Town, 1922.

Afr 8063.30   South Africa. Martial Law Inquiry Judicial Commission. Report. Pretoria, 1922.

Afr 8667.55   Spoelstra, B. Ons volkslewe. Pretoria, 1922.

Afr 9175.15   Statham, J.C.B. Through Angola, a coming colony. Edinburgh, 1922.

Afr 9710.8   Stirke, D.E.C.R. Barotseland. London, 1922.

Afr 1738.20F   Tangier, Africa. Registos paroquiais da se de Tanger. Lisboa, 1922.

Afr 6280.18.2   Temple, Charles L. Notes on the tribes, provinces, emirates and states of the northern provinces of Nigeria. 2d ed. Lagos, 1922.

Afr 4105.8   Thuile, H. Commentaires sur l'atlas historique d'Alexandrie. Le Caire, 1922.

Afr 2530.15   Tumedei, C. La questione tunisina e l'Italia. Bologna, 1922.

Afr 1658.52   Vivero, Augusto. El derrumbamiento. Madrid, 1922.

Afr 2609.22   Voligny, R.B. de. Behind Tunisian walls by L.E. Douglas. London, 1922.

1923

Afr 3725.14   Ade, H.C. Pioniere im Osten. Stuttgart, 1923.

Afr 4700.23   Agostino Orsini, P.D. Espansionismo italiano odierno. Salerno, 1923.

Afr 609.23   Akeley, Carl E. In brightest Africa. Garden City, 1923. 2v.

Afr 609.23.2   Akeley, Carl E. In brightest Africa. Garden City, 1923.

Afr 7377.25   Allen, Gardner M. The trustees of donations for education in Liberia. Boston, 1923.

1923 - cont.

Afr 1571.22   Babin, Gustave. La mystérieuse Ouaouizert. Casablanca, 1923.

Afr 8292.4   Badenhorst, A.M. Tant' Alie of Transvaal, her diary 1880-1902. London, 1923.

Afr 1658.16   Basallo, Francisco. Memorias del sargento Basallo. Madrid, 1923?

Afr 1750.30   Bauer Y Landauer, Ignacio. Papeles de mi archivo. Madrid, 1923.

Afr 1435.5   Baule y Landauer. Consecuencias de la campana de 1860. Madrid, 1923. 4v.

Afr 555.5.5   Bazin, René. Charles de Foucauld. N.Y., 1923.

Afr 150.4.5   Beazley, C.R. Prince Henry the Navigator. London, 1923.

Afr 500.35   Beer, George Louis. African questions at the Paris Peace Conference. N.Y., 1923.

Afr 4180.3.10A   Belgrave, C.D. Siwa. London, 1923.

Afr 1755.49   Berenguer, Damaso. Campanas en el rif y Yebala 1921-1922. Madrid, 1923.

Afr 7809.21.10   Bradley, Mary. On the gorilla trail. N.Y., 1923.

Afr 5245.10   Brevie, J. Islamisme contre naturisme au Soudan français. Paris, 1923.

Afr 6408.5   British Indian Colony. Merchants Association, Bombay. The Kenya decision. Bombay, 1923.

Afr 8846.17   Brownlee, F. The Transkeian native territories. n.p., 1923.

Afr 3979.10.20   Butcher, E.L. Things seen in Egypt. London, 1923.

Afr 1609.23.20   Cansino-Roldan, Luis. Recuerdos de Marruecos. Malaga, 1923.

Afr 3979.23   Carpenter, F.G. Cairo to Kisumu. Garden City, 1923.

Afr 1259.23   Carpenter, F.G. From Tangier to Tripoli. 1st ed. Garden City, 1923.

Afr 1609.23.15   Celarie, H. Un mois au Maroc. Paris, 1923.

Afr 7309.23   Chamberlain, G.A. African hunting among the Thongas. N.Y., 1923.

Afr 2938.20.2   Coletti, Francesco. La Tripolitania settentrionale e la sua vita sociale, studiate dal vero. 2a ed. Bologna, 1923.

Afr 5749.23   Cros, Louis. Madagascar pour tous. Paris, 1923.

Afr 7809.22   Daye, Pierre. L'empire colonial belge. Bruxelles, 1923.

Afr 2224.20   Delmonte, Fabien R.S. Les pouvoirs financiers des assemblées algériennes et le contrôle de la métropole. Thèse. Alger, 1923.

Afr 2308.17   Delvert, C.L. Le port d'Alger. Paris, 1923.

Afr 3215.3   Douin, Georges. Une mission militaire française auprès de Mohamed Aly. Caire, 1923.

Afr 1570.52   Dutaillis, J. Le nouveau Maroc. Paris, 1923.

Afr 1259.04   Eberhardt, I. Dans l'ombre chaude de l'islam. Paris, 1923.

Afr 2209.00.5   Eberhardt, I. Mes journaliers. Paris, 1923.

Afr 1259.04.5   Eberhardt, I. Notes de route, Maroc-Algérie-Tunisie. Paris, 1923.

Afr 3979.23.10   Edgar, H.M. Dahaheah days, an Egyptian winter holiday. Toronto, 1923.

Afr 1955.40   Esquer, G. La prise d'Alger, 1830. Alger, 1923.

Afr 5869.23   Foucque, Hippolyte. L'Ile de la Réunion. Paris, 1923.

Afr 6738.13   France. Commissariat de la République Française au Cameroun. Guide de la colonisation au Cameroun. Paris, 1923.

Afr 5056.123   French West Africa. Catalogue des positions géographiques provisoirement admises par le Service géographique de l'A.O.F. Laval, 1923-24.

Afr 5190.10.5   French West Africa. Notice sur le plan de Dakar et environs d'après photo-aérienne. Gorée, 1923.

Afr 609.23.10   Frobenius, Leo. Das unbekannte Afrika. München, 1923.

Afr 628.223   Garvey, Marcus. Philosophy and opinions of Marcus Garvey. 1st ed. N.Y., 1923.

Afr 2749.23   Gautier, E.F. Le Sahara. Paris, 1923.

Afr Doc 1807.321   Gold Coast (Colony). Census Office. Census report, 1921, for the Gold Coast and Colony. Accra, 1923.

Afr 5585.20   Grandidier, G. Le Myre de Vilers. Paris, 1923.

Afr 1259.11.7   Grant, Cyril F. Studies in North Africa. N.Y., 1923.

Afr 1658.17   Guardiola Cardellach, E. El Rif en Espana. Barcelona, 1923.

Afr 2749.22   Haardt, G.M. Le raid Citroen. Paris, 1923.

Afr 1069.23   Hamet, I. Histoire du Maghreb. Paris, 1923.

Afr 9345.10.8   Harris, J.C. Khama, the great African chief. 4. ed. London, 1923.

Afr 5235.55.5   Hewitt, William Henry. Mungo Park. London, 1923.

Afr 4937.10   Jardine, D. The Mad Mullah of Somaliland. London, 1923.

Afr 7803.48   Jeanroy, V. Vingt-cinq ans de mission au Congo. Bruxelles, 1923.

Afr 7567.12   Landbeck, P. Kongoerinnerungen. Berlin, 1923.

Afr 3978.71.4   Lane, E.W. The manners and customs of modern Egyptians. London, 1923.

Afr 7540.38   Lippens, Maurice. Notes sur le gouvernement du Congo, 1921-22. Gand, 1923.

Afr 1769.18.5   Lopez Rienda, R. Frente al fracaso, Raisuni. De silvestre a burguete. Madrid, 1923.

Afr 6010.10   Lugard, F.D. The dual mandate in British Tropical Africa. 2d ed. Edinburgh, 1923.

Afr 609.23.5   Lyell, Denis D. Memories of an African hunter. London, 1923.

Afr 1487.25   Maestre, Pedro. Divulgacion y orientacion. Granada, 1923.

Afr 6460.10   Mallet, M. A white woman among the Masai. London, 1923.

Afr 2945.15   Marinelli, O. La Cirenaica. Milano, 1923.

Afr 2719.23   Martin, A.G.P. Quatre siècles d'histoire marocaine. Paris, 1923.

Afr 1369.23   Martin, Alfred G.P. Quatre siècles d'histoire marocaine. Paris, 1923.

Afr 3979.23.5A   Martin, P.F. Egypt old and new. London, 1923.

Afr 9700.10   Melland, F.H. In witch-bound Africa. London, 1923.

Afr 9700.10.2   Melland, F.H. In witch-bound Africa. Philadelphia, 1923.

Afr 718.37   Migeod, F.W.H. Across equatorial Africa. London, 1923.

Afr 1390.6   Millet, Rene. Les Almohades, histoire dune dynastie berbère. Paris, 1923.

Afr 8252.5.10   Molteno, J.T. The dominion of Afrikanderdom. London, 1923.

Afr 2220.12   Monmarche, Marcel. Algérie, Tunisie. Paris, 1923.

Afr 1721.7   Moreno Gilabert, Andres. La Ciudad Dormida. Madrid, 1923.

Afr 5342.15   Neveux, M. Religion des noirs...fétiches de la Côte-d'Ivoire. Alencon, 1923.

Afr 1609.23.5   Oconnor, V.C.S. A vision of Morocco. London, 1923.

Afr 3138.10.5   O'Leary, De Lacy. A short history of the Fatimid khalifate. London, 1923.

Afr 4732.15   Petazzi, E. Egitto e Sudan nei loro rapporti economici con la colonia Eritrea. Roma, 1923.

1923 - cont.

Afr 550.8.30   Philippe, A. Le Cardinal Lavigerie, 1825-1892. Dijon, 1923.

Afr 6194.10   Rattray, R.S. Ashanti. Oxford, 1923.

Afr 1570.50   Raynaud, Robert. En marge du livre jaune. Le Maroc. Paris, 1923.

Afr 7459.23   Reeve, H.F. The Black Republic, Liberia. London, 1923.

Afr 4559.23   Rey, Charles F. Unconquered Abyssinia as it is today. London, 1923.

Afr 7809.23.5   Robert, M. Le Congo physique. Bruxelles, 1923.

Afr 8252.17   Ronan, B. Forty South African years. London, 1923.

Afr 6540.12   Roscoe, John. The Bakitara or Banyoro. Cambridge, 1923.

Afr 6540.13   Roscoe, John. The Banyankole. Cambridge, 1923.

Afr 550.31   Rowling, F. Bibliography of Christian literature. London, 1923.

Afr 1609.23.25   Sadler, Georges. A travers le Maghreb. Paris, 1923.

Afr 3040.5   Salem, M.S. Les principes du self-government local dans les democraties modernes et leur application au régime administratif égyptien. Thèse. Dijon, 1923.

Afr 7175.16   Schachtzabel, A. Im Hochland von Angola. Dresden, 1923.

Afr 8175.13   Schreiner, O. Thoughts on South Africa. N.Y., 1923.

VAfr 618.50   Shorthose, William John Townsend. Sport and adventure in Africa. Philadelphia, 1923.

Afr 555.2.101   Socété des Missions Evangéliques, Paris. Un siècle en Afrique et en Océanie. Paris, 1923.

Afr 8678.230   South Africa. Commission on Rebellion of the Bondelzwarts. Report, 1923. Cape Town, 1923.

Afr 4095.25   Stigand, C.H. Equatoria, the Lado Enclave. London, 1923.

Afr 6280.11.5   Talbot, P.A. Life in southern Nigeria. London, 1923.

Afr 5758.23   Tananarive, 1923, Madagascar économique. Tananarive, 1923.

Afr 1609.23   Tarde, Alfred de. Le Maroc, ecole d'energie. Paris, 1923.

Afr 1609.23.10   Tharaud, J. Le Maroc. Paris, 1923.

Afr 1570.49   Touron, Max. Notre protectorat marocain. Thèse. Poitiers, 1923.

Afr 7809.23   Verlaine, Louis. Notre colonie, contribution à la recherche de la méthode de colonisation. Bruxelles, 1923.

Afr 4582.20   Vinassa de Regny, P. Dancalia. Roma, 1923.

Afr 2209.21   Warren, Lady. Through Algeria and Tunisia on a motor-bicycle. Boston, 1923.

Afr 630.10A   Willoughby, W.C. Race problems in the new Africa. Oxford, 1923.

Afr 8252.10.5   Worsfold, B. Sir Bartle Frere. London, 1923.

Afr 3740.12   Yatin, Fernand. Une mise au point, la vérité sur Fachoda. Chaumont, 1923.

Afr 3230.15   Zananiri, G. Le khedive Ismail et l'Egypte, 1830-1894. Alexandrie, 1923.

1924

Afr 2223.65   Algeria. Direction de l'Agriculture, du Commerce et de l'Industrie. Notes sur la vie commerciale et industrielle de l'Algérie en 1923-1924. Alger, 1924.

Afr 575.21   Andre, Pierre J. L'islam noir. Paris, 1924.

Afr 3267.5   Arabi, Ahmed. Memoire d'Arabi-Pacha à ses avocats. Thése. Photoreproduction. Paris, 1924.

Afr 1490.11.15   Azan, Paul. L'expédition de Fez. Paris, 1924.

Afr 2308.19   Baeza, H.L. Le rôle économique du port d'Alger. Thèse. Alger, 1924.

Afr 1271.10F   Bargone, Chas. L'Afrique du Nord, Tunisie, Algérie, Maroc. Paris, 1924.

Afr 2618.28   Bernard, Augustin. Enquête sur l'habitation rurale des indigènes de la Tunisie. Tunis, 1924.

Afr 6879.24   British Empire Exhibition, Wembley, 1924. Central commission of Tanganyika exhibition handbook. London, 1924.

Afr 6565.24   British Empire Exhibition, Wembley, 1924. Zanzibar, an account of its people. Zanzibar, 1924.

Afr 8135.15   Brookes, E.H. The history of native policy in South Africa from 1830 to the present day. Cape Town, 1924.

Afr 8252.25   Buxton, Earl. General Botha. London, 1924.

Afr 1609.24.10   Cabrera Lattore. Magreb-el-aksai. Madrid, 1924.

Afr 4700.24   Capra, G. L'Africa centro-australe e l'emigrazione italiana. Torino, 1924.

Afr 2220.10   Celarie, Henriette. Un mois en Algérie et en Tunisie. Paris, 1924.

Afr 1609.24.5   Champion, P. Tanger, fes et meknes. Paris, 1924.

Afr 9599.24   Christy, C. Big game and Pygmies. London, 1924.

Afr 1965.20   Cockenpot, C. Le traité Desmichels. Paris, 1924.

Afr 9489.24   Colquhoun, A.R. The real Rhodesia. London, 1924.

Afr 7812.224   Congrès Colonial National. La politique économique au Congo belge. Bruxelles, 1924.

Afr 7188.269   Cunha Leal, Francisco Pinto da. Caligula em Brazil. Lisboa, 1924.

Afr 2336.5   Dennis, H.V.M. Hippo Regius from the earliest times to the Arab conquest. Diss. Princeton, 1924.

Afr 8658.49   Dolman, Alfred. In the footsteps of Livingstone, being...our travel notes. London, 1924.

Afr 1753.10.2   Dornellas, Affonso De. Alleo, gloriosa epopeia portuguezaum Ceuta. Lisboa, 1924.

Afr 1753.10.4   Dornellas, Affonso de. Os jogos floraes de 1923 em Ceuta. Lisboa, 1924.

Afr 1753.10   Dornellas, Affonso De. Santissima virgem d'Africa, padroeira de Ceuta. Lisboa, 1924.

Afr 1753.10.3   Dornellas, Affonso de. O tercio de extranjeros do exercito espanhol. Lisboa, 1924.

Afr 4070.35   Dugmore, AR. The vast Sudan. London, 1924.

Afr 6879.24.9   Dundas, A.L.H. Beneath African glaciers. London, 1924.

Afr 6887.10   Dundas, C. Kilimanjaro and its people. London, 1924.

Afr 3193.10   Edmonds, J. L'Egypte indépendante. Projet de 1801. Caire, 1924.

Afr 3300.15   Elgood, P.G. Egypt and the army. London, 1924.

Afr 1080.20   Fagnan, Edmond. Extraits inédits rélatifs au Maghreb. Alger, 1924.

Afr 8125.10   Fairbridge, D. Lady Anne Barnard at the Cape of Good Hope, 1797-1802. Oxford, 1924.

Afr 8252.18   Flemming, L. The call of the Veld. 2d ed. London, 1924.

Afr 1769.18   Forbes, Rosita. El Raisuni, the sultan of the mountains. London, 1924.

Afr 6685.10   France. Commissariat au Togo. Guide de la colonisation au Togo. Paris, 1924.

Afr 1200.67   Gasser, J. Role social de la France dans l'Afrique du Nord. Paris, 1924.

Afr 6192.25   Gold Coast handbook. 2d ed. Accra, 1924.

Afr 3295.4   Hayter, William Goodenough. Recent constitutional developments in Egypt. Cambridge, Eng., 1924.

Afr 555.23.20   Hensey, Andrew F. My children of the forest. N.Y., 1924.

252

Afr 1620.15.5 Heywood, C. Morocco. Paris, 1924.
Afr 9614.4 Hine, John Edward. Days gone by. London, 1924.
Afr 2525.10 Huc, Paul. L'oeuvre politique et économique du protectorat français en Tunisie. Thèse. Toulouse, 1924.
Afr 6455.39 Johnson, M. Camera trails in Africa. N.Y., 1924.
Afr 2223.924.5 Juving, Alex. Le socialisme en Algérie. Thèse. Alger, 1924.
Afr 4115.6.15 Lane-Poole, S. The story of Cairo. London, 1924.
Afr 870.15 Lionnet, J.G. L'ile d'Agalega. Paris, 1924.
Afr 1703.3.10 Lopes, David. Historia de arzila durante o dominio portugues (1471-1550 e 1577-1589). Coimbra, 1924.
Afr 6738.15A Mackenzie, J.K. African clearings. Boston, 1924.
Afr 510.20 Mangin, J.E. Regards sur la France d'Afrique. Paris, 1924.
Afr 3978.76.10 Manning, S. The land of the pharaohs. N.Y., 1924.
Afr 7190.45 Mantero Velarde, A. de. L'espansione politica e coloniale portoghese. Roma, 1924.
Afr 4070.36 Millais, John Guille. Far away up the Nile. London, 1924.
Afr 5243.125.5 Monteil, Charles. Les Bambara du Ségou et du Kaarta. Paris, 1924.
Afr 5035.5 Monteil, P.L. Souvenirs vécus. Quelques feuillets de l'histoire coloniale. Paris, 1924.
Afr 8969.24 Natal. Volksraad. Voortrekker wetgewing, notule van die natalse Volksraad, 1839-1845. Pretoria, 1924.
Afr 8340.3.5 Newton, A.P. Select documents relating to the unification of South Africa. London, 1924. 2v.
Afr 9510.11 Nobles, E.A. Guide to the Matapos. Cape Town, 1924.
Afr 1259.24.5F Nordafrika, Tripolis, Tunis, Algier, Marokko. Berlin, 1924.
Afr 7809.24.10 Norden, H. Fresh tracks in the Belgian Congo. London, 1924.
Afr 659.24F North Africa, Tripoli, Tunis. N.Y., 1924.
Afr 5749.24 Osborn, C.S. Madagascar, land of the man-eating tree. N.Y., 1924.
Afr 3040.18 Osman, Amin. Le mouvement constitutionnel en Egypte et la constitution de 1923. Thèse. Paris, 1924.
Afr 6455.43.5 Percival, A.B. A game ranger's note book. N.Y., 1924.
Afr 2938.15 Persellini, Mario. La Tripolitania: il presente e l'avvenire. Milano, 1924.
Afr 1571.8 Peyris, G. Randonnées au Maroc, 1911-1913. Paris, 1924.
Afr 8252.19 Phillips, L. Some reminiscences. London, 1924.
Afr 5049.100.7 Ponet, Marthe Bordeaux. Hyacinthe Jalabert. 2.éd. Paris, 1924.
Afr 3979.24 Powers, H.H. Egypt. N.Y., 1924.
Afr 6455.42 Powys, L. Black laughter. N.Y., 1924.
Afr 1259.24F Ricard, Prosper. Les merveilles de l'autre France. Paris, 1924.
Afr 2762.10 Richer, A. Les Touareg du Niger. Paris, 1924.
Afr 6540.14 Roscoe, John. The Bagesu and other tribes of the Uganda protectorate. Cambridge, Eng., 1924.
Afr 6540.4.7 Roscoe, John. Immigrants and their influence. Cambridge, Eng., 1924.
Afr 724.15.5 Rosen, Eric von Greve. Vom Kap nach Kairo. Stuttgart, 1924.
Afr 3230.12 Sabry, Mohammed. La genèse de l'esprit national égyptien (1863-1882). Thèse. Paris, 1924.
Afr 2632.6 Sarfatti, M.G. Tunisiaca. Milano, 1924.
Afr 9599.24.5 Savile, F. The high grass trail. London, 1924.
Afr 2209.12.15 Schmitthenner, H. Tunisien und Algerien. Stuttgart, 1924.
Afr 5765.15 Sibree, James. Fifty years in Madagascar. London, 1924.
Afr 555.115 Skolaster, Hermann. Die Pallottiner in Kamerun. Limburg an der Lahn, 1924.
Afr 1570.58 Sloane, Wm.M. Greater France in Africa. N.Y., 1924.
Afr 630.13 Société de Géographie d'Egypte. Catalogue of the Ethnographical Museum of the Royal Geographical Society of Egypt. Le Caire, 1924.
Afr 2731.4 Société d'Etudes du Chemin de Fer Transafricain. Mission du Transafricain. v.1-2 et atlas. Paris, 1924-25. 3v.
Afr 8677.30 South Africa. Parliament. House of Assembly. Select Committee on Public Accounts. 1924. Report. Cape Town, 1924. 2v.
Afr 8678.37 South Africa. Parliament. House of Assembly. Select Committee on Native Affairs. First and second (third and fourth [final]) reports of the Select Committee on Native Affairs. Cape Town, 1924.
Afr 8250.19 Stent, Vere. A personal record of some incidents in the life of Cecil Rhodes. Cape Town, 1924.
Afr 5285.277.7 Tauxier, Louis. Nouvelles notes sur le Mossi et le Gourounsi. Paris, 1924.
Afr 1609.24 Tranchant de Lunel, M. Au pays du paradoxe, Maroc. Paris, 1924.
X Cg Afr 1955.42 Valet, René. L'Afrique du nord devant le Parlement au XIXme siecle. Alger, 1924.
Afr 7809.24.15 Wauters, Joseph. Le Congo au travail. Bruxelles, 1924.
Afr 555.39 Witte, Jehan. Un explorateur et un apôtre du Congo français. Paris, 1924.

1925

Afr 609.25 Akeley, Carl E. In brightest Africa. Garden City, N.Y., 1925.
Afr 609.07.12 Albertis, Enrico Alberto d'. Periplo dell'Africa. 2d ed. Genova, 1925.
Afr 1609.20.5 Amic, Henri. Le Maroc, hier et aujourd hui. Paris, 1925.
Afr 4420.5 Arce, L. L'Abyssinie. Avignon, 1925.
Afr 1047.15 Azan, Paul. L'armée indigène nord-africaine. Paris, 1925.
Afr 1965.12.10 Azan, Paul. L'émir Abd el-Kader, 1808-1883. Paris, 1925.
Afr 1575.2.10F Baiao, Antonio. Documentos do corpo chronologico relativo a Marrocos, 1488 a 1514. Coimbra, 1925.
Afr 6194.20.15 Balmer, W.T. A history of the Akan peoples of the Gold Coast. London, 1925.
Afr 3040.10 Barkouky, El. Les rapports entre le pouvoir judiciaire et le pouvoir exécutif en Egypte. Thèse. Paris, 1925.
Afr 1583.17 Bartels, Albert. Auf eigene Faust meine Erlebnisse vor und während des Weltkrieges in Marokko. Leipzig, 1925.
Afr 2819.25 Bergna, C. Tripoli dal 1510 al 1850. Tripoli, 1925.
Afr 1273.2 Bernard, Paul. Les anciens impôts de l'Afrique du Nord. St. Raphael, 1925.
Afr 8210.12 Botha, P.R. Die staatkundige ontwikkeling van den Zuid Afrikanse Republiek onder Krueger en Leyds. Amsterdam, 1925.
Afr 609.25.5 Boyce, W.D. Illustrated Africa. Chicago, 1925.
Afr 5960.2.5 Bravo Carbonell, J. En la selva virgen del Muni. Madrid, 1925.

Afr 5405.109.5 Brousseau, G. Souvenirs de la mission Savorgnan de Brazza. Paris, 1925.
Afr 6455.40 Curtis, Charles. P. Hunting in Africa east and west. Boston, 1925.
Afr 9614.2.3 Dale, Godfrey. Darkness or light. 3rd ed. London, 1925.
Afr 8659.25 Dawson, Wm. South Africa, people, places, problems. N.Y., 1925.
Afr 2223.60 Dobrenn, Rene. L'apport économique de l'Algérie pendant la guerre. Thèse. Oran, 1925.
Afr 9400.10.5 Dornan, S.S. Pygmies and bushmen of the Kalahari. London, 1925.
Afr 1753.10.12 Dornellas, Affonso de. As armas de Ceuta. Lisboa, 1925.
Afr 1753.10.8 Dornellas, Affonso de. De Ceuta a alacacer kibir em 1923. Lisboa, 1925.
Afr 3193.25 Douin, Georges. L'Egypte de 1802 à 1804. Caire, 1925.
Afr 3207.15 Driault, E. Mohamed Aly et Napoléon, 1807-1814. Le Caire, 1925.
Afr 4070.35.5 Dugmore, A.R. The vast Sudan. N.Y., 1925.
Afr 4559.25.3 Forbes, R.T. From Red Sea to blue Nile. N.Y., 1925.
Afr 9748.582 Fraser, D. The autobiography of an African. London, 1925.
Afr 5056.123.5 French West Africa. Supplément au Catalogue des positions géographiques de l'A.O.F. Laval, 1925.
Afr 1493.76 Garcia Figueras, Tomás. Recuerdos de la campaña. Jeréz, 1925.
Afr 6143.25 Goddard, T.N. The handbook of Sierra Leone. London, 1925.
Afr 6780.10.25 Goebel, J. Afrika zu unsern Füssen. Leipzig, 1925.
Afr 2850.10F Gonni, G. Nel centenario della spedizione navale di Tripoli. Genova, 1925.
Afr 4700.20 Governo fascista nelle colonie (Somalia-Eritrea-Libia). Milano, 1925.
Afr 1738.25 Graevenitz, K.F.H.A.R. Die Tanger-Frage. Berlin, 1925.
Afr 2448.5 Grandchamp, P. Documents relatifs aux corsaires tunisiens (2 octobre 1777-4 mai 1824). Tunis, 1925.
Afr 6420.37 Great Britain. East Africa Commission. East Africa. London, 1925.
Afr 5406.225 Grossard, Jacques H. Mission de délimitation de l'Afrique. Text and plates. Paris, 1925. 2v.
Afr 7567.20 Habran, Louis. Coup d'oeil sur le problème politique et militaire du Congo belge. Bruxelles, 1925.
Afr 3300.17 Harris, Murray G. Egypt under the Egyptians. London, 1925.
Afr 3979.25.20 Harry, Myriam. La vallée des rois et des reines. Paris, 1925.
Afr 4050.15 Hassanein, A.M. The lost oases. London, 1925.
Afr 4050.15.5 Hassanein, A.M. The lost oases. N.Y., 1925.
Afr 6275.109 Hastings, Archibald Charles Gardner. Nigerian days. London, 1925.
Afr 3817.6.5 Hofmayr, Wilhelm. Die Schilluk. St. Gabriel, 1925.
X Cg Afr 1609.25.10 Horne, John. Many days in Morocco. London, 1925.
Afr 1080.1.5 Ibn Khaldun. Histoire des Berbéres et des dynasties musulmanes. Paris, 1925-27. 4v.
Afr 6565.25 Ingrams, W.H. A school history of Zanzibar. London, 1925.
Afr 2223.925 Jones, C.L. Algeria, a commercial handbook. Washington, 1925.
Afr 2749.25.10 Kerillis, Henri de. De l'Algérie au Dahomey en automobile. Paris, 1925.
Afr 2749.22.5 Killian, Conrad. Au Hoggar, mission de 1922. Paris, 1925.
Afr 2929.25 King, William Joseph Harding. Mysteries of the Libyan desert. London, 1925.
Afr 8230.3 Kruger, S.J.P. Paul Kruger amptelike briewe, 1851-1877. Pretoria, 1925.
Afr 1769.1.80 Ladreit de Lacharriere, Jacques. Le reve d'Aabd el Kerim. Paris, 1925.
Afr 5051.15.2 Lebel, A.R. L'Afrique occidentale dans la littérature française depuis 1870. Paris, 1925.
Afr 5051.15 Lebel, A.R. L'Afrique occidentale dans la littérature française depuis 1870. Thèse. Paris, 1925.
Afr 3979.25 LeCarpentier, Georges. L'Egypte moderne. Paris, 1925.
Afr 6455.45.2 Leys, Norman MacLean. Kenya. 2d ed. London, 1925.
Afr 618.10 Lindblom, G. Jakt- och faengst metoder bland afrikanska folk. Stockholm, 1925-26.
Afr 6455.135 Lloyd-Jones, William. Havash. London, 1925.
Afr 1658.48 Lopez Rienda, R. Abd-el-krim contra francia. Madrid, 1925.
Afr 6128.3.2 Luke, H.C. A bibliography of Sierra Leone. 2d ed. London, 1925.
Afr 9610.5 Mackenzie, D.R. The spirit-ridden Konde. Philadelphia, 1925.
Afr 6738.42 Mackenzie, Jean Kenyon. Black sheep. New ed. Boston, 1925.
Afr 3040.14 Mahmoud, Ibrahim Choukri. Règlements intérieurs des Chambres en Egypte. Thèse. Paris, 1925.
Afr 4559.23.10 Maydon, H.C. Simen, its heights and abysses. London, 1925.
Afr 6280.20 Meek, C.K. The northern tribes of Nigeria. London, 1925. 2v.
Afr 2974.5 Meriano, F. La questione di Giarabub. Bologna, 1925.
Afr 11572.50.180 Millin, S.G.(L). God's stepchildren. N.Y., 1925.
Afr 11572.50.110 Millin, S.G.(L). Mary Glenn. N.Y., 1925.
Afr 5765.20.5 Mission de Madagascar betsileo. Lille, 1925.
Afr 5753.7 Mondain, G. Raketaka, tableau de moeurs féminines malgaches dressé à l'aide de proverbes et de Fady. Paris, 1925.
Afr 11010.2 Nathan, Manfred. South African literature. Cape Town, 1925.
Afr 4095.18.15 Omar Toussoun, Prince. Mémoire sur l'histoire du Nil. Le Caire, 1925.
Afr 6460.15.2 Orde-Browne, G.S. The vanishing tribes of Kenya. London, 1925.
Afr 6460.15A Orde-Browne, G.S. The vanishing tribes of Kenya. Philadelphia, 1925.
Afr 5758.25F Paulin, H. Madagascar. Paris, 1925.
Afr 4259.25 Pierre-Alype, L.M. Sous la couronne de Salomon. L'empire des Negus. Paris, 1925.
Afr 1635.15 Piquet, Victor. Le peuple marocain. Paris, 1925.
Afr 1750.28.5 Pita, Carlos. Marruecos. Melilla, 1925.
Afr 2500.10.2 Poiron, M. Mémoires concernant l'état présent du Royaume de Tunis. Paris, 1925.
Afr 2500.10 Poiron, M. Mémoires concernant l'état présent du Royaume de Tunis. Thèse complémentaire présentée par Jean Serres. Paris, 1925.
Afr 4559.25 Powell, E.A. Beyond the utmost purple rim. N.Y., 1925.
Afr 718.39 Powell, E.A. The map that is half unrolled. N.Y., 1925.
Afr 628.225.15 Price, W. The Negro around the world. N.Y., 1925.
Afr 5056.125 Proust, Louis. Visions d'Afrique. Paris, 1925.

1925 - cont.

Afr 1493.70 — Rebellon Dominguez, G. Seis meses en Yebala. Madrid, 1925.
Afr 2260.16 — René-Eugène, P. Les grandes sociétés et la colonisation dans l'Afrique du Nord. Thèse. Alger, 1925.
Afr 1620.15 — Ricard, Prosper. Le Maroc. 3e ed. Paris, 1925.
Afr 3275.17.5 — Rotshtein, F.A. Zakhvat i zakabalenie Egipta. Moscow, 1925.
Afr 1738.23F — Rouard De Card, E. Le statut de Tanger d'après la convention du 18 decembre 1923. Paris, 1925.
Afr 5180.31 — Rouch, J. Sur les côtes du Sénégal et de la Guinée. Paris, 1925.
Afr 5119.25 — Sabatie, A. Le Sénégal. Saint-Louis, 1925.
Afr 715.3.25 — Schweinfurth, G. Afrikanisches Skizzenbuch. Berlin, 1925.
Afr 8340.18.5 — Selborne, W.W.P. The Selborne memorandum. London, 1925.
Afr 1550.33 — Semard, Pierre. Marokko. Hamburg, 1925.
Afr 1200.63 — Serres, Jean. La politique turque en Afrique du Nord sous la Monarchie de Juillet. Paris, 1925.
Afr 1200.63.2 — Serres, Jean. La politique turque en Afrique du Nord sous le Monarchie de Juillet. Thèse. Paris, 1925.
Afr 6720.25.5 — Sholaster, H. Bischof Heinrich Vieter. Limburg, 1925.
Afr 11797.41.100A — Smith, Pauline. The little karoo. N.Y., 1925.
Afr 2223.55 — Société des Fermes Françaises de Tunisie. Vingt-cinq ans de colonisation nord-africaine. Paris, 1925.
Afr Doc 4312.125 — South Africa. Parliament. Official language of the Union Bill. Cape Town, 1925.
Afr 1753.13 — Sureda Blanes, F. Aby la herculana. Calpe, 1925.
Afr 1826.5.9 — Taillart, C. L'Algerie dans la litterature française, essai de bibliog. Paris, 1925.
Afr 1826.5.7 — Taillart, C. L'Algerie dans la litterature française. Paris, 1925.
Afr 1826.5 — Taillart, C. L'Algerie dans la litterature française. Thèse. Paris, 1925.
Afr 1826.5.5 — Taillart, C. L'Algerie dans la litterature française. Thèse. Paris, 1925.
Afr 7815.14 — Torday, Emil. On the trail of the Bushongo. London, 1925.
Afr 5406.225.5 — Vassal, Gabrielle M. Life in French Congo. London, 1925.
Afr 8252.20 — Walker, E.A. Lord de Villiers and his times. London, 1925.
Afr 6541.12 — Willis, John Jameson. An African church in building. London, 1925.
Afr 8045.10 — Winship, Thomas. Law and practice of arbitration in South Africa. Durban, 1925.

1926

Afr 6292.9.5 — Ahmed ibn Fartua. History of the first twelve years of the reign of Mai Idris Alooma of Bornu. Lagos, 1926.
Afr 7809.26 — Barns, T.A. An African eldorado, the Belgian Congo. London, 1926.
Afr 1273.926 — Bernard, A. L'Afrique du Nord pendant la guerre. Paris, 1926.
Afr 555.39.10 — Bestier, G.G. L'apôtre du Congo, Monseigneur Augouard. Paris, 1926.
Afr 5247.25 — Bonnier, Gaetan. L'occupation de Tombouctou. Paris, 1926.
Afr 8110.10A — Botha, C.G. Social life in the Cape colony in the 18th century. Cape Town, 1926.
Afr 7809.17 — Briey, Renaud de. Le sphinx noir. Paris, 1926.
Afr 9400.5 — Brown, John. Among the Bantu nomads. London, 1926.
Afr 575.22 — Brunel, René. Essai sur la confrérie religieuse des Aissaoua au Maroc. Thèse. Paris, 1926.
Afr 2749.22.10 — Buchanan, Angus. Sahara. London, 1926.
Afr 6138.26 — Butt-Thompson, F.W. Sierra Leone in history and tradition. London, 1926.
Afr 5760.7 — Cailliet, E. Essai sur la psychologie du Hovas. Thèse. Paris, 1926.
Afr 2929.26.5F — Calzini, R. Da Leptis Magna a Gadames. Milano, 1926.
Afr 8835.5 — Cape Town. The Cape of Good Hope. 4. ed. Cape Town, 1926.
Afr 4368.12 — Cassinari, E. Il beato Ghebre-Michael. Roma, 1926.
Afr 4368.12.5 — Catholic Church. Litterae apostolicae quibus venerabilis dei Fain Abba Ghebec Michael. Romae, 1926.
Afr 3745.20 — Cheibany, A.K. La situation administrative et économique du Soudan anglo-égyptien. These. Paris, 1926.
Afr 555.50 — Cooksey, J.J. The land of the vanished church. London, 1926.
Afr 4368.10 — Coulbeaux, J.B. Vers la lumière. 2e ed. Paris, 1926.
Afr 4559.26 — Darley, Henry. Slaves and ivory. London, 1926.
Afr 5054.25 — Delafosse, M. Histoire de l'Afrique occidentale française. Paris, 1926.
Afr 3069.26 — Devonshire, H.C. L'Egypte musulmane et les fondateurs de ses monuments. Paris, 1926.
Afr 3207.13 — Douin, Georges. Mohamed Aly, pacha du Caire, 1805-1807. Caire, 1926.
Afr 3215.3.5 — Douin, Georges. Les premières frégates de Mohamed Aly (1824-27). Caire, 1926.
Afr 1738.26 — Durand, Raphael. Le probleme de Tanger. Thèse. Aix-en-provence, 1926.
Afr 3978.69.15 — Eca de Queiroz, J.M. O Egypto, notas de viagem. Porto, 1926.
Afr 1573.24 — España, Juan de. La actuacion de España en Marruecos. Madrid, 1926.
Afr 4700.26 — Federzoni, L. Venti mesi di azione coloniale. Milano, 1926.
Afr 7175.17 — Ferreira Pinto, J. Angola. Lisboa, 1926.
Afr 6275.28 — Fraser, Douglas C. Impressions - Nigeria 1925. London, 1926.
Afr 6109.10 — Gambia. Laws, statutes, etc. A revised edition of the ordinances of the colony of Gambia. London, 1926. 2v.
Afr 1721.9 — Garcia Figueras, T. Temas de protectorado. Ceuta, 1926.
Afr 1750.6.5 — Garcia Pérez, Antonio. Heroicos infantes en Marruecos. Madrid, 1926.
Afr 628.225.10 — Garvey, Marcus. Philosophy and opinions, or Africa for the Africans. v.2. 2d ed. N.Y., 1926.
Afr 1750.32 — Ghirelli, A. El norte de Marruecos. Melilla, 1926.
Afr 4700.26.5 — Gibello Socca, G. Colonie d italia e colonie ex-germaniche d'Africa. Milano, 1926.
Afr 5074.25 — Gillier, L. La pénétration en Mauritanie. Paris, 1926.
Afr 555.39.15 — Goyan, Georges. Monseigneur Augouard. Paris, 1926.
Afr 6887.11 — Gutmann, B. Das Recht der Dschagga. München, 1926.
Afr 6275.6 — Hastings, A.C.G. The voyage of the Dayspring. London, 1926.
Afr 1259.26 — Hawkes, C.P. Mauresques, with some Basque and Spanish cameos. London, 1926.
Afr 1658.28 — Hernandez Mir, F. Del desastre à la victoria 1921-1926. v.1-4. Madrid, 1926-27. 4v.
Afr 2220.12.5 — Heywood, C. Algeria and Tunisia. Paris, 1926.

1926 - cont.

Afr 9445.15 — Hole, Hugh Marshall. The making of Rhodesia. London, 1926.
Afr 2285.20 — Hull, E.M. Camping in the Sahara. London, 1926.
Afr 4700.26.10 — Italy. Ministero delle Colonie. Notizia generali sulla colonie italiane. Roma, 1926.
Afr 3718.15 — Jackson, H.C. Osman Digna. London, 1926.
Afr 9165.42 — Johannesburg Publicity Association. Johannesburg's 40th birthday, Sept. 22, 1926. Johannesburg, 1926.
Afr 9854.10 — Johnson, William Percival. My African reminiscences. Westminster, 1926.
Afr 6498.30 — Jones, Herbert G. Uganda in transformation, 1876-1926. London, 1926.
Afr 2438.21 — Jung, Eugene. Les réformes en Tunisie. Paris, 1926.
Afr 4280.15 — Kammerer, A. Essai sur l'histoire antique d'Abyssinie. Paris, 1926.
Afr 8835.35 — Laidler, Percy Ward. A tavern of the ocean. Cape Town, 1926.
Afr 2508.10 — Langer, W.L. The European power and the French occupation of Tunis, 1878-1881. n.p., 1926.
Afr 555.23.12 — Laveille, E. L'évangile au centre de l'Afrique. Louvain, 1926.
Afr 6455.45.3 — Leys, Norman MacLean. Kenya. 3d ed. London, 1926.
Afr 6314.25 — Lloyd-Jones, W. K.A.R.; being an unofficial account of...the King's African Rifles. London, 1926.
Afr 3979.26 — Lorin, Henri. L'Egypte d'aujourd hui, le pays et les hommes. Cairo, 1926.
Afr 1609.25.5 — Magrini, L. Marocco. Milano, 1926.
Afr 6192.32 — Marie Louise, Princess. Letters from the Gold Coast. London, 1926.
Afr 5051.25 — Martonne, E. de. Inventaire méthodique des cartes et croquis...relatifs á l'Afrique occidentale. Laval, 1926.
Afr 5392.2 — Marty, Paul. Etudes sur l'islam au Dahomey. Paris, 1926.
Afr 8110.22 — Merwe, J.P. van der. Die kaap onder die Bataafse republiek, 1803-1806. Amsterdam, 1926.
Afr 1658.18 — Michaux-Bellaire, Ed. Apuntes para la historia del Rif. Madrid, 1926.
Afr 6143.26 — Migeod, Frederick W. A view of Sierra Leone. London, 1926.
Afr 8659.26.5 — Millin, S.G. The South Africans. London, 1926.
Afr 7459.26 — Mills, Dorothy. Through Liberia. London, 1926.
Afr 3040.1.5 — Moharram, H. Modes de l'acquisition de la nationalité égyptienne. Thèse. Paris, 1926.
Afr 8252.5.15 — Molteno, J.T. Further South African recollections. London, 1926.
Afr 7175.18 — Morton de Matas. A provincia de Angola. Porto, 1926.
Afr 1990.4.10 — Moulis, R.F. Le ministère de l'Algérie (24 juin 1858-24 nov. 1860). Thèse. Alger, 1926.
Afr 9446.33 — Mziki. 'Mlimo. Pietermaritzburg, 1926.
Afr 8659.26 — Nathan, M. South Africa from within. London, 1926.
Afr 1658.39 — Nearing, Scott. Stopping at war. N.Y., 1926.
Afr 1609.26.15 — Odinot, Paul. Le monde marocain. Paris, 1926.
Afr 8305.10 — Omeara, W.A.J. Kekewich in Kimberley. London, 1926.
Afr 1609.26.10 — Ossendowski, F. The fire of desert folk. London, 1926.
Afr 1571.19 — Perrot, Raymond de. The golden road. London, 1926.
Afr 4394.3.11 — Pini, Cesare G. Adua, brevi cenni sulla guerra italo-etiopica mahdista degli anni 1895-96. Torino, 1926.
Afr 4559.26.5 — Pollera, Alberto. Lo stato etiopico e la sua chiesa. Roma, 1926.
Afr 1259.25.10 — Powell, E.A. In Barbary, Tunisia, Algeria, Morocco, and the Sahara. N.Y., 1926.
Afr 3979.26.5 — Quibell, Annie. A wayfarer in Egypt. Boston, 1926.
Afr 550.8.40 — Renard, E. Lavigerie. Paris, 1926.
Afr 9489.26 — Rhodesia, Southern. Department of Agriculture and Lands. Southern Rhodesia. Salisbury, 1926.
Afr 2870.11 — Rinascita della Tripolitania. Milano, 1926.
Afr 2762.12 — Rodd, Francis R. People of the veil. London, 1926.
Afr 861.10 — Rogers, Rose A. The lonely island. London, 1926.
Afr 555.55 — Roome, William J.W. London, 1926.
Afr 8252.21 — Sampson, Victor. My reminiscences. London, 1926.
Afr 6686.25 — Samuel, Ferjus. La muse en valeur du Togo sous le mandat français. Thèse. Paris, 1926.
Afr 1750.22 — Sangroniz, Jose Antonio De. Marruecos, sus condiciones fisicas. 2 ed. Madrid, 1926.
Afr 1658.49 — Santiago Guerrero, M. La columna saro en la campana de alhucemas. Barcelona, 1926.
Afr 1609.25 — Sheean, V. Adventures among the Riffi. London, 1926.
Afr 1609.25.3A — Sheean, V. An american among the Riffi. N.Y., 1926.
Afr 4559.26.13 — Simertz, S. En färd tell Abessinien. 2a upp. Stockholm, 1926.
Afr 609.26 — Smith, Edwin. The golden stool, some aspects of the conflict of cultures in modern Africa. London, 1926.
Afr 550.16 — Smith, Edwin W. The Christian mission in Africa. London, 1926.
Afr 6599.2 — Smith, Herbert Maynard. Frank, bishop of Zanzibar. London, 1926.
Afr 4790.10.30F — Somaliland, Italian. Monografia delle regioni della Somalia. v.1-3 and plates. Torino, 1926-27.
Afr Doc 4312.126 — South Africa. Parliament. Mines and work act. Cape Town, 1926.
Afr 7175.15.10 — Statham, J.C.B. With my wife across Africa by canoe and caravan. 2d. ed. London, 1926.
Afr 1200.70 — Steeg, Theodore. La paix française en Afrique du Nord, en Algérie, au Maroc. Paris, 1926.
Afr 6455.44 — Streeter, D.W. Denatured Africa. N.Y., 1926.
Afr 7809.26.5 — Strickland, Diana. Through the Belgian Congo. London, 1926.
Afr 3674.2 — Sudan. The sub-mamur's handbook. Khartoum, 1926.
Afr 6280.11.10 — Talbot, P.A. The peoples of southern Nigeria. London, 1926. 4v.
Afr 1609.26.5 — Terhorst, Bernd. With the Riff Kabyles. London, 1926.
Afr 1658.23 — Thyen, Maurice. Trois mois de colonne sur le front riffian, juin a sept. 1925. Paris, 1926.
Afr 2929.26 — Traglia, Gustavo. Il Duce libico. Bari, 1926.
Afr 3979.26.12 — Traz, Robert de. Le depaysement oriental. 7.ed. Paris, 1926.
Afr 2710.10 — Vermale, Paul. Au Sahara pendant la guerre europèenne. Alger, 1926.
Afr 6879.26 — White, Stewart E. Lions in the path. Garden City, 1926.
Afr 2209.26 — Wilson, Albert. Rambles in North Africa. Boston, 1926.
Afr 2438.15 — Winkler, Pierre. Essai sur la nationalité dans les protectorats de Tunisie et du Maroc. Thèse. Paris, 1926.
Afr 2948.16 — Zoli, Corrado. Nel Fezzan. Milano, 1926.

1927

Afr 5260.20 Abadie, Maurice. La colonie du Niger. Paris, 1927.
Afr 1769.1.5 Abd Al-Karim. Memoiren. Dresden, 1927.
Afr 1769.1 Abd El-Krim. Memoires d'Abd-el-Krim. 5e ed. Paris, 1927.
Afr 1259.27.10F Afrique du Nord, Algérie, Tunisie, Maroc. Paris, 1927.
Afr 2209.27.40 Algerian State Railways. The mountain, the sea, Roman ruins, the desert. Algiers, 1927.
Afr 1259.27 Anderson, I. From Corsair to Riffian. Boston, 1927.
Afr 4700.27.15 Angelini, G. La politica coloniale italiana dalle sue origini ad oggi. Messina, 1927.
Afr 7176.7.10 Angola. Governor General, 1923-1927 (Ferreira). A situação de Angola. Luanda, 1927.
Afr 6292.82.10 Backwell, H.F. The occupation of Hausaland, 1900-1904. Lagos, 1927.
Afr 7565.14 Banning, Emile. Mémoires politiques et diplomatiques. Paris, 1927.
Afr 1635.8 Barrows, D.P. Berbers and blacks. N.Y., 1927.
Afr 7570.15 Belgium. Ministère de la Défense Nationale. Etat-Major Général de l'Armée. Les campagnes coloniales belges, 1914-1918. Bruxelles, 1927-1929. 2v.
Afr 609.27 Bernard, Marc. En hydravion au-dessus du continent noir. Paris, 1927.
Afr 3988.5A Blackman, Winifred Susan. The fellahin of Upper Egypt. London, 1927.
Afr 2209.27.10 Bodley, R.V.C. Algeria from within. London, 1927.
Afr 7809.24.5 Bradley, M.H. Caravans and cannibals. N.Y., 1927.
Afr 8140.15 Brookes, E.H. The history of native policy in South Africa. 2d ed. Pretoria, 1927.
Afr 8140.19 Brookes, E.H. The political future of South Africa. Pretoria, 1927.
Afr 9614.10 Bulley, Mary Winifred. Kabanza; a story of Africa. Westminster, 1927.
Afr 6455.46 Buxton, Mary Aline B. Kenya days. London, 1927.
Afr 4747.1 Calciatti, C. Nel paese dei Cunama, 1922-23. Milano, 1927.
Afr 6192.23 Cardinall, Allan W. In Ashanti and beyond. London, 1927.
Afr 2209.27.35 Chevrillon, A. Les puritains du désert. Paris, 1927.
Afr 6333.27 Church, Archibald. East Africa, a new dominion. London, 1927.
Afr 7188.109 O coronel João de Almeida. Lisboa, 1927.
Afr 609.26.15 Court Treatt, S. Cape to Cairo. Boston, 1927.
Afr 9500.5 Cripps, A.S. An Africa for Africans. London, 1927.
Afr 6390.32 Czernin, Ottokar G. Mein afrikanisches Tagebuch. Zürich, 1927.
Afr 630.8.10 Delafosse, Maurice. Les Nègres. Paris, 1927.
Afr 2749.27.5 Deloncle, P.E.M.J. La caravane aux éperons verts (Mission Alger-Niger). Paris, 1927.
Afr 4070.39 Domville Fife, C.W. Savage life in the dark Sudan. London, 1927.
Afr 3215.3.10 Douin, Georges. La maison du baron de Boislecomte. Cairo, 1927.
Afr 3215.2 Driault, E. La formation de l'empire de Mohamed Aly de l'Arabie au Sudan (1814-1823). Paris, 1927.
Afr 8808.61.5 Duff-Gordon, Lucie. Letters from the Cape. London, 1927.
Afr 6455.45.10 Eastman, G. Chronicles of an African trip. Rochester, 1927.
Afr 6282.6 Ellis, James Joseph. Two missionary heroines in Africa. Kilmarnock, 1927.
Afr 1259.27.20A Erskine, Beatrice. Vanished cities of northern Africa. Boston, 1927.
Afr 8160.16 Ewart, J.S. British foreign policy and the next war. The Zulu war. Ottawa, 1927.
Afr 8252.194 Fairbridge, K. The autobiography of Kingsley Fairbridge. London, 1927.
Afr 2819.27 Firaud, L.C. Annales tripolitaines. Tunis, 1927.
Afr 7809.27 Fraser, D.C. Through the Congo basin. London, 1927.
Afr 550.15 Fraser, Donald. The new Africa. London, 1927.
Afr 2209.27 Gajon, Edmond. En Algérie avec la France. Paris, 1927.
Afr 1080.10 Gautier, Emile F. L'islamisation de l'Afrique du Nord. Les siècles obscures du Maghreb. Paris, 1927.
Afr 2232.8 Goichon, A. La vie féminine au Mzab. Paris, 1927. 2v.
Afr 9078.50 Goldman, P.L.A. Transvaal Archief. Pretoria, 1927.
Afr 1640.5 Goulven, J. Les Mellah de Rabat-Sale. Paris, 1927.
Afr 6460.85 Great Britain. Colonial Office. Indians in Kenya. London, 1927.
Afr 1869.27 Gsell, S. Histoire d'Algerie. Paris, 1927.
Afr 4700.27.10 Guyot, Georges. L'Italie devant le problème colonial. Roma, 1927.
Afr 715.15 Haardt, G.M. The black journey across central Africa. N.Y., 1927.
Afr 715.15.5 Haardt, G.M. La croisière noire, expédition citroen central-Afrique. Paris, 1927.
Afr 2209.27.5 Hafsa. Desert winds. N.Y., 1927.
Afr 5247.20A Hall, Leland. Timbuctoo. N.Y., 1927.
Afr 500.11.5 Harris, N.D. Europe and Africa. Boston, 1927.
Afr 1658.50 Harris, W.B. France, Spain and the rif. London, 1927.
Afr 6275.29 Hayward, A.H.W. Sport and service in Africa. Philadelphia, 1927.
Afr 4790.10.15 Haywood, C.W. To the mysterious Lorian Swamp. London, 1927.
Afr 6095.38 Henry, Warren. The confessions of a tenderfoot coaster, a trader's chronicle of life on the west African coast. London, 1927.
Afr 4559.27.5 Hodson, A.W. Seven years in southern Abyssinia. London, 1927.
Afr 11456.77.814 Horn, Alfred A. Life and works of Alfred A. Horn. London, 1927. 5v.
Afr 11456.77.810A Horn, Alfred A. Trader Horn. N.Y., 1927.
Afr 11456.77.812 Horn, Alfred A. Trader Horn. N.Y., 1927.
Afr 1658.27 Hubert, Jacques. L'aventure riffaine et ses dessous politiques. Paris, 1927.
Afr 1738.01 Hudson, Manley O. The international mixed court of Tangier. n.p., 1927.
Afr 4700.27.5 Istituto Agricolo Coloniale Italiano. Per le nostre colonie. Firenze, 1927.
Afr 550.8.35 Jammes, F. Lavigerie. Paris, 1927.
Afr 7315.20.5 Junod, H.A. The life of a South African tribe. 2d ed. London, 1927. 2v.
Afr 3269.15 Kleine, Mathilde. Deutschland und die ägyptische Frage. Greifswald, 1927.
Afr 8677.25.5 Koch, M.H. An analysis of the finances of the Union of South Africa. Cape Town, 1927.
Afr 4025.18 Lachanokardes, E. Palaia kai nea Alexandreia. Alexandreia, 1927.
Afr 679.27 Larsen, K. Krøniker fra Guines. Hellerup, 1927.

1927 - cont.

Afr 1658.25 Laure, August M.E. La victoire franco-espagnole dans le Rif. Paris, 1927.
Afr 1571.18 Leclerc, Max. Au Maroc avec Lyautey. Paris, 1927.
Afr 8835.25.2 Lewis, C. Cape Town. Cape Town, 1927.
Afr 555.24.9 Light and darkness in East Africa. London, 1927.
Afr 1571.17.2 Lyautey, L.H.G. Paroles d'action. Paris, 1927.
Afr 8250.21 McDonald, J.G. Rhodes, a life. London, 1927.
Afr 1259.27.5 McLaurin, Hamish. What about North Africa. N.Y., 1927.
Afr 8678.32 MacMillan, W.M. The Cape colour question, a historical survey. London, 1927.
Afr 3040.20 Makram, Hilmy. Problèmes soulevés par la constitution égyptienne. Thèse. Dijon, 1927.
Afr 1878.10 Marchika, Jean. La peste en Afrique septentrionale. Alger, 1927.
Afr 6460.20 Massam, J.A. The cliff dwellers of Kenya. London, 1927.
Afr 555.20.7 Maxwell, J. Lowry. Nigeria, the land, the people and Christian progress. London, 1927.
Afr 2929.27 Mori, Attilio. L'esplorazione geografica della Libia. Firenze, 1927.
Afr 8809.27 Mossop, E.E. Old Cape highways. Cape Town, 1927.
Afr 4559.27.10 Mueller, Otto. Rings um den Tschertischer. Hannover, 1927.
Afr 8678.28 Olivier, S.H.O. The anatomy of African misery. London, 1927.
Afr 2209.27.34 Ossendowski, F.A. Oasis and simoon. N.Y., 1927.
Afr 1658.29 Pech Soff, Zinovi. La legion étrangere au Maroc. Paris, 1927.
Afr 6390.43 Pulitzer, Ralph. Diary of two safaris. N.Y., 1927.
Afr 6194.10.5 Rattray, R.S. Religion and art in Ashanti. Oxford, 1927.
Afr 1738.24 Raymond, Chas. Le statut de Tanger. Alger, 1927.
Afr 4559.27 Rey, Charles F. In the country of the blue Nile. London, 1927.
Afr Doc 3807.326.5 Rhodesia, Southern. Census Office. Report of the director of Census regarding the Census taken on the 4th May 1926. Salisbury, 1927.
Afr 861.10.2 Rogers, Rose A. The lonely island. London, 1927.
Afr 550.17 Roome, W.J.W. Can Africa be won? London, 1927.
Afr 6420.5 Ross, W.M. Kenya from within. London, 1927. 2v.
Afr 1573.25 Ruiz Albeniz, V. Tanger y la colaboracion franco-española en Marruecos. Madrid, 1927.
Afr 3979.27 Rydh, H. Solskivans land. Stockholm, 1927.
Afr 6720.10 Seitz, Theodor. Vom Aufstieg und Niederbruck deutscher Kolonialmacht. Karlsruhe, 1927-29. 3v.
Afr 1738.27 Sibieude, Jean. La question de Tanger. Thèse. Montpellier, 1927.
Afr 8678.30 Silburn, P.A. South Africa, white and black or brown. London, 1927.
Afr 1280.50 Slouschz, Nahum. Travels in North Africa. Philadelphia, 1927.
Afr 7330.10 Sousa e Silva, Pedro. Distrito de Tete. Lisboa, 1927.
Afr Doc 4312.127 South Africa. Parliament. Precious stones bill. Cape Town, 1927.
Afr 4070.37.2 Streeter, D.W. Camels. N.Y., 1927.
Afr 4070.38 Streeter, D.W. Camels. N.Y., 1927.
Afr 6455.44.5 Streeter, D.W. Denatured Africa. N.Y., 1927.
Afr 6280.11.15 Talbot, P.A. Some Nigerian fertility cults. London, 1927.
Afr 5243.125.15 Tauxier, Louis. La religion bambara. Paris, 1927.
Afr 2285.21 The Paris Lyons and Mediterranean Railway Co. Algeria...season 1927-28. Algiers, 1927.
Afr 5758.27 Thorel, Jean. La mise en valeur des richesses économiques de Madagascar. Thèse. Paris, 1927.
Afr 4700.27.20 Vecchi, B.V. Satto il soffio del monsone. Milano, 1927.
Afr 1259.27.25 Vernon, M. Sands, palms and minarets. London, 1927.
Afr 1609.27 Vernon, Paul E. Morocco from a motor. London, 1927.
Afr 4700.27 Virgilli, Filippo. Le colonie italiane. Milano, 1927.
Afr 1083.10 Vonderheyden, M. La Berbérie orientale sous la dynastie des Benou'l-Arlab (800-909). Thèse. Paris, 1927.
Afr 8235.14 Wued, Johannes Andreas. Die Rolle der Biurenrepubliken in der auswaertigen und kolonialen Politik des deutschen Reiches, 1883-1900. Nürnberg, 1927.
Afr 3285.22 Yeghen, Foulad. Saad Zaghloul. Paris, 1927.
NEDL Afr 3199.27 Young, George. Egypt. N.Y., 1927.
Afr 8659.25.8 Zachariah, O. Travel in South Africa. 3d ed. Johannesburg, 1927.
Afr 4790.10.27 Zoli, C. Oltre Giuba. Roma, 1927.
Afr 4790.10.25 Zoli, C. Oltre Giuba. Roma, 1927.
Afr 4790.10.26 Zoli, C. Oltre Giuba. Supplemento. Roma, 1927.

1928

Afr 8180.20A Agar-Hamilton, J.A. von. The native policy of the Voortrekkers. Cape Town, 1928.
Afr 609.28.15 Appel, Joseph Herbert. Africa's white magic. N.Y., 1928.
Afr 4070.49 Assher, B. A nomad in the south Sudan. London, 1928.
Afr 7809.28 Auric, Henri. L'avenir du Congo et du Congo-océan. Thèse. Paris, 1928.
Afr 7020.30 Ayres d'Ornellas. Viagem do principe real julho-setembro 1907. Lisboa, 1928.
Afr 4742.22 Baralta, M. Atlante delle colonie italiane. Novara, 1928.
Afr 7175.20 Barns, T. Alexander. Angolian sketches. London, 1928.
Afr 4559.28.5 Baum, James E. Savage Abyssinia. London, 1928.
Afr 2731.5 Becker, Georges. La pénétration française au Sahara. Un transsaharien? Paris, 1928.
Afr 4700.28 Beguinot, F. La nostra aurora coloniale. Imperia, 1928.
Afr 1200.75.4 Benoist, Charles. La question méditerranéenne. Paris, 1928.
Afr 9400.10.10 Bleek, D.F. The Naron, a bushman tribe of central Kalahari. Cambridge, 1928.
Afr 8028.200 Botha, C.G. The public archives of South Africa, 1652-1910. Cape Town, 1928.
Afr 555.23.51 Boucher, A. Au Congo français. Les missions catholiques. Paris, 1928.
Afr 4259.28 Budge, E.A. A history of Ethiopia, Nubia and Abyssinia. London, 1928. 2v.
Afr 6333.28 Buell, R.L. The destiny of East Africa. N.Y., 1928.
Afr 210.28A Buell, Raymond Lesley. The native problem in Africa. N.Y., 1928. 2v.
Afr 9502.10 Bullock, Charles. The Mashona. Cape Town, 1928.
Afr 1408.2.10 Busnot, F.D. Récits d'aventures au temps de Louis XIV. Paris, 1928.
Afr 2749.27 Cameron, Donald R. A Saharan venture. London, 1928.
Afr 5749.28 Camo, Pierre A. Peinture de Madagascar. Paris, 1928.
Afr 4700.25 Cantalupe, R. L'Italia musulmana. Roma, 1928.

1928 - cont.

Afr 4025.10 Carnoy, Norbert. La colonie française du Caire. These. Paris, 1928.
Afr 4559.28.10 Cerulli, E. Etiopia occidentale. Roma, 1928. 2v.
Afr 5993.20 Ceruti, Frorencio. Africa la virgen. Santander, 1928.
Afr 4700.28.10 Cesari, Cesare. I nostri precursori coloniale. Roma, 1928.
Afr 4259.28.5F Conti Rossini, Carlo. Storia d'Etiopia. Pt.1. Milano, 1928.
Afr 9558.85 Coupland, R. Kirk on the Zambesi. Oxford, 1928.
Afr 7122.50 Cruz, D. da. A crise de Angola. Lisboa, 1928.
Afr 2945.35 Cyrenaica. Camera di Commercio, Industria ed Agricultura. La Cirenaica. Bengasi, 1928.
Afr 1658.30 Damidaux, C. Combats au Maroc 1925-1926. Paris, 1928.
Afr 6196.10 Danquah, J.B. The Akim Abwakwa handbook. London, 1928.
Afr 6194.20 Danquah, J.B. Gold Coast, Akan laws and customs. London, 1928.
Afr 2618.10 Darmon, Raoul. La situation des cultes en Tunisie. Thèse. Paris, 1928.
Afr 6420.80 Davis, Alexander. Chronicles of Kenya. London, 1928.
Afr 2025.31.5 Depont, O. L'Algerie du centenaire. Paris, 1928.
Afr 3207.17 Douin, Georges. L'Angleterre et l'Egypte. Paris, 1928.
Afr 8678.9F Duggan-Cronin, A.M. The Bantu tribes of South Africa. Cambridge, Eng., 1928- 3v.
Afr 3275.41 Elgood, P.G. The transit of Egypt. London, 1928.
Afr 1609.28 Elsner, Eleanor. The magic of Morocco. London, 1928.
Afr 5749.28.5 Esmenard, J. L'ile rouge. Paris, 1928.
Afr 8659.28 Fairbridge, D. The pilgrims' way in South Africa. London, 1928.
Afr 1550.37 Felix, Lucien. Le statut international du Maroc d'après les traités. Thèse. Paris, 1928.
Afr 6720.28 Ferrandi, Jean. Conquête du Cameroun-Nord, 1914-1915. Paris, 1928.
Afr 2313.5 Ferrendier, M. La population musulmane de Blida. Thèse. Blois, 1928.
Afr 9149.28 Figulus, Jiri V. J.V. Figulus a jeho Africka dobrodruzstvi. Praha, 1928. 2 pam.
Afr 9558.55 Finger, Charles J. David Livingstone, explorer and prophet. Garden City, N.Y., 1928.
Afr 2755.2 Foucaucourt, J. de. De l'Algérie au Soudan par le Sahara. 5000 kilomètres en automobile dans le désert et la brousse. Paris, 1928.
Afr 2280.10 Franc, Julien. La colonisation de la Milidja. Thèse. Paris, 1928.
Afr 1830.30.4 Franc, Julien. La colonisation de la Mitidja. Paris, 1928.
Afr 1826.25 Franc, Julien. L'histoire de la colonie de l'Algérie, sources d'archives. Thèse. Alger, 1928.
Afr 7809.28.5 Franck, Louis. Le Congo belge. Bruxelles, 1928. 2v.
Afr 1878.5 Gallico, Augusto. Tunisi i berberi e l'Italia nei secoli. Ancona, 1928.
Afr 5640.15.5 Gallieni, J.S. Lettres de Madagascar, 1896-1905. Paris, 1928.
Afr 8355.20 Gandhi, Mohandas K. Satyagraha in South Africa. Madras, 1928.
Afr 2945.26.10 Gaslini, Mario dei. Col generale Cantore alla caccia del Gran Senusso. Milano, 1928.
Afr 2230.35 Gaudry, Mathéa. La femme Chaouia de l'Aurès. Thèse. Paris, 1928.
Afr 2749.23.5 Gautier, E.F. Le Sahara avec 10 figures et 26 illustrations hors texte. Paris, 1928.
Afr 3040.45 Georges-Gaulis, B. Le nationalisme égyptien. Nancy, 1928.
Afr 2819.28 Ghisleri, A. La Libia nella storia e nei viaggiatori dai tempi omerici all'occupazione italiana. Torino, 1928.
Afr 3193.15 Ghorbal, Shafik. The beginnings of the Egyptian question and the rise of Mehemet Ali. London, 1928.
Afr 6192.25.5 Gold Coast handbook, 1928. London, 1928.
Afr 55.34 Gollock, Georgina Anne. Sons of Africa. London, 1928.
Afr 1750.35 Gomez, Vitaliano. En la hora de la paz, Marruecos, 1924-29. Tetuan, 1928.
Afr 1608.98.10 Graham, R.B.C. Mogreb-el-Acksa. London, 1928.
Afr 609.28.10 Gray, Frank. My two African journeys. London, 1928.
Afr 3204.18 Guenard, Gabriel. Aventuriers mameluks d'Egypte. Toulouse, 1928.
Afr 3979.28A Hall, Trowbridge. Egypt in silhouette. N.Y., 1928.
Afr 4559.28.20 Hentze, W. Volldampf unter Palmen. Leipzig, 1928.
Afr 9489.28 Hole, Hugh Marshall. Old Rhodesian days. London, 1928.
Afr 11456.77.800 Horn, Alfred A. Trader horn. N.Y., 1928.
Afr 11456.77.805 Horn, Alfred A. Trader Horn. v.2. "Harold the Webbed." N.Y., 1928.
Afr 1035.5 Institut des Hautes Etudes Marocaines. Memorial Henri Basset. v.1-2. Paris, 1928. 2v.
Afr 4700.28.15 Italy. Ministero delle Colonie. Ordinamento amministrativo-contabile per l'Eritrea e per la Somalia. Roma, 1928.
Afr 608.91.3 Jaeger, F. Afrika. 3. Aufl. Leipzig, 1928.
Afr 699.28 Jaelson, F.S. Eastern Africa to-day. London, 1928.
Afr 6455.39.5 Johnson, M. Safari. N.Y., 1928.
Afr 5235.128.25 Lamande, André. La vie de René Caillié. Paris, 1928.
Afr 3026.15 Larin, Henri. Bibliographie géographique de l'Egypte. Cairo, 1928-29.
Afr 5640.9 Lebon, A. La pacification de Madagascar, 1896-98. Paris, 1928.
Afr 1493.35 Loustaunau-Lacau, G. Au Maroc français en 1925. Paris, 1928.
Afr 8659.28.5 Lowth, Alys. South Africa calling. 1st ed. London, 1928.
Afr 6670.928 Luce, Edmond P. L'acte de naissance d'une république africaine autonome. Paris, 1928.
Afr 1623.927 Lucien-Graux. Le Maroc économique. Paris, 1928.
Afr 550.55 Mackenzie, J.K. Friends of Africa. Cambridge, Mass., 1928.
Afr 1340.9 Maestacci, Noel. Le Maroc contemporain. Paris, 1928.
Afr 9510.9 Maie, B. Voortrekkerslawe in donker Afrika. 2. druk. Pretoria, 1928.
Afr 3275.39 Marshall, J.E. The Egyptian enigma, 1890-1928. London, 1928.
Afr 1550.35 Martin, Alfred G.P. Le Maroc et l'Europe. Paris, 1928.
Afr 6738.20 Masson, Georges. La mise en valeur des territoires des Cameroun placés sous le mandat français. Thèse. Paris, 1928.
Afr 11572.50.150 Millin, S.G.(L). The coming of the Lord. N.Y., 1928.
Afr 7549.28 Monheim, A. Le Congo et les livres. Bruxelles, 1928.
Afr 5045.40 Morand, Paul. Paris, Tombouctou, documentaire. Paris, 1928.
Afr 6985.1 Native tribes of Southwest Africa. Cape Town, 1928.
Afr 5045.24 Ossendowski, F.A. Slaves of the sun. London, 1928.

1928 - cont.

Afr 555.29.24 Padwick, Constance Evelyn. MacKay of the great lake. London, 1928.
Afr 5219.28 Palmer, H.R. Sudanese memoirs. Lagos, 1928. 3v.
Afr 2948.10 Petragnani, Enrico. Il Sahara tripolitano. Roma, 1928.
Afr 4025.15.5 Polites, Athanasios G. O hellynismos kai i neotera Aigyptos. Alexandreia, 1928. 2v.
Afr 4394.3.8 Pollera, Alberto. La battaglia di Adua del 1 marzo 1896. Firenze, 1928.
Afr 8135.27 Preller, Gustav S. Ekelse en opstelle. Pretoria, 1928.
Afr 9499.5 Rhodesia, Southern. Progress of southern Rhodesia, 1920-27. Salisbury, 1928.
Afr 609.28 Ross, C. Mit Kamera, Kind und Kegel durch Afrika. Leipzig, 1928.
Afr 4500.20 Rouard de Card, E. L'Ethiopie auPoint de vue du droit international. Paris, 1928.
Afr 2438.30 Saada, Raoul. Essai sur l'oeuvre de la justice française en Tunisie. Paris, 1928.
Afr 7320.17 Saldanha, Eduardo d'Almeida. O Sul do Save. Lisboa, 1928-31. 2v.
Afr 1830.40.5 Schefer, Christian. La politique coloniale de la monarchie de juillet. Paris, 1928.
Afr 4559.28.15 Schrenzel, E.H. Abessinien. Berlin, 1928.
Afr 9400.10.15 Schwarz, E.H.L. The Kalahari and its native races. London, 1928.
Afr 5426.100.5 Schweitzer, Albert. On the edge of the primeval forest. London, 1928.
Afr 7459.28 Sibley, James L. Liberia, old and new. London, 1928.
Afr 7219.28 Silva, J. Guides. Colonização. Lourenço Marques, 1928.
Afr 609.26.4 Smith, Edwin. The golden stool, some aspects of the conflict of cultures in modern Africa. Garden City, N.Y., 1928.
Afr 555.22.28 Smith, Edwin W. The way of the white fields in Rhodesia. London, 1928.
Afr 4700.28.5 Stefanini, G. Le colonie. Torino, 1928.
Afr 3725.9 Symons, A.J.A. Emin, the governor of Equatoria. London, 1928.
Afr 4236.928 Symons, R. What Christianity has done for Abyssinia. London, 1928.
Afr 2288.10 Thinières, A.F.C. Le régime de la répression dans les territoires du sud de l'Algérie. Thèse. Alger, 1928.
Htn Afr 1395.25* Tratado da vida e martirio dos cinco martires de Marrocos. Coimbra, 1928.
Afr 2938.30 Tripolitania. Ufficio Studi e Propaganda. Vigor di vita in Tripolitania (anno 1928). Tripoli, 1928.
Afr 3818.4 Veenstra, Johanna. Pioneering for Christ in the Sudan. London, 1928.
Afr 8089.28A Walker, E.A. A history of South Africa. London, 1928.
Afr 8110.13 Walt, A.J.H. Die Ausdehnung der Kolonie am Kap der Guten Hoffnung (1700-1779). Inaug. Diss. Berlin, 1928.
Afr 2880.10 Zoli, C. Le operazioni libiche sul 29 parallelo nord. Roma, 1928.

1929

Afr 6390.26.10 Akeley, Mary L. Carl Akeley's Africa. N.Y., 1929.
Afr 2288.15.5 Algeria. Commissariat Général du Centenaire. Les territoires du sud de l'Algérie. 2d ed. Pt.1-3,5 et cartes. Alger, 1929-30. 5v.
Afr 8659.29 Alston, M. From an old Cape homestead. London, 1929.
Afr 609.29.20 Anderson, I. Circling Africa. Boston, 1929.
Afr 1957.8 Azan, Paul. L'expédition d'Alger. Paris, 1929.
Afr 1830.50.4 Basset, André. La langue berbère. Paris, 1929.
Afr 3280.10 Beaman, Ardern H. The dethronement of the khedive. London, 1929.
Afr 1570.54 Begue, Leon. Le secret d'une conquête. Paris, 1929.
Afr 1869.29 Bernard, Augustin. L'Algerie. Paris, 1929.
Afr 8110.18 Beyers, C. Die kaapse patriotte, 1779-1791. Kaapstad, 1929.
Afr 1609.29.5 Bickerstaffe, Lovelyn Elaine. Things seen in Morocco. N.Y., 1929.
Afr 7369.29 Boone, C.C. Liberia as I know it. Richmond, Va., 1929.
Afr 3979.29.5 Borchardt, Ludwig. Agypten. Berlin, 1929.
Afr 1658.31 Bordes, Pierre. Dans le Rif (Cornet de route d'un marsouin). Orne de gravures et de cartes. Lyon, 1929.
Afr 550.7.10 Bouniol, Joseph. The White Fathers and their missions. London, 1929.
Afr 5955.4 Bravo Carbonell, J. Territorios españoles del Golfo de Guinea. Madrid, 1929.
Afr 9045.10 Bryant, Alfred T. Olden times in Zululand and Natal. London, 1929.
Afr 6214.8 Burns, Alan C. History of Nigeria. London, 1929.
Afr 628.229.5 Cameron, Norman E. The evolution of the Negro. Georgetown, 1929-34. 2v.
Afr 9558.57 Campbell, R.J. Livingstone. London, 1929.
Htn Afr 1407.2.5* Carteret, George. The Barbary voyage of 1638. Philadelphia, 1929.
Afr 1922.10 Celarie, H. La prise d'Alger. Paris, 1929.
Afr 8659.29.5 Chelvers, H.A. The seven wonders of southern Africa. Johannesburg, 1929.
Afr 4700.29.10 Ciarlantini, F. Antologia coloniale. Roma, 1929.
Afr 1408.8 Colin, E.R. Le grand Ismail. Paris, 1929.
Afr 1738.29 Comite de Propagande et de Tourisme, Paris. Tanger. Paris, 1929.
Afr 2224.25 Common, Jacques. Le budget et le fisc algériens. Thèse. Paris, 1929.
Afr 4559.29 Conti Rossini, C. L'Abissinia. Roma, 1929.
Afr 4259.29 Coulbeaux, J.B. Histoire politique et religieuse d'Abyssinie depuis les temps les plus reculés jusqu'à l'avènement. T.1-3. Paris, 1929. 3v.
Afr 7809.29 Crokaert, J. Boula-matari. Bruxelles, 1929.
Afr 1100.2.5 Currey, E.H. Sea wolves of the Mediterranean. N.Y., 1929.
Afr 8687.174.5 Cursons, William E. Joseph Doke. Johannesburg, 1929.
Afr 5749.29 Dandouau, A. Manuel de geographie de Madagascar. 2e ed. Paris, 1929.
Afr 3193.20 Douin, Georges. L'Angleterre et l'Egypte. Caire, 1929-30. 2v.
Afr 6465.5 Dutton, E.H.T. Kenya mountain. London, 1929.
Afr 6333.29 East Africa in transition, being a review of the principles and proposals of the Commission on closer union...Eastern and Central Africa. London, 1929.
Afr 8252.25.5 Engelenburg, Frans V. General Louis Botha. London, 1929.
Afr 1550.39A Enthoven, Henri Emile. Van Tanger tot Agadir. Utrecht, 1929.
Afr 1955.47 Esquer, G. Les commencements d'un empire. Paris, 1929.
Afr 1955.40.2 Esquer, G. La prise d'Alger, 1830. Paris, 1929.

Afr 6019.29	Evans, Ifor Leslie. British in tropical Africa. Cambridge, Eng., 1929.
Afr 2870.15	Federzoni, Luigi. Rinascita dell'Africa romana. Bologna, 1929.
Afr 45.29	Fidel, Camille. Les conseils représentatifs. Bruxelles, 1929.
Afr 715.20	Flaudrau, G.C. Then I saw the Congo. N.Y., 1929.
Afr 6720.25	Franceschi, Roger. Le mandat français au Cameroun. Thèse. Paris, 1929.
Afr 7183.40	Galvão, Henrique. Huíla; relatório de governo. Vila Nova de Famalicão? 1929[1930].
Afr 1955.46	Gautherat, Gustave. La conquête de l'Alger. Paris, 1929.
Afr 3700.8	Gordon, John. My six years with the Black Watch, 1881-1887. Boston, 1929.
Afr 555.3.22	Goyan, George. Mère Javouhey, apôtre des Noirs. Paris, 1929.
Afr 9446.29	Hale, H.M. Lobengula. London, 1929.
Afr 3979.29	Hanotaux, G. Regards sur l'Egypte et la Palestine. Paris, 1929.
Afr 6292.41	Hermon-Hodge, Harry Baldwin. Gazetteer of Ilarin Province. London, 1929.
Afr 1573.29F	Hernandez de Herrera, C. Accion de España en Marruecos. v.1-2. Madrid, 1929-30. 2v.
Afr 6415.10	Hobley, C.W. Kenya, from chartered company to crown colony. London, 1929.
Afr 3300.20	Howell, Joseph M. Egypt's past, present and future. Dayton, O., 1929.
Afr 609.29	Humphrey, Seth. Loafing through Africa. Philadelphia, 1929.
Afr 7560.10	Ihle, Alexander. Das Alte Königreich Kongo. Inaug. Diss. Leipzig, 1929.
Afr 4719.29	Italy. Marina Stato Maggiore. Officio Storico. L'opera della marina in Eritrea e Somalia della occupazione...1928. Roma, 1929.
Afr 4700.29.5	Italy. Ufficio Studi e Propaganda. Le colonie italiane di diretto dominio. Roma, 1929.
Afr 7175.23	Jaspert, Willem. Through unknown Africa. London, 1929.
Afr 6879.29A	Johnson, M.E. Lion, African adventure with the king of beasts. N.Y., 1929.
Afr 2209.28	Kerr, Alfred. Die Allgier trieb nach Algier...Ausflug nach Afrika. 1.Aufl. Berlin, 1929.
Afr 8140.17	Kiewiet, C.W. de. British colonial policy and the South African republics. London, 1929.
Afr 8678.34	Kirk, J. The economic aspects of native segregation in South Africa. London, 1929.
Afr 635.20	Kroll, Hubert. Die Haustiere der Bantu. Inaug. Diss. Berlin, 1929.
Afr 5054.29.5	Lassalle-Séré, R. Le recrutement de l'armée noire. Paris, 1929.
Afr 5054.29	Lassalle-Séré, R. Le recrutement de l'armée noire. Thèse. Paris, 1929.
Afr 1965.7.5	Legras, J. Abd el-Kader. Paris, 1929.
Afr 4559.29.10	Liano, A. Ethiopie, empire des nègres blancs. Paris, 1929.
Afr 5045.15	Londres, Albert. A very naked people. N.Y., 1929.
Afr 1609.29.2	Lowth, Alys. A wayfarer in Morocco. Boston, 1929.
Afr 1609.29	Lowth, Alys. A wayfarer in Morocco. London, 1929.
Afr 4559.29.15	Lubinski, Kurt. Hochzeitreise nach Abessinien. Leipzig, 1929.
Afr 8678.32.3	MacMillan, W.M. Bantu, Boer, and Briton, the making of the South African native problem. London, 1929.
Afr 2929.29	Mandosio, Mario. Tripolitania d'oggi. Milano, 1929.
Afr 9599.29	Maugham, R.C.F. Africa as I have known it. London, 1929.
Afr 11572.50.170	Millin, S.G.(L). The fiddler. N.Y., 1929.
Afr 679.29	Mills, D.R.M. The golden land. London, 1929.
Afr 2505.10	Monchicourt, C. Relations inédites de Nyssen. Paris, 1929.
Afr 628.229	Montenegro, Alvaro de. A raça negra perante a civilisação. Lisboa, 1929.
Afr 8055.30	Neame, L.E. Some South African politicians. Cape Town, 1929.
Afr 6740.10	Nicol, Yves. La tribu des Bakoko. Thèse. Paris, 1929.
Afr 1869.29.5	Paris. Ecole Libre des Sciences Politiques. Société des Anciens Elèves. Une oeuvre française d'Algérie. Paris, 1929.
Afr 6541.27	Philippe, Antony. Au coeur de l'Afrique. Paris, 1929.
Afr 4025.15	Polites, Athanasios G. L'hellénisme et l'Egypte moderne. T.1-2. Paris, 1929-30.
Afr 7045.20	Rates, J. Carlos. Angola, Moçambique, San Tome. Edição do autor. Lisboa, 1929.
Afr 8289.29	Reitz, Deneys. Commando. London, 1929.
Afr 4320.7	Rey, Charles. The romance of the Portuguese in Abyssinia. London, 1929.
Afr 3740.16	Riker, T.W. A survey of British policy in the Fashoda crisis. N.Y., 1929.
Afr 555.150	Roome, William John Waterman. Through Central Africa for the Bible. London, 1929.
Afr 8670.9	Royal Automobile Club Of South Africa. In and out of town. Cape Town, 1929.
Afr 2710.6	Salvati, Cesare. Italia e Francia nel Sahara orientale. Milano, 1929.
Afr 3978.38.5	Sammarco, A. Il viaggio di Mohammed Ali al Sudan. Caire, 1929.
Afr 8155.12	Samuelson, Robert Charles Azariah. Long, long ago. Durban, 1929.
Afr 4559.29.5	Sander, Erich. Das Hochland von Abessinien, Habesch. Heidelberg, 1929.
Afr 7309.29F	Santos Rufino, Jose dos. Albuns fotograficos e descritivos da...colonia de Mocambique. v.1-10. Hamburgo, 1929. 5v.
Afr 5426.100.20	Schweitzer, Albert. A l'orée de la forêt vierge. Paris, 1929.
Afr 555.30	Shepherd, A. Tucker of Uganda. London, 1929.
Afr 4180.3.15	Simpson, G.E. The heart of Libya, the Siwa Oasis, its people, customs and sport. London, 1929.
Afr 679.29.5F	Singer, Caroline. White Africans and black. N.Y., 1929.
Afr 550.18.1	Smith, Edwin. Aggrey of Africa. N.Y., 1929.
Afr Doc 4312.129	South Africa. Parliament. Natives parliamentary representation bill. Cape Town, 1929.
Afr 632.18	Spannaus, Gunther. Züge aus der politischen Organisation afrikanischer Staaten und Völker. Leipzig, 1929.
Afr 4700.29	Stefanini, Giuseppe. I possedimenti italiani in Africa. 2 ed. Firenze, 1929.
Afr 8847.83	Stellenbosch. Stadsraad. Stellenbosch, 1679-1929. Stellenbosch, 1929.
Afr 6455.44.10	Streeter, D.W. Denatured Africa. Garden City, 1929.

Afr 9854.3	Tilsley, George E. Dan Crawford, missionary and pioneer in Central Africa. London, 1929.
Afr 555.12.10	Vanlande, René. Chez les pères blancs, Tunisie, Kabylie Sahara. Paris, 1929.
Afr 590.58	Verhoeven, J.C.M. Jacques de Dixmude. Bruxelles, 1929.
Afr 609.29.5	Vonhoffman, Carl. Jungle gods. London, 1929.
Afr 6198.405.5	Walker, Frank Diaville. Thomas Birch Freeman. London, 1929.
Afr 7809.29.5	Wauters, Arthur. D'Anvers à Bruxelles via le Lac Kivu. Bruxelles, 1929.
Afr 8252.326	Weinthal, Leo. Memories. London, 1929.
Afr 6879.28	Wells, Carveth. In coldest Africa. Garden City, 1929.
Afr 6883.8	Wohlab, Karl. Die Christliche Missionspredigt unter den Schambala. Inaug. Diss. Tübingen, 1929.
Afr 4226.1.10	Zanutto, Silvio. Bibliografia etiopica. v.1-2. Roma, 1929. 2v.

193-

Afr 6196.3	Adjaye, Annor. Nzima land. London, 193-?
Afr 2875.41	Dietrich, Richard. Die Tripolis-Krise, 1911-12, und die erneuerung des Dreibundes 1912. Würzburg, 193-
Afr 8659.30.20	Jannasch, Hans. Unter Buren, Briten, Bantus. Berlin, 193-.
Afr 8252.251.5	Kotze, J.G. Biographical memoirs and reminiscences. v.1. Cape Town, 193-
Afr 9165.42.41	Macmillan, Allister. Environs of the golden city and Pretoria. Capetown, 193-.
Afr 9165.42.40	Macmillan, Allister. The golden city. London, 193-.
Afr 505.43	Padmore, George. Afrika unter dem Joch der Weissen. Zürich, 193-.
Afr 4753.5	Palieri, M. Contributo alla bibliografia e cartografia della Somalia italiana. Roma, 193-.
Afr 9070.5	Pietermaritzburg. Corporation. Pietermaritzburg, Natal, South Africa. Pietermaritzburg, 193-.
Afr 3300.39.5	Sammarco, Angelo. Egitto moderno. Roma, 193-.
Afr 825.10	Sinclair, J.H. Dodging hippopotami and crocodiles in Africa. Rochester, 193- .

1930

Afr 3300.22	Abbas II Hilmi, Khedive of Egypt. A few words on the Anglo-Egyptian settlement. London, 1930.
Afr 2438.17	Aguesse, L.C.P. Le problème de la nationalité en Tunisie. Thèse. Paris, 1930.
Afr 609.26.10	Akeley, Carl E. Adventures in the African jungle. N.Y., 1930.
Afr 609.30.10	Akeley, D.J. Jungle portraits. N.Y., 1930.
Afr 1830.50.5	Alazard, Jean. L'orient et la peinture française au XIXe siècle. Paris, 1930.
Afr 3038.27	Albrecht, W. Die völkerrechtliche Stellung Ägyptens. Inaug. Diss. Würzburg, 1930.
Afr 2819.30	Aleo, G.M. Turchi, senussi e italiani in Libia. Bengasi, 1930.
Afr 1830.110	Algeria. Commissariat General du Centenaire. Les parcs nationaux en Algérie. Alger, 1930.
Afr 1830.20.53	Algeria. Service des Postes, Télégraphes. Exposé du développement des services postaux. Alger, 1930.
Afr 2308.21	Algiers. Chambre de Commerce. Le port d'Alger,1930. Alger, 1930.
Afr 3040.35.5	Amad, P.E. Les pouvoirs des tribunaux mixtes d'Egypte. Thèse. Paris, 1930.
Afr 1470.5	Anderson, Eugene Newton. The first Moroccan crisis, 1904-1906. Chicago, 1930.
Afr 5635.18	Anthouard, Albert. L'expedition de Madagascar en 1895. Paris, 1930.
Afr 2318.1.15	Antoine, L.F. Constantine, centre économique. Thèse. Toulouse, 1930.
Afr 5962.6	Arija, Julio. La Guinea española y sus riquezas. Madrid, 1930.
Afr 4559.30.25	Armandy, A. La désagréable partie de campagne. Paris, 1930.
Afr 1573.27	Armiñan, J.M. Francia, el dictador y el moro. Madrid, 1930.
Afr 9161.8F	Asiatic land tenure (amendement) bill, commonly known as the Transvaal Asiatic bill, 1930. Johannesburg, 1930.
Afr 7175.22F	Associação Comercial de Lajistas de Lisboa. Alguns aspectos psicologicos de nossa colonização en Angola. Lisboa, 1930.
Afr 2749.30	Augieras, Ernest M. Chronique de l'ouest saharien (1900-1930). Paris, 1930.
Afr 1965.4.10	Azan, Paul. Bugeaud et l'Algérie. Paris, 1930.
Afr 1965.12.5	Azan, Paul. Sidi-Brahim. Paris, 1930.
Afr 8678.35	Barnes, L. Caliban in Africa. London, 1930.
Afr 530.20	Bassi, Ugo. Note sui diritti dell'Italia in Africa. Modena, 1930.
Afr 4700.30	Battistelle, V. Africa italiana. Firenze, 1930.
Afr 1621.10	Beaurieux, Remy. Le Maroc. Marseille, 1930.
Afr 4392.4.5	Berkeley, G.F.H. The campaign of Adowa and the rise of Menelik. New ed. London, 1930.
Afr 1609.30.20	Berthel, J. Impressions marocaines. Paris, 1930.
Afr 1830.20.51	Billiard, Louis. Les ports et la navigation de l'Agérie. Paris, 1930.
Afr 6883.9	Boesch, F. Les Banyamwezi, peuple de l'Afrique orientale. Münster, 1930.
Afr 8095.15	Bosman, F.C.L. Hollandse joernalistieks in Suid-Afrika. Kaapstad, 1930.
Afr 2975.7	Brezzi, G. Cento giorni di prigionia nell'oasi di Cufra. Milano, 1930.
Afr 5249.7	Briault, Maurice. La prodigieuse vie de René Caillié. Paris, 1930.
Afr 3040.35	Brinton, Jasper Y. The mixed courts of Egypt. New Haven, 1930.
Afr 698.68	Broomfield, S.S. Kachalola, or The early life and adventures of Sidney Spencer Broomfield. London, 1930.
Afr 1830.40.10F	Broussard, M.E.A. Les carreaux de faience peints dans l'Afrique du nord. Paris, 1930.
Afr 5406.230	Bruel, Georges. L'Afrique équatoriale française (A.E.F.). Paris, 1930.
Afr 609.30.15	Buckley, W. Big game hunting in Central Africa. London, 1930.
Afr 8659.30.5	Butterfield, Fred. Passing notes of a visit to the Cape (1930). London, 1930.
Afr 8659.30	Camacho, Brito. Gente Bóer, aspectos d'Africa. Lisboa, 1930.

Afr 5056.130   Campbell, Dugald. Wanderings in widest Africa. London, 1930.
Afr 2530.17   Caniglia, R. Il dramma di Tunisi. Napoli, 1930.
Afr 6455.47   Carnegie, V.M. A Kenyan farm diary. Edinburgh, 1930.
Afr 4700.30.10   Cesari, Cesare. L'evoluzione della coscienza e dell'attività coloniale italiana. Roma, 1930.
Afr 5405.109.10   Chambrun, J.A. de P. Brazza. Paris, 1930.
Afr 1955.51   Changarnier, N.A.T. Campagnes d'Afrique, 1830-1848. Paris, 1930.
Afr 1957.9   Chaudau de Raynal, P. L'expédition d'Alger, 1830. Paris, 1930.
Afr 8659.30.15   Chilvers, H.A. The seven lost trails of Africa. London, 1930.
Afr 4559.30.5   Ciravegna, G. Nell impero del negus neghest. Torino, 1930.
Afr 4559.30.20   Civinini, G. Sotto le pioggie equatoriali. Roma, 1930.
Afr 2940.10   Cohen, M. Gli Ebrei in Libia. Roma, 1930.
Afr 1570.55   Colliez, A. Notre protectorat marocain. Paris, 1930.
Afr 1955.7.5   Constantin-Weyer, M. La vie du général Yusuf. 10e éd. Paris, 1930.
Afr 4742.10   Corni, Guido. Tra Gasc e Setit. Roma, 1930.
Afr 6720.30   Costedoat, René. Le français et la réorganisation des territoires du Cameroun. Thèse. Besançon, 1930.
Afr 609.30.25   Court Treatt, Chaplin. Out of the beaten track. London, 1930.
Afr 8252.14.10   Cronwright-Schreiner, S.C. Her South African ancestors. London, 1930.
Afr 1957.15   Debu-Bridel, J. La guerre qui paye, Alger, 1830. Paris, 1930.
Afr 5045.30   Delafosse, M. Enquête coloniale dans l'Afrique française occidentale et équatoriale. Paris, 1930.
Afr 7459.30   Delarue, S. The land of the pepper bird. N.Y., 1930.
Afr 1830.20.56   Demontes, Victor. L'Algérie agricole. Paris, 1930.
Afr 1830.20.57   Demontes, Victor. L'Algerie industrielle et commercante. Paris, 1930.
Afr 3035.2   Deny, Jean. Sommaire des archives turques du Caire. Caire, 1930.
Afr 2609.30.15   Despois, Jean. La Tunisie. Paris, 1930.
Afr 1609.30.30   Desvallieres, Jean. Le Maroc. Paris, 1930.
Afr 8931.53.5   Dieterlen, H. Adolphe Mabile. Paris, 1930.
Afr 1830.10.2   Donec, Martial. Un siècle de finances coloniales. Paris, 1930.
Afr 1957.11   Douin, Georges. Mohamed Aly et l'expédition d'Alger (1829-1830). Aire, 1930.
Afr 3215.3.15   Driault, E. L'Égypte et l'Europe. Caire, 1930-31. 3v.
Afr 6310.5   Driberg, J.H. The East African problem. London, 1930.
Afr 1957.25   Dufestre, Henri. Les conquérants de l'Algérie (1830-1857). Paris, 1930.
Afr 555.9.36   Duplessis, Johannes. The evangelisation of pagan Africa. Cape Town, 1930.
Afr 1830.20.61   Ernest-Picard, P. La monnaie et le crédit en Algérie depuis 1830. Alger, 1930.
Afr 2731.3   Esquer, G. Un saharien, le colonel Ludovic de Polignac, 1827-1904. Paris, 1930.
Afr 626.9   Etesse, M. Les grands produits africains. Paris, 1930.
Afr 3040.25   Fahmy, Ahmed. Vers l'unité de juridiction en Egypte. Thèse. Paris, 1930.
Afr 2223.930.5   Falck, Felix. L'Algérie, un siécle de colonisation française. Paris, 1930.
Afr 2929.30A   Fatuzzo, Giacomo. Notiziario geografico del Sud-Tripolitano. Tripoli, 1930.
Afr 4199.37   Fergusson, V.H. The story of Fergie Bey. London, 1930.
Afr 5477.930   Ferrandi, Jean. Le Centre-africain français. Paris, 1930.
Afr 1259.30   Foster, Harry L. A vagabond in Barbary. N.Y., 1930.
Afr 1869.30   France. Comite National. Cahiers du centenaire de l'Algerie. Alger, 1930. 2v.
Afr 1026.10   France. Etat-Major de l'Armée. Service Historique. L'Afrique française du Nord. T.1-4. Paris, 1930-35. 4v.
Afr 4582.10   Franchetti, R. Nella Dancalia etiopica. Milano, 1930.
Afr 4559.30.10   Fulgenzio da Vecchieto, Padre. Il contributo alla geografia dell'Abissinia nelle memorie del cardinale Guglielmo Massaia. Tivoli, 1930.
Afr 4392.9   Gaibi, A. La guerra d'Africa (1895-96). Roma, 1930.
Afr 1487.28   Garcia Figueras, T. Del Marruecos feudal, episodios de la vida del cherif Raisuri. Madrid, 1930.
Afr 1830.40.13   Gautier, E.F. Un siècle de colonisation, études au microscope. Paris, 1930.
Afr 4700.30.5   Giaccone, E. Le colonie d'Italia. Torino, 1930.
Afr 3740.8   Giffen, Morrison B. Fashoda, the incident and its diplomatic setting. Chicago, 1930.
Afr 2315.5   Gojon, Edmond. Cent ans d'effort français en Algérie. Paris, 1930.
Afr 5912.2   Gonzalez Jimenez, E. Territorios del sur de Marruecos y Sahara occidental. Toledo, 1930.
Afr 6620.55   Gorges, E.H. The great war in West Africa. London, 1930.
Afr 9506.1   Gray, S. Douglas. Frontiers of the kingdom. London, 1930.
Afr 6310.8   Great Britain. Colonial Office. Statement of the conclusions of His Majesty's government in the United Kingdom...East Africa. London, 1930.
Afr 6455.49   Great Britain. Oversea Settlement Department. Kenya Colony and Protectorate. London, 1930.
Afr 4390.10   Guebre Sellassie. Chronique du règne de Menelik II, roi des rois d'Ethiopie. Paris, 1930-31. 2v.
Afr 2438.23   Guiga, Bahri. Essai sur l'évolution du Charaa et son application judiciaire en Tunisie. Thèse. Paris, 1930.
Afr 8283.20   Hale, Hugh M. The Jameson raid. London, 1930.
Afr 630.12   Hambly, Wilfrid D. Ethnology of Africa. Chicago, 1930.
Afr 1609.30.5   Hardy, Georges. Le Maroc. Paris, 1930.
Afr 8685.30   Herman, L. A history of the Jews in South Africa. London, 1930.
Afr 1573.26   Hernandez Mir, Francisco. La dictadura en Marruecos. Madrid, 1930.
Afr 6214.10   Hoghen, S.J. The Muhammadan emigrants of Nigeria. London, 1930.
Afr 500.38   Hoskins, Halford Lancaster. European imperialism in Africa. N.Y., 1930.
Afr 1259.30.5   Hulme, K.C. Arab interlude. Philadelphia, 1930.
Afr 3040.50   Israel-Meyer, G. L'Egypte contemporaine et les capitulations. Thése. Paris, 1930.
Afr 6390.20   Jackson, F.J. Early days in East Africa. London, 1930.
Afr 4559.30.15   Jannasch, Hans. Im Schatten des Negus. Berlin, 1930.
Afr 7180.15   Jaspert, Fritz. Die Völkerstämme Mittel-Angolas. Frankfurt a.M., 1930.
Afr 5257.5   Joalland. Le drame de Dankori. Paris, 1930.

Afr 28.8F   Johannesburg. University of the Witwatersrand. Gubbins Library. Preliminary list of Africana, mainly from the Gubbins Library. Johannesburg, 1930.
Afr 575.23   Jung, Eugène. L'islam et les musulmans dans l'Afrique du Nord. Paris, 1930.
Afr 3745.25   Keun, Odette. Foreigner looks at the British Sudan. London, 1930.
Afr 2749.29.5   Khun de Prorok, B. Mysterious Sahara, the land of gold, of sand, and of ruin. London, 1930.
Afr 8710.10   Kilpin, Ralph. The romance of a colonial parliament. London, 1930.
Afr 6850.7   Koch, Ludwig. Ostafrika in der Geschichte der Weltwirtschaft. Berlin, 1930.
Afr 4060.15   Kraus, J. Die Anfänge des Christentums in Nubien. Inaug. Diss. Mödling, 1930.
Afr 7809.30   Landbeck, Paul. Malu Malu; Erlebnisse aus der Sturm- und Drangperiode des Kongostaates. Berlin, 1930.
Afr 8252.54   Laurence, P.M. The life of John Xavier Merriman. London, 1930.
Afr 9073.467   Lee, Albert William. Charles Johnson of Zululand. Westminster, Eng., 1930.
Afr 2224.929   Lejeune, André. Le role du crédit dans le développement économique de l'Algérie depuis la fin de la guerre. Thèse. Paris, 1930.
Afr 1830.30.2   Lespes, René. Alger, étude de géographie et d'histoire urbaines. Paris, 1930.
Afr 1878.8   Lespes, Rene. Alger, étude de geographie et d'histoire urbaines. Thèse. Paris, 1930.
Afr 6780.24   Letcher, O. Cohort of the tropics. London, 1930.
Afr 8278.99.35   Leyds, W.J. Tweede verzameling (Correspondentie 1899-1900). v.1-2. Dordrecht, 1930. 3v.
Afr 8190.10   Mackeurtan, G. The cradle days of Natal, 1497-1845. London, 1930.
Afr 8678.32.5   MacMillan, W.M. Complex South Africa, an economic foot-note to history. London, 1930.
Afr 1609.30.15   Manue, G. R. Sur les marches du Maroc insoumis. 3e ed. Paris, 1930.
Afr 1830.20.58   Marc, H. Notes sur les forets de l'Algeria. Paris, 1930.
Afr 1830.40.11   Marcais, Georges. Le costume musulman d'Alger. Paris, 1930.
Afr 2000.12   Margueritte, V. Un grand Français, le général Margueritte. Paris, 1930.
Afr 4742.15   Martinelli, Renzo. Sud. Firenze, 1930.
Afr 1259.30.10   Maunier, R. Mélanges de sociologie nord-africaine. Paris, 1930.
Afr 1955.49   Maze, Jules. La conquête de l'Algérie. Tours, 1930.
Afr 1957.20.5   Merle, J.T. La prise d'Alger. Paris, 1930.
Afr 1830.10.1   Milliot, Louis. L'oeuvre legislative de la France en Algérie. Paris, 1930.
Afr 2220.12.3   Monmarche, Marcel. Algérie, Tunisie. Paris, 1930.
Afr 1635.6   Montagne, R. Les Berberes et le Makhzen dans le sud du Maroc. Thèse. Paris, 1930.
Afr 1635.21   Montagne, R. Villages et kasbas berberes. Paris, 1930.
Afr 1680.50   Montagne, Robert. Un magasin collectif de l'anti-atlas. Thèse. Paris, 1930.
Afr 2609.30.5   Mori, Attilio. La Tunisia. Roma, 1930.
Afr 8145.10   Mother Cecile in South Africa, 1883-1906. London, 1930.
Afr 609.30   Mott-Smith, M. Africa from port to port. N.Y., 1930.
Afr 6738.22   Mueller, Arno. Die kameruner Waldländer. Inaug. Diss. Ohlau in Schlesien, 1930.
Afr 4742.4   Mulazzani, A. Geografia della colonia Eritrea. Firenze, 1930.
Afr 3204.15   Munier, Jules. La presse en Egypte, 1799-1900. Le Caire, 1930.
Afr 2945.20   Mura, Nicolo. La terra delle donne tenebrose. Bologna, 1930.
Afr 1609.30.25   Nahon, Moise. Propos d'un vieux marocain. Paris, 1930.
Afr 5960.8   Najera y Angulo. La Guinea española y su riqueza forestal. Madrid, 1930.
Afr 8659.30.10   Narath, R. Die Union von Südafrika und ihre Bevölkerung. Leipzig, 1930.
Afr 8252.37   Neame, L.E. General Hertzog, Prime Minister of the Union of South Africa since 1924. London, 1930.
Afr 5758.30   Nemours, C.P. Madagascar et ses richesses. Paris, 1930.
Afr 4582.15   Nesbitt, L.M. La Dancalia esplorata. Firenze, 1930.
Afr 4559.30   Norden, Hermann. Africa's last empire. London, 1930.
Afr 210.30.10   Oldham, J.H. White and black in Africa. London, 1930.
Afr 7222.30   Ornellas, Ayres D. Campanha do Gungunhana, 1895. Lisboa, 1930.
Afr 590.27   Owen, Nicholas. Journal of a slave-dealer. London, 1930.
Afr 7309.30   Paes Mamede. Nas costas d'Africa. Lisboa, 1930.
Afr 2224.30   Peraldi, Geo. L'organisation financiére de l'Algérie du nord. Thèse. Alger, 1930.
Afr 1830.20.8   Petitjean, L. Le temps et la prevision du temps en Algerie et auSahara. Paris, 1930.
Afr 2000.10   Piquet, V. L'Algérie française. Paris, 1930.
Afr 4095.21   Piva, Gino. Un pioniere italiano delle scoperte del Nilo, Giovanni Miani, il Leone Bianco. Firenze, 1930.
Afr 9502.12   Plaatje, S.T. Uhudi. Kimberley, 1930.
Afr 1915.9   Plantet, Eugène. Les consuls de France à Alger avant la conquête, 1579-1830. Paris, 1930.
Afr 1830.20.2F   Pouget. Agrologie du Sahel. Paris, 1930.
Afr 1658.32   Queipo De Llano, G. El general. 7a ed. Madrid, 1930.
Afr 1658.54   Ramos Charco-Villaseñor, Aniceto. El Rif. Toledo, 1930.
Afr 1955.57   Rasteil, M. Le calvaire des colons de 48. Paris, 1930.
Afr 8289.29.3   Reitz, Deneys. Commando. N.Y., 1930.
Afr 8289.29.5   Reitz, Deneys. La guerre des Boers. Paris, 1930.
Afr 1635.10   Ribaut, A.J. Les djemaas judiciaires berberes. Thèse. Alger, 1930.
Afr 5056.130.5   Rondet-Saint, M. Un voyage en A.O.F. Paris, 1930.
Afr 609.30.5   Roome, William J.W. Tramping through Africa. N.Y., 1930.
Afr 555.150.5   Roome, William John Waterman. Through the lands of Nyanka, Central Africa. London, 1930.
Afr 4559.30.30   Roth-Roesthof, A. von. Ba Menelik. Leipzig, 1930.
Afr 8252.77   Rowbotham, A.F. Perilous moments, a true story. London, 1930.
Afr 3215.15   Roy, H. La vie héroïque et romantique du docteur Charles Cuny. Paris, 1930.
Afr 3205.7   Sabry, Mohammed. L'empire égyptien sous Mohamed-Ali et la question d'Orient, 1811-1849. Paris, 1930.
Afr 3038.25   Sabry, Mohammed. Le pouvoir législatif et le pouvoir exécutif en Egypte. Paris, 1930.
Afr 3038.25.5   Sabry, Mohammed. Le pouvoir législatif et le pouvoir exécutif en Egypte. Thèse. Paris, 1930.

1930 - cont.

Afr 1570.39 — Saint-Rene-Taillaudier, Georges. Les origines du Maroc français. Paris, 1930.

Afr 3205.17 — Sammarco, Angelo. Il regno di Mohammed Ali nei documenti diplomatici italiani inediti. v.1,8,9,10. Caire, 1930-32. 4v.

Afr 1658.40 — Sanchez, J.G. Nuestro protectorado. Madrid, 1930.

Afr 1550.41 — Schaettle, Hermann. Die Times in der ersten Marokkokrise mit besonderer Berücksichtigung der englisch-deutschen Beziehungen. Berlin, 1930.

Afr 8678.39 — Schapera, I. The Khoisan peoples of South Africa. London, 1930.

Afr 630.14 — Seligman, C.G. Races of Africa. London, 1930.

Afr 2223.930 — Selnet, F.P.V. Colonisation officielle et crédit agricole en Algérie. Thèse. Alger, 1930.

Afr 5056.130.10 — Semaines Sociales de France. Le problème social aux colonies. Lyon, 1930.

Afr 1830.20.6 — Seurat, L.G. Exploration zoologique de l'Algérie. Paris, 1930.

Afr 1571.39 — Simon, H.J. Un officer d'Afrique, le commandant Verlet-Hanus. Paris, 1930.

Afr 1957.7 — Sixte, Prince of Bourbon-Parma. La dernière conquête du roi, Alger, 1830. V.1-2. Paris, 1930. 2v.

Afr 550.18 — Smith, Edwin. Aggrey of Africa. N.Y., 1930.

Afr 210.30 — Smuts, J.C. Africa and some world problems. Oxford, 1930.

Afr 8678.13.20 — Soga, J.H. The south-eastern Bantu Abe-Nguni, Aba-Mbo, Ama-Lala. Johannesburg, 1930.

Afr Doc 4312.130 — South Africa. Parliament. Natives Parliamentary Representation Bill. Cape Town, 1930.

Afr 635.7.15F — Stow, G. William. Rock-paintings in South Africa. London, 1930.

Afr 6193.5 — Tete-Ansa, W. Africa at work. N.Y., 1930.

Afr 1655.4 — Tharaud, J. Fez, ou les bourgeois de l'islam. Paris, 1930.

Afr 2609.30.10F — Thomas, Jean. A travers le sud Tunisie. Paris, 1930.

Afr 718.44 — Tweedy, Owen. By way of the Sahara. London, 1930.

Afr 6489.12F — Uganda. Local Government Committee. Report, 1930. Entebbe, 1930.

Afr 5406.60 — Vaucaire, Michel. Paul Duchaillu. N.Y., 1930.

Afr 4785.37 — Vecchi, B.V. Vecchio Benadir. Milano, 1930.

Afr 8095.3 — Walker, E.A. The frontier tradition in South Africa. London, 1930.

Afr 6282.40 — Walker, Frank Deaville. The romance of the Black River. London, 1930.

Afr 2609.30 — Warsfold, W.B. France in Tunis and Algeria. N.Y., 1930.

Afr 6196.5 — Welman, C.W. The native states of the Gold Coast. London, 1930.

Afr 1609.30.10 — Willette, H. Au Maroc. Paris, 1930.

Afr 580.10 — Williams, Joseph J. Hebrewisms of West Africa, from Nile to Niger with the Jews. London, 1930.

Afr 580.10.3 — Williams, Joseph J. Hebrewisms of West Africa. N.Y., 1930.

Afr 609.29.10 — Willis, Bailey. Living Africa. N.Y., 1930.

Afr 6280.24 — Wilson-Haffenden, J.R. The red men of Nigeria. London, 1930.

Afr 6645.10 — Zoeller, Hugo. Als Jurnalist und Forscher in Deutschlands grosser Kolonialzeit. Leipzig, 1930.

Afr 4430.25 — Zoli, Corrado. Cronache etiopiche. Roma, 1930.

1931

Afr 2025.29 — Abbas, F. Le jeune Algérien. Paris, 1931.

Afr 5045.28 — Abensour, Leon. La France noire, ses peuples. Paris, 1931.

Afr 7110.5 — Abreu e Brito, D. de. Um inquerito a vida administrativa e economica de Angola e doBrasil. Coimbra, 1931.

Afr 3204.17 — Ahmed, Chafik Bey. L'Egypte moderne et les influences étrangères. Le Caire, 1931.

Afr 1830.40.15 — Alazard, J. Histoire et historiens de l'Algérie. Paris, 1931.

Afr 1830.105 — Algeria. Commissariat General du Centenaire. Le centenaire de l'Algérie. Alger, 1931. 2v.

Afr 3695.7A — Allen, B.M. Gordon and the Sudan. London, 1931.

Afr 2748.57.20 — Assollant, Georges. Eugène Fromentin, un été dans le Sahara. Paris, 1931.

Afr 1844.5 — Azan, Paul. Les grands soldats de l'Algérie. Paris, 1931.

Afr 7320.6 — Azevedo Coutinho, João de. Do Nyassa a Pemba. Lisboa, 1931.

Afr 8860.5 — Ballinger, M.L. Basutoland. Lovedale, 1931.

Afr 9345.50.5 — Ballinger, M.L. Bechuanaland protectorate. Lovedale, 1931.

Afr 1494.37 — Barbau, Muslim. Tempête sur le Maroc. Paris, 1931.

Afr 5540.8 — Barrel, G.P. Le code des 305 articles de Madagascar. Thèse. Paris, 1931.

Afr 1571.17.30 — Barthou, Louis. Lyautey et le Maroc. Paris, 1931.

Afr 4394.3.14 — Bellavita, E. Adua, i precedenti, la battaglia. Genova, 1931.

Afr 3700.11 — Bermann, R.A. Mahdi of Allah. London, 1931.

Afr 2209.31.10 — Bernard, A. L'Algérie. Paris, 1931.

Afr 2209.31.15 — Bernard, A. L'Algérie. Paris, 1931.

Afr 1609.13.2.3 — Bernard, A. Le Maroc. 7. ed. Paris, 1931.

Afr 3040.55 — Bertolini, V.C. La légitime défense dans la doctrine du droit musulman en Egypte. Thèse. Paris, 1931.

Afr 2880.15 — Bignami, Paolo. Tra i colonizzatori in Tripolitania. Bologna, 1931.

Afr 555.77 — Billy, E. de. En Côte d'Ivoire, mission protestante d'A.O.F. Paris, 1931.

Afr 8252.354 — Bosman, J.D. Dr. George McCall theal as die geskiedskrywer van Suid-Afrika. Amsterdam, 1931.

Afr 1840.6 — Bounichon, A. La conversion au christianisme de l'indigène musulman algérien. Thèse. Paris, 1931.

Afr 9225.15 — Brauer, A. Der Oranje-Freistaat, 1854-1888. Emsdetten, 1931.

Afr 5342.66 — Brétignère, Amédée. Aux temps héroïques de la Côte-d'Ivoire. Paris, 1931.

Afr 630.31 — Buxton, Charles R. The race problem in Africa. London, 1931.

Afr 6153.5 — Cardinall, A.W. A bibliography of the Gold Coast. Accra, 1931.

Afr 4766.5 — Caroselli, F.S. Ferro e fuoco in Somalia. Roma, 1931.

Afr 1100.3 — Carranza, F. de. La guerra santa por mar de los corsarios berberiscos. Ceuta, 1931.

Afr 3069.31.10 — Cattaui, Joseph. Coup d'oeil sur la chronologie de la nation égyptienne. Paris, 1931.

Afr 3205.15 — Cattaui, René. Le règne de Mohamed Aly d'après les archives russes en Egypte. v.1-3. Caire, 1931-1936. 4v.

Afr 1609.27.5F — Celarie, H. Behind moroccan walls. N.Y., 1931.

1931 - cont.

Afr 1609.31 — Celerier, Jean. Le Maroc. Paris, 1931.

Afr 8685.25 — Chatterjee, M.N. Auswanderung aus Indien. I. Inaug. Diss. Leipzig, 1931.

Afr 6685.8 — Chazelas, V. Territoires africains sous mandat de la France. Paris, 1931.

Afr 6738.23 — Chazelas, Victor. Territoires africains sous mandat de la France. Paris, 1931.

Afr 1369.31 — Coissac de Chavrebiere. Histoire du Maroc. Paris, 1931.

Afr 555.3.12 — Cooksey, J.J. Religion and civilization in West Africa. London, 1931.

Afr 1422.10 — Cosse Brissac, P. de. Les rapports de la France et du Maroc pendant la conquête de l'Algérie (1830-1847). Paris, 1931.

Afr 8678.49 — Cotton, W.A. Racial segregation in South Africa. London, 1931.

Afr 510.23 — Coty, F. Sauvons nos colonies. Paris, 1931.

Afr 5403.20 — Dairiam, Emmanuel. La subdivision en Afrique équatoriale française. Lyon, 1931.

Afr 9700.15 — Dake, C.M. The Lambas of Northern Rhodesia. London, 1931.

Afr 1340.17 — Decroux, Paul. La vie municipale au Maroc. Thèse. Lyon, 1931.

Afr 630.8.5 — Delafosse, Maurice. The Negroes of Africa. Washington, 1931.

Afr 5056.131.10 — Delavignette, R. Afrique occidentale française. Paris, 1931.

Afr 5640.20 — Delelee-Desloges, J.G. Madagascar et dependances. Paris, 1931.

Afr 4700.31 — Della Valle, Carlo. I pionieri italiani nelle nostre colonie. Roma, 1931.

Afr 5540.10 — Delteil, Pierre. Le fokon'olona (commune malgache) et les conventions de fokon'olona. Thèse. Paris, 1931.

Afr 5765.20 — Derville, Leon. Ils ne sont que quarante...les jésuites chez les Betsileos. Paris, 1931.

Afr 2223.931 — Desfeuilles, P. L'Algérie. Paris, 1931.

Afr 3205.13 — Dodwell, Henry. The founder of modern Egypt. Cambridge, Eng., 1931.

Afr 1573.30 — Donnadieu, M. Les relations diplomatiques de l'Espagne et du Maroc de janvier 1592 a juillet 1926. Montpellier, 1931.

Afr 1571.17.13 — Dubly, H.L. Lyautey-le-magicien. Lille, 1931.

Afr 1609.31.20 — Dumas, P. Le Maroc. Grenoble, 1931.

Afr 2209.31.5 — Dumas, Pierre. L'Algérie. Grenoble, 1931.

Afr 4050.20 — Dumreicher, A. von. Trackers and smugglers in the deserts of Egypt. London, 1931.

Afr 1830.20.85 — Dussert, D. Les mines et les carrieres en Algerie. Paris, 1931.

Afr 3979.31.5 — Egypt. Survey Department. Views of typical desert scenery in Egypt. Giza, 1931.

Afr 555.149.10 — Fauré, Édouard. Les vingt-cinq ans de Coillard au Lessouto. Paris, 1931.

Afr 6720.28.3 — Ferrandi, Jean. De la Benoue à l'Atlantique à la poursuite des allemands. Paris, 1931.

Afr 2632.8 — Ficaya, P. Le peuplement italien en Tunisie. Thèse. Paris, 1931.

Afr 2500.15 — Fiennes, J.B. Une mission tunisienne à Paris en 1743. Tunis, 1931.

Afr 2438.1.25 — Fitoussi, Elie. L'état tunisien et le protectorat français. Paris, 1931. 2v.

Afr 609.30.20 — Fort, T. A vacation in Africa. Boston, 1931.

Afr 4259.31 — Gabre-Hiot, A. La vérité sur l'Ethiopie révélée après le couronnement du roi des rois. Lausanne, 1931.

Afr 1609.31.10 — Gadala, M.T. La feerie marocaine. Grenoble, 1931.

Afr 7122.38 — Galvao, Henrique. Historia de nosso tempo. Lisboa, 1931.

Afr 4700.31.5 — Gaslini, Mario dei. L'oltremare d'Italia in terra d'Africa. Bergamo, 1931.

Afr 2731.12.5 — Gautier, E.F. Figures de conquêtes coloniales. Paris, 1931.

Afr 4368.5.20 — Gentile, Lorenzo. L'apostolo dei Galla. 3 ed. Torino, 1931.

Afr 5640.8 — Gheuse, P.B. Gallieni et Madagascar. Paris, 1931.

Afr 609.16 — Gilligan, Edmund. One lives to tell the tale. N.Y., 1931.

Afr 7182.15 — Graham, Robert Haldane Carson. Under seven Congo kings. London, 1931.

Afr 2514.5 — Grandchamp, P. Les différends de 1832-1833 entre la régence de Tunis et les royaumes de Sardaigne et des Deus-Siciles. Tunis, 1931.

Afr 5640.14.10 — Grandidier, Guillaume. Gallieni. Paris, 1931.

Afr 6310.10F — Great Britain. Colonial Office. Papers relating to the question of the closer union of Kenya. London, 1931.

Afr 5846.2 — Great Britain. Imperial Shipping Commission. Report on the harbour of Port Louis. London, 1931.

Afr 1750.47 — Guanner, Vicente. El Sahara y Sur Marroqui españoles. Toledo, 1931.

Afr 4892.8 — Hachette, R. Djibouti, au seuil de l'Orient. Paris, 1931.

Afr 9599.28 — Haefler, P.L. Africa speaks, a story of adventure. London, 1931.

Afr 3069.31 — Hanotaux, G. Histoire de la nation égyptienne. Paris, 1931-40. 7v.

Afr 8252.36 — Harris, D. Pioneer, soldier and politician. London, 1931.

Afr 9858.10 — Hetherwick, Alexander. The romance of Blantyre. London, 1931.

Afr 8089.31 — Hofmeyer, J.H. South Africa. London, 1931.

Afr 2731.12 — Howe, S.E. Les héros du Sahara. Paris, 1931.

Afr 4093.62 — Huffman, Ray. Nuer customs and folk-lore. London, 1931.

Afr 6390.18A — Huxley, Julian S. Africa view. N.Y., 1931.

Afr 6565.31.2 — Ingrams, W.H. Zanzibar. London, 1931.

Afr 7461.30 — International Commission of Inquiry into the Existence of Slavery and Forced Labor in the Republic of Liberia. Report. Washington, 1931.

Afr 530.22 — Italy. Ufficio Studi e Propaganda. Voyageurs italiens en Afrique. Roma, 1931.

Afr 7809.31.5 — Johnson, Martin. Congorilla. N.Y., 1931.

Afr 1069.31 — Julien, Charles A. Histoire de l'Afrique du Nord. Paris, 1931.

Afr 6455.55 — Kenya and Uganda Rail Road and Harbours. Travel guide to Kenya and Uganda. London, 1931.

Afr 5257.5.5 — Klobb, Un drame colonial. Paris, 1931.

Afr 5053.5 — Labouret, Henri. A la recherche d'une politique indigène dans l'Ouest africain. Paris, 1931.

Afr 1848.5 — Lacoste, L. La marine algerienne sous les Turcs. Paris, 1931.

Afr 1830.20.80 — Lacoste, Louis. La colonisation maritime en Algerie. Paris, 1931.

Afr 5874.15 — Lebband, M. Ile de la Réunion...côte française des Somalis. Paris, 1931.

X Cg

1931 - cont.

Afr 11517.84.100   Letscher, O. Africa unveiled. London, 1931.
Afr 8659.31   Leubuscher, C. Der südafrikanische Eingeborne als Industriearbeiter und als Stadtherrscher. Jena, 1931.
Afr 8278.99.36   Leyds, W.J. Derde verzameling. Deel 1-21. Dordrecht, 1931.
Afr 6455.45.5   Leys, Norman MacLean. A last chance in Kenya. London, 1931.
Afr 2665.5   Mabille de Poncheville, A. Carthage. Paris, 1931.
Afr 5406.231   Maigret, Julien. Afrique équatoriale française. Paris, 1931.
Afr 1830.20.5   Maire, Rene. Les progres des connaissances botaniques en Algerie depuis 1830. Paris, 1931.
Afr 2508.15   Mallon, Jean. L'influence française dans la régence de Tunis. Paris, 1931.
Afr 2209.31   Malo, Pierre. Palmes et burnous. Paris, 1931.
Afr 3986.931PF   Manchester Guardian Commercial, March 19, 1931. Egypt. London, 1931.
Afr 1583.14.15   Mannesmann, C.H. Die unternehmungen des brüder mannesmann in Marokko. Würzburg, 1931.
Afr 5480.231   Maran, René. Le Tchad de sable et d'or. Paris, 1931.
Afr 555.70   Marie-Germaine, Soeur. Le Christ au Gabon. Louvain, 1931.
NEDL   Afr 5045.17.5   Martin du Gard, M. Courrier d'Afrique. Paris, 1931.
Afr 1571.17.10A   Maurois, A. Lyautey. N.Y., 1931.
Afr 1571.17.6   Maurois, A. Lyautey. Paris, 1931.
Afr 1571.17.8   Maurois, A. Lyautey. Paris, 1931.
Afr 6280.21   Meek, C.K. A Sudanese kingdom. London, 1931.
Afr 6280.22   Meek, C.K. Tribal studies in Northern Nigeria. London, 1931. 2v.
Afr 5227.15   Meniaud, Jacques. Les pionniers du Soudan. Paris, 1931. 2v.
Afr 1571.1.10   Messal, R. La genèse de notre victoire marocaine. Paris, 1931.
Afr 7809.31   Miller, Janet. Jungles preferred. Boston, 1931.
Afr 8252.8.10   Milner, A.M. The Milner papers...1897-1905. London, 1931-33. 2v.
Afr 9345.10   Mockford, J. Khama, king of the Bamangwato. London, 1931.
Afr 609.28.5   Monson, R.A. Across Africa on foot. N.Y., 1931.
Afr 3675.9   Mustafa, O.M. Le Soudan égyptien. Thèse. Neuville-sur-Saone, 1931.
Afr 6990.6   Naude, C.P. Ongebaande wee. Kaapstad, 1931.
Afr 8095.35   Nederlandisch-Zuid-Afrikaansche Vereeniging. Nederland-Zuid-Afrika. Amsterdam, 1931.
Afr 1830.10.3   Nores, Edmond. L'oeuvre de la france en Algerie, la justice. Paris, 1931.
Afr 6686.30   Och, Helmut. Die wirtschaftsgeographische Entwicklung...Togo und Kamerun. Königsberg, 1931.
Afr 5640.25   Olivier, Marcel. Six ans de politique sociale a Madagascar. Paris, 1931.
Afr 628.231   Padmore, George. The life and struggles of Negro toilers. London, 1931.
Afr 5749.31.5   Paris, Pierre. Madagascar. Paris, 1931.
Afr 555.12.15   Philippe, A. Missions des pères blancs en Tunisie. Paris, 1931.
Afr 2438.25   Pinon, J.P.M. Les attributions des contrôleurs civils en Tunisie. Thèse. Tunis, 1931.
Afr 1830.20.52   Poggi, Jacques. Les chemins de fer...de l'Algérie. Paris, 1931.
Afr 3252.10   Politis, A.G. Un projet d'alliance entre l'Egypte et la Grèce en 1867. Caire, 1931.
Afr 2870.12   Ravizza, A. La Libia nel suo ordinamento giuridico. Padova, 1931.
Afr 1573.28   Reparaz, G. de. Alfonso XIII y sus complices. Madrid, 1931.
Afr 575.47   Reusch, Richard. Der Islam in Ost-Afrika. Leipzig, 1931.
Afr 1550.43   Rheinlaender, G. Deutschland, England und die Marokkokrise. Inaug. Diss. Bochum-Langendreer, 1931.
Afr 3285.15A   Richter, Erhard. Lord Cromer, Ägypten und die Entstehung der französisch-englischen Entente von 1904. Inaug. Diss. Leipzig, 1931.
Htn   Afr 1258.18.31*   Robbins, A. Robbins journal, comprising an account of the loss of the brig Commerce of Hartford, Conn. Greenwich, 1931.
Afr 7222.90   Saldanha, Eduardo d'Almeida. Moçambique perante genébra. Porto, 1931.
Afr 8289.31   Sampson, V. Anti-commando. London, 1931.
Afr 1830.20.1   Savornin, J. La géologie algérienne et nord-africaine depuis 1830. Paris, 1931.
Afr 2438.19   Scemama, A. De l'influence du mariage sur la nationalité tunisienne. Thèse. Paris, 1931.
Afr 5426.100.15   Schweitzer, Albert. The forest hospital at Lambaréné. N.Y., 1931.
Afr 5056.131   Seabrook, W.B. Jungle ways. London, 1931.
Afr 5056.131.20   Seabrook, W.B. Jungle ways. N.Y., 1931.
Afr 5056.131.5   Societe de Géographie, Paris. D'Algérie au Sénégal, mission Augieras-Draper, 1927-1928. Texte et plates. Paris, 1931. 2v.
Afr 5045.42   Société d'Editions Géographiques. Afrique française. Paris, 1931.
Afr 2223.57   Société des Fermes Françaises de Tunisie. Trente-deux ans de colonisation nord-africaine. Paris, 1931.
Afr 8028.100   South Africa. Parliament. Library. Afrikaanse publikasies. Kaapstad, 1931.
Afr 8678.13.30   Stayt, H.A. The Bavenda. London, 1931.
Afr 1738.30   Stuart, G.H. The international city of Tanger. Stanford, calif., 1931.
Afr 6194.25   Tamakloe, E.F. A brief history of the Daybamba people. Accra, 1931.
Afr 6879.31   Tanganyika Railways and Harbours. Travel guide to Tanganyika and Central Africa. London, 1931.
Afr 1609.31.15   Terrier, A. Le Maroc. Paris, 1931.
Afr 2945.24   Teruzzi, Attilo. Cirenaica verde. Milano, 1931.
Afr 4384.10   Traversi, L. Let-Marefia. Milano, 1931.
Afr 2975.5F   Tripolitania. L'occupazione di Cufra. Tripoli, 1931.
Afr 6138.31   Utting, F.A.J. The story of Sierra Leone. London, 1931.
Afr 3979.31   Vandyke, J.C. In Egypt, studies and sketches along the Nile. N.Y., 1931.
Afr 5056.83   Veistroffer, Albert. Vingt ans dans la brousse africaine. Lille, 1931.
Afr 8145.34   Victor, Osmund. The salient of South Africa. London, 1931.
Afr 1609.31.5   Vicuna, Alejandro. Bajo cielo africano. Paris, 1931.
Afr 2000.14   Viollette, M. L'Algérie vivra-t-elle? Paris, 1931.
Afr 609.31   Weulersse, Jacques. Noirs et blancs. Paris, 1931.
Afr 1571.17.25   Willette, H. Au Maroc avec Lyautey. Paris, 1931.
Afr 3745.30   Yardley, J. Parengon, or eddies in Equatoria. London, 1931.

1931 - cont.

Afr 5749.31   You, André. Madagascar, colonie française, 1896-1930. Paris, 1931.

1932

Afr 55.36   African yearly register. 1st ed. Johannesburg, 1932.
Afr 4700.32   Agostino Orsini, P. Le colonie italiane. Roma, 1932.
Afr 8676.32   Barnes, L. The new Boer war. London, 1932.
Afr 109.32   Berger, A. Afrika, schwarz oder weiss. Berlin, 1932.
Afr 4559.32.10   Bergsma, S. Rainbow empire, Ethiopia stretches out her hands. Grand Rapids, 1932.
Afr 1609.13.2.5   Bernard, A. Le Maroc. 8e ed. Paris, 1932.
Afr 8235.16   Bixler, R.W. Anglo-German imperialism in South Africa, 1880-1900. Baltimore, 1932.
Afr 8235.15   Bixler, R.W. Anglo-German imperialism in South Africa 1880-1900. Diss. Columbus, Ohio, 1932.
Afr 1625.12   Bourrilly, J. Elements d'ethnographie marocaine. Paris, 1932.
Afr 510.25F   Burthe d'Annelet, Anarie. A travers l'Afrique française. Paris, 1932. 2v.
Afr 550.25   Callaway, Godfrey. The soul of an African padré. London, 1932.
Afr 1830.40.20   Charles-Roux, François. France et Afrique du nord avant 1830, les precurseurs de la conquete. Paris, 1932.
Afr 8686.3   Chirgwin, Arthur Mitchell. An African pilgrimage. London, 1932.
Afr 724.6   Cipriani, Lidio. In Africa dal Capo al Cairo. Firenze, 1932.
Afr 6218.7   Crozier, F.P. Five years hard. N.Y., 1932.
Afr 5130.20.5   Demaison, A. Faidherbe. Paris, 1932.
Afr 1623.932.10   Desfeuilles, Paul. Les colonies françaises, le Maroc. Paris, 1932.
Afr 5058.5   Dim Delobsom, A.A. L'empire du Mogho-Naba. Paris, 1932.
Afr 210.32   Dix, Arthur. Weltkrise und Kolonialpolitik. Berlin, 1932.
Afr 2532.2   Droulers, C. Le marquis de Mores, 1858-1896. Paris, 1932.
Afr 9599.32   Duff, Hector Livingston. A small chop. London, 1932.
Afr 3032.1   Egypt. Les codes mixtes d'Egypte. Ibrahimieh, 1932.
Afr 555.152   F.S. Arnot Jubilee Conference, Muchacha, 1931. A Central African jubilee. London, 1932.
Afr 8252.80   Fitzpatrick, J.P. South African memories. London, 1932.
Afr 1568.3   Flournoy, F.R. Political relations of Great Britain with Morocco from 1830 to 1841. N.Y., 1932.
Afr 8252.56   Fort, G.S. Alfred Beit. London, 1932.
Afr 626.19   Frankel, Sally H. Africa in the re-making. Johannesburg, 1932.
Afr 1830.20.40   Fraynaud, Lucien. Hygiène et pathologie nord-africaines. v.1-2. Paris, 1932. 2v.
Afr 7176.27   Galvão, Henrique. Informação económia sobre Angola. Lisboa, 1932.
Afr 861.30   Gane, Douglas M. Tristan da Cunha. London, 1932.
Afr 1830.50.15   Giacobetti, R.P. Les tapis et tissages du Djebel-amour. Paris, 1932.
Afr 4368.5.5   Gianozza, E. Guglielmo Massaia. Torino, 1932.
Afr 575.50   Giglio, Carlo. La confraternità senussita dalle sue origini ad oggi. Padova, 1932.
Afr 1493.72   Goded, M. Marruecos, las etapas de la pacificacion. Madrid, 1932.
Afr Doc 1807.331   Gold Coast (Colony). Census Office. The Gold Coast 1931. A review of conditions in the Gold Coast in 1931 as compared with those of 1921. Accra, 1932. 4v.
Afr 2945.28   Graziani, Rodolfo. Cirenaica pacificata. Milano, 1932.
Afr 6310.12   Great Britain. Colonial Office. Correspondence (1931-1932) arising from the report of the Joint Select Commission on East Africa. London, 1932.
Afr 6457.27   Great Britain. Financial Commissioner to Kenya. Report by the Financial commissioner. n.p., 1932.
Afr 4559.32.5   Gruehl, Max. The citadel of Ethiopia. London, 1932.
Afr 2624.932   Guenee, Georges. Les finances tunisiennes. Thèse. Tunis, 1932.
Afr 6887.11.9   Gutmann, B. Die Stammeslehren der Dschagga. München, 1932. 3v.
Afr 1623.932.5   Hoffher, René. L'économie marocaine. Paris, 1932.
Afr 8089.32   Hole, Hugh Marshall. The passing of the black kings. London, 1932.
Afr 4199.20   Ibn Tagribandi. Les biographies du Manhal Safi. Le Caire, 1932.
Afr 8045.14   Jabavu, D.D.T. Native disabilities in South Africa. Lovedale, 1932.
Afr 626.17   Jussiaume, E. Reflexions sur l'économie africaine. Paris, 1932.
Afr 2875.43   Kalbskopf, W. Die Aussenpolitik der Mittelmächte im Tripoliskrieg...1911-1912. Erlangen, 1932.
Afr Doc 3207.331   Kenya. Census Office. Report on the non-native census enumeration made in the colony and protectorate of Kenya. Nairobi, 1932.
Afr 8846.15   Kenyon, J.T. An address delivered at the University of Stellenbosch on 12th, 13th, 14th Oct. 1932. n.p., 1932.
Afr 3740.10   Labatut, Guy de. Fachoda. 4e ed. Paris, 1932.
Afr 1609.32F   Ladreit de Lacharrière, J. Au Maroc en suivant Foucauld. Paris, 1932.
Afr 5585.25   Launois, Pierre. L'Etat Malgache et ses transformations avant le régime français. Thèse. Paris, 1932.
Afr 5318.20   Lecoeur, C. Le culte de la génération. Paris, 1932.
Afr 2731.10   Lehuraux, L.J. Au Sahara avec le commandant Charlet. Paris, 1932.
Afr 7119.32   Lemos, A. de. Historia de Angola. Lisboa, 1932.
Afr 9549.32   Letcher, Owen. South central Africa. Johannesburg, 1932.
Afr 8657.90.51   Le Vaillant, F. Voyages de F. Le Vaillant dans l'intérieur de l'Afrique, 1781-1785. v.1-2. Paris, 1932.
Afr 5765.24   Lhande, P. Madagascar, 1832-1932. Paris, 1932.
Afr 820.15   Luigi, Duke of the Abruzzi. La esplorazione dello Uabi-Uebi Scebeli. Milano, 1932.
Afr 620.3   Martens, Otto. African handbook and traveller's guide. London, 1932.
Afr 4368.5.25   Massaia, G. I miei trentacinque anni di missione. Torino, 1932.
Afr 9632.5F   Maugham, F.H. North Charterland concession inquiry. Report, July, 1932. London, 1932.
Afr 1840.22   Maunier, R. Loi française et coutume indigene en Algerie. Paris, 1932.
Afr 1571.17.12A   Maurois, A. Lyautey. N.Y., 1932.
Afr 1571.17.9   Maurois, A. Lyautey. Paris, 1932.
Afr 609.32   Maydon, H.C. Big game shooting in Africa. London, 1932.

1932 - cont.

Afr 2875.45	Meyer, Paul. Die Neutralität Deutschlands und Österreich-Ungarns im italienischer Krieg, 1911-1912. Inaug. Diss. Göttingen, 1932.
Afr 1340.20	Michel, Andre. Traité du contentieux administratif au Maroc. Thèse. Paris, 1932.
Afr 3994.932	Michel, Bernard. L'évolution du budget égyptien. n.p., 1932.
Afr 1624.932	Milleron, Jacques. Le controle des engagements de depenses au Maroc. Thèse. Paris, 1932.
Afr 2480.5	Mirot, Leon. Une expédition française en Tunisie au XIVe siècle. Paris, 1932.
Afr 4785.29	Monile, F. Somalia (ricordi e visioni). Bologna, 1932.
Afr 5248.10	Monteil, Charles. Une cité soudanaise, Djénné. Paris, 1932.
Afr 9839.22.5	Murray, S.S. A handbook of Nyasaland. London, 1932.
Afr 4719.32	Pantano, G. Ventitre anni di vita africana. Firenze, 1932.
Afr 2798.5	Perret, Robert. Itinéraire d'In-Salah au Tahat à travers l'Ahaggar. Paris, 1932.
Afr 2870.16	Piccioli, A. Tripolitania scuola di energia. Roma, 1932.
Afr 7815.37	Plancquaert, M. Les Jaga et les Bayaka du Kwango. Bruxelles, 1932.
Afr 1623.932	Pourquier, Rene. L'impôt sur les plus-values immobilieres au Maroc. Thèse. Paris, 1932.
Afr 3069.32A	Précis de l'histoire d'Egypte. Caire, 1932-35. 4v.
Afr 1609.32.5	Rabat, Maroc. Institut des Hautes Etudes Marocaines. Initiation au Maroc. Rabat, 1932.
Afr 1724.7	Ricard, Robert. Un document portugais sur la place de Mazagrn au début du XVIIe siècle. Thèse. Paris, 1932.
Afr 8678.13.40	Richards, A.I. Hunger and work in a savage tribe. London, 1932.
Afr 5832.5.5	Roubaud, L. La Bourdonnais. Paris, 1932.
Afr 500.40	Salvador, M. La penetrazione demografica europea in Africa. Torino, 1932.
Afr 2749.32	Sanchez, J.G.R. El Sahara occidental. 1. ed. Madrid, 1932.
Afr 3725.7.5	Schweitzer, G. Von Khartum zum Kongo. Berlin, 1932.
Afr 4000.15	Seligman, C.G. Pagan tribes of the Nilotic Sudan. London, 1932.
Afr 2870.14	Sillani, T. La Libia in venti anni di occupazione italiana. Roma, 1932.
Afr 8678.33F	South Africa. Native Economic Committee. Report of Native Economic Committee 1930-1932. Pretoria, 1932.
Afr 8656.85	Stel, Simon van der. Journal of his expedition to Namaqualand. London, 1932.
Afr 9149.32	Stevenson-Hamilton, James. The Kruger national park. Johannesburg, South Africa, 1932.
Afr 3993.932	Sulayman, Ali. L'industrialisation de l'Egypte. London, 1932.
Afr 6280.11.20	Talbot, P.A. Tribes of the Niger delta. London, 1932.
Afr Doc 3407.331F	Tanganyika. Secretariat. Census of the native population of Tanganyika territory, 1931. Dar es Salaam, 1932.
Afr 6850.9F	Tanganyika Territory. Secretariat. Census of the native population of Tanganyika territory, 1931. Dar es Salaam, 1932.
Afr 2819.32	Taraschi, T.M. La Libia italiana, nella preparazione diplomatica e nella conquista. Napoli, 1932.
Afr 1713.15	Tharaud, Jerome. La nuit de Fes. Paris, 1932.
Afr 8659.32	Trevor, Tudor Gruffydd. Forty years in Africa. London, 1932.
Afr 640.5.35	Trilled, H. Le Pygmées de la forêt équatoriale. Paris, 1932.
Afr 5235.194.5	Triviet, E. Au Soudan français. Paris, 1932.
Afr 3300.25	Vandenbosch, F. Vingt années d'Egypte. Paris, 1932.
Afr 2446.5	Varloud. La Tunisie d'il y a cinquante ans. Paris, 1932.
Afr 1750.8	Vieuchange, M. Smara, the forbidden city. N.Y., 1932.
Afr 718.2.120	Wassermann, J. Bula Matari. Berlin, 1932.
Afr 6420.30	Weigt, Ernst. Die Kolonisation Kenias. Inaug. Diss. Leipzig, 1932.
Afr 9170.20	Wood, Clement. The man who killed Kitchener, the life of Fritz Joubert Duquesne, 1879. N.Y., 1932.
Afr 4785.35	Zammarano, V. Tedesco. Impressioni di caccia in Somalia italiana. 3a ed. Milano, 1932.
Afr 4390.30	Zintgraff, Alfred. Der Tod des Löwen von Juda. Berlin, 1932.

1933

Afr 6280.26	Abraham, R.C. The Tiv people. Lagos, 1933.
Afr 3285.20	Adams, Charles C. Islam and modernism in Egypt. London, 1933.
Afr 609.33.5	African Safaris, N.Y. A new motor route through Africa. N.Y., 1933.
Afr 7122.12	Albuquerque Felner, A. De. Angola. Coimbra, 1933.
Afr 609.33.10	Anstein, H. Afrika, wie ich es erlebte. Stuttgart, 1933.
Afr 2209.33	Arnaud, R. Les compagnons du jardin. Paris, 1933.
Afr 8687.248	Barnes, Bertram Herbert. Johnson of Nyasaland. Westminster, 1933.
Afr 609.33.15	Behn, Fritz. Kwa heri Afrika. Stuttgart, 1933.
Afr 9560.15	Belgium. Treaties. Great Britain, 1933. Exchange of notes between His Majesty's government in the United Kingdon...Belgian government. London, 1933.
Afr 6465.56	Bellingham, B.L. Mombasa. Nairobi, 1933.
Afr 7073.3	Bernatzik, Hugo. Geheimnisvolle Inseln Tropen-Afrikas. Berlin, 1933.
Afr 5874.20	Besant, Walter. Bourbon journal, August, 1863. London, 1933.
Afr 6535.17	Bland-Sutton, J. Men and creatures in Uganda. London, 1933.
Afr 5344.7	Boulnois, Jean. Gnon-Sua, dieu des Guéré. Paris, 1933.
Afr 5346.11	Bouys, P. Le bas Cavally (Afrique occidentale française) et son avenir. Thèse. Montpellier, 1933.
Afr 5054.33	Bovill, E.W. Caravans of the old Sahara. London, 1933.
Afr 11230.92.100	Bowditch, L. Peter, a tale of the Greek trek. Pretoria, 1933.
Afr 8140.35	Braak, K. Zuid-Afrika en Engeland. Utrecht, 1933.
Afr 1555.3.15	Brugmans, H. Pantersprong. 's-Gravenhage, 1933.
Afr 7175.27	Burr, Malcolm. A fossicker in Angola. London, 1933.
Afr 8678.339	Campbell, Dugald. Blazing trails in Bantu land. London, 1933.
Afr 2950.15	Cerrata, L. Sirtis, studio geografico-storico. Avellino, 1933.
Afr 4700.33	Cesari, Cesare. Gli italiani nella conoscenza dell'Africa. Roma, 1933.
Afr 4700.33.5	Cesari, Cesare. Pionieri italiani in Africa. Rome, 1933.

1933 - cont.

Afr 6620.60	Charbonneau, J. On se bat sous l'équateur. Paris, 1933.
Afr 1609.33F	Chevrillon, A. Visions du Maroc. Marseille, 1933.
Afr 8175.24	Chilvers, Hedley A. The yellow man looks on, being the story of the Anglo-Dutch conflict in Southern Africa. London, 1933.
Afr 4389.11.20	Cipolla, A. In Etiopia. 4a ed. Torino, 1933.
Afr 4559.24.9	Civimini, G. Ricordi di carovana. 2 ed. Milano, 1933.
Afr 5947.10	Coll, A. Villa-cisneros. Madrid, 1933.
Afr 6420.20.5	Commission Regarding the Boundary Between Kenya and Italian Somaliland. Agreement between the local commission appointed to settle certain points...boundary...Kenya and Italian Somaliland. London, 1933.
Afr 6420.20	Commission Regarding the Boundary Between Kenya and Italian Somaliland. Agreement recording the decisions of the commission appointed and treaty between the United Kingdom and Italy of July 15, 1924. London, 1933.
Afr 3230.17	Crabitès, Pierre. Ismail, the maligned khedive. London, 1933.
Afr 555.9.60A	Davis, John Merle. Modern industry and the African. London, 1933.
Afr 5780.5	Decary, Raymond. L'Androy, extreme sud de Madagascar. Paris, 1933. 2v.
Afr 3230.20A	Douin, Georges. Histoire du règne du khedive Ismail. Roma, 1933-34. 5v.
Afr 6879.25.6	Dugmore, Arthur R. The wonderland of big game, being an account of two trips through Tanganyika and Kenya. London, 1933.
Afr 5620.15	Durand, Alfred. Les derniers jours de la cour hova. Paris, 1933.
Afr 1623.933.5	Evin, Guy. L'industrie au Maroc et ses problemes. Thèse. Paris, 1933.
Afr 1573.35	Fernandez Arias, Adelardo. Visperas de sangre en Marruecos. Madrid, 1933.
Afr 5190.12	Gaffiot, R. Gorée, capitale déchue. Paris, 1933.
Afr 609.33	Gatti, Attilio. Hidden Africa. London, 1933.
Afr 3979.33	Géographie du bassin du Nil. Paris, 1933.
Afr 5765.26	Goyau, G. Les grands desseins missionaires d'Henri de Solages (1786-1832). Paris, 1933.
Afr 4700.33.15	Gravelli, A. Africa. Roma, 1933.
Afr 9345.50	Great Britain. Commission on the Financial Position of Bechuanaland Protectorate. Financial and economic position of Bechuanaland protectorate. London, 1933.
Afr 1635.17	Guennoun, S. La montagne berbere les ait oumalon et le pays zaian. Rabat, 1933.
Afr 626.7	Guernier, E.L. L'Afrique, champ d'expansion de l'Europe. Paris, 1933.
Afr 8252.227.15	Halle, G. Mayfair to Maritzburg. London, 1933.
Afr 510.10.5	Hanotaux, G. Pour l'empire colonial français. Paris, 1933.
Afr 8252.227	Harding, C. Far bugles. London, 1933.
Afr 3128.15	Hassan, Z.M. Les Tuluenides, étude de l'Egypte musulmane à fin du IXe siècle 868-905. Thèse. Paris, 1933.
Afr 8089.33	Hattersley, A.F. South Africa, 1652-1933. London, 1933.
Htn Afr 6275.32.5*	Hives, Frank. Ju-Ju and justice in Nigeria. London, 1933.
Afr 9689.33	Hughes, Joseph Edward. Eighteen years on Lake Bangweulu. London, 1933.
Afr 1915.11	Hutin, Paul. La doctrine de l'Association des indigènes et des Français en Algérie. Thèse. Paris, 1933.
Afr 4766.10	Italy. Treaties. Great Britain. 1933. Agreement concerning claims of certain British and Italian protected persons. London, 1933.
Afr 4430.27	Jacoby, C.M. On special mission to Abyssinia. N.Y., 1933.
Afr 6118.2.7	Jobson, R. The golden trade, 1620-21. London, 1933.
Afr 590.36	Kessel, Joseph. Marchés d'esclaves. Paris, 1933.
Afr 5749.33.5	Laurence, A. Madagascar. Paris, 1933.
Afr 4766.10.15	Lefebvre, R. Politica somala. Bologna, 1933.
Afr 1571.15	Leglay, M. Chronique marocaine. Paris, 1933.
Afr 3275.17.85	Lloyd, G.A.L. Egypt since Cromer. London, 1933-34. 2v.
Afr 8250.29	Lockhart, J.G. Cecil Rhodes. London, 1933.
Afr 7812.233	Louwers, Octave. Le problème financier et le problème économique au Congo belge en 1932. Bruxelles, 1933.
Afr 5955.5	Madrid, F. La Guinea incognita. Madrid, 1933.
Afr 9632.5.5F	Maugham, F.H. North charterland concession inquiry. Report, May 30, 1933. London, 1933.
Afr 500.50	Mendelssohn-Bartholdy, A. Europäische Mandatgemeinschaft in Mittelafrika. Roma, 1933.
Afr 590.40	Mercier, René. Le travail obligatoire dans les colonies africaines. Vesoul, 1933.
Afr 4513.15	Micaletti, K. Sangue italiano in Etiopia. Firenze, 1933.
Afr 8250.25	Millin, S.G. Rhodes. London, 1933.
Afr 555.3.27	Missionaires en Afrique française. Paris, 1933.
Afr 4559.33	Monfried, Henri de. Vers les terres hostiles de l'Ethiopie. Paris, 1933.
Afr 4785.933.5	Monile, F. Africa orientale. Bologna, 1933.
Afr 2223.933	Münnich, H. Der Verkehr Algeriens-Tunesiens mit Frankreich. Inaug. Diss. Leipzig, 1933.
Afr 3986.33	Naldoni, Nardo. L'Egitto economico e le sue relazioni con l'Italia. Genova, 1933.
Afr 3979.33.3	Oliver, Mildred Alice. Letters from Egypt. London, 1933.
Afr 5130.22.3	Peter, G. L'effort français au Sénégal. Paris, 1933.
Afr 5130.22	Peter, G. L'effort français au Sénégal. Thèse. Paris, 1933.
Afr 5749.33.10	Petit, G. Madagascar. Paris, 1933.
Afr 4700.33.10	Piccioli, A. La nuova Italia d'oltremare. Verona, 1933. 2v.
Afr 4500.5	Pigli, Mario. L'Etiopia moderna nelle sue relazioni internazionali, 1859-1931. Padova, 1933.
Afr 1750.28	Pita, F. Del protectorado español en Marruecos. Melilla, 1933.
Afr 8250.27	Plomer, W. Cecil Rhodes. London, 1933.
Afr 4700.13	Pollera, Alberto. Piccola bibliografia dell'Africa orientale con speciale riguardo all'Eritrea e paesi confinanti. Asmara, 1933.
Afr 4785.27	Pomilio, Marco. Un giornalista all'equatore. Firenze, 1933.
Afr 1658.37	Reguert, P.T. L'agression riffaine en 1925. Paris, 1933.
Afr 6620.70	Reitz, Deneys. Africander. N.Y., 1933.
Afr 8289.29.4	Reitz, Deneys. Commando. London, 1933.
Afr 6620.75.5	Reitz, Deneys. Trekking on. London, 1933.
Afr 2230.40	Remond, Martial. Au coeur du pays kabyle. Alger, 1933.
Afr 6898.2	Roegels, Fritz Carl. Mit Carl Peters in Afrika. Berlin, 1933.
Afr 8140.21	Rogers, Howard. Native administration in the Union of South Africa. Johannesburg, 1933.
Afr 3809.33	Roulet, Edouard. La mission Roulet. Paris, 1933.
Afr 5749.33	Rusillon, H. Un petit continent, Madagascar. Paris, 1933.

1933 - cont.

Afr 1570.65 Sabin, Mony. La paix au Maroc. Paris, 1933.
Afr 3230.12.5 Sabry, Mohammed. L'empire égyptien sous Ismail et l'ingérence anglo-française (1863-1879). Paris, 1933.
Afr 2945.26 Serra, F. Italia e Senussia. Milano, 1933.
Afr 4732.17 Sillani, Tomaso. L'Affrica orientale italiana. Roma, 1933.
Afr Doc 4307.331F South Africa. Report with summaries and analysis, number, sex, geographical distribution and ages of the European population. Pretoria, 1933.
Afr 8659.33 Stackpole, E.J. South Africa, impressions of an American, 1933. Harrisburg, 1933.
Afr 2632.11 Sulla questione tunisina. Roma, 1933.
Afr 718.2.101 Symons, A.J.A. H.M. Stanley. London, 1933.
Afr 7565.8 Thomson, R.S. Fondation de l'état indépendant du Congo. Bruxelles, 1933.
Afr 555.40.5 Tucker, J.T. Angola, the land of the blacksmith prince. London, 1933.
Afr 8140.25 Uys, C.J. In the era of Shepstone, being a study of British expansion in South Africa (1842-1877). Lovedale, 1933.
Afr 4785.25 Vecchi, B.V. Migiurtinia. Torino, 1933.
Afr 718.2.115 Wassermann, J. Bula Matari, Stanley, conqueror of a continent. N.Y., 1933.
Afr 6738.25 Weiler, Carlos. Wirtschaftsgeographie des britischen Mandats Kamerun. Inaug. Diss. Berlin, 1933.
Afr 530.12.5 Welk, E. Die schwarze Sonne. Berlin, 1933.
Afr 8687.386 Wilder, George Albert. The white African. Bloomfield, 1933.
Afr 6535.33 Worthington, S. Inland waters of Africa. London, 1933.

1934

Afr 8135.17 Agar-Hamilton, J.A.I. South Africa. London, 1934.
Afr 3979.34 Aveline, Claude. La promenade égyptienne. Paris, 1934.
Afr 7377.34 Azikiwe, Nnamdi. Liberia in world politics. London, 1934.
Afr 8250.31 Baker, H. Cecil Rhodes. London, 1934.
Afr 8676.34 Ballinger, W.G. Race and economics in South Africa. London, 1934.
Afr 710.68 Barasiola, Carlo. Sulle orme di Roma. Milano, 1934.
Afr 2748.32 Bargagli-Petrucci, O. Nel Fezzan, aprile, maggio 1932. Firenze, 1934.
Afr 8095.80 Barnouw, Adrian. Language and race problems in South Africa. Nijhoff, 1934.
Afr 4559.34.35 Bartleet, Eustace John. In the land of Sheda. Birmingham, 1934.
Afr 7809.34 Belgium. Commission du Parc National Albert. Parc National Albert. Bruxelles, 1934.
Afr 6979.34 Beumhagen, H., O Südwestafrika Einst und Jetzt. Berlin, 1934.
Afr 2609.34.5 Bonniard, F. Le tell septentrional en Tunisie. Thèse. Paris, 1934.
Afr 2609.34 Bonniard, F. La Tunisie du nord. Paris, 1934. 2v.
Afr 1571.27 Bordeaux, Henry. Le miracle du Maroc. Paris, 1934.
Afr 6488.5 Brendel, Horst. Die Kolonisation Ugandas. Inaug. Diss. Grossenhain, 1934.
Afr 1550.45 Brenning, H.E. Die grossen Mächte und Marokko in den Jahren vor dem Marokko-Abkommen von 8. Apr. 1904 (1898-1904). Berlin, 1934.
Afr 8140.16 Brookes, E.H. The colour problems of South Africa. Lovedale, 1934.
Afr 3705.12 Buchan, John. Gordon at Khartoum. Edinburgh, 1934.
Afr 1990.30 Bugeaud de la Piconnerie, T.R. Le peuplement français de l'Algérie. Tunis, 1934.
Afr 4700.34.5 Castelbarco, G. L'ordinamento sindacale-corporativo nell organizzazione delle colonie italiane. Milano, 1934.
Afr 4559.34.25 Celarie, H. Ethiopie XXe siècle. Paris, 1934.
Afr 4764.934 Cesari, Cesare. La Somalia italiana. Roma, 1934-35.
Afr 4115.18 Clerget, Marcel. Le Caire. v.1-2. Le Caire, 1934. 2v.
Afr 5045.20 Clerisse, Henry. Trente mille kilomètres à travers l'Afrique française. Paris, 1934.
Afr 1494.5.2 Comité d'Action Marocaine. Annexes au plan de réformes marocaines. n.p., 1934.
Afr 1494.5 Comité d'Action Marocaine. Plan de réformes marocaines. n.p., 1934.
Afr 4719.34 Cortese, Guido. Eritrea. Roma, 1934.
Afr 3675.11 Crabitès, Pierre. The winning of the Sudan. London, 1934.
Afr 5054.34 Davis, S.C. Reservoirs of men, a history of the black troops of French West Africa. Thèse. Chambéry, 1934.
Afr 7175.33 Delachaux, T. Pays et peuples d'Angola. Neuchatel, 1934.
Afr 1623.934.10 Ecorcheville, C. Production et protection au Maroc. Paris, 1934.
Afr 609.29.15 Edschmid, Kasimir. Afrika nackt und Angezogen. Frankfurt a.M., 1934.
Afr 8735.5.10 Edwards, I.E. Eighteen-twenty settlers in South Africa. London, 1934.
Afr 3035.10 Egypt. Laws, statutes, etc. Recueil de firmans impériaux ottomans. Le Caire, 1934.
Afr 8140.23 Evans, I.L. Native policy in Southern Africa. Cambridge, Eng., 1934.
Afr 7809.34.5 Fondation pour favoriser l'étude scientifique des parcs nationaux du Congo belge. Brussels, 1934.
Afr 555.146 Fraser, A.R. Donald Fraser of Livingstonia. London, 1934.
Afr 609.34.5 Gatti, Attilio. Black mist. London, 1934.
Afr 2609.34.10 Geniaux, C. L'âme musulmane en Tunisie. Paris, 1934.
Afr 4700.34 Giaccardi, A. Dieci anni di fascismo nelle colonie italiane. Verona, 1934.
Afr 2948.14 Graziani, Rodolfo. La riconquista del Fezzan. Milano, 1934.
Afr 6310.34F Great Britain. Commission. Administration of Justice in Kenya. Commission of inquiry into the administration of justice in Kenya, Uganda...in criminal matters, May, 1933. London, 1934.
Afr 4559.34.10 Griaule, M. Les flambeurs d'hommes. Paris, 1934.
Afr 1635.19 Guennoun, J. La voix des monts. Rabat, 1934.
Afr 28.20 Hache, J. Bibliographie africaine de périodiques. Bruxelles, 1934.
Afr 6118.7 Hardinge, Rex. Gambia and beyond. London, 1934.
Afr 1623.934.5 Hoffherr, Rene. Revenus et niveaux de vie indigenes au Maroc. Paris, 1934.
Afr 5405.270 Homet, Marcel. Congo, terre de souffrances. Paris, 1934.
Afr 2209.34F Horizons de France, Paris. Algérie. Paris, 1934.
Afr 4070.45 Howard-Williams, E.G. Something new out of Africa. London, 1934.
Afr 7309.34 Hubbard, M.C. No one to blame. N.Y., 1934.

1934 - cont.

Afr 1095.25 Ilter Aziz Samih. Şimalî Afrikada Türkler. Istanbul, 1934-37.
Afr 7176.28 Informação económica sôbre o Império e alguns elementos de informação geral. Pôrto, 1934.
Afr 7125.2 Jesuits. Relações de Angola. Coimbra, 1934.
Afr 8040.15 Kayser, H. Demokratie und Föderalismus in der südafrikanischen Union. Düsseldorf, 1934.
NEDL Afr 12131.5.100 Khayat, Georges. Riad. Caire, 1934.
Afr 555.17.15 Koehler, Henry. L'église chrétienne du Maroc et la mission franciscaine, 1221-1790. Paris, 1934.
Afr 7377.34.5 Koren, W. Liberia, the league and the United States. N.Y., 1934.
Afr 3740.14 Kossatz, Heinz. Untersuchungen über den französisch-englischen Weltgegensatz im Faschodajahr (1898). Breslau, 1934.
Afr 1640.10 Lachapelle, F. Les Tekna du sud Marocain. Paris, 1934.
Afr 2305.1 Lapalud, P. Le douar Aghbal: monographie économique. Thèse. Alger, 1934.
Afr 4785.20 Lavagetto, A. La vita eroica del Capitano Bottego (1893-1897). Milano, 1934.
Afr 9854.12 Laws, Robert. Reminiscences of Livingstonia. Edinburgh, 1934.
Afr 5640.27 Leblond, M. Madagascar, creation française. Paris, 1934.
Afr 5887.5 Leguat, F. Voyages et aventures de François Leguat et de ses compagnons en deux îles désertes 1690-1698. Paris, 1934.
Afr 9689.34 Letcher, Owen. When life was rusted through. Johannesburg, 1934.
Afr 8835.25 Lewis, C. Cape Town. Cape Town, 1934.
Afr 8145.18 Lewis, Cecil. Historical records of the Church of the province of South Africa. London, 1934.
Afr 8278.99.37 Leyds, W.J. Vierde verzameling (Correspondentie 1900-1902. Deel 1-2. 's-Gravenhage, 1934. 3v.
Afr 8235.17A Lovell, R.I. The struggle for South Africa, 1875-1899. N.Y., 1934.
Afr 3675.15 MacMichael, H. The Anglo-Egyptian Sudan. London, 1934.
Afr 2632.9 Maggio, G. di. Gli Italiani e le professioni liberali in Tunisia. Tunis, 1934.
Afr 6540.6.5 Mair, L.P. An African people in the twentieth century. London, 1934.
Afr 718.2.110 Malcorps, A. De reus van Kongo. Brugge, 1934.
Afr 3138.10 Mamour, P.H. Polemics on the origin of the Fatimi caliphs. London, 1934.
Afr 1555.3.25 Mann, Walter. Die Agadirkrisis des Jahres 1911. Inaug. Diss. Giessen, 1934.
Afr 5056.134.7 Martet, Jean. Les batisseurs de royaumes. Paris, 1934.
Afr 590.48 Martin, Gaston. Negriers et bois d'ébène. Grenoble, 1934.
Afr 1733.5.15 Mauclair, Camille. Rabat et Sale. Paris, 1934.
Afr 1571.17.11 Maurois, A. Lyautey. Paris, 1934.
Afr 4559.34 Mittelholzer, W. Abessinienflug. Zürich, 1934.
Afr 4060.6F Monneret de Villard, U. I vescovi giacobiti della Nubia. Le Caire, 1934.
Afr 6780.26 Moulaert, Georges. La campagne du Tanganika (1916-1917). Bruxelles, 1934.
Afr 2945.40 Narducci, G. La colonizzazione della Cirenaica nell antichita e nel presente. Bengasi, 1934.
Afr 9839.34.5 Ntara, S.Y. Man of Africa. London, 1934.
Afr 2749.34 Paris. Musée d'Ethnographie du Trocadero. Exposition du Sahara, 15 mai-28 oct. 1934. Paris, 1934.
Afr 2929.34.5 Paris. Musée d'Ethnographie du Trocadéro. Exposition du Sahara, Le Sahara italien. Rome, 1934.
Afr 4700.33.12 Piccioli, A. La nuova Italia d'oltremare. Milano, 1934. 2v.
Afr 8846.19 Pim, H. A Transkei enquiry, 1933. Lovedale, 1934.
Afr 5758.34 Prunieres, A. Madagascar et la crise. Thèse. Paris, 1934.
Afr 4559.34.30 Pucci, Generoso. Coi 'Negadi' in Etiopia. Firenze, 1934.
Afr 6688.4 Puig, F. Etude sur les coutumes des Cabrais (Togo). Thèse. Toulouse, 1934.
Afr 4559.34.5 Rebeaud, Henri. Chez le roi des rois d'Ethiopie. Neuchâtel, 1934.
Afr 7015.15 Republica Portuguesa. Aires de Ornelas. Lisboa, 1934. 3v.
Afr 5872.7 Réunion. Conseil Supérieur. Correspondance du conseil supérieur de Bourbon et de la Compagnie des Indes...1724-1741. V.1-3. Saint-Denis, 1934-37. 4v.
Afr 555.65 Richter, Julius. Tanganyika and its future. London, 1934.
Afr 9548.7 Robert, Maurice. L'Afrique centrale. Paris, 1934.
Afr 628.234 Rogers, J.A. Hundred amazing facts about the Negro with complete proof. N.Y., 1934.
Afr 1623.934 Romanus, H. Eine wirtschaftsgeographische darstellung...Marokkos und Tunesiens. Inaug. Diss. Königsberg, 1934.
Afr 5058.11 Roseberry, R.S. The Niger vision. Harrisburg, 1934.
Afr 679.34 Rossi, V.G. Tropici Senegal all Angola. Milano, 1934.
Afr 2948.12 Scarin, Emilio. Le oasi del Fezzan. v.1-2. Bologna, 1934.
Afr 5249.5 Seabrook, William Buehler. The white monk of Timbuctoo. N.Y., 1934.
Afr 635.30.15 Seligman, C.G. Egypt and Negro Africa. London, 1934.
Afr 2929.34 Siciliani, D. Paesaggi libici. Tripolitania. Tripoli, 1934.
Afr 9149.34 South Africa. National Parks Board of Trustees. A brief description of the Union's national parks. Pretoria, 1934.
Afr 8028.101 South Africa. Parliament. Library. Afrikanse publikasies. 2. uitg. Pretoria, 1934.
Afr 8678.43 Studies and types of South African native life. Durban, 1934.
Afr 7119.34 Teixeira, Alberto de Almeida. Angola intangivel. Pôrto, 1934.
Afr 1571.33 Vallerie, Pierre. Conquérants et conquis au Maroc. Thèse. Paris, 1934.
Afr 8180.10 Walker, E.A. The great trek. London, 1934.
Afr 1609.34 Wattenavyl, R. Von. Ein land, menschen in Marokko. Zürich, 1934.
Afr 699.31.6 Waugh, E. Remote people. London, 1934.
Afr 6218.9 Wellesley, D.A. Sir George Goldie, founder of Nigeria. London, 1934.
Afr 630.34 Westermann, D. The African to-day. London, 1934.
Afr 609.34.10 Weulersse, Jacques. L'Afrique noire. Paris, 1934.
Afr 6738.30 Wilbois, J. La Cameroun. Paris, 1934.
Afr 3988.4 Winkler, Hans Alexander. Baueren zwischen Wasser und Wüste. Stuttgart, 1934.
Afr 9599.34 Wood and iron, a story of Africa written in memory of H.U.C. London, 1934.
Afr 7369.34 Yancy, E.J. Historical lights of Liberia's yesterday and today. Xenia, 1934.
Afr 7565.12.15 Yarnall, H.E. The great powers and the Congo Conference in the year 1884 and 1885. Inaug. Diss. Göttingen, 1934.

1934 - cont.

Afr 7377.30 Young, James C. Liberia rediscovered. Garden City, 1934.

Afr 3994.934 Yunus, Muhammed Tawfig. The preparation of the Egyptian budget. Cairo, 1934.

Afr 4730.15A Zaghi, Carlo. Le origini della colonia Eritrea. Bologna, 1934.

Afr 3695.3.81 Zanaboni, G. Gessi, l'eroe del Bahr-el-Ghazal. Roma, 1934.

1935

Afr 4513.35.125 Abissinia, problema italiano. Roma, 1935.

Afr 4430.35.19 Africanus. (Pseud.). Etiopia, 1935. 4 ed. Roma, 1935.

Afr 4513.35.60F Aloise, P. Speech of Baron Aloise, head of the Italian delegation to the League of Nations. n.p., 1935.

Afr 9525.877 Andrews, Charles. John White of Mashonaland. London, 1935.

Afr 4259.35.7 Arcuno, Irma. Abissinia ieri ed oggi. 2a ed. Napoli, 1935.

Afr 4393.5 L'Assedio di Macallè. Milano, 1935.

Afr 5832.15.2F Austen, H.C.M. Sea fights and corsairs of the Indian Ocean. Port Louis, 1935.

Afr 3305.3 Awad, Fawzi Tadrus. La souveraineté égyptienne et la déclaration du 28 février 1922. Paris, 1935.

Afr 4050.35 Bagnold, R.A. Libyan sands, travel in a dead world. London, 1935.

Afr 4559.35.60.5 Baravelli, G.C. The last stronghold of slavery, what Abyssinia is. Roma, 1935.

Afr 4559.35.60 Baravelli, G.C. The last stronghold of slavery, what Abyssinia is. Roma, 1935.

Afr 4568.15 Baravelli, G.C. The last stronghold of slavery. Roma, 1935.

Afr 4559.35.58 Baravelli, G.C. L'ultimo baluardo della schiavitù, l'Abyssinia. Roma, 1935.

Afr 820.15.12 Basile, C. Uebi-Scebeli nella spedizione di S.A.R. Luigi di Savoia. Bologna, 1935.

Afr 7809.35 Belgian Luxembourg Touring Office. Travel in the Belgian Congo. Brussels, 1935.

Afr 2710.12 Benedetti, Achille. Dal Sahara al Ciad. Milano, 1935.

Afr 2209.35.10 Berenson, Mary. Across the Mediterranean. Prato, 1935.

Afr 4700.35.10 Bermasconi, G. Le guerre e la politica dell'Italia nell'Africa orientale. Milano, 1935.

Afr 5119.35 Beslier, G.G. Le Sénégal. Paris, 1935.

Afr 4513.35.83 Bonardi, Pierre. Brassard amarante. Paris, 1935.

Afr 8710.15 Botha, C.G. An eighteenth century law library. Cape Town, 1935.

Afr 4394.5 Bronzuoli, A. Adua. Roma, 1935.

Afr 5406.218.5 Bruel, Georges. La France équatoriale africaine. Paris, 1935.

Afr 4513.35.55 Burns, Emile. Abyssinia and Italy. London, 1935.

Afr 4559.35.85 Caimpenta, U. L'impero abissino. 10. ed. Milano, 1935.

Afr 2929.35.15 Campbell, D. Camels through Libya. Philadelphia, 1935.

Afr 4700.35 Canevari, E. Il generale Tommaso Salsa e la sue campagne coloniali. Milano, 1935.

Afr 4513.35.20 Carnegie Endowment for International Peace. Division of Intercourse and Education. The Abyssinian dispute. N.Y., 1935.

Afr 4513.35.30 Carter, Boak. Black shirt, black skin. Harrisburg, 1935.

Afr 4513.35.33 Carter, Boak. Black shirt, black skin. London, 1935.

Afr 2880.20 Casetti, F. Restauratio libyca. Roma, 1935.

Afr 4513.36.55 Ciccarelli, Socrate. L'Italia fascista e l'Abissinia. Torino, 1935.

Afr 590.38 Cicognani, D. La questione della schiavetà coloniale dal Congresso di Vienna a oggi. Firenze, 1935.

Afr 4430.35.25 Collombet, E. L'Ethiopie moderne et son avènement à la communauté internationale. Thèse. Dijon, 1935.

Afr 4559.35.80 Comyn-Platt, Thomas. The Abyssinian storm. London, 1935.

Afr 4513.19 Conti Rossini, C. Italia ed Etiopia dal trattato d'Ucciali alla battaglia di Adua. Roma, 1935.

Afr 4559.35.50 Coon, C.S. Measuring Ethiopia and flight into Arabia. Boston, 1935.

Afr 5860.15 Cornu, Henri. Une expérience législative à la Réunion. Thèse. Paris, 1935.

Afr 3217.15 Crabitès, Pierre. Ibrahim of Egypt. London, 1935.

Afr 1445.10.5 Cruikshank, E.F. Morocco at the parting of the ways. Philadelphia, 1935.

Afr 1445.10 Cruikshank, E.F. Morocco at the parting of the ways. Diss. Philadelphia, 1935.

Afr 6883.11 Culwick, A.F. Ubena of the rivers. London, 1935.

Afr 4559.26.3 Darley, Henry. Slaves and ivory. London, 1935.

Afr 4559.26.4 Darley, Henry. Slaves and ivory in Abyssinia. N.Y., 1935.

Afr 4155.5 Decosson, A. Mareotis. London, 1935.

Afr 5235.235 Delavignette, R.L. Soudan, Paris, Boulogne. Paris, 1935.

Afr 3705.14 Delebecque, J. Gordon et le drame de Khartoum. Paris, 1935.

Afr 1571.31 Deschamps, Jean L. Souvenirs des premiers temps du Maroc français (1912-1915). Paris, 1935.

Afr 609.35 Desmond, Shaw. African log. London, 1935.

Afr 2870.20 Despois, Jean. La colonisation italienne en Libye. Thèse. Paris, 1935.

Afr 2949.7 Despois, Jean. Le djebel Nefousa (Tripolitaine). Paris, 1935.

Afr 2949.7.3 Despois, Jean. Le djebel Nefousa (Tripolitaine). Thèse. Paris, 1935.

Afr 8089.35 Dietzel, K.H. Die Südafrikanische Union...Abhandlung. Berlin, 1935.

Afr 4700.35.30 Dotti, Ernesto. Aspetti attuoli dell'economia delle colonie italiane dell'Africa orientale. Roma, 1935.

Afr 3215.3.20 Douin, Georges. L'Egypte de 1828 à 1930. Roma, 1935.

Afr 4559.35.75 Dunckley, F.C. Eight years in Abyssinia. London, 1935.

Afr 3215.3.30 Durand-Viel, G.C. Les campagnes navales de Mohammed Aly et d'Ibrahim. Paris, 1935. 2v.

Afr 8045.16 Edelman, H. Vorming en ontvoogding van de Unie van Zuid-Africa. Proefschrift. Rotterdam, 1935.

Afr 699.28.5 Edward, Duke of Windsor. Sport and travel in East Africa, an account of two visits, 1928 and 1930. N.Y., 1935.

Afr 8055.25 Emden, P.H. Randlords. London, 1935.

Afr 4390.60 Fanelli, Armando. Taitù e Manelik. Milano, 1935.

Afr 4559.35.30 Farago, L. Abyssinia on the eve. London, 1935.

Afr 4513.36.85 Fasci Italiani all'Estero. L'Abissinia e noi. Roma, 1935.

Afr 1680.9 Felze, Jacques. Au Maroc inconnu dans le haut-atlas et le sud Marocain. Grenoble, 1935.

Afr 4340.5 Ferreira, F. Palyart Pinto. Os Portugueses na Ethiópia. Lisboa, 1935.

Afr 1568.5 Flournoy, F.R. British policy towards Morocco in the age of Palmerston (1830-1865). London, 1935.

1935 - cont.

Afr 4559.25.5 Forbes, R.T. From Red Sea to blue Nile. N.Y., 1935.

Afr 4513.35.160 Ford, J.W. War in Africa. N.Y., 1935.

Afr 1571.17.22 Franchet Desperey, L.F.M.F. Discours de réception. 2e ed. Paris, 1935.

Afr 3978.69.25 Fromentin, E. Voyage en Egypte (1869). Paris, 1935.

Afr 6685.7 Full, August. Fünfzig Jahre Togo. Berlin, 1935.

Afr 9439.35.5 Gale, W.D. One man's vision. London, 1935.

Afr 2510.10 Gallico, A. Tunisi e i consoli Sardi, 1816-1834. Bologna, 1935.

Afr 2749.23.10A Gautier, E.F. Sahara. N.Y., 1935.

Afr 4700.35.25 Giglio, V. Le guerre coloniali d'Italia. Milano, 1935.

Afr 6060.20F Gold Coast (Colony). Memorandum on the revision of salaries and other conditions...West Africa. Accra, 1935.

Afr 4559.35.55 Goldmann, Wilhelm. Das ist Abessinien. Bern, 1935.

Afr 5056.135 Gorer, G. Africa dances, West African Negroes. London, 1935.

Afr 4559.34.15 Griaule, M. Abyssinian journal. London, 1935.

Afr 4559.34.20 Griaule, M. Burners of men, modern Ethiopia. Philadelphia, 1935.

Afr 1340.25 Grillet, M. Les alignements en droit marocain. Thèse. Paris, 1935.

Afr 4559.35 Gruehl, Max. Abessinien, ahoi. Berlin, 1935.

Afr 4559.35.65 Gruehl, Max. Abessinien. Berlin, 1935.

Afr 4559.35.3 Gruehl, Max. L'impero del Negus Neghesti. Milano, 1935.

Afr 5235.55.10 Gwynn, Stephen. Mungo Park and the quest of the Niger. N.Y., 1935.

Afr 1609.31.30 Hall, Leland. Salah and his American. N.Y., 1935.

Afr 4070.53A Hamilton, J.A. de C. The Anglo-Egyptian Sudan from within. London, 1935.

Afr 4430.35 Harmsworth, G. Abyssinian adventure. London, 1935.

Afr 4559.35.95 Hayter, Frank Edward. The quest of Sheba's mines. London, 1935.

Afr 9489.35 Hemans, H.N. The log of a native commissioner. London, 1935.

Afr 2209.35.4 Henriot, Emile. Vers l'oasis, en Algérie. Paris, 1935.

Afr 8685.30.2 Herman, L. A history of the Jews in South Africa from the earliest times to 1895. Johannesburg, 1935.

Afr 4513.35.120 Hernandez Alfonso, L. Abisinia. Madrid, 1935.

Afr 4559.35.70 Herrmann, Gerhard. Abessinien; Raum als Schicksal. Leipzig, 1935.

Afr 718.2.106 Hird, Frank. H.M. Stanley. London, 1935.

Afr 4559.35.107 Huyn, Ludwig. Abessinien, Afrikas Unruhe-Herd. Salzburg, 1935.

Afr 4259.35F Istituto della Enciclopedia Italiana. L'Etiopia. Roma, 1935.

Afr 4700.35.20 Italia in Africa. Torino, 1935.

Afr 4513.35.15 Italo-Ethiopian dispute. Roma, 1935.

Afr 4513.35.17 Italy. Il conflitto italo-etiopico. Roma, 1935.

Afr 4513.35.16 Italy. Italo-Ethiopian dispute. Roma, 1935.

Afr 4513.35.70F Italy. Memorandum of the Italian government on the situation in Abyssinia. n.p., 1935.

Afr 4513.35.65F Italy. Memoria del governo italiano circa la situazione in Etiopia. II. n.p., 1935.

Afr 4719.35 Italy. Escrito. Corpo di stato maggiore. Officio Storico. Storia militare della colonia Eritrea. v.1-2, 2 bis. Roma, 1935-36. 3v.

Afr 4513.35.25 Italy. Historical Society. The Italo-Ethiopian controversy. n.p., 1935.

Afr 4513.35.27 Italy. Historical Society. The Italo-Ethiopian controversy. N.Y., 1935.

Afr 4559.35.18 Jansen, P.G. Abisinia di oggi. 8a ed. Milano, 1935.

Afr 609.35.9 Johnson, Martin. Over African jungles. N.Y., 1935.

Afr 8040.12 Kennedy, W.P.M. The law and custom of the South African constitution. London, 1935.

Afr 2285.22 Kenny, H.T. In lightest Africa. London, 1935.

Afr 1259.35 Khum de Prorok, B. In quest of lost worlds. N.Y., 1935.

Afr 4513.35.115 Klein, Fritz. Warum Krieg um Abessinien. Leipzig, 1935.

Afr 4513.35.100 Lachin, M. L'Ethiopie et son destin. 5e ed. Paris, 1935.

Afr 1573.31 Laget, Paul de. Au Maroc espagnol. Marseille, 1935.

Afr 4389.35.7 Lahse, Erich. Abessinien. 2e Aufl. Leipzig, 1935.

Afr 5190.14 Leca, N. Les pêcheurs de Guet N'Dar. Paris, 1935.

Afr 4513.35.10 Legionarius (pseud.). The grounds for the serious charges brought by Italy against Abyssinia. Roma, 1935.

Afr 4513.35.10.2 Legionarius (pseud.). The grounds for the serious charges brought by Italy against Abyssinia. Rome, 1935.

Afr 1622.5F Levi-Provencal, E. Maroc, atlas historique, geographique et économique. Paris, 1935.

Afr 4559.35.5 Lieberenz, P.K. Das Rätsel Abessinien. Berlin, 1935.

Afr 4559.35.130 Littmann, Enno. Abessinien. Hamburg, 1935.

Afr 9705.5 Lusaka, the new capital of Northern Rhodesia, opened Jubilee Week, 1935. London, 1935.

Afr 5640.4.51 Lyautey, L.H.G. Lettres du sud de Madagascar, 1900-1902. Paris, 1935.

Afr 4500.15 MacCallum, Elizabeth P. Rivalries in Ethiopia. Boston, 1935.

Afr 4559.28.3 MacCreagh, Gordon. The last of free Africa. 2d ed. N.Y., 1935.

Afr 7815.17 Maes, J. Volkenkunde van Belgisch Kongo. Antwerpen, 1935.

Afr 4513.35.50 Makin, W.J. War over Ethiopia. London, 1935.

Afr 4513.35.105 Malizia, N. L'Africa orientale italiana e l'Abissinia. Napoli, 1935.

Afr 4559.35.125 Manzini, Luigi. Panorama etiopico. Milano, 1935.

Afr 4513.35.110 Marino, A. Italia ed Abissinia. Bengasi, 1935.

Afr 7540.25 Menache, Albert. L'administration du Congo belge. Thèse. Nancy, 1935.

Afr 7815.24 Mertens, Joseph. Les Ba Dzing de la Kamtsha. Bruxelles, 1935-39.

Afr 3710.13.5 Messedaglia, Luigi. Uomini d'Africa. Bologna, 1935.

Afr 2268.3 Michel, E. Esuli italiani in Algeria, 1815-1861. Bologna, 1935.

Afr 4559.35.92 Monfried, H. de. Le drame éthiopien. Paris, 1935.

Afr 4869.35 Monfried, H. de. Le lepreux. Paris, 1935.

Afr 1340.20.10 Monier, R. Le contentieux administratif au Maroc. Thèse. Paris, 1935.

Afr 7222.70 Mousinha de Albuquerque. Mousinho de Albuquerque. Lisboa, 1935. 2v.

Afr 4559.35.87 Muehlen, Leo. Im Banne des äthiopischen Hochlandes. 2e Aufl. Berlin, 1935.

Afr 4012.1 Murray, G.W. Sons of Ishmael. London, 1935.

Afr 4559.35.35 Nanni, Ugo. Che cosa è l'Etiopia. Milano, 1935.

Afr 4513.35.150 Nenni, P. Il delitto africano del fascismo. Paris, 1935.

Afr 4582.15.5 Nesbitt, L.M. Hell-hole of creation. N.Y., 1935.

Afr 4259.35.15 Nomado, R. Abissinia. Napoli, 1935.

Afr 9603.10 Nyabongo, Akiki K. The story of an African chief. N.Y., 1935.

1935 - cont.

Afr 4394.9.5 — Oriani, A. L'Ora d'Africa. 2a ed. Bologna, 1935.
Afr 3040.65.5 — O'Rourke, V.A. The juristic status of Egypt and the Sudan. Baltimore, 1935.
Afr 3040.65 — O'Rourke, V.A. The juristic status of EgyptAnd the Sudan. Diss. Baltimore, 1935.
Afr 4513.35.135 — Ortega y Gasset, E. Etiopia, el conflicto italo-abisinio. Madrid, 1935.
Afr 4572.15 — Padoan, L. L'Abissinia nella geografia dell'Africa orientale. Milano, 1935.
Afr 8045.12 — Perham, M. The protectorates of South Africa. London, 1935.
Afr 4785.935 — Perricone, V.A. Ricordi somali. Bologna, 1935.
Afr 2929.35.3 — Piccioli, Angelo. The magic gate of the Sahara. London, 1935.
Afr 4500.5.5 — Pigli, Mario. L'Etiopia, l'incognita africana. 2a ed. Padova, 1935.
Afr 1571.29 — Pinon, Rene. Au Maroc, fin des temps héroiques. Paris, 1935.
Afr 530.24 — Pittaluga, Rosetta. Rievocazioni africane. Brescia, 1935.
Afr 6097.7 — Platt, William James. From fetish to faith. London, 1935.
Afr 3150.9 — Poliak, A.N. Les revoltes populaires en Egypte à l'époque des Mamelouks. Paris, 1935.
Afr 3215.20 — Politçs, Athanasios G. Les rapports de la Grèce et de l'Égypte pendant le regne de Mohamed Aly, 1833-1849. Roma, 1935.
Afr 4710.7 — Pollera, A. Le popolazioni indigene dell'Eritrea. Bologna, 1935.
Afr 6455.38 — Preston, R.O. The genesis of Kenya colony. Nairobi, 1935.
Afr 4430.35.5 — Prochazka, R. von. Abessinien, die schwarze Gefahr. Wien, 1935.
Afr 4430.35.8 — Prochazka, R. von. Abissinia pericolo nero. Milano, 1935.
Afr 3040.70 — Ramadan, A.M.S. Evolution de la législation sur la presse en Egypte. Thèse. Le Caire, 1935.
Afr 4559.35.117 — Rebeaud, Henri. Au service du négus. 2e ed. Paris, 1935.
Afr 5635.20 — Reibell, Emile. Le calvaire de Madagascar. Paris, 1935.
Afr 4559.35.45 — Rey, C.F. The real Abyssinia. London, 1935.
Afr 4513.35.90 — Ridley, F.A. Mussolini over Africa. London, 1935.
Afr 1609.35 — Rigo Derighi, E. Holiday in Morocco. London, 1935.
Afr 4559.35.40 — Rocchi, A. Etiopia ed etiopia. Milano, 1935.
Afr 1942.5 — Ross, F.E. The mission of Joseph Donaldson, Jr. to Algiers, 1795-97. n.p., 1935.
Afr 4259.35.30 — Rossi, Corrado. Abissinia. Milano, 1935.
Afr 5346.5.5 — Roussier, Paul. L'établissement d'Issiny, 1687-1702. Paris, 1935.
Afr 4513.35 — Rowan-Robinson, H. England, Italy, Abyssinia. London, 1935.
Afr 4513.20 — Royal Institute of International Affairs. Abyssinia and Italy. N.Y., 1935.
Afr 6570.3 — Russell, L.M.R. General Rigby, Zanzibar and the slave trade. London, 1935.
Afr 635.7.20 — Sadler, M.E. Arts of West Africa, excluding music. London, 1935.
Afr 1658.42 — Sanchez Javaloy, Roque. El Manco de Tikun. Murcia, 1935.
Afr 4742.26 — Santagata, F. La colonia Eritrea. Napoli, 1935.
Afr 4513.17 — Sapelli, A. Memorie d'Africa 1883-1906. Bologna, 1935.
Afr 555.65.5 — Schappi, F.S. Die katholischen Missionsschulen des Tanganyika-Gebietes. Inaug. Diss. Obergininingen, 1935.
Afr 8252.342.5 — Smithers, E.D. March hare. London, 1935.
Afr 4700.35.15 — Societa Geografica Italiana, Roma. L'Africa orientale. Bologna, 1935.
Afr 8678.9.50 — Sonnabend, E.H. Il fattore demografico nell'organizzazione sociale del Bantu. Roma, 1935.
Afr 8659.35 — South Africa. Railways and Harbours Administration, Johannesburg. The sunshine route. London, 1935.
Afr 520.14 — Spain. Servicio Historico Militar. Acción de España en Africa. Madrid, 1935. 3v.
Afr 4389.35.10 — Sperduti, G. Aspetti della questione etiopica. Roma, 1935.
Afr 9439.35 — Standing, T.G. A short history of Rhodesia and her neighbours. London, 1935.
Afr 4559.35.110 — Stuessy, J. Mit dem Faltboot nach Abessinien. Frauenfeld, 1935.
Afr 6455.59.7 — Szechenyi, Z. Land of elephants, Kenya. London, 1935.
Afr 6498.35 — Thomas, H.B. Uganda. London, 1935.
Afr 6310.35 — Thurnwald, R. Black and white in East Africa. London, 1935.
Afr 1623.935 — Tomas Perez, V. Marruecos. Barcelona, 1935.
Afr 4513.35.130 — Traversi, L. L'Italia e l'Etiopia. Bologna, 1935.
Afr 4513.25 — Varanini, Varo. L'Abissinia attuale sotto tutti i suoi aspetti. Torino, 1935.
Afr 4513.35.44 — Vare, Daniele. Italy, Great Britain and the League in the Italo-Ethiopian conflict. N.Y., 1935.
Afr 4513.35.41 — Vare, Daniele. Italy, Great Britain and the League in the Italo-Ethiopian conflict. N.Y., 1935.
Afr 4700.35.5 — Vecchi, B.V. L'Italia ai margini d'Etiopia. Milano, 1935.
Afr 4766.20 — Vecchi di Val Cismon, C.M. Orizzonti d'impero. Milano, 1935.
Afr 6738.35 — Vereet, E.P.A. Het zwarte leven van Mabumba. n.p., 1935.
Afr 8095.10 — Welch, S.R. Europe's discovery of South Africa. Cape Town, 1935.
Afr 4513.35.78 — Wencker-Wiedberg, F. Abessinien, das Pulverfass Afrikas. 3e Aufl. Düsseldorf, 1935.
Afr 8676.35 — Werle, G. Landwirtschaft und Industrie in der Südafrikanischen Union unter Berücksichtigung der deutschen Pionierarbeit. Inaug. Diss. Eisfeld, 1935.
Afr 4513.35.155 — West, J. War and the workers. N.Y., 1935.
Afr 4513.35.5 — White, F. The Abyssinian dispute. London, 1935.
Afr 4500.10 — Work, Ernest. Ethiopia, a pawn in European diplomacy. New Concord, 1935.
Afr 625.15F — Yusuf Kamal, Prince. Quelques éclaircissements épars sur mes Monumenta cartographica Africae et Aegypti. Leiden, 1935.
Afr 4389.35 — Zischka, A. Abessinien, das letzte ungelöste Problem Afrikas. Bern, 1935.
Afr 4389.35.18 — Zoli, Corrado. Etiopia d'oggi. 3a ed. Roma, 1935.

1936

Afr 4513.36.50 — Abbati, A.H. Italy and the Abyssinian war. London, 1936.
Afr 1254.62 — Abd al-Busit ibn Khalil. Douze récits de voyage inédits en Afrique du nord au XVe siècle. Paris, 1936.
Afr 1259.36 — Adrian, W. Friedliches Afrika. Bern, 1936.
Afr 4512.15 — Agostino Orsini, P. D. Perche andiamo in Etiopia. Roma, 1936.

1936 - cont.

Afr 7130.15.2 — Almeida, João de. Sul de Angola, relatório de um govêrno de distrito, 1908-1910. 2. ed. Lisboa, 1936.
Afr 4430.36 — Asfa Yilma, Princess. Haile Selassie. London, 1936.
Afr 6720.28.15 — Aymerich, J.G. La conquête du Cameroun. Paris, 1936.
Afr 1846.13 — Azan, Paul. L'armee d'Afrique de 1830 à 1852. Paris, 1936.
Afr 4513.36.68 — Badoglio, P. La guerra d'Etiopia. Milano, 1936.
Afr 4199.100 — Bahay, Muhammad. Muhammed Abduh. Hamburg, 1936.
Afr 4559.35.62 — Baravelli, G.C. The last stronghold of slavery. London, 1936.
Afr 4700.36.25 — Bardi, Pietro M. Pionieri e soldati d'Africa orientale dall'acquisto di Assab all'impero romano d'Etiopia. Milano, 1936.
Afr 8285.15 — Barthold, U. Studien zur englischen Vorbereitung des Burenkriegs. Inaug. Diss. Köln, 1936.
Afr 6588.2 — Bartlett, C. Statistics of the Zanzibar Protectorate. 8th ed. Zanzibar, 1936.
Afr 6879.36 — Bent, Newell. Jungle giants. Norwood, Mass., 1936.
Afr 609.36 — Birch-Reynardson, H. High street, Africa. Edinburgh, 1936.
Afr 8659.36.3 — Birkby, Carel. Thirstland treks. London, 1936.
Afr 7803.45 — Bittremieux, Leo. La société secrète des Bakhimba au Mayombe. Bruxelles, 1936.
Afr 609.36.10 — Boehmer, H. Mit 14 ps durch Afrika. Wien, 1936.
Afr 4700.36.5 — Bollati, A. Enciclopedia dei nostri combattimenti coloniali fino al 2 ottobre 1935. Torino, 1936.
Afr 500.55 — Borba za svero-vostochnuice, Afrika. Moscow, 1936.
Afr 5045.38.5 — Bordeaux, H. Nos Indes noires. Paris, 1936.
Afr 5054.36.10 — Bordeaux, W. L'épopée noire. Paris, 1936.
Afr 4513.36.35 — Bourcier, E. L'aventure abyssine. Paris, 1936.
Afr 6455.82 — Brodhurst-Hill, Evelyn. So this is Kenya. London, 1936.
Afr 4559.36.20 — Brusati, G.C. Etiopia, studio geografico-economico. Milano, 1936.
Afr 4513.36.95 — Cabiati, A. La conquista dell impero. Milano, 1936.
Afr 4513.36 — Canada. Department of External Affairs. Documents relating to the Italo-Ethiopian conflict. Ottawa, 1936.
Afr 1609.36.10 — Capriles, Georges. La promenade marocaine. Paris, 1936.
Afr 6160.7 — Carbon Ferrière, J. L'organisation politique, administratif et financière de la colonie britannique de la Gold Coast. Thèse. Paris, 1936.
Afr 1576.5.2 — Carvalho, V. de. La domination portugaise au Maroc du XV. Lisbonne, 1936.
Afr 4559.36.25 — Castro, Lincoln de. Etiopia terra, uomini e cose. 2. ed. Milano, 1936.
Afr 4513.36.20 — Chaplin, W.W. Blood and ink. N.Y., 1936.
Afr 5405.112 — Chavannes, Charles de. Avec Brazza. Paris, 1936.
Afr 4688.15.5 — Cheesman, R.E. Lake Tana and the blue Nile. London, 1936.
Afr 4513.36.70 — Cimmaruta, R. Ual ual. Milano, 1936.
Afr 4513.35.145 — Cipolla, A. Da Baldissera a Badoglio. 4a ed. Firenze, 1936.
Afr 9525.288 — Clark, Percy M. The autobiography of an old drifter. London, 1936.
Afr 8160.19 — Clements, W.H. The glamour and tragedy of the Zulu war. London, 1936.
Afr 3745.35 — Colin, Hugues. La condition internationale du Soudan anglo-égyptien et du Haut-Nil. Thèse. Paris, 1936.
Afr 4513.35.165 — Coppola, Francesco. La vittoria bifronte. Milano, 1936.
Afr 7565.12.20 — Courcel, G. de. L'influence de la Conférence de Berlin de 1885. Paris, 1936.
Afr 6210.5 — Crocker, W.R. Nigeria, a critique of British colonial administration. London, 1936.
Afr 3993.1 — Crouchley, Arthur Edwin. The investment of foreign capital in Egyptian companies and public debt. Cairo, 1936.
Afr 4513.36.25 — Currey, M. A woman at the Abyssinian war. London, 1936.
Afr 3740.6.35 — Delebecque, J. Vie du Général Marchand. Paris, 1936.
Afr 3740.6.30 — Delebecque, J. Vie du Général Marchand. Paris, 1936.
Afr 5780.88 — Deschamps, N. Les Antaisaka. Thèse. Tananarive, 1936. 2 pam.
Afr 6280.28F — Dittel, Paul. Die Besiedlung Sudnigeriens von den Anfangen bis zur britischen Kolonisation. Inaug. Diss. Leipzig, 1936.
Afr 6143.27 — Eberl-Elber, Ralph. Westafrikas letztes Rätsel. Salzburg, 1936.
Afr 9289.5 — Engelbrecht, J.A. The Korana. Cape Town, 1936.
Afr 2209.36 — Faci, S. L'Algérie sous l'égide de la France contre la féodalité algérienne. Toulouse, 1936.
Afr 4375.17 — Fanton, A. L'Abyssinie lors de l'expedition anglaise, 1867-1868. Paris, 1936.
Afr 4700.36 — Federzoni, L. A.O., Africa orientale, il posto al sole. Bologna, 1936.
Afr 609.34.2 — Fitzgerald, Walter. Africa. 2d ed. London, 1936.
Afr 7307.98.10 — Fonseca, Q. Vulgarização de episodios coloniais. Famalição, 1936.
Afr 4559.35.102 — Frangipani, A. L'equivoco abissino. 2a ed. Milano, 1936.
Afr 4513.36.115 — Frusci, L. In Somalia sul fronte meridionale. Bologna, 1936.
Afr 4513.36.120 — Fuller, J.F.C. The first of the League wars. London, 1936.
Afr 4513.36.60 — Gentizon, Paul. La conquête de l'Ethiopie. Paris, 1936.
Afr 4238.5 — Ghersi, E. L'organizzazione politica dell Etiopia. Padova, 1936.
Afr 4240.5 — Giannini, A. La costituzione etiopica. 2. ed. Roma, 1936.
Afr 4700.36.20 — Giardini, C. Italiani in Africa orientale, pagine di pionieri. Milano, 1936.
Afr 2731.15.10 — Gorrée, Georges. Sur les traces de Charles de Foucauld. Paris, 1936.
Afr 8250.44 — Green, Jolin Eric Sidney. Rhodes goes north. London, 1936.
Afr 2798.5.5 — Grevin, Emmanuel. Voyage au Hoggar. Paris, 1936.
Afr 3205.19 — Guemard, G. Les réformes en Egypte. Thèse. Le Caire, 1936.
Afr 3193.5 — Guemard, Gabriel. Bibliographie critique de la Commission des sciences et arts et de l'Institut d'Egypte. Thèse complémentaire. Le Caire, 1936.
Afr 4513.5 — Haskell, D.C. Ethiopia, and the Italo-Ethiopian conflict, 1928-1936. N.Y., 1936.
Afr 8983.8.5 — Hattersley, A.F. More annals of Natal. London, 1936.
Afr 4559.36.10 — Hayter, Frank Edward. Gold of Ethiopia. London, 1936.
Afr 6988.52.230 — Hodge, A.L. Angra Pequeña. Inaug. Diss. München, 1936.
Afr 4700.31.8 — Holmboe, Knud. Desert encounter. London, 1936.
Afr 1609.25.12 — Horne, John. Many days in Morocco. 2d ed. Rev. London, 1936.
Afr 4513.36.10 — Hubbard, W.D. Fiaşco in Ethiopia. N.Y., 1936.
Afr 1309.3 — Institut des Hautes Etudes Marocaines. Publications (1915-1935). Tables et index. Rochefort-sur-Mer, 1936. 2v.

264

1936 - cont.

Afr 4700.36.17	Istituto per gli Studi di Politica Internazionale, Milan. L'Africa orientale. 2e ed. Milano, 1936. 2v.
Afr 4513.36.33	Istituto per gli Studi di Politica Internazionale, Milan. Breve storia del conflitto italo-etiopico. Milano, 1936.
Afr 4513.36.30	Istituto per gli Studi di Politica Internazionale, Milan. Il conflitto italo-etiopico. Milano, 1936. 2v.
Afr 4513.36.34	Istituto per gli Studi di Politica Internazionale, Milan. The Italian empire in Africa, present and future. Milano, 1936.
Afr 2308.22	Janon, R. Hommes de peine et filles de joie. Alger, 1936.
Afr 4050.36.5	Jarvis, C.S. Three deserts. London, 1936.
Afr 7175.36	Jessen, O. Reisen und Forschungen in Angola. Berlin, 1936.
Afr 11053.2	Johannesburg University of the Witwatersrand. Songs and war cries. Johannesburg, 1936.
Afr 9165.42.10F	Johannesburg Publicity Association. Johannesburg, city of achievement. Johannesburg, 1936.
Afr 679.36	Jones, G.H. The earth goddess. London, 1936.
Afr 8678.9.65	Junod, H.A. Moeurs et coutumes des Bantous. Paris, 1936. 2v.
Afr 618.7	Keller, E. Verbreitung der Fallenjagd in Afrika. Inaug.-Diss. Berlin, 1936.
Afr 8676.36	Kock, M.H. The economic development of South Africa. London, 1936.
Afr 9045.15	Krige, E.J. The social system of the Zulus. London, 1936.
Afr 4700.36.30	Laccetti, B. Le nostre colonie e cenni geografici generali. Napoli, 1936.
Afr 7309.36	Lacerda e Almeida, Francisco José de. Travessia da Africa. Lisboa, 1936.
Afr 1571.37	Ladreit Delacharriere, J. La pacification du Maroc, 1907-1934. Paris, 1936.
Afr 4513.36.5	Lapradelle, A.G. Le conflit italo-ethiopien. Paris, 1936.
Afr 4513.36.75	Lauro, R. Tre anni a Gondar. Milano, 1936.
Afr 4688.15.15	Lauro, R. di. Le terre del Lago Tsana. Roma, 1936.
Afr 7020.15	Lavradio, Marques do. Portugal em Africa depois de 1851. Lisboa, 1936.
Afr 6739.236	Lawless, L.G. Le principe de l'égalité économique au Cameroun. Paris, 1936.
Afr 8659.36.5	Lea, Henry. A veld farmer's adventures. London, 1936.
Afr 6455.61	Leakey, L.S.B. Kenya. London, 1936.
Afr 1326.7	Lebel, Roland. Les voyageurs français du Maroc. Paris, 1936.
Afr 4559.36	Leichner, G. Gefahrvolles Abessinien. Leipzig, 1936.
X Cg Afr 8110.3.5	Leipoldt, C.L. Jan van Riebeeck. London, 1936. (Changed to XP 3705)
Afr 5057.12	Lenoir, Robert. Les concessions foncières en Afrique occidentale française et équatoriale. Thèse. Paris, 1936.
Afr 4389.36.10	Levin, I.D. Sovremennaia Abissinia. Moscow, 1936.
Afr 6549.251.5	Lloyd, Albert B. Apolo of the Pygmy forest. London, 1936.
Afr 1069.36	Luigi, G. de. La Francia nord-africana. Padova, 1936.
Afr 4430.36.5	MacLean, R. John Hay ofEthiopia. N.Y., 1936.
Afr 630.36.5	Mair, L.P. Native policies in Africa. London, 1936.
Afr 4226.3	Manetti, C. Il contributo italiano all esplorazione ed allo studio del Etiopia. Roma, 1936.
Afr 510.27	Mangin, C.M.E. Souvenirs d'Afrique. Paris, 1936.
Afr 4688.15.10	Marchi, Giulio de. Il Lago Tana e le sue possibilità di sfruttamento. Milano, 1936.
NEDL Afr 4259.36	Markoff, A. Los siete mil anos de Etiopia. Barcelona, 1936.
Afr 4512.10.3	Marotta, Renato. L'Abissinia nelle questioni internazionali. 3a ed. Torino, 1936.
Afr 2025.13.10	Martin, Claude. La commune d'Alger, 1870-1871. Paris, 1936.
Afr 2025.13.12	Martin, Claude. La commune d'Alger, 1870-1871. Thèse. Paris, 1936.
Afr 2274.5	Martin, Claude. Les israélites algériens de 1830 à 1902. Thèse. Paris, 1936.
Afr 4050.36	Mason, M.H. The paradise of fools. London, 1936.
Afr 210.36	Mathews, Basil. Consider Africa. N.Y., 1936.
Afr 6720.28.10	Mentzel, H. Die Kämpfe in Kamerun, 1914-1916. Vorbereitung und Verlauf. Inaug. Diss. Berlin, 1936.
Afr 2840.5	Micacchi, Rodolfo. La Tripolitania sotto il dominio dei Caramànli. Intra, 1936.
Afr 500.43	Middleton, Lamar. The rape of Africa. London, 1936.
Afr 8252.341.5	Millin, S.G.L. General Smuts. Boston, 1936.
Afr 8252.341.75	Millin, S.G.L. General Smuts. London, 1936. 2v.
Afr 7815.15.5	Moeller, Alfred. Les grandes lignes des migrations des Bantous de la province orientale du Congo belge. Bruxelles, 1936.
Afr 4430.36.20	Monfreid, H. de. Masque d'or, ou, Le dernier Negus. 11e éd. Paris, 1936.
Afr 4513.36.130	Montfreid, Henri de. Les guerriers de l'Ogaden. Paris, 1936.
Afr 7320.4.5	Moreira, E. Portuguese East Africa. London, 1936.
Afr 4392.20	Navarotto, Adriano. Il contegno della Santa Sede nel conflitto italo-etiopico. Vicenza, 1936.
Afr 609.36.5	Nebel, Heinrich C. Ein Journalist erzählt. Stuttgart, 1936.
Afr 4389.36A	Newman, E.W.P. Ethiopian realities. London, 1936.
Afr 3150.7	Niemeyer, W. Ägypten zur Zeit der Mamluken. Berlin, 1936.
Afr 6535.36	Nyabongo, A.K. Africa answers back. London, 1936.
Afr 6738.46	L'oeuvre de la France au Cameroun. Yaoundé, 1936.
Afr 1915.13	Orient, N. La question algérienne. Paris, 1936.
Afr 6010.13	Padmore, George. How Britain rules Africa. London, 1936.
Afr 6292.9.10	Palmer, Herbert Richmond. Bornu Sahara and Sudan. London, 1936.
Afr 555.75	Philip, H.R.A. The new day in Kenya. London, 1936.
Afr 4513.36.150	Pinti, Luigi. Le vie dell'impero. Roma, 1936.
Afr 7065.515	Pinto, João Teixeira. A ocupação militar da Guiné. Lisboa, 1936.
Afr 4513.36.110	Po di posto al sole. Milano, 1936.
Afr 2929.36.5	Rava, C.E. Ai margini del Sahara. Bologna, 1936.
Afr 6558.10F	Reports on Zanzibar. Zanzibar, 1936. 3 pam.
Afr 9489.36	Rhodesia, Southern. Bureau of Publicity. Southern Rhodesia. 4. ed. Salisbury, 1936.
Afr 8659.36	Rippmann, Ernst. Weisses und schwarzes Südafrika heute und morgen. Gotha, 1936.
Afr 820.5	Robertson, W. Zambezi days. London, 1936.
Afr 6775.5	Robinson, A.E. Some historical notes on East Africa. n.p., 1936.
Afr 4559.36.5	Roussan, S.M. Seule en Ethiopie. Paris, 1936.
Afr 4700.13.10	Royal Empire Society. London. A bibliography of Italian colonisation in Africa...Abyssinia. London, 1936.
Afr 4259.36.5	Sabelli, L. Storia di Abissinia. v.1-4. Livorno, 1936-38. 4v.

1936 - cont.

Afr 6590.5	Saleh, Ibuni. A short history of the Comorians in Zanzibar. Tanganyika, 1936.
Afr 4513.36.100	Salemi, L. Politica estera. Palermo, 1936.
Afr 4513.36.45	Salvemini, G. Can Italy live at home. N.Y., 1936.
Afr 4700.36.10	Sangiorgi, G.M. L'impero italiano nell'Africa orientale. Bologna, 1936.
Afr 4390.40	Scarforglio, E. Abissinia (1888-1896). v.1. Roma, 1936.
Afr 2719.36	Schiffers-Davringhausen, H. Stumme Front. Leipzig, 1936.
Afr 9225.20	Scholtz, G.D. Die konstitusie en die staatsinstellings van die Oranje-Vrystaat, 1854-1902. Amsterdam, 1936.
Afr 8846.25	Schroth, H. Die Transkei-Territorien, ihre Entstehung. Inaug. Diss. Bottropi, 1936.
Afr 6925.10	Schuessler, W. Adolf Luederitz, ein deutscher Kanipf um Südafrika 1883-1886. Bremen, 1936.
Afr 3305.16	Shah, Ikbal Ali. Fuad, king of Egypt. London, 1936.
Afr 4389.36.5	Shaw, John H. Ethiopia. N.Y., 1936.
Afr 8678.9.85	Shepherd, Robert Henry Wishart. Literature for the South African Bantu. Pretoria, 1936.
Afr 2209.36.5	Sheridan, C.F. Arab interlude. London, 1936.
Afr 4732.17.3	Sillani, Tomaso. L'Affrica orientale italiana. Roma, 1936.
Afr 4513.36.105	Societa Editrice de Novissima, Roma. Facts Geneva refuses to see. Roma, 1936.
Afr 9558.59	Somervell, D.C. Livingstone. London, 1936.
Afr 4236.936	Sottochiesa, G. La religione in Etiopia. Torino, 1936.
Afr 8040.20	Steyn, J.H. Ein Beitrag zu der Geschichte des Föderalismus. Inaug. Diss. Würzburg, 1936.
Afr 8100.40	Strangman, Edward. Early French callers at the Cape. Cape Town, 1936.
Afr 2209.36.10	Stuart, B. Adventure in Algeria. London, 1936.
Afr 4556.60.10	Tellez, B. Historia geral de Ethiopia. Porto, 1936.
Afr 4430.36.15	Tharaud, J. Le passant d'Ethiopie. Paris, 1936.
Afr 8252.354.20	Thompson, F.R. Matabele Thompson. London, 1936.
Afr 1609.36.5	Thornton, P. The voice of atlas, in search of music in Morocco. London, 1936.
Afr 630.36	Thwaite, Daniel. The seething African pot. London, 1936.
Afr 2260.18	Tiquet, J.E.P. Une expérience de petite colonisation indigène en Algèrie. Thèse. Maison-Carrée, 1936.
Afr 5846.3	Toussaint, Auguste. Port-Louis, deux siècles d'histoire, 1735-1935. Port-Louis, 1936.
Afr 6926.11.10	Trew, H.F. Botha treks. London, 1936.
Afr 5003.2	Tuaillon, J.L. Bibliographie critique de l'Afrique occidentale française. Paris, 1936.
Afr 5003.2.3	Tuaillon, J.L. Bibliographie critique de l'Afrique occidentale française. Thèse. Paris, 1936.
Afr 5054.36.5	Tuaillon, J.L.G. L'Afrique occidentale française par l'Atlantique ou par le Sahara. Paris, 1936.
Afr 5054.36.3	Tuaillon, J.L.G. L'Afrique occidentale française par l'Atlantique ou par le Sahara. Thèse. Paris, 1936.
Afr 4513.36.135	Ultima barbarie, come Tafari lascio Addis Abeba. n.p., 1936.
Afr 5219.36	Urvoy, Yves François Marie Aimé. Histoire des populations du Soudan central (colonie du Niger). Paris, 1936.
Afr 1550.50	Usborne, C.V. The conquest of Morocco. London, 1936.
Afr 4700.36.35	Vademecum per l'Africa orientale. Milano, 1936.
Afr 4513.36.40	Vecchi, B.V. La conquista del Tigrai. Milano, 1936.
Afr 4766.15.4	Vecchi, Bernardo V. Somalia. 4a ed. Milano, 1936.
Afr 7812.236	Velde, M.W. Economie belge et Congo belge. Thèse. Nancy, 1936.
Afr 8289.36.5	Verme, L. dal. La guerra anglo-boera. Roma, 1936.
Afr 7062.10	Viegas, Luis A.C. Guiné portuguesa. Lisboa, 1936. 2v.
Afr 4513.36.15	Villari, Luigi. Italy, Abyssinia and the League. Rome, 1936.
Afr 4430.36.10	Virgin. The Abyssinia I knew. London, 1936.
Afr 4513.36.145	Volta, Sandro. Graziani a Neghelli. 2 ed. Firenze, 1936.
Afr 8835.30	Wagner, O.J.M. Poverty and dependency in Cape Town. Cape Town, 1936.
Afr 6988.16.120	Wallis, J.P.R. Fortune may fall, the story of Charles John Anderson, African explorer, 1827-1867. London, 1936.
Afr 3046.10	Weygand, Maxime. Histoire militaire de Mohammed Aly et de ses fils. Paris, 1936. 2v.
Afr 2762.15	The white Tuareg by operator 1384. London, 1936.
Afr 555.105	Wilson, George H. The history of the Universities Mission to Central Africa. Westminster, 1936.
Afr 8844.5	Wilson, M. Hunter. Reaction to conquest. London, 1936.
Afr 109.36A	Woodson, C.G. The African background outlined, or Handbook for the study of the Negro. Washington, 1936.
Afr 3823.2	Wyndham, Richard. The gentle savage. London, 1936.
Afr 3079.36	Zananiri, Gaston. Egypte et léquilibre du Levant. Marseille, 1936.
Afr 4559.36.15F	Zervos, A. L'empire d'Ethiopie. Athens, 1936.
Afr 4389.35.3	Zischka, A. Abissinia, l'ultimo problema insoluto dell'Africa. Firenze, 1936.

1937

Afr 1069.37	Albertini, E. L'Afrique du Nord française dans l'histoire. Lyon, 1937.
Afr 2209.37F	Algeria. Les arts et la technique moderne. Algérie, 1937.
Afr 3275.47	Ambrosini, G. La situazione internazionale dell'Egitto. Firenze, 1937.
Afr 7103.20	Angola; catálogo do documentário coligido pela Comissão de Luanda. Luanda, 1937.
Afr 4513.37.55	Appelius, M. Il crollo dell'impero dei Negus. Milano, 1937.
Afr 4513.37.70	Armellini, Quirino. Con Badoglio in Ethiopia. Milano, 1937.
Afr 8252.341.10	Armstrong, H.C. Grey steel, J.C. Smuts, a study in arrogance. London, 1937.
Afr 6925.5A	Aydelotte, W.O. Bismarck and British colonial policy, the problem of South West Africa, 1883-1885. Philadelphia, 1937.
Afr 609.37	Azikiwe, Nnamdi. Renascent Africa. Accra, 1937.
Afr 4513.36.69	Badoglio, P. War in Abyssinia. London, 1937.
Afr 4513.36.69.5	Badoglio, P. War in Abyssinia. N.Y., 1937.
Afr 715.22	Balfour, P. Lords of the equator, an African journey. London, 1937.
Afr 4513.37.30	Bastin, J. L'affaire d'Ethiopie et les diplomates, 1934-1937. Bruxelles, 1937.
Afr 4513.37.65	Benedetti, A. La guerra equatoriale. Milano, 1937.
Afr 2209.37.5	Berque, A. L'Algérie, terre d'art et d'histoire. Alger, 1937.
Afr 7020.20	Blake, J.W. European beginnings in West Africa, 1454-1578. London, 1937.

1937 - cont.

Afr 3740.6.25   Bobichon, H. Contribution a l'histoire de la mission Marchand. Paris, 1937.

Afr 4513.36.83   Bono, E. La preparazione e le primi operazioni. 3a ed. Roma, 1937.

Afr 4513.36.84   Bono, E. de. Anno XIIII, the conquest of an empire. London, 1937.

Afr 4392.25   Bono, Giulio del. Da Assab ad Adua. Roma, 1937.

Afr 1571.17.45   Borely, J. Le tombeau de Lyautey. Paris, 1937.

Afr 5180.37.6   Bosshard, J.M. Ces routes qui ne menent à rien. 6e éd. Paris, 1937.

Afr 8028.200.5   Botha, C.G. The science of archives in South Africa. Johannesburg, 1937.

Afr 5235.128.10   Caillié, René. Le voyage de René Caillié à Tombouctou. Paris, 1937.

Afr 6883.34   Carnochan, Frederic Grosvenor. Out of Africa. London, 1937.

Afr 1326.12   Cenival, Pierre de. Bibliographie marocaine, 1923-33. Paris, 1937.

Afr 2618.20   Chatelain, Yves. La vie littéraire et intellectuelle en Tunisie de 1900 à 1937. Paris, 1937.

Afr 5405.112.2   Chavannes, Charles de. Le Congo français. Paris, 1937.

Afr 1609.37   Ciarlantine, T. Il marocco com e. Milano, 1937.

Afr 4509.19   Cito de Bitetto, Carlo. Méditerranée, Mer Rouge. Paris, 1937.

Afr 2025.23.10   Cordier, E.W. Napoleon III et l'Algérie. Thèse. Alger, 1937.

Afr 4785.39   Corni, G. Somalia italiana. Milano, 1937. 2v.

Afr 2845.5   Coro, F. Settantasei anni di dominazione turca in Libia, 1835-1911. Tripoli, 1937.

Afr 7119.37   Correa, E.A. da Silva. Historia de Angola. Lisboa, 1937. 2v.

Afr 609.37.5   Daly, Marcus. Big game hunting and adventure, 1897-1936. London, 1937.

Afr 5792.3   Decary, Raymond. L'établissement de Sainte-Marie de Madagascar. Paris, 1937.

Afr 626.11F   Denuce, J. L'Afrique au XVI siècle et le commerce anversois. Anvers, 1937.

Afr 6410.6   Dilley, Marjorie Ruth. British policy in Kenya colony. N.Y., 1937.

Afr 6455.67   Dower, K.G. The spotted lion, in Kenya. Boston, 1937.

Afr 5090.14   Du Puigaudeau, Odette. Barefoot through Mauritania. London, 1937.

Afr 7222.5.10   Durao, Antonio. Cercos de Moçambique. Lisboa, 1937.

Htn   Afr 674.93.14*   Eannes de Azurara, G. Cronica do descobrimento da Guiné. Porto, 1937. 2v.

Afr 7815.13.15   Evans-Pritchard, E.E. Witchcraft, oracles and magic among the Azande. Oxford, 1937.

Afr 4513.37.10   Farfaglio, S. Le bande autocarrate dei fedelissimi da Roma ad Addis Ababa. Paris, 1937.

Afr 718.1.25   Foran, W.R. African odyssey, the life of Verney Lovett Cameron. London, 1937.

Afr 4700.37.15   Fornaciari, J. Nel piano dell'impero. Bologna, 1937.

Afr 4513.37.75   Franchini, M. Ogadèn dal II parallelo al cuore dell'Impero. Bologna, 1937.

Afr 8289.37.5   Fuller, J.F.C. The last of the gentlemen's wars. London, 1937.

Afr 5765.28   Gale, William K. Church planting in Madagascar. London, 1937.

Afr 1623.937   Garcin, Pierre. La politique des contingents dans les relations franco-marocaines. Thèse. Lyon, 1937.

Afr 7809.37   Gatti, A. Great mother forest. N.Y., 1937.

Afr 2870.25.5   Gaziani, R. Pace romana in Libia. Milano, 1937.

Afr 8676.37   Gerich, K.H.A. Aussenhandel und Handelspolitik der Südafrikanischen Union unter besonderer Berücksichtigung der Wirtschafts der Union. Düsseldorf, 1937.

Afr 8110.3.35   Godee Molsbergen, Everhardus Cornelis. Jan van Riebeeck en zijn tijd. Amsterdam, 1937.

Afr 6192.25.19   Gold Coast handbook. London, 1937.

Afr 4700.13.15   Gorresio, V. Paesi e problemi africani. Milano, 1937.

Afr 1493.55   Goulven, Joseph. La France au Maroc. Paris, 1937.

Afr 5003.1.5   Grandidier, G. Bibliographie de l'Afrique occidentale française. Paris, 1937.

Afr 2880.22   Gray, E.M. Il Duce in Libia. Milano, 1937.

Afr 6979.29.5   Grimm, H. Das deutsche Südwester-buch. Muenchen, 1937.

Afr 1550.54   El-Hajoui, M.O. Histoire diplomatique du Maroc (1900-1912). Paris, 1937.

Afr 6979.37   Hardinge, Rex. South African cinderella, a trip through ex-German West Africa. London, 1937.

Afr 5054.37   Hardy, Georges. L'Afrique occidentale française. Paris, 1937.

Afr 2731.15.3   Herisson, R. Avec le père de Foucauld et le général Laperrine, 1909-11. Paris, 1937.

Afr 4513.37.80   Italy. Comando delle Forze Armate della Somalia. La guerra italo-etiopica. Addis Abeba, 1937.

Afr 7549.37   Jentgen, Pierre. La terre belge du Congo. Bruxelles, 1937.

Afr 8230.10.10   Juta, M. The pace of the ox, the life of Paul Kruger. London, 1937.

Afr 6720.37   Kemner, W. Kamerun. Berlin, 1937.

Afr 3230.25   Khedive Ismail and slavery in the Sudan. Cairo, 1937.

Afr 8140.27   Kiewiet, C.W. The imperial factor in South Africa, a study of politics and economics. Cambridge, Eng., 1937.

Afr 3243.10   Kilberg, K.I. Vosstanie Arabi-Pashi v Egipte. Moscow, 1937.

Afr 1555.3.30   Kleinknecht, W. Die englische Politik in der Agadirkrise (1911). Berlin, 1937.

Afr 1571.35A   Knight, M.M. Morocco as a French economic venture. N.Y., 1937.

Afr 4513.37.15   Konovalov, T.E. Con le armate del Negus. Bologna, 1937.

Afr 5035.5.10   Labouret, H. Monteil, explorateur et soldat. Paris, 1937.

Afr 6739.236.5   Lawless, L.G. Le principe de l'égalité économique au Cameroun. Paris, 1937.

Afr 5758.37   Lebel, Charles. La standardisation à Madagascar. Paris, 1937.

Afr 2209.37.10   Lespes, René. Pour comprendre l'Algérie. Alger, 1937.

Afr 8252.7.7   Lewinsohn, R. Barney Barnato, from Whitechapel clown to diamond king. London, 1937.

Afr 1713.11   Lucas, Georges. Fes dans la Maroc moderne. Paris, 1937.

Afr 3979.36.5A   Ludwig, Emil. The Nile, the life story of a river. N.Y., 1937.

Afr 718.25.12   Lukas, J. Zentralsudanische Studien, Wörterverzeichnisse der Deutschen Zentral-Afrika-Expedition 1910-11. Hamburg, 1937.

Afr 4513.37.60   Luongo, G. L'Etiopia, dalla vigilia di sangue alla conquista dell'impero. Napoli, 1937.

1937 - cont.

Afr 1571.16   Lyautey, L.H.G. Vers le Maroc, lettres du Sud-Oranais, 1903-1906. Paris, 1937.

Afr 4394.7   Mansueti, C. Le due Adue, 1896-1936. Milano, 1937.

Afr 2609.37   Margueritte, L.P. Tunisiennes. Paris, 1937.

Afr 5054.37.5   Mary, Gaston. Précis historique de la colonisation française. Paris, 1937.

Afr 4368.5.30   Massaia, G. Lettere del Cardinale Massaia dal 1846 al 1886. Torino, 1937.

Afr 626.13   Massi, E. L'Africa nell'economia mondiale. Milano, 1937.

Afr 9165.42.30   Maud, J.P.R. Johannesburg and the art of self-government. Johannesburg, 1937.

Afr 500.44   Mazzucconi, R. Storia della conquista dell'Africa. Milano, 1937.

Afr 505.40   Melland, Frank Hulme. African dilemma. London, 1937.

Afr 1555.5   Melzer, F. Die Bedeutung der Marokkofrage für die englisch-französischen Beziehungen von 1901. Inaug.-Diss. Dresden, 1937.

Afr 8180.22.3   Merwe, P.J. Die noordwaartse beweging van die Boere voor die groot trek, 1770-1842. Proefschrift. Den Haag, 1937.

Afr 8180.22   Merwe, P.J. Die noordwaartse beweging van die Boere voor die groot trek, 1770-1842. Den Haag, 1937.

Afr 1333.5.5   Morocco. Laws, statutes, etc. Treaties, codes...Supplément pour 1937. Paris, 1937.

Afr 7850.62   Muller, Emmanuel. Les troupes du Katange et les campagnes d'Afrique 1914-1918. v.1-2. Bruxelles, 1937.

Afr 4431.30   Mussolini, Vittorio. Voli sulle ambe. Firenze, 1937.

Afr 8719.37   Nathan, M. The Voortrekkers of South Africa. Johannesburg, 1937.

Afr 4785.934.5   Neuhaus, V. Nella piu lontana terra dell'impero. Bologna, 1937.

Afr 4513.37.47   Newman, E.W.P. Italy's conquest of Abyssinia. London, 1937.

Afr 6214.12   Niven, C.R. A short history of Nigeria. London, 1937.

Afr 1571.17.40   Ormesson, W. Adieux, souvenirs sur Lyautey. Paris, 1937.

Afr 115.25   Padmore, G. Africa and world peace. London, 1937.

Afr 1571.43   Paluel-Marmont, A.P.H.J. Le général Gouraud. Paris, 1937.

Afr 4390.47   Pariset, Dante. Al tempo di Menelik. Milano, 1937.

Afr 4730.20   Passamonti, E. Dall'eccidio di Beilul alla questione di Raheita. Roma, 1937.

Afr 718.46   Pedroso Gamitto, Antonio Candido. O muata cazembe e os povos Maraves. Lisboa, 1937. 2v.

Afr 699.37F   Peiner, Werner. Das Gesicht Ostafrikas. Frankfurt, 1937.

Afr 8289.37   Penner, C.D. England, Germany, and the Transvaal. Chicago, 1937.

Afr 6210.7   Perham, M. Native administration in Nigeria. London, 1937.

Afr 4513.37.25   Pesenti, G. Storia della prima divisione Eritrea, (8 aprile 1935-XIII - 1 maggio XIV). Milano, 1937.

Afr 4700.37.5   Pistolese, G.E. L'economia dell'impero. Roma, 1937.

Afr 2929.37.5   Pottier, R. La Tripolitaine vue par un Français. Paris, 1937.

Afr 8089.37   Preller, G.S. Daglemier in Suid-Afrika. Pretoria, 1937.

Afr 8030.12   Pretorius, H.S. Voortrekker-argiefstukke, 1829-1849. Pretoria, 1937.

Afr 4788.4   Puccioni, Nello. Le popolazioni indigene della Somalia italiana. Bologna, 1937.

Afr 1609.32.7   Rabat. Maroc. Institut des Hautes Études Marocaines. Initiation au Maroc. Paris, 1937.

Afr 3979.37   Rameses (pseud.). Oriental spotlight. London, 1937.

Afr 6850.11   Redeker, D. Die Geschichte der Tagespresse Deutsch-Ostafrikas, 1899-1916. Inaug. Diss. Berlin, 1937.

Afr 4500.22   Reischies, S. Abessinien als Kampfobjekt der grossen Mächte von 1880-1916. Bleicherode am Harz, 1937.

Afr 1573.10.5   Reparaz, G. de. Lo que pudo hacer España en Marruecos. Barcelona, 1937.

Afr 3040.30   Riad, Mohamed Abdel Moneim. La nationalité égyptienne. Paris, 1937.

Afr 1579.5   Ricard, R. Contribution a l'étude du commerce genois au Maroc durant la periode portugaise, 1415-1550. Paris, 1937.

Afr 3199.37   Sammarco, Angelo. Histoire de l'Egypte moderne depuis Mohammed Ali jusqu'à l'occupation britannique. Le Caire, 1937.

Afr 4025.20.25   Sammarco, Angelo. Gli italiani in Egitto. Alessandria, 1937.

Afr 3258.11   Sandes, E.W.C. The Royal Engineer in Egypt and the Sudan. Chatham, 1937.

Afr 8140.31   Sauer, H. Ex Africa. London, 1937.

Afr 4500.24   Schwarz, H. Die Entwicklung der völkerrechtlichen Beziehungen äthiopiens zu den Mächten seit 1885. Breslau, 1937.

Afr 718.4.15   Serpa Pinto, Carlota de. A vida breve e ardente de Serpa Pinto. Lisboa, 1937.

Afr 8678.13.15   Shepherd, R.H.W. Children of the Veld, Bantu vignettes. London, 1937.

Afr 4700.37   Silbani, T. L'impero (A.O.I.). Roma, 1937.

Afr 4513.37.37   Simon, Yves. La campagne d'Ethiopie et la pensée politique française. 2e éd. Lille, 1937.

Afr 2929.37   Società Geografica Italiana, Rome. Il Sahara italiano. Pt.1. Rome, 1937.

Afr 4513.37.5   Steer, G. Caesar in Abyssinia. Boston, 1937.

Afr 555.110   Steinmetz, T. Cinquante ans d'apostolat au Dahomey. Lyon, 1937.

Afr 555.23.55   Stonedake, A.R. Congo, past and present. London, 1937.

Afr 8745.15   Strydom, C.J.S. Kaapland en die Tweede Vryheidsoorlog. Kaapstad, 1937.

Afr 6535.7.51   Synge, P.M. Mountains of the moon. London, 1937.

Afr 2290.12   Thurin, Guy. Le rôle agricole des espagnols en Oranie. Thèse. Lyon, 1937.

Afr 3300.45   Times, London. The Times book of Egypt... 26 Jan. 1937. London, 1937.

Afr 3740.18   Treves, P. Il dramma di Fascioda. Milano, 1937.

Afr 4700.37.20   Vecchi, B.V. Nel sud dell'impero. Milano, 1937.

Afr 6850.13   Vitzthum von Eckstaedt, B. Tanganjikas wirtschaftliche Bedeutung für Deutschland. Abhandlung. München, 1937.

Afr 8252.335.5   Walker, E.A. W.P. Schreiner, a South African. London, 1937.

Afr 530.4   Westermann, D. Beiträge zur deutschen Kolonialfrage. Essen, 1937.

Afr 1584.9   Williamson, F.T. Germany and Morocco before 1905. Baltimore, 1937.

Afr 1584.9.2   Williamson, F.T. Germany and Morocco before 1905. Diss. Baltimore, 1937.

Afr 9489.37   Windram, Foster. Night over Africa. London, 1937.

1937 - cont.

Afr 4513.37.22 Xylander, R. von. La conquista dell Abissinia. Milano, 1937.
Afr 6390.23 Young, T.C. African ways and wisdom. London, 1937.
Afr 625.17F Yusuf Kamal, Prince. Hallucinations scientifiques. Les Portulans. Leiden, 1937.
Afr 6612.5 Zamengof, M. Kolonialnye Pritiazanie germanskogo fashizma v Afrike. Moscow, 1937.

1938

Afr 630.38.5 Abercrombie, Hugh R. Africa's peril. London, 1938.
Afr 3199.38 Amad, E.S. La question d'Egypte, 1841-1938. Thèse. Paris, 1938.
Afr 1609.38.10 Arques, Enrique. Tierra de moros, estampas de folklore v.1-2. Ceuta, 1938-53. 2v.
Afr 3979.38.10 Ayrout, H.H. Moeurs et coutumes des fellahs. Thèse. Paris, 1938.
Afr 7062.5 Barreto, João. Historia da Guiné, 1418-1918. Lisboa, 1938.
Afr 6280.9.10 Basden, George Thomas. Niger Ibos, life, customs. London, 1938.
Afr 6019.38 Batten, T.R. Tropical Africa in world history. London, 1938. 4v.
Afr 575.19.25 Bel, Alfred. La religion musulmane en Berberie. Paris, 1938.
Afr 1069.38.5 Berenson, Mary. A vicarious trip to the Barbary coast. London, 1938.
Afr 109.38 Berger, Arthur. Kampf um Afrika. Berlin, 1938.
Afr 5340.10 Binger, G. Une vie d'explorateur. Paris, 1938.
Afr 8140.29 Blackwell, L. African occasions, reminiscences of thirty years of bar, bench and politics in South Africa. London, 1938.
Afr 6455.65.5A Blixen Finecke, K. Out of Africa. N.Y., 1938.
Afr 8110.4 Boeseken, A.J. Nederlandsche commissarissen aan de Kaap, 1657-1700. 's-Gravenhage, 1938.
Afr 9493.38 Boggie, Jeannie M. Experiences of rHodesia's pioneer women. Bulawayo, 1938.
Afr 4770.5 Bollati, Ambiogio. Somalia italiana. Roma, 1938.
Afr 4513.38.30 Bollati, Ambiogio. La campagne italo-etiopica. Roma, 1938.
Afr 1271.5 Bories, H. Avenir de l'Afrique du Nord. Paris, 1938.
Afr 3275.12.100 Boyle, C.A. A servant of the Empire, a memoir of Harry Boyle. London, 1938.
Afr 2287.5 Brenot, H.E.L. Le douar. Alger, 1938.
Afr 4115.22 Cairo, Egypt. Coptic Museum. A brief guide to the Coptic Museum. Cairo, 1938.
Afr 3300.32 Centre d'Etudes de Politique Etrangère, Paris. L'Egypte indépendante. Paris, 1938.
Afr 1570.67 Charbonneau, J. Maroc, vingt-troisième heure. Paris, 1938.
Afr 4700.38.20 Cobolli Gigli, G. Strade imperiali. Milano, 1938.
Afr 9089.38 Coetzee, A. Die opkoms van die Afrikaanse Kultuurgedagte aan die rand. Johannesburg, 1938.
Afr 7540.39 Congo. Laws, statutes, etc. Les circonscriptions indigènes. Bruxelles, 1938.
Afr 6320.4A Coupland, R. East Africa and its invaders. Oxford, 1938.
Afr 3252.22 Crabitès, Pierre. Americans in the Egyptian army. London, 1938.
Afr 3986.938A Crouchley, A.E. The economic development of modern Egypt. London, 1938.
Afr 555.2.50 Cunha, A. Jornadas e outros trabalhos do missionario Barroso. Lisboa, 1938.
Afr 5058.7 Desbordes, J.G. L'immigration libano-syrienne en Afrique occidentale française. Thèse. Poitiers, 1938.
Afr 632.45 Deutsche Arbeitsfront. Sozialpolitik im afrikanischen Kolonialraum. Berlin, 1938.
Afr 7820.6 Devroey, E. Le Bas-Congo, artère vitale de notre colonie. Bruxelles, 1938.
Afr 5055.6 Duboc, E. L'épopée coloniale en Afrique occidentale française. Paris, 1938.
Afr 6743.50 Egerton, F.C.C. African majesty, a record of refuge at the court of the king of Bangangte in the French Cameroons. London, 1938.
Afr 8928.2 Ellenberger, Victor. A century of mission work in Basutoland, 1833-1933. Morija, 1938.
Afr 675.07.5 Fernandes, V. Description de la côte d'Afrique de Ceuta au Sénégal...1506-1507. Paris, 1938.
Afr 1826.6 Fiori, H. Bibliographie des ouvrages imprimes à Alger. Alger, 1938.
Afr 2731.15.8 Foucauld, Charles, Vicomte de. Memories of Charles de Foucauld. London, 1938.
Afr 555.5.6 Foucauld, Charles de. Lettres è Henry de Castries. 10. éd. Paris, 1938.
Afr 6143.38 Fowler-Lunn, K. The gold missus. N.Y., 1938.
Afr 630.38 Frazer, J.G. The native races of Africa and Madagascar. London, 1938.
Afr 6640.17 Freytagh Loringhoven, Axel F. Das Mandatsrecht in den Deutschen Kolonien. München, 1938.
Afr 4700.38.15 Gaslini, M. L'Italia sul Mar Rosso. Milano, 1938.
Afr 3040.52 Gemayel, P. Un régime qui meurt, les capitulations en Egypte. Thèse. Paris, 1938.
Afr 1571.17.35 Georges-Gaulis, B. Lyautey, intime. Paris, 1938.
Afr 4700.38.5 Giaccardi, A. L'opera del fascismo in Africa. Milano, 1938-39. 2v.
Afr 855.14 Gosse, P. St. Helena, 1502-1938. London, 1938.
Afr 1571.17.55 Gouraud, H.J.E. Lyautey. Paris, 1938.
Afr 4513.38.12 Graziani, R. Il fronte sud. 2a ed. Milano, 1938.
Afr 5243.174.5 Griaule, Marcel. Jeux dogons. Thèse complementaire. Paris, 1938.
Afr 5243.174 Griaule, Marcel. Masques dogons. Thèse. Paris, 1938.
Afr 6640.10 Grosclaude, P. Menaces Allemandes sur l'Afrique. Paris, 1938.
Afr 1550.52 Guernier, E.L. Pour une politique d'empire. Paris, 1938.
Afr 210.38 Hailey, W.M.H. An African survey. London, 1938.
Afr 8983.10 Hattersley, A.F. Later annals of Natal. London, 1938.
Afr 9070.7 Hattersley, A.F. Pietermaritzburg panorama. Pietermaritzburg, 1938.
Afr 12928.3.100 Hazoumé, Paul. Doguicimi. Paris, 1938.
Afr 3822.2 Henriques, Robert. Death by moonlight. London, 1938.
Afr 3979.38.5 Herriot, E. Sanctuaires. Roma, 1938.
Afr 5385.25 Herskovits, M.J. Dahomey, an ancient West African kingdom. N.Y., 1938. 2v.
Afr 2623.938.10 Housset, L. Le statut des terres collectives et la fixation au sol des indigènes en Tunisie. Thèse. Paris, 1938.

1938 - cont.

Afr 1571.17.50 Howe, S.E. Lyautey du Tonkin au Maroc par Madagascar et le Sud-Oranais. Paris, 1938.
Afr 5549.38 Howe, Sonia Elizabeth. The drama of Madagascar. London, 1938.
Afr 724.20 Hoyningen-Huene, G. African mirage. London, 1938.
Afr 8252.257 Huninsohn, Richard. Barney Barnato. 1st ed. N.Y., 1938.
Afr 7809.38 Institut des Parcs Nationaux du Congo Belge. National parks in the Belgian Congo. Brussels, 1938.
Afr 4764.938 Italy. Esercito. Corpo di Stato Maggiore. Ufficio Storico. Somalia. Roma, 1938. 2v.
Afr 4700.38.10 Jaeger, N. Diritto di Roma nelle terre africane. Padova, 1938.
Afr 628.238 James, C.L.R. A history of Negro revolt. London, 1938.
Afr 3979.38 Jarvis, C.S. Desert and delta. London, 1938.
Afr 8710.10.5 Kilpin, Ralph. The parliament of the Cape. London, 1938.
Afr 7565.12.25 Koenigk, G. Die Berliner Kongo-Konferenz, 1884-1885. Essen, 1938.
Afr 3675.17 Kraemer, W. Die koloniale Entwicklung des Anglo-Ägyptischen Sudans. Berlin, 1938.
Afr 1840.3.15 Lazard, Claude. L'accession des indigènes algériens à la citoyenneté française. Thèse. Paris, 1938.
Afr 6390.24.3 Leigh, W.R. Frontiers of enchantment. N.Y., 1938.
Afr 5580.3.9 Lepecki, M.B. Maurycy August Beniowski. Lwow, 1938.
Afr 1830.30.5 Lespes, Rene. Oran. Paris, 1938.
Afr 8278.99.33 Leyds, W.J. Eenige correspondentie uit 1899. 2e druk. Amsterdam, 1938.
Afr 4700.37.12 Lischi, D. Nell'impero liberato. 2a ed. Pisa, 1938.
Afr 505.7 Macmillan, W.M. Africa emergent, a survey of social trends in British Africa. London, 1938.
Afr 4513.38.35 Marchese, Aldo. G.M. Giulietti. Milano, 1938.
Afr 6670.25 Maroix, J.E.P. Le Togo. Paris, 1938.
Afr 2525.15 Marpurgo, G. Italia, Francia, Tunisia. Livorno, 1938.
Afr 4513.37.42A Martelli, G. Italy against the world. N.Y., 1938.
Afr 5758.38 Martin, A. Les delegations économiques et financieres de Madagascar. Thèse. Paris, 1938.
Afr 4513.38A Matthews, H.L. Two wars and more to come. N.Y., 1938.
Afr 3993.538 Mboria, L. La population de l'Egypte. Thèse. Le Caire, 1938.
Afr 6275.107 Miller, W.R.S. Yesterday and tomorrow in Northern Nigeria. London, 1938.
Afr 11572.50.130 Millin, S.G.(L). What hath a man. 1st ed. N.Y., 1938.
Afr 4658.5 Monti della Corte, A.A. I castelli di Gondar. Roma, 1938.
Afr 8325.68.5 Mostert, D. Slegtkamp van Spioenkap. 2. druk. Kaapstad, 1938.
Afr 7309.38.5 Mozambique. Repartição Teenica de Estatistica. Game hunting in Mozambique. Lourenço Marques, 1938.
Afr 7309.38 Mozambique. Repartição Teenica de Estatistica. The ports and lighthouses of Moçambique. Lourenço Marques, 1938.
Afr 7309.38.10 Mozambique. Repartição Teenica de Estatistica. The roads of Moçambique. Lourenço Marques, 1938.
Afr 11598.85.100 Nathan, Manfred. Sarie Marais. London, 1938.
Afr 4559.38 Newman, E.W.P. The new Abyssinia. London, 1938.
Afr 6275.36 Oakley, R.R. Treks and palavers. London, 1938.
Afr 2357.5 Offrey, R. Oran-Mers-el-Kebir. Thèse. Bourg, 1938.
Afr 1609.38 Orano, E. A traverso il Marocco. Napoli, 1938.
Afr 1838.8 Paillard, Jean. Faut-il faire de l'Algérie un dominion. Paris, 1938.
Afr 4559.38.10 Papini, I. La produzione dell'Etiopia. Roma, 1938.
Afr 2223.938 Pasquier Bronde, P.M.E. La coopération et les fellahs algériens. Thèse. Alger, 1938.
Afr 2459.38 Pellegrin, A. Histoire de la Tunisie depuis les origines jusqu'à nos jours. Paris, 1938.
Afr 1575.14 Periale, Marise. Maroc lusitanien, 1415-1769. Paris, 1938.
Afr 4700.38 Pesenti del Thei, F. Clima, acqua, terreno, dove e cosa si produce e si alleva in A.O.I. Venezia, 1938.
Afr 1738.38.5 Petzet, H.W. Tanger und die britische Reichsbildung. Berlin, 1938.
Afr 1738.38.4 Petzet, H.W. Tanger und die britische Reichsbildung. Inaug. Diss. Berlin, 1938.
Afr 8678.13.10 Phillips, Ray E. The Bantu in the city; a study of...cultural adjustment on the Witwatersrand. Diss. Lovedale, 1938.
Afr 9854.22 Pineau, Henry. Evêque roi des brigands. Paris, 1938.
Afr 4513.38.25 Poggiali, Ciro. Albori dell'impero; l'Etiopia come è e come sarà. Milano, 1938.
Afr 9700.16 Poole, Edward Humphry Lane. The native tribes of the eastern province of Northern Rhodesia. 2nd ed. Lusaka, 1938.
Afr 1571.17.80 Postal, R. Présence de Lyautey. Paris, 1938.
Afr 8230.38 Potgieter, C. Kommandant-generaal Hendrik Potgieter. Johannesburg, 1938.
Afr 2731.17.3 Pottier, René. Un prince saharien méconnu, Henri Duveyrier. Paris, 1938.
Afr 8089.38 Preller, G.S. Day-dawn in South-Africa. Pretoria, 1938.
Afr 5385.27.2 Quenum, M. Au pays des Fons. 2me éd. Paris, 1938.
Afr 2248.10 Regnier, Yves. Les Chaamba sous le régime français, leure transformation. Thèse. Paris, 1938.
Afr 590.65 Rinchon, D. Le trafic negrier. Bruxelles, 1938.
Afr 2731.15.15 Robert, C.M. L'ermite du Hoggar...Charles de Foucauld. Alger, 1938.
Afr 530.50 Rosenthal, Eric. Stars and stripes in Africa. London, 1938.
Afr 6720.3 Rudin, H.R. Germans in the Cameroons, 1814-1914. London, 1938.
Afr 6420.30.5 Salvadori, M. La colonisation européenne au Kenya. Paris, 1938.
Afr 2623.938.3 Scemama, R. La Tunisie agricole et rurale. Paris, 1938.
Afr 2623.938 Scemama, R. La Tunisie agricole et rurale et l'oeuvre de la France. Thèse. Paris, 1938.
Afr 8110.20 Schmidt-Pretoria, W. Der Kulturanteil des Deutschtums am Aufbau des Burenvolkes. Hannover, 1938.
Afr 5426.100.10 Schweitzer, Albert. From my African note-book. London, 1938.
Afr 4313.6 Sequeira, D.L. Carta das novas que vieram. Lisboa, 1938.
Afr 4313.5F Sequeira, D.L. The discovery of Abyssinia by the Portuguese in 1520. London, 1938.
Afr 1487.32 Sermaye, J. L'oeuvre française en terre marocaine. Casablanca, 1938.
Afr 8678.9.75 Shropshire, D.W.T. The church and primitive peoples...southern Bantu. London, 1938.
Afr 609.38.5 Sieburg, F. Afrikanischer Frühling, eine Reise. Frankfurt, 1938.
Afr 608.46.7 Silva Porto, Antonio Francisco Ferreira da. Silva Porto e a travessia do continente africano. Lisboa, 1938.

1938 - cont.

Afr 730.10   Smith, C.F. All the way round, sea roads to Africa. London, 1938.

Afr 1069.38   Soames, Jane. The coast of Barbary. London, 1938.

Afr 7020.35   Sociedade de Geografia de Lisboa. Boletim. Numero comemorativo da entrega a S. Ex. a Presidente da republica. Lisboa, 1938.

Afr 4513.38.20A   Società Editrice di Novissima, Rome. The social and economic system of Italian East Africa. Roma, 1938.

Afr 1259.38   Sorrel, J. Pages africaines, l'Afrique du Nord vue par les littérateurs. Paris, 1938.

Afr Doc 4307.336   South Africa. Bureau of Statistics. Sixth census of the population of the Union of South Africa, 1936. v.1-10. Pretoria, 1938- 12v.

Afr 8055.13   South African woman's who's who. v.1. Johannesburg, 1938.

Afr 628.5.10   Spingarn, A.B. Collecting a library of Negro literature. n.p., 1938.

Afr 1340.30   Stefani, P. Les libertés publiques au Maroc. Paris, 1938.

Afr 9047.25   Thompson, Leonard Monteath. Indian immigration into Natal. Pretoria, 1938.

Afr 609.38   Tilman, H.W. Show on the equator. N.Y., 1938.

Afr 4700.38.25   Touring Club italiano...Africa orientale italiana. Milano, 1938.

Afr 8659.38   Trew, H.F. African man hunts. London, 1938.

Afr 1609.38.5   Turnbull, P. Black barbary. London, 1938.

Afr 8710.17   Vanlille, A.J. The native council system with special reference to the Transvaal local councils. Pretoria, 1938.

Afr 6919.34.5   Vedder, H. South-west Africa in early times. London, 1938.

Afr 550.138   Verwimp, E. Thirty years in the African wilds. London, 1938.

Afr 1493.45   Vial, Jean. Le Maroc héroique. Paris, 1938.

Afr 8278.101   Vulliamy, C.E. Outlanders, a study of imperial expansion in South Africa, 1877-1902. London, 1938.

Afr 8369.38   Webster, W.A. Real union in South Africa. Cape Town, 1938.

Afr 4513.38.5   Wienholt, A. The African's last stronghold in Nabath's vineyard. London, 1938.

Afr 609.36.15   Wilson, James C. Three-wheeling through Africa. N.Y., 1938.

Afr 8678.82   Ziervogel, C. Brown South Africa. Cape Town, 1938.

1939

Afr 3675.19   Anchiere, E. Storia della politica inglese nel Sudan, 1882-1938. Milano, 1939.

Afr 2525.13   Ardenne de Tizao. Notre Tunisie. Paris, 1939.

Afr 4869.39.12   Aubert de la Rue, E. La Somalie française. Paris, 1939.

Afr 4236.936.5   Barsotti, G. Etiopia cristiana. Milano, 1939.

Afr 626.15   Barth von Wehrenalp, E. Europa blickt nach Afrika. Leipzig, 1939.

Afr 7540.27   Baumer, Guy. Les centres indigènes extra-coutumiers au Congo belge. Thèse. Paris, 1939.

Afr 7459.39   Becker-Donner, Etta. Hinterland Liberia. London, 1939.

Afr 555.84   Benham, Phyllis. In Livingstone's trail, the quest of the mighty. Westminster, 1939.

Afr 6926.22   Bennett, Benjamin. Hitler over Africa. London, 1939.

Afr 9700.40   Bigland, Eileen. The lake of the royal crocodiles. London, 1939.

Afr 9149.39   Birkley, C. Limpopo journey. London, 1939.

Afr 4199.15   Bland, J. Prince Ahmad of Egypt. London, 1939.

Afr 6926.18   Blumhagen, H. Entscheidungsjahre in Deutsch-Südwestafrika. Berlin, 1939.

Afr 7549.39   Bollati, A. Il Congo belga. Milano, 1939.

Afr 3040.74   Bourgeois, A. La formation de l'Egypte moderne. Paris, 1939.

Afr 6879.39   Braun, Hans. Die Reise nach Ostafrika. Berlin, 1939.

Afr 4513.39.30   Brown, S.H. Für das Rote Kreuz in äthiopien. Zürich, 1939.

Afr 510.26F   Burthe d'Annelet, Anarie. A travers l'Afrique française. Paris, 1939. 2v.

Afr 8844.10   Callaway, G. Pioneers in Pondoland. Lovedale, 1939.

Afr 6780.28   Cameron, D. My Tanganyika service and some Nigeria. London, 1939.

Afr 3994.938   Casson, L. Nine papyrus texts in the New York University collection. Diss. N.Y., 1939.

Afr 2530.23   Cataluccio, F. Italia e Francia in Tunisia, 1878-1939. Roma, 1939.

Afr 5342.20   Chivas-Baron, C. Côte-d'Ivoire. Paris, 1939.

Afr 4394.11   Conti Rossini, C. La battaglia di Adua. Roma, 1939.

Afr 6570.7A   Coupland, R. The exploitation of East Africa, 1856-1890. London, 1939.

Afr 6455.21.5   Cranworth, B.F.G. Kenya chronicles. London, 1939.

Afr 4688.15.20   Dainelli, G. La regione del Lago Tana. Milano, 1939.

Afr 1830.20.7   Dalloni, Marius. Geologie appliquee de l'Algerie. Paris, 1939.

Afr 5078.18   Dandin, Georges. Journal historique de Georges Dandin, 1777-1812. Tananarive, 1939.

Afr 510.105   Delavignette, Robert Louis. Les vrais chefs de l'empire. 7. éd. Paris, 1939.

Afr 5403.10   Demetz, Henri. Le régime foncier en Afrique équatoriale française. Annecy, 1939.

Afr 2218.12   Desparment, Joseph. Coutumes, institutions, croyances, des indigènes de l'Algérie. Alger, 1939.

Afr 4513.39.25   Diel, Louise. Behold our new empire, Mussolini. London, 1939.

Afr 11327.90.2100A   Divine, Arthur D. Wine of good hope. N.Y., 1939.

Afr 628.239   Dubois, W.E.B. Black folk, then and now. N.Y., 1939.

Afr 3979.39.5   Fedden, H.R. The land of Egypt. N.Y., 1939.

Afr 1738.55   Un folleto inglés del siglo XVII referente a Tánger. Larache, 1939.

Afr 1493.25   Franco, Francisco. Marruecos, diario de una bandera, 1922. Sevilla, 1939.

Afr 4892.9   Francolini, B. Djibuti. Rome, 1939.

Afr 8160.20   French, G. Lord Chelmsford and the Zulu war. London, 1939.

Afr 1369.39   Garcia Figueras, T. Marruecos. Barcelona, 1939.

Afr 1259.39   Gautier, E.F. L'Afrique blanche. Paris, 1939.

Afr 609.39.5   Gedat, Gustav A. Wunderwege durch ein Wunderland. 2. Aufl. Stuttgart, 1939.

Afr 1571.41   Gorrée, Georges. Au service du Maroc: Charles de Foucauld. Paris, 1939.

Afr 2530.19.10   Gray, E.M. Italy and the question of Tunis. Milano, 1939.

Afr 2530.19   Gray, E.M. Noi e Tunisi. 4a ed. Milano, 1939.

1939 - cont.

Afr 500.60   Gunzert, T. Kolonialprobleme der Gegenwart in Beitragen. Berlin, 1939.

Afr 6196.27   Hall, Wynyard Montagu. The great drama of Kumasi. London, 1939.

Afr 4559.39   Hayter, Frank Edward. African adventurer. London, 1939.

Afr 5257.10   Herbart, Pierre. La chancre du Niger. Paris, 1939.

Afr 3673.5   Hill, R.L. A bibliography of the Anglo-Egyptian Sudan, from the earliest times to 1937. London, 1939.

Afr 8678.41   Hoernle, R.F.A. South African native policy and the liberal spirit. Cape Town, 1939.

Afr 510.17   Homet, M. Afrique noire, terre inquiète. Paris, 1939.

Afr 2224.939   Houdiard, Y. Les problèmes financiers du Protectorat tunisien. Thèse. Paris, 1939.

Afr 4513.39.40   Italy. Esercito. Corpo di stato maggiore. Ufficio storico. La campagna 1935-46 in Africa orientale. Roma, 1939.

Afr 635.35   Jackson, John G. Ethiopia and the origin of civilization. N.Y., 1939.

Afr 8846.15.5   Kenyon, J.T. An address on the general council administration system of the Transkeian territories, rev. 1939. n.p., 1939.

Afr 6686.201   Kuczynski, R.R. The Cameroons and Togoland. London, 1939.

Afr 6685.12   Kueas, Richard. Togo-Erinnerungen. Berlin, 1939.

Afr 8835.41   Laidler, Percy Ward. The growth and government of Cape Town. Cape Town, 1939.

Afr 1326.10   Lebel, Roland. Le Maroc chez les auteurs anglais du XVIe au XIXe siècle. Paris, 1939.

Afr 3979.39.10   Leprette, Fernand. Egypte, terre du Nil. Paris, 1939.

Afr 4513.39   Lessona, A. Verso l'impero. Firenze, 1939.

Afr 530.6.5   Lewin, Evans. The Germans and Africa. London, 1939.

Afr 8210.14   Leyds, W.J. Kruger days, reminiscences of Dr. W.J. Leyds. London, 1939.

Afr 4513.39.20   Marabini, A. La barbarie dell'imperialismo fascista nelle colonie italiane. Parigi, 1939.

Afr 8678.31   Marais, J.S. The Cape coloured people, 1652-1937. London, 1939.

Afr 635.86   Marie André du Sacre Coeur, Sister. La femme noire en Afrique occidentale. Paris, 1939.

Afr 3285.15.4   Mathews, J.J. Egypt and the formation of the Anglo-French entente of 1904. Thesis. Philadelphia, 1939.

Afr 4513.39.35   Mattioli, Guido. L'aviazione fascista e la conquista dell'impero. Roma, 1939.

Afr 8846.16   Mbeki, Govan Archibald Mrunyelwa. Transkei in the making. n.p., 1939.

Afr 1493.30   Mellor, F.H. Morocco awakes. London, 1939.

Afr 628.5   Mills, C.H. Selective annotated bibliography on the Negro and foreign languages. n.p., 1939.

Afr 7812.236.10   Moulaert, G. Problèmes coloniaux d'hier et d'aujourd'hui. Bruxelles, 1939.

Afr 8115.12   Nathan, M. The Huguenots in South Africa. Johannesburg, 1939.

Afr 8028.110   Nederlandsch-Zuid-Afrikansche Vereeniging. Bibliothek. Catalogues. Amsterdam, 1939.

Afr 4513.39.10   Neri, Italo. La questione del Nilo. Roma, 1939.

Afr 2530.21   Occhipinti, D. Tunisi oggi. Roma, 1939.

Afr 8250.33   Oudard, G. Cecil Rhodes. Paris, 1939.

Afr 6670.939   Pechoux, L. Le mandat français sur le Togo. Paris, 1939.

Afr 8063.20   Perridge, Frank. The history of Prince Alfred's Guard. Port Elizabeth, 1939.

Afr 5056.139   Perrot, Emile. Où en est l'Afrique occidentale française. Paris, 1939.

Afr 3040.72   Poliak, A.N. Feudalism in Egypt, Syria, Palestine, and the Lebanon, 1250-1900. London, 1939.

Afr 2731.15.20   Pottier, René. La vocation saharienne du père de Foucauld. Paris, 1939.

Afr 4513.39.15A   Quaranta, F. Ethiopia. London, 1939.

Afr 2530.25   Question italienne en Tunisie (1868-1938). Paris, 1939.

Afr 3986.939   Raja'i, Nur al-Din. De la condition légale des sociétés anonymes étrangères en Egypte. Thèse. Paris, 1939.

Afr 1555.7   Regendanz, W. Searchlight on German Africa. London, 1939.

Afr 9700.17   Richards, A.I. Land labour and diet in Northern Rhodesia. London, 1939.

Afr 500.46   Rohrbach, P. Afrika heute und morgen. Berlin, 1939.

Afr 4892.11   Salata, F. Il nodo di Gibuti, storia diplomatica su documenti inediti. Milano, 1939.

Afr 3040.67   Saleh, Diaeddine. Les pouvoirs du roi dans la constitution égyptienne. Paris, 1939.

Afr 9769.39   Schwerin, W. Nyassaland. Neudamm, 1939.

Afr 8931.53   Smith, E.W. The Mabilles of Basutoland. London, 1939.

Afr 10916.2   Snelling, John. Fifty years of Rhodesian verse. Oxford, 1939.

Afr 2609.39   Steer, G.L. Date in the desert. London, 1939.

Afr 6620.65   Steer, G.L. Judgment on German Africa. London, 1939.

Afr 2609.39.5   Stephens, E. En Tunisie. Paris, 1939.

Afr 2749.39.5   Symons, H.E. Two roads to Africa. London, 1939.

Afr 3979.39F   Temps. Numéro special. L'Egypte. Paris, 1939.

Afr 618.9   Terweer, M.C. Altruisme bij enkele natuurvolken van Afrika en Australie. Academisch proefschrift. Amsterdam, 1939.

Afr 5322.5   Vieillard, G. Notes sur les coutumes des Peuls au Fouta Djallon. Paris, 1939.

Afr 49742.41.100   Vilakazi, B.W. Udingiswayo kajobe. London, 1939.

Afr 6280.30   Ward-Price, H.L. Dark subjects. London, 1939.

Afr 5235.128.30   Welch, Galbraith. The unveiling of Timbuctoo. N.Y., 1939.

Afr 609.39   Wollschlaeger, Alfred. Gross ist Afrika. Berlin, 1939.

Afr 55.40   Woodson, Carter Godwin. African heroes and heroines. Washington, 1939.

Afr 3695.3.85   Zaghi, Carlo. Vita di Romolo Gessi. Milano, 1939.

194-

Afr 7809.42F   Belgian Information Center. Belgian Congo at war. N.Y., 194-.

Afr 8230.35   Boey, Marcel. Paul Kruger. Tielt, 194-.

Afr 3204.24   Briffauet, Robert. L'Angleterre et l'Egypte. Paris, 194-.

Afr 679.40.10   Ca da Mosto, A. Viagens. Lisboa, 194-.

Afr 8659.40   Green, Lawrence George. To the river's end. Cape Town, 194-.

Afr 2308.23   Palais d'Eté, résidence du gouverneur général de l'Algérie. Alger, 194-.

Afr 150.17   Sanceau, Elaine. Henry the Navigator. London, 194-.

Afr 7190.35   Viagem de Lisboa a ilha de San Tome,...tradução da lingua italiana para a portugues (Seculo XVI). Lisboa, 194-.

1940

Afr 1738.40 — Abbey, W.B.T. Tangier under british rule, 1661-1684. Jersey, Channel Islands, British Isles, 1940.

Afr 6390.26 — Akeley, Mary L. The wilderness lives again, Carl Akeley and the great adventure. N.Y., 1940.

Afr 6275.34 — Anderson, David. Surveyors trek. London, 1940.

Afr 2223.940 — Apiotti, Angelo. Sei milioni di affamati. Milan, 1940.

Afr 7222.40 — Axelson, E.V. South-east Africa, 1488-1530. London, 1940.

Afr 5962.2 — Banciella y Barcena, José Cesar. Rutas de imperio. Madrid, 1940.

Afr 1555.3.35 — Barlow, I.C. The Agadir crisis. Chapel Hill, 1940.

Afr 630.40 — Bigland, Eileen. Pattern in black and white. London, 1940.

Afr 6883.20 — Boehrenz, Wolfgang. Beiträge zur materiellen Kultur der Nyamwezi. Hamburg, 1940.

Afr 5765.30 — Boudou, Adrien. Les Jesuites à Madagascar au XIXe siècle. v.1-2. Paris, 1940. 2v.

Afr 861.20 — Brander, J. Tristan da Cunha, 1506-1902. London, 1940.

Afr 2482.10 — Brunschvig, R. La Berbèrie orientale sous les Hafsides. Paris, 1940-47. 2v.

Afr 861.15.5 — Christophersen, E. Tristan da Cunha. London, 1940.

Afr 699.40 — Courtney, R. A greenhorn in Africa. London, 1940.

Afr 7175.28 — Cruz, José Ribeiro da. Geografia de Angola. Lisboa, 1940.

Afr 7180.40 — Cruz, José Ribeiro da. Notas de etnografia angolana. Lisboa, 1940.

Afr 7119.40 — Cruz, José Ribeiro da. Resumo da história de Angola. Lisboa, 1940.

Afr 9689.40 — Cullen, Lucy P. Beyond the smoke that thunders. N.Y., 1940.

Afr 7809.38.5 — Davis, W.E. Ten years in the Congo. N.Y., 1940.

Afr 4513.40A — Delvalle, P.A. Roman eagles over Ethiopia. Harrisburg, 1940.

Afr 679.40 — Demaison, A. The new Noah's ark. N.Y., 1940.

Afr 2609.40 — Despois, Jean. La Tunisie orientale, Sahel et Basse Steppe, étude géographique. Paris, 1940.

Afr 6715.10 — Drews, Max. Frankreich versagt in Kamerun. Berlin, 1940.

Afr 3817.8 — Evans-Pritchard, Edward Evan. The Nuer. Oxford, 1940.

Afr 675.07.10F — Fernandes, V. O manuscrito Valentim Fernandes. Lisboa, 1940.

Afr 6194.27 — Field, Margaret Joyce. Social organization of the Ga people. London, 1940.

Afr 50.5 — Fortes, Meyer. African political systems. London, 1940.

Afr 2630.5 — Galinier, P. La France tunisienne. Tunis, 1940.

Afr 2525.5 — Giaccardi, A. La conquista di Tunisi. Milano, 1940.

Afr 7175.60 — Granado, Antonio C. Mucandos, ou cartos de Angola. Lisboa, 1940.

Afr 6113.10 — Gray, J.M. A history of the Gambia. Cambridge, Eng., 1940.

Afr 3275.49 — Halassie, S. Democracy on the Nile. Scotch Plains, N.J., 1940.

Afr 7459.40 — Handbook of Liberia. N.Y., 1940.

Afr 8983.8.10 — Hattersley, A.F. The Natalians, further annals of Natal. Pietermaritzburg, 1940.

Afr 9029.40 — Hattersley, A.F. Portrait of a colony, the story of Natal. Cambridge, 1940.

Afr 7803.20 — Hildebrand. Le martyr Georges de Geel et les débuts de la mission du Congo. Anvers, 1940.

Afr 500.48 — Italian Library of Information, N.Y. Colonialism in Africa. N.Y., 1940.

Afr 2870.35A — Italian Library of Information, N.Y. The Italian empire: Libya. N.Y., 1940.

Afr 4700.40 — Italian Library of Information. Development of Italian East Africa. N.Y., 1940.

Afr 1390.7.5F — Jimenez de la Espada, Marcos. La guerra del Moro a fines del siglo XVI. Ceuta, 1940.

Afr 8252.248 — Johnson, F. Great days, the autobiography of an empire pioneer. London, 1940.

Afr 6780.30 — Kock, Nis. Blockade and jungle. London, 1940.

Afr 8135.25 — Kuit, Albert. Transvaalse verskeidenheid. Pretoria, 1940.

Afr 1703.3.15 — Ladron De Guevara, A. Arcila durante la ocupacion portuguesa. Tanger, 1940.

Afr 605.56.10 — Leo Africanus, J. De la descripción de Africa. n.p., 1940.

Afr 9558.14 — Livingstone, D. Some letters from Livingstone, 1840-1872. London, 1940.

Afr 9558.61 — MacNair, James I. Livingstone the liberator. London, 1940.

Afr 679.40.5 — Meek, Charles K. Europe and West Africa, some problems and adjustments. London, 1940.

Afr 5960.14 — Miranda, Agustin. Cartas de la Guinea. Madrid, 1940.

Afr 2870.30 — Moore, M. Fourth shore, Italy's mass colonization of Libya. London, 1940.

Afr 505.9 — Newman, E.W.P. Britain and North-east Africa. London, 1940.

Afr 609.46 — Ojike, Nbonu. My Africa. N.Y., 1940.

Afr 7122.41 — Oliveira de Cadornega, A. Historia geral das guerras angolanas. Lisboa, 1940-42. 3v.

Afr 6777.7.8 — Peters, Karl. Wie Deutsch-Ostafrika entstand. Leipzig, 1940.

Afr 8230.25.5 — Preller, G.S. Andries pretorius. 2. verb. uitg. Johannesburg, 1940.

Afr 609.40 — Rainier, P.W. African hazard. London, 1940.

Afr 8252.322 — Rainier, P.W. My vanished Africa. New Haven, 1940.

Afr 6640.12 — Ritchie, E.M. The unfinished war, the drama of Anglo-German conflict in Africa. London, 1940.

Afr 1755.19 — Sablotny, R. Legionnaire in Morocco. Los Angeles, 1940.

Afr 4660.5 — Santagata, Fernando. L'Harar. Milano, 1940.

Afr 7322.8 — Santos, Joaquim Rodriques dos. Alguns muzimos da Zambezia e o culto dos mortos. Lisboa, 1940.

Afr 9400.10.20 — Schapera, I. Married life in an African tribe. London, 1940.

Afr 628.240 — Sell, Manfred. Die schwarze Völkerwanderung. Wien, 1940.

Afr 8145.14 — Shepherd, R.H.W. Lovedale, South Africa. Lovedale, 1940.

Afr 4559.40A — Shortridge, G.C. A gazetteer of Abyssinia. Pts.1-3. n.p., 1940.

Afr 1259.40 — Sitwell, S. Mauretania, warrior, man and woman. London, 1940.

Afr 8252.341.70 — Smuts, J.C. Greater South Africa. Johannesburg, 1940.

Afr 8676.40F — South Africa. Rural Industries Commission. Report of the Rural Industries Commission. Pretoria, 1940.

Afr 2749.40 — Turnbull, P. Sahara unveiled, a great story of French colonial conquest. London, 1940.

Afr 6538.5 — Uganda. Agricultural Department. Agriculture in Uganda. London, 1940.

1940 - cont.

Afr 5806.5 — Visdelou-Guimbeau, G. La découverte des Iles Mascareignes par les Portugais. N.Y., 1940.

Afr 6926.26 — Visser, P.G. Herinneringe van suidwes-voortrekkers. Kaapstad, 1940.

Afr 8279.40.5A — Vroom, E. The hapless Boers. Scotch Plains, N.J., 1940.

Afr 4070.47 — Worsley, A. Land of the blue veil. Sudan. Birmingham, 1940.

Afr 3300.41 — Youssef Bey, A. Independent Egypt. London, 1940.

1941

Afr 4234.2 — Almagia, R. Contributi alla storia della conscenza dell Etiopia. Padova, 1941.

Afr 520.9 — Aveilza, J.M.De. Reivindicaciones de espana. 2.Ed. Madrid, 1941.

Afr 1493.40 — Bermudo-Soriano, E. El Raisuni (caudillo de Yebala). Madrid, 1941.

Afr 8687.132 — Besselaar, Gerrit. Sestig jaar belewenis van dietse kultuur. Pretoria, 1941.

Afr 609.41.15 — Bohner, Theodor. Africa. Leipzig, 1941.

Afr 8678.150 — Brentz, Paul Lenert. Die politischen und gesellschaftlichen Verhältnisse der Sotho-Tswana in Transvaal und Betschauanaland. Hamburg, 1941.

Afr 7461.37 — Brown, G.W. The economic history of Liberia. Washington, 1941.

Afr 210.41 — Cary, Joyce. The case for African freedom. London, 1941.

Afr 609.41 — Childers, J.S. Mumbo Jumbo, esquire. N.Y., 1941.

Afr 8050.10 — Coetzee, Jan A. Politieke groepering in die wording van die afrikanernasie. Thesis. Johannesburg, 1941.

Afr 861.21 — Crawford, A.B. I went to Tristan. London, 1941.

Afr 8089.41.5 — Dekiewiet, Cornelis Willem. A history of South Africa, social and economic. Oxford, 1941.

Afr 1680.14 — Dresch, Jean. Commentaire des cartes sur les genres de vie de montagne dans le massif central du grand atlas. Tours, 1941.

Afr 609.40.10A — Farson, Negley. Behind God's back. N.Y., 1941.

Afr 2945.33 — Fritz, Egon. Romantische Cyrenaika. Hamburg, 1941.

Afr 7175.39 — Galvao, H. Outras terras, outras gentes. Lisboa, 1941. 2v.

Afr 8210.16 — Gey van Pittius, E.F.W. Staatsopvattings van die voortrekkers en die Boere. Pretoria, 1941.

Afr 2870.32 — Grothe, Hugo. Libyen. Leipzig, 1941.

Afr 7459.41 — Harley, G. Native African medicine. Cambridge, 1941.

Afr 7465.10 — Harley, George W. Notes on the Poro in Liberia. Cambridge, 1941.

Afr 8667.5 — Heever, C.M. van den. Die stryjd om ewewig. Kaapstad, 1941.

Afr 9699.41 — Hinden, Rita. Plan for Africa, a report prepared for the colonial bureau of the Fabian Society. London, 1941.

Afr 4700.41.5 — Hollis, Christopher. Italy in Africa. London, 1941.

Afr 4178.10 — Hueber, Reinhard. Der Suezkanal einst und heute. Berlin, 1941.

Afr 3069.41 — Istituto per gli Studi di Politica Internazionale, Milan. Egitto, moderno e antico. Milano, 1941.

Afr 6390.73 — Johnson, Asa Helen. Four years in paradise. London, 1941.

Afr 609.41.5 — Kearton, Cherry. Cherry Kearton's travels. London, 1941.

Afr 7809.41.5 — Kellersberger, J.L.S. God's ravens. N.Y., 1941.

Afr 5057.14.5 — Labouret, Henri. Paysans d'Afrique occidentale. Paris, 1941.

Afr 674.93.25 — Leite, D. A cerca da cronica dos feitos de Guiné. Lisboa, 1941.

Afr 5190.10.9 — Lengyel, Emil. Dakar, outpost of two hemispheres. N.Y., 1941.

Afr 6395.6 — Leys, N.M. The colour bar in East Africa. London, 1941.

Afr 609.41.10 — Light, Richard V. Focus on Africa. N.Y., 1941.

Afr 8252.156 — Long, B.K. Drummond chaplin. London, 1941.

Afr 1571.17.57 — Lyautey, L.H.G. Rayonnement de Lyautey. Paris, 1941.

Afr 3988.3 — McPherson, Joseph Williams. The Moulids of Egypt. Cairo, 1941.

Afr 8680.20 — Meihuizen, Jan. Dat vrije volk. Amsterdam, 1941.

Afr 8809.41 — Merwe, Petrus J. van der. Pioniers van die Dorsland. Kaapstad, 1941.

Afr 6686.35 — Metzger, O.F. Unsere alte Kolonie Togo. Neudamm, 1941.

Afr 8089.41 — Millin, S.G. South Africa. London, 1941.

Afr 11572.50.100 — Millin, S.G.(L). The night is long. London, 1941.

Afr 11577.50.160 — Millin, S.G.(L). The dark gods. 1st ed. N.Y., 1941.

Afr 11040.3 — Partridge, A.C. Readings in South African English prose. Pretoria, 1941.

Afr 6019.41 — Perham, Margery. Africans and British rule. London, 1941.

Afr 6919.41 — Preller, G.S. Voortrekkers van suidwes. Kaapstad, 1941.

Afr 4513.41 — Rodeno, Franz. Frankreichs Stellung im Abessinienkonflikt. Berlin, 1941.

Afr 5405.285 — Saurat, Denis. Watch over Africa. London, 1941.

Afr 8678.1 — Schapera, I. Select bibliography of South African native life and problems. London, 1941.

Afr 9047.27 — Shropshire, Denys William Tinniswood. The Bantu woman under the Natal code of native law. Lovedale, 1941.

Afr 5849.82 — Société de l'Histoire de l'Ile Maurice. Dictionnaire de biographie mauricienne. Dictionary of Mauritian biography. v.1-30- Saint Louis, 1941- 5v.

Afr 9225.25 — Spies, François Jacobus du Toit. Hamelberg en die Oranje-Vrystaat. Amsterdam, 1941.

Afr 555.30.10 — Thoonen, J.P. Black martyrs. N.Y., 1941.

Afr 1705.5 — Thouvenot, R. Une colonie romaine de Mauretanie Tingitane. Paris, 1941.

Afr 630.41 — Tritonj, Romolo. Politica indigena africana. Milano, 1941.

Afr 5190.10.15 — Vanlande, René. Dakar. Paris, 1941.

Afr 6919.41.5 — Vedden, H. Inleiding tot die geskiedenis van Suidwes-Afrika. Kaapstad, 1941.

Afr 8289.31.9 — Visagie, L.A. Terug na kommando...krygs gebangenes. 3. druk. Kaapstad, 1941.

Afr 8135.21 — Walker, E.A. Britain and South Africa. London, 1941.

Afr 8252.124 — Wallis, J.P.R. Thomas Baines of Kings Lynn. London, 1941.

1942

Afr 7219.42 — Alberto, Manuel Simoes. O oriente africano portugues. Lourenç Marques, 1942.

Afr 115.115 — Amedeo, Duke of Aosta. Studi africani. Bologna, 1942.

Afr 1750.13 — Arques, Enrique. El momento de Espana en Marruecos. Madrid, 1942.

Afr 2875.60 — Askew, W.C. Europe and Italy's acquisition of Libya, 1911-1912. Durham, N.C., 1942.

Afr 3979.38.11.2 — Ayrout, H.H. Fellahs. 2. ed. Le Caire, 1942.

Afr 6455.71 — Baker, R.St.B. Africa drums. London, 1942.

1942 - cont.

Afr 6535.40   Beaufaere, Abel. Ouganda. Paris, 1942.

Afr 150.14   Bensaude, J. A cruzada do Infante Dom Henrique. Lisboa, 1942.

Afr 609.42.10   Bonacelli, B. L'Africa nella concezione geografica degli antichi. Verbania, 1942.

Afr 4700.42   Borelli, Gioranni. Albori coloniali d'Italia (1891-1895). Modena, 1942.

Afr 3979.42.5   Bowman, H.E. Middle east window. London, 1942.

Afr 1259.42   Bremond, Edouard. Berbères et Arabes. Paris, 1942.

Afr 1576.5   Carvalho, V. de. La domination portugaise au Maroc du XVeme au XVIIIeme siècle. Lisbonne, 1942.

Afr 5749.43   Chapman, O.M. Across Madagascar. London, 1942.

Afr 550.37   Church Conference on African Affairs. Christian action in Africa. N.Y., 1942.

Afr 7809.42.5   Comeliau, Marie. Blancs et noirs. Paris, 1942.

Afr 1574.9   Cordero Torres, J.M. Organizacion del protectorado español en Marruecos. v.1-2. Madrid, 1942 43.

Afr 150.16   Costa, Brochado. Infante Dom Henrique. Lisboa, 1942.

Afr 7312.5   Costa, D. Moçambique, nossa terra. Lisboa, 1942.

Afr 7565.12.30   Crowe, S.E. The Berlin West African Conference, 1884-1885. London, 1942.

Afr 1750.11.6   Domenech Lafuente, A. Apuntes sobre geografia de la zona norte del protectorado de Espana en Marruecos. 3. ed. Madrid, 1942.

Afr 6740.20   Duisbung, Adolf von. In Lande des Cheghu von Bornu. Berlin, 1942.

Afr 674.93.12   Eannes de Azurara, G. Cronica dos feitos de Guiné. Lisboa, 1942.

Afr 590.60   Edwards, I.E. Towards emancipation, a study in South African slavery. Cardiff, 1942.

Afr 8680.5   Eloff, Gerhardus. Rasse en rassevermenging. Bloemfontein, 1942.

Afr 550.21   Farânha, A.L. A espansao da fe na Africa e no Brasil. v.1-3. Lisboa, 1942-46. 3v.

Afr 609.34.3   Fitzgerald, Walter. Africa. N.Y., 1942.

Afr 3979.42   Florence, L.S. My goodness. My passport. London, 1942.

Afr 5243.174.10   Ganay, Solange de. Le Binou Yébéné. Paris, 1942.

Afr 1069.42   Ghirelli, Angelo. El pais berebere. Madrid, 1942.

Afr 8089.27.5   Gie, S.F.N. Geskiedenis van Suid Afrika af ons verlede. Stellenbosch, 1942. 2v.

Afr 6390.30   Gontard, E.P.U. Other people. Hollywood, 1942.

Afr 5406.242   Great Britain. Naval Intelligence Division. French Equatorial Africa and Cameroons. London, 1942.

Afr 659.42   Jackson, Mabel V. European powers and south-east Africa. London, 1942.

Afr 8685.40   Joshi, Pranshankar S. The tyranny of colour. Durban, 1942.

Afr 4559.42A   Khun de Prorok, Byron. Dead men do tell tales. N.Y., 1942.

Afr 8325.70   Kotzé, C.R. My bollingskap (St. Helena). Bloemfontein, 1942.

Afr 9089.42   Kuit, Albent. Transvaalse gister. Pretoria, 1942.

Afr 1088.7   Levi-Provencal, E. Un recueil de lettres officielles almohades. Paris, 1942.

Afr 6303.5   Library of Congress. Division of Bibliography. British East and Central Africa, a selected list of references. Washington, 1942.

Afr 505.44   Library of Congress. Division of Bibliography. The British empire in Africa. Washington, 1942-43.

Afr 8028.3   Library of Congress. Division of Bibliography. The British empire in Africa. v.9. Washington, 1942-43.

Afr 510.30A   Library of Congress. Division of Bibliography. French colonies in Africa. Washington, 1942.

Afr 7353.5   Library Of Congress. Division of Bibliography. Liberia, a selected list of references. Photostat. Washington, 1942.

Afr 8369.42.20   Malherbe, D.Y. Afrikaner-volkseeheid. Bloemfontein, 1942.

Afr 6390.28A   Markham, B.C. West with the night; autobiography. Boston, 1942.

Afr 1623.942   Massa, Jose L. Economia marroqui. Tetuan, 1942.

Afr 5049.100   Masseguin, Christiane. A l'ombre des palmes, l'oeuvre familiale et missionaire des soeurs du Saint-Esprit. Paris, 1942.

Afr 500.52   Mbadiwe, K.O. British and Axis aims in Africa. N.Y., 1942.

Afr 150.15   Mendes de Brito, Francisco. O infante Dom Henrique, 1394-1460. Lisboa, 1942.

Afr 8110.28   Milo, Taco H. De geheime onderhandelingen tusschen de Bataafshe en Fransche Republieken. Den Helder, 1942.

Afr 7530.7   Monheim, Christian. Congo - bibliographie. Antwerpen, 1942.

Afr 1609.42   Morocco. Casablanca, 1942.

Afr 5346.5.10   Mouezy, Henri. Histoire et coutumes du pays d'Assinie et du royaume de Krinjabo (fondation de la Côte-d'Ivoire). Paris, 1942.

Afr Doc 9207.340   Mozambique. Repartição Tecnica de Estastistica. Censo da população em 1940. Lourenço Marques, 1942. 4v.

Afr 6280.62   Nadel, Siegfried F. A black Byzantium; the Kingdom of Nupe. London, 1942.

Afr 5074.30   Otton Loyewski, S.W.C. Rezzons sur l'Adrar. Rufisque, 1942.

Afr 609.42   Perham, M.F. African discovery, an anthology of exploration. London, 1942.

Afr 6780.37   Pienaar, M.J.P. Baanbrekers in die maalstroom. Kaapstad, 1942.

Afr 1623.942.5   Piersius. Etude sur les communautés rurales en Beni-Ahsen. Rabat, 1942.

Afr 8252.188.5   Preller, Gustav S. Talana, die drie generaals-slag. Kaapstad, 1942.

Afr 8360.10   Scholtz, G.D. Die rebellie, 1914-15. Johannesburg, 1942.

Afr 608.46.5   Silva Porto, Antonio Francisco Ferreira da. Viagems e apontamentos de um Portuense em Africa. Lisboa, 1942.

Afr 6455.69   Smeaton-Stuart, J.A. Safari for gold. London, 1942.

Afr 8369.42.1   Smuts, J.C. Investing in friendship. London, 1942.

Afr 8369.42.2   Smuts, J.C. Plans for a better world. London, 1942.

Afr 8678.88   Smuts, Jan Christian. The basis of trusteeship in African native policy. Johannesburg, 1942.

Afr 3205.20   Tagher, Jacques. Mohamed Ali jugé par les Européens de son temps. Le Caire, 1942.

Afr 5243.125.35   Tauxier, Louis. Histoire des Bambara. Paris, 1942.

Afr 1713.10   Terrasse, Henri. La mosquee des andalous a Fes. Text and atlas. v.1-2. Paris, 1942. 2v.

Afr 8676.42.5   Tinley, J.M. The native labor problem of South Africa. Chapel Hill, 1942.

Afr 3977.91   Trecourt, Jean Baptiste. Memoires sur l'Egypte. Le Caire, 1942.

1942 - cont.

Afr 5243.10   Urvoy, Y.F.M.A. Petit atlas ethno-démographique du Soudan. Paris, 1942.

Afr 8676.42   Vanderhorst, S.T. Native labor in South Africa. London, 1942.

Afr 609.42.5   Viera, Josef. Ein Kontinent rückt näher. München, 1942.

Afr 8252.8.15   Walker, E.A. Lord Milner and South Africa. London, 1942.

Afr 6397.17   Walker, Frank Deaville. A hundred years in Nigeria: the story of the Methodist Mission in the Western Nigeria district, 1842-1942. London, 1942.

Afr 8320.13   Weeber, E.J. Op die Transvaalse front 1 junie 1900-31 oktober 1900. Bloemfontein, 1942.

Afr 550.44   Wrong, Margaret. Five points for Africa. London, 1942.

1943

Afr 4555.40.3.5   Alvares, Francisco. Verdadeira informação das terras do Preste Joao das Indias. Lisboa, 1943.

Afr 7809.43   Banks, Emily. White woman on the Congo. N.Y., 1943.

Afr 530.28.5   Banse, Ewald. Unsere grossen Afrikaner. Berlin, 1943.

Afr 555.5.3   Bazin, René. Charles de Foucauld, hermit. London, 1943.

Afr 6455.66   Blixen Finecke, K. Den afrikanske farm. København, 1943.

Afr 5600.7   Boudon, A. Le complot de 1857. Tananarive, 1943.

Afr 9689.38   Bradley, K. The diary of district officer. London, 1943.

Afr 630.43   Briault, Maurice. Les sauvages d'Afrique. Paris, 1943.

Afr 1259.43   Brodrick, A.H. North Africa. London, 1943.

Afr 1259.43.5   Brodrick, A.H. Parts of Barbary. London, 1943.

Afr 6048.2   Broomfield, Gerald Webb. Colour conflict; race relations in Africa. London, 1943.

Afr 1270.5   Broutz, Charles. Victory across French North Africa. Alger, 1943.

Afr 8252.341.40   Burbidge, W. Frank. Field Marshal Smuts. Bognor Regis, 1943.

Afr 8369.43.7   Campbell, Alex. Smuts and swastika. London, 1943.

Afr 2929.43   Casairey, G. Tripolitania. London, 1943.

Afr 1040.10F   Centre des Hautes Etudes. Six conférences d'initiation à la politique musulmane de la France en Afrique du Nord. n.p., 1943.

Afr 555.23.65   Chilson, E. H. Ambassador of the king. Wichita, Kan., 1943.

Afr 8289.43   Conradie, Francois. Met cronjé aan die wesfront (1899-1900) en waarom het die boere die oorlog verloor. Kaapstad, 1943.

Afr 6218.11   Cook, Arthur. British enterprise in Nigeria. Philadelphia, 1943.

Afr 8252.341.20   Crafford, F.S. Jan Smuts, a biography. 1st ed. N.Y., 1943.

Afr 10624.3.100   Danqush, Joseph B. The third woman. London, 1943.

Afr 7567.28   Daye, Pierre. Problèmes congolais. Bruxelles, 1943.

Afr 6689.5   Faure, Jean. Togo; champ de mission. Paris, 1943.

Afr 28226.41.100   Fiawoo, F. Kwasi. The fifth landing stage. London, 1943.

Afr 9710.12   Fintan. Life and laughter in darkest Africa. Dublin, 1943.

Afr 1571.45   France. Journal du consulat général de France à Maroc. Casablanca, 1943.

Afr 7809.43.5   Franssen, F. La vie du noir. Liège, 1943.

Afr 7176.24   Freitas Morna, Alvaro de. Problemas económicos da colónia. Luanda, 1943.

Afr 1069.43   Garcia, F.T. Presencia de España en Berberia central y oriental. Madrid, 1943.

Afr 609.43   Gatti, E.M. Here is Africa. N.Y., 1943.

Afr 6095.343A   Graves, A.M. Benvenuto Cellini had no prejudice against bronze, letters from West Africans. Baltimore, 1943.

Afr 5056.143.5   Great Britain. Naval Intelligence Division. French West Africa. v.1-2. London, 1943.

Afr 555.23.63   Grubb, N.P. Alfred Buxton of Abyssinia and Congo. London, 1943.

Afr 5549.43   Haenel, Karl. Madagaskar. Leipzig, 1943.

Afr 7369.43   Hayman, A.I. Lighting up Liberia. N.Y., 1943.

Afr 8252.228.2   Heever, Christiaan. General J.B.M. Hertzog. Johannesburg, 1943.

Afr 21059.5.2   Hinos escolhidos. 2. ed. Bela Vista, Angola, 1943.

Afr 7809.43.10   Hove, Julien van. Regards sur notre Congo. Bruxelles, 1943.

Afr 630.43.5F   Koloniale Völkerkunde. Berlin, 1943.

Afr 9161.10   Krige, E. (Jensen). The realm of a rain-queen. London, 1943.

Afr 7322.5   Lacerda, F.G. de. Figuras c episodios da Zambezia. 2.ed. Lisboa, 1943.

Afr 4389.43A   Lambie, T.A. Boot and saddle in Africa. Philadelphia, 1943.

Afr 5480.243   Lapie, Pierre O. Mes tournées au tchad. London, 1943.

Afr 5480.243.3   Lapie, Pierre O. My travels through Chad. London, 1943.

Afr 5190.10.12   Lengyel, Emil. Dakar avant-poste de deux hémisphères. N.Y., 1943.

Afr 8250.21.5   McDonald, J.G. Rhodes, a heritage. London, 1943.

Afr 115.5   Maisel, A.Q. Africa, facts and forecasts. N.Y., 1943. 2v.

Afr 8678.64   Manuel, G. The coloured people. Cape Town, 1943.

Afr 8659.43.10   Marquard, Leopold. The black man's burden. London, 1943.

Afr 2675.1.5   Martin, D.B. I know Tunisia. N.Y., 1943.

Afr 5843.6   Mauritius. Commission of Enquiry into the Disturbances Which Occurred in the North of Mauritius in 1943. Report. London, 1943.

Afr 6777.9   Peters, Karl. Gesammelte Schriften. München, 1943-44. 3v.

Afr 7320.20   Pires de Lima, Americo. Exploraçães em Moçambique. Lisboa, 1943.

Afr 2731.14   Pottier, René. Laperrine, conquérant pacifique du Sahara. Paris, 1943.

Afr 8325.66   Preller, G.S. Ons parool. 2. druk. Kaapstad, 1943.

Afr 28.25   Ragatz, L.J. A bibliography for the study of African history in the 19th and 20th centuries. Washington, 1943.

Afr 1259.43.10   Ragatz, L.J. Introduction to French North Africa. N.Y., 1943.

Afr 8369.43.15   Reitz, Deneys. No outspan. London, 1943.

Afr 28.91   Royal Commonwealth Society, London. Annotated bibliography of recent publications on Africa. London, 1943.

Afr 4178.5   Sammarco, Angelo. Suez, storia e problemi. Milano, 1943.

Afr 4320.10   Sanceau, Elaine. Portugal in quest of Prester John. London, 1943.

Afr 210.43   Selwyn, James. South of the Congo. N.Y., 1943.

Afr 8369.43   Sowden, L. The Union of South Africa. Garden City, N.Y., 1943.

Afr 555.85   Therol, J. Sous l'armure de laine blanche. Paris, 1943.

Afr 4513.43   Villani, Luigi. Storia diplomatica del conflitto italo-etiopico. Bologna, 1943.

Afr 1259.43.15F   Wrage, W. Nordafrika. Leipzig, 1943.

1943 - cont.

Afr 5342.62   Young, T. Rex. West African agent. London, 1943.

1944

Afr 4199.105   Amin, Osman. Muhammad Abduh. Le Caire, 1944.
Afr 109.44   Bidou, Henry. L'Afrique. Paris, 1944.
Afr 2749.44   Bodley, R.V.C. Wind in the Sahara. N.Y., 1944.
Afr 5960.12   Bonelli Rubio, J.M. Notas sobra la geográfica humana. Madrid, 1944-45.
Afr 2669.5   Bordin, P. Les populations arabes du contrôle civil de Gafsa et leurs genres de vie. Tunis, 1944.
Afr 8055.20   Brett, B.L.W. Makers of South Africa. London, 1944.
Afr 6095.23   British Information Service. Introducing West Africa. N.Y., 1944.
Afr 8685.50.5   Calpin, G.H. There are no South Africans. London, 1944.
Afr 609.44.5   Campbell, Alexander. Empire in Africa. London, 1944.
Afr 1259.44.5   Campbell, D. With the bible in North Africa. Kilmarnock, 1944.
Afr 8685.26   Chatterjee, Santosh Kumar. Indians in South Africa. Calcutta, 1944.
Afr 2209.44   Collier, Joy. Algerian adventure. London, 1944.
Afr 5920.1.15   Cordero Torres, J.M. Iradier. Madrid, 1944.
Afr 7175.35   Costa, Ferreira da. Na pista do marfim e da morte. Porto, 1944.
Afr 1259.44.10   Costa Leite, P. da. Africa do Norte, impressões de viagem. Rio de Janeiro, 1944.
Afr 8369.44   Coulter, C.W.A. Empire unity. Cape Town, 1944.
Afr 40.44   Council on African Affairs, Inc. Proceedings of the Conference on Africa. N.Y. 1944.
Afr 8252.341.21   Crafford, F. Jan Smuts, a biography. Garden City, 1944.
Afr 7182.5   Cushman, W.S. Missionary doctor, the story of twenty years in Africa. 1st ed. N.Y., 1944.
Afr 6194.20.5   Danquah, J.B. The Akan doctrine of God, a fragment of Gold Coast ethics and religion. London, 1944.
Afr 5635.22   David Bernard, Eugene. La conquête de Madagascar. Paris, 1944.
Afr 510.90   Delaporte, Maurice. La vie coloniale. Paris, 1944.
Afr 7068.11   Dias de Carvalho. Guiné. Lisboa, 1944.
Afr 3675.70   Douin, Georges. Histoire du Soudan égyptien. Le Caire, 1944.
Afr 8825.15   Duplessis, I.D. The Cape Malays. Cape Town, 1944.
Afr 1259.44   Elderkin, K.D. (McKnight). From Tripoli to Marrakesh. Springfield, Mass., 1944.
Afr 9165.42.35   Erasmus, J.L.P. Die rand en sy goud. Pretoria, 1944.
Afr 1403.6   Esaguy, Jose de. O minuto vitorioso de Alacer-Quibir. Lisboa, 1944.
Afr 4180.3.25F   Fakhry, Ahmed. Siwa Oasis. Cairo, 1944.
Afr 7048.15   Ferreira, Vincente. Colonização etnica da Africa portuguesa. Lisboa, 1944.
Afr 5749.44   Fiedler, Arkady. Zarliwa wispa Beniowskiego. Letchworth, 1944.
Afr 7119.5   Freitas Morna, A. de. Angola, um ano no governo geral (1942-43). Lisboa, 1944.
Afr 7175.39.5F   Galvao, H. Outras terras, outras gentes (viagens em Africa). v.1- . Porto, 1944- .
Afr 1571.17.70   Garrick, Robert. Le message de Lyautey. Paris, 1944.
Afr 7809.44   Gatti, Ellen M. (Woddill). Exploring we would go. N.Y., 1944.
Afr 8678.10.15   Gavicho de Lacerda, T. Os Cafres, seus usos e costumes. Lisboa, 1944.
Afr 2209.44.5   Great Britain. Naval Intelligence Division. Algeria. v.2. London, 1944.
Afr 7809.44.5   Great Britain. Naval Intelligence Division. The Belgian Congo. London, 1944.
Afr 6010.3   Hailey, William Malcolm H. Native administration and political development in British tropical Africa. London, 1944.
Afr 6275.35   Hanny, Erich Robert. Vom Sudan zum Mittelmeer. St. Gallen, 1944.
Afr 6143.44   Hargrave, C.G. African primitive life as I saw it in Sierra Leone. Wilmington, N.C., 1944.
Afr 1571.17.60   Heidsieck, P. Rayonnement de Lyautey. Paris, 1944.
Afr 6435.5   Huxley, Elspeth Grant. Race and politics in Kenya. London, 1944.
Afr 8659.43.5   James, S. South of the Congo. London, 1944.
Afr 8252.341.30   Kiernan, R.H. General Smuts. London, 1944.
Afr 8252.341.25A   Kraus, Rene. Old master, the life of Jan Christian Smuts. 1st ed. N.Y., 1944.
Afr 8678.42   Krieger, Heinrich. Das Rassenrecht in Südafrika. Berlin, 1944.
Afr 6295.44   Leith-Ross, Sylvia. African conversation piece. London, 1944.
Afr 6780.42   Leubuscher, Charlotte. Tanganyika territory. Oxford, 1944.
Afr 8659.44   Malherbe, J.A. Complex country. London, 1944.
Afr 8105.25   Marais, Johannes S. Maynier and the first Boer republic. Cape Town, 1944.
Afr 8678.40.5   Marquand, Leopold. The native in South Africa. 2. ed. Johannesburg, 1944.
Afr 6979.44   Marsh, John H. Skeleton coast. London, 1944.
Afr 150.15.5   Mendes De Brito, Francisco. Nota carminativa, uma resposta ão Sr. Dr. Duarte Leite. Lisboa, 1944.
Afr 8089.44   Morkford, G. There are South Africans. London, 1944.
Afr 630.44   Negro types, 65 pictures. London, 1944.
Afr 210.44   Orizu, A.A.N. Without bitterness. N.Y., 1944.
Afr 8289.44   Pohl, V. Adventures of a Boer family. London, 1944.
Afr 8230.10.15   Postma, F. Paul Kruger. Stellenbosch, 1944.
Afr 8687.144   Roux, Edward. S.P. Bunting. Cape Town, 1944.
Afr 4320.10.5   Sanceau, Elaine. The land of Prester John. 1st American ed. N.Y., 1944.
Afr 9093.22   Sandberg, Christoph Georg. Twintig jaren onder Kugers Boeren in voor-en tegenspoed. Amsterdam, 1944.
Afr 8369.42.10A   Smuts, J.C. Toward a better world. N.Y., 1944.
Afr 8676.44   Spino, Richard B. Rationalisation of South African industry. Durban, 1944.
Afr 1259.44.15   Tefri (Pseud.) Sonnen-Bilder aus Nord-Afrika. Bulle, 1944.
Afr 550.57   Weeks, Nan F. Builders of a new Africa. Nashville, 1944.
Afr 609.44   Wells, Carveth. Introducing Africa. N.Y., 1944.

1945

Afr 40.45   Batten, T.R. Thoughts on African citizenship. London, 1945.
Afr 5426.115   Briault, Maurice. Sur les pistes de l'AEF. Paris, 1945.

1945 - cont.

Afr 8676.45   Bruwer, A.J. South Africa. Johannesburg, 1945.
Afr 555.81   Callaway, Godfrey. Godfrey Callaway, missionary in Kaffraria, 1892-1942, his life and writings. London, 1945.
Afr 8230.10.12   Cloete, Stuart. Against these three, a biography of Paul Kruger. Boston, 1945.
Afr 4568.20   Conti Rossini, C. Studi etiopici. Roma, 1945.
Afr 6535.45   Cook, Albert R. Uganda memories, 1897-1940. Kampala, 1945.
Afr 6883.13   Cory, Hans. Customary law of the Haya tribe. London, 1945.
Afr 7175.37   Costa, Ferreira da. Pedro do feitico. Porto, 1945.
Afr 9558.86   Coupland, R. Livingstone's last journey. London, 1945.
Afr 8678.47   Cronje, G. 'N truiste vir die nageslag. Johannesburg, 1945.
Afr 555.83   Dekorne, J.C. To who I now send thee, mission work of the Christian Reformed Church in Nigeria. Grand Rapids, Mich., 1945.
Afr 7540.29   Delvaux, Roger. L'organisation administrative du Congo belge. Anvers, 1945.
Afr 2731.19   Dervil, Guy. Trois grands Africains. Paris, 1945.
Afr 7567.44   Dettes de guerre. Elisabethville, 1945.
Afr 5406.51.12   Duchaillu, Paul Belloni. Explorations and adventures in Equatorial Africa. London, 1945.
Afr 659.45   Dumaine, J. D'Ulysse à Eisenhower. Alger, 1945.
Afr 609.45.5   Estailleur-Chanteraine, P. Ciels d'Afrique, 1931-1945. Paris, 1945.
Afr 1703.5.7   Figanier, Joaquim. Historia de Santa Cruz do cabo de gue (Agadir). Lisboa, 1945.
Afr 550.59   Floyd, Olive B. Partners in Africa. N.Y., 1945.
Afr 6194.30   Fortes, Meyer. The dynamics of clanship among the Tallensi. London, 1945.
Afr 5405.109.15   Froment-Guieysse, G. Brazza. Paris, 1945.
Afr 210.45   Garcia Figueras, Thomas. La puesta en valor del continente africano. Barcelona, 1945.
Afr 9599.45   Gatti, Attilio. South of the Sahara. N.Y., 1945.
Afr 7320.25   Gomes de Amorim, F. Colonizacao. Lisboa, 1945.
Afr 2609.45   Great Britain. Naval Intelligence Division. Tunisia. London, 1945.
Afr 510.35   Guy, M., of Tours. Batisseurs d'empire. Paris, 1945.
Afr 210.38.2   Hailey, W.M.H. An African survey. 2d ed. London, 1945.
Afr 8667.5.10   Heever, C.M. van der. Kultur geskiedenis van die Afrikaner. Kaapstad, 1945. 3v.
Afr 8678.45   Hoernle, R.F.A. Race and reason. Johannesburg, 1945.
Afr 8678.41.5   Hoernle, R.F.A. South African native policy and the liberal spirit. Johannesburg, 1945.
Afr 3163.20.10   Ibn Iyas. Histoire des Mamlouks circassiens. v.2. Le Caire, 1945.
Afr 8685.10F   Jacobson, Evelyn. The cape coloured. Rondebosch, 1945.
Afr 8685.27.5   Joshi, Pranshankar S. Verdict on South Africa. Bombay, 1945.
Afr 8135.25.5   Kuit, Albert. Transvaalse terugblikke. Pretoria, 1945.
Afr 7809.45   Latouche, J.T. Congo. N.Y., 1945.
Afr 2749.45.5   Lelong, Maurice H., Père. Le Sahara aux cent visages. Paris, 1945.
Afr 3993.15   Little, Thomas. High dam at Aswan. London, 1945.
Afr 628.245   Logan, Rayford W. The Negro and the post-war world. Washington, 1945.
Afr 8369.45   Long, Basil K. In Smuts's camp. London, 1945.
Afr 4719.45   Longrigg, S.H. A short history of Eritrea. Oxford, 1945.
Afr 632.20   Malinowski, B. The dynamics of culture change. New Haven, 1945.
Afr 8180.24   Merwe, P.J. Trek. Kaapstad, 1945.
Afr 1573.34   Millas y Vallicrosa, J.M. España y Marruecos. Barcelona, 1945.
Afr 7459.45   Mitchell, Francis. Grown up Liberia. n.p., 1945.
Afr 8037.30   Mockford, Julian. Overseas reference book of the Union of South Africa. London, 1945.
Afr 555.20.10   Naw, Henry. We move into Africa. Saint Louis, Mo., 1945.
Afr 4230.4.3   Paez, P. Historia de Etiopia. Livro 1-3. Porto, 1945. 3v.
Afr 5962.4   Perpina Grau, Ramon. De colonización y economia en la Guinea española. Barcelona, 1945.
Afr 2870.40   Pichon, Jean. La question de Libye dans le règlement de la paix. Paris, 1945.
Afr 9525.529   Posselt, Friedrich Wilhelm Traugott. Uppengula the scatterer. Bulawayo, 1945.
Afr 8289.45.4   Raal, Sarah. Met die Boere in die veld. 4. druk. Kaapstad, 1945.
Afr 1609.32.9   Rabat. Maroc. Institut des Hautes Études Marocaines. Initiation au Maroc. Nouvelle ed. Paris, 1945.
Afr 609.45   Robeson, Eslanda G. African journey. N.Y., 1945.
Afr 7175.30   Santos, Afonso C.V.T. dos. Angola coração do imperio. Lisboa, 1945.
Afr 7180.20   Sarmento, Alexandre. O negro de Menongue, notas antropologicas e etnograficas. Lisboa, 1945.
Afr 8089.45.10   Sepulchre, J. Gens et choses de l'Afrique du Sud. Elisabethville, 1945.
Afr Doc 4307.341.5F   South Africa. Bureau of Statistics. Census of Europeans, 6 May, 1941: report on dwellings. Pretoria, 1945.
Afr Doc 4307.341.10F   South Africa. Bureau of Statistics. Census of Europeans, 6th May, 1941: report on structure and income on families. Pretoria, 1945.
Afr 8659.45   South Africa. Government Information Office. This is South Africa. N.Y., 1945.
Afr 8369.43.20   Sowden, Lewis. The South African Union. London, 1945.
Afr 8089.45.5   Sowden, Lewis. The South African union. London, 1945.
Afr 28.52   Spain. Dirección General de Plazas. Catalogo de autores y obras anonimas. Madrid, 1945.
Afr 7175.54.5   Tams, Georg. Die portugiesischen Besitzungen in Süd-West-Afrika. Hamburg, 1945.
Afr 6538.38   Uganda. Standing Finance Committee. Joint report of the Standing Finance Committee and the Development and Welfare Committee on post-war development. 2d ed. Entebbe, 1945.
Afr 854.10   Unzueta y Yuste, A. de. Islas del Golfo de Guinea. Madrid, 1945.
Afr 6460.25   Wilson, C.J. One African colony, the native races of Kenya. London, 1945.
Afr 715.25A   Wilson, Godfrey. The analysis of social change, based on observations in central Africa. Cambridge, Eng., 1945.
Afr 4008.1   Worrell, William H. A short account of the Copts. Ann Arbor, 1945.
Afr 2230.43   Wysner, Glora May. The Kabyle people. N.Y., 1945.

1946

Afr 7122.61	Angola. Govêrno Geral, 1943-1947 (Alves). Discursos do governador geral de Angola, capitão de mar e guerra Vasco Lopes Alves, 1943-1946. Luanda, 1946.
Afr 8685.46	Anjar, P.L. Conflict of races in South Africa. Durban, 1946.
Afr 6685.9	Armattoe, R.E.G. The golden age of West African civilization. Londonderry, 1946.
Afr 8703.5	Barker, Mary. Sir Benjamin d'Urbans administration. Cape Town, 1946.
Afr 9060.2F	Bee, Barbara M. Historical bibliography of the city of Durban, or Port Natal. Cape Town, 1946.
Afr 5243.343.5	Berand-Villars, J.M.E. L'empire de Gao. Paris, 1946.
Afr 8140.29.5	Blackwell, L. Farewell to parliament. Pietermaritzburg, 1946.
Afr 679.46	Blanchod, F.G. La randonnée africaine. Lausanne, 1946.
Afr 3979.46.10	Bordeaux, Henri. Le sphinx sans visage. Marseille, 1946.
Afr 9428.3F	Carpenter, Olive. The development of Southern Rhodesia from the earliest times to the year 1900. Rondebosch, 1946.
Afr 6069.46	Cary, Joyce. Britain and West Africa. London, 1946.
NEDL Afr 6069.46	Cary, Joyce. Britain and West Africa. London, 1946.
Afr 1368.78.5	Castellanos, M.P. Historia de Marruecos. Madrid, 1946. 2v.
Afr 3979.46.5	Choudhary, M.L. Roy. Egypt in 1945. Calcutta, 1946.
Afr 8230.10.13	Cloete, Stuart. African portraits. London, 1946.
Afr 7567.19	Cornet, Rene. Katanga. 3 ed. Bruxelles, 1946.
Afr 7203.5	Costa, Mario A. do. Bibliografia geral de Moçambique. Lisboa, 1946-
Afr 8685.35	Cronje, Geoffrey. Afrika soder die asiaat. Johannesburg, 1946.
Afr 718.4.80	Cunha, Amadeu. Serpa Pinto e o apelo de Africa. Lisboa, 1946.
Afr 7560.12	Cuvelier, Jean. L'ancien royaume de Congo. Bruges, 1946.
Afr 7812.246	Dehoux, Emile. Le problème de demain. Bruxelles, 1946.
Afr 8089.41.6	Dekiewiet, Cornelis Willem. A history of South Africa, social and economic. London, 1946.
Afr 7065.5	Dias Dinis, A.J. O quinto centenario do descobrimento da Guiné portuguesa a luz da critica historica. Braga, 1946.
Afr 5944.15	Domenech Lafuente, A. Algo sobre Rio de Oro. Madrid, 1946.
Afr 9165.5	Engelbrecht, S.P. Die nederduitsch hervormde gemeente zurust (Marico). n.p., 1946.
Afr 8230.30	Engelbrecht, S.P. Thomas François Burgers, a biography. Pretoria, 1946.
Afr 7218.93.5	Ennes, Antonio. Moçambique, relatorio apresentado ao governo. Lisboa, 1946.
Afr 2609.46	Eparvier, Jean. Tunisie vivante. Paris, 1946.
Afr 5749.46	Fiedler, Arkady. The Madagascar I love. London, 1946.
Afr 628.246	Fleming, Beatrice (Jackson.) Distinguished Negroes abroad. Washington, 1946.
Afr 28.30	Fontan Lobé, Juan de. Bibliografia colonial. Madrid, 1946.
Afr 7459.46	Furbay, Elizabeth J. Top hats and tom-toms. London, 1946.
Afr 8089.47.5	Geen, M.S. The making of the Union of South Africa, a brief history, 1487-1939. London, 1946.
Afr 5056.146	Gentil, P. Confins libyens, lac Tchad, fleuve Niger. Paris, 1946.
Afr 555.5.9	Gorrée, Georges. Les amitiés sahariennes du Père de Foucauld. Grenoble, 1946. 2v.
Afr 6280.50.5	Greenberg, Joseph Harold. The influence of Islam on a Sudanese religion. N.Y., 1946.
Afr 8853.2F	Groen, Julie. Bibliography of Basutoland. Cape Town, 1946.
Afr 1347.5	Guillaume, A. Les Berberes marocains et la pacification de l'Atlas central (1912-1933). Paris, 1946.
Afr 8687.225	Guthrie, F.H. Frontier magistrate. Cape Town, 1946.
Afr 8110.3.10	Haantjes, Jacob. Verkenner in koopmansland. Amsterdam, 1946.
Afr 8252.228	Heever, Christiaan. General J.B.M. Hertzog. Johannesburg, 1946.
Afr 3745.40A	Henderson, K.D.D. Survey of the Anglo-Egyptian Sudan, 1898-1944. N.Y., 1946.
Afr 8676.46	Horwitz, Ralph. South Africa's business. Cape Town, 1946.
Afr 8331.10	Hutton, James. The constitution of the Union of South Africa. Cape Town, 1946.
Afr 6019.46	Kam, Josephine. African challenge, story of the British in tropical Africa. London, 1946.
Afr 9070.9	Karlson, Esmc D. Pattern of wings. Pietermaritzburg, 1946.
Afr 8135.29	Kemp, J.C.G. Die pad van die veroweraar. 2. druk. Kaapstad, 1946.
Afr 8135.29.10	Kemp, J.C.G. Vir vryheid en vir reg. 3 druk. Kaapstad, 1946.
Afr 2000.20	Khaldi, Abd al-Aziz. Le problème algérien devant la conscience démocratique. Alger, 1946.
Afr 8685.27.10	Khan, Shafa At A. The Indian in South Africa. Allahabad, 1946.
Afr 8687.251	Kohler, C.W.H. The memoirs of Kohler of the K.W.V. London, 1946.
Afr 6210.11	Launders, J. Report to the Muffidd Foundation on a visit to Nigeria. London, 1946.
Afr 5874.16	Leblond, Marius. Les îles soeurs ou Le paradis retrouvé. Paris, 1946.
Afr 609.46.10	Lefebvre-Despeaux, Maxime. Croquis d'Afrique; voyages. Paris, 1946.
Afr 7815.36	Lelong, M.H. Mes frères du Congo. Alger, 1946. 2v.
Afr 2532.7	Livre blanc tunisien des évènements qui amenèrent la déposition. Tunis, 1946.
Afr 8252.341.60	Macdonald, Tom. Ouma Smuts. London, 1946.
Afr 8678.55	Malherbe, E. Race attitudes and education. Johannesburg, 1946.
Afr 1080.15	Marcais, Georges. La Berbérie musulmane et l'Orient au moyen age. Paris, 1946.
Afr 8089.46F	Masson, D. A scrapbook of the Cape. Cape Town, 1946.
Afr 7809.46	Michiels, A. Notre colonie. 14.ed. Bruxelles, 1946.
Afr 8809.46	Middlemiss, E. Cape country. Cape Town, 1946.
Afr 4199.66	Mohamed Ali, Prince. Souvenirs d'enfance. Pts.1-3. Le Caire, 1946.
Afr 109.46	Monod, Theodore. L'hippopotame et le philosophe. Paris, 1946.
Afr 8685.20	Morris, G.R. A bibliography of the Indian question in South Africa. Cape Town, 1946.

1946 - cont.

Afr 8230.10.20	Nathan, Manfred. Paul Kruger, his life and times. 5. ed. Durban, 1946.
Afr 6214.12.5A	Niven, C.R. Nigeria, outline of a colony. London, 1946.
Afr 4513.46	Pankhurst, E.S. The Ethiopian people. Woodford, 1946.
Afr 7369.46	Phillips, H.A. Liberia's place in Africa's sun. N.Y., 1946.
Afr 11705.39.645	Pohl, V. Land of distant horizons. Johannesburg, 1946.
Afr 6275.38	Quinn-Young, C.T. Geography of Nigeria. London, 1946.
Afr 8687.323	Reitz, Hjalmar. The conversion of a South African nationalist. Cape Town, 1946.
Afr 628.246.5	Rogers, Joel Augustus. World's great men of color. 1st ed. N.Y., 1946-47. 2v.
Afr 9165.42.15	Rosenthal, E. Gold bricks and mortar, 60 years of Johannesburg history. Johannesburg, 1946.
Afr 8252.172	Rosenthal, Eric. General De Wet, a biography. Cape Town, 1946.
Afr 7567.24	Ryckmans, Pierre. Etapes et jalons. Bruxelles, 1946.
Afr 4430.46A	Sandford, C.L. Ethiopia under Haile Selassie. London, 1946.
Afr 6455.73.5	Schwarzenbel, A. A Kenya farmer looks at his colony. N.Y., 1946.
Afr 11790.58.110	Sinclair, F.D. The cold veld. Wynberg, 1946.
Afr 7065.7	Sociedade de Geografia de Lisboa. Congresso comemorativo do quinto centenario do descobrimento da Guinea. Lisboa, 1946. 2v.
Afr Doc 4307.341F	South African. Bureau of Statistics. Census of Europeans, 6th May, 1941: report on the wages of domestic servants. Pretoria, 1946.
Afr 6926.21F	South Africa. Government Information Office. Southwest Africa and Union of South Africa, history of a mandate. N.Y., 1946.
Afr 8703.10	Southery, N. Monica. Kimberley and the diamond fields of Griqualand West. Cape Town, 1946.
Afr 8687.278	Spies, F.J. du T. N Nederlander in diens van-die Oranjevrystaat. (Mueller, H.P.N.). Amsterdam, 1946.
Afr 3979.46	Spring, Frieda. Hell-dunkel Agyptenfahrt. Bern, 1946.
Afr 5425.20	Trujeda Incerna, Luis. Los pámues de nuestra Guin. Madrid, 1946.
Afr 2875.62	Volpe, Grocchino. L'impresa de Tripoli, 1911-12. Roma, 1946.
Afr 9070.10F	Vowles, Margaret. The city of Pietermaritzburg. Capetown, 1946.
Afr 8028.4	Wagner, Mary Saint Clair. The 1st British occupation of the Cape of Good Hope, 1795-1803; a bibliography. Cape Town, 1946.
Afr 609.46.5	Waldeck, T.J. On safari. London, 1946.
Afr 6903.5F	Welch, F.J. South-west Africa. Cape Town, 1946.
Afr 8100.30	Welch, Sidney R. South Africa under King Manuel, 1495-1521. Cape Town, 1946.
Afr 550.63	West Central Africa Regional Conference, Leopoldville, 1946. Abundant life in changing Africa. N.Y., 1946.
Afr 8685.27	Wetherell, V. The Indian question in South Africa. Cape Town, 1946.
Afr 8135.23	Williams, Basil. Botha, Smuts and South Africa. London, 1946.
Afr 8252.341.35	Wilson, Dorothy F. Smuts of South Africa. London, 1946.

1947

Afr 6420.40A	Aaronovitch, S. Crisis in Kenya. London, 1947.
Afr 7122.60	Angola. Governo. Despachas do governador geral de Angola. Luanda, 1947.
Afr 6210.9	Awolowo, Olafemi. Path to Nigerian freedom. London, 1947.
Afr 510.55	Benazet, H. L'Afrique française en danger. Paris, 1947.
Afr 8659.47	Blackwell, L. This is South Africa. Pietermaritzburg, 1947.
Afr 11229.5	Bosman, Herman. Mafeking road. Johannesburg, 1947.
Afr 606.24.1	Braun, Samuel. Schiffahrten. Facsimile-Ausgabe. Basel, 1947.
Afr 9699.47	Brelsford, W.V. Copperbelt markets. Lusaka, 1947.
Afr 8849.7.5	Brooke, A. Robert Gray. Cape Town, 1947.
Afr 1425.5	Caille, Jacques. Une mission de Leon Roches à Rabat en 1845. Thèse. Casablanca, 1947.
Afr 8676.47	Campbell, Alexander. South Africa, what now? Cape Town, 1947.
Afr 500.57	Crocker, Walter R. On governing colonies. London, 1947.
Afr 5405.109.25	Croidys, Pierre. Brazza. Paris, 1947.
Afr 8678.47.5	Cronje, G. Regverdige rasse-apartheid. Stellenbosch, 1947.
Afr 8659.47.5	Delius, Anthony. The young traveller in South Africa. London, 1947.
Afr 5749.47.5	Deschamps, H. Madagascar. Paris, 1947.
Afr 4115.20.7	Devonshire, H.C. Rambles in Cairo. 3d ed. Cairo, 1947.
Afr Doc 1407.344.10	Egypt. Department of Statistics and Census. Census of industrial production, 1944. Cairo, 1947.
Afr 1571.17.18	Esperandieu, Pierre. Lyautey et le protectorat. Paris, 1947.
Afr 1965.25	Estailleur-Chanteraine, Phillippe d'. Abd-el-Kader. Paris, 1947.
Afr 1750.21	Garcia Figueras, Tomas. España en Marruecos. Madrid, 1947.
Afr 6280.9.15	Green, Margaret M. Ibo village affairs. London, 1947.
Afr 5130.20.10	Hardy, Georges. Faidherbe. Paris, 1947.
Afr 6540.15	Hayley, T.T.S. The anatomy of Lango religion and groups. Cambridge, Eng., 1947.
Afr 7369.47	Huberich, Charles Henry. The political and legislative history of Liberia. N.Y., 1947. 2v.
Afr 3300.55	Hussein, Ahmad. The story of Egypt and Anglo-Egyptian relations. N.Y., 1947.
Afr 3300.50A	Issawi, Charles. Egypt. London, 1947.
Afr 7803.5	Kellersberger, Julia L.S. A life for the Congo. N.Y., 1947.
Afr 8369.47.2	Keppel-Jones, A.M. When Smuts goes. London, 1947.
Afr 9198.5	Kuper, H. The uniform of color... Swaziland. Johannesburg, 1947.
Afr 5749.47	Launois, Pierre. Madagascar, hier et aujourd'hui. Paris, 1947.
Afr 11057.3	Leary, E.N. South African short stories. Capetown, 1947.
Afr 7119.47	Lefebvre, G. L'Angola. Liège, 1947.
Afr 8045.20	Lewin, Julius. Studies in African native law. Cape Town, 1947.
Afr 1571.17.62	Lyautey, L.H.G. Rayonnement de Lyautey. Paris, 1947.
Afr 3725.12.10	Manning, Olivia. The reluctant rescue. 1st ed. Garden City, N.Y., 1947.

1947 - cont.

Afr 3725.12.5   Manning, Olivia. The remarkable expedition. London, 1947.
Afr 4719.47   Martini, Ferdinando. Il diario eritreo. Firenze, 1947. 4v.
Afr 4259.47A   Mathew, David. Ethiopia, the study of a polity, 1540-1935. London, 1947.
Afr 7803.33   Meeus, F. de. Les missions religieuses au Congo belge. Anvers, 1947.
Afr 755.5   Meynier, O.F. La mission Joalland-Meynier. Paris, 1947.
Afr 6214.15   Miller, W.R.S. Have we failed in Nigeria? London, 1947.
Afr 2650.4   Moreau, Pierre. Le pays des Nefezaouas. Tunis, 1947.
Afr 3979.47   Mosharrafa, M. Cultural survey of modern Egypt. v.1-2. London, 1947.
Afr Doc 9207.345   Mozambique. Repartição Tecnica de Estatistica. Recenseamento da população mão indigena, em 12 de junho de 1945. Lourenço Marques, 1947.
Afr 5408.16   Muraz, Gaston. Satyres illustrées de l'Afrique noire. Paris, 1947.
Afr 8055.15   Nienaber, P.J. Afrikaanse biografiese woordeboek. Johannesburg, 1947.
Afr 6390.74   Ostrowski, W. Safari przez czarny lad. Londyn, 1947.
Afr 8678.44   Peattie, R. Struggle on the Veld. N.Y., 1947.
Afr 200.15   Pesenti, Gustavo. Le guerre coloniali. Bologna, 1947.
Afr 6498.47   Postlethwaite, John R. I look back. London, 1947.
Afr 2719.47   Pottier, René. Histoire du Sahara. Paris, 1947.
Afr 679.47   Psichari, Ernest. Terres de soleil, et de sommeil. Paris, 1947.
Afr 8845.10   Redgrave, J.J. Port Elizabeth in bygone days. Wynberg, 1947.
Afr 8678.51   Rey, Charles F. The Union of South Africa and some of its problems. N.Y., 1947.
Afr Doc 3707.346   Rhodesia, Northern. Census. Census, 1946. Lusaka, 1947.
Afr 9432.7   Rhodesia, Southern. Central African Archives. Central African Archives in retrospect and prospect. Salisbury, 1947.
Afr 3199.47   Rifaat, M. The awakening of modern Egypt. London, 1947.
Afr 8369.47.5   Roberts, Michael. The South African opposition, 1939-1945. London, 1947.
Afr 3675.50   Sabry, Mohammed. Le Soudan égyptien. Le Caire, 1947.
Afr 8849.3   Sachs, W. Black anger. Boston, 1947.
Afr 150.17.5   Sanceau, Elaine. Henry the Navigator. N.Y., 1947.
Afr 9400.3.5   Schapera, J. Migrant labour and tribal life. London, 1947.
Afr 8659.47.10   Shepherd, Robert H.W. African contrasts. Cape Town, 1947.
Afr 9327.47F   Stevens, Pamela. Bibliography of Bechuanaland. Cape Town, 1947.
Afr 3745.45   Sudan, Egyptian. The Sudan. Khartoum, 1947.
Afr 1487.10   Taillard, Fulbert, Le nationalisme marocain. Paris, 1947.
Afr 8250.2   Thomson, D.W. Cecil John Rhodes. Cape Town, 1947.
Afr 9488.89   Vaughan-Williams, H. A visit to Lobengula in 1889. Pietermaritzburg, 1947.
Afr 2731.15.45   Vignaud, Jean. Frère Charles. Paris, 1947.
Afr 9489.47   Wadio, A.S.N. The romance of Rhodesia. London, 1947.
Afr 1453.11   Weisgerber, F. Au seuil du Maroc moderne. Rabat, 1947.
Afr 8659.39.15   Wells, Arthur W. South Africa. London, 1947.
Afr 6160.10   Wight, M. The Gold Coast legislative council. London, 1947.
Afr 7369.47.5A   Wilson, Charles M. Liberia. N.Y., 1947.
Afr 8089.47   Wolton, D.G. Whither South Africa. London, 1947.
Afr 10118.2A   Young, T. Cullen. African new writing. London, 1947.
Afr 3695.3.86   Zaghi, Carlo. Gordon, Gessi e la riconquista del Sudan, 1874-1881. Firenze, 1947.

1948

Afr 505.13   Batten, T.R. Problems of African development. London, 1948.
Afr 6455.105   Benzon, Boeje. Mine afrikanshe udfinger. København, 1948.
Afr 3979.48   Bigland, E. Journey to Egypt. London, 1948.
Afr 3988.5.5   Blackman, Winifred Susan. Les fellahs de la Haute-Egypte. Paris, 1948.
Afr 2209.48   Blottiere, J.E. L'Algérie. Paris, 1948.
Afr 609.48   Bolinder, Gustaf. Nykypaivan Afrikka. Helsinki, 1948.
Afr 1618.28   Bonjean, François. L'ame marocaine, une à travers les croyances et la politesse. Paris, 1948.
Afr 8687.174   Boreham, Frank W. The man who saved Gandhi, John Joseph Doke. London, 1948.
Afr 8289.48   Breytenbach, J.H. Die Tweede Vryheidsoorlog. Kaapstad, 1948. 2v.
Afr 628.248   Burns, A. Colour prejudice. London, 1948.
Afr 6214.8.10   Burns, Alan C. History of Nigeria. 4th ed. London, 1948.
Afr 2459.48   Cambon, H. Histoire de la régence de Tunis. Paris, 1948.
Afr 8835.10   Cape Town. Foreshore Joint Technical Committee. The Cape Town Foreshore plan. Cape Town, 1948.
Afr 7870.7   Capelle, Emmanuel. La cité indigène de Léopoldville. Léopoldville, 1948.
Afr 5969.157   Cencillo de Pineda, Manuel. El brigadier Conde de Argelejo. Madrid, 1948.
Afr 9165.42.20   Chilvers, Hedley A. Out of the crucible. Johannesburg, 1948.
Afr 1735.5   Coindreau, Roger. Corsaires de Sale. Paris, 1948.
Afr 7549.48.10   Cornet, Rene Jules. Sommaire de l'histoire du Congo belge. Bruxelles, 1948.
Afr 8160.18   Coupland, R. Zulu battle piece, Isandhlwana. London, 1948.
Afr 9165.71   Cross, K.G. Bibliography of Pretoria. Pretoria, 1948.
Afr 9635.5   Davidson, J.W. The Northern Rhodesian legislative council. London, 1948.
Afr 7119.48   Delgado, Ralph. História de Angola. Bereguela, 1948-53. 4v.
Afr 7188.5   Dias, Gastão Sousa. Julgareis qual e mas excelente. Lisboa, 1948[1949].
Afr 2749.48   Etherton, P.T. Across the great deserts. N.Y., 1948.
Afr 4700.48   Fabian Society. Colonial Bureau. The fate of Italy's colonies. London, 1948.
Afr 8676.48   Franklin, N.N. Economics in South Africa. Cape Town, 1948.
Afr 7103.25   Granado, António Coxito. Dicionário corográfico comercial de Angola Atonito. 2. ed. Luanda, 1948.
Afr 2870.25.10   Graziani, R. Libia redenta. Napoli, 1948.
Afr 6145.4F   Great Britain. Commissioners of Inquiry into the Subject of Emigration from Sierra Leone to the West Indies. Copy of the reports made in 1844-1845. London, 1948.
Afr 8095.65   Green, Laurence G. So few are free. Cape Town, 1948.
Afr 550.68   Groves, C.P. The planting of Christianity in Africa. London, 1948. 4v.

1948 - cont.

Afr 4430.48   Haile Selassie. The eighteenth anniversary of the coronation of His Imperial Majesty Haile Selassie I. Addis Ababa, 1948.
Afr 7803.36   Heyse, T. Associations religieuses au Congo belge. Bruxelles, 1948.
Afr 21059.5.3   Hinos escolhidos. 3. ed. Bela Vista, Angola, 1948.
Afr 8735.5.15A   Hockly, H.E. The story of the British settlers of 1820 in South Africa. Cape Town, 1948.
Afr 6390.25   Huxley, Elspeth J.G. The sorcerer's apprentice, a journey through East Africa. London, 1948.
Afr 3993.8   Jiritli, Ali. The structure of modern industry in Egypt. Cairo, 1948.
Afr 5426.100.40   Joy, Charles Rhind. The Africa of Albert Schweitzer. N.Y., 1948.
Afr 2948.13   Lethielleux, J. Le Fezzan. Tunis, 1948.
Afr 13332.53.100   Lomami-Tshibamba, Paul. Ngando (Le crocodile). Bruxelles, 1948.
Afr 8687.230   Macdonald, Tom. Jan Hofmeyer. London, 1948.
Afr 7549.48   Marvel, T. The new Congo. N.Y., 1948.
Afr Doc 2807.344F   Mauritius. Final report on the census enumeration made in the colony of Mauritius. Port Louis, 1948.
Afr 6275.107.5   Miller, W.R.S. Success in Nigeria; assets and possibilities. London, 1948.
Afr 5949.5   Monteil, Vincent. Notes sur Ifni et les Ait Ba-e Amran. Paris, 1948.
Afr 1640.10.5   Monteil, Vincent. Notes sur les Tekna. Paris, 1948.
Afr 7809.48   Moulaert, George. Souvenirs d'Alfrique, 1902-1919. Bruxelles, 1948.
Afr 11675.87.110A   Paton, Alan. Cry, the beloved country. N.Y., 1948.
Afr 4238.10   Perham, M.F. The government of Ethiopia. London, 1948.
Afr 4559.48   Philip, H. Abyssinian memories. Santa Barbara, Calif., 1948.
Afr 9047.10   Reyher, R.H. Zulu woman. N.Y., 1948.
Afr 8678.13.41A   Richards, A.I. Hunger and work in a savage tribe. Glencoe, Ill., 1948.
Afr 28.35   Robinson, A. A bibliography of African bibliographies. Cape Town, 1948.
Afr 7817.25   Roelens, Victor. Notre vieux Congo, 1891-1917. v.1-2. Namur, 1948.
Afr 11040.2   Rosenthal, E. The South African Saturday book. Cape Town, 1948.
Afr 8919.49.5   Rosenthal, Eric. African Switzerland. Cape Town, 1948.
Afr 3669.5   Santandrea, S. Bibliografia di studi africani. Verona, 1948.
Afr 8279.48   Scholtz, Gert D. Die oorsake van die tweede vryheids-oorlog. Johannesburg, 1948-49. 2v.
Afr 12016.2   Senghor, L.S. Anthologie de la nouvelle poésie nègre. 1st ed. Paris, 1948.
Afr 8687.342   Solomon, W.E. Saul Solomon, the member for Cape Town. Cape Town, 1948.
Afr 6879.36.5   Tanganyika guide. 2d ed. Dar es Salaam, 1948.
Afr 3818.7   Trimingham, John Spencer. The Christian approach to Islam in the Sudan. London, 1948.
Afr 630.48   Turner, Walter L. Under the skin of the African. Birmingham, Ala., 1948.
Afr 1640.15   Vainot, L. Pelerinages judeo-musulmans du Maroc. Paris, 1948.
Afr 8180.10.3   Walker, E.A. The great trek. 3d ed. London, 1948.
Afr 6164.9   Ward, W.E.F. A history of the Gold Coast. London, 1948.
Afr 6465.58F   White, L.W.T. Nairobi, master plan for a colonial capital. London, 1948.

1949

Afr 7203.10   Almeida de Eca, F.G. Achegas para a bibliografia de Moçambique. Lisboa, 1949.
Afr 7803.44   Anciaux, Leon. Le problème musulman dans l'Afrique belge. Bruxelles, 1949.
Afr 9558.15   Appleyard, M.E. Doctor David Livingstone. Cape Town, 1949.
Afr 620.1   Automobile Association of South Africa. Trans-African highways. Cape Town, 1949.
Afr 5829.49.5   Barnwell, P.J. A short history of Mauritius. London, 1949.
Afr 7812.249   Belgium. Ministère des Colonies. Plan décennal pour le développement économique et social du Congo belge. Bruxelles, 1949.
Afr 6455.115   Bell, W.D.M. Karamojo safari. 1st ed. N.Y., 1949.
Afr 2030.449   Bennabi, Malek. Discours sur les conditions de la renaissance algérienne. Alger, 1949.
Afr 6164.10   Bourret, F.M. The Gold Coast, 1919-46. Stanford, 1949.
Afr 9029.49   Braatvedt, H. Roaming Zululand with a native commissioner. Pietermaritzburg, 1949.
Afr 1340.35   Bremard, F. L'organisation régionale du Maroc. Paris, 1949.
Afr 8289.49   Breytenbach, J.H. Gedenkalbum van die Tweede Vryheidsoorlog. Kaapstad, 1949.
Afr 4559.49   Buxton, D.R. Travels in Ethiopia. London, 1949.
Afr 1733.5.25   Caille, Jacques. La ville de Rabat. Vanoest, 1949. 3v.
Afr 8685.50   Calpin, G.H. Indians in South Africa. Pietermaritzburg, 1949.
Afr 575.24   Cardaire, M.P. Contribution à l'étude de l'islam noir. Donala, 1949.
Afr 7180.30   Childs, Gladwyn Murray. Umbundu kinship and character. London, 1949.
Afr 1609.49   Coindreau, R. Le Maroc. Paris, 1949.
Afr 7809.49   Congo, Belgian. Guide de voyageur au Congo belge et au Ruanda-Urundi. 1.ed. Bruxelles, 1949.
Afr 9538.5   Cox, D.L. A bibliography of the Federation of the Rhodesias and Nyasaland. Cape Town, 1949.
Afr 6162.15   Cudjoe, S.D. Aids to African autonomy. London, 1949.
Afr 510.40A   Despois, J. L'Afrique blanche française. Paris, 1949. 2v.
Afr 674.93.30   Eannes de Azurara, G. Vida e obras de Gomes Eanes de Zurara. Lisboa, 1949. 2v.
Afr 1990.32   Emerit, Marcel. La révolution de 1848 en Algérie. Paris, 1949.
Afr 2945.26.20   Evans-Pritchard, Edward Evan. The Sanusi of Cyrenaica. Oxford, 1949.
Afr 6455.75   Farson, N. Last chance in Africa. London, 1949.
Afr 3069.49   Francis, René. Agriculture in Egypt. Le Caire, 1949.
Afr 3069.49.5   Francis, René. Egypt in evolution. Le Caire, 1949.
Afr 8180.30   Franken, J.L.M. Piet retief. Kaapstad, 1949.
Afr 2731.15.25   Fremantle, A.J. Desert calling. N.Y., 1949.
Afr 7122.39   Galvao, H. Por Angola. Lisboa, 1949.

1949 - cont.

Afr 5404.15 — Gamache, Pierre. Géographie et histoire de l'Afrique équatoriale française. Paris, 1949.

Afr 4513.49 — Gandar Dower, K. Abyssinian patchwork. London, 1949.

Afr 1369.49.5 — Garcia Figueras, T. Miscelanea de estudios historicos sobre Marruecos. Larache, 1949.

Afr 8095.20 — Gibbs, H. Twilight in South Africa. London, 1949.

Afr 11433.74.125 — Gordimer, N. Face to face. Johannesburg, 1949.

Afr 6410.2F — Great Britain. Colonial Office. Political and social aspects of the development of municipal government in Kenya with special reference to Nairobi. Nairobi, 1949.

Afr 5969.8 — Guinea Lopez, Emilio. En el pais de los Bubis. Madrid, 1949.

Afr 8825.10 — Halford, S.J. The Griquas of Griqualand. Cape Town, 1949.

Afr 8292.14.5 — Hall, David Oswald William. The New Zealanders in South Africa. Wellington, 1949.

Afr 1571.17.75 — Hardy, G. Portrait de Lyautey. Paris, 1949.

Afr 5392.3 — Hardy, Georges. Un apôtre d'aujourd'hui. Paris, 1949.

Afr 8980.10 — Hattersley, Alan Frederick. The Natal settlers, 1849-1951. Pietermaritzburg, 1949.

Afr 8678.57 — Hellmann, E. Handbook on race relations in South Africa. Cape Town, 1949.

Afr 8680.10 — Hettema, H.H. De Nederlandse stam in Zuid-Afrika. Zutphen, 1949.

Afr 3979.49 — Hughes, Pennethorne. While Shepheard's watched. London, 1949.

Afr 8687.238 — Innes, James Rose. Autobiography. Cape Town, 1949.

Afr 3979.42.13 — Jarvis, C.S. Scattered shots. London, 1949.

Afr 115.100 — Jensen, Johannes V. Afrika, opdagelsesrejserne. København, 1949.

Afr 1609.48.5 — Joly, Fernand. Geographie du Maroc. Paris, 1949.

Afr 6298.785 — Jordan, John P. Bishop Shanahan of Southern Nigeria. Dublin, 1949.

Afr 8089.49 — Keppel-Jones, A. South Africa, a short history. London, 1949.

Afr 1635.27 — Koller Angelus, Father. Essai sur l'esprit du berbere marocain. 2 ed. Fribourg, 1949.

Afr 7815.43 — Lamal. Essai d'étude démographique d'une population de Kwango. Bruxelles, 1949.

Afr 1338.20 — Laubadere, A. de. Les réformes des pouvoirs publics au Maroc. Paris, 1949.

Afr 1713.4.5 — Letourneau, Roger. Fez avant le protectorat. Casablanca, 1949.

Afr 7324.19 — Lobato, A. Historia do presidio de Lourenço. Lisboa, 1949-60. 2v.

Afr 115.6 — Louwers, Octave. Le Congrès Volta de 1938 et ses travaux sur l'Afrique. Bruxelles, 1949.

Afr 505.7.5 — Macmillan, W.M. Africa emergent, a survey of social, political and economic trends in British Africa. Harmondsworth, 1949.

Afr 7549.48.3 — Marvel, T. The new Congo. 1st British ed. London, 1949.

Afr 1259.49 — Maugham, R.C.R. North African notebook. N.Y., 1949.

Afr 8045.22.5 — May, Henry John. The South African constitution. 2d. ed. Cape Town, 1949.

Afr 4095.8.6 — Middleton, D. Baker of the Nile. London, 1949.

Afr 4259.49 — Mikael, K. Ethiopia and Western civilization. n.p., 1949.

Afr 11572.50.120 — Millin, S.G.(L). King of the bastards. N.Y., 1949.

Afr 8659.49.5 — Mockford, Julian. The golden land. London, 1949.

Afr 8180.26 — Muller, Christoffel Frederik Jakobus. Die Britse owerheid en de groot trek. Thesis. Kaapstad, 1949.

Afr 6210.8 — Nigeria. Legislative Council. Review of the constitution. Lagos, 1949.

Afr 505.46 — Padmore, George. Africa, Britain's third empire. London, 1949.

Afr 115.120 — Pedrals, Denis Pierre. Manuel scientifique de l'Afrique noire. Paris, 1949.

Afr 8095.25F — Ploegers, J. Plate-atlas von geskiedenis van die Unie von Suid-Afrika. Pretoria, 1949.

Afr 8845.5 — Price, G.N. Port Elizabeth, a bibliography. Cape Town, 1949.

Afr 8687.322 — Ralls, Alice M. Glory which is yours. Pietermaritzburg, 1949.

Afr 5056.149 — Richard Malard, J. Afrique occidentale française. Paris, 1949.

Afr 6883.35 — Robert, J.M. Croyances et coutumes magico-religieuses des Wafipa païens. Tabora, 1949.

Afr 8180.32 — Rooseboom, H. The romance of the great trek. Johannesburg, 1949.

Afr 8919.49 — Rosenthal, Eric. African Switzerland, Basutoland of today. London, 1949.

Afr 4199.25 — Russell, T.W. Egyptian service. 1st ed. London, 1949.

Afr 2026.5 — Sarrasin, P.C. La crise algérienne. Paris, 1949.

Afr 545.10A — Schlosser, Katesa. Propheten in Afrika. Braunschweig, 1949.

Afr 5426.100.12 — Schweitzer, Albert. Zwischen Wasser und Urwald. München, 1949.

Afr 12639.24.110 — Senghor, L.S. Chants pour Naëtt. Paris, 1949.

Afr 6585.9 — Shelswell-White, Geoffrey Henry. A guide to Zanzibar. Zanzibar, 1949.

Afr 8659.49 — Siegfried, A. Afrique du Sud. Paris, 1949.

Afr 8659.49.10 — South Africa. Commission for the Preservation of Natural and Historical Monuments, Relics and Antiques. The monuments of South Africa. 2d ed. Johannesburg, 1949.

Afr Doc 4307.346 — South Africa. Office of Census and Statistics. Population census 7th May 1946. Bevolkinsensus, 7 Mai 1946. Pretoria, 1949. 2v.

Afr 8105.30 — Spilhaus, M.W. The first South Africans and the laws which governed them. Cape Town, 1949.

Afr 8030.15 — Suid-afrikaanse argiefstukke. v.1- Cape Town, 1949. 7v.

Afr 1369.49 — Terrasse, Henri. Histoire du Maroc des origines a l'établissement du protectorat français. v.1-2. Casablanca, 1949-50. 2v.

Afr 8180.28 — Thom, H.B. Die geloftekerk. Kaapstad, 1949.

Afr 3675.66 — Trimingham, J.S. Islam in the Sudan. London, 1949.

Afr 5829.49 — Unienville, N. L'ile Maurice et sa civilisation. Paris, 1949.

Afr 8028.151 — Varley, D.H. Adventures in Africana. Cape Town, 1949.

Afr 6460.50 — Wagner, Guenter. The Bantu of North Kavirondo. London, 1949-56. 2v.

Afr 659.49A — Welch, Galbraith. North African prelude. N.Y., 1949.

Afr 8100.32 — Welch, Sidney R. South Africa under King Sebastian and the cardinal, 1557-1580. Cape Town, 1949.

Afr 7020.40 — Welsch, S.R. South Africa under John III. Capetown, 1949.

Afr 8238.4 — Williams, Alpheus Fuller. Some dreams come true. Cape Town, 1949.

Afr 2000.13 — Wisner, S. L'Algérie dans l'impasse. Paris, 1949.

1949 - cont.

Afr 5426.100.25 — Woyott-Secretan, Marie. Albert Schweitzer. Munich, 1949.

195-

Afr 6218.15 — Azikiwe, Nnamdi. The evolution of federal government in Nigeria. Orlu, 195-. 4 pam.

Afr 7815.34 — Benoit, J. La population africaine à Elisabethville. Elisabethville, 195-.

Afr 12972.41.100 — Biyidi, Alexandre. Ville cruelle. Paris, 195-.

Afr Doc 7708.5 — Congo. Secretariat Général. La population congolaise en 1953. n.p., 195-?

Afr 8687.166 — Creswell, Margaret. An epoch of the political history of South Africa. Cape Town, 195-.

Afr 3163.15 — Darrag, Ahmad. L'Égypte sous le règne de Barsbay. Thèse. Paris, 195-. 2v.

Afr 6540.4.10A — Fallers, Lloyd A. Bantu bureaucracy. Cambridge, Eng., 195-.

Afr 5406.250.5 — France. Direction de la Documentation. French Equatorial Africa. Levallois, 195-.

Afr 6155.3 — Gold Coast (Colony). The Volta River project. Accra, 195-? 4v.

Afr 8045.40 — Kirkwood, Kenneth. The group areas act. Johannesburg, 195-.

Afr 7940.5 — Lyr, Claude. Ruanda Urundi. Brussels, 195-.

Afr 9289.6 — Molema, S. Chief Moroka. Cape Town, 195-.

Afr 3310.10.5 — Nasser, G.A. The philosophy of the revolution. Cairo, 195-.

Afr 10685.67.120 — Okoye, Mokwugo. Some men and women. Onitsha, 195-.

Afr 7183.15 — Pires, Rui. Luanda. Porto, 195-.

Afr 3986.959.5 — Register of Egyptian economy. v.1. n.p., 195-.

Afr 8676.50.5 — Routh, Guy. Industrial relations and race relations. Johannesburg, 195-.

Afr 8659.50.15 — South Africa. State Information Office. South African scene. Pretoria, 195-.

1950

Afr Doc 5307.348 — Algeria. Service de la Statistique Générale. Resultats statistique du dénombrement de la population effective le 31 octobre 1948. Alger, 1950? 2v.

Afr 7222.50 — Almeida de Eca, O.G. De degredado a governado. Lisboa, 1950.

Afr 8028.20 — Amyat, D.L. Background material for the tercentenary of the landing of Jan van Riebeeck. Cape Town, 1950.

Afr 9191.5 — Arnheim, J. Swaziland. Cape Town, 1950.

Afr 7549.50.5 — Bevel, M.L. Le dictionnaire colonial (Encyclopédie). Bruxelles, 1950-51. 2v.

Afr 3979.50 — Bilainkin, G. Cairo to Riyadh diary. London, 1950.

Afr 8063.10 — Birkby, C. The saga of the Transval Scottish Regiment. Cape Town, 1950.

Afr 6198.405 — Birtwhistle, Allen. Thomas Birch Freeman. London, 1950.

Afr 9291.15 — Bloemfontein. City Council. The city of Bloemfontein. Cape Town, 1950.

Afr 1609.50 — Bonn, G. Marokko. 1. Aufl. Stuttgart, 1950.

Afr 520.12 — Borras, T. La España completa. Madrid, 1950.

Afr 2218.9 — Bouteméne, Yahia. La Zaouia des Ouled Sidi Bénamar près de Nédroma. Tlemcen, 1950.

Afr 8659.50.5 — Brady, Cyrus T. Africa astir. Melbourne, 1950.

Afr 9502.14 — Bullock, C. The Mashona and Matabele. Cape Town, 1950.

Afr 8252.228.6 — Burger, M.J. General J.B.M. Hertzog. Kaapstad, 1950.

Afr 8095.70 — Burton, Alfred. Sparks from the border anvil. King Williams Town, 1950.

Afr 4559.49.5 — Buxton, D.R. Travels in Ethiopia. N.Y., 1950.

Afr 1733.5.20 — Caille, Jacques. La petite histoire de Rabat. Casablanca, 1950.

Afr 1369.50 — Caille, Jacques. La petite histoire du Maroc. Casablanca, 1950. 2v.

Afr 7175.40 — Cardoso, A.J.A. Angola. Johannesburg, 1950.

Afr 3205.16 — Cattaui, René. Mohamed-Aly et l'Europe. Paris, 1950.

Afr 5640.7 — Charbonneau, Jean. Gallieni à Madagascar. Paris, 1950.

Afr 6277.45.5 — Chukwuemeka, N. African dependencies, a challenge to Western democracy. N.Y., 1950.

Afr 7850.55F — Comité Spécial du Katanga. Comité spécial du Katanga, 1900-1950. Bruxelles, 1950.

Afr 7850.3 — Cornet, R.J. Terre katangaise. Bruxelles, 1950.

Afr 6460.80.10 — Crazzolara, J. Pasquale. The Lwoo. Verona, 1950-54. 3v.

Afr 5053.7 — Delavignette, R. Freedom and authority in French West Africa. London, 1950.

Afr 8676.50 — Duplessis, J.C. Economic fluctuations in South Africa, 1910-1949. Stellenbosch, 1950.

Afr Doc 3407.348.10 — East Africa High Commission. East African Statistical Department. African population of Tanganyika Territory; geographical and tribal studies. Source: East African population census, 1948. Nairobi, 1950.

Afr Doc 3307.348.10 — East Africa High Commission. East African Statistical Department. African population of Uganda Protectorate; geographical and tribal studies. Nairobi, 1950.

Afr 8815.10 — East London, Cape of Good Hope. City Council. The city of East London. Cape Town, 1950.

Afr 3979.50.5 — Egypt. Cairo, 1950.

Afr 7549.50 — Encyclopedie du Congo belge. Bruxelles, 1950. 3v.

Afr 1955.48 — Esquer, G. Histoire de l'Algérie. 1. ed. Paris, 1950.

Afr 8659.50 — Flavin, Martin. Black and white. 1st ed. N.Y., 1950.

Afr 5404.20 — France. Agence de la France d'Outre-mer. Afrique équatoriale française. v.1-4. Paris, 1950.

Afr 5045.44 — France. Agence de la France d'Outre-Mer. France d'outre-mer. Paris, 1950. 6 pam.

Afr 2731.15.26 — Fremantle, A.J. Desert calling. London, 1950.

Afr 5057.27 — French West Africa. L'équipement de l'A.O.F. Paris, 1950.

Afr 9073.413 — Fynn, Henry Francis. Diary. Malcolm, 1950.

Afr 9439.50 — Gale, W.D. Heritage of Rhodes. Cape Town, 1950.

Afr 7045.26F — Galvao, Henrique. Ronda de Africa. Porto, 1950. 2v.

Afr 8355.20.5A — Gandhi, Mohandas K. Satyagraha in South Africa. 2. ed. Ahmedabad, 1950.

Afr Doc 1807.348 — Gold Coast (Colony). Census Office. Census of populations 1948. Report and tables. London, 1950.

Afr 8289.50 — Graaf, H. de. Boere op St. Helena. Kaapstad, 1950.

Afr 6314.29 — Great Britain. Colonial Office. The British territories in East and Central Africa. London, 1950.

Afr 6390.21 — Great Britain. Colonial Office. Introducing East Africa. London, 1950.

Afr 11435.22.100 — Green, George L. Where men still dream. Cape Town, 1950.

Afr 1200.90 — Guernier, E.L. La Berberie. v.1-2. Paris, 1950. 2v.

1950 - cont.

Afr 505.15 Hailey, W.M.H. Native administration in the British African territories. v.1-5. London, 1950-51. 5v.
Afr 8335.8F Halfeen van afrikaner-prestasie, 1900-1950. Johannesburg, 1950.
Afr 8969.50 Hattersley, A. The British settlement of Natal. Cambridge, Eng., 1950.
Afr 609.50.5A Haynes, G.E. Africa. N.Y., 1950.
Afr 3305.12.5 Heyworth-Dunne, James. Religious and political trends in modern Egypt. Washington, 1950.
Afr 6460.40F Huntingford, G.W.B. Nandi work and culture. London, 1950.
Afr 2609.50 Initiation à la Tunisie. Paris, 1950.
Afr 8678.170 Joshi, Pranshankar. Apartheid in South Africa. Kimberley, 1950.
Afr 5565.2.2 Kammerer, A. La decouverte de Madagascar. Lisboa, 1950.
Afr 4008.2 Kammerer, M. A Coptic bibliography. Ann Arbor, 1950.
Afr 6463.6 Kenya. Commission of Inquiry into the Affray at Kolloa, Baringo. Report. Nairobi, 1950.
Afr 8045.24 Kilpin, R.P. Parliamentary procedure in South Africa. 2d. ed. Juta, 1950.
Afr 8825.25 Kock, V. de. Those in bondage. Cape Town, 1950.
Afr 630.50 Labouret, Henri. Histoire des Noirs d'Afrique. 2. éd. Paris, 1950.
Afr 1609.50.5 Landau, R. Invitation to Morocco. London, 1950.
Afr 4070.51 Langley, M. No woman's country. London, 1950.
Afr 11050.2 MacNab, R.M. Towards the sun. London, 1950.
Afr 8140.33 Malan, D.F. Foreign policy of the Union of South Africa. Pretoria, 1950.
Afr 2373.4 Marcais, Georges. Tlemcen. Paris, 1950.
Afr 4180.3.20 Maugham, R.C.R. Journey to Siwa. N.Y., 1950.
Afr 1609.50.10 Miege, Jean L. Le Maroc. 1. ed. Paris, 1950.
Afr 9345.20 Mockford, J. Seretse Khama and the Bamongwato. London, 1950.
Afr 5040.5 Monmarson, R. L'Afrique noire et son destin. Paris, 1950.
Afr 7881.2 Moulaert, G. Vingt années à Kilo-Moto, 1920-40. Bruxelles, 1950.
Afr 2225.18 Muracciole, Luc. L'émigration algérienne. Alger, 1950.
Afr 6210.8.10 Nigeria. General Conference. Proceedings of the General conference on review of the constitution. Lagos, 1950.
Afr 7332.12 Pedro, E.R. Resenha geografica do distrito da Beira. Lisboa, 1950.
Afr 8659.50.10 Reed, D. Somewhere south of Suez. London, 1950.
Afr 9499.10 Rhodesia, Southern. Public Relations Department. Southern Rhodesia, a field for investment. n.p., 1950.
Afr 1620.15.10 Ricard, Prosper. Maroc. 7. ed. Paris, 1950.
Afr 12288.63.100 Robert, Georges. Incidences 50. Tunis, 1950.
Afr 2225.16 Roger, J.J. Les Musulmans algériens en France et dans les pays islamiques. Paris, 1950.
Afr 6390.60 Roux, Louis. L'Est Africain britannique. Paris, 1950.
Afr 2223.950 Saint Germes, Jean. Economie algérienne. Alger, 1950.
Afr 575.22.5 Sangroniz, José A. Modalidades del islamismo marroqui. Madrid, 1950.
Afr 8678.1.5 Schapera, I. Select bibliography of South African native life and problems. Supplement. Cape Town, 1950.
Afr 2749.50 Schiffers, H. Die Sahara und die Syrten-Länder. 1. Aufl. Stuttgart, 1950.
Afr 8685.80 Sen, Dhirendra Kumar. The position of Indians in South Africa. Calcutta, 1950.
Afr 545.5 Smith, E.W. African ideas of God. London, 1950.
Afr 10916.3 Snelling, John. A new anthology of Rhodesian verse. Oxford, 1950.
Afr 11005.3 South African Public Library, Cape Town. Union list of South African newspapers, Nov. 1949. Cape Town, 1950.
Afr 11802.92.120 Sowden, Lewis. Lady of Coventry. London, 1950.
Afr 1432.25 Spain. Comision del Tesoro. Relato de las gestiones para el cumplimiento de la clausula de indemnizacion del tratado de paz con el Imperio de Marruecos (1860). Madrid, 1950.
Afr 8028.42 Spohr, Otto. Catalogue of books. Cape Town, 1950.
Afr 6760.20F Tanganyika. Africanisation Commission. Report of the Africanisation Commission, 1962. Dar es Salaam, 1950.
Afr 8835.20 Tonder, I.W. Van Riebeecksestad. 1. uitg. Kaapstad, 1950.
Afr 6985.4 Troup, Freda. In face of fear. London, 1950.
Afr 8865.10 Tylden, G. The rise of the Basuto. Cape Town, 1950.
Afr 609.50 Vansinderen, A. Africa, land of many lands. 3d ed. Syracuse, N.Y., 1950.
Afr 7809.50 Verleyen, E.J.B. Congo. Bruxelles, 1950.
Afr 9445.20 Wallis, J.P.R. One man's hand. London, 1950.
Afr 8100.35 Welch, Sidney R. Portuguese rule and Spanish crown in South America. Cape Town, 1950.
Afr 6210.12 Wheare, J. The Nigerian legislative council. London, 1950.
Afr 6850.15 Wood, Alan. The groundnut affair. London, 1950.

1951

Afr 8678.59 Adamastor, (pseud.). White man boss. Boston, 1951.
Afr 5337.3 Amon d'Aby, F. La Côte-d'Ivoire dans la cité africaine. Paris, 1951.
Afr 8089.51.5 Ardizzone, Michael. The mistaken land. London, 1951.
Afr 505.17 Attitude to Africa. Middlesex, Eng., 1951.
Afr 5342.25 Avice, E. La Côte-d'Ivoire. Paris, 1951.
Afr 7315.25 Belchior, M.D. Comprendamos os negros. Lisboa, 1951.
Afr 7812.251F Belgium. Plan décennal pour le développement. Bruxelles, 1951.
Afr 6075.10 Belshan, H. Facing the future in West Africa. London, 1951.
Afr 1869.51 Berthier, A. L'Algérie et son passé. Paris, 1951.
Afr 1408.7 Blunt, Wilfrid. Black sunrise. London, 1951.
Afr 3745.70 British Information Services. The Anglo-Egyptian Sudan. N.Y., 1951.
Afr 1571.50 Caille, Jacques. La représentation diplomatique de la France au Maroc. Paris, 1951.
Afr 1555.10 Campoamor, J.M. La actitud de España ante la cuestion de Marruecos. Madrid, 1951.
Afr 6410.5 Carson, J.B. The administration of Kenya Colony and Protectorate. Rev. ed. Nairobi, 1951.
Afr 7875.5.5 Chapelier, Alice. Elisabethville. Bruxelles, 1951.
Afr 3183.25 Charles-Roux, François. France, Egypte et mer Rouge, de 1715 à 1798. Le Caire, 1951.
Afr 3215.3.25 Charles-Roux, François. Thiers et Méhémet-Ali. Paris, 1951.
Afr 2798.5.15 Couvert, Léon. Tourisme en zigzag vers le Hoggar. Bourg, 1951.
Afr 8045.34 Cowen, D.V. Parliamentary sovereignty and the entrenched sections of the South Africa act. Cape Town, 1951.

1951 - cont.

Afr 4180.4 Crawford, O.G.S. The Fung Kingdom of Sennar. Gloucester, 1951.
Afr 8289.51 Curtis, Lionel. With Milner in South Africa. Oxford, 1951.
Afr 555.7.10 Davies, Horton. Great South African Christians. Cape Town, 1951.
Afr 49724.100 Dube, John. Jeqe, the bodyservant of King Tshaka (Insila Ka Tshaka). Lovedale, 1951.
Afr 3300.60 Egypt. Ministry of Foreign Affairs. Records of conversation, notes and papers. Cairo, 1951.
Afr 3275.55 Egyptian Information Bureau. The Egyptian question. Washington, 1951.
Afr Doc 307.20 Ethiopia. Ministry of Commerce and Industry. Economic handbook of Ethiopia. Addis Ababa, 1951,
Afr 7815.25 Fédération des Associations de Colons du Congo. L'opinion publique coloniale devant l'assimilation des indigènes. Bruxelles, 1951.
Afr 1406.9 Fernandez Alvarez, Manuel. Felipe II, Isabel de Inglaterra y Marruecos. Madrid, 1951.
Afr 5183.951 Fouquet, Joseph. La traite des Arachides dans le pays de Kaolack. Montpelier, 1951.
Afr 5056.151 Gautier Walter, André. Afrique noire. Paris, 1951.
Afr 8667.45 Gerard, Francis. Springbok rampant. London, 1951.
Afr 7815.13.20 Giorgetti, Filiberto. Note di musica zande. Verona, 1951.
Afr 6193.21F Gold Coast (Colony). The development plan, 1951. Accra, 1951.
Afr 6192.24 Gold Coast (Colony). Public Relations Department. Achievement in the Gold Coast. Accra, 1951.
Afr 5426.100.45 Gollomb, Joseph. Albert Schweitzer. London, 1951.
Afr 3042.5 Great Britain. Foreign Office. Anglo-Egyptian conversations. London, 1951.
Afr 6198.436 Griffith, William Brandford. The far horizon. Devon, 1951.
Afr 7219.51 Hamilton, G. In the wake of Da Gama. London, 1951.
Afr 6455.77 Hennings, R.O. African morning. London, 1951.
Afr 4198.5 Hill, Richard Leslie. A biographical dictionary of the Anglo-Egyptian Sudan. Oxford, 1951.
Afr 679.51.5 Howard, C. West African explorers. London, 1951.
Afr 4969.51F Hurt, John A. A general survey of the Somaliland Protectorate, 1944-1950. Harquisa, 1951.
Afr 9506.8 In god's white-robed army. Cape Town, 1951.
Afr 9093.10 Jaarsveld, F.A. van. Die eenheidstrewe van die republikeinse Afrikaners. Johannesburg, 1951.
Afr 6890.2 Jacobsen, Axel. Paa Afrikas vilkaar. København, 1951.
Afr 8685.27.7A Joshi, Pranshankar S. The struggle for equality. Bombay, 1951.
Afr 1069.31.5 Julien, Charles A. Histoire de l'Afrique du Nord. v.1-2. 2. ed. Paris, 1951. 2v.
Afr 8285.20 Kieser, A. President Steijn in die krisesjare. Kaapstad, 1951.
Afr 530.28.10 Lancellatti, A. Pionieri italiane in Africa. Brescia, 1951.
Afr 1494.6 Landau, Rom. The Sultan of Morocco. London, 1951.
Afr 2308.20 Laye, Yves. Le port d'Alger. Alger, 1951.
Afr 6275.114 Leith Ross, Sylvia. Beyond the Niger. London, 1951.
Afr 6903.10 Loening, L.S.E. A bibliography of the states of South-west Africa. Rondebosch, 1951.
Afr 8809.51 Luckhoff, C.A. Table mountain. Cape Town, 1951.
Afr 2285.12 Mackworth, C. The destiny of Isabelle Eberhardt. London, 1951.
Afr 6210.50F Maddocks, K.P. Report on local government in the Northern provinces of Nigeria. Kaduna, 1951.
Afr 5405.109.20 Maran, René. Savorgnan de Brazza. Paris, 1951.
Afr 6460.35F Mayer, Philip. Two studies in applied anthropology in Kenya. London, 1951.
Afr 7820.7F Meessen, J.M.T. Monographie de l'Ituri (nord-est du Congo belge) histoire. Bruxelles, 1951.
Afr 8659.26.5.5 Millin, S.G. The people of South Africa. London, 1951.
Afr 7108.15 Miralles de Imperial y Gomez, C. Angola en tiempos de Felipe II y de Felipe III. Madrid, 1951.
Afr 6542.5 Munger, E.S. Relational patterns of Kampala. Chicago, 1951.
Afr 6280.62.3 Nadel, Siegfried F. A black Byzantium; the Kingdom of Nupe. London, 1951.
Afr 8846.20 National Union of South African Students. The Transkei survey. Cape Town, 1951.
Afr 7309.51 Oliveira Boléo, José de. Moçambique. Lisboa, 1951.
Afr 4766.30 Pankhurst, E. Ex-Italian Somaliland. London, 1951.
Afr 4766.31A Pankhurst, E. Ex-Italian Somaliland. N.Y., 1951.
Afr 6410.12 Parker, Mary. How Kenya is governed. Nairobi, 1951.
Afr 679.51 Pedler, F.J. West Africa. London, 1951.
Afr 1703.6 Peres, Damiao. Conquista de azamor pelo duque de braganca don jaime. Lisboa, 1951.
Afr 11026.2 Raester, Olga. Curtain up. Cape Town, 1951.
Afr 8659.50.10.2 Reed, D. Somewhere south of Suez. N.Y., 1951.
Afr 6168.20 Reindorf, Carl Christian. The history of the Gold Coast and Asante. 2d. ed. Basel, 1951.
Afr 11752.65.100 Rooke, Daphne. A grove of fever trees. London, 1951.
Afr 1739.3.10 Ruiz De Cuevas, T. Apuntes para la historia de Tetuan. Tetuan, 1951.
Afr 9748.807 Rukavina, Kathaleen (Stevens). Jungle pathfinder. London, 1951.
Afr 7815.28 Schebesta, Paul. Baba wa Bambuti. Moedling, 1951.
Afr 3258.8.10 Shukri, M.F. Gordon at Khartoum. Cairo, 1951.
Afr 7809.51.5 Sinderen, A. van. The country of the mountains of the moon. N.Y., 1951.
Afr 1259.40.5 Sitwell, S. Mauretania. London, 1951.
Afr 8252.341.18 Smuts, J.C. The thoughts of General Smuts. Cape Town, 1951.
Afr 11005.5F Snyman, J.P.L. A bibliography of South African novels in English. Potchefstroom, 1951.
Afr 115.10 South Africa. Institute on International Affairs. Africa south of the Sahara. Cape Town, 1951.
Afr 5903.5 Spain. Curso de conferencias sobre la politica africana de los reyes catolicos. V.1-6. Madrid, 1951-53. 3v.
Afr 7312.15 Spence, C.F. The Portuguese colony of Moçambique. Cape Town, 1951.
Afr 550.134 Storme, Marcel. Evangelisatiepogingen. Bruxelles, 1951.
Afr 609.29.25.5 Suggate, L.S. Africa. 4th ed. London, 1951.
Afr 3675.20 Theobald, A.B. The Mahdiya. London, 1951.
Afr 7809.51 Tourist Bureau for the Belgian Congo and Ruanda-Urundi. Travelers guide to the Belgian Congo and Ruanda-Urundi. 1st ed. Brussels, 1951.
Afr 5813.5 Toussaint, Auguste. Select bibliography of Mauritius. Port Louis, 1951.

1951 - cont.

Afr 8283.21   Van der Poel, Jean. The Jameson raid. Cape Town, 1951.
Afr 9839.51A   Vanderpost, L. Venture to the interior. N.Y., 1951.
Afr 8110.30   Welch, Sidney R. Portuguese and Dutch in South Africa. Cape Town, 1951.
Afr 6095.351   Wills, Colin. White traveller in black Africa. London, 1951.
Afr 626.20   Zischka, A. Afrika. Oldenburg, 1951.

1952

Afr 3675.21   Abbas, Mekki. The Sudan question. London, 1952.
Afr 8687.101   Abercrombie, H.R. The secret history of South Africa. 2. ed. Johannesburg, 1952.
Afr 7935.1   Afrianoff, A. Histoire des Bagesera. Bruxelles, 1952.
Afr 679.52   Agyeman, N.Y.T.D. West Africa on the march. N.Y., 1952.
Afr 7369.52   Anderson, R.E. Liberia. Chapel Hill, 1952.
Afr 1430.2   Arnaud, L. Au temps de Mehallas. Casablanca, 1952.
Afr 8925.10   Ashton, H. The Basuto. London, 1952.
Afr 3979.38.11   Ayrout, H.H. Fellahs d'Egypte. 6. ed. Le Caire, 1952.
Afr 3310.50   Barawi, Rashid. The military coup in Egypt. Cairo, 1952.
Afr 8687.126   Barlow, Arthur G. Almost in confidence. Cape Town, 1952.
Afr 7809.52.5   Belgian Information Services. The Belgian Congo appraised. N.Y., 1952.
Afr 7549.52   Belgium. Force Publique. Etat-Major. Le force publique de sa naissance à 1914. Bruxelles, 1952.
Afr 8685.5   Bleek, W.H.I. Zulu legends. 1st ed. Pretoria, 1952.
Afr 8110.3.25   Bosman, D. Brienie van Johanna Maria van Riebeeck. Amsterdam, 1952.
Afr 8110.32F   Botha, Colin G. Three hundred years. Johannesburg, 1952.
Afr 6164.10.2   Bourret, F.M. The Gold Coast. 2d ed. Stanford, 1952.
Afr 555.15.10   Brownlee, M. The lives and work of South African missionaries. Cape Town, 1952.
Afr 11249.86.100   Butler, Guy. Stranger to Europe; poems, 1939-1949. Capetown, 1952.
Afr 1333.15   Cagigas, I. Tratados y convenios referentes a Marruecos. Madrid, 1952.
Afr 1369.52   Cambon, H. Histoire du Maroc. Paris, 1952.
Afr 8028.125   Cape Town. Van Riebeek Festival Book Exhibition. South Africa in print. Cape Town, 1952.
Afr 4150.2.5F   Caton-Thompson, G. Kharga Oasis in prehistory. London, 1952.
Afr 1571.17.85   Catroux, G. Lyautey. Paris, 1952.
Afr 9499.75F   Central African Statistical Office. Report on Southern Rhodesia family expenditure survey. Salisbury, 1952.
Afr 1280.30   Chouraqui, A. Marche vers l'Occident. 1. ed. Paris, 1952.
Afr 6277.45   Chukwuemeka, N. Industrialization of Nigeria. N.Y., 1952.
Afr 9510.5.5   Clark, John Desmond. The Victoria Falls. Lusaka, 1952.
Afr 8252.8.20   Crankshaw, E. The forsaken idea. London, 1952.
Afr 5549.52.5   Damantsoha. Histoire politique et religieuse des Malgaches. Tananarive?, 1952.
Afr 8659.52   Davidson, B. Report on southern Africa. London, 1952.
Afr 710.15   Deschamps, H.J. L'éveil politique africain. 1 ed. Paris, 1952.
Afr 3675.22   Duncan, J.S.R. The Sudan. Edinburgh, 1952.
Afr 8695.5   Dundas, Charles C.F. Problem territories of southern Africa. Cape Town, 1952.
Afr 8678.60   Dvorin, E.P. Racial separation in South Africa. Chicago, 1952.
Afr 2459.52F   Encyclopédie Mensuelle d'Outre-Mer. Tunisie 53. Paris, 1952.
Afr 628.252   Fanon, F. Peau noire. Paris, 1952.
Afr 1709.5   Flamand, P. Demnate, un mellah en pays berbere. Paris, 1952.
Afr 1259.52   France. Président Du Conseil. Facts and figures about French North Africa. Paris, 1952.
Afr 5749.52   France de l'ocean Indien. Paris, 1952.
Afr 8252.9.20   Fraser, Barbara Davidson. John William Colenso. Cape Town, 1952.
Afr 1069.37.5   Gautier, Emile F. Le passé de l'Afrique du Nord. Paris, 1952.
Afr 630.52.5   Ghurye, G.S. Race relations in Negro Africa. Bombay, 1952.
Afr 11433.74.110   Gordimer, N. The soft voice of the serpent. N.Y., 1952.
Afr 11433.75.100   Gordon, Gerald. Let the day perish. London, 1952.
Afr 5058.10   Gouilly, A. L'islam dans l'Afrique occidentale française. Paris, 1952.
Afr 6470.145   Gregory, J.R. Under the sun. Nairobi, 1952.
Afr 609.52.5   Guernier, E.L. L'apport de l'Afrique à la pensée humaine. Paris, 1952.
Afr Doc 8707.350   Guinea, Spanish. Delegacion Colonial de Estadistica. Resúmenes estadisticos del anso general de poblacion del Gobcerno General de los Españoles del Golfo de Guinea al 31 de diciembrre de 1950. Madrid, 1952.
Afr Doc 9407.350   Guinea. Portuguese. Secção Tecnica de Estatistica. Censo da população de 1950. Lisboa, 1952? 2v.
Afr 609.52.10   Hanzelka, Jiri. Africa. 1st ed. Prague, 1952. 3v.
Afr 8028.25   Heerden, J. van. Closer union movement. Cape Town, 1952.
Afr 3026.26   Heyworth-Dunne, J. Select bibliography on modern Egypt. Cairo, 1952.
Afr 8089.52   Hintrager, O. Geschichte von Südafrika. München, 1952.
Afr 8089.31.5   Hofmeyer, J.H. South Africa. 2d ed. N.Y., 1952.
Afr 8809.52   Hondius, J. Klare besgryving van Cabo de Bona Esperança. Kaapstad, 1952.
Afr 2609.52   Hoppenot, Hélène. Tunisie. Lausanne, 1952.
Afr 609.52A   Hunter, J.A. Hunter. 1st ed. N.Y., 1952.
Afr 1494.15   Hure, A.J.J. La pacification du Maroc. Paris, 1952.
Afr 8678.66   India. Information Service. World opinion on apartheid. New Delhi, 1952.
Afr 7809.52.10   Jentgen, P. Les frontières du Congo belge. Bruxelles, 1952.
Afr 1095.5   Julien, C.A. L'Afrique du Nord en marche. Paris, 1952.
Afr 7459.52   Junge, Werner. Bolahun. N.Y., 1952.
Afr 42731.2.700   Kagame, A. La divine pastorale. Bruxelles, 1952.
Afr 7937.9   Kagame, Alexis. Le code des institutions politiques du Rwanda précolonial. Bruxelles, 1952.
Afr 8659.52.15   Kaptein, De Unie van Zuid-Afrika. Amsterdam, 1952.
Afr 9050.54   Keiskammahoek rural survey. Pietermaritzburg, 1952.
Afr 8840.10   Kimberley, South Africa. The city of Kimberley. Cape Town, 1952.
Afr 8095.30   Kock, V. de. Ons drie eeue. Our three centuries. Kaapstad, 1952.
Afr 626.30   Krueger, Karl. Afrika. Berlin, 1952.
Afr 1609.52   Landau, R. Moroccan journal. London, 1952.
Afr 9854.16   Langworthy, Emily (Booth). This Africa was mine. Stirling, Scotland, 1952.

1952 - cont.

Afr 626.26   Laure, René. Le continent africain au milieu du siècle. Paris, 1952.
Afr 605.56.11   Leo Africanus, J. De la descripción de Africa y de las cosas notables que ella se encuentran. n.p., 1952.
Afr 7459.52.5   Liberia. Department of State. Bureau of Information. Liberia. Monrovia, 1952.
Afr 28.7.5   Library of Congress. European Affairs Division. Continuing sources for research on Africa. Washington, 1952.
Afr 28.7   Library of Congress. European Affairs Division. Introduction to Africa. Washington, 1952.
Afr 7567.15   Luwel, Marcel. De limburgers in Congo. Hasselt, 1952.
Afr 5783.5   Madagascar. Tananarive. Tananarive, 1952.
Afr 9760.5F   Mair, L.P. Native administration in central Nyasaland. London, 1952.
Afr 1755.55   Maldonado, E. El rogui. Tetuan, 1952.
Afr 3026.20F   Maple, H.L. A bibliography of Egypt consisting of work printed before A.D. 1801. Pieter-Maritzburg, 1952.
Afr 8095.60   Marguard, Leopold. Blame it on Van Riebeeck. Cape Town, 1952.
Afr 1493.60   Maridalyn, H. Présence française au Maroc. Monte carlo, 1952.
Afr 8678.62   Marquard, L. The peoples and policies of South Africa. London, 1952.
Afr 8110.3.40   Mees, W.C. Maria quevellerius. Assen, 1952.
Afr 1609.50.12   Miege, Jean L. Morocco. Paris, 1952.
Afr 8250.25.10   Millin, S.G. Rhodes. London, 1952.
Afr 11572.50.140   Millin, S.G.(L). The burning man. London, 1952.
Afr 1273.5F   Monde Economique. North Africa, a world in fusion. Tunis, 1952.
Afr 5426.100.30   Monestier, Marianne. Le grand docteur blanc. Paris, 1952.
Afr 5955.2   Moreno Moreno, José A. Reseña histórica de la presencia de España en el Golfo de Guinea. Madrid, 1952.
Afr 630.52   Mylius, N. Afrika Bibliographie. Wien, 1952.
Afr 8680.40   Neame, Lawrence Elvin. White man's Africa. Cape Town, 1952.
Afr 8110.3.30   Nederlandsch Genootschap voor Geslacht, The Hague. Jan van Riebeeck. 's-Gravenhage, 1952.
Afr 6210.48   Nigeria. Northern Legislature. Report of the Joint Select Committee of the Northern Regional Council, 20th and 21st July, and Northern legislature, 7th, 8th and 9th, August, 1951. Kaduna, 1952.
Afr 6385.5   Oliver, R. The missionary factor in East Africa. London, 1952.
Afr 4719.52   Pankhurst, E.S. Eritrea on the eve. Essex, 1952.
Afr 1571.48   Parent, Pierre. The truth about Morocco. N.Y., 1952.
Afr 5501.3.10   Poisson, Henri. Le cinquantenaire de l'Academie malgache. Tananarive, 1952.
Afr 5915.5   Prieto y Llovera, P. Politica aragonesa en Africa hasta la muerte de Fernando el Catolico. Madrid, 1952.
Afr 5549.52   Rabemananjara, R.W. Madagascar. Paris, 1952.
Afr 8110.3.20   Riebeeck, Jan van. Daghregister gehouden by den oppercoopman Jan Anthonisz van Riebeeck. v.1-. Kaapstad, 1952. 3v.
Afr 8110.3.15   Riebeeck, Jan van. Journal. Cape Town, 1952. 3v.
Afr 11752.65.120   Rooke, Daphne. Mittee. Boston, 1952.
Afr 2533.1   Rous, Jean. Tunisie...attention. Paris, 1952.
Afr 1571.17.90   Roux, F. de. La jeunesse de Lyautey. Paris, 1952.
Afr 3305.8   Royal Institute of International Affairs. Great Britain and Egypt, 1914-1951. London, 1952.
Afr 8369.52   Sachs, E.S. The choice before South Africa. London, 1952.
Afr 5260.25   Séré de Rivières, Edmond. Le Niger. Paris, 1952.
Afr 7809.52   Severn, M. Congo pilgrim. London, 1952.
Afr 3715.5A   Shibeika, Mekki. British policy in the Sudan, 1882-1902. London, 1952.
Afr 9345.55   Sillery, A. The Bechuanaland protectorate. Cape Town, 1952.
Afr 6455.80   Simpson, Alyse. Red dust of Africa. London, 1952.
Afr 8687.258   Smith, E.W. The life and times of Daniel Lindley. N.Y., 1952.
Afr 11797.41.102   Smith, Pauline. The little karoo. N.Y., 1952.
Afr 8252.341.45   Smuts, J.C. Jan Christian Smuts. London, 1952.
Afr 8252.341.47   Smuts, J.C. Jan Christian Smuts. N.Y., 1952.
Afr 8659.45.2   South Africa. Government Information Office. This is South Africa. N.Y., 1952.
Afr 6113.15   Southorn, B.S.W. The Gambia. London, 1952.
Afr 3695.3.83   Stocchetti, F. Romolo Gessi. Milano, 1952.
Afr 4559.52   Talbot, D.A. Contemporary Ethiopia. N.Y., 1952.
Afr 1369.49.3   Terrasse, Henri. Histoire du Maroc. Casablanca, 1952.
Afr 2533.8   Tunisian Office for National Liberation. An account of the Tunisian question and its most recent developments. N.Y., 1952.
Afr 11853.88.110   Tutuola, Amos. The palm-wine drinkard and his dead palm-wine tapster. London, 1952.
Afr 7850.5   Verdick, E. Les premiers jours au Katanga. Bruxelles, 1952.
Afr 699.31.3   Waugh, E. They were still dancing. N.Y., 1952.
Afr 109.52   Westermann, Diedrich. Geschichte Afrikas. Köln, 1952.
Afr 11572.50.5   Whyte, Moray. Bibliography of the works of Sarah Gertrude Millin. Cape Town, 1952.
Afr 7850.5   Young, F.B. In South Africa. London, 1952.
Afr 5406.252   Ziegle, Henri. Afrique equatoriale française. Paris, 1952.

1953

Afr 8678.311   Abrahams, Peter. Return to Goli. London, 1953.
Afr 7322.6   Almeida de Eça, Felipe Gastão. Historia das guerras no Zambeze. Lisboa, 1953-54. 2v.
Afr 1369.53   American Committee for Moroccan Independence. The case for Morocco. Washington, 1953.
Afr 4199.105.5   Amin, Osman. MuhammadAbduh. Washington, 1953.
Afr Doc 9307.350   Angola. Segundo recenseamento geral da população, 1950. Luanda, 1953-1956. 5v.
Afr 7176.7   Angola. Direcção dos Serviços de Economia. Angola. Luanda, 1953.
Afr 6415.40   Askwith, Tom G. The story of Kenya's progress. Nairobi, 1953.
Afr 5871.53   Barassin, Jean. Naissance d'une chrétienté. Saint-Denis, 1953.
Afr 1494.10   Barrat, Robert. Justice pour le Maroc. Paris, 1953.
Afr 630.53   Bartlett, V. Struggle for Africa. London, 1953.
Afr 9439.53   Bate, Henry M. Report from the Rhodesias. London, 1953.
Afr 8690.20   Birkby, Carel. In the sun I'm rich. Cape Town, 1953.
Afr 2731.15.30   Bodley, R.V.C. The warrior saint. 1st ed. Boston, 1953.

1953 - cont.

Afr 9439.40.2	Boggie, Jeannie M. First steps in civilizing Rhodesia. Bulawayo, 1953.
Afr 8678.108	Brayshaw, E. Russell. The racial problems of South Africa. London, 1953.
Afr 3745.55	British Information Service. The Sudan, 1899-1953. N.Y., 1953.
Afr 8250.40	Bulawayo, South Africa. Central African Rhodes Centenary Exhibition. The story of Cecil Rhodes. Bulawayo, 1953.
Afr 9093.20	Bulpin, T.V. The golden republic. Cape Town, 1953.
Afr 8658.22.5	Burchell, W.J. Travels in the interior of southern Africa. London, 1953. 2v.
Afr 1608.08	Burel, Antoine. La mission du capitaine Burel au Maroc en 1808. Paris, 1953.
Afr 8252.228.5	Burger, M.J. General J.B.M. Hertzog in Batilio. Kaapstad, 1953.
Afr 11249.86.140	Butler, Guy. The dam. Cape Town, 1953.
Afr 5549.08.12	Callet, F. Histoire des rois. V.1-3. Tananarive, 1953. 2v.
Afr 8667.20	Calpin, G.H. The South African way of life. London, 1953.
Afr 7803.38	Carpenter, G.W. Les chemins du seigneur du Congo. Leopoldville, 1953.
Afr 1200.80	Carpentier, J.A. Les problèmes nord-africains. Paris, 1953.
Afr 9170.11	Carr, W.S. Pioneers' path. Cape Town, 1953.
Afr 628.253	Caruthers, J.C. The African mind in health and disease. Geneva, 1953.
Afr 5585.30	Chapus, G.S. Rainilaiarivony, un homme d'Etat Malgache. Paris, 1953.
Afr 7068.5	Coelho, F. de L. Duas descrições seiscentistas da Guiné. Lisbon, 1953.
Afr 8659.53.5	Coetzee, Abel. Die Afrikaanse volkskultuur. Kaapstad, 1953.
Afr 11397.50.100	Collin-Smiths, J. Locusts and wild honey. London, 1953.
Afr 8675.5	Conseil Scientifique pour l'Afrique au Sud du Sahara. Cartographie de l'Afrique au sud du Sahara. Bukavu, 1953.
Afr 1703.2	Cortocero Hanares, H.F. Alcazarquiver 1950. Tetuan, 1953.
Afr 2798.5.10	Couvert, Léon. Contact avec l'Afrique noire par le Hoggar. Paris, 1953.
Afr 6570.10	Crafton, R.H. Zanzibar affairs, 1914-1933. London, 1953.
Afr 7803.30	Cuvelier, J. Documents sur une mission française au Kakongo 1766-1776. Bruxelles, 1953.
Afr 500.65	Datlin, S. Afrika unter dem Joch des Imperialismus. Berlin, 1953.
Afr 679.53	Davidson, Basil. The new West Africa. London, 1953.
Afr 7369.53	Davis, S.A. This is Liberia. N.Y., 1953.
Afr 2533.10	Day, Georges. Les affaires de la Tunisie et du Maroc devant les Nations Unies. Paris, 1953.
Afr 9609.5	Deane, Phyllis. Colonial social accounting. Cambridge, England, 1953.
Afr 9389.53	Debenham, F. Kalahari sand. London, 1953.
Afr 13324.7.100	Debertry, Leon. Kitawala. Elisabethville, 1953.
Afr 8659.53	Deguingand, F.W. African assignment. London, 1953.
Afr 2618.26.5	Demeerseman, A. Vocation culturelle de la Tunisie. Tunis, 1953.
Afr 2336.10	Despais, J. Le Hodna. 1. ed. Paris, 1953.
Afr 4365.2	Duchesne, Albert. Le consul Blondeel en Abyssinie. Bruxelles, 1953.
Afr 626.24	Dujonchay, I. L industrialisation de l'Afrique. Paris, 1953.
Afr 8835.15	Duplessis, I.D. The Malay quarter and its people. Cape Town, 1953.
Afr 8676.53	Eck, H.J. van. Some aspects of the South African industrial revolution. 2d ed. Johannesburg, 1953.
Afr 5406.253F	Encyclopédie Mensuelle d'Outre-Mer. AEF 53. Paris, 1953.
Afr 2459.53F	Encyclopédie Mensuelle d'Outre-Mer. Tunisie 54. Paris, 1953.
Afr 9635.10F	Epstein, A.L. The administration of justice and the urban African. London, 1953.
Afr 2929.53	Epton, N.C. Oasis kingdom. N.Y., 1953.
Afr 1750.5	Et-Tabyi. Miscelanea marroqui. Ceuta, 1953.
Afr 699.53	Fontaine, Pierre. Alger-Tunis-Rabat. Paris, 1953.
Afr 6397.15	Frank, Cedric N. The life of Bishop Steere. Dar es Salaam, 1953.
Afr 5872.10	Freon, L.S. Un ardennais conseiller du roi. Verviers, 1953.
Afr 1493.50	Gabrielli, L. Abd-el-Krim et les événements du Rif. Casablanca, 1953.
Afr 1409.17	Garcia Figueras, T. Apoyo de España a Mawlay Hisam. Tetuan, 1953.
Afr 2285.23	Gardi, René. Blue veils, red tents. London, 1953.
Afr 3300.75	Ghali, M.B. The policy of tomorrow. Washington, 1953.
Afr 6162.5	Gold Coast (Colony). The government's proposals for constitutional reform. Accra, 1953.
Afr 8369.53.5	Goosen, D.P. Die triomf van nasionalisme in Suid-Afrika, 1910-1953. Johannesburg, 1953.
Afr 11433.74.100	Gordimer, N. The lying days. N.Y., 1953.
Afr 3695.6	Gordon, C.G. Equatoria under Egyptian rule. Cairo, 1953.
Afr 7942.2	Gourou, Pierre. La densité de la population au Ruanda-Urundi. Bruxelles, 1953.
Afr 6979.53	Green, Laurence G. Lords of the last frontier. London, 1953.
Afr 6122.5F	Haswell, Margaret Rosary. Economics of agriculture in a savannah village. London, 1953.
Afr 6565.35	Hollingsworth, L.W. Zanzibar under the Foreign Office. London, 1953.
Afr 5318.30	Hovis, Maurice. La Guinée française. Paris, 1953.
Afr 6420.35.3	Huxley, Elspeth. White man's country. London, 1953. 2v.
Afr 8678.380	India. Ministry of External Affairs. Disabilities of the non-white peoples in the Union of South Africa. Delhi, 1953.
Afr 8369.53	Joekoms, Jan. When Malan goes. Johannesburg, 1953.
Afr 6146.5	Johnson, T.S. The story of a mission, the Sierra Leone church. London, 1953.
Afr 9439.53.5	Jones, Neville. Rhodesian genesis. Bulawayo, 1953.
Afr 4559.53	Kamil, M. Das Land der Negus. Innsbruck, 1953.
Afr 3300.70	Kamil, M. Tomorrow's Egypt. 1st English ed. Cairo, 1953.
Afr 6395.2.15	Kenyatta, Jona. Facing Mt. Kenya. London, 1953.
Afr 3979.53	Khalid, K.M. From here we start. 3d. ed. Washington, 1953.
Afr 11501.89.100	Kruger, Rayne. The spectacle. London, 1953.
Afr 11501.89.110	Kruger, Rayne. Young villain with wings. London, 1953.
Afr 3038.10	Landau, J.M. Parliaments and parties in Egypt. Tel-Aviv, 1953.
Afr 11510.60.100	Lanham, Peter. Blanket boy's moon. London, 1953.
Afr 12832.5.110	Laye, Camara. L'enfant noir. Paris, 1953.
Afr 6395.2.10	Leakey, L.S.B. Mau Mau and the Kikuyu. London, 1953.

1953 - cont.

Afr 6740.15.10	Lecoq, Raymond. Les Bamileke. Paris, 1953.
Afr 3823.6	Lemaire, Charles. Journal de route de Charles Lemaire. Bruxelles, 1953.
Afr 1753.12	Leria, C. Don Francisco y don dionisio. Tetuan, 1953.
Afr 4875.5	Lippmann, A. Guerriers et sorciers en Somalie. Paris, 1953.
Afr 7803.28	Lorenzo da Lucca. Relations sur le Congo du père Lament de Lucques. Bruxelles, 1953.
Afr 1571.17.3	Lyautey, L.H.G. Lyautey l'Africain. v.1-4. Paris, 1953. 4v.
Afr 6760.5	MacKenzie, William James Millar. Report of the Special Commissioner appointed to examine matters arising out of the report of the Committee on Constitutional Development. Dar es Salaam, 1953.
Afr 1571.17.105	Madras, Didier. Dans l'ombre du maréchal Lyautey. Rabat, 1953.
Afr 9499.20	Mai, Erwin. Die Wirtschaft von Britisch-Zentral Afrika. Köln, 1953.
Afr 6883.15A	Malcolm, D.W. Sukumaland. London, 1953.
Afr 609.53	Marie André du Sacre Coeur, Sister. La condition humaine en Afrique noire. Paris, 1953.
Afr 605.73.5F	Marmol Carvajal, L. del. Descripción general de Africa. Madrid, 1953.
Afr 7110.10	Matos, J.M.R.N. A nação una. Lisboa, 1953.
Afr 7018.10	Matos, José Mendes Ribeiro Norton de. Africa nossa. Porto, 1953.
Afr Doc 2807.352F	Mauritius. Census 1952 of Mauritius and of its dependencies. Port Louis, 1953. 3 pam.
Afr 8250.35.2	Maurois, Andre. Cecil Rhodes. London, 1953.
Afr 8250.35	Maurois, Andre. Cecil Rhodes. N.Y., 1953.
Afr 1723.15	Mayne, Peter. The alleys of Marrakesh. 1st ed. Boston, 1953.
Afr 4743.10	Metodio da Nembro. La missione dei Minori Cappuccini in Eritrea (1894-1952). Rome, 1953.
Afr 9149.53	Middelberg, Gerrit Adrian Arnold. Briewe uit Transvaal. Pretoria, 1953.
Afr 9195.15	Miller, A.M. Mamisa, the Swazi warrior. Pietermaritzburg, 1953.
Afr 6282.2	Miller, Walter Richard Samuel. Walter Miller, 1872-1952. Zaria, 1953.
Afr 5247.40	Miner, Horace Mitchell. The primitive city of Timbuctoo. Princeton, 1953.
Afr 1369.53.5	Montagne, Robert. Révolution au Maroc. Paris, 1953.
Afr 1494.7	Moroccan Office of Information and Documentation, N.Y. Morocco under the protectorate. N.Y., 1953.
Afr 5346.5.15	Mouezy, Henri. Assinie et le royaume de Krinjabo. 2. ed. Paris, 1953.
Afr Doc 9207.350	Mozambique. Repartição Tecnica de Estatistica. Recenseamento geral da população em 1950. Lourenço Marques, 1953-1955. 2v.
Afr 8690.5	Muller, D.J. The Orange river. Cape Town, 1953.
Afr 11586.77.100	Murray, M. The fire-raisers. London, 1953.
Afr 1620.25	Nagel, Publishers. Morocco. Paris, 1953.
Afr 8657.10	Natal. Town and Regional Planning Commission. Tugela basin, a regional survey. Pietermaritzburg, 1953.
Afr 3745.50	Newbold, D. The making of modern Sudan. London, 1953.
Afr 1609.53	Newman, B. Morocco today. London, 1953.
Afr 8028.35	Nicholson, G. German settlers in South Africa. Cape Town, 1953.
Afr 9855.2F	Nyasaland. Commission of Inquiry into Disturbances at Mangunda Estate. Report. Zomba, 1953.
Afr 626.28	Organization for European Economic Cooperation in Africa. Energy in overseas territories south of the Sahara and in Surinam. Paris, 1953.
Afr 6164.11	Padmore, G. The Gold Coast revolution. London, 1953.
Afr 4430.40.5	Pankhurst, Estelle S. Ethiopia and Eritrea. Woodford, 1953.
Afr 1494.12	Parent, P. The truth about Morocco. N.Y., 1953.
Afr 6294.2	Parrinder, Edward Geoffrey. Religion in an African city. London, 1953.
Afr 11675.87.100A	Paton, Alan. Too late the phalarope. N.Y., 1953.
Afr 8685.55	Patterson, S. Colour and culture in South Africa. London, 1953.
Afr 500.62	Pesenti, G. Euraffrica. Borgo S. Dalmazzo, 1953.
Afr 6277.25	Prest, A.R. The national income of Nigeria. London, 1953.
Afr 1494.30F	Quarante ans de présence française au Maroc. Casablanca, 1953.
Afr 5640.30	Rabemananjara, R.W. Madagascar sous la revolution Malgache. Paris, 1953.
Afr 1739.3.5	Al-Rahuni, A. Ben M. Historia de Tetuan. Tetuan, 1953.
Afr 5853.2	Réunion. Archives Departementales. Documents concernant les iles de Bourbon et de France. Nerac, 1953.
Afr 9515.7	Rixom, Frank. History of the Salisbury club. Salisbury, 1953.
Afr 8687.265.5	Robins, Eric. This man Malan. Cape Town, 1953.
Afr 6390.29	Ruark, R.C. Harm of the hunter. 1st ed. Garden City, 1953.
Afr 6192.60	Ryan, Isobel. Black man's town. London, 1953.
Afr 7937.4	Ryckmans, P. Une page d'histoire coloniale. Bruxelles, 1953.
Afr 1069.53	Schaefer, Rene. Drame et chances de l'Afrique du Nord. Paris, 1953.
Afr 9050.15	Schimlek, Francis. Mariannhill. Mariannhill, 1953.
Afr 5180.33	Sere de Rivières, E. Le Sénégal. Paris, 1953.
Afr Doc 4312.153	South Africa. Parliament. South Africa Act Amendment Act. v.1-2. Cape Town, 1953.
Afr 626.22	Stamp, L.D. Africa. N.Y., 1953.
Afr 8656.85.2	Stel, Simon van der. Simon van der Stel's journal. Supplement. Dublin, 1953.
Afr 6395.10	Stoneham, C.T. Mau Mau. London, 1953.
Afr 9610.10	Taylor, Don. Rainbow on the Zambezi. London, 1953.
Afr 7809.53	Thibaut, J. Sous l'ombre des volcans africains. Bruxelles, 1953.
Afr 8252.354.25	Thompson, F.R. Matabele Thompson. Johannesburg, 1953.
Afr Doc 3307.348	Uganda. Report on the census of the non-native population of Uganda Protectorate. Nairobi, 1953.
Afr 11865.59.100	Vanderpost, Laurens. The face beside the fire. N.Y., 1953.
Afr 11865.59.110	Vanderpost, Laurens. In a province. London, 1953.
Afr 7850.53	Verbeken, A. La première traversée du Katanga en 1806. Bruxelles, 1953.
Afr 8687.265	Walker, O. Sailor Malan. London, 1953.
Afr 6484.21	Wallis, C.A.G. Report of an inquiry into African local government in the protectorate of Uganda. Uganda, 1953.
Afr 6420.45	Wills, Colin. Who killed Kenya. N.Y., 1953.

Afr 6420.82	Wilson, Christopher James. Before the dawn in Kenya. Nairobi, 1953.
Afr 7549.53	Ydewalle, Charles D. Le Congo du fétiche à l'uranium. Bruxelles, 1953.

1954

Afr 3979.55.5	Aafjes, Bertus. Morgen bloeien de abrikozen. Amsterdam, 1954.
Afr 11108.74.120	Abrahams, Peter. Tell freedom. 1st American ed. N.Y., 1954.
Afr 659.48A	Alal al Fasi. The independence movements in Arab North Africa. Washington, 1954.
Afr 2288.15.3	Algeria. Direction des Territoires du Sud. Les territoires du sud de l'Algérie. Alger, 1954.
Afr 4180.5	Ammar, H. Growing up in an Egyptian village. London, 1954.
Afr 618.15	Arbuthnot, T.S. African hunt. 1st ed. N.Y., 1954.
Afr 10621.76.100	Armattoe, Raphael E.G. Deep down the blackman's mind. Ilfracombe, 1954.
Afr 8095.40	Axelson, Eric Victor. South African explorers. London, 1954.
Afr 3979.38.12	Ayrout, H.H. The fellaheen. 7th ed. Cairo, 1954.
Afr 8680.47	Bantu. An informal publication of the Department of Native Affairs of the Union of South Africa. Pretoria, 1954.
Afr 9700.20	Barnes, J.A. Politics in changing society. Cape Town, 1954.
Afr 6280.26.5F	Bohannan, Paul. Tiv farm and settlement. London, 1954.
Afr 1571.17.95	Boisboissel, Y. de. Dans l'ombre de Lyautey. Paris, 1954.
Afr 5243.343.10	Boulnois, Jean. L'empire de Gao. Paris, 1954.
Afr 2536.10.10	Bourguiba, H. La Tunisie et la France. Paris, 1954.
Afr 679.54.5	Bowen, E.S. Return to laughter. N.Y., 1954.
Afr 550.70	Brasio, A.D. Monumenta missionaria africana. Lisboa, 1954. 10v.
Afr 1494.20	Bridel, T. Le Maroc. Lausanne, 1954.
Afr 8659.54.5	Brown, John. The thirsty land. London, 1954.
Afr 7815.39	Bulck, Gaston van. Orthographie des noms ethniques au Congo belge. Bruxelles, 1954.
Afr 4158.5	Burmester, O.H.E. A guide to the monasteries of the Wadi Natrun. Le Caire, 1954.
Afr 9523.275	Burrows, Edmund Hartford. The moodies of Melsetter. Cape Town, 1954.
Afr 1571.17.100	Cahiers Charles de Foucauld. Lyautey. Grenoble, 1954.
Afr 3003.2.5	Cahiers d'histoire égyptienne. Index, ser.1-5 (1948-53). Le Caire, 1954.
Afr 8659.54	Campbell, A. The heart of Africa. 1st ed. N.Y., 1954.
Afr 7183.33	Cardoso, Manuel da Costa Lobo. Subsidios para a historia de Luanda. Luanda, 1954.
Afr 2749.54.10	Carl, Louis. Tefedest. London, 1954.
Afr 609.54.30	Cecchi, Emilio. Appunti per un periplo dell'Africa. Milano, 1954.
Afr 1609.48	Celerier, Jean. Maroc. 2. ed. Paris, 1954.
Afr Doc 3807.351	Central African Statistical Office. Census of population 1951. Salisbury, 1954.
Afr 609.54.15	Cintas, Pierre. Contribution à l'étude de l'expansion carthagenoise au Maroc. Paris, 1954.
Afr 1618.15	Cola Alberich, Julio. Cultos primitivos de Marruecos. Madrid, 1954.
Afr 609.54.10	Considine, J.J. Africa, world of new men. N.Y., 1954.
Afr 1826.30	Constantine, Algeria. Archives Départmentals. Répertoire de documentation nord-africaine. v.1-2. Constantine, 1954.
Afr 6883.13.5	Cory, Hans. Sukuma law and customs. London, 1954.
Afr 8145.16	Davies, H. South African missions. London, 1954.
Afr 6295.5F	Davies, J.G. The Biu book, a collection and reference book on Biu division (Northern Nigeria). Norla, 1954-56.
Afr 109.54	Degraff Johnson, J.C. African glory. London, 1954.
Afr 11320.50.150	Delius, Anthony. An unknown border; poems. Cape Town, 1954.
Afr 7549.54	Dellicour, Fernand. Les propos d'un colonial belge. Bruxelles, 1954.
Afr 626.35	Dia, Mamadou. Reflexions sur l'économie de l'Afrique noire. Paris, 1954.
Afr 11327.90.100	Divine, David. The golden fool. 1st ed. London, 1954.
Afr 5056.154	Du Puigaudeau, Odette. La piste Maroc-Sénégal. Paris, 1954.
Afr 8680.30	Dutch Reformed Conference of Church Leaders, Pretoria, 1953. Christian principles in multiracial South Africa. Pretoria, 1954.
Afr Doc 3407.352	East Africa High Commission. East African Statistical Department. Report on the census of the non-African population taken on the night of 13 february 1952. Dar es Salaam, 1954.
Afr 3310.15	Egyptian Information Bureau. Egypt in two years. Washington, 1954.
Afr 10675.47.140	Ekwensi, Cyprian. People of the city. London, 1954.
Afr 6210.20	Elias, Taslim O. Groundwork of Nigerian law. London, 1954.
Afr 2209.54	Encyclopédie Mensuelle d'Outre-Mer. Algérie 54. Paris, 1954.
Afr 1609.54.5	Encyclopedie Mensuelle d'Outre-Mer. Morocco 54. Paris, 1954.
Afr 4570.5	Ethiopia. Chamber of Commerce. Guide book of Ethiopia. Addis Ababa, 1954.
Afr 3986.954	Fahmy, M. La révolution de l'industrie en Egypte et ses conséquences sociales au 19. siècle. Leiden, 1954.
Afr 9489.54	Federation of Rhodesia and Nyasaland. Federal Information Services. The new federation of Rhodesia and Nyasaland. Salisbury, 1954.
Afr 2731.15.40	Federici, Emidio. L'eremità del Sahara. Roma, 1954.
Afr 630.54	Forde, C.D. African worlds. London, 1954.
Afr 2731.15.6	Foucauld, Charles, Vicomte de. Lettres inédites au général Laperrine. Paris, 1954.
Afr 1273.954	France. Commission d'Etude. Deuxième plan de modernisation. n.p., 1954. 2 pam.
Afr 2223.954	France. Commission d'Etude et de Coordination des Plans. Deuxième plan de modernisation. n.p., 1954.
Afr 5057.16	France. Direction de la Documentation. French West Africa. Rennes, 1954.
Afr 5342.30	France. Service de Documentation Economique. Côte-d'Ivoire, 1954. Paris, 1954.
Afr 8676.48.2	Franklin, N.N. Economics in South Africa. 2d ed. Cape Town, 1954.
Afr 5320.5	Gaisseau, P.D. The sacred forest. 1st Amer.ed. N.Y., 1954.

Afr 6395.2.40	Garothers, John C. The psychology of Mau Mau. Nairobi, 1954.
Afr 8089.54	Gibbs, H. Background to bitterness. London, 1954.
Afr 6176.45F	Gold Coast (Colony). Commission of Enquiry into Mr. Braimah's Resignation and Allegations Arising therefrom. Report. Accra, 1954.
Afr 6310.44	Great Britain. Commissions. Civil Services of the East African Territories. Report, 1953-54. London, 1954.
Afr 5385.24	Grivot, René. Réactions dahoméennes. Paris, 1954.
Afr 630.54.5	Hafter, Rudolf. Schwarz und Weiss in Afrika. Zürich, 1954.
Afr 7815.42	Haveaux, O.L. La tradition historique des Bapende orientaux. Bruxelles, 1954.
Afr 8676.54.5	Hesse, K. Wirtschaftswunder Südafrika. Düsseldorf, 1954.
Afr 1609.54	Honel, C. Mes aventures marocaines. Casablanca, 1954.
Afr 7549.54.5	Hostelet, Georges. L'oeuvre civilisatrice de la Belgique au Congo. Bruxelles, 1954. 2v.
Afr 699.54	Hunter, J.A. Tales of the African frontier. 1st ed. N.Y., 1954.
Afr 575.30	Hurries, Lyndon. Islam in East Africa. London, 1954.
Afr 679.54	Huxley, E.G. Four Guineas. London, 1954.
Afr 6415.30	Huxley, Elspeth. Grant. Kenya today. London, 1954.
Afr 3160.5	Ibn Tagribardi. History of Egypt. Berkeley, 1954. 2v.
Afr 28.40	International Social Science Council. International Research Office on Social Implications of Technological Change. Conséquences sociales de l'industrialisation et problèmes urbains enAfrique. Paris, 1954.
Afr 115.42	International West African Conference, 4th, Santa Isabel. Conferencia internacional de africanistas occident. v.2. Madrid, 1954.
Afr 3300.51	Issawi, Charles. Egypt at mid-century. London, 1954.
Afr 8667.30	Jackmann, S.B. The numbered day. London, 1954.
Afr 3675.25	Jackson, H.C. The fighting Sudanese. London, 1954.
Afr 4070.57	Jackson, Henry Cecil. Sudan days and ways. N.Y., 1954.
Afr 6143.54	Jarrett, H.R. A geography of Sierra Leone and Gambia. London, 1954.
Afr 1635.23	Justinard, L.V. Un petit royaume berbere. Paris, 1954.
Afr 9439.54	Kane, N.S. The world's view. London, 1954.
Afr 505.20	Kartun, D. Africa, Africa. N.Y., 1954.
Afr 6454.26	Kenya. Committee on African Wages. Report. Nairobi, 1954.
Afr 8100.15	Kock, Victor de. By strength of heart. Cape Town, 1954.
Afr 2533.2	Laitman, L. Tunisia today. N.Y., 1954.
Afr 8668.5	Lake, Alexander. Hunter's choice. 1st ed. Garden City, 1954.
Afr 1635.25	Laredo, A.I. Bereberes y hebreos en Marruecos. Madrid, 1954.
Afr 5320.10	Laye, Camara. The dark child. N.Y., 1954.
Afr 12832.5.120	Laye, Camara. Le regard du roi. Paris, 1954.
Afr 6395.2.14A	Leakey, L.S.B. Defeating Mau Mau. London, 1954.
Afr 6395.2.12	Leakey, L.S.B. Mau Mau and the Kikuyu. 1. American ed. N.Y., 1954.
Afr 2719.54	Lecler, René. Sahara. 1st ed. Garden City, 1954.
Afr 2762.20	Lede, Marie Louise. Seule avec les Touareg du Hoggar. Paris, 1954.
Afr 6019.54	Legum, Colin. Must we lose Africa. London, 1954.
Afr 6420.55	Leigh, Ione. In the shadow of the Mau Mau. London, 1954.
Afr 4199.5.5	Lemandowski, H. Ein Leben für Afrika. Zürich, 1954.
Afr 6715.20	Lembezat, Bertrand. Le Cameroun. Paris, 1954.
Afr 6138.54	Lewis, Roy. Sierra Leone. London, 1954.
Afr 7459.54	Liberia. n.p., 1954.
Afr 7183.18	Lopes, Francisco Xavier. Tres fortalezas de Luanda em 1846. Luanda, 1954.
Afr 9160.5	Lowveld Regional Development Association. A survey of the resources and development of the southern region of the eastern Transvaal. Barberton, 1954.
Afr 5585.35	Lyall, R. Le journal de Robert Lyall. Tananarive, 1954.
Afr 2749.54	MacArthur, D.W. The desert watches. 1st Amer. ed. Indianapolis, 1954.
Afr 6390.35	McDougall, Jan. African turmoil. London, 1954.
Afr 3675.15.5	MacMichael, H. The Sudan. London, 1954.
Afr 5749.54	Madagascar à travers ses provinces. Paris, 1954.
Afr 5969.462	Majo Framis, R. Las generosas y primitivas empresas de Manuel Iradier Bulfy en la Guinea española. Madrid, 1954.
Afr 13333.51.100	Malonga, Jean. La légende de MiPfoumou Ma Mazono. Paris, 1954.
Afr 3199.54.10	Marlowe, J. Anglo-Egyptian relations, 1800-1953. London, 1954.
Afr 3199.54	Marlowe, J. A history of modern Egypt and Anglo-Egyptian relations. N.Y., 1954.
Afr 1571.17.130	Maroc-Medical, Publishers, Casablanca. Lydutey et le médecin. Casablanca, 1954.
Afr 5405.300	Maurice, Albert. Félix Eboué, sa vie et son oeuvre. Bruxelles, 1954.
Afr 609.54	Meeker, Oden. Report on Africa. N.Y., 1954.
Afr 6277.5	Meniru, G.U. African-American cooperation. Glen Gardner, N.J., 1954.
Afr 4760.10	Meregazzi, R. L'amministrazione fiduciaria italiana della Somalia. Milano, 1954.
Afr 8667.90	Meyer, Pieter Johannes. Nog nie die einde nie. Kaapstad, 1954.
Afr 1706.5	Miege, Jean L. Les Européens à Casablanca au XIXe siècle. Paris, 1954.
Afr 8658.02	Mist, Augusta Uitenhage de. Diary of a journey to the Cape of Good Hope and the interior of Africa in 1802 and 1803. Capetown, 1954.
Afr 6333.54	Mitchell, Philip Euen. African afterthoughts. London, 1954.
Afr 4390.50	Monfreid, H. de. Menelik. 7. ed. Paris, 1954.
Afr 1259.54	Monnink, G. Gastvriend van vrije volken. Amsterdam, 1954.
Afr 3300.80	Moore, A.L. Farewell Farouk. Chicago, 1954.
Afr 1623.954.5	Morocco. Division du Commerce et de la Marine Marchande. Maroc, cinq ans de realisation du programme d'equipement. Rabat, 1954.
Afr 7068.9	Mota, Avelino Teixeira da. Guiné portuguesa. v.2. Lisboa, 1954.
Afr 9291.5	Murray, Emma (Rutherford). Young Mrs. Murray goes to Bloemfontein, 1856-1869. Cape Town, 1954.
Afr 3079.54	al-Muwaylihi, Ibrahim. Le paysan d'Egypte à travers l'histoire. Le Caire, 1954.
Afr Doc 2407.352.105	Nigeria. Department of Statistics. Population census of the Northern Region of Nigeria, 1952 Bulletins. Lagos, 1954.
Afr 4592.1	Nowack, Ernst. Land und Volk der Konso. Bonn, 1954.
Afr 8289.54	Otto, J.C. Die konsentrasiekampe. Kaapstad, 1954.

Afr 6415.15	Pankhurst, R.K.P. Kenya. London, 1954.
Afr 4015.5	Paul, Andrew. A history of the Beja tribes of the Sudan. Cambridge, 1954.
Afr 5320.16	Paulme, Denise. Le gens du riz. Paris, 1954.
Afr 7468.4	Price, Frederick A. Liberian odyssey by hammock and surfboat. 1st ed. N.Y., 1954.
Afr 1571.17.125	Proust, L. Le maréchal Lyautey tel que je l'ai connu. Vichy, 1954.
Afr 7809.54	Putnam, A.E. Madami. N.Y., 1954.
Afr 6420.50	Rancliffe, D.H. The struggle for Kenya. London, 1954.
Afr 5857.15	Réunion. Archives Départementales. Répertoire numérique de la série L; Révolution, Empire, régime anglais, 1789-1815. Nérac, 1954.
Afr 699.54.5	Reusch, Richard. History of East Africa. Stuttgart, 1954.
Afr 9433.14.13	Rhodesia and Nyasaland. Report to the federal assembly. Salisbury, 1954. 2 pam.
Afr Doc 3707.351	Rhodesia and Nyasaland. Central Statistical Office. Report on the census of population, 1951. Lusaka, 1954.
Afr 6541.16	Richards, A.I. Economic development and tribal change. Cambridge, Eng., 1954.
Afr 6540.24	Richards, Audrey Isabel. Economic development and tribal change, a study of immigrant labour in Baganda. Cambridge, Eng., 1954.
Afr 1623.954F	Ripoche, Paul. Problemes économiques au Maroc. Rabat, 1954.
Afr 150.18	Rumbucher, K. Heinrich der Seefahrer. München, 1954.
Afr 8369.54	Saint John, Robert. Through Malan's Africa. London, 1954.
Afr 8685.65	Schaltz, Gert D. Het die afrikaanse volk n toekoms. 3. druk. Johannesburg, 1954.
Afr 43393.2	Schapera, I. Ditirafalô tsa merafe ya BaTswana ba lefatshe la Tshireletsô. Tswana, 1954.
Afr 115.20	Schiffers, H. Wilder Ersteil Afrika. Bonn, 1954.
Afr 8685.60	Schnell, E.L.G. For men must work. Capetown, 1954.
Afr 8089.54.10	Scholtz, G.H. Suid-Afrika en die wereldpolitiek 1652-1952. Johannesburg, 1954.
Afr 715.3.30	Schweinfurth, G. Georg Schweinfurth. Stuttgart, 1954.
Afr 6455.85	Scott, R.L. Between the elephant's eyes. N.Y., 1954.
Afr 11780.31.100	Segal, R. Johannesburg Friday. N.Y., 1954.
Afr 9345.60	Sillery, A. Sechele. Oxford, 1954.
Afr 1750.15	Silveira, L. Documentos portugueses sobre la accion de Espana en Africa. Madrid, 1954.
Afr 6455.86	Simonen, Seppo. Mau Mau iskee. Helsinki, 1954.
Afr 7809.54.5	Sion, Georges. Voyages aux quartre coins du Congo, 1949-1952. 3.ed. Bruxelles, 1954.
Afr 618.12	Sommer, F. Man and beast in Africa. 1st American ed. N.Y., 1954.
Afr 5869.54	Souris, Eugène. Histoire abrégée de l'Ile de la Réunion. Saint-Denis, 1954.
Afr 8659.54.15	South Africa. South Africa. Pretoria, 1954.
Afr 8678.96F	South Africa. Commission of Enquiry on Separate Training Facilities for Non-Europeans at Universities. Report. Pretoria, 1954.
Afr Doc 4312.154	South Africa. Parliament. Separate representation of voters act validation and amendment bill, 1954. Cape Town, 1954.
Afr 8659.54.10	South Africa. State Information Office. South African quiz. Pretoria, 1954.
Afr 5640.35	Stibbe, Pierre. Justice pour les Malgaches. Paris, 1954.
Afr 4389.54	Stradal, Otto. Der Weg zum letzten Pharao. Wien, 1954.
Afr 2749.54.5	Stuart, B. Desert adventure. London, 1954.
Afr 3826.5	Sudan. Gezira Board. The Gezira scheme from within. Khartoum, 1954.
Afr 9609.10	Thompson, C.H. Economic development in Rhodesia and Nyassaland. London, 1954.
Afr 609.54.5	Thompson, E.B. Africa, land of my fathers. Garden City, 1954.
Afr 10690.89.100	Tutuola, Amos. My life in the bush of ghosts. London, 1954.
Afr 11853.88.100	Tutuola, Amos. My life in the bush of ghosts. N.Y., 1954.
Afr 8060.5	Tylden, G. The armed forces of South Africa. Johannesburg, 1954.
Afr 6538.45	Uganda. A five year capital development plan, 1955-1960. Uganda, 1954.
Afr 6310.49	Uganda. Proposals for the implementation of the recommendations contained in the report of the Commission on the Civil Services of the East African territories and the East Africa High Commission, 1953-1954. Entebbe, 1954.
Afr 6535.18	Uganda. Department of Information. A guide to Uganda. Entebbe, 1954.
Afr 8825.20	United Party. The Cape coloured vote. Cape Town, 1954.
Afr 8676.54	United States. Bureau of Foreign Commerce. Investment in Union of South Africa. Washington, 1954.
Afr 9500.10	Unyanda, B.J. In search of truth. Bombay, 1954.
Afr 1739.5	Valderrama Martinez, P. El palacio califal de Tetuan. Tetuan, 1954.
Afr 7176.34	Ventura, Reis. O após-guerra em Angola. Luanda, 1954.
Afr 9599.54	Verbeken, Auguste. Contribution à la géographie historique du Katanga et de régions voisines. Bruxelles, 1954.
Afr 7820.8	Verstraeten, E. Six années d'action sociale au Maniema, 1948-1953. Bruxelles, 1954.
Afr 7850.2	Walraet, Marcel. Bibliographie du Katanga. Bruxelles, 1954.
Afr 7530.5	Walraet, Marcel. Bibliographie du Katanga. Fasc.1. Bruxelles, 1954.
Afr 8252.172.10	Wet, Izak J.C. de. Met general De Wet op kommando. Johannesburg, 1954.
Afr 6497.16	Wild, John Vernon. The Uganda mutiny. London, 1954.
Afr 6455.79	Wilson, C.J. Kenya's warning. Nairobi, 1954.
Afr 6192.30	Wright, R. Black power. 1st ed. N.Y., 1954.

1955

Afr 5385.30	Akindele, Adolphe. Le Dahomey. Paris, 1955.
Afr 659.55	Albertini, Eugène. L'Afrique du Nord française dans l'histoire. Lyon, 1955.
Afr 2030.5	Algeria. Gouverneur Général, 1951-55. Quatre ans en Algérie. Alger, 1955.
Afr 2220.14	Algérie, Tunisie. Paris, 1955.
Afr 6415.25	Altrimcham, E.G. Kenya's opportunity. London, 1955.
Afr 6210.14	Aluko, S.A. The problems of self-government for Nigeria. Ilfracombe, 1955.
Afr 609.55.15	American Academy of Political and Social Science, Philadelphia. Contemporary Africa. Philadelphia, 1955.
Afr 8687.111	Anderson, Kenneth. Heroes of South Africa. Cape Town, 1955.

Afr 7320.8	Andrade, Antonio Alberto de. Relações de Moçambique setecentista. Lisboa, 1955.
Afr 6196.20	Ansah, J.K. The centenary history of the Larteh Presbyterian Church, 1853-1953. Larteh, 1955.
Afr 6162.10A	Apter, D.E. The Gold Coast in transition. Princeton, 1955.
Afr 3675.28	Arkell, A.J. A history of the Sudan. London, 1955.
Afr 3040.80	al-Attar, Fuad Abdallah. Le marché de travaux publics. Thèse. Le Caire, 1955.
Afr 6280.35	Baba. Baba of Karo. N.Y., 1955.
Afr 6395.2.20	Baker, R.St.B. Kabongo. 1st ed. Wheatley, Eng., 1955.
Afr 5408.15.2	Balandier, Georges. Sociologie actuelle de l'Afrique noire, changements sociaux au Gabon et au Congo. Paris, 1955.
Afr 5408.15	Balandier, Georges. Sociologie actuelle de l'Afrique noire. Paris, 1955.
Afr 7565.14.5	Banning, E. Textes inédits. Bruxelles, 1955.
Afr 2719.55	Banque Dambert-Blitz. L'avenir du Sahara. Paris, 1955.
Afr 5749.55	Bastian, Georges. Madagascar. Tananarive, 1955.
Afr 7812.255.5	Belgium. Office de l'Information et des Relations Publiques pour le Congo Belge. L'économie du Congo belge et du Ruanda-Urundi. Bruxelles, 1955.
Afr 1680.10	Berque, Jacques. Structures sociales du haut-atlas. 1 ed. Paris, 1955.
Afr 2209.55	Blottière, J.E. L'Algérie. 2. ed. Paris, 1955.
Afr 1338.15	Bonjean, Jacques. L'unité de l'empire chérifien. Paris, 1955.
Afr 5053.30	Bourcart, Robert. Le grand conseil de l'Afrique occidentale. Paris, 1955.
Afr 609.55.25	Brockway, A.F. African journeys. London, 1955.
Afr 6277.15	Buchanan, K.M. Land and people in Nigeria. London, 1955.
Afr 9093.20.5	Bulpin, T.V. Storm over the Transvaal. 2. ed. Cape Town, 1955.
Afr 6214.8.15	Burns, Alan C. History of Nigeria. 5th ed. London, 1955.
Afr 1609.55.5	Buttin, Paul. Le drame du Maroc. Paris, 1955.
Afr 1721.5	Cabanas, Rafael. Rasgos fisiograficos y geologicos. Madrid, 1955.
Afr 5944.10	Carnero Ruiz, Ismael. Vocabulario geográfico-saharico. Madrid, 1955.
Afr 6460.70	Carothers, John C. The psychology of Mau Mau. Nairobi, 1955.
Afr 8659.55	Carter, G.M. South Africa. N.Y., 1955.
Afr 2209.55.5	Charbonneau, Jean. Des Africains s'interrogent. Paris, 1955.
Afr 1570.70	Charles-Roux, François. Missions diplomatiques françaises à Fès. Paris, 1955.
Afr 609.55.5	Cloete, Stuart. The African giant. Boston, 1955.
Afr 7809.55.10	Congo. Service de l'Information. Congo: Belgique d'outre-mer. Léopoldville, 1955?
Afr 11299.69.100	Cope, Jack. The fair house. London, 1955.
Afr 7855.1	Cornet, René Jules. Maniema. 2.ed. Bruxelles, 1955.
Afr 6760.10	Datta, A.K. Tanganyika. n.p., 1955.
Afr 710.20	Davidson, B. The African awakening. London, 1955.
Afr 9839.55	Debenham, F. Nyasaland. London, 1955.
Afr 9558.90	Debenham, F. The way to Ilala. London, 1955.
Afr 2358.5	Debia, René Yves. Orléansville. Alger, 1955.
Afr 1571.17.120	Deloncle, Pierre. Lyautey. Paris, 1955.
Afr 2618.26	Demeersman, A. Soixante ans de pensée tunisienne à travers les revues. Tunis, 1955.
Afr 1268.6	Denti Di Pirajno, Alberto. A cure for serpents. London, 1955.
Afr 7809.55F	Derhinderen, G. Atlas du Congo belge et du Ruanda-Urundi. Paris, 1955.
Afr 2609.40.5	Despois, Jean. La Tunisie orientale. 2.ed. Paris, 1955.
Afr 628.265	Diop, Cheikh Anta. Nations nègres et culture. 2. éd. Paris, 1955.
Afr 5190.18	Duchemin, G. Saint-Louis du Sénégal. Saint-Louis, 1955.
Afr 6333.55	Dundas, Charles C.F. African crossroads. London, 1955.
Afr 1618.22	Duran Pulis, Guillermo. La caza en Marruecos. Las Palmas de Gran Canaria, 1955.
Afr 7048.20	Durieux, Andre. Essai sur le statut. Bruxelles, 1955.
Afr 6300.21.35	East African Institute of Social Research. A report on three years' work, 1950-1953. Kampala, 1955.
Afr 710.20.2	Egerton, F. Clement C. Angola without prejudice. Lisbon, 1955.
Afr 510.50F	Encyclopédie Mensuelle d'Outre-Mer. Le tourisme en Afrique française. Paris, 1955.
Afr 5266.3	Epelle, Emanuel Tobiah. The church in the Niger Delta. Aba, Nigeria, 1955.
Afr 4573.10	Ethiopia. Ministry of Commerce and Industry. Economic progress of Ethiopia. Addis Ababa, 1955.
Afr 2030.320.2	Fanon, Frantz. Studies in a dying colonialism. N.Y., 1955.
Afr 1571.17.115	Farrere, Claude. Lyautey. Paris, 1955.
Afr 9499.15	Federation of Rhodesia and Nyasaland. Federal Information Services. Opportunity in Rhodesia and Nyasaland. Salisbury, 1955.
Afr 4766.23	Finkelstein, L.S. Somaliland under Italian administration. N.Y., 1955.
Afr 11394.88.100	Fitzroy, V.M. Dark bright land. Cape Town, 1955.
Afr 7309.55	Fonseca, M. da. Na fogueira do jornalismo. Lourenço Marques, 1955.
Afr 6883.26	Fouquet, Roger. Irakou. Paris, 1955.
Afr 2762.17	Fuchs, Peter. The land of veiled men. London, 1955.
Afr 8089.54.2A	Gibbs, H. Background to bitterness. N.Y., 1955.
Afr 4430.55.15	Gingold Duprey, A. De l'invasion à la libération de l'Ethiopie. Paris, 1955.
Afr 635.45	Gluckman, Max. Custom and conflict in Africa. Glencoe, 1955.
Afr 9700.25	Gluckman, Max. The judicial process among the Barotse. Manchester, 1955.
Afr 6155.4	Gold Coast (Colony). Report. Accra, 1955.
Afr 6194.40F	Gold Coast (Colony). Committee on Asanteman-Brong Dispute. Report. Accra, 1955.
Afr 6160.23	Gold Coast (Colony). Legislative Assembly. Select Committee on Federal System. Report, and an appendix. Accra, 1955.
Afr 6390.45	Great Britain. East Africa Royal Commission. Report. London, 1955.
Afr 8830.12	Green, Lawrence George. Karoo, the story of the Karoos of South Africa - the great Karoo. Cape Town, 1955.
Afr 7530.10	Grieken-Taverniers, M. van. Inventaire des archives des affaires étrangères de l'état du Congo. Bruxelles, 1955.
Afr 1573.33	Guastavino Gallant, Guillermo. De ambos lados del estrecho. Tetuan, 1955.

1955 - cont.

Afr 1623.955	Guillaume, Albert. L'evolution economique de la societe rurale marocaine. Paris, 1955.
Afr 6395.8	Gulliver, P.H. The family herds. London, 1955.
Afr 609.55.10A	Gunther, John. Inside Africa. 1st ed. N.Y., 1955.
Afr 210.55A	Haines, C.G. Africa today. Baltimore, 1955.
Afr 3310.40	Hasan Abd al-Razik Muhammad. Krizis ekonomiki Egipta. Moscow, 1955.
Afr 8678.57.10	Hellmann, E. Racial laws versus economic and social forces. Johannesburg, 1955.
Afr 6927.5	Hintrager, O. Südwestafrika in der deutschen Zeit. München, 1955.
Afr 6214.5	Historical Society of Nigeria. Memorandum and articles of associations. n.p., 1955.
Afr 8331.15	Hodge, Gillian M.M. South African politics, 1933-1939. Cape Town, 1955.
Afr 8678.84	Houghton, D. Hobart. Life in the Ciskei. Johannesburg, 1955.
Afr 1494.25	Howe, Marvine. The prince and I. N.Y., 1955.
Afr 1088.10	Huici Miranda, Ambrosio. Historia politica del imperio almohade. v.1. Tetuan, 1955.
Afr 1380.5	Ibn Azzuz, M. Historia de Marruecos hasta la dominacion almoravide. Madrid, 1955.
Afr 3163.20A	Ibn Iyas. Journal d'un bourgeois du Caire. Paris, 1955. 2v.
Afr 9599.55	Ingerman, Karel J.J. Een slavenband als ereteken. 2. druk. Amsterdam, 1955.
Afr 8145.20	Inter-Racial Conference of Church Leaders, Johannesburg. God's kingdom in multi-racial South Africa. Johannesburg, 1955.
Afr 6277.30	International Bank for Reconstruction and Development. The economic development of Nigeria. Baltimore, 1955.
Afr 5549.55	Isnard, Hildebert. Madagascar. Paris, 1955.
Afr 109.55	Istituto Italiano per l'Africa. L'Africa nei suoi aspetti geografici. Roma, 1955.
Afr 4700.3.5	Italy. Comitato per la documentazione dell'opera dell'Italia in Africa. L'Italia in Africa. Roma, 1955.
Afr 3745.60	Jackson, H.C. Behind the modern Sudan. London, 1955.
Afr 3069.55	Jarvis, H.W. Pharaoh to Farouk. London, 1955.
Afr 2030.175	Jeanson, Colette. L'Algérie hors la loi. Paris, 1955.
Afr 4259.35.21	Jones, A.H. A history of Ethiopia. Oxford, 1955.
Afr 7945.2	Kagame, Alexis. La philosophie bantu-rwandaise de être. Bruxelles, 1955.
Afr 5285.277.35	Kassoum, Congo. Conséquences de la colonisation sur la vie coutumière en pays mossi. Thèse. Montepellier, 1955.
Afr 8680.45	Katzew, Henry. Solution for South Africa. Cape Town, 1955.
Afr 6415.35	Koinange, M. The people of Kenya speak for themselves. Detroit, 1955.
Afr 3979.55F	Kusch, E. Ägypten im Bild. Nürnberg, 1955.
Afr 5840.20	Lagesse, Lois. Le père Laval. Port-Louis, 1955.
Afr 7812.255	Lefebvre, J. Structures économiques duCongo belge et du Ruanda-Urundi. Bruxelles, 1955.
Afr 8687.271	Lehmann, Olga. Look beyond the wind; the life of Hans Merensky. Capetown, 1955?
Afr 718.43	Lemboum, Hans Jorgen. Hvide mand-hvad nu. København, 1955.
Afr 7947.7	Lestrade, A. La médecine indigène au Ruanda et lexique des termes médicaux français-urunyarwanda. Bruxelles, 1955.
Afr 1880.10	Lewicki, J. Etudes ibadites nord-africaines. v.1. Warszawa, 1955.
Afr 1493.65	Leyris de Campredon. Lyautey. Paris, 1955.
Afr 1738.21	Lilius, Aleko E. Tapahtui tangerissa. Helsingissa, 1955.
Afr 6460.30	Lipscomb, J.F. White Africans. London, 1955.
Afr 3986.955	Little, Arthur D. Opportunities for industrial development in Egypt. Cairo, 1955.
Afr 9558.7	Livingstone, D. Livingstone's travels. London, 1955.
Afr 710.30	London. University. School of Oriental and African Studies. History and archaeology in Africa. London, 1955.
Afr 820.4	Mcdonald, J.F. Zambesi river. London, 1955.
Afr 5755.2	Madagascar. Camores, Reunion, ile Maurice. Paris, 1955.
Afr 8089.55	Marquard, L. The story of South Africa. London, 1955.
Afr 6333.55.5	Mason, Philip. A new deal in East Africa. London, 1955.
Afr 8045.22.6	May, Henry John. The South African constitution. 3d ed. Cape Town, 1955.
Afr 11563.98.100	Mayne, Frederick. The slaughter of an innocent. Johannesburg, 1955.
Afr 1609.55	Mensching, Horst. Zwischen rif und draa. Leipzig, 1955.
Afr 1750.25	Mensua Fernandez, Salvador. Bibliografia geografica de Marruecos español y zona internacional de Tanger. Aragoza, 1955.
Afr 609.55.30	Migliorini, Elio. L'Africa. Torino, 1955.
Afr 11572.50.190	Millin, S.G.(L). The measure of my days. London, 1955.
Afr 5760.14	Molet, Louis. Demographie de l'Ankaizinana. Paris, 1955.
Afr 555.9.25	Morshead, A.E. The history of the Universities' Mission to Central Africa. London, 1955-62. 3v.
Afr 3305.5	Moussa, F. Les négociations anglo-égyptiennes de 1950-1951 sur Suez et le Soudan. Genève, 1955.
Afr 1069.55	Naci, Hikmet. Tarih hoyunca kujey Afrika. Istanbul, 1955?
Afr 3310.10	Nasser, G.A. Egypt's liberation. Washington, 1955.
Afr 3310.5	Neguib, M. Egypt's destiny. London, 1955.
Afr 3310.5.2	Neguib, M. Egypt's destiny. 1st American ed. Garden City, 1955.
Afr 1259.55	Newman, B. North African journey. London, 1955.
Afr 6210.39	Nigeria. Commission on the Public Services of the Governments in the Federation of Nigeria. Report of the Commission on public services of the governments of Nigeria, 1954-1955. Lagos, 1955.
Afr Doc 2560.725.5	Nigeria. Department of Statistics. Population census of the Eastern Region of Nigeria, 1953. Bulletins. Lagos, 1955.
Afr Doc 2520.725.5	Nigeria. Department of Statistics. Population census of the Western region of Nigeria, 1952. Bulletins. Lagos, 1955.
Afr 510.75A	Nord, Pierre. L'Eurafrique. Paris, 1955.
Afr 710.25	Oldham, J.H. New hope in Africa. London, 1955.
Afr 1409.15	Oliver Asin, J. Vida de Don Felipe de Africa. Madrid, 1955.
Afr 4259.55	Pankhurst, E.S. Ethiopia. Essex, 1955.
Afr 6096.5	Pedler, F.J. Economic geography of West Africa. London, 1955.
Afr 9161.23	Potgieter, E.F. The disappearing Bushmen of Lake Clirissie. Pretoria, 1955.
Afr 9291.10	Prinsloo, A. Die geskiedenis van Smithfield en die Caledonrivierdistrik. Bloemfontein, 1955.

1955 - cont.

Afr 8340.25	Pyrah, G.B. Imperial policy and South Africa, 1902-10. Oxford, 1955.
Afr 13438.1.150	Rabemananjara, Jacques. Rites millénaires. Photocopy. Paris, 1955.
Afr 9345.10.10	Redfern, John. Ruth and Seretse. London, 1955.
Afr 609.55	Reynolds, Reginald. Cairo to Cape Town. 1st ed. Garden City, N.Y., 1955.
Afr 1575.12	Ricard, Robert. Etudes sur l'histoire des Portugals au Maroc. Coimbra, 1955.
Afr 9047.15	Ritter, E.A. Shaka Zulu. London, 1955.
Afr 6392.32	Robinson, Edward A.G. Report on the needs for economic research and investigation in East Africa. Entebbe, Uganda, 1955.
Afr 7560.14.15	Roeykens, A. Les débuts de l'oeuvre de Léopold II, 1875-1876. Bruxelles, 1955.
Afr 2223.950.2	Saint Germes, Jean. Economie algérienne. Alger, 1955. 2 pam.
Afr 4430.55.6	Sandford, C.L. The Lion of Judah hath prevailed. London, 1955.
Afr 4430.55.5	Sandford, C.L. The Lion of Judah hath prevailed. N.Y., 1955.
Afr 1769.7	Santamaria Quesada, R. Quien es el glani. Tetuan, 1955.
Afr 5190.15	Savonnet, G. Le ville de Thiès. St. Louis, 1955.
Afr 6738.40	Schmidt, Agathe. Die rote Landenschnur. Berlin, 1955.
Afr 8685.70	Schmidt-Pretoria, W. Deutsche Wanderung nach Südafrika im 19. Jahrhundert. Berlin, 1955.
Afr 8252.341.50	Scott, J.A.S. Jan Christian Smuts. Cape Town, 1955.
Afr 2283.4	Servier, Jean. Dans l'Aurès sur les pas des rébelles. Paris, 1955.
Afr 609.55.20	Seymour, John. One man's Africa. London, 1955.
Afr 6541.17	Shephard, G.W. They wait in darkness. N.Y., 1955.
Afr 6134.2	Sierra Leone. Collected statements of constitutional proposals. Freetown, 1955.
Afr 6147.8	Sierra Leone. Commission of Inquiry into the Strike and Riots in Freetown, Sierra Leone. Report. Freetown, 1955.
Afr 6280.50F	Smith, M.G. The economy of Hausa communities of Zaria. London, 1955.
Afr 11572.50.800	Snyman, J.P.L. The works of Sarah Gertrude Millin. South Africa, 1955.
Afr Doc 4307.351	South Africa. Bureau of Statistics. Population census, 8th May 1951. Pretoria, 1955. 2v.
Afr 8678.71A	South Africa. Commission for the Socio-Economic Development of the Bantu Areas. Summary of the report. Pretoria, 1955.
Afr 8676.55.5	South African Institute of Race Relations. South Africa's changing economy. Johannesburg, 1955.
Afr 9196.5	South African Institute of Race Relations. Swaziland. Johannesburg, 1955.
Afr 28.73	South African Public Library, Cape Town. A bibliography of african bibliographies. 3d ed. Cape Town, 1955.
Afr 11802.92.130	Sowden, Lewis. The crooked bluegum. London, 1955.
Afr 11802.92.110	Sowden, Lewis. Poems with flute. London, 1955.
Afr 5920.12	Spain. Consejo Superior de Investigaciones Científicas. Instituto de Estudios Africanos. Manuales del Africa española. Madrid, 1955- 2v.
Afr 5235.255	Spitz, Georges. Le Soudan français. Paris, 1955.
Afr 718.2.10	Stanley, H.M. Lettres inédites. Bruxelles, 1955.
Afr 1095.10A	Stevens, E. North African powder keg. N.Y., 1955.
Afr 6415.20	Stoneham, C.T. Out of barbarism. London, 1955.
Afr 8676.55	Strand, D. The financial and statistical digest of South Africa. Cape Town, 1955.
Afr 1738.30.2	Stuart, G.H. The international city of Tanger. 2d ed. Stanford, calif., 1955.
Afr Doc 1307.353	Sudan. Department of Statistics. The 1953 pilot population census for the first population census in Sudan. Khartoum, 1955.
Afr 9445.25	Tabler, Edward C. The far interior. Cape Town, 1955.
Afr 4430.55	Talbot, D.A. Haile Selassie I. The Hague, 1955.
Afr 9525.875	Taylor, Don. The Rhodesian, the life of Sir Roy Welensky. London, 1955.
Afr 13340.13.120	Tchichaya U Tamsi, Gerald Felix. Le mauvais sang, poèmes. Paris, 1955.
Afr 6176.5	Timothy, B. Kwame Nkrumah. London, 1955.
Afr 8680.15	Tingsten, Herbert. The problem of South Africa. London, 1955.
Afr 6196.28	Trans-Volta Togoland. Trans-Volta Togoland handbook, 1955. Accra, 1955.
Afr Doc 4812.5.10	Transkeian Territories. General Council. Prodeedings of a special session of the United Transkeian Territories General Council held on 23rd and 24th Nov., 1955. Umtata, 1955.
Afr 4055.5	Tregenza, L.A. The Red Sea mountains of Egypt. London, 1955.
Afr 5406.250.3	Trezenem, Edouard. L'Afrique équatoriale française. Paris, 1955.
Afr 11853.88.120	Tutuola, Amos. Simbi and the satyr of the dark jungle. London, 1955.
Afr 6780.40	United Nations Review. Tanganyika. N.Y., 1955.
Afr 8369.54.5	United Party, South Africa. The native policy of the United Party. Johannesburg, 1955.
Afr 7809.55.5	Vallotton, Henry. Voyage au Congo et au Ruanda-Urundi. Bruxelles, 1955.
Afr 630.55	Vanderpost, Laurens. The dark eye in Africa. N.Y., 1955.
Afr 11865.59.120	Vanderpost, Laurens. Flamingo feather. N.Y., 1955.
Afr 1738.35	Vernier, Victor. La singuliere zone de Tanger. Paris, 1955.
Afr 2525.20	Villiers, G. Derriére le rideau tunisien. Paris, 1955.
Afr 2357.10	Villot, Roland. Jules Du Pré de Saint Maur. 2. ed. Oran, 1955.
Afr 8230.6.10	Vys, C.J. Paul Kruger. Kaapstad, 1955.
Afr 8687.200A	Wallis, John P.R. Fitz. London, 1955.
Afr 8089.55.5	Walt, A.S.H. Geskiedenes van Suid-Afrika. 2 verb. druk. Kaapstad, 1955. 2v.
Afr 9293.2	Walton, J. Vroee plase en nedersettings in die Oranje Vrystaat. Amsterdam, 1955.
Afr 11874.87.100	Watson, J.C. Shadow over the Rand. Johannesburg, 1955.
Afr 8659.55.5	Wellington, J.H. Southern Africa. Cambridge, Eng., 1955. 2v.
Afr 3158.5	Wiet, Gaston. Les marchands d'épices sous les sultans mamlouks. Le Caire, 1955.
Afr 11878.49.100	Wiles, John. The moon to play with. 1st American ed. N.Y., 1955.
Afr 1259.55.5	Wohlfahrt, M. Nordafrika. Berlin, 1955.
Afr 6881.1	Wright, Fergus C. African consumers in Nyasaland and Tanganyika. London, 1955.
Afr 2250.5	Yacono, Xavier. La colonisation des plaines du Chélif. Alger, 1955-56. 2v.

1955 - cont.

Afr 8063.15   Young, P.J. Boot and saddle. Cape Town, 1955.
Afr 2609.55   Zeraffa, Michel. Tunisie. Paris, 1955.

1956

Afr 11108.74.100A   Abrahams, Peter. A wreath for Udomo. 1st American ed. N.Y., 1956.
Afr 6333.56.5   Africa Bureau, London. Reflections on the report of the Royal Commission on East Africa. London, 1956.
Afr 7809.56   Ahl, Frances Norene. Wings over the Congo. Boston, 1956.
Afr 6010.14   Akpan, N.U. Epitaph to indirect rule. London, 1956.
Afr 8667.60   Alberts, Andries. Die Afrikaanse wêreldbeskouing. Kaapstad, 1956.
Afr 2030.275   Algeria. Programme et action du gouvernement en Algérie. Alger, 1956.
Afr 2396.2   Algérie biographique. Sidi-bel-Abbès, 1956.
Afr 210.56.10   American Academy of Political and Social Sciences. Africa and the Western world. Philadelphia, 1956.
Afr 7815.19   Association des Intérêts Coloniaux Belges. Des relations de travail entre européens et africains. Bruxelles, 1956.
Afr 3258.20   Ata, M.M. Egypt between two revolutions. Cairo, 1956.
Afr 1369.56A   Ayache, Albert. Le Maroc. Paris, 1956.
Afr 3990.20   Band, Marcelle. Egypte. Paris, 1956.
Afr 628.256   Bartah, Ernst. Neger, Jazz und tiefer Süden. Leipzig, 1956.
Afr 8369.56   Bate, H.M. South Africa without prejudice. London, 1956.
Afr 9148.43   Bennie, John. An account of a journey into Transorangia and the Potchefstroom-Winburg Trekker Republic in 1843. Cape Town, 1956.
Afr 6739.256   Binet, Jacques. Budgets familiaux des planteurs de Cacao au Cameroun. Paris, 1956.
Afr 12972.41.120   Biyidi, Alexandre. Le pauvre Christ de Bomba. Paris, 1956.
Afr 6463.5   Blakeslee, H. Beyond the Kikuyu curtain. Chicago, 1956.
Afr 8089.56   Bond, J. They were South Africans. Cape Town, 1956.
Afr 11045.2   Booysen, C. Footprints. Johannesburg, 1956.
Afr 1390.8   Bosch Vila, Jacinto. Los Almoravidas. Tetuan, 1956.
Afr 5053.30.2   Bourcart, Robert. Le grand conseil de l'Afrique occidentale. 2. ed. Paris, 1956.
Afr 500.67   Bowles, Chester. Africa's challenge to America. Berkeley, 1956.
Afr 1110.10   Boyer de Latour, Pierre. Vérités sur l'Afrique du Nord. Paris, 1956.
Afr 2749.56   Britsch, Jacques. Perspectives sahariennes. Limoges, 1956.
Afr 6395.2.25   Brom, John L. Mau-Mau. Paris, 1956.
Afr 8250.42   Brookner, Anita. An iconography of Cecil Rhodes. n.p., 1956.
Afr 7812.256.5   Brussels. Université Libre. Vers la promotion de l'économie indigène. Bruxelles, 1956.
Afr 8155.10   Bulpin, J. Victor. Shakas country. 3d ed. Cape Town, 1956. 2v.
Afr 6390.50F   Bulpin, T.V. East Africa and the islands. Cape Town, 1956.
Afr 8678.86   Buskes, Johannes Jacobus. South Africa's apartheid policy - unacceptable. Heidelberg, 1956.
Afr 7815.41   Caeneghem, R. La notion de Dieu chez les Baluba du Kasai. Bruxelles, 1956.
Afr 6390.40   Cameron, R.W. Equator farm. N.Y., 1956.
Afr 1401.80   Caro Baroja, Julio. Una vision de Marruecos a mediados del siglo XVI. Madrid, 1956.
Afr 3979.33.5   Carre, Jean Marie. Voyageurs et ecrivains français en Egypte. 2. éd. Le Caire, 1956. 2v.
Afr 2731.15.35   Carrouges, Michel. Soldier of the spirit. N.Y., 1956.
Afr 7119.56   Chela, João da. Africa lusiada. Alges-Lisboa, 1956.
Afr 8252.25.10   Clark, E.M. Louis Botha, a bibliography. Cape Town, 1956.
Afr 6460.65   Cloete, Stuart. Storm over Africa. Cape Town, 1956.
Afr 9149.56   Cole, Monica M. Land use studies in the Transvaal Lowveld. London, 1956.
Afr 2623.956   Colloque international sur les niveaux de vie en Tunisie. Travaux du colloque international les niveaux de vie en Tunisie. Paris, 1956-58. 3 pam.
Afr 626.58   Commission for Technical Cooperation in Africa South of Sahara. Inter-African scientific and technical cooperation, 1948-1955. Bukavu, 1956.
Afr 4178.25   Compagnie Universelle du Canal Maritime de Suez. La Compagnie Universelle du Canal Maritime de Suez et la décision. v.1-2. Paris, 1956.
Afr 1494.35   Conférence Nationale pour la Solution du Problème Franco-Marocain. Compte-rendu. v.1. Paris, 1956.
Afr 3986.956A   Cooke, M.L. Nasser's High Aswan Dam. Washington, 1956.
Afr 3979.56.5   Cordan, Wolfgang. DerNil. Düsseldorf, 1956.
Afr 1570.75   Corval, Pierre. Le Maroc en révolution. Paris, 1956.
Afr 618.20   Cunha, Joaquim M. da S. Movimentos associativos na Africa negra. Lisboa, 1956.
Afr 1259.56F   Dans la lumière des cités africaines. v.1. Paris, 1956.
Afr 8678.76   Dekiewiet, C.W. The anatomy of South African misery. London, 1956.
Afr 5045.11   Demaison, Andre. La vie des noirs d'Afrique. 4. ed. Paris, 1956.
Afr 6218.10A   Dike, K.O. Trade and politics in the Niger Delta. Oxford, 1956.
Afr 4559.56F   Doresse, Jean. Au pays de la ruine de Saba. Paris, 1956.
Afr 2030.456   Douxey, Jean. S.O.S. Algérie. Paris, 1956.
Afr 1571.17.110   Durasoy, M. Lyautey. Paris, 1956.
Afr 1609.52.5   Durham, Eng. University. Exploration society expedition to French Morocco. Report of the expedition to French Morocco. Durham, 1956.
Afr 609.56.10   Dutton, Geoffrey. Africa in black and white. London, 1956.
Afr 6392.5   East Africa High Commission. Some notes on industrial development in East Africa. Nairobi, 1956.
Afr 11347.82.100   Eastwood, C. The estranged face. London, 1956.
Afr 3069.56   Egypt. Ministry of Education. Egypt. Cairo, 1956.
Afr 3335.12   Egypt. Ministry of Education. Cultural Relations Department. Cultural agreements between Egypt and other countries. Cairo, 1956.
Afr 6420.65   Evans, Peter. Law and disorder. London, 1956.
Afr 6280.40   Forde, C.D. Efik traders of old Calabar. London, 1956.
Afr 8838.2   Fourie, S. Jansenville yesterday and today. Jansenville, 1956.
Afr 5580.4   Foury, B. Mandove et la colonisation de Madagascar. Paris, 1956.

1956 - cont.

Afr Doc 6307.355   France. Ministère de la France d'Outre-Mer. Service des Statistiques. Mission démographique de Guinée. Etude démographique par sondage, Guinée, 1954-1955. Paris, 1956.
Afr 6715.15   Froelich, Jean Claude. Cameroun, 1956.
Afr 2536.10   Garas, Felix. Bourguiba et la naissance d'une nation. Paris, 1956.
Afr 2030.385   Gaschet-Veyret de la Tour, E. L'erreur du siècle et l'homme des civilisations agricoles. Paris, 1956.
Afr 6160.22   Gold Coast (Colony). Government proposals in regard to the future constitution and control of statutory boards and corporations in the Gold Coast. Accra, 1956.
Afr 6194.32   Goody, J.R. The social organization of the Lo Wiili. London, 1956.
Afr 11433.74.115   Gordimer, N. Six feet of the country. London, 1956.
Afr 1571.55   Grandval, G. Ma mission au Maroc. Paris, 1956.
Afr 6174.7   Great Britain. Central Office of Information. Reference Division. The making of Ghana. London, 1956.
Afr 38.4   Grieken, Emil. Les archives inventoriées au Ministère des colonies. Bruxelles, 1956.
Afr 8250.37   Gross, Felix. Rhodes of Africa. London, 1956.
Afr 7068.7   Guerra, M. dos S. Terras da Guiné e Cabo Verde. Lisboa, 1956.
Afr 14665.5   Guerra, Mario Lopes. Dumba e a bangala. la cancão. Sá da Bandeira, 1956.
Afr 550.80   Guilcher, René F. La société des missions africaines. 2. éd. Lyon, 1956.
Afr 3040.79   Hafiz, Mahamid. La délégation législative en France et en Egypte. Le Caire, 1956.
Afr 8252.341.65   Hancock, William Keith. The Smuts papers. London, 1956.
Afr 9775.2   Hanna, Alexander John. The beginnings of Nyasaland and north-eastern Rhodesia. Oxford, 1956.
Afr Doc 3309.227   Harris, Douglas Gordon. Development in Uganda, 1947 to 1956. Wisbech?, Eng., 1956.
Afr 505.25   Hatch, J.C. New from Africa. London, 1956.
Afr 6984.5   Haythornthwaite, Frank. All the way to Abenab. London, 1956.
Afr 8678.57.5   Hellmann, E. In defence of a shared society. Johannesburg, 1956.
Afr 210.56   Hodgkin, Thomas. Nationalism in colonial Africa. London, 1956.
Afr 8678.74   Holloway, J.E. The problems of race relations in South Africa. N.Y., 1956.
Afr 8685.75   Horrell, Muriel. The group areas act. Johannesburg, 1956.
Afr 8678.80   Horrell, Muriel. South Africa's non-white workers. Johannesburg, 1956.
Afr 4238.15   Howard, W.E.H. Public administration in Ethiopia. Groningen, 1956.
Afr 8678.70   Huddleston, T. Naught for your comfort. Garden City, 1956.
Afr 6420.35.7   Huxley, E. Grant. Race and politics in Kenya. London, 1956.
Afr 6203.5   Ibadan, Nigeria. University. Library. Nigerian periodicals and newspapers, 1950-1955. Ibadan, 1956.
Afr 3310.20   India. Information Services. The Suez Canal crisis and India. New Delhi, 1956.
Afr 3315.115   India. Parliament. Hok Sabha. Suez Canal. New Delhi, 1956.
Afr 9599.56   Ingerman, Karel J.J. Dreigend drennen de tam-tams. Amsterdam, 1956.
Afr 626.85.3   Inter-African Labour Institute. Les facteurs humains de la productivité. Bumako, 1956.
Afr 626.56   International African Institute, London. Social implications of industrialization and urbanization in Africa, south of the Sahara. Paris, 1956.
Afr 626.38   International Geographical Union. London, 1956.
Afr 9.7.3   International West African Conference. Proceedings of the third International West African Conference. Lagos, 1956.
Afr 4178.20   Istituto Italiano per l'Africa. Il Congresso di Trento per il centenario del progetto italiano per il taglio dell istmo di Suez. Roma, 1956.
Afr 6283.11   Jackson, I.C. Advance in Africa. London, 1956.
Afr 1769.20   Jalade, Max. Mohammed ben Youssef. Paris, 1956.
Afr 9165.42.55   Johannesburg. City Council. The city of Johannesburg. 2. ed. Cape Town, 1956.
Afr 609.56   Jones, Schuyler. Under the African sun. London, 1956.
Afr 8678.78   Keet, B.B. Whither South Africa. Stellenbosch, 1956.
Afr 8028.150   Kesting, J.G. The Anglo-Boer war, 1899-1902. Cape Town, 1956.
Afr 2808.5A   Khalidi, I.R. Constitutional development in Libya. Beirut, 1956.
Afr 6060.56   Kimble, David. The machinery of self government. London, 1956.
Afr 9497.5F   King, Ralph W. The Rhodesias and Nyasaland. 2. ed. Cape Town, 1956.
Afr 6460.55   Koenig, Oskar. The Maisai story. London, 1956.
Afr 8350.25   Kuper, Leo. Passive resistance in South Africa. London, 1956.
Afr 3300.85   Lacouture, Jean. L'Egypte en mouvement. Paris, 1956.
Afr 1487.5   Landau, Rom. Moroccan drama, 1900-1955. San Francisco, 1956.
Afr 3310.25   Laqueur, W.Z. Nasser's Egypt. London, 1956.
Afr 510.60   Lavergne, B. Afrique du Nord et Afrique Noire. Paris, 1956.
Afr 2030.45   Lavie, Louis. Le drame algérien. 3 ed. Alger, 1956.
Afr 12832.5.700   Laye, Camara. The radiance of the King. London, 1956.
Afr 12421.2   Lebel, Roland. Les poètes français du Maroc. Tanger, 1956.
Afr 2719.56   Lefevre, Georges. Notre Sahara. Paris, 1956.
Afr 605.56.12   Leo Africanus, J. Description de l'Afrique. Paris, 1956. 2v.
Afr Doc 9983.1.73   Liberia. Department of Agriculture and Commerce. Bureau of Statistics. Census of population of Monrovia 1956; general characteristics. Report. Monrovia, 1956.
Afr 28.70   Library of Congress. African newspapers currently received in selected American libraries. Washington, 1956.
Afr 6430.15   Lipscomb, J.F. We built a country. London, 1956.
Afr 5944.5   Lodwick, John. The forbidden coast. London, 1956.
Afr 5857.2   Lougnon, Albert. Classement et inventaire du fonds de la Compagnie des Indes aux archives. Thèse. Nerac, 1956.
Afr 5872.12   Lougnon, Albert. L'Ile Bourbon pendant la régence. Paris, 1956.
Afr 210.56.15   Lovato, Antonio. Le ultime colonie. Roma, 1956.
Afr 115.15   Ly, A. Les masses africaines. Paris, 1956.
Afr 7119.56.5   Machado, Ernesto. No sul de Angola. Lisboa, 1956.
Afr 3310.30   Manchester Guardian, Manchester, Eng. The record on Suez. Manchester, 1956.

Afr 5813.10 — Mauritius. Archives Department. Bibliography of Mauritius. Port Louis, 1956.

Afr Doc 2808.5 — Mauritius. Central Statistical Office. Natality and fertility in Mauritius. Port Louis? 1956?

Afr Doc 2809.305 — Mauritius. Central Statistical Office. The national income and national accounts of Mauritius, 1948-1954. Port Louis, 1956.

Afr 590.78 — Mbotela, J.J. The freeing of the slaves in Eat Africa. London, 1956.

Afr 8848.3 — Meintjes, J. Frontier family. n.p., 1956.

Afr 1915.14 — Meningaud, Jean. La France à l'heure algérienne. Paris, 1956.

Afr 5753.12 — Molet, Louis. Le bain royal à Madagascar. Tananarive, 1956.

Afr 2530.40FA — Monde Economique. Tunisia faces the future. Tunis, 1956.

Afr 510.65 — Monmarson, R. L'Afrique franco-africaine. Paris, 1956.

Afr 6333.56 — Moyse-Bartlett, Hubert. The King's African Rifles. Aldershot, 1956.

Afr 6720.56 — Nguini, Marcel. La valeur politique et sociale de la tutelle française au Cameroun. Thèse. Aix-en-Provence, 1956.

Afr 6210.35F — Nigeria, Western. Executive and Higher Technical Grading Team. Western region executive and higher technical grading team report. Ibadan, 1956.

Afr 6277.70 — Nigeria. Cocoa Marketing Board. Nigerian cocoa farmers. London, 1956.

Afr Doc 2520.725 — Nigeria. Department of Statistics. Population census of the Western region of Nigeria, 1952. Lagos, 1956.

Afr 10685.67.100 — Okoye, Mokwugo. African cameos. Onitsha, 1956.

Afr 6585.7 — Ommanney, F.D. Isle of Cloves. Philadelphia, 1956.

Afr 9285.5 — Orange Free State. The Orange Free State. Cape Town, 1956.

Afr 12985.65.120 — Oyono, Ferdinand. Une vie de boy, roman. Paris, 1956.

Afr 12985.65.110 — Oyono, Ferdinand. Le vieux Nègre et la médaille. Paris, 1956.

Afr 11669.13 — Packer, Joy (P). Valley of the vines. Philadelphia, 1956.

Afr 630.56 — Padmore, George. Pan-Africanism or Communism. N.Y., 1956.

Afr 8688.5.10 — Pama, C. Heraldiek in Suid-Africa. Kaapstad, 1956.

Afr 6280.32 — Parrinder, E.G. The story of Ketu. Ibadan, 1956.

Afr 8145.30 — Pellissier, S.H. Jean Pierre Pellissier van Bethulie. Pretoria, 1956.

Afr 9165.42.50 — Picton-Seymour, Desirée. Transvaal republican. Cape Town, 1956.

Afr 630.56.5 — Pidoux, Edmond. L'Afrique à l'âge ingrat. Neuchâtel, 1956.

Afr Doc 5402.5 — Pilipenko, Helene. Recapitulation des periodiques officiels parus en Tunisie de 1881 à 1955. Tunis, 1956.

Afr 7540.44 — Piron, Pierre. L'indépendance de la magistrature et la statut des magistrats. Bruxelles, 1956.

Afr 3315.35 — Port Said, nouveau Stalingrad. Paris, 1956.

Afr 13438.1.120 — Rabemananjara, Jacques. Antsa. Paris, 1956.

Afr 9853.5 — Read, Margaret. The Ngoni of Nyasaland. London, 1956.

Afr 5407.12F — Réalités africaines. La mise en valeur de l'A.E.F. Casablanca, 1956.

Afr 5857.10 — Réunion. Archives Departementales. Classement et inventaire du fonds de la Compagnie des Indes (Série C.), 1665-1767. Nerac, 1956.

Afr 9432.5 — Rhodesia, Southern. Central African Archives. A guide to the public records of Southern Rhodesia under the regime of the British South Africa Company. Cape Town, 1956.

Afr 9700.45F — Rhodesia. Northern. Committee Appointed to Investigate the Extent to which Racial Discrimination is Practised in Shops and in Other Similar Business Premises. Report. Lusaka, 1956.

Afr Doc 3507.356.15 — Rhodesia and Nyasaland. Central Statistical Office. Report on the census of Africans in employment. Salisbury, 1956.

Afr 1069.56 — Ricard, Robert. Etudes hispano-africaines. Tetuan, 1956.

Afr 590.56.5 — Rinchon, Dieudonne. Les armements negriers au XVIIIe siècle. Bruxelles, 1956.

Afr 1623.956F — Ripoche, Paul. Problemes économiques au Maroc. 2. ed. Rabat, 1956.

Afr 3979.55.10 — Robichon, C. Eternal Egypt. Reprinted. London, 1956.

Afr 7560.14 — Roeykens, A. Le dessein africain de Léopold II. Bruxelles, 1956.

Afr 7808.76 — Roeykens, Aug. Leopold II et la conférence géographique. Bruxelles, 1956.

Afr 8045.36 — Rogers, Mirabel. The black sash. Johannesburg, 1956.

Afr 6194.20.20 — Rouch, Jean. Migrations au Ghana (Gold Coast). Paris, 1956.

Afr 8045.26 — Royal Institute of International Affairs. The high commission territories and the Union of South Africa. London, 1956.

Afr 2929.56 — Royal Institute of International Affairs. Libya. London, 1956.

Afr 5900.5 — Rumeu de Armas, Antonio. España en el Africa atlantica. V.1-2. Madrid, 1956-57.

Afr 3155.5 — Sadeque, Syedah. Baybars I of Egypt. 1st ed. Dacca, 1956.

Afr 4390.55 — Salimbeni, A., Conte. Crispi e Menelick nel diario inedito del Conte Augusto Salimbeni. Torino, 1956.

Afr 8678.72 — Sampson, Anthony. Drum. London, 1956.

Afr 550.72 — Sandoval, Alonso de. De instauranda Aethiopum salute. Bogatà, 1956.

Afr 2030.15 — Schaefer, René. Révolution en Algérie. Paris, 1956.

Afr 8678.9.80 — Schapera, I. The Bantu-speaking tribes of South Africa. London, 1956.

Afr 8045.32 — Schapera, Isaac. Government and politics in tribal societies. London, 1956.

Afr 1571.52 — Selous, G.H. Appointment to Fez. London, 1956.

Afr 12639.24.100 — Senghor, L.S. Ethiopiques, poèmes. Paris, 1956.

Afr 2209.56 — Service de Propagande, d'Edition et d'Information, Paris. A survey of Algeria. Paris, 1956.

Afr 7812.256 — Sion, Georges. Soixante-quinze ans de Congo. Gand, 1956.

Afr 2285.25 — Skolle, John. Azalai. 1st ed. N.Y., 1956.

Afr 9165.42.25F — Smith, Anna H. Pictorial history of Johannesburg. Johannesburg, 1956.

Afr 11797.41.111 — Smith, Pauline. The beadle. Cape Town, 1956.

Afr 7540.42 — Sohier, Jean. Essai sur les transformations des coutumes. Bruxelles, 1956.

Afr 7815.40 — Sousberghe, Léon de. Les danses rituelles mungonge et kela des Ba-pende. Bruxelles, 1956.

Afr 2030.10 — Soustelle, Jacques. Aimée et souffrante Algérie. Paris, 1956.

Afr 8678.296 — South Africa. Commission for the Social Economic Development. The Tomlinson report. Johannesburg, 1956.

Afr Doc 4312.156 — South Africa. Parliament. South Africa Act Amendment Bill. v.1-2. Cape Town, 1956.

Afr 8678.316 — South African Digest, Pretoria. The pattern of race policy in South Africa. Pretoria, 1956.

Afr 8355.35 — South African Institute of Race Relations. The Indian as a South African. Johannesburg, 1956.

Afr 6540.20 — Southall, A.W. Alur society. Cambridge, Eng., 1956.

Afr 3315.45 — Soviet News. Suez. London, 1956.

Afr 3315.128 — Soviet News. Suez and the Middle East; documents. London, 1956.

Afr 5924.240 — Spain. Consejo Superior de Investigaciones. Iradier. Madrid, 1956.

Afr 630.56.10 — Spinola, Francisco Elias de Tejada. Sociologia del Africa negra. Madrid, 1956.

Afr 8678.70.10 — Steward, Alex. You are wrong. 1. ed. London, 1956.

Afr 210.55.10 — Stillman, Calvin W. Africa in the modern world. Chicago, 1956.

Afr 2719.56.5 — Strasser, Daniel. Réalités et promesses sahariennes. Paris, 1956.

Afr Doc 1307.356.11 — Sudan. Population Census Office. First population census of Sudan, 1955-56. Supplement. Khartoum, 1956.

Afr Doc 4107.356 — Swaziland. Census, 1956. Mbabane, 1956?

Afr 3310.10.80 — Taylor, Edmond. The real case against Nasser. n.p., 1956.

Afr 2681.2 — Territoire des Ouled Ali ben-Aoun. 1. ed. Paris, 1956.

Afr 7850.15 — Thier, Franz M. Le centre extra-coutumier de Coquilhatville. Bruxelles, 1956.

Afr 7873.5 — Thier, Franz M. de. Le centre extra-coutumier de Coquilhatville. Bruxelles, 1956.

Afr 7809.51.2 — Tourist Bureau for the Belgian Congo and Ruanda-Urundi. Travellers guide to theBelgianCongo andRuanda-Urundi. 2d ed. Brussels, 1956.

Afr 5813.12 — Toussaint, Auguste. Répertoire des archives de l'Ile de France. Nerac, 1956.

Afr 9510.11.5 — Tredgold, Robert Clarksen. The Matapos. Salisbury, 1956.

Afr 8687.359 — Tremlett, Rex. Road to Ophir. London, 1956.

Afr 2530.3 — Tunisia. Secrétariat d'Etat à l'Information. Six mois de gouvernement Bourguiba. 4 pts. Tunis, 1956.

Afr 1620.30 — U.S. Office of Armed Forces Information and Education. A pocket guide to French Morocco. Washington, 1956.

Afr 9499.25A — United States. Bureau of Foreign Commerce (1953-). Investment in Federation of Rhodesia and Nyasaland. Washington, 1956.

Afr 3315.10 — United States. Department of State. The Suez Canal problem. Washington, 1956.

Afr 11865.59.150 — Vanderpost, Laurens. A bar of shadow. N.Y., 1956.

Afr 5968.2 — Veciana Vilaldach, Antonio de. Los Bujeba. Madrid, 1956.

Afr 7176.36 — Ventura, Reis. Os problemas de Angola, no Primeiro Congresso dos Economistas Portugueses. Lisboa, 1956.

Afr 7913.5 — Verbeken, A. Msiri. Bruxelles, 1956.

Afr 2885.5 — Villard, H.S. Libya. Ithaca, 1956.

Afr 3979.56F — Viollet, Roger. Regards sur l'Egypte. Paris, 1956.

Afr 8678.430 — Volkskongres oon die toekoms van Bantoe, referate en besluite. Stellenbosch, 1956.

Afr 210.56.5 — Wallbank, T.W. Contemporary Africa. Princeton, 1956.

Afr 8659.39.20 — Wells, Arthur W. Southern Africa. London, 1956.

Afr 7870.5 — Whyms. Leopoldville, son histoire, 1881-1956. Bruxelles, 1956.

Afr 7850.10 — Whyms. Léopoldville, son histoire, 1881-1956. Bruxelles, 1956.

Afr 6195.5 — Wiltgen, R.M. Gold Coast mission history, 1471-1880. Techny, Ill., 1956.

Afr 6060.56.5 — Wraith, R.E. Local government. London, 1956.

1957

Afr 3979.57.10 — Abreu, Paradela De. Reportagens no Egipto. Lisboa, 1957.

Afr 9435.12 — Africa Bureau, London. Central Africa and the British Parliament. London, 1957.

Afr 3315.145 — Akademiia Nauk SSSR. Institut Mirovoi Ekonomiki i Mezhdunarodnykh Otnoshenii. Suetskii vopros i imperialisticheskaia agressiia protiv Egipta. Moskva, 1957.

Afr 6664.5 — Alcandre, Sylvine. La république autonome du Togo. Paris, 1957.

Afr 2030.276 — Algeria. Cabinet du Gouverneur Général. Action du gouvernement en Algérie. Alger, 1957.

Afr 2209.57.5 — Algeria. Cabinet du Gouverneur Général. Algérie. Alger, 1957.

Afr 575.25 — Algeria. Direction de l'Intérieur et des Beaux-Arts. Mélanges d'histoire et d'archéologie de l'Occident musulman. v.1-2. Alger, 1957.

Afr Doc 5307.354 — Algeria. Service de la Statistique Générale. Resultats statistiques du denombrement de la population effective le 31 octobre 1954. Alger, 1957. 3v.

Afr 7309.57 — Almeida, Eugenio Ferreira de. Governo do distrito de Moçambique. Lisboa, 1957.

Afr 2030.130 — Alquier, Jean Yves. Nous avons pacifié Tazalt. Paris, 1957.

Afr 3817.12 — American Jewish Congress. Committee on International Affairs and on Israel. The black record, Nasser's persecution. N.Y., 1957.

Afr 3315.60 — Amir, Adil. Le complot continué. Caire, 1957.

Afr 1869.57.10 — Amrouche, Marcel. Terres et hommes d'Algérie. v.1. Alger, 1957.

Afr 8145.38 — Anderson, Theophilus. The story of Pacaltsdorp. Port Elizabeth, 1957.

Afr 5753.9 — Andoiamanjato, Richard. Le Tsiny et le Tody dans la pensée malgache. Paris, 1957.

Afr 718.2.130 — Anstruther, Ian. Dr. Livingstone, I presume. 1st American ed. N.Y., 1957.

Afr 2030.25A — Aron, Raymond. La tragédie algérienne. Paris, 1957.

Afr 6212.5 — Azihiwe, Nrandi. The development of political parties in Nigeria. London, 1957.

Afr 6420.60 — Baldwin, W.W. Mau Mau man-hunt. 1st ed. N.Y., 1957.

Afr 6147.5 — Banton, M.P. West African city. London, 1957.

Afr 2030.30 — Barberot, Roger. Malaventure en Algérie avec le général Paris de Ballardiére. Paris, 1957.

Afr 4155.10 — Barque, Jacques. Histoire sociale d'un village égyptien au XXème siècle. Paris, 1957.

Afr 10516.2 — Bassir, O. An anthology of West African verse. Nigeria, 1957.

Afr 555.95 — Baudu, Paul. Vieil empire. Paris, 1957.

Afr 609.57.10 — Baumann, Hermann. Les peuples et les civilisations de l'Afrique. Paris, 1957.

1957 - cont.

Afr 2030.65 Beau de Lomenie, Emmanuel. L'Algérie trahie par l'argent. Paris, 1957.
Afr 11197.5.100 Beaumont, John H. Poems. Cape Town, 1957.
Afr 9525.201 Beit, Alfred. The will and the way. London, 1957.
Afr 710.55 Belandier, Georges. Afrique ambigue. Paris, 1957.
Afr 3040.76 Berger, Morroe. Bureaucracy and society in modern Egypt. Princeton, 1957.
Afr 6160.15 Bernard, Jane. Black mistress. London, 1957.
Afr 3979.57.5 Besancon, Jacques. L'homme et le Nil. Paris, 1957.
Afr 7812.257 Bezy, Fernand. Problèmes structurels de l'économie congolaise. Louvain, 1957.
Afr 6280.45 Biobaku, S.O. The Egba and their neighbors. Oxford, 1957.
Afr 4199.90A Bird, Michael. Samuel Shepheard of Cairo. London, 1957.
Afr 7369.57 Bixler, R.W. The foreign policy of the United States in Liberia. 1st ed. N.Y., 1957.
Afr 855.18 Blakeston, O. Isle of St. Helena. London, 1957.
Afr 861.25 Boay, D.M. Rock of exile. London, 1957.
Afr 6280.26.6 Bohannan, Paul. Justice and judgment among the Tiv. London, 1957.
Afr 11229.10 Bosman, Herman. A cask of jerepigo. Johannesburg, 1957.
Afr 1280.60 Bousquet, G.H. Les Berbères. 1st ed. Paris, 1957.
Afr 2749.57 Bowles, Paul Frederic. Yallah. N.Y., 1957.
Afr 2326.5 Bresson, Gilbert. Histoire d'un centre rural algérien. Alger, 1957.
Afr 8860.10 Brockway, Tenner. British protectorates. London, 1957.
Afr 3315.15.5 Bromberger, M. Les secrets de l'expédition d'Egypte. Paris, 1957.
Afr 3315.15 Bromberger, M. Secrets of Suez. London, 1957.
Afr 8678.155 Bruwer, J.P. Die Bantö van Suid-Africa. Johannesburg, 1957.
Afr 9510.12 Bulawayo, Southern Rhodesia. City Council. The city of Bulawayo. 2. ed. Cape Town, 1957.
Afr 4559.57 Busk, Douglas L. The fountain of the sun. London, 1957.
Afr 3315.50 Byford-Jones, Wilfred. Oil on troubled waters. London, 1957.
Afr 1585.5 Caille, Jacques. Une ambassade autrichienne au Maroc en 1805. Paris, 1957.
Afr 3026.27 Cairo, Egypt. National Library. Egypt subject catalogue. Cairo, 1957.
Afr 3315.70 Camille, Paul. Suez. Paris, 1957.
Afr 2030.135 Candas, Maurice F.M. Plaidoyer pour l'Algérie. Paris, 1957.
Afr 1069.57.5 Caro Baroja, Julio Estudios mogrebies. Madrid, 1957.
Afr 4764.957 Cerulli, Enrico. Somalia. v.1-2. Roma, 1957-64. 3v.
Afr 2030.125 Ceux d'Algérie, lettres de rappelés. Paris, 1957.
Afr 5048.15 Chapelle, Jean. Nomades noirs du Sahara. Paris, 1957.
Afr 5420.257 Charbonnier, François. Gabon, terre d'avenir. Paris, 1957.
Afr 2749.57.5 Christopher, Robert. Ocean of fire. London, 1957.
Afr 6095.357 Church, R.J.H. West Africa. N.Y., 1957.
Afr 7815.20 Cleene, Natal de. Introduction à l'ethnographie du Congo belge et du Ruanda-Burundi. 2.éd. Anvers, 1957.
Afr 4236.957 Cleret, Maxime. Ethiopie. Paris, 1957.
Afr 8028.130 Coke, R.M. South Africa as seen by the French, 1610-1850. Cape Town, 1957.
Afr 10003.4 Conference of Writers, Publishers, Editors, and University Teachers of English. Proceedings. Johannesburg, 1957.
Afr 2749.57.10 Cornet, Pierre. Sahara. Paris, 1957.
Afr 8678.160 Crijns, Arthur. Race relations and race attitudes in South Africa. Nijmegen, 1957.
Afr 8355.42 Currie, J.C. A bibliography of material published during the period 1946-56. Cape Town, 1957.
Afr 2223.957 Dalmulder, J.J.J. De economische problematiek van Algerije. Leiden, 1957.
Afr 4070.55 Davies, R.T. The camel's back. London, 1957.
Afr 2630.7 Debbasch, Yvan. La nation française en Tunisie, 1577-1835. Paris, 1957.
Afr 5190.20 Delmas, Robert. Des origines de Dakar et ses relations avec l'Europe. Dakar, 1957.
Afr 2618.15 Demeerseman, A. Tunisie: sève nouvelle. Tournai, 1957.
Afr 2310.3 Despois, Jean. Le djebel amour. Paris, 1957.
Afr 626.36 Dia, Mamadou. L'économie africaine. 1. éd. Paris, 1957.
Afr 626.35.5 Dia, Mamadou. Reflexions sur l'économie de l'Afrique noire. Paris, 1957.
Afr 6282.5 Dike, Kenneth. Origins of the Niger mission. Nigeria, 1957.
Afr 6164.15 Diplomatic Bulletin. Ghana. London, 1957.
Afr 150.19 Domingues, Mario. O Infante Dom Henrique. Lisboa, 1957.
Afr 7815.44 Domont, Jean Marie. La prise de conscience de l'individu en milieu rural Kongo. Bruxelles, 1957.
Afr 7815.22 Dooent, Jean. Elite noire. Bruxelles, 1957.
Afr 4259.57 Doresse, Jean. L'empire du Prêtre-Jean. v.1-2. Paris, 1957. 2v.
Afr 3675.22.5 Duncan, J.S.R. The Sudan's path to independence. Edinburgh, 1957.
Afr 510.70 Durand, Huguette. Essai sur la conjoncture de l'Afrique noire. Paris, 1957.
Afr 3315.65 Dzelepy, E.N. Le complot de Suez. Bruxelles, 1957.
Afr 6538.10 Economist (London). Power in Uganda, 1957-1970. London, 1957.
Afr 7119.57 Egerton, F.C.C. Angola in perspective. London, 1957.
Afr 1869.57 Egretaud, Marcel. Réalité de la nation algérienne. Paris, 1957.
Afr 3310.10.22 Egypt. President. Address by the President of the Republic of Egypt. Cairo, 1957.
Afr 510.85 Ehrhard, Jean. Le destin du colonialisme. Paris, 1957.
Afr 1869.57.7 Esquer, Gabriel. Histoire de l'Algérie. 2. ed. Paris, 1957.
Afr 718.2.125 Farwell, Byron. The man who presumed. 1st ed. N.Y., 1957.
Afr 8355.30 Ferguson-Davie, C.J. The early history of Indians in Natal. Johannesburg, 1957.
Afr 5406.257 Fieret, Jeannette. L'enfant blanc de l'Afrique noire. Paris, 1957.
Afr 9525.393.2 Finaughty, William. The recollections of William Finaughty, elephant hunter. 2nd ed. Cape Town, 1957.
Afr 1200.110 Fisher, G. Barbary legend. Oxford, 1957.
Afr 1095.20 Fontaine, Pierre. Dossier secret de l'Afrique du Nord. Paris, 1957.
Afr 3315.90 Foot, Michael. Guilty men. N.Y., 1957.
Afr 2731.15.58 Foucauld, Charles de. Père de Foucauld. Abbé Huvelin. Correspondance inédite. Tournai, 1957.
Afr 2030.85 Fournier, Christiane. Nous avons encore des héros. Paris, 1957.
Afr 2223.957.5 France. Embassy. Algeria at work. N.Y., 1957.

1957 - cont.

Afr 1623.957 France. Institut National de la Statistique et des Études Économiques. Dix ans d'économie marocaine, 1945-1955. Paris, 1957.
Afr 5051.10 French West Africa. Archives. Répertoire des archives. Rufisque, 1957. 2v.
Afr 5057.22F French West Africa. Direction Générale des Services Economiques et du Plan. Le financement du plan. Paris, 1957.
Afr 8678.357 Fuller, Basil. South Africa - not guilty. London, 1957.
Afr 2749.58 Furon, Raymond. Le Sahara. Paris, 1957.
Afr 9339.57 Gabatshwane, S.M. Introduction to the Bechuanaland protectorate history and administration. Kanye, 1957.
Afr 1750.20 Garcia Figueras, Tomas. Espana y su protectorado en Marruecos. Madrid, 1957.
Afr 4178.15 Gaslini, Mario. Suez. Milano, 1957.
Afr 28.50 Geographical Association. Library of the Geographical Association. Sheffield, 1957.
Afr 6160.28 Ghana. Commission Appointed to Enquire into Salaries and Wages of the Civil Service and Non-Government Teaching Service. Report. Accra, 1957.
Afr 8289.57 Gibbs, Peter. Death of the last republic. London, 1957.
Afr 6465.56.5 Gray, J.M. The British in Mombasa, 1824-1826. London, 1957.
Afr 6192.35 Great Britain. Central Office of Information. Britain and the Gold Coast. London, 1957.
Afr 8830.10 Green, L.G. Beyond the city lights. Cape Town, 1957.
Afr 8045.30 Green, L.P. History of local government in South Africa. Cape Town, 1957.
Afr 8310.11 Grineell-Milne, D.W. Baden-Powell at Mafeking. London, 1957.
Afr 6395.12 Grubbe, Peter. Die Trommeln verstummen. Wiesbaden, 1957.
Afr 210.38.5A Hailey, W.M.H. An African survey. London, 1957.
Afr 8089.51 Halt, A.G.H. von der. Geskiedenis von Suid-Afrika. v.1-2. Kaapstad, 1957.
Afr 6570.12 Hamilton, Genesta. Princes of Zinj. London, 1957.
Afr 3979.57 Harris, G.L. Egypt. New Haven, 1957.
Afr 7812.257.5F Hauzeur de Fooz, C. Un demi-siècle avec l'économie du Congo belge. Bruxelles, 1957.
Afr 3315.5 Henriques, R.D.Q. A hundred hours to Suez. N.Y., 1957.
Afr 8735.5.15.2 Hockly, H.E. The story of the British settlers of 1820 in South Africa. 2. ed. Cape Town, 1957.
Afr 609.58.37 Hornman, W. Het masker af. Leiden, 1957.
Afr 8680.35 Horwitz, Ralph. Expand or explode. Cape Town, 1957.
Afr 109.57 Hunton, William A. Decision in Africa. N.Y., 1957.
Afr 4199.10.5 Hussain, Tacha. Kindheitstage in Agypten. München, 1957.
Afr 2209.57.10 Initiation à l'Algérie. Paris, 1957.
Afr 3315.55 International Review Service. The Suez Canal. N.Y., 1957.
Afr 8175.20 Jaarsveld, F.A. van. Die ontwaking van die afrikaanse nasionale bewussyn. Johannesburg, 1957.
Afr 11465.14.100 Jacobson, Dan. The price of diamonds. London, 1957.
Afr 4559.57.5 Jenny, Hans. Äthiopien, Land im Aufbruch. Stuttgart, 1957.
Afr 7933.2 Jentgen, P. Les frontiéres du Ruanda-Urundi et le régime international de Tutelle. Bruxelles, 1957.
Afr 3315.85 Johnson, Paul. Suez war. London, 1957.
Afr 6176.43 Jopp, Keith. Ghana, 1957. Accra, 1957.
Afr 1095.15 Juin, A.P. Le Maghreb en feu. Paris, 1957.
Afr 6715.25 El Kamerun. n.p., 1957?
Afr 4045.12 Kienitz, Ernst. Der Suezkanal. Berlin, 1957.
Afr 635.50 King-Hall, Stephen. Letters from Africa. London, 1957.
Afr 8100.10 Kock, W.J. de. Portugese ontdekkers om die Kaap. Kaapstad, 1957.
Afr 2749.57.15 Kollmannsperger, Fr. Drohende Wüste. Wiesbaden, 1957.
Afr 8678.336 Kuper, Leo. Passive resistance in South Africa. New Haven, 1957.
Afr 1494.6.5 Landau, Rom. Mohammed V. Rabat, 1957.
Afr 6455.130 Lander, Cherry. My Kenya acres. London, 1957.
Afr 5055.57 Laroche, Jean de. Le gouverneur général Felix Ebane. Paris, 1957.
Afr 1487.15 Larteguy, Jean. La tragédie du Maroc interdit. Paris, 1957.
Afr 626.42 Lefebvre, Jacques. Afrique et communauté européenne. Bruxelles, 1957.
Afr 5056.157 Legras, Paul. Voyages et aventures en Afrique française. Nancy, 1957.
Afr 3310.35 Lengyel, Emil. Egypt's role in world affairs. Washington, 1957.
Afr 1069.57 Leone, Enrico de. La colonizzazione dell'Africa del Nord. Padova, 1957.
Afr 2030.75 Leprevost, Jacques. La bataille d'Alger. Alger, 1957.
Afr 2030.77 Leprevost, Jacques. Défense de l'Algérie. Alger, 1957.
Afr 9489.57 Lessing, Doris M. Going home. London, 1957.
Afr 6780.10.7 Lettow-Vorbeck, P.E. von. East African campaigns. N.Y., 1957.
Afr 6780.10.23 Lettow-Vorbeck, P.E. von. Mein Leben. Biberach an der Riss, 1957.
Afr 28.89 Library of Congress. General Reference and Bibliography Division. Africa South of the Sahara. Washington, 1957.
Afr 1026.15 Library of Congress. General Reference and Bibliography Division. North and Northeast Africa. Washington, 1957.
Afr 11523.32.100 Lighton, R.E. Out of the strong. London, 1957.
Afr 7210.10 Lobato, Alexandre. Evolução administrativa e economica de Moçambique, 1752-1763. v.1-. Lisboa, 1957.
Afr 6670.957 Luchaire, Fr. Le Togo français. Paris, 1957.
Afr 8680.25 MacCrone, Ian Douglas. Race attitudes in South Africa. Johannesburg, 1957.
Afr 6385.10 McFarlan, D.M. Calabar. Rev. ed. London, 1957.
Afr 6282.10 McFarlan, Donald. Calabar. Rev. ed. London, 1957.
Afr 11546.13.60 McNeile, Michael. This Africa of ours. Johannesburg, 1957.
Afr 5758.57F Madagascar. Haut Commissariat. Plan de developpement économique et social, programme, 1958-1962. Tananarive, 1957.
Afr 635.55 Maistriaux, Robert. L'intélligence noire et son destin. Bruxelles, 1957.
Afr 8685.22F Mann, John William. The problem of the marginal personality. Durban, 1957.
Afr 8678.31.5 Marais, J.S. The Cape coloured people, 1652-1937. Johannesburg, 1957.
Afr 2209.57 Marcais, Georges. Algérie médiévale. Paris, 1957.
Afr 699.57A Marsh, Zoe. An introduction to the history of East Africa. Cambridge, Eng., 1957.
Afr 6988.58.268 Martin, H. The sheltering desert. London, 1957.
Afr 2030.20 Massenet, Michel. Contrepoison, ou la morale en Algérie. Paris, 1957.

1957 - cont.

Afr 9165.7 — Mathewson, J. Edw. The establishment of an urban Bantu township. Pretoria, 1957.
Afr 6455.90 — Meinertzhagen, R. Kenya diary. Edinburg, 1957.
Afr 2300.6 — Merlo, Manuel. Les personnels des communes algériennes. Blida, 1957.
Afr 5183.957 — Mersadier, Yvon. Budgets familiaux africains. St. Louis du Sénégal, 1957.
Afr 2030.120 — Michelet, Edmond. Contre la guerre civile. Paris, 1957.
Afr 11021.2 — Miller, G.M. A critical survey of South African poetry in English. Cape Town, 1957.
Afr 11572.50.200 — Millin, S.G.(L). Two bucks without hair. London, 1957.
Afr 5343.4F — Mission d'Etude des Groupements. Mission d'étude des groupements immigrés en Côte-d'Ivoire. Paris, 1957.
Afr 5320.15 — Modupe, Prince. I was a savage. N.Y., 1957.
Afr 1609.57 — Nebel, Gerhard. An den Saulen des Herakles. Hamburg, 1957.
Afr 8676.57 — Neumark, S.D. Economic influences of the South African frontier. Stanford, 1957.
Afr Doc 2309.305F — Nigeria. Department of Statistics. Urban consumer surveys in Nigeria. Lagos, 1957.
Afr 6208.20 — Nigeria. Federal Information Service. Federal Nigeria, annual report. London, 1957.
Afr Doc 2343.5 — Nigeria. Nigerianisation Office. Annual report of the Nigerianisation Office. Lagos, 1957.
Afr 3715.10 — Nigumi, M.A. A great trusteeship. London, 1957.
Afr 6174.8 — Nkrumah, Kwame. Ghana. N.Y., 1957.
Afr 2731.15.50 — Nord, Pierre. Le père de Foucauld. Paris, 1957.
Afr 2749.57.20 — Normand, S. Sahara. Paris, 1957.
Afr 9850.10 — Nyasaland. Capital development plan, 1957-1961. Zomba, 1957.
Afr 9445.30 — Olivier, C.P. Many treks made Rhodesia. Cape Town, 1957.
Afr 5245.5 — Ouane, Ibrahima Mamadou. L'islam et la civilisation française. Avignon, 1957.
Afr 12785.89.120 — Ousmane, Sembene. O pays, mon beau peuple; roman. Paris, 1957.
Afr 5243.125.20 — Pageard, Robert. Notes sur l'histoire des Bambaras de Ségou. Paris, 1957.
Afr 8688.5.15 — Pama, C. Die univevlag. Kaapstad, 1957.
Afr 10397.2 — Passion in Africa. 1st ed. London, 1957.
Afr 8667.40 — Paton, Alan. South Africa and her people. London, 1957.
Afr 8685.55.5 — Patterson, S. The last trek. London, 1957.
Afr 3315.68 — Pearson, Lester B. The crisis in the Middle East. Ottawa, 1957.
Afr 6455.95 — Pickering, Elsa. When the windows were opened. London, 1957.
Afr 5385.32 — Pires, Vicente F. Viagem de Africa em o reino de Dahome. São Paulo, 1957.
Afr 5057.28 — Poquin, Jean. Les relations économiques extérieures des pays d'Afrique. Paris, 1957.
Afr 3315.110 — Primakov, E.M. Pouchitelnyi urok. Moscow, 1957.
Afr 8360.11 — Quinn, Gerald D. The rebellion of 1914-15, a bibliography. Cape Town, 1957.
Afr 13438.1.140 — Rabemananjara, Jacques. Les boutriers de l'aurore. Paris, 1957.
Afr 9405.5 — Randall, D. Factors and economic development and the Okovanggo Delta. Chicago, 1957.
Afr 6192.40 — Redmayne, P. Gold Coast to Ghana. London, 1957.
Afr 9428.5F — Rhodes-Livingstone Institute, Lusaka, Northern Rhodesia. A selected bibliography of the federation of Rhodesia and Nyasaland. Lusaka, 1957.
Afr 9436.12.5 — Rhodesia, Southern. Franchise Commission. Report. Salisbury, 1957.
Afr 9436.12 — Rhodesia and Nyasaland. The franchise for federal elections in Rhodesia and Nyasaland. Salisbury, 1957.
Afr 8369.57 — Robertson, H.M. South Africa. Durham, N.C., 1957.
Afr 3315.20 — Robertson, J.H. The most important country. London, 1957.
Afr 7560.14.10 — Roeykens, A. La période initiale de l'oeuvre africaine de Lépold II. Bruxelles, 1957.
Afr 555.73 — Rognes, Louis. Le pionnier du Gabon. Paris, 1957.
Afr 8690.15 — Rosenthal, E. River of diamonds. Cape Town, 1957.
Afr 8710.19 — Rosenthal, Eric. The changing years. Cape Town, 1957.
Afr 6164.17 — Royal Institute of International Affairs. Ghana. London, 1957.
Afr 3305.10.1 — Sadat, Anwar. Geheimtagebuch der ägyptischen Revolution. Düsseldorf, 1957.
Afr 3305.10 — Sadat, Anwar. Revolt on the Nile. London, 1957.
Afr 9515.5.2 — Salisbury. The city ofSalisbury. Cape Town, 1957.
Afr 7130.10 — Santos, Ernesto Moreira dos. Combate de Naulila; cobiça de Angola. Cuimarães, 1957.
Afr 7119.57.5 — Sarmento, Alexandre. Temas angolanos. Lisboa, 1957.
Afr 115.20.5 — Schiffers, H. The quest for Africa. London, 1957.
Afr 609.57 — Schiffers, Heinrich. Afrika. 4. Aufl. Frankfurt, 1957.
Afr 9225.20.5 — Scholtz, G.D. President Johannes Henricus Brand, 1823-1888. Johannesburg, 1957.
Afr 609.57.5 — Schomburgk, Hans Hermann. Zelte in Afrika. 1. Aufl. Berlin, 1957.
Afr 9558.95 — Seaver, George. David Livingstone. N.Y., 1957.
Afr 630.14.3 — Seligman, C.G. Races of Africa. 3d ed. London, 1957.
Afr 2030.35.2 — Servan-Schreiber, Jean Jacques. Lieutenant en Algérie. Paris, 1957.
Afr 2030.35 — Servan-Schreiber, Jean Jacques. Lieutenant in Algeria. 1st Amer. ed. N.Y., 1957.
Afr 6134.3F — Sierra Leone. Report, 1957. Sierra Leone, 1957.
Afr 6145.3.5F — Sierra Leone. Commission of Enquiry into the Conduct of Certain Chiefs. Further reports of the commissioners of enquiry into the conduct of certain chiefs and the government statement thereon. Sierra Leone, 1957.
Afr 6145.3F — Sierra Leone. Commissioners of Enquiry into the Conduct of Certain Chiefs. Reports of the commissioners of enquiry into the conduct of certain chiefs and the government statement thereon. Freetown, 1957.
Afr 11790.58.100 — Sinclair, F.D. Lovers and hermits. Cape Town, 1957.
Afr 5056.157.10 — Siriex, Paul. Une nouvelle Afrique. Paris, 1957.
Afr 9345.65 — Smith, E.W. Great lion of Bechuanaland. London, 1957.
Afr 2362.5 — Solal, Edouard. Philippeville et sa région. Alger, 1957.
Afr 2030.10.5 — Soustelle, Jacques. Le drame algérien et la décadence française. Paris, 1957.
Afr 718.2.12 — Stanley, H.M. Unpublished letters. N.Y., 1957.
Afr 7812.257.10 — Stengers, Jean. Combien le Congo a-t-il couté à la Belgique? Bruxelles, 1957.
Afr 7803.40 — Storme, Marcel. Rapports du père Planque. Bruxelles, 1957.
Afr 8252.348 — Struben, Charles. Vein of gold. Cape Town, 1957.

1957 - cont.

Afr Doc 1307.356.10 — Sudan. Population Census Office. First population census of Sudan, 1955-56. Interim report. Khartoum, 1957.
Afr 8030.15.15 — Suid-afrikaanse argiefstukke. v.1- Kaapstad, 1957- 6v.
Afr 6881.257 — Tanganyika Territory. Department of Commerce and Industry. Commerce and industry in Tanganyika. Dar es Salaam, 1957.
Afr 9689.57 — Tapson, Winifred (Haw). Old timer. Cape Town, 1957.
Afr 550.75 — Taylor, John Vernon. Christianity and politics in Africa. Harmondsworth, 1957.
Afr 13340.12.100 — Tchicaya U Tamsi, Gerald Felix. Feu de brousse. Paris, 1957.
Afr 5056.157.5 — Thompson, V.M. French West Africa. Stanford, Calif., 1957.
Afr 2030.50 — Tillion, G. L'Algérie en 1957. Paris, 1957.
Afr 2623.957 — Tlatli, S.E. Tunisie nouvelle. Tunis, 1957.
Afr 6390.55 — Trawell, M. African tapestry. London, 1957.
Afr 9389.57 — Tshekedi Khama. Bechuanaland. Johannesburg, 1957.
Afr 2928.18.5 — Tully, R. Letters written during a ten years' residence at the court of Tripoli. London, 1957.
Afr 9705.10A — Turner, O.W. Schism and continuity in African society. Manchester, 1957.
Afr 5426.100.35 — Urquhart, Clara. With Dr. Schweitzer in Lambaréné. London, 1957.
Afr 1040.5 — Vassenhove, Leon van. Une solution fédéraliste du problème nord-africain. Neuchâtel, 1957.
Afr 3138.10.10 — Vatikiotis, P.J. The Fatimid theory of state. Lahore, 1957.
Afr 6990.90.20 — Vedder, Heinrich. Kort verhale uit 'n lang lewe. Kaapstad, 1957.
Afr 1380.8 — Vernet Gines, Juan. Historia de Marruecos, la islamizacion. Tetuan, 1957.
Afr 2030.40 — Vialet, Georges. L'Algérie restera française. Paris, 1957.
Afr 14692.41.1110 — Vieira, Luandino. A cidade e a infância. Lisboa, 1957?
Afr 1550.56 — Vieleux, Christian. Aspects marocains. La Rochelle, 1957.
Afr 3979.56.10F — Viollet, Roger. Egypt. N.Y., 1957.
Afr 8063.25 — Vrdoljak, M.K. The history of South African regiments. Cape Town, 1957.
Afr 8089.28.15 — Walker, E.A. A history of Southern Africa. 3rd ed. London, 1957.
Afr 6465.58.5 — Walmsley, Ronald W. Nairobi. Kampala, 1957.
Afr 8919.57 — Walton, James. Historic buildings of Basutoland. Morija, 1957.
Afr 6164.9.7 — Ward, W.E.F. A short history of Ghana. 7th ed. London, 1957.
Afr 3315.25 — Watt, Donald C. Documents on the Suez crisis. London, 1957.
Afr 11878.24.100 — Wiesmar, Chriss. The lowly and the worldly. South Africa, 1957.
Afr 6484.10 — Wild, John V. The story of the Uganda Agreement. London, 1957.
Afr 628.257 — Wright, Richard. White man, listen. 1st ed. Garden City, 1957.
Afr 1110.5 — Ziadek, Nicola A. Whither North Africa. 1st ed. Aligarh, 1957.
Afr 7175.45 — Zwilling, Ernst. Angola-safari. 2.Aufl. Mödling, 1957.

1958

Afr 6196.15 — Acquah, Ioné. Accra survey. London, 1958.
Afr 9435.12.5 — Africa Bureau, London. Central Africa and the franchise. London, 1958.
Afr 609.58.40 — Africa seen by American Negroes. Paris, 1958.
Afr 5019.58.5 — Africanus. L'Afrique noire devant l'indépendance. Paris, 1958.
Afr 550.135 — Afrique chrétienne. Christliches Afrika. Lezay, 1958-1961. 2v.
Afr 5056.158.5 — Afrique occidentale française. Togo. Paris, 1958.
Afr 5425.5 — Alexandre, Pierre. Le groupe dit Pahouin. Paris, 1958.
Afr 2223.958.5 — Algeria. Perspectives décennales de développement économique de l'Algérie. Alger, 1958.
Afr Doc 5307.354.5 — Algeria. Service de la Statistique Générale. Résultats statistiques du denombrement de la population effective le 31 octobre, 1954. Alger, 1958.
Afr 2223.958 — Algérie françise. Sidi-bel-Abbès, 1958.
Afr 2030.60 — Alleg, Henri. The question. N.Y., 1958.
Afr 2030.60.2 — Alleg, Henri. Texte intégral du livre "La question." Paris, 1958.
Afr 6176.10 — Amamoo, J.G. The new Ghana. London, 1958.
Afr 210.58A — American Assembly. The United States and Africa. N.Y., 1958.
Afr 2030.95 — Aron, Raymond. L'Algérie et la République. Paris, 1958.
Afr 8028.135 — Ashpol, R. A select bibliography of South African auto-biographies. Cape Town, 1958.
Afr 6415.40.2 — Askwirth, Tom G. Kenya's progress. 2nd ed. Kampala, 1958.
Afr 628.258.5 — Aspects de la culture noire. Paris, 1958.
Afr 1273.958 — Avakov, R.M. Frantsuzskii monopolisticheskii kapital v severnoi Afrike. Moscow, 1958.
Afr 2533.4 — Aymard, C.E. Tragédie française en Afrique du nord. Paris, 1958.
Afr 7176.9 — Azevedo, João M.C. de. Angola. Luanda, 1958.
Afr 5829.58 — Babaju, Esno. A concise history of Mauritius. Bombay, 1958.
Afr 5048.10 — Bascom, W.R. Continuity and change in African cultures. Chicago, 1958.
Afr Doc 4207.356 — Basutoland. Census Office. 1956 population census, 8th April 1956. Maseru, 1958.
Afr 8860.15 — Basutoland. Council. Report on constitutional reform. Maseru, 1958.
Afr 7575.5A — Bilsen, Antoine. Vers l'indépendance du Congo et du Ruanda-Urundi. Kraainem, 1958.
Afr 12972.41.700 — Biyidi, Alexandre. Mission accomplished. N.Y., 1958.
Afr 12972.41.130 — Biyidi, Alexandre. Le roi miraculé. Paris, 1958.
Afr 5019.58.10 — Blanchet, Andre. L'itinéraire des partis africains depuis Bamoko. Paris, 1958.
Afr 5640.40 — Boiteau, Pierre. Contribution à l'histoire de la nation Malgache. Paris, 1958.
Afr 2225.14 — Bourdieu, Pierre. Sociologie de l'Algérie. 1. ed. Paris, 1958.
Afr 5054.58 — Bovill, E.W. The golden trade of the Moors. London, 1958.
Afr 150.1 — Brasio, A.D. A acção missionaria no periodo henriquino. Lisboa, 1958.
Afr 550.70.2 — Brasio, A.D. Monumenta missionaria africana. 2d serie. Lisboa, 1958-64. 4v.

Afr 2030.100	Bromberger, Serge. Les rébelles algériens. Paris, 1958.
Afr 8045.38	Brookes, Edgar H. Civil liberty in South Africa. Cape Town, 1958.
Afr 6214.8.18	Burns, Alan C. History of Nigeria. London, 1958.
Afr 6310.39	Bustin, Edouard. La décentralisation administrative et l'évolution des structures. Liège, 1958.
Afr 2000.6	Camus, Albert. Actuelles, III. Paris, 1958.
Afr 5057.24	Capet, Marcel F. Traité d'économie tropicale. Paris, 1958.
Afr 2731.15.34	Carrouges, Michel. Charles de Foucauld. 3 ed. Paris, 1958.
Afr 8369.58	Carter, G.M. The politics of inequality. N.Y., 1958.
Afr 6010.16	Carter, G.M. Transition in Africa. Boston, 1958.
Afr 8055.35	Cartwright, A.P. South Africa's hall of fame. Cape Town, 1958.
Afr 7122.35	Casimiro, Augusto. Angola e o futuro. Lisboa, 1958.
Afr 2731.15.60	Charbonneau, Jean. La destinée paradoxale de Charles de Foucauld. Paris, 1958.
Afr 5190.16	Charpy, Jacques. La fondation de Dakar. Paris, 1958.
Afr 2030.458	Chevallier, Jacques. Nous. Paris, 1958.
Afr 6214.20	Coleman, J.S. Nigeria. Berkeley, 1958.
Afr 8252.9.10	Colenso, F.B. Colenso letters from Natal. Pietermaritzburg, 1958.
Afr 1494.64	Communist Party of Morocco. Le parti communiste marocain. Paris, 1958.
Afr 3.20	Conference of Independent African States, 1st, Accra, 1958. Konferenz der unabhängigen Staaten Afrikas, April 15-22, 1958. London, 1958.
Afr 7809.59	Congo belge. Genève, 1958.
Afr 11299.69.110	Cope, Jack. The golden oriole. London, 1958.
Afr 3026.25	Coult, L.H. An annotated research bibliography of studies in Arabic. Coral Gables, Fla., 1958.
Afr 8210.18	Cowan, L.G. Local government in West Africa. N.Y., 1958.
Afr 1623.958.10	Cowan, Laing. The economic development of Morocco. Santa Monica, 1958.
Afr 5053.25	Cowan, Laing G. Local government in West Africa. N.Y., 1958.
Afr 618.20.5	Cunha, Joaquim M. da S. Aspectos dos movimentos associativos na Africa negra. Lisboa, 1958.
Afr 718.25.15	Czekanowski, Jan. W głab lasów Aruwimi. Wrocław, 1958.
Afr 609.58.30	Damme, Fred van. Kaapstad-Kairo per auto-stop. Antwerpen, 1958.
Afr 11319.76.1130	Darlow, David John. African heroes. Lovedale, 1958.
Afr 9446.32	Davidson, A.B. Matabele i Mashona v bor'be protiv angliiskoi kolonizatsii, 1888-1897. Moscow, 1958.
Afr 3979.58.10	Davy, Andre. Four thousand miles of adventure. London, 1958.
Afr 650.5	Denis, Jacques. Le phénomène urbain en Afrique Centrale. Bruxelles, 1958.
Afr 650.3	Denis, Jacques. Le phénomène urbain en Afrique Centrale. Namur, 1958.
Afr 626.52	Denis, Jacques. Le phénomène urbain en Afrique Centrale. Namur, 1958.
Afr 5448.10	Devauges, Roland. Le chômage à Brazzaville en 1957. Paris, 1958.
Afr 210.58.10	Diop, Majhemout. Contribution à l'étude des problèmes politiques en Afrique noire. Paris, 1958.
Afr 11058.2	Dodd, A.D. Anthology of short stories. Cape Town, 1958.
Afr 8045.42	Dodd, Anthony D. South African citizenship. Cape Town, 1958.
Afr 2030.90	Dronne, Raymond. La révolution d'Alger. Paris, 1958.
Afr 5342.12	Dupire, Marguerite. Le pays Adioukrou et sa palmeraie. Paris, 1958.
Afr 8678.104	Duplessis, W.C. Highway to harmony. N.Y., 1958.
Afr 2030.110	Duquesne, Jacques. L'Algérie. Bruges, 1958.
Afr 6193.10	Dusantoy, Peter. Community development in Ghana. London, 1958.
Afr Doc 3284.1.73	East Africa High Commission. Kenya; sample population census of Nairobi, 1957-1958, an experiment on sampling methods. Nairobi, 1958.
Afr Doc 3407.357.10	East Africa High Commission. East African Statistical Department. General African census August 1957. Tribal analysis. Nairobi, 1958.
Afr Doc 3407.357.15	East Africa High Commission. East African Statistical Department. Tanganyika population census, 1957. Dar es Salaam, 1958. 2 pam.
Afr Doc 3407.357	East African High Commission. East African Statistical Department. Report on the census of the non-African population taken 20-21 February 1957. Dar es Salaam, 1958.
Afr 3818.2	Elder, Earl. Vindicating a vision. Philadelphia, 1958.
Afr 725.6.5	Elton, J.F. Elton and the East African coast slave-trade. London, 1958.
Afr 9693.5	Epstein, A.L. Politics in an urban African community. Manchester, 1958.
Afr 1609.58	Epton, Nina C. Saints and sorcerers. London, 1958.
Afr 6192.65	Eskelund, Karl. Black man's country. London, 1958.
Afr 2030.55	Fabre-Luce, Alfred. Demain en Algérie. Paris, 1958.
Afr 609.58.20	Favrod, Charles. Le poids de l'Afrique. Paris, 1958.
Afr 2749.58.5	Favrod, Charles F. Sahara. Lausanne, 1958.
Afr 7119.58	Felgas, Helio A. Historia do Congo (Esteres) portugues. Carmona, 1958.
Afr 1259.58	Fielding, Xan. Corsair country. London, 1958.
Afr 1571.17.27	Figueras, André. Lyautey assassine. Paris, 1958.
Afr 1340.40	Filizzola, Sabine. L'organisation de l'état civil au Maroc. Paris, 1958.
Afr 2030.200	Folliet, Joseph. Guerre et paix en Algérie. Lyon, 1958.
Afr 1493.50.5	Fontaine, Pierre. Abd-el-Krim. Paris, 1958.
Afr 8369.58.5	Forman, Lionel. The South African treason trial. N.Y., 1958.
Afr 50.7	Fortes, Meyer. African political systems. London, 1958.
Afr 2731.15.55	Foucauld, Charles de. Oeuvres spirituelles. Paris, 1958.
Afr 5183.958	Fouquet, Joseph. La traite des Arachides dans le pays de Kaolack. St. Louis du Sénégal, 1958.
Afr 2209.58.5	France. Délégation Générale en Algérie. Documents algériens. Paris, 1958.
Afr 5057.26	France. Embassy. U.S. French Africa. N.Y., 1958.
Afr 609.58.25	François, Charles. Eléments du problème africain. Buhavu, 1958.
Afr Doc 6274.4.73	French West Africa. Service des Etudes et Coordination Statistiques et Mécanographiques. Recensement, démographique de Dakar, 1955: résultats définitifs. Paris, 1958-62. 2v.
Afr 8659.58.10	Friend, M.L. Without fear or favour. Cape Town, 1958.

Afr 9439.58	Gale, W.D. Zambezi sunrise. Cape Town, 1958.
Afr 3315.75	Gallean, Georges. Des deux côtés du Canal. Paris, 1958.
Afr 9645.5	Gann, L.H. The birth of a plural society. Manchester, 1958.
Afr 3986.7	Garzonzi, Eva. Old ills and new remedies in Egypt. Cairo, 1958.
Afr 609.58	Gasset, Pierre. L'Afrique, les Africains. v.1-2. Paris, 1958.
Afr 8089.47.10	Geen, M.S. The making of South Africa. Cape Town, 1958.
Afr 2030.205	Gerin, Paul. L'Algérie du 13 mai. Paris, 1958.
Afr 6176.15	Ghana. Information Service Department. Ghana is born, 6th March 1957. London, 1958.
Afr 10615.2	Ghana. Ministry of Information and Broadcasting. Voices of Ghana. Accra, 1958.
Afr 6160.30	Ghana. Regional Constitutional Commission. Regional assemblies. Accra, 1958.
Afr 6196.7	Ghana. Town and Country Planning Division. Accra, a plan for the town. Accra, 1958.
Afr 6460.45	Gicaru, Muga. Land of sunshine. London, 1958.
Afr 4700.5.10	Giglio, Carlo. Etiopia Mar rosso. Roma, 1958. 3v.
Afr 2030.140	Girard, Henri Georges. Pour Djamila Bouhired. Paris, 1958.
Afr 3305.15	Goldobin, A. M. Egipetskaia revoliutsiia 1919 goda. Leningrad, 1958.
Afr 6395.14	Goldthorpe, J.E. Outlines of East African society. Kampala, 1958.
Afr 11433.74.120	Gordimer, N. A world of strangers. N.Y., 1958.
Afr 609.58.15	Goss, Hilton P. Africa, present and potential. Santa Barbara, 1958.
Afr 3143.10	Gottschalk, Hans L. Al-Malik al-Kamil von Egypten und seine Zeit. Wiesbaden, 1958.
Afr 5549.58F	Grandidier, G. Histoire politique et coloniale. V.3. Tananarive, 1958.
Afr 6280.61	Great Britain. Commissions. Nigeria, report. London, 1958.
Afr 679.54.10	Green, Lawrence G. Under a sky like a flame. 2d ed. Cape Town, 1958.
Afr 8659.58.15	Green, Lawrence George. South Africa beachcomber. 1st ed. Cape Town, 1958.
Afr 9493.58	Griffiths, James. Livingstone's Africa. London, 1958.
Afr 630.58.5	Grobler, Jan H. Africa's destiny. 2. ed. Johannesburg, 1958.
Afr 2533.6	Gros, Simone. La politique de Carthage. Paris, 1958.
Afr 626.40	Hance, W.A. African economic development. 1st ed. N.Y., 1958.
Afr 6750.4.2	Handbook of Tanganyika. 2d ed. Dar es Salaam, 1958.
Afr 6060.58	Hansard Society for Parliamentary Government. What are the problems of parliamentary government in West Africa. London, 1958.
Afr 3986.958.15A	Harbison, F.H. Human resources for Egyptian enterprise. N.Y., 1958.
Afr 6149.257.5	Hargreaves, J.D. A life of Sir Samuel Lewis. London, 1958.
Afr 510.80	Harmand, Jack. L'Afrique à l'heure française. Paris, 1958.
Afr 6460.60	Henderson, Ian. The hunt for Kimathi. London, 1958.
Afr 150.20	Henrique, o Navegador, Infante of Portugal. Conselho do Infante Dom Henrique a seu sobrinho El-Rei Dom Afonso V. Lisboa, 1958.
Afr 618.22	Heusch, Luc de. Essais sur le symbolisme de l'inceste royal en Afrique. Bruxelles, 1958.
Afr 5057.20	Hoffherr, Rene. Coopération économique franco-africaine. Paris, 1958.
Afr 8678.98	Hogarth, Paul. People like us. London, 1958.
Afr 8688.7	Hoge, J. Bydraes tot die genealogie van ou afrikaanse families. Amsterdam, 1958.
Afr 870.20	Holdgate, M.W. Mountains in the sea. N.Y., 1958.
Afr 9502.15	Holleman, J.F. African interlude. Cape Town, 1958.
Afr 8289.58	Holt, Edgar. The Boer war. London, 1958.
Afr 3700.16	Holt, P.M. The Mahdist state in the Sudan, 1881-1898. Oxford, 1958.
Afr 1080.25	Hopkins, J.F.P. Medieval Muslim government in Barbary. London, 1958.
Afr 609.58.35	Hornman, W. Sabonjo de onstuimige. Leiden, 1958.
Afr 28.10	Howard University, Washington, D.C. Library. Moorland Foundation. Catalogue of the African collection in the Moorland Foundation. Washington, 1958.
Afr 679.58.5	Howe, R.W. Black star rising. London, 1958.
Afr 150.27	Ibn Al Hatib. El Africa del Norte en El a mal o a lam de Ibn al Jatib. Madrid, 1958.
Afr 6488.10	Ingham, Kenneth. The making of modern Uganda. London, 1958.
Afr 8678.390	Institute of Administrators of Non-European Affairs. The tightrope dancers; report on the 7th Annual Conference, Institute of Administrators of Non-European Affairs. Durban, 1958.
Afr 109.58	Italiaander, Rolf. Der ruhelose Kontinent. 1. Aufl. Düsseldorf, 1958.
Afr Doc 707.353	Italy. Istituto Centrali di Statistica. Censimento della popolazione Italiana e straniera della Somalia 4 novembre 1953. Roma, 1958.
Afr 5343.7	Ivory Coast. Ministère du Plan. Troisieme plan quadriennal de développement économique et social. Abidjan, 1958.
Afr 5343.5	Ivory Coast. Service de la Statistique Générale et de la Mécanographie. Les budgets familiaux des salariés africains en Abidjan. Paris, 1958.
Afr 5343.6	Ivory Coast. Service de la Statistique Générale et de la Mécanographie. Inventaire économique de la Côte-d'Ivoire. Abidjan, 1958.
Afr 8687.245.10	Jackson, Albert. Trader on the veld. Cape Town, 1958.
Afr 11465.14.110	Jacobson, Dan. A long way from London. London, 1958.
Afr 11465.14.100.2	Jacobson, Dan. The price of diamonds. 1st ed. N.Y., 1958.
Afr 609.58.10	Jahn, Janheinz. Muntu. Düsseldorf, 1958.
Afr 4396.15	Jesman, Czesław. The Russians in Ethiopia. London, 1958.
Afr 6392.10	Joelson, F.S. Rhodesia and East Africa. London, 1958.
Afr 8152.73.5	Johannesburg. Public Library. General index of the first edition of King's Campaigning in Kaffirland. Johannesburg, 1958.
Afr 8095.70.2	Johannesburg. Public Library. Index to items of South African interest in Dr. A.W. Burton's sparks from the border anvil. Johannesburg, 1958.
Afr 8678.102	Joshi, Pranshankar Someshwar. Unrest in South Africa. Bombay, 1958.

1958 - cont.

Afr 7812.258 Journées d'Etudes Coloniales, Institut Universitaire des Territoires d'Outre Mer, Antwerp, 1957. Promotion de la société rurale du Congo belge et du Ruanda-Urundi. Bruxelles, 1958.
Afr 8678.110 Jurgens, Isabel. Why cry beloved country. Ilfracombe, 1958.
Afr 9389.58 Kantor, Cyril. The big thirst. London, 1958.
Afr 5248.15 Kaufmann, Herbert. Reiten durch Iforas. Munich, 1958.
Afr 2030.115 Kernmayr, Erich. Algerien in Flammen. 2.Aufl. Göttingen, 1958.
Afr 11005.2 Kiersen, S. English and Afrikaans novels on South African history. Cape Town, 1958.
Afr 8659.58.5 Kirby, Percival Robson. Jacob van Reenen and the Grosvenor expedition of 1790-1791. Johannesburg, 1958.
Afr 6292.1 Kirk-Greene, Anthony. Adamawa, past and present. London, 1958.
Afr 3745.65 Kiselev, V.I. Put sudana v nezavisimosti. Moscow, 1958.
Afr 8338.326 Kock, Willem J. de. Jacob de Villiers Roos, 1869-1940. Kaapstad, 1958.
Afr 3979.58.5 Kondrashov, S.N. Na beregakh Nila. Moscow, 1958.
Afr 8745.20 Krueger, D.W. The age of the generals. Johannesburg, 1958.
Afr 9060.10A Kuper, Leo. Durban. London, 1958.
Afr 3300.85.2A Lacouture, Jean. Egypt in transition. London, 1958.
Afr 1623.958 Lacouture, Jean. Le Maroc a l'epreuve. Paris, 1958.
Afr 609.58.50 Laidley, Fernando. Roteiro africano; primeira volta a Africa en automovel. 3. ed. Lisboa, 1958.
Afr 3986.958 Landes, David S. Bankers and pashas. Cambridge, 1958.
Afr 3986.958.2 Landes, David S. Bankers and pashas. London, 1958.
Afr 6542.10 Larimore, Ann Evans. The alien town. Chicago, 1958.
Afr 2209.58.10 Laurent, Jacques. L'Algérie. Paris, 1958.
Afr 626.47 Leduc, Gaston. Cours d'économie d'outre-mer et du développement. Paris, 1958.
Afr 510.95 Leger, Jean M. Afrique française. Montréal, 1958.
Afr 3.15 Legum, Colin. Bandung, Cairo and Accra. London, 1958.
Afr 2030.145 Lentin, Albert Paul. L'Algérie des colonels. Paris, 1958.
Afr 3069.58 Little, Tom. Egypt. London, 1958.
Afr 28.55 Loewenthal, R. Russian materials on Africa. Washington, 1958.
Afr 2030.150 Lombard, Pierre. Crise algérienne vue d'Alger. Alger, 1958.
Afr 550.95 Lory, Marie Joseph. Hacia el futuro. Andorra, 1958.
Afr 8687.262 Louw, Abraham F. My eerste neentig jaar. Kaapstad, 1958.
Afr 1738.22 Luke, John. Tangier at high tide. Geneva, 1958.
Afr 4389.58 Luther, E.W. Ethiopia today. Stanford, Calif., 1958.
Afr 1487.20 Lutskaia, N.S. Marokko vnovobretaet nezavisimost'. Moscow, 1958.
Afr 5130.25 Ly, Abdoulaye. La compagnie du Sénégal. Paris, 1958.
Afr 5183.2 Ly, Abdoulays. L'état et la production paysanne. Paris, 1958.
Afr 5832.12 Ly-Tio-Fane, Madeleine. Mauritius and the spice trade. Port Louis, 1958. 2v.
Afr 11051.6 MacNab, R.M. Poets in South Africa. Cape Town, 1958.
Afr 2030.165 Mainguy, M. Le pétrole et l'Algérie. Paris, 1958.
Afr 2357.15 Marchand, Max. Guide touristique de l'Oranie agréé par la municipalité. Oran, 1958.
Afr 2623.958 Marini, Fr. Population et production en Tunisie. Auch, 1958.
Afr 1623.958.15F Maroc. Division de la Coordination Économique et du Plan. Plan biennal d'equipement, 1958-1959. Rabat, 1958.
Afr 3315.80 Marshall, S.L.A. Sinai victory. N.Y., 1958.
Afr 8325.33.5 Martin, A.C. The concentration camps, 1900-02. Cape Town, 1958.
Afr 7815.50 Martins, Manuel Alfredo de Morais. Contacto de culturas no Congo Português. Lisboa, 1958.
Afr 9645.10 Mason, Philip. The birth of a dilemma. London, 1958.
Afr 8110.3.37 Merwe, H.J.J.M. van der. Scheepsjournael en de daghregister. Pretoria, 1958-
Afr 7809.58 Meyer, Roger. Introducing the Belgian Congo and the Ruanda-Urundi. Bruxelles, 1958.
Afr 6194.20.15 Meyerowitz, Eva. The Akan of Ghana. London, 1958.
Afr 2030.80 Mezerik, Avrahn G. The Algerian-French conflict. N.Y., 1958.
Afr 50.10 Middleton, John. Tribes without rulers. London, 1958.
Afr 5055.58A Milcent, Ernest. L'A.O.F. entre en scène. Paris, 1958.
Afr 6192.50 Mitchison, Naomi (Haldane). Other peoples' worlds. London, 1958.
Afr 2539.2 Montety, H. Femmes de Tunisie. Paris, 1958.
Afr 2030.155 Montpeyroux, André Brousse de. Autour d'une erreur politique. Alger, 1958.
Afr 1623.958.5 Morocco. L'evolution économique du Maroc dans le cadre du deuxieme plan quadriennal. Casablanca, 1958.
Afr 1609.58.5F Morocco. Ministere des Affaires Etrangeres. Morocco. Rabat, 1958.
Afr 8659.58 Morris, James. South African winter. N.Y., 1958.
Afr 679.58 Mosley, Nicholas. African switchback. London, 1958.
Afr 7815.38 Mueller, Ernst Wilhelm. Le droit de propriété chez les Mongo-bokote. Bruxelles, 1958.
Afr 8678.143 Mueren, K. van der. Apartheid zonder vooroordelen. Antwerpen, 1958.
Afr 1494.40 Muhammad V, Sultan of Morocco. Le Maroc à l'heure de l'indépendance. v.1. Rabat, 1958.
Afr 6280.56 Nigeria. Commission Appointed to Enquire into the Fears of Minorities and the Means of Allaying Them. Report. London, 1958.
Afr 3715.10.2 Nigumi, M.A. A great trusteeship. 2d ed. London, 1958.
Afr 6095.358 Niven, C.R. The land and people of West Africa. London, 1958.
Afr 7176.5 Oliveira Boleo, Jose de. Ensaio sobre geografia agraria. Lisboa, 1958.
Afr 2209.58 Olivier, Claude. Institutrice en Algérie. Paris, 1958.
Afr 2030.400 Pajaud, Henri. La révolution d'Alger. Paris, 1958.
Afr 630.58 Paraf, Pierre. L'ascension des peuples noirs. Paris, 1958.
Afr 8678.100 Paton, Alan. Hope for South Africa. London, 1958.
Afr 8678.90 Paton, D.M. Church and race in South Africa. London, 1958.
Afr 7946.5 Pauwels, M. Imana et le culte des Manes au Rwanda. Bruxelles, 1958.
Afr 8369.58.15 Paver, Bertram G. His own oppressor. London, 1958.
Afr 628.258 Piguion, René. Reveil de culture. Port au Prince, 1958.
Afr 8252.228.10 Pirow, Oswald. James Barry Munnik Hertzog. London, 1958.
Afr 3986.958.5 Platt, Raye R. Egypt, a compendium. N.Y., 1958.
Afr 626.45 Potekhin, I.I. Afrika iuzhnee Sakhary. Moscow, 1958.

1958 - cont.

Afr 5056.158 Pouquet, Jean. L'Afrique occidentale française. 2.ed. Paris, 1958.
Afr 530.30 Premesse al lavoro italiano in Africa. Roma, 1958.
Afr 626.49 Princeton University Conference. Emerging sub-Sahara Africa. Princeton, 1958.
Afr 1869.58 Question algerienne. Paris, 1958.
Afr 1618.5F Rackow, Ernst. Beiträge zur kenntnis der Materiellen kultur nordwest-marokkos. Wiesbaden, 1958.
Afr 9854.18 Retief, Malcolm. William Murray of Nyasaland. Lovedale, 1958.
Afr 9603.5 Rhodes-Livingstone Institute, Lusaka, Northern Rhodesia. 11th Conference, Lusaka, 1958. Present interrelations in Central African rural and urban life. Lusaka, 1958.
Afr 9515.5.5F Rhodesia and Nyasaland. Report on urban African budget survey in Salisbury, 1957/58. Salisbury, 1958. 2v.
Afr Doc 3889.358 Rhodesia and Nyasaland. Central Statistical Office. Preliminary report on the Salisbury African Demographic survey, August/September, 1958. Salisbury, 1958.
Afr 9435.14.5 Rhodesia and Nyasaland. Commission Appointed to Divide the Territory of Northern Rhodesia into Electoral Districts. Report. Salisbury, 1958.
Afr 9435.14.10 Rhodesia and Nyasaland. Commission Appointed to Divide the Territory of Southern Rhodesia into Electoral Districts. Report. Salisbury, 1958.
Afr 9435.14 Rhodesia and Nyasaland. Commission Appointed to Divide the Territory of Nyasaland into Electoral Districts. Report. Salisbury, 1958..
Afr 9500.35 Rhodesian Institute of African Affairs, Bulawayo, South Africa. The progress of Africans in Southern Rhodesia. Bulawayo, 1958.
Afr 679.58.10 Richard Molard, Jacques. Problèmes humains en Afrique occidentale. 2. éd. Paris, 1958.
Afr 2030.240 Rispy, Franz. Sie klagen an. Zürich, 1958.
Afr 5749.58F Robequain, Chas. Madagascar et les bases dispersees de l'union française. Paris, 1958. 2v.
Afr 7560.14.5 Roeykens, A. Léopold II et l'Afrique, 1855-1880. Bruxelles, 1958.
Afr 10115.2 Rutherfoord, Peggy. Darkness and light. London, 1958.
Afr 7565.19 Ruytjens, E. Historisch ontstaan der grens van de onafhankelijke. Bruxelles, 1958.
Afr 6275.46 Ryan, Isobel. Black man's palaver. London, 1958.
Afr 8369.58.10A Sampson, Anthony. The treason cage. London, 1958.
Afr 679.58.15 Santarem, Manuel Francisco de B. Memoria sobre a prioridade dos descobrimentos. Lisboa, 1958.
Afr 8678.1.10F Schapera, I. Select bibliography of South African native life and problems. 2nd supplement. Cape Town, 1958.
Afr 4571.3 Schneiders, Toni. L'Ethiopie. Paris, 1958.
Afr 8685.70.5 Schwaer, J. Deutsche in Kaffraria. King Williams Town, 1958.
Afr 8678.94 Scott, Michael. A time to speak. London, 1958.
Afr 2030.105 Serigny, Alain de. La révolution du 13 mai. Paris, 1958.
Afr 2030.160 Servier, Jean. Adieu Djebels. Paris, 1958.
Afr 9860.276.5 Shepperson, George. Independent African; John Chilembwe and the origins, setting and significance of the Nyasaland native rising of 1915. Edinburgh, 1958.
Afr 2731.15.65 Six, Jean F. Itinéraire spirituel de Charles de Foucauld. Paris, 1958.
Afr 8659.50.20 Sledzinski, Waclaw. Rzeka Limpopo wpada do Tamizy. Warszawa, 1958.
Afr 2438.32 Snoussi, Mohamed. Les collectivités locales en Tunisie. Paris, 1958.
Afr 4753.10 Somaliland, Italian. Camera di commercio, industria ed agricoltura. Bibliografia somala. Mogadiscio, 1958.
Afr 6277.20 Stapleton, G.B. The wealth of Nigeria. London, 1958.
Afr 2536.10.5 Stephane, R. La Tunisie de Bourguiba. Paris, 1958.
Afr 630.59.5 Stephens, Richard W. Population pressures in Africa, south of the Sahara. Washington, 1958.
Afr 3199.58 Stewart, D.S. Young Egypt. London, 1958.
Afr Doc 1307.356.15 Sudan. Population Census Office. 21 facts about the Sudanese. First population census of Sudan, 1955-56. Khartoum? 1958.
Afr 8030.15.10 Suid-afrikaanse argiefstukke. v.1- Parow, 1958. 5v.
Afr 3986.958.10 Sultanov, A.F. Polozhenie egipetskogo krestianstvo pered zemelskoi reformoi 1952 goda. Moscow, 1958.
Afr 10015.3 Sulzer, Peter. Christ erscheint am Kongo. Heilbronn, 1958.
Afr 609.58.45 Summer, Roger. Inyanga. Cambridge, 1958.
Afr 5019.58 Suret-Canale, Jean. Afrique noire, occidentale et centrale. Paris, 1958. 2v.
Afr 9192.15F Swaziland. Treasury. Revenue and expenditure, 1947-1957. Mababane, 1958.
Afr 5396.2 Tardits, C. Porto-Novo. Paris, 1958.
Afr 6541.30 Taylor, John Vernon. The growth of the church in Buganda. London, 1958.
Afr 210.58.5 Tevoedjre, Albert. L'Afrique revoltée. Paris, 1958.
Afr 2030.50.5 Tillion, G. Algeria. 1st Amer. ed. N.Y., 1958.
Afr 550.85 Toppenberg, Valdemar E. Africa has my heart. Mountain View, 1958.
Afr 5183.958.5 Touze, R.L. Mieux vivre dans notre village; lettres a Seydon. Dakar?, 1958.
Afr 630.58.10 Traore, Bakary. Le théâtre négro-africain. Paris, 1958.
Afr 3979.58 Tregenza, L.A. Egyptian years. London, 1958.
Afr 10690.89.110 Tutuola, Amos. The brave African huntress. London, 1958.
Afr 1270.2 United States. Department of Defense. A pocket guide to North Africa. Washington, 1958.
Afr 2000.8 Uzighan, 'Ammar. Le meilleur combat. Paris, 1958.
Afr 9400.10.25 Vanderpost, Laurens. The lost world of the Kalahari. N.Y., 1958.
Afr 210.58.15 Van Nguen. Les carnets d'un diplomate. Paris, 1958.
Afr 6192.55 Varley, W.J. The geography of Ghana. London, 1958.
Afr 5967.2 Veciana Vilaldach, Antonio de. La secta del Bwiti en la Guinea española. Madrid, 1958.
Afr 7815.32 Verbeken, A. La révolte des Batetela en 1895. Bruxelles, 1958.
Afr 14692.41.100 Victor, Geraldo Bessa. Cubata abandonada. Lisboa, 1958.
Afr 2030.225 Vidal-Naquet, Pierre. L'affaire Audin. Paris, 1958.
Afr 2025.11.15 Vignes, Kenneth. Le gouverneur général Tirman. Paris, 1958. 2v.
Afr 6164.9.2 Ward, W.E.F. A history of Ghana. 2d ed. London, 1958.
Afr 9700.30 Watson, W. Tribal cohesion in a money economy. Manchester, 1958.
Afr 6192.45 Wolfson, Freda. Pageant of Ghana. London, 1958.
Afr 8252.8.25 Wrench, Evelyn. Alfred Lord Milner. London, 1958.
Afr 2945.26.25 Ziadeh, N. Abdo. Sanusiyah. Leiden, 1958.

1958 - cont.

Afr 11899.98.100   Zyl, Tania. Shadow and wall. Cape Town, 1958.

1959

Afr 11211.5   Achebe, Chinua. Things fall apart. N.Y., 1959.
Afr 3986.959   Addison, Herbert. Sun and shadow at Aswan. London, 1959.
Afr 609.52.15   Agundis, T. Campamentos en Africa. México, 1959.
Afr 6470.106   Ainsworth, J.D. John Ainsworth. London, 1959.
Afr 6193.7   Akwawuah, Kwadwo A. Prelude to Ghana's industrialization. London, 1959.
Afr 2030.310   Algeria. Délégation Générale. Algeria's development. Algiers, 1959.
Afr 2030.340.5   Algerian Front of National Liberation. Miscellaneous papers. n.p., 1959-1961. 43 pam.
Afr 8687.109   Altmann, Hendrik. Overdrafts and overwork. Cape Town, 1959.
Afr 10671.52.110   Aluko, Timothy Mofolorunso. One man, one wife. Lagos, 1959.
Afr 2030.230   Alwan, Mohamed. Algeria before the United Nations. N.Y., 1959.
Afr 6218.8   Anyiam, F.U. Men and matters in Nigerian politics 1934-58. Yaba, 1959.
Afr 10005.2A   Approaches to African literature. Ibadan, 1959.
Afr 1409.18   Arribas Palau, Mariano. Cartas arabes de Marruecos en tiempo de Mawlay al Yazid, 1790-1792. Tetuan, 1959.
Afr 8925.20   Auin, P.J. Foods and feeding habits of the Pedi. Johannesburg, 1959.
Afr 2030.459.5   Aumeran, Adolphe. Paix en Algérie. Paris, 1959.
Afr 7812.259   Baeck, Louis. Economische ontwikkeling en sociale structuur in Belgisch-Kongo. Leuven, 1959.
Afr 5056.159   Balez, Eugene. Vagabondage en Afrique noire. Toulouse, 1959.
Afr 9389.59   Balsan, Francois. Nouvelles aventures au Kalahari. Paris, 1959.
Afr 1069.59   Barbour, Nevill. A survey of North-west Africa. London, 1959.
Afr 9038.5   Barker, Anthony. Giving and receiving. London, 1959.
Afr 555.125   Barker, Anthony. The man next to me. N.Y., 1959.
Afr 7309.59   Barreiros, Pinho. Africa, mae e madrasta. Coimbra, 1959.
Afr 38.2F   Baxter, T.W. Archival facilities in sub-Saharan Africa. n.p., 1959.
Afr 555.120   Beach, Peter. Benedictine and Moor. N.Y., 1959.
Afr 6276.4   Beier, Vlli. A year of sacred festivals in one Yoruba town. Marina, 1959.
Afr 7850.52F   Belgium. Chambre des Représentants. Commission parlementaire chargée de faire une enquête. Bruxelles, 1959.
Afr 7809.59.10   Belgium. Office de l'Information et des Relations. Belgian Congo. Brussels, 1959.
Afr 1494.50   Ben Barka el Mehdi. Problèmes d'édification du Maroc et du Moghreb. Paris, 1959.
Afr 628.259   Betancourt, J.R. El Negro. La Habana, 1959.
Afr 2030.215   Beuchard, Georges. L'équivoque algérienne. Paris, 1959.
Afr 6470.135   Binks, H.K. African rainbow. London, 1959.
Afr 11219.66.100   Bloom, Harry. Transvaal episode. Berlin, 1959.
Afr 6192.70   Boateng, E.A. A geography of Ghana. Cambridge, Eng., 1959.
Afr 9525.224   Boggie, Jeannie. A husband and a farm in Rhodesia. Gwelo, S.R., 1959.
Afr 710.35   Booth, Newall S. This is Africa south of the Sahara. N.Y., 1959.
Afr 1609.59   Bourgeois, Paul. L'univers de l'ecolier marocain. v.1-5. Rabat, 1959-60.
Afr 2536.10.15   Bourguiba, H. La bataille de l'évacuation, 17 avril 1956-17 février 1959. Tunis, 1959.
Afr 505.35   Bradley, K. Britain's purpose in Africa. N.Y., 1959.
Afr 6195.10   Braun, Richard. Letters from Ghana. Philadelphia, 1959.
Afr 8028.115   Brett, E.A. Tentative list of books and pamphlets on South Africa. Johannesburg, 1959.
Afr 6310.42   British Information Services. Regional cooperation in British East Africa. N.Y., 1959.
Afr 8095.58   Brookes, E.H. The relationships between history and political science. Natal, 1959.
Afr 8678.120   Brown, William O. Race relations in the American South and in South Africa. Boston, 1959.
Afr 4969.59   Buchholzer, John. The Horn of Africa. London, 1959.
Afr 9748.193   Bulpin, Thomas Victor. Trail of the copper king. Cape Town, 1959.
Afr 11051.7   Butler, G. A book of South African verse. London, 1959.
Afr 635.75F   C.S.A. Meeting of Specialists on the Basic Psychology of African and Madagascan Populations, Tannarvio, Madagascar, 1959. Recommendations and reports. London, 1959.
Afr 4513.59   Caffo, Aventino. Il genio militare nella campagna in Africa orientale. Roma, 1959.
Afr 6879.59   Cairns, John C. Bush and boma. London, 1959.
Afr 6720.59   Cameroons, French. Cameroun. Paris, 1959.
Afr 9700.3   Cannison, Ian. The Luapula people of Northern Rhodesia. Manchester, 1959.
Afr 7850.20   Caprasse, P. Leaders africains en milieu urbain. Bruxelles, 1959.
Afr 7875.5   Caprasse, Pierre. Leaders africains en milieu urbain, Elisabethville. Bruxelles, 1959.
Afr 6979.59   Carnegie, Sacha. Red dust of Africa. London, 1959.
Afr 609.59   Carpenter, G.W. The way in Africa. N.Y., 1959.
Afr 3979.59   Carrington, R. The tears of Isis. London, 1959.
Afr Doc 7207.360   Central African Republic. Service de la Statistique Generale. Enquête démographique. n.p., 1959-60.
Afr 7815.26   Ceulemans, P. La question arabe et le Congo, 1883-1892. Bruxelles, 1959.
Afr 7911.5   Chome, Jules. La passion de Simon Kimbangu. 2. ed. Bruxelles, 1959.
VAfr 5225.6   Clair, Andrée. Le fabuleur empire du Mali. Paris, 1959.
Afr 2030.210   Clark, Michael. Algeria in turmoil. N.Y., 1959.
Afr 1680.12   Clarke, Bryan. Berber village. London, 1959.
Afr 9506.4   Clinton, Iris. 'These vessels' the story of Inyati, 1859-1959. Bulawayo, 1959.
Afr 9795.15   Cluston-Brock, Guy. Down in Nyasaland. London, 1959.
Afr 505.30   Cohen, Andrew. British policy in changing Africa. Evanston, 1959.
Afr 6420.70   Cole, Keith. Kenya. London, 1959.
Afr 8847.83.5   Collier, Joy. Stellenbosch revisited. Stellenbosch, 1959.
Afr 9610.15   Colson, Elizabeth. Seven tribes of BritishCentral Afrika. Manchester, 1959.
Afr 7183.25   Companhia de Diamantes de Angola. Breve noticia sobre o Museu do Dundo. Lisbon, 1959.

1959 - cont.

Afr 500.70F   Conférence des Institutions Européennes, Rome, 1958. Documentation des travaux de la première conférence. Rome, 1959.
Afr 115.90   Conference on History and Archaeology. History and archaeology in Africa. London, 1959.
Afr 7535.15   Congo, Belgian. Laws, statutes, etc. Codes et lois du Congo belge. V.1-3 (V.1, 1960) 8.ed. Bruxelles, 1959. 3v.
Afr 6664.10   Cornevin, Robert. Histoire du Togo. Paris, 1959.
Afr 6535.20   Cott, Hugh B. Uganda in black and white. London, 1959.
Afr 9029.59   Cowles, Raymond Bridgman. Zulu journal. Berkeley, 1959.
Afr 4008.5   Cramer, Maria. Das christlich-koptische Ägypten einst und heute. Wiesbaden, 1959.
Afr 6055.5   Crowder, Michael. Pagans and politicians. London, 1959.
Afr 2030.220   Darboy, Marcel. Jeunesse de France en Algérie. Paris, 1959.
Afr 2209.59   Davezies, Robert. Le front. Paris, 1959.
Afr 609.59.5   Davidson, Basil. The lost cities of Africa. 1st ed. Boston, 1959.
Afr 5753.20   Decary, Raymond. Les ordalies et sacrifices rituels chez les Anains Malgaches. Pau, 1959.
Afr 210.59A   Decraene, Philippe. Le panafricanisme. Paris, 1959.
Afr 626.60   Degraft-Johnson, John C. An introduction to the African economy. Bombay, 1959.
Afr 1494.45   Dehedin, Charles. Adieu Maroc. Paris, 1959.
Afr 11320.50.100   Delius, Anthony. The last division. Cape Town, 1959.
Afr 7809.59.5   Delooz, Eugenus. Zwarte handen en blank kapitaal. Antwerpen, 1959.
Afr 7575.67   Demany, Fernand. S.O.S. Congo. Bruxelles, 1959.
Afr 5760.18   Deschamps, H.J. Les migrations. Paris, 1959.
Afr 7575.45   Dessart, C. Le Congo à tombeau ouvert. Bruxelles, 1959.
Afr 5448.12F   Devauges, Roland. Les conditions sociologiques d'une politique d'urbanisme à Brazzaville. Paris, 1959.
Afr 1723.20   Deverdun, G. Marrakech, des origines à 1912. Rabat, 1959. 2v.
Afr 2030.180   Dion, Michel. Armée d'Algérie et la pacification. Paris, 1959.
Afr 109.59.25   Diop, Cheikh A. Etude comparée des systèmes politiques et sociaux de l'Europe et de l'Afrique, de l'antiquité à la formation des états modernes. Paris 1959.
Afr 109.60   Diop, Cheikh A. L'unité culturelle de l'Afrique. Paris, 1959.
Afr 4559.56.2   Doresse, Jean. Ethiopia. London, 1959.
Afr 7015.20A   Duffy, James Edward. Portuguese Africa. Cambridge, 1959.
Afr 2223.959.5   Dumoulin, Roger. La structure asymétrique de l'économie algérienne. Paris, 1959.
Afr 9445.35   Dunn, Cyril. Central African witness. London, 1959.
Afr 8678.200   Dupreez, Andries B. Inside the South African crucible. Kaapstad, 1959.
Afr 7540.43   Durieux, André. Souveraineté et communauté belgo-congolaise. Bruxelles, 1959.
Afr 626.66   East Africa High Commission. Domestic income and product in Kenya. Nairobi, 1959.
Afr 6392.15   East Africa High Commission. Some notes on industrial development in East Africa. 2nd ed. Nairobi, 1959.
Afr 6881.259   East Africa High Commission. East Africa Statistical Division. Tanganyika Office. The gross domestic product of Tanganyika. v.1-2. Dar es Salaam, 1959.
Afr Doc 3284.1.75   East Africa High Commission. East African Statistical Department. Kenya Unit. The patterns of income, expenditure and consumption of Africans in Nairobi, 1957-1958. Nairobi, 1959.
Afr 5055.59   Ehrhard, Jean. Communauté ou sécession. Paris, 1959.
Afr 2308.16   Espel, Françoise. Alger. Paris, 1959.
Afr 1965.25.5   Estailleur-Chanteraine, Phillippe d'. L'émir magnanime. Paris, 1959.
Afr 6164.12   Fage, J. Ghana. Madison, Wis., 1959.
Afr 2030.320   Fanon, Frantz. L'an cinq de la révolution algérienne. Paris, 1959.
Afr 2030.190   Favrod, Charles. La révolution algérienne. Paris, 1959.
Afr 1110.20   Fernan, F.W. Arabischer Westen. 1. Aufl. Stuttgart, 1959.
Afr 2030.265F   Flament, Marc. Aucune bête au monde. Paris, 1959.
Afr 2948.18   Fontaine, Pierre. La mort étrange de C. Kilian. Paris, 1959.
Afr 6098.5   Fortes, Meyer. Oedipus and Job in West African religion. Cambridge, Eng., 1959.
Afr 626.62   France. Centre National du Commerce Extérieur. Memento commercial. Paris, 1959.
Afr 5426.100.50   Franck, Frederick. Days with Albert Schweitzer. N.Y., 1959.
Afr 2030.270   Franza, Angelo. La rivoluzione algerina. Milano, 1959.
Afr 5407.8   French Equatorial Africa. Service de Coordination des Affaires Economiques. L'A.E.F. économique et sociale, 1947-1958. Paris, 1959.
Afr 3826.2   Gaitskell, Arthur. Gezira. London, 1959.
Afr 6541.5   Gale, Hubert Philip. Uganda and Mill Hill fathers. London, 1959.
Afr 5053.20   Gandolfi, Alain. L'administration territoriale en Afrique noire de langue française. Aix-en-Provence, 1959.
Afr 2030.295   Gangrène. Paris, 1959.
Afr 6212.25   Gaskiya Corporation, Zaria, Nigeria. Federation of Nigeria. Zaria, 1959.
Afr 49016.5   Gbadamosi, Bakare. Yoruba poetry. Ibadan, 1959.
Afr 6193.20   Ghana. Second development plans. Accra, 1959.
Afr 6176.44F   Ghana. Commission Appointed to Enquire into the Matters Disclosed at the Trial of Captain Benjamin Awhaitey, before a Court Martial, and the Surrounding Circumstances. Proceedings and report, with minutes of evidence taken before the commission, January-March, 1959. Accra, 1959.
Afr 5316.5   Gigon, Fernand. Guinée, état pilote. Paris, 1959.
Afr 5312.5A   Guinée. Paris, 1959.
Afr 710.22   Gunther, John. Meet central Africa. London, 1959.
Afr 4108.2   Habachi, Labib. Aswan. Le Caire, 1959.
Afr 2618.25   Hammerton, Thomas. Tunisia unveiled. London, 1959.
Afr 6160.20   Hansard Society for Parliamentary Government. The parliament of Ghana. London, 1959.
Afr 1200.120   Hart, W. Annet. Poker om Noord-Afrika. Den Haag, 1959.
Afr 109.59.10   Hatch, John C. Everyman's Africa. London, 1959.
Afr 8055.45   Hattersley, Alan H. Oliver the spy. Cape Town, 1959.
Afr 109.59.15   Healy, A.M. The map approach to African history. London, 1959.
Afr 8657.67   Hemmy, Gysbert. De Promontorio Bonae Spei, a Latin oration. Cape Town, 1959.
Afr 3675.45   Hill, R.L. Egypt in the Sudan. London, 1959.
Afr 609.58.36   Hornman, W. De gesel van angst. Leiden, 1959.

Afr 7575.17 Hostelet, Georges. Pour éviter l'anarchie puis là. Bruxelles, 1959.

Afr 7575.15A Hostelet, Georges. Le problème politique capital au Congo et en Afrique noire. Burxelles, 1959.

Afr 8687.308 Huenermann, Wilhelm. Der gehorsame Rebell. Innsbruck, 1959.

Afr 6470.231 Huxley, Elspeth Grant. The flame trees of Thika. London, 1959.

Afr 1085.3 Idris, Hady R. LaBerbérie orientale sous les Zirides, Xe-XIIe siècles. v.1-2. Paris, 1959.

Afr 9599.59 Ingerman, Karel J.J. Sluimerend paradijs. Amsterdam, 1959.

Afr 530.52 Instituto Italiano per l'Africa. Permesse al lavoro italiano in Africa. Roma, 1959.

Afr 1020.5F International African Institute. North-east Africa. London, 1959.

Afr 8847.53F Irving, James. Macleantown. Grahamstown, 1959.
Afr 7312.20 Italy. Istituto Nazionale per il Commercio Estero. Mozambico. Roma, 1959.

Afr 2535.2 Ivanov, N.A. Sovremennyi Tunis. Moscow, 1959.
Afr 8057.5 Jaarsveld, F.A. van. Die afrikaner en sy geskiedenis. Kaapstad, 1959.

Afr 11465.14.120 Jacobson, Dan. The Zulu and the zeide. 1st ed. Boston, 1959.

Afr 13305.5 Jadot, Joseph. Les écrivains africains du Congo belge et du Ruanda-Urundi. Bruxelles, 1959.

Afr 7809.57.5 Jonchleere, K. Kongo, met het blote oog. Amsterdam, 1959.
Afr 6192.75 Joslin, Mike. Im Tempel der bösen Geister. Wiesbaden, 1959.

Afr 5460.10 Kalck, Pierre. Réalités oubanguiennes. Paris, 1959.
Afr 7815.23 Kanza, Thomas. Tot ou tard. Bruxelles, 1959.
Afr 9510.10.10 Kariba. Kariba. Bloemfontein, 1959.
Afr 6455.100 Keller, W.P. Africa's wild glory. London, 1959.
Afr 8687.260 Kentridge, Morris. I recall. Johannesburg, 1959.
Afr 6455.50 Kenya Colony and Protectorate. Kenya. 3d ed. London, 1959.

Afr 555.100 Keys, Clara E. We pioneered in Portuguese East Africa. 1st ed. N.Y., 1959.

Afr 9506.7 King, Paul. Mission in Southern Rhodesia. Inyati, 1959.
Afr 710.40 Kittler, Glenn D. Equatorial Africa. N.Y., 1959.
Afr 8678.255 Krishna Mevor, Vengalil Kreshnan. Question of race conflict resulting from the policies of apartheid. New Delhi, 1959.

Afr 8289.59 Kruger, Rayne. Good-bye Dolly Gray. London, 1959.
Afr 109.46.10 Labouret, H. L'Afrique précoloniale. Paris, 1959.
Afr 7549.59.15 Lacger, L. de. Ruanda. Kabgayi, 1959.
Afr 5057.30 Lacroix, Alain. Les conditions de la mise en valeur de l'Afrique occidentale française. Paris, 1959.

Afr 3979.59.5 Laporte, Jean. Première descente du Nil de l'Equateur à la Méditerranée. Paris, 1959.

Afr 28.45F Lavanaux, Maurice. A selected annotated bibliography on Africa. n.p., 1959.

Afr 5485.5 Lebeuf, Annie M.D. Les populations du Tchad. Paris, 1959.
Afr 2030.147 Lentin, Albert Paul. L'Algérie des colonels. Paris, 1959.
Afr 5580.3.10 Lepecky, M.B. Maurycy August Beniowski, zdob. Madagaskaru. Warszawa, 1959.

Afr 11517.76.100 Lerner, Laurence. Domestic interior. London, 1959.
Afr 11517.76.110 Lerner, Laurence. The Englishmen. London, 1959.
Afr 1635.20 Lesne, Marcel. Evolution d'un groupement berbere. Rabat, 1959.

Afr 7549.59.5 Lévêque, Robert J. Le Congo belge. Bruxelles, 1959.
Afr 9436.5 Leys, Colin. European politics in Southern Rhodesia. Oxford, 1959.

Afr Doc 807.354 Libya. Census and Statistical Department. General population census of Libya, 1954; report and tables. Tripoli, 1959.

Afr 9558.14.5 Livingstone, D. Family letters, 1841-1856. London, 1959. 2v.
Afr 7012.5 Lobiano do Rego. Patria Morena da vista da maior epopeia lusiada. Macierra de Cambra, 1959.

Afr 1658.45 Lutskaia, N.S. Respublika rif. Moscow, 1959.
Afr 3079.59 Lutskii, V.B. Ocherki po istorii arabskikh stran. Moscow, 1959.

Afr 5640.12 Lyautey, Pierre. Gallieni. 6. ed. Paris, 1959.
Afr 8028.30F Macdonald, A.M. A contribution to a bibliography on university apartheid. Cape Town, 1959.

Afr 7945.3 Makarakiza, André. La dialectique des Barundi. Bruxelles, 1959.

Afr 7933.3 Maquet, J.J. Elections en société féodale. Bruxelles, 1959.

Afr 7912.15.35 Maquet-Tombu, Jeanne. Le siècle marche; vie du chef congolais Lutunu. 2. éd. Bruxelles, 1959?

Afr 510.100 Marchard, Jean Paul. Vérités sur l'Afrique noire. Paris, 1959.

Afr 11558.76.100 Markowitz, A. Market street. Johannesburg, 1959.
Afr 7812.259.5 Martynov, Vladimir A. Kongo pod gnetom imperializma. Moskva, 1959.

Afr 175.5 Matep, Benjamin. Heurts et malheurs des rapports Europe-Afrique. Paris, 1959.

Afr 6397.2 Matheson, Elizabeth Mary. An enterprise so perilous. London, 1959.

Afr 8667.65 Meyer, P.J. Trek verder. Kaapstad, 1959.
Afr 6275.100 Miller, E.P. Change here for Kano. Zaria, 1959.
Afr 6883.25 Molohan, M.J.B. Detribalization. Dar es Salaam, 1959.
Afr 609.60 Moorehead, Alan. No room in the ark. N.Y., 1959.
Afr 626.54 Morgaut, Marc E. Un dialogue nouveau. Paris, 1959.
Afr 7575.10 Morres, Jacques. L'équinoxe de janvier. Bruxelles, 1959.
Afr 5406.259 Motley, Mary. Devils in waiting. London, 1959.
Afr 2030.370 Moureau, Maurice. Des Algériens accusent. Paris, 1959.
Afr 8849.10 Mphahlele, E. Down Second avenue. London, 1959.
Afr 8340.40 Mukherji, S.B. Indian minority in South Africa. New Delhi, 1959.

Afr 8355.40 Mukherji, S.B. Indian minority in South Africa. New Delhi, 1959.

Afr 2804.5 Murabet, Mohammed. A bibliography of Libya. Valetta, 1959.

Afr 630.59 Murdock, George. Africa. N.Y., 1959.
Afr 8849.12 Murray, Andrew. The political philosophy of J.A. de Mist. Cape Town, 1959.

Afr 635.60 Muthesius, A. Die Afrikanerin. Düsseldorf, 1959.
Afr 6484.8 Namirembe Conference. Agreed recommendations of the Namirembe Conference. Entebbe, 1959? 2 pam.

Afr 3310.10.5.5 Nasser, G.A. The philosophy of the revolution. Buffalo, 1959.

Afr 9040.7 Natal. Natal official guide. Cape Town, 1959.

Afr 150.2.20 Nemesio, Vitorino. Vida e obra do Infante Dom Henrique. Lisboa, 1959. 2v.

Afr 4259.59 Neubacher, Hermann. Die Festung der Löwen. Olten, 1959.
Afr 5252.5 Niger. Constitution. Constitution. Paris, 1959.
Afr 6277.35 Nigeria. Economic Council. Economic survey of Nigeria, 1959. Lagos, 1959.

Afr Doc 2308.300F Nigeria. Federal Office of Statistics. Report on employment and ear-nings inquiry, Sept., 1959. Lagos, 1959?

Afr 2731.15.52 Nord, Pierre. Charles de Foucauld. Paris, 1959.
Afr 3986.959.10 Nour, Mustafa M. Les rapports entre l'évolution économique en Egypte. Fribourg, 1959.

Afr 6195.15 Oelschner, Walter. Landung in Osu. Stuttgart, 1959.
Afr 2030.250 Oppermann, Thomas. Die algerische Frage. Stuttgart, 1959.
Afr 11669.13.5 Packer, Joy (P). The high roof. 1st ed. Philadelphia, 1959.

Afr 4559.59 Pakenham, T. The mountains of Rasselas. N.Y., 1959.
Afr 8688.5 Pama, C. Die wapens van die ou afrikaanse families. Kaapstad, 1959.

Afr 8687.105 Paton, Alan. The people wept. Kloop, 1959.
Afr 7045.25 Pattec, Richard. Portugal em Africa. Lisboa, 1959.
Afr 530.32 Pattee, Richard. Portugal na Africa contemporanea. Coimbra, 1959.

Afr 210.53.2 Paulme, Denise. Les civilisations africaines. 2. ed. Paris, 1959.

Afr 7540.41 Paulus, Jean Pierre. Droit public du Congo belge. Bruxelles, 1959.

Afr 8687.380 Pretorius, G. Man van die daad. Kaapstad, 1959.
Afr 2030.315 Priester, Eva. In Algerien sprechen die Gewehre. 1. Aufl. Berlin, 1959.

Afr 5640.45 Rabemananjara, Jacques. Nationalisme et problemes Malgaches. Paris, 1959.

Afr 8676.59 Rabie, Zacharias Johannes. Der Staat als Unternehmer in der Union von Südafrika. Köln, 1959.

Afr 2030.245 Rahmani, Abd el-Kader. L'affaire des officiers algériens. Paris, 1959.

Afr 1869.59 Rainero, Romain. Storia dell Algeria. Firenze, 1959.
Afr 699.59 Randles, W.G. L'image du sud-est Africain dans la littérature. Lisboa, 1959.

Afr 7549.59.10 Ranieri, Liane. Les relations entre l'état indépendant du Congo et l'Italie. Bruxelles, 1959.

Afr 6194.10.6 Rattray, R.S. Religion and art in Ashanti. London, 1959.
Afr 9545.5 Rhodes-Livingston Institute, Lusaka. From tribal rule to modern government. Lusaka, 1959.

Afr 9435.15 Rhodesia and Nyasaland. The constitution of the federation of Rhodesia and Nyasaland. Salisbury, 1959.

Afr 9609.15F Rhodesia and Nyasaland. Report on a economic survey of Nyasaland. Salisbury, 1959.

Afr Doc 3808.7F Rhodesia and Nyasaland. Central Statistical Office. The 1953-55 demographic sample survey of the indigenous African population of Southern Rhodesia. Salisbury, 1959.

Afr 7809.59.15 Rhodius, Georges. Congo 1959. Bruxelles, 1959.
Afr 7369.59.5 Richardson, N.R. Liberia's past and present. London, 1959.

Afr 5960.9 Rios, Mateos. La España ignorada. Barcelona, 1959.
Afr 4559.55 Rittlinger, H. Ethiopian adventure. London, 1959.
Afr 8089.59 Robertaggi, C. Breve storia del Sud Africa. Firenze, 1959.

Afr 8028.7F Roberts, E.S. Preliminary finding-list of Southern African pamphlets. Cape Town, 1959.

Afr 8847.90 Rosenthal, Eric. One hundred years of Victoria West, 1859-1959. Victoria West, 1959.

Afr 2030.170 Rosfelder, André. L'Algérie à bâtir. Alger, 1959.
Afr 609.59.10 Ross, Emory. Africa distributed. N.Y., 1959.
Afr 3275.17.5.2 Rotshtein, F.A. Zakhvat i zakabalenie Egipta. Moscow, 1959.

Afr 11764.12.100 Sachs, Bernard. South African personalities and places. Johannesburg, 1959.

Afr 200.16 Santa-Rita, José. A Africa nas relações. Lisboa, 1959.
Afr 7176.16 Santos, A.L.F. dos. Estrutura do comercio externo de Angola. Lisboa, 1959.

Afr 2030.459 Scheer, Maximillian. Algerien. 1. Aufl. Berlin, 1959.
Afr 8687.335.5 Schonegevel, Bernardo. This much I'll tell. Cape Town, 1959.

Afr 109.59.5 Scott, John. Africa, world's last frontier. N.Y., 1959.
Afr 2223.959.2 Secrétariat Social d'Alger. La micro-industrie Alger, 1959.

Afr 2223.959 Secrétariat Social d'Alger. Le sous-développement en Algérie. Alger, 1959.

Afr 5055.59.10 Senghor, Leopold. African socialism. N.Y., 1959.
Afr 5053.15 Senghor, Leopold. Congrès constitutif de P.F.A. Paris, 1959.

Afr 2030.390 Servier, Jean. Demain en Algérie. Paris, 1959.
Afr 1494.60 Session d'études administratives. Rabat, 1959.
Afr 3675.30 Shibeika, Mekki. The independent Sudan. N.Y., 1959.
Afr 609.58.5 Sholomir, Jack. Beachcombers of the African jungle. 1st ed. N.Y., 1959.

Afr 626.70 Shpirt, A.I. Afrika vo Vtoroi Mirovoi Voine. Moscow, 1959.

Afr 150.25 Simões Mueller, Adolfo. O principe do mar. Porto, 1959.
Afr 6984.10 Simon, J.M. Bishop for the Hottentots. N.Y., 1959.
Afr 115.30 Sithole, N. African nationalism. Cape Town, 1959.
Afr 7803.25 Slade, Ruth. English-speaking missions in the Congo Independent State (1878-1908). Bruxelles, 1959.

Afr 2030.235 Sneider, Bertrand. La Cinquième République et l'Algérie. Paris, 1959.

Afr 150.2.15 Soares, Ernesto. Iconografia do Infante Dom Henrique. Lisboa, 1959.

Afr 710.45 Soret, Marcel. Les Kongo nord-occidentaux. Paris, 1959.
Afr 7119.59 Sousa Dias, G. Portugueses em Angola. Lisboa, 1959.
Afr 710.76 South African Broadcasting Corporation. Ons Buurstate op die Afrikaanse vasteland. Johannesburg, 1959.

Afr 3710.15 Stacey, Charles. Records of the Nile voyagers. Toronto, 1959.

Afr 6292.9 Stenning, Derrick J. Savannah nomads...the Wodaabe pastural Fulani. London, 1959.

Afr 5055.59.5 Subbotin, V.A. Kolonialnaia politika Frantsii v Zapadnoi Afrike, 1880-1900. Moscow, 1959.

Afr 8678.106 Thomas, E.M. The harmless people. 1st ed. N.Y., 1959.
Afr 5185.8 Thomas, L.V. Les Diola. Macon, 1959. 2v.
Afr 5316.10 Touré, Sékou. L'action politique du parti démocratique de guinée. Paris, 1959.

Afr 5314.10 Touré, Sékou. Expérience guinéenne et unité africaine. Paris, 1959.

1959 - cont.

Afr 8028.15   Towert, A.M.F. Constitutional development in South Africa. Cape Town, 1959.

Afr 575.35   Trimingham, J.S. Islam in West Africa. Oxford, 1959.

Afr 7377.59   Tubman, William. President Tubman of Liberia speaks. London, 1959.

Afr 2438.35   Tunisia. Constitution. Constitution of the Tunisian Republic. Tunis, 1959.

Afr 2442.2   Tunisia. Secrétariat d'Etat à l'Information. Les congrès du Néo-Destour. Tunis, 1959.

Afr 2650.5   Tunisia. Secrétariat d'Etat à l'Information. Land development in the Medjerda valley. n.p., 1959.

Afr 6484.5   Uganda. Constitutional Committee. Report of the constitutional committee, 1957. Entebbe, 1959.

Afr 3313.103   United Arab Republic. The United Arab Republic on the seventh anniversary. n.p., 1959.

Afr 3335.10   United Arab Republic. Information Department. The United Arab Republic in world public opinion. Cairo, 1959.

Afr 626.118F   United Kingdom aid to Africa. London, 1959.

Afr 45.59   Vanderlinden, Jacques. Essai sur les juridictions de droit coutumier. Bruxelles, 1959.

Afr 3310.55   Vauchu, Georges. General Abdel Nasser. Paris, 1959. 2v.

Afr 2030.300   Verges, Jacques. Les disparus. Lausanne, 1959.

Afr 5760.20   Vianes, S. Contribution à l'étude des migrations antesaka. Paris, 1959.

Afr 8934.277.2   Williams, John Grenfell. Moshesh, the man on the mountain. 2nd ed. London, 1959.

Afr 545.15   Wilson, M.H. Divine kings and the breath of men. Cambridge, Eng., 1959.

Afr 6540.21   Winter, Edward. Beyond the mountains of the moon. London, 1959.

Afr 6193.15   Wittman, G.H. The Ghana report. N.Y., 1959.

Afr 6392.20   Wraith, Ronald E. East African citizen. London, 1959.

Afr 7815.18   Wuig, J. Van. Etudes Bakongo. 2.ed. Bruges, 1959.

Afr 724.22   Wymer, Norman. The man from the Cape. London, 1959.

Afr 3310.45   Wynn, Wilton. Nasser of Egypt. Cambridge, Mass., 1959.

Afr 7369.59   Yancy, Ernest Jerome. The Republic of Liberia. London, 1959.

Afr 3315.138   Yanguas Messia, José de. El clima politico de ayer y de hoy en Africa. Escorial, 1959.

Afr 109.59   Zierer, Otto. Geschichte Afrikas. v.1-2. Murnau, 1959. 2v.

Afr 500.69   Zusmanovich, A.Z. Imperialisticheskii razdel Afriki. Moscow, 1959.

Afr 7549.59   Zuylen, Pierre van. L'échiquier congolais. Bruxelles, 1959.

Afr 6390.63   Zwilling, Ernst. Tierparadies Ostafrika. Mödling, 1959.

196

Afr Doc 6807.364   Mali. Service de la Statistique de la Coruptabilité Nationale et de la Mécanographie. Rapport définitif de l'enquête agricole, 1964. Mali, 196 .

196-

Afr 28.97   L'Afrique. Paris, 196-.

Afr 2221.3F   Algeria. Service de l'Information. Direction de la Documentation Générale. Aspects of Algeria. Algiers. 196-.

Afr 10005.7   Bol, Victor P. Littérateurs et poètes noirs. Léopoldville, 196-.

Afr 2030.464.30   Boudiaf, M. Notre révolution. Paris, 196-.

Afr 210.62.43   Braginskii, M.I. Africa wins freedom. Moscow, 196-.

Afr 5343.30   Bureau pour le Developpement de la Production Agricole outre-mer. Etude générale de la région de Man. Paris, 196-? 6v.

Afr 6463.7   Conference on the Role of the Church in Independent Kenya Limuru. Report of the conference held at Limuru Conference Centre, Kenya. Nairobi, 196- .

Afr 4571.8F   Ethiopia. Ministry of Information. Notre terre. Addis Ababa, 196-.

Afr Doc 7108.5   France. Institut National de la Statistique et des Etudes Economiques. La situation démographique au Tchad, résultats provisoires. Paris, 196-.

Afr 5343.3   France. Ministère de la Coopération. Direction des Affaires Economiques. Economie et plan de développement. Paris, 196-.

Afr 7135.12   Gauzes, Anne. Angola, 1961-1963. Luanda? 196-.

Afr 2459.60   Histoire de la Tunisie. Tunis, 196-?

Afr 11509.35.110   LaGuma, Alex. A walk in the night. Ibadan, 196-?

Afr Doc 9919.5   Liberia. The Declaration of Independence and the Constitution of the Republic of Liberia as amended through May, 1955. Monrovia, 196-?

Afr 8678.354   Mahabahe, Zaccheus R. The good fight. Evanston, 196-.

Afr 5758.60.10   Malagasy Republic. Commissariat Général au Plan. The economy of Madagascar. Tananarive, 196-.

Afr 1623.963.5   Morocco. Delegation Generale a la Promotion Nationale et au Plan. Promotion nationale au Maroc. Casa, 196-.

Afr 3310.10.5.25   Nasser, G.A. The philosophy of the revolution. Cairo, 196-.

Afr 6295.60.15   Nigeria, Eastern. Ministry of Economic Planning. Speech by G.E. Ohehe on the presentation of Eastern Nigeria development. Enugu, 196-.

Afr Doc 2524.5   Nigeria, Western. Laws, statutes, etc. Local government manual incorporationg the Local government law, cop.68, the chiefs law, cop.19 staff regulations. Ibadan, 196-.

Afr 6210.30   Nigeria. Constitution. n.p., 196-.

Afr 6275.126   Nigeria. Federal Information Service. Nigeria 1960. Lagos, 196-.

Afr 6280.9.45   Olisah, Okenua. The Ibo native law and custom. Onitsha, 196-.

Afr 7309.60.5   Overseas Companies of Portugal. Mozambique. N.Y., 196-.

Afr Doc 3808.12   Rhodesia (British Colony). European life table no. 2 and Analysis of deaths by causes, 1961-63. Salisbury, 196-.

Afr 7065.10   Terra, Branco da. Guiné do século XV. Lisboa?, 196-.

Afr 5312.18   Toré, Sékou. The doctrine and methods of the Democratic Party of Guinea. v.1-2. Conakry, 196-.

Afr 4108.5   United Arab Republic. Aswan. Cairo, 196-.

Afr 3993.10   United Arab Republic. Mining, food, and textile industries in the second five-year industrial plan. Cairo, 196-. 2 pam.

1960

Afr 7803.10   Abel, Armand. Les Musulmans noirs du Maniema. Bruxelles, 1960.

Afr 210.60.40   Abranches, Esther. Afrique. Luanda, 1960.

1960 - cont.

Afr 626.80   Ady, Peter. System of national accounts in Africa. Paris, 1960.

Afr 9448.70   Africa Bureau, London. Britains dilemma in central Africa. London, 1960.

Afr 210.60.35   Afrika 1960. Moscow, 1960.

Afr 212.56   Afrikanische Gegenwartsfragen. Berlin, 1960.

Afr 3199.60   Ahmed Jamal, M. The intellectual origins of Egyptian nationalism. London, 1960.

Afr Doc 2560.602   Ajuluchukee, M.C.K. Profiles of the ministers of Eastern Nigeria. Enugu, 1960.

Afr 9555.5   Akademiia Nauk SSSR. Institut Etnografii. Arabskie istochniki VII-X vekov. Moscow, 1960. 2v.

Afr 632.25   Akademiia Nauk SSSR. Institut Narodov Azii. Rasovaia diskriminatsiia v stranakh Afriki. Moscow, 1960.

Afr 6193.40   Akwawuah, Kwadwo A. Preludes to Ghana's industrialisation. London, 1960.

Afr 8659.60.10   Albertyn, J.R. Land en stad. Kaapstad, 1960.

Afr 2030.460.25A   Algeria. White paper on the application of the Geneva Convention of 1949. N.Y., 1960.

Afr 2223.960   Algeria. Conseil Supérieur de la Promotion Sociale en Algérie. Pour une promotion dans la coopération. Alger, 1960.

Afr 2209.60   Algeria. Délégation Générale du Gouvernement en Algérie. Algerian documents, 1960. Paris, 1960.

Afr 2223.960.20   Algeria. Direction du Plan et des Etudes Economiques. Plan de Constantine, 1959-1963. Alger, 1960.

Afr 2223.960.10   Algeria. Secrétariat Général Adjoint pour les Affaires Economiques. Leé comptes économiques de l'Algérie et du Sahara pour les années 1957 et 1958. Alger, 1960.

Afr 1840.23   Algeria. Service de l'Information. Elections cantonales en Algérie. Alger, 1960.

Afr 2030.340   Algerian Front of National Liberation. Algeria. N.Y., 1960.

Afr 1955.61   Algiers. Université. Faculté de Droit. Recherches sur la colonisation de l'Algérie au XIXe siècle. Alger, 1960.

Afr 8089.60   Allighan, H. Curtain-up on South Africa. London, 1960.

Afr 7180.25   Amaral, I. do. Aspectos do povoamento branco de Angola. Lisboa, 1960.

Afr 2397.2   Amrani, Djamal. Le témoin. Paris, 1960.

Afr 210.60.45   Andrianov, B.V. Naselenie Afriki. Moscow, 1960.

Afr 5000.11   Annales africaines. Tables quinquennales, 1954-58. Dakar, 1960.

Afr 6298.3   Anyiam, F.U. Among Nigerian celebrities. Yaba, 1960.

Afr 109.59.20   Arbeitstagung über Neuere und Neueste Geschichte. Geschichte und Geschichtsbild Afrikas. Berlin, 1960.

Afr 6275.55   Ardener, Edwin. Plantation and village in the Cameroons. London, 1960.

Afr 6196.25   Arthur, John. Brong Ahafo handbook. Accra, 1960.

Afr 3986.960A   Austry, J. Structure économique et civilisation. Paris, 1960.

Afr 150.2.25   Aveiro, Portugal. Museu. Iconografia do Infante Dom Henrique. Aveiro, 1960.

Afr 6298.181   Awolowo, Obaf. Awo. Cambridge, 1960.

Afr 7015.25   Axelson, Eric V. Portuguese in South East Africa. Johannesburg, 1960.

Afr 3675.35   Baddur, Abd al-Fattah Ibrahim al-Sayid. Sudanese-Egyptian relations. The Hague, 1960.

Afr 6192.80   Balk, Theodor. Unter dem schwarzen Stern. Berlin, 1960.

Afr 6685.11   Banque Centrale des Etats de l'Afrique de l'Ouest. Togo, 1960. Paris, 1960.

Afr 2223.960.5   Banque Nationale pour le Commerce et l'Industrie, Algiers. Les entreprises industrielles en Algérie et au Sahara. Alger, 1960.

Afr 9489.60.5   Barber, F.H. Zambezia andMatabeleland in the seventies. London, 1960.

Afr 3315.100   Barer, Schlomo. The weekend war. N.Y., 1960.

Afr 6390.47   Barker-Benfield, M.A. The lands and peoples of East Africa. London, 1960.

Afr 8369.60   Barlow, A.G. That we may tread safely. Cape Town, 1960.

Afr 2030.365   Barricades et colonels, 24 janvier 1960 par Bromberger. Paris, 1960.

Afr 8325.22   Barry, A. Ons japie. Johannesburg, 1960.

Afr Doc 4218.5   Basutoland constitutional handbook. Maseru, 1960.

Afr 505.13.3   Batten, T.R. Problems of African development. 3d ed. London, 1960.

Afr 635.70   Beart, Charles. Recherche des éléments d'une sociologie des peuples africains. Paris, 1960.

Afr 6540.16   Beattie, John. Bunyoro, an African kingdom. N.Y., 1960.

Afr 718.18.50F   Belgium. Ministère des Affaires Africaines. Document notte. Bruxelles, 1960.

Afr 7533.10   Belgium. Office de l'Information et des Relations Politiques pour le Congo Belge et le Ruanda-Urundi. Ruanda-Urundi. Brussels, 1960. 4 pam.

Afr 7575.65   Belgo-Congolese Round Table Conference, Brussels, 1960. De historische dagen von februari 1960. Brussels, 1960.

Afr 9424.360   Benson, Mary. Tshekedi Khama. London, 1960.

Afr 609.60.30   Bensted-Smith, Richard. Turn left for Tangier. Coventry, 1960.

Afr 8673.15   Bensusan, A.D. South Africa. Cape Town, 1960.

Afr 12922.7.100   Bhely-Quenum, Olympe. Un piège sans fin. Paris, 1960.

Afr 12972.41.110   Biyidi, Alexandre. King Lazarus. London, 1960.

Afr 9389.60   Bjerre, Jens. Kalahari. London, 1960.

Afr 9489.60   Blake, W.T. Rhodesia and Nyasaland journey. London, 1960.

Afr 2704.5   Blaudin de The, Bernard M.S. Essai de bibliographie du Sahara. Paris, 1960. 2v.

Afr 9291.15.2   Bloemfontein. City Council. The city of Bloemfontein. Cape Town, 1960.

Afr 2030.415   Boisson, Jean. Essai sur le problème algérien. Paris, 1960.

Afr 5257.15   Bonardi, Pierre. La république du Niger. Paris, 1960.

Afr 28.100   Boston University. Library. Catalog of African government documents and African area index. Boston, 1960.

Afr 8678.306   Botha, David P. Die opkoms van ons derde stand. Kaapstad, 1960.

Afr 6164.10.5   Bourret, F.M. Ghana. Rev. ed. Stanford, 1960.

Afr 5346.15   Boutillier, J.L. Bongouanou. Paris, 1960.

Afr 6465.56.10   Boxer, Charles R. Fort Jesus and the Portuguese in Mombasa. London, 1960.

Afr 6465.56.9   Boxer, Charles R. A fortaleza de Jesus e os portugueses em Mombaça. Lisboa, 1960.

Afr 8659.59.3   Boydell, T. My beloved country. Cape Town, 1960.

Afr 2000.11   Boyer, Pierre. L'évolution de l'Algérie mediane. Paris, 1960.

Afr 2030.345   Brace, Richard M. Ordeal in Algeria. Princeton, 1960.

Afr 150.40   Bradford, Ernle. A wind from the north. N.Y., 1960.

1960 - cont.

Afr 2760.5 — Briggs, Lloyd C. Tribes of the Sahara. Cambridge, 1960.

Afr 6212.35 — British Information Service. Nigeria, the making of a nation. N.Y., 1960.

Afr 6412.5 — British Information Services. Kenya, progress and problems. N.Y., 1960.

Afr 6140.15 — British Information Services. Sierra Leone. N.Y., 1960.

Afr 150.35 — British Museum. Prince Henry the Navigator. London, 1960.

Afr 6283.12 — Bryan, K.J. Nigeria, guidebooks. Zaria, 1960. 3 pam.

Afr 8657.11F — Buetner, Johan Daniel. Beschrijving van Cabo de Goede Hoop en Rio de la Goa. Pietermaritzburg, 1960.

Afr 3986.960.10 — Bughdadi, A. Address on the five year plan. Cairo, 1960.

Afr 44622.89.112 — al-Buhry, Hemed Abdallah. Utenzi wa vita vya wadachi kutamalaki mrima 1307 A.H. 2. ed. Dar es Salaam, 1960.

Afr 8817.2 — Bulpin, Thomas V. The Cape province. Cape Town, 1960.

Afr 9606.2 — Bulpin, Thomas Victor. Rhodesia and Nyasaland. Cape Town, 1960.

Afr 1713.12F — Burckhardt, Titus. Fes, Stadt des Islam. Alten, 1960.

Afr 8678.175 — Burger, Jan. The gulf between. Cape Town, 1960.

Afr 6390.53 — Burger, John F. My forty years in Africa. London, 1960.

Afr 11249.86.110 — Butler, Guy. Stranger to Europe, with additional poems. Capetown, 1960.

Afr 1333.10 — Caille, Jacques. Les accords internationaux du sultan Sidi Mohammed ben Abdallah (1757-1790). Tanger, 1960.

Afr 8667.70 — Caltex (Africa). South Africa's heritage. Cape Town, 1960.

Afr 150.2.50 — Camacho Pereira, João. O Infante Dom Henrique do 5. centenario da sua morte. Lisboa, 1960.

Afr 8710.20 — Cape of Good Hope. Die administrasie van Kaapland, 1910-1960. Kaapstad, 1960.

Afr 8055.40F — Cape Town. University. Library. Biographical index to men of the times. Cape Town, 1960.

Afr 210.60.10 — Carter, G.M. Independence for Africa. N.Y., 1960.

Afr 718.2.140 — Castries, R. de la Croix. Les rencontres de Stanley. Paris, 1960.

Afr Doc 7207.361 — Central African Republic. Service de la Statistique Générale. Enquête agricole en République centrafricaine. n.p., 1960-61.

Afr 1268.5 — Centre d'Accueil Nord-Africain de Saint-Louis, Marseilles. Eléments d'introduction à la vie moderne. Paris, 1960.

Afr 2248.15 — Centre d'Etudes et d'Informations des Problèmes Humaines dans les Zones Arides. Les Mekhadma. Paris, 1960.

Afr 5405.109.35 — Cerbelaud-Salagnac, Georges. Savorgnan de Brazza. Paris, 1960.

Afr 2030.460.20 — Cercle d'Études Algériennes. Lettres à un métropolitain. Alger, 1960.

Afr 609.60.65 — Chatterji, Suniti. Africanism. Calcutta, 1960.

Afr 4008.8 — Chauleur, S. Histoire des Coptes d'Egypte. Paris, 1960.

Afr 6095.357.2 — Church, R.J.H. West Africa. 2. ed. London, 1960.

Afr 2030.211 — Clark, Michael. Algeria in turmoil. N.Y., 1960.

Afr 6147.5.3 — Clark, William R.E. The morning star of Africa. London, 1960.

Afr 6769.60 — Clarke, P.H.C. A short history of Tanganyika. London, 1960.

Afr 9439.60 — Clegg, E.M. Race and politics. London, 1960.

Afr 8659.53.5.2 — Coetzee, Abel. Die Afrikaanse volkskultuur. 2. druk. Amsterdam, 1960.

Afr 8045.45 — Coetzee, G.A. The Republic. Johannesburg, 1960.

Afr 4513.60 — Cohen, Armand. La Société des Nations devant le conflit italo-éthiopien. Genève, 1960.

Afr 6149.162.5 — Cole, R.W. Kossoh town boy. Cambridge, Eng., 1960.

Afr 10215.5F — Committee for Inter-African Relations, Ibadan, Nigeria. Report on the press in West Africa. Ibadan, 1960.

Afr 6192.57 — Cone, Virginia. Africa, a world in progress. 1st ed. N.Y., 1960.

Afr 210.60.55 — Conférence de l'Action Positive pour la Paix et la Sécurité. Conférence de l action positive pour la paix. Accra, 1960.

Afr 45.60.10 — Conference on the Future of Law in Africa. The future of law in Africa. London, 1960.

Afr 7812.260.10 — Congo, Belgian. Commissariat au Plan Décennal. Le plan décennal pour le développement économique et social du Congo belge. Bruxelles, 1960.

Afr 11298.5 — Conton, William. The African. Boston, 1960.

Afr 11299.69.120 — Cope, Jack. The tame ox. London, 1960.

Afr 6395.2.30 — Corfield, F.D. Historical survey of the origins and growth of Mau Mau. London, 1960.

Afr 109.60.5.2 — Cornevin, Robert. Histoire des peuples de l'Afrique Noire. Paris, 1960.

Afr 109.60.5 — Cornevin, Robert. Histoire des peuples de l'Afrique Noire. Paris, 1960.

Afr 626.125 — Council of Europe. Europe and Africa. Strasbourg, 1960.

Afr 9448.60 — Creighton, P.R. The anatomy of partnership. London, 1960.

Afr 2731.15.75 — Cristiani, L. Pèlerin de l'absolu. Paris, 1960.

Afr 2623.960.5 — Cuisenier, Jean. L'Ansarine; contribution à la sociologie du développement. Paris, 1960.

Afr 7809.60.10 — Cuypers, J.P. Alphonse Vangele (1848-1939). Bruxelles, 1960.

Afr 609.60.10 — Dainelli, Giotto. Gli esploratori italiani in Africa. Torino, 1960.

Afr 5749.60.5 — Dandouau, André. Manuel de geographie de Madagascar. Paris, 1960.

Afr 2030.380 — Darboise, Jean M. Officiers en Algérie. Paris, 1960.

Afr 11319.76.1100 — Darlow, David John. Paths of peace in Africa. Lovedale, 1960.

Afr 210.60.15 — Datlin, S.V. Afrika sbrasyvaet tsepi. Moscow, 1960.

Afr 2030.355 — Debatty, Andre. Le treize mai et la presse. Paris, 1960.

Afr 5794.5 — Decary, Raymond. L'ile Nosy-Bé de Madagascar. Paris, 1960.

Afr 5874.18 — Defos du Rau, J. L'Ile de la Réunion. Bordeaux, 1960.

Afr 10624.2.100 — Dei-Anang, M. Africa speaks. 2d ed. Accra, 1960.

Afr 11320.41.100 — Dei-Anang, Michael. Africa speaks. 2. ed. Accra, 1960.

Afr 210.60.25 — Dekiewiet, C. Can Africa come of age? Johannesburg, 1960.

Afr 500.75 — Dekiewiet, Cornelis W. America's role in Africa. v. 1-2. Durban, 1960.

Afr 11320.50.110 — Delius, Anthony. The fall. Cape Town, 1960.

Afr 2285.30 — Dermenghem, Emile. Le pays d'Abel. Paris, 1960.

Afr 115.60 — Des africanistes russes parlent de l'Afrique. Paris, 1960.

Afr 5549.60 — Deschamps, H.J. Histoire de Madagascar. Paris, 1960.

Afr 545.20 — Deschamps, H.J. Les religions de l'Afrique noire. 2. éd. Paris, 1960.

Afr 109.60.15 — Dia, Mamadou. Nations africaines et solidarité mondiale. Paris, 1960.

Afr 150.55 — Dias, A. Infante de Sagres. Porto, 1960.

Afr 150.72 — Dias Dinis, Antonio J. Estudos henriquinos. Coimbra, 1960.

1960 - cont.

Afr 6275.33 — Dickson, Mora. New Nigerians. London, 1960.

Afr 630.60.5 — Diderot, Toussaint. A la recherche de la personnalité négro-africaine. Monte-Carlo, 1960.

Afr 12624.41.35 — Diop, Birago. Les contes d'Amadou-Koumba. Paris, 1960.

Afr 12624.41.20 — Diop, Birago. Leurres et lueurs, poèmes. Photoreproduction. Paris, 1960.

Afr 109.60.3 — Diop, Cheikh A. L'Afrique noire pré-coloniale. Paris, 1960.

Afr 45.60.5 — Diop, Cheikh Anta. Les fondements culturels, techniques et industriels d'un futur état fédéral d'Afrique noire. Paris, 1960.

Afr 8678.220 — Dison, L.R. Group areas and their development. Durban, 1960.

Afr 550.105 — Doell, E.W. A mission doctor sees the wind of change. London, 1960.

Afr 1618.10 — Dolinger, Jane. Behind harem walls. London, 1960.

Afr 109.60.20 — Drachoussoff, V. L'Afrique decolonisée. Bruxelles, 1960.

Afr 9689.60 — Duffy, Kevin. Black elephant hunter. London, 1960.

Afr 7580.2 — Duyzings, Martin. Mensen en machten in Congo. Amsterdam, 1960.

Afr 3979.60 — Dynkin, A.V. Na drevnei zemle. Stalingrad, 1960.

Afr Doc 3207.359.10 — East Africa. High Commission. East Africa Statistical Department. Kenya Unit. Agricultural census 1959 (non African). Nairobi? 1960.

Afr Doc 3376.5F — East Africa High Commission. East African Statistical Department. Uganda Unit. The patterns of income, expenditure...of workers in Fort Portal, February 1960. Entebbe, 1960.

Afr Doc 3307.359.10 — East Africa High Commission. East African Statistical Department. Uganda: General African Census, 1959. Nairobi, 1960. 2v.

Afr Doc 3307.359 — East Africa High Commission. East African Statistical Department. Uganda census, 1959; non-African population. Nairobi, 1960.

Afr 6295.60.10 — Egharevba, Jacob. A short history of Benin. 3rd ed. Ibadan, 1960.

Afr 3986.960.20 — Egypt. Ministry of Economy. Economic progress in the U.A.R. Cairo, 1960.

Afr 3986.960.15 — Egypt. Ministry of Economy. A statistical portrait. Cairo, 1960.

Afr 3979.60.5 — Egypt. State Tourist Administration. Trends of the travel movement. Cairo, 1960. 2 pam.

Afr 3005.2.5 — Egypte contemporaine. Index, v.1-50 (1909-59). Le Caire, 1960.

Afr 609.60.50 — Ehrenfels, O.R. The light continent. London, 1960.

Afr 3035.15 — Ernst, Hans. Die mamlukischen Sultansurkunden des Sinai-Klosters. Wiesbaden, 1960.

Afr 150.2.70 — Estailleur-Chanteraine, Philippe. L'infant de la mer. Paris, 1960.

Afr 2030.285 — Eulage, André. L'envers des barricades. Paris, 1960.

Afr 6210.25 — Ezera, Kalu. Constitutional development in Nigeria. Cambridge, 1960.

Afr 3675.40 — Fabunmi, L.A. The Sudan in Anglo-Egyptian relations. London, 1960.

Afr 8678.135 — Fagan, Henry Allan. Our responsibility. Stellenbosch, 1960.

Afr 2030.70.5 — Faucher, Jean André. Les barricades d'Alger. Paris, 1960.

Afr 6095.360 — Fax, Elton C. West Africa vignettes. N.Y., 1960.

Afr 7812.260.15 — Fédération des Enterprises Congolaises. The Congolese economy on the eve of independence. Brussels, 1960.

Afr 7183.20 — Felgas, H.A. As populações nativas do Congo portugues. Luanda, 1960.

Afr 6298.432 — Flint, John E. Sir George Goldie and the making of Nigeria. London, 1960.

Afr 8849.16 — Folliott, Pamela. One titan at a time. Cape Town, 1960.

Afr 8678.222 — Forman, L. From the notebooks of Lionel Forman, black and white in South African history. Cape Town, 1960.

Afr 609.60.60 — Forrest, Alfred C. Not tomorrow, now. Toronto, 1960.

Afr 5460.15 — France. Embassy. U.S. The Central African Republic. N.Y., 1960.

Afr 5090.10 — France. Embassy. U.S. The Islamic Republic of Mauritania. N.Y., 1960.

Afr 5645.5 — France. Embassy. U.S. Madagascar, birth of a new republic. N.Y., 1960.

Afr 5385.36 — France. Embassy. U.S. The Republic of Dahomey. N.Y., 1960.

Afr 5180.42 — France. Embassy. U.S. The Republic of Senegal. N.Y., 1960.

Afr 5342.55 — France. Embassy. U.S. The Republic of the Ivory Coast. N.Y., 1960.

Afr 5260.30 — France. Embassy. U.S. The Republic of the Niger. N.Y., 1960.

Afr 5280.5 — France. Embassy. U.S. The Republic of the Upper Volta. N.Y., 1960.

Afr 5749.60 — France. Institut Geographique National. Service Geographique a Tananarive. Expose des travaux exécutes en 1959 sur le territoire de la Republique Malgache. Paris, 1960.

Afr 9500.15 — Franck, Thomas M. Race and nationalism. N.Y., 1960.

Afr 8676.60.25 — Franzsen, David G. Economic growth and stability in a developing economy. Pretoria, 1960.

Afr 8676.60.10 — Franzsen, David G. Die ekonomiese lewe van Suid-Africa. Pretoria, 1960.

Afr 7182.3 — Freyre, Gilberto. Em torno de alguns tumulos afro-cristaos. Bahia, 1960.

Afr 8659.60.25F — Friend, Bloemfontein. Union jubilee, 1910-1960. Bloemfontein, 1960.

Afr 7122.75 — Front Revolutionnaire Africain pour l'Indépendence Nationale des Colonies Portugaises. La repression colonialiste en Angola. 2d ed. Anvers, 1960.

Afr 9060.15 — Frost, R.K. No other foundation. Durban, 1960.

Afr 9439.60.10 — Gale, W.D. Deserve to be great. Bulawayo, 1960.

Afr 5074.35 — Garnier, C. Désert fertile. Paris, 1960.

Afr 6455.120 — Gatti, Attilio. Africa is adventure. London, 1960.

Afr 609.60.5 — Gatti, Ellen. The new Africa. N.Y., 1960.

Afr 2749.60.10 — Gaudio, Attilio. Le Sahara des Africaines. Paris, 1960.

Afr 5318.35 — Gavrilov, N.I. Gvineiskaia Respublika. Moscow, 1960.

Afr 5758.60.5 — Gendarme, René. L'économie de Madagascar. Paris, 1960.

Afr 2749.60.5 — Gerster, Georg. Sahara. London, 1960.

Afr 8145.32A — Geyser, A.S. Delayed action. Pretoria, 1960.

Afr 6160.36 — Ghana. Commissioner for Local Government Enquiries. Report, June, 1957. Accra, 1960.

1960 - cont.

Afr Doc 1812.7	Ghana. Constituent Assembly. Proceedings of the Constituent assembly. Accra, 1960.
Afr 7911.5.5	Gilis, Charles A. Kimbangu, fondateur d'église. Bruxelles, 1960.
Afr 2030.330	Gillespie, Joan. Algeria. London, 1960.
Afr 6910.5	Goldblatt, Israel. The conflict between the United Nations and the Union of South Africa in regard to Southwest Africa. Windhoek, 1960.
Afr 550.132	Gonçalves, José. Protestantismo em Africa. Lisboa, 1960. 2v.
Afr 11433.74.130	Gordimer, N. Friday's footprint. London, 1960.
Afr 6275.39	Grant, James. A geography of Western Nigeria. Cambridge, 1960.
Afr 9500.25	Gray, Richard. The two nations. Oxford, 1960.
Afr 9435.7	Great Britain. Advisory Commission on the Review of Constitution. Report. (With appendix 1-5, appendix 6-8). London, 1960.
Afr 6455.110	Great Britain. Central Office of Information. Kenya. London, 1960.
Afr 6275.70	Great Britain. Central Office of Information. Nigeria. London, 1960.
Afr 6275.50	Great Britain. Central Office of Information. Nigeria today. London, 1960.
Afr 6310.47	Great Britain. Commissions. Public Services of the East African Territories and the East Africa High Commission. Report. Entebbe, 1960.
Afr 8923.2	Great Britain. High Commissioner for Basutoland, the Bechuanaland Protectorate and Swaziland. Basutoland, Bechuanaland protectorate and Swaziland, report of an economic survey mission. London, 1960.
Afr 7809.60	Gruenebaum, Kurt. Kongo im Umbruch. Bruxelles, 1960.
Afr 1618.20	Guillaume, A. La propriété collective au Maroc. Rabat, 1960.
Afr 6540.9	Gurling, F.K. The Acholi of Uganda. London, 1960.
Afr 2030.425	Habart, Michel. Histoire d'un parjure. Paris, 1960.
Afr 9499.40	Haglewood, Arthur. Nyasaland. Oxford, 1960.
Afr 1110.15	Hahn, Lora. North Africa. Washington, 1960.
Afr 4640.3	Haile Selassie I University. Social survey of Addis Ababa, 1960. Addis Ababa, 1960.
Afr 609.60.20	Haller, Albert. Die Welt des Afrikaners. Düsseldorf, 1960.
Afr 9439.60.15	Hanna, A.J. The story of the Rhodesias and Nyasaland. London, 1960.
Afr 609.60.40	Harcourt, François. L'Afrique à l'heure. Paris, 1960.
Afr 6203.4	Harris, John. Books about Nigeria. 2. ed. Nigeria, 1960.
Afr 6210.15	Harris, Philip. Local government in southern Nigeria. Cambridge, 1960.
Afr 6275.65	Harrison, Godfrey. To the new Nigeria. London, 1960.
Afr 9500.30	Haw, Richard C. No other home. Bulawayo, 1960.
Afr 1609.60	Heinemeijir, W.F. Marokko. Meppel, 1960.
Afr 2030.395	Hermans, Fons. Algerije. Amsterdam, 1960.
Afr 2749.60	Heseltine, Nigel. From Libyan sands to Chad. London, 1960.
Afr 626.90	Hesse, Kurt. Wirtschaftliche Entwecklungstendenzen in West-, Mittel- und Ostafrika. Bad Homburg, 1960.
Afr 9435.8	Hickman, A.S. Men who made Rhodesia. Salisbury, 1960.
Afr 6214.25	Hodgkin, Thomas. Nigerian perspectives. London, 1960.
Afr 5342.40	Holas, Bohumil. Cultures matérielles de la Côte-d'Ivoire. Paris, 1960.
Afr 635.65	Hollingworth, L.W. The Asians of East Africa. London, 1960.
Afr 8369.60.5	Holm, Erik. Erik Holm, man en standpunt. Potgietersrus, 1960.
Afr 9161.21	Hooper, Charles. Brief authority. London, 1960.
Afr 625.20	Horrabin, James F. An atlas of Africa. London, 1960.
Afr 7575.35	Houart, P. La pénétration communiste au Congo. Bruxelles, 1960.
Afr 2030.280	Houart, Pierre. L attitude de l eglise dans la guerre d algerie. Bruxelles, 1960.
Afr 8820.5	Houghton, D. Hobart. Economic development in a plural society. Cape Town, 1960.
Afr 8687.308.5	Huenermann, G. Le rebelle obéissant. 2. ed. Mulhouse, 1960.
Afr 10309.60	Hughes, Langston. An African treasury. N.Y., 1960.
Afr 109.57.3	Hunton, William A. Decision in Africa, sources of current conflict. N.Y., 1960.
Afr 1369.60	Husson, Philippe. La question des frontières terrestres du Maroc. Paris, 1960.
Afr 8678.125	Hutchinson, Alfred. Road to Ghana. London, 1960.
Afr 8678.125.5	Hutchinson, Alfred. Road to Ghana. 1st Amer. ed. N.Y., 1960.
Afr 6420.36	Huxley, Elspeth. A new earth. London, 1960.
Afr 6225.3	Independent Nigeria. Yaba, 1960.
Afr 150.45	Infante Dom Henrique. Lisboa, 1960.
Afr 6486.5	Ingrams, William. Uganda. London, 1960.
Afr 7580.3	Institut Royal des Relations Internationales. La crise congolaise. Brussels, 1960.
Afr 626.85	Inter-African Labour Institute. The human factors of productivity in Africa. 2d ed. Brazzaville, 1960.
Afr 626.64	International Bank for Reconstruction and Development. The economic development of Libya. Baltimore, 1960.
Afr 8678.180	International Commission of Jurists. South Africa and the rule of law. Geneva, 1960.
Afr 3310.10.15	International Studies Association, Cairo. Afro-Asian solidarity. Cairo, 1960.
Afr 3986.960.5	International Studies Association, Cairo. Progress in United Arab Republic. Cairo, 1960.
Afr 3310.75	International Studies Association. Nasser. Cairo, 1960.
Afr 55.15	Italiaander, Rolf. Die neuen Männer Afrikas. Düsseldorf, 1960.
Afr 4700.26.18	Italy. Comitato per la Documentazione dell'Opera dell'Italia in Africa. L'Italia in Africa. T.1-5. Roma, 1960- 8v.
Afr 3813.8	Italy. Instituto Nazionale per il Commercio Estero. Sudan. Roma, 1960.
Afr 6193.45	Italy. Istituto Nazionale per il Commercio Estero. Ghana. Roma, 1960.
Afr 5758.60	Italy. Istituto Nazionale per il Commercio Estero. Madagascar. Roma, 1960.
Afr 6277.60	Italy. Istituto Nazionale per il Commercio Estero. Nigeria. Roma, 1960.
Afr 5343.6.3	Ivory Coast. Inventaire économique et social de la Côte-d'Ivoire, 1958. Abidjan, 1960.
Afr Doc 6471.1.73	Ivory Coast. Direction de la Statistique et des Etudes economiques et démographiques. Recensement d'Abidjan 1955. Paris, 1960.

1960 - cont.

Afr Doc 6471.10	Ivory Coast. Direction de la Statistique et des Etudes Economiques et Démographiques. Recensement des centres urbains d'Abengoonon, Aghoville, Dunboko et Man, 1956, 1957. Résultats définitif. Paris, 1960.
Afr 5337.5	Ivory Coast. Ministère de l'Education Nationale. Nation, société, travail. Abidjan, 1960.
Afr 8687.245	Jabavu, N. Drawn in colour. London, 1960.
Afr 11465.14.130	Jacobson, Dan. Evidence of love, a novel. 1st ed. Boston, 1960.
Afr 6095.360.5	Jahn, Janheinz. Durch afrikanische Türen. 1.Aufl. Düsseldorf, 1960.
Afr 3310.65	Joesten, Joachim. Nasser. London, 1960.
Afr 8152.76.2	Johannesburg. Public Library. General index to Narrative of the Kaffir war. Johannesburg, 1960.
Afr 28.58	Joint Secretariat C.C.T.A./C.S.A. Inventory of economic studies concerning Africa South of the Sahara. London, 1960.
Afr 4259.35.23	Jones, A.H. A history of Ethiopia. Oxford, 1960.
Afr 609.60.55	Jones, H.W. Africa in perspective. London, 1960.
Afr 2819.60.5	Karasapan, Celâ Tevfik. Libya; trablusgarp, bingazi ve fizan. Ankara, 1960.
Afr 4787.5	Karp, Mark. The economics of trusteeship in Somalia. Boston, 1960.
Afr 28.9	Kelly, Douglas C. Africa in paperbacks. East Lansing, Michigan, 1960.
Afr 6395.2.16	Kenyatta, Jona. Au pied du Mont Kenya. Paris, 1960.
Afr 2030.460.10	Keramane, Hadif. La pacification. Lausanne, 1960.
Afr 710.50	Kimble, George. Tropical Africa. N.Y., 1960. 2v.
Afr 8659.60.15	Kirby, Percival Robson. The true story of the Grosvenor. N.Y., 1960.
Afr 6420.57	Kitson, Frank. Gangs and counter-gangs. London, 1960.
Afr 8095.75	Kock, Victor de. Ons erfenis. Kaapstad, 1960.
Afr 8050.15.5	Krueger, Daniel. South African parties and policies, 1910-1960. London, 1960.
Afr 8050.15	Krueger, Daniel. South African parties and policies. Cape Town, 1960.
Afr 210.60.20	Kummernuss, Adolph. Wohin geht Afrika. Frankfurt a.M., 1960.
Afr 9047.20	Kuper, Hilda. Indian people in Natal. Natal, 1960.
Afr 11505.69.100	Kuper, Leo. The college brew. Durban, 1960.
Afr 6710.5	Kwayeb, E.K. Les institutions de droit public du pays Bamileke. Paris, 1960.
Afr 4155.15	Lackany, Radames Sany. Mersa Matruh and its environments. 2nd ed. Alexandria, 1960.
Afr 1869.60	Lacoste, Yves. L'Algérie. Paris, 1960.
Afr 115.50	Langenhove, F. Consciences tribales et nationales en Afrique noire. Bruxelles, 1960.
Afr 2030.460.15	Larteguy, J. Les dieux meurent en Algérie. Paris, 1960.
Afr 2030.460.5	Lauriol, M. Au service de l'Algérie française nouvelle. Alger, 1960.
Afr 3315.95	Lauterpacht, E. The Suez Canal settlement. London, 1960.
Afr 555.130	Lawman, Tony. From the hands of the wicked. London, 1960.
Afr 7818.5.5	Leblanc, Maria. Personnalité de la femme katangaise. Louvain, 1960.
Afr 609.60.25	Lenenberger, Hans. Die Stunde des schwarzen Mannes. München, 1960.
Afr 2749.60.15	Lerumeur, Guy. Le Sahara avant le pétrole. Paris, 1960.
Afr 7812.260	Leurquin, Philippe. Le niveau de vie des populations rurales du Ruanda-Urundi. Louvain, 1960.
Afr 7812.260.2	Leurquin, Philippe. Le niveau de vie des populations rurales du Ruanda-Urundi. Louvain, 1960.
Afr 9436.6	Leys, Colin. A new deal in central Africa. London, 1960.
Afr 7459.69	Liberia. Information Service. Liberia, story of progress. London? 1960.
Afr Doc 3002.5	Library of Congress. African Section. Official publications of British East Africa. Washington, 1960-1963.
Afr 9488.91	Lippert, Marie. The Matabeleland travel letters of Marie Lippert. Cape Town, 1960.
Afr 8687.258.5	Lister, Georgina. Reminiscences. Johannesburg, 1960.
Afr 725.10.10	Livingstone, David. Private journals. London, 1960.
Afr 7222.60	Lobato, A. A expansão portuguesa em Moçambique de 1498 a 1530. Lisboa, 1960. 3v.
Afr 8680.22	Loedolff, J.F. Nederlandse immigrante. Kaapstad, 1960.
Afr 6988.58.260	Logan, R.F. The central Namib Desert. Washington, 1960.
Afr 630.60	Lomax, Louis. The reluctant African. 1st ed. N.Y., 1960.
Afr 150.31	Lopes, F.F. A figura e a obra do Infante Dom Henrique. Lisboa, 1960.
Afr 9439.60.5	Loveday, A.F. Three stages of history in Rhodesia. Cape Town, 1960.
Afr 6497.18A	Low, D.A. Buganda and British overrule. London, 1960.
Afr 7015.30	Lupi, Luis C. Quem incendion o Congo. Lisboa, 1960.
Afr 50.15A	Mackenzie, William. Five elections in Africa. Oxford, 1960.
Afr 11546.58.100	MacNab, Roy M. The man of grass. London, 1960.
Afr 3305.20	Makarius, R. La jeunesse intellectuelle d'Egypte. Paris, 1960.
Afr 6395.2.35	Makorere College, Kampala, Uganda. Round Mount Kenya. Kampala, 1960.
Afr 2030.325	Manevy, Alain. L'Algérie à vingt ans. Paris, 1960.
Afr 2228.10	Marchand, Henri. La musulmane algérienne. Rodez, 1960.
Afr 626.68	Marcus, Edward. Investment and development possibilities in tropical Africa. N.Y., 1960.
Afr 8678.62.2	Marquard, L. The peoples and policies of South Africa. 2d. ed. London, 1960.
Afr 5437.5	Martynov, V.A. Zagovor protiv Kongo. Moscow, 1960.
Afr 2030.375	Maschino, Maurice. Le refus. Paris, 1960.
Afr 630.46	Mason, Philip. Race relations in Africa. London, 1960.
Afr 9445.40	Mason, Philip. Year of decision. London, 1960.
Afr 1957.30	Matterer, Amable. Journal de la prise d'Alger. Paris, 1960.
Afr 5090.12	Mauritania. La République islamique de Mauritanie. Paris, 1960.
Afr 8809.60	Meintzis, Johannes. Complex canvas. Johannesburg, 1960.
Afr 150.15.2	Mendes de Brito, Francisco. O Infante Dom Henrique e a civilização ocidental. Santarém, 1960.
Afr 7575.20	Mendiaux, Edouard. Moscou, Accra et le Congo. Bruxelles, 1960.
Afr 6194.20.16	Meyerowitz, Eva. The divine kingship in Ghana. London, 1960.
Afr 7575.25	Mezerik, A.G. Congo and the United Nations. N.Y., 1960. 3v.
Afr 2030.255	Mezerik, Avrahm G. Algerian developments, 1959. N.Y., 1960.
Afr 8678.145	Mezerik, Avrahm G. Apartheid in the Union of South Africa. N.Y., 1960.

Afr 6540.7   Middleton, J. Lugbara religion. London, 1960.
Afr Doc 7207.359   Mission Socioéconomique Centre Oubanqui. Enquête démographique Centre-Oubanqui 1959; méthodologie, résultats provisiores. Paris, 1960.
Afr 632.35   Mitchell, J.C. Tribalism and the plural society. London, 1960.
Afr 6212.10   Mitchison, Lois. Nigeria. London, 1960.
Afr 8283.24   Moggridge, Ann. The Jameson raid. Cape Town, 1960.
Afr 8678.205   Moodie, Donald. The record. Amsterdam, 1960.
Afr 150.68   Moreira de Sa, Artur. O Infante D. Henrique e a universidade. Paris, 1960.
Afr 1623.960.5   Morocco. Division de la Coordination Économique et du Plan. Plan quinquennal, 1960-1964. Rabat, 1960.
Afr 1623.960   Morocco. Division de la Coordination Economique et du Plan. Tableaux économiques du Maroc. Rabat, 1960.
Afr 1340.42   Morocco. Ministère de l'Information et du Tourisme. Documents sur la constitution. Rabat, 1960.
Afr 5074.37   Morocco. Ministère des Affaires Etrangères. Livre blanc sur la Mauritanie. Rabat, 1960.
Afr 9635.22A   Morris, Colin. Colin Morris and Kenneth Haunda. London, 1960.
Afr 150.2.40   Moura, J.J.N. O Infante Dom Henrique na conquista das Canarias. Villa Real de Santo Antonio, 1960.
Afr 8125.15   Mueller, C.F.J. Johannes Frederick Kirsten oor die toestand van die Kaapkolonie in 1795. Pretoria, 1960.
Afr 2819.60   Murabet, Mohammed. Some facts about Libya. Malta, 1960.
Afr 2209.60.5   Muslim Students Federation. Life in Algeria. 3 ed. London, 1960.
Afr 2030.460   Mustapha G. Barberousse. Paris, 1960.
Afr 3310.10.20   Nasser, G.A. On peace. (Cairo I.S.A.). Cairo, 1960. 2 pam.
Afr 9165.42.45   Neame, Lawrence. City built on gold. Johannesburg, 1960.
Afr 1110.25   Near East Conference. Current problems in North Africa. Princeton, 1960.
Afr 4115.17   Nelson, Nina. Shepheard's hotel. London, 1960.
Afr 5219.60   Niane, D.T. Soundjata. Paris, 1960.
Afr 7575.12   Niedergang, M. Tempête sur le Congo. Paris, 1960.
Afr 6295.185   Nigeria, Eastern. Commission of Inquiry into the Administration of the Affairs of the Enugu Municipal Council. Report of the inquiry into the administration of the affairs of the Enugu Municipal Council. v.1-2. Enugu, 1960.
Afr 6275.75   Nigeria, Eastern. Ministry of Information. Eastern Nigeria. Enugu, 1960.
Afr 6210.34   Nigeria. Electoral Committee. Report on the Nigeria federal election. Lagos, 1960.
Afr 6298.60A   Nigeria Broadcasting Corporation. Eminent Nigerians of the nineteenth century. Cambridge, 1960.
Afr 6277.50   Nigeria trade journal, Lagos. Special independence issue, 1960. Lagos, 1960.
Afr 6457.24   Njuguna Wa Gakuo, E. Bedeutung und Möglichkeiten. Freiburg, 1960.
Afr 6176.30.5   Nkrumah, Kwame. Hands off Africa. Accra, 1960.
Afr 7122.66   Nogueira, Jofre A. Angola na epoca pombalina. Lisboa, 1960.
Afr 2030.405   Noureddine, Meziane. Un Algérien raconte. Paris, 1960.
Afr 9858.5   Nyasaland. Southworth Commission. Report on the incident which took place outside Ryalls Hotel. Zomba, 1960.
Afr 9760.15   Nyasaland Constitutional Conference, London, 1960. Report. London, 1960.
Afr 609.60.70   Ottenberg, Simon. Cultures and societies of Africa. N.Y., 1960.
Afr 8659.60   Our first half-century, 1910-1960. Johannesburg, 1960.
Afr 12785.89.130   Ousmane, Sembene. Les bouts de bois de Dieu, Banty Mam Yall. Photoreproduction. Paris, 1960.
Afr 12985.65.100   Oyono, Ferdinand. Chemin d'Europe. Paris, 1960.
Afr 8283.23   Pakenham, E.H.P. Jameson's raid. London, 1960.
Afr 6210.43   Palau Marti, Montserrat. Essai sur la notion de roi chez les Yoraba et les Aja-fon. Paris, 1960.
Afr 8688.5.5   Pama, C. Simbole van die Unie. Kaapstad, 1960.
Afr 150.37   Paris. Musée National du Louvre. Musée de Marine. Henri le navigateur et les decouvreurs portugais. Paris, 1960.
Afr 7812.260.20   Parisis, A. Les finances communales et urbaines au Congo belge. Bruxelles, 1960.
Afr 9500.20   Parker, Franklin. African development and education in Southern Rhodesia. Columbus, 1960.
Afr 150.50   Passos, Vergilio. A projecção do infante no mundo. Lisboa, 1960.
Afr 11675.87.112   Paton, Alan. Cry, the beloved country. N.Y., 1960.
Afr 635.62   Paulme, D. Femmes d'Afrique noire. Paris, 1960.
Afr 8145.25   Pauw, Barthold. Religion in a Tswana chiefdom. London, 1960.
Afr 6295.60   Pedraza, Howard. Dirrioboola-Gha. London, 1960.
Afr 718.46.5   Pedroso Gamitto, Antonio Candido. King Kazembe and the Marave, Cheva, Bisa, Bemba,Lundo. v.1-2. Lisboa, 1960.
Afr 7540.30   Perin, François. Les institutions politiques du Congo...30 juin 1960. Bruxelles, 1960.
Afr 8687.309   Philipps, T. Philipps, 1820 settler. Pietermaritzburg, 1960.
Afr 9448.65   Phillips, Cecil E.L. The vision splendid. London, 1960.
Afr 6176.20   Phillips, John F. Kwame Nkrumah and the future of Africa. London, 1960.
Afr 8678.165   Phillips, Norman. The tragedy of apartheid. N.Y., 1960.
Afr 9499.74   Phoenix Group. Planning the development of the wealth of three nations. Salisbury, 1960.
Afr 8678.130   Pienaar, S. South Africa. London, 1960.
Afr 8845.15   Port Elizabeth Publicity Association. Port Elizabeth municipal centenary. Port Elizabeth, 1960.
Afr 150.70   Portugal. Comissão Executiva das Comemorações do V. Centenario da Morte do Infante Dom Henrique. Exposição Henriquina. Lisboa, 1960.
Afr 150.64   Portugal. Comissão Executiva das Comemorações do V. Centenario da Morte do Infante Dom Henrique. Monumenta Henricina. Coimbra, 1960. 9v.
Afr 150.62   Portugal. Comissão Executiva das Comemorações do V Centenario da Morte do Infante Dom Henrique. Bibliografia Henriquino. Lisboa, 1960. 2v.
Afr 150.2.65   Portugal. Comissão Executiva das Comemorações do V Centenario da Morte do Infante Dom Henrique. Henri le Navigateur. Lisboa, 1960.
Afr 150.2.80   Portugal. Comissão Executiva das Comemorações do V Centenario da Morte do Infante Dom Henrique. Programa das comemorações. Lisboa, 1960.
Afr 609.60.85   Potekhin, I.I. Afrika smotrit v budushchee. Moscow, 1960.
Afr 7540.34   Poupart, R. Première esquisse de l'évolution du syndicalisme au Congo. Bruxelles, 1960.

Afr 50.20   Prasad, Bisheshwar. Contemporary Africa. N.Y., 1960.
Afr 8045.54   Progressive Party of South Africa. Molteno report. Johannesburg, 1960-62.
Afr 609.60.80   Ragusin Righi, Livio. Viaggio nell Africa nera in fermento. Trieste, 1960.
Afr 4732.21   Rainero, R. I primi tentativi di colonizzazione agricola. Milano, 1960.
Afr 210.60.65   Rainero, Romain. Il risveglio dell'Africa nera. Bari, 1960.
Afr 9549.60   Raven, Faith. Central Africa. London, 1960.
Afr 8678.185   Reeves, Ambrose. Shooting at Sharpville. London, 1960.
Afr 150.2.30F   Reis-Santos, Luiz. Iconografia henriquina. Coimbra, 1960.
Afr 9165.71.5   Rex, H.M. Pretoria van kerkplaas tot regeringsetel. Kaapstad, 1960.
Afr 2030.360   Reygasse, René. Témoinage d'un ultra sur le drame algérien. Paris, 1960.
Afr 210.60.60   Rhodes-Livingstone Institute, Lusaka, Northern Rhodesia. Conference, 14th, Lusaka, 1960. Myth in modern Africa. Lusaka, 1960.
Afr 9635.15   Rhodesia, Northern. Commission to Inquire into the Participation of Africans in Local Government. Report. Lusaka, 1960.
Afr 9699.59   Rhodesia, Northern. Special Commissioner for the Western Province. First report on a regional survey of the copperbelt, 1959. Lusaka, 1960.
Afr 9609.20F   Rhodesia and Nyasaland. National accounts of the federation. Salisbury, 1960.
Afr 9499.35   Rhodesia and Nyasaland. Report. Salisbury, 1960.
Afr Doc 3872.2   Rhodesia and Nyasaland. Report on Bulawayo African demographic survey, held in May 1959. Salisbury, 1960.
Afr Doc 3807.359F   Rhodesia and Nyasaland. Report on Umtali and Gwelo African demographic surveys held in August and September, 1959. Salisbury, 1960.
Afr 9510.12.5F   Rhodesia and Nyasaland. Report on urban African budget survey in Bulawayo, 1958/59. Salisbury, 1960.
Afr Doc 3507.356   Rhodesia and Nyasaland. Central Statistical Office. Census of population, 1956. Salisbury, 1960.
Afr 9538.12   Rhodesia and Nyasaland. National Archives. A select bibliography of recent publications. Salisbury, 1960.
Afr 8678.68.5   Rhoodie, N.J. Apartheid. Cape Town, 1960.
Afr 8678.68   Rhoodie, N.J. Die apartheidsgedougte. Kaapstad, 1960.
Afr 2030.305   Ribaud, Paul. Barricades pour un drapeau. Paris, 1960.
Afr 6310.36   Richards, Audrey. East African chiefs. London, 1960.
Afr 6390.65   Richards, C.G. East African explorers. London, 1960.
Afr 150.2.90   Rio de Janeiro. Cabinete Portugues de Leitura. Catálogo henriquino do Real Cabinete Português de Leitura do Rio de Janeiro. Lisboa, 1960.
Afr 210.60   Ritner, Peter. The death of Africa. N.Y., 1960.
Afr 718.45   Rogers, M. When rivers meet. London, 1960.
Afr 5243.343.15   Ronch, Jean. La religion et la magie songhay. Paris, 1960.
Afr 8678.140   Roskam, Karel Lodewijk. Apartheid and discrimination. Leyden, 1960.
Afr 6019.60   Rothchild, Donald. Toward unity in Africa. Washington, 1960.
Afr 8847.83.10   Rothmann, M.E. The drostdy at Swellendam. Swellendam, 1960.
Afr 8685.327   Rousseau, Francois. Handbook on the Group Areas Act. Cape Town, 1960.
Afr 2030.350   Roy, Jules. La guerre d'Algérie. Paris, 1960.
Afr 6212.15   Royal Institute of International Affairs. Nigeria. Oxford, 1960.
Afr 150.4.10   Russell, Peter E. Prince Henry the Navigator. London, 1960.
Afr 10115.2.2   Rutherfoord, Peggy. African voices. N.Y., 1960.
Afr 5753.15   Ruud, Joergen. Taboo. Oslo, 1960.
Afr 8678.190   Sabloniere, Margrit. Apartheid. Amsterdam, 1960.
Afr 5405.179   Saintoyant, J.F. L'affaire du Congo 1905. Paris, 1960.
Afr 210.60.5   Sampson, Anthony. Common sense about Africa. London, 1960.
Afr 9448.50   Sanger, Clyde. Central African emergency. London, 1960.
Afr 2030.260   Savary, Alain. Nationalisme algérien et grandeur française. Paris, 1960.
Afr 8659.60.5   Savoy, Alan. Thunder in the air. London, 1960.
Afr 5480.260   Scheid, T. Journal d'un safari au Tchad. Bruxelles, 1960.
Afr 2609.60   Schleinitz, E.G. Tunisien. Frankfurt a.M., 1960.
Afr 8045.50   Schoor, M.C.E. Republieke en republikeine. Kaapstad, 1960.
Afr 3143.15   Schregle, Goetz. Die Sultanin Sagarat ad-Durr. Inaug.-Diss. Erlangen, 1960.
Afr 2687.1   Sebag, Paul. Un faubourg de Tunis, Saida Manoubia. Paris, 1960.
Afr 3340.5   Sedar, Irving. Behind the Egyptian sphinx. Philadelphia, 1960.
Afr 11780.51.100   Sellier, Richard. Twin-brother hell. London, 1960.
Afr 150.2.45   Selvagem, Carlos (pseud.) Infante Dom Henrique. Lisboa, 1960.
Afr 8676.60.20   Serton, P. Suid-Afrika en Brasilie. Kaapstad, 1960.
Afr 5892.5   Seychelles. A plan for Seychelles. Victoria, 1960? 5 pam.
Afr 6134.8   Sierra Leone. Constitutional Conference, London, 1960. Report. Freetown, 1960.
Afr 550.115   Silva Rego, Antonio da. Alguns problemas sociologicos missionarios da Africa negra. Lisboa, 1960.
Afr 4575.6   Simoons, Frederick. Northwest Ethiopia. Madison, 1960.
Afr 7815.16   Slade, Ruth. The Belgian Congo, some recent changes. London, 1960.
Afr 6295.60.5   Smith, Michael. Government in Zazzau, 1800-1950. London, 1960.
Afr 6275.60   Smythe, Hugh. The new Nigerian elite. Stanford, 1960.
Afr 6739.260   Societe d'Etudes pour le Developpement. Rapport sur les possibilités de développement industriél. Paris, 1960.
Afr 6739.260.5F   Société Générale d'Etudes et de Planification, Paris. Cameroun. Paris, 1960. 2v.
Afr Doc 4307.8   South Africa. Bureau of Statistics. Uniestatistieke, oor vyftig jaar. Jubileumuitgawe. Pretoria, 1960.
Afr 8028.140   South Africa. Department of Colored Affairs. Consolidated general bibliography. Cape Town, 1960.
Afr 8673.10   South Africa. South African Information Service. South Africa, 1910-1960. Pretoria, 1960.
Afr 8667.71   South Africa. South African Information Service. The South African tradition, a brief survey. N.Y., 1960.
Afr 8676.60   South African Council for Scientific and Industrial Research. A survey of rent paying capacity of urban natives in South Africa. Pretoria, 1960.

1960 - cont.

Afr 8673.17F Souvenir of South Africa. Two hundred thirty-one photographs in full colour. Johannesburg, 1960.

Afr 8676.60.5 Sporner, F.P. South African predicament. London, 1960.

Afr 8678.215 Spottiswoode, Hildegarde. South Africa. 2. ed. Cape Town, 1960.

Afr 8687.345 Spulhaus, Karl Antonio. From Lisbon via Lübeck to Cape Town. Cape Town, 1960.

Afr 8676.60.30 Standard Bank of South Africa. Union of South Africa national income and production. Johannesburg, 1960.

Afr 626.75 Stanford Research Institute. African development. Menlo Park, Calif., 1960.

Afr 718.2.135 Sterling, Thomas. Stanley's way. 1st Amer. ed. N.Y., 1960.

Afr 6720.60 Stoecker, Helmuth. Kamerun unter deutscher Kolonialherrschaft. v.1- Berlin, 1960- 2v.

Afr 9436.10 Stonehouse, John. Prohibited immigrant. London, 1960.

Afr 609.60.45 Storey, H.R. The continent of Africa. London, 1960.

Afr 115.80 Study Congress on International Cooperation in Africa. La cooperazione internazionale in Africa. Milano, 1960.

Afr Doc 1307.356.20 Sudan. Department of Statistics. First population census of Sudan 1955-56; methods report. Khartoum, 1960.

Afr 550.100 Sundklur, Bengt. The Christian ministry in Africa. Uppsala, 1960.

Afr 210.60.50 Sundstroem, Erland. Afrika spronger hojorna. Stockholm, 1960.

Afr 115.40 Symposium on Africa, Wellesley College. 1960 symposium on Africa. Wellesley, 1960.

Afr 5549.60.5 Tananarive. Bibliotheque Universitaire. Madagasihara, regards vers le passe. Tananarive, 1960.

Afr 9769.60 Tanser, George Henry. A history of Nyasaland. Capetown, 1960.

Afr 6740.15 Tardits, Claude. Contribution à l'étude des populations Bamileke de l'Ouest Cameroun. Paris, 1960.

Afr 150.2.60 Tavares, Luis C. O Infante Dom Henrique e os descobrimentos. Braga, 1960.

Afr 6275.85 Taylor Woodrow, ltd. Building for the future in Nigeria. London, 1960.

Afr 1713.14 Al-Tazi, Abd Al- Hali. Eleven centuries in the university of al-qarawiyyin. Mohammedia, 1960.

Afr 28.88 Tenri Central Library, Tanba City, Japan. Africana. Tenri, 1960. 2v.

Afr 7530.12 Tervuren, Belgium. Musée Royale de l'Afrique Centrale. Inventaire des documents provenant de la mission. Bruxelles, 1960.

Afr 2719.60 Thomas, Marc-Robert. Sahara et communauté. Paris, 1960.

Afr 8340.30 Thompson, Leonard. The unification of South Africa. Oxford, 1960.

Afr 5404.10 Thompson, V.M. The emerging states of French Equatorial Africa. Stanford, Calif., 1960.

Afr 2030.50.15 Tillion, G. Les ennemis complémentaires. Paris, 1960.

Afr Doc 6781.735 Togo. Service de la Statistique Général. Etude démographique du pays Kabre, 1957. Paris, 1960.

Afr 609.60.75 Torres, Joaquin. Viaje por Africa. Buenos Aires, 1960.

Afr 9499.27 Tow, Leonard. The manufacturing economy of Southern Rhodesia, problems and prospects. Washington, 1960.

Afr 9155.10 Transvaal. Provincial Council. Official guide. Cape Town, 1960.

Afr 4732.20 Trevaskis, G.K.N. Eritrea. London, 1960.

Afr 11848.87.100 Trotter, W.M. Radiance of the veld. Ilfracombe, 1960.

Afr 2623.960F Tunisia. Secrétariat d'Etat à l'Information. Tunisia works. Tunis, 1960.

Afr 6542.4 Uganda. Commission of Inquiry into Disturbances in the Eastern Province. Report. Entebbe, 1960.

Afr 4559.60 Ullendorff, Edward. The Ethiopians. London, 1960.

Afr 6720.60.5 Union des Peuples Camerounais. Memoire soumis à la Conférence des états africains indépendants. Le Caire, 1960.

Afr 2030.410 Union Nationale des Étudiants de France. Le syndicalisme étudiant et le problème algérien. Paris, 1960.

Afr 5212.2 Union Soudanaise. Congrès extraordinaire de l'U.S.R.D.A. le 22 septembre 1960, le Mali continue. Bamako? 1960?

Afr 3986.12F United Arab Republic. Cadre du plan quinquennal général. Le Caire, 1960.

Afr 3986.9 United Arab Republic. The economy of the U.A.R. Cairo, 1960.

Afr 3986.11 United Arab Republic. Overall five year plan for economic and social development. n.p., 1960.

Afr 3340.10 United Arab Republic. The United Arab Republic. Cairo, 1960.

Afr 3986.960.25 United Arab Republic. National Planning Committee. General frame of the five year plan. Cairo, 1960.

Afr 3979.60.10 United Arab Republic. State Tourist Administration. Bases of tourist statistics. Cairo, 1960?

Afr 9499.30 United States. Trade Mission to the Federation of Rhodesia and Nyasaland. Report. Washington, 1960.

Afr 3335.5 United States Trade Mission to the United Arab Republic. Seven Americans in theUnited Arab Republic. Washington, 1960.

Afr 5272.2 Upper Volta. Laws, statutes, etc. Le drame de la Haute-Volta. Paris, 1960.

Afr 5282.2 Upper Volta. Ministère des Finances, des Affaires Economiques et du Plan. Rapport économique, 1959. Ouagadougou, 1960.

Afr 2285.31 Vanney, Jean-René. Pluie et crue dans le Sahara nord-occidental. Alger, 1960.

Afr 8659.60.20 Varley, Douglas. South African reading in earlier days. Johannesburg, 1960.

Afr 150.60 Vasconcellos, Joaquim de. Taboas da pintura portugueza no seculo XV. Lisboa, 1960.

Afr 609.60.15 Vaulx, Bernard de. En Afrique. Paris, 1960.

Afr 7809.60.15 Verbung, C. Afscheid van Kongo. Antwerpen, 1960.

Afr 8688.6 Villiers, Daniel P. A history of the de Villiers family. Cape Town, 1960.

Afr 8678.291 Waetberg, Per. På svarta listan. Stockholm, 1960.

Afr 5415.5 Walker, A.R. Notes d'histoire du Gabon. Montpellier, 1960.

Afr 8180.10.4 Walker, E.A. The great trek. 4th ed. London, 1960.

Afr 109.60.10 Ward, William. A history of Africa. London, 1960. 2v.

Afr 6275.136 Watson, George Derek. A human geography of Nigeria. London, 1960.

Afr 9050.10 Watson, R.G.T. Tongaati. London, 1960.

Afr 6390.37 Waugh, Evelyn. A tourist in Africa. London, 1960.

Afr 7369.60 Welch, Galbraith. The jet lighthouse. London, 1960.

Afr 609.60.35 Westphal, Clarence. African heritage. Minneapolis, 1960.

1960 - cont.

Afr 3675.60 Wharton, William M. The Sudan in pre-history and history. Khartoum, 1960.

Afr 3310.60A Wheelock, K. Nasser's new Egypt. N.Y., 1960.

Afr 8676.60.17 Wijnholds, Heiko. Gren, goud en goedere. Pretoria, 1960.

Afr 2929.60 Willimot, St. G. Field studies in Libya. Durham, Eng., 1960.

Afr 210.60.30 Woddis, Jack. Africa, the roots of revolt. London, 1960.

Afr 6420.25 Wood, Susan B. Kenya. London, 1960.

Afr 11057.7 Wright, David. South African stories. London, 1960.

Afr 5933.2 Yanguas Mirarete, José. Antecedentes históricos. Sidi Infi, 1960.

Afr 6887.12.5 Young, Roland A. Land and politics among the Luguru of Tanganyika. London, 1960.

Afr 6887.12.10 Young, Roland A. Smoke in the hills. Evanston, 1960.

Afr 5243.125.25 Zahan, Dominique. Sociétés d'initiation bambara. v.1. Paris, 1960.

Afr 6562.2 Zanzibar National Party. Whither Zanzibar. Cairo, 1960.

1961

Afr 4559.61 Abu al-Hajjaj, Y. A contribution to the physiography of northern Ethiopia. London, 1961.

Afr 10671.12.110 Achebe, Chinua. No longer at ease. N.Y., 1961.

Afr 109.61.30 Adiko, A. Histoire des peuples noirs. Abidjan, 1961.

Afr 45.61 African Conference on the Rule of Law, Lagos, Nigeria. A report on the proceedings of the conference. Genève, 1961.

Afr 626.120 Agostino Orsini, P. I problemi economici dell'Africa e l'Europa. Roma, 1961.

Afr 210.61.65 Akademiia Nauk SSSR. Institut Afriki. Afrika, 1956-1961. Moscow, 1961.

Afr 2221.2 Algeria, a synthesis of civilizations. n.p., 1961.

Afr 2223.960.15 Algeria. Caisse D'Equipement pour Le Développement de l'Algérie. Rapport sur l'exécution du programme d'équipement en 1960. Alger, 1961.

Afr 2209.61.20 Algeria. Conseil Supérieur de la Promotion Sociale en Algérie. Compte rendu analytique de la troisième session. Alger, 1961.

Afr 2030.340.10 Algerian Front of National Liberation. La révolution algérienne par les textes. Paris, 1961.

Afr 2030.461.15 Alleg, Henri. Prisionniers de guerre. Paris, 1961.

Afr 8378.379.5 Allighan, Garry. Verwoerd - the end, a look-back from the future. London, 1961.

Afr 5040.2 Ansprenger, Franz. Politik im schwarzen Afrika. Köln, 1961.

Afr 6498.61A Apter, David E. The political kingdom in Uganda. Princeton, N.J., 1961.

Afr 45.61.10 Arboussier, Gabriel. L'Afrique vers l'unité. Issy, 1961.

Afr 2623.961.5 Ardant, G. La Tunisie d'aujourd'hui et de demain. Paris, 1961.

Afr 3675.28.2 Arkell, A.J. A history of the Sudan. 2.ed. London, 1961.

Afr 1409.18.2 Arribas Palau, Mariano. Cartas arabes de Marruecos en tiempo de Mawlay al Yazid, 1790-1792. Tetuan, 1961.

Afr 1369.61A Ashford, Douglas. Political change in Morocco. Princeton, 1961.

Afr 2223.961.5 Association pour la Recherche. La consommation des familles d'Algérie. Paris, 1961.

Afr 3295.5 Atiyah, S. Razvitie natsionalno-osvoboditelnogo dvizheniia v Egipte. Moscow, 1961.

Afr 1369.61.5 Avakov, R.M. Marokko. Moscow, 1961.

Afr 6212.20 Azikiwe, N. Zik. Cambridge, 1961.

Afr 5243.207 Ba, A.H. Koumen. Paris, 1961.

Afr 3986.961.10 Bahig, A.F. Selected passages for students of commerce. 4th ed. Alexandria, 1961.

Afr 5235.261 Bamako. Chambre de Commerce, d'Agriculture et d'Industrie. Mali. Bamako, 1961.

Afr 9499.50 Barber, W.J. The economy of British Central Africa. Stanford, 1961.

Afr 4070.62 Barbour, K.M. The Republic of the Sudan. London, 1961.

Afr 7122.80 Barreiros, Americo. A verdade sobre os acontecimentos de Angola. T.1-2. 2.ed. Angola, 1961.

Afr 2970.5 Bary, Erica de. Ghadames, Ghadames. München, 1961.

Afr 2030.461.5 Bedjaoui, Mohammed. La révolution algérienne et le droit. Bruxelles, 1961.

Afr 2030.461.45 Behr, Edward. The Algerian problem. London, 1961.

Afr 9170.7 Behrman, F. My fifty-odd years in Johannesburg. Johannesburg, 1961.

Afr 7937.2 Belgium. Centre de Recherche et d'Information. Rwanda politique (1958-1960). Bruxelles, 1961.

Afr 6192.85 Bell, Willis. The roadmakers. Accra, 1961.

Afr 5844.2 Benedict, B. Indians in a plural society. London, 1961.

Afr 6420.72 Bennett, G. The Kenyatta election. London, 1961.

Afr 6210.32 Berelt, Lionel. Constitutional problems of federalism in Nigeria. Lagos, 1961.

Afr 545.32 Bernardi, Bernardo. Le religioni in Africa. Torino, 1961.

Afr 9149.61.10 Bigalke, Rudolph. Let's visit the Kruger park. Johannesburg, 1961.

Afr 9439.61 Black, Colin. The lands and peoples of Rhodesia and Nyasaland. London, 1961.

Afr 626.95 Black, Eugene Robert. Tales of two continents. Athens, Ga., 1961.

Afr 9448.55 Blake, W.T. Central African survey. London, 1961.

Afr 11216.5 Bley, J. Benibengor. Thoughts of youth. Aboso, 1961.

Afr 1955.63 Bloch, P. Algérie, terre des occasions perdues. Paris, 1961.

Afr 11219.66.110 Bloom, Harry. King Kong. London, 1961.

Afr 5318.40 Bochkarev, I.A. Gvineia segodnia. Moscow, 1961.

Afr 2749.61.5 Bodington, Nicolas. The awakening Sahara. London, 1961.

Afr 5019.61 Boubacar, Diabete. Porte ouverte sur la communauté franco-africaine. Bruxelles, 1961.

Afr 2030.420 Boudot, Pierre. L'Algérie mal enchaînée. Paris, 1961.

Afr 8089.61 Boyce, Arnold N. Europe and South Africa. 2d ed. Cape Town, 1961.

Afr 150.40.5 Bradford, Ernle. Southward the caravels. London, 1961.

Afr 7540.36 Brausch, G. Belgian administration in the Congo. London, 1961.

Afr 6879.61 British Information Services. Tanganyika. N.Y., 1961.

Afr 6879.61.10 British Information Services. Tanganyika. N.Y., 1961.

Afr 8369.61.5 Broughton, M. Press and politics of South Africa. Cape Town, 1961.

Afr 6164.19 Brown, G.N. An active history of Ghana. London, 1961. 2v.

Afr 6979.61 Bruwer, Johannes Petrus. Ons mandate: Suidwes-Afrika. Johannesburg, 1961.

Afr 210.61.35 Bryan, G. McLeod. Whither Africa. Richmond, 1961.

Afr 530.13 Buettner, Kurt. Die Anfänge der deutschen Kolonial-Politik in Ostafrika. Berlin, 1961.

Afr 44622.89.100   al-Buhry, Hemed Abdallah. Utenzi wa AbdirRahmani na Sufiyani. Dar es Salaam, 1961.

Afr 11246.51.100   Bulpin, Thomas U. The white whirlwind. Johannesburg, 1961.

Afr 5240.12   Bureau pour le Développement de la Production Agricole Outre-Mer. La modernisation rurale dans la haute-vallée du Niger. Paris, 1961? 3v.

Afr 650.2F   C.S.A. Meeting of Specialists on Urbanisation and Its Social Aspects Abidjan, Ivory Coast, 1961. Reports and recommendations. London, 1961.

Afr 7122.54   Caio, H. Angola. 3.ed. Lisboa, 1961.

Afr 3326.3   Cairo. Institute of National Planning. Institute of National Planning. Cairo, 1961.

Afr 7575.30   Calder, Ritchie. Agony of the Congo. London, 1961.

Afr 8369.61A   Calvocoressi, P. South Africa and world opinion. London, 1961.

Afr 6109.15   Cameron, Ian Donald. The West African councillor. 2d ed. London, 1961.

Afr 109.61   Cameron, James. The African revolution. London, 1961.

Afr 109.61.1   Cameron, James. The African revolution. N.Y., 1961.

Afr 6705.5   Cameroon, West. Constitution. West Cameroon Constitution, 1961. Buea, 1961.

Afr 6739.261F   Cameroon. Ministère des Finances et du Plan. Premier plan quinquennal économique. Yaounde, 1961.

Afr 5488.12   Capot-Rey, R. Borkou et Ounianga. Alger, 1961.

Afr 7812.261.10   Carbonnelle, C. L'économie des deux Ueles. Bruxelles, 1961.

Afr 109.61.15   Cardot, Vera. Belles pages de l'histoire africaine. Paris, 1961.

Afr 6096.10   Carney, David E. Government and economy in British West Africa. N.Y., 1961.

Afr 2731.15.70   Carrouges, Michel. Foucauld devant l'Afrique du nord. Paris, 1961.

Afr 9549.61   Cerulli, Ernesta. Nel paese dei Bantu. Torino, 1961.

Afr 7122.52   Cesar, A. Angola, 1961. 3. ed. Verbo, 1961.

Afr 5549.61   Chapus, Georges. Manuel d'histoire de Madagascar. Paris, 1961.

Afr 626.106   Charbonneau, J. Marches et marchands d'Afrique noire. Paris, 1961.

Afr 2030.461.35   Charby, J. L'Algérie en prison. Paris, 1961.

Afr 6333.61A   Chidzero, B.T.G. Tanganyika and international trusteeship. London, 1961.

Afr 500.80   Chinese-African People's Friendship Association. The Chinese people resolutely support the just struggle of the African people. Peking, 1961.

Afr 7575.80.5   Chome, Jules. A propos d'un livre posthume de Patrice Lumumba. Bruxelles, 1961.

Afr 7886.5   Choprix, Guy. La naissance d'une ville; étude géographique de Paulis, 1934-1957. Bruxelles, 1961.

Afr 6280.9.20   Chubb, L.T. Ibo land tenure. 2. ed. Ibadan, 1961.

Afr 10673.48.100   Clark, John Pepper. Song of a goat. Ibadan, 1961.

Afr 28.82   Coisel. L'Afrique à travers les publications. Paris, 1961.

Afr 8676.61   Cole, M.M. South Africa. London, 1961.

Afr 8847.34   Collier, Joy. Frontier post, the story of Grahamstown. Grahamstown, 1961.

Afr 6275.80   Collis, Robert. African encounter. N.Y., 1961.

Afr 6328.3   Collister, Peter. The last days of slavery, England and the East African slave trade, 1870-1900. Dar es Salaam, 1961.

Afr 2030.460.30   Comité pour la Paix en Algérie. La Belgique devant le problème algérien. Chênée, 1961.

Afr Doc 7386.5.73   Congo (Brazzaville). Statistique Générale. Recensement démographique de Pointe-Noire, 1958. Paris, 1961.

Afr 45.61.5   Constitutions des états africains d'expression française. Paris, 1961.

Afr 699.61   Cornet, Jacques. Pharaons d'hier et Fellahs d'aujourd'hui. Lyon, 1961.

Afr 7122.70   Cotta, Goncalves. Grito de Angola. Luanda, 1961.

Afr 8040.8   Cowen, D.V. The foundations of freedom. Cape Town, 1961.

Afr 9193.2   Cowen, D.V. Swaziland, report on constitutional reform. n.p., 1961.

Afr 6144.5A   Cox-George, N.A. Finance and development in West Africa. London, 1961.

Afr 2224.961   Cumunel, G. Guide administratif. Paris, 1961.

Afr 2224.961.2   Cumunel, G. Guide administratif. Mise à jour au 15. juin 1961. Paris, 1961.

Afr 2030.461.25   Darbois, Dominique. Les Algériens en guerre. Milano, 1961.

Afr 11317.76.100   Darks, D. Offei. Friends today, enemies tomorrow. Akropong, 1961.

Afr 3163.15.5   Darrag, Ahmad. L'Egypte sous le règne de Barsbay. Damas, 1961.

Afr 5645.10   Datlin, S.V. Malgashskaia republika. Moscow, 1961.

Afr 7815.29   Dauer, Alfonsus. Studien zur Ethnogenese bei den Mangbetu. Mainz, 1961.

Afr 2030.461.20   Davezies, Robert. Le temps de la justice. Lausanne, 1961.

Afr 590.75   Davidson, B. Black mother. Boston, 1961.

Afr 6218.12   Davies, H.O. Nigeria. London, 1961.

Afr 8678.240   Debeer, Zacharias Johannes. Multi-racial South Africa. London, 1961.

Afr 550.146   Dehoney, Wayne. African diary. Nashville, 1961.

Afr 6470.250   Delf, George. Jomo Kenyatta. London, 1961.

Afr 6470.250.10   Delf, George. Jomo Kenyatta. 1st ed. Garden City, 1961.

Afr 8676.61.5F   Denys, A. Land of apartheid, an introduction to the word "apartheid." Natal, 1961.

Afr 8678.245   Deridder, J.C. The personality of the urban African in South Africa. London, 1961.

Afr 555.135   Desallues, Elisabeth. Toumliline. Paris, 1961.

Afr 2209.61.5   Descloitres, R. L'Algérie des Bidonvilles. Paris, 1961.

Afr 2609.61   Despois, Jean. La Tunisie. Paris, 1961.

Afr 210.61.10   Dessarre, Eve. Que sera le destin de l'Afrique? Paris, 1961.

Afr 626.37   Dia, Mamadou. The African nations and world solidarity. N.Y., 1961.

Afr 5920.14   Diaz de Villegas, José. Africa septentrional: Marruecos, el nexo del Estrecho. Madrid, 1961.

Afr 150.2.35   Diaz de Villegas, José. La epopeya de Enrique el Navegante. Madrid, 1961.

Afr 1494.55F   Diplomatist. In memoriam, His Majesty King Mohammed V. London, 1961.

Afr 8678.210   Doxey, G.V. The industrial colour bar in South Africa. London, 1961.

Afr 210.61   Duffy, James. Africa speaks. Princeton, N.J., 1961.

Afr 2030.461.10   Dufresnay, Claude. Des officiers parlent. Paris, 1961.

Afr 7809.61   Dugauquier, D.P. Congo cauldron. London, 1961.

Afr 7575.66   Dumont, G.H. La table ronde belgo-congolaise. Paris, 1961.

Afr 9060.25   Durban, Natal. Durban. Johannesburg, 1961.

Afr 6457.10   East Africa High Commission. Capital formation in Kenya, 1954-1960. Nairobi, 1961. 2 pam.

Afr 6457.15   East Africa High Commission. Reported employment and wages in Kenya. Nairobi, 1961.

Afr Doc 3307.359.5   East Africa High Commission. East African Statistical Department. Uganda census, 1959; African population. Entebbe, 1961.

Afr 1869.57.2   Egretaud, Marcel. Réalité de la nation algérienne. Paris, 1961.

Afr 3986.961.15   Egypt. Information Administration. Assouan. Le Caire, 1961.

Afr 10675.47.160   Ekwensi, Cyprian. Jagua Nana. London, 1961.

Afr 40.61   Elias, T.O. Government and politics in Africa. N.Y. 1961.

Afr 6538.25   Elkan, Walter. The economic development of Uganda. London, 1961.

Afr 6149.99.5   Eminent Sierra Leoneans in the nineteenth century. Freetown, 1961.

Afr 609.61.5   Eskelund, Karl. While God slept. London, 1961.

Afr Doc 309.502   Ethiopia. Ministry of Education and Fine Arts Government, mission, private, community and church schools, 1959-1960. Addis Ababa, 1961?

Afr 530.15   Etinger, J. Bonn greift nach Afrika. Berlin, 1961.

Afr 2030.461.95   Extraditions d'Algériens, ou le chemin de la guillotine. Bruxelles, 1961.

Afr 7175.52   Falcato, J. Angola do meu coração. Lisboa, 1961.

Afr 210.61.55A   Fanon, Franz. Les damnés de la terre. Paris, 1961.

Afr 2030.461.65   Fauvet, J. La Fronde des généraux. Paris, 1961.

Afr 109.61.20   Favrod, Ch.H. L'Afrique seule. Paris, 1961.

Afr 6457.5   Fearn, Hugh. An African economy. London, 1961.

Afr 40.61.5   Feireira, Oliverio. Ordem publica e liberdades politicas na Africa negra. Belo Horizonte, 1961.

Afr 7122.48   Felgas, Helio. Guerra em Angola. Lisboa, 1961.

Afr 7176.12   Ferreira, Eugenio. Sob o signo do real. Luanda, 1961.

Afr 6194.28   Field, Margaret Joyce. Religion and medicine of the Ga people. Accra, 1961.

Afr 8931.29   Forssman, Alric. Chevalier Oscar Wilhelm Alric Forssman. Pretoria, 1961.

Afr 4105.10   Forster, E.M. Alexandria. 3d ed. Garden City, 1961.

Afr 6390.58   Foster, Paul. White to move. London, 1961.

Afr 2731.15.105   Foucauld, Charles. Schriften. Einsiedeln, 1961.

Afr 5420.261   France. Embassy. U.S. The Gabon Republic. N.Y., 1961.

Afr 5480.261   France. Embassy. U.S. The Republic of Chad. N.Y., 1961.

Afr 5440.10   France. Embassy. U.S. The Republic of Congo. N.Y., 1961.

Afr 2223.961.15   France. Embassy. United States. The Constantine plan for Algeria, opening new frontiers in development. N.Y., 1961.

Afr 5285.260   France. Institut National de la Statistique et des Etudes Economiques. Une enquête de ménage en pays Lobi. Paris, 1961.

Afr Doc 5507.356   France. Institut National de la Statistique et des Etudes Economiques. Recensement de la population de la Cote française des Somalis, population non originaire, 1956. Paris, 1961.

Afr 609.61.20   Franck, F. African sketchbook. 1. ed. N.Y., 1961.

Afr 8678.284   Freeland, Sydney Percy. The Christian gospel and the doctrine of separate development. Pretoria, 1961.

Afr 2218.8   Frère, Suzanne. Sons et images dans le bled algérien. Alger, 1961.

Afr 11406.41.100   Friedmann, M.V. The slap. London, 1961.

Afr 2749.61.10   Frison-Roche, Roger. Sahara de l'aventure. Paris, 1961.

Afr 9424.360.5   Gabatshwane, S.M. Tshekedi Khama of Bechuanaland. Cape Town, 1961.

Afr 1273.961   Gallissot, Rene. L'économie de l'Afrique du Nord. Paris, 1961.

Afr 1432.26   Garcia Figueras, T. Recuerdos centenarios de una guerra romantica. Madrid, 1961.

Afr 5190.10.20   Garnier, C. Dakar. Paris, 1961.

Afr 2218.6   Gaudry, Mathéa. La société féminine au Djebel amour et au Ksel. Alger, 1961.

Afr 609.61.45   Gauld, Peter. Africa, continent of change. Belmont, 1961.

Afr 5057.25   Gavrilov, N.I. Zapadnaia Afrika pod gnetom Frantsii. Moscow, 1961.

Afr 28.4.5   Gay, Jean. Bibliographie des ouvrages relatifs à l'Afrique et à l'Arabie. Amsterdam, 1961.

Afr 9445.45   Gelfand, M. Northern Rhodesia. Oxford, 1961.

Afr 8678.305   Gereformeerde Kerke in Suid-Afrika. Algemene Sinode. Uit een bloed. Potchefstroom, 1961.

Afr 6176.35   Ghana. Statement by the government on the recent conspiracy. Accra, 1961.

Afr 3976.86   Giacomo d'Albano, Father. Historia della missione francescana in alto Egitto-Fungi-Etiopia, 1686-1720. Cairo, 1961.

Afr 9599.61   Gibbs, Peter. Avalanche in central Africa. London, 1961.

Afr 8678.275   Giniewski, P. Bantustans. Cape Town, 1961.

Afr 6910.3   Goldblatt, Israel. The mandated territory of Southwest Africa in relation to the United States. CapeTown, 1961.

Afr 7071.5   Gonçalves, J.J. O islamismo na Guiné portuguesa. Lisboa, 1961.

Afr 3705.3.15   Gordon, C.G. General Gordon's Khartoum journal. London, 1961.

Afr 3705.3.16   Gordon, C.G. General Gordon's Khartoum journal. N.Y., 1961.

Afr 210.61.45   Goss, H.P. The political future of the independent nations of Africa. Santa Barbara, Calif., 1961.

Afr 6176.39   Grammens, Mark. Kwame Nkrumah, leider van Afrika. Tielt, 1961.

Afr 5187.16   Gravrand, Henri. Visage africain de l'Eglise. Paris, 1961.

Afr 3685.9   Gray, Richard. A history of the southern Sudan. London, 1961.

Afr 6138.61   Great Britain. Central Office of Information. Sierra Leone. London, 1961.

Afr 6310.9   Great Britain. Colonial Office. The future of East Africa High Commission Services: reports of the London discussions. London, 1961.

Afr 9635.25   Great Britain. Colonial Office. Northern Rhodesia. London, 1961.

Afr 6392.34   Great Britain. Colonial Office. East Africa Economic and Financial Commission. East Africa. London, 1961.

Afr 6484.4   Great Britain. Commissions. Uganda Relationship. Report, 1961. Entebbe, 1961.

Afr 9432.15   Great Britain. Commonwealth Relations Office. Southern Rhodesia constitution. London, 1961. 2 pam.
Afr 11435.22.110   Green, George L. Eight bells at Salamander. 2d ed. Cape Town, 1961.
Afr 609.61.40   Green, Lawrence G. Great north road. Capetown, 1961.
Afr 8667.66   Grense,'n simposium oor rasse- en ander verhoudinge. Stellenbosch, 1961.
Afr 2623.961   Guen, Moncef. La Tunisie indépendante face à son économie. Paris, 1961.
Afr 150.2.75   Guerreiro, Amaro D. Panorama economico dos descobrimentos henriquinos. Lisboa, 1961.
Afr 1625.15   Guiho, Pierre. La nationalité marocaine. Rabat, 1961.
Afr 679.61.10   Halpern, Jan. Na potudnie od Sahary. Warszawa, 1961.
Afr 6535.61   Harwick, Christopher. Red dust. London, 1961.
Afr 550.110   Hatton, Desmond J. Missionlogy in Africa today. Dublin, 1961.
Afr 1623.961.10   Hauet, Daniel. La formation professionnelle par ses propres moyens dans les pays en voie. Rabat, 1961.
Afr 626.100   Hazlewood, Arthur. The economy of Africa. London, 1961.
Afr 9149.61   Helbling, Margrit. Tshakhuma. Zürich, 1961.
Afr 210.61.15   Hempstone, Smith. The new Africa. London, 1961.
Afr 7549.61.5   Hennessy, Maurice N. The Congo. London, 1961.
Afr 3230.26   Hesseltine, W.B. The Blue and the Gray on the Nile. Chicago, 1961.
Afr 6390.72   Hickman, G.M. The lands and peoples of East Africa. London, 1961.
Afr 2938.32   Hilli, Abbas Hilmi. Grundlagen. Köln, 1961.
Afr 50.25   Hodgkin, Thomas. African political parties. Harmondsworth, 1961.
Afr 5342.60   Holas, Bohumil. Changements sociaux en Côte-d'Ivoire. Paris, 1961.
Afr 28.56   Holdsworth, M. Soviet African studies. pt.1-2. Oxford, 1961.
Afr 3675.55   Holt, P.M. A modern history of the Sudan. London, 1961.
Afr 9161.20   Hooper, Charles. Brief authority. N.Y., 1961.
Afr 210.61.80   Houart, Pierre. L'Afrique aux trois visages. Bruxelles, 1961.
Afr 7575.60   Houart, Pierre. Les évènements du Congo. Bruxelles, 1961.
Afr 9502.18   Howarth, David. The shadow of the dam. N.Y., 1961.
Afr 210.61.30   Hughes, John. The new face of Africa south of the Sahara. 1st ed. N.Y., 1961.
Afr 8180.35   Hugo, M. Piet retief. Johannesburg, 1961.
Afr 7175.76   Iglesias, Luis. A verdade sobre Angola. Rio de Janeiro, 1961.
Afr 6277.55   Industrial Development Conference, Lagos, 1961. Nigeria. London, 1961.
Afr 7580.4   Institut Royal des Relations Internationales. Evolution de la crise congolaise de septembre 1960 à avril 1961. Brussels, 1961.
Afr 9538.10F   International African Institute, London. South-east central Africa and Madagascar. London, 1961.
Afr 632.30   International African Seminar. Social change in modern Africa. London, 1961.
Afr 6392.30   International Bank for Reconstruction and Development. The economic development of Tanganyika. Baltimore, 1961.
Afr 626.65   International Bank for Reconstruction and Development. The World Bank in Africa. Washington, 1961.
Afr 630.61   Isaacs, H.R. Emergent Americans. N.Y., 1961.
Afr 28.68   Italiaander, Rolf. Africana. Holland, Michigan, 1961.
Afr 55.16   Italiaander, Rolf. The new leaders of Africa. Englewood Cliffs, 1961.
Afr 4787.6   Italy. Ministero degli Affari Esteri. L'amministrazione fiduciaria della Somalia. Roma, 1961.
Afr Doc 6472.5   Ivory Coast. Direction de la Statistique et des Etudes Economiques et Démographiques. Recensement démographique de Bruehe, 1958. Résultats définitifs. Paris, 1961.
Afr 8175.20.4   Jaarsveld, F.A. van. The awakening of Afrikaner nationalism, 1868-1881. Cape Town, 1961.
Afr 8089.61.5   Jaarsveld, Floris Albertus. Illustrated history for senior certificate. Johannesburg, 1961.
Afr 609.58.12   Jahn, Janheinz. Muntu. London, 1961.
Afr 6194.22   Jahoda, Gustav. White man. London, 1961.
Afr 7540.40A   Janssens, E. J'étais le général Janssens. Bruxelles, 1961.
Afr 3310.70   Jassen, Raul. Nasser. Buenos Aires, 1961.
Afr 5465.3   Jean, S. Les Langbas, population d'Oubangui-Chari. Paris, 1961.
Afr 8659.61.5   Jenny, H. Afrika ist nicht nur schwarz. Düsseldorf, 1961.
Afr 6153.10   Johnson, A.F. Books about Ghana. Accra, 1961.
Afr 109.61.35   Joos, L.C.D. Brève histoire à l'Afrique noire. v.1-2. Issy-les-Moulineaux, 1961-64. 2v.
Afr 2749.61   Joos, Louis D. Through the Sahara to the Congo. London, 1961.
Afr 7812.261.5   Joye, Pierre. Les trusts au Congo. Bruxelles, 1961.
Afr 1069.31.10   Julien, Charles A. Histoire de l'Afrique du Nord. v.1-2. Paris, 1961.
Afr 7947.8   Kagame, Alexis. L'histoire des armées-bovines dans l'ancien Rwanda. Bruxelles, 1961.
Afr Doc 3207.361   Kenya. Economics and Statistics Division. Agriculture census, 1961. Nairobi, 1961.
Afr 8089.49.3   Keppel-Jones, A. South Africa. 3d ed. London, 1961.
Afr 7918.5   Kestergat, Jean. Andre Ryckmans. Paris, 1961.
Afr 7369.61   Khodosh, I.A. Liberiia. Moscow, 1961.
Afr 7575.50   Khokhlov, N.P. Tragediia Kongo. Moscow, 1961. 2 pam.
Afr 6291.5   Kingsley, John Donald. Staff development; Eastern Nigeria public service. Enugu, 1961.
Afr 3813.5   Kleve, Jacob Geert. Capital formation and increase in national income in Sudan in 1955-1959. Rotterdam, 1961.
Afr 8145.35   Knietoch, Clemens M. Nur einer von Vielen, aus dem Leben eines Missionsarztes. Frankfurt, 1961.
Afr 8678.250   Knoob, Willi. Die afrikanisch-christlichen Bewegungen unter den Bantu. Köln, 1961.
Afr 6883.32   Komba, J.J. God and man. Rome, 1961.
Afr 2030.461.50   Kraft, Joseph. The struggle for Algeria. 1st ed. Garden City, 1961.
Afr 8230.6.15   Krueger, D.W. Paul Kruger. Johannesburg, 1961. 2v.
Afr 8378.349   Kruger, D.J. President C.R. Swart. Kaapstad, 1961.
Afr 6140.10   Kup, A.P. A history of Sierra Leone. Cambridge, Eng., 1961.
Afr 9198.10   Kuper, H. An African aristocracy. London, 1961.
Afr 1623.961   Lahaye, R. Les entreprises publiques au Maroc. Rabat, 1961.
Afr 5488.14   Laigret-Pascault, Denyse E. Fort-lamy. Fort-Lamy, 1961.
Afr 2030.461.70   Landa, R.G. Alzhir sbrasyvaet okovy. Moscow, 1961.

Afr Doc 5.8   Landskron, William A. Official serial publications relating to economic development in Africa South of the Sahara. Cambridge, 1961.
Afr 8678.270   Lardon, Naphail. Noirs et blancs. Paris, 1961.
Afr 5787.5   Lavondes, Henrni. Problemes humains dans la region de la Sakay. Tananarive, 1961.
Afr 32.2   Lavroff, D.G. Les constitutions africaines. v.1-2. Paris, 1961-64. 2v.
Afr 626.133   Lazic, Branko M. L'Afrique et les leçons de l'expérience communiste. Paris, 1961.
Afr 6990.90   Leben für Südwestafrika. Windhoek, 1961.
Afr 6740.35   Lebeuf, J.P. L'habitation des Fati. Paris, 1961.
Afr 2030.461.85   Legaillarde, Pierre. On a triché avec l'honneur. Paris, 1961.
Afr 7575.4   Legum, Cohn. Congo disaster. Harmondsworth, 1961.
Afr 609.61.60   Legum, Colin. Africa, a handbook. London, 1961.
Afr 6740.30   Lembezat, Bertrand. Les populations paiennes. Paris, 1961.
Afr 210.59.11   Lengyel, Emil. Africa in ferment. N.Y., 1961.
Afr 1753.14   Leria, Manuel. Un siglo medieval en la historia de Ceuta, 931-1031. Ceuta, 1961.
Afr 1713.4   Letourneau, Roger. Fez in the age of marinides. 1st ed. Norman, 1961.
Afr 6919.61   Levinson, O. The ageless land. Capetown, 1961.
Afr 4788.2   Lewis, I.M. A pastoral democracy. London, 1961.
Afr 3817.10   Lienharot, Godfrey. Divinity and experience, the religion of the Dinka. Oxford, 1961.
Afr 609.61.50   Ligne, Eugene. Africa. Bruxelles, 1961.
Afr 679.61   Linkhovoin, L.L. Po stranam Afriki. Ulan-Ude, 1961.
Afr 9558.14.10   Livingstone, D. Livingstone's missionary correspondence. London, 1961.
Afr 7324.19.5   Lobato, A. Quatro estudos e uma evocação para a historia de Lourenço Marques. Lisboa, 1961.
Afr 7575.80   Lumumba, Patrice. Le Congo. Bruxelles, 1961.
Afr 11542.87   Lytton, David. The goddam white man. N.Y., 1961.
Afr 11542.87.110   Lytton, David. A place apart. London, 1961.
Afr 9149.61.5   MacDonald, Tom. Transvaal story. Cape Town, 1961.
Afr 5758.61   Madagascar, birth of a new republic. N.Y., 1961.
Afr 6138.61.5   Mador, Iulii P. Sierra-Leone vchera i segodnia. Moscow, 1961.
Afr 3028.7   Mahmud, Rajab. Progress on high dam in Aswan. Washington, 1961.
Afr 632.40   Mair, Lucy Philip. Studies in applied anthropology. London, 1961.
Afr 8369.61.20   Malan, Daniel François. Afrikaner-volkseenheid en my ervarings op die pad daarheen. 3. druk. Kaapstad, 1961.
Afr 5240.6   Mali. Ministère du Plan. Rapport sur le plan quinquennal de développement économique. Paris, 1961.
Afr 632.20.5   Malinowski, B. The dynamics of culture change. New Haven, 1961.
Afr 2030.461.30   Mansell, G. Tragedy in Algeria. London, 1961.
Afr 6193.46   Manshard, W. Die geographischen Grundlagen der Wirtschaft Ghanas. Wiesbaden, 1961
Afr 7947.2   Maquet, J.J. The premise of inequality in Ruanda. London, 1961.
Afr 8279.61   Marais, Johannes. The fall of Kruger's republic. Oxford, 1961.
Afr 7175.70F   Marjay, Frederico Pedro. Angola. Lisbon, 1961.
Afr 6275.90   Marris, P. Family and social change in an African city. London, 1961.
Afr 6314.31   Marsh, Zoe. East Africa through contemporary records. Cambridge, Eng., 1961.
Afr 699.57.2   Marsh, Zoe. An introduction to the history of East Africa. 2. ed. Cambridge, Eng., 1961.
Afr 2030.461.75   Martin-Chauffier, L. L'examen des consciences. Paris, 1961.
Afr 2030.376   Maschino, Maurice. L'engagement. Paris, 1961.
Afr 2030.461.40   Maspero, Francois. Le droit à l'insoumission. Paris, 1961.
Afr 5247.30   Maugham, R. The slaves of Timbuktu. 1.Am.ed. N.Y., 1961.
Afr 8825.30   Mayer, Philip. Xhosa in town. Cape Town, 1961-63. 3v.
Afr 5843.2   Meade, James E. The economic and social structure of Mauritius. London, 1961.
Afr 55.20   Melady, T.P. Profiles of African leaders. N.Y., 1961.
Afr 626.112   Mendes, C.B. do Quental. A cooperação em Africa. Lisboa, 1961.
Afr 7565.17   Mendiaux, E. Histoire du Congo. Bruxelles, 1961.
Afr 8678.147   Merwe, Hendrik J.J.M. Segregeer of Sterf. Johannesburg, 1961.
Afr 2535.4   Mezerik, A. Tunisian-French dispute. N.Y., 1961.
Afr 1623.961.5   Middle East Research Association. Washington, D.C. Morocco, a politico-economic analysis, 1956-60. Washington, 1961.
Afr 1550.58   Miege, J.L. Le Maroc et l'Europe. v.1-4. Paris, 1961. 4v.
Afr 2749.61.15   Migliorini, Elio. L'esplorazione del Sahara. Torino, 1961.
Afr 1609.61   Mikesell, M.W. Northern Morocco, a cultural geography. Berkeley, 1961.
Afr 9502.22   Mitchell, J.C. An outline of the sociological background to African labour. Salisbury, 1961.
Afr 2030.461   Moch, J.S. En 1961, paix en Algérie. Paris, 1961.
Afr 3199.61.5   Mommsen, Wolfgang. Imperialismus in Agypten. München, 1961.
Afr 609.61.15   Money, David Charles. Africa. 2d ed. London, 1961.
Afr 7912.15.10   Monheim, Francis. Réponse à père De Vos au sujet...Lumumba. Anvers, 1961.
Afr 725.22   Moorehead, Alan. The White Nile. N.Y., 1961.
Afr 8688.10F   Morkel, Philip William. The Morkels; family history and family tree. Cape Town, 1961. 2v.
Afr 1623.960.6   Morocco. Division de la Coordination Économique et du Plan. Plan quinquennal, 1960-1964. Rabat, 1961.
Afr 5078.22   Morocco. Ministère de l'Information et du Tourisme. La libération de la province mauritanienne et l'opinion international. Rabat, 1961.
Afr Doc 5207.360   Morocco. Service Central des Statistiques. Recensement demographique juin 1960. Population legale du Maroc. Rabat, 1961-62. 2v.
Afr 9645.15   Morris, Colin M. The hour after midnight. London, 1961.
Afr 28.65   Moscow. Gosudarstvennaia Biblioteka SSSR imeni V.I. Lenina. Strany Afriki. Moscow, 1961.
Afr 550.120   Mosmans, G. L'Église à l'heure de l'Afrique. Tournai, 1961.
Afr 109.61.40   Mukarovsky, H. Afrika. Wien, 1961.
Afr 210.61.20   Munger, E. African field report. Cape Town, 1961.
Afr 2030.461.55   Mus, Paul. Guerre sans visage. Paris, 1961.

Afr 7850.40   Musini, P. Kantanga, pelli di fuoco. Parma, 1961.
Afr 3310.10.10   Nasser, G.A. Speeches delivered. Cairo, 1961.
Afr 8369.61.15   Natal Convention. University of Natal. Proceedings. Natal, 1961.
Afr 609.61.10   National Research Council. Human environments in middle Africa. Washington, 1961. 2v.
Afr 2030.461.80   Nazoun, Amar. Ferhat Abbas. Paris, 1961.
Afr 6280.9.40   Ndem, Eyo B.E. Ibos in contemporary nigerian politics. Onitsha, 1961.
Afr 5183.961   Ndiaye, M. Le Sénégal à l'heure de l'indépendance. Doullens, 1961.
Afr 7803.15   Nelson, Robert G. Congo crisis and Christian mission. St. Louis, 1961.
Afr 7575.95   Netherlands. Department van Buitenlandse Zaken. Kongo en de Verenigde Naties. 's-Gravenhage, 1961- 2v.
Afr 6075.15   Newbury, C.W. The western Slave Coast and its rulers. Oxford, 1961
Afr 679.61.5   Niane, D.T. Histoire de l'Afrique occidentale. Paris, 1961.
Afr 8687.284   Nicholls, G.H. South Africa in my time. London, 1961.
Afr 1069.61   Nickerson, J.S. A short history of North Africa. N.Y., 1961.
Afr 6203.7.5   Nigeria. National Archives. An index to organisation and reorganisation reports in record group CS0.26. Ibadan, 1961.
Afr 6295.61.5F   Nigeria. National Archives. An inventory of the administrative records. Ibadan, 1961.
Afr 6295.61F   Nigeria. National Archives. An inventory of the administrative records. Ibadan, 1961.
Afr 6210.58   Nigeria. Nigerianisation Office. Guide to careers in the federal public service of Nigeria. Lagos, 1961.
Afr 6176.30   Nkrumah, Kwame. I speak of freedom. N.Y., 1961.
Afr 2285.12.5   Noel, Jean. Isabelle Eberhardt. Algers, 1961.
Afr 2260.20   Nora, Pierre. Les français d'Algérie. Paris, 1961.
Afr 9525.578   Northcott, C. Robert Moffat. London, 1961.
Afr 28.72   Northern Rhodesia and Nyasaland. Publications Bureau. A descriptive and classified list of books published by or in association with the Northern Rhodesia and Nyasaland Publication Bureau. n.p., 1961.
Afr 10684.99.120   Nzekwu, Onuora. Wand of noble wood. London, 1961.
Afr 210.61.5   Oakes, John B. The edge of freedom. 1st ed. N.Y., 1961.
Afr 6095.361   Oboli, H.O.N. An outline geography of West Africa. New ed. rev. London, 1961.
Afr 10685.67.130   Okoye, Mokwugo. Vistas of life. Enugu, 1961.
Afr 6295.66   Old Calabar. Provincial union Oshogbo constitution. Oshogbo, 1961.
Afr 7309.61   Oliveira Bolio, Jose de. Moçambique. Lisboa, 1961.
Afr 109.61.5   Oliver, Roland A. The dawn of African history. London, 1961.
Afr 2030.252   Oppermann, Thomas. Le problème algérien. Paris, 1961.
Afr 6176.25   Orestov, O.L. V Respublike Gana. Moscow, 1961.
Afr 5580.3.15   Ortowski, Leon. Maurycy August Beniowski. Warszawa, 1961.
Afr 4573.2   Ouannou, J. L'Ethiopie et son économie. 2. ed. Paris, 1961.
Afr 810.17   Owen, Richard. Saga of the Niger. London, 1961.
Afr 2885.10   Owen, Roger. Libya, a brief political and economic survey. London, 1961.
Afr 2030.461.60   Paillat, Claude. Dossier secret de l'Algérie. Paris, 1961. 2v.
Afr 4573.4   Pankhurst, R.K.P. An introduction to the economic history of Ethiopia from early times to 1800. London, 1961.
Afr 6098.10   Parrinder, E.G. West African religion. London, 1961.
Afr 7575.90   Parti Socialiste Belge. Congo. Brussels, 1961.
Afr 9050.7   Paton, A. The Charlestown story. Pietermaritzburg, 1961.
Afr 11675.87.130   Paton, Alan. Debbie go home. London, 1961.
Afr 11675.87.120   Paton, Alan. Tales from a troubled land. N.Y., 1961.
Afr 7575.97   Paulus, J.P. Congo, 1956-1960. Bruxelles, 1961.
Afr 210.62.2   Perham, M.F. The colonial reckoning. London, 1961.
Afr 6119.2   Petch, G.A. Economic development and modern West Africa. London, 1961.
Afr 210.61.75   Pierson-Mathy, P. Evolution politique de l'Afrique. Bruxelles, 1961.
Afr 4430.61   Pignatelli, L. La guerra dei sette mesi. Napoli, 1961.
Afr 2300.8   Planhol, Xavier de. Nouveaux villages algérois. Paris, 1961.
Afr 635.62.10   Plisnier-Ladame, F. La condition de l'Africaine en Afrique noire. Bruxelles, 1961.
Afr 210.61.40   Pomikkar, Kavalam M. Revolution in Africa. London, 1961.
Afr 109.61.50   Portella, Eduardo. Africa, colonos e cumplices. Rio de Janeiro, 1961.
Afr 150.2.66   Portugal. Comissão Executiva das Comemorações do V Centenario da Morte do Infante Dom Henrique. Comemoracoe do V centenario da morte do Infante Dom Henrique. Lisboa, 1961-1963. 4v.
Afr 9060.20   Praechter, Vallmar. Durban. Hamburg, 1961.
Afr 6222.1   Pribytkavskii, L.N. Nigeriia v bor'be za nezqvisimost'. Moskva, 1961.
Afr 150.32   Principe, S. Rectificação historica a memoria do Infante Dom Henrique. Lobito, 1961.
Afr 2753.3   Problèmes humains posés. Paris, 1961.
Afr 4785.961   Prozhogin, N.P. Dobrogo utra, Afrika. Moscow, 1961.
Afr 13438.1.110   Rabemananjara, Jacques. Antidote. Paris, 1961.
Afr 13438.1.132   Rabemananjara, Jacques. Lamba. 2. éd. Paris, 1961.
Afr 609.61.25   Rakhmatov, M. Afrika idet k svoboda. Moscow, 1961.
Afr 2530.71A   Raymond, André. La Tunisie. Paris, 1961.
Afr 1727.5   Raynal, R. Plaines et piedmonts du bassin de la Moulouya. Rabat, 1961.
Afr 7175.50   Rebelo, Horacio de la Viara. Angola na Africa deste tempo. Lisboa, 1961.
Afr 8685.85   Reeves, Ambrose. The pass laws and slavery. London, 1961.
Afr 9689.61.5   Rhodes-Livingston Institute, Lusaka, Northern Rhodesia. Social research and community development. Lusaka, 1961.
Afr 9635.20   Rhodesia, Northern. Northern Rhodesia proposal for constitutional change. London, 1961.
Afr Doc 3893.361F   Rhodesia and Nyasaland. Report on Wankie urban African budget survey held in April/May 1960. Salisbury, 1961.
Afr Doc 3507.359.10   Rhodesia and Nyasaland. Central Statistical Office. The censuses of production of the Federation of Rhodesia and Nyasaland, 1958-1959. Salisbury, 1961.
Afr Doc 3509.510   Rhodesia and Nyasaland. Central Statistical Office. Income tax statistics.v.2. Salisbury, 1961.
Afr 9499.60F   Rhodesia and Nyasaland. Central Statistical Office. National accounts of the Federation of Rhodesia and Nyasaland. Salisbury, 1961.

Afr 7575.40   Ribeaud, P. Adieu Congo. Paris, 1961.
Afr 6390.65.5   Richards, C.G. Some historic journeys in East Africa. London, 1961.
Afr 8735.5.20   Rivett-Carnac, D. Thus came the English in 1820. 2. ed. Cape Town, 1961.
Afr 6420.10   Robertson, J.W. The Kenya coastal strip. London, 1961.
Afr 8687.175   Rose, Walter. Bushman, whale and dinosaur. Cape Town, 1961.
Afr 30.6   Rosenthal, E. Encyclopaedia of Southern Africa. London, 1961
Afr 8809.61   Rosenthal, Eric. The story of Table mountain. Cape Town, 1961.
Afr 8678.140.5   Roskam, Karel Lodewijk. Alleen voor blanken. Amsterdam, 1961.
Afr 7912.10   Rouch, Jane. En cage avec Lumumba. Paris, 1961.
Afr 6903.15   Roukens de Lange, E. South-west Africa, 1946-1960. Bibliography. Cape Town, 1961.
Afr 2609.61.5   Roy, Claude. Tunisie. Paris, 1961.
Afr 2030.352   Roy, Jules. Autour du drame. Paris, 1961.
Afr 2030.350.2   Roy, Jules. The war in Algeria. N.Y., 1961.
Afr 210.61.85   Royal African Society. The Africa of 1961. London, 1961.
Afr 6160.25   Rubin, L. The constitution and government of Ghana. London, 1961.
Afr 7182.10   Ruiz de Arcaute, H. Por tierras de Angola. Victoria, 1961.
Afr 8678.142F   Russell, Margo. A study of a South African interracial neighbourhood. Durban, 1961.
Afr 2209.61.10   Saadia. L'aliénation colonialiste et la résistance de la famille algérienne. Lausanne, 1961.
Afr 8369.61.10   Sachs, Bernard. The road from Sharpeville. London, 1961.
Afr 3199.61A   Safran, N. Egypt in search of political community. Cambridge, 1961.
Afr 7230.5   Santos, Ernesto Moreira dos. Combate de Negomano. Guimarães, 1961.
Afr 2230.42   Sas, Pierre. Vie d'un peuple mort. Paris, 1961.
Afr 7850.25   Sauvy, Jean. Le Katanga, cinquante ans décisifs. Paris, 1961.
Afr 115.101   Savage, K. The history of Africa south of the Sahara. London, 1961.
Afr 4513.61   Schaefer, Ludwig F. The Ethiopian crisis, touchstone of appeasement. Boston, 1961.
Afr 210.61.70   Schatten, Fritz. Afrika. München, 1961.
Afr 3979.61   Scheer, M. Von Afrika nach Kuba. Berlin, 1961.
Afr 6985.7   Scheer, Maximillian. Schwarz und weiss am Waterberg. Schwerin, 1961.
Afr 5055.61   Schnapper, Bernard. La politique et le commerce français dans le Golfe de Guinée. Paris, 1961.
Afr 7575.55   Scholl-Latour, Peter. Matata am Kongo. Stuttgart, 1961.
Afr 3143.18   Schregle, Goetz. Die Sultanin von Ägypten. Wiesbaden, 1961.
Afr 5847.5   Scott, Robert. Limuria, the lesser dependencies of Mauritius. London, 1961.
Afr 2223.961   Secretariat Social d'Alger. Les commissaires du développement. Alger, 1961.
Afr 2209.61   Secrétariat Social d'Alger. De l'Algérie originelle à l'Algérie moderne. Alger, 1961.
Afr 7912.20   Semenov, M.G. Ubiitsa s list-river. Moscow, 1961.
Afr 5183.961.5   Senegal. Plan quadriennal de développement, 1961-1964. Dakar, 1961.
Afr 12639.24.120A   Senghor, L.S. Nocturnes. Paris, 1961.
Afr 2030.106   Serigny, Alain de. Un procès. Paris, 1961.
Afr Doc 2707.360   Seychelles. Population census of the Seychelles Colony. Victoria? 1961?
Afr 626.72   Shpirt, A.I. Syrevye resursy Afriki. Moscow, 1961.
Afr 7122.56   Sidenko, V.P. Angola v ogne. Moscow, 1961.
Afr Doc 1719.5   Sierra Leone. Constitution. The Sierra Leone Constitution, Order in Council, 1961. Freetown, 1961.
Afr 109.61.25   Sik, Endre. Histoire de l'Afrique noire. v.1- Budapest, 1961. 2v.
Afr 1609.61.5   Simoes, Antonio. Marruecos, ayer-hoy. Buenos Aires, 1961.
Afr 7377.61   Simpson, C.L. The memoirs of C.L. Simpson. London, 1961.
Afr 11790.59.100   Singh, A.R. Behold the earth mourns. Johannesburg, 1961.
Afr 7575.75   Slade, R. The Belgian Congo. 2. ed. London, 1961.
Afr 9071.41   Slayter, Eric. Isipingo, village in the sun. Durban, 1961.
Afr 11796.41.100   Smit, Lillian. The wind's wing. Bloemfontein, 1961.
Afr 609.61   Smith, Anthony. High street, Africa. London, 1961.
Afr 7176.14   Soares, Amaden. Politica de bem e estoi rival en Angola. Lisbon, 1961.
Afr 5091.10   Société d'Etudes pour le Développement Economique et Social, Paris. Analyse de l'économie de la République islamique de Mauritanie en 1959. Paris, 1961.
Afr 7912.5   Soiuz Zhurnalistov SSSR. Patris Lumumba. Moscow, 1961.
Afr 5312.10   Solonitskii, A.S. Gvineiskaia Respublika. Moscow, 1961.
Afr 28.74   South African Public Library, Cape Town. A bibliography of African bibliographies covering territories South of the Sahara. 4th ed. Cape Town, 1961.
Afr 9435.11   Southern Rhodesia Constitutional Conference, London, 1961. Report. London, 1961.
Afr 8847.32   Staes, E.L.P. George, die verhaal van die dorp en distrik. George, 1961.
Afr 718.2.30   Stanley, H.M. The exploration diaries of H.M. Stanley. London, 1961.
Afr 8659.61   Stanton, Hannah. Go well. London, 1961.
Afr 7580.5   Stenmans, Alain. Les premiers mois de la République du Congo. Bruxelles, 1961.
Afr 8677.35   Steyn, Daniel. Inleiding tot die Suid-Afrikaanse Staatsfinansies. Pretoria, 1961.
Afr 609.61.30   Stillery, A. Africa. London, 1961.
Afr 7803.40.5   Storme, Marcel. Het ontstaan van die Kasai-missie. Brussels, 1961.
Afr 6320.2.5   Strandes, J. The Portuguese period in East Africa. Nairobi, 1961.
Afr 609.61.55   Stumbuk, Zdenko. Zapiski iz Afrike. Zagreb, 1961.
Afr 3813.15   Sudan. Treaties, etc. 1961. Administration agreement (Roseires irrigation project) between the Republic of the Sudan and Kreditanstalt für Wiederaufbau and International Development Association and International Bank for Reconstruction and Development dated as of June 14, 1961. n.p., 1961.
Afr 2260.22   Suffert, Georges. Les perspectives d'emploi des européens en Algérie. Paris, 1961.
Afr 5019.58.2   Suret-Canale, Jean. Afrique noire occidentale et centrale. 2 ed. v.1. Paris, 1961.

1961 - cont.

Afr 210.61.100	Sutton, Francis Xavier. Africa today; lecture at Cornell University, Nov. 2, 1961. Ithaca? 1961.
Afr 8095.86	Swart, Charles. Kinders van Suid-Afrika. Kaapstad, 1961.
Afr 9092.5	Swart, Marius Johannes. Geloftedag. Kaapstad, 1961.
Afr 6194.36	Tait, David. The Konkomba of northern Ghana. London, 1961.
Afr 6881.261	Tanganyika. Development plan for Tanganyika, 1961/62-1963/64. Dar es Salaam, 1961.
Afr Doc 3408.300	Tanganyika. Tresury. Economics and Statistics Division. Employment and earnings in Tanganyika. Dar es Salaam, 1961-1963.
Afr Doc 3407.361.10	Tanzania. Central Statistical Bureau. Census of industrial production in Tanganyika. Tanganyika, 1961.
Afr 20136.2	Tescaroli, Livio. Poesia sudanese. Bologna, 1961.
Afr 7889.2	Thier, F.M. Singhitini, la Stanleyville musulmane. Bruxelles, 1961.
Afr 5749.61	Thiout, Michel. Madagascar et l'ame malgache. Paris, 1961.
Afr 2030.50.10	Tillion, G. France and Algeria. 1st Amer. ed. N.Y., 1961.
Afr 109.61.10	Tillion, Germaine. L'Afrique bascule vers l'avenir. Paris, 1961.
Afr 5842.20	Titmuss, R.M. Social policies and population growth in Mauritius. London, 1961.
Afr 6664.16	Togo. Bühl-boden, 1961.
Afr 8095.82	Tonder, Johannes. Veertien gedenktekens van Suid-Afrika. Kaapstad, 1961.
Afr 5314.10.2	Touré, Sékou. Expérience guinéenne et unité africaine. Paris, 1961.
Afr 5183.961.10	Touze, R.L. Nouvelles lettres à Seydon. Dakar, 1961.
Afr 575.35.2	Trimingham, J.S. Islam in West Africa. 2nd ed. Oxford, 1961.
Afr 109.61.45	Tunis. Secretariat d'Etat à l'Information. New Africa. Tunis, 1961.
Afr 7815.28.10	Turnbull, Colin M. The forest people. N.Y., 1961.
Afr Doc 3377.5F	Uganda. Ministry of Economic Development. Statistics Branch. The patterns of income, expenditure and consumption of African unskilled workers in Gulu, February 1961. Entebbe, 1961.
Afr 4559.60.1	Ullendorff, Edward. The Ethiopians. London, 1961.
Afr 3986.961.5	United Arab Republic. Economic Research Department. Indicators of economic development. Cairo, 1961.
Afr 3325.5	United Arab Republic. Information Department. The United Arab Republic, nine years. Cairo, 1961.
Afr 210.61.60	United States. National Commission for UNESCO. Africa and the U.S. Washington, 1961.
Afr 4753.15	United States. Operations Mission to the Somali Republic. Inter-river economic exploration. Washington, 1961.
Afr 630.55.2	Vanderpost, Laurens. The dark eye in Africa. N.Y., 1961.
Afr 8809.61.5	Vanonsden, L. Trekboer. Cape Town, 1961.
Afr 8835.40F	Varley, Vera. Index to the growth and government of Cape Town. Cape Town, 1961.
Afr 6879.61.5	Varma, Shanti Narayan. Tanganyika. 1st. ed. New Delhi, 1961.
Afr 3330.5	Vatikiotis, P.J. Egyptian army in politics. Bloomington, 1961.
Afr 2223.961.10	Vaucher, G. Le plan de Constantine et la République Algérienne de demain. Neuchâtel, 1961.
Afr 210.61.90	Vianney, J.J. The new states of Africa. 1st ed. n.p. 1961.
Afr 7122.45	Vinhas, Manuel. Aspectos actuais de Angola. Lisboa, 1961.
Afr 4389.61	Voblikov, D.R. Efiopiia v borbe za sokhranenie nezavisimosti. Moscow, 1961.
Afr 7575.85	Volodin, L.D. Trudnye dni Kongo. Moscow, 1961.
Afr 7912.15	Vos, Pierre de. Vie et mort de Lumumba. Paris, 1961.
Afr 10065.2	Waestberg, Per. Afrika beraettar. Malmoe, 1961.
Afr 9161.21.20	Wall, M.A. The Dominee and the Dom-Pas. Cape Town, 1961.
Afr 210.61.50	Wallerstein, I. Africa. N.Y., 1961.
Afr 6192.27	Warner, Douglas. Ghana and the new Africa. London, 1961.
Afr 3986.961	Warriner, D. Agrarian reform and community development in U.A.R. Cairo, 1961.
Afr 7575.96	Wauters, A. Le norde communiste et la crise du Congo belge. Brussels, 1961.
Afr 6385.15	Welbourn, Frederick B. East African rebels. London, 1961.
Afr 6194.38	Wieke, Ivor. The northern factor in Ashanti history. Achimotu, 1961.
Afr 609.61.35	Williams, C. The rebirth of African civilization. Washington, 1961.
Afr 6460.80	Wilson, Gordon. Luo customary law and marriage laws customs. Nairobi, 1961.
Afr 8844.5.2	Wilson, M. Hunter. Reaction to conquest. London, 1961.
Afr 9854.2	Wishlade, Robert Leonard. Modern sectarian movements in Nyasaland. Durham, 1961.
Afr 210.61.25	Woddis, J. Africa. London, 1961.
Afr 7815.27	Wolfe, A.W. In the Ngombe tradition. Evanston, Ill., 1961.
Afr 9689.61	Wood, Anthony Saint John. Northern Rhodesia. London, 1961.
Afr 7369.59.2	Yancy, Ernest Jerome. The Republic of Liberia. Cairo, 1961.
Afr 6570.14	Zanzibar. Commission of Inquiry into Disturbances in Zanzibar during June 1961. Report. London, 1961.

1962

Afr 2000.15	Abbas, Ferhat. Guerre et révolution d'Algérie. Paris, 1962.
Afr 3310.7	Abdel-Malek, Anouar. Egypte, société militaire. Paris, 1962.
Afr 36.2	Abel, Herbert. Deutsche Afrikawissenschaft. Stand und Aufgaben. Köln, 1962.
Afr 609.62.15	Abraham, W. The mind of Africa. London, 1962.
Afr 3310.85A	Abul-Fath, A. L'affaire Nasser. Paris, 1962.
Afr 7809.62.5	Académie Royale des Sciences d'Outre-Mer. Apport scientifique de la Belgique au développement de l'Afrique centrale. Bruxelles, 1962. 3v.
Afr 5394.2	Adandé, A. Les récades des rois du Dahomey. Dakar, 1962.
Afr 7122.64	Addicott, Len. Cry Angola. London, 1962.
Afr 10665.2	Ademola, F. Reflections, Nigerian prose and verse. Lagos, 1962.
Afr 6218.16	Ademoyega, Wale. The federation of Nigeria from earliest times to independence. London, 1962.
Afr 609.62.5	Afrika segodnia. Moscow, 1962.
Afr 5406.262	Afrique centrale, les républiques d'expression française. Paris, 1962.

1962 - cont.

Afr 575.27	Ahmad, Mubarak. Islam in Africa. Rabwah, 1962.
Afr 2030.462.110	Algeria. Treaties, etc. Les accords d'Evian. Paris, 1962.
Afr 2030.462.112	Algeria. Treaties, etc. Texts of declarations drawn up in common agreement at Evian. N.Y., 1962.
Afr 2030.340.10.5	Algerian Front of National Liberation. La révolution algérienne par les textes. 3. ed. Paris, 1962.
Afr 2030.462.125	Algérie nouvelle et la presse française. Paris, 1962.
Afr 2030.462.55	Allais, Maurice. Les accords d'Evian. Paris, 1962.
Afr 9525.875.10	Allighan, Garry. The Welensky story. Cape Town, 1962.
Afr 45.62.10	Allott, Anthony N. Judicial and legal systems in Africa. London, 1962.
Afr 7175.72	Amaral, I. do. Ensaio de um estudo geografico da rede urbana de Angola. Lisboa, 1962.
Afr 210.62.10	American Society of African Culture. Pan-Africanism reconsidered. Berkeley, 1962.
Afr 7122.62	Angola, a symposium. London, 1962.
Afr 7119.62.5	Angola atraves dos textos. São Paulo, 1962.
Afr 7567.25	Anstey, Roger. Britain and the Congo in the 19th century. Oxford, 1962.
Afr 2030.462.80	Aron, Robert. Les origines de la guerre d'Algérie. Paris, 1962.
Afr 5340.21	Atger, Paul. La France en Côte-d'Ivoire de 1843 à 1893. Dakar, 1962.
Afr 2030.462.20	Azeau, Henri. Révolte militaire, Alger, 22 avril 1961. Paris, 1962.
Afr 5225.7	Ba, Amadou H. L'empire Peul du Macina. Paris, 1962.
Afr 8678.290	Badertscher, Jean. La segregation raciale en Afrique du Sud. Lausanne, 1962.
Afr 6195.16	Baeta, C.G. Prophetism in Ghana. London, 1962.
Afr 3986.962.15	Bahig, A.F. Readings for students of commerce. Alexandria, 1962.
Afr 710.55.5	Balandier, Georges. Afrique ambigue. Paris, 1962.
Afr 5240.10F	Bamako. Chambre de Commerce, d'Agriculture et d'Industrie. Répertoire des représentations exclusives assurées au Mali. Bamako, 1962.
Afr 7312.30	Baptista, J. do Amparo. Moçambique, província portuguesa. Vila Nova de Famalicão, 1962.
Afr 1069.59.2	Barbour, Nevill. A survey of North-west Africa. 2nd ed. London, 1962.
Afr 212.30	Barcata, Louis. Schreie aus dem Dschungel. Stuttgart, 1962.
Afr 6275.95	Barth, H. Travels in Nigeria. London, 1962.
Afr 7575.36	Bartlet, R.E. Communist penetration and subversion of the Belgian Congo, 1946-1960. 1st. ed. Berkeley, 1962.
Afr 8853.3F	Basutoland. Government Archives. Catalogue. n.p., 1962.
Afr 609.62.50	Batson, E. Contemporary dimensions of Africa. Cape Town, 1962.
Afr 1110.35	Baulin, Jacques. The Arab role in Africa. Baltimore, 1962.
Afr 2397.3	Beauvoir, Simone de. Djamila Boupacha. Paris, 1962.
Afr 2397.3.2	Beauvoir, Simone de. Djamila Boupacha. 1st American ed. N.Y., 1962.
Afr 9525.593	Becker, Peter. Path of blood. London, 1962.
Afr 2030.461.45.2	Behr, Edward. The Algerian problem. N.Y., 1962.
Afr 2030.461.46	Behr, Edward. Dramatique Algérie. Paris, 1962.
Afr 6298.202	Bello, Ahmadu. My life. Cambridge, 1962.
Afr 5243.125.30	Benchelt, Eno. Kulturawandel bei den Bambara von Segou. Bonn, 1962.
Afr 6160.26	Bennion, Francis. The constitutional law of Ghana. London, 1962.
Afr 626.104	Benveneste, Guy. Handbook of African economic development. N.Y., 1962.
Afr 2030.462.100	Benzine, A. Le camp. Paris, 1962.
Afr 1110.40	Berque, Jacques. Le Maghreb entre deux guerres. Paris, 1962.
Afr 6153.15	Bibliography of Ghana, 1957-60. Kumasi, 1962.
Afr 7575.6	Bilsen, Antoine. L'indépendance du Congo. Tournai, 1962.
Afr 8659.62.5	Blumberg, Myrna. White madam. London, 1962.
Afr 8809.62	Board, Chr. The border region, natural environment and land use in the eastern Cape. Cape Town, 1962. 2v.
Afr 626.108	Bohannan, Paul. Markets in Africa. Evanston, Ill., 1962.
Afr 7015.40	Bondarevskii, G.L. Portugalskie kolonizatory, vragi narodov Afriki. Moscow, 1962.
Afr 2030.462.140	Bonnaud, R. Itinéraire. Paris, 1962.
Afr 7580.7	Borri, M. Nous, ces affreux, dossier secret de l'ex-Congo belge. Paris, 1962.
Afr 8719.62	Botha, C.G. Collected works. Cape Town, 1962. 3v.
Afr 2030.462.65	Boualam, B. Mon pays, la France. Paris, 1962.
Afr 2225.14.5	Bourdieu, Pierre. The Algerians. Boston, 1962.
Afr 210.62.35	Bow Group Pamphlet. The new Africa. London, 1962.
Afr 8687.141	Bowker, John. Speeches. Cape Town, 1962.
Afr 210.62.50	Boyd, Andrew Kirk Henry. An atlas of African affairs. N.Y., 1962.
Afr 210.62.42	Braginskii, M.I. Osoobozhdenie Afriki. Moscow, 1962.
Afr 6095.362	Braithwaite, E.R. A kind of homecoming. Englewood, N.J., 1962.
Afr 8668.10	Brandel-Syrier, Mia. Black woman in search of God. London, 1962.
Afr 6212.40	Bretton, Henry. Power and stability in Nigeria. N.Y., 1962.
Afr 210.62.20	British Commonwealth Relations. The Commonwealth in Africa. London, 1962.
Afr 6535.62.10	British Information Service. Uganda. N.Y., 1962.
Afr 6535.62.5	British Information Service. Uganda. N.Y., 1962.
Afr 8687.143	Broome, F.N. Not the whole truth. Pietermaritzburg, 1962.
Afr 11237.67.100	Brown, J.A. Seven against the sun. Johannesburg, 1962.
Afr 45.62.5	Buchmann, J. L'Afrique noire indépendante. Paris, 1962.
Afr 8809.62.5	Burman, Jose. Safe to the sea. Kaapstad, 1962.
Afr 50.40	Busia, Kafi A. The challenge of Africa. N.Y., 1962.
Afr 50.46	Bustin, Edouard. Guide des partis politiques africains. Bruxelles, 1962.
Afr 609.62.35	Byford-Jones, N. Africa, journey out of darkness. London, 1962.
Afr 3326.3.10	Cairo. Institute of National Planning. National Planning Institute. Cairo, 1962.
Afr 8687.263.5	Callan, Edward. Albert John Luthuli and the South African race conflict. Kalamazoo, 1962.
Afr 109.62.30	Calle Iturrino, E. De Tutankamen a Nasser. Bilbao, 1962.
Afr Doc 7506.2	Cameroon. Commissariat Général à l'Information. Institutions et Constitution de la République Fédérale du Cameroun. Yaoundé, 1962?
Afr 50.30	Carter, G. African one-party states. Ithaca, 1962.
Afr 8369.58.3	Carter, G.M. The politics of inequality, South Africa since 1948. 3rd ed. London, 1962.
Afr 9149.62	Cartwright, Alan. Valley of gold. Cape Town, 1962.

1962 - cont.

Afr 210.41.10A Cary, Joyce. The case for African freedom. Austin, 1962.

Afr 7543.5 Centre de Recherche et d'Information Socio-Politiques. Documents, 1950-1960. Bruxelles, 1962.

Afr 2223.962 Cercle Taleb-Moumié. Fidel Castro ou tshombe? Paris, 1962.

Afr 4045.14 Cervani, Giulio. Il voyage en Egypte, 1861-1862, di Pasquale Revoltella. Trieste, 1962.

Afr 3180.7A Cezzar, Ahmed. Ottoman Egypt in the eighteenth century. Cambridge, 1962.

Afr 8865.18 Chakela, Koenyama S. The past and present Lesotho (Basutoland). Cairo, 1962.

Afr 5640.15.20 Charbonnel, Henry. De Madagascar à Verdun. Paris, 1962.

Afr 9506.2 Chater, Patricia. Grass roots. London, 1962.

Afr 3315.120A Childers, E.B. The road to Suez. London, 1962.

Afr 44623.40.100 Chum, Haji. Atenji wa vita vya Uhud. Dar es Salaam, 1962.

Afr 8145.42 Church of England in South Africa. Constitution and canons of the Church of the province of South Africa. Cape Town, 1962.

Afr 8678.288 Churchill, Rhona. White man's god. N.Y., 1962.

Afr 10673.48.130 Clark, John Pepper. Poems. Ibadan, 1962.

Afr 2030.462.35 Club Jean-Moulin. Deux pièces du dossier Algérie. Paris, 1962.

Afr 3700.18 Collins, R.O. The southern Sudan. New Haven, 1962.

Afr 2030.462.15 Colloque Internationale sur l'Algérie. Les conditions de l'indépendance. Bruxelles, 1962.

Afr 545.30 Colloque sur les Religions, Abidjan. Colloque sur les religions, Abidjan, 5-12 avril, 1961. Paris, 1962.

Afr 9700.35 Colson, Elizabeth. The plateau Tonga of Northern Rhodesia. Manchester, 1962.

Afr 4640.5 Comhaire-Sylvain, Suzanne. Considerations of migration in Addis Ababa. Addis Ababa, 1962.

Afr 6096.15 Conference on Educational and Occupational Selection in West Africa. Educational and occupational selection in West Africa. London, 1962.

Afr 7580.9 Congo. The Adoula-Tshombe talks. Leopoldville, 1962.

Afr 28.96 Copenhagen. Kongelige Bibliotek. Nyere Africa-litteratur. København, 1962.

Afr 2609.62 Coque, R. La Tunisie présaharienne. Paris, 1962.

Afr 31.12 Cordero Torres, J.M. Textos basicos de Africa. v.1-2. Madrid, 1962. 2v.

Afr 5365.6 Cornevin, R. Histoire du Dahomey. Paris, 1962.

Afr 109.62.20 Cornevin, Robert. Histoire de l'Afrique. Paris, 1962. 2v.

Afr 6664.10.2 Cornevin, Robert. Histoire du Togo. Paris, 1962.

Afr 6214.30 Crowder, M. The story of Nigeria. London, 1962.

Afr 5185.9 Crowder, Michael. Senegal. London, 1962.

Afr 7850.45.5 Cuarenta y seis hombres en colera. Bruselas, 1962.

Afr 8289.51.2 Curtis, Lionel. With Milner in South Africa. Index. Johannesburg, 1962.

Afr 7937.6 Dansina, Jan. L'évolution du royaume Rwanda des origines à 1900. Bruxelles, 1962.

Afr 7850.35 Davister, P. Croisettes et casques bleus, récits. Bruxelles, 1962.

Afr 5055.62 Debay, Jean. Evolutions en Afrique noire. Paris, 1962.

Afr 2535.6 Debbasch, C. La République Tunisienne. Paris, 1962.

Afr 609.62.10 Deblij, Harm. Africa south. Evanston, 1962.

Afr 5753.22 Decary, Raymond. La mort et les coutumes funeraires à Madagascar. Paris, 1962.

Afr 10624.2.700 Dei-Anang, M. Ghana spricht, Gedichte. Herrenalb, 1962.

Afr 5040.6 Delavignette, R.L. L'Afrique noire française et son destin. Paris, 1962.

Afr 11320.50.140 Delius, Anthony. A corner of the world. Cape Town, 1962.

Afr 545.26 Denis, L. Gas de conscience, à l'usage surtout des pays africains. Bruges, 1962-63. 2v.

Afr 2030.462.25 Denoyer, François. Quatre ans de guerre en Algérie. Paris, 1962.

Afr 550.130 Desai, Ram. Christianity in Africa as seen by Africans. Denver, 1962.

Afr 5425.18 Deschamps, H. Traditions orales et archives au Gabon. Paris, 1962.

Afr 40.62 Deschamps, Hubert. Les institutions politiques de l'Afrique Noire. Paris, 1962.

Afr 5078.20 Desire-Vuillemin, G. Contribution à l'histoire de la Mauritanie. Dakar, 1962.

Afr 2397.5 Dessagne, F. Journal d'une mère de famille pied-noir. Paris, 1962.

Afr 12624.41.30 Diop, Birago. Les nouveaux contes d'Amadou Koumba. Paris, 1962.

Afr 7208.2 Documentos sobre os portugueses em Mozambique en na Africa central, 1497-1840. v.1- Lisboa, 1962- 5v.

Afr 635.92 Doherty, Mary A. The role of the African woman, a report. London, 1962.

Afr 2030.462.70 Duchemin, Jacques. Histoire du F.L.N. Paris, 1962.

Afr 2260.24 Ducrocq, Marcel. Notre Algérie. Paris, 1962.

Afr 530.33 Duffy, James. Portugal in Africa. Harmondsworth, 1962.

Afr 7015.35 Duffy, James Edward. Portugal in Africa. Cambridge, 1962.

Afr 5530.4 Duignan, Peter. Madagascar. Stanford, Calif., 1962.

Afr 609.62.40 Dumont, René. L'Afrique noire est mal partie. Paris, 1962.

Afr 5074.20 Du Puigaudeau, Odette. Le passé maghrébin de la Mauritanie. Rabat, 1962.

Afr 9060.26 Durban, Natal. Saint Andrew's Presbyterian Church. The story of Saint Andrew's Presbyterian church. Durban, 1962.

Afr 6176.40 Dzirasa, Stephen. Political thought of Dr. Kwame Nkrumah. Accra, 1962.

Afr 7180.35 Edwards, Adrian. The Ovimbundu under two sovereignties. London, 1962.

Afr 40.62.5 Egyptian Society of International Law. Constitutions of the new African states. n.p., 1962.

Afr 10675.47.100 Ekwensi, Cyprian. Burning grass. London, 1962.

Afr 8673.18 Elionson, Sima. This is South Africa. Cape Town, 1962.

Afr 2030.462.120 Enfants d'Algérie. Paris, 1962.

Afr 5010.12 Etats africains d'expression française et République Malgache. Paris, 1962.

Afr 4573.6 Ethiopia. Second five year development plan, 1955-1959. Addis Ababa, 1962.

Afr 4571.5 Ethiopia. Ministry of Information. Twenty years of work, 1941-1961. Addis Ababa, 1962.

Afr 212.40 Europa-Haus, Marienberg (Westerwald) Ger. Partner Afrika. Hangelar bei Bonn, 1962?

Afr 679.55.5 Fage, J.D. An introduction to the history of West Africa. 3rd ed. Cambridge, Eng., 1962.

Afr 4060.25 Fairservis, W.A. The ancient kingdoms of the Nile and the doomed monuments of Nubia. N.Y., 1962.

Afr 6541.10 Faupel, John. African holocaust. London, 1962.

Afr 6541.10.2 Faupel, John. African holocaust. 2nd ed. London, 1962.

1962 - cont.

Afr 2030.462.95 Favrod, C.H. Le F.L.N. et l'Algérie. Paris, 1962.

Afr 3814.5 Fedorov, T. Finansy i kredit sudana. Moskva, 1962.

Afr 8050.20 Feit, Edward. South Africa. London, 1962.

Afr 2030.462.130A Feraoun, M. Journal, 1955-62. Paris, 1962.

Afr 530.50.5 Fetov, V.P. Amerikanskii imperializm v Afrike. Moscow, 1962.

Afr 2260.25 Figueras, André. Les pieds noirs dans le plat. Paris, 1962.

Afr 626.110 Food and Agriculture Organization of the United Nations. FAO African survey. Rome, 1962.

Afr 6457.20 Forrester, M. Kenya today, social prerequisite for economic development. Monton, 1962.

Afr 618.45 Fort Hare, South Africa. University College. F.S. Malan Museum. Cataloque of the Estelle Hamilton-Welsh collection. Fort Hare, 1962?

Afr 7850.45 Forty-six angry men, the forty-six civilian doctors of Elisabethville denounce U.N. violations in Katanga. Bruxelles, 1962.

Afr 609.62.20 Fox, Frederic. Fourteen Africans vs. one American. N.Y., 1962.

Afr 6277.88 France. Centre National Du Commerce Exterieur. Le marche du Nigeria. Paris, 1962.

Afr 5046.2 France. Direction des Affaires Economiques et Financières. Planification en Afrique. v.2- Paris, 1962- 3v.

Afr Doc 6607.361 France. Institut National de la Statistiqe et des Etudes Economique. Service de Cooperation. Données de base sur la situation démographique au Dahomey en 1961. Paris, 1962.

Afr Doc 6907.360 France. Institut National de la Statistique et des Etudes Economiques. Service de Coopération. Etude démographique du Niger. Paris, 1962-1963. 2v.

Afr 5448.15.10 France. Ministére de la Coopération. Les budgets des ménages africains a Pointe-Noire, 1958-1959. Paris, 1962.

Afr 6320.5 Freeman-Grenville, G. The East-Africa coast, selected documents. Oxford, 1962.

Afr 6775.6F Freeman-Grenville, G.S. The medieval history of the coast of Tanganyika. Berlin, 1962.

Afr 575.32 Froelich, Jean Claude. Les musulmans d'Afrique Noire. Paris, 1962.

Afr 6138.62 Fyfe, Christopher. A history of Sierra Leone. London, 1962.

Afr Doc 7407.361.10 Gabon. Service National de la Statistique. Recensement et enquête démographiques, 1960-1961: Résultats pour Libreville. Paris, 1962.

Afr 10913.2 Gale, W.I. The Rhodesian press. Salisbury, 1962.

Afr 6395.18 Gann, L.H. White settlers in tropical Africa. Harmondsworth, 1962.

Afr 5180.44 Garnier, C. Sénégal, porte de l'Afrique. Paris, 1962.

Afr 9029.62 Gatti, Attilio. Sangoma. London, 1962.

Afr 1658.47 Gaudio, A. Rif, terre marocaine d'epopee et de legende. Paris, 1962.

Afr 9502.13 Gelfand, M. Shona religion. Cape Town, 1962.

Afr 2719.62 Genin, I. A. Imperialisticheskaia bor'ba za Sakharu. Moscow, 1962.

Afr 5480.262F Gentil, Pierre. Les treize préfectures de la République du Tchad. Fort-Lamy, 1962.

Afr 210.62.15 Georgetown Colloquium on Africa. New forces in Africa. Washington, 1962.

Afr 7046.2 Gersdorff, R. von. Wirtschaftsprobleme Portugisisch-Afrikas. Bielefeld, 1962.

Afr 626.150 Giedwidz, Jan. Afryka. Warszawa, 1962.

Afr 8678.285 Giniewski, P. Une autre Afrique du Sud. Paris, 1962.

Afr 2030.462.155 Girardet, R. Pour le tombeau d'un capitaine. Paris, 1962.

Afr 6333.62.5 Glukhov, A.M. Britanskii imperializm v Vostochnoi Afrike. Moscow, 1962.

Afr 150.2.55 Godinho, Vitoriano de Magalhaes. A economia dos descobrimentos henriquinos. Lisboa, 1962.

Afr 8152.76 Godlonton, Robert. Narrative of the Kaffir war, 1850-1851-1852. Cape Town, 1962.

Afr 8028.128 Goldman, F. An index to the colour-plate relating to South Africa appearing in books published before 1850. Johannesburg, 1962.

Afr 1110.41A Gordon, David. North Africa's French legacy, 1954-1962. Cambridge, 1962.

Afr 2030.462.160 Grall, Xavier. La génération du Djebel. Paris, 1962.

Afr 6565.40 Gray, John. History of Zanzibar. London, 1962.

Afr 6542.18 Great Britain. Commission. Dispute Between Buganda and Bunyoro. Uganda. Report of a commission of privy counselors on a dispute between Buganda and Bunyoro presented to Parliament. London, 1962.

Afr 626.103A Green, L. Development in Africa, a study in regional analysis with special reference to southern Africa. Johannesburg, 1962.

Afr 850.6 Green, L.G. Islands time forgot. London, 1962.

Afr 6979.53.2 Green, Laurence G. Lords of the last frontier. Cape Town, 1962.

Afr 4060.20 Greener, Leslie. High Dam over Nubia. N.Y., 1962.

Afr 2030.462.10 Greer, Herb. A scattering of dust. London, 1962.

Afr 6333.62 Gregory, Robert. Sidney Webb and East Africa. Berkeley, 1962.

Afr 8687.294 Gregory, T.E.G. Ernest Oppenheimer and the economic development of southern Africa. Cape Town, 1962.

Afr 12639.24.800 Guibert, A. Léopold Sédar Senghor. Paris, 1962.

Afr 5303.2 Guinea. Archive Nationale. Répertoire des archives nationales. v.1. Conakry, 1962.

Afr 510.110 Gukasian-Gandzaketsi, L.J. Frantsuzskii imperializm i Afrika. Moscow, 1962.

Afr 3326.8 Gulick, Luther Halsey. Government reorganization in the United Arab Republic. Cairo, 1962.

Afr 9500.46 Gussman, Boris. Out in the mid-day sun. London, 1962.

Afr 8678.300 Haigh, Alan. South African tragedy. London, 1962.

Afr 3135.5 Al-Hamdani, Abbas H. The Fatimids. Karachi, 1962.

Afr 8825.35 Hammond-Tooke, W.D. Bhaca society. Cape Town, 1962.

Afr 5012.4 Hamon, Leo. Les partis politiques africains. Paris, 1962.

Afr 8252.341.80A Hancock, William Keith. Smuts. Cambridge, 1962. 2v.

Afr 44616.2 Harries, L. Swahili poetry. Oxford, 1962.

Afr 6203.4.5 Harris, John. Books about Nigeria. Nigeria, 1962.

Afr 6295.101 Hassan, Alhajl. A chronicle of Abuja. Lagos, 1962.

Afr 8687.228 Heerden, Petronella van. Kerssmutsels. Kaapstad, 1962.

Afr 7850.30 Hempstone, Smith. Rebels, mercenaries, and dividends. N.Y., 1962.

Afr 5944.20 Hernandez-Pacheco, Francisco. El Sahara español. Madrid, 1962.

Afr 109.62.10 Herskovits, Melville. The human factor in changing Africa. 1st ed. N.Y., 1962.

Afr 550.140   Hertlein, Siegfried. Christentum und Mission im Urteil der neoafrikanischen Prosaliteratur. Münster, 1962.

Afr 9047.30   Hey, Peter D. The rise of the Natal Indian elite. Pietermaritzburg, 1962.

Afr 210.56.2   Hodgkin, Thomas. Nationalism in colonial Africa. London, 1962.

Afr 5344.9   Holas, Bohumil. Les Toura. Paris, 1962.

Afr 8688.230   Hopkins, Henry Charles. Die Smalberger familieregister. Wynberg, 1962.

Afr 5340.25   Houphouet-Boigny, Felix. Discours à l'assemblée nationale. Abidjan, 1962.

Afr 8925.25   How, Marion Wulsham. The mountain bushmen of Basutoland. Pretoria, 1962.

Afr 10015.2   Hughes, L. Anthologie africaine et malgache. Paris, 1962.

Afr 626.102   Hunter, Guy. The new societies of tropical Africa. London, 1962.

Afr 6740.15.5   Hurault, Jean. La structure sociale des Bamileke. Paris, 1962.

Afr 8676.62.15   Hurwitz, N. Economic framework of South Africa. Pietermaritzburg, 1962.

Afr 6470.231.6   Huxley, Elspeth Grant. The mottled lizard. London, 1962.

Afr 6470.231.5   Huxley, Elspeth Grant. On the edge of the rift, memories of Kenya. N.Y., 1962.

Afr 6280.2.5   Idowu, E. Olodumaie. London, 1962.

Afr 1085.2   Idris, Hady R. La Berbérie orientale sous les Zirides, Xe-XIIe siècles. v.1-2. Paris, 1962.

Afr 3977.19   Ildefonso da Palermo, Father. Cronaca della missione francescana dell'Alto Egitto, 1719-1739. Cairo, 1962.

Afr 6314.33   Ingham, K. A history of East Africa. London, 1962.

Afr 6457.22.2   International Bank for Reconstruction and Development. The economic development of Kenya. Nairobi, 1962.

Afr 6538.20   International Bank for Reconstruction and Development. The economic development of Uganda. Baltimore, 1962.

Afr 212.42   Italiaander, Rolf. Schwarze Haut im roten Griff. Düsseldorf, 1962.

Afr 4700.4.5   Italy. Comitato per la Documentazione dell'Opera dell'Italia in Africa. L'Italia in Africa, le scoperte archeologiche Tripolitania. Roma, 1962. 2v.

Afr 9499.37   Italy. Istituto Nazionale per il Commercio Estero. Federazione delle Rodesia e del Niassaland. Roma, 1962.

Afr 4700.62   Ivanitskii, M.N. Put k nezavisimosti. Kiev, 1962.

Afr 8057.5.5   Jaarsveld, F.A. van. Lewende verlede. Johannesburg, 1962.

Afr 3180.5.5   Jabarti, Abd Al-Rahman. Egipet v period ekspeditsii Bonaparta (1798-1801). Moscow, 1962.

Afr 11465.14.140   Jacobson, Dan. Time of arrival, and other essays. London, 1962.

Afr 679.62   Jahn, Janheinz. Through African doors. N.Y., 1962.

Afr 2223.962.5   Jeanson, F. La révolution algérienne. Milano, 1962.

Afr 5993.17   Jeran, Manuel de. Sintesis geografica de Fernando Poo. Madrid, 1962.

Afr 2025.30   Joesten, Joachim. The red hand. London, 1962.

Afr 8657.90.5   Johannesburg. Public Library. Bibliography of Le Vaillant's "Voyages" and "Oiseaux d'Afrique." Johannesburg, 1962.

Afr 3986.962.5   Johne, Alfred. Die Industrialisierungspolitik des Ägypten unter besonderer Berücksichtigung. Berlin, 1962.

Afr 5749.62.5   Joubert, Elsa. Suid van die wind. Kaapstad, 1962.

Afr 7315.20.6   Junod, H.A. The life of a South African tribe. New Hyde Park, N.Y., 1962. 2v.

Afr 6203.6   Kaduna, Nigeria. Regional Library. An author catalogue of books about Nigeria in the regional library. Kaduna, 1962.

Afr 3979.62.5   Kaesser, Hans. Einiges ägypten. Baden-Baden, 1962.

Afr 8045.52   Kahn, Ellison. The new constitution. London, 1962.

Afr 10066.3   Kaminski-Durocher, B. Poezja czarnej Afryki. Warszawa, 1962.

Afr 7812.262   Katanga. Livre blanc du gouvernement katangais sur les évènements. Elisabethville, 1962.

Afr 8740.46   Katsman, V.I. Tanganika, 1946-61. Moscow, 1962.

Afr 9748.475   Kaunda, Kenneth David. Zambia shall be free. London, 1962.

Afr 5549.62   Kent, R.K. From Madagascar to the Malagasy Republic. N.Y., 1962.

Afr 6410.10   Kenya. Constitutional Conference, London, 1962. Report presented to Parliament by the Secretary of State for the colonies. London, 1962.

Afr Doc 3207.360   Kenya. Economics and Statistics Division. Kenya African agricultural sample census, 1960-1961. Nairobi, 1962.

Afr 2030.462.45   Kessel, Patrick. Le peuple algérien et la guerre. Paris, 1962.

Afr 3155.10   Khawli, Amir. Sviazi mezhdu Nilom i Volgoi v XIII-XIV vv. Moscow, 1962.

Afr 6333.62.10   Khazanov, A.M. Osvoboditel'naia bor'ba narodov Vostochnoi Afriki. Moscow, 1962.

Afr 2030.462.90   Khelifa, L. Manuel du militant algérien. Lausanne, 1962.

Afr 109.62   Kingsnorth, G.W. Africa south of the Sahara. Cambridge, 1962.

Afr 7947.4   Klemke, O. Die Erziehung bei Eingeborenengruppen in Ruanda-Urundi. Bonn, 1962.

Afr 6979.62   Klerk, W.A. Drie swerwers oor die einders. 3. verb. uitg. Kaapstad, 1962.

Afr 7809.62   Knapen, Marie Thérèse. L'enfant Mukongo. Louvain, 1962.

Afr 28.76   Koehler, Jochen. Deutsche Dissertationen über Afrika. Bonn, 1962.

Afr 8678.294   Koos Vorrink Instituut. Zuid-Afrika en de apartheid. Amsterdam, 1962.

Afr 6225.7   Koriavin, L.A. Probudivshaisia Nigeriia. Moscow, 1962.

Afr 8678.298   Kotze, J.C.G. Principle and practice in race relations. Stellenbosch, 1962.

Afr 8028.156   Kuper, B. A bibliography of native law in South Africa, 1941-1961. Johannesburg, 1962.

Afr 6192.95   Kuzvart, Milos. Ghanska cesta. Praha, 1962.

Afr 4180.6   Lackany, Radames Sany. Sollum and its environments. Alexandria, 1962.

Afr 2230.41   Lacoste, Camille. Bibliographie ethnologique de la Grande Kabylie. Paris, 1962.

Afr 3300.85.3   Lacouture, Jean. L'Egypte en mouvement. Paris 1962.

Afr 5010.5   Lamput, Pierre. Les constitutions des états. Paris, 1962.

Afr 1955.62   Lamurière, Marc. Histoire de l'Algérie illustrée de 1830 à nos jours. Paris, 1962.

Afr 2025.32   Landa, R.G. Natsionalno-osvoboditelnoe dvizhenie v Alzhire. Moscow, 1962.

Afr 1495.2   Landau, Rom. Hassan II, King of Morocco. London, 1962.

Afr 6095.362.5F   Lander, H. Westafrikanische Impressionen. Darmstadt, 1962.

Afr 7803.34   Laridan, P. Les martyrs noirs de l'Ouganda. Tournai, 1962.

Afr 6275.103   Laroche, H. La Nigeria. Paris, 1962.

Afr 210.62.30   Legum, Colin. Pan-Africanism. N.Y., 1962.

Afr 109.60.25F   Lenerhulme Inter-Collegiate History Conference, 1960. Historians in tropical Africa. Salisbury, 1962.

Afr 5485.10   Lerouvreur, A. Saheliens et Sahariens du Tchad. Paris, 1962.

Afr 1110.30A   Le Tourneau, Roger. Evolution politique de l'Afrique du Nord musulmane 1920-1961. Paris, 1962.

Afr 28.80   Library of Congress. A list of American doctoral dissertations on Africa. Washington, 1962.

Afr 28.70.5   Library of Congress. Serial Division. African newspapers in selected American libraries. 2d ed. Washington, 1962.

Afr 4559.62   Lipsky, George A. Ethiopia. New Haven, 1962.

Afr 7809.62.10   Liveing, Edward G.D. Across the Congo. London, 1962.

Afr 7222.82   Lobato, Alexandre. Colonização senhorial da Zambezia. Lisboa, 1962.

Afr 6985.5   Loeb, Edwin. In feudal Africa. Bloomington, 1962.

Afr 2676.2   Louis, André. Documents ethnographiques et linguistiques sur les îles Gerkena. Alger, 1962.

Afr 6927.8   Lowenstein, Allard K. Brutal mandate. N.Y., 1962.

Afr 2224.962   Lubell, Harold. A note on the national accounts of Algeria, 1950-1959 and 1964. Santa Monica, Calif., 1962.

Afr 9439.54.5   Lumb, Sybil Victoria. Central and southern Africa. 2. ed. Cambridge, 1962.

Afr 7575.80.10   Lumumba, Patrice. Congo, my country. London, 1962.

Afr 7575.80.11   Lumumba, Patrice. Congo, my country. N.Y., 1962.

Afr 8687.263   Luthuli, A. Let my people go. N.Y., 1962.

Afr 1571.17.65   Lyautey, L.H.G. Les plus belles lettres de Lyautey. Paris, 1962.

Afr 11542.87.120   Lytton, David. The paradise people. London, 1962.

Afr 6295.62.5   Maboganj, A. Yoruba towns. Ibadan, 1962.

Afr 8152.74.2   McKay, James. Reminiscences of the last Kaffir war. General index, excluding appendices. Johannesburg, 1962.

Afr 6535.62   McMaster, D.N. A subsistence agricultural geography of Uganda. Bude, 1962.

Afr 8095.84   Macnab, Roy Martin. Journey into yesterday, South African milestones in Europe. Cape Town, 1962.

Afr 5540.11   Madagascar. Constitution. Constitution et lois organiques de la République Malgache et accords franco-malgaches. Tananarive, 1962.

Afr 6395.16   Mair, J.C. Primitive government. Harmondsworth, 1962.

Afr 6420.73   Majdalany, F. State of emergency, the full story of Mau Mau. London, 1962.

Afr 5230.7   Mali. Embassy. United Arab Republic. Mars 1961-mars 1962. Les relations Mali - République Arabe Unie. Cairo, 1962.

Afr 5240.7   Mali. Ministère du Plan et de l'Economie Rurale. Données économiques. Bamako, 1962.

Afr 590.76   Mannix, Daniel. Black cargoes, a history...1518-1865. N.Y., 1962.

Afr 8335.2   Mansergh, N. South Africa, 1906-1961. N.Y., 1962.

Afr 11555.61.65   Manson, H.W.D. The noose-knot ballad, a play. Cape Town, 1962.

Afr 609.62.25   Maquet, Jacques. Afrique. Paris, 1962.

Afr 9165.42.60   Market Research Africa. An African day. Johannesburg, 1962.

Afr 6275.90.5   Marris, P. Family and social change in an African city. Evanston, Ill., 1962.

Afr 628.262   Mars, Jean. De la préhistoire d'Afrique. Port-au-Prince, 1962.

Afr 7549.62.10   Martelli, George. Leopold to Lumumba. London, 1962.

Afr 9093.25   Mason, Revil. Prehistory of the Transvaal. Johannesburg, 1962.

Afr 2030.462   Matthews, T.S. War in Algeria. N.Y., 1962.

Afr 7549.62.5   Maurice, Albert. Belgique, gouvernante du Congo. Bruxelles, 1962.

Afr 630.62.5   Melady, T.P. The white man's future in black Africa. N.Y., 1962.

Afr 10007.2   Mclonc, Thomas. De la négritude dans la littérature négro-africaine. Paris, 1962.

Afr 545.25   Mendelsohn, J. God, Allah, and Ju Ju. N.Y., 1962.

Afr 6295.62   Mercier, Paul. Civilisation du Benin. Paris, 1962.

Afr 8835.47   Merkens, Alice. Cape Town, Kaapstad, Kapstadt. 2. ed. Cape Town, 1962.

Afr 7567.26   Merlier, Michel. Le Congo de la colonisation belge à l'indépendance. Paris, 1962.

Afr 609.62   Merriam, Alan P. A prologue to the study of the African arts. Yellow Springs, Ohio, 1962.

Afr 8180.23   Merwe, P.J. Nog verder noord. Kaapstad, 1962.

Afr 3986.962.10   Messayer, Mohamed Zaki. Le développement économique de l'Egypte. Lausanne, 1962.

Afr 6198.546   Metcalfe, George. MacLean of the Gold Coast. London, 1962.

Afr 8687.221   Metrowich, F.C. Scotty Smith. Cape Town, 1962.

Afr 6196.26   Meyerowitz, Eva. At the court of an African king. London, 1962.

Afr 30.8   Meyer's Handbuch über Afrika. Mannheim, 1962.

Afr 2030.462.60   Michel, F. Christ et croissant pour l'Algérie nouvelle. Paris, 1962.

Afr 7912.5.5   Michel, Serge. Uhuru Lumumba. Paris, 1962.

Afr 699.62   Miller, Stefan. Vom Nilzum Sambesi. 1. Aufl. Berlin, 1962.

Afr 2250.6   Millet, Jean. La coexistence des communautés en Algérie. Aix-en-Provence, 1962.

Afr 11572.50.210   Millin, S.G.(L). The wizard bird. London, 1962.

Afr 7913.2   Monheim, F. Mobutu, l'homme seul. Paris, 1962.

Afr 11057.2   Moore, G. Seven African writers. London, 1962.

Afr 3979.62   Moorehead, Alan. The Blue Nile. 1st ed. N.Y., 1962.

Afr 11580.75.100   Morgan, Robert. The winds blow red. Ilfracombe, 1962.

Afr 626.121   Morgaut, M.E. Cinq années de psychologies africaines. Paris, 1962.

Afr 9693.7   Morris, Colin. The end of the missionary. London, 1962.

Afr 6542.15   Morris, H.F. A history of Ankole. Nairobi, 1962.

Afr 1869.62   Mouilleseaux, L. Histoire de l'Algerie. Paris, 1962.

Afr 2030.462.150   Moureaux, S. Les accords d'Evian et l'avenir de la révolution algérienne. Paris, 1962.

Afr 5183.962   Moyenne vallée du Sénégal. Paris, 1962.

Afr 6192.90   Mozheiko, I.V. Eto, Gana. Moscow, 1962.

Afr 609.62.45   Mphahlele, E. The African image. N.Y., 1962.

Afr 635.80   Mphahlele, Ezekiel. The African image. London, 1962.

Afr 6640.12   Mueller, F.F. Kolonien unter der Peitsche. Berlin, 1962.

Afr 10013.5   Münster. Universität. Institut für Publizistik. Publizist und Publikum in Afrika. Köln, 1962.

1962 - cont.

Afr 5844.5 — Mukherji, S.B. The indenture system in Mauritius, 1837-1915. 1. ed. Calcutta, 1962.

Afr 11249.86.800 — Muller, G. A bibliography of the poetical works of Guy Butler, Anthony Delius and Roy MacNab. Johannesburg, 1962. 2v.

Afr 6780.43 — Mustafa, Sophia. The Tanganyika way. London, 1962.

Afr 2030.462.30 — Naegelen, Marcel. Mission en Algérie. Paris, 1962.

Afr 8685.27.15 — Narain, I. The politics of racialism. 1. ed. Agra, 1962.

Afr 3669.6 — Nasri, Abdel R. A bibliography of the Sudan, 1938-1958. London, 1962.

Afr 3326.4 — Nasser, G.A. The Charter. Cairo, 1962.

Afr 3310.10.30 — Nasser, G.A. Collection of addresses. Cairo, 1962. 8 pam.

Afr 3322.2 — Nasser, G.A. A draft of the Charter. Cairo, 1962.

Afr 3310.10.5.10 — Nasser, G.A. Historical address on occasion of 4th anniversary of the Union, Feb. 22, 1962. Cairo, 1962.

Afr 8678.260 — Neame, L.E. The history of apartheid. London, 1962.

Afr 8659.62 — Nel, Andries. Stad en dorp. Stellenbosch, 1962.

Afr 5054.62 — Neres, Philip. French-speaking West Africa. London, 1962.

Afr 590.77 — Neuton, John. The journal of a slave trader, John Neuton, 1750-1754. London, 1962.

Afr 550.136 — Newington, D. The shape of personality in African Christian leadership. Nelspruit, 1962.

Afr 550.136.5 — Newington, D. The shape of power in Africa. Nelspruit, 1962.

Afr 5225.8 — Niane, D.T. Recherches sur l'empire du Mali au Moyen Age. Conakry, 1962.

Afr 2030.462.145 — Nicol, A. La bataille de l'O.A.S. Paris, 1962.

Afr 8678.304 — Niekerk, R. Ons uis jon Suid-Afrika. Pretoria, 1962.

Afr 6291.15 — Nigeria, Eastern. Economic Mission. Report of the Economic Mission, 1961. Enugu, 1962.

Afr 6277.75 — Nigeria. Federal government development programme, 1962-68. Lagos, 1962.

Afr 6277.76F — Nigeria. Commission of Inquiry into the Affairs of Certain Statutory Corporations in Western Nigeria. Report of Cokes Commission. V.1-4. Lagos, 1962.

Afr 6277.74 — Nigeria. Federal Ministry of Economic Development. National development plan, 1962-68. Lagos, 1962.

Afr 6203.7 — Nigeria. National Archives. A special list of records in chieftaincy matters. Ibadan, 1962.

Afr 6176.30.35 — Nkrumah, Kwame. Towards colonial freedom. London, 1962.

Afr 11612.100 — Noble, Alex. Boy with a flute. London, 1962.

Afr 1957.29 — Noguères, H. L'expédition d'Alger, 1830. Paris, 1962.

Afr 12884.65.110 — Nokan, Charles. Le soleil noir point. Paris, 1962.

Afr 7461.50 — Northwestern University, Evanston, Ill. Economic survey of Liberia. Evanston, Ill., 1962?

Afr 8676.62.5 — Norval, A. A quarter of a century of industrial progress in South Africa. Cape Town, 1962.

Afr 2000.16 — Nouschi, André. La naissance du nationalisme algérien. Paris, 1962.

Afr 9757.20 — Nyasaland Constitutional Conference. Report of the Nyasaland Constitutional Conference held in London in Nov. 1962. London, 1962.

Afr 9850.7 — Nyasaland development plan, 1962-1965. Zomba, 1962.

Afr 11626.23.110 — Nzekwu, Onuora. Blade among the boys. London, 1962.

Afr 10684.99.110 — Nzekwu, Onuora. Blade among the boys. London, 1962.

Afr 6280.9.25 — Nzimiro, F.I. Family and kinship in Ibo land. Köln, 1962.

Afr 6218.14 — Obi, Chike. Our struggle. V.1-2. Yaba, 1962.

Afr 55.13 — Oeste, Sven. Afrikas ansikte. Stockholm, 1962.

Afr 10685.45.100 — Okigbo, Christopher. Heaven's gate. Ibadan, 1962.

Afr 6277.27 — Okigbo Pius N.C. Nigerian national accounts 1950-57. Nigeria, 1962.

Afr 10685.67.110 — Okoye, Mokwugo. The rebel line. Onitsha, 1962.

Afr 7122.58A — Okuma, T. Angola in ferment. Boston, 1962.

Afr 109.62.15 — Oliver, Roland Anthony. A short history of Africa. Harmondsworth, 1962.

Afr 5920.13 — Ortega Canadell, Rosa. Provincias africanas espanolas. 1.ed. Barcelona, 1962.

Afr 6214.31 — Ottonkwo, D.O. History of Nigeria in a new setting. Onitsha, 1962.

Afr 4559.62.5 — Ouannou, J. L'Ethiopie, pilote de l'Afrique. Paris, 1962.

Afr 12785.89.100 — Ousmane, Sembene. Voltaique; nouvelles. Paris, 1962.

Afr 7119.62 — Panikkar Kavalam Madhusudan. Angola in flames. N.Y., 1962.

Afr 5344.10 — Paulme, Denise. Une société de Côte-d'Ivoire. Paris, 1962.

Afr 2225.20 — Pautard, André. Mohammed, l'Algérien mon ami. Paris, 1962.

Afr 210.62 — Perham, M.F. The colonial reckoning. N.Y., 1962.

Afr 2030.462.85 — Periot, Gerard. Deuxième. Paris, 1962.

Afr 16.10 — Permanent Organization for Afro-Asian Peoples' Solidarity. Dokumenty. V.F. Moskva, 1962. 3v.

Afr 2030.462.75 — Perroux, Francois. L'Algérie de demain. Paris, 1962.

Afr 11683.88.100 — Petrie, A. Saint Andrew's day, 1919-61. Pietermaritzburg, 1962.

Afr 2030.462.5 — Peyrefitte, Alain. Faut-il partager l'Algérie? Paris, 1962.

Afr 8678.167 — Phillips, Norman. La tragedia del apartheid. Mexico, 1962.

Afr 5749.62 — Pidoux, Edmond. Madagascar, maître à son bord. Lausanne, 1962.

Afr 2260.17 — Pieds-noirs et la presse française. Paris, 1962.

Afr 630.62 — Pieto, I. Causas de los conflictos en el Africa del sur. Berriz, 1962.

Afr 109.62.35 — Pirone, Michele. Appunti di storia dell'Africa. Milano, 1962.

Afr 2030.462.40 — Potemkin, Iu. V. Alzhirskii narod v borbe za nezavisimosti. Moscow, 1962.

Afr 2623.962 — Poucet, J. La colonisation et l'agriculture européennes en Tunisie depuis 1881. Paris, 1962.

Afr 9705.15 — Powdermaker, Hortense. Copper town. 1st ed. N.Y., 1962.

Afr 8676.62 — Princeton University. Enterprise and politics in South Africa. Princeton, N.J., 1962.

Afr 6390.70 — Pritchard, J.M. A geography of East Africa. London, 1962.

Afr 210.62.40 — Problemy Mira i Sotsializma. Za natsionalniiu nezavisimost. Praha, 1962.

Afr 13438.1.100 — Rabemananjara, Jacques. Agapes des dieux ou Tritriva. Paris, 1962.

Afr 13438.1.775 — Rabemananjara, Jacques. Insel mit Flammensilben. Herranalb, 1962.

Afr 8230.6.20 — Rademeyer, J.I. Paul Kruger. Johannesburg, 1962.

Afr 6470.269 — Rake, Alan. Tom Mboya. 1st ed. Garden City, N.Y., 1962.

Afr 5426.125 — Raponda-Walker, A. Rites et croyances des peuples du Gabon. Paris, 1962.

Afr 550.125 — Rathe, G. Mud and mosaics. Westminster, Md., 1962.

Afr 9500.40 — Rayner, W. The tribe and its successors. London, 1962.

1962 - cont.

Afr 8678.186 — Reeves, Ambrose. South Africa, yesterday and tomorrow. London, 1962.

Afr 618.31 — Rencontres Internationales, Bouake, Ivory Coast, January 1962. Tradition et modernisme en Afrique noire. Rabat, 1962.

Afr 1338.12 — Reynal, Raoul. Les particularités du droit fiscal par rapport au droit privé. Rabat, 1962.

Afr 9693.8 — Rhodes-Livingstone Institute. The multitribal society. Lusaka, 1962.

Afr 18.5.5 — Rhodes-Livingstone Journal. Index, v.1-30. Manchester, 1962.

Afr 9499.70 — Rhodesia, Southern. Advisory Committee on the Development of the Economic Resources of Southern Rhodesia. The development of the economic resources of Southern Rhodesia. Salisbury, 1962.

Afr 9780.2 — Rhodesia and Nyasaland. The issue of Nyasaland's secession. Salisbury, 1962.

Afr Doc 3507.361 — Rhodesia and Nyasaland. Central Statistical Office. Preliminary results of federal censuses of population and of employees, September, 1961. Salisbury, 1962.

Afr Doc 3809.515 — Rhodesia and Nyasaland. Central Statistical Office. Sample survey of African agriculture, Southern Rhodesia, 1959/60. Salisbury, 1962.

Afr 7803.26 — Richardson, Kenneth. Freedom in Congo. London, 1962.

Afr 28.85 — Rio de Janeiro. Biblioteca Nacionale Bibliografia afro-asiatica. Rio de Janeiro, 1962.

Afr 626.98 — Rivkin, Arnold. Africa and the West. N.Y., 1962.

Afr 11033.2 — Robinson, A.M.L. None daring to make us afraid. Cape Town, 1962.

Afr 210.62.25 — Robinson, James H. Africa at the crossroads. Philadelphia, 1962.

Afr 14505.5 — Rodrigues Junior, Manuel. Literatura ultramarina. Lourenço, 1962.

Afr 9500.45 — Rogers, Cyril A. Racial themes in Southern Rhodesia. New Haven, 1962.

Afr 11752.65.110 — Rooke, Daphne. The Greyling. London, 1962.

Afr 8095.36 — Ross, R.E. van der. History in pictures. 1. ed. Cape Town, 1962.

Afr 1609.62 — Rouze, Michel. Maroc. Lausanne, 1962.

Afr 3255.7 — Rowlatt, Mary. Founders of modern Egypt. London, 1962.

Afr 626.117 — Royal Institue of International Affairs. The African economy. Oxford, 1962.

Afr 9047.21 — Russel, Margo. Unemployment among Indians in Durban, 1962. Durban, 1962.

Afr 4115.24 — Russell, Dorothea. Medieval Cairo and the monasteries of the Wadi Natrun. London, 1962.

Afr 609.62.55 — Rycroft, W.S. A factual study of sub-Saharan Africa. N.Y., 1962.

Afr 7182.20 — Santos, Eduardo dos. Sobre a religião dos Quiocos. Lisboa, 1962.

Afr 8380.2 — Scholtz, Gert. Die Republiek van Suid-Afrika. Johannesburg, 1962.

Afr 7549.62.15 — Schuyler, Philippa. Who killed the Congo? N.Y., 1962.

Afr 28.93 — Scotland. Record Office. Material relating to Africa. Edinburgh, 1962-65.

Afr 55.25 — Segal, Ronald. African profiles. Baltimore, 1962.

Afr 630.62.10 — Seminar on Racialism, Kampala, Uganda. Report. Leiden, 1962.

Afr 2209.62 — Servier, J. Les poètes de l'année, rites et symboles. Paris, 1962.

Afr 3040.78A — Shaw, S.J. The financial and administrative organization and development of Ottoman Egypt, 1517-1798. Princeton, 1962.

Afr 3037.1 — Shayyal, J. al-D. A history of Egyptian historiography in the nineteenth century. Alexandria, 1962.

Afr 50.35 — Shepherd, George. The politics of African nationalism. N.Y., 1962.

Afr 6144.2F — Sierra Leone. Education and economic development in Sierra Leone. Sierra Leone, 1962.

Afr 6144.6F — Sierra Leone. Ten-year plan of economic and social development, 1962/63-1971/72. Freetown, 1962.

Afr 7815.30 — Slade, Ruth. King Leopold's Congo. London, 1962.

Afr 7353.6 — Solomon, Marian D. A general bibliography of the Republic of Liberia. Evanston, 1962.

Afr 5312.10.5 — Solonitskii, A.S. Republik Guinea. Berlin, 1962.

Afr 609.62.30 — Sousa, Daniel. Perspectivas da actualidade africana. n.p., 1962.

Afr Doc 4307.360 — South Africa. Office of Census and Statistics. Population census, 1960. Pretoria, 1962-65. 2v.

Afr 8045.5 — South Africa. Parliament. The parliament of the Republic of South Africa. Cape Town, 1962.

Afr 8676.62.10 — South Africa Foundation. South Africa in the sixties. Johannesburg, 1962.

Afr 11803.21.100 — Spears, D. No common day. Cape Town, 1962.

Afr 210.62.5 — Spiro, Herbert John. Politics in Africa. Englewood Cliffs, N.J., 1962.

Afr 8687.137 — Spohr, Otto H. Wilhelm Heinrich Immanuel Bleek. Cape Town, 1962.

Afr 8678.289 — Steward, Alex. The challenge of change. Cape Town, 1962.

Afr 626.147 — Strasbourg. Université. Centre Universitaire des Hautes Etudes Européennes. L'Europe et l'Afrique noire. Strasbourg, 1962.

Afr 510.111 — Subbotin, V.A. Frantsuzskaia kolonialnaia ekspansiia v kontse XIX v. Ekuatorialnaia Afrika i Idiiskogo Okeana. Moscow, 1962.

Afr 3813.22 — Sudan. Treaties, etc. Kuwait Fund for Arab Economic Development. Loan agreement between the Republic for Sudan and the Kuwait Fund for Arab Economic Development dated March 25th, 1962. Kuwait, 1962?

Afr 45.62 — Summer Conference on Local Government in Africa. Summer conference on local government in Africa, 28 Aug.-9 Sept., 1961. Cambridge, 1962.

Afr 109.62.25 — Svoboda, J. Pet stoleti boju o jizm Afriku. Praha, 1962.

Afr 2533.11 — Szymanski, E. Le problème de l'indépendance de la Tunisie. Warszawa, 1962.

Afr Doc 3419.5 — Tanganyika. Constitution. An act to declare the Constitution of Tanganyika. Dar es Salaam, 1962?

Afr 8678.281 — Tatz, C. Shadow and substance in South Africa. Pietermaritzburg, 1962.

Afr 505.42 — Taylor, Don. The British in Africa. London, 1962.

Afr 13340.13.100 — Tchicaya U Tamsi, Gerald Felix. Epitome. Tunis, 1962.

Afr 7122.68 — Telo, Alencastre. Angola, terra nossa. Lisbon, 1962.

Afr 8658.27.4F — Thompson, George. Travels and adventures in southern Africa. Cape Town, 1962.

1962 - cont.

Afr 6455.3.15 — Thomson, Joseph. Through Masai land with Joseph Thomson. Evanston, Ill., 1962.
Afr 2030.462.50 — Thorez, Maurice. Textes choisis sur l'Algérie. Paris, 1962.
Afr 6225.5 — Tilman, Robert O. The Nigerian political scene. Durham, 1962.
Afr 555.140 — Todd, John Murray. African mission. London, 1962.
Afr Doc 6707.358 — Togo. Service de la Statistique Général. Recensement général de la population du Togo, 1958-1960. Lomé, 1962?
Afr 6664.15 — Tokareva, Z.I. Togolezskaia respublika. Moscow, 1962.
Afr 7580.11 — Tran-Minh Tiet. Congo ex-belge entre l'est et l'ouest. Paris, 1962.
Afr 575.36 — Trimingham, J.S. A history of Islam in West Africa. London, 1962.
Afr 2030.462.135 — Trinquier, R. Le coup d'état du 13 mai. Paris, 1962.
Afr 505.10 — Trofimov, V.A. Politika Anglii i Italii v severo-vostochnoi Afrike. Moscow, 1962.
Afr 2609.62.5 — Tunisia, yesterday and today. Tunis, 1962.
Afr 2623.962.5F — Tunisia. Secretariat. Tunisian development. Tunis, 1962.
Afr 2623.962.10 — Tunisia. Secrétariat d'Etat au Plan et aux Finances. Perspectives décennales de dèveloppement, 1962-1971. Tunis, 1962.
Afr 635.85 — Turnbull, Colin. The lonely African. N.Y., 1962.
Afr 7912.15.25 — Turski, Marian. Lumumba i jego kraj. Warszawa, 1962.
Afr 10690.89.120 — Tutuola, Amos. Feather woman of the jungle. London, 1962.
Afr 6542.3 — Uganda. Commission Appointed to Review the Boundary Between the Districts of Bugisu and Bukedi. Report. Entebbe, 1962.
Afr 6484.20 — Uganda. Commissioners for Africanisation. Report. Entebbe, 1962.
Afr 6538.40F — Uganda. Fiscal Commission. Report. Entebbe, 1962.
Afr Doc 3308.705F — Uganda. Ministry of Economic Development. Statistics Branch. The external trade of Uganda, 1950-1960. Entebbe, 1962.
Afr 6484.15 — Uganda Independence Conference. Report of the Uganda Independence Conference, 1962. London, 1962.
Afr 3340.14 — United Arab Republic. Information report, ten years. Cairo, 1962.
Afr 3340.12 — United Arab Republic. Information Department. The French spy ring in the UAR. Cairo, 1962.
Afr 3986.962.20 — United Arab Republic. Information Department. Ten years of progress...1952-62. Cairo, 1962.
Afr 28.84 — United States. Department of the Army. Africa, its problems and prospects. Washington, 1962?
Afr Doc 6507.361.10 — Upper Volta. Service de Statistique. La situation démographique en Haute-Volta; résultats partiels de l'enquête démographique, 1960-1961. Paris, 1962.
Afr 5282.10 — Upper Volta. Service du Plan. Données actuelles de l'économie voltäique. Paris, 1962.
Afr 6738.44 — Vaast, Pierre. La République fédérale du Cameroun. Paris, 1962.
Afr 5590.12 — Valette, J. Etudes sur le regne de Radama Uer. Tananarive, 1962.
Afr 5792.2 — Valette, Jean. Sainte-Marie et la côte est de Madagascar en 1818. Tananarive, 1962.
Afr 7850.50 — Vandenhang, E. The war in Katanga. N.Y., 1962.
Afr 8678.265 — Vanrensburg, P. Guilty land. London, 1962.
Afr 3986.962 — Vatolina, L.N. Ekonomika Obedinenie Arabskoi Respubliki. Moscow, 1962.
Afr 1495.3 — Vaucher, G. Sous les cèdres d'Ifrane. Paris, 1962.
Afr 2749.58.13 — Verlet, Bruno. Le Sahara. Paris, 1962.
Afr 2030.462.115 — Vidal-Naquet, P. La raison d'état. Paris, 1962.
Afr 9047.35 — Vilakazi, A. Zulu transformations. Pietermaritzburg, 1962.
Afr 49742.41.700 — Vilakazi, B.W. Zulu horizons. Cape Town, 1962.
Afr 8095.89 — Villiers, Anna de. Vrouegalery. Kaapstad, 1962.
Afr 7119.62.10 — Vinhos, Manuel. Para um dialogo sobre Angola. Lisboa, 1962.
Afr 2535.7 — Vokrouhlicky, Zbynek. Napric Tuniskem. Praha, 1962.
Afr 7912.15.5 — Vos, Pierre de. Vida y muerte de Lumumba. Mexico, 1962.
Afr 9560.18 — Warhurst, P.R. Anglo-Portuguese relations in South-Central Africa. London, 1962.
Afr 7122.74 — Waring, R. The war in Angola, 1961. Lisbon, 1962.
Afr 1623.962 — Waterston, A. Planning in Morocco. Washington, 1962.
Afr 8190.15 — Watt, E.P. Febana. London, 1962.
Afr 6277.68 — Wells, Frederick A. Studies in industrialization, Nigeria and the Cameroons. London, 1962.
Afr 8045.55 — Wessels, F.J. Die republikeinse grondwet. Kaapstad, 1962.
Afr 109.62.5 — Wiedner, Donald. A history of Africa. N.Y., 1962.
Afr 8028.132F — Wilkoy, A. Some English writings by non-Europeans in South Africa, 1944-1960. Johannesburg, 1962.
Afr 7567.32 — Willequet, I. Le Congo belge et Weltpolitik. Bruxelles, 1962.
Afr 8135.23.5 — Williams, Basil. Botha. N.Y., 1962.
Afr 6883.30 — Winnus, Edgar. Shambala. Berkeley, 1962.
Afr 3979.62.10 — Wohlfahrt, M. Das neue Agypten. Berlin, 1962.
Afr 6420.26 — Wood, Susan B. Kenya. London, 1962.
Afr 5183.962.5 — Zajadatz, Paul. Probleme und Möglichkeiten der industriellen Entwicklung im Senegal. Köln, 1962.
Afr 6560.2 — Zanzibar Constitutional Conference, 1962. Report of the Zanzibar Constitutional Conference, 1962. London, 1962.
Afr 2459.62 — Ziadeh, N.A. Origins of nationalism in Tunisia. Beirut, 1962.
Afr 7549.62 — Zusmanovich, A.Z. Imperialisticheskii razdel basseina Kongo. Moscow, 1962.

1963

Afr 12371.1.100 — Aba, Noureddine. La Toussaint des énigmes. Paris, 1963.
Afr 109.61.31 — Adiko, A. Histoire des peuples noirs. Abidjan, 1963.
Afr 626.122 — Afrika v tsifrakh. Moscow, 1963.
Afr 8038.5 — Afrikaanse kinderensiklopedi. Kaapstad, 1963. 10v.
Afr 609.63 — Afrique africaine. Lausanne, 1963.
Afr 2030.463.55 — Aguirre, Carlos. Argelia. Año 8. Buenos Aires, 1963.
Afr 35.5 — Akademiia Nauk SSSR. Institut Afriki. Afrikanskii sbornik. v.1-2. Moscow, 1963. 2v.
Afr 40.63 — Akademiia Nauk SSSR. Institut Gosudarstva i Prava. Stanovlenie natsionalnoi gosudarstv v nezavisimykh stranakh Afriki. Moscow, 1963.
Afr 1838.9 — Algeria. Constitution. La constitution. Alger, 1963.
Afr 2037.5 — Algeria. Ministère de l'Orientation Nationale. Une année de révolution socialiste, 1962 - 5 juillet - 1963. Alger, 1963?

1963 - cont.

Afr 545.46 — All-Africa Church Conference, Kampala, Uganda. La conférence de Kampala, 1963. Kitwe, 1963.
Afr 210.58.22 — American Assembly. The United States and Africa. N.Y., 1963.
Afr 109.63.5 — Anders, Robert. L'Afrique africaine. Paris, 1963.
Afr 6192.28 — Antubam, K. Ghana's heritage of culture. Leipzig, 1963.
Afr 6162.10.2 — Apter, D.E. Ghana in transition. N.Y., 1963.
Afr 6470.113 — Archer, G.F. Personal and historical memoirs. Edinburgh, 1963.
Afr 7119.63.10 — Archer, Maria. Brasil, fronteirad Africa. Sao Paulo, 1963.
Afr 3979.38.14 — Ayrout, H.H. The Egyptian peasant. Boston, 1963.
Afr 45.63.10 — Baade, Hans Wolfgang. African law, new law for new nations. N.Y., 1963.
Afr 12672.3.100 — Badlan, J. Sous l'orage. (Italy). Paris, 1963.
Afr 7560.5 — Bal, W. Le royaume du Congo aux XVe et XVIe siècle. Léopoldville, 1963.
Afr 5408.15.5 — Balandier, Georges. Sociologie actuelle de l'Afrique noire. Paris, 1963.
Afr 6176.41 — Balogum, K. Mission to Ghana. 1st ed. N.Y., 1963.
Afr 12351.63 — Barrat, D. Espoir et parole. Paris, 1963.
Afr 2985.2 — Bary, Erica de. Im Oasenkreis. München, 1963.
Afr Doc 4219.5 — Basutoland. Constitutional Commission. Report of the Basutoland Constitutional Commission. Maseru, 1963.
Afr Doc 4207.360 — Basutoland. Department of Agriculture. 1960 agricultural census. v.1-6. Maseru, 1963.
Afr Doc 4207.360F — Basutoland. Department of Agriculture. 1960 agricultural census. v.7. Maseru, 1963.
Afr Doc 4209.500 — Basutoland. Supervisor of Elections. A report on the first general election in Basutoland, 1960. Maseru, 1963.
Afr 626.131 — Bauer, G. Die Wirtschaft Afrikas. Frankfurt a.M., 1963.
Afr 8835.46 — Bax, Dirk. Argitektoniese shoonheid in Kaapstade kompanjiestuin, 1777-1805. Kaapstad, 1963.
Afr 6420.72.5 — Bennett, G. Kenya, a political history. London, 1963.
Afr 6565.42 — Bennett, N.R. Studies in East African history. Boston, 1963.
Afr 8687.263.10 — Benson, M. Chief Albert Lutuli of South Africa. London, 1963.
Afr 8685.90 — Benson, Mary. The African patriots. London, 1963.
Afr 555.153 — Bergner, Gerhard. Heiden, Christen und Politiker. Breklum, 1963.
Afr 4640.2 — Berlan, E. Addis-Abeba. Grenoble, 1963.
Afr 1494.61 — Bernard, S. Le conflit franco-marocain, 1943-56. v.1-2, 3. Bruxelles, 1963. 2v.
Afr 8252.155 — Binns, C.T. The last Zulu king. London, 1963.
Afr 8678.363 — Blaxall, Arthur William. Wake up South Africa, an essay. Johannesburg, 1963.
Afr 8252.1.5 — Borcherds, P.B. An autobiographical memoir. Facsimile reproduction. Cape Town, 1963.
Afr 7175.47 — Borchert, Günter. Südost-Angola. Hamburg, 1963.
Afr 630.63.5 — Borer, M.C. Africa. London, 1963.
Afr 555.148 — Borra, Edoardo. Un meschino di Allah. Torino, 1963.
Afr 2030.463.20 — Boualam, B. Les Harkis au service de la France. Paris, 1963.
Afr 1259.63 — Bowles, Paul. Their heads are green. London, 1963.
Afr 2209.63 — Boyer, P. La vie quotidienne à Alger à la veille de l'intervention française. Paris, 1963.
Afr 109.63.15 — Brentjes, Burchard. Uraltes junges Afrika; 5000 Jahre afrikanischer Geschichte aus zeitgenössischen Quellen. Berlin, 1963.
Afr 8678.299 — Brookes, E.H. Power, law, right and love. Durham, 1963.
Afr 200.17 — Brunschwig, H. L'événement de l'Afrique noire du XIX siècle à nos jours. Paris, 1963.
Afr 7812.263 — Brussels. Université Libre. Centre d'Étude des Questions Economiques Africaines. Le revenu des populations indigènes (du Congo-Léopoldville). Bruxelles, 1963.
Afr 7812.263.1 — Brussels. Université Libre. Centre d'Etudes des Questions Economiques Africaines. Le revenu des populations indigènes du Congo-Léopoldville. Etude élaborée par le Groupe de l'économie africaine. Bruxelles, 1963.
Afr 11240.5 — Brutus, Dennis. Sirens, knuckles, boots. Ibadan, 1963.
Afr 8678.155.2 — Bruwer, J.P. Die Bantoe van Suid-Africa. Johannesburg, 1963.
Afr 630.63 — Bryant, A.T. Bantu origins. Cape Town, 1963.
Afr 210.63.25A — Brzezinski, Z.K. Africa and the communist world. Stanford, Calif., 1963.
Afr 7580.14 — Buccianto, G. Il Congo. Milano, 1963.
Afr 2030.463.15 — Buchard, R. Organisation armée secrète, fév. 14-déc. 1961. Paris, 1963.
Afr 545.21 — Buhlman, Walbert. Afrika. Mainz, 1963.
Afr 8835.21 — Burman, Jose. Peninsula profile, a guide to the fairest cape. Johannesburg, 1963.
Afr 8809.63 — Burman, Jose. So high the road, mountain passes of the western Cape. Cape Town, 1963.
Afr 7580.15 — Cabanes, Bernard. Du Congo belge au Katanga. Paris, 1963.
Afr 3990.22 — Cairo, Alexandria, and environs. Paris, 1963.
Afr 6710.6 — Cameroon. Constitution. Constitution. Buea, 1963.
Afr Doc 7508.5 — Cameroon. Service de la Statistique Général et la Mécanographie. Enquête démographique sur la zone Centre et l'Est. Yaoundé, 1963.
Afr 6210.37 — Campbell, M.J. Law and practice of local government in northern Nigeria. Lagos, 1963.
Afr 210.63.55 — Carter, G.M. Five African states. Ithaca, 1963.
Afr 212.12 — Carvalho, Castro. Africa contemporanea. 2. ed. São Paulo, 1963.
Afr 9435.13 — Central African Conference. Report. London, 1963.
Afr 28.83 — Central Asian Research Centre, London. Soviet writing of Africa, 1959-61. Oxford, 1963.
Afr 6686.20 — Checchi and Company. A development company for Togo. Washington, 1963.
Afr 40.63.5 — Chodak, S. Systemy polityczne czarnej Afryki. Warszawa, 1963.
Afr 5448.14 — Le chômage à Brazzaville. Paris, 1963. 2v.
Afr 679.63 — Church, Ronald J.H. Environment and policies in West Africa. Princeton, 1963.
Afr 8678.282 — Cilliers, Stephanus Petrus. The coloureds of South Africa. Cape Town, 1963.
Afr 6769.60.2 — Clarke, P.H.C. A short history of Tanganyika. 2nd ed. Nairobi, 1963.
Afr 530.50.10 — Collins, Robert O. Americans in Africa. Stanford, Calif., 1963.
Afr 5183.960.8 — Compagnie d'Etudes Industrielles et d'Aménagement du Territoire. Rapport général sur les perspectives de développement du Sénégal. 3. éd. Dakar, 1963.
Afr 5540.14 — Comte, Jean. Les communes malgaches. Tananarive, 1963.

1963 - cont.

Afr 6168.15	Coombs, D. The Gold Coast. London, 1963.
Afr 7549.63	Cornevin, R. Histoire du Congo (Leopoldville). Paris, 1963.
Afr 6664.10.5	Cornevin, Robert. Le Togo, nation-pilote. Paris, 1963.
Afr 11300.83.21	Coster, Vera. Here Everest, and other poems. Grahamstown, 1963.
Afr 2030.463.25	Cretin-Vercel, Michel. Nouvelle Algérie. Paris, 1963.
Afr 8667.68	Cronjé, Geoffrey. Die Westerse kultuur in Suid-Afrika. Pretoria, 1963.
Afr 41906.2	Dampierre, Eric de. Poètes nzakara. Paris, 1963.
Afr 2026.7	Davan, Y.M. La vie politique à Alger de 1940 à 1944. Paris, 1963.
Afr 45.63	Decottignier, R. Les nationalités africaines. Paris, 1963.
Afr 8377.6	Degenaar, Johannes Jacobus. Op weg na 'n nuwe politieke lewenshouding. Kaapstad, 1963.
Afr 10624.2.120	Dei-Anang, M. Okomfo Anakye's golden stool. Accra, 1963.
Afr 6395.20	Delf, George. Asians in East Africa. London, 1963.
Afr 11320.50.120	Delius, Anthony. The day Natal took off. Cape Town, 1963.
Afr 11320.50.130	Delius, Anthony. The day Natal took off. London, 1963.
Afr 5448.15	Devauges, Roland. Les chômeurs de Brazzaville et les perspectives du barrage du Kouilou. Paris, 1963.
Afr 5448.15.5	Devauges, Roland. Les dépenses exceptionnelles dans les budgets de ménage à Pointe-Noire en 1958. Paris, 1963.
Afr 109.60.15.2	Dia, Mamadou. Nations africaines et solidarité mondiale. Paris, 1963.
Afr 12624.41.1100	Diakhaté, Lamine. Primordiale du sixième jour. Paris, 1963.
Afr 12624.4.100	Diop, Birago. Contes et lavanes. Paris, 1963.
Afr 3986.963.10	Dlin, Nikolai A. Obedinennaia Arabskaia Respublika. Moscow, 1963.
Afr 550.143	Dougall, James Watson Cunningham. Christians in the African revolution. Edinburgh, 1963.
Afr 10015.2	Drachler, J. African heritage. N.Y., 1963.
Afr 1110.44	Drame de l'Afrique du Nord et la conscience chrétienne. Paris, 1963.
Afr 626.124	Due, J.F. Taxation and economic development. Cambridge, 1963.
Afr 6588.4	East African Common Services Organization. The pattern of income expenditure and consumption of unskilled workers in Zanzibar. Nairobie, 1963. 2 pam.
Afr 609.63.10	Edinburgh. University. Urbanization in African social change. Edinburgh, 1963.
Afr 8848.5	Efolliott, Pamela. From Moscow to the Cape, the story of the Wienands of Waldeck. Cape Town, 1963.
Afr 7369.63	Egorov, V.V. Liberiia posle Vtoroi Mirovoi Voiny. Moscow, 1963.
Afr 3310.86PF	Egyptian Gazette. Eleven years of achievement. Cairo, 1963.
Afr 7122.72	Ehnmark, Anders. Angola and Mozambique, the case against Portugal. London, 1963.
Afr 3979.63.15	Einmann, E. Pueramiidide maal. Tallinn, 1963.
Afr 10675.47.110	Ekwensi, Cyprian. Beautiful feathers. London, 1963.
Afr 40.61.2	Elias, T.O. Government and politics in Africa. 2.ed. N.Y. 1963.
Afr 40.61.3	Elias, T.O. Government and politics in Africa. 2nd ed. Bombay, 1963.
Afr 6210.21	Elias, Taslim O. The Nigerian legal system. 2nd ed. London, 1963.
Afr 28.101	Englborghs-Bertels, Marthe. Les pays de l'est et la décolonisation particulièrement en Afrique. Bruxelles, 1963.
Afr 626.162F	Etheredge, D.A. Economic development in the newly independent states of Africa. Johannesburg, 1963.
Afr Doc 308.700F	Ethiopia. Central Statistical Office. Summary report on Ethiopia's external trade, 1953-1963. Addis Ababa, 1963.
Afr 210.63.60	Ethiopia. Ministry of Information. Addis Ababa summit. Addis Ababa, 1963.
Afr 4559.63	Ethiopia. Ministry of Information. Ethiopia, a brief sketch. Addis Ababa, 1963.
Afr 7015.42	Evangelista, J. A queixa do Ghana e a conjura contra Portugal. Lisboa, 1963.
Afr 8678.8.10	Fagan, H.A. Co-existence in South Africa. Cape Town, 1963.
Afr 210.63.75	Falcão, F. de S. Quo vadis, Africa. Lisboa, 1963.
Afr 210.61.56A	Fanon, Franz. The damned. Paris, 1963.
Afr 210.63.85	Fanon, Franz. The wretched of the earth. N.Y., 1963.
Afr 6095.360.2	Fax, Elton C. West Africa vignettes. 2 ed. N.Y., 1963.
Afr 676.63.20	Feng, C. Glimpses of West Africa. Peking, 1963.
Afr 679.63.25	Feng, Chi'h-Tan. Glimpses of West Africa. Peking, 1963.
Afr 6919.63	First, Ruth. South West Africa. Baltimore, 1963.
Afr 630.54.2	Forde, C.D. African worlds. London, 1963.
Afr 5091.12	France. Ministère de la Coopération. Economie et plan de développement, République islamique de Mauritanie. 2.éd. Paris, 1963.
Afr Doc 5008.207	France. Ministère de la Cooperation. Perspectives de population dans les pays africains et malgache d'expression française. Paris, 1963.
Afr 5758.63.3	France. Ministère de la Coopération. Direction des Affaires Economiques et Financières. Sous-Direction des Etudes Générales. Economie et plan de développement. 3. éd. Paris, 1963.
Afr 5482.5	France. Ministère de la Coopération. Direction des Affaires Economiques. Economie et plan de développement. Paris, 1963.
Afr 9448.74	Franklin, H. Unholy wedlock. London, 1963.
Afr 3986.963.5	Fridman, L.A. Kapitalisticheskoe razvitie Egipta, 1882-1939. Moscow, 1963.
Afr 8678.301	Friedmann, M.V. I will still be moved. Chicago, 1963.
Afr 6688.5	Froelich, J.C. Les populations du Nord-Togo. Paris, 1963.
Afr 609.63.15	Fromm, Friedrich Karl. Grosswild, Kleinvieh und Touristen. Berlin, 1963.
Afr 8160.24	Furneaux, Rupert. The Zulu war. 1st ed. Philadelphia, 1963.
Afr Doc 7407.361	Gabon. Service de Statistiques. Recensement et enquête démographiques, 1960-1961; résultats provisionelles. Paris, 1963.
Afr 8175.22	Galbraith, J.S. Reluctant empire. Berkeley, 1963.
Afr 1069.63	Gallagher, C.F. The United States and North Africa. Cambridge, 1963.
Afr 7580.8A	Ganshof van der Meersch, W.J. Fin de la souveraineté belge au Congo. Bruxelles, 1963.
Afr 679.63.20	Gardiner, Robert Kweku Atta. The development of social administration. 2nd ed. London, 1963.
Afr 6715.21	Gardinier, D.E. Cameroon, United Nations challenge to French policy. London, 1963.
Afr 6780.10.30	Gardner, B. German east, the story of the First World War in East Africa. London, 1963.
Afr 6780.10.31	Gardner, B. On to Kilimanjaro. Philadelphia, 1963.
Afr 3979.63.10F	Gary, D.H. Sun, stones and silence. N.Y., 1963.
Afr 9499.80	Gedamu, T. Country study on Southern Rhodesia. Addis Ababa? 1963.
Afr 210.62.17	Georgetown Colloquium on Africa. Emerging Africa. Washington, 1963.
Afr 7850.54	Gerard Libois, J. Secession au Katanga. Bruxelles, 1963.
Afr 6295.63	Gervis, P. Of emirs and pagans. London, 1963.
Afr 6160.29	Ghana. Commission Appointed to Enquire into the Circumstances which Led to the Payment of 28,545 Pounds to James Colledge (Cocoa) Ltd. Report. Accra, 1963.
Afr 6193.19	Ghana. Planning Commission. Seven year development plan; a brief outline. Accra? 1963?
Afr 4700.4.15	Girolami, Mario. Contributo dell'Italia alla conocenza della nosografia dell'Africa. Roma, 1963.
Afr 50.41	Gluckman, M. Order and rebellion in tribal Africa. London, 1963.
Afr 9389.63	Goldie, F. Lost city of the Kalahari. Cape Town, 1963.
Afr 8028.128.5	Goldman, Freda Y. An index to South African colour-plates in books, 1851-1899. Johannesburg, 1963.
Afr 5249.6	Gologo, M. Le rescapé de l'Ethylos. Paris, 1963.
Afr 11433.64.100	Goodwin, Harold. Songs from the settler city. Grahamstown, 1963.
Afr 11433.74.140	Gordimer, N. Occasion for loving. N.Y., 1963.
Afr 12002.1	Gras, Jacqueline. Situation de la presse dans les états de l'Union Africaine et Malgache, en Guinée, au Mali, au Togo. Paris, 1963.
Afr 6585.8	Great Britain. Central Office Of Information. Zanzibar. Harrow, 1963.
Afr 6457.28	Great Britain. Fiscal Commission for Kenya. Report of the Fiscal Commission. Nairobi, 1963.
Afr 12005.8	Groos, Almuth. Die Gegenwartsliteratur des Maghreb in französischer Sprache. Frankfurt, 1963.
Afr 9499.76	Guides and Handbooks of Africa. Resources and opportunities in the Rhodesias and Nyasaland. Nairobi, 1963.
Afr 6883.31	Gulliver, P.H. Social control in an African society, a study of the Arusha, agricultural Masai of northern Tanganyika. Boston, 1963.
Afr 6883.31.2	Gulliver, P.H. Social control in an African society. London, 1963.
Afr 6542.5.10	Gutkind, Peter. The royal capital of Buganda. The Hague, 1963.
Afr 8045.53	Hailey, W.M.H. The Republic of South Africa.
Afr 626.157.5	Halpern, Jan. Planowanie w niektorych krajach Afryki. Warszawa, 1963.
Afr 626.157F	Halpern, Jan. Wybrane zagadnienia z historii gospodarczej Afryki. Warszawa, 1963.
Afr 4236.963	Hammerschmidt, E. Stellung und Bedeutung des Sabbats. Stuttgart, 1963.
Afr 679.63.5	Hargreaves, J.D. Prelude to the partition of West Africa. London, 1963.
Afr 6203.4.4	Harris, John. Books about Nigeria. 4th ed. Ibadan, 1963.
Afr 8658.36.7	Harris, W.C. The wild sports of southern Africa. Cape Town, 1963.
Afr 550.131	Hayward, Victor Evelyn William. African independent church movements. London, 1963.
Afr 7855.4	Hecq, J. Agriculture et structures économiques d'un société traditionnelle au Kivu. Bruxelles, 1963.
Afr 6277.81	Helander, Sven. Entwicklungspolitik in Nigeria. Köln, 1963.
Afr 5235.263	Hemmo, Klaus. Zwischen Sahara und Elfenbeinküste. Leipzig, 1963.
Afr 7119.63.15	Hermans, Fons. Angola in opstand. 1. druk. Den Haag, 1963.
Afr 8145.40	Hinchliff, P.B. The Anglican Church in South Africa. London, 1963.
Afr 9689.63	Hock, E. Know your home: Zambia. Chensali? 1963?
Afr 210.63.40	Hodgson, R.D. The changing map of Africa. Princeton, 1963.
Afr 5342.60.5	Holas, Bohumil. Côte-d'Ivoire. Paris, 1963.
Afr 8678.15.2	Holden, W.C. The past and future of the Kaffir races. Cape Town, 1963.
Afr 8088.55.2	Holden, William Clifford. History of the colony of Natal. Cape Town, 1963.
Afr 115.112	Homann, Hermann. Wisser Mann auf heissen Pfaden. Stuttgart, 1963.
Afr 11057.5	Hooper, A.G. Short stories from Southern Africa. Cape Town, 1963.
Afr 8338.284	Hopkins, Henry Charles. Maar één soos hy. Kaapstad, 1963.
Afr 8678.309	Horrell, Muriel. Action, reaction and counteraction. Johannesburg, 1963.
Afr 6333.63	Hughes, Anthony. East Africa. Harmondsworth, 1963.
Afr 10016.2	Hughes, L. Poems from Black Africa. Bloomington, Ind., 1963.
Afr 8676.63.10	Hupkes, G.J. A survey of contemporary economic conditions and prospects for 1964. Stellenbosch, 1963.
Afr 5387.5	Hurault, Jean. Mission d'étude des structures agraires dans le sud Dahomey (février à Nov.1961). Rapport annexe. Paris, 1963.
Afr 8667.72	Idenburg, Petrus Johannes. The Cape of Good Hope. Leiden, 1963.
Afr 12979.44.100	Ikelle-Matiba, J. Cette Afrique-là. Paris, 1963.
Afr 6314.33.2	Ingham, K. A history of East Africa. 2. ed. London, 1963.
Afr 626.116	International Association for Research in Income and Wealth. African studies in income and wealth. Chicago, 1963.
Afr 6457.22	International Bank for Reconstruction and Development. The economic development of Kenya. Baltimore, 1963.
Afr 6280.55	Ismagilova, R.N. Narody Nigerii. Moscow, 1963.
Afr 3986.963	Issawi, C.P. Egypt in revolution. London, 1963.
Afr 55.17	Italiaander, Rolf. Die neuen Männer Afrikas. Düsseldorf, 1963.
Afr 4700.26.20	Italy. Comitato per la Documentazione dell'Opera dell'Italia in Africa. L'Itali in Africa. Roma, 1963.
Afr 1623.963.10	Italy. Instituto Nazionale per il Commercio Estero. Marocco. Roma, 1963.
Afr 5482.20	Italy. Instituto Nazionale per il Commercio Estero. Tchad. Romo, 1963.

1963 - cont.

1963 - cont.

Afr 6739.263 — Italy. Istituto Nazionale per il Commercio Estero. Cameroun. Roma, 1963.
Afr 5343.20 — Italy. Istituto nazionale per il commercio estero Costa d'Avorio. Roma, 1963.
Afr 5342.64 — Ivory Coast. Embassy. U.S. General data on the Republic of the Ivory Coast. Washington, D.C., 1963.
Afr 8687.245.5 — Jabava, N. The Ochre people. N.Y., 1963.
Afr 2030.463.30 — Jacob, A. D'une Algérie à l'autre. Paris, 1963.
Afr 8687.42 — Jaff, Fay. They came to South Africa. Cape Town, 1963.
Afr 10018.2 — Jahn, Janheinz. Das junge Afrika. Wien, 1963.
Afr 3038.12 — Jalal, E.D. Le système unicaméral. Genève, 1963.
Afr 210.63.30 — Jennings, W. Democracy in Africa. Cambridge, Eng., 1963.
Afr 45.63.5 — Jeol, M. La reforme de la justice en Afrique noire. Paris, 1963
Afr 4259.63 — Jesman, Czeslaw. The Ethiopian paradox. London, 1963.
Afr 8673.19 — Johannesburg. Public Library. Some Africana coloured prints and the originals from which they may have been made. Johannesburg, 1963.
Afr 6218.18 — Jones, G.I. The trading states of the oil rivers. London, 1963.
Afr 8369.63 — Joseph, Helen. If this be treason. London, 1963.
Afr 210.62.45 — Judd, P. African independence. N.Y., 1963.
Afr 1869.63 — Juin, A.P. Histoire parallele. Paris, 1963.
Afr 7947.6 — Kagame, A. Les milices du Rwanda précolonial. Bruxelles, 1963.
Afr 6420.74 — Kariuki, Josiah M. Mau Mau detainee. London, 1963.
Afr 4060.30 — Keating, Rex. Nubian twilight. N.Y., 1963.
Afr 9448.72 — Keatley, Patrick. The politics of partnership. Harmondsworth, Middlesex, 1963.
Afr Doc 3207.362.5.5F — Kenya. Economics and Statistics Division. Kenya agricultural census, 1962, scheduled areas and coastal strip. n.p., 1963.
Afr 6410.7 — Kenya Independence Conference, London, 1963. Report presented to Parliament. London, 1963.
Afr 3310.87 — Kerr, M.H. Egypt under Nasser. N.Y., 1963.
Afr 2030.463.40 — Kessel, P. Lettere della rivoluzione algerina. Torino, 1963.
Afr 2885.11A — Khadduri, M. Modern Libya, a study in political development. Baltimore, 1963.
X Cg Afr 3843.5 — Khartum. University. Department of Architecture. El Kereiba village. Khartoum, 1963. (Changed to XP 223)
Afr 609.63.20 — Ki-Zerbo, Joseph. Le monde africain noir. Paris, 1963.
Afr 6164.20 — Kimble, D. A political history of Ghana. Oxford, 1963.
Afr 6390.75.2 — Korabiewicz, Waclaw. Safari mingi. Wyd.2. Warszawa, 1963.
Afr 5645.11 — Korneev, L.A. Obrazovanie Malgashskoi republiki. Moscow, 1963.
Afr 7875.5.10 — Kuitenbrouwer, Joost B.W. Le camp des Balula. Bruxelles, 1963.
Afr 6720.62 — Kuoh Mukouri, J. Doigts noirs. Montreal, 1963.
Afr 9198.2 — Kuper, H. The Swazi, a South African kingdom. N.Y., 1963.
Afr 2875.65 — Kutay, Cemal. Trablus-garbde bir avuc. Istanbul, 1963.
Afr 109.46.5 — Labouret, H. Africa before the white man. N.Y., 1963.
Afr 2030.463.10 — Lancelot, Marie-Thérèse. L'Organisation armée secrète. v.1-2. Paris, 1963.
Afr 2223.963 — Launay, M. Paysans algériens. Paris, 1963.
Afr 4969.63 — Laurence, M. The prophet's camel bell. London, 1963.
Afr 679.63.10 — Lawrence, A.W. Trade castles and forts of West Africa. London, 1963.
Afr 7582.3 — Lawson, Richard G. Strange soldiering. London, 1963.
Afr 5477.963 — Lecornec, J. Histoire politique du Tchad de 1900 à 1962. Paris, 1963.
Afr 5540.1 — Lejamble, George. Le fokonolona et le pouvoir. Tananarive, 1963.
Afr 7459.63 — Lemley, Luther. Liberia. 1st ed. N.Y., 1963.
Afr 11517.76.120 — Lerner, Laurence. The directions of memory. London, 1963.
Afr 5045.46 — Lerumeur, Guy. L'imprévu dans les dunes. Paris, 1963.
Afr 6886.2 — Leslie, J.A.K. A survey of Dar es Salaam. London, 1963.
Afr 8089.63 — Lesourd, J.A. La République d'Afrique du Sud. 2d ed. Paris, 1963.
Afr 109.63.10 — Lewicki, Tadeusz. Dzieje Afryki od czasow najdawniejszych do XIV w. Wyd.1. Warszawa, 1963.
Afr 8678.292 — Lewin, Jilius. Politics and law in South Africa. London, 1963.
Afr 6193.48F — Lewis, William Arthur. Report on industrialisation and the Gold Coast. Accra, 1963.
Afr 28.89.2 — Library of Congress. Africa South of the Sahara. Washington, 1963.
Afr 6128.4 — Library of Congress. African Section. Official publications of Sierra Leone and Gambia. Washington, 1963.
Afr Doc 1702.8 — Library of Congress. African Section. Official publications of Sierra Leone and Gambia. Washington, 1963.
Afr 8808.61.10 — Life at the Cape a hundred years ago. Cape Town, 1963.
Afr 7176.18 — Lima, Manuela. Contribuição para o estudo do comercio externo angolano. Lisboa, 1963.
Afr 115.105 — Lion, J. Od Limpopa k Vltave. Praha, 1963.
Afr 1259.63.5 — Liska, Jiri. The greater Maghreb. Washington, 1963.
Afr 5180.46 — Liubeckis, M. Karsta afrikos saule. Vilnius, 1963.
Afr 725.10.15 — Livingstone, David. African journal, 1853-1856. v.1-2. London, 1963. 2v.
Afr 8250.29.5 — Lockhart, J.G. Cecil Rhodes, the colossus of Southern Africa. N.Y., 1963.
Afr 8250.29.6 — Lockhart, J.G. Rhodes. London, 1963.
Afr 2030.463.35 — Loiseau, J. Pied-noir, mon frère. Paris, 1963.
Afr 6275.104 — London. Commonwealth Institute. The federation of Nigeria. London, 1963.
Afr 7560.18 — Lopes, Duarte. Description du royaume de Congo et des contrées environnantes. Louvain, 1963.
Afr 6984.11 — Loth, H. Die Christliche Mission in Südwestafrika. Berlin, 1963.
Afr 7937.8 — Louis, W.R. Ruanda-Urundi, 1884-1919. Oxford, 1963.
Afr 8678.302 — Louw, E.H. The case of South Africa. N.Y., 1963.
Afr 6549.251 — Luck, Anne. African saint. London, 1963.
Afr 7912.5.100 — Lumumba, Patrice. La pensée politique. Paris, 1963.
Afr 8687.320 — Mcfall, J.L. Trust betrayed, the murder of Sister Mary Aidan. Cape Town, 1963.
Afr 7119.63.5 — Maciel, A. Angola heroica. Lisboa, 1963.
Afr 7119.63 — Maciel, A. Angola heroica. 2.ed. Lisboa, 1963.
Afr 861.31 — Mackay, M.M. Angry island. London, 1963.
Afr 210.63 — McKay, Vernon. Africa in world politics. N.Y., 1963.
Afr 8678.32.4 — MacMillan, W.M. Bantu, Boer, and Briton. Oxford, 1963.
Afr Doc 5609.305 — Malagasy. Republic National de la Statistique et de la Recherche Economique. Series chronologiques et graphiques relatifs a l'économie malgache. Madagascar, 1963.

1963 - cont.

Afr 5530.7 — Malagasy Republic. Service des Archives et de la Documentation. Inventaire de la serié Mi des Archives de la République Malgache. Tananariva, 1963.
Afr Doc 6803.5 — Mali. Gouvernement, assemblée nationale et representations diverses de la République du Mali. Bamalco, 1963.
Afr 7219.63 — Mano, M.L. Entre jente remota. Lourenço Marques, 1963.
Afr 11555.61.100 — Manson, H.W.D. The magnolia tree. Cape Town, 1963.
Afr 7309.63F — Marjay, Frederico. Moçambique. Lisboa, 1963.
Afr 8089.55.2 — Marquard, L. The story of South Africa. London, 1963.
Afr 8089.63.7 — Marquard, L. The story of South Africa. 2d ed. London, 1963.
Afr 2000.7 — Martin, C. Histoire de l'Algérie française, 1830-1962. Paris, 1963.
Afr 7942.5 — Masera, Francesco. Rwanda e Burundi; problemi e prospettive di sviluppo economico. Millano, 1963.
Afr 626.154 — Massachusetts Institue of Technology. Fellows in Africa Program. Managing economic development in Africa. Cambridge, Mass., 1963.
Afr 6392.36 — Massell, B.F. East African economic union. Santa Monica, Calif., 1963.
Afr 7015.45 — Matos, R.J. da Cunha. Compendio historico das possesões de Portugal na Africa. Rio de Janeiro, 1963.
Afr 210.63.35 — Mboya, T. Freedom and after. 1. ed. Boston, 1963.
Afr 12321.2 — Memmi, Albert. La poésie algérienne de 1830 à nos jours. Paris, 1963.
Afr 212.22 — Merwe, H.J.J. Black Africa. Johannesburg, 1963.
Afr 8687.323.25 — Metelerkamp, Sanni. George Rex of Knysna. London, 1963.
Afr 11031.2 — Meurant, L.H. Sixty years ago. Cape Town, 1963.
Afr 1609.58.10 — Miazgowski, Brouirlew. Merakko-Krasnaie zemlia. Moskva, 1963.
Afr 1750.33 — Miranda Diaz, Mario. Espana en el continente africano. Madrid, 1963.
Afr 8687.274 — Modisane, B. Blame me on history. London, 1963.
Afr 8678.13.6 — Molema, S.M. The Bantu. Cape Town, 1963.
Afr 12431.2 — Mollard, P.J. Le régime juridique de la presse au Maroc. Rabat, 1963.
Afr 10066.2A — Moore, Gerald. Modern poetry from Africa. Harmondsworth, 1963.
Afr 1609.63 — Morin-Barde, M. Le Maroc etincelant. Casablanca, 1963.
Afr 1340.41 — Mrejen, Nissim. L'office national marocain du tourisme. Rabat, 1963.
Afr 8180.26.5 — Muller, Christoffel Frederik Jakobus. Die Britse owerheid en die groot trek. 2. uitg. Johannesburg, 1963.
Afr 8028.40 — Musiker, R. Guide to South African reference books. 3d ed. Grahamstown, 1963.
Afr 6715.1 — Mveny, Engelbert. Histoire du Cameroun. Paris, 1963.
Afr 8678.327 — Namgalies, Ursula. Südafrika Zwischen weiss und schwarz. Stuttgart, 1963.
Afr 8678.366 — National Catholic Federation of Students. Moral conflict in South Africa. Johannesburg, 1963.
Afr 7183.27 — Neto, Jose Pereira. O baixo cunene. Lisboa, 1963.
Afr 14518.2 — Neves, João Alves das. Poetas e contistas africanos de expressão portuguesa. São Paulo, 1963.
Afr 8678.428 — Ngubane, Jordan K. An African explains apartheid. N.Y., 1963.
Afr 7858.2F — Nicolai, Henri. Le Kwilu. Bruxelles, 1963.
Afr 8680.50 — Nielsen, Erik W. Afrikanska rasproblem. Stockholm, 1963.
Afr 8678.352 — Nienaber, Gabriel Stefanus. Hottentots. Pretoria, 1963.
Afr 6291.10 — Nigeria, Eastern. Distribution of amenities [in Eastern Nigeria] data and statistics. Enugu, 1963.
Afr Doc 2560.600 — Nigeria, Eastern. Ministry of Information. Know your legislators; biographical notes. Enugu, 1963.
Afr 6277.95 — Nigeria, Northern. Ministry of Trade and Industry. The industrial potentialities of Northern Nigeria. Kaduna, 1963.
Afr 6277.76.5F — Nigeria. Commission of Inquiry into the Affairs of Certain Statutory Corporations in Western Nigeria. An index to the proceedings of the Cokes Commission. Ibadan, 1963.
Afr Doc 2319.5 — Nigeria. Constitution. The consitution of the Federal Republic of Nigeria. Lagos, 1963.
Afr 6210.31 — Nigeria. Constitution. The Constitution of the Federal Republic of Nigeria. Lagos, 1963.
Afr Doc 2309.305.5F — Nigeria. Federal Office of Statistics. Urban Consumer surveys in Nigeria. Lagos, 1963.
Afr 6295.63.5F — Nigeria. National Archives. A preliminary inventory of the administrative records assembled from Endo province. Ibadan, 1963.
Afr 6203.7.10F — Nigeria. National Archives. A special list of annual, half-yearly and quarterly reports. Ibadan, 1963.
Afr 6203.7.15 — Nigeria. National Archives. Kaduna Branch. An inventory of the records of the Secretariat. Kaduna, 1963.
Afr Doc 2307.363.2F — Nigeria. Regional Census Office. Population census of Nigeria, Nov., 1963. 2d ed. Ibadan, 1963.
Afr 210.63.15 — Nkrumah, Kwame. Africa must unite. London, 1963.
Afr 210.63.16 — Nkrumah, Kwame. Africa must unite. N.Y., 1963.
Afr 4070.64 — Odu, Joseph. The problem of the southern Sudan. London, 1963.
Afr 6210.36.5 — Odumosu, O.I. Constitutional crisis: legality and the president's conscience. Ibadan, Nigeria, 1963.
Afr 6210.36 — Odumosu, O.I. The Nigerian constitution. London, 1963.
Afr 49000.89.79F — Ogunsheye, F. Adetowun. A preliminary bibliography of the Yoruba language. Ibadan, 1963.
Afr 7567.30 — Okumu, Washington A. Lumumba's Congo. N.Y., 1963.
Afr 6314.34 — Oliver, R.A. History of East Africa. v.2.
Afr 8028.45 — Olivier, Le Roux. Versamelde Suid-Afrikaanse biografieë. Kaapstad, 1963.
Afr 510.112 — Oplustil, Vaclav. O francouzsko-africkem spolecenstvi. Praha, 1963.
Afr 1571.17.42 — Ormesson, W. Auprès de Lyautey. Paris, 1963.
Afr 4787.8 — Orthner-Heun, Irene. Das Entwicklungsland Somalia. Köln, 1963.
Afr 5758.63 — Ottino, Paul. Les économies paysannes malgaches du Bas Mangoky. Paris, 1963.
Afr 5912.3 — Otto, Archduke of Austria. Européens et Africains. Paris, 1963.
Afr 11669.13.10 — Packer, Joy (P). Home from sea. London, 1963.
Afr 210.63.5 — Padelford, Norman J. Africa and world order. N.Y., 1963.
Afr 210.47.2 — Padmore, G. History of the Pan-African Congress. 2d ed. London, 1963.
Afr 4700.4.10 — Panetta, Ester. Studi italiani di etnografia e di folklore della Libia. Roma, 1963.
Afr 679.63.15 — Panikkar, K.M. The serpent and the crescent. London, 1963.

1963 - cont.

Afr 7937.7 — Papadopoullos, T. Poésie, dynastique du Ruanda et épopée akritique. Paris, 1963.

Afr 5243.174.15 — Parin, Paul. Die Weissen denken zuviel. Zürich, 1963.

Afr 2223.963.5 — Paris. Université. Institut d'Etudes du Développement, etc. Problèmes de l'Algérie indépendante. Paris, 1963.

Afr 6195.17 — Parsons, R.T. The churches and Ghana society, 1918-1955. Leiden, 1963.

Afr 7543.10 — Parti Solidaire Africain. Parti solidaire africain (P.S.A.). Bruxelles, 1963.

Afr 210.63.65 — Passin, H. Africa. Ibadan, 1963.

Afr 9435.9 — Passmore, Gloria. Source book of parliamentary elections and referenda in Rhodesia, 1892-1962. Salisbury, 1963.

Afr 6470.250.20 — Patel, Anubu H. Struggle for Release Jomo and his colleagues. 1st ed. Nairobi, 1963.

Afr 210.63.90 — Paul, Edouard C. Afrique: perspectives, politiques. Port-au-Prince, Haiti, 1963.

Afr 635.62.5 — Paulme, D. Women of tropical Africa. Berkeley, 1963.

Afr 50.42 — Pedersen, O.K. Afrikansk nationalisme. København, 1963.

Afr 609.63.5 — Perham, M.F. African discovery. Evanston, 1963.

Afr 210.62.3 — Perham, M.F. The colonial reckoning. London, 1963.

Afr 6049.63.2 — Perham, M.F. Ten Africans. 2. ed. London, 1963.

Afr 550.137 — Personalité africaine. Paris, 1963.

Afr 6885.15 — Pesce, Geremia. Vitie missionaria nel Tanganika. Bologna, 1963.

Afr 4394.15 — Petrides, Saint Pierre. Le héros d'Adoua. Paris, 1963.

Afr 2030.463 — Pickles, D.M. Algeria and France. N.Y., 1963.

Afr 609.63.25 — Pierce, Samuel R. African journey, 1963. N.Y., 1963?

Afr 7122.76 — Pires, P. Braseiro da morte. Viseu, Portugal, 1963.

Afr 9165.71.15 — Ploeger, Jan. Over-Vaal; the history of an official residence. Pretoria, 1963.

Afr 6025.2 — Pollet, Maurice. L'Afrique du Commonwealth. Paris, 1963.

Afr 8095.37 — Pollock, N.C. An historical geography of South Africa. London, 1963.

Afr 8845.16 — Port Elizabeth Publicity Association. This is Port Elizabeth. Port Elizabeth, 1963.

Afr 6147.5.10 — Porter, A.T. Creoledom. London, 1963.

Afr Doc 9407.360 — Portugal. Missão de Inquerito Agrícola de Cabo Verte, Guiné S. Tomé Principe. Recenseamento agrícola da Guiné, 1960-1961. Lisboa, 1963.

Afr 6218.17 — Post, K.W.J. The Nigerian federal election of 1959. Oxford, 1963.

Afr 1340.10 — Prat, Jean. La responsabilité de la puissance publique au Maroc. Rabat, 1963.

Afr 9525.529.25 — Preller, Gustav Schoeman. Lobengula, the tragedy of a Matabele king. Johannesburg, 1963.

Afr 210.63.10 — Quaison-Sackey, A. Africa unbound. N.Y., 1963.

Afr 9047.16 — Rademeyer, J.I. Shaka. Johannesburg, 1963.

Afr 210.63.80 — Rainero, Romain. Il nuovo volto dell'Africa. Firenze, 1963.

Afr 7870.6 — Raymaekers, P. L'organisation des zones de squatting. Leopoldville, 1963.

Afr 6455.145 — Reece, Alys. To my wife, 50 camels. Leicester, 1963.

Afr 6277.118 — Reinecke, Ulrich. Die industrielle Entwicklung Nigerias. Hamburg, 1963.

Afr 5857.20 — Réunion. Archives Départementales. Répertoire des registres paroissiaux et d'état civil antérieurs à 1849. Nérac, 1963.

Afr 9432.26 — Rhodesia and Nyasaland. Archives in a growing society. Salisbury, 1963.

Afr Doc 3507.360F — Rhodesia and Nyasaland. The census of production in 1960 and 1961: mining, manufacturing, electricity and water supply. Salisbury, 1963.

Afr 9439.63 — Rhodesia and Nyasaland. Legacy of progress. Salisbury, 1963.

Afr Doc 3509.515F — Rhodesia and Nyasaland. Central Statistical Office. Preliminary report on the federal European family expenditure survey, October 1960. Salisbury, 1963.

Afr 9448.73 — Rhodesia and Nyasaland. Prime Minister. The break-up. Salisbury, 1963.

Afr 11057.4 — Rive, Richard. Quartet. N.Y., 1963.

Afr 210.63.50 — Rivkin, A. The African presence in world affairs. N.Y., 1963.

Afr 1340.37 — Robert, Jacques. La monarchie marocaine. Paris, 1963.

Afr 7580.6 — Roberts, John. My Congo adventure. London, 1963.

Afr 3340.13 — Robinson, Nehemiah. Nasser's Egypt. N.Y., 1963.

Afr 6455.17.20 — Roosevelt, K. A sentimental safari. N.Y., 1963.

Afr 8676.63 — Rosenthal, E. Manne en maatskappye. Kaapstad, 1963.

Afr 9060.28 — Rosenthal, Eric. Schooners and sky scrapers. Cape Town, 1963.

Afr 9489.63 — Rotishauser, Josef. Mann in der Mitte. Immensee, 1963.

Afr 8678.250.10 — Roumeguère-Eberhardt, Jacqueline. Pensée et société africaines. Paris, 1963.

Afr 8695.10 — Royal Institute of International Affairs. The high commission territories. London, 1963.

Afr Doc 7819.5 — Rwanda. Constitution. Constitution de la République Rwandaise. Kigali, 1963?

Afr 530.51 — Sablier, E. De l'Oural à l'Atlantique. Paris, 1963.

Afr 10018.3 — Sainville, L. Anthologie de la littérature nègro-africaine. Paris, 1963- 2v.

Afr 555.147 — Sanita, Giuseppe. La Barberia e la Sacra Congregazione. Cairo, 1963.

Afr 10060.2 — Sartre, Jean Paul. Black Orpheus. Paris, 1963.

Afr 9291.18 — Schoor, Marthinus. Edenburg. Edenburg, 1963.

Afr 8678.333 — Schuette, H.G. Weisse ismen, schwarze fakten. Vaterstetten, 1963.

Afr 2609.63 — Schuman, L.O. Tunesie. Meppel, 1963.

Afr 6455.154 — Seaton, Henry. Lion in the morning. London, 1963.

Afr 8378.337 — Segal, Ronald. Into exile. London, 1963.

Afr Doc 6219.14 — Sénégal. Constitution. Constitution de la République du Sénégal. Dakar? 1963

Afr 8659.63 — Serton, P. Zuid-Afrika, land van goede hoop. 3. druk. Meppel, 1963.

Afr 8355.45 — Shastitko, P.M. Sto let bespraviia. Moscow, 1963.

Afr 9165.42.57 — Shaw, T.R. The growth of Johannesburg from 1886-1939. Johannesburg, 1963.

Afr 820.1 — Sherlock, Jill. The Zambesi. Cape Town, 1963.

Afr 8835.36 — Shorten, John R. Cape Town, a record of the mother city from the earliest days to the present. Cape Town, 1963.

Afr 626.71 — Shpirt, A.I. Ekonomika stran Afriki. Moscow, 1963.

Afr 8980.6 — Shuter, C.F. Englishman's inn, 'engelsche logie'. Cape Town, 1963.

1963 - cont.

Afr 6144.8F — Sierra Leone. Commission to Enquire into and Report on the Matters Contained in the Director of Audit's Report on the Accounts of Sierra Leone for the Year 1960-1961. Report of the commission and the government statement thereon. Freetown, 1963.

Afr 6212.42 — Sklar, R.L. Nigerian political parties. Princeton, 1963.

Afr 5282.3 — Société d'Etudes pour le Développement Economique et Social, Paris. Développement économique en Haute-Volta. Paris, 1963. 3v.

Afr 5343.10.2 — Société d'Etudes pour le Développement Economique et Social. Rapport de synthèse. Paris, 1963.

Afr 5343.10 — Société d'Etudes pour le Développement Economique et Social. Le sud-est frontalier. Paris, 1963. 2v.

Afr 555.138 — Soras, Alfred de. Relations de l'église et de l'état dans les pays d'Afrique francophone. Paris, 1963.

Afr 8089.36 — South Africa, Rhodesia and the high commission territories. Cambridge, 1963.

Afr 8019.1.3 — South Africa. Alphabetic index to biographical notices, 1892-1928. Johannesburg, 1963.

Afr Doc 4307.360.5F — South Africa. Bureau of Statistics. Bevolkingsensus, 6 september 1960. Pretoria, 1963. 8v.

Afr 8825.40 — South Africa. Department of Coloured Affairs. Opportunities for the coloureds. Pretoria, 1963.

Afr 8659.63.5 — South Africa. National Parks Board of Trustees. Ons nasionale parke. Pretoria, 1963.

Afr 8333.6 — South Africa. Parliament. House of Assembly. Index to the manuscript annexures and printed papers. Cape Town, 1963.

Afr 8676.3 — South Africa. University, Pretoria. Bureau of Market Research. Buro vir marknavorsing. Pretoria, 1963.

Afr 30.10 — Sovetskaia Entsiklopediia. Afrika. Moscow, 1963. 2v.

Afr 10689.67.110 — Soyinka, W. A dance of the forests. London, 1963.

Afr 10689.67.120 — Soyinka, W. The lion and the jewel. London, 1963.

Afr 10689.67.100 — Soyinka, W. Three plays. Nigeria, 1963.

Afr 7219.63.10 — Spence, C.F. Moçambique. London, 1963.

Afr 7565.9 — Stengers, J. Belgique et Congo. Bruxelles, 1963.

Afr 3979.63.20 — Stevens, G.G. Egypt, yesterday and today. N.Y., 1963.

Afr 6926.27 — Steward, A. The sacred trust. Johannesburg, 1963.

Afr 210.55.12 — Stillman, Calvin W. Africa in the modern world. Chicago, 1963.

Afr 5343.8 — Strasbourg. Université. Centre de Géographie Appliquée. Etude géographique des problèmes de transports en Côte-d'Ivoire. Paris, 1963.

Afr 7580.18 — Sturdza, Michel. World government and international assassination. Belmont, Mass., 1963.

Afr 3834.2 — Sudan. Khartoum, capital. Khartoum, 1963.

Afr 3813.10 — Sudan. Ministry of Finance and Economics. The ten year plan of economic and social development, 1962-1971. Khartoum, 1963.

Afr 40.63.10 — Summit Conference of Independent African States. Summit conference of independent African states, Addis Ababa, 22-25 May 1963. Cairo, 1963.

Afr 2030.463.45 — Susini, J.J. Histoire de l'O.A.S. Paris, 1963.

Afr 8252.144 — Swart, Marius. Hendrik Teodor Buehrmann. Kaapstad, 1963.

Afr 8300.14 — Symons, J. Buller' campaign. London, 1963.

Afr 635.94 — Szyfelbejn-Sokolewicz, Zofia. Tradycyjne zajecia gospodarcze ludow Afryki. Warszawa, 1963.

Afr Doc 3407.357.5 — Tanganyika. Treasury. Central Statistical Bureau. African Census report, 1957. Dar es Salaam, 1963.

Afr Doc 3407.362F — Tanganyika. Treasury. Central Statistical Bureau. Census of large scale commercial farming in Tanganyika, October 1962. Dar es Salaam, 1963.

Afr 8847.45.2 — Tapson, Winifred. Timber and tides; the story of Knysna and Plettenberg Bay. 2. ed. Johannesburg, 1963.

Afr 6769.63 — Taylor, J.C. The political development of Tanganyika. Stanford, 1963.

Afr 5321.5 — Tchidimbo, Raymond-M. L'homme noir dans l'Eglise. Paris, 1963.

Afr 210.63.20 — Thiam, Doudou. La politique étrangère des états africains. Paris, 1963.

Afr 5465.2 — Thomas, Jacqueline M.C. Les Ngbaka de la Lobaye. Paris, 1963.

Afr 9558.500 — Thornton, Richard. The Zambezi papers of Richard Thornton. London, 1963. 2v.

Afr 1623.963 — Tiano, A. La politique économique et financiere du Maroc independant. Paris, 1963.

Afr 5316.10.5 — Toure, Sekou. Guinean revolution and social progress. Cairo, 1963.

Afr 7580.10 — Tournaire, H. Le livre noir du Congo. Paris, 1963.

Afr 7580.12F — Trinquier, R. Notre guerre au Katanga. Paris, 1963.

Afr 2753.4 — Unesco. Nomades et nomadisme au Sahara. Paris, 1963.

Afr 5001.107 — Union africaine et malgache. Documentation: OAMCE (Organisation africaine et malgache de coopération économique). Paris, 1963.

Afr 1273.963A — Union Nationale des Etudiants du Maroc à Alger. Industrialisation au Maghreb. Paris, 1963.

Afr 3326.2 — United Arab Republic. Declaration of the Union accord. Cairo, 1963.

Afr 3326.5 — United Arab Republic. The Revolution in eleven years. Cairo, 1963.

Afr 3979.52.5 — United Arab Republic. Information Department. Eleven years of progress and development. Cairo, 1963.

Afr 3993.963 — United Arab Republic. Information Department. Handbook on U.A.R. economy. Cairo, 1963.

Afr 3979.63 — United Arab Republic. Information Department. Tourism in the U.A.R. Cairo, 1963.

Afr 3979.63.8 — United Arab Republic. Information Department. U.A.R., United Arab Republic. Cairo, 1963.

Afr 3979.63.5 — United Arab Republic. Information Department. United Arab Republic. Cairo, 1963.

Afr 3326.7 — United Arab Republic. Information Service. Ministry of Social Affairs in eleven years from July 23rd, 1952 to July 23rd, 1963. Cairo, 1963.

Afr 3993.563 — United Arab Republic. Ministry of the High Aswan Dam. The High Aswan Dam begins its fourth year of construction. Cairo, 1963.

Afr 3990.28 — United Arab Republic. State Tourist Administration. Tourist information, U.A.R. Egypt. Cairo, 1963.

Afr 8678.355 — United Party (South Africa). Handbook for better race relations. Johannesburg, 1963.

Afr 626.114 — United States. Bureau of International Commerce. Africa, sales frontier for U.S. business. Washington, 1963.

Afr 618.23 — Universities and the Language of Tropical Africa. Language in Africa. Cambridge, 1963.

1963 - cont.

Afr 7183.28 — Urquhart, Alvin W. Patterns of settlement and subsistence in Southwestern Angola. Washington, 1963.

Afr 11865.59.140 — Vanderpost, Laurens. The seed and the sower. London, 1963.

Afr 5219.63 — Vasianin, A.J. Respublika Mali. Moscow, 1963.

Afr 115.109 — Vazquez-Figueros, Alberto. Africa encadenada. 1. ed. Barcelona, 1963.

Afr 5001.109 — Verin, V.P. Prezidentskie respubliki v Afrike. Moscow, 1963.

Afr 12015.15 — Vezinet, Paul. Pages africaines. Paris, 1963-[1966-]. 5v.

Afr 2030.463.5 — Vidal-Naquet, P. Torture, cancer of democracy. Harmondsworth, 1963.

Afr 14692.41.1100 — Vieira, Luandino. Luuanda. Luanda, 1963.

Afr 8950.22 — Vietzen, Colleen. The Natal almanac and yearly register, 1863-1906. Cape Town, 1963.

Afr 6903.17 — Volgis, B. South African imprints. Cape Town, 1963.

Afr 8700.3 — Wackrill, Jill D. Index to the Cape Illustrated Magazine. Johannesburg, 1963.

Afr 5435.2 — Wagret, Jean Michel. Histoire et sociologie politiques de la République du Congo. Paris, 1963.

Afr 609.39.2 — Wallschläger, Alfred. Afrika gestern und heute. 10. Aufl. Gütersloh, 1963.

Afr 6164.9.3 — Ward, W.E.F. A history of Ghana. N.Y., 1963.

Afr 9710.13 — Westbeach, George. Trade and travel in early Barotseland. London, 1963.

Afr 4766.33A — Wettmann, S. Somali nationalism. Cambridge, 1963.

Afr 2945.17 — Williams, Gwyn. Green mountain, an informal guide to Cyrenaica. London, 1963.

Afr 6275.102 — Williams, Harry. Nigeria free. N.Y., 1963.

Afr 7851.58 — Wilmet, Jules. La répartition de la population dans la dépression des rivières Mufuvya et Lufira. Bruxelles, 1963.

Afr 8847.48 — Wilson, M. Langa. Cape Town, 1963.

Afr 210.63.45 — Woddis, J. Africa, the way ahead. London, 1963.

Afr 2030.463.50 — Yacef, Saadi. Souvenirs de la bataille d'Alger déc. 1956-sept. 1957. Paris, 1963.

Afr Doc 2402.2F — Yakuba, Stephen. Publications of the government of the northern region of Nigeria, 1960-1962. Zaria, 1963.

Afr 6194.39 — Zajaczkowski, A. Aszanti, kraj Złotego Tronu. Warszawa, 1963.

Afr 1110.42 — Zartman, I. Government and politics in northern Africa. N.Y., 1963.

Afr 1623.963.15 — Zerilli Marimó, Guido. Maroc économique. Milan, 1963.

Afr 210.63.70 — Ziegler, Jean. La contre-révolution en Afrique. Paris, 1963.

1964

Afr 10671.12.130 — Achebe, Chinua. Arrow of God. London, 1964.

Afr 11211.5.15 — Achebe, Chinua. Arrow of God. London, 1964.

Afr 5056.164 — Adloff, Richard. West Africa. N.Y., 1964.

Afr 109.64.15 — Africa report. A handbook of African affairs. N.Y., 1964.

Afr 210.64.45 — Africa's freedom. London, 1964.

Afr 210.64.55 — Afrika, Colloquium. Afrikas Gegenwart und Zukunft. Hannover, 1964.

Afr 8377.4F — Afro-Asian Solidarity Committee. Memorandum on cooperation between the West German Federal Republic and the Republic of South Africa in the military and atomic fields. Berlin, 1964.

Afr 5262.1 — Agency for International Development. Review of co-operative programme for economic development in Nigeria. Lagos, 1964.

Afr 2000.18 — Ageron, Charles R. Histoire de l'Algérie contemporaine, 1830-1964. Paris, 1964.

Afr 6725.5 — Ahidjo, Ahmado. Contribution à la construction nationale. Paris, 1964.

Afr 2230.38 — Ait Ahmed, Hocine. La guerre et l'après-guerre. Paris, 1964.

Afr 6280.2.15 — Ajayi, J.F.A. de. Yoruba warfare in the nineteenth century. Cambridge, Eng., 1964.

Afr 10005.5 — Akademiia Nauk SSSR Institut Afriki. Literatura stran Afriki. Moskva, 1964-66. 2v.

Afr 212.26 — Akademiia Nauk SSSR. Institut Afriki. Noveishaia istoriia Afriki. Moskva, 1964.

Afr 28.92 — Akaemiia Nauk SSSR. Institut Afriki. Bibliografiia Afriki, do revoliutsionnaia i liberatura na russkom Iazyke. Moscow, 1964.

Afr 6295.64 — Alagoa, E.J. The small brave city-state. Ibadan, 1964.

Afr 1618.24 — Albarracin de Martinez Ruiz, Joaquina. Vestido y adorno de la mujer musulmana de Vêbala (Marruecos). Madrid, 1964.

Afr 2030.464.65 — Algeria. Treaties, etc. Accords passés entre la France et l'Algérie de juillet 1962 au 31 décembre 1963. Paris, 1964.

Afr 2030.464.10 — Algerian Front of National Liberation. La charte d'Alger, ensemble des textes adoptés par le premier congrès du Parti de Front de libération nationale. Alger, 1964.

Afr 10671.52.100 — Aluko, Timothy Mofolorunso. One man, one matchet. London, 1964.

Afr 5316.12 — Ameillon, B. La Guinée. Paris, 1964.

Afr 210.64.70 — American Academy of Political and Social Science. Africa in motion. Philadelphia, 1964.

Afr 4559.64 — American University, Washington, D.C. Area handbook for Ethiopia. 2. ed. Washington, D.C., 1964.

Afr 4070.59.2 — American University, Washington D.C. Foreign Areas Studies Division. Area handbook for the Republic of the Sudan. 2. ed. Washington, 1964.

Afr 3979.64.15 — American University. Foreign Area Studies Division. Area handbook for the United Arab Republic. Washington, 1964.

Afr 7459.64 — American University. Foreign Areas Studies Division. Area handbook for Liberia. Washington, 1964.

Afr 626.134 — Amin Samir. Quelques expériences de décolonisation et de développement économique. v.1-2. Dakar, 1964.

Afr 10050.3 — Amosu, Margaret. A preliminary bibliography of creative African writing in the European languages. Ibadan, 1964.

Afr 8063.32 — Anderson, Ken. Nine flames. Cape Town, 1964.

Afr 4760.12 — Angeloni, Renato. Diritto costituzionale somalo. Milano, 1964.

Afr Doc 9307.360 — Angola. Reparticão de Estatistica Geral. Terceiro recenseamento geral da população, 1960. v.1-5. Luanda, 1964-1969.

Afr 7068.12 — Aquiar, Armando de. Guiné, minha terra. Lisboa, 1964.

Afr 7176.32 — Araujo, A. Correia de. Apectos do desenvolvimento económico e social de Angola. Lisboa, 1964.

Afr 7318.5 — Arcangelo da Barletta. Sulle rive dello Zambesi. Palo del Calle, 1964.

1964 - cont.

Afr 7183.26 — Arriaga, Noel de. Luanda. Lisboa, 1964.

Afr 1494.62 — Ashford, D.E. Perspectives of a Moroccan nationalist. Totowa, N.J., 1964.

Afr 500.53 — Assac, Jacques Ploncard d'. L'erreur africaine. Paris, 1964.

Afr 657.88 — Association for Promoting the Discovery of the Interior Parts of Africa. Records of the African Association, 1788-1831. London, 1964.

Afr 6162.14 — Austin, Dennis. Politics in Ghana, 1946-1960. N.Y., 1964.

Afr 6210.40 — Awa, Eme O. Federal government in Nigeria. Berkeley, 1964.

Afr 28.98 — Axelson, Eric Victor. African history, books and research. Cape Town, 1964.

Afr 3315.126 — Azeau, Henri. Le siège de Suez. Paris, 1964.

Afr 150.2.85 — Azevedo, A.J. da Silva D. Americas, um corolário de sagres. Lisboa, 1964.

Afr 212.16 — Baardseth, Magne. Afrika. 3. Opl. Oslo, 1964.

Afr 6298.110.5 — Balewa, Abubakar Tafawa. Mr. Prime Minister. Lagos, Nigeria, 1964.

Afr 6298.110 — Balewa, Abubakar Tafawa. Nigeria speaks. Ikeja, 1964.

Afr 5240.4F — Bamako. Chambre de Commerce, d'Agriculture et d'Industrie. Répertoire des entreprises financières. Bamako, 1964.

Afr 8825.45 — Banch, Kurt. Deutsche Kultur am Kap. 1st ed. Capetown, 1964.

Afr 3315.140 — Bar-Zohar, Michel. Suez: ultra-secret. Paris, 1964.

Afr 635.87 — Barbe, R. Les classes sociales en Afrique noire. Paris, 1964.

Afr 4070.65 — Barclay, Harold. Buurri al Lamaab. Ithaca, 1964.

Afr 3315.124 — Barker, A.J. Suez, the seven-day war. London, 1964.

Afr 8847.21 — Barker, John P. Industrial development in a border area. Grahamstown, 1964.

Afr 8857.10 — Basutoland. Basutoland records. v.1-3. Facsimile. Cape Town, 1964. 4v.

Afr 8860.16 — Basutoland Constitutional Conference, London, 1964. Basutoland constitutional conference, report. London, 1964.

Afr 5749.64.5 — Battestini, René. Etude geomorphologique de l'Extreme Sud de Madagascar. Paris, 1964.

Afr 5749.64.10 — Battistini, René. Géographie humaine de la plaine côtière Mahafaly. Thèse. Paris, 1964.

Afr 6540.16.2 — Beattie, John. Bunyord, an African kingdom. N.Y., 1964.

Afr 8155.11 — Becker, Peter. Rule of fear. London, 1964.

Afr 8846.26 — Bellwood, W. Whither the Transkei. London, 1964.

Afr 2030.464.45 — Ben Bella, Ahmed. Discours, année 1963. Alger, 1964.

Afr 500.83 — Benítez Cábrera, Jose. Africa, biografia del colonialismo. Habana, 1964.

Afr 718.38 — Berg, Gertrud Wilhelmson. Pori. Stockholm, 1964.

Afr 2035.11 — Bergheaud, Edmond. Le premier quart d'heure. Paris, 1964.

Afr 2030.464.20 — Bergheaud, Edmond. Le premier quart d'heure. Paris, 1964.

Afr 7335.2 — Bermudes, F. A cidade da Beira. Lisboa, 1964.

Afr 115.107 — Bertola, Arnaldo. Storia e istituzioni dei paesi afro-asiatici. Torino, 1964.

Afr 5530.5 — Bibliotheque Nationale, Paris. Periodiques malgaches. Paris, 1964.

Afr 2397.6 — Bittari, Zoubeida. O mes soeurs musulmanes, pleurez Paris, 1964.

Afr 12972.41.705 — Biyidi, Alexandre. Mission to Kala. London, 1964.

Afr 11219.66.120 — Bloom, Harry. Whittaker's wife. London, 1964.

Afr 6420.76 — Blundell, M. So rough a wind. London, 1964.

Afr 2719.64 — Boahen, A.A. Britain, the Sahara. Oxford, 1964.

Afr 8687.347 — Boeeseken, Anna J. Simon van der Stel en sy kinders. Kaapstad, 1964.

Afr 109.64.5 — Bohannan, P. Africa and Africans. 1st ed. Garden City, 1964.

Afr 3818.12.2 — Bonfanti, Adriano. Espulsi dal Sudan. 2. ed. Bologna, 1964.

Afr 1100.6 — Bono, Salvatore. I corsari barbareschi. Torino, 1964.

Afr 8659.64 — Boom, M.J. Reis door Zuid-Afrika. Meppel, 1964.

Afr 11229.81.100 — Bosman, Herman. Unto dust, stories. 2d ed. Cape Town, 1964.

Afr 8849.141 — Bosman di Ravelli, Vere. Saint Theodore and the crocodile. Cape Town, 1964.

Afr Doc 5.2 — Boston University. Library. Catalog of African government documents and African area index. 2d ed. Boston, 1964.

Afr 2030.464.25 — Boualam, Bachaga. L'Algérie sans la France. Paris, 1964.

Afr 626.138 — Bourgaignic, G.E. Jeune Afrique mobilisable. Paris, 1964.

Afr 1069.64 — Brace, R.M. Morocco, Algeria, Tunisia. Englewood Cliffs, N.J., 1964.

Afr 575.45 — Brelvi, Mahmud. Islam in Africa. Lahore, 1964.

Afr 5119.64.5 — Brigaud, Felix. Histoire du Sénégal. Dakar, 1964.

Afr 8678.364 — Brinkman, H.J. Zuidafrikaans samenleven. Zaandijk, 1964.

Afr 8678.312 — Brookes, E.H. The city of God and the city of man in Africa. Lexington, 1964.

Afr 9047.36 — Bryant, A.T. A history of the Zulu and neighboring tribes. Cape Town, 1964.

Afr 8369.64 — Bunting, B.P. The rise of the South African Reich. Harmondsworth, 1964.

Afr 210.64.5 — Burke, Fred. Africa's quest for order. Englewood Cliffs, 1964.

Afr 6542.17 — Burke, Fred. Local government and politics in Uganda. Syracuse, 1964.

Afr 6214.8.19 — Burns, Alan C. History of Nigeria. 6th ed. London, 1964.

Afr 4559.64.5 — Bush och lustgaard. Stockholm, 1964.

Afr 9073.252 — Byron, Lewis. Recollections of an octogenarian. Kloof, 1964.

Afr 212.32 — Calchi Novati, Giampaolo. L'Africa nera non e indipendente. Milano, 1964.

Afr 626.139 — Cambridge Conference on Development Planning. African development planning. Cambridge, England, 1964.

Afr 6739.264F — Cameroon. Ministère des Finances et du Plan. Rapport général du premier plan quinquennal. Yaounde, 1964.

Afr Doc 7509.500 — Cameroon. Service de la Statistique Générale et de la Mécanographie. La niveau de vie des populations de l'Adamaoua. Ircam, 1964. 2v.

Afr 8250.43 — Cape Town. University. Libraries. Pictorial material of Cecil J. Rhodes. Cape Town, 1964.

Afr 6096.16 — Carlson, Sune. International finance and development planning in West Africa. Stockholm, 1964.

Afr 50.30.2 — Carter, G. African one-party states. Ithaca, 1964.

Afr 8678.351F — Carter, G.M. South Africa's international position. Cape Town, 1964.

Afr 1738.50 — Castellani Pastorio, Giovanni. Sviluppi e conclusione della questione di Tangeri. Roma, 1964.

Afr 6397.5 — Catrice, Paul. Un audacieux pionnier de l'église au Afrique. Lyon, 1964.

1964 - cont.

Afr 8678.324 — Cawood, Lesley. The churches and race relations in South Africa. Johannesburg, 1964.

Afr 7503.3.10 — Centre d'Etudes des Problèmes Sociaux Indigènes, Elisabethville, Belgian Congo. Le CEPSI; ses buts, ses activités, ses réalisations. Elisabethville, 1964.

Afr 1494.63 — Cerych, Ladislav. Europeens et Marocains. Bruges, 1964.

Afr 2035.5 — Chaliand, Gérard. L'Algérie est-elle socialiste? Paris, 1964.

Afr 1609.64 — Chalyi, Bohdan I. Marokko, svitanok. Kyiv, 1964.

Afr 4226.4 — Chojnacki, S. List of current periodical publications in Ethiopia. Addis Ababa, 1964.

Afr 609.64.15 — Church, R.J.H. Africa and the islands. N.Y., 1964.

Afr 6164.5.2 — Claridge, W.W. A history of the Gold Coast. London, 1964. 2v.

Afr 3315.122 — Clark, D.M.J. Suez touchdown. London, 1964.

Afr 10673.48.110 — Clark, John Pepper. America, their America. London, 1964.

Afr 10673.48.120 — Clark, John Pepper. Three plays, song of a goat. London, 1964.

Afr 530.50.15 — Clendenen, C.C. Americans in black Africa up to 1865. Stanford, California, 1964.

Afr 8040.22 — Cloete, Jacobus J.N. Sentrale, provinsiale en munisipale instellings van Suid-Afrika. Pretoria, 1964.

Afr 7567.13 — Cola Alberich, Julio. El Congo, 1885-1963. Madrid, 1964.

Afr 210.64.60 — Coleman, J.S. Political parties and national integration in tropical Africa. Berkeley, 1964.

Afr 8095.5.5 — Colenbrander, Herman Theodoor. De afkomst der Boeren. 2. uitg. Kaapstad, 1964.

Afr 6538.35 — Commonwealth Development Corporation. Uganda tea survey, 1964. London, 1964.

Afr 6277.64 — Conference on Attitudes in Development Planning in Local Government, Ahmadu Bello University, 1963. Report. Zaria, Northern Nigeria, 1964.

Afr 626.128 — Conference On Economic Development for Africa. Economic development for Africa south of the Sahara. London, 1964.

Afr 212.2 — Cowan, Laing Gray. The dilemmas of African independence. N.Y., 1964.

Afr 210.64.50 — Cox, R.H.F. Pan-Africanism in practice. London, 1964.

Afr 11303.2.100 — Crafford, Frederick Simon. The place of dragons. Cape Town, 1964.

Afr 14723.1 — Craveirinha, José. Chigubo. Lisboa, 1964.

Afr 9165.42.65 — Crisp, Robert. The outlanders. London, 1964.

Afr 109.64.25 — Currie, D.P. Federalism and the new nations. Chicago, 1964.

Afr 6069.64 — Curtin, P.D. The image of Africa. Madison, 1964.

Afr 609.64.35 — Czyzewski, Krysztof L. W afrykanskiej dzungli, buszu i pustyni. Warszawa, 1964.

Afr 109.64 — Davidson, B. The African past. 1st ed. Boston, 1964.

Afr 210.64.10 — Davidson, Basil. Which way Africa. Harmondsworth, 1964.

Afr 8145.44 — Deblank, J. Out of Africa. London, 1964.

Afr 11319.9.100 — Debruyn, Phillip. The secret place, jazz verse. Cape Town, 1964.

Afr 3817.16 — De Giorgi, Luigi. Culto dei gemelli nel Sudan meridionale. Bologna, 1964.

Afr 6164.21 — Dei-Anang, Michael. Ghana resurgent. Accra, 1964.

Afr 5119.64 — Deschamps, H.J. Le Sénégal et la Gambie. Paris, 1964.

Afr 175.6 — Deschamps, Hubert Jules. L'Afrique tropicale aux XVIIe-XVIIIe siècles. Paris, 1964.

Afr 1259.49.7 — Despois, Jean. L'Afrique blanche. 3. ed. Paris, 1964.

Afr 2260.26 — Dessaigne, Francine. Déraciné. Paris, 1964.

Afr 609.64.30 — Deutsche Afrika-Gesellschaft, Bonn. Afrika im Wandel seiner Gesellschaftsformen. Leiden, 1964.

Afr 1635.30 — Dobo, Nicolas. J'étais le médecin de cent mille Berbères. Paris, 1964.

Afr 626.155 — Dobrska, Zofia. Problemy gospodarcze Afryki. Wyd.1. Warszawa, 1964.

Afr 550.148 — Dodge, Ralph Edward. The unpopular missionary. Westwood, N.J., 1964.

Afr 2030.464.70 — Douence, J.C. La mise en place des institutions algériennes. Paris, 1964.

Afr 724.24 — Douglass, Lillie B. Cape Town to Cairo. Caldwell, 1964.

Afr 11336.41.100 — Drin, Michael. Signpost to fear. Cape Town, 1964.

Afr 4766.34 — Drysdale, J.G.S. The Somali dispute. London, 1964.

Afr 8678.307 — Duncan, P.B. South Africa's rule of violence. London, 1964.

Afr 8676.64.15 — Du Plessis, Eduard Petrus. 'N volk staan op. Kaapstad, 1964.

Afr 10575.82.120 — Easmon, R. Sarif. Dear parent and ogre. London, 1964.

Afr 6390.87 — East Africa, past and present. Paris, 1964.

Afr 3315.121 — Eayrs, James. The Commonwealth and Suez. London, 1964.

Afr 7320.27F — Eca de Queiroz, J.M.D. Santuario bravio. Lisboa, 1964.

Afr 5407.14 — Economist Intelligence Unit, Ltd., London. The states of Equatorial Africa: Gabon, Congo. London, 1964.

Afr 545.35 — Edinburgh. University. Centre Of African Studies. Religion in Africa. Edinburgh, 1964.

Afr 9439.65.11 — Eeden, Guy van. Die vuur brand nader. Kaapstad, 1964.

Afr 10675.10.100 — Egbuna, Obi Benue. Wind versus polygamy. London, 1964.

Afr 30.12 — Encyclopédie africaine et malgache. Paris, 1964.

Afr 5269.24 — Epelle, Emanuel Tobiah. Bishops in the Niger Delta. Aba, Nigeria, 1964.

Afr 4747.7 — Ericksen, E.G. Africa company town. Dubuque, 1964.

Afr 8145.45 — Ervin, Spencer. The polity of the Church of the province of South Africa. Ambler, Pa., 1964.

Afr 2030.464.55 — Estier, Claude. Pour l'Algérie. Paris, 1964.

Afr Doc 303.5F — Ethiopia. Ministry of Interior. Administrative sub-divisions of Ethiopia, as of the end of Sené 1956 e.c. or July 7th, 1964. Addis Ababa, 1964.

Afr 1069.64.10 — Etudes maghrébines. Paris, 1964.

Afr 8678.328 — Eyo, B.E. Apartheid. Jerusalem, 1964.

Afr 6210.25.2 — Ezera, Kalu. Constitutional development in Nigeria. 2d ed. Cambridge, Eng., 1964.

Afr 9510.5.10 — Fagan, Brian M. The Victoria Falls, a handbook to the Victoria Falls, the Batoka Gorge and part of the upper Zambesi river. 2. ed. Lusaka, 1964.

Afr 6210.62 — Fairholm, Gilbert Wayne. Urban government organization in Northern Nigeria. Zaria?, 1964?

Afr 6542.16 — Fallers, Lloyd A. The king's men. London, 1964.

Afr 210.64.20 — Fanon, Frantz. Pour la révolution africaine. Paris, 1964.

Afr 8687.200.20 — Fischer, Maria Adriana. Kampdagboek. Kaapstad, 1964.

Afr 7812.264 — Fonds du Bien-Etre Indigène. A work of cooperation in development. Brussels, 1964.

Afr 40.64 — Foreign Affairs, N.Y. Africa. A Foreign Affairs reader. 1st ed. N.Y., 1964.

Afr 2731.15.67 — Foucauld, Charles, Vicomte de. Spiritual autobiography of Charles de Foucauld. N.Y., 1964.

Afr 6295.64.5 — Fox, A.J. Uzuakoli. London, 1964.

1964 - cont.

Afr 7480.2 — Fraenkel, M. Tribe and class in Monrovia. London, 1964.

Afr 5183.960.3 — France. Ministère de la Coopération. Economie et plan de développement. 3. éd. Paris, 1964.

Afr 510.102 — France. Ministère de la Coopération. Guide pratique sur les républiques. Paris, 1964.

Afr 5046.5 — France. Ministère de la Coopération. Problemes de planification. Paris, 1964. 11v.

Afr 5046.8 — France. Ministère de la Coopération. Rapport sur la coopération franco-africaine. Paris, 1964.

Afr 6930.5 — Freislich, Richard. The last tribal war. Cape Town, 1964.

Afr 7369.64 — Frenkel, Matrei I. SShA i Liberiia. Moscow, 1964.

Afr 6097.8 — Froelich, Jean Claude. Animismes, les religions paiennes de l'Afrique de l'ouest. Paris, 1964.

Afr 6132.12 — Fyfe, Christopher. Sierra Leone inheritance. London, 1964.

Afr 6113.20 — Gailey, Harry A. A history of the Gambia. London, 1964.

Afr 1273.961.2 — Gallissot, Rene. L'economie de l'Afrique du Nord. Paris, 1964.

Afr 1623.964.10 — Gallissot, Rene. Le patronat europeen au Maroc. Rabat, 1964.

Afr 9839.64.5 — Gandu, Madeleine. Matilda, fille du Nyassaland. Paris, 1964.

Afr 9639.64 — Gann, L.H. A history of Northern Rhodesia. London, 1964.

Afr 9525.457 — Gann, L.H. Huggins of Rhodesia. London, 1964.

Afr 5406.264 — Gardi, René. Kiligei. Heitere und ernste Erlebnisse in Afrika. Aarau, 1964.

Afr 6740.18 — Garine, Igor de. Les Massa du Cameroun. Paris, 1964.

Afr 6470.211 — Gatheru, R.M. Child of two worlds. London, 1964.

Afr 1069.37.7 — Gautier, Emile F. Le passé de l'Afrique du Nord. Paris, 1964.

Afr 9506.6 — Gelfand, Michael. Mother Patrick and her nursing sister. Capetown, 1964.

Afr 1609.64.5 — Geographie du Maroc. Paris, 1964.

Afr 4060.36 — Geroter, Georg. Nubien. Zurich, 1964.

Afr Doc 1807.360.5 — Ghana. Census Office. 1960 population census of Ghana. Special report. Accra, 1964.

Afr 6193.19.5 — Ghana. Planning Commission. Seven-year plan for national reconstruction and development. Accra, 1964.

Afr 6194.37 — Gil, B. Tribes in Ghana. Accra, 1964.

Afr 7580.16 — Gilis, Charles A. Kasa-vubu, au coeur du drame congolais. Bruxelles, 1964.

Afr 6390.36F — Gillsaeter, Sven. Pias safari. Stockholm, 1964.

Afr 28.90 — Glazier, K.M. Africa South of the Sahara. Stanford, Calif., 1964-69. 2v.

Afr 9170.34 — Goosen, Willem. On the run. Cape Town, 1964.

Afr 11433.75.110 — Gordon, Gerald. Four people, a novel of South Africa. London, 1964.

Afr 5796.5.10 — Gorse, Jean. Territoire des Comores; bibliographie. Paris, 1964?

Afr 3305.12 — Grant, C. Nationalism and revolution in Egypt. The Hague, 1964.

Afr 5842.19 — Great Britain. Central Office of Information. Mauritius and Seychelles. N.Y., 1964.

Afr 6280.9.17 — Green, Margaret M. Ibo village affairs. 2. ed. London, 1964.

Afr 7312.25 — Grupo de Trabalho de Promoção Social. Promoção social en Moçambique. Lisboa, 1964.

Afr 2035.9.5 — Guérin, Daniel. L'Algérie qui se cherçhe. Paris, 1964.

Afr 4285.6 — Hable-Selassie, Sergew. Beziehungen Athiopiens zur griechisch-römischen Welt. Bonn, 1964.

Afr 609.64.5 — Hahn, E. Africa to me, person to person. 1st ed. Garden City, N.Y., 1964.

Afr 6277.83 — Halpern, Jan. Nigeria i Ghana. Warszawa, 1964.

Afr 8676.64.6 — Hamer, Eberhard. Die Industrialisierung Südafrikas seit dem Zweiten Weltkrieg. Stuttgart, 1964.

Afr 8685.1 — Hampson, Ruth M. Islam in South Africa. Cape Town, 1964.

Afr 609.64.10 — Hance, W.A. The geography of modern Africa. N.Y., 1964.

Afr 8252.341.82 — Hancock, William Keith. Smuts and the shift of world power. London, 1964.

Afr 50.44 — Hanna, W.J. Independent black Africa. Chicago, 1964.

Afr 28.95 — Hanna, W.J. Politics in Black Africa. East Lansing, Michigan, 1964.

Afr 212.3 — Harrigan, Anthony. Red star over Africa. Cape Town, 1964.

Afr 11448.77.100 — Harris, Peter. Some small compassion. London, 1964.

Afr 635.88 — Haselberger, Herta. Bautraditionen der westafrikanischen Negerkulturen. Wien, 1964

Afr 3339.10 — Hatim, Muhammad Abdal-Quadir. Culture and national guidance in twelve years. Cairo, 1964.

Afr 609.64.45 — Hauzeur de Fooz, Carlos. Afrique nouvelle. Bruxelles, 1964.

Afr 10678.61.100 — Henshaw, James Ene. Children of the goddess, and other plays. London, 1964.

Afr 626.129 — Herskovits, Melville J. Economic transition in Africa. Evanston, 1964.

Afr 8678.320 — Hill, C.R. Bantustans. London, 1964.

Afr 8252.9.15 — Hinchliff, Peter Bingham. John William Colenso. London, 1964.

Afr 545.29 — Holas, Bohumil. L'Afrique noire. Paris, 1964.

Afr 5342.60.6 — Holas, Bohumil. La Côte-d'Ivoire. Paris, 1964.

Afr 8678.303 — Holloway, John Edward. Apartheid, a challenge. Johannesburg, 1964.

Afr 6420.77 — Holman, D. Bwana drum. London, 1964.

Afr 14728.1 — Honwana, Luís. Nós matámos o Cão-Tinhoso! Lourenço Marques, 1964.

Afr 8659.64.5 — Hopkinson, T. South Africa. N.Y., 1964.

Afr 8676.64 — Houghton, D. Hobart. The South African economy. Cape Town, 1964.

Afr 210.64.40 — Hughes, L. The first book of Africa. N.Y., 1964.

Afr 3079.64 — Hurst, Harold. A short account of the Nile basin. Cairo, 1964.

Afr 3979.64A — Husayn, Efendi. Ottoman Egypt in the age of French revolution. Cambridge, 1964.

Afr 8678.314 — Hutt, W.H. The economics of the colour bar. London, 1964.

Afr 6390.44 — Huxley, Elspeth Grant. Forks and hope. London, 1964.

Afr 6390.44.2 — Huxley, Elspeth Grant. With forks and hope. N.Y., 1964.

Afr 8820.6 — Illiers, Stephanus. Wes-Kaapland. Stellenbosch, 1964.

Afr 6879.64 — Imperato, Pascal James. Doctor in the land of the lion. 1st ed. N.Y., 1964.

Afr 6275.105 — Institute for International Social Research. The attitudes, hopes and fears of Nigerians. Princeton, 1964.

Afr 710.32 — International African Seminar. The historian in tropical Africa. London, 1964.

Afr 626.136   International Conference on the Organization of Research and Training in Africa in Relation to the Study, Conservation and Utilization of Natural Resources, Lagos, 1964. Final report of the Lagos conference. Lagos, 1964.

Afr 626.136.4   International Conference on the Organization of Research and Training in Africa in Relation to the Study, Conservation and Utilization of Natural Resources, Lagos, 1964. Scientific research in Africa. Lagos, 1964.

Afr 626.136.6   International Conference on the Organization of Research and Training in African in Relation to the Study, Conservation and Utilization of Natural Resources, Lagos, 1964. Outline of a plan for scientific research and training in Africa. Paris, 1964.

Afr 6457.30   Italy. Instituto Nationale Per Il Commercio Estero. Kenya. Roma, 1964.

Afr 5240.8   Italy. Instituto Nazionale per il Commercio Estero. Mali. Roma, 1964.

Afr 5282.4   Italy. Istituto Nazionale per il Commercio Estero. Alto volta. Roma, 1964.

Afr 7461.36   Italy. Istituto Nazionale per il Commercio Estero. Liberia. Roma, 1964.

Afr 5758.60.4   Italy. Istituto Nazionale per il Commercio Estero. Madagascar. Roma, 1964-[1965].

Afr 6538.50   Italy. Istituto Nazionale per il Commercio Estero. Uganda. Roma, 1964.

Afr 8057.6   Jaarsveld, F.A. van. The Afrikaners interpretation. Cape Town, 1964.

Afr 11465.14.150   Jacobson, Dan. Beggar my neighbour, short stories. London, 1964.

Afr 6903.12   Jager, J. de. South-west Africa. Pretoria, 1964.

Afr 6143.54.2   Jarrett, H.R. A geography of Sierra Leone and Gambia. Rev. ed. London, 1964.

Afr 5070.5   Jeol, Michel. Cours de droit administratif mauritanien. Bordeaux, 1964.

Afr 2030.464.15   Joesten, Joachim. The new Algeria. Chicago, 1964.

Afr 10003.5   Johannesburg. Public Library. A list of theatre performances in Johannesburg, 1887-1897. Johannesburg, 1964.

Afr 115.110   Jones, Arthur M. Africa and Indonesia. Leiden, 1964.

Afr 9769.64   Jones, G. Britain and Nyasaland. London, 1964.

Afr 8847.81   Jones, S.M. Personal accounts of visitors to Simon's Town, 1770-1899. Cape Town, 1964.

Afr 2929.64   Jongmans, D.G. Libie, land van de dorst. Meppel, 1964.

Afr 9693.3   Josephine (pseud.) Tell me, Josephine. London, 1964.

Afr 7309.64.5   Joubert, Elsa (pseud.) Die staf van Monomotapa. Kaapstad, 1964.

Afr 2000.17   Julien, Charles A. Histoire de l'Algérie contemporaine. v.1- Paris, 1964-

Afr 3310.94   Karanjia, Rustom Khurshedji. How Nasser did it. Bombay, 1964.

Afr 8676.64.10   Katzen, Leo. Implications of economic and other boycotts for South Africa. Cape Town, 1964.

Afr 550.142   Kaufmann, Robert. Millenarisme et acculturation. Bruxelles, 1964.

Afr 8686.4   Kellermann, Abraham Gerhardus. Profetisme in Suid-Afrika in akkulturasie perspektief. Proefschrift. Voorburg, 1964.

Afr 6457.23   Kenya. Development plan for the period from 1st July, 1964, to 30th June, 1970. Nairobi, 1964.

Afr Doc 3207.362   Kenya. Ministry of Finance and Economic Planning Kenya Population Census, 1962. Nairobi? 1964.

Afr Doc 3202.64F   Kenya. Archives. Archives microfilming programme. Nairobi, 1964.

Afr Doc 3208.468F   Kenya. Directorate of Planning. The pattern of income. Nairobi, 1964.

Afr Doc 3207.362.5F   Kenya. Economics and Statistics Division. Population census, 1962. Nairobi? 1964.

Afr 6457.21   Kenya. Laws, statutes, etc. The Foreign Investments Protection Act, 1964 and rules of procedure. Nairobi, 1964.

Afr 6457.29F   Kenya Tea Development Authority. The operations and development plans of the Kenya Tea Development Authority. Nairobi, 1964.

Afr 6412.6   Kenyatta, J. Harambee. Nairobi, 1964.

Afr 6095.4.3   Kingsley, Mary Henrietta. West African studies. 3d ed. London, 1964.

Afr 6333.64   Kirkman, James S. Men and monuments on the East African coast. London, 1964.

Afr 10118.3   Komey, Ellis A. Modern African stories. London, 1964.

Afr 3986.964.20   Komzin, Ivan V. Svet Asuana. Moscow, 1964.

Afr 10631.58.100   Konadu, Asare. The wizard of Osamang. Accra, 1964.

Afr 698.58   Krapf, J.L. Reisen in Ostafrika. Stuttgart, 1964.

Afr 1623.964.15   Kratz, Achim. Untersuchung der morokkanischen Industriestruktur. Hamburg, 1964.

Afr 626.127   Kreinin, M.E. Israel and Africa. N.Y., 1964.

Afr 6138.64   Kup, A.P. The story of Sierra Leone. Cambridge, Eng., 1964.

Afr 6168.4   Kyereteire, K.O. Bonsu Ashanti heroes. Accra, 1964.

Afr 49032.1.100   Ladipo, Duro. Three Yoruba plays. Ibadan, 1964.

Afr 11509.35.120   LaGuma, Alex. And a threefold cord. Berlin, 1964.

Afr 7122.82   Laidley, Fernando. Missoes de guerra e de paz no norte de Angola. Lisboa, 1964.

Afr 2030.464.75   Laparre, M. de. Journal d'un prêtre en Algérie. Paris, 1964.

Afr 210.64.75   Larsen, Peter. Young Africa. London, 1964.

Afr 679.64.5   Latham, Norah. The heritage of West Africa. London, 1964.

Afr 4969.63.5   Laurence, M. New wind in a dry land. 1. American ed. N.Y., 1964.

Afr 8252.341.68   Lean, Phyllis Scannell. One man in his time. Johannesburg, 1964.

Afr 1733.6   Lecoz, J. Le Rharb, fellahs et colons. Rabat, 1964. 2v.

Afr 1733.6.1   Lecoz, J. Le Rharb. Rabat, 1964. 2v.

Afr 8678.323   Legum, Colin. South Africa, crisis for the West. London, 1964.

Afr 7567.34   Lemarchand, Rene. Political awakening in the Belgian Congo. Berkeley, 1964.

Afr 6988.94.256   Lempp, Ferdinand. Windhoek. 1st ed. Windhoek, 1964.

Afr 2030.464   Lentin, Albert. L'Algérie entre deux mondes. Paris, 1964.

Afr 26719.24.21   Lepoutre, Paul. Contes congolais. Limete, 1964. 2 pam.

Afr 6743.60   Lestringant, Jacques. Les pays de guider au Cameroun. Versailles, 1964.

Afr 2030.464.35   Leulliette, P. St. Michael and the dragon. London, 1964.

Afr 6720.64   Levini, V.T. The Cameroons, from mandate to independence. Berkeley, 1964.

Afr 9165.42.70   Leyds, Gerard A. A history of Johannesburg, the early years. Cape Town, 1964.

Afr Doc 9907.362   Liberia. Office of National Planning. Bureau of Statistics. 1962 population census of Liberia: population characteristics of major areas. Monrovia, 1964? 13v.

Afr Doc 7002.5   Library of Congress. African Section. Official publications of French Equatorial Africa, French Cameroons, and Togo, 1946-1958. Washington, 1964.

Afr Doc 807.364F   Libya. Census and Statistical Department. General population census, 1964. Tripoli, 1964?

Afr Doc 807.364.10   Libya. Census and Statistical Department. Preliminary results of the general population census 1964. Tripoli, 1964.

Afr 2808.6   Libya. Constitution. Constitution of the Kingdom of Libya as modified by Law No.1 of 1963. Benghazi, 1964.

Afr 2938.34   Libya. Ministry of Planning and Development. Five-year economic and social development plan, 1963-1968. Tripoli, 1964.

Afr 5265.5   Ligers, Ziedonis. Les Sorko (Bozo), maîtres du Niger. Paris, 1964-1967. 3v.

Afr 626.132   Little, Ian. Aid to Africa. Oxford, 1964.

Afr 9558.14.15   Livingstone, D. The Zambesi doctors. Edinburgh, 1964.

Afr 10882.41.100   Livingstone, Douglas. Sjambok, and other poems from Africa. London, 1964.

Afr 6168.6   Lloyd, A. The drums of Kumasi. London, 1964.

Afr 8847.56   Lomax, Ambrose. Portret van'n Suid-Afrikaanse dorp. Molteno, 1964.

Afr 6535.64   London. Commonwealth Institute. Uganda. London, 1964.

Afr 7912.15.20   Lopez Alvarez, Luis. Lumumba ou l'Afrique frustrée. Paris, 1964.

Afr 14663.5   Lopo, Júlio de Castro. Jornalismo de Angola. Luanda, 1964.

Afr 7912.5.10   Lumumba, Patrice. Patrice Lumumba. Moscou, 1964.

Afr 7923.5   Luwel, Marcel. Sir Francis de Winton, administrateur général du Congo, 1884-1886. Tervuren, 1964.

Afr 115.17   McCall, D.F. Africa in time-perspective. Boston, 1964.

Afr 5426.100.60   McKnight, G. Verdict on Schweitzer. London, 1964.

Afr 3816.7   McLoughlin, Peter F. Language-switching as an index of socialization. Berkeley, 1964.

Afr 5749.64.15   Madagascar. Tananarive, 1964.

Afr 5758.64F   Madagascar. Commissariat Général au Plan. Plan quinquennal, 1964-1968. Tananarive, 1964.

Afr 8678.315   Magidi, D.T. Black background. London, 1964.

Afr 5765.34   Malagasy. Republic Service des Archives et de la Documentation. Fampisehaana. Tananarive, 1964.

Afr 8050.12   Malan, Daniel Francois. Glo in u volk. D.F. Malan as redenaar, 1908-1954. Kaapstad, 1964.

Afr 8050.8.5   Malan, Maarten Petrus Albertus. Die nasionale party van Suid-Afrika, 1914-1964. Pretoria, 1964.

Afr 9850.5   Malawi - development plan. Zomba, 1964.

Afr 5248.16   Małowist, M. Wielkie państwa sudanu zachodniego w późnym średniowieczu. Warszawa, 1964.

Afr 11555.61.110   Manson, H.W.D. Pat Mulholland's day. Cape Town, 1964.

Afr 212.4   Marais, B.J. The two faces of Africa. Pietermaritzburg, 1964.

Afr 4766.40   Mariam, Mesfin Wolde. The background of the Ethio-Somalia boundary dispute. Addis Ababa, 1964.

Afr 6541.11   Marie André du Sacre Coeur. Uganda. 2.ed. Tournai, 1964.

Afr 7377.64   Marinelli, L.A. The new Liberia. N.Y., 1964. 2v.

Afr 8145.46   Martin, Marie L. The biblical concept of Messianism and Messianism in Southern Africa. Morija, 1964.

Afr 5187.15   Martin, V. La chrétienté africaine de Dakar. Dakar, 1964. 3 pam.

Afr 5187.10   Martin, V. Notes d'introduction à une étude socio-religieuse des populations de Dakar et du Sénégal. Dakar, 1964.

Afr 6392.36.5   Massell, B.F. The distribution of gains in a common market. Santa Monica, Calif., 1964.

Afr 626.129.5   Massell, Benton F. African studies and economic analysis. Santa Monica, 1964.

Afr 3813.20   Massow, Heinrich von. Die Industrie den Republik Sudan. Hamburg, 1964.

Afr Doc 2807.362F   Mauritius. 1962 population census of Mauritius and its dependencies. Port Louis, 1964.

Afr 5843.5   Mauritius. Ministry of Industry, Commerce and industry in Mauritius. Port Louis, 1964.

Afr 8678.319   Mbeki, G.A.M. South Africa. Harmondsworth, 1964.

Afr 5344.8   Meillassoux, Claude. Anthropologie économique des Gouro de Côte-d'Ivoire. Paris, 1964.

Afr 609.64   Melady, T.P. Faces of Africa. N.Y., 1964.

Afr 12015.10   Memmi, Albert. Anthologie des écrivains maghrébins d'expression française. Paris, 1964.

Afr 8380.5   Merwe, Hendrik Johannes Jan Matthijs van der. Gebeure in Afrika. Johannesburg, 1964.

Afr 8110.3.38   Merwe, Hendrik Johannes Jan Matthijs van der. Scheepsjournael en de daghregister. 2.druk. Pretoria, 1964.

Afr 6157.12   Metcalfe, George E. Great Britain and Ghana. London, 1964.

Afr 3315.130   Meyer-Ranke, Peter. Der rote Pharao. Hamburg, 1964.

Afr 7549.64   Meyers, Joseph. Le prix d'un empire. 3.ed. Bruxelles, 1964.

Afr 8678.310   Mezerik, A.G. Apartheid in the Republic of South Africa. N.Y., 1964.

Afr 3979.64.10   Mikhaelides, Gaby. La terre qui berça l'histoire. Bomas-sur-Ourthe, 1964.

Afr 609.64.40   Mikolasek, Vladimir. Africka mozaika. Liberec, 1964.

Afr 11057.6   Millar, Clive. Sixteen stories by South African writers. Cape Town, 1964.

Afr 2623.964   Mission de Productivité en Tunisie. Actions de productivité en Tunisie. Paris, 1964.

Afr 1869.64   Moncade, Noel. Les français d'Algerie. Paris, 1964.

Afr 6385.16   Mondini, A.G. Africa or death. Boston, 1964.

Afr 1069.64.5   Monlau, J. Les états barbaresques. Paris, 1964.

Afr 575.40   Monteil, V. L'islam noir. Paris, 1964.

Afr 10005.15   Morán López, Fernando. Natión y alienación en la literatura negro-africana. Madrid, 1964.

Afr 5053.32   Morgenthau, R.S. Political parties in French-speaking West Africa. Oxford, 1964.

Afr 2030.464.80   Morland. HistoireDe l'organisation de l'armée secrète. Paris, 1964.

Afr Doc 5207.361   Morocco. Service Central des Statistiques. Résultats de l'enquête à objectifs multiples, 1961-1963. Rabat? 1964.

1964 - cont.

Afr Doc 5207.360.5
    Morocco. Service Central des Statistiques. Résultats du recensement de 1960. Rabat, 1964-65.

Afr 41610.2   Morris, H.F. The heroic recitation of the Bahima of Ankole. Oxford, 1964.

Afr 11580.77.100   Morris, Michael. The sweetness and the sadness. Cape Town, 1964

Afr 6403.2   Moses, Larry. Kenya, Uganda, Tanganyika, 1960-1964, a bibliography. Washington, 1964.

Afr 4430.64   Mosley, Leonard O. Haile Selassie, the conquering Lion. London, 1964.

Afr 2218.6.10   Mrabet, F. La femme algérienne. Paris, 1964.

Afr 6218.19   Muffett, D.J.M. Concerning brave captains. London, 1964.

Afr 109.61.41   Mukarovsky, H. Afrique d'hier et d'aujourd'hui. Tournai, 1964.

Afr 9087.8   Mulder, Cornelius Petrus. Die eerste skof van die Nasionale Party in Transvaal, 1914 1964. Johannesburg, 1964.

Afr 9645.17   Mulford, D.C. The Northern Rhodesia general election, 1962. Nairobi, 1964.

Afr 2819.64   Murabet, Mohammed. Facts about Libya. 3rd ed. Malta, 1964.

Afr 8847.34.50   Murray, Marischal. Under lion's head. 2. ed. Cape Town, 1964.

Afr 3310.10.45   Nasser, G.A. President Gamal Abdel Nasser on Palestine. Cairo, 1964.

Afr 9197.2   Natal. University. Institute for Social Research. Experiment in Swaziland. Cape Town, 1964.

Afr 11433.74.800   Nell, Racilla Jilian. Nadine Gordimer. Johannesburg, 1964.

Afr 626.126   Neumark, S.D. Foreign trade and economic development in Africa. Stanford, Calif., 1964.

Afr 6075.16   Newbury, C.W. The West African commonwealth. Durham, N.C., 1964.

Afr 10434.127.100   Ngugi, James. Weep not, child. London, 1964.

Afr 5345.20   Niangoran-Bauah, Georges. La division du temps et le calendrier rituel des peuples lagunaires de Côte-d'Ivoire. Paris, 1964.

Afr 2525.21   Nicaud, C.A. Tunisia. N.Y., 1964.

Afr 109.64.20   Nicol, D. Africa - a subjective view. London, 1964.

Afr 8377.5   Nicol, Margaret. South African protocol, and other formalities. Cape Town, 1964.

Afr 4760.14   Nigam, Shyam Behari Lal. Utilisation of manpower in the public service in Somalia. Mogadiscio, 1964.

Afr 12684.41.100   Niger, Paul. Les grenouilles du mont Kimbo. Paris, 1964.

Afr 6210.46   Nigeria, Midwestern. Ministry of Information. Planting the vineyard. Benin City, 1964.

Afr 6210.45F   Nigeria. Delimitation Commission. Report of the Constituency Delimitation Commission, 1964. Lagos, 1964.

Afr 55.32   Niven, Cecil R. Nine great Africans. London, 1964.

Afr 11611.66.100   Nkosi, Lewis. The rhythm of violence. London, 1964.

Afr 6160.8   Nsarkoh, J.K. Local government in Ghana. Accra, 1964.

Afr 10684.92.100   Nwankwo, Nkem. Danda. London, 1964.

Afr 10684.92.1100   Nwanodi, Okogbule Glory. Icheke and other poems. Ibadan, 1964.

Afr 2030.464.85   OAS parle. Paris, 1964.

Afr 10685.43.100   Okara, Gabriel. The voice. London, 1964.

Afr 115.102   Okoye, M. African responses. Ilfracombe, 1964.

Afr 6280.57   Olinto, A. Brasileiros no Africa. Rio de Janeiro, 1964.

Afr 7225.8   Oliveira Boléo, José de. A campanha de 1783 contra o Vtigulo. Lourenço Marques, 1964.

Afr 5645.12   Ordre National de la République Malgache. Le grand livre de l'Ordre national de la République Malgache. Tananarive, 1964.

Afr 5326.5   Organization for Economic Cooperation and Development. Development Centre. Essai d'une bibliographie sur la Côte-d'Ivoire. Paris, 1964.

Afr 210.64.30   Organization of African Unity. Assembly of the heads of state and government of O.A.U. Cairo, 1964.

Afr 210.64.25   Organization of African Unity. Basic documents and resolutions. Addis Ababa, 1964.

Afr 8849.295   Orpen, Joseph Millerd. Reminiscences of life in South Africa from 1846 to the present day. Cape Town, 1964.

Afr 2030.464.5   Ortiz, Joseph. Mes combats. Paris, 1964.

Afr 5070.10   Ould Daddah, Marie Thérèse. Cours de droit constitutionnel mauritanien. Bordeaux, 1964.

Afr 5368.3   Palau Marti, Montserrat. Le roi-dieu au Bénin. Paris, 1964.

Afr 4388.15   Pankhurst, Richard Keir Patrick. The great Ethiopian famine of 1888-1892, a new assessment. Addis Ababa, 1964.

Afr 6145.2   Parsons, R.T. Religion in an African society. Leiden, 1964.

Afr 212.8   Passos, Inacio de. A grande noite africana. Lisboa, 1964.

Afr 8338.230.5   Paton, Alan. Hofmeyr. London, 1964.

Afr 20756.2   Pawelzik, Fritz. I lie on my mat and pray. N.Y., 1964.

Afr 2223.964   Pawera, J.C. Algeria's infrastructure. N.Y., 1964.

Afr 5912.5   Pelissier, René. Los territorios españoles de Africa. Madrid, 1964.

Afr 626.140   Pelletier, R.A. Mineral resources of South-Central Africa. Capetown, 1964.

Afr 8289.64   Pemberton, W.B. Battles of the Boer war. London, 1964.

Afr 2623.3   Pennec, Pierre. Les transformations des corps de métiers de Tunis. Tunis, 1964.

Afr 10536.69.100   Peters, Lenrie. Poems. Ibadan, 1964.

Afr 6192.72   Pfeffer, Karl Heinz. Ghana. 2. Aufl. Bonn, 1964.

Afr 6225.8   Phillips, C.S. The development of Nigerian foreign policy. Evanston, 1964.

Afr 2510.15   Piano, Lorenzo del. La penetrazione italiana in Tunisia, 1861-1881. Padova, 1964.

Afr 2397.7   Pignal, Jacques. Maurice Cochard, mon ami. Toulouse, 1964.

Afr 7176.6   Pires, Antonio. Angola. Luanda, 1964.

Afr 5266.5   Ploussard, Jean. Carnet de route de Jean Ploussard. Paris, 1964.

Afr 11705.39.641   Pohl, V. The down and after. London, 1964.

Afr 4892.12   Poinsot, Jean Paul. Djibouti et la côte française des Somalis. Paris, 1964.

Afr 6903.8   Poller, Robert Manfred. Swakopmund and Walvis Bay. Cape Town, 1964.

Afr 9839.64.10   Portrait of Malawi. Zomba, 1964.

Afr 7190.16   Portugal. Agencia Geral do Ultramar. San Tome e principe. Lisboa, 1964.

Afr 7219.64   Portugal. Archivo Ultramarino. Historico documentação avulsa moçambicana do arquivo historico ultramarino. Lisboa, 1964. 2v.

1964 - cont.

Afr 679.64   Post, K.W.J. The new states of West Africa. Harmondsworth, 1964.

Afr 8050.21   Potchefstroom. University for Christian Higher Education. Republiek en koninkryk. Potchefstroom, 1964.

Afr 626.156   Prague. Vysoka Skola Ekonomicka. Katedra Ekonomiky Rozvojovych Zemi. Africka Sekce. Nastin ekonomiky rozvojovych zemi Afriky. Praha, 1964.

Afr 2030.464.60   Pravda, Moscow. Nerushimaia druzhba i bratstvo. Moscow, 1964.

Afr 3993.5   Pravda, Moskva. Asuan, simvol sovetsko-arabskoi druzhby. Moskva, 1964.

Afr 609.64.25F   Progrès Egyptien. Afrique d'aujourd'hui. Le Caire, 1964.

Afr 5091.5   Pujos, Jerome. Croissance économique. Paris, 1964.

Afr 11728.41.100   Raik, Lea. Redeemed. 1st ed. Johannesburg, 1964.

Afr 7580.23   La rébellion au Congo. Leopoldville, Congo, 1964.

Afr 8687.323.5   Reitz, Conrad Hjalmar. The Reitz family. Cape Town, 1964.

Afr 9635.26   Rhodesia, Northern. Commission Appointed to Review the Salaries and Conditions of Service. Report. Lusaka, 1964.

Afr Doc 3807.362F   Rhodesia, Southern. Central Statistical Office. Final report of the April/May 1962 census of Africans in Southern Rhodesia. Salisbury, 1964.

Afr Doc 3509.305F   Rhodesia (British Colony). Central Statistical Office. Report on the results of the national income and balance of payments questionaire sent to companies operating in Malaur. v.1. Salisbury, 1964.

Afr 3310.88   Riad, H. L'Egypte nassérienne. Paris, 1964.

Afr 3199.47.2   Rifaat, M. The awakening of modern Egypt. Lahore, 1964.

Afr 11747.90.100   Rive, Richard. Emergency. London, 1964.

Afr 10118.4   Rive, Richard. Modern African prose. London, 1964.

Afr 626.98.5   Rivkin, Arnold. Africa and the European Common Market. Denver, 1964.

Afr 2731.15.85   Roche, Aimé. Charles de Foucauld. Lyon, 1964.

Afr 7175.74   Rodrigues, J. Angola, terra de Portugal. Lourenço Marques, 1964.

Afr 11750.21.100   Roebuck, M.F.C. Nyitso, a novel of West Africa. Cape Town, 1964.

Afr 30.6.1   Rosenthal, Eric. Encyclopaedia of Southern Africa. 2nd ed. London, 1964.

Afr 6192.92   Rouch, Jane. Ghana. Lausanne, 1964.

Afr 5342.63   Rougerie, Gabriel. La Côte-d'Ivoire. Paris, 1964.

Afr 8678.53.2   Roux, Edward. Time longer than rope. 2. ed. Madison, 1964.

Afr 3990.25   Saad, Zaki Yusef. Pharaonic egypt, quick visit. Cairo, 1964.

Afr 3816.4   Santandrea, Stefano. A tribal history. Bologna, 1964.

Afr 7183.34   Santos, Eduardo dos. A questão da Lunda, 1885-1894. Lisboa, 1964.

Afr 7534.1   Santos, Nuno Beja Valdez Thomaz dos. O desconhecido Niassa. Lisboa, 1964.

Afr 7222.72   Sarmento Rodrigues, M.M. Presença de Moçambique na vida da nação. Lisboa, 1964. 3v.

Afr 6277.80   Schatz, Sayre P. Development bank lending in Nigeria. Ibadan, 1964.

Afr 2030.464.40   Scherb, J.D. Le soleil ne chauffe que les vivants. Paris, 1964.

Afr 8289.64.5   Schikkerling, Roland William. Commando courageous. Johannesburg, 1964.

Afr 8289.64.10   Schikkerling, Roland William. Hoe ry die Boere; i 'n kommando-dagboek. Johannesburg, 1964.

Afr 8252.172.16.2   Schoor, Marthinus Cornelius Ellnarius van. Christiaan Rudolph de Wet, 1854-1922. 2. uitg. Bloemfontein, 1964.

Afr 8377.2   Schreiner, Oliver Deneys. The nettle. Johannesburg, 1964.

Afr 9710.15F   Selwyn, P. Report on the economy of Barotseland. n.p., 1964?

Afr 5103.1   Sénégal. Archives Nationales. Centre de Documentation. Eléments de bibliographie sénégalaise. Dakar, 1964.

Afr 5183.964.5   Senegal. Ministère du Développement, et du Plan et l'Economie Generale. Bilan d'execution materielle et financière des investissements publics au 31 dec. 1963. Dakar, 1964.

Afr 12639.24.25   Senghor, L.S. Liberté. Paris, 1964.

Afr 12639.24.130   Senghor, L.S. Poèmes. Paris, 1964.

Afr 12639.24.21   Senghor, L.S. Selected poems. London, 1964.

Afr 545.27   Sharevskaia, Berta I. Starye i novye religii tropicheskoi i iuzhnoi Afriki. Moscow, 1964.

Afr 8847.34.100   Shaw, R.C. Graaff-Reinet, a bibliography. Cape Town, 1964.

Afr 8953.5   Simmonds, Heather A. European immigration into Natal, 1824-1910. Cape Town, 1964.

Afr 5285.277.25   Skinner, Elliott Percival. The Mossi of the Upper Volta. Stanford, 1964.

Afr 8847.89   Smit, Mattheus Theodorus Rehuel. The romance of the village Ugie. Cape Town, 1964.

Afr 7380.5   Smith, Robert A. The emancipation of the hinterland. Monrovia, 1964.

Afr 10839.55.100   Smith, Wilbur Addison. When the lion feeds. N.Y., 1964.

Afr 8678.308   Snethlage, J.L. Meer begrip voor Suid-Afrika. Amsterdam, 1964.

Afr 115.106   Social Sciences Research Conference. Problems of transition. Pietermaritzburg, Natal, 1964.

Afr 4766.36   Somalia. Consiglio dei Ministri. L'attività del governo dall'indipendenza ad oggi. Mogadiscio, 1964.

Afr Doc 719.12   Somalia. Constitution. The Constitution. Mogadiscio, 1964?

Afr 4772.10   Somalia. Council of Ministers. Government activities from independence until today. Mogadiscio, 1964.

Afr 4772.5F   Somalia. Prime Minister. Statement of programme by Abdirizak Hagi Hussen, Prime Minister and President of the Council of Ministers. Mogadiscio, 1964.

Afr 6985.6F   South Africa. Commission of Enquiry into South West African Affairs. Report, 1962-1963. Pretoria, 1964.

Afr 8685.95   South Africa. Department of Bantu Administration and Development. Summary of the report of the Committee on Foreign Affairs. Johannesburg, 1964.

Afr 8380.3   South Africa. South African Information Service. South Africa source books. v.1-4. N.Y., 1964.

Afr 8380.4   South African Communist Party. The road to South African freedom. London, 1964.

Afr 11025.2   Sowden, Lewis. Both sides of the mask. Cape Town, 1964.

Afr 10689.67.130   Soyinka, W. Five plays. London, 1964.

Afr 5953.2   Spain. Consejo Superior de Investigaciones Cientificas. La Guinea ecuatorial y su regimen de Autonomia. Madrid, 1964.

Afr 5921.64   Spain. Servicio Informativo Español. España en el Africa ecuatorial. Madrid, 1964.

1964 - cont.

Afr 626.22.2 — Stamp, L.D. Africa, a study in tropical development. 2d ed. N.Y., 1964.

Afr 9700.50 — Stefaniszyn, Bronislaw. Social and ritual life of the Ambo of Northern Rhodesia. London, 1964.

Afr 626.130 — Steinfield, Jacques. Pour une cooperation économique africaine, vues et perspectives. Bruxelles, 1964.

Afr 3035.7 — Stern, S.M. Fatimid decrees. London, 1964.

Afr 1623.964 — Stewart, C.F. The economy of Morocco, 1912-1962. Cambridge, 1964. 2v.

Afr 8849.347 — Stockenstroem, Andries. The autobiography of the late Sir Andries Stockenstroem. Cape Town, 1964. 2v.

Afr 5749.64 — Stratton, A. The great red island. N.Y., 1964.

Afr 210.64.65 — Strauch, H. Panafrika. Zürich, 1964.

Afr 3745.71 — Sudan. Central Office of Information. Basic facts about the southern provinces of the Sudan. Khartoum, 1964.

Afr 9049.5 — Sundkler, Bengt. Bantu prophets in South Africa. 2. ed. London, 1964.

Afr 5243.207.5 — Suret-Canale, Jean. Essai sur la signification sociale et historique des hégémonies peules. Paris, 1964.

Afr 626.135 — Suslin, P.N. Ekonomika i vneshniaia torgovlia stran Afriki. Moscow, 1964.

Afr 626.149 — Svenska Handelsdelegationen 1963 till Sudan, Ethiopien, Uganda och Tanganyika. Etiopien, Sudan, Tanganyika, Uganda. Stockholm, 1964.

Afr 8676.64.5 — Svermann, Josef. Die weltwirtschaftliche Bedeutung der Südafrikanischen Republik. Göttingen, 1964.

Afr 8028.26 — Taetemeyer, Gerhard. Suedafrika, Suedwestafrika, eine Bibliographie. Freiburg, 1964.

Afr 6881.264 — Tanzania. Tanganyika five-year plan for economic and social development, 1st July, 1964-30th June, 1969. Dar es Salaam, 1964.

Afr 6335.2 — Tanzania. Ministry of Information and Tourism. Meetings and discussions on the proposed East Africa Federation. Dar es Salaam, 1964.

Afr 626.145 — Taufer, Otakar. Vyznam hospodarske spoluprace socialistickych statu s africkymi zeměmi. Praha, 1964.

Afr 13340.13.700 — Tchicaya U Tamsi, Gerald Felix. Brush fire. Ibadan, 1964.

Afr 13340.13.110 — Tchicaya U Tamsi, Gerald Felix. Le ventre. Paris, 1964.

Afr 4392.30 — Tedone, Giovanni. Angerà. Milano, 1964.

Afr 2030.464.50 — Terrenoire, Louis. De Gaulle et l'Algérie. Paris, 1964.

Afr 8089.64 — Theal, G.M. History of South Africa. Cape Town, 1964. 11v.

Afr 8685.82 — Theron, Erika. Die kleurlingbevolking van Suid-Afrika, Stellenbosch, 1964.

Afr 210.64.15 — Thomas, C.M. African national developments. Maxwell, Ala., 1964.

Afr 5243.122 — Thuriaux-Hennebert, Arlette. Les Zande dans l'histoire du Bahr el-Ghazal et de l'Equatoria. Bruxelles, 1964.

Afr 7809.64 — Thurn, Max. Afrika. Wien, 1964.

Afr 5285.277.15 — Tiendrebeogo, Yamba. Histoire et coutumes royales des Mossi de Ouagadougou. Ouagadougou, 1964.

Afr Doc 6708.702 — Togo. Service de la Statistique Générale. Annuaire retrospectif du commerce special du Togo, 1937-1964. Lomé, 1964.

Afr 2749.64 — Toy, Barbara. The way of the chariots. London, 1964.

Afr 4700.4.20 — Traversi, Carlo. Storia della cartografia coloniale italiana. Roma, 1964.

Afr 575.36.10 — Trimingham, J.S. Islam in East Africa. Oxford, 1964.

Afr 7385.5 — Tubman, William. President William V.S. Tubman on African unity. Monrovia, 1964.

Afr 1335.8 — Turin. Museo Civico d'Arte Antica. Il medagliere delle raccolte numismatiche torinesi. Torino, 1964.

Afr 6438.30 — Uganda. The first five-year development plan, 1961-62 to 1965-66. Entebbe, 1964.

Afr 6538.34 — Uganda. Government white paper on the report of the Commonwealth Development Corporation's tea survey team. Uganda, 1964.

Afr 6538.36 — Uganda. Ministry of Planning and Community Development. Statistics Division. The real growth of the economy of Uganda. Entebbe, 1964.

Afr 7309.64 — União Democratica Nacional de Moçambique. Memorandum to 2nd non-aligned conference. Cairo, 1964.

Afr 3986.964.5 — United Arab Republic. The High Aswan Dam. Cairo, 1964.

Afr Doc 1419.2 — United Arab Republic. Constitution. La constitution, 25 mars, 1964. Le Caire, 1964.

Afr 4108.5.2 — United Arab Republic. Information Department. Aswan. Cairo, 1964.

Afr 3979.64.5F — United Arab Republic. Information Department. Culture and arts. Cairo, 1964.

Afr 3990.26 — United Arab Republic. Information Department. Guide book for U.A.R. Cairo, 1964.

Afr 4108.10F — United Arab Republic. Information Department. Le Haut-Barrage d'Assouan. Aswan High Dam. Cairo, 1964?

Afr 3986.964.6 — United Arab Republic. Information Department. The High Dam. Cairo, 1964.

Afr 3326.6 — United Arab Republic. Information Department. The Revolution in twelve years. Cairo, 1964.

Afr 3979.63.6F — United Arab Republic. Information Department. United Arab Republic. Cairo, 1964.

Afr 3339.12 — United Arab Republic. Laws, statutes, etc. Une authentique promotion démocratique. Le Caire, 1964.

Afr 3986.964.10 — United Arab Republic. Ministry of Industry. Twelve years of industrial development, 1952-1964. Cairo, 1964.

Afr 3993.5.5 — United Arab Republic. Ministry of the High Dam. Aswan High Dam, diversion of Nile. Aswan, 1964.

Afr 8678.318 — United Nations. Secretary-General. A new course in South Africa. N.Y., 1964.

Afr 1623.964.5 — United States. Bureau of International Commerce. A market for United States products in Morocco. Washington, 1964.

Afr 3986.964 — United States. Department of Agriculture. Economic Research Service. Development and Trade Analysis Division. Public Law 480 and other economic assistance to United Arab Republic. Washington, 1964.

Afr Doc 6585.1.73 — Upper Volta. Service de la Statistique. Recensement démographique Ouagadougou, 1961-1962. Paris, 1964.

Afr 5874.19 — Vailland, Roger. La Réunion. Lausanne, 1964.

Afr 7580.13 — Valahu, M. The Katanga circus. 1st ed. N.Y., 1964.

Afr 9038.2 — Vandenberghe, P.L. Caneville. 1st. ed. Middletown, Conn., 1964.

Afr 9853.6A — Vanvelsen, J. The politics of kinship. Manchester, 1964. 2v.

Afr 115.85 — Vedovato, Giuseppe. Studi africani e asiatici. Firenze, 1964. 3v.

Afr 7122.79 — Ventura, Reis. O caso de Angola. Braga, 1964.

Afr 609.56.5 — Vergani, Orio. Quarantacinque gradi all'ombra, attraverso l'Africa, dalla Città del Capo al Cairo. Torino, 1964.

1964 - cont.

Afr 590.80 — Verger, Pierre. Bahia and the West Africa trade, 1549-1851. Ibadan, 1964.

Afr 14692.41.110 — Victor, Geraldo Bessa. Mucanda. Braga, 1964.

Afr 8377.10 — Villiers, Hans Heinrich Wicht de. Rivonia, operation Mayibuye. Johannesburg, 1964.

Afr 609.64.20 — Vstrecha s Afrikoi. Moscow, 1964.

Afr 2357.26 — Vulliez, Albert. Mers el-Kebir. Paris, 1964.

Afr 8677.36 — Waasdijk, Tom van. Public expenditure in South Africa. Johannesburg, 1964.

Afr 5057.11 — Wade, Abdoulaye. Economie de l'Ouest africain. Paris, 1964.

Afr 6392.35 — Walker, David. Economic growth in East Africa. Exeter, 1964.

Afr 8678.10.20 — Walker, Oliver. Kaffirs are livelier. London, 1964.

Afr 210.64.35 — Wallbank, T.W. Contemporary Africa. Princeton, N.J., 1964.

Afr 109.64.10 — Wallbank, T.W. Documents on modern Africa. Princeton, N.J., 1964.

Afr 6164.18 — Wallenstein, Immanuel. The road to independence. La Haye, 1964.

Afr 8300.16 — Watkins-Pitchford, Herbert. Besieged in Ladysmith. Pietermaritzburg, 1964.

Afr 115.55 — Wauthier, Claude. L'Afrique des africains. Paris, 1964.

Afr 6282.12 — Webster, James B. The African churches among the Yoruba. Oxford, 1964.

Afr 6392.37 — Weigt, Ernest. Beiträge zur Entwicklungspolitik in Afrika. Köln, 1964.

Afr 3986.964.15 — Weiss, Dieter. Wirtschaftliche Entwicklungsplanung in der Vereinigten Arabischen Republik. Koeln, 1964.

Afr 9448.75 — Welensky, Roy. Welensky's four thousand days. London, 1964.

Afr 2719.64.5 — Wellard, J.H. The great Sahara. London, 1964.

Afr 6460.80.5 — Whisson, Michael. Change and challenge (A study of the social and economic changes among the Kenya Luo). Nairobi, 1964.

Afr 10015.4 — Whiteley, Wilfred H. A selection of African prose. Oxford, 1964. 2v.

Afr 550.133 — Wieland, Robert Julius. For a better Africa. South Africa, 1964.

Afr 4115.25 — Wiet, Gaston. Cairo, city of art and commerce. 1st ed. Norman, 1964.

Afr 9439.64 — Wills, Alfred John. An introduction to the history of central Africa. London, 1964.

Afr 659.64 — Winid, Bogdan. Geografia gospodarcza Afryki, Afryka potnocna. Warszawa, 1964.

Afr 210.64 — Woddis, J. Africa, the way ahead. N.Y., 1964.

Afr 210.64.2 — Woddis, J. L'avenir de l'Afrique. Paris, 1964.

Afr 6060.64 — Wraith, R.E. Local government in West Africa. London, 1964.

Afr 6060.64.2 — Wraith, R.E. Local government in West Africa. N.Y., 1964.

Afr 5318.45 — Youla, Nabi. Mussa; ein Kind aus Guinea. Regensburg, 1964.

Afr 9839.64 — Young, Anthony. A geography of Malawi. London, 1964.

Afr Doc 3707.363.2F — Zambia. Second report of the May/June 1963 census of Africans. Lusaka, 1964.

Afr Doc 3709.305 — Zambia. Central Statistical Office. National accounts and balance of payments of Zambia, 1954-1964. Lusaka, 1964.

Afr 1338.13 — Zartman, I. William. Destiny of dynasty. Columbia, 1964.

Afr 1495.4 — Zartman, I.W. Morocco, problems of new power. N.Y., 1964.

Afr 210.64.80 — Ziegler, Jean. Sociologie de la nouvelle Afrique. Paris, 1964.

Afr 9436.13 — Zimbabwe African Peoples' Union. Zimbabwe. Cairo, 1964.

Afr 5335.2A — Zolberg, Aristide R. One-party government in the Ivory Coast. Princeton, N.J., 1964.

1965

Afr 11108.74.110 — Abrahams, Peter. A night of their own. London, 1965.

Afr 10621.9.100 — Abruquah, Joseph W. The catechist. London, 1965.

Afr 50.43 — Adam, Thomas R. Government and politics in Africa. 3d ed. N.Y., 1965.

Afr 11119.4.100 — Adams, Perseus. The land at my door. Cape Town, 1965.

Afr 45.65 — Adu, A.L. The civil service in new African states. London, 1965.

Afr 8038.10 — Afrikaanse kernensiklopedie. Kaapstad, 1965.

Afr 679.65.20 — Agbodeka, F. The rise of the nation states. London, 1965.

Afr 10621.41.100A — Aidoo, C.A.A. The dilemma of a ghost. Accra, 1965.

Afr 6096.8 — Ajayi, G.B. Introduction to the economics of West Africa. Rev. ed. Ibadan, 1965. 2v.

Afr 679.65.25 — Ajayi, J.F. Ade. A thousand years of West African history. London, 1965.

Afr 6282.15 — Ajayi, J.F. Aoe. Christian missions in Nigeria, 1841-1891. London, 1965.

Afr 626.153 — Akademiia Nauk SSSR. Institut Afriki. Ekonomika Afriki. Moskva, 1965.

Afr 626.148 — Akademiia Nauk SSSR. Institut Afrikii. Nezavisimye strany Afriki. Moskva, 1965.

Afr 6280.26.10 — Akiga. Akiga's story, the Tiv tribe. London, 1965.

Afr 10671.46.100 — Akpan, Ntieyong Udo. The wooden gong. London, 1965.

Afr 6176.42 — Alexander, Henry Templer. African tightrope. London, 1965.

Afr 2037.5.5 — Algeria. Ministère d'Orientation Nationale. Algérie, an II, 1962-1964. Alger, 1965?

Afr 2030.60.5 — Alleg, Henri. La question. Paris, 1965.

Afr 45.65.10 — Allott, Anthony N. Law and language. London, 1965.

Afr 12974.51.100 — Almeida, Modeste d'. Kétéyouli, l'étudiant noir. Lomé, 1965.

Afr 9448.77 — Alport, Cuthbert James McCall. The sudden assignment. London, 1965.

Afr 1869.65 — American University, Washington, D.C. Foreign Area Studies Division. Area handbook for Algeria. Washington, 1965.

Afr 1609.65 — American University, Washington D.C. Foreign Area Studies Division. Area handbook for Morocco. Washington, 1965.

Afr 5240.3 — Amin, Samir. Trois expériences africaines de développement. Paris, 1965.

Afr 6203.2 — Amosu, Margaret. Nigerian theses. Ibadan, 1965.

Afr 6282.22 — Amu, Josiah Wel-Lean Omo. The rise of Christianity in mid-western Nigeria. Lagos, 1965.

Afr 626.158 — Anguile, André G. L'Afrique sans frontières. Monaco, 1965.

Afr 2223.965 — Arcy, François d'. Essais sur l'économie de l'Algérie nouvelle. Paris, 1965.

Afr 6743.5 — Ardener, Edwin. Historical notes on the scheduled monuments of West Cameroon. Buea, 1965.

Afr 6275.110   Ariwoola, Olagoke. The African wife. London, 1965.
Afr 212.18   Armah, Kivesi. Africa's golden road. Kenyatta, 1965.
Afr 2819.65.5   Asal, Muhammad Sami. Die Entstehung Libyens als souveräner Staat. Inaug.-Diss. Berlin, 1965?
Afr 1623.965   Ashford, Douglas Elliott. Marocco-Tunisia. 1st ed. Syracuse, N.Y., 1965.
Afr 3340.25   Assassa, Sami. Die Entstehung der Vereinigten Arabischen Republik und die Entwicklung. Diss. Berlin, 1965.
Afr 11005.6   Astrinsky, Aviva. A bibliography of South African English novels, 1930-1960. Cape Town, 1965.
Afr 210.65.40   Austin, Dennis. Inter-state relations in Africa. 1st ed. Freiburg, 1965.
Afr 12672.3.110   Badian, S. La mort de Chaka. Paris, 1965.
Afr 7560.15   Balandier, Georges. La vie quotidienne au royaume de Kongo du XVI au XVIII siècle. Paris, 1965.
Afr 5396.2.5   Ballard, J.A. The Porto Novo incidents of 1923, politics in the colonial era. Ibadan, 1965.
Afr 4785.965.5   Balsan, Francois. A pied au Nord Somali. Paris, 1965.
Afr 2938.38   Bank of Libya. Economic Research Department. The development of public finance in Libya, 1944-1963. Tripoli, 1965.
Afr 11193.74.100   Baragwanath, Paul. The brave remain. Cape Town, 1965.
Afr 12002.2   Baratte, Thérèse. Bibliographie, auteurs africains et malgaches de langue française. Paris, 1965.
Afr 1369.65   Barbour, N. Morocco. London, 1965.
Afr 2650.3   Bardin, Pierre. La vie d'un douar. Paris, 1965.
Afr 7461.40   Barkay, Richard M. Public sector accounts of Liberia. Monrovia, 1965.
Afr 9196.6   Barker, Dudley. Swaziland. London, 1965.
Afr 6195.7   Bartels, Francis Lodovic. The roots of Ghana Methodism. Cambridge, 1965.
Afr 608.57.5   Barth, H. Travels and discoveries in north and central africa. London, 1965. 3v.
Afr 9149.65F   Battiss, Walter W. Limpopo. 1. ed. Pretoria, 1965.
Afr 6990.90.10   Baumann, Julius. Mission und Ökumene in Südwestafrika, Dargestellt am Lebenswerk. Leiden, 1965.
Afr 618.25   Beard, Peter Hill. The end of the game. N.Y., 1965.
Afr Doc 4007.364   Bechuanaland (Protectorate). Report on the census of the Bechuanaland Protectorate, 1964. Mafeking, South Africa? 1965?
Afr 8155.11.2   Becker, Peter. Dingane, King of the Zulu, 1828-1840. N.Y., 1965.
Afr 11200.21.100   Bee, David. Curse of Magira. 1st ed. N.Y., 1965.
Afr 5842.22   Benedict, Burton. Mauritius. London, 1965.
Afr 11203.59.100   Bennett, J. Main isherman. 1st American ed. Boston, 1965.
Afr 545.34   Benz, Ernst. Messianische Kirchen, Sekten und Bewegungen im heutigen Afrika. Leiden, 1965.
Afr Doc 6208.505   Bernard, Jean. Les industries du Sénégal. Paris, 1965.
Afr 2318.1.20   Berthier, Andre. Constantine. Toulouse, 1965.
Afr 2749.65   Besson, Ferny. Sahara, terre de vérité . Paris, 1965.
Afr 12922.7.110   Bhely-Quenum, Olympe. Le chant du lac. Paris, 1965.
Afr 5540.12   Bilbao, Rene. Le droit malgache de la nationalité. Paris, 1965.
Afr 5056.165   Binet, Jacques. Afrique en question, de la tribu à la nation. Tours, 1965.
Afr 8190.5.2   Bird, John. The annals of Natal, 1495 to 1845. Capetown, 1965. 2v.
Afr 7119.65   Birmingham, D. The Portuguese conquest of Angola. London, 1965.
Afr 8678.334   Black, Margaret. No room for tourists. London, 1965.
Afr 10018.4   Black Orpheus. Black Orpheus. N.Y., 1965.
Afr 626.142   Blair, Thomas Lucien Vincent. Africa, a market profile. N.Y., 1965.
Afr 8687.137.5   Blaxall, Arthur. Suspended sentence. London, 1965.
Afr 8687.137.10   Bleek, Wilhelm Heinrich Immanuel. The Natal diaries of Dr. W.H.I. Bleek, 1855-1856. Cape Town, 1965.
Afr 6210.42   Blitz, L. Franklin. The politics and administration of Nigerian government. N.Y., 1965.
Afr 4431.25   Boca, Angelo del. La guerra d'Abissinia, 1935-1941. Milano, 1965.
Afr 2819.65   Bodianskii, Vadim. Sovremennaia Liviia. Moskva, 1965.
Afr 7817.5   Bormann, Martin. Zwischen Kreuz und Fetisch. Bayreuth, 1965.
Afr 4431.15   Borra, Eduardo. Prologo di un conflitto. Milano, 1965.
Afr 1338.22   Bourely, Michel. Droit public marocain. v.1-2. Rabat, 1965.
Afr 635.90   Boute, Joseph. La démographie de la branche indo-pakistanaise d'Afrique. Louvain, 1965.
Afr 7575.98   Bouvier, Paule. L'accession du Congo belge à l'indépendance. Bruxelles, 1965.
Afr 3275.12.110   Boyle, C.A. Boyle of Cairo, a diplomatist's adventures in the Middle East. Kendal, 1965.
Afr 2030.346   Brace, Richard M. Algerian voices. Princeton, N.J., 1965.
Afr 10018.5   Brambilla, Cristina. Narrativa africana. Bologna, 1965.
Afr 9700.41   Brelsford, William Vernon. Generation of men. Salisbury, 1965.
Afr 9700.41.5.2   Brelsford, William Vernon. The tribes of Zambia. 2nd ed. Lusaka, 1965?
Afr 6738.48   Brendl, Oskar. Die Bundes-Republik Kamerun. Hagen, 1965.
Afr 8687.142   Bresler, Casparus Philippus. Tilt the sack. Pretoria, 1965.
Afr 6603.2   Bridgman, Jon. German Africa. Stanford, 1965.
Afr 8678.330   British Council of Churches. The future of South Africa. London, 1965.
Afr 626.143   Brokensha, David. Ecology and economic development in tropical Africa. Berkeley, 1965.
Afr 8377.3   Brokensha, Miles. The Fourth of July raids. Cape Town, 1965.
Afr 8190.20   Brookes, Edgar Harry. A history of Natal. Pietermaritzburg, 1965.
Afr 11229.67.110   Brown, J.A. The assassins. Johannesburg, 1965.
Afr 6390.86   Browne, Robert. Beyond the Cape of Hope. London, 1965.
Afr 9045.10.1   Bryant, Alfred T. Olden times in Zululand and Natal. Capetown, 1965.
Afr 210.28.2   Buell, Raymond Leslie. The native problem in Africa. London, 1965. 2v.
Afr 6542.16.10   Buganda. Planning Commission. The economic development of kingdom of Buganda. Kampala, 1965.
Afr 44622.89.122   al-Buhry, Hemed Abdallah. Utenzi wa Seyyidna Huseni bin Ali. Dar es Salaam, 1965.
Afr 44622.89.120   al-Buhry, Hemed Abdallah. Utenzi wa Seyyidna Huseni bin Ali. Dar es Salaam, 1965.
Afr 8210.20   Bulpin, Thomas Victor. Lost rails of the Transvaal. Johannesburg, 1965.

Afr 9439.65.5   Bulpin, Thomas Victor. To the banks of the Zambezi. Johannesburg, 1965.
Afr 6881.265   Burke, Fred George. Tanganyika. 1st ed. Syracuse, N.Y., 1965.
Afr 2030.465   Buron, Robert. Carnets politiques de la guerre d'Algérie. Paris, 1965.
Afr 2030.460.35   Buy, François. La République algérienne. Paris, 1965.
Afr 5488.20   Cabot, Jean. Le bassin du moyen Logone. Thèse. Paris, 1965.
Afr 4128.9   Caccia Dominioni di Sillavengo, Paolo. Alamein, 1933-1962. 9. ed. Milano, 1965.
Afr 530.35.3   Caetano, Marcello. Portugal e a internacionalização dos problemas africanos. 3. ed. Lisboa, 1965.
Afr 5235.128.2   Caillié, René. Journal d'un voyage à Temboctou et à Jenne, dans l'Afrique centrale. Paris, 1965?
Afr 4512.20   Caioli, Aldo. L'Italia di Fronte a Gineura, aspetti del conflitto italo-etiopico dalle origini alla conquista dell Impero. Roma, 1965.
Afr 9549.65   Cairns, H. Alan C. The clash of cultures. N.Y., 1965.
Afr 9549.65.5   Cairns, H. Alan C. Prelude to imperialism; British reactions to Central African society, 1840-1890. London, 1965.
Afr 5243.174.25   Calame-Griaule, Geneviève. Ethnologie et langage, la parole chez les Dogon. Paris, 1965.
Afr 40.65.5   California. University. University at Los Angeles. African Studies Center. African law, adaptation and development. Berkeley, 1965.
Afr 679.65.5A   California. University. University at Los Angeles. African Studies Center. Urbanization and migration in West Africa. Berkeley, 1965.
Afr 6720.65.2   Cameroun. Ministère de l'Information et du Tourisme. Les grandes dates du Cameroun. 2. éd. Yaoundé, 1965.
Afr 5053.38   Campbell, Michael J. The structure of local government in West Africa. The Hague, 1965.
Afr 8687.150   Carr, Barbara Comyns. Cherries on my plate. Cape Town, 1965.
Afr 9165.42.75   Cartwright, Alan Patrick. The corner house. Capetown, 1965.
Afr 8918.59.10   Casalis, E. The Basutos, or, Twenty-three years in South Africa. Cape Town, 1965.
Afr 1495.5   Cassaigne, Jean. La situation des Français au Maroc depuis l'indépendance, 1956-1964. Paris, 1965.
Afr 2209.65   Castel, Robert. Inoubliable Algérie. Paris, 1965.
Afr 3315.127   Cavenagh, Sandy. Airborne to Suez. London, 1965.
Afr 7068.4   Cesar, Amandio. Guine 1965, contra-atorque. Braga, 1965.
Afr 5482.10   Chambre de Commerce d'Agriculture et d'Industrie du Tchad. Situation economique de la Republique du Tchad. Fort-Lamy?, 1965.
Afr 2218.11   Charnay, Jean Paul. La vie musulmane en Algérie d'aprés la jurisprudence de la première moitié du XXe siècle. Paris, 1965.
Afr 210.65.35   Chataslnski, Jozef. Blizej afryki. Warszawa, 1965.
Afr 5387.10   Cheminault, R. L'artisanat. Paris, 1965. 2v.
Afr 6392.33   Cherniavsky, Mark. Development prospects in East-Africa: Kenya, Tanzania and Uganda. Bergen, 1965.
Afr 4559.65.10   Choleva, Emil. Etiopska dobrodruzstvi. Praha, 1965.
Afr 1280.30.5   Chouraqui, A. Les Juifs d'Afrique du Nord entre l'Orient et l'Occident. Paris, 1965.
Afr 109.65.25   Chu, Daniel. A glorious age in Africa, the story of three great African empires. 1st ed. Garden City, 1965.
Afr 6689.1   Church between colonial powers. London, 1965.
Afr 109.65.5   Ciba Foundation. Man and Africa. London, 1965.
Afr 5260.32   Clair, Andrée. Le Niger, pays à découvrir. Paris, 1965.
Afr 10673.48.140   Clark, John Pepper. A reed in the tide. London, 1965.
Afr 626.167   Clark, Paul Gordon. Development planning in East Africa. Nairobi, 1965.
Afr 8686.5   Clavier, Henri. Thomas Arbousset. Paris, 1965.
Afr 12016.3   Clive, Wake. An anthology of African and Malagasy poetry in French. London, 1965.
Afr 9165.71.10   Collier, Joy. The purple and the gold. Cape Town, 1965.
Afr 9295.5   Collins, William W. Free statia. Cape Town, 1965.
Afr 12005.2   Colloque sur la littérature africaine d'expression française, actes. Dakar, 1965.
Afr Doc 7372.361   Congo (Brazzaville). Service de Statistique. Recensement de Brazzaville, 1961; résultats définitifs. Paris, 1965.
Afr 6392.45   Conseil National du Patronat Français. Mission industrielle française en Afrique orientale et centrale britannique. Paris, 1965.
Afr 210.65.30   Cook, Arthur Norton. Africa, past and present. Ottowa, 1965.
Afr 10315.5   Cook, David. Origin East Africa. London, 1965.
Afr 8089.65   Cope, John Patrick. South Africa. N.Y., 1965.
Afr 2680.5   Coque, Roger. Nabeul et ses environs, étude d'une population tunisienne. Paris, 1965?
Afr 679.65.40   Coquery, Catherine. La découverte de l'Afrique. Paris, 1965.
Afr 5385.10   Cornevin, Robert. Le Dahomey. Paris, 1965.
Afr 150.66   Cortesão, Jaime. A expansão dos Portugueses no periodo Henriquino. Lisboa, 1965.
Afr 609.65   Cottrell, Kent. Sunburnt Africa, in pencil, paint, and prose. Hollywood, 1965.
Afr 6420.78   Cox, Richard. Kenyatta's country. London, 1965.
Afr 11310.52.100   Culwick, Arthur Theodore. Back to the trees. Cape Town, 1965.
Afr 50.55   Cunha, Joaquim Moreira da Silva. Politische Aspekte des neuen Afrika. Hamburg, 1965.
Afr 4060.8   Curt, Silvio. Nubia, storia di una civilta favolosa. Novara, 1965.
Afr 5183.965   Dakar. Chambre de Commerce. L'économie du Sénégal. 2. éd. Dakar, 1965.
Afr 5183.965.5   Dakar. Chambre de Commerce d'Agriculture et d'Industrie. Catalogue des principales productions industrielles du Sénégal. Dakar, 1965.
Afr 6143.65   Dalton, Kenneth Godfrey. A geography of Sierra Leone. Cambridge, Eng., 1965. 2v.
Afr 7815.35   Danois, Jacques. Mon frère bantu. Bruxelles, 1965.
Afr 11319.76.1120   Darlow, David John. In remembrance. Lovedale, 1965.
Afr 7122.85   Davezies, Robert. Les Angolais. Paris, 1965.
Afr 679.65.30   Davidson, Basil. The growth of African civilisation, West Africa, 1000-1800. London, 1965.
Afr 109.65.10   Davidson, Basil. A guide to African history. 1st ed. Garden City, N.Y., 1965.
Afr 4236.965F   Davis, Asa J. A note on ideological basis of union of church and state in Ethopia. Ibadan, 1965.

Afr 8369.65.5 Dawie (pseud.). Dawie, 1946-1964; 'n bloemlesing uit die geskrifte van Die Burger se politieke kommentator. Kaapstad, 1965.

Afr 10624.2.110 Dei-Anang, M. Ghana glory. London, 1965.

Afr 6455.160 Denis, Michaela. At home with Michaela. London, 1965.

Afr 1620.40 Dennis-Jones, Harold. Your guide to Morocco. London, 1965.

Afr 6210.41 Derrett, John Duncan Martin. Studies in the laws of succession in Nigeria. London, 1965.

Afr 5417.100 Deschamps, Hubert. Quinze ans de Gabon;...1839-1853. Paris, 1965.

Afr 12674.1.100 Dia, Amadou Cissé. Les derniers jours de Lat Dior. Paris, 1965.

Afr 6879.65 Dibble, James Birney. In this land of Eve. N.Y., 1965.

Afr 6277.124 Diejomaoh, Victor Peter. Economic development in Nigeria; its problems, challenges and prospects. Princeton, N.J., 1965.

Afr 20059.5 Dieterlen, Germaine. Textes sacrés d'Afrique noire. Paris, 1965.

Afr 7122.90 Diogo, Alfredo. O Brasil na restauração de Angola. Luanda, 1965.

Afr 5185.12 Diop, Abdoulaye. Société toucouleur et migration. Dakar, 1965.

Afr 4892.15 Djibonti, son port, son arrière-pays. Paris, 1965.

Afr 8678.332 Dominicus, Foort Comelius. Apartheid een wijze voorzorg. Utrecht, 1965.

Afr 7803.42 Dowdy, Homer E. Out of the jaws of the lion. 1st ed. N.Y., 1965.

Afr 11336.41.110 Drin, Michael. McKilty's bride. Cape Town, 1965.

Afr 2260.27 Le droit à indemnisation des Français d'Algérie atteints par des mesures de dépossession. Paris, 1965.

Afr 115.9.2 Dubois, William E. The world and Africa. N.Y., 1965.

Afr 8668.8 Dubow, Rhona. The status of women in South Africa. Cape Town, 1965.

Afr 618.28 Dupin, Henri. Expériences d'éducation sanitaire et nutritionnelle en Afrique. Paris, 1965.

Afr 555.22.17 Duplessis, J. A history of Christian missions in South Africa. Cape Town, 1965.

Afr 2609.65 Duvignaud, Jean. Tunisie. Lausanne, 1965.

Afr 10575.82.100 Easmon, R. Sarif. The new patriots. London, 1965.

Afr 4789.2 Eby, Omar. Sense and license. Scottsdale, 1965.

Afr 650.4 Edinburgh. University. African urbanization. London, 1965.

Afr 590.81 Edinburgh. University. The transatlantic slave trade from West Africa. Edinburgh, 1965.

Afr 590.79 Edressen, Halfdan. Solgt som slave. Oslo, 1965.

Afr 9439.65.10 Eeden, Guy Van. The crime of being white. Cape Town, 1965.

Afr 10675.10.110 Egbuna, Obi Benue. The anthill. London, 1965.

Afr 10675.47.170 Ekwensi, Cyprian. The great elephant-bird. London, 1965.

Afr 10005.6 Eliet, Edouard. Panorama de la littérature négro-africaine, 1921-62. Paris, 1965.

Afr 212.10 Emerson, Rupert. The political awakening of Africa. Englewood Cliffs, N.J., 1965.

Afr 4060.35 Emery, Walter Bryan. Egypt in Nubia. London, 1965.

Afr 6298.363 Enahoro, Anthony. Fugitive offender. London, 1965.

Afr 8686.24F Engelbrecht, Stephanus P. Album vir die geskiedenis van die Nederduitsch Hervormde Kerk van Afrika. Pretoria, 1965.

Afr 6282.20 Epelle, E.T. Writing a local church history, a short guide. Nsukka, Eastern Nigeria, 1965.

Afr 7580.22 Epstein, Howard M. Revolt in the Congo, 1960-64. N.Y., 1965.

Afr 5640.15.10 Esmenard, Jeand D', Vicomte. Gallieni. Paris, 1965.

Afr 3310.93 Estier, Claude. L'Egypte en révolution. Paris, 1965.

Afr 4236.965.5 Ethiopia. Ministry of Information. Religious freedom in Ethiopia. Addis Ababa, 1965.

Afr 609.65.25 Fagan, Brian M. Southern Africa during the Iron Age. London, 1965.

Afr 6277.98 Fairholm, G.W. Native authority finance patterns. Zaria, 1965.

Afr 6540.4.11 Fallers, Lloyd A. Bantu bureaucracy. Chicago, 1965.

Afr 635.89 Fani-Kazode, Remi. Blackism. Lagos, 1965.

Afr 4512.18 Faraci, Giuseppe. Etiopia, guerra epace. Torino, 1965.

Afr 626.144 Farer, Tom J. Financing African development. Cambridge, Mass., 1965.

Afr 7222.80 Faria, Dutra. Portugal do capricornio. Lisboa, 1965.

Afr 6542.45 Farina, Felice. Nel paese di bevitori di sangue; genti nuove alla ribalta! il popolo Karimojòng. Bologna, 1965.

Afr 7180.38.2 Felgas, Hélio. As populacões nativas do norte de Angola. 2. ed. Lisboa, 1965.

VAfr 679.65.35 Fenrych, Wiktor. Zapiski z Afriyki Zachodniej. Szczecin, 1965.

Afr 628.264.5 Fernandes, Florestan. A integrafão do negro na sociedade de classes. v.1-2. São Paulo, 1965.

Afr 2368.5.10 Février, Paul Albert. Fouilles de Sétif, les basiliques chrétiennes du quartier Nord-Ouest. Paris, 1965.

Afr 8378.200 First, Ruth. One hundred and seventeen days. N.Y., 1965.

Afr 6277.91 Fiskvik, Kjell. Development prospects of Nigeria, a draft report. Bergen, 1965.

Afr 505.47 Fokeev, German V. Oni ne khotiat ukhodit. Moskva, 1965.

Afr 5053.34 Foltz, William J. From French West Africa to the Mali federation. New Haven, 1965.

Afr 8110.14 Forbes, Vernon S. Pioneer travellers of South Africa. Cape Town, 1965.

Afr 8110.3.39 Forbes, Vernon Siegfried. Pioneer travellers of South Africa. Cape Town, 1965.

Afr 109.65.15 Fordham, Paul. The geography of African affairs. Baltimore, 1965.

Afr 6096.12 Forrest, Ona B. Financing development plans in West Africa. Cambridge, 1965.

Afr 8659.65.5 Fournier, Gilles. Vérité pour l'Afrique du Sud. Paris, 1965.

Afr Doc 5008.5 France. Institut National de la Statistique et des Etudes Economiques. Service de Cooperation. Afrique noire, Madagascar, Comores; démographie comparée. v.1-5,7,9-10. Paris, 1965-67. 3v.

Afr 5240.14 France. Ministère de la Coopération. Direction des affaires économiques et financières. 2. éd. Paris, 1965.

Afr 6686.40.2 France. Ministère de la Coopération. Economie et plan de développement, Republique Togolaise. 2. ed. Paris, 1965.

Afr 5442.13 France. Ministère de la Coopération. Direction des Affaires Economiques et Financières. Sous-Direction des Etudes Générales. Economie et plan de développement: Republique du Congo-Brazzaville. 3. éd. Paris, 1965.

Afr 6739.262.2 France. Ministère de la Coopération. Direction des Affaires Economiques et Financières. Sous-Direction des Etudes Générales. Economie et plan de développement, République fédérale du Cameroun. 2. éd. Paris, 1965.

Afr 6890.1 Freeman-Grenville, G.S.P. The French at Kilwa Island. Oxford, 1965.

Afr 5422.2F Gabon. Laws, statutes, etc. Loi no. 11-63 du 12/1/63 portant approbation du programme intérimaire de développement. Libreville, 1965.

Afr 5417.702 Gabon. Ministère de l'Information et du Tourisme. Gabon an 5.cinq années de progrès. Libreville, 1965.

Afr Doc 7407.361.15 Gabon. Service Nat+onal de la Statistique. Recensement et enquête demographiques, 1960-1961: ensemble du Gabon. Paris, 1965.

Afr 11907.9.100 Gabre-Medhin, Tsegaye Oda. Oak oracle. London, 1965.

Afr 6113.21 Gailey, Harry A. A history of the Gambia. N.Y., 1965.

Afr 9439.65 Gann, Lewis H. A history of Southern Rhodesia. London, 1965.

Afr 5055.65 Gavrilov, Nikolai Ivanovich. National liberation movement in West Africa. Moscow, 1965.

Afr 6218.5.2 Geary, Nevill. Nigeria under British rule. N.Y., 1965.

Afr 9502.13.5 Gelfand, M. African background. Cape Town, 1965.

Afr 6395.22 Ghai, Dharam P. Portrait of a minority, Asians in East Africa. London, 1965.

Afr Doc 1808.510 Ghana. Central Bureau of Statistics. Area sample survey of small manufacturing establishments, 1963. Accra, 1965.

Afr Doc 1807.362 Ghana. Central Bureau of Statistics. 1962 industrial census report. Accra, 1965.

Afr 6160.32 Ghana. Delimitation Commission. Revised report, 1964. Accra, 1965.

Afr 28.112 Ghana. University. Library. Union list of Africana and related journals, in the Balme Africana Library, Legon, Institute of African Studies Library, Legon, and the Padmore Research Library on African Affairs, Accra. Legon, 1965.

Afr 630.65 Gibbs, J.L. Peoples of Africa. N.Y., 1965.

Afr 6295.65 Gilles, H.M. Akufo, an environmental study of a Nigerian village community. Ibadan, 1965.

Afr 10062.2 Gleason, Judith Illsley. This Africa, novels by West Africans in English and French. Evanston, 1965.

Afr 4308.5 The glorious victories of 'Amda Seyon. Oxford, 1965.

Afr 9710.14 Gluckman, Max. The ideas in Barotse jurisprudence. New Haven, 1965.

Afr 8152.76.05 Godlonton, Robert. A narrative of the irruption of the Kaffir hordes into the eastern province of the Cape of Good Hope. Cape Town, 1965.

Afr 11433.74.150 Gordimer, N. Not for publication, and other stories. N.Y., 1965.

Afr 2731.15.100 Gorrée, Georges. Charles de Foucauld. Paris, 1965.

Afr 9448.76A Great Britain. Prime Minister. Southern Rhodesia. London, 1965.

Afr 11435.22.120 Green, George L. Almost forgotten, never told. Cape Town, 1965.

Afr 11435.22.130 Green, George L. I heard the old men say, secrets of the Cape that has vanished. 2nd ed. Cape Town, 1965.

Afr 4259.65 Greenfield, Richard. Ethiopia, a new political history. London, 1965.

Afr 4559.65.5 Greim, Armin. Im Reich des Negus. Leipzig, 1965.

Afr 5243.174.20 Griaule, Marcel. Conversations with Ogotemmeli. London, 1965.

Afr 2035.9 Guerin, Daniel. L'Algérie caporalisée. Paris, 1965.

Afr 6743.55 Guillard, Joanny. Galenpoui. Paris, 1965.

Afr 5318.3 Guinea (Republic). Secretariat d'Etat à l'Information et au Tourisme. La Guinée et son peuple. Conakry, 1965.

Afr 9748.475.5 Hall, Richard. Kaunda, founder of Zambia. London, 1965.

Afr 9689.65 Hall, Richard Seymour. Zambia. London, 1965.

Afr 715.26 Hallett, Robin. The penetration of Africa. N.Y., 1965.

Afr 8695.11 Halpern, Jack. South Africa's hostages. Harmondsworth, Eng., 1965.

Afr 8252.341.83 Hancock, William Keith. Smuts; study for a portrait. London, 1965.

Afr 9438.165 Hanna, A.J. The story of the Rhodesias and Nyasaland. 2nd ed. London, 1965.

Afr 500.82 Hanna, Alexander John. European rule in Africa. London, 1965.

Afr 3993.965 Hansen, Bent. Development and economic policy in the U.A.R. (Egypt). Amsterdam, 1965.

Afr 7175.77 Hanu, Jose. Quand le vent souffle en Angola. Bruxelles, 1965.

Afr 212.5 Hapgood, D. Africa, from independence to tomorrow. 1st ed. N.Y., 1965.

Afr 8678.337 Harrell, Muriel. Reserves and reservations. Johannesburg, 1965.

Afr 28.1A Harvard University. Library. Widener Library shelflist. No.2. Africa. Cambridge, 1965.

Afr 210.65.5 Hatch, J.C. A history of postwar Africa. London, 1965.

Afr 109.59.12 Hatch, John C. Africa today and tomorrow. 2nd ed. London, 1965.

Afr 8140.40 Hattersley, Alan Frederick. The convict crisis and the growth of unity. Pietermaritzburg, 1965.

Afr 7850.60 Hederén, Olle. Afrikanskt mellanspeli en berättelse om händelserna på Kaminabasen, 1960-1964. Ostra Ryd, 1965.

Afr 8687.228.5 Heerden, Petronella van. Die siestende koppie. Kaapstad, 1965.

Afr 7803.41 Hege, Ruth. We two alone. N.Y., 1965.

Afr 115.91 Heidelberg, Wolfgang. Grundzüge des Niederlassungsrechts in den afrikanischen Staaten. Hamburg, 1965. 2v.

Afr 115.111 Heinrich Barth zum Gedenken. Hamburg, 1965.

Afr 3675.68 Henderson, Kenneth David Driutt. Sudan Republic. London, 1965.

Afr 6095.365 Hennessy, M.N. Africa under my heart. N.Y., 1965.

Afr 7489.37 Henries, Richard A. Speeches of Dr. Richard A. Henries. London, 1965.

Afr 9295.452 Hill, Caroline. Orange days. Pietermaritzburg, 1965.

Afr 3710.16 Hill, R.L. Slatin Pasha. London, 1965.

Afr 1369.65.5 Hoffmann, E. Realm of the evening star. Philadelphia, 1965.

Afr 5342.65 Holas, Bohumil. Industries et cultures en Côte-d'Ivoire. Abidjan, 1965.

Afr 5345.10 Holas, Bohumil. Le séparatisme religieux en Afrique noire. Paris, 1965.

Afr 699.65 Hollingsworth, Lawrence H. A short history of the east coast of Africa. 2nd ed. London, 1965.

1965 - cont.

Afr 5849.2 Hollingworth, Derek. They came to Mauritius. London, 1965.
Afr 8685.96 Holm, Erik. Tier und Gott. Basel, 1965.
Afr 7225.5 Hoppe, Fritz. Portugiesisch-Ostafrika in der Zeit des Marquês de Pombal, 1750-1777. Berlin, 1965.
Afr 9161.24 Horrell, Muriel. Visit to Bantu areas of the northern Transvaal. Johannesburg, 1965.
Afr 7580.17 Hoskyns, Catherine. The Congo since independence. London, 1965.
Afr 212.11 Hugent, John Pear. Call Africa 999. N.Y., 1965.
Afr 5480.265 Hugot, Pierre. Le Tchad. Paris, 1965.
Afr 7175.75 Huibregtse, Pieter Kornelius. Angola is anders. Den Haag, 1965.
Afr 6470.231.20 Hurd, David. Kidnap at Kiunga. London, 1965.
Afr 1727.8 Ibn Talha, Abd al-Wahid. Moulay-Idriss du Zerhoun. Rabat, 1965.
Afr 10679.44.100 Ike, Vincent Chukwuemeka. Toads for supper. London, 1965.
Afr 6930.12 Imeshve, R.W. South West Africa. London, 1965.
Afr 6314.33.3 Ingham, K. A history of East Africa. 3. ed. London, 1965.
Afr 545.28 International African Seminar, 3d, Salisbury, Southern Rhodesia, 1960. African systems of thought. London, 1965.
Afr 626.136.2 International Conference on the Organization of Research and Training in Africa in Relation to the Study, Conservation and Utilization of Natural Resources, Lagos, 1964. Lagos Conference, 28 July to 6 Aug. 1964. Paris, 1965.
Afr 3993.965.5 Issawi, Charles Philip. Egypt in revolution. London, 1965.
Afr 7803.43 Italiaander, Rolf. Im Namen des Herrn im Kongo. Kassel, 1965.
Afr 4700.6 Italy. Comitato per la Documentazione dell'Opera dell'Italia in Africa. L'Italia in Africa; serie civile. Roma, 1965. 2v.
Afr 5343.2 Ivory Coast. Conseil Economique et Social. Rapport sur l'évolution économique et sociale de la Côte-d'Ivoire, 1960-1969. Abidjan, 1965.
Afr 8089.65.10 Jaarsreld, Floris. Die verlede spreek. Pretoria, 1965.
Afr 6979.65.5 Jaeger, Friedrich Robert. Geographische Landschaften Südwestafrikas. Windhoek, 1965.
Afr 10002.1 Jahn, Janheinz. A bibliography of Neo-African literature from Africa, America and the Carribean. London, 1965.
Afr 9704.1 Jamieson, Gladys. Zambia contrasts. London, 1965.
Afr 7580.25 Jarschel, Fritz. Lumumba. Kreuzweingarten/Rhld., 1965.
Afr 9165.82 Johannesburg. Non-European Affairs Department. Cultural change in Soweto. Johannesburg, 1965.
Afr 8331.20F Johannesburg. Public Library. Southern African municipal publications. Johannesburg, 1965.
Afr 8050.22 Johns, S.W. Marxism-Leninism in a multiracial environment. Thesis. Cambridge, 1965.
Afr 6176.30.80 Jones, Peter. Kwame Nkrumah and Africa. London, 1965.
Afr 6298.183 Jones-Quarley, K.A.B. A life of Azikiwe. Baltimore, Maryland, 1965.
Afr 5055.65.5 Jore, Leonce Alphonse Noel Henri. Les établissements français, sur la côte occidentale d'Afrique de 1758 à 1809. Paris, 1965.
Afr 150.42 Kake, Baba Ibrahima. Glossaire critique des expressions geographiques concernant le pays des noirs. Paris, 1965.
Afr 4008.10 Kamil, Murad. Aspects de l'Egypte copte. Berlin, 1965.
Afr 8678.395 Kap ohne Hoffnung; oder, Die Politik der Apartheid. Reinbek bei Hamburg, 1965.
Afr 8369.65 Karis, Thomas. The treason trial in South Africa. Stanford, Calif., 1965.
Afr 8678.331 Katzew, Henry. Apartheid and survival. Cape Town, 1965.
Afr 9639.65 Kay, George. Changing patterns of settlement and land use in the eastern province of Northern Rhodesia. Hull, 1965.
Afr 9860.475 Kayira, Regson. I will try. 1st ed. Garden City, N.Y., 1965.
Afr 6457.25 Kenya. Africa socialism and its application to planning in Kenya. Nairobi, 1965.
Afr 6410.8 Kenya. Committee of Review into the Kenya Institute of Administration. Report, 30th Nov., 1964. Nairobi, 1965.
Afr Doc 3207.364 Kenya. Economics and Statistics Division. Agriculture census, 1964; IV, large farm areas. Nairobi, 1965?
Afr Doc 3207.363 Kenya. Economics and Statistics Division. Census of industrial production, 1963. Nairobi, 1965.
Afr 6457.3 Kenya. Ministry of Economic Planning and Development. High-level manpower. Nairobi, 1965.
Afr 7580.21 Kestergat, Jean. Congo Congo. Paris, 1965.
Afr 10381.2 Kimenye, Barbara. Kalasanda. London, 1965.
Afr 678.97.10 Kingsley, M.H. Travels in West Africa. 3d ed. N.Y., 1965.
Afr 9558.510 Kirk, John. The Zambesi journal and letters of Dr. John Kirk, 1858-63. Edinburg, 1965. 2v.
Afr 6210.10 Kirk-Greene, A.H.M. The principles of native administration in Nigeria. London, 1965.
Afr 505.45 Kirkwood, Kenneth. Britain and Africa. London, 1965.
Afr 210.65.50A Kohn, Hans. African nationalism in the 20th century. Princeton, 1965.
Afr 210.65.15 Kollmannsperger, Franz. Von Afrika nach Afrika. Mainz, 1965.
Afr 4008.14 Koptologische Arbeitskonferenz, Halle, 1964. Koptologische Studien in der DDR. Halle, 1965.
Afr 6218.20 Kopytoff, Jean Herskovits. A preface to modern Nigeria. Madison, 1965.
Afr 6739.265.5 Kratz, Achim. Voraussetzungen und Möglichkeiten einer industriellen Entwicklung in Kamerun. Hamburg, 1965.
Afr 8678.325 Kuper, Leo. An African bourgeoisie. New Haven, 1965.
Afr 6478.2 Kuria, Lucas. A bibliography on politics and government in Uganda. Syracuse, 1965.
Afr 2000.19 Lacheraf, Mostafa. L'Algérie, nation et société. Paris, 1965.
Afr 28716.2 Lacroix, Pierre Francis. Poésie peule de l'Adamawa. Paris, 1965. 2v.
Afr 7580.19 Lafever, E.W. Crisis in the Congo. Washington, 1965.
Afr 12966.2 Lagneau, Lilyan. Neuf poètes camerounais. Yaounde, 1965.
Afr 6460.75 Lambert, H.E. Kikuyu social and political institutions. London, 1965.
Afr 810.2.5 Lander, R. The Niger journal of Richard and John Lander. N.Y., 1965.
Afr 4008.12 Laurent-Taeckholm, Vivi. Faraos barn. Stockholm, 1965.
Afr 7555.51 Lederer, Andre. Histoire de la navigation au Congo. Tervuren, 1965.
Afr 5046.6 Leduc, Michel. Les institutions monétaire africaines, pays francophones. Paris, 1965.
Afr 109.61.57 Legum, Colin. Africa, a handbook. 2d ed. London, 1965.
Afr 8687.271.5 Lehmann, Olga. Hans Merensky. Göttingen, 1965.

1965 - cont.

Afr 8678.350 Leiss, Amelia Catherine. Apartheid and United Nations collective measures. N.Y., 1965.
Afr 6280.9.30 Leith-Ross, Sylvia. African women. N.Y., 1965.
Afr 7850.42 Lekime, Fernand. Katanga, pays du cuirre. Verviers, 1965.
Afr 8289.65 Lemay, Godfrey Hugh Lancelot. British supremacy in South Africa, 1899-1907. Oxford, 1965.
Afr 2662.5 Lepotier, Adolphe Auguste Marie. Bizerte. Paris, 1965.
Afr 5285.277.10 Leroy Ladurie, Marie. Pâques africaines. Paris, 1965.
Afr 1713.4.10 Letourneau, Roger. La vie quotidienne à Fes en 1900. Paris, 1965.
Afr 4559.65 Levine, Donald Nathan. Wax and gold. Chicago, 1965.
Afr 4590.2 Lewis, Herbert Samuel. A Galla monarchy. Madison, Wisconsin, 1965.
Afr 4766.35 Lewis, I.M. The modern history of Somaliland. London, 1965.
Afr 679.65.15 Lewis, William A. Politics in West Africa. London, 1965.
Afr 212.9 Lewis, William Hubert. French-speaking Africa. N.Y., 1965.
Afr Doc 5602.5 Library of Congress. African Section. Madagascar and adjacent islands; a guide to official publications. Washington, 1965.
Afr Doc 3502.5 Library of Congress. African Section. The Rhodesias and Nyasaland. Washington, 1965.
Afr 2938.34.5 Libya. Ministry of Planning and Development. A summary of the evolution of planning institutions in Libya. Tripoli, 1965.
Afr 7582.4 Liège. Université. Fondation pour les Recherches Scientifiques en Afrique Central. Recherches sur le développement rural en Afrique central. Liège, 1965.
Afr 7219.65 Lisbon. Universidade Tecnica. Instituto Superior de Ciências Sociais e Politica Ultramarina. Moçambique; curso de Extensão Universitária, ano lectivo de 1964-1965. Lisboa, 1965.
Afr 6769.65 Listowel, Judith. The making of Tanganyika. London, 1965.
Afr 679.65.10 Little, Kenneth Lindsay. West African urbanization. Cambridge, Eng., 1965.
Afr 109.65.20 Liubimov, Nikolai N. Afrika v mirovoi ekonomike i politike. Moskva, 1965.
Afr 9558.110 Livingstone, David. David Livingstone and the Rovuma. Edinburgh, 1965.
Afr 9489.65.5 Lloyd, Frank. Rhodesian patrol. Ilfracombe, 1965.
Afr 5390.2 Lombard, Jacques. Structures de type féodal en Afrique noire. Paris, 1965.
Afr 7560.18.2 Lopes, Duarte. Description du royaume de Congo et des contrées environnantes parFilippo Pigafetta et Duarte Lopes (1951). 2.ed. Louvain, 1965.
Afr 6565.44A Loschie, Michael F. Zanzibar, background to revolution. Princeton, N.J., 1965.
Afr 7549.65 Loth, Heinrich. Kongo, heisses Herz Afrikas. Geschichte des Landes bis auf unsere Tage. Berlin, 1965.
Afr 8687.262.5 Louw, Andries Andriaan. Andrew Louw van Morgenster. Kaapstad, 1965.
Afr 6010.10.1 Lugard, F.D. The dual mandate in British Tropical Africa. 5th ed. Hamden, Conn., 1965.
Afr 6010.10.2 Lugard, F.D. The dual mandate in British Tropical Africa. 5th ed. London, 1965.
Afr 6214.1.5 Lugard, Flora Louisa. A tropical dependency. N.Y., 1965.
Afr 28.99 Lystad, Robert A. The African world. London, 1965.
Afr 609.65.10 McEwan, Peter J.M. The study of Africa. London, 1965. 4v.
Afr 5749.65.5 Madagascar. v.1-2. Chambéry (Savoie), 1965-1966.
Afr 3675.67 Al-Mahdi, Mandur. A short history of the Sudan. London, 1965.
Afr 3979.59.10 Mahmond, Zaki Naguib. The land and people of Egypt. Rev.Ed. Philadelphia, 1965.
Afr Doc 5607.362 Malagasy Republic. Institut National de la Statistique et de la Recherche Economique. Recensements urbains. Tananarive, 1965- 2v.
Afr 9850.3F Malawi. Ministry of Natural Resources. Development policies and plans, 1965-1969. Zomba, 1965?
Afr 9060.27 Malherbe, Janie. Port Natal. Cape Town, 1965.
Afr 8678.223 Mandela, Nelson Rolihlahla. L'apartheid. Paris, 1965.
Afr 8678.321.5 Mandela, Nelson Rolihlahla. No easy walk to freedom. London, 1965.
Afr 8678.353 Manning, Charles Anthony Woodward. The British churches and South Africa. London, 1965.
Afr 3310.10.85 Mansfield, Peter. Nasser's Egypt. Harmondsworth, 1965.
Afr 3199.54.2 Marlowe, J. A history of modern Egypt and Anglo-Egyptian relations. 2d ed. Hamden, 1965.
Afr 8678.341 Marof, Achkar. Racism in South Africa. N.Y., 1965.
Afr 699.57.3 Marsh, Zoe. An introduction to the history of East Africa. 3. ed. Cambridge, Eng., 1965.
Afr 11558.78.100 Martins, Harper. Nongalazi of the Bemba. Ilfrawmbe, 1965.
Afr 212.6 Marvin, D.K. Emerging Africa in world affairs. San Francisco, 1965.
Afr 9610.16 Marwick, Maxwell Gay. Sorcery in its social setting. Manchester, 1965.
Afr Doc 2809.300 Mauritius. Central Statistical Office. Abstract of economic statistics. Port Louis? 1965?
Afr Doc 2807.364F Mauritius. Central Statistical Office. The census of industrial production, 1964. Port Louis, 1965.
Afr 5417.2 Mba, Léon. Discours, messages. Libreville, 1965.
Afr 8678.320.5 Mbata, J.C.M. Urban Bantu councils. Johannesburg, 1965.
Afr 1105.5 Meinicke-Kleint, Heinz. Algerien, Marokko, Tunesien. Berlin, 1965.
Afr 12002.5 Memmi, Albert. Bibliographie de la littérature nord-africaine d'expression française, 1945-1962. Paris, 1965.
Afr 2030.464.44 Merle, Robert. Ahmed Ben Bella. Paris, 1965.
Afr 212.44 Meyer, Frank S. The African nettle, dilemmas of an emerging continent. N.Y., 1965.
Afr 212.34 Mezu, Sebastian Okeckukure. The philosophy of Pan-Africanism. Washington, 1965.
Afr 9327.65 Middleton, Coral. Bechuanaland. Cape Town, 1965.
Afr 6540.7.5 Middleton, J. The Lugbara of Uganda. N.Y., 1965.
Afr 6585.1 Middleton, John. Zanzibar. London, 1965.
Afr 5119.65 Milcent, Ernest. Au carrefour des options africaines, le Sénégal. Paris, 1965.
Afr 11563.49.100 Miller, Ruth. Floating island, poems. Cape Town, 1965.
Afr 8252.341.85 Mincher, Kathleen. I lived in his shadow. Capetown, 1965.
Afr 5247.35 Miner, H.M. The primitive city of Timbuctoo. Garden City, 1965.
Afr 28715.2 Mohamadou, Eldridge. Contes et poèmes foulbé de la Bénoué-Nord-Cameroun. Yaounde, 1965.
Afr 6743.65 Mohamadou, Eldridge. L'histoire de Tibati, chefferie Foulbé du Cameroun. Yaoundé, 1965.

1965 - cont.

Afr 609.65.15 Mohl, Max. Einmal Afrika und Zurück. Gütersloh, 1965. 4v.

Afr 2030.465.5 Moinet, Bernard. Journal d'une agonie. Paris, 1965.

Afr 212.7 Molnar, T.S. Africa, a political travelogue. N.Y., 1965.

Afr 550.8.50 Montclos, Xavier de. Lavigerie, le saint-siège et l'Église, de l'avènement de Pié IX à l'avènement de Léon XIII, 1846-1878. Paris, 1965.

Afr 10733.66.100 Moore, Bai T. Ebony dust. Liberia, 1965.

Afr 2535.8 Moore, Clement Henry. Tunisia since independence. Berkeley, 1965.

Afr 10055.5 Moore, Gerald. African literature and the universities. Ibadan, 1965.

Afr 210.65 Moraas, Francis Robert. The importance of being black. N.Y., 1965.

Afr 6192.93 Morgan, Clyde. Background to Ghana. 1st ed. London, 1965.

Afr 1623.965.13 Morocco. Division de la Coordination Economique et du Plan. Etude sur le commerce intérieur. Rabat, 1965? 3v.

Afr 1623.965.10 Morocco. Division de la Coordination Economique et du Plan. Three year plan, 1965-1967. Rabat, 1965.

Afr 8160.25 Morris, Donald R. The washing of the spears. N.Y., 1965.

Afr 50.52 Moscow. Universitet Druzhby Narodov. Kafedra Inczhdunarodnogo Prava. Nezavisimaia Afrika v dokumentakh. Moskva, 1965.

Afr 609.65.50 Mountjoy, Alan. Africa, a geographic study. London, 1965.

Afr 6686.48.15F Müller, Julius Otto. Enquête sociologique "Le paysan face au développement". Munich, 1965.

Afr 8685.27.20 Mukhamedova, Dil'bar. Iz istorii rasovoi diskriminatsii indiitsev v Iuzhnoi Afrike. Tashkent, 1965.

Afr 7946.10 Mulago, Vicent. Un visage africain du christianisme. Paris, 1965.

Afr 550.141 Mullin, Joseph. The Catholic Church in modern Africa. London, 1965.

Afr 9339.65 Munger, Edwin S. Bechuanaland. London, 1965.

Afr 8377.1 Munger, Edwin S. Notes on the formation of South African foreign policy. Pasadena, 1965.

Afr 6686.48.40F Munich. Institut für Wirtschaftsforschung. Les finances publiques du Togo, budget-fiscalité; situation, 1965-perspectives, 1970. München, 1965.

Afr 6686.48.20F Munich. Institut für Wirtschaftsforschung. Plan de développement économique et social, 1966-1970; l'artisanat togolais. Munich, 1965.

Afr 6686.48.30F Munich. Institut für Wirtschaftsforschung. Plan de développement économique et social, 1966-1970; le commerce au Togo. Munich, 1965.

Afr 2035.7 Naegelen, Marcel. Une route plus large que longue. Paris, 1965.

Afr 7850.56 Nagy, Laszló. Katanga. Lausanne, 1965.

Afr 3310.10.40 Nasser, G.A. Pre-election speeches in Assiut, March 8, 1965. Cairo, 1965.

Afr 8678.13.45 Natal. University. A study of the social circumstances and characteristics of Bantu in the Durban region. Durban, 1965. 2v.

Afr 11598.89.100 Naude, Adele. Only a setting forth, poems. Cape Town, 1965.

Afr 630.65.10 De Negro-Afrikaanse mens en zijn cultuur. Brugge, 1965.

Afr 2442.5 Néo-Destour Congrès, 7th, Bizerte. Septième congrès. Tunis, 1965.

Afr 6057.65 Newbury, C.W. British policy towards West Africa. Oxford, 1965.

Afr 8659.65 Newman, Bernard. South African journey. London, 1965.

Afr 10434.127.110 Ngugi, James. The river between. London, 1965.

Afr 5219.60.5 Niane, D.T. Sundiata. London, 1965.

Afr 10584.14.100 Nicol, Davidson. The truly married woman. London, 1965.

Afr 10584.14.110 Nicol, Davidson. Two African tales. Cambridge, Eng., 1965.

Afr 8678.329 Nielsen, Waldemar A. African battle line. 1st ed. N.Y., 1965.

Afr 6277.85F Nigeria, Mid-Western. Mid-western Nigeria development plan, 1964-68. Benin City, 1965.

Afr Doc 2307.363.10F Nigeria. Federal Census Office. Population census of Nigeria, 1963. Northern region. Lagos, 1965. 5v.

Afr 6277.120.5 Nigeria. Federal Ministry of Economic Development. Guide to technical assistance in Nigeria. Lagos, 1965.

Afr 6282.37 Nigeria. National Archives. Index for history of Yoruba Mission (CM.S) 1844-1915, in the National Archives at the University of Ibadan, Western Nigeria. Ibadan, 1965? 5v.

Afr 55.32.2 Niven, Cecil R. Nine great Africans. N.Y., 1965.

Afr 11611.66.110 Nkosi, Lewis. Home and exile. London, 1965.

Afr 6176.30.15A Nkrumah, Kwame. Consciencism. N.Y., 1965.

Afr 6176.30.20 Nkrumah, Kwame. Le consciencisme. Paris, 1965.

Afr 626.146 Nkrumah, Kwame. Neo-colonialism. London, 1965.

Afr 609.65.20 Nolan, Cynthia. One traveller's Africa. London, 1965.

Afr 626.152 Nyasaland Economic Symposium. Economic development in Africa. Oxford, 1965.

Afr 6333.65 Nye, Joseph Samuel. Pan-Africanism and East African integration. Cambridge, 1965.

Afr 10684.99.100 Nzekwu, Onuora. High life for lizards. London, 1965.

Afr 13284.99.100 Nzouankeu, Jacques Mariel. Le souffle des ancêtres; nouvelles. Yaoundé, 1965.

Afr 618.30 Obukar, Charles. The modern African. London, 1965.

Afr 210.65.45 Odede, Simon. Nigerian position in the intra-African situation up to May, 1963. The Hague, 1965.

Afr 6210.54 Ohonbamu, Obarogie. The Nigerian constitution and its review. Onitsha, 1965.

Afr 6275.106 Okakor-Omali, Dilim. A Nigerian villager in two worlds. London, 1965.

Afr 6277.73 Okechuku, Ikechuku. Nigeria, socialism or capitalism. Port Harcourt, 1965.

Afr 6277.27.5 Okigbo, Pius N.C. Nigerian public finance. Evanston, 1965.

Afr 6277.77 Oloko, Olatunde. A study of socio-economic factors affecting agricultural productivity in parts of Ondo province of Western Nigeria. Ibadan, 1965. 3 pam.

Afr 650.6 Oram, Nigel. Towns in Africa. London, 1965.

Afr 5303.4 Organization for Economic Cooperation and Development. Development Center. Bibliographie sur la Guinee. Paris, 1965.

Afr 8835.48 Orpen, Neil. Gunners of the Cape. Cape Town, 1965.

Afr 6214.3.2 Orr, Charles William James. The making of Northern Nigeria. 2nd ed. London, 1965.

Afr 2938.35 Ortner-Heun, Irene. Das Entwicklungsland Libyen. Köln, 1965.

Afr 628.265.5 Osei, Gabriel Kingsley. Forgotten great Africans. London, 1965.

1965 - cont.

Afr 6456.5 Osogo, John. Life in Kenya in the olden days, the Baluyia. Nairobi, 1965.

Afr 6470.278 Osogo, John. Nabongo Mumia of the Baluyia. Nairobi, 1965?

Afr 12785.89.110 Ousmane, Sembene. L'harmattan. Paris, 1965.

Afr 12785.89.140 Ousmane, Sembene. Vehi-ciosane, ou Blanche-genèse, suivi du Mandat. Paris, 1965.

Afr 8688.5.20 Pama, C. Lions and virgins. Cape Town, 1965.

Afr 10636.4.100 Parkes, Frank K. Songs from the wilderness. London, 1965.

Afr 5549.65.5 Pascal, Roger. La République Malgache. Paris, 1965.

Afr 8338.230 Paton, Alan. South African tragedy. N.Y., 1965.

Afr 45.65.5 Payne, Denis. African independence and Christian freedom. London, 1965.

Afr 7809.65.5 Peeters, Leo. Les limites forêt-savane dans le nord du Congo en relation avec le milieu géographique. Bruxelles, 1965.

Afr 210.65.10 Pepy, Daniel. Les états africains et leurs problèmes. Paris, 1965. 2v.

Afr 4700.5.5 Perticone, Giacomo. La politica coloniale dell'Italia. Roma, 1965.

Afr 6390.81 Petrov, Valeri. Afrikanski belezhnik. Sofiia, 1965.

Afr 4430.61.2 Pignatelli, L. La guerra dei sette mesi. Milano, 1965.

Afr 9839.65 Pike, John G. Malawi, a geographical study. London, 1965.

Afr 5010.3 Poirier, Jean. Etudes de droit africain et de droit malgache. Paris, 1965.

Afr 3305.25 Politi, Elie I. L'Egypte de 1914 à Suez. Paris, 1965.

Afr 6164.22 Potekhin, Ivan I. Stanovlenie novoi Gany. Moskva, 1965.

Afr 8687.265.10 Pretorius, Gert. Die Malans van Môrewag. Kaapstad, 1965.

Afr 6465.59 Prins, Adriaan Hendrik Johan. Sailing from Lamu. Assen, 1965.

Afr 6277.82 Proehl, Paul O. Foreign enterprise in Nigeria, laws and policies. Chapel Hill, 1965.

Afr 210.65.25 Prokopczuk, Jerzy. Zarys nowozytnej historii Afryki. Warszawa, 1965.

VAfr 6192.98 Pundik, Herbert. Ghana; 20 stammer-én stat. København, 1965.

Afr 609.65.35 Quilici, Folco. I mille fuochi. Bari, 1965.

Afr 8678.340 Rainero, Romain. La segregazione razziale nel Sud Africa. Milano, 1965.

Afr 4575.7 Rait, Mariia V. Narody Efiopii. Moskva, 1965.

Afr 5549.65.10 Ralaimihoatra, Edouard. Histoire de Madagascar. Tananarive, 1965. 2v.

Afr 10005.4 Ramsaran, J.A. New approaches to African literature. Ibadan, 1965.

Afr 5829.65 Rassool, S. Hassam A. Il Maurice, creuset de l'Ocean Indien. Paris, 1965.

Afr 7835.4 Reed, David E. One hundred and eleven days in Stanleyville. 1st ed. N.Y., 1965.

Afr 10016.10 Reed, John. A book of African verse. London, 1965.

Afr 14805.1 Reis, Fernando. Soiá. Braga, 1965.

Afr 618.32 Rencontres Internationales, Bouake, Ivory Coast, January 1962. Tradition et modernisme en Afrique noire. Paris, 1965.

Afr 545.38 Rencontres Internationales, Bouake, Ivory Coast, Oct. 1962. Les religions africaines traditionelles. Paris, 1965.

Afr 9448.56 Rhodesia (British Colony). The demand for independence in Rhodesia. Salisbury, 1965.

Afr Doc 3807.362.5F Rhodesia (British Colony). Central Statistical Office. The census of distribution in 1962 wholesale and retail trade and selected services. Salisbury, 1965.

Afr Doc 3807.361F Rhodesia (British Colony). Central Statistical Office. Final report on the September 1961 census of employees. Salisbury, 1965.

Afr Doc 3809.510 Rhodesia (British Colony). Central Statistical Office. Income tax statistics: income years 1953/54-1962/63. Salisbury, 1965.

Afr Doc 3891.363F Rhodesia (British Colony). Central Statistical Office. Report on the urban African budget survey in Umtali, 1963. Salisbury, 1965.

Afr Doc 3889.363F Rhodesia (British Colony). Central Statistical Office. Report on urban African budget survey in Salisbury, 1963/64. Salisbury, 1965.

Afr Doc 3807.361.5F Rhodesia (British Colony). Central Statistical Office. 1961 census of the European, Asian coloured population. Salisbury, 1965?

Afr Doc 3819.5 Rhodesia (British Colony). Constitution. The Constitution of Rhodesia, 1965. Salisbury, 1965.

Afr Doc 3709.550F Rhodesia and Nyasaland. Central Statistical Office. First report on Urban African budget surveys held in Northern Rhodesia, May to Aug., 1960. Salisbury, 1965. 2 pam.

Afr 1258.17.15 Riley, J. Sufferings in Africa; Captain Riley's narrative. N.Y., 1965.

Afr 3315.125.2 Robertson, Terence. Crisis, the inside story of the Suez conspiracy. London, 1965.

Afr 3315.125 Robertson, Terence. Crisis, the inside story of the Suez conspiracy. 1st ed. N.Y., 1965.

Afr 609.65.45 Rodionov, Viktor N. Afrika na styke stoletii. Leningrad, 1965.

Afr 7309.65 Rodrigues Júnior, José. Moçambique. Lisboa, 1965.

Afr 2035.20 Rogati, Elio. La seconda rivoluzione algeriana. Roma, 1965.

Afr 6095.365.5 Rosenberger, Homer Tope. Letters from Africa. Washington, 1965.

Afr 30.6.3 Rosenthal, Eric. Encyclopaedia of Southern Africa. 3d ed. London, 1965.

Afr 9704.2 Rotberg, Robert Irwin. Christian missionaries and the creation of Northern Rhodesia, 1880-1924. Princeton, N.J., 1965.

Afr 9560.20A Rotberg, Robert Irwin. The rise of nationalism in central Africa. Cambridge, 1965.

Afr 710.60 Rotberg, Robert Irwin. A political history of tropical Africa. N.Y., 1965.

Afr 11764.12.102 Sachs, Bernard. Personalities and places. 2nd series. Johannesburg, 1965.

Afr 8678.356 Sachs, Emil Solomon. The anatomy of apartheid. London, 1965.

Afr 12639.18.100 Sadji, Abdoulaye. Nini, mulâtresse du Sénégal. 2. éd. Paris, 1965.

Afr 12639.18.110 Sadji, Abdoulaye. Tounka, nouvelle. Paris, 1965.

Afr 1069.65 Sahli, Mohamed C. Décoloniser l'histoire. Paris, 1965.

Afr 4070.65.5 Said, Beshir Mohammed. The Sudan. London, 1965.

Afr 3715.12 Sanderson, George Neville. England, Europe and the upper Nile, 1882-1899. Edinburgh, 1965.

Afr 7122.78 Santos, Eduardo dos. Maza. Lisboa, 1965.

Afr 6280.58   Scarritt, J.R. Political change in a traditional African clan. Denver, 1965.

Afr 43316.21   Schapera, Isaac. Praise-poems of Tswana chiefs. Oxford, 1965.

Afr 5869.65   Scherer, André. Histoire de la Réunion. Paris, 1965.

Afr 6886.3   Schneider, Karl-Günther. Dar es Salaam. Wiesbaden, 1965.

Afr 1550.38   Schoettle, Hermann. Die Times in der ersten Marokkokrise. Vaduz, 1965.

Afr 6214.32   Schwarz, Frederick August Otto. Nigeria; the tribes, the nation, or the race. Cambridge, 1965.

Afr 50.45   Scipio. Emergent Africa. Boston, 1965.

Afr 9190.3   Scutt, Joan F. The story of Swaziland. Mbabane, 1965?

Afr 5183.965.10   Senegal. Deuxième plan quadriennal de développement économique et social, 1965-1969. v.1-3. Dakar?, 1965.

Afr 5180.50   Sénégal. Ministére du Développement. Cartes pour servir à l'aménagement du territoire. Dakar, 1965.

Afr 5184.25   Sènégal. Ministére du Développement du Plan et Economie Générale. Deuxième plan quadriennal. Pts. 1-2. Dakar?, 1965.

Afr 12639.24.29   Senghor, L.S. Prose and poetry. London, 1965.

Afr 5255.65   Séré de Rivières, Edmond. Histoire du Niger. Paris, 1965.

Afr 4785.965   Sergeeva, Irina S. Somaliiskaia Respublika. Moskva, 1965.

Afr 1957.31   Serval, Pierre. Alger fut à lui. Paris, 1965.

Afr 9448.78   Shamugawia, Nathan M. Crisis in Rhodesia. London, 1965.

Afr 115.108   Shinnie, Margaret. Ancient African kingdoms. London, 1965.

Afr Doc 1707.363   Sierra Leone. Central Statistics Office. 1963 population census Sierra Leone. Freetown, 1965.

Afr 11005.4   Silbert, Rachel. Southern African drama in English, 1900-1964. Johannesburg, 1965.

Afr 679.65   Simms, R.P. Urbanization in West Africa. Evanston, 1965.

Afr 5385.37   Simon, Marc. Souvenirs de brousse, 1905-1910. Paris, 1965.

Afr 9170.25   Siwundhla, Alice Princess. Alice Princess. Omaha, 1965.

Afr 2731.15.80   Six, Jean F. Witness in the desert, the life of Charles de Foucauld. N.Y., 1965.

VAfr 3675.69   Skuratowicz, Witold. Sudan. Warszawa, 1965.

Afr 6192.71   Sliwka-Szczerbic, W. Harmattan i wielki deszcz. Wyd. 1. Warszawa, 1965.

Afr 8160.26F   Smail, J.L. Historical monuments and battlefields in Natal. Cape Town, 1965.

Afr 10839.55.110   Smith, Wilbur Addison. Iets moet sterf. Johannesburg, 1965.

Afr 5230.8   Snyder, Frank Gregory. One-party government in Mali. New Haven, 1965.

Afr 5282.8   Société d'Aide Technique et de Cooperation. Données critiques sur la campagne depuits villageois encadrée par la SATEC en Haute-Volta. Paris, 1965.

Afr 6739.265   Société d'Etudes pour le Développement Economique et social. Développement industriel au Cameroun. Paris, 1965.

Afr 5488.16F   Société d'Etudes pour le Développement Economique et Social. Etude socio-économique de la ville d'Abéché. Paris, 1965.

Afr 6686.48.25F   Société d'Etudes pour le Développement Économique et Social, Paris. Plan de développement, 1966-1970: organization administrative et développement. Paris, 1965.

Afr 6686.48.35F   Société d'Etudes pour le Développement Économique et Social, Paris. Plan de développement économique et social, 1966-1970: scolarisation. Paris, 1965.

Afr 6686.48.45F   Société d'Etudes pour le Développement Économique et Social, Paris. Plan de développement économique et social, 1966-1970. Paris, 1965.

Afr 5346.6   Société d'Etudes pour le Développement Economique et Social. Région de Korhogo. T.1-8. Paris, 1965. 3v.

Afr 6277.84   Sokolski, Alan. The establishment of manufacturing in Nigeria. N.Y., 1965.

Afr 10689.68.100   Solarin, Tai. Thinking with you. Iheja, 1965.

Afr 1623.965.5   Solonitskii, Aleksandr S. Sotsial'no-ekonomicheskoe razvotie sovremennogo Marokko. Moskva, 1965.

Afr 28.37   Sommer, John W. Bibliography of African geography, 1940-1964. Hanover, N.H., 1965

Afr 626.141   Sousa, Alfredo de. Economia e sociedade em Africa. Lisboa, 1965.

Afr Doc 4308.145   South Africa. Bureau of Statistics. Verslag oor geboortes Suid-Afrikaen suidwes-Afrika, 1958 tot 1963. Report on births. Pretoria, 1965.

Afr 8678.36   South Africa. Department of Information. The progress of the Bantu peoples towards nationhood. Pretoria, 1965?

Afr 8045.3   South Africa. Department of Information. Progress through separate development, South Africa in peaceful transition. N.Y., 1965.

Afr 6979.65   South Africa. Department of Information. South West Africa, the land, its peoples and their future. Pretoria, 1965.

Afr 8045.7   South Africa. Parliament. House of Assembly. Report of the Select Committee on the subject of the constitution amendment bill. Cape Town, 1965.

Afr 8676.62.12   South Africa Foundation. South Africa in the sixties. 2nd ed. Johannesburg, 1965.

Afr 8809.65   South African heritage, from van Riebeeck to nineteenth century times. Cape Town, 1965.

Afr 10689.67.140   Soyinka, W. The interpreters. London, 1965.

Afr 10689.67.150   Soyinka, W. The road. London, 1965.

Afr 8095.88   Spence, J.E. Republic under pressure. London, 1965.

Afr 8088.91.5   Spohr, Otto. Indexes to Limner (R.W. Murray), pen and ink sketches. Cape Town, 1965.

Afr 6498.65   Stacey, T. Summons to Ruwenzori. London, 1965.

Afr 609.65.30   Steffen, Don Carl. The splendour of Africa. N.Y., 1965.

Afr 11807.24.100   Stern, Rhona. The bird flies blind. London, 1965.

Afr 8377.10.10   Strydom, Lauritz. Rivonia unmasked. Johannesburg, 1965.

Afr 9049.7   Sturges, Stanley G. In the valley of seven cities. Washington, D.C., 1965.

Afr Doc 1319.58   Sudan. The National Charter of the Coalition Government. n.p., 1965?

Afr Doc 1385.5F   Sudan. Department of Statistics. Ordurman household budget survey. Khartoum, 1965.

Afr Doc 1307.365   Sudan. Department of Statistics. Population and housing survey, 1964-65. Khartoum, 1965. 11v.

Afr 6930.10   Sweden. Utrikesdepartementet. Faktasamling angaende Sydvaestatrikafra'gan i foerenta nationenna. Stockholm, 1965.

Afr 5010.10   Sy, Seydou Madani. Recherches sur l'exercice du pouvoir politique en Afrique noire. Paris, 1965.

Afr 3708.16   Symons, Julian. England's pride. London, 1965.

Afr 6478.3   Syracuse. University. A bibliography on anthropology and sociology in Uganda. Syracuse, 1965.

Afr 9753.2   Syracuse University. A bibliography of Malawi. Syracuse, N.Y., 1965.

Afr 6193.47   Szcreszewski, R. Structural changes in the economy of Ghana, 1891-1911. London, 1965.

Afr 9515.6   Tanser, George Henry. A scantling of time. Salisbury, 1965.

Afr 6881.264.5   Tanzania. Ministry of Economic Affaires and Development Planning. First year progress report on the implementation of the Five-year Development Plan. Dar-es-Salaam, 1965?

Afr 6785.2   Tanzania. President. President's address to the National assembly, June 8, 1965. Dar es Salaam, 1965.

Afr 6760.15   Tanzania. Presidential Commission on the Establishment of a Democratic One Party State. Report. Dar es Salaam, 1965.

Afr 1338.17   Taraki, Muhammad Insan. Les institutions politiques du Maroc depuis l'indépendance. Thèse. Lyon, 1965.

Afr 7122.77   Teixeira, Bernardo. The fabric of terror, three days in Angola. N.Y., 1965.

Afr 6280.18.7   Temple, Charles Lindsay. Notes on the tribes, provinces, emirates and states of the northern provinces of Nigeria. 2d ed. London, 1965.

Afr 3340.8.2   Terra Viera, Blanca. Egipto en blanco y negro. 2. ed. Madrid, 1965.

Afr 626.160   Tevoedjre, Albert. Contribution à une synthèse sur le problème de la formation des cadres africains en vue de la croissance économique. Paris, 1965.

Afr 3822.5   Theobald, Alan B. Ali Dinar, last sultan of Darfor, 1895-1916. London, 1965.

Afr 210.63.23   Thiam, Doudou. The foreign policy of African states. London, 1965.

Afr 8252.267.2   Thom, Hendrik Bernardus. Die lewe van Gert maritz. 2.druk. Kaapstad, 1965.

Afr 210.65.20   Thomas, Charles Marion. Pan-Africanism. Maxwell Air Force Base, Ala., 1965.

Afr 6540.23   Thomas, Elizabeth Marshall. Warrior herdsmen. 1st ed. N.Y., 1965.

Afr 5749.65   Thompson, Virginia McLean. The Malagasy Republic. Stanford, 1965.

Afr 10105.65   Tibble, Anne (Northgrave). African-English literature. London, 1965.

Afr 6160.35   Tixier, Gilbert. Le Ghana. Paris, 1965.

Afr 6686.48.2   Togo. Five year development plan, 1966-1970. Paris, 1965.

Afr 6686.48.5F   Togo. Plan de développement économique et social, 1966-1970: annexes techniques, développement rural. Paris, 1965.

Afr 6686.48.10   Togo. Plan de développement économique et social, 1966-1970. Annexes techniques: industrie. Paris, 1965.

Afr 6686.48   Togo. Plan quinquennal de développement, 1966-1970. Paris, 1965.

Afr 7580.32   Topuzoglu. Kongo kurtuluş, sowosi. 1. baski. Istanbul, 1965.

Afr 6168.25   Torodoff, William. Ashanti under the Prempehs, 1888-1935. London, 1965.

Afr 5813.12.5   Toussaint, Auguste. L'administration française de l'île Maurice et ses archives, 1721-1810. Fort Luis, 1965.

Afr 659.65   Toynbee, Arnold Joseph. Between Niger and Nile. London, 1965.

Afr 618.26   Traore, Dominic. Comment le Noir se soigne-t-il. Paris, 1965.

Afr 8847.37   Tredgold, Ardeme. Village of the sea. Cape Town, 1965.

Afr 4568.19.2   Trimingham, J.S. Islam in Ethiopia. London, 1965.

Afr 5787.6   Trouchaud, J.P. La basse plaine du Mangoky. Paris, 1965.

Afr 7580.24   Truby, David William. Congo saga. London, 1965.

Afr 6390.79   Truepeney, Charlotte. Our African farm. London, 1965.

Afr 7835.2   Tucker, Angeline. He is in heaven. 1st ed. N.Y., 1965.

Afr 2623.965   Tunisia. Secrétariat d'Etat au Plan et à l'Economie Nationale. Plan guadriennal, 1965-1968. Tunis, 1965?

Afr 2620.2   Tunisie. Paris, 1965.

Afr 8145.22F   Turnbull, C.E.P. The work of the missionaries of Die Nederduits Gereformeerde Kerk van Suid-Afrika up to the year 1910. Johannesburg, 1965.

Afr 7815.28.5   Turnbull, Colin M. Wayward servants. 1st ed. Garden City, N.Y., 1965.

Afr 40.65   Tuzmukhamedov, Rais A. Organizatsiia afrikanskogo edinstva. Moskva, 1965.

Afr 6280.9.35   Uchendu, Victor Chikezie. The Iglo of southwest Nigeria. N.Y., 1965.

Afr 6535.65   Uganda. National Parks Trustees. Uganda national parks handbook. 24th ed. Kampala, 1965.

Afr 6498.32   Uganda. President, 1963-1966 (Mutesa). His Exellency the President's speech from the chair of the National Assembly on 15th Dec., 1965. Uganda, 1965.

Afr 3310.92   United Arab Republic. Diary of the Revolution, 1952-1965. Cairo, 1965.

Afr 3310.90   United Arab Republic. The Revolution in thirteen years, 1952-1965. Cairo, 1965.

Afr 6457.8   United Nations. United Nations mission to Kenya on housing. N.Y., 1965.

Afr 7461.38   United States. Bureau of International Commerce. A market for United States products in Liberia. Washington, 1965.

Afr 28.103   Ustav pro Mezinarodni Politiku a Ekonomii. Bibliograficke prameny the studiv problematiky africkych zemi. Praha, 1965.

Afr 7179.10   Vacchi, Dante. Penteados de Angola. Lisbonne, 1965.

Afr 8095.87   Vandenberghe, Pierre L. South Africa, a study in conflict. Middletown, Conn., 1965.

Afr 618.24   Vandenborghe, P.L. Africa, social problems of change and conflict. San Francisco, 1965.

Afr 710.65   Vansina, Jan. Les anciens royaumes de la savane. Leopoldville, 1965.

Afr 8335.5   Vatcher, William Henry. White laager. London, 1965.

Afr 44615.2   Velten, Carl. Swahili prose texts. London, 1965.

Afr 5440.15   Vennetier, Pierre. Les hommes et leur activitês dans le Nord du Congo-Brazzaville. Paris, 1965.

Afr 7809.65   Verbeck, Roger. Le Congo en question. Paris, 1965.

Afr 6193.50   Volta Resettlement Symposium. Volta Resettlement Symposium papers read at Volta Resettlement Symposium held in Kumasi. Accra, 1965.

Afr 5407.10   Voss, Harald. Kooperation in Afrika. Hamburg, 1965.

Afr 640.7   Walendowska-Zapedowska, Barbara. Problem pigmejow afrykanskich w etnografii europejskiej XIX-XX w. Poznan, 1965.

Afr 9699.65   Wallstorm, Tord. Grying, en bok om Zambia. Stockholm, 1965.

1965 - cont.

Afr 8089.65.5	Walt, Andries Jacobus Hendrik van der. Geskiedenis van Suid-Afrika. 2.uitg. Kaapstad, 1965.
Afr 6060.65	Ward, William Ernest Frank. Government in West Africa. London, 1965.
Afr Doc 4502.2	Webb, C. de B. A guide to the official records of the Colony of Natal. Pietermaritzburg, 1965.
Afr 8686.12	Weber, Karl Friedrich. Kreuz zwischen Weiss und Schwarz. Breklum, 1965.
Afr 555.141	Welbourn, F.B. East African Christian. London, 1965.
Afr 6498.65.5	Welbourn, Frederick Burkewood. Religion and politics in Uganda. Nairobi, 1965.
Afr 609.65.5	Welch, Galbraith. Africa before they came. N.Y., 1965. 4v.
Afr 630.65.5	West, Richard. The white tribes of Africa. London, 1965.
Afr 8678.420	Whitehead, Sylvia. The story of Sarah. London, 1965.
Afr 6210.16	Williams, Babatunde A. Political trends in Nigeria, 1960-1964. Ibadan, 1965.
Afr 2748.26.4	Williams, Harry. Quest beyond the Sahara. London, 1965.
Afr 8835.58	Williams, Roger. Cape Town Africans today. Johannesburg, 1965.
Afr 6195.18	Williamson, Sydney George. Akan religion and the Christian faith. Accra, 1965.
Afr Doc 3802.2	Willson, Francis Michael Glenn. Catalogue of the parliamentary papers of Southern Rhodesia, 1899-1953. Salisbury, 1965.
Afr 9854.2.5	Wishlade, Robert Leonard. Sectarianism in southern Nyasaland. London, 1965.
Afr 7580.20	Young, Crawford. Politics in the Congo. Princeton, N.J., 1965.
Afr 545.33	Zajaczkowski, Andrzej. Pierwotne religie czarnej Afryki. Warszawa, 1965. 10v.
Afr 9699.3	Zambia. Republic of Zambia. Lusaka, 1965.
Afr Doc 3707.362F	Zambia. Central Statistical Office. Census of distribution in 1962; wholesale, retail trade and selected services. Lusaka, 1965.
Afr Doc 3707.363.5	Zambia. Central Statistical Office. The census of production in 1963. Lusaka, 1965.
Afr Doc 3707.361	Zambia. Central Statistical Office. Final report of the Sept. 1961 censuses of non-Africans and employees. Lusaka, 1965.
Afr Doc 3707.363F	Zambia. Central Statistical Office. May/June 1963 census of Africans: v.1 village population. Lusaka, 1965.
Afr 9704.6	Zambia. Commission of Inquiry into the Former Lumpa Church. Report. Lusaka, 1965.
Afr Doc 3703.2	Zambia. Ministry of Foreign Affaires. List of Diplomatic Missions and other Foreign Representatives. Lusaka, 1965.
Afr 3300.90	Zayid, Mahmud Yusuf. Egypt's struggle for independence. 1st ed. Beirut, 1965.
Afr 6192.97	Zeitlin, Arnold. To the Peace Corps, with love. 1st ed. Garden City, 1965.
Afr 2609.65.5	Zeraffa, Michel. Tunisia. N.Y., 1965.
Afr 6535.63	Zwilling, Ernst Alexander. Wildes Karamoja. Mödling bei Wien, 1965.

1966

Afr 3990.27	Abd Allah, Hasan. The handbook of Egypt. Cairo, 1966.
Afr 6277.47	Aboyade, O. Foundations of an African economy. N.Y., 1966.
Afr 590.82	Abramova, Svetlana I. Istoriia rabotorgovli na verkhne-gvineiskom poberezh'e. Moskva, 1966.
Afr 10671.12.100	Achebe, Chinua. A man of the people. London, 1966.
Afr 10671.12.120	Achebe, Chinua. Things fall apart. London, 1966.
Afr 6286.2	Adedeji, Adebayo. An introduction to Western Nigeria. Ibadan?, 1966?
Afr 10671.12.800	Adejumo, Matthew S. Notes and essays on Chinua Achebe's Things fall apart. Ibadan, 1966.
Afr 8380.10	Adstin, Dennis. Britain and South Africa. London, 1966.
Afr 5057.32	Afana, Osende. L'économie de l'Ouest-africain. Paris, 1966.
Afr 212.24	African Conference on Progress through Cooperation. Africa. N.Y., 1966.
Afr 6178.3	Afrifa, A.R. The Ghana coup, 24th February, 1966. London, 1966.
Afr 575.52	L'Afrique islamique. Lezay, 1966.
Afr 210.65.55	Afro-Asian Peoples' Solidarity Conference, 4th, Winneba, Ghana. The Winneba Conference, Ghana, May 1965. Cairo, 1966.
Afr 7817.15	Agwala, Marie Jean. Evènements du Congo à Wamba, 15 août-29 décembre 1964. Clermont-Ferrand, 1966.
Afr 10013.2	Ainslie, Rosalynde. The press in Africa. London, 1966.
Afr 626.153.5	Akademiia Nauk SSSR. Institut Afriki. Ekonomicheskaia istoriia Afriki. Moskva, 1966.
Afr 32.3	Akademiia Nauk SSSR. Institut Gosudarstva i Prava. Konstitutsii gosudarstv Afriki. Moskva, 1966. 2v.
Afr 6176.42.5	Alexander, Henry Templer. African tightrope. N.Y., 1966.
Afr 3818.10	Allison, Oliver Claude. A pilgrim church's progress. London, 1966.
Afr 10671.52.120	Aluko, Timothy Mofolorunso. Kinsman and foreman. London, 1966.
VAfr 2223.966	Alžir. Beograd, 1966.
Afr 10671.53.100	Amadi, Elechi. The concubine. London, 1966.
Afr 6196.13	Amarteifio, Godfrey William. Tema Manhean; a study of resettlement. Kumasi, 1966.
Afr 609.66.25	American Society of African Culture. Southern Africa in transition. London, 1966.
Afr 1273.966	Amin, Samir. L'économie du Maghreb. Paris, 1966.
Afr 1470.5.2	Anderson, Eugene Newton. The first Moroccan crisis, 1904-1906. Hamden, Conn., 1966.
Afr 6282.25	Anderson, Susan. May Perry of Africa. Nashville, 1966.
Afr 630.66.15	Andor, L. Aptitudes and abilities of the black man in sub-Saharan Africa, 1784-1963. Johannesburg, 1966.
Afr 6218.22	Anene, Joseph Christopher. Southern Nigeria in transition, 1885-1906. Cambridge, Eng., 1966.
Afr 7567.36	Anstey, Roger. King Leopold's legacy. London, 1966.
Afr 8678.295	Apartheid, feiten en commentaren. Amsterdam, 1966.
Afr 1105.10	Arene, Joseph C. Africa in the nineteenth and twentieth centuries. Ibadan, 1966.
Afr 5368.8	Argyle, William Johnson. The Fon of Dahomey, a history and ethnography of the Old Kingdom. Oxford, 1966.
Afr 1750.38	Arques, Enrique. Las adelantadas de España. Madrid, 1966.
Afr 6210.9.5	Awolowo, Olafemi. Thoughts on Nigerian constitution. Ibadan, 1966.

1966 - cont.

Afr 6282.8	Ayandele, Emmanuel Ayankammi. The missionary impact on modern Nigeria, 1842-1914, a political and social analysis. London, 1966.
Afr 49019.2	Babalola, S.A. The content and form of Yoruba ijala. Oxford, 1966.
Afr 810.35.2	Baikie, William B. Narrative of an exploring voyage up the rivers Kwóra and Bínue, commonly known as the Niger and Tsádda in 1854. Facsimile. London, 1966.
Afr 2749.66	Baker, Richard Saint Barbe. Sahara conquest. London, 1966.
Afr 710.55.6	Balandier, Georges. Ambiguous Africa, cultures in collision. London, 1966.
Afr 9699.66	Baldwin, Robert Edward. Economic development and export growth. Berkeley, 1966.
Afr 7176.20	Banco de Angola, Lisbon. Economic and financial survey of Angola, 1960-1965. Lisboa, 1966.
Afr 6295.66.15	Barber, C.R. Igbo-Ora; a town in transition. Ibadan, 1966.
Afr 6430.3	Barnett, Donald L. Mau Mau from within, autobiography and analysis of Kenya's peasant revolt. London, 1966.
Afr 6430.3.1	Barnett, Donald L. Mau Mau from within. N.Y., 1966.
Afr 1942.6	Barnly, Henry George. The prisoners of Algiers. London, 1966.
Afr 10013.6	Barton, Frank. The press in Africa. Nairobi, 1966.
Afr 6280.9.8	Basden, George Thomas. Among the Ibos of Nigeria. N.Y., 1966.
Afr 6280.59	Basden, George Thomas. Niger Ibos. 2d ed. N.Y., 1966.
Afr 210.66.20	Bauw, Jean Anatole de. Politique et révolution africaine. Bruxelles, 1966.
Afr 9439.66	Baxter, J.W. Rhodesian epic. Cape Town, 1966.
Afr 7835.5	Bayly, Joseph T. Congo crisis. Grand Rapids, 1966.
Afr 9335.10	Bechuanaland. Commissioner to Consider Localization of Civil Service. Report on localisation and training. Mafeking, 1966.
Afr 9350.66	Bechuanaland Independence Conference, London, 1966. Report. London, 1966.
Afr 9335.5F	Bechuanaland Independence Conference. Report, signed at Marlborough house. n.p., 1966.
Afr 6176.50	Bediako, K.A. The downfall of Kwame Nkrumah. Accra, 1966?
Afr 20016.5	Beier, Ulli. African poetry. Cambridge, Eng., 1966.
Afr 14722.5	Beira, Maria da. Luz no túnel; romane. Porto, 1966.
Afr 630.66.5	Belchior, Manual. Fundamentos para uma politica multicultural em Africa. Lisboa, 1966.
Afr 1495.6.15	Ben Barka, Abdelkader. El Mehdi Ben Barka, mon frère. Paris, 1966.
Afr 1495.6	Benbarka, El Mehdi. Option révolutionnaire au Maroc. Paris, 1966.
VAfr 5580.3.25	Beniowski, M.A. Denník Mórica A. Beňovského. Bratislava, 1966.
Afr 679.63.32	Bennett, Nicholas. Zigzag to Timbuktu. N.Y., 1966.
Afr 1571.17.135	Benoist-Méchin, Jacques. Lyautey l'Africain, ou Le rêve immolé. Lausanne, 1966.
Afr 8685.89	Benson, Mary. South Africa, the struggle for a birthright. London, 1966.
Afr 6542.20	Bere, Rennie Montague. The way to the mountains of the moon. London, 1966.
Afr 8687.131	Berger, Lucy Gough. Where's the madam? Cape Town, 1966.
Afr 609.66.35	Bertacchini, Renato. Continente nero; memorialisti italiani dell'800 in Africa. Parma, 1966.
Afr 109.66.30	Bertaux, Pierre. Afrika. Frankfurt, 1966.
Afr 500.84	Betts, Raymond F. The scramble of Africa, causes and dimensions of empire. Boston, 1966.
Afr 44622.89.124A	Bhalo, Ahmad Nassir Bin Juma. Poems from Kenya. Madison, 1966.
Afr 8808.23.5	Bird, William Wilberforce. State of the Cape of Good Hope in 1822. Cape Town, 1966.
Afr 590.73	Birmingham, David. Trade and conflict in Angola, the Mbundu and their neighbours under the influence of the Portuguese, 1483-1790. Oxford, 1966.
Afr 6193.17	Birmingham, Walter Barr. A study of contemporary Ghana. London, 1966.
Afr 3204.26	Blayland, Gregory. Objective: Egypt. London, 1966.
Afr 7489.8	Blyden, Edward Wilmot. Blyden of Liberia. N.Y., 1966.
Afr 6192.70.2	Boateng, E.A. A geography of Ghana. 2nd ed. Cambridge, 1966.
Afr 679.66.10	Bochen, Albert Adu. Topics in West African history. London, 1966.
Afr 8377.8	Bogaerde, Frans van den. Suid-Afrika in die politiek-ekonomiese proses. Pretoria, 1966.
Afr 109.64.6	Bohannan, P. African outline, a general introduction. Harmondsworth, Middlesex, Eng., 1966.
Afr 5476.5	Boisson, Jacques. L'histoire du Tchad et de Fort Archambault. Besançon, 1966.
Afr 9450.25	Bolze, Louis W. Life with Udi; a cartoon history of independant Rhodesia. v.1-2. Bulawayo, 1966.
Afr 609.65.55	Bonn, Gisela. L'Afrique quitte la brousse. Paris, 1966.
Afr 7535.20	Bontinck, François. Aux origines de l'Etat indépendant du Congo. Louvain, 1966.
Afr 28.110	Boston University. African Studies Center. A list of films on Africa. Boston, 1966.
Afr 9398.2	Botswana. Economic Planning Unit. Transitional plan for social and economic development. Gaberones, 1966.
Afr 8813.2	Bouws, Jan. Die musieklewe van Kaapstad, 1800-1850. Thesis. Kaapstad, 1966.
Afr 6192.96.5	Bowdich, Thomas Edward. Mission from Cape Coast Castle to Ashantee. 3d ed. London, 1966.
Afr 8835.43F	Bowler, Thomas William. Pictorial album of Cape Town. Cape Town, 1966.
Afr 9689.38.4	Bradley, K. The diary of a district officer. 4th ed. London, 1966.
Afr 2235.42	Brauner, Siegmund. Lohrbuch der Hausa-Sprache. München, 1966.
Afr 6176.30.25	Bretton, Henry L. The rise and fall of Kwame Nkrumah; a study of personal rule in Africa. N.Y., 1966.
Afr 7567.40	Bricusse, Georges Henri A. Les carnets de campagne. Bruxelles, 1966.
Afr 6196.20.5	Brokensha, David W. Social change at Larteh, Ghana. Oxford, 1966.
Afr 609.57.16	Brom, John L. African odyssey. 1st ed. N.Y., 1966.
Afr 7582.15	Brookings Institute, Washington, D.C. Foreign Policy Studies Division. United Nations peacekeeping in the Congo: 1960-1964. v.1-4. Washington, 1966. 2v.
Afr 8678.283	Brown, Douglas. Against the world. London, 1966.
Afr 1273.966.5	Brown, Leon Carl. State and society in independent North Africa. Washington, 1966.

Afr 30.14   Brummelkamp, Jacob. Modern Africa. Utrecht, 1966.

Afr 6919.66   Bruwer, Johannes Petrus. South West Africa, the disputed land. Capetown, 1966.

Afr 9047.37   Bryant, Alfred T. Zulu medicine and medicine-men. Cape Town, 1966.

Afr 8969.66   Bulpin, Thomas Victor. Natal and the Zulu country. Cape Town, 1966.

Afr 8668.12   Burman, José. A peak to climb;...mountaineering. Cape Town, 1966.

Afr 550.8.45   Burridge, William. Destiny Africa, Cardinal Lavigerie and the making of the White Fathers. London, 1966.

Afr 4612.1.7   Burton, R.F. First footsteps in East Africa. London, 1966.

Afr 4612.1.6   Burton, R.F. First footsteps in East Africa. N.Y., 1966.

Afr 5385.2.10   Burton, R.F. A mission to Gelele. London, 1966. 2v.

Afr 11249.86.120   Butler, Guy. South of the Zambesi, poems from South Africa. N.Y., 1966.

Afr 8089.66.5   Cadoux, Charles. L'Afrique du Sud. Paris, 1966.

Afr 5228.2   Caioli, Aldo. Esperienza politiche africane; la Federazione del Mali. Milano, 1966.

Afr Doc 7508.6   Cameroon. Service de la Statistique Générale et la Mécanographie. The population of West Cameroon; main findings. Paris, 1966.

Afr 6738.43   Cameroun. 1966, bilan de cinq années d'indépendance. Monaco, 1966.

Afr 8028.148   Cape Town. University. Consolidated list, 1941-1966. Cape Town, 1966.

Afr 6455.122   Carey Jones, N.S. The anatomy of Uhuru, an essay on Kenya's independence. Manchester, 1966.

Afr 1635.35   Carim, Fuat. Yusuf Taşfin; yer yüzünün en Büyük devletlerinden birini kuran Berber imparatoru. Istanbul, 1966.

Afr 8685.61   Carstens, W. Peter. The social structure of a cape coloured reserve. Cape Town, 1966.

Afr 50.31   Carter, G. National unity and regionalism in eight African states. Ithaca, 1966.

Afr 212.25   Carter, Gwendolen Margaret. Politics in Africa. N.Y., 1966.

Afr 8846.30.5   Carter, Gwendolen Margaret. Separate development. Johannesburg, 1966.

Afr 4787.10   Carusoglu, T. Mid-term appraisal of the first five-year plan of Somalia. 1st draft. Mogadiscio, 1966.

Afr 6390.80   Castle, Edgar Bradshaw. Growing up in East Africa. London, 1966.

Afr 659.66.10   Cavallaro, Emanuele. Lo e l'Africa. Palermo, 1966.

Afr 7803.46   Cazlson, Lois. Monganga Paul. N.Y., 1966.

Afr 5282.5   Centre d'Etudes Economiques et Sociales d'Afrique Occidentale. Fonctionnaire et développement. Bobo-Dioulasso, 1966.

Afr Doc 7107.364   Chad. Service de la Statistique Générale. Enquête démographique ou Tchad, 1964 résultats définitifs. v.1-2. Paris, 1966.

Afr 9499.28   Cherkasov, Iurii N. Ekonomicheskie problemy Iuzhnoi Rodezii. Moskva, 1966.

Afr 10663.5   Chick, John D. An exploratory investigation of press readership among selected students in Zaria. Zaria, 1966.

Afr 7920.3   Chome, Jules. Moise Tshombe et l'escroquerie katangaise. Bruxelles, 1966.

Afr 7949.250   Church, John Edward. Forgive them: the story of an African martyr. London, 1966.

Afr 6095.366   Church, R.J.H. Some geographical aspects of West African development. London, 1966.

Afr 6095.357.5   Church, R.J.H. West Africa, a study of the environment and of man's use of it. 5th ed. London, 1966.

VAfr 679.66.25   Cissoko, Sébéné M. Histoire de l'Afrique occidentale. v.1- Paris, 1966-

Afr 9699.66.15   Clairmonte, Frédéric. Rhodesia: National Development Plan, 1965-1968. Addis Abbaba, 1966.

Afr 5962.8   Clairmonte, Frédéric F. Analysis of Spanish Equatorial Guinea Plan, 1964-1967. Addis Ababa, 1966.

Afr 5758.66.5   Clairmonte, Fréderic F. Analysis of the Madagascar Plan, 1964-1968. Addis Ababa, 1966.

Afr 6143.66   Clark, John Innes. Sierra Leone in maps. London, 1966.

Afr 10673.48.160   Clark, John Pepper. Ozidii. London, 1966.

Afr 530.50.20   Clendenen, C.C. Americans in Africa, 1865-1900. Stanford, Calif., 1966.

Afr 8919.66   Coates, Austin. Basutoland. London, 1966.

Afr 1487.36   Cohen, Mark I. Morocco, old land, new nation. N.Y., 1966.

Afr 9545.10   Coissoró, Narana. The customary laws of succession in Central Africa. Thesis. Lisboa, 1966.

Afr 20002.5   Coldham, Geraldine Elizabeth. A bibliography of Scriptures in African languages. London, 1966. 2v.

Afr 8676.61.2   Cole, M.M. South Africa. 2nd ed. London, 1966.

Afr 2037.2   Comité pour la Défense de Ben Bella et des Autres Victimes de la Répression en Algérie. Les torturés d'El Harrach. Paris, 1966.

Afr 2025.34   Confer, Vincent. France and Algeria. 1st ed. N.Y., 1966.

Afr 45.66.10   Conference on African Local Government since Independence, Lincoln University, Pennsylvania, 1966. Proceedings of the Conference on African Local Government since Independence held at Lincoln University, Feb. 3rd and 4th, 1966. Lincoln, 1966.

Afr 36.4   Conference on the Position and Problems of the American Scholar in Africa, White Sulphur Springs, West Va., 1966. Summary report. N.Y., 1966?

Afr 679.66.5   Conton, William F. West Africa in history. London, 1966.

Afr 608.41.5A   Cooley, William Desborough. The Negroland of the Arabs examined and explained. 2nd ed. London, 1966.

Afr 109.62.22   Cornevin, Robert. Histoire de l'Afrique des origines à nos jours. Paris, 1966.

Afr 7549.63.2   Cornevin, Robert. Histoire du Congo: Léopoldville-Kinshassa. 2. éd. Paris, 1966.

Afr 3979.66.15   Cottrell, Leonard. Egypt. N.Y., 1966.

Afr 8687.273   Cowley, Cecil. Kwa Zulu. Cape Town, 1966.

Afr 6214.30.2   Crowder, M. A short history of Nigeria. N.Y., 1966.

Afr 6192.5.2   Cruickshank, B. Eighteen years on the Gold Coast of Africa. 2nd ed. London, 1966. 2v.

Afr 3817.14   Cunnison, Ivan George. Baggara Arabs, power and the lineage in a Sudanese nomad tribe. Oxford, 1966.

Afr 6225.12   Current Issues Society, Kaduna, Nigeria. The Nigerian situation; facts and background. Zaria, 1966.

Afr 6210.52   Dada, Paul O.A. Evaluation of local government courses in relation to careers of staff trained in Zaria, 1954-1964. Zaria, 1966.

Afr 5387.14   Dahomey. Plan de développement économique et social, 1966-1970. Cotohou, 1966.

Afr 5765.31   Dailliez, André. A la découverte d'un diocèse Malgache, Fianarantsoa. Bar-le-Duc, 1966.

Afr 8849.169   Dale, Emmé Ross. Mrs. Dale's diary, 1857-1872. Cape Town, 1966.

Afr 8050.24   Davenport, T.R.H. The Afrikaner bond. Cape Town, 1966.

Afr 109.66F   Davidson, Basil. Africa, history of a continent. London, 1966.

Afr 679.65.30.2   Davidson, Basil. A history of West Africa to the nineteenth century. Garden City, N.Y., 1966. 2v.

Afr 590.75.5   Davidson, Basil. Vom Sklavenhandel zur Kolonialisierung, afrikanisch-europäische Beziehungen zwischen 1500 und 1900. Reinbeck bei Hamburg, 1966.

Afr 6282.35   Davis, Raymond J. Swords in the desert. 5th ed. London, 1966.

Afr 3315.81   Dayan, Moshe. Diary of the Sinai campaign. London, 1966.

Afr 5555.2   Decary, Raymond. Coutumes guerrieres et organisation militaire chez les anciens Malgaches. Paris, 1966. 2v.

Afr 8685.15   Dickie-Clark, H.F. The marginal situation. London, 1966.

Afr 6218.10.1   Dike, K.O. Trade and politics in the Niger Delta. Oxford, 1966.

Afr 6410.6.2   Dilley, Marjorie Ruth. British policy in Kenya colony. 2. ed. London, 1966.

Afr 6203.10   Dipeolu, J.O. Bibliographical sources for Nigerian studies. Evanston, Ill., 1966.

Afr 10674.71.100   Dipoko, Mbella Sonne. A few nights and days. London, 1966.

Afr 50.47   Dodge, Dorothy Rae. African politics in perspective. Princeton, N.J., 1966.

Afr 5112.10   Doll, Peter. Der senegalesische Weg zum afrikanischen Sozialismus. Hamburg, 1966.

Afr 10016.12   Doob, Leonard William. Ants will not eat your fingers. N.Y., 1966.

Afr 609.66.5   Dostent, Pierre Etienne. Africa 1966. Washington, 1966.

Afr 6926.28   Drechsler, Horst. Südwestafrika unter deutscher Kolonialherrschaft. Berlin, 1966.

Afr 1075.5   Duclos, Louis Jean. Les nationalismes maghrébins. Paris, 1966.

Afr 609.62.41   Dumont, René. False start in Africa. London, 1966.

Afr 609.62.41.5   Dumont, René. False start in Africa. N.Y., 1966.

Afr 6168.7.2   Dupuis, J. Journal of a residence in Ashanti. 2d. ed. London, 1966.

Afr 6542.43   Dyson-Hudson, Neville. Karimojong politics. Oxford, 1966.

Afr 6096.6.2   Economics of West Africa. 2. ed. Ibadan, 1966.

Afr 6096.20   Edinburgh. University. Centre of African Studies. Markets and marketing in West Africa. Edinburgh, 1966.

Afr 9450.10   Edwards, Hilton. Rhodesian independence justified. Queenstown, South Africa, 1966.

Afr 10118.5   Edwards, Paul. Modern African narrative, an anthology. London, 1966.

Afr 10015.7   Edwards, Paul Geoffrey. Through African eyes. Cambridge, 1966-

Afr 628.266   Efimov, Aleksei V. Protiv rasizma. Moskva, 1966.

Afr 10675.47.180   Ekwensi, Cyprian. Iska. London, 1966.

Afr 10675.47.150   Ekwensi, Cyprian. Lokotown and other stories. London, 1966.

Afr 6742.5   Endresen, Halfdan. Als Sklave verkauft; Sklaverei und Sklavenhandel im heutigen Afrika und Arabien. Basel, 1966.

Afr 50.51   Entin, Lev M. Natsional'naia gosudarstvennost' narodov Zapadnoi i Tsentral'noi Afriki. Moskva, 1966.

Afr Doc 307.15F   Ethiopia. Central Statistical Office. Report on a survey. Addis Ababa, 1966.

Afr Doc 307.10F   Ethiopia. Central Statistical Office. Report on a survey. Addis Ababa, 1966. 3 pam.

Afr 4559.66   Ethiopia. Ministry Of Information. Ethiopia, Liberation Silver Jubilee, 1941-1966. Addis Ababa, 1966.

Afr 626.185   European Economic Community. Possibilités d'industrialisation des états africains et malgache associés. Paris, 1966. 7v.

Afr 8028.162   Evans, Margaret Jane. Index to pictures of South African interest in the Graphic, 1875-1895. Johannesburg, 1966.

Afr 13275.90.100   Evembe, François Borgia Marie. Sur la terre en passant. Paris, 1966.

Afr 9643.5   Fagan, Brian M. A short history of Zambia. Nairobi, 1966.

Afr 9525.575   Farrant, Jean. Mashonaland martyr. Cape Town, 1966.

Afr 7018.5   Felgas, Hélio Augusto Estevez. Os movimentos terroristos de Angola, Guiné, Moçambique. Lisboa, 1966.

Afr 210.66   Ferkiss, Victor. Africa's search for identity. N.Y., 1966.

Afr 6176.46   Fitch, Robert Beck. Ghana; end of an illusion. N.Y., 1966.

Afr 6282.27   Fletcher, Jesse C. The Wimpy Harper story. Nashville, 1966.

Afr 6214.33   Flint, John E. Nigeria and Ghana. Englewood Cliffs, N.J., 1966.

Afr 1620.35   Fodor, Eugene. Morocco, 1965-66. N.Y., 1966.

Afr 2731.15.7   Foucauld, Charles. Lettres à Mme. de Bondy, de la Trappe à Tamanrasset. Paris, 1966.

Afr 5749.66   France. Institut Geographique National. Annexe de Tananarive. Expose des travaux executes en 1965 sur le territoire de la Republique Malgache. Paris, 1966.

Afr Doc 6907.5   France. Ministère de la Coopération. Mission Economique et Pastorale, 1963. Etude démographique et économique en milieu homade. Paris, 1966.

Afr 8678.360   Francos, Ania. L'Afrique des Afrikaaners. Paris, 1966.

Afr 8676.60.13   Franzsen, D.G. Die ekonomiese lewe van Suid-Afrika, onder redaksie van D.G. Franzsen en H.J.J. Reynders. 3. uitg. Pretoria, 1966.

Afr 6988.66.205   Freyer, E.P.W. Chronik von Otavi und einer Karte. Ötavi, 1966.

Afr 8050.8.2   Fruit of the national regime, 1948-1966. Bloemfontein, 1966.

Afr 11410.31.100   Fugard, Athol. Hello and goodbye; a play in two acts. Cape Town, 1966.

Afr 550.160   Fuller, William Harold. Run while the sun is hot. N.Y., 1966.

Afr 9345.70   Gabatshwane, S.M. Seretse Khama and Botswana. Kanye? 1966.

Afr 5422.5   Gabon. Ministère d'Etat Chargé de l'Economie Nationale du Plan et des Mines. Commissariat au Plan. Résumé du plan de développement économique et social, période 1966-1971. Monaco, 1966.

Afr 210.66.15   Ganiage, Jean. L'Afrique au XXe siècle. Paris, 1966.

Afr 1750.21.5	Garcia Figueras, Tomes. La accion africana de Espana en torno al 98 (1860-1912). Madrid, 1966. 2v.
Afr 9028.36.5	Gardiner, A.F. Narrative of a journey to the Zoolu country in South Africa. Cape Town, 1966.
Afr 8310.12	Gardner, Brian. Mafeking, a Victorian legend. London, 1966.
Afr 1609.66	Garrique, Francois. Maroc enchante. Paris, 1966.
Afr 3993.966.10	Gataullin, Maliuta F. Ekonomika OAR na novom puti. Moskva, 1966.
Afr 630.66.10	Gayre, George Robert. Ethnological elements of Africa. Edinburgh, 1966.
Afr 8849.212	Gearing, Gladys. This was my world. Cape Town, 1966.
Afr 9502.13.10	Gelfand, M. An African's religion, the spirit of Nyajena. Cape Town, 1966.
Afr 7850.54.2	Gerard Libois, J. Katanga secession. Madison, 1966.
Afr 8164.23	Ghana. Information Services Department. Ghana reborn. N.Y., 1966.
Afr 6178.4	Ghana. Ministry of Information and Broadcasting. Nkrumah's subversion in Africa. Accra, 1966.
Afr 6979.66.5	Gíniewski, Paul. Livre noir, livre blanc. Paris, 1966.
Afr 6985.14	Giniewski, Paul. Die stryd om Suidwes-Afrika. Kaapstad, 1966.
Afr 5243.122.5	Giorgetti, Filiberto. La superstizione Zande. Bologna, 1966.
Afr 7549.66	Giovannini, Giovanni. Congo. 2.ed. Milano, 1966.
Afr 8678.425	Glashagen, Ulrich H. Probleme der räumlich getrennten Einbeziehung der Bantu-Bevölkerung Südafrikas in den Wirtschaftsprozes des Landes. Pretoria, 1966.
Afr 2209.66	Gohier, Jacques. Instructeur en Algérie. Rodez, 1966.
Afr 45.66	Gonidec, Pierre François. Cours d'institutions publiques africaines et malgaches. Paris, 1966.
Afr 6395.25	Good, Charles M. Dimensions of East African cultures. East Lansing, 1966.
Afr 8238.2	Goodfellow, Clement Francis. Great Britain and South African confederation, 1870-1881. Cape Town, 1966.
Afr 11433.74.160	Gordimer, N. The late bourgeois world. London, 1966.
Afr 2035.6	Gordon, David. The passing of French Algeria. London, 1966.
Afr 4430.55.10	Gorham, Charles Orson. The Lion of Judah. N.Y., 1966.
Afr 1609.66.10	Gornung, Mikhail B. Marokko. Moskva, 1966.
Afr 6390.90	Grahame, Iain. Jambo effendi: seven years with the King's African Rifles. London, 1966.
Afr 6113.10.2	Gray, J.M. A history of the Gambia. N.Y., 1966.
Afr 9180.2	Great Britain. Colonial Office. Swaziland, constitutional proposals. London, 1966.
Afr 9450.3F	Great Britain. Commonwealth Office. Library. Southern Rhodesia illegal declaration of independence. London, 1966?
Afr 28.118F	Great Britain. Commonwealth Relations Office. Library. African military coups. London, 1966.
Afr 8835.55	Green, Lawrence George. Tavern of the seas. Cape Town, 1966.
Afr 8659.66.25	Green, Lawrence George. Thunder on the Blaauwberg. 1st ed. Cape Town, 1966.
Afr 12377.23.100	Greki, Anna. Temps forts, poèmes. Paris, 1966.
Afr 6282.16	Grimley, John. Church growth in central and southern Nigeria. Grand Rapids, 1966.
Afr 7461.42	Growth without development. Evanston, 1966.
Afr 5135.5	Gueve, Lamine. Itinéraire africain par Lamine Gueve. Paris, 1966.
Afr 6885.5	Gutmann, Bruno. Afrikaner-Europäer in nächstenschaftlicher Entsprechung. Stuttgart, 1966.
Afr 8687.309.5	Gutsche, Thelma. No ordinary woman. Cape Town, 1966.
Afr 9165.42.80	Gutsche, Thelma. Old gold, the history of the Wanderers club. Cape Town, 1966.
Afr 2397.36	Hadj Ali, Bachir. L'Arbitraire. Paris, 1966.
Afr 6741.6	Häberle, Wilhelm. Trommeln, Mächte und ein Ruf. Stuttgart, 1966.
Afr 4630.20.2	Hague. International Court of Justice. Ethiopia and Liberia versus South Africa. 2d ed. Pretoria, 1966.
Afr 710.23	Hallet, Jean Pierre. Congo kitabu. N.Y., 1966.
Afr 679.66	Hallett, Robin. People and progress in West Africa. Oxford, 1966.
Afr 679.66.30	Halpern, Jan. Studia nad gospodarką przedkapitalistyczna no Afryce Gachoancej wieku XIX i XX. Wyd.1. Warszawa, 1966.
Afr 609.66.15	Hama, Boubou. Enquête sur les fondements et la genèse de l'unité africaine. Paris, 1966.
Afr 5285.277.20	Hammond, Peter B. Yatenga. N.Y., 1966.
Afr 7022.2	Hammond, Richard. Portugal and Africa, 1815-1910. Stanford, 1966.
Afr 8667.80	Hancock, William Keith. Are there South Africans? Johannesburg, 1966.
Afr 8659.66	Harrigan, Anthony. The new republic, South Africa's role in the world. Pretoria, 1966.
Afr 9500.38	Harrigan, Anthony. One against the mob. Arlington, 1966.
Afr 6160.27	Harvey, William Burnett. Law and social change in Ghana. Princeton, 1966.
Afr 9489.66	Haw, Richard Claude. Rhodesia. Salisbury, 1966.
Afr 7912.15.40	Heinz, G. Lumumba Patrice: les cinquante derniers jours de sa vie. Bruxelles, 1966.
Afr 6455.150	Heland, Erik von. Mina Afrikaår. Stockholm, 1966.
Afr 6277.90A	Helleiner, Gerald K. Peasant agriculture, government, and economic growth in Nigeria. Homewood, Ill., 1966.
Afr 8089.66.10	Hepple, Alex. South Africa, a political and economic history. London, 1966.
Afr 1609.66.5	Herault, Andre. Le Maroc a visage decouvert. Paris, 1966.
Afr 6885.6	Heremans, Roger. Les établissements de l'Association Internationale Africaine au lac Tanganika et les pères blancs, Mpala et Karema, 1877-1885. Tervuren, 1966.
Afr 628.266.5	Herskovits, Melville Jean. The new world Negro. Bloomington, 1966.
Afr 4766.38	Hess, Robert L. Italian colonialism in Somalia. Chicago, 1966.
Afr 7945.5	Heusch, Luc de. Le Rwanda et la civilisation interlacustre. Bruxelles, 1966.
Afr 10628.37.100	Hihetah, Robert Kofi. Painful road to Kadjebi. Accra, 1966.
Afr 6214.10.5	Hoghen, S.J. The emirates of Northern Nigeria. London, 1966.
Afr 5243.337.2	Holas, Bohumil. Les Senoufo (y compris les minianka). 2nd ed. Paris, 1966.
Afr 8235.20	Holmberg, Ake. African tribes and European agencies. Göteborg, 1966.

Afr 8835.26	Honikman, Alfred Harold. Cape Town, city of Good Hope. Cape Town, 1966.
Afr 9161.24.5	Horrell, Muriel. Group areas; the emerging pattern with illustrative examples from Transvaal. Johannesburg, 1966.
Afr 8678.337.5	Horrell, Muriel. Legislation and race relations. Johannesburg, 1966.
Afr 109.66.15	Howe, Russell Warren. Black Africa, Africa south of the Sahara from pre-history to independence. N.Y., 1966. 2v.
Afr 109.66.5	Howe, Russell Warren. Black Africa, Africa south of the Sahara from prehistory to independence. London, 1966. 2v.
VAfr 109.66.20	Hrbek, Ivan. Dějiny Afriky. Vyd. 1. Praha, 1966. 2v.
Afr 8678.326	Hudson, William. Anatomy of South Africa. Cape Town, 1966.
Afr 9165.42.95	Hughes, Blanche. Personal reminiscences of early Johannesburg in printed books, 1884-1895. Johannesburg, 1966.
Afr 2030.466	Humbaraci, Arslan. Algeria, a revolution that failed. London, 1966.
Afr 31.5	Ibn Batuta. Textes et documents relatifs a l'histoire de l'Afrique. Dakar, 1966.
Afr 3026.22	Ibrahim-Hilmy. The literature of Egypt and theSoudan. Nendeln, 1966. 2v.
Afr 7065.500	Ignat'ev, Oleg K. Pepel i plamia kafina. Moskva, 1966.
Afr 6277.52	Ike, Adelimpe O. Economic development of Nigeria, 1950-1964. Nsukka, 1966.
Afr 545.28.2	International African Seminar, 3rd, Salisbury, Southern Rhodesia, 1960. African systems of thought. London, 1966.
Afr 575.37	International African Seminar, 5th, London, 1966. Islam in tropical Africa, studies presented and discussed at the fifth International African Seminar. London, 1966.
Afr 710.32.6A	International African Seminar, 6th, Ibadan, Nigeria, 1964. The new elites of tropical Africa. London, 1966.
Afr 1623.966	International Bank for Reconstruction and Development. The economic development of Morocco. Baltimore, 1966.
Afr 1259.66	Isnard, Hildebert. Le Maghreb. Paris, 1966.
Afr 3979.66.5	Ivanov, Boris V. 40 vekov i 4 goda. Moskva, 1966.
Afr 8686.22	Ive, Anthony. The Church of England in South Africa. Cape Town, 1966.
Afr 10679.96.100	Iwunze, Godwin Egejuruka. The sting that cures. Enugu, 1966.
Afr 115.117	Izuchenie Afriki v Svetskom Soiuze. Photocopy. Moskva, 1966.
Afr 8089.66.20	Jaarsveld, Floris. Die Republiek van Suid-Afrika. Johannesburg, 1966.
Afr 109.66.10	Jacob, Ernest Gerhard. Grundzüge der Geschichte Afrikas. Darmstadt, 1966.
Afr 11465.14.160	Jacobson, Dan. The beginners. N.Y., 1966.
Afr 10005.3	Jahn, Janheinz. Geschichte der neoafrikanischen Literatur. Düsseldorf, 1966.
Afr 555.132	Jenkins, David E. They led the way. Cape Town, 1966.
Afr 6275.112	Jennings, J.H. A geography of the eastern provinces of Nigeria. Cambridge, 1966.
Afr 6926.32	Jenssen, H.E. Chronik von Deutsch-Südwestafrika. Windhoek, 1966.
Afr 6218.1.5	Johnson, Samuel. The history of the Yorubas; from the earliest times to the beginning of the British protectorate. 1st ed. London, 1966.
Afr 30115.2	Johnston, H.A.S. A selection of Hausa stories. Oxford, 1966.
Afr 8089.66.15	Joos, Louis C.D. Histoire de l'Afrique du Sud. Paris, 1966.
Afr 2209.66.5	Joret, Madeleine. L'Afrique en flânant, de Paris à Tamanrasset. Paris, 1966.
Afr 8678.343	Joseph, Helen. Tomorrow's sun. London, 1966.
Afr 1069.31.12	Julien, Charles A. Histoire de l'Afrique du Nord: Tunisie, Algérie, Maroc. 2e éd. Paris, 1966- 2v.
Afr 659.66	Julien, Charles André. Histoire de l'Afrique blanche. Paris, 1966.
Afr 6535.66	Julsrud, Harald G. Jambo Uganda. Oslo, 1966.
Afr 10831.1.100	Kachingwe, A. No easy task. London, 1966.
Afr 6985.12	Kahn, Carl Hugo Linsingen. The native tribes of South West Africa. 1st ed. London, 1966.
Afr 609.66.30	Kaké, Baba Ibrahima. Terre d'Afrique. Paris, 1966.
Afr 7912.15.30	Kashamura, Anicet. De Lumumba aux colonels. Paris, 1966.
Afr 55.33	Kaula, Edna Mason. Leaders of the new Africa. Cleveland, 1966.
Afr 9748.475.15	Kaunda, Kenneth David. Zambia, independence and beyond, the speeches of Kenneth Kaunda. London, 1966.
Afr 2929.66	Keith, Agnes Newton. Children of Allah. 1st ed. Boston, 1966.
Afr 9700.13	Keith, Grace. The fading colour bar. London, 1966.
Afr 6457.23.5	Kenya. Development plan for the period 1965-1966 to 1966-1970. Nairobi, 1966.
Afr 3285.21	Kerr, Malcolm H. Islamic reform. Berkeley, 1966.
Afr 6134.5	Kilson, Martin Luther. Political change in a West African state. Cambridge, 1966.
Afr 609.66.20	Kimble, George Herbert Tinley. Tropical Africa today. Saint Louis, 1966.
Afr 3979.66.25	Kinross, Patrick. Portrait of Egypt. London, 1966.
Afr 3979.66.20	Kinross, Patrick. Portrait of Egypt. N.Y., 1966.
Afr 7946.12	Kjellberg, Alice. Missionsarbetets början i Burundi. Orebro, 1966.
Afr 4290.5	Kobishchanov, Iurii M. Aksum. Moskva, 1966.
Afr 10631.58.110	Konadu, Asare. Come back Dora, a husband's confession and ritual. Accra, 1966.
Afr 10631.58.120	Konadu, Asare. Shadow of wealth. Accra, 1966.
Afr 5055.66	Kouassigan, Guy Adjéte. L'homme et la terre. Paris, 1966.
Afr 2623.966	Kratz, Achim. Voraussetzungen und Möglichkeiten einer industriellen Entwicklung in Tunesien. Hamburg, 1966.
Afr 6542.52	Kreuer, Werner. Der Wandel der sozialen Struktur in den drei ostafrikanischen Königreichen Ankole, Bunyoro und Buganda. Thesis. Bonn, 1966.
Afr 8686.14	Krueger, Bernhard. The pear tree blossoms; a history of the Moravian mission stations in South Africa, 1737-1869. Thesis. Genadendal, 1966.
Afr 679.66.15	Kubbel', Lev E. Strana zolota. Moskva, 1966.
Afr 3310.95	Kurdgelashvili, Shota N. Revoliutsiia 1952 g. i krakh britanskogo gospodstva v Egipte. Moskva, 1966.
Afr 6303.7	Kuria, Lucas. A bibliography on anthropology and sociology in Tanzania and East Africa. Syracuse, 1966.
Afr 7947.9	Lacroix, Benoît. Le Rwanda: mille heures au pays des mille collines. Montréal, 1966.

1966 - cont.

Afr 6293.2 — Lagos. City Council. Tribunal of Inquiry. Report of the Tribunal ofInquiry into the affairs of the Lagos City Council for the period Oct. 15, 1962 to Apr. 18, 1966. Lagos, 1966.

Afr 9450.5 — Lardner-Burke, Desmond. Rhodesia, the story of the crisis. London, 1966.

Afr 3979.66.30 — Laurent-Täckholm, Vivi. Egyptisk vardag. Stockholm, 1966.

Afr 550.8.500 — Lavigerie, Charles M.A. Ecrits d'Afrique. Paris, 1966.

Afr 5180.48 — Lavroff, Dimitri Georges. La République du Sénégal. Paris, 1966.

Afr 7817.2 — Law, Virginia W. Appointment Congo. Chicago, 1966.

Afr 12832.5.100 — Laye, Camara. Dramouss. Paris, 1966.

Afr 12832.5.112 — Laye, Camara. L'enfant noir. Cambridge, 1966.

Afr 6455.142 — Leakey, Louis S.B. Kenya; contrasts and problems. Cambridge, Mass., 1966.

Afr 8659.66.10 — Lehmann, Emily. Pretoria, Skinnerstraat 295. Wuppertal, 1966.

Afr 8845.8 — Leigh, Ramon Lewis. The city of Port Elizabeth. Johannesburg, 1966.

Afr 7812.266 — Leopoldville. Université Lovanjum. Institut de Recherche Economiques et Sociales. Étude d'orientation pour le plan de développement et de diversification industrielle. Kinshasa, 1966.

Afr Doc 4207.365F — Lesotho. Bureau of Statistics. Lesotho census of production, 1965. Maseru, 1966?

Afr 6280.60 — Levine, Robert A. Dreams and deeds. Chicago, 1966.

Afr 8678.342 — Levinson, Deirdre. Five years. London, 1966.

Afr 6392.17 — Leys, Colin. Federation in East Africa, opportunities. Oxford, 1966.

Afr 7461.45 — Liberia. Policy and Planning Committee on Industry. Liberia manufacturing industry. Monrovia? 1966.

VAfr 2938.39 — Libija. Beograd, 1966.

Afr Doc 2302.5 — Library of Congress. General Reference and Bibliography Division. Nigeria; a guide to official publications. Washington, 1966.

Afr 718.48 — Littell, Blaine. South of the moon. 1st ed. N.Y., 1966.

Afr 49029.41.700 — Ljimere, Obotunde. The imprisonment of Obatala, and other plays. London, 1966.

Afr 7309.66 — Lobato, Alexandre. Ilha de Moçambique: panorama estético. Lisboa, 1966.

Afr 7565.22 — Loth, Heinrich. Kolonialismus und Humanitätsintervention. Berlin, 1966.

Afr 7103.10 — Luanda. Instituto de Investigação Cientifica de Angola. Archivo Histórico. Roteiro topográfico dos códices. Angola, 1966.

Afr 8378.200.10 — Ludi, Gerard. The amazing Mr. Fischer. Cape Town, 1966.

Afr 6210.1 — Lugard, Frederick Dealtry. Instructions to political and other officers. London, 1966.

Afr 2731.15.95 — Lyautey, Pierre. Charles de Foucauld. Paris, 1966.

Afr 11542.87.130 — Lytton, David. The freedom of the cage. London, 1966.

Afr 6333.66 — Lytton, Noel. The stolen desert. London, 1966.

Afr 6879.66 — Macdonald, Alexander. Tanzania, young nation in a hurry. 1st ed. N.Y., 1966.

Afr 210.66.5 — McKay, Vernon. African diplomacy. N.Y., 1966.

Afr 6210.44F — Mackintosh, John P. Nigerian government and politics. London, 1966.

Afr 7561.5 — McLaughlin, Russell U. Foreign investment and development in Liberia. N.Y., 1966.

Afr 6203.18 — McLoughlin, Peter F.M. Eastern region of Nigeria. Santa Clara, Calif., 1966.

Afr Doc 5608.41.5 — Malagasy Republic. Institut National de la Statistique et de la Recherche Economique. Etat civil, année 1965. Tananarive? 1966?

Afr 5540.16 — Malagusy. Republic Institute National de la Statistique et de la Recherche Économique. Des ordinateurs dans l'administration Malgache! Tananarive?, 1966?

Afr 9839.66 — Malawi. Department of Information. Facts from Malawi. Zomba, 1966.

Afr Doc 3607.366F — Malawi. National Statistical Office. Malawi population census, 1966; provisional report. Zomba, 1966?

Afr 8688.14.3 — Malherbe, Daniel François du Toit. Stamregister van die Suid-Afrikaanse volk. 3. uitg. Stellenbosch, 1966.

Afr 1495.6.10 — Mali, Tidiane. Une Philosophie sur l'affaire Ben Barka. Lyon, 1966.

Afr 11555.61.120 — Manson, H.W.D. Captain Smith. Cape Town, 1966.

Afr 1495.6.5 — Marec, Jean Paul. La Ténébreuse affaire Ben Barka. Paris, 1966.

Afr 3979.66 — Marlowe, John. Four aspects of Egypt. London, 1966.

Afr 1620.28.9 — Maroc. 9.ed. Paris, 1966.

Afr 7582.8 — Martelli, George. Experiment in world government, an account of the United Nations operation in the Congo, 1960-1964. London, 1966.

Afr 45.66.5 — Masseron, Jean Paul. Le pouvoir et la justice en Afrique noire francophone et à Madagascar. Paris, 1966.

Afr 3993.966 — Matiukhin, Ivan S. Ob'edinennaia Arabskaia Respublika. Moskva, 1966.

Afr 6143.9.5 — Matthews, J. Voyage to the river Sierra-Leone. London, 1966.

Afr 212.14 — Matthews, Ronald. African powder keg. London, 1966.

Afr 13467.53.100 — Maunick, Edouard. Mascaret ou Le livre de la mer et de la mort. Paris, 1966.

Afr 1769.7.10 — Maxwell, Gavin. Lords of the atlas, the rise and fall of the house of Glaoua, 1893-1956. London, 1966.

Afr 33319.2 — Mbiti, John. Akamba stories. Oxford, 1966.

Afr 6760.25 — Meienberg, Hildebrand. Tanzanian citizen: a civics textbook. Nairobi, 1966[1967]

Afr 8252.323 — Meintjes, Johannes. De la Rey, lion of the west, a biography. Johannesburg, 1966.

Afr 6390.64 — Meister, Albert. L'Afrique peut-elle partir? Paris, 1966.

Afr 6392.25 — Meister, Albert. Le development economique de l'Afrique orientale. Paris, 1966.

Afr 115.114 — Melikian, Ovanes N. Neitralizm gosudarstv Afrikii. Moskva, 1966.

Afr 6979.66 — Mertens, Alice. South West Africa and its indigenous peoples. London, 1966.

Afr 5210.5 — Merzliakov, Nikolai S. Stanovlenie natsional'noi gosudarstvennosti Respubliki Mali. Moskva, 1966.

Afr 10633.13.100 — Mickson, E.K. When the heart decides. Who killed Lucy? v.1-2. Accra, 1966?

Afr 6275.127 — Miller, Stefan. Nigeria zwischen Wüste und Lagune. Berlin, 1966.

Afr 630.66 — Millin, Sarah Gertrude. White Africans are also people. Cape Town, 1966.

1966 - cont.

Afr 9853.8 — Mitchell, James Clyde. The Yao village, a study in the social structure of a Nyasaland tribe. 1st ed. Manchester, 1966.

Afr 545.2 — Mitchell, Robert C. A comprehensive bibliography of modern African religious movements. Evanston, 1966.

Afr 9400.11 — Mitchison, Naomi. Return to the fairy hill. London, 1966.

Afr 9327.66F — Mohome, Paulus. A bibliography on Bechuanaland. Syracuse, 1966.

Afr 8676.66 — Moiseeva, Galina M. Iuzhno-Afrikanskaia Respublika. Moskva, 1966.

Afr 8687.275 — Molema, S.M. Montshiwa, 1815-1896. Cape Town, 1966.

Afr 8659.66.5 — Molnar, Thomas Steven. L'Afrique du Sud. Paris, 1966.

Afr 6985.10 — Molnar, Thomas Steven. South West Africa. N.Y., 1966.

Afr 2025.36 — Montclos, Xavier de. Le toast d'Alger, documents, 1890-1891. Paris, 1966.

Afr 10066.2.2 — Moore, Gerald. Modern poetry from Africa. Harmondsworth, 1966.

Afr Doc 3207.362.10 — Morgan, W.T.W. Population of Kenya; density and distribution; a geographical introduction to the Kenya population census, 1962. Nairobi, 1966.

Afr 1620.42 — Morocco. Paris, 1966.

Afr 609.66.10 — Mueng, Engelbert. Dossier culturel pan-africain. Paris, 1966.

Afr 8028.152 — Muller, Christoffel Frederik Jakobus. A select bibliography of South African history; a guide for historical research. Pretoria, 1966.

Afr 6430.5 — Mungeam, Gordon Hudson. British rule in Kenya, 1895-1912. Oxford, 1966.

Afr 6174.11 — Myatt, Fred. The golden stool. London, 1966.

Afr 1620.25.5 — Nagel, Publishers. Maroc. Genève, 1966.

Afr 21205.5 — National Creative Writers Conference, Salisbury, 1966. African literature in Rhodesia. Rhodesia, 1966.

Afr 609.66 — Nielsen, Waldemar A. Africa. 1st ed. N.Y., 1966.

Afr 6277.100.3 — Nigeria, Eastern. Ministry of Commerce. Investment opportunities in Eastern Nigeria. 3rd ed. Enugu, 1966.

Afr 6225.10 — Nigeria, Eastern. Ministry of Information. Nigerian crisis. Enugu, 1966.

Afr 6225.14 — Nigeria, Eastern. Ministry of Information. Nigerian pogrom; the organized massacre of eastern Nigerians. Enugu, 1966.

Afr 6225.10.5 — Nigeria, Eastern. Ministry of Information. The problem of Nigerian unity. Enugu, 1966?

Afr Doc 2520.950F — Nigeria, Western. Ministry of Economic Planning and Social Development. Statistics Division. Development plan statistics of western group of provinces of Nigeria. Ibadan, 1966.

Afr 6287.2 — Nigeria, Western. Ministry of Economic Planning and Social Development. Statistics Division. Directory of industrial establishments in Western Nigeria. Ibadan, 1966.

Afr 6293.2.5 — Nigeria. Comments of the federal military government on the report of the Tribunal of Inquiry into the affairs of the Lagos City Council for the period Oct. 15, 1962 to Apr. 18, 1966. Lagos, 1966.

Afr 6282.17F — Nigeria. Commission Appointed to Enquire into the Owegbe Cult. Report. Benin City, 1966.

Afr 6277.87 — Nigeria. Federal Ministry of Economic Development. Guidepost for Second National Development Plan, June, 1966. Lagos, 1966.

Afr Doc 2309.305.10F — Nigeria. Federal Office of Statistics. Urban consumer surveys. Lagos, 1966. 3v.

Afr 6210.13F — Nigeria Ad Hoc Conference on the Nigerian Constitution. The ad hoc conference on the Nigerian constitution. Enugu, 1966.

Afr 6225.30 — Nigeria 1965; crisis and criticism. Ibadan, 1966.

Afr 10419.2 — Njururi, Ngumbu. Agikuyu folk tales. London, 1966.

Afr 6166.2 — Noerregaard, Georg. Danish settlements in West Africa, 1658-1850. Boston, 1966.

Afr 12884.65.100 — Nokan, Charles. Violent était le vent. Paris, 1966.

Afr 28.71F — Nordiska Afrikainstitutet, Upsala. Bibliotek. Periodica i Nordiska Afrikainstitutets. Uppsala, 1966.

Afr 6210.28 — North and constitutional developments in Nigeria. Enugu, 1966.

Afr 10684.92.2100 — Nwapa, Flora. Efuru. London, 1966.

Afr 6282.30 — Det nye Nigeria. Adrhus, 1966.

Afr 3993.966.5 — O'brien, Patrick Karl. The revolution in Egypt's economic system, from private enterprise to socialism, 1952-1965. London, 1966.

Afr 6392.18 — O'Connor, Anthony Michael. An economic geography of East Africa. N.Y., 1966.

Afr 10435.34.100 — Ogot, Grace Akinyi. The promised land. Nairobi, 1966.

Afr 7809.66 — Ohm, Sven. Svart folk bygger. Stockholm, 1966.

Afr 6280.2.25 — Ojo, G.J. Afolabi. Yoruba culture, a geographical analysis. Ife, Nigeria, 1966.

Afr 10685.67.140 — Okoye, Mokwugo. The beard of Prometheus. Ilfracombe, 1966.

Afr 8089.66 — Omer-Cooper, John. The Zulu aftermath. London, 1966.

Afr 6277.71 — Onitiri, H.M.A. A preliminary report on the possibilities of price control in Nigeria. Ibadan, 1966.

Afr 6277.46 — Onyemelukwe, Clement Chukwukadibia. Problems of industrial planning and management in Nigeria. London, 1966.

Afr 9489.66.10 — Orcival, Francois d'. Rhodésie, pays des lions fidèles. Paris, 1966.

Afr 6277.108 — Orewa, George Oka. Local government finance in Nigeria. Ibadan, 1966.

Afr 25.104.5 — Organization of African Unity. OAU perspective, Third Regular Assembly, 1966. Addis Ababa, 1966.

Afr 9073.797 — Osborn, Robert F. C.G., a great Natalian; biography of Charles George Smith. Durban, 1966.

Afr 6295.66.10 — Osogo, John. A history of the Baluyia. Nairobi, 1966.

Afr 6298.181.80 — Otubushin, Christopher. The exodus and the return of Chief Obafemi Awolowo. Yala, Nigeria, 1966.

Afr 6538.37 — Overseas Development Institute. Aid in Uganda. London, 1966. 3v.

Afr 3979.66.10 — Owen, Robert. Egypt, United Arab Republic, the country and its people. London, 1966.

Afr 12985.65.700 — Oyono, Ferdinand. House boy. London, 1966.

Afr 12005.5 — Pageard, Robert. Littérature négro-africaine. Paris, 1966.

Afr 5488.22 — Pairault, Claude. Boum-le-Grand, village d'Iro. Paris, 1966.

Afr 9435.16 — Palley, Claire. The constitutional history and law of Southern Rhodesia, 1888-1965. Oxford, 1966.

Afr 8688.5.25 Partridge, A.C. The story of our South African flag. Cape Town, 1966.

Afr 9435.9.5 Passmore, Gloria C. Local government legislation in Southern Rhodesia up to Sept. 30th, 1963. Salisbury, 1966.

Afr 23135.46.30 p'Bitek, Okot. SongOf Lawino. Nairobi, 1966.

Afr 9436.14 Peck, A.J.A. Rhodesia accuses. Salisbury, 1966.

Afr 7188.150 Pereira, Henrique Antonio. Silva Carvalho na provincia portuguêsa de Angola. Montijo, 1966.

Afr 609.65.40 Perham, Margery Freda. African outline. London, 1966.

Afr 6275.119.3 Perkins, William Alfred. Nigeria; a descriptive geography. 3rd ed. Ibadan, 1966.

Afr 545.37 Pettersson, Olof. Afrikas religioner. Stockholm, 1966.

Afr 1069.66 Peyrouton, Bernard Marcel. Histoire générale du Maghreb, Algérie, Maroc, Tunisie. Paris, 1966.

Afr 13286.38.100 Philombe, René. Sola ma chérie. Yaoundé, 1966.

Afr 4574.2 Pischke, J.D. The public sector. Addis Ababa, 1966.

Afr 12936.50.102 Pliya, Jean. Kondo le requin; drame historique en trois actes. 2. éd. Porto-Novo, 1966?

Afr 6740.40 Podlewski, André Michel. La dynamique des principales populations du Nord Cameroun. Paris, 1966.

Afr 2030.466.5 Poerner, Arthur J. Argélia: o caminho da independência. Rio de Janeiro, 1966.

Afr 7176.22 Pössinger, Hermann. Angola als Wirtschaftspartner. Köln, 1966.

Afr 5387.8 Polanyi, Karl. Dahomey and the slave trade; an analysis of an archaic economy. Seattle, 1966.

Afr 7208.8 Portugal. Ministério do Ultramar. Providências legislativas ministeriasis, tomadas em Moçambique em 22 outubro de 1966. Lisboa, 1966.

Afr 10066.4 Présence Africaine. Nouvelle somme de poésie du monde noir. Paris, 1966.

Afr 8658.34.10 Pringle, Thomas. Narrative of a residence in South Africa. Cape Town, 1966.

Afr 1840.24 Purtschet, Christian. Sociologie électorale en Afrique du Nord. Paris, 1966.

Afr 2731.15.90 Quesnel, Roger. Charles de Foucauld, les étapes d'une recherche. Tours, 1966.

Afr 5448.18 Quinze ans de travaux et de recherches dans les pays du Niari. Monaco, 1966-1968.

Afr 109.66.25 Rainero, Romain. Storia dell'Africa dall'epoca coloniale ad oggi. Torino, 1966.

Afr 5549.67 Rajemisa-Raolison, Regis. Dictionnaire historique et geographique de Madagascar. Fianarantsoa, 1966.

Afr 9769.66 Ransford, Oliver. Livingstone's lake, the drama of Nyasa. London, 1966

Afr 9047.38 Reader, Desmond Harold. Zulu tribe in transition. Manchester, 1966.

Afr 8847.34.75 Records of a pioneer family. Capetown, 1966.

Afr 9489.66.5 Reed, Douglas. The battle for Rhodesia. Cape Town, 1966.

Afr 3843.8 Reining, Conrad C. The Zande scheme; an anthropological case study of economic development in Africa. Evanston, 1966.

Afr Doc 3808.505 Rhodesia (British Colony). Central Statistical office. The association of commodities with industries in Rhodesia. Salisbury, 1966.

Afr 8028.133F Richards, Margaret Patricia. Mountaineering in Southern Africa. Johannesburg, 1966.

Afr 8659.66.20 Rip, Colin Melville. Contemporary social pathology. Pretoria, 1966.

Afr 8659.66.17 Rittershaus, Wilhelm. Südafrika, eine Bastion Europas? Tagebuch einer Seereise mit Betrachtung des Rossenproblems. 2. Aufl. Klagenfurt, 1966.

Afr 626.98.6 Rivkin, Arnold. Africa and the European Common Market. 2nd ed. Denver, 1966.

Afr 11749.7.100 Robertson, Olive. The mighty turtle and other poems. Cape Town, 1966.

Afr 200.18 Rooney, Douglas David. The building of modern Africa. London, 1966.

Afr 8089.66.25 Roosenthal, Eric. Vesting van die suide. Kaapstad, 1966.

Afr 6412.7 Rosberg, Carl Gustav. The myth of Mau Mau. Stanford, Calif., 1966.

Afr 6540.6.12 Roscoe, John. The Baganda, an account of their native customs and beliefs. 2d ed. N.Y., 1966.

Afr 8835.49 Rosenthal, Eric. Three hundred years of the castle at Cape Town. Capetown, 1966.

Afr 7835.8 Roseveare, Helen. Doctor among Congo rebels. London, 1966.

Afr 6096.17 Runov, Boris B. Iunaited Afrika kompani. Moskva, 1966.

Afr 6541.28 Russel, John Keith. Men without god. London, 1966.

Afr 8378.331 Sachs, Albert. The jail diary of Albie Sachs. London, 1966.

Afr 5758.66 Sala, G. Les travaux au ras du sol; l'investissement humain à Madagascar. Tananarive, 1966.

Afr 10939.2 Samkange, Stanlake. On trial for my country. London, 1966.

Afr 8678.365 Sampson, Harold Fehrsan. The principle of apartheid. Johannesburg, 1966.

Afr 6460.72 Sangree, Walter H. Age, prayer, and politics Ineriki, Kenya. N.Y., 1966.

Afr 1495.6.20 Sarne, Daniel. L'affaire Ben Barka. Paris, 1966.

Afr 5406.266 Sautter, Gilles. De l'Atlantique au fleuve Congo. Paris, 1966. 2v.

Afr 8678.362 Savage, R.B. A study of Bantu retail traders in certain areas of the eastern Cape. Grahamstown, 1966.

Afr 9400.10.22 Schapera, I. Married life in an African tribe. Evanston, 1966.

Afr 6276.2 Schmoelder, Konstanz. Nigeria, von der traditionellen Gemeinschaft zur angepassten Sozialpolitik. Stuttgart, 1966.

Afr 11774.39.100 Scholefield, Alan. A view of vultures. London, 1966.

Afr 8050.18 Scholtz, Gert Daniel. Die bedreiging van die liberalisme. Pretoria, 1966.

Afr 630.14.4 Seligman, C.G. Races of Africa. 4th ed. London, 1966.

Afr 10639.23.100 Selormey, Francis. The narrow path. London, 1966.

Afr 7180.45 Semana do Ultramar, 1st, Luanda, 1965. Migrações e povoamento. Luanda, 1966.

Afr 3079.66 Semenova, Lidiia Andreevna. Salakh-ad-Din i Mamliuki v Egipte. Moskva, 1966.

Afr 5387.12 Serreau, Jean. Le développement à la base au Dahomey et au Sénégal. Paris, 1966.

Afr 4199.759 Seth, Ronald. Russell pasha. London, 1966.

Afr 4591.2 Shack, William A. The Gurage. London, 1966.

Afr 6455.140 Shaposhnikova, Vera D. Bol'shoe safari. Moskva, 1966.

Afr 6295.66.5 Shell Company Of Nigeria. Uboma, a socio-economic and nutritional survey. Bude, Eng., 1966.

Afr 109.61.26 Sik, Endre. The history of black Africa. Budapest, 1966. 2v.

Afr 7335.5 Silva, Julia. Tavares de Almeida de Sousa e Lupata. Lisboa, 1966.

Afr 9558.520 Simmons, Jack. Livingstone and Africa. London, 1966.

Afr 7025.8 Simões, Martinho. Nos três frentes durante três messes. Lisboa?, 1966.

Afr 9448.79 Skeen, Andrew. Prelude to independence, Skeen's 115 days. Cape Town, 1966.

Afr 6470.250.5 Slater, Montagu. The trial of Jomo Kenyatta. 2d ed. London, 1966.

Afr 8289.66F Smail, John Lees. Monuments and battlefields of the Transvaal War, 1881 and the Spanish American War, 1899. Cape Town, 1966.

Afr 6195.19 Smith, Noel. The Presbyterian Church of Ghana, 1835-1960. Accra, 1966.

Afr 8252.341.48 Smuts, J.C. Selections from the Smuts papers. Cambridge, 1966.

Afr 5343.10.5 Société d'Etudes pour le Développement Economique et Social, Paris. Etudes de petites industries en Côte-d'Ivoire. Paris, 1966.

Afr Doc 707.10.2F Somalia. Ministry of Planning and Coordination. Statistical Department. A multipurpose survey of Afgoi municipality. Mogadiscio, 1966.

Afr 9500.50 Sonius, H.W.J. Rhodesia, een dilemma van ras en grond. Leiden, 1966.

Afr Doc 4308.500 South Africa. Bureau of Statistics. Industrial censuses, 1950-51 to 1960-61. Pretoria, 1966.

Afr Doc 4307.360.10 South Africa. Bureau of Statistics. Sensus van groot en kleindistribusiehandel, 1960-61. Pretoria, 1966. 2v.

Afr 8846.34 South Africa. Department of Information. The Transkei; emancipation without chaos. Pretoria, 1966?

Afr Doc 4314.8F South Africa. Parliament. House of Assembly. Debates of the House of Assembly of the Union of South Africa as reported in the Cape Times. Pretoria, 1966. 8v.

Afr 28715.4 Sow, Alfâ Ibrâhîm. La Femme, la vache, la foi. Paris, 1966.

Afr 5944.22 Spain. Consejo Superior de Investigaciones Cientificas. Instituto de Estudios Africancos. Sahara, provincia española. Madrid, 1966.

Afr 8105.22 Spilhaus, Margaret Whiting. South Africa in the making, 1652-1806. Cape Town, 1966.

Afr 212.28 Spiro, Herbert John. Africa. N.Y., 1966.

Afr 9436.15 Spurling, Basil G. Reluctant rebel. Johannesburg, 1966.

Afr 8658.35.5 Steedman, A. Wanderings and adventures in the interior of southern Africa. Cape Town, 1966. 2v.

Afr 9549.66 Stokes, Eric. The Zambesian past. Manchester, 1966.

Afr 6277.86 Stolper, Wolfgang. Planning without facts. Cambridge, 1966.

Afr 115.113 Subbotin, Vaterii A. Problemy istorii Afriki. Moskva, 1966.

Afr 5019.58.4 Suret-Canale, Jean. Schwarzafrika i Geographie, Bevölkering. Berlin, 1966. 2v.

Afr 9193.3F Swaziland. Development plan. Mababane, 1966.

Afr Doc 4107.366F Swaziland. Census Office. Swaziland population census, 1966. Mbabane, 1966.

Afr Doc 4119.5 Swaziland. Constitutional Committee. Report, 24th March, 1966. Mbabane, 1966.

Afr 9489.65 Symonds, Jane. Southern Rhodesia. Oxford, 1966.

Afr 626.166 Symposium of Industrial Development in Africa, Cairo. Report, Cairo, 27 Jan. to 10 Feb. 1966. N.Y., 1966.

Afr 9619.2 Tabler, Edward C. Pioneers of Rhodesia. Cape Town, 1966.

Afr 6298.181.5 Takande, Latif Kayode. The trial of Obafemi Awolowo. Lagos, 1966.

Afr 1083.15 Talabi, Muhammad. L'Émirat aghlabide. Paris, 1966[1967].

Afr 6212.44 Tamsino, Tekena N. Nigeria and elective representation, 1923-1947. London, 1966.

Afr 6881.266 Tanzania. Presidential Special Committee of Enquiry into the Cooperative Movement and Marketing Boards. Report. Dar-es-Salaam, 1966.

Afr 8050.26 Thompson, Leonard Monteath. Politics in the Republic of South Africa. Boston, 1966.

Afr 6214.17 Thorp, Ellen. Ladder of bones. London, 1966.

Afr 3275.38 Tignor, Robert L. Modernization and British colonial rule in Egypt, 1882-1914. Princeton, 1966.

Afr 9505.2 Todd, Judith. Rhodesia. London, 1966.

Afr 5442.15 Tollet, Marcel. Initiation sociologique à l'Afrique centrale. Anvers, 1966.

Afr 679.66.20 Toulat, Jean. Français d'aujourd'hui en Afrique noire. Paris, 1966.

Afr 5319.5 Toure, Ismael. Parti Dée de Guinée, R.D.A. Le développement économique de la république de Guinée. n.p., 1966.

Afr 5846.3.5 Toussaint, Auguste. Une cite tropicale, Port-Louis de L'île Maurice. Paris, 1966.

Afr 5112.5 Traore, Bakary. Forces politiques en Afrique noire. Paris, 1966.

Afr 6390.78 Travellers guide to East Africa. Oxford, 1966.

Afr 7920.3.5 Tshombe, Moise. Quinze mois de gouvernement du Congo. Paris, 1966.

Afr 609.66.40 Turnbull, Colin. Tradition and change in African tribal life. Cleveland, 1966.

Afr Doc 3302.5 Uganda. Catalogue of government publications published prior to 1st January, 1965. Entebbe, 1966?

Afr 6538.47 Uganda. Work for progress, the second five-year plan, 1966-1971. Entebbe, 1966.

Afr 6484.22 Uganda. Board of Inquiry into a Claim for a Rise in Salaries of "E" Scale Public Officers. Report. Entebbe, 1966. 2 pam.

Afr Doc 3319.5 Uganda. Constitution. The Constitution of Uganda, 15th April, 1966. Entebbe, 1966.

Afr 7580.28 Union des Jeunesses Revolutionaires Congolaises. Memorandum; l'agression armée de l'impérialisme Americano-Belge à Stanleyville et Paulis. Bruxelles, 1966.

Afr 3315.144 United Arab Republic. Information Department. Secrets of the Suez War. Cairo, 1966.

Afr 3335.15 United Arab Republic. Ministry of National Guidance. The U.A.R. and the policy of non-alignment. Cairo, 1966?

Afr 6392.38 United States. Bureau of International Commerce. A market for U.S. products in East Africa. Washington, 1966.

Afr 5343.9 United States. Bureau of International Commerce. A market for U.S. products in the Ivory cOast. Washington, 1966.

Afr Doc 7103.7 United States. Embassy. Chad. Diplomatic list, Fort Lamy. Chad. Fort Lamy? 1966.

1966 - cont.

Afr 9291.20	Uys, Cornelis Janse. Rouxville, 1863-1963. Bloemfontein, 1966.
Afr 8687.375	Van der Spuy, Kenneth R. Chasing the wind. Cape Town, 1966.
Afr 7815.46	Vansina, Jan. Introduction à l'ethnographie du Congo. Kinshasa, 1966.
Afr 710.70	Vansina, Jan. Kingdom of the savanna. Madison, 1966.
Afr 6919.34.6	Vedder, H. South-west Africa in early times. London, 1966.
Afr 5442.5	Vennetier, Pierre. Geographie du Congo-Brazzaville. Paris, 1966.
Afr 5368.15	Verger, Pierre. Le Fort St. Jean-Baptiste d'Ajuda. n.p., 1966.
Afr 7582.5	Verhaegen, Benoit. Rébellions au Congo. Leopoldville, 1966.
Afr 8378.200.11	Vermaak, Christopher J. Braam Fischer. Johannesburg, 1966.
Afr 8050.28	Vermaak, Christopher Johann. The red trap: Communism and violence in South Africa. Johannesburg, 1966.
Afr 8378.379.15	Verwoerd, fotobiografie, pictorial biography, 1901-1966. Johannesburg, 1966.
Afr 8378.379	Verwoerd, Hendrik Frensch. Verwoerd aan die woord. 3. druk. Johannesburg, 1966.
Afr 8688.7.10	Villiers, Christoffel Coetzee de. Geslagsregisters van die ou Kaapse families. Kaapstad, 1966.
Afr 8377.10.5	Villiers, Hans Heinrich Wicht de. Danger en Afrique du Sud. Paris, 1966.
Afr 5447.5	Vincent, Jeanne Françoise. Femmes africaines en milieu urbain. Paris, 1966.
Afr 3310.10.50	La voie égyptienne vers le socialisme. Le Caire, 1966.
Afr 8050.8	Vrugte van die nasionale bewind, 1948-1966. Bloemfontein, 1966.
Afr 6164.9.4	Ward, W.E.F. A history of Ghana. 3rd ed. London, 1966.
Afr 109.60.10.3	Ward, William. A history of Africa. v.1-2. London, 1966.
Afr 9191.7	Warwick, Brian Allan. The Swazi, an ethnographic account of the natives of the Swaziland protectorate. London, 1966.
Afr 11874.86.100	Watling, Cyril. Ink in my blood. Cape Town, 1966.
Afr 115.55.2	Wauthier, Claude. The literature and thought of modern Africa, a survey. London, 1966.
Afr 5417.70.2	Weinstein, Brian. Gabon; nation-building on the Ogooue. Cambridge, Mass., 1966.
Afr 6463.3	Welbourn, Frederick B. A place to feel at home, a study of two independent churches in western Kenya. London, 1966.
Afr 210.66.10	Welch, Claude Emerson. Dream of unity. Ithaca, N.Y., 1966.
Afr 6275.116	White, Stanhope. Dan Bana; the memoirs. London, 1966.
Afr 11878.12.21	Wicht, Hein. The mountain; selected short stories. Cape Town, 1966.
Afr Doc 3803.2	Willson, Francis Michael Glenn. Holders of administrative and ministerial office, 1894-1964. Salisbury, 1966.
Afr 4434.5	Wilsson, Wils Gunnar. Det är ju människor det gäller. Stockholm, 1966.
Afr 6203.9	Wolpe, Howard. A study guide for Nigeria. Boston, 1966.
Afr 6664.12	Wuelker, Gabriele. Togo: Tradition und Entwicklung. Stuttgart, 1966.
Afr Doc 4302.10	Yale Univeristy. Library. South African official publications held by Yale University. New Haven, 1966.
Afr 9389.66	Young, Bertram Alfred. Bechuanaland. London, 1966.
Afr Doc 3703.10	Zambia. General list of chiefs. Lusaka, 1966.
Afr Doc 3708.315	Zambia. Cabinet Office. Manpower report. Lusaka, 1966.
Afr 9699.66.5F	Zambia. Office of National Development and Planning. First national development plan, 1966-1970. Lusaka, 1966.
Afr 212.20	Zartman, I. William. International relations in the new Africa. Englewood Cliffs, 1966.
Afr 5053.36	Zolberg, Aristide R. Creating political order. Chicago, 1966.

1967

Afr 6883.20.10	Abrahams, R.G. The political organization of Unyamwezi. Cambridge, 1967.
Afr 10100.5	Abrash, Barbara. Black African literature in English since 1952; works and criticism. N.Y., 1967.
Afr 6210.57	Ad hoc Conference on Constitutional Proposals, Lagos, 1966. Memoranda submitted by the delegations to the Ad hoc Conference on Constitutional proposals for Nigeria. Apapa, 1967.
Afr 6153.25	Adams, Cynthia. A study guide for Ghana. Boston, 1967.
Afr 6460.90	Adamson, Joy. The peoples of Kenya. London, 1967.
Afr 618.36	L'Africa e la civiltà contemporanea. Firenze, 1967.
Afr 609.67.20	Afrika eshche ne otkryta. Moskva, 1967.
Afr 609.67.45	Afrika-Handbuch für Wirtschaft und Reise. Hamburg, 1967. 2v.
Afr 10671.35.100	Agunwa, Clement. More than once. London, 1967.
Afr 210.61.66	Akademiia Nauk SSSR. Institut Afriki. Afrika, 1961-1965gg. Moskva, 1967.
Afr 212.25.9	Akademiia Nauk SSSR. Institut Afriki. Istoriia Afriki v XIX nachale XX v. Moskva, 1967.
Afr 505.48	Akademiia Nauk SSSR. Institut Narodov Azii. Politika Anglii v Afrike. Moskva, 1967.
Afr 5368.10	Akinjogbin, I.A. Dahomey and its neighbours, 1708-1818. Cambridge, Eng., 1967.
Afr 6277.104F	Alako, Samuel A. Fiscal incentives for industrial development in Nigeria. Ife, 1967.
Afr 40.64.5	Alderfer, Harold Freed. A bibliography of African government, 1950-1966. 2d ed. Lincoln University, 1967.
Afr 8658.38.5	Alexander, James E. An expedition of discovery into the interior of Africa. Cape Town, 1967.
Afr 7175.78	American University, Washington, D.C. Foreign Affairs Studies Division. Area handbook for Angola. Washington, 1967.
Afr 6455.152	American University, Washington, D.C. Foreign Areas Studies Division. Area handbook for Kenya. Washington, 1967.
Afr 6390.100	Ames, Evelyn (Perkins). A glimpse of Eden. Boston, 1967.
Afr 5343.14	Amin, Samir. Le Développement du capitalisme en Côte d'Ivoire. Paris, 1967.
Afr 12871.56.100	Amoi, Fatho. Mon beau pays d'Ivoire. Saint-Genix-sur-Guiers, Savoie, 1967.
Afr 9388.57.5	Anderson, C.J. Lake Ngami, or Explorations and discovery during four years of wanderings in wilds of South Western Africa. Cape Town, 1967.
Afr 3979.67	Andres, Stefan Paul. Agyptisches tagebuch. München, 1967.
Afr 210.67.25	Antiimperialisticheskaia revoliutsiia v Afrike. Moskva, 1967.

1967 - cont.

Afr 6498.61.7	Apter, David E. The political kingdom in Uganda; a study in bureaucratic nationalism. 2nd ed. Princeton, 1967.
Afr 6113.5.2	Archer, F.B. The Gambia colony and protectorate and official handbooks. 1st ed. London, 1967.
Afr 6275.124	Arikpo, Okoi. The development of modern Nigeria. Harmondsworth, 1967.
Afr 9609.25	Arrighi, G. The political economy of Rhodesia. The Hague, 1967.
Afr 10421.79.100	Asalache, Khadambi. A calabash of life. London, 1967.
Afr 1040.15	Ashford, Douglas E. National development and local reform. Princeton, 1967.
Afr 5316.14	Attwood, William. The reds and the blacks, a personal adventure. 1st ed. N.Y., 1967.
Afr 7022.4	Axelson, Eric. Portugal and the scramble for Africa, 1875-1891. Johannesburg, 1967.
Afr 4431.5	Baer, George Webster. The coming of the Italian-Ethiopian war. Cambridge, 1967.
Afr 6741.4	Bahoken, Jean Calvin. Clairières métaphysiques africaines, essai sur la philosophie et la religion chez les Bantu du Sud-Caméroun. Paris, 1967.
Afr 8658.63.4	Baldwin, William C. African hunting and adventure. Facsimile of 3rd ed. Capetown, 1967.
Afr 10822.3.100	Ballinger, W.A. Call it Rhodesia. London, 1967.
Afr 10066.2.15	Balogun, Samuel Idown. Notes and exercises on Modern poetry from Africa. Ibadan, 1967.
Afr 9450.20	Barber, James. Rhodesia: the road to rebellion. London, 1967.
Afr 7072.5	Barbosa, Alexandre. Guinéus; contos, narrativas, crónicas. Lisboa, 1967.
Afr 8378.379.30.3	Barnard, Fred. Dertien jaar in die skadu. 3. druk. Johannesburg, 1967.
Afr 9700.20.5.2	Barnes, J.A. Politics in a changing society. 2nd ed. Manchester, 1967.
Afr 8095.55	Battistini, Rene. L'Afrique australe et Madagascar. Paris, 1967.
Afr 4226.6.2	Baylor, Jim. Ethiopia. 2nd ed. Berkeley, 1967.
Afr 3315.142	Beaufre, Andre. L'Expédition de Suez. Paris, 1967.
Afr 13272.21.100	Bebey, Francis. Le fils d'Agatha Moudio. Yaoundé, 1967.
Afr 8028.149	Beckerling, Joan Letitia. The medical history of the Anglo-Boer war. Cape Town, 1967.
Afr 10622.18.100	Bediako, K.A. A husband for Esi Ellua. Ghana, 1967.
Afr 550.150	Beetham, Thomas Allan. Christianity and the new Africa. London, 1967.
Afr 10005.10	Beier, Ulli. Introduction to Africa literature. Evanston, 1967.
Afr 49017.2	Beier, Ulli. Three Nigerian plays. London, 1967.
Afr 5580.3.30	Beniowski, M.A. Pamigtniki. Wyd. 1. Warszawa, 1967.
Afr 1273.967.5	Benyoussef, Amor. Populations du Maghreb et communauté économique à quatre. Paris, 1967.
Afr 9489.67	Berlyn, Phillippa. Rhodesia, beleaguered country. London, 1967.
Afr 8678.376	Bernstein, Hilda. The world that was ours. London, 1967.
Afr 3290.5	Berque, Jacques. L'Egypte, imperialisme et revolution. Paris, 1967.
Afr 1110.40.5	Berque, Jacques. French North Africa. N.Y., 1967.
Afr 10007.2.5	Berrian, Albert H. Négritude; essays and studies. Hampton, 1967.
Afr 8110.18.2	Beyers, C. Die Kaapse patriotte gedurende die laaste kwart van die agtiende eeu en die voortlewing van hui denkbeelde. 2. uitg. Pretoria, 1967.
Afr 6753.5	Bibliografi over Tanzania. København, 1967.
Afr 6760.22A	Bienen, Henry. Tanzania; party transformation. Princeton, 1967.
VAfr 7580.36	Bin'kowski, Andrzej. Drugi cień mojzesza Czombe. Wyd.1. Warszawa, 1967.
Afr 47619.5	Blacking, John. Venda children's songs. Johannesburg, 1967.
Afr 5343.13	Blokhin, Leonid F. Bereg Slonovoi Kosti. Moskva, 1967.
Afr 7122.95	Boavida, Américo. Angola; cinco séculos de exploracão portuguesa. Rio de Janeiro, 1967.
Afr 9704.10	Bolink, Peter. Towards church union in Zambia. Akademisch Proefschrift. Franeker, 1967.
Afr 1738.45	Bonjean, Jacques. Tanger. Paris, 1967.
Afr 11027.5	Booysen, C. Murray. More tales of South Africa. Cape Town, 1967.
Afr 7176.30	Borchert, Günter. Die Wirtschaftsräume Angolas. Pfaffenhofen/Ilm, 1967.
Afr 11229.81.21	Bosman, Herman. Bosman at his best. Cape Town, 1967.
Afr 5318.2.89.2	Bosman, W. A new and accurate description of the coast of Guinea. London, 1967.
Afr 5758.67	Bostian, Georges. Madagascar, étude géographique et économique. Paris, 1967.
Afr 8028.200.15	Botha, Carol. A catalogue of manuscripts and papers in the Killie Campbell African collection relating to the African peoples. Johannesburg, 1967.
Afr 8378.379.20	Botha, Jan. Verwoerd is dead. Cape Town, 1967.
Afr 12372.67.100	Boukman, Daniel. Chants pour hâter la mort du temps des Orphée ou Madinina île esclave. Honfleur, 1967.
Afr 2035.15	Bourges, Hervé. L'Algérie à l'épreuve du pouvoir (1962-1967). Paris, 1967.
Afr 2536.10.30	Bourguiba, Habib. Articles de presse, 1929-1934. Tunis, 1967.
Afr 2536.10.25	Bourguiba, Habib. Les procès Bourguiba, 9 avril, 1938. Tunis, 1967. 2v.
Afr 6196.14.5	Braiman, Joseph Adam. Salaga: the struggle for power. London, 1967.
Afr 6196.14	Braiman, Joseph Adam. The two Isanwurfos. London, 1967.
Afr 12012.3	Brench, Anthony Cecil. The novelists' inheritance in French Africa. London, 1967.
Afr 12018.5	Brench, Anthony Cecil. Writing in French from Senegal to Cameroon. London, 1967.
Afr 500.86	Britain and Germany in Africa; imperial rivalry and colonial rule. New Haven, 1967.
Afr 6275.120	Brook, Ian. The one eyed man is king. N.Y., 1967.
Afr 8969.67	Brookes, Edgar Harry. A history of Natal. Pietermaritzburg, 1967.
Afr 8846.32	Broster, Joan A. Red blanket valley. Johannesburg, 1967.
Afr 9439.67	Bull, Theodore. Rhodesian perspective. London, 1967.
Afr 9170.126.2	Bulpin, Thomas Victor. The ivory trail. 2nd ed. Capetown, 1967.
Afr 6585.4	Burton, Richard Francis. Zanzibar; city, island, and coast. N.Y., 1967. 2v.
Afr 40.67	Busia, Kofi Abrefa. Africa in search of democracy. N.Y., 1967.
Afr 4559.49.6	Buxton, D.R. Travels in Ethiopia. N.Y., 1967.

Afr 5342.68.2   Cadel, Georges. Noirs et Blances, la lutte contre le racism et le transformation des coutumes africaines. Confances, 1967?

Afr 1571.50.5   Caillé, Jacques. Le consulat de Tanger; des origines à 1830. Paris, 1967.

Afr 210.67.35   Calchi Novati, Giampado. Le rivoluzioni nell'Africa nera. Milano, 1967.

Afr 3315.136   Calvocoressi, Peter. Suez ten years after: broadcasts from the BBC. London, 1967.

Afr 1703.5.10   Cappe, Willy. Agadir, 29 février 1960, histoire et leçons d'une catastrophe. Marseille, 1967.

Afr 2030.467.15   Carréras, Fernand. L'Accord F.L.N.-O.A.S. Paris, 1967.

Afr 6919.67.5   Carroll, Faye. South West Africa and the United Nations. Lexington, 1967.

Afr 8846.30   Carter, Gwendolen Margaret. South Africa's Transkei, the politics of domestic colonialism. Evanston, 1967.

Afr 210.67.15   Castro, Luis Filipe de Oliveira e. A nova Africa, ensaio sociopolitico. Lisboa, 1967.

Afr 1495.6.25   Caviglioli, François. Ben Barka chez les juges. Paris, 1967.

Afr 7068.14   César, Amândio. Em "Chão papel" na terra da Guiné. Lisboa, 1967.

Afr 14505.10   César, Amândio. Parágrafos de literatura ultramarina. Lisboa, 1967.

Afr 5480.267   Chad, President. Terre tchadienne. Paris, 1967.

Afr 5482.15   Chad. Ministère du Plan et de la Coopération. Premier plan quinquennal de développement économique et social, 1966-1970. Fort Lamy?, 1967.

Afr 7025.5   Chaliand, Gérard. Lutte armée en Afrique. Paris, 1967.

Afr 8686.20   Champion, George. Journal of the Reverend George Champion. Cape Town, 1967.

Afr 8808.43.5   Chase, John C. The Cape of Good Hope and the Eastern Province of Algoa Bay. Facsimile. Cape Town, 1967.

Afr 7015.46   Chilcote, Ronald H. Portuguese Africa. Englewood Cliffs, N.J., 1967.

VAfr 6195.20   Chodak, Szymon. Kaplani, czarownicy, wiedźmy. Wyd. 1. Warszawa, 1967.

Afr 7913.2.5   Chomé, Jules. Mobutu et la contre-révolution en Afrique. Waterloo, 1967.

Afr 8686.18   Christofersen, Arthur Fridtjof. Adventuring with God. Durban, 1967.

Afr 609.64.17   Church, R.J.H. Africa and the islands. 2nd ed. London, 1967.

Afr 555.136   The Church in Africa. Maryknoll, 1967.

Afr 12673.41.100   Cissoko, Siriman. Ressac de nous-mêmes, poèmes. Paris, 1967.

Afr 6294.5   The City of Ibadan; series of papers presented to a seminar organized early in 1964 by the Institute of African Studies, University of Ibadan. London, 1967.

Afr 9389.67   Clement, A. John. The Kalahari and its lost city. Cape Town, 1967.

Afr 6785.8   Cliffe, Lionel. One party democracy; the 1965 Tanzania general elections. Nairobi, 1967.

Afr 6390.96   Cloudsley-Thompson, John. Animal twilight. Chester Springs, 1967.

Afr 6280.63   Cohen, Ronald. The Kanuri of Bornu. N.Y., 1967.

Afr 8678.381   Cole, Ernest. House of bondage. N.Y., 1967.

Afr 3069.67   Collins, Robert O. Egypt and the Sudan. Englewood Cliffs, N.J., 1967.

Afr 628.267.5   Colloque sur l'Art Nègre, Dakar. Colloque: fonction et signification de l'art nègre dans la vie du peuple et pour le peuple. Paris, 1967.

Afr 2030.467.25   Comité pour la Défense de Ben Bella et des Autres Victimes de la Répression en Algérie. Qu'est devenu Ben Bella? Paris, 1967.

Afr 6392.31   Conference on Education, Employment and Rural Development, Kericho, Kenya, 1966. Education employment and rural development. Nairobi, 1967.

Afr 1285.5   Cooley, John Kent. Baal, Christ, and Mohammed. London, 1967.

Afr 11299.69.21   Cope, Jack. The man who doubted, and other stories. London, 1967.

Afr 8100.44   Cope, John Patrick. King of the Hottentots. Cape Town, 1967.

Afr 8089.65.2   Cope, John Patrick. South Africa. 2.ed. N.Y., 1967.

Afr 1878.15   Cornaton, Michel. Les regroupements de la décolonisation en Algérie. Thèse. Paris, 1967.

Afr 109.67.30   Cornevin, Robert. Histoire de l'Afrique. Paris, 1967-

Afr 679.67.35   Croce-Spinelli, Michel. Les Enfants de Poto-Poto. Paris, 1967.

Afr 8676.67   Croizat, Victor J. The economic development of South Africa in its political context. Santa Monica, 1967.

Afr 8057.10   Cronjé, Geoffrey. Aspekte van die Suid-Afrikaanse historiografie. Pretoria, 1967.

Afr 5185.9.2   Crowder, Michael. Senegal; a study of French assimilation policy. London, 1967.

Afr 590.66   Curtin, Philip de Armond. Africa remembered. Madison, 1967.

Afr 5365.2.2   Dalzel, A. The history of Dahomey, an inland kingdom of Africa. 1st ed. London, 1967.

Afr 5465.5   Dampierre, Eric de. Un ancien royaume bandia de Haut Oubanqui. Paris, 1967.

Afr 3329.598   Daumal, Jack. Gamal Abd-el-Nasser. Paris, 1967.

Afr 679.65.30.1   Davidson, Basil. The growth of African civilisation. London, 1967.

Afr 109.67.25   Davidson, Basil. The growth of African civilization: East and Central Africa to the late nineteenth century. London, 1967.

Afr 210.64.12   Davidson, Basil. Which way Africa? The search for a new society. Harmondsworth, 1967.

Afr 679.67.25   Davies, Oliver. West Africa before the Europeans: archaeology and prehistory. London, 1967.

Afr 555.9.61   Davis, John Merle. Modern industry and the African. 2nd ed. London, 1967.

Afr 4454.10   Davis, Raymond J. Fire on the mountains, the church in Ethiopia. London, 1967.

Afr 9435.18   Day, John. International nationalism. N.Y., 1967.

Afr 6195.22   Dearunner, Hans Werner. A history of Christianity in Ghana. Accra, 1967.

Afr 5285.277.30   Deniel, Raymond. De la savane à la ville. Aix-en-Provence, 1967.

Afr 679.67.40   Deschamps, Hubert Jules. L'Europe découvre l'Afrique. Paris, 1967.

Afr 11053.4   Desmond, Nerine. Candlelight poets of the Cape. Cape Town, 1967.

Afr 1259.67.5   Despois, Jean. Géographie de l'Afrique du Nord-Ouest. Paris, 1967.

Afr 5190.25   Dessertine, A. Un port secondaire de la côte occidentale d'Afrique, Kaolack; étude historique, juridique et économique des origines à 1958. Kaolack, Sénégal, 1967?

Afr 50.8   Diagné, Patné. Pouvoir politique traditionnel en Afrique occidentale. Paris, 1967.

Afr 12624.41.1110   Diakhaté, Lamine. Temps de mémoire. Paris, 1967.

Afr 12574.5   Diallo, Assane Y. Leyd'am, poèmes. Honfleur, 1967.

Afr 6316.5   Diamond, Stanley. The transformation of East Africa. N.Y., 1967.

Afr 12624.41.25   Diop, Birago. Contes choisis. Cambridge, Eng. 1967.

Afr 12624.41.33   Diop, Birago. Les nouveaux contes d'Amadou Koumba. 3. ed. Paris, 1967.

Afr 628.267   Diop, Cheikh A. Antériorité des civilisations nègres. Paris, 1967.

Afr 10624.42.100   Djoleto, Amu. The strange man. London, 1967.

Afr 1609.67   Dominicus, Johannes. Portret van Marokko. s'Hertogenbosch, 1967.

Afr 7815.48   Doutreloux, Albert. L'ombre des fétiches; société et culture yombe. Louvain, 1967.

Afr 618.34   Drost, Dietrich. Töpferei in Afrika. Technologie. Berlin, 1967.

Afr 8659.67   Drury, Allen. A very strange society. N.Y., 1967.

Afr 5749.67   Dubrau, Louis (pseud.). Les îles du Capricorne: Maurice, La Réunion, Madagascar. Bruxelles, 1967.

Afr 7122.83   Duffy, James Edward. A question of slavery. Cambridge, 1967.

Afr 10624.63.100   Duodu, Cameron. The gab boys. London, 1967.

Afr 5046.12   Duverger, Daniel. La croissance des quantités globales en Afrique de l'ouest de 1947 à 1964. Paris, 1967.

Afr 2623.967   Duwaji, Ghazi. Economic development in Tunisia. N.Y., 1967.

Afr 10575.82.110   Easmon, R. Sarif. The burnt-out marriage. London, 1967.

Afr 28715.6.2   East, Rupert Moultrie. Stories of old Adamawa: a collection of historical texts in the Adamawa dialect of Fulani. Farnborough, 1967.

Afr 210.67.10   East-West confrontation in Africa. Interdoc conference. Cambridge, 22nd and 23rd September 1966. The Hague, 1967.

Afr 4573.13   El'ianov, Aratolu Ia. Efiopiia. Moskva, 1967.

Afr 4205.25   Ethiopia. Chamber of Commerce. Trade directory and guide book to Ethiopia. Addis Abada, 1967.

Afr 4573.35F   Ethiopia. Ministry of Planning and Development. Memorandum on the establishment of appropriate machinery at the central government level for preparation of the third five-year development plan. Addis-Ababa, 1967.

Afr 212.52   Etinger, Iakov Ia. Politicheskie problemy afrikanskogo edinstva. Moskva, 1967.

Afr 49419.4.100   Evans-Pritchard, Edward Evan. The Zande trickster. Oxford, 1967.

Afr 6457.38   Faaland, Just. The economy of Kenya. Bergen, 1967.

Afr 6143.1.5   Falconbridge, Anna Maria. Narrative of two voyages to the River Sierra Leone during the years 1791-1793. Facsimile of 2. ed. London, 1967.

Afr 628.252.5   Fannon, F. Black skin, white masks. N.Y., 1967.

Afr 210.64.22   Fanon, Frantz. Toward the African revolution. N.Y., 1967.

Afr 109.67.40   Farelly, Maurice. Africains d'hier et de demain. Neuchâtel, 1967.

Afr 3700.24   Farwell, Byron. Prisoners of the Mahdi. London, 1967.

Afr 8678.321.20   Feit, Edward. African opposition in South Africa. Stanford, 1967.

Afr 109.64.33   Filesi, Teobaldo. Evoluzione storico-politica dell'Africa. 3. ed. Como, 1967.

Afr 7465.16   Fischer, Eberhard. Der Wandel ökonomischer Rollen bei den westlichen Dan in Liberia. Wiesbaden, 1967.

Afr 6282.27.2   Fletcher, Jesse C. Wimpy Harper of Africa. Nashville, 1967.

Afr 2030.467.20   Fontaine, Pierre. L'Aventure algérienne continue. Paris, 1967.

Afr 679.67   Forde, Cyril Daryll. West African kingdom in the nineteenth century. London, 1967.

Afr 5188.5   Fougeyrollas, Pierre. Modernisation des hommes, l'exemple du Sénégal. Paris, 1967.

Afr 6776.5   Fouquer, Roger. Mirambo, un chief de guerre dans l'Est Africain vers 1830-1884. Paris, 1967.

Afr 6391.5   Fox, Lorene Kimball. East African childhood. Nairobi, 1967.

Afr 55.44   Friedrich-Ebert-Stiftung. Afrika Biographien. Hannover, 1967- 3v.

Afr 2030.467.5   Frolkin, Nikolai M. Krest'ianstvo v alzhirskoi revoliutsii, 1954-1962. Kiev, 1967.

Afr 1493.50.10   Furneaux, Rupert. Abdel Krim: Emir of the Rif. London, 1967.

Afr 6138.62.2   Fyfe, Christopher. A short history of Sierra Leone. London, 1967.

Afr 5422.7   Gabon. Plan de développement économique et social, 1966-1970. Paris, 1967?

Afr 609.67.30   Gailey, Harry A. The history of Africa in maps. Chicago, 1967.

Afr 555.155   Gallesio, Lydia. Un cuore irlandese in Africa. Torino, 1967.

Afr 4431.10   Gallo, Max. L'Affaire d'Ethiopie aux origines de la guerre mondiale. Paris, 1967.

Afr 6103.5F   Gamble, David P. Bibliography of the Gambia. Bathurst, 1967.

Afr 626.190   Gand, Michel. Les premières expériences de planification en Afrique noire. Paris, 1967.

Afr 710.72   Gann, Lewis H. Burden of empire. N.Y., 1967.

Afr 628.225.12   Garvey, Marcus. Philosophy and opinions of Marcus Garvey, or Africa for the Africans. 2nd ed. London, 1967.

Afr 7465.12   Gay, John H. The new mathematics and an old culture. N.Y., 1967.

Afr 9493.67   Gelfand, Michael. The African witch: with particular reference to...Shona of Rhodesia. Edinburgh, 1967.

Afr 7582.6   Germani, Hans. White soldiers in black Africa. Cape Town, 1967.

Afr 8928.5   Germond, Robert Charles. Chronicles of Basutoland. Morija, 1967.

Afr 5090.3   Gerteiny, Alfred G. Mauritania. N.Y., 1967.

Afr 5058.13   Gessain, Monique. Les migrations des Coniagui et Bassari. Paris, 1967.

Afr 6153.20F   Ghana. Bureau of Ghana Languages. Bibliography of works in Ghana languages. Accra, 1967.

1967 - cont.

Afr 6176.40.10 Ghana. Commission Enquire into the Kwame Nkrumah Properties. Report of the comission, appointed under the Commission of Enquiry Act, 1964. Accra, 1967.

Afr Doc 1812.202 Ghana. Commission of Enquiry into Electoral and Local Government Reform. Report. Accra, 1967.

Afr 6160.37 Ghana. Commission of Enquiry on the Commercial Activities. Report. Accra-Tema, 1967?

Afr 6160.40F Ghana. Public Services Structure and Salaries Commission. Report of the commission on the structure and renumeration of the public services in Ghana. Accra, 1967.

Afr 4025.15.10 Gialourakēs, Manōlēs. Ē Egyptos ton Ellenon. Athens, 1967.

Afr Doc 9002.5 Gibson, Mary Jane. Portuguese Africa; a guide to official publications. Washington, 1967.

Afr 4368.20 Giselsson, Emanuel. Med frälsningens budskap; några bilder från den svenskamissionen. Stockholm, 1967.

Afr 9700.25.5.2 Gluckman, Max. The judicial process among the Barotse of Northern Rhodesia. 2. ed. Manchester, 1967.

Afr 9073.263 Goetzsche, Eric. The father of a city, the life and times of George Cato. Pietermaritzburg, 1967.

Afr 7175.80 Gonzaga, Norberto. Angola, a brief survey. Lisbon, 1967.

Afr 6194.32.2 Goody, J.R. The social organization of the Lo Wiili. 2nd ed. London, 1967.

Afr 11055.5 Gordimer, Nadine. South African writing today. Harmondsworth, 1967.

Afr 6010.20 Gower, Laurence Cecil Bartlett. Independent Africa. Cambridge, 1967.

Afr 11435.3.100 Granger, Vivian Hector. Sacred is the breed. Cape Town, 1967.

Afr 6979.67.5 Green, Lawrence George. On wings of fire. Cape Town, 1967.

Afr 626.165 Green, Reginald Herbold. Economic co-operation in Africa, retrospect and prospect. Nairobi, 1967.

Afr 7103.15 Greenwood, Margaret Joan. Angola; a bibliography. Cape Town, 1967.

Afr 628.110.1 Grégoire, Henri. An enquiry concerning the intellectual and moral faculties and literature of Negroes. College Park, 1967.

Afr 555.144 Greschat, Hans-Jürgen. Kitawala. Marburg, 1967.

Afr 609.59.15 Gribaudi, Dino. Profilo geografico dell'Africa. Torino, 1967.

Afr 8028.160 Grivainis, Ilze. Material published after 1925 on the Great Trek until 1854. Thesis. Cape Town, 1967.

Afr 6741.12 Grob, Francis. Témoins camerounais de l'Évangile. Yaoundé, 1967.

Afr 8378.379.10 Grobbelaar, Pieter Willem. This was a man. Cape Town, 1967.

Afr 679.67.15 Grohs, Gerhard. Stufen afrikanischer Emanzipation. Stuttgart, 1967.

Afr 609.67 Grove, Alfred Thomas. Africa South of the Sahara. Oxford, 1967.

Afr 5342.67 Grzimek, Bernhard. He and I and the elephants. London, 1967.

Afr 1583.18 Guillen, Pierre. L'Allemagne et le Maroc de 1870-1905. Thèse. Paris, 1967.

Afr 212.46 Guiton, Raymond. Afrika im Widerspruch. Köln, 1967-

Afr 6738.52 Haeberle, Wilhelm. Kamerun. Stuttgart, 1967.

Afr 659.42.2 Haight, Mabel V. Jackson. European powers and south-east Africa. 2nd ed. N.Y., 1967.

Afr 1493.78A Halstead, John Preston. Rebirth of a nation;...Moroccan nationalism, 1912-1944. Cambridge, 1967.

Afr 6295.221 Hama, Boubou. Histoire du Gobir et de Sokoto. Paris, 1967.

Afr 5243.343.20.5 Hama, Boubou. L'Histoire traditionnelle d'un peuple: les Zarma-Songhay. Paris, 1967.

Afr 2762.22 Hama, Boubou. Recherches sur l'histoire des Touareg sahariens et soudanais. Paris, 1967.

Afr 626.40.2 Hance, W.A. African economic development. N.Y., 1967.

Afr 6166.2.5 Hansen, Thorkild. Slavernes kyst. København, 1967.

Afr 5054.67 Hargreaves, John. West Africa. Englewood Cliffs, 1967.

Afr 6595.5 Harkema, Roelof Cornelius. De stad Zanzibar in de tweede helft van de negentiende eeuw en enkele oudere Oostafrikaanse Kuststeden. Loenen aan de Vecht, 1967.

Afr 5225.10 Hasan, Yūsuf Fadl. The Arabs and the Sundan: from the seventh to the early sixteenth century. Edinburgh, 1967.

Afr 550.155 Hastings, Adrian. Church and mission in modern Africa. London, 1967.

Afr 109.67.10 Hatch, John C. Africa; the rebirth of self-rule. London, 1967.

Afr 109.67.15 Hatch, John C. Africa in the wider world, the inter-relationship of area and comparative studies. Oxford, 1967.

Afr 11026.5 Hatfield, Denis. Cape theatre in the 1940's. Cape Town, 1967.

Afr 8678.367 Hawarden, Eleanor. Prejudice in the classroom. Johannesburg, 1967.

Afr 7835.3 Hayes, Margaret. Missing - believed killed. London, 1967.

Afr 626.100.5 Hazlewood, Arthur. African integration and disintegration. London, 1967.

Afr 109.59.18 Healy, A.M. The map approach to African history. 4th ed. London, 1967.

Afr 715.30 Heinrich Barth. Ein Forscher in Afrika. Eine Sammlung von Beiträgen zum 100. Todestag am 25. Nov. 1965. Wiesbaden, 1967.

Afr 7489.88.5 Henries, A. Doris Banks. A biography of President William V.S. Tubman. London, 1967[1968].

Afr 10678.61.110 Henshaw, James Ene. Dinner for promotion; a comedy in three acts. London, 1967.

Afr 8378.379.25 Hepple, Alexander. Verwoerd. Harmondsworth, 1967.

Afr 500.7.4 Hertslet, E. The map of Africa by treaty. 3rd ed. London, 1967. 3v.

Afr 9073.451 Hey, Peter Drummond. One kind of Phoenix and the story of Peter Hey. Pietermaritzburg, 1967.

Afr 6930.25 Hidayatullah, M. The South-West Africa case. Bombay, 1967.

Afr 4198.5.2 Hill, Richard Leslie. A biographical dictionary of the Anglo-Egyptian Sudan. 2nd ed. London, 1967.

Afr 8828.5 Hinchliff, Peter Brigham. Calendar of Cape missionary correspondence, 1800-1850. Pretoria, 1967.

Afr 8678.432 Hirsch, M.I. For whom the land? Salisbury, 1967.

Afr 1369.67 Histoire du Maroc, par Jean Brignon. Paris, 1967.

Afr 7582.10.4 Hoare, Michael. Congo mercenary. London, 1967.

Afr 109.67 Hodder, Bramwell William. Africa in transition, geographical essays. London, 1967.

1967 - cont.

Afr 1618.26 Hoffman, Bernard G. The structure of traditional Morroccan rural society. The Hague, 1967.

Afr 12628.64.100 Hoffmane, Simone. Envoûtement. Dakar, 1967?

Afr 6214.10.10 Hoghen, S.J. An introduction to the history of the Islamic states of Northern Nigeria. Ibadan, 1967.

Afr 6460.92 Holman, Dennis. The elephant people. London, 1967.

Afr 7353.10 Holsoe, Svend. A study guide for Liberia. Boston, 1967.

Afr 6198.670 Hooker, James R. Black revolutionary; George Padmore. London, 1967.

Afr 8676.67.10 Horwitz, Ralph. The political economy of South Africa. London, 1967.

Afr 500.38.2 Hoskins, Halford Lancaster. European imperialism in Africa. N.Y., 1967.

Afr 8676.64.2 Houghton, D. Hobart. The South African economy. 2. ed. Capetown, 1967.

Afr 6470.250.15F Howarth, Anthony. Kenyatta, a photographic biography. Nairobi, 1967.

Afr 710.63 Hunter, Guy. The best of both worlds? A challenge on development policies in Africa. London, 1967.

Afr 8676.67.5 Hupkes, G.J. A reappraisal of economic prospects for 1967. Stellenbosch, 1967.

Afr 678.61.4 Hutchinson, T.J. Ten years' wanderings among the Ethiopians. London, 1967.

Afr 212.58 Hydén, Göran. Politik och samhälle i Afrika. Stockholm, 1967.

Afr 2875.66 Iakhimovich, Zinaida P. Italo-turetskaia voina, 1911-1912 gg. Moskva, 1967.

Afr 8685.27.25 The Indian South African. Durban, 1967.

Afr 6193.60 International Bank for Reconstruction and Development. Stabilization and development in Ghana. N.Y.?, 1967.

Afr 679.67.20 International Conference on South West Africa, Oxford, 1966. South West Africa: travesty of trust. London, 1967.

Afr 6457.46 International Research Associates. A survey of the Kenyan participant training program. N.Y., 1967.

Afr 6881.267 International Research Associates. A survey of the Tanzanian participant training program. N.Y., 1967.

Afr 10062.3 Irasheva, Valentina V. Literatura stran Zapadnoi Afriki; proza. Moskva, 1967.

Afr 609.67.40 Isnara, Hildebert. Géographie de l'Afrique tropicale et australe. 2. éd. Paris, 1967.

Afr 6277.63 Italy. Embassy. Nigeria. Italiens in Nigeria; a story of successful international co-operation. Lagos, 1967?

Afr 6470.242 Itote, Warohiu. "Mau Mau" general. Nairobi, 1967.

Afr 5343.7.15 Ivory Coast. Loi plan de développement économique, social et culturel pour les années, 1967-1968, 1969-1970. Abidjan, 1967.

Afr 5343.7.6 Ivory Coast. Ministère du Plan. Perspectives decennales...Annexes. Abidjan?, 1967?

Afr 5343.7.5 Ivory Coast. Ministère du Plan. Perspectives decennales de développement èconomic, social et cultural, 1960-1970. Abidjan, 1967.

Afr 5485.15 Jaulin, Robert. La Mort sara, l'ordre de la vie ou la pensée de la mort au Tchad. Paris, 1967.

Afr 6196.29 Johnson, M. The Salaga papers. v.1-2. Legen, 1967-

Afr 6292.82 Johnston, Hugh Anthony St. The Fulani Empire of Sokoto. London, 1967.

Afr 626.161 Kamarck, Andrew Martin. The economics of African development. N.Y., 1967.

Afr 8678.378 Kantor, James. A healthy grave. London, 1967.

Afr 3994.967 Kardouche, George K. The U.A.R. in development, a study in expansionary finance. N.Y., 1967.

Afr 9636.8 Kaunda, Kenneth David. Humanism in Zambia and a guide to its implementation. Lusaka, 1967.

Afr 9748.475.10 Kaunda, Kenneth David. A humanist in Africa. London, 1967.

Afr 590.83 Kay, Frederick George. The shameful trade. London, 1967.

Afr 9699.67 Kay, George. A social geography of Zambia; a survey of population. London, 1967.

Afr 10831.5.100 Kayira, Legson. The looming shadow. Garden City, 1967.

Afr 6435.6 Kenya. Kenya-Somalia relations. Nairobi, 1967.

Afr Doc 3019.5 Kenya. Treaties. Treaty for East African co-operation. Nairobi, 1967.

Afr 10015.5 Kesteloot, Lilyan. Anthologie négro-africaine. Verviers, 1967.

Afr 4115.31 Khodzhash, jvettana I. Kair. Moskva, 1967.

Afr 609.67.25 Khokhlov, Nikolai P. Za vorotami slez. Moskva, 1967.

Afr 7580.30 Kitchen, Helen A. Footnotes to the Congo story. N.Y., 1967.

Afr 6883.10 Kjellberg, Eva. The Ismailis in Tanzania. Photoreproduction. Dar-es-Salaam, 1967.

Afr 44610.5 Knappert, Jan. Traditional Swahili poetry. Leiden, 1967.

Afr 10631.58.130 Konadu, Asare. A woman in her prime. London, 1967.

Afr 3993.967.2 Kornrumpf, Hans-Jurgen. Vereinigte Arabische Republik. Opladen, 1967.

Afr 21107.5 Kunene, Daniel P. The beginning of South African vernacular literature. Los Angeles, 1967.

Afr 10016.15 Kurgantsev, Mikhail. Iz afrikanskoi liriki. Moskva, 1967.

Afr 5343.35 La Côte-d'Ivoire. Chances et risques. Session d'étude 20 juillet-11 août 1966. Bruxelles, 1967. 2v.

Afr 7812.267.5 Lacroix, Jan Louis. Industrialisation au Congo. Paris, 1967.

Afr 11509.35.100 LaGuma, Alex. The stone country. Berlin, 1967.

Afr 659.67 Landa, Robert G. U arabov Afriki. Moskva, 1967.

Afr 210.67.20 Lantier, Jacques. L'Afrique déchirée, de l'anarchie à la dictature, de la magic à la technologie. Paris, 1967.

Afr 6292.82.5 Last, Murray. The Sokoto Caliphate. London, 1967.

Afr 5787.5.5 Lavondes, Henri. Bekoropoka quelques aspects de la vie familiale et sociale d'un village Malgache. Paris, 1967.

Afr 8659.67.10 Leenen, Guillaume A.H. Suid Afrikamoe nie huil nie. Melle, 1967.

Afr Doc 4209.305F Lesotho. Bureau of Statistics. National accounts, 1964/5 and 1965/6. Maseru, 1967.

Afr 12639.24.805 Leusse, Hubert de. Léopold Sédar Senghor, l'Africain. Paris, 1967.

Afr 45.67 Le Vine, Victor T. Political leadership in Africa. Stanford, 1967.

Afr 6879.67 Levitt, Leonard. An African season. N.Y., 1967.

Afr 8670.10.2 Lewis, David. Let's stop here; the pictorial guide to hotels in South Africa, South West Africa, Rhodesia and Moçambique. 2. ed. Durban, 1967.

Afr 6277.102 Lewis, William Arthur. Reflections on Nigeria's economic growth. Paris, 1967.

Afr 6542.22 Leys, Colin. Politicians and policies. Nairobi, 1967.

Afr 6742.8 Libère, Mahend Betind Pierre. Rites et croyances relatifs à l'enfance chez les Banen du Cameroun. Paris, 1967.

Afr 7459.67.5F   Liberia. Department of Information and Cultural Affairs. A collection of useful information on Liberia. Monrovia? 1967?

Afr 7459.67   Liberia. Department of Information and Cultural Affairs. Liberia; open door to travel and investment. Monrovia, 1967.

Afr Doc 6002.2   Library of Congress. African Section. French-speaking West Africa; a guide to official publications. Washington, 1967.

Afr 8658.11.6   Lichtenstein, H. Reisen im südlichen Afrika...1803, 1804, 1805, und 1806. Stuttgart, 1967. 2v.

Afr 6145.6.2   Little, Kenneth. The Mende of Sierra Leone. London, 1967.

Afr 852.5   Lloyd, Peter Gutt. Africa in social change. Harmondsworth, 1967.

Afr 7219.67   Lobato, Alexándre. Ilha de Moçambique, panorama histórico. Lisboa, 1967.

Afr 6295.250.200F   Lock, Max. Kabuna, 1917-1967, 2017. London, 1967.

Afr 8676.67.20   Lombard, Johannes Anthonie. Die ekonomiese politiek van Suid-Afrika. Kaapstad, 1967.

Afr 8676.67.15   Lombard, Johannes Anthonie. Die ekonomiese stelsel van Suid-Afrika. Kaapstad, 1967.

Afr 6203.15   London. Commonwealth Institute. Nigeria. London, 1967.

Afr 6293.7.2   Losi, John B. History of Lagos. Lagos, 1967.

Afr 11534.18.100   Ludi, Gerard. Operation Atlantis. Cape Town, 1967.

Afr 7489.8.5   Lynch, Hollis Ralph. Edward Wilmot Blyden. London, 1967.

Afr 8710.22   McCracken, John Leslie. The Cape parliament, 1854-1910. Oxford, 1967.

Afr 10933.5   McIntosh, John. The thorn trees. 1st ed. N.Y., 1967.

Afr 2218.6.20   M'rabet, Fadéla. Les Algériennes. Paris, 1967.

Afr 50.50   Mair, Lucy Philip. The new Africa. London, 1967.

Afr 150.3.1   Major, R.H. The life of Prince Henry of Portugal. 1st ed. London, 1967.

Afr 8835.50   Manuel, George. District Six. Cape Town, 1967.

Afr 609.67.50   Maquet, Jacques Jérôme. Africanité, traditionnelle et moderne. Paris, 1967.

Afr 8289.67   Marquard, Margaret Murray. Letters from a Boer parsonage: letters of Margaret Marquard during the Boer War. Cape Town, 1967.

Afr 626.202   Mars, John. Afrikanische Wirtschaftsintegration. Wien, 1967.

Afr 9435.20   Marshall, Charles Burton. Crisis over Rhodesia: a skeptical view. Baltimore, 1967.

Afr 8028.164   Matton, Carol Ann. Pictures of South African interest in the Graphic, 1896-1899, a list. Thesis. Johannesburg, 1967.

Afr 5091.14   Mauritania. Ministère des Affaires Etrangères et du Plan. Service de la statistique plan quadriennal, 1963-1966. Nouakchott, 1967.

Afr 6025.5   Mazrui, Ali Al'Amin. The Anglo-African Commonwealth. 1st ed. Oxford, 1967.

Afr 212.36.5   Mazrui, Ali Al'Amin. On heroes and Uhuru worship. London, 1967.

Afr 212.36   Mazrui, Ali Al'amin. Towards a Pax Africana, a study of ideology and ambition. London, 1967.

Afr 3993.967.10   Mead, Donald C. Growth and structural change in the Egyptian economy. Homewood, 1967.

Afr 2030.467.10   Merle, Robert. Ahmed Ben Bella. N.Y., 1967.

Afr 8678.310.5   Mezerik, A.G. Apartheid in the Republic of South Africa. N.Y., 1967.

Afr 6392.2   Mezger, Dorothea. Wirtschaftswissenschaftliche Veröffentlichungen über Ostafrika in englischer Sprache. v.1-3. München, 1967. 2v.

Afr 7180.36.2   Milheiros, Mario. Notas de etnografia angolana. 2. ed. Luanda, 1967.

Afr 6538.60   Milton Obote Foundation. The challenge of Uganda's second five year development plan. Kampala, 1967.

Afr 2026.10   Mirad, Ali. Le réformisme musulman en Algérie de 1925 à 1940. Paris, 1967.

Afr 9489.67.5   Mohn, Albert Henrik. Rhodesia. Oslo, 1967.

Afr 5180.20.5   Mollien, G.T. Travels in the interior of Africa. 1st ed. London, 1967.

Afr 1680.16   Monreal Agustí, Luis. La montaña de los guerrilleros; relato. Barcelona, 1967.

Afr 710.16   Morán Lopez, Fernando. El nuevo reino. Madrid, 1967.

Afr 6390.98   Morgan, Gordon Daniel. African vignettes. Jefferson City, 1967.

Afr 6465.58.10   Morgan, W.T.W. Nairobi, city and region. Nairobi, 1967.

Afr 5316.705   Morrow, John H. First American ambassador to Guinea. New Brunswick, 1967[1968].

Afr 6295.250   Mortimore, M.J. Land and people in the Kano close-settled zone. Zaria, 1967.

Afr 609.67.5   Moscow. Institut Istorii Iskusstvi. Iskusstvo Afriki. Moskva, 1967.

Afr 10002.2   Moscow. Vsesoiuznaia Gosudarstvennaia Biblioteka Inostrannoi Literatury. Khudozhestvennaia literatura stran Afriki v sovetskoi pechati. Moskva, 1967.

Afr 6988.94.277   Mossolow, Nicolai. Windhoek heute. Windhoek to-day. Windhoek, 1967.

Afr 6885.10   Mowinza, Joseph. The human soul. Thesis. Tabora, 1967?

Afr 10015.10   Mphahlele, Ezekiel. African writing today. Harmondsworth, 1967.

Afr 11582.70.21   Mphahlele, Ezekiel. In corner b; short stories. Nairobi, 1967.

Afr 9549.67   Mtshali, B. Valindlela. Rhodesia: background to conflict. N.Y., 1967.

Afr 9636.5   Mulford, David C. Zambia: the politics of independence, 1957-1964. London, 1967.

Afr 212.62   Mungai, Njorge. The independent nations of Africa. Nairobi, 1967.

Afr 8678.370   Munger, Edwin S. Afrikaner and African nationalism. London, 1967.

Afr 1495.6.30   Muratet, Roger. On a tué Ben Barka. Paris, 1967.

Afr 6542.5.15   Mutesa II, King of Buganda. Desecration of my kingdom. London, 1967.

Afr 9860.276   Mwase, George Simeon. Strike a blow and die. Cambridge, 1967.

Afr 39906.5   Le mythe et les contes de sou en pays Mbaï-Moïssala. Paris, 1967.

Afr 9489.67.10   National Federation of Women's Institutes (Rhodesia). Great spaces washed with sun: Rhodesia. Salisbury, 1967.

Afr 212.66   Nationale und soziale Revolution in Afrika. 1. Aufl. n.p., 1967.

Afr 12634.16.100   Ndao, H. Alion. L'Exil d'Albouri. Suivi de La décision. Honfleur, 1967.

Afr 9047.5.40   Neilson, Agnes J. An index to Joseph Shooter: the Kafirs of Natal and the Zulu country. Johannesburg, 1967.

Afr 40.67.10   Nekapitalisticheskii put' razvitiia stran Afriki. Moskva, 1967.

Afr 6883.18   Nelson, Anton. The freemen of Meru. Nairobi, 1967.

Afr 500.85   Neokolonializm v Afrike. Moskva, 1967.

Afr 55.42   The new Africans. 1st American ed. N.Y., 1967.

Afr 10615.5   The new generation: prose and verse from the secondary schools and training colleges of Ghana. Accra, 1967.

Afr 10434.127.120   Ngugi, James. A grain of wheat. London, 1967.

Afr 6225.16   Nigeria, Eastern. Ministry of Information. January 15, before and after. Enugu, 1967.

Afr Doc 2434.10   Nigeria. Committee on the Grading of Duty Posts in Voluntary Agency Educational Institutions. Report. Lagos, 1967.

Afr 6275.117   Nigeria. Federal Ministry of Research and Information. Nigeria, 1966. Apapa, 1967.

Afr 6210.56.5   Nigeria. Supreme Military Council. Meeting of the Nigerian military leaders held at Peduase Lodge. Lagos, 1967.

Afr 6210.56   Nigeria. Supreme Military Council. The meeting of the Supreme Military Council at Aburi, Accra, Ghana 4-5 January 1967. Enugu, 1967.

Afr 6275.122   Niven, Cecil Rex. Nigeria. London, 1967.

Afr 6176.30.30   Nkrumah, Kwame. Axioms of Kwame Nkrumah. London, 1967.

Afr 6176.30.31   Nkrumah, Kwame. Axioms of Kwame Nkrumah. London, 1967.

Afr 7580.26   Nkrumah, Kwame. Challenge of the Congo. London, 1967.

Afr 6178.6   Nkrumah, Kwame. Voice from Conakry. London, 1967.

Afr 609.67.15   Nolen, Barbara. Africa is people, firsthand accounts from contemporary Africa. 1st ed. N.Y., 1967.

Afr 212.54   Nord, Erik. Militärkupper i Afrika. Uppsala, 1967.

Afr 3315.133   Nutting, Anthony. No end of a lesson. London, 1967.

Afr 10516.5   Nwoga, Donatus Ibe. West African verse; an anthology. London, 1967.

Afr 2030.467   O'Ballance, Edgar. The Algerian insurrection, 1954-62. London, 1967.

Afr 6095.361.5   Oboli, H.O.N. An outline geography of West Africa. 5th ed. London, 1967.

Afr 6470.289   Odinga, Ajuma Oginga. Not yet Uhuru, an autobiography. London, 1967.

Afr 6460.80.15   Ogot, Bethwell Allan. History of the southern Luo. Nairobi, 1967.

VAfr 4559.67   Ogrin, Miran. Od Nila do Kartagine. Ljubljana, 1967.

Afr 2026.9   Ohneck, Wolfgang. Die französische Algerienpolitik von 1919-1939. Köln, 1967.

Afr 6225.25   Ohonbamu, Obarogie. Whither Nigeria? Lagos, 1967.

Afr 6280.2.30   Ojo, G.J. Afolabi. Yoruba palaces, a study of Afins of Yorubaland. London, 1967.

Afr 6575.2   Okello, John. Revolution in Zanzibar. Nairobi, 1967.

Afr 626.174   Okigbo, Pius Nwabufo. Africa and the Common Market. London, 1967.

Afr 10316.5   Okola, Lennard. Drum beat; East African poems. Nairobi, 1967.

Afr 7309.61.2   Oliveira Boléo, José de. Mozambique; petite monographie. 2. éd. Lisbonne, 1967.

Afr 1410.2   Oliver, Roland. Africa since 1800. London, 1967.

Afr 109.67.5   Oliver, Roland Anthony. The middle age of African history. London, 1967.

Afr 6463.10   Olivotti, Guiseppe. Verde Kenya. Con presentazione di Giovanni Urbani. Venezia, 1967.

Afr 6225.20   Orbit Publications. Events; a diary of important happenings in Nigeria from 1960-1966. Ebute-Metta, 1967.

Afr 8063.20.10   Orpen, Neil. Prince Alfred's guard, 1856-1966. Port Elizabeth, 1967.

Afr 8377.12   Orpen, Neil. Total defence. 1st ed. Cape Town, 1967.

Afr 609.67.10   Osei, Gabriel Kingsley. The African, his antecedents, his genius and his destiny. London, 1967.

Afr 6457.36   Oser, Jacob. Promoting economie development with illustrations from Kenya. Nairobi, 1967.

Afr 609.67.35   Owen, Roderic Fenwick. Roddy Owen's Africa. Appleford, 1967.

Afr 40.67.5   Oyebola, Areoye. A textbook of government for West Africa. Ibadan, 1967.

Afr 12985.65.701   Oyono, Ferdinand. House boy. London, 1967.

Afr 12985.65.705   Oyono, Ferdinand. The old man and the medal. London, 1967.

Afr 2731.21   Pagès, Louis Jacques Faugère le Saharien. Nérac, 1967.

Afr 5219.28.5   Palmer, H.R. Sudanese memoirs. v.1-3. London, 1967.

Afr 4230.4.15   Pankhurst, Richard Keir Pethick. The Ethiopian royal chronicles. Addis Ababa, 1967.

Afr 5758.67.5   Paproth, Klaus. Voraussetzungen und Möglichkeiten für Industriegründungen in Madagaskar. Hamburg, 1967.

Afr 545.42   Parrinder, E.G. African mythology. London, 1967.

Afr 6280.32.2   Parrinder, E.G. The story of Ketu, an ancient Yoruba kingdom. 2nd ed. Ibadan, Nigeria, 1967.

Afr 1869.67   Pečar, Zdravko. Alžir do nezavisnosti. Beograd, 1967.

Afr 9450.8   Peck, A.J.A. Rhodesia condemns. Salisbury, Rhodesia, 1967.

Afr 6034.2   Perham, Margery Freda. Colonial sequence, 1930 to 1949. London, 1967.

Afr 5190.24   Peterec, Richard J. Dakar and West African economic development. N.Y., 1967.

Afr 10536.69.110   Peters, Lenrie. Satellites. London, 1967.

Afr 7817.10   Petersen, William J. Another hand on mine; the story of Dr. Carl K. Becker of the Africa Inland Mission. 1st ed. N.Y., 1967.

Afr 9565.2   Pitch, Anthony. Inside Zambia - and out. Cape Town, 1967.

Afr 6295.248   Plotnicov, Leonard. Strangers to the city; urban man in Jos, Nigeria. Pittsburgh, 1967.

Afr 659.67.5   Plum, Werner. Sozialer Wandel im Maghreb i Voraussetzungen und Erfahrungen der genossenschaftlichen Entwicklung. Hannover, 1967.

Afr 699.67   Pollard, John. The long safari. London, 1967.

Afr 626.170   Popov, Iurii Nikolaevich. Political economy and African reality. Moscow, 1967.

Afr 3325.10   Powell, Ivor. Disillusion by the Nile: what Nasser has done to Egypt. London, 1967.

Afr 5448.16   Préclin, Louis. Pointe-Noire sous la croix de Lorraine. Paris, 1967.

Afr 679.67.30   Price, Joseph Henry. Political institutions of West Africa. London, 1967.

Afr 8678.69   Prins, Jan. De beknelde kleurling Zuid-Afrika's vierstromenbeld. Assen, 1967.

Afr 3042.8   Quraishi, Zaheer Masood. Liberal nationalism in Egypt; rise and fall of Wafa party. 1st ed. Allahabad, 1967.

1967 - cont.

Afr 9446.37   Ranger, Terence O. Revolt in Southern Rhodesia, 1896-1897. London, 1967.

Afr 9446.40   Ranger, Terence Osborn. Revolt in Southern Rhodesia, 1896-97. Evanston, Ill., 1967.

Afr 8225.15   Ransford, Oliver. The battle of Majuba Hill, the first Boer war. London, 1967.

VAfr 7567.41   Ratajski, Lech. Konge Kinszasa. Wyd. 1. Warszawa, 1967.

Afr 5874.21   Ravat, Yves. La Réunion, terre française. Port Louis, 1967.

Afr 8100.42   Raven-Hart, Rowland. Before Van Riebeeck. Cape Town, 1967.

Afr 36.6   Reconstructing African culture and history. Boston, 1967.

Afr 9489.66.6   Reed, Douglas. Insanity fair '67. London, 1967.

Afr 9839.67   Reed, Frank E. Malawi, land of promise. Blantyre, 1967.

Afr 635.95   Refugee problems in Africa. Uppsala, 1967.

Afr 7580.35   Rétillon, Leon A.M. Témoignage et réflexions. Bruxelles, 1967.

Afr 6919.67.10   Rhoodie, Eschel Mostert. South West: the last frontier in Africa. Johannesburg, 1967.

Afr 6390.65.10   Richards, C.G. East African explorers. Nairobi, 1967.

Afr 210.67   Rivkin, Arnold. The new states of Africa. N.Y., 1967.

Afr 6435.8   Roberts, John S. A land full of people: Kenya today. London, 1967.

Afr 9345.72   Robins, Eric. White Queen in Africa. London, 1967.

Afr 9028.72.1   Robinson, J. Notes on Natal. Pretoria, 1967.

Afr 861.35   Roenne, Arne Falk. Back to Tristan. London, 1967.

Afr 7812.267   Romaniuk, Anatole. La fécondité des populations congolaises. Paris, 1967.

Afr 210.67.30   Rooke, Patrick J. The wind of change in Africa. Glasgow, 1967.

Afr 200.18.2   Rooney, Douglas David. The building of modern Africa. 2nd ed. London, 1967.

Afr 679.67.10   Rosenthal, Ricky. The splendor that was Africa. Dobbs Ferry, 1967.

Afr 2535.10   Rossi, Pierre. La Tunisie de Bourguiba. Tunis, 1967.

Afr 10838.89.100   Rubadiri, David. No bride price. Nairobi, 1967.

Afr 8380.20   Rupert, Anton. Progress through partnership. Cape Town, 1967.

Afr 8678.368   Sacks, Benjamin. South Africa, an imperial dilemma, non-Europeans and the British nation, 1902-1914. 1st ed. Albuquerque, 1967.

Afr 5130.30   Saint-Martin, Yves. L'empire toucouleur et la France un demi-siècle de relation diplomatiques, 1846-1893. Dakar, 1967.

Afr 4558.14.5   Salt, Henry. A voyage to Abyssinia, and travels into the interior of that country. 1st ed. London, 1967.

Afr 7187.2   Santos, Nuno Beja Valdez Thomaz dos. A fortaleza de S. Miguel. Luanda, 1967.

Afr 7188.79   Santos Martins dos. A história de Angola através dos seus personagens principais. Lisboa, 1967.

Afr 6144.10   Saylor, Ralph Gerald. The economic system of Sierra Leone. Durham, 1967.

Afr 8667.75   Schapera, Isaac. Western civilization and the natives of South Africa, studies in culture contrast. 1st ed. London, 1967.

Afr 115.20.10   Schiffers, Heinrich. Afrika, als die Weissen kamen. Düsseldorf, 1967.

Afr 609.57.2   Schiffers, Heinrich. Afrika. 8. Aufl. München, 1967.

Afr 11774.39.110   Scholefield, Alan. Great elephant. London, 1967.

Afr 1270.10   Schramm, Josef. Nordafrika. 2. Aufl. Buchenhain von München, 1967.

Afr 679.67.5   Seck, Assane. L'Afrique occidentale. Paris, 1967.

Afr 210.67.5   Seminar Africa. National and Social Revolution, Cairo, 1966. Seminar Africa, National and Social Revolution, October 24th-29th, 1966, Cairo. Cairo, 1967. 4v.

Afr 626.214   Seminar on Local Government Finance in Africa, Addis Ababa, 1966. Local government finance in Africa. Berlin, 1967.

Afr 618.40   Senghor, Léopold Sédar. Les fondements de l'africanité ou négritude et arabité. Paris, 1967?

Afr 6280.70   Sertorio, Guido. Struttura socialepolitica e ordinamento fondiario Yoruba dall'epoca tradizionale all'odierna. Coma, 1967.

Afr 6293.4   SES Publishers. Your ABC of Lagos and suburbs including guide maps of Benin, Enugu, Ibadan and Kaduna. Lagos, 1967.

Afr 8687.339   Shaw, William. Never a young man: extracts from the letters and journals of the Reverend William Shaw. Cape Town, 1967.

Afr 545.44   Shparhnikov, Genrikh A. Religii stran Afriki. Moskva, 1967.

Afr 109.67.35   Sicard, Maurice Ivan. La contre-révolution africaine. Paris, 1967.

Afr 6141.2F   Sierra Leone. Commission of Inquiry into the Conduct of the 1967 General Elections in Sierra Leone. Report of the Dove-Edwin Commission of inquiry into the conduct of the 1967 general election in Sierra Leone and the government statement thereon. Freetown, 1967.

Afr 590.85   Sierra Leone. Liberated African Department. Notes from Liberated African Department. Uppsala, 1967.

Afr 9203.5   Sinclair, Dorothy Mary. The Orange Free State goldfields; a bibliography. Cape Town, 1967.

Afr 109.67.20   Singleton, F. Seth. Africa in perspective. N.Y., 1967.

Afr 2505.18   Slama, Bice. L'insurrection de 1864 en Tunisie. Tunis, 1967.

Afr 11795.4.100   Slatter, Eve Mary. My leaves are green. Cape Town, 1967.

Afr 635.61   Smirnova, Raisà M. Polozhenre zhenshchin v stranakh Afriki. Moskva, 1967.

Afr 6192.100   Smith, Edward. Where to, black man? Chicago, 1967.

Afr 7489.88.2   Smith, Robert A. William V.S. Tubman. The life and work of an African statesman. 2nd ed. Amsterdam, 1967.

Afr 6095.22.10   Smith, William. A new voyage to Guinea: describing the customs. 1st ed. London, 1967.

Afr 8659.67.5   Somoy, A.G. Paspoort voor Zuid-Afrika. Lier, 1967.

Afr 6457.32   Sorrenson, M.P.K. Land reform in the Kikuyu country. Nairobi, 1967.

Afr 7179.5   Sousa, Gabriel de. A portugalização do suesto de Angola. Lisboa, 1967.

Afr 8378.379.35F   South Africa. Commission of Enquiry Into the Circumstances of the Death of the Late Dr. the Honourable Hendrik Frensch Verwoerd. Report. Pretoria, 1967.

Afr 6979.67   South Africa. Department of Foreign Affairs. South West Africa survey, 1967. Pretoria, 1967.

Afr 1575.15   Souto, A. Meyselles do. Portugal e Marrocos; fostos e notícias. Lisboa, 1967.

1967 - cont.

Afr 9499.78   Sowelem, R.A. Towards financial independance in a developing economy. London, 1967.

Afr 10689.67.21   Soyinka, W. Idanre, and other poems. London, 1967.

Afr 10689.67.160   Soyinka, W. Kongi's harvest. London, 1967.

Afr 9450.15   Sparrow, Gerald. Rhodesia in 'rebellion'. London, 1967.

Afr 4095.13   Speke, John Hanning. What led to the discovery of the source of the Nile. London, 1967.

Afr 6390.92   Spencer, Hope Rockefeller. The way to Rehema's house. N.Y., 1967.

Afr 1487.40   Spillmann, Georges. Du protectorat à l'indépendance, Maroc, 1912-1955. Paris, 1967.

Afr 212.28.5   Spiro, Herbert John. Patterns of African development, five comparisons. Englewood Cliffs, N.J., 1967.

Afr 9488.75   Stabb, Henry. To the Victoria Falls via Matabeleland. Cape Town, 1967.

Afr 28.120.2   Standing Conference on Library Materials on Africa. The SCOLMA directory of libraries and special collections on Africa. 2nd ed. London, 1967.

Afr 6277.20.2   Stapleton, G.B. The wealth of Nigeria. 2nd ed. Ibadan, 1967.

Afr 8865.14   Stevens, Richard P. Lesotho, Botswana, and Swaziland: the former High Commission territoris in Southern Africa. London, 1967.

Afr 626.176   Stokke, Baard Richard. Soviet and Eastern European trade in Africa. N.Y., 1967.

Afr 8678.383   Strydom, Christiaan Johannes Scheepers. Black and white Africans. 1st ed. Cape Town, 1967.

Afr 6879.67.5   Svendsen, Knud Erik. Tanzania vil selv. København, 1967.

Afr 8678.375   Sweden. Utrikesdepartementet. Apartheidfragan i förenta nationerna. Stockholm, 1967.

Afr 10009.5   Taiwo, Oladele. An introduction to West African literature. London, 1967.

Afr 6883.15.5   Tanner, Ralph E.S. Transition in African beliefs. Maryknoll, 1967.

Afr 575.56   Tarverdova, Ekaterina A. Rasprostranenie islama v zapadnoi Afrike, XI-XVI vv. Moskva, 1967.

Afr 50.53   Taylor, Don. Africa, the portrait of power. London, 1967.

Afr 3163.10   Tekindaÿ, M.C. Şehabeddin. Berkuk devrinde Memluk Sultanhgi. Istanbul, 1967.

Afr 3315.132.7   Thomas, Hugh. Suez. N.Y., 1967.

Afr 3315.132   Thomas, Hugh. The Suez affair. London, 1967.

Afr 13240.39.100   Thsinday Lukumbi, Etienne. Marche, pays des espoirs. Paris, 1967.

Afr 1273.967   Tiano, André. Le Maghreb entre les mythes, l'économie nord-africaine. Paris, 1967.

Afr 7817.30   Tielemans, H. Gijzelaars in Congo. Tilburg, 1967?

Afr 626.180   Timmler, Markus. Die Gemeinsame Afrikanisch-Madegassische Organisation. Köln, 1967.

Afr 6785.5   Tordoff, William. Government and politics in Tanzania. Nairobi, 1967.

Afr 5805.5   Toussaint, Auguste. La Route des îles, coutribution à l'histoire maritime des Mascareignes. Paris, 1967.

Afr 6225.35   Toyo, Eskar. The working class and the Nigerian crisis. Ibadan, 1967.

Afr 4785.967   Travis, William. The voice of the turtle. London, 1967.

Afr 7920.3.15   Tshombe, Moise. My fifteen months in government. Plano, Tex., 1967.

Afr 10105.67   Tucker, Martin. Africa in modern literature. N.Y., 1967.

Afr 2688.5F   Turki, Zubayr. Tunis, naguère et aujourd'hui. Tunis, 1967.

Afr 9700.32.5   Turner, Victor Witter. The forest of symbols; aspects of Ndembu ritual. Ithaca, 1967.

Afr 10690.89.130   Tutuola, Amos. Ajaiyi and his inherited poverty. London, 1967.

Afr Doc 3319.15   Uganda. Constitution. The constitution of the Republic of Uganda. Entebbe, 1967?

Afr Doc 3319.10   Uganda. Constitution. The govenment proposals for a new Constitution, 9th June, 1967. Entebbe, 1967.

Afr 6538.55   Uganda. Ministry of Planning and Economic Development. Work for progress. Entebbe, 1967.

Afr 8678.382   UNESCO. Apartheid; its effects on education, science, culture and information. Paris, 1967.

Afr 6277.106   Upton, Martin. Agriculture in South-West Nigeria; a study of the relationships between production and social characteristics in selected villages. Reading, 1967.

Afr 10691.99.100   Uzodinma, Edmund. Our dead speak. London, 1967.

Afr 11865.59.160   Vanderpost, Laurens. The hunter and the whale: a story. London, 1967.

Afr 8685.98   Verner, Beryl Anne. Huguenots in South Africa; a bibliography. Cape Town, 1967.

Afr 14692.41.120   Victor, Geraldo Bessa. Sanzala sem batuque. Braga, 1967.

Afr 7575.99   Vinokurov, Iurii N. Kongo. Moskva, 1967.

Afr 6542.50   Vorlaufer, Karl. Physiognomie, Struktur und Funktion Gross Kampalas. Frankfurt, 1967. 2v.

Afr 9176.5   Wallace, Charles S. Swaziland; a bibliography. Johannesburg, 1967.

Afr 212.38   Wallerstein, Immanuel Maurice. Africa, the politics of unity. N.Y., 1967.

Afr 2929.67   Ward, Philip. Touring Libya. London, 1967.

Afr 6164.9.5   Ward, W.E.F. A history of Ghana. 4th ed. London, 1967.

Afr 175.8   Ward, William Ernest Frank. Emergent Africa. London, 1967.

Afr 3199.67   Waterfield, Gordon. Egypt. London, 1967.

Afr 5055.67   Webster, James B. The revolutionary years: West Africa since 1800. London, 1967.

Afr 6403.5   Webster, John B. A bibliography on Kenya. Syracuse, 1967.

Afr 7543.12   Weiss, Herbert F. Political protest in the Congo. Princeton, 1967.

Afr 1259.67   Wellard, James. Lost worlds of Africa. 1st ed. N.Y., 1967.

Afr 6919.67   Wellington, John Harold. South West Africa and its human issues. Oxford, 1967.

Afr 6460.87   Were, Gideon S. A history of the Abaluyia of western Kenia. Nairobi, 1967.

Afr 6460.87.5   Were, Gideon S. Western Kenya historical texts: Abaluyia, Teso, and Elgon Kalenjin. Nairobi, 1967.

Afr 626.172   Whetham, Edith Holt. Readings in the applied economics of Africa. Cambridge, 1967.

Afr 678.77.2   Whitford, J.F.R.G.S. Trading life in Western and Central Africa. 2nd ed. London, 1967.

Afr 8686.16   Wiberg, Erik. Hundra dagar i Afrika. Jönköping, 1967.

Afr 580.10.4   Williams, Joseph J. Hebrewisms of West Africa, from Nile to Niger with the Jews. N.Y., 1967.

Afr 9439.64.2   Wills, Alfred John. An introduction to the history of central Africa. 2. ed. London, 1967.

1967 - cont.

Afr 7182.17 — Wilson, Thomas E. Angola beloved. Neptune, N.J., 1967.
Afr 9165.42.90 — Winter, James Sydney. First-hand accounts of Johannesburg in English-language periodicals, 1886-1895, a list. Johannesburg, 1967.
Afr 4573.15 — Wohlgemuth, Lennart. Etiopiens ekonomi. Uppsala, 1967.
Afr 3708.20 — Wolseley, Garnet Joseph Wolseley. In relief of Gordon; Lord Wolseley's campaign journal of the Khartoum Relief Expedition, 1884-1885. London, 1967.
Afr 6198.440 — Wraith, Ronald E. Guggisberg. London, 1967.
Afr 9448.51 — Young, Kenneth. Rhodesia and independence, a study in British colonial policy. London, 1967.
Afr 11456.14.1 — Yudelman, Myra. Dan Jacobson, a bibliography. Johannesburg, 1967.
Afr 9699.66.10 — Zambia. Office of National Development and Planning. The building industry and the First National Development Plan. Lusaka, 1967.
Afr 9650.5 — Zambia. Tribunal on Detainees. Report. Lusaka, 1967.
Afr 6128.5 — Zell, Hans M. A bibliography of non-periodical literature on Sierra Leone, 1925-1966. Freetown, 1967?
Afr 2698.5 — Zmerli, Sadok. Les successeurs. Tunis, 1967.
Afr 659.66.7 — Zwischen Mittelmeer und Tschadsee: Reisen deutscher Forscher des 19. 2. Aufl. Berlin, 1967.

1968

Afr 3340.20 — Abdel Malek, Anouar. Egypt: military society; social change under Nasser. 1st American ed. N.Y., 1968.
Afr 4360.10 — Abir, Mordechai. Ethiopia: the era of the princes. London, 1968.
Afr 10671.12.121 — Achebe, Chinua. Things fall apart. London, 1968.
Afr 1706.8 — Adam, André. Casablanca. Thèse. Paris, 1968. 2v.
Afr 6470.103 — Adamson, George. A lifetime with lions. Garden City, 1968.
Afr 6210.60 — Adedeji, Adebayo. Nigerian administration and its political setting. London, 1968.
Afr 710.32.10 — African Population Conference, 1st, University of Ibadan, 1966. The population of tropical Africa; conference held Jan. 3-7, 1966. N.Y., 1968.
Afr 1.32.5 — African studies bulletin. Index, v.1-10 (1958-1967). Boston, 1968.
Afr 2025.38 — Ageron, Charles Robert. Les Algériens musulmans et la France, 1871-1919. Paris, 1968. 2v.
Afr 10013.2.5 — Ainslie, Rosalynde. The press in Africa: communications past and present. N.Y., 1968.
Afr 212.26.2 — Akademiia Nauk SSSR. Institut Afriki. A history of Africa, 1918-1967. Moscow, 1968.
Afr 626.8 — Akinwale, Lydia Oluwafemi. Marxism and African economic development, 1952-1968. Ibadan, 1968.
Afr 6277.126 — Akinyotu, Adetunji. A bibliography on development planning in Nigeria, 1955-1968. Ibadan, 1968.
Afr 10671.53.1100 — Amali, Samson Onyilokwu Onche. The downfall of Ogbúu; a play. Ibadan, 1968?
Afr 6879.68 — American University, Washington, D.C. Foreign Area Studies Division. Area handbook for Tanzania. Washington, 1968.
Afr 2397.8 — Amrouche, Fadhma Aïth Mansour. Histoire de ma vie. Paris, 1968.
Afr 6978.61.2 — Andersson, Carl J. The Okavango River: a narrative of travel, exploration and adventure. Facsimile. Cape Town, 1968.
Afr 5446.5 — Andersson, Efraim. Churches at the grass-roots. London, 1968.
Afr 45.68.5 — Andreski, Stanislav. The African predicament. London, 1968.
Afr 7108.20 — Angolana. Luanda, 1968.
Afr 7183.22 — António, Mário. Luanda, "ilha" criuola. Lisboa, 1968.
Afr 10621.71.100 — Appiah, Peggy. The children of Anause. London, 1968.
Afr 8658.46.5 — Arbousset, Thomas. Narrative of an exploratory tour to the North-East of the Colony of the Cape of Good Hope. Facsimile. Cape Town, 1968.
Afr 10621.53.100 — Armah, Ayi Kwei. The beautyful ones are not yet born. Boston, 1968.
Afr 626.208 — Aromolaran, Adekunie. West African economics today. 1st ed. Ibadan, 1968.
Afr 710.74 — Aspects of Central African history. London, 1968.
Afr 6769.68 — Austen, Ralph Albert. Northwest Tanzania under German and British rule. New Haven, 1968.
Afr 6214.34 — Awdowo Obateni. The people's republic. Ibadan, 1968.
Afr 6298.181.2 — Awolowo, Obaf. My early life. Lagos, 1968.
Afr 6193.52 — Ayatey, Siegfried B.Y. Central banking, international law, and economic development. Dubugre, 1968.
Afr 6212.20.5 — Azikiwe, Nnamdi. Sélection de discours de Nnamdi Azikiwe. Paris, 1968.
Afr 9148.77.5 — Baines, Thomas. The gold regions of south eastern Africa. Bulawayo, 1968.
Afr 8934.123 — Baker, Jeff. African flying journal. London, 1968.
Afr 7560.15.5 — Balandier, Georges. Daily life in the Kingdom of the Kongo from the sixteenth to the eighteenth century. London, 1968.
Afr 30.4 — Balandier, Georges. Dictionnaire des civilisations africaines. Paris, 1968.
Afr 12622.3.100 — Balogun, Ola. Shango, suivi de Le roi-éléphant. Honfleur, 1968.
Afr 8980.3.5 — Bannister, S. Humane policy; or, Justice to the aborigines of new settlements. 1st ed. London, 1968.
Afr 6490.5 — Barber, James P. Imperial frontier. Nairobi, 1968.
Afr 4431.20 — Barker, Arthur J. The civilizing minion; a history of the Italo-Ethiopian War of 1935-1936. N.Y., 1968.
Afr 550.165 — Barrett, David B. Schism and renewal in Africa. Nairobi, 1968.
Afr 8658.01.4 — Barrow, J. An account of travels into the interior of Southern Africa, in the years 1797 and 1798. N.Y., 1968.
Afr 3745.73 — Bashir, Muhammad Umar. The Southern Sudan. London, 1968.
Afr 5275.5 — Bassolet, François Djoby. Evolution de la Haute-Volta de 1898 au 3 janvier 1966. Ouagadougou, 1968.
Afr 13272.21.110 — Bebey, Francis. Embarras et Cie; nouvelles et poèmes. Yaoundé, 1968.
Afr 6739.268 — Bederman, Sanford Harold. The Cameroons Development Corporation. Bota, 1968.
Afr 500.35.2 — Beer, George Louis. African questions at the Paris Peace Conference. 1st ed. London, 1968.
Afr 10013.8 — Behn, Hans Ulrich. Die Presse in Westafrika. Hamburg, 1968.
Afr 6291.42 — Beijbom, Anders. Rapport fran Biafra. Stockholm, 1968.
Afr 1495.6.35 — Ben Barka, el Mehdi. The political thought of Ben Barka. Havana, 1968.

1968 - cont.

Afr 5895.5.2 — Benedict, Burton. People of the Seychelles. 2nd ed. London, 1968.
Afr 590.45.2 — Benezet, Anthony. Some historical account of Guinea, its situation, produce, and the general disposition of its inhabitants. 2nd ed. London, 1968.
Afr 677.71.10 — Benezet, Anthony. Some historical account of Guinea: its situation. 2nd ed. London, 1968.
Afr 6398.10 — Bennett, Norman R. Leadership in eastern Africa. Boston, 1968.
Afr 1326.20 — Bennett, Norman Robert. A study guide for Morocco. Boston, 1968.
Afr 2426.10 — Bennett, Norman Robert. A study guide for Tunisia. Boston, 1968.
Afr 1494.61.5 — Bernard, S. The Franco-Moroccan conflict, 1943-1956. New Haven, 1968.
Afr 5426.100.70 — Bessuges, Jacques. Lambaróné à l'ombre de Schweitzer. Limoges, 1968.
Afr 2030.468.10 — Beyssade, Pierre. La guerre d'Algérie, 1954-1962. Paris, 1968.
Afr 6738.50 — Billard, Pierre. Le Cameroun fédéral. Lyon, 1968. 2v.
Afr 6176.37 — Bing, Geoffrey. Reap the whirlwind: an account of Kwame Nkrumah's Ghana farm 1950 to 1966. London, 1968.
Afr 8985.6 — Binns, C.T. Dinuzuln: the death of the House of Shaka. London, 1968.
Afr 5842.26 — Bissoondoyal, Basdeo. The truth about Mauritius. 1. ed. Bombay, 1968.
Afr 6926.30 — Bley, Helmut. Kolonialherrschaft und Sozialstruktur in Deutsch-Südwestafrika, 1894-1914. Hamburg, 1968.
Afr 2030.468 — Bocca, Geoffrey. The secret army. Englewood Cliffs, 1968.
Afr 2719.68 — Bodley, Ronald V.C. The soundless Sahara. London, 1968.
Afr 6280.26.15 — Bohaman, Pave. TIV economy. Evanston, 1968.
Afr 12639.24.810 — Bonn, Gisela. Léopold Sédar Senghor. Düsseldorf, 1968.
Afr 6291.34 — Bonneville, Floris de. La mort du Biafra. Paris, 1968.
Afr 810.30 — Borill, Edward W. The Niger explored. London, 1968.
Afr 6280.64 — Boston, John Shipway. The Igala Kingdom. Ibadan, 1968.
Afr 9398.4 — Botswana. Republic of Botswana. Ministry of Development Planning. National development plan, 1968-1973. Gaberones, 1968.
Afr 5023.5 — Bouche, Denise. Les villages de liberté en Afrique noire française, 1887-1910. Paris, 1968.
Afr 6314.36 — Bourde, André. L'Afrique orientale. Paris, 1968.
Afr 5054.58.2 — Bovill, E.W. The golden trade of the Moors. 2nd ed. London, 1968.
Afr 550.2.12 — Bowen, T.J. Adventures and missonary labors in several countries in the interior of Africa. 2d ed. London, 1968.
Afr 6198.231 — Boyle, Laura. Diary of a colonial officer's wife. Oxford, 1968.
Afr 6170.11.1 — Brackenbury, H. The Ashanti War: a narrative. 1st ed. London, 1968.
Afr 10622.76.100 — Brew, Kwesi. The shadows of laughter: poems. London, 1968.
Afr 678.43.5 — Bridge, Horatio. Journal of an African cruiser. London, 1968.
Afr 8380.15 — Bringolf, Walther. Gespräche in Südafrika. Zürich, 1968.
Afr 3040.35.2 — Brinton, Jasper Y. The mixed courts of Egypt. New Haven, 1968.
Afr 5183.968 — Brochier, Jacques. La diffusion du progrès technique en milieu rural sénégalais. Paris, 1968.
Afr 8678.415 — Brookes, Edgar Harry. Apartheid. London, 1968.
Afr 8678.392 — Brown, Douglas. Against the world. 1st ed. Garden City, 1968.
Afr 6291.32 — Buhler, Jean. Tuez-les tous. Paris, 1968.
Afr 9439.67.5 — Bull, Theodore. Rhodesia: crisis of color. Chicago, 1968.
Afr 11248.76.100 — Burke, Colin. Elephant across border: a novel. London, 1968.
Afr 6160.45 — Busia, Kofi A. The position of the chief in the modern political system of Ashanti. 1st ed. London, 1968.
Afr 11249.86.130 — Butler, Guy. Cape Charade. Cape Town, 1968. 2v.
Afr 8283.28 — Butler, Jeffrey. The Liberal Party and the Jameson Raid. Oxford, 1968.
Afr 1409.20 — Caillé, Jacques. Une Corse sultane du Maroc, Davia Franceschini et sa famille. Paris, 1968.
Afr 11675.87.800 — Callan, Edward. Alan Paton. N.Y., 1968.
Afr 1723.5 — Canetti, Elias. Die Stimmen von Marrakesch. München, 1968.
Afr 632.50 — Carlston, Kenneth Smith. Social theory and African tribal organization. Urbana, 1968.
Afr 2248.5 — Cauneille, A. Les Chaanba (leur nomadisme). Paris, 1968.
Afr 5957.105 — Cervera Pery, José. La marina española en Guinea Ecuatorial, sentido y grandeza de una aporcacion historica. Santa Isabel, 1968.
Afr 5054.68 — Chaillez, Marcel. Histoire de l'Afrique occidentale française, 1638-1959. Paris, 1968.
Afr 6095.357.6 — Church, R.J.H. West Africa. 6th ed. N.Y., 1968.
Afr 9699.68 — Clausen, Lars. Industrialisierung in Schwarzafrika. Bielefeld, 1968.
Afr 9710.17 — Clay, Gervas. Your friend, Lewanika. London, 1968.
Afr 3745.75 — Collins, Robert O. King Leopold, England and the Upper Nile, 1899-1909. New Haven, 1968.
Afr 109.68.20 — Colloquium on Institution-Building and the African Development Process, University of California at Los Angeles, 1967. Nations by design; institution-building in Africa. 1st ed. Garden City, 1968.
Afr 7920.3.10 — Colvin, Ian Goodhope. The rise and fall of Moise Tshombe: a biography. London, 1968.
Afr 7818.5 — Comhaire-Sylvain, Suzanne. Femmes de Kinshasa hier et aujourd'hui. Paris, 1968.
Afr 115.45 — Conference on the Legal, Economic and Social Aspects of African Refugee Problems. Final report. Uppsala, 1968.
Afr 10317.5 — Cook, David. Short East African plays in English: ten plays in English. Nairobi, 1968.
Afr 7567.42 — Cookey, Sylvanus John Sodienye. Britain and the Congo question, 1885-1913. London, 1968.
Afr 11051.8 — Cope, Jack. The Penguin book of South African verse. Harmondsworth, 1968.
Afr 6570.7.2 — Coupland, R. The exploitation of East Africa, 1856-1890. 2nd ed. London, 1968.
Afr 9558.85.2 — Coupland, R. Kirk on the Zambesi; a chapter of African history. Oxford, 1968.
Afr 2030.468.5 — Courrière, Yves. La guerre d'Algérie. Paris, 1968. 2v.
Afr 9400.12 — Cowley, Olive. Fabled tribe; a voyage to discover the River Bushmen of the Okavango Swamps. 1st ed. N.Y., 1968.
Afr 678.69 — Cox, John George. Cox and the Juju Coast. St. Helier, 1968.

1968 - cont.

Afr 679.68.10 Crowder, Michael. West Africa under colonial rule. London, 1968.

Afr 810.4.5 Crowther, S. The gospel on the banks of the Niger. London, 1968.

Afr 7025.10 Cunha, Manuel. Aquelas longas horas. Lisboa, 1968.

Afr 550.170 Dammann, Ernst. Das Christentum in Afrika. München, 1968.

Afr 659.68 Danasuri, Jamal A.A. Studies in the geography of the Arab world in Africa. Cairo, 1968.

Afr 6194.20.5.2 Danquah, J.B. The Akan doctrine of God: a fragment of Gold Coast ethics and religion. 2nd ed. London, 1968.

Afr 5415.8 Darlington, Charles F. African betrayal. N.Y., 1968.

Afr 109.66.2 Davidson, Basil. Africa in history, themes and outlines. London, 1968.

Afr 9165.70 Davidson, Elizabeth. Pietersburg Magisterial District; a bibliography. Johannesburg, 1968.

Afr 7817.20 Davies, David Michael. The captivity and triumph of Winnie Davies. London, 1968.

Afr 10924.5 Davis, John Gordon. Hold my hand, I'm dying. 1st ed. N.Y., 1968.

Afr 6465.56.15 De Blij, Harm J. Membasa; an African city. Evanston, Ill., 1968.

Afr 6291.40 Debré, François. Biafra, an II. Paris, 1968.

Afr 6753.10 Decalo, Samuel. Tanzania: an introductory bibliography. Kingston?, 1968.

Afr 5322.10.5 Decker, Henry de. Le développement communautaire, une stratégie d'édification de la nation. Paris, 1968.

Afr 5322.10 Decker, Henry de. Nation et développement communautaire en Guinée et au Sénégal. Paris, 1968.

Afr 5046.10 Delavignette, Robert Louis. Du bon usage de la décolonisation. Paris, 1968.

Afr 6280.5.1 Dennett, R.E. Nigerian studies. London, 1968.

Afr 5119.64.2 Deschamps, H.J. Le Sénégal et la Gambie. 2e éd. Paris, 1968.

Afr 5343.40 Development and Resources Corporation. A development plan for the Southwest Region. N.Y., 1968. 4v.

Afr 698.69 Devereux, William Cope. A cruise in the "Gorgon". Reprint of 1869 l. ed. London, 1968.

Afr 210.68.10
Afr Doc 4107.366.6 Diallo, Demba. L'Afrique en question. Paris, 1968.

Distribution and density maps. Mbabane, 1968.

Afr 9502.26 Dotson, Floyd. The Indian minority of Zambia, Rhodesia and Malawi. New Haven, 1968.

Afr 5404.25 Dreux-Brézé, Joachim de. Le Problème du regroupement en Afrique équatoriale, du régime colonial à l'union douanière et économique de l'Afrique centrale. Thèsis. Paris, 1968.

Afr 6285.5A Dudley, Billy J. Parties and politics in Northern Nigeria. London, 1968.

Afr 5385.17.5 Duncan, John. Travels in western African in 1845 and 1846. 1st ed. London, 1968.

Afr 3199.11.2 Duse Muhammad. In the land of the Pharaohs. 2nd ed. London, 1968.

Afr 6193.56 Dutta Roy, D.K. Household budget survey in Ghana. Legon, 1968.

Afr 2687.4 Duvignaud, Jean. Chebika; mutations dans un village du Maghreb. Paris, 1968.

Afr 7315.26.1 Earthy, Emily D. Valenge women; an ethnographic study. London, 1968.

Afr 4789.4 Eby, Omar. A whisper in a dry land. Scottdale, 1968.

Afr 10675.37.100 Echeruo, Michael J.C. Mortality. London, 1968.

Afr 626.209 Ekonomicheskoe sotrudnichestvo SSSR so stranami Afriki. Moskva, 1968.

Afr 8678.320.10 Ellis, Barbaralyn. Religion among the Bantu in South Africa. Johannesburg, 1968.

Afr 725.6.10 Elton, J.F. Travels and researches among the lakes and mountains of eastern and central Africa. 1st ed. London, 1968.

Afr 626.186 Entin, Lev M. Natsional'no-demokraticheskoe gosudarstvo i ekonomicheskii progress. Moskva, 1968.

Afr 618.55 Erny, P. L'Enfant dans la pensée traditionnelle de l'Afrique noire. Paris, 1968.

Afr 5944.24 España en el Sahara. Madrid, 1968.

Afr 6925.20 Esterhuyse, J.H. South West Africa, 1880-1894; the establishment of German authority in South West Africa. Cape Town, 1968.

Afr 4640.7 Ethiopia. Ministry of Information. Africa Hall. Addis Ababa, 1968.

Afr 4226.7 Ethiopia. Press and Information Office. Bibliography of Ethiopia. Addis Ababa, 1968.

Afr 1040.20 Étienne, Bruno. Les Problèmes juridiques des minoritiés européennes au Maghreb. Paris, 1968.

Afr 212.48 Ewandé, Daniel. Vive le Président. La fête africaine. Paris, 1968.

Afr 626.178 Ewing, A.F. Industry in Africa. London, 1968.

Afr 7122.48.5 Felgas, Hélio. Guerra em Angola. 5. ed. Lisboa, 1968.

Afr 2230.44 Feraoun, Mouloud. Jours de Kabylie. (Dessins de Brouty). Paris, 1968.

Afr 1755.60 Fernández de la Reguera, Ricardo. El desastre de Annual. Barcelona, 1968.

Afr 609.34.11 Fitzgerald, Walter. Africa; a social, economic, and political geography of its major regions. 10th ed. n.p., 1968.

Afr 212.61 Fokeev, German V. Vneshniaia politika stran Afriki. Moskva, 1968.

Afr 109.65.16 Fordham, Paul. The geography of African affairs. 2d ed. Harmondsworth, 1968.

Afr 6538.65 Foster, Phillips Wayne. Population growth and rural development in Buganda. College Park, Md., 1968.

Afr 6192.8.3 Freeman, T.B. Journal of various visits to the Kingdoms of Ashanti, Aku, and Dahomi in Western Africa. 3rd ed. London, 1968.

Afr 6147.8.5 Freetown; a symposium. Freetown, 1968.

Afr 718.30.1 Frobenius, Leo. The voice of Africa. N.Y., 1968. 2v.

Afr 8678.410 Frye, William R. In whitest Africa; the dynamics of apartheid. Englewood Cliffs, 1968.

Afr 6164.7.2 Fuller, F. A vanished dynasty. 2. ed. London, 1968.

Afr 11410.51.100 Fulton, Anthony. The dark side of mercy. Cape Town, 1968.

Afr 4559.68 Gal'perin, Georgii L. Ekvatoe riadom. Moskva, 1968.

Afr 2508.20 Ganiage, Jean. Les origines du protectorat français en Tunisie, 1861-1881. 2ème éd. Tunis, 1968.

Afr 1645.5 García Barriuso, Patrocinio. Los derechos del gobierno español en la misión de Marruecos. Madrid, 1968.

Afr 5247.38 Gardner, Brian. The quest for Timbuctoo. London, 1968.

Afr 28.126 Garling, Arthea. Bibliography of African bibliographies. Cambridge, Eng., 1968.

1968 - cont.

Afr 628.268 Garvey, Marcus. Speech presenting the case of the Negro for international racial adjustment. London?, 1968?

Afr 5845.5 Gay, Francois. Ile Maurice, régulation des naissances et action familiale. Lyon, 1968.

Afr 210.68.15 Geiss, Imanuel. Panafrikanismus. Frankfurt am Main, 1968.

Afr 9502.13.15 Gelfand, M. African crucible. Cape Town, 1968.

Afr 9704.12 Gelfland, Michael. Gubulawayo and beyond: letters and journals of the early Jesuit missionaires to Zambesia. London, 1968.

Afr 6193.58F Ghana. Central Bureau of Statistics. Directory of distributive establishments. Accra, 1968.

Afr Doc 1807.360.10 Ghana. Central Bureau of Statistics. Summary of procedures in the 1960 population census of Ghana. Accra, 1968.

Afr Doc 1819.5 Ghana. Constitutional Commission. Memorandum on the proposals for a constitution for Ghana. Accra, 1968.

Afr 6193.64 Ghana. Ministry of Economic Affairs. Two-year development plan: from stabilisation to development. Accra, 1968.

Afr 7122.100 Gilchrist, Sid. Angola awake. Toronto, 1968.

Afr 9446.38 Glass, Stafford. The Matabele War. Harlow, 1968.

Afr 7025.12 Goemaere, Pierre. Le Portugal restera-t-il en Afrique? Bruxelles, 1968.

Afr 6739.268.5 Golubchik, Mark M. Federativnaia Respublika Kamerun. Moskva, 1968.

Afr 45.68.10 Gonidec, Pierre François. Les droits africains. Paris, 1968.

Afr 5110.25 Gonidec, Pierre François. La République du Sénégal. Paris, 1968.

Afr 2218.6.15A Gordon, David C. Women of Algeria; an essay on change. Cambridge, 1968.

Afr 5056.168 Goure, Claude. Les inconnus d'Afrique. Paris, 1968.

Afr 6124.248 Grant, Douglas. The fortunate slave. London, 1968.

Afr 9450.30 Great Britain. Foreign and Commonwealth Office. Rhodesia; report on the discussions held on board H.M.S. Fearless. London, 1968.

Afr 6225.40 Great Britain. Parliament. House of Commons. Extracts from British parliamentary debates on the Nigerian situation in the House of Commons, London, Tuesday, 27th August, 1968. Washington, 1968.

Afr 609.68.10 Green, Lawrence George. Full many a glorious morning. Cape Town, 1968.

Afr 626.165.5 Green, Reginald Herbold. Unity or poverty? The economics of Pan-Africanism. Harmondsworth, 1968.

Afr 5190.26 Groope d'Études Dakaroises. Dakar en devenir. Paris, 1968.

Afr 8687.281 Gutsche, Thelma. Selective index to Not heaven itself; an autobiography. 2. ed. Johannesburg, 1968.

Afr 9689.65.5 Hall, Richard Seymour. Zambia. London, 1968.

Afr 5243.343.20 Hama, Boubou, Histoire des Songhay. Paris, 1968.

Afr 5243.207.10 Hama, Boubou. Contribution à la connaissance de l'histoire des Peul. Paris, 1968.

Afr 2731.15.110 Hamilton, Elizabeth. The desert my dwelling place: a study of Charles de Foucauld, 1858-1916. London, 1968.

Afr 4259.67 Hammerschmidt, Ernst. Äthiopien, christliches Reich zwisches Gestern und Morgen. Wiesbaden, 1968.

Afr 590.88 Hansen, Thorkild. Slavernes skibe. København, 1968.

Afr 6069.68 Harris, John Hobbis. Dawn in darkest Africa. 1st ed. London, 1968.

Afr 4558.44.2.1 Harris, W.C. The highlands of Ethiopia. 1st ed. London, 1968.

Afr 6145.6.5 Harris, William Thomas. The springs of Mende belief and conduct. Freetown, 1968.

Afr 8089.68 Hartmann, Hans Walter. Südafrika. Stuttgart, 1968.

Afr 44628.5.700 Hasani Bin Ismail. The medicine man. Swifa ya ngurumali. Oxford, 1968.

Afr 609.68.5 Heminway, John Hylan. The imminent rains. 1st ed. Boston, 1968.

Afr 6284.5 Heussler, Robert. The British in Northern Nigeria. London, 1968.

Afr 5260.35 Hinkmann, Ulrich. Niger. München, 1968.

Afr 6455.12.5 Hoehnel, Ludwig. Discovery of Lakes Rudolf and Stefanie. 1st English ed. London, 1968. 2v.

Afr 5342.65.2 Holas, Bohumil. Craft and culture in the Ivory Coast. Paris, 1968.

Afr 545.52 Holas, Bohumil. Les dieux d'Afrique noire. Paris, 1968.

Afr 5344.11 Holas, Bonumil. L'Image du monde Bété. Paris, 1968.

Afr 7461.48 Holmsen, Ylva. Lamcos Liberia. Stockholm, 1968.

Afr 3069.68 Holt, Peter M. Political and social change in modern Egypt. London, 1968.

Afr 6739.268.10 Hugon, Philippe. Analyse du sous-développement en Afrique noire. Paris, 1968.

Afr 7309.68 Huibregtse, Pieter Kornelis. Zó is Mozambique. Den Haag, 1968.

Afr 9165.7.5 Humphriss, Deryck. Benoni, son of my sorrow. Benoni, 1968.

Afr 45.68 Hutchison, Thomas W. Africa and law. Madison, 1968.

Afr 555.137 Ijlst, Wim. A present for cold mornings. Dublin, 1968.

Afr 6298.646 Ikime, Obaro. Merchant prince of the Niger Delta; the rise and fall of Nana Olomu. London, 1968.

Afr 6143.68 Ingham, Ernest Graham. Sierra Leone after a hundred years. 1st ed. London, 1968.

Afr 555.151 International African Seminar, 7th, University of Ghana. Christianity in tropical Africa. London, 1968.

Afr 5091.15 International Bank for Reconstruction and Development. Mauritania; guidelines for a four-year development program. Washington, D.C.?, 1968.

Afr 36.8 International Congress of African Historians, University College, Dar-es-Salaam, 1965. Emerging themes of African history; proceedings. Nairobi, 1968.

Afr 626.195 International Monetary Fund. Surveys of African economics. Washington, 1968. 2v.

Afr 6291.38 International observer team in Nigeria. Washington, 1968.

Afr 679.68.15 Iordanskii, Vladimir B. Opnennye ieroglify. Moskva, 1968.

Afr 5316.501 Iordanskii, Vladimir B. Strategiia bor'by za nezavisimost? Moskva, 1968.

Afr 4558.43.5 Isenberg, Karl Wilhelm. The journals of C.W. Isenberg and J.L. Krapt. London, 1968.

Afr 8045.56 Iuzhnoafrikanskii blok Kolonizatorov. Moskva, 1968.

Afr 5343.7.10 Ivory Coast. Ministère du Plan. Première esquisse du plan quinquennal de développement. Paris, 1968.

Afr 11465.14.21 Jacobson, Dan. Through the wilderness, and other stories. N.Y., 1968.

Afr 6919.66.8 Jenny, Hans. Südwestafrika. 3. Aufl. Stuttgart, 1968.

Afr 555.9.65 Jones, David Picton. After Livingstone. The work of a pioneer missionary in Central Africa. London, 1968.

Afr 8678.343.1   Joseph, Helen. Tomorrow's sun. 1. ed. London, 1968.
Afr 679.68   July, Robert William. The origins of modern African thought. London, 1968.
Afr 8678.386   Kahn, Ely Jacques. The separated people; a look at contemporary South Africa. 1st ed. N.Y., 1968.
Afr 3813.18   al-Kammash, Majdi M. Economic development and planning in Egypt. N.Y., 1968.
Afr 6410.14   Kenya. Commission on the Law of Sucession. Report. Nairobi, 1968.
Afr 6465.60F   Kenya. Economics and Statistics Division. Economic survey of Central Province, 1963-1964. Nairobi, 1968.
Afr 6430.10   Kenyatta, Jouro. Suffering without bitterness. Nairobi, 1968.
Afr 12012.6   Khatibi, Abdelkabir. Le roman maghrébin, essai. Paris, 1968.
Afr 10531.61.100   Kinteh, Ramatoulie. Rebellion; a play in three acts. N.Y., 1968.
Afr 6390.93   Kirby, C.P. East Africa: Kenya, Uganda and Tanzania. London, 1968.
Afr 5119.68   Klien, Martin A. Islam and imperialism in Senegal; Sine-Saloum, 1847-1914. Stanford, 1968.
Afr 8659.68.5   Klooster, Willem Simon Brand. Zuid-Africa. Baarn, 1968.
Afr 6277.112   Koch, Bernd. Das Handwerk in ausgewählten Bezirken Westnigerias. Frankfurt, 1968.
Afr 6740.45   Koch, Henri. Magie et chasse dans la forêt camerounaise. Paris, 1968.
Afr 6280.2.35   Kochakova, Nataliie B. Goroda-gosudarstva iorubov. Moskva, 1968.
Afr 12881.67.100   Kourouma, Ahmadou. Les soleils des indépendances. Montréal, 1968.
Afr 6277.110   Kranendonk, H. A preliminary report on rural changes in the Savanna area of the Western State of Nigeria. Ibadan, 1968.
Afr 698.60.3   Krapf, Ludwig. Travels, researches...Eastern Africa. 2. ed. London, 1968.
Afr 6147.8.10   Kreutzinger, Helga. The picture of Krio life, Freetown, 1900-1920. Wien, 1968.
Afr 699.68.5   Laman Trip-de Beaufort, Henriette. Ruimte en zonlicht. Den Haag, 1968.
Afr 609.68.30   Lantier, Jacques. Le destin de l'Afrique. Paris, 1968.
Afr 1840.26   Lapassat, Étienne Jean. La justice en Algérie, 1962-1968. Paris, 1968.
Afr 8678.400   Laurence, John. The seeds of disaster; a guide to the realities, race politics and world-wide propaganda campaigns of the Republic of South Africa. N.Y., 1968.
Afr 8678.322   Laurence, John. The seeds of disaster; a guide to the realities, race politics and world-wide propaganda campaigns of the Republic of South Africa. London, 1968.
Afr 10657.5   Laurence, Margaret. Long drums and cannons. London, 1968.
Afr 12832.5.705   Laye, Camara. A dream of Africa. London, 1968.
Afr Doc 6409.315   Leblan, Pierre Jean. Les comptes de la nation, 1966-1967 (provisoire). Abidjan, 1968.
Afr 5874.22   Leloutre, Jean Claude. La Réunion, departement français. Paris, 1968.
Afr 6280.66   Leonard, Arthur Glyn. The Lower Niger and its tribes. 1st ed. London, 1968.
Afr 11517.76.130   Lerner, Laurence. A free man. London, 1968.
Afr 9489.57.2   Lessing, Doris M. Going home. London, 1968.
Afr 575.58   Leutzion, Nehemia. Muslims and chiefs in West Africa. Oxford, 1968.
Afr 8678.388   Lever, Henry. Ethnic attitudes of Johannesburg youth. Johannesburg, 1968.
Afr 9044.5F   Leverton, Basil James Trewin. Government finance and political development in Natal, 1843 to 1893. Thesis. Pretoria, 1968.
Afr 7459.68   Liberian Trading and Development Bank, Ltd., Monrovia. Liberia: basic data and information, 1968. Monrovia, 1968.
Afr 626.196   Lipets, Iulii G. Strany iugo-vostochne i Afriki. Moskva, 1968.
Afr 10117.10   Litto, Fredric M. Plays from black Africa. 1st ed. N.Y., 1968.
Afr 9558.8.5   Livingstone, David. Dr. Livingstone's Cambridge lectures. Farnborough, Hants., Eng., 1968.
Afr 609.68.25   Llopis, José J. Pueblos y enigmas de Africa. 2a ed. Madrid, 1968.
Afr 6739.268.15   Loginova, Valentina P. Federativnaia Respublika Kamerun. Moskva, 1968.
Afr 9693.10   Long, Norman. Social change and the individual: a study of the social and religious responses to innovation in a Zambian rural community. Manchester, 1968.
Afr 7188.301.800   Lopo, Júlio de Castro. Paiva Couceiro, uma grande figura de Angola. Lisboa, 1968.
Afr 6210.1.5   Lugard, Frederick Dealtry. Lugard and the amalgamation of Nigeria. London, 1968.
Afr 6194.10.11   Lystad, Robert A. The Ashanti; a proud people. N.Y., 1968.
Afr 3305.18   McBride, Barrie St. Clair. Farouk of Egypt; a biography. 1st American ed. South Brunswick, N.J., 1968.
Afr 109.68.5   McEwan, Peter J.M. Readings in African history. London, 1968. 3v.
Afr 109.68   MacGregor-Hastie, Roy. Africa, background for today. London, 1968.
Afr 7817.3   McKinnon, Arch C. Kapitene of the Congo steamship Lapsley. Boston, 1968.
Afr 6099.5.2   Macmillan, Allister. The red book of West Africa. London, 1968.
Afr 8678.32.2   Macmillan, W.M. The Cape colour question. Facsimile. Cape Town, 1968.
Afr 8238.6   McNish, James Thomas. The road to El Dorado. Cape Town, 1968.
Afr 6415.42   MacPhee, Archibald Marshall. Kenya. London, 1968.
Afr 6415.42.2   MacPhee, Archibald Marshall. Kenya. N.Y., 1968.
Afr 109.68.10   The making of modern Africa. N.Y., 1968-
Afr 2875.67   Maltese, Paolo. La terra promessa. Milano, 1968.
Afr 8089.55.3   Marquard, L. The story of South Africa. London, 1968.
Afr 8250.35.5   Maurois, André. Cecil Rhodes. Hamden, Conn., 1968.
Afr 5248.20   Meillassoux, Claude. Urbanization of an African community. Seattle, 1968.
Afr 6390.64.2   Meister, Albert. East Africa; the past in chains, the future in pawn. N.Y., 1968.
Afr 5390.4   Mercier, Paul. Tradition, changement, histoire, les "Somba" du Dahomey septentrional. Paris, 1968.
Afr 609.68.20   Merle, Marcel. L'Afrique noire contemporaine. Paris, 1968.

Afr 12639.24.815   Mezu, Sebastian Okechukwu. Léopold Sédar Senghor et la défense et illustration de la civilisation noire. Paris, 1968.
Afr 699.68.10   Milley, Jacques. L'Afrique orientale, terre des safaris. Paris, 1968.
Afr 6277.116   Mobogunje, Akinlawon Lopide. Urbanization in Nigeria. London, 1968.
Afr 5225.12   Monteil, Charles Victor. Les Empires du Mali. Paris, 1968.
Afr 7175.5.5   Monteiro, J.J. Angola and the River Congo. 1st ed. London, 1968. 2v.
Afr 6280.7.3   Morel, E.D. Nigeria: its peoples and its problems. 3rd ed. London, 1968.
Afr 7560.15.10   Morel, Edmund D. Morel's history of the Congo reform movement. Oxford, 1968.
Afr 6540.25   Morris, H.S. The Indians in Uganda. London, 1968.
Afr 10883.89.100   Mulikita, Fwanyanga Matale. A point of no return. London, 1968.
Afr 4559.68.5   Murphy, Dervla. In Ethiopia with a mule. London, 1968.
Afr 6210.64   Murray, David John. The progress of Nigerian public administration: a report on research. Ibadan, 1968.
Afr 1273.968   Muzikář, Joseph. Les Perspectives de l'intégration des pays maghrébins et leur attitude vis-à-vis du Marché commun. Nancy, 1968.
Afr 3310.10.55   Nasser, G.A. President Gamal Abdel Nasser on consolidation of the cause of world peace. Cairo, 1968?
Afr 2749.68.5   Nau, Christian. La première traversée du Sahara en char a voile. Condé-sur-l'Escaut, 1968.
Afr 115.116   Nekotorye voprosy istorii Afriki. Moskva, 1968.
Afr 6689.10   Nelle, Albrecht. Aufbruch vom Götterberg. Stuttgart, 1968.
Afr 6277.76.10   Nigeria. The policy of the Federal Military Government on statutory corporations and state-owned companies. Lagos, 1968.
Afr 6291.20F   Nigeria. Federal Ministry of Information. The collapse of Ojukwu's rebellion and prospects for lasting peace in Nigeria. Lagos, 1968.
Afr 6293.2.10   Nigeria. Lagos Executive Development Board Tribunal of Inquiry. Report of the tribunal of inquiry into the affairs of the Lagos Executive Development Board for the period 1st October, 1960 to 31st December, 1965. Lagos, 1968.
Afr 718.50   Nils-Magnus. Afrikanska strövtåg. Solna, 1968.
Afr 6178.10   Nkrumah, Kwame. Dark days in Ghana. London, 1968.
Afr 6178.10.2   Nkrumah, Kwame. Dark days in Ghana. London, 1968.
Afr 6176.30.40   Nkrumah, Kwame. Handbook of revolutionary warfare. London, 1968.
Afr 12884.65.120   Nokan, Charles. Les malheurs de Tchakô. Honfleur, 1968.
Afr 3811.5   Nordenstam, Tore. Sudanese ethics. Uppsala, 1968.
Afr 2749.68   Norwich, John Julius Cooper. Sahara. London, 1968.
Afr 212.26.1   Noveishaia istoriia Afriki. 2. izd. Moskva, 1968.
Afr 6899.62   Nyerere, Julius Kambarage. Freedom and socialism. Dar-es-Salaam, 1968.
Afr 3979.68   Ob'edinennaia Arabskaia Respublika. Moskva, 1968.
Afr 5343.25.2   Obermaier, Heinrich. Die Elfenbeinküste als Wirtschaftspartner. 2. Aufl. Köln, 1968.
Afr 6178.20   Ocran, A.K. A myth is broken. Harlow, 1968.
Afr 10385.15.100   Oculi, Okello. Prostitute. Nairobi, 1968.
Afr 7135.1   Oganis'ian, Iulii S. Natsional'naia revoliutsiia v Angole. (1961-1965?). Moskva, 1968.
Afr 699.68   Ogot, Bethwell Allen. Zamani; a survey of East African history. Nairobi, 1968.
Afr 10435.34.102   Ogot, Grace Akinyi. Land without thunder; short stories. Nairobi, 1968.
Afr 6275.130   Okin, Theophilus Adelodum. The urbanized Nigerian. 1st ed. N.Y., 1968.
Afr 109.61.7   Oliver, Roland A. The dawn of African history. 2d ed. London, 1968.
Afr 2609.68   Olivier, Pierre. Tunisie, ma mie. Tunis, 1968.
Afr 679.68.25   Olowokure, Olvsanya. An outline of West African history. Ilesha, 1968.
Afr 6457.34   Ominde, Simeon H. Land and population movements in Kenya. London, 1968.
Afr 545.48   Oosthuizen, Gerhardus Cornelis. Post-Christianity in Africa: a theological and anthropological study. London, 1968.
Afr 7560.19   Orlova, Antonina S. Istoriia gosudarstva Kongo (XVI-XVII vv.). Moskva, 1968.
Afr 500.92   Osei, Gabriel Kingsley. Europe's gift to Africa. London, 1968.
Afr 679.68.5   Osqe, T.A. A short history of West Africa. London, 1968.
Afr 12686.17.100   Owologuem Yambo. Le devoir de violence, roman. Paris, 1968.
Afr 13285.98.700   Oyono, Guillaume. Three suitors: one husband. London, 1968.
Afr 2037.8   Palacio, Léo. Les Pieds-Noirs dans le monde. Paris, 1968.
Afr 4573.20   Pankhurst, Richard Keir Pethick. Economic history of Ethiopia, 1800-1935. 1st ed. Addis Ababa, 1968.
Afr 8659.68   Paton, Alan. The long view. London, 1968.
Afr 6282.42   Peel, John David Yeadon. Aladura: a religious among the Yoruba. London, 1968.
Afr 9073.687   Phipson, Thomas. Letters and other writings of a Natal sheriff. Cape Town, 1968.
Afr 10117.5   Pietense, Cosmo. Ten one-act plays. London, 1968.
Afr 9769.68   Pike, John G. Malawi; a political and economic history. London, 1968.
Afr 9769.68.2   Pike, John G. Malawi; a political and economic history. N.Y., 1968.
Afr 679.68.20   Plessz, Nicolas G. Problems and prospects of economic integration in West Africa. Montreal, 1968.
Afr 3988.8   Poinsenet, Marie Dominique. Rien n'est impossible à l'amour. Paris, 1968.
Afr 609.68   Pollock, Norman Charles. Africa. London, 1968.
Afr 679.64.2   Post, K.W.J. The new states of West Africa. Harmondsworth, 1968.
Afr 626.45.5   Potekhin, I.I. African problems; analysis of eminent Soviet scientist. Moscow, 1968.
Afr 12505.1   Potekhina, Gena I. Ocherki sovremennoi literatury Zapadnoi Afriki. Moskva, 1968.
Afr 6225.50   Pourguoi le Nigéria. Paris, 1968.
Afr 12007.1   Prozhogina, S.V. Literatura Marokko i Tunisa. Moskva, 1968.
Afr 609.66.45   Quilici, Folco. Alla scoperta dell'Africa. 2d ed. Firenze, 1968.

1968 - cont.

Afr 5437.74   Randles, W.G.L. L'ancien royaume du Congo des origines à la fin du XIXE siècle. Paris, 1968.

Afr 9520.10   Ransford, Oliver. Bulawayo: historic battleground of Rhodesia. Cape Town, 1968.

Afr 9439.68   Ransford, Oliver. The rulers of Rhodesia from earliest times to the referendum. London, 1968.

Afr 9853.5.5   Read, Margaret. Children of their fathers...Ngoni of Malawi. N.Y., 1968.

Afr 609.68.15   Religion coloniale et phénomène de déculturation. Paris, 1968.

Afr 5185.10   Reverdy, Jean Claude. Une société rurale au Senegal. Aix-en-Provence, 1968?

Afr 6741.10   Reyburn, William David. Out of the African night. 1st ed. N.Y., 1968.

Afr 9565.5   Rhodesia: the moral issue. Gwelo, 1968.

Afr Doc 3819.10   Rhodesia (British Colony). Constitutional Commission. Report of the Constitutional Commission, 1968. Salisbury, 1968.

Afr 9497.10   La Rhodésie. Paris, 1968.

Afr 8678.68.12   Rhoodie, N.J. Apartheid en partnership. 2. uitg. Pretoria, 1968.

Afr 555.154   Richardson, Kenneth. Garden of miracles; a history of the African Inland Mission. London, 1968.

Afr 6769.68.5   Roberts, Andrew. Tanzania before 1900. Nairobi, 1968.

Afr 626.200   Robson, Peter. Economic integration in Africa. London, 1968.

Afr 10052.5   Rolf, Pamela Gail. An index to the programmes of the Johannesburg repertory players from 1928 to 1959. Johannesburg, 1968.

Afr 8252.172.2   Rosenthal, Eric. General De Wet; a biography. 2. ed. Cape Town, 1968.

Afr 530.50.1   Rosenthal, Eric. Stars and stripes in Africa. Cape Town, 1968.

Afr 6280.68.1   Roth, Henry Ling. Great Benin: its customs, art and horrors. 1st ed. London, 1968.

Afr 6333.68   Rothchild, Donald S. Politics of integration. Nairobi, 1968.

Afr 6881.268   Rutman, Gilbert. The economy of Tanganyika. N.Y., 1968.

Afr 3310.10.95   Saber, Ali. Nasser en procès face à la nation arabe. Paris, 1968.

Afr 8378.331.30   Sachs, Albert. Stephanie on trial. London, 1968.

Afr 212.50   Said, Abd al-Aziz. The African phenomenon. Boston, 1968.

Afr 9072.5   St. Leger-Gordon, Ruth E. Shepstone: the role of the family in the history of South Africa, 1820-1900. Cape Town, 1968.

Afr 9439.68.5   Samkange, Stanlake John Thompson. Origins of Rhodesia. London, 1968.

Afr 6291.66   Santos, Eduardo dos. A questão de Biafra. Porto, 1968.

Afr 210.68   Santos, Eduardo dos. Ideologias politicas africanas. Lisboa, 1968.

Afr 210.68.5   Santos, Eduardo dos. Pan-africanismo de ontem e de hoje. Lisboa, 1968.

Afr 6194.41.2   Sarban, John Mensah. Fanti national constitution; a short treatise. London, 1968.

Afr 3275.12.5   al-Sayyid, Afaf Lutfi. Egypt and Cromer; a study in Anglo-Egyptian relations. London, 1968.

Afr 11774.39.120   Scholefield, Alan. The eagles of malice. N.Y., 1968.

Afr 6214.23   Schwarz, Walter. Nigeria. London, 1968.

Afr 4573.30   Schwarz, William L.K. Industrial investment climate in Ethiopia. Menlo Park, Calif., 1968.

Afr 7809.68   Scotti, Pietro. Il Congo. Ieri, oggi, domani. Genova, 1968.

Afr 6277.114   Seibel, Hans D. Industriearbeit und Kulturwandel in Nigeria. Köln, 1968.

Afr 626.168   Semin, Nikolai S. Strany SEV i Afrika. Moskva, 1968.

Afr 10116.5   Sergeant, Howard. Poetry from Africa. Oxford, 1968.

Afr 10065.5   Shelton, Austin J. The African assertion. N.Y., 1968.

Afr 11057.8   Shore, Herbert L. Come back, Africa! N.Y., 1968.

Afr 6885.20   Sibtain, Nancy de S.P. Dare to look up. Sydney, 1968.

Afr 109.61.25.5   Sik, Endre. Histoire de l'Afrique noire. Budapest, 1968. 2v.

Afr 115.30.2   Sithhole, Ndabaningi. African nationalism. 2d ed. London, 1968.

Afr 7912.15.50   Skurnik, W.A.E. African political thought: Lumumba, Nkrumah and Toure. Denver, 1968.

Afr 8659.68.10F   Smail, John Lees. Monuments and trails of the Voortrekkers. Cape Town, 1968.

Afr 3675.64   Smirnov, Sergei R. Istoriia Sudana (1821-1956). Moskva, 1968.

Afr 9700.5.5   Smith, Edwin William. The Ila-speaking peoples of Northern Rhodesia. New Hyde Park, 1968. 2v.

Afr 6284.8   Smith, John Hilary. Colonial cadet in Nigeria. Durham, N.C., 1968.

Afr 5440.20.5   Soedergren, Sigfried. Sweet smell of mangoes. London, 1968.

Afr 6455.157   Soja, Edward W. The geography of modernization in Kenya. Syracuse, N.Y., 1968.

Afr 4787.12   Somalia. Planning Commission. Short term development programme, 1968-1970. Mogadiscio, 1968.

Afr 6910.8   South Africa. Parliament. Decisions by the government on the financial and administrative relations between the Republic and South West Africa. Cape Town, 1968.

Afr 6275.132   Sowande, Fela. Come now Nigeria. Ibadan, 1968.

Afr 11802.92.100   Sowden, Lewis. The land of afternoon. London, 1968.

Afr 10689.67.170   Soyinka, W. The forest of a thousand demons: a hunter's saga. London, 1968.

Afr 8865.16   Spence, John Edward. Lesotho: the politics of dependence. London, 1968.

Afr 6780.68   Stephens, Hugh W. The political transformation of Tanganyika, 1920-1967. N.Y., 1968.

Afr 4585.1.2   Stern, H.A. Wanderings among the Falashas in Abyssinia. 2d ed. London, 1968.

Afr 632.48   Stevenson, Robert F. Population and political systems in tropical Africa. N.Y., 1968.

Afr 4115.30   Stewart, Desmond Stirling. Cairo, 5500 years. N.Y., 1968.

Afr 9489.68   Stonier, George Walter. Rhodesian spring. London, 1968.

Afr 626.159   Stroitel'stvo natsional'noi ekonomiki v stranakh Afriki. Moskva, 1968.

Afr 49716.5   Stuart, James. Izibongo; Zulu praise-poems. Oxford, 1968.

Afr 5053.40   La succession d'état en Afrique du Nord. Paris, 1968.

Afr 5019.58.3   Suret-Canale, Jean. Afrique noire occidentale et centrale. 3e éd. Paris, 1968.

Afr Doc 4107.366.5   Swaziland. Census Office. Report on the 1966 Swaziland population census. Mbabane, 1968.

1968 - cont.

Afr 6392.8   Symposium on East African Range Problems, Lake Como, Italy, 1968. Report of a symposium on East African range problems held at Villa Serbellani, Lake Como. N.Y.? 1968?

Afr 8678.429   Tairov, Tair F. Apartkheid - prestuplenie veka. Moskva, 1968.

Afr 635.65.5   Tandberg, Olof G. Brun mans Africa. Stockholm, 1968.

Afr Doc 3407.367   Tanzania. Central Census Office. Summary of procedures in the 1967 Tanzania population census. Dar es Salaam, 1968.

Afr 10911.2   Taylor, Charles T.C. The history of Rhodesian entertainment, 1890-1930. Salisbury, 1968.

Afr 6280.17.2   Temple, Charles L. Native races and their rulers. 2nd ed. London, 1968.

Afr 5897.5   Thomas, Athol. Forgotten Eden. London, 1968.

Afr 4819.68   Thompson, Virginia M. Djibonti and the Horn of Africa. Stanford, Calif., 1968.

Afr 725.4.3   Thomson, J. To the Central African lakes and back: the narrative of the Royal Geographical Society's East Central African Expedition, 1878-1880. 2nd ed. London, 1968. 2v.

Afr 6455.3.21   Thomson, Joseph. Through Masai land. London, 1968.

Afr 9549.68   Tindall, P.E.N. A history of central Africa. London, 1968.

Afr 609.68.35   Trappe, Paul. Sozialer Wandel in Afrika südlich der Sahara. Hannover, 1968.

Afr 9489.68.5   Tredgold, Robert Clarkson. The Rhodesia that was my life. London, 1968.

Afr 575.60   Trimingham, John S. The influence of Islam upon Africa. Beirut, 1968.

Afr 9700.32   Turner, Victor Witter. The drums of affliction. Oxford, 1968.

Afr 8687.124   Udeman, Elsa. The published works of Margaret Livingstone Ballinger; a bibliography. Johannesburg, 1968.

Afr 6535.68   Uganda. Ministry of Information. Broadcasting and Tourism. Facts about Uganda. Entebbe, 1968.

Afr Doc 1407.20F   United Arab Republic. Central Agency for Public Mobilization and Statistics. United Arab Republic statistical atlas, 1952-1966. Cairo, 1968.

Afr 9.13   United States. Department of State. Office of External Research. Report on the Second International Congress of Africanists, Dakar, Senegal, Dec. 11-20, 1967. Washington, 1968.

Afr 4798.5   United States. Mission to the Somali Republic. Training Office. A listing of Somalis who participated in a technical assistance training program in the U.S. Mogadiscio, 1968.

Afr 6879.68.10   University Press of Africa. Kilimanjaro country. Nairobi, 1968.

Afr 6888.5   University Press of Africa. Tanga, the central port for East Africa. Nairobi, 1968.

Afr 6879.68.5   University Press of Africa. Tanzania today. Nairobi, 1968.

Afr 6225.45   Unongo, Paul Iyorpuu. The case for Nigeria. Lagos, 1968.

Afr 7175.79   Valahu, Mugur. Angola, chave de Africa. Lisboa, 1968.

Afr 3818.14   Vandevort, Eleanor. A leopard tamed; the story of an African pastor, his people, and his problems. N.Y., 1968.

Afr 3310.100   Vatikiotis, Panayiotis Jerasimof. Egypt since the revolution. London, 1968.

Afr 590.80.5   Verger, Pierre. Flux et reflux de la traité des Nègres entre le Golfe de Boain et Bahia de Todos os Santos de XVIIe au XIXe siècle. Paris, 1968.

Afr 626.206   Vinay, Bernard. L'Afrique commence avec l'Afrique. 1. éd. Paris, 1968.

Afr 7010.8   Visita do Chefe do Estado Almirante Américo Thomaz às províncias da Guiné de Cabo Verde. Lisboa, 1968.

Afr 10443.12.100   Wachira, Godwin. Ordeal in the forest. Nairobi, 1968.

Afr 6457.40   Waller, Peter P. Grundzüge der Raumplanung in der Region Kisumu (Kenia). Berlin, 1968.

Afr 2929.68   Ward, Philip. Touring Libya. London, 1968.

Afr 7465.14   Warner, Esther Sietmann. The crossing fee. Boston, 1968.

Afr 6096.22   West Africa Committee. Foreign investment. London, 1968.

Afr 6457.42   Who controls industry in Kenya? Report of a working party. Nairobi, 1968.

Afr 3290.10   Wilber, Donald Newton. United Arab Republic: Egypt. New Haven, 1968.

Afr 6293.5   Williams, Babatunde A. Urban government for metropolitan Lagos. N.Y., 1968.

Afr 22025.5F   Witahnkenge, E. Panorama de la littérature ntu. Kinshase, 1968.

Afr 7468.2   Woid, Joseph Conrad. God's impatience in Liberia. Grand Rapids, 1968.

Afr 500.20.5   Woolf, Leonard S. Empire and commerce in Africa. N.Y., 1968.

Afr 1493.50.15   Woolman, David J. Rebels in the RF; Abd el Krim and the Rif rebellion. Stanford, 1968.

Afr 6291.46   Yu, Mok Chiu. Nigeria-Biafra; a reading into the problems and peculiarities of the conflict. Adelaide, 1968.

Afr 109.68.15   Zaghi, Carlo. L'Europa devanti all'Africa dai tempi piu antichi alle soglie dell'Ottocento. Napoli, 1968.

Afr 500.88   Zaghi, Carlo. La spartiziche dell'Africa. Napoli, 1968.

Afr 9689.68   Zambia, Rpresident (Kaunda). Zambia's guideline for the next decade. Lusaka, 1968.

Afr 115.121   Zarubezhnye tsentry afrikanistiki. Moskva, 1968.

Afr 3079.68   Ziadeh, Farhat Jacob. Lawyers. Stanford, 1968.

Afr 545.36   Zwernemann, Jürgen. Die Erde in Vorstellungswelt und Kultpraktiken der sudanischen Völker. Berlin, 1968.

1969

Afr 3745.80   Abd al-Rahim, Muddathir. Imperialism and nationalism in the Sudan. Oxford, 1969.

Afr 3204.28   Abdel-Malek, Anouar. Idéologie et renaissance nationale; l'Égypte moderne. Paris, 1969.

Afr 7015.55   Abshire, David M. Portuguese Africa; a handbook. N.Y., 1969.

Afr 6277.122   Adedeji, Adebayo. Nigerian federal finance: its development, problems and prospects. London, 1969.

Afr 6010.22   Adu, Amishadai Lawson. The civil service in Commonwealth Africa. London, 1969.

Afr 115.122   African boundary problems. Stockholm, 1969.

Afr 8678.450   African societies in Southern Africa; historical studies. London, 1969.

Afr 7349.327   Almeida de Eça, Felipe Gastão de. O capitão César Maria de Serpa Rosa. Lisboa, 1969.

Afr 10671.53.110   Amadi, Elechi. The great ponds. London, 1969.

Afr 1940.10   American University, Wahington D.C. Foreign Area Studies. Area handbook for Burundi. Washington, 1969.

1969 - cont.

Afr 6535.69   American University, Washington, D.C. Foreign Area Studies Division. Area handbook for Uganda. Washington, 1969.

Afr 7940.10   American University, Washington, D.C. Foreign Area Studies. Area handbook for Burundi. Washington, 1969.

Afr 7940.15   American University, Washington, D.C. Foreign Area Studies. Area handbook for Rwanda. Washington, 1969.

Afr 9689.69   American University, Washington, D.C. Foreign Area Studies. Area handbook for Zambia. Washington, 1969.

Afr 7309.69   American University, Washington, D.C. Foreign Areas Studies Division. Area handbook for Mozambique. Washington, 1969.

Afr 109.62.41   Ansprenger, Franz. Afrika. Eine politische Länderkunde. 6. Aufl. Berlin, 1969.

Afr 8028.153   Archibald, Jane Erica. The works of Isaac Schapera; a selective bibliography. Johannesburg, 1969.

Afr 555.9.7   Arnot, Frederick Stanley. Garenganze; or, Seven years' pioneer mission work in Central Africa. London, 1969.

Afr 590.90   Asiegbu, Johnson U.J. Slavery and the politics of liberation, 1787-1861. N.Y., 1969.

Afr 575.7.2   Atterbury, Anson Phelps. Islam in Africa. N.Y., 1969.

Afr 115.126.2   Awosika, V.O. An African meditation. 2nd ed. N.Y., 1969.

Afr 609.37.2   Azikiwe, Nnamdi. Renascent Africa. N.Y., 1969.

Afr 28747.5   Ba, Amadou Hampâté. Kaidara. Paris, 1969.

Afr 6292.82.12A   Backwell, H.F. The occupation of Hausaland, 1900-1904. London, 1969.

Afr 5249.123   Badri, Babakr. The memoiris of Babiker Bedu. London, 1969.

Afr 4095.8.3.5   Baker, S.W. Ismailia; a narrative of the expedition to Central Africa for the suppression of the slave trade. N.Y., 1969. 2v.

Afr 8678.444   Ballinger, Margaret. From union to apartheid. N.Y., 1969.

Afr 8335.10   Ballinger, Margaret Livingstone. From union to apartheid; a trek to isolation. Bailey, 1969.

Afr 210.69   Barnes, Leonard. African renaissance. London, 1969.

Afr 6280.2.45   Bascom, William Russell. The Yoruba of Southwestern Nigeria. N.Y., 1969.

Afr 6753.15   Bates, Margaret L. A study guide for Tanzania. Boston, 1969.

Afr 9428.8   Bean, Elizabeth Ann. Political development in Southern Rhodesia. Cape Town, 1969.

Afr 3315.154.1   Beaufre, André. The Suez expedition 1956. N.Y., 1969.

Afr 8934.277.5   Becker, Peter. Hill of destiny. London, 1969.

Afr 8678.448   Beckers, Gerhard. Religiöse Faktoren in der Entwicklung der südafrikanischen Rassenfrage. München, 1969.

Afr 6395.3.2   Beech, M.W.H. The Suk, their language and folklore. N.Y., 1969.

Afr 10018.8   Beier, Ulli. Political spider. London, 1969.

Afr 50.60   Bénot, Yvès. Idéologies des indépendances africaines. Paris, 1969.

Afr 11675.87.2   Bentel, Lea. Alan Paton. Johannesburg, 1969.

Afr 4392.4.10   Berkeley, G.F.H. The campaign of Adowa and the rise of Menelik. N.Y., 1969.

Afr 630.69.10   Bettany, George Thomas. The dark peoples of the land of sunshine. Miami, Fla., 1969.

Afr 545.54   Bibical revelation and African beliefs. London, 1969.

Afr 9558.30.20   Blaikie, W.G. The personal life of David Livingstone. N.Y., 1969.

Afr 4431.25.1   Boca, Angelo del. The Ethiopian War, 1935-1941. Chicago, 1969.

Afr 7015.50   Bosgra, Sietse Jan. Angola, Mozambique, Guinee. Amsterdam, 1969.

Afr 8028.205   Both, Ellen Lisa Marianne. Catalogue of books and pamphlets published in German relating to South Africa and South West Africa as found in the South African Public Library. Cape Town, 1969.

Afr 8735.4.5   Botha, Andries. Trial of Andries Botha. Cape Town, 1969.

Afr 4095.28   Bradham, Frederick. The long walks, journeys to the sources of the White Nile. London, 1969.

Afr 505.3.10   British Africa. 2d ed. N.Y., 1969.

Afr 626.143.5   Brokensha, David W. The anthropology of development in Sub Saharan Africa. Lexington, Ky., 1969.

Afr 11240.89.100   Brutus, Dennis. Letters to Martha, and other poems from a South African prison. London, 1969.

Afr 8369.64.1   Bunting, B.P. The rise of the South African Reich. Harmondsworth, 1969.

Afr 609.69.10   Burke, Fred George. Africa; selected readings. N.Y., 1969.

Afr 8095.90   Burman, José. Who really discovered South Africa? Cape Town, 1969.

Afr 6214.8.20   Burns, Alan C. History of Nigeria. 7th ed. London, 1969.

Afr 7065.526.5   Cabral, Amilcar. Revolution in Guinea: an African people's struggle. London, 1969.

Afr 4115.20.10   Cairo; a life-story of 1000 years, 969-1969. Cairo, 1969.

Afr 8667.97   Calpin, George Harold. At last we have got our country back. 2nd ed. Cape Town, 1969.

Afr 11752.65.1   Camberg, Helen. Daphne Rooke; her works and selected literary criticism. Johannesburg, 1969.

Afr 11865.59.800   Carpenter, Frederic Ives. Laurens Van der Post. N.Y., 1969.

Afr 10005.20   Cartey, Wilfred. Whispers from a continent; the literature of contemporary black Africa. N.Y., 1969.

Afr 9446.47   Cary, Robert. A time to die. 2nd ed. Cape Town, 1969.

Afr 7568.35   Castelein, A. The Congo State; its origin, rights, and duties, the charges of its accusers. N.Y., 1969.

Afr 25.108.2   Červenka, Zdenek. The Organization of African Unity and its charter. 2d ed. London, 1969.

Afr 14518.5   César, Amândio. Contos portugueses do ultramar; antologia. Porto, 1969.

Afr 7065.526   Chaliand, Gérard. Armed struggle in Africa. N.Y., 1969.

Afr 2376.5   Champault, Francine Dominque. Une oasis du Sahara nord-occidental: Tabelbala. Paris, 1969.

Afr 9748.580   Charlton, Leslie. Spark in the stubble: Colin Morris of Zambia. London, 1969.

Afr 7003.2   Chilcote, Ronald H. Emerging nationalism in Portuguese Africa. Stanford, 1969.

Afr 7368.57.5   Christy, David. Ethiopia: her gloom and glory. N.Y., 1969.

Afr 4430.66   Clapham, Christopher S. Hailde-Selassie's government. London, 1969.

Afr 9439.69   Clements, Frank. Rhodesia: the course to collision. London, 1969.

Afr 8230.10.13.2   Cloete, Stuart. African portraits: a biography of Paul Kruger, Cecil Rhodes and Lobengula. Cape Town, 1969.

Afr 6280.69   Cohen, Abner. Custom and politics in urban Africa. Berkeley, 1969.

Afr 10690.89.800   Collins, Harold R. Amos Tutuola. N.Y., 1969.

1969 - cont.

Afr 500.90   Collins, Robert O. The partition of Africa: illusion or necessity? N.Y., 1969.

Afr 590.16.2   Colomb, John Charles Ready. Slave-catching in the Indian Ocean. N.Y., 1969.

Afr 500.94   Colonialism in Africa, 1870-1960. Cambridge, Eng., 1969-

Afr 7812.269   Comeliau, Christian. Conditions de la planification du développement; l'exemple du Congo. Paris, 1969.

Afr 6291.50   Conference on the Nigeria-Biafra Conflict, Washington. The Nigeria-Biafra conflict; report of a one day conference. Washington, 1969.

Afr 715.12   Cooley, William Desborough. Inner Africa laid open. N.Y., 1969.

Afr 6664.10.3   Cornevin, Robert. Histoire du Togo. 3e ed. Paris, 1969.

Afr 7135.14   Costa, Pereira da. Um mês de terrorismo: Angola, março-abril de 1961. Lisboa, 1969.

Afr 8678.49.7   Cotton, Walter Aidan. The race problem in South Africa. N.Y., 1969.

Afr 7368.62.2   Crummell, A. The future of Africa. N.Y., 1969.

Afr 10015.8   Dathorne, Oscar Ronald. Africa in prose. Harmondsworth, 1969.

Afr 115.124   Davidson, Basil. The African genius; an introduction to African cultural and social history. 1st American ed. Boston, 1969.

Afr 109.67.26   Davidson, Basil. A history of East and Central Africa to the late nineteenth century. Garden City, N.Y., 1969.

Afr 7065.520   Davidson, Basil. The liberation of Guiné. Harmondsworth, 1969.

Afr 7065.526.10   Davidson, Basil. Révolution en Afrique; la libération de la Guinée portugaise. Paris, 1969.

Afr 6193.62   Dickson, Kwamina. A historical geography of Ghana. Cambridge, 1969.

Afr 5477.505   Diguimbaye, Georges. L'essor du Tchad. Paris, 1969.

Afr 10674.71.110   Dipoko, Mbella Sonne. Because of women. London, 1969.

Afr 6878.77   Dodgshun, Arthur W. From Zanzibar to Ujiji. Boston, 1969.

Afr 6162.20   Dowse, Robert Edward. Modernization in Ghana and the U.S.S.R., a comparative study. London, 1969.

Afr 8735.10   Dracopoli, J.L. Sir Andries Stockenstrom, 1792-1864; the origin of the racial conflict in South Africa. Cape Town, 1969.

Afr 3978.65.8   Duff-Gordon, Lucie Austin. Letters from Egypt, (1862-1869). London, 1969.

Afr 212.60   Dumoga, John. Africa between East and West. London, 1969.

Afr 6540.30   Edel, May Mandelbaum. The Chiga of western Uganda. London, 1969.

Afr 626.215   Ekonomicheskie i politicheskie problemy Afriki. Moskva, 1969.

Afr 10675.47.171   Ekwensi, Cyprian. Jagua Nana; a novel. Greenwich, Conn., 1969.

Afr 10675.47.141   Ekwensi, Cyprian. People of the city. Greenwich, Conn., 1969.

Afr 10663.10   Elias, Taslim O. Nigerian press law. Lagos, 1969.

Afr 6164.2.5   Ellis, A.B. A history of the Gold Coast of West Africa. N.Y., 1969.

Afr 3725.2   Emin Pasha. Emin Pasha, his life and work. N.Y., 1969. 2v.

Afr 4573.7   Ethiopia. Third five year development plan, 1961-1965 E-C (1968/69-1972/73 G-c). v.1-4. Addis Ababa, 1969.

Afr 8678.434   Evans, Maurice Smethurst. Black and white in South East Africa. N.Y., 1969.

Afr 115.130   Expanding horizons in African studies. Evanston, Ill., 1969.

Afr 679.55.6   Fage, J.D. A history of West Africa. 4th ed. Cambridge, Eng., 1969.

Afr 9193.3.5   Fair, Thomas J.D. Development in Swaziland: a regional analysis. Johannesburg, 1969.

Afr 6214.36   Fajana, A. Nigeria in history. Pkeja, 1969.

Afr 6540.4.15   Fallers, Lloyd A. Law without precedent. Chicago, 1969.

Afr 628.264.2   Fernandes, Florestan. Die Integratión des Negers in die Klassengesellschaft. Bad Homburg, 1969.

Afr 8685.102   Fisher, John. The Afrikaners. London, 1969.

Afr 6291.54   Floyd, Barry. Eastern Nigeria. London, 1969.

Afr 8676.48.2.1   Franklin, N.N. Economics in South Africa. 2nd ed. N.Y., 1969.

Afr 7368.36.5   Freeman, F. Yaradee, a plea for Africa. N.Y., 1969.

Afr 4598.5   Gamst, Frederick C. The Qemant. N.Y., 1969.

Afr 8305.15   Gardner, Brian. The lion's cage. London, 1969.

Afr 1635.40   Gellner, Ernest. Saints of the Atlas. London, 1969.

Afr 3280.5   Ghali, Ibrahim Amin. L'Egypte nationaliste et libérale. La Haye, 1969.

Afr 8658.06.5   Gleanings in Africa; exhibiting a faithful and correct view of the manners and customs of the inhabitants of the Cape of Good Hope, and surrounding country. N.Y., 1969.

Afr 5360.5   Glélé, Maurice A. Naissance d'un état noir, l'évolution politique et constitutionelle du Dahomey, de la colonisation à nos jours. Paris, 1969.

Afr 6460.94   Goldschmidt, Walter Rochs. Kambvya's cattle. Berkeley, 1969.

Afr 55.46   Gollock, Georgina Anne. Lives of eminent Africans. N.Y., 1969.

Afr 7119.69   Gonzaga, Norberto. História de Angola, 1482-1963. Luanda, 1969.

Afr 6291.36   Goodell, Charles Ellsworth. Goodell report on the Biafra study mission. Denver, 1969.

Afr 8678.442   Gorodnov, Valentin P. Iuzhno-afrikanskii rabochii klass v bor'be protiv reaktsii i rasizma. Moskva, 1969.

Afr 9689.11.1   Gouldsbury, C. The great plateau of Northern Rhodesia. N.Y., 1969.

Afr 6879.16.3   Great Britain. Naval Intelligence Division. A handbook of German East Africa. N.Y., 1969.

Afr 3750.1   Griadunov, Iurii S. Novye gorizonty Sudana. Moskva, 1969.

Afr 628.229.12   Guggisberg, Frederick Gordon. The future of the Negro. N.Y., 1969.

Afr 6395.30   Gulliver, Phillip Hugh. Tradition and transition in East Africa. Berkeley, 1969.

Afr 5813.14   Hahn, Lorna. Mauritius; a study and annotated bibliography. Washington, 1969.

Afr 6403.6   Hakes, Jay E. A study guide for Kenya. Boston, 1969.

Afr 6193.66   Halbach, Axel J. Ghana als Wirtschaftspartner. Köln, 1969.

Afr 9650.10   Hall, Richard Seymour. The high price of principles. London, 1969.

Afr 650.8   Hanna, William John. Urban dynamics in Black Africa. N.Y., 1969.

Afr 11797.41.800   Haresnape, Geoffrey. Pauline Smith. N.Y., 1969.

Afr 5052.2   Hargreaves, J.D. France and West Africa. London, 1969.

Afr 630.9.5   Harris, John H. Africa: slave or free? N.Y., 1969.

Afr 7459.30.10A   Harvard African Expedition, 1926-1927. The African republic of Liberia and the Belgian Congo. N.Y., 1969. 2v.

Afr 505.50   Hatch, John C. The history of Britain in Africa. London, 1969.

Afr 8668.14   Hattersley, Alan. An illustrated social history of South Africa. Cape Town, 1969.

Afr 10528.36.100   Hayford, Casely. Ethiopia unbound; studies in race emancipation. 2nd ed. London, 1969.

Afr 6176.52   Hayford, Casely. West African leadership. 1st ed. London, 1969.

Afr 6275.26.5   Hazzledine, George D. The white man in Nigeria. N.Y., 1969.

Afr 10978.5   Head, Bessie. When rain clouds gather. N.Y., 1969.

Afr 7458.98   Heard, William Henry. The bright side of African life. N.Y., 1969.

Afr 109.69   Henries, A. Doris. Africa, our history. London, 1969.

Afr 8849.229   Herschel, John Frederick William. Herschel at the Cape: diaries and correspondence of Sir Jonn Herschel, 1834-1838. Cape Town, 1969.

Afr 678.62.5   Hewett, J.F.N. European settlements on the west coast of Africa. N.Y., 1969.

Afr 6291.64   Hilton, Bruce. Highly irregular. N.Y., 1969.

Afr 679.66.35   A history of West Africa: A.D. 1,000 to to the present day. 2. ed. Ibadan, 1969.

Afr 8279.00.33.1   Hobson, J.A. The war in South Africa. N.Y., 1969.

Afr 6096.24   Hodder, Bramwell William. Markets in West Africa. Ibadan, 1969.

Afr 9435.22   Holleman, Johan Frederik. Chief, council and commissioner: some problems of government in Rhodesia. Assen, 1969.

Afr 3079.69   Hopkins, Harry. Egypt, the crucible: the unfinished revolution of the Arab world. London, 1969.

Afr 6478.5   Hopkins, Terence K. A study guide for Uganda. Boston, 1969.

Afr 6069.69   Horton, James Africanus Beale. West African countries and peoples. Edinburgh, 1969.

Afr 212.64   Howe, Russell Warren. The African revolution. Croydon, Eng., 1969.

Afr 8289.69   Hoyt, Edwin Palmer. The Boer War. London, 1969.

Afr 115.128.2   Huggins, Willis Nathaniel. An introduction to African civilizations. N.Y., 1969.

Afr 550.175   Hughes, W. Dark Africa and the way out. N.Y., 1969.

Afr 3339.14   Hussein, Mahmoud. La Lutte de classes en Égypte de 1945 à 1968. Paris, 1969.

Afr 4433.1   Iag'ia, Vataniar S. Efiopiia v 1941-1954 gg. Moskva, 1969.

Afr 212.68   Ideinye techeniia v tropicheskoi Afrika. Moskva, 1969.

Afr 6778.2   Iliffe, John. Tanganyika under German rule, 1905-1912. London, 1969.

Afr 6275.134   Iloeje, Nwadilibe P. A new geography of Nigeria. London, 1969.

Afr 8678.446   Innes, Duncan. Our country, our responsibility. London, 1969.

Afr 45.66.15   International African Seminar. Ideas and prodedures in African customary law. London, 1969.

Afr 12018.8   Irele, Abiola. Lectures africaines. London, 1969.

Afr 8678.24.7   Jabavu, Davidson Don Tengo. The black problem. N.Y., 1969.

Afr 10005.3.1   Jahn, Janheinz. Neo-African literature. N.Y., 1969.

Afr 6095.369   Johnston, Harry Hamilton. Pioneers in West Africa. N.Y., 1969.

Afr 718.31.2   Johnston, J. Reality versus romance in South Central Africa. 2nd ed. London, 1969.

Afr 5765.8.5   Jordaan, Bee. Splintered cruicifix; early pioneers for Christendom on Madagascar and the Cape of Good Hope. Cape Town, 1969.

Afr 8225.10   Jordan, Robert Alan. The Transvaal War, 1808-1881; a bibliography. Johannesburg, 1969.

Afr 6060.69   Jordan, Robert Smith. Government and power in West Africa. London, 1969.

Afr 2030.469   Jouhaud, Edmond. O mon pays perdu. Paris, 1969.

Afr 6538.70   Kade, Gunnar. Die Stellung der zentralen Orte in der Kulturlandschaftlichen Entwicklung Bugandas (Uganda). Frankfurt, 1969.

Afr 6540.6.10   Kagwa, Apolo. The customs of the Baganoa. N.Y., 1969.

Afr 5227.28   Kanya-Forstner, Alexander Sidney. The conquest of the Western Sedan. Cambridge, Eng., 1969.

Afr 7309.66.5   Karlsson, Elis. Cruising off Mozambique. London, 1969.

Afr 10831.5.110   Kayira, Legson. Jingala. Harlow, 1969.

Afr Doc 3219.5   Kenya. Constitution. The Constitution of Kenya. Nairobi, 1969.

Afr 6277.128   Kilby, Peter. Industrialization in an open economy: Nigeria, 1945-1966. Cambridge, Eng., 1969.

Afr 10671.12.810   Killam, Gordon Douglas. The novels of Chinua Achebe. N.Y., 1969.

Afr 3315.152   Kipping, Norman Victor. The Suez contractors. Havant, Hampshire, 1969.

Afr 10662.5   Klima, Vladimir. Modern Nigerian novels. Prague, 1969.

Afr 635.98   Klineberg, Otto. Nationalism and tribalism among African students. Paris, 1969.

Afr 10631.58.140   Konadu, Asare. Ordained by the oracle. London, 1969.

Afr 626.213   Korendiasov, Evgenii N. Kollektivnyi kolonializm v deistvii. Moskva, 1969.

Afr 6280.2.40   Krapf-Askari, Eve. Yoruba towns and cities. Oxford, 1969.

Afr 679.10   Lang, John. The land of the golden trade, West Africa. N.Y., 1969.

Afr 8658.15.5   Latrole, Christian Ignatius. Journal of a visit to South Africa in 1815 and 1816. Cape Town, 1969.

Afr 11057.10   Lennox-Short, Alan. Stories, South African. Johannesburg, 1969.

Afr 7369.69   Liebenow, J. Gus. Liberia; the evolution of privilege. Ithaca, 1969.

Afr 7560.18.10   Lopes, Duarte. A report of the Kingdom of Congo and of the surrounding countries. N.Y., 1969.

Afr 3315.148   Love, Kenneth. Souez: the twice-fought war; a history. 1st ed. N.Y., 1969.

Afr 7575.80.12   Lumumba, Patrice. Congo, my country. London, 1969.

Afr 8371.5   Lurie, Angela Shulmith. Urban Africans in the Republic of South Africa, 1950-1966. Johannesburg, 1969.

Afr 5040.8   Lusignan, Guy de. French-speaking Africa since independence. London, 1969.

Afr 6570.5   Lyne, Robert Nunez. Zanzibar in contemporary times. N.Y., 1969.

Afr 7912.15.45   McKown, Robin. Lumumba; a biography. 1st ed. Garden City, 1969.

Afr 3305.18.5   McLeave, Hugh. The last Pharaoh: the ten faces of Farouk. London, 1969.

Afr 50.58   Mahiou, Ahmed. L'Avènement du parti unique en Afrique noire. Paris, 1969.

Afr 679.69.5   Małowist, Marian. Europa a Afryka Zachodnia w dobie wezesnej ekspansji kolonialnej. Wyd. 1. Warszawa, 1969.

Afr 630.69   Man in Africa. London, 1969.

Afr 1494.65   Manaserian, Levon P. Marokko v bor'be za nezavisimost'. Erevan, 1969.

Afr 6395.28   Mangat, J.S. A history of the Asians in East Africa, 1886 to 1945. Oxford, 1969.

Afr 3310.10.85.10   Mansfield, Peter. Nasser. London, 1969.

Afr 3310.10.85.5   Mansfield, Peter. Nasser's Egypt. Harmondsworth, 1969.

Afr 7135.4   Marcum, John. The Angolan revolution. Cambridge, 1969.

Afr 5199.337   Markovitz, Irving Leonard. Léopold Sédar Senghor and the politics of Negritude. 1st ed. N.Y., 1969.

Afr 1620.28.12   Maroc. Paris, 1969.

Afr 626.212   Martin, Jane. A bibliography on African regionalism. Boston, 1969.

Afr 8658.69   Mauch, Karl. The journals of Carl Mauch; his travels in the Transvaal and Rhodesia, 1869-1872. Salisbury, 1969.

Afr 2225.22   Mazuni, Abd Allah. Culture et enseignement en Algérie et au Maghreb. Paris, 1969.

Afr 8685.104   Meer, Fatima. Portrait of Indian South Africans. Durban, 1969.

Afr 9404.2   Merriweather, Alfred Musgrave. Desert doctor: medicine and evangelism in the Kalahan Desert. London, 1969.

Afr 6291.68   Metrowich, Frederick Redvers. Nigeria: the Biafran War. Pretoria, 1969.

Afr 9450.40   Metrowich, Frederick Redvers. Rhodesia; birth of a nation. Pretoria, 1969.

Afr 3315.150   Mezerik, Avrahm G. The Suez Canal: 1956 crisis - 1967 war. N.Y., 1969.

Afr Doc 5.10   Michigan. State University, East Lansing. Library. Research sources for African studies. East Lansing, 1969.

Afr 28.130   Michigan. State University, East Lansing. Library. Research sources for African studies. East Lansing, 1969.

Afr 5199.337.5   Milcent, Ernest. Léopold Sédar Senghor et la naissance de l'Afrique moderne. Paris, 1969.

Afr 609.69.5   Miller, Norman N. Research in rural Africa. Montreal, 1969.

Afr 9603.15   Mitchell, J.C. Social networks in urban situations. Manchester, 1969.

Afr 3305.12.10   Mitchell, Richard Paul. The society of the Muslim Brothers. London, 1969.

Afr 5320.15.1   Modupe, Prince. A royal African. N.Y., 1969.

Afr 6291.30A   Mok, Michael. Biafra journal. N.Y., 1969.

Afr 7219.69   Mondlane, Eduardo. The struggle for Mozambique. Harmondsworth, 1969.

Afr 500.19.10   Morel, Edmund D. The black man's burden. N.Y., 1969.

Afr 7568.15.15   Morel, Edmund D. Red rubber. N.Y., 1969.

Afr 3079.68.7   Morenz, Siegfried. Die Begegnung Europas mit Ägypten. 2. Aufl. Zürich, 1969.

Afr 679.69   Morgan, William Basil. West Africa. London, 1969.

Afr 5040.10   Mortimer, Edward. France and the Africans, 1944-1960: a political history. London, 1969.

Afr 8089.68.7   Muller, Christoffel Frederik Jakobus. Vyfhonderd jaar Suid-Afrikaanse Geskiedenis. Pretoria, 1969.

Afr 6210.64.5   Murray, D.J. The work of administration in Nigeria; case studies. London, 1969.

Afr 1268.8   Mutations culturelles et coopération au Maghreb. Paris, 1969.

Afr 9047.39   Mutwa, Vusamazulu Credo. My people, my Africa. 1st American ed. N.Y., 1969.

Afr 41918.5   Mwindo (Nyanga Folk Epic). English and Nyanga. The Mwindo epic from the Banyanga (Congo Republic). Berkeley, 1969.

Afr 679.12   Nassau, Robert Hamill. In an elephant corral, and other tales of West African experiences. N.Y., 1969.

Afr 6003.5   National Book League, London. Commonwealth in Africa. London, 1969.

Afr 632.54   N'Diaye, Jean Pierre. Élites africaines et culture occidentale, assimilation ou resistance? Paris, 1969.

Afr 2532.10   Le Néo-Destour face à la première épreuve, 1934-36. Tunis, 1969.

Afr 6316.10   Ngano; studies in traditional and modern East African history. Nairobi, 1969.

Afr 6210.68   Nicolson, I.F. The administration of Nigeria, 1900-1960: men, methods, and myths. Oxford, 1969.

Afr 212.70   Nielsen, Waldemar A. The great powers and Africa. N.Y., 1969.

Afr 6291.58F   Nigeria, South-Eastern. Ministry of Home Affairs and Information. Information Division. Fact sheets on South-Eastern state of Nigeria. Calabar, 1969.

Afr 6291.48   Nwankwo, Arthur Agwuncha. The making of a nation: Biafra. London, 1969.

Afr 6225.55   Ohonbamu, Obarogie. The psychology of the Nigerian revolution. Ilfracombe, 1969.

Afr 6291.60   Ojukwu, Chukwuemeka Odumeywu. Biafra; selected speeches and random thoughts of C.O. Ojukwu. 1st ed. N.Y., 1969.

Afr 6146.12   Olson, Gilbert W. Church growth in Sierra Leone. Grand Rapids, 1969.

Afr 8089.69   The Oxford history of South Africa. Oxford, 1969.

Afr 10009.10   Pantŭček, Svetozár. La litterature algérienne moderne. Prague, 1969.

Afr 545.50   Parrinder, E.G. Religion in Africa. Harmondsworth, 1969.

Afr 11675.87.140   Paton, Alan. For you departed. N.Y., 1969.

Afr 11675.87.150   Paton, Alan. Kontakion for you departed. London, 1969.

Afr 8685.55.1   Patterson, S. Colour and culture in South Africa. N.Y., 1969.

Afr 628.141   Pennington, James W.C. A text book of the origin and history, (Hartford, 1841). Detroit, 1969?

Afr 4238.10.2   Perham, M.F. The government of Ethiopia. 2nd ed. London, 1969.

Afr 6140.201   Peterson, John. Province of freedom; a history of Sierra Leone, 1787-1870. London, 1969.

Afr 632.52   Pluralism in Africa. Berkeley, 1969.

Afr 7889.5   Pous, Valdo. Stanleyville: an African urban community under Belgian administration. London, 1969.

Afr 6198.71   Priestley, Margaret. West African trade and coast society; a family study. London, 1969.

Afr 609.69   Pritchard, John Malcom. Africa; a study geography for advanced students. London, 1969.

Afr 10007.4   Protest and conflict in African literature. London, 1969.

330

Afr 115.123	Prothero, Ralph Mansell. A geography of Africa; regional essays on fundamental characteristics, issues and problems. London, 1969.
Afr 3315.146	Protopopov, Anatolii S. Sovetskii Soiuz i Suetskii krizis 1956 goda (iiul'-noiabr'). Moskva, 1969.
Afr 8289.04.5	Prussia. Grosser Generalstab. Kriegsgeschichtliche Abteilung. The war in South Africa. N.Y., 1969.
Afr 2030.469.5	Quandt, William B. Revolution and political leadership: Algeria, 1954-1968. Cambridge, 1969.
Afr 5235.269	Radchenko, Galina F. Respublika Mali. Moskva, 1969.
Afr 8325.68.10	Ransford, Oliver. The battle of Spion Kop. London, 1969.
Afr 6194.10.1	Rattray, Robert Sutherland. Ashanti. N.Y., 1969.
Afr 10671.12.805	Ravenscroft, Arthur. Chinua Achebe. Burnt Mill, 1969.
Afr 590.20.2	Read, Hollis. The Negro problem solved. N.Y., 1969.
Afr 6214.38	Renard, Alain. Biafra, naissance d'une nation? Paris, 1969.
Afr 5465.6	Retel-Laurention, Anne. Oracles et ordalies chez les Nzakara. Paris, 1969.
Afr 8678.68.15	Rhoodie, N.J. Apartheid and racial partnership in Southern Africa. Pretoria, 1969.
Afr 6118.10	Rice, Berkeley. Enter Gambia; the birth of and improbable nation. Boston, 1969.
Afr 699.69	Richards, Audrey. The multicultural states of East Africa. Montreal, 1969.
Afr 212.72	Rivkin, A. Nation-building in Africa; problems and prospects. New Brunswick, N.J., 1969.
Afr 8250.45	Roberts, Brian. Cecil Rhodes and the princess. London, 1969.
Afr 626.200.5	Robson, Peter. The economics of Africa. London, 1969.
Afr 626.220	Rowe, David Nelson. The new diplomacy; international technical cooperation projects of the Republic of China in African countries. New Haven, 1969.
Afr 7308.66.2	Rowley, Henry. The story of the universities' mission to Central Africa. 2nd ed. N.Y., 1969.
Afr 718.9.10	Royal Geographical Society. The lands of Cazembe: Lacerda's journey to Cazembe in 1798. N.Y., 1969.
Afr 6282.44	Rubingh, Eugene. Sons of Tiv; a study of the rise of the church among the Tiv of Central Nigeria. Grand Rapids, Michigan, 1969.
Afr 6295.130	Ryder, Alan Frederick Charles. Benin and the Europeans, 1485-1897. London, 1969.
Afr 8678.440	Sachs, Albert. South Africa. London, 1969.
Afr 6198.79.1	Sampson, Magnus John. Makers of modern Ghana. Accra, 1969.
Afr 630.69.5	Santos, Eduardo dos. Elementos de etnologia africana. Lisboa, 1969.
Afr 3275.12.5.2	al-Sayyid, Afaf Lutfi. Egypt and Cromer; a study in Anglo-Egyptian relations. N.Y., 1969.
Afr 5040.12	Scherk, Nikolaus. Dekolonisation und Souveränität. Wien, 1969.
Afr 8225.20	Schreuder, Deryck Marshall. Gladstone and Kruger: liberal government and colonial "home rule". London, 1969.
Afr 7580.38	Scott, Ian. Tumbled house: the Congo at independence. London, 1969.
Afr 6287.4	Search for a place: black separatism and Africa, 1860. Ann Arbor, 1969.
Afr 8289.69.5	Selby, John Millin. The Boer War; a study in cowardice and courage. London, 1969.
Afr 9446.24	Selous, Frederick Courteney. Sunshine and storm in Rhodesia. N.Y., 1969.
Afr 12639.24.700	Senghor, Leopold Sédar. Nocturnes. London, 1969.
Afr 6210.66	Sharwood Smith, Bryan. Recollections of British administration in the Cameroons and Northern Nigeria, 1921-1957. Durham, N.C., 1969.
Afr 8678.438	Simons, Harold. Class and colour in South Africa, 1850-1950. Harmondsworth, 1969.
Afr 4559.06.5	Skinner R.P. Abyssinia of to-day, an account of the first mission sent by the American Government to the court of King of Kings, 1903-1904. N.Y., 1969.
Afr 6410.14.2	Slade, Humphrey. The Parliament of Kenya. 2nd ed. Nairobi, 1969.
Afr 9450.35	Smith, Donald. Rhodesia: the problem. London, 1969.
Afr 679.27.6	Solanke, Ladipo. United West Africa, or Africa, at the bar of the family of nations. London, 1969.
Afr 4226.8	Sommer, John W. A study guide for Ethiopia and the Horn of Africa. Hanover, 1969.
Afr 6878.73.15	Stanley, H.M. My Kalulu, prince, king and slave. N.Y., 1969.
Afr 8235.8.5	Statham, F.R. Blacks, Boers, and British. N.Y., 1969.
Afr 2749.69	Stevens, Jon. The Sahara is yours; a handbook for desert travellers. London, 1969.
Afr 4115.30.1	Stewart, Desmond Stirling. Great Cairo; the world. London, 1969.
Afr 8686.28	Strassberger, Elfriede. The Rhenish Mission Society in South Africa. Cape Town, 1969.
Afr 9489.69	Strauss, Frances. My Rhodesia. Boston, 1969.
Afr 6291.44	Sullivan, John R. Breadless Biafra. Dayton, Ohio, 1969.
Afr 3979.69	Sykes, John. Down into Egypt, a revolution observed. London, 1969.
Afr 2459.69	Sylvester, Anthony. Tunisia. London, 1969.
Afr 6280.11.12	Talbot, P.A. The peoples of southern Nigeria. London, 1969. 4v.
Afr 7175.54.10	Tams, Georg. Visit to the Portuguese possessions in South-Western Africa. N.Y., 1969.
Afr 626.210	Tamuno, Olufunmilayo Grace Esho. Co-operation for development. Ibadan, 1969.
Afr 855.24	Taylor, Margaret Stewart. St. Helens, ocean roadhouse. London, 1969.
Afr 6277.120	Technical Assistance Information Clearing House. Nigeria/Biafrai programs of assistance of U.S. non-profit organizations, March 1969. N.Y., 1969.
Afr 8175.5.1	Theal, G.M. History of the Boers in South Africa. N.Y., 1969.
Afr 8678.13.3	Theal, G.M. The yellow and dark-skinned people of Africa south of the Zambesi. N.Y., 1969.
Afr 7218.96.2	Theal, George McCall. The Portuguese in South Africa. N.Y., 1969.
Afr 8678.436	Thion, Serge. Le pouvoir pâle. Paris, 1969.
Afr 545.56	Thomas, Louis Vincent. Les religions d'Afrique noire. Paris, 1969.
Afr 555.3.2	Thompson, George. The palm land. 2nd ed. London, 1969.
Afr 125.15	Thompson, Lloyd Arthur. Africa in classical antiquity. Ibadan, Nigeria, 1969.
Afr 6178.15	Thompson, William Scott. Ghana's foreign policy, 1957-1966. Princeton, N.J., 1969.

Afr 628.269	Toledo. University. Library. The Black experience; the Negro in America, Africa, and the world. Toledo, Ohio, 1969.
Afr 1088.12	Tourneau, Roger. The Almohad movement in North Africa in the twelfth and thirteenth centuries. Princeton, N.J., 1969.
Afr 6390.102	Townsend, Derek. Wild Africa's silent call. London, 1969.
Afr 14740.76.100	Trindade, Francisco Alberto Cartaxo e. Chinanga, poemas. Lisboa, 1969.
Afr 1555.12	Trout, Frank Emanuel. Morocco's Saharan frontiers. Geneva, 1969.
Afr 6280.9.50	Umeasiegba, Remshna. The way we lived. London, 1969.
Afr 6291.52	Uwechue, Raph. Reflections on the Nigerian civil war; a mall far realism. London, 1969.
Afr 3199.69	Vatikiotis, Panayiotis Jerasimof. The modern history of Egypt. London, 1969.
Afr 7135.10	Venter, Al Johannes. The terror fighters: a profile of guerilla warfare in southern Africa. Cape Town, 1969.
Afr 10443.1.41	Waciuma, Charity. Daughter of Mumbi. Nairobi, 1969.
Afr 8868.10	Wallman, Sandra. Take out hunger; two case studies of rural development in Basutoland. London, 1969.
Afr 7808.90.7	Ward, Herbert. Five years with the Congo cannibals. 3rd ed. N.Y., 1969.
Afr 42208.5	Ward, Philip. The Okefani song of Nij Zitru. London, 1969.
Afr 6291.62	Waugh, Auberon. Biafra; Britain's shame. London, 1969.
Afr 6164.30	Welman, Charles Wellesley. The native states of the Gold Coast. London, 1969.
Afr 6097.10	West African Congress on Evangelism, Ibadan, Nigeria, 1968. West African Congress on Evangelism. n.p., 1969.
Afr 626.172.1	Whetham, Edith Holt. The economics of African countries. London, 1969.
Afr 718.2.95	White, Stanhope. Lost empire on the Nile: H.M. Stanley, Emin Pasha and the imperialists. London, 1969.
Afr 212.74	Williams, G. Mennen. Africa for the Africans. Grand Rapids, 1969.
Afr 6057.69	Wilson, Henry S. Origins of West African nationalism. N.Y., 1969.
Afr 6143.16.2A	Winterbottom, T. An account of the native African in the neighborhood of Sierra Leone. 2nd ed. London, 1969.
Afr 8145.5.5	Wirgman, A.T. The history of the English church and people in South Africa. N.Y., 1969.
Afr Doc 1802.15	Witherell, Julian W. Ghana; a guide to official publications, 1872-1968. Washington, 1969.
Afr 6291.56	Wolf, Jean. La guerre des rapaces, la vérité sur la guerre du Biafra. Paris, 1969.
Afr 2819.69	Wright, John L. Libya. London, 1969.
Afr 8722.2.1	Wright, William. Slavery at the Cape of Good Hope. N.Y., 1969.
Afr 5243.174.30	Zahan, Dominique. La Viande et la graine, mythologie dogon. Paris, 1969.
Afr 5340.505	Zeller, Claus. Elfenbeinküste. 1. Aufl. Freiburg im Breisgau, 1969.
Afr 4573.25	Zerom, Kifle-Mariam. The resources and economy of Ethiopia. Menlo Park, Calif., 1969.
Afr 5335.2.1	Zolberg, Aristide R. One party government in the Ivory Coast. Princeton, N.J., 1969.

1970

Afr 626.218	African development and Europe. 1st ed. Oxford, 1970.
Afr 10621.53.110	Armah, Ayi Kwei. Fragments. Boston, 1970[c1969].
Afr 5187.20	Behrman, Lucy C. Muslim brotherhoods and politics in Senegal. Cambridge, 1970.
Afr 6738.54	Cameroon. Ministère de l'Information et du Tourisme. Cameroun. Paris, 1970.
Afr 10671.12.815	Carroll, David. Chinua Achebe. N.Y., 1970.
Afr 3335.20	Copeland, Miles. The game of nations: the amorality of power politics. London, 1970.
Afr 2687.4.2	Duvignaud, Jean. Changes at Shebika. 1st American ed. N.Y., 1970.
Afr 9838.99.3	Elmslie, Walter Angus. Among the wild Ngoni. 3rd ed. London, 1970.
Afr 109.70.10	Gailey, Harry A. History of Africa, from the earliest times to 1800. N.Y., 1970.
Afr 109.70.5	Hallett, Robin. Africa to 1875; a modern history. Ann Arbor, 1970.
Afr 109.70	July, Robert William. A history of the African people. N.Y., 1970.
Afr 6883.40	Klima, George J. The Barabaig; East African cattle-herders. N.Y., 1970.
Afr 3979.01.10	Page, Thomas Nelson. On the Nile in 1901. Miami, 1970.
Afr 718.2.40	Stanley, Henry Morton. Stanley's despatches to the New York Herald, 1871-1872, 1874-1877. Boston, 1970.
Afr 9445.50	Summers, Roger. The warriors. Cape Town, 1970.
Afr 212.76	Thompson, Vincent Bakpetu. Africa and unity: the evolution of Pan-Africanism. N.Y., 1970.
Afr 6282.46.2	Waddell, Hope Masterton. Twenty-nine years in the West Indies and Central Africa. 2nd ed. London, 1970.
Afr 7459.70	Warner, Esther Sietmann. Trial by sasswood. Oxford, 1970.
Afr 6890.4	Wenner, Kate. Shamba letu. Boston, 1970.
Afr 6284.10	Whitaker, C. Sylvester. The politics of tradition; continuity and change in Northern Nigeria, 1946-1966. Princeton, N.J., 1970.
Afr 6979.69.2	White, Jon Manchip. The land God made in anger: reflections on a journey through South West Africa. London, 1970.

WIDENER LIBRARY SHELFLIST, 34

AFRICAN HISTORY
AND
LITERATURES

AUTHOR AND TITLE LISTING

Afr 5407.8 L'A.E.F. économique et sociale, 1947-1958. (French Equatorial Africa. Service de Coordination des Affaires Economiques.) Paris, 1959.

Afr 555.29.20 A.M. MacKay, pioneer missionary of the Church Missionary Society to Uganda. N.Y., 1896.

Afr 555.29.22 A.M. MacKay, pioneer missionary of the Church Missionary Society to Uganda. N.Y., 1904.

Afr 4700.36 A.O., Africa orientale, il posto al sole. (Federzoni, L.) Bologna, 1936.

Afr 5055.58A L'A.O.F. entre en scène. (Milcent, Ernest.) Paris, 1958.

Afr 1493.5 A la conquête du Maroc sud, 1912-13. (Cornet.) Paris, 1914.

Afr 5318.17 A la côte occidentale d'Afrique. (Laumann, E.M.) Paris, 1890.

Afr 5748.96.5 A la cour de Madagascar. (Cazeneuve, M.) Paris, 1896.

Afr 5765.31 A la découverte d'un diocèse Malgache, Fianarantsoa. (Dailliez, André.) Bar-le-Duc, 1966.

Afr 630.60.5 A la recherche de la personnalité négro-africaine. (Diderot, Toussaint.) Monte-Carlo, 1960.

Afr 5053.5 A la recherche d'une politique indigène dans l'Ouest africain. (Labouret, Henri.) Paris, 1931.

Afr 5426.120 A Lambaréné. (Bonzon, Charles.) Nancy, 1897.

Afr 5049.100 A l'ombre des palmes, l'oeuvre familiale et missionaire des soeurs du Saint-Esprit. (Masseguin, Christiane.) Paris, 1942.

Afr 5426.100.20 A l'orée de la forêt vierge. (Schweitzer, Albert.) Paris, 1929.

Afr 5748.98.3 A Madagascar, hier et aujourd'hui. (Escande, E.) Paris, 1898.

Afr 5749.02 A Madagascar. (Danfreville de la Salle.) Paris, 1902.

Afr 5635.3 A Madagascar. (Orleans, H.P.D.) Paris, 1895.

Afr 2208.97 A pied, le tour de la terre...à travers le sud-algérien. (Grandin.) Paris, 1897.

Afr 4785.965.5 A pied au Nord Somali. (Balsan, Francois.) Paris, 1965.

Afr 2208.88.5 A propos du Transsaharien. (Deporter, Victor.) Alger, 1890.

Afr 7575.80.5 A propos d'un livre posthume de Patrice Lumumba. (Chome, Jules.) Bruxelles, 1961.

Afr 6291.66 A questão de Biafra. (Santos, Eduardo dos.) Porto, 1968.

Afr 1485.5 A travers la Chaouia. (Grasset, Capitaine.) Paris, 1911.

Afr 2230.19F A travers la Kabylie. (Charveriat, F.) n.p.., n.d.

Afr 5090.16 A travers la Mauritanie occidentale. (Gruvel, Abel.) Paris, 1909.

Afr 2929.01 A travers la Tripolitaine. (Mehier de Mathuisieulx, H.) Paris, 1903.

Afr 2929.01.3 A travers la Tripolitaine. 3e ed. (Mehier de Mathuisieulx, H.) Paris, 1912.

Afr 2608.87 A travers la Tunisie. (Baraban, L.) Paris, 1887.

Afr 5045.22 A travers l'Afrique. (Baratier, A.E.A.) Paris, 1910.

Afr 715.6 A travers l'Afrique centrale. (Maistre, C.) Paris, 1895.

Afr 8658.91.7 A travers l'Afrique centrale du Cap au lac Nyassa. 2. éd. (Foà, Édouard.) Paris, 1901.

Afr 510.25F A travers l'Afrique française. (Burthe d'Annelet, Anarie.) Paris, 1932. 2v.

Afr 510.26F A travers l'Afrique française. (Burthe d'Annelet, Anarie.) Paris, 1939. 2v.

Afr 2208.79.3 A travers l'Algérie. (Bourde, P.) Paris, 1880.

Afr 2208.84.2 A travers l'Algérie. (Reuss, L.M.) Paris, 1884.

Afr 5180.4 A travers le Fouta-Diallon et le Bambouc. (Noirot, E.) Paris, n.d.

Afr 1609.23.25 A travers le Maghreb. (Sadler, Georges.) Paris, 1923.

Afr 1608.94.2 A travers le Maroc. (Montbard, G.) Paris, 1894.

Afr 2748.82.6 A travers le Sahara, les missions du colonel Flatters. (Barbier, J.V.) Paris, 1895.

Afr 2609.30.10F A travers le sud Tunisie. (Thomas, Jean.) Paris, 1930.

Afr 2285.7 A travers les oasis sahariennes. (Champeaux, G.) Paris, 1903.

Afr 1609.38 A traverso il Marocco. (Orano, E.) Napoli, 1938.

Afr 3979.55.5 Aafjes, Bertus. Morgen bloeien de abrikozen. Amsterdam, 1954.

Afr 8279.00.37F Aanleiding tot den engelsch-transvaal oorlog. (Achilles, Kort.) 's-Gravenhage, n.d.

Afr 6420.40A Aaronovitch, S. Crisis in Kenya. London, 1947.

Afr 12371.1.100 Aba, Noureddine. La Toussaint des énigmes. Paris, 1963.

Afr 2731.1 Abadie, F. Lettres sur le Trans-saharien. Constantine, 1880.

Afr 5260.20 Abadie, Maurice. La colonie du Niger. Paris, 1927.

Afr 4558.83.5 Abargues de Sosten, J.V. Notas del viaje por Etiopia. Madrid, 1883.

Afr 7815.5.7 Les Abatua. 7. (Halkin, Joseph.) Bruxelles, 1911.

Afr 590.34 Abbadie, A. Sur l'abolition de l'esclavage en Afrique. Paris, 1896.

Afr 2025.29 Abbas, F. Le jeune Algérien. Paris, 1931.

Afr 2000.15 Abbas, Ferhat. Guerre et révolution d'Algérie. Paris, 1962.

Afr 3675.21 Abbas, Mekki. The Sudan question. London, 1952.

Afr 3285.4 Abbas II. (Cromer, E.B.) London, 1915.

Afr 3300.22 Abbas II Hilmi, Khedive of Egypt. A few words on the Anglo-Egyptian settlement. London, 1930.

Afr 4513.36.50 Abbati, A.H. Italy and the Abyssinian war. London, 1936.

NEDL Afr 6275.18 Abbeokuta, or Sunrise within the tropics. (Tucker, Charlotte Maria.) London, 1853.

Afr 6275.18.2 Abbeokuta, or Sunrise within the tropics. (Tucker, Charlotte Maria.) N.Y., 1853.

Afr 6275.18.5 Abbeokuta, or Sunrise within the tropics. (Tucker, Charlotte Maria.) N.Y., 1859.

Afr 6275.18.3 Abbeokuta, or Sunrise within the tropics. 5th ed. (Tucker, Charlotte Maria.) London, 1856.

Afr 1738.40 Abbey, W.B.T. Tangier under british rule, 1661-1684. Jersey, Channel Islands, British Isles, 1940.

Afr 6700.1 Abbia. Yaoundé. 1,1963+ 2v.

Afr 2875.6 Abbott, G.F. The holy war in Tripoli. London, 1912.

Afr 8292.10 Abbott, J.H.M. Tommy Comstalle. (Australian troops). London, 1902.

Afr 1254.62 Abd al-Busit ibn Khalil. Douze récits de voyage inédits en Afrique du nord au XVe siècle. Paris, 1936.

Afr 1769.1.5 Abd Al-Karim. Memoiren. Dresden, 1927.

Afr 3974.00 Abd-Al-Latif. Relation de l'Egypte (XIVe siècle). Paris, 1810.

Afr 3745.80 Abd al-Rahim, Muddathir. Imperialism and nationalism in the Sudan. Oxford, 1969.

Afr 5225.5 Abd al-Rahman ibn Abdallah al-Tonbukti. Tedzkiret en-nisian fi akhbar molouk es-Soudan. Paris, 1901.

Afr 3990.27 Abd Allah, Hasan. The handbook of Egypt. Cairo, 1966.

Afr 1965.23 Abd-el-Kader. (Bellemare, Alex.) Paris, 1863.

Afr 1965.1 Abd-el-Kader. (Dupuch, A.A.) Bordeaux, 1860.

Afr 1965.25 Abd-el-Kader. (Estailleur-Chanteraine, Phillippe d'.) Paris, 1947.

Afr 1965.7.5 Abd el-Kader. (Legras, J.) Paris, 1929.

Afr 1965.7 Abd el-Kader. (Pichon, J.) Tlemcen, n.d.

Afr 1769.1 Abd El-Krim. Memoires d'Abd-el-Krim. 5e ed. Paris, 1927.

Afr 1493.50.5 Abd-el-Krim. (Fontaine, Pierre.) Paris, 1958.

Afr 1658.48 Abd-el-krim contra francia. (Lopez Rienda, R.) Madrid, 1925.

Afr 1493.50 Abd-el-Krim et les événements du Rif. (Gabrielli, L.) Casablanca, 1953.

Afr 3180.5 Abd-el-Rahman, Cheikh. Merveilles biographiques et historiques ou chroniques. Paris 1888. 8v.

X Cg Afr 3180.5 Abd-el-Rahman, Cheikh. Merveilles biographiques et historiques ou chroniques. v.9. Paris, 1888.

Afr 3974.00.5 Abdallatifs Denkwürdigkeiten Egyptens. (Wahl, G.F.G.) Halle, 1790.

Afr 1493.50.10 Abdel Krim: Emir of the Rif. (Furneaux, Rupert.) London, 1967.

Afr 3340.20 Abdel Malek, Anouar. Egypt: military society; social change under Nasser. 1st American ed. N.Y., 1968.

Afr 3310.7 Abdel-Malek, Anouar. Egypte, société militaire. Paris, 1962.

Afr 3204.28 Abdel-Malek, Anouar. Idéologie et renaissance nationale; l'Egypte moderne. Paris, 1969.

Afr 1624.911 Abdesselem, Faleb. L'organisation financiere de l'empire marocain. Paris, 1911.

Afr 7803.10 Abel, Armand. Les Musulmans noirs du Maniema. Bruxelles, 1960.

Afr 36.2 Abel, Herbert. Deutsche Afrikawissenschaft. Stand und Aufgaben. Köln, 1962.

Afr 5045.28 Abensour, Leon. La France noire, ses peuples. Paris, 1931.

Afr 6738.2A Abeokuta and the Camaroons mountains. (Burton, R.F.) London, 1863.

Afr 8687.101 Abercrombie, H.R. The secret history of South Africa. 2. ed. Johannesburg, 1952.

Afr 630.38.5 Abercrombie, Hugh R. Africa's peril. London, 1938.

Afr 1.88 Aberdeen. University. African Studies Group. Bulletin. Aberdeen. 1,1967+

Afr 4559.35.107 Abessinien, Afrikas Unruhe-Herd. (Huyn, Ludwig.) Salzburg, 1935.

Afr 4559.35 Abessinien, ahoi. (Gruehl, Max.) Berlin, 1935.

Afr 4558.69.5 Abessinien, das Alpenland unter den Tropen. (Andree, Richard.) Leipzig, 1869.

Afr 4389.35 Abessinien, das letzte ungelöste Problem Afrikas. (Zischka, A.) Bern, 1935.

Afr 4513.35.78 Abessinien, das Pulverfass Afrikas. 3e Aufl. (Wencker-Wiedberg, F.) Düsseldorf, 1935.

Afr 4430.35.5 Abessinien, die schwarze Gefahr. (Prochazka, R. von.) Wien, 1935.

Afr 4559.18 Abessinien, eine Landeskunde. (Rein, G.K.) Berlin, 1918-20. 3v.

Afr 4559.35.70 Abessinien; Raum als Schicksal. (Herrmann, Gerhard.) Leipzig, 1935.

Afr 4559.35.65 Abessinien. (Gruehl, Max.) Berlin, 1935.

Afr 4559.35.130 Abessinien. (Littmann, Enno.) Hamburg, 1935.

Afr 4558.92.5 Abessinien. (Muenzenberger, E.F.A.) Freiberg, 1892.

Afr 4559.28.15 Abessinien. (Schrenzel, E.H.) Berlin, 1928.

Afr 4389.35.7 Abessinien. 2e Aufl. (Lahse, Erich.) Leipzig, 1935.

Afr 4500.22 Abessinien als Kampfobjekt der grossen Mächte von 1880-1916. (Reischies, S.) Bleicherode am Harz, 1937.

Afr 4559.34 Abessinienflug. (Mittelholzer, W.) Zürich, 1934.

Afr 4580.1 Die Abessinier in Arabien und Afrika. (Glaser, E.) München, 1895.

Afr 4360.10 Abir, Mordechai. Ethiopia: the era of the princes. London, 1968.

Afr 4513.35.120 Abisinia. (Hernandez Alfonso, L.) Madrid, 1935.

Afr 4558.81.5 Abissinia, giornale di un viaggio. (Vigoni, Pippo.) Milano, 1881.

Afr 4389.35.3 Abissinia, l'ultimo problema insoluto dell'Africa. (Zischka, A.) Firenze, 1936.

Afr 4513.35.125 Abissinia, problema italiano. Roma, 1935.

Afr 4559.29 L'Abissinia. (Conti Rossini, C.) Roma, 1929.

Afr 4259.35.15 Abissinia. (Nomado, R.) Napoli, 1935.

Afr 4558.88.5 L'Abissinia. (Parises, N.) Milan, 1888.

Afr 4558.83.2 L'Abissinia. (Rohlfs, G.) Milano, 1885.

Afr 4259.35.30 Abissinia. (Rossi, Corrado.) Milano, 1935.

Afr 4390.40 Abissinia (1888-1896). v.1. (Scarforglio, E.) Roma, 1936.

Afr 4513.25 L'Abissinia attuale sotto tutti i suoi aspetti. (Varanini, Varo.) Torino, 1935.

Afr 4559.35.18 Abissinia di oggi. 8a ed. (Jansen, P.G.) Milano, 1935.

Afr 4513.36.85 L'Abissinia e noi. (Fasci Italiani all'Estero.) Roma, 1935.

Afr 4259.35.7 Abissinia ieri ed oggi. 2a ed. (Arcuno, Irma.) Napoli, 1935.

Afr 4572.15 L'Abissinia nella geografia dell'Africa orientale. (Padoan, L.) Milano, 1935.

Afr 4512.10.3 L'Abissinia nelle questioni internazionali. 3a ed. (Marotta, Renato.) Torino, 1936.

Afr 4430.35.8 Abissinia pericolo nero. (Prochazka, R. von.) Milano, 1935.

Afr 4558.87 L'Abissinia settentrionale. Photoreproduction. (Cecchi, A.) Milano, 1887.

Afr 8678.6 The aborigines of South Africa. (Clarence, W.) Boston, 1860.

Afr 1609.07.3 Abou-Djebel. Tres meses en Marruecos. Madrid, 1907.

Afr 3978.69.5 About, E. Le fellah: souvenirs d'Egypte. Paris, 1869.

Afr 3978.69.5.2 About, E. Le fellah: souvenirs d'Egypte. 2e ed. Paris, 1870.

Afr 3978.69.5.4 About, E. Le fellah: souvenirs d'Egypte. 3e ed. Paris, 1873.

Afr 3978.69.5.6 About, E. Le fellah: souvenirs d'Egypte. 6e ed. Paris, 1896.

Afr 2209.11.5 About Algeria, Algiers. (Thomas-Stanford, C.) London, 1912.

Afr 6277.47 Aboyade, O. Foundations of an African economy. N.Y., 1966.

Afr 6280.26 Abraham, R.C. The Tiv people. Lagos, 1933.

Afr 609.62.15 Abraham, W. The mind of Africa. London, 1962.

Afr 11108.74.110 Abrahams, Peter. A night of their own. London, 1965.

Afr 8678.311 Abrahams, Peter. Return to Goli. London, 1953.

Afr 11108.74.120 Abrahams, Peter. Tell freedom. 1st American ed. N.Y., 1954.

Afr 11108.74.100A Abrahams, Peter. A wreath for Udomo. 1st American ed. N.Y., 1956.

Afr 6883.20.10 Abrahams, R.G. The political organization of Unyamwezi. Cambridge, 1967.

Afr 590.82 Abramova, Svetlana I. Istoriia rabotorgovli na verkhne-gvineiskom poberezh'e. Moskva, 1966.
Afr 210.60.40 Abranches, Esther. Afrique. Luanda, 1960.
Afr 10100.5 Abrash, Barbara. Black African literature in English since 1952; works and criticism. N.Y., 1967.
Afr 8279.00.44 Die Abrechnung mit England. 2. Aufl. (Eisenhart, Karl.) München, 1900.
Afr 3979.57.10 Abreu, Paradela De. Reportagens no Egipto. Lisboa, 1957.
Afr 7110.5 Abreu e Brito, D. de. Um inquerito a vida administrativa e economica de Angola e doBrasil. Coimbra, 1931.
Afr 10621.9.100 Abruquah, Joseph W. The catechist. London, 1965.
Afr 8289.00.3 Absent minded war. London, 1900.
Afr 7015.55 Abshire, David M. Portuguese Africa; a handbook. N.Y., 1969.
Afr 7458.22 Abstract of a journal...to Afrika. (Bacon, E.) Philadelphia, 1822.
Afr Doc 2809.300 Abstract of economic statistics. (Mauritius. Central Statistical Office.) Port Louis? 1965?
Afr Doc 2520.703 Abstract of local government statistics. (Nigeria, Western. Ministry of Economic Planning and Social Development. Statistics Division.) Ibadan. 1,1966+
Afr 7568.25.5 Abstract of the report of the Commission enquiry into a administration of Congo Free State. (Belgium. Commission Chargée de Faire une Enquête dans les Territoires de l'Etat du Congo.) London, 1906.
Afr 1603.80 Abu Al-Feda. Description du pays du Magreb. Alger, 1839.
Afr 4559.61 Abu al-Hajjaj, Y. A contribution to the physiography of northern Ethiopia. London, 1961.
Afr 3977.76 Abu-l-Feda. Descriptio aegypti. Göttingen, 1776.
Afr 1835.1.9 Abu Salem, Called Al-Aiasi. Voyages dans le sud de l'Algérie. Paris, 1846.
Afr 3310.85A Abul-Fath, A. L'affaire Nasser. Paris, 1962.
Afr 550.63 Abundant life in changing Africa. (West Central Africa Regional Conference, Leopoldville, 1946.) N.Y., 1946.
Afr 1753.13 Aby la herculana. (Sureda Blanes, F.) Calpe, 1925.
Afr 4228 Pamphlet box. Abyssinia.
Afr 4228.01 Pamphlet box. Abyssinia.
Afr 4558.68 Abyssinia. (Hotten, J.C.) London, 1868.
Afr 4559.01.5 Abyssinia. (Vivian, H.) N.Y., 1901.
Afr 4513.09F Pamphlet box. Abyssinia. Foreign relations.
Htn Afr 4513.2PF* Pamphlet box. Abyssinia. Foreign relations with Italy.
Afr 4513.05 Pamphlet box. Abyssinia. Foreign relations with Italy.
Afr 4513.07 Pamphlet box. Abyssinia. Foreign relations with Italy.
Afr 4513.35.55 Abyssinia and Italy. (Burns, Emile.) London, 1935.
Afr 4513.20 Abyssinia and Italy. (Royal Institute of International Affairs.) N.Y., 1935.
Afr 4430.36.10 The Abyssinia I knew. (Virgin.) London, 1936.
Afr 4559.06.5 Abyssinia of to-day, an account of the first mission sent by the Americam Government to the court of King of Kings, 1903-1904. (Skinner R.P.) N.Y., 1969.
Afr 4559.06 Abyssinia of to-day. (Skinner, R.P.) London, 1906.
Afr 4559.35.30 Abyssinia on the eve. (Farago, L.) London, 1935.
Afr 4430.35 Abyssinian adventure. (Harmsworth, G.) London, 1935.
Afr 4513.35.20 The Abyssinian dispute. (Carnegie Endowment for International Peace. Division of Intercourse and Education.) N.Y., 1935.
Afr 4513.35.5 The Abyssinian dispute. (White, F.) London, 1935.
Afr 4375.9PF The Abyssinian expedition and the life and the reign of King Theodore. (Acton, Roger.) London, 1868.
Afr 4559.34.15 Abyssinian journal. (Griaule, M.) London, 1935.
Afr 4559.48 Abyssinian memories. (Philip, H.) Santa Barbara, Calif., 1948.
Afr 4513.49 Abyssinian patchwork. (Gandar Dower, K.) London, 1949.
Afr 4559.35.80 The Abyssinian storm. (Comyn-Platt, Thomas.) London, 1935.
Afr 4375.19 The Abyssinian war. (Urquehart, David.) London, 1868.
Afr 4420.5 L'Abyssinie. (Arce, L.) Avignon, 1925.
Afr 4558.76 Abyssinie. (Raffray, A.) Paris, 1876.
Afr 4338.301 L'Abyssinie dans la seconde moitié du XVI siècle. Inaug. Diss. (Saineanu, M.) Leipzig, 1892.
Afr 4557.90.30 L'Abyssinie d'après James Bruce et les voyageurs contemporains. (Drohojowska, Antoinette Joséphine Françoise Anne.) Lille, 1886.
Afr 4558.96 L'Abyssinie en 1896. (Comber, P.) Paris, 1896.
Afr 4375.3 Abyssinie et Angleterre (Theodoros). (Bussidon, C.) Paris, 1888.
Afr 4258.97 L'Abyssinie et les Italiens. (Castonnet des Fosses.) Paris, 1897.
Afr 4375.17 L'Abyssinie lors de l'expedition anglaise, 1867-1868. (Fanton, A.) Paris, 1936.
Afr 4558.83.3 Abyssinien und die übrigen Gebiete des Afrikas. (Hartmann, R.) Leipzig, 1883.
Afr 1753.1.10 Academia das Sciencias de Lisboa. Centenarios de Ceuta e de Afonso de Albuquerque. Lisboa, 1916.
Afr 7015.10 Academia das Sciencias de Lisboa. Conferencias celebradas na Academia Real das Sciencias de Lisboa. Lisboa, 1892.
Afr 5501.3.6 Academie...Tananarivo. Academie Malgache, Tananarivo. Memoires. 1,1926+ 14v.
Afr 5501.3 Academie Malgache. Bulletin. Tananarivo. 1,1902+ 20v.
Afr 7809.62.5 Académie Royale des Sciences d'Outre-Mer. Apport scientifique de la Belgique au développement de l'Afrique centrale. Bruxelles, 1962. 3v.
Afr 7501.5 Académie Royale des Sciences d'Outre Mer. Classe des Sciences Morales et Politiques. Mémoires. 29,1963+ 4v.
Afr 150.1 A acção missionaria no periodo henriquino. (Brasio, A.D.) Lisboa, 1958.
Afr 1840.3.15 L'accession des indigènes algériens à la citoyenneté française. Thèse. (Lazard, Claude.) Paris, 1938.
Afr 7575.98 L'accession du Congo belge à l'indépendance. (Bouvier, Paule.) Bruxelles, 1965.
Afr 1750.21.5 La accion africana de Espana en torno al 98 (1860-1912). (Garcia Figueras, Tomes.) Madrid, 1966. 2v.
Afr 520.14 Acción de España en Africa. (Spain. Servicio Historico Militar.) Madrid, 1935. 3v.
Afr 1573.29F Accion de España en Marruecos. v.1-2. (Hernandez de Herrera, C.) Madrid, 1929-30. 2v.
Afr 1347.3.8 Accion militar...imperio de Marruecos. (Alvarez Cabrera, J.) Madrid, 1898.
Afr 1573.18 La accion militar y politica de España en Africa a traves de los tiempos. (Pita, Federico.) Madrid, 1915.
Afr 2030.467.15 L'Accord F.L.N.-O.A.S. (Carréras, Fernand.) Paris, 1967.
Afr 1325.8F Accords conclus...entre France et l'Angleterre. (France. Ministère des Affaires Etrangères.) Paris, 1904.
Afr 2030.462.150 Les accords d 'Evian et l'avenir de la révolution algérienne. (Moureaux, S.) Paris, 1962.
Afr 2030.462.110 Les accords d'Evian. (Algeria. Treaties, etc.) Paris, 1962.
Afr 2030.462.55 Les accords d'Evian. (Allais, Maurice.) Paris, 1962.
Afr 1333.10 Les accords internationaux du sultan Sidi Mohammed ben Abdallah (1757-1790). (Caille, Jacques.) Tanger, 1960.
Afr 2030.464.65 Accords passés entre la France et l'Algérie de juillet 1962 au 31 décembre 1963. (Algeria. Treaties, etc.) Paris, 1964.
Afr 1570.41 Accords secrets entre la France et l'Italie concernant le Maroc et la Lybie. (Rouard de Card, E.) Paris, 1921.
Afr 1608.09.3 An account...empire of Morocco. (Jackson, J.G.) Philadelphia, 1810.
Afr 1608.09.2 An account...empire of Morocco. 2d ed. (Jackson, J.G.) London, 1811.
Afr 9148.43 An account of a journey into Transorangia and the Potchefstroom-Winburg Trekker Republic in 1843. (Bennie, John.) Cape Town, 1956.
Afr 3978.71.2 An account of manners and customs of modern Egyptians. (Lane, E.W.) London, 1846. 2v.
Afr 3978.71.3 Account of manners and customs of modern Egyptians. (Lane, E.W.) London, 1871. 2v.
Afr 6143.16 An account of native Africans...in Sierra Leone. (Winterbottom, T.) London, 1803. 2v.
Afr 2748.54PF Account of progress of expedition to central Africa, 1850-53. (Petermann, August.) London, 1854.
Htn Afr 1607.13* An account of south-west Barbary. (Ockley, S.) London, 1713.
Afr 8658.04 An account of the Cape of Good Hope. (Percival, R.) London, 1804.
Afr 7808.89.5 Account of the Congo Independent State. (Phillips, Henry.) n.p., 1889.
Afr 7045.2 An account of the discoveries of the Portuguese in the interior of Angola and Mozambique. (Bowdich, T.E.) London, 1824.
Afr 4509.17 An account of the English mission to King Johannis of Abyssinia in 1887. (Portal, G.H.) Winchester, 1888.
Afr 6192.7 Account of the Gold Coast of Africa. (Meredith, H.) London, 1812.
Afr 5842.8 Account of the island of Mauritius. London, 1842.
Afr 3978.37.8 An account of the manners and customs of the modern Egyptians. v.1-2. (Lane, E.W.) London, 1837. 2v.
Afr 6143.16.2A An account of the native African in the neighborhood of Sierra Leone. 2nd ed. (Winterbottom, T.) London, 1969.
Htn Afr 3977.99.3* An account of the present state of Egypt. (Remmey, John.) N.Y., 1799.
Afr 2533.8 An account of the Tunisian question and its most recent developments. (Tunisian Office for National Liberation.) N.Y., 1952.
Afr 1608.20 An account of Timbuctoo and Housa. (Jackson, J.G.) London, 1820.
Afr 8658.01 An account of travels into...South Africa. (Barrow, J.) London, 1801.
Afr 8658.01.2 An account of travels into...South Africa. (Barrow, J.) N.Y., 1802.
Afr 8658.01.4 An account of travels into the interior of Southern Africa, in the years 1797 and 1798. (Barrow, J.) N.Y., 1968.
Afr 2608.11 An account of Tunis. (MacGill, Thomas.) Glasgow, 1811.
Afr Doc 7509.305F The accounts of the government together with a report of the Controller of Accounts. (West Cameroon.) Buea. 1960+
Afr 6196.7 Accra, a plan for the town. (Ghana. Town and Country Planning Division.) Accra, 1958.
Afr 28.86.5F Accra. Research Library on African Affairs. Bibliography Series. Ghana: a current bibliography. Accra. 1,1967+
Afr 6196.15 Accra survey. (Acquah, Ioné.) London, 1958.
Afr 3243.7 L'achat des actions de Suez. (Lesage, C.) Paris, 1906.
Afr 10671.12.130 Achebe, Chinua. Arrow of God. London, 1964.
Afr 11211.5.15 Achebe, Chinua. Arrow of God. London, 1964.
Afr 10671.12.100 Achebe, Chinua. A man of the people. London, 1966.
Afr 10671.12.110 Achebe, Chinua. No longer at ease. N.Y., 1961.
Afr 10671.12.120 Achebe, Chinua. Things fall apart. London, 1966.
Afr 10671.12.121 Achebe, Chinua. Things fall apart. London, 1968.
Afr 11211.5 Achebe, Chinua. Things fall apart. N.Y., 1959.
Afr 7203.10 Achegas para a bibliografia de Moçambique. (Almeida de Eca, F.G.) Lisboa, 1949.
Afr 6192.24 Achievement in the Gold Coast. (Gold Coast (Colony). Public Relations Department.) Accra, 1951.
Afr 8279.00.37F Achilles, Kort. Aanleiding tot den engelsch-transvaal oorlog. 's-Gravenhage, n.d.
Afr 6540.9 The Acholi of Uganda. (Gurling, F.K.) London, 1960.
Afr 5548.33 Ackerman. Histoire des revolutions de Madagascar. Paris, 1833.
Afr 6200.1.10 ACOA Nigeria-Biafra relief memo. (American Committee on Africa.) N.Y. 1,1968+
Afr 7324.21 Os acontecimentos de Lourenço Marques. (Araujo, Antonio José de.) Lisboa, 1889.
Afr 6196.15 Acquah, Ioné. Accra survey. London, 1958.
Afr 609.28.5 Across Africa on foot. (Monson, R.A.) N.Y., 1931.
Afr 6887.5 Across East African glaciers. (Meyer, H.) London, 1891.
Afr 718.37 Across equatorial Africa. (Migeod, F.W.H.) London, 1923.
Afr 5749.43 Across Madagascar. (Chapman, O.M.) London, 1942.
Afr 7809.62.10 Across the Congo. (Liveing, Edward G.D.) London, 1962.
Afr 2749.48 Across the great deserts. (Etherton, P.T.) N.Y., 1948.
Afr 2209.35.10 Across the Mediterranean. (Berenson, Mary.) Prato, 1935.
Afr 2749.06 Across the Sahara. (Vischer, H.) London, 1910.
Afr 9599.07 Across widest Africa. (Landor, A.H.S.) London, 1907. 2v.
Afr Doc 3419.5 An act to declare the Constitution of Tanganyika. (Tanganyika. Constitution.) Dar es Salaam, 1962?
Afr 1550.21 El acta de Algeciras y el porvenir de Espana en Marruecos. (Barclay, T.) Madrid, 1907.
Afr 1550.22 Acta general. (Algeciras. International Conference on Moroccan Affairs, 1906.) Madrid, 1906.
Afr 1335.5 Actas y memorias del primer Congreso Español de Africanistas. Granada, 1894.
Afr 6670.928 L'acte de naissance d'une république africaine autonome. (Luce, Edmond P.) Paris, 1928.
Afr 1325.9F Acte général. (Conférence Internationale d'Algeciras.) La Haye, 1906.
Afr 7565.12 L'acte général de la Conférence de Berlin. (Jooris, J.) Bruxelles, 1885.
Afr 1309.5 Actes du Congrès de l'Institut. (Institut des Hautes Études Marocaines.) Rabat. 1928+ 2v.
Afr 8678.309 Action, reaction and counteraction. (Horrell, Muriel.) Johannesburg, 1963.
Afr 2030.276 Action du gouvernement en Algérie. (Algeria. Cabinet du Gouverneur Général.) Alger, 1957.
Afr 1570.24 L'action française au Maroc. (Jacquin, P.) Paris, 1911.
Afr 5312.15 L'action politique du P.D.G. Conakry. (Parti Démocratique de Guinée.) 1,1961+ 6v.

Afr 5316.10   L'action politique du parti démocratique de guinée. (Touré, Sékou.) Paris, 1959.

Afr 2623.964   Actions de productivité en Tunisie. (Mission de Productivité en Tunisie.) Paris, 1964.

Afr 1555.10   La actitud de España ante la cuestion de Marruecos. (Campoamor, J.M.) Madrid, 1951.

Afr 6164.19   An active history of Ghana. (Brown, G.N.) London, 1961. 2v.

Afr 4375.9PF   Acton, Roger. The Abyssinian expedition and the life and the reign of King Theodore. London, 1868.

Afr 1573.24   La actuacion de España en Marruecos. (España, Juan de.) Madrid, 1926.

Afr 608.95   Actual Africa. (Vincent, F.) N.Y., 1895.

Afr 1801.10   Actualité et documents. 45,1964 (Algeria. Direction Général de l'Information.)

Afr 1.29   Actualités d'Afrique noire. Paris.

Afr 2000.6   Actuelles, III. (Camus, Albert.) Paris, 1958.

Afr 6210.57   Ad hoc Conference on Constitutional Proposals, Lagos, 1966. Memoranda submitted by the delegations to the Ad hoc Conference on Constitutional proposals for Nigeria. Apapa, 1967.

Afr 6210.13F   The ad hoc conference on the Nigerian constitution. (Nigeria Ad Hoc Conference on the Nigerian Constitution.) Enugu, 1966.

Afr 1706.8   Adam, André. Casablanca. Thèse. Paris, 1968. 2v.

Afr 3275.35   Adam, Juliette. L'Angleterre en Egypte. Paris, 1922.

Afr 1583.7   Adam, Paul. Affaires du Maroc, livre blanc allemand. Paris, 1910.

Afr 50.43   Adam, Thomas R. Government and politics in Africa. 3d ed. N.Y., 1965.

Afr 6743.3   Adamana. (Passarge, S.) Berlin, 1895.

Afr 8740.5   Adamantia. (Lindley, A.E.) London, 1873.

Afr 8678.59   Adamastor, (pseud.). White man boss. Boston, 1951.

Afr 6292.1   Adamawa, past and present. (Kirk-Greene, Anthony.) London, 1958.

Afr 3285.20   Adams, Charles C. Islam and modernism in Egypt. London, 1933.

Afr 6153.25   Adams, Cynthia. A study guide for Ghina. Boston, 1967.

Afr 3275.19   Adams, F. The new Egypt. London, 1893.

Afr 6095.12   Adams, J. Remarks on the country...Cape Palmas to the river Congo. London, 1823.

Afr 11119.4.100   Adams, Perseus. The land at my door. Cape Town, 1965.

Afr 1608.16.20   Adams, Robert. Nouveau voyage dans l'interieur de l'Afrique. Paris, 1817.

Afr 6470.103   Adamson, George. A lifetime with lions. Garden City, 1968.

Afr 6460.90   Adamson, Joy. The peoples of Kenya. London, 1967.

Afr 5394.2   Adandé, A. Les récades des rois du Dahomey. Dakar, 1962.

Afr 5180.2   Adanson, M. A voyage to Senegal. London, 1759.

Afr 7122.64   Addicott, Len. Cry Angola. London, 1962.

Afr Doc 303.7   Addis Ababa. Imperial Ethiopian Institute of Public Administration. Administrative directory of the Ethiopian government. Addis Ababa. 5,1965+

Afr 210.63.60   Addis Ababa summit. (Ethiopia. Ministry of Information.) Addis Ababa, 1963.

Afr 4640.2   Addis-Abeba. (Berlan, E.) Grenoble, 1963.

Afr 3986.959   Addison, Herbert. Sun and shadow at Aswan. London, 1959.

Htn   Afr 1738.13*   Addison, L. The Moores baffled. London, 1681.

Htn   Afr 1606.71*   Addison, L. West Barbary. Oxford, 1671.

Afr 8957.6   Additional report. (Natal Regional Survey.) Pietermaritzburg. 1,1951+ 5v.

Afr 7350.5.8   Address...at the annual meeting of the Pennsylvania Colonization Society, Oct. 25, 1838. (Ingersoll, J.R.) Philadelphia, 1838.

Afr 7350.5.10   Address before Pennsylvania Colonization Society, Oct. 25. (Allen, W.H.) Philadelphia, 1863.

Afr 7461.35   An address before the Liberia Union Agricultural Enterprise Co. (Morris, E.D.) Philadelphia, 1863.

Afr Doc 1724.5F   Address by His Excellency the Governor on the occasion of the opening of the Legislative Council. (Sierra Leone. Governor.)

Afr Doc 2324.5   Address by the Governor the the Nigerian council. (Nigeria. Governor General.) 6,1919+

Afr Doc 2324.8   Address by the Governor to the Legislative Council. (Nigeria. Governor General.) 1924+

Afr 3310.10.22   Address by the President of the Republic of Egypt. (Egypt. President.) Cairo, 1957.

Afr 7350.6.10   An address delivered...annual meeting of Maryland State Colonization Society...Annapolis, Jan. 23, 1835. (Harper, C.C.) Baltimore, 1835.

Afr 8846.15   An address delivered at the University of Stellenbosch on 12th, 13th, 14th Oct. 1932. (Kenyon, J.T.) n.p., 1932.

Afr 6210.38   Address delivered at the 7th meeting of Nigeria council held at Lagos. (Nigeria. Governor-General, 1920.) Lagos, 1920.

Afr 7350.5.20   An address delivered before the Middletown Colonization Society at their annual meeting, July 4, 1834. (Whedon, D.D.) Middletown, 1834.

Afr 3986.960.10   Address on the five year plan. (Bughdadi, A.) Cairo, 1960.

Afr 8846.15.5   An address on the general council administration system of the Transkeian territories, rev. 1939. (Kenyon, J.T.) n.p., 1939.

Htn   Afr 7350.3.23*   Address to the American Society for Colonizing the Free People of Colour of the U.S. (Burgess, E.) Washington, 1818.

Afr 7368.52   Addresses...of the House of Representatives. Harrisburg, Pa. (Pettit, W.V.) Philadelphia, 1852.

Afr 3725.14   Ade, H.C. Pioniere im Osten. Stuttgart, 1923.

Afr 6286.2   Adedeji, Adebayo. An introduction to Western Nigeria. Ibadan?, 1966?

Afr 6210.60   Adedeji, Adebayo. Nigerian administration and its political setting. London, 1968.

Afr 6277.122   Adedeji, Adebayo. Nigerian federal finance: its development, problems and prospects. London, 1969.

Afr 10671.12.800   Adejumo, Matthew S. Notes and essays on Chinua Achebe's Things fall apart. Ibadan, 1966.

Afr 1750.38   Las adelantadas de España. (Arques, Enrique.) Madrid, 1966.

Afr 1609.03.6   Adelmann, S. 13 monate in Marokko. Sigmaring, 1903.

Afr 10665.2   Ademola, F. Reflections, Nigerian prose and verse. Lagos, 1962.

Afr 6218.16   Ademoyega, Wale. The federation of Nigeria from earliest times to independence. London, 1962.

Afr 555.15   Adger, J.B. Christian missions and African colonization. Columbia, 1857.

Afr 7575.40   Adieu Congo. (Ribeaud, P.) Paris, 1961.

Afr 2030.160   Adieu Djebels. (Servier, Jean.) Paris, 1958.

Afr 1494.45   Adieu Maroc. (Dehedin, Charles.) Paris, 1959.

Afr 1571.17.40   Adieux, souvenirs sur Lyautey. (Ormesson, W.) Paris, 1937.

Afr 109.61.30   Adiko, A. Histoire des peuples noirs. Abidjan, 1961.

Afr 109.61.31   Adiko, A. Histoire des peuples noirs. Abidjan, 1963.

Afr 6196.3   Adjaye, Annor. Nzima land. London, 193-?

Afr 5056.164   Adloff, Richard. West Africa. N.Y., 1964.

Afr 8710.20   Die administrasie van Kaapland, 1910-1960. (Cape of Good Hope.) Kaapstad, 1960.

Afr 6200.1.12   Administration. Ibadan. 2,1968+

Afr 3813.15   Administration agreement (Roseires irrigation project) between the Republic of the Sudan and Kreditanstalt für Wiederaufbau and International Development Association and International Bank for Reconstruction and Development dated as of June 14, 1961. (Sudan. Treaties, etc. 1961.) n.p., 1961.

Afr 1840.9   Administration de la justice musulmane en Algerie. Thèse. (Gentil, M.) Paris, 1895.

Afr 7540.25   L'administration du Congo belge. Thèse. (Menache, Albert.) Nancy, 1935.

Afr 5130.20   Administration du général Faidherbe au Sénégal. (Gaffarel, P.) Dijon, 188-.

Afr 1.52   Administration et diplomatie d'Afrique Noire et de Madagascar. Paris. 1962+

Afr 5813.12.5   L'administration française de l'île Maurice et ses archives, 1721-1810. (Toussaint, Auguste.) Fort Luis, 1965.

Afr 6400.1   Administration in Kenya. Lower Kabete. 1,1965+

Afr 9635.10F   The administration of justice and the urban African. (Epstein, A.L.) London, 1953.

Afr 6410.5   The administration of Kenya Colony and Protectorate. Rev. ed. (Carson, J.B.) Nairobi, 1951.

Afr 6210.68   The administration of Nigeria, 1900-1960: men, methods, and myths. (Nicolson, I.F.) Oxford, 1969.

Afr Doc 3249.5   Administration report. (Kenya. Survey of Kenya.)

Afr 5053.20   L'administration territoriale en Afrique noire de langue française. (Gandolfi, Alain.) Aix-en-Provence, 1959.

Afr 6460.58F   An administrative and political history. (Sandford, G.R.) London, 1919.

Afr Doc 303.7   Administrative directory of the Ethiopian government. (Addis Ababa. Imperial Ethiopian Institute of Public Administration.) Addis Ababa. 5,1965+

Afr Doc 303.5F   Administrative sub-divisions of Ethiopia, as of the end of Sené 1956 e.c. or July 7th, 1964. (Ethiopia. Ministry of Interior.) Addis Ababa, 1964.

Afr 718.25.4   Adolf, Friedrich. From the Congo to the Niger and the Nile. Philadelphia, 1914. 2v.

Afr 718.25.5   Adolf, Friedrich. From the Congo to the Niger and the Nile. V.1-2. London, 1913. 2v.

Afr 718.25.3   Adolf, Friedrich. In the heart of Africa. London, 1910.

Afr 718.25   Adolf, Friedrich. Ins innerste Afrika. Leipzig, 1909.

Afr 718.25.10   Adolf, Friedrich. Vom Kongo zum Niger und Nil. 3e Aufl. Leipzig, 1921. 2v.

Afr 6925.10   Adolf Luederitz, ein deutscher Kanipf um Südafrika 1883-1886. (Schuessler, W.) Bremen, 1936.

Afr 8931.53.5   Adolphe Mabile. (Dieterlen, H.) Paris, 1930.

Afr 7580.9   The Adoula-Tshombe talks. (Congo.) Leopoldville, 1962.

Afr 1259.36   Adrian, W. Friedliches Afrika. Bern, 1936.

Afr 8380.10   Adstin, Dennis. Britain and South Africa. London, 1966.

Afr 45.65   Adu, A.L. The civil service in new African states. London, 1965.

Afr 6010.22   Adu, Amishadai Lawson. The civil service in Commonwealth Africa. London, 1969.

Afr 4394.3.11   Adua, brevi cenni sulla guerra italo-etiopica mahdista degli anni 1895-96. (Pini, Cesare G.) Torino, 1926.

Afr 4394.3.14   Adua, i precedenti, la battaglia. (Bellavita, E.) Genova, 1931.

Afr 4394.5   Adua. (Bronzuoli, A.) Roma, 1935.

Afr 6283.11   Advance in Africa. (Jackson, I.C.) London, 1956.

Afr 2209.36.10   Adventure in Algeria. (Stuart, B.) London, 1936.

Afr 678.60   Adventures...on west coast of Africa. (Thomas, C.W.) N.Y., 1860.

Afr 1407.1.5   Adventures. (Pellow, J.) London, 1890.

Afr 1609.25   Adventures among the Riffi. (Sheean, V.) London, 1926.

Afr 550.2.12   Adventures and missonary labors in several countries in the interior of Africa. 2d ed. (Bowen, T.J.) London, 1968.

Afr 8659.13.12   Adventures beyond the Zambesi. (Maturin, E.) London, 1913.

Afr 4558.44.3   Adventures in Africa. (Harris, W.C.) Philadelphia, n.d.

Afr 7809.15   Adventures in Africa under the British, Belgian and Portuguese flags. (Thornhill, J.B.) N.Y., 1915.

Afr 8028.151   Adventures in Africana. (Varley, D.H.) Cape Town, 1949.

Afr 9488.93.2   Adventures in Mashonaland. (Blennerhassett.) London, 1893.

Afr 1608.72.8   Adventures in Morocco. (Rohlfs, G.) London, 1874.

Afr 9838.91   Adventures in Nyassaland. (Fotheringham, L.M.) London, 1891.

Afr 9195.10   Adventures in Swaziland. (Oneil, Owen Rowe.) N.Y., 1921.

Afr 609.26.10   Adventures in the African jungle. (Akeley, Carl E.) N.Y., 1930.

Afr 725.15.5   Adventures in the African jungle hunting Pigmies. (Geil, William Edgar.) Garden City, 1917.

Afr 8658.66.5   Adventures in the far interior of South Africa. (Leyland, J.) London, 1866.

Afr 5406.50   Adventures in the great forest of Equatorial Africa. (Duchaillu, Paul Belloni.) N.Y., 1890.

Afr 4050.3   Adventures in the Libyan desert. (Saint John, B.) N.Y., 1849.

Afr 8289.44   Adventures of a Boer family. (Pohl, V.) London, 1944.

Afr 6879.12   The adventures of an elephant hunter. (Sutherland, J.) London, 1912.

Afr 2208.56   The adventures of Gerard, the Lion Killer. (Gerard, Cecile J.B.) N.Y., 1856.

Afr 8686.18   Adventuring with God. (Christofersen, Arthur Fridtjof.) Durban, 1967.

Afr 626.80   Ady, Peter. System of national accounts in Africa. Paris, 1960.

Afr 5406.253F   AEF 53. (Encyclopédie Mensuelle d'Outre-Mer.) Paris, 1953.

Afr 3990.4.2   Ägypten, Reisenhandbuch. 2.Aufl. (Busch, M.) Triest, 1870.

Afr 3038.7   Ägypten, seine staats- und völkerrechtliche Stellung. (Winterei, Hermann.) Berlin, 1915.

Afr 3978.63.15   Aegypten. (Kremer, Alfred, Freiherr von.) Leipzig, 1863.

Afr 3979.55F   Ägypten im Bild. (Kusch, E.) Nürnberg, 1955.

Afr 3199.15.5   Ägypten in Vergangenheit und Gegenwart. (Steindorff, Georg.) Berlin, 1915.

Afr 3275.7   Ägypten unter englischer Okkupation. (Resener, Hans.) Berlin, 1896.

Afr 3150.7   Ägypten zur Zeit der Mamluken. (Niemeyer, W.) Berlin, 1936.

Afr 4434.5   Det är ju människor det gäller. (Wilsson, Wils Gunnar.) Stockholm, 1966.

Afr 4259.67   Äthiopien, christliches Reich zwisches Gestern und Morgen. (Hammerschmidt, Ernst.) Wiesbaden, 1968.

Afr 4559.57.5   Äthiopien, Land im Aufbruch. (Jenny, Hans.) Stuttgart, 1957.

Afr 5057.32   Afana, Osende. L'économie de l'Ouest-africain. Paris, 1966.

Afr 2030.225   L'affaire Audin. (Vidal-Naquet, Pierre.) Paris, 1958.

Afr 1495.6.20   L'affaire Ben Barka. (Sarne, Daniel.) Paris, 1966.

Afr 5635.1   L'affaire de Madagascar. 3e ed. (Hanotaux, G.) Paris, 1896.

Afr 2030.245   L'affaire des officiers algériens. (Rahmani, Abd el-Kader.) Paris, 1959.

Afr 4431.10   L'Affaire d'Ethiopie aux origines de la guerre mondiale. (Gallo, Max.) Paris, 1967.

Afr 4513.37.30   L'affaire d'Ethiopie et les diplomates, 1934-1937. (Bastin, J.) Bruxelles, 1937.

Afr 5405.179   L'affaire du Congo 1905. (Saintoyant, J.F.) Paris, 1960.

Afr 1550.4   L'affaire marocaine. (Berard, V.) Paris, 1906.

Afr 1570.61   L'affaire marocaine. (Berard, Victor.) Paris, 1906.

Afr 3310.85A   L'affaire Nasser. (Abul-Fath, A.) Paris, 1962.

Afr 2533.10   Les affaires de la Tunisie et du Maroc devant les Nations Unies. (Day, Georges.) Paris, 1953.

Afr 3269.1F   Affaires d'Egypte 1884. (France. Ministère des Affaires Etrangères.) Paris, 1884.

Afr 2508.6   Affaires d'orient, la question tunisienne. (Desfosses, Edmond.) Paris, 1881.

Afr 3740.1F   Affaires du Haut-Nil 1897-98. (France. Ministère des Affaires Etrangères.) Paris, 1898.

Afr 1583.7   Affaires du Maroc, livre blanc allemand. (Adam, Paul.) Paris, 1910.

Afr 1570.34   Affaires marocaines...1902-1911. (Cochin, D.) Paris, 1912.

Afr 9405.6   Affairs of Bechuanaland. (Wesleyan Methodist Missionary Society.) London, 1887.

Afr 9192.5F   Affairs of Swaziland. (Great Britain. Colonial Office.) London, 1899.

Afr 1955.5.5   L'Affrica francese. (Christian, P.) Firenze, 1849. 2v.

Afr 4732.17   L'Affrica orientale italiana. (Sillani, Tomaso.) Roma, 1933.

Afr 4732.17.3   L'Affrica orientale italiana. (Sillani, Tomaso.) Roma, 1936.

Afr 8095.5   De afkomst der Boeren. (Colenbrander, Herman Theodoor.) n.p., 1902.

Afr 8095.5.5   De afkomst der Boeren. 2. uitg. (Colenbrander, Herman Theodoor.) Kaapstad, 1964.

Afr 1470.3   Aflalo, M. The truth about Morocco. London, 1904.

Afr 6700.2F   Afri-Cam. Yaoundé. 6,1969+

Afr 7935.1   Afrianoff, A. Histoire des Bagesera. Bruxelles, 1952.

Afr 609.65.50   Africa, a geographic study. (Mountjoy, Alan.) London, 1965.

Afr 609.61.60   Africa, a handbook. (Legum, Colin.) London, 1961.

Afr 109.61.57   Africa, a handbook. 2d ed. (Legum, Colin.) London, 1965.

Afr 626.142   Africa, a market profile. (Blair, Thomas Lucien Vincent.) N.Y., 1965.

Afr 212.7   Africa, a political travelogue. (Molnar, T.S.) N.Y., 1965.

Afr 1.16   Africa; a reference volume on the African continent. Paris. 1,1968+

Afr 609.34.11   Africa; a social, economic, and political geography of its major regions. 10th ed. (Fitzgerald, Walter.) n.p., 1968.

Afr 609.69   Africa; a study geography for advanced students. (Pritchard, John Malcom.) London, 1969.

Afr 626.22.2   Africa, a study in tropical development. 2d ed. (Stamp, L.D.) N.Y., 1964.

Afr 6192.57   Africa, a world in progress. 1st ed. (Cone, Virginia.) N.Y., 1960.

Htn   Afr 606.70F*   Africa, accurate description...regions, Aegypt, Barbary. (Ogilby, John.) London, 1670.

Afr 505.20   Africa, Africa. (Kartun, D.) N.Y., 1954.

Afr 635.4.5   Africa, antropologia della stirpe camitica. (Sergi, Giuseppe.) Torino, 1897.

Afr 1609.03.9   Africa, apuntes de Marruecos. (Irabien Larranaga, E. de.) San Sebastian, 1903.

Afr 109.68   Africa, background for today. (MacGregor-Hastie, Roy.) London, 1968.

Afr 500.83   Africa, biografia del colonialismo. (Benitez Cabrera, José.) Habana, 1964.

Afr 505.46   Africa, Britain's third empire. (Padmore, George.) London, 1949.

Afr 109.61.50   Africa, colonos e cumplices. (Portella, Eduardo.) Rio de Janeiro, 1961.

Afr 609.61.45   Africa, continent of change. (Gauld, Peter.) Belmont, 1961.

Afr 115.5   Africa, facts and forecasts. (Maisel, A.Q.) N.Y., 1943. 2v.

Afr 212.5   Africa, from independence to tomorrow. 1st ed. (Hapgood, D.) N.Y., 1965.

Afr 608.74   Africa, geographical exploration. (Forbes, A.G.) London, 1874.

Afr 109.66F   Africa, history of a continent. (Davidson, Basil.) London, 1966.

Afr 608.88   Africa, its past and future. (Hubbard, G.G.) n.p., 1888.

Afr 28.84   Africa, its problems and prospects. (United States. Department of the Army.) Washington, 1962.

Afr 609.62.35   Africa, journey out of darkness. (Byford-Jones, N.) London, 1968.

Afr 609.50   Africa, land of many lands. 3d ed. (Vansinderen, A.) Syracuse, N.Y., 1950.

Afr 609.54.5   Africa, land of my fathers. (Thompson, E.B.) Garden City, 1954.

Afr 7309.59   Africa, mae e madrasta. (Barreiros, Pinho.) Coimbra, 1959.

Afr 109.69   Africa, our history. (Henries, A. Doris.) London, 1969.

Afr 210.65.30   Africa, past and present. (Cook, Arthur Norton.) Ottowa, 1965.

Afr 608.81.7   Africa, past and present. (Moister, W.) N.Y., 1881.

Afr 609.58.15   Africa, present and potential. (Goss, Hilton P.) Santa Barbara, 1958.

Afr 1.33F   Africa, rivista bimestrale di studi e documentazione. Roma. 14,1959+ 9v.

Afr 626.114   Africa, sales frontier for U.S. business. (United States. Bureau of International Commerce.) Washington, 1963.

Afr 609.69.10   Africa; selected readings. (Burke, Fred George.) N.Y., 1969.

Afr 630.9   Africa, slave or free. (Harris, John H.) London, 1919.

Afr 618.24   Africa, social problems of change and conflict. (Vandenborghe, P.L.) San Francisco, 1965.

Afr 500.9   Africa, su reparto y colonización. (Alzola, Pablo de.) Bilbao, 1901.

Afr 608.75   Africa, the history of exploration. (Jones, C.H.) N.Y., 1875.

Afr 212.38   Africa, the politics of unity. (Wallerstein, Immanuel Maurice.) N.Y., 1967.

Afr 50.53   Africa, the portrait of power. (Taylor, Don.) London, 1967.

Afr 109.67.10   Africa; the rebirth of self-rule. (Hatch, John C.) London, 1967.

Afr 210.60.30   Africa, the roots of revolt. (Woddis, Jack.) London, 1960.

Afr 210.63.45   Africa, the way ahead. (Woddis, J.) London, 1963.

Afr 210.64   Africa, the way ahead. (Woddis, J.) N.Y., 1964.

Afr 210.3   Pamphlet vol. Africa, twentieth century. 10 pam.

Afr 5920.2   Africa, viajes y trabajos de la asociación. (Iradier, Manuel.) Bilbao, 1901. 2v.

Afr 609.54.10   Africa, world of new men. (Considine, J.J.) N.Y., 1954.

Afr 109.59.5   Africa, world's last frontier. (Scott, John.) N.Y., 1959.

Afr 29.6   Pamphlet vol. Africa. 9 pam.

Afr 29.16   Pamphlet vol. Africa. 5 pam.

Afr 29.5   Pamphlet vol. Africa. 7 pam.

Afr 29.12   Pamphlet vol. Africa. 2 pam.

Afr 29.14   Pamphlet vol. Africa.

Afr 29   Pamphlet box. Africa.

Afr 29.4   Pamphlet vol. Africa. 32 pam.

Afr 29.9   Pamphlet vol. Africa. 2 pam.

Afr 29.11   Pamphlet vol. Africa. 3 pam.

Afr 29.13   Pamphlet box. Africa.

Afr 109.63   Pamphlet vol. Africa. 3 pam.

Afr 212.24   Africa. (African Conference on Progress through Cooperation.) N.Y., 1966.

Afr 609.41.15   Africa. (Bohner, Theodor.) Leipzig, 1941.

Afr 630.63.5   Africa. (Borer, M.C.) London, 1963.

Afr 607.96   Africa. (Edrisi, A.A.H.I. el.) Gottingae, 1796.

Afr 609.34.3   Africa. (Fitzgerald, Walter.) N.Y., 1942.

Afr 4700.33.15   Africa. (Gravelli, A.) Roma, 1933.

Afr 609.50.5A   Africa. (Haynes, G.E.) N.Y., 1950.

Afr 5920.1.3   Africa. (Iradier, Manuel.) Madrid, 1878.

Afr 5920.1.5   Africa. (Iradier, Manuel.) Vitoria, 1887. 2v.

Afr 608.95.3   Africa. (Keane, A.H.) London, 1895. 2v.

Afr 108.93.3   Africa. (Keltie, J.S.) Philadelphia, 1907.

Afr 609.61.50   Africa. (Ligne, Eugene.) Bruxelles, 1961.

Afr 609.55.30   L'Africa. (Migliorini, Elio.) Torino, 1955.

Afr 630.59   Africa. (Murdock, George.) N.Y., 1959.

Afr 210.63.65   Africa. (Passin, H.) Ibadan, 1963.

Afr 609.68   Africa. (Pollock, Norman Charles.) London, 1968.

Afr 212.28   Africa. (Spiro, Herbert John.) N.Y., 1966.

Afr 626.22   Africa. (Stamp, L.D.) N.Y., 1953.

Afr 609.61.30   Africa. (Stillery, A.) London, 1961.

Afr 210.61.50   Africa. (Wallerstein, I.) N.Y., 1961.

Afr 210.61.25   Africa. (Woddis, J.) London, 1961.

Afr 29.23   Pamphlet vol. Africa. (Russian). 4 pam.

Afr 29.24   Pamphlet vol. Africa. (Russian). 5 pam.

Afr 29.26   Pamphlet vol. Africa. (Russian). 5 pam.

Afr 29.22   Pamphlet vol. Africa. (Russian). 4 pam.

Afr 6200.1F   Africa. Lagos. 11,1961+

Afr 1.9   Africa. London. 1,1928+ 37v.

Afr 1.14F   Africa. Madrid. 5,1946+ 26v.

Afr 40.64   Africa. A Foreign Affairs reader. 1st ed. (Foreign Affairs, N.Y.) N.Y., 1964.

Afr 29.18   Pamphlet vol. Africa. Economic conditions. (Russian). 6 pam.

Afr 29.10   Pamphlet vol. Africa. Reprints.

Afr 29.7   Pamphlet vol. Africa. Reprints.

Afr 29.8   Pamphlet vol. Africa. Reprints.

Afr 630.9.5   Africa: slave or free? (Harris, John H.) N.Y., 1969.

Afr 608.95.4   Africa. v.2. 2nd ed. (Keane, A.H.) London, 1904.

Afr 609.52.10   Africa. 1st ed. (Hanzelka, Jiri.) Prague, 1952. 3v.

Afr 609.66   Africa. 1st ed. (Nielsen, Waldemar A.) N.Y., 1966.

Afr 609.34.2   Africa. 2d ed. (Fitzgerald, Walter.) London, 1936.

Afr 609.61.15   Africa. 2d ed. (Money, David Charles.) London, 1961.

Afr 608.84   Africa. 3d ed. (Johnston, K.) London, 1884.

Afr 609.29.25.5   Africa. 4th ed. (Suggate, L.S.) London, 1951.

Afr 29.17   Pamphlet vol. Africa. 6 pam.

Afr 109.64.20   Africa - a subjective view. (Nicol, D.) London, 1964.

Afr 29.20   Pamphlet vol. Africa (Russian). 4 pam.

Afr 29.21   Pamphlet vol. Africa (Russian). 4 pam.

Afr 29.19   Pamphlet vol. Africa (Russian). 6 pam.

Afr 109.64.5   Africa and Africans. 1st ed. (Bohannan, P.) Garden City, 1964.

Afr 115.110   Africa and Indonesia. (Jones, Arthur M.) Leiden, 1964.

Afr 626.204   Africa and international co-operation: ILO in Africa. (Tevoedjre, Albert.) n.p., n.d.

Afr 608.91.4   Africa and its exploration. Leipzig, 1891. 2v.

Afr 45.68   Africa and law. (Hutchison, Thomas W.) Madison, 1968.

Afr 210.30   Africa and some world problems. (Smuts, J.C.) Oxford, 1930.

Afr 7458.54   Africa and the American flag. (Foote, A.H.) N.Y., 1854.

Afr 590.24.5   Africa and the American flag. (Foote, Andrew H.) N.Y., 1862.

Afr 626.174   Africa and the Common Market. (Okigbo, Pius Nwabufo.) London, 1967.

Afr 210.63.25A   Africa and the communist world. (Brzezinski, Z.K.) Stanford, Calif., 1963.

Afr 626.98.5   Africa and the European Common Market. (Rivkin, Arnold.) Denver, 1964.

Afr 626.98.6   Africa and the European Common Market. 2nd ed. (Rivkin, Arnold.) Denver, 1966.

Afr 609.64.15   Africa and the islands. (Church, R.J.H.) N.Y., 1964.

Afr 609.64.17   Africa and the islands. 2nd ed. (Church, R.J.H.) London, 1967.

Afr 500.19   Africa and the peace of Europe. Photoreproduction. (Morel, Edmund D.) London, 1917.

Afr 210.61.60   Africa and the U.S. (United States. National Commission for UNESCO.) Washington, 1961.

Afr 210.10   Africa and the war. (Brawley, B.G.) N.Y., 1918.

Afr 626.98   Africa and the West. (Rivkin, Arnold.) N.Y., 1962.

Afr 210.56.10   Africa and the Western world. (American Academy of Political and Social Sciences.) Philadelphia, 1956.

Afr 1.75   Africa and the world. London. 1,1964+ 2v.

Afr 212.76   Africa and unity: the evolution of Pan-Africanism. (Thompson, Vincent Bakpetu.) N.Y., 1970.

Afr Doc 3307.348.10 African population of Uganda Protectorate; geographical and tribal studies. (East Africa High Commission. East African Statistical Department.) Nairobi, 1950.
Afr 8230.10.13 African portraits. (Cloete, Stuart.) London, 1946.
Afr 8230.10.13.2 African portraits: a biography of Paul Kruger, Cecil Rhodes and Lobengula. (Cloete, Stuart.) Cape Town, 1969.
Afr 212.14 African powder keg. (Matthews, Ronald.) London, 1966.
Afr 45.68.5 The African predicament. (Andreski, Stanislav.) London, 1968.
Afr 210.63.50 The African presence in world affairs. (Rivkin, A.) N.Y., 1963.
Afr 6143.44 African primitive life as I saw it in Sierra Leone. (Hargrave, C.G.) Wilmington, N.C., 1944.
Afr 626.45.5 African problems; analysis of eminent Soviet scientist. (Potekhin, I.I.) Moscow, 1968.
Afr 55.25 African profiles. (Segal, Ronald.) Baltimore, 1962.
Afr 500.35 African questions at the Paris Peace Conference. (Beer, George Louis.) N.Y., 1923.
Afr 500.35.2 African questions at the Paris Peace Conference. 1st ed. (Beer, George Louis.) London, 1968.
Afr 6470.135 African rainbow. (Binks, H.K.) London, 1959.
Afr 10665.5 African reader's library. Lagos. 1,1962+
Afr 210.69 African renaissance. (Barnes, Leonard.) London, 1969.
Afr 7350.1 African repository and colonial journal. Washington. 1-68,1825-1892 28v.
Afr 7459.30.10A The African republic of Liberia and the Belgian Congo. (Harvard African Expedition, 1926-1927.) N.Y., 1969. 2v.
Afr 115.102 African responses. (Okoye, M.) Ilfracombe, 1964.
Afr 1.72 African review. Accra. 1,1965+
Afr 109.61 The African revolution. (Cameron, James.) London, 1961.
Afr 109.61.1 The African revolution. (Cameron, James.) N.Y., 1961.
Afr 212.64 The African revolution. (Howe, Russell Warren.) Croydon, Eng., 1969.
Afr 609.33.5 African Safaris, N.Y. A new motor route through Africa. N.Y., 1933.
Afr 6549.251 African saint. (Luck, Anne.) London, 1963.
Afr 1.73 African scholar. Washington. 1,1968+
Afr 6879.67 An African season. (Levitt, Leonard.) N.Y., 1967.
Afr 21.5 African series. (United States. Department of State. Office of Public Services.) Washington.
Afr 609.61.20 African sketchbook. 1. ed. (Franck, F.) N.Y., 1961.
Afr 8658.34 African sketches. (Pringle, Thomas.) London, 1834.
Afr 1.82 African social research. Lusaka. 1,1966+ 2v.
Afr 5055.59.10 African socialism. (Senghor, Leopold.) N.Y., 1959.
Afr 8678.450 African societies in Southern Africa; historical studies. London, 1969.
Afr 10.1 African Society. Journal. London. 1901+ 65v.
Afr 1.86 African statesman. Lagos. 1,1965+
Afr 1.60 African student. Jerusalem.
Afr 630.3 African studies. Johannesburg. 5,1946+ 13v.
Afr 626.129.5 African studies and economic analysis. (Massell, Benton F.) Santa Monica, 1964.
Afr 1.84F African Studies Association. Papers of annual meeting. Philadelphia. 8,1965+ 9v.
Afr 1.94.5 African Studies Association. Committee of Fine Arts and the Humanities. Occasional papers. Bloomington, Ind. 1,1966+
Afr 1.32.5 African studies bulletin. Index, v.1-10 (1958-1967). Boston, 1968.
Afr 1.32 African studies bulletin. N.Y. 1,1958+ 3v.
Afr 626.116 African studies in income and wealth. (International Association for Research in Income and Wealth.) Chicago, 1963.
Afr 1.94 African studies newsletter. N.Y. 1,1968+
Afr 210.38 An African survey. (Hailey, W.M.H.) London, 1938.
Afr 210.38.5A An African survey. (Hailey, W.M.H.) London, 1957.
Afr 210.38.2 An African survey. 2d ed. (Hailey, W.M.H.) London, 1945.
Afr 679.58 African switchback. (Mosley, Nicholas.) London, 1958.
Afr 8919.49 African Switzerland, Basutoland of today. (Rosenthal, Eric.) London, 1949.
Afr 8919.49.5 African Switzerland. (Rosenthal, Eric.) Cape Town, 1948.
Afr 545.28 African systems of thought. (International African Seminar, 3d, Salisbury, Southern Rhodesia, 1960.) London, 1965.
Afr 545.28.2 African systems of thought. (International African Seminar, 3rd, Salisbury, Southern Rhodesia, 1960.) London, 1966.
Afr 630.55 African tapestry. (Trawell, M.) London, 1957.
Afr 6176.42 African tightrope. (Alexander, Henry Templer.) London, 1965.
Afr 6176.42.5 African tightrope. (Alexander, Henry Templer.) N.Y., 1966.
Afr 630.34 The African to-day. (Westermann, D.) London, 1934.
Afr 1.92 African Training and Research Centre in Administration for Development. Nouvelles du CAFRAD. Tanger. 1,1967+
Afr 1.13 African transcripts. Philadelphia. 1,1945+ 2v.
Afr 10309.60 An African treasury. (Hughes, Langston.) N.Y., 1960.
Afr 8235.20 African tribes and European agencies. (Holmberg, Ake.) Göteborg, 1966.
Afr 6390.35 African turmoil. (McDougall, Jan.) London, 1954.
Afr 1.85 African urban notes. Milwaukee. 1,1966+
Afr 1.85.5 African urban notes. Bibliographical supplement. 1,1966+
Afr 650.4 African urbanization. (Edinburgh. University.) London, 1965.
Afr 6390.98 African vignettes. (Morgan, Gordon Daniel.) Jefferson City, 1967.
Afr 10115.2.2 African voices. (Rutherfoord, Peggy.) N.Y., 1960.
Afr 6390.23 African ways and wisdom. (Young, T.C.) London, 1937.
Afr 55.36.3 The African who's who. Johannesburg. 3,1966
Afr 6275.110 The African wife. (Ariwoola, Olagoke.) London, 1965.
Afr 9493.67 The African witch: with particular reference to...Shona of Rhodesia. (Gelfand, Michael.) Edinburgh, 1967.
Afr 6280.9.30 African women. (Leith-Ross, Sylvia.) N.Y., 1965.
Afr 28.99 The African world. (Lystad, Robert A.) London, 1965.
Afr 1.15F African world. London. 1948+ 22v.
NEDL Afr 1.8F African world and Cape Cairo express. London.
Afr 1.15.3F African world annual. London. 1905+ 4v.
Afr 630.54 African worlds. (Forde, C.D.) London, 1954.
Afr 630.54.2 African worlds. (Forde, C.D.) London, 1963.
Afr 10015.10 African writing today. (Mphahlele, Ezekiel.) Harmondsworth, 1967.
Afr 9689.11.5 An African year. (Gouldsbury, C.) London, 1912.
Afr 55.36 African yearly register. 1st ed. Johannesburg, 1932.
Afr 28.68 Africana. (Italiaander, Rolf.) Holland, Michigan, 1961.
Afr 28.88 Africana. (Tenri Central Library, Tanba City, Japan.) Tenri, 1960. 2v.
Afr 6300.2F Africana. Nairobi.

Afr 1.70 Africana bulletin. Warszawa. 1,1964+
Afr 8001.17 Africana Museum, Johannesburg. Annual report. Johannesburg.
Afr 1.47 Africana newsletter. Stanford, Calif.
Afr 8001.15 Africana notes and news. Johannesburg. 1,1943+ 9v.
Afr 8001.16 Africana notes and news. Index v.1-10. (1943-53). Johannesburg, n.d.
Afr 9598.82 Africana or the heart of heathen Africa. (Macdonald, D.) London, 1882. 2v.
Afr 6203.12F Africana pamphlets; microfilm record. (Ibadan, Nigeria. University. Library.) n.p., n.d.
Afr 6620.70 Africander. (Reitz, Deneys.) N.Y., 1933.
Afr 8135.10 The Africander land. (Colquhoun, Archibald.) London, 1906.
Afr 8279.00.54 The Africanders, a century of Dutch-English feud in South Africa. (Hooker, Leroy.) Chicago, 1900.
Afr 8278.96 Africaners en Nederlanders. (Spruyt, C.B.) Amsterdam, 1896.
Afr 609.60.65 Africanism. (Chatterji, Suniti.) Calcutta, 1960.
Afr 1.83.10F The Africanist. Maseru. 1966+
Afr 1.83 Africanist news and views. Cairo. 1,1966+
Afr 609.67.50 Africanité, traditionnelle et moderne. (Maquet, Jacques Jérôme.) Paris, 1967.
Afr 608.61 The Africans at home. (MacBrair, R.M.) London, 1861.
Afr 608.61.2 The Africans at home. (MacBrair, R.M.) London, 1864.
Afr 4513.38.5 The African's last stronghold in Nabath's vineyard. (Wienholt, A.) London, 1938.
Afr 9502.13.10 An African's religion, the spirit of Nyajena. (Gelfand, M.) Cape Town, 1966.
Afr 5019.58.5 Africanus. L'Afrique noire devant l'indépendance. Paris, 1958.
Afr 6615.5 Africanus. The Prussian lash in Africa. London, 1918.
Afr 8210.6 Africanus. The Transvaal Boers. London, 1899.
Afr 4430.35.19 Africanus. (Pseud.). Etiopia, 1935. 4 ed. Roma, 1935.
Afr 500.67 Africa's challenge to America. (Bowles, Chester.) Berkeley, 1956.
Afr 630.58.5 Africa's destiny. 2. ed. (Grobler, Jan H.) Johannesburg, 1958.
Afr 210.64.45 Africa's freedom. London, 1964.
Afr 212.18 Africa's golden road. (Armah, Kivesi.) Kenyatta, 1965.
Afr 1.78 Africa's illustrated news. London. 1,1966+
Afr 4559.30 Africa's last empire. (Norden, Hermann.) London, 1930.
Afr 555.26.3 Africa's mountain valley. (Charlesworth, M.L.) London, 1857.
Afr 1.18 Africa's own library. London.
Afr 630.38.5 Africa's peril. (Abercrombie, Hugh R.) London, 1938.
Afr 210.64.5 Africa's quest for order. (Burke, Fred.) Englewood Cliffs, 1964.
Afr 210.66 Africa's search for identity. (Ferkiss, Victor.) N.Y., 1966.
Afr 609.28.15 Africa's white magic. (Appel, Joseph Herbert.) N.Y., 1928.
Afr 6455.100 Africa's wild glory. (Keller, W.P.) London, 1959.
Afr 609.64.40 Africka mozaika. (Mikolasek, Vladimir.) Liberec, 1964
Afr 6178.3 Afrifa, A.R. The Ghana coup, 24th February, 1966. London, 1966.
Afr 115.20.10 Afrika, als die Weissen kamen. (Schiffers, Heinrich.) Düsseldorf, 1967.
Afr 210.64.55 Afrika, Colloquium. Afrikas Gegenwart und Zukunft. Hannover, 1964.
Afr 115.100 Afrika, opdagelsesrejserne. (Jensen, Johannes V.) København, 1949.
Afr 109.32 Afrika, schwarz oder weiss. (Berger, A.) Berlin, 1932.
Afr 609.33.10 Afrika, wie ich es erlebte. (Anstein, H.) Stuttgart, 1933.
Afr 210.61.65 Afrika, 1956-1961. (Akademiia Nauk SSSR. Institut Afriki.) Moscow, 1961.
Afr 210.61.66 Afrika, 1961-1965gg. (Akademiia Nauk SSSR. Institut Afriki.) Moskva, 1967.
Afr 29.15 Pamphlet vol. Afrika. 3 pam.
Afr 109.66.30 Afrika. (Bertaux, Pierre.) Frankfurt, 1966.
Afr 545.21 Afrika. (Buhlman, Walbert.) Mainz, 1963.
Afr 626.30 Afrika. (Krueger, Karl.) Berlin, 1952.
Afr 109.61.40 Afrika. (Mukarovsky, H.) Wien, 1961.
Afr 210.61.70 Afrika. (Schatten, Fritz.) München, 1961.
Afr 30.10 Afrika. (Sovetskaia Entsiklopediia.) Moscow, 1963. 2v.
Afr 7809.64 Afrika. (Thurn, Max.) Wien, 1964.
Afr 626.20 Afrika. (Zischka, A.) Oldenburg, 1951.
Afr 1.34F Afrika. München. 1-7,1959-1965+ 4v.
Afr 1.46 Afrika. Rotterdam. 16,1962+ 13v.
Afr 608.91 Afrika. Eine allgemeine Landeskunde. (Sievers, W.) Leipzig, 1891.
Afr 109.62.41 Afrika. Eine politische Länderkunde. 6. Aufl. (Ansprenger, Franz.) Berlin, 1969.
Afr 608.91.2 Afrika. 2. Aufl. (Sievers, W.) Leipzig, 1901.
Afr 608.91.3 Afrika. 3. Aufl. (Jaeger, F.) Leipzig, 1928.
Afr 212.16 Afrika. 3. Opl. (Baardseth, Magne.) Oslo, 1964.
Afr 609.57 Afrika. 4. Aufl. (Schiffers, Heinrich.) Frankfurt, 1957.
Afr 609.57.2 Afrika. 8. Aufl. (Schiffers, Heinrich.) München, 1967.
Afr 1.31 Afrika - heute. Bonn. 1957+ 4v.
Afr 10065.2 Afrika beraettar. (Waestberg, Per.) Malmoe, 1961.
Afr 1.80 Afrika-Bericht. (Africa-Verein, Hamburg.) Hamburg. 1963+
Afr 28.104 Afrika-Bibliographie, Verzeichnis der wissenschaftlichen Schrifttum in deutscher Sprache. Bonn. 1,1960+ 2v.
Afr 630.52 Afrika Bibliographie. (Mylius, N.) Wien, 1952.
Afr 55.44 Afrika Biographien. (Friedrich-Ebert-Stiftung.) Hannover, 1967- 3v.
Afr 609.67.20 Afrika eshche ne otkryta. Moskva, 1967.
Afr 609.39.2 Afrika gestern und heute. 10. Aufl. (Wallschläger, Alfred.) Gütersloh, 1963.
Afr 30.5 Afrika Hand-Lexicon. (Heichen, Paul.) Leipzig, 1885-86.
Afr 609.67.45 Afrika-Handbuch für Wirtschaft und Reise. Hamburg, 1967. 2v.
Afr 1.66 Afrika heute. Bonn. 1964+ 5v.
Afr 500.46 Afrika heute und morgen. (Rohrbach, P.) Berlin, 1939.
Afr 609.61.25 Afrika idet k svoboda. (Rakhmatov, M.) Moscow, 1961.
Afr 608.81 Afrika im Lichte unserer Tage. (Chavanne, J.) Wien, 1881.
Afr 609.64.30 Afrika im Wandel seiner Gesellschaftsformen. (Deutsche Afrika-Gesellschaft, Bonn.) Leiden, 1964.
Afr 212.46 Afrika im Widerspruch. (Guiton, Raymond.) Köln, 1967-
Afr 1.42 Afrika-Institut, Pretoria. Bulletin. Pretoria. 2,1962+ 7v.
Afr 1.42.3 Afrika-Institut, Pretoria. Communications. Pretoria.
Afr 8659.61.5 Afrika ist nicht nur schwarz. (Jenny, H.) Düsseldorf, 1961.
Afr 626.45 Afrika iuzhnee Sakhary. (Potekhin, I.I.) Moscow, 1958.
Afr 28.2 Die Afrika-Literatur in der Zeit von 1500 bis 1750 N. Ch. (Paulitschke, P.) Wien, 1882.

Afr 609.65.45 Afrika na styke stoletii. (Rodionov, Viktor N.)
Leningrad, 1965.

Afr 609.29.15 Afrika nackt und Angezogen. (Edschmid, Kasimir.)
Frankfurt a.M., 1934.

Afr 8001.25 Afrika-post. Pretoria. 12,1966+ 5v.

Afr 1.38 Afrika Rundschau, Politik, Wirtschaft, Wissenschaft,
Forschung, Überseedeutschtum. Hamburg. 1,1935+ 7v.

Afr 210.60.15 Afrika sbrasyvaet tsepi. (Datlin, S.V.) Moscow, 1960.

Afr 28.124 Afrika-Schrifttum. Wiesbaden. 1,1966+

Afr 609.62.5 Afrika segodnia. Moscow, 1962.

Afr 609.60.85 Afrika smotrit v budushchee. (Potekhin, I.I.)
Moscow, 1960.

Afr 8685.35 Afrika soder die asiaat. (Cronje, Geoffrey.)
Johannesburg, 1946.

Afr 1.96 Afrika Spectrum. Hamburg. 1,1967+

Afr 210.60.50 Afrika spronger hojorna. (Sundstroem, Erland.)
Stockholm, 1960.

Afr 1.64 Afrika-Studien. Berlin. 1,1964+ 16v.

Afr 1.64.5 Afrika-Studien. Sonderreihe. Berlin. 1,1968+

Afr 505.43 Afrika unter dem Joch der Weissen. (Padmore, George.)
Zürich, 193-.

Afr 500.65 Afrika unter dem Joch des Imperialismus. (Datlin, S.)
Berlin, 1953.

Afr 109.65.20 Afrika v mirovoi ekonomike i politike. (Liubimov, Nikolai
N.) Moskva, 1965.

Afr 626.122 Afrika v tsifrakh. Moscow, 1963.

Afr 626.70 Afrika vo Vtoroi Mirovoi Voine. (Shpirt, A.I.)
Moscow, 1959.

Afr 150.2 Afrika vor den Entdeckungen der Portugiesen. (Kunstmann,
F.) München, 1853.

Afr 6780.10.25 Afrika zu unsern Füssen. (Goebel, J.) Leipzig, 1925.

Afr 210.60.35 Afrika 1960. Moscow, 1960.

Afr 8252.14 Afrikaander. Amsterdam, 1883.

Afr 8055.15 Afrikaanse biografiese woordeboek. (Nienaber, P.J.)
Johannesburg, 1947.

Afr 8038.10 Afrikaanse kernensiklopedie. Kaapstad, 1965.

Afr 8038.5 Afrikaanse kinderensiklopedi. Kaapstad, 1963. 10v.

Afr 8028.100 Afrikaanse publikasies. (South Africa. Parliament.
Library.) Kaapstad, 1931.

Afr 8659.53.5 Die Afrikaanse volkskultuur. (Coetzee, Abel.)
Kaapstad, 1953.

Afr 8659.53.5.2 Die Afrikaanse volkskultuur. 2. druk. (Coetzee, Abel.)
Amsterdam, 1960.

Afr 8667.60 Die Afrikaanse wêreldbeskouing. (Alberts, Andries.)
Kaapstad, 1956.

Afr 679.13.5 Afrikafahrt West. (Grimm, Hans.) Frankfurt, 1913.

Atr 86/8.370 Afrikaner and African nationalism. (Munger, Edwin S.)
London, 1967.

Afr 8283.16 De Afrikaner-Boer en de Jameson-inval. (Hofmeyr, N.J.)
Kaapstad, 1896.

Afr 8050.24 The Afrikaner bond. (Davenport, T.R.H.) Cape Town, 1966.

Afr 8057.5 Die afrikaner en sy geskiedenis. (Jaarsveld, F.A. van.)
Kaapstad, 1959.

Afr 6885.5 Afrikaner-Europäer in nächstenschaftlicher Entsprechung.
(Gutmann, Bruno.) Stuttgart, 1966.

Afr 8369.42.20 Afrikaner-volkseeheid. (Malherbe, D.Y.)
Bloemfontein, 1942.

Afr 8369.61.20 Afrikaner-volkseenheid en my ervarings op die pad daarheen.
3. druk. (Malan, Daniel François.) Kaapstad, 1961.

Afr 635.60 Die Afrikanerin. (Muthesius, A.) Düsseldorf, 1959.

Afr 8685.102 The Afrikaners. (Fisher, John.) London, 1969.

Afr 8057.6 The Afrikaners interpretation. (Jaarsveld, F.A. van.)
Cape Town, 1964.

Afr 8678.250 Die afrikanisch-christlichen Bewegungen unter den Bantu.
(Knoob, Willi.) Köln, 1961.

Afr 212.56 Afrikanische Gegenwartsfragen. Berlin, 1960.

Afr 1.4.5 Afrikanische Gesellschaft in Deutschland.
Correspondenzblatt. Berlin. 1,1873+

Afr 1.4 Afrikanische Gesellschaft in Deutschland. Mittheilungen.
Berlin. 1,1878+ 5v.

Afr 55.10 Afrikanische Köpfe, Charakterskizzen. (Peters, Karl.)
Berlin, 1915.

Afr 7548.85 Die afrikanische Konferenz und der Kongostaat. (Patzig,
Carl Albrecht.) Heidelberg, 1885.

Afr 635.7F Afrikanische Ornamentik. Inaug. Diss. (Heydrich, Martin.)
Leiden, 1914.

Afr 5993.12 Eine afrikanische Tropeninsel. (Baumann, O.) Wien, 1888.

Afr 626.202 Afrikanische Wirtschaftsintegration. (Mars, John.)
Wien, 1967.

Afr 4070.25.2 Die afrikanische Wüste und das Land der Schwarzen am obern
Nil. (Escayrac de Lauture, S.) Leipzig, 1867.

Afr 609.38.5 Afrikanischer Frühling, eine Reise. (Sieburg, F.)
Frankfurt, 1938.

Afr 715.3.25 Afrikanisches Skizzenbuch. (Schweinfurth, G.)
Berlin, 1925.

Afr 8028.101 Afrikanse publikasies. 2. uitg. (South Africa. Parliament.
Library.) Pretoria, 1934.

Afr 50.42 Afrikansk nationalisme. (Pedersen, O.K.) København, 1963.

Afr 8680.50 Afrikanska rasproblem. (Nielsen, Erik W.)
Stockholm, 1963.

Afr 718.50 Afrikanska strövtåg. (Nils-Magnus.) Solna, 1968.

Afr 6455.66 Den afrikanske farm. (Blixen Finecke, K.)
København, 1943.

Afr 6390.81 Afrikanski belezhnik. (Petrov, Valeri.) Sofiia, 1965.

Afr 35.5 Afrikanskii sbornik. v.1-2. (Akademiia Nauk SSSR. Institut
Afriki.) Moscow, 1963. 2v.

Afr 7850.60 Afrikanskt mellanspeli en berättelse om händelserna på
Kaminabasen, 1960-1964. (Hederén, Olle.) Östra Ryd, 1965.

Afr 55.13 Afrikas ansikte. (Oeste, Sven.) Stockholm, 1962.

Afr 210.64.55 Afrikas Gegenwart und Zukunft. (Afrika, Colloquium.)
Hannover, 1964.

Afr 545.37 Afrikas religioner. (Pettersson, Olof.) Stockholm, 1966.

Afr 626.7 L'Afrique, champ d'expansion de l'Europe. (Guernier, E.L.)
Paris, 1933.

Afr 608.87 L'Afrique, choix de lectures. 4th ed. (Lanier, L.)
Paris, 1887.

Afr 609.58 L'Afrique, les Africains. v.1-2. (Gasset, Pierre.)
Paris, 1958.

Afr 210.60.40 Afrique. (Abranches, Esther.) Luanda, 1960.

Afr 125.10 Afrique. (Avezac, A. D.) Paris, 1844.

Afr 109.44 L'Afrique. (Bidou, Henry.) Paris, 1944.

Afr 609.62.25 Afrique. (Maquet, Jacques.) Paris, 1962.

Afr 28.97 L'Afrique. Paris, 196-.

Afr 1.50F Afrique. Paris. 1-69, 1961-1967// 9v.

Afr 210.63.90 Afrique: perspectives, politiques. (Paul, Edouard C.)
Port-au-Prince, Haiti, 1963.

Afr 1.50.5 Afrique. Supplément. 1-9, 1965-1967//

Afr 630.56.5 L'Afrique à l'âge ingrat. (Pidoux, Edmond.)
Neuchâtel, 1956.

Afr 609.60.40 L'Afrique à l'heure. (Harcourt, François.) Paris, 1960.

Afr 510.80 L'Afrique à l'heure française. (Harmand, Jack.)
Paris, 1958.

Afr 109.20 L'Afrique à travers les ages. (Moulin, Alfred.)
Paris, 1920.

Afr 28.82 L'Afrique à travers les publications. (Coisel.)
Paris, 1961.

Afr 109.63.5 L'Afrique africaine. (Anders, Robert.) Paris, 1963.

Afr 609.63 Afrique africaine. Lausanne, 1963.

Afr 710.55.5 Afrique ambigue. (Balandier, Georges.) Paris, 1962.

Afr 710.55 Afrique ambigue. (Belandier, Georges.) Paris, 1957.

Afr 626.11F L'Afrique au XVI siècle et le commerce anversois. (Denuce,
J.) Anvers, 1937.

Afr 210.66.15 L'Afrique au XXe siècle. (Ganiage, Jean.) Paris, 1966.

Afr 608.48.2 Afrique australe, orientale. (Hoefer, J.C.F.)
Paris, 1848.

Afr 8659.01 L'Afrique australe. (Reclus, E.) Paris, 1901.

Afr 8095.55 L'Afrique australe et Madagascar. (Battistini, Rene.)
Paris, 1967.

Afr 210.61.80 L'Afrique aux trois visages. (Houart, Pierre.)
Bruxelles, 1961.

Afr 109.61.10 L'Afrique bascule vers l'avenir. (Tillion, Germaine.)
Paris, 1961.

Afr 1259.39 L'Afrique blanche. (Gautier, E.F.) Paris, 1939.

Afr 1259.49.7 L'Afrique blanche. 3. ed. (Despois, Jean.) Paris, 1964.

Afr 510.40A L'Afrique blanche française. (Despois, J.) Paris, 1949. 2v.

Afr 5406.262 Afrique centrale, les républiques d'expression française.
Paris, 1962.

Afr 715.7 L'Afrique centrale. (Laveleye, E. de.) Paris, 1878.

Afr 9548.7 L'Afrique centrale. (Robert, Maurice.) Paris, 1934.

Afr 550.135 Afrique chrétienne. Christliches Afrika. Lezay, 1958-1961.
2v.

Afr 626.206 L'Afrique commence avec l'Afrique. 1. éd. (Vinay,
Bernard.) Paris, 1968.

Afr 1.48 Afrique contemporaine. Paris. 1,1962+ 4v.

Htn Afr 609.64.25F Afrique d'aujourd'hui. (Progrès Egyptien.) Le
Caire, 1964.

Htn Afr 605.73.6* L'Afrique de Marmol. (Marmol Carvajal, L. del.)
Paris, 1667. 3v.

Afr 210.67.20 L'Afrique déchirée, de l'anarchie à la dictature, de la
magic à la technologie. (Lantier, Jacques.) Paris, 1967.

Afr 109.60.20 L'Afrique decolonisée. (Drachoussoff, V.)
Bruxelles, 1960.

Afr 115.55 L'Afrique des africains. (Wauthier, Claude.) Paris, 1964.

Afr 8678.360 L'Afrique des Afrikaaners. (Francos, Ania.) Paris, 1966.

Afr 109.61.41 Afrique d'hier et d'aujourd'hui. (Mukarovsky, H.)
Tournai, 1964.

Afr 1.40 Afrique documents. Dakar. 1961+ 7v.

Afr 1259.27.10F L'Afrique du Nord, Algérie, Tunisie, Maroc. Paris, 1927.

Afr 1271.10F L'Afrique du Nord, Tunisie, Algérie, Maroc. (Bargone,
Chas.) Paris, 1924.

Afr 659.13 L'Afrique du nord. (Bernard, A.) Paris, 1913.

Afr 1273.922 L'Afrique du nord. (Cosnier, Henri.) Paris, 1922.

Afr 1955.4.5 L'Afrique du nord. (Gerard, J.) Paris, 1860.

Afr 1955.4 L'Afrique du nord. (Gerard, J.) Paris, 1861.

Afr 1259.08 L'Afrique du nord. (Lorin, H.) Paris, 1908.

X Cg Afr 1955.42 L'Afrique du nord devant le Parlement au XIXme siècle.
(Valet, René.) Alger, 1924.

Afr 1095.5 L'Afrique du Nord en marche. (Julien, C.A.) Paris, 1952.

Afr 510.60 Afrique du Nord et Afrique Noire. (Lavergne, B.)
Paris, 1956.

Afr 1200.60 L'Afrique du Nord et la guerre. (Perreau Pradier, P.)
Paris, 1918.

Afr 1069.37 L'Afrique du Nord française dans l'histoire. (Albertini,
E.) Lyon, 1937.

Afr 659.55 L'Afrique du Nord française dans l'histoire. (Albertini,
Eugène.) Lyon, 1955.

Afr 1273.926 L'Afrique du Nord pendant la guerre. (Bernard, A.)
Paris, 1926.

Afr 8658.98.5 L'Afrique du Sud. (Aubert, Georges.) Paris, 1898.

Afr 8089.66.5 L'Afrique du Sud. (Cadoux, Charles.) Paris, 1966.

Afr 8659.66.5 L'Afrique du Sud. (Molnar, Thomas Steven.) Paris, 1966.

Afr 8659.49 Afrique du Sud. (Siegfried, A.) Paris, 1949.

Afr 2209.66.5 L'Afrique en flânant, de Paris à Tamanrasset. (Joret,
Madeleine.) Paris, 1966.

Afr 1.30F Afrique en marche. Paris. 1,1957+ 2v.

Afr 5056.165 Afrique en question. (Diallo, Demba.) Paris, 1968.

Afr 210.68.10 L'Afrique en question. (Binet, Jacques.) Tours, 1965.

Afr 200.12 L'Afrique en 1890. (Kaltbrunner, David.) Paris, 1890.

Afr 5420.175 L'Afrique équatoriale. (Compiegne, Victor D.)
Paris, 1875.

Afr 5406.218 L'Afrique équatoriale française. (Bruel, Georges.)
Paris, 1918.

Afr 5406.231 L'Afrique équatoriale française. (Maigret, Julien.)
Paris, 1931.

Afr 5406.250.3 L'Afrique équatoriale française. (Trezenem, Edouard.)
Paris, 1955.

Afr 5406.252 L'Afrique équatoriale française. (Ziegle, Henri.)
Paris, 1952.

Afr 5404.20 Afrique équatoriale française. v.1-4. (France. Agence de
la France d'Outre-mer.) Paris, 1950.

Afr 5406.211.15.2 L'Afrique équatoriale française. 2. ed. (Rondet-Saint,
Maurice.) Paris, 1911.

Afr 5406.230 L'Afrique équatoriale française (A.E.F.). (Bruel,
Georges.) Paris, 1930.

Afr 5406.213 L'Afrique équatoriale illustrée. (Ranget, Fernand.)
Paris, 1913.

Afr 200.5 Afrique et africains. (Sevin-Deplaces, L.) Paris, 1892.

Afr 626.42 Afrique et communauté européenne. (Lefebvre, Jacques.)
Bruxelles, 1957.

Afr 1.99 Afrique et culture. Paris. 8,1968+

Afr 608.77 L'Afrique et la Conférence géographique de Bruxelles.
(Banning, E.) Bruxelles, 1877.

Afr 500.25 L'Afrique et la Paix de Versailles. (Antonelli, Etienne.)
Paris, 1921.

Afr 500.25.10 L'Afrique et la Paix de Versailles. 4th ed. (Antonelli,
Etienne.) Paris, 1921.

Afr 1.20 L'Afrique et l'Asie. Paris. 1952+ 14v.

Afr 626.133 L'Afrique et les leçons de l'expérience communiste.
(Lazic, Branko M.) Paris, 1961.

Afr 200.7 L'Afrique et l'expansion coloniale. (Chatelain, C.)
Paris, 1901.

NEDL Afr 1.2 Afrique explorée et civilisée. Genève. 1,1879+ 13v.

Afr 6200.1.5   Ahmadu Bello University, Zaria, Nigeria. Institute of Administration. Information memo. Zaria. 4,1963+

Afr 3204.17   Ahmed, Chafik Bey. L'Egypte moderne et les influences étrangères. Le Caire, 1931.

Afr 2030.467.10   Ahmed Ben Bella. (Merle, Robert.) N.Y., 1967.

Afr 2030.464.44   Ahmed Ben Bella. (Merle, Robert.) Paris, 1965.

Afr 6292.9.5   Ahmed ibn Fartua. History of the first twelve years of the reign of Mai Idris Alooma of Bornu. Lagos, 1926.

Afr 3199.60   Ahmed Jamal, M. The intellectual origins of Egyptian nationalism. London, 1960.

Afr 6099.2   Ahuma, S.R.B. Attoh. Memoirs of West African celebrities. Liverpool, 1905.

Afr 2875.11   Ai caduti nella guerra italo-turca. (Facchinetti, P.V.) n.p., 1911.

Afr 4559.13   Ai confini meridionali dell'Etiopia. (Citerni, Carlo.) Milano, 1913.

Afr 2929.36.5   Ai margini del Sahara. (Rava, C.E.) Bologna, 1936.

Afr 6538.37   Aid in Uganda. (Overseas Development Institute.) London, 1966. 3v.

Afr 626.132   Aid to Africa. (Little, Ian.) Oxford, 1964.

Afr 10621.41.100A   Aidoo, C.A.A. The dilemma of a ghost. Accra, 1965.

Afr 6162.15   Aids to African autonomy. (Cudjoe, S.D.) London, 1949.

Afr 2030.10   Aimée et souffrante Algérie. (Soustelle, Jacques.) Paris, 1956.

Afr 10013.2   Ainslie, Rosalynde. The press in Africa. London, 1966.

Afr 10013.2.5   Ainslie, Rosalynde. The press in Africa: communications past and present. N.Y., 1968.

Afr 6470.106   Ainsworth, J.D. John Ainsworth. London, 1959.

Afr 3315.127   Airborne to Suez. (Cavenagh, Sandy.) London, 1965.

Afr 7015.15   Aires de Ornelas. (Republica Portuguesa.) Lisboa, 1934. 3v.

Afr 2230.38   Ait Ahmed, Hocine. La guerre et l'après-guerre. Paris, 1964.

Afr 8088.92.2   Aitton, D. Geschiedenis van Zuid Afrika. 2e druk. Amsterdam, 1897.

Afr 10690.89.130   Ajaiyi and his inherited poverty. (Tutuola, Amos.) London, 1967.

Afr 1609.17   Ajalbert, Jean. Le Maroc sans les boches. Paris, 1917.

Afr 2000.3   Ajam, Maurice. Problèmes algériens. Paris, 1913.

Afr 6096.8   Ajayi, G.B. Introduction to the economics of West Africa. Rev. ed. Ibadan, 1965. 2v.

Afr 679.65.25   Ajayi, J.F. Ade. A thousand years of West African history. London, 1965.

Afr 6282.15   Ajayi, J.F. Aoe. Christian missions in Nigeria, 1841-1891. London, 1965.

Afr 6280.2.15   Ajayi, J.F.A. de. Yoruba warfare in the nineteenth century. Cambridge, Eng., 1964.

Afr Doc 2560.602   Ajuluchukee, M.C.K. Profiles of the ministers of Eastern Nigeria. Enugu, 1960.

Afr 210.61.65   Akademiia Nauk SSSR. Institut Afriki. Afrika, 1956-1961. Moskow, 1961.

Afr 210.61.66   Akademiia Nauk SSSR. Institut Afriki. Afrika, 1961-1965gg. Moskva, 1967.

Afr 35.5   Akademiia Nauk SSSR. Institut Afriki. Afrikanskii sbornik. v.1-2. Moscow, 1963. 2v.

Afr 626.153.5   Akademiia Nauk SSSR. Institut Afriki. Ekonomicheskaia istoriia Afriki. Moskva, 1966.

Afr 626.153   Akademiia Nauk SSSR. Institut Afriki. Ekonomika Afriki. Moskva, 1965.

Afr 212.26.2   Akademiia Nauk SSSR. Institut Afriki. A history of Africa, 1918-1967. Moscow, 1968.

Afr 212.25.9   Akademiia Nauk SSSR. Institut Afriki. Istoriia Afriki v XIX nachale XX v. Moskva, 1967.

Afr 10005.5   Akademiia Nauk SSSR. Institut Afriki. Literatura stran Afriki. Moskva, 1964-66. 2v.

Afr 212.26   Akademiia Nauk SSSR. Institut Afriki. Noveishaia istoriia Afriki. Moskva, 1964.

Afr 626.148   Akademiia Nauk SSSR. Institut Afriki. Nezavisimye strany Afriki. Moskva, 1965.

Afr 9555.5   Akademiia Nauk SSSR. Institut Etnografii. Arabskie istochniki VII-X vekov. Moscow, 1960. 2v.

Afr 32.3   Akademiia Nauk SSSR. Institut Gosudarstva i Prava. Konstitutsii gosudarstv Afriki. Moskva, 1966. 2v.

Afr 40.63   Akademiia Nauk SSSR. Institut Gosudarstva i Prava. Stanovlenie natsionalnoi gosudarstv v nezavisimykh stranakh Afriki. Moscow, 1963.

Afr 3315.145   Akademiia Nauk SSSR. Institut Mirovoi Ekonomiki i Mezhdunarodnykh Otnoshenii. Suetskii vopros i imperialisticheskaia agressiia protiv Egipta. Moskva, 1957.

Afr 505.48   Akademiia Nauk SSSR. Institut Narodov Azii. Politika Anglii v Afrike. Moskva, 1967.

Afr 632.25   Akademiia Nauk SSSR. Institut Narodov Azii. Rasovaia diskriminatsiia v stranakh Afriki. Moscow, 1960.

Afr 28.92   Akaemiia Nauk SSSR. Institut Afriki. Bibliografiia Afriki, do revoliutsionnaia i liberatura na russkom Iazyke. Moscow, 1964.

Afr 6395.4.5   The Akamba in British East Africa. Pt.1-3. Inaug. Diss. (Lindblom, Gerhard.) Uppsala, 1916.

Afr 33319.2   Akamba stories. (Mbiti, John.) Oxford, 1966.

Afr 6194.20.5   The Akan doctrine of God: a fragment of Gold Coast ethics and religion. (Danquah, J.B.) London, 1944.

Afr 6194.20.5.2   The Akan doctrine of God: a fragment of Gold Coast ethics and religion. 2nd ed. (Danquah, J.B.) London, 1968.

Afr 6194.20.15   The Akan of Ghana. (Meyerowitz, Eva.) London, 1958.

Afr 6195.18   Akan religion and the Christian faith. (Williamson, Sydney George.) Accra, 1965.

Afr 609.26.10   Akeley, Carl E. Adventures in the African jungle. N.Y., 1930.

Afr 609.25   Akeley, Carl E. In brightest Africa. Garden City, N.Y., 1925.

Afr 609.23   Akeley, Carl E. In brightest Africa. Garden City, 1923. 2v.

Afr 609.23.2   Akeley, Carl E. In brightest Africa. Garden City, 1923.

Afr 609.30.10   Akeley, D.J. Jungle portraits. N.Y., 1930.

Afr 6390.26.10   Akeley, Mary L. Carl Akeley's Africa. N.Y., 1929.

Afr 6390.26   Akeley, Mary L. The wilderness lives again, Carl Akeley and the great adventure. N.Y., 1940.

Afr 6280.26.10   Akiga. Akiga's story, the Tiv tribe. London, 1965.

Afr 6280.26.10   Akiga's story, the Tiv tribe. (Akiga.) London, 1965.

Afr 6196.10   The Akim Abwakara handbook. (Danquah, J.B.) London, 1928.

Afr 6170.9   Akim-foo, the history of a failure. (Butler, W.F.) London, 1876.

Afr 5385.30   Akindele, Adolphe. Le Dahomey. Paris, 1955.

Afr 5368.10   Akinjogbin, I.A. Dahomey and its neighbours, 1708-1818. Cambridge, Eng., 1967.

Afr 626.8   Akinwale, Lydia Oluwafemi. Marxism and African economic development, 1952-1968. Ibadan, 1968.

Afr 6277.126   Akinyotu, Adetunji. A bibliography on development planning in Nigeria, 1955-1968. Ibadan, 1968.

Afr 6010.14   Akpan, N.U. Epitaph to indirect rule. London, 1956.

Afr 10671.46.100   Akpan, Ntieyong Udo. The wooden gong. London, 1965.

Afr 4290.5   Aksum. (Kobishchanov, Iurii M.) Moskva, 1966.

Afr 1583.3F   Aktenstuecke über Marokko. Berlin, 1908.

Afr 1583.2F   Aktenstuecke über Marokko der Reichstage...8. I. 1906. Berlin, 1906.

Afr 6295.65   Akufo, an environmental study of a Nigerian village community. (Gilles, H.M.) Ibadan, 1965.

Afr 6193.7   Akwawuah, Kwadwo A. Prelude to Ghana's industrialization. London, 1959.

Afr 6193.40   Akwawuah, Kwadwo A. Preludes to Ghana's industrialisation. London, 1960.

Afr 1390.3   Al-bayano'l-mogrib. (Fagnan, E.) Alger, 1901. 2v.

Afr 4688.15   Al Lago Tsana. (Rava, M.) Roma, 1913.

Afr 3143.10   Al-Malik al-Kamil von Egypten und seine Zeit. (Gottschalk, Hans L.) Wiesbaden, 1958.

Afr 3143.5   Al-Qadi al-Fadil, der Wezir Saladins. Inaug.-Diss. (Helbig, Adolph H.) Leipzig, 1908.

Afr 4390.47   Al tempo di Menelik. (Pariset, Dante.) Milano, 1937.

Afr 6282.42   Aladura: a religious among the Yoruba. (Peel, John David Yeadon.) London, 1968.

Afr 6295.64   Alagoa, E.J. The small brave city-state. Ibadan, 1964.

Afr 6277.104F   Alako, Samuel A. Fiscal incentives for industrial development in Nigeria. Ife, 1967.

Afr 659.48A   Alal al Fasi. The independence movements in Arab North Africa. Washington, 1954.

Afr 4128.9   Alamein, 1933-1962. 9. ed. (Caccia Dominioni di Sillavengo, Paolo.) Milano, 1965.

Afr 11675.87.2   Alan Paton. (Bentel, Lea.) Johannesburg, 1969.

Afr 11675.87.800   Alan Paton. (Callan, Edward.) N.Y., 1968.

Afr 4370.5   Alaqa Walda Maryam. History of King Theodore. London, 1906.

Afr 1432.1.2F   Alarcon, P.A. Diario de la guerra de Africa. Madrid, 1860.

Afr 1432.1   Alarcon, P.A. Diario de la guerra de Africa. Madrid, 1880. 3v.

Afr 1830.40.15   Alazard, J. Histoire et historiens de l'Algérie. Paris, 1931.

Afr 1830.50.5   Alazard, Jean. L'orient et la peinture française au XIXe siècle. Paris, 1930.

Afr 1618.24   Albarracin de Martinez Ruiz, Joaquina. Vestido y adorno de la mujer musulmana de Vêbala (Marruecos). Madrid, 1964.

Afr 5385.12   Albeca, A.L. Les établissements français du Golfe de Bénin. Paris, 1889.

Afr 1755.12   Albeniz, R. La Campana del rif, la Verdad de la guerra. n.p., n.d.

Afr 8687.263.5   Albert John Luthuli and the South African race conflict. (Callan, Edward.) Kalamazoo, 1962.

Afr 4095.8.2   The Albert Nyanza. (Baker, S.W.) London, 1866.

Afr 4095.8   The Albert Nyanza. (Baker, S.W.) London, 1867. 2v.

Afr 4095.8.2.10   The Albert Nyanza. (Baker, S.W.) London, 1907.

Afr 4095.8.2.5   The Albert Nyanza. New ed. (Baker, S.W.) London, 1870.

Afr 5426.100.45   Albert Schweitzer. (Gollomb, Joseph.) London, 1951.

Afr 5426.100.25   Albert Schweitzer. (Woyott-Secretan, Marie.) Munich, 1949.

Afr 8830.8   Alberti, J.C.L. Die Kaffern auf der Südküste von Afrika. Gotha, 1815.

Afr 8678.14   Alberti, L. Description physique et historique des Cafres. Amsterdam, 1811.

Afr 1069.37   Albertini, E. L'Afrique du Nord française dans l'histoire. Lyon, 1937.

Afr 659.55   Albertini, Eugène. L'Afrique du Nord française dans l'histoire. Lyon, 1955.

Afr 4785.15   Albertio, Enrico Alberto d'. In Africa, Victoria Nyaza e Benadir. Bergamo, 1906.

Afr 3979.08.10   Albertis, E.A.D. Une croisière sur le Nil, Khartoum-Goudokoro. Le Caire, 1908.

Afr 609.07.12   Albertis, Enrico Alberto d'. Periplo dell'Africa. 2d ed. Genova, 1925.

Afr 7219.42   Alberto, Manuel Simoes. O oriente africano portugues. Lourenç Marques, 1942.

Afr 8667.60   Alberts, Andries. Die Afrikaanse wêreldbeskouing. Kaapstad, 1956.

Afr 8659.60.10   Albertyn, J.R. Land en stad. Kaapstad, 1960.

Afr 1555.3   Albin, P. Le coup d'Agadir. Paris, 1912.

Afr 4700.42   Albori coloniali d'Italia (1891-1895). (Borelli, Gioranni.) Modena, 1942.

Afr 4513.38.25   Albori dell'impero; l'Etiopia come è come sarà. (Poggiali, Ciro.) Milano, 1938.

Afr 3038.27   Albrecht, W. Die völkerrechtliche Stellung Ägyptens. Inaug. Diss. Würzburg, 1919.

Afr 7815.1F   Album...ethnography...Congo-basin. (Schmeltz, J.D.E.) Leyden, n.d.

Afr 1432.8F   Album de la guerra de Africa. Madrid, 1860.

Afr 1965.5.15F   Album militaire d'Afrique. (Batsalle.) Paris, 1846.

Afr 2875.39   Album-portfolio della guerra italo-turca, 1911-12, per la conquista della Libia. Milano, 1913.

Afr 8686.24F   Album vir die geskiedenis van die Nederduitsch Hervormde Kerk van Afrika. (Engelbrecht, Stephanus P.) Pretoria, 1965.

Afr 7309.29F   Albuns fotograficos e descritivos da...colonia de Mocambique. v.1-10. (Santos Rufino, Jose dos.) Hamburg, 1929. 5v.

Afr 7122.12   Albuquerque Felner, A. De. Angola. Coimbra, 1933.

Afr 1990.21   Alby, E. Histoire des prisonniers français en Afrique. Paris, 1849.

Afr 1990.21.5   Alby, E. Les vêpres marocaines. v.1-2. Paris, 1853.

Afr 1736.3   Alcala galiano, pelayo. Memoria sobre la situación de Santa Cruz de Mar Pegueña. 3 in 1. Madrid, 1878. 3 pam.

Afr 1736.4   Alcala Galiano, Pelayo. Santa Cruz de Mar Pequeña. Madrid, 1900.

Afr 6664.5   Alcandre, Sylvine. La république autonome du Togo. Paris, 1957.

Afr 1703.2   Alcazarquiver 1950. (Cortocero Hanares, H.F.) Tetuan, 1953.

Afr 40.64.5   Alderfer, Harold Freed. A bibliography of African government, 1950-1966. 2d ed. Lincoln University, 1967.

Afr 8285.10   Alderson, E.A.H. With the mounted infantry and the Mashona-landfield force, 1896. London, 1898.

Afr 530.7   Alemania en Africa. (Sorela, Luis.) Berlin, 1884.

Afr 1550.30   Alengry, Jean. Les relations franco-espagnoles et l'affaire du Maroc. Paris, 1920.

Afr 1570.43   Alengry, Jean. Les relations franco-espagnoles et l'affaire du Maroc. Thèse. Paris, 1920.

Afr 2819.30	Aleo, G.M. Turchi, senussi e italiani in Libia. Bengasi, 1930.
Afr 7375.5	Alexander, A. History of colonization on the western coast. Philadelphia, 1846.
Afr 718.27	Alexander, Boyd. From the Niger to the Nile. London, 1907.
Afr 718.27.3	Alexander, Boyd. Last journey...memoir by H. Alexander. London, 1912.
Afr 4050.9.5	Alexander, F.G. Wayfarers in the Libyan desert. N.Y., 1912.
Afr 6176.42	Alexander, Henry Templer. African tightrope. London, 1965.
Afr 6176.42.5	Alexander, Henry Templer. African tightrope. N.Y., 1966.
Afr 3275.22	Alexander, J. The truth about Egypt. London, 1911.
Afr 678.40.2	Alexander, J.E. Excursions in western Africa. 2d ed. London, 1840. 2v.
Afr 8658.38.5	Alexander, James E. An expedition of discovery into the interior of Africa. Cape Town, 1967. 2v.
Afr 8658.38	Alexander, James E. An expedition of discovery into the interior of Africa. London, 1835. 2v.
Afr 5425.5	Alexandre, Pierre. Le groupe dit Pahouin. Paris, 1958.
Afr 4105.10	Alexandria. 3d ed. (Forster, E.M.) Garden City, 1961.
Afr 1750.9	Alfaro y Zarabozo, S. de. Geografia de Marruecos y posesiones españolas de Africa. Toledo, 1920.
Afr 1573.28	Alfonso XIII y sus complices. (Reparaz, G. de.) Madrid, 1931.
Afr 3735.5	Alford, H.S.L. The Egyptian Soudan. London, 1898.
Afr 8252.56	Alfred Beit. (Fort, G.S.) London, 1932.
Afr 555.23.63	Alfred Buxton of Abyssinia and Congo. (Grubb, N.P.) London, 1943.
Afr 4390.15	Alfred Ilg. (Keller, Konrad.) Frauenfeld, 1918.
Afr 8252.8.25	Alfred Lord Milner. (Wrench, Evelyn.) London, 1958.
Afr 1258.83	Algarate, I.A. Memoria sobre nuestro poder militar. Madrid, 1883.
Afr 1550.22	Algeciras. International Conference on Moroccan Affairs, 1906. Acta general. Madrid, 1906.
Afr 2208.30.3	Alger, esquisse topographique et historique. (Perrot, A.M.) Paris, 1830.
Afr 1830.30.2	Alger, étude de géographie et d'histoire urbaines. (Lespes, René.) Paris, 1930.
Afr 1878.8	Alger, étude de geographie et d'histoire urbaines. Thèse. (Lespes, Rene.) Paris, 1930.
Afr 2208.30.8	Alger, tableau du royaume. (Renaudot.) Paris, 1830.
Afr 1838.2	Alger, voyage politique. v.1-2. (Bavoux, E.) Paris, 1841.
Afr 2308.4	Alger...son état présent et son avenir. (Pichon.) Paris, 1833.
Afr 2308.16	Alger. (Espel, Françoise.) Paris, 1959.
Afr 2308.1	Alger. (Feydeau, E.) Paris, 1862.
Afr 2308.6	Alger. (Guiauchain, G.) Alger-Mustapha, 1905.
Afr 2308.3	Alger et ses environs. (Piesse, L.) Paris, 1901.
Afr 1957.31	Alger fut à lui. (Serval, Pierre.) Paris, 1965.
Afr 699.53	Alger-Tunis-Rabat. (Fontaine, Pierre.) Paris, 1953.
Afr 2223.925	Algeria, a commercial handbook. (Jones, C.L.) Washington, 1925.
Afr 2030.466	Algeria, a revolution that failed. (Humbaraci, Arslan.) London, 1966.
Afr 2221.2	Algeria, a synthesis of civilizations. n.p., 1961.
Afr 1801.2F	Algeria, revue mensuelle illustrée. Alger. 1,1933+
Afr 1258.80	Algeria, Tunisia e Tripolitania. (Brunialti, A.) Milan, 1881.
Afr 2209.37F	Algeria. Les arts et la technique moderne. Algérie, 1937.
Afr 2223.958.5	Algeria. Perspectives décennales de développement économique de l'Algérie. Alger, 1958.
Afr 2030.275	Algeria. Programme et action du gouvernement en Algérie. Alger, 1956.
Afr 2030.460.25A	Algeria. White paper on the application of the Geneva Convention of 1949. N.Y., 1960.
Afr 2285.21	Algeria...season 1927-28. (The Paris Lyons and Mediterranean Railway Co.) Algiers, 1927.
Afr 2030.340	Algeria. (Algerian Front of National Liberation.) N.Y., 1960.
Afr 2030.330	Algeria. (Gillespie, Joan.) London, 1960.
Afr 2208.54	Algeria. (Morell, J.R.) London, 1854.
Afr 1828.1	Pamphlet vol. Algeria. Bibliography. 7 pam.
Afr 2030.276	Algeria. Cabinet du Gouverneur Général. Action du gouvernement en Algérie. Alger, 1957.
Afr 2209.57.5	Algeria. Cabinet du Gouverneur Général. Algérie. Alger, 1957.
Afr 2223.960.15	Algeria. Caisse D'Equipement pour Le Développement de l'Algérie. Rapport sur l'exécution du programme d'équipement de l'Algérie en 1960. Alger, 1961.
Afr 1830.105	Algeria. Commissariat General du Centenaire. Le centenaire de l'Algérie. Alger, 1931. 2v.
Afr 1830.110	Algeria. Commissariat General du Centenaire. Les parcs nationaux en Algérie. Alger, 1930.
Afr 2288.15.5	Algeria. Commissariat Général du Centenaire. Les territoires du sud de l'Algérie. 2d ed. Pt.1-3,5 et cartes. Alger, 1929-30. 5v.
Afr 2224.862	Algeria. Commission à l'Exposition Universelle de Londres. L'Algérie à l'Exposition universelle de Londres, 1862. Alger, 1862. 2v.
Afr 2209.61.20	Algeria. Conseil Supérieur de la Promotion Sociale en Algérie. Compte rendu analytique de la troisième session. Alger, 1961.
Afr 2223.960	Algeria. Conseil Supérieur de la Promotion Sociale en Algérie. Pour une promotion dans la coopération. Alger, 1960.
Afr 1838.9	Algeria. Constitution. La constitution. Alger, 1963.
Afr 2030.310	Algeria. Délégation Générale. Algeria's development. Algiers, 1959.
Afr 2209.60	Algeria. Délégation Générale du Gouvernement en Algérie. Algerian documents, 1960. Paris, 1960.
Afr 2223.922.5	Algeria. Direction de l agriculture du commerce et de la colonisation. Miscellaneous publications.
Afr 2223.65	Algeria. Direction de l'Agriculture, du Commerce et de l'Industrie. Notes sur la vie commerciale et industrielle de l'Algérie en 1923-1924. Alger, 1924.
Afr 575.25	Algeria. Direction de l'Intérieur et des Beaux-Arts. Mélanges d'histoire et d'archéologie de l'Occident musulman. v.1-2. Alger, 1957.
Afr 2288.15.3	Algeria. Direction des Territoires du Sud. Les territoires du sud de l'Algérie. Alger, 1954.
Afr 2223.960.20	Algeria. Direction du Plan et des Etudes Economiques. Plan de Constantine, 1959-1963. Alger, 1960.
Afr 1801.10	Algeria. Direction Général de l'Information. Actualité et documents. 45,1964+
Afr Doc 5307.15	Algeria. Direction générale du plan et des études économiques. Bulletin de statistiques générales. Alger. 1967+
Afr Doc 5307.10	Algeria. Direction générale du plan et des études économiques. Bulletin mensuel de statistiques générales. Alger. 1956-1965
Afr 2208.46	Pamphlet vol. Algeria. Geography, travels. 6 pam.
Afr 1840.1	Algeria. Gouvernement Général. Exposé de l'état...du gouvernement. Algiers, 1844.
Afr 2030.5	Algeria. Gouverneur Général, 1951-55. Quatre ans en Algérie. Alger, 1955.
Afr 2025.21	Algeria. Gouverneur Général. Etat de l'Algérie au 31 dec. 1882. Alger, 1883.
Afr 1990.18	Pamphlet vol. Algeria. History, 1830-1860. 10 pam.
Afr 1990.14	Pamphlet vol. Algeria. History, 1830-1860. 9 pam.
Afr 1990.20	Pamphlet vol. Algeria. History, 1830-1860. 11 pam.
Afr 1990.17	Pamphlet vol. Algeria. History, 1830-1860. 11 pam.
Afr 1990.19	Pamphlet vol. Algeria. History, 1830-1860. 10 pam.
Afr 2025.9	Pamphlet vol. Algeria. History, 1860- 13 pam.
Afr 2025.12	Pamphlet vol. Algeria. History, 1860- 9 pam.
Afr 2025.8	Pamphlet vol. Algeria. History, 1860- 14 pam.
Afr 2025.11	Pamphlet vol. Algeria. History, 1860- 7 pam.
Afr 2025.10	Pamphlet vol. Algeria. History, 1860- 12 pam.
Afr 2030.290	Pamphlet box. Algeria. History, 1945- .
Afr 2030.292	Pamphlet vol. Algeria. History, 1945 . 6 pam.
Afr 2030.430	Pamphlet vol. Algeria. History, 1945- 8 pam.
Afr 2037.5.5	Algeria. Ministère de l'Orientation Nationale. Algérie, an II, 1962-1964. Alger, 1965?
Afr 2037.5	Algeria. Ministère de l'Orientation Nationale. Une année de révolution socialiste, 1962 - 5 juillet - 1963. Alger, 1963?
Afr 2230.9	Pamphlet vol. Algeria. Races. 8 pam.
Afr 2260.5	Pamphlet vol. Algeria. Races. 8 pam.
Afr 2260.6	Pamphlet vol. Algeria. Races. 10 pam.
Afr 2225.1	Pamphlet vol. Algeria. Races. General. 9 pam.
Afr 2223.960.10	Algeria. Secrétariat Général Adjoint pour les Affaires Economiques. Leé comptes économiques de l'Algérie et du Sahara pour les années 1957 et 1958. Alger, 1960.
Afr 2748.82	Algeria. Service Central des Affaires Indigènes. Deuxième mission Flatters. Algiers, 1882.
Afr Doc 5307.5	Algeria. Service de la Statistique Génerale. Bulletin de statistique generale. Statistiques industrielles. 8,1956+
Afr Doc 5307.348	Algeria. Service de la Statistique Générale. Resultats statistique du dénombrement de la population effective le 31 octobre 1948. Alger, 1950? 2v.
Afr Doc 5307.354	Algeria. Service de la Statistique Générale. Resultats statistiques du denombrement de la population effective le 31 octobre 1954. Alger, 1957. 3v.
Afr Doc 5307.354.5	Algeria. Service de la Statistique Générale. Résultats statistiques du denombrement de la population effective le 31 octobre, 1954. Alger, 1958.
Afr 2223.5	Algeria. Service de la Statistique Générale. Tableaux de l'économie algérienne. 1960+
Afr 1840.23	Algeria. Service de l'Information. Elections cantonales en Algérie. Alger, 1960.
Afr 2221.3F	Algeria. Service de l'Information. Direction de la Documentation Générale. Aspects of Algeria. Algiers. 196-.
Afr 1830.20.53	Algeria. Service des Postes, Télégraphes. Exposé du développement des services postaux. Alger, 1930.
Afr 2030.462.110	Algeria. Treaties, etc. Les accords d'Evian. Paris, 1962.
Afr 2030.464.65	Algeria. Treaties, etc. Accords passés entre la France et l'Algérie de juillet 1962 au 31 décembre 1963. Paris, 1964.
Afr 2030.462.112	Algeria. Treaties, etc. Texts of declarations drawn up in common agreement at Evian. N.Y., 1962.
Afr 2209.44.5	Algeria. v.2. (Great Britain. Naval Intelligence Division.) London, 1944.
Afr 2030.50.5	Algeria. 1st Amer. ed. (Tillion, G.) N.Y., 1958.
Afr 2030.463	Algeria and France. (Pickles, D.M.) N.Y., 1963.
Afr 2209.06.15	Algeria and Tunis. (Nesbitt, Frances E.) London, 1906.
Afr 2208.46.3	Algeria and Tunis in 1845. (Kennedy, J.C.) London, 1846. 2v.
Afr 2220.12.5	Algeria and Tunisia. (Heywood, C.) Paris, 1926.
Afr 2223.957.5	Algeria at work. (France. Embassy.) N.Y., 1957.
Afr 2030.230	Algeria before the United Nations. (Alwan, Mohamed.) N.Y., 1959.
Afr 2209.27.10	Algeria from within. (Bodley, R.V.C.) London, 1927.
Afr 2030.210	Algeria in turmoil. (Clark, Michael.) N.Y., 1959.
Afr 2030.211	Algeria in turmoil. (Clark, Michael.) N.Y., 1960.
Afr 2209.22.10	Algeria to-day. (Casserly, Gordon.) London, 1922.
Afr 2209.44	Algerian adventure. (Collier, Joy.) London, 1944.
Afr 2030.255	Algerian developments, 1959. (Mezerik, Avrahm G.) N.Y., 1960.
Afr 2209.60	Algerian documents, 1960. (Algeria. Délégation Générale du Gouvernement en Algérie.) Paris, 1960.
Afr 2030.80	The Algerian-French conflict. (Mezerik, Avrahn G.) N.Y., 1958.
Afr 2030.340	Algerian Front of National Liberation. Algeria. N.Y., 1960.
Afr 2030.464.10	Algerian Front of National Liberation. La charte d'Alger, ensemble des textes adoptés par le premier congrés du Parti de Front de libération nationale. Alger, 1964.
Afr 2030.461.90	Algerian Front of National Liberation. Documents. N.Y. 1961-62
Afr 2030.340.5	Algerian Front of National Liberation. Miscellaneous papers. n.p., 1959-1961. 43 pam.
Afr 2030.340.10	Algerian Front of National Liberation. La révolution algérienne par les textes. Paris, 1961.
Afr 2030.340.10.5	Algerian Front of National Liberation. La révolution algérienne par les textes. 3. ed. Paris, 1962.
Afr 2030.467	The Algerian insurrection, 1954-62. (O'Ballance, Edgar.) London, 1967.
Afr 2208.95.9	Algerian memories. (Workman, F.B.) London, 1895.
Afr 2030.461.45	The Algerian problem. (Behr, Edward.) London, 1961.
Afr 2030.461.45.2	The Algerian problem. (Behr, Edward.) N.Y., 1962.
Afr 2209.27.40	Algerian State Railways. The mountain, the sea, Roman ruins, the desert. Algiers, 1927.
Afr 2030.346	Algerian voices. (Brace, Richard M.) Princeton, N.J., 1965.
Afr 2225.14.5	The Algerians. (Bourdieu, Pierre.) Boston, 1962.
Afr 2030.310	Algeria's development. (Algeria. Délégation Générale.) Algiers, 1959.
Afr 2223.964	Algeria's infrastruture. (Pawera, J.C.) N.Y., 1964.
Afr 2037.5.5	Algérie, an II, 1962-1964. (Algeria. Ministère de l'Orientation Nationale.) Alger, 1965?
Afr 2208.58.3	L'Algérie, ce qu'elle est. (Duvernois, C.) Alger, 1858.

Afr 1838.1	L'Algérie, des moyens de conserver cette conquête. (Bugeaud.) Paris, 1842.
Afr 1258.50	Algérie, Etats Tripolitains et Tunis. (Rozet.) Paris, 1850.
Afr 2208.83.7	Algérie, géographie générale. 3e ed. (Niel, O.) Paris, 1883.
Afr 2208.83.9	L'Algérie, impressions de voyage. 2e ed. (Clamageran, J.J.) Paris, 1883.
Afr 2000.19	L'Algérie, nation et société. (Lacheraf, Mostafa.) Paris, 1965.
Afr 555.35	Algérie, Sahara, Soudan. Vie travaux, voyages de Mgr. Hacquard. (Marin, Eugène.) Paris, 1905.
Afr 5046.9	Algérie, Sahara, Tchad, réponse à M. Camille Sabatier. (Fock, Andreas.) Paris, 1891.
Afr 2209.37.5	L'Algérie, terre d'art et d'histoire. (Berque, A.) Alger, 1937.
Afr 1933.63	Algérie, terre des occasions perdues. (Bloch, P.) Paris, 1961.
Afr 2220.12	Algérie, Tunisie. (Monmarche, Marcel.) Paris, 1923.
Afr 2220.12.3	Algérie, Tunisie. (Monmarche, Marcel.) Paris, 1930.
Afr 2220.14	Algérie, Tunisie. Paris, 1955.
Afr 2223.930.5	L'Algérie, un siécle de colonisation française. (Falck, Felix.) Paris, 1930.
Afr 2290.8	L'Algérie...deux mois dans province d'Oran. (Lambert, E.) Paris, 1877.
Afr 2209.57.5	Algérie. (Algeria. Cabinet du Gouverneur Général.) Alger, 1957.
Afr 2208.98	L'Algérie. (Battandier.) Paris, 1898.
Afr 2208.65	L'Algérie. (Behaghel, A.) Alger, 1865.
Afr 2209.31.15	L'Algérie. (Bernard, A.) Paris, 1931.
Afr 2209.31.10	L'Algérie. (Bernard, A.) Paris, 1931.
Afr 1869.29	L'Algerie. (Bernard, Augustin.) Paris, 1929.
Afr 2209.48	L'Algérie. (Blottière, J.E.) Paris, 1948.
Afr 2209.20F	L'Algérie. (Bovet, Marie A.) Paris, 1920.
Afr 2209.12.9	Algérie. (Brieux, E.) Vincennes, 1912.
Afr 2223.931	L'Algérie. (Desfeuilles, P.) Paris, 1931.
Afr 2208.72.3	Algérie. (Dubouzet, Charles.) n.p., 1872. 2 pam.
Afr 2209.31.5	L'Algérie. (Dumas, Pierre.) Grenoble, 1931.
Afr 2030.110	L'Algérie. (Duquesne, Jacques.) Bruges, 1958.
Afr 2208.83	L'Algérie. (Gaffarel, P.) Paris, 1883.
Afr 2209.34F	Algérie. (Horizons de France, Paris.) Paris, 1934.
Afr 1869.60	L'Algérie. (Lacoste, Yves.) Paris, 1960.
Afr 2209.58.10	L'Algérie. (Laurent, Jacques.) Paris, 1958.
Afr 2208.83.5	L'Algérie. (Mercier, E.) Paris, 1883.
Afr 2208.84	Algérie. (Niox, G.L.) Paris, 1884.
Afr 2208.94.3	L'Algérie. (Pensa, Henri.) Paris, 1894.
Afr 2208.82	L'Algérie. (Wahl, M.) Paris, 1882.
Afr 2288.5	Algérie. Direction des Territoires du Sud. Les territoires du sud. Exposé de leur situation. (Extrait) Description géographique par E.-F. Gautier. Alger, 1922.
Afr 2288.15	Algérie. Direction des Territoires du Sud. Les territoires du sud. Exposé de leur situation. Pt.1. Alger, 1922.
Afr 2209.55	L'Algérie. 2. ed. (Blottière, J.E.) Paris, 1955.
Afr 2208.85	L'Algérie. 2e ed. (Quesnoy, F.) Paris, 1890.
Afr 2208.82.4	L'Algérie. 4e ed. (Wahl, M.) Paris, 1903.
Afr 2208.82.5	L'Algérie. 5e ed. (Wahl, M.) Paris, 1908.
Afr 2030.170	L'Algérie à bâtir. (Rosfelder, André.) Alger, 1959.
Afr 2035.15	L'Algérie à l'épreuve du pouvoir (1962-1967). (Bourges, Hervé.) Paris, 1967.
Afr 2224.862	L'Algérie à l'Exposition universelle de Londres, 1862. (Algeria. Commission à l'Exposition Universelle de Londres.) Alger, 1862. 2v.
Afr 2030.325	L'Algérie à vingt ans. (Manevy, Alain.) Paris, 1960.
Afr 1830.20.56	L'Algérie agricole. (Demontes, Victor.) Paris, 1930.
Afr 1868.44	L'Algerie ancienne et moderne. (Galibert, L.) Paris, 1844.
Afr 1868.60	L'Algerie ancienne et moderne. 2e ed. (Fillias, A.) Alger, 1875.
Afr 2396.2	Algérie biographique. Sidi-bel-Abbès, 1956.
Afr 2035.9	L'Algérie caporalisée. (Guerin, Daniel.) Paris, 1965.
Afr 2260.10	L'Algérie contemporaine. (Vian, L.) Paris, 1863.
Afr 1826.5.9	L'Algerie dans la litterature française, essai de bibliog. (Taillart, C.) Paris, 1925.
Afr 1826.5.7	L'Algerie dans la litterature française. (Taillart, C.) Paris, 1925.
Afr 1826.5	L'Algerie dans la litterature française. Thèse. (Taillart, C.) Paris, 1925.
Afr 1826.5.5	L'Algerie dans la litterature française. Thèse. (Taillart, C.) Paris, 1925.
Afr 1801.8	Algérie dans le monde. Alger.
Afr 2000.13	L'Algérie dans l'impasse. (Wisner, S.) Paris, 1949.
Afr 2209.02.2	L'Algérie d'aujourd'hui. (Gay, E.) Paris, 1907.
Afr 2030.462.75	L'Algérie de demain. (Perroux, Francois.) Paris, 1962.
Afr 2209.61.5	L'Algérie des Bidonvilles. (Descloitres, R.) Paris, 1961.
Afr 2030.145	L'Algérie des colonels. (Lentin, Albert Paul.) Paris, 1958.
Afr 2030.147	L'Algérie des colonels. (Lentin, Albert Paul.) Paris, 1959.
Afr 2025.4	L'Algérie devant l'empereur. (Warnier, A.) Paris, 1865.
Afr 2025.31.5	L'Algerie du centenaire. (Depont, O.) Paris, 1928.
Afr 2030.205	L'Algérie du 13 mai. (Gerin, Paul.) Paris, 1958.
Afr 2030.461.35	L'Algérie en prison. (Charby, J.) Paris, 1961.
Afr 2260.2	L'Algérie en 1865. (Cosentino.) Paris, 1865.
Afr 2208.80.5	L'Algérie en 1880. (Mercier, E.) Paris, 1880.
Afr 2208.92	L'Algérie en 1891. (Burdeau, A.) Paris, 1892.
Afr 2030.50	L'Algérie en 1957. (Tillion, G.) Paris, 1957.
Afr 2030.464	L'Algérie entre deux mondes. (Lentin, Albert.) Paris, 1964.
Afr 2035.5	L'Algérie est-elle socialiste? (Chaliand, Gérard.) Paris, 1964.
Afr 1915.6	L'Algérie et alliance française. (Wahl, Maurice.) Bordeaux, 1887.
Afr 2026.1	L'Algérie et la guerre (1914-18). (Melia, Jean.) Paris, 1918.
Afr 2025.27	L'Algérie et la métropole. (Gautier, Emile F.) Paris, 1920.
Afr 2030.95	L'Algérie et la République. (Aron, Raymond.) Paris, 1958.
Afr 2208.87.2	L'Algérie et la Tunis. (Leroy-Beaulieu.) Paris, 1897.
Afr 2208.93.4	L'Algérie et la Tunisie à travers les ages. (Boutroue, A.) Paris, 1893.
Afr 1990.15	L'Algérie et l'opinion. (Fabar, Paul.) Paris, 1847.
Afr 2748.82.7	Algérie et Sahara. (Rabourdin, L.) Paris, 1882.
Afr 1869.51	L'Algérie et son passé. (Berthier, A.) Paris, 1951.
Afr 2208.93	Algérie et Tunisie. (Baraudon, A.) Paris, 1893.
Afr 2220.7	Algérie et Tunisie. (Joanne, P.) Paris, 1911.
Afr 1955.12	L'Algérie française, histoire. (Berteuil, A.) Paris, 1856. 2v.
Afr 2025.3	L'Algérie française. (Casteran, A.) Paris, 1900.
Afr 1990.5	L'Algérie française. (Feullide, C. de.) Paris, 1856.
Afr 2000.10	L'Algérie française. (Piquet, V.) Paris, 1930.
Afr 2000.5	L''Algérie française vue par un indigène. (Benhabiles, Cherif.) Alger, 1914.
Afr 2223.958	Algérie françise. Sidi-bel-Abbès, 1958.
Afr 1825.3PF	Algerie historique, pittoresque. (Berbrugger.) Paris, 1843. 3v.
Afr 2030.175	L'Algérie hors la loi. (Jeanson, Colette.) Paris, 1955.
Afr 1830.20.57	L'Algerie industrielle et commercante. (Demontes, Victor.) Paris, 1930.
Afr 2274.3	L'Algérie juive. (Meynie, G.) Paris, 1887.
Afr 2396.1	L'Algérie légendaire. (Trumelet, C.) Alger, 1892.
Afr 2223.25	L'Algérie libre, étude économique sur l'Algérie. (Dessoliers, F.L.) Alger, 1895.
Afr 2030.420	L'Algérie mal enchaînée. (Boudot, Pierre.) Paris, 1961.
Afr 2209.57	Algérie médiévale. (Marçais, Georges.) Paris, 1957.
Afr 2209.14.3	L'Algérie musulmane. (Lavion, H.) Paris, 1914.
Afr 1571.3	Une Algérie nouvelle. (Hess, Jean.) Paris, 1909.
Afr 2030.462.125	Algérie nouvelle et la presse française. Paris, 1962.
Afr 1868.43	Algerie pittoresque. (Clausolles, M.P.) Toulouse, 1845.
Afr 2035.9.5	L'Algérie qui se cherche. (Guérin, Daniel.) Paris, 1964.
Afr 2030.40	L'Algérie restera française. (Vialet, Georges.) Paris, 1957.
Afr 2030.464.25	L'Algérie sans la France. (Boualam, Bachaga.) Paris, 1964.
Afr 2209.36	L'Algérie sous l'égide de la France contre la féodalité algérienne. (Faci, S.) Toulouse, 1936.
Afr 2208.90	L'Algérie telle qu'elle est. (Bergot, Raoul.) Paris, 1890.
Afr 2030.65	L'Algérie trahie par l'argent. (Beau de Lomenie, Emmanuel.) Paris, 1957.
Afr 2000.14	L'Algérie vivra-t-elle? (Viollette, M.) Paris, 1931.
Afr 2209.54	Algérie 54. (Encyclopédie Mensuelle d'Outre-Mer.) Paris, 1954.
Afr 2260.11	Algerien, eine Studie über die Französische Land- und Siedelungspolitik. (Mohr, P.) Berlin, 1907.
Afr 1105.5	Algerien, Marokko, Tunesien. (Meinicke-Kleint, Heinz.) Berlin, 1965.
Afr 2223.35	Algerien, Tunesien, Tripolitanien. (Schanz, M.) Halle, 1905.
Afr 2209.08.5	Algerien. (Kuehnel, Ernst.) Leipzig, 1908.
Afr 2208.81	Algerien. (Schwarz, B.) Leipzig, 1881.
Afr 2030.459	Algerien. 1. Aufl. (Scheer, Maximillian.) Berlin, 1959.
Afr 2030.115	Algerien in Flammen. 2.Aufl. (Kernmayr, Erich.) Göttingen, 1958.
Afr 2030.405	Un Algérien raconte. (Noureddine, Meziane.) Paris, 1960.
Afr 2208.55	Algerien und seine Zukunft unter französischer Herrschaft. (Buvry, L.) Berlin, 1855.
Afr 2218.6.20	Les Algériennes. (M'rabet, Fadéla.) Paris, 1967.
Afr 2030.461.25	Les Algériens en guerre. (Darbois, Dominique.) Milano, 1961.
Afr 2025.38	Les Algériens musulmans et la France, 1871-1919. (Ageron, Charles Robert.) Paris, 1968. 2v.
Afr 2030.395	Algerije. (Hermans, Fons.) Amsterdam, 1960.
Afr 2030.250	Die algerische Frage. (Oppermann, Thomas.) Stuttgart, 1959.
Afr 2208.93.10	Algier og Sahara. Billeder fra nomade- og krigerlivet. (Bruun, Daniel.) Kjøbenhavn, 1893.
Afr 2208.35.10	Algier wie es ist. Stuttgart, 1835.
Afr 2208.35.2	Algiers, notices of neighboring states of Barbary. (Lord, P.B.) London, 1835. 2v.
Afr 3979.12	Algiers, the Sahara and the Nile. (Humphreys, R.) London, 1912.
Afr 1068.17	Algiers...a complete picture of the Barbary states. (Jackson, G.A.) London, 1817.
Afr 2209.06.3	Algiers. (Crouse, M.E.) N.Y., 1906.
Afr 2308.21	Algiers. Chambre de Commerce. Le port d'Alger,1930. Alger, 1930.
Htn Afr 1935.1*	Algiers. Dey. Letter written by the governour...law-counteys. London, 1679.
Afr 1819.3	Algiers. Ecole Supérieure des Lettres d'Alger. Bulletin de correspondance africaine. Alger. 1882+ 4v.
Afr 1955.61	Algiers. Université. Faculté de Droit. Recherches sur la colonisation de l'Algérie au XIXe siècle. Alger, 1960.
Afr 2700.10	Algiers. Université. Institut de Recherches Sahariennes. Documents pour servir à la connaissance du Sahara. 1,1961+
Afr 555.4.10	Algiers (Diocese). Statuts synodaux du diocése d'Alger. Alger, 1853.
Afr 2209.06	Algiers and beyond. (Hilton-Simpson, M.W.) London, 1906.
Afr 2308.11	Algiers as a winter resort. (Gubb, A.S.) London, n.d.
Afr 2308.8	Algiers in 1857. (Davies, E.W.L.) London, 1858.
Afr 5944.15	Algo sobre Rio de Oro. (Domenech Lafuente, A.) Madrid, 1946.
Afr 7175.22F	Alguns aspectos psicologicos de nossa colonização en Angola. (Associação Comercial de Lajistas de Lisboa.) Lisboa, 1930.
Afr 7322.8	Alguns muzimos da Zambezia e o culto dos mortos. (Santos, Joaquim Rodrigues dos.) Lisboa, 1940.
Afr 550.115	Alguns problemas sociologicos missionarios da Africa negra. (Silva Rego, Antonio da.) Lisboa, 1960.
Afr 3822.5	Ali Dinar, last sultan of Darfor, 1895-1916. (Theobald, Alan B.) London, 1965.
Afr 6882.2	Ali Moçambique; Bilder aus dem Leben eines schwarzen Fabeldichters. (Hauer, August.) Berlin, 1922.
Afr 9170.25	Alice Princess. (Siwundhla, Alice Princess.) Omaha, 1965.
Afr 6542.10	The alien town. (Larimore, Ann Evans.) Chicago, 1958.
Afr 2209.61.10	L'aliénation colonialiste et la résistance de la famille algérienne. (Saadia.) Lausanne, 1961.
Afr 1340.25	Les alignements en droit marocain. Thèse. (Grillet, M.) Paris, 1935.
Afr 1400.2	Aljaiyani. Le Maroc de 1631 à 1812. Paris, 1886.
Afr 545.46	All-Africa Church Conference, Kampala, Uganda. La conférence de Kampala, 1963. Kitwe, 1963.
Afr 730.10	All the way round, sea roads to Africa. (Smith, C.F.) London, 1938.
Afr 6984.5	All the way to Abenab. (Haythornthwaite, Frank.) London, 1956.
Afr 4390.20	Alla corte di Menelik. (Piozza, G.) Ancona, 1912.
Afr 609.66.45	Alla scoperta dell'Africa. 2d ed. (Quilici, Folco.) Firenze, 1968.
Afr 2030.462.55	Allais, Maurice. Les accords d'Evian. Paris, 1962.
Afr 6143.12	Alldridge, T.J. A transformed colony. London, 1910.
Afr 6143.3	Alldrige, T.J. The Sherbro and its hinterland. London, 1901.

Afr 4559.20 — Alle sorgenti del Nilo azzurro. (Tedesco Zammarano, V.) Roma, 1920.

Afr 8678.140.5 — Alleen voor blanken. (Roskam, Karel Lodewijk.) Amsterdam, 1961.

Afr 2030.461.15 — Alleg, Henri. Prisionniers de guerre. Paris, 1961.

Afr 2030.60 — Alleg, Henri. The question. N.Y., 1958.

Afr 2030.60.5 — Alleg, Henri. La question. Paris, 1965.

Afr 2030.60.2 — Alleg, Henri. Texte intégral du livre "La question." Paris, 1958.

Afr 7568.27 — Pamphlet box. Alleged conditions in Kongo Free State.

Afr 1583.18 — L'Allemagne et le Maroc de 1870-1905. Thèse. (Guillen, Pierre.) Paris, 1967.

Afr 3695.7A — Allen, B.M. Gordon and the Sudan. London, 1931.

Afr 7377.25 — Allen, Gardner M. The trustees of donations for education in Liberia. Boston, 1923.

Afr 810.9 — Allen, W. Narrative of expedition...river Niger. London, 1848. 2v.

Afr 810.11F — Allen, W. Picturesque views on the river Niger. London, 1840.

Afr 7350.5.10 — Allen, W.H. Address before Pennsylvania Colonization Society, Oct. 25. Philadelphia, 1863.

Afr 1608.95.5 — Allende el estrecho, viajes por Marruecos (1889-94). (Boada y Romeu, J.) Barcelona, 1895.

Afr 1753.10.2 — Alleo, gloriosa epopeia portuguezaum Ceuta. (Dornellas, Affonso De.) Lisboa, 1924.

Afr 5575.10 — Aller neueste Nachricht von Madagascar und dem Leben des jetzigen Beherrschers dieses Insul. (Broke, A. van.) Frankfurt, 1748.

Afr 1723.15 — The alleys of Marrakesh. 1st ed. (Mayne, Peter.) Boston, 1953.

Afr 2209.28 — Die Allgier trieb nach Algier...Ausflug nach Afrika. 1.Aufl. (Kerr, Alfred.) Berlin, 1929.

Afr 1915.5 — L'alliance franco-algérienne. (Heinrich, P.) Lyon, 1898.

Afr 8378.379.5 — Allighan, Garry. Verwoerd - the end, a look-back from the future. London, 1961.

Afr 9525.875.10 — Allighan, Garry. The Welensky story. Cape Town, 1962.

Afr 8089.60 — Allighan, H. Curtain-up on South Africa. London, 1960.

Afr 3818.10 — Allison, Oliver Claude. A pilgrim church's progress. London, 1966.

Afr 45.62.10 — Allott, Anthony N. Judicial and legal systems in Africa. London, 1962.

Afr 45.65.10 — Allott, Anthony N. Law and language. London, 1965.

Afr 6455.9 — Allsopp, Charles. Sport and travel, Abyssinia and British East Africa. London, 1906.

Afr 7190.25 — Almada Negreiros, A.D. Colonies portugaises, ile de San-Thome. Paris, 1901.

Afr 7190.27 — Almada Negreiros, A.D. Historia ethnographica da ilha de San Thome. Lisboa, 1895.

Afr 2945.8 — Almagia, R. Cirenaica. Milano, 1912.

Afr 4234.2 — Almagia, R. Contributi alla storia della conscenza dell Etiopia. Padova, 1941.

Afr Doc 1403.6 — Almanac. (Egypt. Government Press.) Cairo. 1933-1949

Afr 1801.5 — Almanach de l'Algerie. Alger. 1900+

Afr 7309.57 — Almeida, Eugenio Ferreira de. Governo do distrito de Moçambique. Lisboa, 1957.

Afr 150.11 — Almeida, Fortunato. O Infante de Sagres. Porto, 1894.

Afr 7130.15.2 — Almeida, João de. Sul de Angola, relatório de um governo de distrito, 1908-1910. 2. ed. Lisboa, 1936.

Afr 4230.4.5 — Almeida, M. De. Historia Aethiopiae. Liber 1-10. Romae, 1907. 3v.

Afr 4295.2 — Almeida, M. de. Vida de Takla Haymanot. Lisboa, 1899.

Htn Afr 4556.60F* — Almeida, Manoel. Historia geral de Ethiopia. Coimbra, 1660.

Afr 12974.51.100 — Almeida, Modeste d'. Kétéyouli, l'étudiant noir. Lomé, 1965.

Afr 7203.10 — Almeida de Eca, F.G. Achegas para a bibliografia de Moçambique. Lisboa, 1949.

Afr 7322.6 — Almeida de Eca, Felipe Gastão. Historia das guerras no Zambeze. Lisboa, 1953-54. 2v.

Afr 7349.327 — Almeida de Eça, Felipe Gastão de. O capitão César Maria de Serpa Rosa. Lisboa, 1969.

Afr 7222.50 — Almeida de Eca, O.G. De degredado a governado. Lisboa, 1950.

Afr 1088.12 — The Almohad movement in North Africa in the twelfth and thirteenth centuries. (Tourneau, Roger.) Princeton, N.J., 1969.

Afr 1390.6 — Les Almohades, histoire dune dynastie berbère. (Millet, Rene.) Paris, 1923.

Afr 1390.8 — Los Almoravides. (Bosch Vila, Jacinto.) Tetuan, 1956.

Afr 11435.22.120 — Almost forgotten, never told. (Green, George L.) Cape Town, 1965.

Afr 8687.126 — Almost in confidence. (Barlow, Arthur G.) Cape Town, 1952.

Afr 4513.35.60F — Aloise, P. Speech of Baron Aloise, head of the Italian delegation to the League of Nations. n.p., 1935.

Afr 6455.30 — Alone in the sleeping-sickness country. (Oswald, Felix.) London, 1915.

Afr 7809.60.10 — Alphonse Vangele (1848-1939). (Cuypers, J.P.) Bruxelles, 1960.

Afr 9448.77 — Alport, Cuthbert James McCall. The sudden assignment. London, 1965.

Afr 2030.130 — Alquier, Jean Yves. Nous avons pacifié Tazalt. Paris, 1957.

Afr 6645.10 — Als Jurnalist und Forscher in Deutschlands grosser Kolonialzeit. (Zoeller, Hugo.) Leipzig, 1930.

Afr 6742.5 — Als Sklave verkauft; Sklaverei und Sklavenhandel im heutigen Afrika und Arabien. (Endresen, Halfdan.) Basel, 1966.

Afr 8659.29 — Alston, M. From an old Cape homestead. London, 1929.

Afr 8659.16 — Alston, Madeline. From the heart of the veld. London, 1916.

Afr 725.18 — Alte Kenntnis und Kartographie der zentralafrikanischen Seenregion. Inaug. Diss. (Langenmaier, Theo.) Erlangen, 1916.

Afr 7560.10 — Das Alte Königreich Kongo. Inaug. Diss. (Ihle, Alexander.) Leipzig, 1929.

Afr 109.05 — Altere Entdeckungsgeschichte und Kartographie Afrikas. (Hartig, D.) Wien, 1905.

Afr 8687.109 — Altmann, Hendrik. Overdrafts and overwork. Cape Town, 1959.

Afr 5282.4 — Alto volta. (Italy. Istituto Nazionale per il Commercio Estero.) Roma, 1964.

Afr 6415.25 — Altrimcham, E.G. Kenya's opportunity. London, 1955.

Afr 618.9 — Altruisme bij enkele natuurvolken van Afrika en Australie. Academisch proefschrift. (Terweer, M.C.) Amsterdam, 1939.

Afr 6210.14 — Aluko, S.A. The problems of self-government for Nigeria. Ilfracombe, 1955.

Afr 10671.52.120 — Aluko, Timothy Mofolorunso. Kinsman and foreman. London, 1966.

Afr 10671.52.100 — Aluko, Timothy Mofolorunso. One man, one matchet. London, 1964.

Afr 10671.52.110 — Aluko, Timothy Mofolorunso. One man, one wife. Lagos, 1959.

Afr 6540.20 — Alur society. (Southall, A.W.) Cambridge, Eng., 1956.

Htn Afr 4555.40.4* — Alvares, Francisco. Historia de las cosas de Ethiopia. Çragoça, 1561.

Htn Afr 4555.40.5* — Alvares, Francisco. Historia de las cosas de Ethiopia. Toledo, 1588.

Htn Afr 4555.40.8* — Alvares, Francisco. Historiale description de l'Ethiopie. Anvers, 1558.

Htn Afr 4555.40* — Alvares, Francisco. Ho Preste Joam das Indias. Verdadeira informaçam. Lisbon, 1540.

Afr 4555.40.22 — Alvares, Francisco. Kurtze und wahrhafftige Beschreibung der Ethiopie. Eiszlebe, 1567.

Afr 4555.40.3.5 — Alvares, Francisco. Verdadeira informação das terras do Preste Joao das Indias. Lisboa, 1943.

Afr 4555.40.3F — Alvares, Francisco. Verdadeiro informação das terras do Preste João das Indias. Lisboa, 1889.

Afr 5180.14.2 — Alvares d'Almada, Andre. Relação e descripção de Guiné. Lisboa, 1733.

Afr 5180.14 — Alvares d'Almada, Andre. Rios de Guine do Cabo-Verde. Porto, 1841.

Afr 1432.10 — Alvarez, J.A. de. Biografia y retratos de los generales jefes de los cuerpos. Barcelona, 1860.

Afr 1573.20 — Alvarez, Melquiades. El problema de Marruecos. Madrid, 1914.

Afr 1347.3.8 — Alvarez Cabrera, J. Accion militar...imperio de Marruecos. Madrid, 1898.

Afr 1753.6 — Alvarez Cabrera, J. Columnas de operaciones en Marruecos. Tanger, 1909.

Afr 1347.3 — Alvarez Cabrera, J. La guerra en Africa. Madrid, 1893.

Afr 2030.230 — Alwan, Mohamed. Algeria before the United Nations. N.Y., 1959.

Afr 2030.461.70 — Alzhir sbrasyvaet okovy. (Landa, R.G.) Moscow, 1961.

Afr 2030.462.40 — Alzhirskii narod v borbe za nezavisimosti. (Potemkin, Iu. V.) Moscow, 1962.

VAfr 2223.966 — Alžir. Beograd, 1966.

Afr 1869.67 — Alžir do nezavisnosti. (Pečar, Zdravko.) Beograd, 1967.

Afr 500.9 — Alzola, Pablo de. Africa, su reparto y colonización. Bilbao, 1891.

Afr 6275.12 — Am Niger und Benue. (Burda, A.) Leipzig, 1886.

Afr 3199.38 — Amad, E.S. La question d'Egypte, 1841-1938. Thèse. Paris, 1938.

Afr 3040.35.5 — Amad, P.E. Les pouvoirs des tribunaux mixtes d'Egypte. Thèse. Paris, 1930.

Afr 10671.53.100 — Amadi, Elechi. The concubine. London, 1966.

Afr 10671.53.110 — Amadi, Elechi. The great ponds. London, 1969.

Afr 10671.53.1100 — Amali, Samson Onyilokwu Onche. The downfall of Ogbúu; a play. Ibadan, 1968?

Afr 6176.10 — Amamoo, J.G. The new Ghana. London, 1958.

Afr 7180.25 — Amaral, I. do. Aspectos do povoamento branco de Angola. Lisboa, 1960.

Afr 7175.72 — Amaral, I. do. Ensaio de um estudo geografico da rede urbana de Angola. Lisboa, 1962.

Afr 3155.2F — Amari, M. De titoli che usava la cancelleria di sultani di Egitto. Roma, 1886.

Afr 6196.13 — Amarteifio, Godfrey William. Tema Manhean; a study of resettlement. Kumasi, 1966.

Afr 2232.2 — Amat, C. Le Mzab et les Mzabites. Paris, 1888.

Afr 1435.3 — Amaudru, N. Sultane française du Maroc. Paris, 1906.

Afr 8378.200.10 — The amazing Mr. Fischer. (Ludi, Gerard.) Cape Town, 1966.

Afr 8155.7 — Amazulu. The Zulus, their history. (Jenkinson, T.B.) London, 1882.

Afr 1608.87 — Une ambassade au Maroc. (Charmes, G.) Paris, 1887.

Afr 1585.5 — Une ambassade autrichienne au Maroc en 1805. (Caille, Jacques.) Paris, 1957.

Afr 555.23.65 — Ambassador of the king. (Chilson, E. H.) Wichita, Kan., 1943.

Afr 710.55.6 — Ambiguous Africa, cultures in collision. (Balandier, Georges.) London, 1966.

Afr 3275.47 — Ambrosini, G. La situazione internazionale dell'Egitto. Firenze, 1937.

Afr 5243.125 — L'âme d'un peuple africain...les Bambara. (Henry, Joseph.) Münster, 1910.

Afr 1618.28 — L'ame marocaine, une à travers les croyances et la politessc. (Bonjean, François.) Paris, 1948.

Afr 2609.34.10 — L'âme musulmane en Tunisie. (Geniaux, C.) Paris, 1934.

Afr 115.115 — Amedeo, Duke of Aosta. Studi africani. Bologna, 1942.

Afr 5316.12 — Ameillon, B. La Guinée. Paris, 1964.

Afr 1432.19 — Ameller, V. de. Juicio critico de la guerra de Africa. Madrid, 1861.

Afr Doc 9207.5 — Amerário estatistico da colónia de Moçambique. (Mozambique. Repartição Tecnica de Estatistica.) Lourenço Marques. 12,1939+ 13v.

Afr 10673.48.110 — America, their America. (Clark, John Pepper.) London, 1964.

Afr 7368.88 — America and Africa. (Hodge, J.A.) Washington, 1888.

Afr 609.55.15 — American Academy of Political and Social Science. Contemporary Africa. Philadelphia, 1955.

Afr 210.64.70 — American Academy of Political and Social Science. Africa in motion. Philadelphia, 1964.

Afr 210.56.10 — American Academy of Political and Social Sciences. Africa and the Western world. Philadelphia, 1956.

Afr 1609.25.3A — An american among the Riffi. (Sheean, V.) N.Y., 1926.

Afr 210.58A — American Assembly. The United States and Africa. N.Y., 1958.

Afr 210.58.22 — American Assembly. The United States and Africa. N.Y., 1963.

Afr 1567.3 — American claims and the protection of native subjects in Morocco. (Pericaris, I.) n.p., n.d.

Afr 7350.3.21 — The American Colonization Society, 1817-40. Diss. (Fox, Early L.) Baltimore, 1919.

Afr 608.81.3 — American Colonization Society. Annual papers on condition of Africa by the Secretary of the American Colonization Society. Washington. 1881+

NEDL Afr 7350.3 — American Colonization Society. Annual report. Washington. 1,1818+ 9v.

Afr 7350.3.3 — American Colonization Society. Bulletins - Liberia. Washington. 5,1894+

Afr 7458.52 — American Colonization Society. Information about emigration to Liberia. Washington, 1852. 2 pam.

NEDL Afr 7350.3.16 — American Colonization Society. Memorial of the semi-centennial anniversary. Washington, 1867.

Afr 7350.3.20 The American Colonization Society. (Fox, Early L.) Baltimore, 1919.

Afr 1369.53 American Committee for Moroccan Independence. The case for Morocco. Washington, 1953.

Afr 6200.1.10 American Committee on Africa. ACOA Nigeria-Biafra relief memo. N.Y. 1,1968+

Afr 8325.62 American Hospital Ship Fund for South Africa. The concert. Souvenir programme. n.p., n.d.

Afr 3978.42 The American in Egypt. (Cooley, J.E.) N.Y., 1842.

Afr 3817.12 American Jewish Congress. Committee on International Affairs and on Israel. The black record, Nasser's persecution. N.Y., 1957.

Afr 1.68.5 American Society of Africa Culture. AMSAC newsletter. N.Y. 8,1965+

Afr 210.62.10 American Society of African Culture. Pan-Africanism reconsidered. Berkeley, 1962.

Afr 600.66.25 American Society of African Culture. Southern Africa in transition. London, 1966.

Afr 628.10 American Society of African Culture. Summary report, annual conference. N.Y.

Afr 1940.10 American University, Wahington D.C. Foreign Area Studies. Area handbook for Burundi. Washington, 1969.

Afr 4559.64 American University, Washington, D.C. Area handbook for Ethiopia. 2. ed. Washington, D.C., 1964.

Afr 7175.78 American University, Washington, D.C. Foreign Affairs Studies Division. Area handbook for Angola. Washington, 1967.

Afr 1869.65 American University, Washington, D.C. Foreign Area Studies Division. Area handbook for Algeria. Washington, 1965.

Afr 6879.68 American University, Washington, D.C. Foreign Area Studies Division. Area handbook for Tanzania. Washington, 1968.

Afr 6535.69 American University, Washington, D.C. Foreign Area Studies Division. Area handbook for Uganda. Washington, 1969.

Afr 7940.10 American University, Washington, D.C. Foreign Area Studies. Area handbook for Burundi. Washington, 1969.

Afr 7940.15 American University, Washington, D.C. Foreign Area Studies. Area handbook for Rwanda. Washington, 1969.

Afr 9689.69 American University, Washington, D.C. Foreign Area Studies. Area handbook for Zambia. Washington, 1969.

Afr 6455.152 American University, Washington, D.C. Foreign Areas Studies Division. Area handbook for Kenya. Washington, 1967.

Afr 7309.69 American University, Washington, D.C. Foreign Areas Studies Division. Area handbook for Mozambique. Washington, 1969.

Afr 1609.65 American University, Washington D.C. Foreign Area Studies Division. Area handbook for Morocco. Washington, 1965.

Afr 4070.59.2 American University, Washington D.C. Foreign Areas Studies Division. Area handbook for the Republic of the Sudan. 2. ed. Washington, 1964.

Afr 3979.64.15 American University. Foreign Area Studies Division. Area handbook for the United Arab Republic. Washington, 1964.

Afr 7459.64 American University. Foreign Areas Studies Division. Area handbook for Liberia. Washington, 1964.

Afr 8315.5 An American with Lord Roberts. (Ralph, Julian.) N.Y., 1901.

Afr 530.50.20 Americans in Africa, 1865-1900. (Clendenen, C.C.) Stanford, Calif., 1966.

Afr 530.50.10 Americans in Africa. (Collins, Robert O.) Stanford, Calif., 1963.

Afr 530.50.15 Americans in black Africa up to 1865. (Clendenen, C.C.) Stanford, California, 1964.

Afr 3252.22 Americans in the Egyptian army. (Crabitès, Pierre.) London, 1938.

Afr 150.2.85 Americas, un corolario de sagres. (Azevedo, A.J. da Silva D.) Lisboa, 1964.

Afr 500.75 America's role in Africa. v. 1-2. (Dekiewiet, Cornelis W.) Durban, 1960.

Afr 530.50.5 Amerikanskii imperializm v Afrike. (Fetov, V.P.) Moscow, 1962.

Afr 6390.100 Ames, Evelyn (Perkins). A glimpse of Eden. Boston, 1967.
Afr 3069.04 Amherst, L. A sketch of Egyptian history. London, 1904.
Afr 1609.20.5 Amic, Henri. Le Maroc, hier et aujourd hui. Paris, 1925.
Afr 1608.82.4F Amicis, E. de. Marruecos. Barcelona, 1892.
Afr 1608.82.3 Amicis, E. de. Morocco. Milano, 1890.
Afr 1608.82.2 Amicis, E. de. Morocco. N.Y., 1882.
Afr 1608.82 Amicis, E. de. Morocco. N.Y., 1882.
Afr 1608.82.2.5 Amicis, E. de. Morocco. 9 ed. Milano, 1882.
Afr 1947.9.5 Amiet, J.J. Geschichte des Lorenz Arregger von Solothurn. Bern, 1920.

Afr 1947.9 Amiet, J.J. Lorenz Arregger, Sklave in Algier. Bern, 1874.

Afr 4199.105 Amin, Osman. Muhammad Abduh. Le Caire, 1944.
Afr 4199.105.5 Amin, Osman. Muhammad Abduh. Washington, 1953.
Afr 5343.14 Amin, Samir. Le Développement du capitalisme en Côte d'Ivoire. Paris, 1967.
Afr 1273.966 Amin, Samir. L'économie du Maghreb. Paris, 1966.
Afr 5240.3 Amin, Samir. Trois expériences africaines de développement. Paris, 1965.

Afr 626.134 Amin Samir. Quelques expériences de décolonisation et de développement économique. v.1-2. Dakar, 1964.

Afr 3315.60 Amir, Adil. Le continent continué. Caire, 1957.
Afr 4390.35 Les amis de Menelik II, roi des rois d'Ethiopie. (Yaltsasamma.) Paris, 1899.

Afr 555.5.9 Les amitiés sahariennes du Père de Foucauld. (Gorrée, Georges.) Grenoble, 1946. 2v.

Afr 4180.5 Ammar, H. Growing up in an Egyptian village. London, 1954.

Afr 4787.6 L'amministrazione fiduciaria della Somalia. (Italy. Ministero degli Affari Esteri.) Roma, 1961.

Afr 4760.10 L'amministrazione fiduciaria italiana della Somalia. (Meregazzi, R.) Milano, 1954.

Afr 12871.56.100 Amoi, Fatho. Mon beau pays d'Ivoire. Saint-Genix-sur-Guiers, Savoie, 1967.

Afr 5337.3 Amon d'Aby, F. La Côte-d'Ivoire dans la cité africaine. Paris, 1951.

Afr 7815.8 Among Congo cannibals. (Weeks, J.H.) London, 1913.
Afr 6298.3 Among Nigerian celebrities. (Anyiam, F.U.) Yaba, 1960.
Afr 9400.5 Among swamps and giants in Equatorial Africa. (Austin, H.H.) London, 1902.
Afr 2208.68 Among the Arabs. (Naphegyi, G.) Philadelphia, 1868.
Afr 9400.5 Among the Bantu nomads. (Brown, John.) London, 1926.
Afr 2230.5 Among the Berbers of Algeria. (Wilkin, A.) London, 1900.
Afr 2230.30 Among the hill-folk of Algeria. (Hilton-Simpson, M.W.) London, 1921.
Afr 3978.71.8 Among the huts in Egypt. (Whately, Mary L.) London, 1871.
Afr 6280.9.5 Among the Ibos of Nigeria. (Basden, George Thomas.) London, 1921.

Afr 6280.9.8 Among the Ibos of Nigeria. (Basden, George Thomas.) N.Y., 1966.

Afr 6280.9.7 Among the Ibos of Nigeria. (Basden, George Thomas.) Philadelphia, 1921.

Afr 9488.94.2 Among the Matabele. 2. ed. (Carnegie, D.) London, 1894.
Afr 1608.94 Among the Moors. (Montbard, G.) London, 1894.
Afr 1608.94.1 Among the Moors. (Montbard, G.) N.Y., 1894.
Afr 7815.8.5 Among the primitive Bakongo. (Weeks, J.H.) London, 1914.
Afr 9838.99 Among the wild Ngoni. (Elmslie, W.A.) N.Y., 1899.
Afr 9838.99.3 Among the wild Ngoni. 3rd ed. (Elmslie, Walter Angus.) London, 1970.

Afr 9028.75 Among the Zulus and Amatongas. 2. ed. (Leslie, D.) Edinburgh, 1875.

Afr Doc 9271.5 Amorim, Massano de. Relatorio sobre a occupação de Angoche. Lourenço Marques, 1911.

Afr 10690.89.800 Amos Tutuola. (Collins, Harold R.) N.Y., 1969.
Afr 8203.2 Amosu, Margaret. Nigerian theses. Ibadan, 1965.
Afr 10050.3 Amosu, Margaret. A preliminary bibliography of creative African writing in the European languages. Ibadan, 1964.

Afr 3978.44.5 Ampere, J.J. Voyage en Egypte et en Nubie. Paris, 1868.
Afr 2397.2 Amrani, Djamal. Le témoin. Paris, 1960.
Afr 2397.8 Amrouche, Fadhma Aïth Mansour. Histoire de ma vie. Paris, 1968.

Afr 1869.57.10 Amrouche, Marcel. Terres et hommes d'Algérie. v.1. Alger, 1957.

Afr 1.68.5 AMSAC newsletter. (American Society of Africa Culture.) N.Y. 8,1965+

Afr 6282.22 Amu, Josiah Wel-Lean Omo. The rise of Christianity in mid-western Nigeria. Lagos, 1965.

Afr 8028.20 Amyat, D.L. Background material for the tercentenary of the landing of Jan van Riebeeck. Cape Town, 1950.

Afr 2208.87 Un an à Alger. (Baudel, J.) Paris, 1887.
Afr 2030.320 L'an cinq de la révolution algérienne. (Fanon, Frantz.) Paris, 1959.

Afr 1609.57 An den Saulen des Herakles. (Nebel, Gerhard.) Hamburg, 1957.

Afr 1703.3F Anais de arzila, cronica inedita do seculo XVI. (Rodrigues, Bernardo.) Lisboa, 1915-20. 2v.

Afr 2485.1 Anales tunisiennes. (Rousseau, A.) Alger, 1864.
Afr 5091.10 Analyse de l'économie de la République islamique de Mauritanie en 1959. (Société d'Etudes pour le Développement Economique et Social, Paris.) Paris, 1961.

Afr 6739.268.10 Analyse du sous-développement en Afrique noire. (Hugon, Philippe.) Paris, 1968.

Afr Doc 3808.502F An analysis of company accounts. (Rhodesia (British Colony). Central Statistical Office.) Salisbury 1960+

Afr 715.25A The analysis of social change, based on observations in central Africa. (Wilson, Godfrey.) Cambridge, Eng., 1945.

Afr 5962.8 Analysis of Spanish Equatorial Guinea Plan, 1964-1967. (Clairmonte, Frédéric F.) Addis Ababa, 1966.

Afr 8677.25 An analysis of the finances of the Union of South Africa. (Koch, M.H.) Cape Town, 1922.

Afr 8677.25.5 An analysis of the finances of the Union of South Africa. (Koch, M.H.) Cape Town, 1927.

Afr 5758.66.5 Analysis of the Madagascar Plan, 1964-1968. (Clairmonte, Fréderic F.) Addis Ababa, 1966.

Afr 8678.28 The anatomy of African misery. (Olivier, S.H.O.) London, 1927.

Afr 8678.356 The anatomy of apartheid. (Sachs, Emil Solomon.) London, 1965.

Afr 6540.15 The anatomy of Lango religion and groups. (Hayley, T.T.S.) Cambridge, Eng., 1947.

Afr 9448.60 The anatomy of partnership. (Creighton, P.R.) London, 1960.

Afr 8678.326 Anatomy of South Africa. (Hudson, William.) Cape Town, 1966.

Afr 8678.76 The anatomy of South African misery. (Dekiewiet, C.W.) London, 1956.

Afr 6455.122 The anatomy of Uhuru, an essay on Kenya's independence. (Carey Jones, N.S.) Manchester, 1966.

Afr 5054.10.5 Ancelle, Jules. Les explorations au Sénégal et dans les contrées voisines. Paris, 1886.

Afr 1623.919 Ancey, Cesar. Nos interets économiques du Maroc. Paris, 1910.

Afr 3675.19 Anchiere, E. Storia della politica inglese nel Sudan, 1882-1938. Milano, 1939.

Afr 7803.44 Anciaux, Leon. Le problème musulman dans l'Afrique belge. Bruxelles, 1949.

Afr 5465.5 Un ancien royaume bandia de Haut Oubanqui. (Dampierre, Eric de.) Paris, 1967.

Afr 7560.12 L'ancien royaume de Congo. (Cuvelier, Jean.) Bruges, 1946.

Afr 5437.74 L'ancien royaume du Congo des origines à la fin du XIXE siècle. (Randles, W.G.L.) Paris, 1968.

Afr 6979.20 L'ancienne colonie allemande en Sud-ouest Afrique. (Pimienta, R.) Paris, 1920.

Afr 5746.50 Une ancienne relation sur Madagascar (1650). (Chavanon, J.) Paris, 1897.

NEDL Afr 1200.50 Anciennes relations de la France avec la Barbarie, 1515-1830. (Boutin, Abel.) Paris, 1902.

Afr 1273.2 Les anciens impôts de l'Afrique du Nord. (Bernard, Paul.) St. Raphael, 1925.

Afr 710.65 Les anciens royaumes de la savane. (Vansina, Jan.) Leopoldville, 1965.

Afr 115.108 Ancient African kingdoms. (Shinnie, Margaret.) London, 1965.

Afr 4060.25 The ancient kingdoms of the Nile and the doomed monuments of Nubia. (Fairservis, W.A.) N.Y., 1962.

Afr 11509.35.120 And a threefold cord. (LaGuma, Alex.) Berlin, 1964.
Afr 109.63.5 Anders, Robert. L'Afrique africaine. Paris, 1963.
Afr 8658.87.8 Anderson, Andrew Arthur. Twenty-five years in a waggon. London, 1888.

Afr 8658.87.7 Anderson, Andrew Arthur. Twenty-five years in the gold regions of Africa. London, 1887. 2v.

Afr 7458.70 Anderson, B. Narrative of a journey to Musardu. N.Y., 1870.

Afr 9388.57.5 Anderson, C.J. Lake Ngami, or Explorations and discovery during four years of wanderings in wilds of South Western Africa. Cape Town, 1856.

Afr 9388.57 Anderson, C.J. Lake Ngami. N.Y., 1857.
Afr 6988.16.114 Anderson, Charles J. Notes of travel in South Africa. London, 1875.

NEDL Afr 6988.16.116 Anderson, Charles J. Notes of travel in South Africa. N.Y., 1875.

Afr 6275.34 Anderson, David. Surveyors trek. London, 1940.
Afr 1470.5 Anderson, Eugene Newton. The first Moroccan crisis, 1904-1906. Chicago, 1930.

Afr 1470.5.2   Anderson, Eugene Newton. The first Moroccan crisis, 1904-1906. Hamden, Conn., 1966.
Afr 609.29.20   Anderson, I. Circling Africa. Boston, 1929.
Afr 1259.27   Anderson, I. From Corsair to Riffian. Boston, 1927.
Afr 5840.10   Anderson, J.F. Esquisse de l'histoire du protestantisme à l'Ile Mauurice et aux Iles Mascarègnes, 1505 à 1902. Paris, 1903.
Afr 5842.16.2   Anderson, John. Descriptive account of Mauritius. Mauritius, 1858.
Afr 8063.32   Anderson, Ken. Nine flames. Cape Town, 1964.
Afr 8687.111   Anderson, Kenneth. Heroes of South Africa. Cape Town, 1955.
Afr 7369.52   Anderson, R.E. Liberia. Chapel Hill, 1952.
Afr 6282.25   Anderson, Susan. May Perry of Africa. Nashville, 1966.
Afr 8145.38   Anderson, Theophilus. The story of Pacaltsdorp. Port Elizabeth, 1957.
Afr 609.20   Anderson, William A. South of Suez. N.Y., 1920.
Afr 6978.61   Andersson, Carl J. The Okavango River: a narrative of travel, exploration, and adventure. N.Y., 1861.
Afr 6978.61.2   Andersson, Carl J. The Okavango River: a narrative of travel, exploration and adventure. Facsimile. Cape Town, 1968.
Afr 5446.5   Andersson, Efraim. Churches at the grass-roots. London, 1968.
Afr 5753.9   Andoiamanjato, Richard. Le Tsiny et le Tody dans la pensée malgache. Paris, 1957.
Afr 630.66.15   Andor, L. Aptitudes and abilities of the black man in sub-Saharan Africa, 1784-1963. Johannesburg, 1966.
Afr 7183.5   Andrade, Alfredo de. Relatorio da viagem de exploração...de Benguella e Novo Redondo. Lisboa, 1902.
Afr 7320.8   Andrade, Antonio Alberto de. Relações de Moçambique setecentista. Lisboa, 1955.
Htn   Afr 7122.5*   Andrade Leitão, F. de. Copia das proposições e secunda allegaçam. Lisboa, 1642.
Htn   Afr 7122.5.5*   Andrade Leitão, F. de. Copia primae allegationis. n.p., 1642.
Afr 5753.3   Andre, C. De l'esclavage à Madagascar. Paris, 1899.
Afr 575.21   Andre, Pierre J. L'islam noir. Paris, 1924.
Afr 5130.2   André Brue, ou L'Origine. (Berlioux, E.F.) Paris, 1874.
Afr 7918.5   Andre Ryckmans. (Kestergat, Jean.) Paris, 1961.
Afr 4558.69.5   Andree, Richard. Abessinien, das Alpenland unter den Tropen. Leipzig, 1869.
Afr 3979.67   Andres, Stefan Paul. Agyptisches tagebuch. München, 1967.
Afr 45.68.5   Andreski, Stanislav. The African predicament. London, 1968.
Afr 8687.262.5   Andrew Louw van Morgenster. (Louw, Andries Andriaan.) Kaapstad, 1965.
Afr 1609.22   Andrews, C. E. Old Morocco and the forbidden atlas. N.Y., 1922.
Afr 9525.877   Andrews, Charles. John White of Mashonaland. London, 1935.
Afr 210.60.45   Andrianov, B.V. Naselenie Afriki. Moscow, 1960.
Afr 8230.25.5   Andries pretorius. 2. verb. uitg. (Preller, G.S.) Johannesburg, 1940.
Afr 5780.5   L'Androy, extreme sud de Madagascar. (Decary, Raymond.) Paris, 1933. 2v.
Afr 6218.22   Anene, Joseph Christopher. Southern Nigeria in transition, 1885-1906. Cambridge, Eng., 1966.
Afr 6280.14   Anezac, A.D. Notice sur le pays et le peuple des Yebous en Afrique. Paris, 1841.
Afr 530.13   Die Anfänge der deutschen Kolonial-Politik in Ostafrika. (Buettner, Kurt.) Berlin, 1961.
Afr 4060.15   Die Anfänge des Christentums in Nubien. Inaug. Diss. (Kraus, J.) Mödling, 1930.
Afr 5180.24   Anfreville de la Salle. Notre vieux Sénégal, son histoire. Paris, 1909.
Afr 4700.27.15   Angelini, G. La politica coloniale italiana dalle sue origini ad oggi. Messina, 1927.
Afr 4760.12   Angeloni, Renato. Diritto costituzionale somalo. Milano, 1964.
Afr 4392.30   Angerà. (Tedone, Giovanni.) Milano, 1964.
Afr 2749.13   Angieras, E.M. Le Sahara occidental. Paris, 1919.
Afr 3275.13   Les Anglais aux Indes et en Egypte. (Aubin, E.) Paris, 1899.
Afr 3275.13.2   Les Anglais aux Indes et en Egypte. (Aubin, E.) Paris, 1900.
Afr 3243.6   Les Anglais en Egypte. (Hennebert, E.) Paris, 1884.
Afr 3275.18   Les Anglais en Egypte. (Noailles, G. de.) Paris, 1898.
Afr 3275.35   L'Angleterre en Egypte. (Adam, Juliette.) Paris, 1922.
Afr 3204.24   L'Angleterre et l'Egypte. (Briffauet, Robert.) Paris, 194-.
Afr 3193.20   L'Angleterre et l'Egypte. (Douin, Georges.) Caire, 1929-30. 2v.
Afr 3207.17   L'Angleterre et l'Egypte. (Douin, Georges.) Paris, 1928.
Afr 3994.895F   L'Angleterre ruine l'Egypte. (Gavillot, J.C. Aristide.) Paris, 1895.
Afr 8145.40   The Anglican Church in South Africa. (Hinchliff, P.B.) London, 1963.
Afr 55.5   Anglo-African who's who. London. 1905 2v.
Afr 8279.00.3   The Anglo-Boer conflict. (Ireland, A.) Boston, 1900.
Afr 8028.150   The Anglo-Boer war, 1899-1902. (Kesting, J.G.) Cape Town, 1956.
Afr 8289.00.28F   The Anglo-Boer war 1899-1900, an album. (Edwards Dennis and Co.) Cape Town, 190-
Afr 3042.5   Anglo-Egyptian conversations. (Great Britain. Foreign Office.) London, 1951.
Afr 3199.54.10   Anglo-Egyptian relations, 1800-1953. (Marlowe, J.) London, 1954.
Afr 3745.70   The Anglo-Egyptian Sudan. (British Information Services.) N.Y., 1951.
Afr 4070.12   The Anglo-Egyptian Sudan. (Gleichen, Count.) London, 1905. 2v.
Afr 3675.15   The Anglo-Egyptian Sudan. (MacMichael, H.) London, 1934.
Afr 4070.53A   The Anglo-Egyptian Sudan from within. (Hamilton, J.A. de C.) London, 1935.
Afr 8235.16   Anglo-German imperialism in South Africa, 1880-1900. (Bixler, R.W.) Baltimore, 1932.
Afr 8235.15   Anglo-German imperialism in South Africa 1880-1900. Diss. (Bixler, R.W.) Columbus, Ohio, 1932.
Afr 9560.18   Anglo-Portuguese relations in South-Central Africa. (Warhurst, P.R.) London, 1962.
Afr 7103.15   Angola; a bibliography. (Greenwood, Margaret Joan.) Cape Town, 1967.
Afr 7175.80   Angola, a brief survey. (Gonzaga, Norberto.) Lisbon, 1967.
Afr 7122.62   Angola, a symposium. London, 1962.

Afr 7103.20   Angola; catálogo do documentário coligido pela Comissão de Luanda. Luanda, 1937.
Afr 7175.79   Angola, chave de Africa. (Valahu, Mugur.) Lisboa, 1968.
Afr 7122.95   Angola; cinco séculos de exploração portuguesa. (Boavida, Américo.) Rio de Janeiro, 1967.
Afr 7119.20   Angola; memoria. (Trancoso, Francisco.) Lisboa, 1920.
Afr 7045.20   Angola, Moçambique, San Tome. Edição do autor. (Rates, J. Carlos.) Lisboa, 1929.
Afr 7015.50   Angola, Mozambique, Guinee. (Bosgra, Sietse Jan.) Amsterdam, 1969.
Afr 7100.18   Angola; revista de doctrina e propaganda educativa. Luanda. 24,1956+
Afr 7175.74   Angola, terra de Portugal. (Rodrigues, J.) Lourenço Marques, 1964.
Afr 7122.68   Angola, terra nossa. (Telo, Alencastre.) Lisbon, 1962.
Afr 555.40.5   Angola, the land of the blacksmith prince. (Tucker, J.T.) London, 1933.
Afr 7119.5   Angola, um ano no governo geral (1942-43). (Freitas Morna, A. de.) Luanda, 1944.
Afr 7122.52   Angola, 1961. 3. ed. (Cesar, A.) Verbo, 1961.
Afr 7135.12   Angola, 1961-1963. (Gauzes, Anne.) Luanda? 196-.
Afr Doc 9307.350   Angola. Segundo recenseamento geral da população, 1950. Luanda, 1953-1956. 5v.
Afr 7105.1   Pamphlet box. Angola.
Afr 7122.90.5   Pamphlet vol. Angola. 2 pam.
Afr 7122.12   Angola. (Albuquerque Felner, A. De.) Coimbra, 1933.
Afr 7176.7   Angola. (Angola. Direcção dos Serviços de Economia.) Luanda, 1953.
Afr 7176.9   Angola. (Azevedo, João M.C. de.) Luanda, 1958.
Afr 7175.40   Angola. (Cardoso, A.J.A.) Johannesburg, 1950.
Afr 7175.17   Angola. (Ferreira Pinto, J.) Luanda, 1926.
Afr 7119.47   L'Angola. (Lefebvre, G.) Liège, 1947.
Afr 7175.13   Angola. (Marguardsen, H.) Berlin, 1920.
Afr 7175.70F   Angola. (Marjay, Frederico Pedro.) Lisbon, 1961.
Afr 7176.6   Angola. (Pires, Antonio.) Luanda, 1964.
Afr 7176.7   Angola. Direcção dos Serviços de Economia. Angola. Luanda, 1953.
Afr 7122.60   Angola. Governo. Despachas do governador geral de Angola. Luanda, 1947.
Afr 7122.61   Angola. Govêrno Geral, 1943-1947 (Alves). Discursos do governador geral de Angola, capitão de mar e guerra Vasco Lopes Alves, 1943-1946. Luanda, 1946.
Afr 7176.7.10   Angola. Governor General, 1923-1927 (Ferreira). A situação de Angola. Luanda, 1927.
Afr 7100.10   Angola. Instituto de Angola. Bolctim. Luanda. 3,1954 3v.
Afr 7100.12   Angola. Instituto de Angola. Boletim informativo. 61,1964+
Afr Doc 9307.10   Angola. Repartição de Estatistica Geral. Annuario estatistico. Luanda. 1962+
Afr Doc 9307.5   Angola. Repartição de Estatistica Geral. Boletim mensal de estatistica. Luanda. 22,1966+
Afr Doc 9308.703   Angola. Repartição de Estatistica Geral. Comercio exterior. Luanda. 1961+
Afr Doc 9309.505   Angola. Repartição de Estatistica Geral. Estatistica da educação. Luanda. 1951+
Afr Doc 9307.360   Angola. Repartição de Estatistica Geral. Terceiro recenseamento geral da população, 1960. v.1-5. Luanda, 1964-1969.
Afr 7183.10   Angola. Repartição do Gabinete. Relatorio da missao de colonisação no planalto de Benguella em 1909. Loanda, 1910.
Afr Doc 9336.5   Angola. Secretaria Provincial de Formento Rural. Sintese da actividade dos organismos e serviços. Luanda. 1963+
Afr Doc 9345.5   Angola. Secretaria Provincial de Obras Publicas e Comunicações. Sintese da actividade dos serviços. Luanda. 1964+
Afr 7122.54   Angola. 3.ed. (Caio, H.) Lisboa, 1961.
Afr 555.23.15   Angola (Diocese). Visitas pastorais em 1910. Loanda, 1912.
Afr 7122.40   Angola (Dous annos de governo junho 1907 - junho 1909.) (Paiva Couceiro, H.M. de.) Lisboa, 1910.
Afr 7176.22   Angola als Wirtschaftspartner. (Pössinger, Hermann.) Köln, 1966.
Afr 7122.72   Angola and Mozambique, the case against Portugal. (Ehnmark, Anders.) London, 1963.
Afr 7175.5   Angola and the river Congo. (Monteiro, J.J.) London, 1875. 2v.
Afr 7175.5.3   Angola and the river Congo. v.1-2. (Monteiro, J.J.) N.Y., 1876.
Afr 7175.5.5   Angola and the River Congo. 1st ed. (Monteiro, J.J.) London, 1968. 2v.
Afr 7119.62.5   Angola atraves dos textos. São Paulo, 1962.
Afr 7122.100   Angola awake. (Gilchrist, Sid.) Toronto, 1968.
Afr 7182.17   Angola beloved. (Wilson, Thomas E.) Neptune, N.J., 1967.
Afr 7175.30   Angola coração do imperio. (Santos, Afonso C.V.T. dos.) Lisboa, 1961.
Afr 7175.52   Angola do meu coração. (Falcato, J.) Lisboa, 1961.
Afr 7175.42   Angola e Congo. (Pinto, F.A.) Lisboa, 1888.
Afr 7122.35   Angola e o futuro. (Casimiro, Augusto.) Lisboa, 1958.
Afr 7127.5   Angola e os Alemãis. (Paxeco, Fran.) Marahão, 1916.
Afr 7108.15   Angola en tiempos de Felipe II y de Felipe III. (Miralles de Imperial y Gomez, C.) Madrid, 1951.
Afr 7119.63.5   Angola heroica. (Maciel, A.) Lisboa, 1963.
Afr 7119.63   Angola heroica. 2.ed. (Maciel, A.) Lisboa, 1963.
Afr 7122.58A   Angola in ferment. (Okuma, T.) Boston, 1962.
Afr 7119.62   Angola in flames. (Panikkar Kavalam Madhusudan.) N.Y., 1962.
Afr 7119.63.15   Angola in opstand. 1. druk. (Hermans, Fons.) Den Haag, 1963.
Afr 7119.57   Angola in perspective. (Egerton, F.C.C.) London, 1957.
Afr 7119.34   Angola intangivel. (Teixeira, Alberto de Almeida.) Pôrto, 1934.
Afr 7175.75   Angola is anders. (Huibregtse, Pieter Kornelius.) Den Haag, 1965.
Afr 7175.50   Angola na Africa deste tempo. (Rebelo, Horacio de la Viara.) Lisboa, 1961.
Afr 7122.66   Angola na epoca pombalina. (Nogueira, Jofre A.) Lisboa, 1960.
Afr 7175.45   Angola-safari. 2.Aufl. (Zwilling, Ernst.) Mödling, 1957.
Afr 7122.56   Angola v ogne. (Sidenko, V.P.) Moscow, 1961.
Afr 710.20.2   Angola without prejudice. (Egerton, F. Clement C.) Lisbon, 1955.
Afr 7122.85   Les Angolais. (Davezies, Robert.) Paris, 1965.
Afr 7135.4   The Angolan revolution. (Marcum, John.) Cambridge, 1969.
Afr 7108.20   Angolana. Luanda, 1968.
Afr 7175.20   Angolian sketches. (Barns, T. Alexander.) London, 1928.
Afr 8659.10.5   Angore, John. In the early days. Kimberley, 1910.

Afr 4892.5 Angoulvant, G. Djibout, Mer Rouge, Abyssinie. Paris, 1902.

Afr 5340.20 Angoulvant, G.L. La pacification de la Côte-d'Ivoire. Paris, 1916.

Afr 6988.52.230 Angra Pequeña. Inaug. Diss. (Hodge, A.L.) München, 1936.

Afr 861.31 Angry island. (Mackay, M.M.) London, 1963.

Afr 626.158 Anguile, André G. L'Afrique sans frontières. Monaco, 1965.

Afr 6390.96 Animal twilight. (Cloudsley-Thompson, John.) Chester Springs, 1967.

Afr 8685.46 Anjar, P.L. Conflict of races in South Africa. Durban, 1946.

Afr 590.30.15 Annales. (Institut d'Afrique.) Paris.

Afr 5000.10 Annales africaines. Paris. 1958+ 7v.

Afr 5000.11 Annales africaines. Tables quinquennales, 1954-58. Dakar, 1960.

Afr 1955.36 Annales algériennes. (Pellissier de Reynaud, E.) Paris, 1854. 3v.

Afr 1801.12 Annales algériennes de géographie. Alger. 1,1966+

Afr 1990.26 Annales de la colonisation algérienne. Paris. 1-14,1852-1858 14v.

Afr 1390.4 Annales du Maghreb et de l'Espagne. (Ibn al-Atir.) Alger, 1898.

Afr 5501.5 Annales malgaches. Droit. Paris. 2v.

Afr 5501.6 Annales malgaches. Lettres. Paris. 3v.

Afr 1390.1 Annales regum Mauritaniae. v.1-2. Upsaliae, 1843.

Afr 2819.27 Annales tripolitaines. (Firaud, L.C.) Tunis, 1927.

Afr 4700.1.7 Annali dell'Africa italiana. Roma. 1,1938+ 20v.

Afr 8190.5.2 The annals of Natal, 1495 to 1845. (Bird, John.) Capetown, 1965. 2v.

Afr 8190.5 Annals of Natal 1495-1845. v.1 and index. (Bird, John.) Pietermaritzburg, 1888. 2v.

Afr Doc 3835.5 Annaul report. (Rhodesia, Southern. Secretary for African Education.) Salisbury. 1964+

Afr 1.95 Année africaine. Paris. 1,1963+ 5v.

Afr 2280.3 Une année dans le Sahel. 2d ed. (Fromentin, E.) Paris, 1859.

Afr 2280.5 Une année dans le Sahel. 6th ed. (Fromentin, E.) Paris, 1884.

Afr 2037.5 Une année de révolution socialiste, 1962 - 5 juillet - 1963. (Algeria. Ministère de l'Orientation Nationale.) Alger, 1963?

Afr 1.89 L'année politique africaine. Dakar. 1965+

Afr Doc 5409.6 Annexe statistique au rapport sur le budget économique. (Tunisia. Secretariat d'Etat au Plan et à l'Economie Nationale.) Tunis. 1967+

Afr 1494.5.2 Annexes au plan de réformes marocaines. (Comité d'Action Marocaine.) n.p., 1934.

Afr 7567.22 L'annexion du Congo devant Parlement belge. 2d ed. (Flechet, Ferdinand.) Liège, 1909.

Afr 4513.36.84 Anno XIII, the conquest of an empire. (Bono, E. de.) London, 1937.

Afr 20015.5 Annotated African texts. London. 1,1952+ 5v.

Afr 28.91 Annotated bibliography of recent publications on Africa. (Royal Commonwealth Society, London.) London, 1943.

Afr 3026.25 An annotated research bibliography of studies in Arabic. (Coult, L.H.) Coral Gables, Fla., 1958.

Afr 5400.8 Annuaire. (Union Douanière et Economique de l'Afrique Centrale.) Douala. 1,1968+

Afr 1001.10 Annuaire de l'Afrique du Nord. Paris. 1,1962+ 6v.

Afr 1.10 Annuaire de Madagascar et dépendances. Tananarive. 1898+ 6v.

Afr 1.54 Annuaire des états d'Afrique Noire. Paris. 1961+

Afr 555.23.30 Annuaire des missions catholiques au Congo Belge. Paris, 1965.

Afr Doc 7708.705 Annuaire des statistiques du commerce extérieur. (Congo. Diréction de la Statistique et des Etudes Economiques.) Leopoldville. 1963+

Afr 7501.1 Annuaire du Congo belge. Bruxelles.

Afr Doc 6003.5 Annuaire du gouvernement général de l'Afrique occidentale française. (French West Africa.) n.p., n.d.

Afr 1301.2 Annuaire du Maroc. Paris. 1905+ 12v.

Afr Doc 1439.3.5 Annuaire du Ministère de la justice. (Egypt. Ministry of Justice.) Le Caire. 1909

Afr 5100.1 Annuaire du Sénégal et dépendances. St.-Louis, 1869.

Afr Doc 6705.5 L'annuaire du Togo. Lomé, Togo. 1963+

Afr 1301.5 Annuaire économique et financier. (Morocco.) Casablanca. 1917+ 4v.

Afr 5000.5 Annuaire et mémoires. (French West Africa. Comité d'Etudes Historiques et Scientifiques.) Gorée. 1916+ 2v.

Afr 1301.4 Annuaire général du Maroc. Casablanca. 1917+ 5v.

Afr Doc 7505.5 Annuaire national. (Cameroon.) Yaoundé. 1964+

Afr Doc 7405.5 Annuaire national. (Gabon. Ministère de l'Information.) Paris. 1967+

Afr 7540.10 Annuaire officiel. (Belgium. Ministère des Colonies.) Bruxelles. 1914+ 3v.

Afr 5000.1.5 Annuaire politique d'Afrique noire et de Madagascar. Paris. 2,1958+

Afr Doc 6708.702 Annuaire retrospectif du commerce special du Togo, 1937-1964. (Togo. Service de la Statistique Générale.) Lomé, 1964.

Afr Doc 7207.10 Annuaire statistique. (Central African Republic. Direction de la Statistique et de la Conjoncture.) Paris. 1964

Afr Doc 7707.15 Annuaire statistique. (Congo (Brazzaville). Direction du Service National de la Statistique des Etudes Démographiques et Economiques.) 1,1958+

Afr Doc 6607.5 Annuaire statistique. (Dahomey. Haut Commissariat au Plan et au Tourisme.) Cotonou. 1965

Afr Doc 6007.2 Annuaire statistique. (French West Africa. Service des Etudes et Coordination Statistique et Mécanographiques.) Dakar. 3-6,1936-1957 2v.

Afr Doc 7407.5 Annuaire statistique. (Gabon. Service National de la Statistique.) 1964+

Afr Doc 5607.5 Annuaire statistique. (Madagascar. Service de Statistique Generale.) Tananarive. 1,1938+

Afr Doc 6807.5 Annuaire statistique. (Mali. Direction de la Statistique.) Bamako. 1963+

Afr Doc 1407.10 Annuaire statistique. (United Arab Republic. Department of Statistics and Census.) Cairo. 1909+

Afr Doc 7509.510F Annuaire statistique. Enseignement: sécondaire (général et technique), superior, éducation des adultes. (Cameroon. Ministère de l'Education, de la Jeunesse et de la Culture.) Yaoundé. 1964+

Afr Doc 5807.5 Annuaire statistique de la Reunion. (France. Institut National de la Statistique et des Etudes Economiques.) Paris. 1952-1955

Afr Doc 5407.5 Annuaire statistique de Tunisie. (Tunisia. Service des Statistiques.) 1955+ 2v.

Afr Doc 5207.5 Annuaire statistique du Maroc. (Morocco. Service Central des Statistiques.) 1950+

Afr Doc 7107.10 Annuaire statistique du Tchad. (Chad. Service de la Statistique Générale.) Fort Lamy? 2,1968+

Afr 1487.22 Annual. (Ortega y Gasset, Eduardo.) Madrid, 1922.

Afr 6900.35 Annual. (South West Africa.) Windhoek. 1965+

Afr Doc 2520.955 Annual abstract of education statistics. (Nigeria, Western. Ministry of Economic Planning and Community Development. Statistics Division.) 1953+

Afr Doc 2307.5 Annual abstract of statistics. (Nigeria. Federal Office of Statistics.) 1960+

Afr Doc 1408.715 Annual bulletin of foreign trade. (United Arab Republic. Central Agency for Public Mobilisation and Statistics.) Cairo. 1918

Afr Doc 2822.5 Annual departmental reports. (Mauritius.) Port Louis. 1951+

Afr Doc 4322.5 Annual departmental reports. (South Africa. Bureau of Statistics.) Pretoria. 1,1920+

Afr Doc 3326.5 Annual development report. (Uganda.) Entebbe. 1947

Afr Doc 1809.40 Annual estimates. (Ghana.) Accra. 1960+

Afr Doc 308.705F Annual import and export trade statistics. (Ethiopia. Customs Head Office.) Addis Ababa. 1962+

Afr 8028.102 Annual list of Africana added to the Mendelssohn collection. (South Africa. Parliament. Library.) Cape Town. 1-9,1938-1946 2v.

Afr 7350.5.5 Annual meeting. (Pennsylvania Colonization Society.)

Afr Doc 9924.10F Annual message. (Liberia. President.)

Afr 608.81.3 Annual papers on condition of Africa by the Secretary of the American Colonization Society. (American Colonization Society.) Washington. 1881+

Afr 1.44 Annual report. (Africa Bureau, London.) London.

Afr 8001.17 Annual report. (Africana Museum, Johannesburg.) Johannesburg.

NEDL Afr 7350.3 Annual report. (American Colonization Society.) Washington. 1,1818+ 1v.

Afr Doc 4231.5F Annual report. (Basutoland. Department of Agriculture.) 1958+

Afr Doc 4046.5 Annual report. (Bechuanaland. Public Works Department.) Gaberones. 1956+

Afr Doc 4031.5 Annual report. (Botswana. Department of Agriculture.) Gaberones. 1962+

Afr Doc 2643.5 Annual report. (Cameroons, Southern. Marketing Board.) Lagos, Nigeria. 1959+

Afr 8003.2.5 Annual report. (Civil Rights League, Cape Town.)

Afr 6308.5 Annual report. (East Africa High Commission.) Nairobi. 1957+ 2v.

Afr Doc 3049.5 Annual report. (East Africa High Commission. East African Statistical Department.) Nairobi. 1950+

Afr Doc 3005.5 Annual report. (East African Common Services Organization.) London. 1961+

Afr Doc 3039.5 Annual report. (East African Industrial Research Organization.) Nairobi. 1959+

Afr Doc 1830.20F Annual report. (Ghana. Department of Agriculture.) Accra. 1924-1957

Afr Doc 1832.5 Annual report. (Ghana. Department of Cooperation.) Accra. 1949-1950

Afr Doc 1848.5 Annual report. (Ghana. Department of Social Welfare and Community Development.) Accra. 1946+

Afr Doc 1830.5 Annual report. (Ghana. National Archives.) Accra. 1957

Afr Doc 1845.10 Annual report. (Ghana. Police Service.) Accra. 1959+

Afr Doc 1845.5 Annual report. (Ghana. Public Works Department.) Accra. 1953+

Afr 9.17 Annual report. (Indian Council for Africa.) New Delhi. 1963+

Afr Doc 3231.15 Annual report. (Kenya. African Affairs Department.)

Afr Doc 3238.20 Annual report. (Kenya. Central Housing Board.) 1964+

Afr Doc 3233.20 Annual report. (Kenya. Central Land Board.) Nairobi. 1963+

Afr Doc 3212.15 Annual report. (Kenya. Council of State.) Nairobi. 1958+

Afr Doc 3233.10 Annual report. (Kenya. Department of Co-operative Development.)

Afr Doc 3233.35 Annual report. (Kenya. Department of Community Development and Rehabilitation.) Nairobi. 1951-1955

Afr Doc 3239.15 Annual report. (Kenya. Department of Immigration.)

Afr Doc 3239.3 Annual report. (Kenya. Department of Information.) Nairobi. 1955+

Afr Doc 3242.5.20 Annual report. (Kenya. Department of Lands, Mines and Surveys.) Nairobi. 1945

Afr Doc 3242.5.10 Annual report. (Kenya. Department of Lands.) Nairobi. 1926

Afr Doc 3249.10 Annual report. (Kenya. Department of Settlement.)

Afr Doc 3234.5 Annual report. (Kenya. Development and Reconstruction Authority.)

Afr Doc 3236.10 Annual report. (Kenya. Forest Department.) 1964+

Afr Doc 3237.5 Annual report. (Kenya. Game Department.) 1953-1954

Afr Doc 3239.5 Annual report. (Kenya. Information Services.) 1960+

Afr Doc 3239.30 Annual report. (Kenya. Inland Revenue Department.) Nairobi. 1953-1954

Afr 6408.25 Annual report. (Kenya. Kenya Regiment.) Nairobi. 1957-58

Afr Doc 3242.5 Annual report. (Kenya. Lands Department.)

Afr Doc 3242.20 Annual report. (Kenya. Local Government. Loans Authority.) 1964+

Afr Doc 3233.30 Annual report. (Kenya. Ministry of Community Development.) Nairobi. 1957+

Afr Doc 3238.5 Annual report. (Kenya. Ministry of Health and Social Affairs.) 1960+

Afr Doc 3238.15 Annual report. (Kenya. Ministry of Housing.) Nairobi. 1,1958+

Afr Doc 3239.10 Annual report. (Kenya. Ministry of Information, Broadcasting and Tourism.)

Afr Doc 3242.25 Annual report. (Kenya. Ministry of Labour.) Nairobi. 1965+

Afr Doc 3242.30 Annual report. (Kenya. Ministry of Labour and Housing. Housing Section.) Nairobi? 1961

Afr Doc 3231.5F Annual report. (Kenya. Native Affairs Department.) 3v.

Afr Doc 3246.5 Annual report. (Kenya. Printing and Stationery Department.)

Afr Doc 3233.25 Annual report. (Kenya. Registrar of Co-operation Societies.) Nairobi. 1953-1957

Afr Doc 3248.10F Annual report. (Kenya. Road Authority.) Nairobi. 1955+

Afr Doc 3253.5F Annual report. (Kenya. Water Development Department.) Nairobi. 1965+

Afr 628.2.257 Annual report. (League Of Coloured Peoples.) London.

Afr Doc 4231.10F Annual report. (Lesotho. Ministry of Agriculture, Co-ops, and Marketing.) 1,1966+

Afr Doc 9944.5 Annual report. (Liberia. Bureau of Natural Resources and Surveys.) Monrovia. 1965+

Afr Doc 3731.6F Annual report. (Zambia. Ministry of Agriculture.) Lusaka. 2,1965+

Afr Doc 3733.15 Annual report. (Zambia. Ministry of Commerce and Industry.) Lusaka. 1964+

Afr Doc 3735.5 Annual report. (Zambia. Ministry of Education.) Lusaka. 1964+

Afr Doc 3742.10 Annual report. (Zambia. Ministry of Local Government.) Lusaka. 1963+

Afr Doc 3750.20 Annual report. (Zambia. Ministry of Transport and Works.) Lusaka. 1964+

Afr Doc 3731.25 Annual report. (Zambia. National Archives.) Lusaka. 1964+

Afr Doc 3743.10 Annual report. (Zambia. National Museums Board.) Lusaka. 1,1967+

Afr Doc 3746.25 Annual report. (Zambia. Printing and Stationery Department.) Lusaka. 1964+

Afr Doc 3746.20 Annual report. (Zambia. Provincial and District Government.) Lusaka. 1964+

Afr Doc 3746.15 Annual report. (Zambia. Public Service Commission.) Lusaka. 1964+

Afr Doc 3732.10 Annual report. (Zambia. Registrar of Banks.) Lusaka. 1965+

Afr Doc 3732.5 Annual report. (Zambia. Registrar of Building Societies.) Lusaka. 1959+

Afr Doc 3749.12 Annual report. (Zambia. Survey Department.) Lusaka. 1964+

Afr Doc 3750.30 Annual report. (Zambia. Teaching Service Commission.) Lusaka. 1964+

Afr Doc 3750.15 Annual report. (Zambia. Town and Country Planning Service.) Lusaka. 1964+

Afr Doc 3149.5 Annual report. (Zanibar. Social Welfare Department.) Zanibar. 1961+

Afr 7350.3.7 Annual report. Philadelphia. 2,1934 (Ladies Association, Auxiliary to the American Colonization Society.)

Afr Doc 1830.10 Annual report and accounts. (Ghana. Agricultural Produce Marketing Board.) Accra. 1947-1956

Afr Doc 1832.20 Annual report and accounts. (Ghana. State Cocoa Marketing Board.) Accra. 1964+

Afr Doc 3250.5 Annual report and accounts. (Kenya. Tea Development Authority.) Nairobi. 1965+

Afr Doc 2547.5 Annual report and accounts. (Nigeria, Mid-Western. Housing Corporation.) Benin City. 1,1963+

Afr Doc 2527.5 Annual report and accounts. (Western Region Housing Corporation.) Ibadan. 2,1959+

Afr Doc 3634.5 Annual report and statement of accounts. (Malawi Development Corporation.) Blantyre. 1967+

Afr Doc 2709.300 Annual report by the Accountant General. (Seychelles. Treasury.) 1963+

Afr Doc 4146.5F Annual report by the Director of Public Works. (Swaziland. Public Works Department.)

Afr Doc 2846.15 Annual report for the financial year. (Mauritius. Public Works and Surveys Department.) Port Louis. 1946-1948

Afr Doc 9946.10F Annual report of Postmaster General on the operation of the Liberian Postal Administration. (Liberia. Postmaster General.) Monrovia. 1961+

Afr Doc 3242.7 Annual report of the commissioner. (Kenya. Department of Local Government, Lands and Settlement.) Nairobi. 1930-1934

Afr Doc 3242.5.15 Annual report of the Commissioner. (Kenya. Ministry of Lands and Settlement.) Nairobi. 1938

Afr Doc 3633.5 Annual report of the Controller. (Malawi. Department of Customs and Excise.) Zomba. 1964

Afr Doc 2833.5 Annual report of the cooperative credit societies. (Mauritius. Registrar of Co-operative Credit Societies.)

Afr Doc 3533.13F Annual report of the general officer commanding, Central Africa Command. (Rhodesia and Nyasaland. Central Africa Command.) Salisbury. 1,1954

Afr Doc 3640.5 Annual report of the Ministry of Justice including the Department of the Registrar General. (Malawi. Ministry of Justice.) Zomba. 1966+

Afr Doc 2343.5 Annual report of the Nigerianisation Office. (Nigeria. Nigerianisation Office.) Lagos, 1957.

Afr Doc 3546.25 Annual report of the Postmaster-General. (Rhodesia and Nyasaland. Ministry of Posts.) Salisbury. 1954+

Afr Doc 3746.5 Annual report of the Postmaster-General. (Zambia. General Post Office.) Lusaka. 1963+

Afr Doc 3538.5F Annual report of the public health. (Rhodesia and Nyasaland. Ministry of Health.) Zomba. 1,1954+

Afr Doc 3248.5 Annual report of the Registrar-General. (Kenya. Department of the Registrar-General.)

Afr Doc 3648.10 Annual report of the Road Traffic Commissioner. (Malawi. Road Traffic Department.) Zomba. 1965+

Afr Doc 4330.10 Annual report of the secretary for agricultural economics and marketing. (South Africa. Department of Agricultural Economics and Marketing.) Pretoria. 1959+

Afr Doc 3534.5 Annual report of the Secretary for Defence and the Chief of Air Staff. (Rhodesia and Nyasaland. Ministry of Defense.) Salisbury. 1955+

Afr Doc 4332.15F Annual report of the Statistics council. (South Africa. Office of Census and Statistics.) 1951+

Afr Doc 3553.5 Annual report of the Under Secretary. (Rhodesia and Nyasaland. Ministry of Works.)

Afr 8865.12 Annual report on Basutoland. (Great Britain. Commonwealth Relations Office.) 1947+ 3v.

Afr Doc 3433.5 Annual report on co-operative development. (Tanganyika. Co-operative Development Department.) Dar es Salaam. 1956-63

Afr Doc 844.5 Annual report on development activities. (Libya. National Planning Council.) Tripoli. 1,1963+

Afr Doc 3535.5 Annual report on education, 1954-1963. (Rhodesia and Nyasaland. Ministry of Education.)

Afr 9192.10 Annual report on Swaziland. (Great Britain. Commonwealth Relations Office.) n.p. 1946+ 6v.

Afr Doc 2305.10F Annual report on the colony. (Nigeria. Commissioner.) Lagos.

Afr 6308.10 Annual report on the East Africa High Commission. (Great Britain. Colonial Office.) 1948+

Afr Doc 9939.10 Annual report on the operation. (Liberia. Interior Department.) Monrovia. 1961+

Afr Doc 3546.5 Annual report on the operation and financial position of the Federal Pension Fund. (Rhodesia and Nyasaland. Pension Fund Board.) Salisbury. 1956+

Afr Doc 3546.10 Annual report on the operation and financial position of the Federal Provident Fund. (Rhodesia and Nyasaland. Pension Fund Board.) Salisbury. 1961+

Afr Doc 3546.20 Annual report on the Post Office Savings Bank and Savings Certificates. (Rhodesia and Nyasaland. Ministry of Posts.) Salisbury. 1954+

Afr Doc 2305.5 Annual report on the social and economic progress of the people of Nigeria. (Nigeria.) Lagos.

Afr Doc 2449.5 Annual report on the social welfare services. (Nigera, Northern. Ministry of Social Welfare and Cooperatives.) Kaduna. 1961+

Afr Doc 2500.505 Annual reports. (Nigeria, Southern.) Lagos. 1906

Afr Doc 2305.15 Annual reports for the western, northern, eastern provinces and the colony. (Nigeria. Commissioner.) Lagos.

Afr Doc 3305.5 Annual reports on the Kingdom of Buganda, Eastern Province, Western Province and Northern Province. (Uganda.) Entebbe. 1947+

Afr Doc 3608.705 Annual statement of external trade. (Malawi. National Statistical Office.) Zomba. 1,1964+

Afr Doc 3808.706 Annual statement of external trade. (Rhodesia (British Colony). Central Statistical Office.) Salisbury. 1964+

Afr Doc 3508.707F Annual statement of external trade. (Rhodesia and Nyasaland. Central Statistical Office.) Salisbury. 1954+ 4v.

Afr Doc 3708.700 Annual statement of external trade. (Zambia. Central Statistical Office.) Lusaka. 1,1964+

Afr Doc 3808.710 Annual statement of the trade of Southern Rhodesia with British countries and foreign countries. (Central African Statistical Office.) Salisbury. 22-24,1951-1953

Afr Doc 4009.305F Annual statements of account. (Bechuanaland (Protectorate).) Gaberones? 1964+

Afr Doc 4207.5 Annual statistical bulletin. (Lesotho. Bureau of Statistics.) Maseru. 1965+

Afr Doc 1409.500 Annual statistical report. (United Arab Republic. State Tourist Administration.) Cairo. 1960+

Afr Doc 708.731F Annual trade report of Northern Region. (Somalia. Customs and Excise Department.) Mogadisco. 1960+

Afr Doc 3008.700 Annual trade report of Tanganyika, Uganda and Kenya. (East African Common Services Organization. East African Customs and Excise Department.) Mombasa. 1962+ 2v.

Afr 1750.7 Annuario estadistico. Zona de protectorado y de los territorios de soberania de España en el norte de Africa. (Spain. Dirección General de Estadistica.) 1,1941+ 3v.

Afr Doc 9307.10 Annuario estatistico. (Angola. Repartição de Estatistica Geral.) Luanda. 1962+

Afr 7817.10 Another hand on mine; the story of Dr. Carl K. Becker of the Africa Inland Mission. 1st ed. (Petersen, William J.) N.Y., 1967.

Afr 6196.20 Ansah, J.K. The centenary history of the Larteh Presbyterian Church, 1853-1953. Larteh, 1955.

Afr 2623.960.5 L'Ansarine; contribution à la sociologie du développement. (Cuisenier, Jean.) Paris, 1960.

Afr 1755.45 Ansart, F.B. El desastre de annual. Barcelona, 1921.

Afr 6535.4 Ansorge, W.J. Under the African sun. N.Y., 1899.

Afr 109.62.41 Ansprenger, Franz. Afrika. Eine politische Länderkunde. 6. Aufl. Berlin, 1969.

Afr 5040.2 Ansprenger, Franz. Politik im schwarzen Afrika. Köln, 1961.

Afr 609.33.10 Anstein, H. Afrika, wie ich es erlebte. Stuttgart, 1933.

Afr 7567.25 Anstey, Roger. Britain and the Congo in the 19th century. Oxford, 1962.

Afr 7567.36 Anstey, Roger. King Leopold's legacy. London, 1966.

Afr 718.2.130 Anstruther, Ian. Dr. Livingstone, I presume. 1st American ed. N.Y., 1957.

Afr 6200.1.14 ANSWA publication. Ibadan. 1,1968+

Afr 7377.5.5 Answer of the agent of the Indiana Colonization Society. (Colonization Society of the State of Indiana.) Indianapolis, 1852.

Afr 5780.88 Les Antaisaka. Thèse. (Deschamps, N.) Tananarive, 1936. 2 pam.

Afr 5501.2 Antananarivo annual. Antananarivo. 1,1885+ 4v.

Afr 5501.2.5 Antananarivo annual and Madagascar magazine. Antananarivo. 2,1876+ 2v.

Afr 5933.2 Antecedentes históricos. (Yanguas Mirarete, José.) Sidi Infi, 1960.

Afr 628.267 Antériorité des civilisations nègres. (Diop, Cheikh A.) Paris, 1967.

Afr 3978.00.10 Antes, J. Beobachtungen über die Sitten und Gebräuche der Ägypter. Gera, 1801.

Afr 10675.10.110 The anthill. (Egbuna, Obi Benue.) London, 1965.

Afr 12015.2 Anthologie africaine et malgache. (Hughes, L.) Paris, 1962.

Afr 10018.3 Anthologie de la littérature nègro-africaine. (Sainville, L.) Paris, 1963- 2v.

Afr 12016.2 Anthologie de la nouvelle poésie nègre. 1st ed. (Senghor, L.S.) Paris, 1948.

Afr 12015.10 Anthologie des écrivains maghrébins d'expression française. (Memmi, Albert.) Paris, 1964.

Afr 10015.5 Anthologie négro-africaine. (Kesteloot, Lilyan.) Verviers, 1967.

Afr 12016.3 An anthology of African and Malagasy poetry in French. (Clive, Wake.) London, 1965.

Afr 11058.2 Anthology of short stories. (Dodd, A.D.) Cape Town, 1958.

Afr 10516.2 An anthology of West African verse. (Bassir, O.) Nigeria, 1957.

Afr 5635.18 Anthouard, Albert. L'expedition de Madagascar en 1895. Paris, 1930.

Afr 6280.12 Anthropological report on...peoples of Nigeria. (Thomas, N.W.) London, 1910. 2v.

Afr 6280.9 Anthropological report on the Ibo speaking peoples. V.1-6. (Thomas, N.W.) London, 1913-14.

Afr 5344.8 Anthropologie économique des Gouro de Côte-d'Ivoire. (Meillassoux, Claude.) Paris, 1964.

Afr 626.143.5 The anthropology of development in Sub-Saharan Africa. (Brokensha, David W.) Lexington, Ky., 1969.

VAfr 8001.30PF The anti-apartheid news. London. 1,1964

Afr 8289.31 Anti-commando. (Sampson, V.) London, 1931.

Afr 2274.1 L'anti-sémitisme à Alger. (Aumerat, J.F.) Alger, 1885.

Afr 2628.2 Antichan, P.H. Le pays des Khroumirs. Paris, 1883.

Afr 13438.1.110 Antidote. (Rabemananjara, Jacques.) Paris, 1961.

Afr 210.67.25 Antiimperialisticheskaia revoliutsiia v Afrike. Moskva, 1967.

Afr 3977.37.10F The antiquities, natural history, ruins... of Egypt, Nubia and Thebes. (Norden, Frederik L.) London, 1780.

Afr 2318.1.15 Antoine, L.F. Constantine, centre économique. Thèse. Toulouse, 1930.

Afr 4700.29.10 Antologia coloniale. (Ciarlantini, F.) Roma, 1929.

Afr 7549.11.7 Anton, G.K. Kongostaat und Kongoreform. Leipzig, 1911.

Afr 1625.6 Anton Y Ferrandiz, M. Razas y tribus de Marruecos. Madrid, 1903.

Afr 4386.8 Antona-Traversi, Camillo. Sahati e Dogali. Roma, 1887.

Afr 500.25   Antonelli, Etienne. L'Afrique et la Paix de Versailles. Paris, 1921.

Afr 500.25.10   Antonelli, Etienne. L'Afrique et la Paix de Versailles. 4th ed. Paris, 1921.

Afr 7183.22   António, Mário. Luanda, "ilha" crioula. Lisboa, 1968.

Afr 10016.12   Ants will not eat your fingers. (Doob, Leonard William.) N.Y., 1966.

Afr 13438.1.120   Antsa. (Rabemananjara, Jacques.) Paris, 1956.

Afr 6192.28   Antubam, K. Ghana's heritage of culture. Leipzig, 1963.

Afr 7324.7.2   Anuaria de Lourenço Marques. Lourenço Marques. 18,1931+ 3v

Afr Doc 9405.5   Anuário. (Guinea. Portuguese.) Lisbon. 1-2,1946-1948 2v.

Afr 7100.5   Anuario de Angola. Lisboa. 1,1923+

Afr 1301.3   Anuario español de Marruecos. Madrid. 1913+

Afr 6298.3   Anyiam, F.U. Among Nigerian celebrities. Yaba, 1960.

Afr 6218.8   Anyiam, F.U. Men and matters in Nigerian politics 1934-58. Yaba, 1959.

Afr 8678.303   Apartheid, a challenge. (Holloway, John Edward.) Johannesburg, 1964.

Afr 8678.295   Apartheid, feiten en commentaren. Amsterdam, 1966.

Afr 8678.382   Apartheid; its effects on education, science, culture and information. (UNESCO.) Paris, 1967.

Afr 8678.415   Apartheid. (Brookes, Edgar Harry.) London, 1968.

Afr 8678.328   Apartheid. (Eyo, B.E.) Jerusalem, 1964.

Afr 8678.223   L'apartheid. (Mandela, Nelson Rolihlahla.) Paris, 1965.

Afr 8678.68.5   Apartheid. (Rhoodie, N.J.) Cape Town, 1960.

Afr 8678.190   Apartheid. (Sabloniere, Margrit.) Amsterdam, 1960.

Afr 8678.140   Apartheid and discrimination. (Roskam, Karel Lodewijk.) Leyden, 1960.

Afr 8678.68.15   Apartheid and racial partnership in Southern Africa. (Rhoodie, N.J.) Pretoria, 1969.

Afr 8678.331   Apartheid and survival. (Katzew, Henry.) Cape Town, 1965.

Afr 8678.350   Apartheid and United Nations collective measures. (Leiss, Amelia Catherine.) N.Y., 1965.

Afr 8678.332   Apartheid een wijze voorzorg. (Dominicus, Foort Comelius.) Utrecht, 1965.

Afr 8678.68.12   Apartheid en partnership. 2. uitg. (Rhoodie, N.J.) Pretoria, 1968.

Afr 8678.170   Apartheid in South Africa. (Joshi, Pranshankar.) Kimberley, 1950.

Afr 8678.310   Apartheid in the Republic of South Africa. (Mezerik, A.G.) N.Y., 1964.

Afr 8678.310.5   Apartheid in the Republic of South Africa. (Mezerik, A.G.) N.Y., 1967.

Afr 8678.145   Apartheid in the Union of South Africa. (Mezerik, Avrahm G.) N.Y., 1960.

Afr 8678.143   Apartheid zonder vooroordelen. (Mueren, K. van der.) Antwerpen, 1958.

Afr 8678.375   Apartheidfragan i förenta nationerna. (Sweden. Utrikesdepartementet.) Stockholm, 1967.

Afr 8678.68   Die apartheidsgedougte. (Rhoodie, N.J.) Kaapstad, 1960.

Afr 8678.429   Apartkheid - prestuplenie veka. (Tairov, Tair F.) Moskva, 1968.

Afr 7176.32   Apectos do desenvolvimento ecónomico e social de Angola. (Araujo, A. Correia de.) Lisboa, 1964.

Afr 4378.1   Apel, F.H. Drei Monate en Abyssinien. Zürich, 1866.

Afr 2208.30   Aperçu...sur l'état d'Alger. 2e ed. Paris, 1830.

Afr 3978.40   Aperçu général sur l'Egypte. (Clat-Bey, A.) Bruxelles, 1840. 2v.

Afr 3978.40.2   Aperçu général sur l'Egypte. v.1-2. (Clat-Bey, A.) Paris, 1840.

Afr 555.10   Aperçu historique sur l'église d'Afrique. (Barges, Jean Joseph Léandre.) Paris, 1848.

Afr 2223.940   Apiotti, Angelo. Sei milioni di affamati. Milan, 1940.

Afr 6549.251.5   Apolo of the Pygmy forest. (Lloyd, Albert B.) London, 1936.

Afr 7332.5   Apontamentos de um ex-governador de Sofalla. (Brandao Cro de Castro Ferreri, Alfredo.) Lisboa, 1886.

Afr 7176.34   O após-guerra em Angola. (Ventura, Reis.) Luanda, 1954.

Afr 555.17   Apostolado serafico en Marruecos. (Castellanos, M.P.) Madrid, 1896.

Afr 550.11   Apostolat en Afrique. Québec, 1911.

Afr 4368.5.20   L'apostolo dei Galla. 3 ed. (Gentile, Lorenzo.) Torino, 1931.

Afr 5392.3   Un apôtre d'aujourd'hui. (Hardy, Georges.) Paris, 1949.

Afr 555.39.10   L'apôtre du Congo, Monseigneur Augouard. (Bestier, G.G.) Paris, 1926.

Afr 1409.17   Apoyo de España a Mawlay Hisam. (Garcia Figueras, T.) Tetuan, 1953.

Afr 810.8   An appeal...Niger expedition and sequel. (Jamieson, R.) London, 1840-43.

Afr 550.22   Appeal to the churches in behalf of Africa. N.Y., 1834.

Afr 609.28.15   Appel, Joseph Herbert. Africa's white magic. N.Y., 1928.

Afr 4513.37.55   Appelius, M. Il crollo dell'impero dei Negus. Milano, 1937.

Afr 8288.99.10F   Appendices evidence on war in South Africa. (Great Britain. Commissions. South African War.) London, 1903.

Afr 3978.42.3   Appendix to the American in Egypt. (Gliddon, G.R.) Philadelphia, 1842.

Afr 10621.71.100   Appiah, Peggy. The children of Anause. London, 1968.

Afr 8278.99.27   Appleton, L. Britain and the Boers. London, 1899.

Afr 3978.76   Appleton, T.G. A Nile journal. Boston, 1876.

Afr 9558.15   Appleyard, M.E. Doctor David Livingstone. Cape Town, 1949.

Afr 7817.2   Appointment Congo. (Law, Virginia W.) Chicago, 1966.

Afr 1571.52   Appointment to Fez. (Selous, G.H.) London, 1956.

Afr 609.52.5   L'apport de l'Afrique à la pensée humaine. (Guernier, E.L.) Paris, 1952.

Afr 2223.60   L'apport économique de l'Algérie pendant la guerre. Thèse. (Dobrenn, Rene.) Oran, 1925.

Afr 7809.62.5   Apport scientifique de la Belgique au développement de l'Afrique centrale. (Académie Royale des Sciences d'Outre-Mer.) Bruxelles, 1962. 3v.

Afr 10005.2A   Approaches to African literature. Ibadan, 1959.

Afr Doc 3409.310F   The appropriation accounts, revenue statements, accounts of the funds and other public accounts together with the report thereon by the Controller and Auditor-General. (Tanzania.) Dar es Salaam. 1966+

Afr Doc 3609.310F   The appropriation accounts; revenue statements and other public accounts. (Malawi.) Zomba. 1967+

Afr Doc 3209.112   The appropriation accounts. (Kenya.) Nairobi. 1957+

Afr Doc 2709.10   Approved estimates of expenditure. (Seychelles.) Victoria. 1964+

Afr Doc 2709.15   Approved estimates of revenue. (Seychelles.) Victoria. 1964+

Afr Doc 3209.30   Approved estimates of revenue and expenditure. (Kenya. African District Councils.) Nairobi. 1962+

Afr 109.62.35   Appunti di storia dell'Africa. (Pirone, Michele.) Milano, 1962.

Afr 609.54.30   Appunti per un periplo dell'Africa. (Cecchi, Emilio.) Milano, 1954.

Afr 6162.10.2   Apter, D.E. Ghana in transition. N.Y., 1963.

Afr 6162.10A   Apter, D.E. The Gold Coast in transition. Princeton, 1955.

Afr 6498.61.7   Apter, David E. The political kingdom in Uganda; a study in bureaucratic nationalism. 2nd ed. Princeton, 1967.

Afr 6498.61A   Apter, David E. The political kingdom in Uganda. Princeton, N.J., 1961.

Afr 630.66.15   Aptitudes and abilities of the black man in sub-Saharan Africa, 1784-1963. (Andor, L.) Johannesburg, 1966.

Afr 1608.77   Apuntes biograficas de el hach mohamed el Bagdady, Don José Maria de Murqa, segui dos de otros varios para idea de los usas. (Fernandez Duro, Cesareo.) Madrid, 1877.

Htn Afr 1368.60*   Apuntes para la historia de Marruecos. (Canovas del Castello, A. de.) Madrid, 1860.

Afr 1368.60.6   Apuntes para la historia de Marruecos. (Canovas del Castello, A. de.) Madrid, 1913.

Afr 1739.3.10   Apuntes para la historia de Tetuan. (Ruiz De Cuevas, T.) Tetuan, 1951.

Afr 1658.18   Apuntes para la historia del Rif. (Michaux-Bellaire, Ed.) Madrid, 1926.

Afr 1326.3   Apuntes para una bibliografia de Marruecos. (Bauer y Landauer, I.) Madrid, 1922.

Afr 5920.3   Apuntes sobre el estado de la costa occidental. (Navarro, J.J.) Madrid, 1859.

Afr 1750.11.6   Apuntes sobre geografia de la zona norte del protectorado de Espana en Marruegos. 3. ed. (Domenech Lafuente, A.) Madrid, 1942.

Afr 500.21   Apuntes sobre la expansion colonial en Africa. (Yanguas Messia, José.) Madrid, 1915.

Afr 1608.95.7   Apuntes sobre Marruecos. (Canizares y Moyano, ed.) Madrid, 1895.

Afr 7025.10   Aquelas longas horas. (Cunha, Manuel.) Lisboa, 1968.

Afr 7068.12   Aquiar, Armando de. Guiné, minha terra. Lisboa, 1964.

Afr 6455.10   The Arab and the African. (Pruen, S.R.) London, 1891.

Afr 3125.5   The Arab conquest of Egypt. (Butler, A.J.) Oxford, 1902.

Afr 1259.30.5   Arab interlude. (Hulme, K.C.) Philadelphia, 1930.

Afr 2209.36.5   Arab interlude. (Sheridan, C.F.) London, 1936.

Afr 3322.4   Arab political encyclopedia. Cairo. 10,1961+ 2v.

Afr 3320.10F   Arab review. Cairo. 1,1960+ 5v.

Afr 1110.35   The Arab role in Africa. (Baulin, Jacques.) Baltimore, 1962.

Afr 2228.7   L'arabe tel qu'il est. (Robert, A.) Alger, 1900.

Afr 1089.5   Les Arabes en Berbérie du XIe au XIVe siècle. (Marcais, Georges.) Constantine, 1913.

Afr 2228.4   Arabes et Kabyles. (Caix de St. Aymour, A. de.) Paris, 1891.

Afr 2228.6   Arabes et Kabyles. (Guimet, E.) Lyon, 1873.

Afr 3267.5   Arabi, Ahmed. Memoire d'Arabi-Pacha à ses avocats. Thése. Photoreproduction. Paris, 1924.

Afr 1110.20   Arabischen Westen. 1. Aufl. (Fernan, F.W.) Stuttgart, 1959.

Afr 5225.10   The Arabs and the Sundan: from the seventh to the early sixteenth century. (Hasan, Yūsuf Fadl.) Edinburgh, 1967.

Afr 5048.5   Les Arabs dans l'Afrique centrale. (Burdo, A.) Paris, 1885.

Afr 590.19   Arabs in Central Africa and at Lake Nyassa. (Stevenson, J.) Glasgow, 1888.

Afr 2875.15   The Arabs in Tripoli. (Ostler, A.) London, 1912.

Afr 9555.5   Arabskie istochniki VII-X vekov. (Akademiia Nauk SSSR. Institut Etnografii.) Moscow, 1960. 2v.

Afr 5920.11   Arambilet, S. Posesiones españolas del Africa occidental. Madrid, 1903.

Afr 1947.2   Aranda, E.D. Relation de la captivité...esclave à Alger. Bruxelles, 1662.

Afr 1947.2.3   Aranda, E.D. Relation de la captivité...esclave à Alger. Paris, 1657.

Afr 7176.32   Araujo, A. Correia de. Apectos do desenvolvimento ecónomico e social de Angola. Lisboa, 1964.

Afr 7324.21   Araujo, Antonio José de. Os acontecimentos de Lourenço Marques. Lisboa, 1889.

Afr 109.59.20   Arbeitstagung über Neuere und Neueste Geschichte. Geschichte und Geschichtsbild Afrikas. Berlin, 1960.

Afr 2397.36   L'Arbitraire. (Hadj Ali, Bachir.) Paris, 1966.

Afr 8658.46.5   Arbousset, Thomas. Narrative of an exploratory tour to the North-East of the Colony of the Cape of Good Hope. Facsimile. Cape Town, 1968.

Afr 8658.42   Arbousset, Thomas. Relation d'un voyage...au cap de Bonne-Espérance. Paris, 1842.

Afr 45.61.10   Arboussier, Gabriel. L'Afrique vers l'unité. Issy, 1961.

Afr 618.15   Arbuthnot, T.S. African hunt. 1st ed. N.Y., 1954.

Afr 7318.5   Arcangelo da Barletta. Sulle rive dello Zambesi. Palo del Calle, 1964.

Afr 4420.5   Arce, L. L'Abyssinie. Avignon, 1925.

Afr 5833.4   Archer, Edward. A letterTo the right honourable Lord John Russell. London, 1848.

Afr 6113.5   Archer, F.B. Gambia colony and protectorate. London, 1906.

Afr 6113.5.2   Archer, F.B. The Gambia colony and protectorate and official handbooks. 1st ed. London, 1967.

Afr 6470.113   Archer, G.F. Personal and historical memoirs. Edinburgh, 1963.

Afr 7119.63.10   Archer, Maria. Brasil, fronteirada Africa. Sao Paulo, 1963.

Afr 3258.6   Archer, T. War in Egypt and the Soudan. London, 1887. 2v.

Afr 8028.153   Archibald, Jane Erica. The works of Isaac Schapera; a selective bibliography. Johannesburg, 1969.

Afr 4368.16   L'archimandrite Paisi et l'ataman Achinoff. (Constantin, Jean R.) Paris, 1891.

Afr 38.2F   Archival facilities in sub-Saharan Africa. (Baxter, T.W.) n.p., 1959.

Afr 29.25   Pamphlet vol. Archives - Africa. 3 pam.

Afr 1001.2   Archives berbères. Rabat. 1,1915+ 3v.

Afr 7501.3F   Archives du Congo belge. Leopoldville. 2+

Afr 1915.2   Les archives du consulat général de France. (Devoulx, A.) Alger, 1865.

Afr 1026.4   Les archives espagnoles du gouvernement de l'Algérie. (Jacqueton, G.) Alger, 1894.

Afr 1330.5.9   Archives et bibliothèques d'Angleterre, 1661-1757. (France, t.1-3). (Castries, H. de.) Paris, 1918-1925. 3v.

Afr 1330.5.12   Archives et bibliothèques de Portugal. 1,1939+ 6v.

Afr 9432.26   Archives in a growing society. (Rhodesia and Nyasaland.) Salisbury, 1963.

Afr 6170.11	The Ashanti war. (Brackenbury, H.) Edinburgh, 1874. 2v.
Afr 6170.11.1	The Ashanti War: a narrative. 1st ed. (Brackenbury, H.) London, 1968.
Afr 2426.5	Ashbee, H.S. A bibliography of Tunisia...to 1888. London, 1889.
Afr 8305.6	Ashe, E.O. Besieged by the Boers. N.Y., 1900.
Afr 8160.22	Ashe, Major. The story of the Zulu campaign. London, 1880.
Afr 6497.5	Ashe, R.P. Chronicles of Uganda. N.Y., 1895.
Afr 1494.62	Ashford, D.E. Perspectives of a Moroccan nationalist. Totowa, N.J., 1964.
Afr 1369.61A	Ashford, Douglas. Political change in Morocco. Princeton, 1961.
Afr 1040.15	Ashford, Douglas E. National development and local reform. Princeton, 1967.
Afr 1623.965	Ashford, Douglas Elliott. Marocco-Tunisia. 1st ed. Syracuse, N.Y., 1965.
Afr 1490.2	Ashmead-Bartlett, E. Passing of the shereefian empire. Edinburgh, 1910.
Afr 1490.2.5	Ashmead-Bartlett, E. Passing of the shereefian empire. N.Y., 1910.
Afr 7375.4	Ashmun, J. History of the American colony in Liberia. Washington, 1826.
Afr 8028.135	Ashpol, R. A select bibliography of South African auto-biographies. Cape Town, 1958.
Afr 8925.10	Ashton, H. The Basuto. London, 1952.
Afr 6395.20	Asians in East Africa. (Delf, George.) London, 1963.
Afr 635.65	The Asians of East Africa. (Hollingworth, L.W.) London, 1960.
Afr 9161.8F	Asiatic land tenure (amendement) bill, commonly known as the Transvaal Asiatic bill, 1930. Johannesburg, 1930.
Afr 590.90	Asiegbu, Johnson U.J. Slavery and the politics of liberation, 1787-1861. N.Y., 1969.
Afr 2875.60	Askew, W.C. Europe and Italy's acquisition of Libya, 1911-1912. Durham, N.C., 1942.
Afr 6415.40.2	Askwirth, Tom G. Kenya's progress. 2nd ed. Kampala, 1958.
Afr 6415.40	Askwith, Tom G. The story of Kenya's progress. Nairobi, 1953.
Afr 5318.14	Aspe-Fleurimont, L. La Guinée française. Paris, 1900.
Afr 7122.45	Aspectos actuais de Angola. (Vinhas, Manuel.) Lisboa, 1961.
Afr 7180.25	Aspectos do povoamento branco de Angola. (Amaral, I. do.) Lisboa, 1960.
Afr 618.20.5	Aspectos dos movimentos associativos na Africa negra. (Cunha, Joaquim M. da S.) Lisboa, 1958.
Afr 628.258.5	Aspects de la culture noire. Paris, 1958.
Afr 4008.10	Aspects de l'Egypte copte. (Kamil, Murad.) Berlin, 1965.
Afr Doc 6607.20	Aspects éonomiques. (Dahomey. Ministère des Finances et des Affaires Economiques.) Cotonou. 1962+
Afr 1550.56	Aspects marocains. (Vieleux, Christian.) La Rochelle, 1957.
Afr 2221.3F	Aspects of Algeria. (Algeria. Service de l'Information. Direction de la Documentation Générale.) Algiers. 196-.
Afr 2209.12	Aspects of Algeria historical. (Devereux, R.) London, 1912.
Afr 710.74	Aspects of Central African history. London, 1968.
Afr 8057.10	Aspekte van die Suid-Afrikaanse historiografie. (Cronjé, Geoffrey.) Pretoria, 1967.
Afr 4700.35.30	Aspetti attuoli dell'economia delle colonie italiane dell'Africa orientale. (Dotti, Ernesto.) Roma, 1935.
Afr 4389.35.10	Aspetti della questione etiopica. (Sperduti, G.) Roma, 1935.
Afr 4746.15	Assab e i suoi critici. (Sapeto, G.) Genova, 1879.
Afr 4746.10F	Assab et les limites de la souveraineté turco-égyptienne dans la Mer Rouge. (Italy.) Rome, 1882.
Afr 500.53	Assac, Jacques Ploncard d'. L'erreur africaine. Paris, 1964.
Afr 3340.25	Assassa, Sami. Die Entstehung der Vereinigten Arabischen Republik und die Entwicklung. Diss. Berlin, 1965.
Afr 11239.67.110	The assassins. (Brown, J.A.) Johannesburg, 1965.
Afr 4393.5	L'Assedio di Macallè. Milano, 1935.
Afr Doc 3414.10	Assembly debates; official report. (Tanganyika. National Assembly.) 27,1952+ 13v.
Afr 6757.10	Assembly debates, official report. (Tanganyika. National Assembly.) 27,1952+ 12v.
Afr 210.64.30	Assembly of the heads of state and government of O.A.U. (Organization of African Unity.) Cairo, 1964.
Afr 4070.49	Assher, B. A nomad in the south Sudan. London, 1928.
Afr 1609.30	Assher, Ben. A nomad in Morocco. London, n.d.
Afr 5346.5.15	Assinie et le royaume de Krinjabo. 2. éd. (Mouezy, Henri.) Paris, 1953.
Afr 7175.22F	Associação Comercial de Lajistas de Lisboa. Alguns aspectos psicologicos de nossa colonização en Angola. Lisboa, 1930.
Afr 7815.19	Association des Intérêts Coloniaux Belges. Des relations de travail entre européens et africains. Bruxelles, 1956.
Afr 10104.5F	Association for African Literature in English. Bulletin. Freetown. 2,1965+
Afr 657.90F	Association for Promoting the Discovery of the Interior Parts of Africa. Proceedings. London, 1790.
Afr 657.90.5	Association for Promoting the Discovery of the Interior Parts of Africa. Proceedings of the Association for Promoting the Discovery of the Interior Parts of Africa. London, 1810. 2v.
Afr 657.88	Association for Promoting the Discovery of the Interior Parts of Africa. Records of the African Association, 1788-1831. London, 1964.
Afr 2290.2	Association Française pour l'Avancement des Sciences. Oran et l'Algérie en 1887. Oran, 1888. 2v.
Afr 6700.4	Association Française pour les Recherches et Études Camerounaises. Bulletin. Bordeaux. 1,1965+
Afr 1.6F	Association Internationale Africaine. Compte rendu. Bruxelles. 1877+
Afr 6878.79	Association Internationale Africaine. Rapports sur les marchés de la première éxpedition. v.1-4. Bruxelles, 1879-80.
Afr 1.6.7F	Association Internationale Africaine. Comité Naional. Belge. Séance. Bruxelles.
Afr Doc 3808.505	The association of commodities with industries in Rhodesia. (Rhodesia (British Colony). Central Statistical office.) Salisbury, 1966.
Afr 2223.961.5	Association pour la Recherche. La consommation des familles d'Algérie. Paris, 1961.
Afr 7803.36	Associations religieuses au Congo belge. (Heyse, T.) Bruxelles, 1948.
Afr 1.108	Associazione degli Africanisti Italiani. Bollettino. Paria. 1,1968+
Afr 2748.57.20	Assollant, Georges. Eugène Fromentin, un été dans le Sahara. Paris, 1931.
Afr 3986.961.15	Assouan. (Egypt. Information Administration.) Le Caire, 1961.
Afr 11005.6	Astrinsky, Aviva. A bibliography of South African English novels, 1930-1960. Cape Town, 1965.
Afr 3993.5	Asuan, simvol sovetsko-arabskoi druzhby. (Pravda, Moskva.) Moskva, 1964.
Afr 4392.7	Asunto delle relazione sul servizio sanitario...in occasione delle campagna d'Africa, 1895-1896. (Red Cross, Italy (Croce Rossa).) Roma, 1899.
Afr 3046.5.3	Asuntos militares en Egipto. (Stone, Charles. P.) Habana, 1884.
Afr 4108.2	Aswan. (Habachi, Labib.) Le Caire, 1959.
Afr 4108.5	Aswan. (United Arab Republic.) Cairo, 196-.
Afr 4108.5.2	Aswan. (United Arab Republic. Information Department.) Cairo, 1964.
Afr 3993.5.5	Aswan High Dam, diversion of Nile. (United Arab Republic. Ministry of the High Dam.) Aswan, 1964.
Afr 6194.39	Aszanti, kraj Złotego Tronu. (Zajaczkowski, A.) Warszawa, 1963.
Afr 6455.160	At home with Michaela. (Denis, Michaela.) London, 1965.
Afr 8667.97	At last we have got our country back. 2nd ed. (Calpin, George Harold.) Cape Town, 1969.
Afr 5445.5	At the back of the black man's mind. (Dennett, R.E.) London, 1906.
Afr 6196.26	At the court of an African king. (Meyerowitz, Eva.) London, 1962.
Afr 1738.8	At the strait's mouth. (Furlong, C.W.) N.Y., 1904.
Afr 3258.20	Ata, M.M. Egypt between two revolutions. Cairo, 1956.
Afr 44623.40.100	Atenji wa vita vya Uhud. (Chum, Haji.) Dar es Salaam, 1962.
Afr 7501.8	Atennes. Leopoldville. 3,1964+
Afr 5340.21	Atger, Paul. La France en Côte-d'Ivoire de 1843 à 1893. Dakar, 1962.
Afr 3295.5	Atiyah, S. Razvitie natsionalno-osvoboditelnogo dvizheniia v Egipte. Moscow, 1961.
Afr 6095.6	Atkins, J. Voyage to Guinea, Brasil. London, 1735.
Afr 6095.6.2	Atkins, J. Voyage to Guinea, Brasil. 2nd ed. London, 1737.
Afr 8300.8	Atkins, J.B. The relief of Ladysmith. London, 1900.
Afr 4742.22	Atlante delle colonie italiane. (Baralta, M.) Novara, 1928.
Afr 1200.58	L'Atlantide, pays de l'Atlas. (Reclus, Onesime.) Paris, 1918.
Afr 2622.1	Atlas de Tunisie. (Mager, Henri.) Paris, n.d.
Afr 1.100	Atlas des structures agraires au Sud du Sahara. Paris. 1,1967+ 2v.
Afr 7809.55F	Atlas du Congo belge et du Ruanda-Urundi. (Derhinderen, G.) Paris, 1955.
Afr 5920.7.3	Atlas icono-geografico-estadistico del Africa occidental española. (Rio Joan, F. del.) Madrid, 1915.
Afr 1680.2.5	L'atlas marocain d'apres les documents originaux. (Schnell, P.) Paris, 1898.
Afr 625.20	An atlas of Africa. (Horrabin, James F.) London, 1960.
Afr 210.62.50	An atlas of African affairs. (Boyd, Andrew Kirk Henry.) N.Y., 1962.
Afr 3275.16	Atrocities of justice under British rule in Egypt. (Blunt, W.S.) London, 1906.
Afr 3040.80	al-Attar, Fuad Abdallah. Le marché de travaux publics. Thèse. Le Caire, 1955.
Afr 575.7	Atterbury, Anson Phelps. Islam in Africa. N.Y., 1899.
Afr 575.7.2	Atterbury, Anson Phelps. Islam in Africa. N.Y., 1969.
Afr 3735.8	Atteridge, A.H. Towards Khartoum. ondon, 1897.
Afr 3978.95	Attfield, D.H. Private journal in Egypt. London, 1895.
Afr 4700.17	Atti. v.1. (Congresso Coloniale Italiano, Asmara.) Roma, 1906.
Afr 505.17	Attitude to Africa. Middlesex, Eng., 1951.
Afr 6275.105	The attitudes, hopes and fears of Nigerians. (Institute for International Social Research.) Princeton, 1964.
Afr 4743.5	Le attitudini della colonia Eritrea all'agricoltura. (Bartolommei-Gioli, G.) Firenze, 1902.
Afr 4766.36	L'attività del governo dall'indipendenza ad oggi. (Somalia. Consiglio dei Ministri.) Mogadiscio, 1964.
Afr 2945.9	Attraverso la Cirenaica. (Checchi, S.) Roma, 1912.
Afr 2438.25	Les attributions des contrôleurs civils en Tunisie. Thèse. (Pinon, J.P.M.) Tunis, 1931.
Afr 5316.14	Attwood, William. The reds and the blacks, a personal adventure. 1st ed. N.Y., 1967.
Afr 6275.11	Au Bas-Niger. 3. ed. (Viard, E.) Paris, 1886.
Afr 5119.65	Au carrefour des options africaines, le Sénégal. (Milcent, Ernest.) Paris, 1965.
Afr 6541.27	Au coeur de l'Afrique. (Philippe, Antony.) Paris, 1929.
Afr 1680.5	Au coeur de l'atlas. (Segonzac, De.) Paris, 1910.
Afr 1609.13.8	Au coeur du Maroc. (Botte, L.) Paris, 1913.
Afr 2230.40	Au coeur du pays kabyle. (Remond, Martial.) Alger, 1933.
Afr 7808.89.9	Au Congo. (Michaux, Oscar.) Namur, 1913.
Afr 7808.99.3	Au Congo belge. (Mille, P.) Paris, 1899.
Afr 555.23.7	Au Congo et aux Indes. Bruxelles, 1906.
Afr 555.23.51	Au Congo français. Les missions catholiques. (Boucher, A.) Paris, 1928.
Afr 5420.222	Au Gabon, Afrique. (Grebert, F.) Paris, 1922.
Afr 2749.22.5	Au Hoggar, mission de 1922. (Killian, Conrad.) Paris, 1925.
Afr 6887.2	Au Kilima-ndjaro. (Leroy, A.) Paris, 1893.
Afr 1571.29	Au Maroc, fin des temps héroiques. (Pinon, Rene.) Paris, 1935.
Afr 1675.2	Au Maroc, marrakech et les ports du sud. Paris, 1918 (Perigny, Maurice.)
Afr 1608.90	Au Maroc. (Viaud, J.) Paris, 1890.
Afr 1609.30.10	Au Maroc. (Willette, H.) Paris, 1930.
Afr 1713.9	Au Maroc. Fes la capitale du nord. (Erigny, Maurice.) Paris, 191- .
Afr 1609.22.5	Au Maroc. Sur les rives. (Rabbe, P.) Paris, 1922.
Afr 1571.18	Au Maroc avec Lyautey. (Leclerc, Max.) Paris, 1927.
Afr 1571.17.25	Au Maroc avec Lyautey. (Willette, H.) Paris, 1931.
Afr 1450.1	Au Maroc dans l'intimité du sultan. (Veyre, Gabriel.) Paris, n.d.
Afr 1609.32F	Au Maroc en suivant Foucauld. (Ladreit de Lacharrière, J.) Paris, 1932.
Afr 1573.31	Au Maroc espagnol. (Laget, Paul de.) Marseille, 1935.
Afr 1493.35	Au Maroc français en 1925. (Loustaunau-Lacau, G.) Paris, 1928.
Afr 1680.9	Au Maroc inconnu dans le haut-atlas et le sud Marocain. (Felze, Jacques.) Grenoble, 1935.
Afr 1570.35	Au Maroc par les camps et par les villes. (Babin, G.) Paris, 1912.

Afr 1258.96   Au nord de l'Afrique. (Drouet, F.) Nice, 1896.
Afr 2527.7   Au pays de Kroumers et au Maroc. (Benoyts, F. de.) Lille, 1913.
Afr 5635.17   Au pays de la fièvre. (Darricarrere, J.) Paris, 1904.
Afr 1490.12   Au pays de la poudre. (Ceccaldi, C.) Paris, 1914.
Afr 4559.56F   Au pays de la ruine de Saba. (Doresse, Jean.) Paris, 1956.
Afr 5842.2   Au pays de Paul et Virginie. (Leclercq, J.) Paris, 1895.
Afr 659.11   Au pays de Salammbo. (Douel, Martial.) Paris, 1911.
Afr 9710.5.7   Au pays des Barotsi, Haut-Zambèze. (Bertrand, Alfred.) Paris, 1898.
Afr 2208.98.3   Au pays des Burnous. (Barbet, Charles.) Alger, 1898.
Afr 5385.27.2   Au pays des Fons. 2me éd. (Quenum, M.) Paris, 1938.
Afr 6455.3.10   Au pays des Massai. (Thomson, Joseph.) Paris, 1886.
Afr 2209.11.7   Au pays des mirages. (Roy, R.) Paris, 1911.
Afr 2312.4   Au pays des palmes, Biskra. (Hautfort, Felix.) Paris, 1897.
Afr 2312.4.2   Au pays des palmes, Biskra. 2e ed. (Hautfort, Felix.) Paris, 1897.
Afr 4869.01   Au pays des Somalis et des Comoriens. (Heudebert, L.) Paris, 1901.
Afr 1609.24   Au pays du paradoxe, Maroc. (Tranchant de Lunel, M.) Paris, 1924.
Afr 5748.96.10   Au pays Malgache. (Blavet, Emile.) Paris, 1897.
Afr 5748.96.9   Au pays Malgache de Paris à Tananarive et retour. 2e ed. (Blavet, Emile.) Paris, 1897.
Afr 6395.2.16   Au pied du Mont Kenya. (Kenyatta, Jona.) Paris, 1960.
Afr 2731.10   Au Sahara avec le commandant Charlet. (Lehuraux, L.J.) Paris, 1932.
Afr 2710.10   Au Sahara pendant la guerre europèenne (Vermale, Paul.) Alger, 1926.
Afr 1490.11   Au secours de Fès. (Capperon, L.) Paris, 1912.
Afr 2030.460.5   Au service de l'Algérie française nouvelle. (Lauriol, M.) Alger, 1960.
Afr 1571.41   Au service du Maroc: Charles de Foucauld. (Gorrée, Georges.) Paris, 1939.
Afr 4559.35.117   Au service du négus. 2e ed. (Rebeaud, Henri.) Paris, 1935.
Afr 1453.11   Au seuil du Maroc moderne. (Weisgerber, F.) Rabat, 1947.
Afr 5235.189   Au Soudan français. (Peroz, Etienne.) Paris, 1889.
Afr 5235.194.5   Au Soudan français. (Triviet, E.) Paris, 1932.
Afr 2374.1   Au sujet du Touat. (Vivarez, M.) Alger, 1896.
Afr 5480.211   Au Tchad. (Cornel, Charles J.H.) Paris, 1911.
Afr 1430.2   Au temps de Mehallas. (Arnaud, L.) Casablanca, 1952.
Afr 8289.02.35   Au Transvaal, et dans le Sud-Afrique avec les attachés militaires. (Raoul-Duval, R.) Paris, 1902.
Afr 8658.98.5   Aubert, Georges. L'Afrique du Sud. Paris, 1898.
Afr 4869.39.12   Aubert de la Rue, E. La Somalie française. Paris, 1939.
Afr 3275.13   Aubin, E. Les Anglais aux Indes et en Egypte. Paris, 1899.
Afr 3275.13.2   Aubin, E. Les Anglais aux Indes et en Egypte. Paris, 1900.
Afr 1609.04   Aubin, Eugene. Le Maroc d'aujourd hui. Paris, 1904.
Afr 1609.03.12   Aubin, Eugene. Morocco of today. London, 1906.
Afr 5365.4   Aublet, E. La guerre au Dahomey. Paris, 1894.
Afr 2230.14   Aucapitaine, H. Les confins militaires de la Grande Kabylie. Paris, 1857.
Afr 2230.7   Aucapitaine, H. Les Kabyles. Paris, 1864.
Afr 9610.1   Aucapitaine, L.B.H. Les Yem-Yem tribu anthropophage de l'Afrique centrale. Paris, 1857.
Afr 2228.9   Auclert, Hubertine. Les femmes arabes. Paris, 1900.
Afr 2030.265F   Aucune bête au monde. (Flament, Marc.) Paris, 1959.
Afr 6397.5   Un audacieux pionnier de l'église au Afrique. (Catrice, Paul.) Lyon, 1964.
Afr 5748.83   Audebert, J. Madagaskar und das Hovareich. Berlin, 1883.
Afr 1609.06.7   Auer, Grethe. Marokkanische sittenbilder. Bern, 1906.
Afr 5056.110   Auf dem Wege nach Atlantis. (Frobenius, Leo.) Berlin, 1911.
Afr 1583.17   Auf eigene Faust meine Erlebnisse vor und während des Weltkrieges in Marokko. (Bartels, Albert.) Leipzig, 1925.
Afr 8659.03   Auf und ab in Süd-Afrika. (Braun, D.E.) Berlin, 1903.
Afr 6689.10   Aufbruch vom Götterberg. (Nelle, Albrecht.) Stuttgart, 1968.
Afr 2749.30   Augieras, Ernest M. Chronique de l'ouest saharien (1900-1930). Paris, 1930.
Afr 555.39.20   Augouard, Prosper P. Vingt-huit années au Congo. Vienne, 1905.
Afr 5448.13   Augouard, Prosper Philippe. Notes historiques sur la fondation de Brazzaville. Paris, 1917.
Afr 1608.38   Augustin, F. von. Erinnerungen aus Marokko. Wien, 1838.
Afr 8925.20   Auin, P.J. Foods and feeding habits of the Pedi. Johannesburg, 1959.
Afr 1957.2   Ault-Dumesnil, E.D. De l'expédition d'Afrique en 1830. Paris, 1832.
Afr 2030.459.5   Aumeran, Adolphe. Paix en Algérie. Paris, 1959.
Afr 2274.1   Aumerat, J.F. L'anti-sémitisme à Alger. Alger, 1885.
Afr 1571.17.42   Auprès de Lyautey. (Ormesson, W.) Paris, 1963.
Afr 3204.10   Auriant, L. L'Egypte. Paris, 1920.
Afr 7809.28   Auric, Henri. L'avenir du Congo et du Congo-océan. Thèse. Paris, 1928.
Afr 1955.32   Aus Africa und Spanien. Jena, 1870.
Afr 3978.64   Aus dem Orient. (Mainly Egypt). (Brugsch, H.K.F.) Berlin, 1864.
Afr 6878.88.5PF   Aus Deutsch-Ost-Afrika. (Hellgrewe, Rudolf.) Berlin, 1888.
Afr 3978.68.5   Aus Egypten. (Frankl, L.A.) Wien, 1868.
Afr 3978.44   Aus Mehemed Alis Reich. (Pueckler-Muskau.) Stuttgart, 1844.
Afr 8678.12   Aus Namaland und Kalahari. (Schultze, L.) Jena, 1907.
Afr 8110.13   Die Ausdehnung der Kolonie am Kap der Guten Hoffnung (1700-1779). Inaug. Diss. (Walt, A.J.H.) Berlin, 1928.
Afr 1608.46   Ausflug von Lissabon nach Andalusien und...Marokko. (Löwenherz, W. Zu.) Dresden, 1846.
Afr 8676.37   Aussenhandel und Handelspolitik der Südafrikanischen Union unter besonderer Berücksichtigung der Wirtschafts der Union. (Gerich, K.H.A.) Düsseldorf, 1937.
Afr 2875.43   Die Aussenpolitik der Mittelmächte im Tripoliskrieg...1911-1912. (Kalbskopf, W.) Erlangen, 1932.
Afr 5832.15.2F   Austen, H.C.M. Sea fights and corsairs of the Indian Ocean. Port Louis, 1935.
Afr 6769.68   Austen, Ralph Albert. Northwest Tanzania under German and British rule. New Haven, 1968.
Afr 210.65.40   Austin, Dennis. Inter-state relations in Africa. 1st ed. Freiburg, 1965.
Afr 6162.14   Austin, Dennis. Politics in Ghana, 1946-1960. N.Y., 1964.

Afr 6390.5   Austin, H.H. Among swamps and giants in Equatorial Africa. London, 1902.
Afr 6535.11   Austin, H.H. MacDonald in Uganda. London, 1903.
Afr 9388.87   Austral Africa. (Mackenzie, J.) London, 1887. 2v.
Afr 8292.11   Australia at the front, colonial view of Boer war. (Wilkinson, F.) London, 1901.
Afr 1585.3F   Austro-Hungarian Monarchy. Ministerium des Aüssern. Diplomatische Aktenstücken über die Internationale Konferenz von Algeciras, 1905-06. Wien, 1906.
Afr 3986.960A   Austry, J. Structure économique et civilisation. Paris, 1960.
Afr 8685.25   Auswanderung aus Indien. I. Inaug. Diss. (Chatterjee, M.N.) Leipzig, 1931.
Afr 1258.17.2   An authentic narrative of the loss of the American brig Commerce. (Riley, J.) Hartford, 1817.
Afr 1258.17.5   An authentic narrative of the loss of the American brig Commerce. (Riley, J.) Hartford, 1833.
Afr 1258.17.8   An authentic narrative of the loss of the American brig Commerce. (Riley, J.) Hartford, 1844.
Afr 1258.17.10   An authentic narrative of the loss of the American brig Commerce. (Riley, J.) Hartford, 1847.
Afr 3339.12   Une authentique promotion démocratique. (United Arab Republic. Laws, statutes, etc.) Le Caire, 1964.
Afr 6203.6   An author catalogue of books about Nigeria in the regional library. (Kaduna, Nigeria. Regional Library.) Kaduna, 1965.
Afr 8252.1   An autobiographical memoir. (Boreherds, P.B.) Cape Town, 1861.
Afr 8252.1.5   An autobiographical memoir. Facsimile reproduction. (Borcherds, P.B.) Cape Town, 1963.
Afr 4555.86A   Autobiography, account of ten years' life in Abyssinia. (Waldmeier, T.) London, 1886.
Afr 9028.64.5   Autobiography. (Grout, Lewis.) Brattleboro, 1905.
Afr 8687.238   Autobiography. (Innes, James Rose.) Cape Town, 1949.
Afr 9748.582   The autobiography of an African. (Fraser, D.) London, 1925.
Afr 9525.288   The autobiography of an old drifter. (Clark, Percy M.) London, 1936.
Afr 718.2.81A   Autobiography of Henry Morton Stanley. (Grant, J.H.) Boston, 1909.
Afr 8252.194   The autobiography of Kingsley Fairbridge. (Fairbridge, K.) London, 1927.
Afr 8849.347   The autobiography of the late Sir Andries Stockenstroem. (Stockenstroem, Andries.) Cape Town, 1964. 2v.
Afr 620.1   Automobile Association of South Africa. Trans-African highways. Cape Town, 1949.
Afr 5874.8   Autour de l'Ile Bourbon et de Madagascar. (Mahy, F. de.) Paris, 1891.
Afr 2030.352   Autour du drame. (Roy, Jules.) Paris, 1961.
Afr 2030.155   Autour d'une erreur politique. (Montpeyroux, André Brousse de.) Alger, 1958.
Afr 3183.15   Autour d'une route. (Charles-Roux, François.) Paris, 1922.
Afr 8678.285   Une autre Afrique du Sud. (Giniewski, P.) Paris, 1962.
Afr 2875.18   Aux camps turco-arabes. (Remond, G.) Paris, 1913.
Afr 8658.95.5   Aux chutes du Zambèze. (Leclercq, Jules.) Paris, 1936.
Afr 7535.20   Aux origines de l'Etat indépendant du Congo. (Bontinck, François.) Louvain, 1966.
Afr 4070.30   Aux pays du Soudan, Bagos, Mensah, Souakim. (Rivoyre, D. De.) Paris, 1885.
Afr 5342.66   Aux temps héroïques de la Côte-d'Ivoire. (Brétignère, Amédée.) Paris, 1931.
Afr 1273.958   Avakov, R.M. Frantsuzskii monopolisticheskii kapital v severnoi Afrike. Moscow, 1958.
Afr 1369.61.5   Avakov, R.M. Morokko. Moscow, 1961.
Afr 9599.61   Avalanche in central Africa. (Gibbs, Peter.) London, 1961.
Afr 1583.12   Ave caesar. Deutsche Luftschiffe...Marokko. (Maurus, Pseud.) Leipzig, 1909.
Afr 5405.112   Avec Brazza. (Chavannes, Charles de.) Paris, 1936.
Afr 2731.15.3   Avec le père de Foucauld et le général Laperrine, 1909-11. (Herisson, R.) Paris, 1937.
Afr 6780.20   Avec les Vainqueures de Tahora. 2. ed. (Daye, P.) Paris, 1918.
Afr 520.9   Aveilza, J.M.De. Reivindicaciones de espana. 2.Ed. Madrid, 1941.
Afr 150.2.25   Aveiro, Portugal. Museu. Iconografia do Infante Dom Henrique. Aveiro, 1960.
Afr 3979.34   Aveline, Claude. La promenade égyptienne. Paris, 1934.
Afr 200.17   L'avénement de l'Afrique noire du XIX siècle à nos jours. (Brunschwig, H.) Paris, 1963.
Afr 50.58   L'Avènement du parti unique en Afrique noire. (Mahiou, Ahmed.) Paris, 1969.
Afr 1658.10   Avenia Taure, I. Memorias sobre el riff, su conquista y colonizacion. Zaragoza, 1859.
Afr 2609.03.2   L'avenir de la Tunisie. (Pensa, H.) Paris, 1903.
Afr 210.64.2   L'avenir de l'Afrique. (Woddis, J.) Paris, 1964.
Afr 1271.5   Avenir de l'Afrique du Nord. (Bories, H.) Paris, 1938.
Afr 7809.21   L'avenir du Congo belge menacé. 2e ed. (Delcommune, A.) Bruxelles, 1921. 2v.
Afr 7809.28   L'avenir du Congo et du Congo-océan. Thèse. (Auric, Henri.) Paris, 1928.
Afr 2719.55   L'avenir du Sahara. (Banque Dambert-Blitz.) Paris, 1955.
Afr 678.86   Aventuras de un piloto en el Golfo de Guinea. (Donacuige.) Madrid, 1886.
Afr 4513.36.35   L'aventure abyssine. (Bourcier, E.) Paris, 1936.
Afr 2030.467.20   L'Aventure algérienne continue. (Fontaine, Pierre.) Paris, 1967.
Afr 2208.17   Aventure e osservazioni. (Pananti, F.) Firenze, 1817. 2v.
Afr 1658.27   L'aventure riffaine et ses dessous politiques. (Hubert, Jacques.) Paris, 1927.
Afr 1915.3   Aventures de dona ines de la Cisternas. (Frousseaux.) Utrecht, 1737.
Afr 1450.3   Aventures d'un français au Maroc. (Sarnette, F.) Paris, 1905.
Afr 3204.18   Aventuriers mameluks d'Egypte. (Guenard, Gabriel.) Toulouse, 1928.
Afr 5832.9   Averbeck, Franz. Geschichte und Physiographie der Kolonie Mauritius. Metz, 1905.
Afr 125.10   Avezac, A. D. Afrique. Paris, 1844.
Afr 850.2   Avezac-Macayo, M.A.P. Iles de l'Afrique. Paris, 1848.
Afr 4513.39.35   L'aviazione fascista e la conquista dell'impero. (Mattioli, Guido.) Roma, 1939.
Afr 5342.25   Avice, E. La Côte-d'Ivoire. Paris, 1951.
Afr 6210.40   Awa, Eme O. Federal government in Nigeria. Berkeley, 1964.

Afr 3305.3   Awad, Fawzi Tadrus. La souveraineté égyptienne et la déclaration du 28 février 1922. Paris, 1935.
Afr 8175.20.4   The awakening of Afrikaner nationalism, 1868-1881. (Jaarsveld, F.A. van.) Cape Town, 1961.
Afr 3199.47.2   The awakening of modern Egypt. (Rifaat, M.) Lahore, 1964.
Afr 3199.47   The awakening of modern Egypt. (Rifaat, M.) London, 1947.
Afr 2749.61.5   The awakening Sahara. (Bodington, Nicolas.) London, 1961.
Afr 6214.34   Awdowo Obateni. The people's republic. Ibadan, 1968.
Afr 6298.181   Awo. (Awolowo, Obaf.) Cambridge, 1960.
Afr 6298.181   Awolowo, Obaf. Awo. Cambridge, 1960.
Afr 6298.181.2   Awolowo, Obaf. My early life. Lagos, 1968.
Afr 6210.9   Awolowo, Olafemi. Path to Nigerian freedom. London, 1947.
Afr 6210.9.5   Awolowo, Olafemi. Thoughts on Nigerian constitution. Ibadan, 1966.
Afr 115.126.2   Awosika, V.O. An African meditation. 2nd ed. N.Y., 1969.
Afr 7222.40   Axelson, E.V. South-east Africa, 1488-1530. London, 1940.
Afr 7022.4   Axelson, Eric. Portugal and the scramble for Africa, 1875-1891. Johannesburg, 1967.
Afr 7015.25   Axelson, Eric V. Portuguese in South East Africa. Johannesburg, 1960.
Afr 28.98   Axelson, Eric Victor. African history, books and research. Cape Town. 1964.
Afr 8095.40   Axelson, Eric Victor. South African explorers. London, 1954.
Afr 6176.30.31   Axioms of Kwame Nkrumah. (Nkrumah, Kwame.) London, 1967.
Afr 6176.30.30   Axioms of Kwame Nkrumah. (Nkrumah, Kwame.) London, 1967.
Afr 1369.56A   Ayache, Albert. Le Maroc. Paris, 1956.
Afr 6282.8   Ayandele, Emmanuel Ayankammi. The missionary impact on modern Nigeria, 1842-1914, a political and social analysis. London, 1966.
Afr 6193.52   Ayatey, Siegfried B.Y. Central banking, international law, and economic development. Dubugre, 1968.
Afr 6925.5A   Aydelotte, W.O. Bismarck and British colonial policy, the problem of South West Africa, 1883-1885. Philadelphia, 1937.
Afr 8152.90   Aylward, A. The Transvaal of to-day. Edinburgh, 1878.
Afr 2762.6   Aymard, C. Les Touareg. Paris, 1911.
Afr 2533.4   Aymard, C.E. Tragédie française en Afrique du nord. Paris, 1958.
Afr 6720.28.15   Aymerich, J.G. La conquête du Cameroun. Paris, 1936.
Afr 2025.23   Aynard, R. L'oeuvre française en Algérie. Paris, 1912.
Afr 7320.2   Ayres de Carvalho Soveral. Breve estudio,--ilha de Moçambique. Porto, 1887.
Afr 7020.30   Ayres d'Ornellas. Viagem do principe real julho-setembro 1907. Lisboa, 1928.
Afr 3979.38.14   Ayrout, H.H. The Egyptian peasant. Boston, 1963.
Afr 3979.38.12   Ayrout, H.H. The fellaheen. 7th ed. Cairo, 1954.
Afr 3979.38.11.2   Ayrout, H.H. Fellahs. 2. ed. Le Caire, 1942.
Afr 3979.38.11   Ayrout, H.H. Fellahs d'Egypte. 6. ed. Le Caire, 1952.
Afr 3979.38.10   Ayrout, H.H. Moeurs et coutumes des fellahs. Thèse. Paris, 1938.
Afr 2285.25   Azalai. 1st ed. (Skolle, John.) N.Y., 1956.
Afr 1846.13   Azan, Paul. L'armee d'Afrique de 1830 à 1852. Paris, 1936.
Afr 1047.15   Azan, Paul. L'armée indigène nord-africaine. Paris, 1925.
Afr 1965.4.10   Azan, Paul. Bugeaud et l'Algérie. Paris, 1930.
Afr 1965.12.10   Azan, Paul. L'émir Abd el-Kader, 1808-1883. Paris, 1925.
Afr 1957.8   Azan, Paul. L'expédition d'Alger. Paris, 1929.
Afr 1490.11.15   Azan, Paul. L'expédition de Fez. Paris, 1924.
Afr 1844.5   Azan, Paul. Les grands soldats de l'Algerie. Paris, 1931.
Afr 1965.12   Azan, Paul. Récits d'Afrique Sidi-Brahim. Paris, 1905.
Afr 1965.12.5   Azan, Paul. Sidi-Brahim. Paris, 1930.
Afr 1490.14   Azan, Paul. Souvenirs de Casablanca. Paris, 1911.
Afr 2225.11   Azan, Paul J.L. Recherche d une solution de la question indigène en Algérie. Paris, 1903.
Afr 7815.13   Azande, introduction à une ethnographie générale des bassins de l'Ubangi-Uele et de l'Arvwimi. (Colonne-Beaufaict, A. de.) Bruxelles, 1921.
Afr 1.93F   Azania news. Lusaka. 1,1966+
Afr 2030.462.20   Azeau, Henri. Révolte militaire, Alger, 22 avril 1961. Paris, 1962.
Afr 3315.126   Azeau, Henri. Le siège de Suez. Paris, 1964.
Afr 5868.59   Azema, Georges. Histoire de l'Ile Bourbon depuis 1643 jusqu'au 20 décembre 1848. Paris, 1859.
Afr 5868.59.5   Azema, Georges. Histoire de l'Ile Bourbon depuis 1643 jusqu'au 20 décembre 1848. Paris, 1859.
Afr 150.2.85   Azevedo, A.J. da Silva D. Americas, un corolario de sagres. Lisboa, 1964.
Afr 7176.9   Azevedo, João M.C. de. Angola. Luanda, 1958.
Afr 1575.2F   Azevedo, Pedro de. Documentos das chancelarias reais anteriores a 1531. v.1-2. Lisboa, 1915. 2v.
Afr 7320.6   Azevedo Coutinho, João de. Do Nyassa a Pemba. Lisboa, 1931.
Afr 6212.5   Azihiwe, Nrandi. The development of political parties in Nigeria. London, 1957.
Afr 6212.20   Azikiwe, N. Zik. Cambridge, 1961.
Afr 6218.15   Azikiwe, Nnamdi. The evolution of federal government in Nigeria. Orlu, 195-. 4 pam.
Afr 7377.34   Azikiwe, Nnamdi. Liberia in world politics. London, 1934.
Afr 609.37   Azikiwe, Nnamdi. Renascent Africa. Accra, 1937.
Afr 609.37.2   Azikiwe, Nnamdi. Renascent Africa. N.Y., 1969.
Afr 6212.20.5   Azikiwe, Nnamdi. Sélection de discours de Nnamdi Azikiwe. Paris, 1968.
Afr 6212.16   Pamphlet vol. Azikiwe addresser. 4 pam.
Afr 1750.10   Azpeitua, Antonio. Marruecos, la mala semilla. Madrid, 1921.
Afr 8252.7   B.I. Barnato. (Raymond, H.) London, 1897.
Afr 5243.207   Ba, A.H. Koumen. Paris, 1961.
Afr 5225.7   Ba, Amadou H. L'empire Peul du Macina. Paris, 1962.
Afr 28747.5   Ba, Amadou Hampâté. Kaidara. Paris, 1969.
Afr 7815.24   Les Ba Dzing de la Kamtsha. (Mertens, Joseph.) Bruxelles, 1935-39.
Afr 4559.30.30   Ba Menelik. (Roth-Roesthof, A. von.) Leipzig, 1930.
Afr 7315.3   Les Ba-ronga. (Junod, H.A.) Neuchatel, 1898.
Afr 45.63.10   Baade, Hans Wolfgang. African law, new law for new nations. N.Y., 1963.
Afr 2376.2   Baader, Walter. Nach der Oase Tugurt in der Wüste Sahara. Basel, 1903.
Afr 1285.5   Baal, Christ, and Mohammed. (Cooley, John Kent.) London, 1967.
Afr 6780.37   Baanbrekers in die maalstroom. (Pienaar, M.J.P.) Kaapstad, 1942.
Afr 212.16   Baardseth, Magne. Afrika. 3. Opl. Oslo, 1964.
Afr 6280.35   Baba. Baba of Karo. N.Y., 1955.
Afr 6280.35   Baba of Karo. (Baba.) N.Y., 1955.
Afr 7815.28   Baba wa Bambuti. (Schebesta, Paul.) Moedling, 1951.

Afr 5829.58   Babaju, Esno. A concise history of Mauritius. Bombay, 1958.
Afr 49019.2   Babalola, S.A. The content and form of Yoruba ijala. Oxford, 1966.
Afr 3979.02.15   Babcock, M.D. Letters from Egypt and Palestine. N.Y., 1902.
Afr 1570.35   Babin, G. Au Maroc par les camps et par les villes. Paris, 1912.
Afr 1571.22   Babin, Gustave. La mystérieuse Ouaouizert. Casablanca, 1923.
Afr 1609.01.5   Bacheracht, Mme A. de. Une mission à la cour cherifienne. Genève, 1901.
Afr 555.21.15   Back to the long grass. (Crawford, D.) N.Y., n.d.
Afr 11310.52.100   Back to the trees. (Culwick, Arthur Theodore.) Cape Town, 1965.
Afr 861.35   Back to Tristan. (Roenne, Arne Falk.) London, 1967.
Afr 8028.20   Background material for the tercentenary of the landing of Jan van Riebeeck. (Amyat, D.L.) Cape Town, 1950.
Afr 4766.40   The background of the Ethio-Somalia boundary dispute. (Mariam, Mesfin Wolde.) Addis Ababa, 1964.
Afr 8089.54   Background to bitterness. (Gibbs, H.) London, 1954.
Afr 8089.54.2A   Background to bitterness. (Gibbs, H.) N.Y., 1955.
Afr 6192.93   Background to Ghana. 1st ed. (Morgan, Clyde.) London, 1965.
Afr Doc 3309.7   Background to the budget. (Uganda. Ministry of Finance.) 1955+
Afr 8658.44   Backhouse, J. Visit to the Mauritius and South Africa. London, 1844.
Afr 6292.82.10   Backwell, H.F. The occupation of Hausaland, 1900-1904. Lagos, 1927.
Afr 6292.82.12A   Backwell, H.F. The occupation of Hausaland, 1900-1904. London, 1969.
Afr 7458.22   Bacon, E. Abstract of a journal...to Afrika. Philadelphia, 1822.
Afr 3979.01.2   Bacon, Lee. Our houseboat on the Nile. Boston, 1901.
Afr 3979.01.5A   Bacon, Lee. Our houseboat on the Nile. Boston, 1901.
Afr 6283.9   Bacon, R.H. Benin, the city of blood. London, 1897.
Afr 3675.35   Baddur, Abd al-Fattah Ibrahim al-Sayid. Sudanese-Egyptian relations. The Hague, 1960.
Afr 6172.1   Baden-Powell, R. The downfall of Prempeh. London, 1898.
Afr 8310.10F   Baden-Powell, R.S.S. Sketches in Mafeking and East Africa. London, 1907.
Afr 9446.26   Baden-Powell. The Matabele campaign, 1896. London, 1897.
Afr 8310.11   Baden-Powell at Mafeking. (Grineell-Milne, D.W.) London, 1957.
Afr 8292.4   Badenhorst, A.M. Tant' Alie of Transvaal, her diary 1880-1902. London, 1923.
Afr 8678.290   Badertscher, Jean. La segregation raciale en Afrique du Sud. Lausanne, 1962.
Afr 1258.16   Badia y Leyblick. Travels of Ali Bey in Morocco, Tripoli. Philadelphia, 1816. 2v.
Afr 12672.3.110   Badian, S. La mort de Chaka. Paris, 1965.
Afr 12672.3.100   Badian, S. Sous l'orage (Kany). Paris, 1963.
Afr 4513.36.68   Badoglio, P. La guerra d'Etiopia. Milano, 1936.
Afr 4513.36.69   Badoglio, P. War in Abyssinia. London, 1937.
Afr 4513.36.69.5   Badoglio, P. War in Abyssinia. N.Y., 1937.
Afr 5249.123   Badri, Babakr. The memoiris of Babiker Bedu. London, 1969.
Afr 7812.259   Baeck, Louis. Economische ontwikkeling en sociale structuur in Belgisch-Kongo. Leuven, 1959.
Afr 7948.5   Baeck, Louis. Etude socio-économique du centre extra-coutumier d'Usumbura. Bruxelles, n.d.
Afr 3990.2   Baedeker, K. Egypt. 5th ed. Leipzig, 1902.
Afr 1403.4   Baena Parada, J. Epitome de la vida y hechos de Don Sebastian. Madrid, 1692.
Afr 4431.5   Baer, George Webster. The coming of the Italian-Ethiopian war. Cambridge, 1967.
Afr 6195.16   Baeta, C.G. Prophetism in Ghana. London, 1962.
Afr 1432.24   Baeumen, A. von. Nach Marokko. Berlin, 1861.
Afr 2308.19   Baeza, H.L. Le rôle économique du port d'Alger. Thèse. Alger, 1924.
X Cg   Afr 6540.6A   The Baganda, account of their customs. (Roscoe, John.) London, 1911.
Afr 6540.6.12   The Baganda, an account of their native customs and beliefs. 2d ed. (Roscoe, John.) N.Y., 1966.
Afr 6540.14   The Bagesu and other tribes of the Uganda protectorate. (Roscoe, John.) Cambridge, Eng., 1924.
Afr 3817.14   Baggara Arabs, power and the lineage in a Sudanese nomad tribe. (Cunnison, Ivan George.) Oxford, 1966.
Afr 4050.35   Bagnold, R.A. Libyan sands, travel in a dead world. London, 1935.
Afr 8325.17   Bagot, Dosia. Shadows of the war. London, 1900.
Afr 2530.1   Bahar, J. Le protectorat tunisien. Paris, 1904.
Afr 4199.100   Bahay, Muhammad. Muhammed Abduh. Hamburg, 1936.
Afr 590.80   Bahia and the West Africa trade, 1549-1851. (Verger, Pierre.) Ibadan, 1964.
Afr 3986.962.15   Bahig, A.F. Readings for students of commerce. Alexandria, 1962.
Afr 3986.961.10   Bahig, A.F. Selected passages for students of commerce. 4th ed. Alexandria, 1961.
Afr 6741.4   Bahoken, Jean Calvin. Clairières métaphysiques africaines, essai sur la philosophie et la religion chez les Bantu du Sud-Caméroun. Paris, 1967.
Afr 7815.5.9   Les Baholoholo. 9. (Schmitz, Robert.) Bruxelles, 1912.
Afr 1575.2.10F   Baiao, Antonio. Documentos do corpo chronologico relativo a Marrocos, 1488 a 1514. Coimbra, 1925.
Afr 810.35.2   Baikie, William B. Narrative of an exploring voyage up the rivers Kwóra and Bínue, commonly known as the Niger and Tsádda in 1854. Facsimile. London, 1966.
Afr 7808.94   Bailey, Henry. Travel and adventures in Congo Free State. London, 1894.
Afr 6069.12   Bailland, E. La politique indigène de l'Angleterre en Afrique occidentale. Paris, 1912.
Afr 1990.11   Baillet, Noël Bernard. Nécessité de la colonisation de l'Algerie. Paris, 1857.
Afr 1990.11.5   Baillet, Noël Bernard. Rapport...sur son voyage de 1852 en Algérie. Rouen, 1852.
Afr 8310.5   Baillie, F.D. Mafeking. N.Y., 1900.
Afr 5753.12   Le bain royal à Madagascar. (Molet, Louis.) Tananarive, 1956.
Afr 6978.64   Baines, T. Exploration in South-west Africa. London, 1864.
Afr 9148.77.5   Baines, Thomas. The gold regions of south eastern Africa. Bulawayo, 1968.
Afr 9148.77   Baines, Thomas. The gold regions of southeast Africa. London, 1877.

Afr 9510.5PF — Baines, Thomas. The Victoria Falls, Zambesi River. London, 1865.

Afr 608.78 — Bainier, P.F. La géographie appliquée à la marine, au commerce. Paris, 1878.

Afr 7183.27 — O baixo cunene. (Neto, Jose Pereira.) Lisboa, 1963.

Afr 1609.31.5 — Bajo cielo africano. (Vicuna, Alejandro.) Paris, 1931.

Afr 555.9.4 — Baker, Ernest. The life and exploration of Frederick Stanley Arnot. London, 1921.

Afr 8250.31 — Baker, H. Cecil Rhodes. London, 1934.

Afr 8934.123 — Baker, Jeff. African flying journal. London, 1968.

Afr 6455.71 — Baker, R.St.B. Africa drums. London, 1942.

Afr 6395.2.20 — Baker, R.St.B. Kabongo. 1st ed. Wheatley, Eng., 1955.

Afr 2749.66 — Baker, Richard Saint Barbe. Sahara conquest. London, 1966.

Afr 4095.8.2 — Baker, S.W. The Albert Nyanza. London, 1866.

Afr 4095.8 — Baker, S.W. The Albert Nyanza. London, 1867. 2v.

Afr 4095.8.2.10 — Baker, S.W. The Albert Nyanza. London, 1907.

Afr 4095.8 2.5 — Baker, S.W. The Albert Nyanza. New ed. London, 1870.

Afr 4095.8.3.5 — Baker, S.W. Ismailia; a narrative of the expedition to Central Africa for the suppression of the slave trade. N.Y., 1969. 2v.

NEDL Afr 4095.8.3 — Baker, S.W. Ismailia. N.Y., 1875.

Afr 4558.67.4 — Baker, S.W. The Nile tributaries of Abyssinia. Hartford, 1868.

Afr 4558.67.6 — Baker, S.W. The Nile tributaries of Abyssinia. London, 1883.

Afr 4558.67.7 — Baker, S.W. The Nile tributaries of Abyssinia. London, 1886.

Afr 4558.67.3 — Baker, S.W. The Nile tributaries of Abyssinia. 3rd ed. London, 1868.

Afr 4558.67.5.4 — Baker, S.W. The Nile tributaries of Abyssinia. 4th ed. London, 1871.

Afr 4558.67.5A — Baker, S.W. The Nile tributaries of Abyssinia. 4th ed. Philadelphia, 1868.

Afr 4095.8.6 — Baker of the Nile. (Middleton, D.) London, 1949.

Afr 6540.12 — The Bakitara or Banyoro. (Roscoe, John.) Cambridge, 1923.

Afr 7560.5 — Bal, W. Le royaume du Congo aux XVe et XVIe siècle. Léopoldville, 1963.

Afr Doc 808.715 — Balance of payments. (Libya. Census and Statistical Department.) 1956+

Afr Doc 3508.705 — Balance of payments. (Rhodesia and Nyasaland. Central Statistical Office.) Salisbury. 1954+

Afr Doc 3708.710F — Balance of payments. (Zambia. Central Statistical Office.) Lusaka. 1,1964+

Afr Doc 1808.715F — Balance of payments estimates. (Ghana. Central Bureau of Statistics.) 1,1950+

Afr Doc 1808.715.5F — Balance of payments estimates. v.2. Definitions, sources and methods of estimation. (Ghana. Central Bureau of Statistics.) 1,1950+

Afr 710.55.5 — Balandier, Georges. Afrique ambigue. Paris, 1962.

Afr 710.55.6 — Balandier, Georges. Ambiguous Africa, cultures in collision. London, 1966.

Afr 7560.15.5 — Balandier, Georges. Daily life in the Kingdom of the Kongo from the sixteenth to the eighteenth century. London, 1968.

Afr 30.4 — Balandier, Georges. Dictionnaire des civilisations africaines. Paris, 1968.

Afr 5408.15.2 — Balandier, Georges. Sociologie actuelle de l'Afrique noire, changements sociaux au Gabon et au Congo. Paris, 1955.

Afr 5408.15 — Balandier, Georges. Sociologie actuelle de l'Afrique noire. Paris, 1955.

Afr 5408.15.5 — Balandier, Georges. Sociologie actuelle de l'Afrique noire. Paris, 1963.

Afr 7560.15 — Balandier, Georges. La vie quotidienne au royaume de Kongo du XVI au XVIII siècle. Paris, 1965.

Afr 3199.06 — Balboni, L.A. Gl'Italiani nella civiltà egiziana del secolo XIX. Alessandria, 1906. 3v.

Afr 1200.55 — Balch, T.W. France in North Africa, 1906. Philadelphia, 1906.

Afr 4731.5 — Baldissera. Rapport...de la campagne d'Afrique (1895-96) Paris, n.d.

Afr 3180.6 — Baldwin, G. Political recollections related to Egypt. London, 1801.

Afr 9699.66 — Baldwin, Robert Edward. Economic development and export growth. Berkeley, 1966.

Afr 6420.60 — Baldwin, W.W. Mau Mau man-hunt. 1st ed. N.Y., 1957.

Afr 8658.63.4 — Baldwin, William C. African hunting and adventure. Facsimile of 3rd ed. Capetown, 1967.

Afr 8658.63 — Baldwin, William C. African hunting from Natal to the Zambesi. N.Y., 1863.

Afr 6298.110.5 — Balewa, Abubakar Tafawa. Mr. Prime Minister. Lagos, Nigeria, 1964.

Afr 6298.110 — Balewa, Abubakar Tafawa. Nigeria speaks. Ikeja, 1964.

Afr 5056.159 — Balez, Eugene. Vagabondage en Afrique noire. Toulouse, 1959.

Afr 8658.95 — Balfour, A.B. Twelve hundred miles in a waggon. London, 1895.

Afr 715.22 — Balfour, P. Lords of the equator, an African journey. London, 1937.

Afr 6192.80 — Balk, Theodor. Unter dem schwarzen Stern. Berlin, 1960.

Afr 4115.8 — Ball, E.A. Reynold. The city of the caliphs. London, 1898.

Afr 8808.79 — Ballantyne, R.M. Six months at the Cape. London, 1879.

Afr 5396.2.5 — Ballard, J.A. The Porto Novo incidents of 1923, politics in the colonial era. Ibadan, 1965.

Afr 8860.5 — Ballinger, M.L. Basutoland. Lovedale, 1931.

Afr 9345.50.5 — Ballinger, M.L. Bechuanaland protectorate. Lovedale, 1931.

Afr 8678.444 — Ballinger, Margaret. From union to apartheid. N.Y., 1969.

Afr 8335.10 — Ballinger, Margaret Livingstone. From union to apartheid; a trek to isolation. Bailey, 1969.

Afr 10822.3.100 — Ballinger, W.A. Call it Rhodesia. London, 1967.

Afr 8676.34 — Ballinger, W.G. Race and economics in South Africa. London, 1934.

Afr 3979.15 — Balls, W.L. Egypt of the Egyptians. London, 1915.

Afr 6194.20.10 — Balmer, W.T. A history of the Akan peoples of the Gold Coast. London, 1925.

Afr 6176.41 — Balogun, K. Mission to Ghana. 1st ed. N.Y., 1963.

Afr 12622.3.100 — Balogun, Ola. Shango, suivi de Le roi-éléphant. Honfleur, 1968.

Afr 10066.2.15 — Balogun, Samuel Idown. Notes and exercises on Modern poetry from Africa. Ibadan, 1967.

Afr 4785.965.5 — Balsan, Francois. A pied au Nord Somali. Paris, 1965.

Afr 9389.59 — Balsan, Francois. Nouvelles aventures au Kalahari. Paris, 1959.

Afr 7815.5.10 — Les Baluta. 10-11. (Colle, R.P.) Bruxelles, 1913. 2v.

Afr 5240.5F — Bamako. Chambre de Commerce, d'Agriculture et d'Industrie. Eléments du bilan économique. 1962+ 2v.

Afr 5235.261 — Bamako. Chambre de Commerce, d'Agriculture et d'Industrie. Mali. Bamako, 1961.

Afr 5240.4F — Bamako. Chambre de Commerce, d'Agriculture et d'Industrie. Répertoire des entreprises financières. Bamako, 1964.

Afr 5240.10F — Bamako. Chambre de Commerce, d'Agriculture et d'Industrie. Répertoire des représentations exclusives assurées au Mali. Bamako, 1962.

Afr 5243.125.5 — Les Bambara du Ségou et du Kaarta. (Monteil, Charles.) Paris, 1924.

Afr 5243.125.10 — Les Bambaras. (Lebarbier, Louis.) Paris, 1918.

Afr 6740.15.10 — Les Bamileke. (Lecoq, Raymond.) Paris, 1953.

Afr 590.5.8 — Banani, the transition of slavery. (Newman, Henry S.) London, 1898.

Afr 8143.18 — Banbury, G.A.L. Sierra Leone; or The white man's grave. London, 1888.

Afr 8825.45 — Banch, Kurt. Deutsche Kultur am Kap. 1st ed. Capetown, 1964.

Afr 5962.2 — Banciella y Barcena, José Cesar. Rutas de imperio. Madrid, 1940.

Afr 7176.20 — Banco de Angola, Lisbon. Economic and financial survey of Angola, 1960-1965. Lisboa, 1966.

Afr 3990.20 — Band, Marcelle. Egypte. Paris, 1956.

Afr 1573.17 — Bande, Nicasio. La cuestion del dia: desenlace del problema norte-africano y el porvenir de España. Barcelona, 1909.

Afr 4513.37.10 — Le bande autocarrate dei fedelissimi da Roma ad Addis Ababa. (Farfaglio, S.) Paris, 1937.

Afr 2230.16 — Le banditisme en Kabylie. (Violard, Emile.) Paris, 1895.

Afr 3.15 — Bandung, Cairo and Accra. (Legum, Colin.) London, 1958.

Afr 7815.2 — Les Bangala. 1. (Overbergh, C. van.) Bruxelles, 1907.

Afr 3986.5 — Bank Misr. Economic bulletin. Cairo. 3,1959

Afr 2938.38 — Bank of Libya. Economic Research Department. The development of public finance in Libya, 1944-1963. Tripoli, 1965.

Afr 3986.958 — Bankers and pashas. (Landes, David S.) Cambridge, 1958.

Afr 3986.958.2 — Bankers and pashas. (Landes, David S.) London, 1958.

Afr 7809.43 — Banks, Emily. White woman on the Congo. N.Y., 1943.

Afr 3979.13.12 — The banks of the Nile. (Todd, J.A.) London, 1913.

Afr 608.77 — Banning, E. L'Afrique et la Conférence géographique de Bruxelles. Bruxelles, 1877.

Afr 590.13 — Banning, E. La Conférence de Bruxelles. Bruxelles, 1890.

Afr 200.2 — Banning, E. Le partage politique de l'Afrique. Bruxelles, 1888.

Afr 7565.14.5 — Banning, E. Textes inédits. Bruxelles, 1955.

Afr 7565.14 — Banning, Emile. Mémoires politiques et diplomatiques. Paris, 1927.

Afr 8980.3.5 — Bannister, S. Humane policy; or, Justice to the aborigines of new settlements. 1st ed. London, 1968.

Afr 8980.3 — Bannister, S. Humane policy. 2. ed. London, n.d.

Afr 5050.6 — Banque Centrale des Etats de l'Afrique de l'Ouest. Etudes économiques ouest africaines. Paris. 3,1961+ 2v.

Afr 6685.11 — Banque Centrale des Etats de l'Afrique de l'Ouest. Togo, 1960. Paris, 1960.

Afr 2719.55 — Banque Dambert-Blitz. L'avenir du Sahara. Paris, 1955.

Afr Doc 7709.305F — Banque Nationale du Congo. Bulletin. Kinhasa. 7,1968+

Afr 2223.960.5 — Banque Nationale pour le Commerce et l'Industrie, Algiers. Les entreprises industrielles en Algérie et au Sahara. Alger, 1966.

Afr 3979.09 — Banse, E. Agypten. Halle, 1909.

Afr 530.28.5 — Banse, Ewald. Unsere grossen Afrikaner. Berlin, 1943.

Afr 8678.155 — Die Bantô van Suid-Africa. (Bruwer, J.P.) Johannesburg, 1957.

Afr 8678.155.2 — Die Bantoe van Suid-Africa. (Bruwer, J.P.) Johannesburg, 1963.

Afr 6147.5 — Banton, M.P. West African city. London, 1957.

Afr 8678.32.3 — Bantu, Boer, and Briton, the making of the South African native problem. (MacMillan, W.M.) London, 1929.

Afr 8678.32.4 — Bantu, Boer, and Briton. (MacMillan, W.M.) Oxford, 1963.

Afr 8678.13.5 — The Bantu, past and present. (Molema, S.M.) Edinburgh, 1920.

Afr 8680.47 — Bantu. An informal publication of the Department of Native Affairs of the Union of South Africa. Pretoria, 1954.

Afr 8678.13.6 — The Bantu. (Molema, S.M.) Cape Town, 1963.

Afr 6540.4.10A — Bantu bureaucracy. (Fallers, Lloyd A.) Cambridge, Eng., 195-.

Afr 6540.4.11 — Bantu bureaucracy. (Fallers, Lloyd A.) Chicago, 1965.

Afr 8678.13.10 — The Bantu in the city; a study of...cultural adjustment on the Witwatersrand. Diss. (Phillips, Ray E.) Lovedale, 1938.

Afr 6460.50 — The Bantu of North Kavirondo. (Wagner, Guenter.) London, 1949-56. 2v.

Afr 630.63 — Bantu origins. (Bryant, A.T.) Cape Town, 1963.

Afr 9049.5 — Bantu prophets in South Africa. 2. ed. (Sundkler, Bengt.) London, 1964.

Afr 8678.9.80 — The Bantu-speaking tribes of South Africa. (Schapera, I.) London, 1956-.

Afr 630.2.5 — Bantu studies, monograph series. Johannesburg.

Afr 630.2 — Bantu studies. Johannesburg. 2,1923+ 8v.

Afr 8678.9F — The Bantu tribes of South Africa. (Duggan-Cronin, A.M.) Cambridge, Eng., 1928- 3v.

Afr 9047.27 — The Bantu woman under the Natal code of native law. (Shropshire, Denys William Tinniswood.) Lovedale, 1941.

Afr 8678.335 — Pamphlet vol. Bantus. 4 pam.

Afr 8678.275 — Bantustans. (Giniewski, P.) Cape Town, 1961.

Afr 8678.320 — Bantustans. (Hill, C.R.) London, 1964.

Afr 6883.9 — Les Banyamwezi, peuple de l'Afrique orientale. (Boesch, F.) Münster, 1930.

Afr 6540.13 — The Banyankole. (Roscoe, John.) Cambridge, 1923.

Afr 7312.30 — Baptista, J. do Amparo. Moçambique, província portuguesa. Vila Nova de Famalicão, 1962.

Afr 11865.59.150 — A bar of shadow. (Vanderpost, Laurens.) N.Y., 1956.

Afr 3315.140 — Bar-Zohar, Michel. Suez: ultra-secret. Paris, 1964.

Afr 6883.40 — The Barabaig; East African cattle-herders. (Klima, George J.) N.Y., 1970.

Afr 2608.87 — Baraban, L. A travers la Tunisie. Paris, 1887.

Afr 11193.74.100 — Baragwanath, Paul. The brave remain. Cape Town, 1965.

Afr 4742.22 — Baralta, M. Atlante delle colonie italiane. Novara, 1928.

Afr 710.68 — Barasiola, Carlo. Sulle orme di Roma. Milano, 1934.

Afr 5871.53 — Barassin, Jean. Naissance d'une chrétienté. Saint-Denis, 1953.

Afr 5045.22 — Baratier, A.E.A. A travers l'Afrique. Paris, 1910.

Afr 5055.50 — Baratier, A.E.A. Epopées africaines, ouvrage inédit. Paris, 1912.

Afr 4392.3.5 Baratieri, O. Mémoires d'Afrique (1892-1896). Paris, 1899.

Afr 4392.3 Baratieri, O. Memorie d'Africa (1892-1896). Torino, 1898.

Afr 12002.2 Baratte, Thérèse. Bibliographie, auteurs africains et malgaches de langue française. Paris, 1965.

Afr 2208.93 Baraudon, A. Algérie et Tunisie. Paris, 1893.

Afr 4559.35.60 Baravelli, G.C. The last stronghold of slavery, what Abyssinia is. Roma, 1935.

Afr 4559.35.60.5 Baravelli, G.C. The last stronghold of slavery, what Abyssinia is. Roma, 1935.

Afr 4559.35.62 Baravelli, G.C. The last stronghold of slavery. London, 1936.

Afr 4568.15 Baravelli, G.C. The last stronghold of slavery. Roma, 1935.

Afr 4559.35.58 Baravelli, G.C. L'ultimo baluardo della schiavitù, l'Abyssinia. Roma, 1935.

Afr 3310.50 Barawi, Rashid. The military coup in Egypt. Cairo, 1952.

Afr 1609.08.3 Die barbaren von Marokko. (Sternberg, Adalb.) Wien, 1908.

Afr 1103.15 Barbareschi e i cristiani. Ginevra, 1822.

Htn Afr 1407.3* Barbarian cruelty. (Brooks, F.) London, 1693.

Afr 4513.39.20 La barbarie dell'imperialismo fascista nelle colonie italiane. (Marabini, A.) Parigi, 1939.

Afr 1259.21 Barbary. (Scott, A. Maccallum.) London, 1921.

Afr 1259.21.2 Barbary. (Scott, A. Maccallum.) N.Y., 1921.

Afr 1259.13A The Barbary coast. (Bullard, A.) N.Y., 1913.

Afr 1258.93 The Barbary coast. (Field, Henry M.) N.Y., 1893.

Afr 1258.93.2 The Barbary coast. 2nd ed. (Field, Henry M.) N.Y., 1894.

Afr 1200.110 Barbary legend. (Fisher, G.) Oxford, 1957.

Htn Afr 1407.2.5* The Barbary voyage of 1638. (Carteret, George.) Philadelphia, 1929.

Afr 1494.37 Barbau, Muslim. Tempête sur le Maroc. Paris, 1931.

Afr 635.87 Barbe, R. Les classes sociales en Afrique noire. Paris, 1964.

Afr 6295.66.15 Barber, C.R. Igbo-Ora; a town in transition. Ibadan, 1966.

Afr 9489.60.5 Barber, F.H. Zambezia andMatabeleland in the seventies. London, 1960.

Afr 9450.20 Barber, James. Rhodesia: the road to rebellion. London, 1967.

Afr 6490.5 Barber, James P. Imperial frontier. Nairobi, 1968.

Afr 9499.50 Barber, W.J. The economy of British Central Africa. Stanford, 1961.

Afr 555.147 La Barberia e la Sacra Congregazione. (Sanita, Giuseppe.) Cairo, 1963.

Afr 2030.30 Barberot, Roger. Malaventure en Algérie avec le général Paris de Ballardiére. Paris, 1957.

Afr 2030.460 Barberousse. (Mustapha G.) Paris, 1960.

Afr 2208.98.3 Barbet, Charles. Au pays des Burnous. Alger, 1898.

Afr 2373.1 Barbet, Charles. La perle du Maghreb (Tlemeen). Alger, n.d.

Afr 5548.59 Barbie du Bocage, V.A. Madagascar, possession française depuis 1642. Paris, 1859.

Afr 2220.4 Barbier, J. Itinéraire...de l'Algérie. Paris, 1855.

Afr 2748.82.6 Barbier, J.V. A travers le Sahara, les missions du colonel Flatters. Paris, 1895.

Afr 7072.5 Barbosa, Alexandre. Guinéus; contos, narrativas, crónicas. Lisboa, 1967.

Afr 4070.62 Barbour, K.M. The Republic of the Sudan. London, 1961.

Afr 1369.65 Barbour, N. Morocco. London, 1965.

Afr 1069.59 Barbour, Nevill. A survey of North-west Africa. London, 1959.

Afr 1069.59.2 Barbour, Nevill. A survey of North-west Africa. 2nd ed. London, 1962.

Afr 500.81 Barboux, H.M. Opinion. Paris, 1903.

Afr 212.30 Barcata, Louis. Schreie aus dem Dschungel. Stuttgart, 1962.

Afr 1957.32 Barchou de Penhoen, Auguste Theodore Hitaire, Baron. Mémoires d'un officier d'état-major. Paris, 1835.

Afr 2230.17 Barclay, E. Mountain life in Algeria. London, 1882.

Afr 4070.65 Barclay, Harold. Buurri al Lamaab. Ithaca, 1964.

Afr 1550.21 Barclay, T. El acta de Algeciras y el porvenir de Espana en Marruecos. Madrid, 1907.

Afr 2875.8 Barclay, T. The Turco-Italian war and its problems. London, 1912.

Afr 4700.36.25 Bardi, Pietro M. Pionieri e soldati d'Africa orientale dall'acquisto di Assab all'impero romano d'Etiopia. Milano, 1936.

Afr 2650.3 Bardin, Pierre. La vie d'un douar. Paris, 1965.

Afr 1868.86 Bardon, Xavier. Histoire nationale de l'Algérie. Paris, 1886.

Afr 5090.14 Barefoot through Mauritania. (Du Puigaudeau, Odette.) London, 1937.

Afr 1955.26 Barehou-Penhoen. Souvenirs de l'expédition d'Afrique. Paris, 1832.

Afr 3315.100 Barer, Schlomo. The weekend war. N.Y., 1960.

Afr 2748.32 Bargagli-Petrucci, O. Nel Fezzan, aprile, maggio 1932. Firenze, 1934.

Afr 1885.2 Barges, J.J.L. Complement de l'histoire des Beni-Zeiyan. Paris, 1887.

Afr 2373.5 Barges, J.J.L. Tlemcen, ancienne capitale du royaume. Paris, 1859.

Afr 555.10 Barges, Jean Joseph Léandre. Aperçu historique sur l'église d'Afrique. Paris, 1848.

Afr 2290.6 Barges, l'Abbé. Excursion à Sebdon. Paris, 1849.

Afr 1271.10F Bargone, Chas. L'Afrique du Nord, Tunisie, Algérie, Maroc. Paris, 1924.

Afr 4742.28 I Baria e i Cunama. (Pollera, Alberto.) Roma, 1913.

Afr 7461.40 Barkay, Richard M. Public sector accounts of Liberia. Monrovia, 1965.

Afr 3315.124 Barker, A.J. Suez, the seven-day war. London, 1964.

Afr 9038.5 Barker, Anthony. Giving and receiving. London, 1959.

Afr 555.125 Barker, Anthony. The man next to me. N.Y., 1959.

Afr 4431.20 Barker, Arthur J. The civilizing minion; a history of the Italo-Ethiopian War of 1935-1936. N.Y., 1968.

Afr 9196.6 Barker, Dudley. Swaziland. London, 1965.

Afr 8847.21 Barker, John P. Industrial development in a border area. Grahamstown, 1964.

Afr 8703.5 Barker, Mary. Sir Benjamin d'Urbans administration. Cape Town, 1946.

Afr 6390.47 Barker-Benfield, M.A. The lands and peoples of East Africa. London, 1960.

Afr 5897.2 Barkly, Fanny Alexandra. From the tropics to the North Sea. London, 1897.

Afr 3040.10 Barkouky, El. Les rapports entre le pouvoir judiciaire et le pouvoir exécutif en Egypte. Thèse. Paris, 1925.

Afr 8369.60 Barlow, A.G. That we may tread safely. Cape Town, 1960.

Afr 8687.126 Barlow, Arthur G. Almost in confidence. Cape Town, 1952.

Afr 1555.3.35 Barlow, I.C. The Agadir crisis. Chapel Hill, 1940.

Afr 8658.01.5 Barnard, Anne. South Africa a century ago. London, 1901.

Afr 8658.01.8 Barnard, Anne. South Africa a century ago. London, 1901.

Afr 8378.379.30.3 Barnard, Fred. Dertien jaar in die skadu. 3. druk. Johannesburg, 1967.

Afr 590.14 Barnard, R.N. Three years cruise...for suppression of slave trade. London, 1848.

Afr 8687.248 Barnes, Bertram Herbert. Johnson of Nyasaland. Westminster, 1933.

Afr 9700.20.5.2 Barnes, J.A. Politics in a changing society. 2nd ed. Manchester, 1967.

Afr 9700.20 Barnes, J.A. Politics in changing society. Cape Town, 1954.

Afr 718.40 Barnes, James. Through central Africa from coast to coast. N.Y., 1915.

Afr 8678.35 Barnes, L. Caliban in Africa. London, 1930.

Afr 8676.32 Barnes, L. The new Boer war. London, 1932.

Afr 575.5 Barnes, L.C. Shall Islam rule Africa? Boston, 1890.

Afr 210.69 Barnes, Leonard. African renalssance. London, 1969.

Afr 6430.3 Barnett, Donald L. Mau Mau from within, autobiography and analysis of Kenya's peasant revolt. London, 1966.

Afr 6430.3.1 Barnett, Donald L. Mau Mau from within. N.Y., 1966.

Afr 8252.7.7 Barney Barnato, from Whitechapel clown to diamond king. (Lewinsohn, R.) London, 1937.

Afr 8252.257 Barney Barnato. 1st ed. (Huninsohn, Richard.) N.Y., 1938.

Afr 1942.6 Barnly, Henry George. The prisoners of Algiers. London, 1966.

Afr 8095.80 Barnouw, Adrian. Language and race problems in South Africa. Nijhoff, 1934.

Afr 7175.20 Barns, T. Alexander. Angolian sketches. London, 1928.

Afr 7809.26 Barns, T.A. An African eldorado, the Belgian Congo. London, 1926.

Afr 7809.22.5 Barns, T.A. The wonderland of the eastern Congo. London, 1922.

Afr 5829.49.5 Barnwell, P.J. A short history of Mauritius. London, 1949.

Afr 6878.59 Baron Carl Claus von der Decken's Reisen in Ost Afrika in den Jahren 1859 bis 1865. (Decken, Carl Claus, Baron von der.) Leipzig, 1869-79. 6v.

Afr 9710.6 Les Barotse. (Beguin, E.) Lausanne, 1903.

Afr 9710.8 Barotseland. (Stirke, D.E.C.R.) London, 1922.

Afr 4155.10 Barque, Jacques. Histoire sociale d'un village égyptien au XXème siècle. Paris, 1957.

Afr 4230.4.4 Barradas, M. Tractatus tres historico-geographico. Porto, 1906.

Afr 12351.63 Barrat, D. Espoir et parole. Paris, 1963.

Afr 1494.10 Barrat, Robert. Justice pour le Maroc. Paris, 1953.

Afr 3740.3 Barre, P. Fachoda. Paris, n.d.

Afr 7122.80 Barreiros, Americo. A verdade sobre os acontecimentos de Angola. T.1-2. 2.ed. Angola, 1961.

Afr 7309.59 Barreiros, Pinho. Africa, mae e madrasta. Coimbra, 1959.

Afr 5540.8 Barrel, G.P. Le code des 305 articles de Madagascar. Thèse. Paris, 1931.

Afr 5960.4 Barrera y Luyando. Lo que son y lo que deben ser las posesiones. Madrid, 1907.

Afr 6095.18 Barret, P.M.V. Sénégambie et Guinée...l'Afrique occidentale. Paris, 1888. 2v.

Afr 7062.5 Barreto, João. Historia da Guiné, 1418-1918. Lisboa, 1938.

Afr 550.165 Barrett, David B. Schism and renewal in Africa. Nairobi, 1968.

Afr 2030.70.5 Les barricades d'Alger. (Faucher, Jean André.) Paris, 1960.

Afr 2030.365 Barricades et colonels, 24 janvier 1960 par Bromberger. Paris, 1960.

Afr 2030.305 Barricades pour un drapeau. (Ribaud, Paul.) Paris, 1960.

Afr 679.00.10 Barrow, Alfred Henry. Fifty years in Western Africa. London, 1900.

Afr 8658.01 Barrow, J. An account of travels into...South Africa. London, 1801.

Afr 8658.01.2 Barrow, J. An account of travels into...South Africa. N.Y., 1802.

Afr 8658.01.4 Barrow, J. An account of travels into the interior of Southern Africa, in the years 1797 and 1798. N.Y., 1968.

Afr 8658.01.3 Barrow, J. Travels into the interior of South Africa. London, 1806. 2v.

Afr 861.1 Barrow, K.M. Three years in Tristan da Cunha. London, 1910.

Afr 1635.8 Barrows, D.P. Berbers and blacks. N.Y., 1927.

Afr 8325.22 Barry, A. Ons japie. Johannesburg, 1960.

Afr 4236.936.5 Barsotti, G. Etiopia cristiana. Milano, 1939.

Afr 628.256 Bartah, Ernst. Neger, Jazz und tiefer Süden. Leipzig, 1956.

Afr 1583.17 Bartels, Albert. Auf eigene Faust meine Erlebnisse vor und während des Weltkrieges in Marokko. Leipzig, 1925.

Afr 6195.7 Bartels, Francis Lodovic. The roots of Ghana Methodism. Cambridge, 1965.

Afr 9028.52 Barter, Charles. The dorp and the veld or Six months in Natal. London, 1852.

NEDL Afr 608.57 Barth, H. Reisen und Entdeckungen in Nord- und Central-Afrika. Gotha, 1857-58. 5v.

Afr 608.57.5 Barth, H. Travels and discoveries in north and central africa. London, 1965. 3v.

NEDL Afr 608.57.3 Barth, H. Travels and discoveries in North and Central Africa. N.Y., 1857-59. 3v.

Afr 6275.95 Barth, H. Travels in Nigeria. London, 1962.

Afr 626.15 Barth von Wehrenalp, E. Europa blickt nach Afrika. Leipzig, 1939.

Afr 8285.15 Barthold, U. Studien zur englischen Vorbereitung des Burenkriegs. Inaug. Diss. Köln, 1916.

Afr 1570.44 Barthou, Louis. La bataille du Maroc. 3e ed. Paris, 1919.

Afr 1571.17.30 Barthou, Louis. Lyautey et le Maroc. Paris, 1931.

Afr 4559.34.35 Bartleet, Eustace John. In the land of Sheda. Birmingham, 1934.

Afr 7575.36 Bartlet, R.E. Communist penetration and subversion of the Belgian Congo, 1946-1960. 1st ed. Berkeley, 1962.

Afr 6588.2 Bartlett, C. Statistics of the Zanzibar Protectorate. 8th ed. Zanzibar, 1936.

Afr 630.53 Bartlett, V. Struggle for Africa. London, 1953.

Afr 3978.49.6 Bartlett, W.H. The Nile boat, glimpses of Egypt. 2d ed. London, 1850.

Afr 3978.49.5 Bartlett, W.H. The Nile boat. London, 1849.

Afr 3978.51 Bartlett, W.H. The Nile boat. N.Y., 1851.

Afr 3978.49.8 Bartlett, W.H. The Nile boat. 4th ed. London, 1861.

Afr 4743.5 Bartolommei-Gioli, G. Le attitudini della colonia Eritrea all'agricoltura. Firenze, 1902.

Afr 10013.6 Barton, Frank. The press in Africa. Nairobi, 1966.

Afr 5842.24   Bartram, Alfred, Lady. Recollections of seven years' residence at the Mauritius. London, 1830.
Afr 718.14   Barttelot, E.M. Life of E.M. Barttelot. London, 1890.
Afr 6883.2.5   Die Barundi. (Meyer, Hans.) Leipzig, 1916.
Afr 2970.5   Bary, Erica de. Ghadames, Ghadames. München, 1961.
Afr 2985.2   Bary, Erica de. Im Oasenkreis. München, 1963.
Afr 2870.10.65   Barzilai, Salvatore. La impresa libica e la situazione parlamentare esaurita. Roma, 1914. 3 pam.
Afr 5346.11   Le bas Cavally (Afrique occidentale française) et son avenir. Thèse. (Bouys, P.) Montpellier, 1933.
Afr 7820.6   Le Bas-Congo, artère vitale de notre colonie. (Devroey, E.) Bruxelles, 1938.
Afr 810.25   Bas-Niger, Benoue, Dahomey. (Mattei, Antonio.) Grenoble, 1890.
Afr 1658.16   Basallo, Francisco. Memorias del sargento Basallo. Madrid, 1923?
Afr 5048.10   Bascom, W.R. Continuity and change in African cultures. Chicago, 1958.
Afr 6280.2.45   Bascom, William Russell. The Yoruba of Southwestern Nigeria. N.Y., 1969.
Afr 6280.9.5   Basden, George Thomas. Among the Ibos of Nigeria. London, 1921.
Afr 6280.9.8   Basden, George Thomas. Among the Ibos of Nigeria. N.Y., 1966.
Afr 6280.9.7   Basden, George Thomas. Among the Ibos of Nigeria. Philadelphia, 1921.
Afr 6280.9.10   Basden, George Thomas. Niger Ibos, life, customs. London, 1938.
Afr 6280.59   Basden, George Thomas. Niger Ibos. 2d ed. N.Y., 1966.
Afr 3979.60.10   Bases of tourist statistics. (United Arab Republic. State Tourist Administration.) Cairo, 1960?
Afr 3745.73   Bashir, Muhammad Umar. The Southern Sudan. London, 1968.
Afr 210.64.25   Basic documents and resolutions. (Organization of African Unity.) Addis Ababa, 1964.
Afr 3745.71   Basic facts about the southern provinces of the Sudan. (Sudan. Central Office of Information.) Khartoum, 1964.
Afr Doc 1407.12   Basic statistics. (United Arab Republic. Central Agency for Public Mobilisation and Statistics.) Cairo. 1964+
Afr 820.15.12   Basile, C. Uebi-Scebeli nella spedizione di S.A.R. Luigi di Savoia. Bologna, 1935.
Afr 8678.88   The basis of trusteeship in African native policy. (Smuts, Jan Christian.) Johannesburg, 1942.
Afr 7815.4   Les Basonge. 3. (Overbergh, C. van.) Bruxelles, 1908.
Afr 5787.6   La basse plaine du Mangoky. (Trouchaud, J.P.) Paris, 1965.
Afr 1830.50.4   Basset, André. La langue berbère. Paris, 1929.
Afr 5640.6   Basset, Charles. Madagascar et l'oeuvre du Général Gallieni. Thèse. Paris, 1903.
Afr 2748.98.5   Basset, R. Documents géographiques sur l'Afrique septentrional. Paris, 1898.
Afr 2010.7   Basset, R. L'insurrection algérienne de 1871. Louvain, 1892.
Afr 2357.20   Basset, René. Fastes chronologiques de la ville d'Oran. Paris, 1892.
Afr 2355.5   Basset, René. Nedromah et les Traras. Paris, 1901.
Afr 4115.11   Bassi, Alessandro. Santuario della sacra famiglia in Cairo vecchio. Torino, 1862.
Afr 530.20   Bassi, Ugo. Note sui diritti dell'Italia in Africa. Modena, 1914.
Afr 5488.20   Le bassin du moyen Logone. Thèse. (Cabot, Jean.) Paris, 1965.
Afr 5440.5   Les bassins de l'Ubangi. (Wauters, Alphonse Jules.) Brussels, 1902.
Afr 10516.2   Bassir, O. An anthology of West African verse. Nigeria, 1957.
Afr 5275.5   Bassolet, François Djoby. Evolution de la Haute-Volta de 1898 au 3 janvier 1966. Ouagadougou, 1968.
Afr 8918.59   Le Bassoutos. (Casalis, E.) Paris, 1859.
Afr 7185.3   Bastian, A. Ein Besuch in San Salvador. Bremen, 1859.
Afr 5448.5A   Bastian, Adolf. Die deutsche Expedition an der Loango-Küste. Jena, 1874.
Afr 5749.55   Bastian, Georges. Madagascar. Tananarive, 1955.
Afr 2368.1   Bastide, L. Sidi-bel-Abbès et son arrondissement. Oran, 1881.
Afr 4513.37.30   Bastin, J. L'affaire d'Ethiopie et les diplomates, 1934-1937. Bruxelles, 1937.
Afr 8925.10   The Basuto. (Ashton, H.) London, 1952.
Afr 8925.2   Basuto traditions. (MacGregor, J.C.) n.p., n.d.
Afr 8923.2   Basutoland, Bechuanaland protectorate and Swaziland, report of an economic survey mission. (Great Britain. High Commissioner for Basutoland, the Bechuanaland Protectorate and Swaziland.) London, 1960.
Afr Doc 4205.5   Basutoland; report for the years 1947-1965. London, n.d.
Afr 8857.10   Basutoland. Basutoland records. v.1-3. Facsimile. Cape Town, 1964. 4v.
Afr Doc 4209.12F   Basutoland. Estimates of revenue and expenditure. 1967+
Afr Doc 4209.13F   Basutoland. Memorandum on the estimates of revenue and expenditure. 1967+
Afr 8860.5   Basutoland. (Ballinger, M.L.) Lovedale, 1931.
Afr 8919.66   Basutoland. (Coates, Austin.) London, 1966.
Afr Doc 4207.356   Basutoland. Census Office. 1956 population census, 8th April 1956. Maseru, 1958.
Afr Doc 4219.5   Basutoland. Constitutional Commission. Report of the Basutoland Constitutional Commission. Maseru, 1963.
Afr 8860.15   Basutoland. Council. Report on constitutional reform. Maseru, 1958.
Afr Doc 4231.5F   Basutoland. Department of Agriculture. Annual report. 1958+
Afr Doc 4207.360   Basutoland. Department of Agriculture. 1960 agricultural census. v.1-6. Maseru, 1963.
Afr Doc 4207.360F   Basutoland. Department of Agriculture. 1960 agricultural census. v.7. Maseru, 1963.
Afr 8853.3F   Basutoland. Government Archives. Catalogue. n.p., 1962.
Afr Doc 4224.5   Basutoland. High Commissioner. Basutoland proclamations and notices.
Afr Doc 4212.5   Basutoland. National Council. Legislative Council. Debates. 1,1960+
Afr Doc 4209.500   Basutoland. Supervisor of Elections. A report on the first general election in Basutoland, 1960. Maseru, 1963.
Afr Doc 4209.5F   Basutoland. Treasury. Report of the finances and accounts for the financial year. Maseru. 1962+
Afr 8860.16   Basutoland Constitutional Conference, London, 1964. Basutoland constitutional conference, report. London, 1964.
Afr 8860.16   Basutoland constitutional conference, report. (Basutoland Constitutional Conference, London, 1964.) London, 1964.
Afr Doc 4218.5   Basutoland constitutional handbook. Maseru, 1960.

Afr 8850.6F   Basutoland newsletter. Cairo. 1,1963+
Afr Doc 4224.5   Basutoland proclamations and notices. (Basutoland. High Commissioner.)
Afr 8857.5   Basutoland records. Cape Town, 1883. 3v.
Afr 8857.10   Basutoland records. v.1-3. Facsimile. (Basutoland.) Cape Town, 1964. 4v.
Afr 8918.59.10   The Basutos, or, Twenty-three years in South Africa. (Casalis, E.) Cape Town, 1965.
Afr 8918.59.5   The Basutos. (Casalis, E.) London, 1861. 2v.
Afr 8865.5   The Basutos. (Lagden, G.) N.Y., 1909. 2v.
Afr 2030.75   La bataille d'Alger. (Leprevost, Jacques.) Alger, 1957.
Afr 2536.10.15   La bataille de l'évacuation, 17 avril 1956-17 février 1959. (Bourguiba, H.) Tunis, 1959.
Afr 2030.462.145   La bataille de l'O.A.S. (Nicol, A.) Paris, 1962.
Afr 1570.44   La bataille du Maroc. 3e ed. (Barthou, Louis.) Paris, 1919.
Afr 9838.89   Batalha Reis, Jayme. Os portuguezes na região do Nyassa. Lisboa, 1889.
Afr 8369.56   Bate, H.M. South Africa without prejudice. London, 1956.
Afr 9439.53   Bate, Henry M. Report from the Rhodesias. London, 1953.
Afr 7808.89.7   Bateman, C.S.L. The first ascent of the Kasai. London, 1889.
Afr 6753.15   Bates, Margaret L. A study guide for Tanzania. Boston, 1969.
Afr 4180.3.3   Bates, O. Siwan superstitions. Alexandria, 1911.
Afr 5056.134.7   Les batisseurs de royaumes. (Martet, Jean.) Paris, 1934.
Afr 510.35   Batisseurs d'empire. (Guy, M., of Tours.) Paris, 1945.
Afr 1965.5.15F   Batsalle. Album militaire d'Afrique. Paris, 1846.
Afr 609.62.50   Batson, E. Contemporary dimensions of Africa. Cape Town, 1962.
Afr 4394.14   La battaglia di Abba Garima. (Bourelly, G.) Milano, 1901.
Afr 4394.11   La battaglia di Adua. (Conti Rossini, C.) Roma, 1939.
Afr 4394.3.8   La battaglia di Adua del 1 marzo 1896. (Pollera, Alberto.) Firenze, 1928.
Afr 4394.3.5   La battaglia di Adua e il popola italiano. 2a ed. (Guarniere, L.) Torino, 1947.
Afr 2875.58   La battaglia di Tripoli (26 ottobre 1911). (Marinette, F.T.) Milano, 1912.
Afr 2208.98   Battandier. L'Algérie. Paris, 1898.
Afr 505.13   Batten, T.R. Problems of African development. London, 1948.
Afr 505.13.3   Batten, T.R. Problems of African development. 3d ed. London, 1960.
Afr 40.45   Batten, T.R. Thoughts on African citizenship. London, 1945.
Afr 6019.38   Batten, T.R. Tropical Africa in world history. London, 1948. 4v.
Afr 8315.13   Battersby, H.F.P. In the web of a war. London, 1900.
Afr 4937.2   Battersby, H.F.P. Richard Corfield of Somaliland. London, 1914.
Afr 5749.64.5   Battestini, René. Etude geomorphologique de l'Extreme Sud de Madagascar. Paris, 1964.
Afr 9149.65F   Battiss, Walter W. Limpopo. 1. ed. Pretoria, 1965.
Afr 4700.30   Battistelle, V. Africa italiana. Firenze, 1936.
Afr 5749.58.5F   Battistini, R. Population et économie paysanne du Bas-Mangoky. Paris, n.d.
Afr 8095.55   Battistini, Rene. L'Afrique australe et Madagascar. Paris, 1967.
Afr 5749.64.10   Battistini, René. Géographie humaine de la plaine côtière Mahafaly. Thèse. Paris, 1964.
Afr 9489.66.5   The battle for Rhodesia. (Reed, Douglas.) Cape Town, 1966.
Afr 8225.15   The battle of Majuba Hill, the first Boer war. (Ransford, Oliver.) London, 1967.
Afr 8325.68.10   The battle of Spion Kop. (Ransford, Oliver.) London, 1969.
Afr 3700.14   The battle of Tofrek fought near Suakin. (Galloway, W.) London, 1887.
Afr 8289.64   Battles of the Boer war. (Pemberton, W.B.) London, 1964.
Afr 8315.14   Batts, H.J. Pretoria from within...1899-1900. London, 1901.
Afr 2208.87   Baudel, J. Un an à Alger. Paris, 1887.
Afr 2250.1   Baudicour, L. Histoire de la colonization de l'Agérie. Paris, 1860.
Afr 1955.16   Baudicour, L. de. La guerre et le gouvernement de l'Algérie. Paris, 1853.
Afr 5318.12   Baudin, P.N. Fetichism and fetich worshipers. N.Y., 1885.
Afr 1432.2   Baudoz, A. Histoire de la guerre de l'Espagne. Paris, 1860.
Afr 555.95   Baudu, Paul. Vieil empire. Paris, 1957.
Afr 626.131   Bauer, G. Die Wirtschaft Afrikas. Frankfurt a.M., 1963.
Afr 31.10   Bauer Landauer, I. Papeles de mi archivo, relaciones de Africa. Madrid, 1922-23. 4v.
Afr 1326.3   Bauer y Landauer, I. Apuntes para una bibliografia de Marruecos. Madrid, 1922.
Afr 1750.30   Bauer Y Landauer, Ignacio. Papeles de mi archivo. Madrid, 1923.
Afr 3988.4   Baueren zwischen Wasser und Wüste. (Winkler, Hans Alexander.) Stuttgart, 1934.
Afr 1435.5   Baule y Landauer. Consecuencias de la campana de 1860. Madrid, 1923. 4v.
Afr 1110.35   Baulin, Jacques. The Arab role in Africa. Baltimore, 1962.
Afr 4559.28.5   Baum, James E. Savage Abyssinia. London, 1928.
Afr 609.57.10   Baumann, Hermann. Les peuples et les civilisations de l'Afrique. Paris, 1957.
Afr 6990.90.10   Baumann, Julius. Mission und Ökumene in Südwestafrika, Dargestellt am Lebenswerk. Leiden, 1965.
Afr 5993.12   Baumann, O. Eine afrikanische Tropeninsel. Wien, 1888.
Afr 6888.2   Baumann, O. Usambara und seine Nachbargebiete. Berlin, 1891.
Afr 6878.94   Baumann, Oscar. Durch Massailand zur Nilquelle. Berlin, 1894.
Afr 6888.3   Baumann, Oscar. In Deutsch-Ostafrika wahrend Aufstandes. Wien, 1890.
Afr 7540.27   Baumer, Guy. Les centres indigènes extra-coutumiers au Congo belge. Thèse. Paris, 1939.
Afr 550.8.10   Baunard, Louis. Le Cardinal Lavigerie. Paris, 1912. 2v.
Afr 550.8.12   Baunard, Louis. Léon XIII et le toast d'Alger. Paris, 1914.
Afr 2990.2   Bause, E. Tripoli. Weimar, 1912.
Afr 635.88   Bautraditionen der westafrikanischen Negerkulturen. (Haselberger, Herta.) Wien, 1964.
Afr 210.66.20   Bauw, Jean Anatole de. Politique et révolution africaine. Bruxelles, 1966.
Afr 8678.13.30   The Bavenda. (Stayt, H.A.) London, 1931.
Afr 1838.2   Bavoux, E. Alger, voyage politique. v.1-2. Paris, 1841.

Afr 9161.6 The Bawenda of the Spelonken. (Werrmann, R.) London, 1908.
Afr 8835.46 Bax, Dirk. Argitektoniese shoonheid in Kaapstadse kompanjiestuin, 1777-1805. Kaapstad, 1963.
Afr 9439.66 Baxter, J.W. Rhodesian epic. Cape Town, 1966.
Afr 38.2F Baxter, T.W. Archival facilities in sub-Saharan Africa. n.p., 1959.
Afr 3155.5 Baybars I of Egypt. 1st ed. (Sadeque, Syedah.) Dacca, 1956.
Afr 6926.17 Bayer, M.G.S. Mit dem Hauptquartier in Südwestafrika. Berlin, 1909.
Afr 4226.6.2 Baylor, Jim. Ethiopia. 2nd ed. Berkeley, 1967.
Afr 7835.5 Bayly, Joseph T. Congo crisis. Grand Rapids, 1966.
Afr 8300.10 Baynes, A.H. My diocese during the war. London, 1909.
Afr 3265.5 Baynes, K.S. Narrative of the part taken by the 79th Queen's Own Cameron Highlanders, in the Egyptian campaign, 1882. London, 1883.
Afr 555.5.3 Bazin, René. Charles de Foucauld, hermit. London, 1943.
Afr 555.5.5 Bazin, René. Charles de Foucauld. N.Y., 1923.
Afr 555.5 Bazin, René. Charles de Foucauld. Paris, 1921.
Afr 555.120 Beach, Peter. Benedictine and Moor. N.Y., 1959.
Afr 609.58.5 Beachcombers of the African jungle. 1st ed. (Sholomir, Jack.) N.Y., 1959.
Afr 11797.41.111 The beadle. (Smith, Pauline.) Cape Town, 1956.
Afr 4150.2 Beadnell, H.J.L. An Egyptian oasis. London, 1909.
Afr 9230.2 Beak, George B. The aftermath of war. London, 1906.
Afr 3280.10 Beaman, Ardern H. The dethronement of the khedive. London, 1929.
Afr 3978.60 Beamont, William. To Sinai and Syene and back in 1860 and 1861. 2nd ed. London, 1871.
Afr 9428.8 Bean, Elizabeth Ann. Political development in Southern Rhodesia. Cape Town, 1969.
Afr 618.25 Beard, Peter Hill. The end of the game. N.Y., 1965.
Afr 10685.67.140 The beard of Prometheus. (Okoye, Mokwugo.) Ilfracombe, 1966.
Afr 635.70 Beart, Charles. Recherche des éléments d'une sociologie des peuples africains. Paris, 1960.
Afr 4368.12 Il beato Ghebre-Michael. (Cassinari, E.) Roma, 1926.
Afr 5842.10 Beaton, P. Creoles and coolies. London, 1859.
Afr 5874.12 Beaton, P. Six months in Réunion. London, 1860. 2v.
Afr 855.11 Beatson, A. Tracts relative to the island of St. Helena. London, 1816.
Afr 6540.16 Beattie, John. Bunyord, an African kingdom. N.Y., 1960.
Afr 6540.16.2 Beattie, John. Bunyord, an African kingdom. N.Y., 1964.
Afr 6143.20 Beatty, K.J. Human leopards...with note on Sierra Leone. London, 1915.
Afr 2030.65 Beau de Lomenie, Emmanuel. L'Algérie trahie par l'argent. Paris, 1957.
Afr 6535.40 Beaufaere, Abel. Ouganda. Paris, 1942.
Afr 3315.142 Beaufre, Andre. L'Expédition de Suez. Paris, 1967.
Afr 3315.154.1 Beaufre, André. The Suez expedition 1956. N.Y., 1969.
Afr 11197.5.100 Beaumont, John H. Poems. Cape Town, 1957.
Afr 1621.10 Beaurieux, Remy. Le Maroc. Marseille, 1930.
Afr 10675.47.110 Beautiful feathers. (Ekwensi, Cyprian.) London, 1963.
Afr 10621.53.100 The beautyful ones are not yet born. (Armah, Ayi Kwei.) Boston, 1968.
Afr 2397.3 Beauvoir, Simone de. Djamila Boupacha. Paris, 1962.
Afr 2397.3.2 Beauvoir, Simone de. Djamila Boupacha. 1st American ed. N.Y., 1962.
Afr 2010.1 Beauvois, E. En colonne dans la Grande Kabylie...1871. Paris, 1872.
Afr 7073.4 Beaver, Philip. African memoranda. London, 1805.
Afr 150.4.5 Beazley, C.R. Prince Henry the Navigator. London, 1923.
Afr 150.4 Beazley, C.R. Prince Henry the Navigator. N.Y., 1895.
Afr 13272.21.110 Bebey, Francis. Embarras et Cie; nouvelles et poèmes. Yaoundé, 1968.
Afr 13272.21.100 Bebey, Francis. Le fils d'Agatha Moudio. Yaoundé, 1967.
Afr 10674.71.110 Because of women. (Dipoko, Mbella Sonne.) London, 1969.
Afr 4230.4 Beccari, C. Rerum aethiopicarum scriptores occidentales. Introductio generalis. Roma, 1903.
Afr 5235.189.10 Bechet, Eugène. Cinq ans de séjour au Soudan français. Paris, 1889.
Afr 2875.5 Bechler, W.H. The history of the Italian war. Annapolis, 1913.
Afr 4375.7 Bechtinger, J. Ost Afrika. Wien, 1870.
Afr 9400.3 The Bechuana of South Africa. (Crisp, W.) London, 1896.
Afr 9327.65 Bechuanaland. (Middleton, Coral.) Cape Town, 1965.
Afr 9339.65 Bechuanaland. (Munger, Edwin S.) London, 1965.
Afr 9389.57 Bechuanaland. (Tshekedi Khama.) Johannesburg, 1957.
Afr 9389.66 Bechuanaland. (Young, Bertram Alfred.) London, 1966.
Afr 9335.10 Bechuanaland. Commissioner to Consider Localization of Civil Service. Report on localisation and training. Mafeking, 1966.
Afr Doc 4046.5 Bechuanaland. Public Works Department. Annual report. Gaberones. 1956+
Afr Doc 4009.305F Bechuanaland (Protectorate). Annual statements of account. Gaberones? 1964+
Afr Doc 4007.364 Bechuanaland (Protectorate). Report on the census of the Bechuanaland Protectorate, 1964. Mafeking, South Africa? 1965?
Afr Doc 4014.5 Bechuanaland (Protectorate). Legislative Assembly. Official report of the debates. Lobatsi. 1,1965+
Afr Doc 4014.7 Bechuanaland (Protectorate). Legislative Assembly. Papers. Lobatsi. 21,1965+
Afr Doc 4012.5F Bechuanaland (Protectorate). Legislative Council. Official report of the debates. 1,1961+
Afr 9350.66 Bechuanaland Independence Conference, London, 1966. Report. London, 1966.
Afr 9335.5F Bechuanaland Independence Conference. Report, signed at Marlborough house. n.p., 1966.
Afr 9325.2F Bechuanaland newsletter. Cairo. 2,1965+
Afr 9332.5 Bechuanaland protectorate, report for the year. (Great Britain. Commonwealth Relations Office.) 1946+ 6v.
Afr 9345.50.5 Bechuanaland protectorate. (Ballinger, M.L.) Lovedale, 1931.
Afr 9345.55 The Bechuanaland protectorate. (Sillery, A.) Cape Town, 1952.
Afr 8089.06 Beck, Henry. History of South Africa and the Boer-British war. Philadelphia, 1900.
Afr 6640.20 Becker, A. Hermann von Wissmann. Berlin, 1914.
Afr 3132.5 Becker, C.H. Beiträge zur Geschichte Ägyptens unter den Islam. Strassburg, 1902. 2v.
Afr 3132.6F Becker, C.H. Papyri Schott-Reinhardt I. Heidelberg, 1906.
Afr 2731.5 Becker, Georges. La pénétration française au Sahara. Un transsaharien? Paris, 1928.
Afr 1573.8 Becker, J. España y Marruecos. Madrid, 1903.
Afr 1369.15 Becker, Jeronimo. Historia de Marruecos. Madrid, 1915.
Afr 1658.12 Becker, Jeronimo. El Rif. Madrid, 1909.
Afr 8155.11.2 Becker, Peter. Dingane, King of the Zulu, 1828-1840. N.Y., 1965.
Afr 8934.277.5 Becker, Peter. Hill of destiny. London, 1969.
Afr 9525.593 Becker, Peter. Path of blood. London, 1962.
Afr 8155.11 Becker, Peter. Rule of fear. London, 1964.
Afr 7459.39 Becker-Donner, Etta. Hinterland Liberia. London, 1939.
Afr 8028.149 Beckerling, Joan Letitia. The medical history of the Anglo-Boer war. Cape Town, 1967.
Afr 8678.448 Beckers, Gerhard. Religiöse Faktoren in der Entwicklung der südafrikanischen Rassenfrage. München, 1969.
Afr 6739.268 Bederman, Sanford Harold. The Cameroons Development Corporation. Bota, 1968.
Afr 530.10 Bedeutung Afrikas für die deutsche Weltpolitik. (Zimmermann, E.) Berlin, 1917.
Afr 1550.28 Die Bedeutung der Algeciras-Konferenz. (Ruediger, Georg von.) München, 1920.
Afr 1550.28.5 Die Bedeutung der Algeciras-Konferenz. Inaug.-Diss. (Ruediger, Georg von.) Altenburg, 1917.
Afr 1555.5 Die Bedeutung der Marokkofrage für die englisch-französischen Beziehungen von 1901. Inaug.-Diss. (Melzer, F.) Dresden, 1937.
Afr 6457.24 Bedeutung und Möglichkeiten. (Njuguna Wa Gakuo, E.) Freiburg, 1960.
Afr 6176.50 Bediako, K.A. The downfall of Kwame Nkrumah. Accra, 1966?
Afr 10622.18.100 Bediako, K.A. A husband for Esi Ellua. Ghana, 1967.
Afr 2030.461.5 Bedjaoui, Mohammed. La révolution algérienne et le droit. Bruxelles, 1961.
Afr 8050.18 Die bedreiging van die liberalisme. (Scholtz, Gert Daniel.) Pretoria, 1966.
Afr 9060.2F Bee, Barbara M. Historical bibliography of the city of Durban, or Port Natal. Cape Town, 1946.
Afr 11200.21.100 Bee, David. Curse of Magira. 1st ed. N.Y., 1965.
Afr 6395.3.2 Beech, M.W.H. The Suk, their language and folklore. N.Y., 1969.
Afr 6395.3 Beech, M.W.H. The Suk, their language and folklore. Oxford, 1911.
Afr 6164.3.5 Beecham, John. Ashantee and the Gold Coast. London, 1874.
Afr 2802.5 Beechey, F.W. Proceedings of the expedition to explore the northern coast of Africa, from Tripoly eastward. London, 1828.
Afr 500.35 Beer, George Louis. African questions at the Paris Peace Conference. N.Y., 1923.
Afr 500.35.2 Beer, George Louis. African questions at the Paris Peace Conference. 1st ed. London, 1968.
Afr 550.150 Beetham, Thomas Allan. Christianity and the new Africa. London, 1967.
Afr 6420.82 Before the dawn in Kenya. (Wilson, Christopher James.) Nairobi, 1953.
Afr 8100.42 Before Van Riebeeck. (Raven-Hart, Rowland.) Cape Town, 1967.
Afr 6540.2 The Beganda at home. (Hattersley, C.W.) London, 1908.
Afr 3079.68.7 Die Begegnung Europas mit Ägypten. 2. Aufl. (Morenz, Siegfried.) Zürich, 1969.
Afr 11465.14.150 Beggar my neighbour, short stories. (Jacobson, Dan.) London, 1964.
Afr 11465.14.160 The beginners. (Jacobson, Dan.) N.Y., 1966.
Afr 8100.5 The beginning of South African history. (Theal, G.M.) London, 1902.
Afr 21107.5 The beginning of South African vernacular literature. (Kunene, Daniel P.) Los Angeles, 1967.
Afr 9775.2 The beginnings of Nyasaland and north-eastern Rhodesia. (Hanna, Alexander John.) Oxford, 1956.
Afr 3193.15 The beginnings of the Egyptian question and the rise of Mehemet Ali. (Ghorbal, Shafik.) London, 1928.
Afr Doc 4409.5F Begrooting van uitgaaf te worden gedekt gedurende net jaar. (Cape of Good Hope. Department of Treasurer.) 1890-1910 2
Afr Doc 4309.5 Begroting van die addisionele uitgawes wat bestry moet word uit in komste en leningsrekemings. (South Africa. Finance Department.) Pretoria. 1965+
Afr 1570.54 Begue, Leon. Le secret d'une conquête. Paris, 1929.
Afr 9710.6 Beguin, E. Les Barotse. Lausanne, 1903.
Afr 4700.28 Beguinot, F. La nostra aurora coloniale. Imperia, 1928.
Afr 2208.65 Behaghel, A. L'Algérie. Alger, 1865.
Afr 609.40.10A Behind God's back. (Farson, Negley.) N.Y., 1941.
Afr 1618.10 Behind harem walls. (Dolinger, Jane.) London, 1960.
Afr 1609.27.5F Behind moroccan walls. (Celarie, H.) N.Y., 1931.
Afr 3340.5 Behind the Egyptian sphinx. (Sedar, Irving.) Philadelphia, 1960.
Afr 3745.60 Behind the modern Sudan. (Jackson, H.C.) London, 1955.
Afr 9149.01 Behind the scenes in the Transvaal. (Wilson, D.M.) London, 1901.
Afr 2609.22 Behind Tunisian walls by L.E. Douglas. (Voligny, R.B. de.) London, 1922.
Afr 609.33.15 Behn, Fritz. Kwa heri Afrika. Stuttgart, 1933.
Afr 10013.8 Behn, Hans Ulrich. Die Presse in Westafrika. Hamburg, 1968.
Afr 4513.39.25 Behold our new empire, Mussolini. (Diel, Louise.) London, 1939.
Afr 11790.59.100 Behold the earth mourns. (Singh, A.R.) Johannesburg, 1961.
Afr 2030.461.45 Behr, Edward. The Algerian problem. London, 1961.
Afr 2030.461.45.2 Behr, Edward. The Algerian problem. N.Y., 1962.
Afr 2030.461.46 Behr, Edward. Dramatique Algérie. Paris, 1962.
Afr 6777.2 Behr, H.F. von. Kriegsbilder aus dem Araberaupland. Leif, 1891.
Afr 9170.7 Behrman, F. My fifty-odd years in Johannesburg. Johannesburg, 1961.
Afr 5187.20 Behrman, Lucy C. Muslim brotherhoods and politics in Senegal. Cambridge, 1970.
Afr 20016.5 Beier, Ulli. African poetry. Cambridge, Eng., 1966.
Afr 10005.10 Beier, Ulli. Introduction to Africa literature. Evanston, 1967.
Afr 10018.8 Beier, Ulli. Political spider. London, 1969.
Afr 49017.2 Beier, Ulli. Three Nigerian plays. London, 1967.
Afr 6276.4 Beier, Vlli. A year of sacred festivals in one Yoruba town. Marina, 1959.
Afr 6291.42 Beijbom, Anders. Rapport fran Biafra. Stockholm, 1968.
Afr 555.22.5 Beijer, J. Journal gehouden van Port Elisabeth (Algoabaai) naar Reddersburg. Kaapstad, 1862. 2 pam.
Afr 2208.78 Beijerman, H. Drie maanden in Algerie. 's-Gravenhage, 1878.
Htn Afr 4730.4F* Beilul-Zula-Massaua-Sudan. (Italy. Ministero di Affari Esteri.) Rome, 1885.
Afr 2875.19 Beim roten Halbmond vor Tripolis. (Theilhaber, F.A.) Cöln, 1912.
Afr 14722.5 Beira, Maria da. Luz no túnel; romane. Porto, 1966.

Afr Doc 9272.5   Beira. Intendente do Governo. Relatorio. Lourenço Marques. 1908

Afr 9525.201   Beit, Alfred. The will and the way. London, 1957.

Afr 6985.3F   Beiträge...zur Landskunde des deutschen Namalandes. (Range, Paul.) Hamburg, 1914.

Afr 530.4   Beiträge zur deutschen Kolonialfrage. (Westermann, D.) Essen, 1937.

Afr 608.73   Beiträge zur Entdeckungsgeschichte Afrikas. v.1-4. (Kiepert, H.) Berlin, 1873-81. 2v.

Afr 6392.37   Beiträge zur Entwicklungspolitik in Afrika. (Weigt, Ernest.) Köln, 1964.

Afr 3132.5   Beiträge zur Geschichte Ägyptens unter den Islam. (Becker, C.H.) Strassburg, 1902. 2v.

Afr 1618.5F   Beiträge zur kenntnis der Materiellen kultur nordwest-marokkos. (Rackow, Ernst.) Wiesbaden, 1958.

Afr 4559.11   Beiträge zur Landeskunde von Abessinien These. (Rathjens, Carl.) Erlangen, 1911.

Afr 6883.20   Beiträge zur materiellen Kultur der Nyamwezi. (Boehrenz, Wolfgang.) Hamburg, 1940.

Afr 6648.3F   Beitraege zur Völkerkunde. (Luschan, F. Von.) Berlin, 1897.

Afr 6688.2   Beitraege zur Völkerkunde des Togogebietes. (Phehn, R.) Halle, 1898.

Afr 6460.1   Beiträge zur Völkerkunde von Östafrika. (Freitag, C.) n.p., 1908.

Afr 8040.20   Ein Beitrag zu der Geschichte des Föderalismus. Inaug. Diss. (Steyn, J.H.) Würzburg, 1936.

Afr 5760.2   Beitrag zur ethnographie Madagaskars. (Schnackenberg, H.) Strassburg, 1888.

Afr 8678.115   Beitrage zur Kunde der Hottentotten. (Hahn, Theophilus.) Durban, 19-

Afr 4095.4   Beke, C.T. Enquiry into N.D. Abbadie's journey to Kaffa. London, 1851.

Afr 4095.12.5   Beke, C.T. A lecture on the sources of the Nile. London, 1864.

Afr 4095.12   Beke, C.T. The sources of the Nile. London, 1860.

Afr 4509.15.3   Beke, Charles F. The British captives in Abyssinia. 2nd ed. London, 1867.

Afr 8678.69   De beknelde kleurling Zuid-Afrika's vierstromenbeld. (Prins, Jan.) Assen, 1967.

Afr 1608.03   Beknopt dag-journaal van Marocco. (Haringman, H.) Haag, 1803.

Afr 5787.5.5   Bekoropoka quelques aspects de la vie familiale et sociale d'un village Malgache. (Lavondes, Henri.) Paris, 1967.

Afr 1088.6   Bel, A. Les Benou Ghanya. Paris, 1903.

Afr 575.19   Bel, Alfred. Coup d'oeil sur l'islam en Berberie. Paris, 1917.

Afr 575.19.25   Bel, Alfred. La religion musulmane en Berberie. Paris, 1938.

Afr 2373.10.2   Bel, Alfred. Tlemcen et ses environs. 2e ed. Toulouse, 192-

Afr 710.55   Belandier, Georges. Afrique ambigue. Paris, 1957.

Afr 7315.25   Belchior, M.D. Comprendamos os negros. Lisboa, 1951.

Afr 630.66.5   Belchior, Manuel. Fundamentos para uma politica multicultural em Africa. Lisboa, 1966.

Afr 530.36   Belges dans l'Afrique centrale. Bruxelles, 1886. 3v.

Afr 7540.36   Belgian administration in the Congo. (Brausch, G.) London, 1961.

Afr 7502.7   Belgian Congo, monthly information bulletin. Brussels. 1959

Afr 7815.16   The Belgian Congo, some recent changes. (Slade, Ruth.) London, 1960.

Afr 7809.59.10   Belgian Congo. (Belgium. Office de l'Information et des Relations.) Brussels, 1959.

Afr 7809.44.5   The Belgian Congo. (Great Britain. Naval Intelligence Division.) London, 1944.

Afr 7575.75   The Belgian Congo. 2. ed. (Slade, R.) London, 1961.

Afr 7549.19A   The Belgian Congo and the Berlin Act. (Keith, Arthur B.) Oxford, 1919.

Afr 7809.52.5   The Belgian Congo appraised. (Belgian Information Services.) N.Y., 1952.

Afr 7809.42F   Belgian Congo at war. (Belgian Information Center.) N.Y., 194-.

Afr 7502.5   Belgian Congo to-day. Bruxelles. 1+ 6v.

Afr 7809.42F   Belgian Information Center. Belgian Congo at war. N.Y., 194-.

Afr 7809.52.5   Belgian Information Services. The Belgian Congo appraised. N.Y., 1952.

Afr 7809.35   Belgian Luxembourg Touring Office. Travel in the Belgian Congo. Brussels, 1935.

Afr 8360.7.89   A Belgian mission to the Boers. (Standaert, E.H.G.) London, 1917.

Afr 8360.8   A Belgian mission to the Boers. (Standaert, E.H.G.) N.Y., 1917.

Afr 7549.62.5   Belgique, gouvernante du Congo. (Maurice, Albert.) Bruxelles, 1962.

Afr 2030.460.30   La Belgique devant le problème algérien. (Comité pour la Paix en Algérie.) Chênée, 1961.

Afr 7565.9   Belgique et Congo. (Stengers, J.) Bruxelles, 1963.

Afr 7567.10   Belgique et Congo (Une carte itinéraire). (Payen, Edouard.) Paris, 1917.

Afr 7549.11   La Belgique et le Congo. (Vandervelde, E.) Paris, 1911.

Afr 7812.251F   Belgium. Plan décennal pour le développement. Bruxelles, 1951.

Afr 7937.2   Belgium. Centre de Recherche et d'Information. Rwanda politique (1958-1960). Bruxelles, 1961.

Afr 7850.52F   Belgium. Chambre des Représentants. Commission parlamentaire chargée de faire une enquête. Bruxelles, 1959.

Afr 7568.25.5   Belgium. Commission Chargée de Faire une Enquête dans les Territoires de l'Etat du Congo. Abstract of the report of the Commission enquiry into a administration of Congo Free State. London, 1906.

Afr 7809.34   Belgium. Commission du Parc National Albert. Parc National Albert. Bruxelles, 1934.

Afr 7549.52   Belgium. Force Publique. Etat-Major. Le force publique de sa naissance à 1914. Bruxelles, 1952.

Afr 7570.15   Belgium. Ministère de la Défense Nationale. Etat-Major Général de l'Armée. Les campagnes coloniales belges, 1914-1918. Bruxelles, 1927-1929. 3v.

Afr 718.18.50F   Belgium. Ministère des Affaires Africaines. Document notte. Bruxelles, 1960.

Afr 7812.4   Belgium. Ministère des Affaires Africaines. Firmes, établissements particuliers d'activité économique.

Afr Doc 7705.5F   Belgium. Ministère des Affaires Africaines. Rapport annuel sur l'administration de la colonie du Congo Belge. 1921-1956 6v.

Afr 7812.6F   Belgium. Ministère des Affaires Africaines. Secretariat du Plan Décennal. Rapport sur l'execution du plan décennal pour le développment...du Congo Belge, 1956-1958. n.p., n.d.

Afr 7540.10   Belgium. Ministère des Colonies. Annuaire officiel. Bruxelles. 1914+ v.

Afr 7812.249   Belgium. Ministère des Colonies. Plan décennal pour le développement économique et social du Congo belge. Bruxelles, 1949.

Afr 7502.6.5   Belgium. Ministère des Colonies. Direction des Etudes Economiques. De economische toestand van Belgisch-Congo. 1950+ 3v.

Afr 7502.6   Belgium. Ministère des Colonies. Direction des Etudes Economiques. La situation économique du Congo belge. La Louvière. 1951+ 2v.

Afr 7800.50.10   Belgium. Office de l'Information et des Relations. Belgian Congo. Brussels, 1959.

Afr 7533.10   Belgium. Office de l'Information et des Relations Politiques pour le Congo Belge et le Ruanda-Urundi. Ruanda-Urundi. Brussels, 1960. 4 pam.

Afr 7812.255.5   Belgium. Office de l'Information et des Relations Publiques pour le Congo Belge. L'économie du Congo belge et du Ruanda-Urundi. Bruxelles, 1955.

Afr 9560.15   Belgium. Treaties. Great Britain. 1933. Exchange of notes between His Majesty's government in the United Kingdon...Belgian government. London, 1933.

Afr 7575.65   Belgo-Congolese Round Table Conference, Brussels, 1960. De historische dagen von februari 1960. Brussels, 1960.

Afr 4180.3.10A   Belgrave, C.D. Siwa. London, 1923.

Afr 7568.25   Belguim. Commission Chargée de Faire une Enquête dans les Territoires de l'Etat du Congo. The Congo. N.Y., 1906.

Afr 3255.3   Bell, C.F.M. Khedives and pashas. London, 1884.

Afr 8279.00.13   Bell, F.W. The South African conspiracy. London, 1900.

Afr 9155.5   Bell, H.T.M. A guide to the Transvaal and map. Johannesburg, 1905. 2v.

Afr 8687.7   Bell, Nancy R.E. (Mevgens). Heroes of discovery in South Africa. London, 1899.

Afr 6455.115   Bell, W.D.M. Karamojo safari. 1st ed. N.Y., 1949.

Afr 6192.85   Bell, Willis. The roadmakers. Accra, 1961.

Afr 2875.12   La bella guerra. (Gray, E.M.) Firenze, 1912.

Afr 8225.5   Bellairs, Blanche St. John. The Transvaal war 1880-81. Edinburg, 1885.

Afr 4394.3.14   Bellavita, E. Adua, i precedenti, la battaglia. Genova, 1931.

Afr 1965.23   Bellemare, Alex. Abd-el-Kader. Paris, 1863.

Afr 109.61.15   Belles pages de l'histoire africaine. (Cardot, Vera.) Paris, 1961.

Afr 6465.56   Bellingham, B.L. Mombasa. Nairobi, 1933.

Afr 775.5   Bellingham, W. The diary of a working man in central Africa. London, n.d.

Afr 6298.202   Bello, Ahmadu. My life. Cambridge, 1962.

Afr 2209.06.2   Belloc, E. Esto perpetua. London, 1906.

Afr 8279.01.15   Bellows, J. The truth about the Transvaal war and the truth about war. 2d. ed. London, 1901.

Afr 8846.26   Bellwood, W. Whither the Transkei. London, 1964.

Afr 3979.07   Below the Cataracts. (Tyndale, W.) Philadelphia, 1907.

Afr 6075.10   Belshan, H. Facing the future in West Africa. London, 1951.

Afr 555.9.50   Beltrame, G. Il sennaar e lo sciangallah. Verona, 1879. 2v.

Afr 2929.12.20   Beltramelli, A. Paesi di conquista. Ferrara, 1915.

Afr 1432.13   Beltran, F.C. Historia de la guerra de Africa. T.1. Madrid, 1860.

Afr 5960.13   Beltran y Rozpide, Ricardo. La Guinea española. Barcelona, 1901.

Afr 3240.3   Bemmelen, P.V. L'Egypte et l'Europe. Leiden, 1882. 2v.

Afr 1495.6.15   Ben Barka, Abdelkader. El Mehdi Ben Barka, mon frère. Paris, 1966.

Afr 1495.6.35   Ben Barka, el Mehdi. The political thought of Ben Barka. Havana, 1968.

Afr 1495.6.25   Ben Barka chez les juges. (Caviglioli, François.) Paris, 1967.

Afr 1494.50   Ben Barka el Mehdi. Problèmes d'édification du Maroc et du Moghreb. Paris, 1959.

Afr 2030.464.45   Ben Bella, Ahmed. Discours, année 1963. Alger, 1964.

Afr 4785.16   Il Benadir...con 16 fotografie originali. (Piazza, G.) Roma, 1913.

Afr 4766.27   Il Benadir. (Mantegazza, Vico.) Milano, 1908.

Afr 510.55   Benazet, H. L'Afrique française en danger. Paris, 1947.

Afr 1495.6   Benbarka, El Mehdi. Option révolutionnaire au Maroc. Paris, 1966.

Afr 5243.125.30   Benchelt, Eno. Kulturwandel bei den Bambara von Segou. Bonn, 1962.

Afr 6879.24.9   Beneath African glaciers. (Dundas, A.L.H.) London, 1924.

Afr 4513.37.65   Benedetti, A. La guerra equatoriale. Milano, 1937.

Afr 2710.12   Benedetti, Achille. Dal Sahara al Ciad. Milano, 1935.

Afr 5844.2   Benedict, B. Indians in a plural society. London, 1961.

Afr 5842.22   Benedict, Burton. Mauritius. London, 1965.

Afr 5895.5.2   Benedict, Burton. People of the Seychelles. 2nd ed. London, 1968.

Afr 555.120   Benedictine and Moor. (Beach, Peter.) N.Y., 1959.

Afr 3990.5   Benedite, G. Aaron. Egypte. Paris, 1900.

Htn   Afr 590.44*   Benezet, A. Eine kurtze Vorstellung des Theils von Africa. Ephrata, 1763.

Afr 590.45.2   Benezet, Anthony. Some historical account of Guinea, its situation, produce, and the general disposition of its inhabitants. 2nd ed. London, 1968.

Htn   Afr 677.71.5*   Benezet, Anthony. Some historical account of Guinea. London, 1772.

Htn   Afr 677.71*   Benezet, Anthony. Some historical account of Guinea. Philadelphia, 1771. 2 pam.

Afr 677.71.10   Benezet, Anthony. Some historical account of Guinea: its situation. 2nd ed. London, 1968.

Afr 2000.5   Benhabiles, Cherif. L'"Algérie française vue par un indigène. Alger, 1914.

Afr 8849.8   Benham, M.S. Henry Callaway. London, 1896.

Afr 555.84   Benham, Phyllis. In Livingstone's trail, the quest of the mighty. Westminster, 1909.

Afr 2762.4   Benhazera, M. Six Mois chez Les touaregDu Ahaggar. Alger, 1908.

Afr 6283.9   Benin, the city of blood. (Bacon, R.H.) London, 1897.

Afr 6295.130   Benin and the Europeans, 1485-1897. (Ryder, Alan Frederick Charles.) London, 1969.

Afr 6283.3   The Benin massacre. (Boisragon, A.) London, 1897.

VAfr 5580.3.25   Beniovski, M.A. Denník Mórica A. Beňovského. Bratislava, 1966.

Afr 5580.3.20   Beniowski, M.A. Memoirs and travels of Mauritius Augustus. London, 1790. 2v.

Afr 5580.3.30   Beniowski, M.A. Pamigtniki. Wyd. 1. Warszawa, 1967.
Afr 5056.99   Benitez, Cristobal. Mi viaje por el interior del Africa. Tangier, 1899.
Afr 500.83   Benitez Cabrera, José. Africa, biografia del colonialismo. Habana, 1964.
Afr 608.89   Benko, J.F.V. Reise S.M. Schiffes. Albatros...Süd-Amerika dem Caplande und West Afrika, 1885-1886. Pola, 1889.
Afr 2030.449   Bennabi, Malek. Discours sur les conditions de la renaissance algérienne. Alger, 1949.
Afr 6455.33   Bennet, Edward. Shots and snapshots in British East Africa. London, 1914.
Afr 6926.22   Bennett, Benjamin. Hitler over Africa. London, 1939.
Afr 3735.6   Bennett, E.N. The downfall of the Dervishes. London, 1898.
Afr 8325.56   Bennett, E.N. With Methuen's column on an ambulance train. London, 1900.
Afr 2875.14   Bennett, E.N. With the Turks in Tripoli. London, 1912.
Afr 6420.72.5   Bennett, G. Kenya, a political history. London, 1963.
Afr 6420.72   Bennett, G. The Kenyatta election. London, 1961.
Afr 11203.59.100   Bennett, J. Mister fisherman. 1st American ed. Boston, 1965.
Afr 6565.42   Bennett, N.R. Studies in East African history. Boston, 1963.
Afr 679.63.32   Bennett, Nicholas. Zigzag to Timbuktu. N.Y., 1966.
Afr 6398.10   Bennett, Norman R. Leadership in eastern Africa. Boston, 1968.
Afr 1326.20   Bennett, Norman Robert. A study guide for Morocco. Boston, 1968.
Afr 2426.10   Bennett, Norman Robert. A study guide for Tunisia. Boston, 1968.
Afr 9148.43   Bennie, John. An account of a journey into Transorangia and the Potchefstroom-Winburg Trekker Republic in 1843. Cape Town, 1956.
Afr 6160.26   Bennion, Francis. The constitutional law of Ghana. London, 1962.
Afr 2025.14   Benoist, Charles. Enquête algérienne. Paris, 1892.
Afr 1200.75.4   Benoist, Charles. La question méditerranéenne. Paris, 1928.
Afr 1571.17.135   Benoist-Méchin, Jacques. Lyautey l'Africain, ou Le rêve immolé. Lausanne, 1966.
Afr 5748.95.25   Benoit, Felix. Madagascar, étude economique, geographique et ethnographique. Dijon, 1895.
Afr 7815.34   Benoit, J. La population africaine à Elisabethville. Elisabethville, 195-.
Afr 9165.7.5   Benoni, son of my sorrow. (Humphriss, Deryck.) Benoni, 1968.
Afr 50.60   Bénot, Yvès. Idéologies des indépendances africaines. Paris, 1969.
Afr 1088.6   Les Benou Ghanya. (Bel, A.) Paris, 1903.
Afr 2527.7   Benoyts, F. de. Au pays de Kroumers et au Maroc. Lille, 1913.
Afr 150.14   Bensaude, J. A cruzada do Infante Dom Henrique. Lisboa, 1942.
Afr 8687.263.10   Benson, M. Chief Albert Lutuli of South Africa. London, 1963.
Afr 8685.90   Benson, Mary. The African patriots. London, 1963.
Afr 8685.89   Benson, Mary. South Africa, the struggle for a birthright. London, 1966.
Afr 9424.360   Benson, Mary. Tshekedi Khama. London, 1960.
Afr 609.60.30   Bensted-Smith, Richard. Turn left for Tangier. Coventry, 1960.
Afr 8673.15   Bensusan, A.D. South Africa. Cape Town, 1960.
Afr 1609.04.10A   Bensusan, S.L. Morocco. London, 1904.
Afr 4642.1   Bent, J.J. The sacred city of the Ethiopians. London, 1893.
Afr 6879.36   Bent, Newell. Jungle giants. Norwood, Mass., 1936.
Afr 11675.87.2   Bentel, Lea. Alan Paton. Johannesburg, 1969.
Afr 6484.6   Bentley, E.L. British East Africa and Uganda. London, 1892.
Afr 555.23.10   Bentley, H.M. (Mrs.). W. Holman Bentley, the life and adventures of a Congo pioneer. London, 1907.
Afr 7809.00.5   Bentley, W.H. Pioneering on the Congo. N.Y., 1900. 2v.
Afr 7808.87   Bentley, William Holman. Life on the Congo. London, 1887.
Afr 626.104   Benveneste, Guy. Handbook of African economic development. N.Y., 1962.
Afr 1273.967.5   Benyoussef, Amor. Populations du Maghreb et communauté économique à quatre. Paris, 1967.
Afr 545.34   Benz, Ernst. Messianische Kirchen, Sekten und Bewegungen im heutigen Afrika. Leiden, 1965.
Afr 2662.1.5F   Benzert. (Ludwig Salvator.) Prag, 1897.
Afr 2030.462.100   Benzine, A. Le camp. Paris, 1962.
Afr 6455.105   Benzon, Boeje. Mine afrikanshe udfingter. København, 1948.
Afr 3978.00.10   Beobachtungen über die Sitten und Gebräuche der Ägypter. (Antes, J.) Gera, 1801.
Afr 5243.343.5   Berand-Villars, J.M.E. L'empire de Gao. Paris, 1946.
Afr 1550.4   Berard, V. L'affaire marocaine. Paris, 1906.
Afr 1570.61   Berard, Victor. L'affaire marocaine. Paris, 1906.
Afr 1680.12   Berber village. (Clarke, Bryan.) London, 1959.
NEDL Afr 1258.45   Die Berberei. (London, F.H.) Frankfurt, 1845.
Afr 1280.60   Les Berbères. (1st ed. (Bousquet, G.H.) Paris, 1957.
Afr 1259.42   Berbères et Arabes. (Bremond, Edouard.) Paris, 1942.
Afr 1635.6   Les Berberes et le Makhzen dans le sud du Maroc. Thèse. (Montagne, R.) Paris, 1930.
Afr 1347.5   Les Berberes marocains et la pacification de l'Atlas central (1912-1933). (Guillaume, A.) Paris, 1946.
Afr 1200.90   La Berberie. v.1-2. (Guernier, E.L.) Paris, 1950. 2v.
Afr 1080.15   La Berbérie musulmane et l'Orient au moyen age. (Marcais, Georges.) Paris, 1946.
Afr 1083.10   La Berbérie orientale sous la dynastie des Benou'l-Arlab (800-909). Thèse. (Vonderheyden, M.) Paris, 1927.
Afr 2482.10   La Berbérie orientale sous les Hafsides. (Brunschvig, R.) Paris, 1940-47. 2v.
Afr 1085.3   La Berbérie orientale sous les Zirides, Xe-XIIe siècles. v.1-2. (Idris, Hady R.) Paris, 1959.
Afr 1085.2   La Berbérie orientale sous les Zirides, Xe-XIIe siècles. v.1-2. (Idris, Hady R.) Paris, 1962.
Afr 1635.8   Berbers and blacks. (Barrows, D.P.) N.Y., 1927.
Afr 2230.12   Berbrugger, A. Les époques militaires de la Grande Kabilie. Alger, 1857.
Afr 2397.1   Berbrugger, A. Geronimo. Alger, 1854.
Afr 1965.27   Berbrugger, L.A. Négociation entre monseigneur l'évêque d'Alger et Abd el-qader. Paris, 1844.
Afr 1825.3PF   Berbrugger. Algerie historique, pittoresque. Paris, 1843. 3v.
Afr 4045.1   Berchere, N. Le desert de Suez. Paris, n.d.

Afr 6542.20   Bere, Rennie Montague. The way to the mountains of the moon. London, 1966.
Afr 1635.25   Berebres y hebreos en Marruecos. (Laredo, A.I.) Madrid, 1954.
Afr 5343.13   Bereg Slonovoi Kosti. (Blokhin, Leonid F.) Moskva, 1967.
Afr 6210.32   Berelt, Lionel. Constitutional problems of federalism in Nigeria. Lagos, 1961.
Afr 5185.6   Berenger-Ferand, L.J.B. Les peuples de la Sénégambie. Paris, 1879.
Afr 1755.49   Berenguer, Damaso. Campanas en el rif y Yebala 1921-1922. Madrid, 1923.
Afr 1490.20   Berenguer. La guerra en Marruecos. Madrid, 1918.
Afr 2209.35.10   Berenson, Mary. Across the Mediterranean. Prato, 1935.
Afr 1069.38.5   Berenson, Mary. A vicarious trip to the Barbary coast. London, 1938.
Afr 718.38   Berg, Gertrud Wilhelmson. Pori. Stockholm, 1964.
Afr 109.32   Berger, A. Afrika, schwarz oder weiss. Berlin, 1932.
Afr 109.38   Berger, Arthur. Kampf um Afrika. Berlin, 1938.
Afr 8687.131   Berger, Lucy Gough. Where's the madam? Cape Town, 1966.
Afr 3040.76   Berger, Morroe. Bureaucracy and society in modern Egypt. Princeton, 1957.
Afr 2035.11   Bergheaud, Edmond. Le premier quart d'heure. Paris, 1964.
Afr 2030.464.20   Bergleaud, Edmond. Le premier quart d'heure. Paris, 1964.
Afr 2819.25   Bergna, C. Tripoli dal 1510 al 1850. Tripoli, 1925.
Afr 555.153   Bergner, Gerhard. Heiden, Christen und Politiker. Breklum, 1963.
Afr 2208.90   Bergot, Raoul. L'Algérie telle qu'elle est. Paris, 1890.
Afr 4559.32.10   Bergsma, S. Rainbow empire, Ethiopia stretches out her hands. Grand Rapids, 1932.
Afr 6979.04   Bergtouren und Steppenfahrten in Kererolande. (Seiner, F.) Berlin, 1904.
Afr 4558.55F   Bericht über C. Reitz und seine Reise. (Fenzl, E.) Vienna, 1855.
Afr 4392.4.10   Berkeley, G.F.H. The campaign of Adowa and the rise of Menelik. N.Y., 1969.
NEDL Afr 4392.4   Berkeley, G.F.H. The campaign of Adowa and the rise of Menelik. Westminster, 1902.
Afr 4392.4.5   Berkeley, G.F.H. The campaign of Adowa and the rise of Menelik. New ed. London, 1930.
Afr 3163.10   Berkuk devrinde Memluk Sultanhgi. (Tekindaÿ, M.C. Şehabeddin.) Istanbul, 1967.
Afr 4640.2   Berlan, E. Addis-Abeba. Grenoble, 1963.
Afr 7565.12.5F   Berlin. Conference, 1884-85. Protocoles et acte général de la Conférence de Berlin, 1884-85. n.p., (1885).
Afr 7565.12.30   The Berlin West African Conference, 1884-1885. (Crowe, S.E.) London, 1942.
Afr 7565.12.25   Die Berliner Kongo-Konferenz, 1884-1885. (Koenigk, G.) Essen, 1938.
Afr 5130.2   Berlioux, E.F. André Brue, ou L'Origine. Paris, 1874.
Afr 125.5   Berlioux, E.F. La terre habitable vers l'équator. Paris, 1884.
Afr 9489.67   Berlyn, Phillippa. Rhodesia, beleaguered country. London, 1967.
Afr 3700.11   Bermann, R.A. Mahdi of Allah. London, 1931.
Afr 4700.35.10   Bermasconi, G. Le guerre e la politica dell'Italia nell'Africa orientale. Milano, 1935.
Afr 7335.2   Bermudes, F. A cidade da Beira. Lisboa, 1964.
Afr 1493.40   Bermudo-Soriano, E. El Raisuni (caudillo de Yebala). Madrid, 1941.
Afr 659.13   Bernard, A. L'Afrique du nord. Paris, 1913.
Afr 1273.926   Bernard, A. L'Afrique du Nord pendant la guerre. Paris, 1926.
Afr 2209.31.15   Bernard, A. L'Algérie. Paris, 1931.
Afr 2209.31.10   Bernard, A. L'Algérie. Paris, 1931.
Afr 1571.4   Bernard, A. Les confins algéro-marocains. Paris, 1911.
Afr 1571.4.8   Bernard, A. La France au Maroc. Paris, 1917.
Afr 1609.13   Bernard, A. Le Maroc. Paris, 1913.
Afr 1609.13.2   Bernard, A. Le Maroc. 4. ed. Paris, 1916.
Afr 1609.13.2.3   Bernard, A. Le Maroc. 7. ed. Paris, 1931.
Afr 1609.13.2.5   Bernard, A. Le Maroc. 8e ed. Paris, 1932.
Afr 2719.06   Bernard, A. La pénétration saharienne, 1830-1906. Alger, 1906.
Afr 1869.29   Bernard, Augustin. L'Algerie. Paris, 1929.
Afr 2618.28   Bernard, Augustin. Enquête sur l'habitation rurale des indigènes de la Tunisie. Tunis, 1924.
Afr 2762.9   Bernard, F. Deux missions françaises chez les Touareg en 1880-81. Alger, 1896.
Afr 1493.6   Bernard, Francois. Le Maroc économique et agricole. Paris, 1917
Afr 4045.5   Bernard, H. Itinéraire pour l'isthme de Suez et les grandes villes d'Egypte. Paris, 1869.
Afr 6160.15   Bernard, Jane. Black mistress. London, 1957.
Afr Doc 6208.505   Bernard, Jean. Les industries du Sénégal. Paris, 1965.
Afr 2608.92   Bernard, M. De Tripoli à Tunis. Paris, 1925.
Afr 609.27   Bernard, Marc. En hydravion au-dessus du continent noir. Paris, 1927.
Afr 2208.93.6   Bernard, Marius. De Tunis à Alger. Paris, 1893.
Afr 2209.06.10   Bernard, P. Histoire, colonization, géographie et administration de l'Algérie. 2e ed. Alger, 1906.
Afr 1273.2   Bernard, Paul. Les anciens impôts de l'Afrique du Nord. St. Raphael, 1925.
Afr 1494.61   Bernard, S. Le conflit franco-marocain, 1943-56. v.1-2, 3. Bruxelles, 1963. 2v.
Afr 1494.61.5   Bernard, S. The Franco-Moroccan conflict, 1943-1956. New Haven, 1968.
Afr 545.32   Bernardi, Bernardo. Le religioni in Africa. Torino, 1961.
Afr 7073.3   Bernatzik, Hugo. Geheimnisvolle Inseln Tropen-Afrikas. Berlin, 1933.
Afr 8678.376   Bernstein, Hilda. The world that was ours. London, 1967.
Afr 2209.37.5   Berque, A. L'Algérie, terre d'art et d'histoire. Alger, 1937.
Afr 3290.5   Berque, Jacques. L'Egypte, imperialisme et revolution. Paris, 1967.
Afr 1110.40.5   Berque, Jacques. French North Africa. N.Y., 1967.
Afr 1110.40   Berque, Jacques. Le Maghreb entre deux guerres. Paris, 1962.
Afr 1680.10   Berque, Jacques. Structures sociales du haut-atlas. 1 ed. Paris, 1955.
Afr 10007.2.5   Berrian, Albert H. Négritude; essays and studies. Hampton, 1967.
Afr 609.66.35   Bertacchini, Renato. Continente nero; memorialisti italiani dell'800 in Africa. Parma, 1966.
Afr 109.66.30   Bertaux, Pierre. Afrika. Frankfurt, 1966.
Afr 1955.12   Berteuil, A. L'Algérie française, histoire. Paris, 1856. 2v.
Afr 1609.30.20   Berthel, J. Impressions marocaines. Paris, 1930.
Afr 1957.5   Berthezene. Dix-huit mois à Alger. Montpellier, 1834.
Afr 1869.51   Berthier, A. L'Algérie et son passé. Paris, 1951.

Afr 2318.1.20   Berthier, Andre. Constantine. Toulouse, 1965.
Afr 1635.1   Bertholon, L. Les premiers colons. v.1-2. Tunis, 1898.
Afr 1280.25F   Bertholon, Lucien. Recherches anthropologiques dans la Berbérie orientale. Lyon, 1913. 2v.
Afr 115.107   Bertola, Arnaldo. Storia e istituzioni dei paesi afro-asiatici. Torino, 1964.
Afr 3040.55   Bertolini, V.C. La légitime défense dans la doctrine du droit musulman en Egypte. Thèse. Paris, 1931.
Afr 9710.5.7   Bertrand, Alfred. Au pays des Barotsi, Haut-Zambèze. Paris, 1898.
Afr 8919.08   Bertrand, Alfred. Dans le Sud-Africain et au serial de l'Afrique centrale. Genève, 1911.
Afr 555.149.5   Bertrand, Alfred. En Afrique avec le missionnaire Coillard. Genève, 1899.
Afr 9710.5   Bertrand, Alfred. The kingdom of the Barotsi. London, 1899.
Afr 3979.37.3   Besancon, Jacques. L'homme et le Nil. Paris, 1957.
Afr 5874.20   Besant, Walter. Bourbon journal, August, 1863. London, 1933.
Afr 5746.09   Beschreibung...insul Madagascar. (Megiserum, H.) Altenburg, 1609.

Htn   Afr 8657.85*   Beschreibung des Vorgebirges der Guten Hoffnung. (Mentzel, O.) Glogau, 1885-87. 2v.
Afr 8657.11F   Beschrijving van Cabo de Goede Hoop en Rio de la Goa. (Buetner, Johan Daniel.) Pietermaritzburg, 1960.
Afr 6280.28F   Die Besiedlung Sudnigeriens von den Anfangen bis zur britischen Kolonisation. Inaug. Diss. (Dittel, Paul.) Leipzig, 1936.
Afr 8305.6   Besieged by the Boers. (Ashe, E.O.) N.Y., 1900.
Afr 8300.16   Besieged in Ladysmith. (Watkins-Pitchford, Herbert.) Pietermaritzburg, 1964.
Afr 8310.9   Besieged with Baden-Powell. Record of siege. (Neilly, J.E.) London, 1900.
Afr 5119.35   Beslier, G.G. Le Sénégal. Paris, 1935.
Afr 1570.33   Besnard, R. L'oeuvre française au Maroc. Paris, 1914.
Afr 5385.13   Besolow, T.E. From the darkness of Africa to light of America. Boston, 1891.
Afr 8028.6   Besselaar, G. Zuid-Afrika in de letterkunde. Amsterdam, 1914.
Afr 8687.132   Besselaar, Gerrit. Sestig jaar belewenis van dietse kultuur. Pretoria, 1941.
Afr 2749.65   Besson, Ferny. Sahara, terre de vérité . Paris, 1965.
Afr 5760.10   Besson, L. Voyage au pays des Tanala indépendants. n.p., n.d.
Afr 5426.100.70   Bessuges, Jacques. Lambaréné à l'ombre de Schweitzer. Limoges, 1968.
Afr 710.63   The best of both worlds? A challenge on development policies in Africa. (Hunter, Guy.) London, 1967.
Afr 555.39.10   Bestier, G.G. L'apôtre du Congo, Monseigneur Augouard. Paris, 1926.
Afr 7185.3   Ein Besuch in San Salvador. (Bastian, A.) Bremen, 1859.
Afr 628.259   Betancourt, J.R. El Negro. La Habana, 1959.
Afr 1550.8   Betegon, T. La conferencia de Algeciras. Madrid, 1906.
Afr 2209.12.7   Betham-Edwards, M. In French-Africa. Scenes and memories. London, 1912.
Afr 8658.87.15   Bethell, Alfred J. Notes on South African hunting and notes on a ride to the Victoria Falls of the Zambesi. York, 1887.
Afr 1584.7F   Bethmann, H. Denkschrift über deutsche bergwerksinteressen in Marokko. Berlin, 1910.
Afr 8175.19   De betrekkingen tusschen Nederland en Zuid-Africa sedert de verovering van de Kaapkolonie door de Engelschen. (Mansvelt, Nicolas.) Utrecht, 1902.
Afr 630.69.10   Bettany, George Thomas. The dark peoples of the land of sunshine. Miami, Fla., 1966.
Afr 500.84   Betts, Raymond F. The scramble of Africa, causes and dimensions of empire. Boston, 1966.
Afr 659.65   Between Niger and Nile. (Toynbee, Arnold Joseph.) London, 1965.
Afr 6455.85   Between the elephant's eyes. (Scott, R.L.) N.Y., 1954.
Afr 2030.215   Beuchard, Georges. L'équivoque algérienne. Paris, 1959.
Afr 6979.34   Beumhagen, H., O Südwestafrika Einst und Jetzt. Berlin, 1934.
Afr 3978.49.20   Bevan, Samuel. Sand and canvas, a narrative of adventures in Egypt. London, 1849.
Afr 7549.50.5   Bevel, M.L. Le dictionnaire colonial (Encyclopédie). Bruxelles, 1950-51. 2v.
Afr 8825.4   Beverley, R.M. The wrongs of the Caffre nation. London, 1837.
Afr 2875.10   Bevione, G. Come siamo andati a Tripoli. Torino, 1912.
Afr 6640.3   Bevölkerung und Aufenthaltsrecht in den Department schutzgebieten Afrikas. (Luecke, J.H.) Hamburg, 1913.
Afr 6640.4   Bevölkerung und Aufenthaltsrecht in den Department schutzgebieten Afrikas. Inaug. Diss. (Luecke, J.H.) Hamburg, 1913.
Afr Doc 4307.360.5F   Bevolkingsensus, 6 september 1960. (South Africa. Bureau of Statistics.) Pretoria, 1963. 8v.
Afr 500.16   Beyens, N.E.L. La question africaine. Bruxelles, 1918.
Afr 8110.18   Beyers, C. Die kaapse patriotte, 1779-1791. Kaapstad, 1929.
Afr 8110.18.2   Beyers, C. Die Kaapse patriotte gedurende die laaste kwart van die agtiende eeu en die voortlewing van hui denkbeelde. 2. uitg. Pretoria, 1967.
Afr 5748.95.20   Beylie, Leon De. Itineraire de Majunga à Tananarive. Paris, 1895.
Afr 6390.86   Beyond the Cape of Hope. (Browne, Robert.) London, 1965.
Afr 8830.10   Beyond the city lights. (Green, L.G.) Cape Town, 1957.
Afr 6463.5   Beyond the Kikuyu curtain. (Blakeslee, H.) Chicago, 1956.
Afr 6540.21   Beyond the mountains of the moon. (Winter, Edward.) London, 1959.
Afr 6275.114   Beyond the Niger. (Leith Ross, Sylvia.) London, 1951.
Afr 9689.40   Beyond the smoke that thunders. (Cullen, Lucy P.) N.Y., 1940.
Afr 4559.25   Beyond the utmost purple rim. (Powell, E.A.) N.Y., 1925.
Afr 2030.468.10   Beyssade, Pierre. La guerre d'Algérie, 1954-1962. Paris, 1968.
Afr 4285.6   Beziehungen Athiopiens zur griechisch-römischen Welt. (Hable-Selassie, Sergew.) Bonn, 1964.
Afr 7812.257   Bezy, Fernand. Problèmes structurels de l'économie congolaise. Louvain, 1957.
Afr 8825.35   Bhaca society. (Hammond-Tooke, W.D.) Cape Town, 1962.
Afr 44622.89.124A   Bhalo, Ahmad Nassir Bin Juma. Poems from Kenya. Madison, 1966.
Afr 12922.7.110   Bhely-Quenum, Olympe. Le chant du lac. Paris, 1965.
Afr 12922.7.100   Bhely-Quenum, Olympe. Un piège sans fin. Paris, 1960.
Afr 6291.25   Pamphlet vol. Biafa. Miscellaneous pamphlets. 5 pam.

Afr 6291.40   Biafra, an II. (Debré, François.) Paris, 1968.
Afr 6291.62   Biafra; Britain's shame. (Waugh, Auberon.) London, 1969.
Afr 6200.2.10   Biafra; le journal des damnés. Paris. 1,1968+
Afr 6214.38   Biafra, naissance d'une nation? (Renard, Alain.) Paris, 1968.
Afr 6291.60   Biafra; selected speeches and random thoughts of C.O. Ojukwu. 1st ed. (Ojukwu, Chukwuemeka Odumeywu.) N.Y., 1969.
Afr 6291.30A   Biafra journal. (Mok, Michael.) N.Y., 1969.
Afr 6200.2.5   Biafra newsletter. Enugu. 2,1968+
Afr 4558.80.25   Bianchi, G. In Abissinia. Milano, 1896.
Afr 1957.27   Bianchi, Thomas. Relation de l'arrivée dans la rade d'Alger du vaisseau. Paris, 1830.
Afr 5765.6   Bianquis, J. L'oeuvre des missions protestantes à Madagascar. Paris, 1907.
Afr 545.54   Bibical revelation and African beliefs. London, 1969.
Afr 8145.46   The biblical concept of Messianism and Messianism in Southern Africa. (Martin, Marie L.) Morija, 1964.
Afr 6753.5   Bibliografi over Tanzania. København, 1967.
Afr 28.85   Bibliografia afro-asiatica. (Rio de Janeiro. Biblioteca Nacionale) Rio de Janeiro, 1962.
Afr 28.30   Bibliografia colonial. (Fontan Lobé, Juan de.) Madrid, 1946.
Afr 1026.5.15   Bibliografia della Libia. (Ceccherini, Ugo.) Roma, 1915.
Afr 1026.5   Bibliografia della Libia. (Minutilli, F.) Torino, 1903.
Afr 3669.5   Bibliografia di studi africani. (Santandrea, S.) Verona, 1948.
Afr 4226.1   Bibliografia etiopica. (Fumagalli, G.) Milan, 1893.
Afr 4226.1.10   Bibliografia etiopica. v.1-2. (Zanutto, Silvio.) Roma, 1929. 2v.
Afr 1750.25   Bibliografia geografica de Marruecos español y zona internacional de Tanger. (Mensua Fernandez, Salvador.) Aragoza, 1955.
Afr 7203.5   Bibliografia geral de Moçambique. (Costa, Mario A. do.) Lisboa, 1946-
Afr 150.62   Bibliografia Henriquino. (Portugal. Comissão Executiva das Comemorações do V Centenario da Morte do Infante Dom Henrique.) Lisboa, 1960. 2v.
Afr 1326.14   Bibliografia marroque. Tetuan.
Afr 4753.10   Bibliografia somala. (Somaliland, Italian. Camera di commercio, industria ed agricultura.) Mogadiscio, 1958.
Afr 28.103   Bibliograficke prameny the studiv problematiky africkych zemi. (Ustav pro Mezinarodni Politiku a Ekonomii.) Praha, 1965.
Afr 28.92   Bibliografiia Afriki, do revoliutsionnaia i liberatura na russkom Iazyke. (Akaemiia Nauk SSSR. Institut Afriki.) Moscow, 1964.
Afr 6203.10   Bibliographical sources for Nigerian studies. (Dipeolu, J.O.) Evanston, Ill., 1966.
Afr 12002.2   Bibliographie, auteurs africains et malgaches de langue française. (Baratte, Thérèse.) Paris, 1965.
Afr 28.20   Bibliographie africaine de périodiques. (Hache, J.) Bruxelles, 1934.
Afr 5530.6   Bibliographie annuelle de Madagascar. Tananarive. 1,1964+
Afr 7530.4   Bibliographie congolaise 1895-1910. (Simar, T.) Uccle, 1912. 2v.
Afr 3193.5   Bibliographie critique de la Commission des sciences et arts et de l'Institut d'Egypte. Thèse complémentaire. (Guemard, Gabriel.) Le Caire, 1936.
Afr 5003.2   Bibliographie critique de l'Afrique occidentale française. (Tuaillon, J.L.) Paris, 1936.
Afr 5003.2.3   Bibliographie critique de l'Afrique occidentale française. Thèse. (Tuaillon, J.L.) Paris, 1936.
Afr 12002.5   Bibliographie de la littérature nord-africaine d'expression française, 1945-1962. (Memmi, Albert.) Paris, 1965.
Afr 28.4.2   Bibliographie de l'Afrique. (Gay, Jean.) San Remo, 1875.
Afr 28.3   Bibliographie de l'Afrique. (Kayser, A.) Bruxelles, 1887.
Afr 5401.5   Bibliographie de l'Afrique équatoriale française. (Bruel, Georges.) Paris, 1914.
Afr 5003.1.5   Bibliographie de l'Afrique occidentale francaise. (Grandidier, G.) Paris, 1937.
Afr 5003.1   Bibliographie de l'Afrique occidentale française. (Joucla, E.) Paris, 1912.
Afr 7103.5   Bibliographie de l'Angola. (Borchardt, P.) Bruxelles, n.d.
Afr 5530.2   Bibliographie de Madagascar. (Grandidier, G.) Paris, 1905. 4v.
Afr 1826.6   Bibliographie des ouvrages imprimes à Alger. (Fiori, H.) Alger, 1938.
Afr 5203.3   Bibliographie des ouvrages relatifs à la Sénégambie. (Clozel, M.) Paris, 1891.
Afr 5051.30   Bibliographie des ouvrages relatifs à la Sénégambie et au Soudan occidental. (Clozel, M.F.J.) Paris, 1891.
Afr 28.4.5   Bibliographie des ouvrages relatifs à l'Afrique et à l'Arabie. (Gay, Jean.) Amsterdam, 1961.
Afr 550.8.5   Bibliographie du Cardinal Lavigerie. (Tournier, M.J.) Paris, 1913.
Afr 7530.3   Bibliographie du Congo 1880-1895. (Wauters, A.J.) Bruxelles, 1895.
Afr 7850.2   Bibliographie du Katanga. (Walraet, Marcel.) Bruxelles, 1895.
Afr 7530.5   Bibliographie du Katanga. Fasc.1. (Walraet, Marcel.) Bruxelles, 1956.
Afr 3026.10   Bibliographie économique. (Maunier, René.) Le Caire, 1918.
Afr 28.102   Bibliographie éthnographique de l'AfriqueSud-Saharienne. Tervuren. 1960+ 7v.
Afr 2230.41   Bibliographie ethnologique de la Grande Kabylie. (Lacoste, Camille.) Paris, 1962.
Afr 3026.15   Bibliographie géographique de l'Egypte. (Larin, Henri.) Cairo, 1928-29.
Afr 1326.12   Bibliographie marocaine, 1923-33. (Cenival, Pierre de.) Paris, 1937.
Afr 1326.16   Bibliographie nationale marocaine. Rabat. 1,1962+
Afr 5303.4   Bibliographie sur la Guinee. (Organization for Economic Cooperation and Development. Development Center.) Paris, 1965.
Afr 28.25   A bibliography for the study of African history in the 19th and 20th centuries. (Ragatz, L.J.) Washington, 1943.
Afr 28.126   Bibliography of African bibliographies. (Garling, Arthea.) Cambridge, Eng., 1968.
Afr 28.35   A bibliography of African bibliographies. (Robinson, A.) Cape Town, 1948.
Afr 28.73   A bibliography of african bibliographies. 3d ed. (South African Public Library, Cape Town.) Cape Town, 1955.

Afr 28.74 — A bibliography of African bibliographies covering territories South of the Sahara. 4th ed. (South African Public Library, Cape Town.) Cape Town, 1961.

Afr 28.37 — Bibliography of African geography, 1940-1964. (Sommer, John W.) Hanover, N.H., 1965

Afr 40.64.5 — A bibliography of African government, 1950-1966. 2d ed. (Alderfer, Harold Freed.) Lincoln University, 1967.

Afr 1826.1 — Bibliography of Algeria and supplement. (Playfair, R.L.) London, 1888.

Afr 8853.2F — Bibliography of Basutoland. (Groen, Julie.) Cape Town, 1946.

Afr 9327.47F — Bibliography of Bechuanaland. (Stevens, Pamela.) Cape Town, 1947.

Afr 550.31 — Bibliography of Christian literature. (Rowling, F.) London, 1923.

Afr 3026.20F — A bibliography of Egypt consisting of work printed before A.D. 1801. (Maple, H.L.) Pieter-Maritzburg, 1952.

Afr 4226.7 — Bibliography of Ethiopia. (Ethiopia. Press and Information Office.) Addis Ababa, 1968.

Afr 6153.15 — Bibliography of Ghana, 1957-60. Kumasi, 1962.

Afr 4700.13.10 — A bibliography of Italian colonisation in Africa...Abyssinia. (Royal Empire Society. London.) London, 1936.

Afr 8657.90.5 — Bibliography of Le Vaillant's "Voyages" and "Oiseaux d'Afrique." (Johannesburg. Public Library.) Johannesburg, 1962.

Afr 2804.5 — A bibliography of Libya. (Murabet, Mohammed.) Valetta, 1959.

Afr 9753.2 — A bibliography of Malawi. (Syracuse University.) Syracuse, N.Y., 1965.

Afr 8355.42 — A bibliography of material published during the period 1946-56. (Currie, J.C.) Cape Town, 1957.

Afr 5813.10 — Bibliography of Mauritius. (Mauritius. Archives Department.) Port Louis, 1956.

Afr 1326.1 — Bibliography of Morocco. (Playfair, L.) London, 1892.

Afr 8028.156 — A bibliography of native law in South Africa, 1941-1961. (Kuper, B.) Johannesburg, 1962.

Afr 10002.1 — A bibliography of Neo-African literature from Africa, America and the Carribean. (Jahn, Janheinz.) London, 1965.

Afr 9165.71 — Bibliography of Pretoria. (Cross, K.G.) Pretoria, 1948.

Afr 20002.5 — A bibliography of Scriptures in African languages. (Coldham, Geraldine Elizabeth.) London, 1966. 2v.

Afr 11005.6 — A bibliography of South African English novels, 1930-1960. (Astrinsky, Aviva.) Cape Town, 1965.

Afr 11005.5F — A bibliography of South African novels in English. (Snyman, J.P.L.) Potchefstroom, 1951.

Afr 3673.5 — A bibliography of the Anglo-Egyptian Sudan, from the earliest times to 1937. (Hill, R.L.) London, 1939.

Afr 2804.1 — Bibliography of the Barbary states. Pt.1. Tripoli and the Cyrenaica. (Playfair, R.L.) London, 1889.

Afr 9538.5 — A bibliography of the Federation of the Rhodesias and Nyasaland. (Cox, D.L.) Cape Town, 1949.

Afr 6153.5 — A bibliography of the Gold Coast. (Cardinall, A.W.) Accra, 1931.

Afr 8685.20 — A bibliography of the Indian question in South Africa. (Morris, G.R.) Cape Town, 1946.

Afr 11249.86.800 — A bibliography of the poetical works of Guy Butler, Anthony Delius and Roy MacNab. (Muller, G.) Johannesburg, 1962. 2

Afr 6903.10 — A bibliography of the states of South-west Africa. (Loening, L.S.E.) Rondebosch, 1951.

Afr 3669.6 — A bibliography of the Sudan, 1938-1958. (Nasri, Abdel R.) London, 1962.

Afr 11572.50.5 — Bibliography of the works of Sarah Gertrude Millin. (Whyte, Moray.) Cape Town, 1952.

Afr 2426.5 — A bibliography of Tunisia...to 1888. (Ashbee, H.S.) London, 1889.

Afr 6153.20F — Bibliography of works in Ghana languages. (Ghana. Bureau of Ghana Languages.) Accra, 1967.

Afr 626.212 — A bibliography on African regionalism. (Martin, Jane.) Boston, 1969.

Afr 6303.7 — A bibliography on anthropology and sociology in Tanzania and East Africa. (Kuria, Lucas.) Syracuse, 1966.

Afr 6478.3 — A bibliography on anthropology and sociology in Uganda. (Syracuse. University.) Syracuse, 1965.

Afr 9327.66F — A bibliography on Bechuanaland. (Mohome, Paulus.) Syracuse, 1966.

Afr 6277.126 — A bibliography on development planning in Nigeria, 1955-1968. (Akinyotu, Adetunji.) Ibadan, 1968.

Afr 6403.5 — A bibliography on Kenya. (Webster, John B.) Syracuse, 1967.

Afr 6478.2 — A bibliography on politics and government in Uganda. (Kuria, Lucas.) Syracuse, 1965.

Afr 8028.2 — Bibliography related to South Africa. (Suhnnke Hollnay, H.C.) Cape Town, 1898.

Afr 28.87 — Bibliography series. Acquisitions lists. (Padmore Research Library on African Affairs, Accra.) Accra. 1-11,1962-1965//?

Afr 28.86 — Bibliography series. Special subject bibliography. (Padmore Research Library on African Affairs, Accra.) Accra. 2-5,1963-1965//?

Afr 500.3 — Biblioteca di studi coloniale. Firenze. 1,1936+ 11v.

Afr 28.71F — Bibliotek. Periodica i Nordiska Afrikainstitutets. (Nordiska Afrikainstitutet, Upsala.) Uppsala, 1966.

Afr 3026.3 — Bibliotheca Agyptiaca. (Jolowicz, Hermann.) Leipzig, 1858.

Afr 3026.4 — Bibliotheca Agyptiaca. Supplement I. (Jolowicz, Hermann.) Leipzig, 1861.

Afr 1002.5 — Bibliothèque des questions nord-africaines. Paris. 1,1937+ 2v.

Afr 5530.5 — Bibliotheque Nationale, Paris. Periodiques malgaches. Paris, 1964.

Afr 1609.29.5 — Bickerstaffe, Lovelyn Elaine. Things seen in Morocco. N.Y., 1929.

Afr 555.27 — Bickersteth, E. Memoirs of S. Wilhelm, a native of West Africa. New Haven, 1819.

Afr 109.44 — Bidou, Henry. L'Afrique. Paris, 1944.
Afr 4618.5 — Bieber, Friedrich J. Kaffa. Münster, 1920-23. 2v.
Afr 5635.7 — Bienaime. L'expedition de Madagascar de 1895. n.p., n.d. 4 pam.

Afr 6760.22A — Bienen, Henry. Tanzania; party transformation. Princeton, 1967.

Afr Doc 3105.5 — Biennial report. (Zanzibar. District Administration.) Zanzibar. 1,1961+

Afr 9599.24 — Big game and Pygmies. (Christy, C.) London, 1924.
Afr 609.37.5 — Big game hunting and adventure, 1897-1936. (Daly, Marcus.) London, 1937.

Afr 609.30.15 — Big game hunting in Central Africa. (Buckley, W.) London, 1930.

Afr 6390.16 — The big game of Africa. (Tjader, Richard.) N.Y, 1910.
Afr 609.32 — Big game shooting in Africa. (Maydon, H.C.) London, 1932.
Afr 9389.58 — The big thirst. (Kantor, Cyril.) London, 1958.
Afr 9149.61.10 — Bigalke, Rudolph. Let's visit the Kruger park. Johannesburg, 1961.

Afr 8658.97.7 — Bigelow, P. White man's Africa. N.Y., 1898.
Afr 8658.97.10 — Bigelow, P. White man's Africa. N.Y., 1900.
Afr 8278.99.19 — Bigger, E.B. The Boer war, its causes. Toronto, 1899.
Afr 3979.48 — Bigland, E. Journey to Egypt. London, 1948.
Afr 9700.40 — Bigland, Eileen. The lake of the royal crocodiles. London, 1939.

Afr 630.40 — Bigland, Eileen. Pattern in black and white. London, 1939.

Afr 2880.15 — Bignami, Paolo. Tra i colonizzatori in Tripolitania. Bologna, 1931.

Afr 555.9.1 — Bihe and Garenaganze, or, Four years' further work and travel in Central Africa. (Arnot, Frederick Stanley.) London, 1893.

Afr 3979.50 — Bilainkin, G. Cairo to Riyadh diary. London, 1950.
Afr 2224.865 — Bilan de l'Algérie à la fin de l'an 1864 ou de la crise financiére commerciale et agricole. (Leblanc de Prebois, F.) Alger, 1865.

Afr 5183.964.5 — Bilan d'execution materielle et financière des investissements publics au 31 dec. 1963. (Senegal. Ministère du Développement, et du Plan et l'Économie Génerale.) Dakar, 1964.

Afr Doc 709.5 — Bilancio di previsione per l'esercizio finanziario. (Somalia.) Mogadiscio. 1962+

Afr 5540.12 — Bilbao, Rene. Le droit malgache de la nationalité. Paris, 1965.

Afr 6878.91 — Bilder aus Ostafrika. (Coelln, Daniel.) Berlin, 1891.
Afr 3978.67 — Billard, F.L. Les moeurs et le gouvernemnt de l'egypte. Milan, 1867.

Afr 6738.50 — Billard, Pierre. Le Cameroun fédéral. Lyon, 1968. 2v.
Afr 5842.9 — Billiard, A. Voyage aux colonies orientales. Paris, 1822.
Afr 1830.20.51 — Billiard, Louis. Les ports et la navigation de l'Agérie. Paris, 1930.

Afr 555.77 — Billy, E. de. En Côte d'Ivoire, mission protestante d'A.O.F. Paris, 1931.

Afr 7575.6 — Bilsen, Antoine. L'indépandance du Congo. Tournai, 1962.
Afr 7575.5A — Bilsen, Antoine. Vers l'indépendance du Congo et du Ruanda-Urundi. Kraainem, 1958.

Afr 6205.5 — Pamphlet vol. Binder's title. Nigeria. 4 pam.
Afr 4070.9 — The binding of the Nile and the new Soudan. (Peel, Sidney.) London, 1904.

Afr 6275.9 — Bindloss, H. In the Niger country. Edinburgh, 1898.
Afr 5056.165 — Binet, Jacques. Afrique en question, de la tribu à la nation. Tours, 1965.

Afr 6739.256 — Binet, Jacques. Budgets familiaux des planteurs de Cacao au Cameroun. Paris, 1956.

Afr 6176.37 — Bing, Geoffrey. Reap the whirlwind: an account of Kwame Nkrumah's Ghana farm 1950 to 1966. London, 1968.

Afr 5340.10 — Binger, G. Une vie d'explorateur. Paris, 1938.
Afr 5235.189.5 — Binger, Gustave. Du Niger au golfe de Guinée par le pays de Konge le Mossi. Paris, 1892. 2v.

VAfr 7580.36 — Bin'kowski, Andrzej. Drugi cień mojzesza Czombe. Wyd.1. Warszawa, 1967.

Afr 6470.135 — Binks, H.K. African rainbow. London, 1959.
Afr 8985.6 — Binns, C.T. Dinuzuln: the death of the House of Shaka. London, 1968.

Afr 8252.155 — Binns, C.T. The last Zulu king. London, 1963.
Afr 5243.174.10 — Le Binou Yébéné. (Ganay, Solange de.) Paris, 1942.
Afr 6280.45 — Biobaku, S.O. The Egba and their neighbors. Oxford, 1957.
Afr 1432.10 — Biografia y retratos de los generales jefes de los cuerpos. (Alvarez, J.A. de.) Barcelona, 1860.

Afr 8289.01.14 — The biograph in battle. (Dickson, W.K.L.) London, 1901.
Afr 4198.5 — A biographical dictionary of the Anglo-Egyptian Sudan. (Hill, Richard Leslie.) Oxford, 1951.

Afr 4198.5.2 — A biographical dictionary of the Anglo-Egyptian Sudan. 2nd ed. (Hill, Richard Leslie.) London, 1967.

Afr 8055.40F — Biographical index to men of the times. (Cape Town. University. Library.) Cape Town, 1960.

Afr 8735.3 — Biographical memoir of John Montagu. (Newman, W.A.) London, 1855.

Afr 8252.251.5 — Biographical memoirs and reminiscences. v.1. (Kotze, J.G.) Cape Town, 193-

Afr 7900.5 — Biographie coloniale belgc. (Brussels. Institut Royal Colonial Belge.) 1,1948+ 5v.

Afr 4199.20 — Les biographies du Manhal Safi. (Ibn Tagribandi.) Le Caire, 1932.

Afr 7375.8 — Biography of Elder Lott Cary. (Taylor, J.B.) Baltimore, 1852.

Afr 590.18 — Biography of Mahommah G. Baquaqua. (Moore, S.) Detroit, 1854.

Afr 7489.88.5 — A biography of President William V.S. Tubman. (Henries, A. Doris Banks.) London, 1967[1968].

Afr 3248.6 — Bioves, Achille. Français et Anglais en Egypte, 1881-1882. Paris, 1910.

Afr 1084.1 — Birago, G.B. Historia africana della divisione dell'imperi degli Arabi. Venetia, 1650.

NEDL Afr 8288.99.23 — Birch, J.H. History of the war in South Africa. London, Ont., 1899.

Afr 609.36 — Birch-Reynardson, H. High street, Africa. Edinburgh, 1936.

Afr 8190.5.2 — Bird, John. The annals of Natal, 1495 to 1845. Capetown, 1965. 2v.

Afr 8190.5 — Bird, John. Annals of Natal 1495-1845. v.1 and index. Pietermaritzburg, 1888. 2v.

Afr 4199.90A — Bird, Michael. Samuel Shepheard of Cairo. London, 1957.
Afr 8808.23.5 — Bird, William Wilberforce. State of the Cape of Good Hope in 1822. Cape Town, 1966.

Afr 11807.24.100 — The bird flies blind. (Stern, Rhona.) London, 1965.
Afr 8063.10 — Birkby, C. The saga of the Transval Scottish Regiment. Cape Town, 1950.

Afr 8690.20 — Birkby, Carel. In the sun I'm rich. Cape Town, 1953.
Afr 8659.36.3 — Birkby, Carel. Thirstland treks. London, 1936.
Afr 9149.39 — Birkley, C. Limpopo journey. London, 1939.
Afr 7119.65 — Birmingham, D. The Portuguese conquest of Angola. London, 1965.

Afr 590.73 — Birmingham, David. Trade and conflict in Angola, the Mbundu and their neighbours under the influence of the Portuguese, 1483-1790. Oxford, 1966.

Afr 6193.17 — Birmingham, Walter Barr. A study of contemporary Ghana. London, 1966.

Afr 9645.10 — The birth of a dilemma. (Mason, Philip.) London, 1958.

	Afr 9645.5	The birth of a plural society. (Gann, L.H.) Manchester, 1958.
	Afr 6198.405	Birtwhistle, Allen. Thomas Birch Freeman. London, 1950.
	Afr 6720.25.5	Bischof Heinrich Vieter. (Sholaster, H.) Limburg, 1925.
	Afr 6984.10	Bishop for the Hottentots. (Simon, J.M.) N.Y., 1959.
	Afr 6298.785	Bishop Shanahan of Southern Nigeria. (Jordan, John P.) Dublin, 1949.
	Afr 5269.24	Bishops in the Niger Delta. (Epelle, Emanuel Tobiah.) Aba, Nigeria, 1964.
	Afr 2209.10	Biskra, Sidi-Okba and the desert. 1st ed. (Hyam, Joseph C.) Algiers, 1910.
	Afr 6925.5A	Bismarck and British colonial policy, the problem of South West Africa, 1883-1885. (Aydelotte, W.O.) Philadelphia, 1937.
	Afr 2438.12	Bismut, Victor. Essai sur la dualité législative et judiciaire en Tunisie. Dijon, 1922.
	Afr 6174.9	Biss, Harold C. The relief of Kumasi. London, 1901.
	Afr 8658.75	Bisset, John J. Sport and war...1834-1867. London, 1875.
	Afr 5842.26	Bissoondoyal, Basdeo. The truth about Mauritius. 1. ed. Bombay, 1968.
	Afr 2710.4	Bissuel, H. Le Sahara français. Alger, 1891.
	Afr 2762.2	Bissuel, H. Les Touareg de l'ouest. Algiers, 1888.
	Afr 2397.6	Bittari, Zoubeida. O mes soeurs musulmanes, pleurez Paris, 1964.
	Afr 7803.45	Bittremieux, Leo. La société secrète des Bakhimba au Mayombe. Bruxelles, 1936.
	Afr 6295.5F	The Biu book, a collection and reference book on Biu division (Northern Nigeria). (Davies, J.G.) Norla, 1954-56.
	Afr 8235.16	Bixler, R.W. Anglo-German imperialism in South Africa, 1880-1900. Baltimore, 1932.
	Afr 8235.15	Bixler, R.W. Anglo-German imperialism in South Africa 1880-1900. Diss. Columbus, Ohio, 1932.
	Afr 7369.57	Bixler, R.W. The foreign policy of the United States in Liberia. 1st ed. N.Y., 1957.
	Afr 12972.41.110	Biyidi, Alexandre. King Lazarus. London, 1960.
	Afr 12972.41.700	Biyidi, Alexandre. Mission accomplished. N.Y., 1958.
	Afr 12972.41.705	Biyidi, Alexandre. Mission to Kala. London, 1964.
	Afr 12972.41.120	Biyidi, Alexandre. Le pauvre Christ de Bomba. Paris, 1956.
	Afr 12972.41.130	Biyidi, Alexandre. Le roi miraculé. Paris, 1958.
	Afr 12972.41.100	Biyidi, Alexandre. Ville cruelle. Paris, 195-.
	Afr 2662.1	Bizerta und seine Zukunft. (Ludwig Salvator.) Prag, 1881.
	Afr 2662.5	Bizerte. (Lepotier, Adolphe Auguste Marie.) Paris, 1965.
	Afr 4718.97.5F	Bizzoni, A. L'Eritrea nel passato e nel presente. Milano, 1897.
	Afr 9389.60	Bjerre, Jens. Kalahari. London, 1960.
	Afr 9439.61	Black, Colin. The lands and peoples of Rhodesia and Nyasaland. London, 1961.
	Afr 626.95	Black, Eugene Robert. Tales of two continents. Athens, Ga., 1961.
	Afr 8678.334	Black, Margaret. No room for tourists. London, 1965.
	Afr 109.66.15	Black Africa, Africa south of the Sahara from pre-history to independence. (Howe, Russell Warren.) N.Y., 1966. 2v.
	Afr 109.66.5	Black Africa, Africa south of the Sahara from prehistory to independence. (Howe, Russell Warren.) London, 1966. 2v.
	Afr 212.22	Black Africa. (Merwe, H.J.J.) Johannesburg, 1963.
	Afr 10100.5	Black African literature in English since 1952; works and criticism. (Abrash, Barbara.) N.Y., 1967.
	Afr 8659.50	Black and white. 1st ed. (Flavin, Martin.) N.Y., 1950.
	Afr 8678.383	Black and white Africans. 1st ed. (Strydom, Christiaan Johannes Scheepers.) Cape Town, 1967.
	Afr 6310.35	Black and white in East Africa. (Thurnwald, R.) London, 1935.
	Afr 8678.434	Black and white in South East Africa. (Evans, Maurice Smethurst.) N.Y., 1969.
	Afr 8849.3	Black anger. (Sachs, W.) Boston, 1947.
	Afr 8678.315	Black background. (Magidi, D.T.) N.Y., 1964.
	Afr 1609.38.5	Black barbary. (Turnbull, P.) London, 1938.
	Afr 6280.62	A black Byzantium; the Kingdom of Nupe. (Nadel, Siegfried F.) London, 1942.
	Afr 6280.62.3	A black Byzantium; the Kingdom of Nupe. (Nadel, Siegfried F.) London, 1951.
	Afr 590.76	Black cargoes, a history...1518-1865. (Mannix, Daniel.) N.Y., 1962.
	Afr 9689.60	Black elephant hunter. (Duffy, Kevin.) London, 1960.
	Afr 628.269	The Black experience; the Negro in America, Africa, and the world. (Toledo. University. Library.) Toledo, Ohio, 1969.
	Afr 628.239	Black folk, then and now. (Dubois, W.E.B.) N.Y., 1939.
	Afr 715.15	The black journey across central Africa. (Haardt, G.M.) N.Y., 1927.
	Afr 6455.42	Black laughter. (Powys, L.) N.Y., 1924.
	Afr 8659.43.10	The black man's burden. (Marquard, Leopold.) London, 1943.
	Afr 500.19.5	The black man's burden. (Morel, Edmund D.) N.Y., 1920.
	Afr 500.19.10	The black man's burden. (Morel, Edmund D.) N.Y., 1969.
	Afr 6192.65	Black man's country. (Eskelund, Karl.) London, 1958.
	Afr 6275.46	Black man's palaver. (Ryan, Isobel.) London, 1958.
	Afr 8678.25	The black man's place in South Africa. (Nielsen, P.) Cape Town, 1922.
	Afr 6192.60	Black man's town. (Ryan, Isobel.) London, 1953.
	Afr 555.30.10	Black martyrs. (Thoonen, J.P.) N.Y., 1941.
	Afr 609.34.5	Black mist. (Gatti, Attilio.) London, 1934.
	Afr 6160.15	Black mistress. (Bernard, Jane.) London, 1957.
	Afr 590.75	Black mother. (Davidson, B.) Boston, 1961.
	Afr 10018.4	Black Orpheus. Black Orpheus. N.Y., 1965.
	Afr 10018.4	Black Orpheus. (Black Orpheus.) N.Y., 1965.
	Afr 10060.2	Black Orpheus. (Sartre, Jean Paul.) Paris, 1963.
	Afr 11008.10	Black Orpheus. Ibadan. 5v.
	Afr 6192.30	Black power. 1st ed. (Wright, R.) N.Y., 1954.
	Afr 8678.24.7	The black problem. (Jabavu, Davidson Don Tengo.) N.Y., 1969.
	Afr 8678.24.2	The black problem. 2d ed. (Jabavu, D.D.T.) Lovedale, 1921.
	Afr 3817.12	The black record, Nasser's persecution. (American Jewish Congress. Committee on International Affairs and on Israel.) N.Y., 1957.
	Afr 7459.23	The Black Republic, Liberia. (Reeve, H.F.) London, 1923.
	Afr 6198.670	Black revolutionary; George Padmore. (Hooker, James R.) London, 1967.
	Afr 8045.36	The black sash. (Rogers, Mirabel.) Johannesburg, 1956.
	Afr 628.9	The black scholar. San Francisco. 1,1969+
	Afr 6738.42	Black sheep. New ed. (Mackenzie, Jean Kenyon.) Boston, 1925.
	Afr 4513.35.30	Black shirt, black skin. (Carter, Boak.) Harrisburg, 1935.
	Afr 4513.35.33	Black shirt, black skin. (Carter, Boak.) London, 1935.
	Afr 628.252.5	Black skin, white masks. (Fannon, F.) N.Y., 1967.
	Afr 6780.32	The black slaves of Prussia. (Weston, F.) Boston, 1918.
	Afr 679.58.5	Black star rising. (Howe, R.W.) London, 1958.
	Afr 1408.7	Black sunrise. (Blunt, Wilfrid.) London, 1951.
	Afr 8668.10	Black woman in search of God. (Brandel-Syrier, Mia.) London, 1962.
	Afr 8659.11.3	Blackburn, D. Secret service in South Africa. London, 1911.
	Afr 11216.10	Blackburn, Douglas. Prinsloo of Prinsloosdorp. London, 1899.
	Afr 2208.74	Blackburn, H. Artists and Arabs. Boston, 1874.
Htn	Afr 3979.13*	Blackburne, D. Journals of my African travels. Maidstone, 1913.
	Afr 47619.5	Blacking, John. Venda children's songs. Johannesburg, 1967.
	Afr 635.89	Blackism. (Fani-Kazode, Remi.) Lagos, 1965.
	Afr 3988.5A	Blackman, Winifred Susan. The fellahin of Upper Egypt. London, 1927.
	Afr 3988.5.5	Blackman, Winifred Susan. Les fellahs de la Haute-Egypte. Paris, 1948.
	Afr 8235.8.5	Blacks, Boers, and British. (Statham, F.R.) N.Y., 1969.
	Afr 8235.8	Blacks, Boers and British. (Statham, F.R.) London, 1881.
	Afr 8140.29	Blackwell, L. African occasions, reminiscences of thirty years of bar, bench and politics in South Africa. London, 1938.
	Afr 8140.29.5	Blackwell, L. Farewell to parliament. Pietermaritzburg, 1946.
	Afr 8659.47	Blackwell, L. This is South Africa. Pietermaritzburg, 1947.
	Afr 10684.99.110	Blade among the boys. (Nzekwu, Onuora.) London, 1962.
	Afr 11626.23.110	Blade among the boys. (Nzekwu, Onuora.) London, 1962.
	Afr 9558.30	Blaikie, W.G. Personal life of David Livingstone. London, 1880.
	Afr 9558.30.2A	Blaikie, W.G. Personal life of David Livingstone. N.Y., 1881.
	Afr 9558.30.15	Blaikie, W.G. Personal life of David Livingstone. N.Y., 1895.
	Afr 9558.30.20	Blaikie, W.G. The personal life of David Livingstone. N.Y., 1969.
	Afr 626.142	Blair, Thomas Lucien Vincent. Africa, a market profile. N.Y., 1965.
	Afr 7020.20	Blake, J.W. European beginnings in West Africa, 1454-1578. London, 1937.
	Afr 8289.03.20	Blake, J.Y.D. A West Pointer with the Boers. Boston, 1903.
	Afr 9448.55	Blake, W.T. Central African survey. London, 1961.
	Afr 9489.60	Blake, W.T. Rhodesia and Nyasaland journey. London, 1960.
	Afr 6463.5	Blakeslee, H. Beyond the Kikuyu curtain. Chicago, 1956.
	Afr 2208.59.5	Blakesley, J.W. Four months in Algeria. Cambridge, 1859.
	Afr 855.18	Blakeston, O. Isle of St. Helena. London, 1957.
	Afr 8095.60	Blame it on Van Riebeeck. (Marguard, Leopold.) Cape Town, 1952.
	Afr 8687.274	Blame me on history. (Modisane, B.) London, 1963.
	Afr 4375.4	Blanc, H. Ma captivité en Abyssinie. Paris, 1870.
	Afr 4375.4.5	Blanc, H. A narrative of captivity in Abyssinia. London, 1868.
	Afr 7567.8	Blanc, J. Le droit de préférence de la France sur le Congo belge (1884-1911). Thèse. Paris, 1921.
	Afr 5748.72	Blanchard, Emile. L'ile de Madagascar. Paris, 1872.
	Afr 5019.58.10	Blanchet, Andre. L'itinéraire des partis africains depuis Bamoko. Paris, 1958.
	Afr 679.46	Blanchod, F.G. La randonnée africaine. Lausanne, 1946.
	Afr 1280.3	Les blancs d'Afrique. (Weisgerber, H.) Paris, 1910.
	Afr 7809.42.5	Blancs et noirs. (Comeliau, Marie.) Paris, 1942.
	Afr 4199.15	Bland, J. Prince Ahmad of Egypt. London, 1939.
	Afr 6535.17	Bland-Sutton, J. Men and creatures in Uganda. London, 1933.
	Afr 11510.60.100	Blanket boy's moon. (Lanham, Peter.) London, 1953.
	Afr 2704.5	Blaudin de The, Bernard M.S. Essai de bibliographie du Sahara. Paris, 1960- 2v.
	Afr 5748.96.10	Blavet, Emile. Au pays Malgache. Paris, 1897.
	Afr 5748.96.9	Blavet, Emile. Au pays Malgache de Paris à Tananarive et retour. 2e ed. Paris, 1897.
	Afr 8687.137.5	Blaxall, Arthur. Suspended sentence. London, 1965.
	Afr 8678.363	Blaxall, Arthur William. Wake up South Africa, an essay. Johannesburg, 1963.
	Afr 3204.26	Blayland, Gregory. Objective: Egypt. London, 1966.
	Afr 8678.339	Blazing trails in Bantu land. (Campbell, Dugald.) London, 1933.
	Afr 9400.10.10	Bleek, D.F. The Naron, a bushman tribe of central Kalahari. Cambridge, 1928.
	Afr 8685.5	Bleek, W.H.I. Zulu legends. 1st ed. Pretoria, 1952.
	Afr 8687.137.10	Bleek, Wilhelm Heinrich Immanuel. The Natal diaries of Dr. W.H.I. Bleek, 1855-1856. Cape Town, 1965.
	Afr 8340.7	Bleloch, W. The new South Africa. N.Y., 1901.
	Afr 9488.93.2	Blennerhassett. Adventures in Mashonaland. London, 1893.
	Afr 2010.6	Bletterie, A. Le 9me régiment des mobiles de l'Allier. 1870-71. Lapalisse, 1900.
	Afr 6926.30	Bley, Helmut. Kolonialherrschaft und Sozialstruktur in Deutsch-Südwestafrika, 1894-1914. Hamburg, 1968.
	Afr 11216.5	Bley, J. Benibengor. Thoughts of youth. Aboso, 1961.
	Afr 2313.1	Blida. v.1-2. (Trumelet, C.) Alger, 1887.
	Afr 5748.67.4	Een blik in Madagaskar. (Pollen, F.P.L.) Leyden, 1867.
	Afr 9028.87	Blink, H. Door Natal in het hart van Zuid-Afrika. Amsterdam, 1887.
	Afr 8658.89	Blink, Hendrik. Transvaal en omliggende landen. Amsterdam, 1889.
	Afr 8658.90	Blink, Hendrik. De Zuid-Afrikaansche Republiek en hare bewoners. Amsterdam, 1890.
	Afr 6210.42	Blitz, L. Franklin. The politics and administration of Nigerian government. N.Y., 1965.
	Afr 6455.66	Blixen Finecke, K. Den afrikanske farm. København, 1943.
	Afr 6455.65.5A	Blixen Finecke, K. Out of Africa. N.Y., 1938.
	Afr 210.65.35	Blizej afryki. (Chataslnski, Jozef.) Warszawa, 1965.
	Afr 1955.63	Bloch, P. Algérie, terre des occasions perdues. Paris, 1961.
	Afr 6780.30	Blockade and jungle. (Kock, Nis.) London, 1940.
	Afr 9291.15	Bloemfontein. City Council. The city of Bloemfontein. Cape Town, 1950.
	Afr 9291.15.2	Bloemfontein. City Council. The city of Bloemfontein. Cape Town, 1960.
	Afr 5343.13	Blokhin, Leonid F. Bereg Slonovoi Kosti. Moskva, 1967.
	Afr 1960.1	Blondel, L. Nouvel aperçu sur l'Algérie. Paris, 1838.
	Afr 4513.36.20	Blood and ink. (Chaplin, W.W.) N.Y., 1936.
	Afr 11219.66.110	Bloom, Harry. King Kong. London, 1961.
	Afr 11219.66.100	Bloom, Harry. Transvaal episode. Berlin, 1959.
	Afr 11219.66.120	Bloom, Harry. Whittaker's wife. London, 1964.

Afr 2209.48 Blottière, J.E. L'Algérie. Paris, 1948.
Afr 2209.55 Blottière, J.E. L'Algérie. 2. ed. Paris, 1955.
Afr 3230.26 The Blue and the Gray on the Nile. (Hesseltine, W.B.) Chicago, 1961.
Afr Doc 2403.5F Blue book, 1908-1913. (Nigeria, Northern.) Lagos, 1909.
Afr Doc 1603.5 Blue book. (Gambia.) London. 1904-1914
Afr Doc 1803.5 Blue book. (Gold Coast (Colony).) Accra. 1910-1913 4v.
Afr Doc 3203.3F Blue book. (Kenya.)
Afr Doc 2803.5F Blue book. (Mauritius.) 8v.
Afr Doc 2500.605 Blue book. (Nigeria, Southern.) Calabar. 1905-1913 9v.
Afr Doc 2303.5 Blue book. (Nigeria.) Lagos. 1914-1924
Afr Doc 3603.5F Blue book. (Nyasaland.) 11v.
Afr Doc 2703.5F Blue book. (Seychelles.) 10v.
Afr Doc 1703.5F Blue book. (Sierra Leone.) 7v.
Afr Doc 3303.5F Blue book. (Uganda.) 9v.
Afr Doc 3103.5F Blue book. (Zanzibar.) 4v.
Afr 6208.5F Blue book 1904, 1905. (Lagos.) Lagos, 1905.
Afr 3979.62 The Blue Nile. 1st ed. (Moorehead, Alan.) N.Y., 1962.
Afr 2285.23 Blue veils, red tents. (Gardi, René.) London, 1953.
Afr 1885.3 Blum, N. La croisade de XImenes en Afrique. Oran, 1898.
Afr 8659.62.5 Blumberg, Myrna. White madam. London, 1962.
Afr 6926.18 Blumhagen, H. Entscheidungsjahre in Deutsch-Südwestafrika. Berlin, 1939.
Afr 6420.76 Blundell, M. So rough a wind. London, 1964.
Afr 3275.16 Blunt, W.S. Atrocities of justice under British rule in Egypt. London, 1906.
Afr 3258.8.5 Blunt, W.S. Gordon at Khartoum. London, 1911.
Afr 3258.8.3A Blunt, W.S. Secret history of the English occupation of Egypt. N.Y., 1922.
Afr 1408.7 Blunt, Wilfrid. Black sunrise. London, 1951.
Afr 7368.56 Blyden, E.W. Brief account...retirement of President J.J. Roberts. Liberia, 1856.
Afr 550.3 Blyden, E.W. Christianity, Islam and the Negro race. London, 1887.
Afr 7458.62.5 Blyden, E.W. Liberia's offering. N.Y., 1862.
Afr 7368.65 Blyden, E.W. Our origin, dangers, and duties. N.Y., 1865.
Afr 7489.8 Blyden, Edward Wilmot. Blyden of Liberia. N.Y., 1966.
Afr 7489.8 Blyden of Liberia. (Blyden, Edward Wilmot.) N.Y., 1966.
Afr 8002.2F Blythswood review. Butterworth, South Africa. 3,1926+ 2v.
Afr 1608.95.5 Boada y Romeu, J. Allende el estrecho, viajes por Marruecos (1889-94). Barcelona, 1895.
Afr 2719.64 Boahen, A.A. Britain, the Sahara. Oxford, 1964.
Afr 8809.62 Board, Chr. The border region, natural environment and land use in the eastern Cape. Cape Town, 1962. 2v.
Afr 3978.57 Boat life in Egypt and Nubia. (Prime, W.C.) N.Y., 1857.
Afr 3978.57.2 Boat life in Egypt and Nubia. (Prime, W.C.) N.Y., 1868.
Afr 6192.70 Boateng, E.A. A geography of Ghana. Cambridge, Eng., 1959.
Afr 6192.70.2 Boateng, E.A. A geography of Ghana. 2nd ed. Cambridge, 1966.
Afr 550.20 Boavida, A.J. Missões e missionarios portuguezes...17 de abril 1893. Lisboa, 1893.
Afr 7122.95 Boavida, Américo. Angola; cinco séculos de exploracão portuguesa. Rio de Janeiro, 1967.
Afr 861.25 Boay, D.M. Rock of exile. London, 1957.
Afr 3740.6.25 Bobichon, H. Contribution a l'histoire de la mission Marchand. Paris, 1937.
Afr 4431.25.1 Boca, Angelo del. The Ethiopian War, 1935-1941. Chicago, 1969.
Afr 4431.25 Boca, Angelo del. La guerra d'Abissinia, 1935-1941. Milano, 1965.
Afr 2030.468 Bocca, Geoffrey. The secret army. Englewood Cliffs, 1968.
Afr 679.66.10 Bochen, Albert Adu. Topics inWest African history. London, 1966.
Afr 5318.40 Bochkarev, I.A. Gvineia segodnia. Moscow, 1961.
Afr 2608.85 Boddy, A.A. To Kairwan the Holy. London, 1885.
Afr 8045.18 Bodenstein, H.D.J. Engelse invloeden op het gemeenrecht van Zuid Afrika. Amsterdam, 1912.
Afr 2669.1 Bodereau, P. La Capsa ancienne, la Gafsa moderne. Paris, 1907.
Afr 2819.65 Bodianskii, Vadim. Sovremennaia Liviia. Moskva, 1965.
Afr 2220.2 Bodichon, E. Guide book. London, 1858.
Afr 1258.47 Bodichon. Etudes sur l'Algérie et l'Afrique. Alger, 1847.
Afr 2749.61.5 Bodington, Nicolas. The awakening Sahara. London, 1961.
Afr 2209.27.10 Bodley, R.V.C. Algeria from within. London, 1927.
Afr 2731.15.30 Bodley, R.V.C. The warrior saint. 1st ed. Boston, 1953.
Afr 2749.44 Bodley, R.V.C. Wind in the Sahara. N.Y., 1944.
Afr 2719.68 Bodley, Ronald V.C. The soundless Sahara. London, 1968.
Afr 8687.347 Boeseken, Anna J. Simon van der Stel en sy kinders. Kaapstad, 1964.
Afr 6878.88.10 Boehm, Richard. Von Sansibar zum Tanganjika. Leipzig, 1888.
Afr 609.36.10 Boehmer, H. Mit 14 ps durch Afrika. Wien, 1936.
Afr 6883.20 Boehrenz, Wolfgang. Beiträge zur materiellen Kultur der Nyamwezi. Hamburg, 1940.
Afr 8278.96.3 Boer and Uitlander. (Regan, W.F.) London, 1896.
Afr 8289.02.8 The Boer fight for freedom. (Davitt, Michael.) N.Y., 1902.
Afr 8659.00.11 The Boer in peace and war. (Mann, Arthur M.) London, 1900.
Afr 8279.00.25 Boer politics. (Guyot, Yves.) London, 1900.
Afr 8175.9 The Boer states. (Keane, A.H.) London, 1900.
NEDL Afr 8289.01 Boer version of the Transvaal war. London, 1901.
Afr 8289.69.5 The Boer War; a study in cowardice and courage. (Selby, John Millin.) London, 1969.
Afr 8278.99.19 The Boer war, its causes. (Bigger, E.B.) Toronto, 1899.
Afr 8288.1 Pamphlet vol. The Boer war. 26 pam.
Afr 8288.2 Pamphlet vol. The Boer war. 12 pam.
Afr 8277.4 Pamphlet vol. Boer war. 17 pam.
Afr 8289.58 The Boer war. (Holt, Edgar.) London, 1958.
Afr 8289.69 The Boer War. (Hoyt, Edwin Palmer.) London, 1969.
Afr 8277.2 Pamphlet vol. Boer war. Causes. 5 pam.
Afr 8277.5 Pamphlet vol. Boer war. Causes. 9 pam.
Afr 8277.1 Pamphlet vol. Boer war. Causes. 7 pam.
Afr 8277.6 Pamphlet box. Boer war. Causes.
Afr 8277.3 Pamphlet vol. Boer war. Causes. 60 pam.
Afr 8289.50 Boere op St. Helena. (Graaf, H. de.) Kaapstad, 1950.
Afr 8289.01.35F Die boeren-kampen. (Veber, Jean.) Amsterdam, 1901.
Afr 8089.01.5 De boeren-republieken in Zuid-Afrika, hun ontstaan. (Klok, J.) Utrecht, 1901.
Afr 8278.97 Boers and little Englanders. (Procter, John.) London, 1897.
Afr 8325.18 Boers and the war, from the impartial foreigner's point of view. London, 1902.
Afr 8278.99.23 Boers et Anglais. (Demolins, E.) Paris, 1899.
Afr 9086.17 Boers et Anglais. Autours des mines d'or. (Roels, E.) Paris, 1897.
Afr 8289.00.5 The Boers in war. (Hillegas, H.C.) N.Y., 1900.
Afr 6883.9 Boesch, F. Les Banyamwezi, peuple de l'Afrique orientale. Münster, 1930.
Afr 8110.4 Boeseken, A.J. Nederlandsche commissarissen aan de Kaap, 1657-1700. 's-Gravenhage, 1938.
Afr 8230.35 Boey, Marcel. Paul Kruger. Tielt, 194-.
Afr 8377.8 Bogaerde, Frans van den. Suid-Afrika in die politiek-ekonomiese proses. Pretoria, 1966.
Afr 9525.224 Boggie, Jeannie. A husband and a farm in Rhodesia. Gwelo, S.R., 1959.
Afr 9493.38 Boggie, Jeannie M. Experiences of rHodesia's pioneer women. Bulawayo, 1938.
Afr 9439.40.2 Boggie, Jeannie M. First steps in civilizing Rhodesia. Bulawayo, 1953.
Afr 6280.26.15 Bohaman, Pave. TIV economy. Evanston, 1968.
Afr 109.64.5 Bohannan, P. Africa and Africans. 1st ed. Garden City, 1964.
Afr 109.64.6 Bohannan, P. African outline, a general introduction. Harmondsworth, Middlesex, Eng., 1966.
Afr 6280.26.6 Bohannan, Paul. Justice and judgment among the Tiv. London, 1957.
Afr 626.108 Bohannan, Paul. Markets in Africa. Evanston, Ill., 1962.
Afr 6280.26.5F Bohannan, Paul. Tiv farm and settlement. London, 1954.
Afr 609.41.15 Bohner, Theodor. Africa. Leipzig, 1941.
Afr 5180.16 Boilat, P.D. Esquisses sénégalaises. Paris, 1853.
Afr 7809.04.5 Boillat-Robert, I. Léopold II et le Congo. Neuchâtel, 1904.
Afr 3991.2 Boinet, Bey, A. Dictionnaire géographique de l'Egypte. Le Caire, 1899.
Afr 2527.5 Bois, M. Expédition française en Tunisie (1881-82). Paris, 1886.
Afr 1571.17.95 Boisboissel, Y. de. Dans l'ombre de Lyautey. Paris, 1954.
Afr 6283.3 Boisragon, A. The Benin massacre. London, 1897.
Afr 8279.00.26 Boissevain, Charles. The struggle of the Dutch republics, open letter to an American lady. Amsterdam, 1900.
Afr 5476.5 Boisson, Jacques. L'histoire du Tchad et de Fort Archambault. Besançon, 1966.
Afr 2030.415 Boisson, Jean. Essai sur le probléme algérien. Paris, 1960.
Afr 5640.40 Boiteau, Pierre. Contribution à l'histoire de la nation Malgache. Paris, 1958.
Afr 10005.7 Bol, Victor P. Littérateurs et poètes noirs. Léopoldville, 196-.
Afr 7459.52 Bolahun. (Junge, Werner.) N.Y., 1952.
Afr 7050.15PF Bolamense, orgao de propaganda regional de cultura e de turismo. Bolama.
Afr 8320.6 Boldingh, G. Een hollandsch officier in Zuid-Afrika. Rotterdam, 1903.
Afr 7100.10 Boletim. (Angola. Instituto de Angola.) Luanda. 3,1954 3v.
Afr 7020.35 Boletim. Numero comemorativo da entrega a S. Ex. a Presidente da republica. (Sociedade de Geografia de Lisboa.) Lisboa, 1938.
Afr 7050.5 Boletim cultural da Guiné Portuguesa. Bissau. 3,1948+ 18v.
Afr 7100.12 Boletim informativo. (Angola. Instituto de Angola.) 61,1964+
Afr Doc 9207.20 Boletim mensal. (Mozambique. Direcção Provincial dos Serviços de Estatistica Geral.) 5,1964+ 5v.
Afr Doc 9307.5 Boletim mensal de estatistica. (Angola. Repartição de Estatistica Geral.) Luanda. 22,1966+
Afr Doc 9207.10 Boletim trimestral de estatistica. (Mozambique. Repartição Tecnica de Estatistica.) 16-23,1940-1947
Afr 1325.3F Boletin de la Sociedad Union Hispano-Mauritanica 1894. Granada, 1894. 2v.
Afr 1302.1 Boletin oficial de la zona de influencia española en Marruecos. Madrid. 1913+ 6v.
Afr 1302.1.5 Boletin oficial de la zona de influencia española en Marruecos. Anexo. Madrid. 1,1914+
Afr 3978.69.1 Bolgiani, V.M.V. Im Lande der Pharaonen. Wien, 1869.
Afr 3978.69 Bolgiani, V.M.V. Pharaonernas land. Resebilder fraan egypten. Stockholm, 1869.
Afr 609.48 Bolinder, Gustaf. Nykypaivan Afrikka. Helsinki, 1948.
Afr 9704.10 Bolink, Peter. Towards church union in Zambia. Akademisch Proefschrift. Franeker, 1967.
Afr 7549.39 Bollati, A. Il Congo belga. Milano, 1939.
Afr 4700.36.5 Bollati, A. Enciclopedia dei nostri combattimenti coloniali fino al 2 ottobre 1935. Torino, 1936.
Afr 4770.5 Bollati, Ambiogio. Somalia italiana. Roma, 1938.
Afr 4513.38.30 Bollati, Ambrogio. La campagne italo-etiopica. Roma, 1938.
Afr 1.108 Bollettino. (Associazione degli Africanisti Italiani.) Paria. 1,1968+
Afr Doc 707.15F Bollettino trimestralle di statistica. (Somalia. Ministry of Planning and Coordination. Statistical Department.) Mogadiscio. 1,1966+
Afr 1947.11 Bologna. Arciconfraternità di Santa Maria. Ragguaglio della schiavitù in Algeri di Giuseppe Giovanni Nicola Albertazzi. Bologna, 1772.
Afr 6455.140 Bol'shoe safari. (Shaposhnikova, Vera D.) Moskva, 1966.
Afr 9450.25 Bolze, Louis W. Life with Udi; a cartoon history of independant Rhodesia. v.1-2. Bulawayo, 1966.
Afr 609.42.10 Bonacelli, B. L'Africa nella concezione geografica degli antichi. Verbania, 1942.
Afr 2209.12.3 Bonand, R. de. La France de l'Afrique du nord. Paris, 1912.
Afr 5832.3 Bonaparte, R. Le premier établissement des Neerlandais à Maurice. Paris, 1890.
Afr 3275.27 Bonaparte in Egypt. (Browne, A.) London, 1907.
Afr 4513.35.83 Bonardi, Pierre. Brassard amarante. Paris, 1935.
Afr 5257.15 Bonardi, Pierre. La république du Niger. Paris, 1960.
Afr 8089.56 Bond, J. They were South Africans. Cape Town, 1956.
Afr 7015.40 Bondarevskii, G.L. Portugalskie kolonizatory, vragi narodov Afriki. Moscow, 1962.
Afr 2748.87 Bonelli, D.E. El Sahara. Madrid, 1887.
Afr 1608.82.5 Bonelli, E. El imperio de Marruecos y su constitucion. Madrid, 1882.
Afr 5960.12 Bonelli Rubio, J.M. Notas sobra la geográfica humana. Madrid, 1944-45.
Afr 550.6 Bonet-Maury, G. L'islamisme et le christianisme en Afrique. Paris, 1906.
Afr 3818.12.2 Bonfanti, Adriano. Espulsi dal Sudan. 2. ed. Bologna, 1964.
Afr 6645.5 Bongard, Oscar. Wie wandere ich nach Deutschen Kolonien aus. 3. Aufl. Berlin, 1910.
Afr 5346.15 Bongouanou. (Boutillier, J.L.) Paris, 1960.
Afr 1618.28 Bonjean, François. L'ame marocaine, une à travers les croyances et la politesse. Paris, 1948.
Afr 1738.45 Bonjean, Jacques. Tanger. Paris, 1967.

Afr 1338.15 Bonjean, Jacques. L'unité de l'empire chérifien. Paris, 1955.

Afr 1609.50 Bonn, G. Marokko. 1. Aufl. Stuttgart, 1950.

Afr 609.65.55 Bonn, Gisela. L'Afrique quitte la brousse. Paris, 1966.

Afr 12639.24.810 Bonn, Gisela. Léopold Sédar Senghor. Düsseldorf, 1968.

Afr 530.15 Bonn greift nach Afrika. (Etinger, J.) Berlin, 1961.

Afr 1955.11 Bonnafont, Jean Pierre. Douze ans en Algérie, 1830-1842. Paris, 1880.

Afr 2295.8 Bonnafont, Jean Pierre. Réflexions sur l'Algérie. Paris, 1846.

Afr 2030.462.140 Bonnaud, R. Itinéraire. Paris, 1962.

Afr 5758.2 Bonnavoy De Premoti, F.H. Rapport a l'empereur sur la question malgache. Paris, 1856.

NEDL Afr 200.10 Bonnefon, E.L. L'Afrique politique en 1900. Paris, 1900.

Afr 7332.15 Bonnefont de Varinay, P. de. La compagnie de Mozambique. Lisboa, 1899.

Afr 3480.3 Bonnel de Mezières, A. Rapport sur le Haut Oubangui. Paris, 1901.

Afr 5247.17 Bonnel de Mézières, Albert. Le Major A. Gordon Laing, Tomboucton (1826). Paris, 1912.

Afr 5620.4 Bonnemaison, J. Historique de Madagascar. Tarbes, 1894.

Afr 5235.194 Bonnetain, Raymonde. Une française au Soudan. Paris, 1894.

Afr 6291.34 Bonneville, Floris de. La mort du Biafra. Paris, 1968.

Afr 2609.34.5 Bonniard, F. Le tell septentrional en Tunisie. Thèse. Paris, 1934.

Afr 2609.34 Bonniard, F. La Tunisie du nord. Paris, 1934. 2v.

Afr 5247.25 Bonnier, Gaetan. L'occupation de Tombouctou. Paris, 1926.

Afr 4513.36.83 Bono, E. La preparazione e le primi operazioni. 3a ed. Roma, 1937.

Afr 4513.36.84 Bono, E. de. Anno XIIII, the conquest of an empire. London, 1937.

Afr 4392.25 Bono, Giulio del. Da Assab ad Adua. Roma, 1937.

Afr 1100.6 Bono, Salvatore. I corsari barbareschi. Torino, 1964.

Afr 1608.93 Bonsal, S. Jr. Morocco as it is. London, 1893.

Afr 6168.4 Bonsu Ashanti heroes. (Kyereteire, K.O.) Accra, 1964.

Afr 7535.20 Bontinck, François. Aux origines de l'Etat indépendant du Congo. Louvain, 1966.

Afr 2224.899 Bonzom, Lucien. Du régime fiscal en Algérie. Paris, 1899.

Afr 5426.120 Bonzon, Charles. A Lambaréné. Nancy, 1897.

Afr 10016.10 A book of African verse. (Reed, John.) London, 1965.

Afr 11051.7 A book of South African verse. (Butler, G.) London, 1959.

Afr 608.48 The book of travels in Africa. (Frost, John.) N.Y., 1848.

Afr 6153.10 Books about Ghana. (Johnson, A.F.) Accra, 1961.

Afr 6203.4.5 Books about Nigeria. (Harris, John.) Nigeria, 1962.

Afr 6203.4 Books about Nigeria. 2. ed. (Harris, John.) Nigeria, 1960.

Afr 6203.4.4 Books about Nigeria. 4th ed. (Harris, John.) Ibadan, 1963.

Afr 8659.64 Boom, M.J. Reis door Zuid-Afrika. Meppel, 1964.

Afr 2260.12 Booms, P.G. Studien over Algerie. 's-Gravenhage, 1878.

Afr 1975.4 Booms, P.G. Veldtogt van het fransch-afrikaansche leger tegen Klein-Kabylie in 1851. Hertogenbosch, 1852.

Afr 9225.10 Boon, M.J. The history of the Orange Free State. London, 1885.

Afr 8088.85.5 Boon, Martin J. The immortal history of South Africa. London, 1885.

Afr 7369.29 Boone, C.C. Liberia as I know it. Richmond, Va., 1929.

Afr 8055.5 Boonzaier, D.C. Owlographs, a collection of South African celebrities in caricature. Cape Town, 1901.

Afr 8063.15 Boot and saddle. (Young, P.J.) Cape Town, 1955.

Afr 4389.43A Boot and saddle in Africa. (Lambie, T.A.) Philadelphia, 1943.

Afr 8678.405 Booth, Joseph. Africa for the African. Photoreproduction. n.p., 1897?

Afr 710.35 Booth, Newall S. This is Africa south of the Sahara. N.Y., 1959.

Afr 11045.2 Booysen, C. Footprints. Johannesburg, 1956.

Afr 11027.5 Booysen, C. Murray. More tales of South Africa. Cape Town, 1967.

Afr 500.55 Borba za svero-vostochnuice, Afrika. Moscow, 1936.

Afr 3979.29.5 Borchardt, Ludwig. Agypten. Berlin, 1929.

Afr 7103.5 Borchardt, P. Bibliographie de l'Angola. Bruxelles, n.d.

Afr 8252.1.5 Borcherds, P.B. An autobiographical memoir. Facsimile reproduction. Cape Town, 1963.

Afr 7175.47 Borchert, Günter. Südost-Angola. Hamburg, 1963.

Afr 7176.30 Borchert, Günter. Die Wirtschaftsräume Angolas. Pfaffenhofen/Ilm, 1967.

Afr 3230.8 Bordeano, N. L'Egypte d'après les traités de 1840-41. Constantine, 1869.

Afr 9489.00 Bordeaux, A. Rhodesia et Transvaal. Paris, 1900.

Afr 5045.38.5 Bordeaux, H. Nos Indes noires. Paris, 1936.

Afr 3979.46.10 Bordeaux, Henri. Le sphinx sans visage. Marseille, 1946.

Afr 1571.27 Bordeaux, Henry. Le miracle du Maroc. Paris, 1934.

Afr 5054.36.10 Bordeaux, W. L'épopée noire. Paris, 1936.

Afr 8809.62 The border region, natural environment and land use in the eastern Cape. (Board, Chr.) Cape Town, 1962. 2v.

Afr 1658.31 Bordes, Pierre. Dans le Rif (Cornet de route d'un marsouin). Orne de gravures et de cartes. Lyon, 1929.

Afr 2669.5 Bordin, P. Les populations arabes du contrôle civil de Gafsa et leurs genres de vie. Tunis, 1944.

Afr 8687.174 Boreham, Frank W. The man who saved Gandhi, John Joseph Doke. London, 1948.

Afr 8252.1 Boreherds, P.B. An autobiographical memoir. Cape Town, 1861.

Afr 4700.42 Borelli, Gioranni. Albori coloniali d'Italia (1891-1895). Modena, 1942.

Afr 4605.1F Borelli, Jules. Ethiopie meridionale, Amhara. Paris, 1890.

Afr 1571.17.45 Borely, J. Le tombeau de Lyautey. Paris, 1937.

Afr 630.63.5 Borer, M.C. Africa. London, 1963.

Afr 1271.5 Bories, H. Avenir de l'Afrique du Nord. Paris, 1938.

Afr 810.30 Borill, Edward W. The Niger explored. London, 1968.

Afr 5488.12 Borkou et Ounianga. (Capot-Rey, R.) Alger, 1961.

Afr 7817.5 Bormann, Martin. Zwischen Kreuz und Fetisch. Bayreuth, 1965.

Afr 6292.9.10 Bornu Sahara and Sudan. (Palmer, Herbert Richmond.) London, 1936.

Afr 1665.5 Boron De Segonzac, R. De. Excursion au sous. Paris, 1901.

Afr 555.148 Borra, Edoardo. Un meschino di Allah. Torino, 1963.

Afr 4431.15 Borra, Eduardo. Prologo di un conflitto. Milano, 1965.

Afr 520.12 Borras, T. La España completa. Madrid, 1950.

Afr 1975.6 Borrer, D. Narrative of a campaign against Kabailes of Algeria. London, 1848.

Afr 7580.7 Borri, M. Nous, ces affreux, dossier secret de l'ex-Congo belge. Paris, 1962.

Afr 2945.5 Borsari, F. Geografia etnologica e storica della Tripolitania, Cirenaica e Fezzan. Naples, 1888.

Afr 3978.56 Borthelemy Saint-Hilaire. Lettres sur l'Egypte. Paris, 1856.

Afr 1390.8 Bosch Vila, Jacinto. Los Almoravidas. Tetuan, 1956.

Afr 7015.50 Bosgra, Sietse Jan. Angola, Mozambique, Guinee. Amsterdam, 1969.

Afr 8110.3.25 Bosman, D. Brienie van Johanna Maria van Riebeeck. Amsterdam, 1952.

Afr 8095.15 Bosman, F.C.L. Hollandse joernalisticks in Suid-Afrika. Kaapstad, 1930.

Afr 11229.81.21 Bosman, Herman. Bosman at his best. Cape Town, 1967.

Afr 11229.10 Bosman, Herman. A cask of jerepigo. Johannesburg, 1957.

Afr 11229.5 Bosman, Herman. Mafeking road. Johannesburg, 1947.

Afr 11229.81.100 Bosman, Herman. Unto dust, stories. 2d ed. Cape Town, 1964.

Afr 8252.251 Bosman, I.D. Dr. George McCall theal as die geskiedskrywer van Suid-Afrika. Amsterdam, 1931.

Afr 8985.2 Bosman, W. The Natal rebellion of 1906. London, 1907.

Afr 5318.3.5 Bosman, W. Neuwkeurige beschryning van de Guinese. Amsterdam, 1737.

Afr 5318.2.89 Bosman, W. A new accurate description of the coast of Guinea. London, 1705.

Afr 5318.2.89.2 Bosman, W. A new and accurate description of the coast of Guinea. London, 1967.

Afr 5318.3.9 Bosman, W. Voyage de Guinée. Utrecht, 1705.

Afr 11229.81.21 Bosman at his best. (Bosman, Herman.) Cape Town, 1967.

Afr 8849.141 Bosman di Ravelli, Vere. Saint Theodore and the crocodile. Cape Town, 1964.

Afr 5180.37.6 Bosshard, J.M. Ces routes qui ne menent à rien. 6e éd. Paris, 1937.

Afr 5758.67 Bostian, Georges. Madagascar, étude géographique et économique. Paris, 1967.

Afr 6280.64 Boston, John Shipway. The Igala Kingdom. Ibadan, 1968.

Afr 28.4.10 Boston Public Library. List of works on Africa. Boston, 1894.

Afr 28.110 Boston University. African Studies Center. A list of films on Africa. Boston, 1966.

Afr 28.100 Boston University. Library. Catalog of African government documents and African area index. Boston, 1960.

Afr Doc 5.2 Boston University. Library. Catalog of African government documents and African area index. 2d ed. Boston, 1964.

Afr 2.5 Boston University papers in African history. Boston. 1,1964+ 3v.

Afr 4700.14.25 Botarelli, A. Compendio di storia coloniale italiana. Roma, 1914.

Afr 7308.35 Botelho, S.X. Memoria estatistica portuguezes na Africa oriental. Lisboa, 1835-37. 2v.

Afr 7308.34 Botelho, S.X. Resumo para servir de introdução a memoria estatistica sobre os dominios portuguezes na Africa oriental. Lisboa, 1834.

Afr 8028.205 Both, Ellen Lisa Marianne. Catalogue of books and pamphlets published in German relating to South Africa and South West Africa as found in the South African Public Library. Cape Town, 1969.

Afr 11025.2 Both sides of the mask. (Sowden, Lewis.) Cape Town, 1964.

Afr 8278.99.50 Both sides of the South African question. v.2. (Britain and the Boers.) N.Y., 1899-1900.

Afr 8735.4.5 Botha, Andries. Trial of Andries Botha. Cape Town, 1969.

Afr 8735.4 Botha, Andries. Trial of Andries Botha for high treason. Cape Town, 1852.

Afr 8028.200.10 Botha, C.G. A brief guide to the various classes of documents in the Cape archives for 1652-1806. Cape Town, 1918.

Afr 8719.62 Botha, C.G. Collected works. Cape Town, 1962. 3v.

Afr 8710.15 Botha, C.G. An eighteenth century law library. Cape Town, 1935.

Afr 8028.200 Botha, C.G. The public archives of South Africa, 1652-1910. Cape Town, 1928.

Afr 8028.200.5 Botha, C.G. The science of archives in South Africa. Johannesburg, 1937.

Afr 8110.10A Botha, C.G. Social life in the Cape colony in the 18th century. Cape Town, 1926.

Afr 8028.200.15 Botha, Carol. A catalogue of manuscripts and papers in the Killie Campbell African collection relating to the African peoples. Johannesburg, 1967.

Afr 8115.10 Botha, Colin G. The French refugees at the Cape. Cape Town, 1919.

Afr 8110.32F Botha, Colin G. Three hundred years. Johannesburg, 1952.

Afr 8678.306 Botha, David P. Die opkoms van ons derde stand. Kaapstad, 1960.

Afr 8378.379.20 Botha, Jan. Verwoerd is dead. Cape Town, 1967.

Afr 8210.12 Botha, P.R. Die staatkundige ontwikkeling van den Zuid Afrikanse Republiek onder Krueger en Leyds. Amsterdam, 1925.

Afr 8135.23 Botha, Smuts and South Africa. (Williams, Basil.) London, 1946.

Afr 8135.23.5 Botha. (Williams, Basil.) N.Y., 1962.

Afr 6926.11.10 Botha treks. (Trew, H.F.) London, 1936.

Afr 555.9.45 Botha Vlok, T.C. Elf jaren in Midden Afrika. Neerbosch, 1901.

Afr Doc 4009.5F Botswana. Estimates for the development fund. Gaberones. 1966+

Afr Doc 4009.10F Botswana. Estimates of revenue and expenditures. Gaberones. 1967+

Afr Doc 4003.5F Botswana. Central government organization chart. Gaberones. 1968+

Afr Doc 4007.5F Botswana. Central Statistics Office. Statistical abstract. Gaberones. 2,1967+

Afr Doc 4031.5 Botswana. Department of Agriculture. Annual report. Gaberones. 1962+

Afr 9398.2 Botswana. Economic Planning Unit. Transitional plan for social and economic development. Gaberones, 1966.

Afr Doc 4014.6F Botswana. National Assembly. Official report of the debates. Gaberones. 1,1966+

Afr Doc 4014.205 Botswana. National Assembly. Public Accounts Committee. Report. Gaberones. 1966+

Afr 9398.4 Botswana. Republic of Botswana. Ministry of Development Planning. National development plan, 1968-1973. Gaberones, 1968.

Afr 1609.13.8 Botte, L. Au coeur du Maroc. Paris, 1913.

Afr 2315.1 Bou-Farik. 2e ed. (Trumelet, C.) Alger, 1887.

Afr 2030.463.20 Boualam, B. Les Harkis au service de la France. Paris, 1963.

Afr 2030.462.65 Boualam, B. Mon pays, la France. Paris, 1962.

Afr 2030.464.25 Boualam, Bachaga. L'Algérie sans la France. Paris, 1964.

Afr 5019.61   Boubacar, Diabete. Porte ouverte sur la communauté franco-africaine. Bruxelles, 1961.

Afr 5023.5   Bouche, Denise. Les villages de liberté en Afrique noire française, 1887-1910. Paris, 1968.

Afr 590.28   Bouche, P.B. Sept ans en Afrique occidentale, la côte des esclaves. Paris, 1885.

Afr 555.23.51   Boucher, A. Au Congo français. Les missions catholiques. Paris, 1928.

Afr 2030.464.30   Boudiaf, M. Notre révolution. Paris, 196-.

Afr 5600.7   Boudon, A. Le complot de 1857. Tananarive, 1943.

Afr 1432.9   Boudot, P. Une mission militaire prussienne. Paris, 1908.

Afr 2030.420   Boudot, Pierre. L'Algérie mal enchaînée. Paris, 1961.

Afr 5765.30   Boudou, Adrien. Les Jesuites à Madagascar au XIXe siècle. v.1-2. Paris, 1940. 2v.

Afr 852.3   Boudyck Bastiaanse, J. Voyage à la côte de Guinée. La Haye, 1853.

Afr 678.46   Bouet-Willaumez, Edouard, Comte. Des nautiques des côtes de l'Afrique. Paris, 1846.

Afr 1825.2   Bougie, die perle nord afrikas. (Ludwig, Salvator.) Leipzig, 1900.

Afr 1623.30   Bouissi, R. Etude sur la colonisation capitaliste au Maroc. Thèse. Paris, 1921.

Afr 12372.67.100   Boukman, Daniel. Chants pour hâter la mort du temps des Orphée ou Madinina île esclave. Honfleur, 1967.

Afr 7809.29   Boula-matari. (Crokaert, J.) Bruxelles, 1929.

Afr 1400.3   Boulet. Histoire de l'empire des chérifs en Afrique. Paris, 1733.

Afr 1550.1   Un boulevard de l'islam. (Kerdec Cheny, A.) Tanger, 1895.

Afr 7548.98   Boulger, D.C. The Congo state. London, 1898.

Afr 1990.22   Boulle, L. La France et les Beni-Snassen. Paris, n.d.

Afr 5243.343.10   Boulnois, Jean. L'empire de Gao. Paris, 1954.

Afr 5344.7   Boulnois, Jean. Gnon-Sua, dieu des Guéré. Paris, 1933.

Afr 5488.22   Boum-le-Grand, village d'Iro. (Pairault, Claude.) Paris, 1966.

Afr 1840.6   Bounichon, A. La conversion au christianisme de l'indigène musulman algérien. Thèse. Paris, 1931.

Afr 550.7.10   Bouniol, Joseph. The White Fathers and their missions. London, 1929.

Afr 1570.7   Bourassin, R. La question du Maroc. Paris, 1904.

Afr 2945.26.15   Bourbon del Monte Santa Maria, G. L'islamismo e la Confraternità dei Senussi. Città di Castello, 1912.

Afr 5874.20   Bourbon journal, August, 1863. (Besant, Walter.) London, 1933.

Afr 5053.30   Bourcart, Robert. Le grand conseil de l'Afrique occidentale. Paris, 1955.

Afr 5053.30.2   Bourcart, Robert. Le grand conseil de l'Afrique occidentale. 2. ed. Paris, 1956.

Afr 4513.36.35   Bourcier, E. L'aventure abyssine. Paris, 1936.

Afr 6314.36   Bourde, André. L'Afrique orientale. Paris, 1968.

Afr 2208.79.3   Bourde, P. A travers l'Algérie. Paris, 1880.

Afr 2225.14.5   Bourdieu, Pierre. The Algerians. Boston, 1962.

Afr 2225.14   Bourdieu, Pierre. Sociologie de l'Algérie. 1. ed. Paris, 1958.

Afr 1485.6   Bourdon, G. Les journees de Casablanca. Paris, 1908.

Afr 5832.5.5   La Bourdonnais. (Roubaud, L.) Paris, 1932.

Afr 2209.04   Bourdonnaye. Dans le Bled. Paris, 1904.

Afr 2290.4   Bourdonnaye. Le moral algérien. Paris, n.d.

Afr 4394.14   Bourelly. La battaglia di Abba Garima. Milano, 1901.

Afr 1338.22   Bourely, Michel. Droit public marocain. v.1-2. Rabat, 1965.

Afr 626.138   Bourgaignie, G.E. Jeune Afrique mobilisable. Paris, 1964.

Afr 3040.74   Bourgeois, A. La formation de l'Egypte moderne. Paris, 1939.

Afr 1609.59   Bourgeois, Paul. L'univers de l'ecolier marocain. v.1-5. Rabat, 1959-60.

Afr 2035.15   Bourges, Hervé. L'Algérie à l'épreuve du pouvoir (1962-1967). Paris, 1967.

Afr 3248.3   Bourguet, A. La France et l'Angleterre en Egypte. Paris, 1897.

Afr 2536.10.15   Bourguiba, H. La bataille de l'évacuation, 17 avril 1956-17 février 1959. Tunis, 1959.

Afr 2536.10.10   Bourguiba, H. La Tunisie et la France. Paris, 1954.

Afr 2536.10.30   Bourguiba, Habib. Articles de presse, 1929-1934. Tunis, 1967.

Afr 2536.10.25   Bourguiba, Habib. Les procès Bourguiba, 9 avril, 1938. Tunis, 1967. 2v.

Afr 2536.10.20   Pamphlet vol. Bourguiba, Habib. Collection of speeches, 1963-64. 22 pam.

Afr 2536.10   Bourguiba à la naissance d'une nation. (Garas, Felix.) Paris, 1956.

Afr 7568.7   Bourne, H.R.F. Civilisation in Congoland. London, 1903.

Afr 718.20   Bourne, H.R.F. The other side of Emin Pasha relief expedition. London, 1891.

Afr 1609.12.11   Bourote, M. Pour coloniser au Maroc. Paris, 1912.

Afr 2208.81.7   Bourquelot, E. En Algérie. Paris, 1881.

Afr 6164.10.5   Bourret, F.M. Ghana. Rev. ed. Stanford, 1960.

Afr 6164.10   Bourret, F.M. The Gold Coast, 1919-46. Stanford, 1949.

Afr 6164.10.2   Bourret, F.M. The Gold Coast. 2d ed. Stanford, 1952.

Afr 1625.12   Bourrilly, J. Elements d'ethnographie marocaine. Paris, 1932.

Afr 7368.87   Bourzeix, R.P.P. La république de Liberia. Paris, 1887.

Afr 1280.60   Bousquet, G.H. Les Berbères. 1st ed. Paris, 1957.

Afr 635.90   Boute, Joseph. La démographie de la branche indo-pakistanaise d'Afrique. Louvain, 1965.

Afr 2218.9   Boutemène, Yahia. La Zaouia des Ouled Sidi Bénamar près de Nédroma. Tlemcen, 1950.

Afr 5346.15   Boutillier, J.L. Bongouanou. Paris, 1960.

NEDL Afr 1200.50   Boutin, Abel. Anciennes relations de la France avec la Barbarie, 1515-1830. Paris, 1902.

Afr 13438.1.140   Les boutriers de l'aurore. (Rabemananjara, Jacques.) Paris, 1957.

Afr 2208.93.4   Boutroue, A. L'Algérie et la Tunisie à travers les ages. Paris, 1893.

Afr 12785.89.130   Les bouts de bois de Dieu, Banty Mam Yall. Photoreproduction. (Ousmane, Sembene.) Paris, 1960.

Afr 7575.98   Bouvier, Paule. L'accession du Congo belge à l'indépendance. Bruxelles, 1965.

Afr 8813.2   Bouws, Jan. Die musieklewe van Kaapstad, 1800-1850. Thesis. Kaapstadt, 1966.

Afr 5346.11   Bouys, P. Le bas Cavally (Afrique occidentale française) et son avenir. Thèse. Montpellier, 1933.

Afr 2209.20F   Bovet, Marie A. L'Algérie. Paris, 1920.

Afr 5054.33   Bovill, E.W. Caravans of the old Sahara. London, 1933.

Afr 5054.58   Bovill, E.W. The golden trade of the Moors. London, 1958.

Afr 5054.58.2   Bovill, E.W. The golden trade of the Moors. 2nd ed. London, 1968.

Afr 9161.5   Bovill, J.H. Natives under the Transvaal flag. London, 1900.

Afr 210.62.35   Bow Group Pamphlet. The new Africa. London, 1962.

Afr 6168.5   Bowdich, E.T. Mission from Cape Coast Castle to Ashanti. London, 1873.

Afr 7045.2   Bowdich, T.E. An account of the discoveries of the Portuguese in the interior of Angola and Mozambique. London, 1824.

Afr 6192.14F   Bowdich, T.E. Mission from Cape Coast Castle to Ashantee. London, 1819.

Afr 6192.96   Bowdich, Thomas Edward. Mission der englisch-afrikanischen Compagnie von Cape Coast Castle nach Ashantee. Weimar, 1820.

Afr 6192.96.5   Bowdich, Thomas Edward. Mission from Cape Coast Castle to Ashantee. 3d ed. London, 1966.

Afr 6168.30   Bowdich, Thomas Edward. Voyage dans le pays d'Aschantie. Paris, 1819.

Afr 11230.92.100   Bowditch, L. Peter, a tale of the Greek trek. Pretoria, 1933.

Afr 7568.26   The Bowdoin argument in the Bowdoin-Clark debate. (Bowdoin-Clark Debate.) n.p., 1906.

Afr 7568.26   Bowdoin-Clark Debate. The Bowdoin argument in the Bowdoin-Clark debate. n.p., 1906.

Afr 679.54.5   Bowen, E.S. Return to laughter. N.Y., 1954.

Afr 3198.87   Bowen, J.E. Conflict of East and West in Egypt. N.Y., 1887.

Afr 550.2.12   Bowen, T.J. Adventures and missionary labors in several countries in the interior of Africa. 2d ed. London, 1968.

Afr 550.2   Bowen, T.J. Missionary labors in the interior of Africa. Charleston, 1857.

Afr 550.2.5   Bowen, T.J. Missionary labors in the interior of Africa. N.Y., 1857.

Afr 8687.141   Bowker, John. Speeches. Cape Town, 1962.

Afr 6192.16   Bowler, Louis P. Gold Coast palaver. London, 1911.

Afr 8835.43F   Bowler, Thomas William. Pictorial album of Cape Town. Cape Town, 1966.

Afr 500.67   Bowles, Chester. Africa's challenge to America. Berkeley, 1956.

Afr 1259.63   Bowles, Paul. Their heads are green. London, 1963.

Afr 2749.57   Bowles, Paul Frederic. Yallah. N.Y., 1957.

Afr 3979.42.5   Bowman, H.E. Middle east window. London, 1942.

Afr 6465.56.10   Boxer, Charles R. Fort Jesus and the Portuguese in Mombasa. London, 1960.

Afr 6465.56.9   Boxer, Charles R. A fortaleza de Jesus e os portugueses em Mombaça. Lisboa, 1960.

Afr 9598.84.5   The boy travellers in the Far East. (Knox, T.W.) N.Y., 1884.

Afr 3978.82.10   The boy travellers in the Far East. Pt. 4 - Egypt and the Holy Land. (Knox, T.W.) N.Y., 1883.

Afr 11612.100   Boy with a flute. (Noble, Alex.) London, 1962.

Afr 8089.61   Boyce, Arnold N. Europe and South Africa. 2d. ed. Cape Town, 1961.

Afr 609.25.5   Boyce, W.D. Illustrated Africa. Chicago, 1925.

Afr 555.22.25   Boyce, William B. Memoir of the Rev. William Shaw. London, 1874.

Afr 210.62.50   Boyd, Andrew Kirk Henry. An atlas of African affairs. N.Y., 1962.

Afr 7815.7   Boyd, F.R. Les races indigènes du Congo belge. Paris, 1913.

Afr 8659.59.3   Boydell, T. My beloved country. Cape Town, 1960.

Afr 2209.63   Boyer, P. La vie quotidienne à Alger à la veille de l'intervention française. Paris, 1963.

Afr 2000.11   Boyer, Pierre. L'évolution de l'Algérie mediane. Paris, 1960.

Afr 1110.10   Boyer de Latour, Pierre. Vérités sur l'Afrique du Nord. Paris, 1956.

Afr 6395.2.5   Boyes, John. A white king of East Africa. N.Y., 1912.

Afr 3275.12.110   Boyle, C.A. Boyle of Cairo, a diplomatist's adventures in the Middle East. Kendal, 1965.

Afr 3275.12.100   Boyle, C.A. A servant of the Empire, a memoir of Harry Boyle. London, 1938.

Afr 5842.14   Boyle, C.J. Far away, scenery and society in Mauritius. London, 1867.

Afr 6170.6   Boyle, F. Through Fanteeland to Coomassie. London, 1874.

Afr 8235.11   Boyle, Frederick. To the Cape for diamonds. London, 1873.

Afr 6198.231   Boyle, Laura. Diary of a colonial officer's wife. Oxford, 1968.

Afr 3275.12.110   Boyle of Cairo, a diplomatist's adventures in the Middle East. (Boyle, C.A.) Kendal, 1965.

Afr 8140.35   Braak, K. Zuid-Afrika en Engeland. Utrecht, 1933.

Afr 8378.200.11   Braam Fischer. (Vermaak, Christopher J.) Johannesburg, 1966.

Afr 9029.49   Braatvedt, H. Roaming Zululand with a native commissioner. Pietermaritzburg, 1949.

Afr 1069.64   Brace, R.M. Morocco, Algeria, Tunisia. Englewood Cliffs, N.J., 1964.

Afr 2030.346   Brace, Richard M. Algerian voices. Princeton, N.J., 1965.

Afr 2030.345   Brace, Richard M. Ordeal in Algeria. Princeton, 1960.

Afr 6170.11   Brackenbury, H. The Ashanti war. Edinburgh, 1874. 2v.

Afr 6170.11.1   Brackenbury, H. The Ashanti War: a narrative. 1st ed. London, 1968.

Afr 6170.15   Brackenbury, H. Fanti and Ashanti. Edinburgh, 1873.

Afr 3708.8   Brackenbury, H. The river column. Edinburgh, 1885.

Afr 150.40.5   Bradford, Ernle. Southward the caravels. London, 1961.

Afr 150.40   Bradford, Ernle. A wind from the north. N.Y., 1960.

Afr 4095.28   Bradham, Frederick. The long walks, journeys to the sources of the White Nile. London, 1969.

Afr 505.35   Bradley, K. Britain's purpose in Africa. N.Y., 1959.

Afr 9689.38.4   Bradley, K. The diary of a district officer. 4th ed. London, 1966.

Afr 9689.38   Bradley, K. The diary of district officer. London, 1943.

Afr 7809.24.5   Bradley, M.H. Caravans and cannibals. N.Y., 1927.

Afr 7809.21.10   Bradley, Mary. On the gorilla trail. N.Y., 1923.

Afr 5842.11F   Bradshaw, T. Views in the Mauritius, or Isle of France. London, 1832.

Afr 8659.50.5   Brady, Cyrus T. Africa astir. Melbourne, 1950.

Afr 210.62.43   Braginskii, M.I. Africa wins freedom. Moscow, 196-.

Afr 210.62.42   Braginskii, M.I. Osoobozhdenie Afriki. Moscow, 1962.

Afr 1848.7   Braibant, Charles. Inventaire des archives de l'amiraute d'Alger. Alger, 1922.

Afr 6196.14.5   Braiman, Joseph Adam. Salaga: the struggle for power. London, 1967.

Afr 6196.14   Braiman, Joseph Adam. The two Isanwurfos. London, 1967.

Afr 1408.1.5   Braithwaite, Capt. Histoire des révolutions de l'empire de Maroc. Amsterdam, 1731.

Afr 1408.1   Braithwaite, Capt. History of revolution upon death of Ishmail. London, 1729.

Afr 6095.362 | Braithwaite, E.R. A kind of homecoming. Englewood, N.J., 1962.
Afr 10018.5 | Brambilla, Cristina. Narrativa africana. Bologna, 1965.
Afr 8340.9A | Brand, R.H. The Union of South Africa. Oxford, 1909.
Afr 4555.00.5 | Brandao, Zephyrino. Pero da Borilhan. Lisboa, 1897.
Afr 7332.5 | Brandao Cro de Castro Ferreri, Alfredo. Apontamentos de um ex-governador de Sofalla. Lisboa, 1886.
Afr 8668.10 | Brandel-Syrier, Mia. Black woman in search of God. London, 1962.
Afr 6168.10 | Brandenburg-Preussen auf der West-Küste von Afrika. Leipzig, 1912.
Afr 861.20 | Brander, J. Tristan da Cunha, 1506-1902. London, 1940.
Afr 7122.76 | Braseiro da morte. (Pires, P.) Viseu, Portugal, 1963.
Afr 7119.63.10 | Brasil, fronteirada Africa. (Archer, Maria.) Sao Paulo, 1963.
Afr 7122.90 | O Brasil na restauração de Angola. (Diogo, Alfredo.) Luanda, 1965.
Afr 6280.37 | Brasileiros no Africa. (Olinto, A.) Rio de Janeiro, 1964.
Afr 150.1 | Brasio, A.D. A acção missionaria no periodo henriquino. Lisboa, 1958.
Afr 550.70 | Brasio, A.D. Monumenta missionaria africana. Lisboa, 1954. 10v.
Afr 550.70.2 | Brasio, A.D. Monumenta missionaria africana. 2d serie. Lisboa, 1958-64. 4v.
Afr 4513.35.83 | Brassard amarante. (Bonardi, Pierre.) Paris, 1935.
Afr 7809.14 | Bratier, Albert Ernest Augustin. Souvenirs de la mission marchande. Paris, 1914.
Afr 9225.15 | Brauer, A. Der Oranje-Freistaat, 1854-1888. Emsdetten, 1931.
Afr 8659.03 | Braun, D.E. Auf und ab in Süd-Afrika. Berlin, 1903.
Afr 2929.14 | Braun, Ethel. The new Tripoli. London, 1914.
Afr 6879.39 | Braun, Hans. Die Reise nach Ostafrika. Berlin, 1939.
Afr 6195.10 | Braun, Richard. Letters from Ghana. Philadelphia, 1959.
Afr 606.24.1 | Braun, Samuel. Schiffahrten. Facsimile-Ausgabe. Basel, 1947.
Afr 2235.42 | Brauner, Siegmund. Lohrbuch der Hausa-Sprache. München, 1966.
Afr 7540.36 | Brausch, G. Belgian administration in the Congo. London, 1961.
Afr 10690.89.110 | The brave African huntress. (Tutuola, Amos.) London, 1958.
Afr 11193.74.100 | The brave remain. (Baragwanath, Paul.) Cape Town, 1965.
Afr 5960.2.5 | Bravo Carbonell, J. En la selva virgen del Muni. Madrid, 1925.
Afr 5960.2 | Bravo Carbonell, J. Fernando Poo y el Muni. Madrid, 1917.
Afr 5955.4 | Bravo Carbonell, J. Territorios españoles del Golfo de Guinea. Madrid, 1929.
Afr 210.10 | Brawley, B.G. Africa and the war. N.Y., 1918.
Afr 8678.108 | Brayshaw, E. Russell. The racial problems of South Africa. London, 1953.
Afr 5405.109.10 | Brazza. (Chambrun, J.A. de P.) Paris, 1930.
Afr 5405.109.25 | Brazza. (Croidys, Pierre.) Paris, 1947.
Afr 5405.109.15 | Brazza. (Froment-Guieysse, G.) Paris, 1945.
Afr 6291.44 | Breadless Biafra. (Sullivan, John R.) Dayton, Ohio, 1969.
Afr 9448.73 | The break-up. (Rhodesia and Nyasaland. Prime Minister.) Salisbury, 1963.
Afr 6143.17 | Bref innehaallande beskrifning oefver Sierra Leona. (Padenheim, D.W.) Stockholm, 1801.
Afr 3199.01 | Brehier, L. L'Egypte de 1798 à 1900. Paris, 1901.
Afr 9699.47 | Brelsford, W.V. Copperbelt markets. Lusaka, 1947.
Afr 9700.41 | Brelsford, William Vernon. Generation of men. Salisbury, 1965.
Afr 9700.41.5.2 | Brelsford, William Vernon. The tribes of Zambia. 2nd ed. Lusaka, 1965?
Afr 575.45 | Brelvi, Mahmud. Islam in Africa. Lahore, 1964.
Afr 1340.35 | Bremard, F. L'organisation régionale du Maroc. Paris, 1949.
Afr 1259.42 | Bremond, Edouard. Berbères et Arabes. Paris, 1942.
Afr 4610.4F | Bremond, L.A. Expedition scientifique et commerciale au...Choa...Gallas. Paris, 1883.
Afr 12012.3 | Brench, Anthony Cecil. The novelists' inheritance in French Africa. London, 1967.
Afr 12018.5 | Brench, Anthony Cecil. Writing in French from Senegal to Cameroon. London, 1967.
Afr 6488.5 | Brendel, Horst. Die Kolonisation Ugandas. Inaug. Diss. Grossenhain, 1934.
Afr 6738.48 | Brendl, Oskar. Die Bundes-Republik Kamerun. Hagen, 1965.
Afr 5615.5 | Brenier, J. La question de Madagascar. Paris, 1882.
Afr 1550.45 | Brenning, H.E. Die grossen Mächte und Marokko in den Jahren vor dem Marokko-Abkommen von 8. Apr. 1904 (1898-1904). Berlin, 1934.
Afr 2287.5 | Brenot, H.E.L. Le douar. Alger, 1938.
Afr 109.63.15 | Brentjes, Burchard. Uraltes junges Afrika; 5000 Jahre afrikanischer Geschichte nach zeitgenössischen Quellen. Berlin, 1963.
Afr 8678.150 | Brentz, Paul Lenert. Die politischen und gesellschaftlichen Verhältnisse der Sotho-Tswana in Transvaal und Betschauanaland. Hamburg, 1941.
Afr 8687.142 | Bresler, Casparus Philippus. Tilt the sack. Pretoria, 1965.
Afr 5057.10 | Bressolles, H. Organisation financière locale de l'Afrique. Thèse. Bordeaux, 1922.
Afr 2326.5 | Bresson, Gilbert. Histoire d'un centre rural algérien. Alger, 1957.
Afr 5342.66 | Brétignère, Amédée. Aux temps héroiques de la Côte-d'Ivoire. Paris, 1931.
Afr 3978.14 | Breton, M. L'Egypte et la Syrie. v.1-6. Paris, 1814. 3v.
Afr 1550.18 | Bretschger, J. Die Marokko-Konferenz. Zürich, 1913.
Afr 8055.20 | Brett, B.L.W. Makers of South Africa. London, 1944.
Afr 8028.115 | Brett, E.A. Tentative list of books and pamphlets on South Africa. Johannesburg, 1959.
Afr 6212.40 | Bretton, Henry. Power and stability in Nigeria. N.Y., 1962.
Afr 6176.30.25 | Bretton, Henry L. The rise and fall of Kwame Nkrumah; a study of personal rule in Africa. N.Y., 1966.
Afr 2484.4 | Breve, ma distintissima relatione alla Santa Fede del primogenito del re di Tunisi, Mamet Celebi hoggi detto D. Filippo Dai. Roma, 1646.
Afr 7806.92 | Breve e succinta relatione del viaggio nel regno. (Merolla da Sorrento.) Napoli, 1692.
Afr 1608.60.7 | Breve escursion por el imperio de Marruecos. Malaga, 1860.
Afr 7320.2 | Breve estudio,--ilha de Moçambique. (Ayres de Carvalho Soveral.) Porto, 1887.
Afr 109.61.35 | Brève histoire à l'Afrique noire. v.1-2. (Joos, L.C.D.) Issy-les-Moulineaux, 1961-64. 2v.
Afr 1753.4.5 | Breve noticia da gloriosa Vitoria...1732. Lisboa, 1732.

Afr 7183.25 | Breve noticia sobre o Museu do Dundo. (Companhia de Diamantes de Angola.) Lisbon, 1959.
Afr 4513.36.33 | Breve storia del conflitto italo-etiopico. (Istituto per gli Studi di Politica Internazionale, Milan.) Milano, 1936.
Afr 8089.59 | Breve storia del Sud Africa. (Robertaggi, C.) Firenze, 1959.
Afr 5993.16 | Breves apuntes sobre la isla de Fernando Poo en el Golfo de Guinea. (Martinez y Sanz, M.) Madrid, 1859.
Afr 5245.10 | Brevie, J. Islamisme contre naturisme au Soudan français. Paris, 1923.
Afr 10622.76.100 | Brew, Kwesi. The shadows of laughter: poems. London, 1968.
Afr 3974.83.9 | Breydenbach, B. von. Les saintes pérégrinations... Texte ... Par F. Larrinaz. Le Caire, 1904.
Afr 8289.49 | Breytenbach, J.H. Gedenkalbum van die Tweede Vryheidsoorlog. Kaapstad, 1949.
Afr 8289.48 | Breytenbach, J.H. Die Tweede Vryheidsoorlog. Kaapstad, 1948. 2v.
Afr 2975.7 | Brezzi, G. Cento giorni di prigionia nell'oasi di Cufra. Milano, 1930.
Afr 3979.06 | Brianchaninov, N. Skitaniia, Nubiia, Sudan. Moscow, 1908.
Afr 5249.7 | Briault, Maurice. La prodigieuse vie de René Caillié. Paris, 1930.
Afr 630.43 | Briault, Maurice. Les sauvages d'Afrique. Paris, 1943.
Afr 5426.115 | Briault, Maurice. Sur les pistes de l'AEF. Paris, 1945.
Afr 7567.40 | Bricusse, Georges Henri A. Les carnets de campagne. Bruxelles, 1959.
Afr 1494.20 | Bridel, T. Le Maroc. Lausanne, 1954.
Htn Afr 678.45.3* | Bridge, H. Journal of an African cruiser. London, 1845.
Htn Afr 678.45* | Bridge, H. Journal of an African cruiser. N.Y., 1845. 2 pam.
Htn Afr 678.45.6* | Bridge, H. Journal of an African cruiser. N.Y., 1848.
Afr 678.43.5 | Bridge, Horatio. Journal of an African cruiser. London, 1968.
Afr 2208.90.3 | Bridgman, F.A. Winters in Algeria. London, 1890.
Afr 6603.2 | Bridgman, Jon. German Africa. Stanford, 1965.
Afr 7368.56 | Brief account...retirement of President J.J. Roberts. (Blyden, E.W.) Liberia, 1856.
Afr 9161.21 | Brief authority. (Hooper, Charles.) London, 1960.
Afr 9161.20 | Brief authority. (Hooper, Charles.) N.Y., 1961.
Afr 9149.34 | A brief description of the Union's national parks. (South Africa. National Parks Board of Trustees.) Pretoria, 1934.
Afr 4115.22 | A brief guide to the Coptic Museum. (Cairo, Egypt. Coptic Museum.) Cairo, 1938.
Afr 8028.200.10 | A brief guide to the various classes of documents in the Cape archives for 1652-1806. (Botha, C.G.) Cape Town, 1918.
Afr 6194.25 | A brief history of the Daybamba people. (Tamakloe, E.F.) Accra, 1931.
Afr 8160.12 | Brief history of the 13th Regiment...1877-78-79. (McToy, E.D.) Devonport, 1880.
Afr 3978.53.6 | Briefe aus Agypten und Nubien. (Gentz, W.) Berlin, 1853.
Afr 8110.3.25 | Brienie van Johanna Maria van Riebeeck. (Bosman, D.) Amsterdam, 1952.
Afr 2209.12.9 | Brieux, L. Algérie. Vincennes, 1912.
Afr 9149.53 | Briewe uit Transvaal. (Middelberg, Gerrit Adrian Arnold.) Pretoria, 1953.
Afr 7809.17 | Briey, Renaud de. Le sphinx noir. Paris, 1926.
Afr 3204.24 | Briffauet, Robert. L'Angleterre et l'Egypte. Paris, 194-.
Afr 5969.157 | El brigadier Conde de Argelejo. (Cencillo de Pineda, Manuel.) Madrid, 1948.
Afr 3275.24 | Brigands in Egypt. (Pierre l'Ermite.) London, 1882.
Afr 5119.64.5 | Brigaud, Felix. Histoire du Sénégal. Dakar, 1964.
Afr 2760.5 | Briggs, Lloyd C. Tribes of the Sahara. Cambridge, 1960.
Afr 3979.18.5 | Briggs, Martin. Through Egypt in war time. London, 1918.
Afr 7458.98 | The bright side of African life. (Heard, William Henry.) N.Y., 1969.
Afr 8658.92.5 | Brighter South Africa. (Ritchie, James Ewing.) London, 1892.
Afr 1609.09.5 | Brines, A. Voyages au Maroc (1901-1907). Alger, 1909.
Afr 8380.15 | Bringolf, Walther. Gespräche in Südafrika. Zürich, 1968.
Afr 8678.364 | Brinkman, H.J. Zuidafrikaans samenleven. Zaandijk, 1964.
Afr 3040.35 | Brinton, Jasper Y. The mixed courts of Egypt. New Haven, 1930.
Afr 3040.35.2 | Brinton, Jasper Y. The mixed courts of Egypt. New Haven, 1968.
Afr 5240.2 | Bris, Alexis. Sénégal et Soudan. Paris, 1887.
Afr 5090.6 | Brisson, P.R. de. Histoire du naufrage et de la captivité. Genève, 1789.
Afr 2719.64 | Britain, the Sahara. (Boahen, A.A.) Oxford, 1964.
Afr 505.5 | Britain across the seas - Africa. (Johnston, H.) London, n.d.
Afr 505.45 | Britain and Africa. (Kirkwood, Kenneth.) London, 1965.
Afr 500.86 | Britain and Germany in Africa; imperial rivalry and colonial rule. New Haven, 1967.
Afr 505.9 | Britain and North-east Africa. (Newman, E.W.P.) London, 1940.
Afr 9769.64 | Britain and Nyasaland. (Jones, G.) London, 1964.
Afr 8380.10 | Britain and South Africa. (Adstin, Dennis.) London, 1966.
Afr 8135.21 | Britain and South Africa. (Walker, E.A.) London, 1941.
Afr 8278.99.50 | Britain and the Boers. Both sides of the South African question. v.2. N.Y., 1899-1900.
Afr 8278.99.27 | Britain and the Boers. (Appleton, L.) London, 1899.
Afr 7567.25 | Britain and the Congo in the 19th century. (Anstey, Roger.) Oxford, 1962.
Afr 7567.42 | Britain and the Congo question, 1885-1913. (Cookey, Sylvanus John Sodienye.) London, 1968.
Afr 6192.35 | Britain and the Gold Coast. (Great Britain. Central Office of Information.) London, 1957.
Afr 9448.70 | Britains dilemma in central Africa. (Africa Bureau, London.) London, 1960.
Afr 505.35 | Britain's purpose in Africa. (Bradley, K.) N.Y., 1959.
Afr 8719.01 | Britain's title in South Africa. (Cappon, James.) London, 1901.
Afr 3275.6 | Britain's work in Egypt. Edinburgh, 1892.
Afr 6333.62.5 | Britanskii imperializm v Vostochnoi Afrike. (Glukhov, A.M.) Moscow, 1962.
Afr 505.3.10 | British Africa. 2d ed. London, 1962.
Afr 2.3F | British Africa monthly. Johannesburg.
Afr 500.52 | British and Axis aims in Africa. (Mbadiwe, K.O.) N.Y., 1942.
Afr 6333.2 | British and German East Africa. (Brode, Heinrich.) N.Y., 1911.
Afr 6390.15 | A British borderland, service and sport in Equatoria. (Wilson, H.A.) London, 1913.
Afr 6390.22 | A British borderland. (Wilson, H.A.) London, 1913.

Afr 6620.51 British campaigns in Africa and...Pacific. (Dane, Edmond.) London, 1919.
Afr 4509.15.3 The British captives in Abyssinia. 2nd ed. (Beke, Charles F.) London, 1867.
Afr 8175.17 The British case against the Boer republics. (Imperial South African Association.) Westminster, 1900.
Afr 5407.5 The British case in French Congo. (Marel, Edmund D.) London, 1903.
Afr 9548.3 British central Africa. (Johnston, H.H.) N.Y., 1897.
Afr 9548.5 British central Africa. 2. ed. (Johnston, H.H.) London, 1898.
Afr 8678.353 The British churches and South Africa. (Manning, Charles Anthony Woodward.) London, 1965.
Afr 8140.17 British colonial policy and the South African republics. (Kiewiet, C.W. de.) London, 1929.
Afr 210.62.20 British Commonwealth Relations. The Commonwealth in Africa. London, 1962.
Afr 8678.330 British Council of Churches. The future of South Africa. London, 1965.
Afr 6328.2 British East Africa, or Ibea. New ed. (McDermott, P.L.) London, 1895.
Afr 6455.25 British East Africa. The Uganda railway. London, 1911.
Afr 6328.1 British East Africa. (McDermott, P.L.) London, 1893.
Afr 6484.6 British East Africa and Uganda. (Bentley, E.L.) London, 1892.
Afr 6303.5 British East and Central Africa, a selected list of references. (Library of Congress. Division of Bibliography.) Washington, 1942.
Afr 6879.24 British Empire Exhibition, Wembley, 1924. Central commission of Tanganyika exhibition handbook. London, 1924.
Afr 6565.24 British Empire Exhibition, Wembley, 1924. Zanzibar, an account of its people. Zanzibar, 1924.
Afr 505.44 The British empire in Africa. (Library of Congress. Division of Bibliography.) Washington, 1942-43.
Afr 8028.3 The British empire in Africa. v.9. (Library of Congress. Division of Bibliography.) Washington, 1942-43.
Afr 505.3.5 British empire series. v.2. 2d ed. London, 1901.
Afr 6218.11 British enterprise in Nigeria. (Cook, Arthur.) Philadelphia, 1943.
Afr 4375.1 British expedition to Abyssinia. (Hozier, H.M.) London, 1869.
Afr 8160.16 British foreign policy and the next war. The Zulu war. (Ewart, J.S.) Ottawa, 1927.
Afr 505.42 The British in Africa. (Taylor, Don.) London, 1962.
Afr 6465.56.5 The British in Mombasa, 1824-1826. (Gray, J.M.) London, 1957.
Afr 6284.5 The British in Northern Nigeria. (Heussler, Robert.) London, 1968.
Afr 6408.5 British Indian Colony. Merchants Association, Bombay. The Kenya decision. Bombay, 1923.
Afr 6095.23 British Information Service. Introducing West Africa. N.Y., 1944.
Afr 6212.35 British Information Service. Nigeria, the making of a nation. N.Y., 1960.
Afr 3745.55 British Information Service. The Sudan, 1899-1953. N.Y., 1953.
Afr 6535.62.5 British Information Service. Uganda. N.Y., 1962.
Afr 6535.62.10 British Information Service. Uganda. N.Y., 1962.
Afr 3745.70 British Information Services. The Anglo-Egyptian Sudan. N.Y., 1951.
Afr 6412.5 British Information Services. Kenya, progress and problems. N.Y., 1960.
Afr 6310.42 British Information Services. Regional cooperation in British East Africa. N.Y., 1959.
Afr 6140.15 British Information Services. Sierra Leone. N.Y., 1960.
Afr 6879.61.10 British Information Services. Tanganyika. N.Y., 1961.
Afr 6879.61 British Information Services. Tanganyika. N.Y., 1961.
Afr 6300.10 British Institute of History and Archaeology in East Africa. Memoir. Nairobi. 1,1966+
Afr 6300.9 British Institute of History and Archaeology in East Africa. Report. London.
Afr 8140.6F British Kaffaria, the people's blue book. (Committee of Observation on All Matters Connected with Attainment of Independence of British Kaffraria.) King Williams Town, 1863.
Afr 6497.14 The British mission to Uganda, 1893. (Portal, Gerald H.) London, 1894.
Afr 150.35 British Museum. Prince Henry the Navigator. London, 1960.
Afr 6275.5 British Nigeria. (Mockler-Ferryman, A.F.) London, 1902.
Afr 505.30 British policy in changing Africa. (Cohen, Andrew.) Evanston, 1959.
Afr 6410.6 British policy in Kenya colony. (Dilley, Marjorie Ruth.) N.Y., 1937.
Afr 6410.6.2 British policy in Kenya colony. 2. ed. (Dilley, Marjorie Ruth.) London, 1966.
Afr 8278.99.15 British policy in South Africa. (Wilkinson, S.) London, 1899.
Afr 3715.5A British policy in the Sudan, 1882-1902. (Shibeika, Mekki.) London, 1952.
Afr 1568.5 British policy towards Morocco in the age of Palmerston (1830-1865). (Flournoy, F.R.) London, 1935.
Afr 8860.10 British protectorates. (Brockway, Tenner.) London, 1957.
Afr 6430.5 British rule in Kenya, 1895-1912. (Mungeam, Gordon Hudson.) Oxford, 1966.
Afr 8969.50 The British settlement of Natal. (Hattersley, A.) Cambridge, Eng., 1950.
Afr 9435.5.5 British South Africa Company. Director's report and accounts. London. 1896+
Afr 9435.5.10 British South Africa Company. Report of general meeting. London.
Afr 9435.5 British South Africa Company. Reports. London. 1896+
Afr 9489.05 British South Africa Company. Southern Rhodesia. London, 1905.
Afr 590.15 The British squadron on the coast of Africa. (Wilson, J.L.) London, 1851.
Afr 8289.65 British supremacy in South Africa, 1899-1907. (Lemay, Godfrey Hugh Lancelot.) Oxford, 1965.
Afr 6314.29 The British territories in East and Central Africa. (Great Britain. Colonial Office.) London, 1950.
Afr 6055.1 Pamphlet box. British West Africa.
Afr 6075.17 Pamphlet vol. British West Africa. History. 10 pam.
Afr 8279.00A Briton and Boer. (Bryce, J.) N.Y., 1900.
Afr 8279.00.2 Briton and Boer. New ed. (Bryce, J.) N.Y., 1900.
Afr 8325.30 Britons and Boers. (Ives, Herbert.) London, n.d.
Afr 2749.56 Britsch, Jacques. Perspectives sahariennes. Limoges, 1956.

Afr 8180.26 Die Britse owerheid en de groot trek. Thesis. (Muller, Christoffel Frederik Jakobus.) Kaapstad, 1949.
Afr 8180.26.5 Die Britse owerheid en die groot trek. 2. uitg. (Muller, Christoffel Frederik Jakobus.) Johannesburg, 1963.
NEDL Afr 2527.1 Broadley, A.M. Tunis, past and present. Edinburgh, 1882. 2v.
X Cg Afr 3267.1 Broadley, S.M. How we defended Arabi. London, 1884.
Afr 5183.968 Brochier, Jacques. La diffusion du progrès technique en milieu rural sénégalais. Paris, 1968.
Afr 609.55.25 Brockway, A.F. African journeys. London, 1955.
Afr 8860.10 Brockway, Tenner. British protectorates. London, 1957.
Afr 718.19 Brode, H. Tippoo Tib; story of his career in Central Africa. London, 1907.
Afr 6333.2 Brode, Heinrich. British and German East Africa. N.Y., 1911.
Afr 6455.82 Brodhurst-Hill, Evelyn. So this is Kenya. London, 1936.
Afr 1259.43 Brodrick, A.H. North Africa. London, 1943.
Afr 1259.43.5 Brodrick, A.H. Parts of Barbary. London, 1943.
Afr 1990.13 Broglie, A. de. Une réforme administrative en Afrique. Paris, 1860.
Afr 5575.10 Broke, A. van. Aller neueste Nachricht von Madagascar und dem Leben des jetzigen Beherrschers dieses Insul. Frankfurt, 1748.
Afr 626.143 Brokensha, David. Ecology and economic development in tropical Africa. Berkeley, 1965.
Afr 626.143.5 Brokensha, David W. The anthropology of development in Sub-Saharan Africa. Lexington, Ky., 1969.
Afr 6196.20.5 Brokensha, David W. Social change at Larteh, Ghana. Oxford, 1966.
Afr 8377.3 Brokensha, Miles. The Fourth of July raids. Cape Town, 1965.
Afr 609.57.16 Brom, John L. African odyssey. 1st ed. N.Y., 1966.
Afr 6395.2.25 Brom, John L. Mau-Mau. Paris, 1956.
Afr 3315.15.5 Bromberger, M. Les secrets de l'expédition d'Egypte. Paris, 1957.
Afr 3315.15 Bromberger, M. Secrets of Suez. London, 1957.
Afr 2030.100 Bromberger, Serge. Les rébelles algériens. Paris, 1958.
Afr 6196.25 Brong Ahafo handbook. (Arthur, John.) Accra, 1960.
Afr 6455.34 Bronson, Edgar B. In closed territory. Chicago, 1910.
Afr 4394.5 Bronzuoli, A. Adua. Roma, 1935.
Afr 6275.120 Brook, Ian. The one eyed man is king. N.Y., 1967.
Afr 8849.7.5 Brooke, A. Robert Gray. Cape Town, 1947.
Afr 855.8 Brooke, T.H. History..island of St. Helena...1823. London, 1824.
Afr 8289.01.20 Brooke-Hunt, V. A woman's memories of the war in South Africa. London, 1901.
Afr 8678.312 Brookes, E.H. The city of God and the city of man in Africa. Lexington, 1964.
Afr 8140.16 Brookes, E.H. The colour problems of South Africa. Lovedale, 1934.
Afr 8140.15 Brookes, E.H. The history of native policy in South Africa. 2d ed. Pretoria, 1927.
Afr 8135.15 Brookes, E.H. The history of native policy in South Africa from 1830 to the present day. Cape Town, 1924.
Afr 8140.19 Brookes, E.H. The political future of South Africa. Pretoria, 1927.
Afr 8678.299 Brookes, E.H. Power, law, right and love. Durham, 1963.
Afr 8095.58 Brookes, E.H. The relationships between history and political science. Natal, 1959.
Afr 8045.38 Brookes, Edgar H. Civil liberty in South Africa. Cape Town, 1958.
Afr 8678.415 Brookes, Edgar Harry. Apartheid. London, 1968.
Afr 8190.20 Brookes, Edgar Harry. A history of Natal. Pietermaritzburg, 1965.
Afr 8969.67 Brookes, Edgar Harry. A history of Natal. Pietermaritzburg, 1967.
Afr 7582.15 Brookings Institute, Washington, D.C. Foreigin Policy Studies Division. United Nations peacekeeping in the Congo: 1960-1964. v.1-4. Washington, 1966. 2v.
Afr 8250.42 Brookner, Anita. An iconography of Cecil Rhodes. n.p., 1956.
Htn Afr 1407.3* Brooks, F. Barbarian cruelty. London, 1693.
Afr 8968.76 Brooks, Henry. Natal, a history and description of the colony. London, 1876.
Afr 8687.143 Broome, F.N. Not the whole truth. Pietermaritzburg, 1962.
Afr 6048.2 Broomfield, Gerald Webb. Colour conflict; race relations in Africa. London, 1943.
Afr 698.68 Broomfield, S.S. Kachalola, or The early life and adventures of Sidney Spencer Broomfield. London, 1930.
Afr 5190.2 Brosselard-Faidherbe, H. Casamance et Mellacorée. Paris, 1892.
Afr 2748.82.5 Brosselard-Faidherbe, H. Les deux missions Flatters. 2e ed. Paris, 1889.
Afr 2748.82.4 Brosselard-Faidherbe, H. Voyage de la mission Flatters au pays des Touareg Azdjers. Paris, 1883.
Afr 8846.32 Broster, Joan A. Red blanket valley. Johannesburg, 1967.
Afr 590.46.3 Brougham And Vaux, H. Brougham, 1st Baron. A concise statement of the question regarding the abolition of the slave trade. 2d ed. London, 1804.
Afr 8369.61.5 Broughton, M. Press and politics of South Africa. Cape Town, 1961.
Afr 2308.12 Broughton. Six years residence in Algiers. London, 1839.
Afr 1830.40.10F Broussard, M.E.A. Les carreaux de faience peints dans l'Afrique du nord. Paris, 1930.
Afr 5405.109.5 Brousseau, G. Souvenirs de la mission Savorgnan de Brazza. Paris, 1925.
Afr 1270.5 Broutz, Charles. Victory across French North Africa. Alger, 1943.
Afr 8230.7 Brouwer, W. Paul Kruger. Amsterdam, 1900.
Afr 8670.5 Brown, A.S. South Africa. London. 1893+ 48v.
Afr 8678.283 Brown, Douglas. Against the world. London, 1966.
Afr 8678.392 Brown, Douglas. Against the world. 1st ed. Garden City, 1968.
Afr 8658.55 Brown, G. Personal adventure in South Africa. London, 1855.
Afr 6164.19 Brown, G.N. An active history of Ghana. London, 1961. 2v.
Afr 7461.37 Brown, G.W. The economic history of Liberia. Washington, 1941.
Afr 11239.67.110 Brown, J.A. The assassins. Johannesburg, 1965.
Afr 11237.67.100 Brown, J.A. Seven against the sun. Johannesburg, 1962.
Afr 9400.5 Brown, John. Among the Bantu nomads. London, 1926.
Afr 8659.54.5 Brown, John. The thirsty land. London, 1954.
Afr 1273.966.5 Brown, Leon Carl. State and society in independent North Africa. Washington, 1966.
Afr 4513.39.30 Brown, S.H. Für das Rote Kreuz in äthiopien. Zürich, 1939.
Afr 9488.99 Brown, W.H. On the South African frontier. N.Y., 1899.

Afr 8678.120	Brown, William O. Race relations in the American South and in South Africa. Boston, 1959.
Afr 8678.82	Brown South Africa. (Ziervogel, C.) Cape Town, 1938.
Afr 3275.27	Browne, A. Bonaparte in Egypt. London, 1907.
Afr 8659.05.8	Browne, J.H. Balfour. South Africa. London, 1905.
Afr 6390.86	Browne, Robert. Beyond the Cape of Hope. London, 1965.
Afr 3977.98.6	Browne, W.G. Travels in Africa, Egypt, and Syria, 1792-98. London, 1806.
Afr 3977.98.5	Browne, W.G. Travels in Africa, Egypt, and Syria. London, 1799.
Afr 8152.98	Browning, F.G. Fighting and farming in South Africa. London, 1880.
Afr 8167.5	Brownlee, Charles. A chapter on the Basuto war, a lecture. Lovedale, 1889.
Afr 8658.96	Brownlee, Chas. Reminiscences of Kaffir life. Lovedale, 1896.
Afr 8846.17	Brownlee, F. The Transkeian native territories. n.p., 1923.
Afr 555.15.10	Brownlee, M. The lives and work of South African missionaries. Cape Town, 1952.
Afr 8230.10	Bruce, C.T. The real Kruger and the Transvaal. N.Y., 1900.
Afr 4557.90.14	Bruce, J. Travels, between the years 1765 and 1773. London, 1822?
Afr 4557.90F	Bruce, J. Travels. Edinburgh, 1790. 5v.
Afr 4557.90.2F	Bruce, J. Travels to discover source of the Nile. 2nd ed. v.1-8. Plates and maps. Edinburgh, 1805. 8v.
Afr 4557.90.12	Bruce, J. Travels to discover the source of the Nile. Abridged. Boston, 1798.
Afr 2209.08	Bruchard, H. de. La France au soleil, notes sur l'Algérie. Paris, 1908.
Afr 5406.218	Bruel, Georges. L'Afrique équatoriale française. Paris, 1918.
Afr 5406.230	Bruel, Georges. L'Afrique équatoriale française (A.E.F.). Paris, 1930.
Afr 5401.5	Bruel, Georges. Bibliographie de l'Afrique équatoriale française. Paris, 1914.
Afr 5406.218.5	Bruel, Georges. La France équatoriale africaine. Paris, 1935.
Afr 825.5	Bruel, Georges. Notes géographiques sur le bassin de l'Ogooue. Paris, 1911.
Afr 1555.3.15	Brugmans, H. Pantersprong. 's-Gravenhage, 1933.
Afr 3978.64	Brugsch, H.K.F. Aus dem Orient. (Mainly Egypt). Berlin, 1864.
Afr 3978.55	Brugsch-Bey, H. Reiseberichte aus Ägypten. Leipzig, 1855.
Afr 30.14	Brummelkamp, Jacob. Modern Africa. Utrecht, 1966.
Afr 698.38	Brun, C. De redding der bemanning van het...nijverheid. Rotterdam, 1838.
Afr 635.65.5	Brun mans Africa. (Tandberg, Olof G.) Stockholm, 1968.
Afr 5480.194	Brunache, Paul. Le centre de l'Afrique. Paris, 1894.
Afr 575.22	Brunel, René. Essai sur la confrérie religieuse des Aissaoua au Maroc. Thèse. Paris, 1926.
Afr 1868.47	Brunet, Jean B. La question algerienne. Paris, 1847.
Afr 5385.7	Brunet, L. Dahomey et dépendances. Paris, 1901.
Afr 5548.95.3	Brunet, L. La France à Madagascar. 2e ed. Paris, 1895.
Afr 5635.5	Brunet, L. L'oeuvre de la France à Madagascar. Paris, 1903.
Afr 5585.15	Brunet, Louis. La France à Madagascar, 1815-1895. Paris, 1895.
Afr 115.7F	Brunet, P. Les explorateurs de l'Afrique. Tours, 1889.
Afr 1258.80	Brunialti, A. Algeria, Tunisia e Tripolitania. Milan, 1881.
Afr 1733.5.10	Brunot, Louis. La mer dans les traditions et les industries indigenes a Rabat et Sale. Paris, 1920.
Afr 2482.10	Brunschvig, R. La Berbèrie orientale sous les Hafsides. Paris, 1940-47. 2v.
Afr 200.17	Brunschwig, H. L'avénement de l'Afrique noire du XIX siècle à nos jours. Paris, 1963.
Afr 8325.15	The brunt of the war (refugee camps). (Hobhouse, Emily.) London, 1902.
Afr 4559.36.20	Brusati, G.C. Etiopia, studio geografico-economico. Milano, 1936.
Afr 13340.13.700	Brush fire. (Tchicaya U Tamsi, Gerald Felix.) Ibadan, 1964.
Afr 7900.5	Brussels. Institut Royal Colonial Belge. Biographie coloniale belge. 1,1948+ 5v.
Afr 7812.256.5	Brussels. Université Libre. Vers la promotion de l'économie indigène. Bruxelles, 1956.
Afr 7812.263	Brussels. Université Libre. Centre d'Etude des Questions Economiques Africaines. Le revenu des populations indigènes (du Congo-Léopoldville). Bruxelles, 1963.
Afr 7812.263.1	Brussels. Université Libre. Centre d'Etudes des Questions Economiques Africaines. Le revenu des populations indigènes du Congo-Léopoldville. Etude élaborée par le Groupe de l'économie africaine. Bruxelles, 1963.
Afr 6927.8	Brutal mandate. (Lowenstein, Allard K.) N.Y., 1962.
Afr 11240.89.100	Brutus, Dennis. Letters to Martha, and other poems from a South African prison. London, 1969.
Afr 11240.5	Brutus, Dennis. Sirens, knuckles, boots. Ibadan, 1963.
Afr 2608.95.8	Bruun, D. Cave dwellers of southern Tunisia. London, 1898.
Afr 2208.93.10	Bruun, Daniel. Algier og Sahara. Billeder fra nomade- og krigerlivet. Kjøbenhavn, 1893.
Afr 8676.45	Bruwer, A.J. South Africa. Johannesburg, 1945.
Afr 8678.155	Bruwer, J.P. Die Bantö van Suid-Africa. Johannesburg, 1957.
Afr 8678.155.2	Bruwer, J.P. Die Bantoe van Suid-Africa. Johannesburg, 1963.
Afr 6979.61	Bruwer, Johannes Petrus. Ons mandaat: Suidwes-Afrika. Johannesburg, 1961.
Afr 6919.66	Bruwer, Johannes Petrus. South West Africa, the disputed land. Capetown, 1966.
Afr 210.61.35	Bryan, G. McLeod. Whither Africa. Richmond, 1961.
Afr 6283.12	Bryan, K.J. Nigeria, guidebooks. Zaria, 1960. 3 pam.
Afr 630.63	Bryant, A.T. Bantu origins. Cape Town, 1963.
Afr 9047.36	Bryant, A.T. A history of the Zulu and neighboring tribes. Cape Town, 1964.
Afr 9045.10.1	Bryant, Alfred T. Olden times in Zululand and Natal. Capetown, 1965.
Afr 9045.10	Bryant, Alfred T. Olden times in Zululand and Natal. London, 1929.
Afr 9047.37	Bryant, Alfred T. Zulu medicine and medicine-men. Cape Town, 1966.
Afr 8279.00A	Bryce, J. Briton and Boer. N.Y., 1900.
Afr 8279.00.2	Bryce, J. Briton and Boer. New ed. N.Y., 1900.
Afr 8088.97.3	Bryce, James. Impressions of South Africa. London, 1899.
Afr 8088.97A	Bryce, James. Impressions of South Africa. N.Y., 1897.
Afr 8088.97.2	Bryce, James. Impressions of South Africa. N.Y., 1898.
Afr 8088.97.4A	Bryce, James. Impressions of South Africa. N.Y., 1900.
Afr 9388.93.3	Bryden, H.A. Gun and camera in South Africa. London, 1893.
Afr 8089.04	Bryden, H.A. A history of South Africa. Edinburgh, 1904.
Afr 8808.89	Bryden, H.A. Kloof and Karoo...in Cape colony. London, 1889.
Afr 210.63.25A	Brzezinski, Z.K. Africa and the communist world. Stanford, Calif., 1963.
Afr 7580.14	Buccianto, G. Il Congo. Milano, 1963.
Afr 8340.5	Buchan, J. The African colony. Edinburgh, 1903.
Afr 3705.12	Buchan, John. Gordon at Khartoum. Edinburgh, 1934.
Afr 6780.15	Buchanan, A. Three years of war in East Africa. London, 1919.
Afr 2780.5	Buchanan, Angus. Exploration of Air. London, 1921.
Afr 2749.22.10	Buchanan, Angus. Sahara. London, 1926.
Afr 8828.85	Buchanan, J. The Shire Highlands. Edinburgh, 1885.
Afr 6277.15	Buchanan, K.M. Land and people in Nigeria. London, 1955.
Afr 2030.463.15	Buchard, R. Organisation armée secrète, fév. 14-déc. 1961. Paris, 1963.
Afr 678.80	Buchholz, R. Reisen in West Afrika. Leipzig, 1880.
Afr 4969.59	Buchholzer, John. The Horn of Africa. London, 1959.
Afr 45.62.5	Buchmann, J. L'Afrique noire indépendante. Paris, 1962.
Afr 3675.3	Buchta, R. Der Sudan. Leipzig, 1888.
Afr 609.30.15	Buckley, W. Big game hunting in Central Africa. London, 1930.
Afr 4259.28	Budge, E.A. A history of Ethiopia, Nubia and Abyssinia. London, 1928. 2v.
Afr 3990.1	Budge, E.A.W. Cook's handbook. Egypt and the sudan. London, 1906.
Afr 3990.1.7	Budge, E.A.W. Cook's handbook. Egypt and the sudan. 4th ed. Suppl. 1925. London, 1921-25.
Afr 3675.4	Budge, E.A.W. The Egyptian Sudan. London, 1907. 2v.
Afr 3978.93	Budge, E.A.W. The Nile. London, 1893.
Afr 3978.97	Budge, E.A.W. The Nile. 5th ed. London, 1897.
Afr 3978.93.15	Budge, E.A.W. The Nile. 7th. ed. London, 1901.
Afr 3979.10.8A	Budge, E.A.W. The Nile. 11th ed. London, 1910.
Afr 3979.10.9	Budge, E.A.W. The Nile. 12th ed. London, 1912.
Afr Doc 3609.5	Budget; background information. (Malawi. National Statistical Office.) Zomba. 1966
Afr Doc 7509.5	Budget. (Cameroon.) Yaoundé. 1961+ 2v.
Afr Doc 1809.10	Budget. (Ghana. Ministry of Finance.) Accra. 1963+
Afr Doc 3209.5	Budget. (Kenya. Ministry for Finance and Development.) Nairobi. 1959+
Afr Doc 7409.5	Budget de développement. (Gabon. Ministère d'état chargé de l'économie nationale, du plan et des mines.) 1964+
Afr Doc 7209.44	Budget de l'état. (Central African Republic.) 1959+ 8v.
Afr Doc 6809.2F	Budget d'état. (Mali. Ministère des Finances et du Commerce.) Bamako. 1962+
Afr 3994.891F	Budget du gouvernement égyptien. (Egypt. Ministère des Finances.) Le Caire. 1909+
Afr 2224.25	Le budget et le fisc algériens. Thèse. (Common, Jacques.) Paris, 1929.
Afr 5402.5F	Budget général. (French Equatorial Africa. Direction des Finances.) 1948+ 2v.
Afr Doc 5609.5	Budget général de l'état. (Malagasy Republic. Ministère des Finances et du Commerce.) Tananarive. 1964+
Afr 5388.5F	Budget national. (Dahomey.)
Afr Doc 6609.5F	Budget national. (Dahomey.) 1960+
Afr Doc 7709.3F	Budget ordinaire. (Congo. Service du Budget-Contrôle.) 1966+
Afr Doc 1409.3F	Budget report. (United Arab Republic. Ministry of Treasury.) Cairo. 1961+
Afr 2224.922.2	Le budget spécial de l'Algérie. (Capot de Quissac.) Paris, 1922.
Afr 2224.922	Le budget spécial de l'Algérie. Thèse. (Capot de Quissac.) Paris, 1922.
Afr Doc 2319.15	Budget speech. (Nigeria. Federal Ministry of Finance.) Lagos? 1962+
Afr Doc 1709.5	Budget speech. (Sierra Leone.) Freetown. 1962+
Afr Doc 3309.5	Budget speech delivered in the National Assembly by the Minister of Finance. (Uganda. Ministry of Finance.) Entebbe. 1963+
Afr Doc 1809.15	Budget statement. (Ghana. Ministry of Finance.) Accra. 1963+
Afr Doc 3609.20	Budget statement. (Malawi. Ministry of Finance.) Zomba. 3,1967+
Afr Doc 3809.15F	Budget statements by the minister of Finance. (Rhodesia, Southern.) Salisbury? 1964+
Afr Doc 3409.44	Budget survey. (Tanganyika.) 1956-1957
Afr 2624.912	Le budget tunisien. (Sala, R.) Paris, 1912.
Afr 5448.15.10	Les budgets des ménages africains a Pointe-Noire, 1958-1959. (France. Ministére de la Coopération.) Paris, 1962.
Afr 5183.957	Budgets familiaux africains. (Mersadier, Yvon.) St. Louis du Sénégal, 1957.
Afr 6739.256	Budgets familiaux des planteurs de Cacao au Cameroun. (Binet, Jacques.) Paris, 1956.
Afr 5343.5	Les budgets familiaux des salariés africains en Abidjan. (Ivory Coast. Service de la Statistique Générale et de la Mécanographie.) Paris, 1958.
NEDL Afr 108.89	Buel, J.W. Heroes of the dark continent and How Stanley found Emin Pasha. Philadelphia, 1889.
Afr 6333.28	Buell, R.L. The destiny of East Africa. N.Y., 1928.
Afr 210.28A	Buell, Raymond Lesley. The native problem in Africa. N.Y., 1928. 2v.
Afr 210.28.2	Buell, Raymond Leslie. The native problem in Africa. London, 1965. 2v.
Afr 1583.9	Buelow, J. von. Marocco Deutsch. Berlin, 1911.
Afr 5748.83.10	Buet, Charles. Madagascar, la reine des iles africaines. Paris, 1883.
Afr 5748.84.10	Buet, Charles. Six mois à Madagascar. Paris, 1884.
Afr 8657.11F	Buetner, Johan Daniel. Beschrijving van Cabo de Goede Hoop en Rio de la Goa. Pietermaritzburg, 1960.
Afr 7458.90	Buettikofer, J. Reisebilder aus Liberia. Leiden, 1890. 2v.
Afr 530.13	Buettner, Kurt. Die Anfänge der deutschen Kolonial-Politik in Ostafrika. Berlin, 1961.
Afr 1608.10	Buffa, J. Travels through the empire of Morocco. London, 1810.
Afr 6542.16.10	Buganda. Planning Commission. The economic development of kingdom of Buganda. Kampala, 1965.
Afr 6497.18A	Buganda and British overrule. (Low, D.A.) London, 1960.
Afr 2260.7	Bugeaud, M. De l'établissement de légions de colons. Paris, 1838.
Afr 1838.1	Bugeaud. L'Algérie, des moyens de conserver cette conquête. Paris, 1842.

Afr 1990.30   Bugeaud de la Piconnerie, T.R. Le peuplement français de l'Algérie. Tunis, 1934.

Afr 1965.4.10   Bugeaud et l'Algérie. (Azan, Paul.) Paris, 1930.

Afr 3986.960.10   Bughdadi, A. Address on the five year plan. Cairo, 1960.

Afr 6291.32   Buhler, Jean. Tuez-les tous. Paris, 1968.

Afr 545.21   Buhlman, Walbert. Afrika. Mainz, 1963.

Afr 6780.18   Buhrer, J. L'Afrique orientale allemande et la guerre. Paris, 1922.

Afr 44622.89.100   al-Buhry, Hemed Abdallah. Utenzi wa AbdirRahmani na Sufiyani. Dar es Salaam, 1961.

Afr 44622.89.120   al-Buhry, Hemed Abdallah. Utenzi wa Seyyidna Huseni bin Ali. Dar es Salaam, 1965.

Afr 44622.89.122   al-Buhry, Hemed Abdallah. Utenzi wa Seyyidna Huseni bin Ali. Dar es Salaam, 1965.

Afr 44622.89.112   al-Buhry, Hemed Abdallah. Utenzi wa vita vya wadachi kutamalaki mrima 1307 A.H. 2. ed. Dar es Salaam, 1960.

Afr 550.57   Builders of a new Africa. (Weeks, Nan F.) Nashville, 1944.

Afr 6275.85   Building for the future in Nigeria. (Taylor Woodrow, ltd.) London, 1960.

Afr 9699.66.10   The building industry and the First National Development Plan. (Zambia. Office of National Development and Planning.) Lusaka, 1967.

Afr 200.18   The building of modern Africa. (Rooney, Douglas David.) London, 1966.

Afr 200.18.2   The building of modern Africa. 2nd ed. (Rooney, Douglas David.) London, 1967.

Afr 8288.99F   Buitengewone staat-courant 1899-00. Pretoria, 1899-00.

Afr 8289.01.7   Bujac, E. Precis de...campagnes contemporaines d'Afrique centrale. Paris, 1901.

Afr 3700.6   Bujac, E. Précis de quelques campagnes contemporaines. Pt. III - Egypte et Soudan. Paris, 1899.

Afr 5968.2   Los Bujeba. (Veciana Vilaldach, Antonio de.) Madrid, 1956.

Afr 718.2.115   Bula Matari, Stanley, conqueror of a continent. (Wassermann, J.) N.Y., 1933.

Afr 718.2.120   Bula Matari. (Wassermann, J.) Berlin, 1932.

Afr 7073.2   Bulam Association. Report of the institution...Dec. 11, 1792. London, 1792.

Afr 4392.2   Bulatovitch, A.K. S voiskami Menelika II. St. Petersburg, 1900.

Afr 8250.40   Bulawayo, South Africa. Central African Rhodes Centenary Exhibition. The story of Cecil Rhodes. Bulawayo, 1953.

Afr 9510.12   Bulawayo, Southern Rhodesia. City Council. The city of Bulawayo. 2. ed. Cape Town, 1957.

Afr 9520.10   Bulawayo: historic battleground of Rhodesia. (Ransford, Oliver.) Cape Town, 1968.

Afr 7815.39   Bulck, Gaston van. Orthographie des noms ethniques au Congo belge. Bruxelles, 1954.

Afr 9439.67.5   Bull, Theodore. Rhodesia: crisis of color. Chicago, 1968.

Afr 9439.67   Bull, Theodore. Rhodesian perspective. London, 1967.

Afr 1259.13A   Bullard, A. The Barbary coast. N.Y., 1913.

Afr 8300.9   Buller' campaign. (Knox, E.B.) London, 1902.

Afr 8300.14   Buller' campaign. (Symons, J.) London, 1963.

Afr 6125.12   Bulletin, the journal of the Sierra Leone Geographical Association. Freetown. 9,1965+

Afr 1.88   Bulletin. (Aberdeen. University. African Studies Group.) Aberdeen. 1,1967+

Afr 5501.3   Bulletin. (Academie Malgache.) Tananarivo. 1,1902+ 20v.

Afr 1.42   Bulletin. (Afrika-Institut, Pretoria.) Pretoria. 2,1962+ 7v.

Afr 10104.5F   Bulletin. (Association for African Literature in English.) Freetown. 2,1965+

Afr 6700.4   Bulletin. (Association Française pour les Recherches et Études Camerounaises.) Bordeaux. 1,1965+

Afr Doc 7709.305F   Bulletin. (Banque Nationale du Congo.) Kinhasa. 7,1968+

Afr 5000.5.3   Bulletin. (French West Africa. Comité d'Etudes Historiques et Scientifiques.) 1919+ 19v.

Afr 6150.32.15   Bulletin. (Ghana Geographical Association.) Kumasi.

Afr 9.18   Bulletin. (Institut d'Enseignement Supérieur du Bénin, Lomé.) Lomé. 8,1969+

Afr 1309.1   Bulletin. (Institut des Hautes Études Marocaines.) Paris. 1,1920+

Afr 9.4   Bulletin. (Institut Français d'Afrique Noire.) Paris. 1,1939+ 12v.

Afr 3005.7   Bulletin. (London. Egyptian Education Bureau.)

Afr 6392.39F   Bulletin. (Nairobi. University College. Institute for Development Studies. Social Science Division.) Nairobi. 1,1966+

Afr 1818.2   Bulletin. (Réunion d'Etudes Algériennes.) Paris.

Afr 1819.1   Bulletin. (Société de Géographie d'Alger et de l'Afrique du Nord.) Alger. 1,1896+ 32v.

Afr 2368.5   Bulletin. (Société Historique et Géographique de la Région de Sétif.) Sétif.

Afr 19.20   Bulletin. (Society for African Church History.) London. 2,1965+

Afr 9625.40   Bulletin. (Zambia. University. Institute of Social Research.) 1,1966+

Afr 9.4.2   Bulletin. Sér. A. Sciences naturelles. (Institut Français d'Afrique Noire.) Paris. 16,1954+ 28v.

Afr 9.4.3   Bulletin. Sér. B. Sciences humaines. (Institut Français d'Afrique Noire.) Paris. 16,1954+ 16v.

Afr 9.4.4   Bulletin. Tables. (Institut Français d'Afrique Noire.) Dakar. 1,1952+

Afr 1819.3   Bulletin de correspondance africaine. (Algiers. Ecole Supérieure des Lettres d'Alger.) Alger. 1882+ 4v.

Afr 1826.33   Bulletin de documentation. (France. Ministère d'Etat Chargé des Affaires Algériennes.) Paris. 11-44,1961-1965

Afr Doc 7507.5.2   Bulletin de la statistique general. Supplement. (Cameroon. Service de la Statistique Générale et de la Mécanographie.) 1,1958+

Afr 2700.7   Bulletin de liaison saharienne. Alger. 33,1959+ 2v.

Afr Doc 7907.5   Bulletin de statistique. (Burundi. Institut Rundi des Statistiques.) Bujumbura. 1,1966+

Afr Doc 6607.10   Bulletin de statistique. (Dahomey. Service Central de la Statistique et de la Mécanographie.) Cotonou. 2,1965+

Afr Doc 6907.10   Bulletin de statistique. (Niger. Service de la Statistique.) Niamey. 8,1966+

Afr Doc 7807.5   Bulletin de statistique. (Rwanda. Direction de l'Office Général des Statistiques.) Kigali. 1,1964+ 2v.

Afr Doc 6707.2   Bulletin de statistique. (Togoland. Service de la Statistique Générale.) Lomé 7,1964+

Afr Doc 7907.5.5   Bulletin de statistique. Supplement. (Burundi. Institut Rundi des Statistiques.) 1,1966+

Afr Doc 5307.5   Bulletin de statistique generale. Statistiques industrielles. (Algeria. Service de la Statistique Génerale.) 8,1956+

Afr Doc 5307.15   Bulletin de statistiques générales. (Algeria. Direction générale du plan et des études économiques.) Alger. 1967+

Afr Doc 5635.5   Bulletin d'information. (Malagasy Republic. Ministere de l'Equipement et des Communications.) Tananarive. 8,1963+

Afr 19.16   Bulletin d'information. (Société des Africanistes, Paris. Centre de Documentation et d'Information.) Paris. 1-6,1964-1965//

Afr 5430.5   Bulletin d'information. (United Nations. Delegation from the Congo (Brazzaville).)

Afr 1313.2   Bulletin d'information du Maroc. (Morocco. Service Général de l'Information.) Rabat.

Afr 1313.1F   Bulletin d'information et documentation. (Morocco. Service Général de l'Information.) Rabat.

Afr 1814.6   Bulletin d'information NRA. (Nouvelles Realites Algériennes.) Alger. 1,1958+

Afr 2.1   Bulletin du Comite de l'Afrique française. Paris. 1891+ 47v.

Afr 5502.2   Bulletin economique. (Madagascar.) Tananarive. 1923+ 2v.

Afr 1302.2F   Bulletin économique du Maroc. (Morocco.) Rabat. 1,1934+ 4v.

Afr Doc 6607.15   Bulletin économique et statistique. (Dahomey. Direction des Affaires Economiques.) 1961+ 3v.

Afr 5502.2.5   Bulletin economique mensuel. (Madagascar.) Tananarive. 1,1926+

Afr 5050.5   Bulletin mensuel. (French West Africa. Agence Economique.) Paris. 5,1924+ 4v.

Afr 1819.4.6   Bulletin mensuel. (Société Archéologique, Historique et Géographique du Département de Constantine.) Constantine. 35,1930+

Afr Doc 7107.5   Bulletin mensuel de la statistique. (Chad. Service de la Statistique Générale.) Fort-Lamy. 127,1965+

Afr Doc 7507.9   Bulletin mensuel de statistique. (Cameroon. Direction de la Statistique et de la Comptabilité Nationale.) 5,1967+

Afr Doc 7207.5   Bulletin mensuel de statistique. (Central African Republic. Service de la Statistique et de la Conjoncture.) Bangui. 14,1965+

Afr Doc 7407.10   Bulletin mensuel de statistique. (Gabon. Service National de la Statistique.) 5,1963+ 4v.

Afr Doc 6407.3   Bulletin mensuel de statistique. (Ivory Coast. Direction de la Statistique et des Etudes Economiques et Démographiques.) 12,1959+ 3v.

Afr Doc 5607.10   Bulletin mensuel de statistique. (Malagasy Republic. Institut National de la Statistique et de la Recherche Economique.) Tananarive. 64,1961+

Afr Doc 6807.10   Bulletin mensuel de statistique. (Mali. Service de la Statistique Générale et de la Comptabilité Economique Nationale.) Bamako. 1964+

Afr Doc 5207.10   Bulletin mensuel de statistique. (Morocco. Service Central des Statistiques.) 1,1957+

Afr Doc 6507.5   Bulletin mensuel de statistique. (Upper Volta. Ministère du Developpement et du Tourisme.) Ouagadougou. 7,1966+

Afr Doc 7407.10.2   Bulletin mensuel de statistique. Supplement. (Gabon. Service National de la Statistique.) 5,1962+ 2v.

Afr Doc 5207.11   Bulletin mensuel de statistique. Supplement. (Morocco. Service Central des Statistiques.) 1958+

Afr Doc 6407.3.2   Bulletin mensuel de statistique. Supplement trimestriel. Etudes et rapports. (Ivory Coast. Direction de la Statistique et des Etudes Economiques et Démographiques.) 5v.

Afr Doc 7007.5   Bulletin mensuel de statistique de l'Afrique equatoriale française. (French Equatorial Africa. Service de la Statistique Générale.) 4-11,1950-1957 3v.

Afr Doc 5307.10   Bulletin mensuel de statistiques générales. (Algeria. Direction générale du plan et des études économiques.) Alger. 1956-1965

Afr Doc 7307.5   Bulletin mensuel des statistiques. (Congo (Brazzaville). Direction du Service National de la Statistique, des Etudes Démographiques et Economiques.) Brazzaville. 1962+

Afr Doc 7607.3   Bulletin mensuel des statistiques générales du Congo belge et du Ruanda-Urundi. Série speciale. (Congo. Direction de la Statistique.) Leopoldville. 1,1959+

Afr Doc 1408.725   Bulletin mensuel du commerce extérieur de l'Egypte. (Egypt. Customs Administration.) 1899+

Afr Doc 6107.10   Bulletin mensuel statistique. (Mauritania. Ministere de la Planification et du Developpement Rural. Direction de la Statistique.) Nouakchott. 1968

Afr Doc 3709.516F   Bulletin of agricultural statistics. (Zambia. Ministry of Rural Development.) Lusaka. 1969+

Afr 6200.2   Bulletin of rural economics and sociology. Ibadan. 2,1966+

Afr Doc 4307.15   Bulletin of statistics. (South African Bureau of Statistics.) Pretoria. 1,1967+

Afr 2.4F   Bulletin on African affairs. Accra. 2+ 4v.

Afr 1326.18   Bulletin signalétique. (Rabat. Université. Centre Universitaire de la Recherche Scientifique.) Rabat. 1,1963+

Afr 5001.100   Bulletin statistique. (Organisation Commune Africaine et Malgache. Departement des Affaires Economiques, Financieres et des Transports.) Yaounde. 2,1966+

Afr Doc 6207.5   Bulletin statistique bimestriel. (Sénégal. Service de la Statistique Generale.) 3,1959+

Afr Doc 6107.5   Bulletin statistique et economique. (Maurtiania. Service de la Statistique.) Nouakchott. 2,1964+

Afr Doc 6007.5   Bulletin statistique et economique mensuel. (French West Africa. Service des Etudes et Coordination Statistiques et Mécanographiques.) 1955-1959 8v.

Afr Doc 6207.10   Bulletin statistique et économique mensuel. (Sénégal. Service de la Statistique et de la Mécanographie.) 1,1960+

Afr 7503.3   Bulletin trimestriel. (Centre d'Etudes des Problèmes Sociaux Indigènes, Elizabethville, Belgian Congo.) 17,1951+ 17v.

Afr 1018.2   Bulletin trimestriel. (Société de Géographie de la Province d'Oran.) Paris. 7,1887+ 55v.

Afr 6739.5   Bulletin trimestriel d'information. (Cameroon. Ministère des Finances et du Plan. Direction du Plan et de la Coopération Technique.) Yaounde. 4,1964+

Afr 7350.3.3   Bulletins - Liberia. (American Colonization Society.) Washington. 5,1894+

Afr 9614.10   Bulley, Mary Winifred. Kabanza; a story of Africa. Westminster, 1927.

Afr 9502.14   Bullock, C. The Mashona and Matabele. Cape Town, 1950.

Afr 9502.10   Bullock, Charles. The Mashona. Cape Town, 1928.

Afr 9502.25 — Bullock, Charles. Mashona laws and customs. Salisbury, 1913.
Afr 4070.18 — Bulpett, C.W.L. A picnic party in wildest Africa. London, 1907.
Afr 8155.10 — Bulpin, J. Victor. Shakas country. 3d ed. Cape Town, 1956. 2v.
Afr 6390.50F — Bulpin, T.V. East Africa and the islands. Cape Town, 1956.
Afr 9093.20 — Bulpin, T.V. The golden republic. Cape Town, 1953.
Afr 9093.20.5 — Bulpin, T.V. Storm over the Transvaal. 2. ed. Cape Town, 1955.
Afr 11246.51.100 — Bulpin, Thomas U. The white whirlwind. Johannesburg, 1961.
Afr 8817.2 — Bulpin, Thomas V. The Cape province. Cape Town, 1960.
Afr 9170.126.2 — Bulpin, Thomas Victor. The ivory trail. 2nd ed. Capetown, 1967.
Afr 8210.20 — Bulpin, Thomas Victor. Lost rails of the Transvaal. Johannesburg, 1965.
Afr 8969.66 — Bulpin, Thomas Victor. Natal and the Zulu country. Cape Town, 1966.
Afr 9606.2 — Bulpin, Thomas Victor. Rhodesia and Nyasaland. Cape Town, 1960.
Afr 9439.65.5 — Bulpin, Thomas Victor. To the banks of the Zambezi. Johannesburg, 1965.
Afr 9748.193 — Bulpin, Thomas Victor. Trail of the copper king. Cape Town, 1959.
Afr 7808.99.5 — Buls, Charles. Croquis congolais. Bruxelles, 1899.
Afr 8808.48 — Bunbury, C.J.F. Journal of a residence at Cape of Good Hope. London, 1848.
Afr 6738.48 — Die Bundes-Republik Kamerun. (Brendl, Oskar.) Hagen, 1965.
Afr 8369.64 — Bunting, B.P. The rise of the South African Reich. Harmondsworth, 1964.
Afr 8369.64.1 — Bunting, B.P. The rise of the South African Reich. Harmondsworth, 1969.
Afr 6540.16 — Bunyord, an African kingdom. (Beattie, John.) N.Y., 1960.
Afr 6540.16.2 — Bunyord, an African kingdom. (Beattie, John.) N.Y., 1964.
Afr 8252.341.40 — Burbidge, W. Frank. Field Marshal Smuts. Bognor Regis, 1943.
Afr 8658.22 — Burchell, W.J. Travels in...southern Africa. London, 1822. 2v.
Afr 8658.22.5 — Burchell, W.J. Travels in the interior of southern Africa. London, 1953. 2v.
Afr 3978.30F — Burckhardt, J.L. Manners and customs of modern Egyptians. London, 1830.
Afr 4060.4 — Burckhardt, J.L. Travels in Nubia. London, 1819.
Afr 4060.4.2 — Burckhardt, J.L. Travels in Nubia. 2d ed. London, 1822.
Afr 1713.12F — Burckhardt, Titus. Fes, Stadt des Islam. Alten, 1960.
Afr 6275.12 — Burda, A. Am Niger und Benue. Leipzig, 1886.
Afr 2208.92 — Burdeau, A. L'Algérie en 1891. Paris, 1892.
Afr 710.72 — Burden of empire. (Gann, Lewis H.) N.Y., 1967.
Afr 8325.55 — Burdett-Coretts, W. The sick and wounded in South Africa. London, 1900.
Afr 5048.5 — Burdo, A. Les Arabs dans l'Afrique centrale. Paris, 1885.
Afr 810.19 — Burdo, Adolphe. The Niger and the Benueh. London, 1880.
Afr 718.2.93 — Burdo, Adolphe. Stanley, sa vie, ses voyages et ses aventures. Paris, 1889.
Afr 5343.30 — Bureau pour le Developpement de la Production Agricole outre-mer. Etude générale de la région de Man. Paris, 196-? 6v.
Afr 5240.12 — Bureau pour le Développement de la Production Agricole Outre-Mer. La modernisation rurale dans la haute-vallée du Niger. Paris, 1961? 3v.
Afr 3040.76 — Bureaucracy and society in modern Egypt. (Berger, Morroe.) Princeton, 1957.
Afr 1608.08 — Burel, Antoine. La mission du capitaine Burel au Maroc en 1808. Paris, 1953.
Afr 8289.02.28 — Die Buren in der Kap Kolonie im Kriege mit England. (Schowalter, A.) München, 1902.
Afr 8278.97.3 — Die Buren und Jamesons Einfall. (Hofmeyr, N.J.) Bremen, 1897.
Afr 8325.37F — Der Burenkrieg. (Thoma, Ludwig.) München, 1900.
Afr 1990.10 — Buret, Eugène. Question d'Afrique. Paris, 1842.
Afr 8678.175 — Burger, Jan. The gulf between. Cape Town, 1960.
Afr 6390.53 — Burger, John F. My forty years in Africa. London, 1960.
Afr 8252.228.6 — Burger, M.J. General J.B.M. Hertzog. Kaapstad, 1950.
Afr 8252.228.5 — Burger, M.J. General J.B.M. Hertzog in Batilio. Kaapstad, 1953.
Htn — Afr 7350.3.23* — Burgess, E. Address to the American Society for Colonizing the Free People of Colour of the U.S. Washington, 1818.
Afr 11248.76.100 — Burke, Colin. Elephant across border: a novel. London, 1968.
Afr 210.64.5 — Burke, Fred. Africa's quest for order. Englewood Cliffs, 1964.
Afr 6542.17 — Burke, Fred. Local government and politics in Uganda. Syracuse, 1964.
Afr 609.69.10 — Burke, Fred George. Africa; selected readings. N.Y., 1969.
Afr 6881.265 — Burke, Fred George. Tanganyika. 1st ed. Syracuse, N.Y., 1965.
Afr 3708.5 — Burleigh, B. Desert warfare, being the chronicle of the Eastern Soudan campaign. London, 1884.
Afr 3735.3 — Burleigh, B. Khartoum campaign, 1898. London, 1899.
Afr 8300.6 — Burleigh, B. The Natal campaign. London, 1900.
Afr 3735.2 — Burleigh, B. Sirdar and Khalifa. London, 1898.
Afr 3735.2.5 — Burleigh, B. Sirdar and Khalifa. 3rd ed. London, 1898.
Afr 5635.13 — Burleigh, B. Two campaigns, Madagascar and Ashantee. London, 1896.
Afr 8668.12 — Burman, José. A peak to climb;...mountaineering. Cape Town, 1966.
Afr 8835.21 — Burman, Jose. Peninsula profile, a guide to the fairest cape. Johannesburg, 1963.
Afr 8809.62.5 — Burman, Jose. Safe to the sea. Kaapstad, 1962.
Afr 8809.63 — Burman, Jose. So high the road, mountain passes of the western Cape. Cape Town, 1963.
Afr 8095.90 — Burman, José. Who really discovered South Africa? Cape Town, 1969.
Afr 4158.5 — Burmester, O.H.E. A guide to the monasteries of the Wadi Natrun. Le Caire, 1954.
Afr 4559.34.20 — Burners of men, modern Ethiopia. (Griaule, M.) Philadelphia, 1935.

Afr 8292.50 — Burnett, C. The 18th Hussars in South Africa. Winchester, Eng., 1905.
Afr 10675.47.100 — Burning grass. (Ekwensi, Cyprian.) London, 1962.
Afr 11572.50.140 — The burning man. (Millin, S.G.(L).) London, 1952.
Afr 628.248 — Burns, A. Colour prejudice. London, 1948.
Afr 6214.8 — Burns, Alan C. History of Nigeria. London, 1929.
Afr 6214.8.18 — Burns, Alan C. History of Nigeria. London, 1958.
Afr 6214.8.10 — Burns, Alan C. History of Nigeria. 4th ed. London, 1948.
Afr 6214.8.15 — Burns, Alan C. History of Nigeria. 5th ed. London, 1955.
Afr 6214.8.19 — Burns, Alan C. History of Nigeria. 6th ed. London, 1964.
Afr 6214.8.20 — Burns, Alan C. History of Nigeria. 7th ed. London, 1969.
Afr 4513.35.55 — Burns, Emile. Abyssinia and Italy. London, 1935.
Afr 10575.82.110 — The burnt-out marriage. (Easmon, R. Sarif.) London, 1967.
Afr 8676.3 — Buro vir marknavorsing. (South Africa. University, Pretoria.-Bureau of Market Research.) Pretoria, 1963.
Afr 2030.465 — Buron, Robert. Carnets politiques de la guerre d'Algérie. Paris 1965.
Afr 7175.27 — Burr, Malcolm. A fossicker in Angola. London, 1933.
Afr 550.8.45 — Burridge, William. Destiny Africa, Cardinal Lavigerie and the making of the White Fathers. London, 1966.
Afr 9523.275 — Burrows, Edmund Hartford. The moodies of Melsetter. Cape Town, 1954.
Afr 7568.5 — Burrows, G. The curse of Central Africa. London, 1903.
Afr 7808.98 — Burrows, G. The land of the pigmies. London, 1898.
Afr 7808.98.2 — Burrows, G. The land of the pigmies. N.Y., 1898.
Afr 510.25F — Burthe d'Annelet, Anarie. A travers l'Afrique française. Paris, 1932. 2v.
Afr 510.26F — Burthe d'Annelet, Anarie. A travers l'Afrique française. Paris, 1939. 2v.
Afr 8095.70 — Burton, Alfred. Sparks from the border anvil. King Williams Town, 1950.
Afr 6738.2A — Burton, R.F. Abeokuta and the Camaroons mountains. London, 1863.
Afr 4612.1 — Burton, R.F. First-footsteps...or Exploration of Harrar. London, 1856.
Afr 4612.1.7 — Burton, R.F. First footsteps in East Africa. London, 1966.
Afr 4612.1.6 — Burton, R.F. First footsteps in East Africa. N.Y., 1966.
Afr 4612.1.5 — Burton, R.F. First footsteps in East Africa. Memorial ed. London, 1894. 2v.
Afr 725.2 — Burton, R.F. The lake regions of central Africa. London, 1860. 2v.
Afr 5385.1 — Burton, R.F. A mission to Gelele, king of Dahome, with notices. v.1-2. London, 1864. 2v.
Afr 5385.2 — Burton, R.F. Mission to Gelele, king of Dahome. v.1. 2d ed. London, 1864.
Afr 5385.2.5 — Burton, R.F. A mission to Gelele. London, 1893. 2v.
Afr 5385.2.10 — Burton, R.F. A mission to Gelele. London, 1966. 2v.
NEDL — Afr 4095.7 — Burton, R.F. The Nile basin. London, 1864.
Afr 6192.13 — Burton, R.F. To the Gold Coast for gold. London, 1883. 2v.
Afr 678.63 — Burton, R.F. Wanderings in West Africa from Liverpool. London, 1863. 2v.
Afr 5406.176 — Burton, Richard F. Two trips to gorilla land. London, 1876. 4v.
Afr 6585.4 — Burton, Richard Francis. Zanzibar; city, island, and coast. N.Y., 1967. 2v.
Afr Doc 7907.5 — Burundi. Institut Rundi des Statistiques. Bulletin de statistique. Bujumbura. 1,1966+
Afr Doc 7907.5.5 — Burundi. Institut Rundi des Statistiques. Bulletin de statistique. Supplement. 1,1966+
Afr Doc 7909.505F — Burundi. Service des Statistiques et de la Planification. Statistiques de l'enseignement. 1966+
Afr 10304.5 — Dusara. Nairobi. 1,1968+
Afr 3990.4.2 — Busch, M. Ägypten, Reisenhandbuch. 2.Aufl. Triest, 1870.
Afr 9400.10 — Die Buschmänner der Kalahari. (Passarge, S.) Berlin, 1907.
Afr 6879.59 — Bush and boma. (Cairns, John C.) London, 1959.
Afr 4559.64.5 — Bush och lustgaard. Stockholm, 1964.
Afr 8687.175 — Bushman, whale and dinosaur. (Rose, Walter.) Cape Town, 1961.
Afr 50.40 — Busia, Kafi A. The challenge of Africa. N.Y., 1962.
Afr 6160.45 — Busia, Kofi A. The position of the chief in the modern political system of Ashanti. London, 1968.
Afr 40.67 — Busia, Kofi Abrefa. Africa in search of democracy. N.Y., 1967.
Afr 6300.10.5 — Business and economy of Central and East Africa. Ndola. 1-2,1966-1967// 2v.
Afr 4559.57 — Busk, Douglas L. The fountain of the sun. London, 1957.
Afr 8678.86 — Buskes, Johannes Jacobus. South Africa's apartheid policy - unacceptable. Heidelberg, 1956.
Afr 1408.2.5 — Busnot, F.D. Histoire du regne de mouley Ismael. Rouen, 1714.
Afr 1408.2.10 — Busnot, F.D. Récits d'aventures au temps de Louis XIV. Paris, 1928.
Afr 4375.3 — Bussidon, C. Abyssinie et Angleterre (Theodoros). Paris, 1888.
Afr 6310.39 — Bustin, Edouard. La décentralisation administrative et l'évolution des structures. Liège, 1958.
Afr 50.46 — Bustin, Edouard. Guide des partis politiques africains. Bruxelles, 1962.
Afr 3979.11 — Butcher, E.L. Egypt as we knew it. London, 1911.
Afr 3979.10.20 — Butcher, E.L. Things seen in Egypt. London, 1923.
Afr 3125.5 — Butcher, G. The Arab conquest of Egypt. Oxford, 1902.
Afr 11051.7 — Butler, A.J. A book of South African verse. London, 1959.
Afr 11249.86.130 — Butler, Guy. Cape Charade. Cape Town, 1968. 2v.
Afr 11249.86.120 — Butler, Guy. The dam. Cape Town, 1953.
Afr 11249.86.100 — Butler, Guy. South of the Zambesi, poems from South Africa. N.Y., 1966.
Afr 11249.86.110 — Butler, Guy. Stranger to Europe; poems, 1939-1949. Capetown, 1952.
— Butler, Guy. Stranger to Europe, with additional poems. Capetown, 1960.
Afr 9161.7 — Butler, J.E. Native races and the war. London, 1900.
Afr 8283.28 — Butler, Jeffrey. The Liberal Party and the Jameson Raid. Oxford, 1968.

Afr 6170.9	Butler, W.F. Akim-foo, the history of a failure. London, 1876.
Afr 3708.4	Butler, W.F. The campaign of the Cataracts. London, 1887.
Afr 8225.7	Butler, W.F. Life of Sir George Pomeroy-Colley. London, 1899.
Afr 9689.8	Butt, G.E. My travels in north west Rhodesia. London, 1908.
Afr 6138.26	Butt-Thompson, F.W. Sierra Leone in history and tradition. London, 1926.
Afr 8659.30.5	Butterfield, Fred. Passing notes of a visit to the Cape (1930). London, 1930.
Afr 8279.00.27	Buttery, J.A. Why Kruger made war. London, 1900.
Afr 1609.55.5	Buttin, Paul. Le drame du Maroc. Paris, 1955.
Afr 4070.65	Buurri al Lamaab. (Barclay, Harold.) Ithaca, 1964.
Afr 2208.55	Buvry, L. Algerien und seine Zukunft unter französischer Herrschaft. Berlin, 1855.
Afr 630.31	Buxton, Charles R. The race problem in Africa. London, 1931.
Afr 4559.49	Buxton, D.R. Travels in Ethiopia. London, 1949.
Afr 4559.49.5	Buxton, D.R. Travels in Ethiopia. N.Y., 1950.
Afr 4559.49.6	Buxton, D.R. Travels in Ethiopia. N.Y., 1967.
Afr 8252.25	Buxton, Earl. General Botha. London, 1924.
Afr 6333.02	Buxton, Edward North. Two African trips, with notes and suggestions. London, 1902.
Afr 6455.46	Buxton, Mary Aline B. Kenya days. London, 1927.
Afr 2030.460.35	Buy, François. La République algérienne. Paris, 1965.
Afr 6420.77	Bwana drum. (Holman, D.) London, 1964.
Afr 8100.15	By strength of heart. (Kock, Victor de.) Cape Town, 1954.
Afr 6397.10	By the equator's snowy peak. (Crawford, E.M.) London, 1913.
Afr 6397.11	By the equator's snowy peak. 2d ed. (Crawford, E.M.) London, 1914.
Afr 6390.76	By the waters of Africa. (Lorimer, Norma Octavia.) London, 1917.
Afr 2609.06.6	By the waters of Carthage. (Lorimer, Norma.) London, 1906.
Afr 3979.09.10	By the waters of Egypt. (Lorimer, Norma.) N.Y., 1909.
Afr 718.44	By way of the Sahara. (Tweedy, Owen.) London, 1930.
Afr 8688.7	Bydraes tot die genealogie van ou afrikaanse families. (Hoge, J.) Amsterdam, 1958.
Afr 609.62.35	Byford-Jones, N. Africa, journey out of darkness. London, 1962.
Afr 3315.50	Byford-Jones, Wilfred. Oil on troubled waters. London, 1957.
Afr 9073.252	Byron, Lewis. Recollections of an octogenarian. Kloof, 1964.
Afr 9073.797	C.G., a great Natalian; biography of Charles George Smith. (Osborn, Robert F.) Durban, 1966.
Afr 635.75F	C.S.A. Meeting of Specialists on the Basic Psychology of African and Madagascan Populations, Tannarvio, Madagascar, 1959. Recommendations and reports. London, 1959.
Afr 650.2F	C.S.A. Meeting of Specialists on Urbanisation and Its Social Aspects Abidjan, Ivory Coast, 1961. Reports and recommendations. London, 1961.
Afr Doc 3814.15F	C.S.R. [papers]. (Rhodesia (British Colony). Parliament.) Salisbury. 1901+
Afr 679.40.10	Ca da Mosto, A. Viagens. Lisboa, 194-.
Afr 1573.11	Caballero de Puga. Marruecos, politica e interes de España en este imperio. Madrid, 1907.
Afr 1721.5	Cabanas, Rafael. Rasgos fisiograficos y geologicos. Madrid, 1955.
Afr 7580.15	Cabanes, Bernard. Du Congo belge au Katanga. Paris, 1963.
Afr 4513.36.95	Cabiati, A. La conquista dell'impero. Milano, 1936.
Afr 2230.23	Les Cabiles et Boudgie. (Pharaon, J.) Alger, 1835.
Afr 5488.20	Cabot, Jean. Le bassin du moyen Logone. Thèse. Paris, 1965.
Afr Doc 9208.700	Cabotagem. (Mozambique. Direcção Provincial dos Serviços de Estatistica Geral.) Laurenço Marques. 35,1962+
Afr 7065.526.5	Cabral, Amilcar. Revolution in Guinea: an African people's struggle. London, 1969.
Afr 7326.5	Cabral, Augusto. Racas, usos e costumes dos indigenas do districto de Inhambane. Laurenço Marques, 1910.
Afr 1609.24.10	Cabrera Lattore. Magreb-el-aksai. Madrid, 1924.
Afr 7190.18F	O cacau de S. Thomé. Lisboa, 1907.
Afr 4128.9	Caccia Dominioni di Sillavengo, Paolo. Alamein, 1933-1962. 9. ed. Milano, 1965.
Afr 8175.7	Cachet, F.L. De worstelstrijd der transvalers. Amsterdam, 1900.
Afr 678.95	Cadamosto, A. de. Voyages à la côte occidentale d'Afrique. Paris, 1895.
NEDL Afr 7045.5.2	Cadbury, W.A. Labour in Portuguese West Africa. 2d ed. N.Y., 1910.
Afr 7190.32	Cadbury, William A. Os serviças de S. Thomé. Lisboa, 1910.
Afr 725.14	Caddick, Helen. A white woman in central Africa. London, 1900.
Afr 5342.68.2	Cadel, Georges. Noirs et Blances, la lutte contre le racism et le transformation des coutumes africaines. Confances, 1967?
Afr 7100.15	Cadernos culturais. (Sociedade Cultural De Angola.) Luanda.
Afr 8089.66.5	Cadoux, Charles. L'Afrique du Sud. Paris, 1966.
Afr 3986.12F	Cadre du plan quinquennal général. (United Arab Republic.) Le Caire, 1960.
Afr 7815.41	Caeneghem, R. La notion de Dieu chez les Baluba du Kasai. Bruxelles, 1956.
Afr 4513.37.5	Caesar in Abyssinia. (Steer, G.) Boston, 1937.
Afr 530.35.3	Caetano, Marcello. Portugal e a internacionalização dos problemas africanos. 3. ed. Lisboa, 1965.
Afr 4513.59	Caffo, Aventino. Il genio militare nella campagna in Africa orientale. Roma, 1959.
Afr 555.22.7	Caffres and Caffres missions. (Calderwood, H.) London, 1858.
Afr 8678.10.15	Os Cafres, seus usos e costumes. (Gavicho de Lacerda, T.) Lisboa, 1944.
Afr 1333.15	Cagigas, I. Tratados y convenios referentes a Marruecos. Madrid, 1952.
Afr 2608.94	Cagnat. Voyage en Tunisie. Paris, 1894.
Afr 4045.10	Cahiers. (Societe d'Etudes Historiques et Géographiques de l'isthme de Suez.) Le Caire. 1,1955 4v.
Afr 3.32	Cahiers africains. Paris. 1+ 4v.
Afr 1571.17.100	Cahiers Charles de Foucauld. Lyautey. Grenoble, 1954.
Afr 1003.5	Cahiers Charles de Foucauld. Grenoble. 2,1946+ 13v.
Afr 4105.15	Cahiers d'Alexandrie. Alexandrie. 2,1964+
Afr 3.9	Cahiers de l'Afrique et l'Asie. Paris. 1+ 4v.
Afr 5470.5	Cahiers de l'unité. Fort-Lamy. 1,1966+
Afr 2403.5	Cahiers de Tunisie, revue de sciences humaines. Tunis. 5,1957+ 9v.
Afr 3.22	Cahiers d'études africaines. Paris. 1,1960+ 19v.
Afr 3003.2	Cahiers d'histoire égyptienne. Le Caire. 1,1948+ 6v.
Afr 3003.2.5	Cahiers d'histoire égyptienne. Index, ser.1-5 (1948-53). Le Caire, 1954.
Afr 2420.26	Cahiers du C.E.R.E.S. Série démographique. (Tunis (City). Université. Centré d'Etudes et de Recherches Economiques et Sociales.) Tunis. 1,1967+
Afr 2420.25	Cahiers du C.E.R.E.S. Série économique. (Tunis (City). Université. Centre d'Etudes et de Recherches Economiques et Sociales.) Tunis. 1966+
Afr 2420.28	Cahiers du C.E.R.E.S. Série géographique. (Tunis (City). Université. Centre d'Etudes et de Recherches Economiques et Sociales.) Tunis. 1,1968+
Afr 2420.30	Cahiers du C.E.R.E.S. Série linguistique. (Tunis (City). Université. Centre d'Etudes et de Recherches Economiques et Sociales.) Tunis. 1,1968+
Afr 2420.27	Cahiers du C.E.R.E.S. Série sociologique. (Tunis (City). Université. Centre d'Etudes et de Recherches Economiques et Sociales.) Tunis. 1,1968+
Afr 1869.30	Cahiers du centenaire de l'Algerie. (France. Comite National.) Alger, 1930. 2v.
Afr 3.30F	Cahiers économiques et de liaison des comités eurafrique. Paris. 1,1959+ 2v.
Afr 7512.15	Cahiers économiques et sociaux. (Leopoldville. Université Lovanium.) Leopoldville. 3v.
Afr 1555.3.10	Caillaux, J. Agadir. Paris, 1919.
Afr 1333.10	Caille, Jacques. Les accords internationaux du sultan Sidi Mohammed ben Abdallah (1757-1790). Tanger, 1960.
Afr 1585.5	Caille, Jacques. Une ambassade autrichienne au Maroc en 1805. Paris, 1957.
Afr 1571.50.5	Caillé, Jacques. Le consulat de Tanger; des origines à 1830. Paris, 1967.
Afr 1409.20	Caillé, Jacques. Une Corse sultane du Maroc, Davia Franceschini et sa famille. Paris, 1968.
Afr 1425.5	Caille, Jacques. Une mission de Leon Roches à Rabat en 1845. Thèse. Casablanca, 1947.
Afr 1733.5.20	Caille, Jacques. La petite histoire de Rabat. Casablanca, 1950.
Afr 1369.50	Caille, Jacques. La petite histoire du Maroc. Casablanca, 1950. 2v.
Afr 1571.50	Caille, Jacques. La représentation diplomatique de la France au Maroc. Paris, 1951.
Afr 1733.5.25	Caille, Jacques. La ville de Rabat. Vanoest, 1949. 3v.
Afr 4070.23	Cailliaud, F. Voyage à Meroe, au Fleuve Blanc. Paris, 1823-27. 5v.
Afr 5235.128.2	Caillié, René. Journal d'un voyage à Temboctou et à Jenne, dans l'Afrique centrale. Paris, 1965?
Afr 5235.128	Caillié, René. Journal d'un voyage à Tembouctou. Paris, 1830. 3v.
Afr 5235.128.5	Caillié, René. Travels through central Africa to Timbuctoo. London, 1830. 2v.
Afr 5235.128.10	Caillié, René. Le voyage de René Caillié à Tombouctou. Paris, 1937.
Afr 5760.7	Cailliet, E. Essai sur la psychologie du Hovas. Thèse. Paris, 1926.
Afr 4559.35.85	Caimpenta, U. L'impero abissino. 10. ed. Milano, 1935.
Afr 7122.54	Caio, H. Angola. 3.ed. Lisboa, 1961.
Afr 5228.2	Caioli, Aldo. Esperienza politiche africane; la Federazione del Mali. Milano, 1966.
Afr 4512.20	Caioli, Aldo. L'Italia di Fronte a Gineura, aspetti del conflitto italo-etiopico dalle origini alla conquista dell Impero. Roma, 1965.
Afr 4115.18	Le Caire. v.1-2. (Clerget, Marcel.) Le Caire, 1934. 2v.
Afr 3978.83.10	Le Caire et ses environs. (Vaujany, H.) Paris, 1883.
Afr 9549.65	Cairns, H. Alan C. The clash of cultures. N.Y., 1965.
Afr 9549.65.5	Cairns, H. Alan C. Prelude to imperialism; British reactions to Central African society, 1840-1890. London, 1965.
Afr 6879.59	Cairns, John C. Bush and boma. London, 1959.
Afr 4115.20.10	Cairo; a life-story of 1000 years, 969-1969. Cairo, 1969.
Afr 3990.22	Cairo, Alexandria, and environs. Paris, 1963.
Afr 4115.25	Cairo, city of art and commerce. 1st ed. (Wiet, Gaston.) Norman, 1964.
Afr 4115.22	Cairo, Egypt. Coptic Museum. A brief guide to the Coptic Museum. Cairo, 1938.
Afr 3026.27	Cairo, Egypt. National Library. Egypt subject catalogue. Cairo, 1957.
Afr 4115.14A	Cairo, Jerusalem, and Damascus. (Margoliouth, D.S.) N.Y., 1907.
Afr 4115.30	Cairo, 5500 years. (Stewart, Desmond Stirling.) N.Y., 1968.
NEDL Afr 4115.6	Cairo. (Lane-Poole, S.) London, 1892.
Afr 3326.3	Cairo. Institute of National Planning. Institute of National Planning. Cairo, 1961.
Afr 3326.3.10	Cairo. Institute of National Planning. National Planning Institute. Cairo, 1962.
Afr 4115.6.3	Cairo. 3d ed. (Lane-Poole, S.) London, 1898.
Afr 4115.12	Cairo and its environs. (Lamplough, A.O.) London, 1909.
Afr 609.55	Cairo to Cape Town. 1st ed. (Reynolds, Reginald.) Garden City, N.Y., 1955.
Afr 3979.23	Cairo to Kisumu. (Carpenter, F.G.) Garden City, 1923.
Afr 3979.50	Cairo to Riyadh diary. (Bilainkin, G.) London, 1950.
Afr 2223.10	Caisse d'Equipement pour le Développement de l'Algérie. Programme d'équipement. Alger. 1960+
NEDL Afr 3740.4	Caix, R. de. Fachoda. Paris, 1899.
Afr 2228.4	Caix de St. Aymour, A. de. Arabes et Kabyles. Paris, 1891.
Afr 4515.1	Caix de St. Aymour. Histoire des relations de la France avec abyssinie. Paris, 1886.
Afr 4515.1.2	Caix de St. Aymour. Histoire des relations de la France avec l'Abyssinie. Paris, 1892.
Afr 6385.10	Calabar. Rev. ed. (McFarlan, D.M.) London, 1957.

Afr 1422.6	Campagne du Maroc (1844). (Warnier, A.H.) Paris, 1899.	Afr 4700.35	Canevari, E. Il generale Tommaso Salsa e la sue campagne coloniali. Milano, 1935.
Afr 6780.26	La campagne du Tanganika (1916-1917). (Moulaert, Georges.) Bruxelles, 1934.	Afr 9038.2	Caneville. 1st. ed. (Vandenberghe, P.L.) Middletown, Conn., 1964.
Afr 4513.38.30	La campagne italo-etiopica. (Bollati, Ambrogio.) Roma, 1938.	Afr 2530.17	Caniglia, R. Il dramma di Tunisi. Napoli, 1930.
Afr 7570.15	Les campagnes coloniales belges, 1914-1918. (Belgium. Ministère de la Défense Nationale. Etat-Major Général de l'Armée.) Bruxelles, 1927-1929. 2v.	Afr 1608.95.7	Canizares y Moyano, ed. Apuntes sobre Marruecos. Madrid, 1895.
		Afr 7565.20	Cannart d'Hamale, Art. Quelques pages sur le Congo. Bruxelles, 1908.
Afr 1955.51	Campagnes d'Afrique, 1830-1848. (Changarnier, N.A.T.) Paris, 1930.	Afr 9700.3	Cannison, Ian. The Luapula people of Northern Rhodesia. Manchester, 1959.
Afr 1955.30	Campagnes d'Afrique, 1830-1910. (Piquet, V.) Paris, 1912.	Htn Afr 8718.42*	Cannon, R. History of Cape Mounted Riflemen. London, 1842.
Afr 1965.2.10	Campagnes de l'armée d'Afrique, 1835-1839. 2e éd. (Orleans, F.P.L.C.H., Duc.) Paris, 1870.	Htn Afr 1368.60*	Canovas del Castello, A. de. Apuntes para la historia de Marruecos. Madrid, 1860.
Afr 3215.3.30	Les campagnes navales de Mohammed Aly et d'Ibrahim. (Durand-Viel, G.C.) Paris, 1935. 2v.	Afr 1368.60.6	Canovas del Castello, A. de. Apuntes para la historia de Marruecos. Madrid, 1913.
Afr 4375.5	The campaign in Abyssinia. (Shepherd, A.F.) Bombay, 1868.	Afr 1609.23.20	Cansino-Roldan, Luis. Recuerdos de Marruecos. Malaga, 1923.
Afr 4392.4.10	The campaign of Adowa and the rise of Menelik. (Berkeley, G.F.H.) N.Y., 1969.	Afr 4700.25	Cantalupe, R. L'Italia musulmana. Roma, 1928.
NEDL Afr 4392.4	The campaign of Adowa and the rise of Menelik. (Berkeley, G.F.H.) Westminster, 1902.	Afr 115.3.25F	Canti, Cesare. L'incivilimento dell Africa, memoria. n.p., 18- .
Afr 4392.4.5	The campaign of Adowa and the rise of Menelik. New ed. (Berkeley, G.F.H.) London, 1930.	Afr 4392.8.5	Canuti, Giuseppe. L'Italia in Africa e le guerre con l'Abissinia. Firenze, 1911.
Afr 3708.4	The campaign of the Cataracts. (Butler, W.F.) London, 1887.	Afr 8105.20	Le Cap de Bonne-Espérance au XVIIe siècle. (Deherain, Henri.) Paris, 1909.
Afr 8289.00.40	Campaign pictures of the war in South Africa (1899-1900). (Hales, A.G.) London, 1900.	Afr 8808.69	The Cape and its people, and other essays. (Noble, R.) Cape Town, 1869.
Afr 8152.73.2	Campaigning in Kaffirland...1851-52. 2d ed. (King, W.R.) London, 1855.	Afr 8152.72	The Cape and the Kaffirs. (Ward, H.) London, 1851.
Afr 8160.5	Campaigning in South Africa. (Montague, W.E.) Edinburgh, 1880.	Afr 8808.52.2	The Cape and the Kafirs. (Cole, A.W.) London, 1852.
Afr 8152.93	Campaigning in South Africa and Egypt. (Molyneux, W.C.F.) London, 1896.	Afr 11249.86.130	Cape Charade. (Butler, Guy.) Cape Town, 1968. 2v.
Afr 6170.5	Campaigning in West Africa and the Ashantee invasion. (Rogers, E.) London, 1874.	Afr 8678.32	The Cape colour question, a historical survey. (MacMillan, W.M.) London, 1927.
Afr 609.52.15	Campamentos en Africa. (Agundis, T.) México, 1959.	Afr 8678.32.2	The Cape colour question. Facsimile. (Macmillan, W.M.) Cape Town, 1968.
Afr 1432.23	La campaña de Marruecos. (Landa, Nicasio de.) Madrid, 1860.	Afr 8685.10F	The cape coloured. (Jacobson, Evelyn.) Rondebosch, 1945.
Afr 1755.12	La Campana del rif, la Verdad de la guerra. (Albeniz, R.) n.p., n.d.	Afr 8678.31.5	The Cape coloured people, 1652-1937. (Marais, J.S.) Johannesburg, 1957.
Afr 1755.10	La Campana del rif. (Gallego Ramos, E.) Madrid, 1909.	Afr 8678.31	The Cape coloured people, 1652-1937. (Marais, J.S.) London, 1939.
Afr 1755.8	La Campana del rif en 1909. (Urquijo, F. De.) Madrid, n.d.	Afr 8825.20	The Cape coloured vote. (United Party.) Cape Town, 1954.
Afr 1755.49	Campanas en el rif y Yebala 1921-1922. (Berenguer, Damaso.) Madrid, 1923.	Afr 8809.46	Cape country. (Middlemiss, E.) Cape Town, 1946.
		Afr 8835.60	Cape directory. Cape Town, 1800.
Afr 7225.8	A campanha de 1783 contra o Vtigulo. (Oliveira Boléo, José de.) Lisboa, 1964.	Afr 8825.15	The Cape Malays. (Duplessis, I.D.) Cape Town, 1944.
Afr 7187.5	A campanha do Bailundo em 1902. (Moncada, Francisco C.) Lisboa, 1918.	Afr 8657.1	The cape of adventure. (Colvin, Ian D.) London, 1912.
Afr 7222.30	Campanha do Gungunhana, 1895. (Ornellas, Ayres D.) Lisboa, 1930.	Afr 8710.20	Cape of Good Hope. Die administrasie van Kaapland, 1910-1960. Kaapstad, 1960.
Afr 7130.5	Campanha do sul de Angola em 1915. (Eça, Antonio Julio da Costa Pereira de.) Lisboa, 1921.	Afr Doc 4407.291F	Cape of Good Hope. Results of a census of the colony of the Cape of Good Hope. Cape Town, 1892.
Afr 8659.54	Campbell, A. The heart of Africa. 1st ed. N.Y., 1954.	Afr Doc 4407.5	Cape of Good Hope. Statistical register. Cape Town. 1886-1909 23v.
Afr 1608.97.5	Campbell, A. A ride in Morocco. Toronto, 1897.		
Afr 8369.43.7	Campbell, Alex. Smuts and swastika. London, 1943.	Afr 8808.43	The Cape of Good Hope...Algoa bay. (Chase, John C.) London, 1843.
Afr 609.44.5	Campbell, Alexander. Empire in Africa. London, 1944.	Afr 8835.3	The Cape of Good Hope. (Cape Town.) Cape Town, 1911.
Afr 8676.47	Campbell, Alexander. South Africa, what now? Cape Town, 1947.	Afr 8667.72	The Cape of Good Hope. (Idenburg, Petrus Johannes.) Leiden, 1963.
Afr 2929.35.15	Campbell, D. Camels through Libya. Philadelphia, 1935.	Afr 8658.20	Cape of Good Hope. (Stout, Benjamin.) London, 1820.
Afr 710.10	Campbell, D. In the heart of Bantuland. London, 1922.	Afr 8030.7	Cape of Good Hope. Archives. Kaapse archiefstukken, lopende over het jaar 1778- Cape Town. 1926+ 6v.
Afr 1259.44.5	Campbell, D. With the bible in North Africa. Kilmarnock, 1944.	Afr 8030.5	Cape of Good Hope. Archives. Precis. Cape Town. 1,1896+ 13v.
Afr 8678.339	Campbell, Dugald. Blazing trails in Bantu land. London, 1933.	Afr 8177.5	Cape of Good Hope. Archives. The rebellion of 1815. Cape Town, 1902.
Afr 5056.130	Campbell, Dugald. Wanderings in widest Africa. London, 1930.	Afr Doc 4409.5F	Cape of Good Hope. Department of Treasurer. Begrooting van uitgaaf te worden gedekt gedurende net jaar. 1890-1910 27v.
Afr 8658.16	Campbell, J. Travels in South Africa. Andover, 1816.		
Afr 8658.15	Campbell, J. Travels in South Africa. London, 1815.	Afr Doc 4409.6F	Cape of Good Hope. Department of Treasurer. Estimates of the expenditure to be defrayed during the year 1899/1900.
Afr 555.19	Campbell, John. The life of Africaner. Philadelphia, 1827.	Afr 8283.25F	Cape of Good Hope. Parliament. House of Commons. Report of the Select Committee of the Cape of Good Hope. London, 1897.
Afr 6210.37	Campbell, M.J. Law and practice of local government in northern Nigeria. Lagos, 1963.		
Afr 5053.38	Campbell, Michael J. The structure of local government in West Africa. The Hague, 1965.	Afr 8835.5	The Cape of Good Hope. 4. ed. (Cape Town.) Cape Town, 1926.
Afr 6275.19.10	Campbell, R. A few facts, relating to Lagos...Africa. Philadelphia, 1860.	Afr 8707.12	Cape of Good Hope almanac and register. Cape Town. 1849+ 5v.
NEDL Afr 6275.19	Campbell, R. A pilgrimage to my mother land (Central Africa). London, 1861.	Afr 8808.43.5	The Cape of Good Hope and the Eastern Province of Algoa Bay. Facsimile. (Chase, John C.) Cape Town, 1967.
Afr 6275.19.3	Campbell, R. A pilgrimage to my mother land (Central Africa). N.Y., 1861.	Afr 8707.10	Cape of Good Hope civil service list. Cape Town. 1888+ 3v.
Afr 9558.57	Campbell, R.J. Livingstone. London, 1929.	Afr 8710.22	The Cape parliament, 1854-1910. (McCracken, John Leslie.) Oxford, 1967.
Afr 2208.36	Campbell, Thomas. Letters from the south, written during a journey to Algiers. Philadelphia, 1836.	Afr 8809.10	The Cape peninsula. (Juta, Rene.) Cape Town, 1910.
Afr 2208.36.5	Campbell, Thomas. Letters from the south. London, 1837. 2v.	Afr 8817.2	The Cape province. (Bulpin, Thomas V.) Cape Town, 1960.
		Afr 11026.5	Cape theatre in the 1940's. (Hatfield, Denis.) Cape Town, 1967.
Afr 2285.20	Camping in the Sahara. (Hull, E.M.) London, 1926.	Afr 609.26.15	Cape to Cairo. (Court Treatt, S.) Boston, 1927.
Afr 1609.08.6	Campo Angulo, G. Geografia de Marruecos. Madrid, 1908.	Afr 8835.36	Cape Town, a record of the mother city from the earliest days to the present. (Shorten, John R.) Cape Town, 1963.
Afr 1555.10	Campoamor, J.M. La actitud de España ante la cuestion de Marruecos. Madrid, 1951.	Afr 8835.26	Cape Town, city of Good Hope. (Honikman, Alfred Harold.) Cape Town, 1966.
Afr 1608.86.5	Campos, L. de. Un empire qui croule. Paris, 1886.	Afr 8835.47	Cape Town, Kaapstad, Kapstadt. 2. ed. (Merkens, Alice.) Cape Town, 1962.
Afr 2000.6	Camus, Albert. Actuelles, III. Paris, 1958.	Afr 8835.3	Cape Town. The Cape of Good Hope. Cape Town, 1911.
Afr 550.17	Can Africa be won? (Roome, W.J.W.) London, 1927.	Afr 8835.5	Cape Town. The Cape of Good Hope. 4. ed. Cape Town, 1926.
Afr 210.60.25	Can Africa come of age? (Dekiewiet, C.) Johannesburg, 1960.	Afr 8835.25.2	Cape Town. (Lewis, C.) Cape Town, 1927.
Afr 4513.36.45	Can Italy live at home. (Salvemini, G.) N.Y., 1936.	Afr 8835.25	Cape Town. (Lewis, C.) Cape Town, 1934.
Afr 8135.5	Cana, F.R. South Africa from the great trek to the union. London, 1909.	Afr 8835.10	Cape Town Foreshore Joint Technical Committee. The Cape Town Foreshore plan. Cape Town, 1948.
Afr 4513.36	Canada. Department of External Affairs. Documents relating to the Italo-Ethiopian conflict. Ottawa, 1936.	Afr 8028.148	Cape Town. University. Consolidated list, 1941-1966. Cape Town, 1966.
Afr 8292.5.10	Canada. Department of Militia and Defence. Organization, equipment, despatch and service of the Canadians during war in South Africa. Ottawa, 1901. 2 pam.	Afr 8250.43	Cape Town. University. Libraries. Pictorial material of Cecil J. Rhodes. Cape Town, 1964.
		Afr 8055.40F	Cape Town. University. Library. Biographical index to men of the times. Cape Town, 1960.
Afr 8325.50	The Canadian contingents and Canadian imperialism. (Evans, W.S.) Toronto, 1901.	Afr 3.42	Cape Town. University. School of African Studies. Communications. Cape Town. 2,1942+ 4v.
Afr 3.17	Canadian journal of African studies. Montreal. 1,1967+		
Afr 1325.2F	Canal, J. Géographie générale du Maroc. Paris, 1902.	Afr 8028.125	Cape Town. Van Riebeek Festival Book Exhibition. South Africa in print. Cape Town, 1952.
Afr 678.81	Canale, M.G. Memoria. Genova, 1881.	Afr 8835.58	Cape Town Africans today. (Williams, Roger.) Johannesburg, 1965.
Afr 2030.135	Candas, Maurice F.M. Plaidoyer pour l'Algérie. Paris, 1957.	Afr 8835.10	The Cape Town Foreshore plan. (Cape Town. Foreshore Joint Technical Committee.) Cape Town, 1948.
Afr 8279.00.19	The candidates of Cain. (Stead, W.J.) London, 1900.		
Afr 11053.4	Candlelight poets of the Cape. (Desmond, Nerine.) Cape Town, 1967.		
Afr 1723.5	Canetti, Elias. Die Stimmen von Marrakesch. München, 1968.		

Afr 1409.18	Cartas arabes de Marruecos en tiempo de Mawlay al Yazid, 1790-1792. (Arribas Palau, Mariano.) Tetuan, 1959.
Afr 1409.18.2	Cartas arabes de Marruecos en tiempo de Mawlay al Yazid, 1790-1792. (Arribas Palau, Mariano.) Tetuan, 1961.
Afr 5960.14	Cartas de la Guinea. (Miranda, Agustin.) Madrid, 1940.
Afr 7814.1	Carte de l'Etat. (Congo Free State (1887).) Bruxelles, 1887.
Afr 4513.35.30	Carter, Boak. Black shirt, black skin. Harrisburg, 1935.
Afr 4513.35.33	Carter, Boak. Black shirt, black skin. London, 1935.
Afr 50.30	Carter, G. African one-party states. Ithaca, 1962.
Afr 50.30.2	Carter, G. African one-party states. Ithaca, 1964.
Afr 50.31	Carter, G. National unity and regionalism in eight African states. Ithaca, 1966.
Afr 210.63.55	Carter, G.M. Five African states. Ithaca, 1963.
Afr 210.60.10	Carter, G.M. Independence for Africa. N.Y., 1960.
Afr 8369.58.3	Carter, G.M. The politics of inequality, South Africa since 1948. 3rd ed. London, 1962.
Afr 8369.58	Carter, G.M. The politics of inequality. N.Y., 1958.
Afr 8659.55	Carter, G.M. South Africa. N.Y., 1955.
Afr 8678.351F	Carter, G.M. South Africa's international position. Cape Town, 1964.
Afr 6010.16	Carter, G.M. Transition in Africa. Boston, 1958.
Afr 212.25	Carter, Gwendolen Margaret. Politics in Africa. N.Y., 1966.
Afr 8846.30.5	Carter, Gwendolen Margaret. Separate development. Johannesburg, 1966.
Afr 8846.30	Carter, Gwendolen Margaret. South Africa's Transkei, the politics of domestic colonialism. Evanston, 1967.
Afr 8225.4.2	Carter, T.F. A narrative of the Boer war. London, 1896.
Htn Afr 1407.2.5*	Carteret, George. The Barbary voyage of 1638. Philadelphia, 1929.
Afr 5180.50	Cartes pour servir à l'aménagement du territoire. (Sénégal. Ministére du Développement.) Dakar, 1965.
Afr 10005.20	Cartey, Wilfred. Whispers from a continent; the literature of contemporary black Africa. N.Y., 1969.
Afr 2665.5	Carthage. (Mabille de Poncheville, A.) Paris, 1931.
NEDL Afr 2608.69	Carthage and Tunis. (Perry, Amos.) Providence, 1869.
Afr 2609.06	Carthage and Tunis. (Sladin, D.) London, 1906. 2v.
Afr 8675.5	Cartographie de l'Afrique au sud du Sahara. (Conseil Scientifique pour l'Afrique au Sud du Sahara.) Bukavu, 1953.
Afr 5757.5	La cartographie de Madagascar. (Gravier, Gabriel.) Rouen, 1896.
Afr 7809.00.10	Carton de Wiart, H. Mes vacances au Congo. Bruges, 19- .
Htn Afr 8325.35*	Pamphlet box. Cartoons.
Afr 8055.35	Cartwright, A.P. South Africa's hall of fame. Cape Town, 1958.
Afr 9149.62	Cartwright, Alan. Valley of gold. Cape Town, 1962.
Afr 9165.42.75	Cartwright, Alan Patrick. The corner house. Capetown, 1965.
Afr 4787.10	Carusoglu, T. Mid-term appraisal of the first five-year plan of Somalia. 1st draft. Mogadiscio, 1966.
Afr 628.253	Caruthers, J.C. The African mind in health and disease. Geneva, 1953.
Afr 1573.7	Carvajal, Jose de. España y Marruecos. Madrid, 1884.
Afr 212.12	Carvalho, Castro. Africa contemporanea. 2. ed. São Paulo, 1963.
Afr 1576.5.2	Carvalho, V. de. La domination portugaise au Maroc du XV. Lisbonne, 1936.
Afr 1576.5	Carvalho, V. de. La domination portugaise au Maroc du XVeme au XVIIIeme siècle. Lisbonne, 1942.
Afr 7175.25	Carvalho e Menezes, A. Memoria geografica. Lisboa, 1834.
Afr 6069.46	Cary, Joyce. Britain and West Africa. London, 1946.
NEDL Afr 6069.46	Cary, Joyce. Britain and West Africa. London, 1946.
Afr 210.41.10A	Cary, Joyce. The case for African freedom. Austin, 1962.
Afr 210.41	Cary, Joyce. The case for African freedom. London, 1941.
Afr 9446.47	Cary, Robert. A time to die. 2nd ed. Cape Town, 1969.
Afr 1706.2	Casablanca. (Lapeyre.) Paris, 1918.
Afr 1706.8	Casablanca. Thèse. (Adam, André.) Paris, 1968. 2v.
Afr 2929.43	Casairey, G. Tripolitania. London, 1943.
Afr 8918.59	Casalis, E. Le Bassoutos. Paris, 1859.
Afr 8918.59.10	Casalis, E. The Basutos, or, Twenty-three years in South Africa. Cape Town, 1965.
Afr 8918.59.5	Casalis, E. The Basutos. London, 1861.
Afr 5190.2	Casamance et Mellacorée. (Brosselard-Faidherbe, H.) Paris, 1892.
X Cg Afr 3725.4	Casati, G. Ten years in Equatoria. London, 1891. (Changed to XP 3865) 2v.
Afr 3725.4.5	Casati, G. Zehn Jahre in Äquatoria. Hamburg, 1891. 3v.
Afr 210.41.10A	The case for African freedom. (Cary, Joyce.) Austin, 1962.
Afr 210.41	The case for African freedom. (Cary, Joyce.) London, 1941.
Afr 1369.53	The case for Morocco. (American Committee for Moroccan Independence.) Washington, 1953.
Afr 6225.45	The case for Nigeria. (Unongo, Paul Iyorpuu.) Lagos, 1968.
Afr 7073.6F	Case in support of the claim of Great Britain to the Island of Bulama. (Great Britain.) London, 1869.
Afr 8678.302	The case of South Africa. (Louw, E.H.) N.Y., 1963.
Afr 2880.20	Casetti, F. Restauratio libyca. Roma, 1935.
Afr 7122.35	Casimiro, Augusto. Angola e o futuro. Lisboa, 1958.
Afr 11229.10	A cask of jerepigo. (Bosman, Herman.) Johannesburg, 1957.
Afr 7122.79	O caso de Angola. (Ventura, Reis.) Braga, 1964.
Afr 1495.5	Cassaigne, Jean. La situation des Français au Maroc depuis l'indépendance, 1956-1964. Paris, 1965.
Afr 3700.10	Cassell's history of the war in the Soudan. v.1-6. (Grant, James.) London, n.d. 2v.
Afr 2209.22.10	Casserly, Gordon. Algeria to-day. London, 1922.
Afr 4368.12	Cassinari, E. Il beato Ghebre-Michael. Roma, 1926.
Afr 3994.938	Casson, L. Nine papyrus texts in the New York University collection. Diss. N.Y., 1939.
Afr 4335.1	Castanhoso, M. de. Dos feitos de D. Christovam da Gama. Lisboa, 1898.
Afr 4335.2	Castanhoso, M. de. Die Heldentaten des Dom Christoph da Gama. Berlin, 1907.
Afr 4335.3	Castanhoso, M. de. Historia das cousas que o muy esforçado Christovam da Gama. Lisboa, 1855.
Afr 2370.1	Castel, P. Tébessa, histoire et description d'un territoireAlgérien. Paris, 1905. 2v.
Afr 2209.65	Castel, Robert. Inoubliable Algérie. Paris, 1965.

Afr 1432.7F	Castelar, E. Cronica de la guerra de Africa. Madrid, 1859.
Afr 4700.34.5	Castelbarco, G. L'ordinamento sindacale-corporativo nell organizzazione delle colonie italiane. Milano, 1934.
Afr 7568.35	Castelein, A. The Congo State; its origin, rights, and duties, the charges of its accusers. N.Y., 1969.
Afr 1955.17	Castellane, P. de. Military life in Algeria. London, 1853. 2v.
Afr 1955.17.5	Castellane, P. de. Souvenirs de la vie militaire en Afrique. Paris, 1852.
Afr 1570.17	Castellane. Maroc. Paris, 1907.
Afr 3740.5	Castellani, C. Marchand l'africain. Paris, n.d.
Afr 5406.198	Castellani, Charles. Vers le Nil français. Paris, 1898.
Afr 5408.10	Castellani, Charles. Das Weib am Kongo. Minden, 1902.
Afr 1738.50	Castellani Pastorio, Giovanni. Sviluppi e conclusione della questione di Tangeri. Roma, 1964.
Afr 555.17	Castellanos, M.P. Apostolado serafico en Marruecos. Madrid, 1896.
Afr 1368.78	Castellanos, M.P. Descripcion historica de Marruecos. Santiago, 1878.
Afr 1368.78.5	Castellanos, M.P. Historia de Marruecos. Madrid, 1946. 2v.
Afr 1368.78.3	Castellanos, M.P. Historia de Marruecos. Tanger, 1898.
Afr 4658.5	I castelli di Gondar. (Monti della Corte, A.A.) Roma, 1938.
Afr 2875.16	Castellini, G. Nelle trincee di Tripoli. Bologna, 1912.
Afr 2609.11	Castellini, G. Tunisi, e Tripoli. Torino, 1911.
Afr 2025.3	Casteran, A. L'Algérie française. Paris, 1900.
Afr 678.66	Castilho, A.M. de. Descripção...costa occidental de Africa. v.1-2. Lisboa, 1866.
Afr 150.2.5F	Castilho, A.M. de. Os padrões dos descobrimentos portuguezes em Africa. 2a memoria. Lisboa, 1871.
Afr 7320.4	Castilho, S. de. La province portugaise de Mosambique. n.p., 1890.
Afr 7322.10	Castilho Barreto e Noronha, Augusto de. Relatorio da guerra da Zambezia em 1888. Lisboa, 1891.
Afr 1432.12	Castillo, R. del. España y Marruecos, historia de la guerra de Africa. Cadiz, 1859.
Afr 6390.80	Castle, Edgar Bradshaw. Growing up in East Africa. London, 1966.
Afr 5548.84.10	Castonnet des Fosses, H. Madagascar. Paris, 1884. 2 pam.
Afr 1575.5	Castonnet Des Fosses, H. Les Portugais au Maroc. Paris, 1886.
Afr 4258.97	Castonnet des Fosses. L'Abyssinie et les Italiens. Paris, 1897.
Afr 1406.16	Castries, H. de. Agents et voyageurs français au Maroc, 1530-1660. Paris, 1911.
Afr 1330.5.9	Castries, H. de. Archives et bibliothèques d'Angleterre, 1661-1757. (France, t.1-3). Paris, 1918-1925. 3v.
Afr 1605.96	Castries, H. de. Une description du Maroc. Paris, 1909.
Afr 1408.6	Castries, H. de. Moulay Ismail et Jacques II. Paris, 1903.
Afr 1688.5	Castries, H. De. Notes sur figuig. Paris, 1882.
Afr 1330.6	Castries, H. de. Les sources inédites de l'histoire du Maroc. Dynastie filalienne. v.1-6. Paris, 1922-31. 6v.
Afr 1330.5	Castries, H. de. Les sources inédites de l'histoire du Maroc. Dynastie saadienne. Paris, 1905-26. 4v.
Afr 1330.5.7	Castries, H. de. Les sources inédites de l'histoire du Maroc. Dynastie Saadienne. (Espagne, t.1-3). Paris, 1921. 3v.
Afr 1330.5.3	Castries, H. de. Les sources inédites de l'histoire du Maroc. Dynastie saadienne. (Pays-bas, t.1-6). Paris, 1906-23. 6v.
Afr 718.2.140	Castries, R. de la Croix. Les rencontres de Stanley. Paris, 1960.
Afr 4559.36.25	Castro, Lincoln de. Etiopia terra, uomini e cose. 2. ed. Milano, 1936.
Afr 4559.15	Castro, Lincoln de. Nella terra dei negies. Milano, 1915. 2v.
Afr 210.67.15	Castro, Luis Filipe de Oliveira e. A nova Africa, ensaio sociopolitico. Lisboa, 1967.
Afr 3978.70.5	Castro y Serrano, Jose de. La novela del Egipto. Madrid, 1870.
Afr 6143.14	Caswall, H. The martyr of the Pongas. N.Y., 1857.
Afr 555.3.8	Caswall, Henry. The martyr of the Pongas. London, 1857.
Afr 1903.1	Cat, E. Mission bibliog. En Espagne. Paris, 1891.
Afr 825.4	Cat, E. Notice sur la carte de l'Ogooue. Paris, 1890.
Afr 1868.88	Cat, Edouard. Petite histoire de l'Algérie, Tunisie, Maroc. v.1-2. Alger, 1888-91. 2v.
Afr 28.100	Catalog of African government documents and African area index. (Boston University. Library.) Boston, 1960.
Afr Doc 5.2	Catalog of African government documents and African area index. 2d ed. (Boston University. Library.) Boston, 1964.
Afr 28.52	Catalogo de autores y obras anonimas. (Spain. Dirección General de Plazas.) Madrid, 1945.
Afr 150.2.90	Catálogo henriquino do Real Cabinete Português de Leitura do Rio de Janeiro. (Rio de Janeiro. Gabinete Português de Leitura.) Lisboa, 1960.
Afr 8853.3F	Catalogue. (Basutoland. Government Archives.) n.p., 1962.
Afr 5056.123	Catalogue des positions géographiques provisoirement admises par le Service géographique de l'A.O.F. (French West Africa.) Laval, 1923-24.
Afr 5183.965.5	Catalogue des principales productions industrielles du Sénégal. (Dakar. Chambre de Commerce d'Agriculture et d'Industrie.) Dakar, 1965.
Afr 8028.42	Catalogue of books. (Spohr, Otto.) Cape Town, 1950.
Afr 8028.205	Catalogue of books and pamphlets published in German relating to Africa and South West Africa as found in the South African Public Library. (Both, Ellen Lisa Marianne.) Cape Town, 1969.
Afr Doc 3302.5	Catalogue of government publications published prior to 1st January, 1965. (Uganda.) Entebbe, 1966?
Afr 8028.200.15	A catalogue of manuscripts and papers in the Killie Campbell African collection relating to the African peoples. (Botha, Carol.) Johannesburg, 1967.
Afr 28.10	Catalogue of the African collection in the Moorland Foundation. (Howard University, Washington, D.C. Library. Moorland Foundation.) Washington, 1958.

Afr Doc 3802.2	Catalogue of the parliamentary papers of Southern Rhodesia, 1899-1953. (Willson, Francis Michael Glenn.) Salisbury, 1965.
Afr 3978.87.5	Catalogue of views in Egypt and Nubia. (Sebah, P.) Caire, 1887.
Afr 9.4.8	Catalogues. (Institut Français d'Afrique Noire.) Dakar. 5+ 34v.
Afr 8028.110	Catalogues. (Nederlandsch-Zuid-Afrikansche Vereeniging. Bibliothek.) Amsterdam, 1939.
Afr 8028.1.3	Catalogues of books and pamphlets. (Theal, G.M.) Cape Town, 1912.
Afr 618.45	Cataloque of the Estelle Hamilton-Welsh collection. (Fort Hare, South Africa. University College. F.S. Malan Museum.) Fort Hare, 1962?
Afr 630.13	Cataloque of the Ethnographical Museum of the Royal Geographical Society of Egypt. (Société de Géographie d'Egypte.) Le Caire, 1924.
Afr 2530.23	Cataluccio, F. Italia e Francia in Tunisia, 1878-1939. Roma, 1939.
Afr 5748.95.3F	Catat, Louis. Voyage à Madagascar (1889-1890). Paris, 1895.
Afr 10621.9.100	The catechist. (Abruquah, Joseph W.) London, 1965.
Afr 8152.81	Cathcart, G. Correspondence. 2nd ed. London, 1857.
Afr 1947.1	Cathcart, J.L. The captives. La Porte, 1902.
Afr 4368.12.5	Catholic Church. Litterae apostolicae quibus venerabilis dei Fain Abba Ghebec Michael. Romae, 1926.
Afr 550.141	The Catholic Church in modern Africa. (Mullin, Joseph.) London, 1965.
Afr 6497.9	Catholic Union of Great Britain. Memorandum on war in Uganda, 1892. London, 1894.
Afr 5466.5	Le catholicisme et la vapeur au centre de l'Afrique. (Remy.) Poitiers, 1901.
Afr 4150.2.5F	Caton-Thompson, G. Kharga Oasis in prehistory. London, 1952.
Afr 1753.5	Catorce meses enCeuta. (Relosillas, J.J.) Malaga, 1886.
Afr 6397.5	Catrice, Paul. Un audacieux pionnier de l'église au Afrique. Lyon, 1964.
Afr 1571.17.85	Catroux, G. Lyautey. Paris, 1952.
Afr 3069.31.10	Cattaui, Joseph. Coup d'oeil sur la chronologie de la nation égyptienne. Paris, 1931.
Afr 3205.8	Cattaui, Joseph E. Histoire des rapports de l'Egypte avec la Sublime Porte. Thèse. Paris, 1919.
Afr 3205.16	Cattaui, René. Mohamed-Aly et l'Europe. Paris, 1950.
Afr 3205.15	Cattaui, René. Le règne de Mohamed Aly d'après les archives russes en Egypte. v.1-3. Caire, 1931-1936. 4v.
Afr 7568.28	Cattier, F. Etude sur la situation de l'état...Congo. Bruxelles, 1906.
Afr 2248.5	Cauneille, A. Les Chaanba (leur nomadisme). Paris, 1968.
Afr 630.62	Causas de los conflictos en el Africa del sur. (Pieto, I.) Berriz, 1962.
Afr 5868.81	Causeries historiques. (Crestien, G.F.) Paris, 1881.
Afr 1570.47	Caussin. Vers Taza. Paris, 1922.
Afr 659.66.10	Cavallaro, Emanuele. Lo e l'Africa. Palermo, 1966.
Afr 2929.12.25	Cavazza, F. La Libia italiana e il campo che offre a ricerche scientifiche. Bologna, 1912.
Htn Afr 7015.2.2*	Cavazzi, G.A. Istorica descrittione de tre regni Congo, Matamba. n.p., 1690.
Afr 7015.2.1	Cavazzi, G.A. Istorica descrizione de tre regni Congo, Matamba. Bologna, 1687.
Afr 7015.2	Cavazzi, G.A. Relation historique de l'Ethiopie occidentale. Paris, 1732. 5v.
Afr 2608.95.8	Cave dwellers of southern Tunisia. (Bruun, D.) London, 1898.
Afr 3315.127	Cavenagh, Sandy. Airborne to Suez. London, 1965.
Afr 1495.6.25	Caviglioli, François. Ben Barka chez les juges. Paris, 1967.
Afr 8678.324	Cawood, Lesley. The churches and race relations in South Africa. Johannesburg, 1964.
Afr 1618.22	La caza en Marruecos. (Duran Pulis, Guillermo.) Las Palmas de Gran Canaria, 1955.
Afr 2260.1	Cazenave, J. La colonization en Algérie. Alger, 1900.
Afr 5748.96.5	Cazeneuve, M. A la cour de Madagascar. Paris, 1896.
Afr 7803.46	Cazlson, Lois. Monganga Paul. N.Y., 1966.
Afr 2532.6	Ce que la Tunisie demande à la France. (Duran-Angliviel, André.) Paris, 1921.
Afr 2527.2	Cealis, E. De Sousse à Gafsa. Lettres, 1881-84. Paris, n.d.
Afr 1490.12	Ceccaldi, C. Au pays de la poudre. Paris, 1914.
Afr 1026.5.15	Ceccherini, Ugo. Bibliografia della Libia. Roma, 1915.
Afr 4558.87	Cecchi, A. L'Abissinia settentrionale. Photoreproduction. Milano, 1887.
Afr 4610.3	Cecchi, A. Da Zeila alle frontiere del Caffa. Roma, 1886-87. 3v.
Afr 609.54.30	Cecchi, Emilio. Appunti per un periplo dell'Africa. Milano, 1954.
Afr 3285.7	Cecil, E. The leisure of an Egyptian official. London, 1921.
Afr 3285.7.5	Cecil, E. The leisure of an Egyptian official. 2d ed. London, 1921.
Afr 8279.00.23	Cecil, Evelyn. On the eve of the war. London, 1900.
Afr 8250.2	Cecil John Rhodes. (Thomson, D.W.) Cape Town, 1947.
Afr 8250.10	Cecil Rhodes, his political life and speeches 1881-1900. (Verschoyle, F.) London, 1900.
Afr 8250.12	Cecil Rhodes, man and empire-maker. (Radziwill, E.) London, 1918.
Afr 8250.29.5	Cecil Rhodes, the colossus of Southern Africa. (Lockhart, J.G.) N.Y., 1963.
Afr 8250.9A	Cecil Rhodes, the man and his work. (Lesueur, G.) London, 1913.
Afr 8250.9.5	Cecil Rhodes, the man and his work. (Lesueur, G.) N.Y., 1914.
Afr 8250.1	Pamphlet box. Cecil Rhodes.
Afr 8250.31	Cecil Rhodes. (Baker, H.) London, 1934.
Afr 8250.5	Cecil Rhodes. (Hensman, H.) Edinburg, 1901.
Afr 8250.8.5	Cecil Rhodes. (Jourdan, P.) London, 19- .
Afr 8250.8.2	Cecil Rhodes. (Jourdan, P.) London, 1911.
Afr 8250.8	Cecil Rhodes. (Jourdan, P.) London, 1911.
Afr 8250.29	Cecil Rhodes. (Lockhart, J.G.) London, 1933.
Afr 8250.35.5	Cecil Rhodes. (Maurois, André.) Hamden, Conn., 1968.
Afr 8250.35.2	Cecil Rhodes. (Maurois, André.) London, 1953.
Afr 8250.35	Cecil Rhodes. (Maurois, Andre.) N.Y., 1953.
Afr 8250.33	Cecil Rhodes. (Oudard, G.) Paris, 1939.
Afr 8250.27	Cecil Rhodes. (Plomer, W.) London, 1933.

Afr 8250.17A	Cecil Rhodes. (Williams, B.) London, 1921.
Afr 8250.17.2	Cecil Rhodes. (Makers of the 19th century). (Williams, B.) N.Y., 1921.
Afr 8250.3	Cecil Rhodes. London, 1897.
Afr 8250.45	Cecil Rhodes and the princess. (Roberts, Brian.) London, 1969.
Afr 1609.27.5F	Celarie, H. Behind moroccan walls. N.Y., 1931.
Afr 4559.34.25	Celarie, H. Ethiopie XXe siècle. Paris, 1934.
Afr 1609.23.15	Celarie, H. Un mois au Maroc. Paris, 1923.
Afr 1922.10	Celarie, H. La prise d'Alger. Paris, 1929.
Afr 2220.10	Celarie, Henriette. Un mois en Algérie et en Tunisie. Paris, 1924.
Afr 1609.31	Celerier, Jean. Le Maroc. Paris, 1931.
Afr 1609.48	Celerier, Jean. Maroc. 2. ed. Paris, 1954.
Afr 2928.19	Cella, Paolo della. Viaggio da Tripoli di Barberia. Genova, 1819.
Afr 2928.19.2	Cella, Paolo della. Viaggio da Tripoli di Barberia. 3e ed. Città di Castello, 1912.
Afr 5969.157	Cencillo de Pineda, Manuel. El brigadier Conde de Argelejo. Madrid, 1948.
Afr 1326.12	Cenival, Pierre de. Bibliographie marocaine, 1923-33. Paris, 1937.
Afr 4368.5.3	Cenni biografici dell'eminentissimo Cardinale Guglielmo Massaja. Milano, 1889.
Afr Doc 707.353	Censimento della popolazione Italiana e straniera della Somalia 4 novembre 1953. (Italy. Istituto Centrali di Statistica.) Roma, 1958.
Afr Doc 9407.350	Censo da população de 1950. (Guinea. Portuguese. Secção Tecnica de Estatistica.) Lisboa, 1952? 2v.
Afr Doc 9207.340	Censo da população em 1940. (Mozambique. Repartição Tecnica de Estatistica.) Lourenço Marques, 1942. 4v.
Afr Doc 3707.346	Census, 1946. (Rhodesia, Northern. Census.) Lusaka, 1947.
Afr Doc 4107.356	Census, 1956. (Swaziland.) Mbabane, 1956?
Afr Doc 3707.362F	Census of distribution in 1962; wholesale, retail trade and selected services. (Zambia. Central Statistical Office.) Lusaka, 1965.
Afr Doc 3807.362.5F	The census of distribution in 1962 wholesale and retail trade and selected services. (Rhodesia (British Colony). Central Statistical Office.) Salisbury, 1965.
Afr Doc 1407.307	The census of Egypt taken in 1907. (Egypt. Department of Statistics and Census.) Cairo, 1909.
Afr Doc 1407.317	The census of Egypt taken in 1917. (Egypt. Department of Statistics and Census.) Cairo, 1920-21. 2v.
Afr Doc 4307.341.5F	Census of Europeans, 6 May, 1941: report on dwellings. (South Africa. Bureau of Statistics.) Pretoria, 1945.
Afr Doc 4307.341.10F	Census of Europeans, 6th May, 1941: report on structure and income on families. (South Africa. Bureau of Statistics.) Pretoria, 1945.
Afr Doc 4307.341F	Census of Europeans, 6th May, 1941: report on the wages of domestic servants. (South Africa. Bureau of Statistics.) Pretoria, 1946.
Afr Doc 1407.344.10	Census of industrial production, 1944. (Egypt. Department of Statistics and Census.) Cairo, 1947.
Afr Doc 3207.363	Census of industrial production, 1963. (Kenya. Economics and Statistics Division.) Nairobi, 1965.
Afr Doc 2807.364F	The census of industrial production, 1964. (Mauritius. Central Statistical Office.) Port Louis, 1965.
Afr Doc 3608.505	Census of industrial production. (Malawi. National Statistical Office.) Zomba. 1962+
Afr Doc 3407.361.10	Census of industrial production in Tanganyika. (Tanzania. Central Statistical Bureau.) Tanganyika, 1961.
Afr Doc 3407.362F	Census of large scale commercial farming in Tanganyika, October 1962. (Tanganyika. Treasury. Central Statistical Bureau.) Dar es Salaam, 1963.
Afr Doc 3507.356	Census of population, 1956. (Rhodesia and Nyasaland. Central Statistical Office.) Salisbury, 1960.
Afr Doc 9983.1.73	Census of population of Monrovia 1956; general characteristics. Report. (Liberia. Department of Agriculture and Commerce. Bureau of Statistics.) Monrovia, 1956.
Afr Doc 3807.351	Census of population 1951. (Central African Statistical Office.) Salisbury, 1954.
Afr Doc 1807.348	Census of populations 1948. Report and tables. (Gold Coast (Colony). Census Office.) London, 1950.
Afr Doc 3507.360F	The census of production in 1960 and 1961: mining, manufacturing, electricity and water supply. (Rhodesia and Nyasaland.) Salisbury, 1963.
Afr Doc 3707.363.5	The census of production in 1963. (Zambia. Central Statistical Office.) Lusaka, 1965.
Afr Doc 3808.510F	The census of production mining manufacturing construction, electricity, and water supply. (Rhodesia (British Colony). Central Statistical Office.) Salisbury. 1962+
Afr Doc 4307.318	Census of the European or White races of the Union of South Africa, 1918. (South Africa. Office of Census and Statistics.) Cape Town, 1919-1920.
Afr Doc 4307.318.5	Census of the European or white races of the Union of South Africa 1918. Final report and supplementary tables. (South Africa. Office of Census and Statistics.) Cape Town, 1920.
Afr Doc 3407.331F	Census of the native population of Tanganyika territory, 1931. (Tanganyika. Secretariat.) Dar es Salaam, 1932.
Afr 6850.9F	Census of the native population of Tanganyika territory, 1931. (Tanganyika Territory. Secretariat.) Dar es Salaam, 1932.
Afr Doc 4307.311	Census of the Union of South Africa, 1911. (South Africa. Office of Census and Statistics.) Pretoria, 1913. 2v.
Afr Doc 1807.321	Census report, 1921, for the Gold Coast and Colony. (Gold Coast (Colony). Census Office.) Accra, 1923.
Afr Doc 4707.304F	Census report of the Orange River Colony. (Orange Free State.) Bloemfontein, 1904.
Afr Doc 3307.321	Census returns, 1921. (Uganda.) Uganda, 1921.
Afr Doc 2807.352F	Census 1952 of Mauritius and of its dependencies. (Mauritius.) Port Louis, 1953. 3 pam.

Afr Doc 3507.359.10
The censuses of production of the Federation of Rhodesia and Nyasaland, 1958-1959. (Rhodesia and Nyasaland. Central Statistical Office.) Salisbury, 1961.

Afr 2315.5
Cent ans d'effort français en Algérie. (Gojon, Edmond.) Paris, 1930.

Afr 1830.105
Le centenaire de l'Algerie. (Algeria. Commissariat General du Centenaire.) Alger, 1931.
2v.

Afr 1753.1.10
Centenarios de Ceuta e de Afonso de Albuquerque. (Academia das Sciencias de Lisboa.) Lisboa, 1916.

Afr 6196.20
The centenary history of the Larteh Presbyterian Church, 1853-1953. (Ansah, J.K.) Larteh, 1955.

Afr 2975.7
Cento giorni di prigionia nell'oasi di Cufra. (Brezzi, G.) Milano, 1930.

Afr Doc 7209.505
Central Africn Republic. Ministère l'Education Nationale, de la Jeunesse et des Sports. Statistiques scolaires. Bangui. 1964+

Afr 9540.1
Pamphlet box. Central Africa.

NEDL Afr 4095.11
Central Africa. (Long, C.C.) N.Y., 1877.

Afr 9549.60
Central Africa. (Raven, Faith.) London, 1960.

Afr 9435.12
Central Africa and the British Parliament. (Africa Bureau, London.) London, 1957.

Afr 9435.12.5
Central Africa and the franchise. (Africa Bureau, London.) London, 1958.

Afr 9535.12F
Central Africa Historical Association. Local series pamphlet. Salisbury, Rhodesia. 2,1960+

Afr 9535.12.5
Central Africa research bulletin. London. 1,1968+

Afr 9432.7
Central African Archives in retrospect and prospect. (Rhodesia, Southern. Central African Archives.) Salisbury, 1947.

Afr 9435.13
Central African Conference. Report. London, 1963.

Afr 9448.50
Central African emergency. (Sanger, Clyde.) London, 1960.

Afr 9425.15
Central African examiner. Salisbury, Southern Rhodesia. 1,1957+
10v.

Afr 555.152
A Central African jubilee. (F.S. Arnot Jubilee Conference, Muchacha, 1931.) London, 1932.

Afr Doc 7209.44
Central African Republic. Budget de l'état. 1959+
8v.

Afr 5460.15
The Central African Republic. (France. Embassy. U.S.) N.Y., 1960.

Afr Doc 7207.10
Central African Republic. Direction de la Statistique et de la Conjoncture. Annuaire statistique. Paris. 1964

Afr Doc 7207.5
Central African Republic. Service de la Statistique et de la Conjoncture. Bulletin mensuel de statistique. Bangui. 14,1965+

Afr Doc 7207.361
Central African Republic. Service de la Statistique Générale. Enquête agricole en République centrafricaine. n.p., 1960-61.

Afr Doc 7207.360
Central African Republic. Service de la Statistique Generale. Enquête démographique. n.p., 1959-60.

Afr Doc 3808.710
Central African Statistical Office. Annual statement of the trade of Southern Rhodesia with British countries and foreign countries. Salisbury. 22-24,1951-1953

Afr Doc 3807.351
Central African Statistical Office. Census of population 1951. Salisbury, 1954.

Afr 9499.75F
Central African Statistical Office. Report on Southern Rhodesia family expenditure survey. Salisbury, 1952.

Afr 9448.55
Central African survey. (Blake, W.T.) London, 1961.

Afr 9445.35
Central African witness. (Dunn, Cyril.) London, 1959.

Afr 55.30
Central and East African who's who. Salisbury.

Afr 9439.54.5
Central and southern Africa. 2. ed. (Lumb, Sybil Victoria.) Cambridge, 1962.

Afr 28.83
Central Asian Research Centre, London. Soviet writing of Africa, 1959-61. Oxford, 1963.

Afr 6193.52
Central banking, international law, and economic development. (Ayatey, Siegfried B.Y.) Dubugre, 1968.

Afr 9542.8
Central Bantu historical texts. Lusaka. 1+

Afr Doc 1309.15
The central budget; estimates of revenue and expenditure. (Sudan.) Khartoum? 1966+

Afr 6879.24
Central commission of Tanganyika exhibition handbook. (British Empire Exhibition, Wembley, 1924.) London, 1924.

Afr 6988.58.260
The central Namib Desert. (Logan, R.F.) Washington, 1960.

Afr 5477.930
Le Centre-africain français. (Ferrandi, Jean.) Paris, 1930.

Afr 1268.5
Centre d'Accueil Nord-Africain de Saint-Louis, Marseilles. Eléments d'introduction à la vie moderne. Paris, 1960.

Afr 3.50
Centre d'Analyse et de Recherche Documentaires pour l'Afrique Noire. Recherche, enseignement, documentation africanistes francophones. Paris. 1,1969+

Afr 28.1.5
Centre de Documentation Economique et Sociale Africaine. Enquêtes bibliographiques. 7-15
2v.

Afr 5000.25
Centre de Documentation et de Diffusion des Industries, des Mines et de l'Energie Outre-Mer. Colloques. Paris. 1,1963+
4v.

Afr 5480.194
Le centre de l'Afrique. (Brunache, Paul.) Paris, 1894.

Afr 7503.5
Centre de Recherche et d'Information Socio-Politiques. Courrier africain. Bruxelles. 1,1960+
8v.

Afr 7543.5
Centre de Recherche et d'Information Socio-Politiques. Documents, 1950-1960. Bruxelles, 1962.

Afr 3.46F
Centre de Recherche et d'Information Socio-Politiques. Travaux africains. Dossier documentaire. Bruxelles. 1,1964+

Afr 1040.10F
Centre des Hautes Etudes. Six conférences d'initiation à la politique musulmane de la France en Afrique du Nord. n.p., 1943.

Afr 3300.32
Centre d'Etudes de Politique Etrangère, Paris. L'Egypte indépendante. Paris, 1938.

Afr 7503.3.10
Centre d'Etudes des Problèmes Sociaux Indigènes, Elisabethville, Belgian Congo. Le CEPSI; ses buts, ses activités, ses réalisations. Elisabethville, 1964.

Afr 7503.3
Centre d'Etudes des Problèmes Sociaux Indigènes, Elisabethville, Belgian Congo. Bulletin trimestriel. 17,1951+
17v.

Afr 7503.3.5
Centre d'Etudes des Problèmes Sociaux Indigènes, Elisabethville, Belgian Congo. Collection de mémoires. 1+
14v.

Afr 5282.5
Centre d'Etudes Economiques et Sociales d'Afrique Occidentale. Fonctionnaire et développement. Bobo-Dioulasso, 1966.

Afr 6650.5
Centre d'Études et de Recherches de Kara. Documents. Lama-Kara, Togo. 1,1967+

Afr 2248.15
Centre d'Etudes et d'Informations des Problèmes Humaines dans les Zones Arides. Les Mekhadma. Paris, 1960.

Afr 2030.335
Centre d'Études Régionales de Kabylie. Publication. Mémoires et travaux. Alger.

Afr 1803.5
Centre d'Information pour les Problèmes de l'Algérie et du Sahara. Publications. Paris. 1+

Afr 7850.15
Le centre extra-coutumier de Coquilhatville. (Thier, Franz M.) Bruxelles, 1956.

Afr 7873.5
Le centre extra-coutumier de Coquilhatville. (Thier, Franz M. de.) Bruxelles, 1956.

Afr 7540.27
Les centres indigènes extra-coutumiers au Congo belge. Thèse. (Baumer, Guy.) Paris, 1939.

Afr 7050.10
Centro de Estudos da Guiné Portuguesa. Publicações. 1,1947+
9v.

Afr 8928.2
A century of mission work in Basutoland, 1833-1933. (Ellenberger, Victor.) Morija, 1938.

Htn Afr 8279.00.41*
A century of wrong. (Reitz, Francois W.) London, 1900.

Afr 7503.3.10
Le CEPSI; ses buts, ses activités, ses réalisations. (Centre d'Etudes des Problèmes Sociaux Indigènes, Elisabethville, Belgian Congo.) Elisabethville, 1964.

Afr 5405.109.35
Cerbelaud-Salagnac, Georges. Savorgnan de Brazza. Paris, 1960.

Afr 674.93.25
A cerca da cronica dos feitos de Guiné. (Leite, D.) Lisboa, 1941.

Afr 2030.460.20
Cercle d'Études Algériennes. Lettres à un métropolitain. Alger, 1960.

Afr 2223.962
Cercle Taleb-Moumié. Fidel Castro ou tshombe? Paris, 1962.

Afr 7222.5.10
Cercos de Moçambique. (Durao, Antonio.) Lisboa, 1937.

Htn Afr 7222.5*
Cercos de Moçambique. (Durao, Antonio.) Madrid, 1633.

Afr 2950.15
Cerrata, L. Sirtis, studio geografico-storico. Avellino, 1933.

Afr 4559.28.10
Cerulli, E. Etiopia occidentale. Roma, 1928.
2v.

Afr 4764.957
Cerulli, Enrico. Somalia. v.1-2. Roma, 1957-64.
3v.

Afr 9549.61
Cerulli, Ernesta. Nel paese dei Bantu. Torino, 1961.

Afr 5993.20
Ceruti, Frorencio. Africa la virgen. Santander, 1928.

Afr 4045.14
Cervani, Giulio. Il voyage in Egypte, 1861-1862, di Pasquale Revoltella. Trieste, 1962.

Afr 25.108.2
Červenka, Zdenek. The Organization of African Unity and its charter. 2d ed. London, 1969.

Afr 1608.85.8
Cervera Baviera, J. Expedicion geografico-militar...Marruecos. Barcelona, 1885.

Afr 5957.105
Cervera Pery, José. La marina española en Guinea Ecuatorial, sentido y grandeza de una aportacion historica. Santa Isabel, 1968.

Afr 1494.63
Cerych, Ladislav. Europeens et Marocains. Bruges, 1964.

Afr 5180.37.6
Ces routes qui ne menent à rien. 6e éd. (Bosshard, J.M.) Paris, 1937.

Afr 7122.52
Cesar, A. Angola, 1961. 3. ed. Verbo, 1961.

Afr 14518.5
César, Amândio. Contos portugueses do ultramar; antologia. Porto, 1969.

Afr 7068.14
César, Amândio. Em "Chão papel" na terra da Guiné. Lisboa, 1967.

Afr 7068.4
Cesar, Amandio. Guine 1965, contra-atorque. Braga, 1965.

Afr 14505.10
César, Amândio. Parágrafos de literatura ultramarina. Lisboa, 1967.

Afr 4700.30.10
Cesari, Cesare. L'evoluzione della coscienza e dell'attività coloniale italiana. Roma, 1930.

Afr 4700.33
Cesari, Cesare. Gli italiani nella conoscenza dell'Africa. Roma, 1933.

Afr 4700.28.10
Cesari, Cesare. I nostri precursori coloniale. Roma, 1928.

Afr 4700.33.5
Cesari, Cesare. Pionieri italiani in Africa. Rome, 1933.

Afr 4764.934
Cesari, Cesare. La Somalia italiana. Roma, 1934-35.

Afr 8160.6
Cetshwayo's Dutchman. (Vijn, Cornelius.) London, 1880.

Afr 12979.44.100
Cette Afrique-là. (Ikelle-Matiba, J.) Paris, 1963.

Afr 8235.7
Cetywayo and his white neighbours. (Haggard, H.R.) London, 1888.

Afr 8160.7
Cetywayo and the three generals. (Dunn, John.) Pietermaritzburg, 1886.

Afr 7815.26
Ceulemans, P. La question arabe et le Congo, 1883-1892. Bruxelles, 1959.

Afr 1753.1
Pamphlet box. Ceuta.

Afr 1753.8
Ceuta llave principal del Estrecho. (Tello Amondareyn, M.) Madrid, 1897.

Afr 2030.125
Ceux d'Algérie, lettres de rappelés. Paris, 1957.

Afr 3180.7A
Cezzar, Ahmed. Ottoman Egypt in the eighteenth century. Cambridge, 1962.

Afr 2248.10
Les Chaamba sous le régime français, leure transformation. Thèse. (Regnier, Yves.) Paris, 1938.

Afr 2248.5
Les Chaanba (leur nomadisme). (Cauneille, A.) Paris, 1968.

Afr 3988.6
Chabral de Volvic. Essai sur les mours des habitans modernes de l'Egypte. Paris, 1826.

Afr 5480.267
Chad, President. Terre tchadienne. Paris, 1967.

Afr Doc 7109.305
Chad. Comptes économiques. Paris. 1961-1963

Afr Doc 7114.5F
Chad. Assemblée Territoriale. Procès-verbaux, etc. 1951-1953

Afr Doc 7135.5
Chad. Ministère de l'Economie et des Transports. Rapport annuel. 1965+

Afr 5482.15
Chad. Ministère du Plan et de la Coopération. Premier plan quinquennal de développement économique et social, 1966-1970. Fort Lamy?, 1967.

Afr Doc 7107.10
Chad. Service de la Statistique Générale. Annuaire statistique du Tchad. Fort Lamy? 2,1968+

Afr Doc 7107.5
Chad. Service de la Statistique Générale. Bulletin mensuel de la statistique. Fort-Lamy. 127,1965+

Afr Doc 7107.364
Chad. Service de la Statistique Générale. Enquête démographique ou Tchad, 1964 résultats définitifs. v.1-2. Paris, 1966.

Afr Doc 7176.5
Chad. Service de la Statistique Générale. Recensement démographique de Fort Lamy. Paris. 1965

Afr 7065.510
Chagas, Frederico Pinheiro. Na Guiné, 1907-1908. Lisboa, 1910.

Afr 4095.19
Chaille-Long, C. My life in four continents. v.1-2. London, 1912.
2v.

Afr 5054.68
Chaillez, Marcel. Histoire de l'Afrique occidentale française, 1638-1959. Paris, 1968.

Afr 1422.3
Chais, G. De la convention de Tangier. n.p., 1845.

Afr 8865.18
Chakela, Koenyama S. The past and present Lesotho (Basutoland). Cairo, 1962.

Afr 2035.5 — Chaliand, Gérard. L'Algérie est-elle socialiste? Paris, 1964.
Afr 7065.526 — Chaliand, Gérard. Armed struggle in Africa. N.Y., 1969.
Afr 7025.5 — Chaliand, Gérard. Lutte armée en Afrique. Paris, 1967.
Afr 5405.112.5 — Challaye, Felicien. Le Congo français. Paris, 1909.
Afr 50.40 — The challenge of Africa. (Busia, Kafi A.) N.Y., 1962.
Afr 8678.289 — The challenge of change. (Steward, Alex.) Cape Town, 1962.
Afr 7580.26 — Challenge of the Congo. (Nkrumah, Kwame.) London, 1967.
Afr 6538.60 — The challenge of Uganda's second five year development plan. (Milton Obote Foundation.) Kampala, 1967.
Afr 9446.20 — Chalmers, James. Fighting the Matabele. London, 1898.
Afr 1609.64 — Chalyi, Bohdan I. Marokko, svitanok. Kyiv, 1964.
Afr 635.4 — Cham et Zaphet. 2e éd. (Chaneel, A. de.) Paris, 186-.
Afr 7309.23 — Chamberlain, G.A. African hunting among the Thongas. N.Y., 1923.
Afr 8325.25 — Chamberlain, J. Defence of the British troops in South Africa. London, 1902.
Afr 9558.32 — Chambliss, J.E. The lives and travels of Livingstone and Stanley. Boston, 1881.
Afr 5482.10 — Chambre de Commerce d'Agriculture et d'Industrie du Tchad. Situation économique de la Republique du Tchad. Fort-Lamy?, 1965.
Afr 5405.109.10 — Chambrun, J.A. de P. Brazza. Paris, 1930.
Afr 2376.5 — Champault, Francine Dominque. Une oasis du Sahara nord-occidental: Tabelbala. Paris, 1969.
Afr 2285.7 — Champeaux, G. A travers les oasis sahariennes. Paris, 1903.
Afr 8686.20 — Champion, George. Journal of the Reverend George Champion. Cape Town, 1967.
Afr 1609.24.5 — Champion, P. Tanger, fes et meknes. Paris, 1924.
Afr 5343.35 — Chances et risques. Session d'étude 20 juillet-11 août 1966. (La Côte-d'Ivoire.) Bruxelles, 1967. 2v.
Afr 5257.10 — La chancre du Niger. (Herbart, Pierre.) Paris, 1939.
Afr 635.4 — Chaneel, A. de. Cham et Zaphet. 2e éd. Paris, 186-.
Afr 1955.51 — Changarnier, N.A.T. Campagnes d'Afrique, 1830-1848. Paris, 1930.
Afr 6460.80.5 — Change and challenge (A study of the social and economic changes among the Kenya Luo). (Whisson, Michael.) Nairobi, 1964.
Afr 6275.100 — Change here for Kano. (Miller, E.P.) Zaria, 1959.
Afr 5342.60 — Changements sociaux en Côte-d'Ivoire. (Holas, Bohumil.) Paris, 1961.
Afr 2687.4.2 — Changes at Shebika. 1st American ed. (Duvignaud, Jean.) N.Y., 1970.
Afr 210.63.40 — The changing map of Africa. (Hodgson, R.D.) Princeton, 1963.
Afr 9639.65 — Changing patterns of settlement and land use in the eastern province of Northern Rhodesia. (Kay, George.) Hull, 1965.
Afr 8710.19 — The changing years. (Rosenthal, Eric.) Cape Town, 1957.
Afr 6455.4 — Chanler, W.A. Through jungle and desert. 1 vol. and maps. N.Y., 1896. 2v.
Afr 12922.7.110 — Le chant du lac. (Bhely-Quenum, Olympe.) Paris, 1965.
Afr 4000.10F — Chantre, E. Recherches anthropologiques dans l'Afrique orientale. Lyon, 1904.
Afr 12372.67.100 — Chants pour hâter la mort du temps des Orphée ou Madinina île esclave. (Boukman, Daniel.) Honfleur, 1967.
Afr 12639.24.110 — Chants pour Naëtt. (Senghor, L.S.) Paris, 1949.
Afr 7548.94.5 — Chapaux, Albert. Le Congo historique. Bruxelles, 1894.
Afr 7875.5 — Chapelier, Alice. Elisabethville. Bruxelles, 1951.
Afr 5048.15 — Chapelle, Jean. Nomades noirs du Sahara. Paris, 1957.
Afr 1258.64 — Chapitres de géographie sur le nord-ouest de l'Afrique. (Faidherbe, L.L.C.) Paris, 1864.
Afr 4513.36.20 — Chaplin, W.W. Blood and ink. N.Y., 1936.
Afr 4070.43 — Chapman, Abel. Savage Sudan. London, 1921.
Afr 4070.43.5 — Chapman, Abel. Savage Sudan. N.Y., 1922.
Afr 8808.72 — Chapman, Charles. A voyage from Southhampton to Cape Town. London, 1872.
NEDL Afr 8658.68 — Chapman, J. Travels in the interior of South Africa. London, 1868. 2v.
Afr 5749.43 — Chapman, O.M. Across Madagascar. London, 1942.
Afr 9704.3 — Chapman, William. A pathfinder in south Central Africa. London, 1909.
Afr 8167.5 — A chapter on the Basuto war, a lecture. (Brownlee, Charles.) Lovedale, 1889.
Afr 9425.30 — Chapupu, independent Southern Rhodesia. Salisbury. 1,1962+
Afr 5585.30 — Chapus, G.S. Rainilaiarivony, un homme d'Etat Malgache. Paris, 1953.
Afr 5549.61 — Chapus, Georges. Manuel d'histoire de Madagascar. Paris, 1961.
Afr 626.106 — Charbonneau, J. Marches et marchands d'Afrique noire. Paris, 1961.
Afr 1570.67 — Charbonneau, J. Maroc, vingt-troisième heure. Paris, 1938.
Afr 6620.60 — Charbonneau, J. On se bat sous l'équateur. Paris, 1933.
Afr 2209.55.5 — Charbonneau, Jean. Des Africains s'interrogent. Paris, 1955.
Afr 2731.15.60 — Charbonneau, Jean. La destinée paradoxale de Charles de Foucauld. Paris, 1958.
Afr 5640.7 — Charbonneau, Jean. Gallieni à Madagascar. Paris, 1950.
Afr 5640.15.20 — Charbonnel, Henry. De Madagascar au Verdun. Paris, 1962.
Afr 5420.257 — Charbonnier, François. Gabon, terre d'avenir. Paris, 1957.
Afr 2030.461.35 — Charby, J. L'Algérie en prison. Paris, 1961.
Afr 9558.36 — Charles, Elizabeth. Three martyrs of the nineteenth century... Livingstone, Gordon, and Patteson. N.Y., 1886.
Afr 555.5.3 — Charles de Foucauld, hermit. (Bazin, René.) London, 1943.
Afr 2731.15.90 — Charles de Foucauld, les étapes d'une recherche. (Quesnel, Roger.) Tours, 1966.
Afr 555.5.5 — Charles de Foucauld. (Bazin, René.) N.Y., 1923.
Afr 555.5 — Charles de Foucauld. (Bazin, René.) Paris, 1921.
Afr 2731.15.100 — Charles de Foucauld. (Gorrée, Georges.) Paris, 1965.
Afr 2731.15.95 — Charles de Foucauld. (Lyautey, Pierre.) Paris, 1966.
Afr 2731.15.52 — Charles de Foucauld. (Nord, Pierre.) Paris, 1959.
Afr 2731.15.85 — Charles de Foucauld. (Roche, Aimé.) Lyon, 1964.
Afr 2731.15.34 — Charles de Foucauld. 3 ed. (Carrouges, Michel.) Paris, 1958.
Afr 9073.467 — Charles Johnson of Zululand. (Lee, Albert William.) Westminster, Eng., 1930.
Afr 3183.15 — Charles-Roux, François. Autour d'une route. Paris, 1922.
Afr 3183.25 — Charles-Roux, François. France, Egypte et mer Rouge, de 1715 à 1798. Le Caire, 1951.

Afr 1830.40.20 — Charles-Roux, François. France et Afrique du nord avant 1830, les precurseurs de la conquete. Paris, 1932.
Afr 1570.70 — Charles-Roux, François. Missions diplomatiques françaises a Fès. Paris, 1955.
Afr 3215.3.25 — Charles-Roux, François. Thiers et Méhémet-Ali. Paris, 1951.
Afr 8252.4 — Charles Tennant Jones, M.L.A., and our government. (Cowen, Charles.) Wynberg, 1884.
Afr 9050.7 — The Charlestown story. (Paton, A.) Pietermaritzburg, 1961.
Afr 555.26.3 — Charlesworth, M.L. Africa's mountain valley. London, 1857.
Afr 9748.580 — Charlton, Leslie. Spark in the stubble: Colin Morris of Zambia. London, 1969.
Afr 1608.87 — Charmes, G. Une ambassade au Maroc. Paris, 1887.
Afr 2218.11 — Charnay, Jean Paul. La vie musulmane en Algérie d'aprés la jurisprudence de la premiére moitié du XXe siècle. Paris, 1965.
Afr 5190.16 — Charpy, Jacques. La fondation de Dakar. Paris, 1958.
Afr 2030.464.10 — La charte d'Alger, ensemble des textes adoptés par le premier congrés du Parti de Front de libération nationale. (Algerian Front of National Liberation.) Alger, 1964.
Afr 3326.4 — The Charter. (Nasser, G.A.) Cairo, 1962.
Afr 9445.10 — The chartered millions. (Harris, John H.) London, 1920.
Afr 2230.19F — Charveriat, F. A travers la Kabylie. n.p., n.d.
Afr 8808.43 — Chase, John C. The Cape of Good Hope...Algoa bay. London, 1843.
Afr 8808.43.5 — Chase, John C. The Cape of Good Hope and the Eastern Province of Algoa Bay. Facsimile. Cape Town, 1967.
Afr 8320.5 — The chase of De Wet. (Howland, F.H.) Providence, 1901.
Afr 8687.375 — Chasing the wind. (Van der Spuy, Kenneth R.) Cape Town, 1966.
Afr 5840.15 — Chassagnon, H., Abbé. Le frère Scubilion de l'Institut des frères des écoles chrétiennes. Paris, 1902.
Afr 718.34 — Chasses aux grandes fauves pendant la traversée du continent noir. (Foa, Edouard.) Paris, 1899.
Afr 4559.03 — Chasses et gens d'Abyssinie. (Leroux, H.) Paris, 1903.
Afr 1570.26 — Chastaud, P. Les conditions d'établissement du protectorat français au Maroc. Paris, 1913.
Afr 210.65.35 — Chataslnski, Jozef. Blizej afryki. Warszawa, 1965.
Afr 200.7 — Chatelain, C. L'Afrique et l'expansion coloniale. Paris, 1901.
Afr 2618.20 — Chatelain, Yves. La vie littéraire et intellectuelle en Tunisie de 1900 à 1937. Paris, 1937.
Afr 1625.5 — Chatelier, A. Le. Tribus du sud-ouest Marocain. Paris, 1891.
Afr 9506.2 — Chater, Patricia. Grass roots. London, 1962.
Afr 1680.7 — Chatinieres, P. Dans le grand atlas marocain. Paris, 1919.
Afr 2208.93.3 — Chatrieux, E. Etudes algériennes. Paris, 1893.
Afr 8685.25 — Chatterjee, M.N. Auswanderung nach Indien. I. Inaug. Diss. Leipzig, 1931.
Afr 8685.26 — Chatterjee, Santosh Kumar. Indians in South Africa. Calcutta, 1944.
Afr 609.60.65 — Chatterji, Suniti. Africanism. Calcutta, 1960.
Afr 1957.9 — Chaudau de Raynal, P. L'expédition d'Alger, 1830. Paris, 1930.
Afr 5385.21 — Chaudoin, E. Trois mois de captivité au Dahomey. Paris, 1891.
Afr 4008.8 — Chauleur, S. Histoire des Coptes d'Egypte. Paris, 1960.
Afr 5600.6 — Chauvot, H. Madagascar et la France. Paris, 1848.
Afr 608.81 — Chavanne, J. Afrika im Lichte unserer Tage. Wien, 1881.
Afr 625.10 — Chavanne, J. Erleuterungen zur Wandkarte von Afrika. Wien, 1882.
Afr 2748.79 — Chavanne, J. Die Sahara. Vienna, 1879.
Afr 5405.112 — Chavannes, Charles de. Avec Brazza. Paris, 1936.
Afr 5405.112.2 — Chavannes, Charles de. Le Congo français. Paris, 1937.
Afr 5746.50 — Chavanon, J. Une ancienne relation sur Madagascar (1650). Paris, 1897.
Afr 6685.8 — Chazelas, V. Territoires africains sous mandat de la France. Paris, 1931.
Afr 6738.23 — Chazelas, Victor. Territoires africains sous mandat de la France. Paris, 1931.
Afr 4559.35.35 — Che cosa è l'Etiopia. (Nanni, Ugo.) Milano, 1935.
Afr 2687.4 — Chebika: mutations dans un village du Maghreb. (Duvignaud, Jean.) Paris, 1968.
Afr 2945.9 — Checchi, S. Attraverso la Cirenaica. Roma, 1912.
Afr 6686.20 — Checchi and Company. A development company for Togo. Washington, 1963.
Afr 8687.354 — Cheeseman, Thomas. The story of William Threlfall. Cape Town, 1910.
Afr 4688.15.5 — Cheesman, R.E. Lake Tana and the blue Nile. London, 1936.
Afr 3745.20 — Cheibany, A.K. La situation administrative et économique du Soudan anglo-égyptien. These. Paris, 1926.
Afr 7119.56 — Chela, João da. Africa lusiada. Alges-Lisboa, 1956.
Afr 8659.29.5 — Chelvers, H.A. The seven wonders of southern Africa. Johannesburg, 1929.
Afr 12985.65.100 — Chemin d'Europe. (Oyono, Ferdinand.) Paris, 1960.
Afr 5387.10 — Cheminault, R. L'artisanat. Paris, 1965. 2v.
Afr 1830.20.52 — Les chemins de fer...de l'Algérie. (Poggi, Jacques.) Paris, 1931.
Afr 7803.38 — Les chemins du seigneur du Congo. (Carpenter, G.W.) Leopoldville, 1953.
Afr 1607.87.5 — Chenier, L.S. Present state of Morocco. London, 1788. 2v.
Afr 1367.87 — Chenier, L.S. de. Recherches historiques sur les Maures. Paris, 1787. 3v.
Afr 5056.108 — Cheran, Georges. La société noire de l'Afrique occidentale française. Paris, 1908.
Afr 9499.28 — Cherkasov, Iurii N. Ekonomicheskie problemy Iuzhnoi Rodezii. Moskva, 1966.
Afr 6392.33 — Cherniavsky, Mark. Development prospects in East-Africa: Kenya, Tanzania and Uganda. Bergen, 1965.
Afr 8687.150 — Cherries on my plate. (Carr, Barbara Comyns.) Cape Town, 1966.
Afr 609.41.5 — Cherry Kearton's travels. (Kearton, Cherry.) London, 1941.
Afr 8215.5 — Chesson, Frederick William. The Dutch Boers and slavery. London, 1869.
Afr 8215.6 — Chesson, Frederick William. The Dutch Republic of South Africa. London, 1871.
Afr 5480.207 — Chevalier, Auguste. Mission Chari, lac Tchad, 1902-1904. Paris, 1907.
Afr 8931.29 — Chevalier Oscar Wilhelm Alric Forssman. (Forssman, Alric.) Pretoria, 1961.

Afr 2030.458 Chevallier, Jacques. Nous. Paris, 1958.
Afr 2753.1 Les chevaux du Sahara. (Daumas, E.) Paris, 1858.
Afr 1609.13.15 Chevrillon, A. Marrakech dans les palmes. Paris, 1919.
Afr 2209.27.35 Chevrillon, A. Les puritains du désert. Paris, 1927.
Afr 1609.33F Chevrillon, A. Visions du Maroc. Marseille, 1933.
Afr 1655.1 Chevrillon, Andre. Un crepuscule d'islam-Maroc. Paris, 1906.
Afr 2025.17 Chez ceux qui guettent. Islam saharien. (Pommerol, J.) Paris, 1902.
Afr 4259.17 Chez la reine de Saba. (Leroux, Hughes.) Paris, 1917.
Afr 4559.34.5 Chez le roi des rois d'Ethiopie. (Rebeaud, Henri.) Neuchâtel, 1934.
Afr 6194.4 Chez les Ashanti. (Perregaux, E.) n.p., n.d.
Afr 5760.6 Chez les Hovas (au pays rouge). (Carol, Jean.) Paris, 1898.
Afr 5760.6.2 Chez les Hovas (au pays rouge). 2e ed. (Carol, Jean.) Paris, 1898.
Afr 2228.5 Chez les Moumenins. (Mule, A.) Paris, 1906.
Afr 555.12.10 Chez les pères blancs, Tunisie, Kabylie Sahara. (Vanlande, René.) Paris, 1929.
Afr 4384.2 Chiala, L. Discorso sul credito di 20 milioni per l'azione militare in Africa. Roma, 1887.
Afr 2505.5A Chiala, L. Tunisi. Torino, 1895.
Afr 4394.2 Chiala, Valentino. Il Generale Dabormida nella giornata del 1 marzo 1896. Roma, 1897.
Afr 4730.5 Chicala, L. La spedizione di Massaua. Torino, 1888.
Afr 10663.5 Chick, John D. An exploratory investigation of press readership among selected students in Zaria. Zaria, 1966.
Afr 6333.61A Chidzero, B.T.G. Tanganyika and international trusteeship. London, 1961.
Afr 9435.22 Chief, council and commissioner: some problems of government in Rhodesia. (Holleman, Johan Frederik.) Assen, 1969.
Afr 8687.263.10 Chief Albert Lutuli of South Africa. (Benson, M.) London, 1963.
Afr 9289.6 Chief Moroka. (Molema, S.) Cape Town, 195-.
Afr 5445.10 Chiefs and cities of Central Africa. (Macleod, Olive.) Edinburgh, 1912.
Afr 6540.30 The Chiga of western Uganda. (Edel, May Mandelbaum.) London, 1969.
Afr 14723.1 Chigubo. (Craveirinha, José.) Lisboa, 1964.
Afr 7003.2 Chilcote, Ronald H. Emerging nationalism in Portuguese Africa. Stanford, 1969.
Afr 7015.46 Chilcote, Ronald H. Portuguese Africa. Englewood Cliffs, N.J., 1967.
Afr 3978.63.8 Child life in Egypt. (Whately, M.L.) Philadelphia, 1866.
Afr 6470.211 Child of two worlds. (Gatheru, R.M.) London, 1964.
Afr 8289.00.21 Childers, E. In the ranks of the C.I.V. London, 1901.
Afr 3315.120A Childers, E. The road to Suez. London, 1962.
Afr 609.41 Childers, J.S. Mumbo Jumbo, esquire. N.Y., 1941.
Afr 2929.66 Children of Allah. 1st ed. (Keith, Agnes Newton.) Boston, 1966.
Afr 10621.71.100 The children of Anause. (Appiah, Peggy.) London, 1968.
Afr 5748.87 The children of Madagascar. (Standing, H.F.) London, 1887.
Afr 10678.61.100 Children of the goddess, and other plays. (Henshaw, James Ene.) London, 1964.
Afr 8678.13.15 Children of the Veld, Bantu vignettes. (Shepherd, R.H.W.) London, 1937.
Afr 9853.5.5 Children of their fathers...Ngoni of Malawi. (Read, Margaret.) N.Y., 1968.
Afr 7180.30 Childs, Gladwyn Murray. Umbundu kinship and character. London, 1949.
Afr 555.23.65 Chilson, E. H. Ambassador of the king. Wichita, Kan., 1943.
Afr 8659.30.15 Chilvers, H.A. The seven lost trails of Africa. London, 1930.
Afr 9165.42.20 Chilvers, Hedley A. Out of the crucible. Johannesburg, 1948.
Afr 8175.24 Chilvers, Hedley A. The yellow man looks on, being the story of the Anglo-Dutch conflict in Southern Africa. London, 1933.
Afr 14740.76.100 Chinanga, poemas. (Trindade, Francisco Alberto Cartaxo e.) Lisboa, 1969.
Afr 500.80 Chinese-African People's Friendship Association. The Chinese people resolutely support the just struggle of the African people. Peking, 1961.
Afr 500.80 The Chinese people resolutely support the just struggle of the African people. (Chinese-African People's Friendship Association.) Peking, 1961.
Afr 10671.12.815 Chinua Achebe. (Carroll, David.) N.Y., 1970.
Afr 10671.12.805 Chinua Achebe. (Ravenscroft, Arthur.) Burnt Mill, 1969.
Afr 8686.3 Chirgwin, Arthur Mitchell. An African pilgrimage. London, 1932.
Afr 10904.5 Chirimo. Salisbury. 1,1968+
Afr 3285.10 Chirol, Valentine. The Egyptian problem. London, 1920.
Afr 5342.20 Chivas-Baron, C. Côte-d'Ivoire. Paris, 1939.
Afr 40.63.5 Chodak, S. Systemy polityczne czarnej Afryki. Warszawa, 1963.
VAfr 6195.20 Chodak, Szymon. Kaplani, czarownicy, wiedźmy. Wyd. 1. Warszawa, 1967.
Afr 8369.52 The choice before South Africa. (Sachs, E.S.) London, 1952.
Afr 2285.3 Choisy, A. Le Sahara, souvenirs d'une mission à Goléah. Paris, 1881.
Afr 4226.4 Chojnacki, S. List of current periodical publications in Ethiopia. Addis Ababa, 1964.
Afr 4559.65.10 Choleva, Emil. Etiopska dobrodruzstvi. Praha, 1965.
Afr 5448.14 Le chômage à Brazzaville. Paris, 1963. 2v.
Afr 5448.10 Le chômage à Brazzaville en 1957. (Devauges, Roland.) Paris, 1958.
Afr 7575.80.5 Chome, Jules. A propos d'un livre posthume de Patrice Lumumba. Bruxelles, 1961.
Afr 7913.2.5 Chomé, Jules. Mobutu et la contre-révolution en Afrique. Waterloo, 1967.
Afr 7920.3 Chome, Jules. Moise Tshombe et l'escroquerie katangaise. Bruxelles, 1966.
Afr 7911.5 Chome, Jules. La passion de Simon Kimbangu. 2. ed. Bruxelles, 1959.
Afr 5448.15 Les chômeurs de Brazzaville et les perspectives du barrage du Kouilou. (Devauges, Roland.) Paris, 1963.
Afr 7886.5 Choprix, Guy. La naissance d'une ville; étude géographique de Paulis, 1934-1957. Bruxelles, 1961.
Afr 3295.6 Choses d'Egypte. (Gallini, Fahmy.) Le Caire, 1917.
Afr 1200.100 Chotin, A.G. Histoire des expéditions maritimes de Charles-Quint en Barbarie. Bruxelles, 1849.

Afr 3979.46.5 Choudhary, M.L. Roy. Egypt in 1945. Calcutta, 1946.
Afr 1280.30.5 Chouraqui, A. Les Juifs d'Afrique du Nord entre l'Orient et l'Occident. Paris, 1965.
Afr 1280.30 Chouraqui, A. Marche vers l'Occident. 1. ed. Paris, 1952.
Afr 5187.15 La chrétienté africaine de Dakar. (Martin, V.) Dakar, 1964. 3 pam.
Afr 555.70 Le Christ au Gabon. (Marie-Germaine, Soeur.) Louvain, 1931.
Afr 10015.3 Christ erscheint am Kongo. (Sulzer, Peter.) Heilbronn, 1958.
Afr 2030.462.60 Christ et croissant pour l'Algérie nouvelle. (Michel, F.) Paris, 1962.
Afr 550.170 Das Christentum in Afrika. (Dammann, Ernst.) München, 1968.
Afr 550.140 Christentum und Mission im Urteil der neoafrikanischen Prosaliteratur. (Hertlein, Siegfried.) Münster, 1962.
Afr 8252.17.10 Christiaan de wet'n lewensbeskrywing. (Kestell, J.D.) Beperkt, 1920.
Afr 8252.172.16.2 Christiaan Rudolph de Wet, 1854-1922. 2. uitg. (Schoor, Marthinus Cornelius Ellnarius van.) Bloemfontein, 1964.
Afr 1955.5.5 Christian, P. L'Affrica francese. Firenze, 1849. 2v.
Afr 1955.5 Christian, P. L'Afrique française. Paris, 1845.
Afr 1965.4 Christian, P. Souvenirs du maréchal Bugeaud. Bruxelles, 1845.
Afr 550.37 Christian action in Africa. (Church Conference on African Affairs.) N.Y., 1942.
Afr 555.7.5 Christian adventures in South Africa. (Taylor, William.) London, 1868.
Afr 3818.7 The Christian approach to Islam in the Sudan. (Trimingham, John Spencer.) London, 1948.
Afr 8289.02.39 Christian de Wet, de held van Zuid-Afrika. (Klinck-Luetetsburg, F.) Zutphen, 1902.
Afr 8678.284 The Christian gospel and the doctrine of separate development. (Freeland, Sydney Percy.) Pretoria, 1961.
Afr 7458.79 Christian Liberia. (Dyer, A.S.) London, 1879.
Afr 550.100 The Christian ministry in Africa. (Sundklur, Bengt.) Uppsala, 1960.
Afr 550.16 The Christian mission in Africa. (Smith, Edwin W.) London, 1926.
Afr 9704.2 Christian missionaries and the creation of Northern Rhodesia, 1880-1924. (Rotberg, Robert Irwin.) Princeton, N.J., 1965.
Afr 555.15 Christian missions and African colonization. (Adger, J.B.) Columbia, 1857.
Afr 5765.32 Christian missions in Madagascar. (McMahon, Edward Oliver.) Westminster, 1914.
Afr 6282.15 Christian missions in Nigeria, 1841-1891. (Ajayi, J.F. Aoe.) London, 1965.
Afr 8680.30 Christian principles in multiracial South Africa. (Dutch Reformed Conference of Church Leaders, Pretoria, 1953.) Pretoria, 1954.
Afr 555.7 Christian work in zulae land. 2d ed. N.Y., 1870 (Lloyd, Mrs.)
Afr 550.3 Christianity, Islam and the Negro race. (Blyden, E.W.) London, 1887.
Afr 550.75 Christianity and politics in Africa. (Taylor, John Vernon.) Harmondsworth, 1957.
Afr 550.150 Christianity and the new Africa. (Beetham, Thomas Allan.) London, 1967.
Afr 550.130 Christianity in Africa as seen by Africans. (Desai, Ram.) Denver, 1962.
Afr 555.151 Christianity in tropical Africa. (International African Seminar, 7th, University of Ghana.) London, 1968.
Afr 6195.24 Pamphlet vol. Christians in Ghana. 5 pam.
Afr 550.143 Christians in the African revolution. (Dougall, James Watson Cunningham.) Edinburgh, 1963.
Afr 8687.202 Christina Forsyth of Fingoland. (Livingstone, William.) London, 1918.
Afr 4008.5 Das christlich-koptische Ägypten einst und heute. (Cramer, Maria.) Wiesbaden, 1959.
Afr 6984.11 Die Christliche Mission in Südwestafrika. (Loth, H.) Berlin, 1963.
Afr 6883.8 Die Christliche Missionspredigt unter den Schambala. Inaug. Diss. (Wohlab, Karl.) Tübingen, 1929.
Afr 8686.18 Christofersen, Arthur Fridtjof. Adventuring with God. Durban, 1967.
Afr 555.45 Christol, Frank. Quatre ans au Cameroun. Paris, 1922.
Afr 635.7.5 Christol, Frederic. L'art dans l'Afrique australe. Paris, 1911.
Afr 2749.57.5 Christopher, Robert. Ocean of fire. London, 1957.
Afr 861.15.5 Christophersen, E. Tristan da Cunha. London, 1940.
Afr 550.14 Christus liberator. (Parsons, E.C.) N.Y., 1905.
Afr 9599.24 Christy, C. Big game and Pygmies. London, 1924.
Afr 590.6 Christy, D. Lecture on African civilization. Cincinnati, 1850.
Afr 7368.57 Christy, David. Ethiopia. Cincinnati, 1857.
Afr 7368.57.5 Christy, David. Ethiopia: her gloom and glory. N.Y., 1969.
Afr 7375.13 Christy, David. A lecture on African colonization. Cincinnati, 1849.
Afr 674.93.2 Chronica de descobrimento e conquista de Guiné. (Eannes de Azurara, G.) Paris, 1841.
Afr 1432.11 Chronica de la guerra de Africa. Madrid, 1860.
Afr 4349.1 Chronica de Susenyos, rei de Ethiopia. (Esteves Pereira, F.M.) Lisbon, 1892. 2v.
Afr 674.93F Chronica do descobrimento e conquista de Guiné. (Eannes de Azurara, G.) Paris, 1841.
Afr 6295.101 A chronicle of Abuja. (Hassan, Alhajl.) Lagos, 1962.
Afr 6455.45.10 Chronicles of an African trip. (Eastman, G.) Rochester, 1927.
Afr 8928.5 Chronicles of Basutoland. (Germond, Robert Charles.) Morija, 1967.
Afr 6420.80 Chronicles of Kenya. (Davis, Alexander.) London, 1928.
Afr 2285.9 The chronicles of the Sid. (Orpen, A.E.) N.Y., n.d.
Afr 6497.5 Chronicles of Uganda. (Ashe, R.P.) N.Y., 1895.
Afr 6926.32 Chronik von Deutsch-Südwestafrika. (Jenssen, H.E.) Windhoek, 1966.
Afr 6988.66.205 Chronik von Otavi und einer Karte. (Freyer, E.P.W.) Otavi, 1966.
Afr 4370.2 Chronique. (Theodoros II.) Paris, 1905.
Afr 1555.3.5 La chronique de l'an 1911. (Ferrail, Gabriel.) Paris, 1912.

Afr 2749.30 Chronique de l'ouest saharien (1900-1930). (Augieras, Ernest M.) Paris, 1930.
Afr 4390.10 Chronique du règne de Menelik II, roi des rois d'Ethiopie. (Guebre Sellassie.) Paris, 1930-31. 2v.
Afr 1571.15 Chronique marocaine. (Leglay, M.) Paris, 1933.
Afr 5074.36 Chroniques de la Mauritanie sénégalaise. (Hamet, Ismael.) Paris, 1911.
Afr 4309.1 Les chroniques de Zara Yaeqob. (Perruchon, J.) Paris, 1893.
Afr 5190.22 Chroniques du Foûta senegalais. Traduit. (Siré-Abbâs-Soh.) Paris, 1913.
Afr 3.34 Chronologie politique africaine. Paris. 2,1961+ 7v.
Afr 109.65.25 Chu, Daniel. A glorious age in Africa, the story of three great African empires. 1st ed. Garden City, 1965.
Afr 6280.9.20 Chubb, L.T. Ibo land tenure. 2. ed. Ibadan, 1961.
Afr 6277.45.5 Chukwuemeka, N. African dependencies, a challenge to Western democracy. N.Y., 1950.
Afr 6277.45 Chukwuemeka, N. Industrialization of Nigeria. N.Y., 1952.
Afr 44623.40.100 Chum, Haji. Atenji wa vita vya Uhud. Dar es Salaam, 1962.
Afr 6333.27 Church, Archibald. East Africa, a new dominion. London, 1927.
Afr 7949.250 Church, John Edward. Forgive them: the story of an African martyr. London, 1966.
Afr 6143.6 Church, Mary. Sierra Leone, or The liberated Africans. London, 1835.
Afr 609.64.15 Church, R.J.H. Africa and the islands. N.Y., 1964.
Afr 609.64.17 Church, R.J.H. Africa and the islands. 2nd ed. London, 1967.
Afr 6095.366 Church, R.J.H. Some geographical aspects of West African development. London, 1966.
Afr 6095.357.5 Church, R.J.H. West Africa, a study of the environment and of man's use of it. 5th ed. London, 1966.
Afr 6095.357 Church, R.J.H. West Africa. N.Y., 1957.
Afr 6095.357.2 Church, R.J.H. West Africa. 2. ed. London, 1960.
Afr 6095.357.6 Church, R.J.H. West Africa. 6th ed. N.Y., 1968.
Afr 679.63 Church, Ronald J.H. Environment and policies in West Africa. Princeton, 1963.
Afr 550.155 Church and mission in modern Africa. (Hastings, Adrian.) London, 1967.
Afr 8678.9.75 The church and primitive peoples...southern Bantu. (Shropshire, D.W.T.) London, 1938.
Afr 8678.90 Church and race in South Africa. (Paton, D.M.) London, 1958.
Afr 6689.1 Church between colonial powers. London, 1965.
Afr 550.37 Church Conference on African Affairs. Christian action in Africa. N.Y., 1942.
Afr 6282.16 Church growth in central and southern Nigeria. (Grimley, John.) Grand Rapids, 1966.
Afr 6146.12 Church growth in Sierra Leone. (Olson, Gilbert W.) Grand Rapids, 1969.
Afr 555.136 The Church in Africa. Maryknoll, 1967.
Afr 5266.3 The church in the Niger Delta. (Epelle, Emanuel Tobiah.) Aba, Nigeria, 1955.
Afr 8145.42 Church of England in South Africa. Constitution and canons of the Church of the province of South Africa. Cape Town, 1962.
Afr 8686.22 The Church of England in South Africa. (Ive, Anthony.) Cape Town, 1966.
Afr 6143.11 Church of England mission in Sierra Leone. (Walker, S.A.) London, 1847.
Afr 5765.28 Church planting in Madagascar. (Gale, William K.) London, 1937.
Afr 6195.17 The churches and Ghana society, 1918-1955. (Parsons, R.T.) Leiden, 1963.
Afr 8678.324 The churches and race relations in South Africa. (Cawood, Lesley.) Johannesburg, 1964.
Afr 5446.5 Churches at the grass-roots. (Andersson, Efraim.) London, 1968.
Afr 1965.30 Churchill, Charles Henry. The life of Abdel Kader. London, 1867.
Afr 8658.92 Churchill, R.S. Men, mines and animals in South Africa. London, 1892.
Afr 8678.288 Churchill, Rhona. White man's god. N.Y., 1962.
Afr 8315.6 Churchill, W.S. Jan Hamilton's march. London, 1900.
Afr 8300.7A Churchill, W.S. London to Ladysmith. London, 1900.
Afr 8300.7.3 Churchill, W.S. London to Ladysmith. Toronto, 1900.
Afr 8300.7.5 Churchill, W.S. London to Ladysmith via Pretoria. London, 1900.
Htn Afr 699.08.4* Churchill, Winston S. My African journey. London, 1908.
Afr 699.08.4.5 Churchill, Winston S. My African journey. N.Y., 1909.
Htn Afr 3735.7* Churchill, Winston S. The river war. London, 1899. 2v.
Afr 3735.7.5 Churchill, Winston S. The river war. London, 1902.
Afr 3978.53.8 Churi, J.H. Sea Nile, the desert, and Nigritia, travels. London, 1853.
Afr 5219.02.5 La chute de l'empire du Rabah. (Gentil, E.) Paris, 1902.
Afr 1609.37 Ciarlantine, T. Il marocco com e. Milano, 1937.
Afr 4700.29.10 Ciarlantini, F. Antologia coloniale. Roma, 1929.
Afr 109.65.5 Ciba Foundation. Man and Africa. London, 1965.
Afr 4513.36.55 Ciccarelli, Socrate. L'Italia fascista e l'Abissinia. Torino, 1935.
Afr 2875.25 Cicerone, G. La terza colonia italiana. Roma, 1913.
Afr 3978.86 Cicerone durch das Süd und Nord Agypten. (Ebers, G.) Stuttgart, 1886.
Afr 590.38 Cicognani, D. La questione della schiavetà coloniale dal Congresso di Vienna a oggi. Firenze, 1935.
Afr 7335.2 A cidade da Beira. (Bermudes, F.) Lisboa, 1964.
Afr 7187.10 A cidade do Huambo. (Roma Machado de Faria e Maria, Carlos.) Lisboa, 1913.
Afr 14692.41.1110 A cidade e a infância. (Vieira, Luandino.) Lisboa, 1957?
Afr 609.45.5 Ciels d'Afrique, 1931-1945. (Estailleur-Chanteraine, P.) Paris, 1945.
Afr 1750.40 Ciges Aparicio, Manuel. Entre la paz y la guerra: Marruecos. Madrid, 1912.
Afr 8678.282 Cilliers, Stephanus Petrus. The coloureds of South Africa. Cape Town, 1963.
Afr 1570.23 Cimbali, E. L'Europa fa opera di civilta nel Marocco. Roma, 1907.
Afr 4513.36.70 Cimmaruta, R. Ual ual. Milano, 1936.
Afr 1750.44 Cinco años en Marruecos. (Triviño Valdivia, Francisco.) Madrid, 1906.
Afr 626.121 Cinq années de psychologies africaines. (Morgaut, M.E.) Paris, 1962.
Afr 5235.189.10 Cinq ans de séjour au Soudan français. (Bechet, Eugène.) Paris, 1889.

Afr 5781.5 Cinq jours à Tamatave. (Pooka.) Maurice, 1888.
Afr 1609.01.8 Cinq mois au Maroc. (Hamet, Ismael.) Alger, 1901.
Afr 555.110 Cinquante ans d'apostolat au Dahomey. (Steinmetz, T.) Lyon, 1937.
Afr 5501.3.10 Le cinquantenaire de l'Academie malgache. (Poisson, Henri.) Tananarive, 1952.
Afr 2030.235 La Cinquième République et l'Algérie. (Sneider, Bertrand.) Paris, 1959.
Afr 609.54.15 Cintas, Pierre. Contribution à l'étude de l'expansion carthagenoise au Maroc. Paris, 1954.
Afr 4513.35.145 Cipolla, A. Da Baldissera a Badoglio. 4a ed. Firenze, 1936.
Afr 4389.11.20 Cipolla, A. In Etiopia. 4a ed. Torino, 1933.
Afr 724.6 Cipriani, Lidio. In Africa dal Capo al Cairo. Firenze, 1932.
Afr 4559.30.5 Ciravegna, G. Nell impero del negus neghest. Torino, 1930.
Afr 609.29.20 Circling Africa. (Anderson, I.) Boston, 1929.
Afr 7540.39 Les circonscriptions indigènes. (Congo. Laws, statutes, etc.) Bruxelles, 1938.
Afr 7324.8 Circumscripções de Lourenço Marques. Lourenço Marques, 1909.
Afr 2945.8 Cirenaica. (Almagia, R.) Milano, 1912.
Afr 2945.35 La Cirenaica. (Cyrenaica. Camera di Commercio, Industria ed Agricultura.) Bengasi, 1928.
Afr 2945.1 Cirenaica. (Haimann, G.) Roma, 1882.
Afr 2945.15 La Cirenaica. (Marinelli, O.) Milano, 1923.
Afr 2945.1.2 Cirenaica. 2a ed. (Haimann, G.) Milan, 1886.
Afr 2945.22 La Cirenaica ed i suoi servizi civile. (Salvadori, Alessandro.) Roma, 1914.
Afr 2945.28 Cirenaica pacificata. (Graziani, Rodolfo.) Milano, 1932.
Afr 2945.24 Cirenaica verde. (Teruzzi, Attilo.) Milano, 1931.
Afr 1713.7 Cisotti-Ferrara, M. Nel marocco. Milano, 1912.
VAfr 679.66.25 Cissoko, Sébéné M. Histoire de l'Afrique occidentale. v.1- Paris, 1966-
Afr 12673.41.100 Cissoko, Siriman. Ressac de nous-mêmes, poèmes. Paris, 1967.
Afr 4559.32.5 The citadel of Ethiopia. (Gruehl, Max.) London, 1932.
Afr 7870.7 La cité indigène de Léopoldville. (Capelle, Emmanuel.) Léopoldville, 1948.
Afr 5248.10 Une cité soudanaise, Djénné. (Monteil, Charles.) Paris, 1932.
Afr 5846.3.5 Une cite tropicale, Port-Louis de L'île Maurice. (Toussaint, Auguste.) Paris, 1966.
Afr 4559.13 Citerni, Carlo. Ai confini meridionali dell'Etiopia. Milano, 1913.
Afr 4098.2 The cities of Egypt. (Poole, R.S.) London, 1882.
Afr 8003.10F Citizen annual. Claremont, South Africa.
Afr 4509.19 Cito de Bitetto, Carlo. Méditerranée, Mer Rouge. Paris, 1937.
Afr 9165.42.45 City built on gold. (Neame, Lawrence.) Johannesburg, 1960.
Afr 9291.15 The city of Bloemfontein. (Bloemfontein. City Council.) Cape Town, 1950.
Afr 9291.15.2 The city of Bloemfontein. (Bloemfontein. City Council.) Cape Town, 1960.
Afr 9510.12 The city of Bulawayo. 2. ed. (Bulawayo, Southern Rhodesia. City Council.) Cape Town, 1957.
Afr 8815.10 The city of East London. (East London, Cape of Good Hope. City Council.) Cape Town, 1950.
Afr 8678.312 The city of God and the city of man in Africa. (Brookes, E.H.) Lexington, 1964.
Afr 6294.5 The City of Ibadan; series of papers presented to a seminar organized early in 1964 by the Institute of African Studies, University of Ibadan. London, 1967.
Afr 9165.42.55 The city of Johannesburg. 2. ed. (Johannesburg. City Council.) Cape Town, 1956.
Afr 8840.10 The city of Kimberley. (Kimberley, South Africa.) Cape Town, 1952.
Afr 9070.10F The city of Pietermaritzburg. (Vowles, Margaret.) Capetown, 1946.
Afr 8845.8 The city of Port Elizabeth. (Leigh, Ramon Lewis.) Johannesburg, 1966.
Afr 9515.5.2 The city of Salisbury. 2. ed. (Salisbury.) Cape Town, 1957.
Afr 4115.8 The city of the caliphs. (Ball, E.A. Reynold.) London, 1898.
Afr 555.29 A city of the dawn. Uganda. (Keable, Robert.) London, 1915.
Afr 1721.7 La Ciudad Dormida. (Moreno Gilabert, Andres.) Madrid, 1923.
Afr Doc 1809.510F Civil aviation statistics. (Ghana. Central Bureau of Statistics.) Accra. 1954+
Afr Doc 1409.505F Civil aviation statistics. (United Arab Republic. Ministry of War. Civil Aviation Department.) Cairo? 1966+
Afr 8045.38 Civil liberty in South Africa. (Brookes, Edgar H.) Cape Town, 1958.
Afr Doc 3333.10 Civil reabsorption. Progress report. (Uganda.) Entebbe. 1947-1948
Afr 8003.2 Civil rights. Cape Town. 1958+ 3v.
Afr 8003.2.5 Civil Rights League, Cape Town. Annual report.
Afr 45.65 The civil service in new African states. (Adu, A.L.) London, 1965.
Afr 7565.5 La civilisation africaine, 1876-1888. (Kassai, Pierre.) Bruxelles, 1888.
Afr 6295.62 Civilisation du Benin. (Mercier, Paul.) Paris, 1962.
Afr 7568.7 Civilisation in Congoland. (Bourne, H.R.F.) London, 1903.
Afr 2232.4 La civilisation urbaine au Mzab. (Mercier, Marcel.) Alger, 1922.
Afr 4259.04 Les civilisations africaines. (Morie, L.J.) Paris, 1904. 2v.
Afr 210.53.2 Les civilisations africaines. 2. ed. (Paulme, Denise.) Paris, 1959.
Afr 1069.09 Les civilisations de l'Afrique du Nord. (Piquet, V.) Paris, 1909.
Afr 1069.09.3 Les civilisations de l'Afrique du Nord. 2d ed. (Piquet, V.) Paris, 1917.
Afr 2625.6 Les civilisations tunisiennes. (Lapie, P.) Paris, 1898.
Afr 4431.20 The civilizing minion; a history of the Italo-Ethiopian War of 1935-1936. (Barker, Arthur J.) N.Y., 1968.
Afr 4559.24.9 Civinini, G. Ricordi di carovana. 2a ed. Milano, 1933.
Afr 4559.30.20 Civinini, G. Sotto le pioggie equatoriali. Roma, 1930.
VAfr 5225.6 Clair, Andrée. Le fabuleux empire du Mali. Paris, 1959.
Afr 5260.32 Clair, Andrée. Le Niger, pays à découvrir. Paris, 1965.

Afr 6741.4   Clairières métaphysiques africaines, essai sur la philosophie et la religion chez les Bantu du Sud-Caméroun. (Bahoken, Jean Calvin.) Paris, 1967.

Afr 9699.66.15   Clairmonte, Frédéric. Rhodesia: National Development Plan, 1965-1968. Addis Abbaba, 1966.

Afr 5962.8   Clairmonte, Frédéric F. Analysis of Spanish Equatorial Guinea Plan, 1964-1967. Addis Ababa, 1966.

Afr 5758.66.5   Clairmonte, Frédéric F. Analysis of the Madagascar Plan, 1964-1968. Addis Ababa, 1966.

Afr 2208.83.9   Clamageran, J.J. L'Algérie, impressions de voyage. 2e ed. Paris, 1883.

Afr 7549.09   Claparède, René. L'évolution d'un état philanthropique. Genève, 1909.

Afr 4430.66   Clapham, Christopher S. Hailde-Selassie's government. London, 1969.

Afr 6275.3   Clapperton, Hugh. Journal of second expedition into interior of Africa. London, 1829.

Afr 8678.6   Clarence, W. The aborigines of South Africa. Boston, 1860.

Afr 2609.01   Claretie, G. De Syracuse à Tripoli. Paris, 1901.

Afr 7180.10   Claridge, G.C. Wild bush tribes of tropical Africa. Philadelphia, 1922.

Afr 6164.5.2   Claridge, W.W. A history of the Gold Coast. London, 1964. 2v.

Afr 6164.5   Claridge, W.W. History of the Gold Coast and Ashanti. London, 1915. 2v.

Afr 2458.83   Clarin de la Rive, Abel. Histoire générale de la Tunisie. Tunis, 1883.

Afr 3315.122   Clark, D.M.J. Suez touchdown. London, 1964.
Afr 8252.25.10   Clark, E.M. Louis Botha, a bibliography. Cape Town, 1956.
Afr 8279.00.52   Clark, G.B. The official correspondence between the governments of Great Britain, the South African Republic. London, 1900.

Afr 9510.5.5   Clark, John Desmond. The Victoria Falls. Lusaka, 1952.
Afr 6143.66   Clark, John Innes. Sierra Leone in maps. London, 1966.
Afr 10673.48.110   Clark, John Pepper. America, their America. London, 1964.
Afr 10673.48.160   Clark, John Pepper. Ozidii. London, 1966.
Afr 10673.48.130   Clark, John Pepper. Poems. Ibadan, 1962.
Afr 10673.48.140   Clark, John Pepper. A reed in the tide. London, 1965.
Afr 10673.48.100   Clark, John Pepper. Song of a goat. Ibadan, 1961.
Afr 10673.48.120   Clark, John Pepper. Three plays, song of a goat. London, 1964.

Afr 2030.210   Clark, Michael. Algeria in turmoil. N.Y., 1959.
Afr 2030.211   Clark, Michael. Algeria in turmoil. N.Y., 1960.
Afr 626.167   Clark, Paul Gordon. Development planning in East Africa. Nairobi, 1965.

Afr 9525.288   Clark, Percy M. The autobiography of an old drifter. London, 1936.

Afr 6147.5.3   Clark, William R.E. The morning star of Africa. London, 1960.

Afr 1680.12   Clarke, Bryan. Berber village. London, 1959.
Afr 6769.60   Clarke, P.H.C. A short history of Tanganyika. London, 1960.

Afr 6769.60.2   Clarke, P.H.C. A short history of Tanganyika. 2nd ed. Nairobi, 1963.

Afr 6192.12   Clarke, R. Remarks on the topography and diseases of the Gold Coast. n.p., n.d.

Afr 6143.10   Clarke, R. Sierra Leone. London, n.d.
Afr 550.7   Clarke, R.F. Cardinal Lavigerie and African slave trade. London, 1889.

Afr 9549.65   The clash of cultures. (Cairns, H. Alan C.) N.Y., 1965.
Afr 8678.438   Class and colour in South Africa, 1850-1950. (Simons, Harold.) Harmondsworth, 1969.

Afr 5857.10   Classement et inventaire du fonds de la Compagnie des Indes (Série C.), 1665-1767. (Réunion. Archives Departementales.) Nerac, 1956.

Afr 5857.2   Classement et inventaire du fonds de la Compagnie des Indes des archives. Thèse. (Lougnon, Albert.) Nerac, 1956.

Afr Doc 2409.510F   Classes, enrollments and teachers in schools and colleges of Northern Nigeria. (Nigeria, Northern. Ministry of Education. Planning and Development Division.) Kaduna. 1967+

Afr Doc 2409.505F   Classes, enrollments and teachers in the primary schools of Northern Nigeria. (Nigeria, Northern. Ministry of Education. Planning and Development Division.) Kaduna. 2,1965+

Afr 635.87   Les classes sociales en Afrique noire. (Barbe, R.) Paris, 1964.
Afr 3.28   Classiques africains. Aalter.
Afr 3978.40   Clat-Bey, A. Aperçu général sur l'Egypte. Bruxelles, 1840. 2v.

Afr 3978.40.2   Clat-Bey, A. Aperçu général sur l'Egypte. v.1-2. Paris, 1840.

Afr 4095.2   Claudius Ptolemy and the Nile. (Cooley, W.D.) London, 1854.

Afr 9699.68   Clausen, Lars. Industrialisierung in Schwarzafrika. Bielefeld, 1968.
Afr 1868.43   Clausolles, M.P. Algerie pittoresque. Toulouse, 1845.
Afr 2260.9   Clauzel, B. Observations...sur quelques actes. Paris, 1831.

Afr 1955.28   Clauzel, M. Explications. Paris, 1837.
Afr 8686.5   Clavier, Henri. Thomas Arbousset. Paris, 1965.
Afr 9710.17   Clay, Gervas. Your friend, Lewanika. London, 1968.
Afr 1965.2.25   Claye, A. Essai bibliographique sur le "Journal de l'expédition au portes de fer" (Paris, 1844). Paris, 1902.

Afr 8325.60   Cleaver, M.M. A young South African. Johannesburg, 1913.
Afr 7815.20   Cleene, Natal de. Introduction à l'ethnographie du Congo belge et du Ruanda-Burundi. 2.éd. Anvers, 1957.

Afr 9439.60   Clegg, E.M. Race and politics. London, 1960.
Htn   Afr 7568.13*   Clemens, S.L. King Leopold's soliloquy. Boston, 1905.
Afr 9389.67   Clement, A. John. The Kalahari and its lost city. Cape Town, 1967.

Afr 1490.16   Clement-Grandcourt, A. Croquis marocains, sur la Moulouya. Paris, 1912.

Afr 635.6   Clemente d'Assis, F. Estudos indianos e africanos. Lisboa, 1889.

Afr 9439.69   Clements, Frank. Rhodesia: the course to collision. London, 1969.

Afr 8160.19   Clements, W.H. The glamour and tragedy of the Zulu war. London, 1936.

Afr 530.50.20   Clendenen, C.C. Americans in Africa, 1865-1900. Stanford, Calif., 1966.

Afr 530.50.15   Clendenen, C.C. Americans in black Africa up to 1865. Stanford, California, 1964.

Afr 4236.957   Cleret, Maxime. Ethiopie. Paris, 1957.

Afr 4115.18   Clerget, Marcel. Le Caire. v.1-2. Le Caire, 1934. 2v.

Afr Doc 1703.7   Clerical staff list. (Sierra Leone.) Freetown. 1963+
Afr 5045.20   Clerisse, Henry. Trente mille kilomètres à travers l'Afrique française. Paris, 1934.

Afr 6460.20   The cliff dwellers of Kenya. (Massam, J.A.) London, 1927.
Afr 6785.8   Cliffe, Lionel. One party democracy; the 1965 Tanzania general elections. Nairobi, 1967.

Afr 6192.20   Clifford, Elizabeth. Our days on the Gold Coast. London, 1919.

Afr 6095.30   Clifford, Elizabeth de la P. Our days on the Gold Coast, in Ashanti, in the northern territories, and...in Togoland. Accra, 1918.

Afr 6780.22   Clifford, H. The Gold Coast regiment in the East African campaign. London, 1920.

Afr 4700.38   Clima, acqua, terreno, dove e cosa si produce e si alleva in A.O.I. (Pesenti del Thei, F.) Venezia, 1938.

Afr 3315.138   El clima politico de ayer y de hoy en Africa (Yanguas Messia, José de.) Escorial, 1959.

Afr 7175.6   Os clinas e as producções...Malenge a Lunda. (Marques, A.S.) Lisboa, 1889.

Afr 9506.4   Clinton, Iris. 'These vessels' the story of Inyati, 1859-1959. Bulawayo, 1959.

Afr 12016.3   Clive, Wake. An anthology of African and Malagasy poetry in French. London, 1965.

Afr 8180.5   Cloete, Henry. The history of the great Boer trek. London, 1899.

Afr 8180.5.3   Cloete, Henry. The history of the great Boer trek. N.Y., 1899.

Afr 8180.5.4   Cloete, Henry. Vijf voorlezingen over de landverhuizing der hollandsche Boeren. Kaapstad, 1856.

Afr 8040.22   Cloete, Jacobus J.N. Sentrale, provinsiale en munisipale instellings van Suid-Afrika. Pretoria, 1964.

Afr 609.55.5   Cloete, Stuart. The African giant. Boston, 1955.
Afr 8230.10.13   Cloete, Stuart. African portraits. London, 1946.
Afr 8230.10.13.2   Cloete, Stuart. African portraits: a biography of Paul Kruger, Cecil Rhodes and Lobengula. Cape Town, 1969.

Afr 8230.10.12   Cloete, Stuart. Against these three, a biography of Paul Kruger. Boston, 1945.

Afr 6460.65   Cloete, Stuart. Storm over Africa. Cape Town, 1956.
Afr 6926.7   Close, P.L. Prisoner of the Germans in South-west Africa. London, 1916.

Afr 8028.25   Closer union movement. (Heerden, J. van.) Cape Town, 1952.

Afr 6390.96   Cloudsley-Thompson, John. Animal twilight. Chester Springs, 1967.

Afr 635.7.6   Clouzot, Henri. L'art nègre et l'art océanien. Paris, 1919.

Htn   Afr 5333.2*   Clozel, F.J. Coutumes indigènes de la Côte-d'Ivoire. Paris, 1902.

Afr 5342.6   Clozel, F.J. Dix ans à la Côte-d'Ivoire. Paris, 1906.
Afr 5235.212   Clozel, F.J. Haut-Sénégal-Niger (Soudan français). Paris, 1912. 5v.

Afr 5203.3   Clozel, M. Bibliographie des ouvrages relatifs à la Sénégambie. Paris, 1891.

Afr 5051.30   Clozel, M.F.J. Bibliographie des ouvrages relatifs à la Sénégambie et au Soudan occidental. Paris, 1891.

Afr 2030.462.35   Club Jean-Moulin. Deux pièces du dossier Algérie. Paris, 1962.

Afr 9795.15   Cluston-Brock, Guy. Down in Nyasaland. London, 1959.
Afr 8678.8.10   Co-existence in South Africa. (Fagan, H.A.) Cape Town, 1963.

Afr 626.210   Co-operation for development. (Tamuno, Olufunmilayo Grace Esho.) Ibadan, 1969.

Afr 1069.38   The coast of Barbary. (Soames, Jane.) London, 1938.
Afr 8919.66   Coates, Austin. Basutoland. London, 1966.
Afr 4050.9   Cobbold, E. Wayfarers in the Libyan desert. London, 1912.
Afr 4700.38.20   Cobolli Gigli, G. Strade imperiali. Milano, 1938.
Afr 1608.21   Cochelet, C. Naufrage du brick français la sophie. v.1-2. Paris, 1821. 2v.

Afr 1570.34   Cochin, D. Affaires marocaines...1902-1911. Paris, 1912.
Afr 1608.16   Cock, S. The narrative of Robert Adams. London, 1816.
Afr 1965.20   Cockenpot, C. Le traité Desmichels. Paris, 1924.
Afr 7937.9   Le code des institutions politiques du Rwanda précolonial. (Kagame, Alexis.) Bruxelles, 1952.

Afr 5540.8   Le code des 305 articles de Madagascar. Thèse. (Barrel, G.P.) Paris, 1931.

Afr 7540.4   Les codes du Congo. (Hebette, L.) Bruxelles, 1892.
Afr 7535.15   Codes et lois du Congo belge. V.1-3 (V.1, 1960) 8.ed. (Congo, Belgian. Laws, statutes, etc.) Bruxelles, 1959. 3v.

Afr 3032.1   Les codes mixtes d'Egypte. (Egypt.) Ibrahimieh, 1932.
Afr 6155.1   Codrington, W.J. Lecture on...defence of...Gold Coast. n.p., n.d.

Afr 7068.5   Coelho, F. de L. Duas descrições seiscentistas da Guiné. Lisbon, 1953.

Afr 6878.91   Coelln, Daniel. Bilder aus Ostafrika. Berlin, 1891.
Afr 1573.13   Coello y Quesada, Francisco. Intereses de España en Marruecos. Madrid, 1884.

Afr 2870.7   Coen, G. L'Italia a Tripoli. Livorno, 1912.
Afr 9089.38   Coetzee, A. Die opkoms van die Afrikaanse Kultuurgedagte aan die rand. Johannesburg, 1938.

Afr 8659.53.5   Coetzee, Abel. Die Afrikaanse volkskultuur. Kaapstad, 1953.

Afr 8659.53.5.2   Coetzee, Abel. Die Afrikaanse volkskultuur. 2. druk. Amsterdam, 1960.

Afr 8045.45   Coetzee, G.A. The Republic. Johannesburg, 1960.
Afr 8050.10   Coetzee, Jan A. Politieke groepering in die wording van die afrikanernasie. Thesis. Johannesburg, 1941.

Afr 2250.6   La coexistence des communautés en Algérie. (Millet, Jean.) Aix-en-Provence, 1962.

Afr 6280.69   Cohen, Abner. Custom and politics in urban Africa. Berkeley, 1969.

Afr 505.30   Cohen, Andrew. British policy in changing Africa. Evanston, 1959.

Afr 4513.60   Cohen, Armand. La Société des Nations devant le conflit italo-éthiopien. Genève, 1960.

Afr 8840.5   Cohen, L. Reminiscences of Kimberley. London, 1911.
Afr 2940.10   Cohen, M. Gli Ebrei in Libia. Roma, 1930.
Afr 1487.36   Cohen, Mark I. Morocco, old land, new nation. N.Y., 1966.
Afr 6280.63   Cohen, Ronald. The Kanuri of Bornu. N.Y., 1967.
Afr 6780.24   Cohort of the tropics. (Letcher, O.) London, 1930.
Afr 4559.34.30   Coi 'Negadi' in Etiopia. (Pucci, Generoso.) Firenze, 1934.

Afr 820.3.3 Coillard, F. On the threshold of central Africa. London, 1897.

Afr 820.3.6 Coillard, F. Sur le Haut-Zambèze. Paris, 1898.

Afr 555.22 Coillard of the Zambesi. South Africa. 2d ed. (Mackintosh, C.W.) London, 1907.

Afr 1493.9 Un coin de la guerre, la France au Maroc. (Lichtenberger, A.) Paris, 1918.

Afr 1609.49 Coindreau, R. Le Maroc. Paris, 1949.

Afr 1735.5 Coindreau, Roger. Corsaires de Sale. Paris, 1948.

Afr 3979.05 Coins d'Egypte ignorés. (Gayet, A.) Paris, 1905.

Afr 28.82 Coisel. L'Afrique à travers les publications. Paris, 1961.

Afr 1369.31 Coissac de Chavrebiere. Histoire du Maroc. Paris, 1931.

Afr 9545.10 Coissoró, Narana. The customary laws of succession in Central Africa. Thesis. Lisboa, 1966.

Afr 8028.130 Coke, R.M. South Africa as seen by the French, 1610-1850. Cape Town, 1957.

Afr 6146.10 Coke, Thomas. An interesting narrative of a mission sent to Sierra Leone. Paris, 1812.

Afr 2945.26.10 Col generale Cantore alla caccia del Gran Senusso. (Gaslini, Mario dei.) Milano, 1928.

Afr 7567.13 Cola Alberich, Julio. El Congo, 1885-1963. Madrid, 1964.

Afr 1618.15 Cola Alberich, Julio. Cultos primitivos de Marruecos. Madrid, 1954.

Afr 4700.14 Colajanni, N. Politica coloniale. Palermo, 1891.

Afr 3710.3.2 Colborne, J. With Hicks Pasha in the Soudan. 2d ed. London, 1885.

Afr 11790.58.110 The cold veld. (Sinclair, F.D.) Wynberg, 1946.

Afr 20002.5 Coldham, Geraldine Elizabeth. A bibliography of Scriptures in African languages. London, 1966. 2v.

Afr 8808.52.2 Cole, A.W. The Cape and the Kafirs. London, 1852.

Afr 8678.381 Cole, Ernest. House of bondage. N.Y., 1967.

Afr 6420.70 Cole, Keith. Kenya. London, 1959.

Afr 8676.61 Cole, M.M. South Africa. London, 1961.

Afr 8676.61.2 Cole, M.M. South Africa. 2nd ed. London, 1966.

Afr 9149.56 Cole, Monica M. Land use studies in the Transvaal Lowveld. London, 1956.

Afr 6149.162.5 Cole, R.W. Kossoh town boy. Cambridge, Eng., 1960.

Afr 14654.5 Colecção imbondeiro. Angola. 3v.

Afr 1753.9 Coleccion Ceuta. Ceuta. 1,1961+ 4v.

Afr 1574.10 Coleccion completa de tratados y convenios entre Espana y Marruecos, 1799 a 1895. (Spain. Treaties. Morocco.) Melilla, 1904.

Afr 3.48 Coleccion monografica africana. Madrid. 1,1967+

Afr 6214.20 Coleman, J.S. Nigeria. Berkeley, 1958.

Afr 210.64.60 Coleman, J.S. Political parties and national integration in tropical Africa. Berkeley, 1964.

Afr 8095.5 Colenbrander, Herman Theodoor. De afkomst der Boeren. n.p., 1902.

Afr 8095.5.5 Colenbrander, Herman Theodoor. De afkomst der Boeren. 2. uitg. Kaapstad, 1964.

Afr 8252.9.10 Colenso, F.B. Colenso letters from Natal. Pietermaritzburg, 1958.

Afr 8160.11 Colenso, F.E. History of the Zulu war and its origin. London, 1880.

Afr 8163.2 Colenso, Frances Ellen. The ruin of Zululand, an account of British doings in Zululand since the invasion of 1879. London, 1884-85. 2v.

Afr 8980.5 Colenso, J.W. Defence of Langalibalele. n.p., 187-.

Afr 9028.55 Colenso, J.W. Ten weeks in Natal. Cambridge, 1855.

Afr 8252.9.10 Colenso letters from Natal. (Colenso, F.B.) Pietermaritzburg, 1958.

Afr 3275.32 Coles, Charles E. Recollections and reflections. London, 1918.

Afr 2938.20.2 Coletti, Francesco. La Tripolitania settentrionale e la sua vita sociale, studiate dal vero. 2a ed. Bologna, 1923.

Afr 5765.10 Colin, E. Madagascar et la mission catholique. Paris, 1895.

Afr 1408.8 Colin, E.R. Le grand Ismail. Paris, 1929.

Afr 3745.35 Colin, Hugues. La condition internationale du Soudan anglo-égyptien et du Haut-Nil. Thèse. Paris, 1936.

Afr 2025.16 Colin, M. Quelques questions algériennes. Paris, 1899.

Afr 9635.22A Colin Morris and Kenneth Haunda. (Morris, Colin.) London, 1960.

Afr 5947.10 Coll, A. Villa-cisneros. Madrid, 1933.

Afr 5993.2 Coll, Armengol. Segunda memoria de las misiones. Madrid, 1899.

Afr 3.10 Collana di studi di storia e politica africana. Roma. 1+ 4v.

Afr 6291.20F The collapse of Ojukwu's rebellion and prospects for lasting peace in Nigeria. (Nigeria. Federal Ministry of Information.) Lagos, 1968.

Afr 7815.5.10 Colle, R.P. Les Baluta. 10-11. Bruxelles, 1913. 2v.

Afr Doc 9018.5 Collecção de legeslação relativa ás colonias portuguezas em Africa. (Portugal. Laws, statutes, etc.) 2v.

Afr 8658.99.5 Collectanea. (Laurence, Percival M.) London, 1899.

Afr 8719.62 Collected works. (Botha, C.G.) Cape Town, 1962. 3v.

Afr 628.5.10 Collecting a library of Negro literature. (Spingarn, A.B.) n.p., 1938.

Afr 7503.7 Collection carrefours africains. Bruxelles. 1+ 3v.

Afr 3.12 Collection connaissance de l'Afrique française. Oran, Algeria.

Afr 1835.4.2 Collection de documents inédits...après 1830. Sér.2. Paris. 1,1912+ 5v.

Afr 1835.4.3 Collection de documents inédits sur l'histoire de l'Algérie. Sér.3. Paris.

Afr 1835.4 Collection de documents inédits sur l'histoire de l'Algérie après 1830. 1. Serie. Paris. 1-6,1914-1954 7v.

Afr 7503.3.5 Collection de mémoires. (Centre d'Etudes des Problèmes Sociaux Indigènes, Elizabethville, Belgian Congo.) 1+ 14v.

X Cg Afr 5538.2 Collection des ouvrages anciens concernant Madagascar. v.1-9. (Grandidier, A.) Paris, 1903-20. (Changed to XP 3889) 9v.

Afr 12.20 Collection d'études économiques. (Leopoldville. Université Lovanium. Institut de Recherches Economiques et Sociales.) Léopoldville. 1,1965+

Afr 7512.16 Collection d'études politiques. (Leopoldville. Université Lovanium. Cahiers Economiques et Sociaux.) Léopoldville. 4,1964+

Afr 7503.6 Collection études congolaises. Bruxelles. 1+ 8v.

Afr 1309.2 Collection Hesperis. (Institut des Hautes Etudes Marocaines.) Paris. 1+ 4v.

Afr 3.11 Collection le colonialisme. Paris.

Afr 3310.10.30 Collection of addresses. (Nasser, G.A.) Cairo, 1962. 8 pam.

Htn Afr 8325.35.10* Pamphlet vol. A collection of forty-one stereopticon views of the Boer war.

Afr 1550.19 Collection of magazine articles on...Morocco's relations with foreign countries. Zürich, 1904.

Afr 3035.5 Collection of official correspondence. (Paris. Peace Conference, 1919. Egyptian Delegation.) Paris, 1919.

Afr 7320.1.3 Pamphlet vol. A collection of pamphlets on Mozambique published by the colonial exposition at Paris, 1931. 26 pam.

Afr 8300.3F Pamphlet vol. Collection of South Africa war illustrations, Dec. 1899-Mar. 1900, cut from periodicals and pasted in scrapbook.

Afr 6291.28 Pamphlet vol. A collection of speeches. 2 pam.

Afr 7459.67.5F A collection of useful information on Liberia. (Liberia. Department of Information and Cultural Affairs.) Monrovia? 1967?

Afr 2438.32 Les collectivités locales en Tunisie. (Snoussi, Mohamed.) Paris, 1958.

Afr 11505.69.100 The college brew. (Kuper, Leo.) Durban, 1960.

Afr 2209.44 Collier, Joy. Algerian adventure. London, 1944.

Afr 8847.34 Collier, Joy. Frontier post, the story of Grahamstown. Grahamstown, 1961.

Afr 9165.71.10 Collier, Joy. The purple and the gold. Cape Town, 1965.

Afr 8847.83.5 Collier, Joy. Stellenbosch revisited. Stellenbosch, 1959.

Afr 2209.11 Colliez, A. La frontière algéro-marocaine. Paris, 1911.

Afr 1570.55 Colliez, A. Notre protectorat marocain. Paris, 1930.

Afr 1581.5 Collin, V. Le maroc et les intérêts belges. Louvain, 1900.

Afr 11397.50.100 Collin-Smiths, J. Locusts and wild honey. London, 1953.

Afr 10690.89.800 Collins, Harold R. Amos Tutuola. N.Y., 1969.

Afr 3700.18 Collins, R.O. The southern Sudan. New Haven, 1962.

Afr 530.50.10 Collins, Robert O. Americans in Africa. Stanford, Calif., 1963.

Afr 3069.67 Collins, Robert O. Egypt and the Sudan. Englewood Cliffs, N.J., 1967.

Afr 3745.75 Collins, Robert O. King Leopold, England and the Upper Nile, 1899-1909. New Haven, 1968.

Afr 500.90 Collins, Robert O. The partition of Africa: illusion or necessity? N.Y., 1969.

Afr 9295.5 Collins, William W. Free statia. Cape Town, 1965.

Afr 6275.80 Collis, Robert. African encounter. N.Y., 1961.

Afr 6328.3 Collister, Peter. The last days of slavery, England and the East African slave trade, 1870-1900. Dar es Salaam, 1961.

Afr 4430.35.25 Collombet, E. L'Ethiopie moderne et son avènement à la communauté internationale. Thèse. Dijon, 1935.

Afr 628.267.5 Colloque: fonction et signification de l'art nègre dans la vie du peuple et pour le peuple. (Colloque sur l'Art Nègre, Dakar.) Paris, 1967.

Afr 2623.956 Colloque international sur les niveaux de vie en Tunisie. Travaux du colloque international les niveaux de vie en Tunisie. Paris, 1956-58. 3 pam.

Afr 2030.462.15 Colloque Internationale sur l'Algérie. Les conditions de l'indépendance. Bruxelles, 1962.

Afr 12005.2 Colloque sur la littérature africaine d'expression française, actes. Dakar, 1965.

Afr 628.267.5 Colloque sur l'Art Nègre, Dakar. Colloque: fonction et signification de l'art nègre dans la vie du peuple et pour le peuple. Paris, 1967.

Afr 545.30 Colloque sur les religions, Abidjan, 5-12 avril, 1961. (Colloque sur les Religions, Abidjan.) Paris, 1962.

Afr 545.30 Colloque sur les Religions, Abidjan. Colloque sur les religions, Abidjan, 5-12 avril, 1961. Paris, 1962.

Afr 5000.25 Colloques. (Centre de Documentation et de Diffusion des Industries, des Mines et de l'Energie Outre-Mer.) Paris. 1,1963+ 4v.

Afr 109.68.20 Colloquium on Institution-Building and the African Development Process, University of California at Los Angeles, 1967. Nations by design; institution-building in Africa. 1st ed. Garden City, 1968.

Afr 1624.914 Colomb, Jean. Le regime financier du Maroc. Paris, 1914.

Afr 590.16.2 Colomb, John Charles Ready. Slave-catching in the Indian Ocean. N.Y., 1969.

Afr 590.16 Colomb, Philip Howard. Slave catching in the Indian Ocean. London, 1873.

Afr 4718.99 La colonia Eritrea. (Melli, T.B.) Parma, 1899.

Afr 4718.99.2 La colonia Eritrea. (Melli, T.B.) Parma, 1900.

Afr 4742.26 La colonia Eritrea. (Santagata, F.) Napoli, 1935.

Afr 4742.3 La colonia Eritrea. Fasc.1 (Societa Italiana per il Progresso delle Scienze, Rome.) Roma, 1913.

Afr 4730.3 La colonia italiana di Assab. (Italy. Ministero di Affari Esteri.) Roma, 1882.

Afr 4700.14.20 Colonia italiana in Africa e Francesco Crispi; il parlamento ed il paese per un Italiano. Roma, 1896.

Afr 6284.8 Colonial cadet in Nigeria. (Smith, John Hilary.) Durham, N.C., 1968.

Afr Doc 4109.20 Colonial development and welfare schemes. Estimates. (Swaziland.) 1954+

Afr 210.62 The colonial reckoning. (Perham, M.F.) N.Y., 1962.

Afr 210.62.2 The colonial reckoning. (Perham, M.F.) London, 1961.

Afr 210.62.3 The colonial reckoning. (Perham, M.F.) London, 1963.

Afr 678.44 Colonial settlements, western coast of Africa. (Perry, M.C.) Washington, 1844.

Afr 9609.5 Colonial social accounting. (Deane, Phyllis.) Cambridge, England, 1953.

Afr 500.94 Colonialism in Africa, 1870-1960. Cambridge, Eng., 1969-

Afr 500.48 Colonialism in Africa. (Italian Library of Information, N.Y.) N.Y., 1940.

Afr 8292.3 The colonials in South Africa 1899-1902. (Stirling, John.) Edinburgh, 1907.

Afr 4700.28.5 Le colonie. (Stefanini, G.) Torino, 1928.
Afr 6777.5 La colonie allemande de l'Afrique Orientale. (Plumon, E.) Heidelberg, 1906.
Afr 4700.26.5 Colonie d italia e colonie ex-germaniche d'Africa. (Gibello Socca, G.) Milano, 1926.
Afr 4700.30.5 Le colonie d'Italia. (Giaccone, E.) Torino, 1930.
Afr 5260.20 La colonie du Niger. (Abadie, Maurice.) Paris, 1927.
Afr 4025.10 La colonie française du Caire. These. (Carnoy, Norbert.) Paris, 1928.
Afr 4700.32 Le colonie italiane. (Agostino Orsini, P.) Roma, 1932.
Afr 4700.27 Le colonie italiane. (Virgilli, Filippo.) Milano, 1927.
Afr 4700.29.5 Le colonie italiane de diretto dominio. (Italy. Ufficio Studi e Propaganda.) Roma, 1929.
Afr 1705.5 Une colonie romaine de Mauretanie Tingitane. (Thouvenot, R.) Paris, 1941.
Afr 7808.95 Les colonies et l'état indépendant du Congo. (Wincxtenhoven.) Bruxelles, 1895.
Afr 1623.932.10 Les colonies françaises, le Maroc. (Desfeuilles, Paul.) Paris, 1932.
Afr 5180.15 Colonies françaises, Sénégal-Soudan. Paris, 1900.
Afr 7190.25 Colonies portugaises, ile de San-Thome. (Almada Negreiros, A.D.) Paris, 1901.
Afr 7324.10 Colonisação de Lourenço Marques. (Freire d'Andrade, Alfredo.) Porto, 1897.
Afr 2608.99.3 La colonisation agricole en Tunisie. (Zolla, D.) Paris, 1899.
Afr 2280.10 La colonisation de la Milidja. Thèse. (Franc, Julien.) Paris, 1928.
Afr 1830.30.4 La colonisation de la Mitidja. (Franc, Julien.) Paris, 1928.
Afr 5548.44 Colonisation de Madagascar. (Laverdant, D.) Paris, 1844.
Afr 5580.2 La colonisation de Madagascar sous Louis XV. (Ponget de St. Andre.) Paris, 1886.
Afr 2250.5 La colonisation des plaines du Chélif. (Yacono, Xavier.) Alger, 1955-56. 2v.
Afr 2623.962 La colonisation et l'agriculture européennes en Tunisie depuis 1881. (Poucet, J.) Paris, 1962.
Afr 6420.30.5 La colonisation européenne au Kenya. (Salvadori, M.) Paris, 1938.
Afr 2260.13 La colonisation française dans l'Afrique du nord. (Piquet, V.) Paris, 1912.
Afr 2260.13.3 La colonisation française dans l'Afrique du nord. (Piquet, V.) Paris, 1914.
Afr 2870.20 La colonisation italienne en Libye. Thèse. (Despois, Jean.) Paris, 1935.
Afr 1830.20.80 La colonisation maritime en Algerie. (Lacoste, Louis.) Paris, 1931.
Afr 1955.34 La colonisation militaire du maréchal Bugeaud, 1841-47. Thèse. (Ferrand, G.) Paris, 1909.
Afr 1965.4.5 La colonisation militaire sous Bugeaud. Thèse. (Demontes, Victor.) Paris, 1916.
Afr 2223.930 Colonisation officielle et crédit agricole en Algérie. Thèse. (Selnet, F.P.V.) Alger, 1930.
Afr 7320.25 Colonizacao. (Gomes de Amorim, F.) Lisboa, 1945.
Afr 7219.28 Colonização. (Silva, J. Guides.) Lourenço Marques, 1928.
Afr 7048.15 Colonização etnica da Africa portuguesa. (Ferreira, Vincente.) Lisboa, 1944.
Afr 7222.82 Colonização senhorial da Zambezia. (Lobato, Alexandre.) Lisboa, 1962.
Afr 7458.51 Colonization. Notice of V. Hugo's views of slavery. (Latrobe, J.H.B.) Baltimore, 1851.
Afr 7458.51.3 Colonization and abolition. (Latrobe, J.H.B.) Baltimore, 1852.
Afr 2230.6 Colonization de la Kabylie. Alger, 1871.
Afr 2260.1 La colonization en Algérie. (Cazenave, J.) Alger, 1900.
Afr 7350.3.25 Colonization herald and general register. Philadelphia. 1839+
Afr 2250.01 Pamphlet box. Colonization in Algeria.
Afr 7353.1 Pamphlet box. Colonization of Negroes.
Afr 7368.32 Colonization Society of Free Colored Population. Maryland. (Maryland State Colonization Society.) Baltimore, 1852.
Afr 7377.5.5 Colonization Society of the State of Indiana. Answer of the agent of the Indiana Colonization Society. Indianapolis, 1852.
Afr 7355.6 Pamphlet vol. Colonization 1837-62. 3 pam.
Afr 7350.2 Colonizationist and journal of freedom. Boston. 1834+
Afr 2945.40 La colonizzazione della Cirenaica nell antichita e nel presente. (Narducci, G.) Bengasi, 1934.
Afr 1069.57 La colonizzazione dell'Africa del Nord. (Leone, Enrico de.) Padova, 1957.
Afr 2929.12.17 Colonizzazione e proprietà fondiaria in Libia. (Franzoni, A.) Roma, 1912.
Afr 7815.13 Colonne-Beaufaict, A. de. Azande, introduction à une ethnographie générale des bassins de l'Ubangi-Uele et de l'Arvwimi. Bruxelles, 1921.
Afr 1490.19 La colonne du Haut-Guir en Sept. 1908. (Lechartier, G.G.) Paris, 1908.
Afr 1665.7 La colonne du sous, janvrier-juin, 1917. (Dugard, Henry.) Paris, 1918.
Afr 6455.21 A colony in the making. (Cranworth, B.F.G.) London, 1912.
Afr 9028.95 The colony of Natal. (Ingram, J.F.) London, 1895.
Afr 9028.59 The colony of Natal. (Mann, R.J.) London, 1859.
Afr 1738.15 Color. (Garcia, S.F.) Madrid, 1919.
Afr 8685.55 Colour and culture in South Africa. (Patterson, S.) London, 1953.
Afr 8685.55.1 Colour and culture in South Africa. (Patterson, S.) N.Y., 1969.
Afr 6395.6 The colour bar in East Africa. (Leys, N.M.) London, 1941.
Afr 628.248 Colour prejudice. (Burns, A.) London, 1948.
Afr 8140.16 The colour problems of South Africa. (Brookes, E.H.) Lovedale, 1934.
Afr 8678.64 The coloured people. (Manuel, G.) Cape Town, 1943.
Afr 8678.282 The coloureds of South Africa. (Cilliers, Stephanus Petrus.) Cape Town, 1963.
Afr 9445.5 Colquhoun, A.R. Matabeleland, the war, and our position in South Africa. London, 1894.
Afr 8135.10 Colquhoun, Archibald. The Africander land. London, 1906.
Afr 9489.24 Colquhoun, E.C. The real Rhodesia. London, 1924.
Afr 9700.35 Colson, Elizabeth. The plateau Tonga of Northern Rhodesia. Manchester, 1962.
Afr 9610.15 Colson, Elizabeth. Seven tribes of BritishCentral Afrika. Manchester, 1959.
Afr 1658.49 La columna saro en la campana de alhucemas. (Santiago Guerrero, M.) Barcelona, 1926.

Afr 1753.6 Columnas de operaciones en Marruecos. (Alvarez Cabrera, J.) Tanger, 1909.
Afr 6497.10 Colvile, H. The land of the Nile springs. London, 1895.
Afr 3708.6 Colvile, H.E. History of the Sudan campaign. London, 1889. 3v.
Afr 1608.80.2 Colvile, H.E. A ride in petticoats and slippers. London, 1880.
Afr 8315.8 Colvile, H.E. Work of the Ninth Division. London, 1901.
Afr 608.93 Colvile, Zelie. Round the black man's garden. Edinburgh, 1893.
Afr 9599.11 Colville, A. One thousand miles in a Machilla. London, 1911.
Afr 3275.15A Colvin, A. The making of modern Egypt. 3d ed. London, 1906.
Afr 8292.48 Colvin, F.F. Diary of the 9th Lancers. So. Kensington, 1904.
Afr 8657.1 Colvin, Ian D. The cape of adventure. London, 1912.
Afr 8283.19 Colvin, Ian D. The life of Jameson. London, 1922. 2v.
Afr 7920.3.10 Colvin, Ian Goodhope. The rise and fall of Moise Tshombe: a biography. London, 1968.
Afr 8089.09 Colvin, Jan Duncan. South Africa. London, 19-
Afr 7200.3 Combate. Cairo. 2v.
Afr 7130.10 Combate de Naulila; cobiça de Angola. (Santos, Ernesto Moreira dos.) Cuimarães, 1957.
Afr 7230.5 Combate de Negomano. (Santos, Ernesto Moreira dos.) Guimarães, 1916.
Afr 1658.30 Combats au Maroc 1925-1926. Paris, 1928 (Damidaux, C.)
Afr 4558.96 Comber, P. L'Abyssinie en 1896. Paris, 1896.
Afr 4558.37.2 Combes, Edmond. Voyage en Abyssinie...1835-37. Paris, 1839. 4v.
Afr 3978.46.3 Combes, Edmond. Voyage en Egypte. Paris, 1846.
Afr 7812.257.10 Combien le Congo a-t-il couté à la Belgique? (Stengers, Jean.) Bruxelles, 1957.
Afr 11057.8 Come back, Africa! (Shore, Herbert L.) N.Y., 1968.
Afr 10631.58.110 Come back Dora, a husband's confession and ritual. (Konadu, Asare.) Accra, 1966.
Afr 2875.13 Come conquistammo Tripoli. (Piazza, G.) Roma, 1912.
Afr 6275.132 Come now Nigeria. (Sowande, Fela.) Ibadan, 1968.
Afr 2875.10 Come siamo andati a Tripoli. (Bevione, G.) Torino, 1912.
Afr 2870.10.50 Come siamo andati in Libia. Firenze, 1914.
Afr 7812.269 Comeliau, Christian. Conditions de la planification du développement; l'exemple du Congo. Paris, 1969.
Afr 7809.42.5 Comeliau, Marie. Blancs et noirs. Paris, 1942.
Htn Afr 1947.3* Comelin, F. Voyage pour la rédemption des captives...1720. Paris, 1721.
Afr 150.2.66 Comemoracoes do V centenario da morte do Infante Dom Henrique. (Portugal. Comissão Executiva das Comemorações do V Centenario da Morte do Infante Dom Henrique.) Lisboa, 1961-1963. 4v.
Afr Doc 9308.703 Comercio exterior. (Angola. Repartição de Estatistica Geral.) Luanda. 1961+
Afr Doc 9208.710 Comercio externo. (Mozambique. Direcção Provincial dos Serviços de Estatistica Geral.) 1951+ 2v.
NEDL Afr 6050.3.5 Comet. Lagos, Nigeria.
Afr 4640.5 Comhaire-Sylvain, Suzanne. Considerations of migration in Addis Ababa. Addis Ababa, 1962.
Afr 7818.5 Comhaire-Sylvain, Suzanne. Femmes de Kinshasa hier et aujourd'hui. Paris, 1968.
Afr 4431.5 The coming of the Italian-Ethiopian war. (Baer, George Webster.) Cambridge, 1967.
Afr 11572.50.150 The coming of the Lord. (Millin, S.G.(L).) N.Y., 1928.
Afr 1494.5.2 Comité d'Action Marocaine. Annexes au plan de réformes marocaines. n.p., 1934.
Afr 1494.5 Comité d'Action Marocaine. Plan de réformes marocaines. n.p., 1934.
Afr 1738.29 Comite de Propagande et de Tourisme, Paris. Tanger. Paris, 1929.
Afr 2749.05 Comité du Maroc. Dans l'ouest de la Saoura. Paris, 1905.
Afr 2037.2 Comité pour la Défense de Ben Bella et des Autres Victimes de la Répression en Algérie. Les torturés d'El Harrach. Paris, 1966.
Afr 2030.467.25 Comité pour la Défense de Ben Bella et des Autres Victimes de la Répression en Algérie. Qu'est devenu Ben Bella? Paris, 1967.
Afr 2030.460.30 Comité pour la Paix en Algérie. La Belgique devant le problème algérien. Chênée, 1961.
Afr 7850.55F Comité spécial du Katanga, 1900-1950. (Comité Spécial du Katanga.) Bruxelles, 1950.
Afr 7850.55F Comité Spécial du Katanga. Comité spécial du Katanga, 1900-1950. Bruxelles, 1950.
Afr 3.7F Comité Spéciale du Katanga. Rapports et balans. Bruxelles.
Afr 510.12 Le commandant Lamy. (Reibell, Le Commandant.) Paris, 1903.
Afr 8289.29 Commando. (Reitz, Deneys.) London, 1929.
Afr 8289.29.4 Commando. (Reitz, Deneys.) London, 1933.
Afr 8289.29.3 Commando. (Reitz, Deneys.) N.Y., 1930.
Afr 8289.64.5 Commando courageous. (Schikkerling, Roland William.) Johannesburg, 1964.
Afr 4700.2 Commemorazione dell'esploratore africano. (Marson, Luigi.) Mantova, 1902.
Afr 1955.47 Les commencements d'un empire. (Esquer, G.) Paris, 1929.
Afr 1955.6.5 Les commencements d'une conquête. (Rousset, C.) Paris, 1887. 2v.
Afr 1955.6.2 Les commencements d'une conquête. (Rousset, C.) Paris, 1900. 2v.
Afr 618.26 Comment le Noir se soigne-t-il. (Traore, Dominic.) Paris, 1965.
Afr 1570.25 Comment nous avons conquis le Maroc. (Dupuy, E.) Paris, n.d.
Afr 1680.14 Commentaire des cartes sur les genres de vie de montagne dans le massif central du grand atlas. (Dresch, Jean.) Tours, 1941.
Afr 4105.8 Commentaires sur l'atlas historique d'Alexandrie. (Thuile, H.) Le Caire, 1922.
Afr 8021.5 Commentary on politics today. Pretoria.

Afr 6293.2.5	Comments of the federal military government on the report of the Tribunal of Inquiry into the affairs of the Lagos City Council for the period Oct. 15, 1962 to Apr. 18, 1966. (Nigeria.) Lagos, 1966.
Afr 1878.1	Le commerce...de l'Algerie. (Laprimaudie, F.E. de.) Paris, 1861.
Afr 5843.5	Commerce and industry in Mauritius. (Mauritius. Ministry of Industry.) Port Louis, 1964.
Afr 6881.257	Commerce and industry in Tanganyika. (Tanganyika Territory. Department of Commerce and Industry.) Dar es Salaam, 1957.
Afr Doc 6508.705	Commerce extérieur de la Haute-Volta. (Upper Volta. Ministère de l'Economie Nationale.) Ouagadougou. 1961+
Afr Doc 1408.705	Commerce extérieur de l'Egypte. Statistique comparée. (Egypt. Customs Administration.) Roma. 1884-1903 2v.
Afr Doc 5008.700	Commerce exterieur des etats d'Afrique et de Madagascar. (France. Institut National de la Statistique et des Etudes Economique. Service de Coopération.) Paris. 1949+
Afr Doc 6208.705PF	Commerce extérieur du Sénégal. Commerce special. (Sénégal. Service de la Statistique Generale.) 1966+
Afr Doc 6408.707	Commerce exterieur et balance commerciale. (Ivory Coast. Direction du Commerce Extérieur.) Abidjan. 1964+
Afr Doc 4108.705F	Commerce report. (Swaziland.) 1955+
Afr 3998.10	Commercial directory of Egypt. Cairo. 1964+ 2v.
Afr 2223.961	Les commissaires du développement. (Secretariat Social d'Alger.) Alger, 1961.
Afr 7182.8	Commissão africana missões de Angola. (Sociedade de Geographia de Lisboa.) Lisboa, 1892.
Afr 626.58	Commission for Technical Cooperation in Africa South of Sahara. Inter-African scientific and technical cooperation, 1948-1955. Bukavu, 1956.
Afr 3040.60F	Commission Internationale pour l'Examen des Réformes, Egypte. Rapport de la Commission internationale réunie au Caire pour l'examen des réformes proposées...dans l'administration de la justice en Egypte. Alexandrie, 1870.
Afr 8289.03.9	Commission of H.M.S. Terrible. (Crowe, George.) London, 1903.
Afr 6310.34F	Commission of inquiry into the administration of justice in Kenya, Uganda...in criminal matters, May, 1933. (Great Britain. Commission. Administration of Justice in Kenya.) London, 1934.
Afr 7850.52F	Commission parlementaire chargée de faire une enquête. (Belgium. Chambre des Représentants.) Bruxelles, 1959.
Afr 6420.20.5	Commission Regarding the Boundary Between Kenya and Italian Somaliland. Agreement between the local commission appointed to settle certain points...boundary...Kenya and Italian Somaliland. London, 1933.
Afr 6420.20	Commission Regarding the Boundary Between Kenya and Italian Somaliland. Agreement recording the decisions of the commission appointed and treaty between the United Kingdom and Italy of July 15, 1924. London, 1933.
Afr 10215.5F	Committee for Inter-African Relations, Ibadan, Nigeria. Report on the press in West Africa. Ibadan, 1960.
NEDL Afr 1303.2	Committee for Moroccan Studies and Survey. Newsletter. Rabat.
Afr 608.60	Committee of General Literature and Education. Sketches of the African kingdoms and peoples. London, 1860.
Afr 8140.6F	Committee of Observation on All Matters Connected with Attainment of Independence of British Kaffraria. British Kaffaria, the people's blue book. King Williams Town, 1863.
Afr 2224.25	Common, Jacques. Le budget et le fisc algériens. Thèse. Paris, 1929.
Afr 8003.5	Common sense. Johannesburg.
Afr 210.60.5	Common sense about Africa. (Sampson, Anthony.) London, 1960.
Afr 3315.121	The Commonwealth and Suez. (Eayrs, James.) London, 1964.
Afr 6538.35	Commonwealth Development Corporation. Uganda tea survey, 1964. London, 1964.
Afr 210.62.20	The Commonwealth in Africa. (British Commonwealth Relations.) London, 1962.
Afr 6003.5	Commonwealth in Africa. (National Book League, London.) London, 1969.
Afr 5055.59	Communauté ou sécession. (Ehrhard, Jean.) Paris, 1959.
Afr 2025.13.10	La commune d'Alger, 1870-1871. (Martin, Claude.) Paris, 1936.
Afr 2025.13.12	La commune d'Alger, 1870-1871. Thèse. (Martin, Claude.) Paris, 1936.
Afr 5540.14	Les communes malgaches. (Comte, Jean.) Tananarive, 1963.
Afr 9625.25	Communication. (Zambia. University. Institute for Social Research.) Lusaka. 1,1966+
Afr 1.42.3	Communications. (Afrika-Institut, Pretoria.) Pretoria.
Afr 3.42	Communications. (Cape Town. University. School of African Studies.) Cape Town. 2,1942+ 4v.
Afr 1494.64	Communist Party of Morocco. Le parti communiste marocain. Paris, 1958.
Afr 7575.36	Communist penetration and subversion of the Belgian Congo, 1946-1960. 1st. ed. (Bartlet, R.E.) Berkeley, 1962.
Afr 6193.10	Community development in Ghana. (Dusantoy, Peter.) London, 1958.
Afr 718.4.6	Como eu atravessei Africa. vol.1-2. (Serpa Pinto, Alexander de.) Londres, 1881. 2v.
Afr 7332.15	La compagnie de Mozambique. (Bonnefont de Varinay, P. de.) Lisboa, 1899.
Afr 5874.11	Compagnie des Indes Orientales. Isle de Bourbon (Réunion); documents, 1701-1710. N.Y., 1909.
Afr 5183.960.8	Compagnie d'Etudes Industrielles et d'Aménagement du Territoire. Rapport général sur les perspectives de développement du Sénégal. 3. éd. Dakar, 1963.
Afr 5130.25	La compagnie du Sénégal. (Ly, Abdoulaye.) Paris, 1958.
Afr 4178.25	La Compagnie Universelle du Canal Maritime de Suez et la décision. v.1-2. (Compagnie Universlle du Canal Maritime de Suez.) Paris, 1956.
Afr 4178.25	Compagnie Universlle du Canal Maritime de Suez. La Compagnie Universelle du Canal Maritime de Suez et la décision. v.1-2. Paris, 1956.
Afr 2209.33	Les compagnons du jardin. (Arnaud, R.) Paris, 1933.
Afr 7183.25	Companhia de Diamantes de Angola. Breve noticia sobre o Museu do Dundo. Lisbon, 1959.
Afr 7210.15	Companhia de Moçambique. Decretos. Lisboa, 1891.

Afr 1367.64	Compendio de la historia de la España. v.1-2. (Sagarra, J. de.) Barcelona, 1764. 2v.
Afr 4700.14.25	Compendio di storia coloniale italiana. (Botarelli, A.) Roma, 1914.
Afr 7015.45	Compendio historico das possesões de Portugal na Africa. (Matos, R.J. da Cunha.) Rio de Janeiro, 1963.
Afr Doc 707.5	Compendio statistico. (Somalia. Planning Directorate. Statistical Department.) Mogadiscio. 2,1965+
Afr Doc 5008.705	Compendium des statistiques du commerce extérieur de pays africains et Malgache. (France. Institut National de la Statistique et des Etudes Economiques.) 1960+
Afr 8825.4.3	A compendium of Kafir laws and customs. (Maclean, J.) Mount Cape, 1858. 2 pam.
Afr 8088.77.5	Compendium of South African history and geography. 3d ed. (Theal, G.M.) Lovedale, 1877.
Afr Doc 3607.8F	Compendium of statistics for Malawi. (Malawi. National Statistical Office.) Zomba. 1965+
Afr 5420.175	Compiegne, Victor D. L'Afrique équatoriale. Paris, 1875.
Afr 2207.25.3	Compleat history of the piratical states of Barbary. (Laugier de Tassy, N.) London, 1750.
Afr 1885.2	Complement de l'histoire des Beni-Zeiyan. (Barges, J.J.L.) Paris, 1887.
Afr 1867.28	Complete history of Algiers. (Morgan, John.) London, 1728. 2v.
Afr 8289.02.45	Complete history of the South African war in 1899-1902. (Stevens, F.T.) London, 1902.
Afr 8210.3	The complete story of the Transvaal. (Nixon, John.) London, 1885.
Afr 8809.60	Complex canvas. (Meintzis, Johannes.) Johannesburg, 1960.
Afr 8659.44	Complex country. (Malherbe, J.A.) London, 1944.
Afr 8678.32.5	Complex South Africa, an economic foot-note to history. (MacMillan, W.M.) London, 1930.
Afr 3315.60	Le complot continué. (Amir, Adil.) Caire, 1957.
Afr 3315.65	Le complot de Suez. (Dzelepy, E.N.) Bruxelles, 1957.
Afr 545.2	A comprehensive bibliography of modern African religious movements. (Mitchell, Robert C.) Evanston, 1966.
Afr 7315.25	Comprendamos os negros. (Belchior, M.D.) Lisboa, 1951.
Afr 3994.891.3F	Compte général. (Egypt. Ministère des Finances.) Le Caire. 1922/23- 2v.
Afr 1.6F	Compte rendu. (Association Internationale Africaine.) Bruxelles. 1877+
Afr 1494.35	Compte-rendu. v.1. (Conférence Nationale pour la Solution du Problème Franco-Marocain.) Paris, 1956.
Afr Doc 7714.5	Compte rendu analytique. (Congo. Chambre des Representants.) Leopoldville. 1962+ 5v.
Afr 2209.61.20	Compte rendu analytique de la troisième session. (Algeria. Conseil Supérieur de la Promotion Sociale en Algérie.) Alger, 1961.
Afr Doc 7714.10	Compte rendu analytique officiel. (Congo. Chambre des Députés.) Leopoldville. 1966+
Afr Doc 7716.5F	Compte rendu officiel. (Congo. Parlement. Senat.) Leopoldville. 1965+
Afr Doc 6409.315	Les comptes de la nation, 1966-1967 (provisoire). (Leblan, Pierre Jean.) Abidjan, 1968.
Afr Doc 7109.305	Comptes économiques. (Chad.) Paris. 1961-1963
Afr Doc 7409.305	Comptes economiques. (Gabon. Commissariat au Plan.) Libreville. 1964+
Afr Doc 6409.307	Les comptes économiques. (Ivory Coast. Direction de la Statistique et des Etudes Economiques et Démographiques.) 1958+
Afr Doc 6209.305	Comptes économiques. (Sénégal. Ministère du Développement du Plan et de l'Economie.) Paris. 1959+
Afr Doc 5508.614	Comptes économiques de la Cote française des Somalis. (France. Institut National de la Statistique et des Etudes Economiques.) Paris. 1959+
Afr Doc 6509.305	Comptes économiques de la Haute-Volta. (Upper Volta. Service de la Statistique.) Paris. 1964+
Afr Doc 5409.305	Les comptes économiques de la Tunisie. (Tunisia. Service des Statistiques.) 1,1953
Afr Doc 5709.303	Comptes économiques du territoire des Comores. (France. Institut National de la Statistique et des Etudes Economiques.) Paris. 1959+
Afr Doc 6709.305	Comptes nationaux. (Togo. Haut Commissariat au Plan.) Lomé. 1963+
Afr 9.7	Comptes rendus. (International West African Conference, 1st, Dakar, 1945.) Paris. 1+ 2v.
Afr 5045.9	Comptoirs de l'Afrique française occidentale. (Gaffarel, Paul.) Dijon, 1910.
Afr 4868.79	Comptoirs français de l'Afrique orientale. Paris, 1879.
Afr 5540.14	Comte, Jean. Les communes malgaches. Tananarive, 1963.
Afr 4070.29	Comyn, D.C.E. Service and sport in the Sudan. London, 1911.
Afr 1608.22	Comyn, T. De. Ligera ojeada o breve idea...de Marruecos en 1822. Barcelona, 1825.
Afr 4559.35.80	Comyn-Platt, Thomas. The Abyssinian storm. London, 1935.
Afr 4513.37.70	Con Badoglio in Ethiopia. (Armellini, Quirino.) Milano, 1937.
Afr 4513.37.15	Con le armate del Negus. (Konovalov, T.E.) Bologna, 1937.
Afr 8325.33	Het concentratie-kamp van Irene. (Warmelo, J.B.V.) Amsterdam, 1905.
Afr 8325.33.5	The concentration camps, 1900-02. (Martin, A.C.) Cape Town, 1958.
Afr 6218.19	Concerning brave captains. (Muffett, D.J.M.) London, 1964.
Afr 8325.62	The concert. Souvenir programme. (American Hospital Ship Fund for South Africa.) n.p., n.d.
Afr 5057.12	Les concessions foncières en Afrique occidentale française et équatoriale. Thèse. (Lenoir, Robert.) Paris, 1936.
Afr 10004.20	The conch. Paris. 1,1969+
Afr 7375.12	A concise history of...the American colonies in Liberia. (Wilkeson, Samuel.) Washington, 1839.
Afr 5829.58	A concise history of Mauritius. (Babaju, Esno.) Bombay, 1963.
Afr 590.46.3	A concise statement of the question regarding the abolition of the slave trade. 2d ed. (Brougham And Vaux, H. Brougham, 1st Baron.) London, 1804.
Afr 9425.10	Concord, the journal of the interracial association of Southern Rhodesia. Salisbury, Southern Rhodesia. 13+
Afr 10671.53.100	The concubine. (Amadi, Elechi.) London, 1966.
Afr 635.62.10	La condition de l'Africaine en Afrique noire. (Plisnier-Ladame, F.) Bruxelles, 1961.

Afr 1550.9 La condition du Maroc d'après l'accord de 1904. (Lapradelle, A. de.) Paris, 1905.

Afr 609.53 La condition humaine en Afrique noire. (Marie André du Sacre Coeur, Sister.) Paris, 1953.

Afr 3300.1 La condition internationale de l'Egypte depuis 1914. Thèse. (Himaya, Latif.) Paris, 1922.

Afr 3745.35 La condition internationale du Soudan anglo-égyptien et du Haut-Nil. Thèse. (Colin, Hugues.) Paris, 1936.

Afr 575.18 Condition juridique des sujets musulmans. Thèse. (Korei, Aly.) Paris, 1913.

Afr 2225.3 La condition sociale des indigènes algériens. (Drapier, H.) Paris, 1899.

Afr 5057.30 Les conditions de la mise en valeur de l'Afrique occidentale française. (Lacroix, Alain.) Paris, 1959.

Afr 7812.269 Conditions de la planification du développement; l'exemple du Congo. (Comeliau, Christian.) Paris, 1969.

Afr 2030.462.15 Les conditions de l'indépendance. (Colloque Internationale sur l'Algérie.) Bruxelles, 1962.

Afr 1570.26 Les conditions d'établissement du protectorat français au Maroc. (Chastaud, P.) Paris, 1913.

Afr 1738.6 Conditions d'existence à Tanger. Paris, 1906.

Afr 5448.12F Les conditions sociologiques d'une politique d'urbanisme à Brazzaville. (Devauges, Roland.) Paris, 1959.

Htn Afr 2850.12.5* Le condizioni militari della Tripolitania. (Italy. Ministero della Marina.) Rome, 1885.

Afr 6192.57 Cone, Virginia. Africa, a world in progress. 1st ed. N.Y., 1960.

X Cg Afr 3230.6 A Confederate soldier in Egypt. (Loring, W.W.) N.Y., 1884.

Afr 2025.34 Confer, Vincent. France and Algeria. 1st ed. N.Y., 1966.

Afr 6200.12.5F Conference and seminar reports. (Lagos, Nigeria (City). University. Continuing Education Center.) Lagos. 1,1968+

Afr 2530.10 La conférence consultative tunisienne. Thèse. (Dauphin, M.) Paris, 1919.

Afr 1550.11 La conférence d'Algésiras. (Tardier, A.) Paris, 1908.

Afr 1570.12 Conférence d'Algésiras. Paris, 1906.

Afr 590.13 La Conférence de Bruxelles. (Banning, E.) Bruxelles, 1890.

Afr 3255.6 La conférence de Constantinople et la question égyptienne 1882. (Kamel, S.) Paris, 1913.

Afr 545.46 La conférence de Kampala, 1963. (All-Africa Church Conference, Kampala, Uganda.) Kitwe, 1963.

Afr 210.60.55 Conférence de l action positive pour la paix. (Conférence de l'Action Positive pour la Paix et la Sécurité.) Accra, 1960.

Afr 210.60.55 Conférence de l'Action Positive pour la Paix et la Sécurité. Conférence de l action positive pour la paix. Accra, 1960.

Afr 500.70F Conférence des Institutions Européennes, Rome, 1958. Documentation des travaux de la première conférence. Rome, 1959.

Afr 590.13.5F Conférence international de Bruxelles, 18 nov. 1889-2 juil. 1890. v.1-3. (France. Ministère des Affaires Estrangères.) Bruxelles, 1890.

Afr 1325.9F Conférence Internationale d'Algeciras. Acte général. La Haye, 1906.

Afr 1325.9.5F Conférence Internationale d'Algeciras. Despatches from British delegate. London, 1906.

Afr 1494.35 Conférence Nationale pour la Solution du Problème Franco-Marocain. Compte-rendu. v.1. Paris, 1956.

Afr 3.25 Pamphlet vol. Conference of Independent African States, Accra, 1958. 6 pam.

Afr 3.20 Conference of Independent African States, 1st, Accra, 1958. Konferenz der unabhängigen Staaten Afrikas, April 15-22, 1958. London, 1958.

Afr 10003.4 Conference of Writers, Publishers, Editors, and University Teachers of English. Proceedings. Johannesburg, 1957.

Afr 45.66.10 Conference on African Local Government since Independence, Lincoln University, Pennsylvania, 1966. Proceedings of the Conference on African Local Government since Independence held at Lincoln University, Feb. 3rd and 4th, 1966. Lincoln, 1966.

Afr 6277.64 Conference on Attitudes in Development Planning in Local Government, Ahmadu Bello University, 1963. Report. Zaria, Northern Nigeria, 1964.

Afr 626.128 Conference On Economic Development for Africa. Economic development for Africa south of the Sahara. London, 1964.

Afr 6392.31 Conference on Education, Employment and Rural Development, Kericho, Kenya, 1966. Education employment and rural development. Nairobi, 1967.

Afr 6096.15 Conference on Educational and Occupational Selection in West Africa. Educational and occupational selection in West Africa. London, 1962.

Afr 115.90 Conference on History and Archaeology. History and archaeology in Africa. London, 1959.

Afr 6277.130 Conference on National Reconstruction and Development in Nigeria, University of Ibadan 1969. Papers presented at the conference. Ibadan. 1,1969+

Afr 45.60.10 Conference on the Future of Law in Africa. The future of law in Africa. London, 1960.

Afr 115.45 Conference on the Legal, Economic and Social Aspects of African Refugee Problems. Final report. Uppsala, 1968.

Afr 6291.50 Conference on the Nigeria-Biafra Conflict, Washington. The Nigeria-Biafra conflict; report of a one day conference. Washington, 1969.

Afr 36.4 Conference on the Position and Problems of the American Scholar in Africa, White Sulphur Springs, West Va., 1966. Summary report. N.Y., 1966?

Afr 6463.7 Conference on the Role of the Church in Independent Kenya Limuru. Report of the conference held at Limuru Conference Centre, Kenya. Nairobi, 196- .

Afr 6200.14.45F Conference proceedings. (Nigerian Institute of Social and Economic Research, Ibadan, Nigeria.) Ibadan. 1,1952+ 3v.

Afr 5405.109.30 Conférences et lettres sur ses trois explorations dans l'ouest africain de 1875 à 1886. (Savorgnan de Brazza, Pierre.) Paris, 1887.

Afr 7808.86 Conférences sur le Congo. Bruxelles, 1886.

Afr 2438.5 Conférences sur les administrations tunisiennes, 1902. 2.ed. (Tunis.) Sousse, 1902.

Afr 1550.8 La conferencia de Algeciras. (Betegon, T.) Madrid, 1906.

Afr 1574.12 Conferencia del Excmo. Sr. conde de Romanones sobre el problema de Marruecos, Pronunciada en al Teatro de San Fernando de Sevilla el 26 de abril de 1922. (Romanones, Álvaro Figueroa y Torres.) Sevilla, 1922.

Afr 115.42 Conferencia internacional de africanistas occident. v.2. (International West African Conference, 4th, Santa Isabel.) Madrid, 1954.

Afr 7015.10 Conferencias celebradas na Academia Real das Sciencias de Lisboa. (Academia das Sciencias de Lisboa.) Lisboa, 1892.

Afr 718.4.10 As conferencias e o itinerario do viajante Serpa Pinto. (Ribeiro, M.F.) Lisboa, 1879.

Afr 1571.4 Les confins algéro-marocains. (Bernard, A.) Paris, 1911.

Afr 5056.146 Confins libyens, lac Tchad, fleuve Niger. (Gentil, P.) Paris, 1946.

Afr 2230.14 Les confins militaires de la Grande Kabylie. (Aucapitaine, H.) Paris, 1857.

Afr 6910.5 The conflict between the United Nations and the Union of South Africa in regard to Southwest Africa. (Goldblatt, Israel.) Windhoek, 1960.

Afr 3198.87 Conflict of East and West in Egypt. (Bowen, J.E.) N.Y., 1887.

Afr 8685.46 Conflict of races in South Africa. (Anjar, P.L.) Durban, 1946.

Afr 1494.61 Le conflit franco-marocain, 1943-56. v.1-2, 3. (Bernard, S.) Bruxelles, 1963. 2v.

Afr 4513.36.5 Le conflit italo-ethiopien. (Lapradelle, A.G.) Paris, 1936.

Afr 4513.36.30 Il conflitto italo-etiopico. (Istituto per gli Studi di Politica Internazionale, Milan.) Milano, 1936. 2v.

Afr 4513.35.17 Il conflitto italo-etiopico. (Italy.) Roma, 1935.

Afr 1303.5 Confluent, revue marocaine. Rabat. 1,1956+ 13v.

Afr 575.50 La confraternità senussita dalle sue origini ad oggi. (Giglio, Carlo.) Padova, 1932.

Afr 575.11 Les confréries islamiques. (Simian, M.) Alger, 1910.

Afr 575.38 Confréries religieuses musulmanes et marabouts. (Layer, E.) Rouen, 1916.

Afr 7549.61 Congo, background of conflict. (Merriam, Alan P.) Evanston, Ill., n.d.

Afr 7809.49 Congo, Belgian. Guide de voyageur au Congo belge et au Ruanda-Urundi. 1.ed. Bruxelles, 1949.

Afr 7812.260.10 Congo, Belgian. Commissariat au Plan Décennal. Le plan décennal pour le développement économique et social du Congo belge. Bruxelles, 1960.

Afr 7535.15 Congo, Belgian. Laws, statutes, etc. Codes et lois du Congo belge. V.1-3 (V.1, 1960) 8.ed. Bruxelles, 1959. 3v.

Afr 7503.4 Congo, documents belges et africains. Bruxelles. 1959+ 7v.

Afr 7575.80.10 Congo, my country. (Lumumba, Patrice.) London, 1962.

Afr 7575.80.12 Congo, my country. (Lumumba, Patrice.) London, 1969.

Afr 7575.80.11 Congo, my country. (Lumumba, Patrice.) N.Y., 1962.

Afr 555.23.55 Congo, past and present. (Stonedake, A.R.) London, 1937.

Afr 5400.5 Congo, revue générale de la colonie belge. Bruxelles. 1,1920+ 41v.

Afr 5400.5.5 Congo, revue générale de la colonie belge. Tables de Congo. Bruxelles. 1920+

Afr 7540.15 Congo, suite à mes souvenirs d'Afrique. (Liebrechts, C.) Bruxelles, 1920.

Afr 5405.270 Congo, terre de souffrances. (Homet, Marcel.) Paris, 1934.

Afr 7567.13 El Congo, 1885-1963. (Cola Alberich, Julio.) Madrid, 1964.

Afr 7575.97 Congo, 1956-1960. (Paulus, J.P.) Bruxelles, 1961.

Afr 7580.9 Congo. The Adoula-Tshombe talks. Leopoldville, 1962.

Afr Doc 7707.10 Congo. Statistiques relatives à l'année. 1957-1958

Afr 7568.25 The Congo. (Belguim. Commission Chargée de Faire une Enquête dans les Territoires de l'Etat du Congo.) N.Y., 1906.

Afr 7580.14 Il Congo. (Buccianto, G.) Milano, 1963.

Afr 7549.61.5 The Congo. (Hennessy, Maurice N.) London, 1961.

Afr 7809.45 Congo. (Latouche, J.T.) N.Y., 1945.

Afr 7560.3.2 Le Congo. (Lopes, D.) Bruxelles, 1883.

Afr 7575.80 Le Congo. (Lumumba, Patrice.) Bruxelles, 1961.

Afr 7540.21 The Congo. (Mares, R. de.) Brussels, 1904.

Afr 7575.90 Congo. (Parti Socialiste Belge.) Brussels, 1961.

Afr 7808.92 Le Congo. (Ramaix, M.M. de.) Anvers, 1892.

NEDL Afr 7808.85 The Congo. (Stanley, H.M.) London, 1885. 2v.

Afr 7809.50 Congo. (Verleyen, E.J.B.) Bruxelles, 1950.

Afr 7809.55.10 Congo: Belgique d'outre-mer. (Congo. Service de l'Information.) Léopoldville, 1955?

Afr Doc 7714.10 Congo. Chambre des Députés. Compte rendu analytique officiel. Leopoldville. 1966+

Afr Doc 7714.5 Congo. Chambre des Representants. Compte rendu analytique. Leopoldeville. 1962+ 5v.

Afr Doc 7607.3 Congo. Direction de la Statistique. Bulletin mensuel des statistiques générales du Congo belge et du Ruanda-Urundi. Série speciale. Leopoldville. 1,1959+

Afr Doc 7708.705 Congo. Diréction de la Statistique et des Etudes Economiques. Annuaire des statistiques du commerce extérieur. Leopoldville. 1963+

Afr Doc 7724.5 Congo. Gouverneur Général. Discours. 1949-1959 4v.

Afr 7809.68 Il Congo. Ieri, oggi, domani. (Scotti, Pietro.) Genova, 1968.

Afr 7540.39 Congo. Laws, statutes, etc. Les circonscriptions indigènes. Bruxelles, 1938.

Afr Doc 7716.5F Congo. Parlement. Senat. Compte rendu officiel. Leopoldville. 1965+

Afr Doc 7708.5 Congo. Secretariat Général. La population congolaise en 1953. n.p., 195-?

Afr 7809.55.10 Congo. Service de l'Information. Congo: Belgique d'outre-mer. Léopoldville, 1955?

Afr Doc 7709.3F Congo. Service du Budget-Contrôle. Budget ordinaire. 1966+

Afr 7808.85.5 The Congo. v.1-2. (Stanley, H.M.) N.Y., 1885.

Afr 7568.11 Congo. Vice-Governor General. Report to Secretary of State. Brussels, 1904.

Afr 7549.66 Congo. 2.ed. (Giovannini, Giovanni.) Milano, 1966.

Afr 7530.7 Congo - bibliographie. (Monheim, Christian.) Antwerpen, 1942.

Afr 5430.10 Congo (Brazzaville). Plan interimaire de développement économique et social. Paris. 1964-1968

Afr Doc 7312.5F Congo (Brazzaville). Assemblée Nationale. Journal des debats.

Afr Doc 7335.5 Congo (Brazzaville). Conseil Economique et Social. Rapport annuel. 1964+

Afr Doc 7307.5 Congo (Brazzaville). Direction du Service National de la Statistique, des Etudes Démographiques et Economiques. Bulletin mensuel des statistiques. Brazzaville. 1962+

Afr Doc 7307.361 Congo (Brazzaville). Direction du Service National de la Statistique, des Etudes Démographiques et Economiques. Enquête démographique, 1960-1961. Résultats définitifs. n.p., n.d.

Afr Doc 7707.15 Congo (Brazzaville). Direction du Service National de la Statistique des Etudes Démographiques et Economiques. Annuaire statistique. 1,1958+

Afr Doc 7372.361 Congo (Brazzaville). Service de Statistique. Recensement de Brazzaville, 1961; résultats définitifs. Paris, 1965.

Afr Doc 7386.5.73 Congo (Brazzaville). Statistique Générale. Recensement démographique de Pointe Noire, 1958. Paris, 1961.

Afr 7575.45 Le Congo à tombeau ouvert. (Dessart, C.) Bruxelles, 1959.

Afr 7503.8 Congo-Afrique; économie, culture, vie sociale. Kinshasa. 7,1967+ 2v.

Afr 7809.08.5 The Congo and coasts of Africa. (Davis, R.H.) London, 1908.

Afr 7575.25 Congo and the United Nations. (Mezerik, A.G.) N.Y., 1960. 3v.

Afr 7809.24.15 Le Congo au travail. (Wauters, Joseph.) Bruxelles, 1924.

Afr 7560.3.10 Le Congo au XVIe siècle d'après la relation de Lopez-Pigafetta. (Simar, T.) Bruxelles, 1919.

Afr 7549.39 Il Congo belga. (Bollati, A.) Milano, 1939.

Afr 7548.90 Le Congo belge. (Desoer, F.) Liège, 1890.

Afr 7809.28.5 Le Congo belge. (Franck, Louis.) Bruxelles, 1928. 2v.

Afr 7549.59.5 Le Congo belge. (Lévèque, Robert J.) Bruxelles, 1959.

Afr 7503.1F Congo belge. Bruxelles. 1896+ 2v.

Afr 7809.59 Congo belge. Genève, 1958.

Afr 7567.32 Le Congo belge et Weltpolitik. (Willequet, I.) Bruxelles, 1962.

Afr 7809.61 Congo cauldron. (Dugauquier, D.P.) London, 1961.

Afr 7580.21 Congo Congo. (Kestergat, Jean.) Paris, 1965.

Afr 7835.5 Congo crisis. (Bayly, Joseph T.) Grand Rapids, 1966.

Afr 7803.15 Congo crisis and Christian mission. (Nelson, Robert G.) St. Louis, 1961.

Afr 7567.26 Le Congo de la colonisation belge à l'indépendance. (Merlier, Michel.) Paris, 1962.

Afr 7575.4 Congo disaster. (Legum, Cohn.) Harmondsworth, 1961.

Afr 7349.53 Le Congo du fétiche à l'uranium. (Ydewalle, Charles D.) Bruxelles, 1953.

Afr 7809.65 Le Congo en question. (Verbeck, Roger.) Paris, 1965.

Afr 7549.28 Le Congo et les livres. (Monheim, A.) Bruxelles, 1928.

Afr 7580.11 Congo ex-belge entre l'est et l'ouest. (Tran-Minh Tiet.) Paris, 1962.

Afr 5405.112.5 Le Congo français. (Challaye, Felicien.) Paris, 1909.

Afr 5405.112.2 Le Congo français. (Chavannes, Charles de.) Paris, 1937.

Afr 5406.189 Le Congo français du Gabon à Brazzaville. (Guiral, Léon.) Paris, 1889.

Afr 7533.01 Pamphlet box. Congo Free State.

Afr 7533.2 Pamphlet vol. Congo Free State. 6 pam.

Afr 7530.6 Pamphlet vol. Congo Free State. 10 pam.

Afr 7530.6.5 Pamphlet vol. Congo Free State. 5 pam.

Afr 7568F Pamphlet box. Congo Free State.

Afr 7808.86.2F The Congo Free State. (Dewinton, F.W.) London, 1886.

Afr 7814.1 Congo Free State (1887). Carte de l'Etat. Bruxelles, 1887.

Afr 7548.94.5 Le Congo historique. (Chapaux, Albert.) Bruxelles, 1894.

Afr 7503.2F Congo illustré. Bruxelles. 1,1892+ 2v.

Afr 7567.14 The Congo Independent State. (Mountmorres, W.S.B. de M.) London, 1906.

Afr 710.23 Congo kitabu. (Hallet, Jean Pierre.) N.Y., 1966.

Afr 7815.10 Congo life and folklore. (Weeks, John H.) London, 1911.

Afr 7582.10.4 Congo mercenary. (Hoare, Michael.) London, 1967.

Afr 3.5 Congo mission news. Bolenge.

Afr 555.23.25 Congo Missionary Conference. Reports. 7,1918 2v.

Afr 7809.23.5 Le Congo physique. (Robert, M.) Bruxelles, 1923.

Afr 7809.52 Congo pilgrim. (Severn, M.) London, 1952.

Afr 7568.16 Congo Reform Association. Memorial concerning conditions...in Kongo. Washington, 1904.

Afr 7580.24 Congo saga. (Truby, David William.) London, 1965.

Afr 7580.17 The Congo since independence. (Hoskyns, Catherine.) London, 1965.

Afr 7568.35 The Congo State; its origin, rights, and duties, the charges of its accusers. (Castelein, A.) N.Y., 1969.

Afr 7548.98 The Congo state. (Boulger, D.C.) London, 1898.

Afr 7809.59.15 Congo 1959. (Rhodius, Georges.) Bruxelles, 1959.

Afr 7812.260.15 The Congolese economy on the eve of independence. (Fédération des Enterprises Congolaises.) Brussels, 1960.

Afr 7809.31.5 Congorilla. (Johnson, Martin.) N.Y., 1931.

Afr 5765.7.10 Congregation of Priests of the Mission. Memoires. v.9. Paris, 1866.

Afr 7812.224 Congrès Colonial National. La politique économique au Congo belge. Bruxelles, 1924.

Afr 5053.15 Congrès constitutif de P.F.A. (Senghor, Leopold.) Paris, 1959.

Afr 2209.09 Congrès de l'Afrique du nord. Paris, 1909. 2v.

Afr 699.12.5 Congrés de l'Afrique Orientale, Paris, 1911. Congrés de l'Afrique Orientale. Paris, 1912.

Afr 699.12.5 Congrès de l'Afrique Orientale. (Congrés de l'Afrique Orientale, Paris, 1911.) Paris, 1912.

Afr 2442.2 Les congrès du Néo-Destour. (Tunisia. Secrétariat d'Etat à l'Information.) Tunis, 1959.

Afr 5212.2 Congrès extraordinaire de l'U.S.R.D.A. le 22 septembre 1960, mais le Mali continue. (Union Soudanaise.) Bamako? 1960?

Afr 1803.1 Congrès National des Sciences Historiques. Proceedings. Alger. 2,1930+

Afr 115.6 Le Congrès Volta de 1938 et ses travaux sur l'Afrique. (Louwers, Octave.) Bruxelles, 1949.

Afr 1750.4.4 Congreso Africanista. Cuarto congreso africanista. IVth. Barcelona, 1910.

Afr 1750.4.3 Congreso Africanista. Tercer congreso africanista. Barcelona, 1908.

Afr 4700.17 Congresso Coloniale Italiano, Asmara. Atti. v.1. Roma, 1906.

Afr 7065.7 Congresso comemorativo do quinto centenario do descobrimento da Guinea. (Sociedade de Geografia de Lisboa.) Lisboa, 1946. 2v.

Afr 4178.20 Il Congresso di Trento per il centenario del progetto italiano per il taglio dell'istmo di Suez. (Istituto Italiano per l'Africa.) Roma, 1956.

Afr 3.44 Connaissance de l'Afrique. Paris. 13,1965+

Afr 5548.63 Connaissance de Madagascar. (Lacaille, L.P.) Paris, 1863.

Afr 1957.25 Les conquérants de l'Algérie (1830-1857). (Dufestre, Henri.) Paris, 1934.

Afr 1571.33 Conquérants et conquis au Maroc. Thèse. (Vallerie, Pierre.) Paris, 1934.

Afr 1955.3 Conquest and colonization in North Africa. (Cooke, G.W.) Edinburgh, 1860.

Afr 1550.50 The conquest of Morocco. (Usborne, C.V.) London, 1936.

Afr 5227.28 The conquest of the Western Sedan. (Kanya-Forstner, Alexander Sidney.) Cambridge, Eng., 1969.

Afr 674.93.9 Conquests and discoveries of Henry the Navigator. (Eannes de Azurara, G.) London, 1906.

Afr 1957.3 La conquête d'Alger. (Perrot, A.M.) Paris, 1830.

Afr 1955.6 La conquête d'Alger. (Rousset, C.) Paris, 1880.

Afr 1955.6.4 La conquête d'Alger. (Rousset, C.) Paris, 1899.

Afr 200.8 La conquête de l'Afrique. (Darcy, Jean.) Paris, 1900.

Afr 1955.46 La conquête de l'Alger. (Gautherat, Gustave.) Paris, 1929.

Afr 1955.10 La conquête de l'Algérie. (Hennequin, A.) Paris, 1857.

Afr 1955.49 La conquête de l'Algérie. (Maze, Jules.) Tours, 1930.

Afr 1955.6.3 La conquête de l'Algérie. v.1,2 and atlas. (Rousset, C.) Paris, 1904. 3v.

Afr 1960.5 La conquête de l'Algérie jusqu'à la prise de Constantine. (Gaffarel, Paul.) Paris, 1887.

Afr 4513.36.60 La conquête de l'Ethiopie. (Gentizon, Paul.) Paris, 1936.

Afr 5635.22 La conquête de Madagascar. (David Bernard, Eugene.) Paris, 1944.

Afr 5635.16 Conquete de Madagascar (1895-1896). (Poirier, Jules.) Paris, 1902.

Afr 6720.28.15 La conquête du Cameroun. (Aymerich, J.G.) Paris, 1936.

Afr 6720.28 Conquête du Cameroun-Nord, 1914-1915. (Ferrandi, Jean.) Paris, 1928.

Afr 1570.29 La conquête du Maroc. (Millet, R.) Paris, 1913.

Afr 1570.31 La conquête du Maroc (mai 1911-mars 1913). (Sainte-Chapelle, A.M.G.) Paris, 1913.

Afr 2749.10 La conquête du Sahara. (Gautier, E.F.) Paris, 1910.

Afr 2290.10 Conquête du sud-oranais; la colonne d'Igli en 1900. (Guillaume.) Paris, 1910.

Afr 2748.89 La conquête pacifique de l'intérieur africain. (Philebert, C.) Paris, 1889.

Afr 1703.6 Conquista de azamor pelo duque de bragança don jaime. (Peres, Damiao.) Lisboa, 1951.

Afr 1727.2 La conquista de la Mehedia. (Servando Marenco, D.) Madrid, 1908.

Afr 1485.4 La conquista del Mogreb. (Morote, L.) Valencia, n.d.

Afr 4513.36.40 La conquista del Tigrai. (Vecchi, B.V.) Milano, 1936.

Afr 4513.37.22 La conquista dell'Abissinia. (Xylander, R. von.) Milano, 1937.

Afr 4513.36.95 La conquista dell'impero. (Cabiati, A.) Milano, 1936.

Afr 2870.5 La conquista di Tripoli. (Corradini, E.) Milano, 1912.

Afr 2525.5 La conquista di Tunisi. (Giaccardi, A.) Milano, 1940.

Afr 4315.1 La conquista mussulmana dell'Etiopia. (Shihab al-Din Ahmad Ibn Abd al-Kadir.) Rome, 1891.

Afr 8289.43 Conradie, Francois. Met cronjé aan die wesfront (1899-1900) en waarom het die boere die oorlog verloor verloor. Kaapstad, 1943.

Afr 1608.80 Conring, A. von. Marroco, das Land und die Leute. Berlin, 1880.

Afr 1608.80.05 Conring, A. von. Marroco, das Land und die Leute. Berlin, 1884.

Afr 1608.80.1 Conring, A. von. Marroco, el pais y los habitantes. 2e ed. Madrid, 1881.

Afr 115.50 Consciences tribales et nationales en Afrique noire. (Langenhove, F.) Bruxelles, 1960.

Afr 6176.30.15A Conscientism. (Nkrumah, Kwame.) N.Y., 1965.

Afr 6176.30.20 Le consciencisme. (Nkrumah, Kwame.) Paris, 1965.

Afr 1846.7 La conscription des indigenes d'Algérie. (Sibe, J.) Paris, 1912.

Afr 1435.5 Consecuencias de la campana de 1860. (Baule y Landauer.) Madrid, 1923. 4v.

Afr 6392.45 Conseil National du Patronat Français. Mission industrielle française en Afrique orientale et centrale britannique. Paris, 1965.

Afr 8675.5 Conseil Scientifique pour l'Afrique au Sud du Sahara. Cartographie de l'Afrique au sud du Sahara. Bukavu, 1953.

Afr 45.29 Les conseils représentatifs. (Fidel, Camille.) Bruxelles, 1929.

Afr 150.20 Conselho do Infante Dom Henrique a seu sobrinho El-Rei Dom Afonso V. (Henrique, o Navegador, Infante of Portugal.) Lisboa, 1958.

Afr 5285.277.35 Conséquences de la colonisation sur la vie coutumière en pays mossi. Thèse. (Kassoum, Congo.) Montepellier, 1955.

Afr 3994.2 Les conséquences financières de l'occupation de l'Egypte par l'Angleterre. (Kamil, Ali.) Alexandrie, 1911.

Afr 28.40 Conséquences sociales de l'industrialisation et problèmes urbains en Afrique. (International Social Science Council. International Research Office on Social Implications of Technological Change.) Paris, 1954.

Afr 210.36 Consider Africa. (Mathews, Basil.) N.Y., 1936.

Afr 4640.5 Considerations of migration in Addis Ababa. (Comhaire-Sylvain, Suzanne.) Addis Ababa, 1962.

Afr 1957.6 Considerations sur la régence d'Alger. (Jucherau de St. Denis, A.) Paris, 1831.

Afr 3252.20 Considerazioni sul discorso da Layard...Riforma giudiziaria in Egitto. (Lenghi, N.) Alexandria, 1868.

Afr 609.54.10 Considine, J.J. Africa, world of new men. N.Y., 1954.

Afr 3183.20 Consilium Aegyptiacum. (Leibniz, G.W.) Paris, 1842.

Afr Doc 1419.2 La constitution, 25 mars, 1964. (United Arab Republic. Constitution.) Le Caire, 1964.

Afr Doc 2319.5 The constitution of the Federal Republic of Nigeria. (Nigeria. Constitution.) Lagos, 1963.

Afr 8028.140 Consolidated general bibliography. (South Africa. Department of Colored Affairs.) Cape Town, 1960.

Afr 8028.148 Consolidated list, 1941-1966. (Cape Town. University.) Cape Town, 1966.

Afr Doc 1809.35 The consolidation development plan. (Ghana.) Accra. 1,1957+

Afr 2223.961.5 La consommation des familles d'Algérie. (Association pour la Recherche.) Paris, 1961.

Afr 6200.3 Consortium for the Study of Nigerian Rural Development. Report. East Lansing, Michigan. 1,1965+ 10v.

Afr 4368.16 Constantin, Jean R. L'archimandrite Paisi et l'ataman Achinoff. Paris, 1891.

Afr 4368.17 Constantin, N. Une expédition religieuse en Abyssinie. Paris, 1891.

Afr 1955.7.5 Constantin-Weyer, M. La vie du général Yusuf. 10e éd. Paris, 1930.

Afr 1826.30 Constantine, Algeria. Archives Départmentals. Répertoire de documentation nord-africaine. v.1-2. Constantine, 1954.

Afr 2318.1.15 Constantine, centre économique. Thèse. (Antoine, L.F.) Toulouse, 1930.

Afr 2318.1.20 Constantine. (Berthier, Andre.) Toulouse, 1965.

Afr 2318.1 Constantine avant la conquête française. (Mercier, E.) Constantine, 1879.

Afr 2223.961.15 The Constantine plan for Algeria, opening new frontiers in development. (France. Embassy. United States.) N.Y., 1961.

Htn Afr 7360.15* Constitution, government and digest of the laws of Liberia. (Liberia. Constitution.) Washington, 1825.

Afr 1838.9 La constitution. (Algeria. Constitution.) Alger, 1963.

Afr 6710.6 Constitution. (Cameroon. Constitution.) Buea, 1963.

Afr 5252.5 Constitution. (Niger. Constitution.) Paris, 1959.

Afr 6210.30 Constitution. (Nigeria.) n.p., 196-.

Afr Doc 719.12 The Constitution. (Somalia. Constitution.) Mogadiscio, 1964?

Afr 9086.5 Constitution. (South Africa.) London, 1899.

Afr 8145.42 Constitution and canons of the Church of the province of South Africa. (Church of England in South Africa.) Cape Town, 1962.

Afr 6160.25 The constitution and government of Ghana. (Rubin, L.) London, 1961.

Afr Doc 6219.14 Constitution de la République du Sénégal. (Sénégal. Constitution.) Dakar? 1963

Afr Doc 7819.5 Constitution de la République Rwandaise. (Rwanda. Constitution.) Kigali, 1963?

Afr 5540.11 Constitution et lois organiques de la République Malgache et accords franco-malgaches. (Madagascar. Constitution.) Tananarive, 1962.

Afr Doc 3219.5 The Constitution of Kenya. (Kenya. Constitution.) Nairobi, 1969.

Afr Doc 3819.5 The Constitution of Rhodesia, 1965. (Rhodesia (British Colony). Constitution.) Salisbury, 1965.

Afr 6210.31 The Constitution of the Federal Republic of Nigeria. (Nigeria. Constitution.) Lagos, 1963.

Afr 9435.15 The constitution of the federation of Rhodesia and Nyasaland. (Rhodesia and Nyasaland.) Salisbury, 1959.

Afr 2808.6 Constitution of the Kingdom of Libya as modified by Law No.1 of 1963. (Libya. Constitution.) Benghazi, 1964.

Afr Doc 3319.15 The constitution of the Republic of Uganda. (Uganda. Constitution.) Entebbe, 1967?

Afr 2438.35 Constitution of the Tunisian Republic. (Tunisia. Constitution.) Tunis, 1959.

Afr 8331.10 The constitution of the Union of South Africa. (Hutton, James.) Cape Town, 1946.

Afr Doc 3319.5 The Constitution of Uganda, 15th April, 1966. (Uganda. Constitution.) Entebbe, 1966.

Afr 6210.36.5 Constitutional crisis: legality and the president's conscience. (Odumosu, O.I.) Ibadan, Nigeria, 1963.

Afr 2808.5A Constitutional development in Libya. (Khalidi, I.R.) Beirut, 1956.

Afr 6210.25 Constitutional development in Nigeria. (Ezera, Kalu.) Cambridge, 1960.

Afr 6210.25.2 Constitutional development in Nigeria. 2d ed. (Ezera, Kalu.) Cambridge, Eng., 1964.

Afr 8028.15 Constitutional development in South Africa. (Towert, A.M.F.) Cape Town, 1959.

Afr 9435.16 The constitutional history and law of Southern Rhodesia, 1888-1965. (Palley, Claire.) Oxford, 1966.

Afr 6160.26 The constitutional law of Ghana. (Bennion, Francis.) London, 1962.

Afr 6210.32 Constitutional problems of federalism in Nigeria. (Berelt, Lionel.) Lagos, 1961.

Afr 32.2 Les constitutions africaines. v.1-2. (Lavroff, D.G.) Paris, 1961-64. 2v.

Afr 5010.5 Les constitutions des états. (Lamput, Pierre.) Paris, 1962.

Afr 45.61.5 Constitutions des états africains d'expression française. Paris, 1961.

Afr 40.62.5 Constitutions of the new African states. (Egyptian Society of International Law.) n.p., 1962.

Afr 5050.20 Construire ensemble. Bobo-Dioulasso. 1966+

Afr 4365.2 Le consul Blondeel en Abyssinie. (Duchesne, Albert.) Bruxelles, 1953.

Afr 1571.50.5 Le consulat de Tanger; des origines à 1830. (Caillé, Jacques.) Paris, 1967.

Afr 1915.9 Les consuls de France à Alger avant la conquête, 1579-1830. (Plantet, Eugène.) Paris, 1930.

Afr 8003.3F Contact; for united non-racial action. Cape Town. 1958+ 4v.

Afr 2798.5.10 Contact avec l'Afrique noire par le Hoggar. (Couvert, Léon.) Paris, 1953.

Afr 8003.4 Contact pamphlet. Cape Town.

Afr 7815.50 Contacto de culturas no Congo Português. (Martins, Manuel Alfredo de Morais.) Lisboa, 1958.

Afr 4392.20 Il contegno della Santa Sede nel conflitto italo-etiopico. (Navarotto, Adriano.) Vicenza, 1936.

Afr 609.55.15 Contemporary Africa. (American Academy of Political and Social Science, Philadelphia.) Philadelphia, 1955.

Afr 50.20 Contemporary Africa. (Prasad, Bisheshwar.) N.Y., 1960.

Afr 210.64.35 Contemporary Africa. (Wallbank, T.W.) Princeton, N.J., 1964.

Afr 210.56.5 Contemporary Africa. (Wallbank, T.W.) Princeton, 1956.

Afr 6300.14.5 Contemporary African monograph series. Nairobi. 1,1965+

Afr 609.62.50 Contemporary dimensions of Africa. (Batson, E.) Cape Town, 1962.

Afr 4559.52 Contemporary Ethiopia. (Talbot, D.A.) N.Y., 1952.

Afr 8659.66.20 Contemporary social pathology. (Rip, Colin Melville.) Pretoria, 1966.

Afr 49019.2 The content and form of Yoruba ijala. (Babalola, S.A.) Oxford, 1966.

Afr 1340.20.10 Le contentieux administratif au Maroc. Thèse. (Monier, R.) Paris, 1935.

Afr 2438.8 Le contentieux administratif en Tunisie. (Richon, Jean.) Paris, 1916.

Afr 12624.41.25 Contes choisis. (Diop, Birago.) Cambridge, Eng. 1967.

Afr 26719.24.21 Contes congolais. (Lepoutre, Paul.) Limete, 1964. 2 pam.

Afr 12624.41.35 Les contes d'Amadou-Koumba. (Diop, Birago.) Paris, 1960.

Afr 12624.4.100 Contes et lavanes. (Diop, Birago.) Paris, 1963.

Afr 28715.2 Contes et poèmes foulbé de la Bénoué-Nord-Cameroun. (Mohamadou, Eldridge.) Yaounde, 1965.

Afr 4559.29 Conti Rossini, C. L'Abissinia. Roma, 1929.

Afr 4394.11 Conti Rossini, C. La battaglia di Adua. Roma, 1939.

Afr 4360.5 Conti Rossini, C. La cronaca reale Abissinia dall'anno 1800 all'anno 1840. Roma, 1917.

Afr 4513.19 Conti Rossini, C. Italia ed Etiopia dal trattato d'Uccialli alla battaglia di Adua. Roma, 1935.

Afr 4300.1 Conti Rossini, C. Note etiopiche. Una guerra fra la Nubia. Roma, 1897.

Afr 4575.5 Conti Rossini, C. Popoli dell'Ethiopia occidentale. Roma, 1919.

Htn Afr 4742.24* Conti Rossini, C. Ricordi di un soggiorno in Eritrea. Fasc.1. Asmara, 1903.

Afr 4568.20 Conti Rossini, C. Studi etiopici. Roma, 1945.

Afr 4259.28.5F Conti Rossini, Carlo. Storia d'Etiopia. Pt.1. Milano, 1928.

Afr 626.26 Le continent africain au milieu du siècle. (Laure, René.) Paris, 1952.

Afr 609.60.45 The continent of Africa. (Storey, H.R.) London, 1960.

Afr 609.66.35 Continente nero; memorialisti italiani dell'800 in Africa. (Bertacchini, Renato.) Parma, 1966.

Afr 1905.3 Continorazione del diario e relazione. Firenze, 1733.

Afr 28.7.5 Continuing sources for research on Africa. (Library of Congress. European Affairs Division.) Washington, 1952.

Afr 5048.10 Continuity and change in African cultures. (Bascom, W.R.) Chicago, 1958.

Afr 11298.5 Conton, William. The African. Boston, 1960.

Afr 679.66.5 Conton, William F. West Africa in history. London, 1966.

Afr 14518.5 Contos portugueses do ultramar; antologia. (César, Amândio.) Porto, 1969.

Afr 11008.8 Contrast. Cape Town. 1,1960+ 4v.

Afr 2030.120 Contre la guerre civile. (Michelet, Edmond.) Paris, 1957.

Afr 109.67.35 La contre-révolution africaine. (Sicard, Maurice Ivan.) Paris, 1967.

Afr 210.63.70 La contre-révolution en Afrique. (Ziegler, Jean.) Paris, 1963.

Afr 2020.2 Un contre-rezzou au Hoggar. (Lohan, Guillo.) Paris, 1903.

Afr 1947.15 Contremoulins, C. Souvenirs d'un officier français. Paris, 1830.

Afr 2030.20 Contrepoison, ou la morale en Algérie. (Massenet, Michel.) Paris, 1957.

Afr 7176.18 Contribuição para a estudo do comercio externo angolano. (Lima. Manuela.) Lisboa, 1963.

Afr 7315.5 Contribuição para o estudo antropologico indigenas de Moçambique. (Pires de Lima, A.) Porto, 1918.

Afr 4234.2 Contributi alla storia della conscenza dell Etiopia. (Almagia, R.) Padova, 1941.

Afr 5243.207.10 Contribution à la connaissance de l'histoire des Peul. (Hama, Boubou.) Paris, 1968.

Afr 6725.5 Contribution à la construction nationale. (Ahidjo, Ahmado.) Paris, 1964.

Afr 9599.54 Contribution à la géographie historique du Katanga et de régions voisines. (Verbeken, Auguste.) Bruxelles, 1954.

Afr 1840.17 Contribution a l'étude de la réforme administrative de l'Algérie. Thèse. (Duclos, Marcel.) Alger, 1921.

Afr 609.54.15 Contribution à l'étude de l'expansion carthagenoise au Maroc. (Cintas, Pierre.) Paris, 1954.

Afr 575.24 Contribution à l'étude de l'islam noir. (Cardaire, M.P.) Donala, 1949.

Afr 5760.20 Contribution à l'étude des migrations antesaka. (Vianes, S.) Paris, 1959.

Afr 6740.15 Contribution à l'étude des populations Bamileke de l'Ouest Cameroun. (Tardits, Claude.) Paris, 1960.

Afr 210.58.10 Contribution à l'étude des problèmes politiques en Afrique noire. (Diop, Majhemout.) Paris, 1958.

Afr 1579.5 Contribution a l'étude du commerce genois au Maroc durant la periode portugaise, 1415-1550. (Ricard, R.) Paris, 1937.

Afr 2608.92.10 Contribution à l'étude médicale de la Tunisie. (Lafitte, Fernand.) Bordeaux, 1892.

Afr 5078.20 Contribution à l'histoire de la Mauritanie. (Desire-Vuillemin, G.) Dakar, 1962.

Afr 3740.6.25 Contribution a l'histoire de la mission Marchand. (Bobichon, H.) Paris, 1937.

Afr 5640.40 Contribution à l'histoire de la nation Malgache. (Boiteau, Pierre.) Paris, 1958.

Afr 626.160 Contribution à une synthèse sur le problème de la formation des cadres africains en vue de la croissance économique. (Tevoedjre, Albert.) Paris, 1965.

Afr 8028.30F A contribution to a bibliography on university apartheid. (Macdonald, A.M.) Cape Town, 1959.

Afr 4559.61 A contribution to the physiography of northern Ethiopia. (Abu al-Hajjaj, Y.) London, 1961.

Afr 4753.5 Contributo alla bibliografia e cartografia della Somalia italiana. (Palieri, M.) Roma, 193-.

Afr 4559.30.10 Il contributo alla geografia dell'Abissinia nelle memorie del cardinale Guglielmo Massaia. (Fulgenzio da Vecchieto, Padre.) Tivoli, 1930.

Afr 4700.4.15 Contributo dell'Italia alla conocenza della nosografia dell'Africa. (Girolami, Mario.) Roma, 1963.

Afr 4226.3 Il contributo italiano all esplorazione ed allo studio dell Etiopia. (Manetti, C.) Roma, 1936.

Afr 1624.932 Le controle des engagements de depenses au Maroc. Thèse. (Milleron, Jacques.) Paris, 1932.

Afr 1570.42 El convenio entre España by francia relativo a Marruecos. (Maura y Gamazo, Gabriel.) Madrid, 1912.

Afr 500.8 Conventions internationales. (Ortray, F. van.) Bruxelles, 1898.

Afr 3978.82 Conversations and journals in Egypt. (Senior, N.W.) London, 1882. 2v.

Afr 5243.174.20 Conversations with Ogotemmeli. (Griaule, Marcel.) London, 1965.

Afr 1840.6 La conversion au christianisme de l'indigène musulman algérien. Thèse. (Bounichon, A.) Paris, 1931.

Afr 8687.323 The conversion of a South African nationalist. (Reitz, Hjalmar.) Cape Town, 1946.

Afr 8140.40 — The convict crisis and the growth of unity. (Hattersley, Alan Frederick.) Pietermaritzburg, 1965.

Afr 6535.45 — Cook, Albert R. Uganda memories, 1897-1940. Kampala, 1945.

Afr 6218.11 — Cook, Arthur. British enterprise in Nigeria. Philadelphia, 1943.

Afr 210.65.30 — Cook, Arthur Norton. Africa, past and present. Ottowa, 1965.

Afr 10315.5 — Cook, David. Origin East Africa. London, 1965.
Afr 10317.5 — Cook, David. Short East African plays in English: ten plays in English. Nairobi, 1968.

Afr 8279.01.8 — Cook, Edward T. Rights and wrongs of the Transvaal war. London, 1902.

Afr 3979.00 — Cook, J. Programme for visiting Egypt. London, 1900.
Afr 8825.6 — Cook, R.A.W. Social organisation and ceremonial institutions of the Bomvana. Cape Town, 19-

Afr 1955.3 — Cooke, G.W. Conquest and colonization in North Africa. Edinburgh, 1860.

Afr 3986.956A — Cooke, M.L. Nasser's High Aswan Dam. Washington, 1956.

Afr 7567.42 — Cookey, Sylvanus John Sodienye. Britain and the Congo question, 1885-1913. London, 1968.

Afr 3990.1 — Cook's handbook. Egypt and the sudan. (Budge, E.A.W.) London, 1906.

Afr 3990.1.7 — Cook's handbook. Egypt and the sudan. 4th ed. Suppl. 1925. (Budge, E.A.W.) London, 1921-25.

Afr 555.50 — Cooksey, J.J. The land of the vanished church. London, 1926.

Afr 555.3.12 — Cooksey, J.J. Religion and civilization in West Africa. London, 1931.

Afr 3978.42 — Cooley, J.E. The American in Egypt. N.Y., 1842.
Afr 1285.5 — Cooley, John Kent. Baal, Christ, and Mohammed. London, 1967.

Afr 4095.2 — Cooley, W.D. Claudius Ptolemy and the Nile. London, 1854.
Afr 715.12 — Cooley, William Desborough. Inner Africa laid open. N.Y., 1969.

Afr 608.41.5A — Cooley, William Desborough. The Negroland of the Arabs examined and explained. 2nd ed. London, 1966.

Afr 1069.12.5A — Coolidge, A.C. The European reconquest of North Africa. n.p., 1912.

NEDL Afr 6170.13 — Coomassie and Magdala. (Stanley, H.M.) London, 1874.
Afr 6168.15 — Coombs, D. The Gold Coast. London, 1963.
Afr 4559.35.50 — Coon, C.S. Measuring Ethiopia and flight into Arabia. Boston, 1935.

Afr 3979.13.15 — Cooper, Clayton Sedwick. The man of Egypt. London, 1913.
Afr 3988.10 — Cooper, Elizabeth. The women of Egypt. London, 1914.
Afr 590.7 — Cooper, J. The lost continent. London, 1875.
Afr 8658.94 — Cooper-Chadwick, J. Three years with Lobengula. London, 1894.

Afr 626.112 — A cooperação em Africa. (Mendes, C.B. do Quental.) Lisboa, 1961.

Afr 5057.20 — Coopération économique franco-africaine. (Hoffherr, Rene.) Paris, 1958.

Afr 626.6 — Coopération et développement. Paris. 1,1964+ 3v.

Afr 2223.938 — La coopération et les fellahs algériens. Thèse. (Pasquier Bronde, P.M.E.) Alger, 1938.

Afr 115.80 — La cooperazione internazionale in Africa. (Study Congress on International Cooperation in Africa.) Milano, 1960.

Afr 11299.69.100 — Cope, Jack. The fair house. London, 1955.
Afr 11299.69.110 — Cope, Jack. The golden oriole. London, 1958.
Afr 11299.69.21 — Cope, Jack. The man who doubted, and other stories. London, 1967.

Afr 11051.8 — Cope, Jack. The Penguin book of South African verse. Harmondsworth, 1968.

Afr 11299.69.120 — Cope, Jack. The tame ox. London, 1960.
Afr 8100.44 — Cope, John Patrick. King of the Hottentots. Cape Town, 1967.

Afr 8089.65 — Cope, John Patrick. South Africa. N.Y., 1965.
Afr 8089.65.2 — Cope, John Patrick. South Africa. 2.ed. N.Y., 1967.
Afr 3335.20 — Copeland, Miles. The game of nations: the amorality of power politics. London, 1970.

Afr 28.96 — Copenhagen. Kongelige Bibliotek. Nyere Africa-litteratur. København, 1962.

Afr 555.17.10 — Copia d'huma carta escrita pelo Padre Guardiam do Real Convento de Maquinés. Lisboa, 1756.

Htn Afr 7122.5* — Copia das proposições e secunda allegaçam. (Andrade Leitão, F. de.) Lisboa, 1642.

Htn Afr 4349.3.5F* — Copia de una del padre A. Fernandez. (Fernandez, A.) Madrid, 1627.

Htn Afr 7122.5.5* — Copia primae allegationis. (Andrade Leitão, F. de.) n.p., 1642.

Afr 5548.22 — Copland, Samuel. A history of the island of Madagascar. London, 1822.

Afr 9705.15 — Copper town. 1st ed. (Powdermaker, Hortense.) N.Y., 1962.
Afr 9699.47 — Copperbelt markets. (Brelsford, W.V.) Lusaka, 1947.
Htn Afr 1403.2* — Coppia d'una litera venuta di Spagna. Mantova, 1578.
Afr 4513.35.165 — Coppola, Francesco. La vittoria bifronte. Milano, 1936.
Afr 4008.2 — A Coptic bibliography. (Kammerer, M.) Ann Arbor, 1950.
Afr 3275.23 — Copts and Moslems under British control. (Mikhail, K.) London, 1911.

Afr 6145.4F — Copy of the reports made in 1844-1845. (Great Britain. Commissioners of Inquiry into the Subject of Emigration from Sierra Leone to the West Indies.) London, 1948.

Afr 2609.62 — Coque, R. La Tunisie présaharienne. Paris, 1962.
Afr 2680.5 — Coque, Roger. Nabeul et ses environs, étude d'une population tunisienne. Paris, 1965?

Afr 679.65.40 — Coquery, Catherine. La découverte de l'Afrique. Paris, 1965.

Afr 7808.88.5 — Coquilhat, Camille. Sur le Haut-Congo. Paris, 1888.
Afr 3979.56.5 — Cordan, Wolfgang. DerNil. Düsseldorf, 1956.
Afr 5920.1.15 — Cordero Torres, J.M. Iradier. Madrid, 1944.
Afr 1574.9 — Cordero Torres, J.M. Organizacion del protectorado español en Marruecos. v.1-2. Madrid, 1942-43.

Afr 31.12 — Cordero Torres, J.M. Textos basicos de Africa. v.1-2. Madrid, 1962. 2v.

Afr 2025.23.10 — Cordier, E.W. Napoleon III et l'Algérie. Thèse. Alger, 1937.

Afr 6395.2.30 — Corfield, F.D. Historical survey of the origins and growth of Mau Mau. London, 1960.

Afr 1878.15 — Cornaton, Michel. Les regroupements de la décolonisation en Algérie. Thèse. Paris, 1967.

Afr 5480.211 — Cornel, Charles J.H. Au Tchad. Paris, 1911.
Afr 8292.46 — Corner, William. The story of the 34th Company. London, 1902.

Afr 9165.42.75 — The corner house. (Cartwright, Alan Patrick.) Capetown, 1965.

Afr 11320.50.140 — A corner of the world. (Delius, Anthony.) Cape Town, 1962.

Afr 699.61 — Cornet, Jacques. Pharaons d'hier et Fellahs d'aujourd'hui. Lyon, 1961.

Afr 2749.57.10 — Cornet, Pierre. Sahara. Paris, 1957.
Afr 7850.3 — Cornet, R.J. Terre katangaise. Bruxelles, 1950.
Afr 7567.19 — Cornet, Rene. Katanga. 3 ed. Bruxelles, 1946.
Afr 7855.1 — Cornet, René Jules. Maniema. 2.ed. Bruxelles, 1955.
Afr 7549.48.10 — Cornet, Rene Jules. Sommaire de l'histoire du Congo belge. Bruxelles, 1948.

Afr 1493.5 — Cornet. A la conquête du Maroc sud, 1912-13. Paris, 1914.
Afr 7549.63 — Cornevin, R. Histoire du Congo (Leopoldville). Paris, 1963.

Afr 5365.6 — Cornevin, R. Histoire du Dahomey. Paris, 1962.
Afr 5385.10 — Cornevin, Robert. Le Dahomey. Paris, 1965.
Afr 109.62.20 — Cornevin, Robert. Histoire de l'Afrique. Paris, 1962. 2v.

Afr 109.67.30 — Cornevin, Robert. Histoire de l'Afrique. Paris, 1967-
Afr 109.62.22 — Cornevin, Robert. Histoire de l'Afrique des origines à nos jours. Paris, 1966.

Afr 109.60.5.2 — Cornevin, Robert. Histoire des peuples de l'Afrique Noire. Paris, 1960.
Afr 109.60.5 — Cornevin, Robert. Histoire des peuples de l'Afrique Noire. Paris, 1960.

Afr 7549.63.2 — Cornevin, Robert. Histoire du Congo: Léopoldville-Kinshassa. 2. éd. Paris, 1966.

Afr 6664.10 — Cornevin, Robert. Histoire du Togo. Paris, 1959.
Afr 6664.10.2 — Cornevin, Robert. Histoire du Togo. Paris, 1962.
Afr 6664.10.3 — Cornevin, Robert. Histoire du Togo. 3e ed. Paris, 1969.
Afr 6664.10.5 — Cornevin, Robert. Le Togo, nation-pilote. Paris, 1963.
Afr 4785.39 — Corni, G. Somalia italiana. Milano, 1937. 2v.

Afr 4742.10 — Corni, Guido. Tra Gasc e Setit. Roma, 1930.
Afr 5860.15 — Cornu, Henri. Une expérience législative à la Réunion. Thèse. Paris, 1935.

Afr 1955.19 — Cornulier-Lucinière, Comte de. La prise de Bône et Bougie...1832-33. Paris, 1895.

Afr 2845.5 — Coro, F. Settantasei anni di dominazione turca in Libia, 1835-1911. Tripoli, 1937.

Afr 7190.15 — Corographia historica das ilhas de San Thome, Anno Bom, e Fernando Po. (Cunha Mattos, R.J. da.) Porto, 1842.

Afr 7188.109 — O coronel João de Almeida. Lisboa, 1927.
Afr 4232.1F — Corpus juris abessinorum. Berlin, 1889.
Afr 2870.5 — Corradini, E. La conquista di Tripoli. Milano, 1912.
Afr 2929.11.2 — Corradini, E. Ora di tripoli. Milano, 1911.
Afr 2929.11 — Corradini, E. L'ora di Tripoli. Milano, 1911.
Afr 1755.6 — Corral Caballe, M. del. Cronica de la guerra de Africa en 1909. Barcelona, 1909.

Afr 7119.37 — Correa, E.A. da Silva. Historia de Angola. Lisboa, 1937. 2v.

Afr 5180.13 — Correard, A. Naufrage de la frigate La Méduse. Paris, 1818.

Afr 2500.1 — Correspondance des beys de Tunis. (Plantet, E.) Paris, 1893-4. 3v.

Afr 1900.3 — Correspondance des deys d'Alger, 1579-1833. (Plantet, E.) Paris, 1889.

Afr 5872.7 — Correspondance du conseil supérieur de Bourbon et de la Compagnie des Indes...1724-1741. V.1-3. (Réunion. Conseil Supérieur.) Saint-Denis, 1934-37. 4v.

Afr 8152.81 — Correspondence. 2nd ed. (Cathcart, G.) London, 1857.
Afr 6310.12 — Correspondence (1931-1932) arising from the report of the Joint Select Commission on East Africa. (Great Britain. Colonial Office.) London, 1932.

Afr 8283.6F — Correspondence related to South Africa Republic. (Great Britain. Colonial Office.) London, 1896.

Afr 3740.2F — Correspondence with the French government. (Great Britain. Parliament.) London, 1898.

Afr 1432.18 — Correspondencia..Guerra de Africa. (Spain. Ministerio de Estado.) Madrid, 1860.

Afr 1.4.5 — Correspondenzblatt. (Afrikanische Gesellschaft in Deutschland.) Berlin. 1,1873+

Afr 6143.8 — Corry, J. Observations upon the windward coast of Africa. London, 1807.

Afr 1259.58 — Corsair country. (Fielding, Xan.) London, 1958.
Afr 1735.5 — Corsaires de Sale. (Coindreau, Roger.) Paris, 1948.
Afr 1100.6 — I corsari barbareschi. (Bono, Salvatore.) Torino, 1964.
Afr 1409.20 — Une Corse sultane du Maroc, Davia Franceschini et sa famille. (Caillé, Jacques.) Paris, 1968.

Afr 8658.58 — Cortambert, M.E. Esquisse...d'une partie de l'Afrique australe. Paris, 1858.

Afr 1739.3 — La corte de Tetuan. (Munoz, I.) Madrid, 1913.
Htn Afr 1406.1* — Cortende waerachlich verhail...1607. Hague, 1607.
Afr 150.66 — Cortesão, Jaime. A expansão dos Portugueses no periodo Henriquino. Lisboa, 1965.

Afr 5748.87.10 — Cortese, Emilio. Sei mesi al Madagascar. Roma, 1888.
Afr 4719.34 — Cortese, Guido. Eritrea. Roma, 1934.
Afr 2749.08 — Cortier, M. D'une rive à l'autre du Sahara. Paris, 1908.
Afr 1703.2 — Cortocero Hanares, H.F. Alcazarquiver 1950. Tetuan, 1953.
Afr 1570.75 — Corval, Pierre. Le Maroc en révolution. Paris, 1956.
Afr 8089.10 — Cory, G.E. The rise of South Africa. v.1- London, 1910- 6v.

Afr 6883.13 — Cory, Hans. Customary law of the Haya tribe. London, 1945.

Afr 6883.13.5 — Cory, Hans. Sukuma law and customs. London, 1954.
Afr 1609.06.6 — Cosas de los moros. (Diez De Tejada, V.) Barcelona, 1906.
Afr 4732.2 — Cose africane, da Saati ad Abba Carima. (Martini, F.) Milano, 1897.

Afr 2260.2 — Cosentino. L'Algérie en 1865. Paris, 1865.
X Cg Afr 5057.8 — Cosmier, Henri. L'Ouest africain français. Paris, 1921. (Changed to XP 9038).

Afr 1273.922 — Cosnier, Henri. L'Afrique du Nord. Paris, 1922.
Afr 1422.10 — Cosse Brissac, P. de. Les rapports de la France et du Maroc pendant la conquête de l'Algérie (1830-1847). Paris, 1931.

Afr 150.16 — Costa, Brochado. Infante Dom Henrique. Lisboa, 1942.
Afr 7312.5 — Costa, D. Moçambique, nossa terra. Lisboa, 1942.
Afr 7175.35 — Costa, Ferreira da. Na pista do marfim e da morte. Porto, 1944.

Afr 7175.37 — Costa, Ferreira da. Pedro do feitico. Porto, 1945.
Afr 7203.5 — Costa, Mario A. do. Bibliografia geral de Moçambique. Lisboa, 1946-

Afr 7135.14 — Costa, Pereira da. Um mês de terrorismo; Angola, março-abril de 1961. Lisboa, 1969.

Afr 1259.44.10 — Costa Leite, P. da. Africa do Norte, impressões de viagem. Rio de Janeiro, 1944.

Afr 6720.30 Costedoat, René. Le français et la réorganisation des territoires du Cameroun. Thèse. Besançon, 1930.

Afr 11300.83.21 Coster, Vera. Here Everest, and other poems. Grahamstown, 1963.

Afr 4240.5 La costituzione etiopica. 2. ed. (Giannini, A.) Roma, 1936.

Afr 3978.31 Il costume antico e moderno. (Ferrario, G.) Livorno, 1831. 3 pam.

Afr 1830.40.11 Le costume musulman d'Alger. (Marcais, Georges.) Paris, 1930.

Afr 2208.80.6 Côte barbaresque et le Sahara. (Lubomirski, J.) Paris, 1880.

Afr 5342.10 La Côte-d'Ivoire, l'homme des deserts. (Jacolliot, L.) Paris, 1877.

Afr 5342.30 Côte-d'Ivoire, 1954. (France. Service de Documentation Economique.) Paris, 1954.

Afr 5342.25 La Côte-d'Ivoire. (Avice, E.) Paris, 1951.
Afr 5342.20 Côte-d'Ivoire. (Chivas-Baron, C.) Paris, 1939.
Afr 5342.7 La Côte-d'Ivoire. (Gaston, Joseph.) Paris, 1917.
Afr 5342.60.5 Côte-d'Ivoire. (Holas, Bohumil.) Paris, 1963.
Afr 5342.60.6 La Côte-d'Ivoire. (Holas, Bohumil.) Paris, 1964.
Afr 5342.50 La Côte-d'Ivoire. (Lebarbier, Louis.) Paris, 1916.
Afr 5342.63 La Côte-d'Ivoire. (Rougerie, Gabriel.) Paris, 1964.
Afr 5345.17 La Côte-d'Ivoire chrétienne. 2. éd. (Gorju, Joseph.) Lyon, 1915.

Afr 5337.3 La Côte-d'Ivoire dans la cité africaine. (Amon d'Aby, F.) Paris, 1951.

Afr 2208.81.15 La côte et les ports de l'Algérie. (Mouchez, E.) Paris, 1881.

Afr 6535.20 Cott, Hugh B. Uganda in black and white. London, 1959.
Afr 7122.70 Cotta, Goncalves. Grito de Angola. Luanda, 1961.
Afr 2870.8 Cottafari, V. Nella Libia italiana. Bologna, 1912.
Afr 1608.60.5 Cotte, N. Le Maroc contemporain. Paris, 1860.
Afr 5406.211.10 Cottes, A. La mission Cottes au Sud-Cameroun. Paris, 1911.

Afr 8678.49 Cotton, W.A. Racial segregation in South Africa. London, 1931.

Afr 8678.49.7 Cotton, Walter Aidan. The race problem in South Africa. N.Y., 1969.

Afr 609.65 Cottrell, Kent. Sunburnt Africa, in pencil, paint, and prose. Hollywood, 1965.

Afr 3979.66.15 Cottrell, Leonard. Egypt. N.Y., 1966.
Afr 510.23 Coty, F. Sauvons nos colonies. Paris, 1931.
Afr 2640.1 Couche, L. Pourquoi devenir propriétaire en Tunisie. Lille, 1900.

Afr 1570.32 Couillieaux. Le programme de la France au Maroc. Paris, 1912.

Afr 4259.29 Coulbeaux, J.B. Histoire politique et religieuse d'Abyssinie depuis les temps les plus reculés jusqu'à l'avènement. T.1-3. Paris, 1929. 3v.

Afr 4368.10 Coulbeaux, J.B. Vers la lumière. 2e ed. Paris, 1926.
Afr 3026.25 Coult, L.H. An annotated research bibliography of studies in Arabic. Coral Gables, Fla., 1958.

Afr 8369.44 Coulter, C.W.A. Empire unity. Cape Town, 1944.
Afr 626.125 Council of Europe. Europe and Africa. Strasbourg, 1960.
Afr 40.44 Council on African Affairs, Inc. Proceedings of the Conference on Africa. N.Y. 1944.

Afr Doc 2501.5 Council papers. (Nigeria, Southern. Legislative Council.) Lagos. 1909-1911 3v.

Afr 5406.57 The country of the dwarfs. (Duchaillu, Paul Belloni.) N.Y., 1874.

Afr 2608.77 The country of the Moors. (Rae, Edward.) London, 1877.
Afr 7809.51.5 The country of the mountains of the moon. (Sinderen, A. van.) N.Y., 1951.

Afr 9499.80 Country study on Southern Rhodesia. (Gedamu, T.) Addis Ababa? 1963.

Afr 1555.3 Le coup d'Agadir. (Albin, P.) Paris, 1912.
Afr 2030.462.135 Le coup d'état du 13 mai. (Trinquier, R.) Paris, 1962.
Afr 3215.5 Coup-d'oeil...sur l'état présent de l'Egypte. (Jomard, E.F.) Paris, 1836.

Afr 1828.2 Pamphlet vol. Coup d'oeil rapide sur bougie. 9 pam.

Afr 3069.31.10 Coup d'oeil sur la chronologie de la nation égyptienne. (Cattaui, Joseph.) Paris, 1931.

Afr 2802.6F Coup d'oeil sur la Cyrénaique. (Vattier de Bourville, T.) n.p., n.d.

Afr 7567.20 Coup d'oeil sur le problème politique et militaire du Congo belge. (Habran, Louis.) Bruxelles, 1918.

Afr 7549.21 Coup d'oeil sur l'histoire du Congo. (Pirenne, Jacques.) Bruxelles, 1921.

Afr 575.19 Coup d'oeil sur l'islam en Berberie. (Bel, Alfred.) Paris, 1917.

Afr 11302.89.100 Couper, J.K. Mixed humanity. Cape Colony, 1892.
Afr 1259.21.10 Couperus, Louis. Met Louis Couperus in Afrika. Amsterdam, 1921.

Afr 6320.4A Coupland, R. East Africa and its invaders. Oxford, 1938.
Afr 6570.7A Coupland, R. The exploitation of East Africa, 1856-1890. London, 1939.

Afr 6570.7.2 Coupland, R. The exploitation of East Africa, 1856-1890. 2nd ed. London, 1968.

Afr 9558.85.2 Coupland, R. Kirk on the Zambesi; a chapter of African history. Oxford, 1968.
Afr 9558.85 Coupland, R. Kirk on the Zambesi. Oxford, 1928.
Afr 9558.86 Coupland, R. Livingstone's last journey. London, 1945.
Afr 8160.18 Coupland, R. Zulu battle piece, Isandhlwana. London, 1948.

Afr 1390.5 Cour, Auguste. La dynastie marocaine des Beni Wattas (1420-1554). Constantine, 1920.

Afr 1400.6 Cour, Auguste. L'établissement des dynasties des chérif au Maroc. Paris, 1904.

Afr 5620.9 Courand, Charles J. Madagascar, son avenir colonial. La Rochelle, 1895.

Afr 7565.12.20 Courcel, G. de. L'influence de la Conférence de Berlin de 1885. Paris, 1936.

Afr 5753.5 Cournot, M. La famille à Madagascar. Angers, 1897.
Afr 7503.5 Courrier africain. (Centre de Recherche et d'Information Socio-Politiques.) Bruxelles. 1,1960+ 8v.

NEDL Afr 5045.17.5 Courrier d'Afrique. (Martin du Gard, M.) Paris, 1931.
Afr 2030.468.5 Courrière, Yves. La guerre d'Algérie. Paris, 1968. 2v.

Afr 5070.5 Cours de droit administratif mauritanien. (Jeol, Michel.) Bordeaux, 1964.

Afr 5070.10 Cours de droit constitutionnel mauritanien. (Ould Daddah, Marie Thérèse.) Bordeaux, 1964.

Afr 626.47 Cours d'économie d'outre-mer et du développement. (Leduc, Gaston.) Paris, 1958.

Afr 45.66 Cours d'institutions publiques africaines et malgaches. (Gonidec, Pierre François.) Paris, 1966.

Afr 609.30.25 Court Treatt, Chaplin. Out of the beaten track. London, 1930.
Afr 609.26.15 Court Treatt, S. Cape to Cairo. Boston, 1927.
Afr 8292.39 Courtenay, A.H. With the 4th Battalion, the Cameronians (Scottish Rifles) in South Africa. Edinburg, 1905.

Afr 699.40 Courtney, R. A greenhorn in Africa. London, 1940.
Afr 1609.05.10 Cousin, A. Le Maroc. Paris, 1905.
Afr 1738.5 Cousin, A. Tanger. 1st ed. Paris, 1902.
Afr 1738.5.3 Cousin, A. Tanger. 3d ed. Paris, 1903.
Afr 5548.95 Cousins, W.E. Madagascar of to-day. London, 1895.
Afr 1724.1.2 Coutinho, Goncalo. Discurso da jornada de D. Goncalo Coutinho. (Another issue). Lisboa, 1629.

Afr 1724.1 Coutinho, Goncalo. Discurso da jornada de D. Goncalo Coutinho. Lisboa, 1629.

Afr 2218.12 Coutumes, institutions, croyances, des indigènes de l'Algérie. (Desparment, Joseph.) Alger, 1939.

Afr 5333.4 Les coutumes Agni. (Villamur, R.) Paris, 1904.
Afr 5555.2 Coutumes guerrieres et organisation militaire chez les anciens Malgaches. (Decary, Raymond.) Paris, 1966. 2v.

Htn Afr 5333.2* Coutumes indigènes de la Côte-d'Ivoire. (Clozel, F.J.) Paris, 1902.

Afr 2798.5.10 Couvert, Léon. Contact avec l'Afrique noire par le Hoggar. Paris, 1953.

Afr 2798.5.15 Couvert, Léon. Tourisme en zigzag vers le Hoggar. Bourg, 1951.

Afr 3978.70.15 Couvidou, Henri. Etude sur l'Egypte contemporaine. Le Caire, 187-.

Afr 8210.18 Cowan, L.G. Local government in West Africa. N.Y., 1958.
Afr 1623.958.10 Cowan, Laing. The economic development of Morocco. Santa Monica, 1958.

Afr 5053.25 Cowan, Laing G. Local government in West Africa. N.Y., 1958.

Afr 212.2 Cowan, Laing Gray. The dilemmas of African independence. N.Y., 1964.

Afr 8252.4 Cowen, Charles. Charles Tennant Jones, M.L.A., and our government. Wynberg, 1884.

Afr 8252.3 Cowen, Charles. The honorable Lt. Col. Frederick Schermbrucker, M.L.C., at the Cape of Good Hope. Wynberg, 1884.

Afr 8040.8 Cowen, D.V. The foundations of freedom. Cape Town, 1961.
Afr 8045.34 Cowen, D.V. Parliamentary sovereignty and the entrenched sections of the South Africa act. Cape Town, 1951.

Afr 9193.2 Cowen, D.V. Swaziland, report on constitutional reform. n.p., 1961.

Afr 8686.26 Cowie, Margaret J. South African missionary bibliography. n.p., n.d. 2 pam.

Afr 9029.59 Cowles, Raymond Bridgman. Zulu journal. Berkeley, 1959.
Afr 8687.273 Cowley, Cecil. Kwa Zulu. Cape Town, 1966.
Afr 9400.12 Cowley, Olive. Fabled tribe; a voyage to discover the River Bushmen of the Okavango Swamps. 1st ed. N.Y., 1968.

Afr 9538.5 Cox, D.L. A bibliography of the Federation of the Rhodesias and Nyasaland. Cape Town, 1949.

Afr 8252.9 Cox, G.W. Life of John William Colenso. London, 1888. 2v.

Afr 678.69 Cox, John George. Cox and the Juju Coast. St. Helier, 1968.

Afr 210.64.50 Cox, R.H.F. Pan-Africanism in practice. London, 1964.
Afr 6420.78 Cox, Richard. Kenyatta's country. London, 1965.
Afr 678.69 Cox and the Juju Coast. (Cox, John George.) St. Helier, 1968.

Afr 6144.5A Cox-George, N.A. Finance and development in West Africa. London, 1961.

Afr 2232.3A Coyne, A. Le Mzab. Alger, 1879.
Afr 3252.22 Crabitès, Pierre. Americans in the Egyptian army. London, 1938.

Afr 3217.15 Crabitès, Pierre. Ibrahim of Egypt. London, 1935.
Afr 3230.17 Crabitès, Pierre. Ismail, the maligned khedive. London, 1933.

Afr 3675.11 Crabitès, Pierre. The winning of the Sudan. London, 1934.
Afr 8190.10 The cradle days of Natal, 1497-1845. (Mackeurtan, G.) London, 1930. 2v.

Afr 4558.77 The cradle of the Blue Nile. (Decosson, E.A.) London, 1877. 2v.

Afr 8252.341.21 Crafford, F. Jan Smuts, a biography. Garden City, 1944.
Afr 8252.341.20 Crafford, F.S. Jan Smuts, a biography. 1st ed. N.Y., 1943.

Afr 11303.2.100 Crafford, Frederick Simon. The place of dragons. Cape Town, 1964.

Afr 5342.65.2 Craft and culture in the Ivory Coast. (Holas, Bohumil.) Paris, 1968.

Afr 6570.10 Crafton, R.H. Zanzibar affairs, 1914-1933. London, 1953.
Afr 4008.5 Cramer, Maria. Das christlich-koptische Agypten einst und heute. Wiesbaden, 1959.

Afr 6475.5 Crane. Kampala.
Afr 8252.8.20 Crankshaw, E. The forsaken idea. London, 1952.
Afr 6455.21 Cranworth, B.F.G. A colony in the making. London, 1912.
Afr 6455.21.5 Cranworth, B.F.G. Kenya chronicles. London, 1939.
Afr 6592.1 Craster, J.E.E. Pemba, the spice island of Zanzibar. London, 1913.

Afr 14723.1 Craveirinha, José. Chigubo. Lisboa, 1964.
Afr 861.21 Crawford, A.B. I went to Tristan. London, 1941.
Afr 555.21.15 Crawford, D. Back to the long grass. N.Y., n.d.
Afr 555.21 Crawford, D. Thinking black. 2d ed. London, 1914.
Afr 6397.10 Crawford, E.M. By the equator's snowy peak. London, 1913.
Afr 6397.11 Crawford, E.M. By the equator's snowy peak. 2d ed. London, 1914.

Afr 4180.4 Crawford, O.G.S. The Fung Kingdom of Sennar. Gloucester, 1951.

Afr 6460.80.10 Crazzolara, J. Pasquale. The Lwoo. Verona, 1950-54. 3v.

Afr 5053.36 Creating political order. (Zolberg, Aristide R.) Chicago, 1966.

Afr 9448.60 Creighton, P.R. The anatomy of partnership. London, 1960.
Afr 5748.83.5 Cremazy, L. Notes sur Madagascar. Pt.1-3. Paris, 1883-84.
Afr 5538.3 Cremazy, P. Notice bibliographique sur Madagascar. St. Denis, 1884.

Afr 6147.5.10 Creoledom. (Porter, A.T.) London, 1963.
Afr 5842.10 Creoles and coolies. (Beaton, P.) London, 1859.

Afr 1655.1	Un crepuscule d'islam-Maroc. (Chevrillon, Andre.) Paris, 1906.
Afr 2208.59	The crescent and French crusaders. (Ditson, G.L.) N.Y., 1859.
Afr 2208.59.2	The crescent and French crusaders. (Ditson, G.L.) N.Y., 1860.
Afr 3275.26	Cressaty. L'Egypte d'aujourd'hui. Paris, 1912.
Afr 5868.81	Crestien, G.F. Causeries historiques. Paris, 1881.
Afr 8687.166	Creswell, Margaret. An epoch of the political history of South Africa. Cape Town, 195-.
Afr 8289.00.20	Creswicke, L. South Africa and the Transvaal war. London, n.d. 4v.
Afr 2030.463.25	Cretin-Vercel, Michel. Nouvelle Algérie. Paris, 1963.
Afr 628.108.10	Cri des colons contre un ouvrage de M. L'Evêque. (Tussac, R. de.) Paris 1810
Afr 8678.160	Crijns, Arthur. Race relations and race attitudes in South Africa. Nijmegen, 1957.
Afr 9439.65.10	The crime of being white. (Eeden, Guy Van.) Cape Town, 1965.
Afr 7568.29	The crime of the Congo. (Doyle, A.C.) N.Y., 1909.
Afr 9500.5	Cripps, A.S. An Africa for Africans. London, 1927.
Afr 1990.3	Cris de conscience de l'Algérie. (Rozey, A.G.) Paris, 1840.
Afr 2026.5	La crise algérienne. (Sarrasin, P.C.) Paris, 1949.
Afr 2030.150	Crise algérienne vue d'Alger. (Lombard, Pierre.) Alger, 1958.
Afr 7580.3	La crise congolaise. (Institut Royal des Relations Internationales.) Brussels, 1960.
Afr 7122.50	A crise de Angola. (Cruz, D. da.) Lisboa, 1928.
Afr 8279.00.15	La crise sud-africaine. (Kuyper, A.) Paris, 1900.
Afr 3315.125.2	Crisis, the inside story of the Suez conspiracy. (Robertson, Terence.) London, 1965.
Afr 3315.125	Crisis, the inside story of the Suez conspiracy. 1st ed. (Robertson, Terence.) N.Y., 1965.
Afr 3.36	Crisis and change. London. 1,1965+
Afr 3275.3	The crisis in Egypt, a letter to Mr. Gladstone. (Harrison, F.) London, 1882.
Afr 6420.40A	Crisis in Kenya. (Aaronovitch, S.) London, 1947.
Afr 9448.78	Crisis in Rhodesia. (Shamugawia, Nathan M.) London, 1965.
Afr 7580.19	Crisis in the Congo. (Lafever, E.W.) Washington, 1965.
Afr 3315.68	The crisis in the Middle East. (Pearson, Lester B.) Ottawa, 1957.
Afr 9435.20	Crisis over Rhodesia: a skeptical view. (Marshall, Charles Burton.) Baltimore, 1967.
Afr 9165.42.65	Crisp, Robert. The outlanders. London, 1964.
Afr 9400.3	Crisp, W. The Bechuana of South Africa. London, 1896.
Afr 4390.55	Crispi e Menelick nel diario inedito del Conte Augusto Salimbeni. (Salimbeni, A., Conte.) Torino, 1956.
Afr 2731.15.75	Cristiani, L. Pèlerin de l'absolu. Paris, 1960.
Afr 11021.2	A critical survey of South African poetry in English. (Miller, G.M.) Cape Town, 1957.
Afr 679.67.35	Croce-Spinelli, Michel. Les Enfants de Poto-Poto. Paris, 1967.
Afr 6210.5	Crocker, W.R. Nigeria, a critique of British colonial administration. London, 1936.
Afr 500.57	Crocker, Walter R. On governing colonies. London, 1947.
Afr 5405.109.25	Croidys, Pierre. Brazza. Paris, 1947.
Afr 1885.3	La croisade de XImenes en Afrique. (Blum, N.) Oran, 1898.
Afr 7850.35	Croisettes et casques bleus, récits. (Davister, P.) Bruxelles, 1962.
Afr 715.15.5	La croisière noire, expédition citroen central-Afrique. (Haardt, G.M.) Paris, 1927.
Afr 3979.08.10	Une croisière sur le Nil, Khartoum-Goudokoro. (Albertis, E.A.D.) Le Caire, 1908.
Afr 5046.12	La croissance des quantités globales en Afrique de l'ouest de 1947 à 1964. (Duverger, Daniel.) Paris, 1967.
Afr 5091.5	Croissance économique. (Pujos, Jerome.) Paris, 1964.
Afr 8676.67	Croizat, Victor J. The economic development of South Africa in its political context. Santa Monica, 1967.
Afr 7809.29	Crokaert, J. Boula-matari. Bruxelles, 1929.
Afr 4513.37.55	Il crollo dell'impero dei Negus. (Appelius, M.) Milano, 1937.
Afr 3285.4	Cromer, E.B. Abbas II. London, 1915.
Afr 3275.17.2A	Cromer, E.B. Modern Egypt. London, 1908. 2v.
Afr 3275.17.4.5	Cromer, E.B. Modern Egypt. London, 1911.
Afr 3275.17.4A	Cromer, E.B. Modern Egypt. N.Y., 1908. 2v.
Afr 3275.17A	Cromer, E.B. Modern Egypt. N.Y., 1908. 2v.
Afr 3275.17.4.10	Cromer, E.B. Modern Egypt. N.Y., 1916.
Afr 3275.60	Cromer, E.B. The situation in Egypt. London, 1908.
Afr 3977.19	Cronaca della missione francescana dell'Alto Egitto, 1719-1739. (Ildefonso da Palermo, Father.) Cairo, 1962.
Afr 4360.5	La cronaca reale Abissinia dall'anno 1800 all'anno 1840. (Conti Rossini, C.) Roma, 1913.
Afr 4360.3	Cronaca reale Abissinia dall'anno 1800 all'anno 1840. Rome, 1916.
Afr 4430.25	Cronache etiopiche. (Zoli, Corrado.) Roma, 1930.
Afr 1755.17	Cronica artillera...Campana de Melilla. Text and plates. Madrid, 1911.
Afr 1753.2FA	Cronica da tomada de Ceuta. (Eannes de Zurara, G.) Coimbra, 1915.
Afr 1432.7F	Cronica de la guerra de Africa. (Castelar, E.) Madrid, 1859.
Afr 1755.6	Cronica de la guerra de Africa en 1909. (Corral Caballe, M. del.) Barcelona, 1909.
Htn	Afr 674.93.14*	Cronica do descobrimento da Guiné. (Eannes de Azurara, G.) Porto, 1937. 2v.
Afr 674.93.12	Cronica dos feitos de Guiné. (Eannes de Azurara, G.) Lisboa, 1942.
Afr 8678.47.5	Cronje, G. Regverdige rasse-apartheid. Stellenbosch, 1947.
Afr 8678.47	Cronje, G. 'N truiste vir die nageslag. Johannesburg, 1945.
Afr 8685.35	Cronje, Geoffrey. Afrika soder die asiaat. Johannesburg, 1946.
Afr 8057.10	Cronjé, Geoffrey. Aspekte van die Suid-Afrikaanse historiografie. Pretoria, 1967.
Afr 8667.68	Cronjé, Geoffrey. Die Westerse kultuur in Suid-Afrika. Pretoria, 1963.
Afr 8252.14.10	Cronwright-Schreiner, S.C. Her South African ancestors. London, 1938.
Afr 11802.92.130	The crooked bluegum. (Sowden, Lewis.) London, 1955.

Afr 6138.5	Crooks, John J. A history of the colony of Sierra Leone. Dublin, 1903.
Afr 7808.99.5	Croquis congolais. (Buls, Charles.) Bruxelles, 1899.
Afr 609.46.10	Croquis d'Afrique; voyages. (Lefebvre-Despeaux, Maxime.) Paris, 1946.
Afr 1490.16	Croquis marocains, sur la Moulouya. (Clement-Grandcourt, A.) Paris, 1912.
Afr 1609.13.7	Cros, L. Le Maroc pour tous. Paris, 1913.
Afr 5749.23	Cros, Louis. Madagascar pour tous. Paris, 1923.
Afr 9165.71	Cross, K.G. Bibliography of Pretoria. Pretoria, 1948.
Afr 6280.3	Cross river natives. (Partridge, Charles.) London, 1905.
Afr 7465.14	The crossing fee. (Warner, Esther Sietmann.) Boston, 1968.
Afr 3979.13.8	Crossland, Cyril. Desert and water gardens of the Red Sea. Cambridge, 1913.
Afr 678.80	Crouch, A.P. Glimpses of Feverland. London, 1889.
Afr 5045.7	Crouch, Archer P. On a surf-bound coast. London, 1887.
Afr 11051.4	Crouch, E.H. Gold dust. London, 1917.
Afr 11052.3	Crouch, E.H. Sonnets of South Africa. London, 1911.
Afr 11051.5	Crouch, E.H. A treasury of South African poetry and verse. 2. ed. London, 1909.
Afr 3986.938A	Crouchley, A.E. The economic development of modern Egypt. London, 1938.
Afr 3993.1	Crouchley, Arthur Edwin. The investment of foreign capital in Egyptian companies and public debt. Cairo, 1936.
Afr 2209.06.3	Crouse, M.E. Algiers. N.Y., 1906.
Afr 1340.15	Crouzet-Rayssac, A. de. Le régime des capitulations et la condition des étrangers au Maroc. Thèse. Paris, 1921.
Afr 678.30	Crow, Hugh. Memoirs of the late Captain Hugh Crow. London, 1830.
Afr 6214.30.2	Crowder, M. A short history of Nigeria. N.Y., 1966.
Afr 6214.30	Crowder, M. The story of Nigeria. London, 1962.
Afr 6055.5	Crowder, Michael. Pagans and politicians. London, 1959.
Afr 5185.9.2	Crowder, Michael. Senegal; a study of French assimilation policy. London, 1967.
Afr 5185.9	Crowder, Michael. Senegal. London, 1962.
Afr 679.68.10	Crowder, Michael. West Africa under colonial rule. London, 1968.
Afr 8289.03.9	Crowe, George. Commission of H.M.S. Terrible. London, 1903.
Afr 6780.6	Crowe, J.H. General Smuts campaign in East Africa. London, 1918.
Afr 7565.12.30	Crowe, S.E. The Berlin West African Conference, 1884-1885. London, 1942.
Afr 810.4.5	Crowther, S. The gospel on the banks of the Niger. London, 1968.
Afr 810.4	Crowther, S. Journal of an expedition up the Niger. London, 1855.
Afr 555.20	Crowthers, S.A. Niger mission, report of overland journey. London, 1872.
Afr 6883.35	Croyances et coutumes magico-religieuses des Wafipa païens. (Robert, J.M.) Tabora, 1949.
Afr 6218.7	Crozier, F.P. Five years hard. N.Y., 1932.
Afr 1947.14	Cruelties of the Algerine pirates shewing the present dreadful state of the English slaves. 4th ed. London, 1816.
Afr 6192.5	Cruickshank, B. Eighteen years on the Gold Coast of Africa. London, 1853. 2v.
Afr 6192.5.2	Cruickshank, B. Eighteen years on the Gold Coast of Africa. 2nd ed. London, 1966. 2v.
Afr 1445.10.5	Cruikshank, E.F. Morocco at the parting of the ways. Philadelphia, 1935.
Afr 1445.10	Cruikshank, E.F. Morocco at the parting of the ways. Diss. Philadelphia, 1935.
Afr 698.69	A cruise in the "Gorgon". Reprint of 1869 1. ed. (Devereux, William Cope.) London, 1968.
Afr 7309.66.5	Cruising off Mozambique. (Karlsson, Elis.) London, 1969.
Afr 7368.56.5	Crummell, A. The duty of a rising Christian state. Boston, 1857. 3 pam.
Afr 7368.62	Crummell, A. The future of Africa. N.Y., 1862.
Afr 7368.62.2	Crummell, A. The future of Africa. N.Y., 1969.
Afr 7458.61	Crummell, A. Relations and duties of free colored men in America. Hartford, 1861.
Afr 7122.50	Cruz, D. da. A crise de Angola. Lisboa, 1928.
Afr 7175.28	Cruz, José Ribeiro da. Geografia de Angola. Lisboa, 1940.
Afr 7180.40	Cruz, José Ribeiro da. Notas de etnografia angolana. Lisboa, 1940.
Afr 7119.40	Cruz, José Ribeiro da. Resumo da história de Angola. Lisboa, 1940.
Htn	Afr 7122.10*	Cruz, L.F. da. Manifesto das ostilidades que a gente. Lisboa, 1651.
Afr 150.14	A cruzada do Infante Dom Henrique. (Bensaude, J.) Lisboa, 1942.
Afr 11675.87.110A	Cry, the beloved country. (Paton, Alan.) N.Y., 1948.
Afr 11675.87.112	Cry, the beloved country. (Paton, Alan.) N.Y., 1960.
Afr 7122.64	Cry Angola. (Addicott, Len.) London, 1962.
Afr 3.8	Cuadernos de estudios africanos. Madrid. 1,1946+ 11v.
Afr 7850.45.5	Cuarenta y seis hombres en colera. Bruselas, 1962.
Afr 1750.4.4	Cuarto congreso africanista. IVth. (Congreso Africanista.) Barcelona, 1910.
Afr 14692.41.100	Cubata abandonada. (Victor, Geraldo Bessa.) Lisboa, 1958.
Afr 6162.15	Cudjoe, S.D. Aids to African autonomy. London, 1949.
Afr 1550.3	La cuestion de Marruecos. (Maura y Gamazo, Gabriel.) Madrid, 1905.
Afr 1442.5	Cuestion de Marruecos. (Taviel de Andrade, E.) Madrid, 1888.
Afr 1608.93.7	La cuestion de Marruecos y el conflicto de melilla. (Villaescusa, M.H.) Barcelona, 1893.
Afr 1550.24	La cuestion de Marruecos y su honrada solucion. (Camarasa, M. de.) Madrid, 1911.
Afr 1490.21	La cuestion de Marruecos y su solucion...1911. (Camarasa, M. de.) Barcelona, 1911.
Afr 1573.17	La cuestion del dia: desenlace del problema norte-africano y el porvenir de España. (Bande, Nicasio.) Barcelona, 1909.
Afr 607.90	Cuhn, E.W. Sammlung merkwüdiger Reisen in dem Innre von Afrika. Leipzig, 1790.
Afr 2623.960.5	Cuisenier, Jean. L'Ansarine; contribution à la sociologie du développement. Paris, 1960.
Afr 9689.40	Cullen, Lucy P. Beyond the smoke that thunders. N.Y., 1940.
Afr 5318.20	Le culte de la génération. (Lecoeur, C.) Paris, 1932.

Afr 5753.4 Un culte dynast. Avec évocation des morts. (Rusillon, H.) Paris, 1912.

Afr 555.4 Culte protestante en Algérie. Alger, 1867.

Afr 3817.16 Culto dei gemelli nel Sudan meridionale. (De Giorgi, Luigi.) Bologna, 1964.

Afr 1618.15 Cultos primitivos de Marruecos. (Cola Alberich, Julio.) Madrid, 1954.

Afr 5580.3 Cultru, P. De colonia in...Madagascar. Paris, 1901.

Afr 5580.3.5 Cultru, P. Un empereur de Madagascar au XVIIIe siècle, Benyowszky. Paris, 1906.

Afr 5119.10 Cultru, P. Histoire du Sénégal du XV siècle à 1870. Paris, 1910.

Afr 3335.12 Cultural agreements between Egypt and other countries. (Egypt. Ministry of Education. Cultural Relations Department.) Cairo, 1956.

Afr 9165.82 Cultural change in Soweto. (Johannesburg. Non-European Affairs Department.) Johannesburg, 1965.

Afr 3.40 Cultural events in Africa. London. 1,1964+

Afr 3979.47 Cultural survey of modern Egypt. v.1-2. (Mosharrafa, M.) London, 1947.

Afr 3320.143.10 The cultural yearbook. (United Arab Republic. Ministry of Culture and National Guidance.) Cairo. 1959+ 2v.

Afr 3979.64.5F Culture and arts. (United Arab Republic. Information Department.) Cairo, 1964.

Afr 3339.10 Culture and national guidance in twelve years. (Hatim, Muhammad Abdal-Quadir.) Cairo, 1964.

Afr 2225.22 Culture et enseignement en Algérie et au Maghreb. (Mazuni, Abd Allah.) Paris, 1969.

Afr 609.60.70 Cultures and societies of Africa. (Ottenberg, Simon.) N.Y., 1960.

Afr 5342.40 Cultures matérielles de la Côte-d'Ivoire. (Holas, Bohumil.) Paris, 1960.

Afr 6883.11 Culwick, A.F. Ubena of the rivers. London, 1935.

Afr 11310.52.100 Culwick, Arthur Theodore. Back to the trees. Cape Town, 1965.

Afr 8658.96.3 Cumberland, S. What I think of South Africa. London, 1896.

Afr 2224.961 Cumunel, G. Guide administratif. Paris, 1961.

Afr 2224.961.2 Cumunel, G. Guide administratif. Mise à jour au 15. juin 1961. Paris, 1961.

Afr 555.2.50 Cunha, A. Jornadas e outros trabalhos do missionario Barroso. Lisboa, 1938.

Afr 718.4.80 Cunha, Amadeu. Serpa Pinto e o apelo de Africa. Lisboa, 1946.

Afr 618.20.5 Cunha, Joaquim M. da S. Aspectos dos movimentos associativos na Africa negra. Lisboa, 1958.

Afr 618.20 Cunha, Joaquim M. da S. Movimentos associativos na Africa negra. Lisboa, 1956.

Afr 50.55 Cunha, Joaquim Moreira da Silva. Politische Aspekte des neuen Afrika. Hamburg, 1965.

Afr 1103.8 Cunha, Jorge da. Relaçam do successo, que no dia do prezenre mez de julho tiverao os navios. Lisbon, 17-

Afr 7025.10 Cunha, Manuel. Aquelas longas horas. Lisboa, 1968.

Afr 7188.269 Cunha Leal, Francisco Pinto da. Caligula em Brazil. Lisboa, 1924.

Afr 7190.15 Cunha Mattos, R.J. da. Corographia historica das ilhas de San Thome, Anno Bom, e Fernando Po. Porto, 1842.

Afr 6540.1 Cunningham, J.F. Uganda and its peoples. London, 1905.

Afr 3817.14 Cunnison, Ivan George. Baggara Arabs, power and the lineage in a Sudanese nomad tribe. Oxford, 1966.

Afr 4070.24 Cuny, Charles. Journal de voyage...de Siout à El-Obeid. Paris, 1863.

Afr 8152.91 Cunynghame, A.T. My command in South Africa 1874-8. London, 1879.

Afr 555.155 Un cuore irlandese in Africa. (Gallesio, Lydia.) Torino, 1967.

Afr 1268.6 A cure for serpents. (Denti Di Pirajno, Alberto.) London, 1955.

Afr 5408.5.5 Cureau, Adolphe L. Savage man in Central Africa. London, 1915.

Afr 5408.5 Cureau, Adolphe L. Les sociétés primitives de l'Afrique. Paris, 1912.

Afr 7806.66.10F A curious and exact account of a voyage to Congo...1666 and 1667. (Guattini, M.A.) London, 1704. 2 pam.

Afr 6225.12 Current Issues Society, Kaduna, Nigeria. The Nigerian situation; facts and background. Zaria, 1966.

Afr 1110.25 Current problems in North Africa. (Near East Conference.) Princeton, 1960.

Afr 1100.2 Currey, E.H. Sea-wolves of the Mediterranean. London, 1910.

Afr 1100.2.5 Currey, E.H. Sea wolves of the Mediterranean. N.Y., 1929.

Afr 4513.36.25 Currey, M. A woman at the Abyssinian war. London, 1936.

Afr 109.64.25 Currie, D.P. Federalism and the new nations. Chicago, 1964.

Afr 8355.42 Currie, J.C. A bibliography of material published during the period 1946-56. Cape Town, 1957.

Afr 7568.5 The curse of Central Africa. (Burrows, G.) London, 1903.

Afr 11200.21.100 Curse of Magira. 1st ed. (Bee, David.) N.Y., 1965.

Afr 5903.5 Curso de conferencias sobre la politica africana de los reyes catolicos. V.1-6. (Spain.) Madrid, 1951-53. 3v.

Afr 8687.174.5 Cursons, William E. Joseph Doke. Johannesburg, 1929.

Afr 5842.12 Cursory notes on the Isle of France. (Stirling, E.) Calcutta, 1833.

Afr 4060.8 Curt, Silvio. Nubia, storia di una civilta favolosa. Novara, 1965.

Afr 11026.2 Curtain up. (Raester, Olga.) Cape Town, 1951.

Afr 8089.60 Curtain-up on South Africa. (Allighan, H.) London, 1960.

Afr 6069.64 Curtin, P.D. The image of Africa. Madison, 1964.

Afr 590.66 Curtin, Philip de Armond. Africa remembered. Madison, 1967.

Afr 6455.40 Curtis, Charles. P. Hunting in Africa east and west. Boston, 1925.

Afr 3978.51.5 Curtis, G.W. Nile notes. N.Y., 1851.

Afr 3978.51.6 Curtis, G.W. Nile notes. N.Y., 1852.

Htn Afr 3978.51.4* Curtis, G.W. Nile notes of a howadji. N.Y., 1851.

Afr 8289.51 Curtis, Lionel. With Milner in South Africa. Oxford, 1951.

Afr 8289.51.2 Curtis, Lionel. With Milner in South Africa. Index. Johannesburg, 1962.

Afr 3979.05.5 Curtis, W.E. Egypt, Burma and British Malaysia. Chicago, 1905.

Afr 7182.5 Cushman, W.S. Missionary doctor, the story of twenty years in Africa. 1st ed. N.Y., 1944.

Afr 2475.5 Cusson, C. Histoire du royaume de Tunis. Oran, 1863.

Afr 550.4.5 Cust, R.N. Africa rediviva. London, 1891.

Afr 550.4 Cust, R.N. L'occupation de l'Afrique. Genève, 1891.

Afr 635.45 Custom and conflict in Africa. (Gluckman, Max.) Glencoe, 1955.

Afr 6280.69 Custom and politics in urban Africa. (Cohen, Abner.) Berkeley, 1969.

Afr 6883.13 Customary law of the Haya tribe. (Cory, Hans.) London, 1945.

Afr 9545.10 The customary laws of succession in Central Africa. Thesis. (Coissoró, Narana.) Lisboa, 1966.

Afr 6540.6.10 The customs of the Baganoa. (Kagwa, Apolo.) N.Y., 1969.

Afr 7803.30 Cuvelier, J. Documents sur une mission française au Kakongo 1766-1776. Bruxelles, 1953.

Afr 7560.12 Cuvelier, Jean. L'ancien royaume de Congo. Bruges, 1946.

Afr 7809.60.10 Cuypers, J.P. Alphonse Vangele (1848-1939). Bruxelles, 1960.

Afr 3730.4 Cuzzi, G. Fünfzehn Jahre Gefangener des falschen Propheten. Leipzig, 1900.

Afr 2945.35 Cyrenaica. Camera di Commercio, Industria ed Agricultura. La Cirenaica. Bengasi, 1928.

Afr 2945.3 Cyrenaika als Gebiet künftiger Besiedlung. (Hildebrand, G.) Bonn, 1904.

Afr 718.25.15 Czekanowski, Jan. W głab lasów Aruwimi. Wrocław, 1958.

Afr 6390.32 Czernin, Ottokar G. Mein afrikanisches Tagebuch. Zürich, 1927.

Afr 609.64.35 Czyzewski, Kraysztof L. W afrykanskiej dzungli, buszu i pustyni. Warszawa, 1964.

Afr 718.42 Da Angola a Contra-Costa. v.I,II. (Capello, H.) Lisboa, 1886. 2v.

Afr 4392.25 Da Assab ad Adua. (Bono, Giulio del.) Roma, 1937.

Afr 4730.10 Da Assab al Mareb. Roma, 1891.

Afr 4513.35.145 Da Baldissera a Badoglio. 4a ed. (Cipolla, A.) Firenze, 1936.

Afr 2929.26.5F Da Leptis Magna a Gadames. (Calzini, R.) Milano, 1926.

Afr 4610.3 Da Zeila alle frontiere del Caffa. (Cecchi, A.) Roma, 1886-87. 3v.

Afr 6210.52 Dada, Paul O.A. Evaluation of local government courses in relation to careers of staff trained in Zaria, 1954-1964. Zaria, 1966.

Afr 8180.34 Dagboek. (Trigerdt, L.) Bloemfontein, 1917.

Afr 8110.3.20 Daghregister gehouden by den oppercoopman Jan Anthonisz van Riebeeck. v.1-. (Riebeeck, Jan van.) Kaapstad, 1952. 3v.

Afr 8089.37 Daglemier in Suid-Afrika. (Preller, G.S.) Pretoria, 1937.

Afr 3979.23.10 Dahaheah days, an Egyptian winter holiday. (Edgar, H.M.) Toronto, 1923.

Afr 5260.5 Dahomé, Niger, Touareg. (Toutée, Georges Joseph.) Paris, 1897.

Afr 5385.14.2 Le Dahomé - souvenirs de voyage et de mission. (Laffitte, J.) Tours, 1873.

Afr 5385.14 Le Dahomé - souvenirs de voyage et de mission. 4 ed. (Laffitte, J.) Tours, 1876.

Afr 5385.25 Dahomey, an ancient West African kingdom. (Herskovits, M.J.) N.Y., 1938. 2v.

Afr 5385.19 Le Dahomey, histoire, géographie, moeurs (1891-94). (Foa, Edouard.) Paris, 1895.

Afr 5388.5F Dahomey. Budget national.

Afr Doc 6609.5F Dahomey. Budget national. 1960+

Afr 5387.14 Dahomey. Plan de développement économique et social, 1966-1970. Cotohou, 1966.

Afr 5385.30 Le Dahomey. (Akindele, Adolphe.) Paris, 1955.

Afr 5385.10 Le Dahomey. (Cornevin, Robert.) Paris, 1965.

Afr Doc 6607.15 Dahomey. Direction des Affaires Economiques. Bulletin économique et statistique. 1961+ 3v.

Afr Doc 6607.5 Dahomey. Haut Commissariat au Plan et au Tourisme. Annuaire statistique. Cotonou. 1965

Afr Doc 6607.20 Dahomey. Ministère des Finances et des Affaires Economiques. Aspects éonomiques. Cotonou. 1962+

Afr Doc 6607.10 Dahomey. Service Central de la Statistique et de la Mécanographie. Bulletin de statistique. Cotonou. 2,1965+

Afr Doc 6634.5 Dahomey. Service du Développement Rural. Rapport annuel. Porto-Novo. 1962+

Afr 5368.10 Dahomey and its neighbours, 1708-1818. (Akinjogbin, I.A.) Cambridge, Eng., 1967.

Afr 5385.3 Dahomey and the Dahomans. (Forbes, F.E.) London, 1851. 2v.

Afr 5385.3.5 Dahomey and the Dahomans. (Forbes, F.E.) Paris, 1857.

Afr 5387.8 Dahomey and the slave trade; an analysis of an archaic economy. (Polanyi, Karl.) Seattle, 1966.

Afr 5385.15 Dahomey as it is. (Skertchly, J.A.) London, 1874.

Afr 5385.7 Dahomey et dépendances. (Brunet, L.) Paris, 1901.

Afr 5765.31 Dailliez, André. A la découverte d'un diocèse Malgache, Fianarantsoa. Bar-le-Duc, 1966.

Afr 7560.15.5 Daily life in the Kingdom of the Kongo from the sixteenth to the eighteenth century. (Balandier, Georges.) London, 1968.

Afr 4688.15.20 Dainelli, G. La regione del Lago Tana. Milano, 1939.

Afr 609.60.10 Dainelli, Giotto. Gli esploratori italiani in Africa. Torino, 1960.

Afr 4742.5.5 Dainelli, Giotto. In Africa, lettere dall'Eritrea. v.1. Bergamo, 1908.

Afr 4742.5 Dainelli, Giotto. Risultati scientifici di un viaggio nella colonia Eritrea. Firenze, 1912.

Afr 5403.20 Dairiam, Emmanuel. La subdivision en Afrique équatoriale française. Lyon, 1931.

Afr 5190.10.9 Dakar, outpost of two hemispheres. (Lengyel, Emil.) N.Y., 1941.

Afr 5190.10.20 Dakar. (Garnier, C.) Paris, 1961.

Afr 5190.10.15 Dakar. (Vanlande, René.) Paris, 1941.

Afr 5183.965 Dakar. Chambre de Commerce. L'économie du Sénégal. 2. éd. Dakar, 1965.

Afr 5183.965.5 Dakar. Chambre de Commerce d'Agriculture et d'Industrie. Catalogue des principales productions industrielles du Sénégal. Dakar, 1965.

Afr 5050.15 Dakar. Université. Département de Géographie. Travaux.

Afr 5190.24 Dakar and West African economic development. (Peterec, Richard J.) N.Y., 1967.

Afr 5190.10.12 Dakar avant-poste de deux hémisphères. (Lengyel, Emil.) N.Y., 1943.

Afr 5190.26 Dakar en devenir. (Groope d'Études Dakaroises.) Paris, 1968.

Afr 9700.15 Dake, C.M. The Lambas of Northern Rhodesia. London, 1931.

Afr 2710.12 Dal Sahara al Ciad. (Benedetti, Achille.) Milano, 1935.

Afr 5635.22   David Bernard, Eugene. La conquête de Madagascar. Paris, 1944.

Afr 9558.55   David Livingstone, explorer and prophet. (Finger, Charles J.) Garden City, N.Y., 1928.

Afr 9558.65   David Livingstone. (Horne, C.S.) N.Y., 1913.

Afr 9558.38A   David Livingstone. (Hughes, T.) London, 1889.

Afr 9558.43   David Livingstone. (MacLachlan, T.B.) Edinburgh, 1901.

Afr 9558.95   David Livingstone. (Seaver, George.) N.Y., 1957.

Afr 9558.100   David Livingstone. (Sharp, J.A.) London, 1920.

Afr 9558.29   David Livingstone. (Vattemare, H.) Paris, 1879.

Afr 9558.110   David Livingstone and the Rovuma. (Livingstone, David.) Edinburgh, 1965.

Afr 9446.32   Davidson, A.B. Matabele i Mashona v bor'be protiv angliiskoi kolonizatsii, 1888-1897. Moscow, 1958.

Afr 710.20   Davidson, B. The African awakening. London, 1955.

Afr 109.64   Davidson, B. The African past. 1st ed. Boston, 1964.

Afr 590.75   Davidson, B. Black mother. Boston, 1961.

Afr 8659.52   Davidson, B. Report on southern Africa. London, 1952.

Afr 109.66F   Davidson, Basil. Africa, history of a continent. London, 1966.

Afr 109.66.2   Davidson, Basil. Africa in history, themes and outlines. London, 1968.

Afr 115.124   Davidson, Basil. The African genius; an introduction to African cultural and social history. 1st American ed. Boston, 1969.

Afr 679.65.30   Davidson, Basil. The growth of African civilisation, West Africa, 1000-1800. London, 1965.

Afr 679.65.30.1   Davidson, Basil. The growth of African civilisation. London, 1967.

Afr 109.67.25   Davidson, Basil. The growth of African civilization: East and Central Africa to the late nineteenth century. London, 1967.

Afr 109.65.10   Davidson, Basil. A guide to African history. 1st ed. Garden City, N.Y., 1965.

Afr 109.67.26   Davidson, Basil. A history of East and Central Africa to the late nineteenth century. Garden City, N.Y., 1969.

Afr 679.65.30.2   Davidson, Basil. A history of West Africa to the nineteenth century. Garden City, N.Y., 1966. 2v.

Afr 7065.520   Davidson, Basil. The liberation of Guiné. Harmondsworth, 1969.

Afr 609.59.5   Davidson, Basil. The lost cities of Africa. 1st ed. Boston, 1959.

Afr 679.53   Davidson, Basil. The new West Africa. London, 1953.

Afr 7065.526.10   Davidson, Basil. Révolution en Afrique; la libération de la Guinée portugaise. Paris, 1969.

Afr 590.75.5   Davidson, Basil. Vom Sklavenhandel zur Kolonialisierung, afrikanisch-europäische Beziehungen zwischen 1500 und 1900. Reinbeck bei Hamburg, 1966.

Afr 210.64.10   Davidson, Basil. Which way Africa. Harmondsworth, 1964.

Afr 210.64.12   Davidson, Basil. Which way Africa? The search for a new society. Harmondsworth, 1967.

Afr 9165.70   Davidson, Elizabeth. Pietersburg Magisterial District; a bibliography. Johannesburg, 1968.

Afr 555.7.12   Davidson, H. Frances. South and South Central Africa. Elgin, 1915.

Afr 1608.39   Davidson, J. Notes taken during travels in Africa. London, 1839.

Afr 9635.5   Davidson, J.W. The Northern Rhodesian legislative council. London, 1948.

Afr 7817.20   Davies, David Michael. The captivity and triumph of Winnie Davies. London, 1968.

Afr 2308.8   Davies, E.W.L. Algiers in 1857. London, 1858.

Afr 8145.16   Davies, H. South African missions. London, 1954.

Afr 6218.12   Davies, H.O. Nigeria. London, 1961.

Afr 555.7.10   Davies, Horton. Great South African Christians. Cape Town, 1951.

Afr 6295.5F   Davies, J.G. The Biu book, a collection and reference book on Biu division (Northern Nigeria). Norla, 1954-56.

Afr 679.67.25   Davies, Oliver. West Africa before the Europeans: archaeology and prehistory. London, 1967.

Afr 4070.55   Davies, R.T. The camel's back. London, 1957.

Afr 8678.19   Davis, A. The native problem in South Africa. London, 1903.

Afr 6420.80   Davis, Alexander. Chronicles of Kenya. London, 1928.

Afr 4236.965F   Davis, Asa J. A note on ideological basis of union of church and state in Ethopia. Ibadan, 1965.

Afr 10924.5   Davis, John Gordon. Hold my hand, I'm dying. 1st ed. N.Y., 1968.

Afr 555.9.60A   Davis, John Merle. Modern industry and the African. London, 1933.

Afr 555.9.61   Davis, John Merle. Modern industry and the African. 2nd ed. London, 1967.

Afr 2608.54   Davis, N. Evenings in my tent. London, 1854. 2v.

Afr 2300.2   Davis, N. Ruined cities within Numidian and Carthaginian territories. London, 1862.

Afr 575.9   Davis, N. A voice from North Africa. Edinburgh, 1844.

NEDL Afr 9148.99   Davis, Nathaniel Newnham. The Transvaal under the Queen. London, 1899.

Afr 7809.08.5   Davis, R.H. The Congo and coasts of Africa. London, 1908.

Afr 8283.9.2   Davis, R.H. Dr. Jameson's raiders. N.Y., 1897.

Afr 8289.00.7   Davis, R.H. With both armies in South Africa. N.Y., 1900.

Afr 4454.10   Davis, Raymond J. Fire on the mountains, the church in Ethiopia. London, 1967.

Afr 6282.35   Davis, Raymond J. Swords in the desert. 5th ed. London, 1966.

Afr 7369.53   Davis, S.A. This is Liberia. N.Y., 1953.

Afr 5054.34   Davis, S.C. Reservoirs of men, a history of the black troops of French West Africa. Thèse. Chambéry, 1934.

Afr 8279.01   Davis, W. John Bull's crime. N.Y., 1901.

Afr 7809.38.5   Davis, W.E. Ten years in the Congo. N.Y., 1940.

Afr 7850.35   Davister, P. Croisettes et casques bleus, récits. Bruxelles, 1962.

Afr 8289.02.8   Davitt, Michael. The Boer fight for freedom. N.Y., 1902.

Afr 3979.58.10   Davy, Andre. Four thousand miles of adventure. London, 1958.

Afr 8369.65.5   Dawie, 1946-1964; 'n bloemlesing uit die geskrifte van Die Burger se politieke kommentaar. (Dawie (pseud.).) Kaapstad, 1965.

Afr 8369.65.5   Dawie (pseud.). Dawie, 1946-1964; 'n bloemlesing uit die geskrifte van Die Burger se politieke kommentaar. Kaapstad, 1965.

Afr 9488.99.3   Dawkins, C.T. Precis of information concerning Southern Rhodesia. London, 1899.

Afr 6550.5   Dawn in Zanzibar. Cairo.

Afr 109.61.5   The dawn of African history. (Oliver, Roland A.) London, 1961.

Afr 109.61.7   The dawn of African history. 2d ed. (Oliver, Roland A.) London, 1968.

Afr 1609.04.9   Dawson, A.J. Things seen in Morocco. London, 1904.

Afr 8659.25   Dawson, Wm. South Africa, people, places, problems. N.Y., 1925.

Afr 608.76   Day, George T. African adventure and adventures. Boston, 1876.

Afr 2533.10   Day, Georges. Les affaires de la Tunisie et du Maroc devant les Nations Unies. Paris, 1953.

Afr 9435.18   Day, John. International nationalism. N.Y., 1967.

Afr 550.9   Day dawn in Africa. (Scott, A.M.) N.Y., 1858.

Afr 9388.84   Day dawn in dark places. (Mackenzie, John.) London, 1884.

Afr 8089.38   Day-dawn in South-Africa. (Preller, G.S.) Pretoria, 1938.

Afr 11320.50.120   The day Natal took off. (Delius, Anthony.) Cape Town, 1963.

Afr 11320.50.130   The day Natal took off. (Delius, Anthony.) London, 1963.

Afr 3315.81   Dayan, Moshe. Diary of the Sinai campaign. London, 1966.

Afr 550.33.5   Daybreak in the dark continent. 2d ed. (Naylor, W.S.) Boston, 1905.

Afr 6780.20   Daye, P. Avec les Vainqueures de Tahora. 2. ed. Paris, 1918.

Afr 7809.22   Daye, Pierre. L'empire colonial belge. Bruxelles, 1923.

Afr 7567.28   Daye, Pierre. Problèmes congolais. Bruxelles, 1943.

Afr 9148.88   Days and nights by the desert. (Gillmore, Parker.) London, 1888.

Afr 9614.4   Days gone by. (Hine, John Edward.) London, 1924.

Afr 5426.100.50   Days with Albert Schweitzer. (Franck, Frederick.) N.Y., 1959.

Afr 9088.8   De... Zuid-Afrikaansche Republiek. (Loo, C.J. van der.) Zwolle, 1896.

Afr 1573.33   De ambos lados del estrecho. (Guastavino Gallant, Guillermo.) Tetuan, 1955.

Afr 2208.65.3   De batna à Tuggurt et au Souf. (Zaccone, J.) Paris, 1865.

Afr 7175.2.5   De Benguella às terras de Iacca. (Capello, H.) Lisboa, 1881. 2v.

Afr 2608.85.7   De Bone à Tunis. (Cambon, Victor.) Lyon, 1885.

Afr 5406.211   De Bordeaux au Tchad par Brazzaville. (Deschamps, Jean Leopold.) Paris, 1911.

Afr 1753.10.8   De Ceuta a alacacer kibir em 1923. (Dornellas, Affonso de.) Lisboa, 1925.

Afr 5580.3   De colonia in...Madagascar. (Cultru, P.) Paris, 1901.

Afr 5962.4   De colonización y economia en la Guinea española. (Perpina Grau, Ramon.) Barcelona, 1945.

Afr 7222.50   Degredado a governado. (Almeida de Eca, O.G.) Lisboa, 1950.

Afr 2030.464.50   De Gaulle et l'Algérie. (Terrenoire, Louis.) Paris, 1964.

Afr 150.2.3   De iis qui ante Vascum A Gama Africam legere tentaverunt. Thesis. (Lepitre, J.M.A.) Parisis, 1880.

Afr 550.72   De instauranda Aethiopum salute. (Sandoval, Alonso de.) Bogatà, 1956.

Afr 810.7   De Koulikoro à Tombouctou. (Jaime, G.) Paris, 1894.

Afr 6720.28.3   De la Benoue à l'Atlantique à la poursuite des allemands. (Ferrandi, Jean.) Paris, 1931.

Afr 3986.939   De la condition légale des sociétés anonymes étrangères en Egypte. Thèse. (Raja'i, Nur al-Din.) Paris, 1939.

Afr 1840.15   De la condition politique des indigenes musulmans d'Algerie. Thèse. (Elie-Edmond, A.) Alger, 1921.

Afr 1422.3   De la convention de Tangier. (Chais, G.) n.p., 1845.

Afr 5342.8.3   De la Côte-d'Ivoire au Soudan. 3e éd. (Ollone, C.A.) Paris, 1901.

Afr 605.56.10   De la descripción de Africa. (Leo Africanus, J.) n.p., 1940.

Afr 605.56.11   De la descripción de Africa y de las cosas notables que ella se encuentran. (Leo Africanus, J.) n.p., 1952.

Afr 1990.2   De la domination française en Afrique. Paris, 1832.

Afr 1880.5   De la domination turque. (Esterhazy, W.) Paris, 1840.

Afr 1965.10.5   De la guerra en 1851. (Yusuf.) Madrid, 1859.

Afr 628.108   De la littérature des Nègres. (Gregoire, Henri.) Paris, 1808.

Afr 10007.2   De la négritude dans la littérature négro-africaine. (Melone, Thomas.) Paris, 1962.

Afr 628.108.7   De la noblesse de la peau. (Gregoire, Henri.) Paris, 1826.

Afr 2748.88   De la Peña al Sahara. (Lara, Juan F. de.) Madrid, 1888.

Afr 628.262   De la préhistoire d'Afrique. (Mars, Jean.) Port-au-Prince, 1962.

Afr 575.9.10   De la propagande musulmane en Afrique et dans les Indes. (Faugere, A.P.) Paris, 1851.

Afr 8252.323   De la Rey, lion of the west, a biography. (Meintjes, Johannes.) Johannesburg, 1966.

Afr 5285.277.30   De la savane à la ville. (Deniel, Raymond.) Aix-en-Provence, 1967.

Afr 5180.52   De la Sénégambie française. (Carrére, Frédéric.) Paris, 1855.

Afr 5110.20   De la situation politique des sénégalais. (Gueye, L.) Paris, 1922.

Afr 2749.25.10   De l'Algérie au Dahomey en automobile. (Kerillis, Henri de.) Paris, 1925.

Afr 2755.2   De l'Algérie au Soudan par le Sahara. 5000 kilomètres en automobile dans le désert et la brousse. (Foucaucourt, J. de.) Paris, 1928.

Afr 2209.61   De l'Algérie originelle à l'Algérie moderne. (Secrétariat Social d'Alger.) Alger, 1961.

Afr 5406.266   De l'Atlantique au fleuve Congo. (Sautter, Gilles.) Paris, 1966. 2v.

Afr 5235.180.2   De l'Atlantique au Niger. (Sanderval, A.O., vicomte de.) Paris, 1883.

Afr 5235.180   De l'Atlantique au Niger par le Foutah-Djallon. (Sanderval, A.O., vicomte de.) Paris, 1882.

Afr 5753.3   De l'esclavage à Madagascar. (Andre, C.) Paris, 1899.

Afr 2260.7   De l'établissement de légions de colons. (Bugeaud, M.) Paris, 1838.

Afr 1990.8   De l'établissement des Français. 2e éd. (Genty de Bussy, P.) Paris, 1839. 2v.

Afr 1570.36   De l'établissement du protectorat de la France au Maroc. (Lebre, G.) Paris, 1914.

Afr 2508.5   De l'évolution du protectorat de la France sur la Tunisie. Thèse. (Foucher, Louis.) Paris, 1897.

Afr 1957.2   De l'expédition d'Afrique en 1830. (Ault-Dumesnil, E.D.) Paris, 1832.

Afr 1835.2   De l'hygiene en Algerie. v.1-2. (Perier, J.A.N.) Paris, 1847. 2v.

Afr 2260.8   De l'impossibilité de fonder des colonies...en Algerie. (Lasnavères.) Paris, 1866.

Afr 2438.19   De l'influence du mariage sur la nationalité tunisienne. Thèse. (Scemama, A.) Paris, 1931.

Afr 4430.55.15   De l'invasion à la libération de l'Ethiopie. (Gingold Duprey, A.) Paris, 1955.

Afr 718.29   De l'océan Indien à l'océan Atlantique, la traversée de l'Afrique. (Foa, Edouard.) Paris, 1900.

Afr 7540.6   De l'organisation judiciaire et de la compétence en matière civile et commerciale au Congo. (Gohr, Albrecht.) Liège, 1910.

Afr 5425.15   De l'origine des Pahouins. (France, Louis.) Paris, 1905.

Afr 530.51   De l'Oural à l'Atlantique. (Sablier, E.) Paris, 1963.

Afr 7912.15.30   De Lumumba aux colonels. (Kashamura, Anicet.) Paris, 1966.

Afr 5640.15.20   De Madagascar à Verdun. (Charbonnel, Henry.) Paris, 1962.

Afr 2209.13   De Madrid a Uxda. (Lara, Juan F. de.) Madrid, 1913.

Afr 1570.21   De Marruecos. (Palacios, C.M.) Badajoz, 1908.

Afr 3976.17   De natura et incremento nili. (Scortia, J.B.) Lugduni, 1617.

Afr 8657.67   De Promontorio Bonae Spei, a Latin oration. (Hemmy, Gysbert.) Cape Town, 1959.

Afr 530.34   De rebus Africanis. (Mayor, D.R.W.) London, 1886.

Afr 2702.1F   De Saint-Louis à Tripoli. (Monteil, P.L.) Paris, 1895.

Afr 5235.191   De Saint-Louis au port de Temboctou. (Caran, Edmond.) Paris, 1891.

Afr 2527.2   De Sousse à Gafsa. Lettres, 1881-84. (Cealis, E.) Paris, n.d.

Afr 2609.01   De Syracuse à Tripoli. (Claretie, G.) Paris, 1901.

Afr 1608.86   De Tanger a fas et meknas en 1885. (Duveyrier, H.) Paris, 1886.

Afr 3155.2F   De titoli che usava la cancelleria de sultani di Egitto. (Amari, M.) Roma, 1886.

Afr 2608.92   De Tripoli a Tunis. (Bernard, M.) Paris, 1892.

Afr 2208.93.6   De Tunis à Alger. (Bernard, Marius.) Paris, 1893.

Afr 109.62.30   De Tutankamen a Nasser. (Calle Iturrino, E.) Bilbao, 1962.

Afr 9438.96   De Zuid-Afrikaansche Republiek en Rhodesia. (Muller, H.P.N.) 's-Gravenhage, 1896.

Afr 4559.42A   Dead men do tell tales. (Khun de Prorok, Byron.) N.Y., 1942.

Afr 9609.5   Deane, Phyllis. Colonial social accounting. Cambridge, England, 1953.

Afr 10575.82.120   Dear parent and ogre. (Easmon, R. Sarif.) London, 1964.

Afr 6195.22   Dearunner, Hans Werner. A history of Christianity in Ghana. Accra, 1967.

Afr 3822.2   Death by moonlight. (Henriques, Robert.) London, 1938.

Afr 210.60   The death of Africa. (Ritner, Peter.) N.Y., 1960.

Afr 8289.57   Death of the last republic. (Gibbs, Peter.) London, 1957.

Afr Doc 3212.2   Debates; official report. (Kenya. Legislative Council.) Nairobi. 28-91,1947-1963 51v.

Afr Doc 7516.8   Debates; official report. (West Cameroon. House of Assembly.) Buea. 1963+

Afr Doc 4212.5   Debates. (Basutoland. National Council. Legislative Council.) 1,1960+

Afr Doc 2614.5   Debates. (Cameroons, Southern. House of Assembly.) Buea. 1931-1959

Afr Doc 1812.6   Debates. (Gold Coast (Colony). Legislative Assembly.) 1953-1958 8v.

Afr Doc 1812.5   Debates. (Gold Coast (Colony). Legislative Council.) 1925-1928 3v.

Afr Doc 2812.12   Debates. (Mauritius. Legislative Assembly.) Port Louis. 1,1964+

Afr Doc 2812.10   Debates. (Mauritius. Legislative Council.) Port Louis. 2-4,1957-1963

Afr Doc 2563.5   Debates. (Nigeria, Eastern. House of Assembly.) 1,1956+
Afr Doc 2523.5   Debates. (Nigeria, Western. House of Assembly.) 1956+
Afr Doc 2522.5   Debates. (Nigeria, Western. House of Chiefs.) 1,1952+
Afr Doc 2312.5F   Debates. (Nigeria. Legislative Council.) Lagos.
Afr Doc 3714.5   Debates. (Rhodesia, Northern. Legislative Assembly.) 1,1964+

Afr Doc 3712.5   Debates. (Rhodesia, Northern. Legislative Council.) 15v.

Afr Doc 3514.5   Debates. (Rhodesia and Nyasaland. Assembly.) 20v.

Afr Doc 1714.5   Debates. (Sierra Leone. House of Representatives.) 1958+
Afr Doc 1712.15   Debates. (Sierra Leone. Legislative Council.) 3v.

Afr Doc 4314.4   Debates. (South Africa. Parliament. House of Assembly.) 1,1936+

Afr Doc 4314.6   Debates. (South Africa. Parliament. House of Assembly.) 1962+

Afr Doc 4814.5   Debates. (Transkeian Territories. Legislative Assembly.) Umtata. 1,1963+

Afr Doc 7516.5   Debates. (West Cameroon. House of Chiefs.) Buea. 2,1962+
Afr Doc 3714.10   Debates. (Zambia. National Assembly.) 1,1964+
Afr Doc 2416.5   Debates. Official report. (Nigeria, Western. House of Chiefs.)

Afr Doc 2314.5   Debates. Official report. (Nigeria. Parliament. House of Representatives.)

Afr Doc 4314.8F   Debates of the House of Assembly of the Union of South Africa as reported in the Cape Times. (South Africa. Parliament. House of Assembly.) Pretoria, 1966. 8v.

Afr 2030.355   Debatty, Andre. Le treize mai et la presse. Paris, 1960.
Afr 5055.62   Debay, Jean. Evolutions en Afrique noire. Paris, 1962.
Afr 2535.6   Debbasch, C. La République Tunisienne. Paris, 1962.
Afr 2630.7   Debbasch, Yvan. La nation française en Tunisie, 1577-1835. Paris, 1957.

Afr 11675.87.130   Debbie go home. (Paton, Alan.) London, 1961.
Afr 8678.240   Debeer, Zacharias Johannes. Multi-racial South Africa. London, 1961.

Afr 9389.53   Debenham, F. Kalahari sand. London, 1953.
Afr 9839.55   Debenham, F. Nyasaland. London, 1955.
Afr 9558.90   Debenham, F. The way to Ilala. London, 1955.
Afr 13324.7.100   Debertry, Leon. Kitawala. Elisabethville, 1953.
Afr 2358.5   Debia, René Yves. Orléansville. Alger, 1955.
Afr 8145.44   Deblank, J. Out of Africa. London, 1964.
Afr 5794.6   Deblenne, Paul. Essai de géographie medicale de Nosi-Bé. Thèse. Paris, 1883.

Afr 609.62.10   Deblij, Harm. Africa south. Evanston, 1962.
Afr 6465.56.15   De Blij, Harm J. Membasa; an African city. Evanston, Ill., 1968.

Afr 6291.40   Debré, François. Biafra, an II. Paris, 1968.

Afr 11319.9.100   Debruyn, Phillip. The secret place, jazz verse. Cape Town, 1964.

Afr 1957.15   Debu-Bridel, J. La guerre qui paye, Alger, 1830. Paris, 1930.

Afr 5829.10   Deburgh Edwardes, S.B. L'histoire de l'ile Maurice d'après les documents les plus authentiques, 1507-1895. Paris, 1910.

Afr 5829.10.7   Deburgh Edwardes, S.B. The history of Mauritius (1507-1914). London, 1921.

Afr 7560.14.15   Les débuts de l'oeuvre de Léopold II, 1875-1876. (Roeykens, A.) Bruxelles, 1955.

Afr 6753.10   Decalo, Samuel. Tanzania: an introductory bibliography. Kingston?, 1968.

Afr 1333.1   Decard, R. Les traités de commerce conclus par le Maroc.

Afr 5780.5   Decary, Raymond. L'Andray, extreme sud de Madagascar. Paris, 1933. 2v.

Afr 5555.2   Decary, Raymond. Coutumes guerrieres et organisation militaire chez les anciens Malgaches. Paris, 1966. 2v.

Afr 5792.3   Decary, Raymond. L'établissement de Sainte-Marie de Madagascar. Paris, 1937.

Afr 5794.5   Decary, Raymond. L'ile Nosy-Bé de Madagascar. Paris, 1960.

Afr 5753.22   Decary, Raymond. La mort et les coutumes funeraires à Madagascar. Paris, 1962.

Afr 5753.20   Decary, Raymond. Les ordalies et sacrifices rituels chez les Anains Malgaches. Pau, 1959.

Afr 6310.39   La décentralisation administrative et l'évolution des structures. (Bustin, Edouard.) Liège, 1958.

Afr 109.57.3   Decision in Africa, sources of current conflict (Hunton, William A.) N.Y., 1960.

Afr 109.57   Decision in Africa. (Hunton, William A.) N.Y., 1957.

Afr 6910.8   Decisions by the government on the financial and administrative relations between the Republic and South West Africa. (South Africa. Parliament.) Cape Town, 1968.

Afr 6878.59   Decken, Carl Claus, Baron von der. Baron Carl Claus von der Decken's Reisen in Ost Afrika in den Jahren 1859 bis 1865. Leipzig, 1869-79. 6v.

Afr 5322.10.5   Decker, Henry de. Le développement communautaire, une stratégie d'édification de la nation. Paris, 1968.

Afr 5322.10   Decker, Henry de. Nation et développement communautaire en Guinée et au Sénégal. Paris, 1968.

Afr Doc 9919.5   The Declaration of Independence and the Constitution of the Republic of Liberia as amended through May, 1955. (Liberia.) Monrovia, 196-?

Afr 590.42   Declaration of the objects. (Society for Abolishing Slavery All over the World, Newcastle-Upon-Tyne.) Newcastle, 1836.

Afr 3326.2   Declaration of the Union accord. (United Arab Republic.) Cairo, 1963.

Afr 725.12   Decle, Lionel. Three years in savage Africa. London, 1898.

Afr 3275.5   Decline of British prestige in the East. (Faris, Selim.) London, 1887.

Afr 1069.65   Décoloniser l'histoire. (Sahli, Mohamed C.) Paris, 1965.
Afr 5219.05   Decorse, J. Rabah et les Arabes du Chari. Paris, 1905.
Afr 4155.5   Decosson, A. Mareotis. London, 1935.
Afr 4558.77   Decosson, E.A. The cradle of the Blue Nile. London, 1877. 2v.

Afr 45.63   Decottignier, R. Les nationalités africaines. Paris, 1963.

Afr 679.65.40   La découverte de l'Afrique. (Coquery, Catherine.) Paris, 1965.

Afr 5565.2.2   La decouverte de Madagascar. (Kammerer, A.) Lisboa, 1950.
Afr 5565.2   La découverte de Madagascar. (Kammerer, A.) n.p., n.d.
Afr 5806.5   La découverte des Iles Mascareignes par les Portugais. (Visdelou-Guimbeau, G.) N.Y., 1940.

Afr 2650.2   La découverte du bassin hydrographique de la Tunisie centrale. (Roulre, A.M.F.) Paris, 1887.

Afr 718.2.35   La découverte du Congo. (Stanley, H.M.) Paris, 18-
Afr 210.59A   Decraene, Philippe. Le panafricanisme. Paris, 1959.
Afr 7210.15   Decretos. (Companhia de Moçambique.) Lisboa, 1891.
Afr 1340.17   Decroux, Paul. La vie municipale au Maroc. Thèse. Lyon, 1931.

Afr 1940.5   Deducção das votas no Supremo Conselho provizorio. (Ferreira Lobo, R.J.) Londres, 1817.

Afr 10621.76.100   Deep down the blackman's mind. (Armattoe, Raphael E.G.) Ilfracombe, 1954.

Afr 1738.1   La defaite des Anglais à Tanger, 1664. (Rouard de Card, E.) n.p., 1912.

Afr 6395.2.14A   Defeating Mau Mau. (Leakey, L.S.B.) London, 1954.
Afr 1960.2   Défence et occupation de la colonie d'Alger. (Grand, E.) Toulon, 1837.

Afr 8325.38   The defence of Duffer's Drift. (Swinton, Ernest.) London, 1911.

Afr 8980.5   Defence of Langalibalele. (Colenso, J.W.) n.p., 187-.
Afr 8325.25   Defence of the British troops in South Africa. (Chamberlain, J.) London, 1902.

Afr 8160.3   A defence of Zululand and its king. (Dixie, Florence Douglas.) London, 188-

Afr 8300.12   Defender. Sir Charles Warren and Spion Kop, a vindication. London, 1902.

Afr 2030.77   Défense de l'Algérie. (Leprevost, Jacques.) Alger, 1957.
Afr 5874.18   Defos du Rau, J. L'Ile de la Réunion. Bordeaux, 1960.
Afr 8377.6   Degenaar, Johannes Jacobus. Op weg na 'n nuwe politieke lewenshouding. Kaapstad, 1963.

Afr 3817.16   De Giorgi, Luigi. Culto dei gemelli nel Sudan meridionale. Bologna, 1964.

Afr 109.54   Degraff Johnson, J.C. African glory. London, 1954.
Afr 626.60   Degraft-Johnson, John C. An introduction to the African economy. Bombay, 1959.

Afr 3979.05.2   Deguervile, A.B. New Egypt. London, 1905.
Afr 8659.53   Deguingand, F.W. African assignment. London, 1953.
Afr 1494.45   Dehedin, Alexis. Adieu Maroc. Paris, 1955.
Afr 609.04   Deherain, H. Etudes sur l'Afrique. Paris, 1904.
Afr 8175.10   Deherain, H. L'expansion des Boers au XIXe siècle. Paris, 1905.

Afr 3685.5   Deherain, H. Le Soudan égyptien sous Mehemet Ali. Paris, 1898.

Afr 8105.20   Deherain, Henri. Le Cap de Bonne-Espérance au XVIIe siècle. Paris, 1909.

Afr 850.5   Deherain, Henri. Dans l'Atlantique. Paris, 1912.
Afr 603.23.10   Deherain, Henri. Quid Schems Eddin el dimashqui geographus de Africa cognitum habuerit. Thesis. Paris, 1897.

Afr 5045.5 Deherme, G. L'Afrique occidentale française. Paris, 1908.
Afr 550.146 Dehoney, Wayne. African diary. Nashville, 1961.
Afr 7812.246 Dehoux, Emile. Le problème de demain. Bruxelles, 1946.
Afr 10624.2.100 Dei-Anang, M. Africa speaks. 2d ed. Accra, 1960.
Afr 10624.2.110 Dei-Anang, M. Ghana glory. London, 1965.
Afr 10624.2.700 Dei-Anang, M. Ghana spricht, Gedichte. Herrenalb, 1962.
Afr 10624.2.120 Dei-Anang, M. Okomfo Anakye's golden stool. Accra, 1963.
Afr 11320.41.100 Dei-Anang, Michael. Africa speaks. 2. ed. Accra, 1960.
Afr 6164.21 Dei-Anang, Michael. Ghana resurgent. Accra, 1964.
VAfr 109.66.20 Dějiny Afriky. Vyd. 1. (Hrbek, Ivan.) Praha, 1966.
 2v.
Afr 210.60.25 Dekiewiet, C. Can Africa come of age? Johannesburg, 1960.
Afr 8678.76 Dekiewiet, C.W. The anatomy of South African misery. London, 1956.
Afr 500.75 Dekiewiet, Cornelis W. America's role in Africa. v. 1-2. Durban, 1960.
Afr 8089.41.6 Dekiewiet, Cornelis Willem. A history of South Africa, social and economic. London, 1946.
Afr 8089.41.5 Dekiewiet, Cornelis Willem. A history of South Africa, social and economic. Oxford, 1941.
Afr 5040.12 Dekolonisation und Souveränität. (Scherk, Nikolaus.) Wien, 1969.
Afr 555.83 Dekorne, J.C. To who I now send thee, mission work of the Christian Reformed Church in Nigeria. Grand Rapids, Mich., 1945.
Afr 1658.28 Del desastre à la victoria 1921-1926. v.1-4. (Hernandez Mir, F.) Madrid, 1926-27.
 4v.
Afr 1493.74 Del desastre al fracaso. (Hernandez Mir, F.) Madrid, 1922.
Afr 1750.12 Del Marruecos español. (Trivino Valdura, F.) Melilla, 1920.
Afr 1487.28 Del Marruecos feudal, episodios de la vida del cherif Raisuri. (Garcia Figueras, T.) Madrid, 1930.
Afr 1750.28 Del protectorado español en Marruecos. (Pita, F.) Melilla, 1933.
Afr 7175.33 Delachaux, T. Pays et peuples d'Angola. Neuchatel, 1934.
Afr 5045.30 Delafosse, M. Enquête coloniale dans l'Afrique française occidentale et équatoriale. Paris, 1930.
Afr 5054.25 Delafosse, M. Histoire de l'Afrique occidentale française. Paris, 1926.
Afr 7465.3 Delafosse, M. Les Libériens et les Baoule. Paris, 1901.
Afr 630.8.10 Delafosse, Maurice. Les Nègres. Paris, 1927.
Afr 630.8.5 Delafosse, Maurice. The Negroes of Africa. Washington, 1931.
Afr 630.8 Delafosse, Maurice. Les Noires de l'Afrique. Paris, 1922.
Afr 7324.2 Delagoa Bay. (Monteiro, R.) London, 1891.
Afr 7324.7 Delagoa directory, a year book of information. Lourenço Marques. 1917+
 4v.
Afr 510.90 Delaporte, Maurice. La vie coloniale. Paris, 1944.
Afr 2945.13 Delaporte. Relations inédites de la Cyrénaique. Paris, 1825.
Afr 7459.30 Delarue, S. The land of the pepper bird. N.Y., 1930.
Afr 5056.131.10 Delavignette, R. Afrique occidentale française. Paris, 1931.
Afr 5053.7 Delavignette, R. Freedom and authority in French West Africa. London, 1950.
Afr 5040.6 Delavignette, R.L. L'Afrique noire française et son destin. Paris, 1962.
Afr 5235.235 Delavignette, R.L. Soudan, Paris, Boulogne. Paris, 1935.
Afr 5046.10 Delavignette, Robert Louis. Du bon usage de la décolonisation. Paris, 1968.
Afr 510.105 Delavignette, Robert Louis. Les vrais chefs de l'empire. 7. éd. Paris, 1939.
Afr 8145.32A Delayed action. (Geyser, A.S.) Pretoria, 1960.
Afr 1658.8 Delbrel, G. Geografia general de la provincia del Rif. Melilla, 1911.
Afr 3978.79.3 Delchevalerie, G. L'Egypte. Paris, 1879.
Afr 7809.21 Delcommune, A. L'avenir du Congo belge menacé. 2e ed. Bruxelles, 1921.
 2v.
Afr 7808.74 Delcommune, A. Vingt années de vie africaine. Bruxelles, 1922.
 2v.
Afr 8658.79.5 Deleage, Paul. Trois mois chez les Zoulous et les derniers jours du prince impérial. Paris, 1879.
Afr 3705.14 Delebecque, J. Gordon et le drame de Khartoum. Paris, 1935.
Afr 3740.6.35 Delebecque, J. Vie du Général Marchand. Paris, 1936.
Afr 3740.6.30 Delebecque, J. Vie du Général Marchand. Paris, 1936.
Afr 3040.79 La délégation législative en France et en Egypte. (Hafiz, Mahamid.) Le Caire, 1956.
Afr 5758.38 Les delegations économiques et financieres de Madagascar. Thèse. (Martin, A.) Paris, 1938.
Afr 8658.47 Delegorgue, A. Voyage dans l'Afrique australe...1838-44. Paris, 1847.
 2v.
Afr 5640.20 Delelee-Desloges, J.G. Madagascar et dependances. Paris, 1931.
Afr 500.5 De Leon, D. The West African question. n.p., 1886.
Afr 3198.82 DeLeon, E. Egypt under its khedives. London, 1882.
Afr 3978.78 Deleon, E. The khedives Egypt. N.Y., 1878.
Afr 6275.16 Delevoye. En Afrique centrale. Paris, 1906.
Afr 6395.20 Delf, George. Asians in East Africa. London, 1963.
Afr 6470.250 Delf, George. Jomo Kenyatta. London, 1961.
Afr 6470.250.10 Delf, George. Jomo Kenyatta. 1st ed. Garden City, 1961.
Afr 7119.48 Delgado, Ralph. História de Angola. Bereguela, 1948-53.
 4v.
Afr 7815.5.5 Delhaise, C.G. Les Warega (Congo belge). 5. Bruxelles, 1909.
Afr 7809.09 Delhaise, C.G.F.F. Les Warega (Congo belge) par le commandant Delhaise. Bruxelles, 1909.
Afr 28.114F Delhi. University. Library. Documentation list, Africa. Delhi. 5,1966+
Afr 4513.35.150 Il delitto africano del fascismo. (Nenni, P.) Paris, 1935.
Afr 11320.50.140 Delius, Anthony. A corner of the world. Cape Town, 1962.
Afr 11320.50.120 Delius, Anthony. The day Natal took off. Cape Town, 1963.
Afr 11320.50.130 Delius, Anthony. The day Natal took off. London, 1963.
Afr 11320.50.110 Delius, Anthony. The fall. Cape Town, 1960.
Afr 11320.50.100 Delius, Anthony. The last division. Cape Town, 1959.
Afr 11320.50.150 Delius, Anthony. An unknown border; poems. Cape Town, 1954.
Afr 8659.47.5 Delius, Anthony. The young traveller in South Africa. London, 1947.

Afr 4700.31 Della Valle, Carlo. I pionieri italiani nelle nostre colonie. Roma, 1931.
Afr 7549.54 Dellicour, Fernand. Les propos d'un colonial belge. Bruxelles, 1954.
Afr 3978.96 Delmas, E. Egypte et Palestine. Paris, 1896.
Afr 5190.20 Delmas, Robert. Des origines de Dakar et ses relations avec l'Europe. Dakar, 1957.
Afr 2224.20 Delmonte, Fabien R.S. Les pouvoirs financiers des assemblées algériennes et le contrôle de la métropole. Thèse. Alger, 1923.
Afr 2749.27.5 Deloncle, P.E.M.J. La caravane aux éperons verts (Mission Alger-Niger). Paris, 1927.
Afr 1571.17.120 Deloncle, Pierre. Lyautey. Paris, 1955.
Afr 7809.59.5 Delooz, Eugenus. Zwarte handen en blank kapitaal. Antwerpen, 1959.
Afr 1975.3 Delorme, A. Sous la chéchia. Paris, 1901.
Afr 5540.10 Delteil, Pierre. Le fokon'olona (commune malgache) et les conventions de fokon'olona. Thèse. Paris, 1931.
Afr 4513.40A Delvalle, P.A. Roman eagles over Ethiopia. Harrisburg, 1940.
Afr 7540.29 Delvaux, Roger. L'organisation administrative du Congo belge. Anvers, 1945.
Afr 2308.17 Delvert, C.L. Le port d'Alger. Paris, 1923.
Afr 2030.55 Demain en Algérie. (Fabre-Luce, Alfred.) Paris, 1958.
Afr 2025.15 Demain en Algérie. (Ferriol, M.) Paris, n.d.
Afr 2030.390 Demain en Algérie. (Servier, Jean.) Paris, 1959.
Afr 5130.20.5 Demaison, A. Faidherbe. Paris, 1932.
Afr 679.40 Demaison, A. The new Noah's ark. N.Y., 1940.
Afr 5045.11 Demaison, André. La vie des noirs d'Afrique. 4. ed. Paris, 1956.
Afr 9448.56 The demand for independence in Rhodesia. (Rhodesia (British Colony).) Salisbury, 1965.
Afr 5045.2 Demanet, Abbé. Nouvelle histoire de l'Afrique française. Paris, 1767.
 2v.
Afr 7575.67 Demany, Fernand. S.O.S. Congo. Bruxelles, 1959.
Afr 2438.7 Demay, Jules. L'organisation des communes en Tunisie. Tunis, 1915.
Afr 2618.26 Demeerseman, A. Soixante ans de pensée tunisienne à travers les revues. Tunis, 1955.
Afr 2618.15 Demeerseman, A. Tunisie: sève nouvelle. Tournai, 1957.
Afr 2618.26.5 Demeerseman, A. Vocation culturelle de la Tunisie. Tunis, 1953.
Afr 5403.10 Demetz, Henri. Le régime foncier en Afrique équatoriale française. Annecy, 1939.
Afr 7812.257.5F Un demi-siècle avec l'économie du Congo belge. (Hauzeur de Fooz, C.) Bruxelles, 1957.
Afr 4365.1 Demimuid, M. Vie...Justin de Jacobis. 2 ed. Paris, 1906.
Afr 1709.5 Demnate, un mellah en pays berbere. (Flamand, P.) Paris, 1952.
Afr 210.63.30 Democracy in Africa. (Jennings, W.) Cambridge, Eng., 1963.
Afr 3275.49 Democracy on the Nile. (Halassie, S.) Scotch Plains, N.J., 1940.
Afr 635.90 La démographie de la branche indo-pakistanaise d'Afrique. (Boute, Joseph.) Louvain, 1965.
Afr 5760.14 Demographie de l'Ankaizinana. (Molet, Louis.) Paris, 1955.
Afr 8040.15 Demokratie und Föderalismus in der südafrikanischen Union. (Kayser, H.) Düsseldorf, 1934.
Afr 8278.99.23 Demolins, E. Boers et Anglais. Paris, 1899.
Afr 2250.3 Demontes, V. Le peuple algérien. Alger, 1906.
Afr 2223.52 Demontes, V. Renseignements sur l'Algérie économique. Paris, 1922.
Afr 1830.20.56 Demontes, Victor. L'Algérie agricole. Paris, 1930.
Afr 1830.20.57 Demontes, Victor. L'Algérie industrielle et commercante. Paris, 1930.
Afr 1965.4.5 Demontes, Victor. La colonisation militaire sous Bugeaud. Thèse. Paris, 1916.
Afr 1990.25.5 Demontes, Victor. Papiers du général Berthezène...colonisation de l'Algérie. Paris, n.d.
Afr 1990.25 Demontes, Victor. Les préventions du général Berthezène. Paris, 1918.
Afr 6883.6 Dempwolff, Otto. Die Sandawe...Material aus deutsch Ostafrika. Hamburg, 1916.
Afr 6455.44.10 Denatured Africa. (Streeter, D.W.) Garden City, 1929.
Afr 6455.44 Denatured Africa. (Streeter, D.W.) N.Y., 1926.
Afr 6455.44.5 Denatured Africa. (Streeter, D.W.) N.Y., 1927.
Afr 2748.26.3 Denham, Dixon. Narration of travels and discoveries in Northern and Central Africa in the years 1822, 1823 and 1824. 3. ed. London, 1828.
Afr 2748.26 Denham. Narration of travels...in central Africa. Boston, 1826.
Afr 2748.26.2 Denham. Narration of travels...in central Africa. London, 1826.
Afr 5285.277.30 Deniel, Raymond. De la savane à la ville. Aix-en-Provence, 1967.
Afr 650.5 Denis, Jacques. Le phénomène urbain en Afrique Centrale. Bruxelles, 1958.
Afr 650.3 Denis, Jacques. Le phénomène urbain en Afrique Centrale. Namur, 1958.
Afr 626.52 Denis, Jacques. Le phénomène urbain en Afrique Centrale. Namur, 1958.
Afr 545.26 Denis, L. Gas de conscience, à l'usage surtout des pays africains. Bruges, 1962-63.
 2v.
Afr 6455.160 Denis, Michaela. At home with Michaela. London, 1965.
Afr 3978.80.5 Denis de Rivoyre, B.L. Mer Rouge et Abyssinie. Paris, 1880.
Afr 4886.7 Denis de Rivoyre, B.L. Obock, Mascate, Bouchire, Bassorah. Paris, 1883.
Afr 6878.92.5 Denkschrift betreffend Deutsch-Ostafrika. Berlin, n.d.
Afr 1584.7F Denkschrift über das bergwerksinteressen in Marokko. (Bethmann, H.) Berlin, 1910.
Afr 7093.5 Dennett, R.C. Seven years among the Fjort. London, 1887.
Afr 5445.5 Dennett, R.E. At the back of the black man's mind. London, 1906.
Afr 6280.5.1 Dennett, R.E. Nigerian studies. London, 1968.
Afr 1955.23 Denniée. Précis historique et administrative de la campagne d'Afrique. Paris, 1836.
VAfr 5580.3.25 Denník Mórica A. Beňovského. (Beniowski, M.A.) Bratislava, 1966.
Afr 2336.5 Dennis, H.V.M. Hippo Regius from the earliest times to the Arab conquest. Diss. Princeton, 1924.
Afr 1620.40 Dennis-Jones, Harold. Your guide to Morocco. London, 1965.
Afr 3978.03A Denon, V.D. Travels in upper and lower Egypt. N.Y., 1803.
 2v.

Afr 2030.462.25 Denoyer, François. Quatre ans de guerre en Algérie. Paris, 1962.

Afr 7942.2 La densité de la population au Ruanda-Urundi. (Gourou, Pierre.) Bruxelles, 1953.

Afr 1268.6 Denti Di Pirajno, Alberto. A cure for serpents. London, 1955.

Afr 626.11F Denuce, J. L'Afrique au XVI siècle et le commerce anversois. Anvers, 1937.

Afr 3035.2 Deny, Jean. Sommaire des archives turques du Caire. Caire, 1930.

Afr 8676.61.5F Denys, A. Land of apartheid, an introduction to the word "apartheid." Natal, 1961.

Afr Doc 4303.5 Department of Foreign Affairs list. (South Africa. Department of Foreign Affairs.) Pretoria. 1966+

Afr Doc 1805.10F Departmental reports. (Gold Coast (Colony).) 1909+ 9v.

Afr 3979.20.12 Le depaysement oriental. 7.ed. (Tharaud, Jerome.) Paris, 1926.

Afr 555.22.3 Depelchin, H. Trois ans dans l'Afrique australe. Bruxelles, 1883.

Afr 5448.15.5 Les dépenses exceptionnelles dans les budgets de ménage à Pointe-Noire en 1958. (Devauges, Roland.) Paris, 1963.

Afr 2025.31.5 Depont, O. L'Algerie du centenaire. Paris, 1928.

Afr 2208.88.5 Deporter, Victor. A propos du Transsaharien. Alger, 1890.

Afr 6780.12 Deppe, L. Mit Lettow-Vorbeck durch Afrika. Berlin, 1919.

Afr 8289.03.2 Der burenkrieg. (Vallentin, W.) Wald-Solingen, 1903. 2v.

Afr 1680.4 Der hohe Atlas. (Ichmann, G.) Marburg, 1891.

Afr 2260.26 Déraciné. (Dessaigne, Francine.) Paris, 1964.

Afr 8278.99.36 Derde verzameling. Deel 1-21. (Leyds, W.J.) Dordrecht, 1931.

Afr 1645.5 Los derechos del gobierno español en la misión de Marruecos. (García Barriuso, Patrocinio.) Madrid, 1968.

Afr 7809.55F Derhinderen, G. Atlas du Congo belge et du Ruanda-Urundi. Paris, 1955.

Afr 8678.245 Deridder, J.C. The personality of the urban African in South Africa. London, 1961.

Afr 2285.30 Dermenghem, Emile. Le pays d'Abel. Paris, 1960.

Afr 6926.25 Dernburg und die Südwestafrikaner. (Rohrbach, P.) Berlin, 1911.

Afr 1957.7 La dernière conquête du roi, Alger, 1830. V.1-2. (Sixte, Prince de Bourbon-Parma.) Paris, 1930. 2v.

Afr 1658.5 La derniere partie...Littoral de la mediterranee-le Rif. (Duveyrier, H.) Paris, 1888.

Afr 1635.4 Les derniers berberes. (Jary, Georges.) Paris, 1912.

Afr 5620.15 Les derniers jours de la cour hova. (Durand, Alfred.) Paris, 1933.

Afr 12674.1.100 Les derniers jours de Lat Dior. (Dia, Amadou Cissé.) Paris, 1965.

Afr 7809.09.10 Les derniers jours de l'Etat du Congo. (Vandervelde, Emile.) Mons, 1909.

Afr 1965.10 Derrecagaix, V.B. Yusuf. Paris, 1907.

Afr 6210.41 Derrett, John Duncan Martin. Studies in the laws of succession in Nigeria. London, 1965.

Afr 2525.20 Derriére le rideau tunisien. (Villiers, G.) Paris, 1955.

Afr 1658.52 El derrumbamiento. (Vivero, Augusto.) Madrid, 1922.

Afr 8378.379.30.3 Dertien jaar in die skadu. 3. druk. (Barnard, Fred.) Johannesburg, 1967.

Afr 2731.19 Dervil, Guy. Trois grands Africains. Paris, 1945.

Afr 5765.20 Derville, Leon. Ils ne sont que quarante...les jésuites chez les Betsileos. Paris, 1931.

Afr 3675.7 I Dervisci nel Sudan egiziano. (Dal Verme, L.) Roma, 1894.

Afr 2209.55.5 Des Africains s'interrogent. (Charbonneau, Jean.) Paris, 1955.

Afr 115.60 Des africanistes russes parlent de l'Afrique. Paris, 1960.

Afr 2030.370 Des Algériens accusent. (Moureau, Maurice.) Paris, 1959.

Afr 3978.67.5F Des cataractes du Nil...Hannek...Kaybar. (Gottberg, E. de.) Paris, 1867.

Afr 3315.75 Des deux côtés du Canal. (Gallean, Georges.) Paris, 1958.

Afr 1990.7 Des moyens d'assurer la domination française en Algérie. (Letang, B.) Paris, 1840-46. 4 pam.

Afr 678.46 Des nautiques des côtes de l'Afrique. (Bouet-Willaumez, Edouard, Comte.) Paris, 1846.

Afr 2030.461.10 Des officiers parlent. (Dufresnay, Claude.) Paris, 1961.

Afr 5540.16 Des ordinateurs dans l'administration Malgache! (Malagusy. Republic Institute National de la Statistique et de la Recherche Economique.) Tananarive.?, 1966?

Afr 5190.20 Des origines de Dakar et ses relations avec l'Europe. (Delmas, Robert.) Dakar, 1957.

Afr 7815.19 Des relations de travail entre européens et africains. (Association des Intérêts Coloniaux Belges.) Bruxelles, 1956.

Afr 4559.30.25 La désagréable partie de campagne. (Armandy, A.) Paris, 1930.

Afr 550.130 Desai, Ram. Christianity in Africa as seen by Africans. Denver, 1962.

Afr 555.135 Desallues, Elisabeth. Toumliline. Paris, 1961.

Afr 1755.45 El desastre de annual. (Ansart, F.B.) Barcelona, 1921.

Afr 1755.60 El desastre de Annual. (Fernández de la Reguera, Ricardo.) Barcelona, 1968.

Afr 5605.5 Desbassayns de Richemont, P. Documents sur la compagnie de Madagascar. Paris, 1867.

Afr 5058.7 Desbordes, J.G. L'immigration libano-syrienne en Afrique occidentale française. Thèse. Poitiers, 1938.

Afr 7565.18 Descamps, E. L'Afrique nouvelle. Paris, 1903.

Afr 5548.46 Descartes, M. Histoire et geographie de Madagascar. Paris, 1846.

Afr 5749.47.5 Deschamps, H. Madagascar. Paris, 1947.

Afr 5425.18 Deschamps, H. Traditions orales et archives au Gabon. Paris, 1962.

Afr 710.15 Deschamps, H.J. L'éveil politique african. 1 ed. Paris, 1952.

Afr 5549.60 Deschamps, H.J. Histoire de Madagascar. Paris, 1960.

Afr 5760.18 Deschamps, H.J. Les migrations. Paris, 1959.

Afr 545.20 Deschamps, H.J. Les religions de l'Afrique noire. 2. éd. Paris, 1960.

Afr 5119.64 Deschamps, H.J. Le Sénégal et la Gambie. Paris, 1964.

Afr 5119.64.2 Deschamps, H.J. Le Sénégal et la Gambie. 2e éd. Paris, 1968.

Afr 40.62 Deschamps, Hubert. Les institutions politiques de l'Afrique Noire. Paris, 1962.

Afr 5417.100 Deschamps, Hubert. Quinze ans de Gabon;...1839-1853. Paris, 1965.

Afr 175.6 Deschamps, Hubert Jules. L'Afrique tropicale aux XVIIe-XVIIIe siècles. Paris, 1964.

Afr 679.67.40 Deschamps, Hubert Jules. L'Europe découvre l'Afrique. Paris, 1967.

Afr 1571.31 Deschamps, Jean L. Souvenirs des premiers temps du Maroc français (1912-1915). Paris, 1935.

Afr 5406.211 Deschamps, Jean Leopold. De Bordeaux au Tchad par Brazzaville. Paris, 1911.

Afr 5780.88 Deschamps, N. Les Antaisaka. Thèse. Tananarive, 1936. 2 pam.

Afr 2209.61.5 Descloitres, R. L'Algérie des Bidonvilles. Paris, 1961.

Afr 7534.1 O desconhecido Niassa. (Santos, Nuno Beja Valdez Thomaz dos.) Lisboa, 1964.

Afr 678.66 Descripção...costa occidental de Africa. v.1-2. (Castilho, A.M. de.) Lisboa, 1866.

Afr 7309.02.5 Descripção da costa de Moçambique de Lourenço Marques ao Bazaruto. (Ferraz, Guilherme Ivens.) Lisboa, 1902.

Afr 7175.6.2 Descripção da viagem a Mussumba do Muatianvua. v.1-4. (Dias de Carvalho, H.A.) Lisboa, 1890.

Afr 1608.60.9 Descripcion del imperio de Marruecos. (Ferreiro, Martin.) Madrid, 1864.

Afr 605.73.5F Descripción general de Africa. (Marmol Carvajal, L. del.) Madrid, 1953.

Htn Afr 605.73F* Descripción général de Africa. Pt.1, 1-2, pt.II. (Marmol Carvajal, L. del.) Granada, 1573. 3v.

Afr 1609.06.3 Descripcion geografica del imperio de Marruecos. (Minguez Y Vicente, M.) Madrid, 1906.

Afr 5960.10 Descripcion geografica y gobierno. (Ramos Izquierdo Y Vivar, L.) Madrid, 1912.

Afr 1368.78 Descripcion historica de Marruecos. (Castellanos, M.P.) Santiago, 1878.

Afr 1608.59.3 Descripcion y mapas de Marruecos. (Gomez de Arteche y Moro, José.) Madrid, 1859.

Afr 3977.76 Descriptio aegypti. (Abu-l-Feda.) Göttingen, 1776.

Afr 1835.1.8 Description...de l'empire de Maroc. (Renou, E.) Paris, 1846.

Afr 675.07.5 Description de la côte d'Afrique de Ceuta au Sénégal...1506-1507. (Fernandes, V.) Paris, 1938.

Afr 5056.9 Description de la Nigritie. (Pruneau de Pommegorge, Antoine Edmé.) Amsterdam, 1789.

Afr 1835.1.12 Description de la régence de Tunis. (Pellissier de Reynaud, E.) Paris, 1853.

Afr 606.86F Description de l'Afrique. (Dapper, D.O.) Amsterdam, 1686.

Afr 605.56.12 Description de l'Afrique. (Leo Africanus, J.) Paris, 1956. 2v.

Afr 3976.92 Description de l'Egypte. (Maillet, B. de.) Paris, 1735.

Afr 8657.19.7 Description du cap de Bonne-Espérance. (Kolbe, Peter.) Amsterdam, 1741. 3v.

Afr 1605.96 Une description du Maroc. (Castries, H. de.) Paris, 1909.

Afr 1603.80 Description du pays du Magreb. (Abu Al-Feda.) Alger, 1839.

Afr 7560.18 Description du royaume de Congo et des contrées environnantes. (Lopes, Duarte.) Louvain, 1963.

Afr 7560.18.2 Description du royaume de Congo et des contrées environnantes parFilippo Pigafetta et Duarte Lopes (1951). 2.ed. (Lopes, Duarte.) Louvain, 1965.

Afr 2674.2 Description et histoire de l'île de Djerba. (Naceur.) Tunis, 1884.

Afr 1608.60.3 Description et histoire du Maroc. v.1-2. (Godard, L.) Paris, 1860.

Htn Afr 6192.1F* Description et récit historique du riche royaume d'or de Guinea. (Marees, Pieter de.) Amsterdamme, 1605.

Afr 855.9 Description of island of St. Helena. London, 1805.

Afr 8678.14 Description physique et historique des Cafres. (Alberti, L.) Amsterdam, 1811.

Htn Afr 605.56.3* Descriptione libri IX. (Leo Africanus, J.) Liguri, 1559.

Afr 2280.8 Les descriptions de Fromentin. (Martino, P.) Alger, 1910.

Afr 5842.16.2 Descriptive account of Mauritius. (Anderson, John.) Mauritius, 1858.

Afr 28.72 A descriptive and classified list of books published by or in association with the Northern Rhodesia and Nyasaland Publication Bureau. (Northern Rhodesia and Nyasaland. Publications Bureau.) n.p., 1961.

Afr 8808.75 Descriptive handbook of the Cape colony. (Noble, John.) Cape Town, 1875.

Afr 3982.2F Descrittori italiani dell'Egitto e di Alessandria. (Lumbroso, Giacomo.) Roma, 1879.

Afr 1432.21.2 Desde Vad-Ras a Sevilla: Acuarelas de la campaña de Africa. 2a ed. (Navarrete, José.) Madrid, 1880.

Afr 6542.5.15 Desecration of my kingdom. (Mutesa II, King of Buganda.) London, 1967.

Afr 2749.54.5 Desert adventure. (Stuart, B.) London, 1954.

Afr 3979.38 Desert and delta. (Jarvis, C.S.) London, 1938.

Afr 3979.13.8 Desert and water gardens of the Red Sea. (Crossland, Cyril.) Cambridge, 1913.

Afr 2731.15.26 Desert calling. (Fremantle, A.J.) London, 1950.

Afr 2731.15.25 Desert calling. (Fremantle, A.J.) N.Y., n.d.

Afr 4045.1 Le desert de Suez. (Berchere, N.) Paris, n.d.

Afr 9404.2 Desert doctor: medicine and evangelism in the Kalahan Desert. (Merriweather, Alfred Musgrave.) London, 1969.

Afr 4700.31.8 Desert encounter. (Holmboe, Knud.) London, 1936.

Afr 4070.25 Le desert et le Soudan. (Escayrac de Lauture, S.) Paris, 1853.

Afr 5074.35 Désert fertile. (Garnier, C.) Paris, 1960.

Afr 2312.2 The desert gateway. (Leeder, S.H.) London, 1910.

Afr 2731.15.110 The desert my dwelling place: a study of Charles de Foucauld, 1858-1916. (Hamilton, Elizabeth.) London, 1968.

Afr 3708.5 Desert warfare, being the chronicle of the Eastern Soudan campaign. (Burleigh, B.) London, 1884.

Afr 2749.54 The desert watches. 1st Amer. ed. (MacArthur, D.W.) Indianapolis, 1954.

Afr 2209.27.5 Desert winds. (Hafsa.) N.Y., 1927.

Afr 9439.60.10 Deserve to be great. (Gale, W.D.) Bulawayo, 1960.

Afr 2223.931 Desfeuilles, P. L'Algérie. Paris, 1931.

Afr 1623.932.10 Desfeuilles, Paul. Les colonies françaises, le Maroc. Paris, 1932.

Afr 2508.6 Desfosses, Edmond. Affaires d'orient, la question tunisienne. Paris, 1881.

Afr 2608.80 Desgodins de Souhesmes, G. Tunis. Paris, 1880.

Afr 5078.20 Desire-Vuillemin, G. Contribution à l'histoire de la Mauritanie. Dakar, 1962.

Afr 1990.6 Desjobert, A. La question d'Alger. Paris, 1837.

Afr 1082.1 Deslane, M.G. Sur les premiers expéditions. n.p., 1844.

Afr 1200.62 Deslinieres, L. La France nord-africaine. Paris, 1920.

Afr 9499.70   The development of the economic resources of Southern Rhodesia. (Rhodesia, Southern. Advisory Committee on the Development of the Economic Resources of Southern Rhodesia.) Salisbury, 1962.

Afr 6193.21F   The development plan, 1951. (Gold Coast (Colony).) Accra, 1951.

Afr 9193.3F   Development plan. (Swaziland.) Mababane, 1966.

Afr 6881.261   Development plan for Tanganyika, 1961/62-1963/64. (Tanganyika.) Dar es Salaam, 1961.

Afr 6457.23   Development plan for the period from 1st July, 1964, to 30th June, 1970. (Kenya.) Nairobi, 1964.

Afr 6457.23.5   Development plan for the period 1965-1966 to 1966-1970. (Kenya.) Nairobi, 1966.

Afr 5343.40   A development plan for the Southwest Region. (Development and Resources Corporation.) N.Y., 1968. 4v.

Afr Doc 2520.950F   Development plan statistics of western group of provinces of Nigeria. (Nigeria, Western. Ministry of Economic Planning and Social Development. Statistics Division.) Ibadan, 1966.

Afr 626.167   Development planning in East Africa. (Clark, Paul Gordon.) Nairobi, 1965.

Afr 9850.3F   Development policies and plans, 1965-1969. (Malawi. Ministry of Natural Resources.) Zomba, 1965?

Afr Doc 1805.5   Development progress report. (Gold Coast (Colony).) Accra. 1951-1953

Afr 6392.33   Development prospects in East-Africa: Kenya, Tanzania and Uganda. (Cherniavsky, Mark.) Bergen, 1965.

Afr 6277.91   Development prospects of Nigeria, a draft report. (Fiskvik, Kjell.) Bergen, 1965.

Afr 5387.12   Le développement à la base au Dahomey et au Sénégal. (Serreau, Jean.) Paris, 1966.

Afr 5000.15   Développement africain. Alger. 1,1958+ 2v.

Afr 5322.10.5   Le développement communautaire, une stratégie d'édification de la nation. (Decker, Henry de.) Paris, 1968.

Afr 5343.14   Le Développement du capitalisme en Côte d'Ivoire. (Amin, Samir.) Paris, 1967.

Afr 5319.5   Le développement économique de la république de Guinée. (Toure, Ismael. Parti Dée de Guinée, R.D.A.) n.p., 1966.

Afr 3986.962.10   Le développement économique de l'Egypte. (Messayer, Mohamed Zaki.) Lausanne, 1962.

Afr 5282.3   Développement économique en Haute-Volta. (Société d'Etudes pour le Développement Economique et Social, Paris.) Paris, 1963. 2v.

Afr 6739.265   Développement industriel au Cameroun. (Société d'Etudes pour le Développement Economique et social.) Paris, 1965.

Afr 1723.20   Deverdun, G. Marrakech, des origines à 1912. Rabat, 1959. 2v.

Afr 2209.12   Devereux, R. Aspects of Algeria historical. London, 1912.

Afr 8658.99   Devereux, Roy. Side lights on South Africa. London, 1899.

Afr 698.69   Devereux, William Cope. A cruise in the "Gorgon". Reprint of 1869. 1 ed. London, 1968.

Afr 698.83   Devic, L. Marcel. Le pays des Zendjs. Paris, 1883.

Afr 200.6   Deville, V. Partage de l'Afrique. Paris, 1898.

Afr 9086.202   De Villiers, John. The Transvaal. London, 1896.

Afr 5406.259   Devils in waiting. (Motley, Mary.) London, 1959.

Afr 12686.17.100   Le devoir de violence, roman. (Owologuem Yambo.) Paris, 1968.

Afr 1973.1   Devoisins, V. Expéditions de Constantine. Paris, 1840.

Afr 1973.1.5   Devoisins, V. Recueil de documents sur l'expédition et la prise de Constantine. Text and atlas. Paris, 1838. 2v.

Afr 3069.26   Devonshire, H.C. L'Egypte musulmane et les fondateurs de ses monuments. Paris, 1926.

Afr 4115.20.7   Devonshire, H.C. Rambles in Cairo. 3d ed. Cairo, 1947.

Afr 4115.26   Devonshire, Henrietta Caroline. Some Cairo mosques. London, 1921.

Afr 1915.2   Devoulx, A. Les archives du consulat général de France. Alger, 1865.

Afr 7820.6   Devroey, E. Le Bas-Congo, artère vitale de notre colonie. Bruxelles, 1938.

Afr 1769.5   Dewazan, Emily. My life story. London, 1911.

Afr 8320.8   Dewet, C.R. De strijd tusschen boer en brit. Amsterdam, 1902.

Afr 8289.02.12A   Dewet, C.R. Three years war. N.Y., 1902.

Afr 7808.86.2F   Dewinton, F.W. The Congo Free State. London, 1886.

X Cg   Afr 590.5   Dhow chasing in Zanzibar waters. (Sulivan, G.L.) London, 1873. (changed to XP 9127)

Afr 12674.1.100   Dia, Amadou Cissé. Les derniers jours de Lat Dior. Paris, 1965.

Afr 626.37   Dia, Mamadou. The African nations and world solidarity. N.Y., 1961.

Afr 626.36   Dia, Mamadou. L'économie africaine. 1. éd. Paris, 1957.

Afr 109.60.15   Dia, Mamadou. Nations africaines et solidarité mondiale. Paris, 1960.

Afr 109.60.15.2   Dia, Mamadou. Nations africaines et solidarité mondiale. Paris, 1963.

Afr 626.35   Dia, Mamadou. Reflexions sur l'économie de l'Afrique noire. Paris, 1954.

Afr 626.35.5   Dia, Mamadou. Reflexions sur l'économie de l'Afrique noire. Paris, 1957.

Afr 50.8   Diagné, Patné. Pouvoir politique traditionnel en Afrique occidentale. Paris, 1967.

Afr 12624.41.1100   Diakhaté, Lamine. Primordiale du sixième jour. Paris, 1963.

Afr 12624.41.1110   Diakhaté, Lamine. Temps de mémoire. Paris, 1967.

Afr 7945.3   La dialectique des Barundi. (Makarakiza, André.) Bruxelles, 1959.

Afr 12574.5   Diallo, Assane Y. Leyd'am, poémes. Honfleur, 1967.

Afr 210.68.10   Diallo, Demba. L'Afrique en question. Paris, 1968.

Afr 626.54   Un dialogue nouveau. (Morgaut, Marc E.) Paris, 1959.

Afr 6316.5   Diamond, Stanley. The transformation of East Africa. N.Y., 1967.

Afr 1658.9   Diana, M.J. Un prisionero en el riff, memorias del ayudante alvarez. Madrid, 1859.

Afr 1432.1.2F   Diario de la guerra de Africa. (Alarcon, P.A.) Madrid, 1860.

Afr 1432.1   Diario de la guerra de Africa. (Alarcon, P.A.) Madrid, 1880. 3v.

Afr 4719.47   Il diario eritreo. (Martini, Ferdinando.) Firenze, 1947. 4v.

Afr 9073.413   Diary. (Fynn, Henry Francis.) Malcolm, 1950.

Afr 8110.6.5A   Diary. (Tas, A.) London, 1914.

Afr 6198.231   Diary of a colonial officer's wife. (Boyle, Laura.) Oxford, 1968.

Afr 9689.38.4   The diary of a district officer. 4th ed. (Bradley, K.) London, 1966.

Afr 8658.02   Diary of a journey to the Cape of Good Hope and the interior of Africa in 1802 and 1803. (Mist, Augusta Uitenhage de.) Capetown, 1954.

Afr 8659.10   Diary of a soldier of fortune. (Hyatt, S.P.) London, 1910.

Afr 8659.12.10   Diary of a tour in South Africa. (Agate, W.) Paisley, 1912.

Afr 775.5   The diary of a working man in central Africa. (Bellingham, W.) London, n.d.

Afr 3265.2   Diary of an American girl in Cairo, 1882. (Stone, Fanny.) N.Y., 1884.

Afr 9689.38   The diary of district officer. (Bradley, K.) London, 1943

Afr 3310.92   Diary of the Revolution, 1952-1965. (United Arab Republic.) Cairo, 1965.

Afr 3315.81   Diary of the Sinai campaign. (Dayan, Moshe.) London, 1966.

Afr 8292.48   Diary of the 9th Lancers. (Colvin, F.F.) So. Kensington, 1904.

Afr 6390.43   Diary of two safaris. (Pulitzer, Ralph.) N.Y., 1927.

Afr 150.55   Dias, A. Infante de Sagres. Porto, 1960.

Afr 7188.5   Dias, Gastão Sousa. Julgareis qual e mas excelente. Lisboa, 1948[1949].

Afr 7175.6.2   Dias de Carvalho, H.A. Descripção da viagem a Mussumba do Muatianvua. v.1-4. Lisboa, 1890.

Afr 7175.6.3   Dias de Carvalho, H.A. Ethnographia e historia tradicional dos povos da Lunda. Lisboa, 1890.

Afr 590.10   Dias de Carvalho, H.A. L'influence de la civilisation latine et surtout portugais en Afrique. Lisbonne, 1889.

Afr 7175.6.4   Dias de Carvalho, H.A. Meteorologia, climalogia e colonisação. Lisboa, 1892.

Afr 7183.35   Dias de Carvalho, Henrique Augusto. Memoria: A. Lunda; ou, Os estados do Muatiânvua. Lisboa, 1890.

Afr 7068.11   Dias de Carvalho. Guiné. Lisboa, 1944.

Afr 7065.5   Dias Dinis, A.J. O quinto centenario do descobrimento da Guiné portuguesa a luz da critica historica. Braga, 1946.

Afr 150.72   Dias Dinis, Antonio J. Estudos henriquinos. Coimbra, 1960.

Afr 5920.14   Diaz de Villegas, José. Africa septentrional: Marruecos, el nexo del Estrecho. Madrid, 1961.

Afr 150.2.35   Diaz de Villegas, José. La epopeya de Enrique el Navegante. Madrid, 1961.

Afr 1450.9   Diaz Moreu, E. Problema de actualidad: la cuestion de Marruecos. Madrid, 1909.

Afr 6879.65   Dibble, James Birney. In this land of Eve. N.Y., 1965.

X Cg   Afr 3243.3   Dicey, E. England and Egypt. London, 1881.

Afr 4389.12   Dichiarazioni...all'eccedio del viaggiatore Gustavo Bianchi. (Maneini, P.S.) Roma, 1885.

Afr 4388.12   Dichiarazioni...intorno all'eccidio di G. Bianchi. (Mancini, P.S.) Roma, 1885.

Afr 6887.11.15   Dichten und Denken der Dschagganeger. (Gutmann, B.) Leipzig, 1909.

Afr 7103.25   Dicionário corográfico comercial de Angola Atonito. 2. ed. (Granado, António Coxito.) Luanda, 1948.

Afr 8685.15   Dickie-Clark, H.F. The marginal situation. London, 1966.

Htn   Afr 6390.7*   Dickinson, F.A. Lake Victoria to Khartoum with rifle and camera. London, 1910.

Afr 6193.62   Dickson, Kwamina. A historical geography of Ghana. Cambridge, 1969.

Afr 6275.33   Dickson, Mora. New Nigerians. London, 1960.

Afr 8289.01.14   Dickson, W.K.L. The biograph in battle. London, 1901.

Afr 1573.26   La dictadura en Marruecos. (Hernandez Mir, Francisco.) Madrid, 1930.

Afr 7549.50.5   Le dictionnaire colonial (Encyclopédie). (Bevel, M.L.) Bruxelles, 1950-51. 2v.

Afr 5849.82   Dictionnaire de biographie mauricienne. Dictionary of Mauritian biography. v.1-30- (Société de l'Histoire de l'Ile Maurice.) Saint Louis, 1941- 5v.

Afr 30.4   Dictionnaire des civilisations africaines. (Balandier, Georges.) Paris, 1968.

Afr 3991.5   Dictionnaire des villes, villages, hameaux. (Egypt. Direction Générale de la Statistique de l'Egypte.) Caire, 1881.

Afr 3991.2   Dictionnaire géographique de l'Egypte. (Boinet, Bey, A.) Le Caire, 1899.

Afr 5549.67   Dictionnaire historique et geographique de Madagascar. (Rajemisa-Raolison, Regis.) Fianarantsoa, 1966.

Afr 630.60.5   Diderot, Toussaint. A la recherche de la personnalité négro-africaine. Monte-Carlo, 1960.

Afr 1608.44.3   Didier, C. Promenade au Maroc. Paris, 1844.

Afr 8685.65   Het die afrikaanse volk n toekoms. 3. druk. (Schaltz, Gert D.) Johannesburg, 1954.

Afr 7175.3   Die Loango. Expedition 1873-76. (Guessfeldt, P.) London, 1879. 2v.

Afr 4700.34   Dieci anni di fascismo nelle colonie italiane. (Giaccardi, A.) Verona, 1934.

Afr 6277.124   Diejomaoh, Victor Peter. Economic development in Nigeria; its problems, challenges and prospects. Princeton, N.j., 1965.

Afr 4513.39.25   Diel, Louise. Behold our new empire, Mussolini. London, 1939.

Afr 5314.3   Les Dieppois en Guinée en 1364. (Hardy, Jules.) Dieppe, 1864.

Afr 1608.94.10   Diercks, G. Marokko...Kenntnis und Beurteilung des Scherifreiches. Berlin, 1894.

Afr 1550.10   Diercks, Gustav. Die Marokkofrage und die Konferenz von Algeciras. Berlin, 1906.

Afr 20059.5   Dieterlen, Germaine. Textes sacrés d'Afrique noire. Paris, 1965.

Afr 8931.53.5   Dieterlen, H. Adolphe Mabile. Paris, 1930.

Afr 2875.41   Dietrich, Richard. Die Tripolis-Krise, 1911-12, und die erneuerung des Dreibundes 1912. Würzburg, 193-

Afr 5406.181   Dietz, Emile. Un explorateur africain, Auguste Stahl. Paris, 1884.

Afr 8089.35   Dietzel, K.H. Die Südafrikanische Union...Abhandlung. Berlin, 1938.

Afr 1713.8   Dieulefils, P. Maroc occidental. Paris, 1916.

Afr 545.52   Les dieux d'Afrique noire. (Holas, Bohumil.) Paris, 1968.

Afr 2030.460.15   Les dieux meurent en Algérie. (Larteguy, J.) Paris, 1960.

Afr 1955.8   Dieuzaide, V.A. Histoire de l'Algérie, 1830-1878. v.1-2. Oran, 1880-83.

Afr 1609.06.6   Diez De Tejada, V. Cosas de los moros. Barcelona, 1906.

Afr 2514.5   Les différends de 1832-1833 entre la régence de Tunis et les royaumes de Sardaigne et des Deus-Siciles. (Grandchamp, P.) Tunis, 1931.

Afr 5183.968   La diffusion du progrès technique en milieu rural sénégalais. (Brochier, Jacques.) Paris, 1968.

Afr Doc 2309.503   Digest of education statistics. (Nigeria. Federal Ministry of Education.) Lagos. 1959

Afr Doc 2307.7   Digest of statistics. (Nigeria. Federal Office of Statistics.) 11,1962+

Afr 5477.505   Diguimbaye, Georges. L'essor du Tchad. Paris, 1969.

Afr 6218.10A   Dike, K.O. Trade and politics in the Niger Delta. Oxford, 1956.

Afr 6218.10.1   Dike, K.O. Trade and politics in the Niger Delta. Oxford, 1966.

Afr 6282.5   Dike, Kenneth. Origins of the Niger mission. Nigeria, 1957.

Afr 10621.41.100A   The dilemma of a ghost. (Aidoo, C.A.A.) Accra, 1965.

Afr 212.2   The dilemmas of African independence. (Cowan, Laing Gray.) N.Y., 1964.

Afr 6410.6   Dilley, Marjorie Ruth. British policy in Kenya colony. N.Y., 1937.

Afr 6410.6.2   Dilley, Marjorie Ruth. British policy in Kenya colony. 2. ed. London, 1966.

Afr 4285.3   Dillmann, A. Über die Anfänge des axumitischen Reiches. Berlin, 1879.

Afr 5058.5   Dim Delobsom, A.A. L'empire du Mogho-Naba. Paris, 1932.

Afr 6395.25   Dimensions of East African cultures. (Good, Charles M.) East Lansing, 1966.

Afr 6926.24   Dincklage-Campe, F. Deutsche reiber in Südwest. Berlin, 1908.

Afr 8155.11.2   Dingane, King of the Zulu, 1828-1840. (Becker, Peter.) N.Y., 1965.

Afr 10678.61.110   Dinner for promotion; a comedy in three acts. (Henshaw, James Ene.) London, 1967.

Afr 8985.6   Dinuzuln: the death of the House of Shaka. (Binns, C.T.) London, 1968.

Afr 7122.90   Diogo, Alfredo. O Brasil na restauração de Angola. Luanda, 1965.

Afr 5185.8   Les Diola. (Thomas, L.V.) Macon, 1959. 2v.

Afr 2030.180   Dion, Michel. Armée d'Algérie et la pacification. Paris, 1959.

Afr 5185.12   Diop, Abdoulaye. Société toucouleur et migration. Dakar, 1965.

Afr 12624.41.25   Diop, Birago. Contes choisis. Cambridge, Eng. 1967.

Afr 12624.41.35   Diop, Birago. Les contes d'Amadou-Koumba. Paris, 1960.

Afr 12624.4.100   Diop, Birago. Contes et lavanes. Paris, 1963.

Afr 12624.41.20   Diop, Birago. Leurres et vains, poèmes. Photoreproduction. Paris, 1960.

Afr 12624.41.30   Diop, Birago. Les nouveaux contes d'Amadou Koumba. Paris, 1962.

Afr 12624.41.33   Diop, Birago. Les nouveaux contes d'Amadou Koumba. 3. ed. Paris, 1967.

Afr 109.60.3   Diop, Cheikh A. L'Afrique noire pré-coloniale. Paris, 1960.

Afr 628.267   Diop, Cheikh A. Antériorité des civilisations nègres. Paris, 1967.

Afr 109.59.25   Diop, Cheikh A. Etude comparée des systèmes politiques et sociaux de l'Europe et de l'Afrique, l'antiquité à la formation des états modernes. Paris 1959.

Afr 109.60   Diop, Cheikh A. L'unité culturelle de l'Afrique. Paris, 1959.

Afr 45.60.5   Diop, Cheikh Anta. Les fondements culturels, techniques et industriels d'un futur état fédéral d'Afrique noire. Paris, 1960.

Afr 628.265   Diop, Cheikh Anta. Nations nègres et culture. 2. éd. Paris, 1955.

Afr 210.58.10   Diop, Majhemout. Contribution à l'étude des problèmes politiques en Afrique noire. Paris, 1958.

Afr 6203.10   Dipeolu, J.O. Bibliographical sources for Nigerian studies. Evanston, Ill., 1966.

Afr Doc 3603.15   Diplomatic and consular. (Malawi. Ministry of External Affairs.) Zomba. 1965

Afr Doc 1703.10   Diplomatic and consular list, and list of Sierra Leone Commonwealth and Foreign Service postings. (Sierra Leone. Department of External Affairs.) Freetown. 1967+

Afr Doc 1603.11   Diplomatic and consular list and office directory. (Gambia. Bathurst. 1966+

Afr 6164.15   Diplomatic Bulletin. Ghana. London, 1957.

Afr Doc 7103.7   Diplomatic list, Fort Lamy. Chad. (United States. Embassy. Chad.) Fort Lamy? 1966.

Afr 6200.4   Diplomatic press directory of the Federation of Nigeria. London. 1960+ 2v.

Afr 6150.18   Diplomatic press directory of the Republic of Ghana, including trade index and biographical section. London. 1959+ 3v.

Afr 3671.5   Diplomatic press directory of the Republic of the Sudan, including trade index and biographical section. London. 1957+ 6v.

Afr 1585.3F   Diplomatische Aktenstücken über die Internationale Konferenz von Algeciras, 1905-06. (Austro-Hungarian Monarchy. Ministerium der Aüssern.) Wien, 1906.

Afr 1494.55F   Diplomatist. In memoriam, His Majesty King Mohammed V. London, 1961.

Afr 10674.71.110   Dipoko, Mbella Sonne. Because of women. London, 1969.

Afr 10674.71.100   Dipoko, Mbella Sonne. A few nights and days. London, 1966.

Afr 5240.14   Direction des affaires économiques et financières. 2. éd. (France. Ministère de la Coopération.) Paris, 1965.

Afr 11517.76.120   The directions of memory. (Lerner, Laurence.) London, 1963.

Afr 9435.5.5   Director's report and accounts. (British South Africa Company.) London. 1896+

Afr 6193.58F   Directory of distributive establishments. (Ghana. Central Bureau of Statistics.) Accra, 1968.

Afr 6150.32.30F   Directory of industrial enterprises and establishments. (Ghana. Central Bureau of Statistics.) Accra. 1963+

Afr 6287.2   Directory of industrial establishments in Western Nigeria. (Nigeria, Western. Ministry of Economic Planning and Social Development. Statistics Division.) Ibadan, 1966.

Afr 4750.10   Directory of Somalia. London. 1,1968+

Afr Doc 3203.10F   Directory of the govenment. (Kenya.) Nairobi. 1965+

Afr 3329.18   Directory of United Arab Republic personages. Cairo. 1966+

Afr 7010.6   Direitos de padroado de Portugal em Africa; memoranda. (Portugal. Ministério da Marinha e Ultramar.) Lisboa, 1883.

Afr 4760.12   Diritto costituzionale somalo. (Angeloni, Renato.) Milano, 1964.

Afr 4700.38.10   Diritto di Roma nelle terre africane. (Jaeger, N.) Padova, 1938.

Afr 6295.60   Dirrioboola-Gha. (Pedraza, Howard.) London, 1960.

Afr 8678.380   Disabilities of the non-white peoples in the Union of South Africa. (India. Ministry of External Affairs.) Delhi, 1953.

Afr 9161.23   The disappearing Bushmen of Lake Clirissie. (Potgieter, E.F.) Pretoria, 1955.

Afr 4384.2   Discorso sul credito di 20 milioni per l'azione militare in Africa. (Chiala, L.) Roma, 1887.

Afr 2030.464.45   Discours, année 1963. (Ben Bella, Ahmed.) Alger, 1964.

Afr 5417.2   Discours, messages. (Mba, Léon.) Libreville, 1965.

Afr Doc 7724.5   Discours. (Congo. Gouverneur Général.) 1949-1959 4v.

Afr 5340.25   Discours à l'assemblée nationale. (Houphouet-Boigny, Felix.) Abidjan, 1962.

Afr 1571.17.22   Discours de réception. 2e ed. (Franchet Desperey, L.F.M.F.) Paris, 1935.

Afr 2030.449   Discours sur les conditions de la renaissance algérienne. (Bennabi, Malek.) Alger, 1949.

Afr 7350.5.12   A discourse before the Young Men's Colonization Society of Pennsylvania. (Tyson, J.R.) Philadelphia, 1834.

Afr 150.3.2   The discoveries of Prince Henry. (Major, R.H.) London, 1877.

Afr 4313.5F   The discovery of Abyssinia by the Portuguese in 1520. (Sequeira, D.L.) London, 1938.

Afr 6455.12   Discovery of Lakes Rudolf and Stefanie. (Hoehnel, Ludwig.) London, 1894. 2v.

Afr 6455.12.5   Discovery of Lakes Rudolf and Stefanie. 1st English ed. (Hoehnel, Ludwig.) London, 1968. 2v.

Afr 1724.1   Discurso da jornada de D. Goncalo Coutinho. (Coutinho, Goncalo.) Lisboa, 1629.

Afr 1724.1.2   Discurso da jornada de D. Goncalo Coutinho. (Another issue . (Coutinho, Goncalo.) Lisboa, 1629.

Htn   Afr 2489.2*   Discurso della Goletta. (Floriani, Pompeo.) Macerata, 1574.

Afr 7122.61   Discursos do governador geral de Angola, capitão de mar e guerra Vasco Lopes Alves, 1943-1946. (Angola. Governo Geral, 1943-1947 (Alves).) Luanda, 1946.

Afr 6300.58F   Discussion paper. (Nairobi. University College. Institute for Development Studies.) Nairobi. 1,1964+

Afr 3325.10   Disillusion by the Nile: what Nasser has done to Egypt. (Powell, Ivor.) London, 1967.

Afr 8678.220   Dison, L.R. Group areas and their development. Durban, 1960.

Afr 2030.300   Les disparus. (Verges, Jacques.) Lausanne, 1959.

Afr 5056.122   Dispositions cartographiques relatives aux cartes et plans de l'A.O.F. (French West Africa.) Laval, 1922.

Afr 810.20   A dissertation on the course and probable termination of the Niger. (Donkin, Rufane.) London, 1829.

Afr 628.246   Distinguished Negroes abroad. (Fleming, Beatrice (Jackson.)) Washington, 1946.

Afr Doc 4107.366.6   Distribution and density maps. Mbabane, 1968.

Afr 6291.10   Distribution of amenities [in Eastern Nigeria] data and statistics. (Nigeria, Eastern.) Enugu, 1963.

Afr 6392.36.5   The distribution of gains in a common market. (Massell, B.F.) Santa Monica, Calif., 1964.

Afr 8835.50   District Six. (Manuel, George.) Cape Town, 1967.

Afr 7324.6F   O districto de Lourenço Marques e a Africa do sul. (Noronha, J.de.) Lisboa, 1895.

Afr 7330.10   Distrito de Tete. (Sousa e Silva, Pedro.) Lisboa, 1927.

Afr 43393.2   Ditirafaló tsa merafe ya BaTswana ba lefatshe la Tshireletsó. (Schapera, I.) Tswana, 1954.

Afr 2208.59   Ditson, G.L. The crescent and French crusaders. N.Y., 1859.

Afr 2208.59.2   Ditson, G.L. The crescent and French crusaders. N.Y., 1860.

Afr 3978.58   Ditson, G.L. The Para papers on France, Egypt and Ethiopia. Paris, 1858.

Afr 6280.28F   Dittel, Paul. Die Besiedlung Sudnigeriens von den Anfangen bis zur britischen Kolonisation. Inaug. Diss. Leipzig, 1936.

Afr 1840.19   Les diverses politiques coloniales. Thèse. (Riols De Fonclare, F. de.) Toulouse, 1919.

Afr 11327.90.2100A   Divine, Arthur D. Wine of good hope. N.Y., 1939.

Afr 11327.90.100   Divine, David. The golden fool. 1st ed. London, 1954.

Afr 545.15   Divine kings and the breath of men. (Wilson, M.H.) Cambridge, Eng., 1959.

Afr 6194.20.16   The divine kingship in Ghana. (Meyerowitz, Eva.) London, 1960.

Afr 42731.2.700   La divine pastorale. (Kagame, A.) Bruxelles, 1952.

Afr 3817.10   Divinity and experience, the religion of the Dinka. (Lienharot, Godfrey.) Oxford, 1961.

Afr 5345.20   La division du temps et le calendrier rituel des peuples lagunaires de Côte-d'Ivoire. (Niangoran-Bauah, Georges.) Paris, 1964.

Afr 1487.25   Divulgacion y orientacion. (Maestre, Pedro.) Granada, 1923.

Afr 210.32   Dix, Arthur. Weltkrise und Kolonialpolitik. Berlin, 1932.

Afr 5342.6   Dix ans à la Côte-d'Ivoire. (Clozel, F.J.) Paris, 1906.

Afr 1623.957   Dix ans d'économie marocaine, 1945-1955. (France. Institut National de la Statistique et des Études Économiques.) Paris, 1957.

Afr 1957.5   Dix-huit mois à Alger. (Berthezene.) Montpellier, 1834.

Afr 8289.01.9   Dix mois de campagne chez les Boers. (Villebois Mareuil.) Paris, 1901.

Afr 8658.82.4   Dixie, Florence. In the land of misfortune. London, 1882.

Afr 8160.3   Dixie, Florence Douglas. A defence of Zululand and its king. London, 188-

Afr 2397.3   Djamila Boupacha. (Beauvoir, Simone de.) Paris, 1962.

Afr 2397.3.2   Djamila Boupacha. 1st American ed. (Beauvoir, Simone de.) N.Y., 1962.

Afr 1660.1   Les djebala du Maroc. (Doutte, E.) Oran, 1899.

Afr 2310.3   Le djebel amour. (Despois, Jean.) Paris, 1957.

Afr 2949.7   Le djebel Nefousa (Tripolitaine). (Despois, Jean.) Paris, 1935.

Afr 2949.7.3   Le djebel Nefousa (Tripolitaine). Thèse. (Despois, Jean.) Paris, 1935.

Afr 1635.10   Les djemaas judiciaires berberes. Thèse. (Ribaut, A.J.) Alger, 1930.

Afr 4892.15   Djibonti, son port, son arrière-pays. Paris, 1965.

Afr 4819.68   Djibonti and the Horn of Africa. (Thompson, Virginia M.) Stanford, Calif., 1968.

Afr 4892.5   Djibout, Mer Rouge, Abyssinie. (Angoulvant, G.) Paris, 1902.

Afr 4892.8   Djibouti, au seuil de l'Orient. (Hachette, R.) Paris, 1931.

Afr 4892.12   Djibouti et la côte française des Somalis. (Poinsot, Jean Paul.) Paris, 1964.

Afr 4892.9   Djibuti. (Francolini, B.) Rome, 1939.

Afr 10624.42.100   Djoleto, Amu. The strange man. London, 1967.

Afr 3986.903.10   Dlin, Nikolai A. Ob'edinennaia Arabskaia Respublika. Moscow, 1963.

Afr 7320.6   Do Nyassa a Pemba. (Azevedo Coutinho, João de.) Lisboa, 1931.

Afr 1635.30   Dobo, Nicolas. J'étais le médecin de cent mille Berbères. Paris, 1964.

Afr 2223.60   Dobrenn, Rene. L'apport économique de l'Algérie pendant la guerre. Thèse. Oran, 1925.

Afr 4785.961   Dobrogo utra, Afrika. (Prozhogin, N.P.) Moscow, 1961.

Afr 626.155   Dobrska, Zofia. Problemy gospodarcze Afryki. Wyd.1. Warszawa, 1964.

Afr 7835.8   Doctor among Congo rebels. (Roseveare, Helen.) London, 1966.

Afr 9558.15   Doctor David Livingstone. (Appleyard, M.E.) Cape Town, 1949.

Afr 6879.64   Doctor in the land of the lion. 1st ed. (Imperpato, Pascal James.) N.Y., 1964.

Afr 6988.16.385   A doctor's diary in Damaraland. (Walker, H.F.B.) London, 1917.

Afr 5312.18   The doctrine and methods of the Democratic Party of Guinea. v.1-2. (Toré, Sékou.) Conakry, 196-.

Afr 1915.11   La doctrine de l'Association des indigènes et des Français en Algérie. Thèse. (Hutin, Paul.) Paris, 1933.

Afr 718.18.50F   Document notte. (Belgium. Ministére des Affaires Africaines.) Bruxelles, 1960.

Afr 1724.7   Un document portugais sur la place de Mazagrn au début du XVIIe siècle. Thèse. (Ricard, Robert.) Paris, 1932.

Afr 500.70F   Documentation des travaux de la première conférence. (Conférence des Institutions Européennes, Rome, 1958.) Rome, 1959.

Afr 28.114F   Documentation list, Africa. (Delhi. University. Library.) Delhi. 5,1966+

Afr 4.12   Documentation pédagogique africaine. Paris. 3v.

Afr 755.2   Documentation scientifique de la mission Tilho. (France. Ministère des Colonies.) Paris, 1910. 4v.

Afr 2430.5F   La documentation tunisienne. (Tunisia. Secrétariat d'Etat à l'Information.) 1957+

Afr 1325.5F   Documenti diplomatici. Successione sceriffiana (Marrocco). (Italy. Ministero degli Affari Esteri.) Roma, 1895.

Afr 4515.5F   Documenti diplomatici presentati al parliamento italiano. (Italy. Ministero degli Affari Esteri.) Roma, 1890.

Afr 7565.10F   Documenti diplomatici presentati al senato. (Italy. Ministero degli Affari Esteri.) Roma, 1885.

Afr 3269.10   Documenti diplomatici relativi alle indennità per danni sofferti. (Italy. Ministero degli Affari Esteriore.) Roma, 1883.

Afr 2458.38   Documenti sulla storia di Tunis. (Niculy, G.) Livorno, 1838.

Afr 1575.2F   Documentos das chancelarias reais anteriores a 1531. v.1-2. (Azevedo, Pedro de.) Lisboa, 1915. 2v.

Afr 520.2F   Documentos diplomaticos. (Spain. Ministerio de Estado.) Madrid, 1888.

Afr 1575.2.10F   Documentos do corpo chronologico relativo a Marrocos, 1488 a 1514. (Baiao, Antonio.) Coimbra, 1925.

Afr 1750.15   Documentos portugueses sobre la accion de Espana in Africa. (Silveira, L.) Madrid, 1954.

Afr 1445.6F   Documentos presentados a las Cortes. (Spain. Ministerio de Estado.) Madrid, 1889.

Afr 1442.10F   Documentos presentados a las Cortes. (Spain. Ministerio de Estado.) Madrid, 1894.

Afr 1550.22.5F   Documentos presentados a las Cortes. (Spain. Ministerio de Estado.) Madrid, 1906.

Afr 1325.10F   Documentos presentados a las Cortes en la legislatura. (Spain. Ministerio de Estado.) Madrid, 1911.

Afr 1750.3F   Documentos presentados a las cortes en la legislatura de 1891 por el Ministro de Estado. (Spain. Ministerio de Estado.) Madrid, 1891. 3v.

Afr 590.23F   Documentos relativos ao apresamento. (Portugal. Ministerio dos Negocios Estrangeiros.) Lisboa, 1858.

Afr 7332.10   Documentos relativos aos acontecimentos de manica. Lisboa, 1891.

Afr 7208.2   Documentos sobre os portugueses em Mozambique en na Africa central, 1497-1840. v.1- Lisboa, 1962-   X Cg 5v.

Afr 7543.5   Documents, 1950-1960. (Centre de Recherche et d'Information Socio-Politiques.) Bruxelles, 1962.

Afr 2030.461.90   Documents. (Algerian Front of National Liberation.) N.Y. 1961-62

Afr 6650.5   Documents. (Centre d'Études et de Recherches de Kara.) Lama-Kara, Togo. 1,1967+

Afr Doc 1826.5F   Documents. (Gold Coast (Colony).) Accra. 1926-1930 4v.

Afr 2209.58.5   Documents algériens. (France. Délégation Générale en Algérie.) Paris, 1958.

Afr 5853.2   Documents concernant les îles de Bourbon et de France. (Réunion. Archives Departementales.) Nerac, 1953.

Afr 1335.7   Documents d'histoire et de géographie marocaines. Paris. 1,1929+ 4v.

Afr 3269.05F   Documents diplomatiques. (France. Ministère des Affaires Etrangères.) Paris, 1881.

Afr 3269.4F   Documents diplomatiques. (France. Ministère des Affaires Etrangères.) Paris, 1881. 4 pam.

Afr 3269.08F   Documents diplomatiques. (France. Ministère des Affaires Etrangères.) Paris, 1883.

Afr 5620.2F   Documents diplomatiques. (France. Ministère des Affaires Etrangères.) Paris, 1883. 4 pam.

Afr 5402.10F   Documents diplomatiques. (France. Ministère des Affaires Etrangères.) Paris, 1885.

Afr 3269.3F   Documents diplomatiques. (France. Ministère des Affaires Etrangères.) Paris, 1885. 5 pam.

Afr 33.10F   Documents diplomatiques. (France. Ministère des Affaires Etrangères.) Paris, 1890. 16 pam.

Afr 3269.2F   Documents diplomatiques. (France. Ministère des Affaires Etrangères.) Paris, 1893.

Afr 5620.3F   Documents diplomatiques. (France. Ministère des Affaires Etrangères.) Paris, 1895.

Afr 2530.5F   Documents diplomatiques. (France. Ministère des Affaires Etrangères.) Paris, 1897.

Afr 200.4.3F   Documents diplomatiques. (France. Ministère des Affaires Etrangères.) Paris, 1898.

Afr 2430.1F   Documents diplomatiques. Affaires de Tunisie, 1870-81, et supplément. (France. Ministère des Affaires Etrangéres.) Paris, 1881. 2v.

Afr 3994.880.5F   Documents diplomatiques. Affaires d'Egypte. (France. Ministère des Affaires Etrangères.) Paris, 1880.

Afr 1570.10F   Documents diplomatiques. Affaires du Maroc. v.1-6. (France. Ministère des Affaires Etrangères.) Paris, 1904. 6v.

Afr 1445.5F   Documents diplomatiques. Conférences de Madrid. Supplément. (Spain. Ministerio de Estado.) Madrid, 1880. 2 pam.

Afr 1550.14   Documents diplomatiques pour servir à l'étude de la question marocaine. (Rouard de Card, E.) n.p., 1911.

Afr 2676.2   Documents ethnographiques et linguistiques sur les îles Gerkena. (Louis, André.) Alger, 1962.

Afr 2748.98.5   Documents géographiques sur l'Afrique septentrional. (Basset, R.) Paris, 1898.

Afr 1100.5   Documents inédits sur l'histoire de l'occupation espagnole en Afrique. (Laprimandaie, F.E.) Alger, 1875.

Afr 109.64.10   Documents on modern Africa. (Wallbank, T.W.) Princeton, N.J., 1964.

Afr 3315.25   Documents on the Suez crisis. (Watt, Donald C.) London, 1957.

Afr 2700.10   Documents pour servir à la connaissance du Sahara. (Algiers. Université. Institut de Recherches Sahariennes.) 1,1961+

Afr 1258.94.5   Documents pour servir à l'étude du nord-ouest Africain. v.1-4 and atlas. (Lamartiniere, Maximilien Poisson de.) Alger, 1894-1897. 5v.

Afr 5432.5   Documents pour servir à l'histoire de l'Afrique équatoriale française. Série 2. Brazza et la fondation du Congo français. Paris. 1,1966+

Afr 2702.2F   Documents rel. à miss. par Flatters. (France. Ministère des Travaux Publiques.) Paris, 1884.

Afr 2448.5   Documents relatifs aux corsaires tunisiens (2 octobre 1777-4 mai 1824). (Grandchamp, P.) Tunis, 1925.

Afr 8278.98.3   Documents relating to judicial crisis in Transvaal. (Kotze, J.G.) London, 1898.

Afr 4513.36   Documents relating to the Italo-Ethiopian conflict. (Canada. Department of External Affairs.) Ottawa, 1936.

Afr 2749.02.2F   Documents scientifiques de la mission saharienne. (Foureau, F.) Paris, 1903.

Afr 5605.5   Documents sur la compagnie de Madagascar. (Desbassayns de Richemont, P.) Paris, 1867.

Afr 1340.42   Documents sur la constitution. (Morocco. Ministère de l'Information et du Tourisme.) Rabat, 1962.

Afr 590.3   Documents sur la fond de l'oeuvre antiésclavagiste. (Lavigerie, Charles Martial Allemand.) Saint-Cloud, 1889.

Afr 5130.5   Documents sur les établissements français. (Machat, J.) Paris, 1906.

Afr 5538.10   Documents sur l'histoire, la géographie...de la partie occidentale de Madagascar. (Guillain, C.) Paris, 1845.

Afr 698.56   Documents sur l'histoire, la géographie et le commerce de l'Afrique orientale. (Guillain, Charles.) Paris, 1856. 4v.

Afr 698.56PF   Documents sur l'histoire, la géographie et le commerce de l'Afrique orientale. Atlas. (Guillain, Charles.) Paris, 1856. 4v.

Afr 7803.30   Documents sur une mission française au Kakongo 1766-1776. (Cuvelier, J.) Bruxelles, 1953.

Afr 11058.2   Dodd, A.D. Anthology of short stories. Cape Town, 1958.

Afr 8045.42   Dodd, Anthony D. South African citizenship. Cape Town, 1958.

Afr 50.47   Dodge, Dorothy Rae. African politics in perspective. Princeton, N.J., 1966.

Afr 550.148   Dodge, Ralph Edward. The unpopular missionary. Westwood, N.J., 1964.

Afr 825.10   Dodging hippopotami and crocodiles in Africa. (Sinclair, J.H.) Rochester, 193- .

Afr 6878.77   Dodgshun, Arthur W. From Zanzibar to Ujiji. Boston, 1969.

Afr 3205.13   Dodwell, Henry. The founder of modern Egypt. Cambridge, Eng., 1931.

Afr 550.105   Doell, E.W. A mission doctor sees the wind of change. London, 1960.

Afr 5318.18.2   Doelter, C. Uber die Capverden nach dem Rio Grande. Leipzig, 1888.

Afr 12928.3.100   Doguicimi. (Hazoumé, Paul.) Paris, 1938.

Afr 635.92   Doherty, Mary A. The role of the African woman, a report. London, 1962.

Afr 6720.62   Doigts noirs. (Kuoh Mukouri, J.) Montreal, 1963.

Afr 8355.10   Doke, Joseph J. An Indian patriot in South Africa. London, 1909.

Afr 16.10   Dokumenty. V.F. (Permanent Organization for Afro-Asian Peoples' Solidarity.) Moskva, 1962. 3v.

Afr 6780.8   Dolbey, R.V. Sketches of the East Africa campaign. London, 1918.

Afr 1618.10   Dolinger, Jane. Behind harem walls. London, 1960.

Afr 5112.10   Doll, Peter. Der senegalesische Weg zum afrikanischen Sozialismus. Hamburg, 1966.

Afr 8658.49   Dolman, Alfred. In the footsteps of Livingstone, being...our travel notes. London, 1924.

Afr 1400.4   Dombay, F. von. Geschichte der Scherifen. Agram, 1801.

Afr 5944.15   Domenech Lafuente, A. Algo sobre Rio de Oro. Madrid, 1946.

Afr 1750.11.6   Domenech Lafuente, A. Apuntes sobre geografia de la zona norte del protectorado de Espana en Marruecos. 3. ed. Madrid, 1942.

Afr 626.66   Domestic income and product in Kenya. (East Africa High Commission.) Nairobi, 1959.

Afr 11517.76.100   Domestic interior. (Lerner, Laurence.) London, 1959.

Afr 1573.12   La dominacion de España en Tanger. (Marenco, S.) Madrid, 1911.

Afr 1905.1   La domination espagñole a Oran. (Ruff, Paul.) Paris, 1900.

Afr 1903.5   La domination espagñole en Algeria. (Froelicher, E.) Paris, 1904.

Afr 1576.5.2   La domination portugaise au Maroc du XV. (Carvalho, V. de.) Lisbonne, 1936.

Afr 1576.5   La domination portugaise au Maroc du XVeme au XVIIIeme siècle. (Carvalho, V. de.) Lisbonne, 1942.

Afr 9161.21.20   The Dominee and the Dom-Pas. (Wall, M.A.) Cape Town, 1961.

Afr 150.19   Domingues, Mario. O Infante Dom Henrique. Lisboa, 1957.

Afr 8110.8   Dominicus, F.C. Het huiselik en maatschappelik leven van de zuid-afrikaner. 's-Gravenhage, 1919.

Afr 8678.332   Dominicus, Foort Cornelius. Apartheid een wijze voorzorg. Utrecht, 1965.

Afr 1609.67   Dominicus, Johannes. Portret van Marokko. s'Hertogenbosch, 1967.

Afr 6738.17   Dominik, Hans. Vom Atlantik zum Tschadsee. Berlin, 1908.

Afr 8252.5.10   The dominion of Afrikanderdom. (Molteno, J.T.) London, 1923.

Afr 2025.19   Dominique, L.C. Gouverneur général de l'Algérie. Alger, 1908.

Afr 7815.44   Domont, Jean Marie. La prise de conscience de l'individu en milieu rural Kongo. Bruxelles, 1957.

Afr 4070.39   Domville Fife, C.W. Savage life in the dark Sudan. London, 1927.

Afr 1753.12   Don Francisco y don dionisio. (Leria, C.) Tetuan, 1953.

Afr 678.86   Donacuige. Aventuras de un piloto en el Golfo de Guinea. Madrid, 1886.

Afr 555.146   Donald Fraser of Livingstonia. (Fraser, A.R.) London, 1934.

Afr 5765.36   Doncaster, Phebe. Faithful unto death;...life...of William and Lucy S. Johnson. London, 1896.

Afr 6979.03   Done, K. Deutsch-Südwest-Afrika. Berlin, 1903.

Afr 6979.03.2   Done, K. Deutsch-Südwest-Afrika. 2e Aufl. Berlin, 1913.

Afr 1830.10.2   Donec, Martial. Un siècle de finances coloniales. Paris, 1930.

Afr 810.20   Donkin, Rufane. A dissertation on the course and probable termination of the Niger. London, 1829.

Afr 4568.17   La donna in Etiopia. (Pollera, A.) Roma, 1922.

Afr 1573.30   Donnadieu, M. Les relations diplomatiques de l'Espagne et du Maroc de janvier 1592 a juillet 1926. Montpellier, 1931.

Afr 5282.10   Données actuelles de l'économie voltaïque. (Upper Volta. Service du Plan.) Paris, 1962.

Afr 5282.8   Données critiques sur la campagne depuits villageois encadrée par la SATEC en Haute-Volta. (Société d'Aide Technique et de Cooperation.) Paris, 1965.

Afr Doc 6607.361   Données de base sur la situation démographique au Dahomey en 1961. (France. Institut National de la Statistiqe et des Etudes Economique. Service de Cooperation.) Paris, 1962.

Afr 5240.7   Données économiques. (Mali. Ministère du Plan et de l'Economie Rurale.) Bamako, 1962.

Afr Doc 7509.300   Données essentielles de l'économie. (Cameroon. Ministère des Finances du Plan et de l'Equipement National.) Yaoundé. 1951+

Afr Doc 5009.505   Données statistiques sur l'enseignment dans les etats africains et malgache d'expression française. (France. Secretariat d'Etat aux affaires étrangeres, Charge de la Cooperation.) Paris. 1965+

Afr 2209.08.2   Donop. Lettres sur l'Algérie, 1907-08. Paris, 1908.

Afr 9446.34   Donovan, Charles Henry Wynne. With Wilson in Matabeleland. London, 1894.

Afr 10016.12   Doob, Leonard William. Ants will not eat your fingers. N.Y., 1966.

Afr 7815.22   Dooent, Jean. Elite noire. Bruxelles, 1957.

Afr 9028.87   Door Natal in het hart van Zuid-Afrika. (Blink, H.) Amsterdam, 1887.

Afr 1957.4   Dopigez. Souvenirs de l'Algérie. Douai, 1840.

Afr 2875.50   Dopo Tripoli. (Tancredi, L.) Lugano, 1913.

Afr 4559.56F   Doresse, Jean. Au pays de la ruine de Saba. Paris, 1956.

Afr 4259.57   Doresse, Jean. L'empire du Prêtre-Jean. v.1-2. Paris, 1957. 2v.

Afr 4559.56.2   Doresse, Jean. Ethiopia. London, 1959.

Afr 4558.97.5   Dorleans, H. Une visite à l'empereur Menelick. Paris, 1913.

Afr 7568.23   Dorman, M.R.P. Journal...tour in the Congo Free State. Brussels, 1905.

Afr 8340.11   Dormer, F.J. Vengeance as a policy in Afrikanderland. London, 1901.

Afr 9400.10.5   Dornan, S.S. Pygmies and bushmen of the Kalahari. London, 1925.

Afr 1753.10.2   Dornellas, Affonso De. Alleo, gloriosa epopeia portuguezaum Ceuta. Lisboa, 1924.

Afr 1753.10.12   Dornellas, Affonso de. As armas de Ceuta. Lisboa, 1925.

Afr 1753.10.8   Dornellas, Affonso de. De Ceuta a alacacer kibir em 1923. Lisboa, 1925.

Afr 1753.10.4   Dornellas, Affonso de. Os jogos floraes de 1923 em Ceuta. Lisboa, 1924.

Afr 1753.10   Dornellas, Affonso De. Santissima virgem d'Africa, padroeira de Ceuta. Lisboa, 1924.

Afr 1753.10.3   Dornellas, Affonso de. O tercio de extranjeros do exercito espanhol. Lisboa, 1924.

Afr 9028.52   The dorp and the veld or Six months in Natal. (Barter, Charles.) London, 1852.

Afr 4335.1   Dos feitos de D. Christovam da Gama. (Castanhoso, M. de.) Lisboa, 1898.

Afr 609.66.10   Dossier culturel pan-africain. (Mueng, Engelbert.) Paris, 1966.

Afr 1095.20   Dossier secret de l'Afrique du Nord. (Fontaine, Pierre.) Paris, 1957.

Afr 2030.461.60   Dossier secret de l'Algérie. (Paillat, Claude.) Paris, 1961. 2v.

Afr 4.7   Dossiers africains. Dakar. 1,1959+ 2v.

Afr 5470.10   Dossiers de la Recherche cooperative sur programme. (France. Centre National de la Recherche Scientifique.) Paris. 2,1968

Afr 609.66.5   Dostent, Pierre Etienne. Africa 1966. Washington, 1966.

Afr 9502.26   Dotson, Floyd. The Indian minority of Zambia, Rhodesia and Malawi. New Haven, 1968.

Afr 4700.35.30   Dotti, Ernesto. Aspetti attuoli dell'economia delle colonie italiane dell'Africa orientale. Roma, 1935.

Afr 2287.5   Le douar. (Brenot, H.E.L.) Alger, 1938.

Afr 2305.1   Le douar Aghbal: monographie économique. Thèse. (Lapalud, P.) Alger, 1934.

Afr 1920.25   Le double bombardement d'Alger par Duquesne. (Misermont, L.) Paris, 1905.

Afr 659.11   Douel, Martial. Au pays de Salammbo. Paris, 1911.

Afr 2030.464.70   Douence, J.C. La mise en place des institutions algériennes. Paris, 1964.

Afr 550.143   Dougall, James Watson Cunningham. Christians in the African revolution. Edinburgh, 1963.

Afr 9854.20   Douglas, Arthur. Arthur Douglas, missionary on Lake Nyasa. Westminster, 1912.

Afr 2609.12.3   Douglas, N. Fountains in the sand...oases of Tunisia. N.Y., n.d.

Afr 724.24   Douglass, Lillie B. Cape Town to Cairo. Caldwell, 1964.

Afr 3193.20   Douin, Georges. L'Angleterre et l'Egypte. Caire, 1929-30. 2v.

Afr 3207.17   Douin, Georges. L'Angleterre et l'Egypte. Paris, 1928.

Afr 3193.25   Douin, Georges. L'Egypte de 1802 à 1804. Caire, 1925.

Afr 3215.3.20   Douin, Georges. L'Egypte de 1828 à 1930. Roma, 1935.

Afr 3230.20A   Douin, Georges. Histoire du règne du khedive Ismail. Roma, 1933-34. 5v.

Afr 3675.70   Douin, Georges. Histoire du Soudan égyptien. Le Caire, 1944.

Afr 3215.3.10   Douin, Georges. La maison du baron de Boislecomte. Cairo, 1927.

Afr 3215.3   Douin, Georges. Une mission militaire française auprès de Mohamed Aly. Caire, 1923.

Afr 3207.13   Douin, Georges. Mohamed Aly, pacha du Caire, 1805-1807. Caire, 1926.

Afr 1957.11   Douin, Georges. Mohamed Aly et l'expédition d'Alger (1829-1830). Aire, 1930.

Afr 3215.3.5   Douin, Georges. Les premières frégates de Mohamed Aly (1824-27). Caire, 1926.

Afr 1609.13.3   Douoso-Cortes, R. Estudio geográfica politico-militar sobre las zonas Españolas. Madrid, 1913.

Afr 7815.48   Doutreloux, Albert. L'ombre des fétiches; société et culture yombe. Louvain, 1967.

Afr 1660.1   Doutte, E. Les djebala du Maroc. Oran, 1899.

Afr 575.8   Doutte, E. L'islam algérien en l'an 1900. Alger, 1900.

Afr 1609.14.3   Doutte, E. Missions au Maroc, en tribu. Paris, 1914.

Afr 1675.1   Doutte, Edmond. Merrakech. Paris, 1905.

Afr 7808.32   Douville, J.B. Voyage au Congo, 1828-1830. Paris, 1832. 4v.

Afr 7808.32.2   Douville, J.B. Voyage au Congo, 1829-1830. Stuttgart, 1832. 3v.

Afr 2030.456   Douxey, Jean. S.O.S. Algérie. Paris, 1956.

Afr 4390.45   Douze ans en Abyssinie. (Lauribar, Paul de.) Paris, 1898.

Afr 1955.11   Douze ans en Algérie, 1830-1842. (Bonnafont, Jean Pierre.) Paris, 1888.

Afr 5748.98.5   Douze leçons à la Sorbonne sur Madagascar. (Piolet, J.B.) Paris, 1898.

Afr 1254.62   Douze récits de voyage inédits en Afrique du nord au XVe siècle. (Abd al-Busit ibn Khalil.) Paris, 1936.

Afr 626.5   Dove, Karl. Wirtschaftsgeographie von Afrika. Jena, 1917.

Afr 635.1A   Dowd, J. The Negro races, a sociological study. N.Y., 1907. 2v.

Afr 7803.42   Dowdy, Homer E. Out of the jaws of the lion. 1st ed. N.Y., 1965.

Afr 6455.67   Dower, K.G. The spotted lion, in Kenya. Boston, 1937.

Afr 11705.39.641   The down and after. (Pohl, V.) London, 1964.

Afr 9795.15   Down in Nyasaland. (Cluston-Brock, Guy.) London, 1959.

Afr 3979.69   Down into Egypt, a revolution observed. (Sykes, John.) London, 1969.

Afr 8849.10   Down Second avenue. (Mphahlele, E.) London, 1959.

Afr 6780.13   Downes, Walter D. With the Nigerians in German East Africa. London, 1919.

Afr 6176.50   The downfall of Kwame Nkrumah. (Bediako, K.A.) Accra, 1966?

Afr 9446.35   The downfall of Lobengula. (Wills, William Arthur.) London, 1894.

Afr 10671.53.1100   The downfall of Ogbúu; a play. (Amali, Samson Onyilokwu Onche.) Ibadan, 1967.

Afr 6172.1   The downfall of Prempeh. (Baden-Powell, R.) London, 1898.

Afr 3735.6   The downfall of the Dervishes. (Bennett, E.N.) London, 1898.

Afr 6162.20   Dowse, Robert Edward. Modernization in Ghana and the U.S.S.R., a comparative study. London, 1969.

Afr 8678.210   Doxey, G.V. The industrial colour bar in South Africa. London, 1961.

Afr 7568.29   Doyle, A.C. The crime of the Congo. N.Y., 1909.

Afr 8289.00.15   Doyle, A.C. The great Boer war. London, 1900.

Afr 8289.00.19.5   Doyle, A.C. The great Boer war. London, 1903.

Afr 8289.00.19A   Doyle, A.C. The great Boer war. N.Y., 1902.

Afr 8289.02.18A   Doyle, A.C. The war in South Africa. London, 1902.

Afr 3725.10   Dr. Emin Pascha. (Reichard, Paul.) Leipzig, 1891.

Afr 8252.354   Dr. George McCall theal als die geskiedskrywer van Suid-Afrika. (Bosman, J.D.) Amsterdam, 1931.

Afr 8283.18   Dr. Jameson. (Fort, G. Seymour.) London, 1918.

Afr 8283.17   Dr. Jameson's raid. (King, James.) London, 1896.

Afr 8283.9.2   Dr. Jameson's raiders. (Davis, R.H.) N.Y., 1897.

Afr 718.2.130   Dr. Livingstone, I presume. 1st American ed. (Anstruther, Ian.) N.Y., 1957.

Afr 9558.8.5   Dr. Livingstone's Cambridge lectures. (Livingstone, David.) Farnborough, Hants., Eng., 1968.

Afr 10015.2   Drachler, J. African heritage. N.Y., 1963.

Afr 109.60.20   Drachoussoff, V. L'Afrique decolonisée. Bruxelles, 1960.

Afr 4790.10   Dracopoli, I.N. Through Jubaland to the Lorian Swamp. London, 1914.

Afr 8735.10   Dracopoli, J.L. Sir Andries Stockenstrom, 1792-1864; the origin of the racial conflict in South Africa. Cape Town, 1969.

Afr Doc 2809.95   Draft capital estimates. (Mauritius.) Port Louis. 1960+

Afr Doc 2809.100   Draft estimates. (Mauritius.) Port Louis. 1959+

Afr 3322:2   A draft of the Charter. (Nasser, G.A.) Cairo, 1962.

Afr 8658.58.5   Draipon, A.W. Sporting scenes amongst the Kaffirs of South Africa. London, 1858.

Afr 5549.38   The drama of Madagascar. (Howe, Sonia Elizabeth.) London, 1938.

Afr 2030.461.46   Dramatique Algérie. (Behr, Edward.) Paris, 1962.

Afr 2030.45   Le drame algérien. 3 ed. (Lavie, Louis.) Alger, 1956.

Afr 2030.10.5   Le drame algérien et la décadence française. (Soustelle, Jacques.) Paris, 1957.

Afr 5257.5.5   Un drame colonial. (Klobb.) Paris, 1931.

Afr 5257.5   Le drame de Dankori. (Joalland.) Paris, 1930.

Afr 5272.2   Le drame de la Haute-Volta. (Upper Volta. Laws, statutes, etc.) Paris, 1960.

Afr 1110.44   Drame de l'Afrique du Nord et la conscience chrétienne. Paris, 1963.

Afr 1609.55.5   Le drame du Maroc. (Buttin, Paul.) Paris, 1955.

Afr 1069.53   Drame et chances de l'Afrique du Nord. (Schaefer, Rene.) Paris, 1953.

Afr 4339.33.92   Le drame éthiopien. (Monfried, H. de.) Paris, 1935.

Afr 3740.18   Il dramma di Fascioda. (Treves, P.) Milano, 1937.

Afr 2530.17   Il dramma di Tunisi. (Caniglia, R.) Napoli, 1930.

Afr 12832.5.100   Dramouss. (Laye, Camara.) Paris, 1966.

Afr 2225.3   Drapier, H. La condition sociale des indigènes algériens. Paris, 1899.

Afr 8687.245   Drawn in colour. (Jabavu, N.) London, 1960.

Afr 8808.65   Drayson, A.W. Tales at the outspan, or adventures in South Africa. London, 1865.

Afr 12832.5.705   A dream of Africa. (Laye, Camara.) London, 1968.

Afr 210.66.10   Dream of unity. (Welch, Claude Emerson.) Ithaca, N.Y., 1966.

Afr 6280.60   Dreams and deeds. (Levine, Robert A.) Chicago, 1966.

Afr 6926.28   Drechsler, Horst. Südwestafrika unter deutscher Kolonialherrschaft. Berlin, 1966.

Afr 4050.10.5   Drei Jahre in der libyschen Wüste. (Falls, J.C.E.) Freiburg, 1911.

Afr 8658.68.5   Drei Jahre in Süd-Afrika. (Fritsch, G.) Breslau, 1868.

Afr 4378.1   Drei Monate in Abyssinien. (Apel, F.H.) Zürich, 1866.

Afr 4050.5   Drei Monate in der libyschen Wüste. (Rohlfs, G.) Cassel, 1875.

Afr 8687.335   Drei-und-zwanzig Jahre Sturm und Sonnenschein in Südafrika. (Schiel, Adolf.) Leipzig, 1902.

Afr 9599.56   Dreigend drennen de tam-tams. (Ingerman, Karel J.J.) Amsterdam, 1956.

Afr 9558.12   Dreissig Jahre Afrika. (Livingstone, D.) Leipzig, 191-.

Afr 1680.14   Dresch, Jean. Commentaire des cartes sur les genres de vie de montagne dans le massif central du grand atlas. Tours, 1941.

Afr 5404.25   Dreux-Brézé, Joachim de. Le Problème du regroupement en Afrique équatoriale, du régime colonial à l'union douanière et économique de l'Afrique centrale. Thèsis. Paris, 1968.

Afr 6715.10   Drews, Max. Frankreich versagt in Kamerun. Berlin, 1940.

Afr 5054.02   Dreyfus, Camille. La France dans l'Afrique occidentale. Paris, 1902.

Afr 3215.3.15   Driault, E. L'Egypte et l'Europe. Caire, 1930-31. 3v.

Afr 3215.2   Driault, E. La formation de l'empire de Mohamed Aly de l'Arabie au Sudan (1814-1823). Paris, 1927.

Afr 3207.15   Driault, E. Mohamed Aly et Napoléon, 1807-1814. Le Caire, 1925.

Afr 6310.5   Driberg, J.H. The East African problem. London, 1930.

Afr 6540.10   Driberg, J.H. The Lango. London, n.d.

Afr 8175.12   Drie en zestig jaren in dienst der vrijheid. (Wormser, J.A.) Amsterdam, 1900.

Afr 2208.78   Drie maanden in Algerie. (Beijerman, H.) 's-Gravenhage, 1878.

Afr 6979.62   Drie swerwers oor die einders. 3. verb. uitg. (Klerk, W.A.) Kaapstad, 1962.

Afr 8105.5.3   Drie voorlezingen over de Kaap de Goede Hoop. (Watermeyer, E.B.) Kaapstad, 1858.

Afr 11336.41.110   Drin, Michael. McKilty's bride. Cape Town, 1965.

Afr 11336.41.100   Drin, Michael. Signpost to fear. Cape Town, 1964.

Afr 2749.57.15   Drohende Wüste. (Kollmannsperger, F.) Wiesbaden, 1957.

Afr 5405.109   Drohojowska, Antoinette J.F.A. M. Savorgnan de Brazza. Lille, 1884.

Afr 4557.90.30   Drohojowska, Antoinette Joséphine Françoise Anne. L'Abyssinie d'après James Bruce et les voyageurs contemporains. Lille, 1886.

Afr 2260.27   Le droit à indemnisation des Français d'Algérie atteints par des mesures de dépossession. Paris, 1965.

Afr 2030.461.40   Le droit à l'insoumission. (Maspero, Francois.) Paris, 1961.

Afr 7567.8   Le droit de préférence de la France sur le Congo belge (1884-1911). Thèse. (Blanc, J.) Paris, 1921.

Afr 7815.38   Le droit de propriété chez les Mongo-bokote. (Mueller, Ernst Wilhelm.) Bruxelles, 1958.

Afr 8279.00.17   Droit des Anglais dans la guerre de Transvaal. Genève, 1900.

Afr 5540.12   Le droit malgache de la nationalité. (Bilbao, Rene.) Paris, 1965.

Afr 7540.41   Droit public du Congo belge. (Paulus, Jean Pierre.) Bruxelles, 1959.

Afr 1338.22   Droit public marocain. v.1-2. (Bourely, Michel.) Rabat, 1965.

Afr 45.68.10   Les droits africains. (Gonidec, Pierre François.) Paris, 1968.

Afr 7010.2   Droits de patronage du Portugal en Afrique. (Portugal. Ministère de la Marine et des Colonies.) Lisbonne, 1883.

Afr 2030.90   Dronne, Raymond. La révolution d'Alger. Paris, 1958.

Afr 7851.3   Droogmans, H. Notices sur le Bas-Congo. Bruxelles, 1901.

Afr 7820.5   Droogmans, Hubert. Notices sur le Bas-Congo. Bruxelles, 1901.

Afr 618.34   Drost, Dietrich. Töpferei in Afrika. Technologie. Berlin, 1967.

Afr 8847.83.10   The drostdy at Swellendam. (Rothmann, M.E.) Swellendam, 1960.

Afr 1258.96   Drouet, F. Au nord de l'Afrique. Nice, 1896.

Afr 2230.18   Drouet, F. Grande-Kabylie. Les Beni Yenni. Rouen, 1887.

Afr 2731.13   Drouilly, J.G. Le général Laperrine, grand saharien. Paris, 1922.

Afr 2532.2   Droulers, C. Le marquis de Mores, 1858-1896. Paris, 1932.

VAfr 7580.36   Drugi cień mojzesza Czombe. Wyd.1. (Bin'kowski, Andrzej.) Warszawa, 1967.

Afr 8678.72   Drum. (Sampson, Anthony.) London, 1956.

Afr 10316.5   Drum beat; East African poems. (Okola, Lennard.) Nairobi, 1967.

Afr 715.5   Drummond, Henry. Tropical Africa. N.Y., 1888.

Afr 715.11   Drummond, Henry. Tropical Africa. 3rd ed. London, 1889.

Afr 8658.75.5   Drummond, William Henry. The large game and natural history of South and South-East Africa. Edinburgh, 1875.

Afr 8252.156   Drummond chaplin. (Long, B.K.) London, 1941.

Afr 9700.32   The drums of affliction. (Turner, Victor Witter.) Oxford, 1968.

Afr 6168.6   The drums of Kumasi. (Lloyd, A.) London, 1964.

Afr 8659.67   Drury, Allen. A very strange society. N.Y., 1967.

Afr 4766.34   Drysdale, J.G.S. The Somali dispute. London, 1964.

Afr 5046.10   Du bon usage de la décolonisation. (Delavignette, Robert Louis.) Paris, 1968.

Afr 7580.15   Du Congo belge au Katanga. (Cabanes, Bernard.) Paris, 1963.

Afr 5260.10   Du Dahomé au Sahara. (Toutée, Georges Joseph.) Paris, 1899.

Afr 5235.189.5   Du Niger au golfe de Guinée par le pays de Konge le Mossi. (Binger, Gustave.) Paris, 1892. 2v.

Afr 1487.40   Du protectorat à l'indépendance, Maroc, 1912-1955. (Spillmann, Georges.) Paris, 1967.

Afr 2224.899   Du régime fiscal en Algérie. (Bonzom, Lucien.) Paris, 1899.

Afr 7809.21.5   Du Tanganika à l'Atlantique. (Leger, L.T.) Bruxelles, 1921.

Afr 7068.5   Duas descrições seiscentistas da Guiné. (Coelho, F. de L.) Lisbon, 1953.

Afr 5385.16   Dubarry, A. Voyage au Dahomey. Paris, n.d.

Afr 49724.100   Dube, John. Jeqe, the bodyservant of King Tshaka (Insila Ka Tshaka). Lovedale, 1951.

Afr 1571.17.13   Dubly, H.L. Lyautey-le-magicien. Lille, 1931.

Afr 5055.6   Duboc, E. L'épopée coloniale en Afrique occidentale française. Paris, 1938.

Afr 5247.10.5   Dubois, Felix. Timbuctoo the mysterious. N.Y., 1896.

Afr 5247.10   Dubois, Felix. Tombouctou la mystérieuse. Paris, 1897.

Afr 1570.6   Dubois, M. Le Maroc et l'intérêt français. Rouen, 1904.

Afr 628.239   Dubois, W.E.B. Black folk, then and now. N.Y., 1939.

Afr 628.215A   Dubois, W.E.B. The Negro. N.Y., 1915.

Afr 115.9.2   Dubois, William E. The world and Africa. N.Y., 1965.

Afr 5874.10.5   Dubois. Les voyages faits...aux isles Dauphine ou Madagascar. Paris, 1674.

Afr 5874.10   Dubois. Voyages made to Dauphine and Bourbon. London, 1897.

Afr 555.16   Dubose, H.C. Memoirs of Rev. John Leighton Wilson, D.D. Richmond, 1895.

Afr 718.35   Dubourg de Bozas, P.M.R. Mission scientifique. De la mer Rouge. Paris, 1906.

Afr 2208.72.3   Dubouzet, Charles. Algérie. n.p., 1872. 2 pam.

Afr 8668.8   Dubow, Rhona. The status of women in South Africa. Cape Town, 1965.

Afr 5749.67   Dubrau, Louis (pseud.). Les îles du Capricorne: Maurice, La Réunion, Madagascar. Bruxelles, 1967.

Afr 1955.14   Le duc d'Aumale et l'Algérie. (Grieu, R. de.) Paris, 1884.

Afr 2880.22   Il Duce in Libia. (Gray, E.M.) Milano, 1937.

Afr 2929.26   Il Duce libico. (Traglia, Gustavo.) Bari, 1926.

Afr 5406.50   Duchaillu, Paul Belloni. Adventures in the great forest of Equatorial Africa. N.Y., 1890.

Afr 5406.57   Duchaillu, Paul Belloni. The country of the dwarfs. N.Y., 1874.

Afr 5406.51.12   Duchaillu, Paul Belloni. Explorations and adventures in Equatorial Africa. London, 1945.

Afr 5406.51.10   Duchaillu, Paul Belloni. Explorations and adventures in Equatorial Africa. N.Y., 1861.

Afr 5406.51   Duchaillu, Paul Belloni. Explorations and adventures in Equatorial Africa. N.Y., 1861.

Afr 5406.51.5   Duchaillu, Paul Belloni. Explorations and adventures in Equatorial Africa. N.Y., 1871.

Afr 5406.52.5   Duchaillu, Paul Belloni. A journey to Ashango-land. N.Y., 1867.

Afr 5406.52   Duchaillu, Paul Belloni. A journey to Ashango-land. N.Y., 1871.

Afr 5406.58   Duchaillu, Paul Belloni. King Mombo. N.Y., 1902.

Afr 5406.53   Duchaillu, Paul Belloni. Lost in the jungle. N.Y., 1873.

Afr 5406.56   Duchaillu, Paul Belloni. My Apingi kingdom. N.Y., 1874.

Afr 5406.55   Duchaillu, Paul Belloni. Stories of the gorilla country. N.Y., 1874.

Afr 5406.54   Duchaillu, Paul Belloni. Wild life under the equator. N.Y., 1869.

Afr 5406.54.5   Duchaillu, Paul Belloni. Wild life under the equator. N.Y., 1871.

Afr 5190.18   Duchemin, G. Saint-Louis du Sénégal. Saint-Louis, 1955.

Afr 2030.462.70   Duchemin, Jacques. Histoire du F.L.N. Paris, 1962.

Afr 4365.2   Duchesne, Albert. Le consul Blondeel en Abyssinie. Bruxelles, 1953.

Afr 5635.8   Duchesne, C. L'expedition de Madagascar...1896. Paris, n.d.

Afr 5635.8.5   Duchesne, C. Rapport sur l'expedition de Madagascar. Text and atlas. Paris, 1897. 2v.

Afr 4559.09   Duchesne-Fournet, J. Mission en Ethiopie (1901-1903). v.1-2 and atlas. Paris, 1909. 3v.

Afr 1075.5   Duclos, Louis Jean. Les nationalismes maghrébins. Paris, 1969.

Afr 1840.17   Duclos, Marcel. Contribution a l'étude de la réforme administrative de l'Algérie. Thèse. Alger, 1921.

Afr 2260.24   Ducrocq, Marcel. Notre Algérie. Paris, 1962.

Afr 6285.5A   Dudley, Billy J. Parties and politics in Northern Nigeria. London, 1968.

Afr 626.124   Due, J.F. Taxation and economic development. Cambridge, 1963.

Afr 4394.7   Le due Adue, 1896-1936. (Mansueti, C.) Milano, 1937.

Afr 1957.25   Dufestre, Henri. Les conquérants de l'Algérie (1830-1857). Paris, 1930.

Afr 9839.03   Duff, H.L. Nyasaland under the Foreign Office. London, 1903.

Afr 9839.05   Duff, H.L. Nyasaland under the Foreign Office. 2. ed. London, 1906.

Afr 9599.32   Duff, Hector Livingston. A small chop. London, 1932.

Afr 8808.61   Duff-Gordon, Lucie. Letters from the Cape. London, 1921.

Afr 8808.61.5   Duff-Gordon, Lucie. Letters from the Cape. London, 1927.

Afr 3978.65.3   Duff-Gordon, Lucie Austin. Last letters from Egypt. London, 1875.

Afr 3978.65.4   Duff-Gordon, Lucie Austin. Last letters from Egypt. 2d ed. London, 1876.

Afr 3978.65.8   Duff-Gordon, Lucie Austin. Letters from Egypt, (1862-1869). London, 1969.

Afr 3978.65.5   Duff-Gordon, Lucie Austin. Letters from Egypt. London, 1902.

Afr 3978.65.6   Duff-Gordon, Lucie Austin. Letters from Egypt. N.Y., 1902.

Afr 3978.65.7   Duff-Gordon, Lucie Austin. Letters from Egypt. N.Y., 1904.

Afr 3978.65   Duff-Gordon, Lucie Austin. Letters from Egypt 1863-65. London, 1865.

Afr 210.61   Duffy, James. Africa speaks. Princeton, N.J., 1961.
Afr 530.33   Duffy, James. Portugal in Africa. Harmondsworth, 1962.
Afr 7015.35   Duffy, James Edward. Portugal in Africa. Cambridge, 1962.
Afr 7015.20A   Duffy, James Edward. Portuguese Africa. Cambridge, 1959.
Afr 7122.83   Duffy, James Edward. A question of slavery. Cambridge, 1967.

Afr 9689.60   Duffy, Kevin. Black elephant hunter. London, 1960.
Afr 2030.461.10   Dufresnay, Claude. Des officiers parlent. Paris, 1961.
Afr 4558.67.9   Dufton, H. Narrative of a journey through Abyssinia. London, 1867.

Afr 1665.7   Dugard, Henry. La colonne du sous, janvrier-juin, 1917. Paris, 1918.

Afr 1493.7.5   Dugard, Henry. Le Maroc de 1917. Paris, 1917.
Afr 1493.7   Dugard, Henry. Le Maroc de 1918. Paris, 1918.
Afr 1493.7.10   Dugard, Henry. Le Maroc de 1919. Paris, 1919.
Afr 7809.61   Dugauquier, D.P. Congo cauldron. London, 1961.
Afr 8678.9F   Duggan-Cronin, A.M. The Bantu tribes of South Africa. Cambridge, Eng., 1928- 3v.

Afr 6455.16   Dugmore, A.R. Camera adventures in the African wilds. N.Y., 1910.

Afr 4070.35   Dugmore, A.R. The vast Sudan. London, 1924.
Afr 4070.35.5   Dugmore, A.R. The vast Sudan. N.Y., 1925.
Afr 6879.25.6   Dugmore, Arthur R. The wonderland of big game, being an account of two trips through Tanganyika and Kenya. London, 1933.

Afr 5530.4   Duignan, Peter. Madagascar. Stanford, Calif., 1962.
Afr 6740.20   Duisbung, Adolf von. In Lande des Cheghu von Bornu. Berlin, 1942.

Afr 9087.5   Duitschland en de Hollandsche Republieken in Zuid-Afrika. (Valter, M.P.C.) Amsterdam, 1918.

Afr 115.2   Dujarday, H. Resumé des voyages des portugais. Paris, 1839. 2v.

Afr 5219.02   Dujarris, G. La vie du sultan Rabah. Paris, 1902.
Afr 626.24   Dujonchay, I. L industrialisation de l'Afrique. Paris, 1953.

Afr 659.45   D'Ulysse à Eisenhower. (Dumaine, J.) Alger, 1945.
Afr 659.45   Dumaine, J. D'Ulysse à Eisenhower. Alger, 1945.
Afr 3978.39   Dumas, A. Impressions of travel in Egypt. N.Y., 1839.
Afr 2208.48.10   Dumas, Alexandre. Tales of Algeria, or Life among the Arabs. Philadelphia, 1868.

Afr 510.4   Dumas, P. Les français d'Afrique. Paris, 1889.
Afr 1609.31.20   Dumas, P. Le Maroc. Grenoble, 1931.
Afr 2209.31.5   Dumas, Pierre. L'Algérie. Grenoble, 1931.
Afr 14665.5   Dumba e a bangala. la cancão. (Guerra, Mario Lopes.) Sá da Bandeira, 1956.

Afr 212.60   Dumoga, John. Africa between East and West. London, 1969.
Afr 7575.66   Dumont, G.H. La table ronde belgo-congolaise. Paris, 1961.

Afr 1947.10   Dumont, P.J. Histoire de l'esclavage de Dumont. Paris, 1819.

Afr 609.62.40   Dumont, René. L'Afrique noire est mal partie. Paris, 1962.
Afr 609.62.41   Dumont, René. False start in Africa. London, 1966.
Afr 609.62.41.5   Dumont, René. False start in Africa. N.Y., 1966.
Afr 8292.22   Dumoulin, L.E. Two years on trek, Royal Sussex Regiment. London, 1907.
Afr 2223.959.5   Dumoulin, Roger. La structure asymétrique de l'économie algérienne. Paris, 1959.

Afr 4050.20   Dumreicher, A. von. Trackers and smugglers in the deserts of Egypt. London, 1931.

Afr 2608.58   Dunant, J.H. Notice sur la régence de Tunis. Genève, 1858.

Afr 3675.22   Duncan, J.S.R. The Sudan. Edinburgh, 1952.
Afr 3675.22.5   Duncan, J.S.R. The Sudan's path to independence. Edinburgh, 1957.

NEDL Afr 5385.17   Duncan, John. Travels in western Africa...through Dahomey. London, 1847. (Changed to KPE 9015)

NEDL Afr 5385.17.2   Duncan, John. Travels in western Africa in 1845 and 1846. London, 1847. (Changed to KPE 9014) 2v.

Afr 5385.17.5   Duncan, John. Travels in western African in 1845 and 1846. 1st ed. London, 1968.

Afr 8678.307   Duncan, P.B. South Africa's rule of violence. London, 1964.

Afr 4559.35.75   Dunckley, F.C. Eight years in Abyssinia. London, 1935.
Afr 6879.24.9   Dundas, A.L.H. Beneath African glaciers. London, 1924.
Afr 6887.10   Dundas, C. Kilimanjaro and its people. London, 1924.
Afr 6333.55   Dundas, Charles C.F. African crossroads. London, 1955.
Afr 8695.5   Dundas, Charles C.F. Problem territories of southern Africa. Cape Town, 1952.

Afr 2030.463.30   D'une Algérie à l'autre. (Jacob, A.) Paris, 1963.
Afr 2749.08   D'une rive à l'autre du Sahara. (Cortier, M.) Paris, 1908.

Afr 9445.35   Dunn, Cyril. Central African witness. London, 1959.
Afr 8160.7   Dunn, John. Cetywayo and the three generals. Pietermaritzburg, 1886.

Afr 3979.05.10A   Dunning, H.W. Today on the Nile. N.Y., 1905.
Htn Afr 1407.2*   Dunton, J. True iournall of the Sally Fleet. London, 1637.

Afr 10624.63.100   Duodu, Cameron. The gab boys. London, 1967.
Afr 1723.10   Dupac, J. Le sud marocain. Marrakech. Safi et Mogador. Paris, 192- .

Afr 2685.1   Dupaty de Clam, A. Fastes chronologiques de la ville de Sfaks. Paris, 1890.

Afr 2689.1   Dupaty de Clam, A. Fastes chronologiques de Tozeur. Paris, 1890.

Afr 618.28   Dupin, Henri. Expériences d'éducation sanitaire et nutritionnelle en Afrique. Paris, 1965.

Afr 5342.12   Dupire, Marguerite. Le pays Adioukrou et sa palmerie. Paris, 1958.

Afr 8278.99.11   Duplessis, C.N.J. The Transvaal Boer speaking for himself. London, 1899.

Afr 8278.98.5   Duplessis, C.N.J. Uit de geschiedenis van de Zuid-Afrikanische Republiek en de afrikaanders. Amsterdam, 1898.

Afr 8676.64.15   Du Plessis, Eduard Petrus. 'N volk staan op. Kaapstad, 1964.

Afr 8825.15   Duplessis, I.D. The Cape Malays. Cape Town, 1944.
Afr 8835.15   Duplessis, I.D. The Malay quarter and its people. Cape Town, 1953.

Afr 555.22.17   Duplessis, J. A history of Christian missions in South Africa. Cape Town, 1965.
Afr 555.22.16   Duplessis, J. A history of Christian missions in South Africa. London, 1911.

Afr 718.36   Duplessis, J. Thrice through the dark continent. London, 1917.

Afr 8676.50   Duplessis, J.C. Economic fluctuations in South Africa, 1910-1949. Stellenbosch, 1950.

Afr 555.9.36   Duplessis, Johannes. The evangelisation of pagan Africa. Cape Town, 1930.

Afr 555.9.33   Duplessis, Johannes. A thousand miles in the heart of Africa. Edinburgh, 1905.

Afr 8678.104   Duplessis, W.C. Highway to harmony. N.Y., 1958.
Afr 7808.89   Dupont, C.F. Lettres sur le Congo. Paris, 1889.
Afr 1422.5   Duprat, P. Peuples anciens et modernes de Maroc. n.p., n.d.

Afr 1280.15*   Duprat, Pascal. Les races anciennes et modernes de l'Afrique septentrionale. Paris, 1845.

Afr 5748.63   Dupre, Jules. Trois mois de sejour à Madagascar. Paris, 1863.

Afr 8678.200   Dupreez, Andries B. Inside the South African crucible. Kaapstad, 1959.

Afr 1965.1   Dupuch, A.A. Abd-el-Kader. Bordeaux, 1860.
Afr 5090.14   Du Puigaudeau, Odette. Barefoot through Mauritania. London, 1937.

Afr 5074.20   Du Puigaudeau, Odette. Le passé maghrébin de la Mauritanie. Rabat, 1962.

Afr 5056.154   Du Puigaudeau, Odette. La piste Maroc-Sénégal. Paris, 1954.

Afr 6168.7   Dupuis, J. Journal of a residence in Ashanti. London, 1824.

Afr 6168.7.2   Dupuis, J. Journal of a residence in Ashanti. 2d ed. London, 1966.

Afr 1570.25   Dupuy, E. Comment nous avons conquis le Maroc. Paris, n.d.

Afr 2030.110   Duquesne, Jacques. L'Algérie. Bruges, 1958.
Afr 4.10   Duquesne University, Pittsburgh. Institute of African Affairs. Publications. Pittsburgh.

Afr 2532.6   Duran-Angliviel, André. Ce que la Tunisie demande à la France. Paris, 1921.

Afr 1618.22   Duran Pulis, Guillermo. La caza en Marruecos. Las Palmas de Gran Canaria, 1955.

Afr 5620.15   Durand, Alfred. Les derniers jours de la cour hova. Paris, 1933.

Afr 698.88   Durand, E. Une exploration française au Zambèze. Paris, 1888.

Afr 8659.11.5   Durand, H.M. A holiday in South Africa. Edinburgh, 1911.
Afr 510.70   Durand, Huguette. Essai sur la conjoncture de l'Afrique noire. Paris, 1957.

Afr 5180.12.5   Durand, J.B.L. Voyage au Sénégal. v.1-2. Paris, 1807.
Htn Afr 5180.12*   Durand, J.B.L. Voyage au Sénégal. v.1-2 and atlas. Paris, 1802. 3v.

Afr 1738.26   Durand, Raphael. Le probleme de Tanger. Thèse. Aix-en-provence, 1926.

Afr 718.28   Durand. Les voyages des Portugais...XVI et XVII siècles. Meaux, 1879.

Afr 3215.3.30   Durand-Viel, G.C. Les campagnes navales de Mohammed Aly et d'Ibrahim. Paris, 1935. 2v.

Afr 7222.5.10   Durao, Antonio. Cercos de Moçambique. Lisboa, 1937.
Htn Afr 7222.5*   Durao, Antonio. Cercos de Moçambique. Madrid, 1633.
Afr 1571.17.110   Durasoy, M. Lyautey. Paris, 1956.
Afr 9060.25   Durban, Natal. Durban. Johannesburg, 1961.
Afr 9060.26   Durban, Natal. Saint Andrew's Presbyterian Church. The story of Saint Andrew's Presbyterian church. Durban, 1962.
Afr 9060.25   Durban. (Durban, Natal.) Johannesburg, 1961.
Afr 9060.10A   Durban. (Kuper, Leo.) London, 1958.
Afr 9060.20   Durban. (Praechter, Vallmar.) Hamburg, 1961.
Afr 718.8F   Durch Afrika von Ost nach West. (Goetzen, G.A.V.) Berlin, 1899.

Afr 6720.2   Durch Busch und Steppe vom Camps. (Zimmermann, Oscar.) Berlin, 1909.
Afr 4050.8   Durch die Libysche. (Steindorff, G.) Leipzig, 1904.
Afr 6738.4.9   Durch Kamerun von sued nach nord. (Morgen, C. Von.) Leipzig, 1893.

Afr 6878.94   Durch Massailand zur Nilquelle. (Baumann, Oscar.) Berlin, 1894.

Afr 555.37   Durch Sand, Sumpf und Wald. (Geyer, F.X.) München, 1902.
Afr 6738.10   Durchs unbekannte Kamerun. (Haase, Lene.) Berlin, 1915.
Afr 2208.38   Dureau de la Malle. Peyssonnel et Desfontaines voyages...d'Alger. Paris, 1838. 2v.

Afr 1609.52.5   Durham, Eng. University. Exploration society expedition to French Morocco. Report of the expedition to French Morocco. Durham, 1956.

NEDL Afr 7458.92   Durham, F.A. Lone star of Liberia. London, 1892.
Afr 1608.81.3   Durier, C. Une excursion au Maroc. Paris, 1882.
Afr 7048.20   Durieux, André. Essai sur le statut. Bruxelles, 1955.
Afr 7540.43   Durieux, André. Souveraineté et communauté belgo-congolaise. Bruxelles, 1959.

Afr 8252.12   Durnford, E. A soldiers life and work in South Africa 1872-1879. London, 1882.

Afr 1608.54   Durrieu, X. Present state of Morocco. 2 in 1. London, 1854. 2 pam.

Afr 1846.6F   Duruy, V. Le 1er regiment de tirailleurs algeriens. Paris, 1899.

Afr 6193.10   Dusantoy, Peter. Community development in Ghana. London, 1958.

Afr 3199.11   Duse Muhammad. In the land of the pharaohs. N.Y., 1911.
Afr 3199.11.2   Duse Muhammad. In the Pharaohs. 2nd ed. London, 1968.

Afr 1830.20.85   Dussert, D. Les mines et les carriere en Algerie. Paris, 1931.

Afr 1609.05.3   Dutaillis, J. Le Maroc pittoresque. Paris, n.d.
Afr 1570.52   Dutaillis, J. Le nouveau Maroc. Paris, 1923.
Afr 8215.5   The Dutch Boers and slavery. (Chesson, Frederick William.) London, 1869.

Afr 8680.30   Dutch Reformed Conference of Church Leaders, Pretoria, 1953. Christian principles in multiracial South Africa. Pretoria, 1954.

Afr 8215.6 The Dutch Republic of South Africa. (Chesson, Frederick William.) London, 1871.

Afr 9488.97 Dutoit, Stephanus Jacobus. Rhodesia. London, 1897.

Afr 6193.56 Dutta Roy, D.K. Household budget survey in Ghana. Legon, 1968.

Afr 6465.5 Dutton, E.H.T. Kenya mountain. London, 1929.

Afr 609.56.10 Dutton, Geoffrey. Africa in black and white. London, 1956.

Afr 7368.56.5 The duty of a rising Christian state. (Crummell, A.) Boston, 1857.
3 pam.

Afr 8658.82 Duval, C. With a show through southern Africa. London, 1882.
2v.

Afr 2025.5 Duval, Jules. Réflexions sur la politique de l'empereur. Paris, 1866.

Afr 2208.99 Duval, P. Heures d'Afrique. Paris, 1899.

Afr 5748.87.5 Duverge. Madagascar et peuplades independantes abandonnées par la France. Paris, 1887.

Afr 5046.12 Duverger, Daniel. La croissance des quantités globales en Afrique de l'ouest de 1947 à 1964. Paris, 1967.

Afr 2208.58.3 Duvernois, C. L'Algérie, ce qu'elle est. Alger, 1858.

Afr 1608.86 Duveyrier, H. De Tanger a fas et meknas en 1885. Paris, 1886.

Afr 1658.5 Duveyrier, H. La derniere partie...Littoral de la mediterranee-le Rif. Paris, 1888.

Afr 2208.57 Duveyrier, H. Journal d'un voyage dans la province. Paris, 1900.

Afr 2749.05.5 Duveyrier, Henri. Sahara algérien et tunisien. Paris, 1905.

Afr 2608.81 Duveyrier, Henri. La Tunisie. Paris, 1881.

Afr 2687.4.2 Duvignaud, Jean. Changes at Shebika. 1st American ed. N.Y., 1970.

Afr 2687.4 Duvignaud, Jean. Chebika; mutations dans un village du Maghreb. Paris, 1968.

Afr 2609.65 Duvignaud, Jean. Tunisie. Lausanne, 1965.

Afr 1990.12 Duvivier. Solution de la question de l'Algérie. Paris, 1841.

Afr 2295.3 Duvivieu. Recherches...sur la portion de l'Algérie au sud de Guelnia. Paris, 1841.

Afr 2623.967 Duwaji, Ghazi. Economic development in Tunisia. N.Y., 1967.

Afr 3700.7 Duyarric, G. L'Etat Mahdiste au Soudan. Paris, 1901.

Afr 7580.2 Duyzings, Martin. Mensen en machten in Congo. Amsterdam, 1960.

Afr 8678.60 Dvorin, E.P. Racial separation in South Africa. Chicago, 1952.

Afr 640.01 Pamphlet box. Dwarfs.

Afr 640.6 Dwarfs of Mount Atlas. (Haliburton, R.G.) London, 1891.

Afr 5406.191 Dybowski, Jean. La route du Tchad. Paris, 1903.

Afr 4382.1 Dye, W.M. Moslem Egypt and Christian Abyssinia. N.Y., 1880.

Afr 7458.79 Dyer, A.S. Christian Liberia. London, 1879.

Afr 6194.30 The dynamics of clanship among the Tallensi. (Fortes, Meyer.) London, 1945.

Afr 632.20 The dynamics of culture change. (Malinowski, B.) New Haven, 1945.

Afr 632.20.5 The dynamics of culture change. (Malinowski, B.) New Haven, 1961.

Afr 6740.40 La dynamique des principales populations du Nord Cameroun. (Podlewski, André Michel.) Paris, 1966.

Afr 1390.5 La dynastie marocaine des Beni Wattas (1420-1554). (Cour, Auguste.) Constantine, 1920.

Afr 3979.60 Dynkin, A.V. Na drevnei zemle. Stalingrad, 1960.

Afr 6542.43 Dyson-Hudson, Neville. Karimojong politics. Oxford, 1966.

Afr 3315.65 Dzelepy, E.N. Le complot de Suez. Bruxelles, 1957.

Afr 109.63.10 Dzieje Afryki od czasow najdawnicjszych do XIV w. Wyd.1. (Lewicki, Tadeusz.) Warszawa, 1963.

Afr 6176.40 Dzirasa, Stephen. Political thought of Dr. Kwame Nkrumah. Accra, 1962.

Afr 1028.4 Pamphlet volume. Morocco, Tunisia.
6 pam.

Afr 6222.2 Pamphlet volume. Nigerian modern history.
4 pam.

Afr 5892.2 Pamphlet volume. Seychelles Peoples' United Party.
3 pam.

Afr 1005.5 E.S.N.A. Cahiers nord-africaines. Paris. 11,1951+
11v.

Afr 4025.15.10 E Egyptos ton Ellenon. (Gialourakès, Manōlès.) Athens, 1967.

Afr 659.66.10 Lo e l'Africa. (Cavallaro, Emanuele.) Palermo, 1966.

Afr 11774.39.120 The eagles of malice. (Scholefield, Alan.) N.Y., 1968.

Afr 674.93.2 Eannes de Azurara, G. Chronica de descobrimento e conquista de Guiné. Paris, 1841.

Afr 674.93F Eannes de Azurara, G. Chronica do descobrimento e conquista de Guiné. Paris, 1841.

Afr 674.93.9 Eannes de Azurara, G. Conquests and discoveries of Henry the Navigator. London, 1906.

Htn Afr 674.93.14* Eannes de Azurara, G. Cronica do descobrimento da Guiné. Porto, 1937.
2v.

Afr 674.93.12 Eannes de Azurara, G. Cronica dos feitos de Guiné. Lisboa, 1942.

Afr 674.93.30 Eannes de Azurara, G. Vida e obras de Gomes Eanes de Zurara. Lisboa, 1949.
2v.

Afr 1753.2FA Eannes de Zurara, G. Cronica da tomada de Ceuta. Coimbra, 1915.

Afr 6303.3F EARIC information circular. (East African Research Information Centre.) Nairobi. 1,1968+

Afr 108.82 Early African exploration up to the 16th century. (Hahn, T.) Cape Town, 1882.

Afr 6390.20 Early days in East Africa. (Jackson, F.J.) London, 1930.

Afr 8100.40 Early French callers at the Cape. (Strangman, Edward.) Cape Town, 1936.

Afr 8355.30 The early history of Indians in Natal. (Ferguson-Davie, C.J.) Johannesburg, 1957.

Afr 679.36 The earth goddess. (Jones, G.H.) London, 1936.

Afr 7315.26.1 Earthy, Emily D. Valenge women; an ethnographic study. London, 1968.

Afr 10575.82.110 Easmon, R. Sarif. The burnt-out marriage. London, 1967.

Afr 10575.82.120 Easmon, R. Sarif. Dear parent and ogre. London, 1964.

Afr 10575.82.100 Easmon, R. Sarif. The new patriots. London, 1965.

Afr 555.3.10 East, D.J. Western Africa, its conditions. London, 1844.

Afr 28715.6.2 East, Rupert Moultrie. Stories of old Adamawa: a collection of historical texts in the Adamawa dialect of Fulani. Farnborough, 1967.

Afr 6333.27 East Africa, a new dominion. (Church, Archibald.) London, 1927.

Afr 6390.87 East Africa, past and present. Paris, 1964.

Afr 6390.64.2 East Africa; the past in chains, the future in pawn. (Meister, Albert.) N.Y., 1968.

Afr 6392.34 East Africa. (Great Britain. Colonial Office. East Africa Economic and Financial Commission.) London, 1961.

Afr 6420.37 East Africa. (Great Britain. East Africa Commission.) London, 1925.

Afr 6333.63 East Africa. (Hughes, Anthony.) Harmondsworth, 1963.

Afr Doc 3207.359.10 East Africa. High Commission. East Africa Statistical Department. Kenya Unit. Agricultural census 1959 (non African). Nairobi? 1960.

Afr 6390.93 East Africa: Kenya, Uganda and Tanzania. (Kirby, C.P.) London, 1968.

Afr 6720.14 East Africa and its invaders. (Coupland, R.) Oxford, 1938.

Afr 6300.21.15F East Africa and Rhodesia, a weekly journal. London. 34,1958+
16v.

Afr 6390.50F East Africa and the islands. (Bulpin, T.V.) Cape Town, 1956.

Afr 6390.13 East Africa and Uganda. (Wason, J.C.) London, 1905.

Afr 6320.5 The East-Africa coast, selected documents. (Freeman-Grenville, G.) Oxford, 1962.

Afr 6308.5 East Africa High Commission. Annual report. Nairobi. 1957+
2v.

Afr 6457.10 East Africa High Commission. Capital formation in Kenya, 1954-1960. Nairobi, 1961.
2 pam.

Afr 626.66 East Africa High Commission. Domestic income and product in Kenya. Nairobi, 1959.

Afr Doc 3284.1.73 East Africa High Commission. Kenya; sample population census of Nairobi, 1957-1958, an experiment on sampling methods. Nairobi, 1958.

Afr 6457.15 East Africa High Commission. Reported employment and wages in Kenya. Nairobi, 1961.

Afr 6392.5 East Africa High Commission. Some notes on industrial development in East Africa. Nairobi, 1956.

Afr 6392.15 East Africa High Commission. Some notes on industrial development in East Africa. 2nd ed. Nairobi, 1959.

Afr Doc 3207.4 East Africa High Commission. East Africa Statistical Department. Kenya Unit. Statistical abstract. Nairobi.

Afr 6881.259 East Africa High Commission. East Africa Statistical Division. Tanganyika Office. The gross domestic product of Tanganyika. v.1-2. Dar es Salaam, 1959.

Afr 6538.16 East Africa High Commission. East African Statistical Department. Uganda Unit. The geographical income of Uganda. Annual.

Afr 6538.15 East Africa High Commission. East African Statistical Department. Uganda Unit. The geographical income of Uganda. Summary.

Afr Doc 3307.348.10 East Africa High Commission. East African Statistical Department. African population of Uganda Protectorate; geographical and tribal studies. Nairobi, 1950.

Afr Doc 3407.348.10 East Africa High Commission. East African Statistical Department. African population of Tanganyika Territory; geographical and tribal studies. Source: East African population census, 1948. Nairobi, 1950.

Afr Doc 3049.5 East Africa High Commission. East African Statistical Department. Annual report. Nairobi. 1950+

Afr Doc 3407.357.10 East Africa High Commission. East African Statistical Department. General African census August 1957. Tribal analysis. Nairobi, 1958.

Afr Doc 3383.5F East Africa High Commission. East African Statistical Department. Uganda Unit. The patterns of income, expenditure and consumption of African unskilled workers in Mbale, February 1958. Entebbe. 1958

Afr Doc 3381.5F East Africa High Commission. East African Statistical Department. Uganda Unit. The patterns of income, expenditure, unskilled workers in Kampala. 1950+

Afr Doc 3376.5F East Africa High Commission. East African Statistical Department. Uganda Unit. The patterns of income, expenditure...of workers in Fort Portal, February 1960. Entebbe, 1960.

Afr Doc 3284.1.75 East Africa High Commission. East African Statistical Department. Kenya Unit. The patterns of income, expenditure and consumption of Africans in Nairobi, 1957-1958. Nairobi, 1959.

Afr Doc 3007.4 East Africa High Commission. East African Statistical Department. Quarterly economic and statistical bulletin. 3-52,1949-1961
3v.

Afr Doc 3407.352 East Africa High Commission. East African Statistical Department. Report on the census of the non-African population taken on the night of 13 february 1952. Dar es Salaam, 1954.

Afr Doc 3407.357.15 East Africa High Commission. East African Statistical Department. Tanganyika population census, 1957. Dar es Salaam, 1958.
2 pam.

Afr Doc 3307.359.10 East Africa High Commission. East African Statistical Department. Uganda: General African Census, 1959. Nairobi, 1960.
2v.

Afr Doc 3307.359 East Africa High Commission. East African Statistical Department. Uganda census, 1959; non-African population. Nairobi, 1960.

Afr Doc 3307.359.5 East Africa High Commission. East African Statistical Department. Uganda census, 1959; African population. Entebbe, 1961.

Afr 6333.29 East Africa in transition, being a review of the principles and proposals of the Commission on closer union...Eastern and Central Africa. London, 1929.

Afr Doc 3009.500 East Africa insurance statistics. (East African Common Services Organization. East African Statistical Department.) Nairobi. 1963+

Afr 6300.21.25 East Africa journal. Nairobi.
5v.

Afr Doc 3709.300 Economic report. (Zambia. Ministry of Finance.) Lusaka. 2,1965+

Afr Doc 1809.315 Economic survey. (Ghana. Central Bureau of Statistics.) Accra. 1955+

Afr Doc 3209.300 Economic survey. (Kenya. Economics and Statistics Division.) 1961+

Afr Doc 1309.305 Economic survey. (Sudan. Ministry of Finance and Economics.) Khartoum. 1959

Afr 6465.60F Economic survey of Central Province, 1963-1964. (Kenya. Economics and Statistics Division.) Nairobi, 1968.

Afr 7461.50 Economic survey of Liberia. (Northwestern University, Evanston, Ill.) Evanston, Ill., 1962?

Afr 6277.35 Economic survey of Nigeria, 1959. (Nigeria. Economic Council.) Lagos, 1959.

Afr 8676.54.10F Economic survey of South Africa. London. 1954+

Afr 6144.10 The economic system of Sierra Leone. (Saylor, Ralph Gerald.) Durham, 1967.

Afr 626.129 Economic transition in Africa. (Herskovitz, Melville J.) Evanston, 1964.

Afr 2623.10 Economic yearbook of Tunisia. Tunis. 1964+

Afr 8676.48 Economics in South Africa. (Franklin, N.N.) Cape Town, 1948.

Afr 8676.48.2 Economics in South Africa. 2d ed. (Franklin, N.N.) Cape Town, 1954.

Afr 8676.48.2.1 Economics in South Africa. 2nd ed. (Franklin, N.N.) N.Y., 1969.

Afr 626.200.5 The economics of Africa. (Robson, Peter.) London, 1969.

Afr 626.172.1 The economics of African countries. (Whetham, Edith Holt.) London, 1969.

Afr 626.161 The economics of African development. (Kamarck, Andrew Martin.) N.Y., 1967.

Afr 8678.314 The economics of the colour bar. (Hutt, W.H.) London, 1964.

Afr 4787.5 The economics of trusteeship in Somalia. (Karp, Mark.) Boston, 1960.

Afr 6096.6.2 Economics of West Africa. 2. ed. Ibadan, 1966.

Afr 626.36 L'économie africaine. 1. éd. (Dia, Mamadou.) Paris, 1957.

Afr 2223.950 Economie algérienne. (Saint Germes, Jean.) Alger, 1950.

Afr 2223.950.2 Economie algérienne. (Saint Germes, Jean.) Alger, 1955. 2 pam.

Afr 7812.236 Economie belge et Congo belge. Thèse. (Velde, M.W.) Nancy, 1936.

Afr 1273.961 L'économie de l'Afrique du Nord. (Gallissot, Rene.) Paris, 1961.

Afr 1273.961.2 L'économie de l'Afrique du Nord. (Gallissot, Rene.) Paris, 1964.

Afr 5057.32 L'économie de l'Ouest-africain. (Atana, Osende.) Paris, 1966.

Afr 5057.11 Economie de l'Ouest africain. (Wade, Abdoulaye.) Paris, 1964.

Afr 5758.60.5 L'économie de Madagascar. (Gendarme, René.) Paris, 1960.

Afr 7812.261.10 L'économie des deux Ueles. (Carbonnelle, C.) Bruxelles, 1961.

Afr 7812.255.5 L'économie du Congo belge et du Ruanda-Urundi. (Belgium. Office de l'Information et des Relations Publiques pour le Congo Belge.) Bruxelles, 1955.

Afr 1273.966 L'économie du Maghreb. (Amin, Samir.) Paris, 1966.

Afr 5183.965 L'économie du Sénégal. 2. éd. (Dakar. Chambre de Commerce.) Dakar, 1965.

Afr 6739.262.2 Economie et plan de développement, République fédérale du Cameroun. 2. éd. (France. Ministère de la Coopération. Direction des Affaires Économiques et Financières. Sous-Direction des Etudes Générales.) Paris, 1965.

Afr 5091.12 Economie et plan de développement, République islamique de Mauritanie. 2.éd. (France. Ministère de la Coopération.) Paris, 1963.

Afr 6686.40.2 Economie et plan de développement, Republique Togolaise. 2. ed. (France. Ministère de la Coopération.) Paris, 1965.

Afr 5343.3 Economie et plan de développement. (France. Ministère de la Coopération. Direction des Affaires Economiques.) Paris, 196-.

Afr 5482.5 Economie et plan de développement. (France. Ministère de la Coopération. Direction des Affaires Économiques.) Paris, 1963.

Afr 5442.13 Economie et plan de développement: Republique du Congo-Brazzaville. 3. éd. (France. Ministère de la Coopération. Direction des Affaires Economiques et Financières. Sous-Direction des Etudes Générales.) Paris, 1965.

Afr 5183.960.3 Economie et plan de développement. 3. éd. (France. Ministère de la Coopération.) Paris, 1964.

Afr 5758.63.3 Economie et plan de développement. 3. éd. (France. Ministère de la Coopération. Direction des Affaires Economiques et Financières. Sous-Direction des Etudes Générales.) Paris, 1963.

Afr 1623.932.5 L'économie marocaine. (Hoffher, René.) Paris, 1932.

Afr 5758.63 Les économies paysannes malgaches du Bas Mangoky. (Ottino, Paul.) Paris, 1963.

Afr 7812.259 Economische ontwikkeling en sociale structuur in Belgisch-Kongo. (Baeck, Louis.) Leuven, 1959.

Afr 2223.957 De economica problematiek van Algerije. (Dalmulder, J.J.J.) Leiden, 1957.

Afr 7502.6.5 De economische toestand van Belgisch-Congo. (Belgium. Ministère des Colonies. Direction des Etudes Economiques.) 1950+ 3v.

Afr 6538.10 Economist (London). Power in Uganda, 1957-1970. London, 1957.

Afr 5407.14 Economist Intelligence Unit, Ltd., London. The states of Equatorial Africa: Gabon, Congo, London, 1964.

Afr 626.100 The economy of Africa. (Hazlewood, Arthur.) London, 1961.

Afr 9499.50 The economy of British Central Africa. (Barber, W.J.) Stanford, 1961.

Afr 6280.50F The economy of Hausa communities of Zaria. (Smith, M.G.) London, 1955.

Afr 6457.38 The economy of Kenya. (Faaland, Just.) Bergen, 1967.

Afr 5758.60.10 The economy of Madagascar. (Malagasy Republic. Commissariat Général au Plan.) Tananarive, 196-.

Afr 1623.964 The economy of Morocco, 1912-1962. (Stewart, C.F.) Cambridge, 1964. 2v.

Afr 6881.268 The economy of Tanganyika. (Rutman, Gilbert.) N.Y., 1968.

Afr 3986.9 The economy of the U.A.R. (United Arab Republic.) Cairo, 1960.

Afr 1623.934.10 Ecorcheville, C. Production et protection au Maroc. Paris, 1934.

Afr 550.8.500 Ecrits d'Afrique. (Lavigerie, Charles M.A.) Paris, 1966.

Afr 10004.25 L'écrivain africain. Kitwe. 11,1968?+

Afr 13305.5 Les écrivains africains du Congo belge et du Ruanda-Urundi. (Jadot, Joseph.) Bruxelles, 1959.

Afr 6540.30 Edel, May Mandelbaum. The Chiga of western Uganda. London, 1969.

Afr 8045.16 Edelman, H. Vorming en ontvoogding van de Unie van Zuid-Africa. Proefschrift. Rotterdam, 1935.

Afr 9291.18 Edenburg. (Schoor, Marthinus.) Edenburg, 1963.

Afr 3979.23.10 Edgar, H.M. Dahaheah days, an Egyptian winter holiday. Toronto, 1923.

Afr 210.61.5 The edge of freedom. 1st ed. (Oakes, John B.) N.Y., 1961.

Afr 6277.2F EDI working papers. (Nigeria. University. Economic Development Institute.) Enugu. 1,1965+

Afr 590.52 Edinburg Society for Effecting the Abolition of African Slave Trade. Two of the petitions form Scotland, presented to last Parliament, praying abolition of African slave trade. Edinburg, 1790.

Afr 650.4 Edinburgh. University. African urbanization. London, 1965.

Afr 590.81 Edinburgh. University. The transatlantic slave trade from West Africa. Edinburgh, 1965.

Afr 609.63.10 Edinburgh. University. Urbanization in African social change. Edinburgh, 1963.

Afr 6096.20 Edinburgh. University. Centre of African Studies. Markets and marketing in West Africa. Edinburgh, 1966.

Afr 545.35 Edinburgh. University. Centre Of African Studies. Religion in Africa. Edinburgh, 1964.

Afr 13315.5 Editions belles-lettres. Kinshasa. 1,196-?+

Afr 3193.10 Edmonds, J. L'Egypte indépandante. Projet de 1801. Caire, 1924.

Afr 4050.16 Edmonstone, A. A journey to two of the oases of Upper Egypt. London, 1822.

Afr 590.79 Edressen, Halfdan. Solgt som slave. Oslo, 1965.

Afr 607.96 Edrisi, A.A.H.I. el. Africa. Gottingae, 1796.

Afr 609.29.15 Edschmid, Kasimir. Afrika nackt und Angezogen. Frankfurt a.M., 1934.

Afr 6144.2F Education and economic development in Sierra Leone. (Sierra Leone.) Sierra Leone, 1960.

Afr Doc 7509.505 Education department statistics. (West Cameroon. Department of Education.) Buea. 1962+

Afr 6392.31 Education employment and rural development. (Conference on Education, Employment and Rural Development, Kericho, Kenya, 1966.) Nairobi, 1967.

Afr Doc 1834.5 Education report. (Ghana. Ministry of Education.) Accra. 1957+

Afr Doc 1809.505 Education statistics. (Ghana. Central Bureau of Statistics.) Accra. 1962+

Afr Doc 1309.505 Education statistics. (Sudan. Bureau of Education Statistics.) Khartoum. 1959+

Afr 699.28.5 Edward, Duke of Windsor. Sport and travel in East Africa, an account of two visits, 1928 and 1930. N.Y., 1935.

Afr 7489.8.5 Edward Wilmot Blyden. (Lynch, Hollis Ralph.) London, 1967.

Afr 3978.77.8A Edwards, A.B. A thousand miles up the Nile. Leipzig, 1878.

Afr 3978.77.11 Edwards, A.B. A thousand miles up the Nile. London, 1890.

Afr 3978.77.13 Edwards, A.B. A thousand miles up the Nile. London, 1891.

Afr 3978.77.15 Edwards, A.B. A thousand miles up the Nile. London, 1899.

Afr 3978.77.10 Edwards, A.B. A thousand miles up the Nile. 2d. ed. London, 1889.

Afr 7180.35 Edwards, Adrian. The Ovimbundu under two sovereignties. London, 1962.

Afr 9450.10 Edwards, Hilton. Rhodesian independence justified. Queenstown, South Africa, 1966.

Afr 8735.5.10 Edwards, I.E. Eighteen-twenty settlers in South Africa. London, 1934.

Afr 590.60 Edwards, I.E. Towards emancipation, a study in South African slavery. Cardiff, 1942.

Afr 8145.10 Edwards, John. Reminiscences of the early life and missionary labours of John Edwards. Grahamstown, 1883.

Afr 2208.67 Edwards, M.B. A winter with the swallows. London, 1867.

Afr 9149.00 Edwards, Neville. The Transvaal in war and peace. London, 1900.

Afr 10118.5 Edwards, Paul. Modern African narrative, an anthology. London, 1966.

Afr 10015.7 Edwards, Paul Geoffrey. Through African eyes. Cambridge, 1966-

Afr 8289.00.28F Edwards Dennis and Co. The Anglo-Boer war 1899-1900, an album. Cape Town, 190-

Afr 9439.65.10 Eeden, Guy Van. The crime of being white. Cape Town, 1965.

Afr 9439.65.11 Eeden, Guy van. Die vuur brand nader. Kaapstad, 1964.

Afr 9093.10 Die eenheidstrewe van die republikeinse Afrikaners. (Jaarsveld, F.A. van.) Johannesburg, 1951.

Afr 8278.99.33 Eenige correspondentie uit 1899. 2e druk. (Leyds, W.J.) Amsterdam, 1938.

Afr 8215.1.3 De eerste annexatie van de Transvaal. v.1. (Leyds, W.J.) Amsterdam, 1906.

Afr 9087.8 Die eerste skof van die Nasionale Party in Transvaal, 1914-1964. (Mulder, Cornelius Petrus.) Johannesburg, 1964.

Afr 5130.22.3 L'effort français au Sénégal. (Peter, G.) Paris, 1933.

Afr 5130.22 L'effort français au Sénégal. Thèse. (Peter, G.) Paris, 1933.

Afr 6280.40 Efik traders of old Calabar. (Forde, C.D.) London, 1956.

Afr 628.266 Efimov, Aleksei V. Protiv rasizma. Moskva, 1966.

Afr 4573.13 Efiopiia. (El'ianov, Aratolu Ia.) Moskva, 1967.

Afr 4389.61 Efiopiia v borbe za sokhranenie nezavisimosti. (Voblikov, D.R.) Moscow, 1961.

Afr 4433.1 Efiopiia v 1941-1954 gg. (Iag'ia, Vataniar S.) Moskva, 1969.

Afr 8848.5 Efolliott, Pamela. From Moscow to the Cape, the story of the Wienands of Waldeck. Cape Town, 1963.

Afr 10684.92.2100 Efuru. (Nwapa, Flora.) London, 1966.

Afr 6280.45 The Egba and their neighbors. (Biobaku, S.O.) Oxford, 1957.

Afr 10675.10.110 Egbuna, Obi Benue. The anthill. London, 1965.

Afr 10675.10.100 Egbuna, Obi Benue. Wind versus polygamy. London, 1964.

Afr 710.20.2 Egerton, F. Clement C. Angola without prejudice. Lisbon, 1955.

Afr 6743.50 Egerton, F.C.C. African majesty, a record of refuge at the court of the king of Bangangte in the French Cameroons. London, 1938.

Afr 7119.57 Egerton, F.C.C. Angola in perspective. London, 1957.

Afr 3735.11 Egerton, G. With the Seventy-Second Highlanders in the Sudan campaign. London, 1909.

Afr 1925.5.5 Episodes de l'histoire des relations de Grande Bretagne. (Playfair, R.L.) Alger, 1879.
Afr 8252.30 Episodes in my life. (Fraser, J.) Cape Town, 1922.
Afr 1432.15 Episodios militares del ejercito de Africa. 2a ed. (Monedero Ordoñez, Dionisio.) Burgos, 1893.
Afr 8289.02.32 The epistles of Atkins. (Milne, J.) London, 1902.
Afr 13340.13.100 Epitome. (Tchicaya U Tamsi, Gerald Felix.) Tunis, 1962.
Afr 1403.4 Epitome de la vida y hechos de Don Sebastian. (Baena Parada, J.) Madrid, 1692.
Afr Doc 3212.20 Epitome of reports and the treasury memoranda thereon and an index. (Kenya. Public Accounts Committee.) Nairobi. 1947-1954
Afr 8687.166 An epoch of the political history of South Africa. (Creswell, Margaret.) Cape Town, 195-.
Afr 5055.6 L'épopée coloniale en Afrique occidentale française. (Duboc, E.) Paris, 1938.
Afr 5054.36.10 L'épopée noire. (Bordeaux, W.) Paris, 1936.
Afr 5055.50 Epopées africaines, ouvrage inédit. (Baratier, A.E.A.) Paris, 1912.
Afr 150.2.35 La epopeya de Enrique el Navegante. (Diaz de Villegas, José.) Madrid, 1961.
Afr 2230.12 Les époques militaires de la Grande Kabilie. (Berbrugger, A.) Alger, 1857.
Afr 9635.10F Epstein, A.L. The administration of justice and the urban African. London, 1953.
Afr 9693.5 Epstein, A.L. Politics in an urban African community. Manchester, 1958.
Afr 7580.22 Epstein, Howard M. Revolt in the Congo, 1960-64. N.Y., 1965.
Afr 2929.53 Epton, N.C. Oasis kingdom. N.Y., 1953.
Afr 1609.58 Epton, Nina C. Saints and sorcerers. London, 1958.
Afr 6390.40 Equator farm. (Cameron, R.W.) N.Y., 1956.
Afr 4095.25 Equatoria, the Lado Enclave. (Stigand, C.H.) London, 1923.
Afr 3695.6 Equatoria under Egyptian rule. (Gordon, C.G.) Cairo, 1953.
Afr 710.40 Equatorial Africa. (Kittler, Glenn D.) N.Y., 1959.
Afr 7575.10 L'équinoxe de janvier. (Morres, Jacques.) Bruxelles, 1959.
Afr 5057.27 L'équipement de l'A.O.F. (French West Africa.) Paris, 1950.
Afr 4559.35.102 L'equivoco abissino. 2a ed. (Frangipani, A.) Milano, 1936.
Afr 2030.215 L'équivoque algérienne. (Beuchard, Georges.) Paris, 1959.
Afr 9165.42.35 Erasmus, J.L.P. Die rand en sy goud. Pretoria, 1944.
Afr 1608.85 Erckmann, J. Le Maroc moderne. Paris, 1885.
Afr 545.36 Die Erde in Vorstellungswelt und Kultpraktiken der sudanischen Völker. (Zwernemann, Jürgen.) Berlin, 1968.
Afr 2731.15.40 L'eremità del Sahara. (Federici, Emidio.) Roma, 1954.
Afr 4747.7 Ericksen, E.G. Africa company town. Dubuque, 1964.
Afr 1713.9 Erigny, Maurice. Au Maroc. Fes la capitale du nord. Paris, 191- .
Afr 8369.60.5 Erik Holm, man en standpunt. (Holm, Erik.) Potgietersrus, 1960.
Afr 555.22.22 Erinnerungen aus dem Missionsleben in Transvaal, 1859-1882. (Merensky, A.) Berlin, 1899.
Afr 1608.38 Erinnerungen aus Marokko. (Augustin, F. von.) Wien, 1838.
Afr 4703.01 Pamphlet box. Eritrea.
Afr 4719.34 Eritrea. (Cortese, Guido.) Roma, 1934.
Afr 4732.20 Eritrea. (Trevaskis, G.K.N.) London, 1960.
Afr 4719.02 L'Eritrea dalle sue origini a tutto l'anno 1901. (Melli, Beniamino.) Milano, 1902.
Afr 4745.5 L'Eritrea economica. (Società di Studi Geografici e Coloniali.) Novara, 1913.
Afr 4708.5 Eritrea economica. Novara, 1913.
Afr 4718.97.5F L'Eritrea nel passato e nel presente. (Bizzoni, A.) Milano, 1897.
Afr 4719.52 Eritrea on the eve. (Pankhurst, E.S.) Essex, 1952.
Afr 625.10 Erleuterungen zur Wandkarte von Afrika. (Chavanne, J.) Wien, 1882.
Afr 2731.15.15 L'ermite du Hoggar...Charles de Foucauld. (Robert, C.M.) Alger, 1938.
Afr 8687.294 Ernest Oppenheimer and the economic development of southern Africa. (Gregory, T.E.G.) Cape Town, 1962.
Afr 1830.20.61 Ernest-Picard, P. La monnaie et le crédit en Algérie depuis 1830. Alger, 1930.
Afr 3035.15 Ernst, Hans. Die mamlukischen Sultansurkunden des Sinai-Klosters. Wiesbaden, 1960.
Afr 618.55 Erny, P. L'Enfant dans la pensée traditionnelle de l'Afrique noire. Paris, 1968.
Afr 500.53 L'erreur africaine. (Assac, Jacques Ploncard d'.) Paris, 1964.
Afr 2030.385 L'erreur du siècle et l'homme des civilisations agricoles. (Gaschet-Veyret de la Tour, E.) Paris, 1956.
Afr 1259.27.20A Erskine, Beatrice. Vanished cities of northern Africa. Boston, 1927.
Afr 8145.45 Ervin, Spencer. The polity of the Church of the province of South Africa. Ambler, Pa., 1964.
Afr 7947.4 Die Erziehung bei Eingeborenengruppen in Ruanda-Urundi. (Klemke, O.) Bonn, 1962.
Afr 1403.6 Esaguy, Jose de. O minuto vitorioso de Alacer-Quibir. Lisboa, 1944.
Afr 5548.84.5 Escamps, H. D. Histoire et geographie de Madagascar. Paris, 1884.
Afr 555.38 Escande, Benj. Souvenirs intimes. Genève, 1898.
Afr 5765.6.10 Escande, Benjamin. Neuf mois à Madagascar. Paris, 1898.
Afr 5748.98.3 Escande, E. A Madagascar, hier et aujourd'hui. Paris, 1898.
Afr 4070.25.2 Escayrac de Lauture, S. Die afrikanische Wüste und das Land der Schwarzen am obern Nil. Leipzig, 1867.
Afr 4070.25 Escayrac de Lauture, S. Le desert et le Soudan. Paris, 1853.
Afr 4070.2 Escayrac de Lauture, S. Mémoire sur le Soudan. Paris, 1855-56.
Afr 4559.09.5 Escherich, G. Im Lande des Negus. Berlin, 1912.
Afr 590.70 Escravatura, beneficios que podem provir as nossas possessoes. (Xavier Botelho, S.) Lisboa, 1840.
Afr 1738.7 Escribano del Pino, E. Tanger y sus alrededores. Madrid, 1903.
Afr 2945.4 Un escursione in Cirenaica. (Pedretti, A.) Rome, 1901.
Afr 6192.65 Eskelund, Karl. Black man's country. London, 1958.
Afr 609.61.5 Eskelund, Karl. While God slept. London, 1961.
Afr 5749.28.5 Esmenard, J. L'ile rouge. Paris, 1928.
Afr 5640.15.10 Esmenard, Jeand D', Vicomte. Gallieni. Paris, 1965.
Afr 2208.80 Espagne,Algérie et Tunisie. (Tchihatchef, P.) Paris, 1880.

Afr 1570.37.2 L'Espagne et la France au Maroc...1911. 2e ed. (Torcy, L.V.V.F.J. de.) Paris, 1911.
Afr 1432.4 L'Espagne et le Maroc en 1860. (Fillias, A.) Paris, 1860.
Afr 1347.2.3 Les espagnols au Maroc en 1909. 2 ed. (Torcy, General de.) Paris, 1911.
Afr 1573.24 España, Juan de. La actuacion de España en Marruecos. Madrid, 1926.
Afr 520.12 La España completa. (Borras, T.) Madrid, 1950.
Afr 520.3 España en Africa. (Reparaz, G.) Madrid, 1891.
Afr 1485.9 España en Africa 1903. (Espinosa de los Monteros, R.) Madrid, 1903.
Afr 5900.5 España en el Africa atlantica. V.1-2. (Rumeu de Armas, Antonio.) Madrid, 1956-57.
Afr 5921.64 España en el Africa ecuatorial. (Spain. Servicio Informativo Español.) Madrid, 1964.
Afr 5920.4 España en el Africa occidental. (Saavedra y Magdalena, D.) Madrid, 1910.
Afr 1750.14 Espana en el Africa septentrional. (Gimenez, S.) Madrid, 1885.
Afr 1750.33 Espana en el continente africano. (Miranda Diaz, Mario.) Madrid, 1963.
Afr 5973.2 España en el Muni. (Granador, Gregorio.) Madrid, 1907.
Afr 1574.1 España en el noroeste de Africa. (Perez del Torro, F.) Madrid, 1892.
Afr 1658.7.2 Espana en el rif. 2a ed. (Ruiz Albeniz, Victor.) Madrid, 1921.
Afr 5944.24 España en el Sahara. Madrid, 1968.
Afr 1573.16 España en Marruecos, historia secreta de la campaña. (Larios de Medrano, Justo.) Madrid, 1916.
Afr 1750.21 España en Marruecos. (Garcia Figueras, Tomas.) Madrid, 1947.
Afr 1573.21 España en Marruecos. El Raisuni. (Ortega, Manuel L.) Madrid, 1917.
Afr 1490.4.7 España en Marruecos. 7a ed. (Riera, A.) Barcelona, 1911.
Afr 1658.6 Espana en Marruecos (1910-1913). (Calvo, G.) Barcelona, 1914.
Afr 5960.9 La España ignorada. (Rios, Mateos.) Barcelona, 1959.
Afr 1574.8 España y las demas naciones. (Gutierrez, F.L.) Madrid, 1906.
Afr 1432.12 España y Marruecos, historia de la guerra de Africa. (Castillo, R. del.) Cadiz, 1859.
Afr 1573.8 España y Marruecos. (Becker, J.) Madrid, 1903.
Afr 1573.7 España y Marruecos. (Carvajal, Jose de.) Madrid, 1884.
Afr 1573.34 España y Marruecos. (Millas y Vallicrosa, J.M.) Barcelona, 1945.
Afr 1750.20 Espana y su protectorado en Marruecos. (Garcia Figueras, Tomas.) Madrid, 1957.
Afr 1432.28 Españoles y Marroquies. (Ventosa, E.) Barcelona, 1860.
Afr 550.21 A espansao da fe na Africa e no Brasil. v.1-3. (Farãnha, A.L.) Lisboa, 1942-46. 3v.
Afr 7190.45 L'espansione politica e coloniale portoghese. (Mantero Velarde, A. de.) Roma, 1924.
Afr 4700.23 Espansionismo italiano odierno. (Agostino Orsini, P.D.) Salerno, 1923.
Afr 2308.16 Espel, Françoise. Alger. Paris, 1959.
Afr 1571.17.18 Esperandieu, Pierre. Lyautey et le protectorat. Paris, 1947.
Afr 5228.2 Esperienza politiche africane; la Federazione del Mali. (Caioli, Aldo.) Milano, 1966.
Afr 2850.8 Un esperimento di colonizzazione nella Tripolitania. (Pisani, F.) Messina, 1904.
Afr 1485.9 Espinosa de los Monteros, R. España en Africa 1903. Madrid, 1903.
Afr 609.60.10 Gli esploratori italiani in Africa. (Dainelli, Giotto.) Torino, 1960.
Afr 2749.61.15 L'esplorazione del Sahara. (Migliorini, Elio.) Torino, 1961.
Afr 820.15 La esplorazione dello Uabi-Uebi Scebeli. (Luigi, Duke of the Abruzzi.) Milano, 1932.
Afr 2929.27 L'esplorazione geografica della Libia. (Mori, Attilio.) Firenze, 1927.
Afr 4050.11 Esplorazioni e prigionia in Libia. (Sforza, Ascanio M.) Milano, 1919.
Afr 4558.80.20 Esplorazioni in Africa di Gustavo Bianchi. (Pesci, Dino.) Milano, 1886.
Afr 12351.63 Espoir et parole. (Barrat, D.) Paris, 1963.
Afr 3818.12.2 Espulsi dal Sudan. 2. ed. (Bonfanti, Adriano.) Bologna, 1964.
Afr 1955.47 Esquer, G. Les commencements d'un empire. Paris, 1929.
Afr 1955.48 Esquer, G. Histoire de l'Algérie. 1. ed. Paris, 1950.
Afr 1955.40 Esquer, G. La prise d'Alger, 1830. Alger, 1923.
Afr 1955.40.2 Esquer, G. La prise d'Alger, 1830. Paris, 1929.
Afr 2731.3 Esquer, G. Un saharien, le colonel Ludovic de Polignac, 1827-1904. Paris, 1930.
Afr 1869.57.7 Esquer, Gabriel. Histoire de l'Algérie. 2. ed. Paris, 1957.
Afr 8658.58 Esquisse...d'une partie de l'Afrique australe. (Cortambert, M.E.) Paris, 1837.
Afr 2208.26.5 Esquisse de l'état d'Alger. (Shaler, William.) Paris, 1830.
Afr 5840.10 Esquisse de l'histoire du protestantisme à l'Ile Mauurice et aux Iles Mascarègnes, 1505 à 1902. (Anderson, J.F.) Paris, 1903.
Afr 608.37 Esquisse générale de l'Afrique. (D'Avezac-Macaya, Marie A.P.) Paris, 1837.
Afr 5180.16 Esquisses sénégalaises. (Boilat, P.D.) Paris, 1853.
Afr 1965.2.25 Essai bibliographique sur le "Journal de l'expédition au portes de fer" (Paris, 1844). (Claye, A.) Paris, 1902.
Afr 2704.5 Essai de bibliographie du Sahara. (Blaudin de The, Bernard M.S.) Paris, 1960- 2v.
Afr 5794.6 Essai de géographie medicale de Nosi-Bé. Thèse. (Deblenne, Paul.) Paris, 1883.
Afr 7815.43 Essai d'étude démographique d'une population de Kwango. (Lamal.) Bruxelles, 1949.
Afr 5326.5 Essai d'une bibliographie sur la Côte-d'Ivoire. (Organization for Economic Cooperation and Development. Development Centre.) Paris, 1964.
Afr 575.22 Essai sur la confrérie religieuse des Aissaoua au Maroc. Thèse. (Brunel, René.) Paris, 1926.
Afr 510.70 Essai sur la conjoncture de l'Afrique noire. (Durand, Huguette.) Paris, 1957.
Afr 2438.12 Essai sur la dualité législative et judiciaire en Tunisie. (Bismut, Victor.) Dijon, 1922.
Afr 2438.15 Essai sur la nationalité dans les protectorats de Tunisie et du Maroc. Thèse. (Winkler, Pierre.) Paris, 1926.

Afr 2000.11 L'évolution de l'Algérie mediane. (Boyer, Pierre.) Paris, 1960.

Afr 3994.932 L'évolution du budget égyptien. (Michel, Bernard.) n.p., 1932.

Afr 2225.4 L'évolution du nomadisme en Algérie. (Lacroix, Bernardo.) Alger, 1906.

Afr 7937.6 L'évolution du royaume Rwanda des origines à 1900. (Dansina, Jan.) Bruxelles, 1962.

Afr 7549.09 L'évolution d'un état philanthropique. (Claparède, René.) Genève, 1909.

Afr 1635.20 Evolution d'un groupement berbere. (Lesne, Marcel.) Rabat, 1959.

Afr 1623.955 L'evolution economique de la societe rurale marocaine. (Guillaume, Albert.) Paris, 1955.

Afr 1623.958.5 L'evolution économique du Maroc dans le cadre du deuxieme plan quadriennal. (Morocco.) Casablanca, 1958.

Afr 6218.15 The evolution of federal government in Nigeria. (Azikiwe, Nnamdi.) Orlu, 195-. 4 pam.

Afr 632.15 The evolution of kinship. (Hartland, Sidney E.) Oxford, 1922.

Afr 8678.26 The evolution of South African native policy. (Gibson, J.Y.) Pietermaritzburg, 1919.

Afr 628.229.5 The evolution of the Negro. (Cameron, Norman E.) Georgetown, 1929-34. 2v.

Afr 210.61.75 Evolution politique de l'Afrique. (Pierson-Mathy, P.) Bruxelles, 1961.

Afr 1110.30A Evolution politique de l'Afrique du Nord musulmane 1920-1961. (Le Tourneau, Roger.) Paris, 1962.

Afr 5055.62 Evolutions en Afrique noire. (Debay, Jean.) Paris, 1962.
Afr 4700.30.10 L'evoluzione della coscienza e dell'attività coloniale italiana. (Cesari, Cesare.) Roma, 1930.

Afr 109.64.33 Evoluzione storico-politica dell'Africa. 3. ed. (Filesi, Teobaldo.) Como, 1967.

Afr 212.48 Ewandé, Daniel. Vive le Président. La fête africaine. Paris, 1968.

Afr 8160.16 Ewart, J.S. British foreign policy and the next war. The Zulu war. Ottawa, 1927.

Afr 635.2 The Ewe-speaking peoples of the Slave Coast of West Africa. (Ellis, A.B.) London, 1890.

Afr 626.178 Ewing, A.F. Industry in Africa. London, 1968.
Afr 8140.31 Ex Africa. (Sauer, H.) London, 1937.
Afr 4766.30 Ex-Italian Somaliland. (Pankhurst, E.) London, 1951.
Afr 4766.31A Ex-Italian Somaliland. (Pankhurst, E.) N.Y., 1951.
Afr 2030.461.75 L'examen des consciences. (Martin-Chauffier, L.) Paris, 1961.

Afr 9558.20 Exams das viagens do Doutor Livingstone. (Lacerda, F.J. de.) Lisbon, 1867.

Afr 9560.15 Exchange of notes between His Majesty's government in the United Kingdon...Belgian government. (Belgium. Treaties. Great Britain, 1933.) London, 1933.

Afr 555.12.20 Excoffon, Ariste. Les pères blancs en Afrique. Paris, 1893.

Afr 2290.6 Excursion à Sebdon. (Barges, l'Abbé.) Paris, 1849.
Afr 1608.81.3 Une excursion au Maroc. (Durier, C.) Paris, 1882.
Afr 1665.5 Excursion au sous. (Boron De Segonzac, R. De.) Paris, 1901.

Afr 2230.1 Excursion dans la Haute Kabylie. Alger, 1859.
Afr 2208.35 Excursions...Algiers and Tunis. (Temple, G.T.) London, 1835. 2v.

Afr 8152.99 Excursions in Southern Africa. (Napier, Elers.) London, 1850. 2v.

Afr 678.40.2 Excursions in western Africa. 2d ed. (Alexander, J.E.) London, 1840. 2v.

Afr 12634.16.100 L'Exil d'Albouri. Suivi de La décision. (Ndao, H. Alion.) Honfleur, 1967.

Afr 6298.181.80 The exodus and the return of Chief Obafemi Awolowo. (Otubushin, Christopher.) Yala, Nigeria, 1966.

Afr 8680.35 Expand or explode. (Horwitz, Ralph.) Cape Town, 1957.
Afr 115.130 Expanding horizons in African studies. Evanston, Ill., 1969.

Afr 150.66 A expansão dos Portugueses no periodo Henriquino. (Cortesão, Jaime.) Lisboa, 1965.

Afr 7222.60 A expansão portuguesa em Moçambique de 1498 a 1530. (Lobato, A.) Lisboa, 1960. 3v.

Afr 5404.5 L'expansion coloniale au Congo français. (Ronget, Fernand.) Paris, 1906.

Afr 8175.10 L'expansion des Boers au XIXe siècle. (Deherain, H.) Paris, 1905.

Afr 5219.10 L'expansion française et la formation territoriale. (Terrier, A.) Paris, 1910.

Afr 3275.8A The expansion of Egypt. (White, A.S.) London, 1899.
Afr 1609.14.5 Una expedicion cientifica por la zona de influencia española en Marruecos. (Dantin Cereceda, J.) Barcelona, 1914.

Afr 1608.85.8 Expedicion geografico-militar...Marruecos. (Cervera Baviera, J.) Barcelona, 1885.

Afr 2005.1 Une expédition algérienne; épisode de l'insurrection de 1864. (Oget, Jules.) Bastia, 1872.

Afr 1957.9 L'expédition d'Alger, 1830. (Chaudau de Raynal, P.) Paris, 1930.

Afr 1957.29 L'expédition d'Alger, 1830. (Noguères, H.) Paris, 1962.
Afr 1957.8 L'expédition d'Alger. (Azan, Paul.) Paris, 1929.
Afr 1490.11.15 L'expédition de Fez. (Azan, Paul.) Paris, 1924.
Afr 5635.8 L'expédition de Madagascar...1896. (Duchesne, C.) Paris, n.d.

Afr 5635.12F L'expedition de Madagascar. (Hocquard, C.E.) Paris, 1897.
Afr 5635.7 L'expedition de Madagascar de 1895. (Bienaime.) n.p., n.d. 4 pam.

Afr 5635.18 L'expédition de Madagascar en 1895. (Anthouard, Albert.) Paris, 1930.

Afr 2532.4 L'expédition de Mores. (Pavy, A.) Paris, 1897.
Afr 3315.142 L'Expedition de Suez. (Beaufre, Andre.) Paris, 1967.
Afr 2748.47 Expédition du général Cavaignac dans le Sahara algérien en avril et mai 1847. (Jacquot, Felix.) Paris, 1849.

Afr 2527.5 Expédition française en Tunisie (1881-82). (Bois, M.) Paris, 1886.

Afr 2480.5 Une expédition française en Tunisie au XIVe siècle. (Mirot, Leon.) Paris, 1932.

Afr 2527.3 Expédition militaire en Tunisia, 1881-82. Paris, n.d.

Afr 8658.38.5 An expedition of discovery into the interior of Africa. (Alexander, James E.) Cape Town, 1967. 2v.

Afr 8658.38 An expedition of discovery into the interior of Africa. (Alexander, James E.) London, 1835. 2v.

Afr 4368.17 Une expédition religieuse en Abyssinie. (Constantin, N.) Paris, 1891.

Afr 4610.4F Expedition scientifique et commerciale au...Choa...Gallas. (Bremond, L.A.) Paris, 1883.

Afr 4095.5 Expedition to sources of White Nile. (Werne, Ferd.) London, 1849.

Afr 4095.5.5 Expedition zur Entdeckung der Quellen des Weissen Nil. (Werne, Ferd.) Berlin, 1848.

Afr 4230.4.6 Expeditiones Aethiopicae. v.1-4. (Mendez S.I., P.A.) Roma, 1909. 2v.

Afr 200.13.5 Les expéditions anglaises en Afrique, Ashantel 1873-1874. (Septans, Albert.) Paris, 1896.

Afr 1973.1 Expéditions de Constantine. (Devoisins, V.) Paris, 1840.
Afr 2260.18 Une expérience de petite colonisation indigène en Algérie. Thèse. (Tiquet, J.E.P.) Maison-Carrée, 1936.

Afr 5314.10 Expérience guinéenne et unité africaine. (Touré, Sékou.) Paris, 1959.

Afr 5314.10.2 Expérience guinéenne et unité africaine. (Touré, Sékou.) Paris, 1961.

Afr 5860.15 Une expérience législative à la Réunion. Thèse. (Cornu, Henri.) Paris, 1935.

Afr 618.28 Expériences d'éducation sanitaire et nutritionnelle en Afrique. (Dupin, Henri.) Paris, 1965.

Afr 9493.38 Experiences of rHodesia's pioneer women. (Boggie, Jeannie M.) Bulawayo, 1938.

Afr 8350.5 An experiment in alien labor. (Payne, E.G.) Chicago, 1912.

Afr 9197.2 Experiment in Swaziland. (Natal. University. Institute for Social Research.) Cape Town, 1964.

Afr 7582.8 Experiment in world government, an account of the United Nations operation in the Congo, 1960-1964. (Martelli, George.) London, 1966.

Afr 5180.11 The expiring continent. (Mitchinson, A.W.) London, 1881.
Afr 1955.28 Explications. (Clauzel, M.) Paris, 1837.
Afr 6570.7A The exploitation of East Africa, 1856-1890. (Coupland, R.) London, 1939.

Afr 6570.7.2 The exploitation of East Africa, 1856-1890. 2nd ed. (Coupland, R.) London, 1968.

Afr 7320.20 Explorações em Moçambique. (Pires de Lima, Americo.) Lisboa, 1943.

Afr 7324.20 Explorações portuguezas em Lourenço Marques e Inhambane. (Portugal. Comissão de Limitação da Fronteira de Lourenço Marques.) Lisboa, 1894.

Afr 5406.181 Un explorateur africain, Auguste Stahl. (Dietz, Emile.) Paris, 1884.

Afr 555.39 Un explorateur et un apôtre du Congo français. (Witte, Jehan.) Paris, 1924.

Afr 115.7F Les explorateurs de l'Afrique. (Brunet, P.) Tours, 1889.
Afr 715.28 Les explorateurs français en Afrique. (Pares, Eugene.) Limoges, 1881.

Afr 698.50 Exploration de la côte orientale d'Afrique. (Guillain, Charles.) Paris, 1850.

Afr 718.2.30 The exploration diaries of H.M. Stanley. (Stanley, H.M.) London, 1961.

Afr 698.88 Une exploration française au Zambèze. (Durand, E.) Paris, 1888.

Afr 6978.64 Exploration in South-west Africa. (Baines, T.) London, 1864.

Afr 2780.5 Exploration of Air. (Buchanan, Angus.) London, 1921.
Afr 1830.20.6 Exploration zoologique de l'Algerie. (Seurat, L.G.) Paris, 1930.

Afr 5406.51.12 Explorations and adventures in Equatorial Africa. (Duchaillu, Paul Belloni.) London, 1945.

Afr 5406.51 Explorations and adventures in Equatorial Africa. (Duchaillu, Paul Belloni.) N.Y., 1861.

Afr 5406.51.10 Explorations and adventures in Equatorial Africa. (Duchaillu, Paul Belloni.) N.Y., 1861.

Afr 5406.51.5 Explorations and adventures in Equatorial Africa. (Duchaillu, Paul Belloni.) N.Y., 1871.

Afr 1609.06.5 Explorations au Maroc. (Gentil, L.) Paris, 1906.
Afr 5054.10.5 Les explorations au Sénégal et dans les contrées voisines. (Ancelle, Jules.) Paris, 1886.

Afr 9558.11 Explorations dans l'Afrique australe. 2. ed. (Livingstone, D.) Paris, 1869.

Afr 10663.5 An exploratory investigation of press readership among selected students in Zaria. (Chick, John D.) Zaria, 1966.

Afr 7809.44 Exploring we would go. (Gatti, Ellen M. (Woddill).) N.Y., 1944.

Afr 1840.1 Exposé de l'état...du gouvernement. (Algeria. Gouvernement Général.) Algiers, 1844.

Afr 5749.60 Expose des travaux executes en 1959 sur le territoire de la Republique Malgache. (France. Institut Geographique National. Service Geographique a Tananarive.) Paris, 1960.

Afr 5749.66 Expose des travaux executes en 1965 sur le territoire de la Republique Malgache. (France. Institut Geographique National. Annexe de Tananarive.) Paris, 1966.

Afr 1830.20.53 Exposé du développement des services postaux. (Algeria. Service des Postes, Télégraphes.) Alger, 1900.

Afr 150.70 Exposição Henriquina. (Portugal. Comissão Executiva das Comemorações do V. Centenario da Morte do Infante Dom Henrique.) Lisboa, 1960.

Afr 2749.34 Exposition du Sahara, 15 mai-28 oct. 1934. (Paris. Musée d'Ethnographie du Trocadero.) Paris, 1934.

Afr 2636.2 L'extension de la juridiction et de la nationalité française en Tunisie. (Smaja, M.) Tunis, 1900.

Afr Doc 808.720 External trade indices. (Libya. Census and Statistical Department.) Tripoli. 1962+

Afr Doc 3308.705F The external trade of Uganda, 1950-1960. (Uganda. Ministry of Economic Development. Statistics Branch.) Entebbe, 1962.

Afr Doc 808.705 External trade statistics. (Libya. Census and Statistical Department.) 1959+ 3v.

Afr Doc 3708.705F External trade statistics. (Zambia. Central Statistical Office.) Lusaka. 1965+

Afr Doc 1808.705 External trade statistics of Ghana. (Ghana. Central Bureau of Statistics.) 13,1963+

Afr 8110.5 Extract from the narrative of his mission, 1803. (Kicheren.) Wiscasset, 1805.

Afr 6225.40   Extracts from British parliamentary debates on the Nigerian situation in the House of Commons, London, Tuesday, 27th August, 1968. (Great Britain. Parliament. House of Commons.) Washington, 1968.

Afr 855.12   Extracts from the St. Helena records. (St. Helena.) St. Helena, 1885.

Afr 855.12.5   Extracts from the St. Helena records. 2 ed. (St. Helena.) St. Helena, 1908.

Afr 590.30.5   Extracts from 18th and 19th reports...May 1824, and May 1825. (African Institution.) Philadelphia, 1826.

Afr 2030.461.95   Extraditions d'Algériens, ou le chemin de la guillotine. Bruxelles, 1961.

Afr 1957.6.10   Extrait du journal d'un officier supérieur attaché à la deuxième division de l'armée d'Afrique. (Loverdo, N.) Paris, 1831.

Afr 1080.20   Extraits inédits rélatifs au Maghreb. (Fagnan, Edmond.) Alger, 1924.

Afr 8135.7   Eybers, G.W. Select constitutional documents...South African history 1795-1910. London, 1918.

Afr 8678.328   Eyo, B.E. Apartheid. Jerusalem, 1964.
Afr 6210.25   Ezera, Kalu. Constitutional development in Nigeria. Cambridge, 1960.

Afr 6210.25.2   Ezera, Kalu. Constitutional development in Nigeria. 2d ed. Cambridge, Eng., 1964.

Afr 2030.462.95   Le F.L.N. et l'Algérie. (Favrod, C.H.) Paris, 1962.
Afr 555.152   F.S. Arnot Jubilee Conference, Muchacha, 1931. A Central African Jubilee. London, 1932.

Afr 6457.38   Faaland, Just. The economy of Kenya. Bergen, 1967.
Afr 1990.15   Fabar, Paul. L'Algérie et l'opinion. Paris, 1847.
Afr 4700.48   Fabian Society. Colonial Bureau. The fate of Italy's colonies. London, 1948.

Afr 9400.12   Fabled tribe; a voyage to discover the River Bushmen of the Okavango Swamps. 1st ed. (Cowley, Olive.) N.Y., 1968.

Afr 2230.15   Fabre, C. Grand Kabylie, légendes et souvenirs. Paris, 1901.

Afr 2030.55   Fabre-Luce, Alfred. Demain en Algérie. Paris, 1958.
Afr 6760.7   Fabri, F. Deutsch-Ostafrica. Köln, 1886.
Afr 7122.77   The fabric of terror, three days in Angola. (Teixeira, Bernardo.) N.Y., 1965.

VAfr 5225.6   Le fabuleux empire du Mali. (Clair, Andrée.) Paris, 1959.
Afr 3675.40   Fabunmi, L.A. The Sudan in Anglo-Egyptian relations. London, 1960.

Afr 2875.11   Facchinetti, P.V. Ai caduti nella guerra italo-turca. n.p., 1911.

Afr 11865.59.100   The face beside the fire. (Vanderpost, Laurens.) N.Y., 1953.

Afr 11433.74.125   Face to face. (Gordimer, N.) Johannesburg, 1949.
Afr 609.64   Faces of Africa. (Melady, T.P.) N.Y., 1964.
Afr 3740.3   Fachoda. (Barre, P.) Paris, n.d.
NEDL Afr 3740.4   Fachoda. (Caix, R. de.) Paris, 1899.
Afr 3740.10   Fachoda. 4e ed. (Labatut, Guy de.) Paris, 1932.
Afr 2209.36   Faci, S. L'Algérie sous l'égide de la France contre la féodalité algérienne. Toulouse, 1936.

Afr 6395.2.15   Facing Mt. Kenya. (Kenyatta, Jona.) London, 1953.
Afr 8678.196F   Fact paper. (South African Institute of Race Relations.) Johannesburg. 3+ 4v.

Afr 6291.58F   Fact sheets on South-Eastern state of Nigeria. (Nigeria, South-Eastern. Ministry of Home Affairs and Information. Information Division.) Calabar, 1969.

Afr 626.85.3   Les facteurs humains de la productivité. (Inter-African Labour Institute.) Bumako, 1956.

Afr 9405.5   Factors and economic development and the Okovanggo Delta. (Randall, D.) Chicago, 1957.

Afr 7122.20.2   Factos e consideraçõs relativas aos direitos de Portugal. (Sa da Bandeira, B. de S.N. de F. da.) Lisboa, 1855.

Afr 2819.64   Facts about Libya. 3rd ed. (Murabet, Mohammed.) Malta, 1964.

Afr 6535.68   Facts about Uganda. (Uganda. Ministry of Information. Broadcasting and Tourism.) Entebbe, 1968.

Afr 1259.52   Facts and figures about French North Africa. (France. Président Du Conseil.) Paris, 1952.

Afr 7350.3.15   Facts and opinions touching the real origin, character...American Colonization Society. (Stebbins, G.B.) Cleveland, 1853.

Afr 7122.20   Facts and statistics concerning the right of the crown of Portugal to the territory of Molembo Cabinda, Ambriz. (Sa da Bandeira, B. de S.N. de F. da.) London, 1877.

Afr 7350.3.35   Facts designed to exhibit the real character and tendency of the American Colonizaton Society. (Smith, G.) Liverpool, 1833.

Afr 9839.66   Facts from Malawi. (Malawi. Department of Information.) Zomba, 1966.

Afr 4513.36.105   Facts Geneva refuses to see. (Societa Editrice de Novissima, Roma.) Roma, 1936.

Afr 609.62.55   A factual study of sub-Saharan Africa. (Rycroft, W.S.) N.Y., 1962.

Afr 9700.13   The fading colour bar. (Keith, Grace.) London, 1966.
Afr 4559.26.13   En färd tell Abessinien. 2a upp. (Simertz, S.) Stockholm, 1926.

Afr 9643.5   Fagan, Brian M. A short history of Zambia. Nairobi, 1966.
Afr 609.65.25   Fagan, Brian M. Southern Africa during the Iron Age. London, 1965.

Afr 9510.5.10   Fagan, Brian M. The Victoria Falls, a handbook to the Victoria Falls, the Batoka Gorge and part of the upper Zambesi River. 2. ed. Lusaka, 1964.

Afr 8678.8.10   Fagan, H.A. Co-existence in South Africa. Cape Town, 1963.

Afr 8678.135   Fagan, Henry Allan. Our responsibility. Stellenbosch, 1960.

Afr 6164.12   Fage, J. Ghana. Madison, Wis., 1959.
Afr 679.55.6   Fage, J.D. A history of West Africa. 4th ed. Cambridge, Eng., 1969.

Afr 679.55.5   Fage, J.D. An introduction to the history of West Africa. 3rd ed. Cambridge, Eng., 1962.

Afr 1088.5.6   Fagnan, E. L'Afrique septentrionale au XIIe siècle de notre ère. Constantine, 1900.

Afr 1390.3   Fagnan, E. Al-bayano'l-mogrib. Alger, 1901. 2v.

Afr 1088.5   Fagnan, E. Histoire des Almohades. Alger, 1893.
Afr 1080.20   Fagnan, Edmond. Extraits inédits rélatifs au Maghreb. Alger, 1924.

Afr 3040.25   Fahmy, Ahmed. Vers l'unité de juridiction en Egypte. Thèse. Paris, n.d.

Afr 3986.954   Fahmy, M. La révolution de l'industrie en Egypte et ses conséquences sociales au 19. siècle. Leiden, 1954.

Afr 555.29.5   Fahs, Sophia L. Uganda's white man of work. Boston, 1907.

Afr 1258.64   Faidherbe, L.L.C. Chapitres de géographie sur le nord-ouest de l'Afrique. Paris, 1864.

Afr 5118.89   Faidherbe, L.L.C. Le Sénégal. Paris, 1889.
Afr 5185.5   Faidherbe, L.L.C. Le Zenaga des tribus sénégalaises. Paris, 1877.

Afr 5130.20.5   Faidherbe. (Demaison, A.) Paris, 1932.
Afr 5130.20.10   Faidherbe. (Hardy, Georges.) Paris, 1947.
Afr 9193.3.5   Fair, Thomas J.D. Development in Swaziland: a regional analysis. Johannesburg, 1969.

Afr 11299.69.100   The fair house. (Cope, Jack.) London, 1955.
Afr 8089.18A   Fairbridge, D. A history of South Africa. London, 1918.
Afr 8125.10   Fairbridge, D. Lady Anne Barnard at the Cape of Good Hope, 1797-1802. Oxford, 1924.

Afr 8659.28   Fairbridge, D. The pilgrims' way in South Africa. London, 1928.

Afr 8252.194   Fairbridge, K. The autobiography of Kingsley Fairbridge. London, 1927.

Afr 6277.02   Fairholm, G W. Native authority finance patterns. Zaria, 1965.

Afr 6210.62   Fairholm, Gilbert Wayne. Urban government organization in Northern Nigeria. Zaria?, 1964?

Afr 4060.25   Fairservis, W.A. The ancient kingdoms of the Nile and the doomed monuments of Nubia. N.Y., 1962.

Afr 5765.36   Faithful unto death;...life...of William and Lucy S. Johnson. (Doncaster, Phebe.) London, 1896.

Afr 5765.3.5   Faithful unto death. (Ellis, William.) London, 1876.
Afr 4559.10   Faitlovitch, J. Quer durch Abessinien. Berlin, 1910.
Afr 6214.36   Fajana, A. Nigeria in history. Pkeja, 1969.
Afr 4180.3.25F   Fakhry, Ahmed. Siwa Oasis. Cairo, 1944.
Afr 6930.10   Faktsamling angaende Sydvaestrikafra'gan i foerenta nationenna. (Sweden. Utrikesdepartementet.) Stockholm, 1965.

Afr 210.63.75   Falcão, F. de S. Quo vadis, Africa. Lisboa, 1963.
Afr 7175.52   Falcão, J. Angola do meu coração. Lisboa, 1961.
Afr 2223.930.5   Falck, Felix. L'Algérie, un siècle de colonisation française. Paris, 1930.

Afr 2223.922   Falck, Felix. Guide économique de l'Algérie. Paris, 1922.
Afr 6143.1.5   Falconbridge, Anna Maria. Narrative of two voyages to the River Sierra Leone during the years 1791-1793. Facsimile of 2. ed. London, 1967.

Afr 6275.21   Falconer, J.D. On horseback through Nigeria. London, 1911.

Afr 7093.4F   Falkenstein. Die Loango Kuste. Berlin, 1876.
Afr 11320.50.110   The fall. (Delius, Anthony.) Cape Town, 1960.
Afr 8279.61   The fall of Kruger's republic. (Marais, Johannes.) Oxford, 1961.

Afr 7567.4   The fall of the Congo Arabs. (Hinde, S.L.) London, 1897.
Afr 7567.4.5   The fall of the Congo Arabs. (Hinde, Sidney L.) N.Y., 1897.

Afr 6540.4.10A   Fallers, Lloyd A. Bantu bureaucracy. Cambridge, Eng., 195-.

Afr 6540.4.11   Fallers, Lloyd A. Bantu bureaucracy. Chicago, 1965.
Afr 6542.16   Fallers, Lloyd A. The king's men. London, 1964.
Afr 6540.4.15   Fallers, Lloyd A. Law without precedent. Chicago, 1969.
Afr 1570.9   Fallot, E. La solution française de la question du Maroc. Paris, 1904.

Afr 1258.62   Fallot, Ernest. Par dela la Méditerranée. Paris, 1887.
Afr 4050.10.5   Falls, J.C.E. Drei Jahre in der libyschen Wüste. Freiburg, 1911.

Afr 4180.3   Falls, J.C.E. Siwah. Mainz, 1910.
Afr 4050.10   Falls, J.C.E. Three years in the Libyan desert. London, 1913.

Afr 609.62.41   False start in Africa. (Dumont, René.) London, 1966.
Afr 609.62.41.5   False start in Africa. (Dumont, René.) N.Y., 1966.
Afr 5318.8   Famechon. Notice sur la Guinée française. Paris, 1900.
Afr 5753.5   La famille à Madagascar. (Cournot, M.) Angers, 1897.
Afr 6280.9.25   Family and kinship in Ibo land. (Nzimiro, F.I.) Köln, 1962.

Afr 6275.90.5   Family and social change in an African city. (Marris, P.) Evanston, Ill., 1962.

Afr 6275.90   Family and social change in an African city. (Marris, P.) London, 1961.

Afr 6395.8   The family herds. (Gulliver, P.H.) London, 1955.
Afr 9558.14.5   Family letters, 1841-1856. (Livingstone, D.) London, 1959. 2v.

Afr 115.70   Famous explorers and adventures in Africa. v.1-2. (Jones, Ch. H.) N.Y., 1881. 2v.

Afr 5765.34   Fampisehaana. (Malagasy. Republic Service des Archives et de la Documentation.) Tananarive, 1964.

Afr 4390.60   Fanelli, Armando. Taitù e Manelik. Milano, 1935.
Afr 635.89   Fani-Kazode, Remi. Blackism. Lagos, 1965.
Afr 628.252.5   Fannon, F. Black skin, white masks. N.Y., 1967.
Afr 628.252   Fanon, F. Peau noire. Paris, 1952.
Afr 2030.320   Fanon, Frantz. L'an cinq de la révolution algérienne. Paris, 1959.

Afr 210.64.20   Fanon, Frantz. Pour la révolution africaine. Paris, 1964.
Afr 2030.320.2   Fanon, Frantz. Studies in a dying colonialism. N.Y., 1955.

Afr 210.64.22   Fanon, Frantz. Toward the African revolution. N.Y., 1967.
Afr 210.61.56A   Fanon, Franz. The damned. Paris, 1961.
Afr 210.61.55A   Fanon, Franz. Les damnés de la terre. Paris, 1963.
Afr 210.63.85   Fanon, Franz. The wretched of the earth. N.Y., 1963.
Afr 6170.15   Fanti and Ashanti. (Brackenbury, H.) Edinburgh, 1873.
Afr 6194.41.2   Fanti national constitution; a short treatise. (Sarban, John Mensah.) London, 1968.

Afr 4375.17   Fanton, A. L'Abyssinie lors de l'expedition anglaise, 1867-1868. Paris, 1936.

Afr 626.110   FAO African survey. (Food and Agriculture Organization of the United Nations.) Rome, 1962.

Afr 5842.14   Far away, scenery and society in Mauritius. (Boyle, C.J.) London, 1867.

Afr 4070.36   Far away up the Nile. (Millais, John Guille.) London, 1924.

Afr 8252.227   Far bugles. (Harding, C.) London, 1933.
Afr 6198.436   The far horizon. (Griffith, William Brandford.) Devon, 1951.

Afr 8658.86   The far interior. (Kerr, W.M.) London, 1886.

Afr 9445.25   The far interior. (Tabler, Edward C.) Cape Town, 1955.
Afr 4512.18   Faraci, Giuseppe. Etiopia, guerra epace. Torino, 1965.
Afr 4559.35.30   Farago, L. Abyssinia on the eve. London, 1935.
Afr 550.21   Farãnha, A.L. A espansao da fe na Africa e no Brasil. v.1-3. Lisboa, 1942-46. 3v.

Afr 4008.12   Faraos barn. (Laurent-Taeckholm, Vivi.) Stockholm, 1965.

Afr 724.2 — Farde, P. Voyages et aventures. Gand, 1878.
Afr 109.67.40 — Farelly, Maurice. Africains d'hier et de demain. Neuchâtel, 1967.
Afr 626.144 — Farer, Tom J. Financing African development. Cambridge, Mass., 1965.
Afr 3300.80 — Farewell Farouk. (Moore, A.L.) Chicago, 1954.
Afr 8140.29.5 — Farewell to parliament. (Blackwell, L.) Pietermaritzburg, 1946.
Afr 4513.37.10 — Farfaglio, S. Le bande autocarrate dei fedelissimi da Roma ad Addis Ababa. Paris, 1937.
Afr 7222.80 — Faria, Dutra. Portugal do capricornio. Lisboa, 1965.
Htn Afr 1398.5* — Faria e Sousa, Manuel de. Africa portuguesa por su autor Manuel de Faria. Lisboa, 1681.
Afr 6542.45 — Farina, Felice. Nel paese dei bevitori di sangue; genti nuove alla ribalta: il popolo Karimojòng. Bologna, 1965.
Afr 2230.11 — Farine, Charles. Kabyles et Kroumirs. Paris, 1882.
X Cg Afr 9388.86 — Farini, G.A. Through the Kalahari desert. London, 1886. (Changed to XP 3879)
Afr 3275.5 — Faris, Selim. Decline of British prestige in the East. London, 1887.
Afr 3305.18 — Farouk of Egypt; a biography. 1st American ed. (McBride, Barrie St. Clair.) South Brunswick, N.J., 1968.
Afr 9525.575 — Farrant, Jean. Mashonaland martyr. Cape Town, 1966.
Afr 8279.00.21 — Farrelly, M.J. The settlement after the war. London, 1900.
Afr 8968.79 — Farrer, J.A. Zululand and the Zulus. 3rd ed. London, 1879.
Afr 1571.17.115 — Farrere, Claude. Lyautey. Paris, 1955.
Afr 6455.75 — Farson, N. Last chance in Africa. London, 1949.
Afr 609.40.10A — Farson, Negley. Behind God's back. N.Y., 1941.
Afr 718.2.125 — Farwell, Byron. The man who presumed. 1st ed. N.Y., 1957.
Afr 3700.24 — Farwell, Byron. Prisoners of the Mahdi. London, 1967.
Afr 4513.36.85 — Fasci Italiani all'Estero. L'Abissinia e noi. Roma, 1935.
Afr 3740.8 — Fashoda, the incident and its diplomatic setting. (Giffen, Morrison B.) Chicago, 1930.
Afr 2685.1 — Fastes chronologiques de la ville de Sfaks. (Dupaty de Clam, A.) Paris, 1890.
Afr 2357.20 — Fastes chronologiques de la ville d'Oran. (Basset, René.) Paris, 1892.
Afr 2689.1 — Fastes chronologiques de Tozeur. (Dupaty de Clam, A.) Paris, 1890.
Afr 4700.48 — The fate of Italy's colonies. (Fabian Society. Colonial Bureau.) London, 1948.
Afr 9073.263 — The father of a city, the life and times of George Cato. (Goetzsche, Eric.) Pietermaritzburg, 1967.
Afr 3035.7 — Fatimid decrees. (Stern, S.M.) London, 1964.
Afr 3138.10.10 — The Fatimid theory of state. (Vatikiotis, P.J.) Lahore, 1957.
Afr 3135.5 — The Fatimids. (Al-Hamdani, Abbas H.) Karachi, 1962.
Afr 1069.12 — Il fato di Tripoli e il fato latino. (Mariam, V.) Roma, 1912.
Afr 8678.9.50 — Il fattore demografico nell'organizzazione sociale del Bantu. (Sonnabend, E.H.) Roma, 1935.
Afr 2929.30A — Fatuzzo, Giacomo. Notiziario geografico del Sud-Tripolitano. Tripoli, 1930.
Afr 2687.1 — Un faubourg de Tunis, Saida Manoubia. (Sebag, Paul.) Paris, 1960.
Afr 2030.70.5 — Faucher, Jean André. Les barricades d'Alger. Paris, 1960.
Afr 2458.93 — Faucon, N. La Tunisie. Paris, 1893. 2v.
Afr 575.9.10 — Faugere, A.P. De la propagande musulmane en Afrique et dans les Indes. Paris, 1851.
Afr 6097.6 — Faulkner, Rose E. Joseph Sidney Hill, first bishop in western Equatorial Africa. London, 1895.
Afr 5184.20 — Faulong, L. Les rapports financiers de la métropole et de l'Afrique occidentale française. Paris, 1910.
Afr 6541.10 — Faupel, John. African holocaust. London, 1962.
Afr 6541.10.2 — Faupel, John. African holocaust. 2nd ed. London, 1962.
Afr 5190.10 — Faure, Claude. Histoire de la presqu'île du Cap Vert et des origines de Dakar. Paris, 1914.
Afr 555.149.10 — Fauré, Edouard. Les vingt-cinq ans de Coillard au Lessouto. Paris, 1931.
Afr 6689.5 — Faure, Jean. Togo; champ de mission. Paris, 1943.
NEDL Afr 1080.3 — Faure-Biguet, G. Histoire de l'Afrique septentrionale. Paris, 1905.
Afr 1838.8 — Faut-il faire de l'Algérie un dominion. (Paillard, Jean.) Paris, 1938.
Afr 2030.462.5 — Faut-il partager l'Algérie? (Peyrefitte, Alain.) Paris, 1962.
Afr 2030.461.65 — Fauvet, J. La Fronde des généraux. Paris, 1961.
Afr 555.149 — Favre, Edouard. François Coillard. Paris, 1908-13. 3v.
Afr 2030.462.95 — Favrod, C.H. Le F.L.N. et l'Algérie. Paris, 1962.
Afr 109.61.20 — Favrod, Charles. L'Afrique seule. Paris, 1961.
Afr 609.58.20 — Favrod, Charles. Le poids de l'Afrique. Paris, 1958.
Afr 2030.190 — Favrod, Charles. La révolution algérienne. Paris, 1959.
Afr 2749.58.5 — Favrod, Charles F. Sahara. Lausanne, 1958.
Afr 6283.7 — Fawckner, J. Narrative of travels on the coast of Benin. London, 1837.
Afr 6095.360 — Fax, Elton C. West Africa vignettes. N.Y., 1960.
Afr 6095.360.2 — Fax, Elton C. West Africa vignettes. 2 ed. N.Y., 1963.
Afr 3040.35.3 — Fayed, Osman. Tribunaux mixtes d'Egypte. Paris, 1912.
Afr 3978.73.5 — The Fayoum, or Artists in Egypt. (Lenoir, Paul.) London, 1873.
Afr 6457.5 — Fearn, Hugh. An African economy. London, 1961.
Afr 10690.89.120 — Feather woman of the jungle. (Tutuola, Amos.) London, 1962.
Afr 8152.75 — Feature in South African frontier life...embracing complete record of Kafir war 1850-51. (Hudson, M.B.) Port Elizabeth, 1852.
Afr 8190.15 — Febana. (Watt, E.P.) London, 1962.
Afr 7812.267 — La fécondité des populations congolaises. (Romaniuk, Anatole.) Paris, 1967.
Afr 3979.39.5 — Fedden, H.R. The land of Egypt. N.Y., 1939.
Afr 6277.75 — Federal government development programme, 1962-68. (Nigeria.) Lagos, 1962.
Afr 6210.40 — Federal government in Nigeria. (Awa, Eme O.) Berkeley, 1964.
Afr 8235.13 — A federal in South Africa. (Molteno, Percy A.) London, 1896.
Afr 6208.20 — Federal Nigeria, annual report. (Nigeria. Federal Information Service.) London, 1957.
Afr 109.64.25 — Federalism and the new nations. (Currie, D.P.) Chicago, 1964.
Afr 7815.25 — Fédération des Associations de Colons du Congo. L'opinion publique coloniale devant l'assimilation des indigènes. Bruxelles, 1951.

Afr 7812.260.15 — Fédération des Enterprises Congolaises. The Congolese economy on the eve of independence. Brussels, 1960.
Afr 3320.46 — Fédération Egyptienne de l'Industrie. Yearbook. Cairo. 1960+ 6v.
Afr 6392.17 — Federation in East Africa, opportunities. (Leys, Colin.) Oxford, 1966.
Afr 6212.25 — Federation of Nigeria. (Gaskiya Corporation, Zaria, Nigeria.) Zaria, 1959.
Afr 6275.104 — The federation of Nigeria. (London. Commonwealth Institute.) London, 1963.
Afr 6218.16 — The federation of Nigeria from earliest times to independence. (Ademoyega, Wale.) London, 1962.
Afr 9489.54 — Federation of Rhodesia and Nyasaland. Federal Information Services. The new federation of Rhodesia and Nyasaland. Salisbury, 1954.
Afr 9499.15 — Federation of Rhodesia and Nyasaland. Federal Information Services. Opportunity in Rhodesia and Nyasaland. Salisbury, 1955.
Afr 6739.268.5 — Federativnaia Respublika Kamerun. (Golubchik, Mark M.) Moskva, 1968.
Afr 6739.268.15 — Federativnaia Respublika Kamerun. (Loginova, Valentina P.) Moskva, 1968.
Afr 9499.37 — Federazione delle Rodesia e del Niassaland. (Italy. Istituto Nazionale per il Commercio Estero.) Roma, 1962.
Afr 2731.15.40 — Federici, Emidio. L'eremità del Sahara. Roma, 1954.
Afr 4700.36 — Federzoni, L. A.O., Africa orientale, il posto al sole. Bologna, 1936.
Afr 4700.26 — Federzoni, L. Venti mesi di azione coloniale. Milano, 1926.
Afr 2870.15 — Federzoni, Luigi. Rinascita dell'Africa romana. Bologna, 1929.
Afr 3814.5 — Fedorov, T. Finansy i kredit sudana. Moskva, 1962.
Afr 1609.31.10 — La feerie marocaine. (Gadala, M.T.) Grenoble, 1931.
Afr 7315.30 — Feio, Manuel Moreira. Estudos sociologicos; indigenas de Moçambique. Lisboa, 1900.
Afr 40.61.5 — Feireira, Oliverio. Ordem publica e liberdades politicas na Africa negra. Belo Horizonte, 1961.
Afr 8678.321.20 — Feit, Edward. African opposition in South Africa. Stanford, 1967.
Afr 8050.20 — Feit, Edward. South Africa. London, 1962.
Afr 7183.20 — Felgas, H.A. As populações nativas do Congo portugues. Luanda, 1960.
Afr 7122.48 — Felgas, Hélio. Guerra em Angola. Lisboa, 1961.
Afr 7122.48.5 — Felgas, Hélio. Guerra em Angola. 5. ed. Lisboa, 1968.
Afr 7180.38.2 — Felgas, Hélio. As populacões nativas do norte de Angola. 2. ed. Lisboa, 1965.
Afr 7119.58 — Felgas, Helio A. Historia do Congo (Esteres) portugues. Carmona, 1958.
Afr 7018.5 — Felgas, Hélio Augusto Estevez. Os movimentos terroristos de Angola, Guiné, Moçambique. Lisboa, 1966.
Afr 1490.15 — Feline, M.H. L'artillerie au Maroc, campagnes en Chaouia. Paris, 1912.
Afr 1406.9 — Felipe II, Isabel de Inglaterra y Marruecos. (Fernandez Alvarez, Manuel.) Madrid, 1951.
Afr 1757.1 — Feliu De La Pena, F. Leyenda historica...del penon de velez de la Gomera. Valencia, 1846.
Afr 1550.37 — Felix, Lucien. Le statut international du Maroc d'après les traités. Thèse. Paris, 1928.
Afr 5405.300 — Félix Eboué, sa vie et son oeuvre. (Maurice, Albert.) Bruxelles, 1954.
Afr 3978.69.5 — Le fellah: souvenirs d'Egypte. (About, E.) Paris, 1869.
Afr 3978.69.5.2 — Le fellah: souvenirs d'Egypte. 2e ed. (About, E.) Paris, 1870.
Afr 3978.69.5.4 — Le fellah: souvenirs d'Egypte. 3e ed. (About, E.) Paris, 1873.
Afr 3978.69.5.6 — Le fellah: souvenirs d'Egypte. 6e ed. (About, E.) Paris, 1876.
Afr 3979.38.12 — The fellaheen. 7th ed. (Ayrout, H.H.) Cairo, 1954.
Afr 3988.5A — The fellahin of Upper Egypt. (Blackman, Winifred Susan.) London, 1927.
Afr 3979.38.11.2 — Fellahs. 2. ed. (Ayrout, H.H.) Le Caire, 1942.
Afr 3988.5.5 — Les fellahs de la Haute-Egypte. (Blackman, Winifred Susan.) Paris, 1948.
Afr 3979.38.11 — Fellahs d'Egypte. 6. ed. (Ayrout, H.H.) Le Caire, 1952.
Afr 1680.9 — Felze, Jacques. Au Maroc inconnu dans le haut-atlas et le sud Marocain. Grenoble, 1935.
Afr 28715.4 — La Femme, la vache, la foi. (Sow, Alfâ Ibrâhîm.) Paris, 1966.
Afr 2218.6.10 — La femme algérienne. (Mrabet, F.) Paris, 1964.
Afr 2230.35 — La femme Chaouia de l'Aurès. Thèse. (Gaudry, Mathéa.) Paris, 1928.
Afr 2749.00 — Une femme chez les sahariennes. (Pommerot, J.) Paris, 1900.
Afr 635.86 — La femme noire en Afrique occidentale. (Marie André du Sacre Coeur, Sister.) Paris, 1939.
Afr 5447.5 — Femmes africaines en milieu urbain. (Vincent, Jeanne Françoise.) Paris, 1966.
Afr 2228.9 — Les femmes arabes. (Auclert, Hubertine.) Paris, 1900.
Afr 635.62 — Femmes d'Afrique noire. (Paulme, D.) Paris, 1960.
Afr 7818.5 — Femmes de Kinshasa hier et aujourd'hui. (Comhaire-Sylvain, Suzanne.) Paris, 1968.
Afr 2539.2 — Femmes de Tunisie. (Montety, H.) Paris, 1958.
Afr 6780.16 — Fendall, C.P. The East African force, 1915-1919. London, 1921.
Afr 676.63.20 — Feng, C. Glimpses of West Africa. Peking, 1963.
Afr 679.63.25 — Feng, Chi'h-Tan. Glimpses of West Africa. Peking, 1963.
Afr 3993.904 — Fenn, George Manville. The khedive's country. London, 1904.
Afr 8152.95 — Fenn, T.E. How I volunteered for the Cape. London, 1879.
VAfr 679.65.35 — Fenrych, Wiktor. Zapiski z Afriyki Zachodniej. Szczecin, 1965.
Afr 4558.55F — Fenzl, E. Bericht über C. Reitz und seine Reise. Vienna, 1855.
Afr 7118.25 — Feo Cardoza de Castellobranco e Torres, J.C. Memorias contendo a biographia do vice almirante Huiz da Motta a Feo e Torres. Paris, 1825.
Afr 3700.5.10 — Fer et feu au Soudan. (Slatin, R.C.) Le Caire, 1898. 2v.
Afr 1846.8 — Ferand, L.C. Les interprètes de l'armée d'Afrique. Alger, 1876.
Afr 2030.462.130A — Feraoun, M. Journal, 1955-62. Paris, 1962.
Afr 2230.44 — Feraoun, Mouloud. Jours de Kabylie. (Dessins de Brouty). Paris, 1968.
Afr 2345.5 — Féraud, Charles. Histoire des villes de la province de Constantine. La Calle. Alger, 1877.

Afr 6988.16.120	Fortune may fall, the story of Charles John Anderson, African explorer, 1827-1867. (Wallis, J.P.R.) London, 1936.
Afr 7850.45	Forty-six angry men, the forty-six civilian doctors of Elisabethville denounce U.N. violations in Katanga. Bruxelles, 1962.
Afr 8252.17	Forty South African years. (Ronan, B.) London, 1923.
Afr 8659.32	Forty years in Africa. (Trevor, Tudor Gruffydd.) London, 1932.
Afr 8006.10	Forum, South Africa's independent journal of opinion. Johannesburg. 8,1959+ 5v.
Afr 7175.27	A fossicker in Angola. (Burr, Malcolm.) London, 1933.
Afr 1259.30	Foster, Harry L. A vagabond in Barbary. N.Y., 1930.
Afr 555.13	Foster, L.R. Historical sketch - African mission. N.Y., 1884.
Afr 6390.58	Foster, Paul. White to move. London, 1961.
Afr 6538.65	Foster, Phillips Wayne. Population growth and rural development in Buganda. College Park, Md., 1968.
Afr 4070.8	Fothergill, E. Five years in the Sudan. London, 1910.
Afr 9838.91	Fotheringham, L.M. Adventures in Nyassaland. London, 1891.
Afr 632.17	Foucart, George. Questionnaire préliminaire d'ethnologie africaine. Le Caire, 1919.
Afr 2755.2	Foucaucourt, J. de. De l'Algérie au Soudan par le Sahara. 5000 kilomètres en automobile dans le désert et la brousse. Paris, 1928.
Afr 2731.15.6	Foucauld, Charles, Vicomte de. Lettres inédites au général Laperrine. Paris, 1954.
Afr 2731.15.8	Foucauld, Charles, Vicomte de. Memories of Charles de Foucauld. London, 1938.
Afr 2731.15.67	Foucauld, Charles, Vicomte de. Spiritual autobiography of Charles de Foucauld. N.Y., 1964.
Afr 2731.15.7	Foucauld, Charles. Lettres à Mme. de Bondy, de la Trappe à Tamanrasset. Paris, 1966.
Afr 2731.15.105	Foucauld, Charles. Schriften. Einsiedeln, 1961.
Afr 555.5.6	Foucauld, Charles de. Lettres è Henry de Castries. 10. éd. Paris, 1938.
Afr 2731.15.55	Foucauld, Charles de. Oeuvres spirituelles. Paris, 1958.
Afr 2731.15.58	Foucauld, Charles de. Père de Foucauld. Abbé Huvelin. Correspondance inédite. Tournai, 1957.
Afr 1325.1F	Foucauld, Charles de. Reconnaissance au Maroc. Paris, 1888. 2v.
Afr 2731.15.70	Foucauld devant l'Afrique du nord. (Carrouges, Michel.) Paris, 1961.
Afr 2508.5	Foucher, Louis. De l'évolution du protectorat de la France sur la Tunisie. Thèse. Paris, 1897.
Afr 5869.23	Foucque, Hippolyte. L'Ile de la Réunion. Paris, 1923.
Afr 5188.5	Fougeyrollas, Pierre. Modernisation des hommes, l'exemple du Sénégal. Paris, 1967.
Afr 2368.5.10	Fouilles de Sétif, les basiliques chrétiennes du quartier Nord-Ouest. (Février, Paul Albert.) Paris, 1965.
Afr 6415.5	Foundation of British East Africa. (Gregory, J.W.) London, 1901.
Afr 6277.47	Foundations of an African economy. (Aboyade, O.) N.Y., 1966.
Afr 8040.8	The foundations of freedom. (Cowen, D.V.) Cape Town, 1961.
X Cg Afr 3205.13	The founder of modern Egypt. (Dodwell, Henry.) Cambridge, Eng., 1931.
Afr 3255.7	Founders of modern Egypt. (Rowlatt, Mary.) London, 1962.
Afr 4559.57	The fountain of the sun. (Busk, Douglas L.) London, 1957.
Afr 2609.12.3	Fountains in the sand...oases of Tunisia. (Douglas, N.) N.Y., n.d.
Afr 6776.5	Fouquer, Roger. Mirambo, un chief de guerre dans l'Est Africain vers 1830-1884. Paris, 1967.
Afr 5183.951	Fouquet, Joseph. La traite des Arachides dans le pays de Kaolack. Montpelier, 1951.
Afr 5183.958	Fouquet, Joseph. La traite des Arachides dans le pays de Kaolack. St. Louis du Sénégal, 1958.
Afr 6883.26	Fouquet, Roger. Irakou. Paris, 1955.
Afr 3979.66	Four aspects of Egypt. (Marlowe, John.) London, 1966.
Afr 679.54	Four Guineas. (Huxley, E.G.) London, 1954.
Afr 8300.5	Four months besieged. Story of Ladysmith. (Pearse, H.H.S.) London, 1900.
Afr 3978.63	Four months in a dahabeeh. (Carey, M.L.M.) London, 1863.
Afr 2208.59.5	Four months in Algeria. (Blakesley, J.W.) Cambridge, 1859.
Afr 11433.75.110	Four people, a novel of South Africa. (Gordon, Gerald.) London, 1964.
Afr 3979.58.10	Four thousand miles of adventure. (Davy, Andre.) London, 1958.
NEDL Afr 3978.75	Four thousand miles of African travel. (Southworth, A.S.) N.Y., 1875.
Afr 6192.4	Four years in Ashante. (Ramseyer, F.A.) London, 1875.
Afr 7458.57	Four years in Liberia. (Williams, S.) Philadelphia, 1857.
Afr 6390.73	Four years in paradise. (Johnson, Asa Helen.) London, 1941.
Afr 8808.24	Four years in southern Africa. (Rose, C.) London, 1829.
Afr 2749.02	Foureau, F. D'Alger au Congo par le Tchad. Paris, 1902.
Afr 2749.02.2F	Foureau, F. Documents scientifiques de la mission saharienne. Paris, 1903.
Afr 2748.90	Foureau, F. Une mission au Tademayt. Paris, 1890.
Afr 2748.95	Foureau, F. Mission chez les Touareg. Paris, 1895.
Afr 2748.98	Foureau, F. Mon neuvième voyage au Sahara. Paris, 1898.
Afr 8838.2	Fourie, S. Jansenville yesterday and today. Jansenville, 1956.
Afr 1025.1F	Fournel, H. Etude sur la conquête de l'Afrique par les Arabes. v.1-2. Paris, 1857.
Afr 2928.87	Fournel, M. La Tripolitaine. Paris, 1887.
Afr 2608.86	Fournel, M. La Tunisie. Paris, 1886.
Afr 2030.85	Fournier, Christiane. Nous avons encore des héros. Paris, 1957.
Afr 8659.65.5	Fournier, Gilles. Vérité pour l'Afrique du Sud. Paris, 1965.
Afr 8289.02.14	Fournier, P.V. La guerre sud-africaine. Paris, 1902. 3v.
Afr 5749.00.15	Fournier, René. Notice sur Madagascar. Paris, 1900.
Afr 609.62.20	Fourteen Africans vs. one American. (Fox, Frederic.) N.Y., 1962.
Afr 8918.91	Fourteen years in Basutoland. (Widdicombe, John.) London, 1891.
Afr 8377.3	The Fourth of July raids. (Brokensha, Miles.) Cape Town, 1965.
Afr 2870.30	Fourth shore, Italy's mass colonization of Libya. (Moore, M.) London, 1940.

Afr 5580.4	Foury, B. Mandove et la colonisation de Madagascar. Paris, 1956.
Afr 2875.56	Fovel, Natale M. Tripoli e i problemi della democrazia. Firenze, 1914.
Afr 6143.38	Fowler-Lunn, K. The gold missus. N.Y., 1938.
Afr 6295.64.5	Fox, A.J. Uzuakoli. London, 1964.
Afr 7350.3.21	Fox, Early L. The American Colonization Society, 1817-40. Diss. Baltimore, 1919.
Afr 7350.3.20	Fox, Early L. The American Colonization Society. Baltimore, 1919.
Afr 609.62.20	Fox, Frederic. Fourteen Africans vs. one American. N.Y., 1962.
Afr 555.3.17	Fox, George T. A memoir of the...missionary to Cape Palmas. N.Y., 1868.
Afr 6391.5	Fox, Lorene Kimball. East African childhood. Nairobi, 1967.
Afr 6097.5	Fox, William. A brief history of the Wesleyan missions on the western coast of Africa. London, 1851.
Afr 3978.70.10	Fra aegyptenes land. (Watt, Robert.) Kjøbenhavn, 1870.
Afr 1258.94	Från orientens forgårdar. (Rogh, J.) Stockholm, 1894.
Afr 7480.2	Fraenkel, M. Tribe and class in Monrovia. London, 1964.
Afr 5180.10.5	Fragmens d'un voyage en Afrique. (Golberry, S.M.X.) Paris, 1802. 2v.
Afr 8868.5	A fragment of Basuto history. (Theal, G.M.) Cape Town, 1886.
Afr 10621.53.110	Fragments. (Armah, Ayi Kwei.) Boston, 1970[c1969].
Afr 3978.57.3	Fragments. (Mainly Egypt). (Tomard, E.F.) Paris, 1857.
Afr 2280.10	Franc, Julien. La colonisation de la Milidja. Thèse. Paris, 1928.
Afr 1830.30.4	Franc, Julien. La colonisation de la Mitidja. Paris, 1928.
Afr 1826.25	Franc, Julien. L'histoire de la colonie de l'Algérie, sources d'archives. Thèse. Alger, 1928.
Afr 5548.87	Le Français à Madagascar. (Hue, Fernand.) Paris, 1887.
Afr 5748.84	Les Français à Madagascar. (Leroy, L.) Paris, 1884.
Afr 1608.94.14	Les français au Maroc, mort du sultan. (Salmon.) Paris, 1894.
Afr 510.6	Les français aux colonies. (Sarzeau, J.) Paris, 1897.
Afr 510.4	Les français d'Afrique. (Dumas, P.) Paris, 1889.
Afr 1869.64	Les français d'Algérie. (Moncade, Noel.) Paris, 1964.
Afr 2260.20	Les français d'Algérie. (Nora, Pierre.) Paris, 1961.
Afr 2285.2	Les français dans le désert. (Trumelet, C.) Paris, 1865.
Afr 679.66.20	Français d'aujourd'hui en Afrique noire. (Toulat, Jean.) Paris, 1966.
Afr 2208.45	Les Français en Algérie. 3e ed. (Veuillot, L.) Tours, 1863.
Afr 3245.5	Les Français en Egypte. 2. ed. (Giffard, Pierre.) Paris, 1883.
Afr 3248.6	Français et Anglais en Egypte, 1881-1882. (Bioves, Achille.) Paris, 1910.
Afr 1955.18	Français et Arabes en Algérie. (Hugonnet, F.) Paris, 1860.
Afr 6720.30	Le français et la réorganisation des territoires du Cameroun. Thèse. (Costedoat, René.) Besançon, 1930.
Afr 1609.08.4	Une française au Maroc. (Zeys, Mathilde.) Paris, 1908.
Afr 5235.194	Une française au Soudan. (Bonnetain, Raymonde.) Paris, 1894.
Afr 3183.25	France, Egypte et mer Rouge, de 1715 à 1798. (Charles-Roux, François.) Paris, 1951.
Afr 1570.18	La France, l'Allemagne au Maroc. (Rolland-Chevillon.) Paris, 1907.
Afr 5425.15	France, Louis. De l'origine des Pahouins. Paris, 1905.
Afr 1658.50	France, Spain and the rif. (Harris, W.B.) London, 1927.
Afr 1570.13	La France, vassale de l'Angleterre. (Polignac.) Alger, 1894.
Afr 1571.45	France. Journal du consulat général de France à Maroc. Casablanca, 1943.
Afr 1325.7F	France. Question de la protection diplomatique au Maroc. Paris, 1880.
Afr 510.9	La France...en Afrique. (Rouard de Card, E.) Paris, 1903.
Afr 5404.20	France. Agence de la France d'Outre-mer. Afrique équatoriale française. v.1-4. Paris, 1950.
Afr 5045.44	France. Agence de la France d'Outre-Mer. France d'outre-mer. Paris, 1950. 6 pam.
Afr 5470.10	France. Centre National de la Recherche Scientifique. Dossiers de la Recherche cooperative sur programme. Paris. 2,1968
Afr 6277.88	France. Centre National Du Commerce Exterieur. Le marche du Nigeria. Paris, 1962.
Afr 626.62	France. Centre National du Commerce Extérieur. Memento commercial. Paris, 1959.
Afr 2223.38	France. Chambre des Députés (1908). Rapport fait...budget spécial de l'Algérie. v.1-2. Paris, 1908.
Afr 1869.30	France. Comite National. Cahiers du centenaire de l'Algerie. Alger, 1930. 2v.
Afr 6685.10	France. Commissariat au Togo. Guide de la colonisation au Togo. Paris, 1924.
Afr 6738.13	France. Commissariat de la République Française au Cameroun. Guide de la colonisation au Cameroun. Paris, 1923.
Afr 1273.954	France. Commission d'Etude. Deuxième plan de modernisation. n.p., 1954. 2 pam.
Afr 2223.954	France. Commission d'Etude et de Coordination des Plans. Deuxiéme plan de modernisation. n.p., 1954.
Afr 2209.58.5	France. Délégation Générale en Algérie. Documents algériens. Paris, 1958.
Afr Doc 5033.5	France. Direction de la coopération culturelle et technique. Rapport d'activité. Paris. 1961+
Afr 5406.250.5	France. Direction de la Documentation. French Equatorial Africa. Levallois, 195-.
Afr 5057.16	France. Direction de la Documentation. French West Africa. Rennes, 1956.
Afr 5046.2	France. Direction des Affaires Economiques et Financières. Planification en Afrique. v.2- Paris, 1962- 3v.
Afr 2223.957.5	France. Embassy. U.S. Algeria at work. N.Y., 1957.
Afr 5460.15	France. Embassy. U.S. The Central African Republic. N.Y., 1960.
Afr 5057.26	France. Embassy. U.S. French Africa. N.Y., 1958.
Afr 5420.261	France. Embassy. U.S. The Gabon Republic. N.Y., 1961.
Afr 5090.10	France. Embassy. U.S. The Islamic Republic of Mauritania. N.Y., 1960.

Afr 5645.5	France. Embassy. U.S. Madagascar, birth of a new republic. N.Y., 1960.
Afr 5480.261	France. Embassy. U.S. The Republic of Chad. N.Y., 1961.
Afr 5440.10	France. Embassy. U.S. The Republic of Congo. N.Y., 1961.
Afr 5385.36	France. Embassy. U.S. The Republic of Dahomey. N.Y., 1960.
Afr 5180.42	France. Embassy. U.S. The Republic of Senegal. N.Y., 1960.
Afr 5342.55	France. Embassy. U.S. The Republic of the Ivory Coast. N.Y., 1960.
Afr 5260.30	France. Embassy. U.S. The Republic of the Niger. N.Y., 1960.
Afr 5280.5	France. Embassy. U.S. The Republic of the Upper Volta. N.Y., 1960.
Afr 2223.961.15	France. Embassy. United States. The Constantine plan for Algeria, opening new frontiers in development. N.Y., 1961.
Afr 1026.10	France. Etat-Major de l'Armée. Service Historique. L'Afrique français du Nord. T.1-4. Paris, 1930-35. 4v.
Afr 5749.66	France. Institut Geographique National. Annexe de Tananarive. Expose des travaux executes en 1965 sur le territoire de la Republique Malgache. Paris, 1966.
Afr 5749.60	France. Institut Geographique National. Service Geographique a Tananarive. Expose des travaux exécutes en 1959 sur le territoire de la Republique Malgache. Paris, 1960.
Afr Doc 6607.361	France. Institut National de la Statistiqe et des Etudes Economique. Service de Cooperation. Données de base sur la situation démographique au Dahomey en 1961. Paris, 1962.
Afr Doc 5008.5	France. Institut National de la Statistique et des Etudes Economiques. Service de Cooperation. Afrique noire, Madagascar, Comores; démographie comparée. v.1-5,7,9-10. Paris, 1965-67. 3v.
Afr Doc 5008.700	France. Institut National de la Statistique et des Etudes Economique. Service de Coopération. Commerce extérieur des états d'Afrique et de Madagascar. Paris. 1949+
Afr Doc 6907.360	France. Institut National de la Statistique et des Etudes Economiques. Service de Coopération. Etude démographique du Niger. Paris, 1962-1963. 2v.
Afr Doc 5807.5	France. Institut National de la Statistique et des Etudes Economiques. Annuaire statistique de la Reunion. Paris. 1952-1955
Afr Doc 5008.705	France. Institut National de la Statistique et des Etudes Economiques. Compendium des statistiques du commerce extérieur de pays africains et Malgache. 1960+
Afr Doc 5508.614	France. Institut National de la Statistique et des Etudes Economiques. Comptes économiques de la Cote française des Somalis. Paris. 1959+
Afr Doc 5709.303	France. Institut National de la Statistique et des Etudes Economiques. Comptes économiques du territoire des Comores. Paris. 1959+
Afr 1623.957	France. Institut National de la Statistique et des Études Economiques. Dix ans d'économie marocaine, 1945-1955. Paris, 1957.
Afr 5285.260	France. Institut National de la Statistique et des Etudes Economiques. Une enquête de ménage en pays Lobi. Paris, 1961.
Afr Doc 5507.356	France. Institut National de la Statistique et des Etudes Economiques. Recensement de la population de la Cote française des Somalis, population non originaire, 1956. Paris, 1961.
Afr Doc 7108.5	France. Institut National de la Statistique et des Etudes Economique. La situation démographique au Tchad, résultats provisoires. Paris, 196-.
Afr Doc 5002.5	France. Institut National de la Statistique et des Etudes Economiques. Situation des enquêtes statistiques et socio-économiques dans les états africains et malgaches. Paris. 1964+
Afr 5448.15.10	France. Ministère de la Coopération. Les budgets des ménages africains a Pointe-Noire, 1958-1959. Paris, 1962.
Afr 5240.14	France. Ministère de la Coopération. Direction des affaires économiques et financières. 2. éd. Paris, 1965.
Afr 5091.12	France. Ministère de la Coopération. Economie et plan de développement, République islamique de Mauritanie. 2.éd. Paris, 1963.
Afr 6686.40.2	France. Ministère de la Coopération. Economie et plan de développement, Republique Togolaise. 2. ed. Paris, 1965.
Afr 5183.960.3	France. Ministère de la Coopération. Economie et plan de développement. 3. éd. Paris, 1964.
Afr 510.102	France. Ministère de la Coopération. Guide pratique sur les républiques. Paris, 1964.
Afr Doc 5008.207	France. Ministère de la Coopération. Perspectives de population dans les pays africains et malgache d'expression française. Paris, 1963.
Afr 5046.5	France. Ministère de la Coopération. Problemes de planification. Paris, 1964. 11v.
Afr 5046.8	France. Ministère de la Coopération. Rapport sur la coopération franco-africaine. Paris, 1964.
Afr 5758.63.3	France. Ministère de la Coopération. Direction des Affaires Economiques et Financières. Sous-Direction des Etudes Générales. Economie et plan de développement. 3. éd. Paris, 1963.
Afr 5442.13	France. Ministère de la Coopération. Direction des Affaires Economiques et Financières. Sous-Direction des Etudes Générales. Economie et plan de développement: Republique du Congo-Brazzaville. 3. éd. Paris, 1965.
Afr 6739.262.2	France. Ministère de la Coopération. Direction des Affaires Economiques et Financières. Sous-Direction des Etudes Générales. Economie et plan de développement, République fédérale du Cameroun. 2. éd. Paris, 1965.
Afr 5343.3	France. Ministère de la Coopération. Direction des Affaires Economiques. Economie et plan de développement. Paris, 196-.
Afr 5482.5	France. Ministère de la Coopération. Direction des Affaires Economiques. Economie et plan de développement. Paris, 1964.
Afr Doc 6907.5	France. Ministère de la Coopération. Mission Economique et Pastorale, 1963. Etude démographique et économique en milieu homade. Paris, 1966.
Afr Doc 6808.90	France. Ministère de la France d'Outre-Mer. Etude démographique du delta vif du Niger. pt.1. v.2. Paris. 1962
Afr 5200.29	France. Ministère de la France d'Outre-Mer. Service des Statistiques. Mission Socio-Economique du Soudan. Rapport provisoire. 2-3,1957-1958
Afr Doc 6307.355	France. Ministère de la France d'Outre-Mer. Service des Statistiques. Mission démographique de Guinée. Etude démographique par sondage, Guinée, 1954-1955. Paris, 1956.
Afr 2208.53	France. Ministère de la Guerre. Rapport sur la situation de l'Algérie en 1853. Paris, 1854.
Afr 590.13.5F	France. Ministère des Affaires Estrangères. Conférence international de Bruxelles, 18 nov. 1889-2 juil. 1890. v.1-3. Bruxelles, 1890.
Afr 1325.8F	France. Ministère des Affaires Etrangères. Accords conclus...entre France et l'Angleterre. Paris, 1904.
Afr 3269.1F	France. Ministère des Affaires Etrangères. Affaires d'Egypte 1884. Paris, 1884.
Afr 3740.1F	France. Ministère des Affaires Etrangères. Affaires du Haut-Nil 1897-98. Paris, 1898.
Afr 3269.4F	France. Ministère des Affaires Etrangères. Documents diplomatiques. Paris, 1881. 4 pam.
Afr 3269.05F	France. Ministère des Affaires Etrangères. Documents diplomatiques. Paris, 1881.
Afr 3269.08F	France. Ministère des Affaires Etrangères. Documents diplomatiques. Paris, 1883.
Afr 5620.2F	France. Ministère des Affaires Etrangères. Documents diplomatiques. Paris, 1883. 4 pam.
Afr 5402.10F	France. Ministère des Affaires Etrangères. Documents diplomatiques. Paris, 1885.
Afr 3269.3F	France. Ministère des Affaires Etrangères. Documents diplomatiques. Paris, 1885. 5 pam.
Afr 33.10F	France. Ministère des Affaires Etrangères. Documents diplomatiques. Paris, 1890. 16 pam.
Afr 3269.2F	France. Ministère des Affaires Etrangères. Documents diplomatiques. Paris, 1893.
Afr 5620.3F	France. Ministère des Affaires Etrangères. Documents diplomatiques. Paris, 1895.
Afr 2530.5F	France. Ministère des Affaires Etrangères. Documents diplomatiques. Paris, 1897.
Afr 200.4.3F	France. Ministère des Affaires Etrangères. Documents diplomatiques. Paris, 1898.
Afr 2430.1F	France. Ministère des Affaires Etrangères. Documents diplomatiques. Affaires de Tunisie, 1870-81, et supplément. Paris, 1881. 2v.
Afr 3994.880.5F	France. Ministère des Affaires Etrangères. Documents diplomatiques. Affaires d'Egypte. Paris, 1880.
Afr 1570.10F	France. Ministère des Affaires Etrangères. Documents diplomatiques. Affaires du Maroc. v.1-6. Paris, 1904. 6v.
Afr 1340.6	France. Ministère des Affaires Etrangères. Rapport général sur...le protectorat du Maroc. Rabat, 192-.
Afr 755.2	France. Ministère des Colonies. Documentation scientifique de la mission Tilho. Paris, 1910. 4v.
Afr 2702.2F	France. Ministère des Travaux Publiques. Documents rel. à miss. Flatters. Paris, 1884.
Afr 1826.33	France. Ministère d'Etat Chargé des Affaires Algériennes. Bulletin de documentation. Paris. 11-44,1961-1965
Afr 1259.52	France. Président Du Conseil. Facts and figures about French North Africa. Paris, 1952.
Afr Doc 5009.505	France. Secretariat d'Etat aux affaires étrangeres, Charge de la Cooperation. Données statistiques sur l'enseignment dans les etats africains et malgache d'expression française. Paris. 1965+
Afr 5342.30	France. Service de Documentation Economique. Côte-d'Ivoire, 1954. Paris, 1954.
Afr 1915.14	La France à l'heure algérienne. (Meningaud, Jean.) Paris, 1956.
Afr 5585.15	La France à Madagascar, 1815-1895. (Brunet, Louis.) Paris, 1895.
Afr 5625.4	La France à Madagascar. (Marield, J.) Paris, 1887.
Afr 5549.09	La France à Madagascar. (Suau, Pierre.) Paris, 1909.
Afr 5548.95.3	La France à Madagascar. 2e ed. (Brunet, L.) Paris, 1895.
Afr 5573.10.5	La France à Madagascar au XVIIe siecle. (Froidevaux, H.) Paris, 1901.
Afr 2030.50.10	France and Algeria. 1st Amer. ed. (Tillion, G.) N.Y., 1961.
Afr 2025.34	France and Algeria. 1st ed. (Confer, Vincent.) N.Y., 1966.
Afr 1570.01	Pamphlet box. France and Morocco.
Afr 5040.10	France and the Africans, 1944-1960: a political history. (Mortimer, Edward.) London, 1969.
Afr 5052.2	France and West Africa. (Hargreaves, J.D.) London, 1969.
Afr 1571.4.8	La France au Maroc. (Bernard, A.) Paris, 1917.
Afr 1571.14	La France au Maroc. (Georges-Gaulis, B.) Paris, 1919.
Afr 1493.55	La France au Maroc. (Goulven, Joseph.) Paris, 1937.
Afr 2209.08	La France au soleil, notes sur l'Algérie. (Bruchard, H. de.) Paris, 1908.
Afr 510.14	La France aux colonies. (Wahl, M.) Paris, 1896.
Afr 555.11	La France catholique en Tunisie. (Guerin, V.) Tours, 1886.
Afr 2025.2	La France d'Afrique et ses destinées. (Marial, W.) Paris, 1883.
Afr 2208.88	La France dans l'Afrique du nord. (Vignon, L.) Paris, 1888.
Afr 5054.02	La France dans l'Afrique occidentale. (Dreyfus, Camille.) Paris, 1902.
Afr 2710.1	La France dans le Sahara. (Mercier, E.) Paris, 1889.
Afr 5749.09	La France dans l'ocean Indien. (Gallois, E.) Paris, 1909.
Afr 2209.12.3	La France de l'Afrique du nord. (Bonand, R. de.) Paris, 1912.
Afr 5749.52	France de l'ocean Indien. Paris, 1952.
Afr 5045.44	France d'outre-mer. (France. Agence de la France d'Outre-Mer.) Paris, 1950. 6 pam.
Afr 510.5	La France en Afrique. (Ferry, E.) Paris, 1905.
Afr 2260.15	La France en Algérie. (Vignon, L.) Paris, 1893.
Afr 5340.21	La France en Côte-d'Ivoire de 1843 à 1893. (Atger, Paul.) Dakar, 1962.
Afr 2485.5	La France en Tunisie. (Grandchamp, P.) Tunis, 1920-33. 10v.
Afr 2494.10	La France en Tunisie à la fin du XVIe siècle. (Grandchamp, P.) Tunis, 1920.

Afr 5406.242 French Equatorial Africa and Cameroons. (Great Britain. Naval Intelligence Division.) London, 1942.
Afr 5305 Pamphlet box. French Guinea.
Afr 5305.1 Pamphlet box. French Guinea.
Afr 1990.1 The French in Algiers. (Lamping, C.) N.Y., 1845.
Afr 1965.13 The French in Algiers. (Lamping, Clemens.) N.Y., 1845.
Afr 5329.1 Pamphlet box. French Ivory Coast.
Afr 1110.40.5 French North Africa. (Berque, Jacques.) N.Y., 1967.
Afr 5625.2.5 French operations in Madagascar, 1883-1885. (Oliver, S. Pasfield.) London, 1885-86.
   2 pam.
Afr 8115.10 The French refugees at the Cape. (Botha, Colin G.) Cape Town, 1919.
Afr 212.9 French-speaking Africa. (Lewis, William Hubert.) N.Y., 1965.
Afr 5040.8 French-speaking Africa since independence. (Lusignan, Guy de.) London, 1969.
Afr Doc 6002.2 French-speaking West Africa; a guide to official publications. (Library of Congress. African Section.) Washington, 1967.
Afr 5054.62 French-speaking West Africa. (Neres, Philip.) London, 1962.
Afr 3340.12 The French spy ring in the UAR. (United Arab Republic. Information Department.) Cairo, 1962.
Afr 5205 Pamphlet box. French Sudan.
Afr 5205.1 Pamphlet box. French Sudan.
Afr 5005.1 Pamphlet box. French Tropical Africa.
Afr Doc 6003.5 French West Africa. Annuaire du gouvernement général de l'Afrique occidentale française. n.p., n.d.
Afr 5056.123 French West Africa. Catalogue des positions géographiques provisoirement admises par le Service géographique de l'A.O.F. Laval, 1923-24.
Afr 5056.122 French West Africa. Dispositions cartographiques relatives aux cartes et plans de l'A.O.F. Laval, 1924.
Afr 5057.27 French West Africa. L'équipement de l'A.O.F. Paris, 1950.
Afr 5056.107 French West Africa. La Maurétanie. Corseil, 1907.
Afr 5190.10.5 French West Africa. Notice sur le plan de Dakar et environs d'après photo-aérienne. Gorée, 1923.
Afr 5056.123.5 French West Africa. Supplément au Catalogue des positions géographiques de l'A.O.F. Laval, 1925.
Afr 5057.16 French West Africa. (France. Direction de la Documentation.) Rennes, 1954.
Afr 5056.157.5 French West Africa. (Thompson, V.M.) Stanford, Calif., 1957.
Afr 5050.5 French West Africa. Agence Economique. Bulletin mensuel. Paris 5,1924+
   4v.
Afr 5051.10 French West Africa. Archives. Répertoire des archives. Rufisque, 1957.
   2v.
Afr 5000.5 French West Africa. Comité d'Etudes Historiques et Scientifiques. Annuaire et mémoires. Gorée. 1916+
   2v.
Afr 5000.5.3 French West Africa. Comité d'Etudes Historiques et Scientifiques. Bulletin. 1919+
   19v.
Afr 5057.22F French West Africa. Direction Générale des Services Economiques et du Plan. Le financement du plan. Paris, 1957.
Afr Doc 6007.2 French West Africa. Service des Etudes et Coordination Statistique et Mécanographiques. Annuaire statistique. Dakar. 3-6,1936-1957
   2v.
Afr Doc 6007.5 French West Africa. Service des Etudes et Coordination Statistiques et Mécanographiques. Bulletin statistique et economique mensuel. 1955-1959
   8v.
Afr Doc 6274.4.73 French West Africa. Service des Etudes et Coordination Statistiques et Mécanographiques. Recensement, démographique de Dakar, 1955: résultats définitifs. Paris, 1958-62.
   2v.
Afr 5056.124 French West Africa. Service Géographique. Rapport annuel, technique et administratif. Laval. 1922+
Afr 5056.143.5 French West Africa. v.1-2. (Great Britain. Naval Intelligence Division.) London, 1943.
Afr 8289.01.31 French's calvary campaign. 2d ed. (Maydon, J.G.)
Afr 7369.64 Frenkel, Matrei I. SShA i Liberiia. Moscow, 1964.
Afr 6926.1 Frenssen, G. Peter Moors fahrt nach Südwest. Berlin, 1907.
Afr 6926.1.2 Frenssen, G. Peter Moor's journey to Southwest Africa. London, 1908.
Afr 1493.71 Frente a Abd-el-Krim. (Osuna Servent, Arturo.) Madrid, 1922.
Afr 1769.18.5 Frente al fracaso, Raisuni. De silvestre a burguete. (Lopez Rienda, R.) Madrid, 1923.
Afr 7200.6 Frente de Libertação de Moçambique. War communiqué. Cairo. 2,1966+
Afr 7212.3 Pamphlet vol. Frente de Libertação de Moçambique. Spanish.
   2 pam.
Afr 5872.10 Freon, L.S. Un ardennais conseiller du roi. Verviers, 1953.
Afr 6390.10 Frere, H.B.E. Eastern Africa as a field for missionary labour. London, 1874.
Afr 2218.8 Frère, Suzanne. Sons et images dans le bled algérien. Alger, 1961.
Afr 2731.15.45 Frère Charles. (Vignaud, Jean.) Paris, 1947.
Afr 5840.15 Le frère Scubilion de l'Institut des frères des écoles chrétiennes. (Chassagnon, H., Abbé.) Paris, 1902.
Afr 7809.24.10 Fresh tracks in the Belgian Congo. (Norden, H.) London, 1924.
Afr 5218.88 Frey, H. Campagne dans le haut Sénégal et dans le haut Niger, 1885-86. Paris, 1888.
Afr 3199.05 Freycinet, C. de. La question d'Egypte. Paris, 1905.
Afr 5480.208 Freydenberg, Henri. Le Tchad et le bassin du Chari. Thèse. Paris, 1908.
Afr 6988.66.205 Freyer, E.P.W. Chronik von Otavi und einer Karte. Otavi, 1966.
Afr 7182.3 Freyre, Gilberto. Em torno de alguns tumulos afro-cristaos. Bahia, 1960.
Afr 6640.17 Freytagh Loringhoven, Axel F. Das Mandatsrecht in den Deutschen Kolonien. München, 1938.
Afr 1200.65 Fribourg, Andre. L'Afrique latine. Paris, 1922.
Afr 11433.74.130 Friday's footprint. (Gordimer, Nadine.) London, 1960.
Afr 3986.963.5 Fridman, L.A. Kapitalisticheskoe razvitie Egipta, 1882-1939. Moscow, 1963.

Afr 1259.36 Friedliches Afrika. (Adrian, W.) Bern, 1936.
Afr 8678.301 Friedmann, M.V. I will still be moved. Chicago, 1963.
Afr 11406.41.100 Friedmann, M.V. The slap. London, 1961.
Afr 55.44 Friedrich-Ebert-Stiftung. Afrika Biographien. Hannover, 1967-
   3v.
Afr 8659.60.25F Friend, Bloemfontein. Union jubilee, 1910-1960. Bloemfontein, 1960.
Afr 8659.58.10 Friend, Bloemfontein. Without fear or favour. Cape Town, 1958.
Afr 6.1 Friend of Africa. ondon. 1,1841+
Afr 8152.96 Friends and foes in the Transkei. (Prichard, A.M.) London, 1880.
Afr 550.55 Friends of Africa. (Mackenzie, J.K.) Cambridge, Mass., 1928.
Afr 11317.76.100 Friends today, enemies tomorrow. (Darks, D. Offei.) Akropong, 1961
Afr 1608.95.3 Frisch, R.J. Le Maroc géographie Organisation politique. Paris, 1895.
Afr 2749.61.10 Frison-Roche, Roger. Sahara de l'aventure. Paris, 1961.
Afr 8658.60.5 Fritsch, G. Drei Jahre in Süd-Afrika. Breslau, 1868.
Afr 8678.5 Fritsch, G. Die Eingeborenen Süd-Afrikas. Atlas und Text. Breslau, 1872.
Afr 2945.33 Fritz, Egon. Romantische Cyrenaika. Hamburg, 1941.
Afr 3816.2 Frobenius, Herman. Die Heiden-Neger des ägyptischen Sudan. Berlin, 1893.
Afr 7809.04 Frobenius, L. Im Schatten des Kongostaates. Berlin, 1907.
Afr 6280.8 Frobenius, L. Und Afrika sprach. Berlin, 1912.
Afr 718.30 Frobenius, L. The voice of Africa. V.1-2. London, 1913.
   2v.
Afr 632.10 Frobenius, L.V. Ursprung der Kultur. Berlin, 1898.
Afr 5056.110 Frobenius, Leo. Auf dem Wege nach Atlantis. Berlin, 1911.
Afr 609.23.10 Frobenius, Leo. Das unbekannte Afrika. München, 1923.
Afr 718.30.1 Frobenius, Leo. The voice of Africa. N.Y., 1968.
   2v.
Afr 8295.5 Frocard. La guerre au Transvaal. Paris, 1900.
   2v.
Afr 6688.5 Froelich, J.C. Les populations du Nord-Togo. Paris, 1963.
Afr 6097.8 Froelich, Jean Claude. Animismes, les religions paiennes de l'Afrique de l'ouest. Paris, 1964.
Afr 6715.15 Froelich, Jean Claude. Cameroun, Togo. Paris, 1956.
Afr 575.32 Froelich, Jean Claude. Les musulmans d'Afrique Noire. Paris, 1962.
Afr 1903.5 Froelicher, E. La domination espagnole en Algeria. Paris, 1904.
Afr 5573.10.5 Froidevaux, H. La France à Madagascar au XVIIe siècle. Paris, 1901.
Afr 5593.2 Froidevaux, H. Les Lazaristes à Madagascar au XVIII siècle. Paris, 1904.
Afr 5573.10 Froidevaux, H. Un mémoire inédit de La Haye sur Madagascar. Paris, 1897.
   4 pam.
Afr 2030.467.5 Frolkin, Nikolai M. Krest'ianstvo v alzhirskoi revoliutsii, 1954-1962. Kiev, 1967.
Afr 8659.29 From an old Cape homestead. (Alston, M.) London, 1929.
Afr 7175.2 From Benguella to the territory of Yacca. (Capello, H.) London, 1882.
   2v.
Afr 8295.7 From Capetown to Ladysmith. (Steevens, S.W.) N.Y., 1900.
Afr 1259.27 From Corsair to Riffian. (Anderson, I.) Boston, 1927.
Afr 3258.7 From Cyprus to Zanzibar. (Vizetelly, E.) London, 1901.
Afr 5053.34 From French West Africa to the Mali federation. (Foltz, William J.) New Haven, 1965.
Afr 718.21 From Hausaland to Egypt. (Kumm, H.K.W.) London, 1910.
Afr 3979.53 From here we start. 3d ed. (Khalid, K.M.) Washington, 1953.
Afr 6174.5 From Kabul to Kumassi. (Willcocks, J.) London, 1904.
Afr 3708.3.2 From Korti to Khartum. (Wilson, C.W.) Edinburgh, 1885.
Afr 3708.3 From Korti to Khartum. (Wilson, C.W.) Edinburgh, 1886.
Afr 2749.60 From Libyan sands to Chad. (Heseltine, Nigel.) London, 1960.
Afr 8687.345 From Lisbon to Lübeck to Cape Town. (Spulhaus, Karl Antonio.) Cape Town, 1960.
Afr 5549.62 From Madagascar to the Malagasy Republic. (Kent, R.K.) N.Y., 1962.
Afr 8848.5 From Moscow to the Cape, the story of the Wienands of Waldeck. (Efolliott, Pamela.) Cape Town, 1963.
Afr 5426.100.10 From my African note-book. (Schweitzer, Albert.) London, 1938.
Afr 8686.2 From Natal to the Upper Zambesi. 2. ed. (Arnot, Frederick Stanley.) Glasgow, 1883.
Afr 6455.24 From Natal to Zanzibar. Durban, 1873.
Afr 8292.33 From Quebec to Pretoria with...Royal Canadian Regiment. (Hart-Matlarg, W.) Toronto, 1902.
Afr 4559.25.3 From Red Sea to blue Nile. (Forbes, R.T.) N.Y., 1925.
Afr 4559.25.5 From Red Sea to blue Nile. (Forbes, R.T.) N.Y., 1935.
Afr 6535.10 From Ruwenzore to the Congo. (Wollaston, A.F.R.) London, 1908.
Afr 6535.10.3 From Ruwenzore to the Congo. (Wollaston, A.F.R.) N.Y., 1908.
Afr 4050.7 From sphinx to oracle. (White, A.S.) London, 1899.
Afr 1259.23 From Tangier to Tripoli. 1st ed. (Carpenter, F.G.) Garden City, 1923.
Afr 724.3A From the Cape to Cairo. (Grogan, E.S.) London, 1900.
Afr 8659.05 From the Cape to the Zambesi. (Hutchinson, G.T.) London, 1905.
Afr 718.25.4 From the Congo to the Niger and the Nile. (Adolf, Friedrich.) Philadelphia, 1914.
   2v.
Afr 718.25.5 From the Congo to the Niger and the Nile. V.1-2. (Adolf, Friedrich.) London, 1913.
   2v.
Afr 5385.13 From the darkness of Africa to light of America. (Besolow, T.E.) Boston, 1891.
Afr 555.130 From the hands of the wicked. (Lawman, Tony.) London, 1960.
Afr 8659.16 From the heart of the veld. (Alston, Madeline.) London, 1916.
Afr 718.27 From the Niger to the Nile. (Alexander, Boyd.) London, 1907.
Afr 8678.222 From the notebooks of Lionel Forman, black and white in South African history. (Forman, L.) Cape Town, 1960.
Afr 5897.2 From the tropics to the North Sea. (Barkly, Fanny Alexandra.) London, 1897.
Afr 9545.5 From tribal rule to modern government. (Rhodes-Livingston Institute, Lusaka, 1959.
Afr 1259.44 From Tripoli to Marrakesh. (Elderkin, K.D. (McKnight.)) Springfield, Mass., 1944.

Afr 8335.10 From union to apartheid; a trek to isolation. (Ballinger, Margaret Livingstone.) Bailey, 1969.
Afr 8678.444 From union to apartheid. (Ballinger, Margaret.) N.Y., 1969.
Afr 11560.85.100 From veld and street. (Matheson, G.E.) London, 1899.
Afr 6878.77 From Zanzibar to Ujiji. (Dodgshun, Arthur W.) Boston, 1969.
Afr 5405.109.15 Froment-Guieysse, G. Brazza. Paris, 1945.
Afr 2280.3 Fromentin, E. Une année dans le Sahel. 2d ed. Paris, 1859.
Afr 2280.5 Fromentin, E. Une année dans le Sahel. 6th ed. Paris, 1884.
Afr 2748.57 Fromentin, E. Un été dans le Sahara. Paris, 1857.
Afr 2748.57.5 Fromentin, E. Un été dans le Sahara. Paris, 1922.
Afr 3978.69.25 Fromentin, E. Voyage en Egypte (1869). Paris, 1935.
Afr 609.63.15 Fromm, Friedrich Karl. Grosswild, Kleinvieh und Touristen. Berlin, 1963.
Afr 2030.461.65 La Fronde des généraux. (Fauvet, J.) Paris, 1961.
Afr 2209.59 Le front. (Davezies, Robert.) Paris, 1959.
Afr 7122.75 Front Revolutionnaire Africain pour l'Indépendence Nationale des Colonies Portugaises. La repression colonialiste en Angola. 2d ed. Anvers, 1960.
Afr 4513.38.12 Il fronte sud. 2a ed. (Graziani, R.) Milano, 1938.
Afr 8848.3 Frontier family. (Meintjes, J.) n.p., 1956.
Afr 8687.225 Frontier magistrate. (Guthrie, F.H.) Cape Town, 1946.
Afr 8847.34 Frontier post, the story of Grahamstown. (Collier, Joy.) Grahamstown, 1961.
Afr 8095.3 The frontier tradition in South Africa. (Walker, E.A.) London, 1930.
Afr 2209.11 La frontière algéro-marocaine. (Colliez, A.) Paris, 1911.
Afr 1571.2 La frontière franco-marocaine...20 july 1901. (Rouard de Card, E.) Toulouse, 1902.
Afr 7809.52.10 Les frontières du Congo belge. (Jentgen, P.) Bruxelles, 1952.
Afr 7933.2 Les frontiéres du Ruanda-Urundi et le régime international de Tutelle. (Jentgen, P.) Bruxelles, 1957.
Afr 6390.24.3 Frontiers of enchantment. (Leigh, W.R.) N.Y., 1938.
Afr 9506.1 Frontiers of the kingdom. (Gray, S. Douglas.) London, 1930.
Afr 608.48 Frost, John. The book of travels in Africa. N.Y., 1848.
Afr 9060.15 Frost, R.K. No other foundation. Durban, 1960.
Afr 8235.9 Froude, J.A. Two lectures on South Africa. London, 1900.
Afr 1915.3 Frousseaux. Aventures de dona ines de la Cisternas. Utrecht, 1737.
Afr 8050.8.2 Fruit of the national regime, 1948-1966. Bloemfontein, 1966.
Afr 7350.3.30 Fruits of colonizationism. n.p., 1833.
Afr 3978.24 Fruits of enterprize, travels in Egypt. Boston, 1824.
Afr 3978.24.5 Fruits of enterprize, travels in Egypt. New ed. N.Y., 1843.
Afr 4513.36.115 Frusci, L. In Somalia sul fronte meridionale. Bologna, 1936.
Afr 8678.410 Frye, William R. In whitest Africa; the dynamics of apartheid. Englewood Cliffs, 1968.
Afr 3305.16 Fuad, king of Egypt. (Shah, Ikbal Ali.) London, 1936.
Afr 2762.17 Fuchs, Peter. The land of veiled men. London, 1955.
Afr 6879.06F Fuellebom, F. Das Deutsche Njassa- und Ruwuma-Gebiet. Atlas. Berlin, 1906.
Afr 6879.06 Fuellebon, F. Das Deutsche Njassa- und Ruwuma-Gebiet. Text. Berlin, 1906.
Afr 2209.11.3 Fünf Jahre Fremdenlegionär in Algier. (Mueller, Charles.) Stuttgart, 1911.
Afr 3730.4 Fünfzehn Jahre Gefangener des falschen Propheten. (Cuzzi, G.) Leipzig, 1900.
Afr 6685.7 Fünfzig Jahre Togo. (Full, August.) Berlin, 1935.
Afr 4513.39.30 Für das Rote Kreuz in äthiopien. (Brown, S.H.) Zürich, 1939.
Afr 11410.31.100 Fugard, Athol. Hello and goodbye; a play in two acts. Cape Town, 1966.
Afr 6298.363 Fugitive offender. (Enahoro, Anthony.) London, 1965.
Afr 6292.82 The Fulani Empire of Sokoto. (Johnston, Hugh Anthony St.) London, 1967.
Afr 4559.30.10 Fulgenzio da Vecchieto, Padre. Il contributo alla geografia dell'Abissinia nelle memorie del cardinale Guglielmo Massaia. Tivoli, 1930.
Afr 6685.7 Full, August. Fünfzig Jahre Togo. Berlin, 1935.
Afr 609.68.10 Full many a glorious morning. (Green, Lawrence George.) Cape Town, 1968.
Afr 8678.357 Fuller, Basil. South Africa - not guilty. London, 1957.
Afr 6164.7 Fuller, F. A vanished dynasty. London, 1921.
Afr 6164.7.2 Fuller, F. A vanished dynasty. 2. ed. London, 1968.
Afr 3275.11 Fuller, F.W. Egypt and the hinterland. London, 1901.
Afr 4513.36.120 Fuller, J.F.C. The first of the League wars. London, 1936.
Afr 8289.37.5 Fuller, J.F.C. The last of the gentlemen's wars. London, 1937.
Afr 8659.08 Fuller, R.H. South Africa at home. London, n.d.
Afr 7458.51.7 Fuller, T. Journal of voyage to Liberia. Baltimore, 1851.
Afr 8250.7 Fuller, T.E. Right Honourable Cecil J. Rhodes. London, 1910.
Afr 550.160 Fuller, William Harold. Run while the sun is hot. N.Y., 1966.
Afr 4115.5 Fullerton, W.M. In Cairo. London, 1891.
Afr 11410.51.100 Fulton, Anthony. The dark side of mercy. Cape Town, 1968.
Afr 4226.1 Fumagalli, G. Bibliografia etiopica. Milan, 1893.
Afr 630.66.5 Fundamentos para uma politica multicultural em Africa. (Belchior, Manual.) Lisboa, 1966.
Afr 4180.4 The Fung Kingdom of Sennar. (Crawford, O.G.S.) Gloucester, 1951.
Afr 7459.46 Furbay, Elizabeth J. Top hats and tom-toms. London, 1946.
Afr 1738.8 Furlong, C.W. At the strait's mouth. N.Y., 1904.
Afr 2929.09 Furlong, C.W. Gateway to the Sahara...Tripoli. N.Y., 1909.
Afr 1493.50.10 Furneaux, Rupert. Abdel Krim: Emir of the Rif. London, 1967.
Afr 8160.24 Furneaux, Rupert. The Zulu war. 1st ed. Philadelphia, 1963.
Afr 3978.50.5 Furniss, William. Waraga, or The charms of the Nile. N.Y., 1850.
Afr 2749.58 Furon, Raymond. Le Sahara. Paris, 1957.
Afr 8285.5F Further correspondence relating to political affairs in the South African Republic. (Great Britain. Foreign Office.) London, 1899.
Afr 8659.13.3 Further reminiscences of a South African pioneer. (Scully, Wm. C.) London, 1913.
Afr 6145.3.5F Further reports of the commissioners of enquiry into the conduct of certain chiefs and the government statement thereon. (Sierra Leone. Commission of Enquiry into the Conduct of Certain Chiefs.) Sierra Leone, 1957.
Afr 8252.5.15 Further South African recollections. (Molteno, J.T.) London, 1926.
Afr 4315.2 Futuh al-Habashah. Pt.1. (Shihab al-Din Ahmad ibn 'Abd al-Kadir.) London, 1894.
Afr 4317.1 Futuh el-Habacha. (Shihab al-Din Ahmad Ibn Abd al-Kadir.) Paris, 1898.
Afr 7368.62 The future of Africa. (Crummell, A.) N.Y., 1862.
Afr 7368.62.2 The future of Africa. (Crummell, A.) N.Y., 1969.
Afr 550.13 The future of Africa. (Fraser, Donald.) London, 1911.
Afr 6310.9 The future of East Africa High Commission Services: reports of the London discussions. (Great Britain. Colonial Office.) London, 1961.
Afr 3275.31A The future of Egypt. (Worsfold, William B.) London, 1914.
Afr 45.60.10 The future of law in Africa. (Conference on the Future of Law in Africa.) London, 1960.
Afr 8678.330 The future of South Africa. (British Council of Churches.) London, 1965.
Afr 7568.15.5 The future of the Congo. (Morel, E.D.) London, 1909.
Afr 628.229.12 The future of the Negro. (Guggisberg, Frederick Gordon.) N.Y., 1969.
Afr 6138.62 Fyfe, Christopher. A history of Sierra Leone. London, 1962.
Afr 6138.62.2 Fyfe, Christopher. A short history of Sierra Leone. London, 1967.
Afr 6132.12 Fyfe, Christopher. Sierra Leone inheritance. London, 1964.
Afr 3979.11.3 Fyfe, H.H. The new spirit in Egypt. Edinburgh, 1911.
Afr 8659.11 Fyfe, H.H. South Africa to-day. London, 1911.
Afr 8659.11.2 Fyfe, H.H. South Africa today. London, 1911.
Afr 9073.413 Fynn, Henry Francis. Diary. Malcolm, 1950.
Afr 3310.10.90 Pamphlet vol. G.A. Nasser, a collection of addresses, November 25, 1961 to May 31, 1965. 10 pam.
Afr 4513.38.35 G.M. Giulietti. (Marchese, Aldo.) Milano, 1938.
Afr 10624.63.100 The gab boys. (Duodu, Cameron.) London, 1967.
Afr 9339.57 Gabatshwane, S.M. Introduction to the Bechuanaland protectorate history and administration. Kanye, 1957.
Afr 9345.70 Gabatshwane, S.M. Seretse Khama and Botswana. Kanye? 1966.
Afr 9424.360.5 Gabatshwane, S.M. Tshekedi Khama of Bechuanaland. Cape Town, 1961.
Afr 5417.70.2 Gabon; nation-building on the Ogooue. (Weinstein, Brian.) Cambridge, Mass., 1966.
Afr 5420.257 Gabon, terre d'avenir. (Charbonnier, François.) Paris, 1957.
Afr 5422.7 Gabon. Plan de développement économique et social, 1966-1970. Paris, 1967?
Afr Doc 7403.3 Le Gabon. Monte-Carlo. 1964
Afr Doc 7409.305 Gabon. Commissariat au Plan. Comptes economiques. Libreville. 1964+
Afr 5410.10 Gabon. Institut Pédagogique National. Arts et lettres. Libreville. 1,1966+
Afr 5422.2F Gabon. Laws, statutes, etc. Loi no. 11-63 du 12/1/63 portant approbation du programme intérimaire de développement. Libreville, 1965.
Afr Doc 7409.505F Gabon. Ministère de l'Education Nationale. Statistiques de l'enseignement au Gabon. Libreville. 1965+
Afr Doc 7405.5 Gabon. Ministère de l'Information. Annuaire national. Paris. 1967+
Afr 5417.702 Gabon. Ministère de l'Information et du Tourisme. Gabon an 5.cinq années de progrès. Libreville, 1965.
Afr Doc 7409.5 Gabon. Ministère d'état chargé de l'économie nationale, du plan et des mines. Budget de développement. 1964+
Afr 5422.5 Gabon. Ministère d'Etat Chargé de l'Economie Nationale du Plan et des Mines. Commissariat au Plan. Résumé du plan de développement économique et social, période 1966-1971. Monaco, 1966.
Afr Doc 7407.361 Gabon. Service de Statistiques. Recensement et enquête démographiques, 1960-1961; résutats provisionelles. Paris, 1963.
Afr Doc 7407.361.15 Gabon. Service Nat+onal de la Statistique. Recensement et enquête demographiques, 1960-1961: ensemble du Gabon. Paris, 1965
Afr Doc 7407.5 Gabon. Service National de la Statistique. Annuaire statistique. 1964+
Afr Doc 7407.10 Gabon. Service National de la Statistique. Bulletin mensuel de statistique. 5,1963+ 4v.
Afr Doc 7407.10.2 Gabon. Service National de la Statistique. Bulletin mensuel de statistique. Supplement. 5,1962+ 2v.
Afr Doc 7407.361.10 Gabon. Service National de la Statistique. Recensement et enquête démographiques, 1960-1961: Résultats pour Libreville. Paris, 1962.
Afr 5417.702 Gabon an 5.cinq années de progrès. (Gabon. Ministère de l'Information et du Tourisme.) Libreville, 1965.
Afr 5410.5F Gabon d'aujourd'hui. Libreville. 66-84,1965-1966
Afr 5420.261 The Gabon Republic. (France. Embassy. U.S.) N.Y., 1961.
Afr 4259.31 Gabre-Hiot, A. La vérité sur l'Ethiopie révélée après le couronnement du roi des rois. Lausanne, 1931.
Afr 11907.9.100 Gabre-Medhin, Tsegaye Oda. Oak oracle. London, 1965.
Afr 1493.50 Gabrielli, L. Abd-el-Krim et les événements du Rif. Casablanca, 1953.
Afr 5180.40 Gaby, Jean B. Relation de la Nigritie. Paris, 1689.
Afr 1609.31.10 Gadala, M.T. La feerie marocaine. Grenoble, 1931.
Afr 5130.20 Gaffarel, P. Administration du général Faidherbe au Sénégal. Dijon, 188-.
Afr 2208.83 Gaffarel, P. L'Algérie. Paris, 1883.
Afr 510.15 Gaffarel, P.L.J. Notre expansion colonial...1870 à nos jours. Paris, 1918.
Afr 5045.9 Gaffarel, Paul. Comptoirs de l'Afrique française occidentale. Dijon, 1910.
Afr 1960.5 Gaffarel, Paul. La conquête de l'Algérie jusqu'à la prise de Constantine. Paris, 1887.
Afr 2208.88.3 Gaffarel, Paul. Lectures...sur l'Algérie. Paris, 1888.
Afr 5180.26 Gaffarel, Paul. La Sénégal et le Soudan français. Paris, 1890.
Afr 5190.12 Gaffiot, R. Gorée, capitale déchue. Paris, 1933.
Afr 4392.9 Gaibi, A. La guerra d'Africa (1895-96). Roma, 1930.
Afr 109.70.10 Gailey, Harry A. History of Africa, from the earliest times to 1800. N.Y., 1970.

Afr 7350.3.10 Garrison, W.L. Thoughts on African colonization. Boston, 1832.
Afr 1869.10 Garrot, Henri. Histoire generale de l'Algerie. Alger, 1910.
Afr 3025.5F Garstin, W. Note on the Soudan. Cairo, 1899.
Afr 628.225.10 Garvey, Marcus. Philosophy and opinions, or Africa for the Africans. v.2. 2d ed. N.Y., 1926.
Afr 628.225.12 Garvey, Marcus. Philosophy and opinions of Marcus Garvey, or Africa for the Africans. 2nd ed. London, 1967.
Afr 628.223 Garvey, Marcus. Philosophy and opinions of Marcus Garvey. 1st ed. N.Y., 1923.
Afr 628.268 Garvey, Marcus. Speech presenting the case of the Negro for international racial adjustment. London?, 1968?
Afr 3979.63.10F Gary, D.H. Sun, stones and silence. N.Y., 1963.
Afr 2489.3 Garzia, G.D. Vera relazione copia di lettera scritta. Venezia, 1677.
Afr 3986.7 Garzonzi, Eva. Old ills and new remedies in Egypt. Cairo, 1958.
Afr 545.26 Gas de conscience, à l'usage surtout des pays africains. (Denis, L.) Bruges, 1962-63. 2v.
Afr 2030.385 Gaschet-Veyret de la Tour, E. L'erreur du siècle et l'homme des civilisations agricoles. Paris, 1956.
Afr 6212.25 Gaskiya Corporation, Zaria, Nigeria. Federation of Nigeria. Zaria, 1959.
Afr 4700.38.15 Gaslini, M. L'Italia sul Mar Rosso. Milano, 1938.
Afr 4178.15 Gaslini, Mario. Suez. Milano, 1957.
Afr 2945.26.10 Gaslini, Mario dei. Col generale Cantore alla caccia del Gran Senusso. Milano, 1928.
Afr 4700.31.5 Gaslini, Mario dei. L'oltremare d'Italia in terra d'Africa. Bergamo, 1931.
Afr 4766.25 Gasparro, A. La Somalia italiana nell antichità classica. Palermo, 1910.
Afr 5874.5 Gassault, A.G. Notice sur la Réunion. Paris, 1900.
Afr 1200.67 Gasser, J. Role social de la France dans l'Afrique du Nord. Paris, 1924.
Afr 609.58 Gasset, Pierre. L'Afrique, les Africains. v.1-2. Paris, 1958.
Afr 5342.7 Gaston, Joseph. La Côte-d'Ivoire. Paris, 1917.
Afr 1259.54 Gastvriend van vrije volken. (Monnink, G.) Amsterdam, 1954.
Afr 3993.966.10 Gataullin, Maliuta F. Ekonomika OAR na novom puti. Moskva, 1966.
Afr 5227.5 Gatelet, A.L.C. Histoire de la conquête du Soudan français. Paris, 1901.
Afr 1608.78.6 Gatell, Joaquin. Viajes por Marruecos. Madrid, 1878-79.
Afr 2929.09 Gateway to the Sahara...Tripoli. (Furlong, C.W.) N.Y., 1909.
Afr 6470.211 Gatheru, R.M. Child of two worlds. London, 1964.
Afr 7809.37 Gatti, A. Great mother forest. N.Y., 1937.
Afr 6455.120 Gatti, Attilio. Africa is adventure. London, 1960.
Afr 609.34.5 Gatti, Attilio. Black mist. London, 1934.
Afr 609.33 Gatti, Attilio. Hidden Africa. London, 1933.
Afr 9029.62 Gatti, Attilio. Sangoma. London, 1962.
Afr 9599.45 Gatti, Attilio. South of the Sahara. N.Y., 1945.
Afr 609.43 Gatti, E.M. Here is Africa. N.Y., 1943.
Afr 609.60.5 Gatti, Ellen. The new Africa. N.Y., 1960.
Afr 7809.44 Gatti, Ellen M. (Woddill). Exploring we would go. N.Y., 1944.
Afr 7815.5.8 Gaud, Fernand. Les Mandja. 8. Bruxelles, 1911.
Afr 2218.5 Gaudefroy-Demombynes, M. Notes de sociologie maghrébine. Paris, 1901.
Afr 1658.47 Gaudio, A. Rif, terre marocaine d'epopee et de legende. Paris, 1962.
Afr 2749.60.10 Gaudio, Attilio. Le Sahara des Africaines. Paris, 1960.
Afr 2230.35 Gaudry, Mathéa. La femme Chaouia de l'Aurès. Thèse. Paris, 1928.
Afr 2218.6 Gaudry, Mathéa. La société féminine au Djebel amour et au Ksel. Alger, 1961.
Afr 618.5 Gaul, Wilhelm. Das Geschenk nach Form und Inhalt. Braunschweig, 1914.
Afr 609.61.45 Gauld, Peter. Africa, continent of change. Belmont, 1961.
Afr 6095.8 Gaunt, M. Alone in West Africa. London, n.d.
Afr 1955.46 Gautherat, Gustave. La conquête de l'Alger. Paris, 1929.
Afr 1259.39 Gautier, E.F. L'Afrique blanche. Paris, 1939.
Afr 2749.10 Gautier, E.F. La conquête du Sahara. Paris, 1910.
Afr 2731.12.5 Gautier, E.F. Figures de conquêtes coloniales. Paris, 1931.
Afr 2749.08.3 Gautier, E.F. Missions du Sahara. Paris, 1908-09. 2v.
Afr 2749.23.10A Gautier, E.F. Sahara. N.Y., 1935.
Afr 2749.23 Gautier, E.F. Le Sahara. Paris, 1923.
Afr 2749.23.5 Gautier, E.F. Le Sahara avec 10 figures et 26 illustrations hors texte. Paris, 1928.
Afr 1830.40.13 Gautier, E.F. Un siècle de colonisation, études au microscope. Paris, 1930.
Afr 2025.27 Gautier, Emile F. L'Algérie et la métropole. Paris, 1920.
Afr 5748.95.5 Gautier, Emile F. Guide pratique du colon et du soldat à Madagascar. Paris, 1895.
Afr 1080.10 Gautier, Emile F. L'islamisation de l'Afrique du Nord. Les siècles obscures du Maghreb. Paris, 1927.
Afr 1069.37.5 Gautier, Emile F. Le passé de l'Afrique du Nord. Paris, 1952.
Afr 1069.37.7 Gautier, Emile F. Le passé de l'Afrique du Nord. Paris, 1964.
Afr 5056.151 Gautier Walter, André. Afrique noire. Paris, 1951.
Afr 7135.12 Gauzes, Anne. Angola, 1961-1963. Luanda? 196-.
Afr 8678.10.15 Gavicho de Lacerda, T. Os Cafres, seus usos e costumes. Lisboa, 1944.
Afr 3994.895F Gavillot, J.C. Aristide. L'Angleterre ruine l'Egypte. Paris, 1895.
Afr 5318.35 Gavrilov, N.I. Gvineiskaia Respublika. Moscow, 1960.
Afr 5057.25 Gavrilov, N.I. Zapadnaia Afrika pod gnetom Frantsii. Moscow, 1961.
Afr 5055.65 Gavrilov, Nikolai Ivanovich. National liberation movement in West Africa. Moscow, 1965.
Afr 2209.02.2 Gay, E. L'Algérie d'aujourd'hui. Paris, 1907.
Afr 5845.5 Gay, Francois. Ile Maurice, régulation des naissances et action familiale. Lyon, 1968.
Afr 28.4.2 Gay, Jean. Bibliographie de l'Afrique. San Remo, 1875.
Afr 28.4.5 Gay, Jean. Bibliographie des ouvrages relatifs à l'Afrique et à l'Arabie. Amsterdam, 1961.
Afr 7465.12 Gay, John H. The new mathematics and an old culture. N.Y., 1967.
Afr 3979.05 Gayet, A. Coins d'Egypte ignorés. Paris, 1905.
Afr 630.66.10 Gayre, George Robert. Ethnological elements of Africa. Edinburgh, 1966.

Afr 3322.6 Gazette fiscale. Alexandrie.
Afr 6283.13 Gazetteer. (Nigeria, Northern.) London, 1920. 2v.
Afr 4559.40A A gazetteer of Abyssinia. Pts.1-3. (Shortridge, G.C.) n.p., 1940.
Afr 6292.41 Gazetteer of Ilarin Province. (Hermon-Hodge, Harry Baldwin.) London, 1929.
Afr 2870.25.5 Gaziani, R. Pace romana in Libia. Milano, 1937.
Afr 49016.5 Gbadamosi, Bakare. Yoruba poetry. Ibadan, 1959.
Afr 8849.212 Gearing, Gladys. This was my world. Cape Town, 1966.
Afr 6218.5.2 Geary, Nevill. Nigeria under British rule. N.Y., 1965.
Afr 8380.5 Gebeure in Afrika. (Merwe, Hendrik Johannes Jan Matthijs van der.) Johannesburg, 1964.
Afr 9499.80 Gedamu, T. Country study on Southern Rhodesia. Addis Ababa? 1963.
Afr 8289.00.38 Gedanken und Erinnerungen an den Krieg Englands gegen die Burenstaaten. (Peinlich, Fuerchtgots.) Berlin, 1900.
Afr 609.39.5 Gedat, Gustav A. Wunderwege durch ein Wunderland. 2. Aufl. Stuttgart, 1939.
Afr 725.11 Geddie, J.F.R.G. The lake regions of central Africa. London, 1881.
Afr 8289.49 Gedenkalbum van die Tweede Vryheidsoorlog. (Breytenbach, J.H.) Kaapstad, 1949.
Afr 8089.47.10 Geen, M.S. The making of South Africa. Cape Town, 1958.
Afr 8089.47.5 Geen, M.S. The making of the Union of South Africa, a brief history, 1487-1939. London, 1946.
Afr 4559.36 Gefahrvolles Abessinien. (Leichner, G.) Leipzig, 1936.
Afr 12005.8 Die Gegenwartsliteratur des Maghreb in französischer Sprache. (Groos, Almuth.) Frankfurt, 1963.
Afr 8110.28 De geheime onderhandelingen tusschen de Bataafshe en Fransche Republieken. (Milo, Taco H.) Den Helder, 1942.
Afr 7073.3 Geheimnisvolle Inseln Tropen-Afrikas. (Bernatzik, Hugo.) Berlin, 1933.
Afr 3305.10.1 Geheimtagebuch der ägyptischen Revolution. (Sadat, Anwar.) Düsseldorf, 1957.
Afr 8687.308 Der gehorsame Rebell. (Huenermann, Wilhelm.) Innsbruck, 1959.
Afr 725.15.5 Geil, William Edgar. Adventures in the African jungle hunting Pigmies. Garden City, 1917.
Afr 725.15 Geil, William Edgar. A Yankee in Pigmyland. London, 1905.
Afr 210.68.15 Geiss, Imanuel. Panafrikanismus. Frankfurt am Main, 1968.
Afr 628.215.10 Die geistige Entwicklung der Neger-Kinder. Inaug. Diss. (Francke, E.) Leipzig, 1915.
Afr 9502.13.5 Gelfand, M. African background. Cape Town, 1965.
Afr 9502.13.15 Gelfand, M. African crucible. Cape Town, 1968.
Afr 9502.13.10 Gelfand, M. An African's religion, the spirit of Nyajena. Cape Town, 1966.
Afr 9445.45 Gelfand, M. Northern Rhodesia. Oxford, 1961.
Afr 9502.13 Gelfand, M. Shona religion. Cape Town, 1962.
Afr 9493.67 Gelfand, Michael. The African witch: with particular reference to...Shona of Rhodesia. Edinburgh, 1967.
Afr 9506.6 Gelfand, Michael. Mother Patrick and her nursing sister. Capetown, 1964.
Afr 9704.12 Gelfland, Michael. Gubulawayo and beyond: letters and journals of the early Jesuit missionaires to Zambesia. London, 1968.
Afr 3978.76.7 Gellion-Dangler, Eugène. Lettres sur l'Egypte. Paris, 1876.
Afr 1635.40 Gellner, Ernest. Saints of the Atlas. London, 1969.
Afr 9092.5 Geloftedag. (Swart, Marius Johannes.) Kaapstad, 1961.
Afr 8180.28 Die geloftekerk. (Thom, H.B.) Kaapstad, 1949.
Afr 3040.52 Gemayel, P. Un régime qui meurt, les capitulations en Egypte. Thèse. Paris, 1938.
Afr 626.180 Die Gemeinsame Afrikanisch-Madegassische Organisation. (Timmler, Markus.) Köln, 1967.
Afr 5758.60.5 Gendarme, René. L'économie de Madagascar. Paris, 1960.
Afr 1658.32 El general. 7a ed. (Queipo De Llano, G.) Madrid, 1930.
Afr 3310.55 General Abdel Nasser. (Vauchu, Georges.) Paris, 1959. 2v.
Afr Doc 3407.357.10 General African census August 1957. Tribal analysis. (East Africa High Commission. East African Statistical Department.) Nairobi, 1958.
Afr 7353.6 A general bibliography of the Republic of Liberia. (Solomon, Marian D.) Evanston, 1962.
Afr 8340.14.2A General Botha, the career and the man. (Spender, H.) Boston, 1916.
Afr 8340.14 General Botha, the career and the man. (Spender, H.) London, 1916.
Afr 8252.25 General Botha. (Buxton, Earl.) London, 1924.
Afr 5342.64 General data on the Republic of the Ivory Coast. (Ivory Coast. Embassy. U.S.) Washington, D.C., 1963.
Afr 8252.172 General De Wet, a biography. (Rosenthal, Eric.) Cape Town, 1946.
Afr 8252.172.2 General De Wet; a biography. 2. ed. (Rosenthal, Eric.) Cape Town, 1968.
Afr 8815.5 General directory and guide book, to Cape of Good Hope. Cape Town, 1872.
Afr 3986.960.25 General frame of the five year plan. (United Arab Republic. National Planning Committee.) Cairo, 1960.
Afr 5640.14 Le Général Gallieni. (Ellie, Paul.) Paris, 1900.
Afr 3705.3.15 General Gordon's Khartoum journal. (Gordon, C.G.) London, 1961.
Afr 3705.3.16 General Gordon's Khartoum journal. (Gordon, C.G.) N.Y., 1961.
Afr 3705.3.10F General Gordon's last journal. (Gordon, C.G.) London, 1885.
Afr 1571.43 Le général Gouraud. (Paluel-Marmont, A.P.H.J.) Paris, 1937.
Afr 8252.37 General Hertzog, Prime Minister of the Union of South Africa since 1924. (Neame, L.E.) London, 1930.
Afr 8152.73.5 General index of the first edition of King's Campaigning in Kaffirland. (Johannesburg. Public Library.) Johannesburg, 1958.
Afr 8152.76.2 General index to Narrative of the Kaffir war. (Johannesburg. Public Library.) Johannesburg, 1960.
Afr 8252.228.6 General J.B.M. Hertzog. (Burger, M.J.) Kaapstad, 1950.
Afr 8252.228.2 General J.B.M. Hertzog. (Heever, Christiaan.) Johannesburg, 1943.
Afr 8252.228 General J.B.M. Hertzog. (Heever, Christiaan.) Johannesburg, 1946.
Afr 8252.228.5 General J.B.M. Hertzog in Batilio. (Burger, M.J.) Kaapstad, 1953.
Afr 1955.24 Général Lapasset. Algérie 1817-1864. Paris, 1897. 2v.
Afr 2731.13 Le général Laperrine, grand saharien. (Drouilly, J.G.) Paris, 1922.

Afr 530.8.5 The German Empire of Central Africa as the basis of a new German world-policy. (Zimmermann, E.) London, 1918.

Afr 8028.35 German settlers in South Africa. (Nicholson, G.) Cape Town, 1953.

Afr 6905 Pamphlet box. German Southwest Africa.

Afr 6905.01 Pamphlet box. German Southwest Africa.

Afr 7582.6 Germani, Hans. White soldiers in black Africa. Cape Town, 1967.

Afr 530.6 The Germans and Africa. (Lewin, Evans.) London, 1915.

Afr 530.6.5 The Germans and Africa. (Lewin, Evans.) London, 1939.

Afr 6720.3 Germans in the Cameroons, 1814-1914. (Rudin, H.R.) London, 1938.

Afr 530.3 Germany. Kolonialamt. Veröffentlichungen. Jena.
6v.

Afr 6926.20 Germany. Reichs-Kolonialamt. The treatment of native and other populations in the colonial possessions of Germany and England. Berlin, 1919.

Afr 1583.1 Pamphlet box. Germany and Morocco.

Afr 1584.9 Germany and Morocco before 1905. (Williamson, F.T.) Baltimore, 1937.

Afr 1584.9.2 Germany and Morocco before 1905. Diss. (Williamson, F.T.) Baltimore, 1937.

Afr 1583.11 Pamphlet vol. Germany's relations with Morocco. Berlin, 1908.
9 pam.

Afr 8928.5 Germond, Robert Charles. Chronicles of Basutoland. Morija, 1967.

Afr 2397.1 Geronimo. (Berbrugger, A.) Alger, 1854.

Afr 4060.36 Geroter, Georg. Nubien. Zurich, 1964.

Afr 7046.2 Gersdorff, R. von. Wirtschaftsprobleme Portugisisch-Afrikas. Bielefeld, 1962.

Afr 2749.60.5 Gerster, Georg. Sahara. London, 1960.

Afr 5090.3 Gerteiny, Alfred G. Mauritania. N.Y., 1967.

Afr 6295.63 Gervis, P. Of emirs and pagans. London, 1963.

Afr 6777.9 Gesammelte Schriften. (Peters, Karl.) München, 1943-44.
3v.

Afr 618.5 Das Geschenk nach Form und Inhalt. (Gaul, Wilhelm.) Braunschweig, 1914.

Afr 3199.17 Geschichte Ägyptens im 19 Jahrhundert, 1798-1914. (Hasenclever, A.) Halle a.S., 1917.

Afr 109.52 Geschichte Afrikas. (Westermann, Diedrich.) Köln, 1952.

Afr 109.59 Geschichte Afrikas. v.1-2. (Zierer, Otto.) Murnau, 1959.
2v.

Afr 109.13 Geschichte der Aufteilung und Kolonisation Afrikas. (Darmstaedter, P.) Berlin, 1913-20.
2v.

Afr 8685.45 Die Geschichte der Buren. (Lenk, Heinrich von.) Leipzig, 1901-3.

Afr 6919.12 Geschichte der deutsch Kolonial-Gesellschaft für Südwest-Afrika. (Sauder, L.) Berlin, 1912.
2v.

Afr 608.41 Geschichte der Entdeckungsreisen. (Kuelb, P.H.) Mainz, 1841.

Afr 4313.3 Geschichte der Galla. (Schleicher, A.W.) Berlin, 1893.

Afr 6777.10 Geschichte der kaiserlichen Schutztruppe für Deutsch-Ostafrika. (Nigmann, Ernst.) Berlin, 1911.

Afr 10005.3 Geschichte der neoafrikanischen Literatur. (Jahn, Janheinz.) Düsseldorf, 1966.

Afr 1400.4 Geschichte der Scherifen. (Dombay, F. von.) Agram, 1801.

Afr 8210.8 Die Geschichte der Süd-Afrikanischen Republiken. (Vallentin, W.) Berlin, 1901.

Afr 6850.11 Die Geschichte der Tagespresse Deutsch-Ostafrikas, 1899-1916. Inaug. Diss. (Redeker, D.) Berlin, 1937.

Afr 6777.3 Geschichte des Araberaufstandes in Ost-Afrika. (Schmidt, R.) Frankfurt, n.d.

Afr 1947.9.5 Geschichte des Lorenz Arregger von Solothurn. (Amiet, J.J.) Bern, 1920.

Afr 8088.97.6 Geschichte Südafrikas. (Wirth, A.) Bonn, 1897.

Afr 109.59.20 Geschichte und Geschichtsbild Afrikas. (Arbeitstagung über Neuere und Neueste Geschichte.) Berlin, 1960.

Afr 5832.9 Geschichte und Physiographie der Kolonie Mauritius. (Averbeck, Franz.) Metz, 1905.

Afr 8089.52 Geschichte von Südafrika. (Hintrager, O.) München, 1952.

Afr 9093.15 Geschiedenis van de emigranten-boeren en van den vrijheids-oorlog. (Weilbach, J.D.) Kaapstad, 1882.

Afr 8088.88.8 Geschiedenis van Zuid-Afrika. (Theal, G.M.) 's-Gravenhage, 1897.

Afr 8088.92.2 Geschiedenis van Zuid Afrika. 2e druk. (Aitton, D.) Amsterdam, 1897.

Afr 609.58.36 De gesel van angst. (Hornman, W.) Leiden, 1959.

Afr 699.37F Das Gesicht Ostafrikas. (Peiner, Werner.) Frankfurt, 1937.

Afr 8089.55.5 Geskiedenes van Suid-Afrika. 2 verb. druk. (Walt, A.S.H.) Kaapstad, 1955.
2v.

Afr 9291.10 Die geskiedenis van Smithfield en die Caledonrivierdistrik. (Prinsloo, A.) Bloemfontein, 1955.

Afr 8089.65.5 Geskiedenis van Suid-Afrika. 2.uitg. (Walt, Andries Jacobus Hendrik van der.) Kaapstad, 1965.

Afr 8089.27.5 Geskiedenis van Suid Afrika af ons verlede. (Gie, S.F.N.) Stellenbosch, 1942.
2v.

Afr 8089.51 Geskiedenis van Suid-Afrika. v.1-2. (Halt, A.G.H. von der.) Kaapstad, 1957.

Afr 8688.7.10 Geslagsregisters van die ou Kaapse families. (Villiers, Christoffel Coetzee de.) Kaapstad, 1966.

Afr 8380.15 Gespräche in Südafrika. (Bringolf, Walther.) Zürich, 1968.

Afr 5058.13 Gessain, Monique. Les migrations des Coniagui et Bassari. Paris, 1967.

Afr 3695.3.81 Gessi, l'eroe del Bahr-el-Ghazal. (Zanaboni, G.) Roma, 1934.

Afr 3695.3A Gessi Pasha, R. Seven years in the Soudan. London, 1892.

Afr Doc 6409.310 Gestion de la dette publique. Gestion des dépôts. (Ivory Coast. Caisse Autonome d'Amortissement.) Abidjan. 1960+

Afr 4730.1 Geullot, M.E. La Mer Rouge et l'Abyssinie. Lille, 1890.

Afr 5796.5 Gevrey, Alfred. Essai sur les Comores. Pondichery, 1870.

Afr 8210.16 Gey van Pittius, E.F.W. Staatsopvattings van die voortrekkers en die Boere. Pretoria, 1941.

Afr 555.37 Geyer, F.X. Durch Sand, Sumpf und Wald. München, 1902.

Afr 8145.32A Geyser, A.S. Delayed action. Pretoria, 1960.

Afr 3826.2 Gezira. (Gaitskell, Arthur.) London, 1959.

Afr 3826.5 The Gezira scheme from within. (Sudan. Gezira Board.) Khartoum, 1954.

Afr 2970.5 Ghadames, Ghadames. (Bary, Erica de.) München, 1961.

Afr 6395.22 Ghai, Dharam P. Portrait of a minority, Asians in East Africa. London, 1965.

Afr 3280.5 Ghali, Ibrahim Amin. L'Egypte nationaliste et libérale. La Haye, 1969.

Afr 3300.75 Ghali, M.B. The policy of tomorrow. Washington, 1953.

Afr Doc 1802.15 Ghana; a guide to official publications, 1872-1968. (Witherell, Julian W.) Washington, 1969.

Afr 6150.36 Ghana; an objective summary. Accra. 1966+

Afr 6176.46 Ghana; end of an illusion. (Fitch, Robert Beck.) N.Y., 1966.

VAfr 6192.98 Ghana; 20 stammer-én stat. (Pundik, Herbert.) København, 1965.

Afr 6176.43 Ghana, 1957. (Jopp, Keith.) Accra, 1957.

Afr Doc 1809.40 Ghana. Annual estimates. Accra. 1960+

Afr Doc 1809.35 Ghana. The consolidation development plan. Accra. 1,1957+

Afr Doc 1809.50 Ghana. Estimates of charged expenditure. Accra. 1963+

Afr Doc 1809.55 Ghana. Estimates of financial service. Accra. 1966+

Afr Doc 1809.45 Ghana. Estimates of statutory boards, corporations, institutions, etc. Accra. 1962+

Afr 6193.20 Ghana. Second development plans. Accra, 1959.

Afr 6176.35 Ghana. Statement by the government on the recent conspiracy. Accra, 1961.

Afr Doc 1822.5 Ghana. White paper. Accra. 1,1958+

Afr 6155.2 Pamphlet vol. Ghana.
8 pam.

Afr 6164.15 Ghana. (Diplomatic Bulletin.) London, 1957.

Afr 6164.12 Ghana. (Fage, J.) Madison, Wis., 1959.

Afr 6193.45 Ghana. (Italy. Istituto Nazionale per il Commercio Estero.) Roma, 1960.

Afr 6174.8 Ghana. (Nkrumah, Kwame.) N.Y., 1957.

Afr 6192.92 Ghana. (Rouch, Jane.) Lausanne, 1964.

Afr 6164.17 Ghana. (Royal Institute of International Affairs.) London, 1957.

Afr 6160.35 Le Ghana. (Tixier, Gilbert.) Paris, 1965.

Afr 6150.32.10 Ghana. Accra.

Afr 28.86.5F Ghana: a current bibliography. (Accra. Research Library on African Affairs. Bibliography Series.) Accra. 1,1967+

Afr Doc 1809.305 Ghana. Accountant general. Report and financial statements. Accra. 1958+

Afr Doc 1830.10 Ghana. Agricultural Produce Marketing Board. Annual report and accounts. Accra. 1947-1956

Afr Doc 1830.15 Ghana. Auditor-General. Report on the account of the Ghana railway and Harbours Administration. Accra. 1956-1957

Afr Doc 1809.300 Ghana. Auditor-General. Report on the accounts of Ghana. Accra. 1958+

Afr 6153.20F Ghana. Bureau of Ghana Languages. Bibliography of works in Ghana languages. Accra, 1967.

Afr Doc 1807.360 Ghana. Census Office. Ghana. 1960 population census. Accra. 3,1960+

Afr Doc 1807.360.5 Ghana. Census Office. 1960 population census of Ghana. Special report. Accra, 1964.

Afr Doc 1808.715F Ghana. Central Bureau of Statisitcs. Balance of payments estimates. 1,1950+

Afr Doc 1808.510 Ghana. Central Bureau of Statistics. Area sample survey of small manufacturing establishments, 1963. Accra, 1965.

Afr Doc 1808.715.5F Ghana. Central Bureau of Statistics. Balance of payments estimates. v.2. Definitions, sources and methods of estimation. 1,1950+

Afr Doc 1809.510F Ghana. Central Bureau of Statistics. Civil aviation statistics. Accra. 1954+

Afr 6193.58F Ghana. Central Bureau of Statistics. Directory of distributive establishments. Accra, 1968.

Afr 6150.32.30F Ghana. Central Bureau of Statistics. Directory of industrial enterprises and establishments. Accra. 1963+

Afr Doc 1809.315 Ghana. Central Bureau of Statistics. Economic survey. Accra. 1955+

Afr Doc 1809.505 Ghana. Central Bureau of Statistics. Education statistics. Accra. 1962+

Afr Doc 1808.705 Ghana. Central Bureau of Statistics. External trade statistics of Ghana. 13,1963+

Afr Doc 1808.505 Ghana. Central Bureau of Statistics. Industrial statistics. Accra. 1958+

Afr Doc 1808.5 Ghana. Central Bureau of Statistics. Migration statistics. Accra. 1953+

Afr Doc 1809.500 Ghana. Central Bureau of Statistics. Motor vehicle statistics. Accra. 1956+

Afr Doc 1807.20 Ghana. Central Bureau of Statistics. Quarterly digest of statistics. Accra. 1,1952+

Afr Doc 1807.15 Ghana. Central Bureau of Statistics. Statistical and economic papers. Accra. 1,1957+

Afr Doc 1807.5 Ghana. Central Bureau of Statistics. Statistical yearbook. Accra. 1961+

Afr Doc 1807.360.10 Ghana. Central Bureau of Statistics. Summary of procedures in the 1960 population census of Ghana. Accra, 1968.

Afr Doc 1808.700 Ghana. Central Bureau of Statistics. Trade report. Accra. 1952+

Afr Doc 1807.362 Ghana. Central Bureau of Statistics. 1962 industrial census report. Accra, 1965.

Afr 6160.28 Ghana. Commission Appointed to Enquire into Salaries and Wages of the Civil Service and Non-Government Teaching Service. Report. Accra, 1957.

Afr 6160.29 Ghana. Commission Appointed to Enquire into the Circumstances which Led to the Payment of 28,545 Pounds to James Colledge (Cocoa) Ltd. Report. Accra, 1963.

Afr 6176.44F Ghana. Commission Appointed to Enquire into the Matters Disclosed at the Trial of Captain Benjamin Awhaitey, before a Court Martial, and the Surrounding Circumstances. Proceedings and report, with minutes of evidence taken before the commission, January-March, 1959. Accra, 1959.

Afr 6176.40.10 Ghana. Commission Enquire into the Kwame Nkrumah Properties. Report of the comission, appointed under the Commission of Enquiry Act, 1964. Accra, 1967.

Afr Doc 1812.202 Ghana. Commission of Enquiry into Electoral and Local Government Reform. Report. Accra, 1967.

Afr 6160.37 Ghana. Commission of Enquiry on the Commercial Activities. Report. Accra-Tema, 1967?

Afr 6160.36 Ghana. Commissioner for Local Government Enquiries. Report, June, 1957. Accra, 1960.

Afr Doc 1812.7 Ghana. Constituent Assembly. Proceedings of the Constituent assembly. Accra, 1960.

Afr Doc 1819.5 Ghana. Constitutional Commission. Memorandum on the proposals for a constitution for Ghana. Accra, 1968.

Afr 6160.32 Ghana. Delimitation Commission. Revised report, 1964. Accra, 1965.

Afr Doc 1830.20F Ghana. Department of Agriculture. Annual report. Accra. 1924-1957

Afr Doc 1832.5 Ghana. Department of Cooperation. Annual report. Accra. 1949-1950

Afr Doc 1848.5 Ghana. Department of Social Welfare and Community Development. Annual report. Accra. 1946+

Afr 6176.15 Ghana. Information Service Department. Ghana is born, 6th March 1957. London, 1958.

Afr 6164.25 Ghana. Information Services Department. Ghana reborn. N.Y., 1966.

Afr 6193.64 Ghana. Ministry of Economic Affairs. Two-year development plan: from stabilisation to development. Accra, 1968.

Afr Doc 1834.5 Ghana. Ministry of Education. Education report. Accra. 1957+

Afr Doc 1809.10 Ghana. Ministry of Finance. Budget. Accra. 1963+

Afr Doc 1809.15 Ghana. Ministry of Finance. Budget statement. Accra. 1963+

Afr Doc 1809.5 Ghana. Ministry of France. The financial statement presented to the National Assembly on budget day. Accra. 1953+

Afr 6178.4 Ghana. Ministry of Information and Broadcasting. Nkrumah's subversion in Africa. Accra, 1966.

Afr 10615.2 Ghana. Ministry of Information and Broadcasting. Voices of Ghana. Accra, 1958.

Afr Doc 1830.5 Ghana. National Archives. Annual report. Accra. 1957

Afr Doc 1814.215 Ghana. National Assembly. Finance Committee. Report. Accra. 1957+

Afr Doc 1814.205 Ghana. National Assembly. Public Accounts Committee. Report. 1959+

Afr 6192.102.2 Ghana: past and present. 2nd ed. (Mayer, Emerico Somassa.) The Hague, n.d.

Afr 6193.19 Ghana. Planning Commission. Seven year development plan; a brief outline. Accra? 1963?

Afr 6193.19.5 Ghana. Planning Commission. Seven-year plan for national reconstruction and development. Accra, 1964.

Afr Doc 1845.10 Ghana. Police Service. Annual report. Accra. 1959+

Afr 6160.40F Ghana. Public Services Structure and Salaries Commission. Report of the commission on the structure and renumeration of the public services in Ghana. Accra, 1967.

Afr Doc 1845.5 Ghana. Public Works Department. Annual report. Accra. 1953+

Afr 6160.30 Ghana. Regional Constitutional Commission. Regional assemblies. Accra, 1958.

Afr Doc 1832.15 Ghana. Registrar of Cooperative Societies. Report. Accra. 1959-1960

Afr 6164.10.5 Ghana. Rev. ed. (Bourret, F.M.) Stanford, 1960.

Afr Doc 1832.20 Ghana. State Cocoa Marketing Board. Annual report and accounts. Accra. 1964+

Afr Doc 1802.10 Ghana. State Publishing Corporation. Publications price list. Accra. 1958+

Afr Doc 1849.5 Ghana. Tema Corporation. Report and accounts. Accra. 1953+

Afr 6196.7 Ghana. Town and Country Planning Division. Accra, a plan for the town. Accra, 1958.

Afr 7.7 Ghana. University, Legon. Institute of African Studies. Research review. Legon. 1,1965+

Afr 6150.35 Ghana. University. Institute of African Studies. Ashanti Research Project; progress report. Legon. 1,1963+

Afr 28.112 Ghana. University. Library. Union list of Africana and related journals, in the Balme Africana Library, Legon, Institute of African Studies Library, Legon, and the Padmore Research Library on African Affairs, Accra. Legon, 1965.

Afr 6192.72 Ghana. 2. Aufl. (Pfeffer, Karl Heinz.) Bonn, 1964.

Afr Doc 1807.360 Ghana. 1960 population census. (Ghana. Census Office.) Accra. 3,1960+

Afr 6193.66 Ghana als Wirtschaftspartner. (Halbach, Axel J.) . Köln, 1969.

Afr 6192.27 Ghana and the new Africa. (Warner, Douglas.) London, 1961.

Afr 6178.3 The Ghana coup, 24th February, 1966. (Afrifa, A.R.) London, 1966.

Afr Doc 1835.15 Ghana foreign affairs. Accra. 1,1961+
Afr 6150.32.15 Ghana Geographical Association. Bulletin. Kumasi.
Afr 10624.2.110 Ghana glory. (Dei-Anang, M.) London, 1965.
Afr 6162.10.2 Ghana in transition. (Apter, D.E.) N.Y., 1963.
Afr 6176.15 Ghana is born, 6th March 1957. (Ghana. Information Service Department.) London, 1958.
Afr 6150.32.20 Ghana notes and queries. Kumasi.
Afr 6164.25 Ghana reborn. (Ghana. Information Services Department.) N.Y., 1966.
Afr 6150.32.25F Ghana reconstructs. Accra. 1,1961+
2v.
Afr 6193.15 The Ghana report. (Wittman, G.H.) N.Y., 1959.
Afr 6164.21 Ghana resurgent. (Dei-Anang, Michael.) Accra, 1964.
Afr 10624.2.700 Ghana spricht, Gedichte. (Dei-Anang, M.) Herrenalb, 1962.
Afr 6150.32 Ghana today. London. 1,1957+
5v.

Afr 10615.10 Pamphlet vol. Ghanaian literature in English. Miscellaneous publications.
8 pam.

Afr 6178.15 Ghana's foreign policy, 1957-1966. (Thompson, William Scott.) Princeton, N.J., 1969.

Afr 6192.28 Ghana's heritage of culture. (Antubam, K.) Leipzig, 1963.
Afr 6192.95, Ghanska cesta. (Kuzvart, Milos.) Praha, 1962.
Afr 1965.8 Gheel Gildemeester. Reis naar Algiers en verblyf by het fransche leger in 1845. Gouda, 1847.

Afr 7.2 Ghent. International Fair. International days for African studies. Ghent. 1952+
4v.

Afr 4238.5 Ghersi, E. L'organizzazione politica dell Etiopia. Padova, 1936.
Afr 5640.8 Gheuse, P.B. Galliéni et Madagascar. Paris, 1931.
Afr 1750.32 Ghirelli, A. El norte de Marruecos. Melilla, 1926.
Afr 1069.42 Ghirelli, Angelo. El pais berebere. Madrid, 1942.
Afr 3725.5 Ghisleri, A. Gl'Italiani nell'Equatoria. Bergamo, 1893.
Afr 2819.28 Ghisleri, A. La Libia nella storia e nei viaggiatori dai tempi omerici all'occupazione italiana. Torino, 1928.
Afr 2929.12.7 Ghisleri, A. Tripolitania e Cirenaica. Milano, 1912.
Afr 3193.15 Ghorbal, Shafik. The beginnings of the Egyptian question and the rise of Mehemet Ali. London, 1928.
Afr 630.52.5 Ghurye, G.S. Race relations in Negro Africa. Bombay, 1952.
Afr 2525.5 Giaccardi, A. La conquista di Tunisi. Milano, 1940.
Afr 4700.34 Giaccardi, A. Dieci anni di fascismo nelle colonie italiane. Verona, 1934.

Afr 4700.38.5 Giaccardi, A. L'opera del fascismo in Africa. Milano, 1938-39.
2v.
Afr 4700.30.5 Giaccone, E. Le colonie d'Italia. Torino, 1930.
Afr 1830.50.15 Giacobetti, R.P. Les tapis et tissages du Djebel-amour. Paris, 1932.
Afr 3976.86 Giacomo d'Albano, Father. Historia della missione francescana in alto Egitto-Fungi-Etiopia, 1686-1720. Cairo, 1961.
Afr 4025.15.10 Gialourakès, Manòlès. È Egyptos ton Ellenon. Athens, 1967.
Afr 4240.5 Giannini, A. La costituzione etiopica. 2. ed. Roma, 1936.
Afr 4368.5.5 Gianozza, E. Guglielmo Massaia. Torino, 1932.
Afr 4700.36.20 Giardini, C. Italiani in Africa orientale, pagine di pionieri. Milano, 1936.
Afr 724.8 Gibbons, A. St.H. Africa from south to north. London, 1904.
2v.
Afr 500.13A Gibbons, H.A. The new map of Africa, 1900-16. N.Y., 1916.
Afr 500.13.5 Gibbons, H.A. The new map of Africa, 1900-16. N.Y., 1918.
Afr 8089.54 Gibbs, H. Background to bitterness. London, 1954.
Afr 8089.54.2A Gibbs, H. Background to bitterness. N.Y., 1955.
Afr 8095.20 Gibbs, H. Twilight in South Africa. London, 1949.
Afr 630.65 Gibbs, J.L. Peoples of Africa. N.Y., 1965.
Afr 9599.61 Gibbs, Peter. Avalanche in central Africa. London, 1961.
Afr 8289.57 Gibbs, Peter. Death of the last republic. London, 1957.
Afr 4700.26.5 Gibello Socca, G. Colonie d italia e colonie ex-germaniche d'Africa. Milano, 1926.
Afr 8678.26 Gibson, J.Y. The evolution of South African native policy. Pietermaritzburg, 1919.
Afr 8155.5.2 Gibson, J.Y. The story of the Zulus. London, 1911.
Afr Doc 9002.5 Gibson, Mary Jane. Portuguese Africa; a guide to official publications. Washington, 1967.
Afr 6460.45 Gicaru, Muga. Land of sunshine. London, 1958.
Afr 8089.27.5 Gie, S.F.N. Geskiedenis van Suid Afrika af ons verlede. Stellenbosch, 1942.
2v.
Afr 626.150 Giedwidz, Jan. Afryka. Warszawa, 1962.
Afr 1280.10 Giesa de Camps, Santiago. Las Kabilas de Bocoya, Beniburiaga y Flemsamana. Barcelona, 1963.
Afr 3245.5 Giffard, Pierre. Les Français en Egypte. 2. ed. Paris, 1883.
Afr 3740.8 Giffen, Morrison B. Fashoda, the incident and its diplomatic setting. Chicago, 1930.
Afr 2308.7 Gifford, R. Relazione. Firenze, 1604.
Afr 575.50 Giglio, Carlo. La confraternità scnussita dalle sue origini ad oggi. Padova, 1932.
Afr 4700.5.10 Giglio, Carlo. Etiopia Mar rosso. Roma, 1958.
3v.
Afr 4700.35.25 Giglio, V. Le guerre coloniali d'Italia. Milano, 1935.
Afr 5316.5 Gigon, Fernand. Guinée, état pilote. Paris, 1959.
Afr 7817.30 Gijzelaars in Congo. (Tielemans, H.) Tilburg, 1967?
Afr 6194.37 Gil, B. Tribes in Ghana. Accra, 1964.
Afr 8289.02.16 Gilbert, G. La guerre sud-africaine. Paris, 1902.
Afr 8292.37 Gilbert, S.H. Rhodesia - and after. London, 1901.
Afr 7122.100 Gilchrist, Sid. Angola awake. Toronto, 1968.
Afr 7580.16 Gilis, Charles A. Kasa-vubu, au coeur du drame congolais. Bruxelles, 1964.
Afr 7911.5.5 Gilis, Charles A. Kimbangu, fondateur d'église. Bruxelles, 1960.
Afr 860.2 Gill, D. Six months in Ascension. London, 1878.
Afr 6295.65 Gilles, H.M. Akufo, an environmental study of a Nigerian village community. Ibadan, 1965.
Afr 2030.330 Gillespie, Joan. Algeria. London, 1960.
Afr 5074.25 Gillier, L. La pénétration en Mauritanie. Paris, 1926.
Afr 609.16 Gilligan, Edmund. One lives to tell the tale. N.Y., 1931.
Afr 7328.2 Gillmore, P. Through Gasa land. London, 1890.
Afr 9148.88 Gillmore, Parker. Days and nights by the desert. London, 1888.
Afr 8658.78 Gillmore, Parker. The great thirst land. London, 1878.
Afr 8658.86.5 Gillmore, Parker. The hunter's arcadia. London, 1886.
Afr 8658.80.4 Gillmore, Parker. On duty, a ride through hostile Africa. London, 1880.
Afr 6390.36F Gillsaeter, Sven. Pias safari. Stockholm, 1964.
Afr 8292.47.5 Gilson, C.J.L. History of the 1st Battalion Sherwood Foresters Boer War. London, 1907.
Afr 1750.14 Gimenez, S. Espana en el Africa septentrional. Madrid, 1885.
Afr 4430.55.15 Gingold Duprey, A. De l'invasion à la libération de l'Ethiopie. Paris, 1955.
Afr 8678.285 Giniewski, P. Une autre Afrique du Sud. Paris, 1962.
Afr 8678.275 Giniewski, P. Bantustans. Cape Town, 1961.
Afr 6979.66.5 Giniewski, Paul. Livre noir, livre blanc. Paris, 1966.
Afr 6985.14 Giniewski, Paul. Die stryd om Suidwes-Afrika. Kaapstad, 1966.
Afr 7306.69 Gioja, Francesco Maria. Maravigliosa conversione alla Santa Fede. Napoli, 1669.
Afr 7815.13.20 Giorgetti, Filiberto. Note di musica zande. Verona, 1951.
Afr 5243.122.5 Giorgetti, Filiberto. La superstizione Zande. Bologna, 1966.
Afr 4785.27 Un giornalista all'equatore. (Pomilio, Marco.) Firenze, 1933.
Afr 7549.66 Giovannini, Giovanni. Congo. 2.ed. Milano, 1966.
Afr 6780.35 Die Giraffe und der König von England. (Regendanz, W.C.) n.p., n.d.
Afr 3978.82.5 Girard, B. Souvenirs d'une campagne dans le Heraut. Paris, 1883.
Afr 2030.140 Girard, Henri Georges. Pour Djamila Bouhired. Paris, 1958.
Afr 1609.04.3 Girard. Etude sur le Maroc. Paris, 1904.
Afr 2030.462.155 Girardet, R. Pour le tombeau d'un capitaine. Paris, 1962.
Afr 2208.81.13 Girault, A. En Algérie. Paris, 1881.
Afr 4700.4.15 Girolami, Mario. Contributo dell'Italia alla conoscenza della nosografia dell'Africa. Roma, 1963.
Afr 4368.20 Giselsson, Emanuel. Med frälsningens budskap; några bilder från med svenskamissions. Stockholm, 1967.
Afr 9038.5 Giving and receiving. (Barker, Anthony.) London, 1959.
Afr 8225.20 Gladstone and Kruger: liberal government and colonial "home rule". (Schreuder, Deryck Marshall.) London, 1969.
Afr 8160.19 The glamour and tragedy of the Zulu war. (Clements, W.H.) London, 1936.
Afr 4580.1 Glaser, E. Die Abessinier in Arabien und Afrika. München, 1895.
Afr 8678.425 Glashagen, Ulrich H. Probleme der räumlich getrennten Einbeziehung der Bantu-Bevölkerung Südafrikas in den Wirtschaftsprozes des Landes. Pretoria, 1966.
Afr 9446.38 Glass, Stafford. The Matabele War. Harlow, 1968.

Afr 4559.36.10 Gold of Ethiopia. (Hayter, Frank Edward.) London, 1936.
Afr 9148.77.5 The gold regions of south eastern Africa. (Baines, Thomas.) Bulawayo, 1968.
Afr 9148.77 The gold regions of southeast Africa. (Baines, Thomas.) London, 1877.
Afr 6910.5 Goldblatt, Israel. The conflict between the United Nations and the Union of South Africa in regard to Southwest Africa. Windhoek, 1960.
Afr 6910.3 Goldblatt, Israel. The mandated territory of Southwest Africa in relation to the United States. CapeTown, 1961.
Afr 150.7.4 The golden age of Henry the Navigator. (Oliveira Martins, J.P.) London, 1914.
Afr 6685.9 The golden age of West African civilization. (Armattoe, R.E.G.) Londonderry, 1946.
Afr 9165.42.40 The golden city. (Macmillan, Allister.) London, 193-.
Afr 11327.00.100 The golden fool. 1st ed. (Divine, David.) London, 1954.
Afr 679.29 The golden land. (Mills, D.R.M.) London, 1929.
Afr 8659.49.5 The golden land. (Mockford, Julian.) London, 1949.
Afr 11299.69.110 The golden oriole. (Cope, Jack.) London, 1958.
Afr 9093.20 The golden republic. (Bulpin, T.V.) Cape Town, 1953.
Afr 1571.19 The golden road. (Perrot, Raymond de.) London, 1926.
Afr 609.26 The golden stool, some aspects of the conflict of cultures in modern Africa. (Smith, Edwin.) London, 1926.
Afr 609.26.4 The golden stool, some aspects of the conflict of cultures in modern Africa. (Smith, Edwin.) Garden City, N.Y., 1928.
Afr 6174.11 The golden stool. (Myatt, Fred.) London, 1966.
Afr 5054.58 The golden trade of the Moors. (Bovill, E.W.) London, 1958.
Afr 5054.58.2 The golden trade of the Moors. 2nd ed. (Bovill, E.W.) London, 1968.
Afr 9389.63 Goldie, F. Lost city of the Kalahari. Cape Town, 1963.
Afr 8028.128 Goldman, F. An index to the colour-plate relating to South Africa appearing in books published before 1850. Johannesburg, 1962.
Afr 8028.128.5 Goldman, Freda Y. An index to South African colour-plates in books, 1851-1899. Johannesburg, 1963.
Afr 9078.50 Goldman, P.L.A. Transvaal Archief. Pretoria, 1927.
Afr 8289.02.21 Goldmann, C.S. With General French and the cavalry in Africa. London, 1902.
Afr 4559.35.55 Goldmann, Wilhelm. Das ist Abessinien. Bern, 1935.
Afr 3305.15 Goldobin, A. M. Egipetskaia revoliutsiia 1919 goda. Leningrad, 1958.
Afr 6460.94 Goldschmidt, Walter Rochs. Kambvya's cattle. Berkeley, 1969.
Afr 6395.14 Goldthorpe, J.E. Outlines of East African society. Kampala, 1958.
Afr 55.46 Gollock, Georgina Anne. Lives of eminent Africans. N.Y., 1969.
Afr 55.34 Gollock, Georgina Anne. Sons of Africa. London, 1928.
Afr 5426.100.45 Gollomb, Joseph. Albert Schweitzer. London, 1951.
Afr 5249.6 Gologo, M. Le rescapé de l'Ethylos. Paris, 1963.
Afr 6739.268.5 Golubchik, Mark M. Federativnaia Respublika Kamerun. Moskva, 1968.
Afr 7320.25 Gomes de Amorim, F. Colonizacao. Lisboa, 1945.
Afr 1750.35 Gomez, Vitaliano. En la hora de la paz, Marruecos, 1924-29. Tetuan, 1928.
Afr 3979.13.5 Gomez Carrillo, E. La sonrisa de la esfinge. Madrid, 1913.
Afr 1608.59.3 Gomez de Arteche y Moro, José. Descripcion y mapas de Marruecos. Madrid, 1859.
Afr 1550.23 Gomez Gonzalez, M. La penetracion en Marruecos. Zaragoza, 1909.
Afr 1493.20 Gomez Hidalgo, F. Marruecos. Madrid, 1921.
Afr 7071.5 Gonçalves, J.J. O islamismo na Guiné portuguesa. Lisboa, 1961.
Afr 550.132 Gonçalves, José. Protestantismo em Africa. Lisboa, 1960. 2v.
Afr 45.66 Gonidec, Pierre François. Cours d'institutions publiques africaines et malgaches. Paris, 1966.
Afr 45.68.10 Gonidec, Pierre François. Les droits africains. Paris, 1968.
Afr 5110.25 Gonidec, Pierre François. La République du Sénégal. Paris, 1968.
Afr 2850.10F Gonni, G. Nel centenario della spedizione navale di Tripoli. Genova, 1925.
Afr 6390.30 Gontard, E.P.U. Other people. Hollywood, 1942.
Afr 7175.80 Gonzaga, Norberto. Angola, a brief survey. Lisbon, 1967.
Afr 7119.69 Gonzaga, Norberto. História de Angola, 1482-1963. Luanda, 1969.
Afr 1570.38 Gonzalez Hontoria, M. El protectorado frances en Marruecos. Madrid, 1915.
Afr 5912.2 Gonzalez Jimenez, E. Territorios del sur de Marruecos y Sahara occidental. Toledo, 1930.
Afr 6395.25 Good, Charles M. Dimensions of East African cultures. East Lansing, 1966.
Afr 8289.59 Good-bye Dolly Gray. (Kruger, Rayne.) London, 1959.
Afr 8678.354 The good fight. (Mahabahe, Zaccheus R.) Evanston, 196-.
Afr 6700.34 Good news from over the sea. Naperville, Illinois. 1920
Afr 6291.36 Goodell, Charles Ellsworth. Goodell report on the Biafra study mission. Denver, 1969.
Afr 6291.36 Goodell report on the Biafra study mission. (Goodell, Charles Ellsworth.) Denver, 1969.
Afr 8238.2 Goodfellow, Clement Francis. Great Britain and South African confederation, 1870-1881. Cape Town, 1966.
Afr 609.12 Goodrich, Joseph K. Africa of to-day. Chicago, 1912.
Afr 11433.64.100 Goodwin, Harold. Songs from the settler city. Grahamstown, 1963.
Afr 555.9.13 Goodwin, Harvey. Memoir of Bishop Mackenzie. 2d ed. Cambridge, 1865.
Afr 6194.32 Goody, J.R. The social organization of the Lo Wiili. London, 1956.
Afr 6194.32.2 Goody, J.R. The social organization of the Lo Wiili. 2nd ed. London, 1967.
Afr 8369.53.5 Goosen, D.P. Die triomf van nasionalisme in Suid-Afrika, 1910-1953. Johannesburg, 1953.
Afr 9170.34 Goosen, Willem. On the run. Cape Town, 1964.
Afr 2749.15 Gordan, H.C. Woman in the Sahara. London, 1915.
Afr 11433.74.125 Gordimer, N. Face to face. Johannesburg, 1949.
Afr 11433.74.130 Gordimer, N. Friday's footprint. London, 1960.
Afr 11433.74.160 Gordimer, N. The late bourgeois world. London, 1966.
Afr 11433.74.100 Gordimer, N. The lying days. N.Y., 1953.
Afr 11433.74.150 Gordimer, N. Not for publication, and other stories. N.Y., 1965.
Afr 11433.74.140 Gordimer, N. Occasion for loving. N.Y., 1963.
Afr 11433.74.115 Gordimer, N. Six feet of the country. London, 1956.
Afr 11433.74.110 Gordimer, N. The soft voice of the serpent. N.Y., 1952.

Afr 11433.74.120 Gordimer, N. A world of strangers. N.Y., 1958.
Afr 11055.5 Gordimer, Nadine. South African writing today. Harmondsworth, 1967.
Afr 3695.6 Gordon, C.G. Equatoria under Egyptian rule. Cairo, 1953.
Afr 3705.3.15 Gordon, C.G. General Gordon's Khartoum journal. London, 1961.
Afr 3705.3.16 Gordon, C.G. General Gordon's Khartoum journal. N.Y., 1961.
Afr 3705.3.10F Gordon, C.G. General Gordon's last journal. London, 1885.
Afr 3705.3A Gordon, C.G. Journals at Khartoum. Boston, 1885.
Afr 3705.3.5 Gordon, C.G. The journals of Major General Gordon. London, 1885.
Afr 3695.4 Gordon, C.G. Provinces of the equator. Cairo, 1877.
Afr 1110.41A Gordon, David. North Africa's French legacy, 1954-1962. Cambridge, 1962.
Afr 2035.6 Gordon, David. The passing of French Algeria. London, 1966.
Afr 2218.6.15A Gordon, David C. Women of Algeria; an essay on change. Cambridge, 1968.
Afr 11433.75.110 Gordon, Gerald. Four people, a novel of South Africa. London, 1964.
Afr 11433.75.100 Gordon, Gerald. Let the day perish. London, 1952.
Afr 3695.3.86 Gordon, Gessi e la riconquista del Sudan, 1874-1881. (Zaghi, Carlo.) Firenze, 1947.
Afr 3700.8 Gordon, John. My six years with the Black Watch, 1881-1887. Boston, 1929.
Afr 3695.7A Gordon and the Sudan. (Allen, B.M.) London, 1931.
Afr 3258.8.5 Gordon at Khartoum. (Blunt, W.S.) London, 1911.
Afr 3705.12 Gordon at Khartoum. (Buchan, John.) Edinburgh, 1934.
Afr 3258.8.10 Gordon at Khartoum. (Shukri, M.F.) Cairo, 1951.
Afr 8658.50 Gordon Cumming, R. Five years of a hunter's life in the far interior of South Africa. London, 1850. 2v.
Afr 3705.14 Gordon et le drame de Khartoum. (Delebecque, J.) Paris, 1935.
Afr 3695.5 Gordon in Central Africa. (Hill, G.B.) London, 1881.
Afr 6218.13 Gordon Lennox, Esme Charles. With the West African frontier force in Southern Nigeria. London, 1905.
Afr 5190.12 Gorée, capitale déchue. (Gaffiot, R.) Paris, 1933.
Afr 5056.135 Gorer, G. Africa dances, West African Negroes. London, 1935.
Afr 2945.10 Goretti, L. In Cirenaica ed in Arabia. Roma, 1912.
Afr 6620.55 Gorges, E.H. The great war in West Africa. London, 1930.
Afr 4430.55.10 Gorham, Charles Orson. The Lion of Judah. N.Y., 1966.
Afr 5345.17 Gorju, Joseph. La Côte-d'Ivoire chrétienne. 2. éd. Lyon, 1915.
Afr 1609.66.10 Gornung, Mikhail B. Marokko. Moskva, 1966.
Afr 6280.2.35 Goroda-gosudarstva iorubov. (Kochakova, Nataliie B.) Moskva, 1968.
Afr 8678.442 Gorodnov, Valentin P. Iuzhno-afrikanskii rabochii klass v bor'be protiv reaktsii i rasizma. Moskva, 1969
Afr 555.5.9 Gorrée, Georges. Les amitiés sahariennes du Père de Foucauld. Grenoble, 1946. 2v.
Afr 1571.41 Gorrée, Georges. Au service du Maroc: Charles de Foucauld. Paris, 1939.
Afr 2731.15.100 Gorrée, Georges. Charles de Foucauld. Paris, 1965.
Afr 2731.15.10 Gorrée, Georges. Sur les traces de Charles de Foucauld. Paris, 1936.
Afr 4700.13.15 Gorresio, V. Paesi e problemi africani. Milano, 1937.
Afr 5796.5.10 Gorse, Jean. Territoire des Comores; bibliographie. Paris, 1964?
Afr 5765.5.10 Gospel in Madagascar. London, 1863.
Afr 810.4.5 The gospel on the banks of the Niger. (Crowther, S.) London, 1968.
Afr 210.61.45 Goss, H.P. The political future of the independent nations of Africa. Santa Barbara, Calif., 1961.
Afr 609.58.15 Goss, Hilton P. Africa, present and potential. Santa Barbara, 1958.
Afr 855.14 Gosse, P. St. Helena, 1502-1938. London, 1938.
Afr 3978.67.5F Gottberg, E. de. Des cataractes du Nil..Hannek...Kaybar. Paris, 1867.
Afr 3143.10 Gottschalk, Hans L. Al-Malik al-Kamil von Egypten und seine Zeit. Wiesbaden, 1958.
Afr 5058.10 Gouilly, A. L'islam dans l'Afrique occidentale française. Paris, 1952.
Afr 3205.2 Gouin, Edouard. L'Egypte au XIXe siècle, histoire militaire et politique. Paris, 1847.
Afr 9689.11.5 Gouldsbury, C. An African year. London, 1912.
Afr 9689.11 Gouldsbury, C. Great plateau of Northern Rhodesia. London, 1911.
Afr 9689.11.1 Gouldsbury, C. The great plateau of Northern Rhodesia. N.Y., 1969.
Afr 1609.19.5 Goulven, J. Le Maroc. Paris, 1919.
Afr 1640.5 Goulven, J. Les Mellah de Rabat-Sale. Paris, 1927.
Afr 1724.2 Goulven, J. La place de mazagan. Paris, 1917.
Afr 1338.10 Goulven, Jos. Traité d'économie et de législation marocaines. v.1-2. Paris, 1921. 2v.
Afr 1493.55 Goulven, Joseph. La France au Maroc. Paris, 1937.
Afr 5171.17.55 Gouraud, H.J.E. Lyautey. Paris, 1938.
Afr 1570.27 Gourdin, A. La politique française au Maroc. Paris, 1906.
Afr 5056.168 Goure, Claude. Les inconnus d'Afrique. Paris, 1968.
Afr 2025.1 Gourgeot, F. Les sept plaies d'Algérie. Alger, 1891.
Afr 2025.1.5 Gourgeot, F. Situation politique de l'Algérie. Paris, 1881.
Afr 7942.2 Gourou, Pierre. La densité de la population au Ruanda-Urundi. Bruxelles, 1953.
Afr Doc 6803.5 Gouvernement, assemblée nationale et representations diverses de la République du Mali. (Mali.) Bamalco, 1963.
Afr 1990.4 Le gouvernement de l'Algérie, 1852-1858. (Ribourt, F.) Paris, 1859.
Afr 1838.7 Le gouvernement de l'Algérie. (Ferry, J.) Paris, 1892.
Afr 1838.5 Le gouvernement general de l'Algerie. (Cambon, Jules.) Paris, 1918.
Afr 2025.19 Gouverneur général de l'Algérie. (Dominique, L.C.) Alger, 1908.
Afr 5055.57 Le gouverneur général Felix Ebane. (Laroche, Jean de.) Paris, 1957.
Afr 2025.11.15 Le gouverneur général Tirman. (Vignes, Kenneth.) Paris, 1958. 2v.
Afr 6719.5 Gouverneursjahre in Kamerun. (Pultkamer, Jesko.) Berlin, 1912.
Afr Doc 3319.10 The govenment proposals for a new Constitution, 9th June, 1967. (Uganda. Constitution.) Entebbe, 1967.

Afr Doc 309.502 Government, mission, private, community and church schools, 1959-1960. (Ethiopia. Ministry of Education and Fine Arts) Addis Ababa, 1961?

Afr Doc 3309.315F The government accounts of Uganda. (Uganda. Ministry of planning and Economic Development. Statistics Division.) Entebbe. 1,1959+

Afr 4772.10 Government activities from independence until today. (Somalia. Council of Ministers.) Mogadiscio, 1964.

Afr 40.61 Government and politics in Africa. (Elias, T.O.) N.Y. 1961.

Afr 40.61.2 Government and politics in Africa. 2.ed. (Elias, T.O.) N.Y. 1963.

Afr 40.61.3 Government and politics in Africa. 2nd ed. (Elias, T.O.) Bombay, 1963.

Afr 50.43 Government and politics in Africa. 3d ed. (Adam, Thomas R.) N.Y., 1965.

Afr 1110.42 Government and politics in northern Africa. (Zartman, I.) N.Y., 1963.

Afr 6785.5 Government and politics in Tanzania. (Tordoff, William.) Nairobi, 1967.

Afr 8045.32 Government and politics in tribal societies. (Schapera, Isaac.) London, 1956.

Afr 9044.5F Government finance and political development in Natal, 1843 to 1893. Thesis. (Leverton, Basil James Trewin.) Pretoria, 1968.

Afr 6295.60.5 Government in Zazzau, 1800-1950. (Smith, Michael.) London, 1960.

Afr 4238.10 The government of Ethiopia. (Perham, M.F.) London, 1948.

Afr 4238.10.2 The government of Ethiopia. 2nd ed. (Perham, M.F.) London, 1969.

Afr 8040.3 Government of South Africa. Cape Town, 1908. 2v.

Afr Doc 3412.5 Government paper. (Tanganyika. National Assembly.) Dar es Salaam. 7,1958

Afr Doc 3412.7 Government paper. (Tanzania.) Dar es Salaam. 2,1966+

Afr Doc 3705.5 Government paper. (Zambia.) Lusaka. 1966+

Afr 6160.22 Government proposals in regard to the future constitution and control of statutory boards and corporations in the Gold Coast. (Gold Coast (Colony).) Accra, 1956.

Afr Doc 3402.5 Government publications. (Tanzania.) Dar es Salaam. 1961+

Afr 3326.8 Government reorganization in the United Arab Republic. (Gulick, Luther Halsey.) Cairo, 1962.

Afr 6162.5 The government's proposals for constitutional reform. (Gold Coast (Colony).) Accra, 1953.

Afr 7309.57 Governo do distrito de Moçambique. (Almeida, Eugenio Ferreira de.) Lisboa, 1957.

Afr 7326.4 Um governo em Africa. (Garrett, T. de A.) Lisboa, 1907.

Afr 4700.20 Governo fascista nelle colonie (Somalia-Eritrea-Libia). Milano, 1925.

Afr 6010.20 Gower, Laurence Cecil Bartlett. Independent Africa. Cambridge, 1967.

Afr 9510.7 Goy, M.K. Dans les solitudes de l'Afrique. Genève, 1901.

Afr 555.3.22 Goyan, George. Mère Javouhey, apôtre des Noirs. Paris, 1929.

Afr 555.39.15 Goyan, Georges. Monseigneur Augouard. Paris, 1926.

Afr 5765.26 Goyau, G. Les grands desseins missionaires d'Henri de Solages (1786-1832). Paris, 1933.

Afr 1608.34 Graaberg Fraan Hemso. Speccio...dell impero di Marocco. Genova, 1834.

Afr 8289.50 Graaf, H. de. Boere op St. Helena. Kaapstad, 1950.

Afr 8847.34.100 Graaff-Reinet, a bibliography. (Shaw, R.C.) Cape Town, 1964.

Afr 7176.26.2 Graça, Joaquim José da. Projecto de uma companhia agricola e comercial africana. 2. ed. Lisboa, 1879.

Afr 1738.25 Graevenitz, K.F.H.A.R. Die Tanger-Frage. Berlin, 1925.

Afr 1608.98 Graham, R B C Mogreb-el-Acksa, a journey in Morocco. London, 1898.

Afr 1608.98.5 Graham, R.B.C. Mogreb-el-Acksa, a journey in Morocco. London, 1921.

Afr 1608.98.10 Graham, R.B.C. Mogreb-el-Acksa. London, 1928.

Afr 7182.15 Graham, Robert Haldane Carson. Under seven Congo kings. London, 1931.

Afr 6390.90 Grahame, Iain. Jambo effendi: seven years with the King's African Rifles. London, 1966.

Afr 10434.127.120 A grain of wheat. (Ngugi, James.) London, 1967.

Afr 2030.462.160 Grall, Xavier. La génération du Djebel. Paris, 1962.

Afr 6176.39 Grammens, Mark. Kwame Nkrumah, leider van Afrika. Tielt, 1961.

Afr 1900.1 Grammont, H.D. Histoire d'Alger. Paris, 1887.

Afr 1900.2 Grammont, H.D. Histoire des rois d'Alger. Alger, 1881.

Afr 1915.1 Grammont, H.D. Relation entre la France et la regime d'Alger au XVIIe siècle. 4 in 1. Algier, 1879.

Afr 7175.60 Granado, Antonio C. Mucandos, ou cartos de Angola. Lisboa, 1940.

Afr 7103.25 Granado, António Coxito. Dicionário corográfico comercial de Angola Atonito. 2. ed. Luanda, 1948.

Afr 5973.2 Granador, Gregorio. España en el Muni. Madrid, 1907.

Afr 1960.2 Grand, E. Défence et occupation de la colonie d'Alger. Toulon, 1837.

Afr 1550.17 Grand-Carteret, J. Une victoire sans guerre. Paris, 1911.

Afr 5053.30 Le grand conseil de l'Afrique occidentale. (Bourcart, Robert.) Paris, 1955.

Afr 5053.30.2 Le grand conseil de l'Afrique occidentale. 2. ed. (Bourcart, Robert.) Paris, 1956.

Afr 2748.48.3 Le grand désert. (Daumas, E.) Paris, 1848.

Afr 5426.100.30 Le grand docteur blanc. (Monestier, Marianne.) Paris, 1952.

Afr 2000.12 Un grand Français, le général Margueritte. (Margueritte, V.) Paris, 1930.

Afr 1408.8 Le grand Ismail. (Colin, E.R.) Paris, 1929.

Afr 2230.15 Grand Kabylie, légendes and souvenirs. (Fabre, C.) Paris, 1901.

Afr 5645.12 Le grand livre de l'Ordre national de la République Malgache. (Ordre National de la République Malgache.) Tananarive, 1964.

Afr 6883.2 Un grand peuple de l'Afrique équatoriale. (Vander Burgt.) Bois le Duc, 1903.

Afr 2514.5 Grandchamp, P. Les différends de 1832-1833 entre la régence de Tunis et les royaumes de Sardaigne et des Deus-Siciles. Tunis, 1931.

Afr 2448.5 Grandchamp, P. Documents relatifs aux corsaires tunisiens (2 octobre 1777-4 mai 1824). Tunis, 1925.

Afr 2485.5 Grandchamp, P. La France en Tunisie. Tunis, 1920-33. 10v.

Afr 2494.10 Grandchamp, P. La France en Tunisie à la fin du XVIe siècle. Tunis, 1920.

Afr 5749.07 La grande ile de Madagascar. (Leblond, M.A.) Paris, 1907.

Afr 1975.2 La grande Kabylie, études historiques. (Daumas.) Paris, 1847.

Afr 2230.18 Grande-Kabylie. Les Beni Yenni. (Drouet, F.) Rouen, 1887.

Afr 212.8 A grande noite africana. (Passos, Inacio de.) Lisboa, 1964.

Afr 5480.205 La grande route du Tchad. (L'Enfant, Eugène A.) Paris, 1905.

Afr 2208.46.8 Les grandes chasses d'Afrique. (Texier, C.) n.p., n.d.

Afr 5403.30 Les grandes concessions au Congo français. (Massion, Jacques.) Paris, 1920.

Afr 6720.65.2 Les grandes dates du Cameroun. 2. éd. (Cameroon. Ministère de l'Information et du Tourisme.) Yaoundé, 1965.

Afr 1369.21 Les grandes étapes de l'histoire du Maroc. (Hardy, Georges.) Paris, 1921.

Afr 1609.22.10 Les grandes lignes de la geographie du Maroc. (Hardy, Georges.) Paris, 1922.

Afr 7815.15.5 Les grandes lignes des migrations des Bantous de la province orientale du Congo belge. (Moeller, Alfred.) Bruxelles, 1936.

Afr 2260.16 Les grandes sociétés et la colonisation dans l'Afrique du Nord. Thèse. (René-Eugène, P.) Alger, 1925.

X Cg Afr 5538.2 Grandidier, A. Collection des ouvrages anciens concernant Madagascar. v.1-9. Paris, 1903-20. (Changed to XP 3889) 9v.

Afr 5760.5F Grandidier, A. L'origine des Malgaches. Paris, 1901.

Afr 5760.12F Grandidier, Alfred. Ethnographie de Madagascar. v.1-4. Paris, 1908-1928. 4v.

Afr 5748.85.5F Grandidier, Alfred. Histoire de la geographie. Text and atlas. Paris, 1892. 2v.

Afr 5003.1.5 Grandidier, G. Bibliographie de l'Afrique occidentale francaise. Paris, 1937.

Afr 5530.2 Grandidier, G. Bibliographie de Madagascar. Paris, 1905. 4v.

Afr 5549.58F Grandidier, G. Histoire politique et coloniale. V.3. Tananarive, 1958.

Afr 5585.20 Grandidier, G. Le Myre de Vilers. Paris, 1923.

Afr 5749.00.10 Grandidier, G. Voyage dans le sud-ouest. Paris, 1900.

Afr 5640.14.10 Grandidier, Guillaume. Gallieni. Paris, 1931.

Afr 2208.97 Grandin. A pied, le tour de la terre...à travers le sud-algérien. Paris, 1897.

Afr 7175.7 Grandpre, S. de. Voyage à la côte occidentale d'Afrique. Paris, 1801. 2v.

Afr 5765.26 Les grands desseins missionaires d'Henri de Solages (1786-1832). (Goyau, G.) Paris, 1933.

Afr 626.9 Les grands produits africains. (Etesse, M.) Paris, 1930.

Afr 1844.5 Les grands soldats de l'Algerie. (Azan, Paul.) Paris, 1931.

Afr 1571.55 Grandval, G. Ma mission au Maroc. Paris, 1956.

Afr 3977.30 Granger, called Tourtechot. Relation du voyage fait en Egypte... En l'annee 1730. Paris, 1745.

Afr 11435.3.100 Granger, Vivian Hector. Sacred is the breed. Cape Town, 1967.

Afr 855.3 Grant, A. A few notes on St. Helena. St. Helena, 1883.

Afr 3305.12 Grant, C. Nationalism and revolution in Egypt. The Hague, 1964.

Afr 5828.01 Grant, Charles. The history of Mauritius. London, 1801.

Afr 5832.5 Grant, Charles. Letters from Mauritius in 18th century. Mauritius, 1886.

Afr 1259.11.7 Grant, Cyril F. Studies in North Africa. N.Y., 1923.

Afr 1259.11.5 Grant, Cyril F. Twixt sand and sea. London, 1911.

Afr 6124.248 Grant, Douglas. The fortunate slave. London, 1968.

Afr 698.64 Grant, J.A. A walk across Africa. Edinburgh, 1864.

Afr 718.2.81A Grant, J.H. Autobiography of Henry Morton Stanley. Boston, 1909.

Afr 718.2.80F Grant, J.H. On Stanley's exploration of S. Victoria. n.p. 1875.

Afr 3700.10 Grant, James. Cassell's history of the war in the Soudan. v.1-6. London, n.d. 2v.

Afr 6275.39 Grant, James. A geography of Western Nigeria. Cambridge, 1960.

Afr 12002.1 Gras, Jacqueline. Situation de la presse dans les états de l'Union Africaine et Malgache, en Guinée, au Mali, au Togo. Paris, 1963.

Afr 9506.2 Grass roots. (Chater, Patricia.) London, 1962.

Afr 1485.5 Grasset, Capitaine. A travers la Chaouia. Paris, 1911.

Afr 4700.33.15 Gravelli, A. Africa. Roma, 1933.

Afr 6095.343A Graves, A.M. Benvenuto Cellini had no prejudice against bronze, letters from West Africans. Baltimore, 1943.

Afr 5640.3 Gravier, G. Madagascar, les Malgaches. Paris, 1904.

Afr 678.78 Gravier, G. Recherches sur les navigations européennes. Paris, 1878.

Afr 5757.5 Gravier, Gabriel. La cartographie de Madagascar. Rouen, 1896.

Afr 5235.179 Gravier, Gabriel. Paul Soleillet. Paris, 1887.

Afr 5096.2 Gravier, Gabriel. Voyage de Paul Soleillet à l'Adrar. Rouen, 1881.

Afr 5187.16 Gravrand, Henri. Visage africain de l'Eglise. Paris, 1961.

Afr 8849.6 Gray, C.N. Life of Robert Gray. London, 1876. 2v.

Afr 8849.7 Gray, C.N. Life of Robert Gray. London, 1883.

Afr 2875.12 Gray, E.M. La bella guerra. Firenze, 1912.

Afr 2880.22 Gray, E.M. Il Duce in Libia. Milano, 1937.

Afr 2530.19.10 Gray, E.M. Italy and the question of Tunis. Milano, 1939.

Afr 2530.19 Gray, E.M. Noi e Tunisi. 4a ed. Milano, 1939.

Afr 609.28.10 Gray, Frank. My two African journeys. London, 1928.

Afr 6465.56.5 Gray, J.M. The British in Mombasa, 1824-1826. London, 1958.

Afr 6113.10 Gray, J.M. A history of the Gambia. Cambridge, Eng., 1940.

Afr 6113.10.2 Gray, J.M. A history of the Gambia. N.Y., 1966.

Afr 6565.40 Gray, John. History of Zanzibar. London, 1962.

Afr 8252.9.5 Gray, R. A statement...in connexion with the consecration of the Right Rev. Dr. Colenso. London, 1867.

Afr 555.22.9 Gray, R., bishop of Cape Town. Three months visitation by the Bishop of Cape Town, in...1855. London, 1856.

Afr 3685.9 Gray, Richard. A history of the southern Sudan. London, 1961.

Afr 9500.25 Gray, Richard. The two nations. Oxford, 1960.

Afr 9506.1 Gray, S. Douglas. Frontiers of the kingdom. London, 1930.

Afr 5235.121 Gray, William. Travels in western Africa. London, 1825.

Afr 4513.38.12 Graziani, R. Il fronte sud. 2a ed. Milano, 1938.

436

Afr 2870.25.10	Graziani, R. Libia redenta. Napoli, 1948.
Afr 2945.28	Graziani, Rodolfo. Cirenaica pacificata. Milano, 1932.
Afr 2948.14	Graziani, Rodolfo. La riconquista del Fezzan. Milano, 1934.
Afr 4513.36.145	Graziani a Neghelli. 2 ed. (Volta, Sandro.) Firenze, 1936.
Afr 5748.80	The great African islands. (Sibree, James.) London, 1880.
X Cg Afr 6283.5	Great Benin. (Roth, H.L.) Halifax, 1903.
Afr 6280.68.1	Great Benin: its customs, art and horrors. 1st ed. (Roth, Henry Ling.) London, 1968.
Afr 8289.00.15	The great Boer war. (Doyle, A.C.) London, 1900.
Afr 8289.00.19.5	The great Boer war. (Doyle, A.C.) London, 1903.
Afr 8289.00.19A	The great Boer war. (Doyle, A.C.) N.Y., 1902.
Afr 7073.6F	Great Britain. Case in support of the claim of Great Britain to the Island of Bulama. London, 1869.
Afr 8340.4.5F	Great Britain. Papers on criminal procedure code of the Transvaal. London, 1903.
Afr 8340.4.3F	Great Britain. Papers on finances of Transvaal and Orange River colony. London, 1903.
Afr 6981.120	Great Britain. Report on the conditions and prospects of trade in the protectorate of South West Africa. London, 1920.
Afr 8279.01.5F	Great Britain. Report on the Transvaal Concession Commission. London, 1901.
Afr 6879.16	Great Britain. Admiralty. A handbook of German East Africa. n.p., 1916.
Afr 6390.11.15	Great Britain. Admiralty. A handbook of Kenya colony (British East Africa). n.p., 1920.
Afr 2929.17	Great Britain. Admiralty. A handbook of Libya. Sept. 1917. Naval Staff. n.p., 1917.
Afr 9839.20	Great Britain. Admiralty. A handbook of Portuguese Nyasaland. Oxford, 1920.
Afr 6535.16.20	Great Britain. Admiralty. A handbook of the Uganda Protectorate. Oxford, 1920.
Afr 7809.20	Great Britain. Admiralty. A manual of Belgian Congo. London, 1920.
Afr 7309.20	Great Britain. Admiralty. A manual of Portuguese East Africa. London, 1920.
Afr 9435.7	Great Britain. Advisory Commission on the Review of Constitution. Report. (With appendix 1-5, appendix 6-8). London, 1960.
Afr 3038.8F	Great Britain. Agent and Consul-General in Egypt. Reports on the finances...of Egypt and the Soudan. London. 1900+ 4v.
Afr 6192.35	Great Britain. Central Office of Information. Britain and the Gold Coast. London, 1957.
Afr 6455.110	Great Britain. Central Office of Information. Kenya. London, 1960.
Afr 5842.19	Great Britain. Central Office of Information. Mauritius and Seychelles. N.Y., 1964.
Afr 6275.70	Great Britain. Central Office of Information. Nigeria. London, 1960.
Afr 6275.50	Great Britain. Central Office of Information. Nigeria today. London, 1960.
Afr 6138.61	Great Britain. Central Office of Information. Sierra Leone. London, 1961.
Afr 6585.8	Great Britain. Central Office Of Information. Zanzibar. Harrow, 1963.
Afr 6174.7	Great Britain. Central Office of Information. Reference Division. The making of Ghana. London, 1956.
Afr 9192.5F	Great Britain. Colonial Office. Affairs ofSwaziland. London, 1899.
Afr 6308.10	Great Britain. Colonial Office. Annual report on the East Africa High Commission. 1948+
Afr 6314.29	Great Britain. Colonial Office. The British territories in East and Central Africa. London, 1950.
Afr 6310.12	Great Britain. Colonial Office. Correspondence (1931-1932) arising from the report of the Joint Select Commission on East Africa. London, 1932.
Afr 8283.6F	Great Britain. Colonial Office. Correspondence related to South Africa Republic. London, 1896.
Afr 6310.9	Great Britain. Colonial Office. The future of East Africa High Commission Services: reports of the London discussions. London, 1961.
Afr 6174.10F	Great Britain. Colonial Office. Gold Coast. London, 1901.
Afr 6460.85	Great Britain. Colonial Office. Indians in Kenya. London, 1927.
Afr 6390.21	Great Britain. Colonial Office. Introducing East Africa. London, 1950.
Afr 9635.25	Great Britain. Colonial Office. Northern Rhodesia. London, 1961.
Afr 9757.5	Great Britain. Colonial Office. Nyasaland protectorate, report for the year. 1946+ 4v.
Afr 6310.10F	Great Britain. Colonial Office. Papers relating to the question of the closer union of Kenya. London, 1931.
Afr 6410.2F	Great Britain. Colonial Office. Political and social aspects of the development of municipal government in Kenya with special reference to Nairobi. Nairobi, 1949.
Afr 5817.5	Great Britain. Colonial Office. Report on Mauritius. 1946+ 5v.
Afr 6208.10	Great Britain. Colonial Office. Report on Nigeria. 1952+
Afr 9632.10	Great Britain. Colonial Office. Report on northern Rhodesia. 4v.
Afr 5893.10	Great Britain. Colonial Office. Report on Seychelles. 1946+ 2v.
Afr 6132.10	Great Britain. Colonial Office. Report on Sierra Leone. 1952+
Afr 855.4	Great Britain. Colonial Office. Report on St. Helena. 3v.
Afr 6107.10	Great Britain. Colonial Office. Report on the Gambia. 1948+
Afr 6157.5	Great Britain. Colonial Office. Report on the Gold Coast. 1948+
Afr 4905.5	Great Britain. Colonial Office. Report on the Somaliland Protectorate. 1948+ 2v.
Afr 6558.5	Great Britain. Colonial Office. Report on Zanzibar. 1946+ 4v.
Afr 8288.99.6F	Great Britain. Colonial Office. South African Republic. Correspondence. London, 1899-03.
Afr 8288.99.4F	Great Britain. Colonial Office. South African Republic. Correspondence. London, 1899-03.

Afr 8288.99.5F	Great Britain. Colonial Office. South African Republic. Correspondence. London, 1899-03.
Afr 6310.8	Great Britain. Colonial Office. Statement of the conclusions of His Majesty's government in the United Kingdom...East Africa. London, 1930.
Afr 9180.2	Great Britain. Colonial Office. Swaziland, constitutional proposals. London, 1966.
Afr 6482.5	Great Britain. Colonial Office. Uganda, report for the year. 1948+ 3v.
Afr Doc 2805.5	Great Britain. Colonial Office. Census Commissioner. Mauritius. London. 1964
Afr 6392.34	Great Britain. Colonial Office. East Africa Economic and Financial Commission. East Africa. London, 1961.
Afr 6310.34F	Great Britain. Commission. Administration of Justice in Kenya. Commission of inquiry into the administration of justice in Kenya, Uganda...in criminal matters, May, 1933. London, 1934.
Afr 6542.18	Great Britain. Commission. Dispute Between Buganda and Bunyoro. Uganda. Report of a commission of privy counselors on a dispute between Buganda and Bunyoro presented to Parliament. London, 1962.
Afr 8340.20F	Great Britain. Commission. War Stores in South Africa. Report of the Royal Commission on War Stores in South Africa. London, 1906.
Afr 9345.50	Great Britain. Commission on the Financial Position of Bechuanaland Protectorate. Financial and economic position of Bechuanaland protectorate. London, 1933.
Afr 6145.4F	Great Britain. Commissioners of Inquiry into the Subject of Emigration from Sierra Leone to the West Indies. Copy of the reports made in 1844-1845. London, 1948.
Afr 6280.61	Great Britain. Commissions. Nigeria, report. London, 1958.
Afr 6310.44	Great Britain. Commissions. Civil Services of the East African Territories. Report, 1953-54. London, 1954.
Afr 6310.47	Great Britain. Commissions. Public Services of the East African Territories and the East Africa High Commission. Report. Entebbe, 1960.
Afr 8288.99.10F	Great Britain. Commissions. South African War. Appendices evidence on war in South Africa. London, 1903.
Afr 8288.99.9F	Great Britain. Commissions. South African War. Minutes of evidence on war in South Africa. London, 1903. 2v.
Afr 8288.99.7F	Great Britain. Commissions. South African War. Report...war in South Africa. London, 1903.
Afr 6484.4	Great Britain. Commissions. Uganda Relationship. Report, 1961. Entebbe, 1961.
Afr 9450.3F	Great Britain. Commonwealth Office. Library. Southern Rhodesia illegal declaration of independence. London, 1966?
Afr 8865.12	Great Britain. Commonwealth Relations Office. Annual report on Basutoland. 1947+ 3v.
Afr 9192.10	Great Britain. Commonwealth Relations Office. Annual report on Swaziland. n.p. 1946+ 6v.
Afr 9332.5	Great Britain. Commonwealth Relations Office. Bechuanaland protectorate, report for the year. 1946+ 6v.
Afr 9432.15	Great Britain. Commonwealth Relations Office. Southern Rhodesia constitution. London, 1961. 2 pam.
Afr 28.118F	Great Britain. Commonwealth Relations Office. Library. African military coups. London, 1966.
Afr 6420.37	Great Britain. East Africa Commission. East Africa. London, 1925.
Afr 6390.45	Great Britain. East Africa Royal Commission. Report. London, 1955.
Afr 6457.27	Great Britain. Financial Commissioner to Kenya. Report by the Financial commissioner. n.p., 1932.
Afr 6457.28	Great Britain. Fiscal Commission for Kenya. Report of the Fiscal Commission. Nairobi, 1963.
Afr 9450.30	Great Britain. Foreign and Commonwealth Office. Rhodesia; report on the discussions held on board H.M.S. Fearless. London, 1968.
Afr 3042.5	Great Britain. Foreign Office. Anglo-Egyptian conversations. London, 1951.
Afr 8285.5F	Great Britain. Foreign Office. Further correspondence relating to political affairs in the South African Republic. London, 1899.
Afr 3745.5	Great Britain. Foreign Office. Report on the finances, administration and condition of the Sudan. London. 1,1932
NEDL Afr 3745.5	Great Britain. Foreign Office. Report on the finances, administration and condition of the Sudan. London. 1908
Afr 6314.27	Great Britain. Foreign Office. History Section. Kenya, Uganda and Zanzibar. London, 1920.
Afr 8923.2	Great Britain. High Commissioner for Basutoland, the Bechuanaland Protectorate and Swaziland. Basutoland, Bechuanaland protectorate and Swaziland, report of an economic survey mission. London, 1960.
Afr 5846.2	Great Britain. Imperial Shipping Commission. Report on the harbour of Port Louis. London, 1931.
Afr 4070.5	Great Britain. Intelligence. Report on Sudan. London, 1884.
Afr 2209.44.5	Great Britain. Naval Intelligence Division. Algeria. v.2. London, 1944.
Afr 7809.44.5	Great Britain. Naval Intelligence Division. The Belgian Congo. London, 1944.
Afr 5406.242	Great Britain. Naval Intelligence Division. French Equatorial Africa and Cameroons. London, 1942.
Afr 5056.143.5	Great Britain. Naval Intelligence Division. French West Africa. v.1-2. London, 1943.
Afr 6879.16.3	Great Britain. Naval Intelligence Division. A handbook of German East Africa. N.Y., 1969.
Afr 2609.45	Great Britain. Naval Intelligence Division. Tunisia. London, 1945.
Afr 6455.49	Great Britain. Oversea Settlement Department. Kenya Colony and Protectorate. London, 1930.
Afr 6926.14F	Great Britain. Parliament, 1918. Report on the natives of South-west Africa. London, 1918.
Afr 3740.2F	Great Britain. Parliament. Correspondence with the French government. London, 1898.
Afr 6926.12F	Great Britain. Parliament. Papers relating to certain trials in German Southwest Africa. London, 1916.
Afr 6926.13F	Great Britain. Parliament. Papers relating to German atrocities. London, 1916. 2v.

Afr 6225.40 — Great Britain. Parliament. House of Commons. Extracts from British parliamentary debates on the Nigerian situation in the House of Commons, London, Tuesday, 27th August, 1968. Washington, 1968.

Afr 8283.26F — Great Britain. Parliament. House of Commons. Second report. London, 1897.

Afr 9448.76A — Great Britain. Prime Minister. Southern Rhodesia. London, 1965.

Afr 3300.48F — Great Britain. Special Mission to Egypt. Report of the Special Mission to Egypt. London, 1921.

Afr 8288.99.15F — Great Britain. War Department. True history of the war, official despatches. v.1-5. London, 1900.

Afr 4935.5 — Great Britain. War Office. Official history of operations in Somaliland, 1901-04. London, 1907. 2v.

Afr 9838.99.5 — Great Britain. War Office. Intelligence Division. Precis of information concerning the British Central Africa protectorate. London, 1899.

Afr 6390.10.59 — Great Britain. War Office. Intelligence Division. Precis of information concerning the British East Africa Protectorate and Zanzibar. London, 1901.

Afr 6535.19 — Great Britain. War Office. Intelligence Division. Precis of information concerning the Uganda Protectorate. London, 1902.

Afr 9028.85.5 — Great Britain. War Office. Intelligence Division. Precis of information concerning Zululand. London, 1895.

Afr 3305.8 — Great Britain and Egypt, 1914-1951. (Royal Institute of International Affairs.) London, 1952.

Afr 6157.12 — Great Britain and Ghana. (Metcalfe, George E.) London, 1964.

Afr 8238.2 — Great Britain and South African confederation, 1870-1881. (Goodfellow, Clement Francis.) Cape Town, 1966.

Htn — Afr 2494.5* — Great Britain and Tunis. Articles of peace betwixt Charles II and Mahamet of Tunis and Osman. Tripoli. 5 october, 1662. n.p., 1662.

Afr 505.4 — Great Britain in modern Africa. (Sanderson, E.) London, 1907.

Afr 4115.30.1 — Great Cairo; the world. (Stewart, Desmond Stirling.) London, 1969.

Afr 8252.248 — Great days, the autobiography of an empire pioneer. (Johnson, F.) London, 1940.

Afr 6196.27 — The great drama of Kumasi. (Hall, Wynyard Montagu.) London, 1939.

Afr 11774.39.110 — Great elephant. (Scholefield, Alan.) London, 1967.

Afr 10675.47.170 — The great elephant-bird. (Ekwensi, Cyprian.) London, 1969.

Afr 4388.15 — The great Ethiopian famine of 1888-1892, a new assessment. (Pankhurst, Richard Keir Patrick.) Addis Ababa, 1964.

Afr 9345.65 — Great lion of Bechuanaland. (Smith, E.W.) London, 1957.

Afr 7809.37 — Great mother forest. (Gatti, A.) N.Y., 1937.

Afr 609.61.40 — Great north road. (Green, Lawrence G.) Capetown, 1961.

Afr 9689.11 — Great plateau of Northern Rhodesia. (Gouldsbury, C.) London, 1911.

Afr 9689.11.1 — The great plateau of Northern Rhodesia. (Gouldsbury, C.) N.Y., 1969.

Afr 10671.53.110 — The great ponds. (Amadi, Elechi.) London, 1969.

Afr 212.70 — The great powers and Africa. (Nielsen, Waldemar A.) N.Y., 1969.

Afr 7565.12.15 — The great powers and the Congo Conference in the year 1884 and 1885. Inaug. Diss. (Yarnall, H.E.) Göttingen, 1934.

Afr 5749.64 — The great red island. (Stratton, A.) N.Y., 1964.

Afr 2748.60 — The great Sahara. (Tristram, H.B.) London, 1860.

Afr 2719.64.5 — The great Sahara. (Wellard, J.H.) London, 1964.

Afr 555.7.10 — Great South African Christians. (Davies, Horton.) Cape Town, 1951.

Afr 9489.67.10 — Great spaces washed with sun: Rhodesia. (National Federation of Women's Institutes (Rhodesia).) Salisbury, 1967.

Afr 8658.78 — The great thirst land. (Gillmore, Parker.) London, 1878.

Afr 8180.10 — The great trek. (Walker, E.A.) London, 1934.

Afr 8180.10.3 — The great trek. 3d ed. (Walker, E.A.) London, 1948.

Afr 8180.10.4 — The great trek. 4th ed. (Walker, E.A.) London, 1960.

Afr 3715.10 — A great trusteeship. (Nigumi, M.A.) London, 1957.

Afr 3715.10.2 — A great trusteeship. 2d ed. (Nigumi, M.A.) London, 1958.

Afr 6620.55 — The great war in West Africa. (Gorges, E.H.) London, 1930.

Afr 1570.58 — Greater France in Africa. (Sloane, Wm.M.) N.Y., 1924.

Afr 1259.63.5 — The greater Maghreb. (Liska, Jiri.) Washington, 1963.

Afr 8252.341.70 — Greater South Africa. (Smuts, J.C.) Johannesburg, 1940.

Afr 5420.222 — Grebert, F. Au Gabon, Afrique. Paris, 1922.

Afr 11435.22.120 — Green, George L. Almost forgotten, never told. Cape Town, 1965.

Afr 11435.22.110 — Green, George L. Eight bells at Salamander. 2d ed. Cape Town, 1961.

Afr 11435.22.130 — Green, George L. I heard the old men say, secrets of the Cape that has vanished. 2nd ed. Cape Town, 1965.

Afr 11435.22.100 — Green, George L. Where men still dream. Cape Town, 1950.

Afr 8292.12 — Green, James. The story of the Australian Bushmen. Sydney, 1903.

Afr 8250.44 — Green, Jolin Eric Sidney. Rhodes goes north. London, 1936.

Afr 626.103A — Green, L. Development in Africa, a study in regional analysis with special reference to southern Africa. Johannesburg, 1962.

Afr 8830.10 — Green, L.G. Beyond the city lights. Cape Town, 1957.

Afr 850.6 — Green, L.G. Islands time forgot. London, 1962.

Afr 8045.30 — Green, L.P. History of local government in South Africa. Cape Town, 1957.

Afr 6979.53.2 — Green, Laurence G. Lords of the last frontier. Cape Town, 1962.

Afr 6979.53 — Green, Laurence G. Lords of the last frontier. London, 1953.

Afr 8095.65 — Green, Laurence G. So few are free. Cape Town, 1948.

Afr 609.61.40 — Green, Lawrence G. Great north road. Capetown, 1961.

Afr 679.54.10 — Green, Lawrence G. Under a sky like a flame. 2d ed. Cape Town, 1958.

Afr 609.68.10 — Green, Lawrence George. Full many a glorious morning. Cape Town, 1968.

Afr 8830.12 — Green, Lawrence George. Karoo, the story of the Karoos of South Africa - the great Karoo. Cape Town, 1955.

Afr 6979.67.5 — Green, Lawrence George. On wings of fire. Cape Town, 1967.

Afr 8659.58.15 — Green, Lawrence George. South Africa beachcomber. 1st ed. Cape Town, 1958.

Afr 8835.55 — Green, Lawrence George. Tavern of the seas. Cape Town, 1966.

Afr 8659.66.25 — Green, Lawrence George. Thunder on the Blaauwberg. 1st ed. Cape Town, 1966.

Afr 8659.40 — Green, Lawrence George. To the river's end. Cape Town, 194-.

Afr 6280.9.15 — Green, Margaret M. Ibo village affairs. London, 1947.

Afr 6280.9.17 — Green, Margaret M. Ibo village affairs. 2. ed. London, 1964.

Afr 626.165 — Green, Reginald Herbold. Economic co-operation in Africa, retrospect and prospect. Nairobi, 1967.

Afr 626.165.5 — Green, Reginald Herbold. Unity or poverty? The economics of Pan-Africanism. Harmondsworth, 1968.

Afr 2945.17 — Green mountain, an informal guide to Cyrenaica. (Williams, Gwyn.) London, 1963.

Afr 6280.50.5 — Greenberg, Joseph Harold. The influence of Islam on a Sudanese religion. N.Y., 1946.

Afr 4060.20 — Greener, Leslie. High Dam over Nubia. N.Y., 1962.

Afr 4259.65 — Greenfield, Richard. Ethiopia, a new political history. London, 1965.

Afr 699.40 — A greenhorn in Africa. (Courtney, R.) London, 1940.

Afr 2818.35 — Greenhow, R. The history of Tripoli. Richmond, 1835.

Afr 7103.15 — Greenwood, Margaret Joan. Angola; a bibliography. Cape Town, 1967.

Afr 2030.462.10 — Greer, Herb. A scattering of dust. London, 1962.

Afr 628.108 — Gregoire, Henri. De la littérature des Nègres. Paris, 1808.

Afr 628.108.7 — Gregoire, Henri. De la noblesse de la peau. Paris, 1826.

Htn — Afr 628.110* — Grégoire, Henri. An enquiry concerning the intellectual and moral faculties...of Negroes. Brooklyn, 1810.

Afr 628.110.1 — Grégoire, Henri. An enquiry concerning the intellectual and moral faculties and literature of Negroes. College Park, 1967.

Afr 6470.145 — Gregory, J.R. Under the sun. Nairobi, 1952.

Afr 6415.5 — Gregory, J.W. Foundation of British East Africa. London, 1901.

Afr 6333.62 — Gregory, Robert. Sidney Webb and East Africa. Berkeley, 1962.

Afr 8687.294 — Gregory, T.E.G. Ernest Oppenheimer and the economic development of southern Africa. Cape Town, 1962.

Afr 3978.59.2 — Gregory, W.H. Egypt 1855-56. Tunis 1857-58. London, 1859. 2v.

Afr 4559.65.5 — Greim, Armin. Im Reich des Negus. Leipzig, 1965.

Afr 12377.23.100 — Greki, Anna. Temps forts, poèmes. Paris, 1966.

Afr 8676.60.17 — Gren, goud en goedere. (Wijnholds, Heiko.) Pretoria, 1960.

Afr 12684.41.100 — Les grenouilles du mont Kimbo. (Niger, Paul.) Paris, 1964.

Afr 8667.66 — Grense,'n simposium oor rasse- en ander verhoudinge. Stellenbosch, 1961.

Afr 555.144 — Greschat, Hans-Jürgen. Kitawala. Marburg, 1967.

Afr 8658.92.3 — Greswall, W.P. Geography of Africa south of Zambesi. Oxford, 1892.

Afr 8088.85 — Greswell, W. Our South African empire. London, 1885. 2v.

Afr 2208.94 — Greville-Nugent. A land of mosques and marabouts. London, 1894.

Afr 2798.5.5 — Grevin, Emmanuel. Voyage au Hoggar. Paris, 1936.

Afr 9446.30 — Grey, A.H.G. Hubert Hervey. London, 1899.

Afr 1453.1 — Grey, H.M. In Moorish captivity. London, 1899.

Afr 3978.69.6 — Grey, W. Journal...visit to Egypt, Constantinople. London, 1869.

Afr 8252.341.10 — Grey steel, J.C. Smuts, a study in arrogance. (Armstrong, H.C.) London, 1937.

Afr 11752.65.110 — The Greyling. (Rooke, Daphne.) London, 1962.

Afr 3750.1 — Griadunov, Iurii S. Novye gorizonty Sudana. Moskva, 1969.

Afr 4559.34.15 — Griaule, M. Abyssinian journal. London, 1935.

Afr 4559.34.20 — Griaule, M. Burners of men, modern Ethiopia. Philadelphia, 1935.

Afr 4559.34.10 — Griaule, M. Les flambeurs d'hommes. Paris, 1934.

Afr 5243.174.20 — Griaule, Marcel. Conversations with Ogotemmeli. London, 1965.

Afr 5243.174.5 — Griaule, Marcel. Jeux dogons. Thèse complementaire. Paris, 1938.

Afr 5243.174 — Griaule, Marcel. Masques dogons. Thèse. Paris, 1938.

Afr 609.59.15 — Gribaudi, Dino. Profilo geografico dell'Africa. Torino, 1960.

Afr 38.4 — Grieken, Emil. Les archives inventoriées au Ministère des colonies. Bruxelles, 1956.

Afr 7530.10 — Grieken-Taverniers, M. van. Inventaire des archives des affaires étrangères de l'état du Congo. Bruxelles, 1955.

Afr 1955.14 — Grieu, R. de. Le duc d'Aumale et l'Algérie. Paris, 1884.

Afr 6198.436 — Griffith, William Brandford. The far horizon. Devon, 1951.

Afr 5765.2.10 — Griffiths, D. The persecuted Christians of Madagascar. London, 1841.

Afr 9493.58 — Griffiths, James. Livingstone's Africa. London, 1958.

Afr 1340.25 — Grillet, M. Les alignements en droit marocain. Thèse. Paris, 1935.

Afr 6282.16 — Grimley, John. Church growth in central and southern Nigeria. Grand Rapids, 1966.

Afr 6979.29.5 — Grimm, H. Das deutsche Südwester-buch. Muenchen, 1937.

Afr 679.13.5 — Grimm, Hans. Afrikafahrt West. Frankfurt, 1913.

Afr 8310.11 — Grineell-Milne, D.W. Baden-Powell at Mafeking. London, 1957.

Afr 8825.10 — The Griquas of Griqualand. (Halford, S.J.) Cape Town, 1949.

Afr 7122.70 — Grito de Angola. (Cotta, Goncalves.) Luanda, 1961.

Afr 8028.160 — Grivainis, Ilze. Material published after 1925 on the Great Trek until 1854. Thesis. Cape Town, 1967.

Afr 5385.24 — Grivot, René. Réactions dahoméennes. Paris, 1954.

Afr 6741.12 — Grob, Francis. Témoins camerounais de l'Evangile. Yaoundé, 1967.

Afr 8378.379.10 — Grobbelaar, Pieter Willem. This was a man. Cape Town, 1967.

Afr 630.58.5 — Grobler, Jan H. Africa's destiny. 2. ed. Johannesburg, 1958.

Afr 8853.2F — Groen, Julie. Bibliography of Basutoland. Cape Town, 1946.

Afr 724.3A — Grogan, E.S. From the Cape to Cairo. London, 1900.

Afr 679.67.15 — Grohs, Gerhard. Stufen afrikanischer Emanzipation. Stuttgart, 1967.

Afr 5190.26 — Groope d'Etudes Dakaroises. Dakar en devenir. Paris, 1968.

Afr 12005.8 — Groos, Almuth. Die Gegenwartsliteratur des Maghreb in französischer Sprache. Frankfurt, 1963.

Afr 6192.17 — Gros, Jules. Voyages, aventures et captivité de J. Bonnat chez les Achantis. Paris, 1884.

Afr 2533.6 — Gros, Simone. La politique de Carthage. Paris, 1958.

Afr 5110.20	Gueye, L. De la situation politique des sénégalais. Paris, 1922.
Afr 679.09	Guggisberg, Decima (Moore). We two in West Africa. London, 1909.
Afr 628.229.12	Guggisberg, Frederick Gordon. The future of the Negro. N.Y., 1969.
Afr 6198.440	Guggisberg. (Wraith, Ronald E.) London, 1967.
Afr 4368.5.5	Guglielmo Massaia. (Gianozza, E.) Torino, 1932.
Afr 1270.3	Guia del norte de Africa y sur de España. (Ortega, M.L.) Cadiz, 1917.
Afr 2308.6	Guiauchain, G. Alger. Alger-Mustapha, 1905.
Afr 12639.24.800	Guibert, A. Léopold Sédar Senghor. Paris, 1962.
Afr 7.1	Guida amministrativa e delle attività economiche dell'impero Africa orientale italiana. Torino. 1938+
Afr 3812.5	Guide - annuaire d'Egypte. Le Caire. 1872-1873
Afr 2224.961	Guide administratif. (Cumunel, G.) Paris, 1961.
Afr 2224.961.2	Guide administratif. Mise à jour au 15. juin 1961. (Cumunel, G.) Paris, 1961.
Afr 2220.2	Guide book. (Bodichon, E.) London, 1858.
Afr 3990.26	Guide book for U.A.R. (United Arab Republic. Information Department.) Cairo, 1964.
Afr 4570.5	Guide book of Ethiopia. (Ethiopia. Chamber of Commerce.) Addis Ababa, 1954.
Afr 6738.13	Guide de la colonisation au Cameroun. (France. Commissariat de la République Française au Cameroun.) Paris, 1923.
Afr 6685.10	Guide de la colonisation au Togo. (France. Commissariat au Togo.) Paris, 1924.
Afr 7808.97	Guide de la section de l'Etat Indépendant du Congo, la Bruxelles exposition. Bruxelles, 1897.
Afr 5748.99	Guide de l'immigrant à Madagascar. V.1-3 and plates. (Madagascar.) Paris, 1899. 4v.
Afr 7809.49	Guide de voyageur au Congo belge et auRuanda-Urundi. 1.ed. (Congo, Belgian.) Bruxelles, 1949.
Afr 50.46	Guide des partis politiques africains. (Bustin, Edouard.) Bruxelles, 1962.
Afr 2220.1	Guide du voyage en Algérie. (Quetin.) Paris, 1847.
Afr 2223.922	Guide économique de l'Algérie. (Falck, Felix.) Paris, 1922.
Afr 3990.24	Guide hotelier et touristique d'Egypte. Cairo. 1962
Afr 5748.95.5	Guide pratique du colon et du soldat à Madagascar. (Gautier, Emile F.) Paris, 1895.
Afr 510.102	Guide pratique sur les républiques. (France. Ministère de la Coopération.) Paris, 1964.
Afr 109.65.10	A guide to African history. 1st ed. (Davidson, Basil.) Garden City, N.Y., 1965.
Afr 6210.58	Guide to careers in the federal public service of Nigeria. (Nigeria. Nigerianisation Office.) Lagos, 1961.
Afr 3990.15	Guide to Egypt and Sudan. 3d ed. (Macmillan, firm, London.) London, 1905.
Afr 3990.15.5	Guide to Egypt and Sudan. 6th ed. (Macmillan, firm, London.) London, 1911.
Afr 8028.40	Guide to South African reference books. 3d ed. (Musiker, R.) Grahamstown, 1963.
Afr 6277.120.5	Guide to technical assistance in Nigeria. (Nigeria. Federal Ministry of Economic Development.) Lagos, 1965.
Afr 8815.2	Guide to the Cape province of South Africa. Cape Town. 3,1960+
Afr 9510.11	Guide to the Matapos. (Nobles, E.A.) Cape Town, 1924.
Afr 4158.5	A guide to the monasteries of the Wadi Natrun. (Burmester, O.H.E.) Le Caire, 1954.
Afr Doc 4502.2	A guide to the official records of the Colony of Natal. (Webb, C. de B.) Pietermaritzburg, 1965.
Afr 9432.5	A guide to the public records of Southern Rhodesia under the regime of the British South Africa Company. (Rhodesia, Southern. Central African Archives.) Cape Town, 1956.
Afr 9155.5	A guide to the Transvaal and map. (Bell, H.T.M.) Johannesburg, 1905. 2v.
Afr 6535.18	A guide to Uganda. (Uganda. Department of Information.) Entebbe, 1954.
Afr 6585.9	A guide to Zanzibar. (Shelswell-White, Geoffrey Henry.) Zanzibar, 1949.
Afr 2357.15	Guide touristique de l'Oranie agréé par la municipalité. (Marchand, Max.) Oran, 1958.
Afr 6277.87	Guidepost for Second National Development Plan, June, 1966. (Nigeria. Federal Ministry of Economic Development.) Lagos, 1966.
Afr 9499.76	Guides and Handbooks of Africa. Resources and opportunities in the Rhodesias and Nyasaland. Nairobi, 1963.
Afr 5758.1	Guides d'initiation active au développement. Tananarive. 1,1966+
Afr 1807.1	Guides Thiolier. Paris. 1+
Afr 28.78	Guides to materials for West African history in European archives. London.
Afr 1408.5	Guidotti, P. Storia dei Mori. Firenze, 1775.
Afr 5050.3	Guid'ouest africain. Paris. 1965+
Afr 2438.23	Guiga, Bahri. Essai sur l'évolution du Charaa et son application judiciaire en Tunisie. Thèse. Paris, 1930.
Afr 1625.15	Guiho, Pierre. La nationalité marocaine. Rabat, 1961.
Afr 550.80	Guilcher, René F. La société des missions africaines. 2. éd. Lyon, 1956.
Afr 5538.10	Guillain, C. Documents sur l'histoire, la géographie...de la partie occidentale de Madagascar. Paris, 1845.
Afr 698.56	Guillain, Charles. Documents sur l'histoire, la géographie et la commerce de l'Afrique orientale. Paris, 1856. 4v.
Afr 698.56PF	Guillain, Charles. Documents sur l'histoire, la géographie et la commerce de l'Afrique orientale. Atlas. Paris, 1856. 4v.
Afr 698.50	Guillain, Charles. Exploration de la côte orientale d'Afrique. Paris, 1850.
Afr 6743.55	Guillard, Joanny. Golempoui. Paris, 1965.
Afr 1347.5	Guillaume, A. Les Berberes marocains et la pacification de l'Atlas central (1912-1933). Paris, 1946.
Afr 1618.20	Guillaume, A. La propriété collective au Maroc. Rabat, 1960.
Afr 1623.955	Guillaume, Albert. L'evolution economique de la societe rurale marocaine. Paris, 1955.
Afr 2290.10	Guillaume. Conquête du sud-oranais; la colonne d'Igli en 1900. Paris, 1910.
Afr 1485.7	Guillaume. Sur la frontière marocaine. Paris, 1913.
Afr 5406.201	Guillemot, Marcel. Notice sur le Congo français. (2e. série). Paris, 1901.

Afr 1583.18	Guillen, Pierre. L'Allemagne et le Maroc de 1870-1905. Thèse. Paris, 1967.
Afr 5992.4	Guillermar de Aragon, Adolfo. Opusculo sobre la colonización de Fernando Poo. Madrid, 1852.
Afr 2749.04	Guilleux, Charles. Journal de route d'un caporal de tirailleurs de la mission saharienne. Belfort, 1904.
Afr 5385.23	Guillevin. Voyage dans l'intérieur du royaume de Dahomey. Paris, 1862.
Afr 3245.3	Guillon, E. L'Egypte contemporaine et intérêts français. Grenoble, 1885.
Afr 5749.15.5	Guilloteaux, E. Madagascar et la côte de Somalie. Paris, 1922.
Afr 8678.265	Guilty land. (Vanrensburg, P.) London, 1962.
Afr 3315.90	Guilty men. (Foot, Michael.) N.Y., 1957.
Afr 2228.6	Guimet, E. Arabes et Kabyles. Lyon, 1873.
Afr 7050.20	Guiné; anuário turístico. Bissau. 1,1963+
Afr 7068.12	Guiné, minha terra. (Aquiar, Armando de.) Lisboa, 1964.
Afr 7068.11	Guiné. (Dias de Carvalho.) Lisboa, 1944.
Afr 7065.10	Guiné do século XV. (Terra, Branco da.) Lisboa?, 196-.
Afr 7062.10	Guiné portuguesa. (Viegas, Luis A.C.) Lisboa, 1936. 2v.
Afr 7068.9	Guiné portuguesa. v.2. (Mota, Avelino Teixeira da.) Lisboa, 1954.
Afr 7068.4	Guine 1965, contra-atorque. (Cesar, Amandio.) Braga, 1965.
Afr 7069.5	Guinea, Portuguese. Governor. Relatório da provincia da Guiné Portugueza referido ao anno económico de 1888-1889. Lisboa, 1890.
Afr Doc 8707.350	Guinea, Spanish. Delegacion Colonial de Estadistica. Resúmenes estadisticos del anso general de poblacion del Gobcerno General de los Españoles del Golfo de Guinea al 31 de diciembre de 1950. Madrid, 1952.
Afr 7053.1	Pamphlet box. Guinea.
Afr 5303.2	Guinea. Archive Nationale. Répertoire des archives nationales. v.1. Conakry, 1962.
Afr 5316.710	Pamphlet vol. Guinea. Language: French. 3 pam.
Afr Doc 9405.5	Guinea. Portuguese. Anuário. Lisbon. 1-2,1946-1948 2v.
Afr Doc 9407.350	Guinea. Portuguese. Secção Tecnica de Estatistica. Censo da população de 1950. Lisboa, 1952? 2v.
Afr 5318.3	Guinea (Republic). Secretariat d'Etat à l'Information et au Tourisme. La Guinée et son peuple. Conakry, 1965.
Afr 5950.5	La Guinea Ecuatorial. Santa Isabel. 1621,1968+
Afr 5953.2	La Guinea ecuatorial y su regimen de Autonomia. (Spain. Consejo Superior de Investigaciones Cientificas.) Madrid, 1964.
Afr 5960.13	La Guinea española. (Beltran y Rozpide, Ricardo.) Barcelona, 1901.
Afr 5960.8	La Guinea española y su riqueza forestal. (Najera y Angulo.) Madrid, 1930.
Afr 5962.6	La Guinea española y sus riquezas. (Arija, Julio.) Madrid, 1930.
Afr 5955.5	La Guinea incognita. (Madrid, F.) Madrid, 1933.
Afr 5969.8	Guinea Lopez, Emilio. En el pais de los Bubis. Madrid, 1949.
Afr 590.17	The Guinea voyage. (Stanfield, J.F.) Edinburgh, 1807.
Afr 5316.10.5	Guinean revolution and social progress. (Toure, Sekou.) Cairo, 1963.
Afr 5316.5	Guinée, état pilote. (Gigon, Fernand.) Paris, 1959.
Afr 5316.12	La Guinée. (Ameillon, B.) Paris, 1964.
Afr 5312.5A	Guinée. Paris, 1953.
Afr 5318.3	La Guinée et son peuple. (Guinea (Republic). Secretariat d'Etat à l'Information et au Tourisme.) Conakry, 1965.
Afr 5318.7	Guinée française. Rapport d'ensemble. Paris, 1900.
Afr 5318.11	La Guinée française. (Arcin, A.) Paris, 1907.
Afr 5318.14	La Guinée française. (Aspe-Fleurimont, L.) Paris, 1900.
Afr 5318.30	La Guinée française. (Hovis, Maurice.) Paris, 1953.
Afr 7072.5	Guinéus; contos, narrativas, crónicas. (Barbosa, Alexandre.) Lisboa, 1967.
Afr 555.9.16	Guinness, Fanny E. The new world of Central Africa. London, 1890.
Afr 5406.189	Guiral, Léon. Le Congo français du Gabon à Brazzaville. Paris, 1889.
Afr 212.46	Guiton, Raymond. Afrika im Widerspruch. Köln, 1967.
Afr 1658.56	Guixé, Juan. El Rif en sombras lo que yo he visto en Melilla. Madrid, 1922.
Afr 510.110	Gukasian-Gandzaketsi, L.J. Frantsuzskii imperializm i Afrika. Moscow, 1962.
Afr 8678.175	The gulf between. (Burger, Jan.) Cape Town, 1960.
Afr 3326.8	Gulick, Luther Halsey. Government reorganization in the United Arab Republic. Cairo, 1962.
Afr 6395.8	Gulliver, P.H. The family herds. London, 1955.
Afr 6883.31	Gulliver, P.H. Social control in an African society, a study of the Arusha, agricultural Masai of northern Tanganyika. Boston, 1963.
Afr 6883.31.2	Gulliver, P.H. Social control in an African society. London, 1963.
Afr 6395.30	Gulliver, Phillip Hugh. Tradition and transition in East Africa. Berkeley, 1969.
Afr 608.53.3	Gumprecht, J.E. Handbuch der Geographie...von Afrika. Leipzig, 1845.
Afr 9388.93.3	Gun and camera in South Africa. (Bryden, H.A.) London, 1893.
Afr 6192.4.3	Gundert, H. Vier Jahre in Asante-Tagebücher der Missionäre Ramseyer und Kühne. Basel, 1875.
Afr 9290.5	Gunn, Hugh. The language question in the Orange River Colony. Johannesburg, 1910.
Afr 8835.48	Gunners of the Cape. (Orpen, Neil.) Cape Town, 1965.
Afr 609.55.10A	Gunther, John. Inside Africa. 1st ed. N.Y., 1955.
Afr 710.22	Gunther, John. Meet central Africa. London, 1959.
Afr 500.60	Gunzert, T. Kolonialprobleme der Gegenwart in Beitragen. Berlin, 1939.
Afr 4591.2	The Gurage. (Shack, William A.) London, 1966.
Afr 7350.3.14	Gurley, R.R. Letter to Hon. H. Clay, president of the American Colonization Society. London, 1841.
Afr 7375.7	Gurley, R.R. Life of Jehudi Ashmun. Washington, 1835.
Afr 7375.7.2	Gurley, R.R. Life of Jehudi Ashmun. 2d. ed. N.Y., 1839.
Afr 7350.3.13	Gurley, R.R. Mission to England...American Colonization Society. Washington, 1841.
Afr 6540.9	Gurling, F.K. The Acholi of Uganda. London, 1960.
Afr 9500.46	Gussman, Boris. Out in the mid-day sun. London, 1962.
Afr 8687.225	Guthrie, F.H. Frontier magistrate. Cape Town, 1946.
Afr 1574.8	Gutierrez, F.L. España y las demas naciones. Madrid, 1906.
Afr 1573.9	Gutierrez Sobral, J. Marruecos. Madrid, 1905.

Afr 6542.5.10 Gutkind, Peter. The royal capital of Buganda. The Hague, 1963.
Afr 6887.11.15 Gutmann, B. Dichten und Denken der Dschagganeger. Leipzig, 1909.
Afr 6887.11 Gutmann, B. Das Recht der Dschagga. München, 1926.
Afr 6887.11.9 Gutmann, B. Die Stammeslehren der Dschagga. München, 1932. 3v.
Afr 6885.5 Gutmann, Bruno. Afrikaner-Europäer in nächstenschaftlicher Entsprechung. Stuttgart, 1966.
Afr 8687.309.5 Gutsche, Thelma. No ordinary woman. Cape Town, 1966.
Afr 9165.42.80 Gutsche, Thelma. Old gold, the history of the Wanderers club. Cape Town, 1966.
Afr 8687.281 Gutsche, Thelma. Selective index to Not heaven itself; an autobiography. 2. ed. Johannesburg, 1968.
Afr 510.35 Guy, M., of Tours. Batisseurs d'empire. Paris, 1945.
Afr 2295.2 Guyon. Voyage d'Alger aux Ziban (Text and atlas). Alger, 1852. 2v.
Afr 4700.27.10 Guyot, Georges. L'Italie devant le problème colonial. Roma, 1927.
Afr 8279.00.25 Guyot, Yves. Boer politics. London, 1900.
Afr 5318.40 Gvineia segodnia. (Bochkarev, I.A.) Moscow, 1961.
Afr 5318.35 Gvineiskaia Respublika. (Gavrilov, N.I.) Moscow, 1960.
Afr 5312.10 Gvineiskaia Respublika. (Solonitskii, A.S.) Moscow, 1961.
Afr 5235.55.10 Gwynn, Stephen. Mungo Park and the quest of the Niger. N.Y., 1935.
Afr 8292.41 The H.A.C. in South Africa. (Williams, Basil.) London, 1903.
Afr 718.2.85 H.M. Stanley, the African explorer. (Montefiore, A.) London, 1889.
Afr 718.2.106 H.M. Stanley. (Hird, Frank.) London, 1935.
Afr 718.2.101 H.M. Stanley. (Symons, A.J.A.) London, 1933.
Afr 8110.3.10 Haantjes, Jacob. Verkenner in koopmansland. Amsterdam, 1946.
Afr 715.15 Haardt, G.M. The black journey across central Africa. N.Y., 1927.
Afr 715.15.5 Haardt, G.M. La croisière noire, expédition citroen central-Afrique. Paris, 1927.
Afr 2749.22 Haardt, G.M. Le raid Citroen. Paris, 1923.
Afr 6738.10 Haase, Lene. Durchs unbekannte Kamerun. Berlin, 1915.
Afr 4108.2 Habachi, Labib. Aswan. Le Caire, 1959.
Afr 2030.425 Habart, Michel. Histoire d'un parjure. Paris, 1960.
Afr 6740.35 L'habitation des Fati. (Lebeuf, J.P.) Paris, 1961.
Afr 4285.6 Hable-Selassie, Sergew. Beziehungen Äthiopiens zur griechisch-römischen Welt. Bonn, 1964.
Afr 7567.20 Habran, Louis. Coup d'oeil sur le problème politique et militaire du Congo belge. Bruxelles, 1925.
Afr 28.20 Hache, J. Bibliographie africaine de périodiques. Bruxelles, 1934.
Afr 4892.8 Hachette, R. Djibouti, au seuil de l'Orient. Paris, 1931.
Afr 550.95 Hacia el futuro. (Lory, Marie Joseph.) Andorra, 1958.
Afr 5247.5 Hacquard, Augustin. Monographie de Tombouctou. Paris, 1900.
Afr 6400.36 Hadith; proceedings of the annual conference of the Historical Association of Kenya. Nairobi. 1,1967+ 2v.
Afr 2397.36 Hadj Ali, Bachir. L'Arbitraire. Paris, 1966.
Afr 6738.52 Haeberle, Wilhelm. Kamerun. Stuttgart, 1967.
Afr 6741.6 Häberle, Wilhelm. Trommeln, Mächte und ein Ruf. Stuttgart, 1966.
Afr 9599.28 Haefler, P.L. Africa speaks, a story of adventure. London, 1931.
Afr 3994.912 Haekal, M.H. La dette publique égyptienne. Paris, 1912.
Afr 5549.43 Haenel, Karl. Madagaskar. Leipzig, 1943.
Afr 3040.79 Hafiz, Mahamid. La délégation législative en France et en Egypte. Le Caire, 1956.
Afr 2209.27.5 Hafsa. Desert winds. N.Y., 1927.
Afr 630.54.5 Hafter, Rudolf. Schwarz und Weiss in Afrika. Zürich, 1954.
Afr 3700.9 Haggard, A.C. Under crescent and star. Edinburgh, 1895.
Afr 8235.7 Haggard, H.R. Cetywayo and his white neighbours. London, 1888.
Afr 8210.5 Haggard, H.R. A history of the Transvaal. N.Y., 1899.
Afr 8210.5.5 Haggard, H.R. A history of the Transvaal. N.Y., 1900.
Afr 8225.8 Haggard, H.R. The last Boer war. London, 1900.
Afr 9499.40 Haglewood, Arthur. Nyasaland. Oxford, 1960.
Afr 6930.20.2 Hague. International Court of Justice. Ethiopia and Liberia versus South Africa. 2d ed. Pretoria, 1966.
Afr 609.64.5 Hahn, E. Africa to me, person to person. 1st ed. Garden City, 1964.
Afr 1110.15 Hahn, Lora. North Africa. Washington, 1960.
Afr 5813.14 Hahn, Lorna. Mauritius; a study and annotated bibliography. Washington, 1969.
Afr 108.82 Hahn, T. Early African exploration up to the 16th century. Cape Town, 1882.
Afr 8825.3 Hahn, T. Tsuni-Goam, the supreme being. London, 1881.
Afr 8678.115 Hahn, Theophilus. Beitrage zur Kunde der Hottentotten. Durban, 19- .
Afr 8678.300 Haigh, Alan. South African tragedy. London, 1962.
Afr 659.42.2 Haight, Mabel V. Jackson. European powers and south-east Africa. 2nd ed. N.Y., 1967.
Afr 4430.66 Hailde-Selassie's government. (Clapham, Christopher S.) London, 1969.
Afr 4430.64 Haile Selassie, the conquering Lion. (Mosley, Leonard O.) London, 1964.
Afr 4430.48 Haile Selassie. The eighteenth anniversary of the coronation of His Imperial Majesty Haile Selassie I. Addis Ababa, 1948.
Afr 4430.36 Haile Selassie. (Asfa Yilma, Princess.) London, 1936.
Afr 4430.55 Haile Selassie I. (Talbot, D.A.) The Hague, 1955.
Afr 4640.3 Haile Selassie I University. Social survey of Addis Ababa, 1960. Addis Ababa, 1960.
Afr 4208.5 Haile Selassie I University. Department of History. Historical studies. Addis Ababa. 1,1964+
Afr 210.38 Hailey, W.M.H. An African survey. London, 1938.
Afr 210.38.5A Hailey, W.M.H. An African survey. London, 1957.
Afr 210.38.2 Hailey, W.M.H. An African survey. 2d ed. London, 1945.
Afr 505.15 Hailey, W.M.H. Native administration in the British African territories. v.1-5. London, 1950-51. 5v.
Afr 8045.53 Hailey, W.M.H. The Republic of South Africa. London, 1963.
Afr 6010.3 Hailey, William Malcolm H. Native administration and political development in British tropical Africa. London, 1944.
Afr 1609.12.3 Haillot. Le Maroc. Vincennes, 1912.
Afr 2945.1 Haimann, G. Cirenaica. Roma, 1882.
Afr 2945.1.2 Haimann, G. Cirenaica. 2a ed. Milan, 1886.
Afr 210.55A Haines, C.G. Africa today. Baltimore, 1955.
Afr 1550.54 El-Hajoui, M.O. Histoire diplomatique du Maroc (1900-1912). Paris, 1937.
Afr 6403.6 Hakes, Jay E. A study guide for Kenya. Boston, 1969.
Afr 3275.49 Halassie, S. Democracy on the Nile. Scotch Plains, N.J., 1940.
Afr 6193.66 Halbach, Axel J. Ghana als Wirtschaftspartner. Köln, 1969.
Afr 8325.36 Haldane, A. How we escaped from Pretoria. Edinburg, 1901.
Afr 9446.29 Hale, H.M. Lobengula. London, 1929.
Afr 8283.20 Hale, Hugh M. The Jameson raid. London, 1930.
Afr 7458.53 Hale, Sarah J. Liberia. N.Y., 1853.
Afr 8289.00.40 Hales, A.G. Campaign pictures of the war in South Africa (1899-1900). London, 1900.
Afr 8335.8F Halfeen van afrikaner-prestasie, 1900-1950. Johannesburg, 1950.
Afr 8825.10 Halford, S.J. The Griquas of Griqualand. Cape Town, 1949.
Afr 640.6 Haliburton, R.G. Dwarfs of Mount Atlas. London, 1891.
Afr 640.6.3 Haliburton, R.G. Holy land of Punt, racial dwarfs in the Atlas and the Pyrenees. London, 1893.
Afr 640.6.5 Haliburton, R.G. How a race of Pigmies was found. Toronto, 1897.
Afr 7815.5.7 Halkin, Joseph. Les Abatua. 7. Bruxelles, 1911.
Afr 8292.14.5 Hall, David Oswald William. The New Zealanders in South Africa. Wellington, 1949.
Afr 1609.31.30 Hall, Leland. Salah and his American. N.Y., 1935.
Afr 5247.20A Hall, Leland. Timbuctoo. N.Y., 1927.
Afr 699.07 Hall, Mary. A woman's trek from the Cape to Cairo. London, 1907.
Afr 9748.475.5 Hall, Richard. Kaunda, founder of Zambia. London, 1965.
Afr 9650.10 Hall, Richard Seymour. The high price of principles. London, 1969.
Afr 9689.65 Hall, Richard Seymour. Zambia. London, 1965.
Afr 9689.65.5 Hall, Richard Seymour. Zambia. London, 1968.
Afr 3979.28A Hall, Trowbridge. Egypt in silhouette. N.Y., 1928.
Afr 6196.27 Hall, Wynyard Montagu. The great drama of Kumasi. London, 1939.
Afr 8830.6 Hallbeck, H.P. Narrative of visit made in 1819 to...Erron. London, 1820.
Afr 4559.13.5 Halle, C. To Menelek in a motor car. London, 1913.
Afr 8252.227.15 Halle, G. Mayfair to Maritzburg. London, 1933.
Afr 609.60.20 Haller, Albert. Die Welt des Afrikaners. Düsseldorf, 1960.
Afr 710.23 Hallet, Jean Pierre. Congo kitabu. N.Y., 1966.
Afr 109.70.5 Hallett, Robin. Africa to 1875; a modern history. Ann Arbor, 1970.
Afr 715.26 Hallett, Robin. The penetration of Africa. N.Y., 1965.
Afr 679.66 Hallett, Robin. People and progress in West Africa. Oxford, 1966.
Afr 625.17F Hallucinations scientifiques. Les Portulans. (Yusuf Kamal, Prince.) Leiden, 1937.
Afr 8695.11 Halpern, Jack. South Africa's hostages. Harmondsworth, Eng., 1965.
Afr 679.61.10 Halpern, Jan. Na potudnie od Sahary. Warsawa, 1961.
Afr 6277.83 Halpern, Jan. Nigeria i Ghana. Warszawa, 1964.
Afr 626.157.5 Halpern, Jan. Planowanie w niektorych krajach Afryki. Warszawa, 1965.
Afr 679.66.30 Halpern, Jan. Studia nad gospodarka przedkapitalistyczna no Afryee Gachoancej wieku XIX i XX. Wyd.1. Warszawa, 1966.
Afr 626.157F Halpern, Jan. Wybrane zagadnienia z historii gospodarczej Afryki. Warszawa, 1963.
Afr 1493.78A Halstead, John Preston. Rebirth of a nation;...Moroccan nationalism. 1912-1944. Cambridge, 1967.
Afr 8089.51 Halt, A.G.H. von der. Geskiedenis von Suid-Afrika. v.1-2. Kaapstad, 1957.
Afr 5243.343.20 Hama, Boubou. Histoire des Songhay. Paris, 1968.
Afr 5243.207.10 Hama, Boubou. Contribution à la connaissance de l'histoire des Peul. Paris, 1968.
Afr 609.66.15 Hama, Boubou. Enquête sur les fondements et la genèse de l'unité africaine. Paris, 1966.
Afr 6295.221 Hama, Boubou. Histoire du Gobir et de Sokoto. Paris, 1967.
Afr 5243.343.20.5 Hama, Boubou. L'Histoire traditionnelle d'un peuple: les Zarma-Songhay. Paris, 1967.
Afr 2762.22 Hama, Boubou. Recherches sur l'histoire des Touareg sahariens et soudanais. Paris, 1967.
Afr 630.12 Hambly, Wilfrid D. Ethnology of Africa. Chicago, 1930.
Afr 3135.5 Al-Hamdani, Abbas H. The Fatimids. Karachi, 1962.
Afr 9225.25 Hamelberg en die Oranje-Vrystaat. (Spies, François Jacobus du Toit.) Amsterdam, 1941.
Afr 8676.64.6 Hamer, Eberhard. Die Industrialisierung Südafrikas seit dem Zweiten Weltkrieg. Stuttgart, 1964.
Afr 1069.23 Hamet, I. Histoire du Maghreb. Paris, 1923.
Afr 2225.5 Hamet, I. Les Musulmans français du nord de l'Afrique. Paris, 1906.
Afr 5074.36 Hamet, Ismael. Chroniques de la Mauritanie sénégalaise. Paris, 1911.
Afr 1609.01.8 Hamet, Ismael. Cinq mois au Maroc. Alger, 1901.
Afr 4935.6 Hamilton, Angus. Somaliland. London, 1911.
Afr 2731.15.110 Hamilton, Elizabeth. The desert my dwelling place: a study of Charles de Foucauld, 1858-1916. London, 1968.
Afr 7219.51 Hamilton, G. In the wake of Da Gama. London, 1951.
Afr 6570.12 Hamilton, Genesta. Princes of Zinj. London, 1957.
Afr 2945.34 Hamilton, J. Wanderings in North Africa. London, 1856.
Afr 8310.8 Hamilton, J.A. Siege of Mafeking. London, 1900.
Afr 4070.53A Hamilton, J.A. de C. The Anglo-Egyptian Sudan from within. London, 1935.
Afr 8160.15 Hamilton-Browne, G. A lost legionary in South Africa. London, 1912.
Afr 3978.71.5 Hamley, W.G. New sea and an old land..visit to Egypt. Edinburgh, 1871.
Afr 4236.963 Hammerschmidt, E. Stellung und Bedeutung des Sabbats. Stuttgart, 1963.
Afr 4259.67 Hammerschmidt, Ernst. Äthiopien, christliches Reich zwisches Gestern und Morgen. Wiesbaden, 1968.
Afr 2618.25 Hammerton, Thomas. Tunisia unveiled. London, 1959.
Afr 7377.6 Hammond, J.H. Regina coeli. Correspondence of J.H.B. Latrobe. Baltimore, 1858.
Afr 8279.00.9 Hammond, J.H. The Transvaal trouble. N.Y., 1900.
Afr 8283.15A Hammond, J.H. The truth about the Jameson raid. Boston, 1918.
Afr 8283.10 Hammond, J.H. A woman's part in a revolution. N.Y., 1897.
Afr 5285.277.20 Hammond, Peter B. Yatenga. N.Y., 1966.

Afr 7022.2   Hammond, Richard. Portugal and Africa, 1815-1910. Stanford, 1966.

Afr 8825.35   Hammond-Tooke, W.D. Bhaca society. Cape Town, 1962.

Afr 5012.4   Hamon, Leo. Les partis politiques africains. Paris, 1962.

Afr 5746.43   Hamond, W. Madagascar, the richest and most fruitful island in the world. London, 1643.

Afr 3205.5   Hamont, P.N. L'Egypte sous Mehemet-Ali. Paris, 1843. 2v.

Afr 8685.1   Hampson, Ruth M. Islam in South Africa. Cape Town, 1964.

Afr 8686.10   Hance, Gertrude Rachel. The Zulu yesterday and today; twenty-nine years in South Africa. N.Y., 1916.

Afr 626.40.2   Hance, W.A. African economic development. N.Y., 1967.

Afr 626.40   Hance, W.A. African economic development. 1st ed. N.Y., 1958.

Afr 609.64.10   Hance, W.A. The geography of modern Africa. N.Y., 1964.

Afr 8667.80   Hancock, William Keith. Are there South Africans? Johannesburg, 1966.

Afr 8252.341.83   Hancock, William Keith. Smuts; study for a portrait. London, 1965.

Afr 8252.341.80A   Hancock, William Keith. Smuts. Cambridge, 1962. 2v.

Afr 8252.341.82   Hancock, William Keith. Smuts and the shift of world power. London, 1964.

Afr 8252.341.65   Hancock, William Keith. The Smuts papers. London, 1956.

Afr 4258.67   Hand-book of Abyssinia. (Peacock, Geo.) London, 1867.

Afr 3978.49   Hand-book to the American panorama of the Nile. (Gliddon, Geo. R.) London, 1849.

Afr 6900.30   Handbook. (South West Africa.) Windhoek. 1964 +

Afr 8678.355   Handbook for better race relations. (United Party (South Africa).) Johannesburg, 1963.

Afr 6390.8   Handbook for East Africa, Uganda and Zanzibar, 1906. Mombasa, 1906.

Afr 626.104   Handbook of African economic development. (Benveniste, Guy.) N.Y., 1962.

Afr 6390.11.3   Handbook of British East Africa. (Ward, H.F.) London, 1912.

Afr 6277.10   Handbook of commerce and industry in Nigeria. Lagos. 2,1954 + 3v.

Afr 3990.27   The handbook of Egypt. (Abd Allah, Hasan.) Cairo, 1966.

Afr 6879.16   A handbook of German East Africa. (Great Britain. Admiralty.) n.p., 1916.

Afr 6879.16.3   A handbook of German East Africa. (Great Britain. Naval Intelligence Division.) N.Y., 1969.

Afr 6390.11.15   A handbook of Kenya colony (British East Africa). (Great Britain. Admiralty.) n.p., 1920.

Afr 7459.40   Handbook of Liberia. N.Y., 1940.

Afr 2929.17   A handbook of Libya. Sept. 1917. Naval Staff. (Great Britain. Admiralty.) n.p., 1917.

Afr 9839.22.5   A handbook of Nyasaland. (Murray, S.S.) London, 1932.

Afr 9839.20   A handbook of Portuguese Nyasaland. (Great Britain. Admiralty.) Oxford, 1920.

Afr 6176.30.40   Handbook of revolutionary warfare. (Nkrumah, Kwame.) London, 1968.

Afr 6143.25   The handbook of Sierra Leone. (Goddard, T.N.) London, 1925.

Afr 6750.4   Handbook of Tanganyika. London, n.d.

Afr 6750.4.2   Handbook of Tanganyika. 2d ed. Dar es Salaam, 1958.

Afr 6535.16.20   A handbook of the Uganda Protectorate. (Great Britain. Admiralty.) Oxford, 1920.

Afr 6535.12   The handbook of Uganda. (Wallis, H.R.) London, 1913.

Afr 8678.57   Handbook on race relations in South Africa. (Hellmann, E.) Cape Town, 1949.

Afr 8685.327   Handbook on the Group Areas Act. (Rousseau, Francois.) Cape Town, 1960.

Afr 3993.963   Handbook on U.A.R. economy. (United Arab Republic. Information Department.) Cairo, 1963.

Afr 608.53.3   Handbuch der Geographie...von Afrika. (Gumprecht, J.E.) Leipzig, 1853.

Afr 28.128   Handlist of sub-Saharan Africana. Darien, Conn. 1,1968 +

Afr 6176.30.5   Hands off Africa. (Nkrumah, Kwame.) Accra, 1960.

Afr 6277.112   Das Handwerk in ausgewählten Bezirken Westnigerias. (Koch, Bernd.) Frankfurt, 1968.

Afr 6850.3   Handwerk und Industrie in Ostafrika. (Stuhlmann, F.) Hamburg, 1910.

Afr 9439.60.15   Hanna, A.J. The story of the Rhodesias and Nyasaland. London, 1960.

Afr 9438.165   Hanna, A.J. The story of the Rhodesias and Nyasaland. 2nd ed. London, 1965.

Afr 9775.2   Hanna, Alexander John. The beginnings of Nyasaland and north-eastern Rhodesia. Oxford, 1956.

Afr 500.82   Hanna, Alexander John. European rule in Africa. London, 1965.

Afr 50.44   Hanna, W.J. Independent black Africa. Chicago, 1964.

Afr 28.95   Hanna, W.J. Politics in Black Africa. East Lansing, Michigan, 1964.

Afr 650.8   Hanna, William John. Urban dynamics in Black Africa. Washington, 1969.

Afr 6275.35   Hanny, Erich Robert. Vom Sudan zum Mittelmeer. St. Gallen, 1944.

Afr 5635.1   Hanotaux, G. L'affaire de Madagascar. 3e ed. Paris, 1896.

Afr 3069.31   Hanotaux, G. Histoire de la nation égyptienne. Paris, 1931-40. 7v.

Afr 510.10   Hanotaux, G. Le partage de l'Afrique - Fachoda. Paris, n.d.

Afr 510.10.5   Hanotaux, G. Pour l'empire colonial français. Paris, 1933.

Afr 3979.29   Hanotaux, G. Regards sur l'Egypte et la Palestine. Paris, 1929.

Afr 2230.2   Hanoteau, A. La Kabylie et les coutumes kabyles. Paris, 1873. 3v.

Afr 8687.271.5   Hans Merensky. (Lehmann, Olga.) Göttingen, 1965.

Afr 6160.20   Hansard Society for Parliamentary Government. The parliament of Ghana. London, 1959.

Afr 6060.58   Hansard Society for Parliamentary Government. What are the problems of parliamentary government in West Africa. London, 1958.

Afr 3993.965   Hansen, Bent. Development and economic policy in the U.A.R. (Egypt). Amsterdam, 1965.

Afr 6166.2.5   Hansen, Thorkild. Slavernes kyst. København, 1967.

Afr 590.88   Hansen, Thorkild. Slavernes skibe. København, 1968.

Afr 7175.77   Hanu, Jose. Quand le vent souffle en Angola. Bruxelles, 1965.

Afr 609.52.10   Hanzelka, Jiri. Africa. 1st ed. Prague, 1952. 3v.

Afr 212.5   Hapgood, D. Africa, from independence to tomorrow. 1st ed. N.Y., 1965.

Afr 8279.40.5A   The hapless Boers. (Vroom, E.) Scotch Plains, N.J., 1940.

Afr 6412.6   Harambee. (Kenyatta, J.) Nairobi, 1964.

Afr 4660.5   L'Harar. (Santagata, Fernando.) Milano, 1940.

Afr 2386.1   Harbillon, M. Relation du siège de Zaatcha. Paris, 1863.

Afr 3986.958.15A   Harbison, F.H. Human resources for Egyptian enterprise. N.Y., 1958.

Afr 1607.51   Harck Olufs aus der Insul amron im stifte ripen in Juetland. (Riese, Otto.) Flensburg, 1751.

Afr 609.60.40   Harcourt, François. L'Afrique à l'heure. Paris, 1960.

Afr 3978.93.20   Harcourt, François. L'Egypte et les Egyptiens. Paris, 1893.

Afr 8252.227   Harding, C. Far bugles. London, 1933.

Afr 9710.7   Harding, C. In remotest Barotseland. London, 1905.

Afr 8288.99.25   Harding, William. War in South Africa and the dark continent from savagery to civilization. Chicago, 1899.

Afr 6118.7   Hardinge, Rex. Gambia and beyond. London, 1934.

Afr 6979.37   Hardinge, Rex. South African cinderella, a trip through ex-German West Africa. London, 1937.

Afr 1432.3   Hardman, F. The Spanish campaign in Morocco. Edinburgh, 1860.

Afr 6455.2   Hardwick, A.A. An ivory trader in North Kenia. London, 1903.

Afr 1571.17.75   Hardy, G. Portrait de Lyautey. Paris, 1949.

Afr 5054.37   Hardy, Georges. L'Afrique occidentale française. Paris, 1937.

Afr 5392.3   Hardy, Georges. Un apôtre d'aujourd'hui. Paris, 1949.

Afr 5130.20.10   Hardy, Georges. Faidherbe. Paris, 1947.

Afr 1369.21   Hardy, Georges. Les grandes étapes de l'histoire du Maroc. Paris, 1921.

Afr 1609.22.10   Hardy, Georges. Les grandes lignes de la geographie du Maroc. Paris, 1922.

Afr 1609.30.5   Hardy, Georges. Le Maroc. Paris, 1930.

Afr 5130.15.5   Hardy, Georges. La mise en valeur du Sénégal de 1817 à 1854. Paris, 1921.

Afr 5130.15   Hardy, Georges. La mise en valeur du Sénégal de 1817 à 1854. Thèse. Paris, 1921.

Afr 109.22   Hardy, Georges. Vue générale de l'histoire d'Afrique. Paris, 1922.

Afr 5314.3   Hardy, Jules. Les Dieppois en Guinée en 1364. Dieppe, 1864.

Afr 1608.96.3   Harem und Moschee. Reiseskizzen aus Marokko. (Schabelsky, E. von.) Berlin, 1896.

Afr 11797.41.800   Haresnape, Geoffrey. Pauline Smith. N.Y., 1969.

Afr 6535.9   Harford-Battersby, P.F. Pilkington of Uganda. London, n.d.

Afr 6143.44   Hargrave, C.G. African primitive life as I saw it in Sierra Leone. Wilmington, N.C., 1944.

Afr 5052.2   Hargreaves, J.D. France and West Africa. London, 1969.

Afr 6149.257.5   Hargreaves, J.D. A life of Sir Samuel Lewis. London, 1958.

Afr 679.63.5   Hargreaves, J.D. Prelude to the partition of West Africa. London, 1963.

Afr 5054.67   Hargreaves, John. West Africa. Englewood Cliffs, 1967.

Afr 1608.03   Haringman, H. Beknopt dag-journaal van Marocco. Haag, 1803.

Afr 6595.5   Harkema, Roelof Cornelius. De stad Zanzibar in de tweede helft van de negentiende eeuw en enkele oudere Oostafrikaanse Kuststeden. Loenen aan de Vecht, 1967.

Afr 2030.463.20   Les Harkis au service de la France. (Boualam, B.) Paris, 1963.

Afr 7459.41   Harley, G. Native African medicine. Cambridge, 1941.

Afr 7465.10   Harley, George W. Notes on the Poro in Liberia. Cambridge, 1941.

Afr 6390.29   Harm of the hunter. 1st ed. (Ruark, R.C.) Garden City, 1953.

Afr 510.80   Harmand, Jack. L'Afrique à l'heure française. Paris, 1958.

Afr 12785.89.110   L'harmattan. (Ousmane, Sembene.) Paris, 1965.

Afr 6192.71   Harmattan i wielki deszcz. Wyd. 1. (Sliwka-Szczerbic, W.) Warszawa, 1965.

Afr 8678.106   The harmless people. 1st ed. (Thomas, E.M.) N.Y., 1959.

Afr 4430.35   Harmsworth, A. Abyssinian adventure. London, 1935.

Afr 9148.99.5F   Harpen, N. van. Nederland-Zuid-Afrika. Amsterdam, 1899.

Afr 7350.6.10   Harper, C.C. An address delivered...annual meeting of Maryland State Colonization Society...Annapolis, Jan. 23, 1835. Baltimore, 1835.

Afr 4612.2   Harrar. (Paulitschke, P.) Leipzig, 1888.

Afr 8678.337   Harrell, Muriel. Reserves and reservations. Johannesburg, 1965.

Afr 44616.2   Harries, L. Swahili poetry. Oxford, 1962.

Afr 8659.66   Harrigan, Anthony. The new republic, South Africa's role in the world. Pretoria, 1966.

Afr 9500.38   Harrigan, Anthony. One against the mob. Arlington, 1966.

Afr 212.3   Harrigan, Anthony. Red star over Africa. Cape Town, 1964.

Afr 8252.36   Harris, D. Pioneer, soldier and politician. London, 1931.

Afr Doc 3309.227   Harris, Douglas Gordon. Development in Uganda, 1947 to 1956. Wisbech?, Eng., 1956.

Afr 3979.57   Harris, G.L. Egypt. New Haven, 1957.

Afr 9345.10.8   Harris, J.C. Khama, the great African chief. 4. ed. London, 1923.

Afr 6203.4.5   Harris, John. Books about Nigeria. Nigeria, 1962.

Afr 6203.4   Harris, John. Books about Nigeria. 2. ed. Nigeria, 1960.

Afr 6203.4.4   Harris, John. Books about Nigeria. 4th ed. Ibadan, 1963.

Afr 630.9   Harris, John H. Africa, slave or free. London, 1919.

Afr 630.9.5   Harris, John H. Africa: slave or free? N.Y., 1969.

Afr 9445.10   Harris, John H. The chartered millions. London, 1920.

Afr 590.25   Harris, John H. Portuguese slavery, Britain's dilemma. London, 1913.

Afr 6069.68   Harris, John Hobbis. Dawn in darkest Africa. 1st ed. London, 1968.

Afr 1490.3.5   Harris, Lawrence. With Mulai Hafid at Fez. Boston, 1910.

Afr 1490.3   Harris, Lawrence. With Mulai Hafid at Fez. London, 1909.

Afr 3300.17   Harris, Murray G. Egypt under the Egyptians. London, 1925.

Afr 500.11.5   Harris, N.D. Europe and Africa. Boston, 1927.

Afr 500.11A   Harris, N.D. Intervention and colonization in Africa. Boston, 1914.

Afr 11448.77.100   Harris, Peter. Some small compassion. Cape Town, 1964.

Afr 6210.15   Harris, Philip. Local government in southern Nigeria. Cambridge, 1960.

Afr 1658.50   Harris, W.B. France, Spain and the rif. London, 1927.

Afr 1608.89   Harris, W.B. The land of an african sultan. London, 1889.

Afr 1685.1   Harris, W.B. Tafilet. Edinburg, 1895.

Afr 4558.44.3   Harris, W.C. Adventures in Africa. Philadelphia, n.d.

Afr 4558.44.2   Harris, W.C. The highlands of Ethiopia. N.Y., n.d.

Afr 4180.3.15 The heart of Libya, the Siwa Oasis, its people, customs and sport. (Simpson, G.E.) London, 1929.
Afr 10685.45.100 Heaven's gate. (Okigbo, Christopher.) Ibadan, 1962.
Afr 608.96 Heawood, E. Geography of Africa. London, 1896.
Afr 7540.4 Hebette, L. Les codes du Congo. Bruxelles, 1892.
Afr 1640.3 Los hebreos en Marruecos. (Ortega, Manuel L.) Madrid, 1919.
Afr 580.10 Hebrewisms of West Africa, from Nile to Niger with the Jews. (Williams, Joseph J.) London, 1930.
Afr 580.10.4 Hebrewisms of West Africa, from Nile to Niger with the Jews. (Williams, Joseph J.) N.Y., 1967.
Afr 580.10.3 Hebrewisms of West Africa. (Williams, Joseph J.) N.Y., 1930.
Afr 9148.82 Heckford, S. A lady trader in the Transvaal. London, 1882.
Afr 7855.4 Hecq, J. Agriculture et structures économiques d'un société traditionnelle au Kivu. Bruxelles, 1963.
Afr 678.49.5 Hecquard, Hyacinthe. Reise an die Küste und in das Innere von West-Africa. Leipzig, 1854.
Afr 678.49 Hecquard, Hyacinthe. Voyage sur la côte et dans l'intérieur de l'Afrique occidentale. Paris, 1853.
Afr 7850.60 Hederén, Olle. Afrikanskt mellanspeli om händelserna på Kaminabasen, 1960-1964. Östra Ryd, 1965.
Afr 8125.5 Heeft Nederland de Kaap verkocht. (Heeres, Jan E.) Amsterdam, 1914.
Afr 8028.25 Heerden, J. van. Closer union movement. Cape Town, 1952.
Afr 8687.228 Heerden, Petronella van. Kerssmutsels. Kaapstad, 1962.
Afr 8687.228.5 Heerden, Petronella van. Die sestiende koppie. Kaapstad, 1965.
Afr 8125.5 Heeres, Jan E. Heeft Nederland de Kaap verkocht. Amsterdam, 1914.
Afr 8667.5 Heever, C.M. van den. Die stryjd om ewewig. Kaapstad, 1941.
Afr 8667.5.10 Heever, C.M. van der. Kultur geskiedenis van die Afrikaner. Kaapstad, 1945. 3v.
Afr 8252.228.2 Heever, Christiaan. General J.B.M. Hertzog. Johannesburg, 1943.
Afr 8252.228 Heever, Christiaan. General J.B.M. Hertzog. Johannesburg, 1946.
Afr 7803.41 Hege, Ruth. We two alone. N.Y., 1965.
Afr 30.5 Heichen, Paul. Afrika Hand-Lexicon. Leipzig, 1885-86.
Afr 115.91 Heidelberg, Wolfgang. Grundzüge des Niederlassungsrechts in den afrikanischen Staaten. Hamburg, 1965. 2v.
Afr 555.153 Heiden, Christen und Politiker. (Bergner, Gerhard.) Breklum, 1963.
Afr 3816.2 Die Heiden-Neger des ägyptischen Sudan. (Frobenius, Herman.) Berlin, 1893.
Afr 1571.17.60 Heidsieck, P. Rayonnement de Lyautey. Paris, 1944.
Afr 1609.60 Heinemeijir, W.F. Marokko. Meppel, 1960.
Afr 2312.5 Heinke, Kurt. Monographie der algerischen Oase Biskra. Inaug. Diss. Halle, 1914.
Afr 1915.5 Heinrich, P. L'alliance franco-algérienne. Lyon, 1898.
Afr 715.30 Heinrich Barth. Ein Forscher in Afrika. Eine Sammlung von Beiträgen zum 100. Todestag am 25. Nov. 1965. Wiesbaden, 1967.
Afr 115.111 Heinrich Barth zum Gedenken. Hamburg, 1965.
Afr 150.18 Heinrich der Seefahrer. (Rumbucher, K.) München, 1954.
Afr 7912.15.40 Heinz, G. Lumumba Patrice: les cinquante derniers jours de sa vie. Bruxelles, 1966.
Afr 6455.150 Heland, Erik von. Mina Afrikaår. Stockholm, 1966.
Afr 6277.81 Helander, Sven. Entwicklungspolitik in Nigeria. Köln, 1963.
Afr 3143.5 Helbig, Adolph H. Al-Qadi al-Fadil, der Wezir Saladins. Inaug.-Diss. Leipzig, 1908.
Afr 9149.61 Helbling, Margrit. Tshakhuma. Zürich, 1961.
Afr 4335.2 Die Heldentaten des Dom Christoph da Gama. (Castanhoso, M. de.) Berlin, 1907.
Afr 3979.46 Hell-dunkel Agyptenfahrt. (Spring, Frieda.) Bern, 1946.
Afr 4582.15.5 Hell-hole of creation. (Nesbitt, L.M.) N.Y., 1935.
Afr 6277.90A Helleiner, Gerald K. Peasant agriculture, government, and economic growth in Nigeria. Homewood, Ill., 1966.
Afr 4025.15 L'hellénisme et l'Egypte moderne. T.1-2. (Polites, Athanasios G.) Paris, 1929-30.
Afr 1089.3 Der Hellenismus in Kleinafrika. (Thieling, W.) Leipzig, 1911.
Afr 6878.88.5PF Hellgrewe, Rudolf. Aus Deutsch-Ost-Afrika. Berlin, 1888.
Afr 8678.57 Hellmann, E. Handbook on race relations in South Africa. Cape Town, 1949.
Afr 8678.57.5 Hellmann, E. In defence of a shared society. Johannesburg, 1956.
Afr 8678.57.10 Hellmann, E. Racial laws versus economic and social forces. Johannesburg, 1955.
Afr 11410.31.100 Hello and goodbye; a play in two acts. (Fugard, Athol.) Cape Town, 1966.
Afr 5640.2 Hellot, F. La pacification de Madagascar. Paris, 1900.
Afr 628.168 Helper, H.R. The Negroes in Negroland. N.Y., 1868.
Afr 9489.35 Hemans, H.N. The log of a native commissioner. London, 1935.
Afr 609.68.5 Heminway, John Hylan. The imminent rains. 1st ed. Boston, 1968.
Afr 5235.263 Hemmo, Klaus. Zwischen Sahara und Elfenbeinküste. Leipzig, 1963.
Afr 8657.67 Hemmy, Gysbert. De Promontorio Bonae Spei, a Latin oration. Cape Town, 1959.
Afr 210.61.15 Hempstone, Smith. The new Africa. London, 1961.
Afr 7850.30 Hempstone, Smith. Rebels, mercenaries, and dividends. N.Y., 1962.
Afr 6460.60 Henderson, Ian. The hunt for Kimathi. London, 1958.
Afr 3745.40A Henderson, K.D.D. Survey of the Anglo-Egyptian Sudan, 1898-1944. N.Y., 1946.
Afr 3675.68 Henderson, Kenneth David Driutt. Sudan Republic. London, 1965.
Afr 8252.144 Hendrik Teodor Buehrmann. (Swart, Marius.) Kaapstad, 1963.
Afr 555.3.14 Hening, E.F. History of the African mission of the Protestant Episcopal Church. N.Y., 1850.
Afr 3243.6 Hennebert, E. Les Anglais en Egypte. Paris, 1884.
Afr 1955.10 Hennequin, A. La conquête de l'Algérie. Paris, 1857.
Afr 6095.365 Hennessy, M.N. Africa under my heart. N.Y., 1965.
Afr 7549.61.5 Hennessy, Maurice N. The Congo. London, 1961.
Afr 6926.16 Hennig, Richard. Deutsch-Südwest im Weltkriege. Berlin, 1920.
Afr 679.00 Henning, G. Samuel Braun. Basel, 1900.
Afr 6455.77 Hennings, R.O. African morning. London, 1951.
Afr 150.6 Henri le Navigateur. (Mees, Jules.) Bruxelles, 1901.

Afr 150.2.65 Henri le Navigateur. (Portugal. Comissão Executiva das Comemorações do V Centenario da Morte do Infante Dom Henrique.) Lisboa, 1960.
Afr 150.13 Henri le Navigateur et l'Académie Portugaise de Sagres. (Wauwermans, Henri.) Bruxelles, 1890.
Afr 150.37 Henri le navigateur et les decouvreurs portugais. (Paris. Musée National du Louvre. Musée de Marine.) Paris, 1960.
Afr 6685.2 Henrici, Ernst. Das deutsche Togogebiet und meine Afrikareise, 1887. Leipzig, 1888.
Afr 109.69 Henries, A. Doris. Africa, our history. 1969.
Afr 7489.88.5 Henries, A. Doris Banks. A biography of President William V.S. Tubman. London, 1967[1968].
Afr 7489.37 Henries, Richard A. Speeches of Dr. Richard A. Henries. London, 1965.
Afr 2209.35.4 Henriot, Emile. Vers l'oasis, en Algérie. Paris, 1935.
Afr 150.20 Henrique, o Navegador, Infante of Portugal. Conselho do Infante Dom Henrique a seu sobrinho El-Rei Dom Afonso V. Lisboa, 1958.
Afr 3315.5 Henriques, R.D.Q. A hundred hours to Suez. N.Y., 1957.
Afr 3822.2 Henriques, Robert. Death by moonlight. London, 1938.
Afr 5243.125 Henry, Joseph. L'âme d'un peuple africain...les Bambara. Münster, 1910.
Afr 6095.38 Henry, Warren. The confessions of a tenderfoot coaster, a trader's chronicle of life on the west African coast. London, 1927.
Afr 8849.8 Henry Callaway. (Benham, M.S.) London, 1896.
Afr 150.17 Henry the Navigator. (Sanceau, Elaine.) London, 194-.
Afr 150.17.5 Henry the Navigator. (Sanceau, Elaine.) N.Y., 1947.
Afr 555.23.20 Hensey, Andrew F. My children of the forest. N.Y., 1924.
Afr 10678.61.100 Henshaw, James Ene. Children of the goddess, and other plays. London, 1964.
Afr 10678.61.110 Henshaw, James Ene. Dinner for promotion; a comedy in three acts. London, 1967.
Afr 8250.5 Hensman, H. Cecil Rhodes. Edinburg, 1901.
Afr 9439.00 Hensman, H. A history of Rhodesia. Edinburgh, 1900.
VAfr 5385.38 Hentsch, Henry. Deux années au Dahomey, 1903-1905. Nancy, 1916.
Afr 6170.8.2 Henty, G.A. The march to Coomassie. 2nd ed. London, 1874.
Afr 4375.6 Henty, G.A. The march to Magdala. London, 1868.
Afr 4559.28.20 Hentze, W. Volldampf unter Palmen. Leipzig, 1928.
Afr 3979.03 Henze, H. Der Nil... Hydrographie und seiner Wirt. Halle, 1903.
Afr 6455.125 Hepburn, Alonzo Barton. The story of an outing. N.Y., 1913.
Afr 9388.95 Hepburn, J.D. Twenty years in Khamas country. London, 1895.
Afr 8089.66.10 Hepple, Alex. South Africa, a political and economic history. London, 1966.
Afr 8378.379.25 Hepple, Alexander. Verwoerd. Harmondsworth, 1967.
Afr 8252.14.10 Her South African ancestors. (Cronwright-Schreiner, S.C.) London, 1930.
Afr 8688.5.10 Heraldiek in Suid-Africa. (Pama, C.) Kaapstad, 1956.
Afr 1609.66.5 Herault, Andre. Le Maroc a visage decouvert. Paris, 1966.
Afr 5257.10 Herbart, Pierre. La chancre du Niger. Paris, 1939.
Afr 4969.07.3 Herbert, A. Two dianas in Somaliland. 2d ed. London, 1908.
Afr 2208.72 Herbert, Lady. A search after sunshine, or Algeria in 1871. London, 1872.
Afr 11300.83.21 Here Everest, and other poems. (Coster, Vera.) Grahamstown, 1963.
Afr 609.43 Here is Africa. (Gatti, E.M.) N.Y., 1943.
Afr 6885.6 Heremans, Roger. Les établissements de l'Association Internationale Africaine au lac Tanganika et les pères blancs, Mpala et Karema, 1877-1885. Tervuren, 1966.
Afr 6926.26 Herinneringe van suidwes-voortrekkers. (Visser, P.G.) Kaapstad, 1940.
Afr 8289.07 Herinneringen. (Larey, M. de.) Amsterdam, 1907.
Afr 2208.65.5 Herinneringen uit Algiers. (Hartevelt, D.) Arnhem, 1865.
Afr 8220.5 Herinneringen uit Zuid Africa. (Tromp, Theo M.) Leiden, 1879.
Afr 2731.15.3 Herisson, R. Avec le père de Foucauld et le général Laperrine, 1909-11. Paris, 1937.
Afr 9439.50 Heritage of Rhodes. (Gale, W.D.) Cape Town, 1950.
Afr 679.64.5 The heritage of West Africa. (Latham, Norah.) London, 1964.
Afr 8685.30 Herman, L. A history of the Jews in South Africa. London, 1930.
Afr 8685.30.2 Herman, L. A history of the Jews in South Africa from the earliest times to 1895. Johannesburg, 1935.
Afr 6640.20 Hermann von Wissmann. (Becker, A.) Berlin, 1914.
Afr 6640.19 Hermann von Wissmann. (Perbandt, C. von.) Berlin, 1906.
Afr 2030.395 Hermans, Fons. Algerije. Amsterdam, 1960.
Afr 7119.63.15 Hermans, Fons. Angola in opstand. 1. druk. Den Haag, 1963.
Afr 6275.27 Hermon-Hodge, H.B. Up against it in Nigeria. London, 1922.
Afr 6292.41 Hermon-Hodge, Harry Baldwin. Gazetteer of Ilarin Province. London, 1929.
Afr 4513.35.120 Hernandez Alfonso, L. Abisinia. Madrid, 1935.
Afr 1573.29F Hernandez de Herrera, C. Accion de España en Marruecos. v.1-2. Madrid, 1929-30. 2v.
Afr 1658.28 Hernandez Mir, F. Del desastre à la victoria 1921-1926. v.1-4. Madrid, 1926-27. 4v.
Afr 1493.74 Hernandez Mir, F. Del desastre al fracaso. Madrid, 1922.
Afr 1573.26 Hernandez Mir, Francisco. La dictadura en Marruecos. Madrid, 1930.
Afr 5944.20 Hernandez-Pacheco, Francisco. El Sahara español. Madrid, 1962.
Afr 555.9.28 A hero of the dark continent, Rev. William A. Scott. (Rankine, W.H.) Edinburgh, 1897.
Afr 8687.7 Heroes of discovery in South Africa. (Bell, Nancy R.E. (Mevgens).) London, 1899.
Afr 8687.111 Heroes of South Africa. (Anderson, Kenneth.) Cape Town, 1955.
NEDL Afr 108.89 Heroes of the dark continent and How Stanley found Erwin Pasha. (Buel, J.W.) Philadelphia, 1889.
Afr 41610.2 The heroic recitation of the Bahima of Ankole. (Morris, H.F.) Oxford, 1964.
Afr 1750.6.5 Heroicos infantes en Marruecos. (Garcia Pérez, Antonio.) Madrid, 1926.
Afr 4394.15 Le héros d'Adoua. (Petrides, Saint Pierre.) Paris, 1963.
Afr 2731.12 Les héros du Sahara. (Howe, S.E.) Paris, 1931.
Afr 3979.38.5 Herriot, E. Sanctuaires. Roma, 1938.
Afr 4559.35.70 Herrmann, Gerhard. Abessinien; Raum als Schicksal. Leipzig, 1935.

	Afr 5620.4	Historique de Madagascar. (Bonnemaison, J.) Tarbes, 1894.
	Afr 7565.19	Historisch ontstaan der grens van de onafhankelijke. (Ruytjens, E.) Bruxelles, 1958.
	Afr 7575.65	De historische dagen von februari 1960. (Belgo-Congolese Round Table Conference, Brussels, 1960.) Brussels, 1960.
	Afr 8808.86	History, productions and resources of Cape of Good Hope. (Noble, John.) Cape Town, 1886.
NEDL	Afr 8808.86.2	History, productions and resources of the Cape of Good Hope. (Noble, John.) Cape Town, 1886.
	Afr 855.8	History..island of St. Helena...1823. (Brooke, T.H.) London, 1824.
	Afr 115.90	History and archaeology in Africa. (Conference on History and Archaeology.) London, 1969.
	Afr 710.30	History and archaeology in Africa. (London. University. School of Oriental and African Studies.) London, 1955.
NEDL	Afr 8088.88.5	History and ethnography of Africa Zambesi. (Theal, G.M.) London, 1907. 3v.
	Afr 8095.36	History in pictures. 1. ed. (Ross, R.E. van der.) Cape Town, 1962.
	Afr 590.26	The history of a slave. (Johnston, H.H.) London, 1889.
Htn	Afr 5318.5*	History of a voyage to the coast of Africa. (Hawkins, J.) Troy, 1797.
	Afr 109.70.10	History of Africa, from the earliest times to 1800. (Gailey, Harry A.) N.Y., 1970.
	Afr 212.26.2	A history of Africa, 1918-1967. (Akademiia Nauk SSSR. Institut Afriki.) Moscow, 1968.
	Afr 109.60.10	A history of Africa. (Ward, William.) London, 1960. 2v.
	Afr 109.62.5	A history of Africa. (Wiedner, Donald.) N.Y., 1962.
	Afr 109.60.10.3	A history of Africa. v.1-2. (Ward, William.) London, 1966.
	Afr 609.67.30	The history of Africa in maps. (Gailey, Harry A.) Chicago, 1967.
	Afr 115.101	The history of Africa south of the Sahara. (Savage, K.) London, 1961.
	Afr 6542.15	A history of Ankole. (Morris, H.F.) Nairobi, 1962.
	Afr 8678.260	The history of apartheid. (Neame, L.E.) London, 1962.
	Afr 109.61.26	The history of black Africa. (Sik, Endre.) Budapest, 1966. 2v.
	Afr 505.50	The history of Britain in Africa. (Hatch, John C.) London, 1969.
Htn	Afr 8718.42*	History of Cape Mounted Riflemen. (Cannon, R.) London, 1842.
	Afr 9549.68	A history of Central Africa. (Tindall, P.E.N.) London, 1968.
	Afr 555.22.17	A history of Christian missions in South Africa. (Duplessis, J.) Cape Town, 1965.
	Afr 555.22.16	A history of Christian missions in South Africa. (Duplessis, J.) London, 1911.
	Afr 6195.22	A history of Christianity in Ghana. (Dearunner, Hans Werner.) Accra, 1967.
	Afr 7375.5	History of colonization on the western coast. (Alexander, A.) Philadelphia, 1846.
	Afr 5365.2.2	The history of Dahomey, an inland kingdom of Africa. 1st ed. (Dalzel, A.) London, 1967.
Htn	Afr 5365.2*	The history of Dahomy. (Dalzel, A.) London, 1793.
	Afr 6314.33	A history of East Africa. (Ingham, K.) London, 1962.
	Afr 6314.34	History of East Africa. (Oliver, R.A.) Oxford, 1963. 2v.
	Afr 699.54.5	History of East Africa. (Reusch, Richard.) Stuttgart, 1954.
	Afr 6314.33.2	A history of East Africa. 2. ed. (Ingham, K.) London, 1963.
	Afr 6314.33.3	A history of East Africa. 3. ed. (Ingham, K.) London, 1965.
	Afr 109.67.26	A history of East and Central Africa to the late nineteenth century. (Davidson, Basil.) Garden City, N.Y., 1969.
	Afr 3160.5	History of Egypt. (Ibn Tagribardi.) Berkeley, 1954. 2v.
	Afr 3037.1	A history of Egyptian historiography in the nineteenth century. (Shayyal, J. al-D.) Alexandria, 1962.
	Afr 4259.28	A history of Ethiopia, Nubia and Abyssinia. (Budge, E.A.) London, 1928. 2v.
	Afr 4259.35.21	A history of Ethiopia. (Jones, A.H.) Oxford, 1955.
	Afr 4259.35.23	A history of Ethiopia. (Jones, A.H.) Oxford, 1960.
	Afr 3199.15	History of events in Egypt from 1798 to 1914. (Weigall, Arthur E.P. Brome.) Edinburgh, 1915.
	Afr 6164.9.3	A history of Ghana. (Ward, W.E.F.) N.Y., 1963.
	Afr 6164.9.2	A history of Ghana. 2d ed. (Ward, W.E.F.) London, 1958.
	Afr 6164.9.4	A history of Ghana. 3rd ed. (Ward, W.E.F.) London, 1966.
	Afr 6164.9.5	A history of Ghana. 4th ed. (Ward, W.E.F.) London, 1967.
	Afr 6164.2	History of Gold Coast of West Africa. (Ellis, A.B.) London, 1893.
	Afr 575.36	A history of Islam in West Africa. (Trimingham, J.S.) London, 1962.
	Afr 9165.42.70	A history of Johannesburg, the early years. (Leyds, Gerard A.) Cape Town, 1964.
	Afr 4370.5	History of King Theodore. (Alaqa Walda Maryam.) London, 1969.
	Afr 6293.7.2	History of Lagos. (Losi, John B.) Lagos, 1967.
	Afr 7368.91	History of Liberia. (McPherson, J.H.T.) Baltimore, 1891.
	Afr 7369.20.5	History of Liberia. (Walker, T.H.B.) Boston, 1921.
	Afr 8045.30	History of local government in South Africa. (Green, L.P.) Cape Town, 1957.
	Afr 1407.1	History of long captivity. (Pellow, J.) London, 1736.
	Afr 1407.1.2	History of long captivity. 2 ed. (Pellow, J.) London, 1740.
	Afr 8292.58	The history of Lumsden's Horse. (Pearse, H.H.S.) London, 1903.
	Afr 5548.38	History of Madagascar. (Ellis, W.) London, 1838. 2v.
	Afr 5828.01	The history of Mauritius. (Grant, Charles.) London, 1801.
	Afr 5829.10.7	The history of Mauritius (1507-1914). (Deburgh Edwardes, S.B.) London, 1921.
	Afr 3199.54	A history of modern Egypt and Anglo-Egyptian relations. (Marlowe, J.) N.Y., 1954.
	Afr 3199.54.2	A history of modern Egypt and Anglo-Egyptian relations. 2d ed. (Marlowe, J.) Hamden, 1965.
	Afr 8190.20	A history of Natal. (Brookes, Edgar Harry.) Pietermaritzburg, 1965.
	Afr 8969.67	A history of Natal. (Brookes, Edgar Harry.) Pietermaritzburg, 1965.
	Afr 8140.15	The history of native policy in South Africa. 2d ed. (Brookes, E.H.) Pretoria, 1927.

	Afr 8135.15	The history of native policy in South Africa from 1830 to the present day. (Brookes, E.H.) Cape Town, 1924.
	Afr 628.238	A history of Negro revolt. (James, C.L.R.) London, 1938.
	Afr 6214.8	History of Nigeria. (Burns, Alan C.) London, 1929.
	Afr 6214.8.18	History of Nigeria. (Burns, Alan C.) London, 1958.
	Afr 6214.8.10	History of Nigeria. 4th ed. (Burns, Alan C.) London, 1948.
	Afr 6214.8.15	History of Nigeria. 5th ed. (Burns, Alan C.) London, 1955.
	Afr 6214.8.19	History of Nigeria. 6th ed. (Burns, Alan C.) London, 1964.
	Afr 6214.8.20	History of Nigeria. 7th ed. (Burns, Alan C.) London, 1969.
	Afr 6214.31	History of Nigeria in a new setting. (Ottonkwo, D.O.) Onitsha, 1962.
	Afr 9639.64	A history of Northern Rhodesia. (Gann, L.H.) London, 1964.
	Afr 9769.60	A history of Nyasaland. (Tanser, George Henry.) Capetown, 1960.
	Afr 9060.5	The history of old Durban and reminiscences of an emigrant of 1850. (Russell, George.) Durban, 1899.
	Afr 8235.5	History of our own times in South Africa 1872-1898. (Wilmot, A.) Cape Town, 1897. 3v.
	Afr 210.65.5	A history of postwar Africa. (Hatch, J.C.) London, 1965.
	Afr 8063.20	The history of Prince Alfred's Guard. (Perridge, Frank.) Port Elizabeth, 1939.
	Afr 1408.1	History of revolution upon death of Ishmail. (Braithwaite, Capt.) London, 1729.
	Afr 9439.00	A history of Rhodesia. (Hensman, H.) Edinburgh, 1900.
	Afr 10911.2	The history of Rhodesian entertainment, 1890-1930. (Taylor, Charles T.C.) Salisbury, 1968.
	Afr 8089.15	History of South Africa, from earliest days to union. (Scully, W.C.) London, 1915.
	Afr 8089.41.6	A history of South Africa, social and economic. (Dekiewiet, Cornelis Willem.) London, 1946.
	Afr 8089.41.5	A history of South Africa, social and economic. (Dekiewiet, Cornelis Willem.) Oxford, 1941.
	Afr 8089.04	A history of South Africa. (Bryden, H.A.) Edinburgh, 1904.
	Afr 8089.18A	A history of South Africa. (Fairbridge, D.) London, 1918.
	Afr 8089.64	History of South Africa. (Theal, G.M.) Cape Town, 1964. 11v.
NEDL	Afr 8088.88	History of South Africa. (Theal, G.M.) London, 1888- 5v.
	Afr 8089.28A	A history of South Africa. (Walker, E.A.) London, 1928.
	Afr 8089.01	The history of South Africa. (Wilmot, Alex.) London, 1901.
	Afr 8089.00.3A	A history of South Africa. (Worsfold, W.B.) London, 1900.
	Afr 8089.06	History of South Africa and the Boer-British war. (Beck, Henry.) Philadelphia, 1900.
	Afr 8088.88.9	History of South Africa from 1795-1872. (Theal, G.M.) London, 1915. 2v.
	Afr 8088.88.10	History of South Africa from 1873-1884. (Theal, G.M.) London, 1919. 2v.
	Afr 8088.88.7	History of South Africa since Sept. 1795. v.1- (Theal, G.M.) London, 1908- 3v.
	Afr 8063.25	The history of South African regiments. (Vrdoljak, M.K.) Cape Town, 1957.
	Afr 8658.36	History of southern Africa. (Martin, R.M.) London, 1836.
	Afr 8658.36.3	History of southern Africa. 2nd ed. (Martin, R.M.) London, 1843.
	Afr 8089.28.15	A history of Southern Africa. 3rd ed. (Walker, E.A.) London, 1957.
	Afr 9439.65	A history of Southern Rhodesia. (Gann, Lewis H.) London, 1965.
	Afr 6460.87	A history of the Abaluyia of western Kenia. (Were, Gideon S.) Nairobi, 1967.
	Afr 555.3.14	History of the African mission of the Protestant Episcopal Church. (Hening, E.F.) N.Y., 1850.
	Afr 109.70	A history of the African people. (July, Robert William.) N.Y., 1970.
	Afr 6194.20.10	A history of the Akan peoples of the Gold Coast. (Balmer, W.T.) London, 1925.
	Afr 7375.4	History of the American colony in Liberia. (Ashmun, J.) Washington, 1826.
	Afr 4010.1	A history of the Arabs in Sudan. v.1-2. (Macmichael, H.A.) Cambridge, 1922.
	Afr 6395.28	A history of the Asians in East Africa, 1886 to 1945. (Mangat, J.S.) Oxford, 1969.
	Afr 6295.66.10	A history of the Baluyia. (Osogo, John.) Nairobi, 1966.
	Afr 1068.35.2	History of the Barbary states. 2d ed. (Russell, M.) Edinburgh, 1835.
	Afr 1068.35.5	History of the Barbary states. 2d ed. (Russell, M.) N.Y., 1837.
	Afr 8865.7	History of the Basuto, ancient, and modern. (Ellenberger, D.F.) London, 1912.
	Afr 8925.15	History of the Basutur of South Africa. (Orpen, Joseph M.) Cape Town, 1857.
	Afr 8088.88.14	The history of the battles and adventures of the British. (Moodie, Duncan C.F.) Cape Town, 1888. 2v.
	Afr 4015.5	A history of the Beja tribes of the Sudan. (Paul, Andrew.) Cambridge, 1954.
	Afr 8175.5	History of the Boers in South Africa. (Theal, G.M.) London, 1887.
	Afr 8175.5.1	History of the Boers in South Africa. (Theal, G.M.) N.Y., 1969.
	Afr 3207.1	History of the British expedition to Egypt. (Wilson, R.J.) London, 1803.
Htn	Afr 1947.8*	History of the captivity and sufferings in Algiers. (Martin, M.) Boston, 1807.
	Afr 108.99	A history of the colonization of Africa. (Johnston, H.H.) Cambridge, 1899.
	Afr 108.99.4A	A history of the colonization of Africa. (Johnston, H.H.) Cambridge, 1905.
	Afr 108.99.6	A history of the colonization of Africa. (Johnston, H.H.) Cambridge, 1913.
	Afr 8088.55.2	History of the colony of Natal. (Holden, William Clifford.) Cape Town, 1963.
	Afr 8718.69	History of the colony of the Cape of Good Hope. (Wilmot, A.) Cape Town, 1869.
	Afr 8688.6	A history of the de Villiers family. (Villiers, Daniel P.) Cape Town, 1960.

Afr 3078.63 History of the Egyptian revolution. (Paton, A.A.) London, 1863. 2v.

Afr 3078.63.3 History of the Egyptian revolution. (Paton, A.A.) London, 1870. 2v.

Afr 8145.5.5 The history of the English church and people in South Africa. (Wirgman, A.T.) N.Y., 1969.

Afr 8145.5 The history of the English Church in South Africa. (Wirgman, A.T.) London, 1895.

Afr 8088.94 History of the expansion of South Africa. (Wilmot, Alex.) London, 1894.

Afr 6292.9.5 History of the first twelve years of the reign of Mai Idris Alooma of Bornu. (Ahmed ibn Fartua.) Lagos, 1926.

Afr 6164.5.2 A history of the Gold Coast. (Claridge, W.W.) London, 1964. 2v.

Afr 6164.9 A history of the Gold Coast. (Ward, W.E.F.) London, 1948.

Afr 6168.20 The history of the Gold Coast and Asante. 2d. ed. (Reindorf, Carl Christian.) Basel, 1951.

Afr 6164.5 History of the Gold Coast and Ashanti. (Claridge, W.W.) London, 1915. 2v.

Afr 6164.2.5 A history of the Gold Coast of West Africa. (Ellis, A.B.) N.Y., 1969.

Afr 8180.5 The history of the great Boer trek. (Cloete, Henry.) London, 1899.

Afr 8180.5.3 The history of the great Boer trek. (Cloete, Henry.) N.Y., 1899.

Afr 5548.22 A history of the island of Madagascar. (Copland, Samuel.) London, 1822.

Afr 2875.5 The history of the Italian war. (Bechler, W.H.) Annapolis, 1913.

Afr 8685.30 A history of the Jews in South Africa. (Herman, L.) London, 1930.

Afr 8685.30.2 A history of the Jews in South Africa from the earliest times to 1895. (Herman, L.) Johannesburg, 1935.

Afr 9225.10 The history of the Orange Free State. (Boon, M.J.) London, 1885.

Afr 210.47.2 History of the Pan-African Congress. 2d ed. (Padmore, G.) London, 1963.

Afr 3183.8A History of the revolt of Ali Bey. (Lusignan, S.) London, 1783.

Afr 9515.7 History of the Salisbury club. (Rixom, Frank.) Salisbury, 1953.

Afr 6160.80.15 History of the southern Luo. (Ogot, Bethwell Allan.) Nairobi, 1967.

Afr 3685.9 A history of the southern Sudan. (Gray, Richard.) London, 1961.

Afr 3675.28 A history of the Sudan. (Arkell, A.J.) London, 1955.
Afr 3675.28.2 A history of the Sudan. 2.ed. (Arkell, A.J.) London, 1961.

Afr 3708.6 History of the Sudan campaign. (Colvile, H.E.) London, 1889. 3v.

Afr 8210.5 A history of the Transvaal. (Haggard, H.R.) N.Y., 1899.
Afr 8210.5.5 A history of the Transvaal. (Haggard, H.R.) N.Y., 1900.
Afr 555.9.23 The history of the Universities Mission to Central Africa. (Morshead, A.E.) London, 1897.

Afr 555.9.24 The history of the Universities Mission to Central Africa. (Morshead, A.E.) London, 1909.

Afr 555.105 The history of the Universities Mission to Central Africa. (Wilson, George H.) Westminster, 1936.

Afr 555.9.25 The history of the Universities' Mission to Central Africa. (Morshead, A.E.) London, 1955-62. 3v.

NEDL Afr 8288.99.23 History of the war in South Africa. (Birch, J.H.) London, Ont., 1899.

Afr 8289.06 History of the war in South Africa 1899-02. v.1-4. (Maurice, F.) London, 1906. 8v.

Afr 6218.1.5 The history of the Yorubas; from the earliest times to the beginning of the British protectorate. 1st ed. (Johnson, Samuel.) London, 1966.

Afr 6218.1 The history of the Yorubas from the earliest times to the beginning of the British protectorate. (Johnson, Samuel.) London, 1921.

Afr 9047.36 A history of the Zulu and neighboring tribes. (Bryant, A.T.) Cape Town, 1964.

Afr 8985.4 A history of the Zulu rebellion 1906. (Stuart, J.) London, 1913.

Afr 8160.10 History of the Zulu war. (Wilmot, A.) London, 1880.
Afr 8160.11 History of the Zulu war and its origin. (Colenso, F.E.) London, 1880.

Afr 8292.47.5 History of the 1st Battalion Sherwood Foresters Boer War. (Gilson, C.J.L.) London, 1907.

Afr 2818.35 The history of Tripoli. (Greenhow, R.) Richmond, 1835.
Afr 679.66.35 A history of West Africa: A.D. 1,000 to to the present day. 2. ed. Ibadan, 1969.

Afr 679.55.6 A history of West Africa. 4th ed. (Fage, J.D.) Cambridge, Eng., 1969.

Afr 679.65.30.2 A history of West Africa to the nineteenth century. (Davidson, Basil.) Garden City, N.Y., 1966. 2v.

Afr 6565.40 History of Zanzibar. (Gray, John.) London, 1962.
Afr 6926.22 Hitler over Africa. (Bennett, Benjamin.) London, 1939.
Htn Afr 6275.32.5* Hives, Frank. Ju-Ju and justice in Nigeria. London, 1933.
Htn Afr 4555.40* Ho Preste Joam das Indias. Verdadeira informaçam. (Alvares, Francisco.) Lisbon, 1540.

Afr 7582.10.4 Hoare, Michael. Congo mercenary. London, 1967.
Afr 8325.15 Hobhouse, Emily. The brunt of the war (refugee camps). London, 1902.

Afr 6540.8 Hobley, C.W. Eastern Uganda. London, 1902.
Afr 6395.4 Hobley, C.W. Ethnology of A-kamba and other East African tribes. Cambridge, 1910.

Afr 6415.10 Hobley, C.W. Kenya, from chartered company to crown colony. London, 1929.

Afr 8325.20 Hobson, J.A. The psychology of jingoism. London, 1902. 2v.

Afr 8279.00.32 Hobson, J.A. The war in South Africa. London, 1900.
Afr 8279.00.34 Hobson, J.A. The war in South Africa. London, 1900.
Afr 8279.00.33 Hobson, J.A. The war in South Africa. N.Y., 1900.
Afr 8279.00.33.1 Hobson, J.A. The war in South Africa. N.Y., 1900.
Afr 6879.07F Das Hochland der Riesenkrater...Deutsch-Ostafrika. (Jaeger, Fritz.) Berlin, 1911.

Afr 4559.29.5 Das Hochland von Abessinien, Habesch. (Sander, Erich.) Heidelberg, 1929.

Afr 4559.29.15 Hochzeitreise nach Abessinien. (Lubinski, Kurt.) Leipzig, 1929.

Afr 9689.63 Hock, E. Know your home: Zambia. Chensali? 1963?
Afr 8735.5.15A Hockly, H.E. The story of the British settlers of 1820 in South Africa. Cape Town, 1948.

Afr 8735.5.15.2 Hockly, H.E. The story of the British settlers of 1820 in South Africa. 2. ed. Cape Town, 1957.

Afr 5635.12F Hocquard, C.E. L'expedition de Madagascar. Paris, 1897.
Afr 109.67 Hodder, Bramwell William. Africa in transition, geographical essays. London, 1967.

Afr 6096.24 Hodder, Bramwell William. Markets in West Africa. Ibadan, 1969.

Afr 6988.52.230 Hodge, A.L. Angra Pequeña. Inaug. Diss. München, 1936.
Afr 8331.15 Hodge, Gillian M.M. South African politics, 1933-1939. Cape Town, 1955.

Afr 7268.88 Hodge, J.A. America and Africa. Washington, 1888.
Afr 7350.3.12 Hodgkin, T. Inquiry into merits of the American Colonization Society. London, 1833.

Afr 1608.66 Hodgkin, T. Narrative of a journey to Morocco. London, 1866.

Afr 50.25 Hodgkin, Thomas. African political parties. Harmondsworth, 1961.

Afr 210.56 Hodgkin, Thomas. Nationalism in colonial Africa. London, 1956.

Afr 210.56.2 Hodgkin, Thomas. Nationalism in colonial Africa. London, 1962.

Afr 6214.25 Hodgkin, Thomas. Nigerian perspectives. London, 1960.
Afr 6174.2 Hodgson, M. The siege of Kumassi. N.Y., 1901.
Afr 210.63.40 Hodgson, R.D. The changing map of Africa. Princeton, 1963.

Afr 2336.10 Le Hodna. 1. ed. (Despois, J.) Paris, 1953.
Afr 4559.27.5 Hodson, A.W. Seven years in southern Abyssinia. London, 1927.

Afr 9389.13.5 Hodson, A.W. Trekking the great thirst. London, 1914.
Afr 9389.13 Hodson, A.W. Trekking the great thirst. 2. ed. London, 1913.

Afr 8289.64.10 Hoe ry die Boere; i 'n kommando-dagboek. (Schikkerling, Roland William.) Johannesburg, 1964.

Afr 608.48.2 Hoefer, J.C.F. Afrique australe, orientale. Paris, 1848.
Afr 6455.12 Hoehnel, Ludwig. Discovery of Lakes Rudolf and Stefanie. London, 1894. 2v.

Afr 6455.12.5 Hoehnel, Ludwig. Discovery of Lakes Rudolf and Stefanie. 1st English ed. London, 1968. 2v.

Afr 6455.12.2 Hoehnel, Ludwig Ritter von. Zum Rudolph-See und Stephanie-See. Wien, 1892.

Afr 8678.45 Hoernle, R.F.A. Race and reason. Johannesburg, 1945.
Afr 8678.41 Hoernle, R.F.A. South African native policy and the liberal spirit. Cape Town, 1939.

Afr 8678.41.5 Hoernle, R.F.A. South African native policy and the liberal spirit. Johannesburg, 1945.

Afr 1607.81 Hoest, G. Nachrichten von Morokos und Fes. Kopenhagen, 1781.

Afr 1623.932.5 Hoffner, René. L'économie marocaine. Paris, 1932.
Afr 5057.20 Hoffherr, Rene. Coopération économique franco-africaine. Paris, 1958.

Afr 1623.934.5 Hoffherr, Rene. Revenus et niveaux de vie indigenes au Maroc. Paris, 1934.

Afr 1618.26 Hoffman, Bernard G. The structure of traditional Morroccan rural society. The Hague, 1967.

Afr 12628.64.100 Hoffmane, Simone. Envoûtement. Dakar, 1967?
Afr 1369.65.5 Hoffmann, E. Realm of the evening star. Philadelphia, 1965.

Afr 3817.6.5 Hofmayr, Wilhelm. Die Schilluk. St. Gabriel, 1925.
Afr 8089.31 Hofmeyer, J.H. South Africa. London, 1931.
Afr 8089.31.5 Hofmeyer, J.H. South Africa. 2d ed. N.Y., 1952.
Afr 8325.10 Hofmeyr, A. The story of my captivity. London, 1900.
Afr 8252.16 Hofmeyr, Jan. The life of Jan Hendrik Hofmeyr. Cape Town, 1913.

Afr 8295.8 Hofmeyr, N. Zes maanden bij de commandos 's-Gravenhage, 1903.

Afr 8283.16 Hofmeyr, N.J. De Afrikaner-Boer en de Jameson-inval. Kaapstad, 1896.

Afr 8278.97.3 Hofmeyr, N.J. Die Buren und Jamesons Einfall. Bremen, 1897.

Afr 8338.230.5 Hofmeyr. (Paton, Alan.) London, 1964.
Afr 2508.3 Hofstetter, Balthasar. Vorgeschichte des französischen Protektorats in Tunis. Bern, 1914.

Afr 8678.98 Hogarth, Paul. People like us. London, 1958.
Afr 8688.7 Hoge, J. Bydraes tot die genealogie van ou afrikaanse families. Amsterdam, 1958.

Afr 6214.10.5 Hoghen, S.J. The emirates of Northern Nigeria. London, 1966.

Afr 6214.10.10 Hoghen, S.J. An introduction to the history of the Islamic states of Northern Nigeria. Ibadan, 1967.

Afr 6214.10 Hoghen, S.J. The Muhammadan emigrants of Nigeria. London, 1930.

Afr 545.29 Holas, Bohumil. L'Afrique noire. Paris, 1964.
Afr 5342.60 Holas, Bohumil. Changements sociaux en Côte-d'Ivoire. Paris, 1961.

Afr 5342.60.5 Holas, Bohumil. Côte-d'Ivoire. Paris, 1963.
Afr 5342.60.6 Holas, Bohumil. La Côte-d'Ivoire. Paris, 1964.
Afr 5342.65.2 Holas, Bohumil. Craft and culture in the Ivory Coast. Paris, 1968.

Afr 5342.40 Holas, Bohumil. Cultures matérielles de la Côte-d'Ivoire. Paris, 1960.

Afr 545.52 Holas, Bohumil. Les dieux d'Afrique noire. Paris, 1968.
Afr 5342.65 Holas, Bohumil. Industries et cultures en Côte-d'Ivoire. Abidjan, 1965.

Afr 5243.337.2 Holas, Bohumil. Les Senoufo (y compris les minianka). 2nd ed. Paris, 1966.

Afr 5345.10 Holas, Bohumil. Le séparatisme religieux en Afrique noire. Paris, 1965.

Afr 5344.9 Holas, Bohumil. Les Toura. Paris, 1962.
Afr 5344.11 Holas, Bohumil. L'Image du monde Bété. Paris, 1968.
Afr 10924.5 Hold my hand, I'm dying. 1st ed. (Davis, John Gordon.) N.Y., 1968.

Afr 8678.15 Holden, W.C. The past and future of Kaffir races. London, 1866.

Afr 8678.15.2 Holden, W.C. The past and future of the Kaffir races. Cape Town, 1963.

Afr 8088.55.2 Holden, William Clifford. History of the colony of Natal. Cape Town, 1963.

Afr Doc 3803.2 Holders of administrative and ministerial office, 1894-1964. (Willson, Francis Michael Glenn.) Salisbury, 1966.

Afr 6455.40 Hunting in Africa east and west. (Curtis, Charles. P.) Boston, 1925.

Afr 6460.40F Huntingford, G.W.B. Nandi work and culture. London, 1950.

Afr 590.24 Huntley, H. Seven year s service on slave coast of Western Africa. London, 1850. 2v.

Afr 109.57.3 Hunton, William A. Decision in Africa, sources of current conflict. N.Y., 1960.

Afr 109.57 Hunton, William A. Decision in Africa. N.Y., 1957.

Afr 8676.67.5 Hupkes, G.J. A reappraisal of economic prospects for 1967. Stellenbosch, 1967.

Afr 8676.63.10 Hupkes, G.J. A survey of contemporary economic conditions and prospects for 1964. Stellenbosch, 1963.

Afr 5387.5 Hurault, Jean. Mission d'étude des structures agraires dans le sud Dahomey (février à Nov.1961). Rapport annexe. Paris, 1963.

Afr 6740.15.5 Hurault, Jean. La structure sociale des Bamileke. Paris, 1962.

Afr 6470.231.20 Hurd, David. Kidnap at Kiunga. London, 1965.

Afr 1494.15 Hure, A.J.J. La pacification du Maroc. Paris, 1952.

Afr 42715.22 Hurel, Eugène. La poésie chez les primitifs, ou Contes, fables, récits et proverbes du Rwanda (Lac Kivu). Bruxelles, 1922.

Afr 575.30 Hurries, Lyndon. Islam in East Africa. London, 1954.

Afr 3079.64 Hurst, Harold. A short account of the Nile basin. Cairo, 1964.

Afr 4969.51F Hurt, John A. A general survey of the Somaliland Protectorate, 1944-1950. Harquisa, 1951.

Afr 8676.62.15 Hurwitz, N. Economic framework of South Africa. Pietermaritzburg, 1962.

Afr 3979.64A Husayn, Efendi. Ottoman Egypt in the age of French revolution. Cambridge, 1964.

Afr 9525.224 A husband and a farm in Rhodesia. (Boggie, Jeannie.) Gwelo, S.R., 1959.

Afr 10622.18.100 A husband for Esi Ellua. (Bediako, K.A.) Ghana, 1967.

Afr 4199.10.5 Hussain, Tacha. Kindheitstage in Ägypten. München, 1957.

Afr 3300.55 Hussein, Ahmad. The story of Egypt and Anglo-Egyptian relations. N.Y., 1947.

Afr 3339.14 Hussein, Mahmoud. La Lutte de classes en Égypte de 1945 à 1968. Paris, 1969.

Afr 1369.60 Husson, Philippe. La question des frontières terrestres du Maroc. Paris, 1960.

Afr 8678.125 Hutchinson, Alfred. Road to Ghana. London, 1960.

Afr 8678.125.5 Hutchinson, Alfred. Road to Ghana. 1st Amer. ed. N.Y., 1960.

Afr 590.56 Hutchinson, E. The slave trade of East Africa. London, 1874.

Afr 8659.05 Hutchinson, G.T. From the Cape to the Zambesi. London, 1905.

Afr 6095.13 Hutchinson, T.J. Impressions of western Africa. London, 1858.

Afr 810.14 Hutchinson, T.J. Narrative of the Niger, Tshadda and Binue exploration. London, 1855. 2 pam.

Afr 678.61.3 Hutchinson, T.J. Ten years wanderings among the Ethiopians. London, 1861.

Afr 678.61.4 Hutchinson, T.J. Ten years' wanderings among the Ethiopians. London, 1967.

Afr 45.68 Hutchison, Thomas W. Africa and law. Madison, 1968.

Afr 7815.11 Hutereau, Armand. Histoire des peuplades de l'Uele et de l'Ubangi. Bruxelles, 1912.

Afr 1915.11 Hutin, Paul. La doctrine de l'Association des indigènes et des Français en Algérie. Thèse. Paris, 1933.

Afr 8678.314 Hutt, W.H. The economics of the colour bar. London, 1964.

Afr 6738.4 Hutter, F. Wanderungen und Forschungen im nordhinterland von Kamerun. Braunschweig, 1902.

Afr 608.19 Hutton, C. The tour of Africa. London, 1819-21. 3v.

Afr 8331.10 Hutton, James. The constitution of the Union of South Africa. Cape Town, 1946.

Afr 6192.6 Hutton, W. A voyage to Africa. London, 1821.

Afr 6420.35.7 Huxley, E. Grant. Race and politics in Kenya. London, 1956.

Afr 679.54 Huxley, E.G. Four Guineas. London, 1954.

Afr 6420.36 Huxley, Elspeth. A new earth. London, 1960.

Afr 6420.35.3 Huxley, Elspeth. White man's country. London, 1953. 2v.

Afr 6415.30 Huxley, Elspeth. Grant. Kenya today. London, 1954.

Afr 6470.231 Huxley, Elspeth Grant. The flame trees of Thika. London, 1959.

Afr 6390.44 Huxley, Elspeth Grant. Forks and hope. London, 1964.

Afr 6470.231.6 Huxley, Elspeth Grant. The mottled lizard. London, 1962.

Afr 6470.231.5 Huxley, Elspeth Grant. On the edge of the rift, memories of Kenya. N.Y., 1962.

Afr 6435.5 Huxley, Elspeth Grant. Race and politics in Kenya. London, 1944.

Afr 6390.44.2 Huxley, Elspeth Grant. With forks and hope. N.Y., 1964.

Afr 6390.25 Huxley, Elspeth J.G. The sorcerer's apprentice, a journey through East Africa. London, 1948.

Afr 6390.18A Huxley, Julian S. Africa view. N.Y., 1931.

Afr 4559.35.107 Huyn, Ludwig. Abessinien, Afrikas Unruhe-Herd. Salzburg, 1935.

Afr 718.43 Hvide mand-hvad nu. (Lemboum, Hans Jorgen.) København, 1965.

Afr 5049.100.7 Hyacinthe Jalabert. 2.éd. (Ponet, Marthe Bordeaux.) Paris, 1924.

Afr 2209.10 Hyam, Joseph C. Biskra, Sidi-Okba and the desert. 1st ed. Algiers, 1910.

Afr 2208.99.11 Hyam, Joseph C. The illustrated guide to Algiers. 6th ed. Algiers, 1908.

Afr 8659.10 Hyatt, S.P. Diary of a soldier of fortune. London, 1910.

Afr 9489.11.3 Hyatt, S.P. Off the main track. London, 1911.

Afr 8659.14.5 Hyatt, Stanley P. The old transport road. London, 1914.

Afr 212.58 Hydén, Göran. Politik och samhälle i Afrika. Stockholm, 1967.

Afr 1830.20.40 Hygiène et pathologie nord-africaines. v.1-2. (Fraynaud, Lucien.) Paris, 1932. 2v.

Afr 2409.5 I.B.L.A., revue de l'Institut des Belles Lettres Arabes. Tunis. 5,1942+ 28v.

Afr 11435.22.130 I heard the old men say, secrets of the Cape that has vanished. 2nd ed. (Green, George L.) Cape Town, 1965.

Afr 2675.1.5 I know Tunisia. (Martin, D.B.) N.Y., 1943.

Afr 20756.2 I lie on my mat and pray. (Pawelzik, Fritz.) N.Y., 1964.

Afr 8252.341.85 I lived in his shadow. (Mincher, Kathleen.) Capetown, 1965.

Afr 6498.47 I look back. (Postlethwaite, John R.) London, 1947.

Afr 8687.250 I recall. (Kentridge, Morris.) Johannesburg, 1959.

Afr 6176.30 I speak of freedom. (Nkrumah, Kwame.) N.Y., 1961.

Afr 5320.15 I was a savage. (Modupe, Prince.) N.Y., 1957.

Afr 861.21 I went to Tristan. (Crawford, A.B.) London, 1941.

Afr 8678.301 I will still be moved. (Friedmann, M.V.) Chicago, 1963.

Afr 9860.475 I will try. 1st ed. (Kayira, Regson.) Garden City, N.Y., 1965.

Afr 4433.1 Iag'ia, Vataniar S. Efiopiia v 1941-1954 gg. Moskva, 1969.

Afr 2875.66 Iakhimovich, Zinaida P. Italo-turetskaia voina, 1911-1912 gg. Moskva, 1967.

Afr 6200.14.10 Ibadan, Nigeria. University. Department of Geography. Research notes. 1,1952+

Afr 9.10 Ibadan, Nigeria. University. Geographical Society. The university geographer. Ibadan.

Afr 6200.9 Ibadan, Nigeria. University. Institute of Education. Occasional publication. Ibadan. 1,u960+

Afr 6203.12F Ibadan, Nigeria. University. Library. Africana pamphlets, microfilm record. n.p., n.d.

Afr 6203.5 Ibadan, Nigeria. University. Library. Nigerian periodicals and newspapers, 1950-1955. Ibadan, 1956.

Afr 575.55 Ibadan, Nigeria. University College. Center of Arabic Documentation. Research bulletin. 1,1944

Afr 1390.4 Ibn al-Atir. Annales du Maghreb et de l'Espagne. Alger, 1898.

Afr 150.27 Ibn Al Hatib. El Africa del Norte en El a mal ol a lam de Ibn al Jatib. Madrid, 1958.

Afr 1380.5 Ibn Azzuz, M. Historia de Marruecos hasta la dominacion almoravide. Madrid, 1955.

Afr 31.5 Ibn Batuta. Textes et documents relatifs a l'histoire de l'Afrique. Dakar, 1966.

Afr 3163.20.10 Ibn Iyas. Histoire des Mamlouks circassiens. v.2. Le Caire, 1945.

Afr 3163.20A Ibn Iyas. Journal d'un bourgeois du Caire. Paris, 1955. 2v.

Afr 1080.1 Ibn Khaldun. Histoire des Berbère. Algiers, 1852-56. 4v.

X Cg Afr 1080.1.5 Ibn Khaldun. Histoire des Berbères et des dynasties musulmanes. Paris, 1925-27. 4v.

Afr 4199.20 Ibn Tagribandi. Les biographies du Manhal Safi. Le Caire, 1932.

Afr 3160.5 Ibn Tagribardi. History of Egypt. Berkeley, 1954. 2v.

Afr 1727.8 Ibn Talha, Abd al-Wahid. Moulay-Idriss du Zerhoun. Rabat, 1965.

Afr 6280.9.20 Ibo land tenure. 2. ed. (Chubb, L.T.) Ibadan, 1961.

Afr 6280.9.45 The Ibo native law and custom. (Olisah, Okenua.) Onitsha, 196-.

Afr 6280.9.15 Ibo village affairs. (Green, Margaret M.) London, 1947.

Afr 6280.9.17 Ibo village affairs. 2. ed. (Green, Margaret M.) London, 1964.

Afr 6280.9.40 Ibos in contemporary nigerian politics. (Ndem, Eyo B.E.) Onitsha, 1961.

Afr 3026.1 Ibrahim-Hilmy. The literature of Egypt. London, 1886. 2v.

Afr 3026.22 Ibrahim-Hilmy. The literature of Egypt and theSoudan. Nendeln, 1966. 2v.

Afr 3217.15 Ibrahim of Egypt. (Crabitès, Pierre.) London, 1935.

Afr 10684.92.1100 Icheke and other poems. (Nwanodi, Okogbule Glory.) Ibadan, 1964.

Afr 1680.4 Ichmann, G. Der hohe Atlas. Marburg, 1891.

Afr 150.2.25 Iconografia do Infante Dom Henrique. (Aveiro, Portugal. Museu.)

Afr 150.2.15 Iconografia do Infante Dom Henrique. (Soares, Ernesto.) Lisboa, 1959.

Afr 150.2.30F Iconografia henriquina. (Reis-Santos, Luiz.) Coimbra, 1960.

Afr 8250.42 An iconography of Cecil Rhodes. (Brookner, Anita.) n.p., 1956.

Afr 10689.67.21 Idanre, and other poems. (Soyinka, W.) London, 1967.

Afr 45.66.15 Ideas and prodedures in African customary law. (International African Seminar.) London, 1969.

Afr 9710.14 The ideas in Barotse jurisprudence. (Gluckman, Max.) New Haven, 1965.

Afr 212.68 Ideinye techeniia v tropicheskoi Afrika. Moskva, 1969.

Afr 8667.72 Idenburg, Petrus Johannes. The Cape of Good Hope. Leiden, 1963.

Afr 210.68 Ideologias politicas africanas. (Santos, Eduardo dos.) Lisboa, 1968.

Afr 3204.28 Idéologie et renaissance nationale; l'Égypte moderne. (Abdel-Malek, Anouar.) Paris, 1969.

Afr 50.60 Idéologies des indépendances africaines. (Bénot, Yvès.) Paris, 1969.

Afr 6280.2.5 Idowu, E. Olodumaie. London, 1962.

Afr 1085.3 Idris, Hady R. LaBerbérie orientale sous les Zirides, Xe-XIIe siècles. v.1-2. Paris, 1959.

Afr 1085.2 Idris, Hady R. La Berbérie orientale sous les Zirides, Xe-XIIe siècles. v.1-2. Paris, 1962.

Afr 10839.55.110 lets moet sterf. (Smith, Wilbur Addison.) Johannesburg, 1965.

Afr 8369.63 If this be treason. (Joseph, Helen.) London, 1963.

Afr 6280.64 The Igala Kingdom. (Boston, John Shipway.) Ibadan, 1968.

Afr 6295.66.15 Igbo-Ora; a town in transition. (Barber, C.R.) Ibadan, 1966.

Afr 7175.76 Iglesias, Luis. A verdade sobre Angola. Rio de Janeiro, 1961.

Afr 6280.9.35 The Iglo of southwest Nigeria. (Uchendu, Victor Chikezie.) N.Y., 1965.

Afr 7065.500 Ignat'ev, Oleg K. Pepel i plamia kafina. Moskva, 1966.

Afr 7560.10 Ihle, Alexander. Das Alte Königreich Kongo. Inaug. Diss. Leipzig, 1929.

Afr 555.137 Ijlst, Wim. A present for cold mornings. Dublin, 1968.

Afr 6277.52 Ike, Adelimpe O. Economic development of Nigeria, 1950-1964. Nsukka, 1966.

Afr 10679.44.100 Ike, Vincent Chukwuemeka. Toads for supper. London, 1965.

Afr 12979.44.100 Ikelle-Matiba, J. Cette Afrique-là. Paris, 1963.

Afr 6298.646 Ikime, Obaro. Merchant prince of the Niger Delta; the rise and fall of Nana Olomu. London, 1968.

Afr 5829.65 Il Maurice; creuset de l'Ocean Indien. (Rassool, S. Hassam A.) Paris, 1969.

Afr 3978.38.5 Il viaggio di Mohammed Ali al Sudan. (Sammarco, A.) Caire, 1929.

Afr 9700.5.5 The Ila-speaking peoples of Northern Rhodesia. (Smith, Edwin William.) New Hyde Park, 1968. 2v.

Afr 3977.19   Ildefonso da Palermo, Father. Cronaca della missione francescana dell'Alto Egitto, 1719-1739. Cairo, 1962.
Afr 5872.5   L'Ile Bourbon de 1789 à 1803. (Trouette, E.) Paris, 1888.
Afr 5872.12   L'Ile Bourbon pendant la régence. (Lougnon, Albert.) Paris, 1956.
Afr 870.15   L'ile d'Agalega. (Lionnet, J.G.) Paris, 1924.
Afr 5993.6   L'île de Fernando Poo. (Janikowski, L.) Paris, 1886.
Afr 5832.10   L'Ile de France. (Pitot, Albert.) Port-Louis, 1899.
Afr 5829.08.5   L'Ile de France contemporaine. (Herve de Rauville.) Paris, 1908.
Afr 5842.18   L'Ile de France légendaire. (Herve de Rauville.) Paris, 1889.
Afr 5833.2   L'Ile de France sous Decaen. (Prentout, H.) Paris, 1901.
Afr 5876.1   Ile de la Réunion, Cilaos. (Macauliffe, J.M.) Saint Denis, 1902.
Afr 5874.15   Ile de la Réunion...côte française des Somalis. (Lebband, M.) Paris, 1931.
Afr 5874.18   L'Ile de la Réunion. (Defos du Rau, J.) Bordeaux, 1960.
Afr 5869.23   L'Ile de la Réunion. (Foucque, Hippolyte.) Paris, 1923.
Afr 5748.72   L'ile de Madagascar. (Blanchard, Emile.) Paris, 1872.
Afr 5832.10.5   L'ile de Maurice. V.1-2. (Pitot, Albert.) Port-Louis, 1910-12.
Afr 5845.5   Ile Maurice, régulation des naissances et action familiale. (Gay, Francois.) Lyon, 1968.
Afr 5829.49   L'ile Maurice et sa civilisation. (Unienville, N.) Paris, 1949.
Afr 5794.5   L'ile Nosy-Bé de Madagascar. (Decary, Raymond.) Paris, 1960.
Afr 5749.28.5   L'ile rouge. (Esmenard, J.) Paris, 1928.
Afr 850.2   Iles de l'Afrique. (Avezac-Macayo, M.A.P.) Paris, 1848.
Afr 5749.67   Les îles du Capricorne: Maurice, La Réunion, Madagascar. (Dubrau, Louis (pseud.).) Bruxelles, 1967.
Afr 5874.16   Les îles soeurs ou Le paradis retrouvé. (Leblond, Marius.) Paris, 1946.
Afr 4835.1   Ilg, Alfred. Über die Verkehrsentwicklung in Äthiopien. Zürich, 1900.
Afr 7219.67   Ilha de Moçambique; panorama histórico. (Lobato, Alexandre.) Lisboa, 1967.
Afr 7309.66   Ilha de Moçambique: panorama estético. (Lobato, Alexandre.) Lisboa, 1966.
Afr 7190.30   A ilha de San Thome. (Nogueira, A.F.) Lisboa, 1893.
Afr 6778.2   Iliffe, John. Tanganyika under German rule, 1905-1912. London, 1969.
Afr 8820.6   Illiers, Stephanus. Wes-Kaapland. Stellenbosch, 1964.
Afr 730.2   Illing, K.E. Der Periplus des Hanno. Dresden, 1899.
Afr 609.25.5   Illustrated Africa. (Boyce, W.D.) Chicago, 1925.
Afr 2208.99.11   The illustrated guide to Algiers. 6th ed. (Hyam, Joseph C.) Algiers, 1908.
Afr 8089.61.5   Illustrated history for senior certificate. (Jaarsveld, Floris Albertus.) Johannesburg, 1961.
Afr 8668.14   An illustrated social history of South Africa. (Hattersley, Alan.) Cape Town, 1969.
Afr 4115.4PF   Illustrations of Cairo. (Hay, Robert.) London, 1840.
Afr 3258.16F   Illustriret Familie-Journals. Krigen i Aegypten. Pt.1-3. Kjøbenhavn, 1882.
Afr 6275.134   Iloeje, Nwadilibe P. A new geography of Nigeria. London, 1969.
Afr 5765.20   Ils ne sont que quarante...les jésuites chez les Betsileos. (Derville, Leon.) Paris, 1931.
Afr 1095.25   Ilter Aziz Samih. Şimalî Afrikada Türkler. Istanbul, 1936-37.
Afr 4559.08   Im Auto zu Kaiser Menelik. (Holts, A.) Berlin, 1908.
Afr 4559.35.87   Im Banne des äthiopischen Hochlandes. 2e Aufl. (Muehlen, Leo.) Berlin, 1935.
Afr 7309.02   Im Goldland des Altertums. (Peters, C.) München, 1902.
Afr 6275.8   Im Herzen der Haussaländer. 2. Aufl. (Standinger, P.) Oldenburg, 1891.
Afr 715.2   Im Herzen von Afrika. (Schweinfurth, G.) Leipzig, 1874. 2v.
Afr 7175.16   Im Hochland von Angola. (Schachtzabel, A.) Dresden, 1923.
Afr 6738.6.5   Im Hochland von Mittel-Kamerun. (Thorbecke, F.) Hamburg, 1914-16. 4v.
Afr 7808.88.3   Im innern Afrikas. (Wissmann, H.V.) Leipzig, 1891.
Afr 3978.69.1   Im Lande der Pharaonen. (Bolgiani, V.M.V.) Wien, 1869.
Afr 3979.12.5   Im Lande des Khedive. (Mielert, Fritz.) Regensburg, 1916.
Afr 4559.09.5   Im Lande des Negus. (Escherich, G.) Berlin, 1912.
Afr 1609.05.11   Im muhammedanischen abendlande. (Zabel, R.) Altenburg, 1905.
Afr 7803.43   Im Namen des Herrn im Kongo. (Italiaander, Rolf.) Kassel, 1965.
Afr 2985.2   Im Oasenkreis. (Bary, Erica de.) München, 1963.
Afr 4559.65.5   Im Reich des Negus. (Greim, Armin.) Leipzig, 1965.
Afr 4559.07   Im Reiche Kaiser Meneliks. (Kulmer, F.) Leipzig, 1910.
Afr 7809.04   Im Schatten des Kongostaates. (Frobenius, L.) Berlin, 1907.
Afr 4559.30.15   Im Schatten des Negus. (Jannasch, Hans.) Berlin, 1930.
Afr 6192.75   Im Tempel der bösen Geister. (Joslin, Mike.) Wiesbaden, 1959.
Afr 5344.11   L'Image du monde Bété. (Holas, Bonumil.) Paris, 1968.
Afr 699.59   L'image du sud-est Africain dans la littérature. (Randles, W.G.) Lisboa, 1959.
Afr 7946.5   Imana et le culte des Manes au Rwanda. (Pauwels, M.) Bruxelles, 1958.
Afr 6930.12   Imeshve, R.W. South West Africa. London, 1965.
Afr 1550.6   Immanuel. Marokko. Berlin, 1903.
Afr 6540.4.7   Immigrants and their influence. (Roscoe, John.) Cambridge, Eng., 1924.
Afr 5058.7   L'immigration libano-syrienne en Afrique occidentale française. Thèse. (Desbordes, J.G.) Poitiers, 1938.
Afr 609.68.5   The imminent rains. 1st ed. (Heminway, John Hylan.) Boston, 1968.
Afr 8088.85.5   The immortal history of South Africa. (Boon, Martin J.) London, 1885.
Afr 4392.1   Imperator Menelik. (Eletz, Yu.) St. Petersburg, 1898.
Afr 8140.27   The imperial factor in South Africa, a study of politics and economics. (Kiewiet, C.W.) Cambridge, Eng., 1937.
Afr 6490.5   Imperial frontier. (Barber, James P.) Nairobi, 1968.
Afr 8340.25   Imperial policy and South Africa, 1902-10. (Pyrah, G.B.) Oxford, 1955.
Afr 8175.17   Imperial South African Association. The British case against the Boer republics. Westminster, 1900.
Afr 3745.80   Imperialism and nationalism in the Sudan. (Abd al-Rahim, Muddathir.) Oxford, 1969.
Afr 3199.61.5   Imperialismus in Ägypten. (Mommsen, Wolfgang.) München, 1961.

Afr 2719.62   Imperialisticheskaia bor'ba za Sakharu. (Genin, I. A.) Moscow, 1962.
Afr 500.69   Imperialisticheskii razdel Afriki. (Zusmanovich, A.Z.) Moscow, 1959.
Afr 7549.62   Imperialisticheskii razdel basseina Kongo. (Zusmanovich, A.Z.) Moscow, 1962.
Afr 1608.59.5   El imperio de Marruecos, su historia etc. (Torrijos, Manuel.) Madrid, 1859.
Afr 1608.79   El imperio de Marruecos. (M. y Rodriganez, T.) Madrid, 1879.
Afr 1608.82.5   El imperio de Marruecos y su constitucion. (Bonelli, E.) Madrid, 1882.
Afr 4700.37   L'impero (A.O.I.). (Silbani, T.) Roma, 1937.
Afr 4559.35.85   L'impero abissino. 10. ed. (Caimpenta, U.) Milano, 1935.
Afr 4559.35.3   L'impero del Negus Neghesti. (Gruehl, Max.) Milano, 1935.
Afr 4700.36.10   L'impero italiano nell'Africa orientale. (Giangiorgi, O.M.) Bologna, 1936.
Afr 6879.64   Imperpato, Pascal James. Doctor in the land of the lion. 1st ed. N.Y., 1964.
Afr 8676.64.10   Implications of economic and other boycotts for South Africa. (Katzen, Leo.) Cape Town, 1964.
Afr 210.65   The importance of being black. (Moraas, Francis Robert.) N.Y., 1965.
Htn   Afr 5130.6*   The importance of the African expedition considered. (Postlethwayt, M.) London, 1758.
Afr 1623.932   L'impôt sur les plus-values immobilieres au Maroc. Thèse. (Pourquier, Rene.) Paris, 1932.
Afr 2875.62   L'impresa de Tripoli, 1911-12. (Volpe, Grocchino.) Roma, 1946.
Afr 2870.10.65   La impresa libica e la situazione parlamentare esaurita. (Barzilai, Salvatore.) Roma, 1914. 3 pam.
Afr 1658.11   Impresiones del Rif. (Zuhueta Y Gomis, J.) Barcelona, 1916.
Afr 4785.35   Impressioni di caccia in Somalia italiana. 3a ed. (Zammarano, V. Tedesco.) Milano, 1932.
Afr 6275.28   Impressions - Nigeria 1925. (Fraser, Douglas C.) London, 1926.
Afr 4582.5   Impressions de voyage en Apharras. (Jousseaume, F.) Paris, 1914. 2v.
Afr 4559.14.10   Impressions d'Ethiopie. (Merab.) Paris, 1921-29. 3v.
Afr 1609.30.20   Impressions marocaines. (Berthel, J.) Paris, 1930.
Afr 8289.01.25   Impressions of a doctor in Khaki. (Fremantle, F.E.) London, 1901.
Afr 8289.03.4   Impressions of a war correspondent. (Lynch, G.) London, 1903.
Afr 8088.97.3   Impressions of South Africa. (Bryce, James.) London, 1899.
Afr 8088.97A   Impressions of South Africa. (Bryce, James.) N.Y., 1897.
Afr 8088.97.2   Impressions of South Africa. (Bryce, James.) N.Y., 1898.
Afr 8088.97.4A   Impressions of South Africa. (Bryce, James.) N.Y., 1900.
Afr 3978.39   Impressions of travel in Egypt. (Dumas, A.) N.Y., 1839.
Afr 5045.46   L'imprévu dans les dunes. (Lerumeur, Guy.) Paris, 1963.
Afr 49029.41.700   The imprisonment of Obatala, and other plays. (Ljimere, Obotunde.) London, 1966.
Afr 1259.25.10   In Barbary, Tunisia, Algeria, Morocco, and the Sahara. (Powell, E.A.) N.Y., 1926.
Afr 11865.59.110   In a province. (Vanderpost, Laurens.) London, 1953.
Afr 4558.80   In Abissinia, viaggio. (Matteucci, P.) Milano, 1880.
Afr 4558.80.25   In Abissinia. (Bianchi, G.) Milano, 1896.
Afr 4742.5.5   In Africa, lettere dall'Eritrea. v.1. (Dainelli, Giotto.) Bergamo, 1908.
Afr 4785.15   In Africa, Victoria Nyaza e Benadir. (Albertio, Enrico Alberto d'.) Bergamo, 1906.
Afr 724.6   In Africa dal Capo al Cairo. (Cipriani, Lidio.) Firenze, 1932.
Afr 6280.2.20   In Afric's [Sic] forest and jungle. (Stone, Richard Henry.) Edinburgh, 1900.
Afr 2030.315   In Algerien sprechen die Gewehre. 1. Aufl. (Priester, Eva.) Berlin, 1959.
Afr 679.12   In an elephant corral, and other tales of West African experiences. (Nassau, Robert Hamill.) N.Y., 1969.
Afr 8670.9   In and out of town. (Royal Automobile Club Of South Africa.) Cape Town, 1929.
Afr 6192.23   In Ashanti and beyond. (Cardinall, Allan W.) London, 1927.
Afr 609.25   In brightest Africa. (Akeley, Carl E.) Garden City, N.Y., 1925.
Afr 609.23   In brightest Africa. (Akeley, Carl E.) Garden City, 1923. 2v.
Afr 609.23.2   In brightest Africa. (Akeley, Carl E.) Garden City, 1923. 2v.
Afr 4115.5   In Cairo. (Fullerton, W.M.) London, 1891.
Afr 2945.10   In Cirenaica e in Arabia. (Goretti, L.) Roma, 1912.
Afr 6455.34   In closed territory. (Bronson, Edgar B.) Chicago, 1910.
Afr 6879.28   In coldest Africa. (Wells, Carveth.) Garden City, 1929.
Afr 11582.70.21   In corner b; short stories. (Mphahlele, Ezekiel.) Nairobi, 1967.
Afr 718.10.2   In darkest Africa. (Stanley, H.M.) London, 1904.
Afr 718.10A   In darkest Africa. (Stanley, H.M.) N.Y., 1890. 2v.
Afr 718.10.1   In darkest Africa. (Stanley, H.M.) N.Y., 1891. 2v.
Afr 8678.57.5   In defence of a shared society. (Hellmann, E.) Johannesburg, 1956.
Afr 6888.3   In Deutsch-Ostafrika wahrend Aufstandes. (Baumann, Oscar.) Wien, 1890.
Afr 6926.15   In Deutsche-Südwestafrika, 1913-15. (Weck, Ruediger.) Berlin, 1919.
Afr 6926.2   In deutschen Diamantenlande, Deutsch-Südwest-Afrika, 1884-1910. (Schwabe, K.) Berlin, 1909.
Afr 7809.00   In dwarf land and cannibal country. (Lloyd, A.B.) London, 1899.
Afr 7809.00.3   In dwarf land and cannibal country. (Lloyd, A.B.) London, 1907.
Afr 3979.31   In Egypt, studies and sketches along the Nile. (Vandyke, J.C.) N.Y., 1931.
Afr 4559.68.5   In Ethiopia with a mule. (Murphy, Dervla.) London, 1968.
Afr 4389.11.20   In Etiopia. 4a ed. (Cipolla, A.) Torino, 1933.
Afr 6985.4   In face of fear. (Troup, Freda.) London, 1950.
Afr 6985.5   In feudal Africa. (Loeb, Edwin.) Bloomington, 1962.
Afr 2209.12.7   In French-Africa. Scenes and memories. (Betham-Edwards, M.) London, 1912.
Afr 9506.8   In god's white-robed army. Cape Town, 1951.
Afr 6740.20   In Lande des Cheghu von Bornu. (Duisburg, Adolf von.) Berlin, 1942.

Afr 6214.10.10 An introduction to the history of the Islamic states of Northern Nigeria. (Hoghen, S.J.) Ibadan, 1967.
Afr 679.55.5 An introduction to the history of West Africa. 3rd ed. (Fage, J.D.) Cambridge, Eng., 1962.
Afr 10009.5 An introduction to West African literature. (Taiwo, Oladele.) London, 1967.
Afr 6286.2 An introduction to Western Nigeria. (Adedeji, Adebayo.) Ibadan?, 1966?
Afr 2632.2 L'invasion sicilienne. (Saurin, J.) Paris, 1900.
Afr 5530.7 Inventaire de la serié Mi des Archives de la République Malgache. (Malagasy Republic. Service des Archives et de la Documentation.) Tananariva, 1963.
Afr 1848.7 Inventaire des archives de l'amiraute d'Alger. (Braibant, Chas.) Alger, 1922.
Afr 7530.10 Inventaire des archives des affaires étrangères de l'état du Congo. (Grieken-Taverniers, M. van.) Bruxelles, 1955.
Afr 7530.15 Inventaire des archives historiques. (Tervuren, Belgium. Musée Royale de l'Afrique Centrale.) 3,1964+ 2v.
Afr 7530.12 Inventaire des documents provenant de la mission. (Tervuren, Belgium. Musée Royale de l'Afrique Centrale.) Bruxelles, 1960.
Afr 5343.6 Inventaire économique de la Côte-d'Ivoire. (Ivory Coast. Service de la Statistique Générale et de la Mécanographie.) Abidjan, 1958.
Afr Doc 6709.300 Inventaire économique du Togo. (Togoland. Service de la Statistique Générale.) Lomé. 1959+
Afr 5343.6.3 Inventaire économique et social de la Côte-d'Ivoire, 1958. (Ivory Coast.) Abidjan, 1960.
Afr 5051.25 Inventaire méthodique des cartes et croquis...relatifs á l'Afrique occidentale. (Martonne, E. de.) Laval, 1926.
Afr 28.58 Inventory of economic studies concerning Africa South of the Sahara. (Joint Secretariat C.C.T.A./C.S.A.) London, 1960.
Afr 6295.61F An inventory of the administrative records. (Nigeria. National Archives.) Ibadan, 1961.
Afr 6295.61.5F An inventory of the administrative records. (Nigeria. National Archives.) Ibadan, 1961.
Afr 6203.7.15 An inventory of the records of the Secretariat. (Nigeria. National Archives. Kaduna Branch.) Kaduna, 1963.
Afr 8369.42.1 Investing in friendship. (Smuts, J.C.) London, 1942.
Afr 626.68 Investment and development possibilities in tropical Africa. (Marcus, Edward.) N.Y., 1960.
Afr 9499.25A Investment in Federation of Rhodesia and Nyasaland. (United States. Bureau of Foreign Commerce (1953-).) Washington, 1956.
Afr 8676.54 Investment in Union of South Africa. (United States. Bureau of Foreign Commerce.) Washington, 1954.
Afr 3993.1 The investment of foreign capital in Egyptian companies and public debt. (Crouchley, Arthur Edwin.) Cairo, 1936.
Afr 6277.100.3 Investment opportunities in Eastern Nigeria. 3rd ed. (Nigeria, Eastern. Ministry of Commerce.) Enugu, 1966.
Afr 1609.50.5 Invitation to Morocco. (Landau, R.) London, 1950.
Afr 609.58.45 Inyanga. (Summer, Roger.) Cambridge, 1958.
Htn Afr 605.56.5* Ioannis Leonis Africani Africae descriptio IX lib. Absoluta. 2 pt. (Leo Africanus, J.) Lugdunum Batavorum, 1632.
Afr 679.68.15 Iordanskii, Vladimir B. Opnennye ieroglify. Moskva, 1968.
Afr 5316.501 Iordanskii, Vladimir B. Strategiia bor'by za nezavisimost? Moskva, 1968.
Afr 6750.8 IPA study. (Dar es Salaam. University College. Institute of Public Administration.) Dar es Salaam. 1,1965+ 2v.
Afr 1609.03.9 Irabien Larranaga, E. de. Africa, apuntes de Marruecos. San Sebastian, 1903.
Afr 2875.7 Irace, C.F. With the Italians in Tripoli. London, 1912.
Afr 5920.2 Iradier, Manuel. Africa, viajes y trabajos de la asociación. Bilbao, 1901. 2v.
Afr 5920.1.3 Iradier, Manuel. Africa. Madrid, 1878.
Afr 5920.1.5 Iradier, Manuel. Africa. Vitoria, 1887. 2v.
Afr 5920.1.15 Iradier. (Cordero Torres, J.M.) Madrid, 1944.
Afr 5924.240 Iradier. (Spain. Consejo Superior de Investigaciones.) Madrid, 1956.
Afr 6883.26 Irakou. (Fouquet, Roger.) Paris, 1955.
Afr 10062.3 Irasheva, Valentina V. Literatura stran Zapadnoi Afriki; proza. Moskva, 1967.
Afr 3978.68 Irby, C.L. Travels in Nubia. London, 1868.
Afr 8279.00.3 Ireland, A. The Anglo-Boer conflict. Boston, 1900.
Afr 9028.65 Ireland, W. Historical sketch of the Zulu mission. Boston, n.d.
Afr 12018.8 Irele, Abiola. Lectures africaines. London, 1969.
Afr 8815.4 Irons, H. The settler's guide to the Cape of Good Hope and colony of Natal. London, 1858.
Afr 9446.28 An irregular corps in Matabeleland. (Plumer, Herbert C.) London, 1897.
Afr 8847.53F Irving, James. Macleantown. Grahamstown, 1959.
Afr 630.61 Isaacs, H.R. Emergent Americans. N.Y., 1961.
Afr 2285.12.5 Isabelle Eberhardt. (Noel, Jean.) Algers, 1961.
Afr 4558.43.5 Isenberg, Karl Wilhelm. The journals of C.W. Isenberg and J.L. Krapt. London, 1968.
Afr 6192.9.2 Isert, P.E. Reise nach Guinea. Kopenhagen, 1788.
Afr 6192.9 Isert, P.E. Voyages en Guinée. Paris, 1793.
Afr 9071.41 Isipingo, village in the sun. (Slayter, Eric.) Durban, 1961.
Afr 10675.47.180 Iska. (Ekwensi, Cyprian.) London, 1966.
Afr 609.67.5 Iskusstvo Afriki. (Moscow. Institut Istorii Iskusstvi.) Moskva, 1967.
Afr 635.7.10 Iskusstvo negrov. (Markov, Vlats.) Sankt Peterburg, 1919.
Afr 575.8 L'islam algérien en l'an 1900. (Doutte, E.) Alger, 1900.
Afr 5119.68 Islam and imperialism in Senegal; Sine-Saloum, 1847-1914. (Klien, Martin A.) Stanford, 1968.
Afr 3285.20 Islam and modernism in Egypt. (Adams, Charles C.) London, 1933.
NEDL Afr 575.6 L'islam dans l'Afrique occidentale. (Lechatelier, A.) Paris, 1899.
Afr 5058.10 L'islam dans l'Afrique occidentale française. (Gouilly, A.) Paris, 1952.
Afr 575.17.25 L'islam e le nostre colonie. (Ruini, M.) Città di Castello, 1922.
Afr 5245.5 L'islam et la civilisation française. (Ouane, Ibrahima Mamadou.) Avignon, 1957.
Afr 575.13 L'islam et le christianisme. (Forget, D.A.) Paris, 1900.
Afr 575.23 L'islam et les musulmans dans l'Afrique du Nord. (Jung, Eugène.) Paris, 1930.
Afr 575.01 Pamphlet box. Islam in Africa.
Afr 575.27 Islam in Africa. (Ahmad, Mubarak.) Rabwah, 1962.
Afr 575.7 Islam in Africa. (Atterbury, Anson Phelps.) N.Y., 1899.
Afr 575.7.2 Islam in Africa. (Atterbury, Anson Phelps.) N.Y., 1969.
Afr 575.45 Islam in Africa. (Brelvi, Mahmud.) Lahore, 1964.
Afr 575.30 Islam in East Africa. (Hurries, Lyndon.) London, 1954.
Afr 575.36.10 Islam in East Africa. (Trimingham, J.S.) Oxford, 1964.
Afr 4568.19.2 Islam in Ethiopia. (Trimingham, J.S.) London, 1965.
Afr 575.47 Der Islam in Ost-Afrika. (Reusch, Richard.) Leipzig, 1931.
Afr 8685.1 Islam in South Africa. (Hampson, Ruth M.) Cape Town, 1964.
Afr 3675.66 Islam in the Sudan. (Trimingham, J.S.) London, 1949.
Afr 575.37 Islam in tropical Africa, studies presented and discussed at the fifth International African Seminar. (International African Seminar, 5th, London, 1966.) London, 1966.
Afr 575.35 Islam in West Africa. (Trimingham, J.S.) Oxford, 1959.
Afr 575.35.2 Islam in West Africa. 2nd ed. (Trimingham, J.S.) Oxford, 1961.
Afr 1259.10 Islam lands, Nubia, the Sudan, Tunisia, and Algeria. (Shoemaker, M.M.) N.Y., 1910.
Afr 575.21 L'islam noir. (Andre, Pierre J.) Paris, 1924.
Afr 575.40 L'islam noir. (Monteil, V.) Paris, 1964.
Afr 3285.21 Islamic reform. (Kerr, Malcolm H.) Berkeley, 1966.
Afr 5090.10 The Islamic Republic of Mauritania. (France. Embassy. U.S.) N.Y., 1960.
Afr 1080.10 L'islamisation de l'Afrique du Nord. Les siècles obscures du Maghreb. (Gautier, Emile F.) Paris, 1927.
Afr 5245.10 Islamisme contre naturisme au Soudan français. (Brevie, J.) Paris, 1923.
Afr 550.6 L'islamisme et le christianisme en Afrique. (Bonet-Maury, G.) Paris, 1906.
Afr 2945.26.15 L'islamismo e la Confraternità dei Senussi. (Bourbon del Monte Santa Maria, G.) Città di Castello, 1912.
Afr 7071.5 O islamismo na Guiné portuguesa. (Gonçalves, J.J.) Lisboa, 1961.
Afr 850.6 Islands time forgot. (Green, L.G.) London, 1962.
Afr 854.10 Islas del Golfo de Guinea. (Unzueta y Yuste, A. de.) Madrid, 1945.
Afr 5874.11 Isle de Bourbon (Réunion); documents, 1701-1710. (Compagnie des Indes Orientales.) N.Y., 1909.
Afr 1731.1 L'isle de Perecil. (Rouard De Card, E.) Toulouse, 1903.
Afr 6585.7 Isle of Cloves. (Ommanney, F.D.) Philadelphia, 1956.
Afr 855.18 Isle of St. Helena. (Blakeston, O.) London, 1957.
Afr 6280.55 Ismagilova, R.N. Narody Nigerii. Moscow, 1963.
Afr 3230.17 Ismail, the maligned khedive. (Crabitès, Pierre.) London, 1933.
Afr 4095.8.3.5 Ismailia; a narrative of the expedition to Central Africa for the suppression of the slave trade. (Baker, S.W.) N.Y., 1969. 2v.
NEDL Afr 4095.8.3 Ismailia. (Baker, S.W.) N.Y., 1875.
Afr 6883.10 The Ismailis in Tanzania. Photoreproduction. (Kjellberg, Eva.) Dar-es-Salaam, 1967.
Afr 609.67.40 Isnara, Hildebert. Géographie de l'Afrique tropicale et australe. 2. éd. Paris, 1967.
Afr 5549.55 Isnard, Hildebert. Madagascar. Paris, 1955.
Afr 1259.66 Isnard, Hildebert. Le Maghreb. Paris, 1966.
Afr 626.127 Israel and Africa. (Kreinin, M.E.) N.Y., 1964.
Afr 1640.1 Israel au Maroc. (Hess, Jean.) Paris, 1907.
Afr 3040.50 Israel-Meyer, G. L'Egypte contemporaine et les capitulations. Thése. Paris, 1930.
Afr 2274.5 Les israélites algériens de 1830 à 1902. Thèse. (Martin, Claude.) Paris, 1936.
Afr 3986.963 Issawi, C.P. Egypt in revolution. London, 1963.
Afr 3300.50A Issawi, Charles. Egypt. London, 1947.
Afr 3300.51 Issawi, Charles. Egypt at mid-century. London, 1954.
Afr 3993.965.5 Issawi, Charles Philip. Egypt in revolution. London, 1965.
Afr 4742.20 Issel, A. Viaggio nel Mar Rosso e tra i Bogos (1870). Milano, 1872.
Afr 9780.2 The issue of Nyasaland's secession. (Rhodesia and Nyasaland.) Salisbury, 1962.
Afr 4559.35.55 Das ist Abessinien. (Goldmann, Wilhelm.) Bern, 1935.
Afr 4045.3 O Isthmo de Suez e as portuguezes. (Juromenha, J.A. de R.P. de Lacerda.) Lisboa, 1870.
Afr 4700.27.5 Istituto Agricolo Coloniale Italiano. Per le nostre colonie. Firenze, 1927.
Afr 4259.35F Istituto della Enciclopedia Italiana. L'Etiopia. Roma, 1935.
Afr 109.55 Istituto Italiano per l'Africa. L'Africa nei suoi aspetti geografici. Roma, 1955.
Afr 4178.20 Istituto Italiano per l'Africa. Il Congresso di Trento per il centenario del progetto italiano per il taglio dell istmo di Suez. Roma, 1956.
Afr 4700.36.17 Istituto per gli Studi di Politica Internazionale, Milan. L'Africa orientale. 2e ed. Milano, 1936. 2v.
Afr 4513.36.33 Istituto per gli Studi di Politica Internazionale, Milan. Breve storia del conflitto italo-etiopico. Milano, 1936.
Afr 4513.36.30 Istituto per gli Studi di Politica Internazionale, Milan. Il conflitto italo-etiopico. Milano, 1936. 2v.
Afr 3069.41 Istituto per gli Studi di Politica Internazionale, Milan. Egitto, moderno e antico. Milano, 1941.
Afr 4513.36.34 Istituto per gli Studi di Politica Internazionale, Milan. The Italian empire in Africa, present and future. Milano, 1936.
Htn Afr 7015.2.2* Istorica descrittione de tre regni Congo, Matamba. (Cavazzi, G.A.) n.p., 1690.
Afr 7015.2.1 Istorica descrizione de tre regni Congo, Matamba. (Cavazzi, G.A.) Bologna, 1687.
Afr 212.25.9 Istoriia Afriki v XIX nachale XX v. (Akademiia Nauk SSSR. Institut Afriki.) Moskva, 1967.
Afr 7560.19 Istoriia gosudarstva Kongo (XVI-XVII vv.). (Orlova, Antonina S.) Moskva, 1968.
Afr 590.82 Istoriia rabotorgovli na verkhne-gvineiskom poberezh'e. (Abramova, Svetlana I.) Moskva, 1966.
Afr 3675.64 Istoriia Sudana (1821-1956). (Smirnov, Sergei R.) Moskva, 1968.
Afr 4700.26.20 L'Itali in Africa. (Italy. Comitato per la Documentazione dell'Opera dell'Italia in Africa.) Roma, 1963.
Afr 2525.15 Italia, Francia, Tunisia. (Marpurgo, G.) Livorno, 1938.
Afr 2870.7 L'Italia a Tripoli. (Coen, G.) Livorno, 1912.
Afr 4700.35.5 L'Italia ai margini d'Etiopia. (Vecchi, B.V.) Milano, 1935.

Afr 4512.20	L'Italia di Fronte a Gineura, aspetti del conflitto italo-etiopico dalle origini alla conquista dell Impero. (Caioli, Aldo.) Roma, 1965.
Afr 2530.23	Italia e Francia in Tunisia, 1878-1939. (Cataluccio, F.) Roma, 1939.
Afr 2710.6	Italia e Francia nel Sahara orientale. (Salvati, Cesare.) Milano, 1929.
Afr 4712.1	L'Italia e la sua colonia africana. (Franchetti, L.) Città di Castello, 1891.
Afr 4513.35.130	L'Italia e l'Etiopia. (Traversi, L.) Bologna, 1935.
Afr 2870.10	Italia e Libia. (Mosca, G.) Milano, 1912.
Afr 575.16	L'Italia e l'islam in Libia. (Malrezzi, A.) Firenze, 1913.
Afr 2945.26	Italia e Senussia. (Serra, F.) Milano, 1933.
Afr 2510.1	Italia e Tunisi. (Santi, F.L.) Milano, 1881.
Afr 4513.35.110	Italia ed Abissinia. (Marino, A.) Bengasi, 1935.
Afr 4513.19	Italia ed Etiopia dal trattato d'Uccialli alla battaglia di Adua. (Conti Rossini, C.) Roma, 1935.
Afr 4513.36.55	L'Italia fascista e l'Abissinia. (Ciccarelli, Socrate.) Torino, 1935.
Afr 4700.4.5	L'Italia in Africa, le scoperte archeologiche Tripolitania. (Italy. Comitato per la Documentazione dell'Opera dell'Italia in Africa.) Roma, 1962. 2v.
Afr 4700.6	L'Italia in Africa; serie civile. (Italy. Comitato per la Documentazione dell'Opera dell'Italia in Africa.) Roma, 1965. 2v.
Afr 4384.1	Pamphlet vol. Italia in Africa, 1887-97. 11 pam.
Afr 4700.3.5	L'Italia in Africa. (Italy. Comitato per la documentazione dell'opera dell'Italia in Africa.) Roma, 1955.
Afr 4700.35.20	Italia in Africa. Torino, 1935.
Afr 4700.26.18	L'Italia in Africa. T.1-5. (Italy. Comitato per la Documentazione dell'Opera dell'Italia in Africa.) Roma, 1960- 8v.
Afr 4392.8.5	L'Italia in Africa e le guerre con l'Abissinia. (Canuti, Giuseppe.) Firenze, 1911.
Afr 4700.25	L'Italia musulmana. (Cantalupe, R.) Roma, 1928.
Afr 4700.38.15	L'Italia sul Mar Rosso. (Gaslini, M.) Milano, 1938.
Afr 28.68	Italiaander, Rolf. Africana. Holland, Michigan, 1961.
Afr 7803.43	Italiaander, Rolf. Im Namen des Herrn im Kongo. Kassel, 1965.
Afr 55.15	Italiaander, Rolf. Die neuen Männer Afrikas. Düsseldorf, 1960.
Afr 55.17	Italiaander, Rolf. Die neuen Männer Afrikas. Düsseldorf, 1963.
Afr 55.16	Italiaander, Rolf. The new leaders of Africa. Englewood Cliffs, 1961.
Afr 109.58	Italiaander, Rolf. Der ruhelose Kontinent. 1. Aufl. Düsseldorf, 1958.
Afr 212.42	Italiaander, Rolf. Schwarze Haut im roten Griff. Düsseldorf, 1962.
Afr 4766.38	Italian colonialism in Somalia. (Hess, Robert L.) Chicago, 1966.
Afr 2870.35A	The Italian empire: Libya. (Italian Library of Information, N.Y.) N.Y., 1940.
Afr 4513.36.34	The Italian empire in Africa, present and future. (Istituto per gli Studi di Politica Internazionale, Milan.) Milano, 1936.
Afr 500.48	Italian Library of Information, N.Y. Colonialism in Africa. N.Y., 1940.
Afr 2870.35A	Italian Library of Information, N.Y. The Italian empire: Libya. N.Y., 1940.
Afr 4700.40	Italian Library of Information. Development of Italian East Africa. N.Y., 1940.
Afr 2632.9	Gli Italiani e le professioni liberali in Tunisia. (Maggio, G. di.) Tunis, 1934.
Afr 4700.36.20	Italiani in Africa orientale, pagine di pionieri. (Giardini, C.) Milano, 1936.
Afr 4025.20.20	Gl italiani in Egitto. (Oddi, F.F.) Alessandria, 1895.
Afr 4025.20.25	Gli italiani in Egitto. (Sammarco, Angelo.) Alessandria, 1937.
Afr 3199.06	Gl'Italiani nella civiltà egiziana del secolo XIX. (Balboni, L.A.) Alessandria, 1906. 3v.
Afr 4700.33	Gli italiani nella conoscenza dell'Africa. (Cesari, Cesare.) Roma, 1933.
Afr 3725.5	Gl'Italiani nell'Equatoria. (Ghisleri, A.) Bergamo, 1893.
Afr 4700.27.10	L'Italie devant le problème colonial. (Guyot, Georges.) Roma, 1927.
Afr 4392.6	Les Italiens en Afrique (1880-1896). (Pellenc, A.J.J.) Paris, 1897.
Afr 4718.97	Les Italiens en Érythrie. (Jaffanel, C. de.) Paris, 1897.
Afr 6277.63	Italiens in Nigeria; a story of successful international co-operation. (Italy. Embassy. Nigeria.) Lagos, 1967?
Afr 4430.5	Pamphlet vol. Italo-Ethiopian conflict. 24 pam.
Afr 4513.35.25	The Italo-Ethiopian controversy. (Italy. Historical Society.) n.p., 1935.
Afr 4513.35.27	The Italo-Ethiopian controversy. (Italy. Historical Society.) N.Y., 1935.
Afr 4513.35.16	Italo-Ethiopian dispute. (Italy.) Roma, 1935.
Afr 4513.35.15	Italo-Ethiopian dispute. Roma, 1935.
Afr 2875.66	Italo-turetskaia voina, 1911-1912 gg. (Iakhimovich, Zinaida P.) Moskva, 1967.
Afr 4513.36.15	Italy, Abyssinia and the League. (Villari, Luigi.) Rome, 1936.
Afr 4513.35.44	Italy, Great Britain and the League in the Italo-Ethiopian conflict. (Vare, Daniele.) N.Y., 1935.
Afr 4513.35.41	Italy, Great Britain and the League in the Italo-Ethiopian conflict. (Vare, Daniele.) N.Y., 1935.
Afr 4746.10F	Italy. Assab et les limites de la souveraineté turco-égyptienne dans la Mer Rouge. Rome, 1882.
Afr 4513.35.17	Italy. Il conflitto italo-etiopico. Roma, 1935.
Afr 4513.35.16	Italy. Italo-Ethiopian dispute. Roma, 1935.
Afr 4513.35.70F	Italy. Memorandum of the Italian government on the situation in Abyssinia. n.p., 1935.
Afr 4513.35.65F	Italy. Memoria del governo italiano circa la situazione in Etiopia. II. n.p., 1935.
Afr 4513.37.80	Italy. Comando delle Forze Armate della Somalia. La guerra italo-etiopica. Addis Abeba, 1937.
Afr 4700.26.20	Italy. Comitato per la Documentazione dell'Opera dell'Italia in Africa. L'Itali in Africa. Roma, 1963.
Afr 4700.4.5	Italy. Comitato per la Documentazione dell'Opera dell'Italia in Africa. L'Italia in Africa, le scoperte archeologiche Tripolitania. Roma, 1962. 2v.
Afr 4700.6	Italy. Comitato per la Documentazione dell'Opera dell'Italia in Africa. L'Italia in Africa; serie civile. Roma, 1965. 2v.
Afr 4700.3.5	Italy. Comitato per la documentazione dell'opera dell'Italia in Africa. L'Italia in Africa. Roma, 1955.
Afr 4700.26.18	Italy. Comitato per la Documentazione dell'Opera dell'Italia in Africa. L'Italia in Africa. T.1-5. Roma, 1960- 8v.
Afr 4731.6	Italy. Commissione d'Inchiesta sulla Colonia Eritrea. Relazione generale. Roma, 1891.
Afr 4700.15F	Italy. Direzione Centrale degli Affari Coloniali. L'Africa italiana al Parlamento nazionale, 1882-1905. Roma, 1907.
Afr 4700.13.5	Italy. Direzione Centrale degli Affari Coloniali. Raccolta di publicazioni coloniali italiane. Roma, 1911.
Afr 500.18.2	Italy. Direzione Centrale degli Affari Coloniali. Trattati, convenzioni, accordi. Supplemento alla raccolta. Roma, 1909.
Afr 500.18	Italy. Direzione Centrale degli Affari Coloniali. Trattati, convenzioni, accordi. v.1,2-3. Roma, 1906. 2v.
Afr 6277.63	Italy. Embassy. Nigeria. Italiens in Nigeria; a story of successful international co-operation. Lagos, 1967?
Afr 4719.35	Italy. Escrito. Corpo di stato maggiore. Officio Storico. Storia militare della colonia Eritrea. v.1-2, 2 bis. Roma, 1935-36. 3v.
Afr 2875.35	Italy. Esercito. Corpo di Stato Maggiore. Ufficio Storico. Campagna di Libia. Roma, 1922-27. 5v.
Afr 4513.39.40	Italy. Esercito. Corpo di stato maggiore. Ufficio storico. La campagna 1935-46 in Africa orientale. Roma, 1939.
Afr 4764.938	Italy. Esercito. Corpo di Stato Maggiore. Ufficio Storico. Somalia. Roma, 1938. 2v.
Afr 4513.35.25	Italy. Historical Society. The Italo-Ethiopian controversy. n.p., 1935.
Afr 4513.35.27	Italy. Historical Society. The Italo-Ethiopian controversy. N.Y., 1935.
Afr 6457.30	Italy. Instituto Nationale Per Il Commercio Estero. Kenya. Roma, 1964.
Afr 5240.8	Italy. Instituto Nazionale per il Commercio Estero. Mali. Roma, 1964.
Afr 1623.963.10	Italy. Instituto Nazionale per il Commercio Estero. Marocco. Roma, 1963.
Afr 3813.8	Italy. Instituto Nazionale per il Commercio Estero. Sudan. Roma, 1960.
Afr 5482.20	Italy. Instituto Nazionale per il Commercio Estero. Tchad. Romo, 1963.
Afr Doc 707.353	Italy. Istituto Centrali di Statistica. Censimento della popolazione Italiana e straniera della Somalia 4 novembre 1953. Roma, 1958.
Afr 5282.4	Italy. Istituto Nazionale per il Commercio Estero. Alto volta. Roma, 1964.
Afr 6739.263	Italy. Istituto Nazionale per il Commercio Estero. Cameroun. Roma, 1963.
Afr 9499.37	Italy. Istituto Nazionale per il Commercio Estero. Federazione delle Rodesia e del Niassaland. Roma, 1962.
Afr 6193.45	Italy. Istituto Nazionale per il Commercio Estero. Ghana. Roma, 1960.
Afr 7461.36	Italy. Istituto Nazionale per il Commercio Estero. Liberia. Roma, 1964.
Afr 5758.60	Italy. Istituto Nazionale per il Commercio Estero. Madagascar. Roma, 1960.
Afr 5758.60.4	Italy. Istituto Nazionale per il Commercio Estero. Madagascar. Roma, 1964-[1965].
Afr 7312.20	Italy. Istituto Nazionale per il Commercio Estero. Mozambico. Roma, 1959.
Afr 6277.60	Italy. Istituto Nazionale per il Commercio Estero. Nigeria. Roma, 1960.
Afr 6538.50	Italy. Istituto Nazionale per il Commercio Estero. Uganda. Roma, 1964.
Afr 5343.20	Italy. Istituto nazionale per il commercio estero Costa d'Avorio. Roma, 1963.
Afr 4719.29	Italy. Marina Stato Maggiore. Officio Storico. L'opera della marina in Eritrea e Somalia della occupazione...1928. Roma, 1929.
Afr 4515.5F	Italy. Ministero degli Affairi Esteri. Documenti diplomatici presentati al parlamento italiano. Roma, 1890.
Afr 4787.6	Italy. Ministero degli Affari Esteri. L'amministrazione fiduciaria della Somalia. Roma, 1961.
Afr 1325.5F	Italy. Ministero degli Affari Esteri. Documenti diplomatici. Successione sceriffiana (Marrocco). Roma, 1895.
Afr 7565.10F	Italy. Ministero degli Affari Esteri. Documenti diplomatici presentati al senato. Roma, 1885.
Afr 2510.5	Italy. Ministero degli Affari Esteri. Intorno ai provvedimenti relativi alla giurisdizione consolare italiana in Tunisia. Roma, 1884.
Afr 4760.3	Italy. Ministero degli Affari Esteri. Rapport du gouvernement italien à l'Assemblée générale des Nations Unies. 1950+ 5v.
Afr 4025.20.10	Italy. Ministero degli Affari Esteri. Sulla politica italiana inEgitto. Roma, 1882.
Afr 4025.20.5	Italy. Ministero degli Affari Esteri. Sulla tutela degli interessi italiani in Egitto. Rome, 1880.
Afr 3269.10	Italy. Ministero degli Affari Esteriore. Documenti diplomatici relativi alle indennità per danni sofferti. Roma, 1883.
Htn Afr 2850.12.5*	Italy. Ministero della Marina. Le condizioni militari della Tripolitania. Rome, 1885.
Htn Afr 2850.12.10*	Italy. Ministero della Marina. Relazione sulla visita fatta dalla R. Corvetta Vettor Pisani alla baia di Tobruch e Dernah. Rome, 1885.
Afr 4700.26.10	Italy. Ministero delle Colonie. Notizia generali sulla colonie italiane. Roma, 1926.
Afr 4700.28.15	Italy. Ministero delle Colonie. Ordinamento amministrativo-contabile per l'Eritrea e per la Somalia. Roma, 1928.

Afr 4732.10F Italy. Ministero delle Colonie. Relazione sulla colonia Eritrea del R. Commissario civile deputato. Ferdinando Martini per gli esercizi 1902-07. v.1-4. Roma, 1913. 2v.

Htn Afr 4730.4F* Italy. Ministero di Affari Esteri. Beilul-Zula-Massaua-Sudan. Rome, 1885.

Afr 4730.3 Italy. Ministero di Affari Esteri. La colonia italiana di Assab. Roma, 1882.

Afr 2850.2 Italy. Parlamento. La Libia. Milano, 1912. 2v.

Afr 4766.10 Italy. Treaties. Great Britain. 1933. Agreement concerning claims of certain British and Italian protected persons. London, 1933.

Afr 4700.29.5 Italy. Ufficio Studi e Propaganda. Le colonie italiane de diretto dominio. Roma, 1929.

Afr 530.22 Italy. Ufficio Studi e Propaganda. Voyageurs italiens en Afrique. Roma, 1931.

Afr 4513.37.42A Italy against the world. (Martelli, G.) N.Y., 1938.

Afr 4513.36.50 Italy and the Abyssinian war. (Abbati, A.H.) London, 1936.

Afr 2530.19.10 Italy and the question of Tunis. (Gray, E.M.) Milano, 1939.

Afr 4700.41.5 Italy in Africa. (Hollis, Christopher.) London, 1941.

Afr 2875.64 Italy in north Africa. (McClare, William K.) London, 1913.

Afr 2850.3 Italy's civilizing mission in africa. (Vecchi, P.) N.Y., 1912.

Afr 4513.37.47 Italy's conquest of Abyssinia. (Newman, E.W.P.) London, 1937.

Afr 2875.21 Italy's war for a desert (Experiences of war correspondent with Italians in Tripoli). (McCullagh, F.) Chicago, 1913.

Afr 2220.4 Itinéraire...de l'Algérie. (Barbier, J.) Paris, 1855.

Afr 2030.462.140 Itinéraire. (Bonnaud, R.) Paris, 1962.

Afr 5135.5 Itinéraire africain par Lamine Gueve. (Gueve, Lamine.) Paris, 1966.

Afr 2220.3 Itinéraire de l'Algérie. (Piesse, L.) Paris, 1862.

Afr 2220.5 Itinéraire de l'Algérie. (Piesse, L.) Paris, 1881.

Afr 2220.6 Itinéraire de l'Algérie. (Piesse, L.) Paris, 1885.

Afr 5748.95.20 Itineraire de Majunga à Tananarive. (Beylie, Leon De.) Paris, 1895.

Afr 5019.58.10 L'itinéraire des partis africains depuis Bamoko. (Blanchet, Andre.) Paris, 1958.

Afr 2798.5 Itinéraire d'In-Salah au Tahat à travers l'Ahaggar. (Perret, Robert.) Paris, 1932.

Afr 4045.5 Itinéraire pour l'isthme de Suez et les grandes villes d'Egypte. (Bernard, H.) Paris, 1869.

Afr 2731.15.65 Itinéraire spirituel de Charles de Foucauld. (Six, Jean F.) Paris, 1958.

Afr 1609.10 Itineraires au Maroc. (Maps). (Segonzac, M. De.) Paris, 1910.

Afr 2608.82.10F Itinéraires en Tunisie, 1881-82. Pt.1-2 and tables. Paris, 1882.

Htn Afr 606.31* Itinerarium ad regiones sub aequinoctrali. (Geraldinus a Merini, A.) Romae, 1631.

Afr 6470.242 Itote, Warohiu. "Mau Mau" general. Nairobi, 1967.

Afr 6740.25 "It's like this" essays. Bali, Cameroon. 2,1964+

Afr 8676.66 Iuzhno-Afrikanskaia Respublika. (Moiseeva, Galina M.) Moskva, 1966.

Afr 8678.442 Iuzhno-afrikanskii rabochii klass v bor'be protiv reaktsii i rasizma. (Gorodnov, Valentin P.) Moskva, 1969.

Afr 8045.56 Iuzhnoafrikanskii blok Kolonizatorov. Moskva, 1968.

Afr 4700.62 Ivanitskii, M.N. Put k nezavisimosti. Kiev, 1962.

Afr 3979.66.5 Ivanov, Boris V. 40 vekov i 4 goda. Moskva, 1966.

Afr 2535.2 Ivanov, N.A. Sovremennyi Tunis. Moscow, 1959.

Afr 8686.22 Ive, Anthony. The Church of England in South Africa. Cape Town, 1966.

Afr 8325.30 Ives, Herbert. Britons and Boers. London, n.d.

Afr 630.7 Ivory, apes, and peacocks. (Waller, N.) London, 1891.

Afr 5343.6.3 Ivory Coast. Inventaire économique et social de la Côte-d'Ivoire, 1958. Abidjan, 1960.

Afr 5343.7.15 Ivory Coast. Loi plan de développement économique, social et culturel pour les années, 1967-1968, 1969-1970. Abidjan, 1967.

Afr 5325.5F Ivory Coast. Abidjan. 25,1966+

Afr Doc 6409.310 Ivory Coast. Caisse Autonome d'Amortissement. Gestion de la dette publique. Gestion des depôts. Abidjan. 1960+

Afr 5343.2 Ivory Coast. Conseil Economique et Social. Rapport sur l'évolution économique et sociale de la Côte-d'Ivoire, 1960-1969. Abidjan, 1965.

Afr Doc 6409.307 Ivory Coast. Direction de la Statistique et des Etudes Economiques et Démographiques. Les comptes économiques. 1958+

Afr Doc 6407.3.2 Ivory Coast. Direction de la Statistique et des Etudes Economiques et Démographiques. Bulletin mensuel de statistique. Supplement trimestriel. Etudes et rapports. 5v.

Afr Doc 6407.3 Ivory Coast. Direction de la Statistique et des Etudes Economiques et Démographiques. Bulletin mensuel de statistique. 12,1959+ 3v.

Afr Doc 6471.1.73 Ivory Coast. Direction de la Statistique et des Etudes economiques et démographiques. Recensement d'Abidjan 1955. Paris, 1960.

Afr Doc 6472.5 Ivory Coast. Direction de la Statistique et des Etudes Economiques et Démographiques. Recensement démographique de Bruehe, 1958. Résultats définitifs. Paris, 1961.

Afr Doc 6471.10 Ivory Coast. Direction de la Statistique et des Etudes Economiques et Démographiques. Recensement des centres urbains d'Abengoonon, Aghoville, Dunboko et Man, 1956, 1957. Résultats définitif. Paris, 1960.

Afr Doc 6409.305 Ivory Coast. Direction de la Statistique et des Etudes Economiques et Démographiques. Situation économique de la Côte d'Ivoire. 1960+ 3v.

Afr Doc 6408.705 Ivory Coast. Direction de la Statistique et des Etudes Economiques et Démographiques. Statistiques du commerce extérieur de la Côte d'Ivoire. 1961+

Afr Doc 6443.5 Ivory Coast. Direction des Mines et de la Geologie. Rapport annuel. Abidjan. 1966+

Afr Doc 6408.707 Ivory Coast. Direction du Commerce Extérieur. Commerce exterieur et balance commerciale. Abidjan. 1964+

Afr Doc 6408.709 Ivory Coast. Direction du Commerce Extérieur. Memento économique. Abidjan. 1964+

Afr 5342.64 Ivory Coast. Embassy. U.S. General data on the Republic of the Ivory Coast. Washington, D.C., 1963.

Afr 5337.5 Ivory Coast. Ministère de l'Education Nationale. Nation, société, travail. Abidjan, 1960.

Afr Doc 6471.5 Ivory Coast. Ministère des Travaux Publics et des Transports. Port d'Abidjan; rapport annuel. Abidjan. 1966+

Afr 5343.7.6 Ivory Coast. Ministère du Plan. Perspectives decennales...Annexes. Abidjan?, 1967?

Afr 5343.7.5 Ivory Coast. Ministère du Plan. Perspectives decennales de développement èconomic, social et cultural, 1960-1970. Abidjan, 1967.

Afr 5343.7.10 Ivory Coast. Ministère du Plan. Première esquisse du plan quinquennal de développement. Paris, 1968.

Afr 5343.7 Ivory Coast. Ministère du Plan. Troisieme plan quadriennal de développement économique et social. Abidjan, 1958.

Afr 5343.5 Ivory Coast. Service de la Statistique Générale et de la Mécanographie. Les budgets familiaux des salariés africains en Abidjan. Paris, 1958.

Afr 5343.6 Ivory Coast. Service de la Statistique Générale et de la Mécanographie. Inventaire économique de la Côte d'Ivoire, Abidjan, 1958.

Afr 6455.2 An ivory trader in North Kenia. (Hardwick, A.A.) London, 1903.

Afr 9170.126.2 The ivory trail. 2nd ed. (Bulpin, Thomas Victor.) Capetown, 1967.

Afr 10679.96.100 Iwunze, Godwin Egejuruka. The sting that cures. Enugu, 1966.

Afr 10016.15 Iz afrikanskoi liriki. (Kurgantsev, Mikhail.) Moskva, 1967.

Afr 8685.27.20 Iz istorii rasovoi diskriminatsii indiitsev v Iuzhnoi Afrike. (Mukhamedova, Dil'bar.) Tashkent, 1965.

Afr 49716.5 Izibongo; Zulu praise-poems. (Stuart, James.) Oxford, 1968.

Afr 115.117 Izuchenie Afriki v Svetskom Soiuze. Photocopy. Moskva, 1966.

Afr 9149.28 J.V. Figulus a jeho Africka dobrodruzstvi. (Figulus, Jiri V.) Praha, 1928. 2 pam.

Afr 8089.65.10 Jaarsreld, Floris. Die verlede spreek. Pretoria, 1965.

Afr 8057.5 Jaarsveld, F.A. van. Die afrikaner en sy geskiedenis. Kaapstad, 1959.

Afr 8057.6 Jaarsveld, F.A. van. The Afrikaners interpretation. Cape Town, 1964.

Afr 8175.20.4 Jaarsveld, F.A. van. The awakening of Afrikaner nationalism, 1868-1881. Cape Town, 1961.

Afr 9093.10 Jaarsveld, F.A. van. Die eenheidstrewe van die republikeinse Afrikaners. Johannesburg, 1951.

Afr 8057.5.5 Jaarsveld, F.A. van. Lewende verlede. Johannesburg, 1962.

Afr 8175.20 Jaarsveld, F.A. van. Die ontwaking van die afrikaanse nasionale bewussyn. Johannesburg, 1957.

Afr 8089.66.20 Jaarsveld, Floris. Die Republiek van Suid-Afrika. Johannesburg, 1966.

Afr 8089.61.5 Jaarsveld, Floris Albertus. Illustrated history for senior certificate. Johannesburg, 1961.

Afr 3180.5.5 Jabarti, Abd Al-Rahman. Egipet v period ekspeditsii Bonaparta (1798-1801). Moscow, 1962.

Afr 8687.245.5 Jabava, N. The Ochre people. N.Y., 1963.

Afr 8678.24.2 Jabavu, D.D.T. The black problem. 2d ed. Lovedale, 1921.

Afr 8045.14 Jabavu, D.D.T. Native disabilities in South Africa. Lovedale, 1932.

Afr 8678.24.7 Jabavu, Davidson Don Tengo. The black problem. N.Y., 1969.

Afr 8687.245 Jabavu, N. Drawn in colour. London, 1960.

Afr 6535.14 Jack, E.M. On the Congo frontier. London, 1914.

Afr 8667.30 Jackmann, S.B. The numbered day. London, 1954.

Afr 8687.245.10 Jackson, Albert. Trader on the veld. Cape Town, 1958.

Afr 855.5 Jackson, E.L. St. Helena, the historic island. N.Y., 1905.

Afr 6390.20 Jackson, F.J. Early days in East Africa. London, 1930.

Afr 1068.17 Jackson, G.A. Algiers...a complete picture of the Barbary states. London, 1817.

Afr 3745.60 Jackson, H.C. Behind the modern Sudan. London, 1955.

Afr 3675.25 Jackson, H.C. The fighting Sudanese. London, 1954.

Afr 3718.15 Jackson, H.C. Osman Digna. London, 1926.

Afr 4180.4.5 Jackson, H.C. Tooth of fire. Oxford, 1912.

Afr 4070.57 Jackson, Henry Cecil. Sudan days and ways. N.Y., 1954.

Afr 6283.11 Jackson, I.C. Advance in Africa. London, 1956.

Afr 1608.09.3 Jackson, J.G. An account...empire of Morocco. Philadelphia, 1810.

Afr 1608.09.2 Jackson, J.G. An account...empire of Morocco. 2d ed. London, 1811.

Afr 1608.20 Jackson, J.G. An account of Timbuctoo and Housa. London, 1820.

Afr 635.35 Jackson, John G. Ethiopia and the origin of civilization. N.Y., 1939.

Afr 3708.14 Jackson, Louis. Our Caughnawagas in Egypt. Montreal, 1885.

Afr 8289.13 Jackson, M.C. A soldier's diary, South Africa 1899-1901. London, 1913.

Afr 659.42 Jackson, Mabel V. European powers and south-east Africa. London, 1942.

Afr 2030.463.30 Jacob, A. D'une Algérie à l'autre. Paris, 1963.

Afr 109.66.10 Jacob, Ernest Gerhard. Grundzüge der Geschichte Afrikas. Darmstadt, 1966.

Afr 5874.7 Jacob de Cordemoy, H. Etude sur l'Ile de la Réunion. Marseille, 1904.

Afr 8338.326 Jacob de Villiers Roos, 1869-1940. (Kock, Willem J. de.) Kaapstad, 1958.

Afr 8659.58.5 Jacob van Reenen and the Grosvenor expedition of 1790-1791. (Kirby, Percival Robson.) Johannesburg, 1958.

Afr 608.62 Jacobs, A. L'Afrique nouvelle. Paris, 1862.

Afr 6890.2 Jacobsen, Axel. Paa Afrikas vilkaar. København, 1951.

Afr 11465.14.150 Jacobson, Dan. Beggar my neighbour, short stories. London, 1964.

Afr 11465.14.160 Jacobson, Dan. The beginners. N.Y., 1966.

Afr 11465.14.130 Jacobson, Dan. Evidence of love, a novel. 1st ed. Boston, 1960.

Afr 11465.14.110 Jacobson, Dan. A long way from London. London, 1958.

Afr 11465.14.100 Jacobson, Dan. The price of diamonds. London, 1957.

Afr 11465.14.100.2 Jacobson, Dan. The price of diamonds. 1st ed. N.Y., 1958.

Afr 11465.14.21 Jacobson, Dan. Through the wilderness, and other stories. N.Y., 1968.

Afr 11465.14.140 Jacobson, Dan. Time of arrival, and other essays. London, 1962.

Afr 11465.14.120 Jacobson, Dan. The Zulu and the zeide. 1st ed. Boston, 1959.

Afr 8685.10F Jacobson, Evelyn. The cape coloured. Rondebosch, 1945.

Afr 4430.27 Jacoby, C.M. On special mission to Abyssinia. N.Y., 1933.

Afr 5342.10 Jacolliot, L. La Côte-d'Ivoire, l'homme des deserts. Paris, 1877.
Afr 590.58 Jacques de Dixmude. (Verhoeven, J.C.M.) Bruxelles, 1929.
Afr 2731.21 Jacques Faugère le Saharien. (Pagés, Louis.) Nérac, 1967.
Afr 1026.4 Jacqueton, G. Les archives espagnoles du gouvernement de l'Algérie. Alger, 1894.
Afr 1570.24 Jacquin, P. L'action française au Maroc. Paris, 1911.
Afr 2748.47 Jacquot, Felix. Expédition du général Cavaignac dans le Sahara algérien en avril et mai 1847. Paris, 1849.
Afr 8292.55 Jacson, M. The record of a regiment of the line. London, 1908.
Afr 13305.5 Jadot, Joseph. Les écrivains africains du Congo belge et du Ruanda-Urundi. Bruxelles, 1959.
Afr 608.91.3 Jaeger, F. Afrika. 3. Aufl. Leipzig, 1928.
Afr 6979.65.5 Jaeger, Friedrich Robert. Geographische Landschaften Südwestafrikas. Windhoek, 1965.
Afr 6887.8 Jaeger, Fritz. Forschungen in den Hochregionen des Kilimand. Berlin, 1909.
Afr 6879.07F Jaeger, Fritz. Das Hochland der Riesenkrater...Deutsch-Ostafrika. Berlin, 1911.
Afr 4700.38.10 Jaeger, N. Diritto di Roma nelle terre africane. Padova, 1938.
Afr 699.28 Jaelson, F.S. Eastern Africa to-day. London, 1928.
Afr 8687.42 Jaff, Fay. They came to South Africa. Cape Town, 1963.
Afr 4718.97 Jaffanel, C. de. Les Italiens en Erythrie. Paris, 1897.
Afr 7815.37 Les Jaga et les Bayaka du Kwango. (Plancquaert, M.) Bruxelles, 1932.
Afr 6903.12 Jager, J. de. South-west Africa. Pretoria, 1964.
Afr 10675.47.171 Jagua Nana; a novel. (Ekwensi, Cyprian.) Greenwich, Conn., 1969.
Afr 10675.47.160 Jagua Nana. (Ekwensi, Cyprian.) London, 1961.
Afr 10002.1 Jahn, Janheinz. A bibliography of Neo-African literature from Africa, America and the Carribean. London, 1965.
Afr 6095.360.5 Jahn, Janheinz. Durch afrikanische Türen. 1.Aufl. Düsseldorf, 1960.
Afr 10005.3 Jahn, Janheinz. Geschichte der neoafrikanischen Literatur. Düsseldorf, 1966.
Afr 10018.2 Jahn, Janheinz. Das junge Afrika. Wien, 1963.
Afr 609.58.10 Jahn, Janheinz. Muntu. Düsseldorf, 1958.
Afr 609.58.12 Jahn, Janheinz. Muntu. London, 1961.
Afr 10005.3.1 Jahn, Janheinz. Neo-African literature. N.Y., 1969.
Afr 679.62 Jahn, Janheinz. Through African doors. N.Y., 1962.
Afr 6194.22 Jahoda, Gustav. White man. London, 1961.
Afr 8135.8 Ein Jahrhundert voller Unrecht. (Reitz, F.W.) Berlin, 1900.
Afr 8378.331 The jail diary of Albie Sachs. (Sachs, Albert.) London, 1966.
Afr 810.7 Jaime, G. De Koulikoro à Tombouctou. Paris, 1894.
Afr 618.10 Jakt- och faengst metoder bland afrikanska folk. (Lindblom, G.) Stockholm, 1925-26.
Afr 1769.20 Jalade, Max. Mohammed ben Youssef. Paris, 1956.
Afr 3038.12 Jalal, E.D. Le système unicaméral. Genève, 1963.
Afr 6390.90 Jambo effendi: seven years with the King's African Rifles. (Grahame, Iain.) London, 1966.
Afr 6535.66 Jambo Uganda. (Julsrud, Harald G.) Oslo, 1966.
Afr 628.238 James, C.L.R. A history of Negro revolt. London, 1938.
Afr 4968.85 James, F.L. Journey through the Somali country. London, 1885.
Afr 4968.88 James, F.L. The unknown hour of Africa. London, 1888.
Afr 3978.83.4 James, F.L. The wild tribes of the Soudan. London, 1883.
Afr 8659.43.5 James, S. South of the Congo. London, 1944.
Afr 8252.228.10 James Barry Munnik Hertzog. (Pirow, Oswald.) London, 1958.
Afr 6541.3 James Hannington, bishop and martyr; the story of a noble life. (Michael, Charles D.) London, 1910.
Afr 718.12 Jameson, J.S. Forschungen und Erlebnisse im dunkelsten Africa. Hamburg, 1891.
Afr 718.11 Jameson, J.S. Story of the rear column. London, 1890.
Afr 608.30 Jameson, R. Narrative of discovery and adventure in Africa. Edinburgh 1830.
Afr 608.30.2 Jameson, R. Narrative of discovery and adventure in Africa. N.Y., 1836.
Afr 8283.20 The Jameson raid. (Hale, Hugh M.) London, 1930.
Afr 8283.24 The Jameson raid. (Moggridge, Ann.) Cape Town, 1960.
Afr 8283.21 The Jameson raid. (Van der Poel, Jean.) Cape Town, 1951.
Afr 8283.22 Jameson's heroic charge. Johannesburg, 1896.
Afr 8283.23 Jameson's raid. (Pakenham, E.H.P.) London, 1960.
Afr 9704.1 Jamieson, Gladys. Zambia contrasts. London, 1965.
Afr 810.8 Jamieson, R. An appeal...Niger expedition and sequel. London, 1840-43.
Afr 550.8.35 Jammes, F. Lavigerie. Paris, 1927.
Afr 8252.341.50 Jan Christian Smuts. (Scott, J.A.S.) Cape Town, 1955.
Afr 8252.341.45 Jan Christian Smuts. (Smuts, J.C.) London, 1952.
Afr 8252.341.47 Jan Christian Smuts. (Smuts, J.C.) N.Y., 1952.
Afr 8315.6 Jan Hamilton's march. (Churchill, W.S.) London, 1900.
Afr 8687.230 Jan Hofmeyer. (Macdonald, Tom.) London, 1948.
Afr 8252.341.21 Jan Smuts, a biography. (Crafford, F.) Garden City, 1944.
Afr 8252.341.20 Jan Smuts, a biography. 1st ed. (Crafford, F.S.) N.Y., 1943.
Afr 8252.341.15 Jan Smuts. (Levi, N.) London, 1917.
Cg Afr 8110.3.5 Jan van Riebeeck. (Leipoldt, C.L.) London, 1936.
Afr 8110.3.30 Jan van Riebeeck. (Nederlandsch Genootschap voor Geslacht, The Hague.) 's-Gravenhage, 1952.
Afr 8110.3.35 Jan van Riebeeck en zijn tijd. (Godee Molsbergen, Everhardus Cornelis.) Amsterdam, 1937.
Afr 5993.6 Janikowski, L. L'île de Fernando Poo. Paris, 1886.
Afr 4559.30.15 Jannasch, Hans. Im Schatten des Negus. Berlin, 1930.
Afr 8659.30.20 Jannasch, Hans. Unter Buren, Briten, Bantus. Berlin, 193-.
Afr 810.12 Jannequin, C. Voyage de Lybie. Paris, 1643.
Afr 2308.22 Janon, R. Hommes de peine et filles de joie. Alger, 1936.
Afr 4559.35.18 Jansen, P.G. Abissinia di oggi. 8a ed. Milano, 1935.
Afr 8838.2 Jansenville yesterday and today. (Fourie, S.) Jansenville, 1956.
Afr 1258.16.5 Janson, William. A view of the present condition of the states of Barbary. London, 1816.
Afr 7540.40A Janssens, E. J'étais le général Janssens. Bruxelles, 1961.
Afr 6225.16 January 15, before and after. (Nigeria, Eastern. Ministry of Information.) Enugu, 1967.
Afr 4937.10 Jardine, D. The Mad Mullah of Somaliland. London, 1923.
Afr 6143.54 Jarrett, H.R. A geography of Sierra Leone and Gambia. London, 1954.
Afr 6143.54.2 Jarrett, H.R. A geography of Sierra Leone and Gambia. Rev. ed. London, 1964.
Afr 7580.25 Jarschel, Fritz. Lumumba. Kreuzweingarten/Rhld., 1965.

Afr 3979.38 Jarvis, C.S. Desert and delta. London, 1938.
Afr 3979.42.13 Jarvis, C.S. Scattered shots. London, 1949.
Afr 4050.36.5 Jarvis, C.S. Three deserts. London, 1936.
Afr 3069.55 Jarvis, H.W. Pharaoh to Farouk. London, 1955.
Afr 1570.30 Jary, G. Les intérêts de la France au Maroc. Paris, 1911.
Afr 1635.4 Jary, Georges. Les derniers berberes. Paris, 1912.
Afr 7180.15 Jaspert, Fritz. Die Völkerstämme Mittel-Angolas. Frankfurt a.M., 1930.
Afr 7175.23 Jaspert, Willem. Through unknown Africa. London, 1929.
Afr 3310.70 Jassen, Raul. Nasser. Buenos Aires, 1961.
Afr 5485.15 Jaulin, Robert. La Mort sara, l'ordre de la vie ou la pensée de la mort au Tchad. Paris, 1967.
Afr 1990.16 Javary, A. Etudes sur le gouvernement. Paris, 1855.
Afr 2208.95.3A Je deviens colon. (Leroux, H.) Paris, 1895.
Afr 2208.98.8 Je deviens colon. 2e ed. (Leroux, H.) Paris, 1895.
Afr 2208.95.5 Je deviens colon. 4e ed. (Leroux, H.) Paris, 1895.
Afr 2762.5 Jean, C. Les Touareg du sud-est l'Air. Leur rôle dans la politique saharienne. Paris, 1909.
Afr 5465.3 Jean, S. Les Langbas, population d'Oubangui-Chari. Paris, 1961.
Htn Afr 1606.31* Jean Armand, Called Mustapha. Voyages d'Afrique faicts par le commandement du roy. Paris, 1631.
Afr 8145.30 Jean Pierre Pellissier van Bethulie. (Pellissier, S.H.) Pretoria, 1956.
Afr 5406.186 Jeannest, Charles. Quatre années au Congo. Paris, 1886.
Afr 1609.07.2 Jeannot, G. Etude sociale...sur le Maroc. Dijon, 1907.
Afr 7803.48 Jeanroy, V. Vingt-cinq ans de mission au Congo. Bruxelles, 1923.
Afr 2030.175 Jeanson, Colette. L'Algérie hors la loi. Paris, 1955.
Afr 2223.962.5 Jeanson, F. La révolution algérienne. Milano, 1962.
Afr 555.132 Jenkins, David E. They led the way. Cape Town, 1966.
Afr 8155.7 Jenkinson, T.B. Amazulu. The Zulus, their history. London, 1882.
Afr 6275.112 Jennings, J.H. A geography of the eastern provinces of Nigeria. Cambridge, 1966.
Afr 4937.1 Jennings, J.W. With the Abyssinians in Somaliland. London, 1905.
Afr 210.63.30 Jennings, W. Democracy in Africa. Cambridge, Eng., 1963.
Afr 8659.61.5 Jenny, H. Afrika ist nicht nur schwarz. Düsseldorf, 1961.
Afr 4559.57.5 Jenny, Hans. Athiopien, Land im Aufbruch. Stuttgart, 1957.
Afr 6919.66.8 Jenny, Hans. Südwestafrika. 3. Aufl. Stuttgart, 1968.
Afr 115.100 Jensen, Adolf E. Im Lande des Gada. Stuttgart, 1936.
Afr 115.100 Jensen, Aksel V. Afrika, opdagelsesrejserne. København, 1949.
Afr 6926.32 Jenssen, H.E. Chronik von Deutsch-Südwestafrika. Windhoek, 1966.
Afr 7809.52.10 Jentgen, P. Les frontières du Congo belge. Bruxelles, 1952.
Afr 7933.2 Jentgen, P. Les frontiéres du Ruanda-Urundi et le régime international de Tutelle. Bruxelles, 1957.
Afr 7549.37 Jentgen, Pierre. La terre belge du Congo. Bruxelles, 1937.
Afr 45.63.5 Jeol, M. La reforme de la justice en Afrique noire. Paris, 1963.
Afr 5070.5 Jeol, Michel. Cours de droit administratif mauritanien. Bordeaux, 1964.
Afr 3725.3.25 Jephson, A.J.M. Emin Pasha and the rebellion at the equator. N.Y., 1891.
Afr 8210.11 Jeppe, Carl. The kaleidoscopic Transvaal. London, 1906.
Afr 49724.100 Jeqe, the bodyservant of King Tshaka (Insila Ka Tshaka). (Dube, John.) Lovedale, 1951.
Afr 5993.17 Jeran, Manuel de. Sintesis geografica de Fernando Poo. Madrid, 1962.
Afr 3230.5 Jerrold, W.B. Egypt under Ismail Pacha. London, 1879.
Afr 4259.63 Jesman, Czeslaw. The Ethiopian paradox. London, 1963.
Afr 4396.15 Jesman, Czeslaw. The Russians in Ethiopia. London, 1958.
Afr 7175.36 Jessen, O. Reisen und Forschungen in Angola. Berlin, 1936.
Afr 7324.4 Jessett, M.G. Key to South Africa, Delagoa Bay. London, 1899.
Afr 5765.30 Les Jesuites à Madagascar au XIXe siècle. v.1-2. (Boudou, Adrien.) Paris, 1940. 2v.
Afr 7803.32 Les jésuites et les fermes-chapelles, à propos d'un débat récent. (Thibaut, Emile.) Bruxelles 1911.
Afr 7125.2 Jesuits. Relações de Angola. Coimbra, 1934.
Htn Afr 4350.2.6* Jesuits. Letters from Missions. (Abyssinia). Carta do patriarcha de Ethiopia. Lisboa, 1631.
Afr 4350.2.5 Jesuits. Letters from Missions. (Abyssinia). Carta do patriarcha de Ethiopia. Lisboa, 1631.
Htn Afr 4349.3* Jesuits. Letters from Missions. (Abyssinia). Histoire d'Ethiopie, en l'année 1626. Paris, 1629.
Afr 4350.2.3 Jesuits. Letters from Missions. (Abyssinia). Relaçam geral do estado da Christandade de Ethiopia. Lisboa, 1628.
Afr 7369.60 The jet lighthouse. (Welch, Galbraith.) London, 1960.
Afr 7540.40A J'étais le général Janssens. (Janssens, E.) Bruxelles, 1961.
Afr 1635.30 J'étais le médecin de cent mille Berbères. (Dobo, Nicolas.) Paris, 1964.
Afr 626.138 Jeune Afrique mobilisable. (Bourgaignie, G.E.) Paris, 1964.
Afr 2025.29 Le jeune Algérien. (Abbas, F.) Paris, 1931.
Afr 2030.220 Jeunesse de France en Algérie. (Darboy, Marcel.) Paris, 1960.
Afr 1571.17.90 La jeunesse de Lyautey. (Roux, F. de.) Paris, 1952.
Afr 3305.20 La jeunesse intellectuelle d'Egypte. (Makarius, R.) Paris, 1960.
Afr 5243.174.5 Jeux dogons. Thèse complementaire. (Griaule, Marcel.) Paris, 1938.
Afr 6193.54 Jevoch, Michael. Voraussetzungen und Möglichkeiten einer industriellen Entwicklung im Ghana. Hamburg, 1907.
Afr 580.5 The Jews of Africa. (Mendelssohn, S.) London, 1920.
Afr 1390.7.5F Jimenez de la Espada, Marcos. La guerra del Moro a fines del siglo XV. Ceuta, 1940.
Afr 10831.5.110 Jingala. (Kayira, Legson.) Harlow, 1969.
Afr 3993.8 Jiritli, Ali. The structure of modern industry in Egypt. Cairo, 1948.
Afr 5257.5 Joalland. Le drame de Dankori. Paris, 1930.
Afr 2208.50 Joanne, A. Voyage en Afrique. Ixelles, 1850.
Afr 2208.7 Joanne, P. Algérie et Tunisie. Paris, 1911.
Afr 6118.2.7 Jobson, R. The golden trade, 1620-21. London, 1933.
Htn Afr 6118.2* Jobson, R. The golden trade. London, 1623.
Afr 8369.53 Joekoms, Jan. When Malan goes. Johannesburg, 1953.
Afr 6392.10 Joelson, F.S. Rhodesia and East Africa. London, 1958.
Afr 6879.20 Joelson, F.S. The Tanganyika territory. London, 1920.
Afr 3310.65 Joesten, Joachim. Nasser. London, 1960.
Afr 2030.464.15 Joesten, Joachim. The new Algeria. Chicago, 1964.

Afr 2025.30   Joesten, Joachim. The red hand. London, 1962.
Afr 5227.10.5   Joffre, J.J.C. My march to Timbuctoo. London, 1915.
Afr 5227.10   Joffre, J.J.C. My march to Timbuctoo. N.Y., 1915.
Afr 1753.10.4   Os jogos floraes de 1923 em Ceuta. (Dornellas, Affonso de.) Lisboa, 1924.
Afr 8125.15   Johannes Frederick Kirsten oor die toestand van die Kaapkolonie in 1795. (Mueller, C.F.J.) Pretoria, 1960.
Afr 9165.42.10F   Johannesburg, city of achievement. (Johannesburg Publicity Association.) Johannesburg, 1936.
Afr 9165.42.55   Johannesburg. City Council. The city of Johannesburg. 2. ed. Cape Town, 1956.
Afr 9165.82   Johannesburg. Non-European Affairs Department. Cultural change in Soweto. Johannesburg, 1965.
Afr 9165.42.85F   Johannesburg. Non-European Affairs Department. Report of the manager. Johannesburg. 1957+
Afr 8657.90.5   Johannesburg. Public Library. Bibliography of Le Vaillant's "Voyages" and "Oiseaux d'Afrique." Johannesburg, 1962.
Afr 8152.73.5   Johannesburg. Public Library. General index of the first edition of King's Campaigning in Kaffirland. Johannesburg, 1958.
Afr 8152.76.2   Johannesburg. Public Library. General index to Narrative of the Kaffir war. Johannesburg, 1960.
Afr 8095.70.2   Johannesburg. Public Library. Index to items of South African interest in Dr. A.W. Burton's sparks from the border anvil. Johannesburg, 1958.
Afr 8028.145F   Johannesburg. Public Library. Index to South African periodicals. Johannesburg. 1,1940+ 7v.
Afr 10003.5   Johannesburg. Public Library. A list of theatre performances in Johannesburg, 1887-1897. Johannesburg, 1964.
Afr 8673.19   Johannesburg. Public Library. Some Africana coloured prints and the originals from which they may have been made. Johannesburg, 1963.
Afr 8331.20F   Johannesburg. Public Library. Southern African municipal publications. Johannesburg, 1965.
Afr 11053.2   Johannesburg. University of the Witwatersrand. Songs and war cries. Johannesburg, 1936.
Afr 8010.5   Johannesburg. University of the Witwatersrand. African Studies Programme. Occasional paper. 2,1967+
Afr 28.8F   Johannesburg. University of the Witwatersrand. Gubbins Library. Preliminary list of Africana, mainly from the Gubbins Library. Johannesburg, 1930.
Afr 9165.42.30   Johannesburg and the art of self-government. (Maud, J.P.R.) Johannesburg, 1937.
Afr 11780.31.100   Johannesburg Friday. (Segal, A.) N.Y., 1954.
Afr 8283.14   Johannesburg in arms, 1895-96. (Thomas, C.G.) London, 1896.
Afr 9165.42.10F   Johannesburg Publicity Association. Johannesburg, city of achievement. Johannesburg, 1936
Afr 9165.42   Johannesburg Publicity Association. Johannesburg's 40th birthday, Sept. 22, 1926. Johannesburg, 1926.
Afr 9165.42   Johannesburg's 40th birthday, Sept. 22, 1926. (Johannesburg Publicity Association.) Johannesburg, 1926.
Afr 6470.106   John Ainsworth. (Ainsworth, J.D.) London, 1959.
Afr 8279.01   John Bull's crime. (Davis, W.) N.Y., 1901.
Afr 4430.36.5   John Hay of Ethiopia. (MacLean, R.) N.Y., 1936.
Afr 8252.6   John Mackenzie. (Mackenzie, W.D.) N.Y., 1902.
Afr 9525.877   John White of Mashonaland. (Andrews, Charles.) London, 1935.
Afr 8252.9.20   John William Colenso. (Fraser, Barbara Davidson.) Cape Town, 1952.
Afr 8252.9.15   John William Colenso. (Hinchliff, Peter Bingham.) London, 1964.
Afr 3986.962.5   Johne, Alfred. Die Industrialisierungspolitik des Ägypten unter besonderer Berücksichtigung. Berlin, 1962.
Afr 8050.22   Johns, S.W. Marxism-Leninism in a multiracial environment. Thesis. Cambridge, 1965.
Afr 6153.10   Johnson, A.F. Books about Ghana. Accra, 1961.
Afr 6390.73   Johnson, Asa Helen. Four years in paradise. London, 1941.
Afr 8252.248   Johnson, F. Great days, the autobiography of an empire pioneer. London, 1940.
Afr 8289.00.30   Johnson, H. With our soldiers at the front. London, 1907.
Afr 6879.02   Johnson, Harry. Night and morning in dark Africa. London, 1902.
Afr 725.9   Johnson, J.B. Tramp around the Mountains of the Moon and through the back gate of the Congo state. London, 1908.
Afr 6455.39   Johnson, M. Camera trails in Africa. N.Y., 1924.
Afr 6455.39.5   Johnson, M. Safari. N.Y., 1928.
Afr 6196.29   Johnson, M. The Salaga papers. v.1-2. Legon, 1967-
Afr 6879.29A   Johnson, M.E. Lion, African adventure with the king of beasts. N.Y., 1929.
Afr 7809.31.5   Johnson, Martin. Congorilla. N.Y., 1931.
Afr 609.35.9   Johnson, Martin. Over African jungles. N.Y., 1935.
Afr 3315.85   Johnson, Paul. Suez war. London, 1957.
Afr 6218.1.5   Johnson, Samuel. The history of the Yorubas; from the earliest times to the beginning of the British protectorate. 1st ed. London, 1966.
Afr 6218.1   Johnson, Samuel. The history of the Yorubas from the earliest times to the beginning of the British protectorate. London, 1921.
Afr 6146.5   Johnson, T.S. The story of a mission, the Sierra Leone church. London, 1953.
Afr 4070.14   Johnson, W. Fliegende blätter...Reise in Nord-Ost-Afrika...1847-49. Stuttgart, 1851.
Afr 775.10   Johnson, W.P. Nyasa, the great water. London, 1922.
Afr 9854.10   Johnson, William Percival. My African reminiscences. Westminster, 1926.
Afr 8687.248   Johnson of Nyasaland. (Barnes, Bertram Herbert.) Westminster, 1933.
Afr 4558.44   Johnston, C. Travels in southern Abyssinia. London, 1844. 2v.
Afr 505.5   Johnston, H. Britain across the seas - Africa. London, n.d.
Afr 7809.08   Johnston, H. George Grenfell and the Congo. London, 1908. 2v.
Afr 7459.06   Johnston, H. Liberia. London, 1906. 2v.
Afr 4095.18   Johnston, H. The Nile quest. N.Y., 1903.
Afr 6535.5.2   Johnston, H. The Uganda Protectorate. London, 1902. 2v.
Afr 6535.5A   Johnston, H. The Uganda Protectorate. N.Y., 1902. 2v.
Afr 30115.2   Johnston, H.A.S. A selection of Hausa stories. Oxford, 1966.
Afr 9548.3   Johnston, H.H. British central Africa. N.Y., 1897.

Afr 9548.5   Johnston, H.H. British central Africa. 2. ed. London, 1898.
Afr 590.26   Johnston, H.H. The history of a slave. London, 1889.
Afr 108.99   Johnston, H.H. A history of the colonization of Africa. Cambridge, 1899.
Afr 108.99.4A   Johnston, H.H. A history of the colonization of Africa. Cambridge, 1905.
Afr 108.99.6   Johnston, H.H. A history of the colonization of Africa. Cambridge, 1913.
Afr 6887.3   Johnston, H.H. The Kilima-njaro expedition. London, 1885.
Afr 9558.35   Johnston, H.H. Livingstone and exploration of central Africa. London, 1891.
Afr 628.210   Johnston, H.H. The Negro in the new world. London, 1910.
Afr 109.11   Johnston, H.H. The opening up of Africa. London, n.d.
Afr 109.11.5   Johnston, H.H. The opening up of Africa. N.Y., 1911.
Afr 8039.14   Johnston, H.H. Pioneers in South Africa. London, 1914.
Afr 7808.84   Johnston, H.H. The river Congo. London, 1884.
Afr 6095.21   Johnston, Harry. Pioneers in West Africa. London, 1912.
Afr 6095.369   Johnston, Harry Hamilton. Pioneers in West Africa. N.Y., 1969.
Afr 6292.82   Johnston, Hugh Anthony St. The Fulani Empire of Sokoto. London, 1967.
Afr 718.31   Johnston, J. Reality versus romance in south central Africa. London, 1893.
Afr 718.31.2   Johnston, J. Reality versus romance in South Central Africa. 2nd ed. London, 1969.
Afr 608.84   Johnston, K. Africa. 3d ed. London, 1884.
Afr 6538.38   Joint report of the Standing Finance Committee and the Development and Welfare Committee on post-war development. 2d ed. (Uganda. Standing Finance Committee.) Entebbe, 1945.
Afr 28.58   Joint Secretariat C.C.T.A./C.S.A. Inventory of economic studies concerning Africa South of the Sahara. London, 1960.
Afr Doc 2521.5   Joint sitting of the House of Chiefs and House of Assembly debates. Official report. (Nigeria, Western. House of Chiefs.) Ibadan. 1,1960+
Afr 3026.3   Jolowicz, Hermann. Bibliotheca Ägyptiaca. Leipzig, 1858.
Afr 3026.4   Jolowicz, Hermann. Bibliotheca Ägyptiaca. Supplement I. Leipzig, 1861.
Afr 1432.17   Joly, A. Historia critica de la guerra...en 1859-60. Madrid, 1910.
Afr 1609.48.5   Joly, Fernand. Geographie du Maroc. Paris, 1949.
Afr 3215.5   Jomard, E.F. Coup-d'oeil...sur l'état présent de l'Egypte. Paris, 1836
Afr 3822.11   Jomard, Edme Francois. Observations sur le voyage au Darfour. Paris, 1845.
Afr 6470.250   Jomo Kenyatta. (Delf, George.) London, 1961.
Afr 6470.250.10   Jomo Kenyatta. 1st ed. (Delf, George.) Garden City, 1961.
Afr 7809.57.5   Jonchleere, K. Kongo, met het blote oog. Amsterdam, 1959.
Afr 4259.35.21   Jones, A.H. A history of Ethiopia. Oxford, 1955.
Afr 4259.35.23   Jones, A.H. A history of Ethiopia. Oxford, 1960.
Afr 115.110   Jones, Arthur M. Africa and Indonesia. Leiden, 1964.
Afr 608.75   Jones, C.H. Africa, the history of exploration. N.Y., 1875.
Afr 2223.925   Jones, C.L. Algeria, a commercial handbook. Washington, 1925.
Afr 115.70   Jones, Ch. H. Famous explorers and adventures in Africa. v.1-2. N.Y., 1881. 2v.
Afr 555.9.65   Jones, David Picton. After Livingstone. The work of a pioneer missionary in Central Africa. London, 1968.
Afr 9769.64   Jones, G. Britain and Nyasaland. London, 1964.
Afr 679.36   Jones, G. The earth goddess. London, 1936.
Afr 6218.18   Jones, G.I. The trading states of the oil rivers. London, 1963.
Afr 609.60.55   Jones, H.W. Africa in perspective. London, 1960.
Afr 6498.30   Jones, Herbert G. Uganda in transformation, 1876-1926. London, 1926.
Afr 9439.53.5   Jones, Neville. Rhodesian genesis. Bulawayo, 1953.
Afr 6176.30.80   Jones, Peter. Kwame Nkrumah and Africa. London, 1965.
Afr 8847.81   Jones, S.M. Personal accounts of visitors to Simon's Town, 1770-1899. Cape Town, 1964.
Afr 609.56   Jones, Schuyler. Under the African sun. London, 1956.
Afr 6298.183   Jones-Quarley, K.A.B. A life of Azikiwe. Baltimore, Maryland, 1965.
Afr 2929.64   Jongmans, D.G. Libie, land van de dorst. Meppel, 1964.
Afr 7565.12   Jooris, J. L'acte général de la Conférence de Berlin. Bruxelles, 1885.
Afr 109.61.35   Joos, L.C.D. Brève histoire à l'Afrique noire. v.1-2. Issy-les-Moulineaux, 1961-64. 2v.
Afr 8089.66.15   Joos, Louis C.D. Histoire de l'Afrique du Sud. Paris, 1966.
Afr 2749.61   Joos, Louis D. Through the Sahara to the Congo. London, 1961.
Afr 6176.43   Jopp, Keith. Ghana, 1957. Accra, 1957.
Afr 5765.8.5   Jordaan, Bee. Splintered cruicifix; early pioneers for Christendom on Madagascar and the Cape of Good Hope. Cape Town, 1969.
Afr 6298.785   Jordan, John P. Bishop Shanahan of Southern Nigeria. Dublin, 1949.
Afr 8225.10   Jordan, Robert Alan. The Transvaal War, 1808-1881; a bibliography. Johannesburg, 1969.
Afr 6060.69   Jordan, Robert Smith. Government and power in West Africa. London, 1969.
Afr 7459.12   Jore, L. La république de Liberia. Paris, 1912.
Afr 5055.65.5   Jore, Leonce Alphonse Noel Henri. Les établissements français, sur la côte occidentale d'Afrique de 1758 à 1809. Paris, 1965.
Afr 2209.66.5   Joret, Madeleine. L'Afrique en flânant, de paris à Tamanrasset. Paris, 1966.
Afr 8278.97.5   Jorissen, E.J.P. Transvaalische herinneringen 1876-96. Amsterdam, 1897.
Htn   Afr 1403.5.5*   Jornada de Africa. (Mendonca, Jeronymo de.) Lisboa, 1607.
Afr 1403.5   Jornada de Africa. (Mendonca, Jeronymo de.) Lisboa, 1785.
Afr 1403.3   Jornada de Africa por el rey Don Sebastian. (Mesa, S. de.) Barcelona, 1630.
Afr 555.2.50   Jornadas e outros trabalhos do missionario Barroso. (Cunha, A.) Lisboa, 1938.
Afr 14663.5   Jornalismo de Angola. (Lopo, Júlio de Castro.) Luanda, 1964.
Afr 8369.63   Joseph, Helen. If this be treason. London, 1963.
Afr 8678.343   Joseph, Helen. Tomorrow's sun. London, 1966.
Afr 8678.343.1   Joseph, Helen. Tomorrow's sun. 1. ed. London, 1968.
Afr 8283.8.5   Joseph Chamberlain, conspirator of statesman. (Stead, W.J.) London, 1900.

Afr 8687.174.5   Joseph Doke. (Cursons, William E.) Johannesburg, 1929.

Afr 725.4.5   Joseph Thomson, African explorer. (Thomson, James B.) London, 1896.

Afr 9693.3   Josephine (pseud.). Tell me, Josephine. London, 1964.

Afr 8678.170   Joshi, Pranshankar. Apartheid in South Africa. Kimberley, 1950.

Afr 8685.27.7A   Joshi, Pranshankar S. The struggle for equality. Bombay, 1951.

Afr 8685.40   Joshi, Pranshankar S. The tyranny of colour. Durban, 1942.

Afr 8685.27.5   Joshi, Pranshankar S. Verdict on South Africa. Bombay, 1945.

Afr 8678.102   Joshi, Pranshankar Someshwar. Unrest in South Africa. Bombay, 1958.

Afr 6192.75   Joslin, Mike. Im Tempel der bösen Geister. Wiesbaden, 1959.

Afr 5749.62.5   Joubert, Elsa. Suid van die wind. Kaapstad, 1962.

Afr 7309.64.5   Joubert, Elsa (pseud.). Die staf van Monomotapa. Kaapstad, 1964.

Afr 5548.95.5   Joubert, J. La question de Madagascar. Paris, 1895.

Afr 8688.12   Joûbert, Joseph. Les armoiries de la République Sud-africaine. Paris, 1903.

Afr 5003.1   Joucla, E. Bibliographie de l'Afrique occidentale française. Paris, 1912.

Afr 2030.469   Jouhaud, Edmond. O mon pays perdu. Paris, 1969.

Afr 8250.8.5   Jourdan, P. Cecil Rhodes. London, 19- .

Afr 8250.8   Jourdan, P. Cecil Rhodes. London, 1911.

Afr 8250.8.2   Jourdan, P. Cecil Rhodes. London, 1911.

Afr 1607.53.4   Journaal Wegens de Rampspoedige Reys-Tocht van H.C. Steenis. Amsterdam, n.d.

Afr 3978.92.5   Journal, Kittar mountains, 1891. (Pretynian, H.E.) London, 1892.

Afr 2030.462.130A   Journal, 1955-62. (Feraoun, M.) Paris, 1962.

Afr 7568.23   Journal...tour in the Congo Free State. (Dorman, M.R.P.) Brussels, 1905.

Afr 3978.69.6   Journal...visit to Egypt, Constantinople. (Grey, W.) London, 1869.

Afr 10.1   Journal. (African Society.) London. 1901+ 65v.

Afr 6200.8   Journal. (Historical Society of Nigeria.) Ibadan. 1,1956+ 3v.

Afr 8110.3.15   Journal. (Riebeeck, Jan van.) Cape Town, 1952. 3v.

Afr 5890.5   Journal. (Seychelles Society.) Victoria. 5,1966+

Afr 19.14   Journal. (Société des Africanistes, Paris.) Paris. 1,1931+ 16v.

Afr 1258.18.8   A journal comprising an account of the loss of the brig Commerce. (Robbins, A.) Hartford, 1833.

Afr 1258.18   A journal comprising an account of the loss of the brig Commerce. 7 ed. (Robbins, A.) Hartford, 1818.

Afr 1258.18.2   A journal comprising an account of the loss of the brig Commerce. 8 ed. (Robbins, A.) Hartford, 1818.

Afr 1258.18.3   A journal comprising an account of the loss of the brig Commerce. 10 ed (Robbins, A.) Hartford, 1819.

Afr 1957.30   Journal de la prise d'Alger. (Matterer, Amable.) Paris, 1960.

Afr 5585.35   Le journal de Robert Lyall. (Lyall, R.) Tananarive, 1954.

Afr 3823.6   Journal de route de Charles Lemaire. (Lemaire, Charles.) Bruxelles, 1953.

Afr 2749.04   Journal de route d'un caporal de tirailleurs de la mission saharienne. (Guilleux, Charles.) Belfort, 1904.

Afr 4070.24   Journal de voyage...de Siout à El-Obeid. (Cuny, Charles.) Paris, 1863.

Afr Doc 7312.5F   Journal des debats. (Congo (Brazzaville). Assemblée Nationale.)

Afr 1018.2.5   Journal des travaux, 1878-1927. (Table générale). (Société de Géographie de la Province d'Oran.) Oran, 1898-1930. 3v.

Afr 1571.45   Journal du consulat général de France à Maroc. (France.) Casablanca, 1943.

Afr 3163.20A   Journal d'un bourgeois du Caire. (Ibn Iyas.) Paris, 1955. 2v.

Afr 1955.25   Journal d'un officier de l'armée d'Afrique. Paris, 1831.

Afr 2030.464.75   Journal d'un prêtre en Algérie. (Laparre, M. de.) Paris, 1964.

Afr 5480.260   Journal d'un safari au Tchad. (Scheid, T.) Bruxelles, 1960.

Afr 4558.35.5   Journal d'un séjour en Abyssinia. (Gobat, Samuel.) Paris, 1835.

Afr 5235.128.2   Journal d'un voyage à Temboctou et à Jenne, dans l'Afrique centrale. (Caillié, René.) Paris, 1965?

Afr 5235.128   Journal d'un voyage à Tembouctou. (Caillié, René.) Paris, 1830. 3v.

Afr 2208.57   Journal d'un voyage dans la province. (Duveyrier, H.) Paris, 1900.

Afr 2030.465.5   Journal d'une agonie. (Moinet, Bernard.) Paris, 1965.

Afr 2397.5   Journal d'une mère de famille pied-noir. (Dessagne, F.) Paris, 1962.

Afr 4050.1   Journal from Cairo to Mourzouk. (Horneman, F.K.) London, 1802.

Afr 555.22.5   Journaal gehouden van Port Elisabeth (Algoabaai) naar Reddersburg. (Beijer, J.) Kaapstad, 1862. 2 pam.

Afr 5078.18   Journal historique de Georges Dandin, 1777-1812. (Dandin, Georges.) Tananarive, 1939.

Afr 8658.76.3   Journal historique du voyage fait au cap de Bonne-Espérance. (Lacaille, N.L.) Paris, 1776.

Afr 6192.8   Journal of...visits to...Ashanti, Aku, and Dahomi. (Freeman, T.B.) London, 1844.

Afr 5235.54   The journal of a mission to the interior of Africa...1805. (Park, Mungo.) Philadelphia, 1815.

Afr 8808.48   Journal of a residence at Cape of Good Hope. (Bunbury, C.J.F.) London, 1848.

Afr 6168.7   Journal of a residence in Ashanti. (Dupuis, J.) London, 1824.

Afr 6168.7.2   Journal of a residence in Ashanti. 2d. ed. (Dupuis, J.) London, 1966.

Afr 1965.5   Journal of a residence in the Esmailla of Abd-el-Kader. (Scott.) London, 1842.

Afr 590.27   Journal of a slave-dealer. (Owen, Nicholas.) London, 1930.

Afr 590.77   The journal of a slave trader, John Neuton, 1750-1754. (Neuton, John.) London, 1962.

Afr 4558.34   Journal of a three years' residence in Abyssinia. (Gobat, Samuel.) London, 1834.

Afr 1608.78   Journal of a tour in Morocco. (Hooker, J.D.) London, 1878.

Afr 2208.47.3   Journal of a trip to the Algerine territory, 1837. (Lumsden, William.) Glasgow, 1847.

Afr 3978.22   Journal of a visit to some parts of Ethiopia. (Waddington, G.) London, 1822.

Afr 8658.15.5   Journal of a visit to South Africa in 1815 and 1816. (Latrole, Christian Ignatius.) Cape Town, 1969.

Htn   Afr 8808.18*   Journal of a visit to South Africa 1815-1816. (Latrobe, C.I.) London, 1818.

Afr 678.53   Journal of a voyage from Boston to the west coast of Africa. (Carnes, J.A.) London, 1853.

Afr 7315.4   Journal of a voyage performed in the Lion Extra Indiaman. (White, William.) London, 1800.

Afr 3978.51.11   Journal of a voyage up the Nile. Buffalo, 1851.

Afr 10.10   Journal of African administration. London. 1,1949+ 7v.

Afr 10.12   Journal of African and Asian studies. Delhi. 1,1967+

Afr 10.4   Journal of African history. London. 1,1960+ 6v.

Htn   Afr 678.45.3*   Journal of an African cruiser. (Bridge, H.) London, 1845.

Htn   Afr 678.45*   Journal of an African cruiser. (Bridge, H.) N.Y., 1845. 2 pam.

Htn   Afr 678.45.6*   Journal of an African cruiser. (Bridge, H.) N.Y., 1848.

Afr 678.45.5   Journal of an African cruiser. (Bridge, Horatio.) London, 1968.

Afr 1608.46.5   Journal of an expedition to court of Morocco in year 1846. (Hay, J.H.D.) Cambridge, Eng., 1848.

Afr 6275.4.5   Journal of an expedition to explore the course and termination of theNiger. (Lander, R.L.) N.Y., 1839.

Afr 810.1   Journal of an expedition to explore the Niger. (Lander, R.) London, 1832. 3v.

Afr 810.2   Journal of an expedition to explore the Niger. (Lander, R.) N.Y., 1837. 2v.

Afr 810.3   Journal of an expedition to explore the Niger. (Lander, R.) N.Y., 1839. 2v.

Afr 810.4   Journal of an expedition up the Niger. (Crowther, S.) London, 1855.

Afr 4095.6   Journal of discovery of source of the Nile. (Speke, J.H.) Edinburgh, 1863.

Afr 4095.6.3   Journal of discovery of source of the Nile. (Speke, J.H.) N.Y., 1864.

Afr 4095.6.10   Journal of discovery of source of the Nile. (Speke, J.H.) N.Y., 1868.

Afr 4210.5   Journal of Ethiopian studies. Addis Ababa. 1,1963+ 2v.

Afr 8656.85   Journal of his expedition to Namaqualand. (Stel, Simon van der.) London, 1932.

Afr 10.6   Journal of modern African studies. Cambridge, Eng. 1,1963+ 5v.

Afr 545.39   The journal of religion in Africa. Leiden. 1,1967+

Afr 6275.3   Journal of second expedition into interior of Africa. (Clapperton, Hugh.) London, 1829.

Afr 8292.15   The journal of the C.I.V. (City Imperial Volunteers) in South Africa. (Mackinnon, W.H.) London, 1901.

Afr 10004.5   Journal of the new African literature. Stanford, Calif. 1966+

Afr 8686.20   Journal of the Reverend George Champion. (Champion, George.) Cape Town, 1967.

Afr 3978.43   Journal of travels in Egypt. (Millard, D.) N.Y., 1843.

Afr 6192.8.3   Journal of various visits to the Kingdoms of Ashanti, Aku, and Dahomi in Western Africa. 3rd ed. (Freeman, T.B.) London, 1968.

Afr 7458.51.7   Journal of voyage to Liberia. (Fuller, T.) Baltimore, 1851.

Afr Doc 1406.5   Journal official du gouvernement egyptien. Cairo, 1909. 2v.

Afr 5400.7F   Journal officiel. (Union Douanière et Économique de l'Afrique Centrale.) Brazzaville. 1,1966+

Afr Doc 6812.5F   Journal officiel. Debats parlementaires. (Mali. Fédération. Assemblée Fédérale.)

Afr 609.36.5   Ein Journalist erzählt. (Nebel, Heinrich C.) Stuttgart, 1936.

Afr 555.145   Journals and papers. (Maples, C.) London, 1899.

Afr 3705.3A   Journals at Khartoum. (Gordon, C.G.) Boston, 1885.

Afr 4558.43.5   The journals of C.W. Isenberg and J.L. Krapt. (Isenberg, Karl Wilhelm.) London, 1968.

Afr 8658.69   The journals of Carl Mauch; his travels in the Transvaal and Rhodesia, 1869-1872. (Mauch, Karl.) Salisbury, 1969.

Afr 3705.3.5   The journals of Major General Gordon. (Gordon, C.G.) London, 1885.

Afr 4558.43   Journals of Messers Isenberg and Krape. London, 1843.

Htn   Afr 3979.13*   Journals of my African travels. (Blackburne, D.) Maidstone, 1913.

Afr 810.13   Journals of Schoen and S. Crowther...expedition up Niger. (Schoen, J.F.) London, 1842.

Afr 9488.92   Journals of the Mashonaland mission. (Knight-Bruce.) London, 1892.

Afr 10.8   Journées africaines. Louvain.

Afr 1485.6   Les journees de Casablanca. (Bourdon, G.) Paris, 1908.

Afr 7812.258   Journées d'Etudes Coloniales, Institut Universitaire des Territoires d'Outre Mer, Antwerp, 1957. Promotion de la société rurale du Congo belge et du Ruanda-Urundi. Bruxelles, 1958.

Afr 1490.11.9   Journées sanglantes de Fez. 4 ed. (Hubert-Jacques.) Paris, 1913.

Afr 9838.84.2   A journey in East Africa. (Pringle, M.) Edinburgh, 1886.

Afr 8095.84   Journey into yesterday, South African milestones in Europe. (Macnab, Roy Martin.) Cape Town, 1962.

Afr 3207.2   Journey of the late campaign in Egypt. (Walsh, T.) London, 1803.

Afr 4968.85   Journey through the Somali country. (James, F.L.) London, 1888.

Afr 5406.52.5   A journey to Ashango-land. (Duchaillu, Paul Belloni.) N.Y., 1867.

Afr 5406.52   A journey to Ashango-land. (Duchaillu, Paul Belloni.) N.Y., 1871.

Afr 718.9   Journey to Cazembe. (Lacerda e Almeida, F.J.M. de.) London, 1873.

Afr 4095.3.3   A journey to central Africa. (Taylor, G.B.) N.Y., 1854.

Afr 4095.3.2   A journey to central Africa. (Taylor, G.B.) N.Y., 1854.

Afr 3979.48   Journey to Egypt. (Bigland, E.) London, 1948.

Htn   Afr 1607.25*   A journey to Mequinez. (Windus, J.) London, 1725.
(Changed to EC7.W7255.725j, 30/6/69)

Afr 4180.3.20   Journey to Siwa. (Maugham, R.C.R.) N.Y., 1950.

Afr 4050.16   A journey to two of the oases of Upper Egypt. (Edmonstone, A.) London, 1822.

Afr 2230.44   Jours de Kabylie. (Dessins de Brouty). (Feraoun, Mouloud.) Paris, 1968.

Afr 4582.5   Jousseaume, F. Impressions de voyage en Apharras. Paris, 1914. 2v.

Afr 5426.100.40   Joy, Charles Rhind. The Africa of Albert Schweitzer. N.Y., 1948.

Afr 7812.261.5   Joye, Pierre. Les trusts au Congo. Bruxelles, 1961.

Afr 7549.00   Jozon, L. L'état indépendant du Congo. Paris, 1900.

Htn   Afr 6275.32.5*   Ju-Ju and justice in Nigeria. (Hives, Frank.) London, 1933.

Afr 555.60   The jubilee volume of the Sierra Leone Native Church. (Sierra Leone. Native Church. Jubilee Committee.) London, 1917.

Afr 1957.6   Juchereau de St. Denis, A. Considerations sur la régence d'Alger. Paris, 1831.

Afr 210.62.45   Judd, P. African independence. N.Y., 1963.

Afr 6620.65   Judgment on German Africa. (Steer, G.L.) London, 1939.

Afr 45.62.10   Judicial and legal systems in Africa. (Allott, Anthony N.) London, 1962.

Afr 9700.25   The judicial process among the Barotse. (Gluckman, Max.) Manchester, 1955.

Afr 9700.25.5.2   The judicial process among the Barotse of Northern Rhodesia. 2. ed. (Gluckman, Max.) Manchester, 1967.

Afr 1432.19   Juicio critico de la guerra de Africa. (Ameller, V. de.) Madrid, 1861.

Afr 1280.30.5   Les Juifs d'Afrique du Nord entre l'Orient et l'Occident. (Chouraqui, A.) Paris, 1965.

Afr 1869.63   Juin, A.P. Histoire parallele. Paris, 1963.

Afr 1095.15   Juin, A.P. Le Maghreb en feu. Paris, 1957.

Afr 2357.10   Jules Du Pré de Saint Maur. 2. ed. (Villot, Roland.) Oran, 1955.

Afr 7188.5   Julgareis qual e mas excelente. (Dias, Gastão Sousa.) Lisboa, 1948[1949].

Afr 1922.15   Julien, A. La question d'Alger devant les Chambres sous la Restauration. Alger, 1922.

Afr 1095.5   Julien, C.A. L'Afrique du Nord en marche. Paris, 1952.

Afr 1069.31   Julien, Charles A. Histoire de l'Afrique du Nord. Paris, 1931.

Afr 1069.31.12   Julien, Charles A. Histoire de l'Afrique du Nord: Tunisie, Algérie, Maroc. 2e éd. Paris, 1966- 2v.

Afr 1069.31.10   Julien, Charles A. Histoire de l'Afrique du Nord. v.1-2. Paris, 1961.

Afr 1069.31.5   Julien, Charles A. Histoire de l'Afrique du Nord. v.1-2. 2. ed. Paris, 1951. 2v.

Afr 2000.17   Julien, Charles A. Histoire de l'Algérie contemporaine. v.1- Paris, 1964-

Afr 659.66   Julien, Charles André. Histoire de l'Afrique blanche. Paris, 1966.

Afr 5540.3   Julien, G. Institutions politiques et socials de Madagascar. V.1-2. Paris, 1908. 2v.

Afr 5758.5   Jully, M.A. Madagascar. Marseille, 1900.

Afr 6535.66   Julsrud, Harald G. Jambo Uganda. Oslo, 1966.

Afr 109.70   July, Robert William. A history of the African people. N.Y., 1970.

Afr 679.68   July, Robert William. The origins of modern African thought. London, 1968.

Afr 575.23   Jung, Eugène. L'islam et les musulmans dans l'Afrique du Nord. Paris, 1930.

Afr 2438.21   Jung, Eugene. Les réformes en Tunisie. Paris, 1926.

Afr 7459.52   Junge, Werner. Bolahun. N.Y., 1952.

Afr 10018.2   Das junge Afrika. (Jahn, Janheinz.) Wien, 1963.

Afr 679.08   Jungle folk of Africa. (Milligan, R.H.) N.Y., 1908.

Afr 6879.36   Jungle giants. (Bent, Newell.) Norwood, Mass., 1936.

Afr 609.29.5   Jungle gods. (Vonhoffman, Carl.) London, 1929.

Afr 9748.807   Jungle pathfinder. (Rukavina, Kathaleen (Stevens).) London, 1951.

Afr 609.30.10   Jungle portraits. (Akeley, D.J.) N.Y., 1930.

Afr 5056.131   Jungle ways. (Seabrook, W.B.) London, 1931.

Afr 5056.131.20   Jungle ways. (Seabrook, W.B.) N.Y., 1931.

Afr 7809.31   Jungles preferred. (Miller, Janet.) Boston, 1931.

Afr 8667.85   Junius, J.H. Het leven in Zuid-Afrika. Amsterdam, 1896.

Afr 608.90   Junker, W. Travels in Africa, 1890-92. 3v.

Afr 608.89.4   Junker, Wilhelm. Reisen in Afrika, 1875-1878. Wien, 1889.

Afr 7315.3   Junod, H.A. Les Ba-ronga. Neuchatel, 1898.

Afr 7315.20.6   Junod, H.A. The life of a South African tribe. New Hyde Park, N.Y., 1962. 2v.

Afr 7315.20.5   Junod, H.A. The life of a South African tribe. 2d ed. London, 1927. 2v.

Afr 8678.9.65   Junod, H.A. Moeurs et coutumes des Bantous. Paris, 1936. 2v.

Afr 7315.20.10   Junod, H.A. A vida d'uma tribu sul-africana. Famalição, 1917.

Afr 8678.110   Jurgens, Isabel. Why cry beloved country. Ilfracombe, 1958.

Afr 7540.17   Jurisprudence de l'état indépendant du Congo. v.2. (Touchard, G.) Bruxelles, 1911.

Afr 3040.65.5   The juristic status of Egypt and the Sudan. (O'Rourke, V.A.) Baltimore, 1935.

Afr 3040.65   The juristic status of EgyptAnd the Sudan. Diss. (O'Rourke, V.A.) Baltimore, 1935.

Afr 4045.3   Juromenha, J.A. de R.P. de Lacerda. O Isthmo de Suez e as portuguezes. Lisboa, 1870.

Afr 626.17   Jussiaume, E. Reflexions sur l'économie africaine. Paris, 1932.

Afr 6280.26.6   Justice and judgment among the Tiv. (Bohannan, Paul.) London, 1957.

Afr 1840.26   La justice en Algérie, 1962-1968. (Lapassat, Étienne Jean.) Paris, 1968.

Afr 1494.10   Justice pour le Maroc. (Barrat, Robert.) Paris, 1953.

Afr 5640.35   Justice pour les Malgaches. (Stibbe, Pierre.) Paris, 1954.

Afr 1635.23   Justinard, L.V. Un petit royaume berbere. Paris, 1954.

Afr 8230.10.10   Juta, M. The pace of the ox, the life of Paul Kruger. London, 1937.

Afr 8809.10   Juta, Rene. The Cape peninsula. Cape Town, 1910.

Afr 2223.924.5   Juving, Alex. Le socialisme en Algérie. Thèse. Alger, 1924.

Afr 6314.25   K.A.R.; being an unofficial account of...the King's African Rifles. (Lloyd-Jones, W.) London, 1926.

Afr 6300.44   K.I.A. occasional papers. (Kenya Institute of Administration.) Lower Kakete, 1,1968+

Afr 8659.12.5F   De Kaap als een nieuw land. 2. druk. (Kock, J.H.M.) Kaapstad, 1912.

Afr 8110.22   Die kaap onder die Bataafse republiek, 1803-1806. (Merwe, J.P. van der.) Amsterdam, 1926.

Afr 8745.15   Kaapland en die Tweede Vryheidsoorlog. (Strydom, C.J.S.) Kaapstad, 1937.

Afr 8030.7   Kaapse archiefstukken, lopende over het jaar 1778- . Cape Town. 1926 (Cape of Good Hope. Archives.) 6v.

Afr 8110.18   Die kaapse patriotte, 1779-1791. (Beyers, C.) Kaapstad, 1929.

Afr 8110.18.2   Die Kaapse patriotte gedurende die laaste kwart van die agtiende eeu en die voortvlewing van hui denkbeelde. 2. uitg. (Beyers, C.) Pretoria, 1967.

Afr 609.58.30   Kaapstad-Kairo per auto-stop. (Damme, Fred van.) Antwerpen, 1958.

Afr 9614.10   Kabanza; a story of Africa. (Bulley, Mary Winifred.) Westminster, 1927.

Afr 1280.10   Las Kabilas de Bocoya, Beniburiaga y Flemsamana. (Giesa de Camps, Santiago.) Barcelona, 1903.

Afr 6395.2.20   Kabongo. 1st ed. (Baker, R.St.B.) Wheatley, Eng., 1955.

Afr 6295.250.200F   Kabuna, 1917-1967, 2017. (Lock, Max.) London, 1967.

Afr 2230.43   The Kabyle people. (Wysner, Glora May.) N.Y., 1945.

Afr 2230.7   Les Kabyles. (Aucapitaine, H.) Paris, 1864.

Afr 2230.11   Kabyles et Kroumirs. (Farine, Charles.) Paris, 1882.

Afr 2230.9.5   La Kabylie. (Monglave, E. de.) n.p., n.d.

Afr 2230.9   Kabylie. Paris, 1846.

Afr 2230.3   Kabylie du Jurjura. (Lionel, J.) Paris, 1892.

Afr 2230.2   La Kabylie et les coutumes kabyles. (Hanoteau, A.) Paris, 1873. 3v.

Afr 698.68   Kachalola, or The early life and adventures of Sidney Spencer Broomfield. (Broomfield, S.S.) London, 1930.

Afr 10831.1.100   Kachingwe, A. No easy task. London, 1966.

Afr 6538.70   Kade, Gunnar. Die Stellung der zentralen Orte in der Kulturlandschaftlichen Entwicklung Bugandas (Uganda). Frankfurt, 1969.

Afr 6203.6   Kaduna, Nigeria. Regional Library. An author catalogue of books about Nigeria in the regional library. Kaduna, 1962.

Afr 6926.4   Die Kämpfe der deutschen Truppen in Südwest Afrika. (Prussia. Grosser Generalität.) Berlin, 1906-08. 2v.

Afr 6720.28.10   Die Kämpfe in Kamerun, 1914-1916. Vorbereitung und Verlauf. Inaug. Diss. (Mentzel, H.) Berlin, 1936.

Afr 6926.3   Die Kämpfe mit Hendrik Witboi 1894 und Witbois Ende. (Leutwein, T.) Leipzig, 1912.

Afr 3979.62.5   Kaesser, Hans. Einiges ägypten. Baden-Baden, 1962.

Afr 4618.5   Kaffa. (Bieber, Friedrich J.) Münster, 1920-23. 2v.

Afr 8830.8   Die Kaffern auf der Südküste von Afrika. (Alberti, J.C.L.) Gotha, 1815.

Afr 8678.10.20   Kaffirs are livelier. (Walker, Oliver.) London, 1964.

Afr 8830.7   Kaffraria, and its inhabitants. (Fleming, F.) London, 1853.

Afr 8145.9   The Kafir, the Hottentot, and the frontier farmer...missionary life. (Merriman, N.J.) London, 1854.

Afr 8678.10.7   Kafir socialism. (Kidd, D.) London, 1908.

Afr 8152.94   Kafirland, a ten months campaign. (Streatfield, F.M.) London, 1879.

Afr 9047.5   The Kafirs of Natal and Zulu country. (Shooter, J.) London, 1857.

Afr 42731.2.700   Kagame, A. La divine pastorale. Bruxelles, 1952.

Afr 7947.6   Kagame, A. Les milices du Rwanda précolonial. Bruxelles, 1963.

Afr 7937.9   Kagame, Alexis. Le code des institutions politiques du Rwanda précolonial. Bruxelles, 1952.

Afr 7947.8   Kagame, Alexis. L'histoire des armées-bovines dans l'ancien Rwanda. Bruxelles, 1961.

Afr 7945.2   Kagame, Alexis. La philosophie bantu-rwandaise de être. Bruxelles, 1956.

Afr 6540.6.10   Kagwa, Apolo. The customs of the Baganoa. N.Y., 1969.

Afr 6985.12   Kahn, Carl Hugo Linsingen. The native tribes of South West Africa. 1st ed. London, 1966.

Afr 8045.52   Kahn, Ellison. The new constitution. London, 1962.

Afr 8678.386   Kahn, Ely Jacques. The separated people; a look at contemporary South Africa. 1st ed. N.Y., 1968.

Afr 28747.5   Kaidara. (Ba, Amadou Hampâté.) Paris, 1969.

Afr 4115.31   Kair. (Khodzhash, jvettana I.) Moskva, 1967.

Afr 1835.1.7A   Kairuani, Al. Histoire de l'Afrique. Paris, 1845.

Afr 150.42   Kake, Baba Ibrahima. Glossaire critique des expressions geographiques concernant le pays des noirs. Paris, 1965.

Afr 609.66.30   Kaké, Baba Ibrahima. Terre d'Afrique. Paris, 1966.

Afr 2352.1   La Kalaa et Tihamamine. (Robert, M.A.) Constantine, 1903.

Afr 9389.60   Kalahari. (Bjerre, Jens.) London, 1960.

Afr 9389.67   The Kalahari and its lost city. (Clement, A. John.) Cape Town, 1967.

Afr 9400.10.15   The Kalahari and its native races. (Schwarz, E.H.L.) London, 1928.

Afr 9389.53   Kalahari sand. (Debenham, F.) London, 1953.

Afr 10381.2   Kalasanda. (Kimenye, Barbara.) London, 1965.

Afr 2875.43   Kalbskopf, W. Die Aussenpolitik der Mittelmächte im Tripoliskrieg...1911-1912. Erlangen, 1932.

Afr 5460.10   Kalck, Pierre. Réalités oubanguiennes. Paris, 1959.

Afr 8210.11   The kaleidoscopic Transvaal. (Jeppe, Carl.) London, 1906.

Afr 9148.99.3   Kalff, S. Onder een worsteland volk. Haarlem, 1899.

Afr 200.12   Kaltbrunner, David. L'Afrique en 1890. Paris, 1890.

Afr 6019.46   Kam, Josephine. African challenge, story of the British in tropical Africa. London, 1946.

Afr 626.161   Kamarck, Andrew Martin. The economics of African development. N.Y., 1967.

Afr 6460.94   Kambvya's cattle. (Goldschmidt, Walter Rochs.) Berkeley, 1969.

Afr 3255.6   Kamel, S. La conférence de Constantinople et la question égyptienne 1882. Paris, 1913.

Afr 6738.8.5   Kamerun, Reise in die Hinterlande der Kolonie. 2e Ausgabe. (Schwarz, B.) Leipzig, 1888.

Afr 6738.52   Kamerun. (Haeberle, Wilhelm.) Stuttgart, 1967.

Afr 6720.37   Kamerun. (Kemner, W.) Berlin, 1937.

Afr 6738.9   Kamerun. (Sembritzki, Emil.) Berlin, 1909.

Afr 6715.25   El Kamerun. n.p., 1957?

Afr 6720.60   Kamerun unter deutscher Kolonialherrschaft. v.1- (Stoecker, Helmuth.) Berlin, 1960- 2v.

Afr 6738.22   Die kameruner Waldländer. Inaug. Diss. (Mueller, Arno.) Ohlau in Schlesien, 1930.

Afr 3994.2   Kamil, Ali. Les conséquences financières de l'occupation de l'Egypte par l'Angleterre. Bruxelles, 1911.

Afr 4559.53   Kamil, M. Das Land der Negus. Innsbruck, 1953.

Afr 3300.70   Kamil, M. Tomorrow's Egypt. 1st English ed. Cairo, 1953.

Afr 4008.10   Kamil, Murad. Aspects de l'Egypte copte. Berlin, 1965.

Afr 3275.42   Kamil, Mustafa. Egyptiens et Anglais. Paris, 1906.

Afr 10066.3   Kaminski-Durocher, B. Poezja czarnej Afryki. Warszawa, 1962.

Afr 3813.18   al-Kammash, Majdi M. Economic development and planning in Egypt. N.Y., 1968.

Afr 5565.2.2   Kammerer, A. La decouverte de Madagascar. Lisboa, 1950.

Afr 5565.2   Kammerer, A. La decouverte de Madagascar. n.p., n.d.

Afr 4280.15   Kammerer, A. Essai sur l'histoire antique d'Abyssinie. Paris, 1926.

Afr 4008.2   Kammerer, M. A Coptic bibliography. Ann Arbor, 1950.

Afr 8687.200.20   Kampdagboek. (Fischer, Maria Adriana.) Kaapstad, 1964.

Afr 109.38   Kampf um Afrika. (Berger, Arthur.) Berlin, 1938.

Afr 2862.5   Der Kampf um Tripolis. (Mehemed Emin Efendi (Pseud.).) Leipzig, 1912.

Afr 1609.03.5   Kampffmeyer, G. Marokko. Halle, 1903.

Afr 1326.2   Kampffmeyer, Georg. Studien und Mitteilungen der deutschen Marokko-bibliothek. Berlin, 1911.

Afr 3979.04.5   Kandt, Richard. Caput Nili, eine Empfindsarne. Berlin, 1905.

Afr 9439.54   Kane, N.S. The world's view. London, 1954.

Afr 1609.21.5   Kann, Reginald. Le protectorat marocain. Nancy, 1921.

Afr 7850.40   Kantanga, pelli di fuoco. (Musini, P.) Parma, 1961.

Afr 9389.58   Kantor, Cyril. The big thirst. London, 1958.

Afr 8678.378   Kantor, James. A healthy grave. London, 1967.

Afr 6280.63   The Kanuri of Bornu. (Cohen, Ronald.) N.Y., 1967.

Afr 5227.28   Kanya-Forstner, Alexander Sidney. The conquest of the Western Sedan. Cambridge, Eng., 1969.

Afr 7815.23   Kanza, Thomas. Tot ou tard. Bruxelles, 1959.

Afr 8678.395   Kap ohne Hoffnung; oder, Die Politik der Apartheid. Reinbek bei Hamburg, 1965.

Afr 3986.963.5   Kapitalisticheskoe razvitie Egipta, 1882-1939. (Fridman, L.A.) Moscow, 1963.

Afr 7817.3   Kapitene of the Congo steamship Lapsley. (McKinnon, Arch C.) Boston, 1968.

VAfr 6195.20   Kaplani, czarownicy, wiedźmy. Wyd. 1. (Chodak, Szymon.) Warszawa, 1967.

Afr 8659.52.15   Kaptein, A. De Unie van Zuid-Afrika. Amsterdam, 1952.

Afr 8325.66.5   Kaptein Hindon. 2nd ed. (Preller, G.S.) Kaapstad, 1921.

Afr 6455.115   Karamojo safari. 1st ed. (Bell, W.D.M.) N.Y., 1949.

Afr 3310.94   Karanjia, Rustom Khurshedji. How Nasser did it. Bombay, 1964.

Afr 2819.60.5   Karasapan, Celâ Tevfik. Libya; trablusgarp, bingazi ve fizan. Ankara, 1960.

Afr 3994.967   Kardouche, George K. The U.A.R. in development, a study in expansionary finance. N.Y., 1967.

Afr 9510.10.10.10   Kariba. Kariba. Bloemfontein, 1959.

Afr 9510.10.10   Kariba. (Kariba.) Bloemfontein, 1959.

Afr 9510.10.5   Kariba studies. Manchester, Eng. 1,1960+ 3v.

Afr 6542.43   Karimojong politics. (Dyson-Hudson, Neville.) Oxford, 1966.

Afr 8369.65   Karis, Thomas. The treason trial in South Africa. Stanford, Calif., 1965.

Afr 6420.74   Kariuki, Josiah M. Mau Mau detainee. London, 1963.

Afr 9070.9   Karlson, Esme D. Pattern of wings. Pietermaritzburg, 1946.

Afr 7309.66.5   Karlsson, Elis. Cruising off Mozambique. London, 1969.

Afr 7369.09   Karnga, A.W. The Negro Republic on West Africa. Monrovia, 1909.

Afr 8830.12   Karoo, the story of the Karoos of South Africa - the great Karoo. (Green, Lawrence George.) Cape Town, 1955.

Afr 1450.6   Karow, K.L. Neun Jahre in marokkanischen Diensten. Berlin, 1909.

Afr 4787.5   Karp, Mark. The economics of trusteeship in Somalia. Boston, 1960.

Afr 5180.46   Karsta afrikos saule. (Liubeckis, M.) Vilnius, 1963.

Afr 505.20   Kartun, D. Africa, Africa. N.Y., 1954.

Afr 7580.16   Kasa-vubu, au coeur du drame congolais. (Gilis, Charles A.) Bruxelles, 1964.

Afr 7912.15.30   Kashamura, Anicet. De Lumumba aux colonels. Paris, 1966.

Afr 7565.5   Kassai, Pierre. La civilisation africaine, 1876-1888. Bruxelles, 1888.

Afr 724.4   Kassner, Theo. My journey from Rhodesia to Egypt. London, 1911.

Afr 5285.277.35   Kassoum, Congo. Conséquences de la colonisation sur la vie coutumière en pays mossi. Thèse. Montepellier, 1955.

Afr 7850.25   Le Katanga, cinquante ans décisifs. (Sauvy, Jean.) Paris, 1961.

Afr 7850.42   Katanga, pays du cuirre. (Lekime, Fernand.) Verviers, 1965.

Afr 7812.262   Katanga. Livre blanc du gouvernement katangais sur les évènements. Elisabethville, 1962.

Afr 7850.56   Katanga. (Nagy, Laszló.) Lausanne, 1965.

Afr 7567.19   Katanga. 3d ed. (Cornet, Rene.) Bruxelles, 1946.

Afr 7580.13   The Katanga circus. 1st ed. (Valahu, M.) N.Y., 1964.

Afr 7850.54.2   Katanga secession. (Gerard Libois, J.) Madison, 1966.

Afr 555.65.5   Die katholischen Missionsschulen des Tanganyika-Gebietes. Inaug. Diss. (Schappi, F.S.) Oberginingen, 1935.

Afr 6780.46   Katsman, V.I. Tanganika, 1946-61. Moscow, 1962.

Afr 8676.64.10   Katzen, Leo. Implications of economic and other boycotts for South Africa. Cape Town, 1964.

Afr 8678.331   Katzew, Henry. Apartheid and survival. Cape Town, 1965.

Afr 8680.45   Katzew, Henry. Solution for South Africa. Cape Town, 1955.

Afr 5248.15   Kaufmann, Herbert. Reiten durch Iforas. Munich, 1958.

Afr 550.142   Kaufmann, Robert. Millenarisme et acculturation. Bruxelles, 1964.

Afr 3994.891.5   Kaufmann, Wilhelm. Das internationale Recht der egyptischen Staatsschuld. Berlin, 1891.

Afr 55.33   Kaula, Edna Mason. Leaders of the new Africa. Cleveland, 1966.

Afr 9748.475.5   Kaunda, founder of Zambia. (Hall, Richard.) London, 1965.

Afr 9636.8   Kaunda, Kenneth David. Humanism in Zambia and a guide to its implementation. Lusaka, 1967.

Afr 9748.475.10   Kaunda, Kenneth David. A humanist in Africa. London, 1967.

Afr 9748.475.15   Kaunda, Kenneth David. Zambia, independence and beyond, the speeches of Kenneth Kaunda. London, 1966.

Afr 9748.475   Kaunda, Kenneth David. Zambia shall be free. London, 1962.

Afr 590.83   Kay, Frederick George. The shameful trade. London, 1967.

Afr 9639.65   Kay, George. Changing patterns of settlement and land use in the eastern province of Northern Rhodesia. Hull, 1965.

Afr 9699.67   Kay, George. A social geography of Zambia; a survey of population. London, 1967.

Afr 8678.18   Kay, S. Travels and researches in Caffraria. London, 1833.

Afr 10831.5.110   Kayira, Legson. Jingala. Harlow, 1969.

Afr 10831.5.100   Kayira, Legson. The looming shadow. Garden City, 1967.

Afr 9860.475   Kayira, Regson. I will try. 1st ed. Garden City, N.Y., 1965.

Afr 28.3   Kayser, G. Bibliographie de l'Afrique. Bruxelles, 1887.

Afr 8040.15   Kayser, H. Demokratie und Föderalismus in der südafrikanischen Union. Düsseldorf, 1934.

Afr 555.29   Keable, Robert. A city of the dawn. Uganda. London, 1915.

Afr 608.95.3   Keane, A.H. Africa. London, 1895. 2v.

Afr 608.95.4   Keane, A.H. Africa. v.2. 2nd ed. London, 1904.

Afr 8175.9   Keane, A.H. The Boer states. London, 1900.

Afr 609.41.5   Kearton, Cherry. Cherry Kearton's travels. London, 1941.

Afr 718.32   Kearton, Cherry. Through central Africa from east to west. London, 1915.

Afr 4060.30   Keating, Rex. Nubian twilight. N.Y., 1963.

Afr 1325.6F   Keatinge, M. Travels through France and Spain to Morocco. London, 1817.

Afr 9448.72   Keatley, Patrick. The politics of partnership. Harmondsworth, Middlesex, 1963.

Afr 3243.4.2   Keay, J.S. Spoiling the Egyptians. N.Y., 1882.

Afr 2230.4   Les Kebailes du Djerdjera. (Devaux, C.) Marseille, 1859.

Afr 5765.17   Keck, Daniel. Histoire des origines du christianisme à Madagascar. Thèse. Paris, 1898.

Afr 8678.78   Keet, B.B. Whither South Africa. Stellenbosch, 1956.

Afr 9050.54   Keiskammahoek rural survey. Pietermaritzburg, 1952.

Afr 2929.66   Keith, Agnes Newton. Children of Allah. 1st ed. Boston, 1966.

Afr 7549.19A   Keith, Arthur B. The Belgian Congo and the Berlin Act. Oxford, 1919.

Afr 9700.13   Keith, Grace. The fading colour bar. London, 1966.

Afr 8305.10   Kekewich in Kimberley. (Omeara, W.A.J.) London, 1926.

Afr 854.2   Keller, C. Die ostafrikanischen Inseln. v.2. Berlin, 1898.

Afr 618.7   Keller, E. Verbreitung der Fallenjagd in Afrika. Inaug.-Diss. Berlin, 1936.

Afr 4390.15   Keller, Konrad. Alfred Ilg. Frauenfeld, 1918.

Afr 698.86   Keller, Konrad. Reisebilder aus Ost-Afrika. Leipzig, 1887.

Afr 6455.100   Keller, W.P. Africa's wild glory. London, 1959.

Afr 4199.5   Keller-Zschokke, J.V. Werner Munzinger-Pascha. Aarau, 1891.

Afr 8686.4   Kellermann, Abraham Gerhardus. Profetisme in Suid-Afrika in akkulturasie perspektief. Proefschrift. Voorburg, 1964.

Afr 7809.41.5   Kellersberger, J.L.S. God's ravens. N.Y., 1941.

Afr 7803.5   Kellersberger, Julia L.S. A life for the Congo. N.Y., 1947.

Afr 28.9   Kelly, Douglas C. Africa in paperbacks. East Lansing, Michigan, 1966.

Afr 3979.02.4   Kelly, R. Talbot. Egypt painted and described. London, 1906.

Afr 3979.02.5   Kelly, R. Talbot. Egypt painted and described. London, 1910.

Afr 3979.02.3   Kelly, R.J. Egypt painted and described. London, 1903.

Afr 108.93.3   Keltie, J.S. Africa. Philadelphia, 1907.

X Cg Afr 108.93.2   Keltie, J.S. The partition of Africa. 2d ed. London, 1895. (changed to XP 9198)

Afr 108.93.2   Keltie, J.S. The partition of Africa. 2d ed. Photoreproduction. London, 1895. 2v.

Afr 6720.37   Kemner, W. Kamerun. Berlin, 1937.

Afr 6192.3   Kemp, Dennis. Nine years at the Gold Coast. London, 1898.

Afr 8135.29   Kemp, J.C.G. Die pad van die veroweraar. 2. druk. Kaapstad, 1946.

Afr 8135.29.10   Kemp, J.C.G. Vir vryheid en vir reg. 3 druk. Kaapstad, 1946.

Afr 8658.79   Kennedy, D. Kennedy at the Cape. Edinburgh, 1879.

Afr 2208.46.3   Kennedy, J.C. Algeria and Tunis in 1845. London, 1846. 2v.

Afr 8040.12   Kennedy, W.P.M. The law and custom of the South African constitution. London, 1935.

Afr 8658.79   Kennedy at the Cape. (Kennedy, D.) Edinburgh, 1879.

Afr 2285.22   Kenny, H.T. In lightest Africa. London, 1935.

Afr 5549.62   Kent, R.K. From Madagascar to the Malagasy Republic. N.Y., 1962.

Afr 8687.250   Kentridge, Morris. I recall. Johannesburg, 1959.

Afr 6420.72.5   Kenya, a political history. (Bennett, G.) London, 1963.

Afr 6455.142   Kenya; contrasts and problems. (Leakey, Louis S.B.) Cambridge, Mass., 1966.

Afr 6415.10   Kenya, from chartered company to crown colony. (Hobley, C.W.) London, 1929.

Afr 6412.5   Kenya, progress and problems. (British Information Services.) N.Y., 1960.

Afr Doc 3205.5   Kenya; report for the year. London. 1947-1962 4v.

Afr Doc 3284.1.73   Kenya; sample population census of Nairobi, 1957-1958, an experiment on sampling methods. (East Africa High Commission.) Nairobi, 1958.

Afr 6403.2   Kenya, Uganda, Tanganyika, 1960-1964, a bibliography. (Moses, Larry.) Washington, 1964.

Afr 6314.27   Kenya, Uganda and Zanzibar. (Great Britain. Foreign Office. History Section.) London, 1920.

Afr 6457.25   Kenya. Africa socialism and its application to planning in Kenya. Nairobi, 1965.

Afr Doc 3209.112   Kenya. The appropriation accounts. Nairobi. 1957+

Afr Doc 3203.3F   Kenya. Blue book.

Afr Doc 3209.1   Kenya. Development estimates. 1958+

Afr 6457.23   Kenya. Development plan for the period from 1st July, 1964, to 30th June, 1970. Nairobi, 1964.

Afr 6457.23.5   Kenya. Development plan for the period 1965-1966 to 1966-1970. Nairobi, 1966.

Afr Doc 3203.10F   Kenya. Directory of the govenment. Nairobi. 1965+

Afr Doc 3209.15   Kenya. Estimates of expenditure. Nairobi. 1,1958+

Afr Doc 3209.20   Kenya. Estimates of recurrent expenditure. Nairobi? 1963+

Afr Doc 3209.10   Kenya. Estimates of revenue. Nairobi. 1,1958+

Afr 6435.6   Kenya. Kenya-Somalia relations. Nairobi, 1967.
Afr Doc 3207.362   Kenya. Ministry of Finance and Economic Planning Kenya Population Census, 1962. Nairobi? 1964.
Afr Doc 3231.10   Kenya. Report on native affairs.
Afr Doc 3226.5   Kenya. Social development report. Nairobi. 1956-1957
Afr Doc 3203.15   Kenya. Stafflist. Nairobi. 1957-1962
Afr 6420.75   Pamphlet vol. Kenya.
     3 pam.
Afr 6405   Pamphlet box. Kenya.
Afr 6405.4   Pamphlet vol. Kenya.
     11 pam.
Afr 6405.3   Pamphlet vol. Kenya.
     6 pam.
Afr 6420.70   Kenya. (Cole, Keith.) London, 1959.
Afr 6455.110   Kenya. (Great Britain. Central Office of Information.) London, 1960.
Afr 6457.30   Kenya. (Italy. Instituto Nationale Per Il Commercio Estero.) Roma, 1961.
Afr 6455.61   Kenya. (Leakey, L.S.B.) London, 1936.
Afr 6415.42   Kenya. (MacPhee, Archibald Marshall.) London, 1968.
Afr 6415.42.2   Kenya. (MacPhee, Archibald Marshall.) N.Y., 1968.
Afr 6415.15   Kenya. (Pankhurst, R.K.P.) London, 1954.
Afr 6420.25   Kenya. (Wood, Susan B.) London, 1960.
Afr 6420.26   Kenya. (Wood, Susan B.) London, 1962.
Afr Doc 3231.15   Kenya. African Affairs Department. Annual report.
Afr Doc 3209.30   Kenya. African District Councils. Approved estimates of revenue and expenditure. Nairobi. 1962+
Afr Doc 3202.64F   Kenya. Archives. Archives microfilming programme. Nairobi, 1964.
Afr Doc 3207.331   Kenya. Census Office. Report on the non-native census enumeration made in the colony and protectorate of Kenya. Nairobi, 1932.
Afr Doc 3238.20   Kenya. Central Housing Board. Annual report. 1964+
Afr Doc 3233.20   Kenya. Central Land Board. Annual report. Nairobi. 1963+
Afr Doc 3233.15   Kenya. Central Land Board. A review of the activities of the Land Development and Settlement Board. Nairobi. 1961+
Afr Doc 3233.5   Kenya. Civil Service Commission. Report on the working of the Civil Service Commission.
Afr 6463.6   Kenya. Commission of Inquiry into the Affray at Kolloa, Baringo. Report. Nairobi, 1950.
Afr 6410.14   Kenya. Commission on the Law of Succession. Report. Nairobi, 1968.
Afr 6410.8   Kenya. Committee of Review into the Kenya Institute of Administration. Report, 30th Nov., 1964. Nairobi, 1965.
Afr 6454.26   Kenya. Committee on African Wages. Report. Nairobi, 1954.
Afr Doc 3219.5   Kenya. Constitution. The Constitution of Kenya. Nairobi, 1969.
Afr 6410.10   Kenya. Constitutional Conference, London, 1962. Report presented to Parliament by the Secretary of State for the colonies. London, 1962.
Afr Doc 3212.15   Kenya. Council of State. Annual report. Nairobi. 1958+
Afr Doc 3208.705   Kenya. Customs Department. Trade report of Kenya and Uganda. 1928-1948
Afr Doc 3209.505   Kenya. Department of Agriculture. Agricultural census. Annual report. Nairobi. 6-15,1925-1934
     2v.
Afr Doc 3233.10   Kenya. Department of Co-operative Development. Annual report.
Afr Doc 3233.35   Kenya. Department of Community Development and Rehabilitation. Annual report. Nairobi. 1951-1955
Afr Doc 3239.15   Kenya. Department of Immigration. Annual report.
Afr Doc 3239.3   Kenya. Department of Information. Annual report. Nairobi. 1955+
Afr Doc 3242.5.20   Kenya. Department of Lands, Mines and Surveys. Annual report. Nairobi. 1945
Afr Doc 3242.5.10   Kenya. Department of Lands. Annual report. Nairobi. 1926
Afr Doc 3242.7   Kenya. Department of Local Government, Lands and Settlement. Annual report of the commissioner. Nairobi. 1930-1934
Afr Doc 3249.10   Kenya. Department of Settlement. Annual report.
Afr Doc 3248.5   Kenya. Department of the Registrar-General. Annual report of the Registrar-General.
Afr Doc 3234.5   Kenya. Development and Reconstruction Authority. Annual report.
Afr Doc 3234.10   Kenya. Development and Reconstruction Authority. Quarterly report.
Afr Doc 3208.468F   Kenya. Directorate of Planning. The pattern of income. Nairobi, 1964.
Afr Doc 3207.361   Kenya. Economics and Statistics Division. Agriculture census, 1961. Nairobi, 1961.
Afr Doc 3207.364   Kenya. Economics and Statistics Division. Agriculture census, 1964; IV, large farm areas. Nairobi, 1965?
Afr Doc 3207.363   Kenya. Economics and Statistics Division. Census of industrial production, 1963. Nairobi, 1965.
Afr Doc 3209.300   Kenya. Economics and Statistics Division. Economic survey. 1961+
Afr 6465.60F   Kenya. Economics and Statistics Division. Economic survey of Central Province, 1963-1964. Nairobi, 1968.
Afr Doc 3207.360   Kenya. Economics and Statistics Division. Kenya African agricultural sample census, 1960-1961. Nairobi, 1962.
Afr Doc 3207.362.5.5F   Kenya. Economics and Statistics Division. Kenya agricultural census, 1962, scheduled areas and coastal strip. n.p., 1963.
Afr Doc 3207.362.5F   Kenya. Economics and Statistics Division. Population census, 1962. Nairobi? 1964.
Afr Doc 3208.700   Kenya. Economics and Statistics Division. Survey of distribution, 1960. Nairobi. 1963
Afr Doc 3208.375   Kenya. Economis and Statistics Division. Reported employment and earnings in Kenya.
Afr Doc 3236.10   Kenya. Forest Department. Annual report. 1964+
Afr Doc 3237.5   Kenya. Game Department. Annual report. 1953-1954
Afr Doc 3239.5   Kenya. Information Services. Annual report. 1960+
Afr Doc 3239.30   Kenya. Inland Revenue Department. Annual report. Nairobi. 1953-1954
Afr 6408.25   Kenya. Kenya Regiment. Annual report. Nairobi. 1957-58
Afr Doc 3242.5   Kenya. Lands Department.
Afr 6457.21   Kenya. Laws, statutes, etc. The Foreign Investments Protection Act, 1964 and rules of procedure. Nairobi, 1964.
Afr Doc 3212.2   Kenya. Legislative Council. Debates; official report. Nairobi. 28-91,1947-1963
     51v.
Afr Doc 3212.25F   Kenya. Legislative Council. Minutes of the proceedings. 1920-1923

Afr Doc 3212.30F   Kenya. Legislative Council. Record of the proceedings. 1923
Afr Doc 3212.35   Kenya. Legislative Council. Sessional paper. 1947+
Afr Doc 3242.20   Kenya. Local Government. Loans Authority. Annual report. 1964+
Afr Doc 3209.5   Kenya. Ministry for Finance and Development. Budget. Nairobi. 1959+
Afr Doc 3231.20   Kenya. Ministry of Agriculture, Animal Husbandry and Water Resources. Three-year report. Nairobi. 1958+
Afr Doc 3233.30   Kenya. Ministry of Community Development. Annual report. Nairobi. 1957+
Afr 6457.3   Kenya. Ministry of Economic Planning and Development. High-level manpower. Nairobi, 1965.
Afr Doc 3207.5   Kenya. Ministry of Economic Planning and Development. Statistics Deevelopment. Statistics Division. Statistical abstract. Nairobi. 1,1961
Afr Doc 3236.5   Kenya. Ministry of Finance and Development. Report on the progress of development projects.
Afr Doc 3238.5   Kenya. Ministry of Health and Social Affairs. Annual report. 1960+
Afr Doc 3238.15   Kenya. Ministry of Housing. Annual report. Nairobi. 1,1958+
Afr Doc 3239.10   Kenya. Ministry of Information, Broadcasting and Tourism. Annual report.
Afr Doc 3242.25   Kenya. Ministry of Labour. Annual report. Nairobi. 1965+
Afr Doc 3242.30   Kenya. Ministry of Labour and Housing. Housing Section. Annual report. Nairobi? 1961
Afr Doc 3242.5.15   Kenya. Ministry of Lands and Settlement. Annual report of the Commissioner. Nairobi. 1938
Afr Doc 3242.15   Kenya. Ministry of Local Government. Report of Nairobi Standing Committee. Nairobi. 1964
Afr Doc 3242.10   Kenya. Ministry of Local Government. Report of the Permanent Secretary for Local Government. 1948-1950
Afr Doc 3214.2   Kenya. National Assembly. House of Representatives. Official report. 1,1963+
     11v.
Afr Doc 3216.2   Kenya. National Assembly. Senate. Official report. Nairobi. 1,1963+
Afr Doc 3231.5F   Kenya. Native Affairs Department. Annual report.
     3v.
Afr Doc 3224.5   Kenya. President. President's circular. Nairobi. 1967+
Afr Doc 3246.5   Kenya. Printing and Stationery Department. Annual report.
Afr Doc 3212.20   Kenya. Public Accounts Committee. Epitome of reports and the treasury memoranda thereon and an index. Nairobi. 1947-1954
Afr Doc 3212.210   Kenya. Public Accounts Committee. Evidence on the report of the Public Accounts Committee on the Government of Kenya accounts. Nairobi. 1965+
Afr Doc 3212.205   Kenya. Public Accounts Committee. Report on the governmetn of Kenya accounts. Nairobi. 1947+
Afr Doc 3246.8   Kenya. Public Service Commission. Report on the working of the Public Service Commission. Nairobi. 1,1963+
Afr Doc 3246.15   Kenya. Public Works Department. Report. Nairobi. 1935-1956
Afr Doc 3233.25   Kenya. Registrar of Co-operation Societies. Annual report. Nairobi. 1953-1957
Afr Doc 3248.10F   Kenya. Road Authority. Annual report. Nairobi. 1955+
Afr 6405.2   Pamphlet vol. Kenya. Social and economic conditions, 1965. 2 pam.
Afr Doc 3249.5   Kenya. Survey of Kenya. Administration report.
Afr Doc 3250.5   Kenya. Tea Development Authority. Annual report and accounts. Nairobi. 1965+
Afr Doc 3019.5   Kenya. Treaties. Treaty for East African co-operation. Nairobi, 1967.
Afr Doc 3253.5F   Kenya. Water Development Department. Annual report. Nairobi. 1965+
Afr 6455.45.2   Kenya. 2d ed. (Leys, Norman MacLean.) London, 1925.
Afr 6455.50   Kenya. 3d ed. (Kenya Colony and Protectorate.) London, 1959.
Afr 6455.45.3   Kenya. 3d ed. (Leys, Norman MacLean.) London, 1926.
Afr Doc 3207.360   Kenya African agricultural sample census, 1960-1961 (Kenya. Economics and Statistics Division.) Nairobi, 1962.
Afr Doc 3207.362.5.5F   Kenya agricultural census, 1962, scheduled areas and coastal strip. (Kenya. Economics and Statistics Division.) n.p., 1963.
Afr 6455.55   Kenya and Uganda Rail Road and Harbours. Travel guide to Kenya and Uganda. London, 1931.
Afr 6455.21.5   Kenya chronicles. (Cranworth, B.F.G.) London, 1939.
Afr 6420.10   The Kenya coastal strip. (Robertson, J.W.) London, 1961.
Afr 6455.50   Kenya Colony and Protectorate. Kenya. 3d ed. London, 1959.
Afr 6455.49   Kenya Colony and Protectorate. (Great Britain. Oversea Settlement Department.) London, 1930.
Afr 6408.10   Kenya Colony and Protectorate. Planning Committee. Report.
Afr 6455.46   Kenya days. (Buxton, Mary Aline B.) London, 1927.
Afr 6408.5   The Kenya decision. (British Indian Colony. Merchants Association, Bombay.) Bombay, 1923.
Afr 6455.90   Kenya diary. (Meinertzhagen, R.) Edinburg, 1957.
Afr Doc 3203.20   Kenya directory of the diplomatic corps. Nairobi. 1966
Afr 6455.73.5   A Kenya farmer looks at his colony. (Schwarzenberg, A.) N.Y., 1946.
Afr 6420.5   Kenya from within. (Ross, W.M.) London, 1927.
     2v.
Afr 6410.7   Kenya Independence Conference, London, 1963. Report presented to Parliament. London, 1963.
Afr 6300.44   Kenya Institute of Administration. K.I.A. occasional papers. Lower Kakete. 1,1968+
Afr 6465.5   Kenya mountain. (Dutton, E.H.T.) London, 1929.
Afr 6435.6   Kenya-Somalia relations. (Kenya.) Nairobi, 1967.
Afr Doc 3207.10   Kenya statistical digest. Nairobi. 1,1963+
Afr 6457.29F   Kenya Tea Development Authority. The operations and development plans of the Kenya Tea Development Authority. Nairobi, 1964.
Afr 6457.20   Kenya today, social prerequisite for economic development. (Forrester, M.) Monton, 1962.
Afr 6415.30   Kenya today. (Huxley, Elspeth. Grant.) London, 1954.
Afr 6400.44   Kenya today. Nairobi.
Afr 6455.47   A Kenyan farm diary. (Carnegie, V.M.) Edinburgh, 1930.
Afr 6415.25   Kenya's opportunity. (Altrimcham, E.G.) London, 1955.
Afr 6415.40.2   Kenya's progress. 2nd ed. (Askwirth, Tom G.) Kampala, 1958.
Afr 6455.79   Kenya's warning. (Wilson, C.J.) Nairobi, 1954.
Afr 6470.250.15F   Kenyatta, a photographic biography. (Howarth, Anthony.) Nairobi, 1967.

Afr 6095.4.3 Kingsley, Mary Henrietta. West African studies. 3d ed. London, 1964.

Afr 109.62 Kingsnorth, G.W. Africa south of the Sahara. Cambridge, 1962.

Afr 8305.5 Kinnear, A. To Modder River with Methuen. Bristol, 1900.

Afr 3979.66.25 Kinross, Patrick. Portrait of Egypt. London, 1966.
Afr 3979.66.20 Kinross, Patrick. Portrait of Egypt. N.Y., 1966.

Afr 500.10.3 Kinsky, Karl. Vade mecum für Diplomatische Arbeit auf dem Afrikanischen Continent. 3. Aufl. Leipzig, 1900.

Afr 10671.52.120 Kinsman and foreman. (Aluko, Timothy Mofolorunso.) London, 1966.

Afr 10531.61.100 Kinteh, Ramatoulie. Rebellion; a play in three acts. N.Y., 1968.

Afr 3315.152 Kipping, Norman Victor. The Suez contractors. Havant, Hampshire, 1969.

Afr 6390.93 Kirby, C.P. East Africa: Kenya, Uganda and Tanzania. London, 1968.

Afr 8659.60.5 Kirby, Percival Robson. Jacob van Reenen and the Grosvenor expedition of 1790-1791. Johannesburg, 1958.

Afr 8659.60.15 Kirby, Percival Robson. The true story of the Grosvenor. N.Y., 1960.

Afr 8678.34 Kirk, J. The economic aspects of native segregation in South Africa. London, 1929.

Afr 9558.510 Kirk, John. The Zambesi journal and letters of Dr. John Kirk, 1858-63. Edinburg, 1965. 2v.

Afr 6210.10 Kirk-Greene, A.H.M. The principles of native administration in Nigeria. London, 1965.

Afr 6292.1 Kirk-Greene, Anthony. Adamawa, past and present. London, 1958.

Afr 9558.85.2 Kirk on the Zambesi; a chapter of African history. (Coupland, R.) Oxford, 1968.

Afr 9558.85 Kirk on the Zambesi. (Coupland, R.) Oxford, 1928.

Afr 699.08 Kirkland, Caroline. Some African highways, journey of two American women to Uganda and the Transvaal. London, 1908.

Afr 6333.64 Kirkman, James S. Men and monuments on the East African coast. London, 1964.

Afr 505.45 Kirkwood, Kenneth. Britain and Africa. London, 1965.

Afr 8045.40 Kirkwood, Kenneth. The group areas act. Johannesburg, 195-.

Afr 679.17 Kirsch, M. Der Fremdenlegionär. N.Y., 1917.

Afr 6275.20 Kisch, M.S. Letters and sketches from northern Nigeria. London, 1910.

Afr 3745.65 Kiselev, V.I. Put sudana v nezavisimosti. Moscow, 1958.
Afr 13324.7.100 Kitawala. (Debertry, Leon.) Elisabethville, 1953.
Afr 555.144 Kitawala. (Greschat, Hans-Jürgen.) Marburg, 1967.
Afr 7580.30 Kitchen, Helen A. Footnotes to the Congo story. N.Y., 1967.

Afr 6540.3 Kitching, A.L. On the backwaters of the Nile. London, 1912.

Afr 6420.57 Kitson, Frank. Gangs and counter-gangs. London, 1960.
Afr 710.40 Kittler, Glenn D. Equatorial Africa. N.Y., 1959.
Afr 44619.5 Kiungani, or Story and history from Central Africa written by boys in the schools. (Madan, Arthur Cornwallis.) London, 1887.

Afr 7946.12 Kjellberg, Alice. Missionsarbetets börgan i Burundi. Orebro, 1966.

Afr 6883.10 Kjellberg, Eva. The Ismailis in Tanzania. Photoreproduction. Dar-es-Salaam, 1967.

Afr 11051.2 Klaas Gezwint en zijn paert and other songs and rijmpjes of South Africa. Cape Town, 1884.

Afr 8809.52 Klare besgryving van Cabo de Bona Esperança. (Hondius, J.) Kaapstad, 1952.

Afr 550.8 Klein, F. Le Cardinal Lavigerie et ses oeuvres africaines. Paris, 1890.

Afr 550.8.3 Klein, F. Le Cardinal Lavigerie et ses oeuvres africaines. 3e éd. Paris, 1893.

Afr 4513.35.115 Klein, Fritz. Warum Krieg um Abessinien. Leipzig, 1935.

Afr 3269.15 Kleine, Mathilde. Deutschland und die ägyptische Frage. Greifswald, 1927.

Afr 1555.3.30 Kleinknecht, W. Die englische Politik in der Agadirkrise (1911). Berlin, 1937.

Afr 2608.88 Kleist, H. Tunis und seine Umgebung. Leipzig, 1888.
Afr 7947.4 Klemke, O. Die Erziehung bei Eingeborenengruppen in Ruanda-Urundi. Bonn, 1962.

Afr 6979.62 Klerk, W.A. Drie swerwers oor die einders. 3. verb. uitg. Kaapstad, 1962.

Afr 8685.82 Die kleurlingbevolking van Suid-Afrika, Stellenbosch. (Theron, Erika.) Grahamstad, 1964.

Afr 3813.5 Kleve, Jacob Geert. Capital formation and increase in national income in Sudan in 1955-1959. Rotterdam, 1961.

Afr 5119.68 Klien, Martin A. Islam and imperialism in Senegal; Sine-Saloum, 1847-1914. Stanford, 1968.

Afr 6883.40 Klima, George J. The Barabaig; East African cattle-herders. N.Y., 1970.

Afr 10662.5 Klima, Vladimir. Modern Nigerian novels. Prague, 1969.
Afr 8289.02.39 Klinck-Luetetsburg, F. Christian de Wet, de held van Zuid-Afrika. Zutphen, 1902.

Afr 635.98 Klineberg, Otto. Nationalism and tribalism among African students. Paris, 1969.

Afr 5257.5.5 Klobb. Un drame colonial. Paris, 1931.
Afr 8210.10 Kloessel, M.H. Die Südafrikanischen Republiken. Leipzig, 1888.

Afr 8089.01.5 Klok, J. De boeren-republieken in Zuid-Afrika, hun ontstaan. Utrecht, 1901.

Afr 8808.89 Kloof and Karoo...in Cape colony. (Bryden, H.A.) London, 1889.

Afr 8659.68.5 Klooster, Willem Simon Brand. Zuid-Africa. Baarn, 1968.
Afr 6685.3 Klose, Heinrich. Togo unter deutschen Flagge. Berlin, 1899.

Afr 4070.17 Klun, V.F. Reise auf dem Weissen Nil. Laibach, 1851. 3 pam.

Afr 4070.6 Klunzinger, C.B. Upper Egypt. N.Y., 1878.
Afr 7809.62 Knapen, Marie Thérèse. L'enfant Mukongo. Louvain, 1962.
Afr 44610.5 Knappert, Jan. Traditional Swahili poetry. Leiden, 1967.
Afr 8145.35 Knietoch, Clemens M. Nur einer von Vielen, aus dem Leben eines Missionsarztes. Frankfurt, 1961.

Afr 3735.9 Knight, E.F. Letters from the Sudan. London, 1897.
Afr 5635.2 Knight, E.F. Madagascar in war time. London, 1896.
Afr 9488.95.5 Knight, E.F. Rhodesia of to-day. London, 1895.
Afr 7375.9.2 Knight, H.C. Africa redeemed. London, 1851.
Afr 7375.9.5 Knight, H.C. The new republic. 2d. ed. Boston, 1851.
Afr 1571.35A Knight, M.M. Morocco as a French economic venture. N.Y., 1937.

Afr 9424.250 Knight-Bruce, Louise (Torr). The story of an African chief. London, 1893.

Afr 9488.92 Knight-Bruce. Journals of the Mashonaland mission. London, 1892.

Afr 9488.95 Knight-Bruce. Memories of Mashonaland. London, 1895.
Afr 8678.250 Knoob, Willi. Die afrikanisch-christlichen Bewegungen unter den Bantu. Köln, 1961.

Afr 3978.73 Knorring, O.V. Tvaa maanader i egypten. Stockholm, 1873.
Afr 9689.63 Know your home: Zambia. (Hock, E.) Chensali? 1963?
Afr Doc 2560.600 Know your legislators; biographical notes. (Nigeria, Eastern. Ministry of Information.) Enugu, 1963.

Afr 2208.81.9 Knox, A.A. The new playground...Algeria. London, 1881.
Afr 8300.9 Knox, E.B. Buller' campaign. London, 1902.
Afr 9598.84.5 Knox, T.W. The boy travellers in the Far East. N.Y., 1884.

Afr 3978.82.10 Knox, T.W. The boy travellers in the Far East. Pt. 4 - Egypt and the Holy Land. N.Y., 1883.

Afr 4290.5 Kobishchanov, Iurii M. Aksum. Moskva, 1966.
Afr 6277.112 Koch, Bernd. Das Handwerk in ausgewählten Bezirken Westnigerias. Frankfurt, 1968.

Afr 6740.45 Koch, Henri. Magie et chasse dans la forêt camerounaise. Paris, 1968.

Afr 6850.7 Koch, Ludwig. Ostafrika in der Geschichte der Weltwirtschaft. Berlin, 1930.

Afr 8677.25 Koch, M.H. An analysis of the finances of the Union of South Africa. Cape Town, 1922.

Afr 8677.25.5 Koch, M.H. An analysis of the finances of the Union of South Africa. Cape Town, 1927.

Afr 6280.2.35 Kochakova, Nataliie B. Goroda-gosudarstva iorubov. Moskva, 1968.

Afr 8659.12.5F Kock, J.H.M. De Kaap als een nieuw land. 2. druk. Kaapstad, 1912.

Afr 8676.36 Kock, M.H. The economic development of South Africa. London, 1936.

Afr 6780.30 Kock, Nis. Blockade and jungle. London, 1940.
Afr 8095.30 Kock, V. de. Ons drie eeue. Our three centuries. Kaapstad, 1952.

Afr 8825.25 Kock, V. de. Those in bondage. Cape Town, 1950.
Afr 8100.15 Kock, Victor de. By strength of heart. Cape Town, 1954.
Afr 8095.75 Kock, Victor de. Ons erfenis. Kaapstad, 1960.
Afr 8100.10 Kock, W.J. de. Portugese ontdekkers om die Kaap. Kaapstad, 1957.

Afr 8338.326 Kock, Willem J. de. Jacob de Villiers Roos, 1869-1940. Kaapstad, 1958.

Afr 1609.17.3 Koechlin, Raymond. Le Maroc en paix. Paris, 1917.
Afr 2762.3 Koehler, A. Verfassung der Tuareg. Gotha, 1903.
Afr 555.17.15 Koehler, Henry. L'église chrétienne du Maroc et la mission franciscaine, 1221-1790. Paris, 1934.

Afr 28.76 Koehler, Jochen. Deutsche Dissertationen über Afrika. Bonn, 1962.

Afr 5324.3 Koeler, H. Einige Notizen über Bonny. Göttingen, 1848.
Afr 7465.5 Koelle, S.W. Narrative of an expedition into the Vy country of West Africa. London, 1849.

Afr 6460.55 Koenig, Oskar. The Maisai story. London, 1956.
Afr 7565.12.25 Koenigk, G. Die Berliner Kongo-Konferenz, 1884-1885. Essen, 1938.

Afr 8658.73 Koerner, F. Süd Afrika. Breslau, 1873.
Afr 8687.251 Kohler, C.W.H. The memoirs of Kohler of the K.W.V. London, 1946.

Afr 210.65.50A Kohn, Hans. African nationalism in the 20th century. Princeton, 1965.

Afr 6415.35 Koinange, M. The people of Kenya speak for themselves. Detroit, 1955.

Afr 8657.19F Kolbe, Peter. Caput Bonae Spei hodiernum. Nurnberg, 1719.
Afr 8657.19.7 Kolbe, Peter. Description du cap de Bonne-Espérance. Amsterdam, 1741. 3v.

Afr 8657.19.3F Kolbe, Peter. Naaukeurige en uitvoerige beschryving van de Kaap de Goede Hoop. Amsterdam, 1727. 2v.

Afr 8657.19.5 Kolbe, Peter. Present state of the Cape of Good Hope. London, 1731. 2v.

Afr 626.213 Kollektivnyi kolonializm v deistvii. (Korendiasov, Evgenii N.) Moskva, 1969.

Afr 1635.27 Koller Angelus, Father. Essai sur l'esprit du berbere marocain. 2. ed. Fribourg, 1949.

Afr 6889.3 Kollmann, P. The Victoria Nyanza. London, 1899.
Afr 2749.57.15 Kollmannsperger, Fr. Drohende Wüste. Wiesbaden, 1957.
Afr 210.65.15 Kollmannsperger, Franz. Von Afrika nach Afrika. Mainz, 1965.

Afr 4559.14 Kolmodin, J. Traditions de Tsazzega et Hazzega. Annales. Uppsala, 1914.

Afr 3675.17 Die koloniale Entwicklung des Anglo-Ägyptischen Sudans. (Kraemer, W.) Berlin, 1938.

Afr 630.43.5F Koloniale Völkerkunde. Berlin, 1943.
Afr 6926.30 Kolonialherrschaft und Sozialstruktur in Deutsch-Südwestafrika, 1894-1914. (Bley, Helmut.) Hamburg, 1968.

Afr 7565.22 Kolonialismus und Humanitätsintervention. (Loth, Heinrich.) Berlin, 1966.

Afr 5055.59.5 Kolonialnaia politika Frantsii v Zapadnoi Afrike, 1880-1900. (Subbotin, V.A.) Moscow, 1959.

Afr 6612.5 Kolonalnye Pritiazanie germanskogo fashizma v Afrike. (Zamengof, M.) Moscow, 1937.

Afr 500.60 Kolonialprobleme der Gegenwart in Beitragen. (Gunzert, T.) Berlin, 1939.

Afr 6640.22 Kolonien unter der Peitsche. (Mueller, F.F.) Berlin, 1962.

Afr 6420.30 Die Kolonisation Kenias. Inaug. Diss. (Weigt, Ernst.) Leipzig, 1932.

Afr 6488.5 Die Kolonisation Ugandas. Inaug. Diss. (Brendel, Horst.) Grossenhain, 1934.

Afr 6883.32 Komba, J.J. God and man. Rome, 1961.
Afr 10118.3 Komey, Ellis A. Modern African stories. London, 1964.
Afr 8230.38 Kommandant-generaal Hendrik Potgieter. (Potgieter, C.) Johannesburg, 1938.

Afr 3986.964.20 Komzin, Ivan V. Svet Asuana. Moscow, 1964.
Afr 10631.58.110 Konadu, Asare. Come back Dora, a husband's confession and ritual. Accra, 1966.

Afr 10631.58.140 Konadu, Asare. Ordained by the oracle. Accra, 1969.
Afr 10631.58.120 Konadu, Asare. Shadow of wealth. Accra, 1966.
Afr 10631.58.100 Konadu, Asare. The wizard of Osamang. Accra, 1964.
Afr 10631.58.130 Konadu, Asare. A woman in her prime. Accra, 1967.
Afr 12936.50.102 Kondo le requin; drame historique en trois actes. 2. éd. (Pliya, Jean.) Porto-Novo, 1966?

Afr 3979.58.5 Kondrashov, S.N. Na beregakh Nila. Moscow, 1958.

Afr 3.20 Konferenz der unabhängigen Staaten Afrikas, April 15-22, 1958. (Conference of Independent African States, 1st, Accra, 1958.) London, 1958.
VAfr 7567.41 Konge Kinszasa. Wyd. 1. (Ratajski, Lech.) Warszawa, 1967.
Afr 10689.67.160 Kongi's harvest. (Soyinka, W.) London, 1967.
Afr 7549.65 Kongo, heisses Herz Afrikas. Geschichte des Landes bis auf unsere Tage. (Loth, Heinrich.) Berlin, 1965.
Afr 7809.57.5 Kongo, met het blote oog. (Jonchleere, K.) Amsterdam, 1959.
Afr 7809.01 Kongo. (Svambera, V.) Praha, 1901.
Afr 7568.30 Kongo. (Tisdel, W.P.) Leipzig, 1886.
Afr 7575.99 Kongo. (Vinokurov, Iurii N.) Moskva, 1967.
Afr 7533.02F Pamphlet box. Kongo (Belgian).
Afr 7575.95 Kongo en de Verenigde Naties. (Netherlands. Department van Buitenlandse Zaken.) 's-Gravenhage, 1961-
2v.
Afr 7809.60 Kongo im Umbruch. (Gruenebaum, Kurt.) Bruxelles, 1960.
Afr 7580.32 Kongo kurtuluş, sowosi. 1. baski. (Topuzoglu.) Istanbul, 1965.
Afr 710.45 Les Kongo nord-occidentaux. (Soret, Marcel.) Paris, 1959.
Afr 7812.259.5 Kongo pod gnetom imperializma. (Martynov, Vladimir A.) Moskva, 1959.
Afr 7567.12 Kongoerinnerungen. (Landbeck, P.) Berlin, 1923.
Afr 7568.3 Der Kongostaat. (Stengel, K.F. von.) München, 1903.
Afr 7549.11.7 Kongostaat und Kongoreform. (Anton, G.K.) Leipzig, 1911.
Afr 6194.36 The Konkomba of northern Ghana. (Tait, David.) London, 1961.
Afr 4513.37.15 Konovalov, T.E. Con le armate del Negus. Bologna, 1937.
Afr 8289.54 Die konsentrasiekampe. (Otto, J.C.) Kaapstad, 1954.
Afr 9225.20 Die konstitusie en die staatsinstellings van die Oranje-Vrystaat, 1854-1902. (Scholtz, G.D.) Amsterdam, 1936.
Afr 32.3 Konstitutsii gosudarstv Afriki. (Akademiia Nauk SSSR. Institut Gosudarstva i Prava.) Moskva, 1966.
2v.
Afr 11675.87.150 Kontakion for you departed. (Paton, Alan.) London, 1969.
Afr 609.42.5 Ein Kontinent rückt näher. (Viera, Josef.) München, 1942.
Afr 5407.10 Kooperation in Afrika. (Voss, Harald.) Hamburg, 1965.
Afr 8678.294 Koos Vorrink Instituut. Zuid-Afrika en de apartheid. Amsterdam, 1965.
Afr 4008.14 Koptologische Arbeitskonferenz, Halle, 1964. Koptologische Studien in der DDR. Halle, 1965.
Afr 4008.14 Koptologische Studien in der DDR. (Koptologische Arbeitskonferenz, Halle, 1964.) Halle, 1965.
Afr 6218.20 Kopytoff, Jean Herskovits. A preface to modern Nigeria. Madison, 1965.
Afr 6390.75.2 Korabiewicz, Waclaw. Safari mingi. Wyd.2. Warszawa, 1963.
Afr 9289.5 The Korana. (Engelbrecht, J.A.) Cape Town, 1936.
Afr 575.18 Korei, Aly. Condition juridique des sujets musulmans. Thèse. Paris, 1913.
Afr 7377.34.5 Koren, W. Liberia, the league and the United States. N.Y., 1934.
Afr 626.213 Korendiasov, Evgenii N. Kollektivnyi kolonializm v deistvii. Moskva, 1969.
Afr 6225.7 Koriavin, L.A. Probudivshaisia Nigeriia. Moscow, 1962.
Afr 5645.11 Korneev, L.A. Obrazovanie Malgashskoi republiki. Moscow, 1963.
Afr 3993.967.2 Kornrumpf, Hans-Jurgen. Vereinigte Arabische Republik. Opladen, 1964.
Afr 1407.5 Kort...verhaal...slavernye onder de Mooren. Amsterdam, 1753.
Afr 6990.90.20 Kort verhale uit 'n lang lewe. (Vedder, Heinrich.) Kaapstad, 1957.
Afr 3740.14 Kossatz, Heinz. Untersuchungen über den französisch-englischen Weltgegensatz im Faschodajahr (1898). Breslau, 1934.
Afr 6149.162.5 Kossoh town boy. (Cole, R.W.) Cambridge, Eng., 1960.
Afr 1258.80.5 Kostenko, L.Th. Puteshestvie v severnuiu Afriku. Izd 2. Sankt Peterburg, 1880.
Afr 8325.70 Kotzé, C.R. My bollingskap (St. Helena). Bloemfontein, 1942.
Afr 8678.298 Kotze, J.C.G. Principle and practice in race relations. Stellenbosch, 1962.
Afr 8252.251.5 Kotze, J.G. Biographical memoirs and reminiscences. v.1. Cape Town, 193-
Afr 8278.98.3 Kotze, J.G. Documents relating to judicial crisis in Transvaal. London, 1898.
Afr 5055.66 Kouassigan, Guy Adjéte. L'homme et la terre. Paris, 1966.
Afr 5243.207 Koumen. (Ba, A.H.) Paris, 1961.
Afr 12881.67.100 Kourouma, Ahmadou. Les soleils des indépendances. Montréal, 1968.
Afr 7465.8 Die Kpelle. (Westermann, D.) Göttingen, 1921.
Afr 3978.66 Kraemer, R. von. En vinter Orienten. Reseanteckingar fraan Egypten. Stockholm, 1866.
Afr 3675.17 Kraemer, W. Die koloniale Entwicklung des Anglo-Ägyptischen Sudans. Berlin, 1938.
Afr 2030.461.50 Kraft, Joseph. The struggle for Algeria. 1st ed. Garden City, 1961.
Afr 6277.110 Kranendonk, H. A prelimenary report on rural changes in the Savanna area of the Western State of Nigeria. Ibadan, 1968.
Afr 698.58 Krapf, J.L. Reisen in Ostafrika. Stuttgart, 1964.
Afr 698.60.2 Krapf, J.L. Travels, researches...eastern Africa. Boston, 1860.
Afr 698.60 Krapf, J.L. Travels, researches...eastern Africa. Boston, 1860.
Afr 698.60.3 Krapf, Ludwig. Travels, researches...Eastern Africa. 2. ed. London, 1968.
Afr 6280.2.40 Krapf-Askari, Eve. Yoruba towns and cities. Oxford, 1969.
Afr 1623.964.15 Kratz, Achim. Untersuchung der morokkanischen Industriestruktur. Hamburg, 1964.
Afr 6739.265.5 Kratz, Achim. Voraussetzungen und Möglichkeiten einer industriellen Entwicklung in Kamerun. Hamburg, 1965.
Afr 2623.966 Kratz, Achim. Voraussetzungen und Möglichkeiten einer industriellen Entwicklung in Tunesien. Hamburg, 1966.
Afr 4060.15 Kraus, J. Die Anfänge des Christentums in Nubien. Inaug. Diss. Mödling, 1930.
Afr 8252.341.25A Kraus, Rene. Old master, the life of Jan Christian Smuts. 1st ed. N.Y., 1944.
Afr 4320.3 Krause, K. Die Portugiesen in Abessinien. Dresden, 1912.
Afr 626.127 Kreinin, M.E. Israel and Africa. N.Y., 1964.
Afr 3978.63.15 Kremer, Alfred, Freiherr von. Aegypten. Leipzig, 1863.
Afr 2030.467.5 Krest'ianstvo v alzhirskoi revoliutsii, 1954-1962. (Frolkin, Nikolai M.) Kiev, 1967.
Afr 8658.53 Kretzschmar, E. Südafrikanische Skizzen. Leipzig, 1853.

Afr 6542.52 Kreuer, Werner. Der Wandel der sozialen Struktur in den drei ostafrikanischen Königreichen Ankole, Bunyoro und Buganda. Thesis. Bonn, 1966.
Afr 1490.5 Kreuter, A. Marokko: wirtschaftliche und soziale Studien in Marokko 1911. Berlin, 1911.
Afr 6147.8.10 Kreutzinger, Helga. The picture of Krio life, Freetown, 1900-1920. Wien, 1968.
Afr 1609.11.6 Kreuz und qür durch Marokko. (Artbauer, O.C.) Stuttgart, 1911.
Afr 8686.12 Kreuz zwischen Weiss und Schwarz. (Weber, Karl Friedrich.) Breklum, 1965.
Afr 8289.00.47 Der Krieg in Süd-afrika, 1899-1900. v.1-5. (Mueller, A. von.) Berlin, 1900.
Afr 8678.42 Krieger, Heinrich. Das Rassenrecht in Südafrika. Berlin, 1944.
Afr 6777.2 Kriegsbilder aus dem Araberaupland. (Behr, H.F. von.) Leif, 1891.
Afr 9161.10 Krige, E. (Jensen). The realm of a rain-queen. London, 1943.
Afr 9045.15 Krige, E.J. The social system of the Zulus. London, 1936.
Afr 3258.16F Krigen i Aegypten. Pt.1-3. (Illustriret Familie-Journals.) Kjøbenhavn, 1882.
Afr 8678.255 Krishna Mevor, Vengalil Kreshnan. Question of race conflict resulting from the policies of apartheid. New Delhi, 1959.
Afr 8289.01.37 Kritische Betrachtungen über den Burenkrieg. (Mueller, Alfred von.) Berlin, 1901.
Afr 3310.40 Krizis ekonomiki Egipta. (Hasan Abd al-Razik Muhammad.) Moscow, 1955.
Afr 679.27 Krøniker fra Guines. (Larsen, K.) Hellerup, 1927.
Afr 635.20 Kroll, Hubert. Die Haustiere der Bantu. Inaug. Diss. Berlin, 1929.
Afr 8686.14 Krueger, Bernhard. The pear tree blossoms; a history of the Moravian mission stations in South Africa, 1737-1869. Thesis. Genadendal, 1966.
Afr 8745.20 Krueger, D.W. The age of the generals. Johannesburg, 1958.
Afr 8230.6.15 Krueger, D.W. Paul Kruger. Johannesburg, 1961. 2v.
Afr 8050.15.5 Krueger, Daniel. South African parties and policies, 1910-1960. London, 1960.
Afr 8050.15 Krueger, Daniel. South African parties and policies. Cape Town, 1960.
Afr 626.30 Krueger, Karl. Afrika. Berlin, 1952.
Afr 8378.349 Kruger, J.J. President C.R. Swart. Kaapstad, 1961.
Afr 8230.6A Kruger, Paul. Memoirs. N.Y., 1902.
Afr 8230.6.5 Kruger, Paul. Memoirs. v.1-2. London, 1902.
Afr 8289.59 Kruger, Rayne. Good-bye Dolly Gray. London, 1959.
Afr 11501.89.100 Kruger, Rayne. The spectacle. London, 1953.
Afr 11501.89.110 Kruger, Rayne. Young villain with wings. London, 1953.
Afr 8230.3 Kruger, S.J.P. Paul Kruger amptelike briewe, 1851-1877. Pretoria, 1925.
Afr 8210.14 Kruger days, reminiscences of Dr. W.J. Leyds. (Leyds, W.J.) London, 1939.
Afr 9149.32 The Kruger national park. (Stevenson-Hamilton, James.) Johannesburg, South Africa, 1932.
Afr 8230.33 Kruger's secret service. London, 1900.
Afr 679.66.15 Kubbel', Lev E. Strana zolota. Moskva, 1966.
Afr 6686.201 Kuczynski, R.R. The Cameroons and Togoland. London, 1939.
Afr 6685.12 Kueas, Richard. Togo-Erinnerungen. Berlin, 1939.
Afr 2209.08.5 Kuehnel, Ernst. Algerien. Leipzig, 1908.
Afr 608.41 Kuelb, P.H. Geschichte der Entdeckungsreisen. Mainz, 1841.
Afr 2975.1 Kufra. (Rohlfs, G.) Leipzig, 1881.
Afr 9089.42 Kuit, Albert. Transvaalse gister. Pretoria, 1942.
Afr 8135.25.5 Kuit, Albert. Transvaalse terugblikke. Pretoria, 1945.
Afr 8135.25 Kuit, Albert. Transvaalse verskeidenheid. Pretoria, 1940.
Afr 7875.5.10 Kuitenbrouwer, Joost B.W. Le camp des Balula. Bruxelles, 1956.
Afr 7815.5.6 Les Kuku. 6. (Plas, J.V.) Bruxelles, 1910.
Afr 4559.07 Kulmer, F. Im Reiche Kaiser Meneliks. Leipzig, 1910.
Afr 8667.5.10 Kultur geskiedenis van die Afrikaner. (Heever, C.M. van der.) Kaapstad, 1945. 3v.
Afr 8110.20 Der Kulturanteil des Deutschtums am Aufbau des Burenvolkes. (Schmidt-Pretoria, W.) Hannover, 1938.
Afr 5243.125.30 Kulturawandel bei den Bambara von Segou. (Benchelt, Eno.) Bonn, 1962.
Afr 2283.2 Ein kulturgeschichtlicher Ausflug in den Aures. (Stuhlmann, F.) Hamburg, 1912.
Afr 8279.01.20 Der Kulturkampf in Süd Afrika. (Elout, Cornelis.) Leipzig, 1901.
Afr 550.12 Kumm, H.K.W. African missionary heroes and heroines. N.Y., 1917.
Afr 718.21 Kumm, H.K.W. From Hausaland to Egypt. London, 1910.
Afr 718.22 Kumm, H.K.W. Khont-Hon-Nofer, lands of Ethiopia. London, 1910.
Afr 4070.21 Kumm, H.K.W. The Sudan. 2d ed. London, 1909.
Afr 210.60.20 Kummernuss, Adolph. Wohin geht Afrika. Frankfurt a.M., 1960.
Afr 21107.5 Kunene, Daniel P. The beginning of South African vernacular literature. Los Angeles, 1967.
Afr 150.2 Kunstmann, F. Afrika vor den Entdeckungen der Portugiesen. München, 1853.
Afr 6720.62 Kuoh Mukouri, J. Doigts noirs. Montreal, 1963.
Afr 6140.10 Kup, A.P. A history of Sierra Leone. Cambridge, Eng., 1961.
Afr 6138.64 Kup, A.P. The story of Sierra Leone. Cambridge, Eng., 1964.
Afr 8028.156 Kuper, B. A bibliography of native law in South Africa, 1941-1961. Johannesburg, 1962.
Afr 9198.10 Kuper, H. An African aristocracy. London, 1961.
Afr 9198.2 Kuper, H. The Swazi, a South African kingdom. N.Y., 1963.
Afr 9198.5 Kuper, H. The uniform of color... Swaziland. Johannesburg, 1947.
Afr 9047.20 Kuper, Hilda. Indian people in Natal. Natal, 1960.
Afr 8678.325 Kuper, Leo. An African bourgeoisie. New Haven, 1965.
Afr 11505.69.100 Kuper, Leo. The college brew. Durban, 1960.
Afr 9060.10A Kuper, Leo. Durban. London, 1958.
Afr 8350.25 Kuper, Leo. Passive resistance in South Africa. London, 1956.
Afr 8678.336 Kuper, Leo. Passive resistance in South Africa. New Haven, 1957.
Afr 3310.95 Kurdgelashvili, Shota N. Revoliutsiia 1952 g. i krakh britanskogo gospodstva v Egipte. Moskva, 1966.
Afr 10016.15 Kurgantsev, Mikhail. Iz afrikanskoi liriki. Moskva, 1967.

Afr 6303.7	Kuria, Lucas. A bibliography on anthropology and sociology in Tanzania and East Africa. Syracuse, 1966.
Afr 6478.2	Kuria, Lucas. A bibliography on politics and government in Uganda. Syracuse, 1965.
Afr 4555.40.22	Kurtze und wahrhaftige Beschreibung der Ethiopie. (Alvares, Francisco.) Eiszlebe, 1567.
Htn Afr 590.44*	Eine kurtze Vorstellung des Theils von Africa. (Benezet, A.) Ephrata, 1763.
Afr 4585.2	Kurze Schilderung...abessinischen Juden. (Flad, M.) Basel, 1869.
Afr 3979.55F	Kusch, E. Ägypten im Bild. Nürnberg, 1955.
Afr 3230.9	Kusel, S.S. de. An Englishman's recollections of Egypt. London, 1915.
Afr 2875.65	Kutay, Cemal. Trablus-garbde bir avuc. Istanbul, 1963.
Afr 9325.11	Kutlwano. Botswana. 4,1965+ 5v.
Afr 8279.00.15	Kuyper, A. Le crise sud africaine. Paris, 1900.
Afr 6192.95	Kuzvart, Milos. Ghanska cesta. Praha, 1962.
Afr 609.33.15	Kwa heri Afrika. (Behn, Fritz.) Stuttgart, 1933.
Afr 8687.273	Kwa Zulu. (Cowley, Cecil.) Cape Town, 1966.
Afr 6176.39	Kwame Nkrumah, leider van Afrika. (Grammens, Mark.) Tielt, 1961.
Afr 6176.5	Kwame Nkrumah. (Timothy, B.) London, 1955.
Afr 6176.30.80	Kwame Nkrumah and Africa. (Jones, Peter.) London, 1965.
Afr 6176.20	Kwame Nkrumah and the future of Africa. (Phillips, John F.) London, 1960.
Afr 6710.5	Kwayeb, E.K. Les institutions de droit public du pays Bamileke. Paris, 1960.
Afr 7858.2F	Le Kwilu. (Nicolai, Henri.) Bruxelles, 1963.
Afr 6168.4	Kyereteire, K.O. Bonsu Ashanti heroes. Accra, 1964.
Afr 2030.280	L attitude de l eglise dans la guerre d algerie. Bruxelles, 1960 (Houart, Pierre.)
Afr 626.24	L industrialisation de l'Afrique. (Dujonchay, I.) Paris, 1953.
Afr 4710.5	L organisation de la colonie de l'Erythrée. (Mondaini, G.) Bruxelles, 1912.
Afr 6095.14.5	Labarthe, P. Reise nach der Küste von Guinea. Weimar, 1805.
Afr 6095.14	Labarthe, P. Voyage à la côte de Guinée. Paris, 1805.
Afr 5180.21	Labarthe, P. Voyage au Sénégal pendant les années 1784 et 1785. Paris, 1802.
Afr 8292.5.15	Labat, G.P. Le livre d'or. Montreal, 1901.
Afr 3708.10	Labat, G.P. Les voyageurs canadiens à l'expédition du Soudan. Québec, 1886.
Afr 3740.10	Labatut, Guy de. Fachoda. 4e ed. Paris, 1932.
Afr 677.28	Labot, J.B. Nouvelles relations de l'Afrique occidentale. Paris, 1728. 5v.
Afr 8678.20	Labour and other questions in South Africa. (Indicus.) London, 1903.
NEDL Afr 7045.5.2	Labour in Portuguese West Africa. 2d ed. (Cadbury, W.A.) N.Y., 1910.
Afr 109.46.5	Labouret, H. Africa before the white man. N.Y., 1963.
Afr 109.46.10	Labouret, H. L'Afrique précoloniale. Paris, 1959.
Afr 5035.5.10	Labouret, H. Monteil, explorateur et soldat. Paris, 1937.
Afr 5053.5	Labouret, Henri. A la recherche d'une politique indigène dans l'Ouest africain. Paris, 1931.
Afr 630.50	Labouret, Henri. Histoire des Noirs d'Afrique. 2. éd. Paris, 1950.
Afr 5057.14.5	Labouret, Henri. Paysans d'Afrique occidentale. Paris, 1941.
Afr 2875.53	Labriola, Arturo. La guerra di Tripoli e l'opinione socialista. Napoli, 1912.
Afr 5548.63	Lacaille, L.P. Connaissance de Madagascar. Paris, 1863.
Afr 8658.76.3	Lacaille, N.L. Journal historique du voyage fait au cap de Bonne-Espérance. Paris, 1776.
Afr 5748.81	Lacaze, H. Souvenirs de Madagascar. Paris, 1881.
Afr 4700.36.30	Laccetti, B. Le nostre colonie e cenni geografici generali. Napoli, 1936.
Afr 7322.5	Lacerda, F.G. de. Figuras e episodios da Zambezia. 2.ed. Lisboa, 1943.
Afr 9558.20	Lacerda, F.J. de. Exams das viagens do Doutor Livingstone. Lisbon, 1867.
Afr 718.9	Lacerda e Almeida, F.J.M. de. Journey to Cazembe. London, 1873.
Afr 7309.36	Lacerda e Almeida, Francisco José de. Travessia da Africa. Lisboa, 1936.
Afr 7549.59.15	Lacger, L. de. Ruanda. Kabgayi, 1959.
Afr 4025.18	Lachanokardes, E. Palaia kai nea Alexandreia. Alexandreia, 1927.
Afr 1640.10	Lachapelle, F. Les Tekna du sud Marocain. Paris, 1934.
Afr 2000.19	Lacheraf, Mostafa. L'Algérie, nation et société. Paris, 1965.
Afr 4513.35.100	Lachin, M. L'Ethiopie et son destin. 5e ed. Paris, 1935.
Afr 510.8	Lachons l'Asie, prenons l'Afrique. (Reclus, O.) Paris, 1904.
Afr 4155.15	Lackany, Radames Sany. Mersa Matruh and its environments. 2nd ed. Alexandria, 1960.
Afr 4180.6	Lackany, Radames Sany. Sollum and its environments. Alexandria, 1962.
Afr 2230.41	Lacoste, Camille. Bibliographie ethnologique de la Grande Kabylie. Paris, 1962.
Afr 1848.5	Lacoste, L. La marine algerienne sous les Turcs. Paris, 1931.
Afr 1830.20.80	Lacoste, Louis. La colonisation maritime en Algerie. Paris, 1931.
Afr 1869.60	Lacoste, Yves. L'Algérie. Paris, 1960.
Afr 5343.35	La Côte-d'Ivoire. Chances et risques. Session d'étude 20 juillet-11 août 1966. Bruxelles, 1967. 2v.
Afr 3978.70	Lacour, Raoul. L'Egypte d'Alexandrie a la Seconde Cataracte. Paris, 1871.
Afr 5180.19.4	Lacourbe, M.J. de. Premier voyage...fait à la côte d'Afrique...1685. Paris, 1913.
Afr 3300.85.2A	Lacouture, Jean. Egypt in transition. London, 1958.
Afr 3300.85	Lacouture, Jean. L'Égypte en mouvement. Paris, 1956.
Afr 3300.85.3	Lacouture, Jean. L'Égypte en mouvement. Paris 1962.
Afr 1623.958	Lacouture, Jean. Le Maroc a l'epreuve. Paris, 1958.
Afr 2290.1	Lacretelle. Etudes sur la province d'Oran. Marseille, 1865.
Afr 5057.30	Lacroix, Alain. Les conditions de la mise en valeur de l'Afrique occidentale française. Paris, 1959.
Afr 7947.9	Lacroix, Benoît. Le Rwanda: mille heures au pays des mille collines. Montréal, 1966.
Afr 2225.4	Lacroix, Bernardo. L'évolution du nomadisme en Algérie. Alger, 1906.
Afr 7812.267.5	Lacroix, Jan Louis. Industrialisation au Congo. Paris, 1967.
Afr 28716.2	Lacroix, Pierre Francis. Poésie peule de l'Adamawa. Paris, 1965. 2v.
Afr 6214.17	Ladder of bones. (Thorp, Ellen.) London, 1966.
Afr 7350.3.7	Ladies Association, Auxiliary to the American Colonization Society. Annual report. Philadelphia. 2,1934+
Afr 49032.1.100	Ladipo, Duro. Three Yoruba plays. Ibadan, 1964.
Afr 1609.32F	Ladreit de Lacharrière, J. Au Maroc en suivant Foucauld. Paris, 1932.
Afr 1769.1.80	Ladreit de Lacharriere, Jacques. Le reve d'Aabd el Kerim. Paris, 1925.
Afr 1609.13.12	Ladreit de Lacharriere, R. Voyage au Maroc, 1910-11. Paris, 1913.
Afr 1571.37	Ladreit Delacharriere, J. La pacification du Maroc, 1907-1934. Paris, 1936.
Afr 1703.3.15	Ladron De Guevara, A. Arcila durante la ocupacion portuguesa. Tanger, 1940.
Afr 8125.10	Lady Anne Barnard at the Cape of Good Hope, 1797-1802. (Fairbridge, D.) Oxford, 1924.
Afr 11802.92.120	Lady of Coventry. (Sowden, Lewis.) London, 1950.
Afr 9148.82	A lady trader in the Transvaal. (Heckford, S.) London, 1882.
Afr 9598.91	A lady's letter from central Africa. (Moir, J.F.) Glasgow, 1891.
Afr 9049.8	A lady's life and travels in Zululand. (Wilkinson.) London, 1882.
Afr 8300.11	Ladysmith, the diary of a siege. (Nevinson, H.W.) London, 1900.
Afr 12.5	Länder Afrikas. Bonn. 1+ 35v.
Afr 1407.4	Lafaye, J. de. Relation en forme de journal...des captifs. Paris, 1726.
Afr 7580.19	Lafever, E.W. Crisis in the Congo. Washington, 1965.
Afr 5385.14.2	Laffitte, J. Le Dahomé - souvenirs de voyage et de mission. Tours, 1873.
Afr 5385.14	Laffitte, J. Le Dahomé - souvenirs de voyage et de mission. 4 ed. Tours, 1876.
Afr 678.76	Laffitte, J. Le pays des Nègres et la Côte des esclaves. Tours, 1876.
Afr 2608.92.10	Lafitte, Fernand. Contribution à l'étude médicale de la Tunisie. Bordeaux, 1892.
Afr 2748.85	Lagarde, Charles. Une promenade dans le Sahara. Paris, 1885.
Afr 8865.5	Lagden, G. The Basutos. N.Y., 1910. 2v.
Afr 5840.20	Lagesse, Lois. Le père Laval. Port-Louis, 1955.
Afr 1573.31	Laget, Paul de. Au Maroc espagnol. Marseille, 1935.
Afr 12966.2	Lagneau, Lilyan. Neuf poètes camerounais. Yaounde, 1965.
Afr 4688.15.10	Il Lago Tana e le sue possibilità di sfruttamento. (Marchi, Giulio de.) Milano, 1936.
Afr 12.25	Lagos, Nigeria (City). University. African Studies Division. Proceedings at the staff seminars. Lagos. 1966+
Afr 6200.12.5F	Lagos, Nigeria (City). University. Continuing Education Center. Conference and seminar reports. Lagos. 1,1968+
Afr 6208.5F	Lagos. Blue book 1904, 1905. Lagos, 1905.
Afr 6293.2	Lagos. City Council. Tribunal of Inquiry. Report of the Tribunal of Inquiry into the affairs of the Lagos City Council for the period Oct. 15, 1962 to Apr. 18, 1966. Lagos, 1966.
Afr 6205.1	Pamphlet box. Lagos and Nigeria.
Afr 626.136.2	Lagos Conference, 28 July to 6 Aug. 1964. (International Conference on the Organization of Research and Training in Africa in Relation to the Study, Conservation and Utilization of Natural Resources, Lagos, 1964.) Paris, 1965.
Afr 12.40	Lagos notes and records. Lagos. 1,1967+
Afr 11509.35.120	LaGuma, Alex. And a threefold cord. Berlin, 1964.
Afr 11509.35.100	LaGuma, Alex. The stone country. Berlin, 1967
Afr 11509.35.110	LaGuma, Alex. A walk in the night. Ibadan, 196-?
Afr 1623.961	Lahaye, R. Les entreprises publiques au Maroc. Rabat, 1961.
Afr 4389.35.7	Lahse, Erich. Abessinien. 2e Aufl. Leipzig, 1935.
Afr 8835.41	Laidler, Percy Ward. The growth and government of Cape Town. Cape Town, 1939.
Afr 8835.35	Laidler, Percy Ward. A tavern of the ocean. Cape Town, 1926.
Afr 7122.82	Laidley, Fernando. Missoes de guerra e de paz no norte de Angola. Lisboa, 1964.
Afr 609.58.50	Laidley, Fernando. Roteiro africano; primeira volta a Africa em automovel. 3. ed. Lisboa, 1958.
Afr 5488.14	Laigret-Pascault, Denyse E. Fort-lamy. Fort-Lamy, 1961.
Afr 6143.5	Laing, A.G. Travels in...western Africa. London, 1825.
Afr 9446.25	Laing, D.J. The Matabele rebellion, 1896. London, 1897.
Afr 810.3.3	Laird, M. Narrative of expedition into Africa by the river Niger. v.1-2. London, 1837. 2v.
Afr 2533.2	Laitman, L. Tunisia today. N.Y., 1954.
Afr 607.48	Lajardière. Reise-Beschreibung nach Africa. Frankfurt, 1748.
Afr 8668.5	Lake, Alexander. Hunter's choice. 1st ed. Garden City, 1954.
Afr 9388.57.5	Lake Ngami, or Explorations and discovery during four years of wanderings in wilds of South Western Africa. (Anderson, C.J.) Cape Town, 1967.
Afr 9388.57	Lake Ngami. (Anderson, C.J.) N.Y., 1856.
Afr 9700.40	The lake of the royal crocodiles. (Bigland, Eileen.) London, 1939.
Afr 725.2	The lake regions of central Africa. (Burton, R.F.) London, 1860. 2v.
Afr 725.11	The lake regions of central Africa. (Geddie, J.F.R.G.) London, 1881.
Afr 725.16	The lake regions of central Africa. (Taylor, Bayard.) N.Y., 1881.
Afr 4688.15.5	Lake Tana and the blue Nile. (Cheesman, R.E.) London, 1936.
Afr 770.3	Lake Tanganyika. Photoreproduction. (Hore, Edw.C.) n.p., 1889.
Htn Afr 6390.7*	Lake Victoria to Khartoum with rifle and camera. (Dickinson, F.A.) London, 1910.
Afr 725.6	Lakes and mountains of eastern and central Africa. (Elton, J.F.) London, 1879.
Afr 2425.1F	Lallemand, C. Tunis et ses environs. Paris, 1890.

Afr 6019.54 Legum, Colin. Must we lose Africa. London, 1954.
Afr 210.62.30 Legum, Colin. Pan-Africanism. N.Y., 1962.
Afr 8678.323 Legum, Colin. South Africa, crisis for the West. London, 1964.
Afr 5385.11 Leherisse, R. Voyage au Dahomey et à la Côte-d'Ivoire. Paris, 1903.
Afr 8676.25 Lehfeldt, R.A. The national resources of South Africa. Johannesburg, 1922.
Afr 8659.66.10 Lehmann, Emily. Pretoria, Skinnerstraat 295. Wuppertal, 1966.
Afr 8687.271.5 Lehmann, Olga. Hans Merensky. Göttingen, 1965.
Afr 8687.271 Lehmann, Olga. Look beyond the wind; the life of Hans Merensky. Capetown, 1955?
Afr 2731.10 Lehuraux, L.J. Au Sahara avec le commandant Charlet. Paris, 1932.
Afr 3183.20 Leibniz, G.W. Consilium Aegyptiacum. Paris, 1843.
Afr 4339.36 Leichner, G. Gefahrvolles Abessinien. Leipzig, 1936.
Afr 6420.55 Leigh, Ione. In the shadow of the Mau Mau. London, 1954.
Afr 8845.8 Leigh, Ramon Lewis. The city of Port Elizabeth. Johannesburg, 1966.
Afr 6390.24.3 Leigh, W.R. Frontiers of enchantment. N.Y., 1938.
Afr 8105.35 Leilebrandt, Hendrik Carel von. Rambles through the archives of the colony of the Cape of Good Hope. Cape Town, 1887.
X Cg Afr 8110.3.5 Leipoldt, C.L. Jan van Riebeeck. London, 1936. (Changed to XP 3705)
Afr 8678.350 Leiss, Amelia Catherine. Apartheid and United Nations collective measures. N.Y., 1965.
Afr 3285.7 The leisure of an Egyptian official. (Cecil, E.) London, 1921.
Afr 3285.7.5 The leisure of an Egyptian official. 2d ed. (Cecil, E.) London, 1921.
Afr 674.93.25 Leite, D. A cerca da cronica dos feitos de Guiné. Lisboa, 1941.
Afr 6295.44 Leith-Ross, Sylvia. African conversation piece. London, 1944.
Afr 6280.9.30 Leith-Ross, Sylvia. African women. N.Y., 1965.
Afr 6275.114 Leith Ross, Sylvia. Beyond the Niger. London, 1951.
Afr 5540.1 Lejamble, George. Le fokonolona et le pouvoir. Tananarive, 1963.
Afr 4370.7 Lejean, G. Theodore II, le nouvel empire d'Abyssinie et les intérêts français dans le sud de la Mer Rouge. Paris, 1865.
Afr 4558.64F Lejean, G. Voyage en Abyssinie executé de 1862 à 1864. Text and atlas. Paris, 1873. 2v.
Afr 2224.929 Lejeune, André. Le role du crédit dans le développement économique de l'Algérie depuis la fin de la guerre. Thèse. Paris, 1930.
Afr 7850.42 Lekime, Fernand. Katanga, pays du cuirre. Verviers, 1965.
Afr 3978.74 Leland, C.G. The Egyptian sketch book. N.Y., 1874.
Afr 7815.36 Lelong, M.H. Mes frères du Congo. Alger, 1946. 2v.
Afr 2749.45.5 Lelong, Maurice H., Père. Le Sahara aux cent visages. Paris, 1945.
Afr 5874.22 Leloutre, Jean Claude. La Réunion, departement français. Paris, 1968.
Afr 2208.81.11 Lelu, P. En Algérie. Paris, 1881.
Afr 8088.90 Lelu, Paul. Histoire de la colonie anglaise du Cap de Bonne-Espérance. Paris, 1890.
Afr 3823.6 Lemaire, Charles. Journal de route de Charles Lemaire. Bruxelles, 1953.
Afr 606.95.2 Lemaire. Les voyages du Sieur Lemaire. Edinburgh, 1887.
Htn Afr 606.95* Lemaire. Les voyages du Sieur Lemaire. Paris, 1695.
Afr 606.95.2.1 Lemaire. Voyages to the Canaries, Cape Verd and the coast of Africa. Edinburgh, 1887.
Afr 4199.5.5 Lemandowski, H. Ein Leben für Afrika. Zürich, 1954.
Afr 7567.34 Lemarchand, Rene. Political awakening in the Belgian Congo. Berkeley, 1964.
Afr 8289.65 Lemay, Godfrey Hugh Lancelot. British supremacy in South Africa, 1899-1907. Oxford, 1965.
Afr 6715.20 Lembezat, Bertrand. Le Cameroun. Paris, 1954.
Afr 6740.30 Lembezat, Bertrand. Les populations paiennes. Paris, 1961.
Afr 718.43 Lemboum, Hans Jorgen. Hvide mand-hvad nu. København, 1955.
Afr 7459.63 Lemley, Luther. Liberia. 1st ed. N.Y., 1963.
Afr 1609.05.8 Lemoine, Paul. Mission dans le Maroc occidental. Paris, 1905.
Afr 7119.32 Lemos, A. de. Historia de Angola. Lisboa, 1932.
Afr 6988.94.256 Lempp, Ferdinand. Windhoek. 1st ed. Windhoek, 1964.
Afr 1607.91.5 Lempriere, G. Voyage dans l'empire de Maroc. Paris, 1801.
Afr 1607.91.7 Lempriere, W. Le Maroc, il y a cent ans. Paris, 1911.
Afr 1607.91.2 Lempriere, W. Tour to Tangier and Morocco. 2nd ed. London, 1793.
Afr 1607.91.3 Lempriere, W. Tour to Tangier and Morocco. 3rd ed. Newport, 1813.
Afr 609.60.25 Lenenberger, Hans. Die Stunde des schwarzen Mannes. München, 1960.
Afr 109.60.25F Lenerhulme Inter-Collegiate History Conference, 1960. Historians in tropical Africa. Salisbury, 1962.
Afr 810.15 Lenfant, E.H. Le Niger, voie ouverte à notre empire africain. Paris, 1903.
Afr 5480.205 L'Enfant, Eugène A. La grande route du Tchad. Paris, 1905.
Afr 3252.20 Lenghi, N. Considerazioni sul discorso da Layard...Riforma giudiziaria in Egitto. Alexandria, 1868.
Afr 210.59.11 Lengyel, Emil. Africa in ferment. N.Y., 1961.
Afr 5190.10.9 Lengyel, Emil. Dakar, outpost of two hemispheres. N.Y., 1941.
Afr 5190.10.12 Lengyel, Emil. Dakar avant-poste de deux hémisphères. N.Y., 1943.
Afr 3310.35 Lengyel, Emil. Egypt's role in world affairs. Washington, 1957.
Afr 8685.45 Lenk, Heinrich von. Die Geschichte der Buren. Leipzig, 1901-3.
Afr 11057.10 Lennox-Short, Alan. Stories, South African. Johannesburg, 1969.
Afr 3978.73.5 Lenoir, Paul. The Fayoum, or Artists in Egypt. London, 1873.
Afr 5057.12 Lenoir, Robert. Les concessions foncières en Afrique occidentale française et équatoriale. Thèse. Paris, 1936.
Afr 2250.2 Lenormend, J. Le peril étranger. 2e ed. Paris, 1899.
Afr 2030.464 Lentin, Albert. L'Algérie entre deux mondes. Paris, 1964.
Afr 2030.145 Lentin, Albert Paul. L'Algérie des colonels. Paris, 1958.
Afr 2030.147 Lentin, Albert Paul. L'Algérie des colonels. Paris, 1959.

Afr 5635.10 Lenure, Jean. Madagascar, l'expedition au point de vue medical. Paris, 1896.
Afr 678.79 Lenz, O. Skizzen aus Westafrika. Berlin, 1879.
Afr 5247.15 Lenz, Oscar. Timbouctou. Paris, 1886-87. 2v.
Afr 605.56.10 Leo Africanus, J. De la descripción de Africa. n.p., 1940.
Afr 605.56.11 Leo Africanus, J. De la descripción de Africa y de las cosas notables que ella se encuentran. n.p., 1952.
Afr 605.56.12 Leo Africanus, J. Description de l'Afrique. Paris, 1956. 2v.
Htn Afr 605.56.3* Leo Africanus, J. Descriptione libri IX. Liguri, 1559.
Htn Afr 605.56.4* Leo Africanus, J. A geographical historie of Africa. Londini, 1600.
Htn Afr 605.56F* Leo Africanus, J. Historiale description de l'Afrique. Lyon, 1556. 2v.
Htn Afr 605.56.5* Leo Africanus, J. Ioannis Leonis Africani Africae descriptio IX lib. Absoluta. 2 pt. Lugdunum Batavorum, 1632.
Afr 550.8.12 Léon XIII et le toast d'Alger. (Baunard, Louis.) Paris, 1914.
Afr 1609.08.5 Leon Y Ramos, E. Marruecos. Madrid, 1908.
Afr 1609.08.5.4 Leon Y Ramos, E. Marruecos. Novisima ed. Madrid, 1915.
Afr 9488.96.2 Leonard, A.G. How we made Rhodesia. 2. ed. London, 1896.
Afr 6280.4 Leonard, A.G. Lower Niger and its tribes. London, 1906.
Afr 6280.66 Leonard, Arthur Glyn. The Lower Niger and its tribes. 1st ed. London, 1968.
Afr 8235.19 Leonard, C. Papers on the political situation in South Africa, 1885-1895. London, 1903.
Afr 678.33.5 Leonard, Peter. Records of a voyage to the western coast of Africa in his Majesty's ship Dryad. Edinburgh, 1833.
Afr 1069.57 Leone, Enrico de. La colonizzazione dell'Africa del Nord. Padova, 1957.
Afr 4620.3 Leontieff. Provinces équatoriales d'Abyssinie. n.p., n.d.
Afr 3818.14 A leopard tamed; the story of an African pastor, his people, and his problems. (Vandevort, Eleanor.) N.Y., 1968.
Afr 7808.76 Leopold II et la conférence géographique. (Roeykens, Aug.) Bruxelles, 1956.
Afr 7560.14.5 Léopold II et l'Afrique, 1855-1880. (Roeykens, A.) Bruxelles, 1958.
Afr 7809.04.5 Léopold II et le Congo. (Boillat-Robert, I.) Neuchâtel, 1904.
Afr 12639.24.805 Léopold Sédar Senghor, l'Africain. (Leusse, Hubert de.) Paris, 1967.
Afr 12639.24.810 Léopold Sédar Senghor. (Bonn, Gisela.) Düsseldorf, 1968.
Afr 12639.24.800 Léopold Sédar Senghor. (Guibert, A.) Paris, 1962.
Afr 5199.337 Léopold Sédar Senghor and the politics of Negritude. 1st ed. (Markovitz, Irving Leonard.) N.Y., 1969.
Afr 12639.24.815 Léopold Sédar Senghor et la défense et illustration de la civilisation noire. (Mezu, Sebastian Okechukwu.) Paris, 1968.
Afr 5199.337.5 Léopold Sédar Senghor et la naissance de l'Afrique moderne. (Milcent, Ernest.) Paris, 1969.
Afr 7549.62.10 Leopold to Lumumba. (Martelli, George.) London, 1962.
Afr 7870.5 Leopoldville, son histoire, 1881-1956. (Whyms.) Bruxelles, 1956.
Afr 7850.10 Léopoldville, son histoire, 1881-1956. (Whyms.) Bruxelles, 1956.
Afr 7512.15 Leopoldville. Université Lovanium. Cahiers économiques et sociaux. Leopoldville. 3v.
Afr 7512.16 Leopoldville. Université Lovanium. Cahiers Economiques et Sociaux. Collection d'études politiques. Léopoldville. 4,1964+
Afr 7812.266 Leopoldville. Université Lovanium. Institut de Recherche Economiques et Sociales. Etude d'orientation pour le plan de développement et de diversification industrielle. Kinshasa, 1966.
Afr 12.20 Leopoldville. Université Lovanium. Institut de Recherches Economiques et Sociales. Collection d'études économiques. Léopoldville. 1,1965+
Afr 7512.20F Leopoldville. Université Lovanium. Institut de Recherches Economiques et Sociales. Lettre mensuelle de l'I.R.E.S. 1,1961+
Afr 7512.10 Leopoldville. Université Lovanium. Institut de Recherches Economiques et Sociales. Notes et documents. 1,1960+ 2v.
Afr 7512.5 Leopoldville. Université Lovanium. Institut de Recherches Economiques et Sociales. Studia Universitatis Lovanium.
Afr 5580.3.9 Lepecki, M.B. Maurycy August Beniowski. Lwow, 1938.
Afr 5580.3.10 Lepecky, M.B. Maurycy August Beniowski, zdob. Madagaskaru. Warszawa, 1959.
Afr 150.2.3 Lepitre, J.M.A. De iis qui ante Vascum A Gama Africam legere tentaverunt. Thesis. Parisis, 1880.
Afr 2662.5 Lepotier, Adolphe Auguste Marie. Bizerte. Paris, 1965.
Afr 26719.24.21 Lepoutre, Paul. Contes congolais. Limete, 1964. 2 pam.
Afr 3979.39.10 Leprette, Fernand. Egypte, terre du Nil. Paris, 1939.
Afr 4869.35 Le lepreux. (Monfried, H. de.) Paris, 1935.
Afr 2030.75 Leprevost, Jacques. La bataille d'Alger. Alger, 1957.
Afr 2030.77 Leprevost, Jacques. Défense de l'Algérie. Alger, 1957.
Afr 3978.53.3 Lepsius, R. Letters from Egypt. London, 1853.
Afr 5748.40 Lequevel de Lacombe, B.F. Voyage à Madagascar...Camores (1825-30). Paris, 1840. 2v.
Afr 550.42F Leri, Primo. Missione nell'Africa settentrionale. Roma, 1908.
Afr 1753.12 Leria, C. Don Francisco y don dionisio. Tetuan, 1953.
Afr 1753.14 Leria, Manuel. Un siglo medieval en la historia de Ceuta, 931-1031. Ceuta, 1961.
Afr 11517.76.120 Lerner, Laurence. The directions of memory. London, 1963.
Afr 11517.76.100 Lerner, Laurence. Domestic interior. London, 1959.
Afr 11517.76.110 Lerner, Laurence. The Englishmen. London, 1959.
Afr 11517.76.130 Lerner, Laurence. A free man. London, 1968.
Afr 5485.10 Lerouvreur, A. Saheliens et Sahariens du Tchad. Paris, 1962.
Afr 4559.03 Leroux, H. Chasses et gens d'Abyssinie. Paris, 1903.
Afr 2208.95.3A Leroux, H. Je deviens colon. Paris, 1895.
Afr 2208.98.8 Leroux, H. Je deviens colon. 2e ed. Paris, 1895.
Afr 2208.95.5 Leroux, H. Je deviens colon. 4e ed. Paris, 1895.
Afr 4559.01.9 Leroux, H. Menelik and us. Paris, 1901.
Afr 4259.17 Leroux, Hughes. Chez la reine de Saba. Paris, 1917.
Afr 6887.2 Leroy, A. Au Kilima-ndjaro. Paris, 1893.
Afr 2230.20 Leroy, J. Deux ans de séjour en Petite Kabilie. Paris, 1911.

Afr 1838.3   Leroy, L. Etat...du royaume et de la ville d'Alger. La Haye, 1750.
Afr 5748.84   Leroy, L. Les Français à Madagascar. Paris, 1884.
Afr 2731.7   Leroy-Beaulieu, P. Le Sahara. Paris, 1904.
Afr 2208.87.2   Leroy-Beaulieu. L'Algérie et la Tunis. Paris, 1897.
Afr 5285.277.10   Leroy Ladurie, Marie. Pâques africaines. Paris, 1965.
Afr 5045.46   Lerumeur, Guy. L'imprévu dans les dunes. Paris, 1963.
Afr 2749.60.15   Lerumeur, Guy. Le Sahara avant le pétrole. Paris, 1960.
Afr 555.12.20   Les pères blancs en Afrique. (Excoffon, Ariste.) Paris, 1893.
Afr 606.95.2   Les voyages du Sieur Lemaire. (Lemaire.) Edinburgh, 1887.
Afr 3243.7   Lesage, C. L'achat des actions de Suez. Paris, 1906.
Afr 9028.75   Leslie, D. Among the Zulus and Amatongas. 2. ed. Edinburgh, 1875.
Afr 6886.2   Leslie, J.A.K. A survey of Dar es Salaam. London, 1963.
Afr 1635.20   Lesne, Marcel. Evolution d'un groupement berbere. Rabat, 1959.
Afr 8865.14   Lesotho, Botswana, and Swaziland: the former High Commission territoris in Southern Africa. (Stevens, Richard P.) London, 1967.
Afr Doc 4205.10   Lesotho; report. Maseru. 1967+
Afr Doc 4209.10F   Lesotho. Estimates of development fund revenue and expenditure. 1966+
Afr Doc 4209.11F   Lesotho. Memorandum on the Estimates of development fund revenue. 1966+
Afr 8850.49   Lesotho. Morija. 1,1959+
Afr Doc 4207.5   Lesotho. Bureau of Statistics. Annual statistical bulletin. Maseru. 1965+
Afr Doc 4207.365F   Lesotho. Bureau of Statistics. Lesotho census of production, 1965. Maseru, 1966?
Afr Doc 4209.305F   Lesotho. Bureau of Statistics. National accounts, 1964/5 and 1965/6. Maseru, 1967.
Afr Doc 4231.10F   Lesotho. Ministry of Agriculture, Co-ops, and Marketing. Annual report. 1,1966+
Afr 8865.16   Lesotho: the politics of dependence. (Spence, John Edward.) London, 1968.
Afr Doc 4207.365F   Lesotho census of production, 1965. (Lesotho. Bureau of Statistics.) Maseru, 1966?
Afr 8850.49.5   Lesotho quarterly. Morija. 2,1967+
Afr 8089.63   Lesourd, J.A. La République d'Afrique du Sud. 2d ed. Paris, 1963.
Afr 1830.30.2   Lespes, René. Alger, étude de géographie et d'histoire urbaines. Paris, 1930.
Afr 1878.8   Lespes, Rene. Alger, étude de géographie et d'histoire urbaines. Thèse. Paris, 1930.
Afr 1830.30.5   Lespes, Rene. Oran. Paris, 1938.
Afr 2209.37.10   Lespes, René. Pour comprendre l'Algérie. Alger, 1937.
Afr 4258.65   Lesseps, F. Principaux faits de l'histoire d'Abyssinie. Paris, 1865.
Afr 9489.57   Lessing, Doris M. Going home. London, 1957.
Afr 9489.57.2   Lessing, Doris M. Going home. London, 1968.
Afr 4513.39   Lessona, A. Verso l'impero. Firenze, 1939.
Afr 8289.00.9   Lessons of the war. (Wilkinson, S.) Westminster, 1900.
Afr 3275.16.2   Lest we forget. (Rifat, M.M.) n.p., 1915.
Afr 7947.7   Lestrade, A. La médecine indigène au Ruanda et lexique des termes médicaux français-urunyarwanda. Bruxelles, 1955.
Afr 6743.60   Lestringant, Jacques. Le pays de guider au Cameroun. Versailles, 1964.
Afr 8250.9A   Lesueur, G. Cecil Rhodes, the man and his work. London, 1913.
Afr 8250.9.5   Lesueur, G. Cecil Rhodes, the man and his work. N.Y., 1914.
Afr 4384.10   Let-Marefia. (Traversi, L.) Milano, 1931.
Afr 8687.263   Let my people go. (Luthuli, A.) N.Y., 1962.
Afr 11433.75.100   Let the day perish. (Gordon, Gerald.) London, 1952.
Afr 1990.7   Letang, B. Des moyens d'assurer la domination française en Algérie. Paris, 1840-46. 4 pam.
Afr 6780.24   Letcher, O. Cohort of the tropics. London, 1930.
Afr 9549.32   Letcher, Owen. South central Africa. Johannesburg, 1932.
Afr 9689.34   Letcher, Owen. When life was rusted through. Johannesburg, 1934.
Afr 2948.13   Lethielleux, J. Le Fezzan. Tunis, 1948.
Afr 1110.30A   Le Tourneau, Roger. Evolution politique de l'Afrique du Nord musulmane 1920-1961. Paris, 1962.
Afr 1713.4.5   Letourneau, Roger. Fez avant le protectorat. Casablanca, 1949.
Afr 1713.4   Letourneau, Roger. Fez in the age of marinides. 1st ed. Norman, 1961.
Afr 1713.4.10   Letourneau, Roger. La vie quotidienne à Fès en 1900. Paris, 1965.
Afr 8670.10.2   Let's stop here; the pictorial guide to hotels in South Africa, South West Africa, Rhodesia and Moçambique. 2. ed. (Lewis, David.) Durban, 1967.
Afr 9149.61.10   Let's visit the Kruger park. (Bigalke, Rudolph.) Johannesburg, 1961.
Afr 11517.84.100   Letscher, O. Africa unveiled. London, 1931.
Afr 5798.5   A letter from a gentleman giving an account of Joanna. London, 1789.
Htn   Afr 1606.70*   Letter from a gentleman of Lt. Howard's retinue. London, 1706.
Afr 7350.3.14   Letter to Hon. H. Clay, president of the American Colonization Society. (Gurley, R.R.) London, 1841.
Afr 5833.4   A letterTo the right honourable Lord John Russell. (Archer, Edward.) London, 1840.
Afr 810.8.10   A letter to the Rt. Hon. Lord John Russell...Niger expedition. (Stephen, George.) London, 1840.
Htn   Afr 1935.1*   Letter written by the governour...law-counteys. (Algiers. Dey.) London, 1679.
Afr 4368.5.30   Lettere del Cardinale Massaia dal 1846 al 1886. (Massaia, G.) Torino, 1937.
Afr 2030.463.40   Lettere della rivoluzione algerina. (Kessel, P.) Torino, 1963.
Afr 1903.6   Lettere istoriche...d'Africa, e d'America. Venezia, 1775.
Afr 2608.67.5   Lettere sulla Tunisia. (Gubernatis, E. de.) Firenze, 1867.
Afr 5815.2F   Letters, patent, 1879-1894. (Mauritius.) n.p., n.d.
Afr 7377.5   Letters...white and African races. (Mitchell, James.) Washington, 1860.
Afr 8135.6   Letters. (Hart-Synnot, F.) London, 1912.
Afr 9073.687   Letters and other writings of a Natal sheriff. (Phipson, Thomas.) Cape Town, 1968.
Afr 6275.20   Letters and sketches from northern Nigeria. (Kisch, M.S.) London, 1910.
Afr 8289.67   Letters from a Boer parsonage: letters of Margaret Marquard during the Boer War. (Marquard, Margaret Murray.) Cape Town, 1967.

Afr 6174.3   Letters from a bush campaign. (Haylings, D.M.) London, 1902.
Afr 635.50   Letters from Africa. (King-Hall, Stephen.) London, 1957.
Afr 3275.20   Letters from an Egyptian...upon the affairs of Egypt. London, 1908.
Afr 8340.6   Letters from an uitlander, 1899-02. London, 1903.
Afr 3978.65.8   Letters from Egypt, (1862-1869). (Duff-Gordon, Lucie Austin.) London, 1969.
Afr 3978.65.5   Letters from Egypt. (Duff-Gordon, Lucie Austin.) London, 1902.
Afr 3978.65.6   Letters from Egypt. (Duff-Gordon, Lucie Austin.) N.Y., 1902.
Afr 3978.65.7   Letters from Egypt. (Duff-Gordon, Lucie Austin.) N.Y., 1904.
Afr 3978.53.3   Letters from Egypt. (Lepsius, R.) London, 1853.
Afr 3979.33.3   Letters from Egypt. (Oliver, Mildred Alice.) London, 1933.
Afr 3979.02.15   Letters from Egypt and Palestine. (Babcock, M.D.) N.Y., 1902.
Afr 3978.65   Letters from Egypt 1863-65. (Duff-Gordon, Lucie Austin.) London, 1865.
Afr 6195.10   Letters from Ghana. (Braun, Richard.) Philadelphia, 1959.
Afr 3705.7   Letters from Khartoum. (Power, Frank.) London, 1885.
Afr 3705.7.2   Letters from Khartoum. 3d ed. (Power, Frank.) London, 1885.
Afr 5832.5   Letters from Mauritius in 18th century. (Grant, Charles.) Mauritius, 1886.
Afr 6275.24   Letters from Nigeria...1899-1900. (Carnegie, David W.) Brechin, 1902.
Afr 8658.93   Letters from South Africa. London, 1893.
Afr 8808.61   Letters from the Cape. (Duff-Gordon, Lucie.) London, 1921.
Afr 8808.61.5   Letters from the Cape. (Duff-Gordon, Lucie.) London, 1927.
Afr 6192.32   Letters from the Gold Coast. (Marie Louise, Princess.) London, 1926.
Afr 2208.36   Letters from the south, written during a journey to Algiers. (Campbell, Thomas.) Philadelphia, 1836.
Afr 2208.36.5   Letters from the south. (Campbell, Thomas.) London, 1837. 2v.
Afr 3735.9   Letters from the Sudan. (Knight, E.F.) London, 1897.
Afr 555.9.19   Letters of Bishop Tozer and his sister. (Tozer, William G.) London, 1902.
Afr 3977.86.5   Letters on Egypt. vol.1. (Savary, C.) Dublin, 1787.
Afr 11240.89.100   Letters to Martha, and other poems from a South African prison. (Brutus, Dennis.) London, 1969.
Afr 2928.18.5   Letters written during a ten years' residence at the court of Tripoli. (Tully, R.) London, 1957.
Afr 2928.18.8   Letters written during a ten years' residence at the court of Tripoli. 3rd ed. (Tully, R.) London, 1819. 2v.
Afr 6780.10.7   Lettow-Vorbeck, P.E. von. East African campaigns. N.Y., 1957.
Afr 6780.10.23   Lettow-Vorbeck, P.E. von. Mein Leben. Biberach an der Riss, 1957.
Afr 6780.10A   Lettow-Vorbeck, P.E. von. Meine Erinnerungen aus Ostafrika. Leipzig, 1920.
Afr 6780.10.5   Lettow-Vorbeck, P.E. von. My reminiscences of East Africa. London, 1920.
Afr 6780.10.20   Lettow-Vorbeck, P.E. von. Um Vaterland und Kolonien. Berlin, 1919.
Afr 2710.2   Lettre...sur la politique saharienne. (Lechatelier, A.)
Afr 7512.20F   Lettre mensuelle de l'I.R.E.S. (Leopoldville. Université Lovanium. Institut de Recherches Economiques et Sociales.) 1,1963+
Afr 2025.7A   Lettre sur la politique de la France en Algérie. (Napoleon III, Empereur.) Paris, 1865. 2 pam.
Afr 2208.40   Lettres...sur l'Algérie. (Suchet.) Tours, 1840.
Afr 2731.15.7   Lettres à Mme. de Bondy, de la Trappe à Tamanrasset. (Foucauld, Charles.) Paris, 1966.
Afr 2030.460.20   Lettres à un métropolitain. (Cercle d'Études Algériennes.) Alger, 1960.
Afr 5640.15.5   Lettres de Madagascar, 1896-1905. (Galliéni, J.S.) Paris, 1928.
Afr 3223.5   Lettres du Dr. Perron du Caire et l'Alexandrie à M. Jules Mohl, à Paris, 1838-54. (Perron, A.) Le Caire, 1911.
Afr 1609.15   Lettres du Maroc, illustrations de E. Stoeckel. (Roulleaux Dugage, G.) Paris, 1915.
Afr 5227.20   Lettres du Soudan. (Lecert, Paul Edmond.) Paris, 1895.
Afr 5640.4.51   Lettres du sud de Madagascar, 1900-1902. (Lyautey, L.H.G.) Paris, 1935.
Afr 1965.22   Lettres d'un soldat. (Montagnac, L.F.) Paris, 1885.
Afr 555.5.6   Lettres è Henry de Castries. 10. éd. (Foucauld, Charles de.) Paris, 1938.
Afr 3977.98   Lettres ecrites d'Egypte. (Geoffroy Saint Hilaire, E.) Paris, 1901.
Afr 2376.1   Lettres familières sur l'Algérie (Tougourt). 2e ed. (Pein, T.) Alger, 1893.
Afr 718.2.10   Lettres inédites. (Stanley, H.M.) Bruxelles, 1955.
Afr 2731.15.6   Lettres inédites au général Laperrine. (Foucauld, Charles, Vicomte de.) Paris, 1954.
Afr 2336.5.5   Lettres sur Hippone. (Papier, Alexander.) Bone, 1887.
Afr 2209.08.2   Lettres sur l'Algérie, 1907-08. (Donop.) Paris, 1908.
Afr 2208.47   Lettres sur l'Algérie. (Marmier, X.) Paris, 1847.
Afr 7808.89   Lettres sur le Congo. (Dupont, C.F.) Paris, 1889.
Afr 2731.1   Lettres sur le Trans-saharien. (Abadie, F.) Constantine, 1880.
Afr 3978.56   Lettres sur l'Egypte. (Borthelemy Saint-Hilaire.) Paris, 1856.
Afr 3978.76.7   Lettres sur l'Egypte. (Gellion-Dangler, Eugène.) Paris, 1876.
Afr 3977.86   Lettres sur l'Egypte. (Savary, C.) Paris, 1786. 3v.
Afr 1973.4   Lettres sur l'expédition de Constantine. (Wagner, M.) n.p., 1838.
Afr 8659.31   Leubuscher, C. Der südafrikanische Eingeborne als Industriearbeiter und als Stadtherrscher. Jena, 1931.
Afr 6780.42   Leubuscher, Charlotte. Tanganyika territory. Oxford, 1944.
Afr 2030.464.35   Leulliette, P. St. Michael and the dragon. London, 1964.
Afr 7812.260   Leurquin, Philippe. Le niveau de vie des populations rurales du Ruanda-Urundi. Louvain, 1960.
Afr 7812.260.2   Leurquin, Philippe. Le niveau de vie des populations rurales du Ruanda-Urundi. Louvain, 1960.

Afr 7459.69	Liberia. Information Service. Liberia, story of progress. London? 1960.
Afr Doc 9939.10	Liberia. Interior Department. Annual report on the operation. Monrovia. 1961+
Afr 7357.2	Liberia. Laws, statutes, etc. The statute laws of the Republic of Liberia. Monrovia, 1856.
Afr Doc 9946.5	Liberia. Office of National Planning. Annual report. Monrovia. 1961+
Afr Doc 9907.362	Liberia. Office of National Planning. Bureau of Statistics. 1962 population census of Liberia: population characteristics of major areas. Monrovia, 1964? 13v.
Afr 7461.45	Liberia. Policy and Planning Committee on Industry. Liberia manufacturing industry. Monrovia? 1966.
Afr Doc 9946.10F	Liberia. Postmaster General. Annual report of Postmaster General on the operation of the Liberian Postal Administration. Monrovia. 1961+
Afr Doc 9924.10F	Liberia. President. Annual message.
Afr Doc 9924.5F	Liberia. President. Inaugural address.
Afr 7459.63	Liberia. 1st ed. (Lemley, Luther.) N.Y., 1963.
Afr 7375.14.5	Liberia. 2d ed. (Innes, William.) Edinburgh, 1833.
Afr 7355.3	Pamphlet vol. Liberia and colonization. 7 pam.
Afr 7369.29	Liberia as I know it. (Boone, C.C.) Richmond, Va., 1929.
Afr 7377.34	Liberia in world politics. (Azikiwe, Nnamdi.) London, 1934.
Afr 7461.45	Liberia manufacturing industry. (Liberia. Policy and Planning Committee on Industry.) Monrovia? 1966.
Afr 7377.30	Liberia rediscovered. (Young, James C.) Garden City, 1934.
Afr 7350.14	Liberian letter. Washington.
Afr 7468.4	Liberian odyssey by hammock and surfboat. 1st ed. (Price, Frederick A.) N.Y., 1954.
Afr 7458.81A	The Liberian Republic as it is. Photoreproduction. (Stetson, G.R.) Boston, 1881.
Afr 7350.18	Liberian studies journal. Greencastle, Ind. 1,1968+
Afr 7459.68	Liberian Trading and Development Bank, Ltd., Monrovia. Liberia: basic data and information, 1968. Monrovia, 1968.
Afr 7350.16	Liberian year book. London. 1956+
Afr 7458.62.5	Liberia's offering. (Blyden, E.W.) N.Y., 1862.
Afr 7369.59.5	Liberia's past and present. (Richardson, N.R.) London, 1959.
Afr 7369.46	Liberia's place in Africa's sun. (Phillips, H.A.) N.Y., 1946.
Afr 7465.3	Les Libériens et les Baoule. (Delafosse, M.) Paris, 1901.
Afr 7369.61	Liberiia. (Khodosh, I.A.) Moscow, 1961.
Afr 7369.63	Liberiia posle Vtoroi Mirovoi Voiny. (Egorov, V.V.) Moscow, 1963.
Htn Afr 1925.1*	Libertas or reliefe to English captives in Algeria. (Robinson, H.) London, 1642.
Afr 12639.24.25	Liberté. (Senghor, L.S.) Paris, 1964.
Afr 1340.30	Les libertés publiques au Maroc. (Stefani, P.) Paris, 1938.
Afr 2850.2	La Libia. (Italy. Parlamento.) Milano, 1912. 2v.
Afr 2929.12.13	Libia. (Podrecca, G.) Roma, 1912.
Afr 2929.13.5	La Libia. (Ricchieri, Giuseppe.) Milano, 1913.
Afr 2870.14	La Libia in venti anni di occupazione italiana. (Sillani, T.) Roma, 1932.
Afr 2819.32	La Libia italiana, nella preparazione diplomatica e nella conquista. (Taraschi, T.M.) Napoli, 1932.
Afr 2929.12.25	La Libia italiana e il campo che offre a ricerche scientifiche. (Cavazza, F.) Bologna, 1912.
Afr 2870.12	La Libia nel suo ordinamento giuridico. (Ravizza, A.) Padova, 1931.
Afr 2819.28	La Libia nella storia e nei viaggiatori dai tempi omerici all'occupazione italiana. (Ghisleri, A.) Torino, 1928.
Afr 2870.25.10	Libia redenta. (Graziani, R.) Napoli, 1948.
Afr 2929.12.15	La Libia romana e l'impresa italiana. (Darkling, L.) Roma, 1912.
Afr 2929.64	Libie, land van de dorst. (Jongmans, D.G.) Meppel, 1964.
VAfr 2938.39	Libija. Beograd, 1966.
Afr 12.10	Library materials on Africa. London. 3v.
Afr 28.89.2	Library of Congress. Africa South of the Sahara. Washington, 1963.
Afr 28.70	Library of Congress. African newspapers currently received in selected American libraries. Washington, 1956.
Afr 28.80	Library of Congress. A list of American doctoral dissertations on Africa. Washington, 1962.
Afr Doc 6002.2	Library of Congress. African Section. French-speaking West Africa; a guide to official publications. Washington, 1967.
Afr Doc 5602.5	Library of Congress. African Section. Madagascar and adjacent islands; a guide to official publications. Washington, 1965.
Afr Doc 3002.5	Library of Congress. African Section. Official publications of British East Africa. Washington, 1960-1963.
Afr Doc 7002.5	Library of Congress. African Section. Official publications of French Equatorial Africa, French Cameroons, and Togo, 1946-1958. Washington, 1964.
Afr Doc 1702.8	Library of Congress. African Section. Official publications of Sierra Leone and Gambia. Washington, 1963.
Afr 6128.4	Library of Congress. African Section. Official publications of Sierra Leone and Gambia. Washington, 1963.
Afr Doc 3502.5	Library of Congress. African Section. The Rhodesias and Nyasaland. Washington, 1965.
Afr 6303.5	Library of Congress. Division of Bibliography. British East and Central Africa, a selected list of references. Washington, 1942.
Afr 505.44	Library of Congress. Division of Bibliography. The British empire in Africa. Washington, 1942-43.
Afr 8028.3	Library of Congress. Division of Bibliography. The British empire in Africa. v.9. Washington, 1942-43.
Afr 6053.5	Library of Congress. Division of Bibliography. British West Africa, a selected list of references. Washington. 1942+ 2v.
Afr 510.30A	Library of Congress. Division of Bibliography. French colonies in Africa. Washington, 1942.
Afr 7353.5	Library Of Congress. Division of Bibliography. Liberia, a selected list of references. Photostat. Washington, 1942.
Afr 28.7.5	Library of Congress. European Affairs Division. Continuing sources for research on Africa. Washington, 1952.
Afr 28.7	Library of Congress. European Affairs Division. Introduction to Africa. Washington, 1952.
Afr 28.89	Library of Congress. General Reference and Bibliography Division. Africa South of the Sahara. Washington, 1957.
Afr Doc 2302.5	Library of Congress. General Reference and Bibliography Division. Nigeria; a guide to official publications. Washington, 1966.
Afr 1026.15	Library of Congress. General Reference and Bibliography Division. North and Northeast Africa. Washington, 1957.
Afr 28.70.5	Library of Congress. Serial Division. African newspapers in selected American libraries. 2d ed. Washington, 1962.
Afr 28.50	Library of the Geographical Association. (Geographical Association.) Sheffield, 1957.
Afr 2885.10	Libya, a brief political and economic survey. (Owen, Roger.) London, 1961.
Afr 2819.60.5	Libya; trablusgarp, bingazi ve fizan. (Karasapan, Celâ Tevfik.) Ankara, 1960.
Afr 2929.56	Libya. (Royal Institute of International Affairs.) London, 1956
Afr 2885.5	Libya. (Villard, H.S.) Ithaca, 1956.
Afr 2819.69	Libya. (Wright, John L.) London, 1969.
Afr 2800.12	Libya. Roma. 1924-1927 3v.
Afr Doc 808.715	Libya. Census and Statistical Department. Balance of payments. 1956+
Afr Doc 808.720	Libya. Census and Statistical Department. External trade indices. Tripoli. 1962+
Afr Doc 808.705	Libya. Census and Statistical Department. External trade statistics. 1959+ 3v.
Afr Doc 807.364F	Libya. Census and Statistical Department. General population census, 1964. Tripoli, 1964?
Afr Doc 807.354	Libya. Census and Statistical Department. General population census of Libya, 1954; report and tables. Tripoli, 1959.
Afr Doc 890.5	Libya. Census and Statistical Department. Monthly cost of living index for Tripoli town.
Afr Doc 807.364.10	Libya. Census and Statistical Department. Preliminary results of the general population census 1964. Tripoli, 1964.
Afr Doc 808.510	Libya. Census and Statistical Department. Report of the annual survey of large manufacturing establishments. Tripoli. 1,1965+
Afr Doc 807.5	Libya. Census and Statistical Department. Statistical abstract. 1,1958+
Afr Doc 808.710	Libya. Census and Statistical Department. Summary of external trade statistics. 1962+
Afr Doc 809.305	Libya. Central Statistics Office. National income estimates. Benghazi. 1958+
Afr 2808.6	Libya. Constitution. Constitution of the Kingdom of Libya as modified by Law No.1 of 1963. Benghazi, 1964.
Afr 2938.34	Libya. Ministry of Planning and Development. Five-year economic and social development plan, 1963-1968. Tripoli, 1964.
Afr 2938.34.5	Libya. Ministry of Planning and Development. A summary of the evolution of planning institutions in Libya. Tripoli, 1965.
Afr Doc 844.5	Libya. National Planning Council. Annual report on development activities. Tripoli. 1,1963+
Afr 2929.13	Libya italica. (Vivassa de Regny, P.) Milano, 1913.
Afr 2230.22F	Libyan notes. (Randall-MacIver, D.) London, 1901.
Afr 4050.35	Libyan sands, travel in a dead world. (Bagnold, R.A.) London, 1935.
Afr 2870.32	Libyen. (Grothe, Hugo.) Leipzig, 1941.
Afr 1493.9	Lichtenberger, A. Un coin de la guerre, la France au Maroc. Paris, 1918.
Afr 8658.11.3	Lichtenstein, H. Reisen im südlichen Africa...1803-06. Berlin, 1811. 2v.
Afr 8658.11.6	Lichtenstein, H. Reisen im südlichen Afrika...1803, 1804, 1805, und 1806. Stuttgart, 1967. 2v.
Afr 8658.11.5	Lichtenstein, H. Travels in southern Africa. London, 1812. 2v.
Afr 7369.69	Liebenow, J. Gus. Liberia; the evolution of privilege. Ithaca, 1969.
Afr 4559.35.5	Lieberenz, P K. Das Rätsel Abessinien. Berlin, 1935.
Afr 7540.15	Liebrechts, C. Congo, suite a mes souvenirs d'Afrique. Bruxelles, 1920.
Afr 7567.38	Liebrechts, Charles. Notre colonie. Bruxelles, 1922.
Afr 7582.4	Liège. Université. Fondation pour les Recherches Scientifiques en Afrique Central. Recherches sur le développement rural en Afrique central. Liège, 1965.
Afr 3817.10	Lienharot, Godfrey. Divinity and experience, the religion of the Dinka. Oxford, 1961.
Afr 2030.35.2	Lieutenant en Algérie. (Servan-Schreiber, Jean Jacques.) Paris, 1957.
Afr 2030.35	Lieutenant in Algeria. 1st Amer. ed. (Servan-Schreiber, Jean Jacques.) N.Y., 1957.
NEDL Afr 6455.27	Life, wanderings, and labours in eastern Africa. (New, Charles.) London, 1873.
Afr 6143.15	Life...in Sierra Leone and the Gambia. (Poole, T.E.) London, 1850. 2v.
Afr 7808.90	Life among the Congo savages. (Ward, Herbert.) N.Y., 1890.
Afr 4555.31	Life and adventures of N. Pearce during residence. (Pearce, N.) London, 1831. 2v.
Afr 8252.10	The life and correspondence of Sir Bartle Frere. (Martineau, John.) London, 1895. 2v.
Afr 555.9.4	The life and exploration of Frederick Stanley Arnot. (Baker, Ernest.) London, 1921.
Afr 9558.26	Life and explorations of Dr. Livingstone. (Roberts, J.S.) Boston, 1875.
Afr 9558.25	Life and explorations of Dr. Livingstone. London, 187-.
Afr 9710.12	Life and laughter in darkest Africa. (Fintan.) Dublin, 1943.
Afr 628.231	The life and struggles of Negro toilers. (Padmore, George.) London, 1931.
Afr 8250.6	Life and times of C.J. Rhodes. (Michell, L.) N.Y., 1910. 2v.
Afr 8687.258	The life and times of Daniel Lindley. (Smith, E.W.) N.Y., 1952.

Afr 8252.5A   Life and times of Sir J.C. Molteno. (Molteno, P.A.) London, 1900. 2v.

Afr 8252.11   The life and times of Sir Richard Southey. (Wilmot, Alex.) London, 1904.

Afr 5235.51   The life and travels of Mungo Park. (Park, Mungo.) N.Y., 1840.

Afr 11456.77.814   Life and works of Alfred A. Horn. (Horn, Alfred A.) London, 1927. 5v.

Afr 8808.61.10   Life at the Cape a hundred years ago. Cape Town, 1963.

Afr 550.144   A life for Africa. (Parsons, Ellen.) Edinburgh, 1899.

Afr 7803.5   A life for the Congo. (Kellersberger, Julia L.S.) N.Y., 1947.

Afr 4558.53   Life in Abyssinia. (Parkyns, M.) London, 1853. 2v.

Afr 4558.53.2   Life in Abyssinia. (Parkyns, M.) London, 1868.

Afr 1550.54   Life in Abyssinia. v.1-2. (Parkyns, M.) N.Y., 1854.

Afr 2209.60.5   Life in Algeria. 3 ed. (Muslim Students Federation.) London, 1960.

Afr 5406.225.5   Life in French Congo. (Vassal, Gabrielle M.) London, 1925.

Afr 6456.5   Life in Kenya in the olden days, the Baluyia. (Osogo, John.) Nairobi, 1965.

Afr 1609.05   Life in Morocco and glimpses beyond. (Meakin, B.) London, 1905.

Afr 6280.11.5   Life in southern Nigeria. (Talbot, P.A.) London, 1923.

Afr 8678.84   Life in the Ciskei. (Houghton, D. Hobart.) Johannesburg, 1955.

Afr 4070.7   Life in the Soudan. (Williams, J.) London, 1884.

NEDL Afr 8658.46.2   Life in the wilderness. 2d ed. (Methuen, H.H.) London, 1848.

Afr 2928.94   Life in Tripoli. (Thompson, G.E.) Liverpool, 1894.

Afr 7315.20.6   The life of a South African tribe. (Junod, H.A.) New Hyde Park, N.Y., 1962. 2v.

Afr 7315.20.5   The life of a South African tribe. 2d ed. (Junod, H.A.) London, 1927. 2v.

Afr 1965.30   The life of Abdel Kader. (Churchill, Charles Henry.) London, 1867.

Afr 555.19   The life of Africaner. (Campbell, John.) Philadelphia, 1827.

Afr 6298.183   A life of Azikiwe. (Jones-Quartey, K.A.B.) Baltimore, Maryland, 1965.

Afr 6397.15   The life of Bishop Steere. (Frank, Cedric N.) Dar es Salaam, 1953.

Afr 4557.90.25   The life of Bruce. (Head, F.B.) London, 1830.

Afr 9854.5   Life of Charles Alan Smythies, bishop of the university mission to Central Africa. (Ward, Gertrude.) London, 1898.

Afr 718.14   Life of E.M. Barttelot. (Barttelot, E.M.) London, 1890.

Afr 8252.15   Life of Frederick Courtenay Selous. (Millais, J.G.) N.Y., 1919.

Afr 555.14   The life of George Grenfell. (Hawker, G.) London, 1909.

Afr 8145.7   Life of James Green...dean of Maritzburg, Natal, 1849-1906. (Wirgman, A.T.) London, 1909. 2v.

Afr 8283.19   The life of Jameson. (Colvin, Ian D.) London, 1922. 2v.

Afr 8252.16   The life of Jan Hendrik Hofmeyr. (Hofmeyr, Jan.) Cape Town, 1913.

Afr 7375.7   Life of Jehudi Ashmun. (Gurley, R.R.) Washington, 1835.

Afr 7375.7.2   Life of Jehudi Ashmun. 2d ed. (Gurley, R.R.) N.Y., 1839.

Afr 8252.9   Life of John William Colenso. (Cox, G.W.) London, 1888. 2v.

Afr 8252.54   The life of John Xavier Merriman. (Laurence, P.M.) London, 1930.

X Cg   Afr 150.3   Life of Prince Henry of Portugal. (Major, R.H.) London, 1868.

Afr 150.3.1   The life of Prince Henry of Portugal. 1st ed. (Major, R.H.) London, 1967.

Afr 8849.6   Life of Robert Gray. (Gray, C.N.) London, 1876. 2v.

Afr 8849.7   Life of Robert Gray. (Gray, C.N.) London, 1883.

Afr 8225.7   Life of Sir George Pomeroy-Colley. (Butler, W.F.) London, 1899.

Afr 6149.257.5   A life of Sir Samuel Lewis. (Hargreaves, J.D.) London, 1958.

Afr 5765.3   Life of William Ellis, missionary. (Ellis, John E.) London, 1873.

Afr 7808.87   Life on the Congo. (Bentley, William Holman.) London, 1887.

Afr 3978.67.3   Life on the Nile. (Warren, W.W.) Paris, 1867.

Afr 3978.67.4   Life on the Nile. 2d ed. (Warren, W.W.) Boston, 1873.

Afr 8983.5   A life time in South Africa. (Robinson, J.) London, 1900.

Afr 4070.20   Life with the Hamran Arabs. (Myers, A.B.R.) London, 1876.

Afr 9028.55.4   Life with the Zulus of Natal, South Africa. (Mason, G.H.) London, 1855.

Afr 9450.25   Life with Udi; a cartoon history of independant Rhodesia. v.1-2. (Bolze, Louis W.) Bulawayo, 1966.

Afr 9525.578.5   A life's labours in South Africa. (Moffat, Robert.) London, 1871.

Afr 6470.103   A lifetime with lions. (Adamson, George.) Garden City, 1968.

Afr 1573.19   Liga Africanista Española. Tratados, convenios y acuerdos referentes a Marruecos. Madrid, 1918.

Afr 1608.22   Ligera ojeada o breve idea...de Marruecos en 1822. (Comyn, T. De.) Barcelona, 1825.

Afr 5265.5   Ligers, Ziedonis. Les Sorko (Bozo), maîtres du Niger. Paris, 1964-1967. 3v.

Afr 3978.18   Light, Henry. Travels in Egypt, Nubia, Holy Land, Mount Lebanon and Cyprus, in the year 1814. London, 1818.

Afr 609.41.10   Light, Richard V. Focus on Africa. N.Y., 1941

Afr 555.24.9   Light and darkness in East Africa. London, 1927.

Afr 609.60.50   The light continent. (Ehrenfels, O.R.) London, 1960.

Afr 8678.17   Light in Africa. (Macdonald, J.) London, 1890.

Afr 7369.43   Lighting up Liberia. (Hayman, A.I.) N.Y., 1943.

Afr 11523.32.100   Lighton, R.E. Out of the strong. London, 1957.

Afr 5765.11   Lights and shadows. (Richardson, James.) Antananarivo, 1877.

Afr 609.61.50   Ligne, Eugene. Afrika. Bruxelles, 1961.

Afr 7809.09.05   Lilbrechts, C. Souvenirs d'Afrique. Congo. Bruxelles, 1909.

Afr 1738.21   Lilius, Aleko E. Tapahtui tangerissa. Helsingissa, 1955.

Afr 7176.18   Lima. Manuela. Contribução para a estudo do comercio externo angolano. Lisboa, 1963.

Afr 7567.15   De limburgers in Congo. (Luwel, Marcel.) Hasselt, 1952.

Afr 7809.65.5   Les limites forêt-savane dans le nord du Congo en relation avec le milieu géographique. (Peeters, Leo.) Bruxelles, 1965.

Afr 9149.65F   Limpopo. 1. ed. (Battiss, Walter W.) Pretoria, 1965.

Afr 9149.39   Limpopo journey. (Birkley, C.) London, 1939.

Afr 5847.5   Limuria, the lesser dependencies of Mauritius. (Scott, Robert.) London, 1961.

Afr 7175.12   Lina Vidal, João Avangelista. Por terras d'Angola. Coimbra, 1916.

Afr 12.35   Lincoln University African Centre quarterly review. Lincoln University, Pa. 1,1968+

Afr 618.10   Lindblom, G. Jakt- och faengst metoder bland afrikanska folk. Stockholm, 1925-26.

Afr 6393.4.3   Lindblom, Gerhard. The Akamba in British East Africa. Pt.1-3. Inaug. Diss. Uppsala, 1916.

Afr 7540.44   L'indépendance de la magistrature et la statut des magistrats. (Piron, Pierre.) Bruxelles, 1956.

Afr 8740.5   Lindley, A.E. Adamantia. London, 1873.

Afr 8295.9.3   Linesman. Words by an eye witness. Edinburg, 1901.

Afr 1990.9   Lingau. La France et Afrique. Paris, 1846.

Afr 679.61   Linkhovoin, L.L. Po stranam Afriki. Ulan-Ude, 1961.

Afr 6879.29A   Lion, African adventure with the king of beasts. (Johnson, M.E.) N.Y., 1929.

Afr 115.105   Lion, J. Od Limpopa k Vltave. Praha, 1963.

Afr 10689.67.120   The lion and the jewel. (Soyinka, W.) London, 1963.

Afr 6455.154   Lion in the morning. (Seaton, Henry.) London, 1963.

Afr 4430.55.10   The Lion of Judah. (Gorham, Charles Orson.) N.Y., 1966.

Afr 4430.55.6   The Lion of Judah hath prevailed. (Sandford, C.L.) London, 1955.

Afr 4430.55.5   The Lion of Judah hath prevailed. (Sandford, C.L.) N.Y., 1955.

Afr 2230.3   Lionel, J. Kabylie du Jurjura. Paris, 1892.

Afr 870.15   Lionnet, J.G. L'ile d'Agalega. Paris, 1924.

Afr 8688.5.20   Lions and virgins. (Pama, C.) Cape Town, 1965.

Afr 8305.15   The lion's cage. (Gardner, Brian.) London, 1969.

Afr 6879.26   Lions in the path. (White, Stewart E.) Garden City, 1926.

Afr 626.196   Lipets, Iulii G. Strany iugo-vostochne i Afriki. Moskva, 1968.

Afr 7540.38   Lippens, Maurice. Notes sur le gouvernement du Congo, 1921-22. Gand, 1923.

Afr 9488.91   Lippert, Marie. The Matabeleland travel letters of Marie Lippert. Cape Town, 1960.

Afr 4875.5   Lippmann, A. Guerriers et sorciers en Somalie. Paris, 1953.

Afr 6430.15   Lipscomb, J.F. We built a country. London, 1956.

Afr 6460.30   Lipscomb, J.F. White Africans. London, 1955.

Afr 4559.62   Lipsky, George A. Ethiopia. New Haven, 1962.

Afr 7010.4   Lisbon. Sociedade Geografica. La question du Zaire, droits de Portugal. Lisbonne. 1883+

Afr 7219.65   Lisbon. Universidade Tecnica. Instituto Superior de Ciências Sociais e Politica Ultramarina. Moçambique; curso de Extensão Universitária, ano lectivo de 1964-1965. Lisboa, 1965.

Afr 4700.37.12   Lischi, D. Nell'impero liberato. 2a ed. Pisa, 1938.

Afr 1259.63.5   Liska, Jiri. The greater Maghreb. Washington, 1963.

Afr 28.80   A list of American doctoral dissertations on Africa. (Library of Congress.) Washington, 1962.

Afr 6203.8   A list of books, articles and government publications on the economy of Nigeria. (Nigerian Institute of Social and Economic Research, Ibadan, Nigeria.) Ibadan. 1,1960+ 2v.

Afr 4226.4   List of current periodical publications in Ethiopia. (Chojnacki, S.) Addis Ababa, 1964.

Afr Doc 3303.15   List of diplomatic missions and other foreign and Commonwealth representatives in Uganda. (Uganda. Ministry of Foreign Affairs.) Entebbe. 1965+

Afr Doc 3703.2   List of Diplomatic Missions and other Foreign Representatives. (Zambia. Ministry of Foreign Affaires.) Lusaka, 1965+

Afr 28.110   A list of films on Africa. (Boston University. African Studies Center.) Boston, 1966.

Afr Doc 3702.5   List of publications. (Zambia.) 1954+

Afr 10003.5   A list of theatre performances in Johannesburg, 1887-1897. (Johannesburg. Public Library.) Johannesburg, 1964.

Afr 28.4.10   List of works on Africa. (Boston Public Library.) Boston, 1894.

Afr 12.30   Liste de livres, brochures et articles consacrés à l'Afrique, publiés en U.R.S.S. Moscou. 1963+

Afr Doc 1403.10   Liste du corps diplomatique au Caire. (United Arab Republic. Ministry of Foreign Affairs.) Cairo. 1964+

Afr 8687.258.5   Lister, Georgina. Reminiscences. Johannesburg, 1960.

Afr 4798.5   A listing of Somalis who participated in a technical assistance training program in the U.S. (United States. Mission to the Somali Republic. Training Office.) Mogadiscio, 1968.

Afr 6769.65   Listowel, Judith. The making of Tanganyika. London, 1965.

Afr 12007.1   Literatura Marokko i Tunisa. (Prozhogina, S.V.) Moskva, 1968.

Afr 10005.5   Literatura stran Afriki. (Akademiia Nauk SSSR. Institut Afriki.) Moskva, 1964-66. 2v.

Afr 10062.3   Literatura stran Zapadnoi Afriki; proza. (Irasheva, Valentina V.) Moskva, 1967.

Afr 14505.5   Literatura ultramarina. (Rodrigues Junior, Manuel.) Lourenço, 1962.

Afr 8678.9.85   Literature for the South African Bantu. (Shepherd, Robert Henry Wishart.) Pretoria, 1936.

Afr 3026.1   The literature of Egypt. (Ibrahim-Hilmy.) London, 1886. 2v.

Afr 3026.22   The literature of Egypt and the Soudan. (Ibrahim-Hilmy.) Nendeln, 1966. 2v.

Afr 718.48   Littell, Blaine. South of the moon. 1st ed. N.Y., 1966.

Afr 4368.12.5   Litterae apostolicae quibus venerabilis dei Fain Abba Ghebec Michael. (Catholic Church.) Romae, 1926.

Afr 10005.7   Littérateurs et poètes noirs. (Bol, Victor P.) Léopoldville, 196-.

Afr 12004.5   Littérature africaine. Paris. 4,1964+ 3v.

Afr 10009.10   La litterature algérienne moderne. (Pantůček, Svetozár.) Prague, 1969.

Afr 12005.5   Littérature négro-africaine. (Pageard, Robert.) Paris, 1966.

Afr 3986.955 — Little, Arthur D. Opportunities for industrial development in Egypt. Cairo, 1955.
Afr 5748.84.5 — Little, H. William. Madagascar, its history and people. Edinburgh, 1884.
Afr 3725.13 — Little, H.W. One man's power. The life and work of Emin Pasha in Equatorial Africa. London, 1889.
Afr 626.132 — Little, Ian. Aid to Africa. Oxford, 1964.
Afr 8658.84.2 — Little, James S. South Africa. 2d ed. London, 1887.
Afr 6145.6.2 — Little, Kenneth. The Mende of Sierra Leone. London, 1967.
Afr 679.65.10 — Little, Kenneth Lindsay. West African urbanization. Cambridge, Eng., 1965.
Afr 3993.15 — Little, Thomas. High dam at Aswan. London, 1945.
Afr 3069.58 — Little, Tom. Egypt. London, 1958.
Afr 8088.99 — Little, W.J.K. Sketches and studies in South Africa. London, 1899.
Afr 11797.41.100A — The little karoo. (Smith, Pauline.) N.Y., 1925.
Afr 11797.41.102 — The little karoo. (Smith, Pauline.) N.Y., 1952.
Afr 4559.35.130 — Littmann, Enno. Abessinien. Hamburg, 1935.
Afr 10117.10 — Litto, Fredric M. Plays from black Africa. 1st ed. N.Y., 1968.
Afr 5180.46 — Liubeckis, M. Karsta afrikos saule. Vilnius, 1963.
Afr 109.65.20 — Liubimov, Nikolai N. Afrika v mirovoi ekonomike i politike. Moskva, 1965.
Afr 7809.62.10 — Liveing, Edward G.D. Across the Congo. London, 1962.
Afr 9558.32 — The lives and travels of Livingstone and Stanley. (Chambliss, J.E.) Boston, 1881.
Afr 555.15.10 — The lives and work of South African missionaries. (Brownlee, M.) Cape Town, 1952.
Afr 55.46 — Lives of eminent Africans. (Gollock, Georgina Anne.) N.Y., 1969.
Afr 609.29.10 — Living Africa. (Willis, Bailey.) N.Y., 1930.
Afr 6200.12 — Living in Nigeria series. Ibadan. 1,1966+
Afr 555.22.89 — Livingston Inland Mission. Manual of the principles and practice. London, 1882.
Afr 9558.8 — Livingstone, D. Cambridge lectures. London, 1860.
Afr 9558.12 — Livingstone, D. Dreissig Jahre Afrika. Leipzig, 191-.
Afr 9558.11 — Livingstone, D. Explorations dans l'Afrique australe. 2. ed. Paris, 1869.
Afr 9558.14.5 — Livingstone, D. Family letters, 1841-1856. London, 1959. 2v.
Afr 9558.14.10 — Livingstone, D. Livingstone's missionary correspondence. London, 1961.
Afr 9558.7 — Livingstone, D. Livingstone's travels. London, 1955.
Afr 9558.6.3 — Livingstone, D. Missionary travels and researches in South Africa. 25 ed. N.Y., 1859.
Afr 9558.6.15 — Livingstone, D. Missionary travels and researches in South Africa. London, 1899.
Afr 9558.6.10 — Livingstone, D. Missionary travels and researches in South Africa. N.Y., 1870.
Afr 9558.6 — Livingstone, D. Missionary travels in South Africa. N.Y., 1858.
NEDL Afr 9558.10 — Livingstone, D. Narrative of an expedition to the Zambesi. London, 1865.
Afr 9558.10.5 — Livingstone, D. Narrative of an expedition to the Zambesi. N.Y., 1866.
Afr 9558.14 — Livingstone, D. Some letters from Livingstone, 1840-1872. London, 1940.
Afr 9558.9 — Livingstone, D. Travels and researches in South Africa. Philadelphia, 1860.
Afr 9558.5A — Livingstone, D. Travels ans researches in South Africa. Philadelphia, 1858.
Afr 9558.14.15 — Livingstone, D. The Zambesi doctors. Edinburgh, 1964.
Afr 725.10.15 — Livingstone, David. African journal, 1853-1856. v.1-2. London, 1963. 2v.
Afr 9558.110 — Livingstone, David. David Livingstone and the Rovuma. Edinburgh, 1965.
Afr 9558.8.5 — Livingstone, David. Dr. Livingstone's Cambridge lectures. Farnborough, Hants., Eng., 1968.
Afr 725.10A — Livingstone, David. The last journals. London, 1874. 2v.
X Cg Afr 725.10.5 — Livingstone, David. The last journals. N.Y, 1875. (Changed to XP 3656)
Afr 725.10.10 — Livingstone, David. Private journals. London, 1960.
Afr 10882.41.100 — Livingstone, Douglas. Sjambok, and other poems from Africa. London, 1964.
Afr 555.20.5 — Livingstone, W.P. Mary Slessor of Calabar. 9th ed. London, 1917.
Afr 8687.202 — Livingstone, William. Christina Forsyth of Fingoland. London, 1918.
Afr 9558.23 — Pamphlet box. Livingstone.
Afr 9558.57 — Livingstone. (Campbell, R.J.) London, 1929.
Afr 9558.59 — Livingstone. (Somervell, D.C.) London, 1936.
Afr 9558.520 — Livingstone and Africa. (Simmons, Jack.) London, 1966.
Afr 9558.35 — Livingstone and exploration of central Africa. (Johnston, H.H.) London, 1891.
Afr 9558.51A — Livingstone and Newstead. (Fraser, A.Z.) London, 1913.
Afr 9558.61 — Livingstone the liberator. (MacNair, James I.) London, 1940.
Afr 9493.58 — Livingstone's Africa. (Griffiths, James.) London, 1958.
Afr 9769.66 — Livingstone's last, the drama of Nyasa. (Ransford, Oliver.) London, 1966.
Afr 9558.86 — Livingstone's last journey. (Coupland, R.) London, 1945.
Afr 9558.14.10 — Livingstone's missionary correspondence. (Livingstone, D.) London, 1961.
Afr 9558.7 — Livingstone's travels. (Livingstone, D.) London, 1955.
Afr 7812.262 — Livre blanc du gouvernement katangais sur les évènements. (Katanga.) Elisabethville, 1962.
Afr 5074.37 — Livre blanc sur la Mauritanie. (Morocco. Ministère des Affaires Etrangères.) Rabat, 1960.
Afr 2532.7 — Livre blanc tunisien des évènements qui amenèrent la déposition. Tunis, 1946.
Afr 8292.5.15 — Le livre d'or. (Labat, G.P.) Montreal, 1901.
Afr 6979.66.5 — Livre noir, livre blanc. (Giniewski, Paul.) Paris, 1966.
Afr 7580.10 — Le livre noir du Congo. (Tournaire, H.) Paris, 1963.
Afr 1026.6.2 — Livres français des XVIIe et XVIIIe siècle. Etats Barbaresques. Supplément. (Rouard de Card, E.) Paris, 1917.
Afr 1026.6 — Livres français des XVIIe et XVIIIe siècles concernant les états Barbaresques. (Rouard de Card, E.) Paris, 1911.
Afr 1753.4F — Livro de guerra de Ceuta. (Mateus de Pisano.) Lisboa, 1915.
Afr 49029.41.700 — Ljimere, Obotunde. The imprisonment of Obatala, and other plays. London, 1966.
Afr 1755.11 — Llanos Y Alcaraz, A. Melilla. Madrid, 1894.
Afr 609.68.25 — Llopis, José J. Pueblos y enigmas de Africa. 2a ed. Madrid, 1968.

Afr 6168.6 — Lloyd, A. The drums of Kumasi. London, 1964.
Afr 7809.00 — Lloyd, A.B. In dwarf land and cannibal country. London, 1899.
Afr 7809.00.3 — Lloyd, A.B. In dwarf land and cannibal country. London, 1907.
Afr 6535.6 — Lloyd, A.B. Uganda to Khartoum. N.Y., 1906.
Afr 6549.251.5 — Lloyd, Albert B. Apolo of the Pygmy forest. London, 1936.
Afr 9345.5 — Lloyd, E. Three great African chiefs. London, 1895.
Afr 9489.65.5 — Lloyd, Frank. Rhodesian patrol. Ilfracombe, 1965.
Afr 3275.17.85 — Lloyd, G.A.L. Egypt since Cromer. London, 1933-34. 2v.
Afr 8292.16.5 — Lloyd, J.B. One thousand miles with the C.I.V. London, 1901.
Afr 555.7 — Lloyd, Mrs. Christian work in zulae land. 2d ed. N.Y., 1870.
Afr 852.5 — Lloyd, Peter Gutt. Africa in social change. Harmondsworth, 1967.
Afr 6314.25 — Lloyd-Jones, W. K.A.R.; being an unofficial account of...the King's African Rifles. London, 1926.
Afr 6455.135 — Lloyd-Jones, William. Havash. London, 1925.
Afr 1573.10.5 — Lo que pudo hacer España en Marruecos. (Reparaz, G. de.) Barcelona, 1937.
Afr 5960.4 — Lo que son y lo que deben ser las posesiones. (Barrera y Luyando.) Madrid, 1907.
Afr 609.29 — Loafing through Africa. (Humphrey, Seth.) Philadelphia, 1929.
Afr 3813.22 — Loan agreement between the Republic for Sudan and the Kuwait Fund for Arab Economic Development dated March 25t 1962. (Sudan. Treaties, etc. Kuwait Fund for Arab Economic Development.) Kuwait, 1962?
Afr 7093.4F — Die Loango Kuste. (Falkenstein.) Berlin, 1876.
Afr 7222.60 — Lobato, A. A expansão portuguesa em Moçambique de 1498 a 1530. Lisboa, 1960. 3v.
Afr 7324.19 — Lobato, A. Historia do presidio de Lourenço. Lisboa, 1949-60. 2v.
Afr 7324.19.5 — Lobato, A. Quatro estudos e uma evocação para a historia de Lourenço Marques. Lisboa, 1961.
Afr 7222.82 — Lobato, Alexandre. Colonização senhorial da Zambezia. Lisboa, 1962.
Afr 7210.10 — Lobato, Alexandre. Evolução administrativa e economica de Moçambique, 1752-1763. v.1-. Lisboa, 1957.
Afr 7219.67 — Lobato, Alexandre. Ilha de Moçambique; panorama histórico. Lisboa, 1967.
Afr 7309.66 — Lobato, Alexandre. Ilha de Moçambique: panorama estético. Lisboa, 1966.
Afr 9525.529.25 — Lobengula, the tragedy of a Matabele king. (Preller, Gustav Schoeman.) Johannesburg, 1963.
Afr 9446.29 — Lobengula. (Hale, H.M.) London, 1929.
Afr 7012.5 — Lobiano do Rego. Patria Morena da vista da maior epopeia lusiada. Macierra de Cambra, 1959.
Afr 4556.59.13 — Lobo, J. Relation historique d'Abissinie. Paris, 1728.
Afr 4556.59.12 — Lobo, J. Voyage historique d'Abyssinie. Paris, 1728.
Htn Afr 4556.59.23* — Lobo, J. Voyage to Abyssinia. London, 1735.
Afr 4556.59.39 — Lobo, J. A voyage to Abyssinia. London, 1789.
Afr 6542.17 — Local government and politics in Uganda. (Burke, Fred.) Syracuse, 1964.
Afr 9435.17F — Local Government Association of Rhodesia. Report of proceedings of the annual conference. Salisbury. 1966+ 2v.
Afr Doc 2560.903F — Local government estimates. (Nigeria, Eastern.) 1960+
Afr 626.214 — Local government finance in Africa. (Seminar on Local Government Finance in Africa, Addis Ababa, 1966.) Berlin, 1967.
Afr 6277.108 — Local government finance in Nigeria. (Orewa, George Oka.) Ibadan, 1966.
Afr 6160.8 — Local government in Ghana. (Nsarkoh, J.K.) Accra, 1964.
Afr 6210.15 — Local government in southern Nigeria. (Harris, Philip.) Cambridge, 1960.
Afr 8210.18 — Local government in West Africa. (Cowan, L.G.) N.Y., 1958.
Afr 5053.25 — Local government in West Africa. (Cowan, Laing G.) N.Y., 1958.
Afr 9435.9.5 — Local government legislation in Southern Rhodesia up to Sept. 30th, 1963. (Passmore, Gloria C.) Salisbury, 1966.
Afr Doc 2524.5 — Local governmentManual incorporating the Local government law, cop.68, the chiefs law, cop.19 staff regulations. (Nigeria, Western. Laws, statutes, etc.) Ibadan.
Afr 6760.30 — Local government memoranda. (Tanganyika.) Dar-es-Salaam. 2,1957
Afr 9535.12F — Local series pamphlet. (Central Africa Historical Association.) Salisbury, Rhodesia. 2,1960+
Afr 5748.96.8 — Locamus, P. Madagascar et l'alimentation européenne. Paris, 1896.
Afr 5748.96.7 — Locamus, P. Madagascar et ses richesses. Paris, 1896.
Afr 6295.250.200F — Lock, Max. Kabuna, 1917-1967, 2017. London, 1967.
Afr 8250.29.5 — Lockhart, J.G. Cecil Rhodes, the colossus of Southern Africa. N.Y., 1963.
Afr 8250.29 — Lockhart, J.G. Cecil Rhodes. London, 1933.
Afr 8250.29.6 — Lockhart, J.G. Rhodes. London, 1963.
Afr 11397.50.100 — Locusts and wild honey. (Collin-Smiths, J.) London, 1953.
Afr 8809.15 — Lodges in the wilderness. (Scully, W.C.) London, 1915.
Afr 5944.5 — Lodwick, John. The forbidden coast. London, 1956.
Afr 6985.5 — Loeb, Edwin. In feudal Africa. Bloomington, 1962.
Afr 8680.22 — Loedolff, J.F. Nederlandse immigrante. Kaapstad, 1960.
Afr 6903.10 — Loening, L.S.E. A bibliography of the states of South-west Africa. Rondebosch, 1951.
Afr 1608.46 — Löwenstein, W. Zu. Ausflug von Lissabon nach Andalusien und...Marokko. Dresden, 1846.
Afr 28.55 — Loewenthal, R. Russian materials on Africa. Washington, 1958.
Afr 9489.35 — The log of a native commissioner. (Hemans, H.N.) London, 1935.
Afr 6988.58.260 — Logan, R.F. The central Namib Desert. Washington, 1960.
Afr 628.245 — Logan, Rayford W. The Negro and the post-war world. Washington, 1945.
Afr 6739.268.15 — Loginova, Valentina P. Federativnaia Respublika Kamerun. Moskva, 1968.
Afr 2020.2 — Lohan, Guillo. Un contre-rezzou au Hoggar. Paris, 1903.
Afr 2235.42 — Lohrbuch der Hausa-Sprache. (Brauner, Siegmund.) München, 1966.
Afr 1840.22 — Loi française et coutume indigene en Algerie. (Maunier, R.) Paris, 1932.
Afr 5422.2F — Loi no. 11-63 du 12/1/63 portant approbation du programme intérimaire de développement. (Gabon. Laws, statutes, etc.) Libreville, 1965.

Afr 5343.7.15   Loi plan de développement économique, social et culturel pour les années, 1967-1968, 1969-1970. (Ivory Coast.) Abidjan, 1967.

Afr 2030.463.35   Loiseau, J. Pied-noir, mon frère. Paris, 1963.

Afr 5758.14   Loisy, F.X. Madagascar, étude économique. Paris, 1914.

Afr 10675.47.150   Lokotown and other stories. (Ekwensi, Cyprian.) London, 1966.

Afr 13332.53.100   Lomami-Tshibamba, Paul. Ngando (Le crocodile). Bruxelles, 1948.

Afr 8847.56   Lomax, Ambrose. Portret van'n Suid-Afrikaanse dorp. Molteno, 1964.

Afr 630.60   Lomax, Louis. The reluctant African. 1st ed. N.Y., 1960.

Afr 5390.2   Lombard, Jacques. Structures de type féodal en Afrique noire. Paris, 1965.

Afr 8676.67.20   Lombard, Johannes Anthonie. Die ekonomiese politiek van Suid-Afrika. Kaapstad, 1967.

Afr 8676.67.15   Lombard, Johannes Anthonie. Die ekonomiese stelsel van Suid-Afrika. Kaapstad, 1967.

Afr 2030.150   Lombard, Pierre. Crise algérienne vue d'Alger. Alger, 1958.

Afr 1947.4   Lomon, A. Captivité de l'Amiral Bonard. Paris, n.d.

NEDL Afr 1258.45   London, F.H. Die Berberei. Frankfurt, 1845.

Afr 555.23   London. Baptist Mission Society. Rise and progress of work on Congo river. London, 1884.

Afr 6275.104   London. Commonwealth Institute. The federation of Nigeria. London, 1963.

Afr 6203.15   London. Commonwealth Institute. Nigeria. London, 1967.

Afr 6535.64   London. Commonwealth Institute. Uganda. London, 1964.

Afr 3005.7   London. Egyptian Education Bureau. Bulletin.

Afr 710.30   London. University. School of Oriental and African Studies. History and archaeology in Africa. London, 1955.

Afr 5765.12   London Missionary Society. Ten years review of mission work in Madagascar, 1870-80. Antananarivo, 1880.

Afr 8300.7A   London to Ladysmith. (Churchill, W.S.) London, 1900.

Afr 8300.7.3   London to Ladysmith. (Churchill, W.S.) Toronto, 1900.

Afr 8300.7.5   London to Ladysmith via Pretoria. (Churchill, W.S.) London, 1900.

Afr 5045.15   Londres, Albert. A very naked people. N.Y., 1929.

NEDL Afr 7458.92   Lone star of Liberia. (Durham, F.A.) London, 1892.

Afr 635.85   The lonely African. (Turnbull, Colin.) N.Y., 1962.

Afr 861.10   The lonely island. (Rogers, Rose A.) London, 1926.

Afr 861.10.2   The lonely island. (Rogers, Rose A.) London, 1927.

Afr 8252.156   Long, B.K. Drummond chaplin. London, 1941.

Afr 8369.45   Long, Basil K. In Smuts's camp. London, 1945.

NEDL Afr 4095.11   Long, C.C. Central Africa. N.Y., 1877.

Afr 3255.5   Long, C.C. The three prophets. N.Y., 1884.

Afr 8155.12   Long, long ago. (Samuelson, Robert Charles Azariah.) Durban, 1929.

Afr 9693.10   Long, Norman. Social change and the individual: a study of the social and religious responses to innovation in a Zambian rural community. Manchester, 1968.

Afr 10657.5   Long drums and cannons. (Laurence, Margaret.) London, 1968.

Afr 699.67   The long safari. (Pollard, John.) London, 1967.

Afr 8659.68   The long view. (Paton, Alan.) London, 1968.

Afr 4095.28   The long walks, journeys to the sources of the White Nile. (Bradham, Frederick.) London, 1969.

Afr 11465.14.110   A long way from London. (Jacobson, Dan.) London, 1958.

Afr 2819.12.3   Longo, G. La Sicilia e Tripoli. Catania, 1912.

Afr 4719.45   Longrigg, S.H. A short history of Eritrea. Oxford, 1945.

Afr 9088.8   Loo, C.J. van der. De... Zuid-Afrikaansche Republiek. Zwolle, 1896.

Afr 8687.271   Look beyond the wind; the life of Hans Merensky. (Lehmann, Olga.) Capetown, 1955?

Afr 10831.5.100   The looming shadow. (Kayira, Legson.) Garden City, 1967.

Afr 7560.3.2   Lopes, D. Le Congo. Bruxelles, 1883.

Htn   Afr 7560.2*   Lopes, D. Relazione del reame del Congo et del circonvisine contrade. Roma, 1591.

Afr 1703.3.10   Lopes, David. Historia de arzila durante o dominio portugués (1471-1550 e 1577-1589). Coimbra, 1924.

Afr 1734.5   Lopes, David. Textas em aljamia portuguesa. Lisboa, 1897.

Afr 7560.18   Lopes, Duarte. Description du royaume de Congo et des contrées environnantes. Louvain, 1963.

Afr 7560.18.2   Lopes, Duarte. Description du royaume de Congo et des contrées environnantes parFilippo Pigafetta et Duarte Lopes (1951). 2.ed. Louvain, 1965.

Afr 7560.18.10   Lopes, Duarte. A report of the Kingdom of Congo and of the surrounding countries. N.Y., 1969.

Afr 150.31   Lopes, F.F. A figura e a obra do Infante Dom Henrique. Lisboa, 1960.

Afr 7183.18   Lopes, Francisco Xavier. Tres fortalezas de Luanda em 1846. Luanda, 1954.

Afr 1755.13   Lopez Alarcon, E. Melilla 1909, diario de la guerra. Madrid, 1913.

Afr 7912.15.20   Lopez Alvarez, Luis. Lumumba ou l'Afrique frustrée. Paris, 1964.

Afr 1573.14   Lopez Pinto, V. Memoria sobre intereses generales del pais y especiales de las colonias africanas. Ceuta, 1877.

Afr 1658.48   Lopez Rienda, R. Abd-el-krim contra francia. Madrid, 1925.

Afr 1769.18.5   Lopez Rienda, R. Frente al fracaso, Raisuni. De silvestre a burguete. Madrid, 1923.

Afr 14663.5   Lopo, Júlio de Castro. Jornalismo de Angola. Luanda, 1964.

Afr 7188.301.800   Lopo, Júlio de Castro. Paiva Couceiro, uma grande figura de Angola. Lisboa, 1968.

Afr 2208.35.2   Lord, P.B. Algiers, notices of neighboring states of Barbary. London, 1835. 2v.

Afr 8160.20   Lord Chelmsford and the Zulu war. (French, G.) London, 1939.

Afr 3285.15A   Lord Cromer, Ägypten und die Entstehung der französisch-englischen Entente von 1904. Inaug. Diss. (Richter, Erhard.) Leipzig, 1931.

Afr 3275.12   LordCromer. (Traill, H.D.) London, 1897.

Afr 8252.20   Lord de Villiers and his times. (Walker, E.A.) London, 1925.

Afr 8252.8   Lord Milner and South Africa. (Mueller, E.B.I.) London, 1902.

Afr 8252.8.15   Lord Milner and South Africa. (Walker, E.A.) London, 1942.

Afr 8252.8.5   Lord Milner's work in South Africa. (Worsfold, W.B.) London, 1906.

Afr 1769.7.10   Lords of the atlas, the rise and fall of the house of Glaoua, 1893-1956. (Maxwell, Gavin.) London, 1966.

Afr 715.22   Lords of the equator, an African journey. (Balfour, P.) London, 1937.

Afr 6979.53.2   Lords of the last frontier. (Green, Laurence G.) Cape Town, 1962.

Afr 6979.53   Lords of the last frontier. (Green, Laurence G.) London, 1953.

Afr 8289.03   Loren van Thernaat, H. Twee jaren in de Boerenoorlog. Haarlem, 1903.

Afr 1947.9   Lorenz Arregger, Sklave in Algier. (Amiet, J.J.) Bern, 1874.

Afr 7803.28   Lorenzo da Lucca. Relations sur le Congo du père Lament de Lucques. Bruxelles, 1953.

Afr 2609.06.6   Lorimer, Norma. By the waters of Carthage. London, 1906.

Afr 3979.09.10   Lorimer, Norma. By the waters of Egypt. N.Y., 1909.

Afr 6390.76   Lorimer, Norma Octavia. By the waters of Africa. London, 1917.

Afr 1259.08   Lorin, H. L'Afrique du Nord. Paris, 1908.

Afr 2630.1   Lorin, H. Le peuplement français de la Tunisie. Paris, 1904.

Afr 3979.26   Lorin, Henri. L'Egypte d'aujourd hui, le pays et les hommes. Cairo, 1926.

X Cg   Afr 3230.6   Loring, W.W. A Confederate soldier in Egypt. N.Y., 1884.

Afr 550.95   Lory, Marie Joseph. Hacia el futuro. Andorra, 1958.

Afr 6565.44A   Loschie, Michael F. Zanzibar, background to revolution. Princeton, N.J., 1965.

Afr 6293.7.2   Losi, John B. History of Lagos. Lagos, 1967.

Afr 1258.17   Loss of the American brig Commerce. (Riley, J.) London, 1817.

Afr 8659.00.25   Losse gedachten over Zuid-Afrika. (Schreiner, O.) Haarlem, 1900.

Afr 609.59.5   The lost cities of Africa. 1st ed. (Davidson, Basil.) Boston, 1959.

Afr 9389.63   Lost city of the Kalahari. (Goldie, F.) Cape Town, 1963.

Afr 590.7   The lost continent. (Cooper, J.) London, 1875.

Afr 718.2.95   Lost empire on the Nile: H.M. Stanley, Emin Pasha and the imperialists. (White, Stanhope.) London, 1969.

Afr 5406.53   Lost in the jungle. (Duchaillu, Paul Belloni.) N.Y., 1873.

Afr 8160.15   A lost legionary in South Africa. (Hamilton-Browne, G.) London, 1912.

Afr 4050.15   The lost oases. (Hassanein, A.M.) London, 1925.

Afr 4050.15.5   The lost oases. (Hassanein, A.M.) N.Y., 1925.

Afr 8210.20   Lost rails of the Transvaal. (Bulpin, Thomas Victor.) Johannesburg, 1965.

Afr 9400.10.25   The lost world of the Kalahari. (Vanderpost, Laurens.) N.Y., 1958.

Afr 1259.67   Lost worlds of Africa. 1st ed. (Wellard, James.) N.Y., 1967.

Afr 8215.7   Het lot der zwarten in Transvaal. (Huet, P.) Utrecht, 1869.

Afr 2609.07   Loth, G. La Tunisie et l'oeuvre du protectorat français. Paris, 1907.

Afr 2458.98   Loth, Gaston. Histoire de la Tunisie. Paris, 1898.

Afr 2268.1   Loth, Gaston. Le peuplement italien en Tunisie et en Algérie. Paris, 1905.

Afr 6984.11   Loth, H. Die Christliche Mission in Südwestafrika. Berlin, 1963.

Afr 7565.22   Loth, Heinrich. Kolonialismus und Humanitätsintervention. Berlin, 1966.

Afr 7549.65   Loth, Heinrich. Kongo, heisses Herz Afrikas. Geschichte des Landes bis auf unsere Tage. Berlin, 1965.

Afr 5857.2   Lougnon, Albert. Classement et inventaire du fonds de la Compagnie des Indes aux archives. Thèse. Nerac, 1956.

Afr 5872.12   Lougnon, Albert. L'Ile Bourbon pendant la régence. Paris, 1956.

Afr 2676.2   Louis, André. Documents ethnographiques et linguistiques sur les îles Gerkena. Alger, 1962.

Afr 7937.8   Louis, W.R. Ruanda-Urundi, 1884-1919. Oxford, 1963.

Afr 8252.25.10   Louis Botha, a bibliography. (Clark, E.M.) Cape Town, 1957.

Afr 5570.1   Louis XIV et la campagne des Indes Orient de 1664. (Pauliat, J.) Paris, 1886.

Afr 8100.25   Loureiro, Manoel José Gomes. Memorias dos estabelecimentos portuguezes a l'este. Lisboa, 1835.

Afr Doc 9282.4   Lourenço Marques (District). Inspecção das Circunscrições. Relatorio. 1909-1915

Afr 1493.35   Loustaunau-Lacau, G. Au Maroc français en 1925. Paris, 1928.

Afr 8289.02.20   Louter, Jan. De guerre sud-africaine. Bruxelles, 1902.

Afr 5049.5   Louveau, E. Essai sur l'influence sociale et économique des religions de l'Afrique occidentale française. Thèse. Paris, 1924.

Afr 8687.262   Louw, Abraham F. My eerste neentig jaar. Kaapstad, 1958.

Afr 8687.262.5   Louw, Andries Andriaan. Andrew Louw van Morgenster. Kaapstad, 1965.

Afr 8678.302   Louw, E.H. The case of South Africa. N.Y., 1963.

Afr 115.6   Louwers, Octave. Le Congrès Volta de 1938 et ses travaux sur l'Afrique. Bruxelles, 1949.

Afr 7540.19   Louwers, Octave. Eléments du droit de l'état indépendant du Congo. Bruxelles, 1907.

Afr 7812.233   Louwers, Octave. Le problème financier et le problème économique au Congo belge en 1932. Bruxelles, 1933.

Afr 210.56.15   Lovato, Antonio. L'ultime colonie. Roma, 1956.

Afr 3315.148   Love, Kenneth. Souez: the twice-fought war; a history. 1st ed. N.Y., 1969.

Afr 8145.14   Lovedale, South Africa. (Shepherd, R.H.W.) Lovedale, 1940.

Afr 8686.8   Lovedale, South Africa. (Stewart, James.) Edinburgh, 1894.

Afr 9439.60.5   Loveday, A.F. Three stages of history in Rhodesia. Cape Town, 1960.

Afr 8235.17A   Lovell, R.I. The struggle for South Africa, 1875-1899. N.Y., 1934.

Afr 1957.6.10   Loverdo, N. Extrait du journal d'un officier supérieur attaché à la deuxième division de l'armée d'Afrique. Paris, 1831.

Afr 11790.58.100   Lovers and hermits. (Sinclair, F.D.) Cape Town, 1957.

Afr 6497.18A   Low, D.A. Buganda and British overrule. London, 1960.

Afr 3979.14   Low, S. Egypt in transition. London, 1914.

Afr 3979.14.2   Low, S. Egypt in transition. N.Y., 1914.

Afr 609.07   Lowensbach, Lothaire. Promenade autour de l'Afrique, 1907. Paris, 1908.

Afr 6927.8   Lowenstein, Allard K. Brutal mandate. N.Y., 1962.

Afr 6280.4   Lower Niger and its tribes. (Leonard, A.G.) London, 1906.

Afr 6280.66   The Lower Niger and its tribes. 1st ed. (Leonard, Arthur Glyn.) London, 1968.

Afr 11878.24.100   The lowly and the worldly. (Wiesmar, Chriss.) South Africa, 1957.

Afr 8292.24   Lowry, E.P. With the Guards Brigade. London, 1902.

	Afr 8659.28.5	Lowth, Alys. South Africa calling. 1st ed. London, 1928.
	Afr 1609.29.2	Lowth, Alys. A wayfarer in Morocco. Boston, 1929.
	Afr 1609.29	Lowth, Alys. A wayfarer in Morocco. London, 1929.
	Afr 9160.5	Lowveld Regional Development Association. A survey of the resources and development of the southern region of the eastern Transvaal. Barberton, 1954.
	Afr 5346.5	Loyer, G. Relation du voyage du royaume d'Issyny. Paris, 1714.
	Afr 659.05	Loyson, H. To Jerusalem through lands of Islam. Chicago, 1905.
	Afr 7183.22	Luanda, "ilha" crioula. (António, Mário.) Lisboa, 1968.
	Afr 7183.26	Luanda. (Arriaga, Noel de.) Lisboa, 1964.
	Afr 7183.15	Luanda. (Pires, Rui.) Porto, 195-.
	Afr 7103.10	Luanda. Instituto de Investigação Cientifica de Angola. Archivo Histórico. Roteiro topográfico dos códices. Angola, 1966.
	Afr 9700.3	The Luapula people of Northern Rhodesia. (Cannison, Ian.) Manchester, 1959.
	Afr 2224.962	Lubell, Harold. A note on the national accounts of Algeria, 1950-1959 and 1964. Santa Monica, Calif., 1962.
	Afr 4559.29.15	Lubinski, Kurt. Hochzeitreise nach Abessinien. Leipzig, 1929.
	Afr 2208.80.6	Lubomirski, J. Côte barbaresque et le Sahara. Paris, 1880.
	Afr 8659.04	Lucas, C.P. Geography of South Africa. Oxford, 1904.
	Afr 500.30	Lucas, C.P. The partition and colonization of Africa. Oxford, 1922.
	Afr 1713.11	Lucas, Georges. Fes dans la Maroc moderne. Paris, 1937.
	Afr 8152.92	Lucas, T.J. Camp life in South Africa. London, 1878.
	Afr 8152.92.5	Lucas, T.J. Pen and pencil reminiscences of campaign in South Africa. London, 1861.
	Afr 8155.9	Lucas, T.J. The Zulus and the British frontiers. London, 1879.
	Afr 6670.928	Luce, Edmond P. L'acte de naissance d'une république africaine autonome. Paris, 1928.
	Afr 6670.957	Luchaire, Fr. Le Togo français. Paris, 1957.
	Afr 1623.927	Lucien-Graux. Le Maroc économique. Paris, 1928.
	Afr 6549.251	Luck, Anne. African saint. London, 1963.
	Afr 8659.02.4	Luck, R.A. A visit to Lewanika, king of the Barotse. London, 1902.
	Afr 8809.51	Luckhoff, C.A. Table mountain. Cape Town, 1951.
	Afr 8378.200.10	Ludi, Gerard. The amazing Mr. Fischer. Cape Town, 1966.
	Afr 11534.18.100	Ludi, Gerard. Operation Atlantis. Cape Town, 1967.
Htn	Afr 4556.81F*	Ludolf, H. Historia aethiopica. Francofurti ad Moenum, 1681.
	Afr 4556.81.2F	Ludolf, H. Historia aethiopica. Francofurti ad Moenum, 1691.
	Afr 4556.81.31	Ludolf, H. Historie van Abissinien. Utrecht, 1687.
	Afr 4556.81.11	Ludolf, H. A new history of Ethiopia. London, 1682.
	Afr 4556.81.21	Ludolf, H. Nouvelle histoire d'Abissinie. Paris, 1684.
	Afr 3979.36.5A	Ludwig, Emil. The Nile, the life story of a river. N.Y., 1937.
	Afr 724.10.2	Ludwig, Emil. Die Reise nach Afrika. Berlin, 1913.
	Afr 1825.2	Ludwig, Salvator. Bougie, die perle nord afrikas. Leipzig, 1900.
	Afr 658.74	Ludwig, Salvator. Yacht-Reise in den Syrten, 1873. Prag, 1874.
	Afr 2662.1.5F	Ludwig Salvator. Benzert. Prag, 1897.
	Afr 2662.1	Ludwig Salvator. Bizerta und seine Zukunft. Prag, 1881.
	Afr 6640.4	Luecke, J.H. Bevölkerung und Aufenthaltsrecht in den Department schutzgebieten Afrikas. Inaug. Diss. Hamburg, 1913.
	Afr 6640.3	Luecke, J.H. Bevölkerung und Aufenthaltsrecht in den Department schutzgebieten Afrikas. Hamburg, 1913.
	Afr 6010.10.1	Lugard, F.D. The dual mandate in British Tropical Africa. 5th ed. Hamden, Conn., 1965.
	Afr 6010.10.2	Lugard, F.D. The dual mandate in British Tropical Africa. 5th ed. London, 1965.
	Afr 6497.8A	Lugard, F.D. The rise of our East African empire. Edinburgh, 1893. 2v.
	Afr 6010.10	Lugard, F.D. The dual mandate in British Tropical Africa. 2d ed. Edinburgh, 1923.
	Afr 6214.1.5	Lugard, Flora Louisa. A tropical dependency. N.Y., 1965.
	Afr 6210.1	Lugard, Frederick Dealtry. Instructions to political and other officers. London, 1966.
	Afr 6210.1.5	Lugard, Frederick Dealtry. Lugard and the amalgamation of Nigeria. London, 1968.
	Afr 6210.1.5	Lugard and the amalgamation of Nigeria. (Lugard, Frederick Dealtry.) London, 1968.
	Afr 6540.7.5	The Lugbara of Uganda. (Middleton, J.) N.Y., 1965.
	Afr 6540.7	Lugbara religion. (Middleton, J.) London, 1960.
	Afr 4785.4	Lugh, emporio commerciale sul Giuba. (Ferrandi, U.) Roma, 1903.
	Afr 820.15	Luigi, Duke of the Abruzzi. La esplorazione dello Uabi-Uebi Scebeli. Milano, 1932.
	Afr 1069.36	Luigi, G. de. La Francia nord-africana. Padova, 1936.
X Cg	Afr 6128.3	Lukach, H.C. A bibliography of Sierra Leone. Oxford, 1910. (Changed to XP 3869)
	Afr 718.25.12	Lukas, J. Zentralsudanische Studien, Wörterverzeichnisse der Deutschen Zentral-Afrika-Expedition 1910-11. Hamburg, 1937.
	Afr 6128.3.2	Luke, H.C. A bibliography of Sierra Leone. 2d ed. London, 1925.
	Afr 1738.22	Luke, John. Tangier at high tide. Geneva, 1958.
	Afr 9439.54.5	Lumb, Sybil Victoria. Central and southern Africa. 2. ed. Cambridge, 1962.
	Afr 3982.2F	Lumbroso, Giacomo. Descrittori italiani dell'Egitto e di Alessandria. Roma, 1879.
	Afr 2208.47.3	Lumsden, William. Journal of a trip to the Algerine territory, 1837. Glasgow, 1847.
	Afr 7912.15.45	Lumumba; a biography. 1st ed. (McKown, Robin.) Garden City, 1969.
	Afr 7575.80.10	Lumumba, Patrice. Congo, my country. London, 1962.
	Afr 7575.80.12	Lumumba, Patrice. Congo, my country. London, 1969.
	Afr 7575.80.11	Lumumba, Patrice. Congo, my country. N.Y., 1962.
	Afr 7575.80	Lumumba, Patrice. Le Congo. Bruxelles, 1961.
	Afr 7912.5.10	Lumumba, Patrice. Patrice Lumumba. Moscou, 1964.
	Afr 7912.5.100	Lumumba, Patrice. La pensée politique. Paris, 1963.
	Afr 7580.25	Lumumba. (Jarschel, Fritz.) Kreuzweingarten/Rhld., 1965.
	Afr 7912.15.25	Lumumba i jego kraj. (Turski, Marian.) Warszawa, 1962.
	Afr 7912.15.20	Lumumba ou l'Afrique frustrée. (Lopez Alvarez, Luis.) Paris, 1964.
	Afr 7912.15.40	Lumumba Patrice: les cinquante derniers jours de sa vie. (Heinz, G.) Bruxelles, 1966.
	Afr 7567.30	Lumumba's Congo. (Okumu, Washington A.) N.Y., 1963.
	Afr 3978.76.11	Lund, Fr. Taflor fraan orienten af hother tolderlund. Stockholm, 1876.
	Afr 6460.80	Luo customary law and marriage laws customs. (Wilson, Gordon.) Nairobi, 1961.
	Afr 4513.37.60	Luongo, G. L'Etiopia, dalla vigilia di sangue alla conquista dell'impero. Napoli, 1937.
	Afr 7015.30	Lupi, Luis C. Quem incendion o Congo. Lisboa, 1960.
	Afr 3823.4	Lupton, Frank. Geographical observations in the Bahr-el-Ghazal region. London, 1884.
	Afr 550.90	The lure of Africa. (Patton, Cornelius H.) N.Y., 1917.
	Afr 8371.5	Lurie, Angela Shulmith. Urban Africans in the Republic of South Africa, 1950-1966. Johannesburg, 1969.
	Afr 9705.5	Lusaka, the new capital of Northern Rhodesia, opened Jubilee Week, 1935. London, 1935.
	Afr 9625.45	Lusaka. Livingstone Museum. Annual report. Lusaka. 1966
	Afr 6648.3F	Luschan, F. Von. Beitraege zur Völkerkunde. Berlin, 1897.
	Afr 5040.8	Lusignan, Guy de. French-speaking Africa since independence. London, 1969.
	Afr 3183.8A	Lusignan, S. History of the revolt of Ali Bey. London, 1783.
	Afr 4389.58	Luther, E.W. Ethiopia today. Stanford, Calif., 1958.
	Afr 8687.263	Luthuli, A. Let my people go. N.Y., 1962.
	Afr 1487.20	Lutskaia, N.S. Marokko vnovobretaet nezavisimost'. Moscow, 1958.
	Afr 1658.45	Lutskaia, N.S. Respublika rif. Moscow, 1959.
	Afr 3079.59	Lutskii, V.B. Ocherki po istorii arabskikh stran. Moscow, 1959.
	Afr 7025.5	Lutte armée en Afrique. (Chaliand, Gérard.) Paris, 1967.
	Afr 3339.14	La Lutte de classes en Égypte de 1945 à 1968. (Hussein, Mahmoud.) Paris, 1969.
	Afr 14692.41.1100	Luuanda. (Vieira, Luandino.) Luanda, 1963.
	Afr 7567.15	Luwel, Marcel. De limburgers in Congo. Hasselt, 1952.
	Afr 7923.5	Luwel, Marcel. Sir Francis de Winton, administrateur général du Congo, 1884-1886. Tervuren, 1964.
	Afr 5620.10	Lux. La verité sur Madagascar. Paris, 1896.
	Afr 3990.29	Luxor; how to see it. Cairo. 14,1965
	Afr 14722.5	Luz no túnel; romane. (Beira, Maria da.) Porto, 1966.
	Afr 1570.4	Luzeux. Notre politique au Maroc. Paris, n.d.
	Afr 3979.11.15	L'vov, A.N. V strane Amon-Ra. Sankt Peterburg, 1911.
	Afr 6460.80.10	The Lwoo. (Crazzolara, J. Pasquale.) Verona, 1950-54. 3v.
	Afr 115.15	Ly, A. Les masses africaines. Paris, 1956.
	Afr 5130.25	Ly, Abdoulaye. La compagnie du Sénégal. Paris, 1958.
	Afr 5183.2	Ly, Abdoulays. L'état et la production paysanne. Paris, 1958.
	Afr 5832.12	Ly-Tio-Fane, Madeleine. Mauritius and the spice trade. Port Louis, 1958. 2v.
	Afr 5585.35	Lyall, R. Le journal de Robert Lyall. Tananarive, 1954.
	Afr 1571.17.35	Lyautey, intime. (Georges-Gaulis, B.) Paris, 1938.
	Afr 5640.4	Lyautey, L.H.G. Dans le sud de Madagascar. Paris, 1903.
	Afr 5640.4.51	Lyautey, L.H.G. Lettres du sud de Madagascar, 1900-1902. Paris, 1935.
	Afr 1571.17.3	Lyautey, L.H.G. Lyautey l'Africain. v.1-4. Paris, 1953. 4v.
	Afr 1571.17.2	Lyautey, L.H.G. Paroles d'action. Paris, 1927.
	Afr 1571.17.65	Lyautey, L.H.G. Les plus belles lettres de Lyautey. Paris, 1962.
	Afr 1571.17.57	Lyautey, L.H.G. Rayonnement de Lyautey. Paris, 1941.
	Afr 1571.17.62	Lyautey, L.H.G. Rayonnement de Lyautey. Paris, 1947.
	Afr 1571.16	Lyautey, L.H.G. Vers le Maroc, lettres du Sud-Oranais, 1903-1906. Paris, 1937.
	Afr 2731.15.95	Lyautey, Pierre. Charles de Foucauld. Paris, 1966.
	Afr 5640.12	Lyautey, Pierre. Gallieni. 6. ed. Paris, 1959.
	Afr 1571.17.100	Lyautey. (Cahiers Charles de Foucauld.) Grenoble, 1954.
	Afr 1571.17.85	Lyautey. (Catroux, G.) Paris, 1952.
	Afr 1571.17.120	Lyautey. (Deloncle, Pierre.) Paris, 1955.
	Afr 1571.17.110	Lyautey. (Durasoy, M.) Paris, 1956.
	Afr 1571.17.115	Lyautey. (Farrere, Claude.) Paris, 1955.
	Afr 1571.17.55	Lyautey. (Gouraud, H.J.E.) Paris, 1938.
	Afr 1493.65	Lyautey. (Leyris de Campredon.) Paris, 1955.
	Afr 1571.17.10A	Lyautey. (Maurois, A.) N.Y., 1931.
	Afr 1571.17.12A	Lyautey. (Maurois, A.) N.Y., 1932.
	Afr 1571.17.6	Lyautey. (Maurois, A.) Paris, 1931.
	Afr 1571.17.8	Lyautey. (Maurois, A.) Paris, 1931.
	Afr 1571.17.9	Lyautey. (Maurois, A.) Paris, 1932.
	Afr 1571.17.11	Lyautey. (Maurois, A.) Paris, 1934.
	Afr 1571.17.27	Lyautey assassine. (Figueras, Andre.) Paris, 1958.
	Afr 1571.17.50	Lyautey du Tonkin au Maroc par Madagascar et le Sud-Oranais. (Howe, S.E.) Paris, 1938.
	Afr 1571.17.30	Lyautey et le Maroc. (Barthou, Louis.) Paris, 1931.
	Afr 1571.17.18	Lyautey et le protectorat. (Esperandieu, Pierre.) Paris, 1947.
	Afr 1571.17.135	Lyautey l'Africain, ou Le rêve immolé. (Benoist-Méchin, Jacques.) Lausanne, 1966.
	Afr 1571.17.3	Lyautey l'Africain. v.1-4. (Lyautey, L.H.G.) Paris, 1953. 4v.
	Afr 1571.17.13	Lyautey-le-magicien. (Dubly, H.L.) Lille, 1931.
	Afr 1571.17.130	Lydutey et le médecin. (Maroc-Medical, Publishers, Casablanca.) Casablanca, 1954.
	Afr 9839.12	Lyell, D.D. Nyasaland for the hunter and settler. London, 1912.
	Afr 609.23.5	Lyell, Denis D. Memories of an African hunter. London, 1923.
	Afr 11433.74.100	The lying days. (Gordimer, N.) N.Y., 1953.
	Afr 8289.03.4	Lynch, G. Impressions of a war correspondent. London, 1903.
	Afr 7489.8.5	Lynch, Hollis Ralph. Edward Wilmot Blyden. London, 1967.
	Afr 7320.5	Lyne, Robert N. Mozambique. London, 1913.
	Afr 6570.5	Lyne, Robert Nunez. Zanzibar in contemporary times. N.Y., 1969.
Htn	Afr 2928.18.3*	Lyon, G.F. Narrative of travels in North Africa, 1818, 1819 and 1820. London, 1821.
	Afr 7940.5	Lyr, Claude. Ruanda Urundi. Brussels, 195-.
	Afr 28.99	Lystad, Robert A. The African world. London, 1965.
	Afr 6194.10.11	Lystad, Robert A. The Ashanti; a proud people. N.Y., 1968.
	Afr 11542.87.130	Lytton, David. The freedom of the cage. London, 1966.
	Afr 11542.87	Lytton, David. The goddam white man. N.Y., 1961.
	Afr 11542.87.120	Lytton, David. The paradise people. London, 1962.
	Afr 11542.87.110	Lytton, David. A place apart. London, 1961.
	Afr 6333.66	Lytton, Noel. The stolen desert. London, 1966.
	Afr 5405.109	M. Savorgnan de Brazza. (Drohojowska, Antoinette J.F.A.) Lille, 1884.
	Afr 1608.79	M. y Rodriganez, T. El imperio de Marruecos. Madrid, 1879.
	Afr 4375.4	Ma captivité en Abyssinie. (Blanc, H.) Paris, 1870.

Afr 5645.5	Madagascar, birth of a new republic. (France. Embassy. U.S.) N.Y., 1960.
Afr 5758.61	Madagascar, birth of a new republic. N.Y., 1961.
Afr 5749.31	Madagascar, colonie française, 1896-1930. (You, André.) Paris, 1931.
Afr 5600.4	Madagascar, combat livre à Tananarive. n.p., 1846.
Afr 5765.15.5	Madagascar, country, people, missions. (Sibree, James.) London, 1880.
Afr 5640.27	Madagascar, creation française. (Leblond, M.) Paris, 1934.
Afr 5748.95.25	Madagascar, étude economique, geographique et ethnographique. (Benoit, Felix.) Dijon, 1895.
Afr 5758.14	Madagascar, étude économique. (Loisy, F.X.) Paris, 1914.
Afr 5758.67	Madagascar, étude géographique et économique. (Bostian, Georges.) Paris, 1967.
Afr 5540.6F	Madagascar, gouvernement générale. Tananarive, 1903.
Afr 5749.47	Madagascar, hier et aujourd'hui. (Launois, Pierre.) Paris, 1947.
Afr 5749.05	Madagascar, histoire, organisation, colonisation. (You, Andre.) Paris, 1905.
Afr 5748.84.5	Madagascar, its history and people. (Little, H. William.) Edinburgh, 1884.
Afr 5765.13	Madagascar, its missionaries and martyrs. 2d ed. (Townsend, William J.) London, 1892.
Afr 5765.4.2	Madagascar, its missions and its martyrs. London, 1863.
Afr 5748.83.10	Madagascar, la reine des iles africaines. (Buet, Charles.) Paris, 1883.
Afr 5635.14	Madagascar, la vie du soldat. (Gallieni, J.S.) Paris, 1905.
Afr 5749.24	Madagascar, land of the man-eating tree. (Osborn, C.S.) N.Y., 1924.
Afr 5640.3	Madagascar, les Malgaches. (Gravier, G.) Paris, 1904.
Afr 5635.10	Madagascar, l'expedition au point de vue medical. (Lenure, Jean.) Paris, 1896.
Afr 5749.62	Madagascar, maître à son bord. (Pidoux, Edmond.) Lausanne, 1962.
Afr 5600.5	Madagascar, past and present. London, 1847.
Afr 5548.59	Madagascar, possession française depuis 1642. (Barbie du Bocage, V.A.) Paris, 1859.
Afr 5620.9	Madagascar, son avenir colonial. (Courand, Charles J.) La Rochelle, 1895.
Afr 5746.43	Madagascar, the richest and most fruitful island in the world. (Hamond, W.) London, 1643.
Afr 5549.12	Madagascar, 1638-1894, établissement des Français dans l'ile. (Villars, E.J.) Paris, 1912.
Afr 5765.24	Madagascar, 1832-1932. (Lhande, P.) Paris, 1932.
Afr 5625.8	Pamphlet vol. Madagascar, 1868-97. 8 pam.
Afr 5502.2	Madagascar. Bulletin economique. Tananarive. 1923+ 2v.
Afr 5502.2.5	Madagascar. Bulletin economique mensuel. Tananarive. 1,1926+
Afr 5755.2	Madagascar. Camores, Reunion, ile Maurice. Paris, 1955.
Afr 5748.99	Madagascar. Guide de l'immigrant à Madagascar. V.1-3 and plates. Paris, 1899. 4v.
NEDL Afr 5514.1	Madagascar. Notes, reconnaissances et explorations. Tananarive. 1,1897+ 5v.
Afr Doc 5609.500	Madagascar. Notice sur les impôts, droits et taxes. Tananarive. 1964+
Afr 5758.58	Madagascar. Plan de developpement economique et social. Tananarive. 1947+ 4v.
Afr Doc 5622.5	Madagascar. Rapport sur la situation générale de la colonie. n.p., n.d.
Afr 5513.2	Madagascar. Revue de geographie. Toulouse. 1,1962+ 5v.
Afr Doc 5607.15F	Madagascar. Statistiques générales. 1906-1908
Afr 5783.5	Madagascar. Tananarive. Tananarive, 1952.
Afr 5625.6	Pamphlet vol. Madagascar. 5 pam.
Afr 5748.94.5	Pamphlet vol. Madagascar. 2 pam.
Afr 5533.5	Pamphlet vol. Madagascar. 7 pam.
Afr 5533.01	Pamphlet box. Madagascar.
Afr 5748.95.12	Pamphlet vol. Madagascar. 3 pam.
Afr 5533.02F	Pamphlet box. Madagascar.
Afr 5749.55	Madagascar. (Bastian, Georges.) Tananarive, 1955.
Afr 5548.84.10	Madagascar. (Castonnet des Fosses, H.) Paris, 1884. 2 pam.
Afr 5749.47.5	Madagascar. (Deschamps, H.) Paris, 1947.
Afr 5530.4	Madagascar. (Duignan, Peter.) Stanford, Calif., 1962.
Afr 5748.86.5	Madagascar. (Genin, E.) Paris, 1886.
Afr 5748.95.10	Madagascar. (Humbert, G.) Paris, 1895.
Afr 5549.55	Madagascar. (Isnard, Hildebert.) Paris, 1955.
Afr 5758.60	Madagascar. (Istituto Nazionale per il Commercio Estero.) Roma, 1960.
Afr 5758.60.4	Madagascar. (Istituto Nazionale per il Commercio Estero.) Roma, 1964-[1965].
Afr 5758.5	Madagascar. (Jully, M.A.) Marseille, 1900.
Afr 5749.33.5	Madagascar. (Laurence, A.) Paris, 1933.
Afr 5748.94	Madagascar. (Martineau, A.) Paris, 1894.
Afr 5548.86	Madagascar. (Oliver, S.P.) London, 1886. 2v.
Afr 5635.4	Madagascar. (Ortus, C.) Paris, 1895.
Afr 5749.31.5	Madagascar. (Paris, Pierre.) Paris, 1931.
Afr 5749.00.5	Madagascar. (Paris. Exposition Universelle (1900).) Paris, 1900.
Afr 5748.86	Madagascar. (Pastel, R.) Paris, 1886.
Afr 5748.84.15	Madagascar. (Pauliat, Louis.) Paris, 1884.
Afr 5758.25F	Madagascar. (Paulin, H.) Paris, 1925.
Afr 5749.33.10	Madagascar. (Petit, G.) Paris, 1933.
Afr 5749.00F	Madagascar. (Piolet, J.B.) Paris, 1900.
Afr 5549.52	Madagascar. (Rabemananjara, R.W.) Paris, 1952.
Afr 5748.66.5	Pamphlet vol. Madagascar. Geography. 4 pam.
Afr 5749.64.15	Madagascar. Tananarive, 1964.
X Cg Afr 5765.16	Pamphlet vol. Madagascar. (Changed to XP 3993) 7 pam.
Afr 5758.64F	Madagascar. Commissariat Général au Plan. Plan quinquennal, 1964-1968. Tananarive, 1964.
Afr 5540.11	Madagascar. Constitution. Constitution et lois organiques de la République Malgache et accords franco-malgaches. Tananarive, 1962.

Afr Doc 5622.10	Madagascar. Gouvernement Général de Madagascar et Dépendances. Madagascar de 1896 à 1905. n.p., n.d. 2v.
Afr 5758.57F	Madagascar. Haut Commissariat. Plan de developpement économique et social, programme, 1958-1962. Tananarive, 1957.
Afr Doc 5608.700.5	Madagascar. Institut National de la Statistique et de la Recherche Economique. Series retrospectives, 1949-1961. n.p., n.d.
Afr Doc 5609.300	Madagascar. Institut National de la Statistique et de la Recherche Economique. Situation économique. Tananarive. 1961+
Afr Doc 5608.700	Madagascar. Institut National de la Statistique et de la Recherche Economique. Statistiques du commerce exterieur. 1964+
Afr Doc 5607.5	Madagascar. Service de Statistique Generale. Annuaire statistique. Tananarive. 1,1938+
Afr 5749.65.5	Madagascar. v.1-2. Chambéry (Savoie), 1965-1966.
Afr 5748.95.30	Madagascar. 2e ed. (Paisant, M.) Paris, 1895.
Afr 5749.54	Madagascar à travers ses provinces. Paris, 1954.
Afr Doc 5602.5	Madagascar and adjacent islands; a guide to official publications. (Library of Congress. African Section.) Washington, 1965.
Afr 5548.85	Madagascar and France. (Shaw, George A.) London, 1885.
Afr 5548.65	Madagascar and its people. (Mcleod, Lyons.) London, 1865.
Afr 5748.70	Madagascar and its people. (Sibree, James.) London, 1870.
Afr 5748.66	Madagascar and the Malagasy. (Oliver, S. Pasfield.) London, 1866.
Afr 5749.02.5	Madagascar au debut du XXe siècle. Paris, 1902.
Afr 5748.96	Madagascar before the conquest. (Sibree, J.) London, 1896.
Afr 5530.1	A Madagascar bibliography. (Sibree, J.) Antananarivo, 1885.
Afr 5530.1.5	A Madagascar bibliography. Mss. Additions and corrections. (Sibree, J.) Antananarivo, 1885.
Afr Doc 5622.10	Madagascar de 1896 à 1905. (Madagascar. Gouvernement Général de Madagascar et Dépendances.) n.p., n.d. 2v.
Afr 5748.88	Madagascar depuis sa decouverte jusqu'a nos jours. (Lechartier, H.) Paris, 1888.
Afr 5620.5	Madagascar en 1894, étude de politique. (Martineau, A.) Paris, 1894.
Afr 5640.20	Madagascar et dependances. (Delelee-Desloges, J.G.) Paris, 1931.
Afr 5749.15.5	Madagascar et la côte de Somalie. (Guilloteaux, E.) Paris, 1922.
Afr 5758.34	Madagascar et la crise. Thèse. (Prunieres, A.) Paris, 1934.
Afr 5600.6	Madagascar et la France. (Chauvot, H.) Paris, 1848.
Afr 5765.10	Madagascar et la mission catholique. (Colin, E.) Paris, 1895.
Afr 5748.96.8	Madagascar et l'alimentation européenne. (Locamus, P.) Paris, 1896.
Afr 5749.61	Madagascar et l'ame malgache. (Thiout, Michel.) Paris, 1961.
Afr 5605.3	Madagascar et le roi Radama II. (Regnon, Henry de.) Paris, 1863.
Afr 5749.58F	Madagascar et les bases dispersees de l'union française. (Robequain, Chas.) Paris, 1958. 2v.
Afr 5748.95.15	Madagascar et les Hova. (Piolet, J.B.) Paris, 1895.
Afr 5640.6	Madagascar et l'oeuvre du Général Gallieni. Thèse. (Basset, Charles.) Paris, 1903.
Afr 5748.87.5	Madagascar et peuplades independantes abandonnées par la France. (Duverge.) Paris, 1887.
Afr 5765.7.20	Madagascar et ses deux premiers évêques. v.1-2. 3. ed. (Maupoint, A.R.) Paris, 1864.
Afr 5748.70.5	Madagascar et ses habitants. (Sibree, James.) Toulouse, 1873.
Afr 5748.96.7	Madagascar et ses richesses. (Locamus, P.) Paris, 1896.
Afr 5758.30	Madagascar et ses richesses. (Nemours, C.P.) Paris, 1930.
Afr 5749.46	The Madagascar I love. (Fiedler, Arkady.) London, 1946.
Afr 5635.2	Madagascar in war time. (Knight, E.F.) London, 1896.
Afr 5514.2F	Madagascar news. Antananarivo.
Afr 5548.95	Madagascar of to-day. (Cousins, W.E.) London, 1895.
Afr 5749.23	Madagascar pour tous. (Cros, Louis.) Paris, 1923.
Afr 5748.67	Madagascar revisited. (Ellis, William.) London, 1867.
Afr 5640.30	Madagascar sous la revolution Malgache. (Rabemananjara, R.W.) Paris, 1953.
Afr 5548.86.5	Madagascar und die Inseln Seychellen. (Hartmann, R.) Leipzig, 1886.
Afr 5549.60.5	Madagasihara, regards vers le passe. (Tananarive. Bibliotheque Universitaire.) Tananarive, 1960.
Afr 5549.43	Madagaskar. (Haenel, Karl.) Leipzig, 1951.
Afr 5748.83	Madagaskar und das Hovareich. (Audebert, J.) Berlin, 1883.
Afr 7809.54	Madami. (Putnam, A.E.) N.Y., 1954.
Afr 44619.5	Madan, Arthur Cornwallis. Kiungani, or Story and history from Central Africa written by boys in the schools. London, 1887.
Afr 3205.6	Madden, R.R. Egypt and Mohammed Ali. 2d ed. London, 1841.
Afr 6210.50F	Maddocks, K.P. Report on local government in the Northern provinces of Nigeria. Kaduna, 1961.
Afr 6138.61.5	Mador, Iulii P. Sierra-Leone vchera i segodnia. Moscow, 1961.
Afr 1571.17.105	Madras, Didier. Dans l'ombre du maréchal Lyautey. Rabat, 1954.
Afr 5955.5	Madrid, F. La Guinea incognita. Madrid, 1933.
Afr 7815.17	Maes, J. Volkenkunde van Belgisch Kongo. Antwerpen, 1935.
Afr 1340.9	Maestacci, Noel. Le Maroc contemporain. Paris, 1928.
Afr 1487.25	Maestre, Pedro. Divulgacion y orientacion. Granada, 1923.
Afr 8310.12	Mafeking, a Victorian legend. (Gardner, Brian.) London, 1966.
Afr 8310.5	Mafeking. (Baillie, F.D.) N.Y., 1900.
Htn Afr 8310.7F*	Mafeking Mail. Special siege edition. Nov. 1, 1899 to May 31, 1900. n.p., n.d.
Afr 11229.5	Mafeking road. (Bosman, Herman.) Johannesburg, 1947.
Afr 1680.50	Un magasin collectif de l'anti-atlas. Thèse. (Montagne, Robert.) Paris, 1930.
Afr 5235.186	Mage, Eugène. Voyage dans le Soudan occidental. Paris, 1868.
Afr 2622.1	Mager, Henri. Atlas de Tunisie. Paris, n.d.
Afr 5748.98.10	Mager, Henri. La vie à Madagascar. Paris, 1898.
Afr 2632.9	Maggio, G. di. Gli Italiani e le professioni liberali in Tunisia. Tunis, 1934.
Afr 1259.66	Le Maghreb. (Isnard, Hildebert.) Paris, 1966.

Afr 1576.3F Marrocos e três mestres da ordem de cristo, memória publicada por ordem da academia das sciências de Lisboa. (Vieira da S. y Guimaraes.) Lisboa, 1916.
Afr 1609.61.5 Marruecos, ayer-hoy. (Simoes, Antonio.) Buenos Aires, 1961.
Afr 1493.25 Marruecos, diario de una bandera, 1922. (Franco, Francisco.) Sevilla, 1939.
Afr 1750.10 Marruecos, la mala semilla. (Azpeitua, Antonio.) Madrid, 1921.
Afr 1493.72 Marruecos, las etapas de la pacificacion. (Goded, M.) Madrid, 1932.
Afr 1573.11 Marruecos, politica e interes de España en este imperio. (Caballero de Puga.) Madrid, 1907.
Afr 1750.22 Marruecos, sus condiciones fisicas. 2 ed. (Sangroniz, Jose Antonio De.) Madrid, 1926.
Afr 1621.5 Marruecos...en 1894 fotografias. (Echague, F.) Madrid, 1906.
Afr 1608.82.4F Marruecos. (Amicis, E. de.) Barcelona, 1892.
Afr 1369.39 Marruecos. (Garcia Figueras, T.) Barcelona, 1939.
Afr 1493.20 Marruecos. (Gomez Hidalgo, F.) Madrid, 1921.
Afr 1573.9 Marruecos. (Gutierrez Sobral, J.) Madrid, 1905.
Afr 1609.08.5 Marruecos. (Leon Y Ramos, E.) Madrid, 1908.
Afr 1608.85.5 Marruecos. (Mercet, A.) Madrid, 1887.
Afr 1573.23 Marruecos. (Merino Alvarez, A.) Madrid, 1921.
Afr 1608.93.5 Marruecos. (Olivie, M.) Barcelona, 1893.
Afr 1750.28.5 Marruecos. (Pita, F.) Melilla, 1925.
Afr 1623.935 Marruecos. (Tomas Perez, V.) Barcelona, 1935.
Afr 1609.08.5.4 Marruecos. Novisima ed. (Leon Y Ramos, E.) Madrid, 1915.
Afr 1607.91.9 Marruecos hace cien anos. Paris, 1911.
Afr 1750.2 Marruecos y plazas españolas. (Martin Y Peinador.) Madrid, 1908.
Afr 628.262 Mars, Jean. De la préhistoire d'Afrique. Port-au-Prince, 1962.
Afr 626.202 Mars, John. Afrikanische Wirtschaftsintegration. Wien, 1967.
Afr 5230.7 Mars 1961-mars 1962. Les relations Mali - République Arabe Unie. (Mali. Embassy. United Arab Republic.) Cairo, 1962.
Afr 6979.44 Marsh, John H. Skeleton coast. London, 1944.
Afr 6314.31 Marsh, Zoe. East Africa through contemporary records. Cambridge, Eng., 1961.
Afr 699.57A Marsh, Zoe. An introduction to the history of East Africa. Cambridge, Eng., 1957.
Afr 699.57.2 Marsh, Zoe. An introduction to the history of East Africa. 2. ed. Cambridge, Eng., 1961.
Afr 699.57.3 Marsh, Zoe. An introduction to the history of East Africa. 3. ed. Cambridge, Eng., 1965.
Afr 9435.20 Marshall, Charles Burton. Crisis over Rhodesia: a skeptical view. Baltimore, 1967.
Afr 3275.39 Marshall, J.E. The Egyptian enigma, 1890-1928. London, 1928.
Afr 3315.80 Marshall, S.L.A. Sinai victory. N.Y., 1958.
Afr 4700.2 Marson, Luigi. Commemorazione dell'esploratore africano. Mantova, 1902.
Afr 4513.37.42A Martelli, G. Italy against the world. N.Y., 1938.
Afr 7582.8 Martelli, George. Experiment in world government, an account of the United Nations operation in the Congo, 1960-1964. London, 1966.
Afr 7549.62.10 Martelli, George. Leopold to Lumumba. London, 1962.
Afr 620.3 Martens, Otto. African handbook and traveller's guide. London, 1932.
Afr 5056.134.7 Martet, Jean. Les batisseurs de royaumes. Paris, 1934.
Afr 8285.20.10 Marthinus Theunis Steijn. (Merwe, N.J.) Kaapstad, 1921. 2v.
Afr 8285.20.5 Marthinus Theunis Steijn. (Rompel, Frederik.) Amsterdam, 1902.
Afr 4590.1 Martial de Salviac, R.P. Les Galla, grande nation africaine. Cahors, 1900.
Afr 4590.1.2 Martial de Salviac, R.P. Les Galla, grande nation africaine. Paris, 1901.
Afr 5758.38 Martin, A. Les delegations économiques et financieres de Madagascar. Thèse. Paris, 1938.
Afr 8830.5 Martin, A. Home life on an ostrich farm. London, 1890.
Afr 8325.33.5 Martin, A.C. The concentration camps, 1900-02. Cape Town, 1958.
Afr 2374.2 Martin, A.G.P. Les oasis sahariennes. Alger, 1908.
Afr 1259.13.5 Martin, A.G.P. Précis de sociologie nord-africaine. Paris, 1913.
Afr 2719.23 Martin, A.G.P. Quatre siècles d'histoire marocaine. Paris, 1923.
Afr 1550.35 Martin, Alfred G.P. Le Maroc et l'Europe. Paris, 1928.
Afr 1369.23 Martin, Alfred G.P. Quatre siècles d'histoire marocaine. Paris, 1923.
Afr 2000.7 Martin, C. Histoire de l'Algérie française, 1830-1962. Paris, 1963.
Afr 2025.13.10 Martin, Claude. La commune d'Alger, 1870-1871. Paris, 1936.
Afr 2025.13.12 Martin, Claude. La commune d'Alger, 1870-1871. Thèse. Paris, 1936.
Afr 2274.5 Martin, Claude. Les israélites algériens de 1830 à 1902. Thèse. Paris, 1936.
Afr 2675.1.5 Martin, D.B. I know Tunisia. N.Y., 1943.
Afr 590.48 Martin, Gaston. Negriers et bois d'ébène. Grenoble, 1934.
Afr 6988.58.268 Martin, H. The sheltering desert. London, 1957.
Afr 626.212 Martin, Jane. A bibliography on African regionalism. Boston, 1969.
Htn Afr 1947.8* Martin, M. History of the captivity and sufferings in Algiers. Boston, 1807.
Afr 8145.46 Martin, Marie L. The biblical concept of Messianism and Messianism in Southern Africa. Morija, 1964.
Afr 3979.23.5A Martin, P.F. Egypt old and new. London, 1923.
Afr 3745.10A Martin, Percy F. The Sudan in evolution. London, 1921.
Afr 9435.6F Martin, R.E.R. Report on native administration of British South Africa Company. London, 1897.
Afr 8658.36 Martin, R.M. History of southern Africa. London, 1836.
Afr 8658.36.3 Martin, R.M. History of southern Africa. 2nd ed. London, 1843.
Afr 5187.15 Martin, V. La chrétienté africaine de Dakar. Dakar, 1964. 3 pam.
Afr 5187.10 Martin, V. Notes d'introduction à une étude socio-religieuse des populations de Dakar et du Sénégal. Dakar, 1964.
Afr 1432.14 Martin Arrue, F. Guerra hispano-marroqui, 1859-60. Madrid, 1915.
Afr 2030.461.75 Martin-Chauffier, L. L'examen des consciences. Paris, 1961.
NEDL Afr 5045.17.5 Martin du Gard, M. Courrier d'Afrique. Paris, 1931.

Afr 1573.22 Martin Peinador, L. El suelo de Marruecos y sus primeros habitantes. Madrid, 1920.
Afr 1750.2 Martin Y Peinador. Marruecos y plazas españolas. Madrid, 1908.
Afr 5748.94 Martineau, A. Madagascar. Paris, 1894.
Afr 5620.5 Martineau, A. Madagascar en 1894, étude de politique. Paris, 1894.
Afr 8278.99.9 Martineau, J. The Transvaal trouble. London, 1899.
Afr 8252.10 Martineau, John. The life and correspondence of Sir Bartle Frere. London, 1895. 2v.
Afr 4742.15 Martinelli, Renzo. Sud. Firenze, 1930.
Afr 1755.47 Martinez de Campos, Arsenio. Melilla, 1921. Ciudad Real, 1922.
Afr 5993.16 Martinez y Sanz, M. Breves apuntes sobre la isla de Fernando Poo en el Golfo de Guinea. Madrid, 1859.
Afr 4732.2 Martini, F. Cose africane, da Saati ad Abba Carima. Milano, 1897.
Afr 4719.47 Martini, Ferdinando. Il diario eritreo. Firenze, 1947. 4v.
Afr 4718.91.20 Martini, Ferdinando. Nell'Africa italiana. Milano, 1895.
Afr 1608.97 Martiniere, H.M.P. de la. Notice sur le Maroc. Paris, 1897.
Afr 2929.12.5 Martino, G. de. Tripoli, Cirene e Cartagine. 2 ed. Bologna, 1912.
Afr 2280.8 Martino, P. Les descriptions de Fromentin. Alger, 1910.
Afr 11558.78.100 Martins, Harper. Nongalazi of the Bemba. Ilfrawmbe, 1965.
Afr 7815.50 Martins, Manuel Alfredo de Morais. Contacto de culturas no Congo Português. Lisboa, 1958.
Afr 5051.25 Martonne, E. de. Inventaire méthodique des cartes et croquis...relatifs á l'Afrique occidentale. Laval, 1926.
Afr 5392.2 Marty, Paul. Etudes sur l'islam au Dahomey. Paris, 1926.
Afr 5187.5 Marty, Paul. Etudes sur l'islam au Sénégal. v.2-3, pt.1-2. Paris, 1917. 2v.
Afr 5345.5 Marty, Paul. Etudes sur l'islam en Côte-d'Ivoire. Paris, 1922.
Afr 5219.20 Marty, Paul. Etudes sur l'islam et les tribus du Soudan. Paris, 1920-21. 4v.
Afr 5094.2 Marty, Paul. Etudes sur l'islam et les tribus maures. Paris, 1921.
Afr 5437.5 Martynov, V.A. Zagovor protiv Kongo. Moscow, 1960.
Afr 7812.259.5 Martynov, Vladimir A. Kongo pod gnetom imperializma. Moskva, 1959.
Afr 7513.5 Martyr. Stanleyville. 1,1964+
Afr 5765.5.2 The martyr church...Christianity in Madagascar. (Ellis, William.) London, n.d.
Afr 5765.5 The martyr church. (Ellis, William.) Boston, 1870.
Afr 7803.20 Le martyr Georges de Geel et les débuts de la mission du Congo. (Hildebrand.) Anvers, 1940.
Afr 6143.14 The martyr of the Pongas. (Caswall, H.) N.Y., 1857.
Afr 555.3.8 The martyr of the Pongas. (Caswall, Henry.) London, 1857.
Afr 7803.34 Les martyrs noirs de l'Ouganda. (Laridan, P.) Tournai, 1962.
Afr 7549.48 Marvel, T. The new Congo. N.Y., 1948.
Afr 7549.48.3 Marvel, T. The new Congo. 1st British ed. London, 1949.
Afr 212.6 Marvin, D.K. Emerging Africa in world affairs. San Francisco, 1965.
Afr 9610.16 Marwick, Maxwell Gay. Sorcery in its social setting. Manchester, 1965.
Afr 555.20.9 Marwick, William. William and Louisa Anderson. Edinburgh, 1897.
Afr 626.8 Marxism and African economic development, 1952-1968. (Akinwale, Lydia Oluwafemi.) Ibadan, 1968.
Afr 8050.22 Marxism-Leninism in a multiracial environment. Thesis. (Johns, S.W.) Cambridge, 1965.
Afr 5054.37.5 Mary, Gaston. Précis historique de la colonisation française. Paris, 1937.
Afr 1840.5 Mary, P. Influence de la conversion...sur la condition...en Algérie. Thèse. Paris, 1910.
Afr 11572.50.110 Mary Glenn. (Millin, S.G.(L.).) N.Y., 1925.
Afr 555.20.5 Mary Slessor of Calabar. 9th ed. (Livingstone, W.P.) London, 1917.
Afr 7350.6 Maryland colonization journal. Baltimore. 2,1843+
Afr 7350.6.3 Maryland State Colonization Society. Annual report. Baltimore. 3,1835+ 2v.
Afr 7368.32 Maryland State Colonization Society. Colonization Society of Free Colored Population. Maryland. Baltimore, 1852.
Afr 1033.3F Mas Latrie, M.L. de. Traités de paix et de commerce et documents diverses...de l'Afrique septentrionale au Moyen Age. Paris, 1865.
Afr 9325.13 Masa. Cairo. 1,1964+
Afr 6883.1 Die Masai. (Merker, M.) Berlin, 1904.
Afr 1753.3F Mascarenhas, J. Historia de la ciudad de Ceuta. Lisboa, 1918.
Afr 13467.53.100 Mascaret ou Le livre de la mer et de la mort. (Maunick, Edouard.) Paris, 1966.
Afr 2030.376 Maschino, Maurice. L'engagement. Paris, 1961.
Afr 2030.375 Maschino, Maurice. Le refus. Paris, 1960.
Afr 7942.5 Masera, Francesco. Rwanda e Burundi; problemi e prospettive di sviluppo economico. Milano, 1963.
Afr 9502.10 The Mashona. (Bullock, Charles.) Cape Town, 1928.
Afr 9502.14 The Mashona and Matabele. (Bullock, C.) Cape Town, 1950.
Afr 9502.25 Mashona laws and customs. (Bullock, Charles.) Salisbury, 1913.
Afr 9488.94.5 Le Mashonaland. (Nadellaic, Jean François Albert du Pouget Marquis de.) Paris, 1894.
Afr 9525.575 Mashonaland martyr. (Farrant, Jean.) Cape Town, 1966.
Afr 609.58.37 Het masker af. (Hornman, A.W.) Leiden, 1957.
Afr 9028.55.4 Mason, G.H. Life with the Zulus of Natal, South Africa. London, 1855.
Afr 4050.36 Mason, M.H. The paradise of fools. London, 1936.
Afr 9645.10 Mason, Philip. The birth of a dilemma. London, 1958.
Afr 6333.55.5 Mason, Philip. A new deal in East Africa. London, 1955.
Afr 630.46 Mason, Philip. Race relations in Africa. London, 1960.
Afr 9445.40 Mason, Philip. Year of decision. London, 1960.
Afr 9093.25 Mason, Rivil. Prehistory of the Transvaal. Johannesburg, 1962.
Afr 2030.461.40 Maspero, Francois. Le droit à l'insoumission. Paris, 1961.
Afr 3979.10.5 Maspero, Gaston. Ruines et paysages d'Egypte. Paris, 1910.
Afr 4430.36.20 Masque d'or, ou, Le dernier Negus. 11e éd. (Monfreid, H. de.) Paris, 1936.

Afr 2300.4   Masqueray, E. Formation des cités chez les populations sédentaires de l'Algérie. Paris, 1886.

Afr 5243.174   Masques dogons. Thèse. (Griaule, Marcel.) Paris, 1938.

Afr 1623.942   Massa, Jose L. Economia marroqui. Tetuan, 1942.

Afr 6740.18   Les Massa du Cameroun. (Garine, Igor de.) Paris, 1964.

Afr 7350.10   Massachusetts Colonization Society. Annual report. Boston.

Afr 626.154   Massachusetts Institue of Technology. Fellows in Africa Program. Managing economic development in Africa. Cambridge, Mass., 1963.

Afr 4368.5.30   Massaia, G. Lettere del Cardinale Massaia dal 1846 al 1886. Torino, 1937.

Afr 4368.5.25   Massaia, G. I miei trentacinque anni di missione. Torino, 1932.

Afr 4368.5F   Massaja, E.G. Missione nell'alta Etiopia. Roma, 1885. 6v.

Afr 6460.20   Massam, J.A. The cliff dwellers of Kenya. London, 1927.

Afr 5049.100   Masseguin, Christiane. A l'ombre des palmes, l'oeuvre familiale et missionaire des soeurs du Saint-Esprit. Paris, 1942.

Afr 6392.36.5   Massell, B.F. The distribution of gains in a common market. Santa Monica, Calif., 1964.

Afr 6392.36   Massell, B.F. East African economic union. Santa Monica, Calif., 1963.

Afr 626.129.5   Massell, Benton F. African studies and economic analysis. Santa Monica, 1964.

Afr 2030.20   Massenet, Michel. Contrepoison, ou la morale en Algérie. Paris, 1957.

Afr 45.66.5   Masseron, Jean Paul. Le pouvoir et la justice en Afrique noire francophone et à Madagascar. Paris, 1966.

Afr 115.15   Les masses africaines. (Ly, A.) Paris, 1956.

Afr 626.13   Massi, E. L'Africa nell'economia mondiale. Milano, 1937.

Afr 1605.50   Massignon, L. Le Maroc dans les premières années du XVIe siècle. Alger, 1906.

Afr 5403.30   Massion, Jacques. Les grandes concessions au Congo français. Paris, 1920.

Afr 6738.20   Masson, Georges. La mise en valeur des territoires des Cameroun placés sous le mandat français. Thèse. Paris, 1928.

Afr 8089.46F   Masson, M. A scrapbook of the Cape. Cape Town, 1946.

Afr 3813.20   Massow, Heinrich von. Die Industrie der Republik Sudan. Hamburg, 1964.

Afr 9502.24   The Matabele at home. (Nielsen, Peter.) Bulawayo, 1913.

Afr 9446.26   The Matabele campaign, 1896. (Baden-Powell.) London, 1897.

Afr 9446.32   Matabele i Mashona v bor'be protiv angliiskoi kolonizatsii, 1888-1897. (Davidson, A.B.) Moscow, 1958.

Afr 9488.81   Matabele land. (Oates, Frank.) London, 1881.

Afr 9446.25   The Matabele rebellion, 1896. (Laing, D.J.) London, 1897.

Afr 8252.354.25   Matabele Thompson. (Thompson, F.R.) Johannesburg, 1953.

Afr 8252.354.20   Matabele Thompson. (Thompson, F.R.) London, 1936.

Afr 9446.38   The Matabele War. (Glass, Stafford.) Harlow, 1968.

Afr 9445.5   Matabeleland, the war, and our position in South Africa. (Colquhoun, A.R.) London, 1894.

Afr 9488.91   The Matabeleland travel letters of Marie Lippert. (Lippert, Marie.) Cape Town, 1960.

Afr 9510.11.5   The Matapos. (Tredgold, Robert Clarksen.) Salisbury, 1956.

Afr 7575.55   Matata am Kongo. (Scholl-Latour, Peter.) Stuttgart, 1961.

Afr 175.5   Matep, Benjamin. Heurts et malheurs des rapports Europe-Afrique. Paris, 1959.

Afr 8028.160   Material published after 1925 on the Great Trek until 1854. Thesis. (Grivainis, Ilze.) Cape Town, 1967.

Afr 28.93   Material relating to Africa. (Scotland. Record Office.) Edinburgh, 1962-65.

Afr 9218.54   Materials for a speech in defense of the policy of abandoning the Orange River Territory, May 1854. (Molesworth, William.) London, 1854.

Afr 6200.13   Materials for the study of Nigerian church history. Nsukka. 1,1964+

Afr 1753.4F   Mateus de Pisano. Livro de guerra de Ceuta. Lisboa, 1915.

Afr 9488.95.7   Mathers, E.P. Zambesia, England's El Dorado in Africa. London, 1895.

Afr 6397.2   Matheson, Elizabeth Mary. An enterprise so perilous. London, 1959.

Afr 11560.85.100   Matheson, G.E. From veld and street. London, 1899.

Afr 4259.47A   Mathew, David. Ethiopia, the study of a polity, 1540-1935. London, 1947.

Afr 210.36   Mathews, Basil. Consider Africa. N.Y., 1936.

Afr 3285.15.4   Mathews, J.J. Egypt and the formation of the Anglo-French entente of 1904. Thesis. Philadelphia, 1939.

Afr 9165.7   Mathewson, J. Edw. The establishment of an urban Bantu township. Pretoria, 1957.

Afr 9839.64.5   Matilda, fille du Nyassaland. (Gandu, Madeleine.) Paris, 1964.

Afr 3993.966   Matiukhin, Ivan S. Ob'edinennaia Arabskaia Respublika. Moskva, 1966.

Afr 7110.10   Matos, J.M.R.N. A nação una. Lisboa, 1953.

Afr 7018.10   Matos, José Mendes Ribeiro Norton de. Africa nossa. Porto, 1953.

Afr 7015.45   Matos, R.J. da Cunha. Compendio historico das possesões de Portugal na Africa. Rio de Janeiro, 1963.

Afr 810.25   Mattei, Antonio. Bas-Niger, Benoue, Dahomey. Grenoble, 1890.

Afr 1957.30   Matterer, Amable. Journal de la prise d'Alger. Paris, 1960.

Afr 4558.80   Matteucci, P. In Abissinia, viaggio. Milano, 1880.

Afr 4070.41   Matteucci, P. Sudan e Gallas. Milano, 1879.

Afr 4513.38A   Matthews, H.L. Two wars and more to come. N.Y., 1938.

Htn   Afr 6143.9.2*   Matthews, J. Voyage to the river Sierra-Leone. London, 1788.

Afr 6143.9.5   Matthews, J. Voyage to the river Sierra-Leone. London, 1966.

Afr 8658.87.4   Matthews, J.W. Incwadi Yami, or twenty years' personal experience in South Africa. N.Y., 1887.

Afr 8235.6   Matthews, J.W. Incwadi Yami, twenty years in South Africa. London, 1887.

Afr 212.14   Matthews, Ronald. African powder keg. London, 1966.

Afr 2030.462   Matthews, T.S. War in Algeria. N.Y., 1962.

Afr 5765.9   Matthews, T.T. Notes of nine years mission work in the province of Vonizongo, N.W., Madagascar. London, 1881.

Afr 555.6.8   Matthews, T.T. Thirty years in Madagascar. 2d ed. London, 1904.

Afr 4513.39.35   Mattioli, Guido. L'aviazione fascista e la conquista dell'impero. Roma, 1939.

Afr 8028.164   Matton, Carol Ann. Pictures of South African interest in the Graphic, 1896-1899, a list. Thesis. Johannesburg, 1967.

Afr 1573.32   Maturana Vargas, C. La tragica realidad: Marruecos, 1921. Barcelona, 1921.

Afr 8659.13.12   Maturin, E. Adventures beyond the Zambesi. London, 1913.

Afr 8659.09   Maturin, Edith. Petticoat pilgrims on trek. London, 1909.

Afr 6395.2.25   Mau-Mau. (Brom, John L.) Paris, 1956.

Afr 6395.10   Mau Mau. (Stoneham, C.T.) London, 1953.

Afr 6395.2.10   Mau Mau and the Kikuyu. (Leakey, L.S.B.) London, 1953.

Afr 6395.2.12   Mau Mau and the Kikuyu. 1. American ed. (Leakey, L.S.B.) N.Y., 1954.

Afr 6420.74   Mau Mau detainee. (Kariuki, Josiah M.) London, 1963.

Afr 6430.3   Mau Mau from within, autobiography and analysis of Kenya's peasant revolt. (Barnett, Donald L.) London, 1966.

Afr 6430.3.1   Mau Mau from within. (Barnett, Donald L.) N.Y., 1966.

Afr 6470.242   "Mau Mau" general. (Itote, Warohiu.) Nairobi, 1967.

Afr 6455.86   Mau Mau iskee. (Simonen, Seppo.) Helsinki, 1954.

Afr 6420.60   Mau Mau man-hunt. 1st ed. (Baldwin, W.W.) N.Y., 1957.

Afr 8658.69   Mauch, Karl. The journals of Carl Mauch; his travels in the Transvaal and Rhodesia, 1869-1872. Salisbury, 1969.

Afr 1733.5.15   Mauclair, Camille. Rabat et Sale. Paris, 1934.

Afr 9165.42.30   Maud, J.P.R. Johannesburg and the art of self-government. Johannesburg, 1937.

Afr 5748.95   Maude, F.C. Five years in Madagascar. London, 1895.

Afr 9632.5F   Maugham, F.H. North Charterland concession inquiry. Report, July, 1932. London, 1932.

Afr 9632.5.5F   Maugham, F.H. North charterland concession inquiry. Report, May 30, 1933. London, 1933.

Afr 5247.30   Maugham, R. The slaves of Timbuktu. 1.Am.ed. N.Y., 1961.

Afr 9599.29   Maugham, R.C.F. Africa as I have known it. London, 1929.

Afr 7332.1   Maugham, R.C.F. Portuguese East Africa. London, 1906.

Afr 7459.20A   Maugham, R.C.F. The Republic of Liberia. London, 1920.

Afr 7322.3   Maugham, R.C.F. Zambezia. London, 1910.

Afr 4180.3.20   Maugham, R.C.R. Journey to Siwa. N.Y., 1950.

Afr 1259.49   Maugham, R.C.R. North African notebook. N.Y., 1949.

Afr 13467.53.100   Maunick, Edouard. Mascaret ou Le livre de la mer et de la mort. Paris, 1966.

Afr 1840.22   Maunier, R. Loi française et coutume indigene en Algerie. Paris, 1932.

Afr 1259.30.10   Maunier, R. Mélanges de sociologie nord-africaine. Paris, 1930.

Afr 3026.10   Maunier, René. Bibliographie économique. Le Caire, 1918.

Afr 5765.7.20   Maupoint, A.R. Madagascar et ses deux premiers évêques. v.1-2. 3. ed. Paris, 1864.

Afr 1570.42   Maura y Gamazo, Gabriel. El convenio entre España by francia relativo a Marruecos. Madrid, 1912.

Afr 1550.3   Maura y Gamazo, Gabriel. La cuestion de Marruecos. Madrid, 1905.

Afr 1550.3.5   Maura y Gamazo, Gabriel. La question du Maroc. Paris, 1911.

Afr 1609.09.3   Mauran. Le maroc d'aujourd hui et de demain. Paris, 1909.

Afr 1609.12.9   Mauran. La societe marocaine. Paris, 1912.

Afr 2235.1   Les Maures de Constantine. (Morelet.) Dijon, 1876.

Afr 5093.2   Les Maures de l'Afrique occidentale française. (Poulet, G.) Paris, 1904.

Afr 1259.26   Mauresques, with some Basque and Spanish cameos. (Hawkes, C.P.) London, 1926.

Afr 1259.40   Mauretania, warrior, man and woman. (Sitwell, S.) London, 1940.

Afr 1259.40.5   Mauretania. (Sitwell, S.) London, 1951.

Afr 5056.107   La Maurétanie. (French West Africa.) Corseil, 1907.

Afr 7549.62.5   Maurice, Albert. Belgique, gouverneur du Congo. Bruxelles, 1962.

Afr 5405.300   Maurice, Albert. Félix Eboué, sa vie et son oeuvre. Bruxelles, 1954.

Afr 8289.06   Maurice, F. History of the war in South Africa 1899-02. v.1-4. London, 1906. 8v.

Afr 6170.16   Maurice, J.F. The Ashantee war. London, 1874.

Afr 1583.15   Maurice, Louis. La politique marocaine de l'allemagne. Paris, 1916.

Afr 2397.7   Maurice Cochard, mon ami. (Pignal, Jacques.) Toulouse, 1964.

Afr 5091.15   Mauritania; guidelines for a four-year development program. (International Bank for Reconstruction and Development.) Washington, D.C.?, 1968.

Afr 5090.12   Mauritania. La République islamique de Mauritanie. Paris, 1960.

Afr 5090.3   Mauritania. (Gerteiny, Alfred G.) N.Y., 1967.

Afr Doc 6107.10   Mauritania. Ministere de la Planification et du Developpement Rural. Direction de la Statistique. Bulletin mensuel statistique. Nouakchott. 1968

Afr Doc 6109.504   Mauritania. Ministère de L'Education Nationale. Statistiques de l'enseignement du premier degré. 1967+

Afr Doc 6109.505   Mauritania. Ministère de l'Education Nationale. Statistiques de l'enseignement du second degré. 1967+

Afr 5091.14   Mauritania. Ministère des Affaires Etrangères et du Plan. Service de statistique plan quadriennal, 1963-1966. Nouackchott, 1967.

Afr 5813.14   Mauritius; a study and annotated bibliography. (Hahn, Lorna.) Washington, 1969.

Afr 5820.15   Mauritius, Mr. Jeremie's case. (Mauritius.) London, 1834.

Afr Doc 2822.5   Mauritius. Annual departmental reports. Port Louis. 1951+

Afr Doc 2803.5F   Mauritius. Blue book. 8v.

Afr Doc 2809.115   Mauritius. Capital budget. Port Louis. 1966+

Afr Doc 2807.352F   Mauritius. Census 1952 of Mauritius and of its dependencies. Port Louis, 1953. 3 pam.

Afr Doc 2809.95   Mauritius. Draft capital estimates. Port Louis. 1960+

Afr Doc 2809.100   Mauritius. Draft estimates. Port Louis. 1959+

Afr Doc 2809.89   Mauritius. Estimates as passed by the Legislative Assembly. Port Louis. 1963+

Afr Doc 2807.344F   Mauritius. Final report on the census enumeration made in the colony of Mauritius. Port Louis, 1948.

Afr Doc 2809.99   Mauritius. Financial report for the year. Port Louis. 1962+

Afr 5815.2F   Mauritius. Letters, patent, 1879-1894. n.p., n.d.

Afr 5820.15   Mauritius. Mauritius, Mr. Jeremie's case. London, 1834.

Afr Doc 2809.100.5   Mauritius. Memorandum on draft estimates. Port Louis.

Afr Doc 2809.90   Mauritius. Memorandum on estimates. Port Louis. 1965+

Afr Doc 2826.5   Mauritius. Report on district administration in Mauritius. Port Louis. 1949

Afr Doc 2807.362F — Mauritius. 1962 population census of Mauritius and its dependencies. Port Louis, 1964.
Afr 5815.1 — Pamphlet box. Mauritius.
Afr 5842.22 — Mauritius. (Benedict, Burton.) London, 1965.
Afr Doc 2805.5 — Mauritius. (Great Britain. Colonial Office. Census Commissioner.) London. 1964
Afr 5813.10 — Mauritius. Archives Department. Bibliography of Mauritius. Port Louis, 1956.
Afr Doc 2838.5 — Mauritius. Central Housing Authority. Report on the activities. Rose Hill. 1,1960+
Afr Doc 2809.300 — Mauritius. Central Statistical Office. Abstract of economic statistics. Port Louis? 1965?
Afr Doc 2807.364F — Mauritius. Central Statistical Office. The census of industrial production, 1964. Port Louis, 1965.
Afr Doc 2808.5 — Mauritius. Central Statistical Office. Natality and fertility in Mauritius. Port Louis? 1956?
Afr Doc 2809.305 — Mauritius. Central Statistical Office. The national income and national accounts of Mauritius, 1948-1954. Port Louis, 1956.
Afr Doc 2807.10 — Mauritius. Central Statistical Office. Quarterly digest of statistics. 1-6,1961-1966
Afr Doc 2808.305F — Mauritius. Central Statistical Office. Survey of employment and earnings in large establishments. Rose Hill. 1,1966
Afr Doc 2807.5 — Mauritius. Central Statistical Office. Year book of statistics. 13,1958+
Afr Doc 2831.5 — Mauritius. Colonial Audit Department. Report of the Principal Auditor on the accounts of the Colony of Mauritius and the Mauritius government railways. Port Louis. 1946-1949
Afr 5843.6 — Mauritius. Commission of Enquiry into the Disturbances Which Occurred in the North of Mauritius in 1943. Report. London, 1943.
Afr Doc 2835.5 — Mauritius. Education Department. Annual report. Port Louis. 1945-1946
Afr Doc 2835.5.5 — Mauritius. Education Department. Triennial survey of education in Mauritius. Port Louis. 1958+
Afr Doc 2812.12 — Mauritius. Legislative Assembly. Debates. Port Louis. 1,1964+
Afr Doc 2812.10 — Mauritius. Legislative Council. Debates. Port Louis. 2-4,1957-1963
Afr 5843.5 — Mauritius. Ministry of Industry. Commerce and industry in Mauritius. Port Louis, 1964.
Afr Doc 2846.10 — Mauritius. Public Assistance Department. Annual report. Port Louis. 1948-1949
Afr Doc 2846.5 — Mauritius. Public Relations Office. Annual report. Port Louis. 1947-1948
Afr Doc 2846.15 — Mauritius. Public Works and Surveys Department. Annual report for the financial year. Port Louis. 1946-1948
Afr Doc 2848.5 — Mauritius. Reabsorption Office. Report on the activities. Port Louis. 1947-1949
Afr Doc 2833.5 — Mauritius. Registrar of Co-operative Credit Societies. Annual report of the co-operative credit societies. 1949
Afr Doc 2850.5 — Mauritius. Transport Control Board. Annual report. 1949
Afr Doc 2806.5 — The Mauritius almanac and commercial handbook. Port Louis. 1923-1941 10v.
Afr 555.6 — Mauritius and Madagascar. (Ryan, V.W.) London, 1864.
Afr 5842.19 — Mauritius and Seychelles. (Great Britain. Central Office of Information.) N.Y., 1964.
Afr 5832.12 — Mauritius and the spice trade. (Ly-Tio-Fane, Madeleine.) Port Louis, 1958. 2v.
Afr 5810.12 — Mauritius register. Mauritius, 1859.
Afr 1571.17.10A — Maurois, A. Lyautey. N.Y., 1931.
Afr 1571.17.12A — Maurois, A. Lyautey. N.Y., 1932.
Afr 1571.17.8 — Maurois, A. Lyautey. Paris, 1931.
Afr 1571.17.6 — Maurois, A. Lyautey. Paris, 1931.
Afr 1571.17.9 — Maurois, A. Lyautey. Paris, 1932.
Afr 1571.17.11 — Maurois, A. Lyautey. Paris, 1934.
Afr 8250.35.5 — Maurois, André. Cecil Rhodes. Hamden, Conn., 1968.
Afr 8250.35.2 — Maurois, Andre. Cecil Rhodes. London, 1953.
Afr 8250.35 — Maurois, Andre. Cecil Rhodes. N.Y., 1953.
Afr Doc 6107.5 — Maurtiania. Service de la Statistique. Bulletin statistique et economique. Nouakchott. 2,1964+
Afr 1583.12 — Maurus, Pseud. Ave caesar. Deutsche Luftschiffe...Marokko. Leipzig, 1909.
Afr 5580.3.10 — Maurycy August Beniowski, zdob. Madagaskaru. (Lepecky, M.B.) Warszawa, 1959.
Afr 5580.3.9 — Maurycy August Beniowski. (Lepecki, M.B.) Lwow, 1938.
Afr 5580.3.15 — Maurycy August Beniowski. (Ortowski, Leon.) Warszawa, 1961.
Afr 13340.13.120 — Le mauvais sang, poèmes. (Tchichaya U Tamsi, Gerald Felix.) Paris, 1955.
Afr 5180.17 — Mavidal, J. Le Sénégal. Paris, 1863.
Afr 1769.7.10 — Maxwell, Gavin. Lords of the atlas, the rise and fall of the house of Glaoua, 1893-1956. London, 1966.
Afr 555.20.7 — Maxwell, J. Lowry. Nigeria, the land, the people and Christian progress. London, 1927.
Afr 8325.13 — May, Edward S. A retrospect on the South African war. London, 1901.
Afr 8045.22.5 — May, Henry John. The South African constitution. 2d. ed. Cape Town, 1949.
Afr 8045.22.6 — May, Henry John. The South African constitution. 3d ed. Cape Town, 1955.
Afr 6282.25 — May Perry of Africa. (Anderson, Susan.) Nashville, 1966.
Afr Doc 3707.363F — May/June 1963 census of Africans: v.1 village population. (Zambia. Central Statistical Office.) Lusaka, 1965.
Afr 609.32 — Maydon, H.C. Big game shooting in Africa. London, 1932.
Afr 4559.23.10 — Maydon, H.C. Simen, its heights and abysses. London, 1925.
Afr 8289.01.31 — Maydon, J.G. French's calvalry campaign. 2d ed. London, 1902.
Afr 6192.102.2 — Mayer, Emerico Somassa. Ghana: past and present. 2nd ed. The Hague, n.d.
Afr 3978.02.1PF — Mayer, L. Views in Egypt, from the original drawings in the possession of Sir Robert Ainslie. London, 1801.
Afr 3978.02.5PF — Mayer, Ludwig. Views in Egypt. London, 1804.
Afr 3978.02PF — Mayer, Ludwig. Vues en Egypte. Londres, 1802.
Afr 6460.35F — Mayer, Philip. Two studies in applied anthropology in Kenya. London, 1951.
Afr 8825.30 — Mayer, Philip. Xhosa in town. Cape Town, 1961-63. 3v.
Afr 2608.84.2 — Mayet, Valery. Voyage dans le sud de la Tunisie. 2e ed. Paris, 1887.
Afr 8252.227.15 — Mayfair to Maritzburg. (Halle, G.) London, 1933.

Afr 11563.98.100 — Mayne, Frederick. The slaughter of an innocent. Johannesburg, 1955.
Afr 1723.15 — Mayne, Peter. The alleys of Marrakesh. 1st ed. Boston, 1953.
Afr 8105.25 — Maynier and the first Boer republic. (Marais, Johannes S.) Cape Town, 1944.
Afr 7815.3 — Les Mayombe. 2. (Overbergh, C. van.) Bruxelles, 1907.
Afr 530.34 — Mayor, D.R.W. De rebus Africanis. London, 1886.
Afr 7122.78 — Maza. (Santos, Eduardo dos.) Lisboa, 1965.
Afr 1955.49 — Maze, Jules. La conquête de l'Algérie. Tours, 1930.
Afr 2628.1 — Die Mazigh-Völker. (Stuhlmann, F.) Hamburg, 1914.
Afr 6025.5 — Mazrui, Ali Al'Amin. The Anglo-African Commonwealth. 1st ed. Oxford, 1967.
Afr 212.36.5 — Mazrui, Ali Al'Amin. On heroes and Uhuru worship. London, 1967.
Afr 212.36 — Mazrui, Ali Al'amin. Towards a Pax Africana, a study of ideology and ambition. London, 1967.
Afr 2225.22 — Mazuni, Abd Allah. Culture et enseignement en Algérie et au Maghreb. Paris, 1969.
Afr 500.44 — Mazzucconi, R. Storia della conquista dell Africa. Milano, 1937.
Afr 5417.2 — Mba, Léon. Discours, messages. Libreville, 1965.
Afr 500.52 — Mbadiwe, K.O. British and Axis aims in Africa. N.Y., 1942.
Afr 8678.320.5 — Mbata, J.C.M. Urban Bantu councils. Johannesburg, 1965.
Afr 8678.319 — Mbeki, G.A.M. South Africa. Harmondsworth, 1964.
Afr 8846.16 — Mbeki, Govan Archibald Mrunyelwa. Transkei in the making. n.p., 1939.
Afr 6750.7 — Mbioni. Dar es Salaam. 2,1965+ 12v.
Afr 33319.2 — Mbiti, John. Akamba stories. Oxford, 1966.
Afr 3993.538 — Mboria, L. La population de l'Egypte. Thèse. Le Caire, 1938.
Afr 590.78 — Mbotela, J.J. The freeing of the slaves in Eat Africa. London, 1956.
Afr 210.63.35 — Mboya, T. Freedom and after. 1. ed. Boston, 1963.
Afr 11336.41.110 — McKilty's bride. (Drin, Michael.) Cape Town, 1965.
Afr 3993.967.10 — Mead, Donald C. Growth and structural change in the Egyptian economy. Homewood, 1967.
Afr 5843.2 — Meade, James E. The economic and social structure of Mauritius. London, 1961.
Afr 1609.01 — Meakin, B. The land of the Moors. London, 1901.
Afr 1609.05 — Meakin, B. Life in Morocco and glimpses beyond. London, 1905.
Afr 1368.99 — Meakin, B. The Moorish empire. London, 1899.
Afr 1609.02 — Meakin, B. The Moors. London, 1902.
Afr 555.9.5 — Means, J.O. The proposed mission in Central Africa. Cambridge, 1879.
Afr 11572.50.190 — The measure of my days. (Millin, S.G.(L).) London, 1955.
Afr 4559.35.50 — Measuring Ethiopia and flight into Arabia. (Coon, C.S.) Boston, 1935.
Afr 4368.20 — Med frälsningens budskap; några bilder från den svenskamissionen. (Giselsson, Emanuel.) Stockholm, 1967.
Afr 2020.1 — Les Medaganat. (Le Chatelier, A.) Alger, 1888.
Afr 1335.8 — Il medagliere delle raccolte numismatiche torinesi. (Turin. Museo Civico d'Arte Antica.) Torino, 1964.
Afr 555.3.5 — Medbery, R.B. Memoir of William G. Crocker...missionary in South Africa. Boston, 1848.
Afr 7947.7 — La médecine indigène au Ruanda et lexique des termes médicaux français-urunyarwanda. (Lestrade, A.) Bruxelles, 1955.
Afr 8028.149 — The medical history of the Anglo-Boer war. (Beckerling, Joan Letitia.) Cape Town, 1967.
Afr 44628.5.700 — The medicine man. Swifa ya ngurumali. (Hasani Bin Ismail.) Oxford, 1968.
Afr 4115.24 — Medieval Cairo and the monasteries of the Wadi Natrun. (Russell, Dorothea.) London, 1962.
Afr 1080.25 — Medieval Muslim government in Barbary. (Hopkins, J.F.P.) London, 1958.
Afr 2928.78 — Medina, G. La reggenza di Tripoli. Cagliari, 1878.
Afr 1013.5 — Mediterranean survey. N.Y.
Afr 4509.19 — Méditerranée, Mer Rouge. (Cito de Bitetto, Carlo.) Paris, 1937.
Afr 6280.20 — Meek, C.K. The northern tribes of Nigeria. London, 1925. 2v.
Afr 6280.21 — Meek, C.K. A Sudanese kingdom. London, 1931.
Afr 6280.22 — Meek, C.K. Tribal studies in Northern Nigeria. London, 1931. 2v.
Afr 679.40.5 — Meek, Charles K. Europe and West Africa, some problems and adjustments. London, 1940.
Afr 609.54 — Meeker, Oden. Report on Africa. N.Y., 1954.
Afr 8685.104 — Meer, Fatima. Portrait of Indian South Africans. Durban, 1969.
Afr 8678.308 — Meer begrip voor Suid-Afrika. (Snethlage, J.L.) Amsterdam, 1964.
Afr 150.6 — Mees, Jules. Henri le Navigateur. Bruxelles, 1901.
Afr 8110.3.40 — Mees, W.C. Maria quevellerius. Assen, 1952.
Afr 7820.7F — Meessen, J.M.T. Monographie de l'Ituri (nord-est du Congo belge) histoire. Bruxelles, 1951.
Afr 710.22 — Meet central Africa. (Gunther, John.) London, 1959.
Afr 9.8 — Meeting. (Inter-African Conference on Social Sciences.) London.
Afr 6210.56.5 — Meeting of the Nigerian military leaders held at Peduase Lodge. (Nigeria. Supreme Military Council.) Lagos, 1967.
Afr 6210.56 — The meeting of the Supreme Military Council at Aburi, Accra, Ghana 4-5 January 1967. (Nigeria. Supreme Military Council.) Enugu, 1967.
Afr 6335.2 — Meetings and discussions on the proposed East Africa Federation. (Tanzania. Ministry of Information and Tourism.) Dar es Salaam, 1964.
Afr 7803.33 — Meeus, F. Les missions religieuses au Congo belge. Anvers, 1947.
Afr 5746.09 — Megiserum, H. Beschreibung...insul Madagascar. Altenburg, 1609.
Afr 2862.5 — Mehemed Emin Efendi (Pseud.). Der Kampf um Tripolis. Leipzig, 1912.
Afr 2929.01 — Mehier de Mathuisieulx, H. A travers la Tripolitaine. Paris, 1903.
Afr 2929.01.3 — Mehier de Mathuisieulx, H. A travers la Tripolitaine. 3e ed. Paris, 1912.
Afr 2929.12.9 — Mehier De Mathuisieulx, H. La Tripolitaine. Paris, 1912.
Afr 3205.3 — Mehmed-Ali. (Prokesch-Osten, A.) Wien, 1877.
Afr 8658.61 — Meidinger, H. Die südafrikanischen Colonien Englands. Frankfurt, 1861.
Afr 6760.25 — Meienberg, Hildebrand. Tanzanian citizen: a civics textbook. Nairobi, 1966[1967].

Afr 8680.20	Meihuizen, Jan. Dat vrije volk. Amsterdam, 1941.
Afr 6390.77	Meikle, R.S. After big game. London, 1917.
Afr 5344.8	Meillassoux, Claude. Anthropologie économique des Gouro de Côte-d'Ivoire. Paris, 1964.
Afr 5248.20	Meillassoux, Claude. Urbanization of an African community. Seattle, 1968.
Afr 2000.8	Le meilleur combat. (Uzighan, 'Ammar.) Paris, 1958.
Afr 6390.32	Mein afrikanisches Tagebuch. (Czernin, Ottokar G.) Zürich, 1927.
Afr 1608.72.3	Mein ersten aufenthalt in Morokko. (Rohlfs, G.) Norden, 1885.
Afr 6780.10.23	Mein Leben. (Lettow-Vorbeck, P.E. von.) Biberach an der Riss, 1957.
Afr 1680.3	Meine dritte forschungsreise im atlas-vorlande von Marokko im Jahre 1901. (Fischer, T.) Hamburg, 1902.
Afr 6780.10A	Meine Erinnerungen aus Ostafrika. (Lettow-Vorbeck, P.E. von.) Leipzig, 1920.
Afr 6780.9	Meine Erlebnisse Während der Kriegszeit in Deutsch-Ostafrika. (Schnee, A.) Leipzig, 1918.
Afr 6720.15	Meine Kriegsfahrt von Kamerun zur Heimat. (Zimmermann, Emil.) Berlin, 1915.
Afr 4558.83	Meine Mission nach Abessinien. (Rohlfs, G.) Leipzig, 1883.
Afr 2208.32.3	Meine Reisen und Gefangenschaft in Algier. 3rd ed. (Pfeiffer, S.F.) Giessen, 1834.
Afr 718.6	Meine zweite Durchquerung Afrikas. (Wissmann, H.) Frankfurt a.M., 1891.
Afr 6455.90	Meinertzhagen, R. Kenya diary. Edinburg, 1957.
Afr 3821.2	Meinhof, Carl. Eine Studienfahrt nach Kordofan. Hamburg, 1916.
Afr 1105.5	Meinicke-Kleint, Heinz. Algerien, Marokko, Tunesien. Berlin, 1965.
Afr 8848.3	Meintjes, J. Frontier family. n.p., 1956.
Afr 8252.323	Meintjes, Johannes. De la Rey, lion of the west, a biography. Johannesburg, 1966.
Afr 8809.60	Meintzis, Johannes. Complex canvas. Johannesburg, 1960.
Afr 6390.64	Meister, Albert. L'Afrique peut-elle partir? Paris, 1966.
Afr 6392.25	Meister, Albert. Le development economique de l'Afrique orientale. Paris, 1966.
Afr 6390.64.2	Meister, Albert. East Africa; the past in chains, the future in pawn. N.Y., 1968.
Afr 2248.15	Les Mekhadma. (Centre d'Etudes et d'Informations des Problèmes Humaines dans les Zones Arides.) Paris, 1960.
Afr 609.64	Melady, T.P. Faces of Africa. N.Y., 1964.
Afr 55.20	Melady, T.P. Profiles of African leaders. N.Y., 1961.
Afr 630.62.5	Melady, T.P. The white man's future in black Africa. N.Y., 1962.
Afr 1259.30.10	Mélanges de sociologie nord-africaine. (Maunier, R.) Paris, 1930.
Afr 575.25	Mélanges d'histoire et d'archéologie de l'Occident musulman. v.1-2. (Algeria. Direction de l'Intérieur et des Beaux-Arts.) Alger, 1957.
Afr 2026.1	Melia, Jean. L'Algérie et la guerre (1914-18). Paris, 1918.
Afr 2025.25	Melia, Jean. La France et l'Algérie. Paris, 1919.
Afr 2308.15	Melia, Jean. La ville blanche, Alger et son département. Paris, 1921.
Afr 115.114	Melikian, Ovanes N. Neitralizm gosudarstv Afrikii. Moskva, 1966.
Afr 1755.47	Melilla, 1921. (Martinez de Campos, Arsenio.) Ciudad Real, 1922.
Afr 1755.01	Pamphlet box. Melilla.
Afr 1755.11	Melilla. (Llanos Y Alcaraz, A.) Madrid, 1894.
Afr 1755.13	Melilla 1909, diario de la guerra. Madrid, 1913 (Lopez Alarcon, E.)
Afr 2310.1	Melix. Le stèle d'Abisae. n.p., n.d.
Afr 1640.5	Les Mellah de Rabat-Sale. (Goulven, J.) Paris, 1927.
Afr 9700.10	Melland, F.H. In witch-bound Africa. London, 1923.
Afr 9700.10.2	Melland, F.H. In witch-bound Africa. Philadelphia, 1923.
Afr 699.12	Melland, F.H. Through the heart of Africa. London, 1912.
Afr 505.40	Melland, Frank Hulme. African dilemma. London, 1937.
Afr 2875.37	Melli, B. La guerra italo-turca. Roma, 1914.
Afr 4719.02	Melli, Beniamino. L'Eritrea dalle sue origini a tutto l'anno 1901. Milano, 1902.
Afr 4718.99	Melli, T.B. La colonia Eritrea. Parma, 1899.
Afr 4718.99.2	Melli, T.B. La colonia Eritrea. Parma, 1900.
Afr 8292.5	Mellish, A.E. Our boys under fire. Charlottetown, 1900.
Afr 855.10	Melliss, J.C. St. Helena. London, 1875.
Afr 1493.30	Mellor, F.H. Morocco awakes. London, 1939.
Afr 3978.51.9	Melly, George. Khartoum, and the blue and white Niles. London, 1851. 2v.
Afr 10007.2	Melone, Thomas. De la négritude dans la littérature négro-africaine. Paris, 1962.
Afr 13.10	Melville, J. Herskovits memorial lecture. Evanston, Ill. 1,1965+
Afr 1555.5	Melzer, F. Die Bedeutung der Marokkofrage für die englisch-französischen Beziehungen von 1901. Inaug.-Diss. Dresden, 1937.
Afr 6465.56.15	Membasa; an African city. (De Blij, Harm J.) Evanston, Ill., 1968.
Afr 626.62	Memento commercial. (France. Centre National du Commerce Extérieur.) Paris, 1959.
Afr Doc 6408.709	Memento économique. (Ivory Coast. Direction du Commerce Extérieur.) Abidjan. 1964+
Afr 5000.29	Memento statistique de l'économie africaine. Paris. 1969+
Afr 12015.10	Memmi, Albert. Anthologie des écrivains maghrébins d'expression française. Paris, 1964.
Afr 12002.5	Memmi, Albert. Bibliographie de la littérature nord-africaine d'expression française, 1945-1962. Paris, 1965.
Afr 12321.2	Memmi, Albert. La poésie algérienne de 1830 à nos jours. Paris, 1963.
Afr 6300.10	Memoir. (British Institute of History and Archaeology in East Africa.) Nairobi. 1,1966+
Afr 555.9.13	Memoir of Bishop Mackenzie. 2d ed. (Goodwin, Harvey.) Cambridge, 1865.
Afr 1608.96	A memoir of Sir John Hay Drummond Hay. (Hay, J.D.) London, 1896.
Afr 555.3.17	A memoir of the...missionary to Cape Palmas. (Fox, George T.) N.Y., 1868.
Afr 555.22.25	Memoir of the Rev. William Shaw. (Boyce, William B.) London, 1874.
Afr 555.3.5	Memoir of William G. Crocker...missionary in South Africa. (Medbery, R.B.) Boston, 1848.

Afr 1200.5.2	Mémoire concernant le système de paix et de guerre que les puissances européennes pratiquent à l'égard des régences barbaresques. Venise, 1788.
Afr 3267.5	Memoire d'Arabi-Pacha à ses avocats. Thèse. Photoreproduction. (Arabi, Ahmed.) Paris, 1924.
Afr 5747.31.10	Memoire inédit de Grossin sur Madagascar. (Marcel, G.) Paris, 1883.
Afr 5573.10	Un mémoire inédit de La Haye sur Madagascar. (Froidevaux, H.) Paris, 1897. 4 pam.
Afr 6720.60.5	Memoire soumis à la Conférence des états africains indépendants. (Union des Peuples Camerounais.) Le Caire, 1960.
Afr 2748.59	Mémoire sur le Sahara oriental. (Laurent, C.) Paris, 1859.
Afr 4070.2	Mémoire sur le Soudan. (Escayrac de Lauture, S.) Paris, 1855-56.
Afr 1955.22	Mémoire sur les opérations de l'armée française. (Pélissier, A.J.J.) Alger, 1863.
Afr 2625.5	Mémoire sur l'ethnographie de la Tunisie. (Schwab, M.) Paris, 1868.
Afr 4095.18.15	Mémoire sur l'histoire du Nil. (Omar Toussoun, Prince.) Le Caire, 1925.
Afr 1769.1.5	Memoiren. (Abd Al-Karim.) Dresden, 1927.
Afr 2607.36	Memoires, historiques qui concernent le gouvernement...de Tunis. (Saint-Gervais, M.) Paris, 1736.
Afr 1835.1.6	Memoires...sur l'Algerie. (Pellissier, E.) Paris, 1844.
Afr 5501.3.6	Memoires. (Academie...Tananarivo. Academie Malgache, Tananarivo.) 1,1926+ 14v.
Afr 7501.5	Mémoires. (Académie Royale des Sciences d'Outre Mer. Classe des Sciences Morales et Politiques.) 29,1963+ 4v.
Afr 9.4.5	Mémoires. (Institut Français d'Afrique Noire.) Paris. 1,1939+ 58v.
Afr 6283.2	Memoires. (Sandolphe, J.F.) Paris, 1823. 2v.
Afr 5765.7.10	Memoires. v.9. (Congregation of Priests of the Mission.) Paris, 1866.
Afr 2500.10.2	Mémoires concernant l'état présent du Royaume de Tunis. (Poiron, M.) Paris, 1925.
Afr 2500.10	Mémoires concernant l'état présent du Royaume de Tunis. Thèse complémentaire présentée par Jean Serres. (Poiron, M.) Paris, 1925.
Afr 1769.1	Memoires d'Abd-el-Krim. 5e ed. (Abd El-Krim.) Paris, 1927.
Afr 4392.3.5	Mémoires d'Afrique (1892-1896). (Baratieri, O.) Paris, 1899.
Afr 1955.27	Mémoires du maréchal Randon. (Randon, J.L.C.A.) Paris, 1875. 2v.
Afr 1955.27.5	Mémoires du maréchal Randon. 2e éd. (Randon, J.L.C.A.) Paris, 1875-77. 2v.
Afr 1957.32	Mémoires d'un officier d'état-major. (Barchou de Penhoen, Auguste Theodore Hitaire, Baron.) Paris, 1835.
Afr 3078.11	Mémoires géographiques et historiques sur l'Egypte. (Quatremère, Etienne Marc.) Paris, 1811. 2v.
Afr 7565.14	Mémoires politiques et diplomatiques. (Banning, Emile.) Paris, 1927.
Afr 3978.00	Memoires sur l'Egypte. (Institut d'Egypte, Cairo.) Paris, 1800.
Afr 3977.91	Memoires sur l'Egypte. (Trecourt, Jean Baptiste.) Le Caire, 1942.
Afr 3978.00.3	Mémoires sur l'Egypte publiés pendant les campagnes de Général Bonaparte dans les annees VI et VII. (Institut d'Egypte, Cairo.) Paris, 1801.
Afr 5249.123	The memoiris of Babiker Bedu. (Badri, Babakr.) London, 1969.
Afr 8230.6A	Memoirs. (Kruger, Paul.) N.Y., 1902.
Afr 8230.6.5	Memoirs. v.1-2. (Kruger, Paul.) London, 1902.
Afr 5580.3.20	Memoirs and travels of Mauritius Augustus. (Beniowski, M.A.) London, 1790. 2v.
Afr 6585.6	Memoirs of an Arabian princess. (Ruete, E.) N.Y., 1888.
Afr 7377.61	The memoirs of C.L. Simpson. (Simpson, C.L.) London, 1961.
Afr 8687.251	The memoirs of Kohler of the K.W.V. (Kohler, C.W.H.) London, 1946.
Afr 555.16	Memoirs of Rev. John Leighton Wilson, D.D. (Dubose, H.C.) Richmond, 1895.
Afr 555.27	Memoirs of S. Wilhelm, a native of West Africa. (Bickersteth, E.) New Haven, 1819.
Afr 678.30	Memoirs of the late Captain Hugh Crow. (Crow, Hugh.) London, 1830.
Afr 5368.5	Memoirs of the reign of Bossa Ahadee, king of Dahomey...country of Guiney. (Norris, Robert.) London, 1789.
Afr 6210.57	Memoranda submitted by the delegations to the Ad hoc Conference on Constitutional proposals for Nigeria. (Ad hoc Conference on Constitutional Proposals, Lagos, 1966.) Apapa, 1966.
Afr 7580.28	Memorandum; l'agression armée de l'impérialisme Americano-Belge à Stanleyville et Paulis. (Union des Jeunesses Revolutionaires Congolaises.) Bruxelles, 1966.
Afr 6214.5	Memorandum and articles of associations. (Historical Society of Nigeria.) n.p., 1955.
Afr 4513.35.70F	Memorandum of the Italian government on the situation in Abyssinia. (Italy.) n.p., 1935.
Afr 8377.4F	Memorandum on cooperation between the West German Federal Republic and the Republic of South Africa in the military and atomic fields. (Afro-Asian Solidarity Committee.) Berlin, 1964.
Afr Doc 2809.100.5	Memorandum on draft estimates. (Mauritius.) Port Louis.
Afr Doc 2809.90	Memorandum on estimates. (Mauritius.) Port Louis. 1965+
Afr Doc 2560.905F	Memorandum on local government estimates. (Nigeria, Eastern.) 1957+
Afr Doc 1309.5	Memorandum on the budget estimates. (Sudan.) Khartoum. 1966+
Afr Doc 1809.25F	Memorandum on the draft estimates. (Gold Coast (Colony).) Accra. 1930+

Afr 4573.35F   Memorandum on the establishment of appropriate machinery at the central government level for preparation of the third five-year development plan. (Ethiopia. Ministry of Planning and Development.) Addis-Ababa, 1967.

Afr Doc 4209.11F   Memorandum on the Estimates of development fund revenue. (Lesotho.) 1966+

Afr Doc 4209.13F   Memorandum on the estimates of revenue and expenditure. (Basutoland.) 1967+

Afr Doc 1819.5   Memorandum on the proposals for a constitution for Ghana. (Ghana. Constitutional Commission.) Accra, 1968.

Afr 6497.9   Memorandum on war in Uganda, 1892. (Catholic Union of Great Britain.) London, 1894.

Afr 7309.64   Memorandum to 2nd non-aligned conference. (União Democratica Nacional de Moçambique.) Cairo, 1964.

Afr 8862.5F   Pamphlet vol. Memorandums, petition, and statements issued by the Basutoland Congress Party and the Marematlou Freedom Party.
  5 pam.

Afr 678.81   Memoria. (Canale, M.G.) Genova, 1881.

Afr 5907.6F   Memoria. (Spain. Comisario Regio en las Posesiones Españoles del Africa Occidental.) Madrid. 1907+

Afr 7183.35   Memoria: A. Lunda; ou, Os estados do Muatiânvua. (Dias de Carvalho, Henrique Augusto.) Lisboa, 1890.

Afr 7320.15   Memoria acerca do districto de Cabo Delgado. (Romero, J.) Lisboa, 1856.

Afr 5993.15   Memoria de la isla de Fernando Poo. (Usera y Alarcon, Gerónimo M.) Madrid, 1848.

Afr 4513.35.65F   Memoria del governo italiano circa la situazione in Etiopia. II. (Italy.) n.p., 1935.

Afr 7308.35   Memoria estatistica portuguezes na Africa oriental. (Botelho, S.X.) Lisboa, 1835-37.
  2v.

Afr 7175.25   Memoria geografica. (Carvalho e Menezes, A.) Lisboa, 1834.

Afr 1753.16   Memoria historica sobre os bispados de Ceuta e Tanger. (Paiva Manso, Levy Maria Jordão.) Lisboa, 1858.

Afr 5907.5F   Memoria que presenta a las cortes...posesiones españolas del Africa occidental. (Spain. Ministerio de Estado.) Madrid. 1902+

Afr 5907.5   Memoria que presenta a las cortes...posesiones españolas del Africa occidental. (Spain. Ministerio de Estado.) Madrid. 1910+

Afr 679.58.15   Memoria sobre a prioridade dos descobrimentos. (Santarem, Manuel Francisco de B.) Lisboa, 1958.

Afr 115.3.10   Memoria sobre a prioridade dos descobrimentos dos portuguezes. Porto, 1842.

Afr 115.1   Memoria sobre a prioridade dos descobrimentos portugueses. (Santarem, M.F. de B.) Porto, 1841.

Afr 1573.14   Memoria sobre intereses generales del pais y especiales de las colonias africanas. (Lopez Pinto, V.) Ceuta, 1877.

Afr 1736.3   Memoria sobre la situación de Santa Cruz de Mar Pegueña. 3 in 1. (Alcala galiano, pelayo.) Madrid, 1878.
  3 pam.

Afr 7324.5   Memoria sobre Lourenço Marques (Delagoa Bay). (Pawa Manso.) Lisboa, 1870.

Afr 1258.83   Memoria sobre nuestro poder militar. (Algarate, I.A.) Madrid, 1883.

Afr 7568.16   Memorial concerning conditions...in Kongo. (Congo Reform Association.) Washington, 1904.

Afr 1035.5   Memorial Henri Basset. v.1-2. (Institut des Hautes Etudes Marocaines.) Paris, 1928.
  2v.

NEDL Afr 7350.3.16   Memorial of the semi-centennial anniversary. (American Colonization Society.) Washington, 1867.

Htn Afr 555.12.5*   Memoriale per li missionarii apostolici de Tunis. Manuscript. n.p. 16-.

Afr 8289.02.37   Memorials of C.D. Kimber. (Thomson, Ada.) London, 1902.

Afr 555.27.8   Memorials of missionary labours in West Africa. 3d ed. (Moister, William.) London, 1866.

Afr 8808.41   Memorials of South Africa. (Shaw, B.) London, 1841.

Afr 8808.41.3   Memorials of South Africa. (Shaw, B.) N.Y., 1841.

Afr 7118.25   Memorias contendo a biographia do vice almirante Hulz da Motta a Feo e Torres. (Feo Cardoza de Castellobranco e Torres, J.C.) Paris, 1825.

Afr 1658.16   Memorias del sargento Basallo. (Basallo, Francisco.) Madrid, 1923?

Afr 8100.25   Memorias dos estabelecimentos portuguezes a l'este. (Loureiro, Manoel Jose Gomes.) Lisboa, 1835.

Afr 1658.10   Memorias sobre el riff, su conquista y colonizacion. (Avenia Taure, I.) Zaragoza, 1859.

Afr 1868.53   Memorias sobre la Argelia. (Ximenez de Sandoval, C.) Madrid, 1853.

Afr 5920.6   Memorias sobre las islas africanas de España. (Moros y Morellon, J. de.) Madrid, 1844.

Afr 4392.3   Memorie d'Africa (1892-1896). (Baratieri, O.) Torino, 1898.

Afr 4513.17   Memorie d'Africa 1883-1906. (Sapelli, A.) Bologna, 1935.

Afr 8252.326   Memories. (Weinthal, Leo.) London, 1929.

Afr 609.23.5   Memories of an African hunter. (Lyell, Denis D.) London, 1923.

Afr 2731.15.8   Memories of Charles de Foucauld. (Foucauld, Charles, Vicomte de.) London, 1938.

Afr 9488.95   Memories of Mashonaland. (Knight-Bruce.) London, 1895.

Afr 8289.01.11   Mempes, M. War impressions. London, n.d.

Afr 8658.92   Men, mines and animals in South Africa. (Churchill, R.S.) London, 1892.

Afr 6535.17   Men and creatures in Uganda. (Bland-Sutton, J.) London, 1933.

Afr 6218.8   Men and matters in Nigerian politics 1934-58. (Anyiam, F.U.) Yaba, 1959.

Afr 6333.64   Men and monuments on the East African coast. (Kirkman, James S.) London, 1964.

Afr 8055.38F   Men of the times. Johannesburg, 1906.

Afr 9435.8   Men who made Rhodesia. (Hickman, A.S.) Salisbury, 1960.

Afr 6541.28   Men without god. (Russel, John Keith.) London, 1966.

Afr 6640.10   Menaces Allemandes sur l'Afrique. (Grosclaude, P.) Paris, 1938.

Afr 7540.25   Menache, Albert. L'administration du Congo belge. Thèse. Nancy, 1935.

Afr 6145.6.2   The Mende of Sierra Leone. (Little, Kenneth.) London, 1967.

Afr 545.25   Mendelsohn, J. God, Allah, and Ju Ju. N.Y., 1962.

Afr 580.5   Mendelssohn, S. The Jews of Africa. London, 1920.

Afr 8028.5   Mendelssohn, S. Mendelssohn's South African bibliography. London, 1910.
  2v.

Afr 500.50   Mendelssohn-Bartholdy, A. Europäische Mandatgemeinschaft in Mittelafrika. Roma, 1933.

Afr 8028.5   Mendelssohn's South African bibliography. (Mendelssohn, S.) London, 1910.
  2v.

Afr 626.112   Mendes, C.B. do Quental. A cooperação em Africa. Lisboa, 1961.

Afr 150.15   Mendes de Brito, Francisco. O infante Dom Henrique, 1394-1460. Lisboa, 1942.

Afr 150.15.2   Mendes de Brito, Francisco. O Infante Dom Henrique e a civilização ocidental. Santarém, 1960.

Afr 150.15.5   Mendes De Brito, Francisco. Nota carminativa, uma resposta ão Sr. Dr. Duarte Leite. Lisboa, 1944.

Afr 4230.4.6   Mendez S.I., P.A. Expeditiones Aethiopicae. v.1-4. Roma, 1909.
  3v.

Afr 7565.17   Mendiaux, E. Histoire du Congo. Bruxelles, 1961.

Afr 7575.20   Mendiaux, Edouard. Moscou, Accra et le Congo. Bruxelles, 1960.

Htn Afr 1403.5.5*   Mendonca, Jeronymo de. Jornada de Africa. Lisboa, 1607.

Afr 1403.5   Mendonca, Jeronymo de. Jornada de Africa. Lisboa, 1785.

Afr 4390.50   Menelik. 7. ed. (Monfreid, H. de.) Paris, 1954.

Afr 4559.01.9   Menelik et nous. (Leroux, H.) Paris, 1901.

Afr 1325.4.5PF   Menendez Pidal, Juan. Misiones catolicas de Marruecos. Barcelona, 1897.

Afr 1738.9F   Menezes, D.F. De. Historia de Tangere. Lisboa, 1732.

Afr 3205.1   Mengin, Felix. Histoire de l'Egypte sous le gouvernement de Mohammed-Aly. v.1-2 and atlas. Paris, 1823.
  3v.

Afr 3205.1.5   Mengin, Felix. Histoire sommaire de l'Egypte. Paris, 1839.

Afr 5227.15   Meniaud, Jacques. Les pionniers du Soudan. Paris, 1931.
  2v.

Afr 1915.14   Meningaud, Jean. La France à l'heure algérienne. Paris, 1956.

Afr 6277.5   Meniru, G.U. African-American cooperation. Glen Gardner, N.J., 1954.

Afr 8013.3   Mens en gemeenskap. Pretoria. 1,1960+

Afr 1609.55   Mensching, Horst. Zwischen rif und atlas. Leipzig, 1955.

Afr 7580.2   Mensen en machten in Congo. (Duyzings, Martin.) Amsterdam, 1960.

Afr 1750.25   Mensua Fernandez, Salvador. Bibliografia geografica de Marruecos español y zona internacional de Tanger. Aragoza, 1955.

Afr 6720.28.10   Mentzel, H. Die Kämpfe in Kamerun, 1914-1916. Vorbereitung und Verlauf. Inaug. Diss. Berlin, 1936.

Htn Afr 8657.85*   Mentzel, O. Beschreibung des Vorgebirges der Guten Hoffnung. Glogau, 1885-87.
  2v.

Afr 1733.5.10   La mer des traditions et les industries indigenes a Rabat et Sale. (Brunot, Louis.) Paris, 1920.

Afr 2280.12   La mer intérieure africaine. (Roudaire, F.E.) Paris, 1883.

Afr 3978.80.5   Mer Rouge et Abyssinie. (Denis de Rivoyre, B.L.) Paris, 1898.

Afr 4730.1   La Mer Rouge et l'Abyssinie. (Geullot, M.E.) Lille, 1890.

Afr 3275.25   Méra. Une page de politique coloniale. Paris, 1913.

Afr 4559.14.10   Merab. Impressions d'Ethiopie. Paris, 1921-29.
  3v.

Afr 1609.58.10   Merakko-Krasnaie zemlia. (Miazgowski, Brouirlew.) Moskva, 1963.

Afr 1608.85.3   Mercet, A. Le Maroc. Paris, 1895.

Afr 1608.85.5   Mercet, A. Marruecos. Madrid, 1887.

Afr 6298.646   Merchant prince of the Niger Delta; the rise and fall of Nana Olomu. (Ikime, Obaro.) London, 1968.

Afr 2208.83.5   Mercier, E. L'Algérie. Paris, 1883.

Afr 2208.83.5   Mercier, E. L'Algérie en 1880. Paris, 1880.

Afr 2318.1   Mercier, E. Constantine avant la conquête française. Constantine, 1879.

Afr 2710.1   Mercier, E. La France dans le Sahara. Paris, 1889.

Afr 2318.1.5   Mercier, E. Histoire de Constantine. Constantine, 1903.

Afr 1068.88   Mercier, E. Histoire de l'Afrique septentrionale. Paris, 1888-91.
  3v.

Afr 1080.4   Mercier, E. Histoire des Arabes dans l'Afrique septentrionale. Alger, 1875.

Afr 2225.9   Mercier, E. La question indigène en Algérie au commencement du XXe siècle. Paris, 1901.

Afr 2232.4   Mercier, Marcel. La civilisation urbaine au Mzab. Alger, 1922.

Afr 6295.62   Mercier, Paul. Civilisation du Benin. Paris, 1962.

Afr 5390.4   Mercier, Paul. Tradition, changement, histoire, les "Somba" du Dahomey septentrional. Paris, 1968.

Afr 590.40   Mercier, René. Le travail obligatoire dans les colonies africaines. Vesoul, 1933.

Afr 7068.3   Merckwurdige Missions und Reise-Beschreibung nach Congo in Ethiopien. (Zucchelli, A.) Frankfurt, 1715.

Afr 555.3.22   Mère Javouhey, apôtre des Noirs. (Goyan, George.) Paris, 1929.

Afr 6192.7   Meredith, H. Account of the Gold Coast of Africa. London, 1812.

Afr 4760.10   Meregazzi, R. L'amministrazione fiduciaria italiana della Somalia. Milano, 1954.

Afr 555.25   Merensky, A. Deutsche Arbeit am Njassa, Deutsch-Ostafrika. Berlin, 1894.

Afr 555.22.22   Merensky, A. Erinnerungen aus dem Missionsleben in Transvaal, 1859-1882. Berlin, 1899.

Afr 2974.5   Meriano, F. La questione di Giarabub. Bologna, 1925.

Afr 8089.13   Merimee, P. La politique anglaise au Transvaal. Toulouse, 1913.

Afr 1573.23   Merino Alvarez, A. Marruecos. Madrid, 1921.

Afr 8835.47   Merkens, Alice. Cape Town, Kaapstad, Kapstadt. 2. ed. Cape Town, 1962.

Afr 6883.1   Merker, M. Die Masai. Berlin, 1904.

Afr 8110.25.5   Merkwaardig verhaal, aangaande het leven en de lotgevallen van Michiel Christiaan Vos. 2. druk. (Vos, Michiel Christiaan.) Amsterdam, 1850.

Afr 1957.20.5   Merle, J.T. La prise d'Alger. Paris, 1930.

Afr 609.68.20   Merle, Marcel. L'Afrique noire contemporaine. Paris, 1968.

Afr 2030.467.10   Merle, Robert. Ahmed Ben Bella. N.Y., 1967.

Afr 2030.464.44   Merle, Robert. Ahmed Ben Bella. Paris, 1965.

Afr 7567.26   Merlier, Michel. Le Congo de la colonisation belge à l'indépendance. Paris, 1962.

Afr 2300.6   Merlo, Manuel. Les personnels des communes algériennes. Blida, 1957.

Afr 7806.92   Merolla da Sorrento. Breve e succinta relatione del viaggio nel regno. Napoli, 1692.

Afr 1675.1   Merrakech. (Doutte, Edmond.) Paris, 1905.

Afr 7549.61   Merriam, Alan P. Congo, background of conflict. Evanston, Ill., n.d.

Afr 609.62   Merriam, Alan P. A prologue to the study of the African arts. Yellow Springs, Ohio, 1962.

Afr 7458.68   Merriam, M.B. Home life in Africa. Boston, 1868.

Afr 8145.9   Merriman, N.J. The Kafir, the Hottentot, and the frontier farmer...missionary life. London, 1854.

Afr 9404.2   Merriweather, Alfred Musgrave. Desert doctor: medicine and evangelism in the Kalahan Desert. London, 1969.

Afr 3198.64   Merruan, P. L'Egypte contemporaine. Paris, 1864.

Afr 1608.64.6   Merry y Colom, F. Mi embajada extraordinaria a Marruecos en 1863. Madrid, 1894.

Afr 1608.64.3   Merry y Colom, F. Relacion del viaje a la ciudad de Marruecos. Madrid, 1894.

Afr 2357.26   Mers el-Kebir. (Vulliez, Albert.) Paris, 1964.

Afr 4155.15   Mersa Matruh and its environments. 2nd ed. (Lackany, Radames Sany.) Alexandria, 1960.

Afr 5183.957   Mersadier, Yvon. Budgets familiaux africains. St. Louis du Sénégal, 1957.

Afr 6979.66   Mertens, Alice. South West Africa and its indigenous peoples. London, 1966.

Afr 7815.24   Mertens, Joseph. Les Ba Dzing de la Kamtsha. Bruxelles, 1935-39.

Afr 3180.5   Merveilles biographiques et historiques ou chroniques. (Abd-el-Rahman, Cheikh.) Paris 1888. 8v.

X Cg   Afr 3180.5   Merveilles biographiques et historiques ou chroniques. v.9. (Abd-el-Rahman, Cheikh.) Paris, 1888.

Afr 1259.24F   Les merveilles de l'autre France. (Ricard, Prosper.) Paris, 1924.

Afr 212.22   Merwe, H.J.J. Black Africa. Johannesburg, 1963.

Afr 8110.3.37   Merwe, H.J.J.M. van der. Scheepsjournael en de daghregister. Pretoria, 1958-

Afr 8678.147   Merwe, Hendrik J.J.M. Segregeer of Sterf. Johannesburg, 1961.

Afr 8380.5   Merwe, Hendrik Johannes Jan Matthijs van der. Gebeure in Afrika. Johannesburg, 1964.

Afr 8110.3.38   Merwe, Hendrik Johannes Jan Matthijs van der. Scheepsjournael en de daghregister. 2.druk. Pretoria, 1961.

Afr 8110.22   Merwe, J.P. van der. Die kaap onder die Bataafse republiek, 1803-1806. Amsterdam, 1926.

Afr 8285.20.10   Merwe, N.J. Marthinus Theunis Steijn. Kaapstad, 1921. 2v.

Afr 8180.23   Merwe, P.J. Nog verder noord. Kaapstad, 1962.

Afr 8180.22.3   Merwe, P.J. Die noordwaartse beweging van die Boere voor die groot trek, 1770-1842. Proefschrift. Den Haag, 1937.

Afr 8180.22   Merwe, P.J. Die noordwaartse beweging van die Boere voor die groot trek, 1770-1842. Den Haag, 1937.

Afr 8180.24   Merwe, P.J. Trek. Kaapstad, 1945.

Afr 8809.41   Merwe, Petrus J. van der. Pioniers van die Dorsland. Kaapstad, 1941.

Afr 5210.5   Merzliakov, Nikolai S. Stanovlenie natsional'noi gosudarstvennosti Respubliki Mali. Moskva, 1966.

Afr 5190.3   Mes aventures au Sénégal. (Verneuil, V.) Paris, 1858.

Afr 1609.54   Mes aventures marocaines. (Honel, C.) Casablanca, 1954.

Afr 2030.464.5   Mes combats. (Ortiz, Joseph.) Paris, 1964.

Afr 7135.14   Um mês de terrorismo; Angola, março-abril de 1961. (Costa, Pereira da.) Lisboa, 1969.

Afr 7815.36   Mes frères du Congo. (Lelong, M.H.) Alger, 1946. 2v.

Afr 2209.00.5   Mes journaliers. (Eberhardt, I.) Paris, 1923.

Afr 5480.243   Mes tournées au tchad. (Lapie, Pierre O.) London, 1943.

Afr 7809.00.10   Mes vacances au Congo. (Carton de Wiart, H.) Bruges, 19-

Afr 1403.3   Mesa, S. de. Jornada de Africa por el rey Don Sebastian. Barcelona, 1630.

Afr 555.148   Un meschino di Allah. (Borra, Edoardo.) Torino, 1963.

Afr 1571.17.70   Le message de Lyautey. (Garrick, Robert.) Paris, 1944.

Afr 1571.1.10   Messal, R. La genèse de notre victoire marocaine. Paris, 1931.

Afr 3986.962.10   Messayer, Mohamed Zaki. Le développement économique de l'Egypte. Lausanne, 1962.

Afr 3710.13.5   Messedaglia, Luigi. Uomini d'Africa. Bologna, 1935.

Afr 545.34   Messianische Kirchen, Sekten und Bewegungen im heutigen Afrika. (Benz, Ernst.) Leiden, 1965.

Afr 8289.43   Met cronjé aan die wesfront (1899-1900) en waarom het die boere die oorlog verlog verloor. (Conradie, Francois.) Kaapstad, 1943.

Afr 8289.02.23   Met de boeren-commandos. (Kestell, J.D.) Amsterdam, 1902.

Afr 8320.7   Met De Wet en Steijn in het veld. (Villiers, O.T. de.) Amsterdam, 1903.

Afr 8289.45.4   Met die Boere in die veld. 4. druk. (Raal, Sarah.) Kaapstad, 1963.

Afr 8252.172.10   Met general De Wet op kommando. (Wet, Izak J.C. de.) Johannesburg, 1954.

Afr 1259.21.10   Met Louis Couperus in Afrika. (Couperus, Louis.) Amsterdam, 1921.

Afr 6198.546   Metcalfe, George. MacLean of the Gold Coast. London, 1962.

Afr 6157.12   Metcalfe, George E. Great Britain and Ghana. London, 1964.

Afr 8687.323.25   Metelerkamp, Sanni. George Rex of Knysna. London, 1963.

Afr 7175.6.4   Meteorologia, climalogia e colonisação. (Dias de Carvalho, H.A.) Lisboa, 1892.

Afr 8279.01.4   Methuen, A.M.M. Peace or war in South Africa. London, 1901.

Afr 8279.01.3   Methuen, A.M.M. Peace or war in South Africa. London, 1901.

Afr 8279.01.2   Methuen, A.M.M. Peace or war in South Africa. 4th ed. London, 1901.

NEDL   Afr 8658.46.2   Methuen, H.H. Life in the wilderness. 2d ed. London, 1848.

Afr 3979.03.3   Metin, A. La transformation de l'Egypte. Paris, 1903.

Afr 4743.10   Metodio da Nembro. La missione dei Minori Cappuccini in Eritrea (1894-1952). Rome, 1953.

Afr 1609.09   Metour, E.P. In the wake of the green banner. N.Y., 1909.

Afr 8687.221   Metrowich, F.C. Scotty Smith. Cape Town, 1962.

Afr 6291.68   Metrowich, Frederick Redvers. Nigeria: the Biafran War. Pretoria, 1969.

Afr 9450.40   Metrowich, Frederick Redvers. Rhodesia; birth of a nation. Pretoria, 1969.

Afr 555.4.2   Mettetal, A. Le péril du protestantisme en Algérie. Paris, 1883.

Afr 6686.35   Metzger, O.F. Unsere alte Kolonie Togo. Neudamm, 1941.

Afr 11031.2   Meurant, L.H. Sixty years ago. Cape Town, 1963.

Afr 212.44   Meyer, Frank S. The African nettle, dilemmas of an emerging continent. N.Y., 1965.

Afr 6887.5   Meyer, H. Across East African glaciers. London, 1891.

Afr 6887.4   Meyer, H. Der Kilimandjaro. Berlin, 1900.

Afr 6887.1F   Meyer, H. Zum Schneedom des Kilmandscharo. Berlin, 1888.

Afr 6883.2.5   Meyer, Hans. Die Barundi. Leipzig, 1916.

Afr 8667.65   Meyer, P.J. Trek verder. Kaapstad, 1959.

Afr 2875.45   Meyer, Paul. Die Neutralität Deutschlands und Österreich-Ungarns im italienischer Krieg, 1911-1912. Inaug. Diss. Göttingen, 1932.

Afr 8667.90   Meyer, Pieter Johannes. Nog nie die einde nie. Kaapstad, 1954.

Afr 7809.58   Meyer, Roger. Introducing the Belgian Congo and the Ruanda-Urundi. Bruxelles, 1958.

Afr 3315.130   Meyer-Ranke, Peter. Der rote Pharao. Hamburg, 1964.

Afr 6194.20.15   Meyerowitz, Eva. The Akan of Ghana. London, 1958.

Afr 6196.26   Meyerowitz, Eva. At the court of an African king. London, 1962.

Afr 6194.20.16   Meyerowitz, Eva. The divine kingship in Ghana. London, 1960.

Afr 7549.64   Meyers, Joseph. Le prix d'un empire. 3.ed. Bruxelles, 1964.

Afr 30.8   Meyer's Handbuch über Afrika. Mannheim, 1962.

Afr 2274.3   Meynie, G. L'Algérie juive. Paris, 1887.

Afr 755.5   Meynier, O.F. La mission Joalland-Meynier. Paris, 1947.

Afr 8278.99.17   Meysey-Thompson, H. The Transvaal crisis. London, 1899.

Afr 2535.4   Mezerik, A. Tunisian-French dispute. N.Y., 1961.

Afr 8678.310   Mezerik, A.G. Apartheid in the Republic of South Africa. N.Y., 1964.

Afr 8678.310.5   Mezerik, A.G. Apartheid in the Republic of South Africa. N.Y., 1967.

Afr 7575.25   Mezerik, A.G. Congo and the United Nations. N.Y., 1960. 3v.

Afr 2030.255   Mezerik, Avrahm G. Algerian developments, 1959. N.Y., 1960.

Afr 8678.145   Mezerik, Avrahm G. Apartheid in the Union of South Africa. N.Y., 1960.

Afr 3315.150   Mezerik, Avrahm G. The Suez Canal: 1956 crisis - 1967 war. N.Y., 1969.

Afr 2030.80   Mezerik, Avrahn G. The Algerian-French conflict. N.Y., 1958.

Afr 6392.2   Mezger, Dorothea. Wirtschaftswissenschaftliche Veröffentlichungen über Ostafrika in englischer Sprache. v.1-3. München, 1967. 2v.

Afr 12639.24.815   Mezu, Sebastian Okechukwu. Léopold Sédar Senghor et la défense et illustration de la civilisation noire. Paris, 1968.

Afr 212.34   Mezu, Sebastian Okeckukure. The philosophy of Pan-Africanism. Washington, 1965.

Afr 1608.64.6   Mi embajada extraordinaria a Marruecos en 1863. (Merry y Colom, F.) Madrid, 1894.

Afr 5056.99   Mi viaje por el interior del Africa. (Benitez, Cristobal.) Tangier, 1899.

Afr 1609.58.10   Miazgowski, Brouirlew. Merakko-Krasnaie zemlia. Moskva, 1963.

Afr 2840.5   Micacchi, Rodolfo. La Tripolitania sotto il dominio dei Caramànli. Intra, 1936.

Afr 4513.15   Micaletti, K. Sangue italiano in Etiopia. Firenze, 1933.

Afr 6541.3   Michael, Charles D. James Hannington, bishop and martyr; the story of a noble life. London, 1910.

Afr 7808.89.9   Michaux, Oscar. Au Congo. Namur, 1913.

Afr 1658.18   Michaux-Bellaire, Ed. Apuntes para la historia del Rif. Madrid, 1926.

Afr 1340.20   Michel, Andre. Traité du contentieux administratif au Maroc. Thèse. Paris, 1932.

Afr 3994.932   Michel, Bernard. L'évolution du budget égyptien. n.p., 1932.

Afr 4615.1   Michel, C. Vers Fachoda. Paris, 1901.

Afr 2268.3   Michel, E. Esuli italiani in Algeria, 1815-1861. Bologna, 1935.

Afr 2030.462.60   Michel, F. Christ et croissant pour l'Algérie nouvelle. Paris, 1962.

Afr 2608.83   Michel, L. Tunis. Paris, 1883.

Afr 7912.5.5   Michel, Serge. Uhuru Lumumba. Paris, 1962.

Afr 2030.120   Michelet, Edmond. Contre la guerre civile. Paris, 1957.

Afr 6143.23   Michell, Harold. An introduction to the geography of Sierra Leone. London, 1919.

Afr 8250.6   Michell, L. Life and times of C.J. Rhodes. N.Y., 1910. 2v.

Afr 590.21   Michiels, A. Le Capitaine Firmin, ou La vie des Nègres en Afrique. Paris, 1853.

Afr 7809.46   Michiels, A. Notre colonie. 14.ed. Bruxelles, 1946.

Afr 28.130   Michigan. State University, East Lansing. Library. Research sources for African studies. East Lansing, 1969.

Afr Doc 5.10   Michigan. State University, East Lansing. Library. Research sources for African studies. East Lansing, 1969.

Afr 10633.13.100   Mickson, E.K. When the heart decides. Who killed Lucy? v.1-2. Accra, 1966?

Afr 2223.959.2   La micro-industrie. (Secrétariat Social d'Alger.) Alger, 1959.

Afr 4787.10   Mid-term appraisal of the first five-year plan of Somalia. 1st draft. (Carusoglu, T.) Mogadiscio, 1966.

Afr 6277.85F   Mid-western Nigeria development plan, 1964-68. (Nigeria, Mid-Western.) Benin City, 1965.

Afr 9149.53   Middelberg, Gerrit Adrian Arnold. Briewe uit Transvaal. Pretoria, 1953.

Afr 109.67.5   The middle age of African history. (Oliver, Roland Anthony.) London, 1967.

Afr 1623.961.5   Middle East Research Association. Washington, D.C. Morocco, a politico-economic analysis, 1956-60. Washington, 1961.

Afr 3979.42.5   Middle east window. (Bowman, H.E.) London, 1942.

Afr 8809.46   Middlemiss, E. Cape country. Cape Town, 1946.

Afr 9327.65   Middleton, Coral. Bechuanaland. Cape Town, 1965.

Afr 4095.8.6   Middleton, D. Baker of the Nile. London, 1949.

Afr 6540.7.5   Middleton, J. The Lugbara of Uganda. N.Y., 1965.

Afr 6540.7   Middleton, J. Lugbara religion. London, 1960.

Afr 50.10   Middleton, John. Tribes without rulers. London, 1958.

Afr 6585.1   Middleton, John. Zanzibar. London, 1965.

Afr 500.43   Middleton, Lamar. The rape of Africa. London, 1936.

Afr 1550.58   Miege, J.L. Le Maroc et l'Europe. v.1-4. Paris, 1961. 4v.

Afr 1706.5   Miege, Jean L. Les Européens à Casablanca au XIXe siècle. Paris, 1954.

Afr 1609.50.10	Miege, Jean L. Le Maroc. 1. ed. Paris, 1950.
Afr 1609.50.12	Miege, Jean L. Morocco. Paris, 1952.
Afr 4368.5.25	I miei trentacinque anni di missione. (Massaia, G.) Torino, 1932.
Afr 3979.12.5	Mielert, Fritz. Im Lande des Khedive. Regensburg, 1916.
Afr 5183.958.5	Mieux vivre dans notre village; lettres a Seydon. (Touze, R.L.) Dakar?, 1958.
Afr 718.37	Migeod, F.W.H. Across equatorial Africa. London, 1923.
Afr 6143.26	Migeod, Frederick W. A view of Sierra Leone. London, 1926.
Afr 11749.7.100	The mighty turtle and other poems. (Robertson, Olive.) Cape Town, 1966.
Afr 4785.25	Migiurtinia. (Vecchi, B.V.) Torino, 1933.
Afr 609.55.30	Migliorini, Elio. L'Africa. Torino, 1955.
Afr 2749.61.15	Migliorini, Elio. L'esplorazione del Sahara. Torino, 1961.
Afr 3820.8	Mignard, E. Etude sur l'établissement de la domination française a Madagascar. Paris, 1900.
Afr 7180.45	Migrações e povoamento. (Semana do Ultramar, 1st, Luanda, 1965.) Luanda, 1966.
Afr 9400.3.5	Migrant labour and tribal life. (Schapera, J.) London, 1947.
Afr Doc 3808.5	Migration report. (Rhodesia, Southern. Central Statistical Office.) Salisbury. 1964+
Afr Doc 3808.10	Migration report. (Rhodesia (British Colony). Central Statistical Office.) Salisbury. 1965+
Afr Doc 3508.255	Migration report. (Rhodesia and Nyasaland. Central Statistical Office.) Salisbury. 1963
Afr Doc 1808.5	Migration statistics. (Ghana. Central Bureau of Statistics.) Accra. 1953+
Afr 5760.18	Les migrations. (Deschamps, H.J.) Paris, 1959.
Afr 6194.20.20	Migrations au Ghana (Gold Coast). (Rouch, Jean.) Paris, 1956.
Afr 5058.13	Les migrations des Coniagui et Bassari. (Gessain, Monique.) Paris, 1967.
Afr 8289.01.10	Mijn commando en guerilla commando-leven. (Warmelo, D.S.) Amsterdam, 1901.
Afr 8289.02.22	Mijne herinneringen...anglo-boeren-oorlog. (Viljoen, B.J.) Amsterdam, 1902.
Afr 4259.49	Mikael, K. Ethiopia and Western civilization. n.p., 1949.
Afr 1609.61	Mikesell, M.W. Northern Morocco, a cultural geography. Berkeley, 1961.
Afr 3979.64.10	Mikhaelides, Gaby. La terre qui berça l'histoire. Bomas-sur-Ourthe, 1964.
Afr 3275.23	Mikhail, K. Copts and Moslems under British control. London, 1911.
Afr 609.64.40	Mikolasek, Vladimir. Africka mozaika. Liberec, 1964
Afr 5055.58A	Milcent, Ernest. L'A.O.F. entre en scène. Paris, 1958.
Afr 5119.65	Milcent, Ernest. Au carrefour des options africaines, le Sénégal. Paris, 1965.
Afr 5199.337.5	Milcent, Ernest. Léopold Sédar Senghor et la naissance de l'Afrique moderne. Paris, 1969.
Afr 7180.36.2	Milheiros, Mario. Notas de etnografia angolana. 2. ed. Luanda, 1967.
Afr 7947.6	Les milices du Rwanda précolonial. (Kagame, A.) Bruxelles, 1963.
Afr 212.54	Militärkupper i Afrika. (Nord, Erik.) Uppsala, 1967.
Afr 1346.2	Militarische und militärgeographische Betrachtungen. (Huebner, Max.) Berlin, 1905.
Afr 3310.50	The military coup in Egypt. (Barawi, Rashid.) Cairo, 1952.
Afr 1955.17	Military life in Algeria. (Castellane, P. de.) London, 1853. 2v.
Afr 8252.15	Millais, J.G. Life of Frederick Courtenay Selous. N.Y., 1919.
Afr 4070.36	Millais, John Guille. Far away up the Nile. London, 1924.
Afr 11057.6	Millar, Clive. Sixteen stories by South African writers. Cape Town, 1964.
Afr 3978.43	Millard, D. Journal of travels in Egypt. N.Y., 1843.
Afr 1573.34	Millas y Vallicrosa, J.M. España y Marruecos. Barcelona, 1945.
Afr 7808.99.3	Mille, P. Au Congo belge. Paris, 1899.
Afr 5342.3	Mille, P. Notice sur la Côte-d'Ivoire. n.p., 1900.
Afr 609.65.35	I mille fuochi. (Quilici, Folco.) Bari, 1965.
Afr 550.142	Millenarisme et acculturation. (Kaufmann, Robert.) Bruxelles, 1964.
Afr 9195.15	Miller, A.M. Mamisa, the Swazi warrior. Pietermaritzburg, 1953.
Afr 9195.15.5	Miller, Allister Mitchell. Swazieland and the Swazieland corporation. London, 1900.
Afr 8289.14	Miller, David S. A captain of the Gordon's Service experience. London, 1914.
Afr 8289.14.2	Miller, David S. A captain of the Gordon's Service experience. London, 1914.
Afr 6275.100	Miller, E.P. Change here for Kano. Zaria, 1959.
Afr 11021.2	Miller, G.M. A critical survey of South African poetry in English. Cape Town, 1957.
Afr 7809.31	Miller, Janet. Jungles preferred. Boston, 1931.
Afr 609.69.5	Miller, Norman N. Research in rural Africa. Montreal, 1969.
Afr 11563.49.100	Miller, Ruth. Floating island, poems. Cape Town, 1965.
Afr 6275.127	Miller, Stefan. Nigeria zwischen Wüste und Lagune. Berlin, 1966.
Afr 699.62	Miller, Stefan. Vom Nilzum Sambesi. 1. Aufl. Berlin, 1962.
Afr 6214.15	Miller, W.R.S. Have we failed in Nigeria? London, 1947.
Afr 6275.107.5	Miller, W.R.S. Success in Nigeria; assets and possibilities. London, 1948.
Afr 6275.107	Miller, W.R.S. Yesterday and tomorrow in Northern Nigeria. London, 1938.
Afr 6282.2	Miller, Walter Richard Samuel. Walter Miller, 1872-1952. Zaria, 1953.
Afr 1624.932	Milleron, Jacques. Le controle des engagements de depenses au Maroc. Thèse. Paris, 1932.
Afr 2250.6	Millet, Jean. La coexistence des communautés en Algérie. Aix-en-Provence, 1962.
Afr 1570.29	Millet, R. La conquête du Maroc. Paris, 1913.
Afr 1390.6	Millet, Rene. Les Almohades, histoire dune dynastie berbère. Paris, 1923.
Afr 699.68.10	Milley, Jacques. L'Afrique orientale, terre des safaris. Paris, 1968.
Afr 679.08	Milligan, R.H. Jungle folk of Africa. N.Y., 1908.
Afr 5426.110	Milligan, Robert H. The fetish folk of West Africa. N.Y., 1912.
Afr 8659.26.5.5	Millin, S.G. The people of South Africa. London, 1951.
Afr 8250.25	Millin, S.G. Rhodes. London, 1933.

Afr 8250.25.10	Millin, S.G. Rhodes. London, 1952.
Afr 8089.41	Millin, S.G. South Africa. London, 1941.
Afr 8659.26.5	Millin, S.G. The South Africans. London, 1926.
Afr 11572.50.100	Millin, S.G. The night is long. London, 1941.
Afr 11572.50.140	Millin, S.G.(L). The burning man. London, 1952.
Afr 11572.50.150	Millin, S.G.(L). The coming of the Lord. N.Y., 1928.
Afr 11572.50.160	Millin, S.G.(L). The dark gods. 1st ed. N.Y., 1941.
Afr 11572.50.170	Millin, S.G.(L). The fiddler. N.Y., 1929.
Afr 11572.50.180	Millin, S.G.(L). God's stepchildren. N.Y., 1925.
Afr 11572.50.120	Millin, S.G.(L). King of the bastards. N.Y., 1949.
Afr 11572.50.110	Millin, S.G.(L). Mary Glenn. N.Y., 1925.
Afr 11572.50.190	Millin, S.G.(L). The measure of my days. London, 1955.
Afr 11572.50.200	Millin, S.G.(L). Two bucks without hair. London, 1957.
Afr 11572.50.130	Millin, S.G.(L). What hath a man. 1st ed. N.Y., 1938.
Afr 11572.50.210	Millin, S.G.(L). The wizard bird. London, 1962.
Afr 8252.341.5	Millin, S.G.L. General Smuts. Boston, 1936.
Afr 8252.341.75	Millin, S.G.L. General Smuts. London, 1936. 2v.
Afr 630.66	Millin, Sarah Gertrude. White Africans are also people. Cape Town, 1966.
Afr 1830.10.1	Milliot, Louis. L'oeuvre legislative de la France en Algérie. Paris, 1930.
Afr 1335.20	Milliot, Louis. Recueil de jurisprudence chérifienne. v.1-4. Paris, 1920-24. 4v.
Afr 628.5	Mills, C.H. Selective annotated bibliography on the Negro and foreign languages. n.p., 1939.
Afr 679.29	Mills, D.R.M. The golden land. London, 1929.
Afr 9854.14	Mills, Dora S. What we do in Nyasaland. London, 1911.
Afr 7459.26	Mills, Dorothy. Through Liberia. London, 1926.
Afr 8289.02.32	Milne, J. The epistles of Atkins. London, 1902.
Afr 3275.14	Milner, A. England in Egypt. London, 1892.
Afr 3275.14.5	Milner, A. England in Egypt. London, 1894.
Afr 8252.8.10	Milner, A.M. The Milner papers...1897-1905. London, 1931-33. 2v.
Afr 8252.8.10	The Milner papers...1897-1905. (Milner, A.M.) London, 1931-33. 2v.
Afr 8110.28	Milo, Taco H. De geheime onderhandelingen tusschen de Bataafshe en Fransche Republieken. Den Helder, 1942.
Afr 6538.60	Milton Obote Foundation. The challenge of Uganda's second five year development plan. Kampala, 1967.
Afr 2209.08.3	Miltoun, F. In the land of mosques and minarets. Boston, 1908.
Afr 6455.150	Mina Afrikaär. (Heland, Erik von.) Stockholm, 1966.
Afr 8252.341.85	Mincher, Kathleen. I lived in his shadow. Capetown, 1965.
Afr 609.62.15	The mind of Africa. (Abraham, W.) London, 1962.
Afr 6455.105	Mine afrikanshe udfingter. (Benzon, Boeje.) København, 1948.
Afr 5247.35	Miner, H.M. The primitive city of Timbuctoo. Garden City, 1965.
Afr 5247.40	Miner, Horace Mitchell. The primitive city of Timbuctoo. Princeton, 1953.
Afr 626.140	Mineral resources of South-Central Africa. (Pelletier, R.A.) Capetown, 1964.
Afr Doc 4312.126	Mines and work act. (South Africa. Parliament.) Cape Town, 1926.
Afr 1830.20.85	Les mines et les carrieres en Algerie. (Dussert, D.) Paris, 1931.
Afr 1609.06.3	Minguez Y Vicente, M. Descripcion geografica del imperio de Marruecos. Madrid, 1906.
Afr 3993.10	Mining, food, and textile industries in the second five-year industrial plan. (United Arab Republic.) Cairo, 196-. 2 pam.
Afr 1990.4.10	Le ministère de l'Algérie (24 juin 1858-24 nov. 1860). Thèse. (Moulis, R.F.) Alger, 1926.
Afr Doc 3207.362	Ministry of Finance and Economic Planning Kenya Population Census, 1962. (Kenya.) Nairobi? 1964.
Afr 3326.7	Ministry of Social Affairs in eleven years from July 23rd, 1952 to July 23rd, 1963. (United Arab Republic. Information Service.) Cairo, 1963.
Afr Doc 1712.5F	Minutes. (Sierra Leone. Legislative Council.) 1922-1925 3v.
Afr Doc 2412.205	Minutes of evidence. (Nigeria, Northern. Legislature. Public Accounts Joint Committee.) Kaduna. 1963+
Afr Doc 2314.205	Minutes of evidence. (Nigeria. Parliament. House of Representatives. Public Accounts Committee.) Lagos. 1960+
Afr 8288.99.9F	Minutes of evidence on war in South Africa. (Great Britain. Commissions. South African War.) London, 1903. 2v.
Afr Doc 4314.5F	Minutes of proceedings. (South Africa. Parliament. House of Assembly.) 3v.
Afr Doc 4316.5F	Minutes of proceedings. (South Africa. Parliament. Senate.)
Afr Doc 3212.25F	Minutes of the proceedings. (Kenya. Legislative Council.) 1920-1923
Afr Doc 4112.5F	Minutes of the 4th Reconstituted European Advisory Council. (Swaziland. European Advisory Council.) 3v.
Afr 1026.5	Minutilli, F. Bibliografia della Libia. Torino, 1903.
Afr 2929.02	Minutilli, F. La Tripolitania. Torino, 1902.
Afr 2929.02.2	Minutilli, F. La Tripolitania. 2 ed. Torino, 1912.
Afr 1403.6	O minuto vitorioso de Alacer-Quibir. (Esaguy, Jose de.) Lisboa, 1944.
Afr 4050.2	Minutoli, H.V. Reise zum Tempel der Jupiter Ammon. Berlin, 1825.
Afr 3978.27	Minutoli. Recollections of Egypt. Philadelphia, 1827.
Afr 1571.27	Le miracle du Maroc. (Bordeaux, Henry.) Paris, 1918.
Afr 2026.10	Mirad, Ali. Le réformisme musulman en Algérie de 1925 à 1940. Paris, 1967.
Afr 7108.15	Miralles de Imperial y Gomez, C. Angola en tiempos de Felipe II y de Felipe III. Madrid, 1951.
Afr 6776.5	Mirambo, un chief de guerre dans l'Est Africain vers 1830-1884. (Fouquer, Roger.) Paris, 1967.
Afr 5960.14	Miranda, Agustin. Cartas de la Guinea. Madrid, 1940.
Afr 1750.33	Miranda Diaz, Mario. Espana en el continente africano. Madrid, 1963.
Afr 2480.5	Mirot, Leon. Une expédition française en Tunisie au XIVe siècle. Paris, 1932.
Afr 1369.49.5	Miscelanea de estudios historicos sobre Marruecos. (Garcia Figueras, T.) Larache, 1949.
Afr 1750.5	Miscelanea marroqui. (Et-Tabyi.) Ceuta, 1953.
Htn Afr 26.5PF*	Pamphlet box. Miscellaneous broadsides.

	Afr 2870.30	Moore, M. Fourth shore, Italy's mass colonization of Libya. London, 1940.
	Afr 590.18	Moore, S. Biography of Mahommah G. Baquaqua. Detroit, 1854.
	Afr 3979.62	Moorehead, Alan. The Blue Nile. 1st ed. N.Y., 1962.
	Afr 609.60	Moorehead, Alan. No room in the ark. N.Y., 1959.
	Afr 725.22	Moorehead, Alan. The White Nile. N.Y., 1961.
Htn	Afr 1738.13*	The Moores baffled. (Addison, L.) London, 1681.
	Afr 1368.99	The Moorish empire. (Meakin, B.) London, 1899.
	Afr 1609.02	The Moors. (Meakin, B.) London, 1902.
	Afr 210.65	Moraas, Francis Robert. The importance of being black. N.Y., 1965.
	Afr 2290.4	Le moral algérien. (Bourdonnaye.) Paris, n.d.
	Afr 8678.366	Moral conflict in South Africa. (National Catholic Federation of Students.) Johannesburg, 1963.
	Afr 1755.5	Morales, G. de. Datos para la historia de Melilla. Melilla, 1909.
	Afr 10005.15	Morán Lopez, Fernando. Nation y alienación en la literatura negro-africana. Madrid, 1964.
	Afr 710.16	Morán Lopez, Fernando. El nuevo reino. Madrid, 1967.
	Afr 5045.40	Morand, Paul. Paris, Tombouctou, documentaire. Paris, 1928.
	Afr 125.6F	Morcelli, S.A. Africa christiana. Brixiae, 1816. 3v.
	Afr 1347.1	Mordacq, J.J.H. La guerre au Maroc. Paris, 1904.
	Afr 1347.1.2	Mordacq, J.J.H. La guerre au Maroc. 2e ed. Paris, 1907.
	Afr 1990.24	Mordacq, J.J.H. La guerre en Afrique. Paris, 1908.
	Afr 8983.8.5	More annals of Natal. (Hattersley, A.F.) London, 1936.
	Afr 11027.5	More tales of South Africa. (Booysen, C. Murray.) Cape Town, 1967.
	Afr 10671.35.100	More than once. (Agunwa, Clement.) London, 1967.
	Afr 2650.4	Moreau, Pierre. Le pays des Nefezaouas. Tunis, 1947.
	Afr 7320.4.5	Moreira, E. Portuguese East Africa. London, 1936.
	Afr 150.68	Moreira de Sa, Artur. O Infante D. Henrique e a universidade. Lisboa, 1960.
	Afr 6095.2	Morel, E.D. Affairs of West Africa. London, 1902.
	Afr 7568.15.5	Morel, E.D. The future of the Congo. London, 1909.
	Afr 7568.15.2	Morel, E.D. King Leopold's rule in Africa. London, 1904.
	Afr 7568.15	Morel, E.D. King Leopold's rule in Africa. N.Y., 1905.
	Afr 1550.16	Morel, E.D. Morocco in diplomacy. London, 1912.
	Afr 6280.7	Morel, E.D. Nigeria; its people and its problems. London, 1911.
	Afr 6280.7.3	Morel, E.D. Nigeria: its peoples and its problems. 3rd ed. London, 1968.
NEDL	Afr 1550.16.5	Morel, E.D. Ten years of secret diplomacy. 3d ed. London, 1915.
	Afr 500.19	Morel, Edmund D. Africa and the peace of Europe. Photoreproduction. London, 1917.
	Afr 500.19.5	Morel, Edmund D. The black man's burden. N.Y., 1920.
	Afr 500.19.10	Morel, Edmund D. The black man's burden. N.Y., 1969.
	Afr 7568.15.10	Morel, Edmund D. Morel's history of the Congo reform movement. Oxford, 1968.
	Afr 7568.15.15	Morel, Edmund D. Red rubber. N.Y., 1969.
	Afr 2235.1	Morelet. Les Maures de Constantine. Dijon, 1876.
	Afr 2208.54	Morell, J.R. Algeria. London, 1854.
	Afr 7568.15.10	Morel's history of the Congo reform movement. (Morel, Edmund D.) Oxford, 1968.
	Afr 1721.7	Moreno Gilabert, Andres. La Ciudad Dormida. Madrid, 1923.
	Afr 5955.2	Moreno Moreno, José A. Reseña histórica de la presencia de España en el Golfo de Guinea. Madrid, 1952.
	Afr 3079.68.7	Morenz, Siegfried. Die Begegnung Europas mit Ägypten. 2. Aufl. Zürich, 1969.
	Afr 6192.93	Morgan, Clyde. Background to Ghana. 1st ed. London, 1965.
	Afr 6390.98	Morgan, Gordon Daniel. African vignettes. Jefferson City, 1967.
	Afr 1867.28	Morgan, John. Complete history of Algiers. London, 1728. 2v.
	Afr 11580.75.100	Morgan, Robert. The winds blow red. Ilfracombe, 1962.
	Afr 6465.58.10	Morgan, W.T.W. Nairobi, city and region. Nairobi, 1967.
	Afr Doc 3207.362.10	Morgan, W.T.W. Population of Kenya; density and distribution; a geographical introduction to the Kenya population census, 1962. Nairobi, 1966.
	Afr 679.69	Morgan, William Basil. West Africa. London, 1969.
	Afr 626.121	Morgaut, M.E. Cinq années de psychologies africaines. Paris, 1962.
	Afr 626.54	Morgaut, Marc E. Un dialogue nouveau. Paris, 1959.
	Afr 6738.4.9	Morgen, C. Von Durch Kamerun von sued nach nord. Leipzig, 1893.
	Afr 3979.55.5	Morgen bloeien de abrikozen. (Aafjes, Bertus.) Amsterdam, 1954.
	Afr 5053.32	Morgenthau, R.S. Political parties in French-speaking West Africa. Oxford, 1964.
	Afr 2929.27	Mori, Attilio. L'esplorazione geografica della Libia. Firenze, 1927.
	Afr 2609.30.5	Mori, Attilio. La Tunisia. Roma, 1930.
	Afr 4259.04	Morie, L.J. Les civilisations africaines. Paris, 1904. 2v.
	Afr 1609.63	Morin-Barde, M. Le Maroc etincelant. Casablanca, 1963.
	Afr 5746.38	Morizot, C.B. Relations véritables et curieuses de l'isle de Madagascar. Paris, 1651.
	Afr 8688.10F	Morkel, Philip William. The Morkels; family history and family tree. Cape Town, 1961. 2v.
	Afr 8688.10F	The Morkels; family history and family tree. (Morkel, Philip William.) Cape Town, 1961. 2v.
	Afr 8089.44	Morkford, G. There are South Africans. London, 1944.
	Afr 2030.464.80	Morland. HistoireDe l'organisation de l'armée secréte. Paris, 1964.
	Afr 2208.56.10	Mornaud, F. La vie arabe. Paris, 1856.
	Afr 8278.99.25	Morning leader leaflets. v.1- London, 1899-1900.
	Afr 6147.5.3	The morning star of Africa. (Clark, William R.E.) London, 1960.
	Afr 1487.5	Moroccan drama, 1900-1955. (Landau, Rom.) San Francisco, 1956.
	Afr 1609.52	Moroccan journal. (Landau, R.) London, 1952.
	Afr 1494.7	Moroccan Office of Information and Documentation, N.Y. Morocco under the protectorate. N.Y., 1953.
	Afr 1623.961.5	Morocco, a politico-economic analysis, 1956-60. (Middle East Research Association. Washington, D.C.) Washington, 1961.
	Afr 1069.64	Morocco, Algeria, Tunisia. (Brace, R.M.) Englewood Cliffs, N.J., 1964.
	Afr 1487.36	Morocco, old land, new nation. (Cohen, Mark I.) N.Y., 1966.
	Afr 1495.4	Morocco, problems of new power. (Zartman, I.W.) N.Y., 1964.
	Afr 1620.35	Morocco, 1965-66. (Fodor, Eugene.) N.Y., 1966.
	Afr 1301.5	Morocco. Annuaire économique et financier. Casablanca. 1917+ 4v.
	Afr 1623.958.5	Morocco. L'evolution économique du Maroc dans le cadre du deuxieme plan quadriennal. Casablanca, 1958.
	Afr 1328.2	Pamphlet vol. Morocco. 10 pam.
	Afr 1328	Pamphlet box. Morocco.
	Afr 1608.82.3	Morocco. (Amicis, E. de.) Milano, 1890.
	Afr 1608.82.2	Morocco. (Amicis, E. de.) N.Y., 1882.
	Afr 1608.82	Morocco. (Amicis, E. de.) N.Y., 1882.
	Afr 1369.65	Morocco. (Barbour, N.) London, 1965.
	Afr 1609.04.10A	Morocco. (Bensusan, S.L.) London, 1904.
	Afr 1620.15.5	Morocco. (Heywood, C.) Paris, 1924.
	Afr 1608.89.3	Morocco. (Lamartiniere, H.M.P. de.) London, 1889.
	Afr 1609.50.12	Morocco. (Miege, Jean L.) Paris, 1952.
	Afr 1609.58.5F	Morocco. (Morocco. Ministere des Affaires Étrangeres.) Rabat, 1958.
	Afr 1620.25	Morocco. (Nagel, Publishers.) Paris, 1953.
	Afr 1609.42	Morocco. Casablanca, 1942.
	Afr 1620.42	Morocco. Paris, 1966.
	Afr 1623.963.5	Morocco. Delegation Generale a la Promotion Nationale et au Plan. Promotion nationale au Maroc. Casa, 196-.
	Afr 1623.965.15	Morocco. Division de la Coordination Economique et du Plan. Etude sur le commerce intérieur. Rabat, 1965? 3v.
	Afr 1623.960.5	Morocco. Division de la Coordination Économique et du Plan. Plan quinquennal, 1960-1964. Rabat, 1960.
	Afr 1623.960.6	Morocco. Division de la Coordination Économique et du Plan. Plan quinquennal, 1960-1964. Rabat, 1961.
	Afr 1623.960	Morocco. Division de la Coordination Economique et du Plan. Tableaux économiques du Maroc. Rabat, 1960.
	Afr 1623.965.10	Morocco. Division de la Coordination Economique et du Plan. Three year plan, 1965-1967. Rabat, 1965.
	Afr 1623.954.5	Morocco. Division du Commerce et de la Marine Marchande. Maroc, cinq ans de realisation du programme d'equipement. Rabat, 1954.
	Afr 1333.5.5	Morocco. Laws, statutes, etc. Treaties, codes...Supplément pour 1937. Paris, 1937.
	Afr 1340.42	Morocco. Ministère de l'Information et du Tourisme. Documents sur la constitution. Rabat, 1960.
	Afr 5078.22	Morocco. Ministère de l'Information et du Tourisme. La libération de la province mauritanienne et l'opinion international. Rabat, 1961.
	Afr 5074.37	Morocco. Ministère des Affaires Etrangères. Livre blanc sur la Mauritanie. Rabat, 1960.
	Afr 1609.58.5F	Morocco. Ministere des Affaires Étrangeres. Morocco. Rabat, 1958.
	Afr Doc 5208.705	Morocco. Ministere du Commerce et de l'Artisanat. Statistiques du mouvement commercial et maritime du Maroc. Maroc. 1960+
	Afr Doc 5207.5	Morocco. Service Central des Statistiques. Annuaire statistique du Maroc. 1950+
	Afr Doc 5207.10	Morocco. Service Central des Statistiques. Bulletin mensuel de statistique. 1,1957+
	Afr Doc 5207.11	Morocco. Service Central des Statistiques. Bulletin mensuel de statistique. Supplement. 1958+
	Afr Doc 5207.360	Morocco. Service Central des Statistiques. Recensement demographique juin 1960. Population legale du Maroc. Rabat, 1961-62. 2v.
	Afr Doc 5207.361	Morocco. Service Central des Statistiques. Résultats de l'enquête à objectifs multiples, 1961-1963. Rabat? 1964.
	Afr Doc 5207.360.5	Morocco. Service Central des Statistiques. Résultats du recensement de 1960. Rabat, 1964-65.
	Afr 1313.2	Morocco. Service Général de l'Information. Bulletin d'information du Maroc. Rabat.
	Afr 1313.1F	Morocco. Service Général de l'Information. Bulletin d'information et de documentation. Rabat.
	Afr 1608.82.2.5	Morocco. 9 ed. (Amicis, E. de.) Milano, 1882.
	Afr 1750.34	Morocco (Spanish Zone). Seleccion de conferencias y trabajos realizados por la Academia de Interventores. Tetuan. 1949+
	Afr 1609.12	Morocco after twenty-five years. (Kerr, Robert.) London, 1912.
	Afr 1608.44.6	Morocco and the Moors. (Hay, J.H.D.) London, 1861.
	Afr 1608.91A	Morocco and the Moors. (Leared, A.) London, 1891.
	Afr 1571.35A	Morocco as a French economic venture. (Knight, M.M.) N.Y., 1937.
	Afr 1608.93	Morocco as it is. (Bonsal, S. Jr.) London, 1893.
	Afr 1445.10.5	Morocco at the parting of the ways. (Cruikshank, E.F.) Philadelphia, 1935.
	Afr 1445.10	Morocco at the parting of the ways. Diss. (Cruikshank, E.F.) Philadelphia, 1935.
	Afr 1493.30	Morocco awakes. (Mellor, F.H.) London, 1939.
	Afr 1328.3	Pamphlet box. Morocco-description.
	Afr 1609.27	Morocco from a motor. (Vernon, Paul E.) London, 1927.
	Afr 1328.4	Pamphlet box. Morocco-history.
	Afr 1550.16	Morocco in diplomacy. (Morel, E.D.) London, 1912.
	Afr 1609.03.12	Morocco of today. (Aubin, Eugene.) London, 1906.
	Afr 1550.01	Pamphlet box. Morocco question.
	Afr 1550	Pamphlet box. Morocco question.
	Afr 1453.10	Morocco that was. (Harris, Walter B.) Edinburgh, 1921.
	Afr 1609.14	Morocco the piquant. (Holt, G.E.) London, 1914.
	Afr 1609.53	Morocco today. (Newman, B.) London, 1953.
	Afr 1313.6	Morocco tourism. Rabat. 42,1966+ 3v.
	Afr 1494.7	Morocco under the protectorate. (Moroccan Office of Information and Documentation, N.Y.) N.Y., 1953.
	Afr 1609.54.5	Morocco 54. (Encyclopedie Mensuelle d'Outre-Mer.) Paris, 1954.
	Afr 1555.12	Morocco's Saharan frontiers. (Trout, Frank Emanuel.) Geneva, 1969.
	Afr 1608.94.4	Moros y cristianos. (Soriano, Rodrigo.) Madrid, 1894.
	Afr 5920.6	Moros y Morellon, J. de. Memorias sobre las islas africanas de España. Madrid, 1844.
	Afr 1485.4	Morote, L. La conquista del Mogreb. Valencia, n.d.
	Afr 7575.10	Morres, Jacques. L'équinoxe de janvier. Bruxelles, 1959.
	Afr 9635.22A	Morris, Colin. Colin Morris and Kenneth Haunda. London, 1960.
	Afr 9693.7	Morris, Colin. The end of the missionary. London, 1962.
	Afr 9645.15	Morris, Colin M. The hour after midnight. London, 1961.
	Afr 8160.25	Morris, Donald R. The washing of the spears. N.Y., 1965.

Afr Doc 9207.345 Mozambique. Repartição Tecnica de Estatistica. Recenseamento da população mão indigena, em 12 de junho de 1945. Lourenço Marques, 1947.

Afr Doc 9207.350 Mozambique. Repartição Tecnica de Estatistica. Recenseamento geral da população em 1950. Lourenço Marques, 1953-1955. 2v.

Afr 7309.38.5 Mozambique. Repartição Teenica de Estatistica. Game hunting in Mozambique. Lourenço Marques, 1938.

Afr 7309.38 Mozambique. Repartição Teenica de Estatistica. The ports and lighthouses of Moçambique. Lourenço Marques, 1938.

Afr 7309.38.10 Mozambique. Repartição Teenica de Estatistica. The roads of Moçambique. Lourenço Marques, 1938.

Afr Doc 9282.10F Mozambique. Repartičo de Agricultura. Reconhecimento agricola-económico do distrito de Lourenço Marques. 1916-1917

Afr Doc 9282.12F Mozambique. Secretaria Geral. Recenseamentos população...de Lourenço Marques. n.p., 1913.

Afr Doc 9209.300 Mozambique. Direcção Provincial des Serviços de Estatistica Geral. Estatistica das contribuições e impostos. Lourenço Marques. 1,1960+

Afr 6192.90 Mozheiko, I.V. Eto, Gana. Moscow, 1962.

Afr 609.62.45 Mphahlele, E. The African image. N.Y., 1962.

Afr 8849.10 Mphahlele, E. Down Second avenue. London, 1959.

Afr 635.80 Mphahlele, Ezekiel. The African image. London, 1962.

Afr 10015.10 Mphahlele, Ezekiel. African writing today. Harmondsworth, 1967.

Afr 11582.70.21 Mphahlele, Ezekiel. In corner b; short stories. Nairobi, 1967.

Afr 6298.110.5 Mr. Prime Minister. (Balewa, Abubakar Tafawa.) Lagos, Nigeria, 1964.

Afr 2218.6.10 Mrabet, F. La femme algérienne. Paris, 1964.

Afr 1340.41 Mrejen, Nissim. L'office national marocain du tourisme. Rabat, 1963.

Afr 8849.169 Mrs. Dale's diary, 1857-1872. (Dale, Emmé Ross.) Cape Town, 1966.

Afr 7913.5 Msiri. (Verbeken, A.) Bruxelles, 1956.

Afr 9549.67 Mtshali, B. Valindlela. Rhodesia: background to conflict. N.Y., 1967.

Afr 718.46 O muata cazembe e os povos Maraves. (Pedroso Gamitto, Antonio Candido.) Lisboa, 1937. 2v.

Afr 14692.41.110 Mucanda. (Victor, Geraldo Bessa.) Braga, 1964.

Afr 7175.60 Mucandos, ou cartos de Angola. (Granado, Antonio C.) Lisboa, 1940.

Afr 550.125 Mud and mosaics. (Rathe, G.) Westminster, Md., 1962.

Afr 4559.35.87 Muehlen, Leo. Im Banne des äthiopischen Hochlandes. 2e Aufl. Berlin, 1935.

Afr 8289.00.47 Mueller, A. von. Der Krieg in Süd-afrika, 1899-1900. v.1-5. Berlin, 1900.

Afr 8289.01.37 Mueller, Alfred von. Kritische Betrachtungen über den Burenkrieg. Berlin, 1901.

Afr 6738.22 Mueller, Arno. Die kameruner Waldländer. Inaug. Diss. Ohlau in Schlesien, 1930.

Afr 8125.15 Mueller, C.F.J. Johannes Frederik Kirsten oor die toestand van die Kaapkolonie in 1795. Pretoria, 1960.

Afr 2209.11.3 Mueller, Charles. Fünf Jahre Fremdenlegionär in Algier. Stuttgart, 1911.

Afr 8252.8 Mueller, E.B.I. Lord Milner and South Africa. London, 1902.

Afr 7815.38 Mueller, Ernst Wilhelm. Le droit de propriété chez les Mongo-bokote. Bruxelles, 1958.

Afr 6640.22 Mueller, F.F. Kolonien unter der Peitsche. Berlin, 1962.

Afr 6686.48.15F Müller, Julius Otto. Enquête sociologique "Le paysan face au développement". Munich, 1965.

Afr 4559.27.10 Mueller, Otto. Rings um den Tschentischer. Hannover, 1927.

Afr 730.4 Mueller, W. Die Umsegelung Afrikas. Rathenau, 1889.

Afr 609.66.10 Mueng, Engelbert. Dossier culturel pan-africain. Paris, 1966.

Afr 2223.933 Münnich, H. Der Verkehr Algeriens-Tunesiens mit Frankreich. Inaug. Diss. Leipzig, 1933.

Afr 10013.5 Münster. Universität. Institut für Publizistik. Publizist und Publikum in Afrika. Köln, 1962.

Afr 4558.92.5 Muenzenberger, E.F.A. Abessinien. Freiberg, 1892.

Afr 8678.143 Mueren, K. van der. Apartheid zonder vooroordelen. Antwerpen, 1958.

Afr 6218.19 Muffett, D.J.M. Concerning brave captains. London, 1964.

Afr 4199.105 Muhammad Abduh. (Amin, Osman.) Le Caire, 1944.

Afr 4199.105.5 MuhammadAbduh. (Amin, Osman.) Washington, 1953.

Afr 5488.5 Muhammad Ibn Omar. Voyage au Ouadaï. Paris, 1851.

Afr 1494.40 Muhammad V, Sultan of Morocco. Le Maroc à l'heure de l'indépendance. v.1. Rabat, 1958.

Afr 6214.10 The Muhammadan emigrants of Nigeria. (Hoghen, S.J.) London, 1930.

Afr 4199.100 Muhammed Abduh. (Bahay, Muhammad.) Hamburg, 1936.

Afr 1400.1 Muhammed al-Segir. Nozhet-Elhadi, histoire de la dynastie saadienne au Maroc, (1511-1670). Paris, 1889.

Afr 1885.1 Muhammed Al-Tunisi. Histoire des Beni Zeiyan. Paris, 1852.

Afr 3150.5A Muir, William. The Mameluke or slave dynasty of Egypt. London, 1896.

Afr 1608.81.5 La mujer Marroqui, estudio social. 2e ed. (Ovilo y Canales, F.) Madrid, 1881.

Afr 1608.86.10 La mujer marroqui. Nueva edicion. (Ovilo y Canales, D.F.) Madrid, 1886.

Afr 109.61.40 Mukarovsky, H. Afrika. Wien, 1961.

Afr 109.61.41 Mukarovsky, H. Afrique d'hier et d'aujourd'hui. Tournai, 1964.

Afr 8685.27.20 Mukhamedova, Dil'bar. Iz istorii rasovoi diskriminatsii indiitsev v Iuzhnoi Afrike. Tashkent, 1965.

Afr 5844.5 Mukherji, S.B. The indenture system in Mauritius, 1837-1915. 1. ed. Calcutta, 1962.

Afr 8340.40 Mukherji, S.B. Indian minority in South Africa. New Delhi, 1959.

Afr 8355.40 Mukherji, S.B. Indian minority in South Africa. New Delhi, 1959.

Afr 7946.10 Mulago, Vicent. Un visage africain du christianisme. Paris, 1965.

Afr 4742.4 Mulazzani, A. Geografia della colonia Eritrea. Firenze, 1924.

Afr 9087.8 Mulder, Cornelius Petrus. Die eerste skof van die Nasionale Party in Transvaal, 1914-1964. Johannesburg, 1964.

Afr 2228.5 Mule, A. Chez les Moumenins. Paris, 1906.

Afr 9645.17 Mulford, D.C. The Northern Rhodesia general election, 1962. Nairobi, 1964.

Afr 9636.5 Mulford, David C. Zambia: the politics of independence, 1957-1964. London, 1967.

Afr 10883.89.100 Mulikita, Fwanyanga Matale. A point of no return. London, 1968.

Afr 5748.75 Mullens, J. Twelve months in Madagascar. London, 1875.

Afr 8180.26 Muller, Christoffel Frederik Jakobus. Die Britse owerheid en de groot trek. Thesis. Kaapstad, 1949.

Afr 8180.26.5 Muller, Christoffel Frederik Jakobus. Die Britse owerheid en die groot trek. 2. uitg. Johannesburg, 1963.

Afr 8028.152 Muller, Christoffel Frederik Jakobus. A select bibliography of South African history; a guide for historical research. Pretoria, 1966.

Afr 8089.68.7 Muller, Christoffel Frederik Jakobus. Vyfhonderd jaar Suid-Afrikaanse Geskiedenis. Pretoria, 1969.

Afr 8690.5 Muller, D.J. The Orange river. Cape Town, 1953.

Afr 7850.62 Muller, Emmanuel. Les troupes du Katange et les compagnes d'Afrique 1914-1918. v.1-2. Bruxelles, 1937.

Afr 11249.86.800 Muller, G. A bibliography of the poetical works of Guy Butler, Anthony Delius and Roy MacNab. Johannesburg, 1962. 2v.

Afr 9438.96 Muller, H.P.N. De Zuid-Afrikaansche Republiek en Rhodesia. 's-Gravenhage, 1896.

Afr 7322.2 Muller, H.P.N. Land und Volk zwischen Zambesi und Limpopo. Giessen, 1894.

Afr 9225.28 Muller, Hendrik Pieter Nicolaas. Oude tyden in den Oranje-Vrystaat. Leiden, 1907.

Afr 550.141 Mullin, Joseph. The Catholic Church in modern Africa. London, 1965.

Afr 6541.24 Mullins, Joseph Dennis. The wonderful story of Uganda. London, 1904.

Afr 8678.240 Multi-racial South Africa. (Debeer, Zacharias Johannes.) London, 1961.

Afr 699.69 The multicultural states of East Africa. (Richards, Audrey.) Montreal, 1969.

Afr Doc 707.10.2F A multipurpose survey of Afgoi municipality. (Somalia. Ministry of Planning and Coordination. Statistical Department.) Mogadiscio, 1966.

Afr 9693.8 The multitribal society. (Rhodes-Livingstone Institute.) Lusaka, 1962.

Afr 609.41 Mumbo Jumbo, esquire. (Childers, J.S.) N.Y., 1941.

Afr 3978.76.6 Mummies and Moslems. (Warner, C.D.) Hartford, 1876.

Afr 212.62 Mungai, Njorge. The independent nations of Africa. Nairobi, 1967.

Afr 6430.5 Mungeam, Gordon Hudson. British rule in Kenya, 1895-1912. Oxford, 1966.

Afr 210.61.20 Munger, E. African field report. Cape Town, 1961.

Afr 6542.5 Munger, E.S. Relational patterns of Kampala. Chicago, 1951.

Afr 8678.370 Munger, Edwin S. Afrikaner and African nationalism. London, 1967.

Afr 9339.65 Munger, Edwin S. Bechuanaland. London, 1965.

Afr 8377.1 Munger, Edwin S. Notes on the formation of South African foreign policy. Pasadena, 1965.

Afr 5235.55.5 Mungo Park. (Hewitt, William Henry.) London, 1923.

Afr 5235.55 Mungo Park. (MacLachlan, T. Banks.) London, 1898.

Afr 5235.55.15 Mungo Park and the Niger. (Thomson, Joseph.) London, 1890.

Afr 5235.55.10 Mungo Park and the quest of the Niger. (Gwynn, Stephen.) N.Y., 1935.

Afr 5235.52.5 Mungo Parks Reise in das Innere von Afrika in den Jahren 1795, 96, und 97. (Park, Mungo.) Hamburg, 1799.

Afr 6686.48.40F Munich. Institut für Wirtschaftsforschung. Les finances publiques du Togo, budget-fiscalité; situation, 1965-perspectives, 1970. München, 1965.

Afr 6686.48.20F Munich. Institut für Wirtschaftsforschung. Plan de développment économique et social, 1966-1970; l'artisanat togolais. Munich, 1965.

Afr 6686.48.30F Munich. Institut für Wirtschaftsforschung. Plan de développment économique et social, 1966-1970; le commerce au Togo. Munich, 1965.

Afr 3204.15 Munier, Jules. La presse en Egypte, 1799-1900. Le Caire, 1930.

Afr 1609.12.4 Munoz, I. La agonia del Mogreb. Madrid, 1912.

Afr 1739.3 Munoz, I. La corte de Tetuan. Madrid, 1913.

Afr 1609.13.6 Munoz, I. En el pais de los cherifes. Madrid, 1913.

Afr 9161.15 Munro, A. The Transvaal (Chinese) labour problem. London, 1906.

Afr 609.58.10 Muntu. (Jahn, Janheinz.) Düsseldorf, 1958.

Afr 609.58.12 Muntu. (Jahn, Janheinz.) London, 1961.

Afr 4070.1 Munzinger, W. Ostafrikanische Studien. Basle, 1883.

Afr 4558.59 Munzinger, W. Über die Sitten und das Recht der Bogos. Winterthur, 1859.

Afr 2945.20 Mura, Nicolo. La terra delle donne tenebrose. Bologna, 1930.

Afr 2804.5 Murabet, Mohammed. A bibliography of Libya. Valetta, 1959.

Afr 2819.64 Murabet, Mohammed. Facts about Libya. 3rd ed. Malta, 1964.

Afr 2819.60 Murabet, Mohammed. Some facts about Libya. Malta, 1960.

Afr 2225.18 Muracciole, Luc. L'émigration algérienne. Alger, 1950.

Afr 1495.6.30 Muratet, Roger. On a tué Ben Barka. Paris, 1967.

Afr 5408.16 Muraz, Gaston. Satyres illustrées de l'Afrique noire. Paris, 1947.

Afr 630.59 Murdock, George. Africa. N.Y., 1959.

Afr 1608.68 Murga, Jose Maria de. Recuerdos marroquies. Madrid, 1906.

Afr 1608.68.5 Murga, José Maria de. Recuerdos marroquies del moro vizcaino. Barcelona, 1913.

Afr 4559.68.5 Murphy, Dervla. In Ethiopia with a mule. London, 1968.

Afr 8849.12 Murray, Andrew. The political philosophy of J.A. de Mist. Cape Town, 1959.

Afr 6210.64.5 Murray, D.J. The work of administration in Nigeria; case studies. London, 1969.

Afr 6210.64 Murray, David John. The progress of Nigerian public administration: a report on research. Ibadan, 1968.

Afr 1608.59 Murray, E. Sixteen years in Morocco. London, 1859. 2v.

Afr 9291.5 Murray, Emma (Rutherford). Young Mrs. Murray goes to Bloemfontein, 1856-1869. Cape Town, 1954.

Afr 4012.1 Murray, G.W. Sons of Ishmael. London, 1935.

Afr 608.53 Murray, H. The African continent. London, 1853.

Afr 608.18 Murray, H. Historical account of discoveries and travels in Africa. Edinburgh, 1818. 2v.

Afr 608.30.3 Murray, H. Narrative of discovery and adventure in Africa. Edinburgh, 1832.

Afr 608.30.5 Murray, H. Narrative of discovery and adventure in Africa. 4th ed. Edinburgh, 1844.

Afr 11586.77.100 Murray, M. The fire-raisers. London, 1953.
Afr 8847.34.50 Murray, Marischal. Under lion's head. 2. ed. Cape Town, 1964.
Afr 8088.91 Murray, R.W. South Africa from Arab domination to British rule. London, 1891.
Afr 9839.22.5 Murray, S.S. A handbook of Nyasaland. London, 1932.
Afr 4095.8.5 Murray, T.D. Sir S.W. Baker, a memoir. London, 1895.
Afr 2030.461.55 Mus, Paul. Guerre sans visage. Paris, 1961.
Afr 6900.25 Muschel. Swakopmund. 1961+
Afr 6686.25 La muse en valeur du Togo sous le mandat français. Thèse. (Samuel, Ferjus.) Paris, 1926.
Afr 608.25 Museum Africanum. (Hulbert, Charles.) London, 1825.
Afr 6196.12 Musgrave, George Clarke. To Kumassi with Scott. London, 1896.
Afr 8813.2 Die musieklewe van Kaapstad, 1800-1850. Thesis. (Bouws, Jan.) Kaapstadt, 1966.
Afr 8028.40 Musiker, R. Guide to South African reference books. 3d ed. Grahamstown, 1963.
Afr 7850.40 Musini, P. Kantanga, pelli di fuoco. Parma, 1961.
Afr 5187.20 Muslim brotherhoods and politics in Senegal. (Behrman, Lucy C.) Cambridge, 1970.
Afr 2209.60.5 Muslim Students Federation. Life in Algeria. 3 ed. London, 1960.
Afr 575.58 Muslims and chiefs in West Africa. (Leutzion, Nehemia.) Oxford, 1968.
Afr 5318.45 Mussa; ein Kind aus Guinea. (Youla, Nabi.) Regensburg, 1964.
Afr 4431.30 Mussolini, Vittorio. Voli sulle ambe. Firenze, 1937.
Afr 4513.35.90 Mussolini over Africa. (Ridley, F.A.) London, 1935.
Afr 3675.9 Mustafa, O.M. Le Soudan égyptien. Thèse. Neuville-sur-Saone, 1931.
Afr 6780.43 Mustafa, Sophia. The Tanganyika way. London, 1962.
Afr 2030.460 Mustapha G. Barberousse. Paris, 1960.
Afr 2228.10 La musulmane algérienne. (Marchand, Henri.) Rodez, 1960.
Afr 5767.2 Les Musulmans à Madagascar. v.1-3. (Ferrand, G.) Paris, 1891-1902. 2v.
Afr 2225.16 Les Musulmans algériens en France et dans les pays islamiques. (Roger, J.J.) Paris, 1950.
Afr 575.32 Les musulmans d'Afrique Noire. (Froelich, Jean Claude.) Paris, 1962.
Afr 2225.5 Les Musulmans français du nord de l'Afrique. (Hamet, I.) Paris, 1906.
Afr 7803.10 Les Musulmans noirs du Maniema. (Abel, Armand.) Bruxelles, 1960.
Afr 1268.8 Mutations culturelles et coopération au Maghreb. Paris, 1969.
Afr 6542.5.15 Mutesa II, King of Buganda. Desecration of my kingdom. London, 1967.
Afr 635.60 Muthesius, A. Die Afrikanerin. Düsseldorf, 1959.
Afr 9047.39 Mutwa, Vusamazulu Credo. My people, my Africa. 1st American ed. N.Y., 1969.
Afr 3079.54 al-Muwaylihi, Ibrahim. Le paysan d'Egypte à travers l'histoire. Le Caire, 1954.
Afr 1273.968 Muzikář, Joseph. Les Perspectives de l'intégration des pays maghrébins et leur attitude vis-à-vis du Marché commun. Nancy, 1968.
Afr 6715.1 Mveny, Engelbert. Histoire du Cameroun. Paris, 1963.
Afr 9860.276 Mwase, George Simeon. Strike a blow and die. Cambridge, 1967.
Afr 6750.10 Mwenge. Dar es Salaam. 2,1962+
Afr 41918.5 Mwindo (Nyanga Folk Epic). English and Nyanga. The Mwindo epic from the Banyanga (Congo Republic). Berkeley, 1969.
Afr 41918.5 The Mwindo epic from the Banyanga (Congo Republic). (Mwindo (Nyanga Folk Epic). English and Nyanga.) Berkeley, 1969.
Afr 7809.11 My adventures in the Congo. (Roby, Marguerite.) London, 1911.
Afr 609.46 My Africa. (Ojike, Nbonu.) N.Y., 1940.
Htn Afr 699.08.4* My African journey. (Churchill, Winston S.) London, 1908.
Afr 699.08.4.5 My African journey. (Churchill, Winston S.) N.Y., 1909.
Afr 9854.10 My African reminiscences. (Johnson, William Percival.) Westminster, 1926.
Afr 5406.56 My Apingi kingdom. (Duchaillu, Paul Belloni.) N.Y., 1874.
Afr 8659.59.3 My beloved country. (Boydell, T.) Cape Town, 1960.
Afr 8325.70 My bollingskap (St. Helena). (Kotzé, C.R.) Bloemfontein, 1942.
Afr 9028.80 My chief and I, or Six months in Natal. (Wylde, A.) London, 1880.
Afr 555.23.20 My children of the forest. (Hensey, Andrew F.) N.Y., 1924.
Afr 8152.91 My command in South Africa 1874-8. (Cunynghame, A.T.) London, 1879.
Afr 7580.6 My Congo adventure. (Roberts, John.) London, 1963.
Afr 8300.10 My diocese during the war. (Baynes, A.H.) London, 1909.
Afr 6298.181.2 My early life. (Awolowo, Obaf.) Lagos, 1968.
Afr 8687.262 My eerste neentig jaar. (Louw, Abraham F.) Kaapstad, 1958.
Afr 8289.01.5 My experiences of the Boer war. (Sternberg, A.) London, 1901. 2v.
Afr 7920.3.15 My fifteen months in government. (Tshombe, Moise.) Plano, Tex., 1967.
Afr 9170.7 My fifty-odd years in Johannesburg. (Behrman, F.) Johannesburg, 1961.
Afr 6390.53 My forty years in Africa. (Burger, John F.) London, 1960.
Afr 3979.42 My goodness. My passport. (Florence, L.S.) London, 1942.
Afr 724.4 My journey from Rhodesia to Egypt. (Kassner, Theo.) London, 1911.
Afr 6878.73.5 My Kalulu, prince, king and slave. (Stanley, H.M.) London, 1873.
Afr 6878.73.10 My Kalulu, prince, king and slave. (Stanley, H.M.) N.Y., 1874.
Afr 6878.73.15 My Kalulu, prince, king and slave. (Stanley, H.M.) N.Y., 1969.
Afr 6455.130 My Kenya acres. (Lander, Cherry.) London, 1957.
Afr 11795.4.100 My leaves are green. (Slatter, Eve Mary.) Cape Town, 1964.
Afr 6298.202 My life. (Bello, Ahmadu.) Cambridge, 1962.
Afr 4095.19 My life in four continents. v.1-2. (Chaille-Long, C.) London, 1912. 2v.
Afr 10690.89.100 My life in the bush of ghosts. (Tutuola, Amos.) London, 1954.
Afr 11853.88.100 My life in the bush of ghosts. (Tutuola, Amos.) N.Y., 1954.
Afr 1769.5 My life story. (Dewazan, Emily.) London, 1911.

Afr 5227.10.5 My march to Timbuctoo. (Joffre, J.J.C.) London, 1915.
Afr 5227.10 My march to Timbuctoo. (Joffre, J.J.C.) N.Y., 1915.
Afr 4558.92.9 My mission to Abyssinia. (Portal, G.H.) London, 1892.
Afr 555.23.5 My Ogowe being a narrative of daily incidents during sixteen years in West Africa. (Nassau, Robert H.) N.Y., 1914.
Afr 9047.39 My people, my Africa. 1st American ed. (Mutwa, Vusamazulu Credo.) N.Y., 1969.
Afr 718.16 My personal experience in equatorial Africa. (Parke, T.H.) London, 1891.
Afr 718.16.3 My personal experience in equatorial Africa. 3d ed. (Parke, T.H.) London, 1891.
Afr 8252.21 My reminiscences. (Sampson, Victor.) London, 1926.
Afr 8289.02.22.2 My reminiscences of Anglo-Boer war. (Viljoen, B.J.) London, 1902.
Afr 6780.10.5 My reminiscences of East Africa. (Lettow-Vorbeck, P.E. von.) London, 1920.
Afr 9489.69 My Rhodesia. (Strauss, Frances.) Boston, 1969.
Afr 718.7 My second journey through Africa. (Wissmann, H.) London, 1891.
Afr 3700.8 My six years with the Black Watch, 1881-1887. (Gordon, John.) Boston, 1929.
Afr 4969.13 My Somali book. (Mosse, A.H.E.) London, 1913.
Afr 4070.28 My Sudan year. (Stevens, E.S.) London, 1912.
Afr 6780.28 My Tanganyika service and some Nigeria. (Cameron, D.) London, 1939.
Afr 555.24.2 My third campaign in East Africa. (Price, William S.) London, 1891.
Afr 9689.8 My travels in north west Rhodesia. (Butt, G.E.) London, 1908.
Afr 5480.243.3 My travels through Chad. (Lapie, Pierre O.) London, 1943.
Afr 609.28.10 My two African journeys. (Gray, Frank.) London, 1928.
Afr 8252.322 My vanished Africa. (Rainier, P.W.) New Haven, 1940.
Afr 4070.19 My wanderings in the Soudan. (Speedy, C.M.) London, 1884. 2v.
Afr 3978.76.4 My winter on the Nile. (Warner, C.D.) Boston, 1876.
Afr 3978.76.4.5 My winter on the Nile. (Warner, C.D.) Boston, 1881.
Afr 3978.76.3 My winter on the Nile. (Warner, C.D.) Hartford, 1876.
Afr 3978.76.5 My winter on the Nile. v.1-2. (Warner, C.D.) Leipzig, 1891.
Afr 6174.11 Myatt, Fred. The golden stool. London, 1966.
Afr 4070.20 Myers, A.B.R. Life with the Hamran Arabs. London, 1876.
Afr 7903.3 Myers, John Brown. Thomas J. Comber, missionary pioneer to the Congo. London, 1888.
Afr 630.52 Mylius, N. Afrika Bibliographie. Wien, 1952.
Afr 5585.20 Le Myre de Vilers. (Grandidier, G.) Paris, 1923.
Afr 1571.5A Le mystère d'Agadir. (Tardieu, A.) Paris, 1912.
Afr 2929.25 Mysteries of the Libyan desert. (King, William Joseph Harding.) London, 1925.
Afr 1571.22 La mystérieuse Ouaouizert. (Babin, Gustave.) Casablanca, 1923.
Afr 2749.29.5 Mysterious Sahara, the land of gold, of sand, and of ruin. (Khun de Prorok, B.) London, 1930.
Afr 210.60.60 Myth in modern Africa. (Rhodes-Livingstone Institute, Lusaka, Northern Rhodesia. Conference, 14th, Lusaka, 1960.) Lusaka, 1960.
Afr 6178.20 A myth is broken. (Ocran, A.K.) Harlow, 1968.
Afr 6412.7 The myth of Mau Mau. (Rosberg, Carl Gustav.) Stanford, Calif., 1966.
Afr 39906.5 Le mythe et les contes de sou en pays Mbaï-Moïssala. Paris, 1967.
Afr 2232.3A Le Mzab. (Coyne, A.) Alger, 1879.
Afr 2232.2 Le Mzab et les Mzabites. (Amat, C.) Paris, 1888.
Afr 2232.1 Le Mzab son annexion. (Robin.) Alger, 1884.
Afr 9446.33 Mziki. 'Mlimo. Pietermaritzburg, 1926.
Afr 8687.278 N Nederlander in diens van-die Oranjevrystaat. (Mueller, H.P.N.) (Spies, F.J. du T.) Amsterdam, 1946.
Afr 3979.58.5 Na beregakin Nila. (Kondrashov, S.N.) Moscow, 1958.
Afr 3979.60 Na drevnei zemle. (Dynkin, A.V.) Stalingrad, 1960.
Afr 7309.55 Na fogueira do jornalismo. (Fonseca, M. da.) Lourenço Marques, 1955.
Afr 7065.510 Na Guiné, 1907-1908. (Chagas, Frederico Pinheiro.) Lisboa, 1910.
Afr 7175.35 Na pista do marfim e da morte. (Costa, Ferreira da.) Porto, 1944.
Afr 679.61.10 Na potudnie od Sahary. (Halpern, Jan.) Warsawa, 1961.
Afr 8657.19.3F Naaukeurige en uitvoerige beschryving van de Kaap de Goede Hoop. (Kolbe, Peter.) Amsterdam, 1727. 2v.
Afr 2680.5 Nabeul et ses environs, étude d'une population tunisienne. (Coque, Roger.) Paris, 1965?
Afr 6470.278 Nabongo Mumia of the Baluyia. (Osogo, John.) Nairobi, 1965?
Afr 7110.10 A nação una. (Matos, J.M.R.N.) Lisboa, 1953.
Afr 2674.2 Naceur. Description et histoire de l'île de Djerba. Tunis, 1884.
Afr 2208.66.5 Nach Algier. (Rasch, Gustav.) Dresden, 1875.
Afr 2208.66.3 Nach den Oasen von Siban. (Rasch, Gustav.) Berlin, 1866.
Afr 2376.2 Nach der Oase Tugurt in der Wüste Sahara. (Baader, Walter.) Basel, 1903.
Afr 6990.79 Nach Kamerun. (Scholl, Carl.) Leipzig, 1886.
Afr 1432.24 Nach Marokko. (Baeumen, A. von.) Berlin, 1861.
Afr 6143.16.5 Nachrichten von der Sierra Leona Küste. (Winterbottom, T.) Weimar, 1805.
Afr 1607.81 Nachrichten von Morokos und Fes. (Hoest, G.) Kopenhagen, 1781.
Afr 658.79 Nachtigal, S. Sahara und Sudan. Berlin, 1879-89.
Afr 1069.55 Naci, Hikmet. Tarih hoyunca kujey Afrika. Istanbul, 1955?
Afr 6280.62 Nadel, Siegfried F. A black Byzantium; the Kingdom of Nupe. London, 1942.
Afr 6280.62.3 Nadel, Siegfried F. A black Byzantium; the Kingdom of Nupe. London, 1951.
Afr 9488.94.5 Nadellaic, Jean François Albert du Pouget Marquis de. Le Mashonaland. Paris, 1894.
Afr 1406.5 Nader tractaet van oredeende vrundtschap...22 marti 1657. Hague, 1659.
Afr 11433.74.800 Nadine Gordimer. (Nell, Racilla Jilian.) Johannesburg, 1964.
Afr 2030.462.30 Naegelen, Marcel. Mission en Algérie. Paris, 1962.
Afr 2035.7 Naegelen, Marcel. Une route plus large que longue. Paris, 1965.
Afr 1620.25.5 Nagel, Publishers. Maroc. Genève, 1966.
Afr 1620.25 Nagel, Publishers. Morocco. Paris, 1953.
Afr 7850.56 Nagy, Laszló. Katanga. Lausanne, 1965.
Afr 3986.1 Nahas, Joseph F. Situation économique et sociale du fellah égyptien. Paris, 1901.
Afr 1609.30.25 Nahon, Moise. Propos d'un vieux marocain. Paris, 1930.

Afr 6164.30 The native states of the Gold Coast. (Welman, Charles Wellesley.) London, 1969.
Afr 6985.12 The native tribes of South West Africa. 1st ed. (Kahn, Carl Hugo Linsingen.) London, 1966.
Afr 6985.1 Native tribes of Southwest Africa. Cape Town, 1928.
Afr 9700.16 The native tribes of the eastern province of Northern Rhodesia. 2nd ed. (Poole, Edward Humphry Lane.) Lusaka, 1938.
Afr 9853.1A Natives of British Central Africa. (Werner, A.) London, 1906.
Afr 6192.22 The natives of northern territories of Gold Coast. (Cardinall, Alan W.) London, 1920.
Afr 8678.7 The natives of South Africa. (South African Native Races Comittee.) London, 1901.
Afr Doc 4312.129 Natives parliamentary representation bill. (South Africa. Parliament.) Cape Town, 1929.
Afr Doc 4312.130 Natives Parliamentary Representation Bill. (South Africa. Parliament.) Cape Town, 1930.
Afr 9161.5 Natives under the Transvaal flag. (Bovill, J.H.) London, 1900.
Afr 50.51 Natsional'naia gosudarstvennost' narodov Zapadnoi i Tsentral'noi Afriki. (Entin, Lev M.) Moskva, 1966.
Afr 7135.1 Natsional'naia revoliutsiia v Angole. (1961-1965gg.). (Oganis'ian, Iulii S.) Moskva, 1968.
Afr 626.186 Natsional'no-demokraticheskoe gosudarstvo i ekonomicheskii progress. (Entin, Lev M.) Moskva, 1968.
Afr 2025.32 Natsionalno-osvoboditelnoe dvizhenie v Alzhire. (Landa, R.G.) Moscow, 1962.
Afr 725.13 A naturalist in mid-Africa. (Elliot, G.F.S.) London, 1896.
Afr 4050.4 Naturgeschichtliche Reisen durch Nord-Afrika und West-Asien. (Ehrenburg, C.G.) Berlin, 1828.
Afr 2749.68.5 Nau, Christian. La première traversée du Sahara en char a voile. Condé-sur-l'Escaut, 1968.
Afr 11598.89.100 Naude, Adele. Only a setting forth, poems. Cape Town, 1965.
Afr 6990.6 Naude, C.P. Ongebaande wee. Kaapstad, 1931.
Afr 8320.10 Naude, J.F. Vechten en vluchten van beyers en kemp. Rotterdam, n.d.
Afr 5180.13 Naufrage de la frigate La Méduse. (Correard, A.) Paris, 1818.
Afr 1608.21 Naufrage du brick français la sophie. v.1-2. (Cochelet, C.) Paris, 1821. 2v.
Afr 8678.70 Naught for your comfort. (Huddleston, T.) Garden City, 1956.
Afr 8160.14 Naval brigade in South Africa during...1877-78-79. (Norbury, H.F.) London, 1880.
Afr 4392.20 Navarotto, Adriano. Il contegno della Santa Sede nel conflitto italo-etiopico. Vicenza, 1936.
Afr 1432.21.2 Navarrete, José. Desde Vad-Ras a Sevilla: Acuarelas de la campaña de Africa. 2a ed. Madrid, 1880.
Afr 5920.3 Navarro, J.J. Apuntes sobre el estado de la costa occidental. Madrid, 1859.
Afr 8279.00.56 Naville, Edouard. L'indépendance des républiques sud-africaines et l'Angleterre. Genève, 1900.
Afr 555.20.10 Naw, Henry. We move into Africa. Saint Louis, Mo., 1945.
Afr 550.33.5 Naylor, W.S. Daybreak in the dark continent. 2d ed. Boston, 1905.
Afr 2929.12.11 Nazari, V. Tripolitania. 2 ed. Roma, 1912.
Afr 2030.461.80 Nazoun, Amar. Ferhat Abbas. Paris, 1961.
Afr 12634.16.100 Ndao, H. Alion. L'Exil d'Albouri. Suivi de La décision. Honfleur, 1967.
Afr 6280.9.40 Ndem, Eyo B.E. Ibos in contemporary nigerian politics. Onitsha, 1961.
Afr 632.54 N'Diaye, Jean Pierre. Élites africaines et culture occidentale, assimilation ou resistance? Paris, 1969.
Afr 5183.961 Ndiaye, M. Le Sénégal à l'heure de l'indépendance. Doullens, 1961.
Afr 8252.37 Neame, L.E. General Hertzog, Prime Minister of the Union of South Africa since 1924. London, 1930.
Afr 8678.260 Neame, L.E. The history of apartheid. London, 1962.
Afr 8055.30 Neame, L.E. Some South African politicians. Cape Town, 1929.
Afr 9165.42.45 Neame, Lawrence. City built on gold. Johannesburg, 1960.
Afr 8680.40 Neame, Lawrence Elvin. White man's Africa. Cape Town, 1952.
Afr 1947.5 Neapolitan captive, interesting narrative of the captivity and sufferings of V. Laranda. (Laranda, V.) N.Y., 1830.
Afr 1110.25 Near East Conference. Current problems in North Africa. Princeton, 1960.
Afr 1658.39 Nearing, Scott. Stopping at war. N.Y., 1926.
Afr 1609.57 Nebel, Gerhard. An den Saulen des Herakles. Hamburg, 1957.
Afr 609.36.5 Nebel, Heinrich C. Ein Journalist erzählt. Stuttgart, 1936.
Afr 1990.11 Nécessité de la colonisation de l'Algérie. (Baillet, Noël Bernard.) Paris, 1857.
Afr 8110.7 Nederburgh, S.C. Echte stukken. Haage, 1803.
Afr 8678.345 Nederduits Gereformeerde Kerk in Suid Afrika. Statements on race relations. Johannesburg. 1,1960//?
Afr 9165.5 Die nederduitsch hervormde gemeente zurust (Marico). (Engelbrecht, S.P.) n.p., 1946.
Afr 9148.99.5F Nederland-Zuid-Afrika. (Harpen, N. van.) Amsterdam, 1899.
Afr 8095.35 Nederland-Zuid-Afrika. (Nederlandisch-Zuid-Afrikaansche Vereeniging.) Amsterdam, 1931.
Afr 8095.35 Nederlandisch-Zuid-Afrikaansche Vereeniging. Nederland-Zuid-Afrika. Amsterdam, 1931.
Afr 8110.3.30 Nederlandsch Genootschap voor Geslacht, The Hague. Jan van Riebeeck. 's-Gravenhage, 1952.
Afr 8028.110 Nederlandsch-Zuid-Afrikansche Vereeniging. Bibliothek. Catalogues. Amsterdam, 1939.
Afr 8028.111 Nederlandsch-Zuid-Afrikansche Vereeniging. Bibliothek. Supplements. 1939+
Afr 8110.4 Nederlandsche commissarissen aan de Kaap, 1657-1700. (Boeseken, A.J.) 's-Gravenhage, 1938.
Afr 8680.22 Nederlandsch immigrante. (Loedolff, J.F.) Kaapstad, 1960.
Afr 8680.10 De Nederlandse stam in Zuid-Afrika. (Hettema, H.H.) Zutphen, 1949.
Afr 2355.5 Nedromah et les Traras. (Basset, René.) Paris, 1901.
Afr 628.256 Neger, Jazz und tiefer Süden. (Bartah, Ernst.) Leipzig, 1956.
Afr 1965.27 Négociation entre monseigneur l'évêque d'Alger et Abd el-qader. (Berbrugger, L.A.) Paris, 1844.
Afr 1550.15 Négociation franco-espagnole de 1902. (Rouard de Card, E.) Paris, 1912.

Afr 3305.5 Les négociations anglo-égyptiennes de 1950-1951 sur Suez et le Soudan. (Moussa, F.) Genève, 1955.
Afr 7309.04 Negreiros, A. Le Mozambique. Paris, 1904.
Afr 630.8.10 Les Nègres. (Delafosse, Maurice.) Paris, 1927.
Afr 5058.6 Les Nègres de l'Afrique sus-équatoriale. (Hovelacque, Abel.) Paris, 1889.
Afr 590.48 Negriers et bois d'ébène. (Martin, Gaston.) Grenoble, 1934.
Afr 10007.2.5 Négritude; essays and studies. (Berrian, Albert H.) Hampton, 1967.
Afr 628.259 El Negro. (Betancourt, J.R.) La Habana, 1959.
Afr 628.215A The Negro. (Dubois, W.E.B.) N.Y., 1915.
Afr 630.65.10 De Negro-Afrikaanse mens en zijn cultuur. Brugge, 1965.
Afr 628.245 The Negro and the post-war world. (Logan, Rayford W.) Washington, 1945.
Afr 628.225.15 The Negro around the world. (Price, W.) N.Y., 1926.
Afr 7465.6 Negro culture in West Africa. (Ellis, G.W.) N.Y., 1914.
Afr 7180.20 O negro de Menongue, notas antropologicas e etnograficas. (Sarmento, Alexandre.) Lisboa, 1945.
Afr 628.210 The Negro in the new world. (Johnston, H.H.) London, 1910.
Afr 590.20 The Negro problem solved. (Read, Hollis.) N.Y., 1864.
Afr 590.20.2 The Negro problem solved. (Read, Hollis.) N.Y., 1969.
Afr 635.1A The Negro races, a sociological study. (Dowd, J.) N.Y., 1907. 2v.
Afr 7369.09 The Negro Republic on West Africa. (Karnga, A.W.) Monrovia, 1909.
Afr 630.44 Negro types, 65 pictures. London, 1944.
Afr 628.168 The Negroes in Negroland. (Helper, H.R.) N.Y., 1868.
Afr 630.8.5 The Negroes of Africa. (Delafosse, Maurice.) Washington, 1931.
Afr 608.41.5A The Negroland of the Arabs examined and explained. 2nd ed. (Cooley, William Desborough.) London, 1966.
Afr 3310.5 Neguib, M. Egypt's destiny. London, 1955.
Afr 3310.5.2 Neguib, M. Egypt's destiny. 1st American ed. Garden City, 1955.
Afr 4558.92 Negus negusti. (Villiers, F.) N.Y., 1892.
Afr 8310.9 Neilly, J.E. Besieged with Baden-Powell. Record of siege. London, 1900.
Afr 9047.5.40 Neilson, Agnes J. An index to Joseph Shooter: the Kafirs of Natal and the Zulu country. Johannesburg, 1967.
Afr 115.114 Neitralizm gosudarstv Afrikii. (Melikian, Ovanes N.) Moskva, 1966.
Afr 40.67.10 Nekapitalisticheskii put' razvitiia stran Afriki. Moskva, 1967.
Afr 115.116 Nekotorye voprosy istorii Afriki. Moskva, 1968.
Afr 8659.62 Nel, Andries. Stad en dorp. Stellenbosch, 1962.
Afr 2850.10F Nel centenario della spedizione navale di Tripoli. (Gonni, G.) Genova, 1925.
Afr 2748.32 Nel Fezzan, aprile, maggio 1932. (Bargagli-Petrucci, O.) Firenze, 1934.
Afr 2948.16 Nel Fezzan. (Zoli, Corrado.) Milano, 1926.
Afr 1713.7 Nel marocco. (Cisotti-Ferrara, M.) Milano, 1912.
Afr 7815.12 Nel paese dei Bango-bango. (Piscelli, M.) Napoli, 1909.
Afr 9549.61 Nel paese dei Bantu. (Cerulli, Ernesta.) Torino, 1961.
Afr 6542.45 Nel paese dei bevitori di sangue; genti nuove alla ribalta: il popolo Karimojòng. (Farina, Felice.) Bologna, 1965.
Afr 4747.1 Nel paese dei Cunama, 1922-23. (Calciatti, C.) Milano, 1927.
Afr 4700.37.15 Nel piano dell'impero. (Fornaciari, J.) Bologna, 1937.
Afr 4700.37.20 Nel sud dell'impero. (Vecchi, B.V.) Milano, 1937.
Afr 11433.74.800 Nell, Racilla Jilian. Nadine Gordimer. Johannesburg, 1964.
Afr 4559.30.5 Nell impero del negus neghest. (Ciravegna, G.) Torino, 1933.
Afr 4742.17.3 Nella colonia Eritrea. (Paoli, Renato.) Milano, 1908.
Afr 4582.10 Nella Dancalia etiopica. (Franchetti, R.) Milano, 1930.
Afr 2870.8 Nella Libia italiana. (Cottafari, V.) Bologna, 1912.
Afr 4785.934.5 Nella piu lontana terra dell'impero. (Neuhaus, V.) Bologna, 1937.
Afr 4559.15 Nella terra del nègès. (Castro, Lincoln de.) Milano, 1915. 2v.
Afr 4718.91.20 Nell'Africa italiana. (Martini, Ferdinando.) Milano, 1895.
Afr 6689.10 Nelle, Albrecht. Aufbruch vom Götterberg. Stuttgart, 1968.
Afr 2875.16 Nelle trincee di Tripoli. (Castellini, G.) Bologna, 1912.
Afr 4700.37.12 Nell'impero liberato. (Lischi, D.) Pisa, 1938.
Afr 6883.18 Nelson, Anton. The freemen of Meru. Nairobi, 1967.
Afr 4115.17 Nelson, Nina. Shepheard's hotel. London, 1960.
Afr 7803.15 Nelson, Robert G. Congo crisis and Christian mission. St. Louis, 1961.
Afr 150.2.20 Nemesio, Vitorino. Vida e obra do Infante Dom Henrique. Lisboa, 1959. 2v.
Afr 5758.30 Nemours, C.P. Madagascar et ses richesses. Paris, 1930.
Afr 4513.35.158 Nenni, P. Il destino africano del fascismo. Paris, 1935.
Afr 10005.3.1 Neo-African literature. (Jahn, Janheinz.) N.Y., 1969.
Afr 626.146 Neo-colonialism. (Nkrumah, Kwame.) London, 1965.
Afr 2442.5 Néo-Destour Congrès, 7th, Bizerte. Septième congrès. Tunis, 1965.
Afr 2532.10 Le Néo-Destour face à la première épreuve, 1934-36. Tunis, 1965.
Afr 500.85 Neokolonializm v Afrike. Moskva, 1967.
Afr 5054.62 Neres, Philip. French-speaking West Africa. London, 1962.
Afr 4513.39.10 Neri, Italo. La questione del Nilo. Roma, 1939.
Afr 2030.464.60 Nerushimaia druzhba i bratstvo. (Pravda, Moscow.) Moscow, 1964.
Afr 2209.06.15 Nesbitt, Frances E. Algeria and Tunis. London, 1906.
Afr 4582.15 Nesbitt, L.M. La Dancalia esplorata. Firenze, 1930.
Afr 4582.15.5 Nesbitt, L.M. Hell-hole of creation. N.Y., 1935.
Afr 7575.95 Netherlands. Department van Buitenlandse Zaken. Kongo en de Verenigde Naties. 's-Gravenhage, 1961- 2v.
Afr 7183.27 Neto, Jose Pereira. O baixo cunene. Lisboa, 1963.
Afr 1957.1 Nettement, A. Histoire de la conquête d'Alger. Paris, 1867.
Afr 8377.2 The nettle. (Schreiner, Oliver Deneys.) Johannesburg, 1964.
Afr 4259.59 Neubacher, Hermann. Die Festung der Löwen. Olten, 1959.
Afr 3979.62.10 Das neue Agypten. (Wohlfahrt, M.) Berlin, 1962.
Afr 8657.77.4 Neue Kurzgefasste Beschreibung des Vorgebirges der guten Hoffnung. Leipzig, 1779.
Afr 8657.90.12 Neue Reise in das Innere von Afrika. (Le Vaillant, F.) Berlin, 1796. 2v.

	Afr 2608.11.5	Neue Reise nach Tunis. (MacGill, Thomas.) Weimar, 1816. 2 pam.
	Afr 8659.05.5	Das neue Südafrika. (Samassa, Paul.) Berlin, 1905.
	Afr 55.15	Die neuen Männer Afrikas. (Italiaander, Rolf.) Düsseldorf, 1960.
	Afr 55.17	Die neuen Männer Afrikas. (Italiaander, Rolf.) Düsseldorf, 1963.
	Afr 5640.15	Neuf ans a Madagascar. (Gallieni, J.S.) Paris, 1908.
	Afr 5765.6.10	Neuf mois à Madagascar. (Escande, Benjamin.) Paris, 1898.
	Afr 12966.2	Neuf poètes camerounais. (Lagneau, Lilyan.) Yaounde, 1965.
	Afr 3730.5	Neufeld, C. A prisoner of the Khaleefa. N.Y., 1899.
	Afr 3730.5.10	Neufeld, C. A prisoner of the Khaleefa. 3d ed. N.Y., 1899.
	Afr 4785.934.5	Neuhaus, V. Nella piu lontana terra dell'impero. Bologna, 1937.
NEDL	Afr 6455.28	Neumann, A.H. Elephant hunting in East Equatorial Africa. London, 1898.
	Afr 1550.27	Neumann, K. Die Internationalität Marokkos. Berlin, 1919.
	Afr 8676.57	Neumark, S.D. Economic influences of the South African frontier. Stanford, 1957.
	Afr 626.126	Neumark, S.D. Foreign trade and economic development in Africa. Stanford, Calif., 1964.
	Afr 1450.6	Neun Jahre in marokkanischen Diensten. (Karow, K.L.) Berlin, 1909.
	Afr 590.77	Neuton, John. The journal of a slave trader, John Neuton, 1750-1754. London, 1962.
	Afr 2875.45	Die Neutralität Deutschlands und Österreich-Ungarns im italienischer Krieg, 1911-1912. Inaug. Diss. (Meyer, Paul.) Göttingen, 1932.
	Afr 5318.3.5	Neuwkeurige beschryning van de Guinese. (Bosman, W.) Amsterdam, 1737.
	Afr 8687.339	Never a young man: extracts from the letters and journals of the Reverend William Shaw. (Shaw, William.) Cape Town, 1967.
	Afr 14518.2	Neves, João Alves das. Poetas e contistas africanos de expressão portuguesa. São Paulo, 1963.
	Afr 2218.10	Neveu, Edouard. Les Khouan. 3. ed. Alger, 1913.
	Afr 5342.15	Neveux, M. Religion des noirs...fétiches de la Côte-d'Ivoire. Alencon, 1923.
	Afr 8300.11	Nevinson, H.W. Ladysmith, the diary of a siege. London, 1900.
	Afr 590.12	Nevinson, H.W. A modern slavery. London, 1906.
NEDL	Afr 6455.27	New, Charles. Life, wanderings, and labours in eastern Africa. London, 1873.
	Afr 4559.38	The new Abyssinia. (Newman, E.W.P.) London, 1938.
Htn	Afr 5318.2*	A new account of parts of Guinea. (Snelgrave, W.) London, 1734.
	Afr 5318.2.89	A new accurate description of the coast of Guinea. (Bosman, W.) London, 1705.
	Afr 210.62.35	The new Africa. (Bow Group Pamphlet.) London, 1962.
	Afr 550.15	The new Africa. (Fraser, Donald.) London, 1927.
	Afr 609.60.5	The new Africa. (Gatti, Ellen.) N.Y., 1960.
	Afr 210.61.15	The new Africa. (Hempstone, Smith.) London, 1961.
	Afr 50.50	The new Africa. (Mair, Lucy Philip.) London, 1967.
	Afr 608.97	The new Africa. (Schulz, A.) London, 1897.
	Afr 109.61.45	New Africa. (Tunis. Secretariat d'Etat à l'Information.) Tunis, 1961.
	Afr 7568.20F	New Africa. Edinburgh, 1904.
	Afr 14.14	New Africa. London. 8,1966+
	Afr 14.5	New Africa. N.Y.
	Afr 14.8	New African. Cape Town. 1,1962+ 4v.
	Afr 55.42	The new Africans. 1st American ed. N.Y., 1967.
	Afr 2030.464.15	The new Algeria. (Joesten, Joachim.) Chicago, 1964.
	Afr 5318.2.89.2	A new and accurate description of the coast of Guinea. (Bosman, W.) London, 1967.
	Afr 10916.3	A new anthology of Rhodesian verse. (Snelling, John.) Oxford, 1950.
	Afr 10005.4	New approaches to African literature. (Ramsaran, J.A.) Ibadan, 1965.
	Afr 8676.32	The new Boer war. (Barnes, L.) London, 1932.
	Afr 7549.48	The new Congo. (Marvel, T.) N.Y., 1948.
	Afr 7549.48.3	The new Congo. 1st British ed. (Marvel, T.) London, 1949.
	Afr 8045.52	The new constitution. (Kahn, Ellison.) London, 1962.
	Afr 8678.318	A new course in South Africa. (United Nations. Secretary-General.) N.Y., 1964.
	Afr 555.75	The new day in Kenya. (Philip, H.R.A.) London, 1936.
	Afr 9436.6	A new deal in central Africa. (Leys, Colin.) London, 1960.
	Afr 6333.55.5	A new deal in East Africa. (Mason, Philip.) London, 1955.
	Afr 626.220	The new diplomacy; international technical cooperation projects of the Republic of China in African countries. (Rowe, David Nelson.) New Haven, 1969.
	Afr 6420.36	A new earth. (Huxley, Elspeth.) London, 1960.
	Afr 3275.19	The new Egypt. (Adams, F.) London, 1893.
	Afr 3979.05.2	New Egypt. (Deguerville, A.B.) London, 1905.
	Afr 710.32.6A	The new elites of tropical Africa. (International African Seminar, 6th, Ibadan, Nigeria, 1964.) London, 1966.
	Afr 8350.30	The new era in South Africa. (Markham, Violet Rosa.) London, 1904.
	Afr 210.61.30	The new face of Africa south of the Sahara. 1st ed. (Hughes, John.) N.Y., 1961.
	Afr 9489.54	The new federation of Rhodesia and Nyasaland. (Federation of Rhodesia and Nyasaland. Federal Information Services.) Salisbury, 1954.
	Afr 210.62.15	New forces in Africa. (Georgetown Colloquium on Africa.) Washington, 1962.
	Afr 505.25	New from Africa. (Hatch, J.C.) London, 1956.
	Afr 10615.5	The new generation: prose and verse from the secondary schools and training colleges of Ghana. Accra, 1967.
	Afr 6275.134	A new geography of Nigeria. (Iloeje, Nwadilibe P.) London, 1969.
	Afr 6176.10	The new Ghana. (Amamoo, J.G.) London, 1958.
	Afr 7350.8	New Hampshire Colonization Society. Report of the board of managers. Concord, N.H.
	Afr 4556.81.11	A new history of Ethiopia. (Ludolf, H.) London, 1682.
	Afr 710.25	New hope in Africa. (Oldham, J.H.) London, 1955.
	Afr 55.16	The new leaders of Africa. (Italiaander, Rolf.) Englewood Cliffs, 1961.
	Afr 7377.64	The new Liberia. (Marinelli, L.A.) N.Y., 1964. 2v.
	Afr 6455.8	New light on dark Africa.%Peters, Carl.) London, 1891.
	Afr 500.13A	The new map of Africa, 1900-16. (Gibbons, H.A.) N.Y., 1916.
	Afr 500.13.5	The new map of Africa, 1900-16. (Gibbons, H.A.) N.Y., 1918.
	Afr 7465.12	The new mathematics and an old culture. (Gay, John H.) N.Y., 1967.
	Afr 609.33.5	A new motor route through Africa. (African Safaris, N.Y.) N.Y., 1933.
	Afr 8340.8	The new nation. A survey of the condition and prospects of South Africa. (Fremantle, H.E.S.) London, 1909.
	Afr 6275.60	The new Nigerian elite. (Smythe, Hugh.) Stanford, 1960.
	Afr 6275.33	New Nigerians. (Dickson, Mora.) London, 1960.
	Afr 679.40	The new Noah' s ark. (Demaison, A.) N.Y., 1940.
	Afr 10575.82.100	The new patriots. (Easmon, R. Sarif.) London, 1965.
	Afr 6200.14.65F	New perspectives. Nsukka, Nigeria. 1,1967+
	Afr 2208.81.9	The new playground...Algeria. (Knox, A.A.) London, 1881.
	Afr 8659.66	The new republic, South Africa's role in the world. (Harrigan, Anthony.) Pretoria, 1966.
	Afr 7375.9.5	The new republic. 2d. ed. (Knight, H.C.) Boston, 1851.
	Afr 3978.71.5	New sea and an old land..visit to Egypt. (Hamley, W.G.) Edinburgh, 1871.
	Afr 626.102	The new societies of tropical Africa. (Hunter, Guy.) London, 1962.
	Afr 8340.7	The new South Africa. (Bleloch, W.) N.Y., 1901.
	Afr 11045.4	New South African writing. Cape Town. 1,1964+ 5v.
	Afr 3979.11.3	The new spirit in Egypt. (Fyfe, H.H.) Edinburgh, 1911.
	Afr 210.67	The new states of Africa. (Rivkin, Arnold.) N.Y., 1967.
	Afr 210.61.90	The new states of Africa. 1st ed. (Vianney, J.J.) n.p. 1961.
	Afr 679.64	The new states of West Africa. (Post, K.W.J.) Harmondsworth, 1964.
	Afr 679.64.2	The new states of West Africa. (Post, K.W.J.) Harmondsworth, 1968.
	Afr 8657.90.11	New travels into the interior parts of Africa. (Le Vaillant, F.) London, 1796. 3v.
	Afr 2929.14	The new Tripoli. (Braun, Ethel.) London, 1914.
	Afr 679.53	The new West Africa. (Davidson, Basil.) London, 1953.
	Afr 4969.63.5	New wind in a dry land. 1. American ed. (Laurence, M.) N.Y., 1964.
	Afr 628.266.5	The new world Negro. (Herskovits, Melville Jean.) Bloomington, 1966.
	Afr 555.9.16	The new world of Central Africa. (Guinness, Fanny E.) London, 1890.
	Afr 10865.5	New writing from Zambia. Lusaka. 1,1966+
	Afr 8028.154	New York (City) Public Library. Works relating to South Africa in the New York Public Library. N.Y., 1899.
	Afr 7350.4	New York Colonization Society (Founded 1823). Report. N.Y. 1,1823+
	Afr 7350.4.10	New York State Colonization Society (Founded 1829). African colonization. Proceedings...of the society. Albany. 1,1829+
	Afr 7350.4.20	New York State Colonization Society (Founded 1832). Annual report. N.Y.
	Afr 7350.4.23	New York State Colonization Society (Founded 1832). Miscellaneous pamphlets. N.Y.
	Afr 7350.4.25	New York State Colonization Society (Founded 1832). Report to board of managers...by O.F.Cook. N.Y.
	Afr 9689.22	The new Zambesi trail. (Mackintosh, Catharine Winkworth.) London, 1922.
	Afr 8292.14.5	The New Zealanders in South Africa. (Hall, David Oswald William.) Wellington, 1949.
	Afr 3745.50	Newbold, D. The making of modern Sudan. London, 1953.
	Afr 6057.65	Newbury, C.W. British policy towards West Africa. Oxford, 1965.
	Afr 6075.16	Newbury, C.W. The West African commonwealth. Durham, N.C., 1964.
	Afr 6075.15	Newbury, C.W. The western Slave Coast and its rulers. Oxford, 1961.
	Afr 550.136	Newington, D. The shape of personality in African Christian leadership. Nelspruit, 1962.
	Afr 550.136.5	Newington, D. The shape of power in Africa. Nelspruit, 1962.
	Afr 6143.21	Newland, H. Sierra Leone, its people, products, and secret societies. London, 1916.
	Afr 6095.322	Newland, M.O. West Africa. London, 1922.
	Afr 1609.53	Newman, B. Morocco today. London, 1953.
	Afr 1259.55	Newman, B. North African journey. London, 1955.
	Afr 8659.65	Newman, Bernard. South African journey. London, 1965.
	Afr 8225.6	Newman, C.L.N. With the Boers in the Transvaal 1880-1. London, 1896.
	Afr 505.9	Newman, E.W.P. Britain and North-east Africa. London, 1940.
	Afr 4389.36A	Newman, E.W.P. Ethiopian realities. London, 1936.
	Afr 4513.37.47	Newman, E.W.P. Italy's conquest of Abyssinia. London, 1937.
	Afr 4559.38	Newman, E.W.P. The new Abyssinia. London, 1938.
	Afr 590.5.8	Newman, Henry S. Banani, the transition of slavery. London, 1898.
	Afr 8735.3	Newman, W.A. Biographical memoir of John Montagu. London, 1855.
	Afr 1.25.10	News. (Africa Bureau, London.) London. 1-5
	Afr 16.13	News bulletin. (Pan-African Cultural Festival.) Algiers. 1,1969+
	Afr 6900.8F	News bulletin. (South West Africa People's Organisation.) Cairo. 4,1965+
	Afr 7458.32	News from Africa. Collection of facts. Baltimore, 1832.
	Afr 628.2.256	News letter. (League of Coloured Peoples.) London.
NEDL	Afr 1303.2	Newsletter. (Committee for Moroccan Studies and Survey.) Rabat.
	Afr 14.12	Newsletter. (Nordiska Afrikainstitutet, Upsala.) Upsala.
	Afr 8340.3.5	Newton, A.P. Select documents relating to the unification of South Africa. London, 1924. 2v.
	Afr 10304.4	Nexus. Nairobi. 1-2,1967-1968//
	Afr 50.52	Nezavisimaia Afrika v dokumentakh. (Moscow. Universitet Druzhby Narodov. Kafedra Inczhdunarodnogo Prava.) Moskva, 1965.
	Afr 626.148	Nezavisimye strany Afriki. (Akademiia Nauk SSSR. Institut Afrikii.) Moskva, 1965.
	Afr 13332.53.100	Ngando (Le crocodile). (Lomami-Tshibamba, Paul.) Bruxelles, 1948.
	Afr 6316.10	Ngano; studies in traditional and modern East African history. Nairobi, 1969.
	Afr 5465.2	Les Ngbaka de la Lobaye. (Thomas, Jacqueline M.C.) Paris, 1963.
	Afr 5405.190	La N'Goko-Sangha. (Violette, M.) Paris, 1914.
	Afr 9853.5	The Ngoni of Nyasaland. (Read, Margaret.) London, 1956.

Afr Doc 2521.10F | Nigeria, Western. House of Chiefs. Report of the Joint Standing Committee on Finance of the Western House of Chiefs and of the Western House of Assembly. Ibadan. 1957+

Afr Doc 2524.5 | Nigeria, Western. Laws, statutes, etc. Local government manual incorporating the Local government law, cop.68, the chiefs law, cop.19 staff regulations. Ibadan, 196-.

Afr Doc 2521.15 | Nigeria, Western. Legislature. Sessional paper. Ibadan. 1955+

Afr Doc 2527.10 | Nigeria, Western. Marketing Board. Annual report. Ibadan. 1,1954+

Afr Doc 2520.955 | Nigeria, Western. Ministry of Economic Planning and Community Development. Statistics Division. Annual abstract of education statistics. 1953+

Afr Doc 2520.703 | Nigeria, Western. Ministry of Economic Planning and Social Development. Statistics Division. Abstract of local government statistics. Ibadan. 1,1966+

Afr Doc 2520.950F | Nigeria, Western. Ministry of Economic Planning and Social Development. Statistics Division. Development plan statistics of western group of provinces of Nigeria. Ibadan, 1966.

Afr 6287.2 | Nigeria, Western. Ministry of Economic Planning and Social Development. Statistics Division. Directory of industrial establishments in Western Nigeria. Ibadan, 1966.

Afr Doc 2520.705 | Nigeria, Western. Ministry of Economic Planning and Social Development. Statistics Division. Statistical bulletin. Ibadan. 1,1959+

Afr 6275.117 | Nigeria, 1966. (Nigeria. Federal Ministry of Research and Information.) Apapa, 1967.

Afr Doc 2305.5 | Nigeria. Annual report on the social and economic progress of the people of Nigeria. Lagos.

Afr Doc 2303.5 | Nigeria. Blue book. Lagos. 1914-1924

Afr 6293.2.5 | Nigeria. Comments of the federal military government on the report of the Tribunal of Inquiry into the affairs of the Lagos City Council for the period Oct. 15, 1962 to Apr. 18, 1966. Lagos, 1966.

Afr 6210.30 | Nigeria. Constitution. n.p., 196-.

Afr 6277.75 | Nigeria. Federal government development programme, 1962-68. Lagos, 1962.

Afr 6277.76.10 | Nigeria. The policy of the Federal Military Government on statutory corporations and state-owned companies. Lagos, 1968.

Afr 6205.2 | Pamphlet vol. Nigeria. 6 pam.

Afr 6214.20 | Nigeria. (Coleman, J.S.) Berkeley, 1958.

Afr 6218.12 | Nigeria. (Davies, H.O.) London, 1961.

Afr 6275.70 | Nigeria. (Great Britain. Central Office of Information.) London, 1960.

Afr 6277.55 | Nigeria. (Industrial Development Conference, Lagos, 1961.) London, 1961.

Afr 6277.60 | Nigeria. (Italy. Istituto Nazionale per il Commercio Estero.) Roma, 1960.

Afr 6275.103 | La Nigeria. (Laroche, H.) Paris, 1962.

Afr 6203.15 | Nigeria. (London. Commonwealth Institute.) London, 1967.

Afr 6212.10 | Nigeria. (Mitchison, Lois.) London, 1960.

Afr 6275.122 | Nigeria. (Niven, Cecil Rex.) London, 1967.

Afr 6212.15 | Nigeria. (Royal Institute of International Affairs.) Oxford, 1960.

Afr 6214.23 | Nigeria. (Schwarz, Walter.) London, 1968.

Afr 6277.70 | Nigeria. Cocoa Marketing Board. Nigerian cocoa farmers. London, 1965.

Afr 6280.56 | Nigeria. Commission Appointed to Enquire into the Fears of Minorities and the Means of Allaying Them. Report. London, 1958.

Afr 6282.17F | Nigeria. Commission Appointed to Enquire into the Owegbe Cult. Report. Benin City, 1966.

Afr 6277.76.5F | Nigeria. Commission of Inquiry into the Affairs of Certain Statutory Corporations in Western Nigeria. An index to the proceedings of the Cokes Commission. Ibadan, 1963.

Afr 6277.76F | Nigeria. Commission of Inquiry into the Affairs of Certain Statutory Corporations in Western Nigeria. Report of Cokes Commission. V.1-4. Lagos, 1962.

Afr 6210.39 | Nigeria. Commission on the Public Services of the Governments in the Federation of Nigeria. Report of the Commission on public services of the governments of Nigeria, 1954-1955. Lagos, 1955.

Afr Doc 2305.10F | Nigeria. Commissioner. Annual report on the colony. Lagos.

Afr Doc 2305.15 | Nigeria. Commissioner. Annual reports for the western, northern, eastern provinces and the colony. Lagos.

Afr Doc 2434.10 | Nigeria. Committee on the Grading of Duty Posts in Voluntary Agency Educational Institutions. Report. Lagos, 1967.

Afr Doc 2319.5 | Nigeria. Constitution. The consitution of the Federal Republic of Nigeria. Lagos, 1963.

Afr 6210.31 | Nigeria. Constitution. The Constitution of the Federal Republic of Nigeria. Lagos, 1963.

Afr Doc 2332.5F | Nigeria. Customs Department. Annual report. Lagos. 1925-1926

Afr Doc 2308.710 | Nigeria. Customs Department. Trade statistical abstract. Lagos. 1-7,1911-1915

Afr 6210.45F | Nigeria. Delimitation Commission. Report of the Constituency Delimitation Commission, 1964. Lagos, 1964.

Afr Doc 2309.305F | Nigeria. Depaartment of Statistics. Urban consumer surveys in Nigeria. Lagos, 1957.

Afr Doc 2330.5 | Nigeria. Department of Antiquities. Annual report. Apapa. 1,1958+

Afr Doc 2307.353 | Nigeria. Department of Statistics. Population census of Nigeria. Lagos. 1952-1953

Afr Doc 2560.725.5 | Nigeria. Department of Statistics. Population census of the Eastern Region of Nigeria, 1953. Bulletins. Lagos, 1955.

Afr Doc 2407.352.105 | Nigeria. Department of Statistics. Population census of the Northern Region of Nigeria, 1952 Bulletins. Lagos, 1954.

Afr Doc 2520.725.5 | Nigeria. Department of Statistics. Population census of the Western region of Nigeria, 1952. Bulletins. Lagos, 1955.

Afr Doc 2520.725 | Nigeria. Department of Statistics. Population census of the Western region of Nigeria, 1952. Lagos, 1956.

Afr 6277.35 | Nigeria. Economic Council. Economic survey of Nigeria, 1959. Lagos, 1959.

Afr 6210.34 | Nigeria. Electoral Committee. Report on the Nigeria federal election. Lagos, 1960.

Afr Doc 2309.310 | Nigeria. Federal Audit Depaartment. Report of the Director of Federal Audit on the accounts of the government. Lagos. 1960

Afr Doc 2307.363.10F | Nigeria. Federal Census Office. Population census of Nigeria, 1963. Northern region. Lagos, 1965. 5v.

Afr 6208.20 | Nigeria. Federal Information Service. Federal Nigeria, annual report. London, 1957.

Afr 6275.126 | Nigeria. Federal Information Service. Nigeria 1960. Lagos, 196-.

Afr Doc 2332.15F | Nigeria. Federal Ministry of Commerce and Industry. Annual report. Lagos. 1958

Afr Doc 2332.10F | Nigeria. Federal Ministry of Commerce and Industry. Annual report. Lagos. 1959+

Afr 6277.120.5 | Nigeria. Federal Ministry of Economic Development. Guide to technical assistance in Nigeria. Lagos, 1965.

Afr 6277.87 | Nigeria. Federal Ministry of Economic Development. Guidepost for Second National Development Plan, June, 1966. Lagos, 1966.

Afr 6277.74 | Nigeria. Federal Ministry of Economic Development. National development plan, 1962-68. Lagos, 1962.

Afr Doc 2309.503 | Nigeria. Federal Ministry of Education. Digest of education statistics. Lagos. 1959

Afr Doc 2309.500 | Nigeria. Federal Ministry of Education. Statistics of education in Nigeria. Lagos. 1,1961+

Afr Doc 2319.15 | Nigeria. Federal Ministry of Finance. Budget speech. Lagos? 1962+

Afr Doc 2309.223 | Nigeria. Federal Ministry of Finance. Report of the accountant-general. Lagos. 1964+

Afr 6291.20F | Nigeria. Federal Ministry of Information. The collapse of Ojukwu's rebellion and prospects for lasting peace in Nigeria. Lagos, 1968.

Afr Doc 2341.15 | Nigeria. Federal Ministry of Labour and Welfare. Social Welfare Division. Annual report. Lagos. 1961+

Afr Doc 2308.524F | Nigeria. Federal Ministry of Research and Information. Estimates. 1962+

Afr 6275.117 | Nigeria. Federal Ministry of Research and Information. Nigeria, 1966. Apapa, 1967.

Afr Doc 2352.3 | Nigeria. Federal Ministry of Works and Surveys. Works Division. Report. Lagos. 1960+

Afr Doc 2307.5 | Nigeria. Federal Office of Statistics. Annual abstract of statistics. 1960+

Afr Doc 2307.7 | Nigeria. Federal Office of Statistics. Digest of statistics. 11,1962+

Afr Doc 2309.300 | Nigeria. Federal Office of Statistics. Economic and functional analysis of government accounts. Lagos. 1958+

Afr Doc 2308.530F | Nigeria. Federal Office of Statistics. Industrial survey. Lagos. 1963+

Afr Doc 2308.300F | Nigeria. Federal Office of Statistics. Report on employment and ear-nings inquiry, Sept., 1959. Lagos, 1959?

Afr Doc 2308.720 | Nigeria. Federal Office of Statistics. Review of external trade. Lagos. 1964

Afr Doc 2309.505F | Nigeria. Federal Office of Statistics. Rural economic survey of Nigeria. Lagos. 1966+

Afr Doc 2308.705 | Nigeria. Federal Office of Statistics. Trade report. Lagos. 1958+

Afr Doc 2309.305.10F | Nigeria. Federal Office of Statistics. Urban consumer surveys. Lagos, 1966. 3v.

Afr Doc 2309.305.5F | Nigeria. Federal Office of Statistics. Urban Consumer surveys in Nigeria. Lagos, 1963.

Afr Doc 2345.10 | Nigeria. Federal Public Service Commission. Report. Lagos. 1959+

Afr Doc 2303.10 | Nigeria. Federal staff list. Lagos. 10,1962+

Afr 6210.8.10 | Nigeria. General Conference. Proceedings of the General conference on review of the constitution. Lagos, 1950.

Afr 6210.38 | Nigeria. Governor-General, 1920. Address delivered at the 7th meeting of Nigeria council held at Lagos. Lagos, 1920.

Afr Doc 2324.5 | Nigeria. Governor General. Address by the Governor the the Nigerian council. 6,1919+

Afr Doc 2324.8 | Nigeria. Governor General. Address by the Governor to the Legislative Council. 1924+

Afr 6280.7.3 | Nigeria: its peoples and its problems. 3rd ed. (Morel, E.D.) London, 1968.

Afr 6293.2.10 | Nigeria. Lagos Executive Development Board Tribunal of Inquiry. Report of the tribunal of inquiry into the affairs of the Lagos Executive Development Board for the period 1st October, 1960 to 31st December, 1965. Lagos, 1968.

Afr Doc 2312.5F | Nigeria. Legislative Council. Debates. Lagos.

Afr 6210.8 | Nigeria. Legislative Council. Review of the constitution. Lagos, 1949.

Afr Doc 2312.10 | Nigeria. Legislative Council. Sessional paper. 1944-1948

Afr Doc 2310.5 | Pamphlet box. Nigeria. Legislative documents.

Afr 6208.8F | Nigeria. National Archives. Annual report.

Afr 6282.37 | Nigeria. National Archives. Index for history of Yoruba Mission (CM.S) 1844-1915, in the National Archives at the University of Ibadan, Western Nigeria. Ibadan, 1965? 5v.

Afr 6203.7.5 | Nigeria. National Archives. An index to organisation and reorganisation reports in record group CS0.26. Ibadan, 1961.

Afr 6295.61F | Nigeria. National Archives. An inventory of the administrative records. Ibadan, 1961.

Afr 6295.61.5F | Nigeria. National Archives. An inventory of the administrative records. Ibadan, 1961.

Afr 6295.63.5F | Nigeria. National Archives. A preliminary inventory of the administrative records assembled from Endo province. Ibadan, 1963.

Afr 6203.7.10F | Nigeria. National Archives. A special list of annual, half-yearly and quarterly reports. Ibadan, 1963.

Afr 6203.7 | Nigeria. National Archives. A special list of records in chieftaincy matters. Ibadan, 1962.

Afr 6203.7.15 | Nigeria. National Archives. Kaduna Branch. An inventory of the records of the Secretariat. Kaduna, 1963.

Afr 6203.20 | Nigeria. National Library. Index to selected Nigerian periodicals. Lagos. 1,1965+

Afr Doc 2342.5 | Nigeria. National Manpower Board. Annual report. Lagos. 1962+

Afr 6277.3 | Nigeria. National Manpower Board. Manpower studies. Lagos. 1,1963+

Afr Doc 2343.5 | Nigeria. Nigerianisation Office. Annual report of the Nigerianisation Office. Lagos, 1957.

Afr 6210.58   Nigeria. Nigerianisation Office. Guide to careers in the federal public service of Nigeria. Lagos, 1961.

Afr 6210.48   Nigeria. Northern Legislature. Report of the Joint Select Committee of the Northern Regional Council, 20th and 21st July, and Northern legislature, 7th, 8th and 9th, August, 1951. Kaduna, 1952.

Afr Doc 2312.15   Nigeria. Parliament. Sessional paper. Lagos. 1958+

Afr Doc 2314.5   Nigeria. Parliament. House of Representatives. Debates. Official report.

Afr Doc 2314.7   Nigeria. Parliament. House of Representatives. Parliamentary debates.

Afr Doc 2314.205   Nigeria. Parliament. House of Representatives. Public Accounts Committee. Minutes of evidence. Lagos. 1960+

Afr Doc 2314.215   Nigeria. Parliament. House of Representatives. Public Accounts Committee. Report. 2,1961+

Afr Doc 2343.20   Nigeria. Petroleum Division. Annual report. Lagos. 1,1962+

Afr Doc 2307.303.2F   Nigeria. Regional Census Office. Population census of Nigeria, Nov., 1963. 2d ed. Ibadan, 1963.

Afr 6210.56.5   Nigeria. Supreme Military Council. Meeting of the Nigerian military leaders held at Peduase Lodge. Lagos, 1967.

Afr 6210.56   Nigeria. Supreme Military Council. The meeting of the Supreme Military Council at Aburi, Accra, Ghana 4-5 January 1967. Enugu, 1967.

Afr 6291.68   Nigeria: the Biafran War. (Metrowich, Frederick Redvers.) Pretoria, 1969.

Afr 6277.2F   Nigeria. University. Economic Development Institute. EDI working papers. Enugu. 1,1965+

Afr 6225.22   Pamphlet vol. Nigeria - Political crisis, 1966-1967. 16 pam.

Afr 6210.13F   Nigeria Ad Hoc Conference on the Nigerian Constitution. The ad hoc conference on the Nigerian constitution. Enugu, 1966.

Afr 6212.44   Nigeria and elective representation, 1923-1947. (Tamsino, Tekena N.) London, 1966.

Afr 6214.33   Nigeria and Ghana. (Flint, John E.) Englewood Cliffs, N.J., 1966.

Afr 6275.42   Nigeria and its tin fields. (Calvert, A.F.) London, 1912.

Afr 6291.46   Nigeria-Biafra; a reading into the problems and peculiarities of the conflict. (Yu, Mok Chiu.) Adelaide, 1968.

Afr 6291.50   The Nigeria-Biafra conflict; report of a one day conference. (Conference on the Nigeria-Biafra Conflict, Washington.) Washington, 1969.

Afr 6298.60A   Nigeria Broadcasting Corporation. Eminent Nigerians of the nineteenth century. Cambridge, 1960.

Afr Doc 2303.15   The Nigeria civil service list. Lagos. 1927

Afr 6291.24   Pamphlet vol. Nigeria civil war. 14 pam.

Afr 6291.22   Pamphlet vol. Nigeria civil war. 9 pam.

Afr 6275.102   Nigeria free. (Williams, Harry.) N.Y., 1963.

Afr 6275.30   Nigeria handbook. Lagos. 6,1925 | 2v.

Afr 6277.83   Nigeria i Ghana. (Halpern, Jan.) Warszawa, 1964.

Afr 6214.36   Nigeria in history. (Fajana, A.) Pkeja, 1969.

Afr 6298.110   Nigeria speaks. (Balewa, Abubakar Tafawa.) Ikeja, 1964.

Afr 6275.50   Nigeria today. (Great Britain. Central Office of Information.) London, 1960.

Afr 6277.50   Nigeria trade journal, Lagos. Special independence issue, 1960. Lagos, 1960.

Afr Doc 2308.715   Nigeria trade summary. Lagos. 1964+

Afr 6218.5.2   Nigeria under British rule. (Geary, Nevill.) N.Y., 1965.

Afr 6200.14.60   Nigeria year book. Apapa. 1963+

Afr 6275.127   Nigeria zwischen Wüste und Lagune. (Miller, Stefan.) Berlin, 1966.

Afr 6275.126   Nigeria 1960. (Nigeria. Federal Information Service.) Lagos, 196-.

Afr 6225.30   Nigeria 1965; crisis and criticism. Ibadan, 1966.

Afr 6200.14.80   Nigeria/Biafra conflict. N.Y. 1,1968

Afr 6277.120   Nigeria/Biafrai programs of assistance of U.S. non-profit organizations, March 1969. (Technical Assistance Information Clearing House.) N.Y., 1969.

Afr 6210.60   Nigerian administration and its political setting. (Adedeji, Adebayo.) London, 1968.

Afr 6277.70   Nigerian cocoa farmers. (Nigeria. Cocoa Marketing Board.) London, 1956.

Afr 6210.36   The Nigerian constitution. (Odumosu, O.I.) London, 1963.

Afr 6210.54   The Nigerian constitution and its review. (Ohonbamu, Obarogie.) Onitsha, 1965.

Afr 6225.10   Nigerian crisis, 1966. (Nigeria, Eastern. Ministry of Information.) Enugu, 1966.

Afr 6275.109   Nigerian days. (Hastings, Archibald Charles Gardner.) London, 1925.

Afr 6218.17   The Nigerian federal election of 1959. (Post, K.W.J.) Oxford, 1963.

Afr 6277.122   Nigerian federal finance: its development, problems and prospects. (Adedeji, Adebayo.) London, 1969.

Afr 6200.14.5   Nigerian field. London. 7,1938+ 3v.

Afr 6200.14.15   Nigerian geographical journal. Ibadan. 3v.

Afr 6210.44F   Nigerian government and politics. (Mackintosh, John P.) London, 1966.

Afr 6200.14.45F   Nigerian Institute of Social and Economic Research, Ibadan, Nigeria. Conference proceedings. Ibadan. 1,1952+ 3v.

Afr 6200.20   Nigerian Institute of Social and Economic Research, Ibadan, Nigeria. Information bulletin. Ibadan. 1,1965+

Afr 6203.8   Nigerian Institute of Social and Economic Research, Ibadan, Nigeria. A list of books, articles and government publications on the economy of Nigeria. Ibadan. 1,1960+ 2v.

Afr 6200.14.46   Nigerian Institute of Social and Economic Research, Ibadan, Nigeria. Publications. Ibadan. 1963+

Afr 6203.13   Nigerian Institute of Social and Economic Research, Ibadan, Nigeria. Research for national development. Ibadan. 1965+

Afr 6200.14.30   Nigerian journal of economics and social studies. Ibadan. 1,1959+ 4v.

Afr 6210.21   The Nigerian legal system. 2nd ed. (Elias, Taslim O.) London, 1963.

Afr 6210.12   The Nigerian legislative council. (Wheare, J.) London, 1950.

Afr 6277.27   Nigerian national accounts 1950-57. (Okigbo Pius N.C.) Nigeria, 1962.

Afr 6200.14.50F   Nigerian newsletter. Cairo. 7,1965+

Afr 6200.14.40
Afr 6203.5   Nigerian opinion. Ibadan. 1,1965+

Afr 6214.25   Nigerian periodicals and newspapers, 1950-1955. (Ibadan, Nigeria. University. Library.) Ibadan, 1956.

Afr 6225.14   Nigerian perspectives. (Hodgkin, Thomas.) London, 1960.

Afr 6212.42   Nigerian pogrom; the organized massacre of eastern Nigerians. (Nigeria, Eastern. Ministry of Information.) Enugu, 1966.

Afr 6225.5   Nigerian political parties. (Sklar, R.L.) Princeton, 1963.

Afr 210.65.45   The Nigerian political scene. (Tilman, Robert O.) Durham, 1962.

Afr 10663.10   Nigerian position in the intra-African situation up to May, 1963. (Odede, Simon.) The Hague, 1965.

Afr 6277.27.5   Nigerian press law. (Elias, Taslim O.) Lagos, 1969. Nigerian public finance. (Okigbo, Pius N.C.) Evanston, 1965.

Afr 6200.14.75   Nigerian record; background notes on the events in the Federal Republic of Nigeria. Washington. 1968+

Afr 6225.12   The Nigerian situation; facts and background. (Current Issues Society, Kaduna, Nigeria.) Zaria, 1966.

Afr 6200.14.35   Nigerian social and economics studies. London. 1+ 3v.

Afr 6200.14.70F   Nigerian socialist. Ibadan. 1,1967+

Afr 6200.14.55   Nigerian students voice. Baltimore. 3,1965+

Afr 6280.5.1   Nigerian studies. (Dennett, R.E.) London, 1968.

Afr 6203.2   Nigerian theses. (Amosu, Margaret.) Ibadan, 1965.

Afr 6275.106   A Nigerian villager in two worlds. (Okakor-Omali, Dilim.) London, 1965.

Afr 6222.1   Nigeriia v bor'be za nezqvisimost'. (Pribytkavskii, L.N.) Moskva, 1961.

Afr 6879.02   Night and morning in dark Africa. (Johnson, Harry.) London, 1902.

Afr 11572.50.100   The night is long. (Millin, S.G.(L.).) London, 1941.

Afr 11108.74.110   A night of their own. (Abrahams, Peter.) London, 1965.

Afr 9489.37   Night over Africa. (Windram, Foster.) London, 1937.

Afr 6777.10   Nigmann, Ernst. Geschichte der kaiserlichen Schutztruppe für Deutsch-Ostafrika. Berlin, 1911.

Afr 6883.33   Nigmann, Ernst. Schwärze. Berlin, 1922.

Afr 630.6   Die Nigritier. (Hartmann, R.) Berlin, 1876.

Afr 3715.10   Nigumi, M.A. A great trusteeship. London, 1957.

Afr 3715.10.2   Nigumi, M.A. A great trusteeship. 2d ed. London, 1958.

Afr 3068.69   Le Nil, son bassin et ses sources. (Lanoye, F. de.) Paris, 1869.

Afr 3979.03   Der Nil... Hydrographie und seiner Wirt. (Henze, H.) Halle, 1903.

Afr 3979.56.5   DerNil. (Cordan, Wolfgang.) Düsseldorf, 1956.

Afr 3979.36.5A   The Nile, the life story of a river. (Ludwig, Emil.) N.Y., 1937.

Afr 3978.93   The Nile. (Budge, E.A.W.) London, 1893.

Afr 3978.97   The Nile. 5th ed. (Budge, E.A.W.) London, 1897.

Afr 3979.93.15   The Nile. 7th. ed. (Budge, E.A.W.) London, 1901.

Afr 3979.10.8A   The Nile. 11th ed. (Budge, E.A.W.) London, 1910.

Afr 3979.10.9   The Nile. 12th ed. (Budge, E.A.W.) London, 1912.

NEDL Afr 4095.7   The Nile basin. (Burton, R.F.) London, 1864.

Afr 3978.49.6   The Nile boat, glimpses of Egypt. 2d ed. (Bartlett, W.H.) London, 1863.

Afr 3978.49.5   The Nile boat. (Bartlett, W.H.) London, 1849.

Afr 3978.51   The Nile boat. (Bartlett, W.H.) N.Y., 1851.

Afr 3978.49.8   The Nile boat. 4th ed. (Bartlett, W.H.) London, 1861.

Afr 3978.76   A Nile journal. (Appleton, T.G.) Boston, 1876.

Afr 3978.51.5   Nile notes. (Curtis, G.W.) N.Y., 1851.

Afr 3978.51.6   Nile notes. (Curtis, G.W.) N.Y., 1852.

Htn Afr 3978.51.4*   Nile notes of a howadji. (Curtis, G.W.) N.Y., 1851.

Afr 4095.18   The Nile quest. (Johnston, H.) N.Y., 1903.

Afr 4558.67.4   The Nile tributaries of Abyssinia. (Baker, S.W.) Hartford, 1868.

Afr 4558.67.6   The Nile tributaries of Abyssinia. (Baker, S.W.) London, 1883.

Afr 4558.67.7   The Nile tributaries of Abyssinia. (Baker, S.W.) London, 1886.

Afr 4558.67.3   The Nile tributaries of Abyssinia. 3rd ed. (Baker, S.W.) London, 1868.

Afr 4558.67.5.4   The Nile tributaries of Abyssinia. 4th ed. (Baker, S.W.) London, 1871.

Afr 4558.67.5A   The Nile tributaries of Abyssinia. 4th ed. (Baker, S.W.) Philadelphia, 1868.

Afr 718.50   Nils-Magnus. Afrikanska strövtåg. Solna, 1968.

Afr 8063.32   Nine flames. (Anderson, Ken.) Cape Town, 1964.

Afr 55.32   Nine great Africans. (Niven, Cecil R.) London, 1964.

Afr 55.32.2   Nine great Africans. (Niven, Cecil R.) N.Y., 1965.

Afr 3994.938   Nine papyrus texts in the New York University collection. Diss. (Casson, L.) N.Y., 1939.

Afr 6192.3   Nine years at the Gold Coast. (Kemp, Dennis.) London, 1898.

Afr 12639.18.100   Nini, mulâtresse du Sénégal. 2. éd. (Sadji, Abdoulaye.) Paris, 1965.

Afr 2208.84   Niox, G.L. Algérie. Paris, 1884.

Afr Doc 7509.500   La niveau de vie des populations de l'Adamaoua. (Cameroon. Service de la Statistique Générale et de la Mécanographie.) Ircam, 1964. 2v.

Afr 7812.260.2   Le niveau de vie des populations rurales du Ruanda-Urundi. (Leurquin, Philippe.) Louvain, 1960.

Afr 7812.260   Le niveau de vie des populations rurales du Ruanda-Urundi. (Leurquin, Philippe.) Louvain, 1960.

Afr 6095.358   Niven, C.R. The land and people of West Africa. London, 1958.

Afr 6214.12.5A   Niven, C.R. Nigeria, outline of a colony. London, 1946.

Afr 6214.12   Niven, C.R. A short history of Nigeria. London, 1937.

Afr 55.32   Niven, Cecil R. Nine great Africans. London, 1964.

Afr 55.32.2   Niven, Cecil R. Nine great Africans. N.Y., 1965.

Afr 6275.122   Niven, Cecil Rex. Nigeria. London, 1967.

Afr 8210.3   Nixon, John. The complete story of the Transvaal. London, 1885.

Afr 6457.24   Njiguna Wa Gakuo, E. Bedeutung und Möglichkeiten. Freiburg, 1960.

Afr 10419.2   Njruri, Ngumbu. Agikuyu folk tales. London, 1966.

Afr 14.11   Nkanga editions. Kampala. 1,1968+

Afr 11611.66.110   Nkosi, Lewis. Home and exile. London, 1965.

Afr 11611.66.100   Nkosi, Lewis. The rhythm of violence. London, 1964.

Afr 210.63.15   Nkrumah, Kwame. Africa must unite. London, 1963.

Afr 210.63.16   Nkrumah, Kwame. Africa must unite. N.Y., 1963.

Afr 6176.30.30   Nkrumah, Kwame. Axioms of Kwame Nkrumah. London, 1967.

Afr 6176.30.31   Nkrumah, Kwame. Axioms of Kwame Nkrumah. London, 1967.

Afr 1608.16.20   Nouveau voyage dans l'interieur de l'Afrique. (Adams, Robert.) Paris, 1817.

Afr 12624.41.30   Les nouveaux contes d'Amadou Koumba. (Diop, Birago.) Paris, 1962.

Afr 12624.41.33   Les nouveaux contes d'Amadou Koumba. 3. ed. (Diop, Birago.) Paris, 1967.

Afr 2300.8   Nouveaux villages algérois. (Planhol, Xavier de.) Paris, 1961.

Afr 1625.10   Nouvel, Suzanne. Nomades et sedentaires au Maroc. Paris, 1919.

Afr 1960.1   Nouvel aperçu sur l'Algérie. (Blondel, L.) Paris, 1838.

Afr 5056.157.10   Une nouvelle Afrique. (Siriex, Paul.) Paris, 1957.

Afr 2030.463.25   Nouvelle Algérie. (Cretin-Vercel, Michel.) Paris, 1963.

Afr 3014.1   Nouvelle Égypte. Paris. 1,1952+

Afr 4115.7   Nouvelle géographie. Cairo. (Reclus, E.) Paris, 1885.

Afr 608.94   Nouvelle géographie universelle Morocco. Maps of Alger. (Reclus, E.) Paris, 1830-94.

Afr 4556.81.21   Nouvelle histoire d'Abissinie. (Ludolf, H.) Paris, 1684.

Afr 5045.2   Nouvelle histoire de l'Afrique française. (Demanet, Abbé.) Paris, 1767. 2v.

Afr 2700.8F   Nouvelle Revue du Sahara. Noisy-le-Sec. (Seine). 1960+

Afr 10066.4   Nouvelle somme de poésie du monde noir. (Présence Africaine.) Paris, 1966.

Afr 9389.59   Nouvelles aventures au Kalahari. (Balsan, Francois.) Paris, 1959.

Afr 1.92   Nouvelles du CAFRAD. (African Training and Research Centre in Administration for Development.) Tanger. 1,1967+

Afr 5183.961.10   Nouvelles lettres à Seydon. (Touze, R.L.) Dakar, 1961.

Afr 5285.277.7   Nouvelles notes sur le Mossi et le Gorounsi. (Tauxier, Louis.) Paris, 1924.

Afr 1814.6   Nouvelles Realites Algériennes. Bulletin d'information NRA. Alger. 1,1958+

Afr 1814.5   Nouvelles realités algériennes. Alger. 1,1955+ 3v.

Afr 677.28   Nouvelles relations de l'Afrique occidentale. (Labot, J.B.) Paris, 1728. 5v.

Afr 1103.9   Nova, e curiosa relaçao, do fatal combate que teve o capitão de mare guerra espanhol D. Joze Ponce de Leon, com huma nao de Mouros argelinos. Lisbon, 1753.

Afr 210.67.15   A nova Africa, ensaio sociopolitico. (Castro, Luis Filipe de Oliveira e.) Lisboa, 1967.

Afr 1103.6   Nova relaçam e curiosa noticia do combate, que tiveram tres caravellas de Vianna de Caminha com os corsarios dos Mouros. Lisboa, 1754.

Afr 212.26   Noveishaia istoriia Afriki. (Akademiia Nauk SSSR. Institut Afriki.) Moskva, 1964.

Afr 212.26.1   Noveishaia istoriia Afriki. 2. izd. Moskva, 1968.

Afr 3978.70.5   La novela del Egipto. (Castro y Serrano, Jose de.) Madrid, 1870.

Afr 12012.3   The novelists' inheritance in French Africa. (Brench, Anthony Cecil.) London, 1967.

Afr 10671.12.810   The novels of Chinua Achebe. (Killam, Gordon Douglas.) N.Y., 1969.

Afr 1814.10   Novembre. Alger. 3v.

Afr 4357.5   Novo triunfo da religiam serafica, ou noticia summaria do martyrio...3 de marco de 1716. (Freire de Monterroyo Mascarenhas, José.) Lisboa, 1718.

Afr 3750.1   Novye gorizonty Sudana. (Griadunov, Iurii S.) Moskva, 1969.

Afr 4592.1   Nowack, Ernst. Land und Volk der Konso. Bonn, 1954.

Afr 590.32   Noyant. Les horreurs de l'esclavage, de la sorcellerie, des sacrifices humains et du cannibalisme en Afrique. Paris, 1891.

Afr 1400.1   Nozhet-Elhadi, histoire de la dynastie saadienne au Maroc, (1511-1670). (Muhammed al-Segir.) Paris, 1889.

Afr 6160.8   Nsarkoh, J.K. Local government in Ghana. Accra, 1964.

Afr 9839.34.5   Ntara, S.Y. Man of Africa. London, 1934.

Afr 3252.5   Nubar-Pacha devant l'histoire. (Holynski, A.) Paris, 1886.

Afr 4060.8   Nubia, storia di una civilta favolosa. (Curt, Silvio.) Novara, 1965.

Afr 4558.33.2   Nubia and Abyssinia. (Russell, M.) N.Y., 1837.

Afr 4558.33.5   Nubia and Abyssinia. (Russell, M.) N.Y., 1840.

Afr 4558.33.3   Nubia and Abyssinia. 2d ed. (Russell, M.) Edinburgh, 1833.

Afr 4060.5   La Nubia e il Sudan. (Rossi, Elia.) Constantinopoli, 1858.

Afr 4060.30   Nubian twilight. (Keating, Rex.) N.Y., 1963.

Afr 4060.36   Nubien. (Geroter, Georg.) Zurich, 1964.

Afr 4093.62   Nuer customs and folk-lore. (Huffman, Ray.) London, 1931.

Afr 1658.40   Nuestro protectorado. (Sanchez, J.G.) Madrid, 1930.

Htn   Afr 1905.4F*   Nuevo blason de los cardenas y elogios del Duque de Maqueda en Oran. Madrid, 1624.

Afr 710.16   El nuevo reino. (Morán Lopez, Fernando.) Madrid, 1967.

Afr 1713.15   La nuit de Fes. (Tharaud, Jerome.) Paris, 1932.

Afr 8667.30   The numbered day. (Jackmann, S.B.) London, 1954.

Afr 4700.33.12   La nuova Italia d'oltremare. (Piccioli, A.) Milano, 1934. 2v.

Afr 4700.33.10   La nuova Italia d'oltremare. (Piccioli, A.) Verona, 1933. 2v.

Afr 210.63.80   Il nuovo volto dell Africa. (Rainero, Romain.) Firenze, 1966.

Afr 8145.35   Nur einer von Vielen, aus dem Leben eines Missionsarztes. (Knietoch, Clemens M.) Frankfurt, 1961.

Afr 3315.133   Nutting, Anthony. No end of a lesson. London, 1967.

Afr 8019.4   Nuusbrief. (Suid-Afrikaanse Buro vir Raase-Anngeleenthede.) Stellenbosch. 10,1954+ 2v.

Afr 6291.48   Nwankwo, Arthur Agwuncha. The making of a nation: Biafra. London, 1969.

Afr 10684.92.100   Nwankwo, Nkem. Danda. London, 1964.

Afr 10684.92.1100   Nwanodi, Okogbule Glory. Icheke and other poems. Ibadan, 1964.

Afr 10684.92.2100   Nwapa, Flora. Efuru. London, 1966.

Afr 10516.5   Nwoga, Donatus Ibe. West African verse; an anthology. London, 1967.

Afr 6535.36   Nyabongo, A.K. Africa answers back. London, 1936.

Afr 9603.10   Nyabongo, Akiki K. The story of an African chief. N.Y., 1935.

Afr 775.10   Nyasa, the great water. (Johnson, W.P.) London, 1922.

Afr Doc 3603.5F   Nyasaland. Blue book. 11v.

Afr 9850.10   Nyasaland. Capital development plan, 1957-1961. Zomba, 1957.

Afr 9839.55   Nyasaland. (Debenham, F.) London, 1955.

Afr 9499.40   Nyasaland. (Haglewood, Arthur.) Oxford, 1960.

Afr Doc 3609.300   Nyasaland. Auditor-General Department. Report on the accounts. Zomba. 1956-1957

Afr 9855.2F   Nyasaland. Commission of Inquiry into Disturbances at Mangunda Estate. Report. Zomba, 1953.

Afr Doc 3612.10   Nyasaland. Legislative Council. Proceedings.

Afr Doc 3631.10   Nyasaland. Secretary for African Affairs. Annual report. 1958

Afr 9858.5   Nyasaland. Southworth Commission. Report on the incident which took place outside Ryalls Hotel. Zomba, 1960.

Afr 9760.15   Nyasaland Constitutional Conference, London, 1960. Report. London, 1960.

Afr 9757.20   Nyasaland Constitutional Conference. Report of the Nyasaland Constitutional Conference held in London in Nov. 1962. London, 1962.

Afr 9850.7   Nyasaland development plan, 1962-1965. Zomba, 1962.

Afr 626.152   Nyasaland Economic Symposium. Economic development in Africa. Oxford, 1965.

Afr 9839.12   Nyasaland for the hunter and settler. (Lyell, D.D.) London, 1912.

Afr 9755.2   Pamphlet vol. Nyasaland government documents. 4 pam.

Afr 9750.5   Nyasaland journal. Blantyre. 4,1951+ 5v.

Afr 9757.5   Nyasaland protectorate, report for the year. (Great Britain. Colonial Office.) 1946+ 4v.

Afr 9839.03   Nyasaland under the Foreign Office. (Duff, H.L.) London, 1903.

Afr 9839.05   Nyasaland under the Foreign Office. 2. ed. (Duff, H.L.) London, 1906.

Afr 9838.77   Nyassa. (Young, Edward Daniel.) London, 1877.

Afr 9769.39   Nyassaland. (Schwerin, W.) Neudamm, 1939.

Afr 6333.65   Nye, Joseph Samuel. Pan-Africanism and East African integration. Cambridge, 1965.

Afr 6282.30   Det nye Nigeria. Adrhus, 1966.

Afr 28.96   Nyere Africa-litteratur. (Copenhagen. Kongelige Bibliotek.) København, 1962.

Afr 6899.62   Nyerere, Julius Kambarage. Freedom and socialism. Dar-es-Salaam, 1968.

Afr 11750.21.100   Nyitso, a novel of West Africa. (Roebuck, M.F.C.) Cape Town, 1964.

Afr 609.48   Nykypaivan Afrikka. (Bolinder, Gustaf.) Helsinki, 1948.

Afr 10684.99.110   Nzekwu, Onuora. Blade among the boys. London, 1962.

Afr 11626.23.110   Nzekwu, Onuora. Blade among the boys. London, 1962.

Afr 10684.99.100   Nzekwu, Onuora. High life for lizards. London, 1965.

Afr 10684.99.120   Nzekwu, Onuora. Wand of noble wood. London, 1961.

Afr 6196.3   Nzima land. (Adjaye, Annor.) London, 193-?

Afr 6280.9.25   Nzimiro, F.I. Family and kinship in Ibo land. Köln, 1962.

Afr 13284.99.100   Nzouankeu, Jacques Mariel. Le souffle des ancêtres; nouvelles. Yaoundé, 1965.

Afr 510.112   O francouzsko-africkem spolecenstvi. (Oplustil, Vaclav.) Praha, 1963.

Afr 4025.15.5   O hellynismos kai i neotera Aigyptos. (Polites, Athanasios G.) Alexandreia, 1928. 2v.

Afr 150.68   O Infante D. Henrique e a universidade. (Moreira de Sa, Artur.) Lisboa, 1960.

Htn   Afr 150.10F*   O Infante Dom Henrique. (Zuental, Anthero de.) Lisboa, 1894.

Afr 2397.6   O mes soeurs musulmanes, pleurez (Bittari, Zoubeida.) Paris, 1964.

Afr 2030.469   O mon pays perdu. (Jouhaud, Edmond.) Paris, 1969.

Afr 12785.89.120   O pays, mon beau peuple; roman. (Ousmane, Sembene.) Paris, 1957.

Afr 11907.9.100   Oak oracle. (Gabre-Medhin, Tsegaye Oda.) London, 1965.

Afr 210.61.5   Oakes, John B. The edge of freedom. 1st ed. N.Y., 1961.

Afr 6275.36   Oakley, R.R. Treks and palavers. London, 1938.

Afr 2030.464.85   OAS parle. Paris, 1964.

Afr 2948.12   Le oasi del Fezzan. v.1-2. (Scarin, Emilio.) Bologna, 1934.

Afr 2209.27.34   Oasis and simoon. (Ossendowski, F.A.) N.Y., 1927.

Afr 2283.3   Les oasis dans la montagne. (Keun, Odette.) Paris, 1919.

Afr 2290.3   Les oasis de la province d'Oran. (Leclerc, L.) Alger, 1858.

Afr 2295.7.3   Oasis de l'Oued Rir' en 1856 et 1880. 3e ed. Paris, 1881.

Afr 2376.5   Une oasis du Sahara nord-occidental: Tabelbala. (Champault, Francine Dominque.) Paris, 1969.

Afr 2929.53   Oasis kingdom. (Epton, N.C.) N.Y., 1953.

Afr 2374.2   Les oasis sahariennes. (Martin, A.G.P.) Alger, 1908.

Afr 9488.81   Oates, Frank. Matabele land. London, 1881.

Afr 25.104.5   OAU perspective, Third Regular Assembly, 1966. (Organization of African Unity.) Addis Ababa, 1966.

Afr 15.5   OAU review. (Organization of African Unity.) Asmara, Ethiopia. 1,1964+ 2v.

Afr 2030.467   O'Ballance, Edgar. The Algerian insurrection, 1954-62. London, 1967.

Afr 3986.963.10   Obedinennaia Arabskaia Respublika. (Dlin, Nikolai A.) Moscow, 1963.

Afr 3993.966   Ob'edinennaia Arabskaia Respublika. (Matiukhin, Ivan S.) Moskva, 1966.

Afr 3979.68   Ob'edinennaia Arabskaia Respublika. Moskva, 1968.

Afr 678.74   Oberlander, R. Westafrika von Senegal bis Benquela. Leipzig, 1874.

Afr 5343.25.2   Obermaier, Heinrich. Die Elfenbeinküste als Wirtschaftspartner. 2. Aufl. Köln, 1968.

Afr 6218.14   Obi, Chike. Our struggle. V.1-2. Yaba, 1962.

Afr 7350.3.11   Objections...report of the African Colonization Society. (Hopkins, E.) Philadelphia, 1833. 2 pam.

Afr 3204.26   Objective: Egypt. (Blayland, Gregory.) London, 1966.

Afr 4886.7   Obock, Mascate, Bouchire, Bassorah. (Denis de Rivoyre, B.L.) Paris, 1883.

Afr 4886.5   Obock. (Salma, L. de.) Paris, 1893.

Afr 6095.361   Oboli, H.O.N. An outline geography of West Africa. New ed. rev. London, 1961.

Afr 6095.361.5   Oboli, H.O.N. An outline geography of West Africa. 5th ed. London, 1967.

Afr 150.12   A obra do Infante. (Macedo, Lino de.) Villafranca de Xira, 1894.

Afr 5645.11   Obrazovanie Malgashskoi republiki. (Korneev, L.A.) Moscow, 1963.

Afr 3993.966.5   O'brien, Patrick Karl. The revolution in Egypt's economic system, from private enterprise to socialism, 1952-1965. London, 1966.

Afr 5335.2A   One-party government in the Ivory Coast. (Zolberg, Aristide R.) Princeton, N.J., 1964.

Afr 5335.2.1   One party government in the Ivory Coast. (Zolberg, Aristide R.) Princeton, N.J., 1969.

Afr 9599.11   One thousand miles in a Machilla. (Colville, A.) London, 1911.

Afr 8292.16.5   One thousand miles with the C.I.V. (Lloyd, J.B.) London, 1901.

Afr 8849.16   One titan at a time. (Folliott, Pamela.) Cape Town, 1960.

Afr 609.65.20   One traveller's Africa. (Nolan, Cynthia.) London, 1965.

Afr 9195.10   Oneil, Owen Rowe. Adventures in Swaziland. N.Y., 1921.

Afr 6620.50   O'Neill, H.C. The war in Africa, 1914-1917. London, 1919.

Afr 6990.6   Ongebaande wee. (Naude, C.P.) Kaapstad, 1931.

Afr 505.47   Oni ne khotiat ukhodit. (Fokeev, German V.) Moskva, 1965.

Afr 6277.71   Onitiri, H.M.A. A preliminary report on the possibilities of price control in Nigeria. Ibadan, 1966.

Afr 10665.08   Pamphlet vol. Onitsha market literature. 13 pam.

Afr 10665.05   Pamphlet vol. Onitsha market literature. 12 pam.

Afr 11598.89.100   Only a setting forth, poems. (Naude, Adele.) Cape Town, 1965.

Afr 710.76   Ons Buurstate op die Afrikaanse vasteland. (South African Broadcasting Corporation.) Johannesburg, 1959.

Afr 8095.30   Ons drie eeue. Our three centuries. (Kock, V. de.) Kaapstad, 1952.

Afr 8095.75   Ons erfenis. (Kock, Victor de.) Kaapstad, 1960.

Afr 8325.22   Ons japie. (Barry, A.) Johannesburg, 1960.

Afr 6979.61   Ons mandaat: Suidwes-Afrika. (Bruwer, Johannes Petrus.) Johannesburg, 1961.

Afr 8659.63.5   Ons nasionale parke. (South Africa. National Parks Board of Trustees.) Pretoria, 1963.

Afr 8325.66   Ons parool. 2. druk. (Preller, G.S.) Kaapstad, 1943.

Afr 8678.304   Ons uis jon Suid-Afrika. (Niekerk, R.) Pretoria, 1962.

Afr 8667.55   Ons volkslewe. (Spoelstra, B.) Pretoria, 1922.

Afr 7803.40.5   Het ontstaan van de Kasai-missie. (Storme, Marcel.) Brussels, 1961.

Afr 8175.20   Die ontwaking van die afrikaanse nasionale bewussyn. (Jaarsveld, F.A. van.) Johannesburg, 1957.

Afr 8015.10   Onward. Johannesburg. 1,1965+

Afr 6277.46   Onyemelukwe, Clement Chukwukadibia. Problems of industrial planning and management in Nigeria. London, 1966.

Afr 7815.54   Onze Kongo. Leuven. 1,1910-1911

Afr 8278.99.13   Oom Paul's people. (Hillegas, H.C.) N.Y., 1899.

Afr 8210.9   Oordt, J.F.V. Paul Kruger en de opkomst van der Zuid Afrikaansche Republiek. Amsterdam, 1898.

Afr 9088.5   Oordt, J.W.G. van. De Transvaalsche Gebeurtenissen en... Suid-Africa. 's-Gravenhage, 1881.

Afr 8289.02.24   De oorlog in Zuid-Afrika. (Everdingen, W.) Delft, 1902.

Afr 8288.99.20   De oorlog in Zuid-Afrika. (Penning, L.) Rotterdam, 1899-03. 3v.

Afr 8279.00.31   De oorlog in Zuid-Afrika. (Wormser, I.A.) Amsterdam, 1900.

Afr 8279.48   Die oorsake van die tweede vryheids-oorlog. (Scholtz, Gert D.) Johannesburg, 1948-49. 2v.

Afr 8825.8   De oorsprong der kaapsch-hollandsche volksoveringen. (Schonken, F.T.) Amsterdam, 1914.

Afr 545.48   Oosthuizen, Gerhardus Cornelis. Post-Christianity in Africa: a theological and anthropological study. London, 1968.

Afr 8320.13   Op die Transvaalse front 1 junie 1900-31 oktober 1900. (Weeber, E.J.) Bloemfontein, 1942.

Afr 8377.6   Op weg na 'n nuwe politieke lewenshouding. (Degenaar, Johannes Jacobus.) Kaapstad, 1963.

Afr 7568.31   An open letter to His Serene Majesty Leopold II. (Williams, G.W.) n.p., n.d. 2 pam.

Afr 109.11   The opening up of Africa. (Johnston, H.H.) London, n.d.

Afr 109.11.5   The opening up of Africa. (Johnston, H.H.) N.Y., 1911.

Afr 4700.38.5   L'opera del fascismo in Africa. (Giaccardi, A.) Milano, 1938-39. 2v.

Afr 4719.29   L'opera della marina in Eritrea e Somalia della occupazione...1928. (Italy. Marina Stato Maggiore. Officio Storico.) Roma, 1929.

Afr 11534.18.100   Operation Atlantis. (Ludl, Gerard.) Cape Town, 1967.

Afr 6457.29F   The operations and development plans of the Kenya Tea Development Authority. (Kenya Tea Development Authority.) Nairobi, 1964.

Afr 2880.10   Le operazioni libiche sul 29 parallelo nord. (Zoli, C.) Roma, 1928.

Afr 2938.25   Le opere pubbliche della Tripolitania e della Cirenaica. (Simonetti, R.) Roma, 1914.

Afr 10066.5   Ophir, an independent magazine. Pretoria. 4,1968+

Afr 500.81   Opinion. (Barboux, H.M.) Paris, 1903.

Afr 7815.25   L'opinion publique coloniale devant l'assimilation des indigènes. (Fédération des Associations de Colons du Congo.) Bruxelles, 1951.

Afr 9089.38   Die opkoms van die Afrikaanse Kultuurgedagte aan die rand. (Coetzee, A.) Johannesburg, 1938.

Afr 8678.306   Die opkoms van ons derde stand. (Botha, David P.) Kaapstad, 1964.

Afr 510.112   Oplustil, Vaclav. O francouzsko-africkem spolecenstvi. Praha, 1963.

Afr 679.68.15   Opnennye ieroglify. (Iordanskii, Vladimir B.) Moskva, 1968.

Afr 5219.02.2   Oppenheim, M.F. von. Rabeh und das Tschadseegebiet. Berlin, 1902.

Afr 9439.10   Oppenheimer series. (Southern Rhodesia. Government Archives.) 1,1945+ 13v.

Afr 2030.250   Oppermann, Thomas. Die algerische Frage. Stuttgart, 1959.

Afr 2030.252   Oppermann, Thomas. Le problème algérien. Paris, 1961.

Afr 3986.955   Opportunities for industrial development in Egypt. (Little, Arthur D.) Cairo, 1955.

Afr 8825.40   Opportunities for the coloureds. (South Africa. Department of Coloured Affairs.) Pretoria, 1963.

Afr 9499.15   Opportunity in Rhodesia and Nyasaland. (Federation of Rhodesia and Nyasaland. Federal Information Services.) Salisbury, 1955.

Afr 8015.5   Optima. Johannesburg. 1-2,1951-1952 8v.

Afr 1495.6   Option révolutionnaire au Maroc. (Benbarka, El Mehdi.) Paris, 1966.

Afr 5992.4   Opusculo sobre la colonización de Fernando Poo. (Guillermar de Aragon, Adolfo.) Madrid, 1852.

Afr 4394.9.5   L'Ora d'Africa. 2a ed. (Oriani, A.) Bologna, 1935.

Afr 2929.11   L'ora di Tripoli. (Corradini, E.) Milano, 1911.

Afr 2929.11.2   Ora di tripoli. (Corradini, E.) Milano, 1911.

Afr 5465.6   Oracles et ordalies chez les Nzakara. (Retel-Laurentin, Anne.) Paris, 1969.

Afr 650.6   Oram, Nigel. Towns in Africa. London, 1965.

Afr 1830.30.5   Oran. (Lespes, Rene.) Paris, 1938.

Afr 2290.2   Oran et l'Algérie en 1887. (Association Française pour l'Avancement des Sciences.) Oran, 1888. 2v.

Afr 2357.5   Oran-Mers-el-Kebir. Thèse. (Offrey, R.) Bourg, 1938.

Afr 2357.25   Oran sous le commandement du général Desmichels. (Desmichels, L.A.) Paris, 1835.

Afr 2290.5   Oran Tlemcen sud-oranais (1899-1900) (Pimodan.) Paris, 1903.

Afr 9295.452   Orange days. (Hill, Caroline.) Pietermaritzburg, 1965.

Afr Doc 4707.304F   Orange Free State. Census report of the Orange River Colony. Bloemfontein, 1904.

Afr 9285.5   Orange Free State. The Orange Free State. Cape Town, 1956.

Afr 9285.5   The Orange Free State. (Orange Free State.) Cape Town, 1956.

Afr 9218.93   Orange Free State (Republic). South Africa. Chicago, 1893.

Afr 9388.76F   Orange Free State Commission. Sketch of the Orange Free State. Philadelphia, 1876.

Afr 9203.5   The Orange Free State goldfields; a bibliography. (Sinclair, Dorothy Mary.) Cape Town, 1967.

Afr 8690.5   The Orange river. (Muller, D.J.) Cape Town, 1953.

Afr 9205.1   Pamphlet box. Orange River cop.

Afr 9225.15   Der Oranje-Freistaat, 1854-1888. (Brauer, A.) Emsdetten, 1931.

Afr 1609.38   Orano, E. A traverso il Marocco. Napoli, 1938.

Afr 6225.20   Orbit Publications. Events; a diary of important happenings in Nigeria from 1960-1966. Ebute-Metta, 1967.

Afr Doc 9207.15   Orçamento geral. (Mozambique.)

Afr Doc 9209.5F   Orçamento geral para o ano economico. (Mozambique.) 1945

Afr Doc 9209.10   Orçamentos das cámaras municipais, edilidades e comissões. (Mozambique.) Louvenço. 1917

Afr 9489.66.10   Orcival, Francois d'. Rhodésie, pays des lions fidèles. Paris, 1966.

Afr 10631.58.140   Ordained by the oracle. (Konadu, Asare.) London, 1969.

Afr 5753.20   Les ordalies et sacrifices rituels chez les Anains Malgaches. (Decary, Raymond.) Paris, 1959.

Afr 6460.15.2   Orde-Browne, G.S. The vanishing tribes of Kenya. London, 1925.

Afr 6460.15A   Orde-Browne, G.S. The vanishing tribes of Kenya. Philadelphia, 1925.

Afr 2030.345   Ordeal in Algeria. (Brace, Richard M.) Princeton, 1960.

Afr 10443.12.100   Ordeal in the forest. (Wachira, Godwin.) Nairobi, 1968.

Afr 40.61.5   Ordem publica e liberdades politicas na Africa negra. (Felreira, Oliverio.) Belo Horizonte, 1961.

Afr 50.41   Order and rebellion in tribal Africa. (Gluckman, M.) London, 1963.

Afr 4700.28.15   Ordinamento amministrativo-contabile per l'Eritrea e per la Somalia. (Italy. Ministero delle Colonie.) Roma, 1928.

Afr 4700.34.5   L'ordinamento sindacale-corporativo nell organizzazione delle colonie italiane. (Castelbarco, G.) Milano, 1934.

Afr 5645.12   Ordre National de la République Malgache. Le grand livre de l'Ordre national de la République Malgache. Tananarive, 1964.

Afr Doc 1385.5F   Ordurman household budget survey. (Sudan. Department of Statistics.) Khartoum, 1965.

Afr 6176.25   Orestov, O.L. V Respublike Gana. Moscow, 1961.

Afr 6277.108   Orewa, George Oka. Local government finance in Nigeria. Ibadan, 1966.

Afr 7540.29   L'organisation administrative du Congo belge. (Delvaux, Roger.) Anvers, 1945.

Afr 5001.110   Organisation Africaine et Malgache de Coopération Economique. Revue trimestrielle. Yaounde.

Afr 2030.463.15   Organisation armée secrète, fév. 14-déc. 1961. (Buchard, R.) Paris, 1963.

Afr 2030.463.10   L'Organisation armée secrète. v.1-2. (Lancelot, Marie-Thérèse.) Paris, 1963.

Afr 5001.100   Organisation Commune Africaine et Malgache. Departement des Affaires Economiques, Financieres et des Transports. Bulletin statistique. Yaounde. 2,1966+

Afr 1340.40   L'organisation de l'état civil au Maroc. (Filizzola, Sabine.) Paris, 1958.

Afr 2438.7   L'organisation des communes en Tunisie. (Demay, Jules.) Tunis, 1915.

Afr 5219.12   L'organisation des troupes indigènes. (Pasquier, G.) Paris, 1912.

Afr 5219.12.3   L'organisation des troupes indigènes en Afrique occidentale française. (Pasquier, G.) Paris, 1912.

Afr 7870.6   L'organisation des zones de squatting. (Raymaekers, P.) Leopoldville, 1963.

Afr 2224.30   L'organisation financière de l'Algérie du nord. Thèse. (Peraldi, Geo.) Alger, 1930.

Afr 1624.911   L'organisation financière de l'empire marocain. (Abdesselem, Faleb.) Paris, 1911.

Afr 5057.10   Organisation financière locale de l'Afrique. Thèse. (Bressolles, H.) Bordeaux, 1922.

Afr 1340.5   L'organisation intérieur des pays de protectorat. (Revilliod, M.) Paris, 1913.

Afr 6160.7   L'organisation politique, administratif et financière de la colonie britannique de la Gold Coast. Thèse. (Carbon Ferrière.) Paris, 1936.

Afr 1340.35   L'organisation régionale du Maroc. (Bremard, F.) Paris, 1949.

Afr 1574.9   Organizacion del protectorado español en Marruecos. v.1-2. (Cordero Torres, J.M.) Madrid, 1942-43.

Afr 8292.5.10   Organization, equipment, despatch and service of the Canadians during war in South Africa. (Canada. Department of Militia and Defence.) Ottawa, 1901. 2 pam.

Afr 5303.4   Organization for Economic Cooperation and Development. Development Center. Bibliographie sur la Guinee. Paris, 1965.

Afr 5326.5   Organization for Economic Cooperation and Development. Development Centre. Essai d'une bibliographie sur la Côte-d'Ivoire. Paris, 1964.

Afr 626.28   Organization for European Economic Cooperation in Africa. Energy in overseas territories south of the Sahara and in Surinam. Paris, 1953.

Afr 210.64.30   Organization of African Unity. Assembly of the heads of state and government of O.A.U. Cairo, 1964.

Afr 210.64.25   Organization of African Unity. Basic documents and resolutions. Addis Ababa, 1964.

Afr 25.104.5   Organization of African Unity. OAU perspective, Third Regular Assembly, 1966. Addis Ababa, 1966.

Afr 15.5   Organization of African Unity. OAU review. Asmara, Ethiopia. 1,1964+ 2v.

Afr 25.160F   Organization of African Unity. Economic and Social Commission. Proceedings and report. Addis Ababa. 1,1963+

Afr 25.108.2   The Organization of African Unity and its charter. 2d ed. (Červenka, Zdenek.) London, 1969.

Afr 40.65   Organizatsiia afrikanskogo edinstva. (Tuzmukhamedov, Rais A.) Moskva, 1965.

Afr 4238.5   L'organizzazione politica dell Etiopia. (Ghersi, E.) Padova, 1936.

Afr 4394.9.5   Oriani, A. L'Ora d'Africa. 2a ed. Bologna, 1935.

Afr 1915.13   Orient, N. La question algérienne. Paris, 1936.

Afr 1830.50.5   L'orient et la peinture française au XIXe siècle. (Alazard, Jean.) Paris, 1930.

Afr 4115.9   Oriental Cairo. (Sladen, D.) London, 1911.

Afr 4115.9.5   Oriental Cairo. (Sladen, D.) Philadelphia, 1911.

Afr 3979.37   Oriental spotlight. (Rameses (pseud.).) London, 1937.

Afr 7219.42   O oriente africano portugues. (Alberto, Manuel Simoes.) Lourenç Marques, 1942.

Afr 10315.5   Origin East Africa. (Cook, David.) London, 1965.

Afr 8279.00.39   Origin of the Anglo-Boer war revealed. (Thomas, C.H.) London, 1900.

Afr 8678.3   Original matter...in Sutherland's memoir...of South Africa. (Sutherland.) Cape Town, 1847.

Afr 5760.5F   L'origine des Malgaches. (Grandidier, A.) Paris, 1901.

Afr 5573.5   Les origines de la colonisation française à Madagascar, 1648-1661. (Malotet, A.) Paris, 1898.

Afr 2030.462.80   Les origines de la guerre d'Algérie. (Aron, Robert.) Paris, 1962.

Afr 5548.88   Les origines de l'Ile Bourbon. (Guet, M.I.) Paris, 1888.

Afr 1570.39   Les origines du Maroc français. (Saint-Rene-Taillaudier, Georges.) Paris, 1930.

Afr 2508.20   Les origines du protectorat français en Tunisie, 1861-1881. 2ème éd. (Ganiage, Jean.) Tunis, 1968.

Afr 4730.15A   Le origini della colonia Eritrea. (Zaghi, Carlo.) Bologna, 1934.

Afr 679.68   The origins of modern African thought. (July, Robert William.) London, 1968.

Afr 2459.62   Origins of nationalism in Tunisia. (Ziadeh, N.A.) Beirut, 1962.

Afr 9439.68.5   Origins of Rhodesia. (Samkange, Stanlake John Thompson.) London, 1968.

Afr 6282.5   Origins of the Niger mission. (Dike, Kenneth.) Nigeria, 1957.

Afr 210.44   Orizu, A.A.N. Without bitterness. N.Y., 1944.

Afr 4766.20   Orizzonti d'impero. (Vecchi di Val Cismon, C.M.) Milano, 1935.

Afr 1965.2.10   Orleans, F.P.L.C.H., Duc. Campagnes de l'armée d'Afrique, 1835-1839. 2e éd. Paris, 1870.

Afr 1965.2   Orleans, F.P.L.C.H., Duc. Récits de campagne 1833-41. Paris, 1890.

Afr 5635.3   Orleans, H.P.D. A Madagascar. Paris, 1895.

Afr 8659.02.6   Orléans-Bragance, L. Tour d'Afrique. Paris, 1902.

Afr 2358.5   Orléansville. (Debia, René Yves.) Alger, 1955.

Afr 7560.19   Orlova, Antonina S. Istoriia gosudarstva Kongo (XVI-XVII vv.). Moskva, 1968.

Afr 1571.17.40   Ormesson, W. Adieux, souvenirs sur Lyautey. Paris, 1937.

Afr 1571.17.42   Ormesson, W. Auprès de Lyautey. Paris, 1963.

Afr 7315.2   Ornellas, A.D. Raças e linguas indigenas em Moçambique. n.p., 1905.

Afr 7222.30   Ornellas, Ayres D. Campanha do Gungunhana, 1895. Lisboa, 1930.

Afr 3040.65.5   O'Rourke, V.A. The juristic status of Egypt and the Sudan. Baltimore, 1935.

Afr 3040.65   O'Rourke, V.A. The juristic status of EgyptAnd the Sudan. Diss. Baltimore, 1935.

Afr 2285.9   Orpen, A.E. The chronicles of the Sid. N.Y., n.d.

Afr 8925.15   Orpen, Joseph M. History of the Basutur of South Africa. Cape Town, 1857.

Afr 8849.295   Orpen, Joseph Millerd. Reminiscences of life in South Africa from 1846 to the present day. Cape Town, 1964.

Afr 8835.48   Orpen, Neil. Gunners of the Cape. Cape Town, 1965.

Afr 8063.20.10   Orpen, Neil. Prince Alfred's guard, 1856-1966. Port Elizabeth, 1967.

Afr 8377.12   Orpen, Neil. Total defence. 1st ed. Cape Town, 1967.

Afr 6214.3.2   Orr, Charles William James. The making of Northern Nigeria. 2nd ed. London, 1965.

Afr 6214.3   Orr, Charles William James. The making of Northern Nigeria. 9 maps. London, 1911.

Afr 1270.3   Ortega, M.L. Guia del norte de Africa y sur de España. Cadiz, 1917.

Afr 1573.21   Ortega, Manuel L. España en Marruecos. El Raisuni. Madrid, 1917.

Afr 1640.3   Ortega, Manuel L. Los hebreos en Marruecos. Madrid, 1919.

Afr 5920.13   Ortega Canadell, Rosa. Provincias africanas espanolas. 1.ed. Barcelona, 1962.

Afr 4513.35.135   Ortega y Gasset, E. Etiopia, el conflicto italo-abisinio. Madrid, 1935.

Afr 1487.22   Ortega y Gasset, Eduardo. Annual. Madrid, 1922.

Afr 4787.8   Orthner-Heun, Irene. Das Entwicklungsland Somalia. Köln, 1963.

Afr 7815.39   Orthographie des noms ethniques au Congo belge. (Bulck, Gaston van.) Bruxelles, 1954.

Afr 2030.464.5   Ortiz, Joseph. Mes combats. Paris, 1964.

Afr 2938.35   Ortner-Heun, Irene. Das Entwicklungsland Libyen. Köln, 1965.

Afr 5580.3.15   Ortowski, Leon. Maurycy August Beniowski. Warszawa, 1961.

Afr 500.8   Ortray, F. van. Conventions internationales. Bruxelles, 1898.

Afr 5635.4   Ortus, C. Madagascar. Paris, 1895.

Afr 9838.89   Os portuguezes na região do Nyassa. (Batalha Reis, Jayme.) Lisboa, 1889.

Afr 5749.24   Osborn, C.S. Madagascar, land of the man-eating tree. N.Y., 1924.

Afr 9073.797   Osborn, Robert F. C.G., a great Natalian; biography of Charles George Smith. Durban, 1966.

Afr 609.67.10   Osei, Gabriel Kingsley. The African, his antecedents, his genius and his destiny. London, 1967.

Afr 500.92   Osei, Gabriel Kingsley. Europe's gift to Africa. London, 1968.

Afr 628.265.5   Osei, Gabriel Kingsley. Forgotten great Africans. London, 1965.

Afr 6457.36   Oser, Jacob. Promoting economie development with illustrations from Kenya. Nairobi, 1967.

Afr 3040.18   Osman, Amin. Le mouvement constitutionnel en Egypte et la constitution de 1923. Thèse. Paris, 1924.

Afr 1583.14   Osman, H.A. Die Mannesmann-Rechte und den Weissbuch. Berlin, 1910.

Afr 3718.15   Osman Digna. (Jackson, H.C.) London, 1926.

Afr 6295.66.10   Osogo, John. A history of the Baluyia. Nairobi, 1966.

Afr 6456.5   Osogo, John. Life in Kenya in the olden days, the Baluyia. Nairobi, 1965.

Afr 6470.278   Osogo, John. Nabongo Mumia of the Baluyia. Nairobi, 1965?

Afr 210.62.42   Osoobozhdenie Afriki. (Braginskii, M.I.) Moscow, 1962.

Afr 679.68.5   Osqe, T.A. A short history of West Africa. London, 1968.

Afr 1609.26.10   Ossendowski, F. The fire of desert folk. London, 1926.

Afr 2209.27.34   Ossendowski, F.A. Oasis and simoon. N.Y., 1927.

Afr 5045.24   Ossendowski, F.A. Slaves of the sun. London, 1928.

Afr 4375.7   Ost Afrika (Rechtinger, J.) Wien, 1870.

Afr 6850.7   Ostafrika in der Geschichte der Weltwirtschaft. (Koch, Ludwig.) Berlin, 1930.

Afr 4070.13   Ostafrikanische Studien. (Munzinger, W.) Basle, 1883.

Afr 2875.15   Ostler, A. The Arabs in Tripoli. London, 1912.

Afr 6390.74   Ostrowski, W. Safari przez czarny lad. Londyn, 1947.

Afr 1493.71   Osuna Servent, Arturo. Frente a Abd-el-Krim. Madrid, 1922.

Afr 6333.62.10   Osvoboditel'naia bor'ba narodov Vostochnoi Afriki. (Khazanov, A.M.) Moscow, 1962.

Afr 6455.30   Oswald, Felix. Alone in the sleeping-sickness country. London, 1915.

Afr 9558.75   Oswell, W.E. William C. Oswell, hunter and explorer. N.Y., 1900. 2v.

Afr 6390.30   Other people. (Gontard, E.P.U.) Hollywood, 1942.

Afr 6192.50   Other peoples' worlds. (Mitchison, Naomi (Haldane).) London, 1958.

Afr 718.20   The other side of Emin Pasha relief expedition. (Bourne, H.R.F.) London, 1891.

Afr 609.60.70   Ottenberg, Simon. Cultures and societies of Africa. N.Y., 1960.

Afr 5758.63   Ottino, Paul. Les économies paysannes malgaches du Bas Mangoky. Paris, 1963.

Afr 5912.3   Otto, Archduke of Austria. Européens et Africains. Paris, 1963.

Afr 8289.54   Otto, J.C. Die konsentrasiekampe. Kaapstad, 1954.

Afr 3979.64A   Ottoman Egypt in the age of French revolution. (Husayn, Efendi.) Cambridge, 1964.

Afr 3180.7A   Ottoman Egypt in the eighteenth century. (Cezzar, Ahmed.) Cambridge, 1962.

Afr 5074.30   Otton Loyewski, S.W.C. Rezzons sur l'Adrar. Rufisque, 1942.

Afr 6214.31   Ottonkwo, D.O. History of Nigeria in a new setting. Onitsha, 1962.

Afr 6298.181.80   Otubushin, Christopher. The exodus and the return of Chief Obafemi Awolowo. Yala, Nigeria, 1966.

Afr 5056.139   Où en est l'Afrique occidentale française. (Perrot, Emile.) Paris, 1939.

Afr 5245.5   Ouane, Ibrahima Mamadou. L'islam et la civilisation française. Avignon, 1957.

Afr 4559.62.5   Ouannou, J. L'Ethiopie, pilote de l'Afrique. Paris, 1962.

Afr 4573.2   Ouannou, J. L'Ethiopie et son économie. 2. ed. Paris, 1961.

Afr 8250.33   Oudard, G. Cecil Rhodes. Paris, 1939.

Afr 9225.28   Oude tyden in den Oranje-Vrystaat. (Muller, Hendrik Pieter Nicolaas.) Leiden, 1907.

Afr 1742.1   Oudjds et l'Amalat (Maroc). (Voinot, L.) Oran, 1912.

Afr 8110.15   De oudste boeren-republieken graaff-reinst en Zwellendam van 1775-1806. (Wieringa, P.A.C.) 's-Gravenhage, 1921.

Afr 5406.204   L'ouest africain. (Renouard, G.) Paris, 1904.

X Cg   Afr 5057.8   L'ouest africain français. (Cosmier, Henri.) Paris, 1921. (Changed to XP 9038).

Afr 6535.40   Ouganda. (Beaufaere, Abel.) Paris, 1942.

Afr 5070.10   Ould Daddah, Marie Thérèse. Cours de droit constitutionnel mauritanién. Bordeaux, 1964.

Afr 8252.341.60   Ouma Smuts. (Macdonald, Tom.) London, 1946.

Afr 6390.79   Our African farm. (Truepeney, Charlotte.) London, 1965.

Afr 8292.5   Our boys under fire. (Mellish, A.E.) Charlottetown, 1900.

Afr 3708.14   Our Caughnawagas in Egypt. (Jackson, Louis.) Montreal, 1885.

Afr 9028.83   Our colony of Natal. (Peace, Walter.) London, 1883.

Afr 8678.446   Our country, our responsibility. (Innes, Duncan.) London, 1969.

Afr 6192.20   Our days on the Gold Coast. (Clifford, Elizabeth.) London, 1919.

Afr 10691.99.100   Our dead speak. (Uzodinma, Edmund.) London, 1967.

Afr 8659.60   Our first half-century, 1910-1960. Johannesburg, 1960.

Afr 3979.01.2   Our houseboat on the Nile. (Bacon, Lee.) Boston, 1901.

Afr 3979.01.5A   Our houseboat on the Nile. (Bacon, Lee.) Boston, 1901.

Afr 1608.81   Our mission to Morocco. (Trotter, P.D.) Edinburg, 1881.

Afr 7368.65   Our origin, dangers, and duties. (Blyden, E.W.) N.Y., 1865.

Afr 8289.03.7   Our regiments in South Africa, 1899-1902. (Stirling, J.) Edinburgh, 1913.

Afr 8678.135   Our responsibility. (Fagan, Henry Allan.) Stellenbosch, 1960.

Afr 8088.85   Our South African empire. (Greswell, W.) London, 1885. 2v.

Afr 6218.14   Our struggle. V.1-2. (Obi, Chike.) Yaba, 1962.

Afr 12785.89.130   Ousmane, Sembene. Les bouts de bois de Dieu, Banty Mam Yall. Photoreproduction. Paris, 1960.

Afr 12785.89.110   Ousmane, Sembene. L'harmattan. Paris, 1965.

Afr 12785.89.120   Ousmane, Sembene. O pays, mon beau peuple; roman. Paris, 1957.

Afr 12785.89.140   Ousmane, Sembene. Vehi-ciosane, ou Blanche-genèse, suivi du Mandat. Paris, 1965.

Afr 12785.89.100   Ousmane, Sembene. Voltaique; nouvelles. Paris, 1962.

Afr 9500.46   Out in the mid-day sun. (Gussman, Boris.) London, 1962.

Afr 6455.65.5A   Out of Africa. (Blixen Finecke, K.) N.Y., 1938.

Afr 6883.34   Out of Africa. (Carnochan, Frederic Grosvenor.) London, 1937.

Afr 8145.44   Out of Africa. (Deblank, J.) London, 1964.

Afr 4415.20   Out of barbarism. (Stoneham, C.T.) London, 1955.

Afr 6741.10   Out of the African night. 1st ed. (Reyburn, William David.) N.Y., 1968.

Afr 609.30.25   Out of the beaten track. (Court Treatt, Chaplin.) London, 1930.

Afr 9165.42.20 — Out of the crucible. (Chilvers, Hedley A.) Johannesburg, 1948.

Afr 7803.42 — Out of the jaws of the lion. 1st ed. (Dowdy, Homer E.) N.Y., 1965.

Afr 11523.32.100 — Out of the strong. (Lighton, R.E.) London, 1957.

Afr 8278.101 — Outlanders, a study of imperial expansion in South Africa, 1877-1902. (Vulliamy, C.E.) London, 1938.

Afr 9165.42.65 — The outlanders. (Crisp, Robert.) London, 1964.

Afr 626.136.6 — Outline of a plan for scientific research and training in Africa. (International Conference on the Organization of Research and Training in African in Relation to the Study, Conservation and Utilization of Natural Resources, Lagos, 1964.) Paris, 1964.

Afr 9502.22 — An outline of the sociological background to African labour. (Mitchell, J.C.) Salisbury, 1961.

Afr 679.68.25 — An outline of West African history. (Olowokure, Olvsanya.) Ilesha, 1968.

Afr 6395.14 — Outlines of East African society. (Goldthorpe, J.E.) Kampala, 1958.

Afr 7175.39 — Outras terras, outras gentes. (Galvao, H.) Lisboa, 1941. 2v.

Afr 7175.39.5F — Outras terras, outras gentes (viagens en Africa). v.1-. (Galvao, H.) Porto, 1944-.

Afr 609.35.9 — Over African jungles. (Johnson, Martin.) N.Y., 1935.

Afr 9165.71.15 — Over-Vaal; the history of an official residence. (Ploeger, Jan.) Pretoria, 1963.

Afr 3986.11 — Overall five year plan for economic and social development. (United Arab Republic.) n.p., 1960.

Afr 7815.2 — Overbergh, C. van. Les Bangala. 1. Bruxelles, 1907.

Afr 7815.4 — Overbergh, C. van. Les Basonge. 3. Bruxelles, 1908.

Afr 7815.5 — Overbergh, C. van. Les Mangbetu (Congo belge). 4. Bruxelles, 1909.

Afr 7815.3 — Overbergh, C. van. Les Mayombe. 2. Bruxelles, 1907.

Afr 8687.109 — Overdrafts and overwork. (Altmann, Hendrik.) Cape Town, 1959.

Afr 7309.60.5 — Overseas Companies of Portugal. Mozambique. N.Y., 196-.

Afr 6538.37 — Overseas Development Institute. Aid in Uganda. London, 1966. 3v.

Afr 8037.30 — Overseas reference book of the Union of South Africa. (Mockford, Julian.) London, 1945.

Afr 1608.86.10 — Ovilo y Canales, D.F. La mujer marroqui. Nueva edicion. Madrid, 1886.

Afr 1608.81.5 — Ovilo y Canales, F. La mujer Marroqui, estudio social. 2e ed. Madrid, 1881.

Afr 7180.35 — The Ovimbundu under two sovereignties. (Edwards, Adrian.) London, 1962.

Afr 590.27 — Owen, Nicholas. Journal of a slave-dealer. London, 1930.

Afr 810.17 — Owen, Richard. Saga of the Niger. London, 1961.

Afr 3979.66.10 — Owen, Robert. Egypt, United Arab Republic, the country and its people. London, 1966.

Afr 609.67.35 — Owen, Roderic Fenwick. Roddy Owen's Africa. Appleford, 1967.

Afr 2885.10 — Owen, Roger. Libya, a brief political and economic survey. London, 1961.

Afr 8055.5 — Owlographs, a collection of South African celebrities in caricature. (Boonzaier, D.C.) Cape Town, 1901.

Afr 12686.17.100 — Owologuem Yambo. Le devoir de violence, roman. Paris, 1968.

Afr 8089.69 — The Oxford history of South Africa. Oxford, 1969.

Afr 40.67.5 — Oyebola, Areoye. A textbook of government for West Africa. Ibadan, 1967.

Afr 12985.65.100 — Oyono, Ferdinand. Chemin d'Europe. Paris, 1960.

Afr 12985.65.700 — Oyono, Ferdinand. House boy. London, 1966.

Afr 12985.65.701 — Oyono, Ferdinand. House boy. London, 1967.

Afr 12985.65.705 — Oyono, Ferdinand. The old man and the medal. London, 1967.

Afr 12985.65.120 — Oyono, Ferdinand. Une vie de boy, roman. Paris, 1956.

Afr 12985.65.110 — Oyono, Ferdinand. Le vieux Nègre et la médaille. Paris, 1956.

Afr 13285.98.700 — Oyono, Guillaume. Three suitors: one husband. London, 1968.

Afr 10673.48.160 — Ozidii. (Clark, John Pepper.) London, 1966.

Afr 6890.2 — Paa Afrikas vilkaar. (Jacobsen, Axel.) København, 1951.

Afr 8678.291 — På svarta listan. (Waetberg, Per.) Stockholm, 1960.

Afr 8230.10.10 — The pace of the ox, the life of Paul Kruger. (Juta, M.) London, 1937.

Afr 2870.25.5 — Pace romana in Libia. (Gaziani, R.) Milano, 1937.

Afr 4557.97 — Pacelli, M. Viaggi in Etiopia. Napoli, 1797.

Afr 2030.460.10 — La pacification. (Keramane, Hadif.) Lausanne, 1960.

Afr 5340.20 — La pacification de la Côte-d'Ivoire. (Angoulvant, G.L.) Paris, 1916.

Afr 5640.9 — La pacification de Madagascar, 1896-98. (Lebon, A.) Paris, 1928.

Afr 5640.2 — La pacification de Madagascar. (Hellot, F.) Paris, 1900.

Afr 1571.37 — La pacification du Maroc, 1907-1934. (Ladreit Delacharriere, J.) Paris, 1936.

Afr 1494.15 — La pacification du Maroc. (Hure, A.J.J.) Paris, 1952.

Afr 11669.13.5 — Packer, Joy (P). The high roof. 1st ed. Philadelphia, 1959.

Afr 11669.13.10 — Packer, Joy (P). Home from sea. London, 1963.

Afr 11669.13 — Packer, Joy (P). Valley of the vines. Philadelphia, 1956.

Afr 8135.29 — Die pad van die veroweraar. 2. druk (Kemp, J.C.G.) Kaapstad, 1949.

Afr 1608.18 — Paddock, J. A narrative...shipwreck of the ship Oswego. N.Y., 1818.

Afr 210.63.5 — Padelford, Norman J. Africa and world order. N.Y., 1963.

Afr 6143.17 — Padenheim, D.W. Bref innehaallande beskrifning oefver Sierra Leona. Stockholm, 1801.

Afr 115.25 — Padmore, G. Africa and world peace. London, 1937.

Afr 6164.11 — Padmore, G. The Gold Coast revolution. London, 1953.

Afr 210.47.2 — Padmore, G. History of the Pan-African Congress. 2d ed. London, 1963.

Afr 505.46 — Padmore, George. Africa, Britain's third empire. London, 1949.

Afr 505.43 — Padmore, George. Afrika unter dem Joch der Weissen. Zürich, 193-.

Afr 6010.13 — Padmore, George. How Britain rules Africa. London, 1936.

Afr 628.231 — Padmore, George. The life and struggles of Negro toilers. London, 1931.

Afr 630.56 — Padmore, George. Pan-Africanism or Communism. N.Y., 1956.

Afr 28.87 — Padmore Research Library on African Affairs, Accra. Bibliography series. Acquisitions lists. Accra. 1-11,1962-1965//?

Afr 28.86 — Padmore Research Library on African Affairs, Accra. Bibliography series. Special subject bibliography. Accra. 2-5,1963-1965//?

Afr 4572.15 — Padoan, L. L'Abissinia nella geografia dell'Africa orientale. Milano, 1935.

Afr 150.2.5F — Os padrões dos descobrimentos portuguezes em Africa. 2a memoria. (Castilho, A.M. De.) Lisboa, 1871.

Afr 555.29.24 — Padwick, Constance Evelyn. MacKay of the great lake. London, 1928.

Afr 7309.30 — Paes Mamede. Nas costas d'Africa. Lisboa, 1930.

Afr 2929.34 — Paesaggi libici. Tripolitania. (Siciliani, D.) Tripoli, 1934.

Afr 2929.12.20 — Paesi di conquista. (Beltramelli, A.) Ferrara, 1915.

Afr 4700.13.15 — Paesi e problemi africani. (Gorresio, V.) Milano, 1937.

NEDL Afr 4230.4.2 — Paez, P. Historia Aethiopiae. v.1-4. Roma, 1905-06. 2v.

Afr 4230.4.3 — Paez, P. Historia de Etiopia. Livro 1-3. Porto, 1945. 3v.

Afr 4000.15 — Pagan tribes of the Nilotic Sudan. (Seligman, C.G.) London, 1932.

Afr 3163.8 — Pagani, Z. Viaggio di Domenico Trevisan, 1512. Venice, 1875.

Afr 3979.01.10 — Page, Thomas Nelson. On the Nile in 1901. Miami, 1970.

Afr 3275.25 — Une page de politique coloniale. (Méra.) Paris, 1913.

Afr 7937.4 — Une page d'histoire coloniale. (Ryckmans, P.) Bruxelles, 1953.

Afr 5340.5 — Un page d'histoire militaire coloniale, la colonne de Kong. (Monteil, P.L.) Paris, n.d.

Afr 6192.45 — Pageant of Ghana. (Wolfson, Freda.) London, 1958.

Afr 12005.5 — Pageard, Robert. Littérature négro-africaine. Paris, 1966.

Afr 5243.125.20 — Pageard, Robert. Notes sur l'histoire des Bambaras de Ségou. Paris, 1957.

Afr 2731.21 — Pagés, Louis. Jacques Faugère le Saharien. Nérac, 1967.

Afr 1259.38 — Pages africaines, l'Afrique du Nord vue par les littérateurs. (Sorrel, J.) Paris, 1938.

Afr 12015.15 — Pages africaines. (Vezinet, Paul.) Paris, 1963-[1966-]. 5v.

Afr 609.18 — Pages choisies d'impressions d'Afrique et de Locus Solus. (Roussel, Raymond.) Paris, 1918.

Afr 7200.16 — Paginas de doutrinação moçambicana. Lisboa.

Afr 1838.8 — Paillard, Jean. Faut-il faire l'Algérie un dominion. Paris, 1938.

Afr 2030.461.60 — Paillat, Claude. Dossier secret de l'Algérie. Paris, 1961. 2v.

Afr 3978.59 — Paine, Caroline. Tent and harem. N.Y., 1859.

Afr 10628.37.100 — Painful road to Kadjebi. (Hihetah, Robert Kofi.) Accra, 1966.

Afr 5488.22 — Pairault, Claude. Boum-le-Grand, village d'Iro. Paris, 1966.

Afr 1069.42 — El pais berebere. (Ghirelli, Angelo.) Madrid, 1942.

Afr 5748.95.30 — Paisant, M. Madagascar. 2e ed. Paris, 1895.

Afr 7175.9 — Paiva Conceiro, H.M. de. Relatorio de viagem entre Bailundo e as terras do Mususso. Lisboa, 1892.

Afr 7122.40 — Paiva Couceiro, H.M. de. Angola (Dous annos de governo junho 1907 - junho 1909.) Lisboa, 1910.

Afr 7188.301.800 — Paiva Couceiro, uma grande figura de Angola. (Lopo, Júlio de Castro.) Lisboa, 1968.

Afr 7108.10 — Paiva Manso, L.M.J. Historia do Congo. Lisboa, 1877.

Afr 555.8 — Paiva Manso, L.M.J. Historia ecclesiastica ultramarina. Lisboa, 1872.

Afr 1753.16 — Paiva Manso, Levy Maria Jordão. Memoria historica sobre os bispados de Ceuta e Tanger. Lisboa, 1858.

Afr 1570.65 — La paix au Maroc. (Sabin, Mony.) Paris, 1933.

Afr 2030.459.5 — Paix en Algérie. (Aumeran, Adolphe.) Paris, 1959.

Afr 1200.70 — La paix française en Afrique du Nord, en Algérie, au Maroc. (Steeg, Theodore.) Paris, 1926.

Afr 2030.400 — Pajaud, Henri. La révolution d'Alger. Paris, 1958.

Afr 5868.87 — Pajot, Elie. Simples renseignements sur l'Ile Bourbon. Paris, 1887.

Afr 8283.23 — Pakenham, E.H.P. Jameson's raid. London, 1960.

Afr 4559.59 — Pakenham, T. The mountains of Rasselas. N.Y., 1959.

Afr 2037.8 — Palacio, Léo. Les Pieds-Noirs dans le monde. Paris, 1968.

Afr 1739.5 — El palacio califal de Tetuan. (Valderrama Martinez, P.) Tetuan, 1954.

Afr 1570.21 — Palacios, C.M. De Marruecos. Badajoz, 1908.

Afr 4025.18 — Palaia kai nea Alexandreia. (Lachanokardes, E.) Alexandreia, 1927.

Afr 2308.23 — Palais d'Eté, résidence du gouverneur général de l'Algérie. Alger, 194-

Afr 4719.14 — Palarnenghi-Crispi, Tommaso. Francesco Crispi, la prima guerra d'Africa. Milano, 1914.

Afr 6210.43 — Palau Marti, Montserrat. Essai sur la notion de roi chez les Yoruba et les Aja-fon. Paris, 1966.

Afr 5368.3 — Palau Marti, Montserrat. Le roi-dieu au Bénin. Paris, 1964.

Afr 4753.5 — Palieri, M. Contributo alla bibliografia e cartografia della Somalia italiana. Roma, 193-.

Afr 3705.4 — Pall Mall Gazette, London. Who is to have the Soudan? London, 1884.

Afr 9435.16 — Palley, Claire. The constitutional history and law of Southern Rhodesia, 1888-1965. Oxford, 1966.

NEDL Afr 4080.4 — Pallme, J. Travels in Kordofan. London, 1844.

Afr 555.115 — Die Pallottiner in Kamerun. (Skolaster, Hermann.) Limburg an der Lahn, 1924.

Afr 555.3 — The palm land. (Thompson, George.) Cincinnati, 1859.

Afr 555.3.2 — The palm land. 2nd ed. (Thompson, George.) London, 1969.

Afr 3978.65.9 — Palm leaves from the Nile. (Wace, A.T.) Shrewsbury, 1865.

Afr 11853.88.110 — The palm-wine drinkard and his dead palm-wine tapster. (Tutuola, Amos.) London, 1952.

Afr 5219.28 — Palmer, H.R. Sudanese memoirs. Lagos, 1928. 3v.

Afr 5219.28.5 — Palmer, H.R. Sudanese memoirs. v.1-3. London, 1967.

Afr 6292.9.10 — Palmer, Herbert Richmond. Bornu Sahara and Sudan. London, 1936.

Afr 2209.31 — Palmes et burnous. (Malo, Pierre.) Paris, 1931.

Afr 3978.82.15 — Palms and temples. (Arnold, J.T.B.) London, 1882.

Afr 1571.43 — Paluel-Marmont, A.P.H.J. Le général Gouraud. Paris, 1937.

Afr 8688.5.10 — Pama, C. Heraldiek in Suid-Africa. Kaapstad, 1956.

Afr 8688.5.20 — Pama, C. Lions and virgins. Cape Town, 1965.

Afr 8688.5.5 — Pama, C. Simbole van die Unie. Kaapstad, 1960.

Afr 8688.5.15 — Pama, C. Wapens en vlae. Kaapstad, 1957.

Afr 8688.5 — Pama, C. Die wapens van die ou afrikaanse families. Kaapstad, 1959.

Afr 5580.3.30 — Pamigtniki. Wyd. 1. (Beniowski, M.A.) Warszawa, 1967.

Afr 6480.6 — Pamphlet vol. Pamphlets on disturbances in Uganda. 3 pam.

Afr 5425.20 — Los pámues de nuestra Guin. (Trujeda Incerna, Luis.) Madrid, 1946.

Afr 4070.18   A picnic party in wildest Africa. (Bulpett, C.W.L.) London, 1907.

Afr 9165.42.50   Picton-Seymour, Desirée. Transvaal republican. Cape Town, 1956.

Afr 8835.43F   Pictorial album of Cape Town. (Bowler, Thomas William.) Cape Town, 1966.

Afr 9165.42.25F   Pictorial history of Johannesburg. (Smith, Anna H.) Johannesburg, 1956.

Afr 8250.43   Pictorial material of Cecil J. Rhodes. (Cape Town. University. Libraries.) Cape Town, 1964.

Afr 6147.8.10   The picture of Krio life, Freetown, 1900-1920. (Kreutzinger, Helga.) Wien, 1968.

Afr 8028.164   Pictures of South African interest in the Graphic, 1896-1899, a list. Thesis. (Matton, Carol Ann.) Johannesburg, 1967.

Afr 810.11F   Picturesque views on the river Niger. (Allen, W.) London, 1840.

Afr 630.56.5   Pidoux, Edmond. L'Afrique à l'âge ingrat. Neuchâtel, 1956.

Afr 5749.62   Pidoux, Edmond. Madagascar, maître à son bord. Lausanne, 1962.

Afr 1922.5   Pièces curieuses, ou Alger en 1802. Paris, 1830.
Afr 2030.463.35   Pied-noir, mon frère. (Loiseau, J.) Paris, 1963.
Afr 2037.8   Les Pieds-Noirs dans le monde. (Palacio, Léo.) Paris, 1968.

Afr 2260.25   Les pieds noirs dans le plat. (Figueras, André.) Paris, 1962.

Afr 2260.17   Pieds-noirs et la presse française. Paris, 1962.
Afr 12922.7.100   Un piège sans fin. (Bhely-Quenum, Olympe.) Paris, 1960.
Afr 6780.37   Pienaar, M.J.P. Baanbrekers in die maalstroom. Kaapstad, 1942.

Afr 8289.02.3   Pienaar, P. With Steijn and De Wet. London, 1902.
Afr 8678.130   Pienaar, S. South Africa. London, 1960.
Afr 7540.3   Pierantoni, R. Il Trattato di Berlino e lo stato del Congo. Roma, 1898.

Afr 609.63.25   Pierce, Samuel R. African journey, 1963. N.Y., 1963?
Afr 1490.17   Pierrat, J. Vingt-six mois au Maroc. Paris, 1916.
Afr 4500.1   Pierre-Alype, L. L'Ethiopie et les convoitises allemandes. Paris, 1917.

Afr 4259.25   Pierre-Alype, L.M. Sous la couronne de Salomon. L'empire des Negus. Paris, 1925.

Afr 3275.24   Pierre l'Ermite. Brigands in Egypt. London, 1882.
Afr 1623.942.5   Piersius. Etude sur les communautés rurales en Beni-Ahsen. Rabat, 1942.

Afr 6146.8   Pierson, Arthur. Seven years in Sierra Leone. N.Y., 1897.
Afr 210.61.75   Pierson-Mathy, P. Evolution politique de l'Afrique. Bruxelles, 1961.

Afr 545.33   Pierwotne religie czarnej Afryki. (Zajaczkowski, Andrzej.) Warszawa, 1965. 10v.

Afr 2308.3   Piesse, L. Alger et ses environs. Paris, 1901.
Afr 2220.3   Piesse, L. Itinéraire de l'Algérie. Paris, 1862.
Afr 2220.5   Piesse, L. Itinéraire de l'Algérie. Paris, 1881.
Afr 2220.6   Piesse, L. Itinéraire de l'Algérie. Paris, 1885.
X Cg   Afr 2373.3   Piesse, Louis. Les villes de l'Algérie, Tlemcen. Paris, 1889. (Changed to XP 3867)

Afr 8180.30   Piet retief. (Franken, J.L.M.) Kaapstad, 1949.
Afr 8180.35   Piet retief. (Hugo, M.) Johannesburg, 1961.
Afr 8180.31   Piet retief. (Preller, G.S.) Pretoria, 1912.
Afr 10117.5   Pietense, Cosmo. Ten one-act plays. London, 1968.
Afr 9070.5   Pietermaritzburg, Natal, South Africa. (Pietermaritzburg. Corporation.) Pietermaritzburg, 193-.

Afr 9070.5   Pietermaritzburg. Corporation. Pietermaritzburg, Natal, South Africa. Pietermaritzburg, 193-.

Afr 9070.7   Pietermaritzburg panorama. (Hattersley, A.F.) Pietermaritzburg, 1938.

Afr 9165.70   Pietersburg Magisterial District; a bibliography. (Davidson, Elizabeth.) Johannesburg, 1968.

Afr 630.62   Pieto, I. Causas de los conflictos en el Africa del sur. Berriz, 1962.

Afr 1608.78.3   Pietsch, L. Marokko-brief von der Deutschen gesand 1877. Leipzig, 1878.

Afr 7560.3   Pigafetta, F. A report on the kingdom of Congo. London, 1881.

Afr 4500.5.5   Pigli, Mario. L'Etiopia, l'incognita africana. 2a ed. Padova, 1935.

Afr 4500.5   Pigli, Mario. L'Etiopia moderna nelle sue relazioni Internazionali, 1859-1931. Padova, 1933.

Afr 2397.7   Pignal, Jacques. Maurice Cochard, mon ami. Toulouse, 1964.

Afr 4430.61.2   Pignatelli, L. La guerra dei sette mesi. Milano, 1965.
Afr 4430.61   Pignatelli, L. La guerra dei sette mesi. Napoli, 1961.
Afr 628.258   Piguion, René. Reveil de culture. Port au Prince, 1958.
Afr 9839.65   Pike, John G. Malawi, a geographical study. London, 1965.
Afr 9769.68   Pike, John G. Malawi; a political and economic history. London, 1968.

Afr 9769.68.2   Pike, John G. Malawi; a political and economic history. N.Y., 1968.

Afr 5842.6   Pike, N. Sub-tropical rambles. London, 1873.
Afr 8325.45   Pilcher, T.D. Some lessons from the Boer War. London, 1903.

Afr 3818.10   A pilgrim church's progress. (Allison, Oliver Claude.) London, 1966.

Afr 3978.52   A pilgrimage to Egypt. (Smith, J.V.C.) Boston, 1852.
NEDL   Afr 6275.19   A pilgrimage to my mother land (Central Africa). (Campbell, R.) London, 1861.

Afr 6275.19.3   A pilgrimage to my mother land (Central Africa). (Campbell, R.) N.Y., 1861.

Afr 8659.28   The pilgrims' way in South Africa. (Fairbridge, D.) London, 1928.

Afr Doc 5402.5   Pilipenko, Helene. Recapitulation des periodiques officiels parus en Tunisie de 1881 à 1955. Tunis, 1956.

Afr 6535.9   Pilkington of Uganda. (Harford-Battersby, P.F.) London, n.d.

Afr 8846.19   Pim, H. A Transkei enquiry, 1933. Lovedale, 1934.
Afr 3700.20   Pimblett, W. Melville. Story of the Soudan war. London, 1885.

Afr 6979.20   Pimienta, R. L'ancienne colonie allemande en Sud-ouest Afrique. Paris, 1920.

Afr 2290.5   Pimodan. Oran Tlemcen sud-oranais (1899-1900). Paris, 1903.

Afr 9854.22   Pineau, Henry. Évêque roi des brigands. Paris, 1938.
Afr 4394.3.11   Pini, Cesare G. Adua, brevi cenni sulla guerra italo-etiopica mahdista degli anni 1895-96. Torino, 1926.

Afr 2438.25   Pinon, J.P.M. Les attributions des contrôleurs civils en Tunisie. Thèse. Tunis, 1931.

Afr 1571.29   Pinon, Rene. Au Maroc, fin des temps héroiques. Paris, 1935.

Afr 1570.5   Pinon, Rene. L'empire de la Méditerranée. Paris, 1904.
Afr 4513.36.150   Pinti, Luigi. Le vie dell'impero. Roma, 1936.
Afr 7175.42   Pinto, F.A. Angola e Congo. Lisboa, 1888.
Afr 7065.515   Pinto, João Teixeira. A ocupação militar da Guiné. Lisboa, 1936.

Afr 5748.98.5   Piolet, J.B. Douze leçons à la Sorbonne sur Madagascar. Paris, 1898.

Afr 5749.00F   Piolet, J.B. Madagascar. Paris, 1900.
Afr 5748.95.15   Piolet, J.B. Madagascar et les Hova. Paris, 1895.
Afr 8252.36   Pioneer, soldier and politician. (Harris, D.) London, 1931.

Afr 8110.14   Pioneer travellers of South Africa. (Forbes, Vernon S.) Cape Town, 1965.

Afr 8110.3.39   Pioneer travellers of South Africa. (Forbes, Vernon Siegfried.) Cape Town, 1965.

Afr 3818.4   Pioneering for Christ in the Sudan. (Veenstra, Johanna.) London, 1928.

Afr 7809.03   Pioneering in Central Africa. (Verner, S.P.) Richmond, 1903.

Afr 1608.94.3   Pioneering in Morocco. (Kerr, Robert.) London, 1894.
Afr 7809.00.5   Pioneering on the Congo. (Bentley, W.H.) N.Y., 1900. 2v.

Afr 8844.10   Pioneers in Pondoland. (Callaway, G.) Lovedale, 1939.
Afr 8659.14   Pioneers in South Africa. (Johnston, H.H.) London, 1914.
Afr 9619.2   Pioneers of Rhodesia. (Tabler, Edward C.) Cape Town, 1966.

Afr 9170.11   Pioneers' path. (Carr, W.S.) Cape Town, 1953.
Afr 3725.14   Pioniere im Osten. (Ade, H.C.) Stuttgart, 1923.
Afr 4095.21   Un pioniere italiano delle scoperte del Nilo, Giovanni Miani, il Leone Bianco. (Piva, Gino.) Firenze, 1930.

Afr 4700.36.25   Pionieri e soldati d'Africa orientale dall'acquisto di Assab all'impero romano d'Etiopia. (Bardi, Pietro M.) Milano, 1936.

Afr 530.28.10   Pionieri italiane in Africa. (Lancellatti, A.) Brescia, 1951.

Afr 4700.33.5   Pionieri italiani in Africa. (Cesari, Cesare.) Rome, 1933.

Afr 4700.31   I pionieri italiani nelle nostre colonie. (Della Valle, Carlo.) Roma, 1931.

Afr 8809.41   Pioniers van die Dorsland. (Merwe, Petrus J. van der.) Kaapstad, 1941.

Afr 555.73   Le pionnier du Gabon. (Rognes, Louis.) Paris, 1957.
Afr 5227.15   Les pionniers du Soudan. (Meniaud, Jacques.) Paris, 1931. 2v.

Afr 4390.20   Piozza, G. Alla corte di Menelik. Ancona, 1912.
Afr 2000.10   Piquet, V. L'Algérie française. Paris, 1930.
Afr 1955.30   Piquet, V. Campagnes d'Afrique, 1830-1910. Paris, 1912.
Afr 1069.09   Piquet, V. Les civilisations de l'Afrique du Nord. Paris, 1909.

Afr 1069.09.3   Piquet, V. Les civilisations de l'Afrique du Nord. 2d ed. Paris, 1917.

Afr 2260.13   Piquet, V. La colonisation française dans l'Afrique du nord. Paris, 1912.

Afr 2260.13.3   Piquet, V. La colonisation française dans l'Afrique du nord. Paris, 1914.

Afr 1609.17.5   Piquet, Victor. Le Maroc, geographie, histoire, mise en valeur. Paris, 1917.

Afr 1609.17.7   Piquet, Victor. Le Maroc, geographie, histoire, mise en valeur. 3 éd. Paris, 1920.

Afr 1635.15   Piquet, Victor. Le peuple marocain. Paris, 1925.
Afr 1840.12   Piquet, Victor. Les reformes en Algerie et le statut des indigenes. Paris, 1919.

Afr 1100.1   La piraterie sur l'Atlantique. (Vignols, L.) Rennes, 1890.

Afr 7549.21   Pirenne, Jacques. Coup d'oeil sur l'histoire du Congo. Bruxelles, 1921.

Afr 7176.6   Pires, Antonio. Angola. Luanda, 1964.
Afr 7122.76   Pires, P. Braseiro da morte. Viseu, Portugal, 1963.
Afr 7183.15   Pires, Rui. Luanda. Porto, 195-.
Afr 5385.32   Pires, Vicente F. Viagem de Africa em o reino de Dahome. São Paulo, 1957.

Afr 7315.5   Pires de Lima, A. Contribuição para o estudo antropologico indigenas de Moçambique. Porto, 1918.

Afr 7320.20   Pires de Lima, Americo. Explorações em Moçambique. Lisboa, 1943.

Afr 7540.44   Piron, Pierre. L'indépendance de la magistrature et la statut des magistrats. Bruxelles, 1956.

Afr 109.62.35   Pirone, Michele. Appunti di storia dell'Africa. Milano, 1962.

Afr 8252.228.10   Pirow, Oswald. James Barry Munnik Hertzog. London, 1958.
Afr 2850.8   Pisani, F. Un esperimento di colonizzazione nella Tripolitania. Messina, 1904.

Afr 7815.12   Piscelli, M. Nel paese dei Bango-bango. Napoli, 1909.
Afr 4574.2   Pischke, J.D. The public sector. Addis Ababa, 1966.
Afr 5056.154   La piste Maroc-Sénégal. (Du Puigaudeau, Odette.) Paris, 1954.

Afr 4700.37.5   Pistolese, G.E. L'economia dell'impero. Roma, 1937.
Afr 1750.28   Pita, F. Del protectorado español en Marruecos. Melilla, 1933.

Afr 1750.28.5   Pita, F. Marruecos. Melilla, 1925.
Afr 1573.18   Pita, Federico. La accion militar y politica de España en Africa a traves de los tiempos. Madrid, 1915.

Afr 9565.2   Pitch, Anthony. Inside Zambia - and out. Cape Town, 1967.
Afr 5832.10   Pitot, Albert. L'Ile de France. Port-Louis, 1899.
Afr 5832.10.5   Pitot, Albert. L'ile de Maurice. V.1-2. Port-Louis, 1910-12.

Afr 5832.10.3   Pitot, Albert. T'eyland Mauritius. Port-Louis, 1905.
Afr 530.24   Pittaluga, Rosetta. Rievocazioni africane. Brescia, 1935.
Afr 4095.21   Piva, Gino. Un pioniere italiano delle scoperte del Nilo, Giovanni Miani, il Leone Bianco. Firenze, 1930.

Afr 550.8.15   Pizzoli, D. Per i funeri del Cardinal Lavigerie. Palermo, 1892.

X Cg   Afr 9700.5   Pla-speaking people of Northern Rhodesia. (Smith, E.) London, 1920. 2v.

Afr 8340.15   Plaatje, S.T. Native life in South Africa. London, 1916.
Afr 9502.12   Plaatje, S.T. Uhudi. Kimberley, 1930.
Afr 11542.87.110   A place apart. (Lytton, David.) London, 1961.
Afr 1724.2   La place de mazagan. (Goulven, J.) Paris, 1917.
Afr 11303.2.100   The place of dragons. (Crafford, Frederick Simon.) Cape Town, 1966.

Afr 6463.3   A place to feel at home, a study of two independent churches in western Kenya. (Welbourn, Frederick B.) London, 1966.

Afr 2030.135	Plaidoyer pour l'Algérie. (Candas, Maurice F.M.) Paris, 1957.
Afr 1727.5	Plaines et piedmonts du bassin de la Moulouya. (Raynal, R.) Rabat, 1961.
Afr 555.40	Plan alto do sul de Angola. (Lecomte, E.) Lisboa, 1897.
Afr 1623.958.15F	Plan biennal d'equipement, 1958-1959. (Maroc. Division de la Coordination Économique et du Plan.) Rabat, 1958.
Afr 2223.960.20	Plan de Constantine, 1959-1963. (Algeria. Direction du Plan et des Etudes Economiques.) Alger, 1960.
Afr 2223.961.10	Le plan de Constantine et la République Algérienne de demain. (Vaucher, G.) Neuchâtel, 1961.
Afr 6686.48.25F	Plan de développement, 1966-1970: organization administrative et développement. (Société d'Etudes pour le Développement Économique et Social, Paris.) Paris, 1965.
Afr 5758.57F	Plan de developpement economique et social, programme, 1958-1962. (Madagascar. Haut Commissariat.) Tananarive, 1957.
Afr 6686.48.20F	Plan de développement économique et social, 1966-1970; l'artisanat togolais. (Munich. Institut für Wirtschaftsforschung.) Munich, 1965.
Afr 6686.48.30F	Plan de développement économique et social, 1966-1970; le commerce au Togo. (Munich. Institut für Wirtschaftsforschung.) Munich, 1965.
Afr 5387.14	Plan de développement économique et social, 1966-1970. (Dahomey.) Cotohou, 1966.
Afr 5422.7	Plan de développement économique et social, 1966-1970. (Gabon.) Paris, 1967?
Afr 6686.48.45F	Plan de développement économique et social, 1966-1970. (Société d'Etudes pour le Développement Économique et Social, Paris.) Paris, 1965.
Afr 6686.48.5F	Plan de développement économique et social, 1966-1970: annexes techniques, développement rural. (Togo.) Paris, 1965.
Afr 6686.48.10	Plan de développement économique et social, 1966-1970. Annexes techniques: industrie. (Togo.) Paris, 1965.
Afr 6686.48.35F	Plan de développement économique et social, 1966-1970: scolarisation. (Société d'Etudes pour le Développement Économique et Social.) Paris, 1965.
Afr 5758.58	Plan de developpement economique et social. (Madagascar.) Tananarive. 1947+ 4v.
Afr 1494.5	Plan de réformes marocaines. (Comité d'Action Marocaine.) n.p., 1934.
Afr 7812.251F	Plan décennal pour le développement. (Belgium.) Bruxelles, 1951.
Afr 7812.249	Plan décennal pour le développement économique et social du Congo belge. (Belgium. Ministère des Colonies.) Bruxelles, 1949.
Afr 7812.260.10	Le plan décennal pour le développement économique et social du Congo belge. (Congo, Belgian. Commissariat au Plan Décennal.) Bruxelles, 1960.
Afr 9699.41	Plan for Africa, a report prepared for the colonial bureau of the Fabian Society. (Hinden, Rita.) London, 1941.
Afr 5892.5	A plan for Seychelles. (Seychelles.) Victoria, 1960? 5 pam.
Afr 2623.965	Plan guadriennal, 1965-1968. (Tunisia. Secrétariat d'Etat au Plan et à l'Economie Nationale.) Tunis, 1965?
Afr 5430.10	Plan interimaire de développement économique et social. (Congo (Brazzaville).) Paris. 1964-1968
Afr 5183.961.5	Plan quadriennal de développement, 1961-1964. (Senegal.) Dakar, 1961.
Afr 1623.960.5	Plan quinquennal, 1960-1964. (Morocco. Division de la Coordination Économique et du Plan.) Rabat, 1960.
Afr 1623.960.6	Plan quinquennal, 1960-1964. (Morocco. Division de la Coordination Économique et du Plan.) Rabat, 1961.
Afr 5758.64F	Plan quinquennal, 1964-1968. (Madagascar. Commissariat Général au Plan.) Tananarive, 1964.
Afr 6686.48	Plan quinquennal de développement, 1966-1970. (Togo.) Paris, 1965.
Afr 5183.964	Plan réorienté. (Senegal.) n.p., n.d.
Afr 7815.37	Plancquaert, M. Les Jaga et les Bayaka du Kwango. Bruxelles, 1932.
Afr 2300.8	Planhol, Xavier de. Nouveaux villages algérois. Paris, 1961.
Afr 5046.2	Planification en Afrique. v.2- (France. Direction des Affaires Economiques et Financières.) Paris, 1962- 3v.
Afr 1623.962	Planning in Morocco. (Waterston, A.) Washington, 1962.
Afr 9499.74	Planning the development of the wealth of three nations. (Phoenix Group.) Salisbury, 1960.
Afr 6277.86	Planning without facts. (Stolper, Wolfgang.) Cambridge, 1966.
Afr 626.157.5	Planowanie w niektorych krajach Afryki. (Halpern, Jan.) Warszawa, 1963.
Afr 8369.42.2	Plans for a better world. (Smuts, J.C.) London, 1942.
Afr 6275.55	Plantation and village in the Cameroons. (Ardener, Edwin.) London, 1960.
Afr 2500.1	Plantet, E. Correspondance des beys de Tunis. Paris, 1893-4. 3v.
Afr 1900.3	Plantet, E. Correspondance des deys d'Alger, 1579-1833. Paris, 1889.
Afr 1408.4	Plantet, E. Mouley Ismael. Paris, 1893.
Afr 1915.9	Plantet, Eugène. Les consuls de France à Alger avant la conquête, 1579-1830. Paris, 1930.
Afr 550.68	The planting of Christianity in Africa. (Groves, C.P.) London, 1948. 4v.
Afr 6210.46	Planting the vineyard. (Nigeria, Midwestern. Ministry of Information.) Benin City, 1964.
Afr 7815.5.6	Plas, J.V. Les Kuku. 6. Bruxelles, 1910.
Afr 8095.25F	Plate-atlas von geskeidenis von die Unie van Suid-Afrika. (Ploegers, J.) Pretoria, 1949.
Afr 5248.5	Le plateau central nigérien. (Desplagnes, Louis.) Paris, 1907.
Afr 9700.35	The plateau Tonga of Northern Rhodesia. (Colson, Elizabeth.) Manchester, 1962.
Afr 3986.958.5	Platt, Raye R. Egypt, a compendium. N.Y., 1958.
Afr 6097.7	Platt, William James. From fetish to faith. London, 1935.
Afr 1326.1	Playfair, L. Bibliography of Morocco. London, 1892.
Afr 1826.1	Playfair, R.L. Bibliography of Algeria and supplement. London, 1888.
Afr 2804.1	Playfair, R.L. Bibliography of the Barbary states. Pt.1. Tripoli and the Cyrenaica. London, 1889.
Afr 1925.5.5	Playfair, R.L. Episodes de l'histoire des relations de Grande Bretagne. Alger, 1879.
Afr 1925.5	Playfair, R.L. The scourge of Christendom. London, 1884.

Afr 10117.10	Plays from black Africa. 1st ed. (Litto, Fredric M.) N.Y., 1968.
Afr 530.26	Plebano, A. I possedimenti italiani in Africa. Roma, 1889.
Afr 679.68.20	Plessz, Nicolas G. Problems and prospects of economic integration in West Africa. Montreal, 1968.
Afr 2500.20	Pleville-le-Pelley, G.R. La mission de Pleville-le-Pelley à Tunis, 1793-1794. Tunis, 1921.
Afr 1609.07	Pleydell, K.M. Sketches of life in Morocco. London, 1907.
Afr 635.62.10	Plisnier-Ladame, F. La condition de l'Africaine en Afrique noire. Bruxelles, 1961.
Afr 12936.50.102	Pliya, Jean. Kondo le requin; drame historique en trois actes. 2. éd. Porto-Novo, 1966?
Afr 9165.71.15	Ploeger, Jan. Over-Vaal; the history of an official residence. Pretoria, 1963.
Afr 8095.25F	Ploegers, J. Plate-atlas von geskeidenis von die Unie von Suid-Afrika. Pretoria, 1949.
Afr 8250.27	Plomer, W. Cecil Rhodes. London, 1933.
Afr 6295.248	Plotnicov, Leonard. Strangers to the city; urban man in Jos, Nigeria. Pittsburgh, 1967.
Afr 5266.5	Ploussard, Jean. Carnet de route de Jean Ploussard. Paris, 1964.
Afr 4558.68.3	Plowden, W.C. Travels in Abyssinia. London, 1868.
Afr 2285.31	Pluie et crue dans le Sahara nord-occidental. (Vanney, Jean-René.) Alger, 1960.
Afr 659.67.5	Plum, Werner. Sozialer Wandel im Maghreb i Voraussetzungen und Erfahrungen der genossenschaftlichen Entwicklung. Hannover, 1967.
Afr 9446.28	Plumer, Herbert C. An irregular corps in Matabeleland. London, 1897.
Afr 6777.5	Plumon, E. La colonie allemande de l'Afrique Orientale. Heidelberg, 1906.
Afr 632.52	Pluralism in Africa. Berkeley, 1969.
Afr 1571.17.65	Les plus belles lettres de Lyautey. (Lyautey, L.H.G.) Paris, 1962.
Afr 4513.36.110	Po di posto al sole. Milano, 1936.
Afr 679.61	Po stranam Afriki. (Linkhovoin, L.L.) Ulan-Ude, 1961.
Afr 1432.20	Poblacion y Fernandez, A. Historia medica de la guerra de Africa. Madrid, 1860.
Afr 3320.143	Pocket book. (United Arab Republic. Information Department.)
Afr 1620.30	A pocket guide to French Morocco. (U.S. Office of Armed Forces Information and Education.) Washington, 1956.
Afr 1270.2	A pocket guide to North Africa. (United States. Department of Defense.) Washington, 1958.
Afr 6740.40	Podlewski, André Michel. La dynamique des principales populations du Nord Cameroun. Paris, 1966.
Afr 2929.12.13	Podrecca, G. Libia. Roma, 1912.
Afr 12639.24.130	Poèmes. (Senghor, L.S.) Paris, 1964.
Afr 11197.5.100	Poems. (Beaumont, John H.) Cape Town, 1957.
Afr 10673.48.130	Poems. (Clark, John Pepper.) Ibadan, 1962.
Afr 10536.69.100	Poems. (Peters, Lenrie.) Ibadan, 1964.
Afr 10016.2	Poems from Black Africa. (Hughes, L.) Bloomington, Ind., 1963.
Afr 44622.89.124A	Poems from Kenya. (Bhalo, Ahmad Nassir Bin Juma.) Madison, 1966.
Afr 11052.2	Poems of South African history. (Petrie, A.) London, 1919.
Afr 11802.92.110	Poems with flute. (Sowden, Lewis.) London, 1955.
Afr 2030.466.5	Poerner, Arthur J. Argélia: o caminho da independência. Rio de Janeiro, 1966.
Afr 20136.2	Poesia sudanese. (Tescaroli, Livio.) Bologna, 1961.
Afr 1432.16	Pamphlet vol. Poesias a la guerra de Africa. 6 pam.
Afr 7937.7	Poésie, dynastique du Ruanda et épopée akritique. (Papadopoullos, T.) Paris, 1963.
Afr 12321.2	La poésie algérienne de 1830 à nos jours. (Memmi, Albert.) Paris, 1963.
Afr 42715.22	La poésie chez les primitifs, ou Contes, fables, récits et proverbes du Rwanda (Lac Kivu). (Hurel, Eugène.) Bruxelles, 1922.
Afr 28716.2	Poésie peule de l'Adamawa. (Lacroix, Pierre Francis.) Paris, 1965. 2v.
Afr 7176.22	Pössinger, Hermann. Angola als Wirtschaftspartner. Köln, 1966.
Afr 14518.2	Poetas e contistas africanos de expressão portuguesa. (Neves, João Alves das.) São Paulo, 1963.
Afr 2209.62	Les poètes de l'année, rites et symboles. (Servier, J.) Paris, 1962.
Afr 12421.2	Les poètes français du Maroc. (Lebel, Roland.) Tanger, 1956.
Afr 41906.2	Poètes nzakara. (Dampierre, Eric de.) Paris, 1963.
Afr 10116.5	Poetry from Africa. (Sergeant, Howard.) Oxford, 1968.
Afr 11051.6	Poets in South Africa. (MacNab, R.M.) Cape Town, 1958.
Afr 10066.3	Poezja czarnej Afryki. (Kaminski-Durocher, B.) Warszawa, 1962.
Afr 1830.20.52	Poggi, Jacques. Les chemins de fer...de l'Algérie. Paris, 1931.
Afr 4513.38.25	Poggiali, Ciro. Albori dell'impero; l'Etiopia come è e come sarà. Milano, 1938.
Afr 8289.44	Pohl, V. Adventures of a Boer family. London, 1944.
Afr 11705.39.641	Pohl, V. The down and after. London, 1944.
Afr 11705.39.645	Pohl, V. Land of distant horizons. Johannesburg, 1946.
Afr 609.58.20	Le poids de l'Afrique. (Favrod, Charles.) Paris, 1958.
Afr 3988.8	Poinsenet, Marie Dominque. Rien n'est impossible à l'amour. Paris, 1968.
Afr 4892.12	Poinsot, Jean Paul. Djibouti et la côte française des Somalis. Paris, 1964.
Afr 10883.89.100	A point of no return. (Mulikita, Fwanyana Matale.) London, 1968.
Afr 5448.16	Pointe-Noire sous la croix de Lorraine. (Préclin, Louis.) Paris, 1967.
Afr 2608.92.3	Poire, Eugene. La Tunisie française. Paris, 1892.
Afr 1257.89.3	Poiret, J.L.M. Travels through Barbary...1785-1786. London, 1790.
Afr 1257.89	Poiret, J.L.M. Voyage en Barbarie. Paris, 1789. 2v.
Afr 5010.3	Poirier, Jean. Etudes de droit africain et de droit malgache. Paris, 1965.
Afr 5635.16	Poirier, Jules. Conquete de Madagascar (1895-1896). Paris, 1902.
Afr 8210.7	Poirier, Jules. Le Transvaal. Paris, 1900.
Afr 2500.10.2	Poiron, M. Mémoires concernant l'état présent du Royaume de Tunis. Paris, 1925.

Afr 2500.10   Poiron, M. Mémoires concernants l'état présent du Royaume de Tunis. Thèse complémentaire présentée par Jean Serres. Paris, 1925.

Afr 630.5   Les poisons de flèches et les poisons d'épreuve des indigènes de l'Afrique. (Vogt, E.F.) Lons-le-Saunier, 1912.

Afr 5501.3.10   Poisson, Henri. Le cinquantenaire de l'Academie malgache. Tananarive, 1952.

Afr 1200.120   Poker om Noord-Afrika. (Hart, W. Annet.) Den Haag, 1959.

Afr 5387.8   Polanyi, Karl. Dahomey and the slave trade; an analysis of an archaic economy. Seattle, 1966.

Afr 3138.10   Polemics on the origin of the Fatimi caliphs. (Mamour, P.H.) London, 1934.

Afr 3040.72   Poliak, A.N. Feudalism in Egypt, Syria, Palestine, and the Lebanon, 1250-1900. London, 1939.

Afr 3150.9   Poliak, A.N. Les revoltes populaires en Egypte à l'époque des Mamelouks. Paris, 1935.

Afr 4070.9.5   Policy for the eastern Soudan. Biarritz, 1885.

Afr 6277.76.10   The policy of the Federal Military Government on statutory corporations and state-owned companies. (Nigeria.) Lagos, 1968.

Afr 3300.75   The policy of tomorrow. (Ghali, M.B.) Washington, 1953.

Afr 1570.13   Polignac. La France, vassale de l'Angleterre. Alger, 1894.

Afr 4025.15   Polites, Athanasios G. L'hellénisme et l'Egypte moderne. T.1-2. Paris, 1929-30.

Afr 4025.15.5   Polites, Athanasios G. O hellynismos kai i neotera Aigyptos. Alexandreia, 1928. 2v.

Afr 3215.20   Polites, Athanasios G. Les rapports de la Grèce et de l'Egypte pendant le regne de Mohamed Aly, 1833-1849. Roma, 1935.

Afr 3305.25   Politi, Elie I. L'Egypte de 1914 à Suez. Paris, 1965.

Afr 5915.5   Politica aragonesa en Africa hasta la muerte de Fernando el Catolico. (Prieto y Llovera, P.) Madrid, 1952.

Afr 4700.14   Politica coloniale. (Colajanni, N.) Palermo, 1891.

Afr 4700.5.5   La politica coloniale dell'Italia. (Perticone, Giacomo.) Roma, 1965.

Afr 4700.27.15   La politica coloniale italiana dalle sue origini ad oggi. (Angelini, G.) Messina, 1927.

Afr 7176.14   Politica de bem e estoi rival en Angola. (Soares, Amaden.) Lisbon, 1961.

Afr 1573.10   Politica de España en Africa. (Reparaz, G. de.) Barcelona, 1907.

Afr 575.16.10   Politica di penetrazione in Africa. (Sabetta, Guido.) Roma, 1913.

Afr 1485.8   Politica ed armi al Marocco. (Marietti, Giovanni.) Torino, 1909.

Afr 4513.36.100   Politica estera. (Salemi, L.) Palermo, 1936.

Afr 630.41   Politica indigena africana. (Tritonj, Romolo.) Milano, 1941.

Afr 7015.8   Politica portugueza na Africa. Lisboa, 1889.

Afr 4766.10.15   Politica somala. (Lefebvre, R.) Bologna, 1933.

Afr 7369.47   The political and legislative history of Liberia. (Huberich, Charles Henry.) N.Y., 1947. 2v.

Afr 6410.2F   Political and social aspects of the development of municipal government in Kenya with special reference to Nairobi. (Great Britain. Colonial Office.) Nairobi, 1949.

Afr 3069.68   Political and social change in modern Egypt. (Holt, Peter M.) London, 1968.

Afr 7567.34   Political awakening in the Belgian Congo. (Lemarchand, Rene.) Berkeley, 1964.

Afr 212.10   The political awakening of Africa. (Emerson, Rupert.) Englewood Cliffs, N.J., 1965.

Afr 6280.58   Political change in a traditional African clan. (Scarritt, J.R.) Denver, 1965.

Afr 1369.61A   Political change in Morocco. (Ashford, Douglas.) Princeton, 1961.

Afr 9428.8   Political development in Southern Rhodesia. (Bean, Elizabeth Ann.) Cape Town, 1969.

Afr 6769.63   The political development of Tanganyika. (Taylor, J.C.) Stanford, 1963.

Afr 626.170   Political economy and African reality. (Popov, Iurii Nikolaevich.) Moscow, 1967.

Afr 9609.25   The political economy of Rhodesia. (Arrighi, G.) The Hague, 1967.

Afr 8676.67.10   The political economy of South Africa. (Horwitz, Ralph.) London, 1967.

Afr 8140.19   The political future of South Africa. (Brookes, E.H.) Pretoria, 1927.

Afr 210.61.45   The political future of the independent nations of Africa. (Goss, H.P.) Santa Barbara, Calif., 1961.

Afr 6164.20   A political history of Ghana. (Kimble, D.) Oxford, 1963.

Afr 710.60   A political history of tropical Africa. (Rotborg, Robert Irwin.) N.Y., 1965.

Afr 679.67.30   Political institutions of West Africa. (Price, Joseph Henry.) London, 1967.

Afr 6498.61.7   The political kingdom in Uganda; a study in bureaucratic nationalism. 2nd ed. (Apter, David E.) Princeton, 1967.

Afr 6498.61A   The political kingdom in Uganda. (Apter, David E.) Princeton, N.J., 1961.

Afr 9086.10   Political laws. (South Africa.) 1896.

Afr 45.67   Political leadership in Africa. (Le Vine, Victor T.) Stanford, 1967.

Afr 6883.20.10   The political organization of Unyamwezi. (Abrahams, R.G.) Cambridge, 1967.

Afr 210.64.60   Political parties and national integration in tropical Africa. (Coleman, J.S.) Berkeley, 1964.

Afr 5053.32   Political parties in French-speaking West Africa. (Morgenthau, R.S.) Oxford, 1964.

Afr 8849.12   The political philosophy of J.A. de Mist. (Murray, Andrew.) Cape Town, 1959.

Afr 7543.12   Political protest in the Congo. (Weiss, Herbert F.) Princeton, 1967.

Afr 3180.6   Political recollections related to Egypt. (Baldwin, G.) London, 1801.

Afr 1568.3   Political relations of Great Britain with Morocco from 1830 to 1841. (Flournoy, F.R.) N.Y., 1932.

Afr 8745.10   The political situation. (Schriener, O.) London, 1896.

Afr 10018.8   Political spider. (Beier, Ulli.) London, 1969.

Afr 1495.6.35   The political thought of Ben Barka. (Ben Barka, el Mehdi.) Havana, 1968.

Afr 6176.40   Political thought of Dr. Kwame Nkrumah. (Dzirasa, Stephen.) Accra, 1962.

Afr 6780.68   The political transformation of Tanganyika, 1920-1967. (Stephens, Hugh W.) N.Y., 1968.

Afr 6212.46   Political trends in Nigeria, 1960-1964. (Williams, Balatunde A.) Ibadan, 1965.

Afr 212.52   Politicheskie problemy afrikanskogo edinstva. (Etinger, Iakov Ia.) Moskva, 1967.

Afr 6542.22   Politicians and policies. (Leys, Colin.) Nairobi, 1967.

Afr 6210.42   The politics and administration of Nigerian government. (Blitz, L. Franklin.) N.Y., 1965.

Afr 8678.292   Politics and law in South Africa. (Lewin, Jilius.) London, 1963.

Afr 9700.20.5.2   Politics in a changing society. 2nd ed. (Barnes, J.A.) Manchester, 1967.

Afr 212.25   Politics in Africa. (Carter, Gwendolen Margaret.) N.Y., 1966.

Afr 210.62.5   Politics in Africa. (Spiro, Herbert John.) Englewood Cliffs, N.J., 1962.

Afr 9693.5   Politics in an urban African community. (Epstein, A.L.) Manchester, 1958.

Afr 28.95   Politics in Black Africa. (Hanna, W.J.) East Lansing, Michigan, 1964.

Afr 9700.20   Politics in changing society. (Barnes, J.A.) Cape Town, 1954.

Afr 6162.14   Politics in Ghana, 1946-1960. (Austin, Dennis.) N.Y., 1964.

Afr 7580.20   Politics in the Congo. (Young, Crawford.) Princeton, N.J., 1965.

Afr 8050.26   Politics in the Republic of South Africa. (Thompson, Leonard Monteath.) Boston, 1966.

Afr 679.65.15   Politics in West Africa. (Lewis, William A.) London, 1965.

Afr 50.35   The politics of African nationalism. (Shepherd, George.) N.Y., 1962.

Afr 8369.58.3   The politics of inequality, South Africa since 1948. 3rd ed. (Carter, G.M.) London, 1962.

Afr 8369.58   The politics of inequality. (Carter, G.M.) N.Y., 1958.

Afr 6333.68   Politics of integration. (Rothchild, Donald S.) Nairobi, 1968.

Afr 9853.6A   The politics of kinship. (Vanvelsen, J.) Manchester, 1964. 2v.

Afr 9448.72   The politics of partnership. (Keatley, Patrick.) Harmondsworth, Middlesex, 1963.

Afr 8685.27.15   The politics of racialism. 1. ed. (Narain, I.) Agra, 1962.

Afr 6284.10   The politics of tradition; continuity and change in Northern Nigeria, 1946-1966. (Whitaker, C. Sylvester.) Princeton, N.J., 1970.

Afr 8050.10   Politieke groepering in die wording van die afrikanernasie. Thesis. (Coetzee, Jan A.) Johannesburg, 1941.

Afr 5040.2   Politik im schwarzen Afrika. (Ansprenger, Franz.) Köln, 1961.

Afr 212.58   Politik och samhälle i Afrika. (Hydén, Göran.) Stockholm, 1967.

Afr 505.10   Politika Anglii i Italii v severo-vostochnoi Afrike. (Trofimov, V.A.) Moscow, 1962.

Afr 505.48   Politika Anglii v Afrike. (Akademiia Nauk SSSR. Institut Narodov Azii.) Moskva, 1967.

Afr 510.7   Politique africaine. (Hubert, L.) Paris, 1904.

Afr 5000.31   La politique africaine. Paris. 1968+

Afr 1583.16   La politique allemand. (Richet, Etienne.) Paris, 1917.

Afr 8089.13   La politique anglaise au Transvaal. (Merimee, P.) Toulouse, 1913.

Afr 1830.40.5   La politique coloniale de la monarchie de juillet. (Schefer, Christian.) Paris, 1928.

Afr 2533.6   La politique de Carthage. (Gros, Simone.) Paris, 1958.

Afr 2508.2   La politique de la France. (Rouard de Card, E.) Toulouse, 1906.

Afr 1623.937   La politique des contingents dans les relations franco-marocaines. Thèse. (Garcin, Pierre.) Lyon, 1937.

Afr 7812.224   La politique économique au Congo belge. (Congrès Colonial National.) Bruxelles, 1924.

Afr 1623.963   La politique économique et financière du Maroc independant. (Tiano, A.) Paris, 1963.

Afr 5055.61   La politique et le commerce français dans le Golfe de Guinée. (Schnapper, Bernard.) Paris, 1961.

Afr 210.66.20   Politique et révolution africaine. (Bauw, Jean Anatole de.) Bruxelles, 1966.

Afr 210.63.20   La politique étrangère des états africains. (Thiam, Doudou.) Paris, 1963.

Afr 1570.27   La politique française au Maroc. (Gourdin, A.) Paris, 1906.

Afr 2508.1   La politique française en Tunisie. (Estourneller de Constant, Paul.) Paris, 1891.

Afr 1583.15   La politique marocaine de l'allemagne. (Maurice, Louis.) Paris, 1916.

Afr 575.10   La politique musulmane dans l'Afrique occidentale française. (Quellien, A.) Paris, 1910.

Afr 1200.63   La politique turque en Afrique du Nord sous la Monarchie de Juillet. (Serres, Jean.) Paris, 1925.

Afr 1200.63.2   La politique turque en Afrique du Nord sous le Monarchie de Juillet. Thèse. (Serres, Jean.) Paris, 1925.

Afr 3252.10   Politis, A.G. Un projet d'alliance entre l'Egypte et la Grèce en 1867. Caire, 1931.

Afr 50.55   Politische Aspekte des neuen Afrika. (Cunha, Joaquim Moreira da Silva.) Hamburg, 1964.

Afr 8678.150   Die politischen und gesellschaftlichen Verhältnisse der Sotho-Tswana in Transvaal und Betschauanaland. (Brentz, Paul Lenert.) Hamburg, 1941.

Afr 8145.45   The polity of the Church of the province of South Africa. (Ervin, Spencer.) Ambler, Pa., 1964.

Afr 699.67   Pollard, John. The long safari. London, 1967.

Afr 3978.98.5   Pollard, Joseph. The land of the monuments. 2nd ed. London, 1898.

Afr 5748.67.4   Pollen, F.P.L. Een blik in Madagaskar. Leyden, 1867.

Afr 6903.8   Poller, Robert Manfred. Swakopmund and Walvis Bay. Cape Town, 1964.

Afr 4568.17   Pollera, A. La donna in Etiopia. Roma, 1922.

Afr 4710.7   Pollera, A. Le popolazioni indigene dell'Eritrea. Bologna, 1935.

Afr 4742.28   Pollera, Alberto. I Baria e i Cunama. Roma, 1913.

Afr 4394.3.8   Pollera, Alberto. La battaglia di Adua del 1 marzo 1896. Firenze, 1928.

Afr 4700.13   Pollera, Alberto. Piccola bibliografia dell'Africa orientale con speciale riguardo all'Eritrea e paesi confinanti. Asmara, 1933.

Afr 4559.26.5   Pollera, Alberto. Lo stato etiopico e la sua chiesa. Roma, 1926.

Afr 6025.2   Pollet, Maurice. L'Afrique du Commonwealth. Paris, 1963.

Afr 8095.37   Pollock, N.C. An historical geography of South Africa. London, 1963.

Afr 609.68   Pollock, Norman Charles. Africa. London, 1968.

Afr 3986.958.10   Polozhenie egipetskogo krestianstvo pered zemelskoi reformoi 1952 goda. (Sultanov, A.F.) Moscow, 1958.

Afr 635.61   Polozhenre zhenshchin v stranakh Afriki. (Smirnova, Raisà M.) Moskva, 1967.

Afr 210.61.40   Pomikkar, Kavalam M. Revolution in Africa. London, 1961.

Afr 4785.27   Pomilio, Marco. Un giornalista all'equatore. Firenze, 1933.

Afr 2025.17   Pommerol, J. Chez ceux qui guettent. Islam saharien. Paris, 1902.

Afr 2749.00   Pommerot, J. Une femme chez les sahariennes. Paris, 1900.

Afr 5049.100.7   Ponet, Marthe Bordeaux. Hyacinthe Jalabert. 2.éd. Paris, 1924.

Afr 5580.2   Ponget de St. Andre. La colonisation de Madagascar sous Louis XV. Paris, 1886.

Afr 5781.5   Pooka. Cinq jours à Tamatave. Maurice, 1888.

Afr 9700.16   Poole, Edward Humphry Lane. The native tribes of the eastern province of Northern Rhodesia. 2nd ed. Lusaka, 1938.

Afr 4098.2   Poole, R.S. The cities of Egypt. London, 1882.

Afr 3978.45.3   Poole, Sophia L. The Englishwoman in Egypt. London, 1845.

Afr 6143.15   Poole, T.E. Life...in Sierra Leone and the Gambia. London, 1850. 2v.

Afr 4788.4   Le popolazioni indigene della Somalia italiana. (Puccioni, Nello.) Bologna, 1937.

Afr 4710.7   Le popolazioni indigene dell'Eritrea. (Pollera, A.) Bologna, 1935.

Afr 4575.5   Popoli dell'Ethiopia occidentale. (Conti Rossini, C.) Roma, 1919.

Afr 626.170   Popov, Iurii Nikolaevich. Political economy and African reality. Moscow, 1967.

Afr 7183.20   As populações nativas do Congo portugues. (Felgas, H.A.) Luanda, 1960.

Afr 7180.38.2   As populacões nativas do norte de Angola. 2. ed. (Felgas, Hélio.) Lisboa, 1965.

Afr 7815.34   La population africaine à Elisabethville. (Benoit, J.) Elisabethville, 195-.

Afr Doc 1307.365   Population and housing survey, 1964-65. (Sudan. Department of Statistics.) Khartoum, 1965. 11v.

Afr 632.48   Population and political systems in tropical Africa. (Stevenson, Robert F.) N.Y., 1968.

Afr Doc 4307.351   Population census, 8th May 1951. (South Africa. Bureau of Statistics.) Pretoria, 1955. 2v.

Afr Doc 4307.360   Population census, 1960. (South Africa. Office of Census and Statistics.) Pretoria, 1962-65. 2v.

Afr Doc 3207.362.5F   Population census, 1962. (Kenya. Economics and Statistics Division.) Nairobi? 1964.

Afr Doc 4107.362F   Population census, 1962. (Swaziland. Census Office.) n.p., n.d.

Afr Doc 2307.363.2F   Population census of Nigeria, Nov., 1963. 2d ed. (Nigeria. Regional Census Office.) Ibadan, 1963.

Afr Doc 2307.363.10F   Population census of Nigeria, 1963. Northern region. (Nigeria. Federal Census Office.) Lagos, 1965. 5v.

Afr Doc 2307.353   Population census of Nigeria. (Nigeria. Department of Statistics.) Lagos. 1952-1953

Afr Doc 2560.725.5   Population census of the Eastern Region of Nigeria, 1953. Bulletins. (Nigeria. Department of Statistics.) Lagos, 1955.

Afr Doc 2407.352.105   Population census of the Northern Region of Nigeria, 1952 Bulletins. (Nigeria. Department of Statistics.) Lagos, 1954.

Afr Doc 2707.360   Population census of the Seychelles Colony. (Seychelles.) Victoria? 1961?

Afr Doc 2520.725   Population census of the Western region of Nigeria, 1952. (Nigeria. Department of Statistics.) Lagos, 1956.

Afr Doc 2520.725.5   Population census of the Western region of Nigeria, 1952. Bulletins. (Nigeria. Department of Statistics.) Lagos, 1955.

Afr Doc 4307.346   Population census 7th May 1946. Bevolkinsensus, 7 Mai 1946. (South Africa. Office of Census and Statistics.) Pretoria, 1949. 2v.

Afr Doc 7708.5   La population congolaise en 1953. (Congo. Secretariat Général.) n.p., 195-?

Afr 3993.538   La population de l'Egypte. Thèse. (Mboria, L.) Le Caire, 1938.

Afr Doc 5608.105F   Population de Madagascar. (Malagasy Republic. Institut National de la Statistique et de la Recherche Economique.) Tananarive. 1962+

Afr 5749.58.5F   Population et économie paysanne du Bas-Mangoky. (Battistini, R.) Paris, n.d.

Afr 2623.958   Population et production en Tunisie. (Marini, Fr.) Auch, 1958.

Afr 6538.65   Population growth and rural development in Buganda. (Foster, Phillips Wayne.) College Park, Md., 1968.

Afr 2313.5   La population musulmane de Blida. Thèse. (Ferrendier, M.) Blois, 1928.

Afr Doc 3207.362.10   Population of Kenya; density and distribution; a geographical introduction to the Kenya population census, 1962. (Morgan, W.T.W.) Nairobi, 1966.

Afr 710.32.10   The population of tropical Africa; conference held Jan. 3-7, 1966. (African Population Conference, 1st, University of Ibadan, 1966.) N.Y., 1968.

Afr Doc 7508.6   The population of West Cameroon; main findings. (Cameroon. Service de la Statistique Générale et la Mécanographie.) Paris, 1966.

Afr 630.59.5   Population pressures in Africa, south of the Sahara. (Stephens, Richard W.) Washington, 1958.

Afr 2669.5   Les populations arabes du contrôle civil de Gafsa et leurs genres de vie. (Bordin, P.) Tunis, 1944.

Afr 1273.967.5   Populations du Maghreb et communauté économique à quatre. (Benyoussef, Amor.) Paris, 1967.

Afr 6688.5   Les populations du Nord-Togo. (Froelich, J.C.) Paris, 1963.

Afr 5485.5   Les populations du Tchad. (Lebeuf, Annie M.D.) Paris, 1959.

Afr 6740.30   Les populations paiennes. (Lembezat, Bertrand.) Paris, 1961.

Afr 2945.30   Le populazioni della Cirenaica. (Agostini, E. de.) Bengasi, 1922-23.

Afr 5057.28   Poquin, Jean. Les relations économiques extérieures des pays d'Afrique. Paris, 1957.

Afr 7122.39   Por Angola. (Galvao, H.) Lisboa, 1949.

Afr 7175.12   Por terras d'Angola. (Lina Vidal, João Avangelista.) Coimbra, 1916.

Afr 7182.10   Por tierras de Angola. (Ruiz de Arcaute, H.) Victoria, 1961.

Afr 1608.89.5   Por todo marruecos descripcion del imperio. (Sestri, J.A. de.) Barcelona, 1889.

Afr 718.38   Pori. (Berg, Gertrud Wilhelmson.) Stockholm, 1964.

Afr Doc 6471.5   Port d'Ahidjan; rapport annuel. (Ivory Coast. Ministère des Travaux Publics et des Transports.) Abidjan. 1966+

Afr 2308.21   Le port d'Alger,1930. (Algiers. Chambre de Commerce.) Alger, 1930.

Afr 2308.17   Le port d'Alger. (Delvert, C.L.) Paris, 1923.

Afr 2308.20   Le port d'Alger. (Laye, Yves.) Alger, 1951.

Afr 8845.5   Port Elizabeth, a bibliography. (Price, G.N.) Cape Town, 1949.

Afr 8815.8   Port Elizabeth directory and guide. Port Elizabeth, 1877.

Afr 8845.10   Port Elizabeth in bygone days. (Redgrave, J.J.) Wynberg, 1947.

Afr 8845.15   Port Elizabeth municipal centenary. (Port Elizabeth Publicity Association.) Port Elizabeth, 1960.

Afr 8845.15   Port Elizabeth Publicity Association. Port Elizabeth municipal centenary. Port Elizabeth, 1960.

Afr 8845.16   Port Elizabeth Publicity Association. This is Port Elizabeth. Port Elizabeth, 1963.

Afr 5846.3   Port-Louis, deux siècles d'histoire, 1735-1935. (Toussaint, Auguste.) Port-Louis, 1936.

Afr 9060.27   Port Natal. (Malherbe, Janie.) Cape Town, 1965.

Afr 3315.35   Port Said, nouveau Stalingrad. Paris, 1956.

Afr 5190.25   Un port secondaire de la côte occidentale d'Afrique, Kaolack; étude historique, juridique et économique des origines à 1958. (Dessertine, A.) Kaolack, Sénégal, 1967?

Afr 4509.17   Portal, G.H. An account of the English mission to King Johannis of Abyssinia in 1887. Winchester, 1888.

Afr 4558.92.9   Portal, G.H. My mission to Abyssinia. London, 1892.

Afr 6497.14   Portal, Gerald H. The British mission to Uganda, 1893. London, 1894.

Afr 5019.61   Porte ouverte sur la communauté franco-africaine. (Boubacar, Diabete.) Bruxelles, 1961.

Afr 109.61.50   Portella, Eduardo. Africa, colonos e cumplices. Rio de Janeiro, 1961.

Afr 6147.5.10   Porter, A.T. Creoledom. London, 1963.

Afr 5396.2   Porto-Novo. (Tardits, C.) Paris, 1958.

Afr 5396.2.5   The Porto Novo incidents of 1923, politics in the colonial era. (Ballard, J.A.) Ibadan, 1965.

Afr 1571.17.75   Portrait de Lyautey. (Hardy, G.) Paris, 1949.

Afr 9029.40   Portrait of a colony, the story of Natal. (Hattersley, A.F.) Cambridge, 1940.

Afr 6395.22   Portrait of a minority, Asians in East Africa. (Ghai, Dharam P.) London, 1965.

Afr 3979.66.25   Portrait of Egypt. (Kinross, Patrick.) London, 1966.

Afr 3979.66.20   Portrait of Egypt. (Kinross, Patrick.) N.Y., 1966.

Afr 8685.104   Portrait of Indian South Africans. (Meer, Fatima.) Durban, 1969.

Afr 9839.64.10   Portrait of Malawi. Zomba, 1964.

Afr 1609.67   Portret van Marokko. (Dominicus, Johannes.) s'Hertogenbosch, 1967.

Afr 8847.56   Portret van'n Suid-Afrikaanse dorp. (Lomax, Ambrose.) Molteno, 1964.

Afr 7309.38   The ports and lighthouses of Moçambique. (Mozambique. Repartição Teenica de Estatistica.) Lourenço Marques, 1938.

Afr 1830.20.51   Les ports et la navigation de l'Agérie. (Billiard, Louis.) Paris, 1930.

Afr 1575.5   Les Portugais au Maroc. (Castonnet Des Fosses, H.) Paris, 1886.

Afr 7073.8F   Portugal. Resposta do governo portuguez a exposição a favor dos direitos que a Gran-Bretanha. Lisboa, 1869.

Afr 7190.16   Portugal. Agencia Geral do Ultramar. San Tome e principe. Lisboa, n.d.

Afr 7219.64   Portugal. Archivo Ultramarino. Historico documentação avulsa moçambicana do arquivo historico ultramarino. Lisboa, 1964. 2v.

Afr 7324.20   Portugal. Comissão de Limitação da Fronteira de Lourenço Marques. Explorações portuguezas em Lourenço Marques e Inhambane. Lisboa, 1894.

Afr 150.70   Portugal. Comissão Executiva das Comemorações do V. Centenario da Morte do Infante Dom Henrique. Exposição Henriquina. Lisboa, 1960.

Afr 150.64   Portugal. Comissão Executiva das Comemorações do V. Centenario da Morte do Infante Dom Henrique. Monumenta Henricina. Coimbra, 1960. 9v.

Afr 150.62   Portugal. Comissão Executiva das Comemorações do V Centenario da Morte do Infante Dom Henrique. Bibliografia Henriquino. Lisboa, 1960. 2v.

Afr 150.2.65   Portugal. Comissão Executiva das Comemorações do V Centenario da Morte do Infante Dom Henrique. Henri le Navigateur. Lisboa, 1960.

Afr 150.2.80   Portugal. Comissão Executiva das Comemorações do V Centenario da Morte do Infante Dom Henrique. Programa das comemorações. Lisboa, 1960.

Afr 150.2.66   Portugal. Comissão Executiva das Comemorações do V Centenario da Morte do Infante Dom Henrique. Comemoracoe do V centenario da morte do Infante Dom Henrique. Lisboa, 1961-1963. 4v.

Afr Doc 9233.5   Portugal. Curadoria dos Indigenas Portugueses no Transvaal. Relatório do curador. Lourenço Marques.

Afr Doc 9018.5   Portugal. Laws, statutes, etc. Collecção de legeslação relativa ás colonias portuguezas em Africa. 2v.

Afr 7010.2   Portugal. Ministère de la Marine et des Colonies. Droits de patronage du Portugal en Afrique. Lisbonne, 1883.

	Afr 7010.6	Portugal. Ministério da Marinha e Ultramar. Direitos de padroado de Portugal em Africa; memoranda. Lisboa, 1883.
	Afr 7208.8	Portugal. Ministério do Ultramar. Providências legislativas ministeriais, tomadas em Moçambique em 22 outubro de 1966. Lisboa, 1966.
	Afr 7320.10	Portugal. Ministério dos Negocios da Marinha e Ultramar. Regimento. Lisboa, 1867.
	Afr 590.23F	Portugal. Ministério dos Negocios Estrangeiros. Documentos relativos ao apresamento. Lisboa, 1858.
	Afr Doc 9407.360	Portugal. Missão de Inquerito Agrícola de Cabo Verte, Guiné S. Tomé Principe. Recenseamento agrícola da Guiné, 1960-1961. Lisboa, 1963.
	Afr Doc 9245.5F	Portugal. Procuradoria. Relatorio da Procuradoria. 1915-1916
	Afr 1724.3F	Portugal. Sovereigns, 1688-1706 (Peter Ii). Regimento da praca de mazagam. Lisboa, 1692.
	Afr 7022.7	Portugal and Africa, 1815-1910. (Hammond, Richard.) Stanford, 1966.
	Afr 7022.4	Portugal and the scramble for Africa, 1875-1891. (Axelson, Eric.) Johannesburg, 1967.
	Afr 7222.80	Portugal do capricornio. (Faria, Dutra.) Lisboa, 1965.
	Afr 530.35.3	Portugal e a internacionalização dos problemas africanos. 3. ed. (Caetano, Marcello.) Lisboa, 1965.
	Afr 1575.15	Portugal e Marrocos; fostos e notícias. (Souto, A. Meyselles do.) Lisboa, 1967.
	Afr 1575.10	Portugal e Marrocos perante a historia e a politica europea. (Testa, Carlos.) Lisboa, 1888.
X Cg	Afr 7000.15.2	Portugal em Africa. Supplemento colonial. Lisboa. 169-235 3v.
	Afr 7020.25	Portugal em Africa. (Oliviera Martins, J.P.) Porto, 1891.
	Afr 7045.25	Portugal em Africa. (Pattec, Richard.) Lisboa, 1959.
X Cg	Afr 7000.15	Portugal em Africa. Lisboa. 1-17,1894-1910 18v.
	Afr 7000.15	Portugal em Africa. Lisboa. 22,1965+ 3v.
	Afr 7020.15	Portugal em Africa depois de 1851. (Lavradio, Marques do.) Lisboa, 1865.
	Afr 7010.3	Portugal et la France au Congo. Paris, 1884.
	Afr 530.33	Portugal in Africa. (Duffy, James.) Harmondsworth, 1962.
	Afr 7015.35	Portugal in Africa. (Duffy, James Edward.) Cambridge, 1962.
	Afr 4320.10	Portugal in quest of Prester John. (Sanceau, Elaine.) London, 1943.
	Afr 530.32	Portugal na Africa contemporanea. (Pattee, Richard.) Coimbra, 1959.
	Afr 7025.12	Le Portugal restera-t-il en Afrique? (Goemaere, Pierre.) Bruxelles, 1968.
	Afr 7179.5	A portugalização do suesto de Angola. (Sousa, Gabriel de.) Lisboa, 1967.
	Afr 7015.40	Portugalskie kolonizatory, vragi narodov Afriki. (Bondarevskii, G.L.) Moscow, 1962.
	Afr 8100.10	Portugese ontdekkers om die Kaap. (Kock, W.J. de.) Kaapstad, 1957.
	Afr 4320.3	Die Portugiesen in Abessinien. (Krause, K.) Dresden, 1912.
	Afr 6320.2	Die Portugiesenzeit von Deutsch- und Englisch-Ostafrika. (Strandes, J.) Berlin, 1899.
	Afr 7225.5	Portugiesisch-Ostafrika in der Zeit des Marquês de Pombal, 1750-1777. (Hoppe, Fritz.) Berlin, 1965.
	Afr 7175.54.5	Die portugiesischen Besitzungen in Süd-West-Afrika. (Tams, Georg.) Hamburg, 1845.
	Afr Doc 9002.5	Portuguese Africa; a guide to official publications. (Gibson, Mary Jane.) Washington, 1967.
	Afr 7015.55	Portuguese Africa; a handbook. (Abshire, David M.) N.Y., 1969.
	Afr 7015.46	Portuguese Africa. (Chilcote, Ronald H.) Englewood Cliffs, N.J., 1967.
	Afr 7015.20A	Portuguese Africa. (Duffy, James Edward.) Cambridge, 1959.
	Afr 8110.30	Portuguese and Dutch in South Africa. (Welch, Sidney R.) Cape Town, 1951.
	Afr 7312.15	The Portuguese colony of Moçambique. (Spence, C.F.) Cape Town, 1951.
	Afr 7119.65	The Portuguese conquest of Angola. (Birmingham, D.) London, 1965.
	Afr 7332.1	Portuguese East Africa. (Maugham, R.C.F.) London, 1906.
	Afr 7320.4.5	Portuguese East Africa. (Moreira, E.) London, 1936.
	Afr 7218.96	The Portuguese in South Africa. (Theal, George McCall.) Cape Town, 1896.
	Afr 7218.96.2	The Portuguese in South Africa. (Theal, George McCall.) N.Y., 1969.
	Afr 7015.25	Portuguese in South East Africa. (Axelson, Eric V.) Johannesburg, 1960.
	Afr 7308.99	Portuguese Nyassaland. (Worsfold, W.B.) London, 1899.
	Afr 6320.2.5	The Portuguese period in East Africa. (Strandes, J.) Nairobi, 1961.
	Afr 7190.50	Portuguese planters and British humanitarians. (Mantero, F.) Lisbon, 1911.
	Afr 8100.35	Portuguese rule and Spanish crown in South America. (Welch, Sidney R.) Cape Town, 1950.
	Afr 590.25	Portuguese slavery, Britain's dilemma. (Harris, John H.) London, 1913.
	Afr 7005.2	Pamphlet vol. Portuguese Tropical Africa. 6 pam.
	Afr 7119.59	Portugueses em Angola. (Sousa Dias, G.) Lisboa, 1959.
	Afr 4340.5	Os Portugueses na Ethiópia. (Ferreira, F. Palyart Pinto.) Lisboa, 1935.
	Afr 1609.16	Porvenir de Espana en Marruecos. (Vera Salas, Antonio.) Toledo, 1916.
	Afr 5920.11	Posesiones españolas del Africa occidental. (Arambilet, S.) Madrid, 1903.
	Afr 5920.5	Posesiones españolas en el Africa occidental. Madrid, 1900.
	Afr 8685.80	The position of Indians in South Africa. (Sen, Dhirendra Kumar.) Calcutta, 1950.
	Afr 6160.45	The position of the chief in the modern political system of Ashanti. 1st ed. (Busia, Kofi A.) London, 1968.
	Afr 530.26	I possedimenti italiani in Africa. (Plebano, A.) Roma, 1889.
	Afr 4700.29	I possedimenti italiani in Africa. 2 ed. (Stefanini, Giuseppe.) Firenze, 1929.
	Afr 9525.529	Posselt, Friedrich Wilhelm Traugott. Uppengula the scatterer. Bulawayo, 1945.
	Afr 5960.6	Les possessions espagñoles du Golfe de Guinée, leur présent et leur avenir. (Sorela, Luis.) Paris, 1884.
	Afr 4818.99	Les possessions françaises de la côte orientale. (Rouard de Card, E.) Paris, 1899.
	Afr 5054.10.2	Les possessions françaises de l'Afrique occidentale. 2e éd. (Lebrun-Renaud, C.G.N.) Paris, 1886.
	Afr 5406.185	Les possessions françaises du...Congo. (Franche, Lucien.) Paris, 1885.
	Afr 626.185	Possibilités d'industrialisation des états africains et malgache associés. (European Economic Community.) Paris, 1966. 7v.
	Afr 679.64	Post, K.W.J. The new states of West Africa. Harmondsworth, 1964.
	Afr 679.64.2	Post, K.W.J. The new states of West Africa. Harmondsworth, 1968.
	Afr 6218.17	Post, K.W.J. The Nigerian federal election of 1959. Oxford, 1963.
	Afr 545.48	Post-Christianity in Africa: a theological and anthropological study. (Oosthuizen, Gerhardus Cornelis.) London, 1968.
	Afr 1571.17.80	Postal, R. Présence de Lyautey. Paris, 1938.
	Afr 6498.47	Postlethwaite, John R. I look back. London, 1947.
Htn	Afr 5130.6*	Postlethwayt, M. The importance of the African expedition considered. London, 1758.
	Afr 8230.10.15	Postma, F. Paul Kruger. Stellenbosch, 1944.
	Afr 8050.21	Potchefstroom. University for Christian Higher Education. Republiek en koninkryk. Potchefstroom, 1964.
	Afr 626.45.5	Potekhin, I.I. African problems; analysis of eminent Soviet scientist. Moscow, 1968.
	Afr 626.45	Potekhin, I.I. Afrika iuzhnee Sakhary. Moscow, 1958.
	Afr 609.60.85	Potekhin, I.I. Afrika smotrit v budushchee. Moscow, 1960.
	Afr 6164.22	Potekhin, Ivan I. Stanovlenie novoi Gany. Moskva, 1965.
	Afr 12505.1	Potekhina, Gena I. Ocherki sovremennoi literatury Zapadnoi Afriki. Moskva, 1968.
	Afr 2030.462.40	Potemkin, Iu. V. Alzhirskii narod v borbe za nezavisimosti. Moscow, 1962.
	Afr 10431.41.100	Potent ash. (Kibera, Leonard.) Nairobi, n.d.
	Afr 8230.38	Potgieter, C. Kommandant-generaal Hendrik Potgieter. Johannesburg, 1938.
	Afr 9161.23	Potgieter, E.F. The disappearing Bushmen of Lake Clirissie. Pretoria, 1955.
	Afr 4785.13PF	Potocki, Jozef. Notatki mysLiwskie z Afryki. Warszawa, 1897.
	Afr 4975.5PF	Potocki, Jozef. Sport in Somaliland. London, 1900.
	Afr 2929.37.5	Pottier, R. La Tripolitaine vue par un Français. Paris, 1937.
	Afr 2719.47	Pottier, René. Histoire du Sahara. Paris, 1947.
	Afr 2731.14	Pottier, René. Laperrine, conquérant pacifique du Sahara. Paris, 1943.
	Afr 2731.17.3	Pottier, René. Un prince saharien méconnu, Henri Duveyrier. Paris, 1938.
	Afr 2731.15.20	Pottier, René. La vocation saharienne du père de Foucauld. Paris, 1939.
	Afr 2630.2	Poublon, G. La terre, projet de petite colonisation. Tunis, 1901.
	Afr 2623.962	Poucet, J. La colonisation et l'agriculture européennes en Tunisie depuis 1881. Paris, 1962.
	Afr 3315.110	Pouchitelnyi urok. (Primakov, E.M.) Moscow, 1957.
	Afr 1830.20.2F	Pouget. Agrologie du Sahel. Paris, 1930.
	Afr 5093.2	Poulet, G. Les Maures de l'Afrique occidentale française. Paris, 1904.
	Afr 16.18	Pount. Djibouti. 1,1966+
	Afr 7540.34	Poupart, R. Première esquisse de l'évolution du syndicalisme au Congo. Bruxelles, 1960.
	Afr 5056.158	Pouquet, Jean. L'Afrique occidentale française. 2.ed. Paris, 1958.
	Afr 1609.12.11	Pour coloniser au Maroc. (Bourote, M.) Paris, 1912.
	Afr 2209.37.10	Pour comprendre l'Algérie. (Lespes, René.) Alger, 1937.
	Afr 7516.10	Pour connaitre le Congo. Bruxelles. 1,1955+ 3v.
	Afr 2030.140	Pour Djamila Bouhired. (Girard, Henri Georges.) Paris, 1958.
	Afr 7575.17	Pour éviter l'anarchie puis là. (Hostelet, Georges.) Bruxelles, 1959.
	Afr 210.64.20	Pour la révolution africaine. (Fanon, Frantz.) Paris, 1964.
	Afr 2030.464.55	Pour l'Algérie. (Estier, Claude.) Paris, 1964.
	Afr 2030.462.155	Pour le tombeau d'un capitaine. (Girardet, R.) Paris, 1962.
	Afr 510.10.5	Pour l'empire colonial français. (Hanotaux, G.) Paris, 1933.
	Afr 8279.00.47	Pour les Boers contre l'impérialisme. (Volkonskii, G.M.) Genève, 1900.
	Afr 2223.916	Pour s'enrichir en Algérie. (Desroches, G.) Paris, 1916.
	Afr 626.130	Pour une cooperation économique africaine, vues et perspectives. (Steinfield, Jacques.) Bruxelles, 1964.
	Afr 1550.52	Pour une politique d'empire. (Guernier, E.L.) Paris, 1938.
	Afr 2223.960	Pour une promotion dans la coopération. (Algeria. Conseil Supérieur de la Promotion Sociale en Algérie.) Alger, 1960.
	Afr 6225.50	Pourguoi le Nigéria. Paris, 1968.
	Afr 1623.932	Pourquier, Rene. L'impôt sur les plus-values immobilieres au Maroc. Thèse. Paris, 1932.
	Afr 2640.1	Pourquoi devenir propriétaire en Tunisie. (Couche, L.) Lille, 1927.
	Afr 7889.5	Pous, Valdo. Stanleyville: an African urban community under Belgian administration. London, 1969.
	Afr 45.66.5	Le pouvoir et la justice en Afrique noire francophone et à Madagascar. (Masseron, Jean Paul.) Paris, 1966.
	Afr 3038.25	Le pouvoir législatif et le pouvoir exécutif en Egypte. (Sabry, Mohammed.) Paris, 1930.
	Afr 3038.25.5	Le pouvoir législatif et le pouvoir exécutif en Egypte. Thèse. (Sabry, Mohammed.) Paris, 1930.
	Afr 8678.436	Le pouvoir pâle. (Thion, Serge.) Paris, 1969.
	Afr 50.8	Pouvoir politique traditionnel en Afrique occidentale. (Diagné, Patné.) Paris, 1967.
	Afr 3040.35.5	Les pouvoirs des tribunaux mixtes d'Egypte. Thèse. (Amad, P.E.) Paris, 1930.
	Afr 3040.67	Les pouvoirs du roi dans la constitution égyptienne. (Saleh, Diaeddine.) Paris, 1939.
	Afr 2224.20	Les pouvoirs financiers des assemblées algériennes et le contrôle de la métropole. (Delmonte, Fabien R.S.) Alger, 1923.
	Afr 8835.30	Poverty and dependency in Cape Town. (Wagner, O.J.M.) Cape Town, 1936.
	Afr 9705.15	Powdermaker, Hortense. Copper town. 1st ed. N.Y., 1962.
	Afr 4559.25	Powell, E.A. Beyond the utmost purple rim. N.Y., 1925.

Afr 1259.25.10 Powell, E.A. In Barbary, Tunisia, Algeria, Morocco, and the Sahara. N.Y., 1926.
Afr 609.13 Powell, E.A. The last frontier. London, 1913.
Afr 609.13.2 Powell, E.A. The last frontier. N.Y., 1914.
Afr 609.13.7 Powell, E.A. The last frontier. N.Y., 1919.
Afr 718.39 Powell, E.A. The map that is half unrolled. N.Y., 1925.
Afr 3325.10 Powell, Ivor. Disillusion by the Nile: what Nasser has done to Egypt. London, 1967.
Afr 6390.14 Powell-Cotton, P.H.G. In unknown Africa. London, 1904.
Afr 3705.7 Power, Frank. Letters from Khartoum. London, 1885.
Afr 3705.7.2 Power, Frank. Letters from Khartoum. 3d ed. London, 1885.
Afr 8678.299 Power, law, right and love. (Brookes, E.H.) Durham, 1963.
Afr 6212.40 Power and stability in Nigeria. (Bretton, Henry.) N.Y., 1962.
Afr 6538.10 Power in Uganda, 1957-1970. (Economist (London).) London, 1957.
Afr 3979.24 Powers, H.H. Egypt. N.Y., 1924.
Afr 6455.42 Powys, L. Black laughter. N.Y., 1924.
Afr 9060.20 Praechter, Vallmar. Durban. Hamburg, 1961.
Afr 8289.02.27 Präsident Steijn. (Rompel, F.) München, 1902.
Afr 626.156 Prague. Vysoka Skola Ekonomicka. Katedra Ekonomiky Rozvojovych Zemi. Africka Sekce. Nastin ekonomiky rozvojovych zemi Afriky. Praha, 1964.
Afr 43316.21 Praise-poems of Tswana chiefs. (Schapera, Isaac.) Oxford, 1965.
Afr 50.20 Prasad, Bisheshwar. Contemporary Africa. N.Y., 1960.
Afr 1340.10 Prat, Jean. La responsabilité de la puissance publique au Maroc. Rabat, 1963.
Afr 8659.13.9 Pratt, A. The real South Africa. Indianapolis, 1913.
Afr 8089.00.8 Pratt, E.A. Leading points in South African history, 1486 to March 30, 1900. London, 1900.
Afr 2030.464.60 Pravda, Moscow. Nerushimaia druzhba i bratstvo. Moscow, 1964.
Afr 3993.5 Pravda, Moskva. Asuan, simvol sovetsko-arabskoi druzhby. Moskva, 1964.
Afr 3310.10.40 Pre-election speeches in Assiut, March 8, 1965. (Nasser, G.A.) Cairo, 1965.
Afr 2260.4 Preaux. Réflexions sur la colonization. Paris, 1832.
Afr Doc 4312.127 Precious stones bill. (South Africa. Parliament.) Cape Town, 1927.
Afr 8030.5 Precis. (Cape of Good Hope. Archives.) Cape Town. 1,1896+ 13v.
Afr 8289.01.7 Precis de...campagnes contemporaines d'Afrique centrale. (Bujac, E.) Paris, 1901.
Afr 1835.1.10 Précis de jurisprudence musulmane. (Hatil Ibn-Ishah.) Paris, 1848. 6v.
Afr 3069.32A Précis de l'histoire d'Egypte. Caire, 1932-35. 4v.
Afr 3700.6 Précis de quelques campagnes contemporaines. Pt. III - Egypte et Soudan. (Bujac, E.) Paris, 1899.
Afr 1259.13.5 Précis de sociologie nord-africaine. (Martin, A.G.P.) Paris, 1913.
Afr 5054.37.5 Précis historique de la colonisation française. (Mary, Gaston.) Paris, 1937.
Afr 1955.23 Précis historique et administrative de la campagne d'Afrique. (Denniée.) Paris, 1830.
Afr 9488.99.3 Precis of information concerning Southern Rhodesia. (Dawkins, C.T.) London, 1899.
Afr 9838.99.5 Precis of information concerning the British Central Africa protectorate. (Great Britain. War Office. Intelligence Division.) London, 1899.
Afr 6390.10.59 Precis of information concerning the British East Africa Protectorate and Zanzibar. (Great Britain. War Office. Intelligence Division.) London, 1901.
Afr 6535.19 Precis of information concerning the Uganda Protectorate. (Great Britain. War Office. Intelligence Division.) London, 1902.
Afr 9028.85.5 Precis of information concerning Zululand. (Great Britain. War Office. Intelligence Division.) London, 1895.
Afr 5585.3 Précis sur les établissements français formés à Madagascar. Paris, 1836.
Afr 5448.16 Préclin, Louis. Pointe-Noire sous la croix de Lorraine. Paris, 1967.
Afr 6218.20 A preface to modern Nigeria. (Kopytoff, Jean Herskovits.) Madison, 1965.
Afr 9093.25 Prehistory of the Transvaal. (Mason, Rivil.) Johannesburg, 1962.
Afr 8678.367 Prejudice in the classroom. (Hawarden, Eleanor.) Johannesburg, 1963.
Afr 6277.110 A prelimenary report on rural changes in the Savanna area of the Western State of Nigeria. (Kranendonk, H.) Ibadan, 1968.
Afr 10050.3 A preliminary bibliography of creative African writing in the European languages. (Amosu, Margaret.) Ibadan, 1964.
Afr 49000.89.79F A preliminary bibliography of the Yoruba language. (Ogunsheye, F. Adetowun.) Ibadan, 1963.
Afr 8028.7F Preliminary finding-list of Southern African pamphlets. (Roberts, E.S.) Cape Town, 1959.
Afr 6295.63.5F A preliminary inventory of the administrative records assembled from Endo province. (Nigeria. National Archives.) Ibadan, 1963.
Afr 28.8F Preliminary list of Africana, mainly from the Gubbins Library. (Johannesburg. University of the Witwatersrand. Gubbins Library.) Johannesburg, 1930.
Afr Doc 3608.700 Preliminary report on the balance of payments 1964. (Malawi. Ministry of Finance.) Zomba.
Afr Doc 3509.515F Preliminary report on the federal European family expenditure survey, October 1960. (Rhodesia and Nyasaland. Central Statistical Office.) Salisbury, 1963.
Afr 6277.71 A preliminary report on the possibilities of price control in Nigeria. (Onitiri, H.M.A.) Ibadan, 1966.
Afr Doc 3889.358 Preliminary report on the Salisbury African Demographic survey, August/September, 1958. (Rhodesia and Nyasaland. Central Statistical Office.) Salisbury, 1958.
Afr Doc 3507.361 Preliminary results of federal censuses of population and of employees, September, 1961. (Rhodesia and Nyasaland. Central Statistical Office.) Salisbury, 1962.
Afr Doc 807.364.10 Preliminary results of the general population census 1964. (Libya. Census and Statistical Department.) Tripoli, 1964.
Afr Doc 3807.311.5 Preliminary returns of a census taken on May 1911, together with comparative figures from the census of 1907 and 1904. (Rhodesia, Southern. Census Office.) Salisbury, 1911. 2 pam.

Afr 8230.25.5 Preller, G.S. Andries pretorius. 2. verb. uitg. Johannesburg, 1940.
Afr 8089.37 Preller, G.S. Daglemier in Suid-Afrika. Pretoria, 1937.
Afr 8089.38 Preller, G.S. Day-dawn in South-Africa. Pretoria, 1938.
Afr 8325.66.5 Preller, G.S. Kaptein Hindon. 2nd ed. Kaapstad, 1921.
Afr 8325.66 Preller, G.S. Ons parool. 2. druk. Kaapstad, 1943.
Afr 8180.31 Preller, G.S. Piet retief. Pretoria, 1912.
Afr 6919.41 Preller, G.S. Voortrekkers van suidwes. Kaapstad, 1941.
Afr 8135.27 Preller, Gustav S. Ekelse en opstelle. Pretoria, 1928.
Afr 8252.188.5 Preller, Gustav S. Talana, die drie generaals-slag. Kaapstad, 1942.
Afr 9525.529.25 Preller, Gustav Schoeman. Lobengula, the tragedy of a Matabele king. Johannesburg, 1963.
Afr 8030.16 Preller, Gustav Schoeman. Voortrek Kermense. Kaapstad, 1920- 5v.
Afr 6193.7 Prelude to Ghana's industrialization. (Akwawuah, Kwadwo A.) London, 1959.
Afr 9549.65.5 Prelude to imperialism; British reactions to Central African society, 1840-1890. (Cairns, H. Alan C.) London, 1965.
Afr 9448.79 Prelude to independence, Skeen's 115 days. (Skeen, Andrew.) Cape Town, 1966.
Afr 679.63.5 Prelude to the partition of West Africa. (Hargreaves, J.D.) London, 1963.
Afr 6193.40 Preludes to Ghana's industrialisation. (Akwawuah, Kwadwo A.) London, 1960.
Afr 530.30 Premesse al lavoro italiano in Africa. Roma, 1958.
Afr 7368.85 Les premices de l'oeuvre d'émancipation africaine. Liberia. (Wauwermans, H.) Bruxelles, 1885.
Afr 5832.3 Le premier établissement des Neerlandais à Maurice. (Bonaparte, R.) Paris, 1890.
Afr 8289.01.42 Premier livre de l'épopée boer. Paris, 1901.
Afr 5482.15 Premier plan quinquennal de développement économique et social, 1966-1970. (Chad. Ministère du Plan et de la Coopération.) Fort Lamy?, 1967.
Afr 6739.261F Premier plan quinquennal économique. (Cameroon. Ministère des Finances et du Plan.) Yaounde, 1961.
Afr 2035.11 Le premier quart d'heure. (Bergheaud, Edmond.) Paris, 1964.
Afr 2030.464.20 Le premier quart d'heure. (Bergleaud, Edmond.) Paris, 1964.
Afr 5180.19.4 Premier voyage...fait à la côte d'Afrique...1865. (Lacourbe, M.J. de.) Paris, 1913.
Afr 3979.59.5 Première descente du Nil de l'Equateur à la Méditerranée. (Laporte, Jean.) Paris, 1959.
Afr 7540.34 Première esquisse de l'évolution du syndicalisme au Congo. (Poupart, R.) Bruxelles, 1960.
Afr 5343.7.10 Première esquisse du plan quinquennal de développement. (Ivory Coast. Ministère du Plan.) Paris, 1968.
Afr 7850.53 La première traversée du Katanga en 1806. (Verbeken, A.) Bruxelles, 1953.
Afr 2749.68.5 La première traversée du Sahara en char a voile. (Nau, Christian.) Condé-sur-l'Escaut, 1968.
Afr 626.190 Les premières expériences de planification en Afrique noire. (Gand, Michel.) Paris, 1967.
Afr 3215.3.5 Les premières frégates de Mohamed Aly (1824-27). (Douin, Georges.) Caire, 1926.
Afr 1635.1 Les premiers colons. v.1-2. (Bertholon, L.) Tunis, 1898.
Afr 5869.67 Les Premiers colons de l'Ile Bourbon. 2. ed. (Prosset, Alfred.) Paris, n.d.
Afr 7850.5 Les premiers jours au Katanga. (Verdick, E.) Bruxelles, 1952.
Afr 7580.5 Les premiers mois de la République du Congo. (Stenmans, Alain.) Bruxelles, 1961.
Afr 7947.2 The premise of inequality in Ruanda. (Maquet, J.J.) London, 1961.
Afr 5833.2 Prentout, H. L'Ile de France sous Decaen. Paris, 1901.
Afr 3994.934 The preparation of the Egyptian budget. (Yunus, Muhammed Tawfig.) Cairo, 1934.
Afr 4513.36.83 La preparazione e le primi operazioni. 3a ed. (Bono, E.) Roma, 1937.
Afr 6195.19 The Presbyterian Church of Ghana, 1835-1960. (Smith, Noel.) Accra, 1966.
Afr 7222.72 Presença de Moçambique na vida da nação. (Sarmento Rodrigues, M.M.) Lisboa, 1964. 3v.
Afr 10066.4 Présence Africaine. Nouvelle somme de poésie du monde noir. Paris, 1966.
Afr 628.6 Présence africaine. Paris. 1,1947+ 23v.
Afr 628.7 Présence africaine. English edition. Paris. 1,1960+ 6v.
Afr 1571.17.80 Présence de Lyautey. (Postal, R.) Paris, 1938.
Afr 1493.60 Présence française au Maroc. (Maridalyn, H.) Monte carlo, 1952.
Afr 1069.43 Presencia de España en Berberia central y oriental. (Garcia, F.T.) Madrid, 1943.
Afr 3198.99 Present-day Egypt. (Penfield, F.C.) N.Y., 1899.
Afr 555.137 A present for cold mornings. (Ijlst, Wim.) Dublin, 1968.
Afr 9603.5 Present interrelations in Central African rural and urban life. (Rhodes-Livingstone Institute, Lusaka, Northern Rhodesia. 11th Conference, Lusaka, 1958.) Lusaka, 1958.
Htn Afr 3976.78* The present state of Egypt. (Vansleb, F.) London, 1678.
Afr 1607.87.5 Present state of Morocco. (Chenier, L.S.) London, 1788. 2v.
Htn Afr 1606.94.5* Present state of Morocco. (St. Olon, P.) London, 1695.
Afr 1608.54 Present state of Morocco. 2 in 1. (Durrieu, X.) London, 1854. 2 pam.
Htn Afr 1738.2* Present state of Tangier. London, 1676.
Afr 8657.19.5 Present state of the Cape of Good Hope. (Kolbe, Peter.) London, 1731. 2v.
Afr 8378.349 President C.R. Swart. (Kruger, J.J.) Kaapstad, 1961.
Afr 3310.10.55 President Gamal Abdel Nasser on consolidation of the cause of world peace. (Nasser, G.A.) Cairo, 1968?
Afr 3310.10.45 President Gamal Abdel Nasser on Palestine. (Nasser, G.A.) Cairo, 1964.
Afr 9225.20.5 President Johannes Henricus Brand, 1823-1888. (Scholtz, G.D.) Johannesburg, 1957.
Afr 7375.11 President Roberts - the Republic of Liberia. N.Y., 1854.
Afr 8285.20 President Steijn in die krisesjare. (Kieser, A.) Kaapstad, 1951.
Afr 7377.59 President Tubman of Liberia speaks. (Tubman, William.) London, 1959.

Afr 7385.5 President William V.S. Tubman on African unity. (Tubman, William.) Monrovia, 1964.
Afr 8678.197 Presidential address. (South African Institute of Race Relations.) Johannesburg.
Afr 6785.2 President's address to the National assembly, June 8, 1965. (Tanzania. President.) Dar es Salaam, 1965.
Afr Doc 3224.5 President's circular. (Kenya. President.) Nairobi. 1967+
Afr 6200.13.5 Press actions. (Markpress News Feature Service. Biafran Overseas Press Division.) Geneva. 1968+ 2v.
Afr 8369.61.5 Press and politics of South Africa. (Broughton, M.) Cape Town, 1961.
Afr 10013.2 The press in Africa. (Ainslie, Rosalynde.) London, 1966.
Afr 10013.6 The press in Africa. (Barton, Frank.) Nairobi, 1966.
Afr 10013.2.5 The press in Africa: communications past and present. (Ainslie, Rosalynde.) N.Y., 1968.
Afr 1568.1 Presse anglaise et le Maroc. n.p., n.d.
Afr 3204.15 La presse en Egypte, 1799-1900. (Munier, Jules.) Le Caire, 1930.
Afr 10013.8 Die Presse in Westafrika. (Behn, Hans Ulrich.) Hamburg, 1968.
Afr 6277.25 Prest, A.R. The national income of Nigeria. London, 1953.
Afr 6455.38 Preston, R.O. The genesis of Kenya colony. Nairobi, 1935.
Afr 8659.66.10 Pretoria, Skinnerstraat 295. (Lehmann, Emily.) Wuppertal, 1966.
Afr 8315.14 Pretoria from within...1899-1900. (Batts, H.J.) London, 1901.
Afr 9165.71.5 Pretoria van kerkplaas tot regeringsetel. (Rex, H.M.) Kaapstad, 1960.
Afr 8687.380 Pretorius, G. Man van die daad. Kaapstad, 1959.
Afr 8687.265.10 Pretorius, Gert. Die Malans van Môrewag. Kaapstad, 1965.
Afr 8030.12 Pretorius, H.S. Voortrekker-argiefstukke, 1829-1849. Pretoria, 1937.
Afr 3978.92.5 Pretynian, H.E. Journal, Kittar mountains, 1891. London, 1889.
Afr 1990.25 Les préventions du général Berthezène. (Demontes, Victor.) Paris, 1918.
Afr 632.9 Preville, A. de. Les sociétés africaines. Paris, 1894.
Afr 2505.2 Prevost, F. La Tunisie devant l'Europe. Paris, 1862.
Afr 5001.109 Prezidentskie respubliki v Afrike. (Verin, V.P.) Moscow, 1963.
Afr 6222.1 Pribytkavskii, L.N. Nigeriia v bor'be za nezqvisimost'. Moskva, 1961.
Afr 7468.4 Price, Frederick A. Liberian odyssey by hammock and surfboat. 1st ed. N.Y., 1954.
Afr 8845.5 Price, G.N. Port Elizabeth, a bibliography. Cape Town, 1961.
Afr 679.67.30 Price, Joseph Henry. Political institutions of West Africa. London, 1967.
Afr 6455.7 Price, Roger. Private journal. Photoreproduction. n.p., 1877.
Afr 628.225.15 Price, W. The Negro around the world. N.Y., 1925.
Afr 555.24.2 Price, William S. My third campaign in East Africa. London, 1891.
Afr 550.19 The price of Africa. (Taylor, S.E.) Cincinnati, 1902.
Afr 11465.14.100 The price of diamonds. (Jacobson, Dan.) London, 1957.
Afr 11465.14.100.2 The price of diamonds. 1st ed. (Jacobson, Dan.) N.Y., 1958.
Afr 8152.96 Prichard, A.M. Friends and foes in the Transkei. London, 1880.
Afr 2030.315 Priester, Eva. In Algerien sprechen die Gewehre. 1. Aufl. Berlin, 1959.
Afr 6198.71 Priestley, Margaret. West African trade and coast society; a family study. London, 1969.
Afr 5915.5 Prieto y Llovera, P. Politica aragonesa en Africa hasta la muerte de Fernando el Catolico. Madrid, 1952.
Afr 4095.8.4 Prikliucheniia v strane rabstva. (Rubakin, N.A.) Moscow, 1918.
Afr 3315.110 Primakov, E.M. Pouchitelnyi urok. Moscow, 1957.
Afr 3978.57 Prime, W.C. Boat life in Egypt and Nubia. N.Y., 1857.
Afr 3978.57.2 Prime, W.C. Boat life in Egypt and Nubia. N.Y., 1868.
Afr 1607.24.3F Primera parte de las chronicas de la provincia de San Diego. (Francisco de Jesus Maria, de San Juan Del Puerto.) Sevilla, 1724.
Afr 4732.21 I primi tentativi di colonizzazione agricola. (Rainero, R.) Milano, 1960.
Afr 5247.35 The primitive city of Timbuctoo. (Miner, H.M.) Garden City, 1965.
Afr 5247.40 The primitive city of Timbuctoo. (Miner, Horace Mitchell.) Princeton, 1953.
Afr 6395.16 Primitive government. (Mair, L.P.) Harmondsworth, 1962.
Afr 4386.5 Primo anniversairio dei combattimenti di Saati e Dogali. (Frassinesi, M.A.) Casale, 1888.
Afr 12624.41.1100 Primordiale du sixième jour. (Diakhaté, Lamine.) Paris, 1963.
Afr 4199.15 Prince Ahmad of Egypt. (Bland, J.) London, 1939.
Afr 8063.20.10 Prince Alfred's guard, 1856-1966. (Orpen, Neil.) Port Elizabeth, 1967.
Afr 1494.25 The prince and I. (Howe, Marvine.) N.Y., 1955.
Afr 510.9.10 Le prince de Bismarck et l'expansion de la France en Afrique. (Rouard de Card, E.) Paris, 1918.
Afr 150.2.10 Pamphlet box. Prince Henry the Navigator.
Afr 150.4.5 Prince Henry the Navigator. (Beazley, C.R.) London, 1923.
Afr 150.4 Prince Henry the Navigator. (Beazley, C.R.) N.Y., 1895.
Afr 150.35 Prince Henry the Navigator. (British Museum.) London, 1960.
Afr 150.4.10 Prince Henry the Navigator. (Russell, Peter E.) London, 1960.
Afr 2731.17.3 Un prince saharien méconnu, Henri Duveyrier. (Pottier, René.) Paris, 1938.
Afr 6570.12 Princes of Zinj. (Hamilton, Genesta.) London, 1957.
Afr 8676.62 Princeton University. Enterprise and politics in South Africa. Princeton, N.J., 1962.
Afr 626.49 Princeton University Conference. Emerging sub-Sahara Africa. Princeton, 1958.
Afr 4258.65 Principaux faits de l'histoire d'Abyssinie. (Lesseps, F.) Paris, 1865.
Afr 150.32 Principe, S. Rectificação historica a memoria do Infante Dom Henrique. Lobito, 1961.
Afr 6739.236 Le principe de l'égalité économique au Cameroun. (Lawless, L.G.) Paris, 1936.
Afr 6739.236.5 Le principe de l'égalité économique au Cameroun. (Lawless, L.G.) Paris, 1937.
Afr 150.25 O principe do mar. (Simões Mueller, Adolfo.) Porto, 1959.

Afr 3040.5 Les principes du self-government local dans les democraties modernes et leur application au régime administratif égyptien. Thèse. (Salem, M.S.) Dijon, 1923.
Afr 8678.298 Principle and practice in race relations. (Kotze, J.C.G.) Stellenbosch, 1962.
Afr 8678.365 The principle of apartheid. (Sampson, Harold Fehrsan.) Johannesburg, 1966.
Afr 6210.10 The principles of native administration in Nigeria. (Kirk-Greene, A.H.M.) London, 1965.
Afr 9838.84.2 Pringle, M. A journey in East Africa. Edinburgh, 1886.
Afr 8658.34 Pringle, Thomas. African sketches. London, 1834.
Afr 8658.34.10 Pringle, Thomas. Narrative of a residence in South Africa. Cape Town, 1966.
Afr 8658.34.5 Pringle, Thomas. Narrative of a residence in South Africa. London, 1835.
Afr 8658.34.2 Pringle, Thomas. Narrative of a residence in South Africa. London, 1840.
Afr 6465.59 Prins, Adriaan Hendrik Johan. Sailing from Lamu. Assen, 1965.
Afr 8678.69 Prins, Jan. De beknelde kleurling Zuid-Afrika's vierstromenbeeld. Assen, 1967.
Afr 9291.10 Prinsloo, A. Die geskiedenis van Smithfield en die Caledonrivierdistrik. Bloemfontein, 1955.
Afr 11216.10 Prinsloo of Prinsloosdorp. (Blackburn, Douglas.) London, 1899.
Afr 698.19 Prior, James. Voyage along the eastern coast of Africa. London, 1819.
Afr 1955.40 La prise d'Alger, 1830. (Esquer, G.) Alger, 1923.
Afr 1955.40.2 La prise d'Alger, 1830. (Esquer, G.) Paris, 1929.
Afr 1922.10 La prise d'Alger. (Celarie, H.) Paris, 1929.
Afr 1957.20.5 La prise d'Alger. (Merle, J.T.) Paris, 1930.
Afr 1955.19 La prise de Bône et Bougie...1832-33. (Cornulier-Lucinière, Comte de.) Paris, 1895.
Afr 7815.44 La prise de conscience de l'individu en milieu rural Kongo. (Domont, Jean Marie.) Bruxelles, 1957.
Afr 1658.9 Un prisionero en el riff, memorias del ayudante alvarez. (Diana, M.J.) Madrid, 1859.
Afr 2030.461.15 Prisionniers de guerre. (Alleg, Henri.) Paris, 1961.
Afr 6926.7 Prisoner of the Germans in South-west Africa. (Close, P.L.) London, 1916.
Afr 3730.5 A prisoner of the Khaleefa. (Neufeld, C.) N.Y., 1899.
Afr 3730.5.10 A prisoner of the Khaleefa. 3d ed. (Neufeld, C.) N.Y., 1899.
Afr 1942.6 The prisoners of Algiers. (Barnly, Henry George.) London, 1845.
Afr 3700.24 Prisoners of the Mahdi. (Farwell, Byron.) London, 1967.
Afr 6390.70 Pritchard, J.M. A geography of East Africa. London, 1962.
Afr 609.69 Pritchard, John Malcom. Africa; a study geography for advanced students. London, 1969.
Afr 1930.2 Private journal...from Portsmouth. Exeter, 1817.
Afr 6455.7 Private journal. Photoreproduction. (Price, Roger.) n.p., 1877.
Afr 3978.95 Private journal in Egypt. (Attfield, D.H.) London, 1895.
Afr 810.10 Private journal kept during the Niger expedition. (Simpson, W.) London, 1843.
Afr 725.10.10 Private journals. (Livingstone, David.) London, 1960.
Afr 7549.64 Le prix d'un empire. 3.ed. (Meyers, Joseph.) Bruxelles, 1964.
Afr 7458.60 Prize essay on political economy of Liberia. (Payne, J.S.) Monrovia, 1860.
Afr 6225.10.5 The problem of Nigerian unity. (Nigeria, Eastern. Ministry of Information.) Enugu, 1966?
Afr 8680.15 The problem of South Africa. (Tingsten, Herbert.) London, 1955.
Afr 8050.5 The problem of South African unity. (Worsfold, W.B.) London, 1900.
Afr 8685.22F The problem of the marginal personality. (Mann, John William.) Durban, 1957.
Afr 4070.64 The problem of the southern Sudan. (Odu, Joseph.) London, 1963.
Afr 640.7 Problem pigmejow afrykanskich w etnografii europejskiej XIX-XX w. (Walendowska-Zapedowska, Barbara.) Poznan, 1965.
Afr 8695.5 Problem territories of southern Africa. (Dundas, Charles C.F.) Cape Town, 1952.
Afr 1450.9 Problema de actualidad: la cuestion de Marruecos. (Diaz Moreu, E.) Madrid, 1909.
Afr 1573.20 El problema de Marruecos. (Alvarez, Melquiades.) Madrid, 1914.
Afr 1573.36 Problema de Marruecos. Madrid, 1914.
Afr 7176.36 Os problemas de Angola, no Primeiro Congresso dos Economistas Portugueses. (Ventura, Reis.) Lisboa, 1956.
Afr 7176.24 Problemas económicos da colónia. (Freitas Morna, Alvaro de.) Luanda, 1943.
Afr 2030.252 Le problème algérien. (Oppermann, Thomas.) Paris, 1961.
Afr 2000.20 Le problème algérien devant la conscience démocratique. (Khaldi, Abd al-Aziz.) Alger, 1946.
Afr 7812.246 Le problème de demain. (Dehoux, Emile.) Bruxelles, 1946.
Afr 2438.17 Le problème de la nationalité en Tunisie. Thèse. (Aguesse, L.C.P.) Paris, 1930.
Afr 2533.11 Le problème de l'indépendance de la Tunisie. (Szymanski, E.) Warszawa, 1962.
Afr 1738.26 Le problème de Tanger. Thèse. (Durand, Raphael.) Aix-en-provence, 1926.
Afr 8678.425 Probleme der räumlich getrennten Einbeziehung der Bantu-Bevölkerung Südafrikas in den Wirtschaftsprozes des Landes. (Glashagen, Ulrich H.) Pretoria, 1966.
Afr 5404.25 Le Problème du regroupement en Afrique équatoriale, du régime colonial à l'union douanière et économique de l'Afrique centrale. Thèsis. (Dreux-Brézé, Joachim de.) Paris, 1968.
Afr 7812.233 Le problème financier et le problème économique au Congo belge en 1932. (Louwers, Octave.) Bruxelles, 1933.
Afr 7803.44 Le problème musulman dans l'Afrique belge. (Anciaux, Leon.) Bruxelles, 1949.
Afr 7575.15A Le problème politique capital au Congo et en Afrique noire. (Hostelet, Georges.) Bruxelles, 1959.
Afr 5056.130.10 Le problème social aux colonies. (Semaines Sociales de France.) Lyon, 1930.
Afr 5183.962.5 Probleme und Möglichkeiten der industriellen Entwicklung im Senegal. (Zajadatz, Paul.) Köln, 1962.
Afr 2000.3 Problèmes algériens. (Ajam, Maurice.) Paris, 1913.
Afr 7812.236.10 Problèmes coloniaux d'hier et d'aujourd'hui. (Moulaert, G.) Bruxelles, 1939.
Afr 7567.28 Problèmes congolais. (Daye, Pierre.) Bruxelles, 1943.
Afr 7516.5 Problèmes d'Afrique centrale. Bruxelles. 5,1952+ 7v.

Afr 2223.963.5 Problèmes de l'Algérie indépendante. (Paris. Université. Institut d'Etudes du Développement, etc.) Paris, 1963.

Afr 5046.5 Problemes de planification. (France. Ministère de la Coopération.) Paris, 1964. 11v.

Afr 1494.50 Problèmes d'édification du Maroc et du Moghreb. (Ben Barka el Mehdi.) Paris, 1959.

Afr 1623.954F Problemes économiques au Maroc. (Ripoche, Paul.) Rabat, 1954.

Afr 1623.956F Problèmes économiques au Maroc. 2. ed. (Ripoche, Paul.) Rabat, 1956.

Afr 2224.939 Les problèmes financiers du Protectorat tunisien. Thèse. (Houdiard, Y.) Paris, 1939.

Afr 5787.5 Problemes humains dans la region de la Sakay. (Lavondes, Henrni.) Tananarive, 1961.

Afr 679.58.10 Problèmes humains en Afrique occidentale. 2. éd. (Richard Molard, Jacques.) Paris, 1958.

Afr 2753.3 Problèmes humains posés. Paris, 1961.

Afr 1040.20 Les Problémes juridiques des minoritiés européennes au Maghreb. (Étienne, Bruno.) Paris, 1968.

Afr 1200.80 Les problèmes nord-africains. (Carpentier, J.A.) Paris, 1953.

Afr 7503.3.4 Problèmes sociaux congolais. Sommaire des bulletins parus 1946-1966. n.p., n.d.

Afr 3040.20 Problèmes soulevés par la constitution égyptienne. Thèse. (Makram, Hilmy.) Dijon, 1927.

Afr 7812.257 Problèmes structurels de l'économie congolaise. (Bezy, Fernand.) Louvain, 1957.

Afr 626.120 I problemi economici dell'Africa e l'Europa. (Agostino Orsini, P.) Roma, 1961.

Afr 679.68.20 Problems and prospects of economic integration in West Africa. (Plessz, Nicolas G.) Montreal, 1968.

Afr 505.13 Problems of African development. (Batten, T.R.) London, 1948.

Afr 505.13.3 Problems of African development. 3d ed. (Batten, T.R.) London, 1960.

Afr 6277.46 Problems of industrial planning and management in Nigeria. (Onyemelukwe, Clement Chukwukadibia.) London, 1966.

Afr 8678.74 The problems of race relations in South Africa. (Holloway, J.E.) N.Y., 1964.

Afr 6210.14 The problems of self-government for Nigeria. (Aluko, S.A.) Ilfracombe, 1955.

Afr 115.106 Problems of transition. (Social Sciences Research Conference.) Pietermaritzburg, Natal, 1964.

Afr 626.155 Problemy gospodarcze Afryki. Wyd.1. (Dobrska, Zofia.) Warszawa, 1964.

Afr 115.113 Problemy istorii Afriki. (Subbotin, Vaterii A.) Moskva, 1966.

Afr 210.62.40 Problemy Mira i Sotsializma. Za natsionalniiu nezavisimost. Praha, 1962.

Afr 6225.7 Probudivshaisia Nigeriia. (Koriavin, L.A.) Moscow, 1962.

Afr 657.90F Proceedings. (Association for Promoting the Discovery of the Interior Parts of Africa.) London, 1790.

Afr 10003.4 Proceedings. (Conference of Writers, Publishers, Editors, and University Teachers of English.) Johannesburg, 1957.

Afr 1803.1 Proceedings. (Congrés National des Sciences Historiques.) Alger. 2,1930+

Afr 9.12 Proceedings. (International Congress of Africanists.) Evanston, Ill. 1,1962+

Afr 8369.61.15 Proceedings. (Natal Convention. University of Natal.) Natal, 1961.

Afr Doc 3612.10 Proceedings. (Nyasaland. Legislative Council.)

Afr Doc 3712.15 Proceedings. (Rhodesia, Northern. African Representative Council.) 1,1946 4v.

Afr Doc 3312.20 Proceedings. Official report. (Uganda. National Assembly.) 1951+ 31v.

Afr 6176.44F Proceedings and report, with minutes of evidence taken before the commission, January-March, 1959. (Ghana. Commission Appointed to Enquire into the Matters Disclosed at the Trial of Captain Benjamin Awhaitey, before a Court Martial, and the Surrounding Circumstances.) Accra, 1959.

Afr 25.160F Proceedings and report. (Organization of African Unity. Economic and Social Commission.) Addis Ababa. 1,1963+

Afr Doc 4812.5F Proceedings and report of select committees. (Transkeian Territories. General Council.) 1928+

Afr 12.25 Proceedings at the staff seminars. (Lagos, Nigeria (City). University. African Studies Division.) Lagos. 1966+

Afr 9625.16 Proceedings of the annual general conference. (United National Independence Party (Zambia).) Luska. 1967

Afr 657.90.5 Proceedings of the Association for Promoting the Discovery of the Interior Parts of Africa. (Association for Promoting the Discovery of the Interior Parts of Africa.) London, 1810. 2v.

Afr 40.44 Proceedings of the Conference on Africa. (Council on African Affairs, Inc.) N.Y. 1944.

Afr 45.66.10 Proceedings of the Conference on African Local Government since Independence held at Lincoln University, Feb. 3rd and 4th, 1966. (Conference on African Local Government since Independence, Lincoln University, Pennsylvania, 1966.) Lincoln, 1966.

Afr Doc 1812.7 Proceedings of the Constituent assembly. (Ghana. Constituent Assembly.) Accra, 1960.

Afr Doc 3012.5 Proceedings of the debates. (East African Common Services Organization. Central Legislative Assembly.) 1,1962+

Afr 2802.5 Proceedings of the expedition to explore the northern coast of Africa, from Tripoly eastward. (Beechey, F.W.) London, 1828.

Afr 6210.8.10 Proceedings of the General conference on review of the constitution. (Nigeria. General Conference.) Lagos, 1950.

Afr 9.7.3 Proceedings of the third International West African Conference. (International West African Conference.) Lagos, 1956.

Afr 2030.106 Un procés. (Serigny, Alain de.) Paris, 1961.

Afr 2536.10.25 Les procès Bourguiba, 9 avril, 1938. (Bourguiba, Habib.) Tunis, 1967. 2v.

Afr Doc 7114.5F Procès-verbaux, etc. (Chad. Assemblée Territoriale.) 1951-1953

Afr 4430.35.5 Prochazka, R. von. Abessinien, die schwarze Gefahr. Wien, 1935.

Afr 4430.35.8 Prochazka, R. von. Abissinia pericolo nero. Milano, 1935.

Afr 8320.3 Proclamation 15th Sept. 1900. (Roberts, Lord.) Lourenço Marques, 1900.

Afr Doc 1826.10 Proclamations, orders-in-council. (Gold Coast (Colony).) Accra. 1928-1936 10v.

Afr 8278.97 Procter, John. Boers and little Englanders. London, 1897.

Afr Doc 4812.5.10 Prodeedings of a special session of the United Transkeian Territories General Council held on 23rd and 24th Nov., 1955. (Transkeian Territories. General Council.) Umtata, 1955.

Afr 5249.7 La prodigieuse vie de René Caillié. (Briault, Maurice.) Paris, 1930.

Afr 1623.934.10 Production et protection au Maroc. (Ecorcheville, C.) Paris, 1934.

Afr 4559.38.10 La produzione dell'Etiopia. (Papini, I.) Roma, 1938.

Afr 6277.82 Proehl, Paul O. Foreign enterprise in Nigeria, laws and policies. Chapel Hill, 1965.

Afr 8686.4 Profetisme in Suid-Afrika in akkulturasie perspektief. Proefschrift. (Kellermann, Abraham Gerhardus.) Voorburg, 1964.

Afr 55.20 Profiles of African leaders. (Melady, T.P.) N.Y., 1961.

Afr Doc 2560.602 Profiles of the ministers of Eastern Nigeria. (Ajuluchukee, M.C.K.) Enugu, 1960.

Afr 609.59.15 Profilo geografico dell'Africa. (Gribaudi, Dino.) Torino, 1967.

Afr 150.2.80 Programa das comemorações. (Portugal. Comissão Executiva das Comemorações do V Centenario da Morte do Infante Dom Henrique.) Lisboa, 1960.

Afr 1570.32 Le programme de la France au Maroc. (Couillieaux.) Paris, 1912.

Afr 2223.10 Programme d'équipement. (Caisse d'Equipement pour le Développement de l'Algérie.) Alger. 1960+

Afr 2030.275 Programme et action du gouvernement en Algérie. (Algeria.) Alger, 1956.

Afr 3979.00 Programme for visiting Egypt. (Cook, J.) London, 1900.

Afr 1830.20.5 Les progres des connaissances botaniques en Algerie depuis 1830. (Maire, Rene.) Paris, 1931.

Afr 609.64.25F Progrès Egyptien. Afrique d'aujourd'hui. Le Caire, 1964.

Afr Doc 1305.5 Progress. Anniversary of the Sudan revolution. (Sudan. Central Office of Information.) Khartoum. 1963+

Afr 3986.960.5 Progress in United Arab Republic. (International Studies Association, Cairo.) Cairo, 1960.

Afr 9500.35 The progress of Africans in Southern Rhodesia. (Rhodesian Institute of African Affairs, Bulawayo, South Africa.) Bulawayo, 1958.

Afr 6210.64 The progress of Nigerian public administration: a report on research. (Murray, David John.) Ibadan, 1968.

Afr 8089.02 Progress of South Africa. (Theal, G.M.) Toronto, 1902.

Afr 9499.5 Progress of southern Rhodesia, 1920-27. (Rhodesia, Southern.) Salisbury, 1928.

Afr 8678.36 The progress of the Bantu peoples towards nationhood. (South Africa. Department of Information.) Pretoria, 1965?

Afr 3028.7 Progress on high dam in Aswan. (Mahmud, Rajab.) Washington, 1961.

Afr 8380.20 Progress through partnership. (Rupert, Anton.) Cape Town, 1967.

Afr 8045.3 Progress through separate development, South Africa in peaceful transition. (South Africa. Department of Information.) N.Y., 1965.

Afr 8045.54 Progressive Party of South Africa. Molteno report. Johannesburg, 1960-62.

Afr 9436.10 Prohibited immigrant. (Stonehouse, John.) London, 1960.

Afr 150.50 A projecção do infante no mundo. (Passos, Vergilio.) Lisboa, 1960.

Afr Doc 9279.10F Projecto de orçamento. (Inhambane.) 1917-1918

Afr Doc 9290.5F Projecto de orçamento. (Tete.) 1917-1918

Afr Doc 9283.5F Projecto de orçamento. (Mozambique.) 1917-1918

Afr 7176.26.2 Projecto de uma companhia agricola e comercial africana. 2. ed. (Graça, Joaquim José da.) Lisboa, 1879.

Afr 3252.10 Un projet d'alliance entre l'Egypte et la Grèce en 1867. (Politis, A.G.) Caire, 1931.

Afr 2260.3 Projets de colonization. (Lamoriciére.) Paris, 1847.

Afr 3205.3 Prokesch-Osten, A. Mehmed-Ali. Wien, 1877.

Afr 210.65.25 Prokopczuk, Jerzy. Zarys nowozytnej historii Afryki. Warszawa, 1965.

Afr 4431.15 Prologo un conflitto. (Borra, Eduardo.) Milano, 1965.

Afr 609.62 A prologue to the study of the African arts. (Merriam, Alan P.) Yellow Springs, Ohio, 1962.

Afr 1608.44.3 Promenade au Maroc. (Didier, C.) Paris, 1844.

Afr 609.07 Promenade autour de l'Afrique, 1907. (Lowensbach, Lothaire.) Paris, 1908.

Afr 2748.85 Une promenade dans le Sahara. (Lagarde, Charles.) Paris, 1885.

Afr 3979.34 La promenade égyptienne. (Aveline, Claude.) Paris, 1934.

Afr 1609.36.10 La promenade marocaine. (Capriles, Georges.) Paris, 1936.

Afr 2230.10 Promenades...chez les Kabyles. (Hun, F.) Alger, 1860.

Afr 5365.3 Promenades au Dahomey. (Heudebert, L.) Paris, 1902.

Afr 3979.11.10 Promenades au pays des pharaons. (Lamoriniere de la Rochecautin.) Paris, 1913.

Afr 10435.34.100 The promised land. (Ogot, Grace Akinyi.) Nairobi, 1966.

Afr 7312.25 Promoção social en Moçambique. (Grupo de Trabalho de Promoção Social.) Lisboa, 1964.

Afr 6457.36 Promoting economie development with illustrations from Kenya. (Oser, Jacob.) Nairobi, 1967.

Afr 7812.258 Promotion de la société rurale du Congo belge et du Ruanda-Urundi. (Journées d'Etudes Coloniales, Institut Universitaire des Territoires d'Outre Mer, Antwerp, 1957.) Bruxelles, 1958.

Afr 1623.963.5 Promotion nationale au Maroc. (Morocco. Delegation Generale a la Promotion Nationale et au Plan.) Casa, 196-.

Afr 545.10A Propheten in Afrika. (Schlosser, Katesa.) Braunschweig, 1949.

Afr 6195.16 Prophetism in Ghana. (Baeta, C.G.) London, 1962.

Afr 4969.63 The prophet's camel bell. (Laurence, M.) London, 1963.

Afr 7549.54 Les propos d'un colonial belge. (Dellicour, Fernand.) Bruxelles, 1963.

Afr 1609.30.25 Propos d'un vieux marocain. (Nahon, Moise.) Paris, 1930.

Afr 6310.49 Proposals for the implementation of the recommendations contained in the report of the Commission on the Civil Services of the East African territories and the East Africa High Commission, 1953-1954. (Uganda.) Entebbe, 1954.

Afr 555.9.5 The proposed mission in Central Africa. (Means, J.O.) Cambridge, 1879.

Afr 590.8 Propositions sur l'organisation d'une emigration. v.1-2. (Carstensen, E.) Paris, 1869.

Afr 1618.20 La propriété collective au Maroc. (Guillaume, A.) Rabat, 1960.

Afr 12639.24.29 Prose and poetry. (Senghor, L.S.) London, 1965.

Afr 5869.67	Prosset, Alfred. Les Premiers colons de l'Ile Bourbon. 2. ed. Paris, n.d.
Afr 10385.15.100	Prostitute. (Oculi, Okello.) Nairobi, 1968.
Afr 1570.38	El protectorado frances en Marruecos. (Gonzalez Hontoria, M.) Madrid, 1915.
Afr 1570.15	Protectorat de la France sur le Maroc. (Rouard de Card, E.) Toulouse, 1905.
Afr 5053.10	Le protectorat en Afrique occidentale française et les chefs indigènes. Thèse. (Forgeron, J.B.) Bordeaux, 1920.
Afr 5365.5	Le protectorat français sur la Côte des Esclaves. (Salinis, A.) Paris, 1908.
Afr 1609.21.5	Le protectorat marocain. (Kann, Reginald.) Nancy, 1921.
Afr 2530.1	Le protectorat tunisien. (Bahar, J.) Paris, 1904.
Afr 8045.12	The protectorates of South Africa. (Perham, M.) London, 1935.
Afr 10007.4	Protest and conflict in African literature. London, 1969.
Afr 550.132	Protestantismo em Africa. (Gonçalves, José.) Lisboa, 1960. 2v.
Afr 115.123	Prothero, Ralph Mansell. A geography of Africa; regional essays on fundamental characteristics, issues and problems. London, 1969.
Afr 628.266	Protiv rasizma. (Efimov, Aleksei V.) Moskva, 1966.
Afr 7565.12.5F	Protocoles et acte général de la Conférence de Berlin, 1884-85. (Berlin. Conference, 1884-85.) n.p., 1885.
Afr 3315.146	Protopopov, Anatolii S. Sovetskii Soiuz i Suetskii krizis 1956 goda (iiul'-noiabr'). Moskva, 1969.
Afr 1571.17.125	Proust, L. Le maréchal Lyautey tel que je l'ai connu. Vichy, 1954.
Afr 5056.125	Proust, Louis. Visions d'Afrique. Paris, 1925.
Afr 3725.11	Prout, H.G. Where Emin is. n.p., 1889.
Afr 3821.5	Prout, Henri Goslee. General report on the province of Kordofan. Cairo, 1877.
Afr 2870.7.35	Provenzal, G. La missione politica dell'Italia nell'Africa mediterranea. Roma, 1913.
Afr 7208.8	Providências legislativas ministeriasis, tomadas em Moçambique em 22 outubro de 1966. (Portugal. Ministério do Ultramar.) Lisboa, 1966.
Afr 2295.1	Province de Constantine. (Lamalle, D. de.) Paris, 1837.
Afr 7320.4	La province portugaise de Mosambique. (Castilho, S. de.) n.p., 1890.
Afr 4620.3	Provinces équatoriales d'Abyssinie. (Leontieff.) n.p., n.d.
Afr 3695.4	Provinces of the equator. (Gordon, C.G.) Cairo, 1877.
Afr 7175.18	A provincia de Angola. (Morton de Matas.) Porto, 1926.
Afr Doc 2405.5	Provincial annual reports. (Nigeria, Northern.) Kaduna. 1952+
Afr 6295.66	Provincial union Oshogbo constitution. (Old Calabar.) Oshogbo, 1961.
Afr 5920.13	Provincias africanas espanolas. 1.ed. (Ortega Canadell, Rosa.) Barcelona, 1962.
Afr 7093.3.5	Proyart, L.B. Histoire de Loango, Kakongo. Paris, 1776.
Afr 7093.3	Proyart, L.B. Histoire de Loango, Kakongo. Paris, 1819.
Afr 4785.961	Prozhogin, N P. Dobrogo utra, Afrika. Moscow, 1961.
Afr 12007.1	Prozhogina, S.V. Literatura Marokko i Tunisa. Moskva, 1968.
Afr 6455.10	Pruen, S.R. The Arab and the African. London, 1891.
Afr 5056.9	Pruneau de Pommegorge, Antoine Edmé. Description de la Nigritie. Amsterdam, 1789.
Afr 5758.34	Prunieres, A. Madagascar et la crise. Thèse. Paris, 1934.
Afr 2208.52	Prus. A residence in Algeria. London, 1852.
Afr 6926.4	Prussia. Grosser Generalität. Die Kämpfe der deutschen Truppen in Südwest Afrika. Berlin, 1906-08. 2v.
Afr 8289.04.5	Prussia. Grosser Generalstab. Kriegsgeschichtliche Abteilung. The war in South Africa. N.Y., 1969.
Afr 8289.04	Prussia-Grosser. The war in South Africa. London, 1904. 2v.
Afr 6615.5	The Prussian lash in Africa. (Africanus.) London, 1918.
Afr 679.47	Psichari, Ernest. Terres de soleil, et de sommeil. Paris, 1947.
Afr 679.20	Psichari, Ernest. Les voix qui crient dans le désert. Paris, 1920.
Afr 8325.20	The psychology of jingoism. (Hobson, J.A.) London, 1902. 2v.
Afr 6460.70	The psychology of Mau Mau. (Carothers, John C.) Nairobi, 1955.
Afr 6395.2.40	The psychology of Mau Mau. (Garothers, John C.) Nairobi, 1954.
Afr 6225.55	The psychology of the Nigerian revolution. (Ohonbamu, Obarogie.) Ilfracombe, 1969.
Afr 695.12	Ptolemaeus und die Handelsstrassen in Central-Africa. (Roscher, A.) Gotha, 1857.
Afr Doc 3309.305	The public accounts of the government of Uganda together with the report thereon by the Controller and Auditor General. (Uganda. Controller and Auditor General.) Entebbe. 1963+
Afr 4238.15	Public administration in Ethiopia. (Howard, W.E.H.) Groningen, 1956.
Afr 8028.200	The public archives of South Africa, 1652-1910. (Botha, C.G.) Cape Town, 1928.
Afr 8677.36	Public expenditure in South Africa. (Waasdijk, Tom van.) Johannesburg, 1964.
Afr 3986.964	Public Law 480 and other economic assistance to United Arab Republic. (United States. Department of Agriculture. Economic Research Service. Development and Trade Analysis Division.) Washington, 1964.
Afr 4574.2	The public sector. (Pischke, J.D.) Addis Ababa, 1966.
Afr 7461.40	Public sector accounts of Liberia. (Barkay, Richard M.) Monrovia, 1965.
Afr 19.12	Publicações. (Salvador, Brazil. Universidade. Centro de Estudos Afro-Orientais.)
Afr 7050.10	Publicações. 1,1947 (Centro de Estudos da Guiné Portuguesa.) 9v.
Afr 9.3	Publication. (Institute for the Study of Man in Africa.) Johannesburg. 1,1965+
Afr 2030.335	Publication. Mémoires et travaux. (Centre d'Etudes Régionales de Kabylie.) Alger.
Afr 1803.5	Publications. (Centre d'Information pour les Problèmes de l'Algérie et du Sahara.) Paris. 1+
Afr 4.10	Publications. (Duquesne University, Pittsburgh. Institute of African Affairs.) Pittsburgh.
Afr 9.6	Publications. (International African Service Bureau.) London.
Afr 6200.14.46	Publications. (Nigerian Institute of Social and Economic Research, Ibadan, Nigeria.) Ibadan. 1963+

Afr 8022.5	Publications. (Van Riebeeck Society.) Cape Town. 2,1919+ 52v.
Afr 2420.5	Publications. Histoire. (Tunis (City). Université. Faculté des Lettres et des Sciences Humaines.) 1,1961+ 6v.
Afr 2420.10	Publications. Sources de l'histoire de la Tunisie. (Tunis (City). Université. Faculté des Lettres et des Sciences Humaines.) 3+ 2v.
Afr 1309.3	Publications (1915-1935). Tables et index. (Institut des Hautes Etudes Marocaines.) Rochefort-sur-Mer, 1936. 2v.
Afr 16.8	Publications afro-asiatiques. (Permanent Organization for Afro-Asian Peoples' Solidarity.) Le Caire. 2v.
Afr Doc 2402.2F	Publications of the government of the northern region of Nigeria, 1960-1962. (Yakuba, Stephen.) Zaria, 1963.
Afr Doc 1802.10	Publications price list. (Ghana. State Publishing Corporation.) Accra. 1958+
Afr 8687.124	The published works of Margaret Livingstone Ballinger; a bibliography. (Udeman, Elsa.) Johannesburg, 1968.
Afr 10013.5	Publizist und Publikum in Afrika. (Münster. Universität. Institut für Publizistik.) Köln, 1962.
Afr 4559.34.30	Pucci, Generoso. Coi 'Negadi' in Etiopia. Firenze, 1934.
Afr 4788.4	Puccioni, Nello. Le popolazioni indigene della Somalia italiana. Bologna, 1937.
Afr 609.68.25	Pueblos y enigmas de Africa. 2a ed. (Llopis, José J.) Madrid, 1968.
Afr 3978.44	Pueckler-Muskau. Aus Mehemed Alis Reich. Stuttgart, 1844.
Afr 3979.63.15	Pueramiidide maal. (Einmann, E.) Tallinn, 1963.
Afr 210.45	La puesta en valor del continente africano. (Garcia Figueras, Thomas.) Barcelona, 1945.
Afr 6688.4	Puig, F. Etude sur les coutumes des Cabrais (Togo). Thèse. Toulouse, 1934.
Afr 5091.5	Pujos, Jerome. Croissance économique. Paris, 1964.
Afr 6390.43	Pulitzer, Ralph. Diary of two safaris. N.Y., 1927.
Afr 2208.81.3	Pulligny, F.A. de. Six semaines en Algérie. Paris, 1881.
Afr 2208.54.3	Pulszky, F. The tricolor on the atlas. London, 1854.
Afr 6719.5	Pultkamer, Jesko. Gouverneursjahre in Kamerun. Berlin, 1912.
VAfr 6192.98	Pundik, Herbert. Ghana; 20 stammer-én stat. København, 1965.
Afr 2209.27.35	Les puritans du désert. (Chevrillon, A.) Paris, 1927.
Afr 9165.71.10	The purple and the gold. (Collier, Joy.) Cape Town, 1965.
Afr 1840.24	Purtschet, Christian. Sociologie électorale en Afrique du Nord. Paris, 1966.
Afr 6455.35	Purvis, J.B. Through Uganda to Mt. Elgon. London, 1909.
Afr 4700.62	Put k nezavisimosti. (Ivanitskii, M.N.) Kiev, 1962.
Afr 3745.65	Put suḍana v nezavisimosti. (Kiselev, V.I.) Moscow, 1958.
Afr 3978.53.10	Puteshestvie po Egiptu i Nubii, v 1834-1835. Izd.2. (Norov, Avraam S.) Sankt Peterburg, 1853. 2v.
Afr 1258.80.5	Puteshestvie v severnuiu Afriku. Izd 2. Sankt Peterburg, 1880 (Kostenko, L.Th.)
Afr 7809.54	Putnam, A.E. Madami. N.Y., 1954.
Afr 640.5	Les Pygmées. (Quatrefages de Bréau, Armand de.) Paris, 1887.
Afr 640.5.35	Le Pygmées de la forêt équatoriale. (Trilled, H.) Paris, 1932.
Afr 640.5.5	The Pygmies. (Quatrefrages de Bréau, Armand de.) Paris, 1895.
Afr 9400.10.5	Pygmies and bushmen of the Kalahari. (Dornan, S.S.) London, 1925.
Afr 8340.25	Pyrah, G.B. Imperial policy and South Africa, 1902-10. Oxford, 1955.
Afr 4598.5	The Qemant. (Gamst, Frederick C.) N.Y., 1969.
Afr 7122.102	Quadros chronologicos dos governadores geraes da provincia d'Angola. (Pereira, Alberto Feliciano Marques.) Loanda, 1889.
Afr 210.63.10	Quaison-Sackey, A. Africa unbound. N.Y., 1963.
Afr 7175.77	Quand le vent souffle en Angola. (Hanu, Jose.) Bruxelles, 1965.
Afr 2030.469.5	Quandt, William B. Revolution and political leadership: Algeria, 1954-1968. Cambridge, 1969.
Afr 4513.39.15A	Quaranta, F. Ethiopia. London, 1939.
Afr 609.56.5	Quarantacinque gradi all'ombra, attraverso l'Africa, dalla Città del Capo al Cairo. (Vergani, Orio.) Torino, 1964.
Afr 1494.30Γ	Quarante ans de présence française au Maroc. Casablanca, 1953.
Afr 8676.62.5	A quarter of a century of industrial progress in South Africa. (Norval, A.) Cape Town, 1962.
Afr Doc 3509.10	Quarterly bulletin of financial statistics. (Rhodesia. Southern. Central Statistical Office.) Salisbury. 1964
Afr Doc 3809.5	Quarterly bulletin of financial statistics. (Rhodesia (British Colony). Central Statistical Office.) Salisbury. 1965+
Afr Doc 3509.5	Quarterly bulletin of financial statistics. (Rhodesia and Nyasaland. Central Statistical Office.) Salisbury. 1963
Afr Doc 1807.20	Quarterly digest of statistics. (Ghana. Central Bureau of Statistics.) Accra. 1,1952+
Afr Doc 3607.5	Quarterly digest of statistics. (Malawi. National Statistical Office.) Zomba. 1,1966+
Afr Doc 2807.10	Quarterly digest of statistics. (Mauritius. Central Statistical Office.) 1-6,1961-1966
Afr Doc 3007.4	Quarterly economic and statistical bulletin. (East Africa High Commission. East African Statistical Department.) 3-52,1949-1961 3v.
Afr Doc 3234.10	Quarterly report. (Kenya. Development and Reconstruction Authority.)
Afr Doc 1707.5	Quarterly statistical bulletin. (Sierra Leone. Central Statistical Office.) Freetown. 1,1963+
Afr Doc 3807.15	Quarterly statistical summary. (Rhodesia. Central Statistical Office.) Salisbury. 1,1967+
Afr Doc 1708.705	Quarterly trade statistics. (Sierra Leone.) Freetown. 41,1962+
Afr 11057.4	Quartet. (Rive, Richard.) N.Y., 1963.
Afr 5406.186	Quatre années au Congo. (Jeannest, Charles.) Paris, 1886.
Afr 555.45	Quatre ans au Cameroun. (Christol, Frank.) Paris, 1922.
Afr 2030.462.25	Quatre ans de guerre en Algérie. (Denoyer, François.) Paris, 1962.
Afr 2030.5	Quatre ans en Algérie. (Algeria. Gouverneur Général, 1951-55.) Alger, 1955.
Afr 2719.23	Quatre siècles d'histoire marocaine. (Martin, A.G.P.) Paris, 1923.
Afr 1369.23	Quatre siècles d'histoire marocaine. (Martin, Alfred G.P.) Paris, 1923.

Afr 640.5 Quatrefages de Bréau, Armand de. Les Pygmées. Paris, 1887.
Afr 640.5.5 Quatrefages de Bréau, Armand de. The Pygmies. Paris, 1895.
Afr 3078.11 Quatremère, Etienne Marc. Mémoires géographiques et historiques sur l'Egypte. Paris, 1811. 2v.
Afr 3078.11.1 Quatremère, Etienne Marc. Observations sur quelques points de la géographie de l'Egypte. Paris, 1812.
Afr 7324.19.5 Quatro estudos e uma evocação para a historia de Lourenço Marques. (Lobato, A.) Lisboa, 1961.
Afr 210.61.10 Que sera le destin de l'Afrique? (Dessarre, Eve.) Paris, 1961.
Afr 8230.9 Queen or president. (Gluckstein, S.M.) London, 1900.
Afr 3979.10 Queer things about Egypt. (Sladen, D.) London, 1910.
Afr 1658.32 Queipo De Llano, G. El general. 7a ed. Madrid, 1930.
Afr 7015.42 A queixa do Ghana e a conjura contra Portugal. (Evangelista, J.) Lisboa, 1963.
Afr Doc 9287.5 Quelimane. Governador. Relatorio. Lourenço Marques 1907-1915
Afr 625.11 Die Quellen Bourguignon d'Anvilles für seine kritische Karte von Afrika. (Vollkommer, Max.) München, 1904.
Afr 575.10 Quellien, A. La politique musulmane dans l'Afrique occidentale française. Paris, 1910.
Afr 625.15F Quelques éclaircissements épars sur mes Monumenta cartographica Africae et Aegypti. (Yusuf Kamal, Prince.) Leiden, 1935.
Afr 626.134 Quelques expériences de décolonisation et de développement économique. v.1-2. (Amin Samir.) Dakar, 1964.
Afr 8100.20 Quelques notes sur l'établissement et les travaux des Portugais au Monomotapa. Lisbonne, 1889.
Afr 7565.20 Quelques pages sur le Congo. (Cannart d'Hamale, Art.) Bruxelles, 1908.
Afr 2025.16 Quelques questions algériennes. (Colin, M.) Paris, 1899.
Afr 7015.30 Quem incendiou o Congo. (Lupi, Luis C.) Lisboa, 1960.
Afr 5385.27.2 Quenum, M. Au pays des Fons. 2me éd. Paris, 1938.
Afr 4559.10 Quer durch Abessinien. (Faitlovitch, J.) Berlin, 1910.
NEDL Afr 2748.74 Quer durch Afrika. (Rohlfs, G.) Leipzig, 1874. 2v.
Afr 2731.15.90 Quesnel, Roger. Charles de Foucauld, les étapes d'une recherche. Tours, 1966.
Afr 2208.85 Quesnoy, F. L'Algérie. 2e ed. Paris, 1890.
Afr 2748.26.4 Quest beyond the Sahara. (Williams, Harry.) London, 1965.
Afr 2030.467.25 Qu'est devenu Ben Bella? (Comité pour la Défense de Ben Bella et des Autres Victimes de la Répression en Algérie.) Paris, 1967.
Afr 115.20.5 The quest for Africa. (Schiffers, H.) London, 1957.
Afr 5247.38 The quest for Timbuctoo. (Gardner, Brian.) London, 1968.
Afr 4559.35.95 The quest of Sheba's mines. (Hayter, Frank Edward.) London, 1935.
Afr 7183.34 A questão da Lunda, 1885-1894. (Santos, Eduardo dos.) Lisboa, 1964.
Afr 2030.60 The question. (Alleg, Henri.) N.Y., 1958.
Afr 2030.60.5 La question. (Alleg, Henri.) Paris, 1965.
Afr 500.16 La question africaine. (Beyens, N.E.L.) Bruxelles, 1918.
Afr 1868.47 La question algerienne. (Brunet, Jean B.) Paris, 1847.
Afr 1915.13 La question algérienne. (Orient, N.) Paris, 1936.
Afr 1869.58 Question algerienne. Paris, 1958.
Afr 7815.26 La question arabe et le Congo, 1883-1892. (Ceulemans, P.) Bruxelles, 1959.
Afr 1990.10 Question d'Afrique. (Buret, Eugène.) Paris, 1842.
Afr 500.14 La question d'Afrique. (Ronze, Raymond.) Paris, 1918.
Afr 1990.6 La question d'Alger. (Desjobert, A.) Paris, 1837.
Afr 1922.15 La question d'Alger devant les Chambres sous la Restauration. (Julien, A.) Alger, 1922.
Afr 1325.7F Question de la protection diplomatique au Maroc. (France.) Paris, 1880.
Afr 2870.40 La question de Libye dans le règlement de la paix. (Pichon, Jean.) Paris, 1945.
Afr 5615.5 La question de Madagascar. (Brenier, J.) Paris, 1882.
Afr 5548.95.5 La question de Madagascar. (Joubert, J.) Paris, 1895.
Afr 1738.27 La question de Tanger. Thèse. (Sibieude, Jean.) Montpellier, 1927.
Afr 3199.38 La question d'Egypte, 1841-1938. Thèse. (Amad, E.S.) Paris, 1938.
Afr 3199.05 La question d'Egypte. (Freycinet, C. de.) Paris, 1905.
Afr 3199.20 La question d'Egypte depuis Bonaparte jusqu'à la révolution de 1919. (Sabry, Mohammed.) Paris, 1920.
Afr 1369.60 La question des frontières terrestres du Maroc. (Husson, Philippe.) Paris, 1960.
Afr 1570.7 La question du Maroc. (Bourassin, R.) Paris, 1904.
Afr 1570.3 La question du Maroc. (Hess, J.) Paris, 1903.
Afr 1550.3.5 La question du Maroc. (Maura y Gamazo, Gabriel.) Paris, 1911.
Afr 2285.1 La question du sud-ouest. (Sabatier, C.) Alger, 1881.
Afr 7010.4 La question du Zaire, droits de Portugal. (Lisbon. Sociedade Geografica.) Lisbonne. 1883+
Afr 3285.2 La question égyptienne et l'Italie. (Saint-Martin, H. de.) Florence, 1884.
Afr 2225.9 La question indigène en Algérie au commencement du XXe siècle. (Mercier, E.) Paris, 1901.
Afr 2530.25 Question italienne en Tunisie (1868-1938). Paris, 1939.
Afr 1570.19 La question marocaine. (Moulin, H.A.) Paris, 1906.
Afr 1550.13 La question marocaine. (Paquot, G.) Paris, 1908.
Afr 1570.16 La question marocaine. (Ternant, V. de.) Paris, 1894.
Afr 1200.75.4 La question méditerranéenne. (Benoist, Charles.) Paris, 1928.
Afr 8678.23 Question of colour, study of South Africa. Edinburgh, 1906.
NEDL Afr 3275.43 The question of Egypt in Anglo-French relations, 1875-1904. (Regatz, L.J.) Edinburgh, 1922.
X Cg Afr 3204.22 Question of Egypt in Anglo-French relations. Edinburgh, 1917.
Afr 8678.255 Question of race conflict resulting from the policies of apartheid. (Krishna Mevor, Vengalil Kreshnan.) New Delhi, 1959.
Afr 7122.83 A question of slavery. (Duffy, James Edward.) Cambridge, 1967.
Afr 7180.5 Questionario ethnographico acerca dos populações indigenas de Angola e Congo. Luanda, 1912.
Afr 4513.39.10 La questione del Nilo. (Neri, Italo.) Roma, 1939.
Afr 590.38 La questione della schiavetà coloniale dal Congresso di Vienna a oggi. (Cicognani, D.) Firenze, 1935.
Afr 2974.5 La questione di Giarabub. (Meriano, F.) Bologna, 1925.
Afr 2505.1 La questione tunisina e l'Europa. (Carta, F.) Roma, 1879.
Afr 2530.15 La questione tunisina e l'Italia. (Tumedei, C.) Bologna, 1922.
Afr 632.17 Questionnaire préliminaire d'ethnologie africaine. (Foucart, George.) Le Caire, 1919.
Afr Doc 4306.7F Questions affecting South Africa at the United Nations. (South Africa.) Pretoria. 1965+
Afr 1017.1 Questions nord-africaines. Paris. 1,1934+
Afr 2220.1 Quetin. Guide du voyage en Algérie. Paris, 1847.
Afr 3979.26.5 Quibell, Annie. A wayfarer in Egypt. Boston, 1926.
Afr 2945.2.3 Quid de natura...Cyrenaicae pentapolis. (Rainaud, A.) Paris, 1894.
Afr 608.86 Quid novi ex Africa. (Rohlfs, G.) Cassel, 1886.
Afr 603.23.10 Quid Schems Eddin el dimashqui geographus de Africa cognitum habuerit. Thesis. (Deherain, Henri.) Paris, 1897.
Afr 1769.7 Quien es el glani. (Santamaria Quesada, R.) Tetuan, 1955.
Afr 609.66.45 Quilici, Folco. Alla scoperta dell'Africa. 2d ed. Firenze, 1968.
Afr 609.65.35 Quilici, Folco. I mille fuochi. Bari, 1965.
Afr 8360.11 Quinn, Gerald D. The rebellion of 1914-15, a bibliography. Cape Town, 1957.
Afr 6275.38 Quinn-Young, C.T. Geography of Nigeria. London, 1946.
Afr 7065.5 O quinto centenario do descobrimento da Guiné portuguesa a luz da critica historica. (Dias Dinis, A.J.) Braga, 1946.
Afr 5417.100 Quinze ans de Gabon;...1839-1853. (Deschamps, Hubert.) Paris, 1965.
Afr 5448.18 Quinze ans de travaux et de recherches dans les pays du Niari. Monaco, 1966-1968.
Afr 7920.3.5 Quinze mois de gouvernement du Congo. (Tshombe, Moise.) Paris, 1966.
Afr 210.63.75 Quo vadis, Africa. (Falcąo, F. de S.) Lisboa, 1963.
Afr 3042.8 Quraishi, Zaheer Masood. Liberal nationalism in Egypt; rise and fall of Wafa party. 1st ed. Allahabad, 1967.
Afr 5765.7.25 Le R.P. Barbe de la compagnie de Jesus. (Lamaigniere.) Poitiers, 1885.
Afr 550.10 Le R.P. Bouchard. (Tetu, H.) Québec, 1897.
Afr 8289.45.4 Raal, Sarah. Met die Boere in die veld. 4. druk. Kaapstad, 1945.
Afr 1965.3 Raasloeff, W. Rückblick auf Algerie (1840-41). Altona, 1845.
Afr 5219.05 Rabah et les Arabes du Chari. (Decorse, J.) Paris, 1905.
Afr 1609.32.5 Rabat, Maroc. Institut des Hautes Études Marocaines. Initiation au Maroc. Rabat, 1932.
Afr 1733.5 Rabat. (Tharaud, Jerome.) Paris, 1918.
Afr 1609.32.7 Rabat. Maroc. Institut des Hautes Études Marocaines. Initiation au Maroc. Paris, 1937.
Afr 1609.32.9 Rabat. Maroc. Institut des Hautes Études Marocaines. Initiation au Maroc. Nouvelle ed. Paris, 1945.
Afr 1326.18 Rabat. Université. Centre Universitaire de la Recherche Scientifique. Bulletin signalétique. Rabat. 1,1963+
Afr 1733.5.15 Rabat et Sale. Paris, 1934 (Mauclair, Camille.)
Afr 1609.22.5 Rabbe, P. Au Maroc. Sur les rives. Paris, 1922.
Afr 5219.02.2 Rabeh und das Tschadseegebiet. (Oppenheim, M.F. von.) Berlin, 1902.
Afr 13438.1.100 Rabemananjara, Jacques. Agapes des dieux ou Tritriva. Paris, 1962.
Afr 13438.1.110 Rabemananjara, Jacques. Antidote. Paris, 1961.
Afr 13438.1.120 Rabemananjara, Jacques. Antsa. Paris, 1956.
Afr 13438.1.140 Rabemananjara, Jacques. Les boutriers de l'aurore. Paris, 1957.
Afr 13438.1.775 Rabemananjara, Jacques. Insel mit Flammensilben. Herranalb, 1962.
Afr 13438.1.132 Rabemananjara, Jacques. Lamba. 2. éd. Paris, 1961.
Afr 5640.45 Rabemananjara, Jacques. Nationalisme et problemes Malgaches. Paris, 1959.
Afr 13438.1.150 Rabemananjara, Jacques. Rites millénaires. Photocopy. Paris, 1955.
Afr 5549.52 Rabemananjara, R.W. Madagascar. Paris, 1952.
Afr 5640.30 Rabemananjara, R.W. Madagascar sous la revolution Malgache. Paris, 1953.
Afr 8676.59 Rabie, Zacharias Johannes. Der Staat als Unternehmer in der Union von Südafrika. Köln, 1959.
Afr 2748.82.7 Rabourdin, L. Algérie et Sahara. Paris, 1882.
Afr 628.229 A raça negra perante a civilisação. (Montenegro, Alvaro de.) Lisboa, 1929.
Afr 7048.10 A raça negra sob o ponto de vista da civilisação da Africa. (Nogueira, A.F.) Lisboa, 1880.
Afr 7326.5 Racas, usos e costumes dos indigenas do districto de Inhambane. (Cabral, Augusto.) Lourenço Marques, 1910.
Afr 7315.2 Raças e linguas indigenas en Moçambique. (Ornellas, A.D.) n.p., 1905.
Afr 4700.13.5 Raccolta di publicazioni coloniali italiane. (Italy. Direzione Centrale degli Affari Coloniali.) Roma, 1911.
Afr 8676.34 Race and economics in South Africa. (Ballinger, W.G.) London, 1934.
Afr 9500.15 Race and nationalism. (Franck, Thomas M.) N.Y., 1960.
Afr 9439.60 Race and politics. (Clegg, E.M.) London, 1960.
Afr 6420.35.7 Race and politics in Kenya. (Huxley, E. Grant.) London, 1956.
Afr 6435.5 Race and politics in Kenya. (Huxley, Elspeth Grant.) London, 1944.
Afr 8678.45 Race and reason. (Hoernle, R.F.A.) Johannesburg, 1945.
Afr 8678.55 Race attitudes and education. (Malherbe, E.) Johannesburg, 1946.
Afr 8680.25 Race attitudes in South Africa. (MacCrone, Ian Douglas.) Johannesburg, 1957.
Afr 630.31 The race problem in Africa. (Buxton, Charles R.) London, 1931.
Afr 8678.49.7 The race problem in South Africa. (Cotton, Walter Aidan.) N.Y., 1969.
Afr 630.10A Race problems in the new Africa. (Willoughby, W.C.) Oxford, 1923.
Afr 8678.160 Race relations and race attitudes in South Africa. (Crijns, Arthur.) Nijmegen, 1957.
Afr 630.46 Race relations in Africa. (Mason, Philip.) London, 1960.
Afr 630.52.5 Race relations in Negro Africa. (Ghurye, G.S.) Bombay, 1952.
Afr 8678.120 Race relations in the American South and in South Africa. (Brown, William O.) Boston, 1959.
Afr 8678.218 Race Relations Journal. Johannesburg. 24,1957+ 2v.
Afr 1280.15 Les races anciennes et modernes de l'Afrique septentrionale. (Duprat, Pascal.) Paris, 1845.
Afr 7815.7 Les races indigènes du Congo belge. (Boyd, F.R.) Paris, 1913.
Afr 630.01 Pamphlet box. Races of Africa.
Afr 630.14 Races of Africa. (Seligman, C.G.) London, 1930.
Afr 630.14.3 Races of Africa. 3d ed. (Seligman, C.G.) London, 1957.
Afr 630.14.4 Races of Africa. 4th ed. (Seligman, C.G.) London, 1966.

Afr 8678.57.10	Racial laws versus economic and social forces. (Hellmann, E.) Johannesburg, 1955.
Afr 8678.108	The racial problems of South Africa. (Brayshaw, E. Russell.) London, 1953.
Afr 8678.49	Racial segregation in South Africa. (Cotton, W.A.) London, 1931.
Afr 8678.60	Racial separation in South Africa. (Dvorin, E.P.) Chicago, 1952.
Afr 9500.45	Racial themes in Southern Rhodesia. (Rogers, Cyril A.) New Haven, 1962.
Afr 8678.341	Racism in South Africa. (Marof, Achkar.) N.Y., 1965.
Afr 1618.5F	Rackow, Ernst. Beiträge zur kenntnis der Materiellen kultur nordwest-marokkos. Wiesbaden, 1958.
Afr 5235.269	Radchenko, Galina F. Respublika Mali. Moskva, 1969.
Afr 8230.6.20	Rademeyer, J.I. Paul Kruger. Johannesburg, 1962.
Afr 9047.16	Rademeyer, J.I. Shaka. Johannesburg, 1963.
Afr 12832.5.700	The radiance of the King. (Laye, Camara.) London, 1956.
Afr 11010.07.100	Radiance of the veld. (Trotter, W.M.) Ilfracombe, 1960.
Afr 8250.12	Radziwill, E. Cecil Rhodes, man and empire-maker. London, 1918.
Afr 9093.5	Rae, C. Malaboch. London, 1898.
Afr 2608.77	Rae, Edward. The country of the Moors. London, 1877.
Afr 3978.92	Rae, W.F. Egypt to-day. London, 1892.
Afr 11026.2	Raester, Olga. Curtain up. Cape Town, 1951.
Afr 4559.35.5	Das Rätsel Abessinien. (Lieberenz, P.K.) Berlin, 1935.
Afr 5180.18	Raffenel, A. Voyage dans l'Afrique occidentale. Text and atlas. Paris, 1846. 2v.
Afr 5180.25	Raffenel, Anne. Nouveau voyage dans le pays des Nègres. Paris, 1856. 2v.
Afr 4558.76	Raffray, A. Abyssinie. Paris, 1876.
Afr 4558.75	Raffray, A. Voyage en Abyssinie, à Zanzibar et aux pays des Ouanika. n.p., 1875.
Afr 28.25	Ragatz, L.J. A bibliography for the study of African history in the 19th and 20th centuries. Washington, 1943.
Afr 1259.43.10	Ragatz, L.J. Introduction to French North Africa. N.Y., 1943.
Afr 3978.63.5	Ragged life in Egypt. (Whately, M.L.) London, 1863.
Afr 1947.11	Ragguaglio della schiavitù in Algeri di Giuseppe Giovanni Nicola Albertazzi. (Bologna. Arciconfraternità di Santa Maria.) Bologna, 1772.
Afr 2295.5	Ragot, W. Le Sahara de la province de Constantine. Constantine, 1874-75.
Afr 609.60.80	Ragusin Righi, Livio. Viaggio nell Africa nera in fermento. Trieste, 1960.
Afr 2030.245	Rahmani, Abd el-Kader. L'affaire des officiers algériens. Paris, 1959.
Afr 1739.3.5	Al-Rahuni, A. Ben M. Historia de Tetuan. Tetuan, 1953.
Afr 8283.13	Raid and reform. (Hillier, A.P.) London, 1898.
Afr 2749.22	Le raid Citroen. (Haardt, G.M.) Paris, 1923.
Afr 11728.41.100	Raik, Lea. Redeemed. 1st ed. Johannesburg, 1964.
Afr 9489.04	Railways in Rhodesia. (Wright, E.H.S.) London, 1904.
Afr 2945.2	Rainaud, A. La pentapole cyrénéenne. Paris, 1893.
Afr 2945.2.3	Rainaud, A. Quid de natura...Cyrenaicae pentapolis. Paris, 1894.
Afr 4559.32.10	Rainbow empire, Ethiopia stretches out her hands. (Bergsma, S.) Grand Rapids, 1932.
Afr 9610.10	Rainbow on the Zambezi. (Taylor, Don.) London, 1953.
Afr 4732.21	Rainero, R. I primi tentativi di colonizzazione agricola. Milano, 1960.
Afr 210.63.80	Rainero, Romain. Il nuovo volto dell Africa. Firenze, 1963.
Afr 210.60.65	Rainero, Romain. Il risveglio dell'Africa nera. Bari, 1960.
Afr 8678.340	Rainero, Romain. La segregazione razziale nel Sud Africa. Milano, 1965.
Afr 1869.59	Rainero, Romain. Storia dell Algeria. Firenze, 1959.
Afr 109.66.25	Rainero, Romain. Storia dell'Africa dall'epoca coloniale ad oggi. Torino, 1966.
Afr 609.40	Rainier, P.W. African hazard. London, 1940.
Afr 8252.322	Rainier, P.W. My vanished Africa. New Haven, 1940.
Afr 5585.30	Rainilaiarivony, un homme d'Etat Malgache. (Chapus, G.S.) Paris, 1953.
Afr 2030.462.115	La raison d'état. (Vidal-Naquet, P.) Paris, 1962.
Afr 1493.40	El Raisuni (caudillo de Yebala). (Bermudo-Soriano, E.) Madrid, 1941.
Afr 4575.7	Rait, Mariia V. Narody Efiopii. Moskva, 1965.
Afr 3986.939	Raja'i, Nur al-Din. De la condition légale des sociétés anonymes étrangères en Egypte. Thèse. Paris, 1939.
Afr 5549.67	Rajemisa-Raolison, Regis. Dictionnaire historique et geographique de Madagascar. Fianarantsoa, 1966.
Afr 6470.269	Rake, Alan. Tom Mboya. 1st ed. Garden City, N.Y., 1962.
Afr 5753.7	Raketaka, tableau de moeurs féminines malgaches dressé à l'aide de proverbes et de Fady. (Mondain, G.) Paris, 1925.
Afr 609.61.25	Rakhmatov, M. Afrika idet k svoboda. Moscow, 1961.
Afr 5549.65.10	Ralaimihoatra, Edouard. Histoire de Madagascar. Tananarive, 1965. 2v.
Afr 8687.322	Ralls, Alice M. Glory which is yours. Pietermaritzburg, 1949.
Afr 8315.5	Ralph, Julian. An American with Lord Roberts. N.Y., 1901.
Afr 8295.6	Ralph, Julian. Towards Pretoria. N.Y., 1900.
Afr 8315.5.5A	Ralph, Julian. War's brighter side. N.Y., 1901.
Afr 7458.62	Ralston, Gerard. On the Republic of Liberia, its products and resources. London, 1862.
Afr 3040.70	Ramadan, A.M.S. Evolution de la législation sur la presse en Egypte. Thèse. Le Caire, 1935.
Afr 7808.92	Ramaix, M.M. de. Le Congo. Anvers, 1892.
Afr 4115.20.7	Rambles in Cairo. 3d ed. (Devonshire, H.C.) Cairo, 1947.
Afr 3978.37.15	Rambles in Egypt and Candia. v.1-2. (Scott, C.R.) London, 1837. 2v.
Afr 2209.26	Rambles in North Africa. (Wilson, Albert.) Boston, 1926.
Afr 8105.35	Rambles through the archives of the colony of the Cape of Good Hope. (Leilebrandt, Hendrik Carel von.) Cape Town, 1887.
Afr 3979.37	Rameses (pseud.). Oriental spotlight. London, 1937.
Afr 1658.54	Ramos Charco-Villaseñor, Aniceto. El Rif. Toledo, 1930.
Afr 5960.10	Ramos Izquierdo Y Vivar, L. Descripción geografica y gobierno. Madrid, 1912.
Afr 10005.4	Ramsaran, J.A. New approaches to African literature. Ibadan, 1965.
Afr 6174.6	Ramseyer, F.A. Dark and stormy days at Kumassi, 1900. London, 1901.
Afr 6192.4	Ramseyer, F.A. Four years in Ashante. London, 1875.
Afr 605.56.7	Ramusio, G.B. Il viaggio di Giovan Leone e le navigazioni. Venezia, 1837.
Afr 550.8.25	Rance-Bourrey, A.J. Les obsèques du Cardinal Lavigerie. Paris, 1893.
Afr 6420.50	Rancliffe, D.H. The struggle for Kenya. London, 1954.
Afr 5180.5	Rancon, A. Dans la Haute-Gambie. Paris, 1894.
Afr 9165.42.35	Die rand en sy gould. (Erasmus, J.L.P.) Pretoria, 1944.
Afr 9405.5	Randall, D. Factors and economic development and the Okovanggo Delta. Chicago, 1957.
Afr 2230.22F	Randall-MacIver, D. Libyan notes. London, 1901.
Afr 699.59	Randles, W.G. L'image du sud-est Africain dans la littérature. Lisboa, 1959.
Afr 5437.74	Randles, W.G.L. L'ancien royaume du Congo des origines à la fin du XIXE siècle. Paris, 1968.
Afr 8055.25	Randlords. (Emden, P.H.) London, 1935.
Afr 1955.27	Randon, J.L.C.A. Mémoires du maréchal Randon. Paris, 1873. 2v.
Afr 1955.27.5	Randon, J.L.C.A. Mémoires du maréchal Randon. 2e éd. Paris, 1875-77. 2v.
Afr 679.46	La randonnée africaine. (Blanchod, F.G.) Lausanne, 1946.
Afr 1571.8	Randonnées au Maroc, 1911-1913. (Peyris, G.) Paris, 1924.
Afr 6985.3F	Range, Paul. Beiträge...zur Landskunde des deutschen Namalandes. Hamburg, 1914.
Afr 9446.37	Ranger, Terence O. Revolt in Southern Rhodesia, 1896-1897. London, 1967.
Afr 9446.40	Ranger, Terence Osborn. Revolt in Southern Rhodesia, 1896-97. Evanston, Ill., 1967.
Afr 5406.213	Ranget, Fernand. L'Afrique équatoriale illustrée. Paris, 1913.
Afr 7549.59.10	Ranieri, Liane. Les relations entre l'état indépendant du Congo et l'Italie. Bruxelles, 1959.
Afr 9598.93	Rankin, D.J. The Zambesi basin and Nyassaland. Edinburgh, 1893.
Afr 6143.7	Rankin, F.H. The white man's grave. London, 1836. 2v.
Afr 1485.2	Rankin, R. In Morocco with General d'Amade. London, 1908.
Afr 555.9.28	Rankine, W.H. A hero of the dark continent, Rev. William A. Scott. Edinburgh, 1897.
Afr 8225.15	Ransford, Oliver. The battle of Majuba Hill, the first Boer war. London, 1967.
Afr 8325.68.10	Ransford, Oliver. The battle of Spion Kop. London, 1969.
Afr 9520.10	Ransford, Oliver. Bulawayo: historic battleground of Rhodesia. Cape Town, 1968.
Afr 9769.66	Ransford, Oliver. Livingstone's lake, the drama of Nyasa. London, 1966.
Afr 9439.68	Ransford, Oliver. The rulers of Rhodesia from earliest times to the referendum. London, 1968.
Afr 8289.02.35	Raoul-Duval, R. Au Transvaal, et dans le Sud-Afrique avec les attachés militaires. Paris, 1902.
Afr 500.43	The rape of Africa. (Middleton, Lamar.) London, 1936.
Afr 6275.23	Raphael, J.R. Through unknown Nigeria. London, 191-.
Afr 5426.125	Raponda-Walker, A. Rites et croyances des peuples du Gabon. Paris, 1962.
Afr 4731.5	Rapport...de la campagne d'Afrique (1895-96). (Baldissera.) Paris, n.d.
Afr 2025.13	Rapport...sur les actes du gouvernement. (Lasicotière.) Versailles, 1874.
Afr 1990.11.5	Rapport...sur son voyage de 1852 en Algérie. (Baillet, Noël Bernard.) Rouen, 1852.
Afr Doc 7533.10	Rapport. (Cameroon. Conseil National de Credit.) Paris. 1962+
Afr Doc 6931.5	Rapport. (Niger. Service de l'Agriculture.) Niamey. 1964+
Afr 5758.2	Rapport a l'empereur sur la question malgache. (Bonnavoy De Premoti, F.H.) Paris, 1856.
Afr 5056.124	Rapport annuel, technique et administratif. (French West Africa. Service Géographique.) Laval. 1922+
Afr Doc 7533.5	Rapport annuel. (Cameroon. Conseil Economique et Social.) 1962+
Afr Doc 7535.5	Rapport annuel. (Cameroun. Direction de l'Elevage et des Industries Animales.) Yaoundé 1,1966+
Afr Doc 7135.5	Rapport annuel. (Chad. Ministère de l'Economie et des Transports.) 1965+
Afr Doc 7335.5	Rapport annuel. (Congo (Brazzaville). Conseil Economique et Social.) 1964+
Afr Doc 6634.5	Rapport annuel. (Dahomey. Service du Développement Rural.) Porto-Novo. 1962+
Afr Doc 6443.5	Rapport annuel. (Ivory Coast. Direction des Mines et de la Geologie.) Abidjan. 1966+
Afr Doc 7705.5F	Rapport annuel sur l'administration de la colonie du Congo Belge. (Belgium. Ministère des Affaires Africaines.) 1921-1956 6v.
Afr Doc 5033.5	Rapport d'activité. (France. Direction de la coopération culturelle et technique.) Paris. 1961+
Afr 3040.60F	Rapport de la Commission internationale réunie au Caire pour l'examen des réformes proposées...dans l'administration de la justice en Egypte. (Commission Internationale pour l'Examen des Réformes, Egypte.) Alexandrie, 1870.
Afr 5343.10.2	Rapport de synthèse. (Société d'Etudes pour le Développement Economique et Social.) Paris, 1963.
Afr Doc 6807.364	Rapport définitif de l'enquête agricole, 1964. (Mali. Service de la Statistique et de la Coruptabilité Nationale et de la Mécanographie.) Mali, 196 .
Afr 5318.7	Rapport d'ensemble. (Guinée française.) Paris, 1900.
Afr 5640.14.5	Rapport d'ensemble du Général Gallieni sur la situation général de Madagascar. (Gallieni, J.S.) Paris, 1899. 2v.
Afr 4760.3	Rapport du gouvernement italien à l'Assemblée générale des Nations Unies. (Italy. Ministero degli Affari Esteri.) 1950+ 5v.
Afr 5282.2	Rapport économique, 1959. (Upper Volta. Ministère des Finances, des Affaires Economiques et du Plan.) Ouagadougou, 1960.
Afr 2223.38	Rapport fait...budget spécial de l'Algérie. v.1-2. (France. Chambre des Députés (1908).) Paris, 1908.
Afr 6291.42	Rapport fran Biafra. (Beijbom, Anders.) Stockholm, 1968.
Afr 6739.264F	Rapport général du premier plan quinquennal. (Cameroon. Ministère des Finances et du Plan.) Yaounde, 1964.
Afr 1340.6	Rapport général sur...le protectorat du Maroc. (France. Ministère des Affaires Etrangères.) Rabat, 192- .

Afr 5183.960.8   Rapport général sur les perspectives de développement du Sénégal. 3. éd. (Compagnie d'Etudes Industrielles et d'Aménagement du Territoire.) Dakar, 1963.

Afr 5200.29   Rapport provisoire. (France. Ministère de la France d'Outre-Mer. Service des Statistiques. Mission Socio-Economique du Soudan.) 2-3,1957-1958

Afr 5046.8   Rapport sur la coopération franco-africaine. (France. Ministère de la Coopération.) Paris, 1964.

Afr 2208.53   Rapport sur la situation de l'Algérie en 1853. (France. Ministére de la Guerre.) Paris, 1854.

Afr Doc 5622.5   Rapport sur la situation générale de la colonie. (Madagascar.) n.p., n.d.

Afr Doc 5605.5   Rapport sur l'activité du gouvernement. (Malagasy Republic.) Tananarive. 1,1963+

Afr Doc 5409.5   Rapport sur le budget économique. (Tunisia. Secretariat d'Etat au Plan et à l'Economie Nationale.) Tunis. 1967+

Afr Doc 1408.710   Rapport sur le commerce extérieur de l'Egypte. (Egypt. Customs Administration.) 1923-1938

Afr 5460.5   Rapport sur le Haut-Oubangui. (Bonnel de Meziéres, A.) Paris, 1901.

Afr 5240.6   Rapport sur le plan quinquennal de développement économique. (Mali. Ministère du Plan.) Paris, 1961.

Afr 6739.260   Rapport sur les possibilités de développement industriél. (Societe d'Etudes pour le Developpement.) Paris, 1960.

Afr 5343.2   Rapport sur l'évolution économique et sociale de la Côte-d'Ivoire, 1960-1969. (Ivory Coast. Conseil Economique et Social.) Abidjan, 1965.

Afr 7812.6F   Rapport sur l'execution du plan décennal pour le développment...du Congo Belge, 1956-1958. (Belgium. Ministère des Affaires Africaines. Secretariat du Plan Décennal.) n.p., n.d.

Afr 2223.960.15   Rapport sur l'exécution du programme d'équipement de l'Algérie en 1960. (Algeria. Caisse D'Equipement pour Le Développement de l'Algérie.) Alger, 1961.

Afr 5635.8.5   Rapport sur l'expedition de Madagascar. Text and atlas. (Duchesne, C.) Paris, 1897. 2v.

Afr 1422.10   Les rapports de la France et du Maroc pendant la conquête de l'Algérie (1830-1847). (Cosse Brissac, P. de.) Paris, 1931.

Afr 3215.20   Les rapports de la Grèce et de l'Égypte pendant le regne de Mohamed Aly, 1833-1849. (Polites, Athanasios G.) Roma, 1935.

Afr 7803.40   Rapports du père Planque. (Storme, Marcel.) Bruxelles, 1957.

Afr 3040.10   Les rapports entre le pouvoir judiciaire et le pouvoir exécutif en Egypte. Thèse. (Barkouky, El.) Paris, 1925.

Afr 3986.959.10   Les rapports entre l'évolution économique en Egypte. (Nour, Mustafa M.) Fribourg, 1959.

Afr 3.7F   Rapports et balans. (Comité Spéciale du Katanga.) Bruxelles.

Afr 5184.20   Les rapports financiers de la métropole et de l'Afrique occidentale française. (Faulong, L.) Paris, 1910.

Afr 2928.62   Rapports officiels. (Mission de Ghadamès.) Alger, 1863.

Afr 6878.79   Rapports sur les marchés de la premiére expédition. v.1-4. (Association Internationale Africaine.) Bruxelles, 1879-80.

Afr 2208.66.5   Rasch, Gustav. Nach Algier. Dresden, 1875.

Afr 2208.66.3   Rasch, Gustav. Nach den Oasen von Siban. Berlin, 1866.

Afr 1721.5   Rasgos fisiograficos y geologicos. (Cabanas, Rafael.) Madrid, 1955.

Afr 632.25   Rasovaia diskriminatsiia v stranakh Afriki. (Akademiia Nauk SSSR. Institut Narodov Azii.) Moscow, 1960.

Afr 575.56   Rasprostranenie islama v zapadnoi Afrike, XI-XVI vv. (Tarverdova, Ekaterina A.) Moskva, 1967.

Afr 4558.69   Rassam, H. Narrative of British mission to Theodore. London, 1869. 2v.

Afr 8680.5   Rasse en rassevermenging. (Eloff, Gerhardus.) Bloemfontein, 1942.

Afr 4222.5   Rassegna di studi etiopici. Roma. 1,1941+ 8v.

Afr 4700.1.74   Rassegna sociale dell'Africa italiana. Roma. 1,1938+

Afr 8678.42   Das Rassenrecht in Südafrika. (Krieger, Heinrich.) Berlin, 1944.

Afr 5829.65   Rassool, S. Hassam A. Il Maurice; creuset de l'Ocean Indien. Paris, 1965.

Afr 1955.57   Rasteil, M. Le calvaire des colons de 48. Paris, 1930.

VAfr 7567.41   Ratajski, Leon. Kongo Kinszasa. Wyd. 1. Warszawa, 1967.

Afr 7045.20   Rates, J. Carlos. Angola, Moçambique, San Tome. Edição do autor. Lisboa, 1929.

Afr 550.125   Rathe, G. Mud and mosaics. Westminster, Md., 1962.

Afr 4559.11   Rathjens, Carl. Beiträge zur Landeskunde von Abessinien. These. Erlangen, 1911.

Afr 8676.44   Rationalisation of South African industry. (Spino, Richard B.) Durban, 1944.

Afr 6194.10   Rattray, R.S. Ashanti. Oxford, 1923.

Afr 6194.10.6   Rattray, R.S. Religion and art in Ashanti. London, 1959.

Afr 6194.10.5   Rattray, R.S. Religion and art in Ashanti. Oxford, 1927.

Afr 6194.10.1   Rattray, Robert Sutherland. Ashanti. N.Y., 1969.

Afr 2929.36.5   Rava, C.E. Ai margini del Sahara. Bologna, 1936.

Afr 4688.15   Rava, M. Al Lago Tsana. Roma, 1913.

Afr 5874.21   Ravat, Yves. La Réunion, terre française. Port Louis, 1967.

Afr 9549.60   Raven, Faith. Central Africa. London, 1960.

Afr 8100.42   Raven-Hart, Rowland. Before Van Riebeeck. Cape Town, 1967.

Afr 10671.12.805   Ravenscroft, Arthur. Chinua Achebe. Burnt Mill, 1969.

Afr 3978.40.5   Ravioli, C. Viaggio della spedizione romana in Egitto. v.1. Roma, 1870.

Afr 2870.12   Ravizza, A. La Libia nel suo ordinamento giuridico. Padova, 1931.

Afr 3978.92.2   Rawnsley, H.D. Notes for the Nile. Leipzig, 1892.

Afr 4730.2   Rawson, R.W. European territorial claims on the Red Sea. London, 1885.

Afr 7870.6   Raymaekers, P. L'organisation des zones de squatting. Leopoldville, 1963.

Afr 2530.71A   Raymond, André. La Tunisie. Paris, 1961.

Afr 1738.24   Raymond, Chas. Le statut de Tanger. Alger, 1927.

Afr 8252.7   Raymond, H. B.I. Barnato. London, 1897.

Afr 1727.5   Raynal, R. Plaines et piedmonts du bassin de la Moulouya. Rabat, 1961.

Afr 1570.50   Raynaud, Robert. En marge du livre jaune. Le Maroc. Paris, 1923.

Afr 4969.21   Rayne, H.A. Sun, sand and Somalis. London, 1921.

Afr 9500.40   Rayner, W. The tribe and its successors. London, 1962.

Afr 1571.17.60   Rayonnement de Lyautey. (Heidsieck, P.) Paris, 1944.

Afr 1571.17.57   Rayonnement de Lyautey. (Lyautey, L.H.G.) Paris, 1941.

Afr 1571.17.62   Rayonnement de Lyautey. (Lyautey, L.H.G.) Paris, 1947.

Afr 1625.6   Razas y tribus de Marruecos. (Anton Y Ferrandiz, M.) Madrid, 1903.

Afr 3295.5   Razvitie natsionalno-osvoboditelnogo dvizheniia v Egipte. (Atiyah, S.) Moscow, 1961.

Afr 8844.5   Reaction to conquest. (Wilson, M. Hunter.) London, 1936.

Afr 8844.5.2   Reaction to conquest. (Wilson, M. Hunter.) London, 1961.

Afr 5385.24   Réactions dahoméennes. (Grivot, René.) Paris, 1954.

Afr 590.20   Read, Hollis. The Negro problcm solved. N.Y., 1864.

Afr 590.20.2   Read, Hollis. The Negro problem solved. N.Y., 1969.

Afr 9853.5.5   Read, Margaret. Children of their fathers...Ngoni of Malawi. N.Y., 1968.

Afr 9853.5   Read, Margaret. The Ngoni of Nyasaland. London, 1956.

Afr 6170.7   Reade, W. Story of the Ashantee campaign. London, 1874.

Afr 6095.11   Reade, W.W. Savage Africa. 2. ed. London, 1864.

Afr 6095.19   Reade, Winwood. The African sketch-book. London, 1873. 2v.

Afr 9047.38   Reader, Desmond Harold. Zulu tribe in transition. Manchester, 1966.

Afr 6095.10   Reading, J.H. The Ogowe band. Philadelphia, 1890.

Afr 3986.962.15   Readings for students of commerce. (Bahig, A.F.) Alexandria, 1962.

Afr 109.68.5   Readings in African history. (McEwan, Peter J.M.) London, 1968. 3v.

Afr 11040.3   Readings in South African English prose. (Partridge, A.C.) Pretoria, 1941.

Afr 626.172   Readings in the applied economics of Africa. (Whetham, Edith Holt.) Cambridge, 1967.

Afr 4559.35.45   The real Abyssinia. (Rey, C.F.) London, 1935.

Afr 2209.14.5   The real Algeria. (Stott, M.D.) London, 1914.

Afr 3310.10.80   The real case against Nasser. (Taylor, Edmond.) n.p., 1956.

Afr 1409.10   Real cedula en que S.M. declara la guerra al rey de Marruecos. (Spain. Sovereigns. Carlos IV.) Madrid, 1791.

Afr 6538.36   The real growth of the economy of Uganda. (Uganda. Ministry of Planning and Community Development. Statistics Division.) Entebbe, 1964.

Afr 8230.10   The real Kruger and the Transvaal. (Bruce, C.T.) N.Y., 1900.

Afr 9489.24   The real Rhodesia. (Colquhoun, E.C.) London, 1924.

Afr 8659.13.9   The real South Africa. (Pratt, A.) Indianapolis, 1913.

Afr 8369.38   Real union in South Africa. (Webster, W.A.) Cape Town, 1938.

Afr 1869.57   Réalité de la nation algérienne. (Egretaud, Marcel.) Paris, 1957.

Afr 1869.57.2   Réalité de la nation algérienne. (Egretaud, Marcel.) Paris, 1961.

Afr 5407.12F   Réalités africaines. La mise en valeur de l'A.E.F. Casablanca, 1956.

Afr 2223.36   Les réalités algériennes. (Macquart, E.) Blida, 1906.

Afr 2719.56.5   Réalités et promesses sahariennes. (Strasser, Daniel.) Paris, 1956.

Afr 5410.15   Réalités gabonaises. 26,1965+

Afr 5325.8   Realités ivoiriennes. Paris. 16,1966+

Afr 1318.6F   Réalités marocaines, revue semestrielle. Casablanca. 6,1954+

Afr 5460.10   Réalités oubanguiennes. (Kalck, Pierre.) Paris, 1959.

Afr 8018.6   Reality; a journal of liberal opinion. Pietermaritzburg. 1,1969+

Afr 718.31   Reality versus romance in south central Africa. (Johnston, J.) London, 1893.

Afr 718.31.2   Reality versus romance in South Central Africa. 2nd ed. (Johnston, J.) London, 1969.

Afr 9161.10   The realm of a rain-queen. (Krige, E. (Jensen).) London, 1943.

Afr 1369.65.5   Realm of the evening star. (Hoffmann, E.) Philadelphia, 1965.

Afr 6176.37   Reap the whirlwind: an account of Kwame Nkrumah's Ghana farm 1950 to 1966. (Bing, Geoffrey.) London, 1968.

Afr 8676.67.5   A reappraisal of economic prospects for 1967. (Hupkes, G.J.) Stellenbosch, 1967.

Afr 4559.35.117   Rebeaud, Henri. Au service du négus. 2e ed. Paris, 1935.

Afr 4559.34.5   Rebeaud, Henri. Chez le roi des rois d'Ethiopie. Neuchâtel, 1934.

Afr 10685.67.110   The rebel lion. (Okoye, Mokwugo.) Onitsha, 1962.

Afr 8687.308.5   Le rebelle obéissant. 2. ed. (Huenermann, G.) Mulhouse, 1966.

Afr 2030.100   Les rébelles algériens. (Bromberger, Serge.) Paris, 1958.

Afr 8360.10   Die rebellie, 1914-15. (Scholtz, G.D.) Johannesburg, 1942.

Afr 10531.61.100   Rebellion; a play in three acts. (Kinteh, Ramatoulie.) N.Y., 1968.

Afr 7580.23   La rébellion au Congo. Leopoldville, Congo, 1964.

Afr 8177.5   The rebellion of 1815. (Cape of Good Hope. Archives.) Cape Town, 1902.

Afr 8360.10   The rebellion of 1914-15, a bibliography. (Quinn, Gerald D.) Cape Town, 1957.

Afr 7582.5   Rébellions au Congo. (Verhaegen, Benoit.) Leopoldville, 1966.

Afr 1493.70   Rebellon Dominguez, G. Seis meses en Yebala. Madrid, 1953.

Afr 7175.50   Rebelo, Horacio de la Viara. Angola na Africa deste tempo. Lisboa, 1961.

Afr 7850.30   Rebels, mercenaries, and dividends. (Hempstone, Smith.) N.Y., 1967.

Afr 1493.50.15   Rebels in the RF; Abd el Krim and the Rif rebellion. (Woolman, David J.) Stanford, 1968.

Afr 1493.78A   Rebirth of a nation;...Moroccan nationalism, 1912-1944. (Halstead, John Preston.) Cambridge, 1967.

Afr 609.61.35   The rebirth of African civilization. (Williams, C.) Washington, 1961.

Afr 5394.2   Les récades des rois du Dahomey. (Adandé, A.) Dakar, 1962.

Afr Doc 5402.5   Recapitulation des periodiques officiels parus en Tunisie de 1881 à 1955. (Pilipenko, Helene.) Tunis, 1955.

Afr Doc 9407.360   Recenseamento agrícola da Guiné, 1960-1961. (Portugal. Missão de Inquerito Agrícola de Cabo Verte, Guiné S. Tomé Principe.) Lisboa, 1963.

Afr Doc 9207.345   Recenseamento da população mão indigena, em 12 de junho de 1945. (Mozambique. Repartição Tecnica de Estatistica.) Lourenço Marques, 1947.

Afr Doc 9207.355   Recenseamento geral da população civilanada em 1955. (Mozambique. Direcção dos Serviços de Economica e de Estatistica Gerel.) Lourenço Marques. 1,1950+

Afr Doc 9207.350   Recenseamento geral da população em 1950. (Mozambique. Repartição Tecnica de Estatistica.) Lourenço Marques, 1953-1955. 2v.

Afr Doc 9282.12F   Recenseamentos população...de Lourenço Marques. (Mozambique. Secretaria Geral.) n.p., 1913.

Afr Doc 6274.4.73   Recensement, démographique de Dakar, 1955: résultats définitifs. (French West Africa. Service des Etudes et Coordination Statistiques et Mécanographiques.) Paris, 1958-62. 2v.

Afr Doc 6471.1.73   Recensement d'Abidjan 1955. (Ivory Coast. Direction de la Statistique et des Etudes economiques et démographiques.) Paris, 1960.

Afr Doc 7372.361   Recensement de Brazzaville, 1961; résultats définitifs. (Congo (Brazzaville). Service de Statistique.) Paris, 1965.

Afr Doc 5507.356   Recensement de la population de la Cote française des Somalis, population non originaire, 1956. (France. Institut National de la Statistique et des Etudes Economiques.) Paris, 1961.

Afr Doc 6472.5   Recensement démographique de Bruehe, 1958. Résultats définitifs. (Ivory Coast. Direction de la Statistique et des Etudes Economiques et Démographiques.) Paris, 1961.

Afr Doc 7176.5   Recensement démographique de Fort Lamy. (Chad. Service de la Statistique Générale.) Paris. 1965

Afr Doc 5207.360   Recensement demographique juin 1960. Population legale du Maroc. (Morocco. Service Central des Statistiques.) Rabat, 1961-62. 2v.

Afr Doc 6585.1.73   Recensement démographique Ouagadougou, 1961-1962. (Upper Volta. Service de la Statistique.) Paris, 1964.

Afr Doc 6471.10   Recensement des centres urbains d'Abengoonon, Aghoville, Dunboko et Man, 1956, 1957. Résultats définitif. (Ivory Coast. Direction des Etudes et Démographiques.) Paris, 1960.

Afr Doc 7407.361   Recensement et enquête démographiques, 1960-1961; résutats provisionelles. (Gabon. Service de Statistiques.) Paris, 1963.

Afr Doc 7407.361.15   Recensement et enquête demographiques, 1960-1961: ensemble du Gabon. (Gabon. Service Nat+onal de la Statistique.) Paris, 1965.

Afr Doc 7407.361.10   Recensement et enquête demographiques, 1960-1961: Résultats pour Libreville. (Gabon. Service National de la Statistique.) Paris, 1962.

Afr Doc 6707.358   Recensement général de la population du Togo, 1958-1960. (Togo. Service de la Statistique Général.) Lomé, 1962?

Afr Doc 5607.362   Recensements urbains. (Malagasy Republic. Institut National de la Statistique et de la Recherche Economique.) Tananarive, 1965- 2v.

Afr 3295.4   Recent constitutional developments in Egypt. (Hayter, William Goodenough.) Cambridge, Eng., 1924.

Afr 6883.4   Reche, O. Zur Ethnographie der abflusslosen Gebietes Deutsch-Ostafrikas. Hamburg, 1914.

Afr 3.50   Recherche, enseignement, documentation africanistes francophones. (Centre d'Analyse et de Recherche Documentaires pour l'Afrique Noire.) Paris. 1,1969+

Afr 2225.11   Recherche d une solution de la question indigène en Algérie. (Azan, Paul J.L.) Paris, 1903.

Afr 635.70   Recherche des éléments d'une sociologie des peuples africains. (Beart, Charles.) Paris, 1960.

Afr 2295.3   Recherches...sur la portion de l'Algérie au sud de Guelnia. (Duvivieu.) Paris, 1841.

Afr 5300.5   Recherches africaines. 1,1960+ 4v.

Afr 1280.25F   Recherches anthropologiques dans la Berbérie orientale. (Bertholon, Lucien.) Lyon, 1913. 2v.

Afr 4000.10F   Recherches anthropologiques dans l'Afrique orientale. (Chantre, A.) Lyon, 1904.

Afr 16.5   Recherches et documents. Série Afrique Noire. (Paris. Université. Centre de Hautes Etudes Administratives sur l'Afrique et l'Asie Modernes.) Paris. 2v.

Afr 6700.75   Recherches et études camerounaises. Yaounde. 2v.

Afr 658.21   Recherches géographiques sur l'intérieur de l'Afrique. (Walckenaer, C.A.) Paris, 1821.

Afr 1367.87   Recherches historiques sur les Maures. (Chenier, L.S. de.) Paris, 1787. 3v.

Afr 3977.73   Recherches philosophiques sur les égyptiens. (Pauw, C.V.) Berlin, 1773. 2v.

Afr 1955.61   Recherches sur la colonisation de l'Algérie au XIXe siècle. (Algiers. Université. Faculté de Droit.) Alger, 1960.

Afr 1835.1.2   Recherches sur la géographie de l'Algérie. (Carette, E.) Paris, 1844.

Afr 7582.4   Recherches sur le développement rural en Afrique central. (Liège. Université. Fondation pour les Recherches Scientifiques en Afrique Central.) Liège, 1965.

Afr 5225.8   Recherches sur l'empire du Mali au Moyen Age. (Niane, D.T.) Conakry, 1962.

Afr 678.78   Recherches sur les navigations européennes. (Gravier, G.) Paris, 1878.

Afr 5010.10   Recherches sur l'exercice du pouvoir politique en Afrique noire. (Sy, Seydou Madani.) Paris, 1965.

Afr 2762.22   Recherches sur l'histoire des Touareg sahariens et soudanais. (Hama, Boubou.) Paris, 1967.

Afr 1835.1.3   Recherches sur l'origine et les migrations. (Carette, E.) Paris, 1853.

Afr 5270.18   Recherches voltaïques; collection de travaux des sciences humaines sur la Haute-Volta. Paris. 3,1966+

Afr 6887.11   Das Recht der Dschagga. (Gutmann, B.) München, 1926.

Afr 1955.9   Récits algériens. (Perret, E.) Paris, n.d. 2v.

Afr 1965.12   Récits d'Afrique Sidi-Brahim. (Azan, Paul.) Paris, 1905.

Afr 1408.2.10   Récits d'aventures au temps de Louis XIV. (Busnot, F.D.) Paris, 1928.

Afr 1965.2   Récits de campagne 1833-41. (Orleans, F.P.L.C.H., Duc.) Paris, 1890.

Afr 1975.1   Récits de Kabylie, campagne de 1857. (Carrey, E.) Paris, 1858.

Afr 2748.82.3   Récits faits par 3 survivants de la mission Flatters. (Patorni, F.) Constantine, 1884.

Afr 8659.01   Reclus, E. L'Afrique australe. Paris, 1901.

Afr 4115.7   Reclus, E. Nouvelle géographie. Cairo. Paris, 1885.

Afr 608.94   Reclus, E. Nouvelle géographie universelle Morocco. Maps of Alger. Paris, 1830-94.

Afr 510.8   Reclus, O. Lachons l'Asie, prenons l'Afrique. Paris, 1904.

Afr 1200.58   Reclus, Onesime. L'Atlantide, pays de l'Atlas. Paris, 1918.

Afr 3275.32   Recollections and reflections. (Coles, Charles E.) London, 1918.

Afr 9073.252   Recollections of an octogenarian. (Byron, Lewis.) Kloof, 1964.

Afr 6210.66   Recollections of British administration in the Cameroons and Northern Nigeria, 1921-1957. (Sharwood Smith, Bryan.) Durham, N.C., 1969.

Afr 3978.27   Recollections of Egypt. (Minutoli.) Philadelphia, 1827.

Afr 5765.8   Recollections of mission life in Madagascar. (Cameron, James.) Antananarivo, 1874.

Afr 5842.24   Recollections of seven years' residence at the Mauritius. (Bartram, Alfred, Lady.) London, 1830.

Afr 9525.393.2   The recollections of William Finaughty, elephant hunter. 2nd ed. (Finaughty, William.) Cape Town, 1957.

Afr 635.75F   Recommendations and reports. (C.S.A. Meeting of Specialists on the Basic Psychology of African and Madagascan Populations, Tannarvio, Madagascar, 1959.) London, 1959.

Afr Doc 9282.10F   Reconhecimento agricola-económico do distrito de Lourenço Marques. (Mozambique. Repartičo de Agricultura.) 1916-1917

Afr 1325.1F   Reconnaissance au Maroc. (Foucauld, Charles de.) Paris, 1888. 2v.

Afr 4375.15   Reconnoitring in Abyssinia. (Wilkins, H. St.C.) London, 1870.

Afr 36.6   Reconstructing African culture and history. Boston, 1967.

Afr 8089.13.3A   The reconstruction of the new colonies under Lord Milner. (Worsfold, W.B.) London, 1913. 2v.

Afr 8678.205   The record. (Moodie, Donald.) Amsterdam, 1960.

Afr 8292.55   The record of a regiment of the line. (Jacson, M.) London, 1908.

Afr 8292.16   Record of mounted infantry of the City Imperial Volunteers. (Scott, G.H.G.) London, 1902.

Afr 4375.8F   Record of the expedition to Abyssinia. v.1-2, and atlas. (Holland, T.J.) London, 1870. 3v.

Afr 4225.5F   Record of the expedition to Abyssinia. v.1-2 and maps. (Holland, T.J.) London, 1870. 3v.

Afr Doc 3212.30F   Record of the proceedings. (Kenya. Legislative Council.) 1923

Afr 3310.30   The record on Suez. (Manchester Guardian, Manchester, Eng.) Manchester, 1956.

Afr Doc 3708.5   Recorded megration. (Zambia. Central Statistical Office.) Lusaka. 1,1964+

Afr 8847.34.75   Records of a pioneer family. Capetown, 1966.

Afr 678.33.5   Records of a voyage to the western coast of Africa in his Majesty's ship Dryad. (Leonard, Peter.) Edinburgh, 1833.

Afr 8707.5   Records of Cape colony. v.1-35 and index. (Theal, G.M.) London, 1897-1905. 36v.

Afr 6275.4   Records of Captain Clapperton's last expedition to Africa. (Lander, R.L.) London, 1830. 2v.

Afr 3300.60   Records of conversation, notes and papers. (Egypt. Ministry of Foreign Affairs.) Cairo, 1951.

Afr 8030.10   Records of South-eastern Africa. v.1- (Theal, G.M.) London, 1898- 9v.

Afr 657.88   Records of the African Association, 1788-1831. (Association for Promoting the Discovery of the Interior Parts of Africa.) London, 1964.

Afr 3710.15   Records of the Nile voyageurs. (Stacey, Charles.) Toronto, 1959.

Afr 5054.29.5   Le recrutement de l'armée noire. (Lassalle-Séré, R.) Paris, 1929.

Afr 5054.29   Le recrutement de l'armée noire. Thèse. (Lassalle-Séré, R.) Paris, 1929.

Afr 150.32   Rectificação historica a memoria do Infante Dom Henrique. (Principe, S.) Lobito, 1961.

Afr 5857.5   Recueil de documents et travaux inédits pour servir à l'histoire de la Réunion. (Réunion. Archives Départementales.) Nerac. 1,1954+ 3v.

Afr 1973.1.5   Recueil de documents sur l'expédition et la prise de Constantine. Text and atlas. (Devoisins, V.) Paris, 1838. 2v.

Afr 3035.10   Recueil de firmans impériaux ottomans. (Egypt. Laws, statutes, etc.) Le Caire, 1934.

Afr 1335.20   Recueil de jurisprudence chérifienne. v.1-4. (Milliot, Louis.) Paris, 1920-24. 4v.

Afr 1088.7   Un recueil de lettres officielles almohades. (Levi-Provencal, E.) Paris, 1942.

Afr 1819.4   Recueil des notices et mémoires. (Societe Archéologique de Constantine.) Constantine. 1,1953+ 7v.

Afr 1432.26   Recuerdos centenarios de una guerra romantica. (Garcia Figueras, T.) Madrid, 1961.

Afr 1753.7   Recuerdos de Africa, historia de la plaza de Ceuta. (Marquez De Prado, J.A.) Madrid, 1859.

Afr 1493.76   Recuerdos de la campaña. (Garcia Figueras, Tomás.) Jeréz, 1925.

Afr 1490.18   Recuerdos de la guerra del Kert de 1911-12. (Serra Orts, A.) Barcelona, 1914.

Afr 1609.23.20   Recuerdos de Marruecos. (Cansino-Roldan, Luis.) Malaga, 1923.

Afr 1608.68   Recuerdos marroquies. (Murga, Jose Maria de.) Madrid, 1906.

Afr 1608.68.5   Recuerdos marroquies del moro vizcaino. (Murga, José Maria de.) Barcelona, 1913.

Afr 8846.32   Red blanket valley. (Broster, Joan A.) Johannesburg, 1967.

Afr 4392.7 Red Cross, Italy (Croce Rossa). Asunto delle relazione sul servizio sanitario...in occasione delle campagna d'Africa, 1895-1896. Roma, 1899.

Afr 6535.61 Red dust. (Harwick, Christopher.) London, 1961.

Afr 6979.59 Red dust of Africa. (Carnegie, Sacha.) London, 1959.

Afr 6455.80 Red dust of Africa. (Simpson, Alyse.) London, 1952.

Afr 2025.30 The red hand. (Joesten, Joachim.) London, 1962.

Afr 6280.24 The red men of Nigeria. (Wilson-Haffenden, J.R.) London, 1930.

Afr 7568.15.15 Red rubber. (Morel, Edmund D.) N.Y., 1969.

Afr 4055.5 The Red Sea mountains of Egypt. (Tregenza, L.A.) London, 1955.

Afr 212.3 Red star over Africa. (Harrigan, Anthony.) Cape Town, 1964.

Afr 8050.28 The red trap: Communism and violence in South Africa. (Vermaak, Christopher Johann.) Johannesburg, 1966.

Afr 698.38 De redding des bemanning van het...nijverheid. (Brun, C.) Rotterdam, 1838.

Afr 11728.41.100 Redeemed. 1st ed. (Raik, Léa.) Johannesburg, 1964.

Afr 6850.11 Redeker, D. Die Geschichte der Tagespresse Deutsch-Ostafrikas, 1899-1916. Inaug. Diss. Berlin, 1937.

Afr 550.5 The redemption of Africa. (Noble, F.P.) Chicago, 1899.
 2v.

Afr 3978.99 The redemption of Egypt. (Worsfold, W.B.) London, 1899.

Afr 9345.10.10 Redfern, John. Ruth and Seretse. London, 1955.

Afr 8845.10 Redgrave, J.J. Port Elizabeth in bygone days. Wynberg, 1947.

Afr 6879.15 Rediscovered country. (White, Stewart E.) Garden City, 1915.

Afr 6192.40 Redmayne, P. Gold Coast to Ghana. London, 1957.

Afr 5316.14 The reds and the blacks, a personal adventure. 1st ed. (Attwood, William.) N.Y., 1967.

Afr 6455.145 Reece, Alys. To my wife, 50 camels. Leicester, 1963.

Afr 8659.50.10 Reed, D. Somewhere south of Suez. London, 1950.

Afr 8659.50.10.2 Reed, D. Somewhere south of Suez. N.Y., 1951.

Afr 7835.4 Reed, David E. One hundred and eleven days in Stanleyville. 1st ed. N.Y., 1965.

Afr 9489.66.5 Reed, Douglas. The battle for Rhodesia. Cape Town, 1966.

Afr 9489.66.6 Reed, Douglas. Insanity fair '67. London, 1967.

Afr 9839.67 Reed, Frank E. Malawi, land of promise. Blantyre, 1967.

Afr 10016.10 Reed, John. A book of African verse. London, 1965.

Afr 10673.48.140 A reed in the tide. (Clark, John Pepper.) London, 1965.

Afr 7459.23 Reeve, H.F. The Black Republic, Liberia. London, 1923.

Afr 6118.6 Reeve, H.F. The Gambia, its history. London, 1912.

Afr 8685.85 Reeves, Ambrose. The pass laws and slavery. London, 1961.

Afr 8678.185 Reeves, Ambrose. Shooting at Sharpville. London, 1960.

Afr 8678.186 Reeves, Ambrose. South Africa, yesterday and tomorrow. London, 1962.

Afr 7548.94 Reeves, J.S. International beginnings of the Congo Free State. Baltimore, 1894.

Afr 8678.92 Referate geleiver op die jaarvergadering. (Suid-Afrikaanse Buro vir Rasse-Angeleenthede.) Stellenbosch. 1,1950+ 6v.

Afr 10665.2 Reflections, Nigerian prose and verse. (Ademola, F.) Lagos, 1962.

Afr 6277.102 Reflections on Nigeria's economic growth. (Lewis, William Arthur.) Paris, 1967.

Afr 6291.52 Reflections on the Nigerian civil war; a call for realism. (Uwechue, Raph.) London, 1969.

Afr 6333.56.5 Reflections on the report of the Royal Commission on East Africa. (Africa Bureau, London.) London, 1956.

Afr 2260.4 Réflexions sur la colonization. (Preaux.) Paris, 1832.

Afr 2025.5 Réflexions sur la politique de l'empereur. (Duval, Jules.) Paris, 1866.

Afr 2295.8 Réflexions sur l'Algérie. (Bonnafont, Jean Pierre.) Paris, 1846.

Afr 626.17 Reflexions sur l'économie africaine. (Jussiaume, E.) Paris, 1932.

Afr 626.35 Reflexions sur l'économie de l'Afrique noire. (Dia, Mamadou.) Paris, 1954.

Afr 626.35.5 Reflexions sur l'économie de l'Afrique noire. (Dia, Mamadou.) Paris, 1957.

Afr 1990.13 Une réforme administrative en Afrique. (Broglie, A. de.) Paris, 1860.

Afr 45.63.5 La reforme de la justice en Afrique noire. (Jeol, M.) Paris, 1963.

Afr 1338.20 Les réformes des pouvoirs publics au Maroc. (Laubadere, A. de.) Paris, 1949.

Afr 1840.12 Les réformes en Algérie et le statut des indigenes. (Piquet, Victor.) Paris, 1919.

Afr 3205.19 Les réformes en Egypte. Thèse. (Guemard, G.) Le Caire, 1936.

Afr 2438.21 Les réformes en Tunisie. (Jung, Eugene.) Paris, 1926.

Afr 2026.10 Le réformisme musulman en Algérie de 1925 à 1940. (Mirad, Ali.) Paris, 1967.

Afr 635.95 Refugee problems in Africa. Uppsala, 1967.

Afr 2030.375 Le refus. (Maschino, Maurice.) Paris, 1960.

Afr 8278.96.3 Regan, W.F. Boer and Uitlander. London, 1896.

Afr 12832.5.120 Le regard du roi. (Laye, Camara.) Paris, 1954.

Afr 510.20 Regards sur la France d'Afrique. (Mangin, J.E.) Paris, 1924.

Afr 3979.56F Regards sur l'Egypte. (Viollet, Roger.) Paris, 1956.

Afr 3979.29 Regards sur l'Egypte et la Palestine. (Hanotaux, G.) Paris, 1929.

Afr 7809.43.10 Regards sur notre Congo. (Hove, Julien van.) Bruxelles, 1943.

NEDL Afr 3275.43 Regatz, L.J. The question of Egypt in Anglo-French relations, 1875-1904. Edinburgh, 1922.

Afr 2608.61 La régence de Tunis au dix-neuvième siècle. (Flaux, A. de.) Paris, 1865.

Afr 1555.7 Regendanz, W. Searchlight on German Africa. London, 1939.

Afr 6780.35 Regendanz, W.C. Die Giraffe und der König von England. n.p., n.d.

Afr 2608.95.2 Die Regentschaft Tunis. (Fitzner, R.) Berlin, 1895.

Afr 2928.78 La reggenza di Tripoli. (Medina, G.) Cagliari, 1878.

Afr 2288.10 Le régime de la répression dans les territoires du sud de l'Algérie. (Thinières, A.F.C.) Alger, 1928.

Afr 1340.15 Le régime des capitulations et la condition des étrangers au Maroc. Thèse. (Crouzet-Rayssac, A. de.) Paris, 1921.

Afr 1624.914 Le regime financier du Maroc. (Colomb, Jean.) Paris, 1914.

Afr 5403.10 Le régime foncier en Afrique équatoriale française. (Demetz, Henri.) Annecy, 1939.

Afr 12431.2 Le régime juridique de la presse au Maroc. (Mollard, P.J.) Rabat, 1963.

Afr 3040.52 Un régime qui meurt, les capitulations en Egypte. Thèse. (Gemayel, P.) Paris, 1938.

Afr 7320.10 Regimento. (Portugal. Ministerio dos Negocios da Marinha e Ultramar.) Lisboa, 1867.

Afr 1724.3F Regimento da praca de mazagam. (Portugal. Sovereigns, 1688-1706 (Peter Ii).) Lisboa, 1692.

Afr 2753.2 Les régiments de dromadaires. (Wolff, H.) Paris, 1884.

Afr 7377.6 Regina coeli. Correspondence of J.H.B. Latrobe. (Hammond, J.H.) Baltimore, 1858.

Afr 5346.6 Région de Korhogo. T.1-8. (Société d'Etudes pour le Développement Economique et Social.) Paris, 1965.
 3v.

Afr 2609.13 La région du Haut Tell en Tunisie. (Monchicourt, C.) Paris, 1913.

Afr 5488.10 La region du Tchad et du Ouadaï. V.1-2. (Carbou, Henri.) Paris, 1912.
 2v.

Afr 6160.30 Regional assemblies. (Ghana. Regional Constitutional Commission.) Accra, 1958.

Afr 6310.42 Regional cooperation in British East Africa. (British Information Services.) N.Y., 1959.

Afr 4688.15.20 La regione del Lago Tana. (Dainelli, G.) Milano, 1939.

Afr 4226.5 Register of current research on Ethiopia and the horn of Africa. Addis Ababa.

Afr 3986.959.5 Register of Egyptian economy. v.1. n.p., 195-.

Afr 1738.20F Registos paroquiais da se de Tanger. (Tangier, Africa.) Lisboa, 1922.

Afr Doc 3709.525F Registration of motor vehicles in Zambia. (Zambia. Central Statistical Office.) Lusaka. 1965+

Afr Doc 3809.525F Registrations of motor vehicles in Rhodesia. (Rhodesia (British Colony). Central Statistical Office.) Salisbury. 1964+

Afr Doc 3809.524F Registrations of motor vehicles in Southern Rhodesia. (Rhodesia (Southern). Central Statistical Office.) Salisbury. 1964+

Afr 1947.13 Registre des prises maritimes. Alger, 1872.

Afr 3040.14 Règlements intérieurs des Chambres en Egypte. Thèse. (Mahmoud, Ibrahim Choukri.) Paris, 1925.

Afr 3205.15 Le règne de Mohamed Aly d'après les archives russes en Egypte. v.1-3. (Cattaui, René.) Caire, 1931-1936.
 4v.

Afr 2248.10 Regnier, Yves. Les Chaamba sous le régime français, leure transformation. Thèse. Paris, 1938.

Afr 3205.17 Il regno di Mohammed Ali nei documenti diplomatici italiani inediti. v.1,8,9,10. (Sammarco, Angelo.) Caire, 1930-32.
 4v.

Afr 5605.3 Regnon, Henry de. Madagascar et le roi Radama II. Paris, 1863.

Afr 1878.15 Les regroupements de la décolonisation en Algérie. Thèse. (Cornaton, Michel.) Paris, 1967.

Afr 1658.37 Reguert, P.T. L'agression riffaine en 1925. Paris, 1933.

Afr 8678.47.5 Regverdige rasse-apartheid. (Cronje, G.) Stellenbosch, 1947.

Afr 1409.9 El rei. (Spain. Sovereigns. Carlos III.) Madrid, 1774.

Afr 5635.20 Reibell, Emile. Le calvaire de Madagascar. Paris, 1935.

Afr 510.12 Reibell, Le Commandant. Le commandant Lamy. Paris, 1903.

Afr 6878.92 Reichard, Paul. Deutsch-Ostafrika. Leipzig, 1892.

Afr 3725.10 Reichard, Paul. Dr. Emin Pascha. Leipzig, 1891.

Afr 6738.41 Reicheon, Anton. Die deutsche Kolonie Kamerun. Berlin, 1884.

Afr 4559.18 Rein, G.K. Abessinien, eine Landeskunde. Berlin, 1918-20.
 3v.

Afr 1608.94.8 Reina, T.B. Geografia de Marruecos. Barcelona, 1894.

Afr 6168.20 Reindorf, Carl Christian. The history of the Gold Coast and Asante. 2d. ed. Basel, 1951.

Afr 6277.118 Reinecke, Ulrich. Die industrielle Entwicklung Nigerias. Hamburg, 1963.

Afr 3843.8 Reining, Conrad C. The Zande scheme; an anthropological case study of economic development in Africa. Evanston, 1966.

Afr 14805.1 Reis, Fernando. Soiá. Braga, 1965.

Afr 8659.64 Reis door Zuid-Afrika. (Boom, M.J.) Meppel, 1964.

Afr 1965.8 Reis naar Algiers en verblyf by het fransche leger in 1845. (Gheel Gildemeester.) Gouda, 1847.

Afr 150.2.30F Reis-Santos, Luiz. Iconografia henriquina. Coimbra, 1960.

Afr 4500.22 Reischies, S. Abessinien als Kampfobjekt der grossen Mächte von 1880-1916. Bleicherode am Harz, 1937.

Afr 678.49.5 Reise an die Küste und in das Innere von West-Africa. (Hecquard, Hyacinthe.) Leipzig, 1854.

Afr 4070.17 Reise auf dem Weissen Nil. (Klun, V.F.) Laibach, 1851.
 3 pam.

Afr 607.48 Reise-Beschreibung nach Africa. (Lajardière.) Frankfurt, 1748.

Afr 4070.10PF Reise des Freiherrn Adalbert von Barnim durch Nord-Ost-Afrika 1859-60. (Hartmann, Robert.) Berlin, 1863.
 2v.

Afr 5180.10 Reise durch das westliche Afrika...1785-87. (Golberry, S.M.X.) Leipzig, 1803.
 2v.

Afr 1608.64 Reise durch Marokko. (Rohlfs, G.) Norden, 1884.

Afr 4558.38 Reise in Abyssinien. (Rueppell, Edward.) Frankfurt, 1838.
 2v.

Afr 4070.3 Reise in das Gebiet des Weissen Nil. (Heuglin, M.T.) Leipzig, 1869.

Afr 8657.90.6 Reise in das Innere von Afrika. v.1, 3-5. (Le Vaillant, F.) Frankfurt, 1799.
 4v.

Afr 2208.62 Reise in das Innere von Algerien. (Hirsch, M.) Berlin, 1862.

Afr 2608.70 Reise in den Regentschaften Tunis und Tripolis. (Maltzan, Heinrich.) Leipzig, 1870.
 3v.

Afr 4095.9.5 Reise in der egyptischen Aequatorial-Provinz. (Marno, Ernst.) Wien, 1878.

Afr 4095.9 Reise in der egyptischen Aequatorial-Provinz. (Marno, Ernst.) Wien, 1879.

Afr 4060.3 Reise in Nordost Afrika. (Heuglin, Th. von.) Braunschweig, 1877.
 2v.

Afr 4558.68.7 Reise nach Abessinien. (Heuglin, T. von.) Jena, 1868.

Afr 724.10.2 Die Reise nach Afrika. (Ludwig, Emil.) Berlin, 1913.

Afr 2208.34 Reise nach Algier in den Jahren 1831-32. (Schimper, W.) Stuttgart, 1834.

Afr 4095.3.4 Eine Reise nach Centralafrika. (Taylor, G.B.) Leipzig, 1855.

Afr 6192.9.2 Reise nach Guinea. (Isert, P.E.) Kopenhagen, 1788.

Afr 6879.39 Die Reise nach Ostafrika. (Braun, Hans.) Berlin, 1939.

Afr Doc 3709.5 Report of the Auditor-General on the public accounts. (Zambia. Audit Office.) Lusaka. 1964+

Afr Doc 4219.5 Report of the Basutoland Constitutional Commission. (Basutoland. Constitutional Commission.) Maseru, 1963.

Afr 7350.8 Report of the board of managers. (New Hampshire Colonization Society.) Concord, N.H.

Afr 6176.40.10 Report of the comission, appointed under the Commission of Enquiry Act, 1964. (Ghana. Commission Enquire into the Kwame Nkrumah Properties.) Accra, 1967.

Afr 8035.10 Report of the commission. (South African Native Affairs Commission.) Cape Town, 1904-05. 5v.

Afr 6144.8F Report of the commission and the government statement thereon. (Sierra Leone. Commission to Enquire into and Report on the Matters Contained in the Director of Audit's Report on the Accounts of Sierra Leone for the Year 1960-1961.) Freetown, 1963.

Afr 6210.39 Report of the Commission on public services of the governments of Nigeria, 1954-1955. (Nigeria. Commission on the Public Services of the Governments in the Federation of Nigeria.) Lagos, 1955.

Afr 6160.40F Report of the commission on the structure and renumeration of the public services in Ghana. (Ghana. Public Services Structure and Salaries Commission.) Accra, 1967.

Afr Doc 3550.5 Report of the Commissioner of Tades. (Rhodesia and Nyasaland. Department of Taxes.) 1954+

Afr 590.30 Report of the committee of the Institution. (African Institution.) London, 1811.

Afr 6463.7 Report of the conference held at Limuru Conference Centre, Kenya. (Conference on the Role of the Church in Independent Kenya Limuru.) Nairobi, 196- .

Afr 6210.45F Report of the Constituency Delimitation Commission, 1964. (Nigeria. Delimitation Commission.) Lagos, 1964.

Afr Doc 3819.10 Report of the Constitutional Commission, 1968. (Rhodesia (British Colony). Constitutional Commission.) Salisbury, 1968.

Afr 6484.5 Report of the constitutional committee, 1957. (Uganda. Constitutional Committee.) Entebbe, 1959.

Afr Doc 4832.5F Report of the Controller and Auditor-General. (South Africa. Control and Audit Office.) Pretoria. 1964+

Afr Doc 3533.10 Report of the Controller of Customs and Excise. (Rhodesia and Nyasaland. Department of Customs and Excise.) Salisbury. 1954+

Afr Doc 3733.20 Report of the controller of customs and excise. (Zambia. Department of Customs and Excise.) Lusaka. 1965+

Afr Doc 3853.5 Report of the Director. (Rhodesia, Southern. Ministry of Water Development.) Salisbury. 1954+

Afr Doc 3853.10 Report of the Director. (Rhodesia (British Colony). Ministry of Water Development.) Salisbury. 1964+

Afr Doc 3533.6 Report of the Director. (Rhodesia and Nyasaland. Department of Civil Aviation.) Salisbury. 1954+

Afr Doc 3543.5 Report of the director. (Rhodesia and Nyasaland. Department of Meteorological Services.) 1954-1955

Afr Doc 1731.5 Report of the Director of Audit on the accounts of Sierra Leone. (Sierra Leone. Audit Department.) Freetown. 1956+

Afr Doc 2409.305 Report of the Director of Audit on the accounts of the government. (Nigeria, Northern. Audit Department.) 1954+

Afr Doc 3807.326.5 Report of the director of Census regarding the Census taken on the 4th May 1926. (Rhodesia, Southern. Census Office.) Salisbury, 1927.

Afr Doc 4535.5F Report of the Director of Education. (Natal. Education Department.) 1899-1929 4v.

Afr Doc 2309.310 Report of the Director of Federal Audit on the accounts of the government. (Nigeria. Federal Audit Depaartment.) Lagos. 1960

Afr 6291.15 Report of the Economic Mission, 1961. (Nigeria, Eastern. Economic Mission.) Enugu, 1962.

Afr 1609.52.5 Report of the expedition to French Morocco. (Durham, Eng. University. Exploration society expedition to French Morocco.) Durham, 1956.

Afr Doc 4209.5F Report of the finances and accounts for the financial year. (Basutoland. Treasury.) Maseru. 1962+

Afr 6457.28 Report of the Fiscal Commission. (Great Britain. Fiscal Commission for Kenya.) Nairobi, 1963.

Afr 6295.185 Report of the inquiry into the administration of the affairs of the Enugu Municipal Council. v.1-2. (Nigeria, Eastern. Commission of Inquiry into the Administration of the Affairs of the Enugu Municipal Council.) Enugu, 1960.

Afr 7073.2 Report of the institution...Dec. 11, 1792. (Bulam Association.) London, 1792.

Afr 6210.48 Report of the Joint Select Committee of the Northern Regional Council, 20th and 21st July, and Northern legislature, 7th, 8th and 9th, August, 1951. (Nigeria. Northern Legislature.) Kaduna, 1952.

Afr Doc 2521.10F Report of the Joint Standing Committee on Finance of the Western House of Chiefs and of the Western House of Assembly. (Nigeria, Western. House of Chiefs.) Ibadan. 1957+

Afr 7560.18.10 A report of the Kingdom of Congo and of the surrounding countries. (Lopes, Duarte.) N.Y., 1969.

Afr 9165.42.85F Report of the manager. (Johannesburg. Non-European Affairs Department.) Johannesburg. 1957+

Afr 7350.5.3 Report of the managers. Appendix. (Pennsylvania Colonization Society.) Philadelphia, 1830.

Afr 7368.50 Report of the Naval Committee. (United States. Congress. House. Committee on Naval Affairs.) Washington, 1850.

Afr 9757.20 Report of the Nyasaland Constitutional Conference held in London in Nov. 1962. (Nyasaland Constitutional Conference.) London, 1962.

Afr Doc 3242.10 Report of the Permanent Secretary for Local Government. (Kenya. Ministry of Local Government.) 1948-1950

Afr Doc 2831.5 Report of the Principal Auditor on the accounts of the Colony of Mauritius and the Mauritius government railways. (Mauritius. Colonial Audit Department.) Port Louis. 1946-1949

Afr 8340.20F Report of the Royal Commission on War Stores in South Africa. (Great Britain. Commission. War Stores in South Africa.) London, 1906.

Afr 8676.40F Report of the Rural Industries Commission. (South Africa. Rural Industries Commission.) Pretoria, 1940.

Afr Doc 3842.10 Report of the Secretary. (Rhodesia, Southern. Ministry of Lands and Natural Resources.) Salisbury. 1963+

Afr Doc 3533.3 Report of the secretary. (Rhodesia and Nyasaland. Ministry of Commerce and Industry.) 1961-1963

Afr Doc 3535.10F Report of the secretary. (Rhodesia and Nyasaland. Ministry of External Affairs.) Salisbury. 1955-1957

Afr Doc 3843.5 Report of the Secretary for Mines and Lands. (Rhodesia (British Colony). Ministry of Mines and Lands.) Salisbury. 1964+

Afr Doc 3546.15 Report of the Secretary for Power. (Rhodesia and Nyasaland. Ministry of Power.) Salisbury. 1955+

Afr Doc 3531.5 Report of the Secretary to the Federal Ministry of Agriculture. (Rhodesia and Nyasaland. Ministry of Agriculture.) Salisbury. 1954+

Afr Doc 3542.5 Report of the secretary to the Ministry of Law. (Rhodesia and Nyasaland. Ministry of Law.) Salisbury. 1,1955+

Afr 8283.25F Report of the Select Committee of the Cape of Good Hope. (Cape of Good Hope. Parliament. House of Commons.) London, 1897.

Afr 8045.7 Report of the Select Committee on the subject of the constitution amendment bill. (South Africa. Parliament. House of Assembly.) Cape Town, 1965.

Afr 6760.5 Report of the Special Commissioner appointed to examine matters arising out of the report of the Committee on Constitutional Development. (MacKenzie, William James Millar.) Dar es Salaam, 1953.

Afr 3300.48F Report of the Special Mission to Egypt. (Great Britain. Special Mission to Egypt.) London, 1921.

Afr 6293.2 Report of the Tribunal ofInquiry into the affairs of the Lagos City Council for the period Oct. 15, 1962 to Apr. 18, 1966. (Lagos. City Council. Tribunal of Inquiry.) Lagos, 1966.

Afr 6293.2.10 Report of the tribunal of inquiry into the affairs of the Lagos Executive Development Board for the period 1st October, 1960 to 31st December, 1965. (Nigeria. Lagos Executive Development Board Tribunal of Inquiry.) Lagos, 1968.

Afr 6484.15 Report of the Uganda Independence Conference, 1962. (Uganda Independence Conference.) London, 1962.

Afr 6560.2 Report of the Zanzibar Constitutional Conference, 1962. (Zanzibar Constitutional Conference, 1962.) London, 1962.

Afr 9609.15F Report on a economic survey of Nyasaland. (Rhodesia and Nyasaland.) Salisbury, 1959.

Afr Doc 307.10F Report on a survey. (Ethiopia. Central Statistical Office.) Addis Ababa, 1966. 3 pam.

Afr Doc 307.15F Report on a survey. (Ethiopia. Central Statistical Office.) Addis Ababa, 1966.

Afr 609.54 Report on Africa. (Meeker, Oden.) N.Y., 1954.

Afr Doc 3872.2 Report on Bulawayo African demographic survey, held in May 1959. (Rhodesia and Nyasaland.) Salisbury, 1960.

Afr 8860.15 Report on constitutional reform. (Basutoland. Council.) Maseru, 1958.

Afr Doc 4308.5F Report on deaths: South Africa and South West Africa. (South Africa. Bureau of Statistics.) Pretoria. 1958+

Afr Doc 2826.5 Report on district administration in Mauritius. (Mauritius.) Port Louis. 1949

Afr Doc 2308.300F Report on employment and ear-nings inquiry, Sept., 1959. (Nigeria. Federal Office of Statistics.) Lagos, 1959?

Afr 6193.48F Report on industrialisation and the Gold Coast. (Lewis, William Arthur.) Accra, 1963.

Afr 6210.50F Report on local government in the Northern provinces of Nigeria. (Maddocks, K.P.) Kaduna, 1951.

Afr 9335.10 Report on localisation and training. (Bechuanaland. Commissioner to Consider Localization of Civil Service.) Mafeking, 1966.

Afr 5817.5 Report on Mauritius. (Great Britain. Colonial Office.) 1946+ 5v.

Afr 9435.6F Report on native administration of British South Africa Company. (Martin, R.E.R.) London, 1897.

Afr Doc 3231.10 Report on native affairs. (Kenya.)

Afr 6208.10 Report on Nigeria. (Great Britain. Colonial Office.) 1952+

Afr 9632.10 Report on northern Rhodesia. (Great Britain. Colonial Office.) 4v.

Afr Doc 3708.7F Report on Northern Rhodesia. (Rhodesia and Nyasaland. Central Statistical Office.) Salisbury. 1961+

Afr 9.2 Report on progress of work. (International Institute of African Languages and Cultures.) London.

Afr 4388.5 Report on seizure by Abyssinians of geological expedition. (Mitchell, I.H.) Cairo, 1878.

Afr 5893.10 Report on Seychelles. (Great Britain. Colonial Office.) 1946+ 2v.

Afr 8659.52 Report on southern Africa. (Davidson, B.) London, 1952.

Afr 9499.75F Report on Southern Rhodesia family expenditure survey. (Central African Statistical Office.) Salisbury, 1952.

Afr 855.4 Report on St. Helena. (Great Britain. Colonial Office.) 3v.

Afr 4070.5 Report on Sudan. (Great Britain. Intelligence.) London, 1884.

Afr Doc 1830.15 Report on the account of the Ghana railway and Harbours Administration. (Ghana. Auditor-General.) Accra. 1956-1957

Afr Doc 3609.300 Report on the accounts. (Nyasaland. Auditor-General Department.) Zomba. 1956-1957

Afr Doc 3309.310 Report on the accounts. (Uganda. Controller and Auditor General.) Entebbe. 1947+

Afr Doc 3409.305F Report on the accounts and finances. (Tanganyika. Treasury.) Dar es Salaam. 1924-1954

Afr Doc 1809.300 Report on the accounts of Ghana. (Ghana. Auditor-General.) Accra. 1958+

Afr Doc 2731.10 Report on the accounts of the Colony of Seychelles. (Seychelles. Audit Department.) Victoria. 1960+

Afr Doc 3109.300 Report on the accounts of the Zanzibar Protectorate. (Zanzibar.) Zanzibar. 1953-1957

Afr Doc 2838.5 Report on the activities. (Mauritius. Central Housing Authority.) Rose Hill. 1,1960+

Afr Doc 2848.5 Report on the activities. (Mauritius. Reabsorption Office.) Port Louis. 1947-1949

Afr Doc 4332.10F Report on the activities. (South Africa. Department of Community Development.) 1961+

Afr Doc 4345.10F Report on the activities. (South Africa. Department of Planning.) Pretoria. 1,1964+

Afr Doc 4336.5 Report on the activities. (South Africa. Group Areas Development Board.) 1959+

Afr Doc 3509.520F Report on the agricultural production of Southern Rhodesia, Northern Rhodesia and Nyasaland. (Rhodesia and Nyasaland. Central Statistical Office.) Salisbury. 1960+

Afr Doc 4131.5	Report on the audit of the accounts. (Swaziland. Director of Audit.) 1964+
Afr Doc 3507.356.15	
	Report on the census of Africans in employment. (Rhodesia and Nyasaland. Central Statistical Office.) Salisbury, 1956.
Afr Doc 3707.351	Report on the census of population, 1951. (Rhodesia and Nyasaland. Central Statistical Office.) Lusaka, 1954.
Afr Doc 4007.364	Report on the census of the Bechuanaland Protectorate, 1964. (Bechuanaland (Protectorate).) Mafeking, South Africa? 1965?
Afr Doc 3407.352	Report on the census of the non-African population taken on the night of 13 february 1952. (East Africa High Commission. East African Statistical Department.) Dar es Salaam, 1954.
Afr Doc 3407.357	Report on the census of the non-African population taken 20 21 February 1957. (East African High Commission. East African Statistical Department.) Dar es Salaam, 1958.
Afr Doc 3307.348	Report on the census of the non-native population of Uganda Protectorate. (Uganda.) Nairobi, 1953.
Afr 1608.86.8	Report on the condition...empire of Morocco. (Mackenzie, Don.) London, 1886.
Afr 6981.120	Report on the conditions and prospects of trade in the protectorate of South West Africa. (Great Britain.) London, 1920.
Afr 9710.15F	Report on the economy of Barotseland. (Selwyn, P.) n.p., 1964?
Afr Doc 3509.15	Report on the finance accounts, appropriation accounts and accounts of miscellaneous funds. (Rhodesia and Nyasaland. Auditor-General.) Salisbury. 1953+
Afr Doc 4109.305F	Report on the finance and accounts. (Swaziland. Treasury.) 1958+
NEDL Afr 3745.5	Report on the finances, administration and condition of the Sudan. (Great Britain. Foreign Office.) London. 1908
Afr 3745.5	Report on the finances, administration and condition of the Sudan. (Great Britain. Foreign Office.) London. 1,1932
Afr Doc 1809.310	Report on the finances and accounts of the Gold Coast. (Gold Coast (Colony). Accountant General's Department.) 1949-1955
Afr Doc 4209.500	A report on the first general election in Basutoland, 1960. (Basutoland. Supervisor of Elections.) Maseru, 1963.
Afr 6157.5	Report on the Gold Coast. (Great Britain. Colonial Office.) 1948+
Afr Doc 3212.205	Report on the governmetn of Kenya accounts. (Kenya. Public Accounts Committee.) Nairobi. 1947+
Afr 5846.2	Report on the harbour of Port Louis. (Great Britain. Imperial Shipping Commission.) London, 1931.
Afr 9858.5	Report on the incident which took place outside Ryalls Hotel. (Nyasaland. Southworth Commission.) Zomba, 1960.
Afr 7560.3	A report on the kingdom of Congo. (Pigafetta, F.) London, 1881.
Afr 6926.14F	Report on the natives of South-west Africa. (Great Britain Parliament, 1918.) London, 1918.
Afr 6392.32	Report on the needs for economic research and investigation in East Africa. (Robinson, Edward A.G.) Entebbe, Uganda, 1955.
Afr 6210.34	Report on the Nigeria federal election. (Nigeria. Electoral Committee.) Lagos, 1960.
Afr Doc 3207.331	Report on the non-native census enumeration made in the colony and protectorate of Kenya. (Kenya. Census Office.) Nairobi, 1932.
Afr 4180.3.5	A report on the Oasis of Siwa. (Stanley, C.V.B.) Cairo, 1911.
Afr 8360.6F	Report on the outbreak of the rebellion. (South Africa.) Pretoria, 1915.
Afr 10215.5F	Report on the press in West Africa. (Committee for Inter-African Relations, Ibadan, Nigeria.) Ibadan, 1960.
Afr 45.61	A report on the proceedings of the conference. (African Conference on the Rule of Law, Lagos, Nigeria.) Genève, 1961.
Afr 9.5	Report on the progress. (Institute for the Study of Man in Africa.) 1,1960+
Afr Doc 3236.5	Report on the progress of development projects. (Kenya. Ministry of Finance and Development.)
Afr Doc 3346.15	Report on the protectorate's accounts. (Uganda. Public Accounts Committee.) Entebbe. 1951
Afr Doc 3509.305F	Report on the results of the national income and balance of payments questionaire sent to companies operating in Malaur. v.1. (Rhodesia (British Colony). Central Statistical Office.) Salisbury, 1964.
Afr 9.13	Report on the Second International Congress of Africanists, Dakar, Senegal, Dec. 11-20, 1967. (United States. Department of State. Office of External Research.) Washington, 1968.
Afr 4905.5	Report on the Somaliland Protectorate. (Great Britain. Colonial Office.) 1948+ 2v.
Afr 8279.01.5F	Report on the Transvaal Concession Commission. (Great Britain.) London, 1901.
Afr Doc 3891.363F	Report on the urban African budget survey in Umtali, 1963. (Rhodesia (British Colony). Central Statistical Office.) Salisbury, 1965.
Afr Doc 4308.10	Report on the vital statistics. (South Africa. Bureau of Statistics.) 1930-1934
Afr Doc 3233.5	Report on the working of the Civil Service Commission. (Kenya. Civil Service Commission.)
Afr Doc 3246.8	Report on the working of the Public Service Commission. (Kenya. Public Service Commission.) Nairobi. 1,1963+
Afr Doc 4107.366.5	
	Report on the 1966 Swaziland population census. (Swaziland. Census Office.) Mbabane, 1968.
Afr 6300.21.35	A report on three years' work, 1950-1953. (East African Institute of Social Research.) Kampala, 1955.
Afr Doc 3307.362	Report on Uganda census of agriculture. (Uganda. Ministry of Agriculture and Co-operatives.) Entebbe. 1966
Afr Doc 3807.359F	Report on Umtali and Gwelo African demographic surveys held in August and September, 1959. (Rhodesia and Nyasaland.) Salisbury, 1960.
Afr 9510.12.5F	Report on urban African budget survey in Bulawayo, 1958/59. (Rhodesia and Nyasaland.) Salisbury, 1960.
Afr 9515.5.5F	Report on urban African budget survey in Salisbury, 1957/58. (Rhodesia and Nyasaland.) Salisbury, 1958. 2v.
Afr Doc 3889.363F	Report on urban African budget survey in Salisbury, 1963/64. (Rhodesia (British Colony). Central Statistical Office.) Salisbury, 1965.

Afr Doc 3893.361F	Report on Wankie urban African budget survey held in April/May 1960. (Rhodesia and Nyasaland.) Salisbury, 1961.
Afr 6558.5	Report on Zanzibar. (Great Britain. Colonial Office.) 1946+ 4v.
Afr 6410.7	Report presented to Parliament. (Kenya Independence Conference, London, 1963.) London, 1963.
Afr 6410.10	Report presented to Parliament by the Secretary of State for the colonies. (Kenya. Constitutional Conference, London, 1962.) London, 1962.
Afr 3285.3.5	Report submitted by the Egyptian delegation to Foreign Secretary of Great Britain. (Egypt. Delegation, 1908.) Alexandria, 1909.
Afr 7350.4.25	Report to board of managers...by O.F.Cook. (New York State Colonization Society (Founded 1832).) N.Y.
Afr 7568.11	Report to Secretary of State. (Congo. Vice-Governor General.) Brussels, 1904.
Afr 9435.14.15	Report to the federal assembly. (Rhodesia and Nyasaland.) Salisbury, 1954. 2 pam.
Afr 6210.11	Report to the Muffidd Foundation on a visit to Nigeria. (Launders, J.) London, 1946.
Afr Doc 2409.300	Report with financial statements. (Nigeria, Northern. Accountant General.) Kaduna. 1964+
Afr Doc 4307.331F	Report with summaries and analysis, number, sex, geographical distribution and ages of the European population. (South Africa.) Pretoria, 1933.
Afr 3979.57.10	Reportagens no Egipto. (Abreu, Paradela De.) Lisboa, 1957.
Afr Doc 3208.375	Reported employment and earnings in Kenya. (Kenya. Economis and Statistics Division.)
Afr 6457.15	Reported employment and wages in Kenya. (East Africa High Commission.) Nairobi, 1961.
Afr 6300.75	Reporter. Nairobi. 1963+ 6v.
Afr 9435.5	Reports. (British South Africa Company.) London. 1896+
Afr 555.23.25	Reports. (Congo Missionary Conference.) 7,1918 2v.
Afr Doc 1439.3F	Reports. (Egypt. Ministry of Justice.) Cairo. 1898-1907 3v.
Afr 650.2F	Reports and recommendations. (C.S.A. Meeting of Specialists on Urbanisation and Its Social Aspects Abidjan, Ivory Coast, 1961.) London, 1961.
Afr 8846.10	Reports of cases decided in the native appeal courts of the Transkeian territories, 1914. (Transkeian Territories. Native Appeal Court.) Cape Town, 1912.
Afr 6145.3F	Reports of the commissioners of enquiry into the conduct of certain chiefs and the government statement thereon. (Sierra Leone. Commissioners of Enquiry into the Conduct of Certain Chiefs.) Freetown, 1957.
Afr 9095.25F	Reports of Transvaal Volunteers Commission. (Transvaal (Colony). Volunteers Commission.) Pretoria, 1906.
Afr 3038.8F	Reports on the finances...of Egypt and the Soudan. (Great Britain. Agent and Consul-General in Egypt.) London. 1900+ 4v.
Afr 6558.10F	Reports on Zanzibar. Zanzibar, 1936. 3 pam.
Afr 1840.2	La représentation des indigènes musulmans dans les conseils de l'Algérie. (Rouard de Card, E.) Paris, 1909.
Afr 1571.50	La représentation diplomatique de la France au Maroc. (Caille, Jacques.) Paris, 1951.
Afr 7122.75	La repression colonialiste en Angola. 2d ed. (Front Revolutionnaire Africain pour l'Indépendance Nationale des Colonies Portugaises.) Anvers, 1960.
Afr 8045.45	The Republic. (Coetzee, G.A.) Johannesburg, 1960.
Afr 8018.8	Republic in a changing world. Johannesburg.
Afr 5480.261	The Republic of Chad. (France. Embassy. U.S.) N.Y., 1961.
Afr 5440.10	The Republic of Congo. (France. Embassy. U.S.) N.Y., 1961.
Afr 5385.36	The Republic of Dahomey. (France. Embassy. U.S.) N.Y., 1960.
Afr 7459.20A	The Republic of Liberia. (Maugham, R.C.F.) London, 1920.
Afr 7375.6	The Republic of Liberia. (Roberts, J.T.) Washington, 1899.
Afr 7368.68	The Republic of Liberia. (Stockwell, G.S.) N.Y., 1868.
Afr 7369.59.2	The Republic of Liberia. (Yancy, Ernest Jerome.) Cairo, 1961.
Afr 7369.59	The Republic of Liberia. (Yancy, Ernest Jerome.) London, 1959.
Afr 5180.42	The Republic of Senegal. (France. Embassy. U.S.) N.Y., 1960.
Afr 8045.53	The Republic of South Africa. (Hailey, W.M.H.) London, 1963.
Afr 5342.55	The Republic of the Ivory Coast. (France. Embassy. U.S.) N.Y., 1960.
Afr 5260.30	The Republic of the Niger. (France. Embassy. U.S.) N.Y., 1960.
Afr 4070.62	The Republic of the Sudan. (Barbour, K.M.) London, 1961.
Afr 5280.5	The Republic of the Upper Volta. (France. Embassy. U.S.) N.Y., 1960.
Afr 9699.3	Republic of Zambia. (Zambia.) Lusaka, 1965.
Afr 8095.88	Republic under pressure. (Spence, J.E.) London, 1965.
Afr 7015.15	Republica Portuguesa. Aires de Ornelas. Lisboa, 1934. 3v.
Afr 8050.21	Republiek en koninkryk. (Potchefstroom. University for Christian Higher Education.) Potchefstroom, 1964.
Afr 8089.66.20	Die Republiek van Suid-Afrika. (Jaarsveld, Floris.) Johannesburg, 1966.
Afr 8380.2	Die Republiek van Suid-Afrika. (Scholtz, Gert.) Johannesburg, 1962.
Afr 8045.50	Republikein en republikeine. (Schoor, M.C.E.) Kaapstad, 1960.
Afr 5312.10.5	Republik Guinea. (Solonitskii, A.S.) Berlin, 1962.
Afr 8045.55	Die republikeinse grondwet. (Wessels, F.J.) Kaapstad, 1962.
Afr 2030.460.35	La République algérienne. (Buy, François.) Paris, 1965.
Afr 6664.5	La république autonome du Togo. (Alcandre, Sylvine.) Paris, 1957.
Afr 8089.63	La République d'Afrique du Sud. 2d ed. (Lesourd, J.A.) Paris, 1963.
Afr 7368.87	La république de Liberia. (Bourzeix, R.P.P.) Paris, 1887.
Afr 7459.12	La république de Liberia. (Jore, L.) Paris, 1912.
Afr 5257.15	La république du Niger. (Bonardi, Pierre.) Paris, 1960.
Afr 5110.25	La République du Sénégal. (Gonidec, Pierre François.) Paris, 1968.

Afr 7065.526.10   Révolution en Afrique; la libération de la Guinée portugaise. (Davidson, Basil.) Paris, 1969.
Afr 2030.15   Révolution en Algérie. (Schaefer, René.) Paris, 1956.
Afr 210.61.40   Revolution in Africa. (Pomikkar, Kavalam M.) London, 1961.
Afr 3993.966.5   The revolution in Egypt's economic system, from private enterprise to socialism, 1952-1965. (O'brien, Patrick Karl.) London, 1966.
Afr 3326.5   The Revolution in eleven years. (United Arab Republic.) Cairo, 1963.
Afr 7065.526.5   Revolution in Guinea: an African people's struggle. (Cabral, Amilcar.) London, 1969.
Afr 3310.90   The Revolution in thirteen years, 1952-1965. (United Arab Republic.) Cairo, 1965.
Afr 3326.6   The Revolution in twelve years. (United Arab Republic. Information Department.) Cairo, 1964.
Afr 6575.2   Révolution in Zanzibar. (Okello, John.) Nairobi, 1967.
Afr 5055.67   The revolutionary years: West Africa since 1800. (Webster, James B.) London, 1967.
Afr 1018.1   Revue africaine. Algiers. 1,1856+ 75v.
Afr 1018.3   Revue africaine. Paris. 1,1836+ 2v.
Afr 1018.1.5   Revue africaine. Table générale 1856-1881, 1882-1921. Algiers, 1885-1924. 2v.
Afr 1818.5   Revue algérienne des sciences juridiques. Alger. 1964 5v.
Afr 7518.15   La revue congolaise. Bruxelles. 1-4,1910-1914
Afr 5513.2   Revue de geographie. (Madagascar.) Toulouse. 1,1962+ 5v.
Afr 1318.10   Revue de géographie du Maroc. Rabat. 7,1965+
Afr 1018.5   Revue de l'Afrique du Nord. Alger. 1,1921+ 2v.
Afr 1018.2.3   Revue de l'Afrique française et des antiquités africaines. Paris. 1-6,1882-1888 3v.
Afr 1018.7   Revue de l'Occident musulman et de la Méditerranee. Aix-en-Provence. 1,1966+
Afr 5518.1F   Revue de Madagascar. Tananarive. 1-27,1933-1939// 14v.
Afr 5518.4F   Revue de Madagascar. Tananarive. 30,1965+
Afr 3018.10   Revue d'Egypte. Le Caire. 2-4,1895-1897// 2v.
Afr 1018.6   Revue d'histoire et de civilisation du Malghreb. Alger. 2,1967+
Afr 18.11F   Revue encyclopédique de l'Afrique. Abidjan. 1,1960+
NEDL Afr 5810.5   Revue historique et litteraire de l'ile Maurice. Archives coloniales. Port-Louis. 1,1887+ 6v.
NEDL Afr 5810.6   Revue historique et litteraire de l'ile Maurice. Variétés et romans. Port Louis. 1,1887+ 6v.
Afr 1018.4   Revue nord-africaine illustrée. v.1-4. Alger, 1902-05. 4v.
Afr 2700.5F   Revue Sahara. Alger. 5,1959+
Afr 5001.110   Revue trimestrielle. (Organisation Africaine et Malgache de Coopération Economique.) Yaounde.
Afr 2418.1   Revue tunisienne. Tunis. 1,1894+ 36v.
Afr 2418.2.2   Revue Tunisienne de Sciences Sociales. Index bibliographique. Tunis. 1964-1968
Afr 2418.2   Revue tunisienne de sciences sociales. Tunis. 3,1966+
Afr 9165.71.5   Rex, H.M. Pretoria van kerkplaas tot regeringsetel. Kaapstad, 1960.
Afr 4559.35.45   Rey, C.F. The real Abyssinia. London, 1935.
Afr 4320.7   Rey, Charles. The romance of the Portuguese in Abyssinia. London, 1929.
Afr 4559.27   Rey, Charles F. In the country of the blue Nile. London, 1927.
Afr 4559.23   Rey, Charles F. Unconquered Abyssinia as it is today. London, 1923.
Afr 8678.51   Rey, Charles F. The Union of South Africa and some of its problems. N.Y., 1947.
Afr 2609.00.3   Rey, R. Voyage d'études en Tunisie. Paris, n.d.
Afr 6741.10   Reyburn, William David. Out of the African night. 1st ed. N.Y., 1968.
Afr 2030.360   Reygasse, René. Témoinage d'un ultra sur le drame algérien. Paris, 1960.
Afr 9047.10   Reyher, R.H. Zulu woman. N.Y., 1948.
Afr 1338.12   Reynal, Raoul. Les particularités du droit fiscal par rapport au droit privé. Rabat, 1962.
Afr 609.55   Reynolds, Reginald. Cairo to Cape Town. 1st ed. Garden City, N.Y., 1955.
Afr 5074.30   Rezzons sur l'Adrar. (Otton Loyewski, S.W.C.) Rufisque, 1942.
Afr 1733.6   Le Rharb, fellahs et colons. (Lecoz, J.) Rabat, 1964. 2v.
Afr 1733.6.1   Le Rharb. (Lecoz, J.) Rabat, 1964. 2v.
Afr 1550.43   Rheinlaender, G. Deutschland, England und die Marokkokrise. Inaug. Diss. Bochum-Langendreer, 1931.
Afr 8686.28   The Rhenish Mission Society in South Africa. (Strassberger, Elfriede.) Cape Town, 1969.
Afr 8250.21.5   Rhodes, a heritage. (McDonald, J.G.) London, 1943.
Afr 8250.21   Rhodes, a life. (McDonald, J.G.) London, 1927.
Afr 8250.29.6   Rhodes. (Lockhart, J.G.) London, 1963.
Afr 8250.25   Rhodes. (Millin, S.G.) London, 1933.
Afr 8250.25.10   Rhodes. (Millin, S.G.) London, 1952.
Afr 8250.44   Rhodes goes north. (Green, Jolin Eric Sidney.) London, 1936.
Afr 9689.61.5   Rhodes-Livingston Institute, Lusaka, Northern Rhodesia. Social research and community development. Lusaka, 1961.
Afr 9545.5   Rhodes-Livingston Institute, Lusaka. From tribal rule to modern government. Lusaka, 1959.
Afr 9428.5F   Rhodes-Livingstone Institute, Lusaka, Northern Rhodesia. A selected bibliography of the federation of Rhodesia and Nyasaland. Lusaka, 1957.
Afr 210.60.60   Rhodes-Livingstone Institute, Lusaka, Northern Rhodesia. Conference, 14th, Lusaka, 1960. Myth in modern Africa. Lusaka, 1960.
Afr 9603.5   Rhodes-Livingstone Institute, Lusaka, Northern Rhodesia. 11th Conference, Lusaka, 1958. Present interrelations in Central African rural and urban life. Lusaka, 1958.
Afr 9693.8   Rhodes-Livingstone Institute. The multitribal society. Lusaka, 1962.

Afr 18.5.5   Rhodes-Livingstone Journal. Index, v.1-30. Manchester, 1962.
Afr 18.5   Rhodes-Livingstone journal. Cape Town. 1,1944+ 2v.
Afr 8250.23   The Rhodes memorial at Oxford. (Watts-Danton, T.) London, 1910.
Afr 8250.37   Rhodes of Africa. (Gross, Felix.) London, 1956.
Afr 8700.10F   Rhodes University, Grahamstown, South Africa. Institute of Social and Economic Research. Report.
Afr 9489.67   Rhodesia, beleaguered country. (Berlyn, Phillippa.) London, 1967.
Afr 9450.40   Rhodesia; birth of a nation. (Metrowich, Frederick Redvers.) Pretoria, 1969.
Afr 9500.50   Rhodesia, een dilemma van ras en grond. (Sonius, H.W.J.) Leiden, 1966.
Afr Doc 3703.5   Rhodesia, Northern. General list of chiefs. Lusaka. 1960+
Afr 9635.20   Rhodesia, Northern. Northern Rhodesia proposal for constitutional change. London, 1961.
Afr Doc 3739.5   Rhodesia, Northern. Advisory Committee on Industrial Development. Report. 1,1946+
Afr Doc 3712.15   Rhodesia, Northern. African Representative Council. Proceedings. 1,1946 4v.
Afr Doc 3731.10   Rhodesia, Northern. Agricultural Marketing Committee. Review of the general economic condition of the agricultural industry. Lusaka. 1963+
Afr Doc 3707.346   Rhodesia, Northern. Census. Census, 1946. Lusaka, 1947.
Afr 9625.10F   Rhodesia, Northern. Central Race Relations Advisory And Conciliation Committee. Annual report. n.p.
Afr 9625.10.5F   Rhodesia, Northern. Central Race Relations Advisory Committee. Annual report. Lusaka. 1-2,1960-1961//
Afr 9635.26   Rhodesia, Northern. Commission Appointed to Review the Salaries and Conditions of Service. Report. Lusaka, 1964.
Afr 9635.15   Rhodesia, Northern. Commission to Inquire into the Participation of Africans in Local Government. Report. Lusaka, 1960.
Afr Doc 3731.4F   Rhodesia, Northern. Department of Agriculture. Annual report. Lusaka. 1956-1959
Afr Doc 3733.10   Rhodesia, Northern. Department of Community Development. Annual report. Lusaka. 1961+
Afr Doc 3733.5   Rhodesia, Northern. Department of Cooperative Societies. Annual report. Lusaka. 1952+
Afr Doc 3737.5   Rhodesia, Northern. Department of Game and Fisheries. Annual report. Lusaka. 1960+
Afr Doc 3742.5   Rhodesia, Northern. Department of Lands. Annual report. Lusaka. 1963+
Afr Doc 3749.3F   Rhodesia, Northern. Department of Social Welfare. Annual report. Lusaka. 1962-1963 3v.
Afr 9632.15F   Rhodesia, Northern. Department of Water Affairs. Annual report.
Afr Doc 3749.14F   Rhodesia, Northern. Department of Welfare and Probation Services. Social welfare; annual report. Lusaka. 1,1952
Afr Doc 3739.30   Rhodesia, Northern. Income Tax Department. Report. Lusaka. 1953-1954
Afr Doc 3739.10   Rhodesia, Northern. Information Department. Annual report. Lusaka. 1963+
Afr Doc 3714.5   Rhodesia, Northern. Legislative Assembly. Debates. 1,1964+
Afr Doc 3712.5   Rhodesia, Northern. Legislative Council. Debates. 15v.
Afr Doc 3731.5   Rhodesia, Northern. Ministry of African Agriculture. Annual report. Lusaka. 1963+
Afr Doc 3744.10   Rhodesia, Northern. Ministry of Native Affairs. African affairs annual report. Lusaka. 1961+
Afr Doc 3744.5   Rhodesia, Northern. Natural Resources Board. Annual report. 1959+
Afr Doc 3746.10   Rhodesia, Northern. Printing and Stationery Department. Annual report. Lusaka. 1963+
Afr Doc 3748.5   Rhodesia, Northern. Roads Department. Annual report. Lusaka. 1963
Afr 9699.59   Rhodesia, Northern. Special Commissioner for the Western Province. First report on a regional survey of the copperbelt, 1959. Lusaka, 1960.
Afr Doc 3749.10   Rhodesia, Northern. Survey Department. Annual report. Lusaka. 1962-1963
Afr Doc 3750.25   Rhodesia, Northern. Teaching Service Commission. Annual report. Lusaka. 1963
Afr Doc 3750.10   Rhodesia, Northern. Town and Country Planning Service. Annual report. Lusaka. 1961+
Afr Doc 3753.5   Rhodesia, Northern. Workmen's Compensation Commissioner. Annual report. Lusaka. 1960+
Afr 9450.30   Rhodesia; report on the discussions held on board H.M.S. Fearless. (Great Britain. Foreign and Commonwealth Office.) London, 1968.
Afr Doc 3809.15F   Rhodesia, Southern. Budget statements by the minister of Finance. Salisbury? 1964+
Afr Doc 3809.10   Rhodesia, Southern. Estimates of expenditure to be defrayed from revenue funds and from loan funds. Salisbury. 1964+
Afr 9499.5   Rhodesia, Southern. Progress of southern Rhodesia, 1920-27. Salisbury, 1928.
Afr 9499.70   Rhodesia, Southern. Advisory Committee on the Development of the Economic Resources of Southern Rhodesia. The development of the economic resources of Southern Rhodesia. Salisbury, 1962.
Afr 9489.36   Rhodesia, Southern. Bureau of Publicity. Southern Rhodesia. 4. ed. Salisbury, 1936.
Afr Doc 3807.311.5   Rhodesia, Southern. Census Office. Preliminary returns of a census taken on May 1911, together with comparative figures from the census of 1907 and 1904. Salisbury, 1911. 2 pam.
Afr Doc 3807.326.5   Rhodesia, Southern. Census Office. Report of the director of Census regarding the Census taken on the 4th May 1926. Salisbury, 1927.
Afr Doc 3807.321.10   Rhodesia, Southern. Census Office. Second and final report of the director of census regarding the census taken on 3rd May 1921. Salisbury, 1922.
Afr 9432.7   Rhodesia, Southern. Central African Archives. Central African Archives in retrospect and prospect. Salisbury, 1947.

542

Afr Doc 3707.351 — Rhodesia and Nyasaland. Central Statistical Office. Report on the census of population, 1951. Lusaka, 1954.

Afr Doc 3809.515 — Rhodesia and Nyasaland. Central Statistical Office. Sample survey of African agriculture, Southern Rhodesia, 1959/60. Salisbury, 1962.

Afr Doc 3808.7F — Rhodesia and Nyasaland. Central Statistical Office. The 1953-55 demographic sample survey of the indigenous African population of Southern Rhodesia. Salisbury, 1959.

Afr 9435.14.5 — Rhodesia and Nyasaland. Commission Appointed to Divide the Territory of Northern Rhodesia into Electoral Districts. Report. Salisbury, 1958.

Afr 9435.14.10 — Rhodesia and Nyasaland. Commission Appointed to Divide the Territory of Southern Rhodesia into Electoral Districts. Report. Salisbury, 1958.

Afr 9435.14 — Rhodesia and Nyasaland. Commission Appointed to Divide the Territory of Nyasaland into Electoral Districts. Report. Salisbury, 1958..

Afr Doc 3533.6 — Rhodesia and Nyasaland. Department of Civil Aviation. Report of the Director. 1954+

Afr Doc 3533.10 — Rhodesia and Nyasaland. Department of Customs and Excise. Report of the Controller of Customs and Excise. Salisbury. 1954+

Afr Doc 3543.5 — Rhodesia and Nyasaland. Department of Meteorological Services. Report of the director. 1954-1955

Afr Doc 3550.5 — Rhodesia and Nyasaland. Department of Taxes. Report of the Commissioner of Tades. 1954+

Afr Doc 3531.5 — Rhodesia and Nyasaland. Ministry of Agriculture. Report of the Secretary to the Federal Ministry of Agriculture. Salisbury. 1954+

Afr Doc 3533.3 — Rhodesia and Nyasaland. Ministry of Commerce and Industry. Report of the secretary. 1961-1963

Afr Doc 3534.5 — Rhodesia and Nyasaland. Ministry of Defense. Annual report of the Secretary for Defence and the Chief of Air Staff. Salisbury. 1955+

Afr Doc 3509.300 — Rhodesia and Nyasaland. Ministry of Economic Affairs. Economic report. Salisbury. 1954+

Afr Doc 3535.5 — Rhodesia and Nyasaland. Ministry of Education. Annual report on education, 1954-1963.

Afr Doc 3535.10F — Rhodesia and Nyasaland. Ministry of External Affairs. Report of the secretary. Salisbury. 1955-1957

Afr Doc 3538.5F — Rhodesia and Nyasaland. Ministry of Health. Annual report of the public health. Zomba. 1,1954+

Afr Doc 3542.5 — Rhodesia and Nyasaland. Ministry of Law. Report of the secretary to the Ministry of Law. Salisbury. 1,1955+

Afr Doc 3546.25 — Rhodesia and Nyasaland. Ministry of Posts. Annual report of the Postmaster-General. Salisbury. 1954+

Afr Doc 3546.20 — Rhodesia and Nyasaland. Ministry of Posts. Annual report on the Post Office Savings Bank and Savings Certificates. Salisbury. 1954+

Afr Doc 3546.15 — Rhodesia and Nyasaland. Ministry of Power. Report of the Secretary for Power. Salisbury. 1955+

Afr Doc 3553.5 — Rhodesia and Nyasaland. Ministry of Works. Annual report of the Under Secretary. Salisbury. 1955+

Afr 9535.75 — Rhodesia and Nyasaland. National Archives. Occasional papers. Salisbury. 1,1963//

Afr 9538.12 — Rhodesia and Nyasaland. National Archives. A select bibliography of recent publications. Salisbury, 1960.

Afr Doc 3546.10 — Rhodesia and Nyasaland. Pension Fund Board. Annual report on the operation and financial position of the Federal Provident Fund. Salisbury. 1961+

Afr Doc 3546.5 — Rhodesia and Nyasaland. Pension Fund Board. Annual report on the operation and financial position of the Federal Pension Fund. Salisbury. 1956+

Afr 9448.73 — Rhodesia and Nyasaland. Prime Minister. The break-up. Salisbury, 1963.

Afr Doc 3546.30F — Rhodesia and Nyasaland. Public Works Department. Annual report. Salisbury. 1955+

Afr Doc 3539.5 — Rhodesia and Nyasaland. Registrar of Insurance. Report.

Afr 9489.60 — Rhodesia and Nyasaland journey. (Blake, W.T.) London, 1960.

Afr 9450.8 — Rhodesia condemns. (Peck, A.J.A.) Salisbury, Rhodesia, 1966.

Afr 9489.00 — Rhodesia et Transvaal. (Bordeaux, A.) Paris, 1900.

Afr 9450.15 — Rhodesia in 'rebellion'. (Sparrow, Gerald.) London, 1967.

Afr 9488.95.5 — Rhodesia of to-day. (Knight, E.F.) London, 1895.

Afr 9489.68.5 — The Rhodesia that was my life. (Tredgold, Robert Clarkson.) London, 1968.

Afr 9525.875 — The Rhodesian, the life of Sir Roy Welensky. (Taylor, Don.) London, 1955.

Afr 9425.5F — Rhodesian annual. Bulawayo. 1927+

Afr 9425.65 — Rhodesian commentary. Salisbury, Rhodesia. 1,1966+

Afr 9425.60 — The Rhodesian community development review. Causeway. 1,1966+

Afr 9439.66 — Rhodesian epic. (Baxter, J.W.) Cape Town, 1966.

Afr 9439.53.5 — Rhodesian genesis. (Jones, Neville.) Bulawayo, 1953.

Afr 9450.10 — Rhodesian independence justified. (Edwards, Hilton.) Queenstown, South Africa, 1966.

Afr 9500.35 — Rhodesian Institute of African Affairs, Bulawayo, South Africa. The progress of Africans in Southern Rhodesia. Bulawayo, 1958.

Afr 9489.65.5 — Rhodesian patrol. (Lloyd, Frank.) Ilfracombe, 1965.

Afr 9439.67 — Rhodesian perspective. (Bull, Theodore.) London, 1967.

Afr 10913.2 — The Rhodesian press. (Gale, W.I.) Salisbury, 1962.

Afr 9489.68 — Rhodesian spring. (Stonier, George Walter.) London, 1968.

Afr 9425.40 — Rhodesiana. Salisbury. 2,1957+ 2v.

Afr Doc 3502.5 — The Rhodesias and Nyasaland. (Library of Congress. African Section.) Washington, 1965.

Afr 9497.5F — The Rhodesias and Nyasaland. 2. ed. (King, Ralph W.) Cape Town, 1956.

Afr 9489.66.10 — Rhodésie, pays des lions fidèles. (Orcival, Francois d'.) Paris, 1966.

Afr 9497.10 — La Rhodésie. Paris, 1968.

Afr 7809.59.15 — Rhodius, Georges. Congo 1959. Bruxelles, 1959.

Afr 6919.67.10 — Rhoodie, Eschel Mostert. South West: the last frontier in Africa. Johannesburg, 1967.

Afr 8678.68.5 — Rhoodie, N.J. Apartheid. Cape Town, 1960.

Afr 8678.68.15 — Rhoodie, N.J. Apartheid and racial partnership in Southern Africa. Pretoria, 1969.

Afr 8678.68.12 — Rhoodie, N.J. Apartheid en partnership. 2. uitg. Pretoria, 1968.

Afr 8678.68 — Rhoodie, N.J. Die apartheidsgedougte. Kaapstad, 1960.

Afr 11611.66.100 — The rhythm of violence. (Nkosi, Lewis.) London, 1964.

Afr 3310.88 — Riad, H. L'Egypte nassérienne. Paris, 1964.

Afr 3040.30 — Riad, Mohamed Abdel Moneim. La nationalité égyptienne. Paris, 1937.

NEDL Afr 12131.5.100 — Riad. (Khayat, Georges.) Caire, 1934.

Afr 2030.305 — Ribaud, Paul. Barricades pour un drapeau. Paris, 1960.

Afr 1635.10 — Ribaut, A.J. Les djemaas judiciaires berberes. Thèse. Alger, 1930.

Afr 7575.40 — Ribeaud, P. Adieu Congo. Paris, 1961.

Afr 718.4.10 — Ribeiro, M.F. As conferencias e o itinerario do viajante Serpa Pinto. Lisboa, 1879.

Afr 115.3.5 — Ribeiro, M.F. Homenagem aõs heróes que precederam. Lisboa, 1885.

Afr 555.4.5 — Ribolet. Un gand évêque, ou Vingt ans d'église d'Afrique sous l'administration de M. Pavy. Alger, 1902. 3v.

Afr 1990.4 — Ribourt, F. Le gouvernement de l'Algérie, 1852-1858. Paris, 1859.

Afr 5180.29 — Ricard, F. Le Sénégal. Paris, 1865.

Afr 1620.15 — Ricard, Prosper. Le Maroc. 3e ed. Paris, 1925.

Afr 1620.15.10 — Ricard, Prosper. Maroc. 7. ed. Paris, 1950.

Afr 1239.24F — Ricard, Prosper. Les merveilles de l'autre France. Paris, 1924.

Afr 1579.5 — Ricard, R. Contribution à l'étude du commerce genois au Maroc durant la periode portugaise, 1415-1550. Paris, 1937.

Afr 1724.7 — Ricard, Robert. Un document portugais sur la place de Mazagrn au début du XVIIe siècle. Thèse. Paris, 1932.

Afr 1069.56 — Ricard, Robert. Etudes hispano-africaines. Tetuan, 1956.

Afr 1575.12 — Ricard, Robert. Etudes sur l'histoire des Portugals au Maroc. Coimbra, 1955.

Afr 2850.1 — Riccheri, G. La Tripolitania e l'Italia. Milan, 1902.

Afr 2929.13.5 — Ricchieri, Giuseppe. La Libia. Milano, 1913.

Afr 6118.10 — Rice, Berkeley. Enter Gambia; the birth of and improbable nation. Boston, 1969.

Afr 4095.10F — Ricerca delle sorgenti del Nilo. (Torelli-Viollier, E.) Milano, 1878.

Afr 1965.6 — Richard, C. Etude sur l'insurrection du Dhara. Alger, 1846.

Afr 2228.2.3 — Richard, C. Scénes de moeurs arabes. 3e ed. Paris, 1876.

Afr 4937.2 — Richard Corfield of Somaliland. (Battersby, H.F.P.) London, 1914.

Afr 5056.149 — Richard Malard, J. Afrique occidentale française. Paris, 1949.

Afr 679.58.10 — Richard Molard, Jacques. Problèmes humains en Afrique occidentale. 2. éd. Paris, 1958.

Afr 2209.05 — Richardot, H. Sept semaines en Tunisie et en Algérie. Paris, 1905.

Afr 6541.16 — Richards, A.I. Economic development and tribal change. Cambridge, Eng., 1954.

Afr 8678.13.41A — Richards, A.I. Hunger and work in a savage tribe. Glencoe, Ill., 1948.

Afr 8678.13.40 — Richards, A.I. Hunger and work in a savage tribe. London, 1932.

Afr 9700.17 — Richards, A.I. Land labour and diet in Northern Rhodesia. London, 1939.

Afr 6310.36 — Richards, Audrey. East African chiefs. London, 1960.

Afr 699.69 — Richards, Audrey. The multicultural states of East Africa. Montreal, 1969.

Afr 6540.24 — Richards, Audrey Isabel. Economic development and tribal change, a study of immigrant labour in Baganda. Cambridge, Eng., 1954.

Afr 6390.65 — Richards, C.G. East African explorers. London, 1960.

Afr 6390.65.10 — Richards, C.G. East African explorers. Nairobi, 1967.

Afr 6390.65.5 — Richards, C.G. Some historic journeys in East Africa. London, 1961.

Afr 8028.133F — Richards, Margaret Patricia. Mountaineering in Southern Africa. Johannesburg, 1966.

Afr 2748.53 — Richardson, J. Narrative of mission to central Africa (1850-51). London, 1853. 2v.

Afr 1608.60 — Richardson, J. Travels in Morocco. v.1-2. London, 1860.

Afr 2748.48 — Richardson, J. Travels in the...Sahara. London, 1848. 2v.

Afr 5765.11 — Richardson, James. Lights and shadows. Antananarivo, 1877.

Afr 7803.26 — Richardson, Kenneth. Freedom in Congo. London, 1962.

Afr 555.154 — Richardson, Kenneth. Garden of miracles; a history of the African Inland Mission. London, 1968.

Afr 7369.59.5 — Richardson, N.R. Liberia's past and present. London, 1959.

Afr 8292.35 — Richardson, W.D. With the Army Service Corps in South Africa. London, 1903.

Afr 2762.10 — Richer, A. Les Touareg du Niger. Paris, 1924.

Afr 1609.12.15 — Richet, E. Voyage au Maroc. Nouvelle ed. Paris, 1912.

Afr 1583.16 — Richet, Etienne. La politique allemand. Paris, 1917.

Afr 2438.8 — Richon, Jean. Le contentieux administratif en Tunisie. Paris, 1916.

Afr 3285.15A — Richter, Erhard. Lord Cromer, Ägypten und die Entstehung der französisch-englischen Entente von 1904. Inaug. Diss. Leipzig, 1931.

Afr 555.65 — Richter, Julius. Tanganyika and its future. London, 1934.

Afr 6168.9 — Ricketts, H. D. Narrative of the Ashantee war. London, 1831.

Afr 2948.14 — La riconquista del Fezzan. (Graziani, Rodolfo.) Milano, 1934.

Afr 4785.14 — Ricordi del Benadir. (Sorrentino, G.) Napoli, 1912.

Afr 4559.24.9 — Ricordi di carovana. 2 ed. (Civimini, G.) Milano, 1933.

Afr 4394.13 — Ricordi di un prigioniero di guerra nello Scioa, marzo 1896-gennaio 1897. 2a ed. (Gamerra, Giovanni.) Firenze, 1897.

Htn Afr 4742.24* — Ricordi di un soggiorno in Eritrea. Fasc.1. (Conti Rossini, C.) Asmara, 1903.

Afr 4785.935 — Ricordi somali. (Perricone, V.A.) Bologna, 1935.

Afr 1608.97.5 — A ride in Morocco. (Campbell, A.) Toronto, 1897.

Afr 1609.02.5 — A ride in Morocco. (Macnab, Frances.) London, 1902.

Afr 1608.80.2 — A ride in petticoats and slippers. (Colvile, H.E.) London, 1880.

Afr 9165.94 — The ridge of the white waters. (Scully, W.C.) London, 1912.

Afr 4513.35.90 — Ridley, F.A. Mussolini over Africa. London, 1935.

Afr 8690.25 — Ridsdale, Benjamin. Scenes and adventures in great Namaqualand. London, 1883.

Afr 8110.3.20 — Riebeeck, Jan van. Daghregister gehouden by den oppercoopman Jan Anthonisz van Riebeeck. v.1-. Kaapstad, 1952. 3v.

Afr 8110.3.15 — Riebeeck, Jan van. Journal. Cape Town, 1952. 3v.

Afr 6883.7 — Ried, H.A. Zur Anthropologie des abflusslosen Rumpfschollenlandes im nordöstlichen Deutsch-Ostafrika. Hamburg, 1915.

Afr 3315.20 Robertson, J.H. The most important country. London, 1957.
Afr 8289.01.39 Robertson, J.M. Wrecking the empire. London, 1901.
Afr 6420.10 Robertson, J.W. The Kenya coastal strip. London, 1961.
Afr 11749.7.100 Robertson, Olive. The mighty turtle and other poems. Cape Town, 1966.
Afr 3315.125.2 Robertson, Terence. Crisis, the inside story of the Suez conspiracy. London, 1965.
Afr 3315.125 Robertson, Terence. Crisis, the inside story of the Suez conspiracy. 1st ed. N.Y., 1965.
Afr 820.5 Robertson, W. Zambezi days. London, 1936.
Afr 609.45 Robeson, Eslanda G. African journey. N.Y., 1945.
Afr 3979.55.10 Robichon, C. Eternal Egypt. Reprinted. London, 1956.
Afr 2010.4 Robin. L'insurrection de la Grande Kabylie en 1871. Paris, n.d.
Afr 2232.1 Robin. Le Mzab et son annexion. Alger, 1884.
Afr 8687.265.5 Robins, Eric. This man Malan. Cape Town, 1953.
Afr 9343.72 Robins, Eric. White Queen in Africa. London, 1967.
Afr 28.35 Robinson, A. A bibliography of African bibliographies. Cape Town, 1948.
Afr 6775.5 Robinson, A.E. Some historical notes on East Africa. n.p., 1936.
Afr 11033.2 Robinson, A.M.L. None daring to make us afraid. Cape Town, 1962.
NEDL Afr 6275.7 Robinson, C.H. Hausaland. London, 1896.
Afr 6275.7.8 Robinson, C.H. Nigeria, our latest protectorate. London, 1900.
Afr 6392.32 Robinson, Edward A.G. Report on the needs for economic research and investigation in East Africa. Entebbe, Uganda, 1955.
Htn Afr 1925.1* Robinson, H. Libertas or reliefe to English captives in Algeria. London, 1642.
Afr 8983.5 Robinson, J. A life time in South Africa. London, 1900.
Afr 9028.72.1 Robinson, J. Notes on Natal. Pretoria, 1967.
Afr 6926.9 Robinson, J.P.K. With Botha's army. London, 1916.
Afr 210.62.25 Robinson, James H. Africa at the crossroads. Philadelphia, 1962.
Afr 3340.13 Robinson, Nehemiah. Nasser's Egypt. N.Y., 1963.
Afr 626.200 Robson, Peter. Economic integration in Africa. London, 1968.
Afr 626.200.5 Robson, Peter. The economics of Africa. London, 1969.
Afr 7809.11 Roby, Marguerite. My adventures in the Congo. London, 1911.
Afr 4559.35.40 Rocchi, A. Etiopia ed etiopia. Milano, 1935.
Afr 2731.15.85 Roche, Aimé. Charles de Foucauld. Lyon, 1964.
Afr 9148.78 Roche, H.A. On trek in the Transvaal. London, 1878.
Afr 1955.2 Roches, Léon. Trente-deux ans à travers l'islam (1832-64). Paris, 1884.
Afr 4610.2 Rochet d'Héricourt, C.E. Second voyage dans...le royaume de Choa. Paris, 1846.
Afr 4610.6 Rochet d'Héricourt, C.E. Voyage sur la côte orientale de la Mer Rouge et...de Choa. Paris, 1841.
Afr 5747.91 Rochon, A.M. Voyage à Madagascar. Paris, 1791.
Afr 861.25 Rock of exile. (Buay, D.M.) London, 1957.
Afr 635.7.15F Rock-paintings in South Africa. (Stow, G. William.) London, 1930.
Afr 2206.75 Rocqueville. Relation des moeurs...des Turcs d'Alger. Paris, 1675.
Afr 2762.12 Rodd, Francis R. People of the veil. London, 1926.
Afr 609.67.35 Roddy Owen's Africa. (Owen, Roderic Fenwick.) Appleford, 1967.
Afr 4593.1.3 Roden, K.G. Le tribu dei Mensa. Stockholm, 1913.
Afr 4513.41 Rodeno, Franz. Frankreichs Stellung im Abessinienkonflikt. Berlin, 1941.
Afr 609.65.45 Rodionov, Viktor N. Afrika na styke stoletii. Leningrad, 1965.
Afr 1703.3F Rodrigues, Bernardo. Anais de arzila, cronica inedita do seculo XVI. Lisboa, 1915-20. 2v.
Afr 7175.74 Rodrigues, J. Angola, terra de Portugal. Lourenço Marques, 1964.
Afr 7309.65 Rodrigues Júnior, José. Moçambique. Lisboa, 1965.
Afr 14505.5 Rodrigues Junior, Manuel. Literatura ultramarina. Lourenço, 1962.
Afr 11750.21.100 Roebuck, M.F.C. Nyitso, a novel of West Africa. Cape Town, 1964.
Afr 6898.2 Roegels, Fritz Carl. Mit Carl Peters in Afrika. Berlin, 1933.
Afr 7817.25 Roelens, Victor. Notre vieux Congo, 1891-1917. v.1-2. Namur, 1948.
Afr 9086.17 Roels, E. Boers en Anglais. Autours des mines d'or. Paris, 1897.
Afr 861.35 Roenne, Arne Falk. Back to Tristan. London, 1967.
Afr 7560.14.15 Roeykens, A. Les débuts de l'oeuvre de Léopold II, 1875-1876. Bruxelles, 1955.
Afr 7560.14 Roeykens, A. Le dessein africain de Léopold II. Bruxelles, 1956.
Afr 7560.14.5 Roeykens, A. Léopold II et l'Afrique, 1855-1880. Bruxelles, 1958.
Afr 7560.14.10 Roeykens, A. La période initiale de l'oeuvre africaine de Lépold II. Bruxelles, 1957.
Afr 7808.76 Roeykens, Aug. Leopold II et la conférence géographique. Bruxelles, 1956.
Afr 2035.20 Rogati, Elio. La seconda rivoluzione algeriana. Roma, 1965.
Afr 2225.16 Roger, J.J. Les Musulmans algériens en France et dans les pays islamiques. Paris, 1950.
Afr 9500.45 Rogers, Cyril A. Racial themes in Southern Rhodesia. New Haven, 1962.
Afr 6170.5 Rogers, E. Campaigning in West Africa and the Ashantee invasion. London, 1874.
Afr 8140.21 Rogers, Howard. Native administration in the Union of South Africa. Johannesburg, 1933.
Afr 628.234 Rogers, J.A. Hundred amazing facts about the Negro with complete proof. N.Y., 1934.
Afr 628.246.5 Rogers, Joel Augustus. World's great men of color. 1st ed. N.Y., 1946-47. 2v.
Afr 718.45 Rogers, M. When rivers meet. London, 1960.
Afr 8045.36 Rogers, Mirabel. The black sash. Johannesburg, 1956.
Afr 2208.65.6 Rogers, P.A. A winter in Algeria. London, 1865.
Afr 861.10 Rogers, Rose A. The lonely island. London, 1926.
Afr 861.10.2 Rogers, Rose A. The lonely island. London, 1927.
Afr 1258.94 Rogh, J. Från orientens förgårdar. Stockholm, 1894.
Afr 555.73 Rognes, Louis. Le pionnier du Gabon. Paris, 1957.
Afr 1755.55 El rogui. (Maldonado, E.) Tetuan, 1952.
Afr 4558.83.2 Rohlfs, G. L'Abissinia. Milano, 1885.
Afr 1608.72.8 Rohlfs, G. Adventures in Morocco. London, 1874.

Afr 4050.5 Rohlfs, G. Drei Monate in der libyschen Wüste. Cassel, 1875.
Afr 2975.1 Rohlfs, G. Kufra. Leipzig, 1881.
Afr 1258.70 Rohlfs, G. Land und Volk in Afrika, 1865-1870. Bremen, 1870.
Afr 1608.72.3 Rohlfs, G. Mein ersten aufenthalt in Morokko. Norden, 1885.
Afr 4558.83 Rohlfs, G. Meine Mission nach Abessinien. Leipzig, 1883.
NEDL Afr 2748.74 Rohlfs, G. Quer durch Afrika. Leipzig, 1874. 2v.
Afr 608.86 Rohlfs, G. Quid novi ex Africa. Cassel, 1886.
Afr 1608.64 Rohlfs, G. Reise durch Marokko. Norden, 1884.
Afr 2928.85 Rohlfs, G. Von Tripolis nach Alexandrien. Norden, 1885.
Afr 500.46 Rohrbach, P. Afrika heute und morgen. Berlin, 1939.
Afr 6926.25 Rohrbach, P. Dernburg und die Südwestafrikaner. Berlin, 1911.
Afr 5368.3 Le roi-dieu au Bénin. (Palau Marti, Montserrat.) Paris, 1964.
Afr 12972.41.130 Le roi miraculé. (Biyidi, Alexandre.) Paris, 1958.
Afr 2290.12 Le rôle agricole des espagnols en Oranie. Thèse. (Thurin, Guy.) Lyon, 1937.
Afr 1570.22 Le role de la France au Maroc. (Romagny, J.) Oran, 1908.
Afr 2224.929 Le role du crédit dans le développement économique de l'Algérie depuis la fin de la guerre. Thèse. (Lejeune, André.) Paris, 1930.
Afr 2308.19 Le rôle économique du port d'Alger. Thèse. (Baeza, H.L.) Alger, 1924.
Afr 635.92 The role of the African woman, a report. (Doherty, Mary A.) London, 1962.
Afr 1200.67 Role social de la France dans l'Afrique du Nord. (Gasser, J.) Paris, 1924.
Afr 10052.5 Rolf, Pamela Gail. An index to the programmes of the Johannesburg repertory players from 1928 to 1959. Johannesburg, 1968.
Afr 1570.18 Rolland-Chevillon. La France, l'Allemagne au Maroc. Paris, 1907.
Afr 8235.14 Die Rolle der Buirenrepubliken in der auswaertigen und kolonialen Politik des deutschen Reiches, 1883-1900. (Wued, Johannes Andreas.) Nürnberg, 1927.
Afr 8289.01.23 Rolleston, Maud. Yeoman service. London, 1901.
Afr 7187.10 Roma Machado de Faria e Maria, Carlos. A cidade do Huambo. Lisboa, 1913.
Afr 1570.22 Romagny, J. Le role de la France au Maroc. Oran, 1908.
Afr 4513.40A Roman eagles over Ethiopia. (Delvalle, P.A.) Harrisburg, 1940.
Afr 12012.6 Le roman maghrébin, essai. (Khatibi, Abdelkabir.) Paris, 1968.
Afr 8710.10 The romance of a colonial parliament. (Kilpin, Ralph.) London, 1930.
Afr 9858.10 The romance of Blantyre. (Hetherwick, Alexander.) London, 1931.
Afr 9489.47 The romance of Rhodesia. (Wadio, A.S.N.) London, 1947.
Afr 6282.40 The romance of the Black River. (Walker, Frank Deaville.) London, 1930.
Afr 8180.32 The romance of the great trek. (Rooseboom, H.) Johannesburg, 1949.
Afr 4320.7 The romance of the Portuguese in Abyssinia. (Rey, Charles.) London, 1929.
Afr 8847.89 The romance of the village Ugie. (Smit, Mattheus Theodoros Rehuel.) Cape Town, 1964.
Afr 7812.267 Romaniuk, Anatole. La fécondité des populations congolaises. Paris, 1967.
Afr 1574.12 Romanones, Alvaro Figueroa y Torres. Conferencia del Excmo. Sr. conde de Romanones sobre el problema de Marruecos, Pronunciada en al Teatro de San Fernando de Sevilla el 26 de abril de 1922. Sevilla, 1922.
Afr 2945.33 Romantische Cyrenaika. (Fritz, Egon.) Hamburg, 1941.
Afr 1623.934 Romanus, H. Eine wirtschaftsgeographische darstellung...Marokkos und Tunesiens. Inaug. Diss. Königsberg, 1934.
Afr 8292.20 Romer, C.F. Second Battalion Royal Dublin Fusiliers in South African war. London, 1908.
Afr 7320.15 Romero, J. Memoria acerca do districto de Cabo Delgado. Lisboa, 1856.
Afr 3695.3.83 Romolo Gessi. (Stocchetti, F.) Milano, 1952.
Afr 8289.02.27 Rompel, F. Präsident Steijn. München, 1902.
Afr 8285.20.5 Rompel, Frederik. Marthinus Theunis Steijn. Amsterdam, 1902.
Afr 8252.17 Ronan, B. Forty South African years. London, 1923.
Afr 2875.22 Roncagli, Giovanni. Guerra italo-turca, 1911-12. Milano, 1918. 2v.
Afr 5243.343.15 Ronch, Jean. La religion et la magie songhay. Paris, 1960.
Afr 7045.26F Ronda de Africa. (Galvao, Henrique.) Porto, 1950. 2v.
Afr 8847.77 Pamphlet vol. Rondebosch, South Africa. 2 pam.
Afr 1259.14.3 Rondet-Saint, M. En France africaine. Paris, 1914.
Afr 5056.130.5 Rondet-Saint, M. Un voyage en A.O.F. Paris, 1930.
Afr 5406.211.15.2 Rondet-Saint, Maurice. L'Afrique equatoriale française. 2. ed. Paris, 1911.
Afr 5045.27 Rondet-Saint, Maurice. Dans notre empire noir. Paris, 1912.
Afr 5404.5 Ronget, Fernand. L'expansion coloniale au Congo français. Paris, 1906.
Afr 500.14 Ronze, Raymond. La question d'Afrique. Paris, 1918.
Afr 11752.65.110 Rooke, Daphne. The Greyling. London, 1962.
Afr 11752.65.100 Rooke, Daphne. A grove of fever trees. London, 1951.
Afr 11752.65.120 Rooke, Daphne. Mittee. Boston, 1952.
Afr 210.67.30 Rooke, Patrick J. The wind of change in Africa. Glasgow, 1967.
Afr 550.17 Roome, W.J.W. Can Africa be won? London, 1927.
Afr 609.30.5 Roome, William J.W. Tramping through Africa. N.Y., 1930.
Afr 555.55 Roome, William J.W. London, 1926.
Afr 555.150 Roome, William John Waterman. Through Central Africa for the Bible. London, 1929.
Afr 555.150.5 Roome, William John Waterman. Through the lands of Nyanka, Central Africa. London, 1930.
Afr 200.18 Rooney, Douglas David. The building of modern Africa. London, 1966.
Afr 200.18.2 Rooney, Douglas David. The building of modern Africa. 2nd ed. London, 1967.
Afr 8180.32 Rooseboom, H. The romance of the great trek. Johannesburg, 1949.
Afr 8089.66.25 Roosenthal, Eric. Vesting van die suide. Kaapstad, 1966.
Afr 6455.17.20 Roosevelt, K. A sentimental safari. N.Y., 1963.

	Afr 6455.17	Roosevelt, T. African game trails. N.Y., 1910.
	Afr 6195.7	The roots of Ghana Methodism. (Bartels, Francis Lodovic.) Cambridge, 1965.
	Afr 6412.7	Rosberg, Carl Gustav. The myth of Mau Mau. Stanford, Calif., 1966.
	Afr 695.12	Roscher, A. Ptolemaeus und die Handelsstrassen in Central-Africa. Gotha, 1857.
X Cg	Afr 6540.6A	Roscoe, John. The Baganda, account of their customs. London, 1911.
	Afr 6540.6.12	Roscoe, John. The Baganda, an account of their native customs and beliefs. 2d ed. N.Y., 1966.
	Afr 6540.14	Roscoe, John. The Bagesu and other tribes of the Uganda protectorate. Cambridge, Eng., 1924.
	Afr 6540.12	Roscoe, John. The Bakitara or Banyoro. Cambridge, 1923.
	Afr 6540.13	Roscoe, John. The Banyankole. Cambridge, 1923.
	Afr 6540.4.7	Roscoe, John. Immigrants and their influence. Cambridge, Eng., 1924.
	Afr 6540.4.5	Roscoe, John. The northern Bantu. Cambridge, 1915.
	Afr 725.20A	Roscoe, John. The soul of central Africa. London, 1922.
	Afr 6455.37	Roscoe, John. Twenty-five years in East Africa. Cambridge, 1921.
	Afr 8808.24	Rose, C. Four years in southern Africa. London, 1829.
	Afr 8687.175	Rose, Walter. Bushman, whale and dinosaur. Cape Town, 1961.
	Afr 8289.01.27	Rose-Innes, C. With Paget's horse to the front. London, 1901.
	Afr 5058.11	Roseberry, R.S. The Niger vision. Harrisburg, 1934.
	Afr 724.15	Rosen, Eric von Greve. Traeskfolket. Stockholm, 1916.
	Afr 724.15.5	Rosen, Eric von Greve. Vom Kap nach Kairo. Stuttgart, 1924.
	Afr 4559.07.10	Rosen, Felix. Eine deutsche Gesandtschaft in Abessinien. Leipzig, 1907.
	Afr 6095.365.5	Rosenberger, Homer Tope. Letters from Africa. Washington, 1965.
	Afr 30.6	Rosenthal, E. Encyclopaedia of Southern Africa. London, 1961
	Afr 9165.42.15	Rosenthal, E. Gold bricks and mortar, 60 years of Johannesburg history. Johannesburg, 1946.
	Afr 8676.63	Rosenthal, E. Manne en maatskappye. Kaapstad, 1963.
	Afr 8690.15	Rosenthal, E. River of diamonds. Cape Town, 1957.
	Afr 11040.2	Rosenthal, E. The South African Saturday book. Cape Town, 1948.
	Afr 8919.49	Rosenthal, Eric. African Switzerland, Basutoland of today. London, 1949.
	Afr 8919.49.5	Rosenthal, Eric. African Switzerland. Cape Town, 1948.
	Afr 8710.19	Rosenthal, Eric. The changing years. Cape Town, 1957.
	Afr 30.6.1	Rosenthal, Eric. Encyclopaedia of Southern Africa. 2nd ed. London, 1964.
	Afr 30.6.3	Rosenthal, Eric. Encyclopaedia of Southern Africa. 3d ed. London, 1965.
	Afr 8252.172	Rosenthal, Eric. General De Wet, a biography. Cape Town, 1946.
	Afr 8252.172.2	Rosenthal, Eric. General De Wet; a biography. 2. ed. Cape Town, 1968.
	Afr 8847.90	Rosenthal, Eric. One hundred years of Victoria West, 1859-1959. Victoria West, 1959.
	Afr 9060.28	Rosenthal, Eric. Schooners and sky scrapers. Cape Town, 1963.
	Afr 530.50.1	Rosenthal, Eric. Stars and stripes in Africa. Cape Town, 1968.
	Afr 530.50	Rosenthal, Eric. Stars and stripes in Africa. London, 1938.
	Afr 8809.61	Rosenthal, Eric. The story of Table mountain. Cape Town, 1961.
	Afr 8835.49	Rosenthal, Eric. Three hundred years of the castle at Cape Town. Capetown, 1966.
	Afr 679.67.10	Rosenthal, Ricky. The splendor that was Africa. Dobbs Ferry, 1967.
	Afr 7835.8	Roseveare, Helen. Doctor among Congo rebels. London, 1966.
	Afr 2030.170	Rosfelder, André. L'Algérie à bâtir. Alger, 1959.
	Afr 8678.140.5	Roskam, Karel Lodewijk. Alleen voor blanken. Amsterdam, 1961.
	Afr 8678.140	Roskam, Karel Lodewijk. Apartheid and discrimination. Leyden, 1960.
	Afr 678.85F	Roskoschny, H. Europas Kolonien, West Afrika vom Senegal zum Kamerun. 3. Aufl. Leipzig, n.d.
	Afr 609.28	Ross, C. Mit Kamera, Kind und Kegel durch Afrika. Leipzig, 1928.
	Afr 609.59.10	Ross, Emory. Africa distributed. N.Y., 1959.
	Afr 1942.5	Ross, F.E. The mission of Joseph Donaldson, Jr. to Algiers, 1795-97. n.p., 1935.
Htn	Afr 1738.3.5*	Ross, John. Tanger's rescue. London, 1681.
	Afr 8289.01.33	Ross, P.T. A yeoman's letters. London, 1901.
	Afr 8095.36	Ross, R.E. van der. History in pictures. 1. ed. Cape Town, 1960.
	Afr 6420.5	Ross, W.M. Kenya from within. London, 1927. 2v.
	Afr 4396.10	Rossetti, Carlo. Storia diplomatica dell'Etiopia durante il regno di Menelik II. Torino, 1910.
	Afr 4259.35.30	Rossi, Corrado. Abissinia. Milano, 1935.
	Afr 4060.5	Rossi, Elia. La Nubia e il Sudan. Constantinopoli, 1858.
	Afr 2535.10	Rossi, Pierre. La Tunisie de Bourguiba. Tunis, 1967.
	Afr 679.34	Rossi, V.G. Tropici Senegal all Angola. Milano, 1934.
	Afr 8289.00.13	Rosslyn, James. Twice captured. Edinburg, 1900.
	Afr 9704.2	Rotberg, Robert Irwin. Christian missionaries and the creation of Northern Rhodesia, 1880-1924. Princeton, N.J., 1965.
	Afr 9560.20A	Rotberg, Robert Irwin. The rise of nationalism in central Africa. Cambridge, 1965.
	Afr 710.60	Rotborg, Robert Irwin. A political history of tropical Africa. N.Y., 1965.
	Afr 6738.40	Die rote Landenschnur. (Schmidt, Agathe.) Berlin, 1955.
	Afr 3315.130	Der rote Pharao. (Meyer-Ranke, Peter.) Hamburg, 1964.
	Afr 609.58.50	Roteiro africano; primeira volta a Africa em automovel. 3. ed. (Laidley, Fernando.) Lisboa, 1958.
	Afr 7103.10	Roteiro topográfico dos códices. (Luanda. Instituto de Investigação Cientifica de Angola. Archivo Histórico.) Angola, 1966.
X Cg	Afr 6283.5	Roth, H.L. Great Benin. Halifax, 1903.
	Afr 6280.68.1	Roth, Henry Ling. Great Benin: its customs, art and horrors. 1st ed. London, 1968.
	Afr 4559.30.30	Roth-Roesthof, A. von. Ba Menelik. Leipzig, 1930.
	Afr 6019.60	Rothchild, Donald. Toward unity in Africa. Washington, 1960.
	Afr 6333.68	Rothchild, Donald S. Politics of integration. Nairobi, 1968.

Afr 8847.83.10	Rothmann, M.E. The drostdy at Swellendam. Swellendam, 1960.
Afr 9489.63	Rotishauser, Josef. Mann in der Mitte. Immensee, 1963.
Afr 3275.21	Rotshtein, F.A. Egypt's ruin. London, 1910.
Afr 3275.17.5	Rotshtein, F.A. Zakhvat i zakabalenie Egipta. Moscow, 1925.
Afr 3275.17.5.2	Rotshtein, F.A. Zakhvat i zakabalenie Egipta. Moscow, 1959.
Afr 1570.41	Rouard de Card, E. Accords secrets entre la France et l'Italie concernant le Maroc et la Lybie. Paris, 1921.
Afr 1738.1	Rouard de Card, E. La defaite des Anglais à Tanger, 1664. n.p., 1912.
Afr 1550.14	Rouard de Card, E. Documents diplomatiques pour servir a l'étude de la question marocaine. n.p., 1911.
Afr 4500.20	Rouard de Card, E. L'Ethiopie auPoint de vue du droit international. Paris, 1928.
Afr 510.9	Rouard de Card, E. La France...en Afrique. Paris, 1903.
Afr 2710.3	Rouard de Card, E. La France et la Turquie dans le Sahara oriental. Paris, 1910.
Afr 2850.5	Rouard de Card, E. La France et l'Italie et l'article 13 du Pacte de Londres. Paris, 1922.
Afr 1571.2	Rouard de Card, E. La frontière franco-marocaine...20 july 1901. Toulouse, 1902.
Afr 1731.1	Rouard De Card, E. L'isle de Perecil. Toulouse, 1903.
Afr 1026.6.2	Rouard de Card, E. Livres français des XVIIe et XVIIIe siècle. Etats Barbaresques. Supplément. Paris, 1917.
Afr 1026.6	Rouard de Card, E. Livres français des XVIIe et XVIIIe siècles concernant les états Barbaresques. Paris, 1911.
Afr 1550.15	Rouard de Card, E. Négociation franco-espagnole de 1902. Paris, 1912.
Afr 2508.2	Rouard de Card, E. La politique de la France. Toulouse, 1906.
Afr 4818.99	Rouard de Card, E. Les possessions françaises de la côte orientale. Paris, 1899.
Afr 510.9.10	Rouard de Card, E. Le prince de Bismarck et l'expansion de la France en Afrique. Paris, 1918.
Afr 1570.15	Rouard de Card, E. Protectorat de la France sur le Maroc. Toulouse, 1905.
Afr 1574.7	Rouard de Card, E. Les relations de l'Espagne et du Maroc. Paris, 1905.
Afr 1840.2	Rouard de Card, E. La réprésentation des indigènes musulmans dans les conseils de l'Algérie. Paris, 1909.
Afr 1738.23F	Rouard De Card, E. Le statut de Tanger d'après la convention du 18 decembre 1923. Paris, 1925.
Afr 505.2	Rouard de Card, E. Les territoires africaines. Paris, 1901.
Afr 1570.2	Rouard de Card, E. Les traités. La France et le Maroc. Paris, 1898.
Afr 510.11.2	Rouard de Card, E. Traités de délimitation concernant l'Afrique franç,aise. Supplément 1910-13. Paris, 1913.
Afr 510.11	Rouard de Card, E. Traités de délimitation concernant l'Afrique française. Paris, 1910.
Afr 510.11.10	Rouard de Card, E. Traités de la France avec les pays de l'Afrique du Nord. Paris, 1906.
Afr 510.2	Rouard de Card, E. Les traités de protectorat. Paris, 1897.
Afr 1570.40	Rouard de Card, E. Traités et accords concernant le protectorat de la France au Maroc. Paris, 1914.
Afr 2525.2	Rouard de Card, E. La Turquie et le protectorat français. Paris, 1916.
Afr 5832.5.5	Roubaud, L. La Bourdonnais. Paris, 1932.
Afr 5180.31	Rouch, J. Sur les côtes du Sénégal et de la Guinée. Paris, 1925.
Afr 7912.10	Rouch, Jane. En cage avec Lumumba. Paris, 1961.
Afr 6192.92	Rouch, Jane. Ghana. Lausanne, 1964.
Afr 6194.20.20	Rouch, Jean. Migrations au Ghana (Gold Coast). Paris, 1956.
Afr 2280.12	Roudaire, F.E. La mer intérieure africaine. Paris, 1883.
Afr 1390.1.5	Roudh el-Kartas. Histoire des souverains du Maghreb. Paris, 1860.
Afr 5342.63	Rougerie, Gabriel. La Côte-d'Ivoire. Paris, 1964.
Afr 2650.2	Rouire, A.M.F. La découverte du bassin hydrographique de la Tunisie centrale. Paris, 1887.
Afr 6903.15	Roukens de Lange, E. South-west Africa, 1946-1960. Bibliography. Cape Town, 1961.
Afr 3809.33	Roulet, Edouard. La mission Roulet. Paris, 1933.
Afr 1609.15	Roulleaux Dugage, G. Lettres du Maroc, illustrations de E. Stoeckel. Paris, 1915.
Afr 8678.250.10	Roumeguère-Eberhardt, Jacqueline. Pensée et société africaines. Paris, 1963.
Afr 6395.2.35	Round Mount Kenya. (Makorere College, Kampala, Uganda.) Kampala, 1960.
Afr 608.93	Round the black man's garden. (Colvile, Zelie.) Edinburgh, 1893.
Afr 2533.1	Rous, Jean. Tunisie...attention. Paris, 1952.
Afr 4559.36.5	Roussan, S.M. Seule en Ethiopie. Paris, 1936.
Afr 2485.1	Rousseau, A. Anales tunisiennes. Alger, 1864.
Afr 8685.327	Rousseau, Francois. Handbook on the Group Areas Act. Cape Town, 1960.
Afr 609.18	Roussel, Raymond. Pages choisies d'impressions d'Afrique et de Locus Solus. Paris, 1918.
Afr 1609.12.5	Rousselet, L. Sur les confins du Maroc. Paris, 1912.
Afr 1955.6.5	Rousset, C. Les commencements d'une conquête. Paris, 1887. 2v.
Afr 1955.6.2	Rousset, C. Les commencements d'une conquête. Paris, 1900. 2v.
Afr 1955.6	Rousset, C. La conquête d'Alger. Paris, 1880.
Afr 1955.6.4	Rousset, C. La conquête d'Alger. Paris, 1899.
Afr 1955.6.3	Rousset, C. La conquête de l'Algerie. v.1,2 and atlas. Paris, 1904. 3v.
Afr 5346.5.5	Roussier, Paul. L'établissement d'Issiny, 1687-1702. Paris, 1935.
Afr 5805.5	La Route des îles, coutribution à l'histoire maritime des Mascareignes. (Toussaint, Auguste.) Paris, 1967.
Afr 5406.191	La route du Tchad. (Dybowski, Jean.) Paris, 1903.
Afr 2035.7	Une route plus large que longue. (Naegelen, Marcel.) Paris, 1956.
Afr 1738.11	Routh, E.M.G. Tangier. London, 1912.
Afr 8676.50.5	Routh, Guy. Industrial relations and race relations. Johannesburg, 195-.
Afr 6395.2	Routledge, W.S. With a prehistoric people, the Akikuyu of British East Africa. London, 1910.
Afr 8687.144	Roux, Edward. S.P. Bunting. Cape Town, 1944.

Afr 8678.53.2 Roux, Edward. Time longer than rope. 2. ed. Madison, 1964.
Afr 1571.17.90 Roux, F. de. La jeunesse de Lyautey. Paris, 1952.
Afr 5758.4 Roux, Jules C. Les voies de communication et les moyens de transport à Madagascar. Paris, 1898.
Afr 6390.60 Roux, Louis. L'Est Africain britannique. Paris, 1950.
Afr 9291.20 Rouxville, 1863-1963. (Uys, Cornelis Janse.) Bloemfontein, 1966.
Afr 1609.62 Rouze, Michel. Maroc. Lausanne, 1962.
Afr 4513.35 Rowan-Robinson, H. England, Italy, Abyssinia. London, 1935.
Afr 8252.77 Rowbotham, A.F. Perilous moments, a true story. London, 1930.
Afr 626.220 Rowe, David Nelson. The new diplomacy; international technical cooperation projects of the Republic of China in African countries. New Haven, 1969.
Afr 3255.7 Rowlatt, Mary. Founders of modern Egypt. London, 1962.
Afr 7308.66.2 Rowley, Henry. The story of the universities' mission to Central Africa. 2nd ed. N.Y., 1969.
Afr 7308.66 Rowley, Henry. Story of the universities' missions to Central Africa. London, 1866.
Afr 555.9.10 Rowley, Henry. Twenty years in Central Africa. 3d ed. London, 1883.
Afr 550.31 Rowling, F. Bibliography of Christian literature. London, 1923.
Afr 2609.61.5 Roy, Claude. Tunisie. Paris, 1961.
Afr 3215.15 Roy, H. La vie héroïque et romantique du docteur Charles Cuny. Paris, 1930.
Afr 1868.59 Roy, J.J.E. Histoire de l'Algérie. Tours, 1859.
Afr 2030.352 Roy, Jules. Autour du drame. Paris, 1961.
Afr 2030.350 Roy, Jules. La guerre d'Algérie. Paris, 1960.
Afr 2030.350.2 Roy, Jules. The war in Algeria. N.Y., 1961.
Afr 2209.11.7 Roy, R. Au pays des mirages. Paris, 1911.
Afr 5320.15.1 A royal African. (Modupe, Prince.) N.Y., 1969.
Afr 210.61.85 Royal African Society. The Africa of 1961. London, 1961.
Afr 8670.9 Royal Automobile Club Of South Africa. In and out of town. Cape Town, 1929.
Afr 6542.5.10 The royal capital of Buganda. (Gutkind, Peter.) The Hague, 1963.
Afr 4360.7 The Royal Chronicle of Abyssinia, 1769-1840. (Royal Chronicle of Abyssinia.) Cambridge, Eng., 1922.
Afr 4360.7 Royal Chronicle of Abyssinia. The Royal Chronicle of Abyssinia, 1769-1840. Cambridge, Eng., 1922.
Afr 28.91 Royal Commonwealth Society, London. Annotated bibliography of recent publications on Africa. London, 1943.
Afr 4700.13.10 Royal Empire Society. London. A bibliography of Italian colonisation in Africa...Abyssinia. London, 1936.
Afr 3258.11 The Royal Engineer in Egypt and the Sudan. (Sandes, E.W.C.) Chatham, 1937.
Afr 8325.52F Royal Engineering Institute, Chatham. Detailed history of railways in South African War. Chatham, 1904. 2v.
Afr 6125.7F Royal gazette. Freetown 3,1821+
Afr 718.9.10 Royal Geographical Society. The lands of Cazembe: Lacerda's journey to Cazembe in 1798. N.Y., 1969.
Afr 626.117 Royal Institue of International Affairs. The African economy. Oxford, 1962.
Afr 4513.20 Royal Institute of International Affairs. Abyssinia and Italy. N.Y., 1935.
Afr 6164.17 Royal Institute of International Affairs. Ghana. London, 1957.
Afr 3305.8 Royal Institute of International Affairs. Great Britain and Egypt, 1914-1951. London, 1952.
Afr 8695.10 Royal Institute of International Affairs. The high commission territories. London, 1963.
Afr 8045.26 Royal Institute of International Affairs. The high commission territories and the Union of South Africa. London, 1956.
Afr 2929.56 Royal Institute of International Affairs. Libya. London, 1956.
Afr 6212.15 Royal Institute of International Affairs. Nigeria. Oxford, 1960.
Afr 7560.5 Le royaume du Congo aux XVe et XVIe siècle. (Bal, W.) Léopoldville, 1963.
Afr 3258.5 Royle, C. The Egyptian campaigns, 1882-85. London, 1886. 2v.
Afr 3258.5.2 Royle, C. The Egyptian campaigns, 1882-85. London, 1900.
Afr 1258.50 Rozet. Algérie, États Tripolitains et Tunis. Paris, 1850.
Afr 2208.33 Rozet. Voyage dans la régence d'Alger. 3 vols. and atlas. Paris, 1833. 4v.
Afr 1990.3 Rozey, A.G. Cris de conscience de l'Algérie. Paris, 1840.
Afr 7549.59.15 Ruanda. (Lacger, L. de.) Kabgayi, 1959.
Afr 7937.8 Ruanda-Urundi, 1884-1919. (Louis, W.R.) Oxford, 1963.
Afr 7533.10 Ruanda-Urundi. (Belgium. Office de l'Information et des Relations Politiques pour le Congo Belge et le Ruanda-Urundi.) Brussels, 1959. 4 pam.
Afr 7940.5 Ruanda Urundi. (Lyr, Claude.) Brussels, 195-.
Afr 6390.29 Ruark, R.C. Harm of the hunter. 1st ed. Garden City, 1953.
Afr 10838.89.100 Rubadiri, David. No bride price. Nairobi, 1967.
Afr 4095.8.4 Rubakin, N.A. Prikliucheniia v strane rabstva. Moscow, 1918.
Afr 6160.25 Rubin, L. The constitution and government of Ghana. London, 1961.
Afr 6282.44 Rubingh, Eugene. Sons of Tiv; a study of the rise of the church among the Tiv of Central Nigeria. Grand Rapids, Michigan, 1969.
Afr 6720.3 Rudin, H.R. Germans in the Cameroons, 1814-1914. London, 1938.
Afr 1965.3 Rückblick auf Algerie (1840-41). (Raasloeff, W.) Altona, 1845.
Afr 1910.10 Rueckblicke auf Algier. (Schwarzenberg, F.) Wien, 1837.
Afr 1550.28 Ruediger, Georg von. Die Bedeutung der Algeciras-Konferenz. München, 1920.
Afr 1550.28.5 Ruediger, Georg von. Die Bedeutung der Algeciras-Konferenz. Inaug.-Diss. Altenburg, 1917.
Afr 4060.2 Rueppell, E. Reisen im Nubien, Kordofan. Text and atlas. Frankfurt, 1829.
Afr 4558.38 Rueppell, Edward. Reise in Abyssinien. Frankfurt, 1838. 2v.
Afr 6585.6 Ruete, E. Memoirs of an Arabian princess. N.Y., 1888.
Afr 1905.1 Ruff, Paul. La domination espagnole à Oran. Paris, 1900.
Afr 109.58 Der ruhelose Kontinent. 1. Aufl. (Italiaander, Rolf.) Düsseldorf, 1958.

Afr 699.68.5 Ruimte en zonlicht. (Laman Trip-de Beaufort, Henriette.) Den Haag, 1968.
Afr 3700.4 The ruin of the Soudan. (Russell, Henry.) London, 1892.
Afr 8163.2 The ruin of Zululand, an account of British doings in Zululand since the invasion of 1879. (Colenso, Frances Ellen.) London, 1884-85. 2v.
Afr 2300.2 Ruined cities within Numidian and Carthaginian territories. (Davis, N.) London, 1862.
Afr 3979.10.5 Ruines et paysages d'Egypte. (Maspero, Gaston.) Paris, 1910.
Afr 575.17.25 Ruini, M. L'islam e le nostre colonie. Città di Castello, 1922.
Afr 1658.7 Ruiz Albeniz, R. El riff, el riff en paz, la guerra del riff. Madrid, 1912.
Afr 1573.25 Ruiz Albeniz, V. Tanger y la colaboración franco española en Marruecos. Madrid, 1927.
Afr 1750.42 Ruiz Albéniz, Víctor. Ecce homo: las responsabilidades del desastre. Madrid, 1922.
Afr 1658.7.2 Ruiz Albéniz, Víctor. Espana en el rif. 2a ed. Madrid, 1921.
Afr 7182.10 Ruiz de Arcaute, H. Por tierras de Angola. Victoria, 1961.
Afr 1739.3.10 Ruiz De Cuevas, T. Apuntes para la historia de Tetuan. Tetuan, 1951.
Afr 9748.807 Rukavina, Kathaleen (Stevens). Jungle pathfinder. London, 1951.
Afr 8155.11 Rule of fear. (Becker, Peter.) London, 1964.
Afr 9439.68 The rulers of Rhodesia from earliest times to the referendum. (Ransford, Oliver.) London, 1968.
Afr 150.18 Rumbucher, K. Heinrich der Seefahrer. München, 1954.
Afr 5900.5 Rumeu de Armas, Antonio. España en el Africa atlantica. V.1-2. Madrid, 1956-57.
Afr 550.160 Run while the sun is hot. (Fuller, William Harold.) N.Y., 1966.
Afr 11757.58.100 Runcie, John. Songs by the stoep. London, 1905.
Afr 6096.17 Runov, Boris B. Iunaited Afrika kompani. Moskva, 1966.
Afr 8380.20 Rupert, Anton. Progress through partnership. Cape Town, 1967.
Afr 18.16 Rural Africana. East Lansing, Mich. 5,1968+
Afr 6277.58 Pamphlet vol. Rural development in eastern Nigeria.
Afr Doc 2309.505F Rural economic survey of Nigeria. (Nigeria. Federal Office of Statistics.) Lagos. 1966+
Afr Doc 2438.5 Rural health report. (Nigeria, Northern. Ministry of Health.) Kaduna. 1963+
Afr 5753.4 Rusillon, H. Un culte dynast. Avec évocation des morts. Paris, 1912.
Afr 5749.33 Rusillon, H. Un petit continent, Madagascar. Paris, 1933.
Afr 6541.28 Russel, John Keith. Men without god. London, 1966.
Afr 9047.21 Russel, Margo. Unemployment among Indians in Durban, 1962. Durban, 1962.
Afr 4558.84 Russel, S. Une mission en Abyssinie. Paris, 1884.
Afr 4115.24 Russell, Dorothea. Medieval Cairo and the monasteries of the Wadi Natrun. London, 1962.
Afr 9060.5 Russell, George. The history of old Durban and reminiscences of an emigrant of 1850. Durban, 1899.
Afr 3700.4 Russell, Henry. The ruin of the Soudan. London, 1892.
Afr 6570.3 Russell, L.M.R. General Rigby, Zanzibar and the slave trade. London, 1935.
Afr 1068.35.2 Russell, M. History of the Barbary states. 2d ed. Edinburgh, 1835.
Afr 1068.35.5 Russell, M. History of the Barbary states. 2d ed. N.Y., 1837.
Afr 4558.33.2 Russell, M. Nubia and Abyssinia. N.Y., 1837.
Afr 4558.33.5 Russell, M. Nubia and Abyssinia. N.Y., 1840.
Afr 4558.33.3 Russell, M. Nubia and Abyssinia. 2d ed. Edinburgh, 1833.
Afr 3068.31 Russell, M. View of ancient and modern Egypt. Edinburgh, 1831.
Afr 3068.31.4 Russell, M. View of ancient and modern Egypt. Edinburgh, 1838.
Afr 3068.31.2 Russell, M. View of ancient and modern Egypt. N.Y., 1836.
Afr 3068.31.6 Russell, M. View of ancient and modern Egypt. 6th ed. Edinburgh, 1844.
Afr 8678.142F Russell, Margo. A study of a South African interracial neighbourhood. Durban, 1961.
Afr 150.4.10 Russell, Peter E. Prince Henry the Navigator. London, 1960.
Afr 4199.25 Russell, T.W. Egyptian service. 1st ed. London, 1949.
Afr 4199.759 Russell pasha. (Seth, Ronald.) London, 1966.
Afr 28.55 Russian materials on Africa. (Loewenthal, R.) Washington, 1958.
Afr 4396.15 The Russians in Ethiopia. (Jesman, Czesław.) London, 1958.
Afr 6455.8.4 Rust. Die deutsche Emin Pascha Expedition. Berlin, 1890.
Afr 5962.2 Rutas de imperio. (Banciella y Barcena, José Cesar.) Madrid, 1944.
Afr 9345.10.10 Ruth and Seretse. (Redfern, John.) London, 1955.
Afr 10115.2.2 Rutherfoord, Peggy. African voices. N.Y., 1960.
Afr 10115.2 Rutherfoord, Peggy. Darkness and light. London, 1958.
Afr 6881.268 Rutman, Gilbert. The economy of Tanganyika. N.Y., 1968.
Afr 5753.15 Ruud, Joergen. Taboo. Oslo, 1960.
Afr 6535.7 Ruwenzori, an account of the expedition of L. Arredo. (Filippi, F. de.) London, 1908.
Afr 6535.7.5 Ruwenzori, an account of the expedition of L. Arredo. (Filippi, F. de.) N.Y., 1908.
Afr 7565.19 Ruytjens, E. Historisch ontstaan der grens van de onafhankelijke. Bruxelles, 1958.
Afr Doc 7819.5 Rwanda. Constitution. Constitution de la République Rwandaise. Kigali, 1963?
Afr Doc 7807.5 Rwanda. Direction de l'Office Général des Statistiques. Bulletin de statistique. Kigali. 1,1964+ 2v.
Afr Doc 7806.5 Rwanda. Embassy. United States. Information bulletin. Washington. 1,1966+
Afr 7947.9 Le Rwanda: mille heures au pays des mille collines. (Lacroix, Benoît.) Montréal, 1966.
Afr 7942.5 Rwanda e Burundi; problemi e prospettive di sviluppo economico. (Masera, Francesco.) Milano, 1963.
Afr 7945.5 Le Rwanda et la civilisation interlacustre. (Heusch, Luc de.) Bruxelles, 1966.
Afr 7937.2 Rwanda politique (1958-1960). (Belgium. Centre de Recherche et d'Information.) Bruxelles, 1961.
Afr 6275.46 Ryan, Isobel. Black man's palaver. London, 1958.
Afr 6192.60 Ryan, Isobel. Black man's town. London, 1958.
Afr 555.6 Ryan, V.W. Mauritius and Madagascar. London, 1864.
Afr 7937.4 Ryckmans, P. Une page d'histoire coloniale. Bruxelles, 1953.

Afr 7567.24   Ryckmans, Pierre. Etapes et jalons. Bruxelles, 1946.
Afr 609.62.55   Rycroft, W.S. A factual study of sub-Saharan Africa. N.Y., 1962.
Afr 6295.130   Ryder, Alan Frederick Charles. Benin and the Europeans, 1485-1897. London, 1969.
Afr 3979.27   Rydh, H. Solskivans land. Stockholm, 1927.
Afr 8659.50.20   Rzeka Limpopo wpada do Tamizy. (Sledzinski, Waclaw.) Warszawa, 1958.
Afr 2030.456   S.O.S. Algérie. (Douxey, Jean.) Paris, 1956.
Afr 7575.67   S.O.S. Congo. (Demany, Fernand.) Bruxelles, 1959.
Afr 8687.144   S.P. Bunting. (Roux, Edward.) Cape Town, 1944.
Afr 8035.5   S.W. Silver and Company's handbook to South Africa. (Silver, S.W.) London, 1880. 2v.
Afr 4392.2   S voiskami Menelika II. (Bulatovitch, A.K.) St. Petersburg, 1900.
Afr 7122.20.2   Sa da Bandeira, B. de S.N. de F. da. Factos e consideraços relativas aos direitos de Portugal. Lisboa, 1855.
Afr 7122.20   Sa da Bandeira, B. de S.N. de F. da. Facts and statistics concerning the right of the crown of Portugal to the territory of Molembo Cabinda, Ambriz. London, 1877.
Afr 3990.25   Saad, Zaki Yusef. Pharaonic egypt, quick visit. Cairo, 1964.
Afr 3285.22   Saad Zaghloul. (Yeghen, Foulad.) Paris, 1927.
Afr 2438.30   Saada, Raoul. Essai sur l'oeuvre de la justice française en Tunisie. Paris, 1928.
Afr 2209.61.10   Saadia. L'aliénation colonialiste et la résistance de la famille algérienne. Lausanne, 1961.
Afr 5920.4   Saavedra y Magdalena, D. España en el Africa occidental. Madrid, 1910.
Afr 5119.25   Sabatie, A. Le Sénégal. Saint-Louis, 1925.
Afr 2285.1   Sabatier, C. La question du sud-ouest. Alger, 1881.
Afr 2748.91   Sabatier, Camille. Touat, Sahara et Soudan. Paris, 1891.
Afr 4259.36.5   Sabelli, L. Storia di Abissinia. v.1-4. Livorno, 1936-38. 4v.
Afr 3310.10.95   Saber, Ali. Nasser en procès face à la nation arabe. Paris, 1968.
Afr 575.16.10   Sabetta, Guido. Politica di penetrazione in Africa. Roma, 1913.
Afr 1570.65   Sabin, Mony. La paix au Maroc. Paris, 1933.
Afr 530.51   Sablier, E. De l'Oural à l'Atlantique. Paris, 1963.
Afr 8678.190   Sabloniere, Margrit. Apartheid. Amsterdam, 1960.
Afr 1755.19   Sablotny, R. Legionnaire in Morocco. Los Angeles, 1940.
Afr 609.58.35   Sabonjo de onstuimige. (Hornman, W.) Leiden, 1958.
Afr 1450.2   Sabran, J. de. Le Maroc rouge. Paris, n.d.
Afr 3230.12.5   Sabry, Mohammed. L'empire égyptien sous Ismail et l'ingérence anglo-française (1863-1879). Paris, 1933.
Afr 3205.7   Sabry, Mohammed. L'empire égyptien sous Mohamed-Ali et la question d'Orient, 1811-1849. Paris, 1930.
Afr 3230.12   Sabry, Mohammed. La genèse de l'esprit national égyptien (1863-1882). Thèse. Paris, 1924.
Afr 3038.25   Sabry, Mohammed. Le pouvoir législatif et le pouvoir exécutif en Egypte. Paris, 1930.
Afr 3038.25.5   Sabry, Mohammed. Le pouvoir législatif et le pouvoir exécutif en Egypte. Thèse. Paris, 1930.
Afr 3199.20   Sabry, Mohammed. La question d'Egypte depuis Bonaparte jusqu'à la révolution de 1919. Paris, 1920.
Afr 3300.10   Sabry, Mohammed. La révolution égyptienne. Paris, 1919. 2v.
Afr 3675.50   Sabry, Mohammed. Le Soudan égyptien. Le Caire, 1947.
Afr 8378.331   Sachs, Albert. The jail diary of Albie Sachs. London, 1966.
Afr 8678.440   Sachs, Albert. South Africa. London, 1969.
Afr 8378.331.30   Sachs, Albert. Stephanie on trial. London, 1968.
Afr 11764.12.102   Sachs, Bernard. Personalities and places. 2nd series. Johannesburg, 1965.
Afr 8369.61.10   Sachs, Bernard. The road from Sharpeville. London, 1961.
Afr 11764.12.100   Sachs, Bernard. South African personalities and places. Johannesburg, 1959.
Afr 8369.52   Sachs, E.S. The choice before South Africa. London, 1952.
Afr 8678.356   Sachs, Emil Solomon. The anatomy of apartheid. London, 1965.
Afr 8849.3   Sachs, W. Black anger. Boston, 1947.
Afr 8678.368   Sacks, Benjamin. South Africa, an imperial dilemma, non-Europeans and the British nation, 1902-1914. 1st ed. Albuquerque, 1967.
Afr 4642.1   The sacred city of the Ethiopians. (Bent, J.J.) London, 1893.
Afr 5320.5   The sacred forest. 1st Amer.ed. (Gaisseau, P.D.) N.Y., 1954.
Afr 11435.3.100   Sacred is the breed. (Granger, Vivian Hector.) Cape Town, 1967.
Afr 6926.27   The sacred trust. (Steward, A.) Johannesburg, 1963.
Afr 3305.10.1   Sadat, Anwar. Geheimtagebuch der ägyptischen Revolution. Düsseldorf, 1957.
Afr 3305.10   Sadat, Anwar. Revolt on the Nile. London, 1957.
Afr Doc 1437.5   Sadd-el-Aali project. (United Arab Republic. Ministry of the High Dam.) n.p., n.d.
Afr 3155.5   Sadeque, Syedah. Baybars I of Egypt. 1st ed. Dacca, 1956.
Afr 5243.343   Sadi, Abd al-Rahman. Tarikh es-Soudan. Paris, 1900.
Afr 12639.18.100   Sadji, Abdoulaye. Nini, mulâtresse du Sénégal. 2. éd. Paris, 1965.
Afr 12639.18.110   Sadji, Abdoulaye. Tounka, nouvelle. Paris, 1965.
Afr 1609.23.25   Sadler, Georges. A travers le Maghreb. Paris, 1923.
Afr 635.7.20   Sadler, M.E. Arts of West Africa, excluding music. London, 1935.
Afr 6455.39.5   Safari. (Johnson, M.) N.Y., 1928.
Afr 6300.79   Safari. Nairobi. 1,1969+
Afr 6455.69   Safari for gold. (Smeaton-Stuart, J.A.) London, 1942.
Afr 6390.75.2   Safari mingi. Wyd.2. (Korabiewicz, Waclaw.) Warszawa, 1963.
Afr 6390.74   Safari przez czarny lad. (Ostrowski, W.) Londyn, 1947.
Afr 8809.62.5   Safe to the sea. (Burman, Jose.) Kaapstad, 1962.
Afr 3199.61A   Safran, N. Egypt in search of political community. Cambridge, 1961.
Afr 810.17   Saga of the Niger. (Owen, Richard.) London, 1961.
Afr 8063.10   The saga of the Transval Scottish Regiment. (Birkby, C.) Cape Town, 1950.
Afr 1367.64   Sagarra, J. de. Compendio de la historia de la España. v.1-2. Barcelona, 1764. 2v.
Afr 5944.22   Sahara, provincia española. (Spain. Consejo Superior de Investigaciones Cientificas. Instituto de Estudios Africanos.) Madrid, 1966.
Afr 2285.3   Le Sahara, souvenirs d'une mission à Goléah. (Choisy, A.) Paris, 1881.
Afr 2749.65   Sahara, terre de vérité . (Besson, Ferny.) Paris, 1965.

Afr 2705   Pamphlet box. Sahara.
Afr 2748.87   El Sahara. (Bonelli, D.E.) Madrid, 1887.
Afr 2749.22.10   Sahara. (Buchanan, Angus.) London, 1926.
Afr 2748.79   Die Sahara. (Chavanne, J.) Vienna, 1879.
Afr 2749.57.10   Sahara. (Cornet, Pierre.) Paris, 1957.
Afr 2749.58.5   Sahara. (Favrod, Charles F.) Lausanne, 1958.
Afr 2749.58   Le Sahara. (Furon, Raymond.) Paris, 1957.
Afr 2749.23.10A   Sahara. (Gautier, E.F.) N.Y., 1935.
Afr 2749.23   Le Sahara. (Gautier, E.F.) Paris, 1923.
Afr 2749.60.5   Sahara. (Gerster, Georg.) London, 1960.
Afr 2731.7   Le Sahara. (Leroy-Beaulieu, P.) Paris, 1904.
Afr 2749.57.20   Sahara. (Norwich, S.) Paris, 1957.
Afr 2749.68   Sahara. (Norwich, John Julius Cooper.) London, 1968.
Afr 2748.93   Le Sahara. (Schirmer, H.) Paris, 1893.
Afr 2749.58.13   Le Sahara. (Verlet, Bruno.) Paris, 1962.
Afr 2719.54   Sahara. 1st ed. (Lecler, René.) Garden City, 1954.
Afr 2285.5   Le Sahara algérien. (Daumas.) Paris, 1845.
Afr 2749.05.5   Sahara algérien et tunisien. (Duveyrier, Henri.) Paris, 1905.
Afr 2749.45.5   Le Sahara aux cent visages. (Lelong, Maurice H., Père.) Paris, 1945.
Afr 2749.60.15   Le Sahara avant le pétrole. (Lerumeur, Guy.) Paris, 1960.
Afr 2749.23.5   Le Sahara avec 10 figures et 26 illustrations hors texte. (Gautier, E.F.) Paris, 1928.
Afr 2749.66   Sahara conquest. (Baker, Richard Saint Barbe.) London, 1966.
Afr 2295.5   Le Sahara de la province de Constantine. (Ragot, W.) Constantine, 1874-75.
Afr 2749.61.10   Sahara de l'aventure. (Frison-Roche, Roger.) Paris, 1961.
Afr 2749.60.10   Le Sahara des Africaines. (Gaudio, Attilio.) Paris, 1960.
Afr 5944.20   El Sahara español. (Hernandez-Pacheco, Francisco.) Madrid, 1962.
Afr 2719.60   Sahara et communauté. (Thomas, Marc-Robert.) Paris, 1960.
Afr 2285.10   Sahara et Laponie. (Goblet D'Alviella.) Paris, 1873.
Afr 2710.4   Le Sahara français. (Bissuel, H.) Alger, 1891.
Afr 2749.69   The Sahara is yours; a handbook for desert travellers. (Stevens, Jon.) London, 1969.
Afr 2929.37   Il Sahara italiano. Pt.1. (Società Geografica Italiana, Rome.) Rome, 1937.
Afr 2929.34.5   Le Sahara italien. (Paris. Musée d'Ethnographie du Trocadéro. Exposition du Sahara, Paris.) Rome, 1934.
Afr 2749.13   Le Sahara occidental. (Angieras, E.M.) Paris, 1919.
Afr 2749.32   El Sahara occidental. 1. ed. (Sanchez, J.G.R.) Madrid, 1932.
Afr 2710.2.3   Sahara-Touat et frontière marocaine. (Lechatelier, A.) n.p., 1901.
Afr 2948.10   Il Sahara tripolitano. (Petragnani, Enrico.) Roma, 1928.
Afr 2749.50   Die Sahara und die Syrten-Länder. 1. Aufl. (Schiffers, H.) Stuttgart, 1950.
Afr 658.79   Sahara und Sudan. (Nachtigal, S.) Berlin, 1879-89.
Afr 2749.40   Sahara unveiled, a great story of French colonial conquest. (Turnbull, P.) London, 1940.
Afr 1750.47   El Sahara y Sur Marroqui españoles. (Guanner, Vicente.) Toledo, 1931.
Afr 2749.27   A Saharan venture. (Cameron, Donald R.) London, 1928.
Afr 2731.3   Un saharien, le colonel Ludovic de Polignac, 1827-1904. (Esquer, G.) Paris, 1930.
Afr 4386.8   Sahati e Dogali. (Antona-Traversi, Camillo.) Roma, 1887.
Afr 5485.10   Saheliens et Sahariens du Tchad. (Lerouvreur, A.) Paris, 1962.
Afr 1069.65   Sahli, Mohamed C. Décoloniser l'histoire. Paris, 1965.
Afr 212.50   Said, Abd al-Aziz. The African phenomenon. Boston, 1968.
Afr 4070.65.5   Said, Beshir Mohammed. The Sudan. London, 1965.
Afr 6465.59   Sailing from Lamu. (Prins, Adriaan Hendrik Johan.) Assen, 1965.
Afr 5585.10   Saillens, R. Nos droits sur Madagascar. Paris, 1885.
Afr 8687.265   Sailor Malan. (Walker, O.) London, 1953.
Afr 4338.301   Saineanu, M. L'Abyssinie dans la seconde moitié du XVI siècle. Inaug. Diss. Leipzig, 1892.
Htn   Afr 1606.96*   St. Amant. Voyage de St. Amant. Lyon, 1698.
Afr 11683.88.100   Saint Andrew's day, 1919-61. (Petrie, J.) Pietermaritzburg, 1962.
Afr 8019.6   Saint Benedicts booklets. Johannesburg. 2+
Afr 2223.950   Saint Germes, Jean. Economie algérienne. Alger, 1950.
Afr 2223.950.2   Saint Germes, Jean. Economie algérienne. Alger, 1955. 2 pam.
Afr 2607.36   Saint-Gervais, M. Memoires, historiques qui concernent le gouvernement...de Tunis. Paris, 1736.
Afr 855.12   St. Helena. Extracts from the St. Helena records. St. Helena, 1885.
Afr 855.12.5   St. Helena. Extracts from the St. Helena records. 2 ed. St. Helena, 1908.
Afr 8808.52   Saint Helena and the Cape of Good Hope. (Hatfield, E.F.) N.Y., 1852.
Afr 3978.57.5   Saint Hilaire, J.B. Egypt and the great Suez Canal. London, 1857.
Afr 4050.3   Saint John, B. Adventures in the Libyan desert. N.Y., 1849.
Afr 3978.56.5   Saint John, B. Two years residence in a Levantine family. London, 1856.
Afr 4105.1   Saint John, B. Two years residence in a Levantine family. Paris, 1850.
Afr 3978.53   Saint John, Bayle. Village life in Egypt. Boston, 1853. 2v.
Afr 3978.34   Saint John, J.A. Egypt, and Mohammed Ali. vol.1-2. London, 1834. 2v.
Afr 3978.45.5   Saint John, J.A. Egypt and Nubia. London, 1845.
Afr 3978.45   Saint John, J.A. Egypt and Nubia. London, 1845.
Afr 8369.54   Saint John, Robert. Through Malan's Africa. London, 1954.
Afr 8289.03.12   Saint Leger, S.E. War sketches in colour. London, 1903.
Afr 9072.5   St. Leger-Gordon, Ruth E. Shepstone: the role of the family in the history of South Africa, 1820-1900. Cape Town, 1968.
Afr 5190.18   Saint-Louis du Sénégal. (Duchemin, G.) Saint-Louis, 1955.
Afr 2208.46.4   Saint-Marie, Count. A visit to Algeria in 1845. London, 1846.
Afr 3285.2   Saint-Martin, H. de. La question égyptienne et l'Italie. Florence, 1884.
Afr 5130.30   Saint-Martin, Yves. L'empire toucouleur et la France un demi-siècle de relation diplomatiques, 1846-1893. Dakar, 1967.
Htn   Afr 1606.94*   St. Olon, P. Etat present de l'empire de Maroc. Paris, 1694.
Htn   Afr 1606.94.5*   St. Olon, P. Present state of Morocco. London, 1695.
Htn   Afr 1606.94.3*   St. Olon, P. Relation de l'empire de Maroc. Paris, 1695.

Afr 2609.04.5   Saint-Paul, Georges. Souvenirs de Tunisie et d'Algérie. Tunis, 1909.

Afr 5842.4.5   Saint-Pierre, J.H.B. de. Viaggi al Madagascar, alle isole Comore ed all'Isola di Francia. Prato, 1844.

Afr 5842.4   Saint-Pierre, J.H.B. de. Voyage à l'Isle de France. Amsterdam, 1773. 2v.

Afr 1570.39   Saint-Rene-Taillaudier, Georges. Les origines du Maroc français. Paris, 1930.

Afr 8849.141   Saint Theodore and the crocodile. (Bosman di Ravelli, Vere.) Cape Town, 1964.

Afr 5765.7   Saint Vincent de Paul et les missions de Madagascar. (Malotet, A.) Paris, 1900.

Afr 1570.31   Sainte-Chapelle, A.M.G. La conquête du Maroc (mai 1911-mars 1913). Paris, 1913.

Afr 555.12   Sainte-Marie, E. de. La Tunisie chrétienne. Lyon, 1878.

Afr 5790.2   Sainte-Marie et la côte est de Madagascar en 1818. (Valette, Jean.) Tananarive, 1962.

Afr 3974.83.9   Les saintes pérégrinations... Texte ... Par F. Larrinaz. (Breydenbach, B. von.) Le Caire, 1904.

Afr 5180.22   Saintlo, A. de. Relation du voyage du Cap-Verd. Paris, 1637.

Afr 5405.179   Saintoyant, J.F. L'affaire du Congo 1905. Paris, 1960.

Afr 1609.58   Saints and sorcerers. (Epton, Nina C.) London, 1958.

Afr 1635.40   Saints of the Atlas. (Gellner, Ernest.) London, 1969.

Afr 10018.3   Sainville, L. Anthologie de la littérature nègro-africaine. Paris, 1963- 2v.

Afr 5758.66   Sala, G. Les travaux au ras du sol; l'investissement humain à Madagascar. Tananarive, 1966.

Afr 2208.66.8   Sala, George A. A trip to Barbary. London, 1866.

Afr 2624.912   Sala, R. Le budget tunisien. Paris, 1912.

Afr 2688.2   Saladin, H. Tunis et Kairouan. Paris, 1908.

Afr 6196.14.5   Salaga: the struggle for power. (Braiman, Joseph Adam.) London, 1967.

Afr 6196.29   The Salaga papers. v.1-2. (Johnson, M.) Legen, 1967-

Afr 1609.31.30   Salah and his American. (Hall, Leland.) N.Y., 1935.

Afr 3079.66   Salakh-ad-Din i Mamliuki v Egipte. (Semenova, Lidiia Andreevna.) Moskva, 1966.

Afr 1930.1   Salame, A. Narrative of the expedition to Algiers in 1816. London, 1819.

Afr 4892.11   Salata, F. Il nodo di Gibuti, storia diplomatica su documenti inediti. Milano, 1939.

Afr 7222.90   Saldanha, Eduardo d'Almeida. Moçambique perante genébra. Porto, 1931.

Afr 7320.17   Saldanha, Eduardo d'Almeida. O Sul do Save. Lisboa, 1928-31. 2v.

Afr 3040.67   Saleh, Diaeddine. Les pouvoirs du roi dans la constitution égyptienne. Paris, 1939.

Afr 6590.5   Saleh, Ibuni. A short history of the Comorians in Zanzibar. Tanganyika, 1936.

Afr 3040.5   Salem, M.S. Les principes du self government local dans les democraties modernes et leur application au régime administratif égyptien. Thèse. Dijon, 1923.

Afr 4513.36.100   Salemi, L. Politica estera. Palermo, 1936.

Afr 8145.34   The salient of South Africa. (Victor, Osmund.) London, 1931.

Afr 4390.55   Salimbeni, A., Conte. Crispi e Menelick nel diario inedito del Conte Augusto Salimbeni. Torino, 1956.

Afr 5365.5   Salinis, A. Le protectorat français sur la Côte des Esclaves. Paris, 1908.

Afr 9425.25   Salisbury, Rhodesia. University College of Rhodesia and Nyasaland. Department of African Studies. Occasional paper. 1+

Afr Doc 3889.5F   Salisbury, Rodesia. City Council. African Administration Department. Annual report. Salisbury. 1964+

Afr 9515.5.2   Salisbury. The city of Salisbury. 2. ed. Cape Town, 1957.

Afr 109.20.10   Salkin, Paul. Etudes africaines. Bruxelles, 1920.

Afr 4886.5   Salma, L. de. Obock. Paris, 1893.

Afr 1453.7   Salmon, Albert. Le Maroc. Paris, 1908.

Afr 3979.15.5   Salmon, P.R. The wonderland of Egypt. N.Y., 1915.

Afr 1608.94.14   Salmon, Les français au Maroc, mort du sultan. Paris, 1894.

Afr 4558.14.5   Salt, Henry. A voyage to Abyssinia, and travels into the interior of that country. 1st ed. London, 1967.

Afr 4558.14.2   Salt, Henry. Voyage to Abyssinia. Philadelphia, 1816.

Afr 19.12   Salvador, Brazil. Universidade. Centro de Estudos Afro-Orientais. Publicações.

Afr 500.40   Salvador, M. La penetración demografica europea in Africa. Torino, 1932.

Afr 2945.22   Salvadori, Alessandro. La Cirenaica ed i suoi servizi civile. Roma, 1914.

Afr 6420.30.5   Salvadori, M. La colonisation européenne au Kenya. Paris, 1938.

Afr 2710.6   Salvati, Cesare. Italia e Francia nel Sahara orientale. Milano, 1929.

Afr 4513.36.45   Salvemini, G. Can Italy live at home. N.Y., 1936.

Afr 8659.05.5   Samassa, Paul. Das neue Südafrika. Berlin, 1905.

Afr 10939.2   Samkange, Stanlake. On trial for my country. London, 1966.

Afr 9439.68.5   Samkange, Stanlake John Thompson. Origins of Rhodesia. London, 1968.

Afr 3978.38.5   Sammarco, A. Il viaggio di Mohammed Ali al Sudan. Caire, 1929.

Afr 3300.39.5   Sammarco, Angelo. Egitto moderno. Roma, 193-.

Afr 3199.37   Sammarco, Angelo. Histoire de l'Égypte moderne depuis Mohammed Ali jusqu'à l'occupation britannique. Le Caire, 1937.

Afr 4025.20.25   Sammarco, Angelo. Gli italiani in Egitto. Alessandria, 1937.

Afr 3205.17   Sammarco, Angelo. Il regno di Mohammed Ali nei documenti diplomatici italiani inediti. v.1,8,9,10. Caire, 1930-32. 4v.

Afr 4178.5   Sammarco, Angelo. Suez, storia e problemi. Milano, 1943.

Afr 607.90   Sammlung merkwüdiger Reisen in dem Innre von Afrika. (Cuhn, E.W.) Leipzig, 1790. 3v.

Afr 7322.12   Sampaio, Matheus Augusto Ribeiro de. Cartas, officios, ordens de serviço lavrada a 23 de dezembro de 1897 e alguns documentos. Lisboa, 1898.

Afr Doc 3809.515   Sample survey of African agriculture, Southern Rhodesia, 1959/60. (Rhodesia and Nyasaland. Central Statistical Office.) Salisbury, 1962.

Afr 210.60.5   Sampson, Anthony. Common sense about Africa. London, 1960.

Afr 8678.72   Sampson, Anthony. Drum. London, 1956.

Afr 8369.58.10A   Sampson, Anthony. The treason cage. London, 1958.
Afr 8678.365

Afr 6198.79.1   Sampson, Harold Fehrsan. The principle of apartheid. Johannesburg, 1966.

Afr 8360.5   Sampson, Magnus John. Makers of modern Ghana. Accra, 1969.

Afr 8289.31   Sampson, P.J. The capture of De Wet. The South African rebellion, 1914. London, 1915.

Afr 8252.21   Sampson, V. Anti-commando. London, 1931.

Afr 6686.25   Sampson, Victor. My reminiscences. London, 1926.

Afr 679.00   Samuel, Ferjus. La muse en valeur du Togo sous le mandat français. Thèse. Paris, 1926.

Afr 4199.90A   Samuel Braun. (Henning, G.) Basel, 1900.

Afr 8685.3   Samuel Shepheard of Cairo. (Bird, Michael.) London, 1957.

Afr 8155.12   Samuelson, L.H. Some Zulu customs and folk-lore. London, n.d.

Afr 8155.12   Samuelson, Robert Charles Azariah. Long, long ago. Durban, 1929.

Htn   Afr 1606.44*   San Francisco, Matias de. Relacion del viage espiritual. Madrid, 1644.

Afr 5993.14   San Javier. Tres años en Fernando Poo. Madrid, 1875.

Afr 7190.40   San Thome, Africa. Direcção dos Portos e Viação. Missão geodesica. Porto, 1917.

Afr 7190.16   San Tome e principe. (Portugal. Agencia Geral do Ultramar.) Lisboa, 1964.

Afr 150.17   Sanceau, Elaine. Henry the Navigator. London, 194-.

Afr 150.17.5   Sanceau, Elaine. Henry the Navigator. N.Y., 1947.

Afr 4320.10.5   Sanceau, Elaine. The land of Prester John. 1st American ed. N.Y., 1944.

Afr 4320.10   Sanceau, Elaine. Portugal in quest of Prester John. London, 1943.

Afr 1658.40   Sanchez, J.G. Nuestro protectorado. Madrid, 1930.

Afr 2749.32   Sanchez, J.G.R. El Sahara occidental. 1. ed. Madrid, 1932.

Afr 1658.42   Sanchez Javaloy, Roque. El Manco de Tikun. Murcia, 1935.

Afr 2945.7   Sanctis, E. de. Dalla Canea a Tripoli. Roma, 1912.

Afr 150.5   Sanctos Firmo, M. Noticia sobre a vida e escriptos do Infante Dom Henrique. Lisboa, 1866.

Afr 3979.38.5   Sanctuaries. (Herriot, E.) Roma, 1938.
Afr 3978.49.20

Afr 6883.6   Sand and canvas, a narrative of adventures in Egypt. (Bevan, Samuel.) London, 1849.

Afr 9093.22   Die Sandawe...Material aus deutsch Ostafrika. (Dempwolff, Otto.) Hamburg, 1916.

Afr 8658.80   Sandberg, Christoph Georg. Twintig jaren onder Kugers Boeren in voor-en tegenspoed. Amsterdam, 1944.

Afr 4559.29.5   Sandeman, E.F. Eight months in an ox-wagon. London, 1880.

Afr 200.9.5   Sander, Erich. Das Hochland von Abessinien, Habesch. Heidelberg, 1929.

Afr 200.9   Sanderson, E. Africa in the 19th century. London, 1898.

Afr 505.4   Sanderson, E. Africa in the 19th century. N.Y., 1898.

Afr 3715.12   Sanderson, E. Great Britain in modern Africa. London, 1907.

Afr 5235.180.2   Sanderson, George Neville. England, Europe and the upper Nile, 1882-1899. Edinburgh, 1965.

Afr 5235.180   Sanderval, A.O., vicomte de. De l'Atlantique au Niger. Paris, 1883.

Afr 5318.10   Sanderval, A.O., vicomte de. De l'Atlantique au Niger par le Foutah-Djallon. Paris, 1882.

Afr 3258.11   Sanderval, C. de. Soudan français...Kahel. Paris, 1893.

Afr 4430.46A   Sandes, E.W.C. The Royal Engineer in Egypt and the Sudan. Chatham, 1937.

Afr 4430.55.6   Sandford, C.L. Ethiopia under Haile Selassie. London, 1946.

Afr 4430.55.5   Sandford, C.L. The Lion of Judah hath prevailed. London, 1955.

Afr 6460.58F   Sandford, C.L. The Lion of Judah hath prevailed. N.Y., 1955.

Afr 6283.2   Sandford, G.R. An administrative and political history. London, 1919.

Afr 550.72   Sandolphe, J.F. Memoires. Paris, 1823. 2v.

Afr 2870.18   Sandoval, Alonso de. De instauranda Aethiopum salute. Bogata, 1956.

Afr 1259.27.25   Sandri, S. Il generale Rodolfo Graziani. Roma, 19-

Afr 9448.50   Sands, palms and minarets. (Vernon, M.) London, 1927.

Afr 4700.36.10   Sanger, Clyde. Central African emergency. London, 1960.

Afr 9029.62   Sangiorgi, G.M. L'impero italiano nell'Africa orientale. Bologna, 1934.

Afr 6460.72   Sangoma. (Gatti, Attilio.) London, 1962.

Afr 575.22.5   Sangree, Walter H. Age, prayer, and politics Ineriki, Kenya. N.Y., 1966.

Afr 1750.22   Sangroniz, José A. Modalidades del islamismo marroqui. Madrid, 1950.

Afr 4513.15   Sangroniz, Jose Antonio De. Marruecos, sus condiciones fisicas. 2 ed. Madrid, 1926.

Afr 555.147   Sangue italiano in Etiopia. (Micaletti, K.) Firenze, 1933.

Afr 1736.4   Sanita, Giuseppe. La Barberia e la Sacra Congregazione. Cairo, 1963.

Afr 200.16   Santa Cruz de Mar Pequeña. (Alcala Galiano, Pelayo.) Madrid, 1900.

Afr 4742.26   Santa-Rita, José. A Africa nas relações. Lisboa, 1959.

Afr 4660.5   Santagata, F. La colonia Eritrea. Napoli, 1935.

Afr 1769.7   Santagata, Fernando. L'Harar. Milano, 1940.

Afr 3669.5   Santamaria Quesada, R. Quien es el glani. Tetuan, 1955.

Afr 3816.4   Santandrea, S. Bibliografia di studi africani. Verona, 1948.

Afr 115.1   Santandrea, Stefano. A tribal history. Bologna, 1964.

Afr 5180.14.10   Santarem, M.F. de B. Memoria sobre a prioridade dos descobrimentos portugueses. Porto, 1841.

Afr 679.58.15   Santarem, M.F. de B. Notice sur André Alvares d'Almada et sa description de la Guinée. Paris, 1842.

Afr 2510.1   Santarem, Manuel Francisco de B. Memoria sobre a prioridade dos descobrimentos. Lisboa, 1958.

Afr 1658.49   Santiago Guerrero, M. La columna saro en la campana de alhucemas. Barcelona, 1926.

Afr 1753.10   Santissima virgem d'Africa, padroeira de Ceuta. (Dornellas, Affonso De.) Lisboa, 1924.

Afr 7176.16   Santos, A.L.F. dos. Estrutura do comercio externo de Angola. Lisboa, 1959.

Afr 7175.30   Santos, Afonso C.V.T. dos. Angola coração do imperio. Lisboa, 1969.

Afr 6291.66   Santos, Eduardo dos. A questão de Biafra. Porto, 1968.

Afr 630.69.5   Santos, Eduardo dos. Elementos de etnologia africana. Lisboa, 1969.

Afr 210.68   Santos, Eduardo dos. Ideologias politicas africanas. Lisboa, 1968.

Afr 115.20.10	Schiffers, Heinrich. Afrika, als die Weissen kamen. Düsseldorf, 1967.
Afr 609.57	Schiffers, Heinrich. Afrika. 4. Aufl. Frankfurt, 1957.
Afr 609.57.2	Schiffers, Heinrich. Afrika. 8. Aufl. München, 1967.
Afr 2719.36	Schiffers-Davringhausen, H. Stumme Front. Leipzig, 1936.
Afr 8289.64.5	Schikkerling, Roland William. Commando courageous. Johannesburg, 1964.
Afr 8289.64.10	Schikkerling, Roland William. Hoe ry die Boere; i 'n kommando-dagboek. Johannesburg, 1964.
Afr 608.91.10	Schilderungen Suaheli. (Velten, Carl.) Göttingen, 1901.
Afr 699.05	Schillings, C.G. Flashlights in the jungle. N.Y., 1905.
Afr 9599.07.5	Schillings, C.G. In wildest Africa. N.Y., 1907.
Afr 3817.6.5	Die Schilluk. (Hofmayr, Wilhelm.) St. Gabriel, 1925.
Afr 9050.15	Schimlek, Francis. Mariannhill. Mariannhill, 1953.
Afr 2208.34	Schimper, W. Reise nach Algier in den Jahren 1831-32. Stuttgart 1834
Afr 6978.91	Sching, H. Deutsch-Südwest-Afrika. Oldenburg, 1891.
Afr 5180.13.3	Schipbreuk van het fregat Medusa. (Savigny, J.B.H.) Haarlem, 1818.
Afr 2748.93	Schirmer, H. Le Sahara. Paris, 1893.
Afr 9705.10A	Schism and continuity in African society. (Turner, O.W.) Manchester, 1957.
Afr 550.165	Schism and renewal in Africa. (Barrett, David B.) Nairobi, 1968.
Afr 1432.6	Schlagintweit, E. Der spanisch-marokkanische Krieg...1859-60. Leipzig, 1863.
Afr 4313.3	Schleicher, A.W. Geschichte der Galla. Berlin, 1893.
Afr 4045.2	Schleiden, M.J. Die Landenge von Suez. Leipzig, 1858.
Afr 2609.60	Schleinitz, E.G. Tunisien. Frankfurt a.M., 1960.
Afr 545.10A	Schlosser, Katesa. Propheten in Afrika. Braunschweig, 1949.
Afr 7815.1F	Schmeltz, J.D.E. Album...ethnography...Congo-basin. Leyden, n.d.
Afr 6738.40	Schmidt, Agathe. Die rote Landenschnur. Berlin, 1955.
Afr 6585.2	Schmidt, K.W. Zanzibar. Leipzig, 1888.
Afr 6777.3	Schmidt, R. Geschichte des Araberaufstandes in Ost-Afrika. Frankfurt, n.d.
Afr 8685.70	Schmidt-Pretoria, W. Deutsche Wanderung nach Südafrika im 19. Jahrhundert. Berlin, 1955.
Afr 8110.20	Schmidt-Pretoria, W. Der Kulturanteil des Deutschtums am Aufbau des Burenvolkes. Hannover, 1938.
Afr 2209.12.15	Schmitthenner, H. Tunisien und Algerien. Stuttgart, 1924.
Afr 7815.5.9	Schmitz, Robert. Les Baholoholo. 9. Bruxelles, 1912.
Afr 6276.2	Schmoelder, Konstanz. Nigeria, von der traditionellen Gemeinschaft zur angepassten Sozialpolitik. Stuttgart, 1966.
Afr 5760.2	Schnackenberg, H. Beitrag zur ethnographie Madagaskars. Strassburg, 1888.
Afr 5055.61	Schnapper, Bernard. La politique et le commerce français dans le Golfe de Guinée. Paris, 1961.
Afr 6780.9	Schnee, A. Meine Erlebnisse Während der Kriegszeit in Deutsch-Ostafrika. Leipzig, 1918.
Afr 6780.14	Schnee, Heinrich. Deutsch-ostafrika Während des Weltkrieges. Berlin, 1919.
Afr 6886.3	Schneider, Karl-Günther. Dar es Salaam. Wiesbaden, 1965.
Afr 2208.65.4	Schneider, O. Tagebuch aus Algier. Dresden, n.d.
Afr 2608.72	Schneider, O. Von Algier nach Tunis und Constantine. Dresden, 1872.
Afr 4571.3	Schneiders, Toni. L'Ethiopie. Paris, 1958.
Afr 8685.60	Schnell, E.L.G. For men must work. Capetown, 1954.
Afr 1680.2.5	Schnell, P. L'atlas marocain d'apres les documents originaux. Paris, 1898.
Afr 3725.3	Schnitzer, E. Emin Pasha in Central Africa. London, 1888.
Afr 5185.7	Schobel, Fred. The world in miniature, Africa. v.2-3. London, n.d. 2v.
Afr 3978.46	Schoelcher, V. L'Egypte en 1845. Paris, 1846.
Afr 6390.4	Schoeller, M. Mitteilungen über Aquatorial-Ost-Afrika, 1896-97. v.1-2. and plates. Berlin, 1901. 3v.
Afr 810.13	Schoen, J.F. Journals of Schoen and S. Crowther...expedition up Niger. London, 1842.
Afr 1550.38	Schoettle, Hermann. Die Times in der ersten Marokkokrise. Vaduz, 1965.
Afr 11774.39.120	Scholefield, Alan. The eagles of malice. N.Y., 1968.
Afr 11774.39.110	Scholefield, Alan. Great elephant. London, 1967.
Afr 11774.39.100	Scholefield, Alan. A view of vultures. London, 1966.
Afr 6990.79	Scholl, Carl. Nach Kamerun. Leipzig, 1886.
Afr 7575.55	Scholl-Latour, Peter. Matata am Kongo. Stuttgart, 1961.
Afr 9225.20	Scholtz, G.D. Die konstitusie en die staatsinstellings van die Oranje-Vrystaat, 1854-1902. Amsterdam, 1936.
Afr 9225.20.5	Scholtz, G.D. President Johannes Henricus Brand, 1823-1888. Johannesburg, 1957.
Afr 8360.10	Scholtz, G.D. Die rebellie, 1914-15. Johannesburg, 1942.
Afr 8089.54.10	Scholtz, G.H. Suid-Afrika en die wereldpolitiek 1652-1952. Johannesburg, 1954.
Afr 8380.2	Scholtz, Gert. Die Republiek van Suid-Afrika. Johannesburg, 1962.
Afr 8279.48	Scholtz, Gert D. Die oorsake van die tweede vryheids-oorlog. Johannesburg, 1948-49. 2v.
Afr 8050.18	Scholtz, Gert Daniel. Die bedreiging van die liberalisme. Pretoria, 1966.
Afr 609.57.5	Schomburgk, Hans Hermann. Zelte in Afrika. 1. Aufl. Berlin, 1957.
Afr 8687.335.5	Schonegevel, Bernardo. This much I'll tell. Cape Town, 1959.
Afr 8825.8	Schonken, F.T. De oorsprong der kaapsch-hollandsche volksoveringen. Amsterdam, 1914.
Afr Doc 309.505	School census for Ethiopia. Addis Ababa. 1961+
Afr 6565.25	A school history of Zanzibar. (Ingrams, W.H.) London, 1925.
Afr 9060.28	Schooners and sky scrapers. (Rosenthal, Eric.) Cape Town, 1963.
Afr 8045.50	Schoor, M.C.E. Republieke en republikeine. Kaapstad, 1960.
Afr 9291.18	Schoor, Marthinus. Edenburg. Edenburg, 1963.
Afr 8252.172.16.2	Schoor, Marthinus Cornelius Ellnarius van. Christiaan Rudolph de Wet, 1854-1922. 2. uitg. Bloemfontein, 1964.
Afr 8289.02.28	Schowalter, A. Die Buren in der Kap Kolonie im Kriege mit England. München, 1902.
Afr 6310.38	Schrader, R. Die Zwangsarbeit in Ostafrika nach deutschen und britischen Kolonialrecht. Hamburg, 1919.
Afr 1270.10	Schramm, Josef. Nordafrika. 2. Aufl. Buchenhain von München, 1967.
Afr 3143.15	Schregle, Goetz. Die Sultanin Sagarat ad-Durr. Inaug.-Diss. Erlangen, 1960.

Afr 3143.18	Schregle, Goetz. Die Sultanin von Ägypten. Wiesbaden, 1961.
Afr 212.30	Schreie aus dem Dschungel. (Barcata, Louis.) Stuttgart, 1962.
Afr 8659.00.5	Schreiner, O. Losse gedachten over Zuid-Afrika. Haarlem, 1900.
Afr 8175.13	Schreiner, O. Thoughts on South Africa. N.Y., 1923.
Afr 8278.99.03	Schreiner, Olive. An English-South African's view of the situation. London, 1899.
Afr 8278.99F	Schreiner, Olive. An English-South African's view of the situation. London, 1899.
Afr 8278.99.29	Schreiner, Olive. The South African question. Chicago, 1899.
Afr 8377.2	Schreiner, Oliver Deneys. The nettle. Johannesburg, 1964.
Afr 4559.28.15	Schrenzel, E.H. Abessinien. Berlin, 1928.
Afr 8326.20	Schreuder, Deryck Marshall. Gladstone and Kruger. liberal government and colonial "home rule". London, 1969.
Afr 8745.10	Schriener, O. The political situation. London, 1896.
Afr 2731.15.105	Schriften. (Foucauld, Charles.) Einsiedeln, 1961.
Afr 4.5	Schriftenreihe. (Deutsche Africa-Gesellschaft, Bonn.) Bonn. 1+
Afr 8846.25	Schroth, H. Die Transkei-Territorien, ihre Entstehung. Inaug. Diss. Bottropi, 1936.
Afr 6925.10	Schuessler, W. Adolf Luederitz, ein deutscher Kanipf um Südafrika 1883-1886. Bremen, 1936.
Afr 8678.333	Schuette, H.G. Weisse ismen, schwarze fakten. Vaterstetten, 1963.
Afr 6292.9.15	Schultze, Arnold. The sultanate of Bornu. London, 1913.
Afr 8678.12	Schultze, L. Aus Namaland und Kalahari. Jena, 1907.
Afr 608.97	Schulz, A. The new Africa. London, 1897.
Afr 2609.63	Schuman, L.O. Tunesie. Meppel, 1963.
Afr 7549.62.15	Schuyler, Philippa. Who killed the Congo? N.Y., 1962.
Afr 2625.5	Schwab, M. Mémoire sur l'ethnographie de la Tunisie. Paris, 1868.
Afr 6926.2	Schwabe, K. In deutschen Diamantenlande, Deutsch-Südwest-Afrika, 1884-1910. Berlin, 1909.
Afr 6978.99	Schwabe, K. Mit Schwert inDeutsch-Südwestafrika. Berlin, 1899.
Afr 8685.70.5	Schwaer, J. Deutsche in Kaffraria. King Williams Town, 1958.
Afr 6883.33	Schwärze. (Nigmann, Ernst.) Berlin, 1922.
Afr 2208.81	Schwarz, B. Algerien. Leipzig, 1881.
Afr 6738.8.5	Schwarz, B. Kamerun, Reise in die Hinterlande der Kolonie. 2e Ausgabe. Leipzig, 1888.
Afr 9400.10.15	Schwarz, E.H.L. The Kalahari and its native races. London, 1928.
Afr 6214.32	Schwarz, Frederick August Otto. Nigeria; the tribes, the nation, or the race. Cambridge, 1965.
Afr 4500.24	Schwarz, H. Die Entwicklung der völkerrechtlichen Beziehungen äthiopiens zu den Mächten seit 1885. Breslau, 1937.
Afr 6214.23	Schwarz, Walter. Nigeria. London, 1968.
Afr 4573.30	Schwarz, William L.K. Industrial investment climate in Ethiopia. Menlo Park, Calif., 1968.
Afr 6985.7	Schwarz und weiss am Waterberg. (Scheer, Maximillian.) Schwerin, 1961.
Afr 630.54.5	Schwarz und Weiss in Afrika. (Hafter, Rudolf.) Zürich, 1954.
Afr 5019.58.4	Schwarzafrika i Geographie, Bevölkering. (Suret-Canale, Jean.) Berlin, 1966. 2v.
Afr 212.42	Schwarze Haut im roten Griff. (Italiaander, Rolf.) Düsseldorf, 1962.
Afr 530.12.5	Die schwarze Sonne. (Welk, E.) Berlin, 1933.
Afr 628.240	Die schwarze Völkerwanderung. (Sell, Manfred.) Wien, 1940.
Afr 6455.73.5	Schwarzenberg, A. A Kenya farmer looks at his colony. N.Y., 1946.
Afr 1910.10	Schwarzschild, F. Rueckblicke auf Algier. Wien, 1837.
Afr 1623.899	Schwegel, H. Marokko. Wien, 1899.
Afr 715.3.25	Schweinfurth, G. Afrikanisches Skizzenbuch. Berlin, 1925.
Afr 715.3.30	Schweinfurth, G. Georg Schweinfurth. Stuttgart, 1954.
Afr 715.3	Schweinfurth, G. The heart of Africa. London, 1873. 2v.
Afr 715.3.3	Schweinfurth, G. The heart of Africa. N.Y., 1874. 2v.
Afr 715.2	Schweinfurth, G. Im Herzen von Afrika. Leipzig, 1874. 2v.
Afr 28.5	Schweinfurth, G. Veröffentliche Briefe,Aufsätze und Werke. Berlin, 1907.
Afr 575.14	Schweinfurth, G. Die Wiedergeburt Ägnptens. Berlin, 1895.
Afr 5426.100.20	Schweitzer, Albert. A l'orée de la forêt vierge. Paris, 1929.
Afr 5426.100.15	Schweitzer, Albert. The forest hospital at Lambaréné. N.Y., 1931.
Afr 5426.100.10	Schweitzer, Albert. From my African note-book. London, 1938.
Afr 5426.100	Schweitzer, Albert. On the edge of the primeval forest. London, 1922.
Afr 5426.100.5	Schweitzer, Albert. On the edge of the primeval forest. London, 1928.
Afr 5426.100.12	Schweitzer, Albert. Zwischen Wasser und Urwald. München, 1949.
Afr 5426.100.65	Pamphlet vol. Schweitzer, Albert. 3 pam.
Afr 3725.7.5	Schweitzer, G. Von Khartum zum Kongo. Berlin, 1932.
Afr 9769.39	Schwerin, W. Nyassaland. Neudamm, 1934.
Afr 6878.90.5	Schynse, August. Mit Stanley und Emin Pascha durch deutsch Öst-Afrika. Köln, 1890.
Afr 7808.89.3	Schynse, P.A. Zwei Jahre am Congo. Köln, 1889.
Afr 8028.200.5	The science of archives in South Africa. (Botha, C.G.) Johannesburg, 1937.
Afr 3993.18	The scientific industrial record. Cairo. 1,1966+
Afr 626.136.4	Scientific research in Africa. (International Conference on the Organization of Research and Training in Africa in Relation to the Study, Conservation and Utilization of Natural Resources, Lagos, 1964.) Lagos, 1964.
Afr 50.45	Scipio. Emergent Africa. Boston, 1965.
Afr 8279.00.11	Scoble, J.B. The rise and fall of Krugerism. London, 1900.
Afr 28.120.2	The SCOLMA directory of libraries and special collections on Africa. 2nd ed. (Standing Conference on Library Materials on Africa.) London, 1967.
Afr 3976.17	Scortia, J.B. De natura et incremento nili. Lugduni, 1617.
Afr 28.93	Scotland. Record Office. Material relating to Africa. Edinburgh, 1962-65.
Afr 1259.21	Scott, A. Maccallum. Barbary. London, 1921.

Afr 1259.21.2   Scott, A. Maccallum. Barbary. N.Y., 1921.
Afr 550.9   Scott, A.M. Day dawn in Africa. N.Y., 1858.
Afr 3978.37.15   Scott, C.R. Rambles in Egypt and Candia. v.1-2. London, 1837. 2v.
Afr 8659.03.5   Scott, Edward Daniel. Some letters from South Africa, 1894-1902. Manchester, Eng., 1903.
Afr 3040.1   Scott, G.H. The law affecting foreigners in Egypt. Edinburgh, 1907.
Afr 8292.16   Scott, G.H.G. Record of mounted infantry of the City Imperial Volunteers. London, 1902.
Afr 7580.38   Scott, Ian. Tumbled house: the Congo at independence. London, 1969.
Afr 8252.341.50   Scott, J.A.S. Jan Christian Smuts. Cape Town, 1955.
Afr 109.59.5   Scott, John. Africa, world's last frontier. N.Y., 1959.
Afr 9435.10   Scott, L. The struggle for native rights in Rhodesia. London, 1918.
Afr 8678.94   Scott, Michael. A time to speak. London, 1958.
Afr 6455.85   Scott, R.L. Between the elephant's eyes. N.Y., 1954.
Afr 5847.5   Scott, Robert. Limuria, the lesser dependencies of Mauritius. London, 1961.
Afr 1965.5   Scott. Journal of a residence in the Esmailla of Abd-el-Kader. London, 1842.
Afr 7809.68   Scotti, Pietro. Il Congo. Ieri, oggi, domani. Genova, 1968.
Afr 8687.221   Scotty Smith. (Metrowich, F.C.) Cape Town, 1962.
Afr 1925.5   The scourge of Christendom. (Playfair, R.L.) London, 1884.
Afr 500.84   The scramble of Africa, causes and dimensions of empire. (Betts, Raymond F.) Boston, 1966.
Htn   Afr 8288.99.3F*   Scrapbook of miscellaneous cuttings, but largely concerned with affairs of South Africa, 1899-1900. n.p., n.d.
Afr 8289.00.55F   Scrapbook of newspaper clippings, chiefly maps, of campaigns in the South African War, Jan. 7, 1900 - June 10, 1900. (South African War.) n.p., n.d.
Afr 8089.46F   A scrapbook of the Cape. (Masson, M.) Cape Town, 1946.
Afr 6455.20   Scull, G.H. Lassoing wild animals in Africa. N.Y., 1911.
Afr 8089.15   Scully, W.C. History of South Africa, from earliest days to union. London, 1915.
Afr 8809.15   Scully, W.C. Lodges in the wilderness. London, 1915.
Afr 9165.94   Scully, W.C. The ridge of the white waters. London, 1912.
Afr 8687.128   Scully, W.C. Sir J.H. Meiring Beck. Cape Town, 1921.
Afr 8659.13.3   Scully, Wm. C. Further reminiscences of a South African pioneer. London, 1913.
Afr 8659.13   Scully, Wm. C. Reminiscences of a South African pioneer. London, 1913.
Afr 9190.3   Scutt, Joan F. The story of Swaziland. Mbabane, 1965?
Afr 5832.15.2F   Sea fights and corsairs of the Indian Ocean. (Austen, H.C.M.) Port Louis, 1935.
Afr 3978.53.8   Sea Nile, the desert, and Nigritia, travels. (Churi, J.H.) London, 1853.
Afr 1100.2   Sea-wolves of the Mediterranean. (Currey, E.H.) London, 1910.
Afr 1100.2.5   Sea wolves of the Mediterranean. (Currey, E.H.) N.Y., 1929.
Afr 5056.131   Seabrook, W.B. Jungle ways. London, 1931.
Afr 5056.131.20   Seabrook, W.B. Jungle ways. N.Y., 1931.
Afr 5249.5   Seabrook, William Buehler. The white monk of Timbuctoo. N.Y., 1934.
Afr 1.6.7F   Séance. (Association Internationale Africaine. Comité Naional. Belge.) Bruxelles.
Afr 9558.48   The search after Livingstone. (A diary.) (Young, E.D.) London, 1868.
Afr 2208.72   A search after sunshine, or Algeria in 1871. (Herbert, Lady.) London, 1872.
Afr 6287.4   Search for a place: black separatism and Africa, 1860. Ann Arbor, 1969.
Afr 2762.7   Search for the masked Tuwareks. (King, W.J.H.) London, 1903.
Afr 1555.7   Searchlight on German Africa. (Regendanz, W.) London, 1939.
Afr 6455.154   Seaton, Henry. Lion in the morning. London, 1963.
Afr 9558.95   Seaver, George. David Livingstone. N.Y., 1957.
Afr 2687.1   Sebag, Paul. Un faubourg de Tunis, Saida Manoubia. Paris, 1960.
Afr 3978.87.5   Sebah, P. Catalogue of views in Egypt and Nubia. Caire, 1887.
Afr 7850.54   Secession au Katanga. (Gerard Libois, J.) Bruxelles, 1963.
Afr 8019.15   Sechaba; official organ of the African National Congress of South Africa. London. 1,1967+
Afr 9345.60   Sechele. (Sillery, A.) Oxford, 1954.
Afr 679.67.5   Seck, Assane. L'Afrique occidentale. Paris, 1967.
Afr Doc 3807.321.10   Second and final report of the director of census regarding the census taken on 3rd May 1921. (Rhodesia, Southern. Census Office.) Salisbury, 1922.
Afr 8292.20   Second Battalion Royal Dublin Fusiliers in South African war. (Romer, C.F.) London, 1908.
Afr 8289.01.3   The second Boer war 1899-1900. (Wisser, J.P.) Kansas City, 1901. 2v.
Afr 6193.20   Second development plans. (Ghana.) Accra, 1959.
Afr 4573.6   Second five year development plan, 1955-1959. (Ethiopia.) Addis Ababa, 1962.
Afr 8283.26F   Second report. (Great Britain. Parliament. House of Commons.) London, 1897.
Afr Doc 3707.363.2F   Second report of the May/June 1963 census of Africans. (Zambia.) Lusaka, 1964.
Afr 4610.2   Second voyage dans...le royaume de Choa. (Rochet d'Héricourt, C.E.) Paris, 1846.
Afr 2035.20   La seconda rivoluzione algeriana. (Rogati, Elio.) Roma, 1965.
Afr 2030.468   The secret army. (Bocca, Geoffrey.) Englewood Cliffs, 1968.
Afr 1570.54   Le secret d'une conquête. (Begue, Leon.) Paris, 1929.
Afr 8687.101   The secret history of South Africa. 2. ed. (Abercrombie, H.R.) Johannesburg, 1952.
Afr 3258.8.3A   Secret history of the English occupation of Egypt. (Blunt, W.S.) N.Y., 1922.
Afr 2975.3   The secret of the Sahara, Kufara. (Forbes, Rosita.) London, 1921.
Afr 2975.3.5   The secret of the Sahara, Kufara. (Forbes, Rosita.) N.Y., 1921.
Afr 11319.9.100   The secret place, jazz verse. (Debruyn, Phillip.) Cape Town, 1964.

Afr 8659.11.3   Secret service in South Africa. (Blackburn, D.) London, 1911.
Afr 2223.961   Secretariat Social d'Alger. Les commissaires du développement. Alger, 1961.
Afr 2209.61   Secrétariat Social d'Alger. De l'Algérie originelle à l'Algérie moderne. Alger, 1961.
Afr 2223.959.2   Secrétariat Social d'Alger. La micro-industrie. Alger, 1959.
Afr 2223.959   Secrétariat Social d'Alger. Le sous-développement en Algérie. Alger, 1959.
Afr 3315.15.5   Les secrets de l'expédition d'Egypte. (Bromberger, M.) Paris, 1957.
Afr 3315.15   Secrets of Suez. (Bromberger, M.) London, 1957.
Afr 3315.144   Secrets of the Suez War. (United Arab Republic. Information Department.) Cairo, 1966.
Afr 5967.2   La secta del Bwiti en la Guinea española. (Veciana Vilaldach, Antonio de.) Madrid, 1958.
Afr 9854.2.5   Sectarianism in southern Nyasaland. (Wishlade, Robert Leonard.) London, 1965.
Afr 3340.5   Sedar, Irving. Behind the Egyptian sphinx. Philadelphia, 1960.
Afr 11865.59.140   The seed and the sower. (Vanderpost, Laurens.) London, 1963.
Afr 8678.400   The seeds of disaster; a guide to the realities, race politics and world-wide propaganda campaigns of the Republic of South Africa. (Laurence, John.) N.Y., 1968.
Afr 8678.322   The seeds of disaster: a guide to the realities, race politics and world-wide propaganda campaigns of the Republic of South Africa. (Laurence, John.) London, 1968.
Afr 630.36   The seething African pot. (Thwaite, Daniel.) London, 1936.
Afr 7570.20   Segairt, Henri. Un terme au Congo belge. Bruxelles, 1919.
Afr 11780.31.100   Segal, A. Johannesburg Friday. N.Y., 1954.
Afr 55.25   Segal, Ronald. African profiles. Baltimore, 1962.
Afr 8378.337   Segal, Ronald. Into exile. London, 1963.
Afr 1680.5   Segonzac, De. Au coeur de l'atlas. Paris, 1910.
Afr 1609.03.3   Segonzac, de. Voyages au Maroc (1899-1901). Paris, 1903.
Afr 1609.10   Segonzac, M. De. Itineraires au Maroc. (Maps.) Paris, 1910.
Afr 8678.290   La segregation raciale en Afrique du Sud. (Badertscher, Jean.) Lausanne, 1962.
Afr 8678.340   La segregazione razziale nel Sud Africa. (Rainero, Romain.) Milano, 1965.
Afr 8678.147   Segreger of Sterf. (Merwe, Hendrik J.J.M.) Johannesburg, 1961.
Afr 2308.2   Seguin, L.G. Walks in Algiers. London, 1878.
Afr 5993.2   Segunda memoria de las misiones. (Coll, Armengol.) Madrid, 1899.
Afr 1335.6   Segundo congreso africanista. Barcelona, 1908.
Afr Doc 9307.350   Segundo recenseamento geral da população, 1950. (Angola.) Luanda, 1953-1956. 5v.
Afr 5748.87.10   Sei mesi al Madagascar. (Cortese, Emilio.) Roma, 1888.
Afr 2223.940   Sei milioni di affamati. (Apiotti, Angelo.) Milan, 1940.
Afr 6277.114   Seibel, Hans D. Industriearbeit und Kulturwandel in Nigeria. Köln, 1968.
Afr 6738.3   Seidel, A. Deutsch-Kamerun wie es ist. Berlin, 1906.
Afr 9148.98   Seidel, A. Transvaal. Berlin, 1898.
Afr 6979.04   Seiner, F. Bergtouren und Steppenfahrten in Kererolande. Berlin, 1904.
Afr 1493.70   Seis meses en Yebala. (Rebellon Dominguez, G.) Madrid, 1925.
Afr 6720.10   Seitz, Theodor. Vom Aufstieg und Niederbruck deutscher Kolonialmacht. Karlsruhe, 1927-29. 3v.
Afr 8340.18.5   Selborne, W.W.P. The Selborne memorandum. London, 1925.
Afr 8340.18.5   The Selborne memorandum. (Selborne, W.W.P.) London, 1925.
Afr 8289.69.5   Selby, John Millin. The Boer War; a study in cowardice and courage. London, 1969.
Afr 1750.34   Seleccion de conferencias y trabajos realizados por la Academia de Interventores. (Morocco (Spanish Zone).) Tetuan. 1949+
Afr 5813.5   Select bibliography of Mauritius. (Toussaint, Auguste.) Port Louis, 1951.
Afr 9538.12   A select bibliography of recent publications. (Rhodesia and Nyasaland. National Archives.) Salisbury, 1960.
Afr 8028.135   A select bibliography of South African auto-biographies. (Ashpol, R.) Cape Town, 1958.
Afr 8028.152   A select bibliography of South African history; a guide for historical research. (Muller, Christoffel Frederik Jakobus.) Pretoria, 1966.
Afr 8678.1   Select bibliography of South African native life and problems. (Schapera, I.) London, 1941.
Afr 8678.1.5   Select bibliography of South African native life and problems. Supplement. (Schapera, I.) Cape Town, 1950.
Afr 8678.1.10F   Select bibliography of South African native life and problems. 2nd supplement. (Schapera, I.) Cape Town, 1958.
Afr 3026.26   Select bibliography on modern Egypt. (Heyworth-Dunne, J.) Cairo, 1952.
Afr 8135.7   Select constitutional documents...South African history 1795-1910. (Eybers, G.W.) London, 1918.
Afr 8340.3.5   Select documents relating to the unification of South Africa. (Newton, A.P.) London, 1924. 2v.
Afr 28.45F   A selected annotated bibliography on Africa. (Lavanaux, Maurice.) n.p., 1959.
Afr 28.6   Selected bibliography of Africana for 1915. (Carroll, R.F.) Cambridge, 1917.
Afr 9428.5F   A selected bibliography of the federation of Rhodesia and Nyasaland. (Rhodes-Livingstone Institute, Lusaka, Northern Rhodesia.) Lusaka, 1957.
Afr 3986.961.10   Selected passages for students of commerce. 4th ed. (Bahig, A.F.) Alexandria, 1961.
Afr 12639.24.21   Selected poems. (Senghor, L.S.) London, 1964.
Afr 8160.13   Selected writings. (Laurence, W.M.) Grahamstown, 1882.
Afr 6212.20.5   Sélection de discours de Nnamdi Azikiwe. (Azikiwe, Nnamdi.) Paris, 1968.
Afr 10015.4   A selection of African prose. (Whiteley, Wilfred H.) Oxford, 1964. 2v.
Afr 30115.2   A selection of Hausa stories. (Johnston, H.A.S.) Oxford, 1966.
Afr 8252.341.48   Selections from the Smuts papers. (Smuts, J.C.) Cambridge, 1966.
Afr 628.5   Selective annotated bibliography on the Negro and foreign languages. (Mills, C.H.) n.p., 1939.

Afr 8687.281 — Selective index to Not heaven itself; an autobiography. 2. ed. (Gutsche, Thelma.) Johannesburg, 1968.
Afr 635.30.15 — Seligman, C.G. Egypt and Negro Africa. London, 1934.
Afr 4000.15 — Seligman, C.G. Pagan tribes of the Nilotic Sudan. London, 1932.
Afr 630.14 — Seligman, C.G. Races of Africa. London, 1930.
Afr 630.14.3 — Seligman, C.G. Races of Africa. 3d ed. London, 1957.
Afr 630.14.4 — Seligman, C.G. Races of Africa. 4th ed. London, 1966.
Afr 628.240 — Sell, Manfred. Die schwarze Völkerwanderung. Wien, 1940.
Afr 11780.51.100 — Sellier, Richard. Twin-brother hell. London, 1960.
Afr 2223.930 — Selnet, F.P.V. Colonisation officielle et crédit agricole en Algérie. Thèse. Alger, 1930.
Afr 10639.23.100 — Selormey, Francis. The narrow path. London, 1966.
Afr 9489.08 — Selous, F.C. African nature notes and reminiscences. London, 1908.
Afr 9488.95.3 — Selous, F.C. A hunter's wanderings in Africa. London, 1895.
Afr 9446.27 — Selous, F.C. Sunshine and storm in Rhodesia. London, 1896.
Afr 9488.93 — Selous, F.C. Travel and adventure in south-east Africa. London, 1893.
Afr 9446.24 — Selous, Frederick Courteney. Sunshine and storm in Rhodesia. N.Y., 1969.
Afr 1571.52 — Selous, G.H. Appointment to Fez. London, 1956.
Afr 150.2.45 — Selvagem, Carlos (pseud.) Infante Dom Henrique. Lisboa, 1960.
Afr 210.43 — Selwyn, James. South of the Congo. N.Y., 1943.
Afr 9710.15F — Selwyn, P. Report on the economy of Barotseland. n.p., 1964?
Afr 5050.10 — Semaine en Afrique occidentale française. Dakar. 1,1958+ 6v.
Afr 5056.130.10 — Semaines Sociales de France. Le problème social aux colonies. Lyon, 1930.
Afr 7180.45 — Semana do Ultramar, 1st, Luanda, 1965. Migrações e povoamento. Luanda, 1966.
Afr 1550.33 — Semard, Pierre. Marokko. Hamburg, 1925.
Afr 6738.9 — Sembritzki, Emil. Kamerun. Berlin, 1909.
Afr 7912.20 — Semenov, M.G. Ubiitsa s Ist-river. Moscow, 1961.
Afr 3079.66 — Semenova, Lidiia Andreevna. Salakh-ad-Din i Mamliuki v Egipte. Moskva, 1966.
Afr 626.168 — Semin, Nikolai S. Strany SEV i Afrika. Moskva, 1968.
Afr 210.67.5 — Seminar Africa, National and Social Revolution, October 24th-29th, 1966, Cairo. (Seminar Africa. National and Social Revolution, Cairo, 1966.) Cairo, 1967. 4v.
Afr 210.67.5 — Seminar Africa. National and Social Revolution, Cairo, 1966. Seminar Africa, National and Social Revolution, October 24th-29th, 1966, Cairo. Cairo, 1967. 4v.
Afr 626.214 — Seminar on Local Government Finance in Africa, Addis Ababa, 1966. Local government finance in Africa. Berlin, 1967.
Afr 630.62.10 — Seminar on Racialism, Kampala, Uganda. Report. Leiden, 1962.
Afr 8658.03 — Semple, Robert. Walks and sketches at the Cape of Good Hope. London, 1803.
Afr 8685.80 — Sen, Dhirendra Kumar. The position of Indians in South Africa. Calcutta, 1950.
Afr 5185.9.2 — Senegal; a study of French assimilation policy. (Crowder, Michael.) London, 1967.
Afr 5180.44 — Sénégal, porte de l'Afrique. (Garnier, C.) Paris, 1962.
Afr 5183.965.10 — Senegal. Deuxième plan quadriennal de développement économique et social, 1965-1969. v.1-3. Dakar?, 1965.
Afr 5183.961.5 — Senegal. Plan quadriennal de développement, 1961-1964. Dakar, 1961.
Afr 5183.964 — Senegal. Plan réorienté. n.p., n.d.
Afr 5105 — Pamphlet box. Senegal.
Afr 5119.35 — Le Sénégal. (Beslier, G.G.) Paris, 1935.
Afr 5185.9 — Senegal. (Crowder, Michael.) London, 1962.
Afr 5118.89 — Le Sénégal. (Faidherbe, L.L.C.) Paris, 1889.
Afr 5180.17 — Le Sénégal. (Mavidal, J.) Paris, 1863.
Afr 5119.07 — Le Sénégal. (Olivier, M.) Paris, 1907.
Afr 5180.29 — Le Sénégal. (Ricard, F.) Paris, 1865.
Afr 5119.25 — Le Sénégal. (Sabatie, A.) Saint-Louis, 1925.
Afr 5180.33 — Le Sénégal. (Sere de Rivières, E.) Paris, 1953.
Afr 5103.1 — Sénégal. Archives Nationales. Centre de Documentation. Eléments de bibliographie sénégalaise. Dakar, 1964.
Afr Doc 6219.14 — Sénégal. Constitution. Constitution de la République du Sénégal. Dakar? 1963
Afr 5183.964.5 — Senegal. Ministère du Développement, et du Plan et l'Economie Génerale. Bilan d'execution materielle et financière des investissements publics au 31 dec. 1963. Dakar, 1964.
Afr 5180.50 — Sénégal. Ministère du Développement. Cartes pour servir à l'aménagement du territoire. Dakar, 1965.
Afr Doc 6209.305 — Sénégal. Ministère du Développement du Plan et de l'Économie. Comptes économiques. Paris. 1959+
Afr 5184.25 — Sénégal. Ministère du Développement du Plan et Economie Générale. Deuxième plan quadriennal. Pts. 1-2. Dakar?, 1965.
Afr Doc 6207.10 — Sénégal. Service de la Statistique et de la Mécanographie. Bulletin statistique et économique mensuel. 1,1960+
Afr Doc 6207.5 — Sénégal. Service de la Statistique Generale. Bulletin statistique bimestriel. 3,1959+
Afr Doc 6208.705PF — Sénégal. Service de la Statistique Generale. Commerce extérieur du Sénégal. Commerce special. 1966+
Afr Doc 6209.300 — Sénégal. Service de la Statistique Generale. Situation économique du Sénégal. Dakar. 1962+
Afr 5183.961 — Le Sénégal à l'heure de l'indépendance. (Ndiaye, M.) Doullens, 1961.
Afr 5100.9 — Senegal d'aujourd'hui. Dakar. 1966+
Afr 5119.64 — Le Sénégal et la Gambie. (Deschamps, H.J.) Paris, 1964.
Afr 5119.64.2 — Le Sénégal et la Gambie. 2e éd. (Deschamps, H.J.) Paris, 1968.
Afr 5180.26 — La Sénégal et le Soudan français. (Gaffarel, Paul.) Paris, 1890.
Afr 5240.2 — Sénégal et Soudan. (Bris, Alexis.) Paris, 1887.
Afr 5100.5F — Senegal magazine. Dakar. 1960+
Afr 5183.900 — Sénégal-Soudan, agriculture, industrie, commerce. (Paris. Exposition Universelle de 1900.) Paris, 1900.
Afr 5112.10 — Der senegalesische Weg zum afrikanischen Sozialismus. (Doll, Peter.) Hamburg, 1966.
Afr 608.47 — Sénégambie, Guinée, Nubie. (Tardieu, E.A.) Paris, 1847.
Afr 12016.2 — Senghor, L.S. Anthologie de la nouvelle poésie nègre. 1st ed. Paris, 1948.
Afr 12639.24.110 — Senghor, L.S. Chants pour Naëtt. Paris, 1949.
Afr 12639.24.100 — Senghor, L.S. Ethiopiques, poèmes. Paris, 1956.

Afr 12639.24.25 — Senghor, L.S. Liberté. Paris, 1964.
Afr 12639.24.120A — Senghor, L.S. Nocturnes. Paris, 1961.
Afr 12639.24.130 — Senghor, L.S. Poèmes. Paris, 1964.
Afr 12639.24.29 — Senghor, L.S. Prose and poetry. London, 1965.
Afr 12639.24.21 — Senghor, L.S. Selected poems. London, 1964.
Afr 5055.59.10 — Senghor, Leopold. African socialism. N.Y., 1959.
Afr 5053.15 — Senghor, Leopold. Congrès constitutif de P.F.A. Paris, 1959.
Afr 618.40 — Senghor, Léopold Sédar. Les fondements de l'afriquanité ou négritude et arabité. Paris, 1967?
Afr 12639.24.700 — Senghor, Léopold Sédar. Nocturnes. London, 1969.
Afr 3978.82 — Senior, N.W. Conversations and journals in Egypt. London, 1882. 2v.
Afr 555.9.50 — Il sennaar e lo sciangallah. (Beltrame, G.) Verona, 1879. 3v.
Afr 5243.337.2 — Les Senoufo (y compris les minianka). 2nd ed. (Holas, Bohumil.) Paris, 1966.
Afr 4789.2 — Sense and license. (Eby, Omar.) Scottsdale, 1965.
Afr Doc 4307.360.10 — Sensus van groot en kleindistribusiehandel, 1960-61. (South Africa. Bureau of Statistics.) Pretoria, 1966. 2v.
Afr 6455.17.20 — A sentimental safari. (Roosevelt, K.) N.Y., 1963.
Afr 8040.22 — Sentrale, provinsiale en munisipale instellings van Suid-Afrika. (Cloete, Jacobus J.N.) Pretoria, 1964.
Afr 8846.30.5 — Separate development. (Carter, Gwendolen Margaret.) Johannesburg, 1966.
Afr Doc 4312.154 — Separate representation of voters act validation and amendment bill, 1954. (South Africa. Parliament.) Cape Town, 1954.
Afr 8678.386 — The separated people; a look at contemporary South Africa. 1st ed. (Kahn, Ely Jacques.) N.Y., 1968.
Afr 5345.10 — Le séparatisme religieux en Afrique noire. (Holas, Bohumil.) Paris, 1965.
Afr 590.28 — Sept ans en Afrique occidentale, la côte des esclaves. (Bouche, P.B.) Paris, 1885.
Afr 2025.1 — Les sept plaies d'Algérie. (Gourgeot, F.) Alger, 1891.
Afr 2209.05 — Sept semaines en Tunisie et en Algérie. (Richardot, H.) Paris, 1905.
Afr 200.13.5 — Septans, Albert. Les expéditions anglaises en Afrique, Ashantel 1873-1874. Paris, 1896.
Afr 2442.5 — Septième congrès. (Néo-Destour Congrès, 7th, Bizerte.) Tunis, 1965.
Afr 8089.45.10 — Sepulchre, J. Gens et choses de l'Afrique du Sud. Elisabethville, 1945.
Afr 4313.6 — Sequeira, D.L. Carta das novas que vieram. Lisboa, 1938.
Afr 4313.5F — Sequeira, D.L. The discovery of Abyssinia by the Portuguese in 1520. London, 1938.
Afr 1258.17.6 — Sequel to Riley's narrative. (Riley, J.) Columbus, 1851.
Afr 2489.1 — Serbellone, G. Serbellone a Tunisi. Sierra, 1880.
Afr 2489.1 — Serbellone a Tunisi. (Serbellone, G.) Sierra, 1880.
Afr 5180.33 — Sere de Rivières, E. Le Sénégal. Paris, 1953.
Afr 5255.65 — Séré de Rivières, Edmond. Histoire du Niger. Paris, 1965.
Afr 5260.25 — Séré de Rivières, Edmond. Le Niger. Paris, 1952.
Afr 9345.70 — Seretse Khama and Botswana. (Gabatshwane, S.M.) Kanye? 1966.
Afr 9345.20 — Seretse Khama and the Bamongwato. (Mockford, J.) London, 1950.
Afr 10116.5 — Sergeant, Howard. Poetry from Africa. Oxford, 1968.
Afr 4785.965 — Sergeeva, Irina S. Somaliiskaia Respublika. Moskva, 1965.
Afr 635.4.5 — Sergi, Giuseppe. Africa, antropologia della stirpe camitica. Torino, 1897.
Afr Doc 5609.305 — Series chronologiques et graphiques relatifs a l'économie malgache. (Malagasy. Republic National de la Statistique et de la Recherche Economique.) Madagascar, 1963.
Htn Afr 3977.49PF* — A series of prints relative to the manner, customs, etc, of the present inhabitants of Egypt. (Dalton, Richard.) London, 1752.
Afr Doc 5608.700.5 — Series retrospectives, 1949-1961. (Madagascar. Institut National de la Statistique et de la Recherche Economique.) n.p., n.d.
Afr 2030.106 — Serigny, Alain de. Un procés. Paris, 1961.
Afr 2030.105 — Serigny, Alain de. La révolution du 13 mai. Paris, 1958.
Afr 2312.1 — Seriziat. Etudes sur l'oasis de Biskra. Paris, 1875.
Afr 1487.32 — Sermaye, J. L'oeuvre française en terre marocaine. Casablanca, 1938.
Afr 718.4.6 — Serpa Pinto, Alexander de. Como eu atravessei Africa. vol.1-2. Londres, 1881. 2v.
Afr 718.4 — Serpa Pinto, Alexander de. How I crossed Africa. Philadelphia, 1881. 2v.
Afr 718.4.3 — Serpa Pinto, Alexander de. Wandering quer durch Afrika. Leipzig, 1881. 2v.
Afr 718.4.15 — Serpa Pinto, Carlota de. A vida breve e ardente de Serpa Pinto. Lisboa, 1937.
Afr 718.4.80 — Serpa Pinto e o apelo de Africa. (Cunha, Amadeu.) Lisboa, 1946.
Afr 679.63.15 — The serpent and the crescent. (Panikkar, K.M.) London, 1963.
Afr 2945.26 — Serra, F. Italia e Senussia. Milano, 1933.
Afr 1490.18 — Serra Orts, A. Recuerdos de la guerra del Kert de 1911-12. Barcelona, 1914.
Afr 5387.12 — Serreau, Jean. Le développement à la base au Dahomey et au Sénégal. Paris, 1966.
Afr 1200.63 — Serres, Jean. La politique turque en Afrique du Nord sous la Monarchie de Juillet. Paris, 1925.
Afr 1200.63.2 — Serres, Jean. La politique turque en Afrique du Nord sous le Monarchie de Juillet. Thèse. Paris, 1925.
Afr 8676.60.20 — Serton, P. Suid-Afrika en Brasilie. Kaapstad, 1960.
Afr 8659.63 — Serton, P. Zuid-Afrika, land van goede hoop. 3. druk. Meppel, 1960.
Afr 6280.70 — Sertorio, Guido. Struttura sociopolitica e ordinamento fondiario Yoruba dall'epoca tradizionale all'odierna. Coma, 1967.
Afr 1957.31 — Serval, Pierre. Alger fut à lui. Paris, 1965.
Afr 2030.35.2 — Servan-Schreiber, Jean Jacques. Lieutenant en Algérie. Paris, 1957.
Afr 2030.35 — Servan-Schreiber, Jean Jacques. Lieutenant in Algeria. 1st Amer. ed. N.Y., 1957.
Afr 1727.2 — Servando Marenco, D. La conquista de la Mehedia. Madrid, 1908.

Afr 3275.12.100 · A servant of the Empire, a memoir of Harry Boyle. (Boyle, C.A.) London, 1938.

Afr 7190.32 · Os serviçaes de S. Thomé. (Cadbury, William A.) Lisboa, 1910.

Afr 4070.29 · Service and sport in the Sudan. (Comyn, D.C.E.) London, 1911.

Afr 5091.14 · Service de la statistique plan quadriennal, 1963-1966. (Mauritania. Ministère des Affaires Etrangères et du Plan.) Nouakchott, 1967.

Afr 2209.56 · Service de Propagande, d'Edition et d'Information, Paris. A survey of Algeria. Paris, 1956.

Afr 575.17 · Servier, A. Le péril de l'avenir. Le nationalisme musulman. Constantine, 1913.

Afr 2209.62 · Servier, J. Les poètes de l'année, rites et symboles. Paris, 1962.

Afr 2030.160 · Servier, Jean. Adieu Djebels. Paris, 1958.

Afr 2283.4 · Servier, Jean. Dans l'Aurès sur les pas des rébelles. Paris, 1955.

Afr 2030.390 · Servier, Jean. Demain en Algérie. Paris, 1959.

Afr 2670.5 · Servonnet, Jean. En Tunisie, le golfe de Gabès en 1888. Paris, 1888.

Afr 6293.4 · SES Publishers. Your ABC of Lagos and suburbs including guide maps of Benin, Enugu, Ibadan and Kaduna. Lagos, 1967.

Afr 1494.60 · Session d'études administratives. Rabat, 1959.

Afr Doc 1612.5 · Sessional paper. (Gambia. Legislative Council.) Bathurst. 1961+

Afr Doc 3212.35 · Sessional paper. (Kenya. Legislative Council.) 1947+

Afr Doc 2521.15 · Sessional paper. (Nigeria, Western. Legislature.) Ibadan. 1955+

Afr Doc 2312.10 · Sessional paper. (Nigeria. Legislative Council.) 1944-1948

Afr Doc 2312.15 · Sessional paper. (Nigeria. Parliament.) Lagos. 1958+

Afr Doc 1712.10F · Sessional paper. (Sierra Leone. Legislative Council.)

Afr Doc 3312.30 · Sessional paper. (Uganda. National Assembly.) Entebbe. 1948+

Afr 8687.228.5 · Die sestiende koppie. (Heerden, Petronella van.) Kaapstad, 1965.

Afr 8687.132 · Sestig jaar belewenis van dietse kultuur. (Besselaar, Gerrit.) Pretoria, 1941.

Afr 1608.89.5 · Sestri, J.A. de. Por todo marruecos descripcion del imperio. Barcelona, 1889.

Afr 4199.759 · Seth, Ronald. Russell pasha. London, 1966.

Afr 8292.30 · Seton-Kaar, H. The call to arms, 1900-01, mounted sharpshooters. London, 1902.

Afr 2845.5 · Settantasei anni di dominazione turca in Libia, 1835-1911. (Coro, F.) Tripoli, 1937.

Afr 8279.00.21 · The settlement after the war. (Farrelly, M.J.) London, 1900.

Afr 6750.3F · Settler, a weekly journal. Dar es Salaam.

Afr 8815.4 · The settler's guide to the Cape of Good Hope and colony of Natal. (Irons, H.) London, 1858.

Afr 2762.20 · Seule avec les Touareg du Hoggar. (Lede, Marie Louise.) Paris, 1954.

Afr 4559.36.5 · Seule en Ethiopie. (Roussan, S.M.) Paris, 1936.

Afr 1830.20.6 · Seurat, L.G. Exploration zoologique de l'Algerie. Paris, 1930.

Afr 11057.2 · Seven African writers. (Moore, G.) London, 1962.

Afr 11237.67.100 · Seven against the sun. (Brown, J.A.) Johannesburg, 1962.

Afr 3335.5 · Seven Americans in theUnited Arab Republic. (United States Trade Mission to the United Arab Republic.) Washington, 1960.

Afr 8659.30.15 · The seven lost trails of Africa. (Chilvers, H.A.) London, 1930.

Afr 9610.15 · Seven tribes of BritishCentral Afrika. (Colson, Elizabeth.) Manchester, 1959.

Afr 8659.29.5 · The seven wonders of southern Africa. (Chelvers, H.A.) Johannesburg, 1929.

Afr 6193.19 · Seven year development plan; a brief outline. (Ghana. Planning Commission.) Accra? 1963?

Afr 6193.19.5 · Seven-year plan for national reconstruction and development. (Ghana. Planning Commission.) Accra, 1964.

Afr 590.24 · Seven year s service on slave coast of Western Africa. (Huntley, H.) London, 1850. 2v.

Afr 7093.5 · Seven years among the Fjort. (Dennett, R.C.) London, 1887.

Afr 7458.66 · Seven years in Africa. (Fitzgerald, J.J.) Columbus, 1866.

Afr 6146.8 · Seven years in Sierra Leone. (Pierson, Arthur.) N.Y., 1897.

Afr 8658.81 · Seven years in South Africa. (Holub, Emil.) London, 1881. 2v.

Afr 4559.27.5 · Seven years in southern Abyssinia. (Hodson, A.W.) London, 1927.

Afr 3695.3A · Seven years in the Soudan. (Gessi Pasha, R.) London, 1892.

Afr 4968.95.4 · Seventeen trips through Somaliland. (Swayne, H.) London, 1895.

Afr 4968.95.5 · Seventeen trips through Somaliland and a visit to Abyssinia. 2d ed. (Swayne, H.) London, 1900.

Afr 6275.17 · Seventeen years in the Yoruba country. (Hinderer, A.) London, 1873.

Afr 1609.02.3 · Seventy-one days camping in Morocco. (Grove, Lady.) London, 1902.

Afr 7809.52 · Severn, M. Congo pilgrim. London, 1952.

Afr 200.5 · Sevin-Deplaces, L. Afrique et africains. Paris, 1892.

Afr Doc 2709.10 · Seychelles. Approved estimates of expenditure. Victoria. 1964+

Afr Doc 2709.15 · Seychelles. Approved estimates of revenue. Victoria. 1964+

Afr Doc 2703.5F · Seychelles. Blue book. 10v.

Afr 5892.5 · Seychelles. A plan for Seychelles. Victoria, 1960? 5 pam.

Afr Doc 2707.360 · Seychelles. Population census of the Seychelles Colony. Victoria? 1961?

Afr Doc 2708.700 · Seychelles. Trade report. Victoria. 1963+

Afr Doc 2731.10 · Seychelles. Audit Department. Report on the accounts of the Colony of Seychelles. Victoria. 1960+

Afr Doc 2731.5 · Seychelles. Department of Agriculture. Annual report. Victoria. 1964+

Afr Doc 2733.5 · Seychelles. Department of Cooperative Development. Annual report. Victoria. 1965+

Afr Doc 2735.5 · Seychelles. Department of Education. Report. Victoria. 1958+

Afr Doc 2750.7F · Seychelles. Department of Tourism, Information, and Broadcasting. Annual report. Victoria. 1966+

Afr Doc 2750.5F · Seychelles. Department of Tourism, Information, and Broadcasting. Report. Victoria. 1960+

Afr Doc 2739.5 · Seychelles. Income Tax Department. Annual report. Victoria. 1957+

Afr Doc 2742.5F · Seychelles. Labour and Welfare Department. Report. Victoria. 1961-1966

Afr Doc 2742.10 · Seychelles. Labour Department. Report. Mahe. 1,1967+

Afr Doc 2743.5F · Seychelles. Medical Department. Report. Victoria. 1964+

Afr Doc 2746.15 · Seychelles. Police Force. Annual report. Victoria. 1966+

Afr Doc 2746.5 · Seychelles. Port and Marine Department. Triennial report. Victoria. 1961+

Afr Doc 2746.10F · Seychelles. Public Works Department. Annual report. Victoria. 1966+

Afr Doc 2733.10 · Seychelles. Registry of Deeds and Civil Status Department. Annual report. Victoria. 1965+

Afr Doc 2709.300 · Seychelles. Treasury. Annual report by the Accountant General. 1963+

Afr Doc 2753.5 · Seychelles. Welfare Department. Report. Victoria. 1968+

Afr 5893.15 · Seychelles annual. Victoria.

Afr 5890.5 · Seychelles Society. Journal. Victoria. 5,1966+

Afr 609.55.20 · Seymour, John. One man's Africa. London, 1955.

Afr 4050.11 · Sforza, Ascanio M. Esplorazioni e prigionia in Libia. Milano, 1919.

Afr 4591.2 · Shack, William A. The Gurage. London, 1966.

Afr 8678.281 · Shadow and substance in South Africa. (Tatz, C.) Pietermaritzburg, 1962.

Afr 11899.98.100 · Shadow and wall. (Zyl, Tania.) Cape Town, 1958.

Afr 9502.18 · The shadow of the dam. (Howarth, David.) N.Y., 1961.

Afr 10631.58.120 · Shadow of wealth. (Konadu, Asare.) Accra, 1966.

Afr 11874.87.100 · Shadow over the Rand. (Watson, J.C.) Johannesburg, 1955.

Afr 10622.76.100 · The shadows of laughter: poems. (Brew, Kwesi.) London, 1968.

Afr 8325.17 · Shadows of the war. (Bagot, Dosia.) London, 1900.

Afr 3305.16 · Shah, Ikbal Ali. Fuad, king of Egypt. London, 1936.

Afr 1400.5 · The shaikhs of Morocco in the XVI century. (Weir, T.H.) Edinburgh, 1904.

Afr 4060.37 · The shaikiya. (Nicholls, W.) Dublin, 1913.

Afr 9047.16 · Shaka. (Rademeyer, J.I.) Johannesburg, 1963.

Afr 9047.15 · Shaka Zulu. (Ritter, E.A.) London, 1955.

Afr 8155.10 · Shakas country. 3d ed. (Bulpin, J. Victor.) Cape Town, 1956. 2v.

Afr 2208.26.5 · Shaler, William. Esquisse de l'état d'Alger. Paris, 1830.

Afr 2208.26 · Shaler, William. Sketches of Algiers. Boston, 1826.

Afr 8278.99.7 · Shall I slay my brother Boer. (Stead, W.T.) London, 1899.

Afr 575.5 · Shall Islam rule Africa? (Barnes, L.C.) Boston, 1890.

Afr 6890.4 · Shamba letu. (Wenner, Kate.) Boston, 1970.

Afr 6883.30 · Shambala. (Winnus, Edgar.) Berkeley, 1962.

Afr 590.83 · The shameful trade. (Kay, Frederick George.) London, 1967.

Afr 9448.78 · Shamugawia, Nathan M. Crisis in Rhodesia. London, 1965.

Afr 12622.3.100 · Shango, suivi de Le roi-éléphant. (Balogun, Ola.) Honfleur, 1968.

Afr 550.136 · The shape of personality in African Christian leadership. (Newington, D.) Nelspruit, 1962.

Afr 550.136.5 · The shape of power in Africa. (Newington, D.) Nelspruit, 196?.

Afr 6455.140 · Shaposhnikova, Vera D. Bol'shoe safari. Moskva, 1966.

Afr 545.27 · Sharevskaia, Berta I. Starye i novye religii tropicheskoi i iuzhnoi Afriki. Moscow, 1964.

Afr 9558.100 · Sharp, J.A. David Livingstone. London, 1920.

Afr 609.21 · Sharpe, Alfred. The backbone of Africa. London, 1921.

Afr 6210.66 · Sharwood Smith, Bryan. Recollections of British administration in the Cameroons and Northern Nigeria, 1921-1957. Durham, N.C., 1969.

Afr 8355.45 · Shastitko, P.M. Sto let bespraviia. Moscow, 1963.

Afr 8808.41 · Shaw, B. Memorials of South Africa. London, 1841.

Afr 8808.41.3 · Shaw, B. Memorials of South Africa. N.Y., 1841.

Afr 6214.1 · Shaw, F.A. A tropical dependency. London, 1906.

Afr 5548.85 · Shaw, George A. Madagascar and France. London, 1885.

Afr 4389.36.5 · Shaw, John H. Ethiopia. N.Y., 1936.

Afr 8847.34.100 · Shaw, R.C. Graaff-Reinet, a bibliography. Cape Town, 1964.

Afr 3040.78A · Shaw, S.J. The financial and administrative organization and development of Ottoman Egypt, 1517-1798. Princeton, 1962.

Afr 9165.42.57 · Shaw, T.R. The growth of Johannesburg from 1886-1939. Johannesburg, 1961.

Afr 2207.38.15 · Shaw, Thomas. Voyage dans la régence d'Alger. Paris, 1830.

Afr 2207.38.10 · Shaw, Thomas. Voyage dans la régence d'Alger. Paris, 1830.

Afr 2207.38.16 · Shaw, Thomas. Voyage dans la régence d'Alger. Cover 1831. Paris, 1830.

Afr 8145.47 · Shaw, William, Rector of Chelvey. The story of my mission among the native tribes of South Eastern Africa. London, 1872.

Afr 8687.339 · Shaw, William. Never a young man: extracts from the letters and journals of the Reverend William Shaw. Cape Town, 1967.

Afr 3037.1 · Shayyal, J. al-D. A history of Egyptian historiography in the nineteenth century. Alexandria, 1962.

Afr 1609.25 · Sheean, V. Adventures among the Riffi. London, 1926.

Afr 1609.25.3A · Sheean, V. An american among the Riffi. London, 1926.

Afr 8735.5.5 · Sheffield, T. The story of the settlement with a sketch of Grahamstown as it was. 2d ed. Grahamstown, 1884.

Afr 8658.88 · Sheldon, L.V. Yankee girls in Zulu land. N.Y., 1888.

Afr 6887.7 · Sheldon, M.F. Sultan to sultan. London, 1892.

Afr 6295.66.5 · Shell Company Of Nigeria. Uboma, a socio-economic and nutritional survey. Bude, Eng., 1966.

Afr 6585.9 · Shelswell-White, Geoffrey Henry. A guide to Zanzibar. Zanzibar, 1949.

Afr 6988.58.268 · The sheltering desert. (Martin, H.) London, 1957.

Afr 10065.5 · Shelton, Austin J. The African assertion. N.Y., 1968.

Afr 6541.17 · Shephard, G.W. They wait in darkness. N.Y., 1955.

Afr 4115.17 · Shepheard's hotel. (Nelson, Nina.) London, 1960.

Afr 555.30 · Shepherd, A. Tucker of Uganda. London, 1929.

Afr 4375.5 · Shepherd, A. The campaign in Abyssinia. Bombay, 1868.

Afr 50.35 · Shepherd, George. The politics of African nationalism. N.Y., 1962.

Afr 8678.13.15 · Shepherd, R.H.W. Children of the Veld, Bantu vignettes. London, 1968.

Afr 8145.14 · Shepherd, R.H.W. Lovedale, South Africa. Lovedale, 1940.

Afr 8659.47.10 · Shepherd, Robert H.W. African contrasts. Cape Town, 1947.

Afr 8678.9.85 · Shepherd, Robert Henry Wishart. Literature for the South African Bantu. Pretoria, 1936.

Afr 555.22.19   A shepherd of the Veld, Bransly Lewis Key, Africa. (Callaway, Godfrey.) London, 1912.

Afr 9860.276.5   Shepperson, George. Independent African; John Chilembwe and the origins, setting and significance of the Nyasaland native rising of 1915. Edinburgh, 1958.

Afr 8678.338   Shepstone, Theophilus. The native question. n.p., n.d.

Afr 9072.5   Shepstone: the role of the family in the history of South Africa, 1820-1900. (St. Leger-Gordon, Ruth E.) Cape Town, 1968.

Afr 3978.25   Sherer, M. Scenes and impressions in Egypt and Italy. London, 1825.

Afr 2209.36.5   Sheridan, C.F. Arab interlude. London, 1936.

Afr 820.1   Sherlock, Jill. The Zambesi. Cape Town, 1963.

Afr 5620.6   Shervinton, Kathleen. The Shervintons, soldiers of fortune. London, 1899.

Afr 5620.6   The Shervintons, soldiers of fortune. (Shervinton, Kathleen.) London, 1899.

Afr 3715.5A   Shibeika, Mekki. British policy in the Sudan, 1882-1902. London, 1952.

Afr 3675.30   Shibeika, Mekki. The independent Sudan. N.Y., 1959.

Afr 4315.1   Shihab al-Din Ahmad Ibn Abd al-Kadir. La conquista mussulmana dell'Etiopia. Rome, 1891.

Afr 4315.2   Shihab al-Din Ahmad ibn 'Abd al-Kadir. Futuh al-Habashah. Pt.1. London, 1894.

Afr 4317.1   Shihab al-Din Ahmad Ibn Abd al-Kadir. Futuh el-Habacha. Paris, 1898.

Afr 4315.3   Shihab al-Din Ahmad Ibn 'Abd al-Kadir. Histoire de la conquête de l'Abyssinie. Texte arabe v.1, française v.2. Paris, 1897-1909. 2v.

Afr 3817.6   The Shilluk people. (Westermann, Diedrich.) Philadelphia, 1912.

Afr 115.108   Shinnie, Margaret. Ancient African kingdoms. London, 1965.

Afr 9838.85   The Shire Highlands. (Buchanan, J.) Edinburgh, 1885.

Afr 1259.10   Shoemaker, M.M. Islam lands, Nubia, the Sudan, Tunisia, and Algeria. N.Y., 1910.

Afr 6720.25.5   Sholaster, H. Bischof Heinrich Vieter. Limburg, 1925.

Afr 609.58.5   Sholomir, Jack. Beachcombers of the African jungle. 1st ed. N.Y., 1959.

Afr 9502.13   Shona religion. (Gelfand, M.) Cape Town, 1962.

Afr 9047.5   Shooter, J. The Kafirs of Natal and Zulu country. London, 1857.

Afr 8678.185   Shooting at Sharpville. (Reeves, Ambrose.) London, 1960.

Afr 11057.8   Shore, Herbert L. Come back, Africa! N.Y., 1968.

Afr 3700.22   Short, Thomas. The wars in Egypt. Bristol, 19- .

Htn   Afr 1900.4*   Short account of Algiers...wars. (Carey, M.) Philadelphia, 1794.

Afr 4008.1   A short account of the Copts. (Worrell, William H.) Ann Arbor, 1945.

Afr 3079.64   A short account of the Nile basin. (Hurst, Harold.) Cairo, 1964.

Htn   Afr 1406.7*   Short and strange relation of some part of the life of Tafiletta. London, 1669.

Afr 10317.5   Short East African plays in English: ten plays in English. (Cook, David.) Nairobi, 1968.

Afr 109.62.15   A short history of Africa. (Oliver, Roland Anthony.) Harmondsworth, 1962.

Afr 1868.05   Short history of Algiers. 3rd ed. N.Y., 1805.

Afr 6295.60.10   A short history of Benin. 3rd ed. (Egharevba, Jacob.) Ibadan, 1960.

Afr 4719.45   A short history of Eritrea. (Longrigg, S.H.) Oxford, 1945.

Afr 6164.9.7   A short history of Ghana. 7th ed. (Ward, W.E.F.) London, 1957.

Afr 5829.49.5   A short history of Mauritius. (Barnwell, P.J.) London, 1949.

Afr 6214.30.2   A short history of Nigeria. (Crowder, M.) N.Y., 1966.

Afr 6214.12   A short history of Nigeria. (Niven, C.R.) London, 1937.

Afr 1069.61   A short history of North Africa. (Nickerson, J.S.) N.Y., 1961.

Afr 9439.35   A short history of Rhodesia and her neighbours. (Standing, T.G.) London, 1935.

Afr 6769.60   A short history of Tanganyika. (Clarke, P.H.C.) London, 1960.

Afr 6769.60.2   A short history of Tanganyika. 2nd ed. (Clarke, P.H.C.) Nairobi, 1963.

Afr 6590.5   A short history of the Comorians in Zanzibar. (Saleh, Ibuni.) Tanganyika, 1936.

Afr 699.65   A short history of the east coast of Africa. 2nd ed. (Hollingsworth, Lawrence H.) London, 1965.

Afr 3138.10.5   A short history of the Fatimid khalifate. (O'Leary, De Lacy.) London, 1923.

Afr 3675.67   A short history of the Sudan. (Al-Mahdi, Mandur.) London, 1965.

Afr 679.68.5   A short history of West Africa. (Osae, T.A.) London, 1968.

Afr 9643.5   A short history of Zambia. (Fagan, Brian M.) Nairobi, 1966.

Afr 11057.5   Short stories from Southern Africa. (Hooper, A.G.) Cape Town, 1963.

Afr 4787.12   Short term development programme, 1968-1970. (Somalia. Planning Commission.) Mogadiscio, 1968.

Afr Doc 4307.6F   Short term economic indicators. (South Africa. Bureau of Statistics.) Pretoria. 1,1967+

Afr 8835.36   Shorten, John R. Cape Town, a record of the mother city from the earliest days to the present. Cape Town, 1963.

VAfr 618.50   Shorthose, William John Townsend. Sport and adventure in Africa. Philadelphia, 1923.

Afr 4559.40A   Shortridge, G.C. A gazetteer of Abyssinia Pts 1-3. n.p., 1940.

Afr 6455.33   Shots and snapshots in British East Africa. (Bennet, Edward.) London, 1914.

Afr 609.38   Show on the equator. (Tilman, H.W.) N.Y., 1938.

Afr 545.44   Shparhnikov, Genrikh A. Religii stran Afriki. Moskva, 1967.

Afr 626.70   Shpirt, A.I. Afrika vo Vtoroi Mirovoi Voine. Moscow, 1959.

Afr 626.71   Shpirt, A.I. Ekonomika stran Afriki. Moscow, 1963.

Afr 626.72   Shpirt, A.I. Syrevye resursy Afriki. Moscow, 1961.

Afr 8678.9.75   Shropshire, D.W.T. The church and primitive peoples...southern Bantu. London, 1938.

Afr 9047.27   Shropshire, Denys William Tinniswood. The Bantu woman under the Natal code of native law. Lovedale, 1941.

Afr 3258.8.10   Shukri, M.F. Gordon at Khartoum. Cairo, 1951.

Afr 8980.6   Shuter, C.F. Englishman's inn, 'engelsche logie'. Cape Town, 1963.

Afr 2010.5   Si-el-Hadj-Mokrani et la révolte de 1871. (Voission, Louis.) Paris, 1905.

Afr 1846.7   Sibe, A. La conscription des indigenes d'Algerie. Paris, 1912.

Afr 1738.27   Sibieude, Jean. La question de Tanger. Thèse. Montpellier, 1927.

Afr 7459.28   Sibley, James L. Liberia, old and new. London, 1928.

Afr 5748.96   Sibree, J. Madagascar before the conquest. London, 1896.

Afr 5530.1   Sibree, J. A Madagascar bibliography. Antananarivo, 1885.

Afr 5530.1.5   Sibree, J. A Madagascar bibliography. Mss. Additions and corrections. Antananarivo, 1885.

Afr 5765.15   Sibree, James. Fifty years in Madagascar. London, 1924.

Afr 5748.80   Sibree, James. The great African islands. London, 1880.

Afr 5765.15.5   Sibree, James. Madagascar, country, people, missions. London, 1880.

Afr 5710.70   Sibree, James. Madagascar and its people. London, 1870.

Afr 5748.70.5   Sibree, James. Madagascar et ses habitants. Toulouse, 1873.

Afr 6885.20   Sibtain, Nancy de S.P. Dare to look up. Sydney, 1968.

Afr 109.67.35   Sicard, Maurice Ivan. La contre-révolution africaine. Paris, 1967.

Afr 2819.12.3   La Sicilia e Tripoli. (Longo, G.) Catania, 1912.

Afr 2929.34   Siciliani, D. Paesaggi libici. Tripolitania. Tripoli, 1934.

Afr 8325.55   The sick and wounded in South Africa. (Burdett-Coretts, W.) London, 1900.

Afr 1609.03.7   Sid el Hach Abd-el-Nabi Ben Ramos. Perlas negras. Madrid, 1903.

Afr 8658.99   Side lights on South Africa. (Devereux, Roy.) London, 1899.

Afr 8315.11   Side lights on the march. (Mackern, H.F.) London, 1901.

Afr 8659.00.8   Side lights on the war in South Africa. (Sykes, Jessica.) London, 1900.

Afr 7122.56   Sidenko, V.P. Angola v ogne. Moscow, 1961.

Afr 2368.1   Sidi-bel-Abbés et son arrondissement. (Bastide, L.) Oran, 1881.

Afr 1965.12.5   Sidi-Brahim. (Azan, Paul.) Paris, 1930.

Afr 6333.62   Sidney Webb and East Africa. (Gregory, Robert.) Berkeley, 1962.

Afr 2030.240   Sie klagen an. (Rispy, Franz.) Zürich, 1958.

Afr 609.38.5   Sieburg, F. Afrikanischer Frühling, eine Reise. Frankfurt, 1938.

Afr 1830.40.13   Un siècle de colonisation, études au microscope. (Gautier, E.F.) Paris, 1930.

Afr 1830.10.2   Un siècle de finances coloniales. (Donec, Martial.) Paris, 1930.

Afr 5765.22   Un siècle de mission protestante à Madagascar. (Mondain, G.) Paris, 1920.

Afr 555.2.101   Un siècle en Afrique et en Océanie. (Socété des Missions Evangéliques, Paris.) Paris, 1923.

Afr 7912.15.35   Le siècle marche; vie du chef congolais Lutunu. 2. éd. (Maquet-Tombu, Jeanno.) Bruxelles, 1952?

Afr 632.11F   Die Siedelungsverhältnisse der Bantu-Niger. (Schachtgabel, A.) Leiden, 1911.

NEDL   Afr 5130.3F   Le siège de Médine, 1857. (Monet, H.) Paris, n.d.

Afr 3315.126   Le siège de Suez. (Azeau, Henri.) Paris, 1964.

Afr 6174.2   The siege of Kumassi. (Hodgson, M.) N.Y., 1901.

Afr 8310.8   Siege of Mafeking. (Hamilton, J.A.) London, 1900.

Afr 8659.93   Siegfried, A. Afrique du Sud. Paris, 1949.

Afr 6143.21   Sierra Leone, its people, products, and secret societies. (Newland, H.) London, 1916.

Afr 6143.18   Sierra Leone, or The white man's grave. (Banbury, G.A.L.) London, 1888.

Afr Doc 1703.5F   Sierra Leone. Blue book. 7v.

Afr Doc 1709.5   Sierra Leone. Budget speech. Freetown. 1962+

Afr Doc 1703.7   Sierra Leone. Clerical staff list. Freetown. 1963+

Afr 6134.2   Sierra Leone. Collected statements of constitutional proposals. Freetown, 1955.

Afr Doc 1709.92   Sierra Leone. Development estimates. Freetown. 1962+

Afr 6144.2F   Sierra Leone. Education and economic development in Sierra Leone. Sierra Leone, 1962.

Afr Doc 1709.89   Sierra Leone. Estimates of revenue and expenditure. Freetown. 1959+

Afr Doc 1708.705   Sierra Leone. Quarterly trade statistics. Freetown. 41,1962+

Afr 6134.3F   Sierra Leone. Report, 1957. Sierra Leone, 1957.

Afr Doc 1705.5   Sierra Leone. Review of government departments. Freetown. 1960+

Afr Doc 1703.7.5   Sierra Leone. The staff list. Freetown. 1960+

Afr 6144.66F   Sierra Leone. Ten-year plan of economic and social development, 1962/63-1971/72. Freetown, 1962.

Afr Doc 1708.710   Sierra Leone. Trade report. Freetown. 1960+

Afr 6143.10   Sierra Leone. (Clarke, R.) London, n.d.

Afr Doc 1731.5   Sierra Leone. Audit Department. Report of the Director of Audit on the accounts of Sierra Leone. Freetown. 1956+

Afr Doc 1709.320F   Sierra Leone. Central Statistical Office. National accounts. Freetown. 2,1963+

Afr Doc 1707.5   Sierra Leone. Central Statistical Office. Quarterly statistical bulletin. Freetown. 1,1963+

Afr Doc 1707.363   Sierra Leone. Central Statistics Office. 1963 population census Sierra Leone. Freetown, 1965.

Afr 6145.3.5F   Sierra Leone. Commission of Enquiry into the Conduct of Certain Chiefs. Further reports of the commissioners of enquiry into the conduct of certain chiefs and the government statement thereon. Sierra Leone, 1957.

Afr 6141.2F   Sierra Leone. Commission of Inquiry into the Conduct of the 1967 General Elections in Sierra Leone. Report of the Dove-Edwin Commission of inquiry into the conduct of the 1967 general election in Sierra Leone and the government statement thereon. Freetown, 1967.

Afr 6147.8   Sierra Leone. Commission of Inquiry into the Strike and Riots in Freetown, Sierra Leone. Report. Freetown, 1955.

Afr 6144.8F   Sierra Leone. Commission to Enquire into and Report on the Matters Contained in the Director of Audit's Report on the Accounts of Sierra Leone for the Year 1960-1961. Report of the commission and the government statement thereon. Freetown, 1963.

Afr 6145.3F   Sierra Leone. Commissioners of Enquiry into the Conduct of Certain Chiefs. Reports of the commissioners of enquiry into the conduct of certain chiefs and the government statement thereon. Freetown, 1957.

Afr Doc 1719.5   Sierra Leone. Constitution. The Sierra Leone Constitution, Order in Council, 1961. Freetown, 1961.

Afr 6134.8   Sierra Leone. Constitutional Conference, London, 1960. Report. Freetown, 1960.

Afr Doc 1703.10 Sierra Leone. Department of External Affairs. Diplomatic and consular list, and list of Sierra Leone Commonwealth and Foreign Service postings. Freetown. 1967+

Afr Doc 1739.5 Sierra Leone. Department of Information. Report. Freetown. 1959+

Afr Doc 1724.5F Sierra Leone. Governor. Address by His Excellency the Governor on the occasion of the opening of the Legislative Council.

Afr Doc 1714.5 Sierra Leone. House of Representatives. Debates. 1958+

Afr Doc 1712.15 Sierra Leone. Legislative Council. Debates.
3v.

Afr Doc 1712.5F Sierra Leone. Legislative Council. Minutes. 1922-1925
3v.

Afr Doc 1712.10F Sierra Leone. Legislative Council. Sessional paper.

Afr 590.85 Sierra Leone. Liberated African Department. Notes from Liberated African Department. Uppsala, 1967.

Afr Doc 1702.5 Sierra Leone. Library Board. Sierra Leone publications. Freetown. 1962+

Afr Doc 1735.5 Sierra Leone. Ministry of Education. Report. Freetown. 1962+

Afr Doc 1743.5 Sierra Leone. Monuments and Relics Commission. Report. Freetown. 1955+

Afr 555.60 Sierra Leone. Native Church. Jubilee Committee. The jubilee volume of the Sierra Leone Native Church. London, 1917.

Afr Doc 1746.10 Sierra Leone. Posts and Telecommunications Deparment. Report. Freetown. 1959+

Afr Doc 1746.5 Sierra Leone. Public Service Commission. Report. Freetown. 1955+

Afr Doc 1746.15 Sierra Leone. Public Works Department. Report. Freetown. 1958+

Afr Doc 1748.5 Sierra Leone. Road Transport Department. Report. Freetown. 1955+

Afr Doc 1749.5 Sierra Leone. Surveys and Lands Department. Annual report. Freetown. 1963+

Afr Doc 1709.300 Sierra Leone. Treasury Department. Financial report. Freetown. 1957+

Afr 6143.68 Sierra Leone after a hundred years. 1st ed. (Ingham, Ernest Graham.) London, 1968.

Afr 6125.9 Sierra Leone bulletin of religion. Freetown. 2,1960+

Htn Afr 6138.2* Sierra Leone Company. Substance of the report delivered by the Court of directors of the Sierra Leone Company. Philadelphia, 1795.

Afr Doc 1719.5 The Sierra Leone Constitution, Order in Council, 1961. (Sierra Leone. Constitution.) Freetown, 1961.

Afr 6125.13 Sierra Leone Geographical Association. Occasional paper. Freetown. 1,1951+

Afr 6143.66 Sierra Leone in maps. (Clark, John Innes.) London, 1966.

Afr Doc 1702.5 Sierra Leone publications. (Sierra Leone. Library Board.) Freetown. 1962+

Afr 6125.5 Sierra Leone studies. Freetown. 5,1922+
7v.

Afr 6139.5 Sierra Leone trade journal. Freetown. 1,1961+
2v.

Afr 1432.22 Siete dias en el campamento de Africa. (Perez Calvo, Juan.) Madrid, 1860.

NEDL Afr 4259.36 Los siete mil anos de Etiopia. (Markoff, A.) Barcelona, 1936.

Afr 608.91 Sievers, W. Afrika. Eine allgemeine Landeskunde. Leipzig, 1891.

Afr 608.91.2 Sievers, W. Afrika. 2. Aufl. Leipzig, 1901.

Afr 1753.14 Un siglo medieval en la historia de Ceuta, 931-1031. (Leria, Manuel.) Ceuta, 1961.

Afr 11336.41.100 Signpost to fear. (Drin, Michael.) Cape Town, 1964.

Afr 109.61.25.5 Sik, Endre. Histoire de l'Afrique noire. Budapest, 1968.
2v.

Afr 109.61.25 Sik, Endre. Histoire de l'Afrique noire. v.1-Budapest, 1961.
2v.

Afr 109.61.26 Sik, Endre. The history of black Africa. Budapest, 1966.
2v.

Afr 4700.37 Silbani, T. L'impero (A.O.I.). Roma, 1937.

Afr 11005.4 Silbert, Rachel. Southern African drama in English, 1900-1964. Johannesburg, 1965.

Afr 8678.30 Silburn, P.A. South Africa, white and black or brown. London, 1927.

Afr 2870.14 Sillani, T. La Libia in venti anni di occupazione italiana. Roma, 1932.

Afr 4732.17 Sillani, Tomaso. L'Affrica orientale italiana. Roma, 1933.

Afr 4732.17.3 Sillani, Tomaso. L'Affrica orientale italiana. Roma, 1936.

Afr 9345.55 Sillery, A. The Bechuanaland protectorate. Cape Town, 1952.

Afr 9345.60 Sillery, A. Sechele. Oxford, 1954.

Afr 7219.28 Silva, J. Guides. Colonização. Lourenço Marques, 1928.

Afr 7335.5 Silva, Julia. Tavares de Almeida de Sousa e Lupata. Lisboa, 1966.

Afr 7188.150 Silva Carvalho na provincia portuguêsa de Angola. (Pereira, Henrique Antonio.) Montijo, 1966.

Afr 608.46.7 Silva Porto, Antonio Francisco Ferreira da. Silva Porto e a travessia do continente africano. Lisboa, 1938.

Afr 608.46.5 Silva Porto, Antonio Francisco Ferreira da. Viagens e apontamentos de um Portuense em Africa. Lisboa, 1942.

Afr 608.46.7 Silva Porto e a travessia do continente africano. (Silva Porto, Antonio Francisco Ferreira da.) Lisboa, 1938.

Afr 550.115 Silva Rego, Antonio da. Alguns problemas sociologicos missionarios da Africa negra. Lisboa, 1960.

Afr 1750.15 Silveira, L. Documentos portugueses sobre la accion de Espana en Africa. Madrid, 1954.

Afr 8035.5 Silver, S.W. S.W. Silver and Company's handbook to South Africa. London, 1880.
2v.

Afr 1095.25 Şimalî Afrikada Türkler. (Ilter Aziz Samih.) Istanbul, 1934-37.

Afr 7530.4 Simar, T. Bibliographie congolaise 1895-1910. Uccle, 1912.
2v.

Afr 7560.3.10 Simar, T. Le Congo au XVIe siècle d'aprés la relation de Lopez-Pigafetta. Bruxelles, 1919.

Afr 11853.88.120 Simbi and the satyr of the dark jungle. (Tutuola, Amos.) London, 1955.

Afr 8688.5.5 Simbole van die Unie. (Pama, C.) Kaapstad, 1960.

Afr 4559.23.10 Simen, its heights and abysses. (Maydon, H.C.) London, 1925.

Afr 4559.26.13 Simertz, S. En färd tell Abessinien. 2a upp. Stockholm, 1926.

Afr 575.11 Simian, M. Les confréries islamiques. Alger, 1910.

Afr 8953.5 Simmonds, Heather A. European immigration into Natal, 1824-1910. Cape Town, 1964.

Afr 9558.520 Simmons, Jack. Livingstone and Africa. London, 1966.

Afr 679.65 Simms, R.P. Urbanization in West Africa. Evanston, 1965.

Afr 1609.61.5 Simoes, Antonio. Marruecos, ayer-hoy. Buenos Aires, 1966.

Afr 7025.8 Simões, Martinho. Nos três frentes durante três messes. Lisboa?, 1966.

Afr 150.25 Simões Mueller, Adolfo. O principe do mar. Porto, 1959.

Afr 4558.85 Simon, Gabriel. Voyage en Abyssinie et chez les Gallas-Raias. Paris, 1885.

Afr 1571.39 Simon, H.J. Un officer d'Afrique, le commandant Verlet-Hanus. Paris, 1930.

Afr 6984.10 Simon, J.M. Bishop for the Hottentots. N.Y., 1959.

Afr 5385.37 Simon, Marc. Souvenirs de brousse, 1905-1910. Paris, 1965.

Afr 4513.37.37 Simon, Yves. La campagne d'Ethiopie et la pensée politique française. 2e éd. Lille, 1937.

Afr 8687.347 Simon van der Stel en sy kinders. (Boeseken, Anna I) Kaapstad, 1964.

Afr 8656.85.2 Simon van der Stel's journal. Supplement. (Stel, Simon van der.) London, 1953.

Afr 6455.86 Simonen, Seppo. Mau Mau iskee. Helsinki, 1954.

Afr 2938.25 Simonetti, R. Le opere pubbliche della Tripolitania e della Cirenaica. Roma, 1914.

Afr 8678.438 Simons, Harold. Class and colour in South Africa, 1850-1950. Harmondsworth, 1969.

Afr 4575.6 Simoons, Frederick. Northwest Ethiopia. Madison, 1960.

Afr 5868.87 Simples renseignements sur l'Ile Bourbon. (Pajot, Elie.) Paris, 1887.

Afr 6455.80 Simpson, Alyse. Red dust of Africa. London, 1952.

Afr 7377.61 Simpson, C.L. The memoirs of C.L. Simpson. London, 1961.

Afr 4180.3.15 Simpson, G.E. The heart of Libya, the Siwa Oasis, its people, customs and sport. London, 1929.

Afr 810.10 Simpson, W. Private journal kept during the Niger expedition. London, 1843.

Afr 7368.33 The sin of slavery and its remedy. (Wright, E.) N.Y., 1833.

Afr 3315.80 Sinai victory. (Marshall, S.L.A.) N.Y., 1958.

Afr 9203.5 Sinclair, Dorothy Mary. The Orange Free State goldfields; a bibliography. Cape Town, 1967.

Afr 11790.58.110 Sinclair, F.D. The cold veld. Wynberg, 1946.

Afr 11790.58.100 Sinclair, F.D. Lovers and hermits. Cape Town, 1957.

Afr 825.10 Sinclair, J.H. Dodging hippopotami and crocodiles in Africa. Rochester, 19- .

Afr 7809.51.5 Sinderen, A. van. The country of the mountains of the moon. N.Y., 1951.

Afr 679.29.5F Singer, Caroline. White Africans and black. N.Y., 1929.

Afr 11790.59.100 Singh, A.R. Behold the earth mourns. Johannesburg, 1961.

Afr 7889.2 Singhitini, la Stanleyville musulmane. (Thier, F.M.) Bruxelles, 1961.

Afr 109.67.20 Singleton, F. Seth. Africa in perspective. N.Y., 1967.

Afr 1738.35 La singuliere zone de Tanger. (Vernier, Victor.) Paris, 1955.

Afr Doc 9336.5 Sintese da actividade dos organismos e serviços. (Angola. Secretaria Provincial de Formento Rural.) Luanda. 1963+

Afr Doc 9345.5 Sintese da actividade dos serviços. (Angola. Secretaria Provincial de Obras Publicas e Comunicações.) Luanda. 1964+

Afr 5993.17 Sintesis geografica de Fernando Poo. (Jeran, Manuel de.) Madrid, 1962.

Afr 7812.256 Sion, Georges. Soixante-quinze ans de Congo. Gand, 1956.

Afr 7809.54.5 Sion, Georges. Voyages aux quartre coins du Congo, 1949-1952. 3.ed. Bruxelles, 1954.

Afr 8735.10 Sir Andries Stockenstrom, 1792-1864; the origin of the racial conflict in South Africa. (Dracopoli, J.L.) Cape Town, 1969.

Afr 8252.10.5 Sir Bartle Frere. (Worsfold, B.) London, 1923.

Afr 8703.5 Sir Benjamin d'Urbans administration. (Barker, Mary.) Cape Town, 1946.

Afr 8300.12 Sir Charles Warren and Spion Kop, a vindication. (Defender.) London, 1902.

Afr 7923.5 Sir Francis de Winton, administrateur général du Congo, 1884-1886. (Luwel, Marcel.) Tervuren, 1964.

Afr 6218.9 Sir George Goldie, founder of Nigeria. (Wellesley, D.A.) London, 1934.

Afr 6298.432 Sir George Goldie and the making of Nigeria. (Flint, John E.) London, 1960.

Afr 8687.128 Sir J.H. Meiring Beck. (Scully, W.C.) Cape Town, 1921.

Afr 4095.8.5 Sir S.W. Baker, a memoir. (Murray, T.D.) London, 1895.

Afr 3735.2 Sirdar and Khalifa. (Burleigh, B.) London, 1898.

Afr 3735.2.5 Sirdar and Khalifa. 3rd ed. (Burleigh, B.) London, 1898.

Afr 5190.22 Siré-Abbâs-Soh. Chroniques du Foûta senegalais. Traduit. Paris, 1913.

Afr 11240.5 Sirens, knuckles, boots. (Brutus, Dennis.) Ibadan, 1963.

Afr 5086.157.10 Siriex, Paul. Une nouvelle Afrique. Paris, 1957.

Afr 2950.15 Sirtis, studio geografico-storico. (Cerrata, L.) Avellino, 1933.

Afr 115.30.2 Sithhole, Ndabaningi. African nationalism. 2d ed. London, 1968.

Afr 115.30 Sithole, N. African nationalism. Cape Town, 1959.

Afr 1721.3 Sitio de San Antonio de alareche en 1689. (Narvaez Pacheco, J.) Madrid, 1893.

Afr 7176.7.10 A situação de Angola. (Angola. Governor General, 1923-1927 (Ferreira).) Luanda, 1927.

Afr 200.14 Situación politica de Africa en 1892. (Molto y Campo-Redondo, P.) Madrid, 1892.

Afr 3745.20 La situation administrative et économique du Soudan anglo-égyptien. These. (Cheibany, A.K.) Paris, 1926.

Afr 12002.1 Situation de la presse dans les états de l'Union Africaine et Malgache, en Guinée, au Mali, au Togo. (Gras, Jacqueline.) Paris, 1963.

Afr Doc 7108.5 La situation démographique au Tchad, résultats provisoires. (France. Institut National de la Statistique et des Etudes Economique.) Paris, 196-.

Afr Doc 6507.361.10 La situation démographique en Haute-Volta; résultats partiels de l'énquête démographique, 1960-1961. (Upper Volta. Service de Statistique.) Paris, 1962.

Afr 2618.10 La situation des cultes en Tunisie. Thèse. (Darmon, Raoul.) Paris, 1928.

Afr Doc 5002.5 Situation des enquêtes statistiques et socio-économiques dans les états africains et malgaches. (France. Institut National de la Statistique et des Etudes Economiques.) Paris. 1964+

Afr 1495.5 La situation des Français au Maroc depuis l'indépendance, 1956-1964. (Cassaigne, Jean.) Paris, 1965.

	Afr 9450.35	Smith, Donald. Rhodesia: the problem. London, 1969.
X Cg	Afr 9700.5	Smith, E. Pla-speaking people of Northern Rhodesia. London, 1920. 2v.
	Afr 545.5	Smith, E.W. African ideas of God. London, 1950.
	Afr 9345.65	Smith, E.W. Great lion of Bechuanaland. London, 1957.
	Afr 8687.258	Smith, E.W. The life and times of Daniel Lindley. N.Y., 1952.
	Afr 8931.53	Smith, E.W. The Mabilles of Basutoland. London, 1939.
	Afr 6192.100	Smith, Edward. Where to, black man? Chicago, 1967.
	Afr 550.18.1	Smith, Edwin. Aggrey of Africa. N.Y., 1929.
	Afr 550.18	Smith, Edwin. Aggrey of Africa. N.Y., 1930.
	Afr 609.26	Smith, Edwin. The golden stool, some aspects of the conflict of cultures in modern Africa. London, 1926.
	Afr 609.26.4	Smith, Edwin. The golden stool, some aspects of the conflict of cultures in modern Africa. Garden City, N.Y., 1928.
	Afr 550.16	Smith, Edwin W. The Christian mission in Africa. London, 1926.
	Afr 555.22.28	Smith, Edwin W. The way of the white fields in Rhodesia. London, 1928.
	Afr 9700.5.5	Smith, Edwin William. The Ila-speaking peoples of Northern Rhodesia. New Hyde Park, 1968. 2v.
	Afr 4558.90	Smith, F.H. Through Abyssinia. London, 1890.
	Afr 7350.3.35	Smith, G. Facts designed to exhibit the real character and tendency of the American Colonizaton Society. Liverpool, 1833.
	Afr 8279.02.5	Smith, Goldwin. Devant le tribunal de l'histoire. Montreal, 1903.
	Afr 8279.02	Smith, Goldwin. In the court of history. Toronto, 1902.
	Afr 7815.6	Smith, H.S. Yakusu. London, 1911.
	Afr 6599.2	Smith, Herbert Maynard. Frank, bishop of Zanzibar. London, 1926.
	Afr 678.51	Smith, J. Trade and travels in the Gulph of Guinea. London, 1851.
	Afr 3978.52	Smith, J.V.C. A pilgrimage to Egypt. Boston, 1852.
	Afr 6284.8	Smith, John Hilary. Colonial cadet in Nigeria. Durham, N.C., 1968.
	Afr 9704.8	Smith, Julia A. Sunshine and shade in Central Africa. London, 1911.
	Afr 6280.50F	Smith, M.G. The economy of Hausa communities of Zaria. London, 1955.
	Afr 6295.60.5	Smith, Michael. Government in Zazzau, 1800-1950. London, 1960.
	Afr 6195.19	Smith, Noel. The Presbyterian Church of Ghana, 1835-1960. Accra, 1966.
	Afr 11797.41.111	Smith, Pauline. The beadle. Cape Town, 1956.
	Afr 11797.41.100A	Smith, Pauline. The little karoo. N.Y., 1925.
	Afr 11797.41.102	Smith, Pauline. The little karoo. N.Y., 1952.
	Afr 7380.5	Smith, Robert A. The emancipation of the hinterland. Monrovia, 1964.
	Afr 7489.88.2	Smith, Robert A. William V.S. Tubman. The life and work of an African statesman. 2nd ed. Amsterdam, 1967.
	Afr 10839.55.110	Smith, Wilbur Addison. Iets moet sterf. Johannesburg, 1965.
	Afr 10839.55.100	Smith, Wilbur Addison. When the lion feeds. N.Y., 1964.
	Afr 6095.22	Smith, William. A new voyage to Guinea. London, 1744.
	Afr 6095.22.10	Smith, William. A new voyage to Guinea: describing the customs. 1st ed. London, 1967.
	Afr 6095.22.5	Smith, William. Nouveau voyage de Guinée. Paris, 1751.
	Afr 8252.342.5	Smithers, E.D. March hare. London, 1935.
	Afr 6887.12.10	Smoke in the hills. (Young, Roland A.) Evanston, 1960.
	Afr 210.30	Smuts, J.C. Africa and some world problems. Oxford, 1930.
	Afr 8252.341.70	Smuts, J.C. Greater South Africa. Johannesburg, 1940.
	Afr 8369.42.1	Smuts, J.C. Investing in friendship. London, 1942.
	Afr 8252.341.45	Smuts, J.C. Jan Christian Smuts. London, 1952.
	Afr 8252.341.47	Smuts, J.C. Jan Christian Smuts. N.Y., 1952.
	Afr 8369.42.2	Smuts, J.C. Plans for a better world. London, 1942.
	Afr 8252.341.48	Smuts, J.C. Selections from the Smuts papers. Cambridge, 1966.
	Afr 8252.341.18	Smuts, J.C. The thoughts of General Smuts. Cape Town, 1951.
	Afr 8369.42.10A	Smuts, J.C. Toward a better world. N.Y., 1944.
	Afr 8678.88	Smuts, Jan Christian. The basis of trusteeship in African native policy. Johannesburg, 1942.
	Afr 8252.341.83	Smuts; study for a portrait. (Hancock, William Keith.) London, 1965.
	Afr 8252.341.80A	Smuts. (Hancock, William Keith.) Cambridge, 1962. 2v.
	Afr 8369.43.7	Smuts and swastika. (Campbell, Alex.) London, 1943.
	Afr 8252.341.82	Smuts and the shift of world power. (Hancock, William Keith.) London, 1964.
	Afr 8252.341.35	Smuts of South Africa. (Wilson, Dorothy F.) London, 1946.
	Afr 8252.341.65	The Smuts papers. (Hancock, William Keith.) London, 1956.
	Afr 6275.60	Smythe, Hugh. The new Nigerian elite. Stanford, 1960.
	Afr 6170.17	Snape, Thomas. The Ashantee war, causes and results...lecture. Manchester, 1874.
	Afr 2030.235	Sneider, Bertrand. La Cinquième République et l'Algérie. Paris, 1959.
Htn	Afr 5318.2*	Snelgrave, W. A new account of parts of Guinea. London, 1734.
	Afr 10916.2	Snelling, John. Fifty years of Rhodesian verse. Oxford, 1939.
	Afr 10916.3	Snelling, John. A new anthology of Rhodesian verse. Oxford, 1950.
	Afr 8678.308	Snethlage, J.L. Meer begrip voor Suid-Afrika. Amsterdam, 1964.
	Afr 2438.32	Snoussi, Mohamed. Les collectivités locales en Tunisie. Paris, 1958.
	Afr 5230.8	Snyder, Frank Gregory. One-party government in Mali. New Haven, 1965.
	Afr 11005.5F	Snyman, J.P.L. A bibliography of South African novels in English. Potchefstroom, 1951.
	Afr 11572.50.800	Snyman, J.P.L. The works of Sarah Gertrude Millin. South Africa, 1955.
	Afr 8095.65	So few are free. (Green, Laurence G.) Cape Town, 1948.
	Afr 8809.63	So high the road, mountain passes of the western Cape. (Burman, Jose.) Cape Town, 1963.
	Afr 6420.76	So rough a wind. (Blundell, M.) London, 1964.
	Afr 6455.82	So this is Kenya. (Brodhurst-Hill, Evelyn.) London, 1936.
	Afr 1069.38	Soames, Jane. The coast of Barbary. London, 1938.
	Afr 7176.14	Soares, Amaden. Politica de bem e estoi rival en Angola. Lisbon, 1961.
	Afr 150.2.15	Soares, Ernesto. Iconografia do Infante Dom Henrique. Lisboa, 1959.
	Afr 7176.12	Sob o signo do real. (Ferreira, Eugenio.) Luanda, 1961.

Afr 7182.20	Sobre a religião dos Quiocos. (Santos, Eduardo dos.) Lisboa, 1962.
Afr 555.2.101	Socété des Missions Evangéliques, Paris. Un siècle en Afrique et en Océanie. Paris, 1923.
Afr 4513.38.20A	The social and economic system of Italian East Africa. (Società Editrice di Novissima, Rome.) Roma, 1938.
Afr 9700.50	Social and ritual life of the Ambo of Northern Rhodesia. (Stefaniszyn, Bronislaw.) London, 1964.
Afr 9693.10	Social change and the individual: a study of the social and religious responses to innovation in a Zambian rural community. (Long, Norman.) Manchester, 1968.
Afr 6196.20.5	Social change at Larteh, Ghana. (Brokensha, David W.) Oxford, 1966.
Afr 632.30	Social change in modern Africa. (International African Seminar.) London, 1961.
Afr 5640.10	Social conditions...in Madagascar. (Peill, J.) n.p., n.d.
Afr 6883.31	Social control in an African society, a study of the Arusha, agricultural Masai of northern Tanganyika. (Gulliver, P.H.) Boston, 1963.
Afr 6883.31.2	Social control in an African society. (Gulliver, P.H.) London, 1963.
Afr Doc 3226.5	Social development report. (Kenya.) Nairobi. 1956-1957
Afr 9699.67	A social geography of Zambia; a survey of population. (Kay, George.) London, 1967.
Afr 626.56	Social implications of industrialization and urbanization in Africa, south of the Sahara. (International African Institute, London.) Paris, 1956.
Afr 3978.84F	Social life in Egypt. (Lane-Poole, S.) London, 1884.
Afr 8110.10A	Social life in the Cape colony in the 18th century. (Botha, C.G.) Cape Town, 1926.
Afr 9603.15	Social networks in urban situations. (Mitchell, J.C.) Manchester, 1969.
Afr 8825.6	Social organisation and ceremonial institutions of the Bomvana. (Cook, R.A.W.) Cape Town, 19- .
Afr 6194.27	Social organization of the Ga people. (Field, Margaret Joyce.) London, 1940.
Afr 6194.32	The social organization of the Lo Wiili. (Goody, J.R.) London, 1956.
Afr 6194.32.2	The social organization of the Lo Wiili. 2nd ed. (Goody, J.R.) London, 1967.
Afr 5842.20	Social policies and population growth in Mauritius. (Titmuss, R.M.) London, 1961.
Afr 9689.61.5	Social research and community development. (Rhodes-Livingston Institute, Lusaka, Northern Rhodesia.) Lusaka, 1961.
Afr 115.106	Social Sciences Research Conference. Problems of transition. Pietermaritzburg, Natal, 1964.
Afr 8685.61	The social structure of a cape coloured reserve. (Carstens, W. Peter.) Cape Town, 1966.
Afr 4640.3	Social survey of Addis Ababa, 1960. (Haile Selassie I University.) Addis Ababa, 1960.
Afr 9045.15	The social system of the Zulus. (Krige, E.J.) London, 1936.
Afr 632.50	Social theory and African tribal organization. (Carlston, Kenneth Smith.) Urbana, 1968.
Afr Doc 3749.14F	Social welfare; annual report. (Rhodesia, Northern. Department of Welfare and Probation Services.) Lusaka. 1,1952
Afr 2223.924.5	Le socialisme en Algérie. Thèse. (Juving, Alex.) Alger, 1924.
Afr 7100.15	Sociedade Cultural De Angola. Cadernos culturais. Luanda.
Afr 7020.35	Sociedade de Geografia de Lisboa. Boletim. Numero comemorativo da entrega a S. Ex. a Presidente da republica. Lisboa, 1938.
Afr 7065.7	Sociedade de Geografia de Lisboa. Congresso comemorativo do quinto centenario do descobrimento da Guinea. Lisboa, 1946. 2v.
Afr 7182.8	Sociedade de Geographia de Lisboa. Commissão africana missões de Angola. Lisboa, 1892.
Afr 4745.5	Società di Studi Geografici e Coloniali. L'Eritrea economica. Novara, 1913.
Afr 4513.36.105	Societa Editrice de Novissima, Roma. Facts Geneva refuses to see. Roma, 1936.
Afr 4513.38.20A	Società Editrice di Novissima, Rome. The social and economic system of Italian East Africa. Rome, 1938.
Afr 4700.35.15	Societa Geografica Italiana, Roma. L'Africa orientale. Bologna, 1935.
Afr 2929.37	Società Geografica Italiana, Rome. Il Sahara italiano. Pt.1. Rome, 1937.
Afr 4742.3	Societa Italiana per il Progresso delle Scienze, Rome. La colonia Eritrea. Fasc.1 Roma, 1913.
Afr 2949.5	Società Italiana per lo Studio della Libia. Missione Franchetti in Tripolitania (Il Gebel). Firenze, 1914.
Afr 1819.4.6	Société Archéologique, Historique et Géographique du Département de Constantine. Bulletin mensuel. Constantine. 35,1930+
Afr 1819.4	Societe Archéologique de Constantine. Recueil des notices et mémoires. Constantine. 1,1953+ 7v.
Afr 5282.8	Société d'Aide Technique et de Cooperation. Données critiques sur la campagne depuis villageois encadrée par la SATEC en Haute-Volta. Paris, 1965.
Afr 5344.10	Une société de Côte-d'Ivoire. (Paulme, Denise.) Paris, 1962.
Afr 5056.131.5	Societe de Géograhie, Paris. D'Algérie au Sénégal, mission Augieras-Draper, 1927-1928. Texte et plates. Paris, 1931. 2v.
Afr 1819.1	Société de Géographie d'Alger et de l'Afrique du Nord. Bulletin. Alger. 1,1896+ 32v.
Afr 1018.2	Société de Géographie de la Province d'Oran. Bulletin trimestriel. Paris. 7,1887+ 55v.
Afr 1018.2.5	Société de Géographie de la Province d'Oran. Journal des travaux, 1878-1927. (Table générale.) Oran, 1898-1930. 3v.
Afr 630.13	Société de Géographie d'Egypte. Catalogue of the Ethnographical Museum of the Royal Geographical Society of Egypt. Le Caire, 1924.
Afr 5849.82	Société de l'Histoire de l'Ile Maurice. Dictionnaire de biographie mauricienne. Dictionary of Mauritian biography. v.1-30- Saint Louis, 1941- 5v.
Afr 5045.42	Société d'Editions Géographiques. Afrique française. Paris, 1931.

Afr 19.14	Société des Africanistes, Paris. Journal. Paris. 1,1931+ 16v.
Afr 19.16	Société des Africanistes, Paris. Centre de Documentation et d'Information. Bulletin d'information. Paris. 1-6,1964-1965//
Afr 2223.57	Société des Fermes Françaises de Tunisie. Trente-deux ans de colonisation nord-africaine. Paris, 1931.
Afr 2223.55	Société des Fermes Françaises de Tunisie. Vingt-cinq ans de colonisation nord-africaine. Paris, 1925.
Afr 550.80	La société des missions africaines. 2. éd. (Guilcher, René F.) Lyon, 1956.
Afr 550.29	Société des Missions Evangéliques, Paris. Nos champs de mission. 3e éd. Paris, 1922.
Afr 4513.60	La Société des Nations devant le conflit italo-éthiopien. (Cohen, Armand.) Genève, 1960.
Afr 2731.4	Société d'Etudes du Chemin de Fer Transafricain. Mission du Transafricain. v.1,2 and atlas. Paris, 1924-25. 3v.
Afr 4045.10	Societe d'Etudes Historiques et Géographiques de l'isthme de Suez. Cahiers. Le Caire. 1,1955
Afr 6739.260	Societe d'Etudes pour le Developpement. Rapport sur les possibilités de développement industriél. Paris, 1960.
Afr 5091.10	Société d'Etudes pour le Développement Economique et Social, Paris. Analyse de l'économie de la République islamique de Mauritanie en 1959. Paris, 1961.
Afr 5282.3	Société d'Etudes pour le Développement Economique et Social, Paris. Développement économique en Haute-Volta. Paris, 1963. 2v.
Afr 6739.265	Société d'Etudes pour le Développement Economique et social. Développement industriel au Cameroun. Paris, 1965.
Afr 5488.16F	Société d'Etudes pour le Développement Economique et Social. Etude socio-économique de la ville d'Abéché. Paris, 1965.
Afr 5343.10.5	Société d'Etudes pour le Développement Economique et Social, Paris. Etudes de petites industries en Côte-d'Ivoire. Paris, 1966.
Afr 6686.48.25F	Société d'Etudes pour le Développement Économique et Social, Paris. Plan de développement, 1966-1970: organization administrative et développement. Paris, 1965.
Afr 6686.48.45F	Société d'Etudes pour le Développement Economique et Social, Paris. Plan de développement économique et social, 1966-1970. Paris, 1965.
Afr 6686.48.35F	Société d'Etudes pour le Développement Économique et Social, Paris. Plan de développement économique et social, 1966-1970: scolarisation. Paris, 1965.
Afr 5343.10.2	Société d'Etudes pour le Développement Economique et Social. Rapport de synthèse. Paris, 1963.
Afr 5346.6	Société d'Etudes pour le Développement Economique et Social. Région de Korhogo. T.1-8. Paris, 1965. 3v.
Afr 5343.10	Société d'Etudes pour le Développement Economique et Social. Le sud-est frontalier. Paris, 1963. 2v.
Afr 2218.6	La société féminine au Djebel amour et au Ksel. (Gaudry, Mathéa.) Alger, 1961.
Afr 6739.260.5F	Société Générale d'Etudes et de Planification, Paris. Cameroun. Paris, 1960. 2v.
Afr 1826.27	Société Historique Algerienne. Vingt cinq ans d'histoire algerienne. 4 in 1. Alger, 1856.
Afr 2368.5	Société Historique et Géographique de la Région de Sétif. Bulletin. Sétif.
Afr 1609.12.9	La societe marocaine. (Mauran.) Paris, 1912.
Afr 5056.108	La société noire de l'Afrique occidentale française. (Cheran, Georges.) Paris, 1908.
Afr 5185.10	Une société rurale au Senegal. (Reverdy, Jean Claude.) Aix-en-Provence, 1968?
Afr 7803.45	La société secrète des Bakhimba au Mayombe. (Bittremieux, Leo.) Bruxelles, 1936.
Afr 5185.12	Société toucouleur et migration. (Diop, Abdoulaye.) Dakar, 1965.
Afr 632.9	Les sociétés africaines. (Preville, A. de.) Paris, 1894.
Afr 7815.15	Les sociétés bantoues du Congo belge. (Kerken, Georges van der.) Bruxelles, 1919.
Afr 5243.125.25	Sociétés d'initiation bambara. v.1. (Zahan, Dominique.) Paris, 1960.
Afr 5408.5	Les sociétés primitives de l'Afrique. (Cureau, Adolphe L.) Paris, 1912.
Afr 590.42	Society for Abolishing Slavery All over the World, Newcastle-Upon-Tyne. Declaration of the objects. Newcastle, 1836.
Afr 19.20	Society for African Church History. Bulletin. London. 2,1965+
Afr 3305.12.10	The society of the Muslim Brothers. (Mitchell, Richard Paul.) London, 1969.
Afr 630.56.10	Sociologia del Africa negra. (Spinola, Francisco Elias de Tejada.) Madrid, 1956.
Afr 5408.15.2	Sociologie actuelle de l'Afrique noire, changements sociaux au Gabon et au Congo. (Balandier, Georges.) Paris, 1955.
Afr 5408.15	Sociologie actuelle de l'Afrique noire. (Balandier, Georges.) Paris, 1955.
Afr 5408.15.5	Sociologie actuelle de l'Afrique noire. (Balandier, Georges.) Paris, 1955.
Afr 210.64.80	Sociologie de la nouvelle Afrique. (Ziegler, Jean.) Paris, 1964.
Afr 2225.14	Sociologie de l'Algérie. 1. ed. (Bourdieu, Pierre.) Paris, 1958.
Afr 1840.24	Sociologie électorale en Afrique du Nord. (Purtschet, Christian.) Paris, 1966.
Afr 3993.903	Socolis, Georges. Notes sur l'Egypte et son histoire économique depuis 30 ans. Paris, 1903.
Afr 5440.20.5	Soedergren, Sigfried. Sweet smell of mangoes. London, 1968.
Afr 11433.74.110	The soft voice of the serpent. (Gordimer, N.) N.Y., 1952.
Afr 8678.13.20	Soga, J.H. The south-eastern Bantu Abe-Nguni, Aba-Mbo, Ama-Lala. Johannesburg, 1930.
Afr 7540.42	Sohier, Jean. Essai sur les transformations des coutumes. Bruxelles, 1956.
Afr 14805.1	Soiá. (Reis, Fernando.) Braga, 1965.
Afr 7912.5	Soiuz Zhurnalistov SSSR. Patris Lumumba. Moscow, 1961.
Afr 2618.26	Soixante ans de pensée tunisienne à travers les revues. (Demeerseman, A.) Tunis, 1955.
Afr 7812.256	Soixante-quinze ans de Congo. (Sion, Georges.) Gand, 1956.

Afr 6455.157	Soja, Edward W. The geography of modernization in Kenya. Syracuse, N.Y., 1968.
Afr 6277.84	Sokolski, Alan. The establishment of manufacturing in Nigeria. N.Y., 1965.
Afr 6292.82.5	The Sokoto Caliphate. (Last, Murray.) London, 1967.
Afr 13286.38.100	Sola ma chérie. (Philombe, René.) Yaoundé, 1966.
Afr 2362.5	Solal, Edouard. Philippeville et sa région. Alger, 1957.
Afr 679.27.6	Solanke, Ladipo. United West Africa, or Africa, at the bar of the family of nations. London, 1969.
Afr 10689.68.100	Solarin, Tai. Thinking with you. Iheja, 1965.
Afr 7567.6	Soldats et missionnaires au Congo de 1891 à 1894. (Gochet, J.B.) Bruxelles, 1896.
Afr 2731.15.35	Soldier of the spirit. (Carrouges, Michel.) N.Y., 1956.
Afr 6535.16	Soldiering and sport in Uganda. (Lardner, E.S.D.) London, 1912.
Afr 6497.12	Soldiering and surveying in British East Africa (MacDonald, J.R.L.) London, 1897.
Afr 8289.13	A soldier's diary, South Africa 1899-1901. (Jackson, M.C.) London, 1913.
Afr 8252.12	A soldiers life and work in South Africa 1872-1879. (Durnford, E.) London, 1882.
Afr 2030.464.40	Le soleil ne chauffe que les vivants. (Scherb, J.D.) Paris, 1964.
Afr 12884.65.110	Le soleil noir point. (Nokan, Charles.) Paris, 1962.
Afr 2748.81	Soleillet, P. Les voyages...dans le Sahara. Paris, 1881.
Afr 2285.4	Soleillet, Paul. L'Afrique occidentale. Paris, 1877.
Afr 4558.84.5	Soleillet, Paul. Voyages en Ethiopie jan. 1882-oct. 1884. Rouen, 1886.
Afr 12881.67.100	Les soleils des indépendances. (Kourouma, Ahmadou.) Montréal, 1968.
Afr 590.79	Solgt som slave. (Edressen, Halfdan.) Oslo, 1965.
Afr 6900.5	Solidarity. Cairo.
Afr 3198.86	Solimar-Pacha...guerres de l'Egypte. (Vingtrinier, A.) Paris, 1886.
Afr 4180.6	Sollum and its environments. (Lackany, Radames Sany.) Alexandria, 1954.
Afr 7353.6	Solomon, Marian D. A general bibliography of the Republic of Liberia. Evanston, 1962.
Afr 8687.342	Solomon, W.E. Saul Solomon, the member for Cape Town. Cape Town, 1948.
Afr 3138.5	Solomon Ben Joseph, Ha-Kohen. The Turcoman defeat at Cairo. Chicago, 1906.
Afr 5312.10	Solonitskii, A.S. Gvineiskaia Respublika. Moscow, 1961.
Afr 5312.10.5	Solonitskii, A.S. Republik Guinea. Berlin, 1962.
Afr 1623.965.5	Solonitskii, Aleksandr S. Sotsial'no-ekonomicheskoe razvotie sovremennogo Marokko. Moskva, 1965.
Afr 3979.27	Solskivans land. (Rydh, H.) Stockholm, 1927.
Afr 1755.15	Una solucion a los conflictos de Melilla. (Marenco, Servando.) Madrid, 1894.
Afr 1990.12	Solution de la question de l'Algérie. (Duvivier.) Paris, 1841.
Afr 1040.5	Une solution fédéraliste du problème nord-africain. (Vassenhove, Léon van.) Neuchâtel, 1957.
Afr 8680.45	Solution for South Africa. (Katzew, Henry.) Cape Town, 1955.
Afr 1570.9	La solution française de la question du Maroc. (Fallot, E.) Paris, 1904.
Afr 4766.9	The Somali dispute. (Drysdale, J.G.S.) London, 1964.
Afr 4766.33A	Somali nationalism. (Wettman, I.M.) Cambridge, 1963.
Afr Doc 709.5	Somalia. Bilancio di previsione per l'esercizio finanziario. Mogadiscio. 1962+
Afr 4764.938	Somalia. (Italy. Esercito. Corpo di Stato Maggiore. Ufficio Storico.) Roma, 1938. 2v.
Afr 4766.36	Somalia. Consiglio dei Ministri. L'attività del governo dall'indipendenza ad oggi. Mogadiscio, 1964.
Afr Doc 719.12	Somalia. Constitution. The Constitution. Mogadiscio, 1964?
Afr 4772.10	Somalia. Council of Ministers. Government activities from independence until today. Mogadiscio, 1964.
Afr Doc 708.731F	Somalia. Customs and Excise Department. Annual trade report of Northern Region. Mogadiscio. 1960+
Afr Doc 707.15F	Somalia. Ministry of Planning and Coordination. Statistical Department. Bollettino trimestralle di statistica. Mogadiscio. 1,1966+
Afr Doc 707.10.2F	Somalia. Ministry of Planning and Coordination. Statistical Department. A multipurpose survey of Afgoi municipality. Mogadiscio, 1966.
Afr 4787.12	Somalia. Planning Commission. Short term development programme, 1968-1970. Mogadiscio, 1968.
Afr Doc 707.5	Somalia. Planning Directorate. Statistical Department. Compendio statistico. Mogadiscio. 2,1965+
Afr Doc 708.733F	Somalia. Planning Directorate. Statistical Department. Statistica del commercio con l'estero. Mogadiscio. 1964+
Afr 4772.5F	Somalia. Prime Minister. Statement of programme by Abdirizak Hagi Hussen, Prime Minister and President of the Council of Ministers. Mogadiscio, 1964.
Afr Doc 708.732F	Somalia. Statistical Service. Statistica del commercio con l'estero (delle Regioni Meridionali). Mogadiscio. 1961+
Afr 4764.957	Somalia. v.1-2. (Cerulli, Enrico.) Roma, 1957-64. 3v.
Afr 4766.15.4	Somalia. 4a ed. (Vecchi, Bernardo V.) Milano, 1936.
Afr 4785.29	Somalia (ricordi e visioni). (Monile, F.) Bologna, 1932.
Afr 4770.5	Somalia italiana. (Bollati, Ambiogio.) Roma, 1938.
Afr 4764.934	La Somalia italiana. (Cesari, Cesare.) Roma, 1934-35.
Afr 4785.39	La Somalia italiana. (Corni, G.) Milano, 1937. 2v.
Afr 4785.6	La Somalia italiana. (Mocchi, L.) Napoli, 1896.
Afr 4766.25	La Somalia italiana nell antichità classica. (Gasparro, A.) Palermo, 1910.
Afr 4869.39.12	La Somalie française. (Aubert de la Rue, E.) Paris, 1939.
Afr 4785.965	Somaliiskaia Respublika. (Sergeeva, Irina S.) Moskva, 1965.
Afr 4760.5	Somaliland, Italian. Manuale per la Somalia italiana, 1912. Roma, 1912.
Afr 4790.10.30F	Somaliland, Italian. Monografia delle regioni della Somalia. v.1-3 and atlas. Torino, 1926-27.
Afr 4753.10	Somaliland, Italian. Camera di commercio, industria ed agricoltura. Bibliografia somala. Mogadiscio, 1958.
Afr 4935.6	Somaliland. (Hamilton, Angus.) London, 1911.
Afr 4969.00	Somaliland. (Peel, C.V.A.) London, 1900.
Afr 4766.23	Somaliland under Italian administration. (Finkelstein, L.S.) N.Y., 1955.
Afr 9525.435	Some account of George Gray and his work in Africa. London, 1914.

Htn Afr 699.08	Some African highways, journey of two American women to Uganda and the Transvaal. (Kirkland, Caroline.) London, 1908.
Afr 8673.19	Some Africana coloured prints and the originals from which they may have been made. (Johannesburg. Public Library.) Johannesburg, 1963.
Afr 8676.53	Some aspects of the South African industrial revolution. 2d ed. (Eck, H.J. van.) Johannesburg, 1953.
Afr 4115.26	Some Cairo mosques. (Devonshire, Henrietta Caroline.) London, 1921.
Afr 8238.4	Some dreams come true. (Williams, Alpheus Fuller.) Cape Town, 1949.
Afr 8028.132F	Some English writings by non-Europeans in South Africa, 1944-1960. (Wilkoy, A.) Johannesburg, 1962.
Afr 2819.60	Some facts about Libya. (Murabet, Mohammed.) Malta, 1960.
Afr 6390.65.5	Some historic journeys in East Africa. (Richards, C.G.) London, 1961.
Afr 590.45.2	Some historical account of Guinea, its situation, produce, and the general disposition of its inhabitants. 2nd ed. (Benezet, Anthony.) London, 1968.
Htn Afr 677.71.5*	Some historical account of Guinea. (Benezet, Anthony.) London, 1772.
Htn Afr 677.71*	Some historical account of Guinea. (Benezet, Anthony.) Philadelphia, 1771. 2 pam.
Afr 677.71.10	Some historical account of Guinea: its situation. 2nd ed. (Benezet, Anthony.) London, 1968.
Afr 6775.5	Some historical notes on East Africa. (Robinson, A.E.) n.p., 1936.
Afr 8325.45	Some lessons from the Boer War. (Pilcher, T.D.) London, 1903.
Afr 9558.14	Some letters from Livingstone, 1840-1872. (Livingstone, D.) London, 1940.
Afr 8659.03.5	Some letters from South Africa, 1894-1902. (Scott, Edward Daniel.) Manchester, Eng., 1903.
Afr 10685.67.120	Some men and women. (Okoye, Mokwugo.) Onitsha, 195-.
Afr 6280.11.15	Some Nigerian fertility cults. (Talbot, P.A.) London, 1927.
Afr 6392.5	Some notes on industrial development in East Africa. (East Africa High Commission.) Nairobi, 1956.
Afr 6392.15	Some notes on industrial development in East Africa. 2nd ed. (East Africa High Commission.) Nairobi, 1959.
Afr 8252.19	Some reminiscences. (Phillips, L.) London, 1924.
Afr 11448.77.100	Some small compassion. (Harris, Peter.) Cape Town, 1964.
Afr 8055.30	Some South African politicians. (Neame, L.E.) Cape Town, 1929.
Afr 8278.99.5	Some South African recollections. (Phillips, F.) London, 1899.
Afr 8685.3	Some Zulu customs and folk-lore. (Samuelson, L.H.) London, n.d.
Afr 9558.59	Somervell, D.C. Livingstone. London, 1936.
Afr 4070.45	Something new out of Africa. (Howard-Williams, E.G.) London, 1934.
Afr 8659.50.10	Somewhere south of Suez. (Reed, D.) London, 1950.
Afr 8659.50.10.2	Somewhere south of Suez. (Reed, D.) N.Y., 1951.
Afr 7549.48.10	Sommaire de l'histoire du Congo belge. (Cornet, Rene Jules.) Bruxelles, 1948.
Afr 3035.2	Sommaire des archives turques du Caire. (Deny, Jean.) Caire, 1930.
Afr 618.12	Sommer, F. Man and beast in Africa. 1st American ed. N.Y., 1954.
Afr 28.37	Sommer, John W. Bibliography of African geography, 1940-1964. Hanover, N.H., 1965
Afr 4226.8	Sommer, John W. A study guide for Ethiopia and the Horn of Africa. Boston, 1969.
Afr 8659.67.5	Somoy, A.G. Paspoort voor Zuid-Afrika. Lier, 1967.
Afr 10673.48.100	Song of a goat. (Clark, John Pepper.) Ibadan, 1961.
Afr 23135.46.30	SongOf Lawino. (p'Bitek, Okot.) Nairobi, 1966.
Afr 11053.2	Songs and war cries. (Johannesburg. University of the Witwatersrand.) Johannesburg, 1936.
Afr 11757.58.100	Songs by the stoep. (Runcie, John.) London, 1905.
Afr 11433.64.100	Songs from the settler city. (Goodwin, Harold.) Grahamstown, 1963.
Afr 10636.4.100	Songs from the wilderness. (Parkes, Frank K.) London, 1965.
Afr 11051.3	Songs of the veld, and other poems. London, 1902.
Afr 9500.50	Sonius, H.W.J. Rhodesia, een dilemma van ras en grond. Leiden, 1966.
Afr 8678.9.50	Sonnabend, E.H. Il fattore demografico nell'organizzazione sociale del Bantu. Roma, 1935.
Afr 1259.44.15	Sonnen-Bilder aus Nord-Afrika. (Tefri (Pseud.)) Bulle, 1944.
Afr 11052.3	Sonnets of South Africa. (Crouch, E.H.) London, 1911.
Afr 3977.99	Sonnini, C.S. Voyage dans ... Egypte. v.1-3 + atlas. Paris, 1799. 4v.
Afr 3979.13.5	La sonrisa de la esfinge. (Gomez Carrillo, E.) Madrid, 1913.
Afr 2218.8	Sons et images dans le bled algérien. (Frère, Suzanne.) Alger, 1961.
Afr 55.34	Sons of Africa. (Gollock, Georgina Anne.) London, 1928.
Afr 4012.1	Sons of Ishmael. (Murray, G.W.) London, 1935.
Afr 6282.44	Sons of Tiv; a study of the rise of the church among the Tiv of Central Nigeria. (Rubingh, Eugene.) Grand Rapids, Michigan, 1969.
Afr 555.138	Soras, Alfred de. Relations de l'église et de l'état dans les pays d'Afrique francophone. Paris, 1963.
Afr 2875.17	Sorbi, R. In Libia. Firenze, n.d.
Afr 6390.25	The sorcerer's apprentice, a journey through East Africa. (Huxley, Elspeth J.G.) London, 1948.
Afr 9610.16	Sorcery in its social setting. (Marwick, Maxwell Gay.) Manchester, 1965.
Afr 530.7	Sorela, Luis. Alemania en Africa. Berlin, 1884.
Afr 5960.6	Sorela, Luis. Les possessions espagñoles du Golfe de Guinée, leur présent et leur avenir. Paris, 1884.
Afr 710.45	Soret, Marcel. Les Kongo nord-occidentaux. Paris, 1959.
Afr 1608.94.4	Soriano, Rodrigo. Moros y cristianos. Madrid, 1894.
Afr 5265.5	Les Sorko (Bozo), maîtres du Niger. (Ligers, Ziedonis.) Paris, 1964-1967. 3v.
Afr 1259.38	Sorrel, J. Pages africaines, l'Afrique du Nord vue par les littérateurs. Paris, 1938.
Afr 6457.32	Sorrenson, M.P.K. Land reform in the Kikuyu country. Nairobi, 1967.
Afr 4785.14	Sorrentino, G. Ricordi del Benadir. Napoli, 1912.
Afr 1623.965.5	Sotsial'no-ekonomicheskoe razvotie sovremennogo Marokko. (Solonitskii, Aleksandr S.) Moskva, 1965.

Afr 4559.30.20	Sotto le pioggie equatoriali. (Civinini, G.) Roma, 1930.
Afr 4236.936	Sottochiesa, G. La religione in Etiopia. Torino, 1936.
Afr 5235.235	Soudan, Paris, Boulogne. (Delavignette, R.L.) Paris, 1935.
Afr 3675.2	The Soudan. (Syndham, Q.) London, 1884.
Afr 3675.50	Le Soudan égyptien. (Sabry, Mohammed.) Le Caire, 1947.
Afr 3675.5	Le Soudan égyptien. (Sarkissian, G.) Paris, 1913.
Afr 3675.9	Le Soudan égyptien. Thèse. (Mustafa, O.M.) Neuville-sur-Saone, 1931.
Afr 3685.5	Le Soudan égyptien sous Mehemet Ali. (Deherain, H.) Paris, 1898.
Afr 5318.10	Soudan français...Kahel. (Sanderval, C. de.) Paris, 1893.
Afr 5235.255	Le Soudan français. (Spitz, Georges.) Paris, 1955.
Afr 5218.83	Le Soudan française. (Hontay, J.) Lille, 1881-83. 2v.
Afr 3315.148	Souez: the twice-fought war; a history. 1st ed. (Love, Kenneth.) N.Y., 1969.
Afr 13284.99.100	Le souffle des ancêtres; nouvelles. (Nzouankeu, Jacques Mariel.) Yaoundé, 1965.
Afr 550.25	The soul of an African padré. (Callaway, Godfrey.) London, 1932.
Afr 725.20A	The soul of central Africa. (Roscoe, John.) London, 1922.
Afr 5219.60	Soundjata. (Niane, D.T.) Paris, 1960.
Afr 2719.68	The soundless Sahara. (Bodley, Ronald V.C.) London, 1968.
Afr 9435.9	Source book of parliamentary elections and referenda in Rhodesia, 1892-1962. (Passmore, Gloria.) Salisbury, 1963.
Afr 4559.05A	The source of the Blue Nile. (Hayes, A.J.) London, 1905.
Afr 1330.6	Les sources inédites de l'histoire du Maroc. Dynastie filalienne. v.1-6. (Castries, H. de.) Paris, 1922-31. 6v.
Afr 1330.5	Les sources inédites de l'histoire du Maroc. Dynastie saadienne. (Castries, H. de.) Paris, 1905-26. 4v.
Afr 1330.5.7	Les sources inédites de l'histoire du Maroc. Dynastie Saadienne. (Espagne, t.1-3). (Castries, H. de.) Paris, 1921. 3v.
Afr 1330.5.3	Les sources inédites de l'histoire du Maroc. Dynastie saadienne. (Pays-bas, t.1-6). (Castries, H. de.) Paris, 1906-23. 6v.
Afr 4095.12	The sources of the Nile. (Beke, C.T.) London, 1860.
Afr 5869.54	Souris, Eugène. Histoire abrégée de l'Ile de la Réunion. Saint-Denis, 1954.
Afr 2223.959	Le sous-développement en Algérie. (Secrétariat Social d'Alger.) Alger, 1959.
Afr 1975.3	Sous la chéchia. (Delorme, A.) Paris, 1901.
Afr 4259.25	Sous la couronne de Salomon. L'empire des Negus. (Pierre-Alype, L.M.) Paris, 1925.
Afr 1432.5	Sous la tente: souvenirs du Maroc. (Yriarte, C.) Paris, 1863.
Afr 555.85	Sous l'armure de laine blanche. (Therol, J.) Paris, 1943.
Afr 1495.3	Sous les cèdres d'Ifrane. (Vaucher, G.) Paris, 1962.
Afr 2230.21	Sous les figuiers de Kabylie. (Geniaux, Charles.) Paris, 1917.
Afr 7809.53	Sous l'ombre des volcans africains. (Thibaut, J.) Bruxelles, 1953.
Afr 12672.3.100	Sous l'orage (Kany). (Badian, S.) Paris, 1963.
Afr 626.141	Sousa, Alfredo de. Economia e sociedade em Africa. Lisboa, 1965.
Afr 609.62.30	Sousa, Daniel. Perspectivas da actualidade africana. n.p., 1962.
Afr 7179.5	Sousa, Gabriel de. A portugalização do suesto de Angola. Lisboa, 1960.
Afr 7119.59	Sousa Dias, G. Portugueses em Angola. Lisboa, 1959.
Afr 7330.10	Sousa e Silva, Pedro. Distrito de Tete. Lisboa, 1927.
Afr 7815.40	Sousberghe, Léon de. Les danses rituelles mungonge et kela des Ba-pende. Bruxelles, 1956.
Afr 2030.10	Soustelle, Jacques. Aimée et souffrante Algérie. Paris, 1956.
Afr 2030.10.5	Soustelle, Jacques. Le drame algérien et la décadence française. Paris, 1957.
Afr 8037.10	South Africa, a chronicle. Cape Town. 1960+
Afr 8089.66.10	South Africa, a political and economic history. (Hepple, Alex.) London, 1966.
Afr 8089.49	South Africa, a short history. (Keppel-Jones, A.) London, 1949.
Afr 8095.87	South Africa, a study in conflict. (Vandenberghe, Pierre L.) Middletown, Conn., 1965.
Afr 8678.368	South Africa, an imperial dilemma, non-Europeans and the British nation, 1902-1914. 1st ed. (Sacks, Benjamin.) Albuquerque, 1967.
Afr 8678.323	South Africa, crisis for the West. (Legum, Colin.) London, 1964.
Afr 8659.33	South Africa, impressions of an American, 1933. (Stackpole, E.J.) Harrisburg, 1933.
Afr 8019.17F	South Africa; information and analysis. Paris. 51,1967+
Afr 8088.99.5	South Africa, its history. (Mackenzie, W.D.) Chicago, 1899.
Afr 8659.00.15	South Africa, past and present. (Markham, Violet Rosa.) London, 1900.
Afr 8659.25	South Africa, people, places, problems. (Dawson, Wm.) N.Y., 1925.
Afr 8089.36	South Africa, Rhodesia and the high commission territories. Cambridge, 1960.
Afr 8685.89	South Africa, the struggle for a birthright. (Benson, Mary.) London, 1966.
Afr 8676.47	South Africa, what now? (Campbell, Alexander.) Cape Town, 1947.
Afr 8678.30	South Africa, white and black or brown. (Silburn, P.A.) London, 1927.
Afr 8678.186	South Africa, yesterday and tomorrow. (Reeves, Ambrose.) London, 1962.
Afr 8089.14.5	South Africa, 1486-1913. (Tilby, A.W.) Boston, 1916.
Afr 8089.33	South Africa, 1652-1933. (Hattersley, A.F.) London, 1933.
Afr 8340.4F	Pamphlet vol. South Africa, 1903. 7 pam.
Afr 8335.2	South Africa, 1906-1961. (Mansergh, N.) N.Y., 1962.
Afr 8673.10	South Africa, 1910-1961. (South Africa. South African Information Service.) Pretoria, 1960.
Afr 9086.5	South Africa. Constitution. London, 1899.
Afr Doc 4309.20F	South Africa. Estimate of the revenue. 1930+
Afr 9086.10	South Africa. Political laws. London, 1896.
Afr Doc 4306.7F	South Africa. Questions affecting South Africa at the United Nations. Pretoria. 1965+
Afr 8360.6F	South Africa. Report on the outbreak of the rebellion. Pretoria, 1915.

Afr Doc 4353.5   South Africa. National Welfare Board. Welfare organisation act no. 40 of 1947 quinquennial report. 1,1957+

Afr Doc 4353.7   South Africa. National Welfare Board. Welfare organizations act no. 40 of 1947. Report on the operation and administration of the act [annual]. 4,1951+

Afr 8035.20F   South Africa. Native Affairs Commission. Report.

Afr 8035.35   South Africa. Native Affairs Department. Report.

Afr 8678.33F   South Africa. Native Economic Committee. Report of Native Economic Committee 1930-1932. Pretoria, 1932.

Afr Doc 4343.5F   South Africa. Natives Resettlement Board. Annual report. 1954+

Afr Doc 4343.10F   South Africa. Natural Resources Development Council. Annual report. Pretoria. 1,1948+

Afr Doc 4309.500   South Africa. Office of Census and Statistics. Agricultural census. Cape Town, 1918.

Afr Doc 4332.15F   South Africa. Office of Census and Statistics. Annual report of the Statistics council. 1951+

Afr Doc 4307.318   South Africa. Office of Census and Statistics. Census of the European or White races of the Union of South Africa, 1918 . Cape Town, 1919-1920.

Afr Doc 4307.318.5   South Africa. Office of Census and Statistics. Census of the European or white races of the Union of South Africa 1918. Final report and supplementary tables. Cape Town, 1920.

Afr Doc 4307.311   South Africa. Office of Census and Statistics. Census of the Union of South Africa, 1911. Pretoria, 1913. 2v.

Afr Doc 4307.360   South Africa. Office of Census and Statistics. Population census, 1960. Pretoria, 1962-65. 2v.

Afr Doc 4307.346   South Africa. Office of Census and Statistics. Population census 7th May 1946. Bevolkinsensus, 7 Mai 1946. Pretoria, 1949. 2v.

Afr Doc 4308.282F   South Africa. Office of Census and Statistics. Statistics of migration. 1927-1934

Afr 6910.8   South Africa. Parliament. Decisions by the government on the financial and administrative relations between the Republic and South West Africa. Cape Town, 1968.

Afr Doc 4312.126   South Africa. Parliament. Mines and work act. Cape Town, 1926.

Afr Doc 4312.129   South Africa. Parliament. Natives parliamentary representation bill. Cape Town, 1929.

Afr Doc 4312.130   South Africa. Parliament. Natives Parliamentary Representation Bill. Cape Town, 1930.

Afr Doc 4312.125   South Africa. Parliament. Official language of the Union Bill. Cape Town, 1925.

Afr 8045.5   South Africa. Parliament. The parliament of the Republic of South Africa. Cape Town, 1962.

Afr Doc 4312.127   South Africa. Parliament. Precious stones bill. Cape Town, 1927.

Afr Doc 4312.154   South Africa. Parliament. Separate representation of voters act validation and amendment bill, 1954. Cape Town, 1954.

Afr Doc 4312.153   South Africa. Parliament. South Africa Act Amendment Act. v.1-2. Cape Town, 1953.

Afr Doc 4312.156   South Africa. Parliament. South Africa Act Amendment Bill. v.1-2. Cape Town, 1956.

Afr Doc 4314.4   South Africa. Parliament. House of Assembly. Debates. 1,1936+

Afr Doc 4314.6   South Africa. Parliament. House of Assembly. Debates. 1962+

Afr Doc 4314.8F   South Africa. Parliament. House of Assembly. Debates of the House of Assembly of the Union of South Africa as reported in the Cape Times. Pretoria, 1966. 8v.

Afr 8333.6   South Africa. Parliament. House of Assembly. Index to the manuscript annexures and printed papers. Cape Town, 1963.

Afr Doc 4314.5F   South Africa. Parliament. House of Assembly. Minutes of proceedings. 3v.

Afr 8045.7   South Africa. Parliament. House of Assembly. Report of the Select Committee on the subject of the constitution amendment bill. Cape Town, 1965.

Afr 8677.30   South Africa. Parliament. House of Assembly. Select Committee on Public Accounts. 1924. Report. Cape Town, 1924. 2v.

Afr 8678.37   South Africa. Parliament. House of Assembly. Select Committee on Native Affairs. First and second (third and fourth [final]) reports of the Select Committee on Native Affairs. Cape Town, 1924.

Afr Doc 4314.205   South Africa. Parliament. House of Assembly. Select Committee on Public Accounts. Report. Cape Town. 1966+

Afr 8028.100   South Africa. Parliament. Library. Afrikaanse publikasies. Kaapstad, 1931.

Afr 8028.101   South Africa. Parliament. Library. Afrikanse publikasies. 2. uitg. Pretoria, 1934.

Afr 8028.102   South Africa. Parliament. Library. Annual list of Africana added to the Mendelssohn collection. Cape Town. 1-9,1938-1946 2v.

Afr Doc 4316.5F   South Africa. Parliament. Senate. Minutes of proceedings.

Afr 8678.317   Pamphlet vol. South Africa. Race question. 8 pam.

Afr 8678.321   Pamphlet vol. South Africa. Race question. 15 pam.

Afr 8678.321.10   Pamphlet vol. South Africa. Race question. 8 pam.

Afr 8678.280   Pamphlet vol. South Africa. Races. 5 pam.

Afr 8659.35   South Africa. Railways and Harbours Administration, Johannesburg. The sunshine route. London, 1935.

Afr Doc 4332.20F   South Africa. Registrar of Building Societies. Annual report. Pretoria. 1964+

Afr 8676.40F   South Africa. Rural Industries Commission. Report of the Rural Industries Commission. Pretoria, 1940.

Afr Doc 4348.3   South Africa. Social and Economic Planning Council. Annual report.

Afr Doc 4348.5F   South Africa. Social and Economic Planning Council. Report. 1-10,1943-1947

Afr 8673.10   South Africa. South African Information Service. South Africa, 1910-1960. Pretoria, 1960.

Afr 8380.3   South Africa. South African Information Service. South Africa source books. v.1-4. N.Y., 1964.

Afr 8667.71   South Africa. South African Information Service. The South African tradition, a brief survey. N.Y., 1960.

Afr 8659.54.10   South Africa. State Information Office. South African quiz. Pretoria, 1954.

Afr 8659.50.15   South Africa. State Information Office. South African scene. Pretoria, 195-.

Afr 8676.3   South Africa. University, Pretoria. Bureau of Market Research. Buro vir marknavorsing. Pretoria, 1963.

Afr 8676.2   South Africa. University, Pretoria. Bureau of Market Research. Research report. 3+ 9v.

Afr 8325.3   South Africa. Vigilance Committee. Vigilance papers. Cape Town. 1,1900+

Afr 8678.215   South Africa. 2. ed. (Spottiswoode, Hildegarde.) Cape Town, 1960.

Afr 8089.65.2   South Africa. 2.ed. (Cope, John Patrick.) N.Y., 1967.

Afr 8089.31.5   South Africa. 2d ed. (Hofmeyer, J.H.) N.Y., 1952.

Afr 8658.84.2   South Africa. 2d ed. (Little, James S.) London, 1887.

Afr 8676.61.2   South Africa. 2nd ed. (Cole, M.M.) London, 1966.

Afr 8089.49.3   South Africa. 3d ed. (Keppel-Jones, A.) London, 1961.

Afr 8088.94.15   South Africa. 8th ed. (Theal, G.M.) London, 1917.

Afr 8659.43.15   Pamphlet vol. South Africa - description. 10 pam.

Afr 8678.357   South Africa - not guilty. (Fuller, Basil.) London, 1957.

Afr 8019.1.5   South Africa (Weekly). The story of South Africa newspaper. London, 1903.

Afr 8658.01.5   South Africa a century ago. (Barnard, Anne.) London, 1901.

Afr 8658.01.8   South Africa a century ago. (Barnard, Anne.) London, 1901.

Afr Doc 4312.153   South Africa Act Amendment Act. v.1-2. (South Africa. Parliament.) Cape Town, 1953.

Afr Doc 4312.156   South Africa Act Amendment Bill. v.1-2. (South Africa. Parliament.) Cape Town, 1956.

Afr 8667.40   South Africa and her people. (Paton, Alan.) London, 1957.

Afr 8658.91   South Africa and its future. Cape Town, 1890.

Afr 555.7.9   South Africa and its mission fields. (Carlyle, J.E.) London, 1878.

Afr 8678.180   South Africa and the rule of law. (International Commission of Jurists.) Geneva, 1960.

Afr 8289.00.20   South Africa and the Transvaal war. (Creswicke, L.) London, n.d. 4v.

Afr 8369.61A   South Africa and world opinion. (Calvocoressi, P.) London, 1961.

Afr 8028.130   South Africa as seen by the French, 1610-1850. (Coke, R.M.) Cape Town, 1957.

Afr 8659.08   South Africa at home. (Fuller, R.H.) London, n.d.

Afr 8659.58.15   South Africa beachcomber. 1st ed. (Green, Lawrence George.) Cape Town, 1958.

Afr 8659.28.5   South Africa calling. 1st ed. (Lowth, Alys.) London, 1928.

Afr 8676.62.10   South Africa Foundation. South Africa in the sixties. Johannesburg, 1962.

Afr 8676.62.12   South Africa Foundation. South Africa in the sixties. 2nd ed. Johannesburg, 1965.

Afr 8088.91   South Africa from Arab domination to British rule. (Murray, R.W.) London, 1891.

Afr 8135.5   South Africa from the great trek to the union. (Cana, F.R.) London, 1909.

Afr 8659.26   South Africa from within. (Nathan, M.) London, 1926.

Afr 8089.00   South Africa handbooks. London, 1903.

Afr 8687.284   South Africa in my time. (Nicholls, G.H.) London, 1961.

Afr 8028.125   South Africa in print. (Cape Town. Van Riebeek Festival Book Exhibition.) Cape Town, 1952.

Afr 8105.22   South Africa in the making, 1652-1806. (Spilhaus, Margaret Whiting.) Cape Town, 1966.

Afr 8676.62.10   South Africa in the sixties. (South Africa Foundation.) Johannesburg, 1962.

Afr 8676.62.12   South Africa in the sixties. 2nd ed. (South Africa Foundation.) Johannesburg, 1965.

Afr 8278.98A   South Africa of to-day. (Younghusband, F.E.) London, 1898.

Afr 8380.3   South Africa source books. v.1-4. (South Africa. South African Information Service.) N.Y., 1964.

Afr 8019.12   South Africa speaks. Cairo.

Afr 8659.11   South Africa to-day. (Fyfe, H.H.) London, 1911.

Afr 8659.11.2   South Africa today. (Fyfe, H.H.) London, 1911.

Afr 8037.25   South Africa today. Johannesburg.

Afr 7020.40   South Africa under John III. (Welsch, S.R.) Capetown, 1949.

Afr 8100.30   South Africa under King Manuel, 1495-1521. (Welch, Sidney R.) Cape Town, 1946.

Afr 8100.32   South Africa under King Sebastian and the cardinal, 1557-1580. (Welch, Sidney R.) Cape Town, 1949.

Afr 8055.10   South Africa who's who. Johannesburg. 1911-1967 12v.

Afr 8369.56   South Africa without prejudice. (Bate, H.M.) London, 1956.

Afr 8369.44.5   South African affairs pamphlets. Johannesburg.

Afr 710.76   South African Broadcasting Corporation. Ons Buurstate op die Afrikaanse vasteland. Johannesburg, 1959.

Afr Doc 4307.15   South African Bureau of Statistics. Bulletin of statistics. Pretoria. 1,1967+

Afr 8160.9F   The South African campaign 1879. (Mackinnon, J.P.) London, 1880.

Afr 6979.37   South African cinderella, a trip through ex-German West Africa. (Hardinge, Rex.) London, 1937.

Afr 8045.42   South African citizenship. (Dodd, Anthony D.) Cape Town, 1958.

Afr 8040.10   The South African commonwealth. (Nathan, Manfred.) Johannesburg, 1919.

Afr 8380.4   South African Communist Party. The road to South African freedom. London, 1964.

Afr 8279.00.13   The South African conspiracy. (Bell, F.W.) London, 1900.

Afr 8045.22.5   The South African constitution. 2d. ed. (May, Henry John.) Cape Town, 1949.

Afr 8045.22.6   The South African constitution. 3d ed. (May, Henry John.) Cape Town, 1955.

Afr 8040.5F   South African constitution bill. n.p., n.d.

Afr 8676.60   South African Council for Scientific and Industrial Research. A survey of rent paying capacity of urban natives in South Africa. Pretoria, 1960.

Afr 8678.316   South African Digest, Pretoria. The pattern of race policy in South Africa. Pretoria, 1956.

Afr 8019.10   South African digest. Pretoria. 6v.

Afr 8676.64	The South African economy. (Houghton, D. Hobart.) Cape Town, 1964.
Afr 8676.64.2	The South African economy. 2. ed. (Houghton, D. Hobart.) Capetown, 1967.
Afr 8095.40	South African explorers. (Axelson, Eric Victor.) London, 1954.
Afr 8809.65	South African heritage, from van Riebeeck to nineteenth century times. Cape Town, 1965.
Afr 6903.17	South African imprints. (Voigts, B.) Cape Town, 1963.
Afr 8678.196F	South African Institute of Race Relations. Fact paper. Johannesburg. 3+ 4v.
Afr 8355.35	South African Institute of Race Relations. The Indian as a South African. Johannesburg, 1956.
Afr 8678.195	South African Institute of Race Relations. Monograph series. Johannesburg.
Afr 8678.197	South African Institute of Race Relations. Presidential address. Johannesburg.
Afr 8676.55.5	South African Institute of Race Relations. South Africa's changing economy. Johannesburg, 1955.
Afr 9196.5	South African Institute of Race Relations. Swaziland. Johannesburg, 1955.
Afr 8029.3F	Pamphlet vol. South African Institute of Race Relations. Miscellaneous publications. 5 pam.
Afr 8659.65	South African journey. (Newman, Bernard.) London, 1965.
Afr 11010.2	South African literature. (Nathan, Manfred.) Cape Town, 1925.
Afr 8252.80	South African memories. (Fitzpatrick, J.P.) London, 1932.
Afr 8289.09	South African memories. (Wilson, S.) London, 1909.
Afr 8686.26	South African missionary bibliography. (Cowie, Margaret J.) n.p., n.d. 2 pam.
Afr 8145.16	South African missions. (Davies, H.) London, 1954.
Afr 8019.3	South African National Union. Annual report. Johannesburg.
Afr 8035.10	South African Native Affairs Commission. Report of the commission. Cape Town, 1904-05. 5v.
Afr 8678.41	South African native policy and the liberal spirit. (Hoernle, R.F.A.) Cape Town, 1939.
Afr 8678.41.5	South African native policy and the liberal spirit. (Hoernle, R.F.A.) Johannesburg, 1945.
Afr 8678.7	South African Native Races Comittee. The natives of South Africa. London, 1901.
Afr 8678.7.5	South African Native Races Committee. The South African natives. Paris, 1909.
Afr 8678.7.5	The South African natives. (South African Native Races Committee.) Paris, 1909.
Afr Doc 4302.10	South African official publications held by Yale University. (Yale Univeristy. Library.) New Haven, 1966.
Afr 8369.47.5	The South African opposition, 1939-1945. (Roberts, Michael.) London, 1947.
Afr 11008.5	South African P.E.N. year book. Johannesburg. 1954-1960// 2v.
Afr 8019.8F	South African panorama. Pretoria. 6,1961+ 9v.
Afr 8050.15.5	South African parties and policies, 1910-1960. (Krueger, Daniel.) London, 1960.
Afr 8050.15	South African parties and policies. (Krueger, Daniel.) Cape Town, 1960.
Afr 11764.12.100	South African personalities and places. (Sachs, Bernard.) Johannesburg, 1959.
Afr 8331.15	South African politics, 1933-1939. (Hodge, Gillian M.M.) Cape Town, 1955.
Afr 8676.60.5	South African predicament. (Sporner, F.P.) London, 1960.
Afr 8377.5	South African protocol, and other formalities. (Nicol, Margaret.) Cape Town, 1964.
Afr 28.73	South African Public Library, Cape Town. A bibliography of african bibliographies. 3d ed. Cape Town, 1955.
Afr 28.74	South African Public Library, Cape Town. A bibliography of African bibliographies covering territories South of the Sahara. 4th ed. Cape Town, 1961.
Afr 11005.3	South African Public Library, Cape Town. Union list of South African newspapers, Nov. 1949. Cape Town, 1950.
Afr 8279.00.5	The South African question. (MacVane, S.M.) Boston, 1900.
Afr 8278.99.29	The South African question. (Schreiner, Olive.) Chicago, 1899.
Afr 8659.54.10	South African quiz. (South Africa. State Information Office.) Pretoria, 1954.
Afr 8678.321.16	Pamphlet vol. South African race question. 4 pam.
Afr 8678.321.15	Pamphlet vol. South African race question. 13 pam.
Afr 8678.321.3	Pamphlet vol. South African race question. 11 pam.
Afr 8678.313	Pamphlet vol. South African race relations. 5 pam.
Afr Doc 4309.18F	South African railways and harbours. Estimates of additional expenditure on capital and betterment works. (South Africa.) Pretoria. 1966+
Afr Doc 4309.15F	South African railways and harbours. Estimates of the additional expenditure to be defrayed from revenue funds. (South Africa.) Pretoria. 1966+
Afr 8659.60.20	South African reading in earlier days. (Varley, Douglas.) Johannesburg, 1960.
Afr 8288.99.6F	South African Republic. Correspondence. (Great Britain. Colonial Office.) London, 1899-03.
Afr 8288.99.5F	South African Republic. Correspondence. (Great Britain. Colonial Office.) London, 1899-03.
Afr 8288.99.4F	South African Republic. Correspondence. (Great Britain. Colonial Office.) London, 1899-03.
Afr 8037.15	South African review. Durban. 1962+ 2v.
Afr 11040.2	The South African Saturday book. (Rosenthal, E.) Cape Town, 1948.
Afr 8659.13.15	The South African scene. (Markham, Violet R.) London, 1913.
Afr 8659.50.15	South African scene. (South Africa. State Information Office.) Pretoria, 195-.
Afr 11057.3	South African short stories. (Leary, E.N.) Capetown, 1947.
Afr 8808.87	South African sketches. (Ellis, A.B.) London, 1887.
Afr Doc 4307.20	South African statistics. (South Africa. Bureau of Statistics.) Pretoria. 1,1968+
Afr 11057.7	South African stories. (Wright, David.) London, 1960.
Afr 8279.00.35	South African studies. (Hillier, A.P.) London, 1900.

Afr 8667.71	The South African tradition, a brief survey. (South Africa. South African Information Service.) N.Y., 1960.
Afr 8678.300	South African tragedy. (Haigh, Alan.) London, 1962.
Afr 8338.230	South African tragedy. (Paton, Alan.) N.Y., 1965.
Afr 8658.87	South African traits. (Mackinnon, J.) Edinburgh, 1887.
Afr 8369.58.5	The South African treason trial. (Forman, Lionel.) N.Y., 1958.
Afr 8369.43.20	The South African Union. (Sowden, Lewis.) London, 1945.
Afr 8089.45.5	The South African union. (Sowden, Lewis.) London, 1945.
Afr 8290.1	Pamphlet vol. South African war, 1899-1902.
Afr 8288.99.14F	Pamphlet vol. South African war, 1899-1902. 11 pam.
Afr 8288.99.12F	Pamphlet vol. South African war, 1899-1902. 18 pam.
Afr 8288.4F	Pamphlet vol. South African war, 1899-1902. 9 pam.
Afr 8288.99.11F	Pamphlet vol. South African war, 1899-1902. 18 pam.
Afr 8288.3	Pamphlet box. South African war, 1899-1902.
Afr 8289.00.55F	South African War. Scrapbook of newspaper clippings, chiefly maps, of campaigns in the South African War, Jan. 7, 1900 - June 10, 1900. n.p., n.d.
Afr 8292.47	South African war record, 1st Battalion. Hongkong, 1904.
Afr 8667.20	The South African way of life. (Calpin, G.H.) London, 1953.
Afr 8659.58	South African winter. (Morris, James.) N.Y., 1958.
Afr 8055.13	South African woman's who's who. v.1. Johannesburg, 1938.
Afr 11055.5	South African writing today. (Gordimer, Nadine.) Harmondsworth, 1967.
Afr 8037.20	South African year-book. London. 1914+ 5v.
Afr 8659.26.5	The South Africans. (Millin, S.G.) London, 1926.
Afr 8678.86	South Africa's apartheid policy - unacceptable. (Buskes, Johannes Jacobus.) Heidelberg, 1956.
Afr 8676.46	South Africa's business. (Horwitz, Ralph.) Cape Town, 1946.
Afr 8676.55.5	South Africa's changing economy. (South African Institute of Race Relations.) Johannesburg, 1955.
Afr 8055.35	South Africa's hall of fame. (Cartwright, A.P.) Cape Town, 1958.
Afr 8667.70	South Africa's heritage. (Caltex (Africa).) Cape Town, 1960.
Afr 8695.11	South Africa's hostages. (Halpern, Jack.) Harmondsworth, Eng., 1965.
Afr 8678.351F	South Africa's international position. (Carter, G.M.) Cape Town, 1964.
Afr 8678.80	South Africa's non-white workers. (Horrell, Muriel.) Johannesburg, 1956.
Afr 8678.307	South Africa's rule of violence. (Duncan, P.B.) London, 1964.
Afr 8846.30	South Africa's Transkei, the politics of domestic colonialism. (Carter, Gwendolen Margaret.) Evanston, 1967.
Afr 555.7.12	South and South Central Africa. (Davidson, H. Frances.) Elgin, 1915.
Afr 9549.32	South central Africa. (Letcher, Owen.) Johannesburg, 1932.
Afr 7222.40	South-east Africa, 1488-1530. (Axelson, E.V.) London, 1940.
Afr 9538.10F	South-east central Africa and Madagascar. (International African Institute, London.) London, 1961.
Afr 8678.13.20	The south-eastern Bantu Abe-Nguni, Aba-Mbo, Ama-Lala. (Soga, J.H.) Johannesburg, 1930.
Afr 609.20	South of Suez. (Anderson, William A.) N.Y., 1920.
Afr 8659.43.5	South of the Congo. (James, S.) London, 1944.
Afr 210.43	South of the Congo. (Selwyn, James.) N.Y., 1943.
Afr 718.48	South of the moon. 1st ed. (Littell, Blaine.) N.Y., 1966.
Afr 9599.45	South of the Sahara. (Gatti, Attilio.) N.Y., 1945.
Afr 11249.86.120	South of the Zambesi, poems from South Africa. (Butler, Guy.) N.Y., 1966.
Afr 6919.67.10	South West: the last frontier in Africa. (Rhoodie, Eschel Mostert.) Johannesburg, 1967
Afr 6919.66	South West Africa, the disputed land. (Bruwer, Johannes Petrus.) Capetown, 1966.
Afr 6979.65	South West Africa, the land, its peoples and their future. (South Africa. Department of Information.) Pretoria, 1965.
Afr 6925.20	South West Africa, 1880-1894; the establishment of German authority in South West Africa. (Esterhuyse, J.H.) Cape Town, 1968.
Afr 6903.15	South-west Africa, 1946-1960. Bibliography. (Roukens de Lange, E.) Cape Town, 1961.
Afr 6900.35	South West Africa. Annual. Windhoek. 1965+
Afr 6900.30	South West Africa. Handbook. Windhoek. 1964+
Afr 6919.15	South-west Africa. (Eveleigh, William.) London, 1915.
Afr 6919.63	South West Africa. (First, Ruth.) Baltimore, 1963.
Afr 6930.12	South West Africa. (Imeshve, R.W.) London, 1965.
Afr 6903.12	South-west Africa. (Jager, J. de.) Pretoria, 1964.
Afr 6985.10	South West Africa. (Molnar, Thomas Steven.) N.Y., 1966.
Afr 6903.5F	South-west Africa. (Welch, F.J.) Cape Town, 1946.
Afr 679.67.20	South West Africa: travesty of trust. (International Conference on South West Africa, Oxford, 1966.) London, 1967.
Afr 6919.67	South West Africa and its human issues. (Wellington, John Harold.) Oxford, 1967.
Afr 6979.66	South West Africa and its indigenous peoples. (Mertens, Alice.) London, 1966.
Afr 6919.67.5	South West Africa and the United Nations. (Carroll, Faye.) Lexington, 1967.
Afr 6930.25	The South-West Africa case. (Hidayatullah, M.) Bombay, 1967.
Afr 6926.5	South-west Africa during German occupation. (Calvert, A.F.) London, 1915.
Afr 6919.34.5	South-west Africa in early times. (Vedder, H.) London, 1938.
Afr 6919.34.6	South-west Africa in early times. (Vedder, H.) London, 1966.
Afr 6900.8F	South West Africa People's Organisation. News bulletin. Cairo. 4,1965+
Afr 6979.67	South West Africa survey, 1967. (South Africa. Department of Foreign Affairs.) Pretoria, 1967.
Afr 6540.20	Southall, A.W. Alur society. Cambridge, Eng., 1956.
Afr 8659.55.5	Southern Africa. (Wellington, J.H.) Cambridge, Eng., 1955. 2v.
Afr 8659.39.20	Southern Africa. (Wells, Arthur W.) London, 1956.
Afr 609.65.25	Southern Africa during the Iron Age. (Fagan, Brian M.) London, 1965.

Afr 7808.85.5 Stanley, H.M. The Congo. v.1-2. N.Y., 1885.

NEDL Afr 6170.13 Stanley, H.M. Coomassie and Magdala. London, 1874.

Afr 718.18.6 Stanley, H.M. Dans les ténébres de l'Afrique. 3 ed. v.1-2. Paris, 1890. 2v.

Afr 718.2.35 Stanley, H.M. La découverte du Congo. Paris, 18- .

Afr 718.2.30 Stanley, H.M. The exploration diaries of H.M. Stanley. London, 1961.

NEDL Afr 6878.73 Stanley, H.M. How I found Livingstone. London, 1873. (Changed to KPE 2829)

Afr 6878.72.2 Stanley, H.M. How I found Livingstone. N.Y., 1872.

Afr 6878.73.3 Stanley, H.M. How I found Livingstone. N.Y., 1902.

Afr 6878.73.2 Stanley, H.M. How I found Livingstone: travels, adventures, and discoveries in Central Africa. London, 1890.

Afr 718.10.2 Stanley, H.M. In darkest Africa. London, 1904.

Afr 718.10A Stanley, H.M. In darkest Africa. N.Y., 1890. 2v.

Afr 718.10.1 Stanley, H.M. In darkest Africa. N.Y., 1891. 2v.

Afr 718.2.10 Stanley, H.M. Lettres inédites. Bruxelles, 1955.

Afr 6878.73.5 Stanley, H.M. My Kalulu, prince, king and slave. London, 1873.

Afr 6878.73.10 Stanley, H.M. My Kalulu, prince, king and slave. N.Y., 1874.

Afr 6878.73.15 Stanley, H.M. My Kalulu, prince, king and slave. N.Y., 1969.

Afr 590.54 Stanley, H.M. Slavery and the slave trade in Africa. N.Y., 1893.

Afr 718.18.3 Stanley, H.M. The story of Emin's rescue as told in Stanley's letters. Boston, 1890.

Afr 718.18 Stanley, H.M. The story of Emin's rescue as told in Stanley's letters. N.Y., 1890.

Afr 8658.98.2 Stanley, H.M. ThroughSouth Africa. London, 1898.

Afr 8658.98 Stanley, H.M. ThroughSouth Africa. N.Y., 1898.

Afr 718.2A Stanley, H.M. Through the dark continent. N.Y., 1878.

Afr 718.2.12 Stanley, H.M. Unpublished letters. N.Y., 1957.

Afr 718.2.40 Stanley, Henry Morton. Stanley's despatches to the New York Herald, 1871-1872, 1874-1877. Boston, 1970.

Afr 718.2.93 Stanley, sa vie, ses voyages et ses aventures. (Burdo, Adolphe.) Paris, 1889.

Afr 718.2.90 Stanley testimonial shield. n.p., n.d.

Afr 718.2.99 Stanley's adventures in the wilds of Africa. (Headley, J.T.) Philadelphia, 1890.

Afr 718.2.40 Stanley's despatches to the New York Herald, 1871-1872, 1874-1877. (Stanley, Henry Morton.) Boston, 1970.

Afr 718.17.2 Stanley's Emin Pascha expedition. (Wauters, A.J.) London, 1890.

Afr 718.17 Stanley's Emin Pascha expedition. (Wauters, A.J.) Philadelphia, 1890.

Afr 718.2.135 Stanley's way. 1st Amer. ed. (Sterling, Thomas.) N.Y., 1960.

Afr 7889.5 Stanleyville: an African urban community under Belgian administration. (Pous, Valdo.) London, 1969.

Afr 40.63 Stanovlenie natsionalnoi gosudarstv v nezavisimykh stranakh Afriki. (Akademiia Nauk SSSR. Institut Gosudarstva i Prava.) Moscow, 1963.

Afr 5210.5 Stanovlenie natsional'noi gosudarstvennosti Respubliki Mali. (Merzliakov, Nikolai S.) Moskva, 1966.

Afr 6164.22 Stanovlenie novoi Gany. (Potekhin, Ivan I.) Moskva, 1965.

Afr 8659.61 Stanton, Hannah. Go well. London, 1961.

Afr 6277.20 Stapleton, G.B. The wealth of Nigeria. London, 1958.

Afr 6277.20.2 Stapleton, G.B. The wealth of Nigeria. 2nd ed. Ibadan, 1967.

Afr 7369.13 Starr, F. Liberia, description, history, problems. Chicago, 1913.

Afr 7568.33 Starr, F. The truth about the Congo. Chicago, 1907.

Afr 530.50.1 Stars and stripes in Africa. (Rosenthal, Eric.) Cape Town, 1968.

Afr 530.50 Stars and stripes in Africa. (Rosenthal, Eric.) London, 1938.

Afr 545.27 Starye i novye religii tropicheskoi i iuzhnoi Afriki. (Sharevskaia, Berta I.) Moscow, 1964.

Afr 1273.966.5 State and society in independent North Africa. (Brown, Leon Carl.) Washington, 1966.

Afr 6420.73 State of emergency, the full story of Mau Mau. (Majdalany, F.) London, 1962.

Afr 8808.23.5 State of the Cape of Good Hope in 1822. (Bird, William Wilberforce.) Cape Town, 1966.

Afr 8808.23 State of the Cape of Good Hope in 1822. London, 1823.

Afr 8037.5 State of the Union, year book for the Union of South Africa. Cape Town. 1957+ 4v.

Afr 8252.9.5 A statement...in connexion with the consecration of the Right Rev. Dr. Colenso. (Gray, R.) London, 1867.

Afr 6176.35 Statement by the government on the recent conspiracy. (Ghana.) Accra, 1961.

Afr 4772.5F Statement of programme by Abdirizak Hagi Hussen, Prime Minister and President of the Council of Ministers. (Somalia. Prime Minister.) Mogadiscio, 1964.

Afr 6310.8 Statement of the conclusions of His Majesty's government in the United Kingdom...East Africa. (Great Britain. Colonial Office.) London, 1930.

Afr Doc 1409.5F Statement on the draft budget. (United Arab Republic. Ministry of Treasury.) Cairo. 1962+

Afr 8678.345 Statements on race relations. (Nederduits Gereformeerde Kerk in Suid Afrika.) Johannesburg. 1,1960//?

Afr 5407.14 The states of Equatorial Africa: Gabon, Congo. (Economist Intelligence Unit, Ltd., London.) London, 1964.

Afr 8235.8.5 Statham, F.R. Blacks, Boers, and British. N.Y., 1969.

Afr 8235.8 Statham, F.R. Blacks, Boers and British. London, 1881.

Afr 8230.5A Statham, F.R. Paul Kruger and his times. London, 1898.

Afr 7175.15 Statham, J.C.B. Through Angola, a coming colony. Edinburgh, 1922.

Afr 7175.15.10 Statham, J.C.B. With my wife across Africa by canoe and caravan. 2d. ed. London, 1926.

Afr Doc 708.733F Statistica del commercio con l'estero. (Somalia. Planning Directorate. Statistical Department.) Mogadisco. 1964+

Afr Doc 708.732F Statistica del commercio con l'estero (delle Regioni Meridionali). (Somalia. Statistical Service.) Mogadisco. 1961+

Afr Doc 4007.5F Statistical abstract. (Botswana. Central Statistics Office.) Gaberones. 2,1967+

Afr Doc 3207.4 Statistical abstract. (East Africa High Commission. East Africa Statistical Department. Kenya Unit.) Nairobi.

Afr Doc 307.5 Statistical abstract. (Ethiopia. Central Statistical Office.) Addis Ababa. 1964+

Afr Doc 3207.5 Statistical abstract. (Kenya. Ministry of Economic Planning and Development. Statistics Deevelopment. Statistics Division.) Nairobi. 1,1961

Afr Doc 807.5 Statistical abstract. (Libya. Census and Statistical Department.) 1,1958+

Afr Doc 3407.5 Statistical abstract. (Tanganyika. Treasury. Central Statistical Bureau.) 1959+

Afr Doc 3407.10 Statistical abstract. (Tanzania. Central Statistical Bureau.) Dar es Salaam. 1,1964+

Afr Doc 3307.5 Statistical abstract. (Uganda. Ministry of Planning and Economic Development. Statistics Division.) Entebbe. 1957+ 2v.

Afr Doc 1807.25 Statistical abstracts. (Gold Coast (Colony). Office of the Government Statistician.) 1,1956

Afr Doc 1807.15 Statistical and economic papers. (Ghana. Central Bureau of Statistics.) Accra. 1,1957+

Afr Doc 2520.705 Statistical bulletin. (Nigeria, Western. Ministry of Economic Planning and Social Development. Statistics Division.) Ibadan. 1,1959+

Afr Doc 3807.8 Statistical handbook of Southern Rhodesia. Salisbury. 1939-1945

Afr Doc 1807.10 Statistical handbook of the Republic of Ghana. Accra. 1967+

Afr Doc 1407.5 Statistical handbook of the UAR. (United Arab Republic. Central Agency for Public Mobilisation and Statistics.) Cairo. 1952+

Afr Doc 1407.8 Statistical pocket year-book. (United Arab Republic. Department of Statistics and Census.) Cairo. 1945+

Afr 3986.960.15 A statistical portrait. (Egypt. Ministry of Economy.) Cairo, 1960.

Afr Doc 4407.5 Statistical register. (Cape of Good Hope.) Cape Town. 1886-1909 23v.

Afr Doc 707.10F Pamphlet vol. Statistical survey of Solali towns. 9 pam.

Afr Doc 4307.4 Statistical year book of the Union of South Africa. (South Africa. Bureau of Statistics.) Pretoria. 1,1913+

Afr Doc 1807.5 Statistical yearbook. (Ghana. Central Bureau of Statistics.) Accra. 1961+

Afr Doc 4507.5 Statistical yearbook. (Natal, Africa.) 1904-1909 6v.

Afr Doc 2407.5 Statistical yearbook. (Nigeria, Northern. Ministry of Economic Planning.) Kaduna. 1965+

Afr Doc 4307.2 Statistical yearbook. (South Africa. Bureau of Statistics.) Pretoria. 1964+

Afr Doc 3807.10 Statistical yearbook of Southern Rhodesia. Salisbury. 1947

Afr Doc 2309.500 Statistics of education in Nigeria. (Nigeria. Federal Ministry of Education.) Lagos. 1,1961+

Afr Doc 4308.282F Statistics of migration. (South Africa. Office of Census and Statistics.) 1927-1934

Afr 6588.2 Statistics of the Zanzibar Protectorate. 8th ed. (Bartlett, C.) Zanzibar, 1936.

Afr Doc 7909.505F Statistiques de l'enseignement. (Burundi. Service des Statistiques et de la Planification.) 1966+

Afr Doc 7409.505F Statistiques de l'enseignement au Gabon. (Gabon. Ministère de l'Education Nationale.) Libreville. 1965+

Afr Doc 6109.504 Statistiques de l'enseignement du premier degré. (Mauritania. Ministère de L'Education Nationale.) 1967+

Afr Doc 6109.505 Statistiques de l'enseignement du second degré. (Mauritania. Ministère de l'Education Nationale.) 1967+

Afr Doc 5608.700 Statistiques du commerce exterieur. (Madagascar. Institut National de la Statistique et de la Recherche Economique.) 1964+

Afr Doc 5408.705 Statistiques du commerce exterieur. (Tunisia. Secretariat d'Etat au Plan et à l'Economie Nationale.) Tunisia. 1965+

Afr Doc 6408.705 Statistiques du commerce extérieur de la Côte d'Ivoire. (Ivory Coast. Direction de la Statistique et des Etudes Economiques et Démographiques.) 1961+

Afr Doc 5208.705 Statistiques du mouvement commercial et maritime du Maroc. (Morocco. Ministere du Commerce et de l'Artisanat.) Maroc. 1960+

Afr Doc 5607.15F Statistiques générales. (Madagascar.) 1906-1908

Afr Doc 7707.10 Statistiques relatives à l'année. (Congo.) 1957-1958

Afr Doc 7209.505 Statistiques scolaires. (Central Afriacn Republic. Ministère l'Education Nationale, de la Jeunesse et des Sports.) Bangui. 1964+

Afr 4559.26.5 Lo stato etiopico e la sua chiesa. (Pollera, Alberto.) Roma, 1926.

Afr 8668.8 The status of women in South Africa. (Dubow, Rhona.) Cape Town, 1965.

Afr 1738.24 Le statut de Tanger. (Raymond, Chas.) Alger, 1927.

Afr 1738.23F Le statut de Tanger d'après la convention du 18 decembre 1923. (Rouard De Card, E.) Paris, 1925.

Afr 2623.938.10 Le statut des terres collectives et la fixation au sol des indigènes en Tunisie. Thèse. (Housset, L.) Paris, 1938.

Afr 1550.37 Le statut international du Maroc d'après les traités. Thèse. (Felix, Lucien.) Paris, 1928.

Afr 7357.2 The statute laws of the Republic of Liberia. (Liberia. Laws, statutes, etc.) Monrovia, 1856.

Afr 555.4.10 Statuts synodaux du diocése d'Alger. (Algiers (Diocese).) Alger, 1853.

Afr 8678.13.30 Stayt, H.A. The Bavenda. London, 1931.

Afr 8279.00.19 Stead, W.J. The candidates of Cain. London, 1900.

Afr 8283.8.5 Stead, W.J. Joseph Chamberlain, conspirator of statesman. London, 1900.

Afr 8283.8 Stead, W.J. The scandal of the South African committee. London, 1899.

Afr 8278.99.7 Stead, W.T. Shall I slay my brother Boer. London, 1899.

Afr 7350.3.15 Stebbins, G.B. Facts and opinions touching the real origin, chracter...American Colonization Society. Cleveland, 1853.

Afr 8658.35 Steedman, A. Wanderings and adventures...of South Africa. London, 1835. 2v.

Afr 8658.35.5 Steedman, A. Wanderings and adventures in the interior of southern Africa. Cape Town, 1966. 2v.

Afr 1200.70 Steeg, Theodore. La paix française en Afrique du Nord, en Algérie, au Maroc. Paris, 1926.

Afr 4513.37.5 Steer, G. Caesar in Abyssinia. Boston, 1937.

Afr 2609.39 Steer, G.L. Date in the desert. London, 1939.

Afr 6620.65 Steer, G.L. Judgment on German Africa. London, 1939.

Afr 3978.98 Steevens, G.W. Egypt in 1898. N.Y., 1898.

Afr 3735.4 Steevens, G.W. With Kitchener to Khartum. Edinburgh, 1898.

Afr 718.18.3 The story of Emin's rescue as told in Stanley's letters. (Stanley, H.M.) Boston, 1890.

Afr 718.18 The story of Emin's rescue as told in Stanley's letters. (Stanley, H.M.) N.Y., 1890.

Afr 4199.37 The story of Fergie Bey. (Fergusson, V.H.) London, 1930.

Afr 6415.40 The story of Kenya's progress. (Askwith, Tom G.) Nairobi, 1953.

Afr 6280.32.2 The story of Ketu, an ancient Yoruba kingdom. 2nd ed. (Parrinder, E.G.) Ibadan, Nigeria, 1967.

Afr 6280.32 The story of Ketu. (Parrinder, E.G.) Ibadan, 1956.

Afr 8325.10 The story of my captivity. (Hofmeyr, A.) London, 1900.

Afr 8145.47 The story of my mission among the native tribes of South Eastern Africa. (Shaw, William, Rector of Chelvey.) London, 1872.

Afr 6214.30 The story of Nigeria. (Crowder, M.) London, 1962.

Afr 8688.5.25 The story of our South African flag. (Partridge, A.C.) Cape Town, 1966.

Afr 8145.38 The story of Pacaltsdorp (Anderson, Theophilus.) Port Elizabeth, 1957.

Afr 9060.26 The story of Saint Andrew's Presbyterian church. (Durban, Natal. Saint Andrew's Presbyterian Church.) Durban, 1962.

Afr 8678.420 The story of Sarah. (Whitehead, Sylvia.) London, 1965.

Afr 8089.55 The story of South Africa. (Marquard, L.) London, 1955.
Afr 8089.55.2 The story of South Africa. (Marquard, L.) London, 1963.
Afr 8089.55.3 The story of South Africa. (Marquard, L.) London, 1968.

Afr 8089.63.7 The story of South Africa. 2d ed. (Marquard, L.) London, 1963.

Afr 8019.1.5 The story of South Africa newspaper. (South Africa (Weekly).) London, 1903.

Afr 9190.3 The story of Swaziland. (Scutt, Joan F.) Mbabane, 1965?

Afr 8809.61 The story of Table mountain. (Rosenthal, Eric.) Cape Town, 1961.

Afr 6170.7 Story of the Ashantee campaign. (Reade, W.) London, 1874.

Afr 8292.12 The story of the Australian Bushmen. (Green, James.) Sydney, 1903.

Afr 8279.00.7 The story of the Boers. (Vanderhoogt, C.V.) N.Y., 1900.

Afr 8735.5.15A The story of the British settlers of 1820 in South Africa. (Hockly, H.E.) Cape Town, 1948.

Afr 8735.5.15.2 The story of the British settlers of 1820 in South Africa. 2. ed. (Hockly, H.E.) Cape Town, 1957.

Afr 7568.18 The story of the Congo Free State. (Wack, H.W.) N.Y., 1905.

Afr 718.11 Story of the rear column. (Jameson, J.S.) London, 1890.

Afr 9439.60.15 The story of the Rhodesias and Nyasaland. (Hanna, A.J.) London, 1960.

Afr 9438.165 The story of the Rhodesias and Nyasaland. 2nd ed. (Hanna, A.J.) London, 1965.

Afr 8735.5.5 The story of the settlement with a sketch of Grahamstown as it was. 2d ed. (Sheffield, T.) Grahamstown, 1884.

Afr 3700.20 Story of the Soudan war. (Pimblett, W. Melville.) London, 1885.

Afr 6484.10 The story of the Uganda Agreement. (Wild, John V.) London, 1957.

Afr 7308.66.2 The story of the universities' mission to Central Africa. 2nd ed. (Rowley, Henry.) N.Y., 1969.

Afr 7308.66 Story of the universities' missions to Central Africa. (Rowley, Henry.) London, 1866.

Afr 8289.00.11 Story of the war in South Africa. (Mahan, A.T.) London, 1900.

Afr 8160.22 The story of the Zulu campaign. (Ashe, Major.) London, 1880.

Afr 8155.5.2 The story of the Zulus. (Gibson, J.Y.) London, 1911.

Afr 8292.46 The story of the 34th Company. (Corner, William.) London, 1902.

Afr 6541.25 The story of Uganda and the Victoria Nyanza Mission. (Stock, Sarah Geraldina.) London, 1892.

Afr 8687.354 The story of William Threlfall. (Cheeseman, Thomas.) Cape Town, 1910.

Afr 2209.14.5 Stott, M.D. The real Algeria. London, 1914.

Afr 8658.20 Stout, Benjamin. Cape of Good Hope. London, 1820.

Htn Afr 8658.00* Stout, Benjamin. Narrative of the loss of the ship Hercules. New Bedford, 1800.

Afr 635.7.15F Stow, G. William. Rock-paintings in South Africa. London, 1930.

Afr 8678.8.1 Stow, G.W. The native races of South Africa. London, 1905.

Afr 8678.8 Stow, G.W. The native races of South Africa. London, 1905.

Afr 4389.54 Stradal, Otto. Der Weg zum letzten Pharao. Wien, 1954.
Afr 4700.38.20 Strade imperiali. (Cobolli Gigli, G.) Milano, 1938.
Afr 679.66.15 Strana zolota. (Kubbel', Lev E.) Moskva, 1966.
Afr 8676.55 Strand, D. The financial and statistical digest of South Africa. Cape Town, 1955.

Afr 6320.2 Strandes, J. Die Portugiesenzeit von Deutsch- und Englisch-Ostafrika. Berlin, 1899.

Afr 6320.2.5 Strandes, J. The Portuguese period in East Africa. Nairobi, 1961.

Afr 10624.42.100 The strange man. (Djoleto, Amu.) London, 1967.
Afr 7582.3 Strange soldiering. (Lawson, Richard G.) London, 1963.
Afr 11249.86.100 Stranger to Europe; poems, 1939-1949. (Butler, Guy.) Capetown, 1952.

Afr 11249.86.110 Stranger to Europe, with additional poems. (Butler, Guy.) Capetown, 1960.

Afr 6295.248 Strangers to the city; urban man in Jos, Nigeria. (Plotnicov, Leonard.) Pittsburgh, 1967.

Afr 8100.40 Strangman, Edward. Early French callers at the Cape. Cape Town, 1936.

Afr 28.65 Strany Afriki. (Moscow. Gosudarstvennaia Biblioteka SSSR imeni V.I. Lenina.) Moscow, 1961.

Afr 626.196 Strany iugo-vostochne i Afriki. (Lipets, Iulii G.) Moskva, 1968.

Afr 626.168 Strany SEV i Afrika. (Semin, Nikolai S.) Moskva, 1968.
Afr 5343.8 Strasbourg. Université. Centre de Géographie Appliquée. Etude géographique des problèmes de transports en Côte-d'Ivoire. Paris, 1963.

Afr 626.147 Strasbourg. Université. Centre Universitaire des Hautes Etudes Européennes. L'Europe et l'Afrique noire. Strasbourg, 1962.

Afr 8686.28 Strassberger, Elfriede. The Rhenish Mission Society in South Africa. Cape Town, 1969.

Afr 2719.56.5 Strasser, Daniel. Réalités et promesses sahariennes. Paris, 1956.

Afr 5316.501 Strategiia bor'by za nezavisimost? (Iordanskii, Vladimir B.) Moskva, 1968.

Afr 5749.64 Stratton, A. The great red island. N.Y., 1964.
Afr 210.64.65 Strauch, H. Panafrika. Zürich, 1964.
Afr 9489.69 Strauss, Frances. My Rhodesia. Boston, 1969.

Afr 9599.14 Streams in the desert. (Morrison, J.H.) London, 1919.
Afr 8252.13 Streatfeild, F.N. Reminiscences of an old 'un. London, 1911.

Afr 8152.94 Streatfield, F.M. Kafirland, a ten months campaign. London, 1879.

Afr 4070.38 Streeter, D.W. Camels. N.Y., 1927.
Afr 4070.37.2 Streeter, D.W. Camels. N.Y., 1927.
Afr 6455.44.10 Streeter, D.W. Denatured Africa. Garden City, 1929.
Afr 6455.44 Streeter, D.W. Denatured Africa. N.Y., 1926.
Afr 6455.44.5 Streeter, D.W. Denatured Africa. N.Y., 1927.
Afr 609.00 Streifzüge der Ost- und Süd-Afrika. (Schanz, M.) Berlin, 1900.

Afr 6455.8.3 Die Streit um die deutsche Emin Pascha Expedition. (Arendt, Otto.) Berlin, 1889.

Afr 8659.11.7 Streitwolf. Der Caprivizipfel. Berlin, 1911.
Afr 7809.26.5 Strickland, Diana. Through the Belgian Congo. London, 1926.

Afr 8320.8 De strijd tusschen boer en brit. (Dewet, C.R.) Amsterdam, 1902.

Afr 9860.276 Strike a blow and die. (Mwase, George Simeon.) Cambridge, 1967.

Afr 626.159 Stroitel'stvo natsional'noi ekonomiki v strankah Afriki. Moskva, 1968.

Afr 8252.348 Struben, Charles. Vein of gold. Cape Town, 1957.
Afr 6193.47 Structural changes in the economy of Ghana, 1891-1911. (Szcreszewski, R.) London, 1965.

Afr 2223.959.5 La structure asymétrique de l'économie algérienne. (Dumoulin, Roger.) Paris, 1959.

Afr 3986.960A Structure économique et civilisation. (Austry, J.) Paris, 1960.

Afr 5053.38 The structure of local government in West Africa. (Campbell, Michael J.) The Hague, 1965.

Afr 3993.8 The structure of modern industry in Egypt. (Jiritli, Ali.) Cairo, 1948.

Afr 1618.26 The structure of traditional Morroccan rural society. (Hoffman, Bernard G.) The Hague, 1967.

Afr 6740.15.5 La structure sociale des Bamileke. (Hurault, Jean.) Paris, 1962.

Afr 5390.2 Structures de type féodal en Afrique noire. (Lombard, Jacques.) Paris, 1965.

Afr 7812.255 Structures économiques duCongo belge et du Ruanda-Urundi. (Lefebvre, J.) Bruxelles, 1955.

Afr 1680.10 Structures sociales du haut-atlas. 1 ed. (Berque, Jacques.) Paris, 1955.

Afr 630.53 Struggle for Africa. (Bartlett, V.) London, 1953.
Afr 2030.461.50 The struggle for Algeria. 1st ed. (Kraft, Joseph.) Garden City, 1961.

Afr 8685.27.7A The struggle for equality. (Joshi, Pranshankar S.) Bombay, 1951.

Afr 6420.50 The struggle for Kenya. (Rancliffe, D.H.) London, 1954.
Afr 7219.69 The struggle for Mozambique. (Mondlane, Eduardo.) Harmondsworth, 1969.

Afr 9435.10 The struggle for native rights in Rhodesia. (Scott, L.) London, 1918.

Afr 6470.250.20 Struggle for Release Jomo and his colleagues. 1st ed. (Patel, Anubu H.) Nairobi, 1963.

Afr 8235.17A The struggle for South Africa, 1875-1899. (Lovell, R.I.) N.Y., 1934.

Afr 8279.00.26 The struggle of the Dutch republics, open letter to an American lady. (Boissevain, Charles.) Amsterdam, 1900.

Afr 8678.44 Struggle on the Veld. (Peattie, R.) N.Y., 1947.
Afr 1033.4 Strupp, K. Urkunden zur Geschichte des völkerrechts. Erg. 1. Gotha, 1942.

Afr 6280.70 Struttura sociaepolitica e ordinamento fondiario Yoruba dall'epoca tradizionale all'odierna. (Sertorio, Guido.) Coma, 1967.

Afr 6985.14 Die stryd om Suidwes-Afrika. (Giniewski, Paul.) Kaapstad, 1966.

Afr 8745.15 Strydom, C.J.S. Kaapland en die Tweede Vryheidsoorlog. Kaapstad, 1937.

Afr 8678.383 Strydom, Christiaan Johannes Scheepers. Black and white Africans. 1st ed. Cape Town, 1967.

Afr 8377.10.10 Strydom, Lauritz. Rivonia unmasked. Johannesburg, 1965.
Afr 8667.5 Die stryjd om ewewig. (Heever, C.M. van den.) Kaapstad, 1941.

Afr 2209.36.10 Stuart, B. Adventure in Algeria. London, 1936.
Afr 2749.54.5 Stuart, B. Desert adventure. London, 1954.
Afr 1738.30 Stuart, G.H. The international city of Tanger. Stanford, calif., 1931.

Afr 1738.30.2 Stuart, G.H. The international city of Tanger. 2d ed. Stanford, calif., 1955.

Afr 3978.83 Stuart, H.V. Egypt after the war. London, 1883.
Afr 3978.83.3 Stuart, H.V. Egypt after the war. London, 1883.
Afr 8985.4 Stuart, J. A history of the Zulu rebellion 1906. London, 1913.

Afr 49716.5 Stuart, James. Izibongo; Zulu praise-poems. Oxford, 1968.
Afr 115.115 Studi africani. (Amedeo, Duke of Aosta.) Bologna, 1942.
Afr 115.85 Studi africani e asiatici. (Vedovato, Giuseppe.) Firenze, 1964. 3v.

Afr 4568.20 Studi etiopici. (Conti Rossini, C.) Roma, 1945.
Afr 4700.4.10 Studi italiani di etnografia e di folklore della Libia. (Panetta, Ester.) Roma, 1963.

Afr 1019.5 Studi magrebini. Napoli. 1,1966+ 2v.

Afr 19.18 Studia Africana. Praha. 1,1966+
Afr 679.66.30 Studia nad gospodarką przedkapitalistyczna no Afryee Gachoancej wieku XIX i XX. Wyd.1. (Halpern, Jan.) Warszawa, 1966.

Afr 7512.5 Studia Universitatis Lovanii. (Leopoldville. Université Lovanium. Institut de Recherches Economiques et Sociales.)

Afr 2260.12 Studien over Algerie. (Booms, P.G.) 's-Gravenhage, 1878.
Afr 1326.2 Studien und Mitteilungen der deutschen Marokko-bibliothek. (Kampffmeyer, Georg.) Berlin, 1911.

Afr 4285.5 Studien zur äthiopischen Reichsordnung. (Varenbergh, Joseph.) Strassbourg, 1915.

Afr 19.5 Studien zur Auslandskunde. Afrika. Berlin.
Afr 8285.15 Studien zur englischen Vorbereitung des Burenkriegs. Inaug. Diss. (Barthold, U.) Köln, 1936.

Afr 7815.29 Studien zur Ethnogenese bei den Mangbetu. (Dauer, Alfonsus.) Mainz, 1961.

Afr 1609.00 Studien zur wirthschaftsgeographie von Marokko. (Arnold, R.S.) Marburg, 1900.

Afr 3821.2 Eine Studienfahrt nach Kordofan. (Meinhof, Carl.) Hamburg, 1916.

Afr 8678.43   Studies and types of South African native life. Durban, 1934.

Afr 2030.320.2   Studies in a dying colonialism. (Fanon, Frantz.) N.Y., 1955.

Afr 626.2   Studies in African economics. Nairobi. 1,1967+

Afr 19.10   Studies in African history. The Hague. 1,1963+ 5v.

Afr 8045.20   Studies in African native law. (Lewin, Julius.) Cape Town, 1947.

Afr 632.40   Studies in applied anthropology. (Mair, Lucy Philip.) London, 1961.

Afr 10004.30   Studies in black literature. Fredericksburg, Va. 1,1970+

Afr 6565.42   Studies in East African history. (Bennett, N.R.) Boston, 1963.

Afr 6277.68   Studies in industrialization, Nigeria and the Cameroons. (Wells, Frederick A.) London, 1962.

Afr 1259.11.7   Studies in North African. (Grant, Cyril F.) N.Y., 1923.

Afr 8145.28   Studies in the evangelisation of South Africa. (Gerdener, Gustav S.A.) London, 1911.

Afr 659.68   Studies in the geography of the Arab world in Africa. (Danasuri, Jamal A.A.) Cairo, 1968.

Afr 6210.41   Studies in the laws of succession in Nigeria. (Derrett, John Duncan Martin.) London, 1965.

Afr 115.80   Study Congress on International Cooperation in Africa. La cooperazione internationale in Africa. Milano, 1960.

Afr 4226.8   A study guide for Ethiopia and the Horn of Africa. (Sommer, John W.) Boston, 1969.

Afr 6153.25   A study guide for Ghina. (Adams, Cynthia.) Boston, 1967.

Afr 6403.6   A study guide for Kenya. (Hakes, Jay E.) Boston, 1969.

Afr 7353.10   A study guide for Liberia. (Holsoe, Svend.) Boston, 1967.

Afr 1326.20   A study guide for Morocco. (Bennett, Norman Robert.) Boston, 1968.

Afr 6203.9   A study guide for Nigeria. (Wolpe, Howard.) Boston, 1966.

Afr 6753.15   A study guide for Tanzania. (Bates, Margaret L.) Boston, 1969.

Afr 2426.10   A study guide for Tunisia. (Bennett, Norman Robert.) Boston, 1968.

Afr 6478.5   A study guide for Uganda. (Hopkins, Terence K.) Boston, 1969.

Afr 8678.142F   A study of a South African interracial neighbourhood. (Russell, Margo.) Durban, 1961.

Afr 609.65.10   The study of Africa. (McEwan, Peter J.M.) London, 1965. 4v.

Afr 8678.362   A study of Bantu retail traders in certain areas of the eastern Cape. (Savage, R.B.) Grahamstown, 1966.

Afr 6193.17   A study of contemporary Ghana. (Birmingham, Walter Barr.) London, 1966.

Afr 6277.77   A study of socio-economic factors affecting agricultural productivity in parts of Ondo province of Western Nigeria. (Oloko, Olatunde.) Ibadan, 1965. 3 pam.

Afr 8678.13.45   A study of the social circumstances and characteristics of Bantu in the Durban region. (Natal University.) Durban, 1965. 2v.

Afr 4559.35.110   Stuessy, J. Mit dem Faltboot nach Abessinien. Frauenfeld, 1935.

Afr 679.67.15   Stufen afrikanischer Emanzipation. (Grohs, Gerhard.) Stuttgart, 1967.

Afr 6850.3   Stuhlmann, F. Handwerk und Industrie in Ostafrika. Hamburg, 1910.

Afr 2283.2   Stuhlmann, F. Ein kulturgeschichtlicher Ausflug in den Aures. Hamburg, 1912.

Afr 2628.1   Stuhlmann, F. Die Mazigh-Völker. Hamburg, 1914.

Afr 3725.6   Stuhlmann, F. Mit EminPasha in Herz von Afrika. Berlin, 1894.

Afr 8283.5F   Stukken betrekking hebbende op den inval der troepen der British South Africa Company. (South Africa.) Pretoria, 1896.

Afr 609.61.55   Stumbuk, Zdenko. Zapiski iz Afrike. Zagreb, 1961.

Afr 2719.36   Stumme Front. (Schiffers-Davringhausen, H.) Leipzig, 1936.

Afr 609.60.25   Die Stunde des schwarzen Mannes. (Lenenberger, Hans.) München, 1960.

Afr 7580.18   Sturdza, Michel. World government and international assassination. Belmont, Mass., 1963.

Afr 9049.7   Sturges, Stanley G. In the valley of seven cities. Washington, D.C., 1965.

Afr 1608.86.3   Stutfield, H.E.M. El Maghreb, 1200 miles ride through Marocco. London, 1886.

Afr 5549.09   Suau, Pierre. La France à Madagascar. Paris, 1909.

Afr 3674.2   The sub-mamur's handbook. (Sudan.) Khartoum, 1926.

Afr 5842.6   Sub-tropical rambles. (Pike, N.) London, 1873.

Afr 8315.7   Subaltern's letters to his wife. London, 1901.

Afr 510.111   Subbotin, V.A. Frantsuzskaia kolonialnaia ekspansiia v kontse XIX v. Ekuatorialnaia Afrika i Idiiskogo Okeana. Moscow, 1962.

Afr 5055.59.5   Subbotin, V.A. Kolonialnaia politika Frantsii v Zapadnoi Afrike, 1880-1900. Moscow, 1959.

Afr 115.113   Subbotin, Vaterii A. Problemy istorii Afriki. Moskva, 1966.

Afr 5403.20   La subdivision en Afrique équatoriale française. (Dairiam, Emmanuel.) Lyon, 1931.

Afr 7183.33   Subsidios para a historia de Luanda. (Cardoso, Manuel da Costa Lobo.) Luanda, 1954.

Afr 6535.62   A subsistence agricultural geography of Uganda. (McMaster, D.N.) Bude, 1962.

Afr 590.11F   Substance of the evidence...on the slave trade. London, 1789.

Afr 2948.9   Subtil, E. Histoire d'Abd-el-Gelil. n.p., 18- .

Afr 6275.107.5   Success in Nigeria; assets and possibilities. (Miller, W.R.S.) London, 1948.

Afr 2698.5   Les successeurs. (Zmerli, Sadok.) Tunis, 1967.

Afr 5053.40   La succession d'état en Afrique du Nord. Paris, 1968.

Afr 2208.40   Suchet. Lettres...sur l'Algérie. Tours, 1840.

Afr 4742.15   Sud. (Martinelli, Renzo.) Firenze, 1930.

Afr 5343.10   Le sud-est frontalier. (Société d'Etudes pour le Développement Economique et Social.) Paris, 1963. 2v.

Afr 1723.10   Le sud marocain. Marrakech. Safi et Mogador. (Dupac, J.) Paris, 192- .

Afr 1571.1   Sud-Oranais et Maroc. (Lechatelier, A.) Paris, 1903.

Afr 3745.45   Sudan, Egyptian. The Sudan. Khartoum, 1947.

Afr 3745.55   The Sudan, 1899-1953. (British Information Service.) N.Y., 1953.

Afr Doc 1309.15   Sudan. The central budget; estimates of revenue and expenditure. Khartoum? 1966+

Afr 3834.2   Sudan. Khartoum, capital. Khartoum, 1963.

Afr Doc 1309.5   Sudan. Memorandum on the budget estimates. Khartoum. 1966+

Afr Doc 1319.58   Sudan. The National Charter of the Coalition Government. n.p., 1965?

Afr 3674.2   Sudan. The sub-mamur's handbook. Khartoum, 1926.

Afr Doc 1309.10F   Sudan. Ten year plan of economic and social development, 1961/62-1970/71. Development budget. Khartoum. 1965+

Afr Doc 1309.10.5   Sudan. Ten year plan of economic and social development. Explanatory memorandum on development budgets. Khartoum. 1965+

Afr 3675.3   Der Sudan. (Buchta, R.) Leipzig, 1888.

Afr 3675.22   The Sudan. (Duncan, J.S.R.) Edinburgh, 1952.

Afr 3813.8   Sudan. (Italy. Instituto Nazionale per il Commercio Estero.) Roma, 1960.

Afr 3675.15.5   The Sudan. (MacMichael, H.) London, 1954.

Afr 4070.65.5   The Sudan. (Said, Beshir Mohammed.) London, 1965.

VAfr 3675.69   Sudan. (Skuratowicz, Witold.) Warszawa, 1965.

Afr 3745.45   The Sudan. (Sudan, Egyptian.) Khartoum, 1947.

Afr Doc 1309.505   Sudan. Bureau of Education Statistics. Education statistics. Khartoum. 1959+

Afr 3745.71   Sudan. Central Office of Information. Basic facts about the southern provinces of the Sudan. Khartoum, 1964.

Afr Doc 1305.5   Sudan. Central Office of Information. Progress. Anniversary of the Sudan revolution. Khartoum. 1963+

Afr Doc 1342.5   Sudan. Department of Land Use and Rural Water Development. Annual report. 1962+

Afr Doc 1307.356.20   Sudan. Department of Statistics. First population census of Sudan 1955-56; methods report. Khartoum, 1960.

Afr Doc 1308.705   Sudan. Department of Statistics. Foreign trade statistics. 1962+

Afr Doc 1307.5F   Sudan. Department of Statistics. Internal statistics. 1,1960+

Afr Doc 1309.310   Sudan. Department of Statistics. The national income of Sudan. 1,1955+

Afr Doc 1385.5F   Sudan. Department of Statistics. Ordurman household budget survey. Khartoum, 1965.

Afr Doc 1307.365   Sudan. Department of Statistics. Population and housing survey, 1964-65. Khartoum, 1965. 11v.

Afr Doc 1307.353   Sudan. Department of Statistics. The 1953 pilot population census for the first population census in Sudan. Khartoum, 1955.

Afr 3826.5   Sudan. Gezira Board. The Gezira scheme from within. Khartoum, 1954.

Afr Doc 1309.305   Sudan. Ministry of Finance and Economics. Economic survey. Khartoum. 1959

Afr 3671.25   Sudan. Ministry of Finance and Economics. Sudan economic and financial review. Khartoum. 1,1961+

Afr 3671.26   Sudan. Ministry of Finance and Economics. Sudan economic and financial review. A special issue. 1,1962+

Afr 3813.10   Sudan. Ministry of Finance and Economics. The ten year plan of economic and social development, 1962-1971. Khartoum, 1963.

Afr Doc 1307.356.10   Sudan. Population Census Office. First population census of Sudan, 1955-56. Interim report. Khartoum, 1957.

Afr Doc 1307.356.11   Sudan. Population Census Office. First population census of Sudan, 1955-56. Supplement. Khartoum, 1956.

Afr Doc 1307.356.15   Sudan. Population Census Office. 21 facts about the Sudanese. First population census of Sudan, 1955-56. Khartoum? 1958.

Afr 3813.22   Sudan. Treaties, etc. Kuwait Fund for Arab Economic Development. Loan agreement between the Republic for Sudan and the Kuwait Fund for Arab Economic Development dated March 25th, 1962. Kuwait, 1962?

Afr 3813.15   Sudan. Treaties, etc. 1961. Administration agreement (Roseires irrigation project) between the Republic of the Sudan and Kreditanstalt für Wiederaufbau and International Development Association and International Bank for Reconstruction and Development dated as of June 14, 1961. n.p., 1961.

Afr 4070.21   The Sudan. 2d ed. (Kumm, H.K.W.) London, 1909.

Afr 3671.10   Sudan almanac. Khartoum. 1958+ 4v.

Afr 3019.5   Sudan almanac. London. 1929+

Afr 3735.10   Sudan campaign 1896-99. London, 1899.

Afr 4070.57   Sudan days and ways. (Jackson, Henry Cecil.) N.Y., 1954.

Afr 4070.41   Sudan e Gallas. (Matteucci, P.) Milano, 1879.

Afr 3671.25   Sudan economic and financial review. (Sudan. Ministry of Finance and Economics.) Khartoum. 1,1961+

Afr 3671.26   Sudan economic and financial review. A special issue. (Sudan. Ministry of Finance and Economics.) 1,1962+

Afr 3675.40   The Sudan in Anglo-Egyptian relations. (Fabunmi, L.A.) London, 1960.

Afr 3745.10A   The Sudan in evolution. (Martin, Percy F.) London, 1921.

Afr 3675.60   The Sudan in pre-history and history. (Wharton, William M.) Khartoum, 1960.

Afr 3715.3F   Sudan intelligence reports. Cairo. 1-111,1892-1903

Afr 3019.1   Sudan notes and records. Khartoum. 1,1918+ 23v.

Afr 3675.21   The Sudan question. (Abbas, Mekki.) London, 1952.

Afr 3675.68   Sudan Republic. (Henderson, Kenneth David Driutt.) London, 1965.

Afr 3671.20   Sudan research information bulletin. Khartoum. 1,1965+

Afr 3671.15   Sudan society. Khartoum.

Afr 3675.35   Sudanese-Egyptian relations. (Baddur, Abd al-Fattah Ibrahim al-Sayid.) The Hague, 1960.

Afr 3811.5   Sudanese ethics. (Nordenstam, Tore.) Uppsala, 1968.

Afr 6280.21   A Sudanese kingdom. (Meek, C.K.) London, 1931.

Afr 5219.28   Sudanese memoirs. (Palmer, H.R.) Lagos, 1928. 3v.

Afr 5219.28.5   Sudanese memoirs. v.1-3. (Palmer, H.R.) London, 1967.

Afr 3675.22.5   The Sudan's path to independence. (Duncan, J.S.R.) Edinburgh, 1957.

Afr 9448.77   The sudden assignment. (Alport, Cuthbert James McCall.) London, 1965.

Afr 8658.73   Süd Afrika. (Koerner, F.) Breslau, 1873.

Afr 8659.66.17   Südafrika, eine Bastion Europas? Tagebuch einer Seereise mit Betrachtung des Rossenproblems. 2. Aufl. (Rittershaus, Wilhelm.) Klagenfurt, 1966.

Afr 8028.26   Suedafrika, Suedwestafrika, eine Bibliographie. (Taetemeyer, Gerhard.) Freiburg, 1964.

Afr 8089.68   Südafrika. (Hartmann, Hans Walter.) Stuttgart, 1968.

Afr 8678.327 Südafrika Zwischen weiss und schwarz. (Namgalies, Ursula.) Stuttgart, 1963.

Afr 8659.31 Der südafrikanische Eingeborne als Industriearbeiter und als Stadtherrscher. (Leubuscher, C.) Jena, 1931.

Afr 8658.53 Südafrikanische Skizzen. (Kretzschmar, E.) Leipzig, 1853.

Afr 8089.35 Die Südafrikanische Union...Abhandlung. (Dietzel, K.H.) Berlin, 1935.

Afr 8658.61 Die Südafrikanischen Colonien Englands. (Meidinger, H.) Frankfurt, 1861.

Afr 8210.10 Die Südafrikanischen Republiken. (Kloessel, M.H.) Leipzig, 1888.

Afr 7175.47 Südost-Angola. (Borchert, Günter.) Hamburg, 1963.

Afr 6919.66.8 Südwestafrika. 3. Aufl. (Jenny, Hans.) Stuttgart, 1968.

Afr 6979.34 Südwestafrika Einst und Jetzt. (Beumhagen, H., O) Berlin, 1934.

Afr 6927.5 Südwestafrika in der deutschen Zeit. (Hintrager, O.) München, 1955.

Afr 6926.28 Südwestafrika unter deutscher Kolonialherrschaft. (Drechsler, Horst.) Berlin, 1966.

Afr 1573.22 El suelo de Marruecos y sus primeros habitantes. (Martin Peinador, L.) Madrid, 1920.

Afr 3315.145 Suetskii vopros i imperialisticheskaia agressiia protiv Egipta. (Akademiia Nauk SSSR. Institut Mirovoi Ekonomiki i Mezhdunarodnykh Otnoshenii.) Moskva, 1957.

Afr 4178.5 Suez, storia e problemi. (Sammarco, Angelo.) Milano, 1943.

Afr 3315.124 Suez, the seven-day war. (Barker, A.J.) London, 1964.

Afr 3315.70 Suez. (Camille, Paul.) Paris, 1957.

Afr 4178.15 Suez. (Gaslini, Mario.) Milano, 1957.

Afr 3315.45 Suez. (Soviet News.) London, 1956.

Afr 3315.132.7 Suez. (Thomas, Hugh.) N.Y., 1967.

Afr 3315.140 Suez: ultra-secret. (Bar-Zohar, Michel.) Paris, 1964.

Afr 3315.132 The Suez affair. (Thomas, Hugh.) London, 1967.

Afr 3315.128 Suez and the Middle East; documents. (Soviet News.) London, 1956.

Afr 3315.115 Suez Canal. (India. Parliament. Hok Sabha.) New Delhi, 1956.

Afr 3315.55 The Suez Canal. (International Review Service.) N.Y., 1957.

Afr 3315.150 The Suez Canal: 1956 crisis - 1967 war. (Mezerik, Avrahm G.) N.Y., 1969.

Afr 3310.20 The Suez Canal crisis and India. (India. Information Services.) New Delhi, 1956.

Afr 3315.10 The Suez Canal problem. (United States. Department of State.) Washington, 1956.

Afr 3315.95 The Suez Canal settlement. (Lauterpacht, E.) London, 1960.

Afr 3315.152 The Suez contractors. (Kipping, Norman Victor.) Havant, Hampshire, 1969.

Afr 3315.154.1 The Suez expedition 1956. (Beaufre, André.) N.Y., 1969.

Afr 3315.136 Suez ten years after: broadcasts from the BBC. (Calvocoressi, Peter.) London, 1967.

Afr 3315.122 Suez touchdown. (Clark, D.M.J.) London, 1964.

Afr 3315.85 Suez war. (Johnson, Paul.) London, 1957.

Afr 4045.12 Der Suezkanal. (Kienitz, Ernst.) Berlin, 1957.

Afr 4178.10 Der Suezkanal einst und heute. (Hueber, Reinhard.) Berlin, 1941.

Afr 6430.10 Suffering without bitterness. (Kenyatta, Jouro.) Nairobi, 1968.

Afr 1258.17.15 Sufferings in Africa; Captain Riley's narrative. (Riley, J.) N.Y., 1965.

Afr 2260.22 Suffert, Georges. Les perspectives d'emploi des européens en Algérie. Paris, 1961.

Afr 609.29.25.5 Suggate, L.S. Africa. 4th ed. London, 1951.

Afr 4025.20.15 Sugli italiani d'Egitto. (Sterlich, R. de.) Cairo, 1888.

Afr 8028.2 Suhnnke Hollnay, H.C. Bibliography related to South Africa. Cape Town, 1898.

Afr 8676.60.20 Suid-Afrika en Brasilie. (Serton, P.) Kaapstad, 1960.

Afr 8089.54.10 Suid-Afrika en die wereldpolitiek 1652-1952. (Scholtz, G.H.) Johannesburg, 1954.

Afr 8377.8 Suid-Afrika in die politiek-ekonomiese proses. (Bogaerde, Frans van den.) Pretoria, 1966.

Afr 8030.15 Suid-afrikaanse argiefstukke. v.1- Cape Town, 1949. 7v.

Afr 8030.15.15 Suid-afrikaanse argiefstukke. v.1- Kaapstad, 1957- 6v.

Afr 8030.15.5 Suid-afrikaanse argiefstukke. v.1- Oranje-Vrystaat. 1952+ 4v.

Afr 8030.15.10 Suid-afrikaanse argiefstukke. v.1- Parow, 1958. 5v.

Afr 8019.4 Suid-Afrikaanse Buro vir Raase-Aanngeleenthede. Nuusbrief. Stellenbosch. 10,1954+ 2v.

Afr 8678.92 Suid-Afrikaanse Buro vir Rasse-Angeleenthede. Referate geleiver op die jaarvergadering. Stellenbosch. 1,1950+ 6v.

Afr 8659.67.10 Suid Afrikamoe nie huil nie. (Leenen, Guillaume A.H.) Melle, 1967.

Afr 5749.62.5 Suid van die wind. (Joubert, Elsa.) Kaapstad, 1962.

Afr 6395.3.2 The Suk, their language and folklore. (Beech, M.W.H.) N.Y., 1969.

Afr 6395.3 The Suk, their language and folklore. (Beech, M.W.H.) Oxford, 1911.

Afr 6883.13.5 Sukuma law and customs. (Cory, Hans.) London, 1954.

Afr 6883.15A Sukumaland. (Malcolm, D.W.) London, 1953.

Afr 4394.1 Sul campo di Adua. (Ximenes, E.) Milan, 1897.

Afr 7130.15.2 Sul de Angola, relatório de um govêrno de distrito, 1908-1910. 2. ed. (Almeida, João de.) Lisboa, 1936.

Afr 7320.17 O Sul do Save. (Saldanha, Eduardo d'Almeida.) Lisboa, 1928-31. 2v.

Afr 1415.01 Pamphlet box. Sulaiman.

Afr 3993.932 Sulayman, Ali. L'industrialisation de l'Egypte. London, 1932.

X Cg Afr 590.5 Sulivan, G.L. Dhow chasing in Zanzibar waters. London, 1873. (changed to XP 9127)

Afr 4025.20.10 Sulla politica italiana inEgitto. (Italy. Ministero degli Affari Esteri.) Roma, 1882.

Afr 2632.11 Sulla questione tunisina. Roma, 1933.

Afr 4025.20.5 Sulla tutela degli interessi italiani in Egitto. (Italy. Ministero degli Affari Esteri.) Rome, 1880.

Afr 710.68 Sulle orme di Roma. (Barasiola, Carlo.) Milan, 1934.

Afr 7318.5 Sulle rive dello Zambesi. (Arcangelo da Barletta.) Palo del Calle, 1964.

Afr 6291.44 Sullivan, John R. Breadless Biafra. Dayton, Ohio, 1969.

Afr 1494.6 The Sultan of Morocco. (Landau, Rom.) London, 1951.

Afr 6887.7 Sultan to sultan. (Sheldon, M.F.) London, 1892.

Afr 6292.9.15 The sultanate of Bornu. (Schultze, Arnold.) London, 1913.

Afr 1435.3 Sultane française du Maroc. (Amaudru, N.) Paris, 1906.

Afr 3143.15 Die Sultanin Sagarat ad-Durr. Inaug.-Diss. (Schregle, Goetz.) Erlangen, 1960.

Afr 3143.18 Die Sultanin von Ägypten. (Schregle, Goetz.) Wiesbaden, 1961.

Afr 3986.958.10 Sultanov, A.F. Polozhenie egipetskogo krestianstvo pered zemelskoi reformoi 1952 goda. Moscow, 1958.

Afr 10015.3 Sulzer, Peter. Christ erscheint am Kongo. Heilbronn, 1958.

Afr Doc 808.710 Summary of external trade statistics. (Libya. Census and Statistical Department.) 1962+

Afr Doc 1807.360.10 Summary of procedures in the 1960 population census of Ghana. (Ghana. Central Bureau of Statistics.) Accra, 1968.

Afr Doc 3407.367 Summary of procedures in the 1967 Tanzania population census. (Tanzania. Central Census Office.) Dar es Salaam, 1968.

Afr 2938.34.5 A summary of the evolution of planning institutions in Libya. (Libya. Ministry of Planning and Development.) Tripoli, 1965.

Afr 8678.71A Summary of the report. (South Africa. Commission for the Socio-Economic Development of the Bantu Areas.) Pretoria, 1955.

Afr 8685.95 Summary of the report of the Committee on Foreign Affairs. (South Africa. Department of Bantu Administration and Development.) Johannesburg, 1964.

Afr 628.10 Summary report, annual conference. (American Society of African Culture.) N.Y.

Afr 36.4 Summary report. (Conference on the Position and Problems of the American Scholar in Africa, White Sulphur Springs, West Va., 1966.) N.Y., 1966?

Afr Doc 308.700F Summary report on Ethiopia's external trade, 1953-1963. (Ethiopia. Central Statistical Office.) Addis Ababa, 1963.

Afr 609.58.45 Summer, Roger. Inyanga. Cambridge, 1958.

Afr 45.62 Summer conference on local government in Africa, 28 Aug.-9 Sept., 1961. (Summer Conference on Local Government in Africa.) Cambridge, 1962.

Afr 45.62 Summer Conference on Local Government in Africa. Summer conference on local government in Africa, 28 Aug.-9 Sept., 1961. Cambridge, 1962.

Afr 9445.50 Summers, Roger. The warriors. Cape Town, 1970.

Afr 40.63.10 Summit conference of independent African states, Addis Ababa, 22-25 May1963. (Summit Conference of Independent African States.) Cairo, 1963.

Afr 40.63.10 Summit Conference of Independent African States. Summit conference of independent African states, Addis Ababa, 22-25 May1963. Cairo, 1963.

Afr 6498.65 Summons to Ruwenzori. (Stacey, T.) London, 1965.

Afr 590.4 Sumner, Charles. White slavery in Barbary states. Boston, 1853.

Afr 4969.21 Sun, sand and Somalis. (Rayne, H.A.) London, 1921.

Afr 3979.63.10F Sun, stones and silence. (Gary, D.H.) N.Y., 1963.

Afr 3986.959 Sun and shadow at Aswan. (Addison, Herbert.) London, 1959.

Afr 609.65 Sunburnt Africa, in pencil, paint, and prose. (Cottrell, Kent.) Hollywood, 1965.

Afr 5219.60.5 Sundiata. (Niane, D.T.) London, 1965.

Afr 9049.5 Sundkler, Bengt. Bantu prophets in South Africa. 2. ed. London, 1964.

Afr 550.100 Sundklur, Bengt. The Christian ministry in Africa. Uppsala, 1960.

Afr 210.60.50 Sundstroem, Erland. Afrika spronger hojorna. Stockholm, 1960.

Afr 9704.8 Sunshine and shade in Central Africa. (Smith, Julia A.) London, 1911.

Afr 9446.27 Sunshine and storm in Rhodesia. (Selous, F.C.) London, 1896.

Afr 9446.24 Sunshine and storm in Rhodesia. (Selous, Frederick Courteney.) N.Y., 1969.

Afr 8659.35 The sunshine route. (South Africa. Railways and Harbours Administration, Johannesburg.) London, 1935.

Afr 5243.122.5 La superstizione Zande. (Giorgetti, Filiberto.) Bologna, 1966.

Afr 5056.123.5 Supplément au Catalogue des positions géographiques de l'A.O.F. (French West Africa.) Laval, 1925.

Afr Doc 3609.25 Supplementary estimates of expenditure on revenue and development account. (Malawi.) Zomba. 1,1965+

X Cg Afr 7000.15.2 Supplemento colonial. (Portugal em Africa.) Lisboa. 169-235 3v.

Afr 8028.111 Supplements. (Nederlandsch-Zuid-Afrikansche Vereeniging. Bibliothek.) 1939+

Afr 1485.7 Sur la frontière marocaine. (Guillaume.) Paris, 1913.

Afr 13275.90.100 Sur la terre en passant. (Evembe, François Borgia Marie.) Paris, 1966.

Afr 590.34 Sur l'abolition de l'esclavage en Afrique. (Abbadie, A.) Paris, 1896.

Afr 7808.88.5 Sur le Haut-Congo. (Coquilhat, Camille.) Paris, 1888.

Afr 820.3.6 Sur le Haut-Zambèze. (Coillard, F.) Paris, 1898.

Afr 1609.12.5 Sur les confins du Maroc. (Rousselet, L.) Paris, 1912.

Afr 5180.31 Sur les côtes du Sénégal et de la Guinée. (Rouch, J.) Paris, 1925.

Afr 1609.30.15 Sur les marches du Maroc insoumis. 3e ed. (Manue, G. R.) Paris, 1930.

Afr 5426.115 Sur les pistes de l'AEF. (Briault, Maurice.) Paris, 1945.

Afr 1082.1 Sur les premiers expéditions. (Deslane, M.G.) n.p., 1844.

Afr 2731.15.10 Sur les traces de Charles de Foucauld. (Gorrée, Georges.) Paris, 1936.

Afr 5185.4 Sur l'ethnologie...du Sénégal. (Tautain, L.) Paris, 1885.

Afr 1973.2 Sur l'expédition et le siège de Constantine. Paris, 1838.

Afr 1753.13 Sureda Blanes, F. Aby la herculana. Calpe, 1925.

Afr 5019.58 Suret-Canale, Jean. Afrique noire, occidentale et centrale. Paris, 1958. 2v.

Afr 5019.58.2 Suret-Canale, Jean. Afrique noire occidentale et centrale. 2 ed. v.1. Paris, 1961.

Afr 5019.58.3 Suret-Canale, Jean. Afrique noire occidentale et centrale. 3e éd. Paris, 1968.

Afr 5243.207.5 Suret-Canale, Jean. Essai sur la signification sociale et historique des hégémonies peules. Paris, 1964.

Afr 5019.58.4 Suret-Canale, Jean. Schwarzafrika i Geographie, Bevölkerung. Berlin, 1966. 2v.

Afr 2209.56 A survey of Algeria. (Service de Propagande, d'Edition et d'Information, Paris.) Paris, 1956.

Afr 3205.20   Tagher, Jacques. Mohamed Ali jugé par les Européens de son temps. Le Caire, 1942.
Afr 6280.6   The tailed head-hunters of Nigeria. (Tremearne, A.J.N.) London, 1912.
Afr 1487.10   Taillard, Fulbert. Le nationalisme marocain. Paris, 1947.
Afr 1826.5.9   Taillart, C. L'Algerie dans la litterature française, essai de bibliog. Paris, 1925.
Afr 1826.5.7   Taillart, C. L'Algerie dans la litterature française. Paris, 1925.
Afr 1826.5.5   Taillart, C. L'Algerie dans la litterature française. Thèse. Paris, 1925.
Afr 1826.5   Taillart, C. L'Algerie dans la litterature française. Thèse. Paris, 1925.
Afr 8678.429   Tairov, Tair F. Apartkheid - prestuplenie veka. Moskva, 1968.
Afr 6194.36   Tait, David. The Konkomba of northern Ghana. London, 1961.
Afr 4390.60   Taitù e Manelik. (Fanelli, Armando.) Milano, 1935.
Afr 10009.5   Taiwo, Oladele. An introduction to West African literature. London, 1967.
Afr 6298.181.5   Takande, Latif Kayode. The trial of Obafemi Awolowo. Lagos, 1966.
Afr 8868.10   Take out hunger; two case studies of rural development in Basutoland. (Wallman, Sandra.) London, 1969.
Afr 1083.15   Talabi, Muhammad. L'Emirat aghlabide. Paris, 1966[1967].
Afr 8252.188.5   Talana, die drie generaals-slag. (Preller, Gustav S.) Kaapstad, 1942.
Afr 4559.52   Talbot, D.A. Contemporary Ethiopia. N.Y., 1952.
Afr 4430.55   Talbot, D.A. Haile Selassie I. The Hague, 1955.
Afr 6280.10   Talbot, D.A. Woman's mysteries of a primitive people, the Ibibios of Southern Nigeria. London, 1915.
Afr 6280.11   Talbot, P.A. In the shadow of the bush. London, 1912.
Afr 6280.11.5   Talbot, P.A. Life in southern Nigeria. London, 1923.
Afr 6280.11.10   Talbot, P.A. The peoples of southern Nigeria. London, 1926.
    4v.
Afr 6280.11.12   Talbot, P.A. The peoples of southern Nigeria. London, 1969.
    4v.
Afr 6280.11.15   Talbot, P.A. Some Nigerian fertility cults. London, 1927.
Afr 6280.11.20   Talbot, P.A. Tribes of the Niger delta. London, 1932.
Afr 8325.40   The tale of a field hospital. (Treves, Frederick.) London, 1900.
Afr 10615.7   Talent for tomorrow; an anthology of creative writing from the training colleges of Ghana. Accra. 1,1966+
Afr 8808.65   Tales at the outspan, or adventures in South Africa. (Drayson, A.W.) London, 1865.
Afr 11675.87.120   Tales from a troubled land. (Paton, Alan.) N.Y., 1961.
Afr 2208.48.10   Tales of Algeria, or Life among the Arabs. (Dumas, Alexandre.) Philadelphia, 1868.
Afr 699.54   Tales of the African frontier. 1st ed. (Hunter, J.A.) N.Y., 1954.
Afr 626.95   Tales of two continents. (Black, Eugene Robert.) Athens, Ga., 1961.
Afr 20.5   Tam-tam. Paris. 1961+
    2v.
Afr 6194.25   Tamakloe, E.F. A brief history of the Daybamba people. Accra, 1931.
Afr 11299.69.120   The tame ox. (Cope, Jack.) London, 1960.
Afr 7175.54.5   Tams, Georg. Die portugiesischen Besitzungen in Süd-West-Afrika. Hamburg, 1945.
Afr 7175.54.10   Tams, Georg. Visit to the Portuguese possessions in South-Western Africa. N.Y., 1969.
Afr 7175.54   Tams, Georg. Visita as possessões portugueses. Porto, 1850.
Afr 6212.44   Tamsino, Tekena N. Nigeria and elective representation, 1923-1947. London, 1966.
Afr 1320.5   Tamuda, revistas de investigaciones marroquies. Tetuan. 1,1953+
    7v.
Afr 626.210   Tamuno, Olufunmilayo Grace Esho. Co-operation for development. Ibadan, 1969.
Afr 5758.23   Tananarive, 1923, Madagascar économique. Tananarive, 1923.
Afr 5783.5   Tananarive. (Madagascar.) Tananarive, 1952.
Afr 5549.60.5   Tananarive. Bibliotheque Universitaire. Madagasihara, regards vers le passe. Tananarive, 1960.
Afr 2875.50   Tancredi, L. Dopo Tripoli. Lugano, 1913.
Afr 635.65.5   Tandberg, Olof G. Brun mans Africa. Stockholm, 1968.
Afr 6888.5   Tanga, the central port for East Africa. (University Press of Africa.) Nairobi, 1968.
Afr 6780.46   Tanganika, 1946-61. (Katsman, V.I.) Moscow, 1962.
Afr 6850.13   Tanganyikas wirtschaftliche Bedeutung für Deutschland. Abhandlung. (Vitzthum von Eckstaedt, B.) München, 1937.
Afr Doc 3409.44   Tanganyika. Budget survey. 1956-1957
Afr 6881.261   Tanganyika. Development plan for Tanganyika, 1961/62-1963/64. Dar es Salaam, 1961.
Afr 6760.30   Tanganyika. Local government memoranda. Dar-es-Salaam. 2,1957
Afr Doc 3407.321   Tanganyika. Non-native census, 1921, report. Report on the native census, 1921. Dar es Salaam, 1921.
    2 pam.
Afr 6879.61.10   Tanganyika. (British Information Services.) N.Y., 1961.
Afr 6879.61   Tanganyika. (British Information Services.) N.Y., 1961.
Afr 6760.10   Tanganyika. (Datta, A.K.) n.p., 1955.
Afr 6881.255   Tanganyika. (Tanganyika Territory.) n.p., n.d.,
Afr 6780.40   Tanganyika. (United Nations Review.) N.Y., 1955.
Afr 6760.20F   Tanganyika. Africanisation Commission. Report of the Africanisation Commission, 1962. Dar es Salaam, 1950.
Afr Doc 3431.5   Tanganyika. Audit Department. Annual report. Dar es Salaam. 1955-1956
Afr Doc 3433.5   Tanganyika. Co-operative Development Department. Annual report on co-operative development. Dar es Salaam. 1956-63
Afr Doc 3419.5   Tanganyika. Constitution. An act to declare the Constitution of Tanganyika. Dar es Salaam, 1962?
Afr 6757.2   Tanganyika. Department of Antiquities. Annual report.
Afr Doc 3453.5   Tanganyika. Department of Water Development and Irrigation. Annual report. 1959+
Afr 770.3.5   Tanganyika. Eleven years...Central Africa. 2nd ed. Photoreproduction. (Hore, Edw.C.) n.p., 1892.
Afr Doc 3439.5   Tanganyika. Immigration and Passport Department. Annual report. Dar es Salaam. 1955
Afr Doc 3442.5   Tanganyika. Labour Department. Annual report.
Afr Doc 3414.10   Tanganyika. National Assembly. Assembly debates; official report. 27,1952+
    13v.

Afr 6757.10   Tanganyika. National Assembly. Assembly debates, official report. 27,1952+
    12v.
Afr Doc 3412.5   Tanganyika. National Assembly. Government paper. Dar es Salaam. 7,1958
Afr Doc 3414.5   Tanganyika. Parliament. National Assembly. Parliamentry debates. 1,1961+
    3v.
Afr 6757.4   Tanganyika. Public Work Department. Annual report.
Afr Doc 3446.5   Tanganyika. Public Works Department. Annual report. 1957+
Afr Doc 3407.331F   Tanganyika. Secretariat. Census of the native population of Tanganyika territory, 1931. Dar es Salaam, 1932.
Afr Doc 3349.3   Tanganyika. Social Development Department. Annual report. 1959+
Afr Doc 3409.305F   Tanganyika. Treasury. Report on the accounts and finances. Dar es Salaam. 1924-1954
Afr Doc 3407.357.5   Tanganyika. Treasury. Central Statistical Bureau. African Census report, 1957. Dar es Salaam, 1963.
Afr Doc 3407.362F   Tanganyika. Treasury. Central Statistical Bureau. Census of large scale commercial farming in Tanganyika, October 1962. Dar es Salaam, 1963.
Afr Doc 3407.5   Tanganyika. Treasury. Central Statistical Bureau. Statistical abstract. 1959+
Afr Doc 3409.300   Tanganyika. Treasury. Central Statistical Bureau. Village economic surveys. Dar es Salaam. 1961-1962
Afr Doc 3408.300   Tanganyika. Tresury. Economics and Statistics Division. Employment and earnings in Tanganyika. Dar es Salaam, 1961-1963.
Afr 6879.61.5   Tanganyika. 1st ed. (Varma, Shanti Narayan.) New Delhi, 1961.
Afr 6881.265   Tanganyika. 1st ed. (Burke, Fred George.) Syracuse, N.Y., 1965.
Afr 6333.61A   Tanganyika and international trusteeship. (Chidzero, B.T.G.) London, 1961.
Afr 555.65   Tanganyika and its future. (Richter, Julius.) London, 1934.
Afr 6881.264   Tanganyika five-year plan for economic and social development, 1st July, 1964-30th June, 1969. (Tanzania.) Dar es Salaam, 1964.
Afr 6879.36.5   Tanganyika guide. 2d ed. Dar es Salaam, 1948.
Afr 6750.6   Tanganyika notes and records. Dar es Salaam. 34,1953+
    6v.
Afr Doc 3407.357.15   Tanganyika population census, 1957. (East Africa High Commission. East African Statistical Department.) Dar es Salaam, 1958.
    2 pam.
Afr 6879.31   Tanganyika Railways and Harbours. Travel guide to Tanganyika and Central Africa. London, 1931.
Afr 6881.255   Tanganyika Territory. Tanganyika. n.p., n.d.,
Afr 6879.20   The Tanganyika territory. (Joelson, F.S.) London, 1920.
Afr 6780.42   Tanganyika territory. (Leubuscher, Charlotte.) Oxford, 1944.
Afr 6881.257   Tanganyika Territory. Department of Commerce and Industry. Commerce and industry in Tanganyika. Dar es Salaam, 1957.
Afr 6850.9F   Tanganyika Territory. Secretariat. Census of the native population of Tanganyika territory, 1931. Dar es Salaam, 1932.
Afr 6750.5   Tanganyika trade bulletin. Dar es Salaam. 6,1957+
Afr Doc 3408.705   Tanganyika trade bulletin. Dar es Salaam. 6,1957+
Afr 6778.2   Tanganyika under German rule, 1905-1912. (Iliffe, John.) London, 1969.
Afr 6780.43   The Tanganyika way. (Mustafa, Sophia.) London, 1962.
Afr 1609.24.5   Tanger, fes et meknes. (Champion, P.) Paris, 1924.
Afr 1738.45   Tanger. (Bonjean, Jacques.) Paris, 1967.
Afr 1738.29   Tanger. (Comite de Propagande et de Tourisme, Paris.) Paris, 1929.
Afr 1738.5   Tanger. 1st ed. Paris, 1902 (Cousin, A.)
Afr 1738.5.3   Tanger. 3d ed. (Cousin, A.) Paris, 1903.
Afr 1738.25   Die Tanger-Frage. (Graevenitz, K.F.H.A.R.) Berlin, 1925.
Afr 1738.38.5   Tanger und die britische Reichsbildung. (Petzet, H.W.) Berlin, 1938.
Afr 1738.38.4   Tanger und die britische Reichsbildung. Inaug. Diss. (Petzet, H.W.) Berlin, 1938.
Afr 1573.25   Tanger y la colaboracion franco-española en Marruecos. (Ruiz Albeniz, V.) Madrid, 1927.
Afr 1738.7   Tanger y sus alrededores. (Escribano del Pino, E.) Madrid, 1903.
Htn   Afr 1738.3.5*   Tanger's rescue. (Ross, John.) London, 1681.
Afr 1738.20F   Tangier, Africa. Registos paroquiais da se de Tanger. Lisboa, 1922.
Afr 1738.11   Tangier. (Routh, E.M.G.) London, 1912.
Afr 1738.22   Tangier at high tide. (Luke, John.) Geneva, 1958.
Afr 1738.40   Tangier under British rule, 1661-1684. (Abbey, W.B.T.) Jersey, Channel Islands, British Isles, 1940.
Afr 8658.96.5   Tangye, H. Lincoln. In new South Africa. London, 1896.
Afr 4070.15   Tangye, H.S. In the torrid Sudan. Boston, 1910.
Afr 6883.15.5   Tanner, Ralph E.S. Transition in African beliefs. Maryknoll, 1967.
Afr 9769.60   Tanser, George Henry. A history of Nyasaland. Capetown, 1960.
Afr 9515.6   Tanser, George Henry. A scantling of time. Salisbury, 1965.
Afr 8292.4   Tant' Alie of Transvaal, her diary 1880-1902. (Badenhorst, A.M.) London, 1923.
Afr 6760.22A   Tanzania; party transformation. (Bienen, Henry.) Princeton, 1967.
Afr 6879.66   Tanzania, young nation in a hurry. 1st ed. (Macdonald, Alexander.) N.Y., 1966.
Afr Doc 3409.310F   Tanzania. The appropriation accounts, revenue statements, accounts of the funds and other public accounts together with the report thereon by the Controller and Auditor-General. Dar es Salaam. 1966+
Afr Doc 3409.40   Tanzania. Estimates of the expenditure of the United Republic of Tanganyika and Zanzibar. Dar es Salaam. 1964+
Afr Doc 3412.7   Tanzania. Government paper. Dar es Salaam. 2,1966+
Afr Doc 3402.5   Tanzania. Government publications. Dar es Salaam. 1961+
Afr 3109.5   Tanzania. Revised approved estimates of the revenue and expenditure for Zanzibar. Zanzibar. 1,1964+
Afr Doc 3403.5   Tanzania. Staff list. Dar es Salaam. 1965+
Afr 6881.264   Tanzania. Tanganyika five-year plan for economic and social development, 1st July, 1964-30th June, 1969. Dar es Salaam, 1964.
Afr Doc 3431.10   Tanzania. Administrator General's Department. Annual report. Dar es Salaam. 1964+

Afr 6753.10 Tanzania: an introductory bibliography. (Decalo, Samuel.) Kingston?, 1968.
Afr Doc 3407.367 Tanzania. Central Census Office. Summary of procedures in the 1967 Tanzania population census. Dar es Salaam, 1968.
Afr Doc 3407.361.10
Tanzania. Central Statistical Bureau. Census of industrial production in Tanganyika. Tanganyika, 1961.
Afr Doc 3407.10 Tanzania. Central Statistical Bureau. Statistical abstract. Dar es Salaam. 1,1964+
Afr Doc 3433.10 Tanzania. Ministry of Commerce and Co-operatives. Annual report. Dar es Salaam. 1964
Afr 6881.264.5 Tanzania. Ministry of Economic Affaires and Development Planning. First year progress report on the implementation of the Five-year Development Plan. Dar-es-Salaam, 1965?
Afr Doc 3435.5 Tanzania. Ministry of Education. Annual report. Dar es Salaam. 1964+
Afr Doc 3436.5 Tanzania. Ministry of Foreign Affairs. Foreign affairs bulletin. Dar es Salaam. 2,1966+
Afr Doc 3439.10 Tanzania. Ministry of Industries, Mineral Resources and Power. Annual report. Dar es Salaam. 1,1964+
Afr 6335.2 Tanzania. Ministry of Information and Tourism. Meetings and discussions on the proposed East Africa Federation. Dar es Salaam, 1964.
Afr 10002.5 Tanzania. Ministry of Information and Tourism. United Republic press directory. Dar es Salaam. 1965+
Afr Doc 3444.5 Tanzania. National Archives. Annual report. Dar es Salaam. 1,1964+
Afr 6750.12 Tanzania. National Museum. Annual report. Dar es Salaam. 1966+
Afr 6785.2 Tanzania. President. President's address to the National assembly, June 8, 1965. Dar es Salaam, 1965.
Afr 6760.15 Tanzania. Presidential Commission on the Establishment of a Democratic One Party State. Report. Dar es Salaam, 1965.
Afr 6881.266 Tanzania. Presidential Special Committee of Enquiry into the Cooperative Movement and Marketing Boards. Report. Dar-es-Salaam, 1966.
Afr Doc 3450.5 Tanzania. Town Planning Division. Annual report. Dar es Salaam. 1964+
Afr 6769.68.5 Tanzania before 1900. (Roberts, Andrew.) Nairobi, 1968.
Afr 6879.68.5 Tanzania today. (University Press of Africa.) Nairobi, 1968.
Afr 6879.67.5 Tanzania vil selv. (Svendsen, Knud Erik.) København, 1967.
Afr 6750.16F Tanzania zamani. Dar-es-Salaam. 1,1967+
Afr 6760.25 Tanzanian citizen: a civics textbook. (Meienberg, Hildebrand.) Nairobi, 1966[1967].
Afr 1738.21 Tapahtui tangerissa. (Lilius, Aleko E.) Helsingissa, 1955.
Afr 1830.50.15 Les tapis et tissages du Djebel-amour. (Giacobetti, R.P.) Paris, 1932.
Afr 8847.45.2 Tapson, Winifred. Timber and tides; the story of Knysna and Plettenberg Bay. 2. ed. Johannesburg, 1963.
Afr 9689.57 Tapson, Winifred (Haw). Old timer. Cape Town, 1957.
Afr 1338.17 Taraki, Muhammad Insan. Les institutions politiques du Maroc depuis l'indépendance. Thèse. Lyon, 1965.
Afr 2819.32 Taraschi, T.M. La Libia italiana, nella preparazione diplomatica e nella conquista. Napoli, 1932.
Afr 1609.23 Tarde, Alfred de. Le Maroc, ecole d'energie. Paris, 1923.
Afr 1550.11 Tardier, A. La conférence d'Algésiras. Paris, 1908.
Afr 1571.5A Tardieu, A. le mystère d'Agadir. Paris, 1912.
Afr 608.47 Tardieu, E.A. Sénégambie, Guinée, Nubie. Paris, 1847.
Afr 5396.2 Tardits. C. Porto-Novo. Paris, 1958.
Afr 6740.15 Tardits, Claude. Contribution à l'étude des populations Bamileke de l'Ouest Cameroun. Paris, 1960.
Afr 1069.55 Tarih hoyunca kujey Afrika. (Naci, Hikmet.) Istanbul, 1955?
Afr 4220.5F Tarik; gazette d'information archéologique, historique et littéraire. Addis Ababa. 2,1963+
Afr 20.10 Tarikh. Ikeja. 1,1965+
Afr 5243.343 Tarikh es-Soudan. (Sadi, Abd al-Rahman.) Paris, 1900.
Afr 3675.65 Tariks el-Jettoch, ou Chronique du chercheur pour servir a l'histoire des villes, des armées et des principaux personnages du Tekrour. (Timbuktu, Mahmud.) Paris, 1913.
Afr 3204.20 Tarman, E.E. Egypt and its betrayal. N.Y., 1908.
Afr 575.56 Tarverdova, Ekaterina A. Rasprostranenie islama v zapadnoi Afrike, XI-XVI vv. Moskva, 1967.
Afr 8110.6.5A Tas, A. Diary. London, 1914.
Afr 9029.11 Tatlow, A.H. Natal province, descriptive guide. Durban, 1911.
Afr 8678.281 Tatz, C. Shadow and substance in South Africa. Pietermaritzburg, 1962.
Afr 626.145 Taufer, Otakar. Vyznam hospodarske spoluprace socialistickych statu s africkymi zememi. Praha, 1964.
Afr 5185.4 Tautain, L. Sur l'ethnologie...du Sénégal. Paris, 1885.
Afr 1280.2 Tauxier, Henri. Etude sur les migrations des nations berbères avant l'islamisme. Paris, 1863.
Afr 5243.125.35 Tauxier, Louis. Histoire des Bambara. Paris, 1942.
NEDL Afr 5344.5 Tauxier, Louis. Le noir de Bondoukou. Paris, 1921.
Afr 5243.12 Tauxier, Louis. Le Noir du Soudan. Paris, 1912.
Afr 5285.277.5 Tauxier, Louis. Le noir du Yatenga-Mossi. Paris, 1917.
Afr 5285.277.7 Tauxier, Louis. Nouvelles notes sur le Mossi et le Gorounsi. Paris, 1924.
Afr 5243.125.15 Tauxier, Louis. La religion bambara. Paris, 1927.
Afr 150.2.60 Tavares, Luis C. O Infante Dom Henrique e os descobrimentos. Braga, 1960.
Afr 7335.5 Tavares de Almeida e Sousa e Lupata. (Silva, Julia.) Lisboa, 1966.
Afr 8835.35 A tavern of the ocean. (Laidler, Percy Ward.) Cape Town, 1926.
Afr 8835.55 Tavern of the seas. (Green, Lawrence George.) Cape Town, 1966.
Afr 1442.5 Taviel de Andrade, E. Cuestion de Marruecos. Madrid, 1888.
Afr 626.124 Taxation and economic development. (Due, J.F.) Cambridge, 1963.
Afr 725.16 Taylor, Bayard. The lake regions of central Africa. N.Y., 1881.
Afr 8658.72.5 Taylor, Bayard. Travels in South Africa. N.Y., 1872.
Afr 8658.72.10 Taylor, Bayard. Travels in South Africa. N.Y., 1881.
Afr 10911.2 Taylor, Charles T.C. The history of Rhodesian entertainment, 1890-1930. Salisbury, 1968.
Afr 50.53 Taylor, Don. Africa, the portrait of power. London, 1967.
Afr 505.42 Taylor, Don. The British in Africa. London, 1962.
Afr 9610.10 Taylor, Don. Rainbow on the Zambezi. London, 1953.
Afr 9525.875 Taylor, Don. The Rhodesian, the life of Sir Roy Welensky. London, 1955.
Afr 3310.10.80 Taylor, Edmond. The real case against Nasser. n.p., 1956.

Afr 4095.3.3 Taylor, G.B. A journey to central Africa. N.Y., 1854.
Afr 4095.3.2 Taylor, G.B. A journey to central Africa. N.Y., 1854.
Afr 4095.3.4 Taylor, G.B. Eine Reise nach Centralafrika. Leipzig, 1855.
Afr 724.9 Taylor, Henry James. Capetown to Kafue. London, 1916.
Afr 608.21.2 Taylor, I. Scenes in Africa. London, 1821.
Afr 3978.88 Taylor, Isaac. Leaves from an Egyptian note-book. London, 1888.
Afr 7375.8 Taylor, J.B. Biography of Elder Lott Cary. Baltimore, 1837.
Afr 6769.63 Taylor, J.C. The political development of Tanganyika. Stanford, 1963.
Afr 550.75 Taylor, John Vernon. Christianity and politics in Africa. Harmondsworth, 1957.
Afr 6541.30 Taylor, John Vernon. The growth of the church in Buganda. London, 1958.
Afr 855.24 Taylor, Margaret Stewart. St. Helena, ocean roadhouse. London, 1969.
Afr 550.19 Taylor, S.E. The price of Africa. Cincinnati, 1902.
Afr 108.98 Taylor, W. The flaming torch in darkest Africa. N.Y., 1898.
Afr 555.7.5 Taylor, William. Christian adventures in South Africa. London, 1868.
Afr 6275.85 Taylor Woodrow, ltd. Building for the future in Nigeria. London, 1960.
Afr 1713.14 Al-Tazi, Abd Al- Hali. Eleven centuries in the university of al-qarawiyyin. Mohammedia, 1960.
Afr 5480.265 Le Tchad. (Hugot, Pierre.) Paris, 1965.
Afr 5482.20 Tchad. (Italy. Instituto Nazionale per il Commercio Estero.) Romo, 1963.
Afr 5480.231 Le Tchad de sable et d'or. (Maran, René.) Paris, 1931.
Afr 5480.208 Le Tchad et le bassin du Chari. Thèse. (Freydenberg, Henri.) Paris, 1908.
Afr 13340.13.700 Tchicaya U Tamsi, Gerald Felix. Brush fire. Ibadan, 1964.
Afr 13340.13.100 Tchicaya U Tamsi, Gerald Felix. Epitome. Tunis, 1962.
Afr 13340.12.100 Tchicaya U Tamsi, Gerald Felix. Feu de brousse. Paris, 1957.
Afr 13340.13.110 Tchicaya U Tamsi, Gerald Felix. Le ventre. Paris, 1964.
Afr 13340.13.120 Tchichaya U Tamsi, Gerald Felix. Le mauvais sang, poèmes. Paris, 1955.
Afr 5321.5 Tchidimbo, Raymond-M. L'homme noir dans l'Eglise. Paris, 1963.
Afr 2208.80 Tchihatchef, P. Espagne, Algérie et Tunisie. Paris, 1880.
Afr 3979.59 The tears of Isis. (Carrington, R.) London, 1959.
Afr 2370.1 Tébessa, histoire et description d'un territoire Algérien. (Castel, P.) Paris, 1905. 2v.
Afr 6277.120 Technical Assistance Information Clearing House. Nigeria/Biafrai programs of assistance of U.S. non-profit organizations, March 1969. N.Y., 1969.
Afr 4559.20 Tedesco Zammarano, V. Alle sorgenti del Nilo azzurro. Roma, 1920.
Afr 4392.30 Tedone, Giovanni Angerà. Milano, 1964.
Afr 5225.5 Tedzkiret en-nisian fi akhbar molouk es-Soudan. (Abd al-Rahman ibn Abdallah al-Tonbukti.) Paris, 1901.
Afr 2749.54.10 Tefedest. (Carl, Louis.) London, 1954.
Afr 1259.44.15 Tefri (Pseud.) Sonnen-Bilder aus Nord-Afrika. Bulle, 1944.
Afr 7119.34 Teixeira, Alberto de Almeida. Angola intangivel. Pôrto, 1934.
Afr 7122.77 Teixeira, Bernardo. The fabric of terror, three days in Angola. N.Y., 1965.
Afr 3163.10 Tekindağ, M.C. Şehabeddin. Berkuk devrinde Memluk Sultanhgi. Istanbul, 1967.
Afr 1640.10 Les Tekna du sud Marocain. (Lachapelle, F.) Paris, 1934.
Afr 11108.74.120 Tell freedom. 1st American ed. (Abrahams, Peter.) N.Y., 1954.
Afr 9693.3 Tell me, Josephine. (Josephine (pseud.).) London, 1964.
Afr 2609.34.5 Le tell septentrional en Tunisie. Thèse. (Bonniard, F.) Paris, 1934.
Htn Afr 4556.60.2* Tellez, B. Historia geral de Ethiopia. (Earlier issue). Coimbra, 1660.
Afr 4556.60.10 Tellez, B. Historia geral de Ethiopia. Porto, 1936.
Afr 1753.8 Tello Amondareyn, M. Ceuta llave principal del Estrecho. Madrid, 1897.
Afr 7122.68 Telo, Alencastre. Angola, terra nossa. Lisbon, 1962.
Afr 6196.13 Tema Manhean; a study of resettlement. (Amarteifio, Godfrey William.) Kumasi, 1966.
Afr 7119.57.5 Temas angolanos. (Sarmento, Alexandre.) Lisboa, 1957.
Afr 1721.9 Temas de protectorado. (Garcia Figueras, T.) Ceuta, 1926.
Afr 7580.35 Témoignage et réflexions. (Rétillon, Leon A.M.) Bruxelles, 1962.
Afr 2397.2 Le témoin. (Amrani, Djamal.) Paris, 1960.
Afr 2030.360 Témoignage d'un ultra sur le drame algérien. (Reygasse, René.) Paris, 1960.
Afr 6741.12 Témoins camerounais de l'Évangile. (Grob, Francis.) Yaoundé, 1967.
Afr 7575.12 Tempête sur le Congo. (Niedergang, M.) Paris, 1960.
Afr 1494.37 Tempête sur le Maroc. (Barbau, Muslim.) Paris, 1931.
Afr 6280.17 Temple, Charles L. Native races and their rulers. London, 1918.
Afr 6280.17.2 Temple, Charles L. Native races and their rulers. 2nd ed. London, 1968.
Afr 6280.18.2 Temple, Charles L. Notes on the tribes, provinces, emirates and states of the northern provinces of Nigeria. 2d ed. Lagos, 1922.
Afr 6280.18.7 Temple, Charles Lindsay. Notes on the tribes, provinces, emirates and states of the northern provinces of Nigeria. 2d ed. London, 1965.
Afr 2208.35 Temple, G.T. Excursions...Algiers and Tunis. London, 1835. 2v.
Afr 3979.39F Temps. Numéro special. L'Egypte. Paris, 1939.
Afr 2030.461.20 Le temps de la justice. (Davezies, Robert.) Lausanne, 1961.
Afr 12624.41.1110 Temps de mémoire. (Diakhaté, Lamine.) Paris, 1967.
Afr 1830.20.8 Le temps et la prevision du temps en Algerie et au Sahara. (Petitjean, L.) Paris, 1930.
Afr 12377.23.100 Temps forts, poèmes. (Greki, Anna.) Paris, 1966.
Afr 10117.5 Ten one-act plays. (Pietense, Cosmo.) London, 1968.
Afr 9028.55 Ten weeks in Natal. (Colenso, J.W.) Cambridge, 1855.
Afr Doc 1309.10F Ten year plan of economic and social development, 1961/62-1970/71. Development budget. (Sudan.) Khartoum. 1965+
Afr 3813.10 The ten year plan of economic and social development, 1962-1971. (Sudan. Ministry of Finance and Economics.) Khartoum, 1963.

Afr 6144.6F   Ten-year plan of economic and social development, 1962/63-1971/72. (Sierra Leone.) Freetown, 1962.

Afr Doc 1309.10.5   Ten year plan of economic and social development. Explanatory memorandum on development budgets. (Sudan.) Khartoum. 1965+

Afr 3730.3   Ten years' captivity in the Mahdi's camp. (Ohrwalder, J.) London, 1893.

Afr 3730.3.5   Ten years' captivity in the Mahdi's camp. (Ohrwalder, J.) N.Y., 1893.

Afr 3730.2   Ten years' captivity in the Mahdi's camp. 7th ed. (Ohrwalder, J.) London, 1892.

Afr 3730.2.5   Ten years' captivity in the Mahdi's camp. 10th ed. (Ohrwalder, J.) Leipzig, 1893.

Afr 555.22.14   Ten years' church work in Natal. (Rivett, A.W.L.) London, 1890.

X Cg   Afr 3725.4   Ten years in Equatoria. (Casati, G.) London, 1891. (Changed to XP 3865) 2v.

Afr 8808.35   Ten years in South Africa. (Moodie, John W D) London, 1835. 2v.

Afr 7809.38.5   Ten years in the Congo. (Davis, W.E.) N.Y., 1940.

Afr 8658.71   Ten years north of the Orange River. (Mackenzie, J.) Edinburgh, 1871.

Afr 3986.962.20   Ten years of progress...1952-62. (United Arab Republic. Information Department.) Cairo, 1962.

NEDL   Afr 1550.16.5   Ten years of secret diplomacy. 3d ed. (Morel, E.D.) London, 1915.

Afr 5765.12   Ten years review of mission work in Madagascar, 1870-80. (London Missionary Society.) Antananarivo, 1880.

Afr 678.61.3   Ten years wanderings among the Ethiopians. (Hutchinson, T.J.) London, 1861.

Afr 678.61.4   Ten years' wanderings among the Ethiopians. (Hutchinson, T.J.) London, 1967.

Afr 1495.6.5   La Ténébreuse affaire Ben Barka. (Marec, Jean Paul.) Paris, 1966.

Afr 28.88   Tenri Central Library, Tanba City, Japan. Africana. Tenri, 1960. 2v.

Afr 3978.59   Tent and harem. (Paine, Caroline.) N.Y., 1859.

Afr 8028.115   Tentative list of books and pamphlets on South Africa. (Brett, E.A.) Johannesburg, 1959.

Afr Doc 9307.360   Terceiro recenseamento geral da população, 1960. v.1-5. (Angola. Repartição de Estatistica Geral.) Luanda, 1964-1969.

Afr 1750.4.3   Tercer congreso africanista. (Congreso Africanista.) Barcelona, 1909.

Afr 1753.10.3   O tercio de extranjeros do exercito espanhol. (Dornellas, Affonso de.) Lisboa, 1924.

Afr 1609.26.5   Terhorst, Bernd. With the Riff Kabyles. London, 1926.

Afr 7570.20   Un terme au Congo belge. (Segairt, Henri.) Bruxelles, 1919.

Afr 7210.5F   Termos de vassallagem nos territorios de machona, etc., 1858 a 1889. Lisboa, 1890.

Afr 1570.16   Ternant, V. de. La question marocaine. Paris, 1894.

Afr 7065.10   Terra, Branco da. Guiné do século XV. Lisboa?, 196-.

Afr 2945.20   La terra delle donne tenebrose. (Mura, Nicolo.) Bologna, 1930.

Afr 2875.67   La terra promessa. (Maltese, Paolo.) Milano, 1968.

Afr 3340.8.2   Terra Viera, Blanca. Egipto en blanco y negro. 2. ed. Madrid, 1965.

Afr 8283.12   Terrail, G. Le Transvaal et la chartered. Paris, 1897.

Afr 7068.7   Terras da Guiné e Cabo Verde. (Guerra, M. dos S.) Lisboa, 1956.

Afr 1369.49.3   Terrasse, Henri. Histoire du Maroc. Casablanca, 1952.

Afr 1369.49   Terrasse, Henri. Histoire du Maroc des origines a l'établissement du protectorat français. v.1-2. Casablanca, 1949-50. 2v.

Afr 1713.10   Terrasse, Henri. La mosquee des andalous a Fes. Text and atlas. v.1-2. Paris, 1942. 2v.

Afr 2630.2   La terre, projet de petite colonisation. (Poublon, G.) Tunis, 1901.

Afr 7549.37   La terre belge du Congo. (Jentgen, Pierre.) Bruxelles, 1937.

Afr 609.66.30   Terre d'Afrique. (Kaké, Baba Ibrahima.) Paris, 1966.

Afr 4688.15.15   Le terre del Lago Tsana. (Lauro, R. di.) Roma, 1936.

Afr 125.5   La terre habitable vers l'équator. (Berlioux, E.F.) Paris, 1884.

Afr 7850.3   Terre katangaise. (Cornet, R.J.) Bruxelles, 1950.

Afr 3979.64.10   La terre qui berça l'histoire. (Mikhaelides, Gaby.) Bomas-sur-Ourthe, 1964.

Afr 5480.267   Terre tchadienne. (Chad, President.) Paris, 1967.

Afr 2030.464.50   Terrenoire, Louis. De Gaulle et l'Algérie. Paris, 1964.

Afr 679.47   Terres de soleil, et de sommeil. (Psichari, Ernest.) Paris, 1947.

Afr 1869.57.10   Terres et hommes d'Algérie. v.1. (Amrouche, Marcel.) Alger, 1957.

Afr 5219.10   Terrier, A. L'expansion française et la formation territoriale. Paris, 1910.

Afr 1609.31.15   Terrier, A. Le Maroc. Paris, 1931.

Afr 5796.5.10   Territoire des Comores; bibliographie. (Gorse, Jean.) Paris, 1964?

Afr 2681.2   Territoire des Ouled Ali ben-Aoun. 1. ed. Paris, 1956.

Afr Doc 7109.5F   Territoire du Tchad; budget local. (French Equatorial Africa.) Fort Lamy. 1952-1953

Afr 505.2   Les territoires africaines. (Rouard de Card, E.) Paris, 1901.

Afr 6685.8   Territoires africains sous mandat de la France. (Chazelas, V.) Paris, 1931.

Afr 6738.23   Territoires africains sous mandat de la France. (Chazelas, Victor.) Paris, 1931.

Afr 2288.5   Les territoires du sud. Exposé de leur situation. (Extrait) Description géographique par E.-F. Gautier. (Algérie. Direction des Territoires du Sud.) Alger, 1922.

Afr 2288.15   Les territoires du sud. Exposé de leur situation. Pt.1. (Algérie. Direction des Territoires du Sud.) Alger, 1922.

Afr 2288.15.3   Les territoires du sud de l'Algérie. (Algeria. Direction des Territoires du Sud.) Alger, 1954.

Afr 2288.15.5   Les territoires du sud de l'Algérie. 2d ed. Pt.1-3,5 et cartes. (Algeria. Commissariat Général du Centenaire.) Alger, 1929-30. 5v.

Afr 5912.2   Territorios del sur de Marruecos y Sahara occidental. (Gonzalez Jimenez, E.) Toledo, 1930.

Afr 5912.5   Los territorios españoles de Africa. (Pelissier, René.) Madrid, 1964.

Afr 5955.4   Territorios españoles del Golfo de Guinea. (Bravo Carbonell, J.) Madrid, 1929.

Afr 7135.10   The terror fighters: a profile of guerilla warfare in southern Africa. (Venter, Al Johannes.) Cape Town, 1969.

Afr 8289.31.9   Terug na kommando...krygs gebangenes. 3. druk. (Visagie, L.A.) Kaapstad, 1941.

Afr 2945.24   Teruzzi, Attilo. Cirenaica verde. Milano, 1931.

Afr 7530.15   Tervuren, Belgium. Musée Royale de l'Afrique Centrale. Inventaire des archives historiques. 3,1964+ 2v.

Afr 7530.12   Tervuren, Belgium. Musée Royale de l'Afrique Centrale. Inventaire des documents provenant de la mission. Bruxelles, 1960.

Afr 618.9   Terweer, M.C. Altruisme bij enkele natuurvolken van Afrika en Australie. Academisch proefschrift. Amsterdam, 1939.

Afr 2875.25   La terza colonia italiana. (Cicerone, G.) Roma, 1913.

Afr 20136.2   Tescaroli, Livio. Poesia sudanese. Bologna, 1961.

Afr 635.5F   Tessmann, Günter. Die Pangew. Berlin, 1913-

Afr 2928.56   Testa, C.E. le. Notice statistique et commerciale. La Haye, 1856.

Afr 1575.10   Testa, Carlos. Portugal e Marrocos perante a historia e a politica europea. Lisboa, 1888.

Afr Doc 9290.5F   Tete. Projecto de orçamento. 1917-1918

Afr Doc 9290.10   Tete. Governador. Relatorio. Lourenço Marques. 1908-1912

Afr 6193.5   Tete-Ansa, W. Africa at work. N.Y., 1930.

Afr 550.10   Tetu, H. Le R.P. Bouchard. Québec, 1897.

Afr 626.204   Tevoedjre, Albert. Africa and international co-operation: ILO in Africa. n.p., n.d.

Afr 210.58.5   Tevoedjre, Albert. L'Afrique revoltée. Paris, 1958.

Afr 626.160   Tevoedjre, Albert. Contribution à une synthèse sur le problème de la formation des cadres africains en vue de la croissance économique. Paris, 1965.

Afr 2208.46.8   Texier, C. Les grandes chasses d'Afrique. n.p., n.d.

Afr 628.141   A text book of the origin and history. (Hartford, 1841). (Pennington, James W.C.) Detroit, 1969?

Afr 1734.5   Textas em aljamia portuguesa. (Lopes, David.) Lisboa, 1897.

Afr 40.67.5   A textbook of government for West Africa. (Oyebola, Areoye.) Ibadan, 1967.

Afr 2030.60.2   Texte intégral du livre "La question." (Alleg, Henri.) Paris, 1958.

Afr 2030.462.50   Textes choisis sur l'Algérie. (Thorez, Maurice.) Paris, 1962.

Afr 31.5   Textes et documents relatifs a l'histoire de l'Afrique. (Ibn Batuta.) Dakar, 1966.

Afr 7565.14.5   Textes inédits. (Banning, E.) Bruxelles, 1955.

Afr 1030.20   Textes relatifs à l'histoire de l'Afrique du Nord. Alger. 1,1916+ 2v.

Afr 20059.5   Textes sacrés d'Afrique noire. (Dieterlen, Germaine.) Paris, 1965.

Afr 5874.9   Textor de Rairsi. Etudes sur...des palmistes....l'Ile de la Réunion. Saint-Denis, 1848.

Afr 31.12   Textos basicos de Africa. v.1-2. (Cordero Torres, J.M.) Madrid, 1962. 2v.

Afr 2030.462.112   Texts of declarations drawn up in common agreement at Evian. (Algeria. Treaties, etc.) N.Y., 1962.

Afr 5832.10.3   T'eylandt Mauritius. (Pitot, Albert.) Port-Louis, 1905.

Afr 1655.4   Tharaud, J. Fez, ou les bourgeois de l'islam. Paris, 1930.

Afr 1609.23.10   Tharaud, J. Le Maroc. Paris, 1923.

Afr 4430.36.15   Tharaud, J. Le passant d'Ethiopie. Paris, 1936.

Afr 1609.20   Tharaud, Jerome. Marrakech. Paris, 1920.

Afr 1713.15   Tharaud, Jerome. La nuit de Fes. Paris, 1932.

Afr 1733.5   Tharaud, Jerome. Rabat. Paris, 1918.

Afr 8369.60   That we may tread safely. (Barlow, A.G.) Cape Town, 1960.

Afr 609.21   The backbone of Africa. (Sharpe, Alfred.) London, 1921.

Afr 115.55.2   The literature and thought of modern Africa, a survey. (Wauthier, Claude.) London, 1966.

Afr 6775.6F   The medieval history of the coast of Tanganyika. (Freeman-Grenville, G.S.) Berlin, 1962.

Afr 3817.8   The Nuer. (Evans-Pritchard, Edward Evan.) Oxford, 1940.

Afr 2285.21   The Paris Lyons and Mediterranean Railway Co. Algeria...season 1927-28. Algiers, 1927.

Afr 8846.34   The Transkei; emancipation without chaos. (South Africa. Department of Information.) Pretoria, 1966?

Afr 9086.20   The Transvaal. (De Villiers, John.) London, 1896.

Afr 8100.5   Theal, G.M. The beginning of South African history. London, 1902.

Afr 8028.1.3   Theal, G.M. Catalogues of books and pamphlets. Cape Town, 1912.

Afr 8088.77.5   Theal, G.M. Compendium of South African history and geography. 3d ed. Lovedale, 1877.

Afr 8100.5.3   Theal, G.M. Ethnography and condition of South Africa. London, 1919.

Afr 8868.5   Theal, G.M. A fragment of Basuto history. Cape Town, 1886.

Afr 8088.88.8   Theal, G.M. Geschiedenis van Zuid-Afrika. 's-Gravenhage, 1897.

NEDL   Afr 8088.88.5   Theal, G.M. History and ethnography of Africa Zambesi. London, 1907. 3v.

Afr 8089.64   Theal, G.M. History of South Africa. Cape Town, 1964. 11v.

NEDL   Afr 8088.88   Theal, G.M. History of South Africa. London, 1888- 5v.

Afr 8088.88.9   Theal, G.M. History of South Africa from 1795-1872. London, 1915. 2v.

Afr 8088.88.10   Theal, G.M. History of South Africa from 1873-1884. London, 1919. 2v.

Afr 8088.88.7   Theal, G.M. History of South Africa since Sept. 1795. v.1- London, 1908- 3v.

Afr 8175.5   Theal, G.M. History of the Boers in South Africa. London, 1887.

Afr 8175.5.1   Theal, G.M. History of the Boers in South Africa. N.Y., 1969.

Afr 8028.1   Theal, G.M. Notes upon books referring to South Africa. Cape Town, 1882.

Afr 8089.02   Theal, G.M. Progress of South Africa. Toronto, 1902.

Afr 8707.5   Theal, G.M. Records of Cape colony. v.1-35 and index. London, 1897-1905. 36v.

Afr 8030.10 Theal, G.M. Records of South-eastern Africa. v.1- London, 1898- 9v.
Afr 8088.94.3 Theal, G.M. South Africa. N.Y., 1894.
Afr 8088.94.15 Theal, G.M. South Africa. 8th ed. London, 1917.
NEDL Afr 8678.13 Theal, G.M. The yellow and dark skinned people...Zambesi. London, 1910.
Afr 8678.13.3 Theal, G.M. The yellow and dark-skinned people of Africa south of the Zambesi. N.Y., 1969.
Afr 7218.96 Theal, George McCall. The Portuguese in South Africa. Cape Town, 1896.
Afr 7218.96.2 Theal, George McCall. The Portuguese in South Africa. N.Y., 1969.
Afr 630.58.10 Le théâtre négro-africain. (Traore, Bakary.) Paris, 1958.
Afr 3207.20 Thedenet-Duvent, P.P. L'Egypte sous Mehemed-Ali. Paris, 1822.
Afr 2875.19 Theilhaber, F.A. Beim roten Halbmond vor Tripolis. Cöln, 1912.
Afr 1259.63 Their heads are green. (Bowles, Paul.) London, 1963.
Afr 715.20 Then I saw the Congo. (Flaudrau, G.C.) N.Y., 1929.
Afr 3675.20 Theobald, A.B. The Mahdiya. London, 1951.
Afr 3822.5 Theobald, Alan B. Ali Dinar, last sultan of Darfor, 1895-1916. London, 1965.
Afr 4370.7 Theodore II, le nouvel empire d'Abyssinie et les intérêts français dans le sud de la Mer Rouge. (Lejean, G.) Paris, 1865.
Afr 4370.2 Theodoros II. Chronique. Paris, 1905.
Afr 8685.50.5 There are no South Africans. (Calpin, G.H.) London, 1944.
Afr 8089.44 There are South Africans. (Morkford, G.) London, 1944.
Afr 555.85 Therol, J. Sous l'armure de laine blanche. Paris, 1943.
Afr 8685.82 Theron, Erika. Die kleurlingbevolking van Suid-Afrika, Stellenbosch. Grahamstad, 1964.
Afr 9506.4 'These vessels' the story of Inyati, 1859-1959. (Clinton, Iris.) Bulawayo, 1959.
Afr 5849.2 They came to Mauritius. (Hollingworth, Derek.) London, 1965.
Afr 8687.42 They came to South Africa. (Jaff, Fay.) Cape Town, 1963.
Afr 555.132 They led the way. (Jenkins, David E.) Cape Town, 1966.
Afr 6541.17 They wait in darkness. (Shephard, G.W.) N.Y., 1955.
Afr 8089.56 They were South Africans. (Bond, J.) Cape Town, 1956.
Afr 699.31.3 They were still dancing. (Waugh, E.) N.Y., 1952.
Afr 210.63.23 Thiam, Doudou. The foreign policy of African states. London, 1965.
Afr 210.63.20 Thiam, Doudou. La politique étrangère des états africains. Paris, 1963.
Afr 7803.32 Thibaut, Emile. Les jésuites et les fermes-chapelles, à propos d'un débat récent. Bruxelles 1911.
Afr 7809.53 Thibaut, J. Sous l'ombre des volcans africains. Bruxelles, 1953.
Afr 1089.3 Thieling, W. Der Hellenismus in Kleinafrika. Leipzig, 1911.
Afr 7889.2 Thier, F.M. Singhitini, la Stanleyville musulmane. Bruxelles, 1961.
Afr 7850.15 Thier, Franz M. Le centre extra-coutumier de Coquilhatville. Bruxelles, 1956.
Afr 7873.5 Thier, Franz M. de. Le centre extra-coutumier de Coquilhatville. Bruxelles, 1956.
Afr 2208.62.4 Thierry-Mieg, C. Six semaines en Afrique. 2e ed. Paris, 1862.
Afr 3215.3.25 Thiers et Méhémet-Ali. (Charles-Roux, François.) Paris, 1951.
Afr 10671.12.120 Things fall apart. (Achebe, Chinua.) London, 1966.
Afr 10671.12.121 Things fall apart. (Achebe, Chinua.) London, 1968.
Afr 11211.5 Things fall apart. (Achebe, Chinua.) N.Y., 1959.
Afr 3979.10.20 Things seen in Egypt. (Butcher, E.L.) London, 1923.
Afr 3979.08.5 Things seen in Egypt. (Holland, Clive.) N.Y., 1908.
Afr 1609.29.5 Things seen in Morocco. (Bickerstaffe, Lovelyn Elaine.) N.Y., 1929.
Afr 1609.04.9 Things seen in Morocco. (Dawson, A.J.) London, 1904.
Afr 2288.10 Thinières, A.F.C. Le régime de la répression dans les territoires du sud de l'Algérie. Thèse. Alger, 1928.
Afr 555.21 Thinking black. 2d ed. (Crawford, D.) London, 1914.
Afr 10689.68.100 Thinking with you. (Solarin, Tai.) Ikeja, 1965.
Afr 8678.436 Thion, Serge. Le pouvoir pâle. Paris, 1969.
Afr 5749.61 Thiout, Michel. Madagascar et l'ame malgache. Paris, 1961.
Afr 4573.7 Third five year development plan, 1961-1965 E-C (1968/69-1972/73 G-c). v.1-4. (Ethiopia.) Addis Ababa, 1969.
Afr 10624.3.100 The third woman. (Danqush, Joseph B.) London, 1943.
Afr 8659.36.3 Thirstland treks. (Birkby, Carel.) London, 1936.
Afr 8659.54.5 The thirsty land. (Brown, John.) London, 1954.
Afr 555.6.8 Thirty years in Madagascar. 2d ed. (Matthews, T.T.) London, 1904.
Afr 550.138 Thirty years in the African wilds. (Verwimp, E.) London, 1938.
Afr 10062.2 This Africa, novels by West Africans in English and French. (Gleason, Judith Illsley.) Evanston, 1965.
Afr 11546.13.60 This Africa of ours. (McNeile, Michael.) Johannesburg, 1957.
Afr 9854.16 This Africa was mine. (Langworthy, Emily (Booth).) Stirling, Scotland, 1952.
Afr 710.35 This is Africa south of the Sahara. (Booth, Newall S.) N.Y., 1959.
Afr 7369.53 This is Liberia. (Davis, S.A.) N.Y., 1953.
Afr 8845.16 This is Port Elizabeth. (Port Elizabeth Publicity Association.) Port Elizabeth, 1963.
Afr 8659.47 This is South Africa. (Blackwell, L.) Pietermaritzburg, 1947.
Afr 8673.18 This is South Africa. (Elionson, Sima.) Cape Town, 1962.
Afr 8659.45 This is South Africa. (South Africa. Government Information Office.) N.Y., 1945.
Afr 8659.45.2 This is South Africa. (South Africa. Government Information Office.) N.Y., 1952.
Afr 8687.265.5 This man Malan. (Robins, Eric.) Cape Town, 1953.
Afr 8687.335.5 This much I'll tell. (Schonegevel, Bernardo.) Cape Town, 1959.
Afr 8378.379.10 This was a man. (Grobbelaar, Pieter Willem.) Cape Town, 1967.
Afr 8849.212 This was my world. (Gearing, Gladys.) Cape Town, 1966.
Afr 8180.28 Thom, H.B. Die geloftekerk. Kaapstad, 1949.
Afr 8252.267.2 Thom, Hendrik Bernardus. Die lewe van Gert maritz. 2.druk. Kaapstad, 1965.
Afr 8325.37F Thoma, Ludwig. Der Burenkrieg. München, 1900.
Afr 5897.5 Thomas, Athol. Forgotten Eden. London, 1968.
Afr 8283.14 Thomas, C.G. Johannesburg in arms, 1895-96. London, 1896.
Afr 8279.00.39 Thomas, C.H. Origin of the Anglo-Boer war revealed. London, 1900.
Afr 210.64.15 Thomas, C.M. African national developments. Maxwell, Ala., 1964.
Afr 678.60 Thomas, C.W. Adventures...on west coast of Africa. N.Y., 1860.
Afr 210.65.20 Thomas, Charles Marion. Pan-Africanism. Maxwell Air Force Base, Ala., 1965.
Afr 9028.94 Thomas, E. Neumann. How thankful should we be. Cape Town, 1894.
Afr 8678.106 Thomas, E.M. The harmless people. 1st ed. N.Y., 1959.
Afr 6540.23 Thomas, Elizabeth Marshall. Warrior herdsmen. 1st ed. N.Y., 1965.
Afr 6498.35 Thomas, H.B. Uganda. London, 1935.
Afr 3315.132.7 Thomas, Hugh. Suez. N.Y., 1967.
Afr 3315.132 Thomas, Hugh. The Suez affair. London, 1967.
Afr 5465.2 Thomas, Jacqueline M.C. Les Ngbaka de la Lobaye. Paris, 1963.
Afr 2609.30.10F Thomas, Jean. A travers le sud Tunisie. Paris, 1930.
Afr 1680.6 Thomas, L. Voyage au goundafa et au sous. Paris, 1918.
Afr 5185.8 Thomas, L.V. Les Diola. Macon, 1959. 2v.
Afr 545.56 Thomas, Louis Vincent. Les religions d'Afrique noire. Paris, 1969.
Afr 2719.60 Thomas, Marc-Robert. Sahara et communauté. Paris, 1960.
Afr 6280.12 Thomas, N.W. Anthropological report on...peoples of Nigeria. London, 1910. 2v.
Afr 6280.9 Thomas, N.W. Anthropological report on the Ibo speaking peoples. V.1-6. London, 1913-14.
Afr 8658.72 Thomas, T.M. Eleven years in central South Africa. London, 1872.
Afr 8686.5 Thomas Arbousset. (Clavier, Henri.) Paris, 1965.
Afr 8252.124 Thomas Baines of Kings Lynn. (Wallis, J.P.R.) London, 1941.
Afr 6198.405 Thomas Birch Freeman. (Birtwhistle, Allen.) London, 1950.
Afr 6198.405.5 Thomas Birch Freeman. (Walker, Frank Diaville.) London, 1929.
Afr 8230.30 Thomas François Burgers, a biography. (Engelbrecht, S.P.) Pretoria, 1946.
Afr 7903.3 Thomas J. Comber, missionary pioneer to the Congo. (Myers, John Brown.) London, 1888.
Afr 2209.11.5 Thomas-Stanford, C. About Algeria, Algiers. London, 1912.
Afr 555.24.6 Thomas Wakefield...in East Africa. 2d ed. (Wakefield, E.S.) London, 1904.
Afr 7350.3.18 Thomasson, W.P. To the citizens of Jefferson County. n.p., 1849.
Afr 1570.1 Thomassy, R. Le Maroc et ses caravanes. Paris, 1845.
Afr 9609.10 Thompson, C.H. Economic development in Rhodesia and Nyassaland. London, 1954.
Afr 609.54.5 Thompson, E.B. Africa, land of my fathers. Garden City, 1954.
Afr 8252.354.25 Thompson, F.R. Matabele Thompson. Johannesburg, 1953.
Afr 8252.354.20 Thompson, F.R. Matabele Thompson. London, 1936.
Afr 550.40 Thompson, G. Africa in a nutshell for the millions. Oberlin, 1886.
Afr 2928.94 Thompson, G.E. Life in Tripoli. Liverpool, 1894.
Afr 555.3 Thompson, George. The palm land. Cincinnati, 1859.
Afr 555.3.2 Thompson, George. The palm land. 2nd ed. London, 1969.
Afr 555.2 Thompson, George. Thompson in Africa. N.Y., 1854.
Afr 8658.27.4F Thompson, George. Travels and adventures in southern Africa. Cape Town, 1962.
Afr 8658.27 Thompson, George. Travels and adventures in southern Africa. London, 1827.
Afr 8658.27.3 Thompson, George. Travels and adventures in Southern Africa. 2d ed. London, 1827. 2v.
Afr 3978.54.2 Thompson, J.P. Photographic views of Egypt. Boston, 1854.
Afr 3978.54.5 Thompson, J.P. Photographic views of Egypt. Boston, 1856.
Afr 3978.54 Thompson, J.P. Photographic views of Egypt. Glasgow, n.d.
Afr 8340.30 Thompson, Leonard. The unification of South Africa. Oxford, 1960.
Afr 9047.25 Thompson, Leonard Monteath. Indian immigration into Natal. Pretoria, 1938.
Afr 8050.26 Thompson, Leonard Monteath. Politics in the Republic of South Africa. Boston, 1966.
Afr 125.15 Thompson, Lloyd Arthur. Africa in classical antiquity. Ibadan, Nigeria, 1969.
Afr 5404.10 Thompson, V.M. The emerging states of French Equatorial Africa. Stanford, Calif., 1960.
Afr 5056.157.5 Thompson, V.M. French West Africa. Stanford, Calif., 1957.
Afr 212.76 Thompson, Vincent Bakpetu. Africa and unity: the evolution of Pan-Africanism. N.Y., 1970.
Afr 4819.68 Thompson, Virginia M. Djibonti and the Horn of Africa. Stanford, Calif., 1968.
Afr 5749.65 Thompson, Virginia McLean. The Malagasy Republic. Stanford, 1965.
Afr 6178.15 Thompson, William Scott. Ghana's foreign policy, 1957-1966. Princeton, N.J., 1969.
Afr 555.2 Thompson in Africa. (Thompson, George.) N.Y., 1854.
Afr 8289.02.37 Thomson, Ada. Memorials of C.D. Kimber. London, 1902.
Afr 8250.2 Thomson, D.W. Cecil John Rhodes. Cape Town, 1947.
Afr 9438.98 Thomson, H.C. Rhodesia and its government. London, 1898.
Afr 6455.3.5 Thomson, J. Through Masai land. London, 1885.
Afr 6455.3 Thomson, J. Through Masai land. Photoreproduction. London, 1895.
Afr 725.4.3 Thomson, J. To the Central African lakes and back: the narrative of the Royal Geographical Society's East Central African Expedition, 1878-1880. 2nd ed. London, 1968. 2v.
NEDL Afr 725.4 Thomson, J. To the central African lakes and back. v.1-2. London, 1881. 2v.
Afr 725.4.2 Thomson, J. To the central African lakes and back. 2d ed. Boston, 1881. 2v.
Afr 1680.1 Thomson, J. Travels in the atlas and southern Morocco. London, 1889.
Afr 725.4.5 Thomson, James B. Joseph Thomson, African explorer. London, 1896.
Afr 6455.3.10 Thomson, Joseph. Au pays des Massai. Paris, 1886.
Afr 5235.55.15 Thomson, Joseph. Mungo Park and the Niger. London, 1890.
Afr 6455.3.21 Thomson, Joseph. Through Masai land. London, 1968.
Afr 6455.3.15 Thomson, Joseph. Through Masai land with Joseph Thomson. Evanston, Ill., 1962.

Afr 8678.53.2 Time longer than rope. 2. ed. (Roux, Edward.)
    Madison, 1964.
Afr 11465.14.140 Time of arrival, and other essays. (Jacobson, Dan.)
    London, 1962.
Afr 9446.47 A time to die. 2nd ed. (Cary, Robert.) Cape Town, 1969.
Afr 8678.94 A time to speak. (Scott, Michael.) London, 1958.
Afr 3300.45 Times, London. The Times book of Egypt... 26 Jan. 1937.
    London, 1937.
Afr 8289.00A Times, London. The Times history of the war in South
    Africa. London, 1900-6.
    7v.
Afr 3300.45 The Times book of Egypt... 26 Jan. 1937. (Times, London.)
    London, 1937.
Afr 8289.00A The Times history of the war in South Africa. (Times,
    London.) London, 1900-6.
    7v.
Afr 1550.38 Die Times in der ersten Marokkokrise. (Schoettle,
    Hermann.) Vaduz, 1965.
Afr 1550.41 Die Times in der ersten Marokkokrise mit besonderer
    Berücksichtigung der englisch-deutschen Beziehungen.
    (Schaettle, Hermann.) Berlin, 1930.
Afr 626.180 Timmler, Markus. Die Gemeinsame Afrikanisch-Madegassische
    Organisation. Köln, 1967.
Afr 6176.5 Timothy, B. Kwame Nkrumah. London, 1955.
Afr 9549.68 Tindall, P.E.N. A history of Central Africa.
    London, 1968.
Afr 8680.15 Tingsten, Herbert. The problem of South Africa.
    London, 1955.
Afr 8676.42.5 Tinley, J.M. The native labor problem of South Africa.
    Chapel Hill, 1942.
Afr 718.19 Tippoo Tib; story of his career in Central Africa. (Brode,
    H.) London, 1907.
Afr 2260.18 Tiquet, J.E.P. Une expérience de petite colonisation
    indigène en Algèrie. Thèse. Maison-Carrée, 1936.
Afr 7568.30 Tisdel, W.P. Kongo. Leipzig, 1886.
Afr 5842.20 Titmuss, R.M. Social policies and population growth in
    Mauritius. London, 1961.
Afr 6280.26.15 TIV economy. (Bohaman, Pave.) Evanston, 1968.
Afr 6280.26.5F Tiv farm and settlement. (Bohannan, Paul.) London, 1954.
Afr 6280.26 The Tiv people. (Abraham, R.C.) Lagos, 1933.
Afr 6160.35 Tixier, Gilbert. Le Ghana. Paris, 1965.
Afr 6390.16 Tjader, Richard. The big game of Africa. N.Y, 1910.
Afr 2623.957 Tlatli, S.E. Tunisie nouvelle. Tunis, 1957.
Afr 2373.5 Tlemcen, ancienne capitale du royaume. (Barges, J.J.L.)
    Paris, 1859.
Afr 2373.4 Tlemcen. (Marcais, Georges.) Paris, 1950.
Afr 2373.10.2 Tlemcen et ses environs. 2e ed. (Bel, Alfred.)
    Toulouse, 192-
Afr 6455.18 To Abyssinia through an unknown land. (Stigand, C.H.)
    London, 1910.
Afr 659.05 To Jerusalem through lands of Islam. (Loyson, H.)
    Chicago, 1905.
Afr 2608.85 To Kairwan the Holy. (Boddy, A.A.) London, 1885.
Afr 6196.12 To Kumassi with Scott. (Musgrave, George Clarke.)
    London, 1896.
Afr 6878.86 To Lake Tanganyika in a bath chair. (Hore, Annie B.)
    London, 1886.
Afr 4559.13.5 To Menelek in a motor car. (Halle, C.) London, 1913.
Afr 8305.5 To Modder River with Methuen. (Kinnear, A.)
    Bristol, 1900.
Afr 6455.145 To my wife, 50 camels. (Reece, Alys.) Leicester, 1963.
Afr 3275.45 To see with others' eyes. Cairo, 1907.
Afr 3978.60 To Sinai and Syene and back in 1860 and 1861. 2nd ed.
    (Beamont, William.) London, 1871.
Afr 9439.65.5 To the banks of the Zambezi. (Bulpin, Thomas Victor.)
    Johannesburg, 1965.
Afr 8235.11 To the Cape for diamonds. (Boyle, Frederick.)
    London, 1873.
Afr 725.4.3 To the Central African lakes and back: the narrative of the
    Royal Geographical Society's East Central African
    Expedition, 1878-1880. 2nd ed. (Thomson, J.)
    London, 1968.
    2v.
NEDL Afr 725.4 To the central African lakes and back. v.1-2. (Thomson,
    J.) London, 1881.
    2v.
Afr 725.4.2 To the central African lakes and back. 2d ed. (Thomson,
    J.) Boston, 1881.
    2v.
Afr 7350.3.18 To the citizens of Jefferson County. (Thomasson, W.P.)
    n.p., 1849.
Afr 6192.13 To the Gold Coast for gold. (Burton, R.F.) London, 1883.
    2v.
Afr 725.8 To the Mountains of the Moon. (Moore, J.E.S.)
    London, 1901.
Afr 4790.10.15 To the mysterious Lorian Swamp. (Haywood, C.W.)
    London, 1927.
Afr 6275.65 To the new Nigeria. (Harrison, Godfrey.) London, 1960.
Afr 6192.97 To the Peace Corps, with love. 1st ed. (Zeitlin, Arnold.)
    Garden City, 1965.
Afr 8659.40 To the river's end. (Green, Lawrence George.) Cape
    Town, 194-
Afr 8658.76 To the Victoria Falls of the Zambesi. (Mohr, Edward.)
    London, 1876.
Afr 9488.75 To the Victoria Falls via Matabeleland. (Stabb, Henry.)
    Cape Town, 1967.
Afr 555.83 To who I now send thee, mission work of the Christian
    Reformed Church in Nigeria. (Dekorne, J.C.) Grand Rapids,
    Mich., 1945.
Afr 10679.44.100 Toads for supper. (Ike, Vincent Chukwuemeka.)
    London, 1965.
Afr 2025.36 Le toast d'Alger, documents, 1890-1891. (Montclos, Xavier
    de.) Paris, 1966.
Afr 4390.30 Der Tod des Löwen von Juda. (Zintgraff, Alfred.)
    Berlin, 1932.
Afr 3979.05.10A Today on the Nile. (Dunning, H.W.) N.Y., 1905.
Afr 3979.13.12 Todd, J.A. The banks of the Nile. London, 1913.
Afr 555.140 Todd, John Murray. African mission. London, 1962.
Afr 9505.2 Todd, Judith. Rhodesia. London, 1966.
Afr 2990.1.2 Todd, M.L. Tripoli the mysterious. Boston, 1912.
Afr 2990.1 Todd, M.L. Tripoli the mysterious. London, 1912.
Afr 7459.10 Toepfer, R. Liberia. Berlin, 1910.
Afr 618.34 Töpferei in Afrika. Technologie. (Drost, Dietrich.)
    Berlin, 1967.
Afr 6689.5 Togo; champ de mission. (Faure, Jean.) Paris, 1943.
Afr 6664.10.5 Le Togo, nation-pilote. (Cornevin, Robert.) Paris, 1963.

Afr 6685.11 Togo, 1960. (Banque Centrale des Etats de l'Afrique de
    l'Ouest.) Paris, 1960.
Afr 6686.48.2 Togo. Five year development plan, 1966-1970. Paris, 1965.
Afr 6686.48.5F Togo. Plan de développement économique et social,
    1966-1970: annexes techniques, développement rural.
    Paris, 1965.
Afr 6686.48.10 Togo. Plan de développement économique et social,
    1966-1970. Annexes techniques: industrie. Paris, 1965.
Afr 6686.48 Togo. Plan quinquennal de développement, 1966-1970.
    Paris, 1965.
Afr 6670.25 Le Togo. (Maroix, J.E.P.) Paris, 1938.
Afr 6664.16 Togo. Bühl-boden, 1961.
Afr Doc 6709.305 Togo. Haut Commissariat au Plan. Comptes nationaux. Lomé.
    1963+
Afr Doc 6707.361 Togo. Service de la Statistique Général. Enquête
    démographique, 1961. Lomé, 1962?
Afr Doc 6781.735 Togo. Service de la Statistique Général. Etude
    démographique du pays Kabre, 1957. Paris, 1960.
Afr Doc 6707.358 Togo. Service de la Statistique Général. Recensement
    général de la population du Togo, 1958-1960. Lomé, 1962?
Afr Doc 6708.702 Togo. Service de la Statistique Générale. Annuaire
    retrospectif du commerce special du Togo, 1937-1964.
    Lomé, 1964.
Afr 6664.12 Togo: Tradition und Entwicklung. (Wuelker, Gabriele.)
    Stuttgart, 1966.
Afr 6685.12 Togo-Erinnerungen. (Kueas, Richard.) Berlin, 1939.
Afr 6670.957 Le Togo français. (Luchaire, Fr.) Paris, 1957.
Afr 6685.3 Togo unter den deutschen Flagge. (Klose, Heinrich.)
    Berlin, 1899.
Afr 6685.5 Togoland. (Calvert, Albert F.) London, 1918.
Afr Doc 6707.2 Togoland. Service de la Statistique Générale. Bulletin de
    statistique. Lomé 7,1964+
Afr Doc 6709.300 Togoland. Service de la Statistique Générale. Inventaire
    économique du Togo. Lomé. 1959+
Afr 6664.15 Togolezskaia respublika. (Tokareva, Z.I.) Moscow, 1962.
Afr 6664.15 Tokareva, Z.I. Togolezskaia respublika. Moscow, 1962.
Afr 628.269 Toledo. University. Library. The Black experience; the
    Negro in America, Africa, and the world. Toledo,
    Ohio, 1969.
Afr 5442.15 Tollet, Marcel. Initiation sociologique à l'Afrique
    centrale. Anvers, 1966.
Afr 6470.269 Tom Mboya. 1st ed. (Rake, Alan.) Garden City, N.Y., 1962.
Afr 3978.57.3 Tomard, E.F. Fragments. (Mainly Egypt). Paris, 1857.
Afr 1623.935 Tomas Perez, V. Marruecos. Barcelona, 1935.
Afr 1571.17.45 Le tombeau de Lyautey. (Borely, J.) Paris, 1937.
Afr 5247.10 Tombouctou la mystérieuse. (Dubois, Felix.) Paris, 1897.
Afr 8678.296 The Tomlinson report. (South Africa. Commission for the
    Social Economic Development.) Johannesburg, 1956.
Afr 8292.10 Tommy Comstalle. (Australian troops). (Abbott, J.H.M.)
    London, 1902.
Afr 3300.70 Tomorrow's Egypt. 1st English ed. (Kamil, M.)
    Cairo, 1953.
Afr 8678.343 Tomorrow's sun. (Joseph, Helen.) London, 1966.
Afr 8678.343.1 Tomorrow's sun. 1. ed. (Joseph, Helen.) London, 1968.
Afr 8835.20 Tonder, I.W. Van Riebeecksestad. 1. uitg. Kaapstad, 1950.
Afr 8095.82 Tonder, Johannes. Veertien gedenktekens van Suid-Afrika.
    Kaapstad, 1961.
Afr 9050.10 Tongaati. (Watson, R.G.T.) London, 1960.
Afr 3705.5 Too late for Gordon and Khartoum. (Macdonald, A.)
    London, 1887.
Afr 11675.87.100A Too late the phalarope. (Paton, Alan.) N.Y., 1953.
Afr 4180.4.5 Tooth of fire. (Jackson, H.C.) Oxford, 1912.
Afr 7459.46 Top hats and tom-toms. (Furbay, Elizabeth J.)
    London, 1946.
Afr 679.66.10 Topics in West African history. (Bochen, Albert Adu.)
    London, 1966.
Afr 3978.35 Topography of Thebes. (Wilkinson, J.G.) London, 1835.
Afr 550.85 Toppenberg, Valdemar E. Africa has my heart. Mountain
    View, 1958.
Afr 7580.32 Topuzoglu. Kongo kurtuluş, sowosi. 1. baski.
    Istanbul, 1965.
Afr 1347.23 Torey, General de. Les espagnols au Maroc en 1909. 2 éd.
    Paris, 1911.
Afr 1570.37.2 Torcy, L.V.V.F.J. de. L'Espagne et la France au
    Maroc...1911. 2e ed. Paris, 1911.
Afr 7809.13 Torday, Emil. Camp and tramp in African wilds.
    Philadelphia, 1913.
Afr 7815.14 Torday, Emil. On the trail of the Bushongo. London, 1925.
Afr 6785.5 Tordoff, William. Government and politics in Tanzania.
    Nairobi, 1967.
Afr 5312.18 Toré, Sékou. The doctrine and methods of the Democratic
    Party of Guinea. v.1-2. Conakry, 196-
Afr 4095.10F Torelli-Viollier, E. Ricerca delle sorgenti del Nilo.
    Milano, 1878.
Afr 6168.25 Torodoff, William. Ashanti under the Prempehs, 1888-1935.
    London, 1965.
Htn Afr 1401.5* Torres, D. de. Relacion del origen y sucesso de los
    karifes. Sevilla, 1586.
Htn Afr 1401.1* Torres, D. de. Relation de l'origine et succez des
    cherifs. Paris, 1636.
Afr 609.60.75 Torres, Joaquin. Viaje por Africa. Buenos Aires, 1960.
Afr 1608.59.5 Torrijos, Manuel. El imperio de Marruecos, su historia
    etc. Madrid, 1859.
Afr 2030.463.5 Torture, cancer of democracy. (Vidal-Naquet, P.)
    Harmondsworth, 1963.
Afr 2037.2 Les torturés d'El Harrach. (Comité pour la Défense de Ben
    Bella et des Autres Victimes de la Répression en Algérie.)
    Paris, 1966.
Afr 7815.23 Tot ou tard. (Kanza, Thomas.) Bruxelles, 1959.
Afr 8377.12 Total defence. 1st ed. (Orpen, Neil.) Cape Town, 1967.
Afr 5425.10 Le totémisme chez les Fan. (Trilles, H.) Münster, 1912.
Afr 2762.6 Les Touareg. (Aymard, C.) Paris, 1911.
Afr 2762.2 Les Touareg de l'ouest. (Bissuel, H.) Algiers, 1888.
Afr 2762.10 Les Touareg du Niger. (Richer, A.) Paris, 1924.
Afr 2762.5 Les Touareg du sud-est l'Air. Leur rôle dans la politique
    saharienne. (Jean, C.) Paris, 1909.
Afr 2748.91 Touat, Sahara et Soudan. (Sabatier, Camille.)
    Paris, 1891.
Afr 7540.17 Touchard, G. Jurisprudence de l'état indépendant du Congo.
    v.2. Bruxelles, 1911.
Afr 1990.27 Touchard-Lafosse, T. Histoire de la gendarmerie d'Afrique.
    Alger, 1860.
Afr 679.66.20 Toulat, Jean. Français d'aujourd'hui en Afrique noire.
    Paris, 1966.
Afr 555.135 Toumliline. (Desallues, Elisabeth.) Paris, 1961.
Afr 12639.18.110 Tounka, nouvelle. (Sadji, Abdoulaye.) Paris, 1965.
Afr 8659.02.6 Tour d'Afrique. (Orléans-Brangance, L.) Paris, 1902.

Afr 555.22.12	Tour in South Africa, with notices of Natal. (Freeman, Joseph J.) London, 1851.
Afr 608.19	The tour of Africa. (Hutton, C.) London, 1819-21. 3v.
Afr 1607.91.2	Tour to Tangier and Morocco. 2nd ed. (Lempriere, W.) London, 1793.
Afr 1607.91.3	Tour to Tangier and Morocco. 3rd ed. (Lempriere, W.) Newport, 1813.
Afr 5344.9	Les Toura. (Holas, Bohumil.) Paris, 1962.
Afr 5319.5	Toure, Ismael. Parti Déé de Guinée, R.D.A. Le développement économique de la république de Guinée. n.p., 1966.
Afr 5316.10	Touré, Sékou. L'action politique du parti démocratique de guinée. Paris, 1959.
Afr 5314.10	Touré, Sékou. Expérience guinéenne et unité africaine. Paris, 1959.
Afr 5314.10.2	Touré, Sékou. Expérience guinéenne et unité africaine. Paris, 1961.
Afr 5316.10.5	Toure, Sekou. Guinean revolution and social progress. Cairo, 1963.
Afr 4700.38.25	Touring Club italiano...Africa orientale italiana. Milano, 1938.
Afr 2929.67	Touring Libya. (Ward, Philip.) London, 1967.
Afr 2929.68	Touring Libya. (Ward, Philip.) London, 1968.
Afr 3979.63	Tourism in the U.A.R. (United Arab Republic. Information Department.) Cairo, 1963.
Afr 510.50F	Le tourisme en Afrique française. (Encyclopédie Mensuelle d'Outre-Mer.) Paris, 1955.
Afr 2798.5.15	Tourisme en zigzag vers le Hoggar. (Couvert, Léon.) Bourg, 1951.
Afr 3320.142	Tourisme in Egypt. (United Arab Republic. State Tourist Administration.) n.p., n.d.
Afr 7809.51	Tourist Bureau for the Belgian Congo and Ruanda-Urundi. Travelers guide to the Belgian Congo and Ruanda-Urundi. 1st ed. Brussels, 1951.
Afr 7809.51.2	Tourist Bureau for the Belgian Congo and Ruanda-Urundi. Travellers guide to the Belgian Congo and Ruanda-Urundi. 2d ed. Brussels, 1956.
Afr 6390.37	A tourist in Africa. (Waugh, Evelyn.) London, 1960.
Afr 3990.28	Tourist information, U.A.R. Egypt. (United Arab Republic. State Tourist Administration.) Cairo, 1963.
Afr 7580.10	Tournaire, H. Le livre noir du Congo. Paris, 1963.
Afr 1088.12	Tourneau, Roger. The Almohad movement in North Africa in the twelfth and thirteenth centuries. Princeton, N.J., 1969.
Afr 550.8.5	Tournier, M.J. Bibliographie du Cardinal Lavigerie. Paris, 1913.
Afr 1570.49	Touron, Max. Notre protectorat marocain. Thèse. Poitiers, 1923.
Afr 5813.12.5	Toussaint, Auguste. L'administration française de l'île Maurice et ses archives, 1721-1810. Fort Luis, 1965.
Afr 5846.3.5	Toussaint, Auguste. Une cite tropicale, Port-Louis de L'île Maurice. Paris, 1966.
Afr 5846.3	Toussaint, Auguste. Port-Louis, deux siècles d'histoire, 1735-1935. Port-Louis, 1936.
Afr 5813.12	Toussaint, Auguste. Répertoire des archives de l'Ile de France. Nerac, 1956.
Afr 5805.5	Toussaint, Auguste. La Route des îles, coutribution à l'histoire maritime des Mascareignes. Paris, 1967.
Afr 5813.5	Toussaint, Auguste. Select bibliography of Mauritius. Port Louis, 1951.
Afr 12371.1.100	La Toussaint des énigmes. (Aba, Noureddine.) Paris, 1963.
Afr 5260.5	Toutée, Georges Joseph. Dahomé, Niger, Touareg. Paris, 1897.
Afr 5260.10	Toutée, Georges Joseph. Du Dahomé au Sahara. Paris, 1899.
Afr 5183.958.5	Touze, R.L. Mieux vivre dans notre village; lettres a Seydon. Dakar?, 1958.
Afr 5183.961.10	Touze, R.L. Nouvelles lettres à Seydon. Dakar, 1961.
Afr 9499.27	Tow, Leonard. The manufacturing economy of Southern Rhodesia, problems and prospects. Washington, 1960.
Afr 8369.42.10A	Toward a better world. (Smuts, J.C.) N.Y., 1944.
Afr 210.64.22	Toward the African revolution. (Fanon, Frantz.) N.Y., 1967.
Afr 212.36	Towards a Pax Africana, a study of ideology and ambition. (Mazrui, Ali A'amin.) London, 1967.
Afr 9704.10	Towards church union in Zambia. Akademisch Proefschrift. (Bolink, Peter.) Franeker, 1967.
Afr 6176.30.35	Towards colonial freedom. (Nkrumah, Kwame.) London, 1962.
Afr 590.60	Towards emancipation, a study in South African slavery. (Edwards, I.E.) Cardiff, 1942.
Afr 9499.78	Towards financial independance in a developing economy. (Sowelem, R.A.) London, 1967.
Afr 3735.8	Towards Khartoum. (Atteridge, A.H.) ondon, 1897.
Afr 8295.6	Towards Pretoria. (Ralph, Julian.) N.Y., 1900.
Afr 11050.2	Towards the sun. (MacNab, R.M.) London, 1950.
Afr 8028.15	Towert, A.M.F. Constitutional development in South Africa. Cape Town, 1959.
Afr 650.6	Towns in Africa. (Oram, Nigel.) London, 1965.
Afr 6390.102	Townsend, Derek. Wild Africa's silent call. London, 1969.
Afr 5765.13	Townsend, William J. Madagascar, its missionaries and martyrs. 2d ed. London, 1892.
Afr 2749.64	Toy, Barbara. The way of the chariots. London, 1964.
Afr 659.65	Toynbee, Arnold Joseph. Between Niger and Nile. London, 1965.
Afr 6225.35	Toyo, Eskar. The working class and the Nigerian crisis. Ibadan, 1967.
Afr 555.9.19	Tozer, William G. Letters of Bishop Tozer and his sister. London, 1902.
Afr 4742.10	Tra Gasc e Setit. (Corni, Guido.) Roma, 1930.
Afr 2880.15	Tra i colonizzatori in Tripolitania. (Bignami, Paolo.) Bologna, 1930.
Afr 2875.65	Trablus-garbde bir avuc. (Kutay, Cemal.) Istanbul, 1963.
Afr 4050.20	Trackers and smugglers in the deserts of Egypt. (Dumreicher, A. von.) London, 1931.
Afr 1406.13	Tractaat susschen Marocco en de Nederlanden. 's-Gravenhage, 1777.
Afr 4230.4.4	Tractatus tres historico-geographico. (Barradas, M.) Porto, 1906.
Afr 7355.2	Pamphlet vol. Tracts on colonization and slavery. 17 pam.
Afr 855.11	Tracts relative to the island of St. Helena. (Beatson, A.) London, 1816.
Afr 6095.15.5	Tracy, J. Colonization and missions, historical examination of the state of society in western Africa. 5th ed. Boston, 1846.

Afr 590.73	Trade and conflict in Angola, the Mbundu and their neighbours under the influence of the Portuguese, 1483-1790. (Birmingham, David.) Oxford, 1966.
Afr 6218.10A	Trade and politics in the Niger Delta. (Dike, K.O.) Oxford, 1956.
Afr 6218.10.1	Trade and politics in the Niger Delta. (Dike, K.O.) Oxford, 1966.
Afr 9710.13	Trade and travel in early Barotseland. (Westbeach, George.) London, 1963.
Afr 678.51	Trade and travels in the Gulph of Guinea. (Smith, J.) London, 1851.
Afr 679.63.10	Trade castles and forts of West Africa. (Lawrence, A.W.) London, 1963.
Afr 4205.25	Trade directory and guide book to Ethiopia. (Ethiopia. Chamber of Commerce.) Addis Abada, 1967.
Afr Doc 4308.715F	Trade of the Union of South Africa, Southern and Northern Rhodesia, British South Africa and the territory of Southwest Africa. (South Africa. Department of Customs and Excise.) Cape Town. 1909+ 21v.
Afr Doc 1808.700	Trade report. (Ghana. Central Bureau of Statistics.) Accra. 1952+
Afr Doc 2308.705	Trade report. (Nigeria. Federal Office of Statistics.) Lagos. 1958+
Afr Doc 2708.700	Trade report. (Seychelles.) Victoria. 1963+
Afr Doc 1708.710	Trade report. (Sierra Leone.) Freetown. 1960+
Afr Doc 3208.705	Trade report of Kenya and Uganda. (Kenya. Customs Department.) 1928-1948
Afr Doc 2308.710	Trade statistical abstract. (Nigeria. Customs Department.) Lagos. 1-7,1911-1915
Afr 11456.77.812	Trader Horn. (Horn, Alfred A.) N.Y., 1927.
Afr 11456.77.810A	Trader Horn. (Horn, Alfred A.) N.Y., 1927.
Afr 11456.77.800	Trader Horn. (Horn, Alfred A.) N.Y., 1928.
Afr 11456.77.805	Trader Horn. v.2. "Harold the Webbed." (Horn, Alfred A.) N.Y., 1928.
Afr 8687.245.10	Trader on the veld. (Jackson, Albert.) Cape Town, 1958.
Afr 678.77	Trading life in Western and Central Africa. (Whitford, J.F.R.G.S.) Liverpool, 1877.
Afr 678.77.2	Trading life in Western and Central Africa. 2nd ed. (Whitford, J.F.R.G.S.) London, 1967.
Afr 6218.18	The trading states of the oil rivers. (Jones, G.I.) London, 1963.
Afr 5390.4	Tradition, changement, histoire, les "Somba" du Dahomey septentrional. (Mercier, Paul.) Paris, 1968.
Afr 609.66.40	Tradition and change in African tribal life. (Turnbull, Colin.) Cleveland, 1966.
Afr 6395.30	Tradition and transition in East Africa. (Gulliver, Phillip Hugh.) Berkeley, 1969.
Afr 618.31	Tradition et modernisme en Afrique noire. (Rencontres Internationales, Bouake, Ivory Coast, January 1962.) Rabat, 1962.
Afr 618.32	Tradition et modernisme en Afrique noire. (Rencontres Internationales, Bouake, Ivory Coast, January 1962.) Paris, 1965.
Afr 7815.42	La tradition historique des Bapende orientaux. (Haveaux, O.L.) Bruxelles, 1954.
Afr 44610.5	Traditional Swahili poetry. (Knappert, Jan.) Leiden, 1967.
Afr 4559.14	Traditions de Tsazzega et Hazzega. Annales. (Kolmodin, J.) Uppsala, 1914.
Afr 5425.18	Traditions orales et archives au Gabon. (Deschamps, H.) Paris, 1962.
Afr 635.94	Tradycyjne zajecia gospodarcze ludow Afryki. (Szyfelbejn-Sokolewicz, Zofia.) Warszawa, 1963.
Afr 724.15	Traeskfolket. (Rosen, Eric von Greve.) Stockholm, 1916.
Afr 590.65	Le trafic negrier. (Rinchon, D.) Bruxelles, 1938.
Afr 8678.167	La tragedia del apartheid. (Phillips, Norman.) Mexico, 1961.
Afr 2030.25A	La tragédie algérienne. (Aron, Raymond.) Paris, 1957.
Afr 1487.15	La tragédie du Maroc interdit. (Larteguy, Jean.) Paris, 1957.
Afr 2533.4	Tragédie française en Afrique du nord. (Aymard, C.E.) Paris, 1958.
Afr 7575.50	Tragediia Kongo. (Khokhlov, N.P.) Moscow, 1961. 2 pam.
Afr 2030.461.30	Tragedy in Algeria. (Mansell, G.) London, 1961.
Afr 8678.165	The tragedy of apartheid. (Phillips, Norman.) N.Y., 1960.
Afr 1573.32	La tragica realidad: Marruecos, 1921. (Maturana Vargas, C.) Barcelona, 1921
Afr 2929.26	Traglia, Gustavo. Il Duce libico. Bari, 1926.
Afr 2929.11.9	Tragni. Tripolitania e Cirenaica. Bologna, 1911.
Afr 9748.193	Trail of the copper king. (Bulpin, Thomas Victor.) Cape Town, 1959.
Afr 3275.9	Traill, H.D. England, Egypt and the Sudan. Westminster, 1900.
Afr 3275.12	Traill, H.D. LordCromer. London, 1897.
Afr 5520.1	Trait d'union. Tananarive.
Afr 1338.10	Traité d'économie et de législation marocaines. v.1-2. (Goulven, Jos.) Paris, 1921. 2v.
Afr 5057.24	Traité d'économie tropicale. (Capet, Marcel F.) Paris, 1958.
Afr 5183.951	La traite des Arachides dans le pays de Kaolack. (Fouquet, Joseph.) Montpelier, 1951.
Afr 5183.958	La traite des Arachides dans le pays de Kaolack. (Fouquet, Joseph.) St. Louis du Sénégal, 1958.
Afr 1965.20	Le traité Desmichels. (Cockenpot, C.) Paris, 1924.
Afr 1340.20	Traité du contentieux administratif au Maroc. Thèse. (Michel, Andre.) Paris, 1932.
Afr 1570.2	Les traités. La France et le Maroc. (Rouard de Card, E.) Paris, 1898.
Afr 1333.1	Les traités de commerce conclus par le Maroc. (Decard, R.) Paris, 1907.
Afr 510.11.2	Traités de délimitation concernant l'Afrique franç,aise. Supplément 1910-13. (Rouard de Card, E.) Paris, 1913.
Afr 510.11	Traités de délimitation concernant l'Afrique française. (Rouard de Card, E.) Paris, 1910.
Afr 510.11.10	Traités de la France avec les pays de l'Afrique du Nord. (Rouard de Card, E.) Paris, 1906.
Afr 1033.3F	Traités de paix et de commerce et documents diverses...de l'Afrique septentrionale au Moyen Age. (Mas Latrie, M.L. de.) Paris, 1865.
Afr 510.2	Les traités de protectorat. (Rouard de Card, E.) Paris, 1897.
Afr 1570.40	Traités et accords concernant le protectorat de la France au Maroc. (Rouard de Card, E.) Paris, 1914.

Afr 3675.66 Trimingham, J.S. Islam in the Sudan. London, 1949.
Afr 575.35 Trimingham, J.S. Islam in West Africa. Oxford, 1959.
Afr 575.35.2 Trimingham, J.S. Islam in West Africa. 2nd ed. Oxford, 1961.
Afr 575.60 Trimingham, John S. The influence of Islam upon Africa. Beirut, 1968.
Afr 3818.7 Trimingham, John Spencer. The Christian approach to Islam in the Sudan. London, 1948.
Afr 14740.76.100 Trindade, Francisco Alberto Cartaxo e. Chinanga, poemas. Lisboa, 1969.
Afr 2030.462.135 Trinquier, R. Le coup d'état du 13 mai. Paris, 1962.
Afr 7580.12F Trinquier, R. Notre guerre au Katanga. Paris, 1963.
Afr 8019.4.5 Triomf, jaarboek van die Suid-afrikaanse Buro vir Raase-aangeleenthede. Pretoria. 1,1966+
Afr 8369.53.5 Die triomf van nasionalisme in Suid-Afrika, 1910-1953. (Goosen, D.P.) Johannesburg, 1953.
Afr 2208.66.8 A trip to Barbary. (Sala, George A.) London, 1866.
Afr 2748.84 Trip to the great Sahara. London, 1884.
Afr 2929.12.5 Tripoli, Cirene e Cartagine. 2 ed. (Martino, G. de.) Bologna, 1912.
Afr 2990.2 Tripoli. (Bause, E.) Weimar, 1912.
Afr 2870.6 Tripoli and young Italy. (Lapworth, Charles.) London, 1912.
Afr 2819.25 Tripoli dal 1510 al 1850. (Bergna, C.) Tripoli, 1925.
Afr 2870.9 Tripoli e i diritti della civiltà. (Mantegazza, V.) Milano, 1912.
Afr 2875.56 Tripoli e i problemi della democrazia. (Fovel, Natale M.) Firenze, 1914.
Afr 2880.5 Tripoli e la guerra. (Scaglione, Emilio.) Napoli, 1918.
Afr 2819.12 Tripoli nella storia marinara d'Italia. (Manfroni, C.) Padova, 1912.
Afr 2990.1.2 Tripoli the mysterious. (Todd, M.L.) Boston, 1912.
Afr 2990.1 Tripoli the mysterious. (Todd, M.L.) London, 1912.
Afr 2875.41 Die Tripolis-Krise, 1911-12, und die erneuerung des Dreibundes 1912. (Dietrich, Richard.) Würzburg, 193-
Afr 2928.87 La Tripolitaine. (Fournel, M.) Paris, 1887.
Afr 2929.12.9 La Tripolitaine. (Mehier De Mathuisieulx, H.) Paris, 1912.
Afr 2984.1 La Tripolitaine interdite: Ghadames. (Pervinquière, L.) Paris, 1912.
Afr 2929.37.5 La Tripolitaine vue par un Français. (Pottier, R.) Paris, 1937.
Afr 2870.01 Pamphlet box. Tripolitan affairs, 1911-
Afr 2975.5F Tripolitania. L'occupazione di Cufra. Tripoli, 1931.
Afr 2929.43 Tripolitania. (Casairey, G.) London, 1943.
Afr 2929.02 La Tripolitania. (Minutilli, F.) Torino, 1902.
Afr 2929.11.7 Tripolitania. (Tumiati, D.) Milano, 1911.
Afr 2938.15 La Tripolitania: il presente e l'avvenire. (Persellini, Mario.) Milano, 1924.
Afr 2938.30 Tripolitania. Ufficio Studi e Propaganda. Vigor di vita in Tripolitania (anno 1928). Tripoli, 1928.
Afr 2929.02.2 La Tripolitania. 2 ed. (Minutilli, F.) Torino, 1912.
Afr 2929.12.11 Tripolitania. 2 ed. (Nazari, V.) Roma, 1912.
Afr 2929.29 Tripolitania d'oggi. (Mandosio, Mario.) Milano, 1929.
Afr 2929.12.7 Tripolitania e Cirenaica. (Ghisleri, A.) Milano, 1912.
Afr 2929.11.9 Tripolitania e Cirenaica. (Tragni, B.) Bologna, 1911.
Afr 2850.1 La Tripolitania e l'Italia. (Riccheri, G.) Milan, 1902.
Afr 2870.16 Tripolitania scuola di energia. (Piccioli, A.) Roma, 1932.
Afr 2938.20.2 La Tripolitania settentrionale e la sua vita sociale, studiata al vero. 2a ed. (Coletti, Francesco.) Bologna, 1923.
Afr 2840.5 La Tripolitania sotto il dominio dei Caramànli. (Micacchi, Rodolfo.) Intra, 1936.
Afr 2929.11.12 Tripolitanien: Grundzüge zu einer Landeskunde. (Vatter, E.) Strassburg, 1912.
Afr 861.20 Tristan da Cunha, 1506-1902. (Brander, J.) London, 1940.
Afr 861.15.5 Tristan da Cunha. (Christophersen, E.) London, 1940.
Afr 861.30 Tristan da Cunha. (Gane, Douglas M.) London, 1932.
Afr 2748.60 Tristram, H.B. The great Sahara. London, 1860.
Afr 630.41 Tritonj, Romolo. Politica indigena africana. Milano, 1941.
Afr 715.9 Trivier, E. Mon voyage au continent noir, "La Gironde" en Afrique. Paris, 1891.
Afr 5235.194.5 Triviet, E. Au Soudan français. Paris, 1932.
Afr 1750.44 Triviño Valdivia, Francisco. Cinco años en Marruecos. Madrid, 1903.
Afr 1750.12 Trivino Valdura, F. Del Marruecos español. Melilla, 1920.
Afr 505.10 Trofimov, V.A. Politika Anglii i Italii v severo-vostochnoi Afrike. Moscow, 1962.
Afr 555.22.3 Trois ans dans l'Afrique australe. (Depelchin, H.) Bruxelles, 1883.
Afr 5240.3 Trois expériences africaines de développement. (Amin, Samir.) Paris, 1965.
Afr 2731.19 Trois grands Africains. (Dervil, Guy.) Paris, 1945.
Afr 8658.79.5 Trois mois chez les Zoulous et les derniers jours du prince impérial. (Deleage, Paul.) Paris, 1879.
Afr 1609.04.5 Trois mois de campagne au Maroc. (Weisgerber, F.) Paris, 1904.
Afr 5385.21 Trois mois de captivité au Dahomey. (Chaudoin, E.) Paris, 1891.
Afr 1658.23 Trois mois de colonne sur le front riffain, juin a sept. 1925. (Thyen, Maurice.) Paris, 1926.
Afr 5748.63 Trois mois de sejour à Madagascar. (Dupre, Jules.) Paris, 1863.
Afr 5180.3 Trois voyages dans l'Afrique. (Marche, A.) Paris, 1879.
Afr 5343.7 Troisieme plan quadriennal de développement économique et social. (Ivory Coast. Ministère du Plan.) Abidjan, 1958.
Afr 6741.6 Trommeln, Mächte und ein Ruf. (Häberle, Wilhelm.) Stuttgart, 1966.
Afr 6395.12 Die Trommeln verstummen. (Grubbe, Peter.) Wiesbaden, 1957.
Afr 8220.5 Tromp, Theo M. Herinneringen uit Zuid Africa. Leiden, 1879.
Afr 8325.34 A trooper's sketch book of Boer War. (Watson, J. Hannan.) Glasgow, 19-
Afr 210.61.95 Pamphlet vol. Tropical Africa. 2 pam.
Afr 715.5 Tropical Africa. (Drummond, Henry.) N.Y., 1888.
Afr 710.50 Tropical Africa. (Kimble, George.) N.Y., 1960. 2v.
Afr 715.11 Tropical Africa. 3rd ed. (Drummond, Henry.) London, 1889.
Afr 609.66.20 Tropical Africa today. (Kimble, George Herbert Tinley.) Saint Louis, 1966.
Afr 6214.1.5 A tropical dependency. (Lugard, Flora Louisa.) N.Y., 1965.
Afr 6214.1 A tropical dependency. (Shaw, F.A.) London, 1906.

Afr 679.34 Tropici Senegal all Angola. (Rossi, V.G.) Milano, 1934.
Afr 8105.15 Trotter, Alys F. (Keatinge). Old Cape colony. Westminster, 1903.
Afr 6143.19 Trotter, James Keith. The Niger sources and the borders of the new Sierra Leone protectorate. London, 1898.
Afr 1608.81 Trotter, P.D. Our mission to Morocco. Edinburg, 1881.
Afr 11848.87.100 Trotter, W.M. Radiance of the veld. Ilfracombe, 1960.
Afr 1442.1 Pamphlet box. Troubles with Spain (about 1894).
Afr 5787.6 Trouchaud, J.P. La basse plaine du Mangoky. Paris, 1965.
Afr 5872.5 Trouette, E. L'Ile Bourbon de 1789 à 1803. Paris, 1888.
Afr 6985.4 Troup, Freda. In face of fear. London, 1950.
Afr 718.13 Troup, J.R. With Stanley's rear column. London, 1890.
Afr 7850.62 Les troupes du Katange et les campagnes d'Afrique 1914-1918. v.1-2. (Muller, Emmanuel.) Bruxelles, 1937.
Afr 1555.12 Trout, Frank Emanuel. Morocco's Saharan frontiers. Geneva, 1969.
Afr 7500.24 Truby, David William. Congo saga. London, 1965.
Afr 7575.85 Trudnye dni Kongo. (Volodin, L.D.) Moscow, 1961.
Htn Afr 1401.7* True historicall discourse of Muley-Hamets rising. London, 1609.
Afr 8288.99.15F True history of the war, official despatches. v.1-5. (Great Britain. War Department.) London, 1900.
Htn Afr 1407.2* True iournall of the Sally Fleet. (Dunton, J.) London, 1637.
Afr 5993.10 A true narrative of the sufferings of David Williamson. (Williamson, David.) London, 1771.
Afr 5625.2 True story of the French dispute in Madagascar. (Oliver, S. Pasfield.) London, 1885.
Afr 8659.60.15 The true story of the Grosvenor. (Kirby, Percival Robson.) N.Y., 1960.
Afr 6390.79 Truepeney, Charlotte. Our African farm. London, 1965.
Afr 8678.47 'N truiste vir die nageslag. (Cronje, G.) Johannesburg, 1945.
Afr 5425.20 Trujeda Incerna, Luis. Los pámues de nuestra Guin. Madrid, 1946.
Afr 10584.14.100 The truly married woman. (Nicol, Davidson.) London, 1965.
Afr 2396.1 Trumelet, C. L'Algérie légendaire. Alger, 1892.
Afr 2313.1 Trumelet, C. Blida. v.1-2. Alger, 1887.
Afr 2315.1 Trumelet, C. Bou-Farik. 2e ed. Alger, 1887.
Afr 2285.2 Trumelet, C. Les français dans le désert. Paris, 1865.
Afr 1955.7 Trumelet, C. Le général Yusuf. Paris, 1890. 2v.
Afr 2005.3 Trumelet, C. Histoire de l'insurrection dans le sud de la province d'Alger, 1864-69. Alger, 1879-84.
Afr 8687.320 Trust betrayed, the murder of Sister Mary Aidan. (Mcfall, J.L.) Cape Town, 1963.
Afr 7377.25 The trustees of donations for education in Liberia. (Allen, Gardner M.) Boston, 1923.
Afr 7812.261.5 Les trusts au Congo. (Joye, Pierre.) Bruxelles, 1961.
Afr 7568.9 Truth about civilisation in Congoland. Brussels, 1903.
Afr 3275.22 Truth about Egypt. (Alexander, J.) London, 1911.
Afr 5842.26 The truth about Mauritius. 1. ed. (Bissoondoyal, Basdeo.) Bombay, 1968.
Afr 1470.3 The truth about Morocco. (Aflalo, M.) London, 1904.
Afr 1494.12 The truth about Morocco. (Parent, P.) N.Y., 1953.
Afr 1571.48 The truth about Morocco. (Parent, Pierre.) N.Y., 1952.
Afr 7568.33 The truth about the Congo. (Starr, F.) Chicago, 1907.
Afr 8283.15A The truth about the Jameson raid. (Hammond, J.H.) Boston, 1918.
Afr 8235.10 The truth about the Portuguese in Africa. (Weale, J.P.M.) London, 1891.
Afr 8279.01.15 The truth about the Transvaal war and the truth about war. 2d. ed. (Johnson, J.) London, 1901.
Afr 8283.7 The truth from Johannesburg. (Mann, A.M.) London, 1897.
Afr 9149.61 Tshakhuma. (Helbling, Margrit.) Zürich, 1961.
Afr 9389.57 Tshekedi Khama. Bechuanaland. Johannesburg, 1957.
Afr 9424.360 Tshekedi Khama. (Benson, Mary.) London, 1960.
Afr 9424.360.5 Tshekedi Khama of Bechuanaland. (Gabatshwane, S.M.) Cape Town, 1961.
Afr 6194.3 The Tshi-speaking peoples of the Gold Coast. (Ellis, A.B.) London, 1887.
Afr 7920.3.15 Tshombe, Moise. My fifteen months in government. Plano, Tex., 1967.
Afr 7920.3.5 Tshombe, Moise. Quinze mois de gouvernement du Congo. Paris, 1966.
Afr 5753.9 Le Tsiny et le Tody dans la pensée malgache. (Andoiamanjato, Richard.) Paris, 1957.
Afr 9750.3 Tsopano, Nyasaland monthly. Salisbury, Southern Rhodesia. 1,1959+
Afr 8825.3 Tsuni-Goam, the supreme being. (Hahn, T.) London, 1881.
Afr 5003.2 Tuaillon, J.L. Bibliographie critique de l'Afrique occidentale française. Paris, 1936.
Afr 5003.2.3 Tuaillon, J.L. Bibliographie critique de l'Afrique occidentale française. Thèse. Paris, 1936.
Afr 5054.36.5 Tuaillon, J.L.G. L'Afrique occidentale française par l'Atlantique ou par le Sahara. Paris, 1936.
Afr 5054.36.3 Tuaillon, J.L.G. L'Afrique occidentale française par l'Atlantique ou par le Sahara. Thèse. Paris, 1936.
Afr 7377.59 Tubman, William. President Tubman of Liberia speaks. London, 1959.
Afr 7385.5 Tubman, William. President William V.S. Tubman on African unity. Monrovia, 1964.
Afr 6535.8 Tucker, A.R. Eighteen years in Uganda and East Africa. London, 1908. 2v.
Afr 7835.2 Tucker, Angeline. He is in heaven. 1st ed. N.Y., 1965.
NEDL Afr 6275.18 Tucker, Charlotte Maria. Abbeokuta, or Sunrise within the tropics. London, 1853.
Afr 6275.18.2 Tucker, Charlotte Maria. Abbeokuta, or Sunrise within the tropics. N.Y., 1853.
Afr 6275.18.5 Tucker, Charlotte Maria. Abbeokuta, or Sunrise within the tropics. N.Y., 1859.
Afr 6275.18.3 Tucker, Charlotte Maria. Abbeokuta, or Sunrise within the tropics. 5th ed. London, 1856.
Afr 555.40.5 Tucker, J.T. Angola, the land of the blacksmith prince. London, 1933.
Afr 10105.67 Tucker, Martin. Africa in modern literature. N.Y., 1967.
Afr 555.30 Tucker of Uganda. (Shepherd, A.) London, 1929.
Afr 7808.18.3 Tuckey, J.K. Narrative of an expedition to explore the River Zaire. London, 1818.
Afr 7808.18.2 Tuckey, J.K. Narrative of an expedition to explore the River Zaire. N.Y., 1818.
Afr 2208.56.5F Le tueur de lions. (Gerard, Jules.) Paris, 1892.
Afr 6291.32 Tuez-les tous. (Buhler, Jean.) Paris, 1968.
Afr 8657.10 Tugela basin, a regional survey. (Natal. Town and Regional Planning Commission.) Pietermaritzburg, 1953.

Afr 2928.18.5 — Tully, R. Letters written during a ten years' residence at the court of Tripoli. London, 1957.

Afr 2928.18.8 — Tully, R. Letters written during a ten years' residence at the court of Tripoli. 3rd ed. London, 1819. 2v.

Htn Afr 2928.18* — Tully, R. Narrative of a ten years'Residence in Tripoli. London, 1816.

Afr 2928.18.2 — Tully, R. Narrative of a ten years' residence in Tripoli. 2d ed. London, 1817.

Afr 3128.15 — Les Tuluenides, étude de l'Egypte musulmane à fin du IXe siècle 868-905. Thèse. (Hassan, Z.M.) Paris, 1933.

Afr 7580.38 — Tumbled house: the Congo at independence. (Scott, Ian.) London, 1969.

Afr 2530.15 — Tumedei, C. La questione tunisina e l'Italia. Bologna, 1922.

Afr 2929.11.7 — Tumiati, D. Tripolitania. Milano, 1911.

Afr 2609.63 — Tunesie. (Schuman, L.O.) Meppel, 1963.

Afr 2688.5F — Tunis, naguère et aujourd'hui. (Turki, Zubayr.) Tunis, 1967.

NEDL Afr 2527.1 — Tunis, past and present. (Broadley, A.M.) Edinburgh, 1882. 2v.

Afr 2438.5 — Tunis. Conférences sur les administrations tunisiennes, 1902. 2.ed. Sousse, 1902.

Afr 2609.03 — Tunis. Notice sur la Tunisie. Tunis, 1903.

Afr 2623.15 — Tunis. Welt-Ausstellung 1873 in Wien. Wien, 1873.

Afr 2428 — Pamphlet box. Tunis.

Afr 2608.80 — Tunis. (Desgodins de Souhesmes, G.) Paris, 1880.

Afr 2608.82 — Tunis. (Hesse-Wartegg, E.) N.Y., 1882.

Afr 2608.83 — Tunis. (Michel, L.) Paris, 1883.

Afr 2609.06.3 — Tunis. Comité. D'Hivernage. La Tunisie. Tunis, 1906.

Afr 2623.01 — Pamphlet box. Tunis. Economic resources.

Afr 109.61.45 — Tunis. Secretariat d'Etat à l'Information. New Africa. Tunis, 1961.

Afr 2420.30 — Tunis (City). Université. Centre d'Etudes et de Recherches Economiques et Sociales. Cahiers du C.E.R.E.S. Série linguistique. Tunis. 1,1968+

Afr 2420.28 — Tunis (City). Université. Centre d'Etudes et de Recherches Economiques et Sociales. Cahiers du C.E.R.E.S. Série géographique. Tunis. 1,1968+

Afr 2420.26 — Tunis (City). Université. Centré d'Etudes et de Recherches Economiques et Sociales. Cahiers du C.E.R.E.S. Série démographique. Tunis. 1,1967+

Afr 2420.27 — Tunis (City). Université. Centre d'Etudes et de Recherches Economiques et Sociales. Cahiers du C.E.R.E.S. Série sociologique. Tunis. 1,1968+

Afr 2420.25 — Tunis (City). Université. Centre d'Etudes et de Recherches Economiques et Sociales. Cahiers du C.E.R.E.S. Série économique. Tunis. 1966+

Afr 2420.5 — Tunis (City). Université. Faculté des Lettres et des Sciences Humaines. Publications. Histoire. 1,1961+ 6v.

Afr 2420.10 — Tunis (City). Université. Faculté des Lettres et des Sciences Humaines. Publications. Sources de l'histoire de la Tunisie. 3+ 2v.

Afr 2000.01 — Pamphlet box. Tunis and Algiers.

Afr 2688.2 — Tunis et Kairouan. (Saladin, H.) Paris, 1908.

Afr 2425.1F — Tunis et ses environs. (Lallemand, C.) Paris, 1890.

Afr 2609.12 — Tunis la blanche. (Harry, M.) Paris, n.d.

Afr 2608.88 — Tunis und seine Umgebung. (Kleist, H.) Leipzig, 1888.

Afr 2609.11 — Tunisi, e Tripoli. (Castellini, G.) Torino, 1911.

Afr 3822.8 — Al-Tunisi, Muhammad Ibn Umar. Voyage au Darfour. Paris, 1845.

Afr 2505.5A — Tunisi. (Chiala, L.) Torino, 1895.

Afr 2510.10 — Tunisi e i consoli Sardi, 1816-1834. (Gallico, A.) Bologna, 1935.

Afr 1878.5 — Tunisi i berberi e l'Italia nei secoli. (Gallico, Augusto.) Ancona, 1928.

Afr 2530.21 — Tunisi oggi. (Occhipinti, D.) Roma, 1939.

Afr 2609.62.5 — Tunisia, yesterday and today. Tunis, 1962.

Afr 2609.45 — Tunisia. (Great Britain. Naval Intelligence Division.) London, 1945.

Afr 2609.30.5 — La Tunisia. (Mori, Attilio.) Roma, 1930.

Afr 2525.21 — Tunisia. (Nicaud, C.A.) N.Y., 1964.

Afr 2459.69 — Tunisia. (Sylvester, Anthony.) London, 1969.

Afr 2608.99 — Tunisia. (Vivian, H.) N.Y., 1899.

Afr 2609.65.5 — Tunisia. (Zeraffa, Michel.) N.Y., 1965.

Afr 2438.35 — Tunisia. Constitution. Constitution of the Tunisian Republic. Tunis, 1959.

Afr 2625.7F — Tunisia. Secrétaire Général du Gouvernement. Nomenclature et répartition des tribus de Tunisie. Chelons-Saône, 1900.

Afr 2623.962.5F — Tunisia. Secretariat. Tunisian development. Tunis, 1962.

Afr 2442.2 — Tunisia. Secrétariat d'Etat à l'Information. Les congrès du Néo-Destour. Tunis, 1959.

Afr 2430.5F — Tunisia. Secrétariat d'Etat à l'Information. La documentation tunisienne. 1957+

Afr 2420.15 — Tunisia. Secrétariat d'Etat à l'Information. Etudes et documents. Tunis. 1,1959+

Afr 2650.5 — Tunisia. Secrétariat d'Etat à l'Information. Land development in the Medjerda valley. n.p., 1959.

Afr 2530.3 — Tunisia. Secrétariat d'Etat à l'Information. Six mois de gouvernement Bourguiba. 4 pts. Tunis, 1956.

Afr 2420.20 — Tunisia. Secrétariat d'Etat à l'Information. Surveys and documents. Tunis. 1,1959+

Afr 2623.960F — Tunisia. Secrétariat d'Etat à l'Information. Tunisia works. Tunis, 1960.

Afr Doc 5409.6 — Tunisia. Secretariat d'Etat au Plan et à l'Economie Nationale. Annexe statistique au rapport sur le budget économique. Tunis. 1967+

Afr 2623.965 — Tunisia. Secrétariat d'Etat au Plan et à l'Economie Nationale. Plan guadriennal, 1965-1968. Tunis, 1965?

Afr Doc 5409.5 — Tunisia. Secretariat d'Etat au Plan et à l'Economie Nationale. Rapport sur le budget économique. Tunis. 1967+

Afr Doc 5408.705 — Tunisia. Secretariat d'Etat au Plan et à l'Economie Nationale. Statistiques du commerce exterieur. Tunisia. 1965+

Afr 2623.962.10 — Tunisia. Secrétariat d'Etat au Plan et aux Finances. Perspectives décennales de dèveloppement, 1962-1971. Tunis, 1962.

Afr Doc 5407.5 — Tunisia. Service des Statistiques. Annuaire statistique de Tunisie. 1955+ 2v.

Afr Doc 5409.305 — Tunisia. Service des Statistiques. Les comptes économiques de la Tunisie. 1,1953

Afr 2530.40FA — Tunisia faces the future. (Monde Economique.) Tunis, 1956.

Afr 2535.8 — Tunisia since independence. (Moore, Clement Henry.) Berkeley, 1965.

Afr 2533.2 — Tunisia today. (Laitman, L.) N.Y., 1954.

Afr 2618.25 — Tunisia unveiled. (Hammerton, Thomas.) London, 1959.

Afr 2623.960F — Tunisia works. (Tunisia. Secrétariat d'Etat à l'Information.) Tunis, 1960.

Afr 2632.6 — Tunisiaca. (Sarfatti, M.G.) Milano, 1924.

Afr 2623.962.5F — Tunisian development. (Tunisia. Secretariat.) Tunis, 1962.

Afr 2535.4 — Tunisian-French dispute. (Mezerik, A.) N.Y., 1961.

Afr 2533.8 — Tunisian Office for National Liberation. An account of the Tunisian question and its most recent developments. N.Y., 1952.

Afr 2609.68 — Tunisie, ma mie. (Olivier, Pierre.) Tunis, 1968.

Afr 2533.1 — Tunisie...attention. (Rous, Jean.) Paris, 1952.

Afr 2609.30.15 — La Tunisie. (Despois, Jean.) Paris, 1930.

Afr 2609.61 — La Tunisie. (Despois, Jean.) Paris, 1961.

Afr 2608.81 — La Tunisie. (Duveyrier, Henri.) Paris, 1881.

Afr 2609.65 — Tunisie. (Duvignaud, Jean.) Lausanne, 1965.

Afr 2458.93 — La Tunisie. (Faucon, N.) Paris, 1893. 2v.

Afr 2608.86 — La Tunisie. (Fournel, M.) Paris, 1886.

Afr 2609.52 — Tunisie. (Hoppenot, Hélène.) Lausanne, 1952.

Afr 2530.71A — La Tunisie. (Raymond, André.) Paris, 1961.

Afr 2609.61.5 — Tunisie. (Roy, Claude.) Paris, 1961.

Afr 2609.06.3 — La Tunisie. (Tunis. Comité. D'Hivernage.) Tunis, 1906.

Afr 2609.55 — Tunisie. (Zeraffa, Michel.) Paris, 1955.

Afr 2620.2 — Tunisie. Paris, 1965.

Afr 2618.15 — Tunisie: sève nouvelle. (Demeerseman, A.) Tournai, 1957.

Afr 2623.938.3 — La Tunisie agricole et rurale. (Scemama, R.) Paris, 1938.

Afr 2623.938 — La Tunisie agricole et rurale et l'oeuvre de la France. Thèse. (Scemama, R.) Paris, 1938.

Afr 2609.04 — Tunisie au début du XXme siècle. Paris, 1904.

Afr 555.12 — La Tunisie chrétienne. (Sainte-Marie, E. de.) Lyon, 1878.

Afr 2623.961.5 — La Tunisie d'aujourd'hui et de demain. (Ardant, G.) Paris, 1961.

Afr 2535.10 — La Tunisie de Bourguiba. (Rossi, Pierre.) Tunis, 1967.

Afr 2536.10.5 — La Tunisie de Bourguiba. (Stephane, R.) Paris, 1958.

Afr 2505.2 — La Tunisie devant l'Europe. (Prevost, F.) Paris, 1862.

Afr 2446.5 — La Tunisie d'il y a cinquante ans. (Varloud.) Paris, 1932.

Afr 2609.34 — La Tunisie du nord. (Bonniard, F.) Paris, 1934. 2v.

Afr 2536.10.10 — La Tunisie et la France. (Bourguiba, H.) Paris, 1954.

Afr 2609.07 — La Tunisie et l'oeuvre du protectorat français. (Loth, G.) Paris, 1907.

Afr 2609.21 — La Tunisie et ses richesses. (Ferdinand-Lop, S.) Paris, 1921.

Afr 2608.92.3 — La Tunisie française. (Poire, Eugene.) Paris, 1892.

Afr 2623.961 — La Tunisie indépendante face à son économie. (Guen, Moncef.) Paris, 1961.

Afr 2623.957 — Tunisie nouvelle. (Tlatli, S.E.) Tunis, 1957.

Afr 2609.40 — La Tunisie orientale, Sahel et Basse Steppe, étude géographique. (Despois, Jean.) Paris, 1940.

Afr 2609.40.5 — La Tunisie orientale. 2.ed. (Despois, Jean.) Paris, 1955.

Afr 2609.62 — La Tunisie présaharienne. (Coque, R.) Paris, 1962.

Afr 2609.46 — Tunisie vivante. (Eparvier, Jean.) Paris, 1946.

Afr 2459.52F — Tunisie 53. (Encyclopédie Mensuelle d'Outre-Mer.) Paris, 1952.

Afr 2459.53F — Tunisie 54. (Encyclopédie Mensuelle d'Outre-Mer.) Paris, 1953.

Afr 2609.60 — Tunisien. (Schleinitz, E.G.) Frankfurt a.M., 1960.

Afr 2209.12.15 — Tunisien und Algerien. (Schmitthenner, H.) Stuttgart, 1924.

Afr 2609.37 — Tunisiennes. (Margueritte, L.P.) Paris, 1937.

Afr 2819.30 — Turchi, senussi e italiani in Libia. (Aleo, G.M.) Bengasi, 1930.

Afr 2875.8 — The Turco-Italian war and its problems. (Barclay, T.) London, 1912.

Afr 2875.3F — Turco-Italian war concerning Tripoli. n.p., 1911.

Afr 3138.5 — The Turcoman defeat at Cairo. (Solomon Ben Joseph, Ha-Kohen.) Chicago, 1906.

Afr 1335.8 — Turin. Museo Civico d'Arte Antica. Il medagliere delle raccolte numismatiche torinesi. Torino, 1964.

Afr 2688.5F — Turki, Zubayr. Tunis, naguère et aujourd'hui. Tunis, 1967.

Afr 609.60.30 — Turn left for Tangier. (Bensted-Smith, Richard.) Coventry, 1960.

Afr 8145.22F — Turnbull, C.E.P. The work of the missionaries of Die Nederduits Gereformeerde Kerk van Suid-Afrika up to the year 1910. Johannesburg, 1965.

Afr 635.85 — Turnbull, Colin. The lonely African. N.Y., 1962.

Afr 609.66.40 — Turnbull, Colin. Tradition and change in African tribal life. Cleveland, 1966.

Afr 7815.28.10 — Turnbull, Colin M. The forest people. N.Y., 1961.

Afr 7815.28.5 — Turnbull, Colin M. Wayward servants. 1st ed. Garden City, N.Y., 1965.

Afr 1609.38.5 — Turnbull, P. Black barbary. London, 1938.

Afr 2749.40 — Turnbull, P. Sahara unveiled, a great story of French colonial conquest. London, 1940.

Afr 9705.10A — Turner, O.W. Schism and continuity in African society. Manchester, 1957.

Afr 9700.32 — Turner, Victor Witter. The drums of affliction. Oxford, 1968.

Afr 9700.32.5 — Turner, Victor Witter. The forest of symbols; aspects of Ndembu ritual. Ithaca, 1967.

Afr 630.48 — Turner, Walter L. Under the skin of the African. Birmingham, Ala., 1948.

Afr 2525.2 — La Turquie et le protectorat français. (Rouard de Card, E.) Paris, 1916.

Afr 7912.15.25 — Turski, Marian. Lumumba i jego kraj. Warszawa, 1962.

Afr 628.108.10 — Tussac, R. de. Cri des colons contre un ouvrage de M. L'Evêque. Paris, 1810.

Afr 10690.89.130 — Tutuola, Amos. Ajaiyi and his inherited poverty. London, 1967.

Afr 10690.89.110 — Tutuola, Amos. The brave African huntress. London, 1958.

Afr 10690.89.120 — Tutuola, Amos. Feather woman of the jungle. London, 1962.

Afr 10690.89.100 — Tutuola, Amos. My life in the bush of ghosts. London, 1954.

Afr 11853.88.100 — Tutuola, Amos. My life in the bush of ghosts. N.Y., 1954.

Afr 11853.88.110 — Tutuola, Amos. The palm-wine drinkard and his dead palm-wine tapster. London, 1952.

Afr 11853.88.120 — Tutuola, Amos. Simbi and the satyr of the dark jungle. London, 1955.

Afr 40.65	Tuzmukhamedov, Rais A. Organizatsiia afrikanskogo edinstva. Moskva, 1965.
Afr 3978.73	Tvaa maanader i egypten. (Knorring, O.V.) Stockholm, 1873.
Afr 8289.03	Twee jaren in de Boerenoorlog. (Loren van Thernaat, H.) Haarlem, 1903.
Afr 8278.99.35	Tweede verzameling (Correspondentie 1899-1900). v.1-2. (Leyds, W.J.) Dordrecht, 1930. 3v.
Afr 8289.48	Die Tweede Vryheidsoorlog. (Breytenbach, J.H.) Kaapstad, 1948. 2v.
Afr 718.44	Tweedy, Owen. By way of the Sahara. London, 1930.
Afr 8658.95	Twelve hundred miles in a waggon. (Balfour, A.B.) London, 1895.
Afr 5748.75	Twelve months in Madagascar. (Mullens, J.) London, 1875.
Afr 7096.061.10	Twelve years of industrial development, 1952-1964. (United Arab Republic. Ministry of Industry.) Cairo, 1964.
Afr 8658.87.8	Twenty-five years in a waggon. (Anderson, Andrew Arthur.) London, 1888.
Afr 6455.37	Twenty-five years in East Africa. (Roscoe, John.) Cambridge, 1921.
Afr 6275.22	Twenty-five years in Qua Iboe. (McKeown, R.L.) London, 1912.
Afr 8658.87.7	Twenty-five years in the gold regions of Africa. (Anderson, Andrew Arthur.) London, 1887. 2v.
Afr 8063.5	Twenty-five years soldiering in South Africa. (Woon, Harry V.) London, 1909.
Afr 6282.46	Twenty-nine years in the West Indies and Central Africa. (Waddell, Hope Masterton.) London, 1863.
Afr 6282.46.2	Twenty-nine years in the West Indies and Central Africa. 2nd ed. (Waddell, Hope Masterton.) London, 1970.
Afr 555.9.10	Twenty years in Central Africa. 3d ed. (Rowley, Henry.) London, 1883.
Afr 9388.95	Twenty years in Khamas country. (Hepburn, J.D.) London, 1895.
Afr 4571.5	Twenty years of work, 1941-1961. (Ethiopia. Ministry of Information.) Addis Ababa, 1962.
Afr 8289.00.13	Twice captured. (Rosslyn, James.) Edinburg, 1900.
Afr 8095.20	Twilight in South Africa. (Gibbs, H.) London, 1949.
Afr 6540.6.15	Twilight tales of the black Baganda. (Fisher, Ruth Hurditch.) London, 1911.
Afr 11780.51.100	Twin-brother hell. (Sellier, Richard.) London, 1960.
Afr 9093.22	Twintig jaren onder Kugers Boeren in voor-en tegenspoed. (Sandberg, Christoph Georg.) Amsterdam, 1944.
Afr 7565.16	Twiss, Travers. An international protectorate of the Congo River. London, 1883.
Afr 1259.11.5	Twixt sand and sea. (Grant, Cyril F.) London, 1911.
Afr 4559.01	Twixt Sirdar and Menelik. (Wellby, M.S.) London, 1901.
Afr 10584.14.110	Two African tales. (Nicol, Davidson.) Cambridge, Eng., 1965
Afr 6333.02	Two African trips, with notes and suggestions. (Buxton, Edward North.) London, 1902.
Afr 11572.50.200	Two bucks without hair. (Millin, S.G.(L).) London, 1957.
Afr 5635.13	Two campaigns, Madagascar and Ashantee. (Burleigh, B.) London, 1896.
Afr 4969.07.3	Two dianas in Somaliland. 2d ed. (Herbert, A.) London, 1908.
Afr 212.4	The two faces of Africa. (Marais, B.J.) Pietermaritzburg, 1964.
Afr 8673.17F	Two hundred thirty-one photographs in full colour. (Souvenir of South Africa.) Johannesburg, 1960.
Afr 6196.14	The two Isanwurfos. (Braiman, Joseph Adam.) London, 1967.
Afr 8235.9	Two lectures on South Africa. (Froude, J.A.) London, 1900.
Afr 6282.6	Two missionary heroines in Africa. (Ellis, James Joseph.) Kilmarnock, 1927.
Afr 9500.25	The two nations. (Gray, Richard.) Oxford, 1960.
Afr 590.52	Two of the petitions form Scotland, presented to last Parliament, praying abolition of African slave trade. (Edinburg Society for Effecting the Abolition of African Slave Trade.) Edinburg, 1790.
Afr 2749.39.5	Two roads to Africa. (Symons, H.E.) London, 1939.
Afr 6460.35F	Two studies in applied anthropology in Kenya. (Mayer, Philip.) London, 1951.
Afr 10916.5	Two tone. Salisbury, Rhodesia. 5,1969+
Afr 5406.176	Two trips to gorilla land. (Burton, Richard F.) London, 1876. 4v.
Afr 4513.38A	Two wars and more to come. (Matthews, H.L.) N.Y., 1938.
Afr 6193.64	Two-year development plan: from stabilisation to development. (Ghana. Ministry of Economic Affairs.) Accra, 1968.
Afr 8315.10	Two years at the front. (Moeller, B.) London, 1903.
Afr 8292.22	Two years on trek, Royal Sussex Regiment. (Dumoulin, L.E.) London, 1907.
Afr 3978.56.5	Two years residence in a Levantine family. (Saint John, B.) London, 1856.
Afr 4105.1	Two years residence in a Levantine family. (Saint John, B.) Paris, 1850.
Afr 2875.20	Two years under the crescent. (Wright, H.C.S.) London, 1913.
Afr 8020.3	Tydskrif vir raase-aangeleenthede. Stellenbosch. 3,1951+ 10v.
Afr 8060.5	Tylden, G. The armed forces of South Africa. Johannesburg, 1954.
Afr 8865.10	Tylden, G. The rise of the Basuto. Cape Town, 1950.
Afr 3979.12.2	Tyndale, W. An artist inEgypt. N.Y., 1912.
Afr 3979.07	Tyndale, W. Below the Cataracts. Philadelphia, 1907.
Afr 8685.40	The tyranny of colour. (Joshi, Pranshankar S.) Durban, 1942.
Afr 7350.5.12	Tyson, J.R. A discourse before the Young Men's Colonization Society of Pennsylvania. Philadelphia, 1834.
Afr 3979.63.8	U.A.R., United Arab Republic. (United Arab Republic. Information Department.) Cairo, 1963.
Afr 3335.15	The U.A.R. and the policy of non-alignment. (United Arab Republic. Ministry of National Guidance.) Cairo, 1966?
Afr Doc 1408.700	U.A.R. foreign trade according to standard international trade classification revised. (United Arab Republic. Central Agency for Public Mobilisation and Statistics.) Cairo, 1966.
Afr 3994.967	The U.A.R. in development, a study in expansionary finance. (Kardouche, George K.) N.Y., 1967.
Afr 3986.14	Pamphlet vol. U.A.R. Pams. 6 pam.
Afr 3320.143.5F	U.A.R. today. Cairo. 1963+

Afr 1620.30	U.S. Office of Armed Forces Information and Education. A pocket guide to French Morocco. Washington, 1956.
Afr 659.67	U arabov Afriki. (Landa, Robert G.) Moskva, 1967.
Afr 4513.36.70	Ual ual. (Cimmaruta, R.) Milano, 1936.
Afr 6883.11	Ubena of the rivers. (Culwick, A.F.) London, 1935.
Afr 7912.20	Ubiitsa s Ist-river. (Semenov, M.G.) Moscow, 1961.
Afr 6295.66.5	Uboma, a socio-economic and nutritional survey. (Shell Company Of Nigeria.) Bude, Eng., 1966.
Afr 6280.9.35	Uchendu, Victor Chikezie. The Iglo of southwest Nigeria. N.Y., 1965.
Afr 8687.124	Udeman, Elsa. The published works of Margaret Livingstone Ballinger; a bibliography. Johannesburg, 1968.
Afr 49742.41.100	Udingiswayo kajobe. (Vilakazi, B.W.) London, 1939.
Afr 4285.3	Uber die Anfänge des axumitischen Reiches. (Dillmann, A.) Berlin, 1879.
Afr 5318.18.2	Über die Canverden nach dem Rio Grande. (Doelter, C.) Leipzig, 1888.
Afr 4558.59	Über die Sitten und das Recht der Bogos. (Munzinger, W.) Winterthur, 1859.
Afr 4835.1	Über die Verkehrsentwicklung in Äthiopien. (Ilg, Alfred.) Zürich, 1900.
Afr 820.15.12	Uebi-Scebeli nella spedizione di S.A.R. Luigi di Savoia. (Basile, C.) Bologna, 1935.
Afr 6482.5	Uganda, report for the year. (Great Britain. Colonial Office.) 1948+ 3v.
Afr 6535.12.2	Uganda, the handbook of Uganda. (Wallis, H.R.) London, 1920.
Afr Doc 3326.5	Uganda. Annual development report. Entebbe. 1947
Afr Doc 3305.5	Uganda. Annual reports on the Kingdom of Buganda, Eastern Province, Western Province and Northern Province. Entebbe. 1947+
Afr Doc 3303.5F	Uganda. Blue book. 9v.
Afr Doc 3302.5	Uganda. Catalogue of government publications published prior to 1st January, 1965. Entebbe, 1966?
Afr Doc 3307.321	Uganda. Census returns, 1921. Uganda, 1921.
Afr Doc 3333.10	Uganda. Civil reabsorption. Progress report. Entebbe. 1947-1948
Afr Doc 3309.15	Uganda. Estimates of development expenditure. Entebbe. 1964+
Afr Doc 3309.10	Uganda. Estimates of recurrent expenditure. Entebbe. 1964+
Afr Doc 3309.189.5	Uganda. Financial summary and revenue estimates. Entebbe. 1961+
Afr 6438.30	Uganda. The first five-year development plan, 1961-62 to 1965-66. Entebbe, 1964.
Afr 6538.45	Uganda. A five year capital development plan, 1955-1960. Uganda, 1954.
Afr 6310.49	Uganda. Proposals for the implementation of the recommendations contained in the report of the Commission on the Civil Services of the East African territories and the East Africa High Commission, 1953-1954. Entebbe, 1954.
Afr Doc 3307.348	Uganda. Report on the census of the non-native population of Uganda Protectorate. Nairobi, 1953.
Afr 6538.47	Uganda. Work for progress, the second five-year plan, 1966-1971. Entebbe, 1966.
Afr 6480	Pamphlet box. Uganda.
Afr 6535.62.10	Uganda. (British Information Service.) N.Y., 1962.
Afr 6535.62.5	Uganda. (British Information Service.) N.Y., 1962.
Afr 6486.5	Uganda. (Ingrams, William.) London, 1960.
Afr 6538.50	Uganda. (Italy. Istituto Nazionale per il Commercio Estero.) Roma, 1964.
Afr 6535.64	Uganda. (London. Commonwealth Institute.) London, 1964.
Afr 6498.35	Uganda. (Thomas, H.B.) London, 1935.
Afr 6475.15	Uganda. Entebbe. 1,1962+ 2v.
Afr 6538.5	Uganda. Agricultural Department. Agriculture in Uganda. London, 1940.
Afr Doc 3331.10	Uganda. Agriculture Department. Annual report. Entebbe. 1947-1956
Afr 6484.22	Uganda. Board of Inquiry into a Claim for a Rise in Salaries of "E" Scale Public Officers. Report. Entebbe, 1966. 2 pam.
Afr 6542.3	Uganda. Commission Appointed to Review the Boundary Between the Districts of Bugisu and Bukedi. Report. Entebbe, 1962.
Afr 6542.4	Uganda. Commission of Inquiry into Disturbances in the Eastern Province, 1960. Report. Entebbe, 1960.
Afr 6484.20	Uganda. Commissioners for Africanisation. Report. Entebbe, 1962.
Afr Doc 3319.15	Uganda. Constitution. The constitution of the Republic of Uganda. Entebbe, 1967?
Afr Doc 3319.5	Uganda. Constitution. The Constitution of Uganda, 15th April, 1966. Entebbe, 1966.
Afr Doc 3319.10	Uganda. Constitution. The govenment proposals for a new Constitution, 9th June, 1967. Entebbe, 1967.
Afr 6484.5	Uganda. Constitutional Committee. Report of the constitutional committee, 1957. Entebbe, 1959.
Afr Doc 3309.305	Uganda. Controller and Auditor General. The public accounts of the government of Uganda together with the report thereon by the Controller and Auditor General. Entebbe. 1963+
Afr Doc 3331.15	Uganda. Controller and Auditor General. Report. Entebbe. 1947+
Afr Doc 3309.310	Uganda. Controller and Auditor General. Report on the accounts. Entebbe. 1947+
Afr Doc 3333.5	Uganda. Department of Community Development. Annual report. Entebbe. 1952+
Afr Doc 3343.5	Uganda. Department of Geological Survey and Mines. Mines Division. Annual report. Entebbe. 1961+
Afr Doc 3339.5	Uganda. Department of Information. Annual report. Entebbe. 1953+
Afr 6535.18	Uganda. Department of Information. A guide to Uganda. Entebbe, 1954.
Afr Doc 3346.10	Uganda. Department of Public Relations and Social Welfare. Annual report. Entebbe. 1947-1948
Afr Doc 3331.5	Uganda. Department of the Administrator General. Annual report. Entebbe. 1947+
Afr 6538.3F	Uganda. Development Commission. Report, 1920. Entebbe, 1920.
Afr Doc 3335.5	Uganda. Economic Development Commission. Report. 1956+
Afr 6538.40F	Uganda. Fiscal Commission. Report. Entebbe, 1962.

Afr 210.61.60   United States. National Commission for UNESCO. Africa and the U.S. Washington, 1961.

Afr 4753.15   United States. Operations Mission to the Somali Republic. Inter-river economic exploration. Washington, 1961.

Afr 9499.30   United States. Trade Mission to the Federation of Rhodesia and Nyasaland. Report. Washington, 1960.

Afr 210.58A   The United States and Africa. (American Assembly.) N.Y., 1958.

Afr 210.58.22   The United States and Africa. (American Assembly.) N.Y., 1963.

Afr 28.60   United States and Canadian publications on Africa. Stanford. 1963+
    4v.

Afr 1069.63   The United States and North Africa. (Gallagher, C.F.) Cambridge, 1963.

Afr 3335.5   United States Trade Mission to the United Arab Republic. Seven Americans in theUnited Arab Republic. Washington, 1960.

Afr 679.27.6   United West Africa, or Africa, at the bar of the family of nations. (Solanke, Ladipo.) London, 1969.

Afr 626.165.5   Unity or poverty? The economics of Pan-Africanism. (Green, Reginald Herbold.) Harmondsworth, 1968.

Afr 1609.59   L'univers de l'ecolier marocain. v.1-5. (Bourgeois, Paul.) Rabat, 1959-60.

Afr 618.23   Universities and the Language of Tropical Africa. Language in Africa. Cambridge, 1963.

Afr 4210.4   University college review. Addis Ababa. 1,1961

Afr 9.10   The university geographer. (Ibadan, Nigeria. University. Geographical Society.) Ibadan.

Afr 6879.68.10   University Press of Africa. Kilimanjaro country. Nairobi, 1968.

Afr 6888.5   University Press of Africa. Tanga, the central port for East Africa. Nairobi, 1968.

Afr 6879.68.5   University Press of Africa. Tanzania today. Nairobi, 1968.

Afr 11320.50.150   An unknown border; poems. (Delius, Anthony.) Cape Town, 1954.

Afr 4968.88   The unknown hour of Africa. (James, F.L.) London, 1888.

Afr 8289.01.29   Unofficial dispatches. (Wallace, E.) London, 1901.

Afr 6225.45   Unongo, Paul Iyorpuu. The case for Nigeria. Lagos, 1968.

Afr 550.148   The unpopular missionary. (Dodge, Ralph Edward.) Westwood, N.J., 1964.

Afr 718.2.12   Unpublished letters. (Stanley, H.M.) N.Y., 1957.

Afr 8678.102   Unrest in South Africa. (Joshi, Pranshankar Someshwar.) Bombay, 1958.

Afr 6686.35   Unsere alte Kolonie Togo. (Metzger, O.F.) Neudamm, 1941.

Afr 530.28.5   Unsere grossen Afrikaner. (Banse, Ewald.) Berlin, 1943.

Afr 8659.30.20   Unter Buren, Briten, Bantus. (Jannasch, Hans.) Berlin, 193-.

Afr 6192.80   Unter dem schwarzen Stern. (Balk, Theodor.) Berlin, 1960.

Afr 718.5   Unter Deutsche Flagge quer durch Afrika. (Wissmann, H.) Berlin, 1889.

Afr 1583.14.15   Die unternehmungen des brüder mannesmann in Marokko. (Mannesmann, C.H.) Würzburg, 1931.

Afr 1623.964.15   Untersuchung der morokkanischen Industriestruktur. (Kratz, Achim.) Hamburg, 1964.

Afr 3740.14   Untersuchungen über den französisch-englischen Weltgegensatz im Faschodajahr (1898). (Kossatz, Heinz.) Breslau, 1934.

Afr 150.8   Untersuchungen üeber die geographischen Entdeckungen der Portugiesen unter Heinrich dem Seefahrer. (Wappaens, J.E.) Göttingen, 1842.

Afr 11229.81.100   Unto dust, stories. 2d ed. (Bosman, Herman.) Cape Town, 1964.

Afr 5235.128.30   The unveiling of Timbuctoo. (Welch, Galbraith.) N.Y., 1939.

Afr 9500.10   Unyanda, B.J. In search of truth. Bombay, 1954.

Afr 854.10   Unzueta y Yuste, A. de. Islas del Golfo de Guinea. Madrid, 1945.

Afr 3710.13.5   Uomini d'Africa. (Messedaglia, Luigi.) Bologna, 1935.

Afr 6275.27   Up against it in Nigeria. (Hermon-Hodge, H.B.) London, 1922.

Afr 810.5   Up the Niger. (Mockler-Ferryman, A.F.) London, 1892.

Afr 9525.529   Uppengula the scatterer. (Posselt, Friedrich Wilhelm Traugott.) Bulawayo, 1945.

Afr 4070.6   Upper Egypt. (Klunzinger, C.B.) N.Y., 1878.

Afr 5272.2   Upper Volta. Laws, statutes, etc. Le drame de la Haute-Volta. Paris, 1960.

Afr Doc 6508.705   Upper Volta. Ministère de l'Economie Nationale. Commerce extérieur de la Haute-Volta. Ouagadougou. 1961+

Afr 5282.2   Upper Volta. Ministère des Finances, des Affaires Economiques et du Plan. Rapport économique, 1959. Ouagadougou, 1960.

Afr Doc 6507.5   Upper Volta. Ministère du Developpement et du Tourisme. Bulletin mensuel de statistique. Ouagadougou. 7,1966+

Afr Doc 6509.305   Upper Volta. Service de la Statistique. Comptes économiques de la Haute-Volta. Paris. 1964+

Afr Doc 6585.1.73   Upper Volta. Service de la Statistique. Recensement démographique Ouagadougou, 1961-1962. Paris, 1964.

Afr Doc 6507.361.10   Upper Volta. Service de Statistique. La situation démographique en Haute-Volta; résultats partiels de l'énquête démographique, 1960-1961. Paris, 1962.

Afr 5282.10   Upper Volta. Service du Plan. Données actuelles de l'économie voltäique. Paris, 1962.

Afr 6277.106   Upton, Martin. Agriculture in South-West Nigeria; a study of the relationships between production and social characteristics in selected villages. Reading, 1967.

Afr 109.63.15   Uraltes junges Afrika; 5000 Jahre afrikanischer Geschichte nach zeitgenössischen Quellen. (Brentjes, Burchard.) Berlin, 1963.

Afr 8371.5   Urban Africans in the Republic of South Africa, 1950-1966. (Lurie, Angela Shulmith.) Johannesburg, 1969.

Afr 8678.320.5   Urban Bantu councils. (Mbata, J.C.M.) Johannesburg, 1965.

Afr Doc 2309.305.10F   Urban consumer surveys. (Nigeria. Federal Office of Statistics.) Lagos, 1966.
    3v.

Afr Doc 2309.305F   Urban consumer surveys in Nigeria. (Nigeria. Depaartment of Statistics.) Lagos, 1957.

Afr Doc 2309.305.5F   Urban Consumer surveys in Nigeria. (Nigeria. Federal Office of Statistics.) Lagos, 1963.

Afr 650.8   Urban dynamics in Black Africa. (Hanna, William John.) Washington, 1969.

Afr 6293.5   Urban government for metropolitan Lagos. (Williams, Babatunde A.) N.Y., 1968.

Afr 6210.62   Urban government organization in Northern Nigeria. (Fairholm, Gilbert Wayne.) Zaria?, 1964?

Afr 679.65.5A   Urbanization and migration in West Africa. (California. University. University at Los Angeles. African Studies Center.) Berkeley, 1965.

Afr 609.63.10   Urbanization in African social change. (Edinburgh. University.) Edinburgh, 1963.

Afr 6277.116   Urbanization in Nigeria. (Mobogunje, Akinlawon Lopide.) London, 1968.

Afr 679.65   Urbanization in West Africa. (Simms, R.P.) Evanston, 1965.

Afr 5248.20   Urbanization of an African community. (Meillassoux, Claude.) Seattle, 1968.

Afr 6275.130   The urbanized Nigerian. 1st ed. (Okin, Theophilus Adelodum.) N.Y., 1968.

Afr Doc 3319.6   Urganda. Constitutional Committe. Report, 1959 and Supplementary Report 1960. n.p., n.d.
    2 pam.

Afr 1033.4   Urkunden zur Geschichte des völkerrechts. Erg. 1. (Strupp, K.) Gotha, 1912.

Afr 4375.19   Urquehart, David. The Abyssinian war. London, 1868.

Afr 7183.28   Urquhart, Alvin W. Patterns of settlement and subsistence in Southwestern Angola. Washington, 1963.

Afr 5426.100.35   Urquhart, Clara. With Dr. Schweitzer in Lambaréné. London, 1957.

Afr 1755.8   Urquijo, F. De. La Campana del rif en 1909. Madrid, n.d.

Afr 1608.75   Urrestarazu, D.T. de A. de. Viajes por Marruecos. Madrid, 18- .

Htn   Afr 4256.10*   Urreta, L. Historia eclesiastica, politica, natural, y moral de los grandes y remotos reynos de la Etiopia. Pt.1. Valencia, 1610.

Htn   Afr 4320.25*   Urreta, Luis de. Historia de la Sagrada Orden de Predicadores. Valencia, 1611.

Afr 632.10   Ursprung der Kultur. (Frobenius, L.V.) Berlin, 1898.

Afr 5243.10   Urvoy, Y.F.M.A. Petit atlas ethno-démographique du Soudan. Paris, 1942.

Afr 5219.36   Urvoy, Yves François Marie Aimé. Histoire des populations du Soudan central (colonie du Niger). Paris, 1936.

Afr 6888.2   Usambara und seine Nachbargebiete. (Baumann, O.) Berlin, 1891.

Afr 1550.50   Usborne, C.V. The conquest of Morocco. London, 1936.

Afr 5993.15   Usera y Alarcon, Gerónimo M. Memoria de la isla de Fernando Poo. Madrid, 1848.

Afr 5992.2   Usera y Alarcon, Gerónimo M. Observaciones al Llamado Opusculo. Madrid, 1852.

Afr 4558.90.5   Usi e costumi. (Pasini, L.) Milano, n.d.

Afr 28.103   Ustav pro Mezinarodni Politiku a Ekonomii. Bibliograficke prameny studiv problematiky africkych zemi. Praha, 193-.

Afr 44622.89.100   Utenzi wa AbdirRahmani na Sufiyani. (al-Buhry, Hemed Abdallah.) Dar es Salaam, 1961.

Afr 44622.89.122   Utenzi wa Seyyidna Huseni bin Ali. (al-Buhry, Hemed Abdallah.) Dar es Salaam, 1965.

Afr 44622.89.120   Utenzi wa Seyyidna Huseni bin Ali. (al-Buhry, Hemed Abdallah.) Dar es Salaam, 1965.

Afr 44622.89.112   Utenzi wa vita vya wadachi kutamalaki mrima 1307 A.H. 2. ed. (al-Buhry, Hemed Abdallah.) Dar es Salaam, 1960.

Afr 4760.14   Utilisation of manpower in the public service in Somalia. (Nigam, Shyam Behari Lal.) Mogadiscio, 1964.

Afr 6138.31   Utting, F.A.J. The story of Sierra Leone. London, 1931.

Afr 6291.52   Uwechue, Raph. Reflections on the Nigerian civil war; a call for realism. London, 1969.

Afr 8140.25   Uys, C.J. In the era of Shepstone, being a study of British expansion in South Africa (1842-1877). Lovedale, 1933.

Afr 9291.20   Uys, Cornelis Janse. Rouxville, 1863-1963. Bloemfontein, 1966.

Afr 2000.8   Uzighan, 'Ammar. Le meilleur combat. Paris, 1958.

Afr 10691.99.100   Uzodinma, Edmund. Our dead speak. London, 1967.

Afr 6295.64.5   Uzuakoli. (Fox, A.J.) London, 1964.

Afr 6176.25   V Respublike Gana. (Orestov, O.L.) Moscow, 1961.

Afr 3979.11.15   V strane Amon-Ra. (L'vov, A.N.) Sankt Peterburg, 1911.

Afr 6738.44   Vaast, Pierre. La République fédérale du Cameroun. Paris, 1962.

Afr 609.30.20   A vacation in Africa. (Fort, T.) Boston, 1931.

Afr 3979.12.3   A vacation on the Nile. (Parkhurst, L.) Boston, 1913.

Afr 7179.10   Vacchi, Dante. Penteados de Angola. Lisbonne, 1965.

Afr 500.10.3   Vade mecum für Diplomatische Arbeit auf dem Afrikanischen Continent. 3. Aufl. (Kinsky, Karl.) Leipzig, 1900.

Afr 4700.36.35   Vademecum per l'Africa orientale. Milano, 1936.

Afr 1259.30   A vagabond in Barbary. (Foster, Harry L.) N.Y., 1930.

Afr 5056.159   Vagabondage en Afrique noire. (Balez, Eugene.) Toulouse, 1959.

Afr 5874.19   Vailland, Roger. La Réunion. Lausanne, 1964.

Afr 1640.15   Vainot, L. Pelerinages judeo-musulmans du Maroc. Paris, 1948.

Afr 7580.13   Valahu, M. The Katanga circus. 1st ed. N.Y., 1964.

Afr 7175.79   Valahu, Mugur. Angola, chave de Africa. Lisboa, 1968.

Afr 1739.5   Valderrama Martinez, P. El palacio califal de Tetuan. Tetuan, 1954.

Afr 7315.26.1   Valenge women; an ethnographic study. (Earthy, Emily D.) London, 1968.

X Cg   Afr 1955.42   Valet, René. L'Afrique du nord devant le Parlement au XIXme siecle. Alger, 1924.

Afr 5590.12   Valette, J. Etudes sur le regne de Radama Uer. Tananarive, 1962.

Afr 5792.2   Valette, Jean. Sainte-Marie et la côte est de Madagascar en 1818. Tananarive, 1962.

Afr 6720.56   La valeur politique et sociale de la tutelle française au Cameroun. Thèse. (Nguini, Marcel.) Aix-en-Provence, 1956.

Afr 4785.12   La vallé du Darrar. (Revoil, G.E.J.) Paris, 1882.

Afr 3979.25.20   La vallée des rois et des reines. (Harry, Myriam.) Paris, 1925.

Afr 8289.03.2   Vallentin, W. Der burenkrieg. Wald-Solingen, 1903.
    2v.

Afr 8210.8   Vallentin, W. Die Geschichte der Süd-Afrikanischen Republiken. Berlin, 1901.

Afr 1571.33   Vallerie, Pierre. Conquérants et conquis au Maroc. Thèse. Paris, 1934.

Afr 9149.62   Valley of gold. (Cartwright, Alan.) Cape Town, 1962.

Afr 11669.13   Valley of the vines. (Packer, Joy (P).) Philadelphia, 1956.

Afr 7809.55.5   Vallotton, Henry. Voyage au Congo et au Ruanda-Urundi. Bruxelles, 1955.

Afr 9087.5   Valter, M.P.C. Duitschland en de Hollandsche Republieken in Zuid-Afrika. Amsterdam, 1918.

Afr 8658.98.7 — Van Amsterdam naar Pretoria. (Wormser, J.A.) Amsterdam, 1898.
Afr 8835.20 — Van Riebeecksestad. 1. uitg. (Tonder, I.W.) Kaapstad, 1950.
Afr 1550.39A — Van Tanger tot Agadir. (Enthoven, Henri Emile.) Utrecht, 1929.
Afr 6018.98 — Vandeleur, S. Campaigning on the upper Nile. London, 1898.
Afr 6460.5 — Vanden Bergh, L.J. On the trail of the Pigmies. N.Y., 1921.
Afr 9038.2 — Vandenberghe, P.L. Caneville. 1st. ed. Middletown, Conn., 1964.
Afr 8095.87 — Vandenberghe, Pierre L. South Africa, a study in conflict. Middletown, Conn., 1965.
Afr 618.24 — Vandenborghe, P.L. Africa, social problems of change and conflict. San Francisco, 1965.
Afr 3300.23 — Vandenbosch, F. Vingt annees d'Egypte. Paris, 1932.
Afr 7850.50 — Vandenhang, E. The war in Katanga. N.Y., 1962.
Afr 6883.2 — Vander Burgt. Un grand peuple de l'Afrique équatoriale. Bois le Duc, 1903.
Afr 8279.00.7 — Vanderhoogt, C.V. The story of the Boers. N.Y., 1900.
Afr 8676.42 — Vanderhorst, S.T. Native labor in South Africa. London, 1942.
Afr 45.59 — Vanderlinden, Jacques. Essai sur les juridictions de droit coutumier. Bruxelles, 1959.
Afr 8283.21 — Van der Poel, Jean. The Jameson raid. Cape Town, 1951.
Afr 9839.51A — Vanderpost, L. Venture to the interior. N.Y., 1951.
Afr 11865.59.150 — Vanderpost, Laurens. A bar of shadow. N.Y., 1956.
Afr 630.55 — Vanderpost, Laurens. The dark eye in Africa. N.Y., 1955.
Afr 630.55.2 — Vanderpost, Laurens. The dark eye in Africa. N.Y., 1961.
Afr 11865.59.100 — Vanderpost, Laurens. The face beside the fire. N.Y., 1953.
Afr 11865.59.120 — Vanderpost, Laurens. Flamingo feather. N.Y., 1955.
Afr 11865.59.160 — Vanderpost, Laurens. The hunter and the whale: a story. London, 1967.
Afr 11865.59.110 — Vanderpost, Laurens. In a province. London, 1953.
Afr 9400.10.25 — Vanderpost, Laurens. The lost world of the Kalahari. N.Y., 1958.
Afr 11865.59.140 — Vanderpost, Laurens. The seed and the sower. London, 1963.
Afr 8687.375 — Van der Spuy, Kenneth R. Chasing the wind. Cape Town, 1966.
Afr 7549.11 — Vandervelde, E. La Belgique et le Congo. Paris, 1911.
Afr 7809.09.10 — Vandervelde, Emile. Les derniers jours de l'Etat du Congo. Mons, 1909.
Afr 3818.14 — Vandevort, Eleanor. A leopard tamed; the story of an African pastor, his people, and his problems. N.Y., 1968.
Afr 3979.31 — Vandyke, J.C. In Egypt, studies and sketches along the Nile. N.Y., 1931.
Afr 8315.9 — Vane, Francis Patrick Fletcher. Pax britannia in South Africa. London, 1905.
Afr 1259.27.20A — Vanished cities of northern Africa. (Erskine, Beatrice.) Boston, 1927.
Afr 6164.7 — A vanished dynasty. (Fuller, F.) London, 1921.
Afr 6164.7.2 — A vanished dynasty. 2. ed. (Fuller, F.) London, 1968.
Afr 6460.15.2 — The vanishing tribes of Kenya. (Orde-Browne, G.S.) London, 1925.
Afr 6460.15A — The vanishing tribes of Kenya. (Orde-Browne, G.S.) Philadelphia, 1925.
Afr 555.12.10 — Vanlande, René. Chez les pères blancs, Tunisie, Kabylie Sahara. Paris, 1929.
Afr 5190.10.15 — Vanlande, René. Dakar. Paris, 1941.
Afr 8710.17 — Vanlille, A.J. The native council system with special reference to the Transvaal local councils. Pretoria, 1938.
Afr 2285.31 — Vanney, Jean-René. Pluie et crue dans le Sahara nord-occidental. Alger, 1960.
Afr 210.58.15 — Van Nguen. Les carnets d'un diplomate. Paris, 1958.
Afr 4785.10 — Vannutelli, L. L'Omo. Viaggio d'esplorazione nell'Africa orientale. Milano, 1899.
Afr 8809.61.5 — Vanonsden, L. Trekboer. Cape Town, 1961.
Afr 8678.265 — Vanrensburg, P. Guilty land. London, 1962.
Afr 8022.5 — Van Riebeeck Society. Publications. Cape Town. 2,1919+ 52v.
Afr 710.65 — Vansina, Jan. Les anciens royaumes de la savane. Leopoldville, 1965.
Afr 7815.46 — Vansina, Jan. Introduction à l'ethnographie du Congo. Kinshasa, 1966.
Afr 710.70 — Vansina, Jan. Kingdom of the savanna. Madison, 1966.
Afr 609.50 — Vansinderen, A. Africa, land of many lands. 3d ed. Syracuse, N.Y., 1950.
Htn   Afr 3976.78* — Vansleb, F. The present state of Egypt. London, 1678.
Afr 9853.6A — Vanvelsen, J. The politics of kinship. Manchester, 1964. 2v.
Afr 1609.13.5 — Van Wincxtenhoven. Le Maroc, rapport général. Bruxelles, 1913.
Afr 4513.25 — Varanini, Varo. L'Abissinia attuale sotto tutti i suoi aspetti. Torino, 1935.
Afr 4513.35.41 — Vare, Daniele. Italy, Great Britain and the League in the Italo-Ethiopian conflict. N.Y., 1935.
Afr 4513.35.44 — Vare, Daniele. Italy, Great Britain and the League in the Italo-Ethiopian conflict. N.Y., 1935.
Afr 4285.5 — Varenbergh, Joseph. Studien zur äthiopischen Reichsordnung. Strassbourg, 1915.
Afr 8028.151 — Varley, D.H. Adventures in Africana. Cape Town, 1949.
Afr 8659.60.20 — Varley, Douglas. South African reading in earlier days. Johannesburg, 1960.
Afr 8835.40F — Varley, Vera. Index to the growth and government of Cape Town. Cape Town, 1961.
Afr 6192.55 — Varley, W.J. The geography of Ghana. London, 1958.
Afr 2446.5 — Varloud. La Tunisie d'il y a cinquante ans. Paris, 1932.
Afr 6879.61.5 — Varma, Shanti Narayan. Tanganyika. 1st. ed. New Delhi, 1961.
Afr 150.60 — Vasconcellos, Joaquim de. Taboas da pintura portugueza no seculo XV. Lisboa, 1960.
Afr 5219.63 — Vasianin, A.J. Respublika Mali. Moscow, 1963.
Afr 5406.225.5 — Vassal, Gabrielle M. Life in French Congo. London, 1925.
Afr 1040.5 — Vassenhove, Leon van. Une solution fédéraliste du problème nord-africain. Neuchâtel, 1957.
Afr 4070.35 — The vast Sudan. (Dugmore, A.R.) London, 1924.
Afr 4070.35.5 — The vast Sudan. (Dugmore, A.R.) N.Y., 1925.
Afr 8335.5 — Vatcher, William Henry. White laager. London, 1965.
Afr 3330.5 — Vatikiotis, P.J. Egyptian army in politics. Bloomington, 1961.
Afr 3138.10.10 — Vatikiotis, P.J. The Fatimid theory of state. Lahore, 1957.
Afr 3310.100 — Vatikiotis, Panayiotis Jerasimof. Egypt since the revolution. London, 1968.

Afr 3199.69 — Vatikiotis, Panayiotis Jerasimof. The modern history of Egypt. London, 1969.
Afr 3986.962 — Vatolina, L.N. Ekonomika Obedinenie Arabskoi Respubliki. Moscow, 1962.
Afr 9558.29 — Vattemare, H. David Livingstone. Paris, 1879.
Afr 2929.11.11 — Vatter, E. Die Grundzüge einer Landeskunde von Tripolitanien. Marburg, 1912.
Afr 2929.11.12 — Vatter, E. Tripolitanien: Grundzüge zu einer Landeskunde. Strassburg, 1912.
Afr 2802.6F — Vattier de Bourville, T. Coup d'oeil sur la Cyrénaique. n.p., n.d.
Afr 5406.60 — Vaucaire, Michel. Paul Duchaillu. N.Y., 1930.
Afr 2223.961.10 — Vaucher, G. Le plan de Constantine et la République Algérienne de demain. Neuchâtel, 1961.
Afr 1495.3 — Vaucher, G. Sous les cèdres d'Ifrane. Paris, 1962.
Afr 3310.55 — Vaucher, Georges. General Abdel Nasser. Paris, 1959. 2v.
Afr 9488.89 — Vaughan-Williams, H. A visit to Lobengula in 1889. Pietermaritzburg, 1947.
Afr 3978.83.10 — Vaujany, H. Le Caire et ses environs. Paris, 1883.
Afr 3068.81 — Vaujany, H. Histoire de l'Egypte, depuis les temps les plus reculés jusqu'à nos jours. Le Caire, 1881.
Afr 1570.8 — Vaulx, A. de. La France et le Maroc. Paris, 1903.
Afr 609.60.15 — Vaulx, Bernard de. En Afrique. Paris, 1960.
Afr 2318.1.10 — Vaysseties, E. Histoire de Constantine. Constantine, 1869.
Afr 115.109 — Vazquez-Figueros, Alberto. Africa encadenada. 1. ed. Barcelona, 1963.
Afr 1658.35 — Vazquez Sastre, G. En tierras del rif. Melilla, 1913.
Afr 8289.01.35F — Veber, Jean. Die boeren-kampen. Amsterdam, 1901.
Afr 4513.36.40 — Vecchi, B.V. La conquista del Tigrai. Milano, 1936.
Afr 4700.35.5 — Vecchi, B.V. L'Italia ai margini d'Etiopia. Milano, 1935.
Afr 4785.25 — Vecchi, B.V. Migiurtinia. Torino, 1933.
Afr 4700.37.20 — Vecchi, B.V. Nel sud dell'impero. Milano, 1937.
Afr 4700.27.20 — Vecchi, B.V. Satto il soffio del monsone. Milano, 1927.
Afr 4785.37 — Vecchi, B.V. Vecchio Benadir. Milano, 1930.
Afr 4766.15.4 — Vecchi, Bernardo V. Somalia. 4a ed. Milano, 1936.
Afr 2850.3 — Vecchi, P. Italy's civilizing mission in africa. N.Y., 1912.
Afr 4766.20 — Vecchi di Val Cismon, C.M. Orizzonti d'impero. Milano, 1935.
Afr 4785.37 — Vecchio Benadir. (Vecchi, B.V.) Milano, 1930.
Afr 8320.10 — Vechten en vluchten van beyers en kemp. (Naude, J.F.) Rotterdam, n.d.
Afr 5968.2 — Veciana Vilaldach, Antonio de. Los Bujeba. Madrid, 1956.
Afr 5967.2 — Veciana Vilaldach, Antonio de. La secta del Bwiti en la Guinea española. Madrid, 1958.
Afr 6919.41.5 — Vedden, H. Inleiding tot die geskiedenis van Suidwes-Afrika. Kaapstad, 1941.
Afr 6919.34.5 — Vedder, H. South-west Africa in early times. London, 1938.
Afr 6919.34.6 — Vedder, H. South-west Africa in early times. London, 1966.
Afr 6990.90.20 — Vedder, Heinrich. Kort verhale uit 'n lang lewe. Kaapstad, 1953.
Afr 115.85 — Vedovato, Giuseppe. Studi africani e asiatici. Firenze, 1964. 3v.
Afr 3818.4 — Veenstra, Johanna. Pioneering for Christ in the Sudan. London, 1928.
Afr 8095.82 — Veertien gedenktekens van Suid-Afrika. (Tonder, Johannes.) Kaapstad, 1965.
Afr 12785.89.140 — Vehi-ciosane, ou Blanche-genèse, suivi du Mandat. (Ousmane, Sembene.) Paris, 1965.
Afr 8252.348 — Vein of gold. (Struben, Charles.) Cape Town, 1957.
Afr 5056.83 — Veistroffer, Albert. Vingt ans dans la brousse africaine. Lille, 1931.
Afr 8659.36.5 — A veld farmer's adventures. (Lea, Henry.) London, 1936.
Afr 7812.236 — Velde, M.W. Economie belge et Congo belge. Thèse. Nancy, 1936.
Afr 1975.4 — Veldtogt van het fransch-afrikaansche leger tegen Klein-Kabylie in 1851. (Booms, P.G.) Hertogenbosch, 1852.
Afr 608.91.10 — Velten, Carl. Schilderungen Suaheli. Göttingen, 1901.
Afr 44615.2 — Velton, Carl. Swahili prose texts. London, 1965.
Afr 47619.5 — Venda children's songs. (Blacking, John.) Johannesburg, 1967.
Afr 8340.11 — Vengeance as a policy in Afrikanderland. (Dormer, F.J.) London, 1901.
Afr 5442.5 — Vennetier, Pierre. Geographie du Congo-Brazzaville. Paris, 1966.
Afr 5440.15 — Vennetier, Pierre. Les hommes et leur activités dans le Nord du Congo-Brazzaville. Paris, 1965.
Afr 7135.10 — Venter, Al Johannes. The terror fighters: a profile of guerilla warfare in southern Africa. Cape Town, 1969.
Afr 4700.26 — Venti mesi di azione coloniale. (Federzoni, L.) Milano, 1926.
Afr 4719.32 — Ventire anni di vita africana. (Pantano, G.) Firenze, 1932.
Afr 1432.28 — Ventosa, E. Españoles y Marroquies. Barcelona, 1860.
Afr 13340.13.110 — Le ventre. (Tchicaya U Tamsi, Gerald Felix.) Paris, 1964.
Afr 7176.34 — Ventura, Reis. O após-guerra em Angola. Luanda, 1954.
Afr 7122.79 — Ventura, Reis. O caso de Angola. Braga, 1964.
Afr 7176.36 — Ventura, Reis. Os problemas de Angola, no Primeiro Congresso dos Economistas Portugueses. Lisboa, 1956.
Afr 9839.51A — Venture to the interior. (Vanderpost, L.) N.Y., 1951.
Afr 1990.21.5 — Les vêpres marocaines. v.1-2. (Alby, E.) Paris, 1853.
Afr 2489.3 — Vera relazione copia di lettera scritta. (Garzia, G.D.) Venezia, 1677.
Afr 1658.15 — Vera Salas, A. El Rif occidental. Melilla, 1918.
Afr 1609.16 — Vera Salas, Antonio. Porvenir de Espana en Marruecos. Toledo, 1916.
Afr 7809.65 — Verbeck, Roger. Le Congo en question. Paris, 1965.
Afr 7913.5 — Verbeken, A. Msiri. Bruxelles, 1956.
Afr 7850.53 — Verbeken, A. La première traversée du Katanga en 1806. Bruxelles, 1953.
Afr 7815.32 — Verbeken, A. La révolte des Batetela en 1895. Bruxelles, 1958.
Afr 9599.54 — Verbeken, Auguste. Contribution à la géographie historique du Katanga et de régions voisines. Bruxelles, 1954.
Afr 618.7 — Verbreitung der Fallenjagd in Afrika. Inaug.-Diss. (Keller, E.) Berlin, 1936.
Afr 7809.60.15 — Verbung, C. Afscheid van Kongo. Antwerpen, 1960.
Afr 7175.76 — A verdade sobre Angola. (Iglesias, Luis.) Rio de Janeiro, 1961.
Afr 7122.80 — A verdade sobre os acontecimentos de Angola. T.1-2. 2.ed. (Barreiros, Americo.) Angola, 1961.

Afr 4555.40.3.5 Verdadeira informação das terras do Preste João das Indias. (Alvares, Francisco.) Lisboa, 1943.

Afr 1103.5 Verdadeira noticia da grande esquadra que do reino de Napoles sahio em corso contra os Mouros de Argel. Lisboa, 1757.

Afr 4555.40.3F Verdadeiro informação das terras do Preste João das Indias. (Alvares, Francisco.) Lisboa, 1889.

Afr 6463.10 Verde Kenya. Con presentazione di Giovanni Urbani. (Olivotti, Guiseppe.) Venezia, 1967.

Afr 7850.5 Verdick, E. Les premiers jours au Katanga. Bruxelles, 1952.

Afr 5426.100.60 Verdict on Schweitzer. (McKnight, G.) London, 1964.
Afr 8685.27.5 Verdict on South Africa. (Joshi, Pranshankar S.) Bombay, 1945.

Afr 6738.35 Vereet, E.P.A. Het zwarte leven van Mabumba. n.p., 1935.
Afr 3993.967.2 Vereinigte Arabische Republik. (Kornrumpf, Hans-Jurgen.) Opladen, 1967.

Afr 2762.3 Verfassung der Tuareg. (Koehler, A.) Gotha, 1903.
Afr 9086.16 Verfassungsentwickelung Transvaals. (Huessen, F.) Karlsruhe, 1909.

Afr 1838.4 Die verfassungsentwicklung von Algerien. (Gmelin, H.) Hamburg, 1911.

Afr 609.56.5 Vergani, Orio. Quarantacinque gradi all'ombra, attraverso l'Africa, dalla Città del Capo al Cairo. Torino, 1964.

Afr 590.80 Verger, Pierre. Bahia and the West Africa trade, 1549-1851. Ibadan, 1964.

Afr 590.80.5 Verger, Pierre. Flux et reflux de la traité des Nègres entre le Golfe de Boain et Bahia de Todos os Santos de XVIIe au XIXe siècle. Paris, 1968.

Afr 5368.15 Verger, Pierre. Le Fort St. Jean-Baptiste d'Ajuda. n.p., 1966.

Afr 2030.300 Verges, Jacques. Les disparus. Lausanne, 1959.
Afr 7582.5 Verhaegen, Benoit. Rébellions au Congo. Leopoldville, 1966.

Afr 590.58 Verhoeven, J.C.M. Jacques de Dixmude. Bruxelles, 1929.
Afr 5001.109 Verin, V.P. Prezidentskie republiki v Afrike. Moscow, 1963.

Afr 1822.2PF Vérité, liberté, cahier d'information sur la guerre d'Algérie. Paris. 2+

Afr 8659.65.5 Vérité pour l'Afrique du Sud. (Fournier, Gilles.) Paris, 1965.

Afr 5635.10.5 Verité sur la guerre de Madagascar par le colonel XXX. Toulouse, 1896.

Afr 2025.6.3 La vérité sur l'Algérie. (Hess, Jean.) Paris, 19- .
Afr 2025.6 La vérité sur l'Algérie. (Hess, Jean.) Paris, 1905.
Afr 4259.31 La vérité sur l'Ethiopie révélée après le couronnement du roi des rois. (Gabre-Hiot, A.) Lausanne, 1931.

Afr 5620.10 La verité sur Madagascar. (Lux.) Paris, 1896.
Afr 1110.10 Vérités sur l'Afrique du Nord. (Boyer de Latour, Pierre.) Paris, 1956.

Afr 510.100 Vérités sur l'Afrique noire. (Marchand, Jean Paul.) Paris, 1959.

Afr 2223.933 Der Verkehr Algeriens-Tunesiens mit Frankreich. Inaug. Diss. (Münnich, H.) Leipzig, 1933.

Afr 8110.3.10 Verkenner in koopmansland. (Haantjes, Jacob.) Amsterdam, 1946.

Afr 7809.23 Verlaine, Louis. Notre colonie, contribution à la recherche de la méthode de colonisation. Bruxelles, 1923.

Afr 8089.65.10 Die verlede spreek. (Jaarsreld, Floris.) Pretoria, 1965.
Afr 2749.58.13 Verlet, Bruno. Le Sahara. Paris, 1962.
Afr 7809.50 Verleyen, E.J.B. Congo. Bruxelles, 1950.
Afr 8378.200.11 Vermaak, Christopher J. Braam Fischer. Johannesburg, 1966.

Afr 8050.28 Vermaak, Christopher Johann. The red trap: Communism and violence in South Africa. Johannesburg, 1966.

Afr 2710.10 Vermale, Paul. Au Sahara pendant la guerre europèenne. Alger, 1926.

Afr 8289.36.5 Verme, L. dal. La guerra anglo-boera. Roma, 1936.
Afr 7350.12 Vermont Colonization Society. Annual report. Montpelier. 40,1859+

Afr 1608.99.3 Verneau, R. Le Maroc et les Canaries. Paris, 1899.
Afr 8685.98 Verner, Beryl Anne. Huguenots in South Africa; a bibliography. Cape Town, 1967.

Afr 7809.03 Verner, S.P. Pioneering in Central Africa. Richmond, 1903.

Afr 3708.12F Verner, Willoughby. Sketches in the Soudan. 2d ed. London, 1886.

Afr 1380.8 Vernet Gines, Juan. Historia de Marruecos, la islamizacion. Tetuan, 1957.

Afr 5190.3 Verneuil, V. Mes aventures au Sénégal. Paris, 1858.
Afr 1738.35 Vernier, Victor. La singuliere zone de Tanger. Paris, 1955.

Afr 1259.27.25 Vernon, M. Sands, palms and minarets. London, 1927.
Afr 1609.27 Vernon, Paul E. Morocco from a motor. London, 1927.
Afr 28.5 Veröffentliche Briefe,Aufsätze und Werke. (Schweinfurth, G.) Berlin, 1907.

Afr 530.3 Veröffentlichungen. (Germany. Kolonialamt.) Jena. 6v.

Afr 4615.1 Vers Fachoda. (Michel, C.) Paris, 1901.
Afr 4368.10 Vers la lumière. 2e ed. (Coulbeaux, J.B.) Paris, 1926.
Afr 7812.256.5 Vers la promotion de l'économie indigène. (Brussels. Université Libre.) Bruxelles, 1956.

Afr 1571.16 Vers le Maroc, lettres du Sud-Oranais, 1903-1906. (Lyautey, L.H.G.) Paris, 1937.

Afr 5406.198 Vers le Nil français. (Castellani, Charles.) Paris, 1898.
Afr 725.17.3F Vers les grands lacs de l'Afrique orientale, d'après les notes de l'explorateur. 3. ed. (Heudebert, Lucien.) Paris, 19- .

Afr 4559.33 Vers les terres hostiles de l'Ethiopie. (Monfried, Henri de.) Paris, 1933.

Afr 7575.5A Vers l'indépendance du Congo et du Ruanda-Urundi. (Bilsen, Antoine.) Kraainem, 1958.

Afr 2209.35.4 Vers l'oasis, en Algérie. (Henriot, Emile.) Paris, 1935.
Afr 3040.25 Vers l'unité de juridiction en Egypte. Thèse. (Fahmy, Ahmed.) Paris, 1930.

Afr 1570.47 Vers Taza. (Caussin.) Paris, 1922.
Afr 8028.45 Versamelde Suid-Afrikaanse biografieë. (Olivier, Le Roux.) Kaapstad, 1963.

Afr 8250.10 Verschoyle, F. Cecil Rhodes, his political life and speeches 1881-1900. London, 1900.

Afr Doc 4308.145 Verslag oor geboortes Suid-Afrikaen suidwes-Afrika, 1958 tot 1963. Report on births. (South Africa. Bureau of Statistics.) Pretoria, 1965.

Afr 4513.39 Verso l'impero. (Lessona, A.) Firenze, 1939.
Afr 7820.8 Verstraeten, E. Six années d'action sociale au Maniema, 1948-1953. Bruxelles, 1954.

Afr 6740.5 Verwald-Dokumente. (Mansfield, Alfred.) Berlin, 1908.

Afr 550.138 Verwimp, E. Thirty years in the African wilds. London, 1938.

Afr 8378.379.15 Verwoerd, fotobiografie, pictorial biography, 1901-1966. Johannesburg, 1966.

Afr 8378.379 Verwoerd, Hendrik Frensch. Verwoerd aan die woord. 3. druk. Johannesburg, 1966.

Afr 8378.379.25 Verwoerd. (Hepple, Alexander.) Harmondsworth, 1967.
Afr 8378.379.5 Verwoerd - the end, a look-back from the future. (Allighan, Garry.) London, 1961.

Afr 8378.379 Verwoerd aan die woord. 3. druk. (Verwoerd, Hendrik Frensch.) Johannesburg, 1966.

Afr 8378.379.20 Verwoerd is dead. (Botha, Jan.) Cape Town, 1967.
Afr 5045.15 A very naked people. (Londres, Albert.) N.Y., 1929.
Afr 8659.67 A very strange society. (Drury, Allen.) N.Y., 1967.
Afr 4060.6F I vescovi giacobiti della Nubia. (Monneret de Villard, U.) Le Caire, 1934.

Afr 1618.24 Vestido y adorno de la mujer musulmana de Vêbala (Marruecos). (Albarracin de Martinez Ruiz, Joaquina.) Madrid, 1964.

Afr 8089.66.25 Vesting van die suide. (Roosenthal, Eric.) Kaapstad, 1966.

Afr 7175.8 Veth, Pieter J. Daniel Veths reizer in Angola. Haarlem, 1887.

Afr 2208.45 Veuillot, L. Les Français en Algérie. 3e ed. Tours, 1863.
Afr 1450.1 Veyre, Gabriel. Au Maroc dans l'intimité du sultan. Paris, n.d.

Afr 12015.15 Vezinet, Paul. Pages africaines. Paris, 1963-[1966-]. 5v.

Afr 9489.11 Via Rhodesia. (Mansfield, C.) London, 1911.
Afr 5385.32 Viagem de Africa em o reino de Dahome. (Pires, Vicente F.) São Paulo, 1957.

Afr 7190.35 Viagem de Lisboa a ilha de San Tome,...tradução da lingua italiana para a portugues (Seculo XVI). Lisboa, 194-.

Afr 7020.30 Viagem do principe real julho-setembro 1907. (Ayres d'Ornellas.) Lisboa, 1928.

Afr 608.46.5 Viagems e apontamentos de um Portuense em Africa. (Silva Porto, Antonio Francisco Ferreira da.) Lisboa, 1942.

Afr 679.40.10 Viagens. (Ca da Mosto, A.) Lisboa, 194-.
Afr 4555.00 Viagens de Pedro da Covilhan. (Ficalho.) Lisboa, 1898.
Afr 115.3 Viagens explorações dos portugueses. (Cardeiro, L. Ed.) Lisboa, 1881.

Afr 5842.4.5 Viaggi al Madagascar, alle isole Comore ed allsola di Francia. (Saint-Pierre, J.H.B. de.) Prato, 1844.

Afr 699.13 Viaggi in Africa. (Elena, Duchess of Aosta.) Milano, 1913.

Afr 4557.97 Viaggi in Etiopia. (Pacelli, M.) Napoli, 1797.
Afr 2928.19 Viaggio da Tripoli di Barberia. (Cella, Paolo della.) Genova, 1819.

Afr 2928.19.2 Viaggio da Tripoli di Barberia. 3e ed. (Cella, Paolo della.) Città di Castello, 1912.

Afr 7806.66.5 Viaggio del P. Michael Angelo de Guattini da Reggio. (Guattini, M.A.) Reggio, 1672.

Afr 3978.40.5 Viaggio della spedizione romana in Egitto. v.1. (Ravioli, C.) Roma, 1870.

Afr 3163.8 Viaggio di Domenico Trevisan, 1512. (Pagani, Z.) Venice, 1875.

Afr 605.56.7 Il viaggio di Giovan Leone e le navigazioni. (Ramusio, G.B.) Venezia, 1837.

Afr 4742.20 Viaggio nel Mar Rosso e tra i Bogos (1870). (Issel, A.) Milano, 1872.

Afr 609.60.80 Viaggio nell'Africa nera in fermento. (Ragusin Righi, Livio.) Trieste, 1960.

Afr 2208.32.5 Viaje a la Argelia. (Malo de Molina, M.) Valencia, 1852.
Afr 3978.83.7 Viaje a oriente. (Malanco, Luis.) Mexico, 1883. 2v.

Afr 609.60.75 Viaje por Africa. (Torres, Joaquin.) Buenos Aires, 1960.
Afr 1608.78.6 Viajes por Marruecos. (Gatell, Joaquin.) Madrid, 1878-79.
Afr 1608.75 Viajes por Marruecos. (Urrestarazu, D.T. de A. de.) Madrid, 18- .

Afr 1493.45 Vial, Jean. Le Maroc héroique. Paris, 1938.
Afr 2030.40 Vialet, Georges. L'Algérie restera française. Paris, 1957.

Afr 2260.10 Vian, L. L'Algérie contemporaine. Paris, 1863.
Afr 5243.174.30 La Viande et la graine, mythologie dogon. (Zahan, Dominique.) Paris, 1969.

Afr 5760.20 Vianes, S. Contribution à l'étude des migrations antesaka. Paris, 1959.

Afr 210.61.90 Vianney, J.J. The new states of Africa. 1st ed. n.p. 1961.

Afr 6275.11 Viard, E. Au Bas-Niger. 3. ed. Paris, 1886.
Afr 1608.90 Viaud, J. Au Maroc. Paris, 1890.
Afr 1608.89.20 Viaud, J. Into Morocco. Chicago, n.d.
Afr 1069.38.5 A vicarious trip to the Barbary coast. (Berenson, Mary.) London, 1938.

Afr 1658.25 La victoire franco-espagnole dans le Rif. (Laure, August M.E.) Paris, 1927.

Afr 1550.17 Une victoire sans guerre. (Grand-Carteret, J.) Paris, 1911.

Afr 1947.6 Victoires de la charité. Paris, 1846.
Afr 14692.41.100 Victor, Geraldo Bessa. Cubata abandonada. Lisboa, 1958.
Afr 14692.41.60 Victor, Geraldo Bessa. Mucanda. Braga, 1964.
Afr 14692.41.120 Victor, Geraldo Bessa. Sanzala sem batuque. Braga, 1967.
Afr 8145.34 Victor, Osmund. The salient of South Africa. London, 1931.

Afr 9510.5.10 The Victoria Falls, a handbook to the Victoria Falls, the Batoka Gorge and part of the upper Zambesi River. 2. ed. (Fagan, Brian M.) Lusaka, 1964.

Afr 9510.5PF The Victoria Falls, Zambesi River. (Baines, Thomas.) London, 1865.

Afr 9510.5.5 The Victoria Falls. (Clark, John Desmond.) Lusaka, 1952.
Afr 765.3 Der Victoria-Njansa. (Perthes, Joachim.) Göttingen, 1913.
Afr 6889.3 The Victoria Nyanza. (Kollmann, P.) London, 1899.
Afr 1270.5 Victory across French North Africa. (Broutz, Charles.) Alger, 1943.

Afr 1609.31.5 Vicuna, Alejandro. Bajo cielo africano. Paris, 1931.
Afr 718.4.15 A vida breve e ardente de Serpa Pinto. (Serpa Pinto, Carlota de.) Lisboa, 1937.

Afr 1409.15 Vida de Don Felipe de Africa. (Oliver Asin, J.) Madrid, 1955.

Afr 4295.2 Vida de Takla Haymanot. (Almeida, M. de.) Lisboa, 1899.
Afr 150.9 Vida do Infante Dom Henrique. (Freire, F.J.) Lisboa, 1758.
Afr 150.3.5 Vida do Infante Dom Henrique de Portugal. (Major, R.H.) Lisboa, 1876.

Afr 7315.20.10 A vida d'uma tribu sul-africana. (Junod, H.A.) Famalição, 1917.

Afr 150.2.20 — Vida e obra do Infante Dom Henrique. (Nemesio, Vitorino.) Lisboa, 1959. 2v.

Afr 674.93.30 — Vida e obras de Gomes Eanes de Zurara. (Eannes de Azurara, G.) Lisboa, 1949. 2v.

Afr 7912.15.5 — Vida y muerte de Lumumba. (Vos, Pierre de.) Mexico, 1962.

Afr 2030.462.115 — Vidal-Naquet, P. La raison d'état. Paris, 1962.

Afr 2030.463.5 — Vidal-Naquet, P. Torture, cancer of democracy. Harmondsworth, 1963.

Afr 2030.225 — Vidal-Naquet, Pierre. L'affaire Audin. Paris, 1958.

Afr 4365.1 — Vie...Justin de Jacobis. 2 ed. (Demimuid, M.) Paris, 1906.

Afr 5748.98.10 — La vie à Madagascar. (Mager, Henri.) Paris, 1898.

Afr 2208.56.10 — La vie arabe. (Mornaud, F.) Paris, 1856.

Afr 2228.8 — La vie arabe et la société musulmane. (Daumas, E.) Paris, 1869.

Afr 510.90 — La vie coloniale. (Delaporte, Maurice.) Paris, 1944.

Afr 12985.65.120 — Une vie de boy, roman. (Oyono, Ferdinand.) Paris, 1956.

Afr 4306.1 — Vie de Lalibala. (Perruchon, J.) Paris, 1892.

Afr 150.9.6 — Vie de l'Infant Dom Henri de Portugal. (Freire, F.J.) Lisbonne, 1781.

Afr 5235.128.25 — La vie de René Caillié. (Lamande, André.) Paris, 1928.

Afr 4513.36.150 — Le vie dell'impero. (Pinti, Luigi.) Roma, 1936.

Afr 5045.11 — La vie des noirs d'Afrique. 4. ed. (Demaison, Andre.) Paris, 1956.

Afr 5340.10 — Une vie d'explorateur. (Binger, G.) Paris, 1938.

Afr 3740.6.30 — Vie du Général Marchand. (Delebecque, J.) Paris, 1936.

Afr 3740.6.35 — Vie du Général Marchand. (Delebecque, J.) Paris, 1936.

Afr 1955.7.5 — La vie du général Yusuf. 10e éd. (Constantin-Weyer, M.) Paris, 1930.

Afr 7809.43.5 — La vie du noir. (Franssen, F.) Liège, 1943.

Afr 5219.02 — La vie du sultan Rabah. (Dujarris, G.) Paris, 1902.

Afr 2650.3 — La vie d'un douar. (Bardin, Pierre.) Paris, 1965.

Afr 2230.42 — Vie d'un peuple mort. (Sas, Pierre.) Paris, 1961.

Afr 7912.15 — Vie et mort de Lumumba. (Vos, Pierre de.) Paris, 1961.

Afr 2232.8 — La vie féminine au Mzab. (Goichon, A.) Paris, 1927. 2v.

Afr 3215.15 — La vie héroïque et romantique du docteur Charles Cuny. (Roy, H.) Paris, 1930.

Afr 2618.20 — La vie littéraire et intellectuelle en Tunisie de 1900 à 1937. (Chatelain, Yves.) Paris, 1937.

Afr 1340.17 — La vie municipale au Maroc. Thèse. (Decroux, Paul.) Lyon, 1931.

Afr 2218.11 — La vie musulmane en Algérie d'après la jurisprudence de la première moitié du XXe siècle. (Charnay, Jean Paul.) Paris, 1965.

Afr 2026.7 — La vie politique à Alger de 1940 à 1944. (Davan, Y.M.) Paris, 1963.

Afr 2209.63 — La vie quotidienne à Alger à la veille de l'intervention française. (Boyer, P.) Paris, 1963.

Afr 1713.4.10 — La vie quotidienne à Fes en 1900. (Letourneau, Roger.) Paris, 1965.

Afr 7560.15 — La vie quotidienne au royaume de Kongo du XVI au XVIII siècle. (Balandier, Georges.) Paris, 1965. X Cg

Afr 7062.10 — Viegas, Luis A.C. Guiné portuguesa. Lisboa, 1936. 2v.

Afr 2308.10 — Vieil Alger. n.p., n.d.

Afr 555.95 — Vieil empire. (Baudu, Paul.) Paris, 1957.

Afr 5322.5 — Vieillard, G. Notes sur les coutumes des Peuls au Fouta Djallon. Paris, 1939.

Afr 14692.41.1110 — Vieira, Luandino. A cidade e a infância. Lisboa, 1957?

Afr 14692.41.1100 — Vieira, Luandino. Luuanda. Luanda, 1963.

Afr 1576.3F — Vieira da S. y Guimaraes. Marrocos e três mestres da ordem de cristo, memória publicada por ordem da academia das sciências de Lisboa. Lisboa, 1916.

Afr 1550.56 — Vieleux, Christian. Aspects marocains. La Rochelle, 1957.

Afr 5796.5.5 — Vienne, Emile. Notice sur Mayotte et les Comores. Paris, 1900.

Afr 6192.4.3 — Vier Jahre in Asante-Tagebücher der Missionäre Ramseyer und Kühne. (Gundert, H.) Basel, 1875.

Afr 6780.11 — Vier jahre Weltkrieg in Deutsche-Ostafrika. (Arning, W.) Hannover, 1919.

Afr 609.42.5 — Viera, Josef. Ein Kontinent rückt näher. München, 1942.

Afr 8278.99.37 — Vierde verzameling (Correspondentie 1900-1902). Deel 1-2. (Leyds, W.J.) 's-Gravenhage, 1934. 3v.

Afr 8950.22 — Vietzen, Colleen. The Natal almanac and yearly register, 1863-1906. Cape Town, 1963.

Afr 1750.8 — Vieuchange, M. Smara, the forbidden city. N.Y., 1932.

Afr 12985.65.110 — Le vieux Nègre et la médaille. (Oyono, Ferdinand.) Paris, 1956.

Afr 3068.31 — View of ancient and modern Egypt. (Russell, M.) Edinburgh, 1831.

Afr 3068.31.4 — View of ancient and modern Egypt. (Russell, M.) Edinburgh, 1838.

Afr 3068.31.2 — View of ancient and modern Egypt. (Russell, M.) N.Y., 1836.

Afr 3068.31.6 — View of ancient and modern Egypt. 6th ed. (Russell, M.) Edinburgh, 1844.

Afr 6143.26 — A view of Sierra Leone. (Migeod, Frederick W.) London, 1926.

Afr 1258.16.5 — A view of the present condition of the states of Barbary. (Janson, William.) London, 1816.

Afr 11774.39.100 — A view of vultures. (Scholefield, Alan.) London, 1966.

Afr 4571.1 — Views in central Abyssinia. London, 1868.

Afr 3978.02.1PF — Views in Egypt, from the original drawings in the possession of Sir Robert Ainslie. (Mayer, L.) London, 1801.

Afr 3978.02.5PF — Views in Egypt. (Mayer, Luigi.) London, 1804.

Afr 5842.11F — Views in the Mauritius, or Isle of France. (Bradshaw, T.) London, 1832.

Afr 1738.12 — Views of tangier. n.p., n.d.

Afr 3979.31.5 — Views of typical desert scenery in Egypt. (Egypt. Survey Department.) Giza, 1931.

Afr 8325.3 — Vigilance papers. (South Africa. Vigilance Committee.) Cape Town. 1,1900+

Afr 2731.15.45 — Vignaud, Jean. Frère Charles. Paris, 1947.

Afr 4558.97 — Vigneras, S. Une mission française en Abyssinie. Paris, 1897.

Afr 4869.00 — Vigneras, S. Notice sur la côte française des Somalis. Paris, 1900.

Afr 2025.11.15 — Vignes, Kenneth. Le gouverneur général Tirman. Paris, 1958. 2v.

Afr 1100.1 — Vignols, L. La piraterie sur l'Atlantique. Rennes, 1890.

Afr 2208.88 — Vignon, L. La France dans l'Afrique du nord. Paris, 1888.

Afr 2260.15 — Vignon, L. La France en Algérie. Paris, 1893.

Afr 4558.81.5 — Vigoni, Pippo. Abissinia, giornale di un viaggio. Milano, 1881.

Afr 2938.30 — Vigor di vita in Tripolitania (anno 1928). (Tripolitania. Ufficio Studi e Propaganda.) Tripoli, 1928.

Afr 8180.5.4 — Vijf voorlezingen over de landverhuizing der hollandsche Boeren. (Cloete, Henry.) Kaapstad, 1856.

Afr 8160.6 — Vijn, Cornelius. Cetshwayo's Dutchman. London, 1880.

Afr 9047.35 — Vilakazi, A. Zulu transformations. Pietermaritzburg, 1965.

Afr 49742.41.100 — Vilakazi, B.W. Udingiswayo kajobe. London, 1939.

Afr 49742.41.700 — Vilakazi, B.W. Zulu horizons. Cape Town, 1962.

Afr 2230.8 — Vilbort, J. En Kabylie. Paris, 1875.

Afr 8289.02.22 — Viljoen, B.J. Mijne herinneringen...anglo-boeren-oorlog. Amsterdam, 1902.

Afr 8289.02.22.2 — Viljoen, B.J. My reminiscences of Anglo-Boer war London, 1902.

Afr 5947.10 — Villa-cisneros. (Coll, A.) Madrid, 1933.

Afr 1608.93.7 — Villaescusa, M.H. La cuestion de Marruecos y el conflicto de melilla. Barcelona, 1893.

Afr Doc 3409.300 — Village economic surveys. (Tanganyika. Treasury. Central Statistical Bureau.) Dar es Salaam. 1961-1962

Afr 3978.53 — Village life in Egypt. (Saint John, Bayle.) Boston, 1853. 2v.

Afr 8847.37 — Village of the sea. (Tredgold, Ardeme.) Cape Town, 1965.

Afr 5023.5 — Les villages de liberté en Afrique noire française, 1887-1910. (Bouche, Denise.) Paris, 1968.

Afr 1635.21 — Villages et kasbas berberes. (Montagne, R.) Paris, 1930.

Afr 5333.4 — Villamur, R. Les coutumes Agni. Paris, 1904.

Afr 5342.2 — Villamur, R. Notre colonie de la Côte-d'Ivoire. Paris, 1903.

Afr 4513.43 — Villani, Luigi. Storia diplomatica del conflitto italo-etiopico. Bologna, 1943.

Afr 2885.5 — Villard, H.S. Libya. Ithaca, 1956.

Afr 4513.36.15 — Villari, Luigi. Italy, Abyssinia and the League. Rome, 1936.

Afr 5549.12 — Villars, E.J. Madagascar, 1638-1894, établissement des Français dans l'île. Paris, 1912.

Afr 676.66 — Villault, N. Relation des côtes d'Afrique, appellées Guinée. Paris, 1669.

Afr 676.66.5 — Villault, N. Relation des côtes d'Afrique, appellées Guinée. Photocopy. Paris, 1669.

Afr 2308.15 — La ville blanche, Alger et son département. (Melia, Jean.) Paris, 1921.

Afr 12972.41.100 — Ville cruelle. (Biyidi, Alexandre.) Paris, 195-.

Afr 1733.5.25 — La ville de Rabat. (Caille, Jacques.) Vanoest, 1949. 3v.

Afr 5190.15 — Le ville de Thiès. (Savonnet, G.) St. Louis, 1955.

Afr 1713.6 — Une ville d'islam, fes. (Gaillard, H.) Paris, 1905.

Afr 8289.02.29 — Villebois-Mareuil. Carnet de campagne. Paris, 1902.

Afr 8289.01.9 — Villebois Mareuil. Dix mois de campagne chez les Boers. Paris, 1901.

Afr 8289.01.8 — Villebois Mareuil. War notes, diary. London, 1901.

Afr 2373.3 — Les villes de l'Algérie, Tlemcen. (Piesse, Louis.) Paris, 1889. (Changed to XP 3867)

Afr 1609.15.3 — Villes et tribus du Maroc. v.1-11. (Mission Scientifique du Maroc.) Paris, 1915-32. 11v.

Afr 8095.89 — Villiers, Anna de. Vrouegalery. Kaapstad, 1962.

Afr 8688.7.10 — Villiers, Christoffel Coetzee de. Geslagsregisters van die ou Kaapse families. Kaapstad, 1966.

Afr 8688.6 — Villiers, Daniel P. A history of the de Villiers family. Cape Town, 1960.

Afr 4558.92 — Villiers, F. Negus negusti. N.Y., 1892.

Afr 2525.20 — Villiers, G. Derrière le rideau tunisien. Paris, 1955.

Afr 8377.10.5 — Villiers, Hans Heinrich Wicht de. Danger en Afrique du Sud. Paris, 1966.

Afr 8377.10 — Villiers, Hans Heinrich Wicht de. Rivonia, operation Mayibuye. Johannesburg, 1964.

Afr 8320.7 — Villiers, O.T. de. Met De Wet en Steijn in het veld. Amsterdam, 1903.

Afr 2208.71.5 — Villot, E. Moeurs, coutumes, de l'Algérie. 3e ed. Alger, 1888.

Afr 2357.10 — Villot, Roland. Jules Du Pré de Saint Maur. 2. ed. Oran, 1955.

Afr 4582.20 — Vinassa de Regny, P. Dancalia. Roma, 1923.

Afr 626.206 — Vinay, Bernard. L'Afrique commence avec l'Afrique. 1. éd. Paris, 1968.

Afr 608.95 — Vincent, F. Actual Africa. N.Y., 1895.

Afr 5447.5 — Vincent, Jeanne Françoise. Femmes africaines en milieu urbain. Paris, 1966.

Afr 3818.2 — Vindicating a vision. (Elder, Earl.) Philadelphia, 1958.

Afr 7881.2 — Vingt années à Kilo-Moto, 1920-40. (Moulaert, G.) Bruxelles, 1950.

Afr 7808.74 — Vingt années de vie africaine. (Delcommune, A.) Bruxelles, 1922. 2v.

Afr 3300.25 — Vingt années d'Egypte. (Vandenbosch, F.) Paris, 1932.

Afr 5748.85 — Vingt ans à Madagascar. (Lavaissiere, C. de.) Paris, 1885.

Afr 5056.83 — Vingt ans dans la brousse africaine. (Veistroffer, Albert.) Lille, 1931.

Afr 555.149.1C — Les vingt-cinq ans de Coillard au Lessouto. (Fauré, Edouard.) Paris, 1931.

Afr 2223.55 — Vingt-cinq de colonisation nord-africaine. (Société des Fermes Françaises de Tunisie.) Paris, 1931.

Afr 7803.48 — Vingt-cinq ans de mission au Congo. (Jeanroy, V.) Bruxelles, 1923.

Afr 1826.27 — Vingt cinq ans d'histoire algerienne. 4 in 1. (Société Historique Algerienne.) Alger, 1931.

Afr 555.39.20 — Vingt-huit années au Congo. (Augouard, Prosper P.) Vienne, 1905.

Afr 1490.17 — Vingt-six mois au Maroc. (Pierrat, J.) Paris, 1916.

Afr 3198.86 — Vingtrinier, A. Solimar-Pacha...guerres de l'Egypte. Paris, 1886.

Afr 7122.45 — Vinhas, Manuel. Aspectos actuais de Angola. Lisboa, 1961.

Afr 7119.62.10 — Vinhos, Manuel. Para um dialogo sobre Angola. Lisboa, 1962.

Afr 7575.99 — Vinokurov, Iurii N. Kongo. Moskva, 1967.

Afr 5748.65 — Vinson, A. Voyage à Madagascar au couronnement de Radama II. Paris, 1865.

Afr 3978.66 — En orienten. Reseanteckingar fraan Egypten. (Kraemer, R. von.) Stockholm, 1866.

Afr 2230.16 — Violand. Le banditisme en Kabylie. Paris, 1895.

Afr 12884.65.100 — Violent était le vent. (Nokan, Charles.) Paris, 1966.

Afr 5405.190 — Violette, M. La N'Goko-Sangha. Paris, 1914.

Afr 3979.56.10F — Viollet, Roger. Egypt. N.Y., 1957.

Afr 3243.10   Vosstanie Arabi-Pashi v Egipte. (Kilberg, K.I.)
Moscow, 1937.

Afr Doc 3814.10F   Votes and proceedings. (Rhodesia, Southern. Legislative
Assembly.)
41v.

Afr Doc 3514.10   Votes and proceedings. (Rhodesia and Nyasaland. Assembly.)
1954-1963
10v.

Afr 9070.10F   Vowles, Margaret. The city of Pietermaritzburg.
Capetown, 1946.

Afr 5180.20   Voyage...aux sources du Sénégal et de la Gambie, 1818.
(Mollien, G.T.) Paris, 1820.

Afr 8657.90   Voyage...dans l'intérieur de l'Afrique. (Le Vaillant, F.)
Lausanne, 1790.
2v.

Afr 852.3   Voyage à la côte de Guinée. (Boudyck Bastiaanse, J.) La
Haye, 1853.

Afr 7175.7   Voyage à la côte occidentale d'Afrique. (Grandpré, 0. de.)
Paris, 1801.
2v.

NEDL Afr 698.66   Voyage à la côte orientale, 1866. (Horner.) Paris, 1872.

Afr 5842.4   Voyage à l'Isle de France. (Saint-Pierre, J.H.B. de.)
Amsterdam, 1773.
2v.

Afr 5748.40   Voyage à Madagascar...Camores (1825-30). (Lequevel de
Lacombe, B.F.) Paris, 1840.
2v.

Afr 5748.84.7   Voyage à Madagascar. (Macquarie, J.L.) Paris, 1884.

Afr 5748.57.10   Voyage à Madagascar. (Pfeiffer, Ida R.) Paris, 1881.

Afr 5747.91   Voyage à Madagascar. (Rochon, A.M.) Paris, 1791.

Afr 5748.95.3F   Voyage à Madagascar (1889-1890). (Catat, Louis.)
Paris, 1895.

Afr 5748.65   Voyage à Madagascar au couronnement de Radama II. (Vinson,
A.) Paris, 1865.

Afr 4070.23   Voyage à Meroe, au Fleuve Blanc. (Cailliaud, F.)
Paris, 1823-27.
5v.

Afr 698.19   Voyage along the eastern coast of Africa. (Prior, James.)
London, 1819.

Afr 4785.3   Voyage au Cap des Aromates (Africa orientale). (Revoil,
G.) Paris, 1880.

Afr 7808.32   Voyage au Congo, 1828-1830. (Douville, J.B.) Paris, 1832.
4v.

Afr 7808.32.2   Voyage au Congo, 1829-1830. (Douville, J.B.)
Stuttgart, 1832.
3v.

Afr 7809.55.5   Voyage au Congo et au Ruanda-Urundi. (Vallotton, Henry.)
Bruxelles, 1955.

Afr 5385.16   Voyage au Dahomey. (Dubarry, A.) Paris, n.d.

Afr 5385.11   Voyage au Dahomey et à la Côte-d'Ivoire. (Leherisse, R.)
Paris, 1903.

Afr 3822.8   Voyage au Darfour. (Al-Tunisi, Muhammad Ibn Umar.)
Paris, 1845.

Afr 1680.6   Voyage au goundafa et au sous. (Thomas, L.) Paris, 1918.

Afr 2798.5.5   Voyage au Hoggar. (Grevin, Emmanuel.) Paris, 1936.

Afr 1609.13.12   Voyage au Maroc, 1910-11. (Ladreit de Lacharriere, R.)
Paris, 1913.

Afr 1609.12.15   Voyage au Maroc. Nouvelle ed. (Richet, E.) Paris, 1912.

Afr 1606.40   Voyage au Maroc (1640-41). (Nathaim, D.A.) La Have, 1866.

Afr 5488.5   Voyage au Ouadaï. (Muhammad Ibn Omar.) Paris, 1851.

Afr 7308.80   Voyage au pays de l'ivoire. (Wauters, Alphonse Jules.)
Bruxelles, 190-.

Afr 2975.2   Voyage au pays des Senoussia. (al-Hashayishi, Muhammad ibn
Uthman.) Paris, 1903.

Afr 2940.15.2   Voyage au pays des Senoussia a travers à Tripolitaine et
les pays touareg. 2.ed. (al-Hashayishi, Muhammad ibn
Uthman.) Paris, 1912.

Afr 5760.10   Voyage au pays des Tanala indépendants. (Besson, L.)
n.p., n.d.

Afr 5180.12.5   Voyage au Sénégal. v.1-2. (Durand, J.B.L.) Paris, 1807.

Htn Afr 5180.12*   Voyage au Sénégal. v.1-2 and atlas. (Durand, J.B.L.)
Paris, 1802.
3v.

Afr 5180.21   Voyage au Sénégal pendant les années 1784 et 1785.
(Labarthe, P.) Paris, 1802.

Afr 5842.9   Voyage aux colonies orientales. (Billiard, A.)
Paris, 1822.

Afr 2295.2   Voyage d'Alger aux Ziban (Text and atlas). (Guyon.)
Alger, 1852.
2v.

Afr 3977.99   Voyage dans ... Egypte. v.1-3 + atlas. (Sonnini, C.S.)
Paris, 1799.
4v.

Afr 2207.38.10   Voyage dans la régence d'Alger. (Shaw, Thomas.)
Paris, 1830.

Afr 2207.38.15   Voyage dans la régence d'Alger. (Shaw, Thomas.)
Paris, 1830.

Afr 2207.38.16   Voyage dans la régence d'Alger. Cover 1831. (Shaw,
Thomas.) Paris, 1830.

Afr 2208.33   Voyage dans la régence d'Alger. 3 vols. and atlas.
(Rozet.) Paris, 1833.
4v.

Afr 8658.47   Voyage dans l'Afrique australe...1838-44. (Delegorgue, A.)
Paris, 1847.
2v.

Afr 5180.18   Voyage dans l'Afrique occidentale. Text and atlas.
(Raffenel, A.) Paris, 1846.
2v.

Afr 5180.28   Un voyage dans le Haut-Sénégal. (Foret, Auguste.)
Paris, 1888.

Afr 6168.30   Voyage dans le pays d'Aschantie. (Bowdich, Thomas Edward.)
Paris, 1819.

Afr 5235.186   Voyage dans le Soudan occidental. (Mage, Eugène.)
Paris, 1868.

Afr 2608.84.2   Voyage dans le sud de la Tunisie. 2e ed. (Mayet, Valery.)
Paris, 1887.

Afr 5749.00.10   Voyage dans le sud-ouest. (Grandidier, G.) Paris, 1900.

Afr 1607.91.5   Voyage dans l'empire de Maroc. (Lempriere, G.)
Paris, 1801.

Afr 1028.1   Voyage dans les déserts du Sahara. (Follie.) Paris, 1792.
4 pam.

Afr 5385.23   Voyage dans l'intérieur du royaume de Dahomey.
(Guillevin.) Paris, 1862.

Afr 5318.3.9   Voyage de Guinée. (Bosman, W.) Utrecht, 1705.

Afr 2748.82.4   Voyage de la mission Flatters aux pays des Touareg Azdjers.
(Brosselard-Faidherbe, H.) Paris, 1883.

Afr 810.12   Voyage de Lybie. (Jannequin, C.) Paris, 1643.

Afr 5746.63   Voyage de Madagascar. (Carpeau du Saussay.) Paris, 1722.

Afr 5096.2   Voyage de Paul Soleillet à l'Adrar. (Gravier, Gabriel.)
Rouen, 1881.

Afr 5235.128.10   Le voyage de René Caillié à Tombouctou. (Caillié, René.)
Paris, 1937.

Htn Afr 1606.96*   Voyage de St. Amant. (St. Amant.) Lyon, 1698.

Afr 2609.00.3   Voyage d'études en Tunisie. (Rey, R.) Paris, n.d.

Afr 5056.130.5   Un voyage en A.O.F. (Rondet-Saint, M.) Paris, 1930.

Afr 4558.75   Voyage en Abyssinie, à Zanzibar et aux pays des Ouanika.
(Raffray, A.) n.p., 1875.

Afr 4558.37.2   Voyage en Abyssinie...1835-37. (Combes, Edmond.)
Paris, 1839.
4v.

Afr 4558.44.11   Voyage en Abyssinie. (Lefebvre, Theophile.) Paris, 1844.

Htn Afr 4558.45.2PF*   Voyage en Abyssinie. (Lefebvre, Theophile.)
Paris, 1845-51.
3v.

Htn Afr 4558.45*   Voyage en Abyssinie. v.1-. (Lefebvre, Theophile.)
Paris, 1845.
8v.

Afr 4558.47   Voyage en Abyssinie dans les provinces. (Ferret, A.)
Paris, 1847-48.
2v.

Afr 4558.47PF   Voyage en Abyssinie dans les provinces. Atlas. (Ferret,
A.) Paris, 1847-48.

Afr 4558.85   Voyage en Abyssinie et chez les Gallas-Raias. (Simon,
Gabriel.) Paris, 1885.

Afr 4558.64F   Voyage en Abyssinie execute de 1862 à 1864. Text and atlas.
(Lejean, G.) Paris, 1873.
2v.

Afr 2208.50   Voyage en Afrique. (Joanne, A.) Ixelles, 1850.

Afr 2945.12   Voyage en Afrique au royaume de Barcah et dans la
Cyrénaique à travers le désert. (Pezant, A.) Paris, 1840.

Afr 1257.89   Voyage en Barbarie. (Poiret, J.L.M.) Paris, 1789.
2v.

Afr 4045.14   Il viaggio in Egypto, 1861-1862, di Pasquale Revoltella.
(Cervani, Giulio.) Trieste, 1962.

Afr 3978.46.3   Voyage en Egypte. (Combes, Edmond.) Paris, 1846.

Afr 3978.69.25   Voyage en Egypte (1869). (Fromentin, E.) Paris, 1935.

Afr 3978.44.5   Voyage en Egypte et en Nubie. (Ampere, J.J.) Paris, 1868.

Afr 4070.27   Voyage en Ethiopie au Soudan oriental et dans la Nigritie.
v.1- (Tremaux, P.) Paris, 1862.
2v.

Afr 2608.94   Voyage en Tunisie. (Cagnat.) Paris, 1894.

Afr 8808.72   A voyage from Southhampton to Cape Town. (Chapman,
Charles.) London, 1872.

Afr 4556.59.12   Voyage historique d'Abyssinie. (Lobo, J.) Paris, 1728.

Afr 6275.6   The voyage of the Dayspring. (Hastings, A.C.G.)
London, 1926.

Htn Afr 1947.3*   Voyage pour la rédemption des captives...1720. (Comelin,
F.) Paris, 1721.

Afr 678.49   Voyage sur la côte et dans l'intérieur de l'Afrique
occidentale. (Hecquard, Hyacinthe.) Paris, 1853.

Afr 4610.6   Voyage sur la côte orientale de la Mer Rouge et...de Choa.
(Rochet d'Héricourt, C.E.) Paris, 1841.

Afr 4558.14.5   A voyage to Abyssinia, and travels into the interior of
that country. 1st ed. (Salt, Henry.) London, 1967.

Htn Afr 4556.59.23*   Voyage to Abyssinia. (Lobo, J.) London, 1735.

Afr 4556.59.39   A voyage to Abyssinia. (Lobo, J.) London, 1789.

Afr 4558.14.2   Voyage to Abyssinia. (Salt, Henry.) Philadelphia, 1816.

Afr 6192.6   A voyage to Africa. (Hutton, W.) London, 1821.

Afr 5385.5   A voyage to Africa. (Macleod, John.) London, 1820.

Afr 5180.2   A voyage to Senegal. (Adanson, M.) London, 1759.

Htn Afr 6143.9.2*   Voyage to the river Sierra-Leone. (Matthews, J.)
London, 1788.

Afr 6143.9.5   Voyage to the river Sierra-Leone. (Matthews, J.)
London, 1966.

Afr 6192.17   Voyages, aventures et captivité de J. Bonnat chez les
Achantis. (Gros, Jules.) Paris, 1884.

Afr 2748.81   Les voyages...dans le Sahara. (Soleillet, P.)
Paris, 1881.

Afr 678.95   Voyages à la côte occidentale d'Afrique. (Cadamosto, A.
de.) Paris, 1895.

Afr 1947.7   Voyages and five years captivity in Algiers. (Pfeiffer,
G.S.F.) Harrisburg, 1836.

Afr 1609.03.3   Voyages au Maroc (1899-1901). (Segonzac, de.)
Paris, 1903.

Afr 1609.09.5   Voyages au Maroc (1901-1907). (Brines, A.) Alger, 1909.

Afr 7809.54.5   Voyages aux quartre coins du Congo, 1949-1952. 3.ed.
(Sion, Georges.) Bruxelles, 1954.

Htn Afr 1606.31*   Voyages d'Afrique faicts par le commandement du roy. (Jean
Armand, Called Mustapha.) Paris, 1631.

Afr 1835.1.9   Voyages dans le sud de l'Algérie. (Abu Salem, Called
Al-Aiasi.) Paris, 1846.

Afr 8657.90.51   Voyages de F. Le Vaillant dans l'intérieur de l'Afrique,
1781-1785. v.1-2. (Le Vaillant, F.) Paris, 1932.

Afr 718.28   Les voyages des Portugais...XVI et XVII siècles. (Durand.)
Meaux, 1879.

Htn Afr 606.95*   Les voyages du Sieur Lemaire. (Lemaire.) Paris, 1695.

Afr 7809.14.5   Voyages en Afrique. (Wauters, Alphones Jules.)
Bruxelles, 1914.

Afr 4558.84.5   Voyages en Ethiopie jan. 1882-oct. 1884. (Soleillet,
Paul.) Rouen, 1886.

Afr 6192.9   Voyages en Guinée. (Isert, P.E.) Paris, 1793.

Afr 724.2   Voyages et aventures. (Farde, P.) Gand, 1878.

Afr 5887.5   Voyages et aventures de François Leguat et de ses
compagnons en deux îles désertes 1690-1698. (Leguat, F.)
Paris, 1934.

Afr 5056.157   Voyages et aventures en Afrique française. (Legras, Paul.)
Nancy, 1957.

Afr 1868.85   Voyages extraordinaires. (Mohammed Abou Ras.)
Alger, 1885.

Afr 5874.10.5   Les voyages faits...aux isles Dauphine ou Madagascar.
(Dubois.) Paris, 1674.

Afr 5874.10   Voyages made to Dauphine and Bourbon. (Dubois.)
London, 1897.

Afr 606.95.2.1   Voyages to the Canaries, Cape Verd and the coast of Africa.
(Lemaire.) Edinburgh, 1887.

Afr 5056.12   Voyages to the coast of Africa. (Saugnier.) London, 1792.

Afr 3708.10   Les voyageurs canadiens à l'expédition du Soudan. (Labat,
G.P.) Québec, 1886.

Afr 3979.33.5   Voyageurs et ecrivains français en Egypte. 2. éd. (Carre,
Jean Marie.) Le Caire, 1956.
2v.

Afr 1326.7   Les voyageurs français du Maroc. (Lebel, Roland.)
Paris, 1936.

Afr 9093.27 Wangemann, H. Maleo und Sekukuni. Berlin, 1868.
Afr 8688.5 Die wapens van die ou afrikaanse families. (Pama, C.) Kaapstad, 1959.
Afr 150.8 Wappaens, J.E. Untersuchungen ueber die geographischen Entdeckungen der Portugiesen unter Heinrich dem Seefahrer. Göttingen, 1842.
Afr 8289.01.17 The war against the Dutch republics in South Africa. (Ogden, H.J.) Manchester, 1901.
Afr 8288.99.18 War against war in South Africa. London, 1899-00.
Afr 4513.35.155 War and the workers. (West, J.) N.Y., 1935.
Afr 7200.6 War communiqué. (Frente de Libertação de Moçambique.) Cairo. 2,1966+
Afr 8289.01.11 War impressions. (Mempes, M.) London, n.d.
Afr 4513.36.69 War in Abyssinia. (Badoglio, P.) London, 1937.
Afr 4513.36.69.5 War in Abyssinia. (Badoglio, P.) N.Y., 1937.
Afr 6620.50 The war in Africa, 1914-1917. (O'Neill, H.C.) London, 1919.
Afr 4513.35.160 War in Africa. (Ford, J.W.) N.Y., 1933.
Afr 2030.462 War in Algeria. (Matthews, T.S.) N.Y., 1962.
Afr 2030.350.2 The war in Algeria. (Roy, Jules.) N.Y., 1961.
Afr 7122.74 The war in Angola, 1961. (Waring, R.) Lisbon, 1962.
Afr 3258.6 War in Egypt and the Soudan. (Archer, T.) London, 1887. 2v.
Afr 7850.50 The war in Katanga. (Vandenhang, E.) N.Y., 1962.
Afr 8289.00.52 The war in South Africa, 1899-1900. (Hudleston, W.H.) London, 1900.
Afr 8289.02.18A The war in South Africa. (Doyle, A.C.) London, 1902.
Afr 8279.00.32 The war in South Africa. (Hobson, J.A.) London, 1900.
Afr 8279.00.34 The war in South Africa. (Hobson, J.A.) London, 1900.
Afr 8279.00.33 The war in South Africa. (Hobson, J.A.) N.Y., 1900.
Afr 8279.00.33.1 The war in South Africa. (Hobson, J.A.) N.Y., 1969.
Afr 8289.04.5 The war in South Africa. (Prussia. Grosser Generalstab. Kriegsgeschichtliche Abteilung.) N.Y., 1969.
Afr 8289.04 The war in South Africa. (Prussia-Grosser.) London, 1904. 2v.
Afr 8288.99.25 War in South Africa and the dark continent from savagery to civilization. (Harding, William.) Chicago, 1899.
Afr 3700.12 The war in the Soudan. (Haultain, T.A.) Toronto, 1885.
Afr 8289.01.8 War notes, diary. (Villebois Mareuil.) London, 1901.
Afr 4513.35.50 War over Ethiopia. (Makin, W.J.) London, 1935.
Afr 8289.03.12 War sketches in colour. (Saint Leger, S.E.) London, 1903.
Afr 1438.1 Pamphlet box. War with Spain (1859-60).
Afr 3978.50.5 Waraga, or The charms of the Nile. (Furniss, William.) N.Y., 1850.
Afr 2209.20.5 Ward, Emily. Three travellers in North Africa. London, 1921.
Afr 9854.5 Ward, Gertrude. Life of Charles Alan Smythies, bishop of the university mission to Central Africa. London, 1898.
Afr 8152.72 Ward, H. The Cape and the Kaffirs. London, 1851.
Afr 8152.72.5 Ward, H. Five years in Kaffirland. London, 1848. 2v.
Afr 7809.10 Ward, H. A voice from the Congo. London, 1910.
Afr 6390.11.3 Ward, H.F. Handbook of British East Africa. London, 1912.
Afr 7808.90.2 Ward, Herbert. Five years with Congo cannibals. London, 1890.
Afr 7808.90.4 Ward, Herbert. Five years with the Congo cannibals. n.p., 1890.
Afr 7808.90.7 Ward, Herbert. Five years with the Congo cannibals. 3rd ed. N.Y., 1969.
Afr 7808.90 Ward, Herbert. Life among the Congo savages. N.Y., 1890.
Afr 42208.5 Ward, Philip. The Okefani song of Nij Zitru. London, 1969.
Afr 2929.67 Ward, Philip. Touring Libya. London, 1967.
Afr 2929.68 Ward, Philip. Touring Libya. London, 1968.
Afr 6164.9.3 Ward, W.E.F. A history of Ghana. N.Y., 1963.
Afr 6164.9.2 Ward, W.E.F. A history of Ghana. 2d ed. London, 1958.
Afr 6164.9.4 Ward, W.E.F. A history of Ghana. 3rd ed. London, 1966.
Afr 6164.9.5 Ward, W.E.F. A history of Ghana. 4th ed. London, 1967.
Afr 6164.9 Ward, W.E.F. A history of the Gold Coast. London, 1948.
Afr 6164.9.7 Ward, W.E.F. A short history of Ghana. 7th ed. London, 1957.
Afr 109.60.10 Ward, William. A history of Africa. London, 1960. 2v.
Afr 109.60.10.3 Ward, William. A history of Africa. v.1-2. London, 1966.
Afr 175.8 Ward, William Ernest Frank. Emergent Africa. London, 1967.
Afr 6060.65 Ward, William Ernest Frank. Government in West Africa. London, 1965.
Afr 6280.30 Ward-Price, H.L. Dark subjects. London, 1939.
Afr 7815.5.5 Les Warega (Congo belge). 5. (Delhaise, C.G.) Bruxelles, 1909.
Afr 7809.09 Les Warega (Congo belge) par le commandant Delhaise. (Delhaise, C.G.F.F.) Bruxelles, 1909.
Afr 9560.18 Warhurst, P.R. Anglo-Portuguese relations in South-Central Africa. London, 1962.
Afr 7122.74 Waring, R. The war in Angola, 1961. Lisbon, 1962.
Afr 8289.01.10 Warmelo, D.S. Mijn commando en guerilla commando-leven. Amsterdam, 1901.
Afr 8289.01.10.5 Warmelo, D.S. On commando. London, 1902.
Afr 8325.33 Warmelo, J.B.V. Het concentratie-kamp van Irene. Amsterdam, 1905.
Afr 3978.76.6 Warner, C.D. Mummies and Moslems. Hartford, 1876.
Afr 3978.76.4 Warner, C.D. My winter on the Nile. Boston, 1876.
Afr 3978.76.4.5 Warner, C.D. My winter on the Nile. Boston, 1881.
Afr 3978.76.3 Warner, C.D. My winter on the Nile. Hartford, 1876.
Afr 3978.76.5 Warner, C.D. My winter on the Nile. v.1-2. Leipzig, 1891.
Afr 6192.27 Warner, Douglas. Ghana and the new Africa. London, 1961.
Afr 7465.14 Warner, Esther Sietmann. The crossing fee. Boston, 1968.
Afr 7459.70 Warner, Esther Sietmann. Trial by sasswood. Oxford, 1970.
Afr 2025.4 Warnier, A. L'Algérie devant l'empereur. Paris, 1865.
Afr 1422.6 Warnier, A.H. Campagne du Maroc (1844). Paris, 1899.
Afr 5600.3 Warnier de Wailly, L.M.A.A. Campagne de Madagascar (1829-1830). Paris, 1895.
Afr 8659.02 Warren, Charles. On the veldt in the seventies. London, 1902.
Afr 2209.21 Warren, Lady. Through Algeria and Tunisia on a motor-bicycle. Boston, 1923.
Afr 3978.67.3 Warren, W.W. Life on the Nile. Paris, 1867.
Afr 3978.67.4 Warren, W.W. Life on the Nile. 2d ed. Boston, 1873.
Afr 3986.961 Warriner, D. Agrarian reform and community development in U.A.R. Cairo, 1961.
Afr 6540.23 Warrior herdsmen. 1st ed. (Thomas, Elizabeth Marshall.) N.Y., 1965.
Afr 2731.15.30 The warrior saint. 1st ed. (Bodley, R.V.C.) Boston, 1953.
Afr 9445.50 The warriors. (Summers, Roger.) Cape Town, 1970.
Afr 8315.5.5A War's brighter side. (Ralph, Julian.) N.Y., 1901.
Afr 3700.22 The wars in Egypt. (Short, Thomas.) Bristol, 19- .

Afr 2609.30 Warsfold, W.B. France in Tunis and Algeria. N.Y., 1930.
Afr 4513.35.115 Warum Krieg um Abessinien. (Klein, Fritz.) Leipzig, 1935.
Afr 9191.7 Warwick, Brian Allan. The Swazi, an ethnographic account of the natives of the Swaziland protectorate. London, 1966.
Afr 6990.21.5 Was Afrika nur gab und nahm. 3. Aufl. (Eckenbrecher, M.) Berlin, 1908.
Afr 8160.25 The washing of the spears. (Morris, Donald R.) N.Y., 1965.
Afr 23.5 Washington notes on Africa. Washington. 1,1969+
Afr 6390.13 Wason, J.C. East Africa and Uganda. London, 1905.
Afr 718.2.115 Wassermann, J. Bula Matari, Stanley, conqueror of a continent. N.Y., 1933.
Afr 718.2.120 Wassermann, J. Bula Matari. Berlin, 1932.
Afr 1973.3 Watbled, E. Souvenirs de l'armée d'Afrique. Paris, 1877.
Afr 5405.285 Watch over Africa. (Saurat, Denis.) London, 1941.
Afr 3199.67 Waterfield, Gordon. Egypt. London, 1967.
Afr 8105.5.3 Watermeyer, E.B. Drie voorlezingen over de Kaap de Goede Hoop. Kaapstad, 1858.
Afr 3068.81.5 Waters, C.E.C. Egypt. Boston, 1881.
Afr 1623.962 Waterston, A. Planning in Morocco. Washington, 1962.
Afr 8300.16 Watkins-Pitchford, Herbert. Besieged in Ladysmith. Pietermaritzburg, 1964.
Afr 11874.86.100 Watling, Cyril. Ink in my blood. Cape Town, 1966.
Afr 4040.5 Watson, Charles R. In the valley of the Nile. N.Y., 1908.
Afr 2285.8 Watson, G. The voice of the south (Algeria). London, 1905.
Afr 6275.136 Watson, George Derek. A human geography of Nigeria. London, 1960.
Afr 8325.34 Watson, J. Hannan. A trooper's sketch book of Boer War. Glasgow, 19- .
Afr 11874.87.100 Watson, J.C. Shadow over the Rand. Johannesburg, 1955.
Afr 9050.10 Watson, R.G.T. Tongaati. London, 1960.
Afr 1745.1 Watson, R.S. A visit to Wazan. London, 1880.
Afr 9700.30 Watson, W. Tribal cohesion in a money economy. Manchester, 1958.
Afr 3315.25 Watt, Donald C. Documents on the Suez crisis. London, 1957.
Afr 8190.15 Watt, E.P. Febana. London, 1962.
Afr 6455.36 Watt, Rachel. In the heart of savagedom. 2d ed. London, 1920.
Afr 3978.70.10 Watt, Robert. Fra aegypternes land. Kjøbenhavn, 1870.
Afr 1609.34 Wattenavyl, R. Von. Ein land, menschen in Marokko. Zürich, 1934.
Afr 2208.77 Wattenwyl, M. von. Zwei Jahre in Algerien. Bern, 1877.
Afr 8250.23 Watts-Danton, T. The Rhodes memorial at Oxford. London, 1910.
Afr 6291.62 Waugh, Auberon. Biafra; Britain's shame. London, 1969.
Afr 699.31.6 Waugh, E. Remote people. London, 1934.
Afr 699.31.3 Waugh, E. They were still dancing. N.Y., 1952.
Afr 6390.37 Waugh, Evelyn. A tourist in Africa. London, 1960.
Afr 7575.96 Wauters, A. Le norde communiste et la crise du Congo belge. Brussels, 1961
Afr 7530.3 Wauters, A.J. Bibliographie du Congo 1880-1895. Bruxelles, 1895.
Afr 7808.99 Wauters, A.J. L'Etat Indépendant du Congo. Bruxelles, 1899.
Afr 7549.11.3 Wauters, A.J. Histoire politique du Congo belge. Bruxelles, 1911.
Afr 3740.9 Wauters, A.J. Souvenirs de Fashoda et de l'expedition Dhanis. Bruxelles, 1910.
Afr 718.17.2 Wauters, A.J. Stanley's Emin Pascha expedition. London, 1890.
Afr 718.17 Wauters, A.J. Stanley's Emin Pascha expedition. Philadelphia, 1890.
Afr 7809.14.5 Wauters, Alphones Jules. Voyages en Afrique. Bruxelles, 1914.
Afr 5440.5 Wauters, Alphonse Jules. Les bassins de l'Ubangi. Brussels, 1902.
Afr 7308.80 Wauters, Alphonse Jules. Voyage au pays de l'ivoire. Bruxelles, 190- .
Afr 7809.29.5 Wauters, Arthur. D'Anvers à Bruxelles via le Lac Kivu. Bruxelles, 1929.
Afr 7809.24.15 Wauters, Joseph. Le Congo au travail. Bruxelles, 1924.
Afr 115.55 Wauthier, Claude. L'Afrique des africains. Paris, 1964.
Afr 115.55.2 Wauthier, Claude. The literature and thought of modern Africa, a survey. London, 1966.
Afr 7368.85 Wauwermans, H. Les premices de l'oeuvre d'émancipation africaine. Liberia. Bruxelles, 1885.
Afr 150.13 Wauwermans, Henri. Henri le Navigateur et l'Académie Portugaise de Sagres. Bruxelles, 1890.
Afr 4559.65 Wax and gold. (Levine, Donald Nathan.) Chicago, 1965.
Afr 609.59 The way in Africa. (Carpenter, G.W.) N.Y., 1959.
Afr 2749.64 The way of the chariots. (Toy, Barbara.) London, 1964.
Afr 555.22.28 The way of the white fields in Rhodesia. (Smith, Edwin W.) London, 1928.
Afr 9558.90 The way to Ilala. (Debenham, F.) London, 1955.
Afr 6390.92 The way to Rehema's house. (Spencer, Hope Rockefeller.) N.Y., 1967.
Afr 6542.20 The way to the mountains of the moon. (Bere, Rennie Montague.) London, 1966.
Afr 6280.9.50 The way we lived. (Umeasiegba, Remshna.) London, 1969.
Afr 3979.26.5 A wayfarer in Egypt. (Quibell, Annie.) Boston, 1926.
Afr 1609.29.2 A wayfarer in Morocco. (Lowth, Alys.) Boston, 1929.
Afr 1609.29 A wayfarer in Morocco. (Lowth, Alys.) London, 1929.
Afr 4050.9.5 Wayfarers in the Libyan desert. (Alexander, F.G.) N.Y., 1912.
Afr 4050.9 Wayfarers in the Libyan desert. (Cobbold, E.) London, 1912.
Afr 7815.28.5 Wayward servants. 1st ed. (Turnbull, Colin M.) Garden City, N.Y., 1965.
Afr 6430.15 We built a country. (Lipscomb, J.F.) London, 1956.
Afr 555.20.10 We move into Africa. (Naw, Henry.) Saint Louis, Mo., 1945.
Afr 555.100 We pioneered in Portuguese East Africa. 1st ed. (Keys, Clara E.) N.Y., 1959.
Afr 7803.41 We two alone. (Hege, Ruth.) N.Y., 1965.
Afr 679.09 We two in West Africa. (Guggisberg, Decima (Moore).) London, 1909.
Afr 8235.10 Weale, J.P.M. The truth about the Portuguese in Africa. London, 1891.
Afr 6277.20 The wealth of Nigeria. (Stapleton, G.B.) London, 1958.
Afr 6277.20.2 The wealth of Nigeria. 2nd ed. (Stapleton, G.B.) Ibadan, 1967.
Afr Doc 4502.2 Webb, C. de B. A guide to the official records of the Colony of Natal. Pietermaritzburg, 1965.

Afr 8686.12 Weber, Karl Friedrich. Kreuz zwischen Weiss und Schwarz. Breklum, 1965.

Afr 3978.30.3 Webster, James. Travels through Egypt. London, 1830. 2v.

Afr 6282.12 Webster, James B. The African churches among the Yoruba. Oxford, 1964.

Afr 5055.67 Webster, James B. The revolutionary years: West Africa since 1800. London, 1967.

Afr 6403.5 Webster, John B. A bibliography on Kenya. Syracuse, 1967.

Afr 8369.38 Webster, W.A. Real union in South Africa. Cape Town, 1938.

Afr 6926.15 Weck, Ruediger. In Deutsche-Südwestafrika, 1913-15. Berlin, 1919.

Afr 8320.13 Weeber, E.J. Op die Transvaalse front 1 junie 1900-31 oktober 1900. Bloemfontein, 1942.

Afr 3315.100 The weekend war. (Barer, Schlomo.) N.Y., 1960.

Afr 7815.8 Weeks, J.H. Among Congo cannibals. London, 1913.

Afr 7815.8.5 Weeks, J.H. Among the primitive Bakongo. London, 1914.

Afr 7815.10 Weeks, John H. Congo life and folklore. London, 1911.

Afr 550.57 Weeks, Nan F. Builders of a new Africa. Nashville, 1944.

Afr 10434.127.100 Weep not, child. (Ngugi, James.) London, 1964.

Afr 4389.54 Der Weg zum letzten Pharao. (Stradal, Otto.) Wien, 1954.

Afr 5408.10 Das Weib am Kongo. (Castellani, Charles.) Minden, 1902.

Afr 530.12 Weidmann, C. Deutsche Männer in Afrika. Lübeck, 1894.

Afr 3979.09.5 Weigall, A.E.P. Travels in the Upper Egyptian deserts. Edinburgh, 1909.

Afr 3199.15 Weigall, Arthur E.P. Brome. History of events in Egypt from 1798 to 1914. Edinburgh, 1915.

Afr 6392.37 Weigt, Ernest. Beiträge zur Entwicklungspolitik in Afrika. Köln, 1964.

Afr 6420.30 Weigt, Ernst. Die Kolonisation Kenias. Inaug. Diss. Leipzig, 1932.

Afr 9093.15 Weilbach, J.D. Geschiedenis van de emigranten-boeren en van den vrijheids-oorlog. Kaapstad, 1882.

Afr 6738.25 Weiler, Carlos. Wirtschaftsgeographie des britischen Mandats Kamerun. Inaug. Diss. Berlin, 1933.

Afr 5417.70.2 Weinstein, Brian. Gabon; nation-building on the Ogooue. Cambridge, Mass., 1966.

Afr 8252.326 Weinthal, Leo. Memories. London, 1929.

Afr 1400.5 Weir, T.H. The shaikhs of Morocco in the XVI century. Edinburgh, 1904.

Afr 1453.11 Weisgerber, F. Au seuil du Maroc moderne. Rabat, 1947.

Afr 1609.04.5 Weisgerber, F. Trois mois de campagne au Maroc. Paris, 1904.

Afr 1280.3 Weisgerber, H. Les blancs d'Afrique. Paris, 1910.

Afr 3986.964.15 Weiss, Dieter. Wirtschaftliche Entwicklungsplanung in der Vereinigten Arabischen Republik. Koeln, 1964.

Afr 7543.12 Weiss, Herbert F. Political protest in the Congo. Princeton, 1967.

Afr 6883.3 Weiss, Max. Die Völkerstämme in nord Deutsch-Ostafrika. Berlin, 1910.

Afr 8678.333 Weisse ismen, schwarze fakten. (Schuette, H.G.) Vaterstetten, 1963.

Afr 5243.174.15 Die Weissen denken zuviel. (Parin, Paul.) Zürich, 1963.

Afr 8659.36 Weisses und schwarzes Südafrika heute und morgen. (Rippmann, Ernst.) Gotha, 1936.

Afr 555.141 Welbourn, F.B. East African Christian. London, 1965.

Afr 6385.15 Welbourn, Frederick B. East African rebels. London, 1961.

Afr 6463.3 Welbourn, Frederick B. A place to feel at home, a study of two independent churches in western Kenya. London, 1966.

Afr 6498.65.5 Welbourn, Frederick Burkewood. Religion and politics in Uganda. Nairobi, 1965.

Afr 210.66.10 Welch, Claude Emerson. Dream of unity. Ithaca, N.Y., 1966.

Afr 6903.5F Welch, F.J. South-west Africa. Cape Town, 1946.

Afr 609.65.5 Welch, Galbraith. Africa before they came. N.Y., 1965. 4v.

Afr 7369.60 Welch, Galbraith. The jet lighthouse. London, 1960.

Afr 659.49A Welch, Galbraith. North African prelude. N.Y., 1949.

Afr 5235.128.30 Welch, Galbraith. The unveiling of Timbuctoo. N.Y., 1939.

Afr 8095.10 Welch, S.R. Europe's discovery of South Africa. Cape Town, 1935.

Afr 8110.30 Welch, Sidney R. Portuguese and Dutch in South Africa. Cape Town, 1951.

Afr 8100.35 Welch, Sidney R. Portuguese rule and Spanish crown in South America. Cape Town, 1950.

Afr 8100.30 Welch, Sidney R. South Africa under King Manuel, 1495-1521. Cape Town, 1946.

Afr 8100.32 Welch, Sidney R. South Africa under King Sebastian and the cardinal, 1557-1580. Cape Town, 1949.

Afr 9448.75 Welensky, Roy. Welensky's four thousand days. London, 1964.

Afr 9525.875.10 The Welensky story. (Allighan, Garry.) Cape Town, 1962.

Afr 9448.75 Welensky's four thousand days. (Welensky, Roy.) London, 1964.

Afr 3275.29 The Welfare of Egypt. (Willmore, J.S.) London, 1917.

Afr Doc 4353.5 Welfare organisation act no. 40 of 1947 quinquennial report. (South Africa. National Welfare Board.) 1,1957+

Afr Doc 4353.7 Welfare organizations act no. 40 of 1947. Report on the operation and administration of the act [annual]. (South Africa. National Welfare Board.) 4,1951+

Afr 530.12.5 Welk, E. Die schwarze Sonne. Berlin, 1933.

Afr 2719.64.5 Wellard, J.H. The great Sahara. London, 1964.

Afr 1259.67 Wellard, James. Lost worlds of Africa. 1st ed. N.Y., 1967.

Afr 4559.01 Wellby, M.S. Twixt Sirdar and Menelik. London, 1901.

Afr 6218.9 Wellesley, D.A. Sir George Goldie, founder of Nigeria. London, 1934.

Afr 8659.55.5 Wellington, J.H. Southern Africa. Cambridge, Eng., 1955. 2v.

Afr 6919.67 Wellington, John Harold. South West Africa and its human issues. Oxford, 1967.

Afr 8659.39.15 Wells, Arthur W. South Africa. London, 1947.

Afr 8659.39.20 Wells, Arthur W. South Africa. London, 1956.

Afr 6879.28 Wells, Carveth. In coldest Africa. Garden City, 1929.

Afr 609.44 Wells, Carveth. Introducing Africa. N.Y., 1944.

Afr 6277.68 Wells, Frederick A. Studies in industrialization, Nigeria and the Cameroons. London, 1962.

Afr 6196.5 Welman, C.W. The native states of the Gold Coast. London, 1930.

Afr 6164.30 Welman, Charles Wellesley. The native states of the Gold Coast. London, 1969.

Afr 7020.40 Welsch, S.R. South Africa under John III. Capetown, 1949.

Afr 2623.15 Welt-Ausstellung 1873 in Wien. (Tunis.) Wien, 1873.

Afr 609.60.20 Die Welt des Afrikaners. (Haller, Albert.) Düsseldorf, 1960.

Afr 210.32 Weltkrise und Kolonialpolitik. (Dix, Arthur.) Berlin, 1932.

Afr 8676.64.5 Die weltwirtschaftliche Bedeutung der Südafrikanischen Republik. (Svermann, Josef.) Göttingen, 1964.

Afr 4513.35.78 Wencker-Wiedberg, F. Abessinien, das Pulverfass Afrikas. 3e Aufl. Düsseldorf, 1935.

Afr 6890.4 Wenner, Kate. Shamba letu. Boston, 1970.

Afr 6460.87 Were, Gideon S. A history of the Abaluyia of western Kenia. Nairobi, 1967.

Afr 6460.87.5 Were, Gideon S. Western Kenya historical texts: Abaluyia, Teso, and Elgon Kalenjin. Nairobi, 1967.

Afr 8676.35 Werle, G. Landwirtschaft und Industrie in der Südafrikanischen Union unter Berücksichtigung der deutschen Pionierarbeit. Inaug. Diss. Eisfeld, 1935.

Afr 1583.5 Werle. Deutschlands beziehungen zu marokko. Coburg, 1902.

Afr 4095.5 Werne, Ferd. Expedition to sources of White Nile. London, 1849.

Afr 4095.5.5 Werne, Ferd. Expedition zur Entdeckung der Quellen des Weissen Nil. Berlin, 1848.

Afr 9853.1A Werner, A. Natives of British Central Africa. London, 1906.

Afr 718.15 Werner, J.R. Visit to stanley s rear guard. Edinburg, 1889.

Afr 4199.5 Werner Munzinger-Pascha. (Keller-Zschokke, J.V.) Aarau, 1891.

Afr 9161.6 Werrmann, R. The Bawenda of the Spelonken. London, 1908.

Afr 6879.15.5 Werth, Emil. Das Deutsch-Ostafrikanische Küstenland. Berlin, 1915. 2v.

Afr 765.4 Werther, Waldemar. Zum Victoria Nyanza. Berlin, 1894.

Afr 8820.6 Wes-Kaapland. (Illiers, Stephanus.) Stellenbosch, 1964.

Afr 9405.6 Wesleyan Methodist Missionary Society. Affairs of Bechuanaland. London, 1887.

Afr 8045.55 Wessels, F.J. Die republikeinse grondwet. Kaapstad, 1962.

Afr 4513.35.155 West, J. War and the workers. N.Y., 1935.

Afr 630.65.5 West, Richard. The white tribes of Africa. London, 1965.

Afr 6050.5F West Africa, a weekly news paper. London. 1956+ 23v.

Afr 5056.164 West Africa. (Adloff, Richard.) N.Y., 1964.

Afr 5054.67 West Africa. (Hargreaves, John.) Englewood Cliffs, 1967.

Afr 679.69 West Africa. (Morgan, William Basil.) London, 1969.

Afr 679.51 West Africa. (Pedler, F.J.) London, 1951.

Afr 6050.15 West Africa annual. London. 1962+ 4v.

Afr 679.67.25 West Africa before the Europeans: archaeology and prehistory. (Davies, Oliver.) London, 1967.

Afr 6096.22 West Africa Committee. Foreign investment. London, 1968.

Afr 679.66.5 West Africa in history. (Conton, William F.) London, 1966.

Afr 679.52 West Africa on the march. (Agyeman, N.Y.T.D.) N.Y., 1952.

Afr 679.68.10 West Africa under colonial rule. (Crowder, Michael.) London, 1968.

Afr 5342.62 West African agent. (Young, T. Rex.) London, 1943.

Afr 6147.5 West African city. (Banton, M.P.) London, 1957.

Afr 6097.10 West African Congress on Evangelism, Ibadan, Nigeria, 1968. West African Congress on Evangelism. n.p., 1968.

Afr 626.208 West African economics today. 1st ed. (Aromolaran, Adekunie.) Ibadan, 1968.

Afr 679.51.5 West African explorers. (Howard, C.) London, 1951.

Afr 852.2 West African islands. (Ellis, A.B.) London, 1885.

Afr 679.67 West African kingdom in the nineteenth century. (Forde, Cyril Daryll.) London, 1967.

Afr 6176.52 West African leadership. 1st ed. (Hayford, Casely.) London, 1969.

Afr 500.5 The West African question. (De Leon, D.) n.p., 1886.

Afr 6050.10 West African review. London. 33,1962+

Afr 6095.5 West African sketches...G.R. Collier. London, 1824.

Afr 6198.71 West African trade and coast society; a family study. (Priestley, Margaret.) London, 1969.

Afr 679.65.10 West African urbanization. (Little, Kenneth Lindsay.) Cambridge, Eng., 1965.

Afr 10516.5 West African verse; an anthology. (Nwoga, Donatus Ibe.) London, 1967.

Htn Afr 1606.71* West Barbary. (Addison, L.) Oxford, 1671.

Afr Doc 7509.305F West Cameroon. The accounts of the government together with a report of the Controller of Accounts. Buea. 1960+

Afr Doc 7509.89 West Cameroon. Estimates. Buea. 1964+

Afr Doc 7509.505 West Cameroon. Department of Education. Education department statistics. Buea. 1962+

Afr Doc 7516.8 West Cameroon. House of Assembly. Debates; official report. Buea. 1963+

Afr Doc 7516.5 West Cameroon. House of Chiefs. Debates. Buea. 2,1962+

Afr Doc 7516.10 West Cameroon. House of Chiefs. Standing orders. Buea. 1962+

Afr 6705.5 West Cameroon Constitution, 1961. (Cameroon, West. Constitution.) Buea, 1961.

Afr 550.63 West Central Africa Regional Conference, Leopoldville, 1946. Abundant life in changing Africa. N.Y., 1946.

Afr 6200.23 The West Coast directory. Lagos. 1968+

Afr 6400.93 West Kenya annual. Kisumu. 1967+

Afr 8289.03.20 A West Pointer with the Boers. (Blake, J.Y.D.) Boston, 1903.

Afr 6390.28A West with the night; autobiography. (Markham, B.C.) Boston, 1942.

Afr 678.74 Westafrika von Senegal bis Benquela. (Oberlaender, R.) Leipzig, 1874.

Afr 6143.27 Westafrikas letztes Rätsel. (Eberl-Elber, Ralph.) Salzburg, 1936.

Afr 9710.13 Westbeach, George. Trade and travel in early Barotseland. London, 1963.

Afr 630.34 Westermann, D. The African to-day. London, 1934.

Afr 530.4 Westermann, D. Beiträge zur deutschen Kolonialfrage. Essen, 1937.

Afr 7465.8 Westermann, D. Die Kpelle. Göttingen, 1921.

Afr 109.52 Westermann, Diedrich. Geschichte Afrikas. Köln, 1952.

Afr 3817.6 Westermann, Diedrich. The Shilluk people. Philadelphia, 1912.

Afr 555.3.10 Western Africa, its conditions. (East, D.J.) London, 1844.

Afr 678.56A Western Africa. (Wilson, T.L.) N.Y., 1856.

Afr 8667.75 Western civilization and the natives of South Africa, studies in culture contrast. 1st ed. (Schapera, Isaac.) London, 1967.

Afr 678.33 The western coast of Africa. Philadelphia, 1833.

Afr 6460.87.5 Western Kenya historical texts: Abaluyia, Teso, and Elgon Kalenjin. (Were, Gideon S.) Nairobi, 1967.

Afr 7809.56 Wings over the Congo. (Ahl, Frances Norene.) Boston, 1956.

Afr 659.64 Winid, Bogdan. Geografia gospodarcza Afryki, Afryka potnocna. Warszawa, 1964.

Afr 3988.4 Winkler, Hans Alexander. Baueren zwischen Wasser und Wüste. Stuttgart, 1934.

Afr 2438.15 Winkler, Pierre. Essai sur la nationalité dans les protectorats de Tunisie et du Maroc. Thèse. Paris, 1926.

Afr 210.65.55 The Winneba Conference, Ghana, May 1965. (Afro-Asian Peoples' Solidarity Conference, 4th, Winneba, Ghana.) Cairo, 1966.

Afr 3675.11 The winning of the Sudan. (Crabitès, Pierre.) London, 1934.

Afr 6883.30 Winnus, Edgar. Shambala. Berkeley, 1962.

Afr 8045.10 Winship, Thomas. Law and practice of arbitration in South Africa. Durban, 1925.

Afr 4558.81 Winstanley, W. A visit to Abyssinia. London, 1861. 2v.

Afr 6540.21 Winter, Edward. Beyond the mountains of the moon. London, 1959.

Afr 9165.42.90 Winter, James Sydney. First-hand accounts of Johannesburg in English-language periodicals, 1886-1895, a list. Johannesburg, 1967.

Afr 2208.65.6 A winter in Algeria. (Rogers, P.A.) London, 1865.

Afr 1608.73 A winter in Morocco. (Perrier, A.) London, 1873.

Afr 1738.4 A winter in Tangier. (Howard-Vyse, L.) London, 1882.

Afr 3978.63.10 A winter in upper and lower Egypt. (Hoskins, G.A.) London, 1863.

Afr 8658.89.5 A winter tour in South Africa. (Young, Frederick.) London, 1890.

Afr 2208.67 A winter with the swallows. (Edwards, M.B.) London, 1867.

Afr 6143.16 Winterbottom, T. An account of native Africans...in Sierra Leone. London, 1803. 2v.

Afr 6143.16.2A Winterbottom, T. An account of the native African in the neighborhood of Sierra Leone. 2nd ed. London, 1969.

Afr 6143.16.5 Winterbottom, T. Nachrichten von der Sierra Leona Küste. Weimar, 1805.

Afr 3038.7 Winterei, Hermann. Ägypten, seine staats- und völkerrechtliche Stellung. Berlin, 1915.

Afr 2208.90.3 Winters in Algeria. (Bridgman, F.A.) London, 1890.

Afr 8145.5.5 Wirgman, A.T. The history of the English church and people in South Africa. N.Y., 1969.

Afr 8145.5 Wirgman, A.T. The history of the English Church in South Africa. London, 1895.

Afr 8145.7 Wirgman, A.T. Life of James Green...dean of Maritzburg, Natal, 1849-1906. London, 1909. 2v.

Afr 1583.8 Wirth, A. Die Entscheidung über Marokko. Stuttgart, 1911.

Afr 8088.97.6 Wirth, A. Geschichte Südafrikas. Bonn, 1897.

Afr 1550.20 Wirth, A. Marokko. Frankfurt, 1908.

Afr 626.131 Die Wirtschaft Afrikas. (Bauer, G.) Frankfurt a.M., 1963.

Afr 9499.20 Die Wirtschaft von Britisch-Zentral Afrika. (Mai, Erwin.) Koln, 1953.

Afr 626.90 Wirtschaftliche Entweeklungstendenzen in West-, Mittel- und Ostafrika. (Hesse, Kurt.) Bad Homburg, 1960.

Afr 3986.964.15 Wirtschaftliche Entwicklungsplanung in der Vereinigten Arabischen Republik. (Weiss, Dieter.) Koeln, 1964.

Afr 6738.25 Wirtschaftsgeographie des britischen Mandats Kamerun. Inaug. Diss. (Weiler, Carlos.) Berlin, 1933.

Afr 626.5 Wirtschaftsgeographie von Afrika. (Dove, Karl.) Jena, 1917.

Afr 1623.934 Eine wirtschaftsgeographische darstellung...Marokkos und Tunesiens. Inaug. Diss. (Romanus, H.) Königsberg, 1934.

Afr 6686.30 Die wirtschaftsgeographische Entwicklung...Togo und Kamerun. (Och, Helmut.) Königsberg, 1931.

Afr 7046.2 Wirtschaftsprobleme Portugisisch-Afrikas. (Gersdorff, R. von.) Bielefeld, 1962.

Afr 7176.30 Die Wirtschaftsräume Angolas. (Borchert, Günter.) Pfaffenhofen/Ilm, 1967.

Afr 6392.2 Wirtschaftswissenschaftliche Veröffentlichungen über Ostafrika in englischer Sprache. v.1-3. (Mezger, Dorothea.) München, 1967. 2v.

Afr 8676.54.5 Wirtschaftswunder Südafrika. (Hesse, K.) Düsseldorf, 1954.

Afr 9854.2 Wishlade, Robert Leonard. Modern sectarian movements in Nyasaland. Durham, 1961.

Afr 9854.2.5 Wishlade, Robert Leonard. Sectarianism in southern Nyasaland. London, 1965.

Afr 2000.13 Wisner, S. L'Algérie dans l'impasse. Paris, 1949.

Afr 715.10 Wissenschaftliche Ergebnisse der Deutschen Zentral-Afrika-Expedition. Leipzig. 5v.

Afr 8289.01.3 Wisser, J.P. The second Boer war 1899-1900. Kansas City, 1901. 2v.

Afr 115.112 Wisser Mann auf heissen Pfaden. (Homann, Hermann.) Stuttgart, 1968.

Afr 718.6 Wissmann, H. Meine zweite Durchquerung Afrikas. Frankfurt a.M., 1891.

Afr 718.7 Wissmann, H. My second journey through Africa. London, 1891.

Afr 718.5 Wissmann, H. Unter Deutsche Flagge quer durch Afrika. Berlin, 1889.

Afr 7808.88.3 Wissmann, H.V. Im innern Afrikas. Leipzig, 1891.

Afr 22025.5F Witahnkenge, E. Panorama de la littérature ntu. Kinshase, 1968.

Afr 7815.13.15 Witchcraft, oracles and magic among the Azande. (Evans-Pritchard, E.E.) Oxford, 1937.

Afr 6395.2 With a prehistoric people, the Akikuyu of British East Africa. (Routledge, W.S.) London, 1910.

Afr 8658.82 With a show through southern Africa. (Duval, C.) London, 1882. 2v.

Afr 8315.12 With Bobs and Kruger. (Unger, F.W.) Philadelphia, 1901.

Afr 8289.00.7 With both armies in South Africa. (Davis, R.H.) N.Y., 1900.

Afr 6926.11.5 With Botha and Smuts in Africa. (Whittall, W.) London, 1917.

Afr 6926.11 With Botha in the field. (Ritchie, Moore.) London, 1915.

Afr 6926.9 With Botha's army. (Robinson, J.P.K.) London, 1916.

Afr 6878.93 With Captain Stairs to Katanga. (Moloney, J.A.) London, 1893.

Afr 5426.100.35 With Dr. Schweitzer in Lambaréné. (Urquhart, Clara.) London, 1957.

Afr 6390.44.2 With forks and hope. (Huxley, Elspeth Grant.) N.Y., 1964.

Afr 8289.02.21 With General French and the cavalry in Africa. (Goldmann, C.S.) London, 1902.

Afr 3710.3.2 With Hicks Pasha in the Soudan. 2d ed. (Colborne, J.) London, 1885.

Afr 3275.30 With Kitchener in Cairo. (Mosely, Sydney R.) London, 1917.

Afr 3735.4 With Kitchener to Khartum. (Steevens, G.W.) Edinburgh, 1898.

Afr 3735.4.6 With Kitchener to Khartum. (Steevens, G.W.) London, 1909.

Afr 3735.4.1 With Kitchener to Khartum. (Steevens, G.W.) N.Y., 1898.

Afr 3735.4.3 With Kitchener to Khartum. (Steevens, G.W.) N.Y., 1899.

Afr 3735.4.2 With Kitchener to Khartum. 12th ed. (Steevens, G.W.) Edinburgh, 1898.

Afr 8325.56 With Methuen's column on an ambulance train. (Bennett, E.N.) London, 1900.

Afr 8289.51 With Milner in South Africa. (Curtis, Lionel.) Oxford, 1951.

Afr 8289.51.2 With Milner in South Africa. Index. (Curtis, Lionel.) Johannesburg, 1962.

Afr 1490.3.5 With Mulai Hafid at Fez. (Harris, Lawrence.) Boston, 1910.

Afr 1490.3 With Mulai Hafid at Fez. (Harris, Lawrence.) London, 1909.

Afr 7175.15.10 With my wife across Africa by canoe and caravan. 2d. ed. (Statham, J.C.B.) London, 1926.

Afr 8289.00.30 With our soldiers at the front. (Johnson, H.) London, 1907.

Afr 8289.01.27 With Paget's horse to the front. (Rose-Innes, C.) London, 1901.

Afr 9446.36 With Plumer in Matabeleland, an account of the operations of the Matabeleland relief force during the rebellion of 1896. (Sykes, Frank W.) Westminster, 1897.

Afr 8250.16 With Rhodes in Mashonaland. (Waal, David C.) Cape Town, 1896.

Afr 8289.02.6 With Rimmington. (Phillipps, L.M.) London, 1902.

Afr 718.13 With Stanley's rear column. (Troup, J.R.) London, 1890.

Afr 8289.02.3 With Steijn and De Wet. (Pienaar, P.) London, 1902.

Afr 4937.1 With the Abyssinians in Somaliland. (Jennings, J.W.) London, 1905.

Afr 8292.35 With the Army Service Corps in South Africa. (Richardson, W.D.) London, 1903.

Afr 1259.44.5 With the bible in North Africa. (Campbell, D.) Kilmarnock, 1944.

Afr 8325.75 With the Boer forces. (Hillegas, H.C.) London, 1900.

Afr 8225.6 With the Boers in the Transvaal 1880-1. (Newman, C.L.N.) London, 1896.

Afr 3708.7 With the Camel Corps up the Nile. (Gleichen, C.) London, 1888.

Afr 8289.00.24F With the flag to Pretoria, history, Boer war 1899-1900. (Wilson, H.W.) London, 1900-01 2v.

Afr 8292.25 With the Green Howards in South Africa, 1899-1902. (Ferrar, M.L.) London, 1904.

Afr 8292.24 With the Guards Brigade. (Lowry, E.P.) London, 1902.

Afr 8292.43 With the Inniskilling Dragoons. (Yardley, J.W.) London, 1904.

Afr 2875.7 With the Italians in Tripoli. (Irace, C.F.) London, 1912.

Afr 4558.98A With the mission to Menelik 1897. (Gleichen, A.E.W.) London, 1898.

Afr 8285.10 With the mounted infantry and the Mashona-landfield force, 1896. (Alderson, E.A.H.) London, 1898.

Afr 6780.13 With the Nigerians in German East Africa. (Downes, Walter D.) London, 1919.

Afr 1609.26.5 With the Riff Kabyles. (Terhorst, Bernd.) London, 1926.

Afr 3735.11 With the Seventy-Second Highlanders in the Sudan campaign. (Egerton, G.) London, 1909.

Afr 6275.25 With the tin gods. (Tremlett, Horace.) London, 1915.

Afr 2875.14 With the Turks in Tripoli. (Bennett, E.N.) London, 1912.

Afr 6218.13 With the West African frontier force in Southern Nigeria. (Gordon Lennox, Esme Charles.) London, 1905.

Afr 8292.39 With the 4th Battalion, the Cameronians (Scottish Rifles) in South Africa. (Courtenay, A.H.) Edinburg, 1905.

Afr 9446.34 With Wilson in Matabeleland. (Donovan, Charles Henry Wynne.) London, 1894.

Afr Doc 1802.15 Witherell, Julian W. Ghana; a guide to official publications, 1872-1968. Washington, 1969.

Afr 8278.96.5 Withers, H. English and Dutch in South Africa. London, 1896.

Afr 210.44 Without bitterness. (Orizu, A.A.N.) N.Y., 1944.

Afr 8659.58.10 Without fear or favour. (Friend, M.L.) Cape Town, 1958.

Afr 2731.15.80 Witness in the desert, the life of Charles de Foucauld. (Six, Jean F.) N.Y., 1965.

Afr 5408.105 Witte, Jehan. Les deux Congo, trente-cinq ans d'apostolat. Paris, 1913.

Afr 555.39 Witte, Jehan. Un explorateur et un apôtre du Congo français. Paris, 1924.

Afr 6193.15 Wittman, G.H. The Ghana report. N.Y., 1959.

Afr 11572.50.210 The wizard bird. (Millin, S.G.(L).) London, 1962.

Afr 10631.58.100 The wizard of Osamang. (Konadu, Asare.) Accra, 1964.

Afr 210.63.45 Woddis, J. Africa, the way ahead. London, 1963.

Afr 210.64 Woddis, J. Africa, the way ahead. N.Y., 1964.

Afr 210.61.25 Woddis, J. Africa. London, 1961.

Afr 210.64.2 Woddis, J. L'avenir de l'Afrique. Paris, 1964.

Afr 210.60.30 Woddis, Jack. Africa, the roots of revolt. London, 1960.

Afr 210.60.20 Wohin geht Afrika. (Kummernuss, Adolph.) Frankfurt a.M., 1960.

Afr 6883.8 Wohlab, Karl. Die Christliche Missionspredigt unter den Schambala. Inaug. Diss. Tübingen, 1928.

Afr 3979.62.10 Wohlfahrt, M. Das neue Ägypten. Berlin, 1962.

Afr 1259.55.5 Wohlfahrt, M. Nordafrika. Berlin, 1955.

Afr 4573.15 Wohlgemuth, Lennart. Etiopiens ekonomi. Uppsala, 1967.

Afr 7468.2 Woid, Joseph Conrad. God's impatience in Liberia. Grand Rapids, 1968.

Afr 1846.9 Wolf, Christian. Der fremdenlegionaer in Krieg und Frieden. Berlin, 1913.

Afr 6291.56 Wolf, Jean. La guerre des rapaces, la vérité sur la guerre du Biafra. Paris, 1969.

Afr 7815.27 Wolfe, A.W. In the Ngombe tradition. Evanston, Ill., 1961.

Afr 2753.2 Wolff, H. Les régiments de dromadaires. Paris, 1884.

Afr 7808.89.2 Wolff, W. Von Banana zum Kiammo. Oldenburg, 1889.

Afr 1609.06.10 Wolfrom, G. Le Maroc. Paris, 1906.

Afr 6192.45 Wolfson, Freda. Pageant of Ghana. London, 1958.

Afr 6535.10 Wollaston, A.F.R. From Ruwenzore to the Congo. London, 1908.

Afr 6535.10.3 Wollaston, A.F.R. From Ruwenzore to the Congo. N.Y., 1908.

Afr 609.39   Wollschlaeger, Alfred. Gross ist Afrika. Berlin, 1939.

Afr 6203.9   Wolpe, Howard. A study guide for Nigeria. Boston, 1966.

Afr 3708.20   Wolseley, Garnet Joseph Wolseley. In relief of Gordon; Lord Wolseley's campaign journal of the Khartoum Relief Expedition, 1884-1885. London, 1967.

Afr 8089.47   Wolton, D.G. Whither South Africa. London, 1947.

Afr 4785.7   Wolverton, Frederick Glyn, 4th Baron. Five months sport in Somaliland. London, 1894.

Afr 4513.36.25   A woman at the Abyssinian war. (Currey, M.) London, 1936.

Afr 10631.58.130   A woman in her prime. (Konadu, Asare.) London, 1967.

Afr 2749.15   Woman in the Sahara. (Gordan, H.C.) London, 1915.

Afr 8289.01.20   A woman's memories of the war in South Africa. (Brooke-Hunt, V.) London, 1901.

Afr 6280.10   Woman's mysteries of a primitive people, the Ibibios of Southern Nigeria. (Talbot, D.A.) London, 1915.

Afr 8283.10   A woman's part in a revolution. (Hammond, J.H.) N.Y., 1897.

Afr 699.07   A woman's trek from the Cape to Cairo. (Hall, Mary.) London, 1907.

Afr 2218.6.15A   Women of Algeria; an essay on change. (Gordon, David C.) Cambridge, 1968.

Afr 3988.10   The women of Egypt. (Cooper, Elizabeth.) London, 1914.

Afr 635.62.5   Women of tropical Africa. (Paulme, D.) Berkeley, 1963.

Afr 6541.24   The wonderful story of Uganda. (Mullins, Joseph Dennis.) London, 1904.

Afr 6879.25.6   The wonderland of big game, being an account of two trips through Tanganyika and Kenya. (Dugmore, Arthur R.) London, 1933.

Afr 3979.15.5   The wonderland of Egypt. (Salmon, P.R.) N.Y., 1915.

Afr 7809.22.5   The wonderland of the eastern Congo. (Barns, T.A.) London, 1922.

Afr 6850.15   Wood, Alan. The groundnut affair. London, 1950.

Afr 9689.61   Wood, Anthony Saint John. Northern Rhodesia. London, 1961.

Afr 9170.20   Wood, Clement. The man who killed Kitchener, the life of Fritz Joubert Duquesne, 1879. N.Y., 1932.

Afr 3275.4   Wood, H.F. Egypt under the British. London, 1896.

Afr 6420.25   Wood, Susan B. Kenya. London, 1960.

Afr 6420.26   Wood, Susan B. Kenya. London, 1962.

Afr 9599.34   Wood and iron, a story of Africa written in memory of H.U.C. London, 1934.

Afr 1259.14   Woodberry, G.E. North Africa and the desert. N.Y., 1914.

Afr 10671.46.100   The wooden gong. (Akpan, Ntieyong Udo.) London, 1965.

Afr 9489.11.6   Woods, M.L. Pastels under the Southern Cross. London, 1911.

Afr 109.36A   Woodson, C.G. The African background outlined, or Handbook for the study of the Negro. Washington, 1936.

Afr 55.40   Woodson, Carter Godwin. African heroes and heroines. Washington, 1939.

Afr 500.20.2   Woolf, Leonard S. Empire and commerce in Africa. N.Y., 1919.

Afr 500.20.5   Woolf, Leonard S. Empire and commerce in Africa. N.Y., 1968.

Afr 500.20   Woolf, Leonard S. Empire and commerce in Africa. Westminster, 1919.

Afr 1493.50.15   Woolman, David J. Rebels in the RF; Abd el Krim and the Rif rebellion. Stanford, 1968.

Afr 8063.5   Woon, Harry V. Twenty-five years soldiering in South Africa. London, 1909.

Afr 7350.7   Worcester County. Auxiliary Colonization Society. Report. Worcester. 1832+

Afr 8295.9.3   Words by an eye witness. (Linesman.) Edinburg, 1901.

Afr 4500.10   Work, Ernest. Ethiopia, a pawn in European diplomacy. New Concord, 1935.

Afr 6538.47   Work for progress, the second five-year plan, 1966-1971. (Uganda.) Entebbe, 1966.

Afr 6538.55   Work for progress. (Uganda. Ministry of Planning and Economic Development.) Entebbe, 1967.

Afr 6210.64.5   The work of administration in Nigeria; case studies. (Murray, D.J.) London, 1969.

Afr 7812.264   A work of cooperation in development. (Fonds du Bien-Etre Indigène.) Brussels, 1964.

Afr 8145.22F   The work of the missionaries of Die Nederduits Gereformeerde Kerk van Suid-Afrika up to the year 1910. (Turnbull, C.E.P.) Johannesburg, 1965.

Afr 8315.8   Work of the Ninth Division. (Colvile, H.E.) London, 1901.

Afr 6225.35   The working class and the Nigerian crisis. (Toyo, Eskar.) Ibadan, 1967.

Afr 2208.95.9   Workman, F.B. Algerian memories. London, 1895.

Afr 8028.153   The works of Isaac Schapera; a selective bibliography. (Archibald, Jane Erica.) Johannesburg, 1969.

Afr 11572.50.800   The works of Sarah Gertrude Millin. (Snyman, J.P.L.) South Africa, 1955.

Afr 8028.154   Works relating to South Africa in the New York Public Library. (New York (City) Public Library.) N.Y., 1899.

Afr 115.9.2   The world and Africa. (Dubois, William E.) N.Y., 1965.

Afr 626.65   The World Bank in Africa. (International Bank for Reconstruction and Development.) Washington, 1961.

Afr 7580.18   World government and international assassination. (Sturdza, Michel.) Belmont, Mass., 1963.

Afr 5185.7   The world in miniature, Africa. v.2-3. (Schobel, Fred.) London, n.d. 2v.

Afr 11433.74.120   A world of strangers. (Gordimer, N.) N.Y., 1958.

Afr 8678.66   World opinion on apartheid. (India. Information Service.) New Delhi, 1952.

Afr 8678.376   The world that was ours. (Bernstein, Hilda.) London, 1967.

Afr 628.246.5   World's great men of color. 1st ed. (Rogers, Joel Augustus.) N.Y., 1946-47. 2v.

Afr 9439.54   The world's view. (Kane, N.S.) London, 1954.

Afr 8175.12   Wormser, J.A. Drie en zestig jaren in dienst der vrijheid. Amsterdam, 1900.

Afr 8279.00.31   Wormser, J.A. De oorlog in Zuid-Afrika. Amsterdam, 1900.

Afr 8658.98.7   Wormser, J.A. Van Amsterdam naar Pretoria. Amsterdam, 1898.

Afr 8658.99.3F   Wormser, J.A. De Zuster-Republieken in Zuid-Afrika. Amsterdam, 1899.

Afr 4008.1   Worrell, William H. A short account of the Copts. Ann Arbor, 1945.

Afr 8252.10.5   Worsfold, B. Sir Bartle Frere. London, 1923.

Afr 3069.01   Worsfold, W.B. Egypt yesterday and to-day. N.Y., 1901.

Afr 8089.00.3A   Worsfold, W.B. A history of South Africa. London, 1900.

Afr 8252.8.5   Worsfold, W.B. Lord Milner's work in South Africa. London, 1906.

Afr 7308.99   Worsfold, W.B. Portuguese Nyassaland. London, 1899.

Afr 8050.5   Worsfold, W.B. The problem of South African unity. London, 1900.

Afr 8089.13.3A   Worsfold, W.B. The reconstruction of the new colonies under Lord Milner. London, 1913. 2v.

Afr 3978.99   Worsfold, W.B. The redemption of Egypt. London, 1899.

Afr 8088.95   Worsfold, W.B. South Africa. London, 1895.

Afr 8659.12   Worsfold, W.B. Union of South Africa. London, 1912.

Afr 3275.31A   Worsfold, William B. The future of Egypt. London, 1914.

Afr 4070.47   Worsley, A. Land of the blue veil. Sudan. Birmingham, 1940.

Afr 8175.7   De worstelstrijd der transvalers. (Cachet, F.L.) Amsterdam, 1900.

Afr 6535.33   Worthington, S. Inland waters of Africa. London, 1933.

Afr 5426.100.25   Woyott-Secretan, Marie. Albert Schweitzer. Munich, 1949.

Afr 1259.43.15F   Wrage, W. Nordafrika. Leipzig, 1943.

Afr 6060.56.5   Wraith, R.E. Local government. London, 1956.

Afr 6060.64   Wraith, R.E. Local government in West Africa. London, 1964.

Afr 6060.64.2   Wraith, R.E. Local government in West Africa. N.Y., 1964.

Afr 6392.20   Wraith, Ronald E. East African citizen. London, 1959.

Afr 6198.440   Wraith, Ronald E. Guggisberg. London, 1967.

Afr 11108.74.100A   A wreath for Udomo. 1st American ed. (Abrahams, Peter.) N.Y., 1956.

Afr 8289.01.39   Wrecking the empire. (Robertson, J.M.) London, 1901.

Afr 8252.8.25   Wrench, Evelyn. Alfred Lord Milner. London, 1958.

Afr 210.63.85   The wretched of the earth. (Fanon, Franz.) N.Y., 1963.

Afr 11057.7   Wright, David. South African stories. London, 1960.

Afr 7368.33   Wright, E. The sin of slavery and its remedy. N.Y., 1833.

Afr 9489.04   Wright, E.H.S. Railways in Rhodesia. London, 1904.

Afr 6881.1   Wright, Fergus C. African consumers in Nyasaland and Tanganyika. London, 1955.

Afr 2875.20   Wright, H.C.S. Two years under the crescent. London, 1913.

Afr 2819.69   Wright, John L. Libya. London, 1969.

Afr 6192.30   Wright, R. Black power. 1st ed. N.Y., 1954.

Afr 628.257   Wright, Richard. White man, listen. 1st ed. Garden City, 1957.

Afr 8722.2.1   Wright, William. Slavery at the Cape of Good Hope. N.Y., 1831.

Afr 6282.20   Writing a local church history, a short guide. (Epelle, E.T.) Nsukka, Eastern Nigeria, 1965.

Afr 12018.5   Writing in French from Senegal to Cameroon. (Brench, Anthony Cecil.) London, 1967.

Afr 550.44   Wrong, Margaret. Five points for Africa. London, 1942.

Afr 8825.4   The wrongs of the Caffre nation. (Beverley, R.M.) London, 1837.

Afr 8235.14   Wued, Johannes Andreas. Die Rolle der Burenrepubliken in der auswaertigen und kolonialen Politik des deutschen Reiches, 1883-1900. Nürnberg, 1927.

Afr 6664.12   Wuelker, Gabriele. Togo: Tradition und Entwicklung. Stuttgart, 1966.

Afr 7815.18   Wuig, J. Van. Etudes Bakongo. 2.ed. Bruges, 1959.

Afr 609.39.5   Wunderwege durch ein Wunderland. 2. Aufl. (Gedat, Gustav A.) Stuttgart, 1939.

Afr 626.157F   Wybrane zagadnienia z historii gospodarczej Afryki. (Halpern, Jan.) Warszawa, 1963.

Afr 9028.80   Wylde, A. My chief and I, or Six months in Natal. London, 1880.

NEDL Afr 3700.2   Wylde, A.B. Eighty-three to eighty-seven in the Soudan. London, 1888. 2v.

Afr 4559.01.15   Wylde, A.B. Modern Abyssinia. London, 1901.

Afr 724.22   Wymer, Norman. The man from the Cape. London, 1959.

Afr 3823.2   Wyndham, Richard. The gentle savage. London, 1936.

Afr 3310.45   Wynn, Wilton. Nasser of Egypt. Cambridge, Mass., 1959.

Afr 2230.43   Wysner, Glora May. The Kabyle people. N.Y., 1945.

Afr 590.70   Xavier Botelho, S. Escravatura, beneficios que podem provir as nossas possessoes. Lisboa, 1840.

Afr 8825.30   Xhosa in town. (Mayer, Philip.) Cape Town, 1961-63. 3v.

Afr 4394.1   Ximenes, E. Sul campo di Adua. Milan, 1897.

Afr 1868.53   Ximenez de Sandoval, C. Memorias sobre la Argelia. Madrid, 1853.

Afr 1080.5   Ximenez de Sandovel, C. Guerras de Africa en la antigüdad. Madrid, 1881.

Afr 4513.37.22   Xylander, R. von. La conquista dell'Abissinia. Milano, 1937.

Afr 2030.463.50   Yacef, Saadi. Souvenirs de la bataille d'Alger déc. 1956-sept. 1957. Paris, 1963.

Afr 658.74   Yacht-Reise in den Syrten, 1873. (Ludwig, Salvator.) Prag, 1874.

Afr 2250.5   Yacono, Xavier. La colonisation des plaines du Chélif. Alger, 1955-56. 2v.

Afr Doc 2402.2F   Yakuba, Stephen. Publications of the government of the northern region of Nigeria, 1960-1962. Zaria, 1963.

Afr 7815.6   Yakusu. (Smith, H.S.) London, 1911.

Afr Doc 4302.10   Yale Univeristy. Library. South African official publications held by Yale University. New Haven, 1966.

Afr 2749.27   Yallah. (Bowles, Paul Frederic.) N.Y., 1957.

Afr 4390.35   Yaltsasamma. Les amis de Menelik II, roi des rois d'Ethiopie. Paris, 1899.

Afr 7369.34   Yancy, E.J. Historical lights of Liberia's yesterday and today. Xenia, 1934.

Afr 7369.59.2   Yancy, Ernest Jerome. The Republic of Liberia. Cairo, 1961.

Afr 7369.59   Yancy, Ernest Jerome. The Republic of Liberia. London, 1959.

Afr 500.21   Yanguas Messia, José. Apuntes sobre la expansion colonial en Africa. Madrid, 1915.

Afr 3315.138   Yanguas Messia, José de. El clima politico de ayer y de hoy en Africa. Escorial, 1959.

Afr 5933.2   Yanguas Mirarete, José. Antecedentes históricos. Sidi Infi, 1960.

Afr 8658.88   Yankee girls in Zulu land. (Sheldon, L.V.) N.Y., 1888.

Afr 725.15   A Yankee in Pigmyland. (Geil, William Edgar.) London, 1905.

Afr 9853.8   The Yao village, a study in the social structure of a Nyasaland tribe. 1st ed. (Mitchell, James Clyde.) Manchester, 1966.

Afr 7368.36.5   Yaradee, a plea for Africa. (Freeman, F.) N.Y., 1969.

Afr 7368.36   Yaradee, plea for Africa. (Freeman, F.) Philadelphia, 1836.

Afr 3745.30   Yardley, J. Parengon, or eddies in Equatoria. London, 1931.

Afr 8292.43   Yardley, J.W. With the Inniskilling Dragoons. London, 1904.

Afr 7565.12.15   Yarnall, H.E. The great powers and the Congo Conference in the year 1884 and 1885. Inaug. Diss. Göttingen, 1934.

Afr 5285.277.20   Yatenga. (Hammond, Peter B.) N.Y., 1966.

Afr 3978.43.5   Yates, W.H. Modern history and condition of Egypt. London, 1843. 2v.

Afr 3740.12   Yatin, Fernand. Une mise au point, la vérité sur Fachoda. Chaumont, 1923.

Afr 7549.53   Ydewalle, Charles D. Le Congo du fétiche à l'uranium. Bruxelles, 1953.

Afr 6300.98   Year book of East Africa. Nairobi. 1953+

Afr Doc 2807.5   Year book of statistics. (Mauritius. Central Statistical Office.) 13,1958+

Afr 9445.40   Year of decision. (Mason, Philip.) London, 1960.

Afr 6276.4   A year of sacred festivals in one Yoruba town. (Beier, Ulli.) Marina, 1959.

Afr 3320.46   Yearbook. (Fédération Egyptienne de l'Industrie.) Cairo. 1960+ 6v.

Afr Doc 1405.5   The yearbook. (United Arab Republic. Ministry of National Guidance.) Cairo. 1959+

Afr 24.5   Yearbook and guide to East Africa. 1950+ 13v.

Afr 3285.22   Yeghen, Foulad. Saad Zaghloul. Paris, 1927.

NEDL Afr 8678.13   The yellow and dark skinned people...Zambesi. (Theal, G.M.) London, 1910.

Afr 8678.13.3   The yellow and dark-skinned people of Africa south of the Zambesi. (Theal, G.M.) N.Y., 1969.

Afr 8175.24   The yellow man looks on, being the story of the Anglo-Dutch conflict in Southern Africa. (Chilvers, Hedley A.) London, 1933.

Afr 9610.1   Les Yem-Yem tribu anthropophage de l'Afrique centrale. (Aucapitaine, L.B.H.) Paris, 1857.

Afr 8289.01.23   Yeoman service. (Rolleston, Maud.) London, 1901.

Afr 8289.01.33   A yeoman's letters. (Ross, P.T.) London, 1901.

Afr 6275.107   Yesterday and tomorrow in Northern Nigeria. (Miller, W.R.S.) London, 1938.

Afr 6280.2.25   Yoruba culture, a geographical analysis. (Ojo, G.J. Afolabi.) Ife, Nigeria, 1966.

Afr 6280.2.45   The Yoruba of Southwestern Nigeria. (Bascom, William Russell.) N.Y., 1969.

Afr 6280.2.30   Yoruba palaces, a study of Afins of Yorubaland. (Ojo, G.J. Afolabi.) London, 1967.

Afr 49016.5   Yoruba poetry. (Gbadamosi, Bakare.) Ibadan, 1959.

Afr 6280.2   The Yoruba-speaking peoples of the Slave Coast of West Africa. (Ellis, A.B.) London, 1894.

Afr 6295.62.5   Yoruba towns. (Maboganj, A.) Ibadan, 1962.

Afr 6280.2.40   Yoruba towns and cities. (Krapf-Askari, Eve.) Oxford, 1969.

Afr 6280.2.15   Yoruba warfare in the nineteenth century. (Ajayi, J.F.A. de.) Cambridge, Eng., 1964.

Afr 5749.31   You, Andre. Madagascar, colonie française, 1896-1930. Paris, 1931.

Afr 5749.05   You, Andre. Madagascar, histoire, organisation, colonisation. Paris, 1905.

Afr 8678.70.10   You are young. 1. ed. (Steward, Alex.) London, 1956.

Afr 5318.45   Youla, Nabi. Mussa; ein Kind aus Guinea. Regensburg, 1964.

Afr 9839.64   Young, Anthony. A geography of Malawi. London, 1964.

Afr 9389.66   Young, Bertram Alfred. Bechuanaland. London, 1966.

Afr 7580.20   Young, Crawford. Politics in the Congo. Princeton, N.J., 1965.

Afr 9558.48   Young, E.D. The search after Livingstone. (A diary). London, 1868.

Afr 9838.77   Young, Edward Daniel. Nyassa. London, 1877.

Afr 8659.52.5   Young, F.B. In South Africa. London, 1952.

Afr 6780.5   Young, F.B. Marching on Tanga. London, 1917.

Afr 8310.6   Young, Filson. The relief of Mafeking. London, 1900.

Afr 8658.89.5   Young, Frederick. A winter tour in South Africa. London, 1890.

NEDL Afr 3199.27   Young, George. Egypt. N.Y., 1927.

Afr 7377.30   Young, James C. Liberia rediscovered. Garden City, 1934.

Afr 9448.51   Young, Kenneth. Rhodesia and independence, a study in British colonial policy. London, 1967.

Afr 8063.15   Young, P.J. Boot and saddle. Cape Town, 1955.

Afr 6887.12.5   Young, Roland A. Land and politics among the Luguru of Tanganyika. London, 1960.

Afr 6887.12.10   Young, Roland A. Smoke in the hills. Evanston, 1960.

Afr 10118.2A   Young, T. Cullen. African new writing. London, 1947.

Afr 5342.62   Young, T. Rex. West African agent. London, 1943.

Afr 6390.23   Young, T.C. African ways and wisdom. London, 1937.

Afr 210.64.75   Young Africa. (Larsen, Peter.) London, 1964.

Afr 3199.58   Young Egypt. (Stewart, D.S.) London, 1958.

Afr 9291.5   Young Mrs. Murray goes to Bloemfontein, 1856-1869. (Murray, Emma (Rutherford).) Cape Town, 1954.

Afr 8325.60   A young South African. (Cleaver, M.M.) Johannesburg, 1913.

Afr 8659.47.5   The young traveller in South Africa. (Delius, Anthony.) London, 1947.

Afr 11501.89.110   Young villain with wings. (Kruger, Rayne.) London, 1953.

Afr 6390.12   Younghusband, E. Glimpses of East Africa and Zanzibar. London, 1910.

Afr 8278.98A   Younghusband, F.E. South Africa of to-day. London, 1898.

Afr 6293.4   Your ABC of Lagos and suburbs including guide maps of Benin, Enugu, Ibadan and Kaduna. (SES Publishers.) Lagos, 1967.

Afr 9710.17   Your friend, Lewanika. (Clay, Gervas.) London, 1968.

Afr 1620.40   Your guide to Morrocco. (Dennis-Jones, Harold.) London, 1965.

Afr 3300.41   Youssef Bey, A. Independent Egypt. London, 1940.

Afr 1432.5   Yriarte, C. Sous la tente: souvenirs du Maroc. Paris, 1863.

Afr 6291.46   Yu, Mok Chiu. Nigeria-Biafra; a reading into the problems and peculiarities of the conflict. Adelaide, 1968.

Afr 11456.14.1   Yudelman, Myra. Dan Jacobson, a bibliography. Johannesburg, 1967.

Afr 3994.934   Yunus, Muhammed Tawfig. The preparation of the Egyptian budget. Cairo, 1934.

Afr 1965.10.5   Yusuf. De la guerra en Africa...en 1851. Madrid, 1859.

Afr 1965.10   Yusuf. (Derrecagaix, V.B.) Paris, 1907.

Afr 625.17F   Yusuf Kamal, Prince. Hallucinations scientifiques. Les Portulans. Leiden, 1937.

Afr 625.15F   Yusuf Kamal, Prince. Quelques éclaircissements épars sur mes Monumenta cartographica Africae et Aegypti. Leiden, 1935.

Afr 1635.35   Yusuf Taşfin; yer yüzünün en Büyük devletlerinden birini kuran Berber imparatoru. (Carim, Fuat.) Istanbul, 1966.

Afr 9625.22   Z; international edition. Lusaka. 1,1969+

Afr 210.62.40   Za natsionalniiu nezavisimost. (Problemy Mira i Sotsializma.) Praha, 1962.

Afr 609.67.25   Za vorotami slez. (Khokhlov, Nikolai P.) Moskva, 1967.

Afr 1609.05.11   Zabel, R. Im muhammendanischen abendlande. Altenburg, 1905.

Afr 1609.13.4   Zabel, R. Zu unruhiger Zeit in Marokko. Cöln am Rhein, 1913.

Afr 2208.65.3   Zaccone, J. De batna à Tuggurt et au Souf. Paris, 1865.

Afr 2608.75   Zaccone, P. Notes sur la régence de Tunis. Paris, 1875.

Afr 8659.25.8   Zachariah, O. Travel in South Africa. 3d ed. Johannesburg, 1927.

Afr 109.68.15   Zaghi, Carlo. L'Europa devanti all'Africa dai tempi piu antichi alle soglie dell'Ottocento. Napoli, 1968.

Afr 3695.3.86   Zaghi, Carlo. Gordon, Gessi e la riconquista del Sudan, 1874-1881. Firenze, 1947.

Afr 4730.15A   Zaghi, Carlo. Le origini della colonia Eritrea. Bologna, 1934.

Afr 500.88   Zaghi, Carlo. La spartiziche dell'Africa. Napoli, 1968.

Afr 3695.3.85   Zaghi, Carlo. Vita di Romolo Gessi. Milano, 1939.

Afr 5437.5   Zagovor protiv Kongo. (Martynov, V.A.) Moscow, 1960.

Afr 5243.125.25   Zahan, Dominique. Sociétés d'initiation bambara. v.1. Paris, 1960.

Afr 5243.174.30   Zahan, Dominique. La Viande et la graine, mythologie dogon. Paris, 1969.

Afr 7526.5   Zaire, revue congolaise. Bruxelles. 4,1950+ 21v.

Afr 6194.39   Zajaczkowski, A. Aszanti, kraj Złotego Tronu. Warszawa, 1963.

Afr 545.33   Zajaczkowski, Andrzej. Pierwotne religie czarnej Afryki. Warszawa, 1965. 10v.

Afr 5183.962.5   Zajadatz, Paul. Probleme und Möglichkeiten der industriellen Entwicklung im Senegal. Köln, 1962.

Afr 3275.17.5   Zakhvat i zakabalenie Egipta. (Rotshtein, F.A.) Moscow, 1925.

Afr 3275.17.5.2   Zakhvat i zakabalenie Egipta. (Rotshtein, F.A.) Moscow, 1959.

Afr 699.68   Zamani; a survey of East African history. (Ogot, Bethwell Allen.) Nairobi, 1968.

Afr 820.1   The Zambesi. (Sherlock, Jill.) Cape Town, 1963.

Afr 9598.93   The Zambesi basin and Nyassaland. (Rankin, D.J.) Edinburgh, 1893.

Afr 9558.14.15   The Zambesi doctors. (Livingstone, D.) Edinburgh, 1964.

Afr 9558.510   The Zambesi journal and letters of Dr. John Kirk, 1858-63. (Kirk, John.) Edinburg, 1965. 2v.

Afr 820.4   Zambesi river. (Mcdonald, J.F.) London, 1955.

Afr 9488.95.7   Zambesia, England's El Dorado in Africa. (Mathers, E.P.) London, 1895.

Afr 9549.66   The Zambesian past. (Stokes, Eric.) Manchester, 1966.

Afr 820.5   Zambezi days. (Robertson, W.) London, 1936.

Afr 9558.500   The Zambezi papers of Richard Thornton. (Thornton, Richard.) London, 1963. 2v.

Afr 9439.58   Zambezi sunrise. (Gale, W.D.) Cape Town, 1958.

Afr 9535.98   Zambezia; a journal of social studies in southern and central Africa. Salisbury. 1,1969+

Afr 7322.3   Zambezia. (Maugham, R.C.F.) London, 1910.

Afr 9489.60.5   Zambezia and Matabeleland in the seventies. (Barber, F.H.) London, 1960.

Afr 9748.475.15   Zambia, independence and beyond, the speeches of Kenneth Kaunda. (Kaunda, Kenneth David.) London, 1966.

Afr 9689.68   Zambia, Rpresident (Kaunda). Zambia's guideline for the next decade. Lusaka, 1968.

Afr Doc 3709.10F   Zambia. Estimates of revenue and expenditure. Lusaka. 1,1964+

Afr Doc 3703.10   Zambia. General list of chiefs. Lusaka, 1966.

Afr Doc 3705.5   Zambia. Government paper. Lusaka. 1966+

Afr Doc 3702.5   Zambia. List of publications. 1954+

Afr 9699.3   Zambia. Republic of Zambia. Lusaka, 1965.

Afr Doc 3707.363.2F   Zambia. Second report of the May/June 1963 census of Africans. Lusaka, 1964.

Afr 9689.65   Zambia. (Hall, Richard Seymour.) London, 1965.

Afr 9689.65.5   Zambia. (Hall, Richard Seymour.) London, 1968.

Afr 9625.20   Zambia. Lusaka. 1965-1969// 3v.

Afr Doc 3731.15   Zambia. Agricultural Marketing Committee. Review of the operations. Lusaka. 1964+

Afr Doc 3709.5   Zambia. Audit Office. Report of the Auditor-General on the public accounts. Lusaka. 1964+

Afr Doc 3708.315   Zambia. Cabinet Office. Manpower report. Lusaka, 1966.

Afr Doc 3709.520F   Zambia. Central Statistical Office. Agricultural and pastoral production statistics (For commercial farms only). Lusaka. 1966+

Afr Doc 3709.505   Zambia. Central Statistical Office. Agriculture production in Zambia. Lusaka. 1963+

Afr Doc 3709.510F   Zambia. Central Statistical Office. Agriculture production statistics. Lusaka. 1964+

Afr Doc 3749.16F   Zambia. Central Statistical Office. Annual report. Lusaka. 1965+

Afr Doc 3708.700   Zambia. Central Statistical Office. Annual statement of external trade. Lusaka. 1,1964+

Afr Doc 3708.710F   Zambia. Central Statistical Office. Balance of payments. Lusaka. 1,1964+

Afr Doc 3707.362F   Zambia. Central Statistical Office. Census of distribution in 1962; wholesale, retail trade and selected services. Lusaka, 1965.

Afr Doc 3707.363.5   Zambia. Central Statistical Office. The census of production in 1963. Lusaka, 1965.

Afr Doc 3708.705F   Zambia. Central Statistical Office. External trade statistics. Lusaka. 1965+

Afr Doc 3707.361   Zambia. Central Statistical Office. Final report of the Sept. 1961 censuses of non-Africans and employees. Lusaka, 1965.

Afr Doc 3709.530F   Zambia. Central Statistical Office. Income tax statistics. Lusaka. 1,1962+

Afr Doc 3709.535F   Zambia. Central Statistical Office. Insurance statistics. Lusaka. 1,1964+

Afr Doc 3707.363F   Zambia. Central Statistical Office. May/June 1963 census of Africans: v.1 village population. Lusaka, 1965.

Afr Doc 3707.56   Zambia. Central Statistical Office. Monthly digest of statistics. 1,1964+